## MAXIMUM FINES FOR DISOBEDIENCE TO COURT ORDERS AND CONTEMPT OF COURT

| | | |
|---|---|---|
| CJ & Immig Act 2008, Sch 2, Part 2, para (2)(*a*) | Breach of requirement of youth rehabilitation order | £2,500 |
| MCA 1980, s 63(3)(*a*) | Disobedience of order other than for payment of money | £5,000 |
| MCA 1980, s 97(4) | Refusal to give evidence | £2,500 |
| CCA 1981, ss 12(2) and 14(2) | Contempt of court | £2,500 |
| PCC(S)A 2000, s 131(1) | Maximum amount payable under a **compensation** order | £5,000 |
| PCC(S)A 2000, s 150 | Maximum **recognizance from parent** or guardian (or fine for refusal) | £1,000 |

BUTTERWORTHS

# STONE'S

# JUSTICES' MANUAL

## VOLUME 3

BUTTERWORTHS

# STONE'S JUSTICES' MANUAL 2017

One Hundred and Forty-Ninth Edition

VOLUME 3

edited by

**A P CARR**

*District Judge (Magistrates' Courts)* and

**A J TURNER**

*Barrister, Chambers of Adrian Turner, Eastbourne*

LexisNexis®

**Members of the LexisNexis Group worldwide**

| | |
|---|---|
| United Kingdom | RELX (UK) Limited, trading as LexisNexis, 1–3 Strand, London, WC2N 5JR |
| Australia | LexisNexis Butterworths, Chatswood, New South Wales |
| Austria | LexisNexis Verlag ARD Orac GmbH & Co KG, Vienna |
| Benelux | LexisNexis Benelux, Amsterdam |
| Canada | LexisNexis Canada, Markham, Ontario |
| China | LexisNexis China, Beijing and Shanghai |
| France | LexisNexis SA, Paris |
| Germany | LexisNexis GmbH, Dusseldorf |
| Hong Kong | LexisNexis Hong Kong, Hong Kong |
| India | LexisNexis India, New Delhi |
| Italy | Giuffrè Editore, Milan |
| Japan | LexisNexis Japan, Tokyo |
| Malaysia | Malayan Law Journal Sdn Bhd, Kuala Lumpur |
| New Zealand | LexisNexis NZ Ltd, Wellington |
| Poland | Wydawnictwo Prawnicze LexisNexis Sp, Warsaw |
| Singapore | LexisNexis Singapore, Singapore |
| South Africa | LexisNexis Butterworths, Durban |
| USA | LexisNexis, Dayton, Ohio |


Published by LexisNexis

This is a Butterworths title


A CIP Catalogue record for this book is available from the British Library.

ISBN 978-1-4743-0402-3

ISBN 978-1-4743-0399-6

ISBN for this volume: 9781474303996

ISBN for the set: 9781474304023

Printed and bound by CPI Group (UK) Ltd, Croydon, CR0 4YY

Visit LexisNexis at www.lexisnexis.co.uk

# CONTENTS

(WITH REFERENCE TO PARAS)

## VOLUME 1



## VOLUME 2

## VOLUME 3



## KEY MATERIALS

## Ready Reference

| | Statutory provision | *KM* = *Key Materials* | Narrative |
|---|---|---|---|
| **Principal police powers** | | | 1.62 |
| **Search warrants** | | | 1.70, 1.70A, 1.70B |
| **Bail** | Bail Act 1976 | 1.455 | 1.166 |
| *Exceptions to right to bail (imprisonable offences)* | Bail Act 1976, Sch 1 Pt 1 | 1.473 | 1.174 |
| *Exceptions to right to bail (summary-only imprisonable offences and low value criminal damage)* | Bail Act 1976, Sch 1 Pt 1A | 1.473 | 1.175 |
| *Special provision for drug users* | | | 1.176 |
| *Exceptions to the right to bail (non-imprisonable offences)* | Bail Act 1976, Sch 1 Pt 2 | 1.473 | 1.177 |
| *Prosecution appeal* | Bail (Amend) Act 1993, s 1 | 1.857 | 1.185 |
| **Remand** | MCA 1980, ss 128–131 | 1.633<br>1.637 | 1.166 |
| *Custody time limits* | PO (CTL) Regs 1987 | 1.2386 | |
| *Live link at preliminary hearing* | CDA 1998, ss 57A–57B | 1.1027 | 1.138 |
| **Disclosure** | CrimPR Pt 22 | *KM* B.14 | |
| *Initial details* | | | 1.139 |
| *Public interest immunity* | | | 1.229 |
| *Initial duty of prosecution* | CPIA 1996, s 3 | 1.905 | 1.224 |
| *Code of Practice* | | 1.2832 | |
| *A-G Guidelines* | | 1.2828 | |
| **Judicial protocol** | | 1.2829 | |
| **Civil legal aid** | LASPO 2012, ss 8–12<br>Civil L A (Proc) R 2012<br>Civil L A (Merits) R 20131 | 1.1738<br>1.1896<br>1.2004 | |
| **Criminal legal aid** | LASPO 2012, ss 13–20<br>Criminal L A (Gen) R 2013 | 1.1742<br>1.1965 | 1.54 |
| **Disqualification and Bias** | | | 1.34, 1.37, 1.38 & 1.39 |
| **Abuse of process** | | | 1.152 |
| **Information and written charge** | | | 1.118 |
| *Time limit* | MCA 1980, s 127 | 1.632 | 1.119 |
| *Allegations* | CrimPR Pt 7, r 7.3 | *KM* B.7 | 1.120 |
| *Several offences* | | | 1.149 |
| *Several defendants* | | | 1.150 |
| *Adults and minors* | | | 1.151 |
| *Duplicity* | CrimPR Pt 7, r 7.3 | *KM* B.7 | 1.121 |
| *Amendment* | MCA 1980, s 123 | 1.620 | 1.147 |
| **Summons** | | | |
| *Issue of* | | | 1.123 |
| *Service* | CrimPR Pt 4, r 4.2 | *KM* B.4 | 1.128 |
| *Proof of service* | CrimPR Pt 4, r 4.11 | *KM* B.4 | |

| | Statutory provision | | Narrative |
|---|---|---|---|
| **Adjournment** | | | 1.164 |
| **Plea before venue** | MCA 1980, ss 17A–17C | 1.508<br>1.510 | 1.191 |
| **Mode of trial** | MCA 1980, s 18–21 | 1.513<br>1.517 | 1.198 |
| *Guidelines* | Sentencing Guidelines | *KM* C.5 | |
| *Adults and youths* | CDA 1998, ss 50A, 51 & 51A | 1.1017 | 1.202<br>5.12 |
| *Criminal damage* | MCA 1980, s 22 | 1.518 | 1.203 |
| **Low value shoplifting** | MCA 1980, s 22A | 1.518A | 1.188A |
| **Sending for trial** | CDA 1998, ss 50A, 51 & 51A | 1.1017 | 1.189, 5.11 ff |
| **Trial** | | | 1.219 |
| *Proceeding in absence of accused* | | | 1.140 |
| *Procedure* | CrimPR Pt 37, r 37.3 | *KM* B.23 | 1.251 |
| **Evidence** | | | |
| *Identification* | PACE Code D | 2.362 | 2.119 |
| *Exclusion of unfairly obtained* | PACE 1984, s 78 | 2.232 | 2.43 |
| *Hearsay* | CJA 2003, ss 114–134 | 2.336<br>2.353 | 2.95 ff |
| | CrimPR Pt 34 | *KM* B.23 | 1.241 |
| *Bad character* | CJA 2003, ss 98–112 | 2.321<br>2.335 | 2.74 ff |
| | CrimPR Pt 35 | *KM* B.21 | 1.242 |
| *Oaths etc* | Oaths Act 1978 | 2.190 | 1.254 |
| *Competence* | YJCEA 1999, s 53 | 2.311 | 2.45<br>2.46 |
| *Compellability* | PACE 1984, s 80 | 2.234 | 2.45<br>2.46 |
| *Hostile* | Crim Proc Act 1865, s 3 | 1.343 | 1.260 |
| *Special measures* | YJCEA 1999, Pt II, Ch I | 2.272 | 2.51A ff<br>1.238 |
| *Protection from cross examination* | YJCEA 1999, Pt II, Ch II | 2.294 | 2.71 |
| | Crim PR Pt 23 | B.23 | |
| *Complainant's sexual history* | YJCEA 1999, Pt II, Ch III | 2.300 | 2.72 |
| | Crim PR Pt 22 | B.21 | 1.243 |
| *Refreshing memory* | CJA 2003, s 139 | 2.356 | 1.262 |
| *Accused – effect of silence of at trial* | CJPOA 1994, s 35 | 2.253 | 2.125 |
| **Submission of no case** | | | 1.269 |
| **Burden and standard of proof** | | | 1.277<br>1.281 |
| **Procedure on conviction** | | | 1.284 |
| **Sentencing** | | | |
| *Purposes* | CJA 2003, s 142 | 3.588 | 3.2 |
| *Sentencing by live link* | CDA 1998, ss 57D, 57E | 1.1030<br>1.1031 | 3.8 |
| *Overarching principles* | | | 3.21 |
| *Credit for guilty plea* | | | 3.25 |

| | Statutory provision | | Narrative |
|---|---|---|---|
| *Available non-custodial sentences (adults)* | | | 3.33 |
| *Magistrates' Courts Sentencing Guidelines* | | *KM* C.1–C.29 | |
| *Fine enforcement* | MCA 1980, ss 75–91 | 1.569<br>1.588 | 3.46<br>3.47 |
| *Imprisonment* | | | |
| *– restrictions on* | CJA 2003, s 152 | 3.599 | 3.55 |
| *– consecutive terms* | MCA 1980, s 133 | 1.639 | 3.59 |
| *– return to* | | | 3.63<br>3.66 |
| *Behaviour orders* | | | 3.109 |
| *Sex offenders* | SOA 2003, Pt 2 | 7.10641 ff | 3.101 ff |
| *Sentencing Guidelines and examples of sentencing for particular offences* | | | 3.110 ff |
| **Costs** | Pros of Offences Act 1985, s 16–19B | 1.815<br>1.821 | 1.301<br><br>3.93 |
| **Road traffic** | | | |
| *Highway Code* | | 4.866 | |
| *Duty to give information as to identity of driver* | RTA 1988, s 172 | 4.411 | 4.16 |
| *NIPs* | RTOA 1988, s 1, Sch 1 | 4.434<br>4.553 | 4.17 |
| *Offences* | | | |
| *– careless driving* | RTA 1988, s 3 | 4.232 | 4.9 |
| *– alcohol (OPL)* | RTA 1988, s 5 | 4.237 | |
| *– fail provide specimen* | RTA 1988, s 7 | 4.244 | |
| *– no insurance* | RTA 1988, s 143 | 4.384 | |
| *– fail to stop/report* | RTA 1988, s 170 | 4.409 | |
| *Driving licences* | RTA 1988, s 87 ff | 4.324 ff | 4.23 |
| *Newly qualified drivers* | RT(ND)A 1995 | | 4.34 |
| *Penalties* | | | |
| *– list of maximum penalties and endorseable offences* | RTOA 1988, Sch 2 | 4.554 | |
| *– codes* | | 4.864 | |
| *Disqualification* | | | 4.19 |
| *– mandatory/special reasons* | RTOA 1988, s 34(1) | 4.466 | |
| *– discretionary* | RTOA 1988, s 34(2) | 4.466 | |
| *– penalty points/mitigating circumstances* | RTOA 1988, s 35 | 4.475 | 4.18 |

# PART VII
# MISCELLANEOUS OFFENCES AND CIVIL PROCEEDINGS (J–W)

## JURIES

### Juries Act 1974
(1974 c 23)

7.7027 **20. Offences: failure to attend, serving while disqualified etc** (1) Subject to the provisions of subsections (2) to (4) below—

(*a*) if a person duly summoned under this Act fails to attend (on the first or any subsequent day on which he is required to attend by the summons or by the appropriate officer) in compliance with the summons, or

(*b*) if a person, after attending in pursuance of a summons, is not available when called on to serve as a juror, or is unfit for service by reason of drink or drugs,

he shall be liable to a fine not exceeding **level 3** on the standard scale.

(2) An offence under subsection (1) above shall be punishable either on summary conviction or as if it were criminal contempt of court committed in the face of the court.

(3) Subsection (1)(*a*) above shall not apply to a person summoned, otherwise than under s 6 of this Act[1], unless the summons was duly served on him on a date not later than fourteen days before the date fixed by the summons for his first attendance.

(4) A person shall not be liable to be punished under the preceding provisions of this section if he can show some reasonable cause for his failure to comply with the summons, or for not being available when called on to serve, and those provisions have effect subject to the provisions of this Act about the withdrawal or alteration of a summons and about the granting of any excusal or deferral.

(5) If any person—

(*a*) having been summoned under this Act makes, or causes or permits to be made on his behalf, any false representation to the appropriate officer with the intention of evading jury service; or

(*b*) makes or causes to be made on behalf of another person who has been so summoned any false representation to that officer with the intention of enabling the other to evade jury service; or

(*c*) when any question is put to him in pursuance of section 2(5) of this Act, refuses without reasonable excuse to answer, or gives an answer he knows to be false in a material particular, or recklessly gives an answer which is false in a material particular; or

(*d*) knowing that he is not qualified for jury service by reason of section 40 of the Criminal Justice and Public Order Act 1994,, serves on a jury, or

(*e*) knowing that he is not qualified for jury service by reason of section 40 of the Criminal Justice and Public Order Act 1994, serves on a jury,

he shall be liable on summary conviction to a fine of not more than **level 5** on the standard scale in the case of an offence of serving on a jury when disqualified and, in any other case, a fine of not more than **level 3** on the standard scale.

[Juries Act 1974, s 20 as amended by the Criminal Justice Act 1982, ss 38 and 46, the Criminal Justice Act 1988, Sch 15, the Criminal Justice and Public Order Act 1994, Sch 10, the Criminal Justice Act 2003, Sch 33 and the Criminal Justice and Courts Act 2015, s 71.]

---

1 Section 6 contains a power to summon a person in exceptional circumstances without any written notice.

7.7027A **20A. Offence: research by jurors** (1) It is an offence for a member of a jury that tries an issue in a case before a court to research the case during the trial period, subject to the exceptions in subsections (6) and (7).

(2) A person researches a case if (and only if) the person—

(*a*) intentionally seeks information, and

(*b*) when doing so, knows or ought reasonably to know that the information is or may be relevant to the case.

(3) The ways in which a person may seek information include—

(*a*) asking a question,

(*b*) searching an electronic database, including by means of the internet,

(*c*) visiting or inspecting a place or object,

(*d*) conducting an experiment, and

(*e*) asking another person to seek the information.

(4) Information relevant to the case includes information about—

(*a*) a person involved in events relevant to the case,

(*b*) the judge dealing with the issue,

(*c*) any other person involved in the trial, whether as a lawyer, a witness or otherwise,

(*d*) the law relating to the case,

(*e*) the law of evidence, and

(*f*) court procedure.

(5) "The trial period", in relation to a member of a jury that tries an issue, is the period—

(*a*) beginning when the person is sworn to try the issue, and

(*b*) ending when the judge discharges the jury or, if earlier, when the judge discharges the person.

(6) It is not an offence under this section for a person to seek information if the person needs the information for a reason which is not connected with the case.

(7) It is not an offence under this section for a person—

(*a*) to attend proceedings before the court on the issue;

(*b*) to seek information from the judge dealing with the issue;

(*c*) to do anything which the judge dealing with the issue directs or authorises the person to do;

(*d*) to seek information from another member of the jury, unless the person knows or ought reasonably to know that the other member of the jury contravened this section in the process of obtaining the information;

(*e*) to do anything else which is reasonably necessary in order for the jury to try the issue.

(8) A person guilty of an offence under this section is liable, on conviction on indictment, to imprisonment for a term not exceeding 2 years or a fine (or both).

(9) Proceedings for an offence under this section may only be instituted by or with the consent of the Attorney General.

[Juries Act 1974, s 20A as inserted by the Criminal Justice and Courts Act 2015, s 71.]

**7.7027B 20B. Offence: sharing research with other jurors** (1) It is an offence for a member of a jury that tries an issue in a case before a court intentionally to disclose information to another member of the jury during the trial period if—

(*a*) the member contravened section 20A in the process of obtaining the information, and

(*b*) the information has not been provided by the court.

(2) Information has been provided by the court if (and only if) it has been provided as part of—

(*a*) evidence presented in the proceedings on the issue, or

(*b*) other information provided to the jury or a juror during the trial period by, or with the permission of, the judge dealing with the issue.

(3) A person guilty of an offence under this section is liable, on conviction on indictment, to imprisonment for a term not exceeding 2 years or a fine (or both).

(4) Proceedings for an offence under this section may not be instituted except by or with the consent of the Attorney General.

(5) In this section, "the trial period" has the same meaning as in section 20A.

[Juries Act 1974, s 20B as inserted by the Criminal Justice and Courts Act 2015, s 72.]

**7.7027C 20C. Offence: jurors engaging in other prohibited conduct** (1) It is an offence for a member of a jury that tries an issue in a case before a court intentionally to engage in prohibited conduct during the trial period, subject to the exceptions in subsections (4) and (5).

(2) "Prohibited conduct" means conduct from which it may reasonably be concluded that the person intends to try the issue otherwise than on the basis of the evidence presented in the proceedings on the issue.

(3) An offence under this section is committed whether or not the person knows that the conduct is prohibited conduct.

(4) It is not an offence under this section for a member of the jury to research the case (as defined in section 20A(2) to (4)).

(5) It is not an offence under this section for a member of the jury to disclose information to another member of the jury.

(6) A person guilty of an offence under this section is liable, on conviction on indictment, to imprisonment for a term not exceeding 2 years or a fine (or both).

(7) Proceedings for an offence under this section may not be instituted except by or with the consent of the Attorney General.

(8) In this section, "the trial period" has the same meaning as in section 20A.

[Juries Act 1974, s 20C as inserted by the Criminal Justice and Courts Act 2015, s 73.]

**7.7027D 20D. Offence: disclosing jury's deliberations** (1) It is an offence for a person intentionally—

(*a*) to disclose information about statements made, opinions expressed, arguments advanced or votes cast by members of a jury in the course of their deliberations in proceedings before a court, or

(*b*) to solicit or obtain such information,

subject to the exceptions in sections 20E to 20G.

(2) A person guilty of an offence under this section is liable, on conviction on indictment, to imprisonment for a term not exceeding 2 years or a fine (or both).

(3) Proceedings for an offence under this section may not be instituted except by or with the consent of the Attorney General.

[Juries Act 1974, s 20D as inserted by the Criminal Justice and Courts Act 2015, s 74.]

**7.7027E 20E. Offence of disclosing jury's deliberations: initial exceptions** (1) It is not an offence under section 20D for a person to disclose information in the proceedings mentioned in section 20D(1) for the purposes of enabling the jury to arrive at their verdict or in connection with the delivery of that verdict.

(2) It is not an offence under section 20D for the judge dealing with those proceedings to disclose information—

(*a*) for the purposes of dealing with the case, or

(*b*) for the purposes of an investigation by a relevant investigator into whether an offence or contempt of court has been committed by or in relation to a juror in the proceedings mentioned in section 20D(1).

(3) It is not an offence under section 20D for a person who reasonably believes that a disclosure described in subsection (2)(*b*) has been made to disclose information for the purposes of the investigation.

(4) It is not an offence under section 20D to publish information disclosed as described in subsection (1) or (2)(*a*) in the proceedings mentioned in section 20D(1).

(5) In this section—

"publish" means make available to the public or a section of the public;

"relevant investigator" means—

(*a*) a police force;

(*b*) the Attorney General;

(*c*) any other person or class of person specified by the Lord Chancellor for the purposes of this section by regulations made by statutory instrument.

(6) The Lord Chancellor must obtain the consent of the Lord Chief Justice before making regulations under this section.

(7) A statutory instrument containing regulations under this section is subject to annulment in pursuance of a resolution of either House of Parliament.

[Juries Act 1974, s 20E as inserted by the Criminal Justice and Courts Act 2015, s 74.]

**7.7027F 20F. Offence of disclosing jury's deliberations: further exceptions** (1) It is not an offence under section 20D for a person to disclose information to a person listed in subsection (2) if—

(*a*) the disclosure is made after the jury in the proceedings mentioned in section 20D(1) has been discharged, and

(*b*) the person making the disclosure reasonably believes that—

(i) an offence or contempt of court has been, or may have been, committed by or in relation to a juror in connection with those proceedings, or

(ii) conduct of a juror in connection with those proceedings may provide grounds for an appeal against conviction or sentence.

(2) Those persons are—

(*a*) a member of a police force;

(*b*) a judge of the Court of Appeal;

(*c*) the registrar of criminal appeals;

(*d*) a judge of the court where the proceedings mentioned in section 20D(1) took place;

(*e*) a member of staff of that court who would reasonably be expected to disclose the information only to a person mentioned in paragraphs (*b*) to (*d*).

(3) It is not an offence under section 20D for a member of a police force to disclose information for the purposes of obtaining assistance in deciding whether to submit the information to a judge of the Court of Appeal or the registrar of criminal appeals, provided that the disclosure does not involve publishing the information.

(4) It is not an offence under section 20D for a judge of the Court of Appeal or the registrar of criminal appeals to disclose information for the purposes of an investigation by a relevant investigator into—

(*a*) whether an offence or contempt of court has been committed by or in relation to a juror in connection with the proceedings mentioned in section 20D(1), or

(*b*) whether conduct of a juror in connection with those proceedings may provide grounds for an appeal against conviction or sentence.

(5) It is not an offence under section 20D for a judge of the Court of Appeal or the registrar of criminal appeals to disclose information for the purposes of enabling or assisting—

(*a*) a person who was the defendant in the proceedings mentioned in section 20D(1), or

(*b*) a legal representative of such a person,

to consider whether conduct of a juror in connection with those proceedings may provide grounds for an appeal against conviction or sentence.

(6) It is not an offence under section 20D for a person who reasonably believes that a disclosure described in subsection (4) or (5) has been made to disclose information for the purposes of the investigation or consideration in question.

(7) It is not an offence under section 20D for a person to disclose information in evidence in—

(*a*) proceedings for an offence or contempt of court alleged to have been committed by or in relation to a juror in connection with the proceedings mentioned in section 20D(1),

(*b*) proceedings on an appeal, or an application for leave to appeal, against a decision in the proceedings mentioned in section 20D(1) where an allegation relating to conduct of or in relation to a juror forms part of the grounds of appeal, or

(*c*) proceedings on any further appeal or reference arising out of proceedings mentioned in paragraph (*a*) or (*b*).

(8) It is not an offence under section 20D for a person to disclose information in the course of taking reasonable steps to prepare for proceedings described in subsection (7)(*a*) to (*c*).

(9) It is not an offence under section 20D to publish information disclosed as described in subsection (7).

(10) In this section—

"publish" means make available to the public or a section of the public;

"relevant investigator" means—

(*a*) a police force;

(*b*) the Attorney General;

(*c*) the Criminal Cases Review Commission;

(*d*) the Crown Prosecution Service;

(*e*) any other person or class of person specified by the Lord Chancellor for the purposes of this section by regulations made by statutory instrument.

(11) The Lord Chancellor must obtain the consent of the Lord Chief Justice before making regulations under this section.

(12) A statutory instrument containing regulations under this section is subject to annulment in pursuance of a resolution of either House of Parliament.

[Juries Act 1974, s 20F as inserted by the Criminal Justice and Courts Act 2015, s 74.]

7.7027G **20G. Offence of disclosing jury's deliberations: exceptions for soliciting disclosures or obtaining information** (1) It is not an offence under section 20D to solicit a disclosure described in section 20E(1) to (4) or section 20F(1) to (9).

(2) It is not an offence under section 20D to obtain information—

(*a*) by means of a disclosure described in section 20E(1) to (4) or section 20F(1) to (9), or

(*b*) from a document that is available to the public or a section of the public.

[Juries Act 1974, s 20G as inserted by the Criminal Justice and Courts Act 2015, s 74.]

# LIBEL

**Contents**



7.7028 **Immunity for informants, witnesses, etc in criminal investigations and proceedings.**—A witness has absolute privilege when giving evidence in court and in relation to prior statements made to the party calling the witness or to that party's lawyers: *Watson v M'Ewan* [1905] AC 480. Immunity for out of court statements is not confined to persons who are subsequently called as witnesses: *Taylor v Director of the Serious Fraud Office* [1999] 2 AC 177, [1998] 4 All ER 801, HL(E). Absolute immunity from suit also applies to those who participate in a criminal investigation whether as informants, investigators, or prosecutors. This is justified by the necessity for the due administration of criminal justice that complaints of alleged criminal conduct should always be capable of being made to the police free from fear that the person accused will subsequently involve the complainant in costly litigation. Such immunity is consistent with art 8 of the European Convention on Human Rights. A person who makes a complaint to the police, thereby instigating a police investigation which does not lead to a prosecution, can shelter behind the defence of absolute privilege if a claim is brought against her in defamation: *Westcott v Westcott* [2008] EWCA Civ 818, [2009] QB 407. The question is whether the oral statement made by a defendant to a libel action and her subsequent written statement can each fairly be said to be part of the process of investigating a crime or a possible crime with a view to a prosecution or possible prosecution in respect of the matter being investigated: *Evans v London Hospital Medical College (University of London)* [1981] 1 All ER 715, [1981] 1 WLR 184. Although immunity for defamatory statements extends to a malicious informer, where malice is established there may be a claim for the different tort of malicious prosecution. The different torts protect different public interests—the wider administration of justice in the case of the making of defamatory statements and the narrower need to prevent abuse of the process of the court in the case of malicious prosecution: *Martin v Watson* [1996] AC 74, [1995] 3 All ER 559.

## Newspapers, Printers, and Reading Rooms Repeal Act 1869

(1869 c 24)

[12th July 1869]

7.7029 1. **Continuance of Acts in second schedule** . . .The provisions of the . . . Acts which are set out in the second schedule to this Act shall continue in force in the same manner as if they were enacted in the body of this Act; . . .

[Newspapers, Printers, and Reading Rooms Repeal Act 1869, s 1.]

7.7030 2. **Short title** This Act may be cited as "The Newspapers, Printers, and Reading Rooms Repeal Act 1869."

[Newspapers, Printers, and Reading Rooms Repeal Act 1869, s 2.]

**7.7030A**

SCHEDULE 1 Section 1

7.7031 . . .

SCHEDULE 2 Section 1

The enactments in this Schedule, with the exception of section 19 of 6 & 7 Will 4 c 76, do not apply to Ireland

7.7032 39 Geo 3 c 79

Section twenty-eight

**Not to extend to papers printed by authority of Parliament** Nothing in this Act contained shall extend or be construed to extend to any papers printed by the authority and for the use of either House of Parliament.

Section twenty-nine

**Printers to keep a copy of every paper they print, and write thereon the name and abode of their employer. Penalty of £20 for neglect or refusing to produce the copy within six months** Every person who shall print any paper for hire, reward, gain, or profit, shall carefully preserve and keep one copy (at least) of every paper so printed by him or her, on which he or she shall write, or cause to be written or printed, in fair and legible characters, the name and place of abode of the person or persons by whom he or she shall be employed to print the same; and every person printing any paper for hire, reward, gain, or profit who shall omit or neglect to write, or cause to be written or printed as aforesaid, the name and place of his or her employer on one of such printed papers, or to keep or preserve the same for the space of six calendar months next after the printing thereof, or to produce and show the same to any justice of the peace who within the said space of six calendar months shall require to see the same, shall for every such omission, neglect, or refusal be liable on summary conviction to a fine of level 2 on the standard scale.

Section thirty-one

**Not to extend to impressions of engravings or the printing names and addresses** Nothing herein contained shall extend . . . to the printing . . . of the name, or the name and address, or business or profession, of any person, and the articles in which he deals, or to any papers for the sale of estates or goods by auction or otherwise.

Section thirty-four

**Prosecutions to be commenced within three months after penalty is incurred** No person shall be prosecuted . . . for any penalty imposed by this Act, unless such prosecution shall be commenced. . . within three calendar months next after such penalty shall have been incurred.

Part of section thirty-five

. . . Section thirty-six

. . . 51 Geo 3 c 65

Section three

**Name and residence of printers not required to be put to bank notes, bills, etc, or to any paper printed by authority of any public board or public office** Nothing in the Unlawful Societies Act 1799, or in this Act contained shall extend or be construed to extend to require the name and residence of the printer to be printed upon any bank note, . . . of the . . . Bank of England, upon any bill of exchange, or promissory note, or upon any bond or other security for payment of money, or upon any bill of lading, policy of insurance, letter of attorney, deed, or agreement, or upon any transfer or assignment of any public stocks, funds, or other securities, or upon any transfer or assignment of the stocks of any public corporation or company authorised or sanctioned by Act of Parliament, or upon any dividend warrant of or for any such public or other stocks, funds, or securities, or upon any receipt for money or goods, or upon any proceeding in any court of law or equity, or in any inferior court, warrant, order, or other papers printed by the authority of any public board or public officer in the execution of the duties of their respective offices, notwithstanding the whole or any part of the said several securities, instruments, proceedings, matters, and things aforesaid shall have been or shall be printed.

6 & 7 Will 4 c 76

Section nineteen

**Discovery of proprietors, printers, or publishers of newspapers may be enforced by bill, etc** If any person shall file any bill in any court for the discovery of the name of any person concerned as printer, publisher, or proprietor of any newspaper, or of any matters relative to the printing or publishing of any newspaper, in order the more effectually to bring or carry on any suit or action for damages alleged to have been sustained by reason of any slanderous or libellous matter contained in any such newspaper respecting such person, it shall not be lawful for the defendant to plead or demur to such bill, but such defendant shall be compellable to make the discovery required; provided always, that such discovery shall not be made use of as evidence or otherwise in any proceeding against the defendant, save only in that proceeding for which the discovery is made.

2 & 3 Vict c 12

Section two

**Penalty upon printers for not printing their name and residence on every paper or book, and on persons publishing the same** Every person who shall print any paper or book whatsoever which shall be meant to be published or dispersed, and who shall not print upon the front of every such paper, if the same shall be printed on one side only, or upon the first or last leaf of every paper or book which shall consist of more than one leaf, in legible characters, his or her name and usual place of abode or business, and every person who shall publish or disperse, or assist in publishing or dispersing, any printed paper or book on which the name and place of abode of the person printing the same shall not be printed as aforesaid, shall for every copy of such paper so printed by him or her be liable on summary conviction to a fine not exceeding level 1 on the standard scale: Provided always, that nothing herein contained shall be construed to impose any penalty upon any person for printing any paper excepted out of the operation of the Unlawful Societies Act 1799 either in the said Act or by any Act made for the amendment thereof.

Section three

**As to books or papers printed at the university presses** In the case of books or papers printed at the University Press of Oxford, or the Pitt Press of Cambridge, the printer, instead of printing his name thereon, shall print the following words, "Printed at the University Press, Oxford," or "The Pitt Press, Cambridge," as the case may be.

Section four

**No actions for penalties to be commenced except in the name of the Attorney or Solicitor General in England or the Queen's Advocate in Scotland**

Provided always, that it shall not be lawful for any person or persons whatsoever to commence, prosecute, enter, or file, or cause or procure to be commenced, prosecuted, entered, or filed, any action, bill, plaint, or information in any of Her Majesty's courts, or before any justice or justices of the peace, against any person or persons for the recovery of any fine, penalty, or forfeiture made or incurred or which may hereafter be incurred under the provisions of this Act, unless the same be commenced, prosecuted, entered, or filed in the name of Her Majesty's Attorney General . . . in . . . England, or Her Majesty's Advocate for Scotland (as the case may be respectively); and if any action, bill, plaint or information shall be commenced, prosecuted, or filed in the name or names of any other person or persons than is or are in that behalf before mentioned, the same and every proceeding thereupon had are hereby declared and the same shall be null and void to all intents and purposes. 9 & 10 Vict c 33

Section one

**Proceedings shall not be commenced unless in the name of the law officers of the Crown** It shall not be lawful for any person or persons to commence, prosecute, enter, or file, or cause or procure to be commenced, prosecuted, entered, or filed, any action, bill, plaint, or information in any of Her Majesty's courts, or before any justice or justices of the peace, against any person or persons for the recovery of any fine which may hereafter be incurred under the provisions of the Unlawful Societies Act 1799 set out in this Act, unless the same be commenced, prosecuted, entered, or filed in the name of Her Majesty's Attorney General . . . in England or Her Majesty's Advocate in Scotland, and every action, bill, plaint or information which shall be commenced, prosecuted, entered, or filed in the name or names of any other person or persons than is in that behalf before mentioned, and every proceeding thereupon had, shall be null and void to all intents and purposes.

## Judicial Proceedings (Regulation of Reports) Act 1926

(16 & 17 Geo 5 c 61)

7.7033 **1. Restriction on publication of reports of judicial proceedings** (1) It shall not be lawful to print or publish, or cause or procure to be printed or published—

(*a*) in relation to any judicial proceedings[1] any indecent matter or indecent medical, surgical or physiological details, being matter or details the publication of which would be calculated to injure public morals;

(*b*) in relation to any judicial proceedings for dissolution of marriage, for nullity of marriage, or for judicial separation[2], or for the dissolution or annulment of a civil partnership or for the separation of civil partners, any particulars other than the following, that is to say:

(i) the names, addresses and occupations of the parties and witnesses;

(ii) a concise statement of the charges, defences and countercharges in support of which evidence has been given;

(iii) submissions on any point of law arising in the course of the proceedings and the decision of the court thereon;

(iv) the summing up of the judge and the finding of the jury (if any) and the judgment of the court and observations made by the judge in giving judgment:

Provided that nothing in this part of this subsection shall be held to permit the publication of anything contrary to the provisions of paragraph (*a*) of this subsection.*

(2) If any person acts in contravention of the provisions of this Act, he shall in respect of each offence be liable, on summary conviction, to imprisonment for a term not exceeding **four months**** or to a fine not exceeding **level 5** on the standard scale, or to both such imprisonment and fine: Provided that no person, other than a proprietor, editor, master printer or publisher, shall be liable to be convicted under this Act.

(3) No prosecution to be commenced without the Attorney-General's sanction.

(4) Nothing in this section shall apply to the printing of any pleading, transcript of evidence or other document for use in connection with any judicial proceedings or the communication thereof to persons concerned in the proceedings, or to the printing or publishing of any notice or report in pursuance of the directions of the court; or to the printing or publishing of any matter in any separate volume or part of any bona fide series of law reports which does not form part of any other publication and consists solely of reports of proceedings in courts of law, or in any publication of a technical character bona fide intended for circulation among members of the legal or medical professions.

(5) *Repealed*.

[Judicial Proceedings (Regulation of Reports) Act 1926, s 1 as amended by the Criminal Justice Act 1982, ss 38 and 46 and the Civil Partnership Act 2004, Sch 27.]

---

* **Amended by the Family Law Act 1996, Sch 8 from a date to be appointed.**

** **Words substituted by the Criminal Justice Act 2003, Sch 26 from a date to be appointed.**

1 Not defined by this Act. Cf Perjury Act 1911, s 1(2), post.

2 For newspaper reports of domestic proceedings, see the Magistrates' Courts Act 1980, s 71 in PART I: MAGISTRATES' COURTS, PROCEDURE, ante.

7.7034 **Minors and Youth Courts** Prohibition against publication of certain matter in newspapers. See Children and Young Persons Act 1933, ss 39, 49 in PART V: YOUTH COURTS.

## Defamation Act 1996[1]

(1996 c 31)

*Statutory privilege*

7.7036 **14. Reports of court proceedings absolutely privileged** (1) A fair and accurate report of proceedings in public before a court to which this section applies, if published contemporaneously with the proceedings, is absolutely privileged.

(2) A report of proceedings which by an order of the court, or as a consequence of any statutory provision, is required to be postponed shall be treated as published contemporaneously if it is published as soon as practicable after publication is permitted.

(3) This section applies to—

(*a*) any court in the United Kingdom,

(*b*) any court established under the law of a country or territory outside the United Kingdom;

(*c*) any international court or tribunal established by the Security Council of the United Nations or by an international agreement;

and in paragraphs (*a*) and (*b*) "court" includes any tribunal or body exercising the judicial power of the State.

[Defamation Act 1996, s 14 as amended by the Defamation Act 2013, s 7.]

---

1 The Defamation Act 1996 amends the law of defamation and amends the law of limitation with respect to actions for defamation or malicious falsehood. Only those provisions of the Act which are relevant to the work of magistrates' courts are included in this manual.

7.7037 **15. Reports, etc. protected by qualified privilege.** (1) The publication of any report or other statement mentioned in Schedule 1 to this Act is privileged unless the publication is shown to be made with malice, subject as follows.

(2) In defamation proceedings in respect of the publication of a report or other statement mentioned in Part II of that Schedule, there is no defence under this section if the plaintiff shows that the defendant—

(*a*) was requested by him to publish in a suitable manner a reasonable letter or statement by way of explanation or contradiction, and

(*b*) refused or neglected to do so.

For this purpose "in a suitable manner" means in the same manner as the publication complained of or in a manner that is adequate and reasonable in the circumstances.

(3) This section does not apply to the publication to the public, or a section of the public, of matter which is not of public interest and the publication of which is not for the public benefit.

(4) Nothing in this section shall be construed—

(*a*) as protecting the publication of matter the publication of which is prohibited by law, or

(*b*) as limiting or abridging any privilege subsisting apart from this section.

[Defamation Act 1996, s 15 as amended by the Defamation Act 2013, s 7.]

*Supplementary provisions*

7.7038 **17. Interpretation** (1) In this Act—

"publication" and "publish", in relation to a statement, have the meaning they have for the purposes of the law of defamation generally, but "publisher" is specially defined for the purposes of section 1;

"statement" means words, pictures, visual images, gestures or any other method of signifying meaning; and

"statutory provision" means—

(*a*) a provision contained in an Act or in subordinate legislation within the meaning of the Interpretation Act 1978, or

(*aa*) a provision contained in an Act of the Scottish Parliament or in an instrument made under such an Act, or

(*b*) a statutory provision within the meaning given by section 1 (*f*) of the Interpretation Act (Northern Ireland) 1954.

(2) In this Act as it applies to proceedings in Scotland—

"costs" means expenses; and

"plaintiff" and "defendant" mean pursuer and defender.

[Defamation Act 1996, s 17 as amended by the Scotland Act 1998, Sch 8.]

*General provisions*

7.7039 **20. Short title and saving** (1) This Act may be cited as the Defamation Act 1996.

(2) *Repealed.*

[Defamation Act 1996, s 20 as amended by the Coroners and Justice Act 2009, Sch 23.]

## SCHEDULES

### SCHEDULE 1
QUALIFIED PRIVILEGE — Section 15

*(Amended by the Scotland Act 1998, Sch 8, SI 2001/2237, SI 2002/808 and 1057, the Government of Wales Act 2006, Sch 10, SI 2009/1941 and the Defamation Act 2013, s 7.)*

#### PART I
STATEMENTS HAVING QUALIFIED PRIVILEGE WITHOUT EXPLANATION OR CONTRADICTION

7.7040 **1.** A fair and accurate report of proceedings in public of a legislature anywhere in the world.

**2.** A fair and accurate report of proceedings in public before a court anywhere in the world.

**3.** A fair and accurate report of proceedings in public of a person appointed to hold a public inquiry by a government or legislature anywhere in the world.

**4.** A fair and accurate report of proceedings in public anywhere in the world of an international organisation or an international conference.

**5.** A fair and accurate copy of or extract from any register or other document required by law to be open to public inspection.

**6.** A notice or advertisement published by or on the authority of a court, or of a judge or officer of a court, anywhere in the world.

**7.** A fair and accurate copy of or extract from matter published by or on the authority of a government or legislature anywhere in the world.

**8.** A fair and accurate copy of or extract from matter published anywhere in the world by an international organisation or an international conference.

#### PART II
STATEMENTS PRIVILEGED SUBJECT TO EXPLANATION OR CONTRADICTION

**9.** (1) A fair and accurate copy of, extract from or summary of a notice or other matter issued for the information of the public by or on behalf of—

(*a*) a legislature or government anywhere in the world;

(*b*) an authority anywhere in the world performing governmental functions;

(*c*) an international organisation or international conference.

(2) In this paragraph "governmental functions" includes police functions.

**10.** A fair and accurate copy of, extract from or summary of a document made available by a court anywhere in the world, or by a judge or officer of such a court.

**11.** (1) A fair and accurate report of proceedings at any public meeting or sitting in the United Kingdom of—

(*a*) a local authority or local authority committee;

(*aa*) in the case of a local authority which are operating executive arrangements, the executive of that authority or a committee of that executive;

(*b*) a justice or justices of the peace acting otherwise than as a court exercising judicial authority;

(*c*) a commission, tribunal, committee or person appointed for the purposes of any inquiry by any statutory provision, by Her Majesty or by a Minister of the Crown a member of the Scottish Executive, the Welsh Ministers or the Counsel General to the Welsh Assembly Government or a Northern Ireland Department;

(*d*) a person appointed by a local authority to hold a local inquiry in pursuance of any statutory provision;

(*e*) any other tribunal, board, committee or body constituted by or under, and exercising functions under, any statutory provision.

(1A) In the case of a local authority which are operating executive arrangements, a fair and accurate record of any decision made by any member of the executive where that record is required to be made and available for public inspection by virtue of section 22 of the Local Government Act 2000 or of any provision in regulations made under that section.

(2) In sub-paragraphs (1)(*a*), (1)(*aa*) and (1A)—

"local authority" means—

(*a*) in relation to England and Wales, a principal council within the meaning of the Local Government Act 1972, any body falling within any paragraph of section 100J(1) of that Act or an authority or body to which the Public Bodies (Admission to Meetings) Act 1960 applies,

(*b*) in relation to Scotland, a council constituted under section 2 of the Local Government etc. (Scotland) Act 1994 or an authority or body to which the Public Bodies (Admission to Meetings) Act 1960 applies,

(*c*) in relation to Northern Ireland, any authority or body to which sections 23 to 27 of the Local Government Act (Northern Ireland) 1972 apply; and

"local authority committee" means any committee of a local authority or of local authorities, and includes—

(*a*) any committee or sub-committee in relation to which sections 100A to 100D of the Local Government Act 1972 apply by virtue of section 100E of that Act (whether or not also by virtue of section 100J of that Act), and

(*b*) any committee or sub-committee in relation to which sections 50A to 50D of the Local Government (Scotland) Act 1973 apply by virtue of section 50E of that Act.

(2A) In sub-paragraphs (1) and (1A)—

"executive" and "executive arrangements" have the same meaning as in Part II of the Local Government Act 2000.

(3) A fair and accurate report of any corresponding proceedings in any of the Channel Islands or the Isle of Man or in another member State.

**11A.** A fair and accurate report of proceedings at a press conference held anywhere in the world for the discussion of a matter of public interest.]

**12.** (1) A fair and accurate report of proceedings at any public meeting held anywhere in the world.

(2) In this paragraph a "public meeting" means a meeting bona fide and lawfully held for a lawful purpose and for the furtherance or discussion of a matter of public interest, whether admission to the meeting is general or restricted.

**13.** (1) A fair and accurate report of proceedings at a general meeting of a listed company.

(2) A fair and accurate copy of, extract from or summary of any document circulated to members of a listed company—

(*a*) by or with the authority of the board of directors of the company,

(*b*) by the auditors of the company, or

(*c*) by any member of the company in pursuance of a right conferred by any statutory provision.

(3) A fair and accurate copy of, extract from or summary of any document circulated to members of a listed company which relates to the appointment, resignation, retirement or dismissal of directors of the company or its auditors.

(4) In this paragraph "listed company" has the same meaning as in Part 12 of the Corporation Tax Act 2009 (see section 1005 of that Act).

**14.** A fair and accurate report of any finding or decision of any of the following descriptions of association, formed anywhere in the world, or of any committee or governing body of such an association—

(*a*) an association formed for the purpose of promoting or encouraging the exercise of or interest in any art, science, religion or learning, and empowered by its constitution to exercise control over or adjudicate on matters of interest or concern to the association, or the actions or conduct of any person subject to such control or adjudication;

(*b*) an association formed for the purpose of promoting or safeguarding the interests of any trade, business, industry or profession, or of the persons carrying on or engaged in any trade, business, industry or profession, and empowered by its constitution to exercise control over or adjudicate upon matters connected with that trade, business, industry or profession, or the actions or conduct of those persons;

(*c*) an association formed for the purpose of promoting or safeguarding the interests of a game, sport or pastime to the playing or exercise of which members of the public are invited or admitted, and empowered by its constitution to exercise control over or adjudicate upon persons connected with or taking part in the game, sport or pastime;

(*d*) an association formed for the purpose of promoting charitable objects or other objects beneficial to the community and empowered by its constitution to exercise control over or to adjudicate on matters of interest or concern to the association, or the actions or conduct of any person subject to such control or adjudication.

**14A.** A fair and accurate—

(*a*) report of proceedings of a scientific or academic conference held anywhere in the world, or

(*b*) copy of, extract from or summary of matter published by such a conference.

**15.** (1) A fair and accurate report or summary of, copy of or extract from, any adjudication, report, statement or notice issued by a body, officer or other person designated for the purposes of this paragraph by order of the Lord Chancellor.

(2) An order under this paragraph shall be made by statutory instrument which shall be subject to annulment in pursuance of a resolution of either House of Parliament.

## Part III
## Supplementary Provisions

**16.** (1) In this Schedule—

"court" includes—

(*a*) any tribunal or body established under the law of any country or territory exercising the judicial power of the State;

(*b*) any international tribunal established by the Security Council of the United Nations or by an international agreement;

(*c*) any international tribunal deciding matters in dispute between States;

"international conference" means a conference attended by representatives of two or more governments;

"international organisation" means an organisation of which two or more governments are members, and includes any committee or other subordinate body of such an organisation;

"legislature" includes a local legislature; and

"member State" includes any European dependent territory of a member State.

# LOCAL GOVERNMENT

**Contents**



## Fixed penalties issued by local authorities

**7.7043** The Environmental Offences (Fixed Penalties) (Miscellaneous Provisions) Regulations 2007, SI 2007/175 amended by SI 2012/1151 fix the range within which local authorities may set fixed penalties under various statutory provisions including discounts for early payment. Provision is also made for destination of receipts to the benefit of authorities performing at the level of "excellent" or "good" or "4 stars", "3 stars" and "2 stars".

## Local Government Act 1972

(1972 c 70)

### Part I

### Local Government Areas and Authorities in England

**7.7044 1. Local government areas in England** With the exception of Greater London[1] and the Isles of Scilly, England is divided into local government areas to be known as counties and in those counties there shall be local government areas known as districts[2]. The counties are either metropolitan counties or non-metropolitan counties.

[Local Government Act 1972, s 1—summarised.]

1 There shall be a council for every London borough (Sch 2).

2 The districts in metropolitan counties are to be known as "metropolitan districts" (Sch 2). Districts in non-metropolitan countries are to be established under Sch 3; and "non-metropolitan district" means any district other than a metropolitan district (s 270(2)).

**7.7045 2. Councils** There shall be a council for each non-metropolitan county and district: the "County Council" and "District Council" respectively.

[Local Government Act 1972, s 2, amended by the Local Government Act 1985, Sch 16 and the Local Government Act 2000, Sch 3—summarised.]

### Part II

### Local Government Areas and Authorities in Wales

**7.7046 20. Local Government areas in Wales** With effect from 1st April 1996 Wales is divided into local government areas to be known as counties and county boroughs ("principal areas") and communities[1].

[Local Government Act 1972, s 20 as substituted by the Local Government (Wales) Act 1994, s 1—summarised.]

1 References in pre-existing legislation to councils or areas of a county or district are to be construed as references to the principal areas (Local Government (Wales) Act 1994, s 17. Other transitional provisions are made by Pt VI of the Act.)

**7.7047 21. Councils in Wales** There shall be a council for every county and county borough.

[Local Government Act 1972, s 21 amended by the Local Government (Wales) Act 1994, s 2 and the Local Government Act 2000, Sch 3—summarised.]

**7.7048 27–35.** *Community Councils.*

PART V

7.7049 **92. Proceedings for disqualification** (1) Proceedings against any person on the ground that he acted or claims to be entitled to act as a member of a local authority while disqualified[1] for so acting within the meaning of this section may be instituted by, and only by, any local government elector for the area concerned—

(*a*) in the High Court or a magistrates' court if that person so acted;
(*b*) in the High Court if that person claims to be entitled so to act;

but proceedings under paragraph (*a*) above shall not be instituted against any person after the expiration of more than six months from the date on which he so acted.

(2) Where in proceedings instituted under this section it is proved that the defendant has acted as a member of a local authority while disqualified for so acting, then—

(*a*) if the proceedings are in the High Court, the High Court may—
(i) make a declaration to that effect and declare that the office in which the defendant has acted is vacant;
(ii) grant an injunction restraining the defendant from so acting;
(iii) order that the defendant shall forfeit to Her Majesty such sum as the court think fit, not exceeding **£50** for each occasion on which he so acted while disqualified;
(*b*) if the proceedings are in a magistrates' court, the magistrates' court may, subject to the provisions of this section, convict the defendant and impose on him a fine not exceeding **level 3** on the standard scale for each occasion on which he so acted while disqualified.

(3) Where proceedings under this section are instituted in a magistrates' court, then—

(*a*) if the court is satisfied that the matter would be more properly dealt with in the High Court, it shall by order discontinue the proceedings;
(*b*) if the High Court, on application made to it by the defendant within fourteen days after service of the summons, is satisfied that the matter would be more properly dealt with in the High Court, it may make an order, which shall not be subject to any appeal, requiring the magistrates' court by order to discontinue the proceedings.

(4) Where in proceedings instituted under this section in the High Court it is proved that the defendant claims to act as a member of a local authority and is disqualified for so acting, the court may make a declaration to that effect and declare that the office in which the defendant claims to be entitled to act is vacant and grant an injunction restraining him from so acting.

(5) No proceedings shall be instituted against a person otherwise than under this section on the ground that he has, while disqualified for acting as a member of a local authority, so acted or claimed to be entitled so to act.

(6) For the purposes of this section a person shall be deemed to be disqualified for acting as a member of a local authority—

(*a*) if he is not qualified to be, or is disqualified for being, a member of the authority; or
(*b*) if by reason of failure to make and deliver the declaration of acceptance of office within the period required, or by reason of resignation or failure to attend meetings of the local authority, he has ceased to be a member of the authority.

(7) In this section "local authority" includes a joint authority, an economic prosperity board and a combined authority; and in relation to a joint authority, an economic prosperity board and a combined authority the reference in subsection (1) above to a local government elector for the area concerned shall be construed as a reference to a local government elector for any local government area in the area for which the authority is established.

(7A) *Repealed.*

(7B) *Repealed.*

(8) In relation to the Broads Authority, the reference in subsection (1) above to a local government elector for the area concerned shall be construed as a reference to a local government elector for the area of any of the local authorities mentioned in section 1(3)(*a*) of the Norfolk and Suffolk Broads Act 1988.

[Local Government Act 1972, s 92 as amended by the Criminal Justice Act 1982, ss 38 and 46, the Local Government Act 1985, Sch 14, the Norfolk and Suffolk Broads Act 1988, Sch 6. the Education Reform Act 1988, Sch 13, the Local Government and Public Involvement in Health Act 2007, Sch 13, the Local Democracy, Economic Development and Construction Act 2009, Sch 6 and the Deregulation Act 2015, Sch 13.]

1 See ss 79 and 80 for provisions as to qualification and disqualification; and see *Bishop v Deakin* [1936] Ch 409, [1936] 1 All ER 255, 100 JP 201, as to time within which proceedings must be commenced.

7.7050 **94. Disability of members of authorities for voting on account of interest in contracts, etc** (1) Subject to the provisions of section 97[1] below, if a member of a local authority has any pecuniary interest[2], direct or indirect, in any contract, proposed contract or other matter, and is present at a meeting of the local authority at which the contract or other matter is the subject of consideration, he shall at the meeting and as soon as practicable after its commencement disclose[3] the fact and shall not take part in the consideration or discussion of the contract or other matter or vote on any question with respect to it.

(2) If any person fails to comply with the provisions of subsection (1) above he shall for each offence be liable on summary conviction to a fine not exceeding **level 4** on the standard scale unless he proves that he did not know that the contract, proposed contract or other matter in which he had

a pecuniary interest was the subject of consideration at that meeting.

(3) A prosecution for an offence under this section shall not be instituted except by or on behalf of the Director of Public Prosecutions.

(4) A local authority may by standing orders provide for the exclusion of a member of the authority from a meeting of the authority while any contract, proposed contract or other matter in which he has a pecuniary interest, direct or indirect, is under consideration.

(5) The following, that is to say—

(*a*) the receipt by the chairman, vice-chairman or deputy chairman of a principal council of an allowance to meet the expenses of his office or his right to receive, or the possibility of his receiving, such an allowance;

(*b*) the receipt by a member of a local authority of an allowance or other payment under any provision of sections 173 to 176 below or under any scheme made by virtue of section 18 of the Local Government and Housing Act 1989 or paragraph 25 of Schedule 2 to the Police Act or his right to receive, or the possibility of his receiving, any such payment;

shall not be treated as a pecuniary interest for the purposes of this section.*

[Local Government Act 1972, s 94 as amended by the Criminal Justice Act 1982, ss 38 and 46, the Local Government and Housing Act 1989, Sch 11, the Police and Magistrates' Courts Act 1994, Sch 4, the Police Act 1996, Sch 7, the Police Act 1997, Sch 6 and the Criminal Justice and Police Act 2001, Sch 7.]

---

* **Repealed by the Local Government Act 2000, Schs 5 and 6 from a date to be appointed.**

1 Section 97, which is not quoted in this work, contains provisions for the removal or exclusion of a disability.

2 See s 95, not quoted in this work, for provisions as to pecuniary interests. See also s 94(5): specified allowances not to be treated as a pecuniary interest. Where a pecuniary interest exists, the disability extends to a vote which is disadvantageous to that interest (*Brown v DPP* [1956] 2 QB 369, [1956] 2 All ER 189, 120 JP 303; *Rands v Oldroyd* [1959] 1 QB 204, [1958] 3 All ER 344, 123 JP 1). For the precise application of exemptions see *Readman v Payne* (1991) 155 JP 884, DC.

3 See s 96, not quoted in this work, containing provisions as to general notice of disclosure.

## PART VA[1]

## ACCESS TO MEETINGS AND DOCUMENTS OF CERTAIN AUTHORITIES, COMMITTEES AND SUB-COMMITTEES

7.7051 **100A. Admission to meetings of principal councils** (1) A meeting of a principal council[2] shall be open to the public except to the extent that they are excluded (whether during the whole or part of the proceedings) under subsection (2) below or by resolution under subsection (4) below.

(2) Public shall be excluded from a meeting of a principal council during an item of business whenever it is likely confidential information would be disclosed in breach of the obligation of confidence; and nothing in this Part shall be taken to authorise or require the disclosure of confidential information in breach of the obligation of confidence (*summarised*).

(3)–(8) *Supplementary provisions as to admission of the public.*

[Local Government Act 1972, s 100A, as inserted by the Local Government (Access to Information) Act 1985, s 1 and amended by SI 2002/715.]

---

1 Part VA contains ss 100A–100K, and was inserted by the Local Government (Access to Information) Act 1985, s 1. Sections 100A to 100D, 100H, 100I of and Sch 12A to this Act are applied, with modifications, to a "joint committee", being a joint consultative committee appointed pursuant to an order under s 22 of the National Health Service Act 1977, or a sub-committee of such a committee, or a joint sub-committee of 2 or more such committees (Health Service Joint Consultative Committees (Access to Information) Act 1986, ss 1 and 2). Sections 100A to 100D are also applied, with modifications, to a Community Health Council, established under s 20 of the National Health Service Act 1977, and the Committees of those Councils (Community Health Councils (Access to Information) Act 1988, ss 1 and 2).

2 For meaning of "principal council", see ss 100J and 270(1), post.

7.7052 **100B. Access to agenda and connected reports** (1) Copies of the agenda for a meeting of a principal council[1] and, subject to subsection (2) below, copies of any report for the meeting shall be open to inspection by members of the public at the offices of the council in accordance with subsection (3) below.

(2) If the proper officer thinks fit, there may be excluded from the copies of reports provided in pursuance of subsection (1) above the whole of any report which, or any part which, relates only to items during which, in his opinion, the meeting is likely not to be open to the public.

(3) Any document which is required by subsection (1) above to be open to inspection shall be so open at least five clear days before the meeting, except that—

(*a*) where the meeting is convened at shorter notice, the copies of the agenda and reports shall be open to inspection from the time the meeting is convened, and

(*b*) where an item is added to an agenda copies of which are open to inspection by the public, copies of the item (or of the revised agenda), and the copies of any report for the meeting relating to the item, shall be open to inspection from the time the item is added to the agenda;

but nothing in this subsection requires copies of any agenda, item or report to be open to inspection by the public until copies are available to members of the council.

(4) An item of business may not be considered at a meeting of a principal council unless either—

(*a*) a copy of the agenda including the item (or a copy of the item) is open to inspection by members of the public in pursuance of subsection (1) above for at least five clear days before the meeting or, where the meeting is convened at shorter notice, from the time the meeting is convened; or

(*b*) by reason of special circumstances, which shall be specified in the minutes, the chairman of the meeting is of the opinion that the item should be considered at the meeting as a matter of urgency.

(5) Where by virtue of subsection (2) above the whole or any part of a report for a meeting is not open to inspection by the public under subsection (1) above—

(*a*) every copy of the report or of the part shall be marked "Not for publication"; and

(*b*) there shall be stated on every copy of the whole or any part of the report the description, in terms of Schedule 12A to this Act, of the exempt information by virtue of which the council are likely to exclude the public during the item to which the report relates.

(6) Where a meeting of a principal council is required by section 100A above to be open to the public during the proceedings or any part of them, there shall be made available for the use of members of the public present at the meeting a reasonable number of copies of the agenda and, subject to subsection (8) below, of the reports for the meeting.

(7) There shall, on request and on payment of postage or other necessary charge for transmission, be supplied for the benefit of any newspaper—

(*a*) a copy of the agenda for a meeting of a principal council and, subject to subsection (8) below, a copy of each of the reports for the meeting;

(*b*) such further statements or particulars, if any, as are necessary to indicate the nature of the items included in the agenda; and

(*c*) if the proper officer thinks fit in the case of any item, copies of any other documents supplied to members of the council in connection with the item.

(8) Subsection (2) above applies in relation to copies of reports provided in pursuance of subsection (6) or (7) above as it applies in relation to copies of reports provided in pursuance of subsection (1) above.

[Local Government Act 1972, s 100B as inserted by the Local Government (Access to Information) Act 1985, s 1 and amended by SI 2002/715.]

[1] For meaning of "principal council", see ss 100J and 270(1), post.

7.7053 **100C. Inspection of minutes and other documents after meetings** (1) After a meeting of a principal council[1] the following documents shall be open to inspection by members of the public at the offices of the council until the expiration of the period of six years beginning with the date of the meeting, namely—

(*a*) the minutes, or a copy of the minutes, of the meeting, excluding so much of the minutes of proceedings during which the meeting was not open to the public as discloses exempt information;

(*b*) where applicable, a summary under subsection (2) below;

(*c*) a copy of the agenda for the meeting; and

(*d*) a copy of so much of any report for the meeting as relates to any item during which the meeting was open to the public.

(2) Where, in consequence of the exclusion of parts of the minutes which disclose exempt information, the document open to inspection under subsection (1)(*a*) above does not provide members of the public with a reasonably fair and coherent record of the whole or part of the proceedings, the proper officer shall make a written summary of the proceedings or the part, as the case may be, which provides such a record without disclosing the exempt information.

[Local Government Act 1972, s 100C as inserted by the Local Government (Access to Information) Act 1985, s 1.]

[1] For meaning of "principal council", see ss 100J and 270(1), post.

7.7054 **100D. Inspection of background papers** (1) Subject, in the case of section 100C(1), to subsection (2) below, if and so long as copies of the whole or part of a report for a meeting of a principal council are required by section 100B(1) or 100C(1) above to be open to inspection by members of the public—

(*a*) those copies shall each include a copy of a list, compiled by the proper officer, of the background papers for the report or the part of the report, and

(*b*) at least one copy of each of the documents included in that list shall also be open to inspection at the offices of the council.

(2) Subsection (1) above does not require a copy of any document included in the list, to be open to inspection after the expiration of the period of four years beginning with the date of the meeting.

(3) Where a copy of any of the background papers for a report is required by subsection (1) above to be open to inspection by members of the public, the copy shall be taken for the purposes of this Part to be so open if arrangements exist for its production to members of the public as soon as is reasonably practicable after the making of a request to inspect the copy.

(4) Nothing in this section—

(*a*) requires any document which discloses exempt information to be included in the list referred to in subsection (1) above; or (*b*) without prejudice to the generality of subsection (2) of section 100A above, requires or authorises the inclusion in the list of any document which, if open to inspection by the public, would disclose confidential information in breach of the obligation of confidence, within the meaning of that subsection.

(5) For the purposes of this section the background papers for a report are those documents relating to the subject matter of the report which—

(*a*) disclose any facts or matters on which, in the opinion of the proper officer, the report or an important part of the report is based, and

(*b*) have, in his opinion, been relied on to a material extent in preparing the report,

but do not include any published works.

[Local Government Act 1972, s 100D as inserted by the Local Government (Access to Information) Act 1985, s 1 and amended by the Local Government Act 2000, s 97 and Sch 6.]

7.7055 **100E. Application to committees and sub-committees** (1) Sections 100A to 100D above shall apply in relation to a committee or sub-committee of a principal council as they apply in relation to a principal council.

(2) In the application by virtue of this section of sections 100A to 100D above in relation to a committee or sub-committee—

(*a*) section 100A(6)(*a*) shall be taken to have been complied with if the notice is given by posting it at the time there mentioned at the offices of every constituent principal council and, if the meeting of the committee or sub-committee to which that section so applies is to be held at premises other than the offices of such a council, at those premises;

(*b*) for the purposes of section 100A(6)(*c*), premises belonging to a constituent principal council shall be treated as belonging to the committee or sub-committee; and

(*c*) for the purposes of sections 100B(1), 100C(1) and 100D(1), offices of any constituent principal council shall be treated as offices of the committee or sub-committee.

(3) Any reference in this Part to a committee or sub-committee of a principal council is a reference to—

(*a*) a committee which is constituted under an enactment specified in section 101(9) below or which is appointed by one or more principal councils under section 102 below; or

(*b*) a joint committee not falling within paragraph (*a*) above which is appointed or established under any enactment by two or more principal councils and is not a body corporate; or

(*bba*) a committee in place by virtue of section 107D(3)(*c*)(ii) of the Local Democracy, Economic Development and Construction Act 2009;

(*bbb*) a joint committee in place by virtue of section 107E of that Act;

(*bb*) the Navigation Committee of the Broads Authority; or

(*c*) a sub-committee appointed or established under any enactment by one or more committees falling within paragraphs (*a*) to (*bb*) above.

(4) Any reference in this Part to a constituent principal council, in relation to a committee or sub-committee, is a reference—

(*a*) in the case of a committee, to the principal council, or any of the principal councils, of which it is a committee; and

(*b*) in the case of a sub-committee, to any principal council which, by virtue of paragraph (*a*) above, is a constituent principal council in relation to the committee, or any of the committees, which established or appointed the sub-committee.

[Local Government Act 1972, s 100E as inserted by the Local Government (Access to Information) Act 1985, s 1 and amended by the Norfolk and Suffolk Broads Act 1988, Sch 6 and the Cities and Local Government Devolution Act 2016, Sch 5.]

7.7056 **100EA. Inspection of records relating to functions exercisable by members** (1) The Secretary of State may by regulations[1] make provision for written records of decisions made or action taken by a member of a local authority, in exercise of a function of the authority by virtue of arrangements made under section 236 of the Local Government and Public Involvement in Health Act 2007, to be made and provided to the authority by the member.

(2) Any written record provided to the authority under regulations under subsection (1) shall be open to inspection by members of the public at the offices of the authority for the period of six years beginning with the date on which the decision was made or action was taken.

(3) A statutory instrument containing regulations under subsection (1) shall be subject to annulment in pursuance of a resolution of either House of Parliament.

[Local Government Act 1972, s 100EA as inserted by the Local Government and Public Involvement in Health Act 2007, s 237.]

---

[1] The Exercise of Functions by Local Councillors (Written Records) Regulations 2009, SI 2009/352 have been made.

7.7057 **100F–100G.** *Additional rights[1] of access to documents for members of principal councils; principal councils to publish additional information.*

---

[1] See also the Local Government (Inspection of Documents) (Summary of Rights) Order 1986, SI 1986/854, which specifies for these purposes additional enactments which confer rights to attend meetings and to inspect, copy and be furnished with documents.

7.7058 **100H. Supplemental provisions and offences** (1) A document directed by any provision of this Part to be open to inspection shall be so open at all reasonable hours and—

(*a*) in the case of a document open to inspection by virtue of section 100D(1) above, upon payment of such reasonable fee as may be required for the facility; and

(*b*) in any other case, without payment.

(2) Where a document is open to inspection by a person under any provision of this Part, the person may, subject to subsection (3) below—

(*a*) make copies of or extracts from the document, or

(*b*) require the person having custody of the document to supply to him a photographic copy of or of extracts from the document,

upon payment of such reasonable fee as may be required for the facility.

(3) Subsection (2) above does not require or authorise the doing of any act which infringes the copyright in any work except that, where the owner of the copyright is a principal council, nothing done in pursuance of that subsection shall constitute an infringement of the copyright.

(4) If, without reasonable excuse, a person having the custody of a document which is required by section 100B(1), 100C(1) or 100EA(2) above to be open to inspection by the public—

(*a*) intentionally obstructs any person exercising a right conferred by this Part to inspect, or to make a copy of or extracts from the document, or

(*b*) refuses to furnish copies to any person entitled to obtain them under any provision of this Part,

he shall be liable on summary conviction to a fine not exceeding **level 1** on the standard scale.

(5) Where any accessible document for a meeting to which this subsection applies—

(*a*) is supplied to, or open to inspection by, a member of the public, or

(*b*) is supplied for the benefit of any newspaper, in pursuance of section 100B(7) above,

the publication thereby of any defamatory matter contained in the document shall be privileged unless the publication is proved to be made with malice.

(6) Subsection (5) above applies to any meeting of a principal council and any meeting of a committee or sub-committee of a principal council; and, for the purposes of that subsection, the "accessible documents" for a meeting are the following—

(*a*) any copy of the agenda or of any item included in the agenda for the meeting;

(*b*) any such further statements or particulars for the purpose of indicating the nature of any item included in the agenda as are mentioned in section 100B(7)(*b*) above;

(*c*) any copy of a document relating to such an item which is supplied for the benefit of a newspaper in pursuance of section 100B(7)(*c*) above;

(*d*) any copy of the whole or part of a report for the meeting;

(*e*) any copy of the whole or part of any background papers for a report for the meeting, within the meaning of section 100D above.

(7) The rights conferred by this Part to inspect, copy and be furnished with documents are in addition, and without prejudice, to any such rights conferred by or under any other enactment.

[Local Government Act 1972, s 100H as inserted by the Local Government (Access to Information) Act 1985, s 1 and amended by the Local Government and Public Involvement in Health Act 2007, s 237.]

7.7059 **100I. Exempt information and power to vary Schedule 12A** (1) In relation to principal councils in England, the descriptions of information which are, for the purposes of this Part, exempt information are those for the time being specified in Part I of Schedule 12A to this Act, but subject to any qualifications contained in Part II of that Schedule; and Part III has effect for the interpretation of Parts 1 to 3 of that Schedule.

(1A) In relation to principal councils in Wales, the descriptions of information which are, for the purposes of this Part, exempt information are those for the time being specified in Part 4 of Schedule 12A to this Act, but subject to any qualifications contained in Part 5 of that Schedule; and Part 6 has effect for the interpretation of Parts 4 to 6 of that Schedule.

(2) The appropriate person may by order vary Schedule 12A to this Act by adding to it any description or other provision or by deleting from it or varying any description or other provision for the time being specified or contained in it.

(3) The appropriate person may exercise the power conferred by subsection (2) above by amending any Part of Schedule 12A to this Act, with or without amendment of any other Part.

(3A) In this section "the appropriate person" means—

(*a*) in relation to England, the Secretary of State;

(*b*) in relation to Wales, the National Assembly for Wales.

(4) Any statutory instrument containing an order under this section made by the Secretary of State shall be subject to annulment in pursuance of a resolution of either House of Parliament.

[Local Government Act 1972, s 100I as inserted by the Local Government (Access to Information) Act 1985, s 1 and amended by SI 2006/88.]

7.7060 **100J. Application to new authorities, Common Council, etc** (1) Except in this section, any reference in this Part to a principal council[1] includes a reference to—

(*a*) *repealed*;

(*b*) a joint authority;

(*ba*) *repealed*;

(*bb*) the London Fire and Emergency Planning Authority;

(*bc*) an economic prosperity board;
(*bd*) a combined authority;
(*be*) Transport for London;
(*bf*) a sub-national transport body;
(*c*) the Common Council;
(*cc*) the Broads Authority;
(*cd*) a National Park authority;
(*d*) a joint board or joint committee falling within subsection (2) below;
(*e*) *repealed*
(*eza*) *repealed*
(*ea*) *repealed*
(*f*) a fire and rescue authority constituted by a scheme under section 2 of the Fire and Rescue Services Act 2004 or scheme to which section 4 of that Act applies.
(*g*) the Homes and Communities Agency so far as it is exercising functions conferred on it in relation to a designated area by virtue of a designation order.
(*h*) a Mayoral development corporation.

(2) A joint board or joint committee falls within this subsection if—
(*a*) it is constituted under any enactment as a body corporate; and
(*b*) it discharges functions of two or more principal councils;
and for the purposes of this subsection any body falling within paragraph (*a*), (*b*), (*bb*), (*bc*), (*bd*) or (*c*) of subsection (1) above shall be treated as a principal council.

(2A) In its application by virtue of subsection (1)(*g*) above in relation to the Homes and Communities Agency, a reference in this Part to the offices of the council (however expressed)—
(*a*) is to be treated as a reference to such premises located within the designated area as the Homes and Communities Agency considers appropriate, and
(*b*) in the application of section 100A(6)(*a*) above to a case where the meeting is to be held at premises other than those mentioned in paragraph (*a*) above, includes a reference to those other premises.

(2B) In section 100A, subsections (5A), (7A) to (7F) and (9) do not apply to—
(*a*) *repealed*
(*b*) the Common Council other than in its capacity as a local authority or police authority;
(*c*) a joint board or a joint committee falling within subsection (2) above;
(*d*) the Homes and Communities Agency; or
(*e*) a Mayoral development corporation.

(3) In its application by virtue of subsection (1) above in relation to a body falling within paragraph (*b*), (*bb*), (*be*),(*bf*), (*cc*), (*cd*), (*d*), (*f*) or (*h*) of that subsection, section 100A(6)(*a*) above shall have effect with the insertion after the word "council" of the words "(and, if the meeting is to be held at premises other than those offices, at those premises)".

(3ZA) In its application by virtue of subsection (1)(*g*) above in relation to the Homes and Communities Agency, section 100E above shall have effect as if—
(*a*) in subsection (2), paragraph (*c*) was omitted, and
(*b*) in subsection (3), for paragraphs (*a*) to (*c*) there were substituted—
"(*a*) a committee established under paragraph 6(1) of Schedule 1 to the Housing and Regeneration Act 2008 for the purpose of exercising functions conferred on the Homes and Communities Agency in relation to a designated area by virtue of a designation order; or
(*b*) a sub-committee of such a committee established under paragraph 6(2) of that Schedule to that Act for that purpose".

(3ZAA) In its application by virtue of subsection (1)(*h*) above in relation to a Mayoral development corporation, section 100E(3) has effect as if for paragraphs (*a*) to (*c*) there were substituted—
"(*a*) a committee which is established under Schedule 21 to the Localism Act 2011 by a principal council, or
(*b*) a sub-committee established under that Schedule by a committee within paragraph (*a*).

(3ZB) In its application by virtue of subsection (1)(*g*) above in relation to the Homes and Communities Agency, section 100G(1) above shall have effect as if paragraph (*a*) was omitted.]

(3A) *Repealed.*

(4) In its application by virtue of subsection (1) above, section 100G(1)(*a*) above shall have effect—
(*a*) in relation to a joint authority, a sub-national transport body, an economic prosperity board or a combined authority, with the substitution for the words after "together with" of the words "the name or description of the body or other person that appointed him"; and
(*aa*) in relation to the Broads Authority or its Navigation Committee or any National Park authority, with the substitution for the words after "together with" of the words "the name of the person who appointed him"; and

(*b*) in relation to a Mayoral development corporation, or a joint board or joint committee falling within subsection (2) above, with the omission of the words after "for the time being"; and

(*c*) in relation to a fire and rescue authority falling within subsection (1)(*f*) above, with the substitution for the words ", in the case of a councillor, the ward or division" of the words "the constituent area".

(4A) In its application by virtue of subsection (1)(*bb*) above in relation to the London Fire and Emergency Planning Authority, section 100G(1)(*a*) shall have effect with the substitution for the words "together with, in the case of a councillor, the ward or division which he represents" of the words "and whether he is an Assembly representative or a borough representative, and—

(i) if he is an Assembly representative, whether he is a London member or a constituency member and, if a constituency member, the Assembly constituency for which he is a member; or

(ii) if he is a borough representative, the council of which he is a member (whether a London borough council or the Common Council).

(4B) In this section "designated area" and "designation order" have the same meanings as in Part 1 of the Housing and Regeneration Act 2008.

(5) *Repealed.*

[Local Government Act 1972, s 100J as inserted by the Local Government (Access to Information) Act 1985, s 1 and amended by the Norfolk and Suffolk Broads Act 1988, Sch 6, the Education Reform Act 1988, Sch 13, the Police and Magistrates' Courts Act 1994, Sch 4, the Environment Act 1995, Sch 7, the Police Act 1996, Sch 7, the Police Act 1997, Sch 6, the Greater London Authority Act 1999, ss 313 and 331, the Criminal Justice and Police Act 2001, Schs 6 and 7, the Fire and Rescue Services Act 2004, Sch 1, the Local Government and Public Involvement in Health Act 2007, Sch 13, the Housing and Regeneration Act 2008, Sch 8, the Local Democracy, Economic Development and Construction Act 2009, Sch 6, the Police Reform and Social Responsibility Act 2011, Sch 16, the Localism Act 2011, Sch 22, SI 2014/2095, the Deregulation Act 2015, Sch 13 and the Cities and Local Government Devolution Act 2016, Sch 5.]

[1] For meaning of "principal council", see also s 270(1), post.

7.7061 **100K. Interpretation and application of Part VA** (1) In this Part—

"committee or sub-committee of a principal council" shall be construed in accordance with section 100E(3) above (and see section 100J(3ZA)(*b*) and (3ZAA) above);

"constituent principal council" shall be construed in accordance with section 100E(4) above;

"copy", in relation to any document, includes a copy made from a copy;

"exempt information" has the meaning given by section 100I above;

"information" includes an expression of opinion, any recommendations and any decision taken;

"newspaper" includes—

(*a*) a news agency which systematically carries on the business of selling and supplying reports or information to newspapers; and

(*b*) any organisation which is systematically engaged in collecting news—

(i) for sound or television broadcasts; or

(ii) for inclusion in programmes to be included in any programme service (within the meaning of the Broadcasting Act 1990) other than a sound or television broadcasting service;

"principal council" shall be construed in accordance with section 100J above.

(2) Any reference in this Part to a meeting is a reference to a meeting held after 1st April 1986.

(3) The Secretary of State may by order amend sections 100A(6)(*a*) and 100B(3) and (4)(*a*) above so as to substitute for each reference to three clear days such greater number of days as may be specified in the order.

(4) Any statutory instrument containing an order under subsection (3) above shall be subject to annulment in pursuance of a resolution of either House of Parliament.

[Local Government Act 1972, s 100K as inserted by the Local Government (Access to Information) Act 1985, s 1 and amended by the Broadcasting Act 1990, Sch 20, the Local Government Act 2000, s 98(1), the Housing and Regeneration Act 2008, Sch 8 and the Localism Act 2011, Sch 22.]

## PART VII

## MISCELLANEOUS POWERS OF LOCAL AUTHORITIES

7.7062 **117. Disclosure by officers of interest in contracts** (1) If it comes to the knowledge of an officer employed, whether under this Act or any other enactment, by a local authority that a contract in which he has any pecuniary interest, whether direct or indirect (not being a contract to which he is himself a party), has been, or is proposed to be, entered into by the authority or any committee thereof, he shall as soon as practicable give notice in writing to the authority of the fact that he is interested therein.

For the purposes of this section an officer shall be treated as having indirectly a pecuniary interest in a contract or proposed contract if he would have been so treated by virtue of section 95[1] above had he been a member of the authority.

(2) An officer of a local authority shall not, under colour of his office or employment, accept any fee or reward whatsoever other than his proper remuneration.

(3) Any person who contravenes the provisions of subsection (1) or (2) above shall be liable on

summary conviction to a fine not exceeding **level 4** on the standard scale.

(4) References in this section to a local authority shall include references to a joint committee appointed under Part VI of this Act or any other enactment.

[Local Government Act 1972, s 117 as amended by the Criminal Justice Act 1982, ss 38 and 46.]

1 Section 95 is not reproduced in this work.

## PART X

## JUDICIAL AND RELATED MATTERS

[See PART I: THE JUSTICES AND THE CLERK, ante.]

## PART XI

## GENERAL PROVISIONS AS TO LOCAL AUTHORITIES

*Legal proceedings*

7.7063 **222. Power of local authorities to prosecute or defend legal proceedings**

(1) Where a local authority consider[1] it expedient for the promotion or protection of the interests of the inhabitants of their area—

(*a*) they may prosecute or defend or appear in any legal proceedings and, in the case of civil proceedings, may institute[2] them in their own name, and

(*b*) they may, in their own name, make representations in the interests of the inhabitants at any public inquiry held by or on behalf of any Minister or public body under any enactment.

(2) In this section "local authority" includes the Common Council and the London Fire and Emergency Planning Authority.

[Local Government Act 1972, s 222 as amended by the Greater London Authority Act 1999, Sch 29.]

1 In certain circumstances a local authority may institute proceedings in its own name seeking an injunction in the civil courts as a means of preventing a breach of the criminal law (*Stoke-on-Trent City Council v B & Q (Retail) Ltd* [1984] AC 754, [1984] 2 All ER 332, HL). This is subject to any legislation specifically designed to deal with the situation for which an injunction is sought such as in relation to anti-social behaviour under the Crime and Disorder Act 1998. An injunction to restrain anti-social behaviour would only be granted in an exceptional case. In such a case the criminal standard of proof applies except where the relief sought is not identical or almost identical to an ASBO where, subject to argument in a particular case, the civil standard might apply: *Birmingham City Council v Shafi* [2008] EWCA Civ 1186, [2009] 1 WLR 1961. A local authority can bring proceedings in public nuisance without having to show it has a special responsibility for enforcement of the criminal law eg against a person arrested for dealing in drugs for an injunction restraining him from entering a housing estate (*Nottingham City Council v Zain (a minor)* [2001] EWCA Civ 1248, [2002] 1 WLR 607). It is the duty of a local planning authority to protect the amenities of its area through a proper observance of planning control, and in order to perform that duty the authority is entitled in appropriate circumstances to seek a civil remedy under this section without first exhausting the processes of the criminal law (*Runnymede Borough Council v Ball* [1986] 1 All ER 629, [1986] 1 WLR 353). Where the conditions in sub-s (1) are met, a local authority is not precluded by s 4 of the Road Traffic Offenders Act 1988 from prosecuting an offence of using a motor vehicle without insurance contrary to s 143 of the Road Traffic Act 1988, (*Middlesborough Borough Council v Safeer* [2001] EWHC Admin 525, [2001] 4 All ER 630, [2002] 1 Cr App Rep 23, [2001] Crim LR 922, DC).

2 In determining whether a local authority has considered whether it is expedient to prosecute, the maxim omnia praesumuntur rite esse acta applies. The burden of displacing this presumption is on the defendant by showing that the local authority made their decision on the basis of facts they should not have taken into account, or failed to take into account matters they should have taken into account (*R v Richards* [1999] Crim LR 598).

7.7064 **223. Appearance of local authorities in legal proceedings** (1) Any member or officer of a local authority who is authorised by that authority to prosecute or defend on their behalf, or to appear on their behalf in, proceedings before a magistrates' court shall be entitled to prosecute or defend or to appear in any such proceedings, and, to conduct any proceedings.

(2) In this section "local authority" includes the Common Council, a joint authority, an economic prosperity board, a combined authority, the Greater London Authority, a police and crime commissioner and the Mayor's Office for Policing and Crime.

[Local Government Act 1972, s 223 as amended by the Local Government Act 1985, Sch 14, the Education Reform Act 1988, Sch 13, the Water Act 1989, Sch 25, the Police and Magistrates' Courts Act 1994, Sch 4, the Environment Act 1995, Sch 22, the Police Act 1996, Sch 7, the Police Act 1997, Sch 6, the Greater London Authority Act 1999, Sch 27, SI 2001/3719, the Criminal Justice and Police Act 2001, Sch 6, the Local Government and Public Involvement in Health Act 2007, Sch 13 the Legal Services Act 2007, Sch 21, the Local Democracy, Economic Development and Construction Act 2009, Sch 6, the Police Reform and Social Responsibility Act 2011, Sch 16 and the Deregulation Act 2015, Sch 13.]

*Documents and Notices, etc*

7.7065 **225. Deposit of documents with proper officer of authority, etc** (1) In any case in which a document of any description is deposited[1] with the proper officer[2] of a local authority[3], or with the chairman of a parish or community council or with the chairman of a parish meeting, pursuant to the standing orders of either House of Parliament or to any enactment or instrument, the proper officer or chairman, as the case may be, shall receive and retain the document in the manner and for the purposes directed by the standing orders or enactment or instrument, and shall make such notes or endorsements on, and give such acknowledgments and receipts in respect of, the document as may be so directed.

(2) All documents required by any enactment or instrument to be deposited with the proper officer[1] of a parish or community shall, in the case of a parish or community not having a separate parish or community council, be deposited in England with the chairman of the parish meeting or in

Wales with the proper officer of the principal council.

(3) In this section "local authority" includes a joint authority, an economic prosperity board and a combined authority.

[Local Government Act 1972, s 225 as amended by the Local Government Act 1985, Sch 14, the Education Reform Act 1988, Sch 13, the Local Government (Wales) Act 1994, Sch 15, the Local Government and Public Involvement in Health Act 2007, Sch 13, the Local Democracy, Economic Development and Construction Act 2009, Sch 6 and the Deregulation Act 2015, Sch 13.]

1 Claim forms submitted to a local authority pursuant to the Local Government (Allowances) Regulations 1974 are not documents deposited with a proper officer within the meaning of s 225(1) of this Act (*Brookman v Green* (1983) 147 JP 555).

2 Any reference in this Act to a proper officer shall, in relation to any purpose and any local authority or other body or any area, be construed as a reference to an officer appointed for that purpose by that body or for that area, as the case may be (s 270(3)).

3 "Local authority" means a county council, a district council, a London borough council or a parish and in relation to Wales, a county council, county borough or community council (s 270(1)).

7.7066 **228. Inspection of documents** (1) The minutes of proceedings of a parish or community council shall be open to the inspection of any local government elector[1] for the area of the council and any such local government elector may make a copy of or extract from the minutes.

(2) A local government elector[1] for the area of a local authority[2] may inspect and make a copy of or extract from an order for the payment of money made by the local authority.

(3) The accounts of a local authority and of any proper officer of a local authority shall be open to the inspection of any member of the authority, and any such member may make a copy of or extract from the accounts.

(4) *Repealed.*

(5) Subject to any provisions to the contrary in any other enactment or instrument, a person interested in any document deposited as mentioned in section 225 above may, at all reasonable hours, inspect and make copies thereof or extracts therefrom on payment to the person having custody thereof of the sum of 10p for every such inspection, and of the further sum of 10p for every hour during which such inspection continues after the first hour.

(6) A document directed by this section to be open to inspection shall be so open at all reasonable hours and, except where otherwise expressly provided, without payment.

(7) If a person having the custody of any such document[3]—

(*a*) obstructs any person entitled to inspect the document or to make a copy thereof or extract therefrom in inspecting the document or making a copy or extract,

(*b*) refuses to give copies or extracts to any person entitled to obtain copies or extracts,[4]

he shall be liable on summary conviction to a fine not exceeding **level 1** on the standard scale.

(7A) This section shall apply to the minutes of proceedings and the accounts of a joint authority, an economic prosperity board, or a combined authority as if that authority were a local authority and as if, references to a local government elector for the area of the authority were a reference to a local government elector for any local government area in the area for which the authority is established.

(7B) *Repealed.*

(8) This section shall apply to the minutes of proceedings and to the accounts of a parish meeting as if that meeting were a parish council.

(9) In relation to the Broads Authority, the references in this section to a local government elector for the area of the authority shall be construed as references to a local government elector for the area of any of the local authorities mentioned in section 1(3)(*a*) of the Norfolk and Suffolk Broads Act 1988.

[Local Government Act 1972, s 228 as amended by the Criminal Justice Act 1982, ss 38 and 46, the Local Government Finance Act 1982, Sch 6, the Local Government (Access to Information) Act 1985, Sch 2, the Local Government Act 1985, Sch 14, the Norfolk and Suffolk Broads Act 1988, Sch 6, the Education Reform Act 1988, Sch 13, the Police and Magistrates' Courts Act 1994, Sch 4, the Police Act 1996, Sch 7, the Police Act 1997, Sch 6, the Greater London Authority Act 1999, Sch 27, the Criminal Justice and Police Act 2001, Sch 6, the Local Government and Public Involvement in Health Act 2007, Sch 13, the Local Democracy, Economic Development and Construction Act 2009, Sch 6, the Police Reform and Social Responsibility Act 2011, Sch 16 and the Deregulation Act 2015, Sch 13.]

1 "Local government elector" means a person registered as a local government elector in the register of electors in accordance with the provisions of the Representation of the People Acts (s 270(1)).

2 For meaning of "local authority", see note 3 at para 7.7065, ante.

3 Claim forms submitted to a local authority pursuant to the Local Government (Allowances) Regulations 1974 are not documents deposited with a proper officer within the meaning of s 225(1) of this Act (*Brookman v Green* (1983) 147 JP 555).

4 There is no longer any obligation to give copies or extracts to any person entitled, since paragraph (*b*) related only to the circumstances in sub-s (4) which has now been repealed; see *Russell-Walker v Gimblett* (1985) 149 JP 448.

7.7067 **229. Photographic copies of documents** (1) Subject to subsections (3) and (7) below, any requirement imposed by any enactment that a local authority or parish meeting shall keep a document of any description shall be satisfied by their keeping a photographic copy of the document.

(2) Subject to subsection (7) below, any requirement imposed by any enactment that a document of any description in the custody or under the control of a local authority or parish meeting shall be made available for inspection shall be satisfied by their making available for inspection a photographic copy of the document.

(3) Subsection (1) above shall not apply to any document deposited with a local authority

under the Public Records Act 1958.

(4) In legal proceedings a photographic copy of a document in the custody of a local authority or parish meeting, or of a document which has been destroyed while in the custody of a local authority or parish meeting, or of any part of any such document, shall, subject to subsection (6) below, be admissible in evidence to the like extent as the original.

(5) A certificate purporting to be signed by the proper officer of the local authority, or the chairman of the parish meeting, concerned that a document is such a photographic copy as is mentioned in subsection (4) above, shall, subject to subsection (7) below, be evidence to that effect.

(6) The court before which a photographic copy is tendered in evidence in pursuance of subsection (4) above may, if the original is in existence, require its production and thereupon that subsection shall not apply to the copy.

(7) A photographic copy of a document in colour where the colours are relevant to the interpretation of the document shall not suffice for the purposes of this section unless it so distinguishes between the colours as to enable the document to be interpreted.

(8) In this section "court" and "legal proceedings" have the same meanings as in the Civil Evidence Act 1968 and "local authority" includes a joint authority, an economic prosperity board, a combined authority, a police and crime commissioner and the Mayor's Office for Policing and Crime.

[Local Government Act 1972, s 229 as amended by the Local Government Act 1985, Sch 14, the Education Reform Act 1988, Sch 13, the Police and Magistrates' Courts Act 1994, Sch 4, the Police Act 1996, Sch 7, the Police Act 1997, Sch 6, the Greater London Authority Act 1999, Sch 27, the Criminal Justice and Police Act 2001, Sch 6, the Local Government and Public Involvement in Health Act 2007, Sch 13, the Local Democracy, Economic Development and Construction Act 2009, Sch 6, the Police Reform and Social Responsibility Act 2011, Sch 16 and the Deregulation Act 2015, Sch 13.]

7.7068 **231. Service of notices on local authorities, etc** (1) Subject to subsection (3) below, any notice, order or other document required or authorised by any enactment or any instrument made under an enactment to be given to or served on a local authority or the chairman or an officer of a local authority shall be given or served by addressing it to the local authority and leaving it at, or sending it by post to, the principal office of the authority or any other office of the authority specified by them as one at which they will accept documents of the same description as that document.

(2) Any notice, order or other document so required or authorised to be given to or served on a parish meeting, or the chairman of the parish meeting, shall be given or served by addressing it to the chairman of the parish meeting and by delivering it to him, or by leaving it at his last known address, or by sending it by post to him at that address.

(3) The foregoing provisions of this section do not apply to a document which is to be given or served in any proceedings in court, but except as aforesaid the method of giving or serving documents provided for by those provisions are in substitution for the methods provided for by any other enactment or any instrument made under an enactment so far as it relates to the giving or service of documents to or on a local authority, the chairman or an officer of a local authority or a parish meeting or the chairman of a parish meeting.

(4) In this section "local authority" includes a joint authority, an economic prosperity board, a combined authority, a police and crime commissioner and the Mayor's Office for Policing and Crime.

[Local Government Act 1972, s 231 as amended by the Local Government Act 1985, Sch 14, the Education Reform Act 1988, Sch 13, the Police and Magistrates' Courts Act 1994, Sch 4, the Police Act 1996, Sch 7, the Police Act 1997, Sch 6, the Greater London Authority Act 1999, Sch 27, the Criminal Justice and Police Act 2001, Sch 7, the Local Government and Public Involvement in Health Act 2007, Sch 13, the Local Democracy, Economic Development and Construction Act 2009, Sch 6, the Police Reform and Social Responsibility Act 2011, Sch 16 and the Deregulation Act 2015, Sch 13.]

7.7069 **233. Service of notices by local authorities** (1) Subject to subsection (8) below, subsections (2) to (5) below shall have effect in relation to any notice, order or other document required or authorised by or under any enactment to be given to or served on any person by or on behalf of a local authority or by an officer of a local authority.

(2) Any such document may be given to or served on the person in question either by delivering it to him, or by leaving it at his proper address, or by sending it by post to him at that address.

(3) Any such document may—

(*a*) in the case of a body corporate, be given to or served on the secretary or clerk of that body;

(*b*) in the case of a partnership, be given to or served on a partner or a person having the control or management of the partnership business.

(4) For the purposes of this section and of section 26 of the Interpretation Act 1889 (service of documents by post) in its application to this section, the proper address of any person to or on whom a document is to be given or served shall be his last known address, except that—

(*a*) in the case of a body corporate or their secretary or clerk, it shall be the address of the registered or principal office of that body;

(*b*) in the case of a partnership or a person having the control or management of the partnership business, it shall be that of the principal office of the partnership;

and for the purposes of this subsection the principal office of a company registered outside the United Kingdom or of a partnership carrying on business outside the United Kingdom shall be their principal office within the United Kingdom.

(5) If the person to be given or served with any document mentioned in subsection (1) above has specified an address within the United Kingdom other than his proper address within the meaning of subsection (4) above as the one at which he or someone on his behalf will accept documents of the same description as that document, that address shall also be treated for the purposes of this section and section 26 of the Interpretation Act 1889 as his proper address.

(6) *Repealed.*

(7) If the name or address of any owner, lessee or occupier of land to or on whom any document mentioned in subsection (1) above is to be given or served cannot after reasonable inquiry be ascertained, the document may be given or served either by leaving it in the hands of a person who is or appears to be resident or employed on the land or by leaving it conspicuously affixed to some building or object on the land.

(8) This section shall apply to a document required or authorised by or under any enactment to be given to or served on any person by or on behalf of the chairman of a parish meeting as it applies to a document so required or authorised to be given to or served on any person by or on behalf of a local authority.

(9) The foregoing provisions of this section do not apply to a document which is to be given or served in any proceedings[1] in court.

(10) Except as aforesaid and subject to any provision of any enactment or instrument excluding the foregoing provisions of this section, the methods of giving or serving documents which are available under those provisions are in addition to the methods which are available under any other enactment or any instrument made under any enactment.

(11) In this section "local authority" includes a joint authority, an economic prosperity board, a combined authority, a police and crime commissioner and the Mayor's Office for Policing and Crime.

[Local Government Act 1972, s 233 as amended by the Local Government (Miscellaneous Provisions) Act 1976, Sch 2, the Local Government Act 1985, Sch 14, the Education Reform Act 1988, Sch 13, the Police and Magistrates' Courts Act 1994, Sch 4, the Police Act 1996, Sch 7, the Police Act 1997, Sch 6, the Greater London Authority Act 1999, Sch 27, the Criminal Justice and Police Act 2001, Sch 6, the Local Government and Public Involvement in Health Act 2007, Sch 13, the Local Democracy, Economic Development and Construction Act 2009, Sch 6, the Police Reform and Social Responsibility Act 2011, Sch 16 and the Deregulation Act 2015, Sch 13.]

1 However, it would seem that these provisions may enable proof of the service of documents which took place before proceedings commenced or were in contemplation, otherwise they would have no purpose.

7.7070 **234. Authentication of documents** (1) Any notice, order or other document which a local authority are authorised or required by or under any enactment (including any enactment in this Act) to give, make or issue may be signed[1] on behalf of the authority by the proper officer of the authority.

(2) Any document purporting to bear the signature of the proper officer of the authority shall be deemed, until the contrary is proved, to have been duly given, made or issued by the authority of the local authority.

In this subsection the word "signature" includes a facsimile of a signature by whatever process reproduced.

(3) Where any enactment or instrument made under an enactment makes, in relation to any document or class of documents, provision with respect to the matters dealt with by one of the two foregoing subsections, that subsection shall not apply in relation to that document or class of documents.

(4) In this section "local authority" includes a joint authority, an economic prosperity board, a combined authority, a police and crime commissioner and the Mayor's Office for Policing and Crime.

[Local Government Act 1972, s 234 as amended by the Local Government Act 1985, Sch 14, the Education Reform Act 1988, Sch 13, the Police and Magistrates' Courts Act 1994, Sch 4, the Police Act 1996, Sch 7, the Police Act 1997, Sch 6, the Greater London Authority Act 1999, Sch 27, the Criminal Justice and Police Act 2001, Sch 6, the Local Government and Public Involvement in Health Act 2007, Sch 13, the Local Democracy, Economic Development and Construction Act 2009, Sch 6, the Police Reform and Social Responsibility Act 2011, Sch 16 and the Deregulation Act 2015, Sch 13.]

1 The requirement of a signature may be satisfied by a facsimile: see *Plymouth City Corpn v Hurrell* [1968] 1 QB 455, [1967] 3 All ER 354, 131 JP 479.

*Bye-laws*

7.7071 **235. Power of councils to make bye-laws for good rule and government and suppression of nuisances** (1) The council of a district, the council of a principal area in Wales and the council of a London borough may make bye-laws[1] for the good rule and government of the whole or any part of the district, principal area or borough, as the case may be, and for the prevention and suppression of nuisances therein[2].

(2) The confirming authority in relation to bye-laws made under this section shall be the Secretary of State.

(3) Bye-laws shall not be made under this section for any purpose as respects any area if provision for that purpose as respects that area is made by, or is or may be made under, any other enactment.

[Local Government Act 1972, s 235 as amended by the Local Government (Wales) Act 1994, Sch 15.]

[1] Justices are bound to decide on any objection to the validity of a bye-law, although it may have been regularly made and confirmed; and they will exceed their jurisdiction if they convict on the mere proof of facts bringing the case within the bye-law without also deciding the bye-law is good (*R v Rose* (1855) 19 JP 676). It was decided in that case that a power to make bye-laws for removal of dust, filth, etc, from streets by occupiers did not authorise the making a bye-law for removal of pure snow. Applied in *R v Crown Court at Reading, ex p Hutchinson* [1988] QB 384, [1988] 1 All ER 333, 152 JP 47, where it was held that it is neither necessary nor appropriate for proceedings before magistrates to be adjourned so that the validity of the byelaw can be determined in the High Court by way of judicial review. If byelaws are to be upheld as good in part notwithstanding that they are bad in part, they must be substantially severable. If textual severance is possible, the test of substantial severability will be satisfied when the valid text is unaffected by, and independent of, the invalid. But when the court must modify the text in order to achieve severance, the test of substantial severability will be satisfied only if the substance of what remains is essentially unchanged in its legislative purpose, operation and effect; see *DPP v Hutchinson* [1990] 2 AC 783, [1990] 2 All ER 836, 155 JP 71, HL. Where a properly constituted criminal court has ruled that byelaws on which a prosecution has been based are invalid, the authority responsible for promulgating those byelaws must have regard to that decision in its dealings with others who were not parties to those proceedings and if it fails to do so it may be acting *Wednesbury* unreasonably even if it is not bound by judicial precedent such as where the decision declaring the byelaw invalid is that of a magistrates' court or the Crown Court. If however there are serious doubts about the correctness of the Criminal court's decision as to the validity of the byelaws, and there are serious reasons of public safety or security which require the retention of the byelaws pending an appeal, a case might be made for retaining them, provided an appeal is pursued with expedition, or other means found urgently to establish their validity in a court. See the remarks of Carnwath J in *Secretary of State for Defence v Percy* [1999] 1 All ER 732, Ch D (a case concerning byelaws made under s 14 of the Military Lands Act 1892).

As to a nuisance caused by a failure to remove snow, see *Slater v Worthington's Cash Stores (1930) Ltd* [1941] 1 KB 488, [1941] 3 All ER 28. As to infraction of bye-laws against collecting a crowd by shouting, etc, see *Phillips v Canham* (1872) 36 JP 310. A bye-law made by the Worcester County Council under the repealed s 16 of the Local Government Act 1888, against using obscene language in a street or public place or on land adjacent thereto without words importing that the language must be used to cause annoyance was held to be invalid, and repugnant to the general law because it was not limited to the use of such language to the annoyance of the public or by any limitation to the like effect (*Strickland v Hayes* [1896] 1 QB 290, 60 JP 164). This case was commented on in a later case, and it was held that a bye-law, made under s 16 of the Local Government Act 1888, which provided that "No person shall in any house, building, garden, land, or other place abutting on or near to a street or public place, make use of any violent, abusive, profane, indecent, or obscene language, gesture, or conduct, to the annoyance of any person in such street or public place", was a valid bye-law, and justified a conviction for using such language in a private house abutting on a street to the annoyance of the persons in the street (*Mantle v Jordan* [1897] 1 QB 248, 61 JP 119). *Strickland v Hayes* seems to conflict with *Kruse v Johnson*, infra, as to reasonableness, and it may be doubted whether it is now good law. Further doubt was thrown in this case in *Gentel v Rapps* [1902] 1 KB 160, 66 JP 117, where it was held that a tramway bye-law was not invalid because it omitted the words "to the annoyance of the passengers". See also *Brabham v Wookey* (1901) 18 TLR 99. A publican using indecent language in a public house to two constables who had entered the house on business does not infringe a bye-law prohibiting the use of indecent language in a "public place to the annoyance of passengers" (*Russon v Dutton (No 2)* (1911) 75 JP 207).

A bye-law relating to betting in a public place which did not make available to a person charged defences for which the public Acts provided, was held to be repugnant to the general law and invalid (*Powell v May* [1946] KB 330, [1946] 1 All ER 444, 110 JP 157). A bye-law against selling any paper devoted wholly or mainly to giving information as to the probable result of races, steeplechases, or other competitions was held by the Divisional Court (Alverstone LCJ and Kennedy J, Phillimore J, diss) to be invalid on the ground of its being uncertain and unreasonable (*Scott v Pilliner* [1904] 2 KB 855, 68 JP 518). Russell LCJ, laid down a general rule with regard to the construction that should be put upon bye-laws, and said in his opinion the courts were bound to support as far as possible bye-laws issued by local authorities unless it could be shown the bye-law was made without jurisdiction or was obviously unreasonable. He said the court ought not willingly to "pick holes" in rules that dealt with local matters and local requirements, which the local authorities were often better able to judge than the courts (*Walker v Stretton* (1896) 60 JP 313). Great regard will be paid to findings of local justices upon a bye-law made by a body with knowledge of local conditions (*Everton v Walker* (1927) 91 JP 125). See also *Friend v Brehout* (1914) 79 JP 25.

A local bye-law at Cambridge rendered liable to a penalty any person making a violent noise or outcry in the street "to the annoyance of the inhabitants". A newsboy cried his papers outside the house of one of the inhabitants for some minutes to the annoyance of that inhabitant. The Queen's Bench Division held the bye-law was reasonable and the defendant was not the less liable to conviction because one particular inhabitant only was annoyed (*Innes v Newman* [1894] 2 QB 292, 58 JP 543; followed in *Raymond v Cook* [1958] 3 All ER 407, 123 JP 35). A bye-law provided that "every person who shall sound or play upon any musical instrument, or sing, or make any noise whatsoever in any street, or near any house within the borough, after having been required by any householder resident in such street or by any police constable to desist from making such sound or noise either on account of the illness of any inmate or from any other reasonable cause", shall be liable, etc. The defendant, a "Captain" in the Salvation Army, played on a concertina on a Sunday morning surrounded by a crowd in a square in Truro, and refused to desist at the request of the superintendent of police, who told him he had reasonable cause for the request by reason of the complaints of the inhabitants. The Queen's Bench Division held there was nothing unreasonable or void in such a bye-law, and it was for the justices to decide whether there was a reasonable cause for requiring the appellant to desist (*R v Powell, etc, Truro Justices* (1884) 48 JP 740). A bye-law at St Albans made liable to a penalty any person blowing a horn "or any other noisy instrument", to the annoyance of any of the inhabitants. The justices found that a concertina was a noisy instrument, and a conviction was upheld. The Queen's Bench Division held it was sufficient to prove the instrument was a nuisance or annoyance to some of the inhabitants (*Booth v Howell* (1889) 53 JP 678); if, indeed, it is found as a fact that the noise in question was calculated to be an annoyance, evidence that inhabitants were annoyed is unnecessary (*Raymond v Cook* [1958] 3 All ER 407, 123 JP 35). Similarly, in relation to the use of obscene language in a street, justices are entitled to infer annoyance in the absence of positive evidence that any person was annoyed (*Nicholson v Glasspool* (1959) 123 JP 229).

A bye-law made by the county council of Kent provided that "No person shall sound or play upon any musical or noisy instrument, or sing in any public place or highway within fifty yards of any dwelling-house, after being required by any constable, or by an inmate of such house personally, or by his or her servant to desist". Defendant was conducting an open-air religious service on a public highway, and persisted in singing within fifty yards of a dwelling-house, after having been requested by a police constable to desist. The case was considered of such great importance that it was heard by a specially constituted court of seven judges and the conviction was upheld. Russell LCJ, made some important observations as to the principles to be applied by the court in deciding as to the validity of bye-laws and held that bye-laws made by local authorities ought to be benevolently interpreted, and credit ought to be given to those who have to administer them that they will be benevolently administered. This case must be looked upon as a leading case (*Kruse v Johnson* [1898] 2 QB 91, 62 JP 469. See also *Brownscombe v Johnson* (1898) 62 JP 326, which led to the case of *Kruse v Johnson*). A bye-law made by the Town Council of Southend under a local Act provided that "No organ or other musical instrument worked by steam or other mechanical means shall be used within the borough provided that this bye-law shall not apply to any locomotive or steam engine in use on any railway within the borough"; (other steam whistles, etc, then permitted by statute were also excluded). A travelling showman erected in a field within the borough a roundabout worked by steam, to which an organ was attached, also worked by steam. The organ was in the centre of a field 116 yards from a public road, and played from 7 a.m. until 9.30 p.m. The Queen's Bench Division held the bye-law was valid (*Southend Corpn v Davis* (1900) 16 TLR 167). A bye-law made by the Town Council of Croydon provided that "No person not being a member of Her Majesty's Army or Auxiliary Forces, under the orders of his commanding officer, shall sound or play upon any musical instrument in any of the streets in the borough on Sunday". The appellant, one of the Salvation Army, played a musical instrument on a Sunday and was fined. The Queen's Bench Division held that as the bye-law stated no qualification or exception in any circumstances, it was unreasonable and void (*Johnson v Croydon Corpn* (1886) 16 QBD 708, 50 JP 487, Treat 163). So also was a bye-law that every person who shall play a noisy instrument or sing or preach in any street without a previously written licence from the mayor shall be fined, etc, as it would enable a mayor to legalise a nuisance or prohibit a lawful act which was not a nuisance (*Munro v Watson* (1887) 51 JP 660). But a bye-law which prohibited the exposure for sale of any commodity, etc, or for hire of any chair, etc, on the sea beach, esplanade, etc, except by direction of the sanitary authority, or in such parts as they might by notice appoint, made under a local Act, which authorised bye-laws to be made for regulation of the esplanade, was upheld (*Gray v Sylvester* (1897) 61 JP 807). The court distinguished a bye-law for the good government of a town from bye-laws for the regulation of an esplanade. See also *Slee v Meadows* (1911) 75 JP 246. A bye-law that no person shall wilfully annoy passengers in the public streets was held to be invalid for uncertainty (*Nash v Finlay* (1901) 66 JP 183). So was a bye-law preventing any person hawking on beach or foreshore except in pursuance of agreement with corporation (*Parker v Bournemouth Corpn* (1902) 66 JP 440). This was followed in *Moorman v Tordoff* (1908) 72 JP 142. But see *Williams v Weston-super-Mare UDC (No 1)* (1907) 72 JP 54, where *Parker v Bournemouth Corpn, supra*, was distinguished; *Williams v Weston-super-Mare UDC (No 2)* (1910) 74 JP 370 and *Cassell v Jones* (1913) 77 JP 197. A bye-law made under s 69 (repealed by the Statute Law (Repeals) Act 1975) of the Town Police Clauses Act 1847, as to bathing, and providing that the prescribed charges should include charges for the use of towels and bathing costume, thus purporting to prohibit any extra charge being made therefore, was declared *ultra vires* (*Parker v Clegg* (1903) 2 LGR 608).

A bye-law at Luton provided that "no person shall to the annoyance or disturbance of residents or passengers keep or manage a shooting gallery, swing boat, roundabout, or other like thing in any street or public place or on land adjoining or near to such street or public place, provided that the bye-law shall not apply to any fair lawfully held". It was contended by the appellant that the bye-law was *ultra vires* on the ground that the town council had no authority to make a bye-law affecting private property, and because it created a new criminal offence. The Queen's Bench Division upheld the bye-law (*Teale v Harris* (1896) 60 JP 744). Where a bye-law prohibited touting for hackney carriages in any public thoroughfare, it was held that the respondent committed an offence though he stood at the time on a piece of land adjoining the street and belonging to private persons (*Dereham v Strickland* (1911) 75 JP 300; *McQuade v Barnes* [1949] 1 All ER 154, 113 JP 89).

A licence proposed to be granted by the Edinburgh magistrates under the provisions of an Act regulating the selling of ice-cream, and professing to limit the days and hours when premises should be kept open, was held by the House of Lords to be *ultra vires* (*Rossi v Edinburgh Corpn* [1905] AC 21). Football had been played many years on open ground crossed by footpaths. Appellants set up that the paths were not streets within the meaning of a bye-law, and claimed a right as sons of freemen to play on the open space. The Queen's Bench Division held that justices properly overruled the claim, as such a right could not possibly exist (*Pearson v Whitfield* (1888) 52 JP Jo 708). As to bye-laws regulating games on a public common, see *Harris v Harrison* (1914) 78 JP 398. A local authority has no power to sanction building plans not in accordance with bye-laws; they have no dispensing power, any purported approval of plans contravening bye-laws is inoperative (*Yabbicom v King* [1899] 1 QB 444, 63 JP 149).

[2] As to offences against bye-laws, and penalties, see s 237 and notes thereto, post.

7.7072 **236. Procedure etc, for bye-laws** (1) Subject to subsection (2) below, the following provisions of this section shall apply to bye-laws[1] to be made by a local authority under this Act and to byelaws made by a local authority, the Greater London Authority, Transport for London or an Integrated Transport Authority for an integrated transport area in England under any other enactment and conferring on the authority, a power to make bye-laws and for which specific provision is not otherwise made.

(2) This section shall not apply to

(*a*) byelaws of a class prescribed by regulations under section 236A, or

(*b*) bye-laws made by the Civil Aviation Authority under section 29 of the Civil Aviation Act 1982 and the Local Government Act 1985, Sch 14.

(3)–(11) *Procedure for making and confirming bye-laws.*

[Local Government Act 1972, s 236 as amended by the Civil Aviation Act 1982, Sch 15, the Local Government Act 1985, Sch 14, the Education Reform Act 1988, Sch 12, the Water Act 1989, Sch 27, the Local Government (Wales) Act 1994, Sch 15, the Greater London Authority Act 1999, ss 76 and 166, SI 2001/3719, the Local Government and Public Involvement in Health Act 2007, s 129 and the Local Transport Act 2008, Sch 4.]

[1] Section 236 is modified by SI 1986/143 in relation to byelaws for marine nature reserves made under ss 36 and 37 of the Wildlife and Countryside Act 1981.

7.7073 **236A. Alternative procedure for certain byelaws** (1) The Secretary of State may, in relation to England, by regulations[1]—

(*a*) prescribe classes of byelaws to which section 236 does not apply, and

(*b*) make provision about the procedure for the making and coming into force of such byelaws.

(2) The regulations may prescribe a class of byelaws by reference, in particular, to one or more of the following—

(*a*) the enactment under which byelaws are made,

(*b*) the subject-matter of byelaws,

(*c*) the authority by whom byelaws are made,

(*d*) the authority or person by whom byelaws are confirmed.

(3) The regulations may, in particular, include provision about—

(*a*) consultation to be undertaken before a byelaw is made,

(*b*) publicising a byelaw after it is made.

(4) The regulations may make—

(*a*) such incidental, consequential, transitional or supplemental provision (including provision amending, repealing or revoking enactments) as the Secretary of State considers appropriate, and

(*b*) different provision for different areas, including different provision for different localities and for different authorities.

(5) Regulations may not be made under subsection (1) unless a draft of the instrument containing the regulations has been laid before, and approved by a resolution of, each House of Parliament.

[Local Government Act 1972, s 236A as inserted by the Local Government and Public Involvement in Health Act 2007, s 129.]

---

1 The Byelaws (Alternative Procedure) (England) Regulations 2016, SI 2016/165 have been made. The Explanatory Note to the regulations outlines the policy background:

"The policy aim is to specify a procedure for making and bringing into force certain byelaws without any central Government confirmation involvement, which decentralises this power to specified local authorities, who then assume complete responsibility for these byelaws and their lawfulness. The Regulations do not give authorities powers to create new categories of byelaws; authorities already have a wide range of byelaw-making powers. What is new is that following leave to proceed to make the byelaw by the Secretary of State, there is no requirement for subsequent confirmation by the Secretary of State – it will be a matter for the authority having taken account of any representations made about the proposed byelaw. The Secretary of State for Communities and Local Government is responsible for byelaws made by local authorities on Good Rule and Government. Under the alternative procedure authorities will undertake a two stage process for byelaw preparation and consultation before advertising and making a new byelaw. As such the resolving of any objections and the bringing into force of certain byelaws will be undertaken locally, instead of by the Secretary of State, as currently happens."

7.7074 **236B. Revocation of byelaws** (1) This section applies to—

(*a*) a local authority;

(*b*) the Greater London Authority;

(*c*) Transport for London;

(*d*) an Integrated Transport Authority for an integrated transport area in England.

(*e*) a combined authority.

(2) Such an authority may make a byelaw under this section to revoke a byelaw made by the authority.

(3) The power under subsection (2) may be exercised only where the authority has no other power to revoke the byelaw.

(4) The confirming authority in relation to a byelaw made under this section shall be—

(*a*) in relation to a byelaw made by a local authority in Wales, the Welsh Ministers;

(*b*) in relation to any other byelaw, the Secretary of State.

(5) The Secretary of State may, in relation to England, by order revoke any byelaw which appears to him to have become spent, obsolete or unnecessary.

(6) The Welsh Ministers may, in relation to Wales, by order revoke any byelaw which appears to them to have become spent, obsolete or unnecessary.

(7) An order under this section may make—

(*a*) such incidental, consequential, transitional or supplemental provision (including provision amending, repealing or revoking enactments) as the person making the order considers appropriate, and

(*b*) different provision for different areas, including different provision for different localities and for different authorities.

(8) A statutory instrument containing an order under this section which amends or repeals any provision of an Act may not be made by the Secretary of State unless a draft of the instrument containing the order has been laid before, and approved by a resolution of, each House of Parliament.

(9) Otherwise, a statutory instrument containing an order made by the Secretary of State under this section shall be subject to annulment in pursuance of a resolution of either House of Parliament.

(10) A statutory instrument containing an order under this section which amends or repeals any provision of an Act may not be made by the Welsh Ministers unless a draft of the instrument containing the order has been laid before, and approved by a resolution of, the National Assembly for Wales.

(11) Otherwise, a statutory instrument containing an order made by the Welsh Ministers under this section shall be subject to annulment in pursuance of a resolution of the National Assembly for Wales.

[Local Government Act 1972, s 236B, as inserted by the Local Government and Public Involvement in Health Act 2007, s 134 and amended by the Local Transport Act 2008, Sch 4 and the Local Democracy, Economic Development and Construction Act 2009, Sch 6.]

7.7075 **237. Offences against bye-laws**[1] Bye-laws to which section 236 above applies and byelaws of a class prescribed by regulations under section 236A may provide that persons contravening the bye-laws shall be liable on summary conviction to a fine not exceeding such sum as may be fixed by the enactment conferring the power to make the bye-laws, or, if no sum is so fixed, the sum of **level 2** on the standard scale[1], and in the case of a continuing offence a further fine not exceeding such sum as may be fixed as aforesaid, or, if no sum is so fixed, the sum of **£5**[2] for each day during which the offence continues after conviction thereof.

[Local Government Act 1972, s 237 as amended by the Criminal Law Act 1977, s 31(3), the Criminal Justice Act 1982, s 46 and the Local Government and Public Involvement in Health Act 2007, s 129.]

[1] Notwithstanding its repeal, byelaws made under the Local Government Act 1933, are by virtue of s 272(2) of the Local Government Act 1972, preserved and remain in force (*DPP v Jackson* (1990) 154 JP 967).

[2] Justices always have jurisdiction to inquire into the validity of a byelaw (*R v Crown Court at Reading, ex p Hutchinson* [1988] QB 384, [1988] 1 All ER 333, 152 JP 47).

A bye-law made by virtue of the Public Health Act 1875, s 183 or the Local Government Act 1933, s 251, or the Local Government Act 1972, s 237, which was in force on 17 July 1978 and specified £20 as the maximum fine (including a bye-law which specified £5 and was increased to £20 by virtue of the Criminal Justice Act 1967 s 92(3) and Sch 3 Part II), had effect as if the bye-law specified a fine of £50 (Criminal Law Act 1977, s 31(2) and (3)). By virtue of s 46 of the Criminal Justice Act 1982 the reference to a maximum of £50 was converted to a reference to level 2 on the standard scale. However, if on 17 July 1978 such bye-law specified an amount less than £20 it remains unchanged (Criminal Law Act 1977, s 31(2) and (3)). In the case of a bye-law made by virtue of an enactment or instrument after 30 April 1984 and before the commencement of s 52 of the Criminal Justice Act 1988, the maximum fine on conviction of a summary offence specified in the bye-law shall be construed as the level in the first column of the standard scale corresponding to that amount (Criminal Justice Act 1988, s 52, when in force).

Byelaws of local authorities made under this section dealing with the burning of straw, stubble or other crop residues on agricultural land have been repealed by the Burning of Crop Residues (Repeal of Byelaws) Order 1992, SI 1992/693. Section 152 of the Environmental Protection Act 1990, title PUBLIC HEALTH, post, enables regulations to be made prohibiting or restricting the burning of crop residue on agricultural land. Where the byelaws were made under ss 36 or 37 of the Wildlife and Countryside Act 1981 for marine nature reserves, the penalty prescribed here by SI 1986/143 is £1,000.

7.7076 **237ZA. Section 235 byelaws: powers of seizure etc** A byelaw made under section 235 may include provision for or in connection with—

(*a*) the seizure and retention of any property in connection with any contravention of the byelaw, and

(*b*) the forfeiture of any such property on a person's conviction of an offence of contravention of the byelaw.*

[Local Government Act 1972, s 237ZA as inserted by the Police Reform and Social Responsibility Act 2011, s 150.]

* **Section in force from 19 December 2011 (insofar as it relates to byelaws made by local authorities in England): see SI 2011/2834, art 2(*k*), and from a date to be appointed for remaining purposes.**

7.7077 **237A. Fixed penalty notices** (1) The Secretary of State may, in relation to England, by regulations prescribe classes of byelaws to which this section applies.

(2) The regulations may prescribe a class of byelaws by reference, in particular, to one or more of the following—

(*a*) the enactment under which byelaws are made,

(*b*) the subject-matter of byelaws,

(*c*) the authority by whom byelaws are made,

(*d*) the authority or person by whom byelaws are confirmed.

(3) Where—

(*a*) an authorised officer of an authority which has made a byelaw to which this section applies has reason to believe that a person has committed an offence against the byelaw, or

(*b*) an authorised officer of a parish council has reason to believe that a person has in its area committed an offence against a byelaw to which this section applies made by an authority other than the parish council,

the officer may give that person a notice offering him the opportunity of discharging any liability to conviction for the offence by payment of a fixed penalty.

(4) A fixed penalty notice under this section is payable to the authority whose officer gave the notice.

(5) Where a person is given a notice under this section in respect of an offence—

(*a*) no proceedings may be instituted for the offence before the end of the period of fourteen days following the date of the notice, and

(*b*) he may not be convicted of the offence if he pays the fixed penalty before the end of that period.

(6) A notice under this section must give such particulars of the circumstances alleged to constitute the offence as are necessary for giving reasonable information about the offence.

(7) A notice under this section must also state—

(*a*) the period during which, by virtue of subsection (5), proceedings will not be taken for the offence,

(*b*) the amount of the fixed penalty, and

(*c*) the person to whom and the address at which the fixed penalty may be paid.

(8) Without prejudice to payment by any other method, payment of the fixed penalty may be made by pre-paying and posting a letter containing the amount of the penalty (in cash or otherwise) to the person mentioned in subsection (7)(*c*) at the address so mentioned.

(9) Where a letter is sent in accordance with subsection (8) payment is to be regarded as having been made at the time at which that letter would be delivered in the ordinary course of post.

(10) The form of a notice under this section may be specified in regulations under subsection (1).

(11) In any proceedings a certificate which—

(*a*) purports to be signed on behalf of the chief finance officer of an authority, and

(*b*) states that payment of a fixed penalty was or was not received by a date specified in the certificate,

is evidence of the facts stated.

(12) In this section—

"authorised officer", in relation to an authority, means—

(*a*) an employee of the authority who is authorised in writing by the authority for the purpose of giving notices under this section,

(*b*) any person who, in pursuance of arrangements made with the authority, has the function of giving such notices and is authorised in writing by the authority to perform the function, and

(*c*) any employee of such a person who is authorised in writing by the authority for the purpose of giving such notices,

"chief finance officer", in relation to an authority, means the person having responsibility for the financial affairs of the authority.

(13) Regulations under subsection (1) may prescribe conditions to be satisfied by a person before a parish council may authorise him in writing for the purpose of giving notices under this section.

[Local Government Act 1972, s 237A as inserted by the Local Government and Public Involvement in Health Act 2007, s 130.]

**7.7078 237B. Amount of fixed penalty** (1) The amount of a fixed penalty payable in pursuance of a notice under section 237A is—

(*a*) the amount specified by the authority which made the byelaw, or

(*b*) if no amount is so specified, £75.

(2) An authority may specify different amounts in relation to different byelaws.

(3) The Secretary of State may by regulations make provision in connection with the powers under subsections (1)(*a*) and (2).

(4) Regulations under subsection (3) may, in particular—

(*a*) require an amount specified under subsection (1)(*a*) to fall within a range prescribed in the regulations,

(*b*) restrict the extent to which, and the circumstances in which, an authority can make provision under subsection (2).

(5) The Secretary of State may by order substitute a different amount for the amount for the time being specified in subsection (1)(*b*).

[Local Government Act 1972, s 237B as inserted by the Local Government and Public Involvement in Health Act 2007, s 130.]

**7.7079 237C. Power to require name and address in connection with fixed penalty**

(1) If an authorised officer proposes to give a person a notice under section 237A, the officer may require the person to give him his name and address.

(2) A person commits an offence if—

(*a*) he fails to give his name and address when required to do so under subsection (1), or

(*b*) he gives a false or inaccurate name or address in response to a requirement under that subsection.

(3) A person guilty of an offence under subsection (2) is liable on summary conviction to a fine not exceeding level 3 on the standard scale.

(4) In this section, "authorised officer" has the same meaning as in section 237A.

[Local Government Act 1972, s 237C as inserted by the Local Government and Public Involvement in Health Act 2007, s 130.]

**7.7080 237D. Use of fixed penalty receipts** (1) "Fixed penalty receipts" means amounts paid to an authority in pursuance of notices under section 237A.

(2) The authority shall have regard to the desirability of using its fixed penalty receipts for the purpose of combating any relevant nuisance.

(3) A "relevant nuisance" is a nuisance in the authority's area for the prevention of which any byelaw to which section 237A applies was made.

[Local Government Act 1972, s 237D as inserted by the Local Government and Public Involvement in Health Act 2007, s 131.]

**7.7081 237E. Guidance relating to sections 236A and 237A to 237D** An authority which makes byelaws of a class prescribed by regulations under section 236A or 237A must have regard to any guidance issued by the Secretary of State about—

(*a*) procedure for which provision is made by regulations under section 236A(1);

(*b*) fixed penalties;

(*c*) anything related to the matters mentioned in paragraph (*a*) or (*b*).

[Local Government Act 1972, s 237E as inserted by the Local Government and Public Involvement in Health Act 2007, s 132.]

**7.7082 237F. Further provision about regulations and orders under section 237A or 237B**

(1) Regulations under section 237A or 237B, and an order under section 237B, may make—

(a) such incidental, consequential, transitional or supplemental provision (including provision amending, repealing or revoking enactments) as the Secretary of State considers appropriate, and

(b) different provision for different areas, including different provision for different localities and for different authorities.

(2) A statutory instrument containing—

(a) regulations under section 237A or 237B which amend or repeal any provision of an Act, or

(b) an order under section 237B which amends or repeals any provision of an Act,

may not be made unless a draft of the instrument containing the regulations or order has been laid before, and approved by a resolution of, each House of Parliament.

(3) Otherwise, a statutory instrument containing regulations under section 237A or 237B, or an order under section 237B, shall be subject to annulment in pursuance of a resolution of either House of Parliament.

[Local Government Act 1972, s 237F as inserted by the Local Government and Public Involvement in Health Act 2007, s 130.]

7.7083 **238. Evidence of bye-laws** The production of a printed copy of a bye-law purporting to be made by a local authority, the Greater London Authority, an Integrated Transport Authority for an integrated transport area in England or a combined authority upon which is endorsed a certificate purporting to be signed by the proper officer of the authority stating—

(a) that the bye-law was made by the authority;

(b) that the copy is a true copy of the bye-law;

(c) that on a specified date the bye-law was confirmed by the authority named in the certificate or, as the case may require, was sent to the Secretary of State and has not been disallowed[1];

(d) the date, if any, fixed by the confirming authority for the coming into operation of the bye-law[1];

shall be prima facie evidence of the facts stated in the certificate and without proof of the handwriting or official position of any person purporting to sign the certificate.

[Local Government Act 1972, s 238 as amended by the Local Government Act 1985, Sch 14, the Education Reform Act 1988, Sch 12, SI 2001/3719, the Local Transport Act 2008, Sch 4 and the Local Democracy, Economic Development and Construction Act 2009, Sch 6.]

---

1 Where the byelaws were made under s 37 of the Wildlife and Countryside Act 1981 for marine nature reserves, paras (c) and (d) are omitted by the operation of SI 1986/143.

7.7084 **265–265A.** *Application of Act to Isles of Scilly; application in relation to the Broads Authority.*

7.7085 **270. General provisions as to interpretation** (1) In the Act, except where the context otherwise requires, the following expressions have the following meanings respectively, that is to say—

"alternative arrangements" has the same meaning as in Part II of the Local Government Act 2000;

"the Broads" has the same meaning as in the Norfolk and Suffolk Broads Act 1988;

"combined authority" means a combined authority established under section 103 of the Local Democracy, Economic Development and Construction Act 2009;

"economic prosperity board" means an economic prosperity board established under section 88 of the Local Democracy, Economic Development and Construction Act 2009;

"joint authority" means an authority established by Part IV of the Local Government Act 1985;

"local authority" means a county council, a district council, a London borough council or a parish council, but in relation to Wales, means a county council, county borough or community council;

"principal area" means a county, Greater London, a district or a London borough;

"principal council" means a council elected for a principal area;

"sub-national transport body" means a sub-national transport body established under section 102E of the Local Transport Act 2008.[1]

(2) In this Act and in any other enactment, whether passed before, at the same time as, or after this Act, the expression "non-metropolitan county" means any county other than a metropolitan county, and the expression "non-metropolitan district" means any district other than a metropolitan district.

(3) Any reference in this Act to a proper officer and any reference which by virtue of this Act is to be construed as such a reference shall, in relation to any purpose and any local authority or other body or any area, be construed as a reference to an officer appointed for that purpose by that body or for that area, as the case may be.

(4) In any provision of this Act which applies to a London borough, except Schedule 2 to this Act,—

(a) any reference to the chairman of the council or of any class of councils comprising the council or to a member of a local authority shall be construed as or, as the case may be, as including a reference to the mayor of the borough;

(*b*) any reference to the vice-chairman of the council or any such class of councils shall be construed as a reference to the deputy mayor of the borough; and

(*c*) any reference to the proper officer of the council or any such class of councils shall be construed as a reference to the proper officer of the borough.

(4A) Where a London borough council are operating executive arrangements which involve a mayor and cabinet executive, subsection (4) above shall have effect with the omission of paragraphs (*a*) and (*b*).

(5) In this Act, except where the context otherwise requires, references to any enactment shall be construed as references to that enactment as amended, extended or applied by or under any other enactment, including any enactment contained in this Act.

[Local Government Act 1972, s 270 as amended by the Local Government Act 1985, Schs 14 and 17, the Norfolk and Suffolk Broads Act 1988, Sch 6, the Local Government (Wales) Act 1994, s 1(5), the Local Government Act 2000, s 46, SI 2001/2237, the Local Government and Public Involvement in Health Act 2007, Sch 13, the Local Democracy, Economic Development and Construction Act 2009, Sch 6, the Localism Act 2011, Sch 3, the Deregulation Act 2015, Sch 13 and the Cities and Local Government Devolution Act 2016, Sch 5.]

---

[1] Only the definitions relevant to the provisions reproduced in Stone are included.

## SCHEDULE 12A

### Access to Information: Exempt Information

*(As substituted by SI 2006/88 and amended by SI 2007/2194 and the Charities Act 2011, Sch 7.)*

### Part 1

### Descriptions of Exempt Information

7.7086 **1.** Information relating to any individual.

**2.** Information which is likely to reveal the identity of an individual.

**3.** Information relating to the financial or business affairs of any particular person (including the authority holding that information).

**4.** Information relating to any consultations or negotiations, or contemplated consultations or negotiations, in connection with any labour relations matter arising between the authority or a Minister of the Crown and employees of, or office holders under, the authority.

**5.** Information in respect of which a claim to legal professional privilege could be maintained in legal proceedings.

**6.** Information which reveals that the authority proposes—

(*a*) to give under any enactment a notice under or by virtue of which requirements are imposed on a person; or

(*b*) to make an order or direction under any enactment.

**7.** Information relating to any action taken or to be taken in connection with the prevention, investigation or prosecution of crime.

### Part 2

### Qualifications: England

**8.** Information falling within paragraph 3 above is not exempt information by virtue of that paragraph if it is required to be registered under—

(*a*) the Companies Acts (as defined in section 2 of the Companies Act 2006);

(*b*) the Friendly Societies Act 1974;

(*c*) the Friendly Societies Act 1992;

(*d*) the Industrial and Provident Societies Acts 1965 to 1978;

(*e*) the Building Societies Act 1986; or

(*f*) the Charities Act 2011.

**9.** Information is not exempt information if it relates to proposed development for which the local planning authority may grant itself planning permission pursuant to regulation 3 of the Town and Country Planning General Regulations 1992.

**10.** Information which—

(*a*) falls within any of paragraphs 1 to 7 above; and

(*b*) is not prevented from being exempt by virtue of paragraph 8 or 9 above,

is exempt information if and so long, as in all the circumstances of the case, the public interest in maintaining the exemption outweighs the public interest in disclosing the information.

### Part 3

### Interpretation: England

**11.** (1) In Parts 1 and 2 and this Part of this Schedule—

"employee" means a person employed under a contract of service;

"financial or business affairs" includes contemplated, as well as past or current, activities;

"labour relations matter" means—

(*a*) any of the matters specified in paragraphs (*a*) to (*g*) of section 218(1) of the Trade Union and Labour Relations (Consolidation) Act 1992 (matters which may be the subject of a trade dispute, within the meaning of that Act); or

(*b*) any dispute about a matter falling within paragraph (*a*) above;

and for the purposes of this definition the enactments mentioned in paragraph (*a*) above, with the necessary modifications, shall apply in relation to office-holders under the authority as they apply in relation to employees of the authority;

"office-holder", in relation to the authority, means the holder of any paid office appointments to which are or may be made or confirmed by the authority or by any joint board on which the authority is represented or by any person who holds any such office or is an employee of the authority;

"registered" in relation to information required to be registered under the Building Societies Act 1986, means recorded in the public file of any building society (within the meaning of that Act).

(2) Any reference in Parts 1 and 2 and this Part of this Schedule to "the authority" is a reference to the principal council or, as the case may be, the committee or sub-committee in relation to whose proceedings or documents the question whether information is exempt or not falls to be determined and includes a reference—

(*a*) in the case of a principal council, to any committee or sub-committee of the council; and

(*b*) in the case of a committee, to—

(i) any constituent principal council;

(ii) any other principal council by which appointments are made to the committee or whose functions the committee discharges; and

(iii) any other committee or sub-committee of a principal council falling within sub-paragraph (i) or (ii) above; and

(*c*) in the case of a sub-committee, to—

(i) the committee, or any of the committees, of which it is a sub-committee; and

(ii) any principal council which falls within paragraph (*b*) above in relation to that committee.

## Part 4

## Descriptions of Exempt Information: Wales

*(As substituted by SI 2007/969.)*

**12.** Information relating to a particular individual.

**13.** Information which is likely to reveal the identity of an individual.

**14.** Information relating to the financial or business affairs of any particular person (including the authority holding that information).

**15.** Information relating to any consultations or negotiations, or contemplated consultations or negotiations, in connection with any labour relations matter arising between the authority or a Minister of the Crown and employees of, or office holders under, the authority.

**16.** Information in respect of which a claim to legal professional privilege could be maintained in legal proceedings.

**17.** Information which reveals that the authority proposes—

(*a*) to give under any enactment a notice under or by virtue of which requirements are imposed on a person; or

(*b*) to make an order or direction under any enactment.

**18.** Information relating to any action taken or to be taken in connection with the prevention, investigation or prosecution of crime.

## Part 5

## Qualifications: Wales

*(As substituted by SI 2007/969 and amended by SI 2007/2194 and the Charities Act 2011, Sch 7.)*

**19.** Information falling within paragraph 14 above is not exempt information by virtue of that paragraph if it is required to be registered under—

(*a*) the Companies Acts (as defined in section 2 of the Companies Act 2006);

(*b*) the Friendly Societies Act 1974;

(*c*) the Friendly Societies Act 1992;

(*d*) the Industrial and Provident Societies Acts 1965 to 1978;

(*e*) the Building Societies Act 1986; or

(*f*) the Charities Act 2011.

**20.** Information is not exempt information if it relates to proposed development for which the local planning authority may grant itself planning permission pursuant to regulation 3 of the Town and Country Planning General Regulations 1992.

**21.** Information which—

(*a*) falls within any of paragraphs 12 to 15, 17 and 18 above; and

(*b*) is not prevented from being exempt by virtue of paragraph 19 or 20 above,

is exempt information if and so long, as in all the circumstances of the case, the public interest in maintaining the exemption outweighs the public interest in disclosing the information.

## Part 6

## Interpretation: Wales

*(As substituted by SI 2007/969.)*

**22.** (1) In Parts 4 and 5 and this Part of this Schedule—

"employee" means a person employed under a contract of service;

"financial or business affairs" includes contemplated, as well as past or current, activities;

"labour relations matter" means—

(*a*) any of the matters specified in paragraphs (*a*) to (*g*) of section 218(1) of the Trade Union and Labour Relations (Consolidation) Act 1992 (matters which may be the subject of a trade dispute, within the meaning of that Act); or

(*b*) any dispute about a matter falling within paragraph (*a*) above;

and for the purposes of this definition the enactments mentioned in paragraph (*a*) above, with the necessary modifications, shall apply in relation to office-holders under the authority as they apply in relation to employees of the authority;

"office-holder", in relation to the authority, means the holder of any paid office appointments to which are or may be made or confirmed by the authority or by any joint board on which the authority is represented or by any person who holds any such office or is an employee of the authority;

"registered" in relation to information required to be registered under the Building Societies Act 1986, means recorded in the public file of any building society (within the meaning of that Act).

(2) Any reference in Parts 4 and 5 and this Part of this Schedule to "the authority" is a reference to the principal council or, as the case may be, the committee or sub-committee in relation to whose proceedings or documents the question whether information is exempt or not falls to be determined and includes a reference—

(*a*) in the case of a principal council, to any committee or sub-committee of the council; and

(*b*) in the case of a committee, to—

(i) any constituent principal council;

(ii) any other principal council by which appointments are made to the committee or whose functions the committee discharges; and

(iii) any other committee or sub-committee of a principal council falling within sub-paragraph (i) or (ii) above; and

(*c*) in the case of a sub-committee, to—

(i) the committee, or any of the committees, of which it is a sub-committee; and

(ii) any principal council which falls within paragraph (*b*) above in relation to that committee.

# Local Government (Miscellaneous Provisions) Act 1976

(1976 c 57)

## PART I
## GENERAL

### *Highways*

7.7092 **7. Control of road-side sales** (1) If a highway authority considers that, for the purpose of avoiding danger on or facilitating the passage of traffic over a highway for which it is the highway authority, it is appropriate to make an order under this subsection in respect of the highway, the authority may make an order (hereafter in this section referred to as a "control order") specifying the highway and providing that, subject to subsection (5) of this section—

(*a*) no person shall sell anything on the highway or offer or expose anything for sale on the highway; and

(*b*) no person shall, for the purpose of selling anything or offering or exposing anything for sale on the highway or of attracting from users of the highway offers to buy anything, put, keep or use on the highway or on land within fifteen metres from any part of the highway any stall or similar structure or any container or vehicle.

(2) The highway authority for a highway in respect of which a control order is in force may vary or revoke the order by a subsequent order.

(3) Paragraphs 20 to 23, paragraph 24 (except so much of it as relates to appeals by district councils) and paragraph 25 of Schedule 9 to the Road Traffic Regulation Act 1984 (which relates to the procedure for making orders under the provisions of that Act mentioned in paragraphs 20(1) and 24(*a*) and (*b*) of that Schedule) shall have effect as if subsections (1) and (2) of this section were included among those provisions[1].

(4) If a person contravenes a control order which is in force for a highway, the highway authority for the highway may by a notice served on him require him not to contravene the order after a date specified in the notice (which must not be before the expiration of the period of 7 days beginning with the date of service of the notice); and—

(*a*) if a person on whom a notice relating to a contravention of a control order is served in pursuance of this subsection contravenes the order after the expiration of that period, or causes, permits or procures another person to contravene it after the expiration of that period, he shall be guilty of an offence and liable on summary conviction to a fine not exceeding **level 3** on the standard scale;

(*b*) if a contravention in respect of which a person is convicted of an offence in pursuance of the preceding paragraph is continued by him after the expiration of the period of 7 days beginning with the date of the conviction he shall, as respects each day on which the contravention is so continued, be guilty of a further offence and liable on summary conviction to a fine not exceeding **£10**.

(5) A control order does not apply—

(*a*) to anything done at premises used as a shop or petrol filling station either—

(i) in pursuance of planning permission granted or deemed to be granted under the Town and Country Planning Act 1990, or

(ii) in a case where the premises are, without such permission, lawfully used as a shop or petrol filling station;

(*b*) to anything done at a market in respect of which tolls, stallages or rents are payable;

(*c*) to the sale, offer or exposure for sale of things from or on a vehicle which is used only for the purposes of itinerant trading with the occupiers of premises or which is used only for that purpose and for purposes other than trading;

(*d*) to such a vehicle as is mentioned in the preceding paragraph or to containers on the vehicle;

(*e*) to, or to containers used in connection with, the sale, offer or exposure for sale, by or on behalf of the occupier of land used for agriculture and on that land, of agricultural produce produced on that land;

(*f*) to the provision, in a lay-by situated on a highway, of facilities for the purchase of refreshments by persons travelling on the highway or on another highway near to the highway;

(*g*) to anything as respects which the control order provides that the order is not to apply to it.

In paragraph (*e*) of this subsection "agriculture" and "agricultural" have the same meanings as in the Agriculture Act 1947.

(6) References in the preceding provisions of this section to a control order are, in the case of a control order which has been varied in pursuance of subsection (2) of this section, references to the order as so varied.

[Local Government (Miscellaneous Provisions) Act 1976, s 7 as amended by the Criminal Justice Act 1982, ss 38 and 46, the Road Traffic Regulation Act 1984, Sch 13, the Planning (Consequential Provisions) Act 1990, Sch 2 and the Planning and Compensation Act 1991, Sch 7.]

---

[1] The Control of Road-side Sales Orders (Procedure) Regulations 1978, SI 1978/932, have been made.

*Heating etc*

7.7093 **11.** *Production and supply of heat etc by local authorities*[1].

---

[1] Under this provision the Sale of Electricity by Local Authorities (England and Wales) Regulations 2010, SI 2010/1910 have been made.

7.7094 **12. Provisions supplementary to section 11** (1) A local authority which supplies or proposes to supply heat, hot air, hot water or steam in pursuance of the preceding section may make byelaws—

(*a*) with respect to the works and apparatus to be provided or used by persons other than the authority in connection with the supply;

(*b*) for preventing waste and unauthorised use of the supply and unauthorised interference with works and apparatus used by the authority or any other person in connection with the supply;

(*c*) providing for any specified contravention of the byelaws to be an offence punishable on summary conviction with a fine of such an amount, not exceeding **level 3** on the standard scale, as is specified in the byelaws.

[Local Government (Miscellaneous Provisions) Act 1976, s 12, as amended by the Criminal Justice Act 1982, ss 40 and 46 and the Building Act 1984, Sch 6.]

*Land*

7.7095 **15. Power of local authorities to survey land which they propose to acquire compulsorily** (1) A person authorised in writing in that behalf by a local authority may at any reasonable time—

(*a*) survey any land in connection with a proposal by the authority to acquire compulsorily an interest in the land or a right over the land which is not such an interest; and

(*b*) for the purpose of surveying any land in pursuance of the preceding paragraph, enter on the land and other land.

(2) The power to survey land conferred by the preceding subsection includes power to search and bore on and in the land for the purpose of ascertaining the nature of the subsoil or whether minerals are present in the subsoil, and the power to enter on land conferred by that subsection includes power to place and leave, on or in the land, apparatus for use in connection with the survey in question and power to remove the apparatus; and it is hereby declared that references to surveying in this section include surveying from the air.

(3) [1]A person authorised by a local authority to enter on land in pursuance of subsection (1) of this section—

(*a*) shall, if so required before or after entering on the land, produce evidence of his authority to enter;

(*b*) may take with him on to the land such other persons and such equipment as are necessary for the survey in question;

(*c*) shall not if the land is occupied demand admission to the land as of right unless notice of the intended entry has been served by the local authority on the occupier not less than fourteen days before the demand;

(*d*) shall, if the land is unoccupied when he enters or the occupier is then temporarily absent, leave the land as effectually secured against trespassers as he found it;

(*e*) shall not place or leave apparatus on or in the land or remove apparatus from the land—

(i) unless notice of his intention to do so has been served by the local authority on an owner of the land, and if the land is occupied on the occupier, not less than fourteen days before he does so, and

(ii) if the land is held by relevant undertakers who within that period serve on the local authority a notice stating that they object to the placing or leaving or removal of the apparatus on the ground that to do so would be seriously detrimental to the carrying on of their undertaking, unless the Secretary of State authorises him in writing to do so;

(*f*) shall not search or bore on or in the land which is the subject of the survey in question if the land is held by relevant undertakers—

(i) unless notice of his intention to do so has been served by the local authority on the undertakers not less than fourteen days before he does so, and

(ii) if within that period the undertakers serve on the local authority a notice stating that they object to the searching or boring on the ground that to do so would be seriously detrimental to the carrying on of their undertaking, unless the Secretary of State authorises him in writing to do so;

and in paragraphs (*e*) and (*f*) of this subsection "relevant undertakers" means any statutory undertakers, any person authorised to carry on a light railway undertaking, a ferry undertaking or an undertaking for supplying district heating, the Civil Aviation Authority and a person who holds a licence under Chapter I of Part I of the Transport Act 2000 (air traffic services).

(3A) For the purposes of subsection (3) of this section—

(*a*) a person who holds a licence under Chapter I of Part I of the Transport Act 2000 shall not be considered to be a relevant undertaker unless the person is carrying out activities authorised by the licence;

(*b*) the person's undertaking shall not be considered to be that of a relevant undertaker except to the extent that it is the person's undertaking as licence holder.

(4)–(6) *Survey in a street or controlled land within the meaning of the New Roads and Street Works Act* 1991*; compensation for damage arising from a survey.*

(7) If a person—

(*a*) wilfully obstructs another person in the exercise of a power conferred on the other person by subsection (1) or (3)(*b*) of this section; or

(*b*) while another person is on any land in pursuance of the said subsection (3)(*b*), wilfully obstructs him in doing things connected with the survey in question; or

(*c*) removes or otherwise interferes with apparatus left on or in land in pursuance of this section,

he shall be guilty of an offence and liable on summary conviction to a fine not exceeding **level 3** on the standard scale.

(8) If a person who has entered on any land in pursuance of this section discloses to another person information obtained by him there about a manufacturing process or trade secret, then, unless the disclosure is made in the course of performing his duty in connection with the purposes for which he was authorised to enter on the land, he shall be guilty of an offence and liable[2], on summary conviction, to a fine not exceeding **the statutory maximum** or, on conviction on indictment, to imprisonment for a term not exceeding **two years** or a fine or both.

(9) A local authority which has power by virtue of section 289(1) of the Highways Act 1980, section 324(6) of the Town and Country Planning Act 1990, section 88(5) of the Planning (Listed Buildings and Conservation Areas) Act 1990, or paragraph 20(1) of Schedule 4 to the Community Land Act 1975 to authorise a person to survey or enter on any land as mentioned in subsection (1) of this section shall not be entitled by virtue of that subsection to authorise a person to survey or enter on the land.

[Local Government (Miscellaneous Provisions) Act 1976, s 15 as amended by the Criminal Law Act 1977, s 28, the Highways Act 1980, Sch 24, the Criminal Justice Act 1982, ss 38 and 46, the Airports Act 1986, Sch 6, the Coal Industry Act 1987, Sch 1, the Planning (Consequential Provisions) Act 1990, Sch 2, the New Roads and Street Works Act 1991, Sch 8, the Coal Industry Act 1994, Sch 9, SI 2001/4050 and SI 2009/1307.]

---

1 For the purposes of s 15(3) of this Act, the holder of a licence under s 6(1) of the Electricity Act 1989 shall be deemed to be a statutory undertaker and his undertaking a statutory undertaking (Electricity Act 1989, Sch 16, para 1).

2 For procedure in respect of this offence which is triable either way, see the Magistrates' Courts Act 1980, ss 17A–21, in PART I: MAGISTRATES' COURTS, PROCEDURE, ante.

**7.7096 16. Power[1] of local authorities to obtain particulars of persons interested in land**

(1) Where, with a view to performing a function conferred on a local authority by any enactment, the authority considers that it ought to have information connected with any land, the authority may serve on one or more of the following persons, namely—

(*a*) the occupier of the land; and

(*b*) any person who has an interest in the land either as freeholder, mortgagee or lessee or who directly or indirectly receives rent for the land; and

(*c*) any person who, in pursuance of an agreement between himself and a person interested in the land, is authorised to manage the land or to arrange for the letting of it,

a notice specifying the land and the function and the enactment which confers the function and requiring the recipient of the notice to furnish to the authority, within a period specified in the notice (which shall not be less than fourteen days beginning with the day on which the notice is served) the nature of his interest in the land and the name and address of each person whom the recipient of the notice believes is the occupier of the land and of each person whom he believes is, as respects the land, such a person as is mentioned in the provisions of paragraphs (*b*) and (*c*) of this subsection.

(2) A person who—

(*a*) fails to comply with the requirements of a notice served on him in pursuance of the preceding subsection; or

(*b*) in furnishing any information in compliance with such a notice makes a statement which he knows to be false in a material particular or recklessly makes a statement which is false in a material particular,

shall be guilty of an offence and liable[2] on summary conviction to a fine not exceeding **level 5** on the standard scale.

[Local Government (Miscellaneous Provisions) Act 1976, s 16 as amended by the Criminal Justice Act 1982, ss 38 and 46.]

1 This power shall not be exercisable with a view to performing any function under Pt I of the Local Government Finance Act 1992 (council tax): Local Government Finance Act 1992, Sch 13.
2 For liability of director, etc, where offence is committed by a body corporate, see s 44(3), post.

*Bathing and boating*

7.7097 17. **Byelaws about bathing and boating** The power of a local authority to make byelaws under section 231 of the Public Health Act 1936 and section 76 of the Public Health Act 1961 may be exercised as respects any area of sea which is outside the area of the authority and within 1,000 metres to seaward of any place where the low water mark is within or on the boundary of the area of the authority; an offence against a byelaw made under the above provision may be dealt with as if committed within the area of the authority.

[Local Government (Miscellaneous Provisions) Act 1976, s 17—summarised.]

*Places of entertainment*

7.7098 19. *Recreational facilities.*

7.7099 20. **Provision of sanitary appliances at places of entertainment** (1) A local authority (other than a county council in England and the Greater London Council[1]) may, by a notice served on an owner or occupier of a relevant place[2] in the area of the authority, require him—

(*a*) to provide, before the expiration of a period specified in the notice and in such positions at the place as are so specified, sanitary appliances[2] of such kinds and numbers as are so specified;

(*b*) to maintain and keep clean the appliances to the reasonable satisfaction of the authority;

(*c*) to provide and maintain a proper supply of such things for use in connection with the appliances as are so specified (which may be or include cold water or hot water or both); and

(*d*) to make the appliances and things available for use by members of the public resorting to the place and, if the notice so requires, to make them so available free of charge.

(2) A notice in pursuance of this section may require the provision of sanitary appliances on such occasions as are specified in the notice but if it does so it shall not also require the provision of sanitary appliances as respects which occasions are not so specified.

(3) A notice in pursuance of this section—

(*a*) shall not require the provision, in connection with any building for which fixed sanitary appliances could be required by virtue of building regulations in force when the notice is served if the building were to be newly constructed then, of fixed sanitary appliances which are of a different kind from, or which as respects a particular kind are more numerous than, those which could be required as aforesaid;

(*b*) shall not require the provision of movable sanitary appliances at a betting office[2];

(*c*) shall, unless it is an occasional notice[2], specify as the period before the expiration of which sanitary appliances are to be provided in pursuance of the notice a period equal to or longer than that during which the recipient of the notice may appeal against it in pursuance of the following section.

(4) It is hereby declared that a notice in pursuance of this section in respect of a relevant place may—

(*a*) be served on an owner or occupier of the place notwithstanding that he is for the time being required to comply with a previous notice served on him in pursuance of this section in respect of the place;

(*b*) require the provision at the place of appliances already provided there.

(5) A person authorised in writing in that behalf by a local authority (other than a county council in England and the Greater London Council) may at any reasonable time, upon producing if so required evidence that he is so authorised, enter any relevant place for the purpose of determining whether the authority should serve a notice in pursuance of this section in respect of the place or of ascertaining whether the requirements of such a notice served on a person who is an owner or occupier of the place are being complied with; and a person who wilfully obstructs another person acting in the exercise of powers conferred on the other person by this subsection shall be guilty of an offence and liable on summary conviction to a fine not exceeding **level 3** on the standard scale.

(6) Subject to subsections (7) and (8) of this section, a person who without reasonable excuse fails to comply with a notice in respect of a relevant place which was served on him in pursuance of this section when he was an owner or occupier of the place shall be guilty of an offence and liable[3] on summary conviction to a fine not exceeding **the prescribed sum** or, on conviction on indictment, to a fine; and if after the conviction of a person of such an offence the failure in question continues he shall, as respects each day on which it continues, be guilty of a further offence and liable on summary conviction to a fine not exceeding **£50** or, on conviction on indictment, to a fine.

(7) In proceedings for an offence under the preceding subsection of failing to comply with a notice it shall be a defence to prove that at the time of the failure the person on whom the notice was served was neither an owner nor an occupier of the relevant place in question and that he did not cease to be an owner or occupier of it by reason of anything done or omitted by him or any other

person with a view to avoiding compliance with the notice.

(8) In proceedings for an offence under subsection (6) of this section which is alleged to have been committed on a particular day it shall be a defence to prove that on that day the relevant place in question was closed to members of the public or was used neither as a betting office nor for any of the purposes mentioned in paragraph (*a*) of the definition of relevant place in the following subsection; and in proceedings for an offence under subsection (6) of this section of failing to comply with an occasional notice it shall be a defence to prove—

(*a*) that the alleged offence is in respect of a requirement of the notice which is unreasonable; or

(*b*) that it would have been fairer to serve the notice on a person, other than the defendant—

(i) who was an owner or occupier of the relevant place in question when the notice was served on the defendant, and

(ii) whose name and address were furnished by the defendant, to the local authority which served the notice, before the expiration of the period specified in the notice in pursuance of subsection (1)(*a*) of this section.

(9) In this section and the following section—

"betting office" means premises, other than a track within the meaning of the Gambling Act 2005, in respect of which a betting premises licence under Part 8 of that Act has effect;

"occasional notice" means a notice in pursuance of this section requiring the provision of sanitary appliances on occasions specified in the notice;

"sanitary appliances" means water closets, other closets, urinals and wash basins;

"relevant place" means any of the following places—

(*a*) a place which is normally used or is proposed to be normally used for any of the following purposes, namely—

(i) the holding of any entertainment, exhibition or sporting event to which members of the public are admitted either as spectators or otherwise,

(ii) the sale of food or drink to members of the public for consumption at the place[4];

(*b*) a place which is used on some occasion or occasions or is proposed to be used on some occasion or occasions for any of the purposes aforesaid; and

(*c*) a betting office.

(10) *Consequential amendment.*

(11) A notice under this section shall draw the attention of the person on whom it is served—

(*a*) to sections 6(1) and 7 of the Chronically Sick and Disabled Persons Act 1970; and

(*b*) to the Code of Practice for Access for the Disabled to Buildings.

(12) In subsection (11) of this section "the Code of Practice for Access for the Disabled to Buildings" means, subject to subsection (13) of this section, the British Standards Institution code of practice referred to as BS 5810: 1979.

(13) Section 28 of the Chronically Sick and Disabled Persons Act 1970 (power to define certain expressions for the purposes of provisions of that Act) shall have effect as if any reference in it to a provision of that Act included a reference to this section.

[Local Government (Miscellaneous Provisions) Act 1976, s 20 as amended by the Criminal Law Act 1977, s 28, the Disabled Persons Act 1981, s 4, the Criminal Justice Act 1982, ss 38 and 46 and the Gambling Act 2005, Sch 16.]

---

1 The Greater London Council was abolished by the Local Government Act 1985, s 1.

2 Defined in sub-s (9), post.

3 For procedure in respect of this offence which is triable either way, see the Magistrates' Courts Act 1980, ss 17A–21, in PART I: MAGISTRATES' COURTS, PROCEDURE, ante. For liability of director, etc, where offence is committed by a body corporate, see s 44(3), post.

4 "Normal use" is not the same as "predominant" use; it is "normal" use of premises for a customer to sit down and eat and drink at a seat provided in the premises for such use even though most customers take away their purchases and do not stay long. Where "advice and guidance" has been issued by a "primary authority" in accordance with s 27(1)(*b*) of the Regulatory Enforcement and Sanctions Act 2008, it must state the law correctly. Any construction of s 20 of the 1976 Act ultimately remains for the court. The discretionary functions under the 1976 Act remain with the authority for the area concerned. It must take the advice very seriously but, as decision-maker, it must satisfy itself that the advice and guidance is satisfactory: *R (Kingston upon Hull City Council) v Secretary of State for Business, Innovation and Skills* [2016] EWHC 1064 (Admin), 181 JP 20.

**7.7100 21.** *Appeal to county court against certain notices under s* 20.

*Dangerous trees and excavations*

**7.7101 23.** *Power of local authorities to deal with dangerous trees.*

**7.7102 24. Provisions supplementary to section 23** (1) A person authorised in writing in that behalf by such a council as is mentioned in subsection (1)[1] of the preceding section may enter on any land for the purpose of—

(*a*) determining whether the council should take steps in pursuance of subsection (2) or (7)[2] or serve a notice in pursuance of subsection (3)[2] of that section in respect of a tree on the land; or

(*b*) exercising on behalf of the council a power conferred on the council by subsection (2) or (7)[2] of that section in respect of a tree on the land.

(2) A person authorised to enter on any land in pursuance of the preceding subsection—

(*a*) shall, if so required before or after entering on the land, produce evidence of his authority to enter;

(*b*) may take with him on to the land such other persons and such equipment as are necessary for achieving the purpose for which he was authorised to enter on the land;

(*c*) shall, if the land is unoccupied when he enters or the occupier is then temporarily absent, leave the land as effectually secured against trespassers as he found it.

(3) If a person—

(*a*) wilfully obstructs another person in the exercise of a power conferred on the other person by subsection (1) or (2)(*b*) of this section; or

(*b*) while another person is on land in pursuance of the said subsection (1) or (2)(*b*), wilfully obstructs the other person in doing things connected with the purpose for which the other person is authorised to be on the land,

he shall be guilty of an offence and liable on summary conviction to a fine not exceeding **level 3** on the standard scale.

(4) If a person interested in any land suffers damage by reason of—

(*a*) the exercise of the power to enter on the land which is conferred by virtue of subsection (1)(*a*) of this section; or

(*b*) the exercise on the land, in connection with the exercise of the power mentioned in the preceding paragraph, of the power conferred by subsection (2)(*b*) of this section; or

(*c*) a failure to perform the duty imposed by subsection (2)(*c*) of this section in respect of the land,

he shall be entitled to recover compensation for the damage from the local authority which authorised the entry in question.

(5)–(6) *Compensation for damage; council to recover expenses with interest.*

[Local Government (Miscellaneous Provisions) Act 1976, s 24 amended by the Local Government, Planning and Land Act 1980, Sch 6, the Criminal Justice Act 1982, ss 38 and 46 and SI 2009/1307.]

---

1 This means a district council, a London borough council or the Common Council (s 23(1)).

2 Where a council receives from an owner or occupier of land a notice requesting that it makes safe a tree on other land which is not owned or occupied by that person, and the council considers that the tree is likely to cause damage, and does not know the name and address of the owner or occupier of the other land, it may take steps on the land, by felling or otherwise, to make the tree safe (s 23(2)—SUMMARISED). Where a council receives such a request to make a tree safe, and considers the tree is likely to cause damage, and knows the name and address of the owner or occupier of the land, the council may serve on such person a notice requiring him within a specified time to make the tree safe (s 23(3)—SUMMARISED). If a person fails to comply with a notice under s 23(3), the council may take the steps specified in the notice and recover from that person the expenses reasonably incurred (s 23(7)—SUMMARISED).

7.7103 25. *Power of certain councils with respect to dangerous excavations.*

7.7104 26. **Provisions supplementary to s 25**[1] (1) A person authorised in writing in that behalf by such a council as is mentioned in subsection (1)[2] of the preceding section may enter on any land in the area of the council for the purpose of—

(*a*) ascertaining whether the land is suitable as the site of works which the council may carry out or for which the council may serve a notice in pursuance of that section[3]; or

(*b*) carrying out, maintaining, repairing or removing in pursuance of that section[3] any works on behalf of the council; or

(*c*) ascertaining whether any works carried out by the council in pursuance of that section[3] should be or have been maintained, repaired or removed.

(2) A person authorised by a council to enter on land in pursuance of the preceding subsection—

(*a*) shall, if so required before or after entering on the land, produce evidence of his authority to enter;

(*b*) may take with him on to the land such other persons and such equipment as are necessary for achieving the purpose for which he was authorised to enter on the land;

(*c*) shall, if the land is unoccupied when he enters or the occupier is then temporarily absent, leave the land as effectually secured against trespassers as he found it.

(3)–(4) *Compensation for damage.*

(5) If a person—

(*a*) wilfully obstructs another person in the exercise of a power conferred on the other person by subsection (1) or (2)(*b*) of this section; or

(*b*) while another person is on land in pursuance of the said subsection (2)(*b*) wilfully obstructs him in doing things connected with the works in question; or

(*c*) without the agreement of the council by which works have been carried out in pursuance of the preceding section, removes or otherwise interferes with the works,

he shall be guilty of an offence and liable on summary conviction to a fine not exceeding **level 3** on the standard scale.

(6) Nothing in the preceding section or the preceding provisions of this section applies to an excavation—

(*a*) on operational land of statutory undertakers; or

(*b*) on land of the Coal Authority of such a description as the Secretary of State may specify by regulations made by statutory instrument;

and the definition of "operational land" in section 263 of the Town and Country Planning Act 1990 shall apply for the purposes of paragraph (*a*) of this subsection as if in that section "statutory undertakers" had the same meaning as in that paragraph and "undertaking" had a corresponding meaning.

[Local Government (Miscellaneous Provisions) Act 1976, s 26, as amended by the Criminal Justice Act 1982, ss 38 and 46, the Coal Industry Act 1987, Sch 1, the Planning (Consequential Provisions) Act 1990, Sch 2 and the Coal Industry Act 1994, Sch 9.]

---

1 For the purposes of s 26 of this Act, the holder of a licence under s 6(1) of the Electricity Act 1989 shall be deemed to be a statutory undertaker and his undertaking a statutory undertaking (Electricity Act 1989, Sch 16, para 1).

2 This means a district council, a London borough council or the Common Council (s 25(1)).

3 Where a council considers that an excavation on land is accessible to the public from a highway or a place of public resort and, by reason of its being unenclosed or inadequately enclosed, is a danger to the public, and the council does not know the name and address of the owner or occupier of the land on which works to remove the danger should be carried out, the council may carry out on that land works for the purpose of removing the danger (s 25(1)—SUMMARISED). Where a council considers that an excavation is as mentioned in s 25(1), and knows the name and address of the owner or occupier of the land on which works to remove the danger should be carried out, the council may serve on the owner or occupier of the land a notice specifying the excavation and stating that the council proposes to carry out works specified in the notice (s 25(2)—SUMMARISED).

*Miscellaneous*

7.7105 35. **Removal of obstructions from private sewers** (1) If a private sewer is obstructed at a point within the area of a local authority (other than a county council in England), the authority may serve on each of the persons who is an owner or occupier of premises served by the sewer, or on each of such of those persons as the authority thinks fit, a notice requiring the recipients of notices in pursuance of this subsection in respect of the obstruction to remove it before a time specified in the notice; and that time shall not be earlier than forty-eight hours after the service of the notice or, if different notices in respect of the same obstruction are served in pursuance of this subsection at different times, shall not be earlier than forty-eight hours after the latest of those times.

(2) If an obstruction in respect of which notices have been served by an authority in pursuance of the preceding subsection is not removed within the period specified in the notices, the authority may remove it.

(3)–(6) *Recovery of expenses incurred in pursuance of subsection* (2).

(7) Expressions used in this section and in Part II of the Public Health Act 1936 have the same meanings in this section as in that Part; and sections 287 and 288 of that Act[1] (which confer power to enter premises and penalise obstruction) shall have effect as if references to that Act included references to this section.

[Local Government (Miscellaneous Provisions) Act 1976, s 35 as amended by the Local Government Act 1985, Sch 17 and SI 1996/3071.]

---

1 See title PUBLIC HEALTH, post.

7.7106 36. *Power of local authorities to appoint times and charges for markets.*

7.7107 41. **Evidence[1] of resolutions and minutes of proceedings etc** (1) A document which—

(*a*) purports to be a copy of—

(i) a resolution, order or report of a local authority or a precursor of a local authority, or

(ii) the minutes of the proceedings at a meeting of a local authority or a precursor of a local authority; and

(*b*) bears a certificate purporting to be signed by the proper officer of the authority or a person authorised in that behalf by him or the authority and stating that the resolution was passed or the order or report was made by the authority or precursor on a date specified in the certificate or, as the case may be, that the minutes were signed in accordance with paragraph 41 of Schedule 12 to the Local Government Act 1972 or the corresponding provision specified in the certificate of the enactments relating to local government which were in force when the minutes were signed,

shall be evidence in any proceedings of the matters stated in the certificate and of the terms of the resolution, order, report or minutes in question.

(2) In the preceding subsection references to a local authority, except the first and second references in paragraph (*b*), include references to a committee of a local authority and a sub-committee of such a committee and references to a precursor of a local authority include references to a committee of such a precursor and a sub-committee of such a committee.

(2A) In the case of a local authority which are operating executive arrangements, a document which—

(*a*) purports to be a copy of a record of any decision made by the executive of that authority or a member of that executive, or any person acting on behalf of that executive, where that record is required to be kept or produced by section 22 of the Local Government Act 2000 or any regulations made under that section; and (*b*) bears a certificate purporting to be signed by the proper officer of the authority or by a person authorised in that behalf by him or any other person who, by virtue of regulations made under section 22 of the Local Government Act 2000, is authorised or required to produce such a record, stating that the decision was made on the date specified in the certificate by that executive, or as the case may be, by the member of that executive or by the person acting on behalf of that executive,

shall be evidence in any proceedings of the matters stated in the certificate and of the terms of the decision in question.

(2B) Subsection (2C) applies to a record if—

(*a*) it records a decision made or action taken by a member of a local authority or of a precursor of a local authority in exercise of a function of the authority or precursor by virtue of arrangements made under section 236 of the Local Government and Public Involvement in Health Act 2007, and

(*b*) it is required to be made by regulations under section 100EA of the Local Government Act 1972.

(2C) If a document which purports to be a copy of a record to which this subsection applies bears a certificate—

(*a*) purporting to be signed by—

(i) the proper officer of the local authority, or

(ii) a person authorised in that behalf by that officer or by the local authority, and

(*b*) stating that the decision was made or the action was taken by the member of the local authority on the date specified in the certificate,

the document shall be evidence in any proceedings of the matters stated in the certificate and of the terms of the decision, or nature of the action, in question.

(3) A document which—

(*a*) purports to be a copy of an instrument by which the proper officer of a local authority appointed a person to be an officer of the authority or authorised a person to perform functions specified in the instrument; and

(*b*) bears a certificate purporting to be signed as mentioned in subsection (1)(*b*) of this section and stating that the document is a copy of the instrument in question,

shall be evidence in any proceedings of the fact that the instrument was made by the said proper officer and of the terms of the instrument.

(4) In the preceding provisions of this section "precursor", in relation to a local authority, means any authority which has ceased to exist but which when it existed was constituted, in pursuance of the enactments relating to local government which were then in force, for an area any part of which is included in the area of the local authority.

[Local Government (Miscellaneous Provisions) Act 1976, s 41 as amended by SI 2001/2237 and the Local Government and Public Involvement in Health Act 2007, s 237.]

---

[1] Note the requirement for strict compliance with s 41(1) when prosecuting an alleged breach of the system of licensing sex establishments (*Smakowski v Westminster City Council* (1989) 154 JP 345).

*Supplemental*

7.7108 **44. Interpretation etc of Part I** (1) In this Part of this Act, except where the contrary intention appears—

"apparatus" includes any structure constructed in order that apparatus may be lodged in it;

"the Common Council" means the Common Council of the City of London;

"executive" and "executive arrangements" have the same meaning as in Part II of the Local Government Act 2000;

"functions" includes powers and duties;

"highway" has the same meaning as in the Highways Act 1980[1];

"local Act" includes a provisional order confirmed by an Act;

"local authority" means a county council, a county borough council, a district council, a London borough council, the Common Council, the Council of the Isles of Scilly and—

(*a*) in sections 13 to 16, 29, 30, 38, 39 and 41 of this Act, a police and crime commissioner, the Mayor's Office for Policing and Crime, a joint authority established by Part IV of the Local Government Act 1985 an economic prosperity board established under section 88 of the Local Democracy, Economic Development and Construction Act 2009, a combined authority established under section 103 of that Act and the London Fire and Emergency Planning Authority;

(*b*) in sections 1, 16, 19, 30, 36, 39 and 41 of this Act, a parish council and a community council;

(*c*) in section 40 of this Act, a joint authority established by Part IV of the Local Government Act 1985, an authority established under section 10 of that Act (waste regulation and disposal authorities), an economic prosperity board established under section 88 of the Local Democracy, Economic Development and Construction Act 2009, a combined authority established under section 103 of that Act, the London Fire and Emergency Planning Authority and the South Yorkshire Pensions Authority;

"notice" means notice in writing;

"owner", in relation to any land, place or premises, means a person who, either on his own account or as agent or trustee for another person, is receiving the rackrent of the land, place or premises or would be entitled to receive it if the land, place or premises were let at a rackrent, and "owned" shall be construed accordingly;

"statutory undertakers"[2] means any of the following bodies, namely, any statutory undertakers within the meaning of the Highways Act 1980; and, a universal service provider in connection with the provision of a universal postal service; and

"traffic sign" has the same meaning as in the Road Traffic Regulation Act 1984;

"universal service provider" has the same meaning as in the Postal Services Act 2000; and references to the provision of a universal postal service shall be construed in accordance with that Act.

(1ZA) The undertaking of a universal service provider so far as relating to the provision of a universal postal service shall be taken to be his statutory undertaking for the purposes of this Part; and references in this Part to his undertaking shall be construed accordingly.

(1A) Sections 13, 15, 16, 29, 30, 32, 38, 39 and 41 of this Act shall have effect as if the Broads Authority were a local authority and the Broads (as defined in the Norfolk and Suffolk Broads Act 1988) were its local government area.

(1B) Section 16 of this Act shall have effect as if the Environment Agency were a local authority.

(2) Section 32[2] of the Highways Act 1980 (which relates to the service of documents) shall apply to the service of any document by or on the Secretary of State in pursuance of section 7 of this Act as if that section were a provision of that Act.

(3) When an offence under this Part of this Act (including an offence under byelaws made by virtue of section 12 of this Act) which has been committed by a body corporate is proved to have been committed with the consent or connivance of, or to be attributable to any neglect on the part of, any director, manager, secretary or other similar officer of the body corporate or any person who was purporting to act in any such capacity, he as well as the body corporate shall be guilty of that offence and be liable to be proceeded against and punished accordingly.

Where the affairs of a body corporate are managed by its members the preceding provisions of this subsection shall apply in relation to the acts and defaults of a member in connection with his functions of management as if he were a director of the body corporate.

(4) Except so far as this Part of this Act expressly provides otherwise and subject to the provisions of section 33 of the Interpretation Act 1889[3] (which relates to offences under two or more laws), nothing in this Part of this Act—

(*a*) confers a right of action in any civil proceedings (other than proceedings for the recovery of a fine) in respect of any contravention of this Part of this Act or an instrument made in pursuance of this Part of this Act;

(*b*) affects any restriction imposed by or under any other enactment, whether public, local or private; or

(*c*) derogates from any right of action or other remedy (whether civil or criminal) in proceedings instituted otherwise than under this Part of this Act.

(5) Nothing in paragraph (*a*) of the preceding subsection applies to the failure of a person to perform a duty imposed on him by section 1(4), 2(5), 25(6) or (7)(*b*) of this Act or section 61(2)(*c*) of the Road Traffic Regulation Act 1984.

(6) References in this Part of this Act to any enactment are references to it as amended by or under any other enactment.

[Local Government (Miscellaneous Provisions) Act 1976, s 44 as amended by the Highways Act 1980, Schs 24 and 25, the British Telecommunications Act 1981, Sch 3, the Road Traffic Regulation Act 1984, Sch 13, the Local Government Act 1985, Schs 14 and 17, the Telecommunications Act 1984, Sch 7, the Norfolk and Suffolk Broads Act 1988, Sch 6, the Education Reform Act 1988, Sch 13, the Water Act 1989, Sch 27, SI 1990/1765, the Police and Magistrates' Courts Act 1994, Sch 4, the Environment Act 1995, Sch 22, the Police Act 1996, Sch 7, the Police Act 1997, Sch 6, the Greater London Authority Act 1999, Schs 27, 29 and 34, SI 2001/1149, the Criminal Justice and Police Act 2001, Sch 6, SI 2002/808, the Local Government and Public Involvement in Health Act 2007, Sch 13, the Local Democracy, Economic Development and Construction Act 2009, Sch 6, the Police Reform and Social Responsibility Act 2011, Sch 16 and the Deregulation Act 2015, Sch 13.]

1 See s 328 of the Highways Act 1980, PART VI: TRANSPORT, title HIGHWAYS.

2 The National Rivers Authority, every water undertaker and every sewerage undertaker is deemed to be a statutory undertaker for the purposes of this Act (Water Act 1989, Sch 25, para 1).

3 Now s 18 of the Interpretation Act 1978.

## PART II[1]
## HACKNEY CARRIAGES AND PRIVATE HIRE VEHICLES

7.7109 **45. Application of Part II** (1) The provisions of this Part of this Act, except this section, shall come into force in accordance with the following provisions of this section.

(2) If the Act of 1847[2] is in force in the area of a district council, the council may resolve that the provisions of this Part of this Act, other than this section, are to apply to the relevant area; and if the

council do so resolve those provisions shall come into force in the relevant area on the day specified in that behalf in the resolution (which must not be before the expiration of the period of one month beginning with the day on which the resolution is passed).

In this subsection "the relevant area", in relation to a council, means—

(*a*) if the Act of 1847 is in force throughout the area of the council, that area; and

(*b*) if the Act of 1847 is in force for part only of the area of the council, that part of that area.

(3) A council shall not pass a resolution in pursuance of the foregoing subsection unless they have—

(*a*) published in two consecutive weeks, in a local newspaper circulating in their area, notice of their intention to pass the resolution; and

(*b*) served a copy of the notice, not later than the date on which it is first published in pursuance of the foregoing paragraph, on the council of each parish or community which would be affected by the resolution or, in the case of such a parish which has no parish council, on the chairman of the parish meeting.

(4) If after a council has passed a resolution in pursuance of subsection (2) of this section the Act of 1847 comes into force for any part of the area of the council for which it was not in force when the council passed the resolution, the council may pass a resolution in accordance with the foregoing provisions of this section in respect of that part as if that part were included in the relevant area for the purposes of subsection (2) of this section.

[Local Government (Miscellaneous Provisions) Act 1976, s 45.]

---

1 Part II of this Act amended and extended the controls over hackney carriages under the Town Police Clauses Act 1847, and introduced new powers to control private hire vehicles and their drivers, proprietors and operators. Part II does not apply to London. Sections 1, 2, and 42 of the Public Passenger Vehicles Act 1981, post, provide certain exemptions from the PSV licensing system; it shall however continue to be treated as such for the purposes of a local Act or Pt II of this Act (Public Passenger Vehicles Act 1981, s 79, post).

Part II of this Act, to the extent to which it is part of the taxi code, subject to modifications and exceptions, shall apply to a licensed taxi which is being used to provide a local service under a special licence under s 12 of the Transport Act 1985 (Local Services (Operation by Taxis) Regulations 1986, SI 1986/567).

Sections 47, 65(5), 66 and 67 of the Act are modified or disapplied in relation to the hiring of taxis at separate fares under ss 10 and 11 of the Transport Act 1985 (Licensed Taxis (Hiring at Separate Fares) Order 1986, SI 1986/1386).

2 "The Act of 1847" means the provisions of the Town Police Clauses Act 1847 with respect to hackney carriages (s 80(1), post). For that Act, see title TOWNS IMPROVEMENTS: TOWN POLICE, post.

7.7110 **46. Vehicle, drivers' and operators' licences** (1) Except as authorised by this Part of this Act—

(*a*) no person being the proprietor[1] of any vehicle, not being a hackney carriage[1] or London cab in respect of which a vehicle licence[1] is in force, shall use or permit the same to be used in a controlled district[1] as a private hire vehicle[1] without having for such a vehicle a current licence under section 48 of this Act[2];

(*b*) no person shall in a controlled district act as driver[3] of any private hire vehicle without having a current licence under section 51 of this Act[4];

(*c*) no person being the proprietor of a private hire vehicle licensed under this Part of this Act shall employ as the driver[3] thereof for the purpose of any hiring any person who does not have a current licence under the said section 51;

(*d*) no person shall in a controlled district operate[1] any vehicle as a private hire vehicle without having a current licence under section 55 of this Act[5];

(*e*) no person licensed under the said section 55 shall in a controlled district operate[1] any vehicle as a private hire vehicle—

(i) if for the vehicle a current licence under the said section 48 is not in force; or

(ii) if the driver does not have a current licence under the said section 51[6].

(2) If any person knowingly contravenes the provisions of this section, he shall be guilty of an offence[7].

[Local Government (Miscellaneous Provisions) Act 1976, s 46 as amended by the Transport Act 1985, Sch 7.]

---

1 For meaning of "proprietor", "hackney carriage", "vehicle licence", "controlled district", "operate" and "private hire vehicle", see s 80(1), post. The fact that a vehicle is licensed as a hackney carriage by one local authority does not preclude its being a private hire vehicle in the area of another local authority (*Kingston upon Hull City Council v Wilson* (1995) Times, 25 July). For the purposes of s 46(1)(*d*) and (*e*), the meaning of "operate" is that provided in s 80(1), post (*Adur District Council v Fry* [1997] RTR 257). See also *Brentwood Borough Council v Gladen* [2004] EWHC 2500 (Admin), [2005] RTR 12; and *R (on the application of Newcastle City Council) v Berwick-Upon-Tweed Borough Council* [2008] EWHC 2369 (Admin), [2009] RTR 34.)

For the purposes of s 46(1)(*d*) and (*e*), the meaning of "operate" is that provided in s 80(1), post (*Adur District Council v Fry* [1997] RTR 257).

It was held in *Stockton-on-Tees Borough Council v Fidler* [2010] EWHC 2430 (Admin), 175 JP 49 that "hackney carriage" in s 80(1) of the 1976 Act, meant a hackney carriage wherever it had been licensed as such. A hackney carriage was always a hackney carriage, no matter what it was doing, or where, and its use, for whatever purpose, could never make it a private hire vehicle in the statutory sense. There were entirely separate and distinct regimes for the licensing of hackney carriages and private hire vehicles, and the regime that regulated private hire vehicles had no application to a vehicle registered as a hackney carriage. The purpose of the 1976 Act was to impose a scheme of licensing on otherwise unlicensed vehicles and their drivers; it was not to impose further regulation on already-regulated hackney carriages. To "operate" within the meaning of the 1976 Act, including for the purposes of ss 46(1)(*d*) and 46(1)(*e*) of that Act, was, as the definition of "operate" in s 80(1) made clear, an activity that could have been carried out only in relation to a private hire vehicle as defined by s 80(1) and that definition explicitly excluded a hackney carriage; it was not an activity carried out, or capable of being carried out, in relation to a hackney carriage, however or wherever it was being used. The provision of a hackney carriage for hire together with the services of the driver pursuant to an advance booking was not a licensable activity. It had always been an activity unregulated under any statute.

[2] Where a hackney carriage, in respect of which a vehicle licence was in force, was used to collect a passenger in a controlled district outside the area of the local authority that had issued the vehicle licence, it was held no offence had been committed (*Britain v ABC Cabs (Camberley) Ltd* [1981] RTR 395).

[3] A short-staffed licensed operator whose wife drove pre-arranged bookings for no cost was "operating" for the purposes of this section and s 80(1) post and thus liable as his wife was not a licensed driver: (*St Albans District Council v Taylor* [1991] RTR 400, DC).

[4] Section 46(1)(*b*) applies to all driving in a controlled district of a vehicle characterised under s 80(1), post, as a private hire vehicle, whatever the specific activity in connection with which the vehicle is in fact being driven. Accordingly, it is no defence in a prosecution under s 46(1)(*b*) that the vehicle was not actually being used for private hire (*Benson v Boyce* [1997] RTR 226). Section 46(2) requires the prosecution, if it is to establish guilt in relation to s 46(1)(*b*), to prove that the defendant knew that: (i) he was driving in a controlled district; (ii) the vehicle he was driving was a private hire vehicle; and (iii) at the time, he was not the holder of a driver's licence to drive such a vehicle. Providing knowledge of those three factors is proved, it matters not that the defendant did not appreciate that he was committing an offence (*Reading Borough Council v Ahmad* (1998) 163 JP 451).

[5] The collection of a passenger within a controlled district in pursuance of a contract for hire made outside the controlled district is not "operating" for the purposes of s 46(1)(*d*) (*Britain v ABC Cabs (Camberley) Ltd* [1981] RTR 395; followed in *Stockton-on-Tees Borough Council v Fidler*, supra.).

[6] Section 46(1)(*e*) must be read subject to the provisions of s 80(2), post, so as to require private hire operators licensed under s 55, post, to make use only of vehicles and drivers licensed by the council of the district by which the operators are licensed when operating in that controlled district (*Dittah v Birmingham City Council* (1993) 157 JP 1110, [1993] RTR 356, [1993] Crim LR 610).

[7] For penalty, see s 76, post, and note possible defences under s 75, post.

7.7111 **47. Licensing of hackney carriages** (1) A district council may attach to the grant of a licence of a hackney carriage under the Act of 1847[1] such conditions[2] as the district council may consider reasonably necessary.

(2) Without prejudice to the generality of the foregoing subsection, a district council may require any hackney carriage licensed by them under the Act of 1847 to be of such design or appearance or bear such distinguishing marks as shall clearly identify it as a hackney carriage.

(3) Any person aggrieved by any conditions attached to such a licence may appeal[3] to a magistrates' court.

[Local Government (Miscellaneous Provisions) Act 1976, s 47.]

---

[1] See note 2 to para 7.7109, ante.

[2] A condition requiring adaptation of vehicles and applying only to new licences is valid (*R v Manchester City Justices, ex p McHugh* [1989] RTR 285—disabled facilities). Conditions cannot be imposed to restrict new licences to certain parts of the District Council's area; such an approach would create a two-tier system that flew in the face of the legislative approach to remove restraints and to allow market forces to take effect (*R (on the application of Maud) v Castle Point Borough Council* [2002] EWCA Civ 1526, [2002] JPN 782, [2003] RTR 122). However, the wide manner in which s 47 is framed empowers a local authority to attach to a hackney carriage licence any condition it considers to be reasonably necessary to further the objectives of the licensing regime provided for in conjunction with the Town Police Clauses Act 1847; it is desirable in principle that licensing authorities are able to restrict the issue of licences to proprietors and drivers intending to ply for hire in its area and to refuse to license those who do not intend to ply for hire in its area to a material extent; therefore, a condition that the licence holder must ensure that full and contemporaneous records are kept of all uses of the vehicle either as a hackney carriage or as a private hire vehicle, such records would be considered by the local authority when determining annual licence renewal applications, is workable, rational and lawful: *R (Shanks and others (trading as Blue Line Taxis)) v Northumberland County Council* [2012] EWHC 1539 (Admin), (2013) PTSR 154.

[3] The procedure shall be in accordance with ss 300–302 of the Public Health Act 1936, title PUBLIC HEALTH, post (s 77, post). See also Magistrates' Court's Rules 1981, r 34, in PART I: MAGISTRATES' COURTS Procedure, ante.

7.7112 **48. Licensing of private hire vehicles** (1) Subject to the provisions of this Part of this Act, a district council may on the receipt of an application from the proprietor[1] of any vehicle for the grant in respect of such vehicle of a licence to use the vehicle as a private hire vehicle[1], grant in respect thereof a vehicle licence:

Provided that a district council shall not grant such a licence unless they are satisfied—

(*a*) that the vehicle is—

(i) suitable[2] in type, size and design for use as a private hire vehicle;

(ii) not of such design and appearance as to lead any person to believe that the vehicle is a hackney carriage;

(iii) in a suitable mechanical condition;

(iv) safe; and

(v) comfortable;

(*b*) that there is in force in relation to the use of the vehicle a policy of insurance or such security as complies with the requirements of Part VI of the Road Traffic Act 1988,

and shall not refuse such a licence for the purpose of limiting the number of vehicles in respect of which such licences are granted by the council.

(2) A district council may attach to the grant of a licence under this section such conditions as they may consider reasonably necessary[3] including, without prejudice to the generality of the foregoing provisions of this subsection, conditions requiring or prohibiting the display of signs on or from the vehicle to which the licence relates.

(3) In every vehicle licence granted under this section there shall be specified—

(*a*) The name and address of—

(i) the applicant; and

(ii) every other person who is a proprietor of the private hire vehicle in respect of which the licence is granted, or who is concerned, either solely or in partnership with any other person, in the keeping, employing or letting on hire of the private hire vehicle;

(*b*) the number of the licence which shall correspond with the number to be painted or marked on the plate or disc to be exhibited on the private hire vehicle in accordance with subsection (6) of this section;

(*c*) the conditions attached to the grant of the licence; and

(*d*) such other particulars as the district council consider reasonably necessary.

(4) Every licence granted under this section shall—

(*a*) be signed by an authorised officer[4] of the council which granted it;

(*b*) relate to not more than one private hire vehicle; and

(*c*) remain in force for such period not being longer than one year as the district council may specify in the licence.

(5) Where a district council grant under this section a vehicle licence in respect of a private hire vehicle they shall issue a plate or disc identifying that vehicle as a private hire vehicle in respect of which a vehicle licence has been granted.

(6)

(*a*) Subject to the provisions of this Part of this Act, no person shall use or permit to be used in a controlled district as a private hire vehicle a vehicle in respect of which a licence has been granted under this section unless the plate or disc issued in accordance with subsection (5) of this section is exhibited on the vehicle in such manner as the district council shall prescribe by condition attached to the grant of the licence.

(*b*) If any person without reasonable excuse contravenes the provisions of this subsection he shall be guilty of an offence[5].

(7) Any person aggrieved[6] by the refusal of a district council to grant a vehicle licence under this section, or by any conditions specified in such a licence, may appeal[7] to a magistrates' court.

[Local Government (Miscellaneous Provisions) Act 1976, s 48 as amended by the Road Traffic (Consequential Provisions) Act 1988, Sch 3.]

---

1 See note 1 to para 7.7110, ante.

2 Safety of the vehicle for use as a private hire vehicle is part of the suitability for such proposed use. "Safe" in para (iv) might refer to whether the vehicle, suitable in other respects, is safe in the sense, for example, that its components are not defective (*Chauffeur Bikes v Leeds City Council* [2005] EWHC 2369 (Admin), 170 JP 24).

3 A condition which prohibited a private hire vehicle to stand in any public place other than in connection with a pre-arranged booking was held to be beyond the purpose envisaged by the statute and to be unenforceable, or alternatively, not "reasonably necessary" (*R v Blackpool Borough Council, ex p Red Cab Taxis Ltd* (1994) 158 JP 1069).

4 For meaning of "authorised officer", see s 80(1), post.

5 For penalty, see s 76, post.

6 A hackney carriage licence holder may be a 'person aggrieved' by a condition imposed on private hire vehicles (*R v Swansea City and County, ex p Davies* [2001] RTR 54, (2000) Times, 7 July, DC).

7 The procedure shall be in accordance with ss 300–302 of the Public Health Act 1936, title PUBLIC HEALTH, post (s 77, post). See also Magistrates' Courts Rules 1981, r 34, in PART I: MAGISTRATES' COURTS PROCEDURE, ante. The size and design of a licence disc or plate cannot be the subject of an appeal, the only exemptions from display are contained in s 75, post, the nature of the appellant's business is irrelevant to the appeal (*Solihull Metropolitan Borough Council v Silverline Cars* (1988) 153 JP 209, [1989] RTR 142 DC).

7.7113 **49. Transfer of hackney carriages and private hire vehicles** (1) If the proprietor[1] of a hackney carriage[1] or of a private hire vehicle[1] in respect of which a vehicle licence has been granted by a district council transfers his interest in the hackney carriage or private hire vehicle to a person other than the proprietor whose name is specified in the licence, he shall within fourteen days after such transfer give notice in writing thereof to the district council specifying the name and address of the person to whom the hackney carriage or private hire vehicle has been transferred.

(2) If a proprietor without reasonable excuse fails to give notice to a district council as provided by subsection (1) of this section he shall be guilty of an offence[2].

[Local Government (Miscellaneous Provisions) Act 1976, s 49.]

---

1 For meaning of "proprietor", "hackney carriage" and "private hire vehicle", see s 80(1), post.

2 For penalty, see s 76 post.

7.7114 **50. Provisions as to proprietors** (1) Without prejudice to the provisions of section 68 of this Act, the proprietor[1] of any hackney carriage[1] or of any private hire vehicle[1] licensed by a district council shall present such hackney carriage or private hire vehicle for inspection and testing by or on behalf of the council within such period and at such place within the area of the council as they may by notice reasonably require:

Provided that a district council shall not under the provisions of this subsection require a proprietor to present the same hackney carriage or private hire vehicle for inspection and testing on more than three separate occasions during any one period of twelve months.

(2) The proprietor of any hackney carriage or private hire vehicle—

(*a*) licensed by a district council under the Act of 1847[2] or under this Part of this Act; or

(*b*) in respect of which an application for a licence has been made to a district council under the Act of 1847 or under this Part of this Act;

shall, within such period as the district council may by notice reasonably require, state in writing the address of every place where such hackney carriage or private hire vehicle is kept when not in use, and shall if the district council so require afford to them such facilities as may be reasonably necessary to enable them to cause such hackney carriage or private hire vehicle to be inspected and tested there.

(3) Without prejudice to the provisions of section 170 of the Road Traffic Act 1988, the proprietor of a hackney carriage or of a private hire vehicle licensed by a district council shall report to them as soon as reasonably practicable, and in any case within seventy-two hours of the occurrence thereof, any accident to such hackney carriage or private hire vehicle causing damage materially affecting the safety, performance or appearance of the hackney carriage or private hire vehicle or the comfort or convenience of persons carried therein.

(4) The proprietor of any hackney carriage or of any private hire vehicle licensed by a district council shall at the request of any authorised officer[3] of the council produce for inspection the vehicle, licence for such hackney carriage or private hire vehicle and the certificate of the policy of insurance or security required by Part VI of the Road Traffic Act 1988 in respect of such hackney carriage or private hire vehicle.

(5) If any person without reasonable excuse contravenes the provisions of this section, he shall be guilty of an offence[4].

[Local Government (Miscellaneous Provisions) Act 1976, s 50 amended by the Road Traffic (Consequential Provisions) Act 1988, Sch 3.]

---

[1] For meaning of "proprietor", "hackney carriage" and "private hire vehicle", see s 80(1), post.

[2] "The Act of 1847" means the provisions of the Town Police Clauses Act 1847 with respect to hackney carriages (s 80(1), post). For that Act, see title TOWNS IMPROVEMENTS: TOWN POLICE, post.

[3] For meaning of "authorised officer", see s 80(1), post.

[4] See note 4 to para 7.7112, ante.

7.7115 **51. Licensing of drivers of private hire vehicles** (1) Subject to the provisions of this Part of this Act, a district council shall, on the receipt of an application from any person for the grant to that person of a licence to drive private hire vehicles, grant to that person a driver's licence: Provided that a district council shall not grant a licence—

(*a*) unless they are satisfied—

(i) that the applicant is a fit and proper person to hold a driver's licence; and

(ii) that the applicant is not disqualified by reason of the applicant's immigration status from driving a private hire vehicle; or

(*b*) to any person who has not for at least twelve months[1] been authorised to drive a motor car, or is not at the date of the application for a driver's licence so authorised.

(1) For the purposes of subsection (1) of this section a person is authorised to drive a motor car if—

(*a*) he holds a licence granted under Part III of the Road Traffic Act 1988 (not being a provisional licence) authorising him to drive a motor car, or

(*b*) he is authorised by virtue of section 99A(1) or section 109(1) of that Act to drive in Great Britain a motor car.*

(1ZA) In determining for the purposes of subsection (1) whether an applicant is disqualified by reason of the applicant's immigration status from driving a private hire vehicle, a district council must have regard to any guidance issued by the Secretary of State.

(2) A district council may attach to the grant of a licence under this section such conditions as they may consider reasonably necessary[2].

(3) It shall be the duty of a council by which licences are granted in pursuance of this section to enter, in a register maintained by the council for the purpose, the following particulars of each such licence, namely—

(*a*) the name of the person to whom it is granted;

(*b*) the date on which and the period for which it is granted; and

(*c*) if the licence has a serial number, that number,

and to keep the register available at its principal offices for inspection by members of the public during office hours free of charge.

[Local Government (Miscellaneous Provisions) Act 1976, s 51 amended by the Road Traffic (Consequential Provisions) Act 1988, Sch 3, the Road Traffic Act 1991, s 47, SI 1996/1974, the Police Act 1997, Sch 9, SI 1998/1946 and the Immigration Act 2016, Sch 5.]

---

* **It would appear that this subsection has been numbered incorrectly by the amending SI 1996/1974.**

[1] A person who has held a licence for 12 months in the past, and does in fact hold a licence at the date of the application, is entitled to qualify, notwithstanding that there is no continuity between the two periods (*Crawley Borough Council v Crabb* [1996] RTR 201).

[2] See note 2 to s 48(2) in para 7.7112.

7.7116 **52. Appeals in respect of drivers' licences** Any person aggrieved[1] by—

(1) the refusal of the district council to grant a driver's licence under section 51 of this Act; or

(2) any conditions attached to the grant of a driver's licence;

may appeal[2] to a magistrates' court.

[Local Government (Miscellaneous Provisions) Act 1976, s 52.]

---

[1] A person is not a "person aggrieved" and cannot bring an appeal under this section unless he has applied for a licence and his application has been refused or granted with conditions and he is aggrieved by that refusal or with those conditions: *Peddubriwny v Cambridge City Council* [2001] EWHC Admin 200, [2001] RTR 461.

[2] See note 2 to para 7.7123, post. Where the holder of a driver's licence in this application for renewal of the licence failed to give details of his conviction, it was held, on an appeal against the refusal of the district council to renew the licence, that the justices in determining whether the appellant was a fit and proper person had to consider whether the false statement was made knowingly or recklessly, in such circumstances, it was not permissible for the justices to review the question of whether or not the convictions recorded in earlier criminal proceedings were incorrectly arrived at (*Nottingham City Council v Farooq* (1998) Times, 28 October). In determining whether a person is "fit and proper" justices are entitled to rely on any evidential material which might reasonably and properly influence the making of a responsible judgment in good faith. Some evidence such as gossip, speculation and hearsay, might by its source, nature and inherent probability carry a greater degree of credibility. The civil standard of proof applies and in seeking to rebut the applicant's contention that he is a fit and proper person the onus on the local authority is to do this on the civil standard of proof even if the substance of what they seek to prove amounts to a criminal offence. (*McCool v Rushcliffe Borough Council* (1998) 163 JP 46, DC).

7.7117 **53. Drivers' licences for hackney carriages and private hire vehicles** (1)

(*a*) Subject to section 53A, every licence granted by a district council under the provisions of this Part of this Act to any person to drive a private hire vehicle[1] shall remain in force for three years from the date of such licence or for such lesser period, specified in the licence, as the district council think appropriate in the circumstances of the case.

(*b*) Notwithstanding the provisions of the Public Health Act 1875 and the Town Police Clauses Act 1889, but subject to section 53A, every licence granted by a district council under the provisions of the Act of 1847[2] to any person to drive a hackney carriage[1] shall remain in force for three years from the date of such licence or for such lesser period, specified in the licence, as the district council think appropriate in the circumstances of the case.

(2) Notwithstanding the provisions of the Act of 1847, a district council may demand and recover for the grant to any person of a licence to drive a hackney carriage, or a private hire vehicle, as the case may be, such a fee as they consider reasonable with a view to recovering the costs of issue and administration and may remit the whole or part of the fee in respect of a private hire vehicle in any case in which they think it appropriate to do so.

(3) The driver of any hackney carriage or of any private hire vehicle licensed by a district council shall at the request of any authorised officer[1] of the council or of any constable produce for inspection his driver's licence either forthwith or—

(*a*) in the case of a request by an authorised officer, at the principal offices of the council before the expiration of the period of five days beginning with the day following that on which the request is made;

(*b*) in the case of a request by a constable, before the expiration of the period aforesaid at any police station which is within the area of the council and is nominated by the driver when the request is made.

(4) If any person without reasonable excuse contravenes the provisions of this section, he shall be guilty of an offence[3].

[Local Government (Miscellaneous Provisions) Act, 1976, s 53 as amended by the Deregulation Act 2015, s 10 and the Immigration Act 2016, Sch 5.]

[1] For meaning of "private hire vehicle", "hackney carriage", and "authorised officer", see s 80(1), post.
[2] See note 2 to para 7.7114, ante.
[3] For penalty, see s 76, post.

7.7117A **53A. Drivers' licences for persons subject to immigration control**

(1) Subsection (2) applies if—

(a) a licence within section 53(1)(a) or (b) is to be granted to a person who has been granted leave to enter or remain in the United Kingdom for a limited period ("the leave period");

(b) the person's leave has not been extended by virtue of section 3C of the Immigration Act 1971 (continuation of leave pending variation decision); and

(c) apart from subsection (2), the period for which the licence would have been in force would have ended after the end of the leave period.

(2) The district council which grants the licence must specify a period in the licence as the period for which it remains in force; and that period must end at or before the end of the leave period.

(3) Subsection (4) applies if—

(a) a licence within section 53(1)(a) or (b) is to be granted to a person who has been granted leave to enter or remain in the United Kingdom for a limited period; and

(b) the person's leave has been extended by virtue of section 3C of the Immigration Act 1971 (continuation of leave pending variation decision).

(4) The district council which grants the licence must specify a period in the licence as the period for which it remains in force; and that period must not exceed six months.

(5) A licence within section 53(1)(a) ceases to be in force if the person to whom it was granted becomes disqualified by reason of the person's immigration status from driving a private hire vehicle.

(6) A licence within section 53(1)(b) ceases to be in force if the person to whom it was granted becomes disqualified by reason of the person's immigration status from driving a hackney carriage.

(7) If a licence granted in accordance with subsection (2) or (4) expires, the person to whom it was granted must, within the period of 7 days beginning with the day after that on which it expired,

return the licence and the person's driver's badge to the district council which granted the licence.

(8) If subsection (5) or (6) applies to a licence, the person to whom it was granted must, within the period of 7 days beginning with the day after the day on which the person first became disqualified, return the licence and the person's driver's badge to the district council which granted the licence.

(9) A person who, without reasonable excuse, contravenes subsection (7) or (8) is guilty of an offence and liable on summary conviction—

(a) to a fine not exceeding level 3 on the standard scale; and

(b) in the case of a continuing offence, to a fine not exceeding ten pounds for each day during which an offence continues after conviction.

(10) The Secretary of State may by regulations made by statutory instrument amend the amount for the time being specified in subsection (9)(b).

(11) Regulations under subsection (10) may make transitional, transitory or saving provision.

(12) A statutory instrument containing regulations under subsection (10) may not be made unless a draft of the instrument has been laid before, and approved by a resolution of, each House of Parliament.

[Local Government (Miscellaneous Provisions) Act, 1976, s 53A as inserted by the Immigration Act 2016, Sch 5.]

7.7118 54. **Issue of drivers' badges** (1) When granting a driver's licence under section 51 of this Act a district council shall issue a driver's badge in such a form as may from time to time be prescribed by them.

(2)

(*a*) A driver shall at all times when acting in accordance with the driver's licence granted to him wear such badge in such position and manner as to be plainly and distinctly visible.

(*b*) If any person without reasonable excuse contravenes the provisions of this subsection, he shall be guilty of an offence[1].

[Local Government (Miscellaneous Provisions) Act 1976, s 54.]

---

1 For penalty, see s 76, post.

7.7119 55. **Licensing of operators of private hire vehicles** (1) Subject to the provisions of this Part of this Act, a district council shall, on receipt of an application from any person for the grant to that person of a licence to operate private hire vehicles grant to that person an operator's licence:

Provided that a district council shall not grant a licence unless they are satisfied—

(a) that the applicant is a fit and proper person to hold an operator's licence;

(b) if the applicant is an individual, that the applicant is not disqualified by reason of the applicant's immigration status from operating a private hire vehicle.

(1A) In determining for the purposes of subsection (1) whether an applicant is disqualified by reason of the applicant's immigration status from operating a private hire vehicle, a district council must have regard to any guidance issued by the Secretary of State.

(2) Subject to section 55ZA, every licence granted under this section shall remain in force for five years or for such lesser period, specified in the licence, as the district council think appropriate in the circumstances of the case.

(3) A district council may attach to the grant of a licence under this section such conditions as they may consider reasonably necessary[1].

(4) Any applicant aggrieved by the refusal of a district council to grant an operator's licence under this section, or by any conditions attached to the grant of such a licence, may appeal[2] to a magistrates' court.

[Local Government (Miscellaneous Provisions) Act 1976, s 55 as amended by the Deregulation Act 2015, s 10.]

---

1 See note 2 to s 48(2) at para 7.7112, ante.

2 See note 5 to para 7.7112, ante.

7.7119ZA 55ZA. **Operators' licences for persons subject to immigration control**

(1) Subsection (2) applies if—

(a) a licence under section 55 is to be granted to a person who has been granted leave to enter or remain in the United Kingdom for a limited period ("the leave period");

(b) the person's leave has not been extended by virtue of section 3C of the Immigration Act 1971 (continuation of leave pending variation decision); and

(c) apart from subsection (2), the period for which the licence would have been in force would have ended after the end of the leave period.

(2) The district council which grants the licence must specify a period in the licence as the period for which it remains in force; and that period must end at or before the end of the leave period.

(3) Subsection (4) applies if—

(a) a licence under section 55 is to be granted to a person who has been granted leave to enter or remain in the United Kingdom for a limited period; and

(b) the person's leave has been extended by virtue of section 3C of the Immigration Act 1971 (continuation of leave pending variation decision).

(4) The district council which grants the licence must specify a period in the licence as the

period for which it remains in force; and that period must not exceed six months.

(5) A licence under section 55 ceases to be in force if the person to whom it was granted becomes disqualified by reason of the person's immigration status from operating a private hire vehicle.

(6) If a licence granted in accordance with subsection (2) or (4) expires, the person to whom it was granted must, within the period of 7 days beginning with the day after that on which it expired, return the licence to the district council which granted the licence.

(7) If subsection (5) applies to a licence, the person to whom it was granted must, within the period of 7 days beginning with the day after the day on which the person first became disqualified, return it to the district council which granted the licence.

(8) A person who, without reasonable excuse, contravenes subsection (6) or (7) is guilty of an offence and liable on summary conviction—

(a) to a fine not exceeding level 3 on the standard scale; and

(b) in the case of a continuing offence, to a fine not exceeding ten pounds for each day during which an offence continues after conviction.

(9) The Secretary of State may by regulations made by statutory instrument amend the amount for the time being specified in subsection (8)(b).

(10) Regulations under subsection (9) may make transitional, transitory or saving provision.

(11) A statutory instrument containing regulations under subsection (9) may not be made unless a draft of the instrument has been laid before, and approved by a resolution of, each House of Parliament.

[Local Government (Miscellaneous Provisions) Act 1976, s 55ZA as inserted by the Immigration Act 2016, Sch 5.]

**7.7119A 55A. Sub-contracting by operators** (1) A person licensed under section 55 who has in a controlled district accepted a booking for a private hire vehicle may arrange for another person to provide a vehicle to carry out the booking if—

(*a*) the other person is licensed under section 55 in respect of the same controlled district and the sub-contracted booking is accepted in that district;

(*b*) the other person is licensed under section 55 in respect of another controlled district and the sub-contracted booking is accepted in that district;

(*c*) the other person is a London PHV operator and the sub-contracted booking is accepted at an operating centre in London; or

(*d*) the other person accepts the sub-contracted booking in Scotland.

(2) It is immaterial for the purposes of subsection (1) whether or not sub-contracting is permitted by the contract between the person licensed under section 55 who accepted the booking and the person who made the booking.

(3) Where a person licensed under section 55 in respect of a controlled district is also licensed under that section in respect of another controlled district, subsection (1) (so far as relating to paragraph (*b*) of that subsection) and section 55B(1) and (2) apply as if each licence were held by a separate person.

(4) Where a person licensed under section 55 in respect of a controlled district is also a London PHV operator, subsection (1) (so far as relating to paragraph (*c*) of that subsection) and section 55B(1) and (2) apply as if the person holding the licence under section 55 and the London PHV operator were separate persons.

(5) Where a person licensed under section 55 in respect of a controlled district also makes provision in the course of a business for the invitation or acceptance of bookings for a private hire car or taxi in Scotland, subsection (1) (so far as relating to paragraph (d) of that subsection) and section 55B(1) and (2) apply as if the person holding the licence under section 55 and the person making the provision in Scotland were separate persons.

In this subsection, "private hire car" and "taxi" have the same meaning as in sections 10 to 22 of the Civic Government (Scotland) Act 1982.

(6) In this section, "London PHV operator" and "operating centre" have the same meaning as in the Private Hire Vehicles (London) Act 1998.

[Local Government (Miscellaneous Provisions) Act 1976, s 55A as inserted by the Deregulation Act 2015, s 11.]

**7.7119B 55B. Sub-contracting by operators: criminal liability** (1) In this section—

"the first operator" means a person licensed under section 55 who has in a controlled district accepted a booking for a private hire vehicle and then made arrangements for another person to provide a vehicle to carry out the booking in accordance with section 55A(1);

"the second operator" means the person with whom the first operator made the arrangements (and, accordingly, the person who accepted the sub-contracted booking).

(2) The first operator is not to be treated for the purposes of section 46(1)(*e*) as operating a private hire vehicle by virtue of having invited or accepted the booking.

(3) The first operator is guilty of an offence if—

(*a*) the second operator is a person mentioned in section 55A(1)(*a*) or (*b*),

(*b*) the second operator contravenes section 46(1)(*e*) in respect of the sub-contracted booking, and

(*c*) the first operator knew that the second operator would contravene section 46(1)(*e*) in respect of the booking.

[Local Government (Miscellaneous Provisions) Act 1976, s 55B as inserted by the Deregulation Act 2015, s 11.]

7.7120 **56. Operators of private hire vehicles** (1) For the purposes of this Part of this Act every contract for the hire of a private hire vehicle licensed under this Part of this Act shall be deemed to be made with the operator who accepted the booking for that vehicle whether or not he himself provided the vehicle.

(2) Every person to whom a licence in force under section 55 of this Act has been granted by a district council shall keep a record in such form as the council may, by condition attached to the grant of the licence, prescribe and shall enter therein, before the commencement of each journey, such particulars of every booking of a private hire vehicle invited or accepted by him, whether by accepting the same from the hirer or by undertaking it at the request of another operator, as the district council may by condition prescribe and shall produce such record on request to any authorised officer[1] of the council or to any constable for inspection.

(3) Every person to whom a licence in force under section 55 of this Act has been granted by a district council shall keep such records as the council may, by conditions attached to the grant of the licence, prescribe of the particulars of any private hire vehicle operated by him and shall produce the same on request to any authorised officer of the council or to any constable for inspection.

(4) A person to whom a licence in force under section 55 of this Act has been granted by a district council shall produce the licence on request to any authorised officer of the council or any constable for inspection.

(5) If any person without reasonable excuse contravenes the provisions of this section, he shall be guilty of an offence[2].

[Local Government (Miscellaneous Provisions) Act 1976, s 56.]

1 For meaning of "authorised officer", see s 80(1), post.
2 For penalty, see s 76, post.

7.7121 **57. Power to require applicants to submit information** (1) A district council may require any applicant for a licence under the Act of 1847[1] or under this Part of this Act to submit to them such information as they may reasonably consider necessary to enable them to determine whether the licence should be granted and whether conditions should be attached to any such licence.

(2) Without prejudice to the generality of the foregoing subsection—

(*a*) a district council may require an applicant for a driver's licence[2] in respect of a hackney carriage[2] or a private hire vehicle[2]—

(i) to produce a certificate signed by a registered medical practitioner to the effect that he is physically fit to be the driver of a hackney carriage or a private hire vehicle; and

(ii) whether or not such a certificate has been produced, to submit to examination by a registered medical practitioner selected by the district council as to his physical fitness to be the driver of a hackney carriage or a private hire vehicle;

(*b*) a district council may require an applicant for an operator's licence to submit to them such information as to—

(i) the name and address of the applicant;

(ii) the address or addresses whether within the area of the council or not from which he intends to carry on business in connection with private hire vehicles licensed under this Part of this Act;

(iii) any trade or business activities he has carried on before making the application;

(iv) any previous application he has made for an operator's licence;

(v) the revocation or suspension of any operator's licence previously held by him;

(vi) any convictions recorded against the applicant;

as they may reasonably consider necessary to enable them to determine whether to grant such licence;

(*c*) in addition to the information specified in paragraph (*b*) of this subsection, a district council may require an applicant for an operator's licence[3] to submit to them—

(i) if the applicant is or has been a director or secretary of a company, information as to any convictions recorded against that company at any relevant time; any trade or business activities carried on by that company; any previous application made by that company for an operator's licence; and any revocation or suspension of an operator's licence previously held by that company;

(ii) if the applicant is a company, information as to any convictions recorded against a director or secretary of that company; any trade or business activities carried on by any such director or secretary; any previous application made by any such director or secretary for an operator's licence; and any revocation or suspension of an operator's licence previously held by such director or secretary;

(iii) if the applicant proposes to operate the vehicle in partnership with any other person, information as to any convictions recorded against that person; any trade or business activities carried on by that person; any previous application made by that person for an operator's licence; and any revocation or suspension of an operator's licence previously held by him.

(3) If any person knowingly or recklessly makes a false statement or omits any material particular in giving information under this section, he shall be guilty of an offence[4].

[Local Government (Miscellaneous Provisions) Act 1976, s 57.]

---

[1] "The Act of 1847" means the provisions of the Town Police Clauses Act 1847 with respect to hackney carriages (s 80(1), post). For that Act, see title TOWNS IMPROVEMENTS: TOWN POLICE, post.

[2] For meaning of "driver's licence", "hackney carriage" and "private hire vehicle", see s 80(1), post.

[3] "Operator's licence" means a licence under s 55 of this Act (s 80(1), post).

[4] For penalty, see s 76, post.

**7.7122 58. Return of identification plate or disc on revocation or expiry of licence etc**

(1) On—

(*a*) the revocation or expiry of a vehicle licence[1] in relation to a hackney carriage[1] or private hire vehicle[1]; or

(*b*) the suspension of a licence under section 68 of this Act;

a district council may by notice require the proprietor of that hackney carriage or private hire vehicle licensed by them to return to them within seven days after the service on him of the notice the plate or disc which—

(*a*) in the case of a hackney carriage, is required to be affixed to the carriage as mentioned in section 38 of the Act of 1847; and

(*b*) in the case of a private hire vehicle, was issued for the vehicle under section 48(5) of this Act.

(2) If any proprietor[1] fails without reasonable excuse to comply with the terms of a notice under subsection (1) of this section—

(*a*) he shall be guilty of an offence and liable on summary conviction to a fine not exceeding **level 3** on the standard scale and to a daily fine[1] not exceeding **£10**; and

(*b*) any authorised officer[1] of the council or constable shall be entitled to remove and retain the said plate or disc from the said hackney carriage or private hire vehicle.

[Local Government (Miscellaneous Provisions) Act 1976, s 58, as amended by the Criminal Justice Act 1982, ss 38 and 46.]

---

[1] For meaning of "vehicle licence", "hackney carriage", "private hire vehicle", "proprietor", "daily fine" and "authorised officer", see s 80(1), post.

**7.7123 59. Qualifications for drivers of hackney carriages** (1) Notwithstanding anything in the Act of 1847[1], a district council shall not grant a licence to drive a hackney carriage—

(*a*) unless they are satisfied—

(i) that the applicant is a fit and proper person[2] to hold a driver's licence; and

(ii) that the applicant is not disqualified by reason of the applicant's immigration status from driving a hackney carriage; or

(*b*) to any person who has not for at least twelve months been authorised to drive a motor car, or is not at the date of the application for a driver's licence so authorised.

(1ZA) In determining for the purposes of subsection (1) whether an applicant is disqualified by reason of the applicant's immigration status from driving a hackney carriage, a district council must have regard to any guidance issued by the Secretary of State.

(1A) For the purposes of subsection (1) of this section a person is authorised to drive a motor car if—

(*a*) he holds a licence granted under Part III of the Road Traffic Act 1988 (not being a provisional licence) authorising him to drive a motor car, or

(*b*) he is authorised by virtue of section 99A(1) or section 109(1) of that Act to drive in Great Britain a motor car.

(2) Any applicant aggrieved by the refusal of a district council to grant a driver's licence on the ground that he is not a fit and proper person to hold such licence may appeal[3] to a magistrates' court.

[Local Government (Miscellaneous Provisions) Act 1976, s 59 amended by the Road Traffic (Consequential Provisions) Act 1988, Sch 3, the Road Traffic Act 1991, s 47, SI 1996/1974, the Police Act 1997, Sch 9, SI 1998/1946 and the Immigration Act 2016, Sch 5.]

---

[1] See note 1 to para 7.7121, ante.

[2] A local authority is entitled in considering whether a person is a fit and proper person to hold a licence to have regard to that person's standard of driving, and to adopt, following proper consultation, a policy to apply in the generality of cases that it will not to regard as fit and proper somebody who has not passed the Driving Standards Agency taxi driver test: *Darlington Borough Council v Kaye* [2004] EWHC (Admin) 2836, [2005] RTR 14.

When deciding, exceptionally, to admit spent convictions under s 7(3) of the Rehabilitation of Offenders Act 1974 (in PART III: SENTENCING, ante) the local authority or justices hearing an appeal should first identify the issue before them to which those convictions must relate. The party furnishing the spent convictions should consider objectively whether any are relevant to that issue, and give a broad indication of the nature, age and seriousness of the offence. The justices will then consider whether to admit some or all of the convictions in the light of the issue before them. Once some or all of the convictions have been admitted, the applicant is entitled to be heard and make representations to persuade the local authority or the justices of the irrelevancy of those convictions to the issue before them (*Adamson v Waveney District Council* [1997] 2 All ER 898, 161 JP 787, DC).

[3] The procedure shall be in accordance with ss 300–302 of the Public Health Act 1936, title PUBLIC HEALTH, post (s 77, post). See also Magistrates' Courts Rules 1981, r 34, in PART I, ante. The appeal is by way of a complete rehearing (*Darlington Borough Council v Wakefield* (1989) 153 JP 481). However, the justices must have regard to the policy of the

local authority and should not lightly reverse the authority's decision: *Cherwell District Council v Anwar* [2011] EWHC 2943 (Admin), [2012] RTR 15. The personal circumstances of the appellant are irrelevant, save, perhaps, in very rare cases to explain or excuse some conduct of the driver: *Leeds City Council v Hussain* [2002] EWHC 1145 (Admin), [2003] RTR 199. However, the justices must have regard to the policy of the local authority and should not lightly reverse the authority's decision: *Cherwell District Council v Anwar* [2011] EWHC 2943 (Admin), [2012] RTR 15. The personal circumstances of the appellant are irrelevant, save, perhaps, in very rare cases to explain or excuse some conduct of the driver: *Leeds City Council v Hussain* [2002] EWHC 1145 (Admin), [2003] RTR 199.

7.7124 **60. Suspension and revocation of vehicle licences** (1) Notwithstanding anything in the Act of 1847[1] or in this Part of this Act, a district council may suspend or revoke, or (on application therefor under section 40 of the Act of 1847 or section 48 of this Act, as the case may be) refuse to renew a vehicle licence[2] on any of the following grounds—

(*a*) that the hackney carriage[2] or private hire vehicle[2] is unfit for use as a hackney carriage or private hire vehicle;

(*b*) any offence under, or non-compliance with, the provisions of the Act of 1847 or of this Part of this Act by the operator or driver; or

(*c*) any other reasonable cause[3].

(2) Where a district council suspend, revoke or refuse to renew any licence under this section they shall give to the proprietor of the vehicle notice of the grounds on which the licence has been suspended or revoked or on which they have refused to renew the licence within fourteen days of such suspension, revocation or refusal.

(3) Any proprietor aggrieved by a decision of a district council under this section may appeal[4] to a magistrates' court.

[Local Government (Miscellaneous Provisions) Act 1976, s 60.]

---

1 See note 1 to para 7.7121, ante.

2 For meaning of "vehicle licence", "hackney carriage", "private hire vehicle", and see s 80(1), post.

3 "Any other reasonable cause" confers a wide discretion on a council; where there is a pending prosecution there is no need for a conclusion to be reached as to the chance of the licence holder being convicted, there is no requirement before deciding to suspend the licence to hear evidence from witnesses to the alleged offence and hearsay evidence is admissible (*Leeds City Council v Hussain* [2002] EWHC 1145 (Admin), [2003] RTR 199). The impact of a suspension on the driver and the absence of compensation if he is ultimately acquitted of the offence are not relevant considerations; personal circumstances are irrelevant save perhaps in very rare cases to explain or to excuse the conduct of the driver (*Leeds City Council v Hussain*, supra).

4 The procedure shall be in accordance with ss 300–302 of the Public Health Act 1936, title PUBLIC HEALTH, post (s 77, post). See also Magistrates' Courts Rules 1981, r 34, in PART I: MAGISTRATES' COURTS, PROCEDURE, ante.

7.7125 **61. Suspension and revocation of drivers' licences** (1) Notwithstanding any thing in the Act of 1847[1] or in this Part of this Act, a district council may suspend or revoke or (on application therefor under section 46 of the Act of 1847 or section 51 of this Act, as the case may be) refuse to renew the licence of a driver of a hackney carriage or a private hire vehicle on any of the following grounds—

(*a*) that he has since the grant of the licence—

(i) been convicted of an offence involving dishonesty, indecency or violence; or

(ii) been convicted of an offence under or has failed to comply with the provisions of the Act of 1847 or of this Part of this Act;

(*aa*) that he has since the grant of the licence been convicted of an immigration offence or required to pay an immigration penalty; or

(*b*) any other reasonable cause[2].

(1A) Subsection (1)(aa) does not apply if—

(a) in a case where the driver has been convicted of an immigration offence, the conviction is a spent conviction within the meaning of the Rehabilitation of Offenders Act 1974, or

(b) in a case where the driver has been required to pay an immigration penalty—

(i) more than three years have elapsed since the date on which the penalty was imposed, and

(ii) the amount of the penalty has been paid in full.

(2)

(*a*) Where a district council suspend, revoke or refuse to renew any licence under this section they shall give to the driver notice of the grounds on which the licence has been suspended or revoked or on which they have refused to renew such licence within fourteen days of such suspension, revocation or refusal and the driver shall on demand return to the district council the driver's badge issued to him in accordance with section 54 of this Act.

(*b*) If any person without reasonable excuse contravenes the provisions of this section he shall be guilty of an offence and liable on summary conviction to a fine not exceeding **level 1** on the standard scale.

(2ZA) The requirement in subsection (2)(a) to return a driver's badge does not apply in a case where section 62A applies (but see subsection (2) of that section).

(2A) Subject to subsection (2B) of this section, a suspension or revocation of the licence of a driver under this section takes effect at the end of the period of 21 days beginning with the day on which notice is given to the driver under subsection (2)(*a*) of this section.

(2B) If it appears that the interests of public safety require the suspension or revocation of the licence to have immediate effect, and the notice given to the driver under subsection (2)(*a*) of this section includes a statement that that is so and an explanation why, the suspension or revocation takes effect when the notice is given to the driver.

(3) Any driver aggrieved by a decision of a district council under subsection (1) of this section may appeal[3] to a magistrates' court.

[Local Government (Miscellaneous Provisions) Act 1976, s 61 as amended by the Criminal Justice Act 1982, ss 38 and 46, the Road Safety Act 2006, s 52 and the Immigration Act 2016, Sch 5.]

[1] See note 1 to para 7.7121, ante.

[2] See note to s 60(1)(*c*), ante.

[3] See note 2 to para 7.7123, ante. On the hearing of an appeal under this section justices should make findings of fact and record reasons for their decision and the appellant is entitled to be so informed (*R v Burton-upon-Trent Justices, ex p Hussain* (1996) 160 JP 808).

7.7126 **62. Suspension and revocation of operators' licences** (1) Notwithstanding anything in this Part of this Act a district council may suspend or revoke, or (on application therefor under section 55 of this Act) refuse to renew an operator's licence[1] on any of the following grounds—

(*a*) any offence under, or non-compliance with, the provisions of this Part of this Act;

(*b*) any conduct on the part of the operator which appears to the district council to render him unfit to hold an operator's licence;

(*c*) any material change since the licence was granted in any of the circumstances of the operator on the basis of which the licence was granted;

(*ca*) that the operator has since the grant of the licence been convicted of an immigration offence or required to pay an immigration penalty; or

(*d*) any other reasonable cause.

(1A) Subsection (1)(ca) does not apply if—

(a) in a case where the operator has been convicted of an immigration offence, the conviction is a spent conviction within the meaning of the Rehabilitation of Offenders Act 1974, or

(b) in a case where the operator has been required to pay an immigration penalty—

(i) more than three years have elapsed since the date on which the penalty was imposed, and

(ii) the amount of the penalty has been paid in full.

(2) Where a district council suspend, revoke or refuse to renew any licence under this section they shall give to the operator notice of the grounds on which the licence has been suspended or revoked or on which they have refused to renew such licence within fourteen days of such suspension, revocation or refusal.

(3) Any operator aggrieved by a decision of a district council under this section may appeal[2] to a magistrates' court.

[Local Government (Miscellaneous Provisions) Act 1976, s 62 as amended by the Immigration Act 2016, Sch 5.]

[1] "Operator's licence" means a licence under s 55 of this Act (s 80(1), post).

[2] See note 2 to para 7.7123, ante. On the hearing of an appeal under this section justices should make findings of fact and record reasons for their decision and the appellant is entitled to be so informed (*R v Burton-upon-Trent Justices, ex p Hussain* (1996) 160 JP 808).

7.7126A **62A. Return of licences suspended or revoked on immigration grounds**

(1) Subsection (2) applies if—

(a) under section 61 a district council suspend, revoke or refuse to renew the licence of a driver of a hackney carriage or a private hire vehicle on the ground mentioned in subsection (1)(aa) of that section, or

(b) under section 62 a district council suspend, revoke or refuse to renew an operator's licence on the ground mentioned in subsection (1)(ca) of that section.

(2) The person to whom the licence was granted must, within the period of 7 days beginning with the relevant day, return to the district council—

(a) the licence, and

(b) in the case of a licence of a driver of a hackney carriage or a private hire vehicle, the person's driver's badge.

(3) In subsection (2) "the relevant day" means—

(a) where the licence is suspended or revoked, the day on which the suspension or revocation takes effect;

(b) where the district council refuse to renew the licence, the day on which the licence expires as a result of the failure to renew it.

(4) A person who, without reasonable excuse, contravenes subsection (2) is guilty of an offence and liable on summary conviction—

(a) to a fine not exceeding level 3 on the standard scale, and

(b) in the case of a continuing offence, to a fine not exceeding ten pounds for each day during which an offence continues after conviction.

(5) The Secretary of State may by regulations made by statutory instrument amend the amount for the time being specified in subsection (4)(b).

(6) Regulations under subsection (5) may make transitional, transitory or saving provision.

(7) A statutory instrument containing regulations under subsection (5) may not be made unless a draft of the instrument has been laid before, and approved by a resolution of, each House of Parliament.

[Local Government (Miscellaneous Provisions) Act 1976, s 62A as inserted by the Immigration Act 2016, Sch 5.]

7.7127 **63. Stands for hackney carriages** (1) For the purposes of their functions under the Act of 1847[1], a district council may from time to time appoint stands for hackney carriages[2] for the whole or any part of a day in any highway in the district which is maintainable at the public expense and, with the consent[3] of the owner, on any land in the district which does not form part of a highway so maintainable and may from time to time vary the number of hackney carriages permitted to be at each stand.

(2) Before appointing any stand for hackney carriages or varying the number of hackney carriages to be at each stand in exercise of the powers of this section, a district council shall give notice to the chief officer of police for the police area in which the stand is situated and shall also give public notice of the proposal by advertisement in at least one local newspaper circulating in the district and shall take into consideration any objections or representations in respect of such proposal which may be made to them in writing within twenty-eight days of the first publication of such notice.

(3) Nothing in this section shall empower a district council to appoint any such stand—

(*a*) so as unreasonably to prevent access to any premises;

(*b*) so as to impede the use of any points authorised to be used in connection with a local service within the meaning of the Transport Act 1985 or PSV operator's licence granted under the Public Passenger Vehicles Act 1981, as points for the taking up or setting down of passengers, or in such a position as to interfere unreasonably with access to any station or depot of any passenger road transport operators, except with the consent of those operators;

(*c*) on any highway except with the consent of the highway authority;

and in deciding the position of stands a district council shall have regard to the position of any bus stops for the time being in use.

(4) Any hackney carriage byelaws[4] for fixing stands for hackney carriages which were made by a district council before the date when this section comes into force in the area of the council and are in force immediately before that date shall cease to have effect, but any stands fixed by such byelaws shall be deemed to have been appointed under this section.

(5) The power to appoint stands for hackney carriages under subsection (1) of this section shall include power to revoke such appointment and to alter any stand so appointed and the expressions "appointing" and "appoint" in subsections (2) and (3) of this section shall be construed accordingly.

[Local Government (Miscellaneous Provisions) Act 1976, s 63, as amended by the Transport Act 1980, Sch 5, the Transport Act 1985, Sch 1 and the Public Passenger Vehicles Act 1981, Sch 7.]

---

1 "The Act of 1847" means the provisions of the Town Police Clauses Act 1847 with respect to hackney carriages (s 80(1), post). For that Act, see title TOWNS IMPROVEMENTS: TOWN POLICE, post.

2 For meaning of "hackney carriage", see s 80(1), post.

3 The landowner is entitled to withhold consent, or to give subject to conditions, for example, of the payment of charges: *Jones v First Greater Western Ltd* [2014] EWCA Civ 301, [2015] RTR 3.

4 For meaning of "hackney carriage byelaws", see s 80(1), post.

7.7128 **64. Prohibition of other vehicles on hackney carriage stands** (1) No person shall cause or permit any vehicle other than a hackney carriage to wait on any stand for hackney carriages during any period for which that stand has been appointed, or is deemed to have been appointed, by a district council under the provisions of section 63 of this Act.

(2) Notice of the prohibition in this section shall be indicated by such traffic signs as may be prescribed or authorised for the purpose by the Secretary of State in pursuance of his powers under section 64 of the Road Traffic Regulation Act 1984[1].

(3) If any person without reasonable excuse contravenes the provisions of this section, he shall be guilty of an offence[2].

(4) In any proceedings under this section against the driver of a public service vehicle it shall be a defence to show that, by reason of obstruction to traffic or for other compelling reason, he caused his vehicle to wait on a stand or part thereof and that he caused or permitted his vehicle so to wait only for so long as was reasonably necessary for the taking up or setting down of passengers.

[Local Government (Miscellaneous Provisions) Act 1976, s 64 as amended by the Road Traffic Regulation Act 1984, Sch 13.]

---

1 See PART VI: TRANSPORT, title ROAD TRAFFIC.

2 For penalty, see s 76, post.

7.7129 **65.** *Fixing of fares for hackney carriages.*

7.7130 **66. Fares for long journeys** (1) No person, being the driver of a hackney carriage[1] licensed by a district council, and undertaking for any hirer a journey ending outside the district[1] and in respect of which no fare and no rate of fare was agreed before the hiring was effected, shall require for such journey a fare greater than that indicated on the taximeter[1] with which the hackney carriage is equipped or, if it is not equipped with a taximeter, greater than that which, if the current byelaws fixing rates or fares and in force in the district in pursuance of section 68 of the Act of 1847[2] or, as the case may be, the current table of fares in force within the district in pursuance of section 65 of this Act had applied to the journey, would have been authorised for the journey by the byelaws or table.

(2) If any person knowingly contravenes the provisions of this section, he shall be guilty of an offence[3].

[Local Government (Miscellaneous Provisions) Act 1976, s 66.]

1 For meaning of "hackney carriage", "district" and "taximeter", see s 80(1), post.
2 See note 1 to para 7.7127, ante.
3 For penalty, see s 76, post.

7.7131 **67. Hackney carriages used for private hire** (1) No hackney carriage[1] shall be used in the district[1] under a contract or purported contract for private hire except at a rate of fares or charges not greater than that fixed by the byelaws or table mentioned in section 66 of this Act, and, when any such hackney carriage is so used, the fare or charge shall be calculated from the point in the district at which the hirer commences his journey.

(2) Any person who knowingly contravenes this section shall be guilty of an offence[2].

(3) In subsection (1) of this section "contract" means—

(*a*) a contract made otherwise than while the relevant hackney carriage is plying for hire in the district or waiting at a place in the district which, when the contract is made, is a stand for hackney carriages appointed by the district council under section 63 of this Act; and

(*b*) a contract made, otherwise than with or through the driver of the relevant hackney carriage, while it is so plying or waiting.

[Local Government (Miscellaneous Provisions) Act 1976, s 67.]

1 For meaning of "hackney carriage", and "district" see s 80(1), post.
2 For penalty, see s 76, post. It is permissible for a hackney carriage to undertake a journey at a fixed price, but it is an offence under s 67(1) to do so at a price in excess of the metered fare; a licensed hackney driver could safely be assumed, unless the contrary was shown, to have sufficiently good knowledge of both his area and the metered fares within it to know that it was unlawful to charge £32 when the metered fare would have been £21.10: *Stratford-on-Avon District Council v Dyde* [2009] EWHC 3011 (Admin), [2010] RTR 13.

7.7132 **68. Fitness of hackney carriages and private hire vehicles** Any authorised officer[1] of the council in question or any constable shall have power at all reasonable times to inspect and test, for the purpose of ascertaining its fitness, any hackney carriage[1] or private hire vehicle[1] licensed by a district council, or any taximeter[1] affixed to such a vehicle, and if he is not satisfied as to the fitness of the hackney carriage or private hire vehicle or as to the accuracy of its taximeter he may by notice in writing require the proprietor[1] of the hackney carriage or private hire vehicle to make it or its taximeter available for further inspection and testing at such reasonable time and place as may be specified in the notice and suspend the vehicle licence[1] until such time as such authorised officer or constable is so satisfied:

Provided that, if the authorised officer or constable is not so satisfied before the expiration of a period of two months, the said licence shall, by virtue of this section, be deemed to have been revoked and subsections (2) and (3) of section 60[2] of this Act shall apply with any necessary modifications.

[Local Government (Miscellaneous Provisions) Act 1976, s 68.]

1 For meaning of "authorised officer", "hackney carriage", "private hire vehicle", "proprietor", "taximeter", and "vehicle licence", see s 80(1), post.
2 Ante.

7.7133 **69. Prolongation of journeys** (1) No person being the driver of a hackney carriage[1] or of a private hire vehicle[1] licensed by a district council shall without reasonable cause unnecessarily prolong, in distance or in time, the journey for which the hackney carriage or private hire vehicle has been hired.

(2) If any person contravenes the provisions of this section, he shall be guilty of an offence[2].

[Local Government (Miscellaneous Provisions) Act 1976, s 69.]

1 For meaning of "hackney carriage", and "private hire vehicle", see s 80(1), post.
2 For penalty, see s 76, post.

7.7134 **70.** *Fees[1] for vehicle and operators' licences.*

1 A local authority is entitled to charge fees for inspections at the time they are carried out and whether or not the vehicle passed the inspection. Furthermore it is lawful for there to be a graduated scale of fees where further tests were required and an additional fee on grant of the licence (*Kelly v Liverpool City Council* [2003] EWCA Civ 197, [2003] 2 All ER 772, [2003] RTR 236).

7.7135 **71. Taximeters** (1) Nothing in this Act shall require any private hire vehicle[1] to be equipped with any form of taximeter[1] but no private hire vehicle so equipped shall be used for hire in a controlled district[1] unless such taximeter has been tested and approved by or on behalf of the district council for the district or any other district council by which a vehicle licence[1] in force for the vehicle was issued.

(2) Any person who—

(*a*) tampers with any seal on any taximeter without lawful excuse; or
(*b*) alters any taximeter with intent to mislead; or
(*c*) knowingly causes or permits a vehicle of which he is the proprietor to be used in contravention of subsection (1) of this section,

shall be guilty of an offence[2].

[Local Government (Miscellaneous Provisions) Act 1976, s 71.]

[1] For meaning of "controlled district", "private hire vehicle", "taximeter", and "vehicle licence", see s 80(1), post.
[2] For penalty, see s 76, post.

7.7136 72. **Offences due to fault of other person etc** (1) Where an offence by any person under this Part of this Act is due to the act or default of another person, then, whether proceedings are taken against the first-mentioned person or not, that other person may be charged with and convicted of that offence, and shall be liable on conviction to the same punishment as might have been imposed on the first-mentioned person if he had been convicted of the offence.

(2) Section 44(3)[1] of this Act shall apply to an offence under this Part of the Act as it applies to an offence under Part I of this Act.

[Local Government (Miscellaneous Provisions) Act 1976, s 72.]

[1] Ante.

7.7137 73. **Obstruction of authorised officer** (1) Any person who—
(*a*) wilfully obstructs an authorised officer[1] or constable acting in pursuance of this Part of this Act or the Act of 1847[2]; or
(*b*) without reasonable excuse fails to comply with any requirement properly made to him by such officer or constable under this Part of this Act; or
(*c*) without reasonable cause fails to give such an officer or constable so acting any other assistance or information which he may reasonably require of such person for the purpose of the performance of his functions under this Part of this Act or the Act of 1847;

shall be guilty of an offence[3].

(2) If any person, in giving any such information as is mentioned in the preceding subsection, makes any statement which he knows to be false, he shall be guilty of an offence[3].

[Local Government (Miscellaneous Provisions) Act 1976, s 73.]

[1] For meaning of "authorised officer", see s 80(1), post.
[2] "The Act of 1847" means the provisions of the Town Police Clauses Act 1847 with respect to hackney carriages (s 80(1), post). For that Act, see title TOWNS IMPROVEMENTS: TOWN POLICE, post.
[3] For penalty, see s 76, post.

7.7138 74. *Saving for certain businesses.*

7.7139 75. **Saving for certain vehicles etc** (1) Nothing in this Part of this Act shall—
(*a*) apply to a vehicle used for bringing passengers or goods within a controlled district[1] in pursuance of a contract for the hire of the vehicle made outside the district if the vehicle is not made available for hire within the district;
(*b*) *repealed*
(*c*) apply to a vehicle while it is being used in connection with a funeral or a vehicle used wholly or mainly, by a person carrying on the business of a funeral director, for the purpose of funerals;
(*cc*) apply to a vehicle while it is being used in connection with a wedding;
(*d*) require the display of any plate, disc or notice in or on any private hire vehicle licensed by a council under this Part of this Act during such period that such vehicle is used for carrying passengers for hire or reward—
  (i) *repealed*
  (ii) under a contract for the hire of the vehicle for a period of not less than 24 hours.

(2) Paragraphs (*a*), (*b*) and (*c*) of section 46(1) of this Act shall not apply to the use or driving of a vehicle or to the employment of a driver of a vehicle while the vehicle is used as a private hire vehicle in a controlled district if a licence issued under section 48 of this Act by the council whose area consists of or includes another controlled district is then in force for the vehicle and a driver's licence issued by such a council is then in force for the driver of the vehicle.

(2A) Where a vehicle is being used as a taxi or private hire car, paragraphs (*a*), (*b*) and (*c*) of section 46(1) of this Act shall not apply to the use or driving of the vehicle or the employment of a person to drive it if—
(*a*) a licence issued under section 10 of the Civic Government (Scotland) Act 1982 for its use as a taxi or, as the case may be, private hire car is then in force, and
(*b*) the driver holds a licence issued under section 13 of that Act for the driving of taxis or, as the case may be, private hire cars.

In this subsection "private hire car" and "taxi" have the same meaning as in sections 10 to 22 of the Civic Government (Scotland) Act 1982.

(2B) Paragraphs (*a*), (*b*) and (*c*) of section 46(1) of this Act shall not apply to the use or driving of a vehicle, or to the employment of a driver of a vehicle, if—

(*a*) a London PHV licence issued under section 7 of the Private Hire Vehicles (London) Act 1998 is in force in relation to that vehicle; and

(*b*) the driver of the vehicle holds a London PHV driver's licence issued under section 13 of that Act.]

(3) Where a licence under section 48 of this Act is in force for a vehicle, the council which issued the licence may, by a notice in writing given to the proprietor of the vehicle, provide that paragraph (*a*) of subsection (6) of that section shall not apply to the vehicle on any occasion specified in the notice or shall not so apply while the notice is carried in the vehicle; and on any occasion on which by virtue of this subsection that paragraph does not apply to a vehicle section 54(2)(*a*) of this Act shall not apply to the driver of the vehicle.

[Local Government (Miscellaneous Provisions) Act 1976, s 75 as amended by the Civic Government (Scotland) Act 1982, s 16, the Transport Act 1985, Sch 7, the Private Hire Vehicles (London) Act 1998, Sch 1 and the Road Safety Act 2006, Sch 7.]

1 For meaning of "controlled district", see s 80(1), post. Section 75(1)(*a*) is concerned with the vehicle which brings passengers into a controlled district; it is not concerned with a vehicle which makes an initial journey within the controlled district; see *Braintree District Council v Howard* [1993] RTR 193.

7.7140 **76. Penalties** Any person who commits an offence against any of the provisions of this Part of this Act in respect of which no penalty is expressly provided shall be liable on summary conviction to a fine not exceeding **level 3** on the standard scale.

[Local Government (Miscellaneous Provisions) Act 1976, s 76 as amended by the Criminal Justice Act 1982, ss 38 and 46.]

7.7141 **77. Appeals** (1) Sections 300 to 302 of the Act of 1936[1], which relate to appeals, shall have effect as if this Part of this Act were part of that Act.

(2) If any requirement, refusal or other decision of a district council against which a right of appeal is conferred by this Act—

(*a*) involves the execution of any work or the taking of any action; or

(*b*) makes it unlawful for any person to carry on a business which he was lawfully carrying on up to the time of the requirement, refusal or decision;

then, until the time for appealing has expired, or, when an appeal is lodged, until the appeal is disposed of or withdrawn or fails for want of prosecution—

(i) no proceedings shall be taken in respect of any failure to execute the work, or take the action; and

(ii) that person may carry on that business.

(3) Subsection (2) of this section does not apply in relation to a decision under subsection (1) of section 61 of this Act which has immediate effect in accordance with subsection (2B) of that section.

(4) On an appeal under this Part of this Act or an appeal under section 302 of the Act of 1936 as applied by this section, the court is not entitled to entertain any question as to whether—

(a) a person should be, or should have been, granted leave to enter or remain in the United Kingdom; or

(b) a person has, after the date of the decision being appealed against, been granted leave to enter or remain in the United Kingdom.

[Local Government (Miscellaneous Provisions) Act 1976, s 77 as amended by the Road Safety Act 2006, s 52 and the Immigration Act 2016, Sch 5.]

1 See title PUBLIC HEALTH, post.

7.7142 **78. Application of provisions of Act of 1936** Subsection (1) of section 283[1] and section 304[2] of the Act of 1936 shall have effect as if references therein to that Act included a reference to this Part of this Act.

[Local Government (Miscellaneous Provisions) Act 1976, s 78.]

1 Section 283(1) of the Public Health Act 1936 provides that all notices, etc shall be in writing.

2 Section 304 of the Public Health Act 1936 provides that judges and justices shall not be disqualified by liability to pay rates.

7.7143 **79. Authentication of licences** Notwithstanding anything in section 43 of the Act of 1847, any vehicle licence or driver's licence granted by a district council under that Act, or any licence granted by a district council under this Part of this Act, shall not be required to be under the common seal of the district council, but if not so sealed shall be signed by an authorised officer of the council.

[Local Government (Miscellaneous Provisions) Act 1976, s 79.]

7.7143A **79A. Persons disqualified by reason of immigration status** (1) For the purposes of this Part of this Act a person is disqualified by reason of the person's immigration status from carrying on a licensable activity if the person is subject to immigration control and—

(a) the person has not been granted leave to enter or remain in the United Kingdom; or

(b) the person's leave to enter or remain in the United Kingdom—

(i) is invalid;

(ii) has ceased to have effect (whether by reason of curtailment, revocation, cancellation, passage of time or otherwise); or

(iii) is subject to a condition preventing the person from carrying on the licensable activity.

(2) Where a person is on immigration bail within the meaning of Part 1 of Schedule 10 to the Immigration Act 2016—

(a) the person is to be treated for the purposes of this Part of this Act as if the person had been granted leave to enter the United Kingdom; but

(b) any condition as to the person's work in the United Kingdom to which the person's immigration bail is subject is to be treated for those purposes as a condition of leave.

(3) For the purposes of this section a person is subject to immigration control if under the Immigration Act 1971 the person requires leave to enter or remain in the United Kingdom.

(4) For the purposes of this section a person carries on a licensable activity if the person—

(a) drives a private hire vehicle;

(b) operates a private hire vehicle; or

(c) drives a hackney carriage.

[Local Government (Miscellaneous Provisions) Act 1976, s 79A as inserted by the Immigration Act 2016, Sch 5.]

7.7143B **79B. Immigration offences and immigration penalties** (1) In this Part of this Act "immigration offence" means—

(a) an offence under any of the Immigration Acts;

(b) an offence under section 1 of the Criminal Attempts Act 1981 of attempting to commit an offence within paragraph (a); or

(c) an offence under section 1 of the Criminal Law Act 1977 of conspiracy to commit an offence within paragraph (a).

(2) In this Part of this Act "immigration penalty" means a penalty under—

(a) section 15 of the Immigration, Asylum and Nationality Act 2006 ("the 2006 Act"); or

(b) section 23 of the Immigration Act 2014 ("the 2014 Act").

(3) For the purposes of this Part of this Act a person to whom a penalty notice under section 15 of the 2006 Act has been given is not to be treated as having been required to pay an immigration penalty if—

(a) the person is excused payment by virtue of section 15(3) of that Act; or

(b) the penalty is cancelled by virtue of section 16 or 17 of that Act.

(4) For the purposes of this Part of this Act a person to whom a penalty notice under section 15 of the 2006 Act has been given is not to be treated as having been required to pay an immigration penalty until such time as—

(a) the period for giving a notice of objection under section 16 of that Act has expired and the Secretary of State has considered any notice given within that period; and

(b) if a notice of objection was given within that period, the period for appealing under section 17 of that Act has expired and any appeal brought within that period has been finally determined, abandoned or withdrawn.

(5) For the purposes of this Part of this Act a person to whom a penalty notice under section 23 of the 2014 Act has been given is not to be treated as having been required to pay an immigration penalty if—

(a) the person is excused payment by virtue of section 24 of that Act; or

(b) the penalty is cancelled by virtue of section 29 or 30 of that Act.

(6) For the purposes of this Part of this Act a person to whom a penalty notice under section 23 of the 2014 Act has been given is not to be treated as having been required to pay an immigration penalty until such time as—

(a) the period for giving a notice of objection under section 29 of that Act has expired and the Secretary of State has considered any notice given within that period; and

(b) if a notice of objection was given within that period, the period for appealing under section 30 of that Act has expired and any appeal brought within that period has been finally determined, abandoned or withdrawn.

[Local Government (Miscellaneous Provisions) Act 1976, s 79B as inserted by the Immigration Act 2016, Sch 5.]

7.7144 **80. Interpretation of Part II** (1) In this Part of this Act, unless the subject or context otherwise requires—

"the Act of 1847" means the provisions of the Town Police Clauses Act 1847 with respect to hackney carriages;

"the Act of 1936" means the Public Health Act 1936;

"authorised officer" means any officer of a district council authorised in writing by the council for the purposes of this Part of this Act;

"contravene" includes fail to comply;

"controlled district" means any area for which this Part of this Act is in force by virtue of—

(*a*) a resolution passed by a district council under section 45 of this Act; or

(*b*) section 255(4) of the Greater London Authority Act 1999;

"daily fine" means a fine for each day during which an offence continues after conviction thereof;

"the district", in relation to a district council in whose area the provisions of this Part of this Act are in force, means—

(*a*) if those provisions are in force throughout the area of the council, that area; and (*b*) if those provisions are in force for part only of the area of the council, that part of that area;

"driver's badge" means, in relation to the driver of a hackney carriage, any badge issued by a district council under byelaws made under section 68 of the Act of 1847 and, in relation to the driver of a private hire vehicle, any badge issued by a district council under section 54 of this Act;

"driver's licence" means, in relation to the driver of a hackney carriage, a licence under section 46 of the Act of 1847 and, in relation to the driver of a private hire vehicle, a licence under section 51 of this Act;

"hackney carriage" has the same meaning as in the Act of 1847;

"hackney carriage byelaws" means the byelaws for the time being in force in the controlled district in question relating to hackney carriages;

"London cab" means a vehicle which is a hackney carriage within the meaning of the Metropolitan Public Carriage Act 1869;

"operate" means in the course of business to make provision for the invitation[1] or acceptance of bookings for a private hire vehicle[2];

"operator's licence" means a licence under section 55 of this Act;

"private hire vehicle" means a motor vehicle constructed or adapted to seat fewer than nine passengers, other than a hackney carriage or public service vehicle or a London cab or tramcar, which is provided for hire[3] with the services of a driver for the purpose of carrying passengers;

"proprietor" includes a part-proprietor and, in relation to a vehicle which is the subject of a hiring agreement or hire-purchase agreement, means the person in possession of the vehicle under that agreement;

"public service vehicle" has the same meaning as in the Public Passenger Vehicles Act 1981;

"taximeter" means any device for calculating the fare to be charged in respect of any journey in a hackney carriage or private hire vehicle by reference to the distance travelled or time elapsed since the start of the journey, or a combination of both; and

"vehicle licence" means in relation to a hackney carriage a licence under sections 37 to 45 of the Act of 1847 in relation to a London cab in a licence under section 6 of the Metropolitan Public Carriage Act 1869 and in relation to a private hire vehicle means a licence under section 48 of this Act.

(2) In this Part of this Act references to a licence, in connection with a controlled district, are references to a licence issued by the council whose area consists of or includes that district, and "licensed" shall be construed accordingly.

(3) Except where the context otherwise requires, any reference in this Part of this Act to any enactment shall be construed as a reference to that enactment as applied, extended, amended or varied by, or by virtue of, any subsequent enactment including this Act.

(4) In this Part of this Act, except where the context otherwise requires, references to a district council shall, in relation to Wales, be construed as references to a county council or county borough council.

[Local Government (Miscellaneous Provisions) Act 1976, s 80 as amended by the Transport Act 1980, Sch 5, Part II, the Public Passenger Vehicles Act 1981, Sch 7, the Transport Act 1985, Sch 7, the Road Traffic (Consequential Provisions) Act 1988, Sch 1, the Transport and Works Act 1992, s 62, SI 1996/3071 and SI 2000/412.]

---

1 The determining factor is not whether any individual booking was accepted, let alone where it was accepted, but whether the defendant had in the area in question made provision for the invitation or acceptance of bookings in general (*Windsor and Maidenhead Royal Borough Council v Khan)* [1994] RTR 87).

2 It would seem that activity taking place outside an operator's premises may come within the definition of "operate"; see *Adur District Council v Fry* [1997] RTR 257.

3 The words "provided for hire" relate to the nature of the vehicle rather than to the nature of the activity (*Benson v Boyce* [1997] RTR 226).

# Local Government, Planning and Land Act 1980

(1980 c 65)

## Part XVI[1]

## Urban Development

*Highways*

7.7145 **157B. Traffic regulation orders for private streets** (1) Where—

(*a*) an urban development corporation[2] submits to the Secretary of State that an order under this section should be made in relation to any road in the urban development area[2] which is a private street; and

(*b*) it appears to the Secretary of State that the traffic authority do not intend to make an order under section 1 or, as the case may be, section 6 of the Road Traffic Regulation Act 1984 (orders concerning traffic regulation) in relation to the road,

the Secretary of State may by order under this section make in relation to the road any such provision as he might have made by order under that section if he had been the traffic authority.

(2) The Road Traffic Regulation Act 1984 applies to an order under this section as it applies to an order made by the Secretary of State under section 1 or, as the case may be, section 6 of that Act

in relation to a road for which he is the traffic authority.

(3) In this section—

"private street" has the same meaning as in Part XI of the Highways Act 1980;

"road" and "traffic authority" have the same meanings as in the Road Traffic Regulation Act 1984.

(4) This section does not extend to Scotland.

[Local Government, Planning and Land Act 1980, s 157B as inserted by the Leasehold Reform, Housing and Urban Development Act 1993, s 178.]

---

[1] Part XVI contains ss 134–172. For the purposes of Pt XVI of this Act, the holder of a licence under s 6(1) of the Electricity Act 1989 shall be deemed to be a statutory undertaker and his undertaking a statutory undertaking (Electricity Act 1989, Sch 16, para 1).

[2] For the meaning of "urban development area" and "urban development corporation", see ss 134 and 135 respectively.

*Miscellaneous*

7.7146 **167. Power to survey land etc** (1) A person to whom this subsection applies may at any reasonable time—

(*a*) survey any land, or estimate its value, in connection with a proposal by an urban development corporation[1] to acquire the land compulsorily;

(*b*) for the purpose of surveying, or estimating the value of, any land in pursuance of paragraph (*a*) above, enter on the land and other land.

(2) Subsection (1) above applies—

(*a*) to a person authorised in writing by the urban development corporation; and

(*b*) to an officer of the Valuation Office.

(3) The power to survey land conferred by subsection (1) above includes power for a person to whom that subsection applies by virtue of subsection (2)(*a*) above to search and bore on and in the land for the purpose of ascertaining the nature of the subsoil or whether minerals are present in the subsoil, and the power to enter on land conferred by that subsection includes power for such a person to place and leave, on or in the land, apparatus for use in connection with the survey in question and to remove the apparatus.

(4) A person authorised by an urban development corporation to enter on land in pursuance of subsection (1) above—

(*a*) shall, if so required before or after entering on the land, produce evidence of his authority to enter;

(*b*) may take with him on to the land such other persons and such equipment as are necessary for the survey in question;

(*c*) shall not (if the land is occupied) demand admission to the land as of right unless notice of the intended entry has been served by the corporation on the occupier not less than 28 days before the demand;

(*d*) shall (if the land is unoccupied when he enters or the occupier is then temporarily absent) leave the land as effectually secured against trespassers as he found it;

(*e*) shall not place or leave apparatus on or in the land or remove apparatus from the land—

  (i) unless notice of his intention to do so has been served by the corporation on an owner of the land, and if the land is occupied on the occupier, not less than 28 days before he does so, and

  (ii) if the land is held by a local authority or statutory undertakers[2] who within that period serve on the corporation a notice stating that they object to the placing or leaving or removal of the apparatus on the ground that to do so would be seriously detrimental to the performance of any of their functions or, as the case may be, the carrying on of their undertakings unless he has a written Ministerial authorisation to do so;

(*f*) shall not search or bore on or in the land which is the subject of the survey in question if the land is held by a local authority or statutory undertakers—

  (i) unless notice of his intention to do so has been served by the corporation on the authority or undertakers not less than 28 days before he does so, and

  (ii) if within that period the authority or undertakers serve on the corporation a notice stating that they object to the searching or boring on the ground that to do so would be seriously detrimental to the performance of any of their functions or, as the case may be, the carrying on of their undertaking, unless he has a written Ministerial authorisation to do so.

(5) In subsection (4) above "Ministerial authorisation" means—

(*a*) in relation to land held by a local authority, the authorisation of the Secretary of State; and

(*b*) in relation to land held by statutory undertakers, the authorisation of the Secretary of State and the appropriate Minister.

(6) In exercising the powers of this section to survey land held by a local authority or statutory

undertakers a person to whom subsection (1) above applies shall comply with all reasonable conditions imposed by the authority or undertakers with regard to the entry on, surveying of, searching or boring on or in the land, or placing or leaving on, or removal of apparatus from the land.

(7) Where it is proposed to search or bore in pursuance of this section in a street within the meaning of Part III of the New Roads and Street Works Act 1991 or, in Scotland, a road within the meaning of Part IV of that Act—

(*a*) section 55 or 114 of that Act (notice of starting date of works), so far as it requires notice to be given to a person having apparatus in the street or road which is likely to be affected by the works,

(*b*) section 69 or 128 of that Act (requirements to be complied with where works likely to affect another person's apparatus in the street or road), and

(*c*) section 82 or 141 of that Act (liability for damage or loss caused),

have effect in relation to the searching or boring as if they were street works within the meaning of the said Part III or (*Scotland*).

(8) If, in connection with such a proposal of a corporation as is mentioned in subsection (1)(*a*) above, a person interested in any land suffers damage in consequence of the exercise of a power conferred by subsection (1) or (4)(*b*) above or a failure to perform the duty imposed by subsection (4)(*d*) above in respect of the land, he shall be entitled to recover compensation for the damage from the corporation.

(9) Any dispute as to a person's entitlement to compensation in pursuance of subsection (8) above or as to the amount of the compensation shall be determined by the Upper Tribunal, and section 4 of the Land Compensation Act 1961 (which relates to costs) shall with the necessary modifications apply in relation to the determination by the Tribunal of such a dispute.

(10) If a person—

(*a*) wilfully obstructs another person in the exercise of a power conferred on the other person by subsection (1) or (4)(*b*) above; or

(*b*) while another person is on any land in pursuance of the said subsection (4)(*b*), wilfully obstructs him in doing things connected with the survey in question; or

(*c*) removes or otherwise interferes with apparatus left on or in land in pursuance of this section,

he shall be guilty of an offence and liable on summary conviction to a fine not exceeding **level 3** on the standard scale.

(11) If a person who has entered on any land in pursuance of this section discloses to another person information obtained by him there about a manufacturing process or trade secret, then, unless the disclosure is made in the course of performing his duty in connection with the purposes for which he was authorised to enter on the land, he shall be guilty of an offence and liable[3], on summary conviction, to a **fine** not exceeding the statutory maximum or, on conviction on indictment, to imprisonment for a term not exceeding **2 years** or a **fine** or both.

(12) It is hereby declared that references to surveying in this section include references to surveying from the air.

(13) *Scotland.*

(14) In this section—

"the Valuation Office" means the Valuation Office of the Inland Revenue Department.

(15) *Repealed.*

[Local Government, Planning and Land Act 1980, s 167 as amended by the Criminal Justice Act 1982, s 46, the New Roads and Street Works Act 1991, Sch 8, the Statute Law (Repeals) Act 1993, Sch 1 and SI 2009/1307.]

1 For meaning of "urban development corporation", see s 135.

2 For meaning of "statutory undertakers", see s 170, post.

3 For procedure in respect of this offence which is triable either way, see the Magistrates' Courts Act 1980, ss 17A–21, in PART I: MAGISTRATES' COURTS, PROCEDURE, ante.

7.7147 **168. Service of notices** (1) This section has effect in relation to any notice required or authorised by this Part of this Act to be served on any person by an urban development corporation.

(2) Any such notice may be served on the person in question either by delivering it to him, or by leaving it at his proper address, or by sending it by post to him at that address.

(3) Any such notice may—

(*a*) in the case of a body corporate, be given to or served on the secretary or clerk of that body;

(*b*) in the case of a partnership, be given to or served on a partner or a person having the control or management of the partnership business.

(4) For the purposes of this section and of section 7 of the Interpretation Act 1978 (service of documents by post) in its application to this section, the proper address of any person to or on whom a notice is to be given or served shall be his last known address, except that—

(*a*) in the case of a body corporate or its secretary or clerk, it shall be the address of the registered or principal office of that body;

(*b*) in the case of a partnership or a person having the control or management of the partnership business, it shall be that of the principal office of the partnership;

and for the purposes of this subsection the principal office of a company registered outside the United Kingdom or of a partnership carrying on business outside the United Kingdom shall be its principal office within the United Kingdom.

(5) If the person to be given or served with any notice mentioned in subsection (1) above has specified an address within the United Kingdom other than his proper address within the meaning of subsection (4) above as the one at which he or someone on his behalf will accept documents of the same description as that notice, that address shall also be treated for the purposes of this section and section 7 of the Interpretation Act 1978 as his proper address.

(6) If the name or address of any owner, lessee or occupier of land to or on whom any notice mentioned in subsection (1) above is to be served cannot after reasonable inquiry be ascertained, the document may be served either by leaving it in the hands of a person who is or appears to be resident or employed on the land or by leaving it conspicuously affixed to some building or object on the land.

[Local Government, Planning and Land Act 1980, s 168.]

7.7148 **170. Interpretation; statutory undertakers etc** (1) In this Part of this Act, unless the context otherwise requires, "statutory undertakers"[1] means—

(*a*) persons authorised by any enactment to carry on any railway, light railway, tramway, road transport, water transport, canal, inland navigation, dock, harbour, pier or lighthouse undertaking, or any undertaking for the supply of hydraulic power,

(*b*) the Civil Aviation Authority, a universal service provider in connection with the provision of a universal postal service and any other authority, body or undertakers which by virtue of any enactment are to be treated as statutory undertakers for any of the purposes of the 1990 Act or of the 1997 Act,

(*c*) any other authority, body or undertakers specified in an order made by the Secretary of State under this paragraph, and

(*d*) any wholly-owned subsidiary within the meaning assigned by section 1159 of the Companies Act 2006) of any person, authority, body or undertakers mentioned in paragraphs (*a*) and (*b*) above or specified in an order made under paragraph (*c*) above,

and "statutory undertaking" shall be construed accordingly.

(2) In section 141 above "statutory undertakers" also includes British Shipbuilders, and any wholly-owned subsidiary as defined by section 1159 of the Companies Act 2006) of any of them.

(2A) The undertaking of a universal service provider so far as relating to the provision of a universal postal service shall be taken to be his statutory undertaking for the purposes of this Part of this Act; and references in this Part of this Act to his undertaking shall be construed accordingly.

(2B) In subsection (1) and (2A) above "universal service provider" has the same meaning as in the Postal Services Act 2000; and references to the provision of a universal postal service shall be construed in accordance with that Act.

(3) In this Part of this Act the expression "the appropriate Minister", and any reference to the Secretary of State and the appropriate Minister—

(*a*) in relation to any statutory undertakers who are also statutory undertakers for the purposes of any provision of Part XI of the 1990 Act or Part X of the 1997 Act, shall have the same meanings as in the said Part XI, and

(*b*) in relation to any other statutory undertakers, shall have the meanings given by an order made by the Secretary of State under this subsection.

(4) If, in relation to anything required or authorised to be done under this Part of this Act, any question arises as to which Minister is the appropriate Minister in relation to any statutory undertakers; that question shall be determined by the Treasury.

(5) An order made under this section shall be made by statutory instrument subject to annulment in pursuance of a resolution of either House of Parliament.

[Local Government, Planning and Land Act 1980, s 170 as amended by the Companies Consolidation (Consequential Provisions) Act 1985, Sch 2, the Airports Act 1986, Sch 6, the Gas Act 1986 Sch 9, the Coal Industry Act 1987, Sch 1, the British Steel Act 1988, Sch 2, the Water Act 1989, Sch 25, the Companies Act 1989, Sch 18, the Electricity Act 1989, Sch 18, the Planning (Consequential Provisions) Act 1990, Sch 2, the British Technology Group Act 1991, Sch 2, the Coal Industry Act 1994, Schs 9 and 11, SI 2001/1149 and SI 2009/1941.]

---

1. The Environment Agency, every water undertaker and every sewerage undertaker is deemed to be a statutory undertaker for the purposes of Part XVI of this Act (Water Act 1989, Sch 25, para 1).

7.7149 **171. Interpretation: general** In this Part of this Act, except in so far as the context otherwise requires—

"ecclesiastical property" means land belonging to an ecclesiastical benefice of the Church of England, or being or forming part of a church subject to the jurisdiction of a bishop, of any diocese of the Church of England or the site of such a church, or being or forming part of a burial ground subject to such jurisdiction;

"the 1981 Act" means the Acquisition of Land Act 1981;

"the 1947 Act" means the Acquisition of Land (Authorisation Procedure) (Scotland) Act 1947;

"the 1990 Act" means the Town and Country Planning Act 1990;

"the 1997 Act" means the Town and Country Planning (Scotland) Act 1997;

"urban development area" means so much of an area designated by an order under subsection (1) of section 134 above as is not excluded from it by an order under subsection (3A) of that section;

"urban development corporation" means a corporation established by an order under section 135 above.

[Local Government, Planning and Land Act 1980, s 171 as amended by the Acquisition of Land Act 1981, Sch 4, the Planning (Consequential Provisions) Act 1990, Sch 2, the Leasehold Reform, Housing and Urban Development Act 1993, s 179 and the Church of England (Miscellaneous Provisions) Measure 2006, s 16.

## PART XIX[1]

### MISCELLANEOUS AND SUPPLEMENTARY

*Pleasure Boats*

7.7150 185. **Pleasure boats bye laws** (1) Subject to the provisions of this section, any of the following authorities, namely—

(i) a district council;

(ii) a London borough council;

(iii) the Common Council of the City of London;

(iv) the council of a Welsh county or county borough,

may make byelaws—

(*a*) for regulating the numbering and naming of pleasure boats and vessels which are let for hire to the public and the mooring places for such boats and vessels; and

(*b*) for fixing the qualifications of the boatmen or other persons in charge of such boats or vessels; and

(*c*) for securing their good and orderly conduct while in charge.

(2) No authority mentioned in subsection (1) above shall have power to make byelaws under that subsection in relation to pleasure boats or vessels operating—

(*a*) on any water owned or managed by the British Waterways Board;

(*b*) on any inland waters (within the meaning of the Water Resources Act 1991) in respect of which the Environment Agency may make byelaws by virtue of paragraph 1 of Schedule 25 to that Act;

(*c*) subject to subsection (3) below, on any canal or other inland navigation which a navigation authority, as defined in section 135(1) of the Water Resources Act 1963[2], are required or empowered to manage or maintain under any enactment; or

(*d*) on any harbour maintained or managed by a harbour authority, as defined in section 57(1) of the Harbours Act 1964.

(3) Subsection 2(*c*) above does not preclude a local authority making byelaws under subsection (1) above in relation to pleasure boats or vessels operating on any canal or inland navigation which they themselves are required or empowered to manage or maintain.

[Local Government, Planning and Land Act 1980, s 18, as amended by the Water Act 1989, Sch 25, the Water Consolidation (Consequential Provisions) Act 1991, Sch 1, the Local Government (Wales) 1994 Act, Sch 16 and SI 1996/593.]

---

1 Part XIX contains ss 180–197.

2 This reference continues to have effect despite the repeal and re-enactment of those provisions: see the Water Consolidation (Consequential Provisions) Act 1991, Sch 1, para 35.

# Local Government (Miscellaneous Provisions) Act 1982

(1982 c 30)

## PART II[1]

### CONTROL OF SEX ESTABLISHMENTS

7.7151 2. **Control of sex establishments** (1) A local authority may resolve that Schedule 3 to this Act is to apply to their area; and if a local authority do so resolve, that Schedule shall come into force in their area on the day specified in that behalf in the resolution (which must not be before the expiration of the period of one month beginning with the day on which the resolution is passed).

(2) A local authority shall publish notice that they have passed a resolution under this section in two consecutive weeks in a local newspaper circulating in their area.

(3) The first publication shall not be later than 28 days before the day specified in the resolution for the coming into force of Schedule 3 to this Act in the local authority's area.

(4) The notice shall state the general effect of that Schedule.

(5) In this Part of this Act "local authority" means—

(*a*) the council of a district;

(*b*) the council of a London borough; and

(*c*) the Common Council of the City of London.

[Local Government (Miscellaneous Provisions) Act 1982, s 2.]

---

1 Part II contains s 2.

## PART III[1]
## STREET TRADING

7.7152 **3. Power of district council to adopt Schedule 4** A district council may resolve that Schedule 4 to this Act shall apply to their district and, if a council so resolve, that Schedule shall come into force in their district on such day as may be specified in the resolution.

[Local Government (Miscellaneous Provisions) Act 1982, s 3.]

[1] Part III contains s 3.

## PART VII[1]
## BYELAWS

7.7153 **12. General provisions relating to byelaws** (1) Notwithstanding anything in section 298 of the Public Health Act 1936 or section 253 of the Public Health Act 1875 or any other enactment, a constable may take proceedings in respect of an offence against a byelaw made by a relevant local authority under any enactment without the consent of the Attorney General.

(2) In subsection (1) above "relevant local authority" means—

(*a*) a local authority, as defined in section 270 of the Local Government Act 1972; and

(*b*) any body that was the predecessor of a local authority as so defined.

(3) It is immaterial for the purposes of this section that a byelaw was made after the passing of this Act.

[Local Government (Miscellaneous Provisions) Act 1982, s 12.]

[1] Part VII contains s 12.

## PART VIII[1]
## ACUPUNCTURE, TATTOOING, EAR-PIERCING AND ELECTROLYSIS

7.7154 **13. Application of Part VIII** (1) The provisions of this Part of this Act, except this section, shall come into force in accordance with the following provisions of this section.

(2) A local authority may resolve that the provisions of this Part of this Act which are mentioned in paragraph (*a*), (*b*) or (*c*) of subsection (3) below are to apply to their area; and if a local authority do so resolve, the provisions specified in the resolution shall come into force in their area on the day specified in that behalf in the resolution (which must not be before the expiration of the period of one month beginning with the day on which the resolution is passed).

(3) The provisions that may be specified in a resolution under subsection (2) above are—

(*a*) sections 14, 16 and 17 below; or

(*b*) sections 15 to 17 below; or

(*c*) sections 14 to 17 below.

(4) A resolution which provides that section 15 below is to apply to the area of a local authority need not provide that it shall apply to all the descriptions of persons specified in subsection (1) of that section; and if such a resolution does not provide that section 15 below is to apply to persons of all of those descriptions, the reference in subsection (2) above to the coming into force of provisions specified in the resolution shall be construed, in its application to section 15 below, and to section 16 below so far as it has effect for the purposes of section 15 below, as a reference to the coming into force of those sections only in relation to persons of the description or descriptions specified in the resolution.

(5) If a resolution provides for the coming into force of section 15 below in relation to persons of more than one of the descriptions specified in subsection (1) of that section, it may provide that that section, and section 16 below so far as it has effect for the purposes of that section, shall come into force on different days in relation to persons of each of the descriptions specified in the resolution.

(6) A local authority shall publish notice that they have passed a resolution under this section in two consecutive weeks in a local newspaper circulating in their area.

(7) The first publication shall not be later than 28 days before the day specified in the resolution for the coming into force of the provisions specified in it in the local authority's area.

(8) The notice shall state which provisions are to come into force in that area.

(9) The notice shall also—

(*a*) if the resolution provides for the coming into force of section 14 below, explain that that section applies to persons carrying on the practice of acupuncture; and

(*b*) if it provides for the coming into force of section 15 below, specify the descriptions of persons in relation to whom that section is to come into force.

(10) Any such notice shall state the general effect, in relation to persons to whom the provisions specified in the resolution will apply, of the coming into force of those provisions.

(11) In this Part of the Act "local authority" means—

(*a*) the council of a district;

(*b*) the council of a London borough; and

(*c*) the Common Council of the City of London.

[Local Government (Miscellaneous Provisions) Act 1982, s 13.]

[1] Part VIII contains ss 13–17.

7.7155 **14. Acupuncture** (1) A person shall not in any area in which this section is in force carry on the practice of acupuncture unless he is registered by the local authority for the area under this section.

(2) A person shall only carry on the practice of acupuncture in any area in which this section is in force in premises registered by the local authority for the area under this section; but a person who is registered under this section does not contravene this subsection merely because he sometimes visits people to give them treatment at their request.

(3) Subject to section 16(8)(*b*) below, on application for registration under this section a local authority shall register the applicant and the premises where he desires to practise and shall issue to the applicant a certificate of registration.

(4) An application for registration under this section shall be accompanied by such particulars as the local authority may reasonably require.

(5) The particulars that the local authority may require include, without prejudice to the generality of subsection (4) above,—

(*a*) particulars as to the premises where the applicant desires to practise; and

(*b*) particulars of any conviction of the applicant under section 16 below,

but do not include information about individual people to whom the applicant has given treatment.

(6) A local authority may charge such reasonable fees as they may determine for registration under this section.

(7) A local authority may make byelaws for the purpose of securing—

(*a*) the cleanliness of premises registered under this section and fittings in such premises;

(*b*) the cleanliness of persons so registered and persons assisting persons so registered in their practice;

(*c*) the cleansing and, so far as is appropriate, the sterilisation of instruments, materials and equipment used in connection with the practice of acupuncture.

(8) Nothing in this section shall extend to the practice of acupuncture by or under the supervision of a person who is registered as a medical practitioner or a dentist or to premises on which the practice of acupuncture is carried on by or under the supervision of such a person.

[Local Government (Miscellaneous Provisions) Act 1982, s 14.]

7.7156 **15. Tattooing, semi-permanent skin-colouring, cosmetic piercing and electrolysis**

(1) A person shall not in any area in which this section is in force carry on the business—

(*a*) of tattooing;

(*aa*) of semi-permanent skin-colouring;

(*b*) of cosmetic piercing; or

(*c*) of electrolysis,

unless he is registered by the local authority for the area under this section.

(2) A person shall only carry on a business mentioned in subsection (1) above in any area in which this section is in force in premises registered under this section for the carrying on of that business; but a person who carries on the business of tattooing, semi-permanent skin-colouring, cosmetic piercing or electrolysis and is registered under this section as carrying on that business does not contravene this subsection merely because he sometimes visits people at their request to tattoo them or, as the case may be, to carry out semi-permanent skin-colouring on them, pierce their bodies or give them electrolysis.

(3) Subject to section 16(8)(*b*) below, on application for registration under this section a local authority shall register the applicant and the premises where he desires to carry on his business and shall issue to the applicant a certificate of registration.

(4) An application for registration under this section shall be accompanied by such particulars as the local authority may reasonably require.

(5) The particulars that the local authority may require include, without prejudice to the generality of subsection (4) above,—

(*a*) particulars as to the premises where the applicant desires to carry on his business; and

(*b*) particulars of any conviction of the applicant under section 16 below,

but do not include information about individual people whom the applicant has tattooed or given electrolysis, whose bodies he has pierced or on whom he has carried out semi-permanent skin-colouring.

(6) A local authority may charge such reasonable fees as they may determine for registration under this section.

(7) A local authority may make byelaws for the purposes of securing—

(*a*) the cleanliness of premises registered under this section and fittings in such premises;

(*b*) the cleanliness of persons so registered and persons assisting persons so registered in the business in respect of which they are registered;

(*c*) the cleansing and, so far as is appropriate, the sterilisation of instruments, materials and equipment used in connection with a business in respect of which a person is registered under this section.

(8) Nothing in this section shall extend to the carrying on of a business such as is mentioned in subsection (1) above by or under the supervision of a person who is registered as a medical practitioner or to premises on which any such business is carried on by or under the supervision of

such a person.

(9) In this section "semi-permanent skin-colouring" means the insertion of semi-permanent colouring into a person's skin.

[Local Government (Miscellaneous Provisions) Act 1982, s 15 as amended by the Local Government Act 2003, s 120.]

7.7157 16. **Provisions supplementary to ss 14 and 15** (1) Any person who contravenes—

(*a*) section 14(1) or (2) above; or

(*b*) section 15(1) or (2) above,

shall be guilty of an offence and liable on summary conviction to a fine not exceeding **level 3** on the standard scale.

(2) Any person who contravenes a byelaw made—

(*a*) under section 14(7) above; or

(*b*) under section 15(7) above,

shall be guilty of an offence and liable on summary conviction to a fine not exceeding **level 3** on the standard scale.

(3) If a person registered under section 14 above is found guilty of an offence under subsection (2)(*a*) above, the court, instead of or in addition to imposing a fine under subsection (2) above, may order the suspension or cancellation of his registration.

(4) If a person registered under section 15 above is found guilty of an offence under subsection (2)(*b*) above, the court, instead of or in addition to imposing a fine under subsection (2) above, may order the suspension or cancellation of his registration.

(5) A court which orders the suspension or cancellation of a registration by virtue of subsection (3) or (4) above may also order the suspension or cancellation of any registration under section 14 or, as the case may be, 15 above of the premises in which the offence was committed, if they are occupied by the person found guilty of the offence.

(6) Subject to subsection (7) below, a court ordering the suspension or cancellation of registration by virtue of subsection (3) or (4) above may suspend the operation of the order until the expiration of the period prescribed by Criminal Procedure Rules for giving notice of appeal to the Crown Court.

(7) If notice of appeal is given within the period so prescribed, an order under subsection (3) or (4) above shall be suspended until the appeal is finally determined or abandoned.

(8) Where the registration of any person under section 14 or 15 above is cancelled by order of the court under this section—

(*a*) he shall within 7 days deliver up to the local authority the cancelled certificate of registration, and, if he fails to do so, he shall be guilty of an offence and liable on summary conviction to a fine not exceeding **level 2** on the standard scale and thereafter to a daily fine not exceeding **£5**; and

(*b*) he shall not again be registered by the local authority under section 14 or, as the case may be, 15 above except with the consent of the magistrates' court which convicted him.

(9) A person registered under this Part of this Act shall keep a copy—

(*a*) of any certificate of registration issued to him under this Part of this Act; and

(*b*) of any byelaws under this Part of this Act relating to the practice or business in respect of which he is so registered,

prominently displayed at the place where he carries on that practice or business.

(10) A person who contravenes subsection (9) above shall be guilty of an offence and liable on summary conviction to a fine not exceeding **level 2** on the standard scale.

(11) It shall be a defence for a person charged with an offence under subsection (1), (2), (8) or (10) above to prove that he took all reasonable precautions and exercised all due diligence to avoid commission of the offence.

(12) Nothing in this Part of this Act applies to anything done to an animal.

[Local Government (Miscellaneous Provisions) Act 1982, s 16 as amended by the Criminal Justice Act 1982, s 46 and SI 2004/2035.]

7.7158 17. **Power to enter premises (acupuncture etc)** (1) Subject to subsection (2) below, an authorised officer of a local authority may enter any premises in the authority's area if he has reason to suspect that an offence under section 16 above is being committed there.

(2) The power conferred by this section may be exercised by an authorised officer of a local authority only if he has been granted a warrant by a justice of the peace.

(3) A justice may grant a warrant under this section only if he is satisfied—

(*a*) that admission to any premises has been refused, or that refusal is apprehended, or that the case is one of urgency, or that an application for admission would defeat the object of the entry; and

(*b*) that there is reasonable ground for entry under this section.

(4) A warrant shall not be granted unless the justice is satisfied either that notice of the intention to apply for a warrant has been given to the occupier, or that the case is one of urgency, or that the giving of such notice would defeat the object of the entry.

(5) A warrant shall continue in force—

(*a*) for seven days; or

(*b*) until the power conferred by this section has been exercised in accordance with the warrant,

whichever period is the shorter.

(6) Where an authorised officer of a local authority exercises the power conferred by this section, he shall produce his authority if required to do so by the occupier of the premises.

(7) Any person who without reasonable excuse refuses to permit an authorised officer of a local authority to exercise the power conferred by this section shall be guilty of an offence and shall for every such refusal be liable on summary conviction to a fine not exceeding **level 3** on the standard scale.

[Local Government (Miscellaneous Provisions) Act 1982, s 17, as amended by the Criminal Justice Act 1982, s 46.]

## PART XII[1]

## MISCELLANEOUS

7.7159 **33. Enforceability by local authorities of certain covenants relating to land**

(1) The provisions of this section shall apply if a principal council (in the exercise of their powers under section 111 of the Local Government Act 1972 or otherwise) and any other person are parties to an instrument under seal which—

(*a*) is executed for the purpose of securing the carrying out of works on land in the council's area in which the other person has an interest; or

(*b*) is executed for the purpose of regulating the use of or otherwise connected with land in or outside the council's area in which the other person has an interest,

and which is neither executed for the purpose of facilitating nor connected with the development of the land in question.

(2) If, in a case where this section applies,—

(*a*) the instrument contains a covenant on the part of any person having an interest in land, being a covenant to carry out any works or do any other thing on or in relation to that land, and

(*b*) the instrument defines the land to which the covenant relates, being land in which that person has an interest at the time the instrument is executed, and

(*c*) the covenant is expressed to be one to which this section or section 126 of the Housing Act 1974 (which is superseded by this section) applies,

the covenant shall be enforceable (without any limit of time) against any person deriving title from the original covenantor in respect of his interest in any of the land defined as mentioned in paragraph (*b*) above and any person deriving title under him in respect of any lesser interest in that land as if that person had also been an original covenanting party in respect of the interest for the time being held by him.

(3) Without prejudice to any other method of enforcement of a covenant falling within subsection (2) above, if there is a breach of the covenant in relation to any of the land to which the covenant relates, then, subject to subsection (4) below, the principal council who are a party to the instrument in which the covenant is contained may—

(*a*) enter on the land concerned and carry out the works or do anything which the covenant requires to be carried out or done or remedy anything which has been done and which the covenant required not to be done; and

(*b*) recover from any person against whom the covenant is enforceable (whether by virtue of subsection (2) above or otherwise) any expenses incurred by the council in exercise of their powers under this subsection.

(4) Before a principal council exercise their powers under subsection (3)(*a*) above they shall give not less than 21 days notice of their intention to do so to any person—

(*a*) who has for the time being an interest in the land on or in relation to which the works are to be carried out or other thing is to be done; and

(*b*) against whom the covenant is enforceable (whether by virtue of subsection (2) above or otherwise).

(5) If a person against whom a covenant is enforceable by virtue of subsection (2) above requests the principal council to supply him with a copy of the covenant, it shall be their duty to do so free of charge.

(6) The Public Health Act 1936 shall have effect as if any reference to that Act in—

(*a*) section 283[2] of that Act (notices to be in writing; forms of notices, etc),

(*b*) section 288[2] of that Act (penalty for obstructing execution of Act), and

(*c*) section 291 of that Act (certain expenses recoverable from owners to be a charge on the premises; power to order payment by instalments),

included a reference to subsections (1) to (4) above and as if any reference in those sections of that Act—

(i) to a local authority were a reference to a principal council; and

(ii) to the owner of the premises were a reference to the holder of an interest in land.

(7) Section 16[3] of the Local Government (Miscellaneous Provisions) Act 1976 shall have effect as if references to a local authority and to functions conferred on a local authority by any enactment included respectively references to such a board as is mentioned in subsection (9) below and to

functions of such a board under this section.

(8) In its application to a notice or other document authorised to be given or served under subsection (4) above or by virtue of any provision of the Public Health Act 1936 specified in subsection (6) above, section 233 of the Local Government Act 1972 (service of notices by local authorities) shall have effect as if any reference in that section to a local authority included a reference to the Common Council of the City of London and such a board as is mentioned in the following subsection.

(9) In this section—

(*a*) "principal council" means the council of a county, district or London borough, the Broads Authority, a board constituted in pursuance of section 2 of the Town and Country Planning Act 1990, the Common Council of the City of London, the London Residuary Body, the London Fire and Emergency Planning Authority, a police authority established under section 3 of the Police Act 1996, the Metropolitan Police Authority, the Residuary Body for Wales (Corff Gweddilliol Cymru), a joint authority established by Part 4 of the Local Government Act 1985, an economic prosperity board established under section 88 of the Local Democracy, Economic Development and Construction Act 2009, or a combined authority established under section 103 of that Act; and

(*b*) "area" in relation to such a board means the district for which the board is constituted in relation to the London Residuary Body means Greater London, in relation to the Residuary Body for Wales (Corff Gweddilliol Cymru) means Wales and in relation to such a joint authority, economic prosperity board or combined authority means the area for which the authority was established.

(10) Section 126 of the Housing Act 1974 (which is superseded by this section) shall cease to have effect; but in relation to a covenant falling within subsection (2) of that section, section 1(1)(*d*) of the Local Land Charges Act 1975 shall continue to have effect as if the reference to the commencement of that Act had been a reference to the coming into operation of the said section 126.

[Local Government (Miscellaneous Provisions) Act 1982, s 33 as amended by the Local Government Act 1985, Schs 14 and 17, the Education Reform Act 1988, Sch 13, the Norfolk and Suffolk Broads Act 1988, Sch 6, the Planning (Consequential Provisions) Act 1990, Sch 2, the Planning and Compensation Act 1991, Sch 7, the Police and Magistrates' Courts Act 1994, Sch 4, the Environment Act 1995, Sch 24, the Police Act 1996, Sch 7, the Police Act 1997, Sch 6, the Greater London Authority Act 1999, Schs 27 and 29, the Criminal Justice and Police Act 2001, Sch 6, the Local Government and Public Involvement in Health 2007, Sch 13, the Local Democracy, Economic Development and Construction Act 2009, Sch 6 and the Deregulation Act 2015, Sch 13.]

---

1 Part XII contains ss 33–46.
2 See title, PUBLIC HEALTH, post.
3 Ante.

7.7160 37. **Temporary markets** (1) The council of a district or a London borough may resolve that the following provisions of this section shall apply to their district or borough; and if a council so resolve and within 14 days of the passing of the resolution give notice of the resolution by advertising in a local newspaper circulating in their area, those provisions shall come into force in their district or borough on the day specified in the resolution.

(2) Subject to subsection (3) below, any person intending to hold a temporary market in a district or London borough where the provisions of this section have come into force, and any occupier of land in such a district or borough who intends to permit the land to be used as the site of a temporary market or for purposes of that market, shall give the council of the district or the borough not less than one month before the date on which it is proposed to hold the market notice of his intention to hold it or to permit the land to be so used, as the case may be.

(3) No notice is required under subsection (2) above if the proceeds of the temporary market are to be applied solely or principally for charitable, social, sporting or political purposes.

(4) Any notice given under subsection (2) above shall state—

(*a*) the full name and address of the person intending to hold the market;

(*b*) the day or days on which it is proposed that the market shall be held and its proposed opening and closing times;

(*c*) the site on which it is proposed that it shall be held;

(*d*) the full name and address of the occupier of that site, if he is not the person intending to hold the market.

(5) A person who without giving the notice required by subsection (2) above holds a temporary market or permits land occupied by him to be used as the site of a temporary market shall be guilty of an offence and liable on summary conviction to a fine not exceeding **level 4** on the standard scale.

(6) In this section "temporary market" means a concourse of buyers and sellers of articles held otherwise than in a building or on a highway, and comprising not less than five stalls, stands, vehicles (whether movable or not) or pitches from which articles are sold, but does not include—

(*a*) a market or fair the right to hold which was acquired by virtue of a grant (including a presumed grant) or acquired or established by virtue of an enactment or order; or

(*b*) a sale by auction of farm livestock or deadstock.

(7) A person holds a temporary market for the purposes of this section if—

(*a*) he is entitled to payment for any space or pitch hired or let on the site of the market to persons wishing to trade in the market; or (*b*) he is entitled, as a person promoting the market, or as the agent, licensee or assignee of a person promoting the market, to payment for goods sold or services rendered to persons attending the market.

(8) This section does not apply to a market held on any land in accordance with planning permission granted on an application made under Part III of the Town and Country Planning Act 1990.

[Local Government (Miscellaneous Provisions) Act 1982, s 37, as amended by the Criminal Justice Act 1982, s 46 and the Planning (Consequential Provisions) Act 1990, Sch 2.]

## PART XIII[1]
### SUPPLEMENTARY

7.7161 **48. Consequential repeal or amendment of local statutory provisions** (1) The Secretary of State may by order—

(*a*) repeal any provision of a local Act passed before or in the same Session as this Act or of an order or other instrument made under or confirmed by any Act so passed if it appears to him that the provision is inconsistent with or has become unnecessary in consequence of any provision of this Act; and

(*b*) amend any provision of such a local Act, order or instrument if it appears to him that the provision requires amendment in consequence of any provision contained in this Act or any repeal made by virtue of paragraph (*a*) above.

(2) An order under subsection (1) above may contain such incidental or transitional provisions as the Secretary of State considers appropriate in connection with the order.

(3) It shall be the duty of the Secretary of State, before he makes an order under subsection (1) above repealing or amending any provision of a local Act, to consult each local authority which he considers would be affected by the repeal or amendment of that provision.

(4) A statutory instrument containing an order under subsection (1) above shall be subject to annulment in pursuance of a resolution of either House of Parliament.

[Local Government (Miscellaneous Provisions) Act 1982, s 48.]

---

1 Part XIII contains ss 47–49.

7.7162 **49. Citation and extent** (1) This Act may be cited as the Local Government (Miscellaneous Provisions) Act 1982.

(2) Subject to sections 38(3) and 47(4) above, and to paragraph 8(2) of Schedule 6 to this Act, this Act extends to England and Wales only.

[Local Government (Miscellaneous Provisions) Act 1982, s 49 as amended by the Statute Law (Repeals) Act 2004.]

## SCHEDULES

### SCHEDULE 3
### CONTROL OF SEX ESTABLISHMENTS

Section 2

*(As amended by the Criminal Justice Act 1982, s 46, SI 1984 No 447, the Cinemas Act 1985, Sch 2, the London Local Authorities Act 1990, s 18, SI 2005/886, the Licensing Act 2005, Sch 6, SI 2005/1541, the Serious Organised Crime and Police Act 2005, Sch 7, SI 2006/484, SI 2009/2999, the Policing and Crime Act 2009, s 27, SI 2010/723 and SI 2015/664.)*

*Saving for existing law*

7.7163 1. Nothing in this Schedule—

(*a*) shall afford a defence to a charge in respect of any offence at common law or under an enactment other than this Schedule; or

(*b*) shall be taken into account in any way—

(i) at a trial for such an offence; or

(ii) in proceedings for forfeiture under section 3 of the Obscene Publications Act 1959 or section 5* of the Protection of Children Act 1978; or

(iii) in proceedings for condemnation under Schedule 3 to the Customs and Excise Management Act 1979 of goods which section 42 of the Customs Consolidation Act 1876 prohibits to be imported or brought into the United Kingdom as being indecent or obscene; or

(*c*) shall in any way limit the other powers exercisable under any of those Acts.

---

* **Words substituted by the Police and Justice Act 2006, Sch 14 from a date to be appointed.**

*Meaning of "sex establishment"*

2. In this Schedule "sex establishment" means a sexual entertainment venue, sex cinema, a hostess bar or a sex shop.

*Meaning of "sexual entertainment venue"*

2A. (1) In this Schedule "sexual entertainment venue" means any premises at which relevant entertainment is provided before a live audience for the financial gain of the organiser or the entertainer.

(2) In this paragraph "relevant entertainment" means—

(*a*) any live performance; or

(*b*) any live display of nudity;

which is of such a nature that, ignoring financial gain, it must reasonably be assumed to be provided solely or principally for the purpose of sexually stimulating any member of the audience (whether by verbal or other means).

(3) The following are not sexual entertainment venues for the purposes of this Schedule—

(*a*) sex cinemas and sex shops;

(*b*) premises at which the provision of relevant entertainment as mentioned in sub-paragraph (1) is such that, at the time in question and including any relevant entertainment which is being so provided at that time—

(i) there have not been more than eleven occasions on which relevant entertainment has been so provided which fall (wholly or partly) within the period of 12 months ending with that time;

(ii) no such occasion has lasted for more than 24 hours; and

(iii) no such occasion has begun within the period of one month beginning with the end of any previous occasion on which relevant entertainment has been so provided (whether or not that previous occasion falls within the 12 month period mentioned in sub-paragraph (i));

(*c*) premises specified or described in an order made by the relevant national authority.

(4) The relevant national authority may by order amend or repeal sub-paragraph (3)(*b*).

(5) But no order under sub-paragraph (4) may—

(*a*) increase the number or length of occasions in any period on which sub-paragraph (3)(*b*) as originally enacted would permit relevant entertainment to be provided; or

(*b*) provide for shorter intervals between such occasions.

(6) The relevant national authority may by order provide for descriptions of performances, or of displays of nudity, which are not to be treated as relevant entertainment for the purposes of this Schedule.

(7) Any power of the relevant national authority to make an order under this paragraph—

(*a*) is exercisable by statutory instrument;

(*b*) may be exercised so as to make different provision for different cases or descriptions of case or for different purposes; and

(*c*) includes power to make supplementary, incidental, consequential, transitional, transitory or saving provision.

(8) A statutory instrument containing an order under sub-paragraph (4) may not be made by the Secretary of State unless a draft of the instrument has been laid before, and approved by a resolution of, each House of Parliament.

(9) A statutory instrument containing an order made under sub-paragraph (3)(*c*) or (6) by the Secretary of State is subject to annulment in pursuance of a resolution of either House of Parliament.

(10) A statutory instrument containing an order under sub-paragraph (4) may not be made by the Welsh Ministers unless a draft of the instrument has been laid before, and approved by a resolution of, the National Assembly for Wales.

(11) A statutory instrument containing an order made under sub-paragraph (3)(*c*) or (6) by the Welsh Ministers is subject to annulment in pursuance of a resolution of the National Assembly for Wales.

(12) For the purposes of this paragraph relevant entertainment is provided if, and only if, it is provided, or permitted to be provided, by or on behalf of the organiser.

(13) For the purposes of this Schedule references to the use of any premises as a sexual entertainment venue are to be read as references to their use by the organiser.

(14) In this paragraph—

"audience" includes an audience of one;

"display of nudity" means—

(*a*) in the case of a woman, exposure of her nipples, pubic area, genitals or anus; and

(*b*) in the case of a man, exposure of his pubic area, genitals or anus;

"the organiser", in relation to the provision of relevant entertainment at premises, means any person who is responsible for the organisation or management of—

(*a*) the relevant entertainment; or

(*b*) the premises;

"premises" includes any vessel, vehicle or stall but does not include any private dwelling to which the public is not admitted;

"relevant national authority" means—

(*a*) in relation to England, the Secretary of State; and

(*b*) in relation to Wales, the Welsh Ministers;

and for the purposes of sub-paragraphs (1) and (2) it does not matter whether the financial gain arises directly or indirectly from the performance or display of nudity.

*Meaning of "sex cinema"*

3. (1) In this Schedule, "sex cinema" means any premises, vehicle, vessel or stall used to a significant degree for the exhibition of moving pictures, by whatever means produced, which—

(*a*) are concerned primarily with the portrayal of, or primarily deal with or relate to, or are intended to stimulate or encourage—

(i) sexual activity; or

(ii) acts of force or restraint which are associated with sexual activity; or

(*b*) are concerned primarily with the portrayal of, or primarily deal with or relate to, genital organs or urinary or excretory functions,

but does not include a dwelling-house to which the public is not admitted.

(2) No premises shall be treated as a sex cinema by reason only—

(*a*) if they may be used for an exhibition of a film (within the meaning of paragraph 15 of Schedule 1 to the Licensing Act 2003) by virtue of an authorisation (within the meaning of section 136 of that Act), of their use in accordance with that authorisation; or

(*b*) of their use for an exhibition to which section 6 of that Act (certain non-commercial exhibitions) applies given by an exempted organisation within the meaning of section 6(6) of the Cinemas Act 1985.

**3A.** *Repealed.**

---

* **New para 3B inserted in relation to the City of Westminster and certain London boroughs by the London Local Authorities Act 2007, s 33. In force for remaining purposes for a date to be appointed.**

*Meaning of "sex shop" and "sex article"*

4. (1) In this Schedule[1] "sex shop" means any premises, vehicle, vessel or stall used for a business which consists to a significant[2] degree of selling, hiring, exchanging, lending, displaying or demonstrating—

(*a*) sex articles; or

(*b*) other things intended for use in connection with, or for the purpose of stimulating or encouraging—

(i) sexual activity; or

(ii) acts of force or restraint which are associated with sexual activity.

(2) No premises shall be treated as a sex shop by reason only of their use for the exhibition of moving pictures by whatever means produced.

(3) In this Schedule "sex article" means—

(*a*) anything made for use in connection with, or for the purpose of stimulating or encouraging—

(i) sexual activity; or

(ii) acts of force or restraint which are associated with sexual activity; and

(*b*) anything to which sub-paragraph (4) below applies.

(4) This sub-paragraph applies—

(*a*) to any article containing or embodying matter to be read or looked at or anything intended to be used, either alone or as one of a set, for the reproduction or manufacture of any such article; and

(*b*) to any recording of vision or sound, which—

(i) is concerned primarily with the portrayal of, or primarily deals with or relates to, or is intended to stimulate or encourage, sexual activity or acts of force or restraint which are associated with sexual activity; or

(ii) is concerned primarily with the portrayal of, or primarily deals with or relates to, genital organs, or urinary or excretory functions.

---

1 This Schedule is additionally amended by the Greater London Council (General Powers) Act 1986, s 12 where a borough council so resolves. This is to enable there to be regulation of sex encounter establishments. See also *McMonagle v Westminster City Council* [1990] 2 AC 716, [1990] 1 All ER 993, 154 JP 854, HL.

2 "Significant" means more than "more than trifling"; in deciding whether an establishment is a "sex shop", the ratio between the sexual and other aspects of the business will always be material, so also will be the absolute quantity of sales, and the character of the remainder of the business. The court must decide which considerations are material to the individual case and what weight is to be attached to them (*Lambeth London Borough Council v Grewal* (1985) 150 JP 138, [1986] Crim LR 260).

*Miscellaneous definitions*

5. (1) In this Schedule—

"the appropriate authority" means, in relation to any area for which a resolution has been passed under section 2 above, the local authority who passed it;

"the chief officer of police", in relation to any locality, means the chief officer of police for the police area in which the locality is situated; and

"vessel" includes any ship, boat, raft or other apparatus constructed or adapted for floating on water.

(2) This Schedule applies to hovercraft as it applies to vessels.

*Requirement for licences for sex establishments*

6. (1) Subject to the provisions of this Schedule, no person shall in any area in which this Schedule is in force use any premises, vehicle, vessel or stall as a sex establishment except under and in accordance with the terms of a licence granted under this Schedule by the appropriate authority.

(2) Sub-paragraph (1) above does not apply to the sale, supply or demonstration of articles which—

(*a*) are manufactured for use primarily for the purposes of birth control; or

(*b*) primarily relate to birth control.

7. (1) Any person who—

(*a*) uses any premises, vehicle, vessel or stall as a sex establishment; or

(*b*) proposes to do so,

may apply to the appropriate authority for them to waive the requirement of a licence.

(2) An application under this paragraph may be made either as part of an application for a licence under this Schedule or without any such application.

(3) An application under this paragraph shall be made in writing and shall contain the particulars specified in paragraph 10(2) to (5) below and such particulars as the appropriate authority may reasonably require in addition.

(4) The appropriate authority may waive the requirement of a licence in any case where they consider that to require a licence would be unreasonable or inappropriate.

(5) A waiver may be for such period as the appropriate authority think fit.

(6) Where the appropriate authority grant an application for a waiver, they shall give the applicant for the waiver notice that they have granted his application.

(7) The appropriate authority may at any time give a person who would acquire a licence but for a waiver notice that the waiver is to terminate on such date not less than 28 days from the date on which they give the notice as may be specified in the notice.

*Grant, renewal and transfer of licences for sex establishments*

8. (1) Subject to sub-paragraph (2) and paragraph 12(1) below, the appropriate authority may grant to any applicant, and from time to time renew, a licence under this Schedule for the use of any premises, vehicle, vessel or stall specified in it for a sex establishment on such terms and conditions and subject to such restrictions as may be so specified.

(2) No term, condition or restriction may be specified under sub-paragraph (1) above in so far as it relates to any matter in relation to which requirements or prohibitions are or could be imposed by or under the Regulatory Reform (Fire Safety) Order 2005 in respect of the premises, vehicle, vessel or stall.

9. (1) Subject to paragraphs 11 and 27 below, any licence under this Schedule shall, unless previously cancelled under paragraph 16 or 27A below or revoked under paragraph 17(1) below, remain in force for one

year or for such shorter period specified in the licence as the appropriate authority may think fit.

(2) Where a licence under this Schedule has been granted to any person, the appropriate authority may, if they think fit, transfer that licence to any other person on the application of that other person.

**10.** (1) An application for the grant, renewal or transfer of a licence under this Schedule shall be made in writing to the appropriate authority.

(2) An application made otherwise than by or on behalf of a body corporate or an unincorporated body shall state—

(*a*) the full name of the applicant;

(*b*) his permanent address; and

(*c*) his age.

(3) An application made by a body corporate or an unincorporated body shall state—

(*a*) the full name of the body;

(*b*) the address of its registered or principal office; and

(*c*) the full names and private addresses of the directors or other persons responsible for its management.

(4) An application relating to premises shall state the full address of the premises.

(5) An application relating to a vehicle, vessel or stall shall state where it is to be used as a sex establishment.

(6) Every application shall contain such particulars as the appropriate authority may reasonably require in addition to any particulars required under sub-paragraphs (2) to (5) above.

(7) An applicant for the grant, renewal or transfer of a licence under this Schedule shall give public notice of the application.

(8) Notice shall in all cases be given by publishing an advertisement in a local newspaper circulating in the appropriate authority's area.

(9) The publication shall not be later than 7 days after the date of the application.

(10) Where the application is in respect of premises, notice of it shall in addition be displayed for 21 days beginning with the date of the application on or near the premises and in a place where the notice can conveniently be read by the public.

(11) Every notice under this paragraph which relates to premises shall identify the premises.

(12) Every such notice which relates to a vehicle, vessel or stall shall specify where it is to be used as a sex establishment.

(13) Subject to sub-paragraphs (11) and (12) above, a notice under this paragraph shall be in such form as the appropriate authority may prescribe.

(14) A copy of an application for the grant, renewal or transfer of a licence under this Schedule shall be sent to the chief officer of police—

(*a*) in a case where the application is made by means of a relevant electronic facility, by the appropriate authority not later than 7 days after the date the application is received by the authority;

(*b*) in any other case, by the applicant not later than 7 days after the date of the application.

(14A) In sub-paragraph (14) above "relevant electronic facility" means—

(*a*) the electronic assistance facility referred to in regulation 38 of the Provision of Services Regulations 2009, or

(*b*) any facility established and maintained by the appropriate authority for the purpose of receiving applications under this Schedule electronically.

(15) Any person objecting to an application for the grant, renewal or transfer of a licence under this Schedule shall give notice in writing of his objection to the appropriate authority, stating in general terms the grounds of the objection, not later than 28 days after the date of the application.

(16) Where the appropriate authority receive notice of any objection under sub-paragraph (15) above, the authority shall, before considering the application, give notice in writing of the general terms of the objection to the applicant.

(17) The appropriate authority shall not without the consent of the person making the objection reveal his name or address to the applicant.

(18) In considering any application for the grant, renewal or transfer of a licence the appropriate authority shall have regard to any observations submitted to them by the chief officer of police and any objections of which notice has been sent to them under subparagraph (15) above.

(19) The appropriate authority shall give an opportunity of appearing before and of being heard by a committee or sub-committee of the authority—

(*a*) before refusing to grant a licence, to the applicant;

(*b*) before refusing to renew a licence, to the holder; and

(*c*) before refusing to transfer a licence, to the holder and the person to whom he desires that it shall be transferred.

(20) Where the appropriate authority refuse to grant, renew or transfer a licence, they shall give him a statement in writing of the reasons for their decision.

**11.** (1) Where, before the date of expiry of a licence, an application has been made for its renewal, it shall be deemed to remain in force notwithstanding that the date has passed until the withdrawal of the application or its determination by the appropriate authority.

(2) Where, before the date of expiry of a licence, an application has been made for its transfer, it shall be deemed to remain in force with any necessary modifications until the withdrawal of the application or its determination, notwithstanding that the date has passed or that the person to whom the licence is to be transferred if the application is granted is carrying on the business of the sex establishment.

*Refusal of licences*

**12.** (1) A licence under this Schedule shall not be granted—

(*a*) to a person under the age of 18; or

(*b*) to a person who is for the time being disqualified under paragraph 17(3) below; or

(*c*) to a person, other than a body corporate, who is not resident in an EEA state or was not so resident throughout the period of six months immediately preceding the date when the application was made; or

(*d*) to a body corporate which is not incorporated in an EEA state; or

(*e*) to a person who has, within a period of 12 months immediately preceding the date when the application was made, been refused the grant or renewal of a licence for the premises, vehicle, vessel or stall in respect of which the application is made, unless the refusal has been reversed on appeal.

(2) Subject to paragraph 27 below, the appropriate authority may refuse—

(*a*) an application for the grant or renewal of a licence on one or more of the grounds specified in sub-paragraph (3) below;

(*b*) an application for the transfer of a licence on either or both of the grounds specified in paragraphs (*a*) and (*b*) of that sub-paragraph.

(3) The grounds mentioned in sub-paragraph (2) above are—

(*a*) that the applicant is unsuitable to hold the licence by reason of having been convicted of an offence or for any other reason;

(*b*) that if the licence were to be granted, renewed or transferred the business to which it relates would be managed by or carried on for the benefit of a person, other than the applicant, who would be refused the grant, renewal or transfer of such a licence if he made the application himself;

(*c*) that the number of sex establishments, or of sex establishments of a particular kind, in the relevant locality at the time the application is determined is equal to or exceeds the number which the authority consider is appropriate for that locality; (*d*) that the grant or renewal[1] of the licence would be inappropriate, having regard—

(i) to the character of the relevant locality; or

(ii) to the use to which any premises in the vicinity are put; or

(iii) to the layout, character or condition of the premises, vehicle, vessel or stall in respect of which the application is made.

(4) Nil may be an appropriate number for the purposes of sub-paragraph (3)(*c*) above.

(5) In this paragraph "the relevant locality" means—

(*a*) in relation to premises, the locality where they are situated; and

(*b*) in relation to a vehicle, vessel or stall, any locality where it is desired to use it as a sex establishment.

---

[1] The licensing authority is entitled to refuse to renew an existing licence on the grounds specified in para 12(3)(*d*), despite the fact that there has not been any change of circumstances, provided it gives due weight to the fact that the licence has previously been granted and gives rational reasons for its refusal (*R v Birmingham City Council, ex p Sheptonhurst Ltd* [1990] 1 All ER 1026, 87 LGR 830, CA). The Sch 3 regime gives a wide discretion to licensing authorities, in particular in forming value judgements as to whether the grant or renewal of a licence would be appropriate having regard to the character of the locality. On an application to renew an SEV licence it is not necessary for an objector to demonstrate that something has changed since the decision granting the licence. But whilst it is open to the local authority to depart from the decision of its predecessor, it has to have due regard to the fact that a licence was previously granted. It is under a duty to take account of the earlier decision, to grasp the nettle of any disagreement with the earlier decision and to state its reasons for coming to a different conclusion: *R (on the application of Thompson) v Oxford City Council (Spearmint Rhino Ventures (UK) Ltd intervening)* [2014] EWCA Civ 94, [2014] 1 WLR 1811.

*Power to prescribe standard conditions*

**13.** (1) Subject to the provisions of this Schedule, the appropriate authority may make regulations prescribing standard conditions applicable to licences for sex establishments, that is to say, terms, conditions and restrictions on or subject to which licences under this Schedule are in general to be granted, renewed or transferred by them.

(1A) No standard condition may be prescribed by regulation under sub-paragraph (1) above in so far as it relates to any matter in relation to which requirements or prohibitions are or could be imposed by or under the Regulatory Reform (Fire Safety) Order 2005.

(2) Regulations under sub-paragraph (1) above may make different provision—

(*a*) for sexual entertainment venues, sex cinemas, hostess bars and sex shops; and

(*b*) for different kinds of sexual entertainment venues, sex cinemas, hostess bars and sex shops.

(3) Without prejudice to the generality of sub-paragraphs (1) and (2) above, regulations under this paragraph may prescribe conditions regulating—

(*a*) the hours of opening and closing of sex establishments;

(*b*) displays or advertisements on or in such establishments;

(*c*) the visibility of the interior of sex establishments to passers-by; and

(*d*) any change from one kind of sex establishment mentioned in sub-paragraph (2)(*a*) above to another kind of sex establishment so mentioned.

(4) Where the appropriate authority have made regulations under sub-paragraph (1) above, every such licence granted, renewed or transferred by them shall be presumed to have been so granted, renewed or transferred subject to any standard conditions applicable to it unless they have been expressly excluded or varied.

(5) Where the appropriate authority have made regulations under sub-paragraph (1) above, they shall, if so requested by any person, supply him with a copy of the regulations on payment of such reasonable fee as the authority may determine.

(6) In any legal proceedings the production of a copy of any regulations made by the appropriate authority under sub-paragraph (1) above purporting to be certified as a true copy by an officer of the authority authorised to give a certificate for the purposes of this paragraph shall be prima facie evidence of such regulations, and no proof shall be required of the handwriting or official position or authority of any person giving such certificate.

*Copies of licences and standard conditions*

**14.** (1) The holder of a licence under this Schedule shall keep exhibited in a suitable place to be specified in the licence a copy of the licence and any regulations made under paragraph 13(1) above which prescribe standard conditions subject to which the licence is held.

(2) The appropriate authority shall send a copy of any licence granted under this Schedule to the chief officer of police for the area where the sex establishment is situated.

*Transmission and cancellation of licences*

**15.** In the event of the death of the holder of a licence granted under this Schedule, that licence shall be deemed to have been granted to his personal representatives and shall, unless previously revoked, remain in force until the end of the period of 3 months beginning with the death and shall then expire; but the appropriate authority may from time to time, on the application of those representatives, extend or further extend the period of three months if the authority are satisfied that the extension is necessary for the purpose of winding up the deceased's estate and that no other circumstances make it undesirable.

**16.** The appropriate authority may, at the written request of the holder of a licence, cancel the licence.

*Revocation of licences*

**17.** (1) The appropriate authority may, after giving the holder of a licence under this Schedule an opportunity of appearing before and being heard by them, at any time revoke the licence—

(*a*) on any ground specified in sub-paragraph (1) of paragraph 12 above; or

(*b*) on either of the grounds specified in sub-paragraph (3)(*a*) and (*b*) of that paragraph.

(2) Where a licence is revoked, the appropriate authority shall, if required to do so by the person who held it, give him a statement in writing of the reasons for their decision within 7 days of his requiring them to do so.

(3) Where a licence is revoked, its holder shall be disqualified from holding or obtaining a licence in the area of the appropriate authority for a period of 12 months beginning with the date of revocation.

*Variation of licences*

**18.** (1) The holder of a licence under this Schedule may at any time apply to the appropriate authority for any such variation of the terms, conditions or restrictions on or subject to which the licence is held as may be specified in the application.

(2) Subject to sub-paragraph (4) below, the appropriate authority—

(*a*) may make the variation specified in the application; or

(*b*) may make such variations as they think fit; or

(*c*) may refuse the application.

(3) The variations that an authority may make by virtue of sub-paragraph (2)(*b*) above include, without prejudice to the generality of that sub-paragraph, variations involving the imposition of terms, conditions or restrictions other than those specified in the application.

(4) No variation is to be made under this paragraph in so far as it relates to any matter in relation to which requirements or prohibitions are or could be imposed by or under the Regulatory Reform (Fire Safety) Order 2005.

*Fees*

**19.** An applicant for the grant, variation, renewal or transfer of a licence under this Schedule shall pay a reasonable fee determined by the appropriate authority[1].

[1] A licensing authority is permitted by this provision to require an applicant for the grant of renewal of a licence to pay a fee to cover the running and enforcement costs of a licensing scheme, and to make this fee payable either: (a) outright, as and when the licence is actually granted, pursuant to the application; or (b) on a refundable basis, at the time when the application is lodged *R (on the application of Hemming (t/a Simply Pleasure Ltd)) v Westminster City Council* [2015] UKSC 25, [2015] 4 All ER 471, [2015] All ER (D) 226 (Apr).

*Enforcement*

**20.** (1) A person who—

(*a*) knowingly[1] uses, or knowingly causes or permits the use of, any premises, vehicle, vessel or stall contrary to paragraph 6 above[2]; or

(*b*) being the holder of a licence for a sex establishment, employs in the business of the establishment any person known to him to be disqualified from holding such a licence; or

(*c*) being the holder of a licence under this Schedule, without reasonable excuse knowingly contravenes, or without reasonable excuse knowingly permits the contravention of, a term, condition or restriction specified in the licence; or

(*d*) being the servant or agent of the holder of a licence under this Schedule, without reasonable excuse knowingly contravenes, or without reasonable excuse knowingly permits the contravention of, a term, condition or restriction specified in the licence,

shall be guilty of an offence.

**21.** Any person who, in connection with an application for the grant, renewal or transfer of a licence under this Schedule, makes a false statement which he knows to be false in any material respect or which he does not believe to be true, shall be guilty of an offence.

**22.** (1) A person guilty of an offence under paragraph 20 or 21 above shall be liable on summary conviction to a fine.

(2) A person who, being the holder of a licence under this Schedule, fails without reasonable excuse to comply with paragraph 14(1) above shall be guilty of an offence and liable on summary conviction to a fine not exceeding **level 3** on the standard scale.

[1] The prosecution must establish not only that the person knew that the premises were used as a sex establishment but also that he knew that they were being so used without a licence. Such knowledge may be proved either by proving actual knowledge or by showing that the defendant had deliberately shut his eyes to the obvious or refrained from inquiry because he suspected the truth but did not want to have his suspicions confirmed (*Westminster City Council v Croyalgrange Ltd* [1986] 2 All ER 353, [1986] 1 WLR 674, HL).

[2] On such a prosecution, the court cannot investigate and determine the validity of a licensing authority's refusal to grant a licence (*Quietlynn Ltd v Plymouth City Council* [1988] QB 114, [1987] 2 All ER 1040, 151 JP 810, DC).

*Offences relating to persons under 18*

**23.** (1) A person who, being the holder of a licence for a sex establishment—

(*a*) without reasonable excuse knowingly permits a person under 18 years of age to enter the establishment; or

(*b*) employs a person known to him to be under 18 years of age in the business of the establishment,

shall be guilty of an offence.

(2) A person guilty of an offence under this paragraph shall be liable on summary conviction to a fine.

*Powers of constables and local authority officers*

**24.** *Repealed.*

**25.** (1) A constable may, at any reasonable time, enter and inspect any sex establishment in respect of which a licence under this Schedule is for the time being in force, with a view to seeing—

(i) whether the terms, conditions or restrictions on or subject to which the licence is held are complied with;

(ii) whether any person employed in the business of the establishment is disqualified from holding a licence under this Schedule;

(iii) whether any person under 18 years of age is in the establishment; and

(iv) whether any person under that age is employed in the business of the establishment.

(2) Subject to sub-paragraph (4) below, a constable may enter and inspect a sex establishment if he has reason to suspect that an offence under paragraph 20, 21 or 23 above has been, is being, or is about to be committed in relation to it.

(3) An authorised officer of a local authority may exercise the powers conferred by sub-paragraphs (1) and (2) above in relation to a sex establishment in the local authority's area.

(4) No power conferred by sub-paragraph (2) above may be exercised by a constable or an authorised officer of a local authority unless he has been authorised to exercise it by a warrant granted by a justice of the peace.

(5) Where an authorised officer of a local authority exercises any such power, he shall produce his authority if required to do so by the occupier of the premises or the person in charge of the vehicle, vessel or stall in relation to which the power is exercised.

(6) Any person who without reasonable excuse refuses to permit a constable or an authorised officer of a local authority to exercise any such power shall be guilty of an offence and shall for every such refusal be liable on summary conviction to a fine not exceeding **level 5** on the standard scale.

**25A.** (1) A person acting under the authority of a warrant under paragraph 25(4) may seize and remove anything found on the premises concerned that the person reasonably believes could be forfeited under sub-paragraph (4).

(2) The person who, immediately before the seizure, had custody or control of anything seized under sub-paragraph (1) may request any authorised officer of a local authority who seized it to provide a record of what was seized.

(3) The authorised officer must provide the record within a reasonable time of the request being made.

(4) The court by or before which a person is convicted of an offence under paragraph 20 or 23 of this Schedule may order anything—

(*a*) produced to the court; and

(*b*) shown to the satisfaction of the court to relate to the offence;

to be forfeited and dealt with in such manner as the court may order.

(5) But the court may not order the forfeiture of anything under sub-paragraph (4) if it (whether alone or taken together with other things being forfeited which appear to the court to have been in the custody or control of the same person) is worth more than the amount of the maximum fine specified in paragraph 22(1).

(6) Sub-paragraph (7) applies if a person claiming to be the owner of, or otherwise interested in, anything that may be forfeited applies to be heard by the court.

(7) The court may not order the forfeiture unless the person has had an opportunity to show why the order should not be made.

*Offences by bodies corporate*

**26.** (1) Where an offence under this Schedule committed by a body corporate is proved to have been committed with the consent or connivance of, or to be attributable to any neglect on the part of, any director, manager, secretary or other similar officer of the body corporate, or any person who was purporting to act in any such capacity, he, as well as the body corporate, shall be guilty of the offence.

(2) Where the affairs of a body corporate are managed by its members sub-paragraph (1) above shall apply to the acts and defaults of a member in connection with his function of management as if he were a director of the body corporate.

*Appeals*

**27.** (1) Subject to sub-paragraphs (2) and (3) below, any of the following persons, that is to say—

(*a*) an applicant for the grant, renewal or transfer of a licence under this Schedule whose application is refused;

(*b*) an applicant for the variation of the terms, conditions or restrictions on or subject to which any such licence is held whose application is refused;

(*c*) a holder of any such licence who is aggrieved by any term, condition or restriction on or subject to which the licence is held; or

(*d*) a holder of any such licence whose licence is revoked,

may at any time before the expiration of the period of 21 days beginning with the relevant date appeal to a magistrates' court

(2) An applicant whose application for the grant or renewal of a licence is refused, or whose licence is revoked, on any ground specified in paragraph 12(1) above shall not have a right to appeal under this paragraph unless the applicant seeks to show that the ground did not apply to him.

(3) An applicant whose application for the grant or renewal of a licence is refused on either ground specified in paragraph 12(3)(*c*) or (*d*) above shall not have the right to appeal under this paragraph.

(4) In this paragraph—

"the relevant date" means the date on which the person in question is notified of the refusal of his application, the imposition of the term, condition or restriction by which he is aggrieved or the revocation of his licence, as the case may be.

(5) An appeal against the decision of a magistrates' court under this paragraph may be brought to the Crown Court.

(6) Where an appeal is brought to the Crown Court under sub-paragraph (5) above, the decision of the Crown Court shall be final.

(7) On an appeal to the magistrates' court or the Crown Court under this paragraph the court may make such order as it thinks fit.

(8) Subject to sub-paragraphs (9) to (12) below, it shall be the duty of the appropriate authority to give effect to an order of the magistrates' court or the Crown Court.

(9) The appropriate authority need not give effect to the order of the magistrates' court until the time for bringing an appeal under sub-paragraph (5) above has expired and, if such an appeal is duly brought, until the determination or abandonment of the appeal.

(10) Where a licence is revoked or an application for the renewal of a licence is refused, the licence shall be deemed to remain in force—

(*a*) until the time for bringing an appeal under this paragraph has expired and, if such an appeal is duly brought, until the determination or abandonment of the appeal; and

(*b*) where an appeal relating to the refusal of an application for such a renewal is successful and no further appeal is available, until the licence is renewed by the appropriate authority.

(10A) Sub-paragraph (10) does not apply if the grounds for refusing an application for the renewal of a licence are those set out in paragraph 12(3)(*c*) or (*d*) of this Schedule.

(11) Where—

(*a*) the holder of a licence makes an application under paragraph 18 above; and

(*b*) the appropriate authority impose any term, condition or restriction other than one specified in the application,

the licence shall be deemed to be free of it until the time for bringing an appeal under this paragraph has expired.

(12) Where an appeal is brought under this paragraph against the imposition of any such term, condition or restriction, the licence shall be deemed to be free of it until the determination or abandonment of the appeal.

*Premises which are deemed sexual entertainment venues*

**27A.** (1) This paragraph applies if—

(*a*) premises are subject to a licence for a sexual entertainment venue; and

(*b*) their use would be use as such a venue but for the operation of paragraph 2A(3)(*b*).

(2) This Schedule applies as if—

(*a*) the premises were a sexual entertainment venue; and

(*b*) the use or business of the premises was use as, or the business of, such a venue.

(3) But the appropriate authority must cancel the licence if the holder of the licence asks them in writing to do so.

(4) In this paragraph "premises" has the same meaning as in paragraph 2A.

*Provisions relating to existing premises*

**28.** (1) Without prejudice to any other enactment it shall be lawful for any person who—

(*a*) was using any premises, vehicle, vessel or stall as a sex establishment immediately before the date of the first publication under subsection (2) of section 2 above of a notice of the passing of a resolution under that section by the local authority for the area; and

(*b*) had before the appointed day duly applied to the appropriate authority for a licence for the establishment,

to continue to use the premises, vehicle, vessel or stall as a sex establishment until the determination of his application.

(2) In this paragraph and paragraph 29 below "the appointed day", in relation to any area, means the day specified in the resolution passed under section 2 above as the date upon which this Schedule is to come into force in that area.

**29.** (1) This paragraph applies to an application for the grant of a licence under this Schedule made before the appointed day.

(2) A local authority shall not consider any application to which this paragraph applies before the appointed day.

(3) A local authority shall not grant any application to which this paragraph applies until they have considered all such applications.

(4) In considering which of several applications to which this paragraph applies should be granted a local authority shall give preference over other applicants to any applicant who satisfies them—

(*a*) that he is using the premises, vehicle, vessel or stall to which the application relates as a sex establishment; and

(*b*) that some person was using the premises, vehicle, vessel or stall as a sex establishment on 22nd December 1981; and

(*c*) that—

(i) he is that person; or

(ii) he is a successor of that person in the business or activity which was being carried on there on that date.

*Commencement of Schedule*

**30.** (1) So far as it relates to sex cinemas, this Schedule shall come into force on such day as the Secretary of State may by order[1] made by statutory instrument appoint.

(2) Subject to sub-paragraph (1) above, this Schedule shall come into force on the day on which this Act is passed.

(3) Where, in relation to any area, the day appointed under sub-paragraph (1) above falls after the day specified in a resolution passed under section 2 above as the day upon which this Schedule is to come into force in that area, the day so appointed shall, for the purposes of paragraphs 28 and 29 above, be the appointed day in relation to sex cinemas in the area.

---

[1] The Local Government (Miscellaneous Provisions) Act 1982 (Commencement No 1) Order 1982, SI 1982/1119, brought into force on 13 October 1982, Sch 3 so far as it relates to sex cinemas.

## SCHEDULE 4
### STREET TRADING

Section 3

*(As amended by the Criminal Justice Act 1982, s 46, the Food Act 1984, Sch 10, the Government of Wales Act 1998, Sch 15 and Sch 18, the Housing and Regeneration Act 2008, Sch 8 and the Localism Act 2011, Schs 19 and 22.)*

*Interpretation*

7.7185 **1.** (1) In this Schedule—

"consent street" means a street in which street trading is prohibited without the consent of the district council;

"licence street" means a street in which street trading is prohibited without a licence granted by the district council;

"principal terms", in relation to a street trading licence, has the meaning assigned to it by paragraph 4(3) below;

"prohibited street" means a street in which street trading is prohibited;

"street" includes—

(*a*) any road, footway, beach or other area to which the public have access without payment; and

(*b*) a service area as defined in section 329 of the Highways Act 1980,

and also includes any part of a street;

"street trading" means, subject to sub-paragraph (2) below, the selling or exposing or offering for sale of any article (including a living thing) in a street; and

"subsidiary terms", in relation to a street trading licence, has the meaning assigned to it by paragraph 4(4) below.

(2) The following are not street trading for the purposes of this Schedule—

(*a*) trading by a person acting as a pedlar[1] under the authority of a pedlar's certificate granted under the Pedlars Act 1871;

(*b*) anything done in a market[2] or fair the right to hold which was acquired by virtue of a grant (including a presumed grant) or acquired or established by virtue of an enactment or order.

(*c*) trading in a trunk road picnic area provided by the Secretary of State under section 112 of the Highways Act 1980;

(*d*) trading as a news vendor;

(*e*) trading which—

(i) is carried on at premises used as a petrol filling station; or

(ii) is carried on at premises used as a shop or in a street adjoining premises so used and as part of the business of the shop;

(*f*) selling things, or offering or exposing them for sale, as a roundsman[3];

(*g*) the use for trading under Part VIIA of the Highways Act 1980 of an object or structure placed on, in or over a highway;

(*h*) the operation of facilities for recreation or refreshment under Part VIIA of the Highways Act 1980;

(*j*) the doing of anything authorised by regulations made under section 5 of the Police, Factories, etc (Miscellaneous Provisions) Act 1916.*

(3) The reference to trading as a news vendor in sub-paragraph (2)(*d*) is a reference to trading where—

(*a*) the only articles sold or exposed or offered for sale are newspapers or periodicals; and

(*b*) they are sold or exposed or offered for sale without a stall or receptacle for them or with a stall or receptacle for them which does not—

(i) exceed one metre in length or width or two metres in height;

(ii) occupy a ground area exceeding 0·25 square metres; or

(iii) stand on the carriageway of a street.

---

* **Para 1(2)(*j*) substituted by the Charities Act 1992, Sch 6 from a date to be appointed. Further substituted by the Charities Act 2006, Sch 8 from a date to be appointed.**

1 See the definition of "pedlar" in s 3 of the 1871 Act in this PART, post. The burden of proving that the defendant was trading as a pedlar with a certificate is on the defendant: *Jones v Bath and North East Somerset Council* [2012] EWHC 1361 (Admin), (2012) 176 JP 530.

2 In the first instance, it is for the defendant to prove that the place where he was trading was a market. The holder of a market right may, however, restrict the holding of the market to an area smaller than that over which his right subsists; see *Jones v Lewis* (1989) Times, 14 June, DC.

3 "Roundsman" means "one who goes the round of his customers for orders and the delivery of goods" and "denotes a person who follows a set route to attend on specific/identifiable customers for the purpose of either taking orders or for the delivery of goods"; the Act clearly envisages that "intermediate sales" may be made, but that is ancillary to the "round": *Kempin (t/a British Bulldog) v Brighton and Hove Council* [2001] EWHC Admin 140, [2001] All ER (D) 125 (Feb)).

*Designation of streets*

2. (1) A district council may by resolution designate any street in their district as—

(*a*) a prohibited street;

(*b*) a licence street; or

(*c*) a consent street.

(2) If a district council pass such a resolution as is mentioned in sub-paragraph (1) above, the designation of the street shall take effect on the day specified in that behalf in the resolution (which must not be before the expiration of the period of one month beginning with the day on which the resolution is passed).

(3) A council shall not pass such a resolution unless—

(*a*) they have published notice of their intention to pass such a resolution in a local newspaper circulating in their area;

(*b*) they have served a copy of the notice—

(i) on the chief officer of police for the area in which the street to be designated by the resolution is situated; and

(ii) on any highway authority responsible for that street; and

(*c*) where sub-paragraph (4) below applies, they have obtained the necessary consent.

(4) This sub-paragraph applies—

(*a*) where the resolution relates to a street which is owned or maintainable by a relevant corporation; and

(*b*) where the resolution designates as a licence street any street maintained by a highway authority;

and in sub-paragraph (3) above "necessary consent" means—

(i) in the case mentioned in paragraph (*a*) above, the consent of the relevant corporation; and

(ii) in the case mentioned in paragraph (*b*) above, the consent of the highway authority.

(5) The following are relevant corporations for the purposes of this paragraph—

(*a*) the British Railways Board;

(*b*) new towns residuary body;

(*ba*) a Mayoral development corporation;

(*c*) a development corporation for a new town; and

(*d*) an urban development corporation established under the Local Government, Planning and Land Act 1980.

(*e*) *repealed.*

(5A) In sub-paragraph (5)(*b*) above "new towns residuary body" means—

(*a*) in relation to England, the Homes and Communities Agency so far as exercising functions in relation to anything transferred (or to be transferred) to it as mentioned in section 52(1)(*a*) to (*d*) of the Housing and Regeneration Act 2008 or the Greater London Authority so far as exercising its new towns and urban development functions; and

(*b*) in relation to Wales, the Welsh Ministers so far as exercising functions in relation to anything transferred (or to be transferred) to them as mentioned in section 36(1)(*a*)(i) to (iii) of the New Towns Act 1981.

(6) The notice referred to in sub-paragraph (3) above—

(*a*) shall contain a draft of the resolution; and

(*b*) shall state that representations relating to it may be made in writing to the council within such period, not less than 28 days after publication of the notice, as may be specified in the notice.

(7) As soon as practicable after the expiry of the period specified under sub-paragraph (6) above, the council shall consider any representations relating to the proposed resolution which they have received before the expiry of that period.

(8) After the council have considered those representations, they may, if they think fit, pass such a resolution relating to the street as is mentioned in sub-paragraph (1) above.

(9) The council shall publish notice that they have passed such a resolution in two consecutive weeks in a local newspaper circulating in their area.

(10) The first publication shall not be later than 28 days before the day specified in the resolution for the coming into force of the designation.

(11) Where a street is designated as a licence street, the council may resolve—

(*a*) in the resolution which so designates the street; or

(*b*) subject to sub-paragraph (12) below, by a separate resolution at any time,

that a street trading licence is not to be granted to any person who proposes to trade in the street for a number of days in every week less than a number specified in the resolution.

(12) Sub-paragraphs (3)(*a*) and (6) to (10) above shall apply in relation to a resolution under sub-paragraph (11)(*b*) above as they apply in relation to a resolution under sub-paragraph (1) above.

(13) Any resolution passed under this paragraph may be varied or rescinded by a subsequent resolution so passed.

*Street trading licences*

**3.** (1) An application for a street trading licence or the renewal of such a licence shall be made in writing to the district council.

(2) The applicant shall state—

(*a*) his full name and address;

(*b*) the street in which, days on which and times between which he desires to trade;

(*c*) the description of articles in which he desires to trade and the description of any stall or container which he desires to use in connection with his trade in those articles; and

(*d*) such other particulars as the council may reasonably require.

(3) If the council so require, the applicant shall submit two photographs of himself with his application.

(4) A street trading licence shall not be granted—

(*a*) to a person under the age of 17 years; or

(*b*) for any trading in a highway in relation to which a control order under section 7 of the Local Government (Miscellaneous Provisions) Act 1976 (road-side sales) is in force, other than trading to which the control order does not apply.

(5) Subject to sub-paragraph (4) above, it shall be the duty of the council to grant an application for a street trading licence or the renewal of such a licence unless they consider that the application ought to be refused on one or more of the grounds specified in sub-paragraph (6) below.

(6) Subject to sub-paragraph (8) below, the council may refuse an application on any of the following grounds—

(*a*) that there is not enough space in the street for the applicant to engage in the trading in which he desires to engage without causing undue interference or inconvenience to persons using the street;

(*b*) that there are already enough traders trading in the street from shops or otherwise in the goods in which the applicant desires to trade;

(*c*) that the applicant desires to trade on fewer days than the minimum number specified in a resolution under paragraph 2(11) above;

(*d*) that the applicant is unsuitable to hold the licence by reason of having been convicted of an offence or for any other reason;

(*e*) that the applicant has at any time been granted a street trading licence by the council and has persistently refused or neglected to pay fees due to them for it or charges due to them under paragraph 9(6) below for services rendered by them to him in his capacity as licence-holder;

(*f*) that the applicant has at any time been granted a street trading consent by the council and has persistently refused or neglected to pay fees due to them for it;

(*g*) that the applicant has without reasonable excuse failed to avail himself to a reasonable extent of a previous street trading licence.

(7) If the council consider that grounds for refusal exist under sub-paragraph (6)(*a*), (*b*) or (*g*) above, they may grant the applicant a licence which permits him—

(*a*) to trade on fewer days or during a shorter period in each day than specified in the application; or

(*b*) to trade only in one or more of the descriptions of goods specified in the application.

(8) If—

(*a*) a person is licensed or otherwise authorised to trade in a street under the provisions of any local Act; and

(*b*) the street becomes a licence street; and

(*c*) he was trading from a fixed position in the street immediately before it became a licence street; and

(*d*) he applied for a street trading licence to trade in the street, his application shall not be refused on any of the grounds mentioned in sub-paragraph (6)(*a*) to (*c*) above.

**4.** (1) A street trading licence shall specify—

(*a*) the street in which, days on which and times between which the licence-holder is permitted to trade; and

(*b*) the description of articles in which he is permitted to trade.

(2) If the district council determine that a licence-holder is to confine his trading to a particular place in the street, his street trading licence shall specify that place.

(3) Matters that fall to be specified in a street trading licence by virtue of sub-paragraph (1) or (2) above are referred to in this Schedule as the "principal terms" of the licence.

(4) When granting or renewing a street trading licence, the council may attach such further conditions (in this Schedule referred to as the "subsidiary terms" of the licence) as appear to them to be reasonable.

(5) Without prejudice to the generality of sub-paragraph (4) above, the subsidiary terms of a licence may include conditions—

(*a*) specifying the size and type of any stall or container which the licence-holder may use for trading;

(*b*) requiring that any stall or container so used shall carry the name of the licence-holder or the number of his licence or both; and

(*c*) prohibiting the leaving of refuse by the licence-holder or restricting the amount of refuse which he may leave or the places in which he may leave it.

(6) A street trading licence shall, unless previously revoked or surrendered, remain valid for a period of 12 months from the date on which it is granted or, if a shorter period is specified in the licence, for that period.

(7) If a district council resolve that the whole or part of a licence street shall be designated a prohibited street, then, on the designation taking effect, any street trading licence issued for trading in that street shall cease to be valid so far as it relates to the prohibited street.

5. (1) A district council may at any time revoke a street trading licence if they consider—

(*a*) that, owing to circumstances which have arisen since the grant or renewal of the licence, there is not enough space in the street for the licence-holder to engage in the trading permitted by the licence without causing undue interference or inconvenience to persons using the street;

(*b*) that the licence-holder is unsuitable to hold the licence by reason of having been convicted of an offence or for any other reason;

(*c*) that, since the grant or renewal of the licence, the licence-holder has persistently refused or neglected to pay fees due to the council for it or charges due to them under paragraph 9(6) below for services rendered by them to him in his capacity as licence-holder; or

(*d*) that, since the grant or renewal of the licence, the licence-holder has without reasonable excuse failed to avail himself of the licence to a reasonable extent.

(2) If the council consider that they have ground for revoking a licence by virtue of sub-paragraph (1)(*a*) or (*d*) above, they may, instead of revoking it, vary its principal terms—

(*a*) by reducing the number of days or the period in any one day during which the licence-holder is permitted to trade; or

(*b*) by restricting the descriptions of goods in which he is permitted to trade.

(3) A licence-holder may at any time surrender his licence to the council and it shall then cease to be valid.

**6.** (1) When a district council receive an application for the grant or renewal of a street trading licence, they shall within a reasonable time—

(*a*) grant a licence in the terms applied for; or

(*b*) serve notice on the applicant under sub-paragraph (2) below.

(2) If the council propose—

(*a*) to refuse an application for the grant or renewal of a licence; or

(*b*) to grant a licence on principal terms different from those specified in the application; or

(*c*) to grant a licence confining the applicant's trading to a particular place in a street; or

(*d*) to vary the principal terms of a licence; or

(*e*) to revoke a licence,

they shall first serve a notice on the applicant or, as the case may be, the licence-holder—

(i) specifying the ground or grounds on which their decision would be based; and

(ii) stating that within 7 days of receiving the notice he may in writing require them to give him an opportunity to make representations to them concerning it.

(3) Where a notice has been served under sub-paragraph (2) above, the council shall not determine the matter until either—

(*a*) the person on whom it was served has made representations to them concerning their decision; or

(*b*) the period during which he could have required them to give him an opportunity to make representations has elapsed without his requiring them to give him such an opportunity; or

(*c*) the conditions specified in sub-paragraph (4) below are satisfied.

(4) The conditions mentioned in sub-paragraph (3)(*c*) above are—

(*a*) that the person on whom the notice under sub-paragraph (2) above was served has required the council to give him an opportunity to make representations to them concerning it, as provided by sub-paragraph (2)(ii) above;

(*b*) that the council have allowed him a reasonable period for making his representations; and

(*c*) that he has failed to make them within that period.

(5) A person aggrieved—

(*a*) by the refusal of a council to grant or renew a licence, where—

(i) they specified in their notice under sub-paragraph (2) above one of the grounds mentioned in paragraph 3(6)(*d*) to (*g*) above as the only ground on which their decision would be based; or

(ii) they specified more than one ground in that notice but all the specified grounds were grounds mentioned in those paragraphs; or

(*b*) by a decision of a council to grant him a licence with principal terms different from those of a licence which he previously held, where they specified in their notice under sub-paragraph (2) above the ground mentioned in paragraph 3(6)(*g*) above as the only ground on which their decision would be based; or

(*c*) by a decision of a council—

(i) to vary the principal terms of a licence; or

(ii) to revoke a licence,

in a case where they specified in their notice under sub-paragraph (2) above one of the grounds mentioned in paragraph 5(1)(*b*) to (*d*) above as the only ground on which their decision would be based or they specified more than one ground in that notice but all the specified grounds were grounds mentioned in those paragraphs,

may, at any time before the expiration of the period of 21 days beginning with the date upon which he is notified of the refusal or decision, appeal to the magistrates' court acting for the petty sessions area in which the street is situated.

(6) An appeal[1] against the decision of a magistrates' court under this paragraph may be brought to the Crown Court.

(7) On an appeal to the magistrates' court or the Crown Court under this paragraph the court may make such order as it thinks fit.

(8) Subject to sub-paragraphs (9) to (11) below, it shall be the duty of the council to give effect to an order of the magistrates' court or the Crown Court.

(9) The council need not give effect to the order of the magistrates' court until the time for bringing an appeal under sub-paragraph (6) above has expired and, if such an appeal is duly brought, until the determination or abandonment of the appeal.

(10) If a licence-holder applies for renewal of his licence before the date of its expiry, it shall remain valid—

(*a*) until the grant by the council of a new licence with the same principal terms; or

(*b*) if—

(i) the council refuse renewal of the licence or decide to grant a licence with principal terms different from those of the existing licence, and

(ii) he has a right of appeal under this paragraph,

until the time for bringing an appeal has expired or, where an appeal is duly brought, until the determination or abandonment of the appeal; or

(*c*) if he has no right of appeal under this paragraph, until the council either grant him a new licence with principal terms different from those of the existing licence or notify him of their decision to refuse his application.

(11) Where—

(*a*) a council decide—

(i) to vary the principal terms of a licence; or

(ii) to revoke a licence; and

(*b*) a right of appeal is available to the licence-holder under this paragraph,

the variation or revocation shall not take effect until the time for bringing an appeal has expired or, where an appeal is duly brought, until the determination or abandonment of the appeal.

---

[1] The position in London is governed by the London County Council (General Powers) Act 1947 and is somewhat different: see *R v Crown Court at Southwark, ex p Watts* (1989) 153 JP 666, 88 LGR 86, DC.

*Street trading consents*

7. (1) An application for a street trading consent or the renewal of such a consent shall be made in writing to the district council.

(2) Subject to sub-paragraph (3) below, the council may grant a consent if they think fit.

(3) A street trading consent shall not be granted—

(*a*) to a person under the age of 17 years; or

(*b*) for any trading in a highway to which a control order under section 7 of the Local Government (Miscellaneous Provisions) Act 1976 is in force, other than trading to which the control order does not apply.

(4) When granting or renewing a street trading consent the council may attach such conditions to it as they consider reasonably necessary.

(5) Without prejudice to the generality of sub-paragraph (4) above, the conditions that may be attached to a street trading consent by virtue of that sub-paragraph include conditions to prevent—

(*a*) obstruction of the street or danger to persons using it; or

(*b*) nuisance or annoyance (whether to persons using the street or otherwise).

(6) The council may at any time vary the conditions of a street trading consent.

(7) Subject to sub-paragraph (8) below, the holder of a street trading consent shall not trade in a consent street from a van or other vehicle or from a stall, barrow or cart.

(8) The council may include in a street trading consent permission for its holder to trade in a consent street—

(*a*) from a stationary van, cart, barrow or other vehicle; or

(*b*) from a portable stall.

(9) If they include such a permission, they may make the consent subject to conditions—

(*a*) as to where the holder of the street trading consent may trade by virtue of the permission; and

(*b*) as to the times between which or periods for which he may so trade.

(10) A street trading consent may be granted for any period not exceeding 12 months but may be revoked at any time.

(11) The holder of a street trading consent may at anytime surrender his consent to the council and it shall then cease to be valid.

*General*

8. The holder of a street trading licence or a street trading consent may employ any other person to assist him in his trading without a further licence or consent being required.

9. (1) A district council may charge such fees as they consider reasonable for the grant or renewal of a street trading licence or a street trading consent.

(2) A council may determine different fees for different types of licence or consent and, in particular, but without prejudice to the generality of this sub-paragraph, may determine fees differing according—

(*a*) to the duration of the licence or consent;

(*b*) to the street in which it authorises trading; and

(*c*) to the descriptions of articles in which the holder is authorised to trade.

(3) A council may require that applications for the grant or renewal of licences or consents shall be accompanied by so much of the fee as the council may require, by way of a deposit to be repaid by the council to the applicant if the application is refused.

(4) A council may determine that fees may be paid by instalments.

(5) Where a consent is surrendered or revoked, the council shall remit or refund, as they consider appropriate, the whole or a part of any fee paid for the grant or renewal of the consent.

(6) A council may recover from a licence-holder such reasonable charges as they may determine for the collection of refuse, the cleansing of streets and other services rendered by them to him in his capacity as licence-holder.

(7) Where a licence—

(*a*) is surrendered or revoked; or

(*b*) ceases to be valid by virtue of paragraph 4(7) above,

the council may remit or refund, as they consider appropriate, the whole or a part—

(i) of any fee paid for the grant or renewal of the licence; or

(ii) of any charges recoverable under sub-paragraph (6) above.

(8) The council may determine—

(*a*) that charges under sub-paragraph (6) above shall be included in a fee payable under sub-paragraph (1) above; or

(*b*) that they shall be separately recoverable.

(9) Before determining charges to be made under sub-paragraph (6) above or varying the amount of such charges the council—

(*a*) shall give notice of the proposed charges to licence-holders; and

(*b*) shall publish notice of the proposed charges in a local newspaper circulating in their area.

(10) A notice under sub-paragraph (9) above shall specify a reasonable period within which representations concerning the proposed charges may be made to the council.

(11) It shall be the duty of a council to consider any such representations which are made to them within the period specified in the notice.

*Offences*

**10.** (1) A person who—

(*a*) engages in street trading in a prohibited street; or

(*b*) engages in street trading in a licence street or a consent street without being authorised[1] to do so under this Schedule; or

(*c*) contravenes any of the principal terms of a street trading licence; or

(*d*) being authorised by a street trading consent to trade in a consent street, trades in that street—

(i) from a stationary van, cart, barrow or other vehicle; or

(ii) from a portable stall,

without first having been granted permission to do so under paragraph 7(8) above; or

(*e*) contravenes a condition imposed under paragraph 7(9) above,

shall be guilty of an offence[2].

(2) It shall be a defence for a person charged with an offence under sub-paragraph (1) above to prove that he took all reasonable precautions and exercised all due diligence to avoid commission of the offence.

(3) Any person who, in connection with an application for a street trading licence or for a street trading consent, makes a false statement which he knows to be false in any material respect, or which he does not believe to be true, shall be guilty of an offence.

(4) A person guilty of an offence under this paragraph shall be liable on summary conviction to a fine not exceeding **level 3** on the standard scale.

---

1 The burden of establishing the statutory exception is on the defendant: *Jones v Bath and North East Somerset Council* [2012] EWHC 1361 (Admin), 176 JP 530.

2 In *Caradon District Council v Cheeseman* [2000] Crim LR 190, it was held that a trader had common law rights, including the right to be treated fairly and that justices rightly held that a public law challenge was available as a defence to a criminal charge for an offence under this Schedule.

*Savings*

**11.** Nothing in this Schedule shall affect—

(*a*) section 13 of the Markets and Fairs Clauses Act 1847 (prohibition of sales elsewhere than in market or in shops etc) as applied by any other Act;

(*b*) section 56 of the Food Act 1984 (prohibition of certain sales during market hours).

# Local Government Act 1986

(1986 c 10)

## PART II[1]

## LOCAL AUTHORITY PUBLICITY

7.7192 **2. Prohibition of political publicity** (1) A local authority shall not publish, or arrange for the publication of, any material which, in whole or in part, appears to be designed to affect public support for a political party.

(2) In determining whether material falls within the prohibition regard shall be had to content and style of the material, the time and other circumstances of publication and the likely effect on those to whom it is directed and, in particular, to the following matters—

(*a*) whether material refers to a political party or to persons identified with a political party or promotes or opposes a point of view on a question of political controversy which is identifiable as the view of one political party and not of another;

(*b*) where the material is part of a campaign, the effect which the campaign appears to be designed to achieve.

(3) A local authority shall not give financial or other assistance to a person for the publication of material which the authority are prohibited by this section from publishing themselves.

[Local Government Act 1986, s 2 as amended by the Local Government Act 1988, s 27 and the Communications Act 2003, s 349.]

[1] Part II contains ss 2–6.

7.7193 **4. Codes of recommended practice as regards publicity** *Secretary of State may issue codes of recommended practice as regards the content, style, distribution and cost of local authority publicity.*

7.7194 **5. Separate account of expenditure on publicity** (1) A local authority shall keep a separate account of their expenditure on publicity.

(2) Any person interested may at any reasonable time and without payment inspect the account and make copies of it or any part of it.

(3) A person having custody of the account who intentionally obstructs a person in the exercise of the rights conferred by subsection (2) commits an offence and is liable on summary conviction to a fine not exceeding **level 3** on the standard scale.

(4) The regulation making power conferred by section 32(1)(e) of the Local Audit and Accountability Act 2014, section 39(1)(e) of the Public Audit (Wales) Act 2004 or section 105(1)(d) of the Local Government (Scotland) Act 1973 (power to make provision as to exercise of right of inspection and as to informing persons of those rights) applies to the right of inspection conferred by subsection (2).

(5) The Secretary of State may by order[2] provide that subsection (1) does not apply to publicity or expenditure of a prescribed description.

(6) Before making an order the Secretary of State shall consult such associations of local authorities as appear to him to be concerned and any local authority with whom consultation appears to him to be desirable.

(7) An order shall be made by statutory instrument which shall be subject to annulment in pursuance of a resolution of either House of Parliament.

[Local Government Act 1986, s 5 as amended by the Public Audit (Wales) Act 2004, Sch 2 and the Local Audit and Accountability Act 2014, Sch 12.]

[1] See this title, post.

[2] The Local Authorities (Publicity Account) (Exemption) Order 1987, SI 1987/2004 has been made.

7.7195 **6. Interpretation and application of Part II** (1) References in this Part to local authorities and to publicity, and related expressions, shall be construed in accordance with the following provisions.

(2) "Local authority" means—

(*a*) in England and Wales—
a county, district or London borough council,
the Common Council of the City of London,
the Broads Authority (except in section 3),
a police and crime commissioner,
the Mayor's Office for Policing and Crime,
a joint authority established by Part IV of the Local Government Act 1985,
an economic prosperity board established under section 88 of the Local Democracy, Economic Development and Construction Act 2009,
a combined authority established under section 103 of that Act,
the London Fire and Emergency Planning Authority
the Council of the Isles of Scilly, or
a parish or community council;

(*b*) *Scotland*;

and includes any authority, board or committee which discharges functions which would otherwise fall to be discharged by two or more such authorities.

(3) This Part applies to the Common Council of the City of London as local authority, police authority or port health authority.

(4) "Publicity", "publish" and "publication" refer to any communication, in whatever form, addressed to the public at large or to a section of the public.

(5) This Part applies to any such publicity expressly or impliedly authorised by any statutory provision, including—

section 111 of the Local Government Act 1972 or section 69 of the Local Government (Scotland) Act 1973 (general subsidiary powers of local authorities),

section 141 of the Local Government Act 1972 or section 87 of the Local Government (Scotland) Act 1973 (research and collection of information), and

section 145(1)(*a*) of the Local Government Act 1972 or section 16(1)(*a*) of the Local Government and Planning (Scotland) Act 1982 (provision of entertainments, etc).

(6) Nothing in this Part shall be construed as applying to anything done by a local authority in the discharge of their duties under Part VA of the Local Government Act 1972 or Part IIIA of the Local Government (Scotland) Act 1973 (duty to afford public access to meetings and certain documents).

(7) Nothing in this Part shall be construed as applying to anything done by a person in the discharge of any duties under regulations made under section 22 of the Local Government Act 2000 (access to information etc).

[Local Government Act 1986, s 6 as amended by the Norfolk and Suffolk Broads Act 1988, Sch 6, the Education Reform Act 1988, Sch 13, the Police and Magistrates' Courts Act 1994, Sch 4, the Police Act 1996, Sch 7, the Police Act 1997, Sch 6, the Greater London Authority Act 1999, Sch 27, SI 2001/2237, the Criminal Justice and Police Act 2001, Sch 7, the Local Democracy, Economic Development and Construction Act 2009, Sch 6 and the Police Reform and Social Responsibility Act 2011, Sch 16.]

## Local Government Finance Act 1988
(1988 c 41)

*Non-domestic rate*

**7.7196** Part III of the 1988 Act and Regulations make provision for the payment of rates for non-domestic hereditaments; see in particular the Non-Domestic Rating (Collection and Enforcement) (Local Lists) Regulations 1989 ("the Regulations"), post. Under reg 12(5) of the Regulations a magistrates' court to whom a charging authority has applied shall make a liability order if satisfied that the sum has become payable and has not been paid, to include costs.

Section 43 deals with liability for occupied hereditaments and s 45 for unoccupied hereditaments. Exemptions are covered by Sch 5, valuation by Sch 6 and administration by Sch 9.

At the liability order hearing, the magistrates' court will need satisfying on the following matters:

(1) The local authority officer conducting proceedings is duly authorised under s 233 of the Local Government Act 1972 (ante).
(2) An entry appears in the local rating list and the sums have been calculated, demanded or notified in accordance with statutory provision.
(3) Full payment has not been made by the due date.
(4) A second notice or reminder has been issued, and the sum not having been paid within 7 days of the service thereof thus making the full sum due.
(5) A summons has been served for the remaining year's rates and the full sum claimed has not been paid.

The following defences may be raised:

(1) The property in respect of which the amount is claimed did not appear for the relevant period in the local rating list.
(2) The amount due has not been demanded or notified in accordance with statutory provisions.
(3) The amount has not been paid.
(4) The amount has not been calculated correctly.
(5) Joint and several liability has been alleged and the defendant's relationship with the defaulting ratepayer was not such at the time the debt was incurred.
(6) The defendant is not in occupation of the hereditament.

Once the liability order has been made, enforcement is under the Regulations alone; reg 14 provides for distress (now warrant of control) (with appeal to a magistrates' courts by a person aggrieved, under reg 15); thereafter imprisonment (see comments on this above in relation to community charge). The authority may consider insolvency (reg 18).

### PART III[1]
### NON-DOMESTIC RATING

*Local rating*

**7.7197 41.** *Local rating lists.*

[1] Part III contains ss 41–67. Part III is extensively amended by the Local Government and Housing Act 1989, Sch 5. Provision for the exchange of information between rating officials is made by the Non-Domestic Rating (Information) Act 1996.

**7.7198 41A.** *Local non-domestic rating lists for Welsh billing authorities.*

**7.7199 42.** *Contents of local lists*[1].

[1] Section 42 is supplemented by SI 1989/1060 amended by SI 1993/616, SI 1994/3122, SI 1996/619 and SI 2009/1307. The Non-Domestic Rating (Alteration of Lists and Appeals) (England) Regulations 2009, SI 2009/2268 amended by SI 2015/427 have also been made.

**7.7200 42A–B.** *Rural settlement list.*

**7.7201 43. Occupied hereditaments: liability** (1) A person (the ratepayer) shall as regards a hereditament be subject to a non-domestic rate in respect of a chargeable financial year if the following conditions are fulfilled in respect of any day in the year—

(*a*) on the day the ratepayer is in occupation[1] of all or part of the hereditament, and
(*b*) the hereditament is shown for the day in a local non-domestic rating list in force for the year.

(2) In such a case the ratepayer shall be liable to pay an amount calculated by—

(*a*) finding the chargeable amount for each chargeable day, and
(*b*) aggregating the amounts found under paragraph (*a*) above.

(3) A chargeable day is one which falls within the financial year and in respect of which the

conditions mentioned in subsection (1) above are fulfilled.

(4) Subject to subsections (4A), (5) and (6A) below, the chargeable amount for a chargeable day shall be calculated in accordance with the formula—

$$\frac{A \times B}{C}$$

(4A) Where subsection (4B) below applies, the chargeable amount for a chargeable day shall be calculated—

(*a*) in relation to England, in accordance with the formula—

$$(A \times D) / (C \times E)$$

(*b*) in relation to Wales, in accordance with the formula—

$$(A \times B) / (C \times E)$$

(4B) This subsection applies—

(*a*) in relation to England, where—

(i) *repealed*

(ii) on the day concerned any conditions prescribed by the Secretary of State by order[2] are satisfied, and

(iii) *repealed*

(*b*) in relation to Wales, where—

(i) the rateable value of the hereditament shown in the local non-domestic rating list for the first day of the chargeable financial year is not more than any amount prescribed by the National Assembly for Wales by order[3], and

(ii) on the day concerned any conditions prescribed by the National Assembly for Wales by order[3] are satisfied.

(4C) *Repealed.*

(4D) If the ratepayer makes an application in order to satisfy a condition prescribed under subsection (4B)(*a*)(ii) above and—

(*a*) makes a statement in the application which he knows to be false in a material particular, or

(*b*) recklessly makes a statement in the application which is false in a material particular,

he shall be liable on summary conviction to imprisonment for a term not exceeding 3 months or to a fine not exceeding level 3 on the standard scale or to both.

(5) Where subsection (6) below applies the chargeable amount for a chargeable day shall be calculated in accordance with the formula—

$$\frac{A \times B}{C \times 5}$$

(6) This subsection applies where on the day concerned—

(*a*) the ratepayer is a charity or trustees for a charity and the hereditament is wholly or mainly used for charitable purposes (whether of that charity or of that and other charities), or

(*b*) the ratepayer is a registered club for the purposes of Schedule 18 to the Finance Act 2002 (community amateur sports clubs) and the hereditament is wholly or mainly used—

(i) for the purposes of that club, or

(ii) for the purposes of that club and of other such registered clubs.

(6A) Where subsection (6B) below applies, or, subject to subsection (6I) below, subsection (6F) below applies, the chargeable amount for a chargeable day shall be calculated in accordance with the formula—

$$\frac{A \times B}{C \times 2}$$

(6B) This subsection applies where—

(*aa*) the hereditament is situated in England,

(*a*) on the day concerned the hereditament is within a settlement identified in the billing authority's rural settlement list for the chargeable financial year,

(*b*) the rateable value of the hereditament shown in the local non-domestic rating list at the beginning of that year is not more than any amount prescribed by the Secretary of State by order[4], and

(*c*) on the day concerned—

(i) the whole or part of the hereditament is used as a qualifying general store, a qualifying food store or qualifying post office, or

(ii) any conditions prescribed by the Secretary of State by order[5] are satisfied;

and subsections (6C) to (6E) below apply for the purposes of this subsection.

(6C) A hereditament, or part of a hereditament, is used as a qualifying general store on any day in a chargeable financial year if—

(*a*) a trade or business consisting wholly or mainly of the sale by retail of both food for human consumption (excluding confectionery) and general household goods is carried on there, and (*b*) such a trade or business is not carried on in any other hereditament, or part of a hereditament, in the settlement concerned.

(6CA) A hereditament, or part of a hereditament, is used as a qualifying food store on any day in a chargeable financial year if a trade or business consisting wholly or mainly of the sale by retail of food for human consumption (excluding confectionery and excluding the supply of food in the course of catering) is carried on there.

(6CB) In subsection (6CA) above the supply of food in the course of catering includes—

(*a*) any supply of food for consumption on the premises on which it is supplied; and

(*b*) any supply of hot food for consumption off those premises;

and for the purposes of paragraph (*b*) above "hot food" means food which, or any part of which—

(i) has been heated for the purposes of enabling it to be consumed at a temperature above the ambient air temperature; and

(ii) is at the time of supply above that temperature.

(6D) A hereditament, or part of a hereditament, is used as a qualifying post office on any day in a chargeable financial year if—

(*a*) it is used for the purposes of a universal service provider (within the meaning of the Postal Services Act 2000) and in connection with the provision of a universal postal service (within the meaning of that Act), and

(*b*) no other hereditament, or part of a hereditament, in the settlement concerned is so used.

(6E) Where a hereditament or part is used as a qualifying general store or qualifying post office on any day in a chargeable financial year, it is not to be treated as ceasing to be so used on any subsequent day in that year merely because the condition in subsection (6C)(*b*) or (6D)(*b*) above ceases to be satisfied.

(6F) This subsection applies where—

(*a*) on the day concerned the condition mentioned in subsection (6G) below is fulfilled in respect of the hereditament; and

(*b*) the rateable value of the hereditament shown in the local non-domestic rating list at the beginning of the chargeable financial year is not more than any amount prescribed by the Secretary of State by order[6].

(6G) The condition is that the hereditament—

(*a*) consists wholly or mainly of land or buildings which were, on at least 183 days during the period of one year ending immediately before this subsection comes into effect, agricultural land or agricultural buildings for the purposes of the exemption under paragraph 1 of Schedule 5 to this Act; and

(*b*) includes land or a building which is not agricultural for the purposes of that exemption but was agricultural for those purposes on at least 183 days during the period mentioned in paragraph (*a*) above.

(6H) For the purposes of subsection (6G) above—

(*a*) in relation to any hereditament which includes property which is domestic within the meaning of section 66 below, paragraph (*a*) has effect as if that part of the hereditament which does not consist of such property were the entire hereditament; and

(*b*) a building which has replaced a building which was an agricultural building for the purposes of the exemption mentioned in that subsection ("the original building") is to be treated as if it were the original building.

(6I) Subsection (6A) above shall not have effect, in relation to a hereditament to which subsection (6F) above applies, on a chargeable day on which paragraph 2A of Schedule 6 to this Act applies in relation to the hereditament.

(6J) Subject to subsection (6K) below, subsections (6F) to (6I) above shall cease to have effect at the end of the period of five years beginning with the day on which those subsections come into effect.

(6K) The Secretary of State may by order extend or further extend the period mentioned in subsection (6J).

(6L) If the period is so extended or further extended—

(*a*) subsection (6F) above cannot apply to a hereditament after the end of the period of five years beginning with the day on which it first applies; and

(*b*) where a hereditament to which subsection (6F) above applies ("the original hereditament") includes land or a building which is subsequently included in a different hereditament, that subsection cannot apply to the different hereditament after the end of the period of five years beginning with the day on which it first applies to the original hereditament.

(7) The amount the ratepayer is liable to pay under this section shall be paid to the billing authority in whose local non-domestic rating list the hereditament is shown.

(8) The liability to pay any such amount shall be discharged by making a payment or payments in accordance with regulations under Schedule 9 below.

(8A) In relation to any hereditament in respect of which both subsections (4A) and (6A) above (but not subsection (5) above) have effect on the day concerned, the chargeable amount—

(*a*) in relation to England, shall be calculated in accordance with subsection (6A) above, (*b*) in relation to Wales, shall be calculated in accordance with whichever of subsections (4A) and (6A) above produces the smaller amount.

(8B) In relation to any hereditament in respect of which—

(*a*) subsections (4A), (5) and (6A) above each have effect on the day concerned,

(*b*) subsections (4A) and (5) above both have effect on that day, or

(*c*) subsections (5) and (6A) above both have effect on that day,

the chargeable amount shall be calculated in accordance with subsection (5) above.

[Local Government Finance Act 1988, s 43 as amended by the Local Government Finance Act 1992, Sch 13, the Local Government and Finance Act 1997, Sch 1, the Rating (Former Agricultural Premises and Rural Shops) Act 2001, ss 1(1), 3(1), the Local Government Act 2003, s 61 and 63 and the Localism Act 2011, s 70 and Sch 25.]

[1] The actions of a receiver and manager in running a company's business do not, without more, amount to rateable occupation of the company's premises by him, since his occupation amounts to occupation by the company; if the company subsequently goes into liquidation (which terminates the receiver's agency by virtue of s 44(1)(*a*) of the Insolvency Act 1986), but the receiver continues to run the company as before, the company remains in rateable occupation and the receiver does not become liable for the rates (*Rees v Boston Borough Council* [2001] EWCA Civ 1934, [2002] 1 WLR 1304).

[2] The Non-Domestic Rating (Reliefs, Thresholds and Amendment) (England) Order 2017, SI 2017/102 has been made.

[3] The Non-Domestic Rating (Small Business Relief) (Wales) Order 2008, SI 2008/2770 amended by SI 2010/273 and 2223, SI 2011/995 and 2085, SI 2012/465, SI 2013/371 and 472, SI 2014/372, SI 2015/229 (as amended by SI 2016/32) and SI 2017/25 has been made.

[4] See the Non-Domestic Rating (Rural Settlements) (England) Order 1997, SI 1997/2792 amended by SI 2000/521, SI 2001/1346, SI 2004/3153 and SI 2009/3176, the Non-Domestic Rating (Rural Settlements) (Wales) Order 1998, SI 1998/2963 amended by SI 2002/331 and the Non-domestic Rating (Rural Rate Relief) (Wales) Order 2002, SI 2002/331.

[5] The Non-domestic Rating Contributions (Public Houses and Petrol Filling Stations) (England) Order 2001, SI 2001/1345 amended by SI 2006/591 and SI 2007/724 has been made.

[6] The Non-domestic Rating (Former Agricultural Premises) (England) Order 2004, SI 2004/3152 has been made.

7.7202 **44. Occupied hereditaments: supplementary** (1) This section applies for the purposes of section 43 above.

(2) A is the rateable value shown for the day under section 42(4) above as regards the hereditament.

(3) *Repealed.*

(4) Subject to subsection (5) below, B is the non-domestic rating multiplier for the financial year.

(5) Where the billing authority is a special authority, B is the authority's non-domestic rating multiplier for the financial year.

(6) C is the number of days in the financial year.

(7) Subject to subsection (8) below, D is the small business non-domestic rating multiplier for the financial year.

(8) Where the billing authority is a special authority, D is the authority's small business non-domestic rating multiplier for the financial year.

(9) E is such amount as may be prescribed—

(*a*) in relation to England, by the Secretary of State by order[1],

(*b*) in relation to Wales, by the National Assembly for Wales by order[2].

[Local Government Finance Act 1988, s 44, as amended by the Local Government and Housing Act 1989, Schs 5 and 12, the Local Government Finance Act 1992, Sch 13 and the Local Government Act 2003, s 61.]

[1] The Non-domestic Rating (Small Business Rate Relief) (England) Order 2012, SI 2012/148 amended by SI 2013/15, SI 2014/43, SI 2015/106 and SI 2016/143 has been made.

[2] The Non-Domestic Rating (Small Business Relief) (Wales) Order 2008, SI 2008/2770 amended by SI 2010/273 and 2223, SI 2011/995 and 2085, SI 2012/465, SI 2013/371 and 472 and SI 2015/106 has been made.

7.7203 **44A. Partly occupied hereditaments** (1) Where a hereditament is shown in a billing authority's local non-domestic rating list and it appears to the authority that part of the hereditament is unoccupied but will remain so for a short time only the authority may require the valuation officer for the authority to apportion the rateable value of the hereditament between the occupied and unoccupied parts of the hereditament and to certify the apportionment to the authority.

(2) The reference in subsection (1) above to the rateable value of the hereditament is a reference to the rateable value shown under section 42(4) above as regards the hereditament for the day on which the authority makes its requirement.

(3) For the purposes of this section an apportionment under subsection (1) above shall be treated as applicable for any day which—

(*a*) falls within the operative period in relation to the apportionment, and

(*b*) is a day for which the rateable value shown under section 42(4) above as regards the hereditament to which the apportionment relates is the same as that so shown for the day on which the authority requires the apportionment.

(4) References in this section to the operative period in relation to an apportionment are references to the period beginning—

(*a*) where requiring the apportionment does not have the effect of bringing to an end the operative period in relation to a previous apportionment under subsection (1) above, with the day on which the hereditament to which the apportionment relates became partly unoccupied, and (*b*) where requiring the apportionment does have the effect of bringing to an end the operative period in relation to a previous apportionment under subsection (1) above, with the day immediately following the end of that period,

and ending with the first day on which one or more of the events listed below occurs.

(5) The events are—

(*a*) the occupation of any of the unoccupied part of the hereditament to which the apportionment relates;

(*b*) the ending of the rate period in which the authority requires the apportionment;

(*c*) the requiring of a further apportionment under subsection (1) above in relation to the hereditament to which the apportionment relates;

(*d*) the hereditament to which the apportionment relates becoming completely unoccupied.

(6) Subsection (7) below applies where—

(*a*) a billing authority requires an apportionment under subsection (1) above, and

(*b*) the hereditament to which the apportionment relates—

(i) does not fall within a class prescribed under section 45(1)(*d*), or

(ii) would (if unoccupied) be zero-rated under section 45A.

(7) In relation to any day for which the apportionment is applicable, section 43 above shall have effect as regards the hereditament as if the following subsections were substituted for section 44(2)—

"(2) A is such part of the rateable value shown for the day under section 42(4) above as regards the hereditament as is assigned by the relevant apportionments to the occupied part of the hereditament.

(2A) In subsection (2) above "the relevant apportionment" means the apportionment under section 44A(1) below which relates to the hereditament and is treated for the purposes of section 44A below as applicable for the day."

(8) Subsection (9) below applies where—

(*a*) a billing authority requires an apportionment under subsection (1) above, and

(*b*) the hereditament to which the apportionment relates—

(i) falls within a class prescribed under section 45(1)(*d*), and

(ii) would (if unoccupied) not be zero-rated under section 45A, and

(*c*) an order under section 45(4A) is in force and has effect in relation to the hereditament.

(9) In relation to any day for which the apportionment is applicable, section 43 above shall have effect as regards the hereditament as if the following subsections were substituted for section 44(2)—

"(2) A is the sum of—

(*b*) such part of that rateable value as is assigned by the relevant apportionment to the unoccupied part of the hereditament, divided by the number prescribed by the order under section 45(4A) as it has effect in relation to the hereditament.

(*b*) one half of such part of that rateable value as is assigned by the relevant apportionment to the unoccupied part of the hereditament.

(2A) In subsection (2) above "the relevant apportionment" means the apportionment under section 44A(1) below which relates to the hereditament and is treated for the purposes of section 44A below as applicable for the day.".

(9A) In relation to a day to which neither subsection (7) nor subsection (9) applies, an apportionment under subsection (1) does not have any effect in relation to the chargeable amount.

(10) References in subsections (1) to (5) above to the hereditament, in relation to a hereditament which is partly domestic property or partly exempt from local non-domestic rating, shall, except where the reference is to the rateable value of the hereditament, be construed as references to such part of the hereditament as is neither domestic property nor exempt from local non-domestic rating.

[Local Government Finance Act 1988, s 44A, as inserted with retrospective effect by the Local Government and Housing Act 1989, s 139, Sch 5, paras 22, 79(3) and amended by the Local Government and Housing Act 1989, Schs 5 and 12, the Local Government Finance Act 1992, Sch 13 and the Rating (Empty Properties) Act 2007, Sch 1.]

7.7204 **45. Unoccupied hereditaments: liability** (1) A person (the ratepayer) shall as regards a hereditament be subject to a non-domestic rate in respect of a chargeable financial year if the following conditions are fulfilled in respect of any day in the year—

(*a*) on the day none of the hereditament is occupied,

(*b*) on the day the ratepayer is the owner[1] of the whole of the hereditament,

(*c*) the hereditament is shown for the day in a local non-domestic rating list in force for the year, and

(*d*) on the day the hereditament falls within a class prescribed by the Secretary of State by regulations[2].

(2) In such a case the ratepayer shall be liable to pay an amount calculated by—

(*a*) finding the chargeable amount for each chargeable day, and

(*b*) aggregating the amounts found under paragraph (*a*) above.

(3) A chargeable day is one which falls within the financial year and in respect of which the

conditions mentioned in subsection (1) above are fulfilled.

(4) Subject to subsection (4A) and to section 45A below, the chargeable amount for a chargeable day shall be calculated in accordance with the formula—

$$(A \times B) / C$$

where A, B and C have the meanings given by section 46.

(4A) An order may provide that subsection (4) shall have effect as if the following formula were substituted—

$$(A \times B) / (C \times N)$$

where N is such number (greater than one but not greater than two) as may be prescribed.

(4B) An order under subsection (4A) may be made—

(*a*) in relation to England, by the Secretary of State;

(*b*) in relation to Wales, by the Welsh Ministers.

(5) *Repealed.*

(6) *Repealed.*

(7) The amount the ratepayer is liable to pay under this section shall be paid to the billing authority in whose local non-domestic rating list the hereditament is shown.

(8) The liability to pay any such amount shall be discharged by making a payment or payments in accordance with regulations under Schedule 9 below.

(9) For the purposes of subsection (1)(*d*) above a class may be prescribed by reference to such factors as the Secretary of State sees fit.

(10) Without prejudice to the generality of subsection (9) above a class may be prescribed by reference to one or more of the following factors—

(*a*) the physical characteristics of the hereditaments;

(*b*) the fact that hereditaments have been unoccupied at any time preceding the day mentioned in subsection (1) above;

(*c*) the fact that the owners of hereditaments fall within prescribed descriptions.

[Local Government Finance Act 1988, s 45, as amended by the Local Government and Housing Act 1989, Sch 5 and the Local Government Finance Act 1992, Sch 13 and the Rating (Empty Properties) Act 2007, s 1, Sch 2.]

---

[1] Where a landlord brings a claim for forfeiture of a lease and the tenant accepts that repudiation of the lease and vacates the premises, it is the landlord who is responsible for the non-domestic rate in respect of the unoccupied premises (*Royal Borough of Kingston upon Thames v Marlow* (1995) 160 JP 502, DC).

[2] The Non-Domestic Rating (Unoccupied Property) (England) Regulations 2008, post, have been made. Provision for Wales is made by the Non-Domestic Rating (Unoccupied Property) (Wales) Regulations 2008, SI 2008/2499 amended by SI 2009/255, SI 2010/272, SI 2011/197 and SI 2015/1641.

7.7205 **45A. Unoccupied hereditaments: zero-rating** (1) Where section 45 applies in relation to a hereditament, the chargeable amount for a chargeable day is zero in the following cases.

(2) The first case is where—

(*a*) the ratepayer is a charity or trustees for a charity, and

(*b*) it appears that when next in use the hereditament will be wholly or mainly used for charitable purposes (whether of that charity or of that and other charities).

(3) The second case is where—

(*a*) the ratepayer is a registered club for the purposes of Schedule 18 to the Finance Act 2002 (community amateur sports clubs), and

(*b*) it appears that when the hereditament is next in use—

(i) it will be wholly or mainly used for the purposes of that club and that club will be such a registered club, or

(ii) it will be wholly or mainly used for the purposes of two or more clubs including that club, and each of those clubs will be such a registered club.

[Local Government Finance Act 1988, s 45A as inserted by the Rating (Empty Properties) Act 2007, s 1.]

7.7206 **46. Unoccupied hereditaments: supplementary** (1) This section applies for the purposes of section 45 above.

(2) A is the rateable value shown for the day under section 42(4) above as regards the hereditament.

(3) Subject to subsection (4) below, B is the non-domestic rating multiplier for the financial year.

(4) Where the billing authority is a special authority, B is the authority's non-domestic rating multiplier for the financial year.

(5) C is the number of days in the financial year.

[Local Government Finance Act 1988, s 46 as amended by the Local Government and Housing Act 1989, Sch 5 and the Local Government Finance Act 1992, Sch 13.]

7.7207 **46A. Unoccupied hereditaments: new buildings** (1) Schedule 4A below (which makes provision with respect to the determination of a day as the completion day in relation to a new building) shall have effect.

(2) Where—

(*a*) a completion notice is served under Schedule 4A below, and

(*b*) the building to which the notice relates is not completed on or before the relevant day,

then for the purposes of section 42 above and Schedule 6 below the building shall be deemed to be completed on that day.

(3) For the purposes of subsection (2) above the relevant day in relation to a completion notice is—

(*a*) where an appeal against the notice is brought under paragraph 4 of Schedule 4A below, the day stated in the notice, and

(*b*) where no appeal against the notice is brought under that paragraph, the day determined under that Schedule as the completion day in relation to the building to which the notice relates.

(4) Where—

(*a*) a day is determined under Schedule 4A below as the completion day in relation to a new building, and

(*b*) the building is not occupied on that day,

it shall be deemed for the purposes of section 45 above to become unoccupied on that day.

(5) Where—

(*a*) a day is determined under Schedule 4A below as the completion day in relation to a new building, and

(*b*) the building is one produced by the structural alteration of an existing building,

the hereditament which comprised the existing building shall be deemed for the purposes of section 45 above to have ceased to exist, and to have been omitted from the list, on that day.

(6) In this section—

(*a*) "building" includes part of a building, and

(*b*) references to a new building include references to a building produced by the structural alteration of an existing building where the existing building is comprised in a hereditament which, by virtue of the alteration, becomes, or becomes part of, a different hereditament or different hereditaments.

[Local Government Finance Act 1988, s 46A inserted with retrospective effect by the Local Government and Housing Act 1989, s 139, Sch 5.]

7.7208 **47. Discretionary relief** (1) Where the condition mentioned in subsection (3) below is fulfilled for a day which is a chargeable day within the meaning of section 43 or 45 above (as the case may be)—

(*a*) the chargeable amount for the day shall be such as is determined by, or found in accordance with rules determined by, the billing authority concerned, and

(*b*) sections 43(4) to (6B) and 44 above, sections 45(4) to (4B) and 46 above, regulations under section 57A or 58 below or any provision of or made under Schedule 7A below (as the case may be) shall not apply as regards the day.

(2) *Repealed.*

(3) The condition is that, during a period which consists of or includes the chargeable day, a decision of the billing authority concerned operates to the effect that this section applies as regards the hereditament concerned.

(3A)–(3D) *Repealed.*

(4) A determination under subsection (1)(*a*) above—

(*a*) must be such that the chargeable amount for the day is less than the amount it would be apart from this section;

(*b*) may be such that the chargeable amount for the day is 0;

(*c*) may be varied by a further determination of the authority under subsection (1)(*a*) above.

(5) In deciding what the chargeable amount for the day would be apart from this section the effect of any regulations under section 57A or 58 below or any provision of or made under Schedule 7A below shall be taken into account but anything which has been done or could be done under section 49 below shall be ignored.

(5A) So far as a decision under subsection (3) above would have effect where none of section 43(6) above, section 43(6B) above and subsection (5B) below applies, the billing authority may make the decision only if it is satisfied that it would be reasonable for it to do so, having regard to the interests of persons liable to pay council tax set by it.

(5B) This subsection applies on the chargeable day if—

(*a*) all or part of the hereditament is occupied for the purposes of one or more institutions or other organisations—

(i) none of which is established or conducted for profit, and

(ii) each of whose main objects are charitable or are otherwise philanthropic or religious or concerned with education, social welfare, science, literature or the fine arts, or

(*b*) the hereditament—

(i) is wholly or mainly used for purposes of recreation, and

(ii) all or part of it is occupied for the purposes of a club, society or other organisation not established or conducted for profit.

(5C) A billing authority in England, when making a decision under subsection (3) above, must have regard to any relevant guidance issued by the Secretary of State.

(5D) A billing authority in Wales, when making a decision under subsection (3) above, must have regard to any relevant guidance issued by the Welsh Ministers.

(6) A decision under subsection (3) above may be revoked by a further decision of the authority.

(7) A decision under subsection (3) above is invalid as regards a day if made more than six months after the end of the financial year in which the day falls.

(8) *Regulations.*[1]

(8A) This section does not apply where the hereditament is an excepted hereditament.

(9) A hereditament is an excepted hereditament if all or part of it is occupied (otherwise than as trustee) by—

(*a*) a billing authority; or

(*b*) a precepting authority, other than the Receiver for the Metropolitan Police District or* charter trustees; or

(*c*) a functional body, within the meaning of the Greater London Authority Act 1999, s 138.

(10) This section does not apply where the hereditament is zero-rated under section 45A.

[Local Government Finance Act 1988, s 47, as amended by the Local Government and Housing Act 1989, Sch 5, the Local Government Finance Act 1992, Sch 13, the Local Government and Rating Act 1997, Schs 1 and 3, the Greater London Authority Act 1999, s 138, the Rating (Former Agricultural Premises and Rural Shops) Act 2001, s 2(1), the Local Government Act 2003, s 63 and Sch 7, the Rating (Empty Properties) Act 2007, Sch 1 and the Localism Act 2011, s 69 and Sch 25.]

---

* **Repealed by the Greater London Authority Act 1999, Sch 34, as from a day to be appointed.**

1 The Non-Domestic Rating (Discretionary Relief) Regulations 1989, SI 1989/1059 amended by SI 1993/616 and SI 2006/3392 (W) have been made. See also the Non Domestic Rating Contributions (England) Regulations 1992, SI 1992/3082 amended by SI 1992/3259, SI 1993/1496 and 3082, SI 1994/421, 1431 and 3139, SI 1995/3181, SI 1996/561 and 3245, SI 1997/3031, SI 1998/3038, SI 2005/3333, SI 2007/3393, SI 2008/3078, SI 2009/1307, 1597 and 3095, SI 2010/2952, SI 2011/995, 1665 and 2993 and SI 2012/664 and 994; and the Non-Domestic Rating Contributions (Wales) Regulations 1992, SI 1992/3238 amended by SI 1993/1505 and 3077, SI 1994/547, 1742 and 3125, SI 1995/3235, SI 1996/3018, SI 1997/3003, SI 1998/2962, SI 2005/3345, SI 2008/2838 and 2929, SI 2009/3147, SI 2010/2889, SI 2011/2610, SI 2012/466 and 3036, SI 2013/3046, SI 2014/3193, SI 2015/1905 and SI 2016/1169.

7.7209 **48. Discretionary relief: supplementary** (1) This section applies for the purposes of section 47 above.

(2) *Repealed.*

(3) A hereditament not in use shall be treated as wholly or mainly used for purposes of recreation if it appears that when next in use it will be wholly or mainly used for purposes of recreation.

(4) A hereditament which is wholly unoccupied shall be treated as an excepted hereditament if it appears that when any of it is next occupied the hereditament will be an excepted hereditament.

(5) If a hereditament is wholly unoccupied but it appears that it or any part of it when next occupied will be occupied for particular purposes, the hereditament or part concerned (as the case may be) shall be treated as occupied for those purposes.

[Local Government Finance Act 1988, s 48 as amended by the Local Government and Rating Act 1997, Sch 1, the Rating (Empty Properties) Act 2007, Sch 2 and the Localism Act 2011, Sch 25.]

7.7210 **48A. Discretionary relief: functions of Mayoral development corporations** (1) The Mayor of London may require a billing authority to provide the Mayor with information to assist the Mayor with making decisions under section 214 of the Localism Act 2011 (Mayor's power to decide that a Mayoral development corporation should have functions under section 47 above).

(2) A Mayoral development corporation which has, or expects to have, functions under section 47 above may require a billing authority to provide the corporation with information to assist the corporation to exercise functions under that section.

(3) A billing authority must comply with a requirement imposed on it under subsection (1) or (2) above so far as the requirement relates to information available to the billing authority.

(4) A person to whom information is provided in response to a requirement imposed under subsection (1) or (2) above may use the information only for the purposes for which it was sought.

(5) The Secretary of State may by regulations make transitional provision in connection with, or in anticipation of, a Mayoral development corporation—

(*a*) beginning to exercise functions under section 47 above, or

(*b*) ceasing to exercise functions under that section.

(6) The Secretary of State may by regulations make provision about payment by a Mayoral development corporation to a billing authority of amounts—

(*a*) as regards the operation of section 47 above in cases where the corporation has exercised functions under that section;

(*b*) as regards costs of collection and recovery in such cases.

[Local Government Finance Act 1988, s 48A as inserted by the Localism Act 2011, Sch 22.]

7.7211 **49. Reduction or remission of liability** (1) A billing authority may—

(*a*) reduce any amount a person is liable to pay to it under section 43 or 45 above, or

(*b*) remit payment of the whole of any amount a person would otherwise be liable to pay to it under section 43 or 45 above.

(2) But an authority may not act under this section unless it is satisfied that—

(*a*) the ratepayer would sustain hardship if the authority did not do so, and (*b*) it is reasonable for the authority to do so, having regard to the interests of persons liable to pay council tax set by it.

(3) The amount as regards which a reduction or remittance may be made under subsection (1) above is the amount the person would be liable to pay (apart from this section) taking account of anything done under section 47 above, the effect of any regulations under section 57A or 58 below, and the effect of any provision of or made under Schedule 7A below.

(4) Where an authority acts under this section, section 43 or 45 above shall be construed accordingly as regards the case concerned.

[Local Government Finance Act 1988, s 49 as amended by the Local Government and Housing Act 1989, Sch 5, the Local Government Finance Act 1992, Sch 13 and the Local Government Act 2003, Sch 7.]

7.7212 **49A. Cancellation of backdated liabilities for days in years 2005 to 2010** (1) The Secretary of State may by regulations[1] provide that, in a prescribed case, the chargeable amount under section 43 or 45 for a hereditament in England for a chargeable day is zero.

(2) The regulations may give that relief in relation to a hereditament and a chargeable day only if—

(*a*) the hereditament is shown for the day in a local non-domestic rating list compiled on 1 April 2005, and

(*b*) it is shown for that day as it is shown as the result of an alteration of the list made after the list was compiled.

(3) The regulations may give that relief in relation to a hereditament and a chargeable day subject to the fulfilment of prescribed conditions.

(4) A prescribed condition may be—

(*a*) a condition to be fulfilled in relation to the hereditament,

(*b*) a condition to be fulfilled in relation to some other hereditament, or

(*c*) some other condition.

(5) The conditions that may be prescribed include, in particular

(*a*) conditions relating to the circumstances in which an alteration of a local non-domestic rating list was made;

(*b*) conditions relating to the consequences of the alteration;

(*c*) conditions relating to the length of the period beginning with the first day from which an alteration had effect and ending with the day on which the alteration was made;

(*d*) conditions relating to a person's liability or otherwise to non-domestic rates at any time.

[Local Government Finance Act 1988, s 49A as inserted by the Localism Act 2011, s 71.]

1 The Non-Domestic Rating (Cancellation of Backdated Liabilities) Regulations 2012, SI 2012/537 have been made.

7.7213 **50. Joint owners or occupiers** (1) The Secretary of State may make such regulations[1] as he sees fit to deal with any case where (apart from the regulations) there would be more than one owner or occupier of a hereditament or part or of land at a particular time.

(2) Nothing in the following provisions of this section shall prejudice the generality of subsection (1) above.

(3) The regulations may provide for the owner or occupier at the time concerned to be taken to be such one of the owners or occupiers as is identified in accordance with prescribed rules.

(4) The regulations may provide that—

(*a*) as regards any time when there is only one owner or occupier, section 43 or 45 above (as the case may be) shall apply;

(*b*) as regards any time when there is more than one owner or occupier, the owners or occupiers shall be jointly and severally liable to pay a prescribed amount by way of non-domestic rate.

(5) The regulations may include provision that prescribed provisions shall apply instead of prescribed provisions of this Part, or that prescribed provisions of this Part shall not apply or shall apply subject to prescribed amendments or adaptations.

[Local Government Finance Act 1988, s 50.]

1 See Part II of the Non-Domestic Rating (Collection and Enforcement) (Miscellaneous Provisions) Regulations 1990, SI 1990/145 amended by SI 1993/616, 774 and 894 and SI 2008/428 (E). The occupier of part of a hereditament is not liable under these Regulations to a liability order being made against him for the whole of the hereditament since it is not the intention of the Regulations themselves to impose such a liability (*Ford v Burnley Borough Council* (1995) 160 JP 541, [1995] RA 205).

7.7214 **51. Exemption** Schedule 5 below shall have effect to determine the extent (if any) to which a hereditament is for the purposes of this Part exempt from local non-domestic rating.

[Local Government Finance Act 1988, s 51.]

*Central rating*

7.7215 **52. Central rating lists** (1) In accordance with this Part the central valuation officer shall compile, and then maintain, lists (to be called central non-domestic rating lists).

(2) A list must be compiled on 1st April 1990 and on 1st April in every fifth year afterwards.

(3) A list shall come into force on the day on which it is compiled and shall remain in force until the next one is compiled five years later.

(4) Before a list is compiled the central valuation officer must take such steps as are reasonably

practicable to ensure that it is accurately compiled on 1st April concerned.

(5) Not later than 30th September preceding a day on which a list is to be compiled the central valuation officer shall send to the Secretary of State a copy of the list he proposes (on the information then before him) to compile.

(6) As soon as is reasonably practicable after receiving the copy the Secretary of State shall deposit it at his principal office.

(6A) As soon as is reasonably practicable after compiling a list the central valuation officer shall send a copy of it to the Secretary of State.

(6B) As soon as is reasonably practicable after receiving the copy the Secretary of State shall deposit it at his principal office.

(7) A list must be maintained for so long as is necessary for the purposes of this Part, so that the expiry of the five year period for which it is in force does not detract from the duty to maintain it.

[Local Government Finance Act 1988, s 52 as amended by the Local Government and Housing Act 1989, Sch 5 and the Local Government Act 2003, s 60.]

7.7216 **53. Contents of central lists** (1) With a view to securing the central rating en bloc of certain hereditaments, the Secretary of State may by regulations[1] designate a person and prescribe in relation to him one or more descriptions of relevant non-domestic hereditament.

(2) Where the regulations so require, a central non-domestic rating list must show, for each day in each chargeable financial year for which it is in force, the name of the designated person and, against it, each hereditament (wherever situated) which on the day concerned—

(*a*) is occupied or (if unoccupied) owned by him, and

(*b*) falls within any description prescribed in relation to him.

(3) For each such day the list must also show against the name of the designated person the rateable value (as a whole) of the hereditaments so shown.

(4) Where regulations are for the time being in force under this section prescribing a description of non-domestic hereditament in relation to a person designated in the regulations ("the previously designated person"), amending regulations altering the designated person in relation to whom that description of hereditament is prescribed may have effect from a date earlier than that on which the amending regulations are made.

(4A) Where, by virtue of subsection (4) above, the designated person in relation to any description of non-domestic hereditament is changed from a date earlier than the making of the regulation,—

(*a*) any necessary alteration shall be made with effect from that date to a central non-domestic rating list on which any hereditament concerned is shown; and

(*b*) an order making the provision referred to in paragraph 3(2) of Schedule 6 below and specifying a description of hereditament by reference to the previously designated person shall be treated, with effect from that date, as referring to the person designated by the amending regulations.*

(5) A central non-domestic rating list must also contain such information about hereditaments shown in it as may be prescribed by the Secretary of State by regulations[2].

[Local Government Finance Act 1988, s 53 as amended by the Local Government and Housing Act 1989, Sch 5.]

---

* **Repealed by the Local Government Act 2003, Sch 8 from a date to be appointed.**

1 The Central Rating List (Wales) Regulations 2005, SI 2005/422 and the Central Rating List (England) Regulations 2005, SI 2005/551 amended by SI 2005/3050, SI 2008/429, SI 2010/456, SI 2011/2743, SI 2012/1292, SI 2013/408 and 2887 and SI 2016/146, 645, 714 and 882 have been made.

2 The Non-Domestic Rating (Alteration of Lists and Appeals) (England) Regulations 2009, SI 2009/2268 amended by SI 2015/427 have been made.

7.7217 **54. Central rating: liability** (1) A person (the ratepayer) shall be subject to a non-domestic rate in respect of a chargeable financial year if for any day in the year his name is shown in a central non-domestic rating list in force for the year.

(2) In such a case the ratepayer shall be liable to pay an amount calculated by—

(*a*) finding the chargeable amount for each chargeable day, and

(*b*) aggregating the amounts found under paragraph (*a*) above.

(3) A chargeable day is one which falls within the financial year and for which the ratepayer's name is shown in the list.

(4) The chargeable amount for a chargeable day shall be calculated in accordance with the formula—

$$\frac{A \times B}{C}$$

(5) A is the rateable value shown for the day in the list against the ratepayer's name.

(6) B is the non-domestic rating multiplier for the financial year.

(7) C is the number of days in the financial year.

(8) The amount the ratepayer is liable to pay under this section shall be paid to the Secretary of State.

(9) The liability to pay any such amount shall be discharged by making a payment or payments in accordance with regulations under Schedule 9 below.

[Local Government Finance Act 1988, s 54.]

*General*

7.7218 **55.** *Alteration of lists.*

7.7219 **62. Administration** Schedule 9 below (which contains provisions about administration, including collection and recovery) shall have effect.*

[Local Government Finance Act 1988, s 62.]

7.7220 **62A. Recovery by taking control of goods** Where a liability order has been made against a person under regulations under Schedule 9, the billing authority may use the procedure in Schedule 12 to the Tribunals, Courts and Enforcement Act 2007 (taking control of goods) to recover the amount in respect of which the order was made, to the extent that it remains unpaid.

[Local Government Finance Act 1988, s 62A as inserted by the Tribunals, Courts and Enforcement Act 2007, Sch 13.]

7.7221 **63.** *Death.*

*Interpretation*

7.7222 **64. Hereditaments** (1) A hereditament is anything which, by virtue of the definition of hereditament in section 115(1) of the 1967 Act, would have been a hereditament for the purposes of that Act had this Act not been passed.

(2) In addition, a right is a hereditament if it is a right to use any land for the purpose of exhibiting advertisements and—

(*a*) the right is let out or reserved to any person other than the occupier[1] of the land, or

(*b*) where the land is not occupied for any other purpose, the right is let out or reserved to any person other than the owner of the land.

(2A) In addition, a right is a hereditament if—

(*a*) it is a right to use any land for the purpose of operating a meter to measure a supply of gas or electricity or such other service as—

(i) the Secretary of State in relation to England, or

(ii) the National Assembly for Wales in relation to Wales,

may by order specify, and

(*b*) the meter is owned by a person other than the consumer of the service.

(3) The Secretary of State may make regulations[2] providing that in prescribed cases—

(*a*) anything which would (apart from the regulations) be one hereditament shall be treated as more than one hereditament;

(*b*) anything which would (apart from the regulations) be more than one hereditament shall be treated as one hereditament[3].

(3A) The Secretary of State may make regulations providing that where on any land there are two or more moorings which—

(*a*) are owned by the same person,

(*b*) are not domestic property, and

(*c*) are separately occupied, or available for separate occupation, by persons other than that person,

a valuation officer may determine that, for the purposes of the compilation or alteration of a local non-domestic rating list, all or any of the moorings, or all or any of them together with any adjacent moorings or land owned and occupied by that person, shall be treated as one hereditament.

(3B) Regulations under subsection (3A) above may provide that—

(*a*) where a valuation officer makes a determination as mentioned in that subsection, he shall, if prescribed conditions are fulfilled, supply prescribed persons with prescribed information;

(*b*) while such a determination is in force—

(i) the person who on any day is the owner of the moorings (or the moorings and land) which constitute the hereditament shall be treated for the purposes of sections 43, 44A and 45 above as being in occupation of all of the hereditament on that day; and

(ii) no other person shall be treated for those purposes as being in occupation of all or any part of the hereditament on that day.

(4) A hereditament is a relevant hereditament if it consists of property of any of the following descriptions—

(*a*) lands;

(*b*) coal mines;

(*c*) mines of any other description, other than a mine of which the royalty or dues are for the time being wholly reserved in kind;

(*d*) *repealed;*

(*e*) any right which is a hereditament by virtue of subsection (2) or (2A) above.

(5)–(7D) *Repealed.*

(8) A hereditament is non-domestic if either—

(*a*) it consists entirely of property which is not domestic, or

(*b*) it is a composite hereditament.

(9) A hereditament is composite if part only of it consists of domestic property.

(10) A hereditament shall be treated as wholly or mainly used for charitable purposes at any time if at the time it is wholly or mainly used for the sale of goods donated to a charity and the proceeds of sale of the goods (after any deduction of expenses) are applied for the purposes of a charity.

(11) In subsection (2) above "land" includes a wall or other part of a building and a sign, hoarding, frame, post or other structure erected or to be erected on land.

(11A) The Secretary of State in relation to England, and the National Assembly in relation to Wales, may by regulations make provision as to what is to be regarded as being a meter for the purposes of subsection (2A) above.

(11B) In subsection (2A) above "land" includes a wall or other part of a building.

(12) In subsections (3A) and (3B) above "owner", in relation to a mooring, means the person who (if the mooring is let) is entitled to receive rent, whether on his own account or as agent or trustee for any other person, or (if the mooring is not let) would be so entitled if the mooring were let, and "owned" shall be construed accordingly.

[Local Government Finance Act 1988, s 64 as amended by the Local Government and Housing Act 1989, Sch 5, the Local Government Finance Act 1992, Sch 10, the Local Government and Rating Act 1997, s 2 and Sch 3 and the Local Government Act 2003, s 66.]

---

1 Where a person has been granted the right to use a flank wall of a building for advertising and place structures thereon, it is the wall on which a fixture is placed that is the "land" and not the fixture so that a hereditament in the advertising structure is created within the terms of s 64(2)(*a*) as the beneficiary of the right is a person other than the occupier of the land (*O'Brien v Secker* [1996] RA 409, CA).

2 See the Non-Domestic Rating (Miscellaneous Provisions) Regulations 1989, SI 1989/1060 amended by SI 1993/616, SI 1994/3122, SI 1996/619 and SI 2009/1307, the Non-Domestic Rating (Caravan Sites) Regulations 1990, SI 1990/673 amended by SI 1991/471, the Non-Domestic Rating (Electricity Generators) Regulations 1991, SI 1991/475, the Non-Domestic Rating (Police Authorities) Order 1995, SI 1995/1679, the Non-Domestic Rating (Communications and Light Railways) (England) Regulations 2005, SI 2005/549 amended by SI 2010/2692, the Central Rating List (Wales) Regulations 2005, SI 2005/422 and the Central Rating List (England) Regulations 2005, SI 2005/551 amended by SI 2005/3050, SI 2008/429, SI 2010/456 and 2692, SI 2011/2743, SI 2012/1292, SI 2013/408 and 2887 and SI 2016/146 and 645 and the Non-Domestic Rating (Waterways) (Wales) Regulations 2015, SI 2015/539.

3 Cross-boundary property is dealt with by SI 1989/1060 amended by SI 1993/616, SI 1994/3122, SI 1996/619 and SI 2009/1307.

7.7223 65. **Owners and occupiers** (1) The owner of a hereditament or land is the person entitled to possession of it[1].

(2) Whether a hereditament or land is occupied, and who is the occupier, shall be determined by reference to the rules which would have applied for the purposes of the 1967 Act had this Act not been passed (ignoring any express statutory rules such as those in sections 24 and 46A of that Act).

(3) Subsections (1) and (2) above shall have effect subject to the following provisions of this section.

(4) Regulations under section 64(3) above may include rules for ascertaining—

(*a*) whether the different hereditaments or the one hereditament (as the case may be) shall be treated as occupied or unoccupied;

(*b*) who shall be treated as the owner or occupier of the different hereditaments or the one hereditament (as the case may be).

(5) A hereditament which is not in use shall be treated as unoccupied if (apart from this subsection) it would be treated as occupied by reason only of there being kept in or on the hereditament plant, machinery or equipment—

(*a*) which was used in or on the hereditament when it was last in use, or

(*b*) which is intended for use in or on the hereditament.

(6) A hereditament shall be treated as unoccupied if (apart from this subsection) it would be treated as occupied by reason only of—

(*a*) the use of it for the holding of public meetings in furtherance of a person's candidature at a parliamentary or local government election, or

(*b*) if it is a house, the use of a room in it by a returning officer for the purpose of taking the poll in a parliamentary or local government election.

(7) In subsection (6) above "returning officer" shall be construed in accordance with section 24 or 35 of the Representation of the People Act 1983 (as the case may be).

(8) A right which is a hereditament by virtue of section 64(2) above shall be treated as occupied by the person for the time being entitled to the right.

(8A) In a case where—

(*a*) land consisting of a hereditament is used (permanently or temporarily) for the exhibition of advertisements or for the erection of a structure used for the exhibition of advertisements,

(*b*) section 64(2) above does not apply, and

(*c*) apart from this subsection, the hereditament is not occupied,

the hereditament shall be treated as occupied by the person permitting it to be so used or, if that person cannot be ascertained, its owner.

(9) *Repealed.*

[Local Government Finance Act 1988, s 65 as amended by the Local Government and Housing Act 1989, Sch 5 and the Local Government and Rating Act 1997, s 2.]

1 If a landlord claims forfeiture of a lease, it is open to the tenant to accept it and thereby terminate all future rights and liabilities under the lease including his right to possession as well as his liability for rent (*Royal Borough of Kingston upon Thames v Marlow* (1995) 160 JP 502, DC). Receivers who were appointed as agents under the terms of the debentures to take possession of the charged properties were held not to be entitled, by reason only of that appointment, to possession of the premises and thus were not "owners" for the purposes of s 65(1) of the Act; accordingly, the receivers were not personally liable for the non-domestic unoccupied property rates (*Brown v City of London Corpn* [1996] 1 WLR 1070).

7.7224 **65A. Crown Property** (1) This Part applies to the Crown as it applies to other persons.

(2) Accordingly, liability to a non-domestic rate in respect of a hereditament is not affected by the fact that—

(*a*) the hereditament is occupied by the Crown or by a person acting on behalf of the Crown or is used for Crown purposes, or

(*b*) the Crown or a person acting on behalf of the Crown is the owner of the hereditament.

(3) If (apart from this subsection) any property would consist of two or more Crown hereditaments, the property is to be treated for the purposes of this Part as if it were a single hereditament occupied by such one of the occupiers as appears to the billing authority to occupy the largest part of the property.

(4) In this section, "Crown hereditament" means a hereditament which—

(*a*) is occupied by a Minister of the Crown or Government department or by any officer or body exercising functions on behalf of the Crown, but

(*b*) is not provided or maintained by a local authority or by a police and crime commissioner.

(5) In this section—

(*a*) references to this Part include any subordinate legislation (within the meaning of the Interpretation Act 1978) made under it, and

(*b*) "local authority" has the same meaning as in the Local Government Act 1972, and includes the Common Council of the City of London.

(6) The Secretary of State may by order amend subsection (4)(*b*) above so as to alter the persons for the time being referred to there.

(7) Subsection (3) above does not affect the power conferred by section 64(3) above.

[Local Government Finance Act 1988, s 65A as inserted by the Local Government and Rating Act 1997, s 3 and amended by the Criminal Justice and Police Act 2001, Sch 6 and the Police Reform and Social Responsibility Act 2011, Sch 16.]

7.7225 **66. Domestic property** (1) Subject to subsections (2), (2B) and (2E) below, property is domestic if—

(*a*) it is used wholly for the purposes of living accommodation,

(*b*) it is a yard, garden, outhouse or other appurtenance belonging to or enjoyed with property falling within paragraph (*a*) above,

(*c*) it is a private garage which either has a floor area of 25 square metres or less or is used wholly or mainly for the accommodation of a private motor vehicle, or

(*d*) it is private storage premises used wholly or mainly for the storage of articles of domestic use.

(2) Property is not domestic property if it is wholly or mainly used in the course of a business for the provision of short-stay accommodation, that is to say accommodation—

(*a*) Which is provided for short periods to individuals whose sole or main residence is elsewhere, and

(*b*) which is not self-contained self-catering accommodation provided commercially.

(2A) Subsection (2) above does not apply if—

(*a*) it is intended that within the year beginning with the end of the day in relation to which the question is being considered, short-stay accommodation will not be provided within the hereditament for more than six persons simultaneously; and

(*b*) the person intending to provide such accommodation intends to have his sole or main residence within that hereditament throughout any period when such accommodation is to be provided, and that any use of living accommodation within the hereditament which would, apart from this subsection, cause any part of it to be treated as non-domestic, will be subsidiary to the use of the hereditament for, or in connection with, his sole or main residence.

(2B) A building or self-contained part of a building is not domestic property if—

(*a*) the relevant person intends that, in the year beginning with the end of the day in relation to which the question is being considered, the whole of the building or self-contained part will be available for letting commercially, as self-catering accommodation, for short periods totalling 140 days or more, and

(*b*) on that day his interest in the building or part is such as to enable him to let it for such periods.

(2C) For the purposes of subsection (2B) the relevant person is—

(*a*) where the property in question is a building and is not subject as a whole to a relevant leasehold interest, the person having the freehold interest in the whole of the building; and (*b*) in any other case, any person having a relevant leasehold interest in the building or self-contained part which is not subject (as a whole) to a single relevant leasehold interest inferior to his interest.

(2D) Subsection (2B) above does not apply where the building or self-contained part is used as the sole or main residence of any person.

(2E) Property is not domestic property if it is timeshare accommodation within the meaning of the Timeshare Act 1992.

(3) Subsection (1) above does not apply in the case of a pitch occupied by a caravan, but if in such a case the caravan is the sole or main residence of an individual, the pitch and the caravan, together with any garden, yard, outhouse or other appurtenance belonging to or enjoyed with them, are domestic property[1].

(4) Subsection (1) above does not apply in the case of a mooring occupied by a boat, but if in such a case the boat is the sole or main residence of an individual, the mooring and the boat, together with any garden, yard, outhouse or other appurtenance belonging to or enjoyed with them, are domestic property.

(4A) Subsection (3) or (4) above does not have effect in the case of a pitch occupied by a caravan, or a mooring occupied by a boat, which is an appurtenance enjoyed with other property to which subsection (1)(*a*) above applies[1].

(5) Property not in use is domestic if it appears that when next in use it will be domestic.

(6) *Repealed.*

(7) Whether anything is a caravan shall be construed in accordance with Part I of the Caravan Sites and Control of Development Act 1960.

(8) *Repealed.*

(8A) In this section—

"business" includes—

(*a*) any activity carried on by a body of persons, whether corporate or unincorporate, and

(*b*) any activity carried on by a charity;

"commercially" means on a commercial basis, and with a view to the realisation of profits; and

"relevant leasehold interest" means an interest under a lease or underlease which was granted for a term of 6 months or more and conferred the right to exclusive possession throughout the term.

(9) The Secretary of State may by order[2] amend, or substitute another definition for, any definition of domestic property for the time being effective for the purposes of this Part.

[Local Government Finance Act 1988, s 66 amended by SI 1990/162, the Caravans (Standard Community Charge and Rating) Act 1991, s 1, SI 1991/474, the Local Government Finance Act 1992, Sch 13, SI 1993/542 and the Rating (Caravan and Boats) Act 1996, s 1.]

---

1 The Rating (Caravan and Boats) Act 1996, s 1(4) and (5) provides that sub-ss (3) and (4) of the 1988 Act as substituted by the 1996 Act are to be treated as having had effect on and after 1 April 1990 and any additional sums payable thereby in respect of non-domestic rates may accordingly be recovered. Exception is made in respect of a hereditament where:

(a) a proposal for the alteration of a local non-domestic rating list in respect of the hereditament has been made, and not withdrawn, before 30 January 1995 in accordance with regulations under s 55 of the Local Government Finance Act 1988;

(b) the ground for the proposal was that the list was inaccurate because the hereditament ought not to be shown in the list or, in the case of a composite hereditament, the rateable value shown in the list was too high; and

(c) the reason or one of the reasons given in the proposal, or on an appeal (in accordance with those regulations) to a tribunal against a refusal to make the proposed alteration, for the list being inaccurate was that any pitch occupied by a caravan or (as the case may be) mooring occupied by a boat was domestic property by virtue of s 66(1)(*a*) or (*b*) of that Act.

It is further provided by subsection (6) that—

Local non-domestic rating lists compiled on 1 April 1990, 1 April 1995 or 1 April 1996 must be altered so far as required in consequence of this section: and the alterations are to be treated as having had effect from 1 April 1990 or, in the case of lists compiled on 1 April 1995 or 1 April 1996, from 1 April 1995 or from such other date as may be applicable in accordance with regulations under s 2.

2 The Non-Domestic Rating (Definition of Domestic Property) (Wales) Order 2010, SI 2010/682 and the Non-Domestic Rating and Council Tax (Definition of Domestic Property and Dwelling) (England) Order 2013, SI 2013/468 have been made.

**7.7226 66A. Unoccupied hereditaments: change of state of property to be disregarded**

(1) Regulations may provide that, for the purposes of this Part as it applies in relation to an unoccupied hereditament, the state of any property comprising or included in the hereditament shall be deemed not to have changed—

(*a*) since before any event of a prescribed description, or

(*b*) by reason of any act done by or on behalf of a prescribed person.

(2) The regulations may make provision as to the circumstances in which, and period for which, that is deemed to be the case.

(3) The regulations may provide for the making of such assumptions or apportionments as may be prescribed in determining whether, or to what extent, the state of any property has changed in comparison with an earlier point in time.

(4) The regulations may—

(*a*) provide that an act is to be treated as done on behalf of a prescribed person if it is done by any person connected with that person, and

(*b*) define in what circumstances persons are to be treated for that purpose as connected.

(5) The regulations may provide that they have effect (with any necessary adaptations) in

relation to omissions as well as to acts.

(6) Regulations under this section may be made—

(*a*) in relation to England, by the Secretary of State;

(*b*) in relation to Wales, by the Welsh Ministers.

[Local Government Finance Act 1988, s 66A as inserted by the Rating (Empty Properties) Act 2007, Sch 1.]

7.7227 **67. Interpretation: other provisions** (1) Unless the context otherwise requires, references to lists are to local and central non-domestic rating lists.

(2) Unless the context otherwise requires, references to valuation officers are to valuation officers for billing authorities and the central valuation officer.

(3) A right or other property is a hereditament on a particular day if (and only if) it is a hereditament immediately before the day ends.

(4) A hereditament is relevant, non-domestic, composite, unoccupied or wholly or partly occupied on a particular day if (and only if) it is relevant, non-domestic, composite, unoccupied or wholly or partly occupied (as the case may be) immediately before the day ends.

(5) For the purpose of deciding the extent (if any) to which a hereditament consists of domestic property on a particular day, or is exempt from local non-domestic rating on a particular day, the state of affairs existing immediately before the day ends shall be treated as having existed throughout the day.

(5A) In subsection (5) above "Crown hereditament" has the same meaning as in section 65A above.

(6) A person is the owner, or in occupation of all or part, of a hereditament on a particular day if (and only if) he is its owner or in such occupation (as the case may be) immediately before the day ends.

(7) A relevant provision applies on a particular day if (and only if) it applies immediately before the day ends; and for this purpose relevant provisions are sections 43(6), 45A(2) and (3) and 47(2) above.

(8) For the purpose of deciding what is shown in a list for a particular day the state of the list as it has effect immediately before the day ends shall be treated as having been its state throughout the day; and "effect" here includes any effect which is retrospective by virtue of an alteration of the list.

(9) A hereditament shall be treated as shown in a central non-domestic rating list for a day if on the day it falls within a class of hereditament shown for the day in the list; and for this purpose a hereditament falls within a class on a particular day if (and only if) it falls within the class immediately before the day ends.

(9A) In subsection (9) above "class" means a class expressed by reference to whether hereditaments—

(*a*) are occupied or owned by a person designated under section 53(1) above, and

(*b*) fall within any description prescribed in relation to him under section 53(1).

(10) A charity is an institution or other organisation established for charitable purposes only or any persons administering a trust established for charitable purposes only.

(10A) The times at which a club is a registered club for the purposes of Schedule 18 to the Finance Act 2002 (community amateur sports clubs)—

(*a*) shall, where it is registered with retrospective effect, be taken to have included those within the period beginning with the date with effect from which it is registered and ending with its registration; but

(*b*) shall, where its registration is terminated with retrospective effect, be taken not to have included those within the period beginning with the date with effect from which its registration is terminated and ending with the termination of its registration.

(11) The 1967 Act is the General Rate Act 1967.

(12) Nothing in a private or local Act passed before this Act shall have the effect that a hereditament is exempt as regards non-domestic rating, or prevent a person being subject to a non-domestic rate, or prevent a person being designated or a description of hereditament being prescribed under section 53 above.

(13) This section and sections 64 to 66 above apply for the purposes of this Part.

[Local Government Finance Act 1988, s 67 as amended by the Local Government Finance Act 1992, Sch 13 and the Local Government and Rating Act 1997, Sch 3, the Local Government Act 2003, s 64 and the Rating (Empty Properties) Act 2007, Sch 1.]

## PART XI[1]
## MISCELLANEOUS AND GENERAL

*General*

7.7228 **138. Judicial review** (1) The matters mentioned in subsection (2) below shall not be questioned except by an application for judicial review.

(2) The matters are—

(*a*)–(*d*) *repealed*,

(*e*) a levy issued under regulations under section 74 above,

(*f*) a special levy issued under regulations under section 75 above,

(*g*) *repealed*,

(*h*) the specification of a non-domestic rating multiplier under paragraph 2 of Schedule 7 below,

(*i*) the specification of a non-domestic rating multiplier under paragraph 7 of Schedule 7 below, and

(*j*) the setting by a special authority of a non-domestic rating multiplier or small business non-domestic rating multiplier under Schedule 7 below, whether originally or by way of substitute.

(3) If on an application for judicial review the court decides to grant relief in respect of the matters mentioned in subsection (2)(*e*) or (*f*) or (*h*) to (*j*) above, it shall quash the levy, special levy, specification or setting (as the case may be).

[Local Government Finance Act 1988, s 138 as amended by the Local Government Finance Act 1992, Sch 13 and the Local Government Act 2003, Sch 7.]

---

1 Part XI contains ss 130–152.

## SCHEDULES

### SCHEDULE 5

NON-DOMESTIC RATING: EXEMPTION Section 51

*(As amended by the Water Act 1989, Sch 25, the Local Government and Housing Act 1989, Sch 5, the Water Consolidation (Consequential Provisions) Act 1991, Sch 1, the Local Government Finance Act 1992, Sch 10, the Merchant Shipping Act 1995 Sch 13, the Local Government and Rating Act 1997, ss 2 and 4 and Sch 3, the Transport Act 2000, s 200, the National Health Service (Consequential Provisions) Act 2006, Sch 1 and SI 2015/914.)*

*Agricultural premises*

7.7229 **1.** A hereditament is exempt to the extent that it consists of any of the following—

(*a*) agricultural land;

(*b*) agricultural buildings.

**2.** (1) Agricultural land is—

(*a*) land used as arable, meadow or pasture ground only,

(*b*) land used for a plantation or a wood or for the growth of saleable underwood.

(*c*) land exceeding 0.10 hectare and used for the purposes of poultry farming,

(*d*) anything which consists of a market garden, nursery ground, orchard or allotment (which here includes an allotment garden within the meaning of the Allotments Act 1922), or

(*e*) land occupied with, and used solely in connection with the use of, a building which (or buildings each of which) is an agricultural building by virtue of paragraph 4, 5, 6 or 7 below.

(2) But agricultural land does not include—

(*a*) land occupied together with a house as a park,

(*b*) gardens (other than market gardens),

(*c*) pleasure grounds,

(*d*) land used mainly or exclusively for purposes of sport or recreation, or

(*e*) land used as a racecourse.

**3.** A building is an agricultural building if it is not a dwelling and—

(*a*) it is occupied together with agricultural land and is used solely in connection with agricultural operations on the land, or

(*b*) it is or forms part of a market garden and is used solely in connection with agricultural operations at the market garden.

**4.** (1) A building is an agricultural building if it is used solely in connection with agricultural operations carried on on agricultural land and sub-paragraph (2) or (3) below applies.

(2) This sub-paragraph applies if the building is occupied by the occupiers of all the land concerned.

(3) This sub-paragraph applies if the building is occupied by individuals each of whom is appointed by the occupiers of the land concerned to manage the use of the building and is—

(*a*) an occupier of some of the land concerned, or

(*b*) a member of the board of directors or other governing body of a person who is both a body corporate and an occupier of the land concerned.

(4) This paragraph does not apply unless the number of occupiers of the land concerned is less than 25.

**5.** (1) A building is an agricultural building if—

(*a*) it is used for the keeping or breeding of livestock, or

(*b*) it is not a dwelling, it is occupied together with a building or buildings falling within paragraph (*a*) above, and it is used in connection with the operations carried on in that building or those buildings.

(2) Sub-paragraph (1)(*a*) above does not apply unless—

(*a*) the building is solely used as there mentioned, or

(*b*) the building is occupied together with agricultural land and used also in connection with agricultural operations on that land, and that other use together with the use mentioned in sub-paragraph (1)(*a*) is its sole use.

(3) Sub-paragraph (1)(*b*) above does not apply unless—

(*a*) the building is solely used as there mentioned, or

(*b*) the building is occupied also together with agricultural land and used also in connection with agricultural operations on that land, and that other use together with the use mentioned in sub-paragraph (1)(*b*) is its sole use.

(4) A building (the building in question) is not an agricultural building by virtue of this paragraph unless it is surrounded by or contiguous to an area of agricultural land which amounts to not less than 2 hectares.

(5) In deciding for the purposes of sub-paragraph (4) above whether an area is agricultural land and what is its size, the following shall be disregarded—

(*a*) any road, watercourse or railway (which here includes the former site of a railway from which railway lines have been removed);

(*b*) any agricultural building other than the building in question;

(c) any building occupied together with the building in question.

**6.** (1) A building is an agricultural building if it is not a dwelling, is occupied by a person keeping bees, and is used solely in connection with the keeping of those bees.

(2) Sub-paragraphs (4) and (5) of paragraph 5 above apply for the purposes of this paragraph as for those of that.

**7.** (1) A building is an agricultural building if it is not a dwelling and—

(a) it is used in connection with agricultural operations carried on on agricultural land, and

(b) it is occupied by a body corporate any of whose members are or are together with the body the occupiers of the land, and

(c) the members who are occupiers of the land together have control of the body.

(2) A building is also an agricultural building if it is not a dwelling and—

(a) it is used in connection with the operations carried on in a building which, or buildings each of which, is used for the keeping or breeding of livestock and is an agricultural building by virtue of paragraph 5 above, and

(b) sub-paragraph (3), (4) or (5) below applies as regards the building first mentioned in this sub-paragraph (the building in question).

(3) This sub-paragraph applies if—

(a) the building in question is occupied by a body corporate any of whose members are, or are together with the body, the occupiers of the building or buildings mentioned in sub-paragraph (2)(*a*) above, and

(b) the members who are occupiers of the land together have control of the body.

(4) This sub-paragraph applies if the building in question, and the building or buildings mentioned in sub-paragraph (2)(*a*) above, are occupied by the same persons.

(5) This sub-paragraph applies if the building in question is occupied by individuals each of whom is appointed by the occupiers of the building or buildings mentioned in sub-paragraph (2)(*a*) above to manage the use of the building in question and is—

(a) an occupier of part of the building, or of part of one of the buildings, mentioned in sub-paragraph (2)(*a*) above, or

(b) a member of the board of directors or other governing body of a person who is both a body corporate and an occupier of the building or buildings mentioned in sub-paragraph (2)(*a*) above.

(6) Sub-paragraph (1) above does not apply unless the use there mentioned, or that use together with the use mentioned in sub-paragraph (2) above, is its sole use.

(7) Sub-paragraph (2) above does not apply unless the use there mentioned, or that use together with the use mentioned in sub-paragraph (1) above, is its sole use.

(8) Sub-paragraph (4) or (5) above does not apply unless the number of occupiers of the building or buildings mentioned in sub-paragraph (2)(*a*) above is less than 25.

(9) In this paragraph "control" shall be construed in accordance with section 416(2) to (6) of the Income and Corporation Taxes Act 1988.

**8.** (1) In paragraphs 1 and 3 to 7 above "agricultural land" shall be construed in accordance with paragraph 2 above.

(2) In paragraphs 1 and 5(5)(*b*) above "agricultural building" shall be construed in accordance with paragraphs 3 to 7 above.

(3) In determining for the purposes of paragraphs 3 to 7 above whether a building used in any way is solely so used, no account shall be taken of any time during which it is used in any other way, if that time does not amount to a substantial part of the time during which the building is used.

(4) In paragraphs 2 to 7 above and sub-paragraph (2) above "building" includes a separate part of a building.

(5) In paragraphs 5 and 7 above "livestock" includes any mammal or bird kept for the production of food or wool or for the purpose of its use in the farming of land.

*Fish farms*

**9.** (1) A hereditament is exempt to the extent that it consists of any of the following—

(a) land used solely for or in connection with fish farming;

(b) buildings (other than dwellings) so used.

(2) In determining whether land or a building used for or in connection with fish farming is solely so used, no account shall be taken of any time during which it is used in any other way, if that time does not amount to a substantial part of the time during which the land or building is used.

(3) "Building" includes a separate part of a building.

(4) "Fish farming" means the breeding or rearing of fish, or the cultivation of shellfish, for the purpose of (or for purposes which include) transferring them to other waters or producing food for human consumption.

(4A) But an activity does not constitute fish farming if the fish or shellfish are or include fish or shellfish which—

(a) are purely ornamental, or

(b) are bred, reared or cultivated for exhibition.

(5) "Shellfish" includes crustaceans and molluscs of any description.

**10.** *Repealed.*

*Places of religious worship etc*

**11.** (1) A hereditament is exempt to the extent that it consists of any of the following—

(a) a place of public religious worship which belongs to the Church of England or the Church in Wales (within the meaning of the Welsh Church Act 1914) or is for the time being certified as required by law as a place of religious worship;*

(b) a church hall, chapel hall or similar building used in connection with a place falling within paragraph (*a*) above for the purposes of the organisation responsible for the conduct of public religious worship in that place.

(2) A hereditament is exempt to the extent that it is occupied by an organisation responsible for the conduct of public religious worship in a place falling within sub-paragraph (1)(*a*) above, and—

(a) is used for carrying out administrative or other activities relating to the organisation of the conduct of public religious worship in such a place;

(*b*) is used as an office or for office purposes, or for purposes ancillary to its use as an office or for office purposes.

(3) In this paragraph "office purposes" include administration, clerical work and handling money; and "clerical work" includes writing, book-keeping, sorting papers or information, filing, typing, duplicating, calculating (by whatever means), drawing and the editorial preparation of matter for publication.

---

* **Substituted by the Local Government Act 2003, s 68 from a date to be appointed.**

*Certain property of Trinity House*

**12.** (1) A hereditament is exempt to the extent that it belongs to or is occupied by the Trinity House and consists of any of the following—

(*a*) a lighthouse;

(*b*) a buoy;

(*c*) a beacon;

(*d*) property within the same curtilage as, and occupied for the purposes of, a lighthouse.

(2) No other hereditament (or part of a hereditament) belonging to or occupied by the Trinity House is exempt, notwithstanding anything in section 221 (1) of the Merchant Shipping Act 1995.

*Sewers*

**13.** (1) A hereditament is exempt to the extent that it consists of any of the following—

(*a*) a sewer;

(*b*) an accessory belonging to a sewer.

(2) "Sewer" has the meaning given by section 343 of the Public Health Act 1936.

(3) "Accessory" means a manhole, ventilating shaft, pumping station, pump or other accessory.

(4) The Secretary of State may by order repeal sub-paragraphs (1) to (3) above.

*Property of drainage authorities*

**14.** (1) A hereditament is exempt to the extent that it consists of any of the following—

(*a*) land which is occupied by a drainage authority and which forms part of a main river or of a watercourse maintained by the authority;

(*b*) a structure maintained by a drainage authority for the purpose of controlling or regulating the flow of water in, into or out of a watercourse which forms part of a main river or is maintained by the authority;

(*c*) an appliance so maintained for that purpose.

(2) "Drainage authority", means the Environment Agency or any internal drainage board and "main river" and "watercourse" have the same meanings, respectively as they have in the Water Resources Act 1991 and the Land Drainage Act 1991.

(3) *Repealed.*

*Parks*

**15.** (1) A hereditament is exempt to the extent that it consists of a park which—

(*a*) has been provided by, or is under the management of, a relevant authority or two or more relevant authorities acting in combination, and

(*b*) is available for free and unrestricted use by members of the public.

(2) The reference to a park includes a reference to a recreation or pleasure ground, a public walk, an open space within the meaning of the Open Spaces Act 1906, and a playing field provided under the Physical Training and Recreation Act 1937.

(3) Each of the following is a relevant authority—

(*aa*) a Minister of the Crown or Government department or any officer or body exercising functions on behalf of the Crown,

(*a*) a county council,

(*aa*) a county borough council;

(*b*) a district council,

(*c*) a London borough council,

(*d*) the Common Council,

(*e*) the Council of the Isles of Scilly,

(*f*) a parish or community council, and

(*g*) the chairman of a parish meeting.

(4) In construing sub-paragraph (1)(*b*) above any temporary close (at night or otherwise) shall be ignored.

*Property used for the disabled*

**16.** (1) A hereditament is exempt to the extent that it consists of property used wholly for any of the following purposes—

(*a*) the provision of facilities for training, or keeping suitably occupied, persons who are disabled or who are or have been suffering from illness;

(*b*) the provision of welfare services for disabled persons;

(*c*) the provision of facilities under section 15 of the Disabled Persons (Employment) Act 1944;

(*d*) the provision of a workshop or of other facilities under section 3(1) of the Disabled Persons (Employment) Act 1958.

(1A) For the purposes of this paragraph in its application to hereditaments in England, a person is disabled if he has a disability within the meaning given by section 6 of the Equality Act 2010.

(2) For the purposes of this paragraph in its application to hereditaments in Wales, a person is disabled if he is blind, deaf or dumb or suffers from mental disorder of any description or is substantially and permanently handicapped by illness, injury, congenital deformity or any other disability for the time being prescribed for the purposes of section 29(1) of the National Assistance Act 1948.

(3) "Illness" has the meaning given by section 275 of the National Health Service Act 2006.

(4) "Welfare services for disabled persons" means services or facilities (by whomsoever provided) of a kind

which a local authority has power to provide under section 29 of the National Assistance Act 1948 or, in the case of a local authority in England, had power to provide under that section immediately before it ceased to apply to local authorities in England.

*Air-raid protection works*

**17.** A hereditament is exempt to the extent that it consists of property which—

(*a*) is intended to be occupied or used solely for the purpose of affording protection in the event of hostile attack from the air, and

(*b*) is not occupied or used for any other purpose.

*Swinging moorings*

**18.** A hereditament is exempt to the extent that it consists of a mooring which is used or intended to be used by a boat or ship and which is equipped only with a buoy attached to an anchor, weight or other device—

(*a*) which rests on or in the bed of the sea or any river or other waters when in use, and

(*b*) which is designed to be raised from that bed from time to time.

*Road crossings over watercourses etc*

**18A.** (1) A hereditament which is occupied (as mentioned in section 65 of this Act) is exempt to the extent that it consists of, or of any of the appurtenances of, a fixed road crossing over an estuary, river or other watercourse.

(2) For the purposes of this paragraph, a fixed road crossing means a bridge, viaduct, tunnel or other construction providing a means for road vehicles or pedestrians or both to cross the estuary, river or other watercourse concerned.

(3) For the purposes of sub-paragraph (2) above—

(*a*) a bridge may be a fixed road crossing notwithstanding that it is designed so that part of it can be swung, raised or otherwise moved in order to facilitate passage across, above or below it; but

(*b*) the expression "bridge" does not include a floating bridge, that is to say, a ferry operating between fixed chains.

(4) The reference in sub-paragraph (1) above to the appurtenances of a fixed road crossing is a reference to—

(*a*) the carriageway and any footway thereof;

(*b*) any building, other than office buildings, used in connection with the crossing; and

(*c*) any machinery, apparatus or works used in connection with the crossing or with any of the items mentioned in paragraphs (*a*) and (*b*) above.

*Property used for road user charging schemes*

**18B.** (1) A hereditament which is occupied (as mentioned in section 65 of this Act) is exempt to the extent that—

(*a*) it consists of a road in respect of which charges are imposed by a charging scheme under Schedule 23 to the Greater London Authority Act 1999 or Part III of the Transport Act 2000, or

(*b*) it is used solely for or in connection with the operation of such a scheme.

(2) But office buildings are not exempt under sub-paragraph (1)(*b*) above.

*Property in enterprise zones*

**19.** (1) A hereditament is exempt to the extent that it is situated in an enterprise zone.

(2) An enterprise zone is an area for the time being designated as an enterprise zone under Schedule 32 to the Local Government, Planning and Land Act 1980.

*Visiting Forces etc.*

**19A.** (1) A hereditament is exempt to the extent that it consists of property which is occupied for the purposes of a visiting force, or a headquarters, in pursuance of arrangements made in that behalf with any Government department.

(2) In this paragraph—

"headquarters" means an international headquarters or defence organisation designated by an Order in Council under section 1 of the International Headquarters and Defence Organisations Act 1964; and

"visiting force" means any such body, contingent or detachment of the forces of any country as is a visiting force for the purposes of any provision of the Visiting Forces Act 1952.

*Power to confer exemption*

**20.** (1) The Secretary of State may make regulations providing that prescribed hereditaments or hereditaments falling within any prescribed description are exempt to such extent (whether as to the whole or some lesser extent) as may be prescribed.

(2) But the power under sub-paragraph (1) above may not be exercised so as to confer exemption which in his opinion goes beyond such exemption or privilege (if any) as fulfils the first and second conditions.

(3) The first condition is that the exemption or privilege operated or was enjoyed in practice, immediately before the passing of this Act, in respect of a general rate in its application to the hereditaments prescribed or falling within the prescribed description.

(4) The second condition is that the exemption or privilege—

(*a*) was conferred by a local Act or order passed or made on or after 22 December 1925, or

(*b*) was conferred by a local Act or order passed or made before 22 December 1925 and was saved by section 117(5)(*b*) of the 1967 Act.

(5) Regulations under sub-paragraph (1) above in their application to a particular financial year (including regulations amending or revoking others) shall not be effective unless they come into force before 1 January in the preceding financial year.

*Interpretation*

**21.** (1) This paragraph applies for the purposes of this Schedule.

(2) "Exempt" means exempt from local non-domestic rating.

(3) Any land, building or property not in use shall be treated as used in a particular way if it appears that when next in use it will be used in that way.

(4) Any land or building which is not occupied shall be treated as occupied in a particular way if it appears that when next occupied it will be occupied in that way.

(5) A person shall be treated as an occupier of any land or building which is not occupied if it appears that when it is next occupied he will be an occupier of it.

## SCHEDULE 6

NON-DOMESTIC RATING: VALUATION[1] Section 56

**7.7245**

*(Amended by the Local Government and Housing Act 1989, Schs 5 and 12, the Local Government Finance Act 1992, Sch 10, SI 1993/544, the Local Government and Rating Act 1997, s 2 and the Rating (Valuation) Act 1999, s 1.)*

[1] See the Non-Domestic Rating (Miscellaneous Provisions) Regulations 1989, SI 1989/1060 amended by SI 1989/2303, SI 1993/616, SI 1994/3122, SI 1996/619, SI 1994/3122, SI 1996/619 and SI 2009/1307, the Non-Domestic Rating (Miscellaneous Provisions) (No 2) Regulations 1989, SI 1989/2303 amended by SI 1991/2906, SI 1993/544 and 616, SI 1994/3122, SI 2000/532 (England) and 908 (Wales), SI 2004/1000 (W) and 1494 (E), SI 2008/2997, SI 2015/1759 (W) and SI 2016/777; Non-Domestic Rating (Material Day for List Alterations) Regulations 1992, SI 1992/556 amended by SI 2005/658 (E) and 758; the Water Undertakers (Rateable Values) (Wales) Order 2000, SI 2000/299 amended by SI 2003/944, the BG plc (Rateable Value) (Wales) Order 2000, amended by SI 2003/944, the Railtrack plc (Rateable Value) (Wales) Order 2000, SI 2003/555 amended by SI 2003/944, the Valuation for Rating (Plant and Machinery) (England) Regulations 2000, SI 2000/540 amended by SI 2001/846 and SI 2008/2332, the Valuation for Rating (Plant and Machinery) (Wales) Regulations 2000, SI 2000/1097 amended by SI 2001/2357 and SI 2010/146; Non-domestic Rating (Stud Farms) (England) Order 2004, SI 2004/3151; Non-Domestic Rating (Communications Hereditaments) (Valuation, Alteration of Lists and Appeals and Material Day) (England) Regulations 2008, SI 2008/2333; Non-Domestic Rating (Communications Hereditaments) (Valuation, Alteration of Lists and Appeals and Material Day) (Wales) Regulations 2008, SI 2008/2671; Non-Domestic Rating (Stud Farms) (England) Order 2009, SI 2009/3177 amended by SI 2017/102; Rating Lists (Valuation Date) (England) Order 2014, SI 2014/2841 and Rating Lists (Valuation Date) (Wales) Order 2014, SI 2014/2917.

## SCHEDULE 9

NON-DOMESTIC RATING: ADMINISTRATION Section 62

*(As amended by the Local Government and Housing Act 1989, Sch 5 and 12, the Local Government Finance Act 1992, Sch 13, the Local Government Act 2003, s 72, the Local Government (Wales) Act 1994, Sch 16, the Local Government and Public Involvement in Health Act 2007, Sch 16, the Tribunals, Courts and Enforcement Act 2007, Sch 13 and SI 2015/982.)*

*Collection and recovery*

**7.7246** **1.** The Secretary of State may make regulations containing such provision as he sees fit in relation to the collection and the recovery, otherwise than under Schedule 12 to the Tribunals, Courts and Enforcement Act 2007 (taking control of goods), of amounts persons are liable to pay under sections 43, 45 and 54 above.

**2–4A.** *Regulations*[1].

[1] See the Non-Domestic Rating (Collection and Enforcement) (Local Lists) Regulations 1989, post, the Non-Domestic Rating (Collection and Enforcement) (Central Lists) Regulations 1989, SI 1989/2260, amended by SI 1991/142, SI 1992/1513, SI 1993/1494, SI 2009/1597, 2154 (W) and 2706 (W) and SI 2012/24, 466 (W) and 994 (E), the Environment Act 1995, Sch 22, para 233(1), SI 1996/1880 and SI 2002/180, the Council Tax and Non-domestic Rating (Demand Notices) (England) Regulations 2003, SI 2003/2613 amended by SI 2003/3081, SI 2004/3389, SI 2006/217, 492 and 3395, SI 2008/387 and 3264, SI 2009/355 and 1597 (which apply to non-domestic rating and (in respect of years 2009 and before), council tax), SI 2010/140 and 187, SI 2012/538 and 994, SI 2013/694, SI 2014/404, SI 2016/316 and SI 2017/39; Non-Domestic Rating (Deferred Payments) (England) Regulations 2009, SI 2009/1597; Non-Domestic Rating (Deferred Payments) (Wales) Regulations 2009, SI 2009/2154; Non-Domestic Rating (Deferred Payments) (Wales) Regulations 2012, SI 2012/466 and SI 2017/113; Non-Domestic Rating (Deferred Payments) (England) Regulations 2012, SI 2012/994 amended by SI 2013/694, SI 2014/404, SI 2016/316 and SI 2017/39; Non-Domestic Rating (Demand Notices) (Wales) Regulations 2017, SI 2017/113 have been made.

*Information*

5. (1) A valuation officer may serve a notice on a person who is an owner or occupier of a hereditament requesting him to supply to the officer information—

(*a*) which is specified in the notice, and

(*b*) which the officer reasonably believes will assist him in carrying out functions conferred or imposed on him by or under this Part.

(1A) A notice under this paragraph must state that the officer believes the information requested will assist him in carrying out functions conferred or imposed on him by or under this Part.

(2) A person on whom a notice is served under this paragraph shall supply the information requested in such form and manner as is specified in the notice.

(3) *Repealed.*

(4) If a notice has been served on a person under this paragraph, and in supplying information in purported compliance with sub-paragraph (2) above he makes a statement which he knows to be false in a material particular or recklessly makes a statement which is false in a material particular, he shall be liable on summary conviction to imprisonment for a term not exceeding **3 months** or to a fine not exceeding **level 3** on the standard scale or to both.

**5A.** (1) If a person on whom a notice is served under paragraph 5 above fails to comply with paragraph 5(2) within the period of 56 days beginning with the day on which the notice is served, he shall be liable to a penalty of £100.

(2) Where a person becomes liable to a penalty under sub-paragraph (1) above, the valuation officer shall serve on him a notice (a "penalty notice") stating—

(*a*) that he has failed to comply with paragraph 5(2) above within the period mentioned in sub-paragraph (1) above,

(*b*) that he is liable to a penalty of £100,
(*c*) the effect of sub-paragraphs (3) and (4) below, and
(*d*) that he has a right of appeal under paragraph 5C below.

(3) If the person on whom a penalty notice is served fails to comply with paragraph 5(2) within the period of 21 days beginning with the day on which the notice is served, he shall be liable—
(*a*) to a further penalty of £100, and
(*b*) subject to sub-paragraph (4) below, to a further penalty of £20 for each day in respect of which the failure continues after the end of that period.

(4) The amount to which a person shall be liable under this paragraph in respect of a failure to comply with a notice served under paragraph 5 above shall not exceed the greater of—
(*a*) the rateable value of the hereditament concerned for the day on which the penalty notice is served, and
(*b*) £500.

(5) For the purposes of sub-paragraph (4)(*a*) above—
(*a*) the hereditament concerned is the hereditament in respect of which the notice under paragraph 5 above was served, and
(*b*) a list compiled under this Part shall be used to find the rateable value of the hereditament for the day concerned.

**5B.** A valuation officer may mitigate or remit any penalty imposed under paragraph 5A above.

**5C.** (1) A person may appeal to a valuation tribunal if he is aggrieved by the imposition on him of a penalty under paragraph 5A above.

(2) An appeal under this paragraph must be made before the end of the period of 28 days beginning with the day on which the penalty notice is served.

(3) An appeal under this paragraph shall not prevent liability to any further penalty or penalties arising under paragraph 5A(3) above.

(4) An appeal under this paragraph shall be treated as an appeal against the penalty imposed under paragraph 5A(1) above and any further penalty which may be imposed under paragraph 5A(3) above.

(5) On an appeal under this paragraph the valuation tribunal may mitigate or remit any penalty under paragraph 5A above if it is satisfied on either or both of the grounds specified in sub-paragraph (6) below.

(6) Those grounds are—
(*a*) that the appellant had a reasonable excuse for not complying with paragraph 5(2) above, or
(*b*) that the information requested is not in the possession or control of the appellant.

(7) In this paragraph "valuation tribunal" means—
(*a*) in relation to England: the Valuation Tribunal for England;
(*b*) in relation to Wales: a valuation tribunal established under paragraph 1 of Schedule 11.

**5D.** (1) Subject to sub-paragraph (2) below, any penalty imposed under paragraph 5A above may be recovered by the valuation officer concerned as a civil debt due to him.

(2) No claim to recover any such penalty may be made—
(*a*) before the end of the period mentioned in paragraph 5C(2) above, or
(*b*) if an appeal is made under paragraph 5C above, before the appeal is finally disposed of.

**5E.** Any sums received by a valuation officer by way of penalty under paragraph 5A above must be paid into the Consolidated Fund.

**5F.** (1) The Secretary of State in relation to England, and the National Assembly of Wales in relation to Wales, may by regulations make provision in relation to notices served under paragraphs 5 and 5A above.

(2) The provision that may be made by regulations under this paragraph includes—
(*a*) provision enabling a valuation officer to request or obtain information for the purpose of identifying the owner or occupier of a hereditament;
(*b*) provision enabling a notice to be served on a person either by name or by such description as may be prescribed.

**5G.** The Secretary of State in relation to England, and the National Assembly in relation to Wales, may by order amend paragraph 5A above to increase or decrease the amount of any penalty under that paragraph.

**5H.** Where a valuation officer requires the name or address of a person on whom a notice under paragraph 5 or 5A above is to be served, he may serve a notice on a billing authority which he reasonably believes may have that information requesting the authority to supply him with that information.

**6.** (1) If in the course of the exercise of its functions any information comes to the notice of a billing authority which leads it to suppose that a list requires alteration it shall be the authority's duty to inform the valuation officer who has the duty to maintain the list.

(1A) *Regulations*[1].

---

[1] The Non-Domestic Rating (Alteration of Lists and Appeals) (England) Regulations 2009, SI 2009/2268 amended by SI 2015/427 have been made.

**6A.** *Regulations may require information to be supplied to the billing authority.*

*Power of entry*

**6B.** (1) If a valuation officer needs to value a hereditament in England for the purpose of carrying out functions conferred or imposed on the officer by or under this Part, the officer and any person authorised by the officer in writing may enter on, survey and value the hereditament if sub-paragraphs (2) and (4) are fulfilled and (where it applies) subparagraph (5) is fulfilled.

(2) The valuation officer must obtain the approval of the tribunal before the officer or a person authorised by the officer exercises the power under sub-paragraph (1).

(3) The tribunal must not give its approval unless it is satisfied that the valuation officer needs to value the hereditament.

(4) After the tribunal has given its approval, at least 3 days' notice in writing must be given of the proposed exercise of the power.

(5) In a case where a person authorised by the valuation officer proposes to exercise the power, the person must if required produce the authorisation.

(6) A person who wilfully delays or obstructs a person in the exercise of a power under this paragraph is liable on summary conviction to a fine not exceeding level 1 on the standard scale.

(7) For the purpose of the requirement under sub-paragraph (4), the following days are to be disregarded—

(*a*) a Saturday, a Sunday, Christmas Day or Good Friday;

(*b*) a day which is a bank holiday under the Banking and Financial Dealings Act 1971 in England and Wales.

(8) The tribunal may—

(*a*) determine any application brought under this paragraph and any question arising from that application;

(*b*) specify the arrangements by which any entry approved by it must be conducted, including whether the entry may occur on more than one day.

(9) In this paragraph "the tribunal" means the First-tier Tribunal.

**7.** (1) If a valuation officer needs to value a hereditament in Wales for the purpose of carrying out functions conferred or imposed on him by or under this Part, he and any person authorised by him in writing may enter on, survey and value the hereditament if sub-paragraph (2) below is fulfilled and (where it applies) sub-paragraph (3) below is fulfilled.

(2) At least 24 hours' notice in writing of the proposed exercise of the power must be given.

(3) In a case where a person authorised by the valuation officer proposes to exercise the power, the person must if required produce his authority.

(4) If a person wilfully delays or obstructs a person in the exercise of a power under this paragraph, he shall be liable on summary conviction to a fine not exceeding **level 1** on the standard scale.

*Inspection*

**8.** (1) A person may require a valuation officer to give him access to such information as will enable him to establish what is the state of a list, or has been its state at any time since it came into force, if—

(*a*) the officer is maintaining the list, and

(*b*) the list is in force or has been in force at any time in the preceding 5 years.

(2) A person may require a billing authority to give him access to such information as will enable him to establish what is the state of a copy of a list, or has been its state at any time since it was deposited, if—

(*a*) the authority has deposited the copy under section 41(6B) or 41A(10) above, and

(*b*) the list is in force or has been in force at any time in the preceding 5 years.

(3) A person may require the Secretary of State to give him access to such information as will enable him to establish what is the state of a copy of a list, or has been its state at any time since it was deposited, if—

(*a*) the Secretary of State has deposited the copy under section 52(6B) above, and

(*b*) the list is in force or has been in force at any time in the preceding 5 years.

(4) A person may require a billing authority to give him access to such information as will enable him to establish what is the state of a copy of a proposed list if—

(*a*) the authority has deposited the copy under section 41(6) above, and

(*b*) the list itself is not yet in force.

(5) A person may require the Secretary of State to give him access to such information as will enable him to establish what is the state of a copy of a proposed list if—

(*a*) the Secretary of State has deposited the copy under section 52(6) above, and

(*b*) the list itself is not yet in force.

(6) A requirement under any of the preceding provisions of this paragraph must be complied with at a reasonable time and place and without payment being sought; but the information may be in documentary or other form, as the person or authority of whom the requirement is made thinks fit.

(7) Where access is given under this paragraph to information in documentary form the person to whom access is given may—

(*a*) make copies of (or of extracts from) the document;

(*b*) require a person having custody of the document to supply to him a photographic copy of (or of extracts from) the document.

(8) Where access is given under this paragraph to information in a form which is not documentary the person to whom access is given may—

(*a*) make transcripts of (or of extracts from) the information;

(*b*) require a person having control of access to the information to supply to him a copy in documentary form of (or of extracts from) the information.

(9) If a reasonable charge is required for a facility under sub-paragraph (7) or (8) above, the sub-paragraph concerned shall not apply unless the person seeking to avail himself of the facility pays the charge.

(10) If without reasonable excuse a person having custody of a document containing, or having control of access to, information access to which is sought under this paragraph—

(*a*) intentionally obstructs a person in exercising a right under sub-paragraph (1), (2), (3), (4), (5), (7)(*a*) or (8)(*a*) above, or

(*b*) refuses to comply with a requirement under sub-paragraph (7)(*b*) or 8(*b*) above,

he shall be liable on summary conviction to a fine not exceeding **level 1** on the standard scale.

**9.** (1) A person may, at a reasonable time and without making payment, inspect any proposal made or notice of appeal given under regulations made under section 55 above, if made or given as regards a list which is in force when inspection is sought or has been in force at any time in the preceding years.

(2) A person may—

(*a*) make copies of (or of extracts from) a document mentioned in sub-paragraph (1) above, or

(*b*) require a person having custody of such a document to supply him a photographic copy of (or of extracts from) the document.

(3) If a reasonable charge is required for a facility under sub-paragraph (2) above, the sub-paragraph shall not apply unless the person seeking to avail himself of the facility pays the charge.

(4) If without reasonable excuse a person having custody of a document mentioned in sub-paragraph (1) above—

(*a*) intentionally obstructs a person in exercising a right under sub-paragraph (1) or (2)(*a*) above, or

(*b*) refuses to supply a copy to a person entitled to it under sub-paragraph (2)(*b*) above,

he shall be liable on summary conviction to a fine not exceeding **level 1** on the standard scale.

# Local Government Finance Act 1992

(1992 c 14)

*Introduction: council tax*

**7.7251** The Local Government Finance Act 1992 ("the Act") and regulations made thereunder establish a system of council tax replacing the community charge ("poll tax") and thus reverting to a property-based liability.

Part I (ss 1–69) is divided into six Chapters. Chapter I gives the main provisions of the council tax, Chapter II sets out provisions relating to valuation lists; intentional delay or obstruction exercising a power of entry following three clear days' notice (excluding Saturday, Sunday, Christmas Day, Good Friday, bank holidays) is punishable by a level 2 fine (s 26); failing to comply with notice requiring information about property is punishable by a level 2 fine (s **27(4)** and knowingly or recklessly making a statement false in a material particular is punishable by 3 months' imprisonment and/or a level 3 fine (s **27(5)**). Chapter III is concerned with the setting of the council tax and Chapter IV with precepts. Limitation of council tax and precepts by the Secretary of State is dealt with in Chapter V and Chapter VI (ss 65–69) covers miscellaneous and supplemental matters including Part I interpretation. Part III (ss 100–102) provides for transition from community charges.

## PART I
## COUNCIL TAX: ENGLAND AND WALES

### CHAPTER I
### MAIN PROVISIONS

*Preliminary*

7.7252 **1. Council tax in respect of dwellings** (1) As regards the financial year beginning in 1993 and subsequent financial years, each billing authority shall, in accordance with this Part, levy and collect a tax, to be called council tax, which shall be payable in respect of dwellings situated in its area.

(2) In this Part "billing authority" means—

(*a*) in relation to England, a district council or London borough council, the Common Council or the Council of the Isles of Scilly, and

(*b*) in relation to Wales, a county council or county borough council.

(3) For the purposes of this Part the Secretary of State may make regulations[1] containing rules for treating a dwelling as situated in a billing authority's area if part only of the dwelling falls within the area.

[Local Government Finance Act 1992, s 1 as amended by the Local Government (Wales) Act 1994, s 35(5).]

---

[1] See Pt II of the Council Tax (Situation and Valuation of Dwellings) Regulations 1992, SI 1992/550 amended by SI 1994/1747 and SI 2008/315.

7.7253 **2. Liability to tax determined on a daily basis** (1) Liability to pay council tax shall be determined on a daily basis.

(2) For the purposes of determining for any day—

(*a*) whether any property is a chargeable dwelling;

(*b*) which valuation band is shown in the billing authority's valuation list as applicable to any chargeable dwelling;

(*c*) the person liable to pay council tax in respect of any such dwelling; or

(*d*) whether any amount of council tax is subject to a discount and (if so) the amount of the discount,

it shall be assumed that any state of affairs subsisting at the end of the day had subsisted throughout the day.

[Local Government Finance Act 1992, s 2.]

*Chargeable dwellings*

7.7254 **3. Meaning of "dwelling"** (1) This section has effect for determining what is a dwelling for the purposes of this Part.

(2) Subject to the following provisions of this section, a dwelling is any property which—

(*a*) by virtue of the definition of hereditament in section 115(1) of the General Rate Act 1967, would have been a hereditament for the purposes of that Act if that Act remained in force; and

(*b*) is not for the time being shown or required to be shown in a local or a central non-domestic rating list in force at that time; and

(*c*) is not for the time being exempt from local non-domestic rating for the purposes of Part III of the Local Government Finance Act 1988 ("the 1988 Act");

and in applying paragraphs (*b*) and (*c*) above no account shall be taken of any rules as to Crown exemption.

(3) A hereditament which—

(*a*) is a composite hereditament for the purposes of Part III of the 1988 Act; and (*b*) would still be such a hereditament if paragraphs (*b*) to (*d*) of section 66(1) of that Act (domestic property) were omitted,

is also, subject to subsection (6) below, a dwelling for the purposes of this Part.

(4) Subject to subsection (6) below, none of the following property, namely—

(*a*) a yard, garden, outhouse or other appurtenance belonging to or enjoyed with property used wholly for the purposes of living accommodation; or

(*b*) a private garage which either has a floor area of not more than 25 square metres or is used wholly or mainly for the accommodation of a private motor vehicle; or

(*c*) private storage premises used wholly or mainly for the storage of articles of domestic use,

is a dwelling except in so far as it forms part of a larger property which is itself a dwelling by virtue of subsection (2) above.

(5) The Secretary of State may by order[1] provide that in such cases as may be prescribed by or determined under the order—

(*a*) anything which would (apart from the order) be one dwelling shall be treated as two or more dwellings; and

(*b*) anything which would (apart from the order) be two or more dwellings shall be treated as one dwelling.

(6) The Secretary of State may by order amend any definition of "dwelling" which is for the time being effective for the purposes of this Part.

[Local Government Finance Act 1992, s 3.]

---

[1] The Council Tax (Chargeable Dwellings) Order 1992, SI 1992/549 amended by SI 1997/656, SI 2003/3121, SI 2004/2921 (W), SI 2012/1915 and SI 2014/2653 (W) has been made.

7.7255 **4. Dwellings chargeable to council tax** (1) Council tax shall be payable in respect of any dwelling which is not an exempt dwelling.

(2) In this Chapter—

"chargeable dwelling" means any dwelling in respect of which council tax is payable;

"exempt dwelling" means any dwelling of a class prescribed[1] by an order made by the Secretary of State.

(3) For the purposes of subsection (2) above, a class of dwellings may be prescribed by reference to such factors as the Secretary of State sees fit.

(4) Without prejudice to the generality of subsection (3) above, a class of dwellings may be prescribed by reference to one or more of the following factors—

(*a*) the physical characteristics of dwellings;

(*b*) the fact that dwellings are unoccupied or are occupied for prescribed purposes or are occupied or owned by persons of prescribed descriptions.

[Local Government Finance Act 1992, s 4.]

---

[1] The Council Tax (Exempt Dwellings) Order 1992, SI 1992/558 amended by SI 1992/2941, SI 1993/150, SI 1994/539, SI 1997/74, SI 1998/291, SI 1996/536, SI 2000/424 and 1025 (Wales), SI 2003/3121, SI 2004/2921 (W), SI 2005/2865 (E) and 3302 (W), SI 2006/2318 (E), SI 2011/2581 and SI 2012/2965 (E).

7.7256 **5. Different amounts for dwellings in different valuation bands** (1) The amounts of council tax payable in respect of dwellings situated in the same billing authority's area (or the same part of such an area) and listed in different valuation bands shall be in the proportion—

6: 7: 8: 9: 11: 13: 15: 18

where 6 is for dwellings listed in valuation band A, 7 is for dwellings listed in valuation band B, and so on.

(1A) For the purposes of the application of subsection (1) to dwellings situated in Wales, for the purposes of financial years beginning on or after 1st April 2005, for the proportion specified in that subsection there is substituted the following proportion:

6: 7: 8: 9: 11: 13: 15: 18: 21

(2) The valuation bands for dwellings in England are set out in the following Table—

| **Range of values** | **Valuation band** |
|---|---|
| Values not exceeding £40,000 | A |
| Values exceeding £40,000 but not exceeding £52,000 | B |
| Values exceeding £52,000 but not exceeding £68,000 | C |
| Values exceeding £68,000 but not exceeding £88,000 | D |
| Values exceeding £88,000 but not exceeding £120,000 | E |
| Values exceeding £120,000 but not exceeding £160,000 | F |
| Values exceeding £160,000 but not exceeding £320,000 | G |
| Values exceeding £320,000 | H |

(3) The valuation bands for dwellings in Wales are set out in the following Table—

| Range of values | Valuation band |
|---|---|
| Values not exceeding £44,000 | A |
| Values exceeding £44,000 but not exceeding £65,000 | B |
| Values exceeding £65,000 but not exceeding £91,000 | C |
| Values exceeding £91,000 but not exceeding £123,000 | D |
| Values exceeding £123,000 but not exceeding £162,000 | E |
| Values exceeding £162,000 but not exceeding £223,000 | F |
| Values exceeding £223,000 but not exceeding £324,000 | G |
| Values exceeding £324,000 but not exceeding £424,000 | H |
| Values exceeding £424,000 | I |

(4) The Secretary of State may by order[1], as regards financial years beginning on or after such date as is specified in the order—

(*a*) substitute another proportion for that which is for the time being effective for the purposes of subsection (1) above;

(*b*) substitute other valuation bands for those which are for the time being effective for the purposes of subsection (2) or (3) above.

(4A) The power under subsection (4)(*b*) above includes power to make provision for a different number of valuation bands from those which are for the time being effective for the purposes of subsection (2) or (3) above.

(5) No order under subsection (4) above shall be made unless a draft of the order has been laid before and approved by resolution of the House of Commons.

(6) Any reference in this Part to dwellings listed in a particular valuation band shall be construed as a reference to dwellings to which that valuation band is shown as applicable in the billing authority's valuation list.

[Local Government Finance Act 1992, s 5 as amended by SI 2003/3046 and the Local Government Act 2003, s 78.]

[1] The Council Tax (Valuation Bands) (Wales) Order 2003, SI 2003/3046 has been made.

*Liability to tax*

7.7257 **6. Persons liable to pay council tax** (1) The person who is liable to pay council tax in respect of any chargeable dwelling and any day is the person who falls within the first paragraph of subsection (2) below to apply, taking paragraph (*a*) of that subsection first, paragraph (*b*) next, and so on.

(2) A person falls within this subsection in relation to any chargeable dwelling and any day if, on that day—

(*a*) he is a resident of the dwelling and has a freehold interest in the whole or any part of it;

(*b*) he is such a resident and has a leasehold interest in the whole or any part of the dwelling which is not inferior to another such interest held by another such resident;

(*c*) he is both such a resident and a statutory, secure or introductory tenant of the whole or any part of the dwelling;

(*d*) he is such a resident and has a contractual licence to occupy the whole or any part of the dwelling;

(*e*) he is such a resident; or

(*f*) he is the owner of the dwelling.

(3) Where, in relation to any chargeable dwelling and any day, two or more persons fall within the first paragraph of subsection (2) above to apply, they shall each be jointly and severally liable to pay the council tax in respect of the dwelling and that day.

(4) Subsection (3) above shall not apply as respects any day on which one or more of the persons there mentioned fall to be disregarded for the purposes of discount by virtue of paragraph 2 of Schedule 1 to this Act (the severely mentally impaired) and one or more of them do not; and liability to pay the council tax in respect of the dwelling and that day shall be determined as follows—

(*a*) if only one of those persons does not fall to be so disregarded, he shall be solely liable;

(*b*) if two or more of those persons do not fall to be so disregarded, they shall each be jointly and severally liable.

(5) In this Part, unless the context otherwise requires—

"owner", in relation to any dwelling, means the person as regards whom the following conditions are fulfilled—

(*a*) he has a material interest in the whole or any part of the dwelling; and

(*b*) at least part of the dwelling or, as the case may be, of the part concerned is not subject to a material interest inferior to his interest;

"resident", in relation to any dwelling, means an individual who has attained the age of 18 years and has his sole or main residence[1] in the dwelling.

(6) In this section—

"introductory tenant" means a tenant under an introductory tenancy within the meaning of Chapter I of Part V of the Housing Act 1996;

"material interest" means a freehold interest or a leasehold interest which was granted for a term of six months or more;

"secure tenant" means a tenant under a secure tenancy within the meaning of Part IV of the Housing Act 1985;

"statutory tenant" means a statutory tenant within the meaning of the Rent Act 1977 or the Rent (Agriculture) Act 1976.

[Local Government Finance Act 1992, s 6 as amended by SI 1997/74.]

---

[1] The words "sole or main residence" in s 6(5) of the 1992 Act refer to premises in which a taxpayer actually resided, and the qualification "sole or main" addresses the fact that a person could reside in more than one place: *Williams v Horsham District Council* [2004] EWCA Civ 39, [2004] 3 All ER 30.

7.7258 7. **Liability in respect of caravans and boats** (1) Subsections (2) to (4) below shall have effect in substitution for section 6 above in relation to any chargeable dwelling which consists of a pitch occupied by a caravan, or a mooring occupied by a boat.

(2) Where on any day the owner of the caravan or boat is not, but some other person is, a resident of the dwelling, that other person shall be liable to pay the council tax in respect of the dwelling and that day.

(3) Where on any day subsection (2) above does not apply, the owner of the caravan or boat shall be liable to pay the council tax in respect of the dwelling and that day.

(4) Where on any day two or more persons fall within subsection (2) or (3) above, they shall each be jointly and severally liable to pay the council tax in respect of the dwelling and that day.

(5) Subsection (4) of section 6 above shall apply for the purposes of subsection (4) above as it applies for the purposes of subsection (3) of that section.

(6) In this section "caravan" shall be construed in accordance with Part I of the Caravan Sites and Control of Development Act 1960.

(7) Any reference in this section to the owner of a caravan or boat shall be construed—

(*a*) in relation to a caravan or boat which is subject to an agreement for hire-purchase or conditional sale, as a reference to the person in possession under the agreement;

(*b*) in relation to a caravan or boat which is subject to a bill of sale or mortgage, as a reference to the person entitled to the property in it apart from the bill or mortgage.

[Local Government Finance Act 1992, s 7.]

7.7259 8. **Liability in prescribed cases** (1) Subsections (3) and (4) below shall have effect in substitution for section 6 or (as the case may be) section 7 above in relation to any chargeable dwelling of a class prescribed[1] for the purposes of this subsection.

(2) Subsections (3) and (4) below shall have effect in substitution for section 6 or (as the case may be) section 7 above in relation to any chargeable dwelling of a class prescribed for the purposes of this subsection, if the billing authority so determines in relation to all dwellings of that class which are situated in its area.

(3) Where on any day this subsection has effect in relation to a dwelling, the owner of the dwelling shall be liable to pay the council tax in respect of the dwelling and that day.

(4) Where on any day two or more persons fall within subsection (3) above, they shall each be jointly and severally liable to pay the council tax in respect of the dwelling and that day.

(5) Subsection (4) of section 6 above shall apply for the purposes of subsection (4) above as it applies for the purposes of subsection (3) of that section.

(6) Regulations prescribing a class of chargeable dwellings for the purposes of subsection (1) or (2) above may provide that, in relation to any dwelling of that class, subsection (3) above shall have effect as if for the reference to the owner of the dwelling there were substituted a reference to the person falling within such description as may be prescribed[1].

(7) Subsections (3) and (4) of section 4 above shall apply for the purposes of subsections (1) and (2) above as they apply for the purposes of subsection (2) of that section.

[Local Government Finance Act 1992, s 8.]

---

[1] The Council Tax (Liability for Owners) Regulations 1992, SI 1992/551 amended by SI 1993/151, SI 1997/74, SI 2000/537 (England) and 1024 (Wales), SI 2003/3125, SI 2004/2920 (W), SI 2012/1915 and SI 2015/643 have been made.

7.7260 9. **Liability of spouses** (1) Where—

(*a*) a person who is liable to pay council tax in respect of any chargeable dwelling of which he is a resident and any day is married, or is the civil partner of, to another person; and*

(*b*) that other person is also a resident of the dwelling on that day but would not, apart from this section, be so liable,

those persons shall each be jointly and severally liable to pay the council tax in respect of the dwelling and that day.

(2) Subsection (1) above shall not apply as respects any day on which the other person there mentioned falls to be disregarded for the purposes of discount by virtue of paragraph 2 of Schedule 1 to this Act (the severely mentally impaired).

(3) For the purposes of this section two persons are married to each other if they are a man and a woman—

(*a*) who are married to each other; or

(*b*) who are not married to each other but are living together as husband and wife.

(4) For the purposes of this section two persons are civil partners of each other if they are of the same sex and either—

(*a*) they are civil partners of each other; or

(*b*) They are not civil partners of each other but are living together as if they were civil partners.

[Local Government Finance Act 1992, s 9 as amended by the Civil Partnership Act 2004, Sch 27.]

*Amounts of tax payable*

7.7261 **10. Basic amounts payable** (1) Subject to sections 11 to 13 below, a person who is liable to pay council tax in respect of any chargeable dwelling and any day shall, as respects the dwelling and the day, pay to the billing authority for the area in which the dwelling is situated an amount calculated in accordance with the formula—

$$\frac{A}{B}$$

where—

A is the amount which, for the financial year in which the day falls and for dwellings in the valuation band listed for the dwelling, has been set by the authority for its area or (as the case may be) the part of its area in which the dwelling is situated;

D is the number of days in the financial year.

(2) For the purposes of this Part the Secretary of State may make regulations containing rules for ascertaining in what part of a billing authority's area a dwelling is situated (whether situated in the area in fact or by virtue of regulations[1] made under section 1(3) above).

[Local Government Finance Act 1992, s 10.]

---

1 See Pt III of the Council Tax (Situation and Valuation of Dwellings) Regulations 1992, SI 1992/550 amended by SI 1994/1747 and SI 2008/315.

7.7262 **11. Discounts** (1) The amount of council tax payable in respect of any chargeable dwelling and any day shall be subject to a discount equal to the appropriate percentage of that amount if on that day—

(*a*) there is only one resident of the dwelling and he does not fall to be disregarded for the purposes of discount; or

(*b*) there are two or more residents of the dwelling and each of them except one falls to be disregarded for those purposes.

(2) Subject to sections 11A and 12 below, the amount of council tax payable in respect of any chargeable dwelling and any day shall be subject to a discount equal to twice the appropriate percentage of that amount if on that day—

(*a*) there is no resident of the dwelling; or

(*b*) there are one or more residents of the dwelling and each of them falls to be disregarded for the purposes of discount.

(3) In this section "the appropriate percentage" means 25 per cent or, if the Secretary of State by order so provides in relation to the financial year in which the day falls, such other percentage as is specified in the order.

(4) No order under subsection (3) above shall be made unless a draft of the order has been laid before and approved by resolution of the House of Commons.

(5) Schedule 1 to this Act shall have effect for determining who shall be disregarded for the purposes of discount.

[Local Government Finance Act 1992, s 11 as amended by the Local Government Act 2003, Schs 7 and 8.]

7.7263 **11A. Discounts: special provision for England** (1) The Secretary of State may for any financial year by regulations[1] prescribe one or more classes of dwelling in England for the purposes of subsection (3) or (4) below.

(2) A class of dwellings may be prescribed under subsection (1) above by reference to such factors as the Secretary of State sees fit and may, in particular, be prescribed by reference to—

(*a*) the physical characteristics of dwellings, or

(*b*) the fact that dwellings are unoccupied.

(3) For any financial year for which a class of dwellings is prescribed for the purposes of this subsection, a billing authority in England may by determination provide in relation to all dwellings of that class in its area, or in such part of its area as it may specify in the determination, that the discount under section 11(2)(*a*) shall be such lesser percentage of at least 10 as it may so specify.

(4) For any financial year for which a class of dwellings is prescribed for the purposes of this subsection, a billing authority in England may by determination provide in relation to all dwellings of that class in its area, or in such part of its area as it may specify in the determination—

(*a*) that the discount under section 11(2)(*a*) above shall not apply, or

(*b*) that the discount under that provision shall be such lesser percentage as it may so specify.

(5) A billing authority may make a determination varying or revoking a determination under

subsection (3) or (4) for a financial year, but only before the beginning of the year.

(6) A billing authority which makes a determination under this section shall publish a notice of it in at least one newspaper circulating in its area and do so before the end of the period of 21 days beginning with the date of the determination.

(7) Failure to comply with subsection (6) above shall not affect the validity of a determination.

[Local Government Finance Act 1992, s 11A as inserted by the Local Government Act 2003, s 75(1).]

---

1 The Council Tax (Prescribed Classes of Dwellings) (England) Regulations 2003, SI 2003/3011 amended by SI 2004/926, SI 2005/416 and 2866 and SI 2012/2964 have been made.

**11B. Higher amount for long-term empty dwellings: England**

7.7264 **12. Discounts: special provision for Wales** (1) Where any class of dwellings in Wales is prescribed[1] for the purposes of this section for any financial year, a Welsh billing authority may determine that for the year subsection (2) or (3) below shall have effect in substitution for section 11(2)(*a*) above in relation to all dwellings of that class which are situated in its area.

(2) Where this subsection has effect for any year in relation to any class of dwellings, the amount of council tax payable in respect of—

(*a*) any chargeable dwelling of that class; and

(*b*) any day in the year on which there is no resident of the dwelling,

shall be subject to a discount equal to the appropriate percentage of that amount.

(3) Where this subsection has effect for any year in relation to any class of dwellings, the amount of council tax payable in respect of—

(*a*) any chargeable dwelling of that class; and

(*b*) any day in the year on which there is no resident of the dwelling,

shall not be subject to a discount.

(4) A determination under subsection (1) above for a financial year may be varied or revoked at any time before the year begins.

(5) Subsections (3) and (4) of section 4 above shall apply for the purposes of subsection (1) above as they apply for the purposes of subsection (2) of that section.

(6) A billing authority which has made a determination under subsection (1) above shall, before the end of the period of 21 days beginning with the day of doing so, publish a notice of the determination in at least one newspaper circulating in the authority's area.

(7) Failure to comply with subsection (6) above does not make the making of the determination invalid.

[Local Government Finance Act 1992, s 12.]

---

1 The Council Tax (Prescribed Class of Dwellings) (Wales) Regulations 1992, SI 1992/3023 amended by SI 1998/105, SI 2004/452, SI 2005/3302, SI 2014/107 and SI 2017/42 have been made.

7.7265 **13. Reduced amounts** (1) The Secretary of State may make regulations[1] as regards any case where—

(*a*) a person is liable to pay an amount to a billing authority in respect of council tax for any financial year which is prescribed; and

(*b*) prescribed conditions are fulfilled.

(2) The regulations may provide that the amount he is liable to pay shall be an amount which—

(*a*) is less than the amount it would be apart from the regulations; and

(*b*) is determined in accordance with prescribed rules.

(3) This section applies whether the amount mentioned in subsection (1) above is determined under section 10 above or under that section read with section 11, 11A or 12 above.

(4) The conditions mentioned in subsection (1) above may be prescribed by reference to such factors as the Secretary of State thinks fit; and in particular such factors may include the making of an application by the person concerned and all or any of—

(*a*) the factors mentioned in subsection (5) below; or

(*b*) the factors mentioned in subsection (6) below.

(5) The factors referred to in subsection (4)(*a*) above are—

(*a*) community charges for a period before 1st April 1993;

(*b*) the circumstances of, or other matters relating to, the person concerned;

(*c*) an amount relating to the authority concerned and specified, or to be specified, for the purposes of the regulations in a report laid, or to be laid, before the House of Commons;

(*d*) such other amounts as may be prescribed or arrived at in a prescribed manner.

(6) The factors referred to in subsection (4)(*b*) above are—

(*a*) a disabled person having his sole or main residence in the dwelling concerned;

(*b*) the circumstances of or other matters relating to, that person;

(*c*) the physical characteristics of, or other matters relating to, that dwelling.

(7) The rules mentioned in subsection (2) above may be prescribed by reference to such factors as the Secretary of State thinks fit; and in particular such factors may include all or any of the factors mentioned in subsection (5) or subsection (6)(*b*) or (*c*) above.

(8) Without prejudice to the generality of section 113(2) below, regulations under this section may include—

(*a*) provision requiring the Secretary of State to specify in a report, for the purposes of the regulations, an amount in relation to each billing authority;

(*b*) provision requiring him to lay the report before the House of Commons;

(*c*) provision for the review of any prescribed decision of a billing authority relating to the application or operation of the regulations;

(*d*) provision that no appeal may be made to a valuation tribunal in respect of such a decision, notwithstanding section 16(1) below.

(9) To the extent that he would not have power to do so apart from this subsection, the Secretary of State may—

(*a*) include in regulations under this section such amendments of any social security instrument as he thinks expedient in consequence of the regulations under this section;

(*b*) include in any social security instrument such provision as he thinks expedient in consequence of regulations under this section.

(10) In subsection (9) above "social security instrument" means an order or regulations made, or falling to be made, by the Secretary of State under the Social Security Acts, that is to say, the Social Security Contributions and Benefits Act 1992 and the Social Security Administration Act 1992.

[Local Government Finance Act 1992, s 13 as amended by the Local Government Act 2003, Sch 7.]

---

1 The Council Tax (Reductions for Disabilities) Regulations 1992, SI 1992/554 amended by SI 1993/195, SI 1999/1004 and SI 2005/702 (W), the Local Government Reorganisation (Wales) (Council Tax Reduction Scheme) Regulations 1996, SI 1996/309, the Local Government Reorganisation (Wales) (Council Tax Reduction Scheme) Regulations 1997, SI 1997/261 and the Council Tax Reduction Scheme (Wales) Regulations 1998, SI 1998/266, the Council Tax Reduction Scheme (Wales) Regulations 1999, SI 1999/347 and the Council Tax (Reduction Scheme) and (Demand Notices Transitional Provisions) (Wales) Regulations 2000, SI 2000/501 have been made. Transitional relief for the year 1993/4 is afforded by the Council Tax (Transitional Reduction Scheme) (England) Regulations 1993, SI 1993/175 amended by SI 1993/253 and 401 for the year 1995/6 by SI 1995/209 and for the year 1996/7 by SI 1996/176 (the 1996 Regulations) amended by SI 1996/333 and SI 1997/215.

The 1996 Regulations are modified by the Local Government Changes for England (Council Tax) (Transitional Reduction) Regulations 1997, SI 1997/215 and 1998, SI 1998/214 and are revoked with savings by the Local Government Changes for England (Council Tax) (Transitional Reduction) Regulations 1999, SI 1999/259 which have effect for the financial year 1999/2000.

The Council Tax (Reductions for Annexes) (England) Regulations 2013, SI 2013/2977 have been made.

7.7266 **13A. Billing authority's power to reduce amount of tax payable** (1) Where a person is liable to pay council tax in respect of any chargeable dwelling and any day, the billing authority for the area in which the dwelling is situated may reduce the amount which he is liable to pay as respects the dwelling and the day to such extent as it thinks fit.

(2) The power under subsection (1) above includes power to reduce an amount to nil.

(3) The power under subsection (1) may be exercised in relation to particular cases or by determining a class of case in which liability is to be reduced to an extent provided by the determination[1].

[Local Government Finance Act 1992, s 13A inserted by the Local Government Act 2003, s 76.]

---

1 Regulations have been made under powers in Sch 1B, post.

7.7267 **13B. Transitional arrangements**[1]

---

1 The Council Tax Reduction Schemes (Transitional Provisions) (Wales) Regulations 2013, SI 2013/111 have been made.

*Administration and appeals*

7.7268 **14. Administration, penalties and enforcement** (1) Schedule 2 to this Act (which contains provisions about administration, including collection) shall have effect.

(2) Schedule 3 to this Act (which contains provisions about civil penalties) shall have effect.

(3) Schedule 4 to this Act (which contains provisions about the recovery of sums due, including sums due as penalties) shall have effect.

(4) Where a liability order has been made against a person under regulations under Schedule 4, the billing authority concerned may use the procedure in Schedule 12 to the Tribunals, Courts and Enforcement Act 2007 (taking control of goods) to recover the amount in respect of which the order was made, to the extent that it remains unpaid.

[Local Government Finance Act 1992, s 14 as amended by the Tribunals, Courts and Enforcement Act 2007, Sch 13.]

7.7268A **14A. Regulations[1] about powers to require information**

---

1 The Council Tax Reduction Schemes (Detection of Fraud and Enforcement) (England) Regulations 2013, SI 2013/501 have been made.

7.7268B **14B. Regulations about offences**

7.7268C **14C. Regulations about penalties**

7.7268D **14D. Sections 14A to 14C: supplementary**

7.7269 **15. Valuation tribunals** (1) Valuation and community charge tribunals established under Schedule 11 to the 1988 Act shall be known as valuation tribunals.

(2) Such tribunals shall exercise, in addition to the jurisdiction conferred on them by or under the 1988 Act, the jurisdiction conferred on them by—

(*a*) section 16 below;

(*b*) regulations made under section 24 below; and

(*c*) paragraph 3 of Schedule 3 to this Act.

[Local Government Finance Act 1992, s 15.]

7.7270 **16. Appeals: general** (1) A person may appeal to a valuation tribunal if he is aggrieved by—

(*a*) any decision of a billing authority that a dwelling is a chargeable dwelling, or that he is liable to pay council tax in respect of such a dwelling; or

(*b*) any calculation made by such an authority of an amount which he is liable to pay to the authority in respect of council tax.

(2) In subsection (1) above the reference to any calculation of an amount includes a reference to any estimate of the amount.

(3) Subsection (1) above shall not apply where the grounds on which the person concerned is aggrieved fall within such category or categories as may be prescribed[1].

(4) No appeal may be made under subsection (1) above unless—

(*a*) the aggrieved person serves a written notice under this subsection; and

(*b*) one of the conditions mentioned in subsection (7) below is fulfilled.

(5) A notice under subsection (4) above must be served on the billing authority concerned.

(6) A notice under subsection (4) above must state the matter by which and the grounds on which the person is aggrieved.

(7) The conditions are that—

(*a*) the aggrieved person is notified in writing, by the authority on which he served the notice, that the authority believes the grievance is not well founded, but the person is still aggrieved;

(*b*) the aggrieved person is notified in writing, by the authority on which he served the notice, that steps have been taken to deal with the grievance, but the person is still aggrieved;

(*c*) the period of two months, beginning with the date of service of the aggrieved person's notice, has ended without his being notified under paragraph (*a*) or (*b*) above.

(8) Where a notice under subsection (4) above is served on an authority, the authority shall—

(*a*) consider the matter to which the notice relates;

(*b*) include in any notification under subsection (7)(*a*) above the reasons for the belief concerned;

(*c*) include in any notification under subsection (7)(*b*) above a statement of the steps taken.

[Local Government Finance Act 1992, s 16.]

---

1 See reg 30 of the Council Tax (Administration and Enforcement) Regulations 1992, in this PART, post.

*Miscellaneous*

7.7271 **17. Completion of new dwellings** (1) Subject to the provisions of this section, Schedule 4A to the 1988 Act (which makes provision with respect to the determination of a day as the completion day in relation to a new building) shall, with the exception of paragraph 6, apply for the purposes of this Part as it applies for the purposes of Part III of that Act.

(2) Any reference in this section to the Schedule is a reference to Schedule 4A to the 1988 Act as it applies for the purposes of this Part.

(3) Where—

(*a*) a completion notice is served under the Schedule; and

(*b*) the building to which the notice relates is not completed on or before the relevant day,

any dwelling in which the building or any part of it will be comprised shall be deemed for the purposes of this Part to have come into existence on that day.

(4) For the purposes of subsection (3) above the relevant day in relation to a completion notice is—

(*a*) where no appeal against the notice is brought under paragraph 4 of the Schedule, the day stated in the notice; and

(*b*) where an appeal against the notice is brought under that paragraph, the day determined under the Schedule as the completion day in relation to the building to which the notice relates.

(5) Where—

(*a*) a day is determined under the Schedule as the completion day in relation to a new building; and

(*b*) the building is one produced by the structural alteration of a building which is comprised in one or more existing dwellings,

the existing dwelling or dwellings shall be deemed for the purposes of this Part to have ceased to exist on that day.

(6) Any reference in this section or the Schedule to a new building includes a reference to a building produced by the structural alteration of an existing building where—

(*a*) the existing building or any part of it is comprised in a dwelling which, by virtue of the alteration, becomes, or becomes part of a different dwelling or different dwellings; or

(*b*) neither the existing building nor any part of it is, except by virtue of the alteration, comprised in any dwelling.

(7) Any reference in this section to a building includes a reference to a part of a building; and any reference in the Schedule to the valuation officer shall be construed as a reference to the listing officer.

[Local Government Finance Act 1992, s 17 as amended by the Local Government Act 2003, Sch 7.]

7.7272 **18. Death of persons liable** *Secretary of State may make regulations*[1]

[Local Government Finance Act 1992, s 18—summarised.]

---

1 See reg 58 of the Council Tax (Administration and Enforcement) Regulations in this PART post.

7.7273 **19.** *Exclusion of Crown exemption in certain cases.*

## SCHEDULES

### SCHEDULE 1

PERSONS DISREGARDED FOR PURPOSES OF DISCOUNT — Sections 11(5) and 79(5)

*(As amended by the Powers of Criminal Courts (Sentencing) Act 2000, Sch 9, the Care Standards Act 2000, Schs 3 and 4, SSI 2005/465, the National Health Service (Consequential Provisions) Act 2006, Sch 1, the Armed Forces Act 2006, Schs 16 and 17 and SI 2015/914.)*

*Persons in detention*

7.7274 **1.** (1) A person shall be disregarded for the purposes of discount on a particular day if on the day—

(*a*) he is detained in a prison, a hospital or any other place by virtue of an order or award to which sub-paragraph (2) below applies;

(*b*) he is detained under paragraph 2 of Schedule 3 to the Immigration Act 1971 (deportation);

(*c*) he is detained under Part II or section 46, 47, 48 or 136 of the Mental Health Act 1983; or

(*d*) he is detained under Parts 5, 6 and 7 or sections 136 or 297 of the Mental Health (Care and Treatment) (Scotland) Act 2003 or sections 52D or 52M or the Criminal Procedure (Scotland) Act 1995;

(2) This sub-paragraph applies to—

(*a*) an order of a court in the United Kingdom;

(*b*) an order or award (whether or not of a court) made (anywhere) in proceedings in respect of a service offence within the meaning of the Armed Forces Act 2006.

(3) If a person—

(*a*) is temporarily discharged under section 28 of the Prison Act 1952, or temporarily released under rules under section 47(5) of that Act;

(*aa*) is temporarily released under rules under section 300 of the Armed Forces Act 2006; or

(*b*) is temporarily discharged under section 27 of the Prisons (Scotland) Act 1989, or temporarily released under rules under section 39(6) of that Act,

for the purposes of sub-paragraph (1) above he shall be treated as detained.

(4) Sub-paragraph (1) above does not apply where the person—

(*a*) is detained under regulations made under paragraph 8 of Schedule 4 to this Act;

(*b*) is detained under section 76 of the Magistrates' Courts Act 1980, or section 108 of the Powers of Criminal Courts (Sentencing) Act 2000,* for default in payment of a fine; or

(*c*) is detained only under section 407 of the Criminal Procedure (Scotland) Act 1975.

(5) In sub-paragraph (1) above "order" includes a sentence, direction, warrant or other means of giving effect to the decision of the court concerned.

(6) The Secretary of State may by order[1] provide that a person shall be disregarded for the purposes of discount on a particular day if—

(*a*) on the day he is in service custody; and

(*b*) such conditions as may be prescribed by the order are fulfilled.

---

* **Repealed by the Criminal Justice and Court Services Act 2000, Sch 8 from a date to be appointed.**

1 The Council Tax (Disregards) Order 1992, SI 1992/548 amended by SI 1994/543, SI 1995/619, SI 1996/636 and 3143, SI 1997/656, SI 1998/291, SI 2003/673 (W), SI 2004/2921 (W), SI 2006/3396 (E), SI 2007/580 (W), SI 2009/2054, SI 2010/2448 (W), SI 2011/948, SI 2013/638 (W), 1048 (W) and SI 2015/971 has been made.

*The severely mentally impaired*

**2.** (1) A person shall be disregarded for the purposes of discount on a particular day if—

(*a*) on the day he is severely mentally impaired;

(*b*) as regards any period which includes the day he is stated in a certificate of a registered medical practitioner to have been or to be likely to be severely mentally impaired; and

(*c*) as regards the day he fulfils such conditions as may be prescribed by order[1] made by the Secretary of State.

(2) For the purposes of this paragraph a person is severely mentally impaired if he has a severe impairment of intelligence and social functioning (however caused) which appears to be permanent.

(3) The Secretary of State may by order substitute another definition for the definition in sub-paragraph (2) above as for the time being effective for the purposes of this paragraph.

---

1 The Council Tax (Disregards) Order 1992, SI 1992/548 has been made. For amending instruments, see note to para 1, ante.

*Persons in respect of whom child benefit is payable*

**3.** (1) A person shall be disregarded for the purposes of discount on a particular day if on the day he—

(*a*) has attained the age of 18 years; but

(*b*) is a person in respect of whom another person is entitled to child benefit, or would be so entitled but for paragraph 1(*c*) of Schedule 9 to the Social Security Contributions and Benefits Act 1992.

(2) The Secretary of State may by order substitute another provision for sub-paragraph (1)(*b*) above as for the time being effective for the purposes of this paragraph.

*Students etc*

**4.** (1) A person shall be disregarded for the purposes of discount on a particular day if—

(*a*) on the day he is a student, student nurse, apprentice or youth training trainee; and

(*b*) such conditions as may be prescribed by order[1] made by the Secretary of State are fulfilled.

(2) In this paragraph "apprentice", "student", "student nurse" and "youth training trainee" have the meanings for the time being assigned to them by order[1] made by the Secretary of State.

---

[1] The Council Tax (Disregards) Order 1992, SI 1992/548 has been made. For amending instruments, see note to para 1, ante.

**5.** (1) An institution shall, on request, supply a certificate under this paragraph to any person who is following or, subject to sub-paragraph (3) below, has followed a course of education at that institution as a student or student nurse.

(2) A certificate under this paragraph shall contain such information about the person to whom it refers as may be prescribed by order[1] made by the Secretary of State.

(3) An institution may refuse to comply with a request made more than one year after the person making it has ceased to follow a course of education at that institution.

(4) In this paragraph—

"institution" means any such educational establishment or other body as may be prescribed by order[1] made by the Secretary of State; and

"student" and "student nurse" have the same meanings as in paragraph 4 above.

---

[1] The Council Tax (Disregards) Order 1992, SI 1992/548 has been made. For amending instruments, see note to para 1, ante.

*Hospital patients*

**6.** (1) A person shall be disregarded for the purposes of discount on a particular day if on the day he is a patient who has his sole or main residence in a hospital.

(2) In this paragraph "hospital" means—

(*a*) a health service hospital within the meaning of the National Health Service Act 2006, the National Health Service (Wales) Act 2006 or section 108(1) (interpretation) of the National Health Service (Scotland) Act 1978; and

(*b*) a military, air-force or naval unit or establishment at or in which medical or surgical treatment is provided for persons subject to service law within the meaning of the Armed Forces Act 2006.

(3) The Secretary of State may by order substitute another definition for the definition in sub-paragraph (2) above as for the time being effective for the purposes of this paragraph.

*Patients in homes in England and Wales*

**7.** (1) A person shall be disregarded for the purposes of discount on a particular day if on the day—

(*a*) he has his sole or main residence in a care home, independent hospital or hostel in England and Wales; and

(*b*) he is receiving care or treatment (or both) in the home, hospital or hostel.

(2) In this paragraph—

"care home" means—

(*a*) a care home within the meaning of the Care Standards Act 2000; or

(*b*) a building or part of a building in which residential accommodation is provided under section 21 of the National Assistance Act 1948;

(*c*) a building or part of a building in which accommodation is provided under Part 1 of the Care Act 2014;

"hostel" means anything which falls within any definition of hostel for the time being prescribed by order made by the Secretary of State under this sub-paragraph;

"independent hospital" has the same meaning as in the Care Standards Act 2000.

(3) The Secretary of State may by order[1] substitute another definition for any definition of "care home" or "independent hospital" for the time being effective for the purposes of this paragraph.

---

[1] The Council Tax (Disregards) Order 1992, SI 1992/548 has been made. For amending instruments, see note to para 1, ante.

**8.** *Scotland*

*Care workers*

**9.** (1) A person shall be disregarded for the purposes of discount on a particular day if—

(*a*) on the day he is engaged in providing care or support (or both) to another person or other persons; and

(*b*) such conditions as may be prescribed[1] are fulfilled.

(2) Without prejudice to the generality of sub-paragraph (1)(*b*) above the conditions may—

(*a*) require the care or support (or both) to be provided on behalf of a charity or a person fulfilling some other description;

(*b*) relate to the period for which the person is engaged in providing care or support (or both);

(*c*) require his income for a prescribed period (which contains the day concerned) not to exceed a prescribed amount;

(*d*) require his capital not to exceed a prescribed amount;

(e) require him to be resident in prescribed premises;
(f) require him not to exceed a prescribed age;
(g) require the other person or persons to fulfil a prescribed description (whether relating to age, disablement or otherwise).

[1] The Council Tax (Additional Provision for Discount Disregards) Regulations 1992, SI 1992/552, amended by SI 1992/2942, SI 1993/149 and 540, SI 1994/540, SI 1996/637, SI 1997/657, SI 1998/294, SI 2005/2866 (E) and 3302 (W), SI 2006/3395 (E), SI 2007/581 (W), SI 2013/639 (W) and 1049 (W) have been made.

*Residents of certain dwellings*

**10.** (1) A person shall be disregarded for the purposes of discount on a particular day if on the day he has his sole or main residence in a dwelling to which sub-paragraph (2) below applies.

(2) This sub-paragraph applies to any dwelling if—

(a) it is for the time being providing residential accommodation, whether as a hostel or night shelter or otherwise; and
(b) the accommodation is predominantly provided—
   (i) otherwise than in separate and self-contained sets of premises;
   (ii) for persons of no fixed abode and no settled way of life; and
   (iii) under licences to occupy which do not constitute tenancies.

*Persons of other descriptions*

**11.** A person shall be disregarded for the purposes of discount on a particular day if—

(a) on the day he falls within such description as may be prescribed[1]; and
(b) such conditions as may be prescribed[1] are fulfilled.

[1] The Council Tax (Additional Provisions for Discount Disregards) Regulations 1992, SI 1992/552 amended by SI 1992/2942, SI 1993/149 and 540, SI 1994/540, SI 1996/637, SI 1997/657, SI 1998/294, SI 2005/2866 (E) and 3302 (W), SI 2006/3395 (E), SI 2007/581 (W) and SI 2013/639 (W) and 1049 (W) have been made and for succeeding years see, SI 2010/2990.

## SCHEDULE 1A

### Council tax reduction schemes: England[1]

[1] The Council Tax Reduction Schemes (Transitional Provision) (England) Regulations 2013, SI 2013/215 have been made.

## SCHEDULE 2

### Administration[1]

Sections 14(1) and 97(3)

[1] This Schedule empowers the Secretary of State to make regulations covering specific matters such as collection, discounts, reduction for lump sum payments, exempt dwellings, supply of information and its use. See Pts I to IV of the Council Tax (Administration and Enforcement) Regulations 1992. Under this provision the following regulations have been made: Council Tax (Demand Notices) (England) Regulations 2011, SI 2011/3038 amended by SI 2012/3087, SI 2016/188 and SI 2017/13 and the Council Tax Reduction Schemes (Prescribed Requirements) (England) Regulations 2012, SI 2012/2885 amended by SI 2013/3181, SI 2014/448, 513, 3255 and 3312, SI 2015/643, 971, 1985 and 2041 and SI 2016/50 and 1262 have been made. The Council Tax (Demand Notices) (Wales) Regulations 1993, SI 1993/255 amended by SI 1995/160, SI 1996/310 and 1880, SI 2004/460, SI 2006/217, SI 2013/63 and SI 2014/122.

## SCHEDULE 3

### Penalties[1]

Sections 14(2) and 97(4)

[1] This Schedule enables a billing authority or levying authority to impose penalties for failure to supply information. Appeal lies to a valuation tribunal. The same conduct shall not lead both to a conviction and a penalty. As to the collection of penalties see reg 29 of the Council Tax (Administration and Enforcement) Regulations 1992 in this Part post.

## SCHEDULE 4

### Enforcement: England and Wales[1]

Section 14(3)

7.7285

*(Amended by Local Government Act 2003, s 76.)*

*Quashing of liability orders*

**12A.** Regulations under paragraph 1(1) above may provide—

(a) that, where on an application by the authority concerned a magistrates' court is satisfied that a liability order should not have been made, it shall quash the order;
(b) that, where on an application to a magistrates' court for the quashing of a liability order, the court is satisfied that, had the original application been for a liability order in respect of a lesser sum payable, such an order could properly have been made, it shall substitute a liability order in respect of the aggregate of—
   (i) that lesser sum, and
   (ii) any sum included in the quashed order in respect of the costs incurred in obtaining it.

[1] This Schedule empowers the Secretary of State to make regulations covering specific matters such as liability orders, attachment of earnings, deductions from income support, distress (now warrant of control), commitment to prison, bankruptcy, winding up, charging orders, admissibility of evidence, costs. See Pt V of the Council Tax (Administration and Enforcement) Regulations 1992 in this Part post.

## Licensing of alcohol, entertainment and late night refreshment

7.7314 **Introduction** The Licensing Act 2003 (LA 2003) has introduced a new regime for the licensing of alcohol (both in premises open to the general public and to qualifying clubs), and has amalgamated it with the licensing of regulated entertainment (previously called "public entertainment" under the provisions of the Local Government (Miscellaneous Provisions) Act 1982, or licensed separately under legislation dealing with theatres and cinemas), and, for the first time, "late night refreshment".

The LA 2003 was intended to provide a "more efficient"; "more responsive" and "flexible" system of licensing which did not interfere unnecessarily. It aimed to give business greater freedom and flexibility to meet the expectations of customers and to provide greater choice for consumers whilst protecting local residents from disturbance and anti-social behaviour. The LA 2003 expects licensable activities to be restricted only where that is necessary to promote the four licensing objectives set out in s 4(2)[1].

1 See the review of the law by Black J in *R (Daniel Thwaites plc) v Wirral Borough Magistrates' Court* [2008] EWCH 838 (Admin), 172 JP 301.

7.7315 *Transfer of responsibilities* The Act removes the responsibility for licensing such activities from the licensing justices (who were previously responsible for the licensing of alcohol) and hands the responsibilities to "licensing authorities". These are defined in the LA 2003, s 3, and include district councils, unitary authorities and London boroughs. The role of magistrates' courts is to act as an appellate court against the myriad of decisions that can be appealed; to deal with the raft of criminal offences under the Act; and to consider closure orders made by the police under Part 8 of the Act. Because primary responsibility for such matters has been removed from licensing justices, what follows is a short commentary by way of an overview of the LA 2003, and a more detailed commentary on those parts of the Act that magistrates' courts retain jurisdiction over.

7.7316 **Licensable activities and qualifying club activities** These are defined as the sale by retail[1] of alcohol[2]; the supply of alcohol by or on behalf of a club to, or to the order of, a member of the club; the provision of regulated entertainment; and the provision of late night refreshment[3]. Regulated entertainment is defined fully in Sch 1, and includes both entertainment and entertainment facilities that are provided for the public or a section of the public, and to entertainment provided exclusively for members of a qualifying club. The previous public entertainment regime did not require entertainment provided for club members to be licensed because it was not "public". Entertainment includes those activities listed in Sch 1, para 2. Certain activities listed in Sch 1, Part 2 are exempt from the definition. The provision of late night refreshment is defined in Sch 2. It involves the provision of hot food or hot drink to members of the public between 11pm and 5am on or from any premises, whether for consumption on or off the premises[4]. Certain supplies, such as to residents in hotels, are exempt[5]. If a licensable activity is taking place, it must be licensed either by virtue of a premises licence issued under Part 3 of the Act or by virtue of it being a "permitted temporary activity" under Part 5[6]. A qualifying club activity can only take place by virtue of a club premises certificate issued under Part 4[7].

1 Defined in the LA 2003, s 192.
2 Defined in the LA 2003, s 191.
3 LA 2003, s 1(1). Qualifying club activities are further defined in ss 1(2) and (3). Activities that are carried on in certain locations are not licensable activities: LA 2003, s 173. However, licensable activities or qualifying club activities that take place on vessels, vehicles or other moveable structures do require a premises licence: LA 2003, s 189. Premises licences that purport to licence roadside service areas or premises used primarily as a garage for the sale or supply of alcohol are invalid: LA 2003, s 176.
4 LA 2003, Sch 2, para 1(1).
5 For a full list, see the LA 2003, Sch 2, paras 3, 4 and 5.
6 LA 2003, s 2(1).
7 LA 2003, s 2(2).

7.7316A Certain entertainments fall outside the definition of "regulated entertainment" such as performances of plays, indoor sport and the exhibition of dance in all locations to audiences of up to 500 people (1000 indoor sport). Other entertainments are exempted from the requirement for licensing including: religious services, places of worship, entertainment at Garden fêtes and Morris dancing. Particular provision is made for activities organised by, or on behalf of, Local Authorities (including parish councils), hospitals and schools on their own premises; activities organised by, or on behalf of hospitals and schools (including sixth form colleges on their own premises) and for live and recorded music at activities held on community premises (such as church halls, village halls and community halls etc)[1]. Various exemptions are provided in respect of live and recorded music at licensed venues. In particular, performances of live music and the playing of recorded music on licensed premises is exempt where the specified conditions are satisfied which include the condition that the maximum number of persons in the audience is 500[2]. Provision is made for the suspension of any licence condition which relates to live music and also applies to licence conditions which relate to recorded music or to both live and recorded music[3].

1 Licensing Act 2003, Sch 1, in this title, post.
2 LA 2003, Sch 1, para 12A, in this title, post.
3 LA 2003, s 177A, in this title, post.

7.7317 **Functions of licensing authorities and licensing objectives** A licensing authority must carry out its functions under the Act with a view to promoting the four licensing objectives of prevention of crime and disorder; public safety; prevention[1] of public nuisance; and the protection of children from harm[2]. In addition, those licensing authorities that are local authorities within the meaning of s 270(1) of the Local Government Act 1972, must have regard to the need to do all that they reasonably can to prevent crime and disorder in their areas[3]. Magistrates' courts dealing with appeals must also have regard to the need to promote the licensing objectives and, because they stand in the feet of licensing authorities when carrying out their appellate functions, it is submitted that they must also have regard to the duty imposed on licensing authorities by the Crime and Disorder Act 1998. Licensing authorities (and magistrates' courts dealing with appeals) must also have regard to the Statement of Licensing Policy issued under s 5 of the Act; and the Secretary of State's guidance issued under s 182 of the Act[4]. A licensing authority must establish a licensing committee of between 10 and 15 members of the authority[5], and most matters are delegated to that committee[6] (or sub-committees consisting of three members[7]) to deal with. Matters can be further delegated to local government officers to determine if they are uncontested[8]. A licensing authority is required to keep a register containing prescribed information[9].

[1] This duty is prospective. It is concerned with prevention and not with whether a crime has been committed, let alone prosecuted: *East Lindsey DC v Hanif (T/A Zaraf Restaurant and Takeaway)* [2016] EWHC 1265 (Admin), [2016] CTLC 81 (where, in any event, crimes had been committed; a chef working at the restaurant was an illegal immigrant and had been paid cash in hand at less than the minimum wage, with "tax" deducted but not forwarded to HMRC).
[2] LA 2003, s 4.
[3] Crime and Disorder Act 1998, s 17(1).
[4] See the Guidance issued under s 182 of the LA 2003 issued by the DCMS in July 2004.
[5] LA 2003, s 6(1).
[6] LA 2003, s 7.
[7] LA 2003, s 9.
[8] LA 2003, s 10.
[9] LA 2003, s 8 and Sch 3.

7.7318 **Late night levy** A licensing authority may, having considered the costs of policing and other arrangements for the reduction or prevention of crime and disorder, decide that the late night levy requirement is to apply in the whole of its area in connection with the supply of alcohol between midnight and 6 am[1]. The levy may apply to a premises licence or club premises certificate which authorises the supply of alcohol at a time or times during the late night supply period on one or more days in the related payment year. The late night supply period is decided by the authority and must begin at or after midnight, and end at or before 6 am. The amount and enforcement of the late night levy is prescribed by regulations[2], and ss 55A and 92A of the LA 2003 (suspension of premises licence or club premises certificate for failure to pay annual fee) apply. The licensing authority must pay a specified proportion being not less that 70 per cent of that amount to the relevant local policing body, and apply the remainder of that amount in accordance with regulations[2].

[1] See the Police Reform and Social Responsibility Act 2011, Part 2 Chapter 2 (ss 125–139).
[2] See the Late Night Levy (Expenses, Exemptions and Reductions) Regulations 2012, SI 2012/2550.

7.7319 **Early morning alcohol restriction order** If a licensing authority considers it appropriate for the promotion of the licensing objectives, it may make an order providing that premises licences and club premises certificates, and temporary event notices do not have effect to the extent that they authorise the sale or supply of alcohol during the period specified in the order which must begin no earlier than midnight, and end no later than 6 am[1]. It is immaterial whether a premises licence or club premises certificate is granted, or a temporary event notice is given, before or after the order is made. The proposed order must be advertised in a manner prescribed by regulations[2], and the authority must hold a hearing to consider any relevant representations, unless the authority and each person who has made such representations agree that a hearing is unnecessary. An early morning alcohol restriction order may be revoked or varied by the authority and is subject to an order under s 172 (relaxation of opening hours for special occasions).

[1] See the LA 2003, s 172A–172E, in this title, post.
[2] See the Licensing Act 2003 (Early Morning Alcohol Restriction Orders) Regulations 2012, SI 2012/2551.

7.7320 **Premises licences** A person listed in s 16 of the Act may apply to a licensing authority for a premises licence which authorises premises to be used for one or more licensable activities[1]. The application must be in the prescribed manner and must be properly advertised[2]. The application must be accompanied by an "operating schedule", which must be in the prescribed form and must summarise, amongst other things, the licensable activities (and the times during which they will take place); details about the "premises supervisor" (if one of the licensable activities is the supply of alcohol); and the steps that the applicant intends to take to promote the licensing objectives[3]. A licensing authority receiving a valid application must grant the licence (subject only to such conditions as are consistent with the operating schedule submitted and any mandatory conditions[4]) unless "relevant representations"[5] have been received. Relevant representations can only be made by an "interested party"[6] or a "responsible authority"[7]. If relevant representations are received, the authority must hold a hearing to consider them (unless all parties to the application agree that a hearing is unnecessary)[8] and, having regard to the representations, must take such of the prescribed steps[9] (if any) as it considers necessary for the promotion of the licensing objectives[10]. Once granted, a premises licence has effect until it is revoked, unless the licence has been granted for a limited period or it has been suspended[11]. Application can be made to vary a premises licence[12], and an interested party or responsible authority may make relevant representations about such an application. An application can also be made to transfer a premises licence into the name of any person who could, by virtue of s 16, apply for a licence in his own right. An applicant can apply for such an application to have interim effect[13], and only the chief officer of police can object to a transfer application[14].

More than one party may simultaneously hold licences in respect of particular premises and the licences need not be in identical or near identical terms; if there are sound policy reasons to take issue with any differences between the terms of a shadow application and the primary application these can be considered at the hearing before the licensing committee[15].

1 LA 2003, s 11. Applications can also be made for provisional statements under s 29 in respect of premises that are being, or are about to be constructed, extended or otherwise altered. There are only limited powers to make relevant representations in respect of an application for a premises licence where the premises already enjoys the benefit of a provisional statement: LA 2003, s 32.

2 LA 2003, s 17(2) and the Licensing Act 2003 (Premises licences and club premises certificates) Regulations 2005, SI 2005/42.

3 LA 2003, s 17(4).

4 LA 2003, s 18(2). Mandatory conditions are those listed in the LA 2003, ss 19–21.

5 Defined in s 18(6) as those which are about the likely effect of the grant of the premises licence on the promotion of the licensing objectives, and which are, in all other requirements, valid.

6 Defined in the LA 2003, s 13(3).

7 Defined in the LA 2003, s 13(4).

8 LA 2003, s 18(3)(*a*).

9 The prescribed steps are listed in the LA 2003, s 18(4). The licensing authority has a wide discretion, including modifying or adding to proposed conditions, excluding certain licensable activities, refusing to specify a person as the premises supervisor, and rejecting the application outright.

10 LA 2003, s 18(3)(*b*).

11 LA 2003, s 26. A premises licence will also lapse in any of the circumstances listed in s 27, and it can be surrendered under s 28. If it has lapsed, s 47 provides for a person with a prescribed interest in the premises or a person connected to the premises licence holder to give an "interim authority notice" to the licensing authority. This has the effect of reinstating the premises licence in the name of the person giving the notice for a maximum period of seven days, during which time an application for transfer must be made. The chief officer of police may object to an interim authority notice, in which case the licensing authority must hold a hearing to consider his representations: LA 2003, s 48. Even if no interim authority notice is given, any person who could apply for a licence by virtue of s 16 of the LA 2003 can apply within 7 days of the lapse or surrender of the licence for a transfer of the premises licence to him: LA 2003, s 50. Where such an application is made, the premises licence is reinstated from the date of receipt of the application by the licensing authority.

12 LA 2003, s 34. There is a separate provision in s 37 to apply to vary a premises licence so as to change the name of the premises supervisor. Such an application can have interim effect if requested: LA 2003, s 38. Only the Chief Officer of Police can object to such an application, and only if he is satisfied that the exceptional circumstances of the case are such that granting the application would undermine the crime prevention licensing objective: LA 2003, s 37(5).

13 LA 2003, s 43.

14 LA 2003, s 42(6).

15 *Extreme Oyster and Star Oyster Ltd v Guildford Borough Council* [2013] EWHC 2174 (Admin), 177 JP 481.

**7.7321** *Reviews of premises licences* An interested party or responsible authority may apply to the licensing authority for a review of a premises licence at any time[1]. Unless the grounds for the application are irrelevant to the licensing objectives, frivolous, vexatious or repetitious, the licensing authority must hold a hearing to consider the application[2], and must, having regard to the application and the relevant representations, take such of a number of steps[3] (if any) as it considers necessary to promote the licensing objectives.

1 LA 2003, s 51(1). Repeated applications based on the same grounds are prohibited by s 51(4)(*b*)(ii).

2 LA 2003, s 52(2).

3 The steps are listed at the LA 2003, s 52(4).

**7.7322 Club premises certificates** A qualifying club[1] may apply to a licensing authority for a club premises certificate in respect of any premises which are occupied by, and habitually used for the purposes of, the club[2]. A club does not need to specify a premises supervisor, and it is not subject to the same powers of the police to close it[3], but in all other respects the regime for the licensing of clubs is very similar to that of other premises. An application for a club premises certificate must be in a prescribed form and must be advertised correctly[4]. The application must be accompanied by a "club operating schedule"[5] listing, amongst other things, the qualifying club activities (and the times during which they are proposed to take place), whether alcohol is to be supplied for consumption on or off the premises (if applicable), and the steps which the club proposes to take to promote the licensing objectives. A licensing authority receiving a valid application must grant the licence (subject only to such conditions as are consistent with the club operating schedule submitted and any mandatory conditions[6]) unless "relevant representations"[7] have been received. Relevant representations can only be made by an "interested party"[8] or a "responsible authority"[9]. If relevant representations are received, the authority must hold a hearing to consider them (unless all parties to the application agree that a hearing is unnecessary)[10] and, having regard to the representations, must take such of the prescribed steps[11] (if any) as it considers necessary for the promotion of the licensing objectives[12]. The licensing authority may not impose conditions restricting the right of a club to sell alcohol to an associate member[13] or their guest[14]; nor may it impose a condition restricting the nature of plays that may be performed at a club premises that is licensed for that form of regulated entertainment[15]. Once granted a club premises certificate has effect until such time as it is withdrawn (following a review or the club ceasing to be a qualifying club[16]) or it is surrendered[17]. Where a justice of the peace is satisfied, on information on oath, that there are reasonable grounds for believing that a club which holds a club premises certificate does not satisfy the conditions for being a qualifying club in relation to a qualifying club activity to which the certificate relates, and that evidence of that fact is to be obtained at the premises to which the certificate relates, he may issue a warrant authorising a constable to enter the premises, if necessary by force, at any time within one month from the time of issue of the warrant, and to seize and retain any documents relating to the business of the club[18]. Application can be made to vary a club premises certificate[19], and there is power for an interested party or responsible authority to make relevant representations about such an application. An interested party, a responsible authority or a member of the club can apply for a review of the certificate at any time[20]. Unless the grounds for the application are irrelevant to the licensing objectives, frivolous, vexatious or repetitious, the licensing authority must hold a hearing to consider the application[21], and must, having regard to the application and the relevant representations, take such of a number of steps[22] (if any) as it considers necessary to promote the licensing objectives.

[1] Section 61 of the LA 2003 defines what is a qualifying club. General conditions (listed in the LA 2003, s 62) must be satisfied as must additional conditions (listed in the LA 2003, s 64) if the club wants to be licensed for the supply of alcohol.
[2] LA 2003, s 71(1).
[3] LA 2003, Part 8. Those powers only exist in relation to premises which have the benefit of a premises licence or a TEN.
[4] LA 2003, s 71.
[5] LA 2003, s 71(5).
[6] LA 2003, s 72(2). Mandatory conditions are those listed in the LA 2003, ss 73(2)–(5) and 74.
[7] Defined in theLA 2003, s 72(7) as those which are about the likely effect of the grant of the premises licence on the promotion of the licensing objectives, and which are, in all other requirements, valid.
[8] Defined in the LA 2003, s 69(3).
[9] Defined in the LA 2003, s 69(4).
[10] LA 2003, s 72(3)(*a*).
[11] The prescribed steps are listed in s 72(4). The licensing authority has a wide discretion, including modifying or adding to proposed conditions, excluding certain licensable activities, and rejecting the application outright.
[12] LA 2003, s 72(3)(*b*).
[13] "Associate member" is defined in the LA 2003, s 67.
[14] LA 2003, s 75.
[15] LA 2003, s 76.
[16] LA 2003, s 90. If the licensing authority is of the opinion that this is the case in relation to one or more of its qualifying club activities, it must give a notice to the club withdrawing the certificate so far as it relates to that activity or those activities.
[17] LAc 2003, s 80(1).
[18] LA 2003, s 90(5) and (6).
[19] LA 2003, s 84.
[20] LA 2003, s 87(1).
[21] LA 2003, s 88(2).
[22] The steps are listed at the LA 2003, s 88(4).

**7.7323** *Mandatory licensing conditions* The Secretary of State has prescribed mandatory conditions applicable to premises licences and club premises certificates which authorise the supply of alcohol[1].

[1] See the Licensing Act 2003 (Mandatory Licensing Conditions) Order 2010, in this title, post.

**7.7324 Permitted temporary activities** Aside from applying for a premises licence, the only other way to receive permission to carry on a licensable activity is for a premises user to apply for a "Temporary Event Notice" ("TEN"). A licensable activity carried out in accordance with a permission given using the TENs procedure is a permitted temporary activity[1]. There are limitations on when the TENs procedure can be used. An activity cannot last more than 96 hours[2]. The maximum number of persons permitted at the event at any one time cannot exceed 499[3]. A TEN is void if the period specified in it starts or ends within 24 hours of another notice given in respect of the same premises by the premises user, or an associate or business colleague of that premises user[4]. A licensing authority must give a "counter notice" (effectively refusing the application for a TEN) if the premises user has already given 50 such notices in the last calendar year (if the premises user is a personal licence holder[5]); or 5 such notices (in the case of anybody else[6]); or if 12 such notices have been given in the last calendar year in respect of the same premises[7]; or if there have been 15 days worth of such events at the premises in the last calendar year[8]. To apply for a permitted temporary activity, the premises user gives a TEN to the licensing authority. The TEN must be in the prescribed form and must contain the prescribed information[9]. A copy of the notice must be served in duplicate on the licensing authority no later than 10 working days before the day on which the event period begins[10], and a copy must be served on the chief officer of police[11]. The chief officer of police must object within 48 hours if he is satisfied that the use of the premises in accordance with the notice would undermine the crime prevention objective[12]. If objection is made the licensing authority must hold a hearing to consider the objection notice[13] and, having regard to the objection notice, must give the premises user a counter notice if it considers it necessary for the promotion of the crime prevention licensing objective[14]. The decision to give or not to give a counter notice under this section can be appealed to the magistrates' court[15], but a decision to give a counter notice because a premises user has exceeded the permitted limits under the TENs procedure cannot.

[1] LA 2003, s 98.
[2] LA 2003, s 100(1).
[3] LA 2003, s 100(5)(*d*).
[4] LA 2003, s 101.
[5] LA 2003, s 107(2).
[6] LA 2003, s 107(3).
[7] LA 2003, s 107(4).

[8] LA 2003, s 107(5).
[9] LA 2003, s 100(5).
[10] LA 2003, s 100(7)(*a*).
[11] LA 2003, s 104(1).
[12] LA 2003, s 104(2) and (3). However, there is provision in s 106 for the premises user and the Police to negotiate away any objections by making modifications to the TEN. If this happens the objection notice is treated as withdrawn: LA 2003, s 106(3).
[13] LA 2003, s 105(2)(*a*).
[14] LA 2003, s 105(2)(*b*).
[15] LA 2003, Sch 5, para 16.

7.7325 **Personal licences** A personal licence is granted by a licensing authority[1] to an individual and authorises that person to supply (whether by retail or by or on behalf of a club to, or to the order of a member of the club) alcohol, or authorise the supply of alcohol, in accordance with a premises licence[2]. Once granted, it has effect for a period of ten years[3] unless it is surrendered[4], revoked, forfeited or suspended. It must be renewed every ten years.

An application must be made in the prescribed form and must be granted if it appears to the licensing authority that the four prescribed conditions are met[5]. If it appears to the licensing authority that any of the first three prescribed conditions are not met, it must reject the application[6]. If it appears to the authority that the fourth condition is not met (because the applicant has been convicted of a "relevant offence[7]" or "foreign offence[8]") it must give notice to that effect to the chief officer of police. If the chief officer of police is satisfied that, because of those convictions, the grant of a personal licence would undermine the crime prevention objective, he must give the licensing authority an objection notice[9], and the authority must hold a hearing to consider the notice[10]. It must refuse the application if it considers it necessary to promote the crime prevention licensing objective[11].

Similar provisions apply on an application for renewal if the applicant has been convicted of a relevant or foreign offence since the grant of the licence[12]. If the licensing authority becomes aware of a conviction of a personal licence holder for a relevant or foreign offence since that individual was granted a personal licence (whether on first application or renewal), it must give a notice to that effect to the chief officer of police. A process akin to that referred to above (on an application for a grant or renewal of a personal licence) then begins, and the licence must be revoked by a licensing authority after a hearing if it considers this necessary to promote the crime prevention licensing objective[13].

[1] Application must be made to the licensing authority for the area in which the applicant is ordinarily resident.
[2] LA 2003, s 111(1).
[3] LA 2003, s 115(1).
[4] LA 2003, s 116.
[5] The prescribed conditions are listed in the LA 2003, s 120(2).
[6] LA 2003, s 120(3).
[7] Relevant offences are listed in Sch 4 of the Act. Offences which are spent within the meaning of the Rehabilitation of Offenders Act 1974 must be disregarded: LA 2003, s 114.
[8] Defined in the LA 2003, s 113(3). Offences which are spent within the meaning of the Rehabilitation of Offenders Act 1974 must be disregarded: LA 2003, s 114.
[9] LA 2003, s 120(5).
[10] LA 2003, s 120(7(*a*).
[11] LA 2003, s 120(7)(*b*)(i).
[12] LA 2003, s 121.
[13] LA 2003, s 124.

7.7326 *Personal licence holders appearing before a magistrates' court* Where a personal licence holder is charged with a relevant offence he must, no later than the time he makes his first appearance in a magistrates' court in connection with that offence, produce his personal licence to the court or, if that is not practicable, notify the court of its existence[1].

A similar obligation is placed on a person who is granted a personal licence after a first court appearance but before the matter is dealt with[2]. A personal licence holder in such a situation must also keep the court notified of any changes in the status of his personal licence[3]. Where a personal licence holder is convicted of a relevant offence, the convicting court may order the forfeiture or suspension for up to 6 months of the personal licence[4]. The convicting court may suspend the operation of any such order pending an appeal[5], as may the court to which an appeal is made[6]. A convicting court must also notify the licensing authority that granted the personal licence of the outcome of the prosecution and the sentence imposed[7].

[1] LA 2003, s 128(1).
[2] LA 2003, s 128(2) and (3).
[3] LA 2003, s 128(4) and (5).
[4] LA 2003, s 129.
[5] LA 2003, s 129(4).
[6] LA 2003, s 130.
[7] LA 2003, s 130(2).

7.7327 **Appeals** The powers of applicants, interested parties and responsible authorities to appeal against decisions of a licensing authority are wide and varied. Essentially, any party to an original decision of the licensing authority following a hearing may appeal against the decision to grant, vary, impose conditions or refuse an application[1]. Magistrates' courts will sit as a final court of appeal, from which appeals will only be permitted on a point of law[2]. Magistrates' courts hearing an appeal are empowered to dismiss the appeal, substitute the decision of the licensing authority with its own decision, or remit the case to the licensing authority to dispose of in accordance with its direction; and can make such order as to costs as it thinks fit[3]. Appeals must be commenced by notice of appeal given to the designated officer of the magistrates' court within the period of 21 days beginning with the day on which the appellant was notified of the decision appealed against[4].

Magistrates must have regard to the licensing objectives, take account of the changed approach to licensing introduced by the LA 2003, the Secretary of State's Guidance and in deciding what regulation was required, look for real evidence that it was required in the circumstances of the case and not give excessive weight to their own views[5].

[1] This right does not extend to certain decisions that can be made by a licensing authority without the need for a hearing. Such decisions would have to be challenged by way of an application for judicial review. Examples include a decision of the licensing authority that a representation is irrelevant, frivolous, vexatious or repetitious; and a decision of a licensing authority to serve a counter notice to a TEN where the permitted limits have been exceeded: LA 2003, s 107. Some appeals may only be brought by the holder of a licence. In such cases where an appeal is brought by a person intending to appeal but having no standing to do so, the court cannot amend the complaint to refer to the holder of the licence as that would be substituting one legal entity for another and is not merely a misnaming of the appellant. Such an amendment is outside the scope of the Magistrates' Courts Act 1980, s 123. The issue for the magistrates' court considering an application to amend the complaint will be whether the matter is one of identity or misdescription. For the approach to deciding this issue, see *R (Essence Bars Ltd) v Wimbledon Magistrates' Court* [2016] EWCA Civ 63, [2016] 1 WLR 3265 and the Magistrates' Courts Act 1980, s 123 and notes thereto in PART I: MAGISTRATES' COURTS, PROCEDURE, ante and also para 1.145 **Objection to the information or charge**.

[2] There is an exception to this rule in the case of closure orders: LA 2003, s 166.

[3] LA 2003, s 181(2). For a more detailed commentary on the award of costs see para 7.7334.

[4] LA 2003, Sch 5, paras 9(2), 15(2), 16(5), 17(7) and 18(5). The Licensing Act (Hearings) Regulations 2005, SI 2005/44 require a notice of determination to be given in writing: reg 34.

[5] See the comments by Black J in *R (Daniel Thwaites plc) v Wirral Borough Magistrates' Court* [2008] EWHC 838 (Admin), [2009] 1 All ER 239, 172 JP 301.

**7.7328** *Appeals in respect of premises licences* Where a licensing authority rejects an application for a premises licence under s 18; rejects an application (in whole or part) to vary a premises licence under s 35; rejects an application under s 35 to vary a premises licence so as to specify a new premises supervisor; or rejects an application to transfer a premises licence under s 44, the applicant may appeal to the magistrates' court[1]. Where a licensing authority grant a premises licence, the applicant may appeal against any decision to impose conditions under s 18(2)(*a*) or (3)(*b*), or to exclude specific licensable activities (s 18(4)(*b*)), or to refuse to specify an individual as the premises supervisor (s 18(4)(*c*))[2]; whilst a person who made relevant representations may appeal on the grounds that the licence ought not to have been granted or that, on granting the licence, different or additional conditions should have been imposed or a decision should have been taken to exclude certain licensable activities or refuse to specify a person as the premises supervisor[3]. Similar rights of appeal exist in relation to the issuing of a provisional statement under s 31[4]; the grant (in whole or part) of an application to vary a premises licence[5]; and a decision on a review of the premises licence under s 52[6]. In addition a chief officer of police may appeal against a decision to vary a premises licence under s 39(2) so as to specify a new premises supervisor[7] or a decision to transfer a licence under s 44[8], so long as, in both cases, he gave a notice objecting to the application in the first place which was not withdrawn. Where an interim authority notice is given under s 47 and a chief officer of police gives a notice under s 48(2), the person given the notice can appeal against a decision to cancel the interim authority and the chief officer of police can appeal against a decision not to cancel it[9]. Where such an appeal is brought, the magistrates' court hearing the appeal may, on such terms as it thinks fit, order the reinstatement of the interim authority notice pending the disposal of the appeal or the expiry of the interim authority period (two months after the notice was given[10]), whichever occurs first[11].

[1] LA 2003, Sch 5, para 1.

[2] LA 2003, Sch 5, para 2(2).

[3] LA 2003, Sch 5, para 2(3).

[4] LA 2003, Sch 5, para 3.

[5] LA 2003, Sch 5, para 4.

[6] LA 2003, Sch 5, para 8.

[7] LA 2003, Sch 5, para 5(2).

[8] LA 2003, Sch 5, para 6(2).

[9] LA 2003, Sch 5, para 7.

[10] LA 2003, s 47(10).

[11] LA 2003, Sch 5, para 7(4).

**7.7329** *Appeals in respect of club premises certificates* Where a licensing authority rejects an application for a club premises certificate or rejects (in whole or part) an application to vary a club premises certificate, the club that made the application may appeal against the decision[1]. Where a licensing authority grants a club premises certificate, the club may appeal against any decision to impose conditions under s 72(2) or (3)(*b*), or to exclude specific qualifying club activities (s 72(4)(*b*)); whilst a person who made relevant representations may appeal on the grounds that the certificate ought not to have been granted or that, on granting the certificate, different or additional conditions should have been imposed or a decision should have been taken to exclude certain qualifying club activities[2]. Similar rights of appeal exist in relation to the grant (in whole or part) of an application to vary a certificate[3]; and a decision on a review of the certificate under s 88[4]. A club may also appeal against a decision of a licensing authority to give a notice under s 90 withdrawing the club premises certificate[5].

[1] LA2003, Sch 5, para 10.
[2] LA 2003, Sch 5, para 11.
[3] LA 2003, Sch 5, para 12.
[4] LA 2003, Sch 5, para 13.
[5] LA 2003, Sch 5, para 14.

**7.7330** *Appeals in respect of permitted temporary activities* A premises user may appeal against a decision of a licensing authority to give a counter notice[1], and a chief officer of police may appeal against a decision of a licensing authority not to give one[2]. No appeal in respect of a permitted temporary activity may be brought later than five working days before the day on which the event period specified in the TEN begins[3].

[1] LA 2003, Sch 5, para 16(2).
[2] LA 2003, Sch 5, para 16(3).
[3] LA 2003, Sch 5, para 16(6).

**7.7331** *Appeals in respect of personal licences* An applicant may appeal against a decision to reject an application for a personal licence[1], or a decision to revoke a licence[2]. A chief officer of police may appeal against a decision to grant an application for a personal licence where he has served an objection notice to the application[3], and a decision not to revoke a personal licence[4].

[1] Whether that decision was made on a first application or on an application for renewal: LA 2003, Sch 5, para 17(1).
[2] LA 2003, Sch 5, para 17(4).
[3] Whether that decision was made on a first application or on an application for renewal: LA 2003, Sch 5, para 17(2) and (3).
[4] LA 2003, Sch 5, para 17(5).

**7.7332** *Appeals in respect of closure orders* The licence holder or any person who made representations in respect of a review of a premises licence under s 167 may appeal against the licensing authority's decision[1].

[1] LA 2003, Sch 5, para 18.

**7.7333** *Procedure on appeals* Appeals to the magistrates' court are to be by way of a rehearing[1] on both the merits and the law, and the magistrates' court is not limited to considering only those grounds of complaint that were raised in the notice application or the representations which were made to the licensing authority; the parties are free to adduce such evidence as they think fit, subject to the control of the court[2]. Although it is a rehearing, justices must pay proper regard to the decision of the local authority and should not exercise their discretion uninfluenced by the local authorities' opinion[3]. This principle is not limited to decisions which can be classified as "policy based". In *R (on the application of Hope and Glory Public House Ltd) v City of Westminster Magistrates' Court (The Lord Mayor and the Citizens of the City of Westminster Intervening)*[4] it was held that the magistrates' court should approach its task in accordance with the following guidance and principles:

> "39. Since (counsel for the appellant) accepted (in our view rightly) that the decision of the licensing authority was a relevant matter for the District Judge to take into consideration, whether or not the decision is classified as 'policy based', the issues are quite narrow. They are:
>
> (1) How much weight was the District Judge entitled to give to the decision of the licensing authority?
>
> (2) More particularly, was he right to hold that he should only allow the appeal if satisfied that the decision of the licensing authority was wrong?
>
> (3) (Compliance with art 6)
>
> 40. We do not consider that it is possible to give a formulaic answer to the first question because it may depend on a variety of factors — the nature of the issue, the nature and quality of the reasons given by the licensing authority and the nature and quality of the evidence on the appeal.
>
> 41. As (was) rightly submitted, the licensing function of a licensing authority is an administrative function. By contrast, the function of the District Judge is a judicial function. The licensing authority has a duty, in accordance with the rule of law, to behave fairly in the decision-making procedure, but the decision itself is not a judicial or quasi-judicial act. It is the exercise of a power delegated by the people as a whole to decide what the public interest requires...
>
> 42. Licensing decisions often involve weighing a variety of competing considerations: the demand for licensed establishments, the economic benefit to the proprietor and to the locality by drawing in visitors and stimulating the demand, the effect on law and order, the impact on the lives of those who live and work in the vicinity, and so on. Sometimes a licensing decision may involve narrower questions, such as whether noise, noxious smells or litter coming from premises amount to a public nuisance. Although such questions are in a sense questions of fact, they are not questions of the 'heads or tails'; variety. They involve an evaluation of what is to be regarded as reasonably acceptable in the particular location. In any case, deciding what (if any) conditions should be attached to a licence as necessary and proportionate to the promotion of the statutory licensing objectives is essentially a matter of judgment rather than a matter of pure fact.
>
> 43. The statutory duty of the licensing authority to give reasons for its decision serves a number of purposes. It informs the public, who can make their views known to their elected representatives if they do not like the licensing sub-committee's approach. It enables a party aggrieved by the decision to know why it has lost and to consider the prospects of a successful appeal. If an appeal

is brought, it enables the magistrates' court to know the reasons which led to the decision. The fuller and clearer the reasons, the more force they are likely to carry.

44. The evidence called on the appeal may, or may not, throw a very different light on matters. Someone whose representations were accepted by the licensing authority may be totally discredited as a result of cross-examination. By contrast, in the present case the District Judge heard a mass of evidence over four days, as a result of which he reached essentially the same factual conclusions as the licensing authority had reached after five hours.

45. Given all the variables, the proper conclusion to the first question can only be stated in very general terms. It is right in all cases that the magistrates' court should pay careful attention to the reasons given by the licensing authority for arriving at the decision under appeal, bearing in mind that Parliament has chosen to place responsibility for making such decisions on local authorities. The weight which the magistrates should ultimately attach to those reasons must be a matter for their judgment in all the circumstances, taking into account the fullness and clarity of the reasons, the nature of the issues and the evidence given on the appeal.

46. As to the second question, we agree with the way in which Burton J dealt with the matter in paras 43–45 of his judgment:

'("43.... What the appellate court will have to do is to be satisfied that the judgment below "is wrong", that is to reach its conclusion on the basis of the evidence put before it and then to conclude that the judgment below is wrong, even if it was not wrong at the time. That is what this District Judge was prepared to do by allowing fresh evidence in, on both sides.

44. The onus still remains on the claimant, hence the correct decision that the claimant should start, one that cannot be challenged as I have indicated.

45. At the end of the day, the decision before the District Judge is whether the decision of the licensing committee is wrong. (Counsel for the appellant) has submitted that the word "wrong" is difficult to understand, or, at any rate, insufficiently clarified. What does it mean? It is plainly not "Wednesbury unreasonable" because this is not a question of judicial review. It means that the task of the District Judge — having heard the evidence which is now before him, and specifically addressing the decision of the court below — is to give a decision whether, because he disagrees with the decision below in the light of the evidence before him, it is therefore wrong.')

47. We do not accept (the) submission that the statement of Lord Goddard in *Stepney BC v Joffe*, applied by Edmund Davies LJ in *Sagnata Investments Ltd v Norwich Corporation* is applicable only in a case where the original decision was based on 'policy considerations'. We doubt whether such a distinction would be practicable, because it involves the unreal assumption that all decisions can be put in one of two boxes, one marked policy and the other not.....

48. It is normal for an appellant to have the responsibility of persuading the court that it should reverse the order under appeal, and the Magistrates' Courts Rules envisage that this is so in the case of statutory appeals to magistrates' courts from decisions of local authorities. We see no indication that Parliament intended to create an exception in the case of appeals under the Licensing Act.

49. We are also impressed by (the) point that in a case such as this, where the licensing sub-committee has exercised what amounts to a statutory discretion to attach conditions to the licence, it makes good sense that the licensee should have to persuade the magistrates' court that the sub-committee should not have exercised its discretion in the way that it did rather than that the magistrates' court should be required to exercise the discretion afresh on the hearing of the appeal."

Justices will need to be familiar with the scheme of the 2003 Act, the licensing objectives, the DCMS Guidance and the statement of policy of the licensing authority whose decision is being appealed. The court must carry out its appellate function with a view to promoting the licensing objectives[5]. Licensing and planning objectives plainly overlap and, except in relation to the protection of children from harm, each of the licensing objectives is also a land use planning objective. However, the framework and substance of the LA 2003, and its underlying rationale, point strongly to operational matters being regulated primarily in the former jurisdiction, though each case must be considered on its own facts; justices should not in involve themselves in planning matters, and in a licensing appeal it is not for them to examine whether a particular variation requires planning consent or to speculate whether, if it does, this will be forthcoming because these are matters exclusively within the competence of the planning authority[6]. The licensing authority will be a respondent to every appeal, with additional named respondents being specified depending on the decision being appealed against[7]. No express right is granted to either an interested party or a responsible authority to appear as a respondent to an appeal, although either may appear in specified circumstances as an appellant. Nevertheless, magistrates may permit an interested party or responsible authority to appear where, balancing the need to protect the appellant from any undue burden, they consider that to do so would further a fair and just resolution of the appeal in accordance with the licensing objectives[8]. No guidance has yet been given to magistrates' courts about the giving of directions, but it would seem to be good practice to issue standardised directions covering disclosure, exchange of evidence (lay and expert) and lodging of appeal bundles. If not resolved between the parties, these should be discussed at a pre-trial review. In considering the appeal, the court will be exercising an administrative function. Accordingly, strict rules of evidence do not apply, hearsay evidence is admissible[9] and there is no burden of proof. Although the LA 2003 does not specify the procedure by which an appeal is brought (referring throughout Sch 5 to "notices of appeal"), r 14 of the Magistrates' Court Rules 1981[10] states that the complainant should present his case first. This may not always be the most appropriate order, since in complex cases it will mean the justices will hear why the decision was allegedly wrong before it hears what the decision was and why it was reached. It is open to a court to vary the order (with the consent of all parties) so that the licensing authority presents its case first. If there is a second respondent then it would be sensible for their case to follow the licensing authority, so that the appellant goes last. Justices are advised to give comprehensive reasons for the decision that they reach[11].

Where a court is considering imposing conditions it will almost always be good practice for the conditions under consideration to be outlined for debate by the parties. Errors of drafting can then be identified, as can improvements and consideration of the underlying propositions behind the conditions themselves[12].

[1] Because of this, fresh evidence may be adduced that was not available at the original hearing (*Rushmoor Borough Council v Richards* (1996) 160 LG Rev 460).

[2] *Khan v Coventry Magistrates' Court, Coventry City Council (Interested Party)* [2011] EWCA Civ 751, (2011) 175 JP 429.

[3] *Sagnata Investments v Norwich Corpn* [1971] 2 All ER 1441. The Court of Appeal expressly approved the approach outlined in *Stepney Borough Council v Joffe* [1949] 1 All ER 256, that the appellate court ought "to pay great attention to the fact that the duly constituted and elected local authority have come to an opinion on the matter and ought not lightly to reverse their opinion . . . the function of a court of appeal is to exercise its powers when it is satisfied that the judgment below is wrong, not merely because it is not satisfied that the judgment was right".

[4] [2011] EWCA Civ 31, [2011] 3 All ER 579, (2011) 175 JP 77.

[5] And, it is submitted, must also have regard to the duty imposed on a licensing authority under s 17 of the Crime and Disorder Act 1998: see para 7.7316.

[6] *R (on the application of Blackwood) v Birmingham Magistrates and Birmingham City Council, Mitchells and Butler Leisure Retail Ltd (Interested Party)* [2006] EWHC 1800 (Admin), 170 JP 613.

[7] LA 2003, Sch 5, paras 9(4), 15(3), 16(7), 17(8) and 18(6).

[8] *R (Chief Constable of Nottinghamshire Police) v Nottingham Magistrates' Court* [2009] EWHC 3182 (Admin), [2010] 2 All ER 342, 174 JP 1.

[9] *Kavanagh v Chief Constable of Devon & Cornwall* [1974] 1QB 624; *Westminster City Council v Zestfair Ltd* (1989) 88 LGR 288.

[10] SI 1981/552 as amended: see para 1.2260.

[11] However, see *R (on the application of Blackwood) v Birmingham Magistrates and Birmingham City Council, Mitchells and Butler Leisure Retail Ltd (Interested Party)*, supra, where the reasons, though "somewhat sparse", were held to be adequate to bring home to anyone familiar with the licensing regime that the proposed variation in respect of opening hours was reasonable in the light of the licensing objectives, particularly those concerning public nuisance.

[12] *R (Westminster City Council) v Metropolitan Stipendiary Magistrate* [2008] EWHC 1202 (Admin), 172 JP 462.

**7.7334** *The role of the DCMS Guidance and the licensing authority's statement of policy in appeal hearings* Chapter 10 of the DCMS Guidance advises that magistrates' courts must have regard to the Guidance and the licensing authority's statement of licensing policy when hearing an appeal[1]. The Guidance says that the court may depart from either document if it considers that it is justified in doing so because of the individual circumstances of the case; or because it finds any part of either document to be ultra vires[2]. It is submitted that, in this last respect, the Guidance is wrong in law and that a proper method of challenging the validity of a statement of licensing policy is by way of an application for judicial review[3].

The court must give reasons where it departs from the guidance. When considering an appeal involving the use of premises for criminal purposes, furtherance of the licensing objectives includes the prevention of crime. In this regard deterrence is an appropriate consideration so that the court must address the guidance on this point[4].

[1] Guidance issued under s 182 of the LA 2003, July 2004, para 10.8.

[2] Guidance issued under s 182 of the LA 2003, July 2004, para 10.8. This would appear to run contrary to the decision of the High Court in *R (Westminster City Council) v Middlesex Crown Court & Chorion plc* [2002] LLR 538.

[3] For an example of a challenge by way of judicial review to a licensing authority's statement of licensing policy, see *R (on the application of British Beer and Pub Association) v Canterbury City Council* [2005] EWHC 1318 (Admin), 6169 JP 521.

[4] *R (Bassetlaw District Council v Worksop Magistrates' Court)* [2008] EWHC 3530 (Admin), 173 JP 599.

**7.7335** *Costs on appeal* A magistrates' court hearing an appeal may make such order as to costs as it thinks fit[1]. This power is in wider terms than that where the costs of an appeal are ordered under other powers[2]. In licensing cases the permutations of result may be frequently more complex than simple success or failure. The court has an unfettered power in relation to costs subject to the requirement that in making such order as is just it must take into account all relevant matters and not take into account irrelevant matters. The court is not limited to ordering costs to follow the event so that where an appellant had succeeded on her appeal but it was hardly a resounding victory, the court was upheld in ordering the appellant to pay the respondent licensing authority's (substantial) costs[3]. As regards ordering a licensing authority to pay costs, existing principles in other areas of administrative law dealt with by magistrates' courts as an appellate body are that costs should not be routinely awarded against an authority that acted honestly, reasonably and properly on sound grounds[4]. Financial prejudice to the successful private party can potentially justify departure from the normal position of no costs against the local authority, but this requires evidence that the private party will suffer exceptional or substantial financial hardship[5]. In relation to the power to order costs under s 181(2) of the LA 2003 whilst there has been emphasis on the very wide nature of the justices' discretion[6], it has been held that although the power to award costs was not confined to cases where the local authority acted unreasonably or in bad faith, the fact that the local authority had acted reasonably and in good faith was plainly a most important factor[7].

[1] Licensing Act 2003, s 181(2).
[2] Ie under s 64 of the Magistrates' Courts Act 1980 where costs may only be claimed by a successful party, see further para 1.310, in PART I: MAGISTRATES' COURTS, PROCEDURE, ante.
[3] *Prasannan v Royal Borough of Kensington and Chelsea* [2010] EWHC 319 (Admin), 174 JP 418.
[4] *Bradford Metropolitan District Council v Booth* (2000) 164 JP 485 (a case concerning the licensing of a private hire operator).
[5] *R (on the application of Newham London Borough Council) v Stratford Magistrates' Court* [2012] All ER (D) 184 (Jan).
[6] *Prasannan*, supra, also *Crawley Borough Council v Attenborough* [2006] EWHC 1278 (Admin), (2006) 170 JP 593.
[7] *R (on the application of Cambridge City Council) v Alex Nesting Ltd* [2006] EWHC 1374 (Admin), 170 JP 539.

7.7336 **Closure of premises** A police officer of the rank of Superintendent or above may apply to a magistrates' court for an order to close premises licensed under a premises licence or TEN[1] for up to 24 hours if there is or is expected to be disorder in the area and the premises concerned are situated at or near the place of disorder or expected disorder[2]. A magistrates' court may make such an order only if it satisfied that it is necessary to prevent disorder[3]. Once an order has been made a constable may use such force as may be necessary to close premises which have been ordered to close[4]. Additionally, a police officer of the rank of Inspector or above may make a "closure order" in relation to premises licensed under a premises licence or TEN if he reasonably believes that there is, or is likely imminently to be, disorder on, or in the vicinity of and related to, the premises and their closure is necessary in the interests of public safety; or that a public nuisance is being caused by noise coming from the premises and the closure of the premises is necessary to prevent that nuisance[5]. The effect of the closure order is to require the premises to be closed for a period not exceeding 24 hours from the moment that notice of the order is given to an appropriate person[6] who is connected with any of the activities to which the disorder or nuisance relates[7]. It is an offence to permit premises to be open in contravention of an order[8]. As soon as reasonably practicable after a closure order has come into force, the police officer that decided to make the order must apply to a magistrates' court for it to consider the order and any extension of it[9]. If the police officer reasonably believes that a magistrates' court will not have determined whether to exercise its powers under s 165(2) by the end of the initial 24 hour closure period he may, before that initial period expires, extend it by a further period of up to 24 hours if certain conditions are satisfied[10]. Equally, the police officer must cancel the order if he does not reasonably believe that the conditions for it remain.

[1] But not a premises that has the benefit of a club premises certificate.
[2] Licensing Act 2003, s 160(1).
[3] LA 2003, s 160(3).
[4] LA 2003, s 160(7).
[5] LA 2003, s 161(1).
[6] Defined in the LA 2003, s 171(5).
[7] LA 2003, s 161(2) and (5).
[8] LA 2003, s 161(6).
[9] LA 2003, s 164(1).
[10] LA 2003, s 162.

7.7337 *Consideration of closure order by magistrates' court* As soon as reasonably practicable after receipt of an application under s 164(1) a magistrates' court must hold a hearing to consider whether it is appropriate to exercise any of its powers in relation to the order[1]. The powers are listed in s 164(2) and are wide ranging. In coming to a determination the court must consider, in particular, whether continued closure is necessary for the same reasons as the order was made in the first place[2]. Offences are committed if, without reasonable excuse, a person permits premises to be open in contravention of the magistrates' order. There is a right of appeal to the Crown Court against the decision of a magistrates' court[3]. Once a decision has been made by a magistrates' court in relation to a premises with the benefit of a premises licence, it must notify the licensing authority of that decision[4]. The licensing authority must then review the premises licence[5].

[1] LA 2003, s 165(1). The court does not need to exercise its powers if the premises have ceased to be licensed (for example, because the premises had the benefit of a TEN that has subsequently expired). The hearing is to be by way of a complaint for an order: LA 2003, s 165(9).
[2] LA 2003, s 165(3).
[3] LA 2003, s 166(1).
[4] LA 2003, s 165(4).
[5] LA 2003, s 167(2).

7.7338 **Offences – introduction** All offences in the LA 2003 are summary only, but the time limit for instituting proceedings is raised to 12 months[1]. Proceedings for offences may be instituted by a licensing authority, the DPP, or (in the case of offences under ss 146 and 147 by a local weights and measures authority[2]). Offences may be committed by bodies corporate, partnerships and unincorporated associations and by individuals in those organisations if the requirements of s 187 are satisfied.

[1] LA 2003, s 186(3).
[2] LA 2003, s 186(2).

7.7339 *"Documentary" offences* Part 7 outlines the substantive offences contained in the Act. However, there are a raft of documentary offences throughout the Act, dealing with such matters as failing to notify a licensing authority of a change in the name or address of a premises licence holder or premises supervisor[1]; a change in the name, rules[2] or address[3] of a club; a conviction of a personal licence holder for a relevant or foreign offence[4]; and the name or address of a personal licence holder[5]. Offences are also committed if a summary of a premises licence or club premises certificate, or a copy of a temporary event notice is not displayed at the premises to which they relate[6]. Furthermore, offences are committed if a premises licence, club premises certificate or personal licence is not provided to the licensing authority to be updated when requested[7]. There are also offences relating to the obstruction of an authorised person who is carrying out his duties in relation to personal licences, club premises certificates or permitted temporary activities[8]; and offences of failing to produce a premises licence, club premises certificate, temporary event notice or personal licence to an authorised officer or police constable[9].

1 LA 2003, s 33(6).
2 LA 2003, s 82(6).
3 LA 2003, s 83(6).
4 Either during the application period for a licence: LA 2003, s 123(2); or after a licence has been granted: LA 2003, s 132(4).
5 LA 2003, s 127(1).
6 See, for example, LA 2003, ss 57(4), 94(5), 94(6) and 109(4).
7 See, for example, LA 2003, ss 41(5), 56(3), 93(3) and 134(5).
8 See, for example, LA 2003, ss 59(5), 96(5) and 108(3). The offence does not apply to obstruction of a police officer because that is already an offence: Police Act 1996, s 89(2).
9 See, for example, LA 2003, ss 57(7), 94(9), 109(8) and 135(4).

**7.7340** *Offences – unauthorised licensable activities* A person commits an offence if he carries on, attempts to carry on or knowingly allows to be carried on a licensable activity on or from any premises otherwise than under and in accordance with a premises licence, club premises certificate or valid temporary event notice[1]. This provision is directed at persons who *as a matter of fact* actually carry on etc a licensable activity on or from the premises. It is not directed at holders of premises licences as such who do not automatically incur liability by the mere fact of holding a licence[2]. It is also an offence to expose alcohol for sale by retail[3] in circumstances where the sale would be an unauthorised licensable activity[4]; and to keep alcohol in one's possession or under one's control with the intention of selling it by retail or supplying it in circumstances where the sale or supply would be an unauthorised licensable activity[5]. A due diligence defence[6] is available for all of these offences except for one committed under s 136(1)(*b*).

1 LA 2003, s 136(1). No offence is committed solely by reason of the person being a performer in an unlicensed performance of regulated entertainment: LA 2003, 136(2). Conviction carries a maximum penalty of six months' imprisonment and/or a £20,000 fine.
2 *Hall & Woodhouse Ltd v Borough and County of the Town of Poole* [2009] EWHC 1587 (Admin), [2010] 1 All ER 425, 173 JP 433.
3 "Sale by retail" is defined in the LA 2003, s 192.
4 LA 2003, s 137(1). Conviction carries a maximum penalty of six months' imprisonment and/or a £20,000 fine. A convicting court may order forfeiture of the alcohol in question: LA 2003, s 137(4).
5 LA 2003, s 138(1). Conviction carries a maximum of a level 2 fine on the standard scale. A convicting court may order forfeiture of the alcohol in question: LA 2003, s 138(5).
6 LA 2003, s 139.

**7.7341** *Offences – drunkenness and disorderly conduct* A large number of people can commit an offence of knowingly[1] allowing disorderly conduct[2] on relevant premises[3]. Those people include any person who works at the premises in a capacity, paid or unpaid, which authorises him to prevent the conduct; the holder of a premises licence; a premises supervisor; any member or officer of a club who is present at the club when the disorder takes place in a capacity which enables him to prevent it; and the premises user in relation to a permitted temporary activity[4]. The same group of people may commit an offence of knowingly[5] selling, attempting to sell or allowing to be sold alcohol to a person who is drunk[6]. It is an offence for a person, on relevant premises[7], to knowingly obtain or attempt to obtain alcohol for consumption on those premises by a person who is drunk[8]; and it is an offence for a drunk or disorderly person, without reasonable excuse, to fail to leave relevant premises[9] when requested to do so by a constable or a person to whom s 143(2) applies[10], or to enter or attempt to enter such premises after that person has requested him not to do so[11].

1 See the case of *R v Winson* [1968] 1 All ER 197. The doctrine of delegation applies to the concept of "knowingly", so that a defendant can be guilty of an offence committed by another if he has delegated responsibility for compliance with the law to that other person who did knowingly allow the offence to occur. See also *Howker v Robinson* [1972] 2 All ER 786.
2 "Disorderly conduct" is not defined.
3 LA 2003, s 140(1). The offence carries a maximum of a level 3 fine on the standard scale. "Relevant premises" are defined in s 159 and include premises covered by a premises licence, club premises certificate or temporary event notice.
4 LA 2003, s 140(2).
5 See note 1, above.
6 LA 2003, 141(1). The offence carries a maximum of a level 3 fine on the standard scale. "Drunk" is not defined, but in the case of *Neale v E (a minor)* (1983) 80 Cr App Rep 20, (a case on the meaning of "drunk" under the offence of drunkenness in a public place, contrary to s 91 of the Criminal Justice Act 1967), it was held that it referred to a person who has taken intoxicating liquor to excess so that he has lost the power of self-control.
7 See note 3, above, for definition of "relevant premises".
8 LA 2003, s 142(1). The offence carries a maximum of a level 3 fine on the standard scale. See note 6, above, for guidance on the meaning of "drunk".
9 See note 3, ante, for definition of "relevant premises".
10 LA 2003, s 143(1)(*a*). The offence carries a maximum of a level 1 fine on the standard scale.

[11] Licensing Act 2003, s 143(1)(*b*). The offence carries a maximum of a level 1 fine on the standard scale.

**7.7342** *Offences – smuggled goods* The same group of people who can commit an offence under s 140(1)[1], can also commit an offence of knowingly[2] keeping or allowing to be kept, on any relevant premises[3], any goods which have been imported without payment of duty or which have otherwise been unlawfully imported[4].

[1] See para 7.7341, ante.

[2] See note 1 to para 7.7341, ante, for discussion of "knowingly". The defendant need only know that the goods are on the premises, not that they are smuggled.

[3] See note 3, to para 7.7341, ante, for meaning of "relevant premises".

[4] LA 2003, s 144(1). The offence carries a maximum of a level 3 fine on the standard scale. A convicting court may order forfeiture of the goods in question: LA 2003, s 144(4).

**7.7343** *Offences – children and alcohol – unaccompanied children on certain premises* It is an offence[1] for a person listed in s 145(3) to allow an unaccompanied child under 16 to be on premises that he knows are exclusively or primarily used for the supply of alcohol for consumption there[2] at a time when they are open for that purpose[3]; or to allow an unaccompanied[4] child under 16 to be on those premises between midnight and 5am when the premises[5] are open for the purposes of being used for the supply of alcohol for consumption there[6]. No offence is committed if the child is on the premises solely for the purpose of passing to or from some other place and there is no other convenient means of getting to or from that place[7]. If a person is charged with the offence by reason of his own conduct, it is a defence[8] that the person believed the child to be 16 or over or the accompanying person (if there was one) to be 18 or over, and he had either taken all reasonable steps[9] to establish the individual's age, or nobody could reasonably have suspected from the individual's appearance that he was aged under 16 or under 18, as the case may be. A person charged because of the act or default of another has a defence if he exercised all due diligence to avoid committing it[10].

[1] The offences carry a maximum of a level 3 fine on the standard scale: LA 2003, s 145(9).

[2] The premises can be licensed by virtue of a premises licence, club premises certificate or temporary event notice: LA 2003, s 145(4) and (10).

[3] LA 2003, s 145(1)(*a*).

[4] "Unaccompanied" means not accompanied by an individual aged 18 or over: LA 2003, s 145(2)(*b*).

[5] See note 1 ante for definition of premises.

[6] LA 2003, s 145(1)(*b*).

[7] LA 2003, s 145(5).

[8] \ls 2003, s 145(6).

[9] A person is deemed to have taken all reasonable steps if he asked the individual for evidence of age and the evidence would have convinced a reasonable person: LA 2003, s 145(7).

[10] LA 2003, s 145(8).

**7.7344** *Offences – children and alcohol – sale or supply of alcohol to children* There are numerous offences involving the sale of alcohol to children. A person commits an offence if he sells alcohol to a child under 18[1]. A club commits an offence[2] if alcohol is supplied by it or on its behalf to, or to the order of, a member of the club who is under 18[3]. A person charged with an offence by reason of his own conduct has the same defence as is available in respect of a s 145 charge[4]; and a person charged because of the act or default of another has a due diligence defence available[5]. It is also an offence to knowingly[6] allow the sale of alcohol, on relevant premises[7], to a child under 18[8]. Further, there are offences in relation to the sale or supply liqueur confectionery[9] to children under 16[10].

[1] LA 2003, s 149(1)(*a*). The offence can be committed anywhere, even on unlicensed premises. A similar offence is created if an under 18 member of a club is supplied with, or attempts to be supplied with, alcohol: LA 2003, s 149(1)(*b*).

[2] LA 2003, s 149(2).

[3] LA 2003, s 149(3)(*a*). A similar offence is committed if the person is a member of a club: LA 2003, s 149(3)(*b*). Both offences carry a defence that the person charged had no reason to suspect that the individual was under 18: LA 2003, s 149(6).

[4] LA 2003, s 149(4)(*a*). A similar offence is committed if the person is a member of a club: LA 2003, s 149(4)(*b*). "Relevant premises" are defined in s 159. Both offences carry a defence that the person charged had no reason to suspect that the individual was under 18: LA 2003, s 149(6).

[5] "The table meal exemption": LA 2003, s 149(5).

[6] So the offence would not be committed if the child unwittingly consumed a spiked drink.

[7] LA 2003, s 150(1). No offence is committed if the "table meal exemption" applies: LA 2003, s 150(4). "Relevant premises" are defined in LA 2003, s 159.

[8] Licensing Act 2003, s 150(2). No offence is committed if the "table meal exemption" applies: LA 2003, s 150(4). "Relevant premises" are defined in s 159.

[9] "Relevant premises" are defined in s 159.

[10] LA 2003, s 151(1).

**7.7345** *Offences – children and alcohol – purchase and consumption of alcohol by children* A child under 18 commits an offence if he buys or attempts to buy alcohol[1], unless that act is committed in the course of him being used for a test purchase operation[2]. A person who acts as an agent for a child under 18 by buying or attempting to buy alcohol on behalf of the child also commits an offence[3], as does a person who acts as agent for a child under 18 and buys or attempts to buy alcohol for him for consumption on relevant premises[4]. However, this last offence does not apply if the person purchasing or attempting to purchase the alcohol is over 18; the child is 16 or 17; the alcohol is beer, wine or cider; the purchase is for consumption at a table meal; and the child is accompanied by an adult[5]. A child also commits an offence if he knowingly[6] consumes alcohol on relevant premises[7], and a person to whom s 150(3) applies commits an offence if he knowingly allows the consumption of alcohol by a child under 18 on relevant premises[8].

[1] LA 2003, s 149(1)(*a*). The offence can be committed anywhere, even on unlicensed premises. A similar offence is created if an under 18 member of a club is supplied with, or attempts to be supplied with, alcohol: LA 2003, s 149(1)(*b*).

[2] LA 2003, s 149(2).

[3] LA 2003, s 149(3)(*a*). A similar offence is committed if the person is a member of a club: LA 2003, s 149(3)(*b*). Both offences carry a defence that the person charged had no reason to suspect that the individual was under 18: LA 2003, 149(6).

[4] LA 2003, s 149(4)(*a*). A similar offence is committed if the person is a member of a club: LA 2003, s 149(4)(*b*). "Relevant premises" are defined in s 159. Both offences carry a defence that the person charged had no reason to suspect that the individual was under 18: LA 2003, 149(6).

[5] "The table meal exemption": LA 2003, s 149(5).

[6] So the offence would not be committed if the child unwittingly consumed a spiked drink.

[7] LA 2003, s 150(1). No offence is committed if the "table meal exemption" applies: LA 2003, s 150(4). "Relevant premises" are defined in LA 2003, s 159.

[8] LA 2003, s 150(2). No offence is committed if the "table meal exemption" applies: LA 2003, s 150(4). "Relevant premises" are defined in s 159.

**7.7346** *Offences – children and alcohol – delivering alcohol to children and sending children to obtain alcohol* A person who works on relevant premises[1] in any capacity commits an offence if he knowingly delivers to a child under 18 alcohol sold on the premises, or supplied on the premises (in the case of a club)[2]. Similar offences are committed by a person who knowingly allows anybody else to deliver the alcohol[3]. The offences are not committed if the alcohol is delivered to a place where the buyer or person supplied lives or works[4]; if the child under 18 is himself working on relevant premises in a capacity that involves the delivery of alcohol; or if the alcohol is sold or supplied for consumption on relevant premises[5]. It is also an offence to knowingly send a child under 18 to obtain alcohol sold or supplied on relevant premises for consumption off those premises[6].

[1] "Relevant premises" are defined in the LA 2003, s 159.

[2] LA 2003, s 151(1).

[3] LA2003, s 151(2) and (4). The person must work in a capacity which authorises him to prevent the delivery: LA 2003, s 151(3) and (5).

[4] This would seem to mean that a child can take delivery of the alcohol on behalf of a parent or employer and no offence is committed.

[5] LA 2003, s 151(6).

[6] LA 2003, s 152(1). An example would be a parent sending a child to collect alcohol which had already been paid for from an off licence, although it is immaterial where the alcohol is actually collected from: LA 2003, s 152(2). Exceptions are provided in the case of test purchase operations (LA 2003, s 152(4)) and where the child works on the relevant premises in a capacity that involves the delivery of alcohol (LA 2003, s 152(3)).

**7.7347** *Offences – children and alcohol – unsupervised sales by children* It is an offence for a responsible person[1] on relevant premises[2] to knowingly allow a child under 18 to make a sale or supply of alcohol on the premises unless the sale or supply has been specifically approved by that or another responsible person[3]. However, no offence is committed if the child serves or supplies alcohol to a person for consumption with a table meal in an area set aside for that purpose[4].

[1] "Responsible person" is defined in the LA 2003, s 153(4).

[2] "Relevant premises" are defined in the LA 2003, s 159.

[3] LA 2003, s 153(1).

[4] LA 2003, s 153(2).

**7.7348** *Offences – vehicles and trains* A person commits an offence if he sells by retail[1] alcohol on or from a vehicle[2] at a time when the vehicle is not permanently or temporarily parked[3]. A magistrates' court, if it is satisfied that it is necessary to prevent disorder, may, on the application of a police officer of the rank of Inspector or above, make an order prohibiting the sale of alcohol during a specified period on any railway vehicle that is at a station or stations in the petty sessional area of the court, or on any railway vehicle that is travelling between such stations, one of which must be in that petty sessional area[4]. It is an offence to knowingly sell, attempt to sell or allow the sale of alcohol in contravention of such an order[5].

[1] "Sale by retail" is defined in the LA 2003, s 192.

[2] "Vehicle" is defined in the LA 2003, s 193 as "a vehicle intended or adapted for use on roads".

[3] LA 2003, s 156(1). The offence carries a maximum penalty of three months' imprisonment and/or a £20,000 fine. A due diligence defence is available: LA 2003, s 156(3).

[4] LA 2003, s 157(1)–(3). The order must be served by the police officer on the train operator(s) affected by the order. It would seem that this power is designed to compliment the power in the LA 2003, s 160 for magistrates to order the closure of premises in an area of ongoing or expected disorder: see para 7.7336, ante.

[5] LA 2003, s 157(5). The offence carries a maximum penalty of three months' imprisonment and/or a £20,000 fine: LA 2003, s 157(6).

**7.7349** *Offences – false statements* It is an offence for a person to knowingly or recklessly make a false statement[1] in or in connection with any of numerous applications under the Act[2].

[1] A person is treated as making a false statement if he produces, furnishes, signs or otherwise makes use of a document that contains a false statement: LA 2003, s 158(2).

[2] LA 2003, s 158(1). The offence carries a maximum of a level 5 fine on the standard scale.

# Licensing Act 2003[1]

(2003 c 17)

## Part 1[2]

## Licensable Activities

7.7350 **1. Licensable activities and qualifying club activities** (1) For the purposes of this Act the following are licensable activities[3]—

(*a*) the sale by retail[4] of alcohol[5],

(*b*) the supply of alcohol by or on behalf of a club to, or to the order of, a member of the club,

(*c*) the provision of regulated entertainment, and

(*d*) the provision of late night refreshment.

(2) For those purposes the following licensable activities are also qualifying club activities—

(*a*) the supply of alcohol by or on behalf of a club to, or to the order of, a member of the club,

(*b*) the sale by retail of alcohol by or on behalf of a club to a guest of a member of the club for consumption on the premises where the sale takes place, and

(*c*) the provision of regulated entertainment where that provision is by or on behalf of a club for members of the club or members of the club and their guests.

(3) In this Act references to the supply of alcohol by or on behalf of a club to, or to the order of, a member of the club do not include a reference to any supply which is a sale by retail of alcohol.

(4) Schedule 1 makes provision about what constitutes the provision of regulated entertainment for the purposes of this Act.

(5) Schedule 2 makes provision about what constitutes the provision of late night refreshment for those purposes (including provision that certain activities carried on in relation to certain clubs or hotels etc, or certain employees, do not constitute provision of late night refreshment and are, accordingly, not licensable activities).

(6) For the purposes of this Act premises are "used" for a licensable activity if that activity is carried on or from the premises.

(7) This section is subject to sections 173 to 175 (which exclude activities from the definition of licensable activity in certain circumstances).

[Licensing Act 2003, s 1.]

---

[1] This Act is to be brought into force in accordance with orders made under s 201. At the date of going to press the following commencement orders have been made:(Commencement) Order 2003, SI 2003/1911; (Commencement No 2) Order 2003, SI 2003/2100; (Commencement No 3) Order 2003, SI 2003/3222; (Commencement No 4) Order 2004, SI 2004/1738; (Commencement No 5) Order 2004, SI 2004/2360; (Commencement No 6) Order 2005, SI 2005/2090; and (Commencement No 7 and Transitional Provisions) Order 2005, SI 2005/3056.

[2] Part 1 comprises ss 1–2 and Schs 1 and 2.

[3] For activities in certain locations which are not licensable, see s 173, post and for exemptions for raffles and tombola, etc., see s 175, post.

[4] For meaning of "sale by retail", see s 192, post.

[5] For meaning of "alcohol", see s 191, post.

7.7351 **2. Authorisation for licensable activities and qualifying club activities** (1) A licensable activity may be carried on—

(*a*) under and in accordance with a premises licence (see Part 3), or

(*b*) in circumstances where the activity is a permitted temporary activity by virtue of Part 5.

(2) A qualifying club activity may be carried on under and in accordance with a club premises certificate (see Part 4).

(3) Nothing in this Act prevents two or more authorisations having effect concurrently in respect of the whole or a part of the same premises or in respect of the same person.

(4) For the purposes of subsection (3) "authorisation" means—

(*a*) a premises licence;

(*b*) a club premises certificate;

(*c*) a temporary event notice.*

[Licensing Act 2003, s 2.]

---

* **Amended by the Deregulation Act 2015, s 67 from a date to be appointed.**

## Part 2[1]

## Licensing Authorities

*The authorities*

7.7352 **3. Licensing authorities** (1) In this Act "licensing authority" means—

(*a*) the council of a district in England,

(*b*) the council of a county in England in which there are no district councils,

(*c*) the council of a county or county borough in Wales,

(*d*) the council of a London borough,

(*e*) the Common Council of the City of London,
(*f*) the Sub-Treasurer of the Inner Temple,
(*g*) the Under-Treasurer of the Middle Temple, or
(*h*) the Council of the Isles of Scilly.

(2) For the purposes of this Act, a licensing authority's area is the area for which the authority acts.

[Licensing Act 2003, s 3.]

[1] Part 2 comprises ss 3–10 and Sch 3.

*Functions of licensing authorities etc*

7.7353 **4. General duties of licensing authorities** (1) A licensing authority must carry out its functions under this Act ("licensing functions") with a view to promoting the licensing objectives.

(2) The licensing objectives are—

(*a*) the prevention of crime and disorder[1];
(*b*) public safety;
(*c*) the prevention of public nuisance; and
(*d*) the protection of children from harm.

(3) In carrying out its licensing functions, a licensing authority must also have regard to—

(*a*) its licensing statement published under section 5, and
(*b*) any guidance issued by the Secretary of State under section 182[2].

[Licensing Act 2003, s 4.]

[1] The council (or magistrates' court on appeal) may take into account issues relating to crime and disorder away from the proposed premises and beyond the direct control of the licensee: *Brooke Leisure Ltd v Luminar Leisure Ltd* [2008] EWHC 1002 (Admin), 172 JP 345.

The terms "crime" and "disorder" are to be regarded disjunctively; thus, evidence of smoking in licensed premises, which is an offence under s 8 of the Health Act 2006, is relevant to the licensing objective of preventing crime even though it does not involve "disorder" and even though the offence did not exist when the Licensing Act 2003 was passed, because the words of a statute can apply to future events: *Blackpool Council v Howitt (Secretary of State for the Culture Media and Sport Intervening)* [2008] EWHC 3300 (Admin), 173 JP 101.

[2] The guidance is not to be construed as if it were a statute: *Blackpool Council v Howitt (Secretary of State for the Culture, Media and Sport Intervening)*, supra.

7.7354 **5. Statement of licensing policy** *Every licensing authority, in accordance with any regulations published, is required to make in consultation with interested parties, publish and keep under review a Statement of licensing policy in respect of each 5 year period[1].*

[1] The Licensing Act 2003 (Licensing statement period) Order 2004, SI 2004/2362 made under s 5(2) appoints 7 January 2005 as the day the first period of three years begins.

7.7355 **6, 7.** *Licensing authority must establish a licensing committee; certain functions may be delegated and exercised at various levels of the authority.*

7.7356 **8. Requirement to keep a register** *Licensing authority must keep a register containing specified information and such other information as may be prescribed by the Secretary of State[1].*

[1] The Licensing Act 2003 (Licensing Authority's Register) (Other Information) Regulations 2005, SI 2005/43 amended by SI 2007/2502 and SI 2009/1809 have been made.

*Licensing committees*

7.7357 **9.** *Power of licensing committee to establish sub-committees and to regulate its own procedure. Power of Secretary of State to make Regulations regarding the proceedings of licensing committees and sub-committees. The Licensing Act 2003 (Hearings) Regulations 2005, SI 2005/44 amended by SI 2005/78, SI 2007/2502 and SI 2014/2341 and the Gambling Act 2005 (Proceedings of Licensing Committees and Sub-committees) (Premises Licences and Provisional Statements) (England and Wales) Regulations 2007, SI 2007/173 amended by SI 2010/2440 have been made.*

## PART 3[1]
## PREMISES LICENCES

*Introductory*

7.7358 **11. Premises licence** In this Act "premises licence" means a licence granted under this Part, in respect of any premises, which authorises the premises[2] to be used for one or more licensable activities.

[Licensing Act 2003, s 11.]

[1] Part 3 comprises ss 11–59.
[2] For meaning of "premises", see s 193, post.

7.7359 **12. The relevant licensing authority** *Determination of relevant licensing authority for a premises is dependent upon the location of the whole, or greater part of the premises.*

7.7360 **13. Authorised persons and responsible authorities** (1) In this Part in relation to any premises each of the following expressions has the meaning given to it by this section—
"authorised person",
"responsible authority".

(2) "Authorised person" means any of the following—

(*a*) an officer of a licensing authority in whose area the premises are situated who is authorised by that authority for the purposes of this Act,

(*b*) an inspector appointed by the fire and rescue authority for the area in which the premises are situated,

(*c*) an inspector appointed under section 19 of the Health and Safety at Work etc Act 1974 (c 37),

(*d*) an officer of a local authority, in whose area the premises are situated, who is authorised by that authority for the purposes of exercising one or more of its statutory functions in relation to minimising or preventing the risk of pollution of the environment or of harm to human health,

(*e*) in relation to a vessel, an inspector, or a surveyor of ships, appointed under section 256 of the Merchant Shipping Act 1995 (c 21),

(*f*) a person prescribed for the purposes of this subsection.

(3) *Repealed.*

(4) "Responsible authority" means any of the following—

(*za*) the relevant licensing authority and any other licensing authority in whose area part of the premises is situated,

(*a*) the chief officer of police for any police area in which the premises are situated,

(*b*) the fire and rescue authority for any area in which the premises are situated,

(*ba*) the Primary Care Trust or Local Health Board for any area in which the premises are situated,

(*c*) the enforcing authority within the meaning given by section 18 of the Health and Safety at Work etc Act 1974 for any area in which the premises are situated,

(*d*) the local planning authority within the meaning given by the Town and Country Planning Act 1990 (c 8) for any area in which the premises are situated,

(*e*) the local authority by which statutory functions are exercisable in any area in which the premises are situated in relation to minimising or preventing the risk of pollution of the environment or of harm to human health,

(*f*) a body which—
 (i) represents those who, in relation to any such area, are responsible for, or interested in, matters relating to the protection of children from harm, and
 (ii) is recognised by the licensing authority for that area for the purposes of this section as being competent to advise it on such matters,

(*g*) *repealed*

(*h*) in relation to a vessel—
 (i) a navigation authority (within the meaning of section 221(1) of the Water Resources Act 1991 (c 57) having functions in relation to the waters where the vessel is usually moored or berthed or any waters where it is, or is proposed to be, navigated at a time when it is used for licensable activities,
 (ii) the Environment Agency,
 (iii) the British Waterways Board, or
 (iv) the Secretary of State,

(*ha*) where the premises (not being a vessel) are being, or are proposed to be, used for a licensable activity within section 1(1)(a) or (d), the Secretary of State,

(*i*) a person prescribed[1] for the purposes of this subsection.

(5) For the purposes of this section, "statutory function" means a function conferred by or under any enactment.

[Licensing Act 2003, s 13 as amended by the Fire and Rescue Services Act 2004, Sch 1, SI 2005/1541, the Policing and Crime Act 2009, s 33, the Police Reform and Social Responsibility Act 2011, ss 103–105 and the Immigration Act 2016, Sch 4.]

[1] See the Licensing Act 2003 (Premises Licences and Club Premises Certificates) Regulations 2005, SI 2005/42 amended by SI 2007/2502, SI 2009/1809,3159, SI 2010/2851, SI 2012/955 and 2290 and SI 2013/432.

7.7361 **14. Meaning of "supply of alcohol"** For the purposes of this Part the "supply of alcohol" means—

(*a*) the sale by retail of alcohol, or

(*b*) the supply of alcohol by or on behalf of a club to, or to the order of, a member of the club.

[Licensing Act 2003, s 14.]

7.7362 **15. Meaning of "designated premises supervisor"** (1) In this Act references to the "designated premises supervisor", in relation to a premises licence, are to the individual for the time being specified in that licence as the premises supervisor.

(2) Nothing in this Act prevents an individual who holds a premises licence from also being specified in the licence as the premises supervisor.

[Licensing Act 2003, s 15.]

*Grant of premises licence*

7.7363 **16. Applicant for premises licence** *Prescribes persons or bodies who can apply for a premises licence. Residual power to Secretary of State to prescribe persons of other descriptions who can also apply (as amended by the Immigration Act 2016, Sch 4)*

7.7364 **17. Application for premises licence** *Application to be in the prescribed form and accompanied by an Operating Schedule; application to be advertised in accordance with regulations.* [1]

---

1 See the Licensing Act 2003 (Premises Licences and Club Premises Certificates) Regulations 2005, SI 2005/42 (for amending instruments, see note to s 13, ante) and the Welsh Language (Gambling and Licensing Forms) Regulations 2010, SI 2010/2440 have been made. Where it is alleged that there has been non-compliance with the procedural requirements in the LA 2003 or the 2005 Regulations, the general modern approach to the consequences of such non-compliance is a purposive one as in *R v Immigration Appeal Tribunal, ex p Jeyeanthan; Ravichandran v Secretary of State for the Home Department* [1999] 3 All ER 231, [2000] 1 WLR 354, [1999] All ER (D) 519, CA. This requires analysis of the statutory intent of the legislation taken as a whole. The questions to be posed and answered are: (1) whether there has been substantial compliance with the requirements, although not strict compliance; (2) whether non-compliance is capable of being waived, and if so, whether it is; (3) if non-compliance is not capable of being waived or is not been waived what are the consequences of non-compliance: *R (on the application of Akin) v Stratford Magistrates Court* [2014] EWHC 4633 (Admin), [2015] 1 WLR 4829 (The advertised notice set out the fact that there was to be a review by the licensing sub-committee; the grounds of review could be read and the period for which representations could be made, the licensing objectives on which representations had to be based, and the penal notice. Review not invalidated where the advertised notice stated the grounds could be read and the court held that there was substantial compliance, that the failure to comply strictly had not and could not be waived, but that the failure did not invalidate the sub-committee's decision because the purpose of the legislation was to give local people an opportunity to know what is going on and to be heard if they wished.)

7.7365 **18. Determination of application for premises licence**[1] (1) This section applies where the relevant licensing authority—

(*a*) receives an application for a premises licence made in accordance with section 17, and

(*b*) is satisfied that the applicant has complied with any requirement imposed on him under subsection (5) of that section.

(2) Subject to subsection (3), the authority must grant the licence in accordance with the application subject only to—

(*a*) such conditions[2] as are consistent with the operating schedule accompanying the application, and

(*b*) any conditions which must under section 19, 20 or 21 be included in the licence.

(3) Where relevant representations are made, the authority must—

(*a*) hold a hearing to consider them, unless the authority, the applicant and each person who has made such representations agree that a hearing is unnecessary, and

(*b*) having regard to the representations, take such of the steps mentioned in subsection (4) (if any) as it considers appropriate for the promotion of the licensing objectives.

(4) The steps are—

(*a*) to grant the licence subject to—

(i) the conditions mentioned in subsection (2)(*a*) modified to such extent as the authority considers appropriate for the promotion of the licensing objectives, and

(ii) any condition which must under section 19, 20 or 21 be included in the licence;

(*b*) to exclude from the scope of the licence any of the licensable activities to which the application relates;

(*c*) to refuse to specify a person in the licence as the premises supervisor;

(*d*) to reject the application.

(5) For the purposes of subsection (4)(*a*)(i) the conditions mentioned in subsection (2)(*a*) are modified if any of them is altered or omitted or any new condition is added.

(6) For the purposes of this section, "relevant representations" means representations which—

(*a*) are about the likely effect of the grant of the premises licence on the promotion of the licensing objectives,

(*b*) meet the requirements of subsection (7),

(*c*) if they relate to the identity of the person named in the application as the proposed premises supervisor, meet the requirements of subsection (9), and

(*d*) are not excluded representations by virtue of section 32 (restriction on making representations following issue of provisional statement).

(7) The requirements of this subsection are—

(*a*) that the representations were made by a responsible authority or other person within the period prescribed under section 17(5)(*c*),

(*b*) that they have not been withdrawn, and

(*c*) in the case of representations made by a person who is not a responsible authority, that they are not, in the opinion of the relevant licensing authority, frivolous or vexatious.

(8) Where the authority determines for the purposes of subsection (7)(*c*) that any representations are frivolous or vexatious, it must notify the person who made them of the reasons for its determination.

(9) The requirements of this subsection are that the representations—

(*a*) were made by a chief officer of police for a police area in which the premises are situated, and

(*b*) include a statement that, due to the exceptional circumstances of the case, he is satisfied that the designation of the person concerned as the premises supervisor under the premises licence would undermine the crime prevention objective.

(10) In discharging its duty under subsection (2) or (3)(*b*), a licensing authority may grant a licence under this section subject to different conditions in respect of—

(*a*) different parts of the premises concerned;

(*b*) different licensable activities.

[Licensing Act 2003, s 18 as amended by the Police Reform and Social Responsibility Act 2011, ss 105, 109.]

---

[1] For appeal to a magistrates' court against a decision of a licensing authority under this section, see s 181 and Sch 5, post.

[2] Where a court is considering imposing conditions it will almost always be good practice for the conditions under consideration to be outlined for debate by the parties. Errors of drafting can then be identified, as can improvements and consideration of the underlying propositions behind the conditions themselves: *R (Westminster City Council) v Metropolitan Stipendiary Magistrate* [2008] EWHC 1202 (Admin), 172 JP 462.

**7.7366 19. Mandatory conditions where licence authorises supply of alcohol** (1) Where a premises licence authorises the supply of alcohol, the licence must include the following conditions.

(2) The first condition is that no supply of alcohol may be made under the premises licence—

(*a*) at a time when there is no designated premises supervisor in respect of the premises licence, or

(*b*) at a time when the designated premises supervisor does not hold a personal licence or his personal licence is suspended.

(3) The second condition is that every supply of alcohol under the premises licence must be made or authorised by a person who holds a personal licence.

(4) The other conditions are any conditions specified in an order under section 19A and applicable to the premises licence.

[Licensing Act 2003, s 19 as amended by the Policing and Crime Act 2009, Sch 4.]

**7.7367 19A. Power of Secretary of State to impose section 19(4) mandatory conditions**

(1) The Secretary of State may by order[1] specify conditions relating to the supply of alcohol and applicable to all relevant premises licences or relevant premises licences of a particular description if the Secretary of State considers it appropriate to do so for the promotion of the licensing objectives.

(2) The number of conditions in force by virtue of subsection (1) in relation to all relevant premises licences and the number of conditions in force by virtue of that subsection in relation to relevant premises licences of particular descriptions must not (when added together) exceed at any time nine.

(3) An order under subsection (1) may—

(*a*) relate to existing or future relevant premises licences,

(*b*) specify conditions which involve, or consist of, the exercise of a discretion by any person.

(4) Any conditions specified by an order under subsection (1) in relation to existing relevant premises licences are to be treated as—

(*a*) included in those licences from the coming into force of the order, and

(*b*) overriding any conditions already included in those licences ("the existing conditions") so far as they are—

(i) identical to the existing conditions, or

(ii) inconsistent with, and more onerous than, the existing conditions.

(5) Any conditions included, or treated as included, in relevant premises licences by virtue of section 19(4) and this section cease to have effect so far as they cease to be specified under this section in relation to those licences.

(6) Any conditions treated as mentioned in subsection (4)(*b*) cease to be so treated so far as they cease to be specified under this section in relation to the relevant premises licences concerned.

(7) So far as conditions cease to be treated as mentioned in subsection (4)(*b*), the existing conditions revive.

(8) Subsections (5) to (7) are subject to any alternative transitional or saving provision made by the order revoking the specification.

(9) In this section—

"existing relevant premises licence", in relation to an order, means a relevant premises licence granted before the coming into force of the order and in effect, or capable of having effect, on its coming into force,

"future relevant premises licence", in relation to an order, means a relevant premises licence granted on or after the coming into force of the order, "relevant premises licence" means a premises licence authorising the supply of alcohol.

[Licensing Act 2003, s 19A as inserted by the Policing and Crime Act 2009, Sch 4.]

1 The Licensing Act 2003 (Mandatory Licensing Conditions) Orders 2010, SI 2010/860 and 2014/1252 have been made, in this title, post.

7.7368 **20. Mandatory condition: exhibition of films** (1) Where a premises licence authorises the exhibition of films, the licence must include a condition requiring the admission of children to the exhibition of any film to be restricted in accordance with this section.

(2) Where the film classification body is specified in the licence, unless subsection (3)(*b*) applies, admission of children must be restricted in accordance with any recommendation made by that body.

(3) Where—

(*a*) the film classification body is not specified in the licence, or

(*b*) the relevant licensing authority has notified the holder of the licence that this subsection applies to the film in question,

admission of children must be restricted in accordance with any recommendation made by that licensing authority.

(4) In this section—

"children" means persons aged under 18; and

"film classification body" means the person or persons designated as the authority under section 4 of the Video Recordings Act 1984 (c 39) (authority to determine suitability of video works for classification).

[Licensing Act 2003, s 20.]

7.7369 **21. Mandatory condition: door supervision** (1) Where a premises licence includes a condition that at specified times one or more individuals must be at the premises to carry out a security activity, the licence must include a condition that each such individual must—

(*a*) be authorised to carry out that activity by a licence granted under the Private Security Industry Act 2001; or

(*b*) be entitled to carry out that activity by virtue of section 4 of that Act.

(2) But nothing in subsection (1) requires such a condition to be imposed—

(*a*) in respect of premises within paragraph 8(3)(*a*) of Schedule 2 to the Private Security Industry Act 2001 (c 12)[1] (premises with premises licences authorising plays or films), or

(*b*) in respect of premises in relation to—

(i) any occasion mentioned in paragraph 8(3)(*b*) or (*c*) of that Schedule (premises being used exclusively by club with club premises certificate, under a temporary event notice authorising plays or films or under a gaming licence), or

(ii) any occasion within paragraph 8(3)(*d*) of that Schedule (occasions prescribed by regulations under that Act).

(3) For the purposes of this section—

(*a*) "security activity" means an activity to which paragraph 2(1)(*a*) of that Schedule applies and which is licensable conduct for the purposes of that Act (see section 3(2) of that Act), and

(*b*) paragraph 8(5) of that Schedule (interpretation of references to an occasion) applies as it applies in relation to paragraph 8 of that Schedule.

[Licensing Act 2003, s 21 as amended by the Violent Crime Reduction Act 2006, s 25.]

1 In this PART, title, INDUSTRY AND COMMERCE, post.

7.7370 **22. Prohibited conditions: plays** (1) In relation to a premises licence which authorises the performance of plays, no condition may be attached to the licence as to the nature of the plays which may be performed, or the manner of performing plays, under the licence.

(2) But subsection (1) does not prevent a licensing authority imposing, in accordance with section 18(2)(*a*) or (3)(*b*), 35(3)(*b*) or 52(3), any condition which it considers appropriate on the grounds of public safety.

[Licensing Act 2003, s 22 as amended by the Police Reform and Social Responsibility Act 2011, s 109.]

7.7371 **23. Grant or rejection of application** (1) Where an application is granted under section 18, the relevant licensing authority must forthwith—

(*a*) give a notice to that effect to—

(i) the applicant,

(ii) any person who made relevant representations in respect of the application, and

(iii) the chief officer of police for the police area (or each police area) in which the premises are situated, and

(*b*) issue the applicant with the licence and a summary of it.

(2) Where relevant representations were made in respect of the application, the notice under subsection (1)(*a*) must state the authority's reasons for its decision as to the steps (if any) to take under section 18(3)(*b*).

(3) Where an application is rejected under section 18, the relevant licensing authority must forthwith give a notice to that effect, stating its reasons for the decision, to—

(*a*) the applicant,
(*b*) any person who made relevant representations in respect of the application, and
(*c*) the chief officer of police for the police area (or each police area) in which the premises are situated.

(4) In this section "relevant representations" has the meaning given in section 18(6).
[Licensing Act 2003, s 23.]

7.7372 **24. Form of licence and summary** *Licence and summary of it to be in prescribed form*[1].

[1] See the Licensing Act 2003 (Premises Licences and Club Premises Certificates) Regulations 2005, SI 2005/42 (for amending instruments, see note to s 13, ante) and the Welsh Language (Gambling and Licensing Forms) Regulations 2010, SI 2010/2440 have been made.

7.7373 **25. Theft, loss, etc of premises licence or summary** *Power to apply for duplicate licence or summary on payment of fee.*

7.7374 **25A. Grant of premises licence: supply of alcohol from community premises** (1) Where a management committee of community premises makes an application under section 17 for a premises licence authorising the supply of alcohol, the application may include an application for the alternative licence condition to be included in the licence instead of the conditions in section 19(2) and (3).

(2) In this section "the alternative licence condition" is the condition that every supply of alcohol under the premises licence must be made or authorised by the management committee.

(3) In a case where an application under section 17 includes an application under subsection (1), sections 17 to 19 are modified as follows.

(4) Section 17 has effect as if subsections (3)(*c*) and (4)(*e*) were omitted.

(5) Section 18 has effect as if—

(*a*) subsection (4)(*c*) were omitted;
(*b*) in subsection (6)(*c*), the reference to the identity of the person named in the application as the proposed premises supervisor were to the inclusion of the alternative licence condition;
(*c*) in subsection (9)(*b*), the reference to the designation of the person concerned as the premises supervisor under the premises licence were to the inclusion of the alternative licence condition.

(6) Section 19 has effect as if at the end there were inserted—

"(5) But where—

(*a*) the relevant licensing authority is satisfied that the arrangements for the management of the premises by the applicant are sufficient to ensure adequate supervision of the supply of alcohol on the premises, and
(*b*) if any representations are made pursuant to section 18(6)(*c*), the authority does not consider the inclusion of the conditions in subsections (2) and (3) to be appropriate to promote the crime prevention objective,

the licence must not include the conditions in subsections (2) and (3) but must include the alternative licence condition referred to in section 25A(2) instead."

[Licensing Act 2003, s 25A as inserted by SI 2009/1724 and amended by the Policing and Crime Act 2009, Sch 7 and the Police Reform and Social Responsibility Act 2011, s 109.]

*Duration of licence*

7.7375 **26. Period of validity of premises licence** *Premises licence to have effect until revoked, lapses, is surrendered, or is for a limited period and comes to an end. Licence of no effect if suspended following a review under s 52.*

7.7376 **27. Death, incapacity, insolvency etc of licence holder** (1) A premises licence lapses if the holder of the licence—

(*a*) dies,
(*b*) becomes a person who lacks capacity (within the meaning of the Mental Capacity Act 2005) to hold the licence,
(*c*) becomes insolvent,
(*d*) is dissolved, or
(*e*) if it is a club, ceases to be a recognised club.

(1A) A premises licence that authorises premises to be used for a licensable activity within section 1(1)(a) or (d) also lapses if the holder of the licence ceases to be entitled to work in the United Kingdom at a time when the holder of the licence is resident in the United Kingdom (or becomes so resident without being entitled to work in the United Kingdom).

(2) This section is subject to sections 47 and 50 (which make provision for the reinstatement of the licence in certain circumstances).

(3) For the purposes of this section, an individual becomes insolvent on—

(*a*) the approval of a voluntary arrangement proposed by him,
(*b*) being adjudged bankrupt or having his estate sequestrated, or
(*c*) entering into a trust deed for his creditors.

(4) For the purposes of this section, a company becomes insolvent on—

(*a*) the approval of a voluntary arrangement proposed by its directors,
(*b*) the appointment of an administrator in respect of the company,
(*c*) the appointment of an administrative receiver in respect of the company, or
(*d*) going into liquidation.

(5) An expression used in this section and in the Insolvency Act 1986 (c 45) has the same meaning in this section as in that Act.

[Licensing Act 2003, s 27 as amended by the Mental Capacity Act 2005, Sch 6, the Deregulation Act 2015, Sch 6 and the Immigration Act 2016, Sch 4.]

7.7377 **28. Surrender of premises licence** *Premises licence holder may surrender licence by giving notice to licensing authority. Licence lapses on receipt of notice.*

*Provisional statement*

7.7378 **29, 30.** *Application for provisional statement to be in the prescribed form and accompanied by a Schedule of Works*[1].

---

1 The Licensing Act 2003 (Premises Licences and Club Premises Certificates) Regulations 2005, SI 2005/42 (for amending instruments, see note to s 13, ante) and the Welsh Language (Gambling and Licensing Forms) Regulations 2010, SI 2010/2440 have been made. Application to be advertised in accordance with Regulations.

7.7379 **31. Determination of application for provisional statement**[1] (1) This section applies where the relevant licensing authority—

(*a*) receives a provisional statement application, and
(*b*) is satisfied that the applicant has complied with any requirement imposed on him by virtue of section 30.

(2) Where no relevant representations are made, the authority must issue the applicant with a statement to that effect.

(3) Where relevant representations are made, the authority must—

(*a*) hold a hearing to consider them, unless the authority, the applicant and each person who has made such representations agree that a hearing is unnecessary,
(*b*) determine whether, on the basis of those representations and the provisional statement application, it would consider it appropriate to take any steps under section 18(3)(*b*) if, on the work being satisfactorily completed, it had to decide whether to grant a premises licence in the form described in the provisional statement application, and
(*c*) issue the applicant with a statement which—
 (i) gives details of that determination, and
 (ii) states the authority's reasons for its decision as to the steps (if any) that it would be appropriate to take under section 18(3)(*b*).

(4) The licensing authority must give a copy of the provisional statement to—

(*a*) each person who made relevant representations, and
(*b*) the chief officer of police for each police area in which the premises are situated.

(5) In this section "relevant representations" means representations—

(*a*) which are about the likely effect on the licensing objectives of the grant of a premises licence in the form described in the provisional statement application, if the work at the premises was satisfactorily completed, and
(*b*) which meet the requirements of subsection (6).

(6) The requirements are—

(*a*) that the representations are made by a responsible authority or other person within the period prescribed under section 17(5)(*c*) by virtue of section 30,
(*b*) that the representations have not been withdrawn, and
(*c*) in the case of representations made by a person who is not a responsible authority, that they are not, in the opinion of the relevant licensing authority, frivolous or vexatious.

(7) Where the authority determines for the purposes of subsection (6)(*c*) that any representations are frivolous or vexatious, it must notify the person who made them of the reasons for its determination.

(8) In this section "provisional statement application" means an application made in accordance with section 29.

[Licensing Act 2003, s 31 as amended by the Police Reform and Social Responsibility Act 2011, ss 105, 109.]

---

1 For appeal to a magistrates' court against a decision of a licensing authority under this section, see s 181 and Sch 5, post.

7.7380 **32. Restriction on representations following provisional statement** (1) This section applies where a provisional statement has been issued in respect of any premises ("the relevant premises") and a person subsequently applies for a premises licence in respect of—

(*a*) the relevant premises or a part of them, or
(*b*) premises that are substantially the same as the relevant premises or a part of them.

(2) Where—

(*a*) the application for the premises licence is an application for a licence in the same form as the licence described in the application for the provisional statement, and (*b*) the work described in the schedule of works accompanying the application for that statement has been satisfactorily completed,

representations made by a person ("the relevant person") in respect of the application for the premises licence are excluded representations for the purposes of section 18(6)(*d*) if subsection (3) applies.

(3) This subsection applies if—

(*a*) given the information provided in the application for the provisional statement, the relevant person could have made the same, or substantially the same, representations about that application but failed to do so, without reasonable excuse, and

(*b*) there has been no material change in circumstances relating either to the relevant premises or to the area in the vicinity of those premises since the provisional statement was made.

[Licensing Act 2003, s 32.]

*Duty to notify certain changes*

7.7381 **33. Notification of change of name or address** (1) The holder of a premises licence must, as soon as is reasonably practicable, notify the relevant licensing authority of any change in—

(*a*) his name or address,

(*b*) unless the designated premises supervisor has already notified the authority under subsection (4), the name or address of that supervisor.

(2) Subsection (1) is subject to regulations under section 55(1) (fee to accompany application).

(3) A notice under subsection (1) must also be accompanied by the premises licence (or the appropriate part of the licence) or, if that is not practicable, by a statement of the reasons for the failure to produce the licence (or part).

(4) Where the designated premises supervisor under a premises licence is not the holder of the licence, he may notify the relevant licensing authority under this subsection of any change in his name or address.

(5) Where the designated premises supervisor gives a notice under subsection (4), he must, as soon as is reasonably practicable, give the holder of the premises licence a copy of that notice.

(6) A person commits an offence if he fails, without reasonable excuse, to comply with this section.

(7) A person guilty of an offence under subsection (6) is liable on summary conviction to a fine not exceeding level 2 on the standard scale.

[Licensing Act 2003, s 33.]

*Variation of licences*

7.7382 **34. Application to vary premises licence** *Application for variation of premises licence to be in the prescribed form and advertised in accordance with regulations*[1].

1 See the Licensing Act 2003 (Premises Licences and Club Premises Certificates) Regulations 2005, SI 2005/42 (for amending instruments, see note to s 13, ante) and the Welsh Language (Gambling and Licensing Forms) Regulations 2010, SI 2010/2440.

7.7383 **35. Determination of application under section 34**[1] (1) This section applies where the relevant licensing authority—

(*a*) receives an application, made in accordance with section 34, to vary a premises licence, and

(*b*) is satisfied that the applicant has complied with any requirement imposed on him by virtue of subsection (5) of that section.

(2) Subject to subsection (3) and section 36(6), the authority must grant the application.

(3) Where relevant representations are made, the authority must—

(*a*) hold a hearing to consider them, unless the authority, the applicant and each person who has made such representations agree that a hearing is unnecessary, and

(*b*) having regard to the representations, take such of the steps mentioned in subsection (4) (if any) as it considers appropriate for the promotion of the licensing objectives.

(4) The steps are—

(*a*) to modify the conditions of the licence;

(*b*) to reject the whole or part of the application;

and for this purpose the conditions of the licence are modified if any of them is altered or omitted or any new condition is added.

(5) In this section "relevant representations" means representations which—

(*a*) are about the likely effect of the grant of the application on the promotion of the licensing objectives, and

(*b*) meet the requirements of subsection (6).

(6) The requirements are—

(*a*) that the representations are made by a responsible authority or other person within the period prescribed under section 17(5)(*c*) by virtue of section 34(5),

(*b*) that they have not been withdrawn, and

(*c*) in the case of representations made by a person who is not a responsible authority, that they are not, in the opinion of the relevant licensing authority, frivolous or vexatious.

(7) Subsections (2) and (3) are subject to sections 19 to 21 (which require certain conditions to be included in premises licences).[2]

[Licensing Act 2003, s 35 as amended by the Policing and Crime Act 2009, Sch 7 and the Police Reform and Social Responsibility Act 2011, ss 105, 109.]

[1] For appeal to a magistrates' court against a decision of a licensing authority under this section, see s 181 and Sch 5, post.

[2] There is no mechanism for amending an application. If representations are made, that triggers the decision-making process of the licensing authority. The authority exercises an administrative function within restrictions imposed by the legislation: an application to vary never triggers a general review of the licence. Where a licensee wishes to modify his application in the light of representations received, whilst not amounting to a formal amendment of the application, the authority is bound to take account of the views of the licensee in exercising its discretion and it is not required to consult local residents and other interested parties in the form of re-advertisement: *Taylor v Manchester City Council* [2012] EWHC 3467 (Admin), [2013] 2 All ER 490, 177 JP 1.

7.7384 **36. Supplementary provision about determinations under section 35** (1) Where an application (or any part of an application) is granted under section 35, the relevant licensing authority must forthwith give a notice to that effect to—

(*a*) the applicant,

(*b*) any person who made relevant representations in respect of the application, and

(*c*) the chief officer of police for the police area (or each police area) in which the premises are situated.

(2) Where relevant representations were made in respect of the application, the notice under subsection (1) must state the authority's reasons for its decision as to the steps (if any) to take under section 35(3)(*b*).

(3) The notice under subsection (1) must specify the time when the variation in question takes effect.

That time is the time specified in the application or, if that time is before the applicant is given that notice, such later time as the relevant licensing authority specifies in the notice.

(4) Where an application (or any part of an application) is rejected under section 35, the relevant licensing authority must forthwith give a notice to that effect stating its reasons for rejecting the application to—

(*a*) the applicant,

(*b*) any person who made relevant representations in respect of the application, and

(*c*) the chief officer of police for the police area (or each police area) in which the premises are situated.

(5) Where the relevant licensing authority determines for the purposes of section 35(6)(*c*) that any representations are frivolous or vexatious, it must notify the person who made them of the reasons for that determination.

(6) A licence may not be varied under section 35 so as—

(*a*) to extend the period for which the licence has effect, or

(*b*) to vary substantially the premises to which it relates.

(7) In discharging its duty under subsection (2) or (3)(*b*) of that section, a licensing authority may vary a premises licence so that it has effect subject to different conditions in respect of—

(*a*) different parts of the premises concerned;

(*b*) different licensable activities.

(8) In this section "relevant representations" has the meaning given in section 35(5).

[Licensing Act 2003, s 36.]

7.7385 **37. Application to vary licence to specify individual as premises supervisor** (1)–(4B) *Application for variation of premises licence to specify individual as premises supervisor to be in the prescribed form and in accordance with regulations*[1].

(5) Where a chief officer of police notified under subsection (4) is satisfied that the exceptional circumstances of the case are such that granting the application would undermine the crime prevention objective, he must give the relevant licensing authority a notice stating the reasons why he is so satisfied.

(6) The chief officer of police must give that notice within the period of 14 days beginning with the day on which he is notified of the application under subsection (4).

[Licensing Act 2003, s 37 as amended by SI 2009/2999.]

[1] See the Licensing Act 2003 (Premises Licences and Club Premises Certificates) Regulations 2005, SI 2005/42 (for amending instruments, see note to s 13, ante) and the Welsh Language (Gambling and Licensing Forms) Regulations 2010, SI 2010/2440.

7.7386 **38. Circumstances in which section 37 application given interim effect** *Section 37 application to have interim effect if requested.*

7.7387 **39. Determination of section 37 application**[1] (1) This section applies where an application is made, in accordance with section 37, to vary a premises licence so as to specify a new premises supervisor ("the proposed individual").

(2) Subject to subsection (3), the relevant licensing authority must grant the application.

(3) Where a notice is given under section 37(5) (and not withdrawn), the authority must—

(*a*) hold a hearing to consider it, unless the authority, the applicant and the chief officer of police who gave the notice agree that a hearing is unnecessary, and

(*b*) having regard to the notice, reject the application if it considers it appropriate for the promotion of the crime prevention objective to do so.

(4) Where an application under section 37 is granted or rejected, the relevant licensing authority must give a notice to that effect to—

(*a*) the applicant,

(*b*) the proposed individual, and

(*c*) the chief officer of police for the police area (or each police area) in which the premises are situated.

(5) Where a chief officer of police gave a notice under subsection (5) of that section (and it was not withdrawn), the notice under subsection (4) of this section must state the authority's reasons for granting or rejecting the application.

(6) Where the application is granted, the notice under subsection (4) must specify the time when the variation takes effect.

That time is the time specified in the application or, if that time is before the applicant is given that notice, such later time as the relevant licensing authority specifies in the notice.

[Licensing Act 2003, s 39 as amended by the Police Reform and Social Responsibility Act 2011, s 109.]

---

[1] For appeal to a magistrates' court against a decision of a licensing authority under this section, see s 181 and Sch 5, post.

7.7388 **40. Duty of applicant following determination under section 39** (1) Where the holder of a premises licence is notified under section 39(4), he must forthwith—

(*a*) if his application has been granted, notify the person (if any) who has been replaced as the designated premises supervisor of the variation, and

(*b*) if his application has been rejected, give the designated premises supervisor (if any) notice to that effect.

(2) A person commits an offence if he fails, without reasonable excuse, to comply with subsection (1).

(3) A person guilty of an offence under subsection (2) is liable on summary conviction to a fine not exceeding level 3 on the standard scale.

[Licensing Act 2003, s 40.]

7.7389 **41. Request to be removed as designated premises supervisor** (1) Where an individual wishes to cease being the designated premises supervisor in respect of a premises licence, he may give the relevant licensing authority a notice to that effect.

(2) Subsection (1) is subject to regulations under section 54 (form etc of notices etc).

(3) Where the individual is the holder of the premises licence, the notice under subsection (1) must also be accompanied by the premises licence (or the appropriate part of the licence) or, if that is not practicable, by a statement of the reasons for the failure to provide the licence (or part).

(4) In any other case, the individual must no later than 48 hours after giving the notice under subsection (1) give the holder of the premises licence—

(*a*) a copy of that notice, and

(*b*) a notice directing the holder to send to the relevant licensing authority within 14 days of receiving the notice—

(i) the premises licence (or the appropriate part of the licence), or

(ii) if that is not practicable, a statement of the reasons for the failure to provide the licence (or part).

(5) A person commits an offence if he fails, without reasonable excuse, to comply with a direction given to him under subsection (4)(*b*).

(6) A person guilty of an offence under subsection (5) is liable on summary conviction to a fine not exceeding level 3 on the standard scale.

(7) Where an individual—

(*a*) gives the relevant licensing authority a notice in accordance with this section, and

(*b*) satisfies the requirements of subsection (3) or (4),

he is to be treated for the purposes of this Act as if, from the relevant time, he were not the designated premises supervisor.

(8) For this purpose "the relevant time" means—

(*a*) the time the notice under subsection (1) is received by the relevant licensing authority, or

(*b*) if later, the time specified in the notice.

[Licensing Act 2003, s 41.]

*Variation of licences: minor variations*

7.7390 **41A. Application for minor variation of premises licence]** (1) Subject to subsection (3), the holder of a premises licence may apply under this section (instead of under section 34) to the relevant licensing authority for variation of the licence.

(2) Subsection (1) is subject to regulations under—

(*a*) section 54 (form etc of applications etc);

(*b*) section 55 (fees to accompany applications etc).

(3) An application may not be made under this section to vary a premises licence so as to—

(*a*) extend the period for which it has effect,

(*b*) vary substantially the premises to which it relates,

(*c*) specify an individual as the premises supervisor,

(*d*) add the supply of alcohol as an activity authorised by the licence,

(*e*) authorise—

(i) the supply of alcohol at any time between 11pm and 7am, or

(ii) an increase in the amount of time on any day during which alcohol may be sold by retail or supplied, or

(*f*) include the alternative licence condition referred to in section 41D(3).

(4) The duty to make regulations imposed on the Secretary of State by subsection (5)(*a*) of section 17 (advertisement etc of application) applies in relation to applications under this section as it applies in relation to applications under that section.

[Licensing Act 2003, s 41A as inserted by SI 2009/1772.]

7.7391 **41B. Determination of application under section 41A** (1) This section applies where the relevant licensing authority receives an application made under section 41A.

(2) In determining the application the authority must—

(*a*) consult such of the responsible authorities as it considers appropriate, and

(*b*) take into account any relevant representations—

(i) made by those authorities, or

(ii) made by any other person and received by the authority within ten working days beginning on the initial day.

(3) If the authority considers that—

(*a*) the variation proposed in the application could not have an adverse effect on the promotion of any of the licensing objectives, or

(*b*) if more than one variation is proposed, none of them, whether considered separately or together could have such an effect,

it must grant the application.

(4) In any other case the authority must reject the application.

(5) A determination under this section must be made within the period of fifteen working days beginning on the initial day.

(6) If at the expiry of the period referred to in subsection (5) the authority has not determined the application—

(*a*) the application is rejected, and

(*b*) the authority must forthwith return the fee that accompanied the application.

(7) But nothing in subsection (6) prevents the authority, with the agreement of the applicant, from treating—

(*a*) an application rejected by virtue of that subsection ("the first application") as a new application made under section 41A,

(*b*) the prescribed fee that accompanied the first application as the prescribed fee accompanying a new application, or

(*c*) both.

(8) A new application of the kind referred to in subsection (7)(*a*) is to be treated as having been made on the date of the agreement referred to in that provision, or on such other date as is specified in the agreement.

(9) Any fee owed to an applicant under subsection (6) may be recovered as a debt due to the applicant.

(10) For the purposes of this section—

"initial day" in relation to an application means the first working day after the day on which the authority receives the application;

"relevant representations" in relation to an application means representations which are about the likely effect of the grant of the application on the promotion of the licensing objectives.

[Licensing Act 2003, s 41B as inserted by SI 2009/1772 and amended by the Police Reform and Social Responsibility Act 2011, s 105.]

7.7392 **41C. Supplementary provision about determinations under section 41B** (1) Where an application is granted under section 41B, the relevant licensing authority must forthwith give a notice to that effect to the applicant.

(2) The notice under subsection (1) must specify—

(*a*) any variation of the premises licence which is to have effect as a result of the grant of the application, and

(*b*) the time at which that variation takes effect.

(3) The time referred to in subsection (2)(*b*) is the time specified in the application or, if that time is before the applicant is given the notice referred to in subsection (2), such later time as the authority specifies in the notice.

(4) Where an application is rejected under section 41B, the relevant licensing authority must

forthwith give a notice to that effect to the applicant.

(5) The notice under subsection (4) must include a statement by the authority of the reasons for its decision.

[Licensing Act 2003, s 41C as inserted by SI 2009/1772.]

7.7393 **41D. Variation of premises licence: supply of alcohol from community premises**

(1) Where a management committee which holds a premises licence in respect of community premises makes an application under section 34 for variation of the licence so as to authorise the supply of alcohol, the application may include an application for the alternative licence condition to be included in the licence instead of the conditions in section 19(2) and (3).

(2) A management committee which holds a premises licence in respect of community premises which includes the conditions in section 19(2) and (3) may make an application under section 34 for (or which includes an application for) variation of the licence to include the alternative licence condition instead of those conditions.

(3) In this section "the alternative licence condition" is the condition that every supply of alcohol under the premises licence must be made or authorised by the management committee.

(4) In a case where an application under section 34 includes an application under subsection (1), or is made pursuant to subsection (2), section 19 (as it applies by virtue of section 35(7)) and section 35 are modified as follows.

(5) Section 19 has effect as if at the end there were inserted—

"(5) But where—

(*a*) the relevant licensing authority is satisfied that the arrangements for the management of the premises by the applicant are sufficient to ensure adequate supervision of the supply of alcohol on the premises, and

(*b*) if any representations are made pursuant to section 35(5)(aa), the authority does not consider the inclusion of the conditions in subsections (2) and (3) to be appropriate to promote the crime prevention objective,

the licence must not include the conditions in subsections (2) and (3) but must include the alternative licence condition referred to in section 41D(3) instead.".

(6) Section 35 has effect as if—

(*a*) after subsection (5)(*a*) there were inserted—

"(*aa*) if they relate to the inclusion of the alternative licence condition referred to in section 41D(3)—

(i) were made by the chief officer of police for a police area in which the premises are situated, and

(ii) include a statement that, due to the exceptional circumstances of the case, he is satisfied that including the alternative licence condition instead of the conditions in section 19(2) and (3) would undermine the crime prevention objective, and", and

(*b*) subsection (6)(*c*) were omitted.

[Licensing Act 2003, s 41D as inserted by SI 2009/1724 and amended by the Policing and Crime Act 2009. Sch 7 and the Police Reform and Social Responsibility Act 2011, ss 105, 109.]

*Transfer of premises licence*

7.7394 **42. Application for transfer of premises licence** (1)–(4) *Application for transfer of premises licence to be in prescribed form and in accordance with regulations*[1].

(5) The relevant person must give notice of the application to the chief officer of police for the police area (or each police area) in which the premises are situated.

(5ZA) Where the premises licence authorises premises to be used for a licensable activity within section 1(1)(a) or (d), the relevant person must also give notice of the application to the Secretary of State.

(5A) In subsections (5) and (5ZA), "relevant person" means—

(*a*) the relevant licensing authority, in a case where the applicant submitted the application to the relevant licensing authority by means of a relevant electronic facility;

(*b*) the applicant, in any other case.

(6) Where a chief officer of police notified under subsection (5) is satisfied that the exceptional circumstances of the case are such that granting the application would undermine the crime prevention objective, he must give the relevant licensing authority a notice stating the reasons why he is so satisfied.

(7) The chief officer of police must give that notice within the period of 14 days beginning with the day on which he is notified of the application under subsection (5).

(8) Where the Secretary of State is given notice under subsection (5ZA) and is satisfied that the exceptional circumstances of the case are such that granting the application would be prejudicial to the prevention of illegal working in licensed premises, the Secretary of State must give the relevant licensing authority a notice stating the reasons for being so satisfied.

(9) The Secretary of State must give that notice within the period of 14 days beginning with the day on which the Secretary of State is notified of the application under subsection (5ZA).

[Licensing Act 2003, s 42 as amended by SI 2009/2999 and the Immigration Act 2016, Sch 4.]

[1] See the Licensing Act 2003 (Premises Licences and Club Premises Certificates) Regulations 2005, SI 2005/42 (for amending instruments, see note to s 13, ante) and the Welsh Language (Gambling and Licensing Forms) Regulations 2010, SI 2010/2440.

7.7395 **43. Circumstances in which transfer application given interim effect** *Transfer application given interim effect if requested and with consent of existing premises licence holder (unless exempted from that requirement by licensing authority).*

7.7396 **44. Determination of transfer application**[1] (1) This section applies where an application for the transfer of a licence is made in accordance with section 42.

(2) Subject to subsections (3) and (5), the authority must transfer the licence in accordance with the application.

(3) The authority must reject the application if none of the conditions in subsection (4) applies.

(4) The conditions are—

(*a*) that section 43(1) (applications given interim effect) applies to the application,

(*b*) that the holder of the premises licence consents to the transfer,

(*c*) that the applicant is exempted under subsection (6) from the requirement to obtain the holder's consent to the transfer.

(5) Where a notice is given under section 42(6) or (8) (and not withdrawn), and subsection (3) above does not apply, the authority must—

(*a*) hold a hearing to consider it, unless the authority, the applicant and the person who gave the notice agree that a hearing is unnecessary, and

(*b*) having regard to the notice—

(i) where the notice is given under section 42(6), reject the application if it considers it appropriate for the promotion of the crime prevention objective to do so, or

(ii) where the notice is given under section 42(8), reject the application if it considers it appropriate for the prevention of illegal working in licensed premises to do so.

(6) The relevant licensing authority must exempt the applicant from the requirement to obtain the holder's consent if the applicant shows to the authority's satisfaction—

(*a*) that he has taken all reasonable steps to obtain that consent, and

(*b*) that, if the application were granted, he would be in a position to use the premises for the licensable activity or activities authorised by the premises licence.

(7) Where the relevant licensing authority refuses to exempt an applicant under subsection (6), it must notify the applicant of its reasons for that decision.

[Licensing Act 2003, s 44 as amended by the Police Reform and Social Responsibility Act 2011, s 109 and the Immigration Act 2016, Sch 4.]

[1] For appeal to a magistrates' court against a decision of a licensing authority under this section, see s 181 and Sch 5, post.

7.7397 **45. Notification of determination under section 44** (1) Where an application under section 42 is granted or rejected, the relevant licensing authority must give a notice to that effect to—

(*a*) the applicant, and

(*b*) the chief officer of police for the police area (or each police area) in which the premises are situated.

(2) Where a chief officer of police gave a notice under subsection (6) of that section or the Secretary of State gave a notice under subsection (8) of that section (which, in either case, was not withdrawn), the notice under subsection (1) of this section must state the licensing authority's reasons for granting or rejecting the application.

(2A) Where the Secretary of State gave a notice under subsection (8) of section 42 (which was not withdrawn), the notice under subsection (1) of this section must also be given to the Secretary of State.

(3) Where the application is granted, the notice under subsection (1) must specify the time when the transfer takes effect.

That time is the time specified in the application or, if that time is before the applicant is given that notice, such later time as the relevant licensing authority specifies in the notice.

(4) The relevant licensing authority must also give a copy of the notice given under subsection (1)—

(*a*) where the application is granted—

(i) to the holder of the licence immediately before the application was granted, or

(ii) if the application was one to which section 43(1) applied, to the holder of the licence immediately before the application was made (if any),

(*b*) where the application is rejected, to the holder of the premises licence (if any).

[Licensing Act 2003, s 45 as amended by the Immigration Act 2016, Sch 4.]

7.7398 **46. Duty to notify designated premises supervisor of transfer** (1) This section applies where—

(*a*) an application is made in accordance with section 42 to transfer a premises licence in respect of which there is a designated premises supervisor, and

(*b*) the applicant and that supervisor are not the same person.

(2) Where section 43(1) applies in relation to the application, the applicant must forthwith notify the designated premises supervisor of the application.

(3) If the application is granted, the applicant must forthwith notify the designated premises supervisor of the transfer.

(4) A person commits an offence if he fails, without reasonable excuse, to comply with this section.

(5) A person guilty of an offence under subsection (4) is liable on summary conviction to a fine not exceeding level 3 on the standard scale.

[Licensing Act 2003, s 46.]

*Interim authority notices*

7.7399 **47. Interim authority notice following death etc of licence holder** *(As amended by the Immigration Act 2016, Sch 4)* Power for a person with a prescribed interest to serve an interim authority notice on licensing authority within 7 days of a licence having lapsed because of death, incapacity or insolvency of licence holder. Application to be in prescribed form and in accordance with regulations[1].

---

[1] See the Licensing Act 2003 (Premises Licences and Club Premises Certificates) Regulations 2005, SI 2005/42 (for amending instruments, see note to s 13, ante) and the Welsh Language (Gambling and Licensing Forms) Regulations 2010, SI 2010/2440.

7.7400 **48. Cancellation of interim authority notice following objections[1]**

(1) Subsection (2) applies where—

(*a*) an interim authority notice by a person ("the relevant person") is given in accordance with section 47,

(*b*) the chief officer of police for the police area (or each police area) in which the premises are situated is given a copy of the interim authority notice before the end of the initial 28 day period (within the meaning of that section), and

(*c*) that chief officer (or any of those chief officers) is satisfied that the exceptional circumstances of the case are such that a failure to cancel the interim authority notice would undermine the crime prevention objective.

(2) The chief officer of police must before the end of the second working day following the day on which he receives the copy of the interim authority notice give the relevant licensing authority a notice stating why he is so satisfied.

(2A) Subsection (2B) applies where—

(a) an interim authority notice by a person ("the relevant person") is given in accordance with section 47,

(b) the Secretary of State is given a copy of the interim authority notice before the end of the initial 28 day period (within the meaning of that section), and

(c) the Secretary of State is satisfied that the exceptional circumstances of the case are such that a failure to cancel the interim authority notice would be prejudicial to the prevention of illegal working in licensed premises.

(2B) The Secretary of State must before the end of the second working day following receipt of the copy of the interim authority notice give the relevant licensing authority a notice stating why the Secretary of State is so satisfied.

(3) Where a notice is given under subsection (2) or (2B) (and not withdrawn), the authority must—

(*a*) hold a hearing to consider it, unless the authority, the relevant person and the person who gave the notice agree that a hearing is unnecessary, and

(*b*) having regard to the notice—

(i) where the notice is given under subsection (2), cancel the interim authority notice if it considers it appropriate for the promotion of the crime prevention objective to do so, or

(ii) where the notice is given under subsection (2B), cancel the interim authority notice if it considers it appropriate for the prevention of illegal working in licensed premises to do so.

(4) An interim authority notice is cancelled under subsection (3)(*b*) by the licensing authority giving the relevant person a notice stating that it is cancelled and the authority's reasons for its decision.

(5) The licensing authority must give a copy of a notice under subsection (4) to the chief officer of police for the police area (or each police area) in which the premises are situated.

(5A) Where an interim authority notice is cancelled under subsection (3)(b)(ii), the licensing authority must also give a copy of the notice under subsection (4) to the Secretary of State.

(6) The premises licence lapses if, and when, a notice is given under subsection (4). This is subject to paragraph 7(5) of Schedule 5 (reinstatement of premises licence where appeal

made against cancellation of interim authority notice).

(7) The relevant licensing authority must not cancel an interim authority notice after a relevant transfer application (within the meaning of section 47) is made in respect of the premises licence.

[Licensing Act 2003, s 48 as amended by SI 2010/2452, the Police Reform and Social Responsibility Act 2011, s 109 and the Immigration Act 2016, Sch 4.]

---

1 For appeal to a magistrates' court against a decision of a licensing authority under this section, see s 181 and Sch 5, post.

7.7401 **49. Supplementary provision about interim authority notices** (1) On receipt of an interim authority notice, the relevant licensing authority must issue to the person who gave the notice a copy of the licence and a copy of the summary (in each case certified by the authority to be a true copy).

(2) The copies issued under this section must be copies of the premises licence and summary in the form in which they existed immediately before the licence lapsed under section 27, except that they must specify the person who gave the interim authority notice as the person who is the holder.

(3) This Act applies in relation to a copy issued under this section as it applies in relation to an original licence or summary.

(4) Where a person becomes the holder of a premises licence by virtue of section 47, he must (unless he is the designated premises supervisor under the licence) forthwith notify the supervisor (if any) of the interim authority notice.

(5) A person commits an offence if he fails, without reasonable excuse, to comply with subsection (4).

(6) A person guilty of an offence under subsection (5) is liable on summary conviction to a fine not exceeding level 3 on the standard scale.

[Licensing Act 2003, s 49.]

*Transfer following death etc of licence holder*

7.7402 **50. Reinstatement of licence on transfer following death etc of holder** *(As amended by the Immigration Act 2016, Sch 4) Power to any person who could apply for a premises licence under s 16(1) to apply for reinstatement of lapsed licence on transfer under s 42.*

*Review of licences*

7.7403 **51. Application for review of premises licence** (1) Where a premises licence has effect, a responsible authority or any other person may apply to the relevant licensing authority for a review of the licence.

(2) Subsection (1) is subject to regulations[1] under section 54 (form etc of applications etc).

(3) The Secretary of State must by regulations under this section—

*(a)* require the applicant to give a notice containing details of the application to the holder of the premises licence and each responsible authority within such period as may be prescribed;

*(b)* require the authority to advertise the application and invite representations about it to be made to the authority by responsible authorities and other persons;

*(c)* prescribe the period during which representations may be made by the holder of the premises licence, any other person;

*(d)* require any notice under paragraph *(a)* or advertisement under paragraph *(b)* to specify that period.

(4) The relevant licensing authority may, at any time, reject any ground for review specified in an application under this section if it is satisfied—

*(a)* that the ground is not relevant to one or more of the licensing objectives, or

*(b)* in the case of an application made by a person other than a responsible authority, that—

(i) the ground is frivolous or vexatious, or

(ii) the ground is a repetition.

(5) For this purpose a ground for review is a repetition if—

*(a)* it is identical or substantially similar to—

(i) a ground for review specified in an earlier application for review made in respect of the same premises licence and determined under section 52, or

(ii) representations considered by the relevant licensing authority in accordance with section 18, before it determined the application for the premises licence under that section, or

(iii) representations which would have been so considered but for the fact that they were excluded representations by virtue of section 32, and

*(b)* a reasonable interval has not elapsed since that earlier application for review or the grant of the licence (as the case may be).

(6) Where the authority rejects a ground for review under subsection (4)*(b)*, it must notify the applicant of its decision and, if the ground was rejected because it was frivolous or vexatious, the authority must notify him of its reasons for making that decision.

(7) The application is to be treated as rejected to the extent that any of the grounds for review

are rejected under subsection (4).

Accordingly the requirements imposed under subsection (3)(*a*) and (*b*) and by section 52 (so far as not already met) apply only to so much (if any) of the application as has not been rejected.

[Licensing Act 2003, s 51 as amended by the Police Reform and Social Responsibility Act 2011, s 106.]

---

1 See the Licensing Act 2003 (Premises Licences and Club Premises Certificates) Regulations 2005, SI 2005/42 (for amending instruments, see note to s 13, ante) and the Welsh Language (Gambling and Licensing Forms) Regulations 2010, SI 2010/2440. For effect of any failure to comply with procedural requirements, see note to s 17, ante.

7.7404 52. **Determination of application for review**[1] (1) This section applies where—

(*a*) the relevant licensing authority receives an application made in accordance with section 51,

(*b*) the applicant has complied with any requirement imposed on him under subsection (3)(*a*) or (*d*) of that section, and

(*c*) the authority has complied with any requirement imposed on it under subsection (3)(*b*) or (*d*) of that section.

(2) Before determining the application, the authority must hold a hearing to consider it and any relevant representations.

(3) The authority must, having regard to the application and any relevant representations, take such of the steps mentioned in subsection (4) (if any) as it considers appropriate for the promotion of the licensing objectives.

(4) The steps are—

(*a*) to modify the conditions of the licence;

(*b*) to exclude a licensable activity from the scope of the licence;

(*c*) to remove the designated premises supervisor;

(*d*) to suspend the licence for a period not exceeding three months;

(*e*) to revoke the licence;

and for this purpose the conditions of the licence are modified if any of them is altered or omitted or any new condition is added.

(5) Subsection (3) is subject to sections 19 to 21 (requirement to include certain conditions in premises licences).

(6) Where the authority takes a step mentioned in subsection (4)(*a*) or (*b*), it may provide that the modification or exclusion is to have effect for only such period (not exceeding three months) as it may specify.

(7) In this section "relevant representations" means representations which—

(*a*) are relevant to one or more of the licensing objectives, and

(*b*) meet the requirements of subsection (8).

(8) The requirements are—

(*a*) that the representations are made—

(i) by the holder of the premises licence, a responsible authority or any other person, and

(ii) within the period prescribed under section 51(3)(*c*),

(*b*) that they have not been withdrawn, and

(*c*) if they are made by a person who is not a responsible authority, that they are not, in the opinion of the relevant licensing authority, frivolous or vexatious.

(9) Where the relevant licensing authority determines that any representations are frivolous or vexatious, it must notify the person who made them of the reasons for that determination.

(10) Where a licensing authority determines an application for review under this section it must notify the determination and its reasons for making it to—

(*a*) the holder of the licence,

(*b*) the applicant,

(*c*) any person who made relevant representations, and

(*d*) the chief officer of police for the police area (or each police area) in which the premises are situated.

(11) A determination under this section does not have effect—

(*a*) until the end of the period given for appealing against the decision, or

(*b*) if the decision is appealed against, until the appeal is disposed of.

[Licensing Act 2003, s 52 as amended by the Policing and Crime Act 2009, Sch 7 and the Police Reform and Social Responsibility Act 2011, ss 105, 109.]

---

1 For appeal to a magistrates' court against a decision of a licensing authority under this section, see s 181 and Sch 5, post.

7.7405 52A. **Review: supply of alcohol from community premises** (1) In a case where an application is made under section 51 for review of a premises licence which—

(*a*) is held by a management committee in respect of community premises, and

(*b*) includes the alternative licence condition,

section 52 is modified as follows.

(2) Subsection (4) has effect as if paragraph (*c*) were omitted.

(3) Subsection (5) has effect as if for that subsection there were substituted—

"(5) Subsection (3) is subject—

(*a*) to the requirement that the licence must include—

(i) the conditions in section 19(2) and (3), or

(i) the alternative licence condition referred to in section 52A(4)

(but not both), and

(*b*) to sections 19(4) and 19A to 21 (requirement to include certain conditions in premises licences)".

(4) In this section "the alternative licence condition" is the condition that every supply of alcohol under the premises licence must be made or authorised by the management committee.

[Licensing Act 2003, s 52A as inserted by SI 2009/1724 and amended by the Policing and Crime Act 2009, Sch 7.]

7.7406 **53. Supplementary provision about review** *Licensing authority able to determine review which has been applied for by itself in its separate capacity as a responsible authority under s 13(4).*

*Summary reviews in serious cases of crime or disorder*

7.7407 **53A. Summary reviews on application of senior police officer** (1) The chief officer of police of a police force for a police area may apply under this section to the relevant licensing authority for a review of the premises licence for any premises wholly or partly in that area if—

(*a*) the premises are licensed premises in relation to the sale of alcohol by retail; and

(*b*) a senior member of that force has given a certificate that it is his opinion that the premises are associated with[1] serious crime or serious disorder or both;

and that certificate must accompany the application.

(2) On receipt of such an application, the relevant licensing authority must—

(*a*) within 48 hours of the time of its receipt, consider under section 53B whether it is necessary to take interim steps pending the determination of a review of the premises licence; and

(*b*) within 28 days after the day of its receipt, review that licence in accordance with section 53C and reach a determination on that review.

(3) The Secretary of State must by regulations[2]—

(*a*) require a relevant licensing authority to whom an application for a review under this section has been made to give notice of the review to the holder of the premises licence and to every responsible authority;

(*b*) prescribe the period after the making of the application within which the notice under paragraph (*a*) must be given;

(*c*) require a relevant licensing authority to advertise the review, inviting representations about it to be made to the authority by the responsible authorities and other persons;

(*d*) prescribe the period after the making of the application within which the advertisement must be published;

(*e*) prescribe the period after the publication of the advertisement during which representations may be made by the holder of the premises licence, any responsible authority or any other person; and

(*f*) require a notice or advertisement under paragraph (*a*) or (*c*) to specify the period prescribed under paragraph (*e*).

(4) In this section—

"senior member", in relation to a police force, means a police officer who is a member of that force and of or above the rank of superintendent; and

"serious crime" has the same meaning as in the Regulation of Investigatory Powers Act 2000 (c 23) (see section 81(2) and (3) of that Act).

(5) In computing the period of 48 hours mentioned in subsection (2)(*a*) time that is not on a working day is to be disregarded.

[Licensing Act 2003, s 53A as inserted by the Violent Crime Reduction Act 2006, s 21 and amended by the Police Reform and Social Responsibility Act 2011, s 106.]

---

1 There must be a connection or link between the premises and serious crime or serious disorder, and this may require more than the fact that serious crime or serious disorder occurred in, or close to, the premises. It is unnecessary, however, to show a pattern of such behaviour; a single incident can suffice. The licensing authority must carry out a review even if it considers that the information available to the senior police officer when he gave the certificate does not establish the required association: *Lalli v Metropolitan Police Commissioner and another* [2015] EWHC 14 (Admin), [2015] All ER (D) 48 (Jan).

2 See the Licensing Act 2003 (Premises Licences and Club Premises Certificates) Regulations 2005, SI 2005/42 (for amending instruments, see note to s 13, ante).

7.7408 **53B. Interim steps pending review** (1) This section applies to the consideration by a relevant licensing authority on an application under section 53A whether it is necessary to take interim steps pending the determination of the review applied for.

(2) The consideration may take place without the holder of the premises licence having been given an opportunity to make representations to the relevant licensing authority.

(3) The interim steps the relevant licensing authority must consider taking are—

(*a*) the modification of the conditions of the premises licence;

(*b*) the exclusion of the sale of alcohol by retail from the scope of the licence;

(*c*) the removal of the designated premises supervisor from the licence;
(*d*) the suspension of the licence.

(4) For the purposes of subsection (3)(*a*) the conditions of a premises licence are modified if any of them is altered or omitted or any new condition is added.

(5) Where on its consideration of whether to take interim steps the relevant licensing authority does take one or more such steps—
(*a*) its decision takes effect immediately or as soon after that as that authority directs; but
(*b*) it must give immediate notice of its decision and of its reasons for making it to—
(i) the holder of the premises licence; and
(ii) the chief officer of police for the police area in which the premises are situated (or for each police area in which they are partly situated).

(6) Subject to subsection (9A), if the holder of the premises licence makes, and does not withdraw, representations against any interim steps taken by the relevant licensing authority, the authority must, within 48 hours of the time of its receipt of the representations, hold a hearing to consider those representations.

(7) The relevant licensing authority must give advance notice of the hearing to—
(*a*) the holder of the premises licence;
(*b*) the chief officer of police for the police area in which the premises are situated (or for each police area in which they are partly situated).

(8) At the hearing, the relevant licensing authority must—
(*a*) consider whether the interim steps are appropriate for the promotion of the licensing objectives; and
(*b*) determine whether to withdraw or modify the steps taken.

(9) In considering those matters the relevant licensing authority must have regard to—
(*a*) the certificate that accompanied the application;
(*b*) any representations made by the chief officer of police for the police area in which the premises are situated (or for each police area in which they are partly situated); and
(*c*) any representations made by the holder of the premises licence.

(9A) Where the relevant licensing authority has determined under subsection (8) whether to withdraw or modify the interim steps taken, the holder of the premises licence may only make further representations under subsection (6) if there has been a material change in circumstances since the authority made its determination.

(10) In computing the period of 48 hours mentioned in subsection (6) time that is not on a working day is to be disregarded.

[Licensing Act 2003, s 53B as inserted by the Violent Crime Reduction Act 2006, s 21 and amended by the Police Reform and Social Responsibility Act 2011, s 109 and the Policing and Crime Act 2017, s 136.]

**7.7409 53C. Review of premises licence following review notice** (1) This section applies to a review of a premises licence which a relevant licensing authority has to conduct on an application under section 53A.

(2) The relevant licensing authority must—
(*a*) hold a hearing to consider the application for the review and any relevant representations; and
(*b*) take such steps mentioned in subsection (3) (if any) as it considers appropriate for the promotion of the licensing objectives.
(*c*) secure that, from the coming into effect of the decision made on the determination of the review, any interim steps having effect pending that determination cease to have effect (except so far as they are comprised in steps taken in accordance with paragraph (*b*)).

(3) Those steps are—
(*a*) the modification of the conditions of the premises licence,
(*b*) the exclusion of a licensable activity from the scope of the licence,
(*c*) the removal of the designated premises supervisor from the licence,
(*d*) the suspension of the licence for a period not exceeding three months, or
(*e*) the revocation of the licence.

(4) For the purposes of subsection (3)(*a*) the conditions of a premises licence are modified if any of them is altered or omitted or any new condition is added.

(5) Subsection (2)(*b*) is subject to sections 19 to 21 (requirement to include certain conditions in premises licences).

(6) Where the authority takes a step within subsection (3)(*a*) or (*b*), it may provide that the modification or exclusion is to have effect only for a specified period (not exceeding three months).

(7) In this section "relevant representations" means representations which—
(*a*) are relevant to one or more of the licensing objectives, and
(*b*) meet the requirements of subsection (8).

(8) The requirements are—
(*a*) that the representations are made by the holder of the premises licence, a responsible authority or any other person within the period prescribed under subsection 53A(3)(*e*),
(*b*) that they have not been withdrawn, and
(*c*) if they are made by a person who is not a responsible authority, that they are not, in the

opinion of the relevant licensing authority, frivolous or vexatious.

(9) Where the relevant licensing authority determines that any representations are frivolous or vexatious, it must notify the person who made them of the reasons for that determination.

(10) Where a relevant licensing authority determines a review under this section it must notify the determination and its reasons for making it to—

(*a*) the holder of the premises licence,

(*b*) any person who made relevant representations, and

(*c*) the chief officer of police for the police area in which the premises are situated (or for each police area in which they are partly situated).

(11) A decision under this section does not have effect until—

(*a*) the end of the period given for appealing against the decision, or

(*b*) if the decision is appealed against, the time the appeal is disposed of.

(12) Section 53D makes provision about the application and review of any interim steps that have been taken under section 53B in relation to a premises licence before a decision under this section comes into effect in relation to the licence.

[Licensing Act 2003, s 53C as inserted by the Violent Crime Reduction Act 2006, s 21 and amended by the Policing and Crime Act 2009, Sch 7, the Police Reform and Social Responsibility Act 2011, ss 106, 109 and the Policing and Crime Act 2017, s 137.]

7.7409A **53D. Interim steps pending section 53C decision coming into effect** (1) At the hearing to consider an application for a review under section 53A, the relevant licensing authority must review any interim steps that have been taken by the relevant licensing authority under section 53B that have effect on the date of the hearing.

(2) In conducting the review under this section, the relevant licensing authority must—

(a) consider whether the interim steps are appropriate for the promotion of the licensing objectives;

(b) consider any relevant representations; and

(c) determine whether to withdraw or modify the interim steps taken.

(3) The power of the relevant licensing authority on a review under this section includes a power to take any of the following interim steps—

(a) the modification of the conditions of the premises licence;

(b) the exclusion of the sale of alcohol by retail from the scope of the licence;

(c) the removal of the designated premises supervisor from the licence;

(d) the suspension of the licence;

and for this purpose the conditions of the licence are modified if any of them is altered or omitted or any new condition is added.

(4) Any interim steps taken under subsection (3) apply until—

(a) the end of the period given for appealing against a decision made under section 53C,

(b) if the decision under section 53C is appealed against, the time the appeal is disposed of, or

(c) the end of a period determined by the relevant licensing authority (which may not be longer than the period of time for which such interim steps could apply under paragraph (a) or (b)).

(5) Any interim steps taken under section 53B in relation to a premises licence cease to have effect when the decision made under section 53C comes into effect.

(6) In subsection (2) "relevant representations" means representations which—

(a) are relevant to one or more of the licensing objectives, and

(b) meet the requirements of subsection (7).

(7) The requirements are—

(a) that the representations are made by the holder of the premises licence, a responsible authority or any other person within the period prescribed under subsection 53A(3)(e),

(b) that they have not been withdrawn, and

(c) if they are made by a person who is not a responsible authority, that they are not, in the opinion of the relevant licensing authority, frivolous or vexatious.

(8) Where the relevant licensing authority determines that any representations are frivolous or vexatious, it must notify the person who made them of the reasons for that determination.

(9) A decision under this section may be appealed (see paragraph 8B of Part 1 of Schedule 5 (appeals: premises licences)).

[Licensing Act 2003, s 53D as inserted by the Policing and Crime Act 2017, s 137.]

7.7410 **55A. Suspension of premises licence for failing to pay annual fee** *Licensing authority must suspend a club premises certificate if the holder of the certificate has failed to pay an annual fee.*

*Production of licence, rights of entry, etc*

7.7411 **56. Licensing authority's duty to update licence document** (1) Where—

(*a*) the relevant licensing authority, in relation to a premises licence, makes a determination or receives a notice under this Part,

(*b*) a premises licence lapses under this Part, or

(c) an appeal against a decision under this Part is disposed of,

the relevant licensing authority must make the appropriate amendments (if any) to the licence and, if necessary, issue a new summary of the licence.

(2) Where a licensing authority is not in possession of the licence (or the appropriate part of the licence) it may, for the purposes of discharging its obligations under subsection (1), require the holder of a premises licence to produce the licence (or the appropriate part) to the authority within 14 days from the date on which he is notified of the requirement.

(3) A person commits an offence if he fails, without reasonable excuse, to comply with a requirement under subsection (2).

(4) A person guilty of an offence under subsection (3) is liable on summary conviction to a fine not exceeding level 2 on the standard scale.

[Licensing Act 2003, s 56.]

7.7412 **57. Duty to keep and produce licence etc** (1) This section applies whenever premises in respect of which a premises licence has effect are being used for one or more licensable activities authorised by the licence.

(2) The holder of the premises licence must secure that the licence or a certified copy of it and a list of any relevant mandatory conditions applicable to the licence are kept at the premises in the custody or under the control of—

(a) the holder of the licence, or

(b) a person who works at the premises and whom the holder of the licence has nominated in writing for the purposes of this subsection.

(3) The holder of the premises licence must secure that—

(a) the summary of the licence or a certified copy of that summary, and

(b) a notice specifying the position held at the premises by any person nominated for the purposes of subsection (2),

are prominently displayed at the premises.

(4) The holder of a premises licence commits an offence if he fails, without reasonable excuse, to comply with subsection (2) or (3).

(5) A constable or an authorised person may require the person who, by virtue of arrangements made for the purposes of subsection (2), is required to have the premises licence (or a certified copy of it) or a list of relevant mandatory conditions in his custody or under his control to produce the licence (or such a copy) or the list for examination.

(6) An authorised person exercising the power conferred by subsection (5) must, if so requested, produce evidence of his authority to exercise the power.

(7) A person commits an offence if he fails, without reasonable excuse, to produce a premises licence or certified copy of a premises licence or a list of relevant mandatory conditions in accordance with a requirement under subsection (5).

(8) A person guilty of an offence under this section is liable on summary conviction to a fine not exceeding level 2 on the standard scale.

(9) In subsection (3) the reference to the summary of the licence is a reference to the summary issued under section 23 or, where one or more summaries have subsequently been issued under section 56, the most recent summary to have been so issued.

(10) Section 58 makes provision about certified copies of documents for the purposes of this section.

(11) In this section "relevant mandatory conditions", in relation to a premises licence, means conditions applicable to the licence by virtue of section 19(4) or 19A.

[Licensing Act 2003, s 57 as amended by the Policing and Crime Act 2009, Sch 7.]

7.7413 **58. Provision supplementary to section 57** (1) Any reference in section 57 to a certified copy of any document is a reference to a copy of that document which is certified to be a true copy by—

(a) the relevant licensing authority,

(b) a solicitor or notary, or

(c) a person of a prescribed[1] description.

(2) Any certified copy produced in accordance with a requirement under section 57(5) must be a copy of the document in the form in which it exists at the time.

(3) A document which purports to be a certified copy of a document is to be taken to be such a copy, and to comply with the requirements of subsection (2), unless the contrary is shown.

(4) In this section "notary" means a person (other than a solicitor) who, for the purposes of the Legal Services Act 2007, is an authorised person in relation to any activity which constitutes a notarial activity (within the meaning of that Act).

[Licensing Act 2003, s 58 as amended by the Legal Services Act 2007, Sch 21.]

---

1. I.e. prescribed by regulations, see s 193, post. At the date of going to press no such regulations had been made.

7.7414 **59. Inspection of premises before grant of licence etc** (1) In this section "relevant application" means an application under—

(a) section 17 (grant of licence),

(b) section 29 (provisional statement),

(c) section 34 (variation of licence), or

(*d*) section 51 (review of licence).

(2) A constable or an authorised person may, at any reasonable time before the determination of a relevant application, enter the premises to which the application relates to assess—

(*a*) in a case within subsection (1)(*a*), (*b*) or (*c*), the likely effect of the grant of the application on the promotion of the licensing objectives, and

(*b*) in a case within subsection (1)(*d*), the effect of the activities authorised by the premises licence on the promotion of those objectives.

(3) An authorised person exercising the power conferred by this section must, if so requested, produce evidence of his authority to exercise the power.

(4) A constable or an authorised person exercising the power conferred by this section in relation to an application within subsection (1)(*d*) may, if necessary, use reasonable force.

(5) A person commits an offence if he intentionally obstructs an authorised person exercising a power conferred by this section.

(6) A person guilty of an offence under this section is liable on summary conviction to a fine not exceeding level 2 on the standard scale.

[Licensing Act 2003, s 59.]

## PART 4[1]
## CLUBS

*Introductory*

7.7415 **60. Club premises certificate** (1) In this Act "club premises certificate" means a certificate granted under this Part—

(*a*) in respect of premises[2] occupied by, and habitually used for the purposes of, a club,

(*b*) by the relevant licensing authority, and

(*c*) certifying the matters specified in subsection (2).

(2) Those matters are—

(*a*) that the premises may be used by the club for one or more qualifying club activities[3] specified in the certificate, and

(*b*) that the club is a qualifying club in relation to each of those activities (see section 61).

[Licensing Act 2003, s 60.]

1. Part 4 comprises ss 60–97.
2. For meaning of "premises", see s 193, post.
3. For meaning of "qualifying club activities", see s 1(2), ante.

*Qualifying clubs*

7.7416 **61. Qualifying clubs** (1) This section applies for determining for the purposes of this Part whether a club is a qualifying club in relation to a qualifying club activity.

(2) A club is a qualifying club in relation to the supply of alcohol to members or guests[1] if it satisfies both—

(*a*) the general conditions in section 62, and

(*b*) the additional conditions in section 64.

(3) A club is a qualifying club in relation to the provision of regulated entertainment[2] if it satisfies the general conditions in section 62.

[Licensing Act 2003, s 61.]

1. For meaning of "supply of alcohol to members or guests", see s 70, post.
2. For meaning of "regulated entertainment, see Sch 1, post.

7.7417 **62. The general conditions** (1) The general conditions which a club must satisfy if it is to be a qualifying club in relation to a qualifying club activity are the following.

(2) Condition 1 is that under the rules of the club persons may not—

(*a*) be admitted to membership, or

(*b*) be admitted, as candidates for membership, to any of the privileges of membership,

without an interval of at least two days between their nomination or application for membership and their admission.

(3) Condition 2 is that under the rules of the club persons becoming members without prior nomination or application may not be admitted to the privileges of membership without an interval of at least two days between their becoming members and their admission.

(4) Condition 3 is that the club is established and conducted in good faith as a club (see section 63).

(5) Condition 4 is that the club has at least 25 members.

(6) Condition 5 is that alcohol is not supplied, or intended to be supplied, to members on the premises otherwise than by or on behalf of the club.

[Licensing Act 2003, s 62.]

7.7418 **63. Determining whether a club is established and conducted in good faith**

(1) In determining for the purposes of condition 3 in subsection (4) of section 62 whether a club is established and conducted in good faith as a club, the matters to be taken into account are

those specified in subsection (2).

(2) Those matters are—

(*a*) any arrangements restricting the club's freedom of purchase of alcohol;

(*b*) any provision in the rules, or arrangements, under which—

(i) money or property of the club, or

(ii) any gain arising from the carrying on of the club,

is or may be applied otherwise than for the benefit of the club as a whole or for charitable, benevolent or political purposes;

(*c*) the arrangements for giving members information about the finances of the club;

(*d*) the books of account and other records kept to ensure the accuracy of that information;

(*e*) the nature of the premises[1] occupied by the club.

(3) If a licensing authority decides for any purpose of this Act that a club does not satisfy condition 3 in subsection (4) of section 62, the authority must give the club notice of the decision and of the reasons for it.

[Licensing Act 2003, s 63.]

1 For meaning of "premises", see s 193, post.

7.7419 **64. The additional conditions for the supply of alcohol** (1) The additional conditions which a club must satisfy if it is to be a qualifying club in relation to the supply of alcohol to members or guests[1] are the following.

(2) Additional condition 1 is that (so far as not managed by the club in general meeting or otherwise by the general body of members) the purchase of alcohol for the club, and the supply of alcohol by the club, are managed by a committee whose members—

(*a*) are members of the club;

(*b*) have attained the age of 18 years; and

(*c*) are elected by the members of the club.

This subsection is subject to section 65 (which makes special provision for industrial and provident societies, friendly societies etc).

(3) Additional condition 2 is that no arrangements are, or are intended to be, made for any person to receive at the expense of the club any commission, percentage or similar payment on, or with reference to, purchases of alcohol by the club.

(4) Additional condition 3 is that no arrangements are, or are intended to be, made for any person directly or indirectly to derive any pecuniary benefit from the supply of alcohol by or on behalf of the club to members or guests, apart from—

(*a*) any benefit accruing to the club as a whole, or

(*b*) any benefit which a person derives indirectly by reason of the supply giving rise or contributing to a general gain from the carrying on of the club.

[Licensing Act 2003, s 64.]

1 For meaning of "supply of alcohol to members or guests", see s 70, post.

7.7420 **65. Industrial and provident societies, friendly societies etc** (1) Subsection (2) applies in relation to any club which is—

(*a*) a registered society, within the meaning of the Industrial and Provident Societies Act 1965 (c 12)(see section 74(1) of that Act),

(*b*) a registered society, within the meaning of the Friendly Societies Act 1974 (c 46) (see section 111(1) of that Act), or

(*c*) a registered friendly society, within the meaning of the Friendly Societies Act 1992 (c 40) (see section 116 of that Act).

(2) Any such club is to be taken for the purposes of this Act to satisfy additional condition 1 in subsection (2) of section 64 if and to the extent that—

(*a*) the purchase of alcohol for the club, and

(*b*) the supply of alcohol by the club,

are under the control of the members or of a committee appointed by the members.

(3) References in this Act, other than this section, to—

(*a*) subsection (2) of section 64, or

(*b*) additional condition 1 in that subsection,

are references to it as read with subsection (1) of this section.

(4) Subject to subsection (5), this Act applies in relation to an incorporated friendly society as it applies in relation to a club, and accordingly—

(*a*) the premises[1] of the society are to be treated as the premises of a club,

(*b*) the members of the society are to be treated as the members of the club, and

(*c*) anything done by or on behalf of the society is to be treated as done by or on behalf of the club.

(5) In determining for the purposes of section 61 whether an incorporated friendly society is a qualifying club in relation to a qualifying club activity[2], the society is to be taken to satisfy the following conditions—

(*a*) condition 3 in subsection (4) of section 62,

(*b*) condition 5 in subsection (6) of that section,

(*c*) the additional conditions in section 64.

(6) In this section "incorporated friendly society" has the same meaning as in the Friendly Societies Act 1992 (see section 116 of that Act).

[Licensing Act 2003, s 65.]

---

[1] For meaning of "premises", see s 193, post.

[2] For "qualifying club activities", see s 1(2), ante.

7.7421 **66. Miners' welfare institutes** (1) Subject to subsection (2), this Act applies to a relevant miners' welfare institute as it applies to a club, and accordingly—

(*a*) the premises of the institute are to be treated as the premises of a club,

(*b*) the persons enrolled as members of the institute are to be treated as the members of the club, and

(*c*) anything done by or on behalf of the trustees or managers in carrying on the institute is to be treated as done by or on behalf of the club.

(2) In determining for the purposes of section 61 whether a relevant miners' welfare institute is a qualifying club in relation to a qualifying club activity, the institute is to be taken to satisfy the following conditions—

(*a*) condition 3 in subsection (4) of section 62,

(*b*) condition 4 in subsection (5) of that section,

(*c*) condition 5 in subsection (6) of that section,

(*d*) the additional conditions in section 64.

(3) For the purposes of this section—

(*a*) "miners' welfare institute" means an association organised for the social well-being and recreation of persons employed in or about coal mines (or of such persons in particular), and

(*b*) a miners' welfare institute is "relevant" if it satisfies one of the following conditions.

(4) The first condition is that—

(*a*) the institute is managed by a committee or board, and

(*b*) at least two thirds of the committee or board consists—

(i) partly of persons appointed or nominated, or appointed or elected from among persons nominated, by one or more licensed operators within the meaning of the Coal Industry Act 1994 (c 21), and

(ii) partly of persons appointed or nominated, or appointed or elected from among persons nominated, by one or more organisations representing persons employed in or about coal mines.

(5) The second condition is that—

(*a*) the institute is managed by a committee or board, but

(*b*) the making of—

(i) an appointment or nomination falling within subsection (4)(*b*)(i), or

(ii) an appointment or nomination falling within subsection (4)(*b*)(ii),

is not practicable or would not be appropriate, and

(*c*) at least two thirds of the committee or board consists—

(i) partly of persons employed, or formerly employed, in or about coal mines, and

(ii) partly of persons appointed by the Coal Industry Social Welfare Organisation or a body or person to which the functions of that Organisation have been transferred under section 12(3) of the Miners' Welfare Act 1952 (c 23).

(6) The third condition is that the premises of the institute are held on trusts to which section 2 of the Recreational Charities Act 1958 (c 17) applies.

[Licensing Act 2003, s 66.]

*Interpretation*

7.7422 **67. Associate members and their guests** (1) Any reference in this Act (other than this section) to a guest of a member of a club includes a reference to—

(*a*) an associate member of the club, and

(*b*) a guest of an associate member of the club.

(2) For the purposes of this Act a person is an "associate member" of a club if—

(*a*) in accordance with the rules of the club, he is admitted to its premises as being a member of another club, and

(*b*) that other club is a recognised club (see section 193).

[Licensing Act 2003, s 67.]

7.7423 **68. The relevant licensing authority** *Determination of relevant licensing authority for a club dependent on location of whole, or greater part of club premises.*

7.7424 **69. Authorised persons, interested parties and responsible authorities** *Authorised persons, interested parties and responsible authorities are the same for club premises as they are for premises licences*[1].

[1] See s 13, ante, for full list.

7.7425 **70. Other definitions relating to clubs** In this Part—

"secretary", in relation to a club, includes any person (whether or not an officer of the club) performing the duties of a secretary;

"supply of alcohol to members or guests" means, in the case of any club,—

(*a*) the supply of alcohol by or on behalf of the club to, or to the order of, a member of the club, or

(*b*) the sale by retail of alcohol by or on behalf of the club to a guest of a member of the club for consumption on the premises where the sale takes place,

and related expressions are to be construed accordingly.

[Licensing Act 2003, s 70.]

*Grant of club premises certificate*

7.7426 **71. Application for club premises certificate** *Application to be in the prescribed form and accompanied by a Club Operating Schedule; application to be advertised in accordance with regulations*[1].

[1] See the Licensing Act 2003 (Premises Licences and Club Premises Certificates) Regulations 2005, SI 2005/42 (for amending instruments, see note to s 13, ante) and the Welsh Language (Gambling and Licensing Forms) Regulations 2010, SI 2010/2440.

7.7427 **72. Determination of application for club premises certificate** (1) This section applies where the relevant licensing authority—

(*a*) receives an application for a club premises certificate made in accordance with section 71, and

(*b*) is satisfied that the applicant has complied with any requirement imposed on the applicant under subsection (6) of that section.

(2) Subject to subsection (3), the authority must grant the certificate in accordance with the application subject only to—

(*a*) such conditions as are consistent with the club operating schedule accompanying the application, and

(*b*) any conditions which must under section 73(2) to (5), 73A or 74 be included in the certificate.

(3) Where relevant representations are made, the authority must—

(*a*) hold a hearing to consider them, unless the authority, the applicant and each person who has made such representations agree that a hearing is unnecessary, and

(*b*) having regard to the representations, take such of the steps mentioned in subsection (4) (if any) as it considers appropriate for the promotion of the licensing objectives.

(4) The steps are—

(*a*) to grant the certificate subject to—

(i) the conditions mentioned in subsection (2)(*a*) modified to such extent as the authority considers appropriate for the promotion of the licensing objectives, and

(ii) any conditions which must under section 73(2) to (5) or 74 be included in the certificate;

(*b*) to exclude from the scope of the certificate any of the qualifying club activities to which the application relates;

(*c*) to reject the application.

(5) Subsections (2) and (3)(*b*) are subject to section 73(1) (certificate may authorise off-supplies only if it authorises on-supplies).

(6) For the purposes of subsection (4)(*a*)(4)(*a*) the conditions mentioned in subsection (2)(*a*) are modified if any of them is altered or omitted or any new condition is added.

(7) For the purposes of this section, "relevant representations" means representations which—

(*a*) are about the likely effect of the grant of the certificate on the promotion of the licensing objectives, and

(*b*) meet the requirements of subsection (8).

(8) The requirements are—

(*a*) that the representations were made by a responsible authority or other person within the period prescribed under section 71(6)(*c*),

(*b*) that they have not been withdrawn, and

(*c*) in the case of representations made by a person who is not a responsible authority, that they are not, in the opinion of the relevant licensing authority, frivolous or vexatious.

(9) Where the authority determines for the purposes of subsection (8)(*c*) that any representations are frivolous or vexatious, it must notify the person who made them of the reasons for its determination.

(10) In discharging its duty under subsection (2) or (3)(*b*) a licensing authority may grant a club premises certificate subject to different conditions in respect of—

(*a*) different parts of the premises concerned;

(*b*) different qualifying club activities.

[Licensing Act 2003, s 72 as amended by the Policing and Crime Act 2009, Sch 7 and the Police Reform and Social Responsibility Act 2011, ss 107, 110.]

**7.7428 73. Certificate authorising supply of alcohol for consumption off the premises**

(1) A club premises certificate may not authorise the supply of alcohol for consumption off the premises unless it also authorises the supply of alcohol to a member of the club for consumption on those premises.

(2) A club premises certificate which authorises the supply of alcohol for consumption off the premises must include the following conditions.

(3) The first condition is that the supply must be made at a time when the premises are open for the purposes of supplying alcohol, in accordance with the club premises certificate, to members of the club for consumption on the premises.

(4) The second condition is that any alcohol supplied for consumption off the premises must be in a sealed container.

(5) The third condition is that any supply of alcohol for consumption off the premises must be made to a member of the club in person.

[Licensing Act 2003, s 73.]

**7.7429 73A. Mandatory conditions relating to the supply of alcohol to members or guests**

Where a club premises certificate authorises the supply of alcohol to members or guests, the certificate must include any conditions specified in an order under section 73B and applicable to the certificate.

[Licensing Act 2003, s 73A as inserted by the Policing and Crime Act 2009, Sch 4.]

**7.7430 73B. Power of Secretary of State to impose section 73A mandatory conditions**

(1) The Secretary of State may by order[1] specify conditions relating to the supply of alcohol to members or guests and applicable to all relevant club premises certificates or relevant club premises certificates of a particular description if the Secretary of State considers it appropriate to do so for the promotion of the licensing objectives.

(2) The number of conditions in force by virtue of subsection (1) in relation to all relevant club premises certificates and the number of conditions in force by virtue of that subsection in relation to relevant club premises certificates of particular descriptions must not (when added together) exceed at any time nine.

(3) An order under subsection (1) may—

(*a*) relate to existing or future relevant club premises certificates,

(*b*) specify conditions which involve, or consist of, the exercise of a discretion by any person.

(4) Any conditions specified by an order under subsection (1) in relation to existing relevant club premises certificates are to be treated as—

(*a*) included in those certificates from the coming into force of the order, and

(*b*) overriding any conditions already included in those certificates ("the existing conditions") so far as they are—

(i) identical to the existing conditions, or

(ii) inconsistent with, and more onerous than, the existing conditions.

(5) Any conditions included, or treated as included, in relevant club premises certificates by virtue of section 73A and this section cease to have effect so far as they cease to be specified under this section in relation to those certificates.

(6) Any conditions treated as mentioned in subsection (4)(*b*) cease to be so treated so far as they cease to be specified under this section in relation to the relevant club premises certificates concerned.

(7) So far as conditions cease to be treated as mentioned in subsection (4)(*b*), the existing conditions revive.

(8) Subsections (5) to (7) are subject to any alternative transitional or saving provision made by the order revoking the specification.

(9) In this section—

"existing relevant club premises certificate", in relation to an order, means a relevant club premises certificate granted before the coming into force of the order and in effect, or capable of having effect, on its coming into force,

"future relevant club premises certificate", in relation to an order, means a relevant club premises certificate granted on or after the coming into force of the order,

"relevant club premises certificate" means a club premises certificate authorising the supply of alcohol to members or guests.

[Licensing Act 2003, s 73B as inserted by the Policing and Crime Act 2009, Sch 4.]

---

[1] The Licensing Act 2003 (Mandatory Licensing Conditions) Orders 2010, SI 2010/860 and 2014/1252 have been made, in this title, post.

**7.7431 74. Mandatory condition: exhibition of films** (1) Where a club premises certificate authorises the exhibition of films, the certificate must include a condition requiring the admission of children to the exhibition of any film to be restricted in accordance with this section.

(2) Where the film classification body is specified in the certificate, unless subsection (3)(*b*) applies, admission of children must be restricted in accordance with any recommendation made by

that body.

(3) Where—

(*a*) the film classification body is not specified in the certificate, or

(*b*) the relevant licensing authority has notified the club which holds the certificate that this subsection applies to the film in question,

admission of children must be restricted in accordance with any recommendation made by that licensing authority.

(4) In this section—

"children" means persons aged under 18; and

"film classification body" means the person or persons designated as the authority under section 4 of the Video Recordings Act 1984 (c 39) (authority to determine suitability of video works for classification).

[Licensing Act 2003, s 74.]

7.7432 **75. Prohibited conditions: associate members and their guests** (1) Where the rules of a club provide for the sale by retail of alcohol on any premises by or on behalf of the club to, or to a guest of, an associate member[1] of the club, no condition may be attached to a club premises certificate in respect of the sale by retail of alcohol on those premises by or on behalf of the club so as to prevent the sale by retail of alcohol to any such associate member or guest.

(2) Where the rules of a club provide for the provision of any regulated entertainment on any premises by or on behalf of the club to, or to a guest of, an associate member of the club, no condition may be attached to a club premises certificate in respect of the provision of any such regulated entertainment on those premises by or on behalf of the club so as to prevent its provision to any such associate member or guest.

[Licensing Act 2003, s 75.]

1 For "associate members" and "guests", see s 67, ante.

7.7433 **76. Prohibited conditions: plays** (1) In relation to a club premises certificate which authorises the performance of plays, no condition may be attached to the certificate as to the nature of the plays which may be performed, or the manner of performing plays, under the certificate.

(2) But subsection (1) does not prevent a licensing authority imposing, in accordance with section 72(2) or (3)(*b*), 85(3)(*b*) or 88(3), any condition which it considers appropriate on the grounds of public safety.*

[Licensing Act 2003, s 76 as amended by the Police Reform and Social Responsibility Act 2011, s 110.]

7.7434 **77. Grant or rejection of application for club premises certificate** (1) Where an application is granted under section 72, the relevant licensing authority must forthwith—

(*a*) give a notice to that effect to—

(i) the applicant,

(ii) any person who made relevant representations in respect of the application, and

(iii) the chief officer of police for the police area (or each police area) in which the premises are situated, and

(*b*) issue the club with the club premises certificate and a summary of it.

(2) Where relevant representations were made in respect of the application, the notice under subsection (1)(*a*) must specify the authority's reasons for its decision as to the steps (if any) to take under section 72(3)(*b*).

(3) Where an application is rejected under section 72, the relevant licensing authority must forthwith give a notice to that effect, stating its reasons for that decision, to—

(*a*) the applicant,

(*b*) any person who made relevant representations in respect of the application, and

(*c*) the chief officer of police for the police area (or each police area) in which the premises are situated.

(4) In this section "relevant representations" has the meaning given in section 72(6).

[Licensing Act 2003, s 77.]

7.7435 **78. Form of certificate and summary** *Licence and summary to be in form prescribed[1].*

1 See the Licensing Act 2003 (Premises Licences and Club Premises Certificates) Regulations 2005, SI 2005/42 (for amending instruments, see note to s 13, ante) and the Welsh Language (Gambling and Licensing Forms) Regulations 2010, SI 2010/2440.

7.7436 **79. Theft, loss, etc of certificate or summary** *Power to apply for duplicate licence or summary on payment of fee.*

*Duration of certificate*

7.7437 **80. Period of validity of club premises certificate** *Club premises certificate to have effect until withdrawn under ss 88 or 90 or until lapses. Certificate of no effect if suspended following a review under s 88.*

7.7438 **81. Surrender of club premises certificate** *Club may surrender certificate by giving notice to licensing authority. Certificate lapses on receipt of notice.*

*Duty to notify certain changes*

7.7439 **82. Notification of change of name or alteration of rules of club** (1) Where a club—

(*a*) holds a club premises certificate, or

(*b*) has made an application for a club premises certificate which has not been determined by the relevant licensing authority,

the secretary[1] of the club must give the relevant licensing authority notice of any change in the name, or alteration made to the rules, of the club.

(2) Subsection (1) is subject to regulations under section 92(1) (power to prescribe fee to accompany application).

(3) A notice under subsection (1) by a club which holds a club premises certificate must be accompanied by the certificate or, if that is not practicable, by a statement of the reasons for the failure to produce the certificate.

(4) An authority notified under this section of a change in the name, or alteration to the rules, of a club must amend the club premises certificate accordingly.

(5) But nothing in subsection (4) requires or authorises the making of any amendment to a club premises certificate so as to change the premises to which the certificate relates (and no amendment made under that subsection to a club premises certificate has effect so as to change those premises).

(6) If a notice required by this section is not given within the 28 days following the day on which the change of name or alteration to the rules is made, the secretary of the club commits an offence.

(7) A person guilty of an offence under subsection (6) is liable on summary conviction to a fine not exceeding level 2 on the standard scale.

[Licensing Act 2003, s 82.]

1 For the secretary of a club, see s 70, ante.

7.7440 **83. Change of relevant registered address of club** (1) A club which holds a club premises certificate may give the relevant licensing authority notice of any change desired to be made in the address which is to be the club's relevant registered address.

(2) If a club which holds a club premises certificate ceases to have any authority to make use of the address which is its relevant registered address, it must as soon as reasonably practicable give to the relevant licensing authority notice of the change to be made in the address which is to be the club's relevant registered address.

(3) Subsections (1) and (2) are subject to regulations under section 92(1) (power to prescribe fee to accompany application).

(4) A notice under subsection (1) or (2) must also be accompanied by the club premises certificate or, if that is not practicable, by a statement of the reasons for the failure to produce the certificate.

(5) An authority notified under subsection (1) or (2) of a change to be made in the relevant registered address of a club must amend the club premises certificate accordingly.

(6) If a club fails, without reasonable excuse, to comply with subsection (2) the secretary commits an offence.

(7) A person guilty of an offence under subsection (6) is liable on summary conviction to a fine not exceeding level 2 on the standard scale.

(8) In this section "relevant registered address" has the meaning given in section 184(7).

[Licensing Act 2003, s 83.]

*Variation of certificates*

7.7441 **84. Application to vary club premises certificate** *Application for variation of club premises certificate to be in the prescribed form and advertised in accordance with Regulations. The Licensing Act 2003 (Premises Licences and Club Premises Certificates) Regulations 2005, SI 2005/42 (for amending instruments, see note to s 13, ante) and the Welsh Language (Gambling and Licensing Forms) Regulations 2010, SI 2010/2440 have been made.*

7.7442 **85. Determination of application under section 84** (1) This section applies where the relevant licensing authority—

(*a*) receives an application, made in accordance with section 84, to vary a club premises certificate, and

(*b*) is satisfied that the applicant has complied with any requirement imposed by virtue of subsection (4) of that section.

(2) Subject to subsection (3) and section 86(6), the authority must grant the application.

(3) Where relevant representations are made, the authority must—

(*a*) hold a hearing to consider them, unless the authority, the applicant and each person who has made such representations agree that a hearing is unnecessary, and

(*b*) having regard to the representations, take such of the steps mentioned in subsection (4) (if any) as it considers appropriate for the promotion of the licensing objectives.

(4) The steps are—

(*a*) to modify the conditions of the certificate;

(*b*) to reject the whole or part of the application;

and for this purpose the conditions of the certificate are modified if any of them is altered or omitted or any new condition is added.

(5) In this section "relevant representations" means representations which—

(*a*) are about the likely effect of the grant of the application on the promotion of the licensing objectives, and

(*b*) meet the requirements of subsection (6).

(6) The requirements are—

(*a*) that the representations are made by a responsible authority or other person within the period prescribed under section 71(6)(*c*) by virtue of section 84(4),

(*b*) that they have not been withdrawn, and

(*c*) in the case of representations made by a person who is not a responsible authority, that they are not, in the opinion of the relevant licensing authority, frivolous or vexatious.

(7) Subsections (2) and (3) are subject to sections 73 to 74 (mandatory conditions relating to alcohol and to exhibition of films).

[Licensing Act 2003, s 85 as amended by the Policing and Crime Act 2009, Sch 7 and the Police Reform and Social Responsibility Act 2011, ss 107, 110.]

7.7443 **86. Supplementary provision about applications under section 84** (1) Where an application (or any part of an application) is granted under section 85, the relevant licensing authority must forthwith give a notice to that effect to—

(*a*) the applicant,

(*b*) any person who made relevant representations in respect of the application, and

(*c*) the chief officer of police for the police area (or each police area) in which the premises are situated.

(2) Where relevant representations were made in respect of the application, the notice under subsection (1) must specify the authority's reasons for its decision as to the steps (if any) to take under section 85(3)(*b*).

(3) The notice under subsection (1) must specify the time when the variation in question takes effect.

That time is the time specified in the application or, if that time is before the applicant is given the notice, such later time as the relevant licensing authority specifies in the notice.

(4) Where an application (or any part of an application) is rejected under section 85, the relevant licensing authority must forthwith give a notice to that effect stating its reasons for rejecting the application to—

(*a*) the applicant,

(*b*) any person who made relevant representations, and

(*c*) the chief officer of police for the police area (or each police area) in which the premises are situated.

(5) Where the relevant licensing authority determines for the purposes of section 85(6)(*c*) that any representations are frivolous or vexatious, it must give the person who made them its reasons for that determination.

(6) A club premises certificate may not be varied under section 85 so as to vary substantially the premises to which it relates.

(7) In discharging its duty under subsection (2) or (3)(*b*) of that section, a licensing authority may vary a club premises certificate so that it has effect subject to different conditions in respect of—

(*a*) different parts of the premises concerned;

(*b*) different qualifying club activities.

(8) In this section "relevant representations" has the meaning given in section 85(5).

[Licensing Act 2003, s 86.]

7.7444 **86A. Application for minor variation of club premises certificate** (1) Subject to subsection (3), a club which holds a club premises certificate may apply under this section (instead of under section 84) to the relevant licensing authority for variation of the certificate.

(2) Subsection (1) is subject to regulations under—

(*a*) section 91 (form etc of applications etc);

(*b*) section 92 (fees to accompany applications etc).

(3) An application may not be made under this section to vary a club premises certificate so as to—

(*a*) vary substantially the premises to which it relates,

(*b*) add the supply of alcohol to members or guests as an activity authorised by the certificate, or

(*c*) authorise—

(i) the supply of alcohol to members or guests at any time between 11pm and 7am, or

(ii) an increase in the amount of time on any day during which alcohol may be supplied to members or guests.

(4) The duty to make regulations imposed on the Secretary of State by subsection (6)(*a*) of section 71 (advertisement etc of application) applies in relation to applications under this section as it applies in relation to applications under that section.

[Licensing Act 2003, s 86A as inserted by SI 2009/1772.]

7.7445 **86B. Determination of application under section 86A** (1) This section applies where the relevant licensing authority receives an application made under section 86A.

(2) In determining the application the authority must—

(*a*) consult such of the responsible authorities as it considers appropriate, and

(*b*) take into account any relevant representations—

(i) made by those authorities, or

(ii) made by any other person and received by the authority within ten working days beginning on the initial day.

(3) If the authority considers that—

(*a*) the variation proposed in the application could not have an adverse effect on the promotion of any of the licensing objectives, or

(*b*) if more than one variation is proposed, none of them, whether considered separately or together could have such an effect,

it must grant the application.

(4) In any other case the authority must reject the application.

(5) A determination under this section must be made within the period of fifteen working days beginning on the initial day.

(6) If at the expiry of the period referred to in subsection (5) the authority has not determined the application—

(*a*) the application is rejected, and

(*b*) the authority must forthwith return the fee that accompanied the application.

(7) But nothing in subsection (6) prevents the authority, with the agreement of the applicant, from treating—

(*a*) an application rejected by virtue of that subsection ("the first application") as a new application made under section 86A,

(*b*) the prescribed fee that accompanied the first application as the prescribed fee accompanying a new application, or

(*c*) both.

(8) A new application of the kind referred to in subsection (7)(*a*) is to be treated as having been made on the date of the agreement referred to in that provision, or on such other date as is specified in the agreement.

(9) Any fee owed to an applicant under subsection (6) may be recovered as a debt due to the applicant.

(10) For the purposes of this section—

"initial day" in relation to an application means the first working day after the day on which the authority receives the application;

"relevant representations" in relation to an application means representations which are about the likely effect of the grant of the application on the promotion of the licensing objectives.

[Licensing Act 2003, s 86B as inserted by SI 2009/1772 and the Police Reform and Social Responsibility Act 2011, s 107.]

7.7446 **86C. Supplementary provision about determinations under section 86B** (1) Where an application is granted under section 86B, the relevant licensing authority must forthwith give a notice to that effect to the applicant.

(2) The notice under subsection (1) must specify—

(*a*) any variation of the club premises certificate which is to have effect as a result of the grant of the application, and

(*b*) the time at which that variation takes effect.

(3) The time referred to in subsection (2)(*b*) is the time specified in the application or, if that time is before the applicant is given the notice referred to in subsection (2), such later time as the authority specifies in the notice.

(4) Where an application is rejected under section 86B, the relevant licensing authority must forthwith give a notice to that effect to the applicant.

(5) The notice under subsection (4) must include a statement by the authority of the reasons for its decision.

[Licensing Act 2003, s 86C as inserted by SI 2009/1772.]

*Review of certificates*

7.7447 **87. Application for review of club premises certificate** (1) Where a club holds a club premises certificate, a responsible authority or any other person may apply to the relevant licensing authority for a review of the certificate.

(2) Subsection (1) is subject to regulations under section 91 (form etc of applications).

(3) The Secretary of State must by regulations[1] under this section—

(*a*) require the applicant to give a notice containing details of the application to the club and each responsible authority within such period as may be prescribed;

(*b*) require the authority to advertise the application and invite representations relating to it to be made to the authority by the club, responsible authorities and other persons;

(*c*) prescribe the period during which representations may be made by the club, any responsible authority and any other person;

(*d*) require any notice under paragraph (*a*) or advertisement under paragraph (*b*) to specify that period.

(4) The relevant licensing authority may, at any time, reject any ground for review specified in an application under this section if it is satisfied—

(*a*) that the ground is not relevant to one or more of the licensing objectives, or

(*b*) in the case of an application made by a person other than a responsible authority, that—

(i) the ground is frivolous or vexatious, or

(ii) the ground is a repetition.

(5) For this purpose a ground for review is a repetition if—

(*a*) it is identical or substantially similar to—

(i) a ground for review specified in an earlier application for review made in respect of the same club premises certificate and determined under section 88, or

(ii) representations considered by the relevant licensing authority in accordance with section 72, before it determined the application for the club premises certificate under that section, and

(*b*) a reasonable interval has not elapsed since that earlier application or that grant.

(6) Where the authority rejects a ground for review under subsection (4)(*b*), it must notify the applicant of its decision and, if the ground was rejected because it was frivolous or vexatious, the authority must notify him of its reasons for making that decision.

(7) The application is to be treated as rejected to the extent that any of the grounds for review are rejected under subsection (4).

Accordingly, the requirements imposed under subsection (3)(*a*) and (*b*) and by section 88 (so far as not already met) apply only to so much (if any) of the application as has not been rejected.

[Licensing Act 2003, s 87 as amended by the Police Reform and Social Responsibility Act 2011, s 108.]

[1] See the Licensing Act 2003 (Premises Licences and Club Premises Certificates) Regulations 2005, SI 2005/42 (for amending instruments, see note to s 13, ante) and the Welsh Language (Gambling and Licensing Forms) Regulations 2010, SI 2010/2440.

7.7448 **88. Determination of application for review** (1) This section applies where—

(*a*) the relevant licensing authority receives an application made in accordance with section 87,

(*b*) the applicant has complied with any requirement imposed by virtue of subsection (3)(*a*) or (*d*) of that section, and

(*c*) the authority has complied with any requirement imposed on it under subsection (3)(*b*) or (*d*) of that section.

(2) Before determining the application, the authority must hold a hearing to consider it and any relevant representations.

(3) The authority must, having regard to the application and any relevant representations, take such of the steps mentioned in subsection (4) (if any) as it considers appropriate for the promotion of the licensing objectives.

(4) The steps are—

(*a*) to modify the conditions of the certificate;

(*b*) to exclude a qualifying club activity from the scope of the certificate;

(*c*) to suspend the certificate for a period not exceeding three months;

(*d*) to withdraw the certificate;

and for this purpose the conditions of the certificate are modified if any of them is altered or omitted or any new condition is added.

(5) Subsection (3) is subject to sections 73 to 74 (mandatory conditions relating to alcohol and to exhibition of films).

(6) Where the authority takes a step within subsection (4)(*a*) or (*b*), it may provide that the modification or exclusion is to have effect for only such period (not exceeding three months) as it may specify.

(7) In this section "relevant representations" means representations which—

(*a*) are relevant to one or more of the licensing objectives, and

(*b*) meet the requirements of subsection (8).

(8) The requirements are—

(*a*) that the representations are made by the club, a responsible authority or any other person within the period prescribed under section 87(3)(*c*),

(*b*) that they have not been withdrawn, and

(*c*) if they are made by a person who is not a responsible authority, that they are not, in the opinion of the relevant licensing authority, frivolous or vexatious.

(9) Where the relevant licensing authority determines that any representations are frivolous or vexatious, it must give the person who made them its reasons for that determination.

(10) Where a licensing authority determines an application for review under this section it must notify the determination and its reasons for making it to—

(*a*) the club,

(*b*) the applicant,

(*c*) any person who made relevant representations, and

(*d*) the chief officer of police for the police area (or each police area) in which the premises are situated.

(11) A determination under this section does not have effect—

(*a*) until the end of the period given for appealing against the decision, or

(*b*) if the decision is appealed against, until the appeal is disposed of.

[Licensing Act 2003, s 88 as amended by the Policing and Crime Act 2009, Sch 7 and the Police Reform and Social Responsibility Act 2011, ss 108, 110.]

7.7449 **89. Supplementary provision about review** *Licensing authority able to determine review which has been applied for by itself in its separate capacity as a responsible authority.*

*Withdrawal of certificates*

7.7450 **90. Club ceasing to be a qualifying club** (1) Where—

(*a*) a club holds a club premises certificate, and

(*b*) it appears to the relevant licensing authority that the club does not satisfy the conditions for being a qualifying club in relation to a qualifying club activity to which the certificate relates (see section 61),

the authority must give a notice to the club withdrawing the certificate, so far as relating to that activity.

(2) Where the only reason that the club does not satisfy the conditions for being a qualifying club in relation to the activity in question is that the club has fewer than the required number of members, the notice withdrawing the certificate must state that the withdrawal—

(*a*) does not take effect until immediately after the end of the period of three months following the date of the notice, and

(*b*) will not take effect if, at the end of that period, the club again has at least the required number of members.

(3) The references in subsection (2) to the required number of members are references to the minimum number of members required by condition 4 in section 62(5) (25 at the passing of this Act).

(4) Nothing in subsection (2) prevents the giving of a further notice of withdrawal under this section at any time.

(5) Where a justice of the peace is satisfied, on information on oath, that there are reasonable grounds for believing—

(*a*) that a club which holds a club premises certificate does not satisfy the conditions for being a qualifying club in relation to a qualifying club activity to which the certificate relates, and

(*b*) that evidence of that fact is to be obtained at the premises to which the certificate relates,

he may issue a warrant authorising a constable to enter the premises, if necessary by force, at any time within one month from the time of the issue of the warrant, and search them.

(6) A person who enters premises under the authority of a warrant under subsection (5) may seize and remove any documents relating to the business of the club in question.

[Licensing Act 2003, s 90.]

*General provision*

7.7451 **91. Form etc of applications and notices under Part 4** *Applications and notices to be in the form prescribed by regulations*[1].

---

1 See the Licensing Act 2003 (Premises Licences and Club Premises Certificates) Regulations 2005, SI 2005/42 (for amending instruments, see note to s 13, ante) and the Welsh Language (Gambling and Licensing Forms) Regulations 2010, SI 2010/2440.

7.7452 **92A. Suspension of premises licence for failing to pay annual fee** *Licensing authority must suspend a club premises certificate if the holder of the certificate has failed to pay an annual fee.*

*Production of certificate, rights of entry, etc*

7.7453 **93. Licensing authority's duty to update club premises certificate** (1) Where—

(*a*) the relevant licensing authority, in relation to a club premises certificate, makes a determination or receives a notice under this Part, or

(*b*) an appeal against a decision under this Part is disposed of,

the relevant licensing authority must make the appropriate amendments (if any) to the certificate and, if necessary, issue a new summary of the certificate.

(2) Where a licensing authority is not in possession of the club premises certificate, it may, for the purpose of discharging its obligations under subsection (1), require the secretary of the club to produce the certificate to the authority within 14 days from the date on which the club is notified of the requirement.

(3) A person commits an offence if he fails, without reasonable excuse, to comply with a requirement under subsection (2).

(4) A person guilty of an offence under subsection (3) is liable on summary conviction to a fine not exceeding level 2 on the standard scale.

[Licensing Act 2003, s 93.]

7.7454 **94. Duty to keep and produce certificate etc** (1) This section applies whenever premises in respect of which a club premises certificate has effect are being used for one or more qualifying club activities authorised by the certificate.

(2) The secretary[1] of the club must secure that the certificate, or a certified copy of it, and a list of any relevant mandatory conditions applicable to the certificate are kept at the premises in the custody or under the control of a person (the "nominated person") who—

(*a*) falls within subsection (3),

(*b*) has been nominated for the purpose by the secretary in writing, and

(*c*) has been identified to the relevant licensing authority in a notice given by the secretary.

(3) The persons who fall within this subsection are—

(*a*) the secretary of the club,

(*b*) any member of the club,

(*c*) any person who works at the premises for the purposes of the club.

(4) The nominated person must secure that—

(*a*) the summary of the certificate or a certified copy of that summary, and

(*b*) a notice specifying the position which he holds at the premises,

are prominently displayed at the premises.

(5) The secretary commits an offence if he fails, without reasonable excuse, to comply with subsection (2).

(6) The nominated person commits an offence if he fails, without reasonable excuse, to comply with subsection (4).

(7) A constable or an authorised person may require the nominated person to produce the club premises certificate (or certified copy) or any list of relevant mandatory conditions for examination.

(8) An authorised person exercising the power conferred by subsection (7) must, if so requested, produce evidence of his authority to exercise the power.

(9) A person commits an offence if he fails, without reasonable excuse, to produce a club premises certificate or any list of relevant mandatory conditions or certified copy of a club premises certificate in accordance with a requirement under subsection (7).

(10) A person guilty of an offence under this section is liable on summary conviction to a fine not exceeding level 2 on the standard scale.

(11) In subsection (4) the reference to the summary of the certificate is a reference to the summary issued under section 77 or, where one or more summaries have subsequently been issued under section 93, the most recent summary to be so issued.

(12) Section 95 makes provision about certified copies of club premises certificates and of summaries of club premises certificates for the purposes of this section.

(13) In this section "relevant mandatory conditions", in relation to a club premises certificate, means conditions applicable to the certificate by virtue of section 73A or 73B.

[Licensing Act 2003, s 94 as amended by the Policing and Crime Act 2009, Sch 7.]

---

1 For the secretary of a club, see s 70, ante.

7.7455 **95. Provision supplementary to section 94** (1) Any reference in section 94 to a certified copy of a document is a reference to a copy of the document which is certified to be a true copy by—

(*a*) the relevant licensing authority,

(*b*) a solicitor or notary, or

(*c*) a person of a prescribed description.

(2) Any certified copy produced in accordance with a requirement under subsection 94(7) must be a copy of the document in the form in which it exists at the time.

(3) A document which purports to be a certified copy of a document is to be taken to be such a copy, and to comply with the requirements of subsection (2), unless the contrary is shown.

(4) In this section "notary" means a person (other than a solicitor) who, for the purposes of the Legal Services Act 2007, is an authorised person in relation to any activity which constitutes a notarial activity (within the meaning of that Act).

[Licensing Act 2003, s 95 as amended by the Legal Services Act 2007, Sch 21.]

7.7456 **96. Inspection of premises before grant of certificate etc** (1) Subsection (2) applies where—

(*a*) a club applies for a club premises certificate in respect of any premises,

(*b*) a club applies under section 84 for the variation of a club premises certificate held by it, or

(*c*) an application is made under section 87 for review of a club premises certificate.

(2) On production of his authority—

(*a*) an authorised person, or

(*b*) a constable authorised by the chief officer of police,

may enter and inspect the premises.

(3) Any entry and inspection under this section must take place at a reasonable time on a day—

(*a*) which is not more than 14 days after the making of the application in question, and (*b*) which is specified in the notice required by subsection (4).

(4) Before an authorised person or constable enters and inspects any premises under this section, at least 48 hours' notice must be given to the club.

(5) Any person obstructing an authorised person in the exercise of the power conferred by this section commits an offence.

(6) A person guilty of an offence under subsection (5) is liable on summary conviction to a fine not exceeding level 2 on the standard scale.

(7) The relevant licensing authority may, on the application of a responsible authority, extend by not more than 7 days the time allowed for carrying out an entry and inspection under this section.

(8) The relevant licensing authority may allow such an extension of time only if it appears to the authority that—

(*a*) reasonable steps had been taken for an authorised person or constable authorised by the applicant to inspect the premises in good time, but

(*b*) it was not possible for the inspection to take place within the time allowed.

[Licensing Act 2003, s 96.]

7.7457 **97. Other powers of entry and search** (1) Where a club premises certificate has effect in respect of any premises, a constable may enter and search the premises if he has reasonable cause to believe—

(*a*) that an offence under section 4(3)(*a*), (*b*) or (*c*) of the Misuse of Drugs Act 1971 (c 38) (supplying or offering to supply, or being concerned in supplying or making an offer to supply, a controlled drug) has been, is being, or is about to be, committed there,

(*aa*) that an offence under section 5(1) or (2) of the Psychoactive Substances Act 2016 (supplying, or offering to supply, a psychoactive substance) has been, is being, or is about to be, committed there, or

(*b*) that there is likely to be a breach of the peace there.

(2) A constable exercising any power conferred by this section may, if necessary, use reasonable force.

[Licensing Act 2003, s 97 as amended by the Psychoactive Substances Act 2015, Sch 5.]

## PART 5[1]
## PERMITTED TEMPORARY ACTIVITIES

*Introductory*

7.7458 **98. Meaning of "permitted temporary activity"** (1) A licensable activity[2] is a permitted temporary activity by virtue of this Part if—

(*a*) it is carried on in accordance with—

(i) a notice given in accordance with section 100, and

(ii) any conditions imposed under section 106A, and

(*b*) the following conditions are satisfied.

(2) The first condition is that the requirements of section 102 (acknowledgement of notice) are met in relation to the notice.

(3) The second condition is that the notice has not been withdrawn under this Part.

(4) The third condition is that no counter notice has been given under this Part in respect of the notice.

[Licensing Act 2003, s 98 as amended by the Police Reform and Social Responsibility Act 2011, ss 113, 114.]

1 Part 5 comprises ss 98–110.

2 For meaning of "licensable activity", see s 1(1), ante.

7.7459 **99. The relevant licensing authority** In this Part references to the "relevant licensing authority", in relation to any premises, are references to—

(*a*) the licensing authority in whose area the premises are situated, or

(*b*) where the premises are situated in the areas of two or more licensing authorities, each of those authorities.

[Licensing Act 2003, s 99.]

7.7460 **99A. Meaning of "relevant person"** In this Part references to a "relevant person", in relation to any premises, are references to the following—

(*a*) the chief officer of police for any police area in which the premises are situated,

(*b*) the local authority by which statutory functions are exercisable in any area in which the premises are situated in relation to minimising or preventing the risk of pollution of the environment or of harm to human health.

[Licensing Act 2003, s 99A as inserted by the Police Reform and Social Responsibility Act 2011, s 112.]

*Temporary event notices*

7.7461 **100. Temporary event notice** (1) Where it is proposed to use premises[1] for one or more licensable activities during a period not exceeding 168 hours, an individual may give to the relevant licensing authority notice of that proposal (a "temporary event notice").

(2) In this Act, the "premises user", in relation to a temporary event notice, is the individual who gave the notice.

(3) An individual may not give a temporary event notice unless he is aged 18 or over.

(4) A temporary event notice must be in the prescribed form and contain—

(*a*) a statement of the matters mentioned in subsection (5),

(*b*) where subsection (6) applies, a statement of the condition mentioned in that subsection, and

(*c*) such other information as may be prescribed[2].

(5) Those matters are—

(*a*) the licensable activities to which the proposal mentioned in subsection (1) relates ("the relevant licensable activities"),

(*b*) the period (not exceeding 168 hours) during which it is proposed to use the premises for those activities ("the event period"),

(*c*) the times during the event period when the premises user proposes that those licensable activities shall take place,

(*d*) the maximum number of persons (being a number less than 500) which the premises user proposes should, during those times, be allowed on the premises at the same time,

(*e*) where the relevant licensable activities include the supply of alcohol, whether supplies are proposed to be for consumption on the premises or off the premises, or both, and

(*f*) such other matters as may be prescribed[2].

(6) Where the relevant licensable activities include the supply of alcohol, the notice must make it a condition of using the premises for such supplies that all such supplies are made by or under the authority of the premises user.

(7) The temporary event notice—

(*a*) must be given in accordance with section 100A, and

(*b*) must be accompanied by the prescribed[3] fee when it is given by the premises user to the relevant licensing authority.

(8) The Secretary of State may, by order—

(*a*) amend subsections (1) and (5)(*b*) so as to substitute any period for the period for the time being specified there;

(*b*) amend subsection (5)(*d*) so as to substitute any number for the number for the time being specified there.

(9) In this section "supply of alcohol" means—

(*a*) the sale by retail of alcohol, or

(*b*) the supply of alcohol by or on behalf of a club to, or to the order of, a member of the club.*

[Licensing Act 2003, s 100 as amended by SI 2009/2999 and the Police Reform and Social Responsibility Act 2011, ss 114, 115.]

1 For meaning of "premises", see s 193, post.

2 The Licensing Act 2003 (Permitted Temporary Activities) (Notices) Regulations 2005, SI 2005/2918 amended by SI 2012/960, SI 2014/2417 and SI 2016/20 and the Welsh Language (Gambling and Licensing Forms) Regulations 2010, SI 2010/2440 have been made.

3 The Licensing Act 2003 (Fees) Regulations 2005, SI 2005/79 amended by SI 2009/1809 have been made.

7.7462 **100A. Standard and late temporary event notices** (1) For the purposes of section 100(7)(*a*), a temporary event notice must be given in accordance with—

(*a*) subsection (2), in which case the notice is a "standard temporary event notice", or

(*b*) subsection (3), in which case the notice is a "late temporary event notice".

(2) A temporary event notice is given in accordance with this subsection if, no later than ten working days before the day on which the event period begins,—

(*a*) it is given to the relevant licensing authority by means of a relevant electronic facility, or

(*b*) it is given to the relevant licensing authority (otherwise than by means of a relevant electronic facility) and to each relevant person.

(3) A temporary event notice is given in accordance with this subsection if—

(*a*) it is given to the relevant licensing authority by means of a relevant electronic facility no later than five working days, but no earlier than nine working days, before the day the event period begins, or

(*b*) both of the following are satisfied—

(i) it is given to the relevant licensing authority (otherwise than by means of a relevant electronic facility) and to each relevant person no later than five working days before the day on which the event period begins;

(ii) it is given to at least one of those persons no earlier than nine working days before the day on which that event period begins.

(4) Where a temporary event notice (the "original notice") is given by the premises user to the relevant licensing authority by means of a relevant electronic facility as referred to in subsection (2)(*a*) or (3)(*a*)—

(*a*) the licensing authority must give a copy of the original notice to each relevant person no later than the end of the first working day after the day on which the original notice was given to the authority, and (*b*) for the purposes of this Act, the copy is to be treated as if it were the original notice.

(5) In this section "event period" in relation to a temporary event notice means the event period specified in the notice.

[Licensing Act 2003, s 100A as inserted by the Police Reform and Social Responsibility Act 2011, s 114.]

7.7463 **101. Minimum of 24 hours between event periods** *Temporary Event Notice void if period specified in it starts or ends within 24 hours of another notice given in respect of the same premises by the premises user, or an associate or business colleague of that premises user.*

7.7464 **102. Acknowledgement of notice** *Licensing authority obliged to acknowledge receipt of Temporary Event Notice within one working day of receipt, unless counter notice served under s 107 because permitted limits have been exceeded.*

7.7465 **103. Withdrawal of notice** (1) A temporary event notice may be withdrawn by the premises user giving the relevant licensing authority a notice to that effect no later than 24 hours before the beginning of the event period specified in the temporary event notice.

(2) Nothing in section 102 or sections 104 to 107 applies in relation to a notice withdrawn in accordance with this section.

[Licensing Act 2003, s 103.]

*Police objections*

7.7466 **104. Objection to notice by the police** *Copy of Temporary Event Notice to be served on Chief Officer of Police no later than 10 working days before event begins. Police must give objection notice no later than 48 hours after the chief officer of police is given a copy of the temporary event notice if satisfied that use of premises in accordance with the Temporary Event Notice would undermine the crime prevention licensing objective.*

7.7467 **104A. Counter notice following objection to late notice** *Where an objection notice is given in respect of a late temporary event notice, the licensing authority must give the premises user a counter notice.*

[Licensing Act 2003, s 104A as inserted by the Police Reform and Social Responsibility Act 2011, s 114.]

7.7468 **105. Counter notice following objection to standard temporary event notice** (1) This section applies where an objection notice is given under section 104(2) in respect of a standard temporary event notice.

(2) The relevant licensing authority must—

(*a*) hold a hearing to consider the objection notice, unless the premises user, the relevant person who gave the objection notice and the authority agree that a hearing is unnecessary, and

(*b*) having regard to the objection notice, give the premises user a counter notice under this section if it considers it appropriate for the promotion of a licensing objective to do so.

(3) The relevant licensing authority must—

(*a*) in a case where it decides not to give a counter notice under this section, give the premises user and each relevant person notice of the decision, and

(*b*) in any other case—

(i) give the premises user the counter notice and a notice stating the reasons for its decision, and

(ii) give each relevant person a copy of both of those notices.

(4) A decision must be made under subsection (2)(*b*), and the requirements of subsection (3) must be met, at least 24 hours before the beginning of the event period specified in the temporary event notice.

(5) Where the premises are situated in the area of more than one licensing authority, the functions conferred on the relevant licensing authority by this section must be exercised by those authorities jointly.

(6) This section does not apply—

(*a*) if the objection notice has been withdrawn (whether by virtue of section 106 or otherwise), or

(*b*) if the premises user has been given a counter notice under section 107.

(7) *Repealed.*

[Licensing Act 2003, s 105 as amended by the Police Reform and Social Responsibility Act 2011, ss 111, 112, 114.]

7.7469 **106. Modification of standard temporary event notice following objection** *Power of relevant person, where an objection notice has been given, to modify the temporary event notice with the agreement of the premises user and each other relevant person.*

7.7470 **106A. Conditions on standard temporary event notice following objection** *Licensing authority may impose one or more conditions on the standard temporary event notice if it considers it appropriate for the promotion of the licensing objectives to do so.*

[Licensing Act 2003, s 106A as inserted by the Police Reform and Social Responsibility Act 2011, s 113.]

*Limits on temporary event notices*

7.7471 **107. Counter notice where permitted limits exceeded** *Duty of licensing authority to give counter notice if permitted limits exceeded. The giving of a counter notice under this section cannot be appealed to the magistrates' court.*

*Rights of entry, production of notice, etc*

7.7472 **108. Right of entry where temporary event notice given** (1) A constable or an authorised officer may, at any reasonable time, enter the premises to which a temporary event notice relates to assess the likely effect of the notice on the promotion of the crime prevention objective.

(2) An authorised officer exercising the power conferred by this section must, if so requested, produce evidence of his authority to exercise the power.

(3) A person commits an offence if he intentionally obstructs an authorised officer exercising a power conferred by this section.

(4) A person guilty of an offence under this section is liable on summary conviction to a fine not exceeding level 2 on the standard scale.

(5) In this section "authorised officer" means—

(*a*) an officer of the licensing authority in whose area the premises are situated, or

(*b*) if the premises are situated in the area of more than one licensing authority, an officer of any of those authorities,

authorised for the purposes of this Act.

[Licensing Act 2003, s 108.]

7.7473 **109. Duty to keep and produce temporary event notice and statement of conditions** (1) This section applies whenever premises are being used for one or more licensable activities which are or are purported to be permitted temporary activities by virtue of this Part.

(2) The premises user must either—

(*a*) secure that a copy of the temporary event notice, together with a copy of any statement of conditions given under section 106A(3) in respect of the notice is prominently displayed at the premises, or

(*b*) meet the requirements of subsection (3).

(3) The requirements of this subsection are that the premises user must—

(*a*) secure that the temporary event notice, together with a copy of any statement of conditions given under section 106A(3) in respect of the notice is kept at the premises in—

(i) his custody, or

(ii) in the custody of a person who is present and working at the premises and whom he has nominated for the purposes of this section, and

(*b*) where the temporary event notice and any statement of conditions are in the custody of a person so nominated, secure that a notice specifying that fact and the position held at the premises by that person is prominently displayed at the premises.

(4) The premises user commits an offence if he fails, without reasonable excuse, to comply with subsection (2).

(5) Where—

(*a*) the temporary event notice or any statement of conditions is not displayed as mentioned in subsection (2)(*a*), and

(*b*) no notice is displayed as mentioned in subsection (3)(*b*),

a constable or authorised officer may require the premises user to produce the temporary event notice or statement of conditions for examination.

(6) Where a notice is displayed as mentioned in subsection (3)(*b*), a constable or authorised officer may require the person specified in that notice to produce the temporary event notice or statement of conditions for examination.

(7) An authorised officer exercising the power conferred by subsection (5) or (6) must, if so requested, produce evidence of his authority to exercise the power.

(8) A person commits an offence if he fails, without reasonable excuse, to produce a temporary event notice or statement of conditions in accordance with a requirement under subsection (5) or (6).

(9) A person guilty of an offence under this section is liable on summary conviction to a fine not exceeding level 2 on the standard scale.

(10) In this section "authorised officer" has the meaning given in section 108(5).

[Licensing Act 2003, s 109 as amended by the Police Reform and Social Responsibility Act 2011, s 113.]

*Miscellaneous*

7.7474 **110. Theft, loss, etc of temporary event notice or statement of conditions** *Power to apply for a duplicate temporary event notice or statement of conditions on payment of a fee.*

## PART 5A

### Sale of alcohol at community events etc and ancillary business sale of alcohol

*Conditions for permitted sales*

7.7474A **110A. General conditions** (1) A sale by retail of alcohol is a permitted sale by virtue of this Part if—

(*a*) the community event conditions (set out in section 110B or in regulations made under that section) or the ancillary business sales conditions (set out in section 110C or in regulations made under that section) are satisfied in relation to it, and

(*b*) the conditions set out in subsections (2) to (5) below are satisfied in relation to it.

(2) The sale must take place on premises specified in a notice that complies with section 110D (a "Part 5A notice").

(3) No counter notice under section 110J must have been given in relation to the Part 5A notice.

(4) The sale must take place during the period of 36 months beginning with the date when the Part 5A notice takes effect.

(5) The sale must take place between 07.00 am and 11.00 pm

[Licensing Act 2003, s 110A as inserted by the Deregulation Act 2015, Sch 17 from a date to be appointed.]

**7.7474B 110B. Community event conditions** (1) The community event conditions, in relation to a sale by retail of alcohol, are the conditions set out in subsections (2) to (6) and any additional conditions set out in regulations under subsection (7).

(2) The sale must be made by or on behalf of a body that—

(*a*) is of a prescribed description,

(*b*) does not trade for profit, and

(*c*) meets any prescribed criteria.

(3) The sale must be ancillary to an event that—

(*a*) is taking place on the premises,

(*b*) is organised by the body by or on whose behalf the sale is made,

(*c*) has been advertised in advance, and

(*d*) meets any prescribed criteria.

(4) The sale must take place on the premises during the course of the event.

(5) The alcohol must be sold for consumption on the premises during the course of the event.

(6) The number of persons present on the premises at the time of the sale must not exceed 300.

(7) Regulations may provide for additional conditions prescribed in the regulations to be community event conditions.

[Licensing Act 2003, s 110B as inserted by the Deregulation Act 2015, Sch 17 from a date to be appointed.]

**7.7474C 110C. Ancillary business sales conditions** (1) The ancillary business sales conditions, in relation to a sale by retail of alcohol, are the conditions set out in subsections (2) to (5) and any additional conditions set out in regulations under subsection (6).

(2) The sale must be made by or on behalf of a body that—

(*a*) is of a prescribed description, and

(*b*) meets any prescribed criteria.

(3) The sale must take place on premises that—

(*a*) are managed by the body by or on whose behalf the sale is made,

(*b*) are of a prescribed description, and

(*c*) meet any prescribed criteria.

(4) The sale must be ancillary to the provision of goods or services to a person on the premises where the sale takes place.

(5) Except in prescribed circumstances, the alcohol must be sold for consumption on those premises.

(6) Regulations may provide for additional conditions prescribed in the regulations to be ancillary business sales conditions.

[Licensing Act 2003, s 110C as inserted by the Deregulation Act 2015, Sch 17 from a date to be appointed.]

*Part 5A notices*

**7.7474D 110D. Conditions for validity of notices** (1) A notice complies with this section if the conditions set out in subsections (2) to (10) are satisfied in relation to the notice.

(2) The notice must specify whether—

(*a*) the community event conditions (set out in section 110B or in regulations under that section), or

(*b*) the ancillary business sales conditions (set out in section 110C or in regulations under that section),

will be satisfied in relation to sales of alcohol on the premises in question.

(3) The notice must specify (for the purposes of section 110A(2))—

(*a*) in the case of a notice that specifies the ancillary business sales conditions, the set of premises to which it relates;

(*b*) in the case of a notice that specifies the community event conditions, no more than three sets of community premises, each of which must be wholly or partly in the area of the same licensing authority.

(4) The notice must be given, on behalf of the body by or on whose behalf the sale of alcohol on the premises would take place, by a person who is aged 18 or over and is concerned in the management of the body.

(5) The notice must be given to the relevant licensing authority, accompanied by the prescribed

fee.

(6) Unless the notice is given to the relevant licensing authority by means of a relevant electronic facility, a copy of the notice must be given to each relevant person.

(7) The notice must be in the prescribed form.

(8) The notice must specify the date when it takes effect.

(9) The specified date must be at least 10 working days, but no more than 3 months, after the day on which the notice is given.

Where subsection (6) applies, the notice is treated as given only when that subsection is complied with.

(10) The notice must contain any other information that regulations require it to contain.

(11) In this Part, "relevant person", in relation to any premises, means—

(*a*) the chief officer of police for any police area in which the premises are situated;

(*b*) the local authority by which statutory functions are exercisable in any area in which the premises are situated in relation to minimising or preventing the risk of pollution of the environment or of harm to human health.

[Licensing Act 2003, s 110D as inserted by the Deregulation Act 2015, Sch 17 from a date to be appointed.]

7.7474E **110E. Special restriction on giving of notices** (1) This section applies where—

(*a*) a Part 5A notice is given on behalf of a body, and

(*b*) a counter notice under section 110J is given in relation to the Part 5A notice.

(2) No further Part 5A notice may be given in respect of any premises specified in the notice, whether on behalf of that body or on behalf of another body that is an associate of it, before the end of the period of 12 months beginning with the day on which the counter notice is given.

(3) However, the restriction in subsection (2) ceases to apply if the counter notice is revoked under section 110K or quashed by a court.

(4) For the purposes of this section, a body is an associate of another body if it would be an associate of the other body for the purposes of the Estate Agents Act 1979 (see section 32(4) to (6) of that Act).

[Licensing Act 2003, s 110E as inserted by the Deregulation Act 2015, Sch 17 from a date to be appointed.]

7.7474F **110F. Date when Part 5A notice takes effect** (1) A Part 5A notice takes effect on the date specified under section 110D(8).

(2) Subsection (1) does not apply if a counter notice is given under section 110J in relation to the notice.

(For the case where a counter notice is revoked or quashed by a court, see section 110K(2).)

[Licensing Act 2003, s 110F as inserted by the Deregulation Act 2015, Sch 17 from a date to be appointed.]

7.7474G **110G. Acknowledgement of notice etc** (1) This section applies where a relevant licensing authority receives a notice that is, or purports to be, a Part 5A notice.

(2) The authority must give written acknowledgement of the receipt of the notice to the person who gave it.

(3) The acknowledgment must be given—

(*a*) before the end of the first working day following the day on which it was received, or

(*b*) if the day on which it was received was not a working day, before the end of the second working day following that day.

(4) If the licensing authority is of the opinion that the notice does not comply with section 110D, the authority must as soon as possible give to the person who gave the notice written notification of the reasons for its opinion.

(5) Subsection (2) does not apply where, before the time by which acknowledgement of the receipt of the notice must be given in accordance with subsection (3), the person who gave the notice has been given a counter notice under section 110J.

[Licensing Act 2003, s 110G as inserted by the Deregulation Act 2015, Sch 17 from a date to be appointed.]

7.7474H **110H. Theft, loss etc of Part 5A notice** (1) Where a Part 5A notice is lost, stolen, damaged or destroyed, the person who gave the notice may apply to the relevant licensing authority for a copy of the notice.

(2) The application must be accompanied by the prescribed fee.

(3) Where an application is made in accordance with this section, the licensing authority must issue the applicant with a copy of the notice (certified by the authority to be a true copy) if it is satisfied that the notice has been lost, stolen, damaged or destroyed.

(4) This Act applies in relation to a copy issued under this section as it applies in relation to an original notice.

[Licensing Act 2003, s 110H as inserted by the Deregulation Act 2015, Sch 17 from a date to be appointed.]

*Objections and counter notices*

7.7474I **110I. Objection to Part 5A notice by a relevant person** (1) Where a relevant person who is given a Part 5A notice is satisfied that allowing alcohol to be sold on the premises (or any of the premises) to which the notice relates would undermine a licensing objective, the relevant person must give a notice stating the reasons for being so satisfied (an "objection notice")—

(*a*) to the relevant licensing authority,

(*b*) to the person who gave the Part 5A notice, and

(*c*) to every other relevant person.

(2) Subsection (1) does not apply at any time after the relevant person has received a copy of a counter notice under section 110J in relation to the Part 5A notice.

(3) An objection notice may be given only during the period beginning with the day on which the relevant person is given the Part 5A notice and ending with the third working day following that day ("the three-day period").

(4) The restriction in subsection (3) does not apply to an objection notice based on—

(*a*) things occurring after the end of the three-day period, or

(*b*) information that the relevant person was unaware of, and could not with reasonable diligence have discovered, until after the end of that period.

[Licensing Act 2003, s 110I as inserted by the Deregulation Act 2015, Sch 17 from a date to be appointed.]

**7.7474J 110J. Counter notices** (1) Where a relevant licensing authority receives a Part 5A notice, the relevant licensing authority may—

(*a*) give the person who gave the Part 5A notice a counter notice under this section;

(*b*) give a copy of the counter notice to each relevant person.

(2) Where the relevant licensing authority receives an objection notice given in compliance with the requirement imposed by section 110I(3), the relevant licensing authority must decide whether to give a counter notice (and, if it does so decide, give that notice) no later than whichever of the following is the earlier—

(*a*) the day before the date when the Part 5A notice would take effect (see section 110D(8));

(*b*) the expiry of the period of 28 days beginning with the day on which the objection notice is received by the relevant licensing authority.

(3) The power conferred by subsection (1) may not be exercised at any time after the Part 5A notice takes effect unless an objection notice under section 110I has been given, by virtue of subsection (4) of that section, in relation to the notice.

(4) The counter notice must—

(*a*) be in the prescribed form, and

(*b*) be given in the prescribed manner.

[Licensing Act 2003, s 110J as inserted by the Deregulation Act 2015, Sch 17 from a date to be appointed.]

**7.7474K 110K. Counter notices: revocation etc** (1) A relevant licensing authority must revoke a counter notice given under section 110J if—

(*a*) the counter notice was given in consequence of one or more objection notices under section 110I, and

(*b*) the objection notice or (as the case may be) each of them is withdrawn by the person who gave it or is quashed by a court.

(2) Where a counter notice is revoked or is quashed by a court—

(*a*) the counter notice is disregarded for the purposes of section 110A(3), except in relation to any time before the day on which it is revoked or quashed,

(*b*) the Part 5A notice takes effect on that day, and

(*c*) the relevant licensing authority must as soon as possible notify the person who gave the Part 5A notice of the date on which it takes effect.

[Licensing Act 2003, s 110K as inserted by the Deregulation Act 2015, Sch 17 from a date to be appointed.]

*Rights of entry, production of notice, etc*

**7.7474L 110L. Right of entry where Part 5A notice given** (1) A constable or an authorised officer may, at any reasonable time, enter premises to which a Part 5A notice relates to assess the likely effect of the notice on the promotion of the crime prevention objective.

(2) An authorised officer exercising the power conferred by this section must, if so requested, produce evidence of the officer's authority to exercise the power.

(3) It is an offence intentionally to obstruct an authorised officer exercising a power conferred by this section.

(4) A person guilty of an offence under this section is liable on summary conviction to a fine not exceeding level 2 on the standard scale.

(5) In this section "authorised officer" means—

(*a*) an officer of the licensing authority in whose area the premises are situated, or

(*b*) if the premises are situated in the area of more than one licensing authority, an officer of any of those authorities,

authorised for the purposes of this Act.

[Licensing Act 2003, s 110L as inserted by the Deregulation Act 2015, Sch 17 from a date to be appointed.]

**7.7474M 110M. Duty to keep and produce Part 5A notice** (1) This section applies whenever premises are being used for sales of alcohol which are, or are purported to be, permitted sales by virtue of this Part.

(2) The person who gave the Part 5A notice must secure that a copy of the notice is either—

(*a*) prominently displayed at the premises, or

(*b*) kept at the premises in the custody of that person or of someone who is present and working at the premises and whom that person has nominated for the purposes of this section (a "nominated person").

(3) Where a copy of the Part 5A notice is kept in the custody of a nominated person (and not prominently displayed at the premises) the person who gave the Part 5A notice must secure that a notice—

(*a*) stating that a copy of the Part 5A notice is in the nominated person's custody, and

(*b*) specifying the position held at the premises by the nominated person,

is prominently displayed at the premises.

(4) It is an offence for the person who gave the Part 5A notice to fail, without reasonable excuse, to comply with subsection (2) or (where it applies) subsection (3).

(5) Where—

(*a*) a copy of the Part 5A notice is not prominently displayed at the premises, and

(*b*) no notice is displayed as mentioned in subsection (3),

a constable or authorised officer may require the person who gave the Part 5A notice to produce a copy of it for examination.

(6) Where a notice is displayed as mentioned in subsection (3), a constable or authorised officer may require the nominated person to produce a copy of the Part 5A notice for examination.

(7) An authorised officer exercising the power conferred by subsection (5) or (6) must, if so requested, produce evidence of the officer's authority to exercise the power.

(8) It is an offence for a person to fail, without reasonable excuse, to produce a copy of a Part 5A notice in accordance with a requirement under subsection (5) or (6).

(9) A person guilty of an offence under this section is liable on summary conviction to a fine not exceeding level 2 on the standard scale.

(10) In this section "authorised officer" has the meaning given in section 110L(5).

[Licensing Act 2003, s 110M as inserted by the Deregulation Act 2015, Sch 17 from a date to be appointed.]

*Supplementary*

7.7474N **110N. The relevant licensing authority** (1) For the purposes of this Part, the "relevant licensing authority", in relation to any premises, is determined in accordance with this section.

(2) In the case of a Part 5A notice that specifies the ancillary business sales conditions or in the case of a Part 5A notice that specifies the community event conditions in relation to only one set of premises, the relevant licensing authority is, subject to subsection (3), the authority in whose area the premises are situated.

(3) Where the premises are situated in the areas of two or more licensing authorities, the relevant licensing authority is—

(*a*) the licensing authority in whose area the greater or greatest part of the premises is situated, or

(*b*) if there is no authority to which paragraph (a) applies, such one of the authorities as the person giving the Part 5A notice may choose.

(4) In the case of a Part 5A notice that specifies the community event conditions in relation to more than one set of premises, the relevant licensing authority is—

(*a*) if there is only one licensing authority in whose area each set of premises is wholly or partly situated, that licensing authority;

(*b*) if each set of premises falls partly in the area of one authority and also partly in the area of another, such one of them as the person giving the Part 5A notice may choose.

[Licensing Act 2003, s 110N as inserted by the Deregulation Act 2015, Sch 17 from a date to be appointed.]

## PART 6[1]

## PERSONAL LICENCES

*Introductory*

7.7475 **111. Personal licence** (1) In this Act "personal licence" means a licence which—

(*a*) is granted by a licensing authority to an individual, and

(*b*) authorises that individual to supply alcohol, or authorise the supply of alcohol, in accordance with a premises licence.

(2) In subsection (1)(*b*) the reference to an individual supplying alcohol is to him—

(*a*) selling alcohol by retail, or

(*b*) supplying alcohol by or on behalf of a club to, or to the order of, a member of the club.

[Licensing Act 2003, s 111.]

[1] Part 6 comprises ss 111–135 and Sch 4.

7.7476 **112. The relevant licensing authority** For the purposes of this Part the "relevant licensing authority", in relation to a personal licence, is the licensing authority which granted the licence.

[Licensing Act 2003, s 112.]

7.7477 **113. Meaning of "relevant offence", "immigration offence", "foreign offence" and "immigration penalty"** (1) In this Part "relevant offence" means an offence listed in Schedule 4.

(2) The Secretary of State may by order amend that list so as to add, modify or omit any entry.

(2A) In this Part "immigration offence" means—

(a) an offence referred to in paragraph 7A of Schedule 4, or

(b) an offence listed in paragraph 24 or 25 of Schedule 4 that is committed in relation to an offence referred to in paragraph 7A of that Schedule.

(3) In this Part "foreign offence" means an offence (other than a relevant offence) under the law of any place outside England and Wales.

(4) In this Part "immigration penalty" means a penalty under—

(a) section 15 of the Immigration, Asylum and Nationality Act 2006 ("the 2006 Act"), or

(b) section 23 of the Immigration Act 2014 ("the 2014 Act").

(5) For the purposes of this Part a person to whom a penalty notice under section 15 of the 2006 Act has been given is not to be treated as having been required to pay an immigration penalty if—

(a) the person is excused payment by virtue of section 15(3) of that Act, or

(b) the penalty is cancelled by virtue of section 16 or 17 of that Act.

(6) For the purposes of this Part a person to whom a penalty notice under section 15 of the 2006 Act has been given is not to be treated as having been required to pay an immigration penalty until such time as—

(a) the period for giving a notice of objection under section 16 of that Act has expired and the Secretary of State has considered any notice given within that period, and

(b) if a notice of objection was given within that period, the period for appealing under section 17 of that Act has expired and any appeal brought within that period has been finally determined, abandoned or withdrawn.

(7) For the purposes of this Part a person to whom a penalty notice under section 23 of the 2014 Act has been given is not to be treated as having been required to pay an immigration penalty if—

(a) the person is excused payment by virtue of section 24 of that Act, or

(b) the penalty is cancelled by virtue of section 29 or 30 of that Act.

(8) For the purposes of this Part a person to whom a penalty notice under section 23 of the 2014 Act has been given is not to be treated as having been required to pay an immigration penalty until such time as—

(a) the period for giving a notice of objection under section 29 of that Act has expired and the Secretary of State has considered any notice given within that period, and

(b) if a notice of objection was given within that period, the period for appealing under section 30 of that Act has expired and any appeal brought within that period has been finally determined, abandoned or withdrawn.

[Licensing Act 2003, s 113 as amended by the Immigration Act 2016, Sch 4.]

7.7478 **114. Spent convictions** For the purposes of this Part a conviction for a relevant offence or a foreign offence must be disregarded if it is spent for the purposes of the Rehabilitation of Offenders Act 1974 (c 53)[1].

[Licensing Act 2003, s 114.]

---

1 In PART III: SENTENCING, ante.

7.7479 **115. Period of validity of personal licence** *(As amended by the Immigration Act 2016, Sch 4) Personal licence to have effect indefinitely. Personal licence ceases to have effect if surrendered under s 116, revoked under s 119, or forfeited under s 129. Also of no effect during period of any suspension under s 129.*

7.7480 **116. Surrender of personal licence** *Personal licence may be surrendered by giving of notice to licensing authority. Licence lapses on receipt of notice.*

*Grant of licences*

7.7481 **117. Application for grant of personal licence** *An application by an individual for the grant of a personal licence must, if the applicant is ordinarily resident in the area of a licensing authority, be made to that authority, and may, in any other case, be made to any licensing authority.*

7.7482 **118.** *Individual permitted to hold one personal licence only.*

7.7483 **120. Determination of application for grant** (1) This section applies where an application for the grant of a personal licence is made to a licensing authority in accordance with section 117.

(2) The authority must grant the licence if it appears to it that—

(*a*) the applicant is aged 18 or over,

(*aa*) he is entitled to work in the United Kingdom,

(*b*) he possesses a licensing qualification or is a person of a prescribed[1] description,

(*c*) no personal licence held by him has been forfeited in the period of five years ending with the day the application was made, and

(*d*) he has not been convicted of any relevant offence[2] or any foreign offence or required to pay an immigration penalty.

(3) The authority must reject the application if it appears to it that the applicant fails to meet the

condition in any of paragraphs (a) to (c) of subsection (2).

(4) If it appears to the authority that the applicant meets the conditions in paragraphs (*a*) to (*c*) of that subsection but fails to meet the condition in paragraph (*d*) of that subsection, the authority must give the chief officer of police for its area a notice to that effect.

(5) Where, having regard to—

(*a*) any conviction of the applicant for a relevant offence,

(*b*) any conviction of his for a foreign offence which the chief officer of police considers to be comparable to a relevant offence, and

(*c*) the applicant having been required to pay any immigration penalty,

the chief officer of police is satisfied that granting the licence would undermine the crime prevention objective, he must, within the period of 14 days beginning with the day he received the notice under subsection (4), give the authority a notice stating the reasons why he is so satisfied (an "objection notice").

(5A) If it appears to the authority that the applicant meets the conditions in paragraphs (a) to (c) of subsection (2) but fails to meet the condition in paragraph (d) of that subsection by virtue of having been—

(a) convicted of an immigration offence,

(b) convicted of a foreign offence that the authority considers to be comparable to an immigration offence, or

(c) required to pay an immigration penalty,

the authority must give the Secretary of State a notice to that effect.

(5B) Where, having regard to—

(a) any conviction of the applicant for an immigration offence,

(b) any conviction of the applicant for a foreign offence which the Secretary of State considers to be comparable to an immigration offence, and

(c) the applicant having been required to pay any immigration penalty,

the Secretary of State is satisfied that granting the licence would be prejudicial to the prevention of illegal working in licensed premises, the Secretary of State must, within the period of 14 days beginning with the day the Secretary of State received the notice under subsection (5A), give the authority a notice stating the reasons for being so satisfied (an "immigration objection notice").

(6) Where no objection notice or immigration objection notice is given within the period of 14 days referred to in subsection (5) or (5B) (as the case may be), or any such notice given is withdrawn, the authority must grant the application.

(7) Where an objection notice or an immigration objection notice is given within the period of 14 days referred to in subsection (5) or (5B) (as the case may be), and not withdrawn, the authority—

(*a*) must hold a hearing to consider the notice, unless the applicant, the person who gave the notice and the authority agree that it is unnecessary, and

(b) having regard to the notice, must—

(i) where the notice is an objection notice, reject the application if it considers it appropriate for the promotion of the crime prevention objective to do so, or

(ii) where the notice is an immigration objection notice, reject the application if it considers it appropriate for the prevention of illegal working in licensed premises to do so.

(7A) An application that is not rejected by the authority under subsection (7)(b) must be granted by it.

(8) In this section "licensing qualification" means—

(*a*) a qualification—

(i) accredited at the time of its award, and

(ii) awarded by a body accredited at that time,

(*b*) a qualification awarded before the coming into force of this section which the Secretary of State certifies is to be treated for the purposes of this section as if it were a qualification within paragraph (*a*), or

(*c*) a qualification obtained in Scotland or Northern Ireland or in an EEA State (other than the United Kingdom) which is equivalent to a qualification within paragraph (*a*) or (*b*).

(9) For this purpose—

"accredited" means accredited by the Secretary of State; and

"EEA State" means a state which is a contracting party to the Agreement on the European Economic Area signed at Oporto on 2nd May 1992, as adjusted by the Protocol signed at Brussels on 17th March 1993.

[Licensing Act 2003, s 120 as amended by the Police Reform and Social Responsibility Act 2011, s 111 and the Immigration Act 2016, Sch 4.]

1 See the Licensing Act 2003 (Personal Licences) Regulations 2005, SI 2005/41 amended by SI 2012/946 and SI 2014/3284 and the Welsh Language (Gambling and Licensing Forms) Regulations 2010, SI 2010/2440.

2 For meaning of "relevant offence", see Sch 4, post.

7.7485 **122. Notification of determinations** (1) Where a licensing authority grants an application—

(*a*) it must give the applicant and the chief officer of police for its area a notice to that effect, and

(*b*) if the chief officer of police gave an objection notice or the Secretary of State gave an immigration objection notice (which, in either case) was not withdrawn), the notice under paragraph (*a*) must contain a statement of the licensing authority's reasons for granting the application.

(2) A licensing authority which rejects an application must give the applicant and the chief officer of police for its area a notice to that effect containing a statement of the authority's reasons for rejecting the application.

(2A) Where the Secretary of State gave an immigration objection notice (which was not withdrawn) the notice under subsection (1)(a) or (2), as the case may be, must also be given to the Secretary of State.

(3) In this section—

"application" means an application for the grant of a personal licence; and

"objection notice" and "immigration objection notice" have the meaning given in section 120.

[Licensing Act 2003, s 122 as amended by the Deregulation Act 2015, Sch 18 and the Immigration Act 2016, Sch 4.]

7.7486 **123. Duty to notify licensing authority of convictions etc during application period** (1) Where an applicant for the grant of a personal licence is convicted of a relevant offence or a foreign offence during the application period, he must as soon as reasonably practicable notify the conviction or the requirement to pay (as the case may be) to the authority to which the application is made.

(2) A person commits an offence if he fails, without reasonable excuse, to comply with subsection (1).

(3) A person guilty of an offence under this section is liable on summary conviction to a fine not exceeding level 4 on the standard scale.

(4) In this section "the application period", or is required to pay an immigration penalty during that period means the period that—

(*a*) begins when the application for grant is made, and

(*b*) ends when the application is determined or withdrawn.

[Licensing Act 2003, s 123 as amended by the Deregulation Act 2015, Sch 18 and the Immigration Act 2016, Sch 4.]

7.7487 **124. Convictions coming to light after grant** (1) This section applies where, after a licensing authority has granted a personal licence, it becomes aware (whether by virtue of section 123(1), 131 or 132 or otherwise) that the holder of a personal licence ("the licence holder") was convicted during the application period of any relevant offence or foreign offence or was required during that period to pay an immigration penalty.

(2) The licensing authority must give a notice to that effect to the chief officer of police for its area.

(3) Where, having regard to—

(*a*) any conviction of the licence holder for a relevant offence which occurred before the end of the application period,

(*b*) any conviction of his for a foreign offence which the chief officer of police considers to be comparable to a relevant offence and which occurred before the end of the application period, and

(*c*) the licence holder having been required before the end of the application period to pay any immigration penalty,

the chief officer of police is satisfied that continuation of the licence would undermine the crime prevention objective, he must, within the period of 14 days beginning with the day he received the notice under subsection (2), give the authority a notice stating the reasons why he is so satisfied (an "objection notice").

(3A) Where the licence holder was (during the application period)—

(a) convicted of an immigration offence,

(b) convicted of a foreign offence that the licensing authority considers to be comparable to an immigration offence, or

(c) required to pay an immigration penalty,

the authority must give the Secretary of State a notice to that effect.

(3B) Where, having regard to—

(a) any conviction of the licence holder for an immigration offence which occurred before the end of the application period,

(b) any conviction of the licence holder for a foreign offence which the Secretary of State considers to be comparable to an immigration offence and which occurred before the end of the application period, and

(c) the licence holder having been required before the end of the application period to pay any immigration penalty,

the Secretary of State is satisfied that continuation of the licence would be prejudicial to the prevention of illegal working in licensed premises, the Secretary of State must, within the period of 14 days beginning with the day the Secretary of State received the notice under subsection (3A), give the authority a notice stating the reasons for being so satisfied (an "immigration objection notice").

(4) Where an objection notice or an immigration objection notice is given within the period of 14 days referred to in subsection (3) or (3B), as the case may be, (and not withdrawn), the authority—

(*a*) must hold a hearing to consider the notice, unless the licence holder, the person who gave the notice and the authority agree it is unnecessary, and

(*b*) having regard to the notice, must—

(i) where the notice is an objection notice, revoke the licence if it considers it appropriate for the promotion of the crime prevention objective to do so, or

(ii) where the notice is an immigration objection notice, revoke the licence if it considers it appropriate for the prevention of illegal working in licensed premises to do so.

(5) Where the authority revokes or decides not to revoke a licence under subsection (4) it must notify the offender and the chief officer of police of the decision and its reasons for making it.

(5A) Where the authority revokes or decides not to revoke a licence under subsection (4)(b)(ii) it must also notify the Secretary of State of the decision and its reasons for making it.

(6) A decision under this section does not have effect—

(*a*) until the end of the period given for appealing against the decision, or

(*b*) if the decision is appealed against, until the appeal is disposed of.

(7) In this section "application period", in relation to the grant of a personal licence, means the period that—

(*a*) begins when the application for the grant is made, and

(*b*) ends at the time of the grant.

[Licensing Act 2003, s 124 as amended by the Police Reform and Social Responsibility Act 2011, s 111, the Deregulation Act 2015, Sch 18 and the Immigration Act 2016, Sch 4.]

7.7488 **125. Form of personal licence** *(as amended by the Immigration Act 2016, Sch 4) Form of personal licence prescribed by regulations*[1].

[1] The Licensing Act 2003 (Personal Licences) Regulations 2005, SI 2005/41 amended by SI 2012/946 and SI 2014/3284 and the Welsh Language (Gambling and Licensing Forms) Regulations 2010, SI 2010/2440 have been made.

7.7489 **126. Theft, loss, etc of personal licence** *Power to apply for duplicate personal licence on payment of fee.*

*Duty to notify certain changes*

7.7490 **127. Duty to notify change of name or address** (1) The holder of a personal licence must, as soon as reasonably practicable, notify the relevant licensing authority of any change in his name or address as stated in the personal licence.

(2) Subsection (1) is subject to regulations under section 133(2) (power to prescribe fee to accompany notice).

(3) A notice under subsection (1) must also be accompanied by the personal licence or, if that is not practicable, by a statement of the reasons for the failure to provide the licence.

(4) A person commits an offence if he fails, without reasonable excuse, to comply with this section.

(5) A person guilty of an offence under subsection (4) is liable on summary conviction to a fine not exceeding level 2 on the standard scale.

[Licensing Act 2003, s 127.]

*Conviction of licence holder for relevant offence*

7.7491 **128. Duty to notify court of personal licence** (1) Where the holder of a personal licence is charged with a relevant offence[1], he must, no later than the time he makes his first appearance in a magistrates' court in connection with that offence—

(*a*) produce to the court the personal licence, or

(*b*) if that is not practicable, notify the court of the existence of the personal licence and the identity of the relevant licensing authority and of the reasons why he cannot produce the licence.

(2) Subsection (3) applies where a person charged with a relevant offence is granted a personal licence—

(*a*) after his first appearance in a magistrates' court in connection with that offence, but

(*b*) before—

(i) his conviction, and sentencing for the offence, or his acquittal, or,

(ii) where an appeal is brought against his conviction, sentence or acquittal, the disposal of that appeal.

(3) At his next appearance in court in connection with that offence, that person must—

(*a*) produce to the court the personal licence, or

(*b*) if that is not practicable, notify the court of the existence of the personal licence and the identity of the relevant licensing authority and of the reasons why he cannot produce the licence.

(4) Where—

(*a*) a person charged with a relevant offence has produced his licence to, or notified, a court under subsection (1) or (3), and

(*b*) before he is convicted of and sentenced for, or acquitted of, that offence, a notifiable event occurs in respect of the licence,

he must, at his next appearance in court in connection with that offence, notify the court of that event.

(5) For this purpose a "notifiable event" in relation to a personal licence means any of the following—

(*a*) *repealed*

(*b*) the surrender of the licence under section 116;

(*c*) *repealed*

(*d*) the revocation of the licence under section 124.

(6) A person commits an offence if he fails, without reasonable excuse, to comply with this section.

(7) A person guilty of an offence under subsection (6) is liable on summary conviction to a fine not exceeding level 2 on the standard scale.

[Licensing Act 2003, s 128 as amended by the Deregulation Act 2015, Sch 18.]

---

1 For meaning of "relevant offence", see Sch 4, post.

**7.7492 129. Forfeiture or suspension of licence on conviction for relevant offence**

(1) This section applies where the holder of a personal licence is convicted of a relevant offence[1] by or before a court in England and Wales.

(2) The court may—

(*a*) order the forfeiture of the licence, or

(*b*) order its suspension for a period not exceeding six months.

(3) In determining whether to make an order under subsection (2), the court may take account of any previous conviction of the holder for a relevant offence.

(4) Where a court makes an order under this section it may suspend the order pending an appeal against it.

(5) Subject to subsection (4) and section 130, an order under this section takes effect immediately after it is made.

[Licensing Act 2003, s 129.]

---

1 For meaning of "relevant offence", see Sch 4, post.

**7.7493 131. Court's duty to notify licensing authority of convictions** (1) This section applies where a person who holds a personal licence ("the relevant person") is convicted, by or before a court in England and Wales, of a relevant offence in a case where—

(*a*) the relevant person has given notice under section 128 (notification of personal licence), or

(*b*) the court is, for any other reason, aware of the existence of that personal licence.

(2) The appropriate officer of the court must (as soon as reasonably practicable)—

(*a*) send to the relevant licensing authority a notice specifying—

(i) the name and address of the relevant person,

(ii) the nature and date of the conviction, and

(iii) any sentence passed in respect of it, including any order made under section 129, and

(*b*) send a copy of the notice to the relevant person.

(3) Where, on an appeal against the relevant person's conviction for the relevant offence or against the sentence imposed on him for that offence, his conviction is quashed or a new sentence is substituted for that sentence, the court which determines the appeal must (as soon as reasonably practicable) arrange—

(*a*) for notice of the quashing of the conviction or the substituting of the sentence to be sent to the relevant licensing authority, and

(*b*) for a copy of the notice to be sent to the relevant person.

(4) Where the case is referred to the Court of Appeal under section 36 of the Criminal Justice Act 1988 (c 33) (review of lenient sentence), the court must cause—

(*a*) notice of any action it takes under subsection (1) of that section to be sent to the relevant licensing authority, and

(*b*) a copy of the notice to be sent to the relevant person.

(5) For the purposes of subsection (2) "the appropriate officer" is—

(*a*) in the case of a magistrates' court, the clerk of the court, and

(*b*) in the case of the Crown Court, the appropriate officer;

and section 141 of the Magistrates' Courts Act 1980 (c 43) (meaning of "clerk of a magistrates' court") applies in relation to this subsection as it applies in relation to that section.

[Licensing Act 2003, s 131.]

**7.7494 132. Licence holder's duty to notify licensing authority of convictions etc**

(1) Subsection (2) applies where the holder of a personal licence—

(*a*) is convicted of a relevant offence, in a case where section 131(1) does not apply, or

(*b*) is convicted of a foreign offence.

(2) The holder must—

(*a*) as soon as reasonably practicable after the conviction, give the relevant licensing authority a notice containing details of the nature and date of the conviction, and any sentence imposed on him in respect of it, and

(*b*) as soon as reasonably practicable after the determination of any appeal against the conviction or sentence, or of any reference under section 36 of the Criminal Justice Act 1988 (c 33) in respect of the case, give the relevant licensing authority a notice containing details of the determination.

(2A) Subsection (2B) applies where the holder of a personal licence is required to pay an immigration penalty.

(2B) The holder must, as soon as reasonably practicable after being required to pay the penalty, give the relevant licensing authority a notice containing details of the penalty, including the date of the notice by which the penalty was imposed.

(3) A notice under subsection (2) or (2B) must be accompanied by the personal licence or, if that is not practicable, a statement of the reasons for the failure to provide the licence.

(4) A person commits an offence if he fails, without reasonable excuse, to comply with this section.

(5) A person guilty of an offence under subsection (4) is liable on summary conviction to a fine not exceeding level 2 on the standard scale.

[Licensing Act 2003, s 132 as amended by the Immigration Act 2016, Sch 4.]

**7.7494A 132A. Convictions etc of licence-holder: powers of licensing authority**

(1) This section applies where a licensing authority has granted a personal licence and it becomes aware (whether by virtue of section 123(1), 131 or 132 or otherwise) that the holder of the licence ("the licence holder") has been, at any time before or after the grant of the licence—

(a) convicted of any relevant offence or foreign offence, or

(b) required to pay an immigration penalty.

(2) But this section does not apply at any time when in the case of a licence holder who has been convicted of any relevant offence or foreign offence—

(a) the licence holder has appealed against a conviction for, or any sentence imposed in relation to, a relevant offence or foreign offence and that appeal has not been disposed of, or

(b) the time limit for appealing against such a conviction or sentence has not expired.

(3) The relevant licensing authority may—

(a) suspend the licence for a period not exceeding six months, or

(b) revoke the licence.

(4) If the relevant licensing authority is considering whether to suspend or revoke the licence, the authority must give notice to the licence holder.

(5) A notice under subsection (4) must invite the licence holder to make representations regarding—

(a) the relevant offence, foreign offence or immigration penalty that has caused the relevant licensing authority to issue the notice,

(b) any decision of a court under section 129 or 130 in relation to the licence, and

(c) any other relevant information (including information regarding the licence holder's personal circumstances).

(6) The licence holder may make representations under subsection (5) to the relevant licensing authority within the period of 28 days beginning with the day the notice was issued.

(7) Before deciding whether to suspend or revoke the licence the relevant licensing authority must take into account—

(a) any representations made by the licence holder under this section,

(b) any decision of a court under section 129 or 130 of which the licensing authority is aware, and

(c) any other information which the authority considers relevant.

(8) Having taken into account the matters described in subsection (7) the relevant licensing authority may make a decision whether to suspend or revoke a licence, unless subsection (9) applies.

(9) This subsection applies where the relevant licensing authority has taken into account the matters described in subsection (7) and proposes not to revoke the licence.

(10) Where subsection (9) applies the authority must—

(a) give notice to the chief officer of police for its area that it proposes not to revoke the licence, and

(b) invite the officer to make representations regarding the issue of whether the licence should be suspended or revoked having regard to the crime prevention objective.

(11) The chief officer of police may make representations under subsection (10)(b) to the relevant licensing authority within the period of 14 days beginning with the day the notice was received.

(12) Where the relevant licensing authority has given notice to the chief officer of police under subsection (10)(a), the authority must take into account—

(a) any representations from the officer, and
(b) the matters described in subsection (7),

and then make a decision whether to suspend or revoke the licence.

(13) The relevant licensing authority must give notice of any decision made under subsection (8) or (12) to the licence holder and the chief officer of police, including reasons for the decision.

(14) A decision under this section does not have effect—
(a) until the end of the period given for appealing against the decision, or
(b) if the decision is appealed against, until the appeal is disposed of.

(15) A decision under subsection (8) or (12) may be appealed (see paragraph 17(5A) of Part 3 of Schedule 5 (appeals: personal licences)).

[Licensing Act 2003, s 132A as inserted by the Policing and Crime Act 2017, s 138.]

*General provision*

**7.7495 133. Form etc of applications and notices under Part 6** *Form of application or notice, manner in which it is to be made or give and information and documents to accompany it and any fee payable to be prescribed by regulations*[1].

---

[1] The Licensing Act 2003 (Personal Licences) Regulations 2005, SI 2005/41 amended by SI 2012/946 and SI 2014/3284, the Licensing Act 2003 (Fees) Regulations 2005, SI 2005/79 amended by SI 2009/1809 and the Welsh Language (Gambling and Licensing Forms) Regulations 2010, SI 2010/2440 have been made.

**7.7496 134. Licensing authority's duty to update licence document** (1) Where—
(*a*) the relevant licensing authority makes a determination under section 124(4),
(*b*) it receives a notice under section 123(1), 127, 131 or 132, or
(*c*) an appeal against a decision under this Part is disposed of,

in relation to a personal licence, the authority must make the appropriate amendments (if any) to the licence.

(2) Where, under section 131, notice is given of the making of an order under section 129, the relevant licensing authority must make an endorsement on the licence stating the terms of the order.

(3) Where, under section 131, notice is given of the quashing of such an order, any endorsement previously made under subsection (2) in respect of it must be cancelled.

(4) Where a licensing authority is not in possession of a personal licence, it may, for the purposes of discharging its obligations under this section, require the holder of the licence to produce it to the authority within 14 days beginning with the day on which he is notified of the requirement.

(5) A person commits an offence if he fails, without reasonable excuse, to comply with a requirement under subsection (4).

(6) A person guilty of an offence under subsection (5) is liable on summary conviction to a fine not exceeding level 2 on the standard scale.

[Licensing Act 2003, s 134 as amended by the Deregulation Act 2015, Sch 18.]

*Production of licence*

**7.7497 135. Licence holder's duty to produce licence** (1) This section applies where the holder of a personal licence is on premises to make or authorise the supply of alcohol, and such supplies—
(*a*) are authorised by a premises licence in respect of those premises, or
(*b*) are a permitted temporary activity on the premises by virtue of a temporary event notice given under Part 5 in respect of which he is the premises user.

(2) Any constable or authorised officer may require the holder of the personal licence to produce that licence for examination.

(3) An authorised officer exercising the power conferred by subsection (2) must, if so requested, produce evidence of his authority to exercise the power.

(4) A person who fails, without reasonable excuse, to comply with a requirement under subsection (2) is guilty of an offence.

(5) A person guilty of an offence under subsection (4) is liable on summary conviction to a fine not exceeding level 2 on the standard scale.

(6) In this section "authorised officer" means an officer of a licensing authority authorised by the authority for the purposes of this Act.

[Licensing Act 2003, s 135.]

## PART 7[1]
## OFFENCES

*Unauthorised licensable activities*

**7.7498 136. Unauthorised licensable activities**[2] (1) A person commits an offence[3] if—
(*a*) he carries on or attempts to carry on[4] a licensable activity[5] on or from any premises otherwise than under and in accordance with an authorisation, or
(*b*) he knowingly allows a licensable activity[5] to be so carried on.

(2) Where the licensable activity[5] in question is the provision of regulated entertainment, a

person does not commit an offence under this section if his only involvement in the provision of the entertainment is that he—

(*a*) performs in a play,
(*b*) participates as a sportsman in an indoor sporting event,
(*c*) boxes or wrestles in a boxing or wrestling entertainment,
(*d*) performs live music,
(*e*) plays recorded music,
(*f*) performs dance, or
(*g*) does something coming within paragraph 2(1)(*h*) of Schedule 1 (entertainment similar to music, dance, etc).

(3) Subsection (2) is to be construed in accordance with Part 3 of Schedule 1.

(4) A person guilty of an offence under this section is liable on summary conviction to imprisonment for a term not exceeding six months or to a fine, or to both.

(5) In this Part "authorisation" means—

(*a*) a premises licence,
(*b*) a club premises certificate, or
(*c*) a temporary event notice in respect of which the conditions of section 98(2) to (4) are satisfied.*

[Licensing Act 2003, s 136 as amended by SI 2015/664.]

---

* **Amended by the Deregulation Act 2015, s 67 from a date to be appointed.**

1 Part 7 comprises ss 136–159.

2 See **para** 7.7340 **Offences – unauthorised licensable activities** ante, for liability under this provision.

3 For defence of due diligence, see s 139, post.

4 In *Hall v Woodhouse Ltd v Borough and County of the Town of Poole* [2009] EWHC 1587 (Admin)the convictions under this provision of a business which let a public house in which the tenant and his manager conducted unauthorised licensable activities were quashed:

> "17. In my judgment, s 136(1)(*a*) is directed at persons who, as a matter of fact, actually carry on or attempt to carry on a licensable activity on or from premises. That is the natural meaning of the language used. The matters referred to in subs (2), namely performing a play, participating as a sportsman and so on, also suggest that the focus is on actual conduct. So does s 139(1) which gives a person a defence where his act was due to a mistake etc and he took all reasonable precautions and exercised all due diligence to avoid committing the offence.
>
> 18. Section 136(1)(*a*) is not directed at holders of premises licences as such. An offence may be committed by carrying on a licensable activity when no premises licence exists at all. Where there is a premises licence but a licensable activity is carried on outside the scope of that licence or in breach of the conditions of the licence, it must, in my view, be a question of fact whether it is carried on by the holder of the licence. The mere fact that he is the holder of a licence does not make him automatically liable in respect of the carrying of a licensable activity on or from the premises to which the licence relates (per Richards LJ)."

5 For meaning of "licensing activity", see s 1(1).

7.7499 **137. Exposing alcohol for unauthorised sale** (1) A person commits an offence[1] if, on any premises, he exposes for sale by retail any alcohol in circumstances where the sale by retail of that alcohol on those premises would be an unauthorised licensable activity.

(2) For that purpose a licensable activity is unauthorised unless it is under and in accordance with an authorisation.

(3) A person guilty of an offence under this section is liable on summary conviction to imprisonment for a term not exceeding six months or to a fine, or to both.

(4) The court by which a person is convicted of an offence under this section may order the alcohol in question, and any container for it, to be forfeited and either destroyed or dealt with in such other manner as the court may order.

[Licensing Act 2003, s 137 as amended by SI 2015/664.]

---

1 For defence of due diligence, see s 139, post.

7.7500 **138. Keeping alcohol on premises for unauthorised sale etc** (1) A person commits an offence[1] if he has in his possession or under his control alcohol which he intends to sell by retail or supply in circumstances where that activity would be an unauthorised licensable activity.

(2) For that purpose a licensable activity is unauthorised unless it is under and in accordance with an authorisation[2].

(3) In subsection (1) the reference to the supply of alcohol is a reference to the supply of alcohol by or on behalf of a club to, or to the order of, a member of the club.

(4) A person guilty of an offence under this section is liable on summary conviction to a fine not exceeding level 2 on the standard scale.

(5) The court by which a person is convicted of an offence under this section may order the alcohol in question, and any container for it, to be forfeited and either destroyed or dealt with in such other manner as the court may order.

[Licensing Act 2003, s 138.]

---

1 For defence of due diligence, see s 139, post.

2 For meaning of "authorisation", see s 136(5), post.

7.7501 **139. Defence of due diligence** (1) In proceedings against a person for an offence to which subsection (2) applies, it is a defence that—

(*a*) his act was due to a mistake, or to reliance on information given to him, or to an act or omission by another person, or to some other cause beyond his control, and

(*b*) he took all reasonable precautions and exercised all due diligence to avoid committing the offence.

(2) This subsection applies to an offence under—

(*a*) section 136(1)(*a*) (carrying on unauthorised licensable activity),

(*b*) section 137 (exposing alcohol for unauthorised sale), or

(*c*) section 138 (keeping alcohol on premises for unauthorised sale).

[Licensing Act 2003, s 139.]

*Drunkenness and disorderly conduct*

7.7502 **140. Allowing disorderly conduct on licensed premises etc** (1) A person to whom subsection (2) applies commits an offence if he knowingly allows disorderly conduct on relevant premises.

(2) This subsection applies—

(*a*) to any person who works at the premises in a capacity, whether paid or unpaid, which authorises him to prevent the conduct,

(*b*) in the case of licensed premises, to—

(i) the holder of a premises licence in respect of the premises, and

(ii) the designated premises supervisor (if any) under such a licence,

(*c*) in the case of premises in respect of which a club premises certificate has effect, to any member or officer of the club which holds the certificate who at the time the conduct takes place is present on the premises in a capacity which enables him to prevent it, and

(*d*) in the case of premises which may be used for a permitted temporary activity by virtue of Part 5, to the premises user in relation to the temporary event notice in question.

(3) A person guilty of an offence under this section is liable on summary conviction to a fine not exceeding level 3 on the standard scale.*

[Licensing Act 2003, s 140.]

* **Amended by the Deregulation Act 2015, s 67 from a date to be appointed.**

7.7503 **141. Sale of alcohol to a person who is drunk** (1) A person to whom subsection (2) applies commits an offence if, on relevant premises, he knowingly—

(*a*) sells or attempts to sell alcohol to a person who is drunk, or

(*b*) allows alcohol to be sold to such a person.

(2) This subsection applies—

(*a*) to any person who works at the premises in a capacity, whether paid or unpaid, which gives him authority to sell the alcohol concerned,

(*b*) in the case of licensed premises, to—

(i) the holder of a premises licence in respect of the premises, and

(ii) the designated premises supervisor (if any) under such a licence,

(*c*) in the case of premises in respect of which a club premises certificate has effect, to any member or officer of the club which holds the certificate who at the time the sale (or attempted sale) takes place is present on the premises in a capacity which enables him to prevent it, and

(*d*) in the case of premises which may be used for a permitted temporary activity by virtue of Part 5, to the premises user in relation to the temporary event notice in question.

(3) This section applies in relation to the supply of alcohol by or on behalf of a club to or to the order of a member of the club as it applies in relation to the sale of alcohol.

(4) A person guilty of an offence under this section is liable on summary conviction to a fine not exceeding level 3 on the standard scale.*

[Licensing Act 2003, s 141.]

* **Amended by the Deregulation Act 2015, s 67 from a date to be appointed.**

7.7504 **142. Obtaining alcohol for a person who is drunk** (1) A person commits an offence if, on relevant premises, he knowingly obtains or attempts to obtain alcohol for consumption on those premises by a person who is drunk.

(2) A person guilty of an offence under this section is liable on summary conviction to a fine not exceeding level 3 on the standard scale.

[Licensing Act 2003, s 142.]

7.7505 **143. Failure to leave licensed premises etc** (1) A person who is drunk or disorderly commits an offence if, without reasonable excuse—

(*a*) he fails to leave relevant premises when requested to do so by a constable or by a person to whom subsection (2) applies, or

(*b*) he enters or attempts to enter relevant premises after a constable or a person to whom subsection (2) applies has requested him not to enter.

(2) This subsection applies—

(*a*) to any person who works at the premises in a capacity, whether paid or unpaid, which authorises him to make such a request,

(*b*) in the case of licensed premises, to—
(i) the holder of a premises licence in respect of the premises, or
(ii) the designated premises supervisor (if any) under such a licence,
(*c*) in the case of premises in respect of which a club premises certificate has effect, to any member or officer of the club which holds the certificate who is present on the premises in a capacity which enables him to make such a request, and
(*d*) in the case of premises which may be used for a permitted temporary activity by virtue of Part 5, to the premises user in relation to the temporary event notice in question.

(3) A person guilty of an offence under subsection (1) is liable on summary conviction to a fine not exceeding level 1 on the standard scale.

(4) On being requested to do so by a person to whom subsection (2) applies, a constable must—
(*a*) help to expel from relevant premises a person who is drunk or disorderly;
(*b*) help to prevent such a person from entering relevant premises[1].*

[Licensing Act 2003, s 143.]

---

* **Amended by the Deregulation Act 2015, s 67 from a date to be appointed.**

[1] Although no provision is made in this section for the use of force, the right of the licence holder to eject a customer arises from common law and he may use at least reasonable force. The licensee may use an agent to assist. Subsection (4) merely requires a constable to assist. Accordingly, a constable exercises a common law power in using reasonable force to eject a customer when required to assist a licence holder. Implicit in a landlord's request for help to eject a customer, is a request to stop him immediately coming back into that public house: *Semple v Luton and South Bedfordshire Magistrates' Court* [2009] EWHC 3241 (Admin), [2010] 2 All ER 353.

*Smuggled goods*

7.7506 **144. Keeping of smuggled goods** (1) A person to whom subsection (2) applies commits an offence if he knowingly keeps or allows to be kept, on any relevant premises, any goods which have been imported without payment of duty or which have otherwise been unlawfully imported.

(2) This subsection applies—
(*a*) to any person who works at the premises in a capacity, whether paid or unpaid, which gives him authority to prevent the keeping of the goods on the premises,
(*b*) in the case of licensed premises, to—
(i) the holder of a premises licence in respect of the premises, and
(ii) the designated premises supervisor (if any) under such a licence,
(*c*) in the case of premises in respect of which a club premises certificate has effect, to any member or officer of the club which holds the certificate who is present on the premises at any time when the goods are kept on the premises in a capacity which enables him to prevent them being so kept, and
(*d*) in the case of premises which may be used for a permitted temporary activity by virtue of Part 5, to the premises user in relation to the temporary event notice in question.

(3) A person guilty of an offence under this section is liable on summary conviction to a fine not exceeding level 3 on the standard scale.

(4) The court by which a person is convicted of an offence under this section may order the goods in question, and any container for them, to be forfeited and either destroyed or dealt with in such other manner as the court may order.*

[Licensing Act 2003, s 144.]

---

* **Amended by the Deregulation Act 2015, s 67 from a date to be appointed.**

*Children and alcohol*

7.7507 **145. Unaccompanied children prohibited from certain premises** (1) A person to whom subsection (3) applies commits an offence if—
(*a*) knowing that relevant premises are within subsection (4), he allows an unaccompanied child to be on the premises at a time when they are open for the purposes of being used for the supply of alcohol for consumption there, or
(*b*) he allows an unaccompanied child to be on relevant premises at a time between the hours of midnight and 5 a.m. when the premises are open for the purposes of being used for the supply of alcohol for consumption there.

(2) For the purposes of this section—
(*a*) "child" means an individual aged under 16,
(*b*) a child is unaccompanied if he is not in the company of an individual aged 18 or over.

(3) This subsection applies—
(*a*) to any person who works at the premises in a capacity, whether paid or unpaid, which authorises him to request the unaccompanied child to leave the premises,
(*b*) in the case of licensed premises, to—
(i) the holder of a premises licence in respect of the premises, and
(ii) the designated premises supervisor (if any) under such a licence,
(*c*) in the case of premises in respect of which a club premises certificate has effect, to any member or officer of the club which holds the certificate who is present on the premises in a capacity which enables him to make such a request, and

(*d*) in the case of premises which may be used for a permitted temporary activity by virtue of Part 5, to the premises user in relation to the temporary event notice in question.

(4) Relevant premises are within this subsection if—

(*a*) they are exclusively or primarily used for the supply of alcohol for consumption on the premises, or

(*b*) they are open for the purposes of being used for the supply of alcohol for consumption on the premises by virtue of Part 5 (permitted temporary activities) and, at the time the temporary event notice in question has effect, they are exclusively or primarily used for such supplies.

(5) No offence is committed under this section if the unaccompanied child is on the premises solely for the purpose of passing to or from some other place to or from which there is no other convenient means of access or egress.

(6) Where a person is charged with an offence under this section by reason of his own conduct it is a defence that—

(*a*) he believed that the unaccompanied child was aged 16 or over or that an individual accompanying him was aged 18 or over, and

(*b*) either—

(i) he had taken all reasonable steps to establish the individual's age, or

(ii) nobody could reasonably have suspected from the individual's appearance that he was aged under 16 or, as the case may be, under 18.

(7) For the purposes of subsection (6), a person is treated as having taken all reasonable steps to establish an individual's age if—

(*a*) he asked the individual for evidence of his age, and

(*b*) the evidence would have convinced a reasonable person.

(8) Where a person ("the accused") is charged with an offence under this section by reason of the act or default of some other person, it is a defence that the accused exercised all due diligence to avoid committing it.

(9) A person guilty of an offence under this section is liable on summary conviction to a fine not exceeding level 3 on the standard scale.

(10) In this section "supply of alcohol" means—

(*a*) the sale by retail of alcohol, or

(*b*) the supply of alcohol by or on behalf of a club to, or to the order of, a member of the club.

[Licensing Act 2003, s 145.]

**7.7508 146. Sale of alcohol to children** (1) A person commits an offence if he sells alcohol to an individual aged under 18.

(2) A club commits an offence if alcohol is supplied by it or on its behalf—

(*a*) to, or to the order of, a member of the club who is aged under 18, or

(*b*) to the order of a member of the club, to an individual who is aged under 18.

(3) A person commits an offence if he supplies alcohol on behalf of a club—

(*a*) to, or to the order of, a member of the club who is aged under 18, or

(*b*) to the order of a member of the club, to an individual who is aged under 18.

(4) Where a person is charged with an offence under this section by reason of his own conduct it is a defence that—

(*a*) he believed that the individual was aged 18 or over, and

(*b*) either—

(i) he had taken all reasonable steps to establish the individual's age, or

(ii) nobody could reasonably have suspected from the individual's appearance that he was aged under 18.

(5) For the purposes of subsection (4), a person is treated as having taken all reasonable steps to establish an individual's age if—

(*a*) he asked the individual for evidence of his age, and

(*b*) the evidence would have convinced a reasonable person.

(6) Where a person ("the accused") is charged with an offence under this section by reason of the act or default of some other person, it is a defence that the accused exercised all due diligence to avoid committing it.

(7) A person guilty of an offence under this section is liable on summary conviction to a fine not exceeding level 5 on the standard scale.

[Licensing Act 2003, s 146.]

**7.7509 147. Allowing the sale of alcohol to children** (1) A person to whom subsection (2) applies commits an offence if he knowingly allows the sale of alcohol on relevant premises to an individual aged under 18.

(2) This subsection applies to a person who works at the premises in a capacity, whether paid or unpaid, which authorises him to prevent the sale.

(3) A person to whom subsection (4) applies commits an offence if he knowingly allows alcohol to be supplied on relevant premises by or on behalf of a club—

(*a*) to or to the order of a member of the club who is aged under 18, or (*b*) to the order of a member of the club, to an individual who is aged under 18.

(4) This subsection applies to—

(*a*) a person who works on the premises in a capacity, whether paid or unpaid, which authorises him to prevent the supply, and

(*b*) any member or officer of the club who at the time of the supply is present on the relevant premises in a capacity which enables him to prevent it.

(5) A person guilty of an offence under this section is liable on summary conviction to a fine not exceeding level 5 on the standard scale.

[Licensing Act 2003, s 147.]

7.7510 **147A. Persistently selling alcohol to children** (1) A person is guilty of an offence if—

(*a*) on 2 or more different occasions within a period of 3 consecutive months alcohol is unlawfully sold on the same premises to an individual aged under 18;

(*b*) at the time of each sale the premises were either licensed premises or premises authorised to be used for a permitted temporary activity by virtue of Part 5; and

(*c*) that person was a responsible person in relation to the premises at each such time.

(2) For the purposes of this section alcohol sold to an individual aged under 18 is unlawfully sold to him if—

(*a*) the person making the sale believed the individual to be aged under 18; or

(*b*) that person did not have reasonable grounds for believing the individual to be aged 18 or over.

(3) For the purposes of subsection (2) a person has reasonable grounds for believing an individual to be aged 18 or over only if—

(*a*) he asked the individual for evidence of his age and that individual produced evidence that would have convinced a reasonable person; or

(*b*) nobody could reasonably have suspected from the individual's appearance that he was aged under 18.

(4) A person is, in relation to premises and a time, a responsible person for the purposes of subsection (1) if, at that time, he is—

(*a*) the person or one of the persons holding a premises licence in respect of the premises; or

(*b*) the person or one of the persons who is the premises user in respect of a temporary event notice by reference to which the premises are authorised to be used for a permitted temporary activity by virtue of Part 5.

(5) The individual to whom the sales mentioned in subsection (1) are made may, but need not be, the same in each case.

(6) The same sale may not be counted in respect of different offences for the purpose—

(*a*) of enabling the same person to be convicted of more than one offence under this section; or

(*b*) of enabling the same person to be convicted of both an offence under this section and an offence under section 146 or 147.

(7) In determining whether an offence under this section has been committed, the following shall be admissible as evidence that there has been an unlawful sale of alcohol to an individual aged under 18 on any premises on any occasion—

(*a*) the conviction of a person for an offence under section 146 in respect of a sale to that individual on those premises on that occasion;

(*b*) the giving to a person of a caution (within the meaning of Part 5 of the Police Act 1997) in respect of such an offence; or

(*c*) the payment by a person of a fixed penalty under Part 1 of the Criminal Justice and Police Act 2001 in respect of such a sale.

(8) A person guilty of an offence under this section shall be liable, on summary conviction, to a fine.

(9) The Secretary of State may by order amend subsection (8) to increase the maximum fine for the time being specified in that subsection.*

[Licensing Act 2003, s 147A as inserted by the Violent Crime Reduction Act 2006, s 23 and amended by the Policing and Crime Act 2009, s 28, the Police Reform and Social Responsibility Act 2011, s 118 and SI 2015/664.]

---

* **Amended by the Deregulation Act 2015, s 67 from a date to be appointed.**

7.7511 **147B. Order suspending a licence in respect of offence under section 147A**

(1) Where the holder of a premises licence is convicted of an offence under section 147A in respect of sales on the premises to which the licence relates, the court may order that so much of the licence as authorises the sale by retail of alcohol on those premises is suspended for a period not exceeding three months.

(2) Where more than one person is liable for an offence under section 147A relating to the same sales, no more than one order under subsection (1) may be made in relation to the premises in question in respect of convictions by reference to those sales.

(3) Subject to subsections (4) and (5), an order under subsection (1) comes into force at the

time specified by the court that makes it.

(4) Where a magistrates' court makes an order under subsection (1), it may suspend its coming into force pending an appeal.

(5) Section 130 (powers of appellate court to suspend section 129 order) applies (with the omission of subsection (9)) where an order under subsection (1) is made on conviction of an offence under section 147A as it applies where an order under section 129 is made on conviction of a relevant offence in Part 6.

[Licensing Act 2003, s 147B as inserted by the Violent Crime Reduction Act 2006, s 23.]

7.7513 **149. Purchase of alcohol by or on behalf of children** (1) An individual aged under 18 commits an offence if—

(*a*) he buys or attempts to buy alcohol, or

(*b*) where he is a member of a club—

(i) alcohol is supplied to him or to his order by or on behalf of the club, as a result of some act or default of his, or

(ii) he attempts to have alcohol supplied to him or to his order by or on behalf of the club.

(2) But subsection (1) does not apply where the individual buys or attempts to buy the alcohol at the request of—

(*a*) a constable, or

(*b*) a weights and measures inspector,

who is acting in the course of his duty.

(3) A person commits an offence if—

(*a*) he buys or attempts to buy alcohol on behalf of an individual aged under 18, or

(*b*) where he is a member of a club, on behalf of an individual aged under 18 he—

(i) makes arrangements whereby alcohol is supplied to him or to his order by or on behalf of the club, or

(ii) attempts to make such arrangements.

(4) A person ("the relevant person") commits an offence if—

(*a*) he buys or attempts to buy alcohol for consumption on relevant premises by an individual aged under 18, or

(*b*) where he is a member of a club—

(i) by some act or default of his, alcohol is supplied to him, or to his order, by or on behalf of the club for consumption on relevant premises by an individual aged under 18, or

(ii) he attempts to have alcohol so supplied for such consumption.

(5) But subsection (4) does not apply where—

(*a*) the relevant person is aged 18 or over,

(*b*) the individual is aged 16 or 17,

(*c*) the alcohol is beer, wine or cider,

(*d*) its purchase or supply is for consumption at a table meal on relevant premises, and

(*e*) the individual is accompanied at the meal by an individual aged 18 or over.

(6) Where a person is charged with an offence under subsection (3) or (4) it is a defence that he had no reason to suspect that the individual was aged under 18.

(7) A person guilty of an offence under this section is liable on summary conviction—

(*a*) in the case of an offence under subsection (1), to a fine not exceeding level 3 on the standard scale, and

(*b*) in the case of an offence under subsection (3) or (4), to a fine not exceeding level 5 on the standard scale.

[Licensing Act 2003, s 149.]

7.7514 **150. Consumption of alcohol by children** (1) An individual aged under 18 commits an offence if he knowingly consumes alcohol on relevant premises.

(2) A person to whom subsection (3) applies commits an offence if he knowingly allows the consumption of alcohol on relevant premises by an individual aged under 18.

(3) This subsection applies—

(*a*) to a person who works at the premises in a capacity, whether paid or unpaid, which authorises him to prevent the consumption, and

(*b*) where the alcohol was supplied by a club to or to the order of a member of the club, to any member or officer of the club who is present at the premises at the time of the consumption in a capacity which enables him to prevent it.

(4) Subsections (1) and (2) do not apply where—

(*a*) the individual is aged 16 or 17,

(*b*) the alcohol is beer, wine or cider,

(*c*) its consumption is at a table meal on relevant premises, and

(*d*) the individual is accompanied at the meal by an individual aged 18 or over.

(5) A person guilty of an offence under this section is liable on summary conviction—

(*a*) in the case of an offence under subsection (1), to a fine not exceeding level 3 on the standard scale, and (*b*) in the case of an offence under subsection (2), to a fine not exceeding level 5 on the standard scale.

[Licensing Act 2003, s 150.]

7.7515 151. **Delivering alcohol to children** (1) A person who works on relevant premises in any capacity, whether paid or unpaid, commits an offence if he knowingly delivers to an individual aged under 18—

(*a*) alcohol sold on the premises, or

(*b*) alcohol supplied on the premises by or on behalf of a club to or to the order of a member of the club.

(2) A person to whom subsection (3) applies commits an offence if he knowingly allows anybody else to deliver to an individual aged under 18 alcohol sold on relevant premises.

(3) This subsection applies to a person who works on the premises in a capacity, whether paid or unpaid, which authorises him to prevent the delivery of the alcohol.

(4) A person to whom subsection (5) applies commits an offence if he knowingly allows anybody else to deliver to an individual aged under 18 alcohol supplied on relevant premises by or on behalf of a club to or to the order of a member of the club.

(5) This subsection applies—

(*a*) to a person who works on the premises in a capacity, whether paid or unpaid, which authorises him to prevent the supply, and

(*b*) to any member or officer of the club who at the time of the supply in question is present on the premises in a capacity which enables him to prevent the supply.

(6) Subsections (1), (2) and (4) do not apply where—

(*a*) the alcohol is delivered at a place where the buyer or, as the case may be, person supplied lives or works, or

(*b*) the individual aged under 18 works on the relevant premises in a capacity, whether paid or unpaid, which involves the delivery of alcohol, or

(*c*) the alcohol is sold or supplied for consumption on the relevant premises.

(7) A person guilty of an offence under this section is liable on summary conviction to a fine not exceeding level 5 on the standard scale.

[Licensing Act 2003, s 151.]

7.7516 152. **Sending a child to obtain alcohol** (1) A person commits an offence if he knowingly sends an individual aged under 18 to obtain—

(*a*) alcohol sold or to be sold on relevant premises for consumption off the premises, or

(*b*) alcohol supplied or to be supplied by or on behalf of a club to or to the order of a member of the club for such consumption.

(2) For the purposes of this section, it is immaterial whether the individual aged under 18 is sent to obtain the alcohol from the relevant premises or from other premises from which it is delivered in pursuance of the sale or supply.

(3) Subsection (1) does not apply where the individual aged under 18 works on the relevant premises in a capacity, whether paid or unpaid, which involves the delivery of alcohol.

(4) Subsection (1) also does not apply where the individual aged under 18 is sent by—

(*a*) a constable, or

(*b*) a weights and measures inspector,

who is acting in the course of his duty.

(5) A person guilty of an offence under this section is liable on summary conviction to a fine not exceeding level 5 on the standard scale.

[Licensing Act 2003, s 152.]

7.7517 153. **Prohibition of unsupervised sales by children** (1) A responsible person commits an offence if on any relevant premises he knowingly allows an individual aged under 18 to make on the premises—

(*a*) any sale of alcohol, or

(*b*) any supply of alcohol by or on behalf of a club to or to the order of a member of the club,

unless the sale or supply has been specifically approved by that or another responsible person.

(2) But subsection (1) does not apply where—

(*a*) the alcohol is sold or supplied for consumption with a table meal,

(*b*) it is sold or supplied in premises which are being used for the service of table meals (or in a part of any premises which is being so used), and

(*c*) the premises are (or the part is) not used for the sale or supply of alcohol otherwise than to persons having table meals there and for consumption by such a person as an ancillary to his meal.

(3) A person guilty of an offence under this section is liable on summary conviction to a fine not exceeding level 1 on the standard scale.

(4) In this section "responsible person" means—

(*a*) in relation to licensed premises—

(i) the holder of a premises licence in respect of the premises,

(ii) the designated premises supervisor (if any) under such a licence, or

(iii) any individual aged 18 or over who is authorised for the purposes of this section by such a holder or supervisor,

(*b*) in relation to premises in respect of which there is in force a club premises certificate, any member or officer of the club present on the premises in a capacity which enables him to prevent the supply in question, and

(*c*) in relation to premises which may be used for a permitted temporary activity by virtue of Part 5—

(i) the premises user, or

(ii) any individual aged 18 or over who is authorised for the purposes of this section by the premises user.*

[Licensing Act 2003, s 153.]

---

* **Amended by the Deregulation Act 2015, s 67 from a date to be appointed.**

7.7518 **154. Enforcement role for weights and measures authorities** (1) It is the duty of every local weights and measures authority in England and Wales to enforce within its area the provisions of sections 146 and 147, so far as they apply to sales of alcohol made on or from premises to which the public have access.

(2) A weights and measures inspector may make, or authorise any person to make on his behalf, such purchases of goods as appear expedient for the purpose of determining whether those provisions are being complied with.

[Licensing Act 2003, s 154.]

*Confiscation of alcohol*

7.7519 **155. Confiscation of sealed containers of alcohol** *Confiscation of Alcohol (Young Persons) Act 1997 amended to remove the requirement for the alcohol to be in a sealed container in certain circumstances.*

*Vehicles and trains*

7.7520 **156. Prohibition on sale of alcohol on moving vehicles** (1) A person commits an offence under this section if he sells by retail alcohol on or from a vehicle at a time when the vehicle is not permanently or temporarily parked.

(2) A person guilty of an offence under this section is liable on summary conviction to imprisonment for a term not exceeding three months or to a fine, or to both.

(3) In proceedings against a person for an offence under this section, it is a defence that—

(*a*) his act was due to a mistake, or to reliance on information given to him, or to an act or omission by another person, or to some other cause beyond his control, and

(*b*) he took all reasonable precautions and exercised all due diligence to avoid committing the offence.

[Licensing Act 2003, s 156 as amended by SI 2015/664.]

7.7521 **157. Power to prohibit sale of alcohol on trains** (1) A magistrates' court acting for the local justice area may make an order prohibiting the sale of alcohol, during such period as may be specified, on any railway vehicle—

(*a*) at such station or stations as may be specified, being stations in that area, or

(*b*) travelling between such stations as may be specified, at least one of which is in that area.

(2) A magistrates' court may make an order under this section only on the application of a senior police officer.

(3) A magistrates' court may not make such an order unless it is satisfied that the order is necessary to prevent disorder.

(4) Where an order is made under this section, the responsible senior police officer must, forthwith, serve a copy of the order on the train operator (or each train operator) affected by the order.

(5) A person commits an offence if he knowingly—

(*a*) sells or attempts to sell alcohol in contravention of an order under this section, or

(*b*) allows the sale of alcohol in contravention of such an order.

(6) A person guilty of an offence under this section is liable on summary conviction to imprisonment for a term not exceeding three months or to a fine, or to both.

(7) In this section—

"railway vehicle" has the meaning given by section 83 of the Railways Act 1993;

"responsible senior police officer", in relation to an order under this section, means the senior police officer who applied for the order or, if the chief officer of police of the force in question has designated another senior police officer for the purpose, that other officer;

"senior police officer" means a police officer of, or above, the rank of inspector;

"specified" means specified in the order under this section;

"station" has the meaning given by section 83 of the Railways Act 1993 (c 43); and

"train operator" means a person authorised by a licence under section 8 of that Act to operate railway assets (within the meaning of section 6 of that Act).

[Licensing Act 2003, s 157, as amended by SI 2005/886 and SI 2015/664.]

*False statement relating to licensing etc*

7.7522 **158. False statements made for the purposes of this Act** (1) A person commits an offence if he knowingly or recklessly makes a false statement in or in connection with—

(*a*) an application for the grant, variation, transfer or review of a premises licence or club premises certificate,

(*b*) an application for a provisional statement,

(*c*) a temporary event notice, an interim authority notice or any other notice under this Act,

(*d*) an application for the grant of a personal licence, or

(*e*) a notice within section 178(1) (notice by freeholder etc conferring right to be notified of changes to licensing register).

(2) For the purposes of subsection (1) a person is to be treated as making a false statement if he produces, furnishes, signs or otherwise makes use of a document that contains a false statement.

(3) A person guilty of an offence under this section is liable on summary conviction to a fine not exceeding level 5 on the standard scale.

[Licensing Act 2003, s 158 as amended by the Deregulation Act 2015, Sch 18.]

*Interpretation*

7.7523 **159. Interpretation of Part 7** In this Part—

"authorisation" has the meaning given in section 136(5);

"relevant premises" means—

(*a*) licensed premises, or

(*b*) premises in respect of which there is in force a club premises certificate, or

(*c*) premises which may be used for a permitted temporary activity by virtue of Part 5;

"table meal" means a meal eaten by a person seated at a table, or at a counter or other structure which serves the purpose of a table and is not used for the service of refreshments for consumption by persons not seated at a table or structure serving the purpose of a table; and

"weights and measures inspector" means an inspector of weights and measures appointed under section 72(1) of the Weights and Measures Act 1985 (c 72).*

[Licensing Act 2003, s 159.]

* **Amended by the Deregulation Act 2015, s 67 from a date to be appointed.**

## PART 8[1]

## CLOSURE OF PREMISES

*Closure of premises in an identified area*

7.7524 **160. Orders to close premises in area experiencing disorder** (1) Where there is or is expected to be disorder in any local justice area, a magistrates' court acting in the area may make an order requiring all premises—

(*a*) which are situated at or near the place of the disorder or expected disorder, and

(*b*) in respect of which a premises licence or a temporary event notice has effect,

to be closed for a period, not exceeding 24 hours, specified in the order.

(2) A magistrates' court may make an order under this section only on the application of a police officer who is of the rank of superintendent or above.

(3) A magistrates' court may not make such an order unless it is satisfied that it is necessary to prevent disorder.

(4) Where an order is made under this section, a person to whom subsection (5) applies commits an offence if he knowingly keeps any premises to which the order relates open, or allows any such premises to be kept open, during the period of the order.

(5) This subsection applies—

(*a*) to any manager of the premises,

(*b*) in the case of licensed premises, to—

(i) the holder of a premises licence in respect of the premises, and

(ii) the designated premises supervisor (if any) under such a licence, and

(*c*) in the case of premises in respect of which a temporary event notice has effect, to the premises user in relation to that notice.

(6) A person guilty of an offence under subsection (4) is liable on summary conviction to a fine not exceeding level 3 on the standard scale.

(7) A constable may use such force as may be necessary for the purpose of closing premises ordered to be closed under this section.

[Licensing Act 2003, s 160, as amended by SI 2005/886.]

1 Part 8 comprises ss 160–171.

*Closure of identified premises*

7.7531 **167. Review of premises licence following closure order** (1) This section applies where—

(*a*) a magistrates' court has made a closure order under section 80 of the Anti-social Behaviour, Crime and Policing Act 2014, or the Crown Court has made a closure order on appeal under section 84 of that Act, in relation to premises in respect of which a premises licence has effect, and

(*b*) the relevant licensing authority has accordingly received a notice under section 80(9) or 84(7) of that Act.

(1A) This section also applies where a court has made an illegal working compliance order under Schedule 6 to the Immigration Act 2016 and the relevant licensing authority has accordingly received a notice under that Schedule.

(2) The relevant licensing authority must review the premises licence.

(3) The authority must reach a determination on the review no later than 28 days after the day on which it receives the notice mentioned in subsection (1)(*b*).

(4) The Secretary of State must by regulations[1]—

(*a*) require the relevant licensing authority to give, to the holder of the premises licence and each responsible authority, notice of the review and of the order mentioned in subsection (1)(*a*);

(*b*) require the authority to advertise the review and invite representations about it to be made to the authority by responsible authorities and other persons;

(*c*) prescribe the period during which representations may be made by the holder of the premises licence, any responsible authority or any other person;

(*d*) require any notice under paragraph (*a*) or advertisement under paragraph (*b*) to specify that period.

(5) The relevant licensing authority must—

(*a*) hold a hearing to consider the order mentioned in subsection (1)(*a*) and any relevant representations; and

(*b*) take such of the steps mentioned in subsection (6) (if any) as it considers appropriate for the promotion of the licensing objectives.

(6) Those steps are—

(*a*) to modify the conditions of the premises licence,

(*b*) to exclude a licensable activity from the scope of the licence,

(*c*) to remove the designated premises supervisor from the licence,

(*d*) to suspend the licence for a period not exceeding three months, or

(*e*) to revoke the licence;

and for this purpose the conditions of a premises licence are modified if any of them is altered or omitted or any new condition is added.

(7) Subsection (5)(*b*) is subject to sections 19 to 21 (requirement to include certain conditions in premises licences).

(8) Where the authority takes a step within subsection (6)(*a*) or (*b*), it may provide that the modification or exclusion is to have effect only for a specified period (not exceeding three months).

(9) In this section "relevant representations" means representations which—

(*a*) are relevant to one or more of the licensing objectives, and

(*b*) meet the requirements of subsection (10).

(10) The requirements are—

(*a*) that the representations are made by the holder of the premises licence, a responsible authority or any other person within the period prescribed under subsection (4)(*c*),

(*b*) that they have not been withdrawn, and

(*c*) if they are made by a person who is not a responsible authority, that they are not, in the opinion of the relevant licensing authority, frivolous or vexatious.

(11) Where the relevant licensing authority determines that any representations are frivolous or vexatious, it must notify the person who made them of the reasons for that determination.

(12) Where a licensing authority determines a review under this section it must notify the determination and its reasons for making it to—

(*a*) the holder of the licence,

(*b*) any person who made relevant representations, and

(*c*) the chief officer of police for the police area (or each police area) in which the premises are situated.

(13) Section 168 makes provision about when the determination takes effect.

(14) In this section "responsible authority" has the same meaning as in Part 3.

[Licensing Act 2003, s 167 as amended by the Policing and Crime Act 2009, Sch 7, the Police Reform and Social Responsibility Act 2011, ss 106, 111, the Anti-social Behaviour, Crime and Policing Act 2014, Sch 11 and the Immigration Act 2016, Sch 6.]

1 See the Licensing Act 2003 (Premises Licences and Club Premises Certificates) Regulations 2005, SI 2005/42 (for amending instruments, see note to s 13, ante) and the Welsh Language (Gambling and Licensing Forms) Regulations 2010, SI 2010/2440.

7.7532 **168. Provision about decisions under section 167** (1) Subject to this section, a decision under section 167 does not have effect until the relevant time.

(2) In this section "the relevant time", in relation to any decision, means—

(*a*) the end of the period given for appealing against the decision, or (*b*) if the decision is appealed against, the time the appeal is disposed of.

(3) Subsections (4) and (5) apply where—

(*a*) the relevant licensing authority decides on a review under section 167 to take one or more of the steps mentioned in subsection (6)(*a*) to (*d*) of that section, and

(*b*) the premises to which the licence relates are closed at the time of the decision by virtue of an closure order made under section 80 or 84 of the Anti-social Behaviour, Crime and Policing Act 2014.

(4) The decision by the relevant licensing authority to take any of the steps mentioned in section 167(6)(*a*) to (*d*) takes effect when it is notified to the holder of the licence under section 167(12).

This is subject to subsection (5) and paragraph 18(3) of Schedule 5 (power of magistrates' court to suspend decision pending appeal).

(5) The relevant licensing authority may, on such terms as it thinks fit, suspend the operation of that decision (in whole or in part) until the relevant time.

(6) Subsection (7) applies where—

(*a*) the relevant licensing authority decides on a review under section 167 to revoke the premises licence, and

(*b*) the premises to which the licence relates are closed at the time of the decision by virtue of an closure order made under section 80 or 84 of the Anti-social Behaviour, Crime and Policing Act 2014.

(7) The premises must remain closed (but the licence otherwise in force) until the relevant time.

This is subject to paragraph 18(4) of Schedule 5 (power of magistrates' court to modify closure order pending appeal).

(8) A person commits an offence if, without reasonable excuse, he allows premises to be open in contravention of subsection (7).

(9) A person guilty of an offence under subsection (8) is liable on summary conviction to imprisonment for a term not exceeding three months or to a fine, or to both.

[Licensing Act 2003, s 168 as amended by the Anti-social Behaviour, Crime and Policing Act 2014, Sch 11 and SI 2015/664.]

*Closure notices*

7.7534 **169A. Closure notices for persistently selling alcohol to children** (1) A relevant officer may give a notice under this section (a "closure notice") applying to any premises if—

(*a*) there is evidence that a person ("the offender") has committed an offence under section 147A in relation to those premises;

(*b*) the relevant officer considers that the evidence is such that, if the offender were prosecuted for the offence, there would be a realistic prospect of his being convicted; and

(*c*) the offender is still, at the time when the notice is given, the holder of a premises licence in respect of those premises, or one of the holders of such a licence.

(2) A closure notice is a notice which—

(*a*) proposes a prohibition, for the period specified in the notice, on sales of alcohol on the premises in question; and

(*b*) offers the opportunity to discharge all criminal liability in respect of the alleged offence by the acceptance of the prohibition proposed by the notice.

(3) A closure notice must—

(*a*) be in the form prescribed by regulations[1] made by the Secretary of State;

(*b*) specify the premises to which it applies;

(*c*) give such particulars of the circumstances believed to constitute the alleged offence (including the sales to which it relates) as are necessary to provide reasonable information about it;

(*d*) specify the length of the period during which it is proposed that sales of alcohol should be prohibited on those premises;

(*e*) specify when that period would begin if the prohibition is accepted;

(*f*) explain what would be the effect of the proposed prohibition and the consequences under this Act (including the maximum penalties) of a sale of alcohol on the premises during the period for which it is in force;

(*g*) explain the right of every person who, at the time of the alleged offence, held or was one of the holders of a premises licence in respect of those premises to be tried for that offence; and

(*h*) explain how that right may be exercised and how (where it is not exercised) the proposed prohibition may be accepted.

(4) The period specified for the purposes of subsection (3)(*d*) must be at least 48 hours but not more than 336 hours; and the time specified as the time from which that period would begin must be not less than 14 days after the date of the service of the closure notice in accordance with subsection (6).

(5) The provision included in the notice by virtue of subsection (3)(*h*) must—

(*a*) provide a means of identifying a police officer or trading standards officer to whom notice exercising the option to accept the prohibition may be given;

(*b*) set out particulars of where and how that notice may be given to that police officer or trading standards officer;

(*c*) require that notice to be given within 14 days after the date of the service of the closure notice; and

(*d*) explain that the right to be tried for the alleged offence will be taken to have been exercised unless every person who, at the time of the notice, holds or is one of the holders of the premises licence for the premises in question accepts the proposed prohibition.

(6) Section 184 (giving of notices) does not apply to a closure notice; but such a notice must be served on the premises to which it applies.

(7) A closure notice may be served on the premises to which it applies—

(*a*) only by being handed by a constable or trading standards officer to a person on the premises who appears to the constable or trading standards officer to have control of or responsibility for the premises (whether on his own or with others); and

(*b*) only at a time when it appears to that constable or trading standards officer that licensable activities are being carried on there.

(8) A copy of every closure notice given under this section must be sent to the holder of the premises licence for the premises to which it applies at whatever address for that person is for the time being set out in the licence.

(9) A closure notice must not be given more than 3 months after the time of the last of the sales to which the alleged offence relates.

(10) No more that one closure notice may be given in respect of offences relating to the same sales; nor may such a notice be given in respect of an offence in respect of which a prosecution has already been brought.

(11) In this section "relevant officer" means—

(*a*) a police officer of the rank of superintendent or above; or

(*b*) an inspector of weights and measures appointed under section 72(1) of the Weights and Measures Act 1985.

[Licensing Act 2003, s 169A as inserted by the Violent Crime Reduction Act 2006, s 24 and amended by the Police Reform and Social Responsibility Act 2011, s 118.]

---

[1] The Licensing Act 2003 (Persistent Selling of Alcohol to Children) (Prescribed Form of Closure Notice) Regulations 2012, SI 2012/963 have been made.

7.7535 **169B. Effect of closure notices** (1) This section applies where a closure notice is given under section 169A in respect of an alleged offence under section 147A.

(2) No proceedings may be brought for the alleged offence or any related offence at any time before the time when the prohibition proposed by the notice would take effect.

(3) If before that time every person who, at the time of the notice, holds or is one of the holders of the premises licence for the premises in question accepts the proposed prohibition in the manner specified in the notice—

(*a*) that prohibition takes effect at the time so specified in relation to the premises in question; and

(*b*) no proceedings may subsequently be brought against any such person for the alleged offence or any related offence.

(4) If the prohibition contained in a closure notice takes effect in accordance with subsection (3)(*a*) in relation to any premises, so much of the premises licence for those premises as authorises the sale by retail of alcohol on those premises is suspended for the period specified in the closure notice.

(5) In this section "related offence", in relation to the alleged offence, means an offence under section 146 or 147 in respect of any of the sales to which the alleged offence relates.

(6) The operation of this section is not affected by any contravention of section 169A(8).

[Licensing Act 2003, s 169B as inserted by the Violent Crime Reduction Act 2006, s 24.]

*Interpretation*

7.7536 **171. Interpretation of Part 8** (1) This section has effect for the purposes of this Part.

(2) Premises are open if a person who is not within subsection (4) enters the premises and—

(*a*) he buys or is otherwise supplied with food, drink or anything usually sold on the premises, or

(*b*) while he is on the premises, they are used for the provision of regulated entertainment.

(3) But in determining whether premises are open the following are to be disregarded—

(*a*) where no premises licence has effect in respect of the premises, any use of the premises for activities (other than licensable activities) which do not take place during an event period specified in a temporary event notice having effect in respect of the premises,

(*b*) any use of the premises for a qualifying club activity under and in accordance with a club premises certificate, and

(*c*) any supply exempted under paragraph 3 of Schedule 2 (certain supplies of hot food and drink by clubs, hotels etc not a licensable activity) in circumstances where a person will neither be admitted to the premises, nor be supplied as mentioned in sub-paragraph (1)(*b*) of that paragraph, except by virtue of being a member of a recognised club or a guest of such a member.

(4) A person is within this subsection if he is—

(*a*) an appropriate person in relation to the premises,

(*b*) a person who usually lives at the premises, or

(*c*) a member of the family of a person within paragraph (*a*) or (*b*).

(5) The following expressions have the meanings given—

"appropriate person", in relation to any premises, means—

(*a*) any person who holds a premises licence in respect of the premises,

(*b*) any designated premises supervisor under such a licence,

(*c*) the premises user in relation to any temporary event notice which has effect in respect of the premises, or

(*d*) a manager of the premises;

"closure notice" has the meaning given in section 169A;

"local weights and measures authority' has the meaning given by section 69 of the Weights and Measures Act 1985;

"manager", in relation to any premises, means a person who works at the premises in a capacity, whether paid or unpaid, which authorises him to close them;

"relevant licensing authority", in relation to any licensed premises, has the same meaning as in Part 3;

"trading standards officer", in relation to any premises to which a premises licence relates, means a person authorised by a local weights and measures authority to act in the area where those premises are situated in relation to proposed prohibitions contained in closure notices.

(6) A temporary event notice has effect from the time it is given in accordance with Part 5 until—

(*a*) the time it is withdrawn,

(*b*) the time a counter notice is given under that Part, or

(*c*) the expiry of the event period specified in the temporary event notice,

whichever first occurs.

[Licensing Act 2003, s 171 as amended by SI 2005/886, the Violent Crime Reduction Act 2006, s 24 and the Anti-social Behaviour, Crime and Policing Act 2014, Sch 11.]

## Part 9[1]

## Miscellaneous and Supplementary

### *Special occasions*

7.7537 **172. Relaxation of opening hours for special occasions** *Power of Secretary of State to make a "Licensing Hours Order" for celebration periods marking an occasion of exceptional international, national or local significance.*

[Licensing Act 2003, s 172.]

1 Part 8 comprises ss 172–201 and Schs 5–8.

7.7538 **172A. Power to make early morning alcohol restriction order** (1) If a licensing authority considers it appropriate for the promotion of the licensing objectives, it may, subject as follows, make an order under this section.

(2) An order under this section is an order providing that—

(*a*) premises licences and club premises certificates granted by the authority, and temporary event notices given to the authority, do not have effect to the extent that they authorise the sale of alcohol during the period specified in the order, and

(*b*) club premises certificates granted by the authority do not have effect to the extent that they authorise the supply of alcohol by or on behalf of a club to, or to the order of, a member of the club during the period specified in the order.

(3) For the purposes of subsection (2)(*a*) and (*b*), the period that may be specified in the order must—

(*a*) begin no earlier than midnight, and

(*b*) end no later than 6am.

(4) It is immaterial for the purposes of an order under this section whether a premises licence or club premises certificate is granted, or a temporary event notice is given, before or after the order is made.

(5) An order under this section may provide that it is to apply—

(*a*) in relation to the same period of every day on which the order is to apply, or in relation to different periods of different days,

(*b*) every day or only on particular days (for example, particular days of the week or year),

(*c*) in relation to the whole or part of a licensing authority's area, or

(*d*) for a limited or unlimited period.

(6) An order under this section must specify—

(*a*) the days on which it is to apply and the period of those days,

(*b*) the area in relation to which it is to apply,

(*c*) if it is to apply for a limited period, that period, and
(*d*) the date from which it is to apply.

(7) An order under this section must—
(*a*) be in the prescribed form, and
(*b*) have the prescribed content.

[Licensing Act 2003, s 172A as inserted by the Police Reform and Social Responsibility Act 2011, s 119.]

**7.7539 172B. Procedural requirements for early morning alcohol restriction order**

(1) A licensing authority proposing to make an order under section 172A must—
(*a*) advertise the proposed order in the prescribed manner, and
(*b*) hold a hearing to consider any relevant representations, unless the authority and each person who has made such representations agree that a hearing is unnecessary.

(2) In this section "relevant representations" means representations which—
(*a*) are about the likely effect of the making of the proposed order on the promotion of the licensing objectives,
(*b*) are made to the licensing authority by an affected person, a responsible authority or any other person,
(*c*) are made in the prescribed form and manner and within the prescribed period,
(*d*) have not been withdrawn, and
(*e*) in the case of representations made by a person who is not a responsible authority, are not, in the opinion of the licensing authority, frivolous or vexatious.

(3) In subsection (2)(*b*), "affected person" means—
(*a*) the holder of the premises licence or club premises certificate in respect of affected premises,
(*b*) the premises user in relation to a temporary event notice in respect of affected premises,
(*c*) a person who has applied for a premises licence or club premises certificate in respect of affected premises (where the application has not been determined), and
(*d*) a person to whom a provisional statement has been issued in respect of affected premises.

(4) In subsection (2)(*b*) and (*e*), "responsible authority" means—
(*a*) the licensing authority and any other licensing authority in whose area part of any affected premises is situated,
(*b*) the chief officer of police for a police area any part of which is in the area specified in the order,
(*c*) the fire and rescue authority for an area any part of which is in the area specified in the order,
(*d*) the Primary Care Trust or Local Health Board for an area any part of which is in the area specified in the order,
(*e*) the local weights and measures authority for any such area,
(*f*) the enforcing authority within the meaning given by section 18 of the Health and Safety at Work etc Act 1974 for any such area,
(*g*) the local planning authority within the meaning given by the Town and Country Planning Act 1990 for any such area,
(*h*) the local authority by which statutory functions are exercisable in the area specified in the order in relation to minimising or preventing the risk of pollution of the environment or of harm to human health,
(*i*) a body which—
(i) represents those who, in relation to the area specified in the order, are responsible for, or interested in, matters relating to the protection of children from harm, and
(ii) is recognised by the licensing authority for the purposes of this section as being competent to advise on such matters,
(*j*) where affected premises are a vessel—
(i) a navigation authority (within the meaning given by section 221(1) of the Water Resources Act 1991) having functions in relation to the waters where the vessel is usually moored or berthed or any waters where it is navigated at a time when it is used for licensable activities to which the proposed order relates,
(ii) the Environment Agency,
(iii) Canal & River Trust, and
(iv) the Secretary of State, and
(*k*) a prescribed person.

(5) Where a licensing authority determines for the purposes of subsection (2)(*e*) that any representations are frivolous or vexatious, it must notify the person who made them of its reasons for its determination.

(6) In this section—

"affected premises", in relation to a proposed order, means premises in respect of which it applies from the date specified in it;

"statutory function" means a function conferred by or under an enactment.

[Licensing Act 2003, s 172B as inserted by the Police Reform and Social Responsibility Act 2011, s 119 and amended by SI 2012/1659.]

7.7540 172C. **Making of early morning alcohol restriction order** (1) A licensing authority may not make an order under section 172A applying in relation to—

(*a*) an area not specified in the proposed order advertised under section 172B,

(*b*) a day not specified in that proposed order, or

(*c*) a period other than the period specified in that proposed order of any day so specified.

(2) After making an order under section 172A a licensing authority must publish it or otherwise make it available—

(*a*) in the prescribed form and manner, and

(*b*) within the prescribed period.

[Licensing Act 2003, s 172C as inserted by the Police Reform and Social Responsibility Act 2011, s 119.]

7.7541 172D. **Variation and revocation of early morning alcohol restriction order** (1) A licensing authority may vary or revoke an order under section 172A.

(2) Sections 172B and 172C apply in relation to the variation or revocation of an order under section 172A as in relation to the making of such an order.

[Licensing Act 2003, s 172D as inserted by the Police Reform and Social Responsibility Act 2011, s 119.]

7.7542 172E. **Exceptions from effect of early morning alcohol restriction order** (1) An order under section 172A does not apply in prescribed cases or circumstances.

(2) The cases referred to in subsection (1) may in particular be defined by reference to—

(*a*) particular kinds of premises, or

(*b*) particular days.

(3) An order under section 172A is subject to an order under section 172 (whether made before or afterwards), unless and to the extent that the order under section 172 provides otherwise.

[Licensing Act 2003, s 172E as inserted by the Police Reform and Social Responsibility Act 2011, s 119.]

*Exemptions etc*

7.7543 173. **Activities in certain locations not licensable** (1) An activity is not a licensable activity if it is carried on—

(*a*) aboard an aircraft, hovercraft or railway vehicle engaged on a journey,

(*b*) aboard a vessel engaged on an international journey,

(*c*) at an approved wharf at a designated port or hoverport,

(*d*) at an examination station at a designated airport,

(*e*) at a royal palace,

(*f*) at premises which, at the time when the activity is carried on, are permanently or temporarily occupied for the purposes of the armed forces of the Crown,

(*g*) at premises in respect of which a certificate issued under section 174 (exemption for national security) has effect, or

(*h*) at such other place as may be prescribed.

(2) For the purposes of subsection (1) the period during which an aircraft, hovercraft, railway vehicle or vessel is engaged on a journey includes—

(*a*) any period ending with its departure when preparations are being made for the journey, and

(*b*) any period after its arrival at its destination when it continues to be occupied by those (or any of those) who made the journey (or any part of it).

(3) The Secretary of State may by order designate a port, hoverport or airport for the purposes of subsection (1), if it appears to him to be one at which there is a substantial amount of international passenger traffic.

(4) Any port, airport or hoverport where section 86A or 87 of the Licensing Act 1964 (c 26) is in operation immediately before the commencement of this section is, on and after that commencement, to be treated for the purposes of subsection (1) as if it were designated.

(5) But provision may by order be made for subsection (4) to cease to have effect in relation to any port, airport or hoverport.

(6) For the purposes of this section—

"approved wharf" has the meaning given by section 20A of the Customs and Excise Management Act 1979 (c 2);

"designated" means designated by an order under subsection (3);

"examination station" has the meaning given by section 22A of that Act;

"international journey" means—

(*a*) a journey from a place in the United Kingdom to an immediate destination outside the United Kingdom, or

(*b*) a journey from a place outside the United Kingdom to an immediate destination in the United Kingdom; and

"railway vehicle" has the meaning given by section 83 of the Railways Act 1993 (c 43).

[Licensing Act 2003, s 173.]

7.7544 **174. Certifying of premises on grounds of national security** (1) A Minister of the Crown may issue a certificate under this section in respect of any premises, if he considers that it is appropriate to do so for the purposes of safeguarding national security.

(2) A certificate under this section may identify the premises in question by means of a general description.

(3) A document purporting to be a certificate under this section is to be received in evidence and treated as being a certificate under this section unless the contrary is proved.

(4) A document which purports to be certified by or on behalf of a Minister of the Crown as a true copy of a certificate given by a Minister of the Crown under this section is evidence of that certificate.

(5) A Minister of the Crown may cancel a certificate issued by him, or any other Minister of the Crown, under this section.

(6) The powers conferred by this section on a Minister of the Crown may be exercised only by a Minister who is a member of the Cabinet or by the Attorney General.

(7) In this section "Minister of the Crown" has the meaning given by the Ministers of the Crown Act 1975 (c 26).

[Licensing Act 2003, s 174.]

7.7545 **175. Exemption for incidental lottery** (1) The promotion of a lottery to which this section applies shall not constitute a licensable activity by reason only of one or more of the prizes in the lottery consisting of or including alcohol, provided that the alcohol is in a sealed container.

(2) *Repealed.*

[Licensing Act 2003, s 175 as substituted by the Gambling Act 2005, Sch 16 and amended by SI 2016/124.]

*Service areas and garages etc*

7.7546 **176. Prohibition of alcohol sales at service areas, garages etc** (1) No premises licence, club premises certificate or temporary event notice has effect to authorise the sale by retail or supply of alcohol on or from excluded premises.

(2) In this section "excluded premises" means—

(*a*) premises situated on land acquired or appropriated by a special road authority, and for the time being used, for the provision of facilities to be used in connection with the use of a special road provided for the use of traffic of class I (with or without other classes); or

(*b*) premises used primarily as a garage or which form part of premises which are primarily so used[1].

(3) The Secretary of State may by order amend the definition of excluded premises in subsection (2) so as to include or exclude premises of such description as may be specified in the order.

(4) For the purposes of this section—

(*a*) "special road" and "special road authority" have the same meaning as in the Highways Act 1980 (c 66), except that "special road" includes a trunk road to which (by virtue of paragraph 3 of Schedule 23 to that Act) the provisions of that Act apply as if the road were a special road,

(*b*) "class I" means class I in Schedule 4 to the Highways Act 1980 as varied from time to time by an order under section 17 of that Act, but if that Schedule is amended by such an order so as to add to it a further class of traffic, the order may adapt the reference in subsection (2)(*a*) to traffic of class I so as to take account of the additional class, and

(*c*) premises are used as a garage if they are used for one or more of the following—

(i) the retailing of petrol,

(ii) the retailing of derv,

(iii) the sale of motor vehicles,

(iv) the maintenance of motor vehicles.

[Licensing Act 2003, s 176.]

---

1 As to the determination of primary use and the entitlement to adjourn to elicit more information and clarification from the applicant, see *R (on the application of Murco Petroleum Ltd) v Bristol City Council* [2010] EWHC 1992 (Admin), 174 JP 425.

*Small premises*

7.7547 **177. Dancing in certain small premises** (1) Subsection (2) applies where—

(*a*) a premises licence authorises—

(i) the supply of alcohol for consumption on the premises, and

(ii) dancing, and

(*b*) the premises—

(i) are used primarily for the supply of alcohol for consumption on the premises, and

(ii) have a permitted capacity of not more than 200 persons.

(2) At any time when—

(*a*) the premises—

(i) are open for the purposes of being used for the supply of alcohol for consumption on the premises, and

(ii) are being used for dancing,

(*b*) *repealed*

any licensing authority imposed condition of the premises licence which relates to dancing does not have effect unless it falls within subsection (5) or (6).

(3) *Repealed.*

(4) *Repealed.*

(5) A condition falls within this subsection if the premises licence specifies that the licensing authority which granted the licence considers the imposition of the condition appropriate on one or both of the following grounds—

(*a*) the prevention of crime and disorder,

(*b*) public safety.

(6) A condition falls within this subsection if, on a review of the premises licence—

(*a*) it is altered so as to include a statement that this section does not apply to it, or

(*b*) it is added to the licence and includes such a statement.

(7) This section applies in relation to a club premises certificate as it applies in relation to a premises licence except that, in the application of this section in relation to such a certificate, the definition of "licensing authority imposed condition" in subsection (8) has effect as if for "section 18(3)(*b*)" to the end there were substituted "section 72(3)(*b*) (but is not referred to in section 72(2)) or which is imposed by virtue of section 85(3)(*b*) or 88(3)".

(8) In this section—

"licensing authority imposed condition" means a condition which is imposed by virtue of section 18(3)(*b*) (but is not referred to in section 18(2)(*a*)) or which is imposed by virtue of 35(3)(*b*), 52(3) or 167(5)(*b*) or in accordance with section 21;

"dancing" means—

(*a*) entertainment of a description falling within, or of a similar description to that falling within, paragraph 2(1)(*g*) of Schedule 1,

(*b*) *repealed*

"permitted capacity", in relation to any premises, means—

(*a*) *repealed*

(*b*) the limit on the number of persons who may be on the premises at any one time in accordance with a recommendation made by, or on behalf of, the fire and rescue authority for the area in which the premises are situated (or, if the premises are situated in the area of more than one fire and rescue authority, those authorities); and

"supply of alcohol" means—

(*a*) the sale by retail of alcohol, or

(*b*) the supply of alcohol by or on behalf of a club to, or to the order of, a member of the club.

[Licensing Act 2003, s 177 as amended by SI 2005/1541, the Police Reform and Social Responsibility Act 2011, s 109 and the Live Music Act 2012, s 1.]

7.7548 **177A. Licence review for live and recorded music** (1) Subsection (2) applies where—

(*a*) music takes place on premises which are authorised by a premises licence or club premises certificate to be used for the supply of alcohol for consumption on the premises,

(*b*) at the time of the music, the premises are open for the purposes of being used for the supply of alcohol for consumption on the premises,

(*c*) if the music is amplified, it takes place in the presence of an audience of no more than 500 persons, and

(*d*) the music takes place between 8am and 11pm on the same day (or, where an order under section 172 has effect in relation to music, during any times specified under that order).

(2) Any condition of the premises licence or club premises certificate which relates to live music, recorded music or both does not have effect in relation to the music unless it falls within subsection (3) or is added to the licence in accordance with subsection (4).

(3) A condition falls within this subsection if, on a review of the premises licence or club premises certificate it is altered so as to include a statement that this section does not apply to it.

(4) On a review of a premises licence or club premises certificate a licensing authority may (without prejudice to any other steps available to it under this Act) add a condition relating to music as if—

(*a*) the music were regulated entertainment, and

(*b*) the licence or certificate licensed the music.

(4A) This section does not apply to music which, by virtue of a provision other than paragraph 12A or 12C of Schedule 1, is not regarded as the provision of regulated entertainment for the purposes of this Act.

(5) In this section—

"condition" means a condition—

(*a*) included in a premises licence by virtue of section 18(2)(*a*) or (3)(*b*), 35(3)(*b*), 52(3) or 167(5)(*b*),
(*b*) included in a club premises certificate by virtue of section 72(2)(*a*) or (3)(*b*), 85(3)(*b*) or 88(3),
(*c*) added to a premises licence by virtue of its inclusion in an application to vary the licence in accordance with section 34 or 41A which is granted under section 35(2) or 41B(3) (as the case may be), or
(*d*) added to a club premises certificate by virtue of its inclusion in an application to vary the certificate in accordance with section 84 or 86A which is granted under section 85(2) or 86B(3) (as the case may be);

"live music" means entertainment of a description falling within, or of a similar description to that falling within, paragraph 2(1)(*e*) of Schedule 1;
"music" means live music or recorded music or both;
"recorded music" means entertainment of a description falling within, or of a similar description to that falling within, paragraph 2(1)(f) of Schedule 1;
"supply of alcohol" means—
(*a*) the sale by retail of alcohol, or
(*b*) the supply of alcohol by or on behalf of a club to, or to the order of, a member of the club.

[Licensing Act 2003, s 177A as inserted by the Live Music Act 2012, s 1 and amended by SI 2014/3253.]

*Rights of freeholders etc*

7.7549 **178. Right of freeholder etc to be notified of licensing matters** *Right of person with a property interest in any premises to notify the licensing authority of that interest and then to be told by the licensing authority of any changes to the licensing register affecting that premises.*

*Rights of entry*

7.7550 **179. Rights of entry to investigate licensable activities** (1) Where a constable or an authorised person has reason to believe that any premises are being, or are about to be, used for a licensable activity, he may enter the premises with a view to seeing whether the activity is being, or is to be, carried on under and in accordance with an authorisation.

(1A) Where an immigration officer has reason to believe that any premises are being used for a licensable activity within section 1(1)(a) or (d), the officer may enter the premises with a view to seeing whether an offence under any of the Immigration Acts is being committed in connection with the carrying on of the activity.

(2) An authorised person or an immigration officer exercising a power conferred by this section must, if so requested, produce evidence of his authority to exercise the power.

(3) A person exercising the power conferred by this section may, if necessary, use reasonable force.

(4) A person commits an offence if he intentionally obstructs an authorised person or an immigration officer exercising a power conferred by this section.

(5) A person guilty of an offence under subsection (4) is liable on summary conviction to a fine not exceeding level 3 on the standard scale.

(6) In this section—
"authorisation" means—
(*a*) a premises licence,
(*b*) a club premises certificate, or
(*c*) a temporary event notice in respect of which the conditions of section 98(2) to (4) are satisfied;

"authorised person" means an authorised person within the meaning of Part 3 or 4 or an authorised officer within the meaning of section 108(5);
"immigration officer" means a person appointed as an immigration officer under paragraph 1 of Schedule 2 to the Immigration Act 1971.

(7) Nothing in this section applies in relation to premises in respect of which there is a club premises certificate but no other authorisation.

[Licensing Act 2003, s 179 as amended by the Immigration Act 2016, Sch 4.]

7.7551 **180. Right of entry to investigate offences** (1) A constable may enter and search any premises in respect of which he has reason to believe that an offence under this Act has been, is being or is about to be committed.

(2) A constable exercising a power conferred by this section may, if necessary, use reasonable force.

[Licensing Act 2003, s 180.]

*Appeals*

7.7552 **181. Appeals against decisions of licensing authorities** (1) Schedule 5 (which makes provision for appeals against decisions of licensing authorities) has effect.

(2) On an appeal in accordance with that Schedule against a decision of a licensing authority, a magistrates' court may—
(*a*) dismiss the appeal,

(*b*) substitute for the decision appealed against any other decision which could have been made by the licensing authority, or

(*c*) remit the case to the licensing authority to dispose of it in accordance with the direction of the court,

and may make such order as to costs as it thinks fit[1].

[Licensing Act 2003, s 181.]

[1] In *Crawley Borough Council v Attenborough* [2006] EWHC 1278 (Admin) it was held that there was no practical distinction between the terms of this section and s 64(1) of the Magistrates' Courts Act 1980 (see para 1.310, in PART I: MAGISTRATES' COURTS, PROCEDURE, ante). But in *Prasannan v Royal Borough of Kensington and Chelsea* [2010] EWHC 319 (Admin), 174 JP 418 it was held that the remarks in the *Crawley Borough Council* case were obiter. There was no scope for fettering the power in s 182(2) by construing it in light of the provisions of s 64(1) of the 1980 Act. The two provisions are entirely independent of each other for good reason. In licensing cases the permutations of result may be frequently more complex than simple success or failure. The court has an unfettered power in relation to costs subject to the requirement that in making such order as is just it must take into account all relevant matters and not take into account irrelevant matters.

*Guidance, hearings etc*

7.7553 **182. Guidance** (1) The Secretary of State must issue guidance ("the licensing guidance") to licensing authorities on the discharge of their functions under this Act.[1].

[1] The "Guidance issued under s 182 of the Licensing Act 2003 and Guidance to Police Officers on the operation of Closure Powers in Part 8 of the Licensing Act 2003" dated July 2004 has been issued by the Secretary of State.

7.7554 **183. Hearings** *Power to make regulations prescribing hearings procedure*[1].

[1] The Licensing Act 2003 (Hearings) Regulations 2005, SI 2005/44 amended by SI 2005/78, SI 2007/2502 and SI 2014/2341 have been made. A licensing authority may not award costs in respect of licensing hearings.

7.7555 **184. Giving of notices, etc** (1) This section has effect in relation to any document required or authorised by or under this Act to be given to any person ("relevant document").

(2) Where that person is a licensing authority, the relevant document must be given by addressing it to the authority and leaving it at or sending it by post to—

(*a*) the principal office of the authority, or

(*b*) any other office of the authority specified by it as one at which it will accept documents of the same description as that document.

(3) In any other case the relevant document may be given to the person in question by delivering it to him, or by leaving it at his proper address, or by sending it by post to him at that address.

(4) A relevant document may—

(*a*) in the case of a body corporate (other than a licensing authority), be given to the secretary or clerk of that body;

(*b*) in the case of a partnership, be given to a partner or a person having the control or management of the partnership business;

(*c*) in the case of an unincorporated association (other than a partnership), be given to an officer of the association.

(5) For the purposes of this section and section 7 of the Interpretation Act 1978 (c 30) (service of documents by post) in its application to this section, the proper address of any person to whom a relevant document is to be given is his last known address, except that—

(*a*) in the case of a body corporate or its secretary or clerk, it is the address of the registered office of that body or its principal office in the United Kingdom,

(*b*) in the case of a partnership, a partner or a person having control or management of the partnership business, it is that of the principal office of the partnership in the United Kingdom, and

(*c*) in the case of an unincorporated association (other than a partnership) or any officer of the association, it is that of its principal office in the United Kingdom.

(6) But if a relevant document is given to a person in his capacity as the holder of a premises licence, club premises certificate or personal licence, or as the designated premises supervisor under a premises licence, his relevant registered address is also to be treated, for the purposes of this section and section 7 of the Interpretation Act 1978 (c 30), as his proper address.

(7) In subsection (6) "relevant registered address", in relation to such a person, means the address given for that person in the record for the licence or certificate (as the case may be) which is contained in the register kept under section 8 by the licensing authority which granted the licence or certificate.

(8) The following provisions of the Local Government Act 1972 (c 70)do not apply in relation to the service of a relevant document—

(*a*) section 231 (service of notices on local authorities etc),

(*b*) section 233 (service of notices by local authorities).

[Licensing Act 2003, s 184.]

7.7556 **185. Provision of information** *Power to share information between responsible authorities and licensing authorities for the purposes of facilitating the exercise of their functions under the Act.*

*General provisions about offences*

**7.7557 186. Proceedings for offences** (1) In this section "offence" means an offence under this Act.

(2) Proceedings for an offence may be instituted—

(*a*) except in the case of an offence under section 147A, by a licensing authority,

(*b*) by the Director of Public Prosecutions, or

(*c*) in the case of an offence under section 146, 147 or 147A (sale of alcohol to children), by a local weights and measures authority (within the meaning of section 69 of the Weights and Measures Act 1985 (c 72)).

(3) In relation to any offence, section 127(1) of the Magistrates' Courts Act 1980 (information to be laid within six months of offence) is to have effect as if for the reference to six months there were substituted a reference to 12 months.

[Licensing Act 2003, s 186 as amended by the Violent Crime Reduction Act 2006, s 23.]

**7.7558 187. Offences by bodies corporate etc** (1) If an offence committed by a body corporate is shown—

(*a*) to have been committed with the consent or connivance of an officer, or

(*b*) to be attributable to any neglect on his part,

the officer as well as the body corporate is guilty of the offence and liable to be proceeded against and punished accordingly.

(2) If the affairs of a body corporate are managed by its members, subsection (1) applies in relation to the acts and defaults of a member in connection with his functions of management as if he were a director of the body.

(3) In subsection (1) "officer", in relation to a body corporate, means—

(*a*) a director, member of the committee of management, chief executive, manager, secretary or other similar officer of the body, or a person purporting to act in any such capacity, or

(*b*) an individual who is a controller of the body.

(4) If an offence committed by a partnership is shown—

(*a*) to have been committed with the consent or connivance of a partner, or

(*b*) to be attributable to any neglect on his part,

the partner as well as the partnership is guilty of the offence and liable to be proceeded against and punished accordingly.

(5) In subsection (4) "partner" includes a person purporting to act as a partner.

(6) If an offence committed by an unincorporated association (other than a partnership) is shown—

(*a*) to have been committed with the consent or connivance of an officer of the association or a member of its governing body, or

(*b*) to be attributable to any neglect on the part of such an officer or member,

that officer or member as well as the association is guilty of the offence and liable to be proceeded against and punished accordingly.

(7) Regulations may provide for the application of any provision of this section, with such modifications as the Secretary of State considers appropriate, to a body corporate or unincorporated association formed or recognised under the law of a territory outside the United Kingdom.

(8) In this section "offence" means an offence under this Act.

[Licensing Act 2003, s 187.]

**7.7559 188. Jurisdiction and procedure in respect of offences** (1) A fine imposed on an unincorporated association on its conviction for an offence is to be paid out of the funds of the association.

(2) Proceedings for an offence alleged to have been committed by an unincorporated association must be brought in the name of the association (and not in that of any of its members).

(3) Rules of court relating to the service of documents are to have effect as if the association were a body corporate.

(4) In proceedings for an offence brought against an unincorporated association, section 33 of the Criminal Justice Act 1925 (c 86) and Schedule 3 to the Magistrates' Courts Act 1980 (c 43) (procedure) apply as they do in relation to a body corporate.

(5) Proceedings for an offence may be taken—

(*a*) against a body corporate or unincorporated association at any place at which it has a place of business;

(*b*) against an individual at any place where he is for the time being.

(6) Subsection (5) does not affect any jurisdiction exercisable apart from this section.

(7) In this section "offence" means an offence under this Act.

[Licensing Act 2003, s 188.]

*Vessels, vehicles and moveable structures*

**7.7560 189. Vessels, vehicles and moveable structures** (1) This Act applies in relation to a vessel which is not permanently moored or berthed as if it were premises situated in the place where it is usually moored or berthed.

(2) Where a vehicle which is not permanently situated in the same place is, or is proposed to be, used for one or more licensable activities while parked at a particular place, the vehicle is to be treated for the purposes of this Act as if it were premises situated at that place.

(3) Where a moveable structure which is not permanently situated in the same place is, or is proposed to be, used for one or more licensable activities while set in a particular place, the structure is to be treated for the purposes of this Act as if it were premises situated at that place.

(4) Where subsection (2) applies in relation to the same vehicle, or subsection (3) applies in relation to the same structure, in respect of more than one place, the premises which by virtue of that subsection are situated at each such place are to be treated as separate premises.

(5) Sections 29 to 31 (which make provision in respect of provisional statements relating to premises licences) do not apply in relation to a vessel, vehicle or structure to which this section applies.

[Licensing Act 2003, s 189.]

*Interpretation*

7.7561 **190. Location of sales** (1) This section applies where the place where a contract for the sale of alcohol is made is different from the place where the alcohol is appropriated to the contract.

(2) For the purposes of this Act the sale of alcohol is to be treated as taking place where the alcohol is appropriated to the contract.

[Licensing Act 2003, s 190.]

7.7562 **191. Meaning of "alcohol"** (1) In this Act, "alcohol" means spirits, wine, beer, cider or any other fermented, distilled or spirituous liquor (in any state), but does not include—

(*a*) alcohol which is of a strength not exceeding 0.5% at the time of the sale or supply in question,

(*b*) perfume,

(*c*) flavouring essences recognised by the Commissioners of Customs and Excise as not being intended for consumption as or with dutiable alcoholic liquor,

(*d*) the aromatic flavouring essence commonly known as Angostura bitters,

(*e*) alcohol which is, or is included in, a medicinal product or a veterinary medicinal product,

(*f*) denatured alcohol,

(*g*) methyl alcohol,

(*h*) naphtha, or

(*i*) alcohol contained in liqueur confectionery.

(2) In this section—

"denatured alcohol" has the same meaning as in section 5 of the Finance Act 1995 (c 4);

"dutiable alcoholic liquor" has the same meaning as in the Alcoholic Liquor Duties Act 1979 (c 4);

"liqueur confectionery" means confectionery which—

(*a*) contains alcohol in a proportion not greater than 0.2 litres of alcohol (of a strength not exceeding 57%) per kilogram of the confectionery, and

(*b*) either consists of separate pieces weighing not more than 42g or is designed to be broken into such pieces for the purpose of consumption;

"medicinal product" has the same meaning as in section 130 of the Medicines Act 1968 (c 67); and

"strength" is to be construed in accordance with section 2 of the Alcoholic Liquor Duties Act 1979

"veterinary medicinal product" has the same meaning as in regulation 2 of the Veterinary Medicines Regulations 2006.

[Licensing Act 2003, s 191 as amended by SI 2006/2407 and the Policing and Crime Act 2017, s 135.]

7.7563 **192. Meaning of "sale by retail"** (1) For the purposes of this Act "sale by retail", in relation to any alcohol, means a sale of alcohol to any person, other than a sale of alcohol that—

(*a*) is within subsection (2),

(*b*) is made from premises owned by the person making the sale, or occupied by him under a lease to which the provisions of Part 2 of the Landlord and Tenant Act 1954 (c 56) (security of tenure) apply, and

(*c*) is made for consumption off the premises.

(2) A sale of alcohol is within this subsection if it is—

(*a*) to a trader for the purposes of his trade,

(*b*) to a club, which holds a club premises certificate, for the purposes of that club,

(*c*) to the holder of a personal licence for the purpose of making sales authorised by a premises licence,

(*d*) to the holder of a premises licence for the purpose of making sales authorised by that licence, or

(*e*) to the premises user in relation to a temporary event notice for the purpose of making sales authorised by that notice.

[Licensing Act 2003, s 192.]

**7.7563A 192A. Entitlement to work in the United Kingdom** (1) For the purposes of this Act an individual is entitled to work in the United Kingdom if—

(a) the individual does not under the Immigration Act 1971 require leave to enter or remain in the United Kingdom, or

(b) the individual has been granted such leave and the leave—

(i) is not invalid,

(ii) has not ceased to have effect (whether by reason of curtailment, revocation, cancellation, passage of time or otherwise), and

(iii) is not subject to a condition preventing the individual from doing work relating to the carrying on of a licensable activity within section 1(1)(a) or (d).

(2) Where an individual is on immigration bail within the meaning of Part 1 of Schedule 10 to the Immigration Act 2016—

(a) the individual is to be treated for the purposes of subsection (1) as if the individual had been granted leave to enter the United Kingdom, but

(b) any condition as to the individual's work in the United Kingdom to which the individual's immigration bail is subject is to be treated for those purposes as a condition of leave.

[Licensing Act 2003, s 192A as inserted by the Immigration Act 2016, Sch 4.]

**7.7564 193. Other definitions** (1) In this Act—

"beer" has the same meaning as in the Alcoholic Liquor Duties Act 1979 (c 4);

"cider" has the same meaning as in that Act;

"community premises" means premises that are or form part of—

(*a*) a church hall, chapel hall or other similar building, or

(*b*) a village hall, parish hall, community hall or other similar building;

"crime prevention objective" means the licensing objective mentioned in section 4(2)(*a*) (prevention of crime and disorder);

"licensed premises" means premises in respect of which a premises licence has effect;

"licensing functions" is to be construed in accordance with section 4(1);

"management committee", in relation to any community premises, means a committee or board of individuals with responsibility for the management of the premises;

"order", except so far as the contrary intention appears, means an order made by the Secretary of State;

"premises" means any place and includes a vehicle, vessel or moveable structure;

"prescribed" means prescribed by regulations;

"recognised club" means a club which satisfies conditions 1 to 3 of the general conditions in section 62;

"regulations" means regulations made by the Secretary of State;

"relevant electronic facility" means—

(*a*) the electronic assistance facility referred to in regulation 38 of the Provision of Services Regulations 2009, or

(*b*) any facility established and maintained by a licensing authority for the purpose of receiving applications, notices or representations electronically;

"vehicle" means a vehicle intended or adapted for use on roads;

"vessel" includes a ship, boat, raft or other apparatus constructed or adapted for floating on water;

"wine" means—

(*a*) "wine" within the meaning of the Alcoholic Liquor Duties Act 1979, and

(*b*) "made-wine" within the meaning of that Act;

"working day" means any day other than a Saturday, a Sunday, Christmas Day, Good Friday or a day which is a bank holiday under the Banking and Financial Dealings Act 1971 (c 80) in England and Wales.

(2) For the purposes of references in this Act to the prevention of illegal working in licensed premises, a person is working illegally if by doing that work at that time the person is committing an offence under section 24B of the Immigration Act 1971.

[Licensing Act 2003, s 193 as amended by SI 2009/1724, SI 2009/2999 and the Immigration Act 2016, Sch 4.]

**7.7565 194. Index of defined expressions** In this Act the following expressions are defined or otherwise explained by the provisions indicated—

| ***Expression*** | ***Interpretation provision*** |
|---|---|
| alcohol | section 191 |
| associate member | section 67(2) |
| authorised person, in Part 3 | section 13 |
| authorised person, in Part 4 | section 69 |
| beer | section 193 |
| cider | section 193 |
| club premises certificate | section 60 |
| community premises | section 193 |
| conviction, in Part 6 | section 114 |
| crime prevention objective | section 193 |
| designated premises supervisor | section 15 |
| entitled to work in the United Kingdom | section 192A |
| foreign offence, in Part 6 | section 113 |
| given, in relation to a notice, etc | section 184 |
| guest | section 67(1) |
| immigration offence | section 113 |
| immigration penalty (and required to pay, in relation to an immigration penalty) | section 113 |
| interim authority notice | section 47 |
| late night refreshment | Schedule 2 |
| late temporary event notice | section 100A(1)(*b*) |
| licensable activity | section 1(1) |
| licensed premises | section 193 |
| licensing authority | section 3(1) |
| licensing authority's area | section 3(2) |
| licensing functions | sections 4(1) and 193 |
| licensing objectives | section 4(2) |
| management committee | section 193 |
| order | section 193 |
| permitted temporary activity | section 98 |
| personal licence | section 111(1) |
| premises | section 193 |
| premises licence | section 11 |
| premises user, in relation to a temporary event notice | section 100(2) |
| prescribed | section 193 |
| provisional statement | section 29(3) |
| qualifying club | section 61 |
| qualifying club activity | section 1(2) |
| recognised club | section 193 |
| regulated entertainment | Schedule 1 |
| regulations | section 193 |
| relevant electronic facility | section 193 |
| relevant licensing authority, in Part 3 | section 12 |
| relevant licensing authority, in Part 4 | section 68 |
| relevant licensing authority, in Part 5 | section 99 |
| relevant licensing authority, in Part 6 | section 112 |
| relevant offence, in Part 6 | section 113 |
| relevant person, in Part 5 | section 99A |
| responsible authority, in Part 3 | section 13 |
| responsible authority, in Part 4 | section 69 |
| sale by retail, in relation to alcohol | section 192 |
| secretary, in Part 4 | section 70 |
| standard temporary event notice | section 100A(1)(*a*) |
| supply of alcohol, in Part 3 | section 14 |
| supply of alcohol to members or guests, in relation to a club, in Part 4 | section 70 |
| temporary event notice | section 100(1) |

| *Expression* | *Interpretation provision* |
|---|---|
| vehicle | section 193 |
| vessel | section 193 |
| wine | section 193 |
| working day | section 193 |
| working illegally, in relation to the prevention of illegal working in licensed premises | section 193* |

[Licensing Act 2003, s 194 as amended by SI 2009/1724, SI 2009/2999, the Police Reform and Social Responsibility Act 2011, ss 105, 107, 112, 114 and the Immigration Act 2016, Sch 4.]

* **Amended by the Deregulation Act 2015, s 67 from a date to be appointed.**

*Supplementary and general*

7.7566 **195. Crown application** (1) This Act binds the Crown and has effect in relation to land in which there is—

(*a*) an interest belonging to Her Majesty in right of the Crown,

(*b*) an interest belonging to a government department, or

(*c*) an interest held in trust for Her Majesty for the purposes of such a department.

(2) This Act also applies to—

(*a*) land which is vested in, but not occupied by, Her Majesty in right of the Duchy of Lancaster, and

(*b*) land which is vested in, but not occupied by, the possessor for the time being of the Duchy of Cornwall.

(3) No contravention by the Crown of any provision made by or under this Act makes the Crown criminally liable; but the High Court may declare unlawful any act or omission of the Crown which constitutes such a contravention.

(4) Provision made by or under this Act applies to persons in the public service of the Crown as it applies to other persons.

(5) But nothing in this Act affects Her Majesty in Her private capacity.

[Licensing Act 2003, s 195.]

7.7567 **196. Removal of privileges and exemptions** No privilege or exemption mentioned in section 199(*a*) or (*b*) of the Licensing Act 1964 (c 26) (University of Cambridge and the Vintners of the City of London) operates to exempt any person from the requirements of this Act.

[Licensing Act 2003, s 196.]

7.7568 **197. Regulations and orders**

7.7568A **198. Minor and consequential amendments**

7.7568B **199. Repeals**

7.7569 **200. Transitional provision etc**

7.7570 **201. Short title, commencement and extent** (1) This Act may be cited as the Licensing Act 2003.

(2) The preceding provisions (and the Schedules) come into force in accordance with provision made by order[1].

(3) Subject to subsections (4) and (5), this Act extends to England and Wales only.

(4) Section 155(1) also extends to Northern Ireland.

(5) An amendment or repeal contained in Schedule 6 or 7 has the same extent as the enactment to which it relates.

[Licensing Act 2003, s 201.]

[1] For commencement orders made at the date of going to press, see the note to the title of this Act, ante.

## SCHEDULE 1

Provision of Regulated Entertainment — Section 1

7.7571

*(Amended by the Gambling Act 2005, Sch 16, the Policing and Crime Act 2009, Sch 7, the Live Music Act 2012, ss 2, 3, SI 2013/1578, SI 2014/3253 and the Deregulation Act 2015, s 76.)*

### Part 1
### General Definitions

*The provision of regulated entertainment*

1. (1) For the purposes of this Act, the "provision of regulated entertainment" means the provision of entertainment of a description falling within paragraph 2 where the conditions in sub-paragraphs (2) and (3) are satisfied.

(2) The first condition is that the entertainment is provided—

(*a*) to any extent for members of the public or a section of the public, (*b*) exclusively for members of a club which is a qualifying club in relation to the provision of regulated entertainment, or for members of such a club and their guests, or

(*c*) in any case not falling within paragraph (*a*) or (*b*), for consideration and with a view to profit.

(3) The second condition is that the premises on which the entertainment is provided are made available for the purpose, or for purposes which include the purpose, of enabling the entertainment concerned to take place.

(4) For the purposes of sub-paragraph (2)(*c*), entertainment is to be regarded as provided for consideration only if any charge—

(*a*) is made by or on behalf of any person concerned in the organisation or management of that entertainment, and

(*b*) is paid by or on behalf of some or all of the persons for whom that entertainment is provided.

(5) In sub-paragraph (4), "charge" includes any charge for the provision of goods or services.

(6) For the purposes of sub-paragraph (4)(*a*), where the entertainment consists of the performance of live music or the playing of recorded music, a person performing or playing the music is not concerned in the organisation or management of the entertainment by reason only that he does one or more of the following—

(*a*) chooses the music to be performed or played,

(*b*) determines the manner in which he performs or plays it,

(*c*) *repealed.*

(7) This paragraph is subject to Part 2 of this Schedule (exemptions).

*Entertainment*

**2.** (1) The descriptions of entertainment are—

(*a*) a performance of a play,

(*b*) an exhibition of a film,

(*c*) an indoor sporting event,

(*d*) a boxing or wrestling entertainment,

(*e*) a performance of live music,

(*f*) any playing of recorded music,

(*g*) a performance of dance,

(*h*) entertainment of a similar description to that falling within paragraph (*e*), (*f*) or (*g*),

the following conditions are satisfied (so far as relevant).

(1A) The first condition is that the entertainment—

(*a*) takes place in the presence of an audience, and

(*b*) is provided for the purpose, or for purposes which include the purpose, of entertaining that audience.

(1B) The second condition is relevant only to a performance of a play, and is that one or more of the following applies—

(*a*) the audience consists of more than 500 persons;

(*b*) the entertainment takes place before 8am on any day;

(*c*) the entertainment takes place after 11pm on any day.

(1C) The third condition is relevant only to an indoor sporting event, and is that one or more of the following applies—

(*a*) the audience consists of more than 1000 persons;

(*b*) the entertainment takes place before 8am on any day;

(*c*) the entertainment takes place after 11pm on any day.

(1D) The fourth condition is relevant only to a performance of dance, and is that one or more of the following applies—

(*a*) the audience consists of more than 500 persons;

(*b*) the entertainment takes place before 8am on any day;

(*c*) the entertainment takes place after 11pm on any day;

(*d*) the entertainment is relevant entertainment within the meaning of paragraph 2A of Schedule 3 to the Local Government (Miscellaneous Provisions) Act 1982 (meaning of "sexual entertainment venue").

(1E) So much of any entertainment of a description specified in paragraphs (*a*) to (*h*) of sub-paragraph (1) as does not satisfy the conditions in sub-paragraphs (1A) to (1D) (so far as relevant) is not to be regarded as falling within sub-paragraph (1).

(2) Any reference in this paragraph to an audience includes a reference to spectators.

(3) This paragraph is subject to Part 3 of this Schedule (interpretation).

**3.** *Repealed.*

*Power to amend Schedule*

**4.** The Secretary of State may by order amend this Schedule for the purposes of modifying the descriptions of entertainment specified in paragraph 2, and for this purpose "modify" includes adding, varying or removing any description.

## Part 2

## Exemptions

*Film exhibitions for the purposes of advertisement, information, education, etc*

**5.** The provision of entertainment consisting of the exhibition of a film is not to be regarded as the provision of regulated entertainment for the purposes of this Act if its sole or main purpose is to—

(*a*) demonstrate any product,

(*b*) advertise any goods or services, or

(*c*) provide information, education or instruction.

*Film exhibitions: museums and art galleries*

**6.** The provision of entertainment consisting of the exhibition of a film is not to be regarded as the provision of regulated entertainment for the purposes of this Act if it consists of or forms part of an exhibit put on show for any purposes of a museum or art gallery.

*Film exhibitions: community premises*

**6A.** (1) The provision of entertainment consisting of the exhibition of a film at community premises is not to be regarded as the provision of regulated entertainment for the purposes of this Act if the following conditions are satisfied.

(2) The first condition is that prior written consent for the entertainment to take place at the community premises has been obtained, by or on behalf of a person concerned in the organisation or management of the entertainment—

(*a*) from the management committee of the community premises, or

(*b*) where there is no management committee, from—

(i) a person who has control of the community premises (as occupier or otherwise) in connection with the carrying on by that person of a trade, business or other undertaking (for profit or not), or

(ii) where there is no such person, an owner of the community premises.

(3) The second condition is that the entertainment is not provided with a view to profit.

(4) The third condition is that the entertainment takes place in the presence of an audience of no more than 500 persons.

(5) The fourth condition is that the entertainment takes place between 8am and 11pm on the same day.

(6) The fifth condition is that the film classification body or the relevant licensing authority has made a recommendation concerning the admission of children to an exhibition of the film and—

(*a*) where a recommendation has been made only by the film classification body, the admission of children is subject to such restrictions (if any) as are necessary to comply with the recommendation of that body;

(*b*) where a recommendation has been made only by the relevant licensing authority, the admission of children is subject to such restrictions (if any) as are necessary to comply with the recommendation of that authority;

(*c*) where recommendations have been made both by the film classification body and the relevant licensing authority, the admission of children is subject to such restrictions (if any) as are necessary to comply with the recommendation of the relevant licensing authority.

(7) In sub-paragraph (6) the reference to the "relevant licensing authority", in relation to the exhibition of a film at particular community premises, is a reference to—

(*a*) the licensing authority in whose area the premises are situated, or

(*b*) where the premises are situated in the areas of two or more licensing authorities, those authorities or (as the context requires) such of those authorities as have made a recommendation.

(8) In this paragraph—

"children" and "film classification body" have the same meaning as in section 20;

"owner", in relation to community premises, means—

(*a*) a person who is for the time being entitled to dispose of the fee simple in the premises, whether in possession or in reversion, or

(*b*) a person who holds or is entitled to the rents and profits of the premises under a lease which (when granted) was for a term of not less than 3 years.

*Music and film incidental to certain other activities*

**7.** The provision of entertainment consisting of the performance of live music, the playing of recorded music or the exhibition of a film is not to be regarded as the provision of regulated entertainment for the purposes of this Act to the extent that it is incidental to some other activity which is not itself a description of entertainment falling within paragraph 2.

*Use of television or radio receivers*

**8.** The provision of any entertainment is not to be regarded as the provision of regulated entertainment for the purposes of this Act to the extent that it consists of the simultaneous reception and playing of a programme included in a programme service within the meaning of the Broadcasting Act 1990 (c 42).

*Religious services, places of worship etc*

**9.** The provision of any entertainment—

(*a*) for the purposes of, or for purposes incidental to, a religious meeting or service, or

(*b*) at a place of public religious worship,

is not to be regarded as the provision of regulated entertainment for the purposes of this Act.

*Garden fêtes, etc*

**10.** (1) The provision of any entertainment at a garden fête, or at a function or event of a similar character, is not to be regarded as the provision of regulated entertainment for the purposes of this Act.

(2) But sub-paragraph (1) does not apply if the fête, function or event is promoted with a view to applying the whole or part of its proceeds for purposes of private gain.

(3) In sub-paragraph (2) "private gain", in relation to the proceeds of a fête, function or event, is to be construed in accordance with section 19(3) of the Gambling Act 2005.

*Morris dancing etc*

**11.** The provision of any entertainment is not to be regarded as the provision of regulated entertainment for the purposes of this Act to the extent that it consists of the provision of—

(*a*) a performance of morris dancing or any dancing of a similar nature or the playing of live or recorded music that forms an integral part of such a performance, or

(*b*) *repealed.*

*Sexual entertainment venues*

**11A.** (1) The provision of relevant entertainment—

(*a*) at premises for which a licence for a sexual entertainment venue is required (or the requirement has been waived) by virtue of Schedule 3 to the Local Government (Miscellaneous Provisions) Act 1982, and (*b*) of a kind, and in a way, by virtue of which the premises qualify as such a venue,

is not to be regarded as the provision of regulated entertainment for the purposes of this Act.

(2) The provision of relevant entertainment—

(*a*) at premises which are subject to a licence for a sexual entertainment venue but are not such a venue merely because of the operation of paragraph 2A(3)(*b*) of Schedule 3 to the Act of 1982, and

(*b*) of a kind, and in a way, by virtue of which the premises would qualify as such a venue but for the operation of that paragraph,

is not to be regarded as the provision of regulated entertainment for the purposes of this Act.

(3) The provision of entertainment consisting of the performance of live music or the playing of recorded music is not to be regarded as the provision of regulated entertainment for the purposes of this Act to the extent that it is an integral part of such provision of relevant entertainment as falls within sub-paragraph (1) or (2).

(4) *Repealed*

(5) In this paragraph—

"premises" has the meaning given by paragraph 2A(14) of Schedule 3 to the Act of 1982;

"relevant entertainment" has the meaning given by paragraph 2A(2) of that Schedule to that Act;

"sexual entertainment venue" has the meaning given by paragraph 2A(1) of that Schedule to that Act.

*Vehicles in motion*

**12.** The provision of any entertainment—

(*a*) on premises consisting of or forming part of a vehicle, and

(*b*) at a time when the vehicle is not permanently or temporarily parked,

is not to be regarded as the provision of regulated entertainment for the purposes of this Act.

*Entertainment provided by health care providers, local authorities and school proprietors*

**12ZA.** (1) The provision of any entertainment by or on behalf of a health care provider, local authority or school proprietor is not to be regarded as the provision of regulated entertainment for the purposes of this Act if the conditions in sub-paragraphs (2) to (5) are satisfied.

(2) The first condition is that the entertainment takes place—

(*a*) if it is provided by or on behalf of a health care provider, on any premises forming part of a hospital—

(i) in which that provider has a relevant property interest, or

(ii) which are lawfully occupied by that provider,

(*b*) if it is provided by or on behalf of a local authority, on any premises in which that authority has a relevant property interest or which are lawfully occupied by that authority, and

(*c*) if it is provided by or on behalf of a school proprietor, on the premises of the school.

(3) The second condition is that the premises are not domestic premises.

(4) The third condition is that the entertainment takes place between 8am and 11pm on the same day (or, where an order under section 172 has effect in relation to that entertainment, during any times specified under that order).

(5) The fourth condition is that the entertainment is not relevant entertainment within the meaning of paragraph 2A(2) of Schedule 3 to the Local Government (Miscellaneous Provisions) Act 1982 (meaning of "sexual entertainment venue").

(6) For the purposes of this paragraph, a person has a relevant property interest in premises if that person—

(*a*) is for the time being entitled to dispose of the fee simple in the premises, whether in possession or in reversion, or

(*b*) holds or is entitled to the rents and profits of the premises under a lease which (when granted) was for a term of not less than 3 years.

(7) In sub-paragraph (3), "domestic premises" means premises occupied as a private dwelling, including any garden, yard, garage, outhouse or other appurtenance of such premises whether or not used in common by the occupants of more than one such dwelling.

*Music at community premises etc.*

**12ZB.** (1) The provision of entertainment consisting of one or both of the following is not to be regarded as the provision of regulated entertainment for the purposes of this Act if the conditions in sub-paragraphs (2) to (6) are satisfied—

(*a*) a performance of live music;

(*b*) the playing of recorded music.

(2) The first condition is that the entertainment takes place at—

(*a*) community premises that are not authorised, by a premises licence or club premises certificate, to be used for the supply of alcohol for consumption on the premises,

(*b*) the premises of a hospital,

(*c*) premises in which a local authority has a relevant property interest or which are lawfully occupied by a local authority, or

(*d*) the premises of a school.

(3) The second condition is that the premises are not domestic premises (within the meaning of paragraph 12ZA(7)).

(4) The third condition is that the entertainment takes place in the presence of an audience of no more than 500 persons.

(5) The fourth condition is that the entertainment takes place between 8am and 11pm on the same day (or, where an order under section 172 has effect in relation to that entertainment, during any times specified under that order).

(6) The fifth condition is that a person concerned in the organisation or management of the entertainment has obtained the prior written consent of a relevant person for the entertainment to take place.

(7) In sub-paragraph (6), "relevant person" means—

(*a*) where the entertainment takes place at community premises—

(i) the management committee of the premises, or

(ii) if there is no management committee, a person who has control of the premises (as occupier or otherwise) in connection with the carrying on by that person of a trade, business or other undertaking (for profit or not) or (in the absence of such a person) a person with a relevant property interest in the premises;

(*b*) where the entertainment takes place at the premises of a hospital, a health care provider which has a relevant property interest in or lawfully occupies those premises;

(*c*) where the entertainment takes place at premises in which a local authority has a relevant property interest or which are lawfully occupied by a local authority, that authority;

(*d*) where the entertainment takes place at the premises of a school, the school proprietor.

(8) Paragraph 12ZA(6) (meaning of "relevant property interest") applies for the purposes of this paragraph as it applies for the purposes of paragraph 12ZA.

*Music in licensed venues*

**12A.** (1) The provision of entertainment consisting of one or both of the following is not to be regarded as the provision of regulated entertainment for the purposes of this Act if the conditions in sub-paragraph (2) are satisfied—

(*a*) a performance of live music;

(*b*) the playing of recorded music.

(2) The conditions referred to in sub-paragraph (1) are that—

(*a*) the requirements of section 177A(1) are satisfied, and

(*b*) conditions are not included in the premises licence or club premises certificate referred to in section 177A(1)(*a*) by virtue of section 177A(3) or (4).

*Live music in workplaces*

**12B.** The provision of entertainment consisting of a performance of live music is not to be regarded as the provision of regulated entertainment for the purposes of this Act, provided that—

(*a*) the place where the performance is provided is not licensed under this Act (or is so licensed only for the provision of late night refreshment) but is a workplace as defined in regulation 2(1) of the Workplace (Health, Safety and Welfare) Regulations 1992,

(*b*) the performance takes place in the presence of an audience of no more than 500 persons, and

(*c*) the performance takes place between 8am and 11pm on the same day.

*Live unamplified music*

**12C.** The provision of entertainment consisting of a performance of live music is not (subject to section 177A(3) and (4)) to be regarded as the provision of regulated entertainment for the purposes of this Act provided that the music—

(*a*) is unamplified; and

(*b*) takes place between 8am and 11pm on the same day.

*Circuses*

**12D.** (1) The provision of any entertainment that consists of or forms part of a performance by a travelling circus is not to be regarded as the provision of regulated entertainment for the purposes of this Act if the conditions in sub-paragraphs (2) to (5) are satisfied.

(2) The first condition is that the entertainment is not of a description falling within paragraph 2(1)(*b*) (exhibition of a film) or paragraph 2(1)(*d*) (boxing or wrestling entertainment).

(3) The second condition is that the entertainment takes place between 8am and 11pm on the same day.

(4) The third condition is that—

(*a*) the entertainment takes place wholly within a moveable structure, and

(*b*) the audience present is accommodated wholly inside that moveable structure.

(5) The fourth condition is that the travelling circus has not been located on the same site for more than 28 consecutive days.

(6) In this paragraph, "travelling circus" means a circus which travels from site to site for the purpose of giving performances.

*Boxing or wrestling entertainment: certain forms of wrestling*

**12E.** The provision of entertainment consisting of a boxing or wrestling entertainment is not to be regarded as the provision of regulated entertainment for the purposes of this Act if—

(*a*) it is a contest, exhibition or display of Greco-Roman wrestling, or of freestyle wrestling, between two participants (regardless of their sex),

(*b*) it takes place in the presence of no more than 1000 spectators,

(*c*) it takes place between 8am and 11pm on the same day,

(*d*) it takes place wholly inside a building, and

(*e*) the spectators present at that entertainment are accommodated wholly inside that building.

## PART 3

## INTERPRETATION

*General*

**13.** This Part has effect for the purposes of this Schedule.

*Plays*

**14.** (1) A "performance of a play" means a performance of any dramatic piece, whether involving improvisation or not,—

(*a*) which is given wholly or in part by one or more persons actually present and performing, and

(*b*) in which the whole or a major proportion of what is done by the person or persons performing, whether by way of speech, singing or action, involves the playing of a role.

(2) In this paragraph, "performance" includes rehearsal (and "performing" is to be construed accordingly).

*Film exhibitions*

15. An "exhibition of a film" means any exhibition of moving pictures.

*Indoor sporting events*

16. (1) An "indoor sporting event" is a sporting event—
(*a*) which takes place wholly inside a building, and
(*b*) at which the spectators present at the event are accommodated wholly inside that building.
(2) In this paragraph—
"building" means any roofed structure (other than a structure with a roof which may be opened or closed) and includes a vehicle, vessel or moveable structure,
"sporting event" means any contest, exhibition or display of any sport, and
"sport" other than a boxing or wrestling entertainment includes—
(*a*) any game in which physical skill is the predominant factor, and
(*b*) any form of physical recreation which is also engaged in for purposes of competition or display.

*Boxing or wrestling entertainments*

17. A "boxing or wrestling entertainment" is any contest, exhibition or display of boxing or wrestling, or which combines boxing or wrestling with one or more martial arts.

*Music*

18. "Music" includes vocal or instrumental music or any combination of the two.

*Health care providers and hospitals*

19. (1) "Health care provider" means a person providing any form of health care services for individuals.
(2) In sub-paragraph (1), "health care" means all forms of health care provided for individuals, whether relating to physical or mental health, and the reference to health care services is to be read accordingly.
(3) "Hospital"—
(*a*) in England, has the same meaning as in section 275 of the National Health Service Act 2006, and
(*b*) in Wales, has the same meaning as in section 206 of the National Health Service (Wales) Act 2006.

*Local authorities*

20. "Local authority" means—
(*a*) a local authority within the meaning of section 270 of the Local Government Act 1972;
(*b*) the Greater London Authority;
(*c*) the Common Council of the City of London;
(*d*) the Council of the Isles of Scilly;
(*e*) a National Park authority established by an order under section 63(1) of the Environment Act 1995 for an area in England or Wales;
(*f*) the Broads Authority; and
(*g*) the Sub-Treasurer of the Inner Temple or the Under-Treasurer of the Middle Temple

*Schools, school proprietors and school premises*

21. (1) "School" means—
(*a*) a maintained school as defined by section 20(7) of the School Standards and Framework Act 1998;
(*b*) an independent school as defined by section 463 of the Education Act 1996 entered on a register of independent schools kept under section 158 of the Education Act 2002;
(*c*) an independent educational institution within section 92(1)(*b*) of the Education and Skills Act 2008 entered on a register of independent educational institutions kept under section 95 of that Act;
(*d*) a pupil referral unit as defined by section 19 of the Education Act 1996;
(*e*) an alternative provision Academy within the meaning of section 1C(3) of the Academies Act 2010, other than an independent school as defined by section 463 of the Education Act 1996;
(*f*) a school approved under section 342 of the Education Act 1996 (non-maintained special schools);
(*g*) a 16 to 19 Academy within the meaning of section 1B(3) of the Academies Act 2010;
(*h*) a sixth form college as defined by section 91(3A) of the Further and Higher Education Act 1992;
(*i*) a maintained nursery school as defined by section 22(9) of the Schools Standards and Framework Act 1998.
(2) "School proprietor" means—
(*a*) in relation to a school (other than a pupil referral unit or a sixth form college), the person or body of persons responsible for the management of the school,
(*b*) in relation to a pupil referral unit—
(i) the committee which is established to act as the management committee for that unit by virtue of paragraph 15 of Schedule 1 to the Education Act 1996, or
(ii) if there is no such committee, the local authority (as defined by section 579(1) of that Act) which maintains that unit,
(*c*) in relation to a sixth form college, the sixth form college corporation as defined in section 90(1) of the Further and Higher Education Act 1992.
(3) In relation to a school, "premises" includes any detached playing fields.

## SCHEDULE 2
## Provision of Late Night Refreshment

*(As amended by the Charities Act 2011, Sch 7 and the Deregulation Act 2015, s 71)* Section 1

*The provision of late night refreshment*

7.7575 1. (1) For the purposes of this Act, a person "provides late night refreshment" if—
(*a*) at any time between the hours of 11.00 p m. and 5.00 a.m., he supplies hot food or hot drink to members of the public, or a section of the public, on or from any premises, whether for consumption on or off the premises, or

(*b*) at any time between those hours when members of the public, or a section of the public, are admitted to any premises, he supplies, or holds himself out as willing to supply, hot food or hot drink to any persons, or to persons of a particular description, on or from those premises, whether for consumption on or off the premises,

unless the supply is an exempt supply by virtue of paragraph 2A, 3, 4 or 5.

(2) References in this Act to the "provision of late night refreshment" are to be construed in accordance with sub-paragraph (1).

(3) This paragraph is subject to the following provisions of this Schedule.

*Hot food or hot drink*

**2.** Food or drink supplied on or from any premises is "hot" for the purposes of this Schedule if the food or drink, or any part of it,—

(*a*) before it is supplied, is heated on the premises or elsewhere for the purpose of enabling it to be consumed at a temperature above the ambient air temperature and, at the time of supply, is above that temperature, or

(*b*) after it is supplied, may be heated on the premises for the purpose of enabling it to be consumed at a temperature above the ambient air temperature.

*Exempt supplies: designated areas, descriptions of premises and times*

**2A.** (1) The supply of hot food or hot drink is an exempt supply for the purposes of paragraph 1(1) if it takes place—

(*a*) on or from premises which are wholly situated in an area designated by the relevant licensing authority;

(*b*) on or from premises which are of a description designated by the relevant licensing authority; or

(*c*) during a period (beginning no earlier than 11.00 pm and ending no later than 5.00 am) designated by the relevant licensing authority.

(2) A licensing authority may designate a description of premises under sub-paragraph (1)(b) only if the description is one that is prescribed by regulations[1].

(3) A designation under sub-paragraph (1) may be varied or revoked by the licensing authority that made it.

(4) A licensing authority that makes, varies or revokes a designation under sub-paragraph (1) must publish the designation, variation or revocation.

(4) In sub-paragraph (1) references to the "relevant licensing authority", in relation to a supply of hot food or hot drink, are references to—

(*a*) the licensing authority in whose area the premises on or from which the food or drink is supplied are situated, or

(*b*) where those premises are situated in the areas of two or more licensing authorities, any of those authorities.

---

[1] The Licensing Act 2003 (Late Night Refreshment) Regulations 2015, SI 2015/1781 have been made.

*Exempt supplies: clubs, hotels etc and employees*

**3.** (1) The supply of hot food or hot drink on or from any premises at any time is an exempt supply for the purposes of paragraph 1(1) if, at that time, a person will neither—

(*a*) be admitted to the premises, nor

(*b*) be supplied with hot food or hot drink on or from the premises,

except by virtue of being a person of a description falling within sub-paragraph (2).

(2) The descriptions are that—

(*a*) he is a member of a recognised club,

(*b*) he is a person staying at a particular hotel, or at particular comparable premises, for the night in question,

(*c*) he is an employee of a particular employer,

(*d*) he is engaged in a particular trade, he is a member of a particular profession or he follows a particular vocation,

(*e*) he is a guest of a person falling within any of paragraphs (*a*) to (*d*).

(3) The premises which, for the purposes of sub-paragraph (2)(*b*), are comparable to a hotel are—

(*a*) a guest house, lodging house or hostel,

(*b*) a caravan site or camping site, or

(*c*) any other premises the main purpose of maintaining which is the provision of facilities for overnight accommodation.

*Exempt supplies: premises licensed under certain other Acts*

**4.** The supply of hot food or hot drink on or from any premises is an exempt supply for the purposes of paragraph 1(1) if it takes place during a period for which—

(*a*) the premises may be used for a public exhibition of a kind described in section 21(1) of the Greater London Council (General Powers) Act 1966 (c xxviii) by virtue of a licence under that section, or

(*b*) the premises may be used as near beer premises within the meaning of section 14 of the London Local Authorities Act 1995 (c x) by virtue of a licence under section 16 of that Act.

*Miscellaneous exempt supplies*

**5.** (1) The following supplies of hot food or hot drink are exempt supplies for the purposes of paragraph 1(1)—

(*a*) the supply of hot drink which consists of or contains alcohol,

(*b*) the supply of hot drink by means of a vending machine,

(*c*) the supply of hot food or hot drink free of charge,

(*d*) the supply of hot food or hot drink by a registered charity or a person authorised by a registered charity,

(*e*) the supply of hot food or hot drink on a vehicle at a time when the vehicle is not permanently or temporarily parked.

(2) Hot drink is supplied by means of a vending machine for the purposes of sub-paragraph (1)(*b*) only if—

(*a*) the payment for the hot drink is inserted into the machine by a member of the public, and
(*b*) the hot drink is supplied directly by the machine to a member of the public.

(3) Hot food or hot drink is not to be regarded as supplied free of charge for the purposes of sub-paragraph (1)(*c*) if, in order to obtain the hot food or hot drink, a charge must be paid—

(*a*) for admission to any premises, or
(*b*) for some other item.

(4) In sub-paragraph (1)(*d*) "registered charity" means—

(*a*) a charity which is registered in accordance with section 30 of the Charities Act 2011, or
(*b*) a charity which by virtue of subsection (2) of that section is not required to be so registered.

*Clubs which are not recognised clubs: members and guests*

**6.** For the purposes of this Schedule—

(*a*) the supply of hot food or hot drink to a person as being a member, or the guest of a member, of a club which is not a recognised club is to be taken to be a supply to a member of the public, and
(*b*) the admission of any person to any premises as being such a member or guest is to be taken to be the admission of a member of the public.

## SCHEDULE 4
### Personal Licence: Relevant Offences

Section 113

*(Amended by SI 2005/2366, the Gambling Act 2005, Sch 16, the Fraud Act 2006, Sch 1, SI 2007/2075, SI 2008/1277, the Police Reform and Social Responsibility Act 2011, s 123, the Psychoactive Substances Act 2015, Sch 5, the Immigration Act 2016, Sch 4 and the Policing and Crime Act 2017, s 139)*

**7.7576** **1.** An offence under this Act.

**2.** An offence under any of the following enactments—

(*a*) Schedule 12 to the London Government Act 1963 (c 33) (public entertainment licensing);
(*b*) the Licensing Act 1964 (c 26);
(*c*) the Private Places of Entertainment (Licensing) Act 1967 (c 19);
(*d*) section 13 of the Theatres Act 1968 (c 54);
(*e*) the Late Night Refreshment Houses Act 1969 (c 53);
(*f*) section 6 of, or Schedule 1 to, the Local Government (Miscellaneous Provisions) Act 1982 (c 30);
(*g*) the Licensing (Occasional Permissions) Act 1983 (c 24);
(*h*) the Cinemas Act 1985 (c 13);
(*i*) the London Local Authorities Act 1990 (c vii).

**3.** An offence under the Firearms Act 1968 (c 27).

**4.** An offence under section 1 of the Trade Descriptions Act 1968 (c 29) (false trade description of goods) in circumstances where the goods in question are or include alcohol.

**5.** An offence under any of the following provisions of the Theft Act 1968 (c 60)—

(*a*) section 1 (theft);
(*b*) section 8 (robbery);
(*c*) section 9 (burglary);
(*d*) section 10 (aggravated burglary);
(*e*) section 11 (removal of articles from places open to the public);
(*f*) section 12A (aggravated vehicle-taking), in circumstances where subsection (2)(*b*) of that section applies and the accident caused the death of any person;
(*g*) section 13 (abstracting of electricity);
(*h*) section 15 (obtaining property by deception);
(*i*) section 15A (obtaining a money transfer by deception);
(*j*) section 16 (obtaining pecuniary advantage by deception);
(*k*) section 17 (false accounting);
(*l*) section 19 (false statements by company directors etc);
(*m*) section 20 (suppression, etc of documents);
(*n*) section 21 (blackmail);
(*o*) section 22 (handling stolen goods);
(*p*) section 24A (dishonestly retaining a wrongful credit);
(*q*) section 25 (going equipped for stealing etc).

**6.** An offence under section 7(2) of the Gaming Act 1968 (c 65) (allowing child to take part in gaming on premises licensed for the sale of alcohol).

**7.** An offence under any of the following provisions of the Misuse of Drugs Act 1971 (c 38)—

(*a*) section 4(2) (production of a controlled drug);
(*b*) section 4(3) (supply of a controlled drug);
(*c*) section 5(3) (possession of a controlled drug with intent to supply);
(*d*) section 8 (permitting activities to take place on premises).

**7A.** An offence under any of the Immigration Acts.

**8.** An offence under either of the following provisions of the Theft Act 1978 (c 31)—

(*a*) section 1 (obtaining services by deception);
(*b*) section 2 (evasion of liability by deception).

**9.** An offence under either of the following provisions of the Customs and Excise Management Act 1979 (c 2)—

(*a*) section 170 (disregarding subsection (1)(*a*)) (fraudulent evasion of duty etc);
(*b*) section 170B (taking preparatory steps for evasion of duty).

**10.** An offence under either of the following provisions of the Tobacco Products Duty Act 1979 (c 7)—

(*a*) section 8G (possession and sale of unmarked tobacco);
(*b*) section 8H (use of premises for sale of unmarked tobacco).

**11.** An offence under the Forgery and Counterfeiting Act 1981 (c 45) (other than an offence under section 18 or 19 of that Act).

**12.** An offence under the Firearms (Amendment) Act 1988 (c 45).

**13.** An offence under any of the following provisions of the Copyright, Designs and Patents Act 1988 (c 48)—

(*a*) section 107(1)(*d*)(iii) (public exhibition in the course of a business of article infringing copyright);
(*b*) section 107(3) (infringement of copyright by public performance of work etc);

(*c*) section 198(2) (broadcast etc of recording of performance made without sufficient consent);
(*d*) section 297(1) (fraudulent reception of transmission);
(*e*) section 297A(1) (supply etc of unauthorised decoder).

**14.** An offence under any of the following provisions of the Road Traffic Act 1988 (c 52)—
(*a*) section 3A (causing death by careless driving while under the influence of drink or drugs);
(*b*) section 4 (driving etc a vehicle when under the influence of drink or drugs);
(*c*) section 5 (driving etc a vehicle with alcohol concentration above prescribed limit);
(*d*) section 6(6) (failing to co-operate with a preliminary test).

**15.** An offence under either of the following provisions of the Food Safety Act 1990 (c 16) in circumstances where the food in question is or includes alcohol—
(*a*) section 14 (selling food or drink not of the nature, substance or quality demanded);
(*b*) section 15 (falsely describing or presenting food or drink).

**16.** An offence under section 92(1) or (2) of the Trade Marks Act 1994 (c 26) (unauthorised use of trade mark, etc in relation to goods) in circumstances where the goods in question are or include alcohol.

**17.** An offence under the Firearms (Amendment) Act 1997 (c 5).

**18.** A sexual offence, being an offence—
(*a*) listed in Part 2 of Schedule 15 to the Criminal Justice Act 2003, other than the offence mentioned in paragraph 95 (an offence under section 4 of the Sexual Offences Act 1967 (procuring others to commit homosexual acts));
(*aa*) listed in Schedule 3 to the Sexual Offences Act 2003 (sexual offences for the purposes of notification and orders);
(*b*) an offence under section 8 of the Sexual Offences Act 1956 (intercourse with a defective);
(*c*) an offence under section 18 of the Sexual Offences Act 1956 (fraudulent abduction of an heiress).

**19.** A violent offence, being any offence which leads, or is intended or likely to lead, to a person's death or to physical injury to a person, including an offence which is required to be charged as arson (whether or not it would otherwise fall within this definition).

**19A.** An offence listed in Part 1 of Schedule 15 to the Criminal Justice Act 2003 (specified violent offences).

**20.** An offence under section 3 of the Private Security Industry Act 2001 (c 12) (engaging in certain activities relating to security without a licence).

**21.** An offence under section 46 of the Gambling Act 2005 if the child or young person was invited, caused or permitted to gamble on premises in respect of which a premises licence under this Act had effect.

**22.** An offence under the Fraud Act 2006.

**22ZA.** An offence under any of the following provisions of the Violent Crime Reduction Act 2006—
(a) section 28 (using someone to mind a weapon);
(b) section 36 (manufacture, import and sale of realistic imitation firearms).

**22A.** An offence under regulation 6 of the Business Protection from Misleading Marketing Regulations 2008 (offence of misleading advertising) in circumstances where the advertising in question relates to alcohol or to goods that include alcohol.

**23.** An offence under regulation 8, 9, 10, 11 or 12 of the Consumer Protection from Unfair Trading Regulations 2008 (offences relating to unfair commercial practices) in circumstances where the commercial practice in question is directly connected with the promotion, sale or supply of alcohol or of a product that includes alcohol.

**23A.** An offence under any of the following provisions of the Psychoactive Substances Act 2016—
(*a*) section 4 (producing a psychoactive substance);
(*b*) section 5 (supplying, or offering to supply, a psychoactive substance);
(*c*) section 7 (possession of psychoactive substance with intent to supply);
(*d*) section 8 (importing or exporting a psychoactive substance).

**23B.** An offence listed in section 41 of the Counter-Terrorism Act 2008 (terrorism offences).

**24.** An offence under section 1 of the Criminal Attempts Act 1981 of attempting to commit an offence that is a relevant offence.

**25.** An offence under section 1 of the Criminal Law Act 1977 of conspiracy to commit an offence that is a relevant offence.

**26.** The offence at common law of conspiracy to defraud.

## SCHEDULE 5
### Appeals

*(Amended by SI 2005/886, the Violent Crime Reduction Act 2006, s 22, the Police Reform and Social Responsibility Act 2011, ss 112, 114, the Deregulation Act 2015, Sch 18, the Immigration Act 2016, Sch 4 and the Policing and Crime Act 2017, ss 137, 138.)* Section 181

### PART 1
### PREMISES LICENCES

*Rejection of applications relating to premises licences*

7.7577 **1.** Where a licensing authority—
(*a*) rejects an application for a premises licence under section 18,
(*b*) rejects (in whole or in part) an application to vary a premises licence under section 35,
(*c*) rejects an application to vary a premises licence to specify an individual as the premises supervisor under section 39, or
(*d*) rejects an application to transfer a premises licence under section 44,

the applicant may appeal against the decision.

*Decision to grant premises licence or impose conditions etc*

**2.** (1) This paragraph applies where a licensing authority grants a premises licence under section 18.

(2) The holder[1] of the licence may appeal against any decision—
(*a*) to impose conditions on the licence under subsection (2)(*a*) or (3)(*b*) of that section, or
(*b*) to take any step mentioned in subsection (4)(*b*) or (*c*) of that section (exclusion of licensable activity or refusal to specify person as premises supervisor).

(3) Where a person who made relevant representations in relation to the application desires to contend—
(*a*) that the licence ought not to have been granted, or

(*b*) that, on granting the licence, the licensing authority ought to have imposed different or additional conditions, or to have taken a step mentioned in subsection (4)(*b*) or (*c*) of that section,

he may appeal against the decision.

(4) In sub-paragraph (3) "relevant representations" has the meaning given in section 18(6).

*Issue of provisional statement*

3. (1) This paragraph applies where a provisional statement is issued under subsection (3)(*c*) of section 31.

(2) An appeal against the decision may be made by—

(*a*) the applicant, or

(*b*) any person who made relevant representations in relation to the application.

(3) In sub-paragraph (2) "relevant representations" has the meaning given in subsection (5) of that section.

*Variation of licence under section 35*

4. (1) This paragraph applies where an application to vary a premises licence is granted (in whole or in part) under section 35.

(2) The applicant may appeal against any decision to modify the conditions of the licence under subsection (4)(*a*) of that section.

(3) Where a person who made relevant representations in relation to the application desires to contend—

(*a*) that any variation made ought not to have been made, or

(*b*) that, when varying the licence, the licensing authority ought not to have modified the conditions of the licence, or ought to have modified them in a different way, under subsection (4)(*a*) of that section,

he may appeal against the decision.

(4) In sub-paragraph (3) "relevant representations" has the meaning given in section 35(5).

*Variation of licence to specify individual as premises supervisor*

5. (1) This paragraph applies where an application to vary a premises licence is granted under section 39(2) in a case where a chief officer of police gave a notice under section 37(5) (which was not withdrawn).

(2) The chief officer of police may appeal against the decision to grant the application.

*Transfer of licence*

6. (1) This paragraph applies where an application to transfer a premises licence is granted under section 44 in a case where a chief officer of police gave a notice under section 42(6) or the Secretary of State gave a notice under section 42(8) (which, in either case, was not withdrawn).

(2) The chief officer of police or the Secretary of State, as the case may be, may appeal against the decision to grant the application.

*Interim authority notice*

7. (1) This paragraph applies where—

(*a*) an interim authority notice is given in accordance with section 47, and

(*b*) a chief officer of police gives a notice under section 48(2) or the Secretary of State gives a notice under section 48(2B) (which, in either case, is not withdrawn).

(2) Where the relevant licensing authority decides to cancel the interim authority notice under subsection (3) of section 48, the person who gave the interim authority notice may appeal against that decision.

(3) Where the relevant licensing authority decides not to cancel the interim authority notice under section 48(3) after the giving of a notice by a chief officer of police under section 48(2), the chief officer of police may appeal against that decision.

(3A) Where the relevant licensing authority decides not to cancel the interim authority notice under section 48(3) after the giving of a notice by the Secretary of State under section 48(2B), the Secretary of State may appeal against that decision.

(4) Where an appeal is brought under sub-paragraph (2), the court to which it is brought may, on such terms as it thinks fit, order the reinstatement of the interim authority notice pending—

(*a*) the disposal of the appeal, or

(*b*) the expiry of the interim authority period,

whichever first occurs.

(5) Where the court makes an order under sub-paragraph (4), the premises licence is reinstated from the time the order is made, and section 47 has effect in a case where the appeal is dismissed or abandoned before the end of the interim authority period as if—

(*a*) the reference in subsection (7)(*b*) to the end of the interim authority period were a reference to the time when the appeal is dismissed or abandoned, and

(*b*) the reference in subsection (9)(*a*) to the interim authority period were a reference to that period disregarding the part of it which falls after that time.

(6) In this paragraph "interim authority period" has the same meaning as in section 47.

*Review of premises licence*

8. (1) This paragraph applies where an application for a review of a premises licence is decided under section 52.

(2) An appeal may be made against that decision by—

(*a*) the applicant for the review,

(*b*) the holder[2] of the premises licence, or

(*c*) any other person who made relevant representations in relation to the application.

(3) In sub-paragraph (2) "relevant representations" has the meaning given in section 52(7).

*Summary review of premises licence*

8A. (1) This paragraph applies where a review of a premises licence is decided under section 53A(2)(*b*) (review of premises licence following review notice).

(2) An appeal may be made against that decision by—

(*a*) the chief officer of police for the police area (or each police area) in which the premises are situated,

(*b*) the holder[1] of the premises licence, or

(*c*) any other person who made relevant representations in relation to the application for the review.

(3) In sub-paragraph (2) "relevant representations" has the meaning given in section 53C(7).

[1] For the position where there has been a mistake as to the identity or description of the premises licence holder in the appeal notice, see *R (Essence Bars Ltd) v Wimbledon Magistrates' Court* [2016] EWCA Civ 63, [2016] 1 WLR 3265 and the Magistrates' Courts Act 1980, s 123 and para 1.145 **Objection to the information or charge** in PART I: MAGISTRATES' COURTS, PROCEDURE, ante.

**8B.** (1) This paragraph applies where a review of interim steps is decided under section 53D (review of interim steps at a summary review of a premises licence).

(2) An appeal may be made against that decision by—

(a) the chief officer of police for the police area (or each police area) in which the premises are situated, or

(b) the holder of the premises licence.

(3) An appeal under this paragraph must be heard by the magistrates' court within the period of 28 days beginning with the day on which the appellant commenced the appeal (see paragraph 9(2)).

*General provision about appeals under this Part*

**9.** (1) An appeal under this Part must be made to a magistrates' court.

(2) An appeal under this Part must be commenced by notice of appeal given by the appellant to the designated officer for the magistrates' court within the period of 21 days beginning with the day on which the appellant was notified by the licensing authority of the decision appealed against.

(3) On an appeal under paragraph 2(3), 3(2)(*b*), 4(3), 5(2), 6(2) or 8(2)(*a*) or (*c*), the holder of the premises licence is to be the respondent in addition to the licensing authority[1].

(4) On an appeal under paragraph 7(3) or (3A), the person who gave the interim authority notice is to be the respondent in addition to the licensing authority.

[1] For the position of interested parties and responsible authorities as respondents, see *R (Chief Constable of Nottinghamshire Police) v Nottingham Magistrates' Court* [2009] EWHC 3182 (Admin), [2010] 2 All ER 342, 174 JP 1 and para 7.7333 **Procedure on appeals**, ante.

## PART 2
## CLUB PREMISES CERTIFICATES

*Rejection of applications relating to club premises certificates*

**10.** Where a licensing authority—

(*a*) rejects an application for a club premises certificate under section 72, or

(*b*) rejects (in whole or in part) an application to vary a club premises certificate under section 85,

the club that made the application may appeal against the decision.

*Decision to grant club premises certificate or impose conditions etc*

**11.** (1) This paragraph applies where a licensing authority grants a club premises certificate under section 72.

(2) The club holding the certificate may appeal against any decision—

(*a*) to impose conditions on the certificate under subsection (2) or (3)(*b*) of that section, or

(*b*) to take any step mentioned in subsection (4)(*b*) of that section (exclusion of qualifying club activity).

(3) Where a person who made relevant representations in relation to the application desires to contend—

(*a*) that the certificate ought not to have been granted, or

(*b*) that, on granting the certificate, the licensing authority ought to have imposed different or additional conditions, or to have taken a step mentioned in subsection (4)(*b*) of that section,

he may appeal against the decision.

(4) In sub-paragraph (3) "relevant representations" has the meaning given in section 72(7).

*Variation of club premises certificate*

**12.** (1) This paragraph applies where an application to vary a club premises certificate is granted (in whole or in part) under section 85.

(2) The club may appeal against any decision to modify the conditions of the certificate under subsection (3)(*b*) of that section.

(3) Where a person who made relevant representations in relation to the application desires to contend—

(*a*) that any variation ought not to have been made, or

(*b*) that, when varying the certificate, the licensing authority ought not to have modified the conditions of the certificate, or ought to have modified them in a different way, under subsection (3)(*b*) of that section,

he may appeal against the decision.

(4) In sub-paragraph (3) "relevant representations" has the meaning given in section 85(5).

*Review of club premises certificate*

**13.** (1) This paragraph applies where an application for a review of a club premises certificate is decided under section 88.

(2) An appeal may be made against that decision by—

(*a*) the applicant for the review,

(*b*) the club that holds or held the club premises certificate, or

(*c*) any other person who made relevant representations in relation to the application.

(3) In sub-paragraph (2) "relevant representations" has the meaning given in section 88(7).

*Withdrawal of club premises certificate*

**14.** Where the relevant licensing authority gives notice withdrawing a club premises certificate under section 90, the club which holds or held the certificate may appeal against the decision to withdraw it.

*General provision about appeals under this Part*

**15.** (1) An appeal under this Part must be made to a magistrates' court.

(2) An appeal under this Part must be commenced by notice of appeal given by the appellant to the designated officer for the magistrates' court within the period of 21 days beginning with the day on which the appellant was notified by the licensing authority of the decision appealed against.

(3) On an appeal under paragraph 11(3), 12(3) or 13(2)(*a*) or (*c*), the club that holds or held the club premises certificate is to be the respondent in addition to the licensing authority.

## PART 3
## OTHER APPEALS

*Temporary event notices*

**16.** (1) This paragraph applies where—

(*a*) a standard temporary event notice is given under section 100, and

(*b*) a relevant person gives an objection notice in accordance with section 104(2).

(2) Where the relevant licensing authority gives a counter notice under section 105(3), the premises user may appeal against that decision.

(3) Where that authority decides not to give such a counter notice, the relevant person may appeal against that decision.

(4) An appeal under this paragraph must be made to a magistrates' court.

(5) An appeal under this paragraph must be commenced by notice of appeal given by the appellant to the designated officer for the magistrates' court within the period of 21 days beginning with the day on which the appellant was notified by the licensing authority of the decision appealed against.

(6) But no appeal may be brought later than five working days before the day on which the event period specified in the temporary event notice begins.

(7) On an appeal under sub-paragraph (3), the premises user is to be the respondent in addition to the licensing authority.

(8) In this paragraph—

"objection notice" has the same meaning as in section 104;

"relevant licensing authority" has the meaning given in section 99; and

"relevant person" has the meaning given in section 99A.

*Personal licences*

**17.** (1) Where a licensing authority rejects an application for the grant of a personal licence under section 120, the applicant may appeal against that decision.

(2) Where a licensing authority grants an application for a personal licence under section 120(7A) after the giving of a notice under section 120(5), the chief officer of police who gave the notice may appeal against that decision.

(2A) Where a licensing authority grants an application for a personal licence under section 120(7A) after the giving of a notice under section 120(5B), the Secretary of State may appeal against that decision.

(3) *Repealed.*

(4) Where a licensing authority revokes a personal licence under section 124(4), the holder of the licence may appeal against that decision.

(5) Where in a case to which section 124 (convictions coming to light after grant) applies—

(*a*) the chief officer of police for the licensing authority's area gives a notice under subsection (3) of that section (and does not later withdraw it), and

(*b*) the licensing authority decides not to revoke the licence,

the chief officer of police may appeal against the decision.

(5A) Where in a case to which section 124 applies—

(a) the Secretary of State gives a notice under subsection (3B) of that section (and does not later withdraw it), and

(b) the licensing authority decides not to revoke the licence,

the Secretary of State may appeal against the decision.

(5A) Where a licensing authority revokes or suspends a personal licence under section 132A(8) or (12) the holder of the licence may appeal against that decision.

(6) An appeal under this paragraph must be made to a magistrates' court.

(7) An appeal under this paragraph must be commenced by notice of appeal given by the appellant to the designated officer for the magistrates' court within the period of 21 days beginning with the day on which the appellant was notified by the licensing authority of the decision appealed against.

(8) On an appeal under sub-paragraph (2), (2A), (5) or (5A), the holder of the personal licence is to be the respondent in addition to the licensing authority.

(9) *Repealed.*

(10) *Repealed.*

(11) *Repealed.*

*Closure orders*

**18.** (1) This paragraph applies where, on a review of a premises licence under section 167, the relevant licensing authority decides under subsection (5)(*b*) of that section—

(*a*) to take any of the steps mentioned in subsection (6) of that section, in relation to a premises licence for those premises, or

(*b*) not to take any such step.

(2) An appeal may be made against that decision by—

(*a*) the holder of the premises licence, or

(*b*) any other person who made relevant representations in relation to the review.

(3) Where an appeal is made under this paragraph against a decision to take any of the steps mentioned in section 167(6)(*a*) to (*d*) (modification of licence conditions etc), the magistrates' court may in a case within section 168(3) (premises closed when decision taken)—

(*a*) if the relevant licensing authority has not made an order under section 168(5) (order suspending operation of decision in whole or part), make any order under section 168(5) that could have been made by the relevant licensing authority, or

(*b*) if the authority has made such an order, cancel it or substitute for it any order which could have been made by the authority under section 168(5).

(4) Where an appeal is made under this paragraph in a case within section 168(6) (premises closed when decision to revoke made to remain closed pending appeal), the magistrates' court may, on such conditions as it thinks fit, order that section 168(7) (premises to remain closed pending appeal) is not to apply to the premises.

(5) An appeal under this paragraph must be commenced by notice of appeal given by the appellant to the designated officer for the magistrates' court within the period of 21 days beginning with the day on which the appellant was notified by the relevant licensing authority of the decision appealed against.

(6) On an appeal under this paragraph by a person other than the holder of the premises licence, that holder is to be the respondent in addition to the licensing authority that made the decision.

(7) In this paragraph—

"relevant licensing authority" has the same meaning as in Part 3 of this Act; and

"relevant representations" has the meaning given in section 167(9).

### Part 4
### Questions about Leave to Enter or Remain in the UK

**19.** On an appeal under this Schedule, a magistrates' court is not entitled to entertain any question as to whether—

(a) an individual should be, or should have been, granted leave to enter or remain in the United Kingdom, or

(b) an individual has, after the date of the decision being appealed against, been granted leave to enter or remain in the United Kingdom.

# Local Democracy, Economic Development and Construction Act 2009[1]

(2009 c 20)

7.7580 **47. Access to information** (1) A person appointed under this Chapter in relation to an entity (in this section referred to as an "auditor") has a right of access at all reasonable times to every document relating to the entity which appears to the auditor necessary for the purpose of the exercise of their functions under section 45.

(2) The right conferred by subsection (1) includes power to inspect, copy or take away the document.

(3) An auditor may—

(*a*) require a person holding or accountable for any document referred to in subsection (1) to give to the auditor such information or explanation as the auditor thinks necessary for the purpose of the exercise of the auditor's functions under section 45, and

(*b*) if the auditor thinks it necessary, require the person to attend before the auditor in person to give the information or explanation or to produce the document.

(4) Without prejudice to subsection (3), an auditor may—

(*a*) require any officer or member of the entity to give to the auditor such information or explanation as the auditor thinks necessary for the purpose of the exercise of the auditor's functions under section 45, and

(*b*) if the auditor thinks it necessary, require the officer or member to attend before the auditor in person to give the information or explanation.

(5) In relation to any document kept in electronic form, the power in subsection (3)(*b*) to require a person to produce a document includes power to require it to be produced in a form in which it is legible and can be taken away.

(6) In connection with inspecting such a document, an auditor—

(*a*) may obtain access to, and inspect and check the operation of, any computer and associated apparatus or material which the auditor considers is or has been used in connection with the document;

(*b*) may require a person within subsection (7) to afford the auditor such reasonable assistance as the auditor may require for that purpose.

(7) The following persons are within this subsection—

(*a*) a person by whom or on whose behalf the computer is or has been used;

(*b*) a person having charge of, or otherwise concerned with the operation of, the computer, apparatus or material.

(8) Without prejudice to subsections (1) to (7), the entity must provide the auditor with every facility and all information which the auditor may reasonably require for the purposes of the exercise of the auditor's functions under section 45.

(9) A person who without reasonable excuse obstructs the exercise of any power conferred by this section or fails to comply with any requirement of an auditor under this section is guilty of an offence.

(10) A person guilty of an offence under subsection (9) is liable on summary conviction—

(*a*) to a fine not exceeding level 3 on the standard scale, and

(*b*) to an additional fine not exceeding £20 for each day on which the offence continues after the person has been convicted of it.

(11) Any expenses incurred by an auditor in connection with proceedings for an offence under this section, so far as not recovered from any other source, are recoverable from the entity in relation to which the auditor is appointed.

(12) The powers under this section are in addition to any other powers which an auditor has in relation to the exercise of the auditor's functions under or pursuant to this Chapter.

[Local Democracy, Economic Development and Construction Act 2009, s 147.]

[1] Chapter 3 (ss 36–54) of Part 2 (ss 31–54) implements recommendations from Lord Sharman's independent review into the audit and accountability of public money *Holding to Account: The Review of Audit and Accountability for Central Government (2001)* in relation to companies, limited liability partnerships and industrial and provident societies that are connected with local authorities. Provision is made for the appointment of an auditor to an entity connected to a local authority and for the auditor to issue a public interest report where it is in the public interest to do so. The entity must be connected with a local authority and meet other conditions specified in regulations made by the Secretary of State in England or by Welsh Ministers in Wales. Smaller parish councils are excluded from the provisions as they are not required to prepare statements of accounts. At the date of going to press s 147 had not been brought into force.

# Police Reform and Social Responsibility Act 2011

(2011 c 13)

## Part 2

## Licensing

### Chapter 1

### Amendments of the Licensing Act 2003

*Early morning alcohol restriction orders*

7.7581 **119. Early morning alcohol restriction orders** (1) The Licensing Act 2003 is amended as set out in subsections (2) and (3).

(2) In section 7 (exercise and delegation of functions), in subsection (2), after paragraph (*a*) (but before the final "or") insert—

"(*aa*) the functions of making, and varying or revoking, an order under section 172A (early morning alcohol restriction order),".

(3) For sections 172A to 172E (early morning alcohol restriction order), as inserted by section 55 of the Crime and Security Act 2010, substitute—

**"172A Power to make early morning alcohol restriction order** (1) If a licensing authority considers it appropriate for the promotion of the licensing objectives, it may, subject as follows, make an order under this section.

(2) An order under this section is an order providing that—

(*a*) premises licences and club premises certificates granted by the authority, and temporary event notices given to the authority, do not have effect to the extent that they authorise the sale of alcohol during the period specified in the order, and

(*b*) club premises certificates granted by the authority do not have effect to the extent that they authorise the supply of alcohol by or on behalf of a club to, or to the order of, a member of the club during the period specified in the order.

(3) For the purposes of subsection (2)(*a*) and (*b*), the period that may be specified in the order must—

(*a*) begin no earlier than midnight, and

(*b*) end no later than 6am.

(4) It is immaterial for the purposes of an order under this section whether a premises licence or club premises certificate is granted, or a temporary event notice is given, before or after the order is made.

(5) An order under this section may provide that it is to apply—

(*a*) in relation to the same period of every day on which the order is to apply, or in relation to different periods of different days,

(*b*) every day or only on particular days (for example, particular days of the week or year),

(*c*) in relation to the whole or part of a licensing authority's area, or

(*d*) for a limited or unlimited period.

(6) An order under this section must specify—

(*a*) the days on which it is to apply and the period of those days,

(*b*) the area in relation to which it is to apply,

(*c*) if it is to apply for a limited period, that period, and

(*d*) the date from which it is to apply.

(7) An order under this section must—

(*a*) be in the prescribed form, and

(*b*) have the prescribed content.

**172B Procedural requirements for early morning alcohol restriction order** (1) A licensing authority proposing to make an order under section 172A must—

(*a*) advertise the proposed order in the prescribed manner, and (*b*) hold a hearing to consider any relevant representations, unless the authority and each person who has made such representations agree that a hearing is unnecessary.

(2) In this section "relevant representations" means representations which—

(*a*) are about the likely effect of the making of the proposed order on the promotion of the licensing objectives,

(*b*) are made to the licensing authority by an affected person, a responsible authority or any other person,

(*c*) are made in the prescribed form and manner and within the prescribed period,

(*d*) have not been withdrawn, and

(*e*) in the case of representations made by a person who is not a responsible authority, are not, in the opinion of the licensing authority, frivolous or vexatious.

(3) In subsection (2)(*b*), "affected person" means—

(*a*) the holder of the premises licence or club premises certificate in respect of affected premises,

(*b*) the premises user in relation to a temporary event notice in respect of affected premises,

(*c*) a person who has applied for a premises licence or club premises certificate in respect of affected premises (where the application has not been determined), and

(*d*) a person to whom a provisional statement has been issued in respect of affected premises.

(4) In subsection (2)(*b*) and (*e*), "responsible authority" means—

(*a*) the licensing authority and any other licensing authority in whose area part of any affected premises is situated,

(*b*) the chief officer of police for a police area any part of which is in the area specified in the order,

(*c*) the fire and rescue authority for an area any part of which is in the area specified in the order,

(*d*) the Primary Care Trust or Local Health Board for an area any part of which is in the area specified in the order,

(*e*) the local weights and measures authority for any such area,

(*f*) the enforcing authority within the meaning given by section 18 of the Health and Safety at Work etc Act 1974 for any such area,

(*g*) the local planning authority within the meaning given by the Town and Country Planning Act 1990 for any such area,

(*h*) the local authority by which statutory functions are exercisable in the area specified in the order in relation to minimising or preventing the risk of pollution of the environment or of harm to human health,

(*i*) a body which—

(i) represents those who, in relation to the area specified in the order, are responsible for, or interested in, matters relating to the protection of children from harm, and

(ii) is recognised by the licensing authority for the purposes of this section as being competent to advise on such matters,

(*j*) where affected premises are a vessel—

(i) a navigation authority (within the meaning given by section 221(1) of the Water Resources Act 1991) having functions in relation to the waters where the vessel is usually moored or berthed or any waters where it is navigated at a time when it is used for licensable activities to which the proposed order relates,

(ii) the Environment Agency,

(iii) the British Waterways Board, and

(iv) the Secretary of State, and

(*k*) a prescribed person.

(5) Where a licensing authority determines for the purposes of subsection (2)(*e*) that any representations are frivolous or vexatious, it must notify the person who made them of its reasons for its determination.

(6) In this section—

"affected premises", in relation to a proposed order, means premises in respect of which it applies from the date specified in it;

"statutory function" means a function conferred by or under an enactment.

**172C Making of early morning alcohol restriction order** (1) A licensing authority may not make an order under section 172A applying in relation to—

(*a*) an area not specified in the proposed order advertised under section 172B,

(*b*) a day not specified in that proposed order, or

(*c*) a period other than the period specified in that proposed order of any day so specified.

(2) After making an order under section 172A a licensing authority must publish it or otherwise make it available—

(*a*) in the prescribed form and manner, and

(*b*) within the prescribed period.

**172D Variation and revocation of early morning alcohol restriction order** (1) A licensing authority may vary or revoke an order under section 172A.

(2) Sections 172B and 172C apply in relation to the variation or revocation of an order under section 172A as in relation to the making of such an order.

**172E Exceptions from effect of early morning alcohol restriction order** (1) An order under section 172A does not apply in prescribed cases or circumstances.

(2) The cases referred to in subsection (1) may in particular be defined by reference to—

(*a*) particular kinds of premises, or

(*b*) particular days.

(3) An order under section 172A is subject to an order under section 172 (whether made before or afterwards), unless and to the extent that the order under section 172 provides otherwise.".

(4) Section 55 of the Crime and Security Act 2010 (power to restrict sale and supply of alcohol) is repealed.

[Police Reform and Social Responsibility Act 2011, s 119.]

*Fees*

7.7582 **121. Power for licensing authorities to set fees** (1) The Licensing Act 2003 is amended as follows.

(2) After section 197 insert—

"**197A Regulations about fees** (1) Subsection (2) applies where the Secretary of State makes regulations under this Act prescribing the amount of any fee.

(2) The Secretary of State may, in determining the amount of the fee, have regard, in particular, to—

(*a*) the costs of any licensing authority to whom the fee is to be payable which are referable to the discharge of the function to which the fee relates, and

(*b*) the general costs of any such licensing authority;

and may determine an amount by reference to fees payable to, and costs of, any such licensing authorities, taken together.

(3) A power under this Act to prescribe the amount of a fee includes power to provide that the amount of the fee is to be determined by the licensing authority to whom it is to be payable.

(4) Regulations which so provide may also specify constraints on the licensing authority's power to determine the amount of the fee.

(5) Subsections (6) and (7)—

(*a*) apply where, by virtue of subsection (3), regulations provide that the amount of a fee is to be determined by a licensing authority, and

(*b*) are subject to any constraint imposed under subsection (4).

(6) The licensing authority—

(*a*) must determine the amount of the fee (and may from time to time determine a revised amount),

(*b*) may determine different amounts for different classes of case specified in the regulations (but may not otherwise determine different amounts for different cases), and

(*c*) must publish the amount of the fee as determined from time to time.

(7) In determining the amount of the fee, the licensing authority must seek to secure that the income from fees of that kind will equate, as nearly as possible, to the aggregate of—

(*a*) the licensing authority's costs referable to the discharge of the function to which the fee relates, and

(*b*) a reasonable share of the licensing authority's general costs;

and must assess income and costs for this purpose in such manner as it considers appropriate.

**197B Regulations about fees: supplementary provision** (1) Subsections (2) and (3) apply for the purposes of section 197A.

(2) References to a licensing authority's costs referable to the discharge of a function include, in particular—

(*a*) administrative costs of the licensing authority so far as they are referable to the discharge of the function, and

(*b*) costs in connection with the discharge of the function which are incurred by the licensing authority acting—

(i) under this Act, but

(ii) in a capacity other than that of licensing authority (whether that of local authority, local planning authority or any other authority).

(3) References to the general costs of a licensing authority are to costs of the authority so far as they are referable to the discharge of functions under this Act in respect of which no fee is otherwise chargeable and include, in particular—

(*a*) costs referable to the authority's functions under section 5;

(*b*) costs of or incurred in connection with the monitoring and enforcement of Parts 7 and 8 of this Act;

(*c*) costs incurred in exercising functions conferred by virtue of section 197A.

(4) To the extent that they prescribe the amount of a fee or include provision made by virtue of section 197A(3) or (4), regulations may—

(*a*) make provision which applies generally or only to specified authorities or descriptions of authority, and

(*b*) make different provision for different authorities or descriptions of authority.

(5) Subsection (4) is not to be taken to limit the generality of section 197.".

(3) In section 10(4) (sub-delegation of functions by licensing committee etc)—

(*a*) omit "or" at the end of paragraph (*c*), and

(*b*) after paragraph (*d*) insert

"or

(*e*) any function conferred by virtue of section 197A (regulations about fees).".

[Police Reform and Social Responsibility Act 2011, s 121.]

## CHAPTER 2
## LATE NIGHT LEVY

*Application of late night levy requirement in licensing authority's area*

**125.** *Chapter 2 (***ss 125–139***) makes provision for licensing authorities to apply a light night levy requirement in its area in accordance with regulations having regard to the costs of policing and other arrangements for the reduction or prevention of crime and disorder, in connection with the supply of alcohol between midnight and 6 am.*

# Localism Act 2011

(2011 c 20)

## CHAPTER 7
## STANDARDS

**7.7583** *Chapter 7* **(26–37)** *makes further provision for standards relating to the conduct of local government members and employees. A relevant authority (which includes county, district and parish councils and fire and rescue authorities) must promote and maintain high standards of conduct by members and co-opted members of the authority. In particular, an authority must adopt a code dealing with the conduct that is expected of members and co-opted members of the authority when they are acting in that capacity* **(27–28)***. The monitoring officer of a relevant authority must establish and maintain a register of interests of members and co-opted members of the authority* **(28)**.

**7.7584 30. Disclosure of pecuniary interests on taking office** (1) A member or co-opted member of a relevant authority must, before the end of 28 days beginning with the day on which the person becomes a member or co-opted member of the authority, notify the authority's monitoring officer of any disclosable pecuniary interests which the person has at the time when the notification is given.

(2) Where a person becomes a member or co-opted member of a relevant authority as a result of re-election or re-appointment, subsection (1) applies only as regards disclosable pecuniary interests not entered in the authority's register when the notification is given.

(3) For the purposes of this Chapter, a pecuniary interest is a "disclosable pecuniary interest" in relation to a person ("M") if it is of a description specified in regulations made by the Secretary of State and either—

(*a*) it is an interest of M's, or

(*b*) it is an interest of—

(i) M's spouse or civil partner,

(ii) a person with whom M is living as husband and wife, or

(iii) a person with whom M is living as if they were civil partners,

and M is aware that that other person has the interest.

(4) Where a member or co-opted member of a relevant authority gives a notification for the purposes of subsection (1), the authority's monitoring officer is to cause the interests notified to be entered in the authority's register (whether or not they are disclosable pecuniary interests).[1]

[Localism Act 2011, s 30.]

---

[1] The Localism Act 2011 (Commencement No 6 and Transitional, Savings and Transitory Provisions) Order 2012, SI 2012/1463 amended by SI 2012/1714 brought into force on 7 June 2012 s 31(10) so far as it enables a relevant authority to make standing orders that will take effect on or after 1 July 2012; and s 33 so far as it enables a relevant authority to grant a dispensation which will take effect on or after 1 July 2012; s 34 on 1 July 2012; ss 30–34 fully in force 1 July 2012.

**7.7585 31. Pecuniary interests in matters considered at meetings or by a single member**

(1) Subsections (2) to (4) apply if a member or co-opted member of a relevant authority—

(*a*) is present at a meeting of the authority or of any committee, sub-committee, joint committee or joint sub-committee of the authority, (*b*) has a disclosable pecuniary interest in any matter to be considered, or being considered, at the meeting, and

(*c*) is aware that the condition in paragraph (*b*) is met.

(2) If the interest is not entered in the authority's register, the member or co-opted member must disclose the interest to the meeting, but this is subject to section 32(3).

(3) If the interest is not entered in the authority's register and is not the subject of a pending notification, the member or co-opted member must notify the authority's monitoring officer of the interest before the end of 28 days beginning with the date of the disclosure.

(4) The member or co-opted member may not—

(*a*) participate, or participate further, in any discussion of the matter at the meeting, or

(*b*) participate in any vote, or further vote, taken on the matter at the meeting,

but this is subject to section 33.

(5) In the case of a relevant authority to which Part 1A of the Local Government Act 2000 applies and which is operating executive arrangements, the reference in subsection (1)(*a*) to a committee of the authority includes a reference to the authority's executive and a reference to a committee of the executive.

(6) Subsections (7) and (8) apply if—

(*a*) a function of a relevant authority may be discharged by a member of the authority acting alone,

(*b*) the member has a disclosable pecuniary interest in any matter to be dealt with, or being dealt with, by the member in the course of discharging that function, and

(*c*) the member is aware that the condition in paragraph (*b*) is met.

(7) If the interest is not entered in the authority's register and is not the subject of a pending notification, the member must notify the authority's monitoring officer of the interest before the end of 28 days beginning with the date when the member becomes aware that the condition in subsection (6)(*b*) is met in relation to the matter.

(8) The member must not take any steps, or any further steps, in relation to the matter (except for the purpose of enabling the matter to be dealt with otherwise than by the member).

(9) Where a member or co-opted member of a relevant authority gives a notification for the purposes of subsection (3) or (7), the authority's monitoring officer is to cause the interest notified to be entered in the authority's register (whether or not it is a disclosable pecuniary interest).

(10) Standing orders of a relevant authority may provide for the exclusion of a member or co-opted member of the authority from a meeting while any discussion or vote takes place in which, as a result of the operation of subsection (4), the member or co-opted member may not participate.

(11) For the purpose of this section, an interest is "subject to a pending notification" if—

(*a*) under this section or section 30, the interest has been notified to a relevant authority's monitoring officer, but

(*b*) has not been entered in the authority's register in consequence of that notification.

[Localism Act 2011, s 31.]

7.7586 32. **Sensitive interests** (1) Subsections (2) and (3) apply where—

(*a*) a member or co-opted member of a relevant authority has an interest (whether or not a disclosable pecuniary interest), and

(*b*) the nature of the interest is such that the member or co-opted member, and the authority's monitoring officer, consider that disclosure of the details of the interest could lead to the member or co-opted member, or a person connected with the member or co-opted member, being subject to violence or intimidation.

(2) If the interest is entered in the authority's register, copies of the register that are made available for inspection, and any published version of the register, must not include details of the interest (but may state that the member or co-opted member has an interest the details of which are withheld under this subsection).

(3) If section 31(2) applies in relation to the interest, that provision is to be read as requiring the member or co-opted member to disclose not the interest but merely the fact that the member or co-opted member has a disclosable pecuniary interest in the matter concerned.

[Localism Act 2011, s 32.]

7.7587 33. **Dispensations from section 31(4)** (1) A relevant authority may, on a written request made to the proper officer of the authority by a member or co-opted member of the authority, grant a dispensation relieving the member or co-opted member from either or both of the restrictions in section 31(4) in cases described in the dispensation.

(2) A relevant authority may grant a dispensation under this section only if, after having had regard to all relevant circumstances, the authority—

(*a*) considers that without the dispensation the number of persons prohibited by section 31(4) from participating in any particular business would be so great a proportion of the body transacting the business as to impede the transaction of the business,

(*b*) considers that without the dispensation the representation of different political groups on the body transacting any particular business would be so upset as to alter the likely outcome of any vote relating to the business, (*c*) considers that granting the dispensation is in the interests of persons living in the authority's area,

(*d*) if it is an authority to which Part 1A of the Local Government Act 2000 applies and is operating executive arrangements, considers that without the dispensation each member of the authority's executive would be prohibited by section 31(4) from participating in any particular business to be transacted by the authority's executive, or

(*e*) considers that it is otherwise appropriate to grant a dispensation.

(3) A dispensation under this section must specify the period for which it has effect, and the period specified may not exceed four years.

(4) Section 31(4) does not apply in relation to anything done for the purpose of deciding whether to grant a dispensation under this section.

[Localism Act 2011, s 33.]

**7.7588 34. Offences** (1) A person commits an offence if, without reasonable excuse, the person—

(*a*) fails to comply with an obligation imposed on the person by section 30(1) or 31(2), (3) or (7),

(*b*) participates in any discussion or vote in contravention of section 31(4), or

(*c*) takes any steps in contravention of section 31(8).

(2) A person commits an offence if under section 30(1) or 31(2), (3) or (7) the person provides information that is false or misleading and the person—

(*a*) knows that the information is false or misleading, or

(*b*) is reckless as to whether the information is true and not misleading.

(3) A person who is guilty of an offence under this section is liable on summary conviction to a fine not exceeding level 5 on the standard scale.

(4) A court dealing with a person for an offence under this section may (in addition to any other power exercisable in the person's case) by order disqualify the person, for a period not exceeding five years, for being or becoming (by election or otherwise) a member or co-opted member of the relevant authority in question or any other relevant authority.

(5) A prosecution for an offence under this section is not to be instituted except by or on behalf of the Director of Public Prosecutions.

(6) Proceedings for an offence under this section may be brought within a period of 12 months beginning with the date on which evidence sufficient in the opinion of the prosecutor to warrant the proceedings came to the prosecutor's knowledge.

(7) But no such proceedings may be brought more than three years—

(*a*) after the commission of the offence, or

(*b*) in the case of a continuous contravention, after the last date on which the offence was committed.

(8) A certificate signed by the prosecutor and stating the date on which such evidence came to the prosecutor's knowledge is conclusive evidence of that fact; and a certificate to that effect and purporting to be so signed is to be treated as being so signed unless the contrary is proved.

(9) The Local Government Act 1972 is amended as follows.

(10) In section 86(1)(*b*) (authority to declare vacancy where member becomes disqualified otherwise than in certain cases) after "2000" insert "or section 34 of the Localism Act 2011".

(11) In section 87(1)(ee) (date of casual vacancies)—

(*a*) after "2000" insert "or section 34 of the Localism Act 2011 or", and

(*b*) after "decision" insert "or order".

(12) The Greater London Authority Act 1999 is amended as follows.

(13) In each of sections 7(*b*) and 14(*b*) (Authority to declare vacancy where Assembly member or Mayor becomes disqualified otherwise than in certain cases) after sub-paragraph (i) insert—

"(ia) under section 34 of the Localism Act 2011,".

(14) In section 9(1)(*f*) (date of casual vacancies)—

(*a*) before "or by virtue of" insert "or section 34 of the Localism Act 2011", and

(*b*) after "that Act" insert "of 1998 or that section".

[Localism Act 2011, s 34.]

## Local Audit and Accountability Act 2014

(2014 c 2)

### Part 2[1]

### Basic Concepts and Requirements

[1] Part 2 comprises ss 2–6 and Sch 2. For commencement, see s 49, post.

**7.7589 2. Relevant authorities** (1) In this Act "relevant authority" means a person or body listed in Schedule 2.

(2) The application of this Act to a relevant authority is subject to any note forming part of the entry for that authority in Schedule 2.

(3) The Secretary of State may by regulations amend Schedule 2 by adding, modifying or

removing an entry relating to a relevant authority.

(4) Regulations under subsection (3) may add an entry relating to a person or body to Schedule 2 only if that person or body exercises functions of a public nature in relation to an area which is—

(*a*) wholly in England, or

(*b*) partly in England and partly in Wales.

(5) The Secretary of State may by regulations or order make provision about the application of this Act or provision made under it to a person or body that comes to fall within Schedule 2 (whether or not as a result of regulations under subsection (3)).

(6) The power in subsection (5) includes power—

(*a*) to amend this Act or provision made under it in its application to that person or body, or

(*b*) to make provision for this Act or provision made under it to apply to that person or body with modifications.

[Local Audit and Accountability Act 2014, s 2.]

7.7590 3. **General requirements for accounts** (1) A relevant authority, other than a health service body, must keep adequate accounting records.

(2) "Adequate accounting records" means records that are sufficient—

(*a*) to show and explain the relevant authority's transactions,

(*b*) to disclose at any time, with reasonable accuracy, the financial position of the authority at that time, and

(*c*) to enable the authority to ensure that any statements of accounts required to be prepared by the authority comply with the requirements imposed by or under this Act.

(3) A relevant authority, other than a health service body, must prepare a statement of accounts in respect of each financial year.

(4) In this Act "financial year" means a period of 12 months ending with 31 March.

(5) The Secretary of State may by regulations—

(*a*) make provision for the financial year of a relevant authority, other than a health service body, for the purposes of this Act to be such period as is specified in the regulations;

(*b*) make provision for any requirement in this section not to apply, or to apply with modifications, in relation to the relevant authorities, other than health service bodies, specified or described in the regulations.

(6) Regulations under subsection (5)(*a*) may—

(*a*) amend this Act or provision made under it in its application to a relevant authority to which the regulations apply, or

(*b*) provide for this Act or provision made under it to apply in relation to such a relevant authority with modifications.

(7) Regulations under subsection (5)(*a*) may make provision in relation to—

(*a*) all relevant authorities (other than health service bodies);

(*b*) the relevant authorities specified or described in the regulations.

(8) Section 32 enables the Secretary of State by regulations to make further provision about accounting records and statements of accounts.

(9) In this Act "health service body" means—

(*a*) a clinical commissioning group;

(*b*) special trustees appointed as mentioned in section 212(1) of the National Health Service Act 2006 (special trustees for a university hospital or teaching hospital) for a hospital in England (referred to in this Act as "special trustees for a hospital").*

[Local Audit and Accountability Act 2014, s 3.]

---

* **Amended by the NHS (Charitable Trusts Etc) Act 2016, Schedule from a date to be appointed.**

7.7591 4. **General requirements for audit** (1) The accounts of a relevant authority for a financial year must be audited—

(*a*) in accordance with this Act and provision made under it, and

(*b*) by an auditor (a "local auditor") appointed in accordance with this Act or provision made under it.

(2) In this Act, references to accounts are to be construed in accordance with the following subsections.

(3) In relation to a relevant authority which is not a health service body, "accounts" means—

(*a*) the authority's accounting records, and

(*b*) the authority's statement of accounts.

(4) In relation to a clinical commissioning group, "accounts" means—

(*a*) the annual accounts of the group prepared under paragraph 17(2) of Schedule 1A to the National Health Service Act 2006 (accounts and audit of clinical commissioning groups);

(*b*) any accounts of the group prepared under paragraph 17(3) of that Schedule in respect of which a direction has been given under paragraph 17(5) of that Schedule.

(5) In relation to special trustees for a hospital, "accounts" means the annual accounts of the trustees prepared under paragraph 3 of Schedule 15 to the National Health Service Act 2006.*

[Local Audit and Accountability Act 2014, s 4.]

* **Amended by the NHS (Charitable Trusts Etc) Act 2016, Schedule from a date to be appointed.**

**7.7592 5. Modification of Act in relation to smaller authorities** (1) The Secretary of State may by regulations[1] make provision about the audit of the accounts of smaller authorities.

(2) Regulations under subsection (1) may, in particular, provide for any provision of or made under this Act not to apply, or to apply with modifications, in relation to smaller authorities.

(3) Subsection (2) applies to a provision of or made under this Act even if it makes specific provision about a smaller authority to which the regulations apply.

(4) Regulations under subsection (1) may, in particular—

- (*a*) provide for the appointment, by a person specified by the Secretary of State, of a local auditor in relation to the audit of the accounts of a smaller authority;
- (*b*) make provision about the persons that may be specified by the Secretary of State;
- (*c*) make provision about the procedure for specifying a person and for a person's specification to come to an end in specified circumstances;
- (*d*) make provision about the consequences of a person's specification coming to an end, including for the exercise of functions by the Secretary of State and the transfer of the person's rights and liabilities arising by virtue of the regulations to the Secretary of State or another specified person;
- (*e*) confer functions on a specified person, including in relation to—
  - (i) the appointment of local auditors under the regulations,
  - (ii) the activities of such auditors, and
  - (iii) the resignation or removal from office of such auditors;
- (*f*) require a specified person to consult such persons as are specified in the regulations before exercising specified functions;
- (*g*) make provision for the appointment of a local auditor in relation to the accounts of a smaller authority to which arrangements within paragraph (*a*) apply where the specified person does not make an appointment under the regulations (and in particular for such an appointment to be made by the authority or the Secretary of State).

(5) Regulations under subsection (1) may, in particular—

- (*a*) make provision about the smaller authorities to which arrangements within subsection (4)(*a*) apply, including provision for them to apply to an authority that has opted into them or has not opted out of them;
- (*b*) make provision about the procedures to be followed in relation to opting into or out of those arrangements;
- (*c*) impose duties on smaller authorities to which those arrangements apply, including duties as to—
  - (i) the payment of fees to a specified person, and
  - (ii) the provision of information to a specified person;
- (*d*) make provision for the making of payments, in specified circumstances and by the smaller authorities to which those arrangements apply, to a fund of a specified kind for the purposes of meeting local auditors' costs of a specified kind.

(6) Provision made by regulations under subsection (1) by virtue of subsection (5)(*c*)(i) may, in particular—

- (*a*) provide for fees to be paid in accordance with a scale or scales of fees determined by a specified person, and
- (*b*) provide for the payment in specified circumstances of a larger or smaller fee than is set out in the appropriate scale.

(7) Regulations under subsection (1) may, in particular—

- (*a*) make provision about the eligibility of a person to be appointed as a local auditor of the accounts of a smaller authority;
- (*b*) make provision about the functions of a local auditor in relation to the accounts of a smaller authority.

(8) Regulations under subsection (1) may, in particular—

- (*a*) provide that, in specified circumstances, the accounts of a smaller authority of a specified description are to be exempt from specified audit requirements;
- (*b*) make provision for an exemption under paragraph (*a*) not to apply or to cease to apply to an authority in specified circumstances.

(9) In this section "specified" (except in the expressions "person specified by the Secretary of State" and "specified person") means specified in regulations under subsection (1).

[Local Audit and Accountability Act 2014, s 5.]

[1] The Local Audit (Smaller Authorities) Regulations 2015, SI 2015/184 have been made.

**7.7593 6. Meaning of "smaller authority"** (1) For the purposes of section 5, a relevant authority is a "smaller authority" for a financial year if—

- (*a*) where that year is the year in which the authority was established, the qualifying condition is met for that year, (*b*) where that year is the year following that in which the authority was established, the qualifying condition is met for that year or the previous year, and

(*c*) where that year is the second or any subsequent year following that in which the authority was established, the qualifying condition is met for that year or either of the two previous years.

(2) The qualifying condition is met for a relevant authority and a financial year if the higher of the authority's gross income for the year and its gross expenditure for the year does not exceed £6.5 million.

(3) For the purpose of determining, at a time when a relevant authority's gross income or expenditure for a financial year cannot be accurately determined, whether subsection (2) applies or will apply to the authority, that subsection is to be read as referring to the authority's estimated gross income or expenditure (as the case may be).

(4) The Secretary of State may by regulations[1] make provision about the application of this Act (including in its application by virtue of section 5) or any provision made under it in a case where—

(*a*) an authority is treated as a smaller authority for a financial year, and

(*b*) the authority was not in fact a smaller authority for that year.

(5) The Secretary of State may by regulations amend this section.

[Local Audit and Accountability Act 2014, s 6.]

---

[1] The Local Audit (Smaller Authorities) Regulations 2015, SI 2015/184 have been made.

## Part 3[1]
## Appointment etc of Local Auditors

---

[1] Part 3 comprises ss 17–17 and Schs 3–4.

7.7594 **7. Appointment of local auditor** (1) A relevant authority must appoint a local auditor to audit its accounts for a financial year not later than 31 December in the preceding financial year.

(2) A relevant authority may appoint a local auditor to audit its accounts for more than one financial year; and in such a case—

(*a*) subsection (1) does not apply in relation to the second or any subsequent year for which the appointment is made, but

(*b*) the authority must make a further appointment of a local auditor at least once every 5 years.

(3) Subsection (2)(*b*) does not prevent the relevant authority from re-appointing a local auditor.

(4) The Secretary of State may by regulations amend subsection (2)(*b*) so as to alter the period for the time being specified in it.

(5) A local auditor appointed under this section—

(*a*) must be eligible for appointment as a local auditor (see Part 4), and

(*b*) must not be prohibited from acting as a local auditor of the accounts of the relevant authority by virtue of section 1214 of the Companies Act 2006 (independence requirement) as it has effect by virtue of Schedule 5.

(6) Two or more local auditors may be appointed to audit the accounts of a relevant authority, and those auditors may be appointed—

(*a*) to act jointly in relation to some or all parts of the accounts;

(*b*) to act separately in relation to different parts of the accounts;

(*c*) to carry out different functions in relation to the audit.

(7) If, as a result of an appointment under subsection (6)(*b*) or (*c*), a function under this Act may be exercised by two or more local auditors—

(*a*) it may be exercised by both or all of them acting jointly or by such one or more of them as they may determine, and

(*b*) references (however expressed) to the local auditor by whom the function is or has been exercised are to the auditors by whom it is or has been exercised.

(8) Schedule 3 makes further provision about the appointment of local auditors; and this section is subject to that Schedule and provision made under it.

[Local Audit and Accountability Act 2014, s 7.]

## Part 5[1]
## Conduct of Local Audit

*Codes of practice and guidance*

7.7595 **19 Codes of audit practice and guidance**

*General powers and duties of auditors*

7.7596 **20. General duties of auditors** (1) In auditing the accounts of a relevant authority other than a health service body, a local auditor must, by examination of the accounts and otherwise, be satisfied—

(*a*) that the accounts comply with the requirements of the enactments that apply to them, (*b*) that proper practices have been observed in the preparation of the statement of accounts, and that the statement presents a true and fair view, and

(*c*) that the authority has made proper arrangements for securing economy, efficiency and effectiveness in its use of resources.

(2) Subject as follows, when a local auditor has completed an audit of the accounts of a relevant authority other than a health service body, the auditor must enter on the statement of accounts—

(*a*) a certificate that the auditor has completed the audit in accordance with this Act, and

(*b*) the auditor's opinion on the statement.

(3) If, for any part of the period for which a relevant authority is required to prepare a statement of accounts, the authority is required to maintain a pension fund under regulations under section 1 of the Public Service Pensions Act 2013 as they relate to local government workers (within the meaning of that Act), the authority's local auditor must give a separate opinion on the part of the statement that relates to the accounts of that pension fund.

(4) A local auditor may enter an opinion on the statement of accounts on that statement before the audit is completed if—

(*a*) the audit has not been completed because an objection has been made under section 27 and that objection has not been disposed of, and

(*b*) the auditor thinks that, if the objection were resolved in the objector's favour, this would not affect the accuracy of the statement of accounts.

(5) A local auditor must, in carrying out the auditor's functions in relation to the accounts of a relevant authority, comply with the code of audit practice applicable to the authority that is for the time being in force.

(6) A local auditor must, in carrying out functions under this Act, have regard to guidance issued by the Comptroller and Auditor General under paragraph 9 of Schedule 6.

[Local Audit and Accountability Act 2014, s 20.]

[1] Part 5 comprises ss 19–32 and Schs 6–8.

7.7597 21. **General duties of auditors of accounts of health service bodies** (1) In auditing the accounts of a clinical commissioning group, a local auditor must, by examination of the accounts and otherwise, be satisfied—

(*a*) that the accounts present a true and fair view, and comply with the requirements of the enactments that apply to them,

(*b*) that proper practices have been observed in the preparation of the accounts,

(*c*) that the group has made proper arrangements for securing economy, efficiency and effectiveness in its use of resources,

(*d*) that money provided by Parliament has been expended for the purposes intended by Parliament,

(*e*) that resources authorised by Parliament to be used have been used for the purposes in relation to which the use was authorised, and

(*f*) that the financial transactions of the group are in accordance with any authority which is relevant to the transactions.

(2) In subsection (1)(*e*) use of resources means their expenditure, consumption or reduction in value.

(3) In auditing the accounts of special trustees for a hospital, a local auditor must, by examination of the accounts and otherwise, be satisfied—

(*a*) that the accounts present a true and fair view, and comply with the requirements of the enactments that apply to them,

(*b*) that proper practices have been observed in the preparation of the accounts, and

(*c*) that the special trustees have made proper arrangements for securing economy, efficiency and effectiveness in their use of resources.

(4) When a local auditor has completed an audit of the accounts of a health service body, the auditor must—

(*a*) enter on the accounts a certificate that the auditor has completed the audit in accordance with this Act, and

(*b*) make a report in accordance with subsection (5).

(5) A report under subsection (4)(*b*)—

(*a*) must contain the auditor's opinion on the accounts, including on the matters in subsection (1) or, as the case may be, subsection (3), but

(*b*) must not contain the auditor's opinion on the matter in subsection (1)(*c*) or (3)(*c*) if the auditor is satisfied as to that matter.*

[Local Audit and Accountability Act 2014, s 21.]

* **Amended by the NHS (Charitable Trusts Etc) Act 2016, Schedule from a date to be appointed.**

7.7598 22. **Auditors' right to documents and information** (1) A local auditor has a right of access at all reasonable times to every document (an "audit document") that—

(*a*) relates to a relevant authority or an entity connected with a relevant authority, and

(*b*) the auditor thinks is necessary for the purposes of the auditor's functions under this Act.

(2) This includes power to inspect, copy or take away an audit document.

(3) A local auditor may—

(*a*) require a person holding or accountable for, or who has at any time held or been accountable for, an audit document to provide such information or explanation as the auditor thinks is necessary for the purposes of this Act, and

(*b*) if the auditor thinks it necessary, require the person to meet the auditor to give the information or explanation or (if the person holds or is accountable for the document) to produce the document.

(4) Where an audit document is in an electronic form, the power to require a person to produce the document includes power to require it to be produced in a form in which it is legible and can be taken away.

(5) For the purpose of inspecting an audit document which is in an electronic form, a local auditor—

(*a*) may have access to, and inspect and check the operation of, any computer and associated apparatus or material which the auditor thinks is or has been used in connection with the document, and

(*b*) may require a person within subsection (6) to give the auditor the reasonable assistance that the auditor needs for that purpose.

(6) A person is within this subsection who—

(*a*) is the person by whom or on whose behalf the computer is or has been used, or

(*b*) is a person in charge of, or otherwise involved in operating, the computer, apparatus or material.

(7) A local auditor may—

(*a*) require any person to whom this subsection applies to provide such information or explanation as the auditor thinks is necessary for the purposes of this Act, and

(*b*) if the auditor thinks it necessary, require the person to meet the auditor to give the information or explanation.

(8) Subsection (7) applies to—

(*a*) a member or officer of a relevant authority,

(*b*) where a relevant authority is a corporation sole, the holder of that office,

(*c*) a person elected or appointed—

(i) as an entity connected with a relevant authority,

(ii) to such an entity, or

(iii) to an office of such an entity,

(*d*) an employee of such an entity,

(*e*) an auditor of the accounts of such an entity, or

(*f*) a person who fell within any of paragraphs (*a*) to (*d*) at a time to which the information or explanation required by the local auditor relates.

(9) A local auditor of the accounts of a parish meeting may only exercise the function in subsection (7), so far as it applies to a person who is or was a member or officer of a relevant authority, in relation to a person who is or was the chairman of the parish meeting or the proper officer of the district council within whose area the parish lies.

(10) A relevant authority or an entity connected with a relevant authority must provide a local auditor with the facilities and information that the auditor reasonably requires for the purposes of the auditor's functions under this Act.

(11) A statement made by a person in response to a requirement under this section may not be used in evidence against that person in criminal proceedings other than proceedings for an offence under section 23.

(12) Nothing in this section compels a person to disclose information in respect of which a claim to legal professional privilege could be maintained in legal proceedings.

[Local Audit and Accountability Act 2014, s 22.]

7.7599 **23. Offences relating to section 22** (1) A person is guilty of an offence if, without reasonable excuse, the person—

(*a*) obstructs the exercise of any power conferred by section 22, or

(*b*) fails to comply with any requirement of a local auditor under that section.

(2) A person guilty of an offence under subsection (1) is liable on summary conviction—

(*a*) to a fine not exceeding level 3 on the standard scale, and

(*b*) to an additional fine of not more than £20 for each day on which the offence continues after conviction for that offence.

(3) The reasonable expenses incurred by a local auditor in connection with proceedings for an offence under subsection (1) alleged to have been committed by a person within subsection (4) in relation to the audit of the accounts of a relevant authority are recoverable from that authority so far as they are not recovered from any other source.

(4) The persons within this subsection are—

(*a*) a member or officer of the relevant authority,

(*b*) a person elected or appointed—

(i) as an entity connected with the relevant authority,

(ii) to such an entity, or

(iii) to an office of such an entity, and

(*c*) an employee of such an entity.

(5) Subsection (3) does not apply in relation to a parish meeting unless the offence is alleged to have been committed by the chairman of the parish meeting or the proper officer of the district council within whose area the parish lies.

(6) In subsection (4)(*a*) the reference to a member of the relevant authority, in relation to a corporation sole, is to the holder of that office.

[Local Audit and Accountability Act 2014, s 23.]

*Public inspection etc and action by auditor*

7.7600 **25. Inspection of statements of accounts etc** (1) A relevant authority other than a health service body must ensure that a local government elector for its area may inspect and make copies of—

(*a*) the statement of accounts prepared by the authority,

(*b*) the local auditor's certificate that the audit of the authority's accounts including that statement has been completed,

(*c*) the local auditor's opinion on the statement of accounts,

(*d*) any public interest report relating to the authority or an entity connected with it, and

(*e*) any recommendation relating to the authority or an entity connected with it.

(2) A relevant authority other than a health service body must ensure that a local government elector for its area may have copies of any document within subsection (1) supplied to the elector at the elector's request on payment of a reasonable sum for each copy.

(3) The relevant authority must ensure that a local government elector may inspect a document within subsection (1) at all reasonable times and without payment.

(4) This section applies in relation to a document only if the relevant authority has prepared the document or it has been made available to the authority.

(5) References in this section to copies of a document include a reference to copies of any part of it.

[Local Audit and Accountability Act 2014, s 25.]

7.7601 **26. Inspection of documents etc** (1) At each audit of accounts under this Act, other than an audit of accounts of a health service body, any persons interested may—

(*a*) inspect the accounting records for the financial year to which the audit relates and all books, deeds, contracts, bills, vouchers, receipts and other documents relating to those records, and

(*b*) make copies of all or any part of those records or documents.

(2) At the request of a local government elector for any area to which the accounts relate, the local auditor must give the elector, or any representative of the elector, an opportunity to question the auditor about the accounting records.

(3) The local auditor's reasonable costs of complying with subsection (2) are recoverable from the relevant authority to which the accounts relate.

(4) This section does not entitle a person—

(*a*) to inspect or copy any part of any record or document containing information which is protected on the grounds of commercial confidentiality, or

(*b*) to require any such information to be disclosed in answer to any question.

(5) Information is protected on the grounds of commercial confidentiality if—

(*a*) its disclosure would prejudice commercial confidentiality, and

(*b*) there is no overriding public interest in favour of its disclosure.

(6) This section does not entitle a person—

(*a*) to inspect or copy any part of any record or document containing personal information, or

(*b*) to require any personal information to be disclosed in answer to any question.

(7) Information is personal information if it identifies a particular individual or enables a particular individual to be identified (but see subsection (8)).

(8) Information is not personal information merely because it relates to a business carried on by an individual as a sole trader.

(9) Information is personal information if it is information about an officer of the relevant authority which relates specifically to a particular individual and is available to the authority because—

(*a*) the individual holds or has held an office or employment with that authority, or

(*b*) payments or other benefits in respect of an office or employment under any other person are or have been made or provided to that individual by that authority.

(10) For the purposes of subsection (9)—

(*a*) "the relevant authority" means the relevant authority whose accounts are being audited, and

(*b*) payments made or benefits provided to an individual in respect of an office or employment include any payment made or benefit provided in respect of the individual ceasing to hold the office or employment.

[Local Audit and Accountability Act 2014, s 26.]

7.7602 **27. Right to make objections at audit** (1) This section applies if, at an audit of accounts under this Act other than an audit of accounts of a health service body, a local government elector for an area to which the accounts relate makes an objection to the local auditor which meets the requirements in subsection (2) and which—

(*a*) concerns a matter in respect of which the auditor could make a public interest report, or

(*b*) concerns a matter in respect of which the auditor could apply for a declaration under section 28.

(2) The requirements are that—

(*a*) the objection is made in writing, and

(*b*) a copy of the objection is sent to the relevant authority whose accounts are being audited.

(3) The local auditor must decide—

(*a*) whether to consider the objection, and

(*b*) if the auditor does so, whether to take action within paragraph (*a*) or (*b*) of subsection (1) in response.

(4) The local auditor may decide not to consider the objection if, in particular, the auditor thinks that—

(*a*) the objection is frivolous or vexatious,

(*b*) the cost of the auditor considering the objection would be disproportionate to the sums to which the objection relates, or

(*c*) the objection repeats an objection already considered—

(i) under this section by a local auditor of the authority's accounts, or

(ii) under section 16 of the Audit Commission Act 1998 by an auditor appointed under that Act in relation to those accounts.

(5) Subsection (4)(*b*) does not entitle the local auditor to refuse to consider an objection which the auditor thinks might disclose serious concerns about how the relevant authority is managed or led.

(6) If the local auditor decides not to take action within paragraph (*a*) or (*b*) of subsection (1), the auditor may recommend that the relevant authority should instead take action in response to the objection.

(7) The local auditor's reasonable costs of exercising functions under this section are recoverable from the relevant authority.

[Local Audit and Accountability Act 2014, s 27.]

## PART 7
## MISCELLANEOUS AND SUPPLEMENTARY[1]

### *Supplementary*

7.7603 **44. Interpretation of Act** (1) In this Act (unless the context otherwise requires)—

"accounts" is to be construed in accordance with section 4(3) to (5);

"area"—

(*a*) in relation to a chief constable, means the police area of the chief constable's police force;

(*b*) in relation to a clinical commissioning group, means the area specified in the group's constitution (see Schedule 1A to the National Health Service Act 2006);

"charter trustees" means charter trustees constituted—

(*a*) under section 246 of the Local Government Act 1972,

(*b*) by the Charter Trustees Regulations 1996 (SI 1996/263), or

(*c*) under Part 1 of the Local Government and Public Involvement in Health Act 2007;

"chief constable" means a chief constable for a police force for a police area;

"code of audit practice" means a code of audit practice under Schedule 6;

"combined authority" means a combined authority established under section 103 of the Local Democracy, Economic Development and Construction Act 2009;

"the Common Council" means the Common Council of the City of London;

"costs", in relation to anything done by a local auditor, means the costs of the auditor's time to do that thing, whether or not the auditor charges on the basis of the time taken to do it;

"enactment" includes an enactment contained in subordinate legislation as defined in section 21(1) of the Interpretation Act 1978;

"executive" and "executive arrangements" have the same meaning as in Part 1A of the Local Government Act 2000;

"expenses", in relation to anything done by a local auditor, means the expenses incurred by the auditor in doing that thing, including the auditor's costs of doing it;

"financial year" has the meaning given by section 3(4) (subject to provision made under section 3(5));

"functional body" has the same meaning as in the Greater London Authority Act 1999 (see section 424(1) of that Act);

"health service body" has the meaning given by section 3(9);
"item of account" has the meaning given by section 28(9);
"local auditor" has the meaning given by section 4(1)(*b*);
"local government elector" means a person registered as a local government elector in the register of electors in accordance with the Representation of the People Acts (but see subsection (6));
"officer", in relation to a relevant authority—
(*a*) includes a member of the staff of the authority, but
(*b*) does not include a local auditor appointed to audit the authority's accounts;
"parish meeting" means a parish meeting of a parish which does not have a separate parish council;
"police area" means a police area listed in Schedule 1 to the Police Act 1996 (police areas outside London);
"public interest report" has the meaning given by paragraph 1(2) of Schedule 7;
"recognised qualifying body" has the meaning given by 1219(12) of the Companies Act 2006 as it has effect by virtue of Schedule 5 to this Act;
"recognised supervisory body" is to be construed in accordance with section 1217(4) of and Schedule 10 to the Companies Act 2006 as they have effect by virtue of Schedule 5 to this Act;
"recommendation" means a recommendation under paragraph 2(1) of Schedule 7;
"related authority" has the meaning given by paragraph 2(6) of Schedule 7;
"relevant authority" has the meaning given by section 2(1);
"special trustees for a hospital" has the meaning given by section 3(9)(*b*);
"sub-national transport body" means a sub-national transport body established under section 102E of the Local Transport Act 2008.

(2) References in this Act to a function under this Act or a Part of this Act include a function under regulations under this Act or that Part.

(3) References in this Act to provision made under it include provision made under Part 42 of the Companies Act 2006 as it has effect by virtue of Schedule 5.

(4) References in this Act to an entity connected with a relevant authority or to a connected entity are to be construed in accordance with paragraph 8 of Schedule 4.

(5) References in this Act to persons for whom a clinical commissioning group is responsible are to be construed in accordance with section 3 of the National Health Service Act 2006 (duties of clinical commissioning groups as to commissioning certain health services).

(6) A reference in this Act to a local government elector for any area—
(*a*) in relation to a Passenger Transport Executive, is a reference to a local government elector for the area of the Integrated Transport Authority or combined authority for the area for which the Executive is established;
(*b*) in relation to the Broads Authority, is a reference to a local government elector for the area of any participating authority (as defined by section 25 of the Norfolk and Suffolk Broads Act 1988);
(*c*) in relation to a National Park authority which is the local planning authority for a National Park, is a reference to a local government elector for any area the whole or any part of which is comprised in that Park.

(7) Any function conferred or imposed on the Greater London Authority under or by virtue of this Act is exercisable by the Mayor of London acting on behalf of the Authority.

(8) Subsection (7) does not apply in relation to any function expressly conferred on—
(*a*) the London Assembly, or
(*b*) the Mayor of London and the London Assembly acting jointly on behalf of the Greater London Authority.

(9) Any function conferred or imposed on a parish meeting under or by virtue of this Act, other than a function expressly conferred on the parish meeting itself, is exercisable by the chairman of the parish meeting acting on behalf of the authority.

(10) References in this Act to accounts, accounting records or statements of account in relation to the Common Council are to its accounts, accounting records or statements of account so far as relating to—
(*a*) the collection fund of the Common Council,
(*b*) the City Fund, or
(*c*) a pension fund maintained and administered by the Common Council under regulations under section 1 of the Public Service Pensions Act 2013.*

[Local Audit and Accountability Act 2014, s 44 as amended by the Cities and Local Government Devolution Act 2016, Sch 5.]

---

* **Amended by the NHS (Charitable Trusts Etc) Act 2016, Schedule from a date to be appointed.**
[1] Part 7 comprises ss 34–50 and Schs 10–13.

7.7604 **48. Extent**

7.7605 **49. Commencement** (1) The provisions of this Act come into force on such day as the Secretary of State may by order[1] appoint, subject to subsections (2) to (4).

(2) Sections 39 and 40 come into force at the end of the period of 2 months beginning with the

day on which this Act is passed.

(3) If this Act is passed before 5 February 2014, section 41 comes into force on the day on which this Act is passed; otherwise that section comes into force on such day as the Secretary of State may by order appoint.

(4) The following provisions come into force on the day on which this Act is passed—

(*a*) section 43;
(*b*) section 44;
(*c*) section 46;
(*d*) section 48;
(*e*) this section;
(*f*) section 50.

(5) An order under this section may—

(*a*) appoint different days for different purposes or different areas;
(*b*) make transitional, transitory or saving provision.

(6) Provision under subsection (5)(*b*) may, in particular, enable a function of the Audit Commission under—

(*a*) a provision that is amended or repealed by this Act, or
(*b*) any of sections 139A to 139C of the Social Security Administration Act 1992,

to be exercised by a person or body, or by the persons or bodies, specified in the order for a period specified in or determined under the order.

(7) Where provision under subsection (5)(*b*) made by virtue of subsection (6) enables a function to be exercised by a Minister of the Crown, an order under this section may enable the Minister to delegate the exercise of that function to another person or body or other persons or bodies.

(8) An order under this section which makes provision under subsection (5)(*b*) by virtue of subsection (6) or (7) may in particular provide for references in an enactment to the Audit Commission to be read as references to the person or body or persons or bodies by whom the function may be exercised.

(9) Provision under subsection (5)(*b*) may, in particular, provide for the first local auditor appointed by a relevant authority under subsection (1) of section 7 to be appointed on a date later than that specified in that subsection.

(10) In this section "the Audit Commission" means the Audit Commission for Local Authorities and the National Health Service in England.

[Local Audit and Accountability Act 2014, s 49.]

[1] All the provisions reproduced in this Manual have been brought fully into force. The following commencement orders had been made: (No 1) SI 2014/900; (No 2) SI 2014/940; (No 3) SI 2014/1596; (No 4) SI 2014/3319; (No 5) SI 2015/179; (No 6) SI 2015/223; (No 7, Transitional Provisions and Savings) SI 2015/841; and (Commencement No 8 and Commencement No 7, Transitional Provisions and Savings (Amendment)) SI 2016/675.

**7.7606 50. Short title**

# Non-Domestic Rating (Collection and Enforcement) (Local Lists) Regulations 1989[1]

(SI 1989/1058 amended by SI 1990/145 and 156, SI 1991/141, SI 1992/474 and 1512, SI 1993/616, 774, 894 and 1493, the Statute Law (Repeals) Act 1995, Sch 1, SI 1996/675 and 1880, SI 1998/3089, SI 2000/2026, SI 2001/362 and 1076, the Courts Act 2003, Sch 8, SI 2003/1714 (W), 2210 (E), 2604 (E) and 3052 (E), SI 2006/237 (E) and 3395 (E), SI 2007/501 (E) and 582 (W), SI 2008/428 (E), SI 2009/204 (E), 1597 (E), 2154 (W), 2706 (W) and SI 2010/187 (E), 752 (E), 1507 (E), 1656 (E), 2222 (W), SI 2011/113 (E), 528 (W), 966 (W), 1665 (E), SI 2012/24 (E), 466 (W) and 994 (E), SI 2014/379 (W), 479 (E) and 600 and SI 2017/39 and 113 (W))

## PART I GENERAL

**7.7607** 1. *Citation, commencement and interpretation* (1) *Citation, commencement.*

(2) In these Regulations—

"the Act" means the Local Government Finance Act 1988;

"the BRS Act" means the Business Rate Supplements Act 2009;

"address" in relation to electronic communications, includes any number or address used for the purposes of such communications;

"business day" means any day except a Saturday or Sunday, Christmas Day, Good Friday or a day which is a bank holiday under the Banking and Financial Dealings Act 1971 in England and Wales;

"demand notice regulations" means the Council Tax and Non-Domestic Rating (Demand Notices) (England) Regulations 1993 or, as the case may be, the Council Tax and Non-Domestic Rating (Demand Notices) (England) Regulations 2003;

"electronic communication" means a communication transmitted (whether from one person to another, from one device to another or from a person to a device or vice versa)—

(*a*) by means of a telecommunications system (within the meaning of section 32(1) of the Communications Act 2003); or
(*b*) by other means but while in electronic form.*

"non-domestic rate" includes a business rate supplement within the meaning of section 1(1) of the BRS Act.

* **Reproduced as in force in England.**

[1] These Regulations made under ss 63, 143(1) and (2) and 146(6) of, and paras 1–4 of Sch 9 to, the Local Government Finance Act 1988, are practically identical in form to the Community Charges (Administration and Enforcement) Regulations, ante. So far as non-domestic ratepayers appearing on central lists are concerned, see the Local Government Finance Act 1988, ss 52 to 54, ante in Part IV: Local Government.

**7.7608** 2. *Service of notices** (1) *Common Council notices to be served as under s 233 Local Government Act 1972.*

(2) Without prejudice to section 233 of the Local Government Act 1972 and paragraph (1) above, where any notice which is required or authorised by these Regulations to be given to or served on a person relates to a hereditament which is (or, where such a notice relates to more than one hereditament, one or more of which is) a place of business of that person, it may be given or served by leaving it at, or by sending it by post to him at, the place of business (or, as the case may be, one of those places of business).

(3) Without prejudice to section 233 of the Local Government Act 1972 and paragraphs (1) and (2) above and subject to paragraphs (4) to (7) below, any notice required or authorised to be given to or served by a billing authority on any person by a provision of Part II of these Regulations, is served:

(*a*) may be so given or served by sending the notice to that person by electronic communication to such address as may be notified by that person for that purpose; or

(*b*) shall be treated as given or served to that person where—

(i) the billing authority and that person have agreed for that purpose that any documents containing the notice may be accessed by that person on a website;

(ii) the document is a document to which that agreement applies;

(iii) the billing authority has published the document on a website; and

(iv) that person is notified, in a manner for the time being agreed for those purposes between him and the billing authority, of—

(*aa*) the publication of the document on a website;

(*bb*) the address of that website; and

(*cc*) the place on the website where the document may be accessed.

(3A) Without prejudice to section 233 of the Local Government Act 1972 and subject to paragraphs (5) and (6) below, any information required by the demand notice regulations to be supplied to any person when a demand notice (within the meaning of Part II of these Regulations) is served—

(*a*) may be so supplied by sending the information to that person by electronic communication to such address as may be notified by that person for that purpose; or

(*b*) subject to paragraph (3B) is treated as supplied to that person where the billing authority has published the information on a website and has notified that person by way of the demand notice of—

(i) the publication of the information on a website;

(ii) the address of that website; and

(iii) the place on the website where the information may be accessed.

(3B) Where a person requests a hard copy of the information, the authority must supply the information in hard copy as soon as practicable following the request.

(4) For the purpose of any legal proceedings, a notice given by a means described in paragraph (3) shall, unless the contrary is proved, be treated as served on the second business day after—

(*a*) it was sent in accordance with paragraph (3)(*a*); or

(*b*) notification of its publication was given in accordance with paragraph (3)(*b*)(iv).

(5) A person who has notified an address for the purpose of paragraphs (3)(*a*) or (3A)(*a*) shall, by notice in writing to the billing authority, advise the billing authority of any change in that address; and the change shall take effect on the third business day after the date on which the notice is received by the billing authority.

(6) A person who has notified an address for the purpose of paragraphs (3)(*a*) or (3A)(*a*) may, by notice in writing to the billing authority, withdraw that notification; and the withdrawal shall take effect on the third business day after the date on which the notice is received by the billing authority.

(7) A person who has entered into an agreement with the billing authority under paragraph (3)(*b*)(i) may, by notice in writing to the billing authority, inform the authority that he no longer wishes to be a party to the agreement; and where such notice is given, the agreement shall be treated as revoked on the third business day after the date on which the notice is received by the billing authority.

* **Reproduced as in force in England.**

## PART II BILLING

**7.7609** 3. *Interpretation and application of Part II** (1) In this Part—

"the amount payable" for a chargeable financial year or part of a chargeable financial year in relation to a ratepayer, a billing authority and a hereditament means—

(*a*) the amount the ratepayer is liable to pay to the authority as regards the hereditament in respect of the year or part under—

(i) section 43 or 45 of the Act, whether calculated by reference to section 43(4) to

(6) or 45(4) or (4A) of the Act (as those provisions are amended or substituted in any case by or under Schedule 7A to the Act) or by reference to an amount or rules determined or prescribed under section 47(1)(*a*), 57A(3)(*a*) or 58(3)(*a*) of the Act; and

(ii) section 11 of the BRS Act, whether calculated by reference to section 13 of the BRS Act (chargeable amount) or determined in accordance with rules set by the levying authority under section 15 of the BRS Act (BRS relief); or(*b*) where an amount falls to be credited by the billing authority against the ratepayer's liability in respect of the year or part, the amount (if any) by which the amount referred to in sub-paragraph (*a*) above exceeds the amount falling to be so credited;

"demand notice" means the notice required to be served by regulation 4(1);

"ratepayer" in relation to a chargeable financial year and a billing authority means a person liable to pay an amount under section 43 or 45 of the Act to the authority in respect of the year; and

"relevant year" in relation to a notice means the chargeable financial year to which the notice relates;

"the 1992 Act" means the Non-Domestic Rating Act 1992;

"the 1993 Act" means the Non-Domestic Rating Act 1993;

"transitional adjustment notice" has the meaning given by paragraph 7A(2)(*b*) of Schedule 1.

(2) For the purposes of this Part the conditions mentioned in section 43(1) or 45(1) of the Act are not to be treated as fulfilled as regards a hereditament on any day on which the chargeable amount for the day in respect of it is 0 under section 45A of the Act or by virtue of a determination to that effect under section 47(1)(*a*) of the Act.

(3) Where references are made in this Part to the day on which a notice is issued, they shall be taken to be references—

(*a*) if the notice is served in the manner described in regulation 2(2) or section 233(2) of the Local Government Act 1972 by being left at, or sent by post to, a person's place of business or proper address, to the day on which it is so left or posted, or

(*b*) in any other case, to the day on which it is served.

(4) The provisions of this Part which provide for the repayment or crediting of any amount or the adjustment of payments due under a notice (including in particular paragraph 7 of Schedule 1) shall have effect subject to paragraph 10(4) of Schedule 7 to the Act.

* **Reproduced as in force in England.**

7.7610 4. *The requirement for demand notices* (1) For each chargeable financial year a billing authority shall, in accordance with regulations 5 to 7, serve a notice in writing on every person who is a ratepayer of the authority in relation to the year.

(2) Different demand notices shall be served for different chargeable financial years.

(3) A demand notice shall be served with respect to the amount payable for every hereditament as regards which a person is a ratepayer of the authority, though a single notice may relate to the amount payable with respect to more than one such hereditament.

(3A) *Revoked.*

(4) If a single demand notice relates to the amount payable with respect to more than one hereditament, subject to paragraphs 5 and 8 of Schedule 1 the amounts due under it, and the times at which they fall due, shall be determined as if separate notices were issued in respect of each hereditament.

(5) *Revoked.*

7.7611 5. *Service of demand notices*[1] (1) Subject to paragraph (2), a demand notice shall be served on or as soon as practicable after—

(*a*) except in a case falling within sub-paragraph (*b*), 1st April in the relevant year, or

(*b*) if the conditions mentioned in section 43(1) or 45(1) of the Act are not fulfilled in respect of that day as regards the ratepayers and the hereditament concerned, the first day after that day in respect of which such conditions are fulfilled as regards them.

(2) Subject to paragraph (3), a demand notice may, if the non-domestic multiplier for the relevant year has been determined or set under Schedule 7 to the Act, be served before the beginning of the relevant year on a person with respect to whom on the day it is issued it appears to the billing authority that the conditions mentioned in section 43(1) or 45(1) of the Act are fulfilled (or would be fulfilled if a list sent under section 41(5) of the Act were in force) as regards the hereditament to which it relates; and if it is so served, references in this Part to a ratepayer shall, in relation to that notice and so far as the context permits, be construed as references to that person.

(3) A demand notice shall not be served before the authority has set amounts for the relevant year under section 30 of the Local Government Finance Act 1992.

[1] Where a boundary order changes the charging authority to that of another one, this regulation is modified by SI 1991/242.

7.7612 6. *Payments under demand notices*[1] (1) If a demand notice is issued before or during the relevant year and it appears to the billing authority that the conditions mentioned in section 43(1) or 45(1) of the Act are fulfilled (or would be fulfilled if a list sent under section 41(5) of the Act were in force) in respect of the day on which the notice is issued as regards the ratepayer and the hereditament to which it relates, the notice shall require payment of an amount equal to the billing authority's estimate of the amount payable for the year, made as respects periods after the issue of the notice on the assumption that the conditions concerned will continue to be fulfilled on every day after that day.

(1A) Where, as a result of the application of article 7 of the Non-Domestic Rating (Small Business Rate Relief) (England) Order 2004 and in accordance with that Order, there is any change to the amount which the ratepayer is liable to pay to the billing authority as regards the hereditament, the authority's estimate under paragraph (1) of the amount payable shall take account of such change.

(1B) Where, as a result of the application of article 11A of the Non-Domestic Rating (Small Business Relief) (Wales) Order 2008 and in accordance with that Order, there is any change to the amount which the ratepayer is liable to pay to the billing authority as regards the hereditament, the authority's estimate under paragraph (1) of the amount payable is to take account of such change.

(2) If a demand notice is issued during the relevant year but paragraph (1) does not apply, the notice shall require payment of an amount equal to the amount payable for the period in the year up to the day on which the conditions mentioned in sections 43(1) and 45(1) were last fulfilled as regards the ratepayer and hereditament concerned.

(3) If, after a notice is served to which paragraph (2) applies, the conditions mentioned in section 43(1) or 45(1) of the Act are fulfilled again in the relevant year as regards the ratepayer and the hereditament concerned, a further notice shall be served on him requiring payments with respect to the amount payable in relation to the hereditament for the period in the relevant year beginning with the day in respect of which the conditions are so fulfilled again; and regulations 5 to 8 (and, so far as applicable, Schedule 1) shall apply to the further notice with respect to that period as if it were a demand notice and the conditions had previously not been fulfilled.

(4) If a demand notice is issued after the end of the relevant year, it shall require payment of the amount payable for the year.

---

[1] Where a boundary order changes the charging authority to that of another one, this regulation is modified by SI 1991/242.

**7.7613** 7. *Payments under demand notices: further provision* (1) Unless an agreement under paragraph (3) in relation to the relevant year has been reached between the ratepayer and the billing authority before the demand notice is issued or paragraph (1A) or paragraph (1B) applies, a notice to which regulation 6(1) applies shall require the estimate of the amount payable to be paid by instalments in accordance with Part I of Schedule 1; and where such instalments are required Part II of the Schedule applies for their cessation or adjustment in the circumstances described in that Part.

(1A) Unless an agreement under paragraph (3) in relation to the relevant year has been reached between the ratepayer and the billing authority before the demand notice is issued, where—

(*a*) the chargeable financial year begins on 1st April 2011;

(*b*) it appears to the billing authority that the estimate of the amount payable for that year would fall to be calculated by reference to section 43(4A) of the Act or by reference to the rules prescribed in regulation 10(6) of the Non-Domestic Rating (Chargeable Amounts) (England) Regulations 2009; and

(*c*) the rateable value of the hereditament concerned is not more than £12,000, a notice to which regulation 6(1) applies shall require the estimate of the amount payable to be paid in instalments in accordance with Schedule 1E.

(1B) Unless an agreement under paragraph (3) in relation to the relevant year has been reached between the ratepayer and the billing authority before the demand notice is issued, where—

(*a*) the chargeable financial year begins on 1 April 2011;

(*b*) it appears to the billing authority that the estimate of the amount payable for that year would fall to be calculated by reference to section 43(4A) of the Act; and

(*c*) the rateable value of the hereditament concerned is not more than £12,000,

a notice to which regulation 6(1) applies must require the estimate of the amount payable to be paid in instalments in accordance with Schedule 1F.

(1C) *Revoked.*

(1D) In this regulation and in paragraph 1 of Schedule 1, "instalment notice" means a notice given by a ratepayer to a billing authority under paragraph (1E).

(1E) Paragraphs (1F) to (1K) apply where a ratepayer gives notice in writing to the billing authority that they wish to pay the estimate of the amount payable for each chargeable financial year by 12 monthly instalments until further notice.

(1F) An instalment notice may be given either before or after a demand notice is issued and may specify that it is to take effect starting in relation to the relevant year or the year following the relevant year.

(1G) Where an instalment notice relates to the relevant year, a demand notice to which regulation 6(1) applies shall be issued as soon as reasonably practicable after the date on which the instalment notice is received by the billing authority and shall require the estimate of the amount payable to be paid in instalments in accordance with paragraph 1(2C) of Schedule 1.

(1H) Where an instalment notice relates to the year following the relevant year, as soon as reasonably practicable after the date on which the instalment notice is received by the billing authority, the billing authority shall write to confirm that the estimate of the amount payable for that year is to be paid in instalments in accordance with paragraph 1(2C) of Schedule 1.

(1I) For each subsequent chargeable financial year for which the billing authority issues a demand notice to the ratepayer in accordance with regulation 6(1) after an instalment notice has been given, the demand notice shall require payment of the estimate of the amount payable for the year in accordance with paragraph 1(2C) of Schedule 1.

(1J) A ratepayer may give notice in writing to the billing authority that paragraph 1(2C) of Schedule 1 is no longer to apply.

(1K) Subject to paragraph (3), a notice given under paragraph (1J) takes effect at the expiry of the chargeable financial year in which it was received.

(2) If an agreement under paragraph (3) in relation to the relevant year has been reached between the billing authority and the ratepayer before the demand notice is issued, a notice to which regulation 6(1) applies shall require the estimate of the amount payable to be paid in accordance with that agreement.

(3) A billing authority and a ratepayer may agree that the estimate of the amount payable which is required to be paid under a notice to which regulation 6(1) applies should be paid in such manner as is provided by the agreement, rather than in accordance with Schedules 1 or 1E or 1F.

(4) Notwithstanding anything in the foregoing provisions of this regulation, such an agreement may be entered into either before or after the demand notice concerned is issued, and may make provision for the cessation or adjustment of payments, and for the making of fresh estimates, in the event of the estimate mentioned in regulation 6(1) turning out to be wrong; and if it is entered into after the demand notice has been issued, it may make provision dealing with the treatment for the purposes of the agreement of any sums paid in accordance with Schedules 1 or 1E or 1F before it was entered into.

(5) A notice to which regulation 6(2) or (4) applies shall require payment of the amount payable on the expiry of such period (being not less than 14 days) after the day of issue of the notice as is specified in it.

(6) No payment in respect of the amount payable by a ratepayer in relation to a hereditament for any chargeable financial year (whether interim, final or sole) need be made unless a notice served under this Part requires it.

**7.7614** *7A. Backdated liability: special provision in relation to 2005 rating lists* Notwithstanding the requirements of a demand notice issued in accordance with regulation 7, a ratepayer and a billing authority may reach an agreement in accordance with Schedule 1A.

**7.7615** *7B. Deferred payments: special provision in relation to financial years beginning on 1st April 2009, 2010 and 2011* Schedules 1B and 1C, which contain special provision in relation to payments under demand notices relating to financial years beginning on 1st April 2009, 1st April 2010 and 1st April 2011, shall have effect.

**7.7616** *7C. Deferred payments: special provision in relation to Wales for the financial years beginning on 1st April 2009, 2010 and 2011* Schedule 1D which contains special provision in relation to payments under demand notices relating to financial years beginning on 1st April 2009, 1st April 2010 and 1st April 2011, must have effect.

**7.7617** *7D. Deferred payments: special provision in relation to England for financial years beginning on 1st April 2012, 2013 and 2014* Schedules 1G and 1H, which contain special provision in relation to payments under demand notices relating to financial years beginning on 1st April 2012, 1st April 2013 and 1st April 2014, shall have effect.

**7.7618** *8. Failure to pay instalments* (1) Where—

(*a*) a demand notice has been served by a billing authority on a ratepayer,

(*b*) instalments are payable under the notice in accordance with Schedules 1 or 1E or 1F, and

(*c*) any such instalment is not paid in accordance with Schedules 1 or 1E or 1F,

the billing authority shall (unless all the instalments have fallen due) serve a further notice on the ratepayer stating the instalments required to be paid.

(2) If, after the service of a further notice under paragraph (1), the ratepayer—

(*a*) fails to pay, before the expiry of the period of 7 days beginning with the day of service of the further notice, any instalments which fall due before the expiry of that period under the demand notice concerned, or

(*b*) fails to pay any instalment which falls due after the expiry of that period under the demand notice concerned on or before the day on which it so falls due,

the unpaid balance of the estimated amount shall become payable by him at the expiry of a further period 7 days beginning with the day of the failure.

(3) If the unpaid balance of the estimated amount has become payable under paragraph (2), and on calculating the amount payable for the relevant year in relation to a hereditament to which the demand notice concerned relates that amount proves to be greater than the estimated amount in relation to the hereditament, an additional sum equal to the difference between the two shall, on the service by the billing authority on the ratepayer of a notice stating the amount payable, be due from the person to the authority on the expiry of such period (being not less than 14 days) after the day of issue of the notice as is specified in it.

(4) If the unpaid balance of the estimated amount has become payable under paragraph (2), and on calculating the amount payable for the relevant year in relation to a hereditament to which the demand notice concerned relates that amount proves to be less than the estimated amount in relation to the hereditament, the billing authority shall notify the ratepayer in writing of the amount payable; and any overpayment in respect of any liability of the ratepayer under this Part—

(*a*) shall be repaid if the ratepayer so requires, or

(*b*) in any other case shall (as the billing authority determines) either be repaid or be credited against any subsequent liability of the ratepayer to pay anything to it by way of non-domestic rate.

(5) If any factor or assumption by reference to which the estimated amount was calculated in relation to a hereditament is shown to be false before the amount payable is capable of final determination for the purposes of paragraphs (3) and (4), the billing authority may, and if so required by the ratepayer shall, make a calculation of the appropriate amount with a view to adjusting the ratepayer's liability in respect of the estimated amount and (as appropriate) to—

(*a*) requiring an interim payment from the ratepayer if the appropriate amount is greater than the estimated amount, or

(*b*) making an interim repayment to the ratepayer if the appropriate amount is less than the amount of the estimated amount paid.

(6) The appropriate amount for the purposes of paragraph (5) is the amount which would be required to be paid under a demand notice if such a notice were issued with respect to the relevant year, the ratepayer and the hereditament on the day that the notice under paragraph (7) is issued or the repayment under paragraph (5)(*b*) is made (as the case may be); and more than one calculation of the appropriate amount and interim payment or repayment may be required or made under paragraph (5) according to the circumstances.

(7) On calculating the appropriate amount the billing authority shall notify the ratepayer in writing of it; and a payment required under paragraph (5)(*a*) shall be due from the ratepayer to the billing authority on the expiry of such period (being not less than 14 days) after the day of issue of the notice as is specified in it.

(8) In this regulation—

"the appropriate amount" has the meaning given in paragraph (6); and

"the estimated amount" means the amount last estimated under regulation 6(1) for the purposes of the demand notice mentioned in paragraph (1)(*a*) or any subsequent notice given under paragraph 7(2) or, as the case may be, paragraph 7A or paragraph 7B or paragraph 7C or paragraph 7D or paragraph 7E of Schedule 1, or under paragraph 7 of that Schedule as modified by paragraph 5(3) of Schedule 1E or paragraph 5(3) of Schedule 1F, prior to the failure mentioned in paragraph (2) above, save that if in any case an interim adjustment has been required or made under paragraph (5) in relation to a hereditament, it means as regards the next payment, repayment or interim adjustment in relation to the hereditament under this regulation (if any), the appropriate amount by reference to which the previous interim adjustment was so made.

**7.7619** 9. *Demand notices: final adjustment* (1) This regulation applies where—

(*a*) a notice has been issued by a billing authority under this Part requiring a payment or payments to be made by a ratepayer in respect of the amount payable in relation to a hereditament for a chargeable financial year or part of a chargeable financial year,

(*b*) the payment or payments required to be paid are found to be in excess of or less than the amount payable in relation to the hereditament for the year or the part, and

(*c*) provision for adjusting the amounts required under the notice and (as appropriate) for the making of additional payments or the repaying or crediting of any amount overpaid is not made by any other provision of this Part, of the Act or of any agreement entered into under regulation 7(3).

(2) the billing authority shall as soon as practicable after the expiry of the year or the part of a year serve a further notice on the ratepayer stating the amount payable for the year or part in relation to the hereditament, and adjusting (by reference to that amount) the amounts required to be paid under the notice referred to in paragraph (1)(*a*).

(3) If the amount stated in the further notice is greater than the amount required to be paid under the notice referred to in paragraph (1)(*a*), the amount of the difference for which such other provision as is mentioned in paragraph (1)(*c*) is not made shall be due from the ratepayer to the billing authority on the expiry of such period (being not less than 14 days) after the day of issue of the notice as is specified in it.

(4) If there has been an overpayment in respect of any liability of the ratepayer under this Part, the amount overpaid for which such other provision as is mentioned in paragraph (1)(*c*) is not made—

(*a*) shall be repaid if the ratepayer so requires, or

(*b*) in any other case shall (as the billing authority determines) either be repaid or be credited against any subsequent liability of the ratepayer to pay anything to it by way of non-domestic rate.

**7.7620** 10. *Interpretation and application of Part III* (1) In this Part—

"debtor" means a person against whom a liability order has been made;

"liability order" means an order under regulation 12; and

"Schedule 12" means Schedule 12 to the Tribunals, Courts and Enforcement Act 2007, "the Schedule 12 procedure" means the procedure in that Schedule (taking control of goods and selling them to recover a sum of money), and "enforcement agent" has the meaning given in that Schedule.

(2) A sum which has become payable to a billing authority under Part II and which has not been paid shall be recoverable under a liability order, or in a court of competent jurisdiction, in accordance with regulations 11 to 21.

(3) References in this Part to a sum which has become payable and which has not been paid include references to a sum forming part of a larger sum which has become payable and the other part of which has been paid.

**7.7621** 11. *Liability orders: preliminary steps* (1) Subject to paragraph (3), before a billing authority applies for a liability order it shall serve on the person against whom the application is to be made a notice ("reminder notice"), which is to be in addition to any notice required to be served under Part II and which is to state every amount in respect of which the authority is to make the application.

(2) A reminder notice may be served in respect of an amount at any time after it has become due.

(3) A reminder notice need not be served on a person who has been served under regulation 8(1)

with a notice in respect of the amount concerned where there has been such a failure as is mentioned in regulation 8(2)(*a*) in relation to the notice.

**7.7622** *12. Application for liability order* (1) Subject to paragraph (3), if an amount which has fallen due under regulation 8(2) in consequence of such a failure as is mentioned in sub-paragraph (*a*) of that provision is wholly or partly unpaid, or (in a case where a reminder notice is required under regulation 11) the amount stated in the reminder notice is wholly or partly unpaid at the expiry of the period of 7 days beginning with the day on which the notice was served, the billing authority may, in accordance with paragraph (2), apply to a magistrates' court for an order against the person by whom it is payable.

(2) The application is to be instituted by making complaint to a justice of the peace, and requesting the issue of a summons directed to that person to appear before the court to show why he has not paid the sum which is outstanding.

(3) Section 127(1) of the Magistrates' Courts Act 1980 does not apply to such an application; but no application may be instituted in respect of a sum after the period of 6 years beginning with the day on which it became due under Part II.

(4) A warrant shall not be issued under section 55(2) of the Magistrates' Courts Act 1980 in any proceedings under this regulation.

(5) The court shall make the order[1] if it is satisfied that the sum has become payable by the defendant and has not been paid.

(6) An order made pursuant to paragraph (5) shall be made in respect of an amount equal to the aggregate of—

(*a*) the sum payable, and

(*b*) a sum of an amount equal to the costs reasonably incurred by the applicant in obtaining the order (which costs, including those of instituting the application under paragraph (2), are not to exceed the prescribed amount of £70).

(7) Where the sum payable is paid after a liability order has been applied for under paragraph (2) but before it is made, the court shall nonetheless (if so requested by the billing authority) make the order in respect of a sum of an amount equal to the costs reasonably incurred by the authority in making the application (which costs, including those of instituting the application under paragraph (2), are not to exceed the prescribed amount of £70).

[1] There are three criteria to be satisfied before an order made by a magistrates' court in its civil jurisdiction can be set aside: there must be a genuine and arguable dispute as to the defendant's liability to the order in question; the order must be made as a result of a substantial procedural error, defect or mishap; and the application to the justices for the order to be set aside is made promptly after a defendant learns that it has been made or has notice that an order may have been made: *R (London Borough of Newham) v Stratford Magistrates' Court* [2008] EWHC 125 (Admin), 173 JP 30. Justices may reopen their decision to make a liability order made in ignorance of the receipt of an application to adjourn so that they may exercise their judicial discretion whether to grant the order or adjourn (*Liverpool City Council v Pleroma Distribution Ltd* [2003] RA 34, [2003] 04 LS Gaz R 33). The appropriate procedure where liability orders were made as a result of incorrect service would be (i) for the individual to inform the justices and the local authority that he or she had not been properly served; (ii) the authority should determine if that assertion was correct, which would entail some co-operation with the individual; (iii) where it was established that the individual was not liable, but he or she was not content to accept the authority's assurance that liability orders would not be enforced, and wished for them to be set aside, the authority should join in an application to the justices to have the orders set aside; (iv) if such an application was refused, then the justices would be acting unreasonably and would be liable for costs (*R (on the application of Tull) v Camberwell Green Magistrates' Court* (2004) 168 JPN 986).

**7.7623** *13. Liability orders: further provision* (1) A single liability order may deal with one person and one such amount (or aggregate amount) as is mentioned in regulation 12(6) and (7), or, if the court thinks fit, may deal with more than one person and more than one such amount (or aggregate amount).

(2) A summons issued under regulation 12(2) may be served on a person—

(*a*) by delivering it to him,

(*b*) by leaving it as his usual or last known place of abode, or in the case of a company, at its registered office,

(*c*) by sending it by post to him at his usual or last known place of abode, or in the case of a company, to its registered office,

(*d*) where all or part of the sum to which it relates is payable with respect to a hereditament which is a place of business of the person, by leaving it at, or by sending it by post to him at, the place of business, or

(*e*) by leaving it at, or by sending it by post to him at, an address given by the person as an address at which service of the summons will be accepted.

(2A) No liability order shall be made in pursuance of a summons issued under regulation 12(2) unless fourteen days have elapsed since the day on which the summons was served.

(3) The amount in respect of which a liability order is made is enforceable in accordance with this part; and accordingly for the purposes of any of the provisions of Part III of the Magistrates' Courts Act 1980 (satisfaction and enforcement) it is not to be treated as a sum adjudged to be paid by order of the court.

**7.7624** *14. Enforcement by taking control of goods* Where a liability order has been made, payment may be enforced by using the Schedule 12 procedure.

**7.7626** *16. Commitment to prison* (1) Where a billing authority has sought to enforce payment by use of the Schedule 12 procedure pursuant to regulation 14, the debtor is an individual, and the enforcement agent reports to the authority that he was unable (for whatever reason) to find any or sufficient goods of the debtor to enforce payment, the authority may apply to a magistrates' court for the issue of a warrant committing the debtor to prison.

(2) On such application being made the court shall (in the debtor's presence) inquire as to his means and inquire whether the failure to pay which led to the liability order concerned being made

against him was due to his wilful refusal or culpable neglect.

(3) If (and only if) the court is of the opinion that his failure was due to his wilful refusal or culpable neglect it may if it thinks fit—

(*a*) issue a warrant of commitment against the debtor, or

(*b*) fix a term of imprisonment and postpone the issue of the warrant until such time and on such conditions (if any) as the court thinks just.

(4) The warrant shall be made in respect of the relevant amount; and the relevant amount for this purpose is the aggregate of—

(*a*) the amount outstanding (within the meaning of Schedule 12), and

(*b*) a sum of an amount equal to the costs reasonably incurred by the applicant in respect of the application.

(5) The warrant—

(*a*) shall state the relevant amount mentioned in paragraph (4),

(*b*) may be directed to the authority making the application and to such other persons (if any) as the court issuing it thinks fit, and

(*c*) may be executed anywhere in England and Wales by any person to whom it is directed.

(6) If—

(*a*) before a warrant has been issued, or a term of imprisonment fixed and the issue of a warrant postponed, an amount determined in accordance with paragraph (6A) is paid or tendered to the authority, or

(*b*) after a term of imprisonment has been fixed and the issue of a warrant postponed, any amount the court has ordered the debtor to pay is paid or tendered to the authority, or

(*c*) after a warrant has been issued, the amount stated in it is paid or tendered to the authority,

the authority shall accept the amount concerned, no further steps shall be taken as regards its recovery, and the debtor, if committed to prison, shall be released.

(6A) The amount referred to in paragraph (6)(*a*) above is the aggregate of—

(*a*) the amount outstanding (within the meaning of Schedule 12), and

(*b*) subject to sub-paragraph (6B) below, the authority's reasonable costs incurred up to the time of payment or tender in making one or more of the applications referred to in Schedule 4.

(6B) For the purposes of paragraph (6A)(*b*) above, the authority's reasonable costs in respect of any application shall not exceed the amount specified in relation to that application in Schedule 4.

(7) The order in the warrant shall be that the debtor be imprisoned for a time specified[1] in the warrant which shall not exceed 3 months, unless the amount stated in the warrant is sooner paid; but—

(*a*) where a warrant is issued after a postponement under paragraph (3)(*b*) and, since the term of imprisonment was fixed but before the issue of the warrant, the amount mentioned in paragraph (4)(*a*) with respect to which the warrant would (but for the postponement) have been made has been reduced by a part payment, the period of imprisonment ordered under the warrant shall be the term (*a*) the appropriate amount mentioned in regulation 14(2) (or so much of it as remains outstanding), and

(*b*) subject to sub-paragraph (6B) below, the authority's reasonable costs incurred up to the time of payment or tender in making one or more of the applications referred to in Schedule 4 fixed under paragraph (3) reduced by such number of days as bears to the total number of days in that term less one day the same proportion as the part paid bears to that amount, and

(*b*) where, after the issue of a warrant, a part payment of the amount stated in it is made, the period of imprisonment shall be reduced by such number of days as bears to the total number of days in the term of imprisonment specified in the warrant less one day the same proportion as the part paid bears to the amount so stated.

(8) In calculating a reduction required under paragraph (7) any fraction of a day shall be left out of account; and rule 55(1), (2) and (3) of the Magistrates' Courts Rules 1981 applies (so far as is relevant) to a part payment as if the imprisonment concerned were imposed for insufficient recovery by way of the Schedule 12 procedure to satisfy a sum adjudged to be paid by a magistrates' court.

---

[1] When determining the period of imprisonment to be specified in the warrant, the justices must have regard to the principle of proportionality. The more serious the case, whether in terms of the amount outstanding or in terms of the degree of culpability or blame to be attached to the debtor for his non-payment, the closer will any period imposed approach the maximum. A finding of wilful refusal, in this respect, represents a more serious state of affairs than culpable neglect (*R v Highbury Corner Magistrates' Court, ex p Uchendu* (1994) 158 JP 409).

**7.7627** 17. *Commitment to prison: further provision* (1) A single warrant may not be issued under regulation 16 against more than one person.

(2) Where an application under regulation 16 has been made, and after the making of the inquiries mentioned in paragraph (2) of that regulation no warrant is issued or term of imprisonment fixed, the court may remit all or part of the appropriate amount mentioned in regulation 14(2) to which the application relates.

(3) Where an application under regulation 16 has been made but no warrant is issued or term of imprisonment fixed, the application may be renewed (except so far as regards any sum remitted under paragraph (2)) on the ground that the circumstances of the debtor have changed.

(4) A statement in writing to the effect that wages of any amount have been paid to the debtor during any period, purporting to be signed by or on behalf of his employer, shall in any

proceedings under regulation 16 be evidence of the facts there stated.
(5) For the purpose of enabling enquiry to be made as to the debtor's conduct and means under regulation 16(2), a justice of the peace may—
(*a*) issue a summons to him to appear before a magistrates' court and (if he does not obey the summons) issue a warrant for his arrest, or
(*b*) issue a warrant for the debtor's arrest without issuing a summons.
(6) A warrant issued under paragraph (5) may be executed anywhere in England and Wales by any person to whom it is directed or by any constable acting within his police area; and section 125(3) of the Magistrates' Courts Act 1980 applies to such a warrant.
(7) Regulation 16 and this regulation have effect subject to Part I of the Criminal Justice Act 1982 (treatment of young offenders).

**7.7628** *18. Insolvency* (1) Where a liability order has been made and the debtor against whom it was made is an individual, the amount due shall be deemed to be a debt for the purposes of section 267 of the Insolvency Act 1986 (grounds of creditor's petition).
(2) Where a liability order has been made and the debtor against whom it was made is a company, the amount due shall be deemed to be a debt for the purpose of section 122(1)(*f*) (winding up of companies by the court) or, as the case may be, section 221(5)(*b*) (winding up of unregistered companies) of that Act.
(3) The amount due for the purposes of this regulation is an amount equal to any outstanding sum which is or forms part of the amount in respect of which the liability order was made.

**7.7629** *19. Relationship between remedies under a liability order* (1) Where a warrant of commitment is issued against (or a term of imprisonment is fixed in the case of) a person under regulation 16(3), no steps, or no further steps, may be taken under this Part by way of the Schedule 12 procedure or bankruptcy in relation to the relevant amount mentioned in regulation 16(4).
(2) Steps under this Part by way of the Schedule 12 procedure, commitment, bankruptcy or winding up may not be taken against a person under a liability order while steps by way of another of those methods are being taken against him under it.
(3) Subject to paragraphs (1) and (2) the Schedule 12 procedure may be resorted to more than once.
(4) Where a step is taken by way of the Schedule 12 procedure for the recovery of an outstanding sum which is or forms part of an amount in respect of which a liability order has been made, any sum recovered thereby which is less than the aggregate of the amount outstanding and any charges arising under Schedule 3 shall be treated as discharging first the charges, the balance (if any) being applied towards the discharge of the outstanding sum.

**7.7630** *20. Recovery in court of competent jurisdiction* (1) A sum which has become payable to a billing authority under Part II, which has not been paid, and in respect of which a liability order has not been made may (as an alternative to recovery under a liability order) be recovered in the court of competent jurisdiction.
(2) A liability order may not be made in respect of any amount in relation to which proceedings have been instituted under paragraph (1) above.

**7.7631** *21. Magistrates' courts* (1) *Revoked.*
(1A) *Revoked.*
(2) Subject to any other enactment authorising a District Judge (Magistrates' Courts) or other person to act by himself, a magistrates' court shall not under this Part hear a summons, entertain an application for a warrant or hold an inquiry as to means on such an application except when composed of at least two justices.
(3) References to a justice of the peace in regulations 12(2) and 15(2) shall be construed subject to rule 3 of the Justices' Clerks Rules 1970 (which authorises certain matters authorised to be done by a justice of the peace to be done by a justices' clerk).
(4) In any proceedings under regulation 12 (application for liability order) or regulation 16 (commitment to prison), a statement contained in a document constituting or forming part of a record compiled by the applicant authority or an authorised person[1] shall be admissible as evidence of any fact stated in it of which direct oral evidence would be admissible.
(5) In proceedings where the applicant authority or an authorised person[1] desires to give a statement in evidence in accordance with paragraph (4), and the document containing that statement is produced by a computer, a certificate—
(*a*) identifying the document containing the statement and the computer by which it was produced;
(*b*) containing a statement that at all material times the computer was operating properly, or if not, that any respect in which it was not operating properly or was out of operation was not such as to affect the production of the document or the accuracy of its contents;
(*c*) giving such explanation as may be appropriate of the content of the document; and
(*d*) purporting to be signed by a person occupying a responsible position in relation to the operation of the computer,

shall be admissible as evidence of anything which is stated in it to the best of the signatory's information and belief.
(6) In paragraph (4) above, "statement" includes any representation of fact, whether made in words or otherwise; and the reference to an application under regulation 16 includes a reference to an application made in the circumstances mentioned in regulation 17(3).
(7) In this regulation and in regulation 23(3), "authorised person" means any person authorised by a billing authority to exercise any functions relating to the collection and enforcement of non-domestic rates[1].

[1] A billing authority may authorise another person, or that person's employees, to exercise functions relating to the administration and enforcement of non-domestic rates: see the Local Authorities (Contracting Out of Tax Billing, Collection and Enforcement Functions) Order 1996, SI 1996/1880.

**7.7632** *22. Repayments* A sum which has become payable (by way of repayment) under Part II to a person other than a billing authority but which has not been paid shall be recoverable in a court of competent jurisdiction.

**7.7633** *23. Miscellaneous provisions* (1) Any matter which could be the subject of an appeal under regulations under section 55 of the Act may not be raised in proceedings under this Part.

(2) The contents of a local non-domestic rating list or an extract from such a list may be proved in proceedings under this Part by production of a copy of the list or relevant part of the list purporting to be certified by the proper officer of the billing authority to which the list or extract relates to be a true copy.

(3) If a liability order has been made and by virtue of—

(*a*) a notification which is given by the billing authority or an authorised person under regulation 8(4) or (7) or 9(2) or paragraph 6(3) or 7(2)(*a*) of Schedule 1 or sub-paragraph (2) of paragraph 7A of that Schedule (including a notification given under that sub-paragraph pursuant to paragraph 7B(2) of that Schedule), or

(*b*) paragraph 10(4) or Schedule 7 to the Act applying in any case,

any part of the amount mentioned in regulation 12(6)(*a*) in respect of which the order was made would (if paid) fall to be repaid or credited against any subsequent liability, that part shall be treated for the purposes of this Part as paid on the day the notification is given or the multiplier in substitution is set under paragraph 10 of Schedule 7 to the Act (as the case may be) and accordingly as no longer outstanding.

(4) If, after a warrant is issued or term of imprisonment is fixed under regulation 16(3), and before the term of imprisonment has begun or been fully served, a billing authority gives such a notification as is mentioned in paragraph (3)(*a*) in the case in question, or sets a multiplier in substitution so that paragraph 10(4) of Schedule 7 to the Act applies in the case in question, it shall forthwith notify accordingly the designated officer for the court which issued the warrant and (if the debtor is detained) the governor or keeper of the prison or place where he is detained or such other person as has lawful custody of him.

## PART IV MISCELLANEOUS

**7.7634** *24. Outstanding liabilities on death** (1) This regulation applies where a person dies and at any time before his death he was (or is alleged to have been) subject to a non-domestic rate.

(2) Where—

(*a*) before the deceased's death a sum has become payable by him under Part II or by way of relevant costs in respect of a non-domestic rate but has not been paid, or

(*b*) after the deceased's death a sum would, but for his death (and whether or not on the service of a notice) become payable by him under Part II in respect of a non-domestic rate,

his executor or administrator shall, subject to paragraph (3) and to the extent that it is not in excess of the deceased's liability under the Act or the BRS Act (including relevant costs payable by him) in respect of the rate, be liable to pay the sum and may deduct out of the assets and effects of the deceased any payments made (or to be made).

(3) Where paragraph (2)(*b*) applies, the liability of the executor or administrator does not arise until the service on him of a notice requiring payment of the sum.

(4) Where before the deceased's death a sum in excess of his liability under the Act or the BRS Act (including relevant costs payable by him) in respect of a non-domestic rate has been paid (whether the excess arises because of his death or otherwise) and has not been repaid or credited under Part II, his executor or administrator shall be entitled to the sum.

(5) Costs are relevant costs for the purposes of paragraphs (2) and (4) if—

(*a*) an order or warrant (as the case may be) was made by the court in respect of them under regulation 12(6)(*b*) or (7) or 16(4)(*b*), or in proceedings under regulation 20, or

(*b*) they are charges connected with the use of the Schedule 12 procedure which may be recovered pursuant to regulations under paragraph 62 of Schedule 12.

(6) A sum payable under paragraph (2) shall be enforceable in the administration of the deceased's estate as a debt of the deceased and accordingly—

(*a*) no liability order need be applied for in respect of it after the deceased's death under regulation 12, and

(*b*) the liability of the executor or administrator is a liability in his capacity as such.

(7) Regulation 23(1) and (2) applies to proceedings to enforce a liability arising under this regulation as it applies to proceedings under Part III.

(8) Insofar as is relevant to his liability under this regulation in the administration of the deceased's estate, the executor or administrator may institute, continue or withdraw proceedings (whether by way of appeal under regulations under section 55 of the Act or otherwise).

* **Reproduced as in force in England.**

SCHEDULE 1
NON-DOMESTIC RATE INSTALMENT SCHEME Regulation 7(1)

SCHEDULE 1A
BACKDATED LIABILITY: SPECIAL PROVISION IN RELATION TO 2005 RATING LISTS Regulation 7A

SCHEDULE 1B Regulation 7B

SCHEDULE 1C
(Form of application) Regulation 7B

SCHEDULE 4
COSTS CONNECTED WITH COMMITTAL Regulation 16(6A) and (6B)

## Council Tax (Administration and Enforcement) Regulations 1992[1]

(SI 1992/613 amended by SI 1992/3008, SI 1993/196 and 773, SI 1994/505, SI 1995/22, the Statute Law (Repeals) Act 1995, Sch 1, SI 1996/675 and 1880, SI 1997/393, SI 1998/295, SI 1999/534, SI 2000/2026, SI 2001/1076 and 2237, SI 2003/552 (W) and 768 (E), 1715 (W), 2211 (E) and 2604 (E), SI 2004/927 (E), 785 (W) and 1013 (W), SI 2005/2866 (E) and 3302 (W), SI 2006/237 (E) and 3395 (E), SI 2007/501 (E) and 582 (W), SI 2009/2706 (W), SI 2010/752 (E), SI 2011/528 (W), SI 2012/672 and 3086 (E), SI 2013/62(W), 570 (W), 590 (E), 630 (E) and 2977 (E), 2014/129 (W) and 600 and SI 2017/41 (W))

### PART I
### *General*

**7.7635** *1. Citation, commencement and interpretation* (1) *Citation and commencement.*

(2) In these Regulations—

"the Act" means the Local Government Finance Act 1992;

"address" in relation to electronic communications, includes any number or address used for the purposes of such communications;

"business day" means any day except a Saturday or Sunday, Christmas Day, Good Friday or a day which is a bank holiday under the Banking and Financial Dealings Act 1971 in England and Wales;

"council tax offence" has the same meaning as in the Detection of Fraud Regulations;

"demand notice regulations" means regulations under paragraph 1(1) of Schedule 2 to the Act making such provision as is mentioned in paragraph 2(4)(*e*) or 2(4)(*j*) of that Schedule; and

"Detection of Fraud Regulations" means the Council Tax Reduction Schemes (Detection of Fraud and Enforcement) (England) Regulations 2013;

"discount" means—

(*a*) a discount under section 11 or section 11A of the Act;

(*b*) a reduction in the amount of council tax payable for a dwelling under the Council Tax (Reductions for Annexes) (England) Regulations 2013; or (*c*) a reduction under section 13A(1)(*a*) or

(*c*) where—

(i) a scheme under section 13A(2) of the Act provides, or

(ii) the billing authority has determined under section 13A(7) of the Act,

that liability shall be reduced otherwise than to nil;

"electronic communication" means a communication transmitted (whether from one person to another, from one device to another or from a person to a device or vice versa)—

(*a*) by means of an electronic communications network within the meaning of section 32(1) of the Communications Act 2003;

(*b*) by other means but while in an electronic form;

"exempt dwelling" means a dwelling which is exempt from council tax under the Exempt Dwellings Order or a dwelling in relation to which no council tax is payable by virtue of a reduction under section 13A(1)(*a*) or section 13A(1)(*c*) of the Act where—

(*a*) a scheme under section 13A(2) of the Act provides; or

(*b*) the billing authority has determined under section 13A(7) of the Act;

that liability shall be reduced otherwise than to nil;

"Exempt Dwellings Order" means the Council Tax (Exempt Dwellings) Order 1992;

"managing agent", in relation to a dwelling, means any person authorised to arrange lettings of the dwelling;

"premium" means an increase in the amount of council tax payable in respect of a dwelling under section 11B(1) of the Act; and

"universal credit" means universal credit under Part 1 of the Welfare Reform Act 2012".

---

[1] Made by the Secretary of State for the Environment, as respects England, and the Secretary of State for Wales, as respects Wales, in exercise of the powers conferred on them by ss 16(3) and 113(1) and (2) of, and paragraphs 1(1), 2(2), (3), (4)(*a*) to (*c*) and (5), 3–11, 13(1)(*a*) and (3), 16 and 18 of Sch 2, paras 1 and 6 of Sch 3 and paras 1–15, and 17–19 of Sch 4 to, the Local Government Finance Act 1992.

**7.7636** *2. Service of notices* (1) Where any notice which is required or authorised by these Regulations to be given to or served on any person falls to be given or served by or on behalf of the Common Council it may be given or served in any manner in which it might be given or served under section 233 of the Local Government Act 1972 if the Common Council were a local authority within the meaning of that section.

(2) If the name of any person on whom a notice is to be served in accordance with regulation 3

(information from residents etc) or regulation 12 (information relating to exempt dwellings etc) cannot after reasonable inquiry be ascertained, the notice may be served by addressing it to "The Resident" or, as the case may be, "The Owner" or "The Managing Agent" of the dwelling concerned (naming the dwelling) without further name or description.

(3) If the name of any person to whom a notice is to be given or on whom a notice is to be served in accordance with any provision of Part V (billing) of these Regulations cannot after reasonable inquiry be ascertained, the notice may be given or served by addressing it to "The Council Tax Payer" of the dwelling concerned (naming the dwelling) without further name or description.

(4) Without prejudice to section 233 of the Local Government Act 1972 and paragraphs (1), (2) and (3) above and subject to paragraphs (5) to (8) below, any notice required or authorised to be given to or served by a billing authority on any person by a provision of Part II, III or V of these Regulations:

(*a*) may be so given, served or supplied by sending the notice or information to that person by electronic communication to such address as may be notified by that person for that purpose; or

(*b*) shall be treated as given, served or supplied to that person where—

(i) the billing authority and that person have agreed for that purpose that any document containing that notice or information may be accessed by that person on a website;

(ii) the document is a document to which that agreement applies;

(iii) the billing authority has published the document on a website; and

(iv) that person is notified, in a manner for the time being agreed for that purpose between him and the billing authority, of—

(*aa*) the publication of the document on a website;

(*bb*) the address of that website; and

(*cc*) the place on the website where the document may be accessed.

(4A) Without prejudice to section 233 of the Local Government Act 1972(*b*) and subject to paragraphs (6) and (7) below, any information required by the demand notice regulations to be supplied to any person when a demand notice (within the meaning of Part V of these Regulations) is served:

(*a*) may be so supplied by sending the information to that person by electronic communication to such address as may be notified by that person for that purpose; or

(*b*) subject to paragraph (4B) shall be treated as supplied to that person where the billing authority has published the information on a website and that person is notified by way of the demand notice of—

(i) the publication of the information on a website;

(ii) the address of that website; and

(iii) the place on the website where the information may be accessed;

(4B) Sub-paragraph (*b*) of paragraph (4A) shall not apply where that person has requested a hard copy of the information.

(4C) Where a person requests a hard copy of the information referred to in paragraph (4A) in writing either before or after the demand notice is issued the authority must supply it as soon as reasonably practicable following receipt of the request.

(5) For the purpose of any legal proceedings, a notice given by a means described in paragraph (4), shall, unless the contrary is proved, be treated as served on the second business day after—

(*a*) it was sent in accordance with sub-paragraph (*a*); or

(*b*) notification of its publication was given in accordance with sub-paragraph (*b*)(iv).

(6) A person who has notified an address for the purposes of paragraph (4)(*a*) or (4A)(*a*) shall, by notice in writing to the billing authority, advise the billing authority of any change in that address; and the change shall take effect on the third business day after the date on which the notice is received by the billing authority.

(7) A person who has notified an address for the purposes of paragraph (4)(*a*) or (4A)(*a*) may, by notice in writing to the billing authority, withdraw that notification; and the withdrawal shall take effect on the third business day after the date on which the notice is received by the billing authority.

(8) A person who has entered into an agreement with the billing authority under paragraph (4)(*b*)(i) may, by notice in writing to the billing authority, inform the authority that he no longer wishes to be party to the agreement; and where such notice is given, the agreement shall be treated as revoked on the third business day after the date on which the notice is received by the billing authority.

## Part II
*Information: General*

## Part III
*Exempt Dwellings, Etc*

## Part IV
*Discounts*

## Part V
*Billing*

**7.7637** 17. *Interpretation and application of Part V* (1) In this Part—

"demand notice" means the notice required to be served by regulation 18(1);

"joint taxpayers" means two or more persons who are, or in the opinion of the billing authority will be, jointly and severally liable to pay to the authority an amount in respect of council tax in respect of a particular dwelling and a day (whether such liability arises by virtue of section 6(3) or (4)(*b*), 7(4) or (5), 8(4) or (5) or 9(1) of the Act);

"joint taxpayers' notice" means a notice served in accordance with regulation 28;

"Part II scheme" means a scheme for the payment of the chargeable amount by instalments in accordance with a scheme complying with the requirements of Part II of Schedule 1 to these Regulations;

"the relevant year", in relation to a notice, means the financial year to which the notice relates.

(1A) Any reference in this Part to the relevant valuation band in relation to a dwelling is a reference to the valuation band shown as applicable to the dwelling—

(*a*) in the billing authority's valuation list; or

(*b*) if no such list is in force—

(i) except in a case to which paragraph (1B) applies, in the copy of the proposed list supplied to the authority under section 22(5)(*b*) of the Act;

(ii) in a case to which paragraph (1B) applies, in information which for the purposes of this paragraph is relevant information.

(1B) This paragraph applies where the listing officer supplies the authority with information relating to property shown in the proposed list (including information relating to the application to such property of article 3 or 4 of the Council Tax (Chargeable Dwellings) Order 1992); and such information is relevant information for the purposes of paragraph (1A)(*b*)(ii) to the extent that it differs from information contained in the proposed list.

(2) Except where the context otherwise requires, and subject to paragraph (5), any reference in this Part to the liable person (however expressed) is a reference—

(*a*) to a person who is, or in the opinion of the billing authority will be, solely liable to pay to the authority, an amount in respect of council tax in respect of a particular dwelling and a day; or

(*b*) where persons are joint taxpayers, to those persons.

(3) Any reference in this Part to the chargeable amount is a reference to the amount the liable person is or will be liable to pay.

(4) Any reference in this Part to the day on or time at which a notice is issued, is a reference—

(*a*) if the notice is served in the manner described in section 233(2) of the Local Government Act 1972 by being left at, or sent by post to, a person's proper address, to the day on or time at which it is so left or posted, or

(*b*) in any other case, to the day on or time at which the notice is served.

(5) This Part applies (amongst other matters) for the making of payments in relation to the chargeable amount for a financial year; but its application as regards persons who are joint taxpayers is subject to the provisions of regulations 27 to 28A.

(6) The provisions of this Part which provide for the repayment or crediting of any amount or the adjustment of payments due under a notice shall have effect subject to section 31(4) of the Act.

**7.7638** 18. *The requirement for demand notices* (1) Subject to paragraph (2), for each financial year a billing authority shall serve a notice in writing[1] on every liable person in accordance with regulations 19 to 21.

(2) Where, but for this paragraph, notices would fall to be served in accordance with this Part—

(*a*) at the same time; and

(*b*) in respect of the same dwelling,

in relation to a financial year not then ended and any preceding financial year, nothing in paragraph (1) shall require a billing authority to serve more than one notice.

(3) If a person is liable in any financial year to pay to the same billing authority different chargeable amounts in respect of different dwellings, a demand notice shall be served in respect of each chargeable amount.

---

[1] The Council Tax and Non-Domestic Rating (Demand Notices) (England) Regulations 1993, SI 1993/191 provide for the content of Council Tax notices and for the information to be supplied with such notices in the financial year beginning on 1 April 1993.

**7.7639** 19. *Service of demand notices* (1) The demand notice is to be served on or as soon as practicable after the day the billing authority first sets an amount of council tax for the relevant year for the category of dwellings which includes the chargeable dwelling to which the notice relates.

(2) For the purposes of paragraph (1), "category" shall be construed in accordance with section 30(4) of the Act; and where a demand notice is served before 1st April 1993, a dwelling shall be treated as included in the category in which, in the opinion of the billing authority, it will be included on 1st April 1993.

**7.7640** *20. Demand notices: payments required* (1) If the demand notice is issued before or during the relevant year, the notice shall require the making of payments on account of the amount referred to in paragraph (2).

(2) The amount is—

(*a*) the billing authority's estimate of the chargeable amount, made as respects the relevant year or part, as the case may be, on the assumptions referred to in paragraph (3); or

(*b*) subject to paragraph (2A), where an amount falls to be credited by the billing authority against the chargeable amount, the amount (if any) by which the amount estimated as mentioned in sub-paragraph (*a*) exceeds the amount falling to be so credited.

(2A) Where the billing authority has made a determination under—

(*a*) paragraph 118(1)(*c*) of the scheme prescribed in the Schedule to the Council Tax Reduction Schemes (Default Scheme) (England) Regulations 2012; or

(*b*) a provision contained in an authority's scheme under section 13A(2) of the Act by virtue of paragraph 14(1)(*c*) of Schedule 8 to the Council Tax Reduction Schemes (Prescribed Requirements) (England) Regulations 2012

paragraph (2)(*b*) shall not apply in relation to that amount.

(3) The assumptions are—

(*a*) that the person will be liable to pay the council tax to which the notice relates on every day after the issue of the notice;

(*b*) that, as regards the dwelling concerned, the relevant valuation band on the day the notice is issued will remain the relevant valuation band for the dwelling as regards every day after the issue of the notice;

(*c*) if on the day the notice is issued the person satisfies conditions prescribed for the purposes of regulations under section 13 of the Act (and consequently the chargeable amount in his case is less than it would otherwise be), that he will continue to satisfy those conditions as regards every day after the issue of the notice;

(*d*) if, by virtue of regulation 9(1), the dwelling to which the notice relates is assumed to be a chargeable dwelling on the day the notice is issued, that it will continue to be a chargeable dwelling as regards every day after the issue of the notice;

(*e*) if, by virtue of regulation 15(1), the chargeable amount is assumed not to be subject to a discount on the day the notice is issued, that it will not be subject to a discount as regards any day after the issue of the notice;

(*f*) if, by virtue of regulation 15(2), the chargeable amount is assumed to be subject to a discount on the day the notice is issued, that it will continue to be subject to the same rate of discount as regards every day after the issue of the notice;

(*fa*) if, by virtue of regulation 15(3) it is assumed that the chargeable amount is not subject to a discount, that it will not be subject to a discount as regards any day after the issue of the notice; and

(*g*) if on the day the notice is issued a determination as to council tax benefit to which the person is entitled is in effect, and by virtue of regulations under section 138(1) of the Social Security Administration Act 1992 the benefit allowed as regards that day takes the form of a reduction in the amount the person is liable to pay in respect of council tax for the relevant year, that as regards every day after that day he will be allowed the same reduction in that amount.

(4) If the demand notice is issued during the relevant year and the liable person is not liable to pay an amount by way of council tax in respect of the day on which the notice is issued, the demand notice shall require payment of—

(*a*) the chargeable amount for the period in the year up to the last day in respect of which he was so liable; or

(*b*) where an amount falls to be credited by the billing authority against that chargeable amount, an amount equal to the amount (if any) by which that chargeable amount exceeds the amount falling to be so credited.

(5) If the demand notice is issued after the end of the relevant year, it shall require payment of—

(*a*) the chargeable amount; or

(*b*) where an amount falls to be credited by the billing authority against the chargeable amount, an amount equal to the amount (if any) by which the chargeable amount exceeds the amount falling to be so credited.

**7.7641** *21. Council tax: payments* (1) Unless—

(*a*) an agreement under paragraph (5) in relation to the relevant year has been reached between the billing authority and the liable person before the demand notice is issued, or

(*b*) the authority has resolved that a Part II scheme shall have effect for the relevant year as regards dwellings of a class which includes the dwelling in respect of which the chargeable amount falls to be paid,

a notice to which paragraph (1) of regulation 20 applies shall require the amount mentioned in paragraph (2) of that regulation to be paid by instalments in accordance with Part I of Schedule 1 hereto.

(1A) Where a liable person requests by notice in writing to the billing authority to pay the amount mentioned in regulation 20(2) by 12 monthly instalments paragraphs (1B), (1C) and (1D) apply.

(1B) Such a request may be made either before or after the demand notice is issued and may be made in relation to the relevant year or the year following the relevant year.

(1C) Where the request relates to the relevant year, a notice to which paragraph (1) of regulation 20 applies shall be issued as soon as reasonably practicable after the date on which the notice in paragraph (1A)is received by the billing authority and shall require the amount mentioned in paragraph (2) of regulation 20 to be paid by instalments in accordance with paragraph 2(3A) of Schedule 1 to these Regulations.

(1D) Where the request relates to the year following the relevant year, as soon as reasonably practicable after the date on which the notice is received by the billing authority, the billing authority shall write to confirm that from such date as is requested in the notice in paragraph (1A) the amount mentioned in paragraph (2) of regulation 20 for that year shall be paid by instalments in accordance with paragraph 2(3A) of Schedule 1 to these Regulations.

(2) Where a billing authority has resolved as mentioned in paragraph (1)(*b*), a notice to which paragraph (1) of regulation 20 applies shall require the amount mentioned in paragraph (2) of that regulation to be paid by instalments in accordance with the provisions of the authority's Part II scheme.

(3) Where instalments are required to be paid in accordance with a Part II scheme or under Part I of Schedule 1, Part III of that Schedule applies for their cessation or adjustment in the circumstances described in that Part (subject, in the case of payments in accordance with a Part II scheme, to provision included in the scheme pursuant to paragraph 8(6) of Part II of that Schedule).

(4) If an agreement under paragraph (5) in relation to the relevant year has been reached between the billing authority and the liable person before the demand notice is issued, a notice to which paragraph (1) of regulation 20 applies shall require the amount mentioned in paragraph (2) of that regulation to be paid in accordance with that agreement.

(5) A billing authority and a liable person may agree that the amount mentioned in regulation 20(2) which is required to be paid under a notice to which regulation 20(1) applies shall be paid in such manner as is provided by the agreement.

(6) Notwithstanding the foregoing provisions of this regulation, such an agreement may be entered into either before or after the demand notice concerned is issued, and may make provision for the cessation or adjustment of payments, and for the making of fresh estimates, in the event of the estimate mentioned in regulation 20(2) turning out to be wrong; and if it is entered into after the demand notice has been issued, it may make provision dealing with the treatment for the purposes of the agreement of any sums paid in accordance with Part I of Schedule 1 or a Part II scheme before it was entered into.

(7) A notice to which regulation 20(4) or (5) applies shall (as the billing authority determines) require payment of the amount concerned—

(*a*) on the expiry of such period (being not less than 14 days) after the day of issue of the notice as is specified in it; or

(*b*) by instalments of such amounts as are specified in the notice, payable at such intervals and on such day in each interval as is so specified.

**7.7642** *21A. Referendums relating to council tax increases: excessive amount not approved*

**7.7643** *22. Notices: further provision* No payment on account of the chargeable amount (whether interim, final or sole) need be made unless a notice served under this Part requires it.

**7.7644** *23. Failure to pay instalments* (1) Subject to paragraph (2), where—

(*a*) a demand notice has been served by a billing authority on a liable person,

(*b*) instalments in respect of the council tax to which the notice relates are payable in accordance with Part I of Schedule 1 or, as the case may be, a Part II scheme or a determination under regulation 21(7), and

(*c*) any such instalment is not paid in accordance with that Schedule or, as the case may be, the relevant scheme or determination

the billing authority shall serve a notice ("reminder notice") on the liable person stating—

(i) the amount which is the aggregate of the instalments which are due under the demand notice or any subsequent notice given under paragraph 10 of Schedule 1 and which are unpaid and the instalments that will become due within the period of seven days beginning with the day on which the reminder notice is issued;

(ii) that the amount mentioned in sub-paragraph (i) above is required to be paid by him within the period mentioned in that sub-paragraph;

(iii) the effect of paragraph (3) below and the amount that will become payable by him in the circumstances mentioned in that paragraph; and

(iv) where the notice is the second such notice as regards the relevant year, the effect of paragraph (4) below.

(2) Nothing in paragraph (1) shall require the service of a reminder notice—

(*a*) where all the instalments have fallen due; or

(*b*) in the circumstances mentioned in paragraphs (3) and (4).

(3) If, within the period of 7 days beginning with the day on which a reminder notice is issued, the liable person fails to pay any instalments which are or will become due before the expiry of that period, the unpaid balance of the estimated amount (or, as the case may be, the chargeable amount) shall become payable by him at the expiry of a further period of 7 days beginning with the

day of the failure.

(4) If, after making a payment in accordance with a reminder notice which is the second such notice as regards the relevant year, the liable person fails to pay any subsequent instalment as regards that year on or before the day on which it falls due, the unpaid balance of the estimated amount (or, as the case may be, the chargeable amount) shall become payable by him on the day following the day of the failure.

**7.7645** 24. *Payments: adjustments*

**7.7646** 25. *Lump sum payments*

**7.7647** 26. *Non-cash payments*

**7.7648** 27. *Joint taxpayers* (1) This regulation applies in the case of joint taxpayers; but its application to joint taxpayers on whom a joint taxpayers' notice is served is subject to regulation 28A.

(2) In a case to which this regulation applies—

(*a*) regulation 18 (the requirement for demand notices) has effect as if in paragraph (1) for the words "every liable person" there were substituted the words "at least one of the joint taxpayers";

(*b*) regulation 20 (demand notices; payments required) has effect as if—

(i) the assumption referred to in sub-paragraph (*c*) of paragraph (3) is made as regards such of the joint taxpayers as on the day of issue of the demand notice satisfy the conditions referred to in that sub-paragraph;

(ii) the assumption referred to in sub-paragraph (*g*) of paragraph (3) is made as regards such of the joint taxpayers in respect of whom on the day of issue of the demand notice a determination has effect as mentioned in that sub-paragraph;

(*c*) regulation 21 (council tax: payments) has effect as if—

(i) in paragraphs (1) and (4), for the words "the liable person" there were substituted the words "one or more of the joint taxpayers";

(ii) in paragraph (3), for the words after "that Part" there were substituted the following—

"subject—

(*a*) in the case of payments in accordance with a Part II scheme, to provision included in the scheme pursuant to paragraph 8(6) of Part II of that Schedule; and

(*b*) in the case of joint taxpayers, to regulations 28 and 28A.";

(iii) in paragraph (5), for the words "a liable person" there were substituted the words "one or more of the joint taxpayers"; and

(iv) in paragraph (5), there were inserted at the end the words ": but, subject to regulation 28A(1), a billing authority may not enter into an agreement after the issue of the demand notice concerned with a joint taxpayer on whom that notice was not served";

(*d*) regulation 23 (failure to pay instalments) has effect as if references to the liable person and to an amount becoming payable by the liable person were references to such of the joint taxpayers as have been served with a demand notice and to an amount becoming payable by them, respectively;

(*e*) regulation 29 (collection of penalties) has effect as if—

(i) for paragraph (1), there were substituted the following—

"(1) Subject to paragraphs (2) and (3), where a penalty is payable to a billing authority under any of sub-paragraphs (1) to (3) of paragraph 1 of Schedule 3 to the Act or under any of regulations 11 to 13 of the Detection of Fraud Regulations by a person who is one of joint taxpayers, it may be collected by the service by the authority on the person of a notice requiring payment of the penalty on the expiry of such period (being not less than 14 days) after the issue of the notice as is specified in it."; and

(ii) paragraph (4) were omitted; and

(*f*) paragraph 9 (cessation of instalments) of Schedule 1 does not apply unless—

(i) every person on whom the demand notice was served has ceased to be a joint taxpayer;

(ii) none of those persons is, as regards any part of the period to which the demand notice relates, solely liable to pay an amount in respect of council tax as regards the dwelling concerned; and

(iii) no other person who, as regards any part of that period, was jointly and severally liable with any of those persons as regards the dwelling concerned, is a liable person (whether his liability is sole or joint and several) as regards the dwelling concerned.

**7.7649** 28. *Joint taxpayers' notice* (1) An amount shall not be payable by a person who is one of joint taxpayers and on whom a demand notice has not been served unless a notice ("joint taxpayers' notice") is served on him in accordance with the following provisions of this regulation.

(2) A joint taxpayers' notice may not be served on a person after the expiry of the period of six years beginning with the first day of the financial year to which the notice relates.

(3) Where—

(*a*) a joint taxpayers' notice is served during the relevant year; and

(*b*) the person on whom (as one of the joint taxpayers) a demand notice for that year was served (or, if more than one person was so served, each of them) is not on the day of issue of the notice one of the joint taxpayers; and (*c*) the unpaid balance of the estimated amount has not become due as mentioned in paragraph (3) or (4) of regulation 23,

the notice shall require the payment of the adjusted amount.

(4) For the purposes of paragraph (3)—

"the adjusted amount" means an amount equal to the lesser of—

(*a*) the billing authority's estimate of the chargeable amount made as respects the period to which the joint taxpayers' notice relates; and regulation 20(3) shall have effect for these purposes as it has effect in a case to which regulation 27 applies and as if references in regulation 27(2)(*b*) to the demand notice were references to the joint taxpayers' notice; and

(*b*) the relevant sum; and

"the relevant sum" means an amount equal to the difference between—

(*a*) the amount estimated or last estimated as regards the dwelling concerned—

(i) for the purposes of an agreement under regulation 21(5); or

(ii) under regulation 20(2) for the purposes of the demand notice or any subsequent notice given under paragraph 10 of Schedule 1; and

(*b*) the aggregate of the amounts paid to the authority under any such agreement or notice before the issue of the joint taxpayers' notice.

(5) Subject to regulation 28A(1), the amount required to be paid under paragraph (3) shall be payable by instalments of such amounts, and at such intervals and on such days in each interval, as are specified in the notice; provided that the number of instalments shall not be less than the number of instalments payable under the agreement, the demand notice or any subsequent notice given under paragraph 10 of Schedule 1, as the case may be, as regards the period beginning on the day on which the joint taxpayers' notice is served and ending on the last day of the relevant year.

(6) A joint taxpayers' notice which is issued after the end of the relevant year, or after the unpaid balance of the estimated amount has become due as mentioned in paragraph (3) or (4) of regulation 23, shall (as the billing authority determines) require payment of the amount concerned—

(*a*) on the expiry of such period (being not less than 14 days) after the issue of the notice as is specified in it; or

(*b*) by instalments of such amounts as are specified in the notice, payable at such intervals and on such day in each interval as is so specified.

**7.7650** 28A. *Joint taxpayers' notice: further provision* (1) A billing authority and a person on whom a joint taxpayers' notice is served may agree that the amount required to be paid under the notice shall be paid in such manner as is provided by the agreement; and paragraph (6) of regulation 21 shall apply with the necessary modifications in relation to an agreement under this paragraph as it applies to an agreement under paragraph (5) of that regulation.

(2) Regulation 23 (failure to pay instalments) shall apply with the necessary modifications in relation to instalments payable in accordance with a joint taxpayers' notice as it applies to instalments payable in accordance with Part I of Schedule 1 or a Part II scheme.

(3) If the amount required to be paid under a joint taxpayers' notice is shown to be incorrect, the billing authority shall serve a further notice on every person on whom the joint taxpayers' notice was served stating the revised sum required to be paid.

(4) If the amount stated in the further notice served under paragraph (3) is greater than the amount required to be paid under the joint taxpayers' notice, the further notice shall also state the revised amount of each remaining instalment or, as the case may be, the period (being not less than 14 days) after the issue of that further notice within which the further sum payable is required to be paid.

(5) If the amount stated in the further notice under paragraph (3) is less than the amount required to be paid under the joint taxpayers' notice, any overpayment—

(*a*) shall be repaid if the person on whom the joint taxpayers' notice was served so requires, or

(*b*) in any other case shall (as the billing authority determines) either be repaid or be credited against any subsequent liability of that person to make a payment in respect of council tax to the authority.

**7.7651** 29. *Collection of penalties* (1) Subject to paragraphs (2) to (4), where a penalty is payable by a person to a billing authority under any of sub-paragraphs (1) to (3) of paragraph 1 of Schedule 3 to the Act or under any of regulations 11 to 13 of the Detection of Fraud Regulations it may be collected, as the authority to which it is payable determines, either—

(*a*) by treating the penalty for the purposes of regulations 20 and 21 and Schedule 1 as if it were part of the amount that the person is or will be liable to pay in respect of council tax as regards any demand notice issued pursuant to regulation 20(2) after the penalty is imposed, or

(*b*) by the service by the authority on the person of a notice requiring payment of the penalty on the expiry of such period (being not less than 14 days) after the issue of the notice as is specified in it.

(2) Where the imposition of a penalty is subject to an appeal or arbitration, no amount shall be payable in respect of the penalty while the appeal or arbitration is outstanding.

(3) The imposition of a penalty is to be treated as subject to an appeal or arbitration for the purposes of this regulation and regulation 27(6) until such time as the matter is finally disposed of in accordance with regulations under paragraph A3 of Schedule 11 to the Local Government Finance Act 1988 (valuable tribunals) or is abandoned or fails for non-prosecution; and the

circumstances in which an appeal is to be treated as failing for non-prosecution include the expiry of any time prescribed under paragraph 8(2)(*a*) of that Schedule in consequence of which any such appeal would be required to be dismissed by a valuation tribunal.

(4) A demand notice making provision for the recovery of a penalty which is subject to appeal or arbitration may not be issued under paragraph (1)(*a*) during the period that the appeal or arbitration concerned is outstanding; and where a penalty becomes subject to appeal or arbitration after the issue of a demand notice which makes such provision, such proportion of the instalments due under it as are attributable to the penalty shall not fall due until the appeal or arbitration is finally disposed of, abandoned or fails for non-prosecution.

(5) Where an amount has been paid by a person in respect of a penalty which is quashed under paragraph 1(6) of Schedule 3 to the Act, regulation 12(4) or regulation 13(6) of the Detection of Fraud Regulations, or pursuant to the order of a valuation tribunal or the High Court, the billing authority which imposed the penalty may allow the amount to him by way of deduction against any other sum which has become due from him under this Part (whether in respect of another penalty or otherwise); and any balance shall be repaid to him.

**7.7652** 30. *Appeals in relation to estimates* Section 16(1) of the Act shall not apply where the ground on which the person concerned is aggrieved is that any assumption as to the future that is required by this Part to be made in the calculation of an amount may prove to be inaccurate.

**7.7653** 31. *Demand notices: final adjustment* (1) This regulation applies where—

(*a*) a notice has been issued by a billing authority under this Part requiring a payment or payments to be made by a person in respect of his liability to pay council tax for a financial year or part of a financial year,

(*b*) the payment or payments required to be made are found to be in excess of or less than his liability for the year or the part, and

(*c*) provision for adjusting the amounts required under the notice and (as appropriate) for the making of additional payments or the repaying or crediting of any amount overpaid is not made by any other provision of this Part, of the Act or of any agreement entered into under regulation 21(5).

(2) The billing authority shall as soon as practicable after the expiry of the year or the part of a year serve a further notice on the person stating the amount of his liability for the year or the part, and adjusting (by reference to that amount) the amounts required to be paid under the notice referred to in paragraph (1)(*a*).

(3) If the amount stated in the further notice is greater than the amount required to be paid under the notice referred to in paragraph (1)(*a*), the amount of the difference for which such other provision as is mentioned in paragraph (1)(*c*) is not made shall be due from the person to the billing authority on the expiry of such period (being not less than 14 days) after the day of issue of the notice as is specified in it.

(4) If there has been an overpayment, the amount overpaid for which such other provision as is mentioned in paragraph (1)(*c*) is not made—

(*a*) shall be repaid if the person so requires, or

(*b*) in any other case shall (as the billing authority determines) either be repaid or be credited against any subsequent liability of the person to make a payment in respect of any council tax of the authority.

## Part VI

## *Enforcement*

**7.7654** 32. *Interpretation and application of Part VI* (1) In this Part—

"attachment of allowances order" means an order under regulation 44;

"attachment of earnings order" means an order under regulation 37;

"authorised person" means any person authorised by a billing authority to exercise any functions relating to the administration and enforcement of the council tax[1];

"charging order" means an order under regulation 50;

"debtor" means a person against whom a liability order has been made;

"earnings" means sums payable to a person—

(*a*) by way of wages or salary (including any fees, bonus, commission, overtime pay or other emoluments payable in addition to wages or salary or payable under a contract of service); or

(*b*) by way of statutory sick pay,

but, in so far as the following would otherwise be treated as earnings, they shall not be treated as such:

(i) sums payable by any public department of the Government of Northern Ireland or of a territory outside the United Kingdom;

(ii) pay or allowances payable to the debtor as a member of Her Majesty's forces other than pay or allowances payable by his employer to him as a special member of a reserve force (within the meaning of the Reserve Forces Act 1996);

(iii) allowances or benefit payable under the Social Security Acts;

(iiia) tax credits within the meaning of the Tax Credits Act 2002;

(iiib) universal credit;

(iv) allowances payable in respect of disablement or disability; and

(v) wages payable to a person as a seaman, other than wages payable to him as a seaman of a fishing boat;

(vi) tax credits within the meaning of the Tax Credits Act 2002.

"the Income Support Regulations" means the Council Tax (Deductions from Income Support) Regulations 1993;

"liability order" means an order under regulation 34 or regulation 36A(5);

"net earnings" in relation to an employment means the residue of earnings payable under the employment after deduction by the employer of—

(*a*) income tax;

(*b*) primary Class 1 contributions under Part I of the Social Security Contributions and Benefits Act 1992; and

(*c*) amounts deductible under any enactment, or in pursuance of a request in writing by the debtor, for the purposes of a superannuation scheme, namely any enactment, rules, deed or other instrument providing for the payment of annuities or lump sum—

(i) to the persons with respect to whom the instrument has effect on their retirement at a specified age or on becoming incapacitated at some earlier age, or

(ii) to the personal representatives or the widows, widowers, surviving civil partners, relatives or dependants of such persons on their death or otherwise,

whether with or without any further or other benefits; and where an order under regulation 32 (making of attachment of earnings order) of the Community Charges (Administration and Enforcement) Regulations 1989 made before the making of the attachment of earnings order concerned remains in force,

(*d*) any amount required to be deducted in accordance with that order; and

"Schedule 12" means Schedule 12 to the Tribunals, Courts and Enforcement Act 2007, and "the Schedule 12 procedure" means the procedure in that Schedule (taking control of goods and selling them to recover a sum of money).

(2) In sub-paragraph (v) of the definition of "earnings" in paragraph (1) above expressions used in the Merchant Shipping Act 1894 have the same meanings as in that Act.

(3) Regulations 33 to 53 apply for the recovery of a sum which has become payable to a billing authority under Part V and which has not been paid; but their application in relation to a sum for which persons are jointly and severally liable under that Part is subject to the provisions of regulation 54 (joint and several liability).

(4) References in this Part to a sum which has become payable and which has not been paid include references to a sum forming part of a larger sum which has become payable and the other part of which has been paid.

(5) Any reference in this Part to the day on or time at which a notice is issued, is a reference—

(*a*) if the notice is served in the manner described in section 233(2) of the Local Government Act 1972 by being left at, or sent by post to, a person's proper address, to the day on or time at which it is so left or posted, or

(*b*) in any other case, to the day on or time at which the notice is served.

---

[1] A billing authority may authorise another person, or that person's employees, to exercise functions relating to the administration and enforcement of the council tax: see the Local Authorities (Contracting Out of Tax Billing, Collection and Enforcement Functions) Order 1996, SI 1996/1880.

**7.7655** *33. Liability orders: preliminary steps* (1) Subject to paragraph (3), before a billing authority applies for a liability order it shall serve on the person against whom the application is to be made a notice ("final notice"), and which is to state every amount in respect of which the authority is to make the application.

(2) A final notice may be served in respect of an amount at any time after it has become due.

(3) Nothing in paragraph (1) shall require the service of a final notice in the circumstances mentioned in paragraph (3) of regulation 23 (including that paragraph as applied as mentioned in regulation 28A(2)).

**7.7656** *34. Application for liability order* (1) If an amount which has fallen due under paragraph (3) or (4) of regulation 23 (including those paragraphs as applied as mentioned in regulation 28A(2)) is wholly or partly unpaid, or (in a case where a final notice is required under regulation 33) the amount stated in the final notice is wholly or partly unpaid at the expiry of the period of 7 days beginning with the day on which the notice was issued, the billing authority may, in accordance with paragraph (2), apply to a magistrates' court for an order against the person by whom it is payable.

(2) The application is to be instituted by making complaint to a justice of the peace, and requesting the issue of a summons directed to that person to appear before the court to show why he has not paid the sum which is outstanding.

(3) Section 127(1) of the Magistrates' Courts Act 1980 does not apply to such an application; but no application may be instituted in respect of a sum after the period of six years beginning with the day on which it became due[1] under Part V.

(4) A warrant shall not be issued under section 55(2) of the Magistrates' Courts Act 1980 in any proceedings under this regulation.

(5) If, after a summons has been issued in accordance with paragraph (2) but before the application is heard, there is paid or tendered to the authority an amount equal to the aggregate of—

(*a*) the sum specified in the summons as the sum outstanding or so much of it as remains outstanding (as the case may be); and

(*b*) a sum of an amount equal to the costs reasonably incurred by the authority in connection with the application up to the time of the payment or tender, the authority shall accept the amount and the application shall not be proceeded with.

(6) The court shall[2] make the order[3] if it is satisfied that the sum has become payable by the defendant and has not been paid.

(7) An order made pursuant to paragraph (6) shall be made in respect of an amount equal to the aggregate of—

(*a*) the sum payable, and

(*b*) a sum of an amount equal to the costs reasonably incurred by the applicant in obtaining the order[4] (which costs, including those of instituting the application under paragraph (2), are not to exceed the prescribed amount of £70)*.

(8) Where the sum payable is paid after a liability order has been applied for under paragraph (2) but before it is made, the court shall nonetheless (if so requested by the billing authority) make the order in respect of a sum of an amount equal to the costs reasonably incurred by the authority in making the application (which costs, including those of instituting the application under paragraph (2), are not to exceed the prescribed amount of £70)*.

---

* **Words underlined in paras (7), (8) inserted in relation to Wales only by SI 2011/528.**

1 Liability to pay council tax arises when the demand is service and not when the amount of tax was set by the billing authority (*Regentford v Thanet District Council* [2004] TLR 143 (whether procedural or substantial prejudice precluded a claim did not arise on the facts where the payer had allowed the proceedings to go by default, see also *Encon Insulation Ltd v Nottingham City Council* [1999] RA 382)).

2 There are three criteria to be satisfied before an order made by a magistrates' court in its civil jurisdiction can be set aside: there must be a genuine and arguable dispute as to the defendant's liability to the order in question; the order must be made as a result of a substantial procedural error, defect or mishap; and the application to the justices for the order to be set aside is made promptly after a defendant learns that it has been made or has notice that an order may have been made (*R (London Borough of Newham) v Stratford Magistrates' Court* [2008] EWHC 125 (Admin), 173 JP 30). Magistrates have to consider not only whether the dispute is genuine but also whether it is arguable. It is also necessary for magistrates to identify specifically the procedural error referred to. If, for example, the magistrates find that defendant had not been served with any summons and did not know about the liability proceedings at the relevant time, they must make an express finding to that effect, explaining briefly upon what material they have relied to reach the finding. Failure to do so constitutes a substantial defect in the reasoning in support of their decision per Kenneth Parker J in *London Borough of Tower Hamlets v Rahman* [2012] EWHC 3428 (Admin), 177 JP 192. (Justices may reopen their decision to make a liability order made in ignorance of the receipt of an application to adjourn so that they may exercise their judicial discretion whether to grant the order or adjourn (*Liverpool City Council v Pleroma Distribution Ltd* [2003] 04 LS Gaz R 33, decided under reg 12(5) of the Non-Domestic Rating (Collection and Enforcement) Regs 1989). The appropriate procedure where liability orders were made as a result of incorrect service would be (i) for the individual to inform the justices and the local authority that he or she had not been properly served; (ii) the authority should determine if that assertion was correct, which would entail some co-operation with the individual; (iii) where it was established that the individual was not liable, but he or she was not content to accept the authority's assurance that liability orders would not be enforced, and wished for them to be set aside, the authority should join in an application to the justices to have the orders set aside; (iv) if such an application was refused, then the justices would be acting unreasonably and would be liable for costs (*R (on the application of Tull) v Camberwell Green Magistrates' Court* (2004) 168 JPN 986) (decided under the Non-Domestic Rating (Collection and Enforcement) etc Regulations 1989, ante).

3 In a case decided under the Community Charge (Administration and Enforcement) Regulations 1989, a liability order may be made for the full amount of the community charge notwithstanding that an application for benefit under the Community Charge Benefits (General) Regulations 1989 is outstanding, or that the local authority is in breach of its statutory duty under those regulations to determine such an application 'within 14 days . . . or as soon as practicable thereafter' (*R v Bristol City Magistrates' Court, ex p Willsman* (1991) 156 JP 409, CA).

4 Regulation 34(7) means that the court must be satisfied:

(i) that the local authority has actually incurred those costs;

(ii) that the costs in question were incurred in obtaining the liability order; and

(iii) that it was reasonable for the local authority to incur them.

The question whether the requirements are satisfied is an issue of mixed fact and law, not a matter of discretion. Once the court is satisfied that the costs have been reasonably incurred, it has no discretion but to award costs in that amount, and that the ability of a particular respondent to pay those costs is not a relevant consideration.

A defendant is entitled to know how the court is able to satisfy itself that the costs claimed do represent the costs reasonably incurred in obtaining the liability order, in the absence of any information as to how that figure was computed. *Guidance to local councils on good practice in the collection of Council Tax arrears* (2013) para 3.4, states:

> "Local Authorities are reminded that they are only permitted to charge reasonable costs for the court summons and liability order. In the interests of transparency, Local Authorities should be able to provide a breakdown, on request, showing how these costs are calculated. While it is likely that authorities will have discussed costs with the Clerk to Justices it should be recognised that the Court may wish to be satisfied that the amount claimed by way of costs in any individual case is no more than that reasonably incurred by the authority."

The provisions in reg 34(7) were considered in *R (on the application of Reverend Nicolson) v Tottenham Magistrates* [2015] EWHC 1252 (Admin), [2015] PTSR 1045, 179 JP 421 and the findings and observations of Andrews J are summarised in what follows.

For the court to be satisfied that the costs were reasonably incurred it is insufficient for the court to rely on general and vague assertions with no supporting particulars. The focus must be not on whether the costs claimed was a reasonable amount but whether those costs were reasonably incurred in obtaining the liability order. There must be a sufficient link between the costs in question and the process of obtaining the liability order. It will be impermissible to include in the costs claimed any element referable to the costs of executing the order after it was obtained, or to the overall administration of council tax in the area concerned.

Costs incurred in obtaining the order encompass costs incurred in connexion with the application for a summons and encompass, but are not confined to, the fee for issuing the summons. In principle the intention in the Regulations is to enable the local authority to recover the actual cost to it of utilising the enforcement process under reg 34, which will include some administrative costs, as well as any legal fees and out of pocket expenses. The Regulations should be construed in such a way as to ensure that the costs recovered are only those which are genuinely attributable to the enforcement process.

Costs do not necessarily have to be incurred on or after the date on which the summons was issued. Once the decision to enforce has been taken there may still need to be checks carried out to ensure that the summons is issued in the correct amount and against the right person. But the costs of taking the decision to exercise the discretion to enforce would appear to fall on the wrong side of the line.

Given the large number of summonses issued, it will not be practical for the local authority to carry out and provide a detailed calculation of the actual costs incurred in each and every case (save possibly where the actual costs are well in excess of the norm, for example if the local authority has to instruct counsel to turn up and argue specific points of law raised by the taxpayer in defence). In principle, therefore, provided that the right types of costs and expenses are taken into account, and provided that due consideration is given to the dangers of double-counting, or of artificial inflation of costs, it may be a legitimate approach for a local authority to calculate and aggregate the relevant costs it has incurred in the previous year, and divide that up by the previous (or anticipated) number of summonses over 12 months so as to provide an average figure which could be levied across the board in "standard" cases, but could be amplified in circumstances where there was justification for incurring additional legal and/or administrative costs. If that approach is adopted, however, it is essential that the magistrates and their clerk are equipped with sufficient readily available information to enable the magistrates to check for themselves without too much difficulty, and relatively swiftly, that a legitimate approach has been taken, and to furnish a respondent with that information on request.

If the necessary causal link is established to the satisfaction of the court then the next question is whether the costs claimed have been "reasonably" incurred. It may be that the method by which the costs are calculated demonstrates this without the need for further evidence; but there may be individual cases in which it will be open to the respondent to argue that the costs were not reasonably incurred, for example, if it is not reasonable for the local authority to take steps to enforce payment, or if the costs which were incurred are excessive – eg if the local authority sends a QC along to argue a simple point of law in the magistrates' court.

Establishing that the costs are reasonably incurred is not the same thing as establishing that the costs are reasonable in amount. The latter may have a bearing on the former, since if the costs appear to be excessive, or disproportionate, there may be legitimate grounds for querying whether it was reasonable of the local authority to incur costs in that amount. So far as proportionality is concerned, in the context where the recoverable sums are relatively small it is inherently likely that there will be a disparity between those sums and the costs of recovering them. On the other hand, the practice of processing applications in bulk could drive the average costs of obtaining liability orders down rather than up.

Given the absence of any independent assessment, the scope for abuse of the system is self-evident, and that makes it all the more important that due process is observed. Therefore, it is incumbent upon the magistrates to reach a proper judicial determination of the amount of costs reasonably incurred by the applicant Council, in obtaining the liability order. They need to have sufficient information as to how the figure was arrived at and that the costs were incurred in obtaining the order and not, for example, in sending out council tax bills to all the taxpayers in the borough. See also *Nicolson v Grant Thornton UK LLP* [2016] EWHC 710 (Admin), [2016] 2 Costs LR 211. There is nothing to prevent a summons from stating on its face the amount of costs claimed by the local authority in connection with the complaint: *Williams v East Northamptonshire DC* [2016] EWHC 470 (Admin), [2016] RA 191. However, in *Ewing v Highbury Corner Magistrates' Court* [2015] EWHC 3788 (Admin), [2016] RVR 174 an order for costs was quashed. The court had not had sufficient relevant information to reach a proper determination of whether the costs claimed represented costs reasonably incurred by the local authority in obtaining the liability order.

**7.7657** *35. Liability orders: further provision* (1) A single liability order may deal with one person and one such amount (or aggregate amount) as is mentioned in regulation 34(7) and (8), or, if the court thinks fit, may deal with more than one person and more than one such amount.

(2) A summons issued under regulation 34(2) may be served on a person—

(*a*) by delivering it to him, or

(*b*) by leaving it at his usual or last known place of abode, or in the case of a company, at its registered office, or

(*c*) by sending it by post to him at his usual or last known place of abode, or in the case of a company, to its registered office, or

(*d*) by leaving it at, or by sending it by post to him at, an address given by the person as an address at which service of the summons will be accepted.

(2A) No liability order shall be made in pursuance of a summons issued under regulation 34(2) unless 14 days have elapsed since the day on which the summons was served.

(3) The amount in respect of which a liability order[1] is made is enforceable in accordance with this Part; and accordingly for the purposes of any of the provisions of Part III of the Magistrates' Courts Act 1980 (satisfaction and enforcement) it is not to be treated as a sum adjudged to be paid by order of the court.

[1] In addition to the remedies available under this Part, where a liability order has been made and the debtor is entitled to income support the billing authority concerned may apply to the Secretary of State asking him to deduct sums from any amounts payable to the debtor by way of income support in order to secure the payment of any outstanding sum which is or forms part of the amount in respect of which the liability order was made (Council Tax (Deductions from Income Support) Regulations 1993, SI 1993/494, reg 2).

**7.7658** *36. Duties of debtors subject to liability order* (1) Where a liability order has been made, the debtor against whom it was made shall, during such time as the amount in respect of which the order was made remains wholly or partly unpaid, be under a duty to supply relevant information to the billing authority on whose application it was made.

(2) For the purposes of paragraph (1), relevant information is such information as fulfils the following conditions—

(*a*) it is in the debtor's possession or control;

(*b*) the billing authority requests him by notice given in writing to supply it; and

(*c*) it falls within paragraph (3).

(3) Information falls within this paragraph if it is specified in the notice mentioned in paragraph (2)(*b*) and it falls within one or more of the following descriptions—

(*a*) information as to the name and address of an employer of the debtor;

(*b*) information as to earnings or expected earnings of the debtor;

(*c*) information as to deductions and expected deductions from such earnings in respect of the matters referred to in paragraphs (*a*) to (*c*) of the definition of "net earnings" in regulation 32 or attachment of earnings orders made under this Part, regulation 32 of the Community Charges (Administration and Enforcement) Regulations 1989, the Attachment of Earnings Act 1971 or the Child Support Act 1991;

(*d*) information as to the debtor's work or identity number in an employment, or such other information as will enable an employer of the debtor to identify him;

(*e*) information as to sources of income of the debtor other than an employer of his;

(*f*) information as to whether another person is jointly and severally liable with the debtor for the whole or any part of the amount in respect of which the order was made.

(4) Information is to be supplied within 14 days of the day on which the request is made.

**7.7659** *36A. Quashing of liability orders* (1) Where—

(*a*) a magistrates' court has made a liability order pursuant to regulation 34(6), and (*b*) the authority on whose application the liability order was made considers that the order should not have been made,

the authority may apply to a magistrates' court to have the liability order quashed.

(2) Where, on an application by an authority in accordance with paragraph (1) above, the magistrates' court is satisfied that the liability order should not have been made, it shall quash the order.

(3) Where an authority makes an application under paragraph (1) for a liability order ("the original order") to be quashed, and a lesser amount than the amount for which the original order was made has fallen due under paragraph (3) or (4) of regulation 23 (including those paragraphs as applied as mentioned in regulation 28A(2)) and is wholly or partly unpaid or (in a case where a final notice is required under regulation 33) the amount stated in the final notice is wholly or partly unpaid at the expiry of the period of seven days beginning with the day on which the notice was issued, the billing authority may also apply to the magistrates' court for an order against the person by whom the lesser amount was payable.

(4) Paragraphs (2) to (5) of regulation 34 shall apply to applications under paragraph (3) above.

(5) Where, having quashed a liability order in accordance with paragraph (2) above, the magistrates' court is satisfied that, had the original application for the liability order been for a liability order in respect of a lesser sum payable, such an order could properly have been made, it shall make a liability order in respect of the aggregate of—

(*a*) that lesser sum payable, and

(*b*) any sum included in the quashed order in respect of the costs reasonably incurred by the authority in obtaining the quashed order.

**7.7660** *37. Making of attachment of earnings order* (1) Where a liability order has been made and the debtor against whom it was made is an individual, the authority which applied for the order may, subject to paragraph (4), make an order under this regulation to secure the payment of the appropriate amount.

(1A) For the purposes of this regulation the appropriate amount is the aggregate of—

(*a*) any outstanding sum which is or forms part of the amount in respect of which the liability order was made.

(*b*) *revoked.*

(2) An order under this regulation—

(*a*) shall be in the form specified in (and accordingly contain the matters specified in) Schedule 3; and

(*b*) shall remain in force until discharged under regulation 41(2) or the whole amount to which it relates has been paid (whether by attachment of earnings or otherwise).

(3) The authority may serve a copy of the order on a person who appears to the authority to have the debtor in his employment; and a person on whom it is so served who has the debtor in his employment shall comply with it.

(4) No order may be made under this regulation by an authority if the effect would be that the number of orders for the time being in force made by that authority in relation to the debtor in question exceeded two.

**7.7661** *38. Deductions under attachment of earnings order* (1) Subject to paragraphs (2) and (3), the sum to be deducted by an employer under an attachment of earnings order on any pay-day shall be—

(*a*) where the debtor's earnings from the employer are payable weekly, a sum equal to the appropriate percentage of the net earnings otherwise payable on that pay-day; and for this purpose the appropriate percentage is the percentage (or percentages) specified in column 2 of Table A in Schedule 4 in relation to the band in column 1 of that Table within which the net earnings fall;

(*b*) where his earnings from the employer are payable monthly, a sum equal to the appropriate percentage of the net earnings otherwise payable on that pay-day; and for this purpose the appropriate percentage is the percentage (or percentages) specified in column 2 of Table B in that Schedule 4 in relation to the band in column 1 of Table within which the net earnings fall;

(*c*) where his earnings from the employer are payable at regular intervals of a whole number of weeks or months, the sum arrived at by—

(i) calculating what would be his weekly or monthly net earnings by dividing the net earnings payable to him by the employer on the pay-day by that whole number (of weeks or months, as the case may be),

(ii) ascertaining the percentage (or percentages) specified in column 2 of Table A (if the whole number is of weeks) or of Table B (if the whole number is of months) in Schedule 4 opposite the band in column 1 of that Table within which the notional net earnings calculated under paragraph (i) fall, and

(iii) calculating the sum which equals the appropriate percentage (or percentages) of the notional net earnings for any of those weeks or months and multiplying that sum by the whole number of weeks or months, as appropriate.

(2) Where paragraph (1) applies and the amount to be paid to the debtor on any pay-day includes an advance in respect of future pay, the sum to be deducted on that pay-day shall be the aggregate of the amount which would otherwise fall to be deducted under paragraph (1) and—

(*a*) where the amount advanced would otherwise have been paid on a single pay-day, the sum which would have been deducted on that pay-day in accordance with paragraph (1) if the amount advanced had been the amount of net earnings on that day; or (*b*) where the amount advanced would otherwise have been paid on more than one pay-day, the sums which would have been deducted on each of the relevant pay-days in accordance with paragraph (1) if—

(i) an equal proportion of the amount advanced had been paid on each of those days; and

(ii) the net earnings of the debtor on each of those days had been an amount equal to that proportion.

(3) Where the amount payable to the debtor on any pay-day is reduced by reason of an earlier advance of pay, the net earnings of the debtor on that day shall, for the purposes of paragraph (1), be the amount defined in regulation 32(1) less the amount of the deduction.

(4) Subject to paragraphs (5) and (6), where the debtor's earnings from the employer are payable at regular intervals other than at intervals to which paragraph (1) applies, the sum to be deducted on any pay-day shall be arrived at by—

(*a*) calculating what would be his daily net earnings by dividing the net earnings payable to him by the employer on the pay-day by the number of days in the interval,

(*b*) ascertaining the percentage (or percentages) specified in column 2 of Table C in Schedule 4 opposite the band in column 1 of that Table within which the notional net earnings calculated under sub-paragraph (*a*) fall, and

(*c*) calculating the sum which equals the appropriate percentage (or percentages) of the notional daily net earnings and multiplying that sum by the number of days in the interval.

(5) Where the debtor's earnings are payable as mentioned in paragraph (4), and the amount to be paid to the debtor on any pay-day includes an amount advanced in respect of future pay, the amount of the debtor's notional net earnings under sub-paragraph (*a*) of that paragraph shall be calculated in accordance with the formula—

$$\frac{A+B}{C+D}$$

where—

A is the amount of net earnings payable to him on that pay-day (exclusive of the amount advanced);

B is the amount advanced;

C is the number of days in the period for which the amount of net earnings is payable; and

D is the number of days in the period for which, but for the agreement to pay in advance, the amount advanced would have been payable.

(6) Paragraph (3) applies in relation to paragraph (4) as it applies in relation to paragraph (1).

(7) Where earnings are payable to a debtor by the employer by 2 or more series of payments at regular intervals—

(*a*) if some or all of the intervals are of different lengths—

(i) for the purpose of arriving at the sum to be deducted, whichever of paragraphs (1), (2), (3), (4), (5) and (6) is appropriate shall apply to the series with the shortest interval (or, if there is more than one series with the shortest interval, such one of those series as the employer may choose), and

(ii) in relation to the earnings payable in every other series, the sum to be deducted shall be 20 per cent of the net earnings or, where on any pay-day an amount advanced is also paid, 20 per cent of the aggregate of the net earnings and the amount advanced;

(*b*) if all of the intervals are of the same length, whichever of paragraphs (1), (2), (3), (4), (5) and (6) is appropriate shall apply to such series as the employer may choose and sub-paragraph (*a*)(ii) shall apply to every other series,

and paragraph (3) shall apply in relation to sub-paragraph (*a*)(ii) above as it applies in relation to paragraph (1).

(8) Subject to paragraphs (9) and (10), where the debtor's earnings from the employer are payable at irregular intervals, the sums to be deducted on any pay-day shall be arrived at by—

(*a*) calculating what would be his daily net earnings by dividing the net earnings payable to him by the employer on the pay-day—

(i) by the number of days since earnings were last payable by the employer to him, or

(ii) if the earnings are the first earnings to be payable by the employer to him with respect to the employment in question, by the number of days since he began the employment;

(*b*) ascertaining the percentage (or percentages) specified in column 2 of Table C of Schedule 4 opposite the band in column 1 of that Table within which the notional net earnings calculated under sub-paragraph (*a*) fall; and

(*c*) calculating the sum which equals the appropriate percentage (or percentages) of the daily net earnings and multiplying that sum by the same number as that of the divisor for the purposes of the calculation mentioned in sub-paragraph (*a*).

(9) Where on the same pay-day there are payable to the debtor by the employer both earnings payable at regular intervals and earnings payable at irregular intervals, for the purpose of arriving at the sum to be deducted on the pay-day under the foregoing provisions of this regulation all the earnings shall be aggregated and treated as earnings payable at the regular interval.

(10) Where there are earnings payable to the debtor by the employer at regular intervals on the pay-day, and earnings are payable by the employer to him at irregular intervals on a different pay-

day, the sum to be deducted on each of the pay-days on which the earnings which are payable at irregular intervals are so payable shall be 20 per cent of the net earnings payable to him on the day.

**7.7662** *39. Attachment of earnings orders: ancillary powers and duties of employers and others served* (1) An employer who deducts and pays amounts under an attachment of earnings order may, on each occasion that he makes such a deduction, also deduct from the debtor's earnings the sum of one pound towards his administrative costs.

(2) An employer who deducts and pays amounts under an attachment of earnings order shall, in accordance with paragraph (3), notify the debtor in writing of—

(*a*) the total amount of the sums (including sums deducted under paragraph (1)) deducted under the order up to the time of the notification; or

(*b*) the total amount of the sums (including sums deducted under paragraph (1)) that will fall to be so deducted after that time.

(3) A notification under paragraph (2) must be given at the time that the pay statement given by the employer to the debtor next after a deduction has been made is so given, or if no such statements are usually issued by the employer, as soon as practicable after a deduction has been made.

(4) A person on whom a copy of an attachment of earnings order has been served shall, in accordance with paragraph (5), notify in writing the authority which made the order if he does not have the debtor against whom it was made in his employment or the debtor subsequently ceases to be in his employment.

(5) A notification under paragraph (4) must be given within 14 days of the day on which the copy of the order was served on him or the debtor ceased to be in his employment (as the case may be).

(6) While an attachment of earnings order is in force, any person who becomes the debtor's employer and knows that the order is in force and by what authority it was made shall notify that authority in writing that he is the debtor's employer.

(7) A notification under paragraph (6) must be given within 14 days of the day on which the debtor became the person's employee or of the day on which the person first knows that the order is in force and the identity of the authority by which it was made, whichever is the later.

**7.7663** *40. Attachment of earnings orders: duties of debtor* (1) While an attachment of earnings order is in force, the debtor in respect of whom the order has been made shall notify in writing the authority which made it of each occasion when he leaves an employment or becomes employed or re-employed, and (in a case where he becomes so employed or re-employed) shall include in the notification a statement of—

(*a*) his earnings and (so far as he is able) expected earnings from the employment concerned,

(*b*) the deductions and (so far as he is able) expected deductions from such earnings—

(i) in respect of income tax;

(ii) in respect of primary Class 1 contributions under Part I of the Social Security Contributions and Benefits Act 1992;

(iii) for the purposes of such a superannuation scheme as is mentioned in the definition of "net earnings" in regulation 32(1),

(*c*) the name and address of the employer, and—

(*d*) his work or identity number in the employment (if any).

(2) A notification under paragraph (1) must be given within 14 days of the day on which the debtor leaves or commences (or recommences) the employment (as the case may be), or (if later) the day on which he is informed by the authority that the order has been made.

**7.7664** *41. Attachment of earnings orders: ancillary powers and duties of authority* (1) Where the whole amount to which an attachment of earnings order relates has been paid (whether by attachment of earnings or otherwise), the authority by which it was made shall give notice of the fact to any person who appears to it to have the debtor in his employment and who has been served with a copy of the order.

(2) The authority by which an attachment of earnings order was made may, on its own account or on the application of the debtor or an employer of the debtor, make an order discharging the attachment of earnings order; and if it does so it shall give notice of that fact to any person who appears to it to have the debtor in his employment and who has been served with a copy of the order.

(3) If an authority serves a copy of an attachment of earnings order in accordance with regulation 37(3), it shall (unless it has previously done so) also serve a copy of the order on the debtor.

**7.7665** *42. Priority as between orders* (1) Where an employer would, but for this paragraph, be obliged to make deductions on any pay-day under more than one attachment of earnings order, he shall—

(*a*) deal with the orders according to the respective dates on which they were made, disregarding any later order until an earlier one has been dealt with; and

(*b*) deal with any later order as if the earnings to which it relates were the residue of the debtor's earnings after the making of any deduction to comply with any earlier order.

(2) Subject to paragraph (3), where an employer would, but for this paragraph, be obliged to comply with one or more attachment of earnings order and with one or more deduction order, he shall deal with the orders according to the respective dates on which they were made in like manner as under paragraph (1).

(3) An employer shall not deal with a deduction order made either wholly or in part in respect of the payment of a judgment debt or payments under an administration order until he has dealt with

the attachment of earnings order or orders and any other deduction order.
(4) In this regulation "deduction order" means an order under the Attachment of Earnings Act 1971 or section 31(2) (deductions from earnings orders) of the Child Support Act 1991.

7.7666 *43. Attachment of earnings orders: persons employed under the Crown* (1) Where a debtor is in the employment of the Crown and an attachment of earnings order is made in respect of him, for the purposes of this Part—

(*a*) the chief officer for the time being of the department, office or other body in which the debtor is employed shall be treated as having the debtor in his employment (any transfer of the debtor from one department, office or body to another being treated as a change of employment); and

(*b*) any earnings paid by the Crown or a Minister of the Crown, or out of the public revenue of the United Kingdom, shall be treated as paid by that chief officer.

(2) If any question arises as to what department, office or other body is concerned for the purposes of this regulation, or as to who for those purposes is its chief officer, the question shall be referred to and determined by the Minister for the Civil Service.
(3) A document purporting to set out a determination of the Minister under paragraph (2) and to be signed by an official of the Office of that Minister shall, in any proceedings arising in relation to an attachment of earnings order, be admissible in evidence and be deemed to contain an accurate statement of such a determination unless the contrary is shown.
(4) This Part shall have effect in relation to attachment of earnings orders notwithstanding any enactment passed before 29th May 1970 and preventing or avoiding the attachment or diversion of sums due to a person in respect of services under the Crown; whether by way of remuneration, pension or otherwise.

7.7667 *44. Attachment of allowances orders* (1) This regulation applies in relation to an elected member of a relevant billing authority or a relevant precepting authority.
(2) For the purposes of this regulation—

(*a*) a relevant billing authority is a billing authority other than the Common Council;

(*b*) a relevant precepting authority is a major precepting authority other than the Receiver for the Metropolitan Police District;

(*c*) a person is an elected member of a relevant precepting authority other than a county council if he is appointed to the authority by a constituent council of which he is an elected member; and

(*d*) references to attachable allowances are references to the allowances referred to in paragraph (7)(*b*).

(3) Where a liability order has been made and the debtor against whom it was made is a person in relation to whom this regulation applies, the authority which applied for the order may make an order under this regulation to secure the payment of any outstanding sum which is or forms part of the amount in respect of which the liability order was made.
(4) An order under this regulation shall be expressed to be directed to the authority of whom the debtor is an elected member and shall operate as an instruction to the authority to make deductions from attachable allowances payable to the debtor and to pay the sums so deducted to the authority by which the order was made.
(5) An order under this regulation shall remain in force until discharged or the whole sum to which it relates has been paid (whether by attachment of allowances or otherwise).
(6) The sum to be deducted by an authority under an order under this regulation on any day shall be a sum equal to 40 per cent of the aggregate of attachable allowances payable to the debtor on that day.
(7) Paragraph (3) of regulation 37, paragraphs (1) to (5) of regulation 39 and paragraphs (1) and (2) of regulation 41 shall apply to orders under this regulation as they apply to attachment of earnings orders as if any reference in those paragraphs—

(*a*) to an employer or a person having the debtor in his employment, were a reference to such an authority as is mentioned in paragraph (1) above having the debtor as an elected member;

(*b*) to the debtor's earnings, were a reference to allowances—

  (i) payable to the debtor in accordance with a scheme under regulations under section 18 (schemes for basic, attendance and special responsibility allowances for local authority members) of the Local Government and Housing Act 1989; or

  (ii) in the nature of an attendance allowance, payable to the debtor under section 175 (allowances for attending conferences and meetings) of the Local Government Act 1972;

(*c*) to an attachment of earnings order, were a reference to an order under this regulation.

7.7668 *45. Enforcement by taking control of goods* Where a liability order has been made, payment may be enforced by using the Schedule 12 procedure.

7.7671 *47. Commitment to prison*[1] (1) Where a billing authority has sought to enforce payment by use of the Schedule 12 procedure pursuant to regulation 45, the debtor is an individual who has attained the age of 18 years, and the enforcement agent reports to the authority that he was unable (for whatever reason) to find any or sufficient goods of the debtor to enforce payment [2], the authority may apply to a magistrates' court for the issue of a warrant committing the debtor to prison[3].
(2) On such application being made the court shall (in the debtor's presence) inquire as to his means and inquire whether the failure to pay which has led to the application is due to his wilful

refusal or culpable neglect[4].

(3) If (and only if) the court is of the opinion that his failure is due to his wilful refusal or culpable neglect[5] it may if it thinks fit[6]—

(*a*) issue a warrant of commitment against the debtor, or

(*b*) fix a term of imprisonment and postpone[7] the issue of the warrant until such time and on such conditions[8] (if any) as the court thinks just.

(4) The warrant shall be made in respect of the relevant amount; and the relevant amount for this purpose is the aggregate of—

(*a*) an amount equal to the amount outstanding (within the meaning of Schedule 12), and

(*b*) a sum of an amount equal to the costs reasonably incurred by the applicant in respect of the application.

(5) The warrant—

(*a*) shall state the relevant amount mentioned in paragraph (4),

(*b*) may be directed to the authority making the application and to such other persons (if any) as the court issuing it thinks fit, and

(*c*) may be executed anywhere in England and Wales by any person to whom it is directed.

(6) If—

(*a*) before a warrant has been issued, or a term of imprisonment fixed and the issue of a warrant postponed, an amount determined in accordance with paragraph (6A) below is paid or tendered to the authority, or

(*b*) after a term of imprisonment has been fixed and the issue of a warrant postponed, the amount (if any) the court has ordered the debtor to pay is paid or tendered to the authority, or

(*c*) after a warrant has been issued, the amount stated in it is paid or tendered to the authority,

the authority shall accept the amount concerned, no further steps shall be taken as regards its recovery, and the debtor, if committed to prison, shall be released.

(6A) The amount referred to in paragraph (6)(*a*) above is the aggregate of—

(*a*) the amount outstanding (within the meaning of Schedule 12), and

(*b*) subject to paragraph (6B) below, the authority's reasonable costs incurred up to the time of payment or tender in making one or more of the applications referred to in Schedule 6.

(6B) For the purposes of paragraph (6A)(*b*) above, the authority's reasonable costs in respect of any application shall not exceed the amount specified for that application in Schedule 6.

(7) The order in the warrant shall be that the debtor be imprisoned for a time specified[9] in the warrant which shall not exceed 3 months, unless the amount stated in the warrant is sooner paid; but—

(*a*) where a warrant is issued after a postponement under paragraph (3)(*b*) and, since the term of imprisonment was fixed but before the issue of the warrant, the amount mentioned in paragraph (4)(*a*) with respect to which the warrant would (but for the postponement) have been made has been reduced by a part payment, the period of imprisonment ordered under the warrant shall be the term fixed under paragraph (3) reduced by such number of days as bears to the total number of days in that term less one day the same proportion as the part paid bears to that amount, and

(*b*) where, after the issue of a warrant, a part payment of the amount stated in it is made, the period of imprisonment shall be reduced by such number of days as bears to the total number of days in the term of imprisonment specified in the warrant less one day the same proportion as the part paid bears to the amount so stated.

(8) In calculating a reduction required under paragraph (7) any fraction of a day shall be left out of account; and rule 55(1), (2) and (3) of the Magistrates' Courts Rules 1981 applies (so far as is relevant) to a part payment as if the imprisonment concerned were imposed for want of sufficient distress to satisfy a sum adjudged to be paid by a magistrates' court.

---

[1] Cases decided under the similarly worded reg 41 of the Community Charge etc Regulations 1989 are still useful sources of reference and have, therefore, been included in the footnotes to this regulation. The power to commit to prison is plainly intended to be used as a weapon to extract payment rather than to punish (*R v Wolverhampton Magistrates' Court, ex p Mould* [1992] RA 309) and is a perfectly proper means of extracting payment from a person possessed of income or assets who has been guilty of wilful refusal (*R v Oldbury Justices, ex p Smith* (1994) 159 JP 316). Justices retain a discretion and the Regulations do not limit the power to commit to prison to those cases in which every other possibility has been exhaustively explored (*R v Newcastle-under-Lyme Justices, ex p K A Massey* (26 May 1993, unreported). Nevertheless, before committing a debtor to prison, it is incumbent upon justices to consider all available alternatives to effect the recovery of the sum due (*R v Middleton Magistrates, ex p Phillips* (29 October 1993, unreported).

[2] It is unnecessary for the justices to determine the existence of these preconditions to the local authority's decision to apply for a warrant of commitment; the procedure adopted by the local authority, however, may be challenged on proceedings for judicial review (*R v Dudley Justices, ex p Blatchford* (1992) 156 JP 846).

[3] It is not necessary for the charging authority to call evidence to establish the requirements of sub-s (1); the application need not be by way of complaint and therefore would not be subject to the time limit contained in s 127 of the Magistrates' Court Act 1980 (*R v Wolverhampton Magistrates' Court* (1992) 157 JP 1017).

[4] This must be a separate inquiry into the circumstances relevant under reg 47 for each separate year of liability: *R (on the application of Aldous) v Dartford Magistrates' Court and Gravesham Borough Council* [2011] EWHC 1919 (Admin), (2011) 175 JP 445.

[5] If the basis of the decision is that the defaulter had earning capacity which he chose not to use, there must at least be clear evidence that gainful employment for which he was fit was on offer to the defaulter which he had rejected; the proper date for assessing his means is when the court hears the application for commitment (See *R v Poole Justices, ex p Benham* (1991) 156 JP 177).

[6] Justices must consider the issue of wilful refusal or culpable neglect separately from the question of the appropriate disposal. Accordingly, where justices find that the debtor has wilfully refused to pay, it does not follow that the court has no alternative other than to order the immediate issue of the warrant of commitment. It is incumbent on the justices, in such circumstances, to consider any offer to pay and if they deem it inappropriate to fix a term of imprisonment and postpone the issue of the warrant on terms, they must give reasons for so deciding (*R v Middleton Magistrates, ex p*

*Phillips* (29 October 1993, unreported)). See also *R v Alfreton Justices, ex p Gratton* (1993)Times, 7 December. However in *R v Oldbury Justices, ex p Smith* (1994) 159 JP 316 Turner J doubted the need to give reasons for making a finding of wilful refusal or culpable neglect given that the appropriate route of appeal was by way of case stated in which the justices' reasons would be made apparent.

[7] The court may take into account the attitude of a spouse where the charge payer is financially dependent upon that spouse (*R v Ramsgate Magistrates' Court, ex p Haddow* (1992) 157 JP 545). In proceedings for recovery of the Community Charge under the Community Charges (Administration and Enforcement) Regulations 1989, SI 1989/712, it was held that the principles governing the exercise of discretion under reg 41(3)(*a*) and (*b*) of the 1989 regs were different; justices were not obliged to exhaust all possibilities of recovering unpaid community charge before making a suspended committal order (*R v Preston Justices, ex p McCosh* (1995) Times, 30 January). We would suggest that this reasoning remains applicable to reg 47(3)(*a*) and (*b*) of the 1992 regulations. Where the court postpones the issue of the warrant of commitment, it will not be lawful for the warrant to be issued without there being a further hearing, on the application of the local authority, of which the debtor must be given notice of the date and purpose of the hearing, and an opportunity of attending. The magistrates must be satisfied that the council tax payer has received notice of the hearing and must carry out an appropriate inquiry to make sure that the notice must have come into his hands. Accordingly the notice should be sent by recorded delivery, see *R v Newcastle upon Tyne Justices, ex p Devine* (1998) 162 JP 602, DC (a case decided under the similarly worded reg 41 of the Community Charge (Administration and Enforcement) Regulations 1989, SI 1989/712). At that hearing the debtor is entitled to put the local authority to proof of non-payment and non-compliance with the conditions of postponement; and to draw the court's attention to any change of circumstances since the decision to fix the terms of imprisonment which renders it inexpedient for the warrant to issue (*R v Faversham and Sittingbourne Magistrates' Court, ex p Ursell* (1992) 156 JP 765). See also *R v Northampton Justices, ex p Newell* (1992) 157 JP 869. Before it can activate the committal order, the court must be satisfied that the debtor has had the ability to pay the instalment order, or otherwise comply with the conditions on which the issue of the warrant was postponed, but has failed to do so; see *R v Felixstowe Justices, ex p Herridge* [1993] RA 83.

[8] When postponing the issue of a warrant on terms as to the repayment of the sum due by instalments, the court should be mindful of the principles applicable to the payment of fines in criminal cases. If satisfied that the particular person in front of the court is a person of limited means and if such an order is contemplated, the appropriate course is to remit such part of the arrears as will reduce the total sum in respect of which the order is made to a sum which can be met by the instalments envisaged within a reasonable period and certainly not a period in excess of three years (*R v Newcastle upon Tyne Justices, ex p Devine* (1998) 162 JP 602, DC (a case decided under the similarly worded reg 41 of the Community Charge (Administration and Enforcement) Regulations 1989, SI 1989/712).

[9] In an application for judicial review of a decision under reg 16 of the Non-Domestic Rating (Collection etc) Regulations 1989, post, the High Court held that, when determining the period of imprisonment to be specified in the warrant, the justices must have regard to the principle of proportionality. The more serious the case, whether in terms of the amount outstanding or in terms of the degree of culpability or blame to be attached to the debtor for his non-payment, the closer will any period imposed approach the maximum. A finding of wilful refusal, in this respect, represents a more serious state of affairs than culpable neglect; see *R v Highbury Corner Magistrates' Court, ex p Uchendu* (1994) 158 JP 409. It follows that, to fix the appropriate term, the court must decide which of culpable neglect or wilful refusal led to the failure to pay: *R (on the application of Aldous) v Dartford Magistrates' Court and Gravesham Borough Council* (supra).

**7.7672** *48. Commitment to prison: further provision* (1) A single warrant may not be issued under regulation 47 against more than one person.

(2) Where an application under regulation 47 has been made, and after the making of the inquiries mentioned in paragraph (2) of that regulation no warrant is issued or term of imprisonment fixed, the court may remit[1] all or part of the appropriate amount mentioned in regulation 45(2) with respect to which the application related.

(3) Where an application under regulation 47 has been made but no warrant is issued or term of imprisonment fixed, the application may be renewed (except so far as regards any sum remitted under paragraph (2)) on the ground that the circumstances of the debtor have changed.

(4) A statement in writing to the effect that wages of any amount have been paid to the debtor during any period, purporting to be signed by or on behalf of his employer, shall in any proceedings under regulation 47 be evidence of the facts there stated.

(5) For the purpose of enabling inquiry to be made as to the debtor's conduct and means under regulation 47, a justice of the peace may—

(*a*) issue a summons to him to appear before a magistrates' court and (if he does not obey the summons) issue a warrant for his arrest, or

(*b*) issue a warrant for the debtor's arrest without issuing a summons.

(6) A warrant issued under paragraph (5) may be executed anywhere in England and Wales by any person to whom it is directed or by any constable acting within his police area; and section 125(3) of the Magistrates' Courts Act 1980 applies to such a warrant.

(7) Regulation 47 and this regulation have effect subject to Part I of the Criminal Justice Act 1982 (treatment of young offenders).

---

[1] In cases decided under the similarly worded reg 42 of the Community Charge etc Regulations 1989 it is maintained that if the court has come to the conclusion that there has been wilful refusal or culpable neglect, then it must proceed accordingly and it is not open to contend that there is a discretion to remit all or part of the appropriate amount (*R v Oldbury Justices, ex p Smith* (1994) 159 JP 316) and that there is no inherent power available to justices to remit a community charge debt once a term of imprisonment has been fixed or a warrant of commitment has been issued (*Harrogate Borough Council v Barker* (1995) 159 JP 809).

**7.7673** *49. Insolvency* (1) Where a liability order has been made and the debtor against whom it was made is an individual, the amount due shall be deemed to be a debt for the purposes of section 267 of the Insolvency Act 1986 (grounds of creditor's petition).

(2) Where a liability order has been made and the debtor against whom it was made is a company, the amount due shall be deemed to be a debt for the purposes of section 122(1)(*f*) (winding up of companies by the court) or, as the case may be, section 221(5)(*b*) (winding up of unregistered companies) of that Act.

(3) For the purposes of this regulation the amount due is an amount equal to any outstanding sum which is or forms part of the amount in respect of which the liability order was made.

**7.7674** *50. Charging orders* (1) An application to the appropriate court may be made under this regulation where—

(*a*) a magistrates' court has made one or more liability orders pursuant to either regulation 34(6) or 36A(5);

(*b*) the amount mentioned in regulation 34(7)(*a*) or 36A(5)(*a*) in respect of which the liability order was made, or, where more than one liability order was made, the aggregate of the amounts mentioned in regulation 34(7)(*a*) or 36A(5)(*a*) in respect of which each such liability order was made, is an amount the debtor is liable to pay under Part V; and

(*c*) at the time that the application under this regulation is made at least £1000 of the amount in respect of which the liability order was made, or, where more than one liability order was made, the aggregate of the amounts in respect of which those liability orders were made, remains outstanding.

(2) The application which may be made to the appropriate court under this regulation is an application by the authority concerned for an order imposing, on any interest held by the debtor beneficially in the relevant dwelling, a charge for securing the due amount; and the court may make such an order on such application.

(3) For the purposes of paragraph (2)—

(*a*) the authority concerned is the authority which applied for the one or more liability orders referred to in paragraph (1)(*a*);

(*b*) the relevant dwelling is the dwelling in respect of which, at the time the application for the liability order was made, or, where more than one liability order was made, at the time the applications for the liability orders were made, the debtor was liable to pay council tax;

(*c*) the due amount is the aggregate of—

(i) an amount equal to any outstanding sum which is or forms part of the amount in respect of which the one or more liability orders were made; and

(ii) a sum of an amount equal to the costs reasonably incurred by the applicant in obtaining the charging order;

(*d*) the appropriate court is the county court for the area in which the relevant dwelling is situated.

**7.7675** 51. *Charging orders: further provision* (1) In deciding whether to make a charging order, the court shall consider all the circumstances of the case, and in particular any evidence before it as to—

(*a*) the personal circumstances of the debtor, and

(*b*) whether any other person would be likely to be unduly prejudiced by the making of the order.

(2) A charging order—

(*a*) shall specify the dwelling concerned and the interest held by the debtor beneficially in it, and

(*b*) may, as the court thinks fit, be made absolutely or subject to conditions as to the time when the charge is to become enforceable or as to other matters.

(3) A charge imposed by a charging order shall have the like effect and shall be enforceable in the same courts and in the same manner as an equitable charge created by the debtor by writing under his hand.

(4) The court by which a charging order was made may at any time, on the application of the debtor, the authority on whose application the order was made or any person interested in the dwelling, make an order discharging or varying the charging order.

(5) The Land Charges Act 1972 and the Land Registration Act 1925 shall apply in relation to charging orders as they apply in relation to orders or writs issued or made for the purposes of enforcing judgments; and in section 49(1)(*g*) of the Land Registration Act 1925, after the words "Local Government Finance Act 1988" there are inserted the words ", or regulations under paragraph 11 of Schedule 4 to the Local Government Finance Act 1992".

(6) Where a charging order has been protected by an entry registered under the Land Charges Act 1972 or the Land Registration Act 1925, an order under paragraph (4) discharging the charging order may direct that the entry be cancelled.

**7.7676** 52. *Relationship between remedies* (1) Where a warrant of commitment is issued against (or a term of imprisonment is fixed in the case of) a person under regulation 47(3), no steps, or no further steps, may be taken under this Part by way of attachment of allowances, attachment of earnings, the Schedule 12 procedure, bankruptcy or charging, or under the Income Support Regulations in relation to the relevant amount mentioned in regulation 47(4).

(2) Steps under this Part by way of attachment of allowances, attachment of earnings, the Schedule 12 procedure, commitment, bankruptcy, winding up or charging may not be taken in relation to a person against whom a liability order has been made while—

(*a*) steps by way of another of those methods are being taken against him under it; or

(*b*) deductions are being made under the Income Support Regulations from any amount payable to him by way of income support, universal credit or jobseeker's allowance; or

(*c*) an application under regulation 2 of the Income Support Regulations has been made in respect of him to the Secretary of State and remains undetermined.

(2A) An application under regulation 2 of the Income Support Regulations may not be made in respect of a person against whom a liability order has been made while steps under this Part are being taken against him for the recovery of an amount equal to any outstanding sum which is or forms part of the amount in respect of which the liability order was made.

(3) Subject to paragraphs (1) and (2)—

(*a*) attachment of allowances, attachment of earnings, deductions under the Income Support Regulations or the Schedule 12 procedure may be resorted to more than once, and

(*b*) attachment of allowances, attachment of earnings, deductions under the Income Support Regulations or the Schedule 12 procedure may be resorted to in any order or alternately (or both).

(4) Where a step is taken for the recovery of an outstanding sum which is or forms part of an amount in respect of which a liability order has been made and under which additional costs or charges with respect to the step are also recoverable in accordance with this Part, any sum recovered thereby which is less than the aggregate of the amount outstanding and such additional costs and charges shall be treated as discharging first the costs and charges, the balance (if any) being applied towards the discharge of the outstanding sum.

**7.7677** *53. Magistrates' courts* (1) *Revoked.*

(1A) *Revoked.*

(2) Subject to any other enactment authorising a District Judge (Magistrates' Courts) or other person to act by himself, a magistrates' court shall not under this Part hear a summons, entertain an application for a warrant or hold an inquiry as to means on such an application except when composed of at least two justices.

(3) References to a justice of the peace in regulations 34(2) and 46(2) shall be construed subject to rule 3 of the Justices' Clerks Rules 1970 (which authorises certain matters authorised to be done by a justice of the pace to be done by a justices' clerk).

(4) In any proceedings under regulation 34 (application for liability order) or regulation 47 (commitment to prison), a statement contained in a document constituting or forming part of a record compiled by the applicant authority or an authorised person[1] shall be admissible as evidence of any fact stated in it of which direct oral evidence would be admissible.

(5) In proceedings where the applicant authority or an authorised person[1] desires to give a statement in evidence in accordance with paragraph (4), and the document containing that statement is produced by a computer, a certificate—

(*a*) identifying the document containing the statement and the computer by which it was produced;

(*b*) containing a statement that at all material times the computer was operating properly, or if not, that any respect in which it was not operating properly or was out of operation was not such as to affect the production of the document or the accuracy of its contents;

(*c*) giving such explanation as may be appropriate of the content of the document; and

(*d*) purporting to be signed by a person occupying a responsible position in relation to the operation of the computer,

shall be admissible as evidence of anything which is stated in it to the best of the signatory's information and belief.

(6) In paragraph (4) above, "statement" includes any representation of fact, whether made in words or otherwise; and the reference to an application under regulation 47 includes a reference to an application made in the circumstances mentioned in regulation 48(3).

[1] A billing authority may authorise another person, or that person's employees, to exercise functions relating to the administration and enforcement of the council tax: see the Local Authorities (Contracting Out of Tax Billing, Collection and Enforcement Functions) Order 1996, SI 1996/1880.

**7.7678** *54. Joint and several liability: enforcement* (1) This regulation has effect with respect to the application of regulations 33 to 53 to a sum for which persons are jointly and severally liable under Part V.

(2) In this regulation, "joint taxpayers" means two or more individuals who are jointly and severally liable to pay an amount in respect of council tax.

(3) A final notice served in accordance with regulation 33 on every person against whom the application for a liability order is to be made may be addressed to two or more joint taxpayers in joint names.

(3A) A summons under regulation 34(2) may be addressed to two or more joint taxpayers in joint names.

(4) A liability order may be made against one or more joint taxpayers in respect of an amount for which they are jointly and severally liable.

(5) Where a liability order has been made against two or more joint taxpayers, subject to paragraphs (6) and 6(A)—

(*a*) an attachment of allowances order or an attachment of earnings order may be made against one of them, or different such orders may be made against more than one;

(*b*) the Schedule 12 procedure may be used against one or more of them;

(*c*) a charging order may be made against one of them, or against more than one jointly, or different such orders may be made against more than one of them (as the circumstances require); and

(*d*) deductions may be made under the Income Support Regulations from any amount payable to one or more of them by way of income support or universal credit.

(6) Where a liability order has been made against two or more joint taxpayers in respect of an amount, steps by way of any method specified in paragraph (5)—

(*a*) may not be taken under it in respect of one of them while steps by way of that or another of those methods are being taken under it in respect of another of them; and

(*b*) may be taken under it in respect of one of them notwithstanding that no steps by way of that or another of those methods have been taken under it in respect of another of them.

(6A) Where a liability order has been made against two or more joint taxpayers and an amount is payable to one of them by way of income support or universal credit and—

(*a*) deductions are being made under the Income Support Regulations from any such amount; or

(*b*) an application under regulation 2 of those Regulations has been made in respect of him to the Secretary of State and remains undetermined.

no steps, or no further steps, by way of attachment of allowances or earnings, distress, commitment, bankruptcy or charging may be taken, under that or any other liability order, against him or any other of those joint taxpayers who is a member of his family.

(6B) In paragraph (6A) above—

"income support" means income support within the meaning of the Social Security Contributions and Benefits Act 1992; and

"family" has the same meaning as in section 137(1) of that Act.

(7) Where the Schedule 12 procedure has been used against two or more joint taxpayers in respect of an amount a warrant of commitment may, subject to paragraph (8), be applied for at any time against one of them or different warrants may be applied for against more than one of them: but no such application may be made in respect of any of them who has not attained the age of 18 years.

(8) Where a liability order has been made against two or more joint taxpayers in respect of an amount, a warrant of commitment may not be applied for unless—

(*a*) distress has been made against all of them; and

(*b*) the person making the distress reports to the authority that, in relation to each of them, he was unable (for whatever reason) to find any or sufficient goods.

(9) Where a liability order has been made against two or more joint taxpayers in respect of an amount, and a warrant of commitment is issued against (or a term of imprisonment is fixed in the case of) one of them under regulation 47(3), no steps, or no further steps, may be taken against any of them by way of attachment of allowances or earnings, the Schedule 12 procedure, bankruptcy or charging in relation to the amount mentioned in regulation 47(4).

(9A) Where a liability order has been made against persons who are joint taxpayers, and a warrant of commitment is issued against (or a term of imprisonment is fixed in the case of) one of them under regulation 47(3), no steps, or further steps, may be taken under the Income Support Regulations in respect of any of them in relation to the amount mentioned in regulation 47(4).

(10) Where a liability order has been made against two or more joint taxpayers in respect of an amount and in using the Schedule 12 procedure against one of them goods jointly owned by both or all of them are found, control may be taken of those goods with respect to that amount; but in any subsequent proceedings under regulation 47 (commitment), charges arising under the Taking Control of Goods (Fees) Regulations 2014 from the use of the Schedule 12 procedure shall be treated as charges relating to the person against whose goods the Schedule 12 procedure was intended to be used when the joint goods were found, and not as charges relating to the other or others.

(11) Where—

(*a*) a liability order has been made against more than one person in respect of an amount; and

(*b*) a charge has arisen against one of them for the enforcement stage within the meaning of regulation 5 of the Taking Control of Goods (Fees) Regulations 2014 in respect of that amount,

no further charge for the enforcement stage or compliance stage (within the meaning of regulation 5 of the Taking Control of Goods (Fees) Regulations 2014) in consequence of any further use or attempted use of the Schedule 12 procedure in respect of that amount may be recovered from any of them; and a charge for the compliance stage shall be treated for those purposes as a charge with respect to the others as well as that one.

**7.7679** *55. Repayments* A sum which has become payable (by way of repayment) under Part V to a person other than a billing authority but which has not been paid shall be recoverable in a court of competent jurisdiction.

**7.7680** *56. Offences* (1) A person shall be guilty of an offence if, following a request under paragraph (2)(*b*) of regulation 36, he is under a duty to supply information and—

(*a*) he fails without reasonable excuse to supply the information in accordance with that regulation, or

(*b*) in supplying information in purported compliance with that regulation he makes a statement which is false in a material particular or recklessly makes a statement which is false in a material particular.

(2) Subject to paragraph (3), a person shall be guilty of an offence if, following the service on him of a copy of an attachment of allowances order or an attachment of earnings order, he is under a duty to comply with the order by virtue of regulation 37(3) (including that provision as applied for the purposes of attachment of allowances orders by regulation 44(7)) and he fails to do so.

(3) It shall be a defence for a person charged with an offence under paragraph (2) to prove that he took all reasonable steps to comply with the order.

(4) A person shall be guilty of an offence if he is under a duty to notify another person under regulation 39(2) and (3) or (4) and (5) (including those provisions as applied for the purposes of attachment of allowances orders by regulation 44(7)), regulation 39(6) and (7) or regulation 40 and—

(*a*) he fails without reasonable excuse to notify the other person in accordance with the provision concerned, or

(*b*) in notifying the other person in purported compliance with the provision concerned he makes a statement which he knows to be false in a material particular or recklessly makes a statement which is false in a material particular.

(5) A person guilty of an offence under paragraph (1)(*a*) or (4)(*a*) shall be liable on summary

conviction to a fine not exceeding level 2 on the standard scale.

(6) A person guilty of an offence under paragraph (1)(*b*), (2) or (4)(*b*) shall be liable on summary conviction to a fine not exceeding level 3 on the standard scale.

7.7681 *57. Miscellaneous provisions* (1) Any matter which could be the subject of an appeal under section 16 of the Act or regulations under section 24 of the Act may not be raised in proceedings under this Part[1].

(2) If a liability order has been made and by virtue of—

(*a*) a notification which is given by the billing authority or an authorised person under regulation 24(2) or (5), 25(5) or (8), 28(3) or (4) or 31(2), or paragraph 9(3) or 10(2)(*a*) of Schedule 1, or

(*b*) section 31(4) of the Act applying in any case,

any part of the amount mentioned in regulation 34(5)(*a*) in respect of which the order was made would (if paid) fall to be repaid or credited against any subsequent liability, that part shall be treated for the purposes of this Part as paid on the day the notification is given or the amount in substitution is set under section 31(2) of the Act and accordingly is no longer outstanding.

(3) If, after a warrant is issued or term of imprisonment is fixed under regulation 47(3), and before the term of imprisonment has begun or been fully served, a billing authority gives such a notification as is mentioned in paragraph (2)(*a*) in the case in question, or sets an amount in substitution so that section 31(4) of the Act applies in the case in question, it shall forthwith notify accordingly the designated officer for the court which issued the warrant and (if the debtor is detained) the governor or keeper of the prison or place where he is detained or such other person as has lawful custody of him.

(4) If the debtor is treated as having paid an amount under paragraph (2) on any day, and

(*a*) that day falls after the completion of the service of a term of imprisonment imposed under regulation 47 in respect of the amount he is treated as having paid, or

(*b*) the debtor is serving a term of imprisonment imposed under regulation 47 on that day and the amount he is treated as having paid exceeds the amount of any part payment which, if made, would cause the expiry of the term of imprisonment pursuant to paragraph (7)(*b*) of that regulation on that day,

the amount mentioned in sub-paragraph (*a*) or excess mentioned in sub-paragraph (*b*) shall be paid to the debtor or credited against any subsequent liability of his, as the debtor requires.

---

[1] The substantial merits of a billing authority's decision regarding an individual's liability are matters for a valuation tribunal and cannot be raised before the magistrates' court in enforcement proceedings; where an issue as to liability is raised it may be sensible to adjourn the enforcement application to await the decision of the valuation tribunal: *Wiltshire Council v Piggin* [2014] EWHC 4386 (Admin), [2015] RVR 45.

## Part VII
### *Miscellaneous*

7.7682 *58. Outstanding liabilities on death* (1) This regulation applies where a person dies and at any time before his death—

(*a*) he was (or is alleged to have been) liable to pay council tax under section 6, 7 or 8 of the Act, or

(*b*) he was (or is alleged to have been) so liable, as spouse or civil partner, under section 9 of the Act, or

(*c*) a penalty was imposed on him under any of sub-paragraphs (1) to (3) of paragraph 1 of Schedule 3 to the Act or under any of regulations 11 to 13 of the Detection of Fraud Regulations.

(2) Where—

(*a*) before the deceased's death a sum has become payable by him under Part V or by way of relevant costs in respect of one of the matters mentioned in paragraph (1) but has not been paid, or

(*b*) after the deceased's death a sum would, but for his death (and whether or not on the service of a notice), become payable by him under Part V in respect of one of those matters,

his executor or administrator shall, subject to paragraph (3) and to the extent that it is not in excess of the deceased's liability under the Act (including relevant costs payable by him) in respect of the matter, be liable to pay the sum and may deduct out of the assets and effects of the deceased any payments made (or to be made).

(3) Where paragraph (2)(*b*) applies, the liability of the executor or administrator does not arise until the service on him of a notice requiring payment of the sum.

(4) Where before the deceased's death a sum in excess of his liability under the Act (including relevant costs payable by him) in respect of one of the matters mentioned in paragraph (1) has been paid (whether the excess arises because of his death or otherwise) and has not been repaid or credited under Part V, his executor or administrator shall be entitled to the sum.

(5) Costs are relevant costs for the purposes of paragraphs (2) and (4) if—

(*a*) an order or warrant (as the case may be) was made by the court in respect of them before the deceased's death under regulation 34(7)(*b*) or (8), 36A(5)(*b*), 47(4)(*b*) or 50(3)(*c*)(ii), or

(*b*) they are charges which may be recovered pursuant to the Taking Control of Goods (Fees) Regulations 2014.

(6) A sum payable under paragraph (2) shall be enforceable in the administration of the deceased's estate as a debt of the deceased and accordingly—

(*a*) no liability order need be applied for in respect of it after the deceased's death under regulation 34, and

(*b*) the liability of the executor or administrator is a liability in his capacity as such.

(7) Regulation 57(1) applies to proceedings to enforce a liability arising under this regulation as it applies to proceedings under Part VI.

(8) Insofar as is relevant to his liability under this regulation in the administration of the deceased's estate, the executor or administrator may institute, continue or withdraw proceedings (whether by way of appeal under section 16 of the Act or otherwise).

SCHEDULE 1
COUNCIL TAX INSTALMENT SCHEMES
Regulation 21

SCHEDULE 3
FORM OF ATTACHMENT OF EARNINGS ORDER
Regulation 37

SCHEDULE 4
DEDUCTIONS TO BE MADE UNDER ATTACHMENT OF EARNINGS ORDER

SCHEDULE 6
COSTS CONNECTED WITH COMMITTAL
Regulation 47(6A) and (6B)

7.7684

| (1) *Application* | (2) *Maximum costs* |
|---|---|
| For making an application for a warrant of commitment: | £305.00. |
| For making an application for a warrant of arrest: | £145.00. |

## Non-Domestic Rating (Unoccupied Property) (England) Regulations 2008[1]

(SI 2008/386 amended by SI 2009/353, SI 2010/408, SI 2015/1641 and SI 2017/102)

**7.7685** 1. *Citation, application and commencement* These Regulations, which apply in relation to England only, may be cited as the Non-Domestic Rating (Unoccupied Property) (England) Regulations 2008 and shall come into force on 1st April 2008.

[1] Made by the Secretary of State, in exercise of the powers conferred by ss 45(1)(*d*), (9) and (10), 143(2) and 146(6) of the Local Government Finance Act 1988.

**7.7686** 2. *Interpretation* In these Regulations—

"qualifying industrial hereditament" means any hereditament other than a retail hereditament in relation to which all buildings comprised in the hereditament are—

(*a*) constructed or adapted for use in the course of a trade or business; and

(*b*) constructed or adapted for use for one or more of the following purposes, or one or more such purposes and one or more purposes ancillary thereto—

(i) the manufacture, repair or adaptation of goods or materials, or the subjection of goods or materials to any process;

(ii) storage (including the storage or handling of goods in the course of their distribution);

(iii) the working or processing of minerals; and

(iv) the generation of electricity;

"relevant non-domestic hereditament" means any non-domestic hereditament consisting of, or of part of, any building, together with any land ordinarily used or intended for use for the purposes of the building or part;

"retail hereditament" means any hereditament where any building or part of a building comprised in the hereditament is constructed or adapted for the purpose of the retail provision of—

(*a*) goods, or

(*b*) services, other than storage for distribution services, where the services are to be provided on or from the hereditament; and

"the Act" means the Local Government Finance Act 1988.

**7.7687** 3. *Hereditaments prescribed for the purposes of section 45(1)(d) of the Act* The class of non-domestic hereditaments prescribed for the purposes of section 45(1)(*d*) of the Act consists of all relevant non-domestic hereditaments other than those described in regulation 4.

**7.7688** 4. *Hereditaments not prescribed for the purposes of section 45(1)(d) of the Act* The relevant non-domestic hereditaments described in this regulation are any hereditament—

(*a*) which, subject to regulation 5, has been unoccupied for a continuous period not exceeding three months;

(*b*) which is a qualifying industrial hereditament that, subject to regulation 5, has been unoccupied for a continuous period not exceeding six months;

(*c*) whose owner is prohibited by law from occupying it or allowing it to be occupied;

(*d*) which is kept vacant by reason of action taken by or on behalf of the Crown or any local or public authority with a view to prohibiting the occupation of the hereditament or to acquiring it;

(*e*) which is the subject of a building preservation notice within the meaning of the Planning (Listed Buildings and Conservation Areas) Act 1990 or is included in a list compiled under section 1 of that Act;

(*f*) which is included in the Schedule of monuments compiled under section 1 of the Ancient Monuments and Archaeological Areas Act 1979;

(*g*) whose rateable value is less than—

(i) in relation to the financial year beginning on 1st April 2008, £2,200;

(ii) in relation to the financial year beginning on 1st April 2009, £15,000;

(iii) in relation to the financial year beginning on 1st April 2010, £18,000;

(iv) in relation to the financial years beginning on 1st April 2011, 1st April 2012, 1st April 2013, 1st April 2014, 1st April 2015 and 1st April 2016, £2,600;

(v) in relation to financial years beginning on or after 1st April 2017, £2,900.

(*h*) whose owner is entitled to possession only in his capacity as the personal representative of a deceased person;

(*i*) where, in respect of the owner's estate, there subsists a bankruptcy order within the meaning of section 381(2) of the Insolvency Act 1986;

(*j*) *revoked*

(*k*) whose owner is a company which is subject to a winding-up order made under the Insolvency Act 1986 or which is being wound up voluntarily under that Act;

(*l*) whose owner is a company in administration within the meaning of paragraph 1 of Schedule B1 to the Insolvency Act 1986 or is subject to an administration order made under the former administration provisions within the meaning of article 3 of the Enterprise Act 2002 (Commencement No 4 andTransitional Provisions and Savings) Order 2003;

(*m*) whose owner is entitled to possession of the hereditament in his capacity as liquidator by virtue of an order made under section 112 or section 145 of the Insolvency Act 1986.

**7.7689** 5. *Continuous occupation* A hereditament which has been unoccupied and becomes occupied on any day shall be treated as having been continuously unoccupied for the purposes of regulation 4(*a*) and (*b*) if it becomes unoccupied again on the expiration of a period of less than six weeks beginning with that day.

**7.7690** 6. *Hereditaments not previously occupied* For the purposes of regulation 4(*a*) and (*b*), a hereditament which has not previously been occupied shall be treated as becoming unoccupied—

(*a*) on the day determined under paragraph 8 of Schedule 1 to the General Rate Act 1967, or on the day determined under Schedule 4A to the Act, whichever day first occurs; or

(*b*) where paragraph (*a*) does not apply, on the day for which the hereditament is first shown in a local rating list.

7. *Revocation and saving*

## Licensing Act 2003 (Mandatory Licensing Conditions) Order 2010[1]

(SI 2010/860 amended by SI 2014/2440)

**7.7691** 1. *Citation and commencement* (1) This Order may be cited as the Licensing Act 2003 (Mandatory Licensing Conditions) Order 2010.

(2) This Order shall come into force on 6th April 2010 other than paragraphs 4 and 5 of the Schedule which shall come into force on 1st October 2010.

[1] Made by the Secretary of State in exercise of the powers conferred by ss 19A, 73B and 197(2) of the Licensing Act 2003.

**7.7692** 2. *Interpretation* In this Order—

"the Act" means the Licensing Act 2003;

"anti-social behaviour" has the meaning given in section 36 of the Anti-social Behaviour Act 2003;

"disability" has the meaning given in section 1 of the Disability Discrimination Act 1995;

"relevant premises" has the meaning given in paragraphs (*a*) and (*b*) of the definition in section 159 of the Act;

"responsible person" has the meaning given in paragraphs (*a*) and (*b*) of the definition in section 153(4) of the Act.

**7.7693** 3. *Mandatory conditions* (1) Subject to paragraph (3), in relation to an existing or future relevant premises licence, the conditions set out in the Schedule are specified for the purposes of section 19(4) of the Act (mandatory conditions where licence authorises supply of alcohol).

(2) Subject to paragraph (3), in relation to an existing or future relevant club premises certificate, the conditions set out in the Schedule are specified for the purposes of section 73A of the Act (mandatory conditions relating to the supply of alcohol to members or guests).

(3) The conditions in paragraphs 1, 2 and 4 of the Schedule do not apply where the licence or certificate authorises the sale by retail or supply of alcohol only for consumption off the premises.

SCHEDULE

MANDATORY LICENSING CONDITIONS Article 3

**7.7694** 1. (1) The responsible person must ensure that staff on relevant premises do not carry out, arrange or participate in any irresponsible promotions in relation to the premises.

(2) In this paragraph, an irresponsible promotion means any one or more of the following activities, or substantially similar activities, carried on for the purpose of encouraging the sale or supply of alcohol for consumption on the premises—

(*a*) games or other activities which require or encourage, or are designed to require or encourage, individuals to—

(i) drink a quantity of alcohol within a time limit (other than to drink alcohol sold or supplied on the premises before the cessation of the period in which the responsible person is authorised to sell or supply alcohol), or

(ii) drink as much alcohol as possible (whether within a time limit or otherwise);

(*b*) provision of unlimited or unspecified quantities of alcohol free or for a fixed or discounted fee to the public or to a group defined by a particular characteristic in a manner which carries a significant risk of undermining a licensing objective;

(*c*) provision of free or discounted alcohol or any other thing as a prize to encourage or reward the purchase and consumption of alcohol over a period of 24 hours or less in a manner which carries a significant risk of undermining a licensing objective;

(*d*) selling or supplying alcohol in association with promotional posters or flyers on, or in the vicinity of, the premises which can reasonably be considered to condone, encourage or glamorise anti-social behaviour or to refer to the effects of drunkenness in any favourable manner;

(*e*) dispensing alcohol directly by one person into the mouth of another (other than where that other person is unable to drink without assistance by reason of disability).

*2.* The responsible person must ensure that free potable water is provided on request to customers where it is reasonably available.

*3.* (1) The premises licence holder or club premises certificate holder must ensure that an age verification policy is adopted in respect of the premises in relation to the sale or supply of alcohol.

(2) The designated premises supervisor in relation to the premises licence must ensure that the supply of alcohol at the premises is carried on in accordance with the age verification policy.

(3) The policy must require individuals who appear to the responsible person to be under 18 years of age (or such older age as may be specified in the policy) to produce on request, before being served alcohol, identification bearing their photograph, date of birth and either—

(*a*) a holographic mark, or

(*b*) an ultraviolet feature.

*4.* he responsible person must ensure that—

(*a*) where any of the following alcoholic drinks is sold or supplied for consumption on the premises (other than alcoholic drinks sold or supplied having been made up in advance ready for sale or supply in a securely closed container) it is available to customers in the following measures—

(i) beer or cider: ½ pint;

(ii) gin, rum, vodka or whisky: 25 ml or 35 ml; and

(iii) still wine in a glass: 125 ml;

(*b*) these measures are displayed in a menu, price list or other printed material which is available to customers on the premises; and

(*c*) where a customer does not in relation to a sale of alcohol specify the quantity of alcohol to be sold, the customer is made aware that these measures are available.

## Licensing Act 2003 (Mandatory Conditions) Order 2014[1]

(SI 2014/1252)

**7.7694A** *1. Citation and commencement* This Order may be cited as the Licensing Act 2003 (Mandatory Conditions) Order 2014 and comes into force 14 days after the day on which it is made.

[1] Made by the Secretary of State in exercise of the powers conferred by ss 19A, 73B and 197(2) of the Licensing Act 2003.

**7.7694B** *2. Mandatory licensing condition* (1) In relation to an existing or future relevant premises licence, the condition set out in the Schedule is specified for the purposes of section 19(4) of the Licensing Act 2003.

(2) In relation to an existing or future relevant club premises certificate, the condition set out in the Schedule is specified for the purposes of section 73A of the Licensing Act 2003.

SCHEDULE

MANDATORY LICENSING CONDITION

Article 2

**7.7694C** *1.* A relevant person shall ensure that no alcohol is sold or supplied for consumption on or off the premises for a price which is less than the permitted price.

*2.* For the purposes of the condition set out in paragraph 1—

(a) "duty" is to be construed in accordance with the Alcoholic Liquor Duties Act 1979;

(b) "permitted price" is the price found by applying the formula—

$P = D + (D \times V)$

where—

(i) P is the permitted price,

(ii) D is the amount of duty chargeable in relation to the alcohol as if the duty were charged on the date of the sale or supply of the alcohol, and

(iii) V is the rate of value added tax chargeable in relation to the alcohol as if the value added tax were charged on the date of the sale or supply of the alcohol;

(c) "relevant person" means, in relation to premises in respect of which there is in force a premises licence—

(i) the holder of the premises licence,

(ii) the designated premises supervisor (if any) in respect of such a licence, or

(iii) the personal licence holder who makes or authorises a supply of alcohol under such a licence;

(d) "relevant person" means, in relation to premises in respect of which there is in force a club premises certificate, any member or officer of the club present on the premises in a capacity which enables the member or officer to prevent the supply in question; and

(e) "value added tax" means value added tax charged in accordance with the Value Added Tax Act 1994.

*3.* Where the permitted price given by Paragraph (b) of paragraph 2 would (apart from this paragraph) not be a whole number of pennies, the price given by that sub-paragraph shall be taken to be the price actually given by that sub-paragraph rounded up to the nearest penny.

4. (1) Sub-paragraph (2) applies where the permitted price given by Paragraph (b) of paragraph 2 on a day ("the first day") would be different from the permitted price on the next day ("the second day") as a result of a change to the rate of duty or value added tax.
(2) The permitted price which would apply on the first day applies to sales or supplies of alcohol which take place before the expiry of the period of 14 days beginning on the second day.

# LONDON

**Contents**



## Public Order

## Metropolitan Police Act 1839

(2 and 3 Vict c 47)

7.7695 54. **Offences in thoroughfares or public places** Every person shall be liable to a penalty not more than **level 2** on the standard scale, who, within the limits of the metropolitan police district shall in any thoroughfare or public place[1], commit any of the following offences; (that is to say,)

1. very person who shall, to the annoyance[2] of the inhabitants or passengers expose for show or sale (except in a market lawfully appointed for that purpose) or feed or fodder any horse or other animal, or show any caravan containing any animal or any other show or public entertainment, or shoe, bleed, or farry any horse or animal (except in cases of accident), or clean, dress, exercise, train, or break any horse or animal, or clean, make, or repair any part of any cart or carriage, except in cases of accident where repair on the spot is necessary:
2. Every person who shall turn loose any horse or cattle, or suffer to be at large any unmuzzled ferocious[3] dog, or set on or urge any dog or other animal to attack, worry, or put in fear any person, horse, or other animal:
3. Every person who by negligence or ill-usage in driving cattle shall cause any mischief to be done by such cattle, or who shall in anywise misbehave himself in the driving, care, or management of such cattle, and also every person not being hired or employed to drive such cattle who shall wantonly and unlawfully, pelt, drive, or hunt any such cattle:
4. Every person having the care of any cart or carriage who shall ride on any part thereof, on the shafts, or on any horse or other animal drawing the same, without having and holding the reins, or who shall be at such a distance from such cart or carriage as not to have the complete control over every horse or other animal drawing the same[4]:

5. Every person who shall ride or drive furiously, or so as to endanger the life or limb of any person, or to the common danger of the passengers in any thoroughfare[5]:

6. Every person who shall cause any cart, public carriage, sledge, truck, or barrow, with or without horses, to stand longer than may be necessary for loading or unloading or for taking up or setting down passengers, except hackney carriages standing for hire in any place not forbidden by law, or who, by means of any cart, carriage, sledge, truck, or barrow or any horse or other animal, shall wilfully interrupt[6] any public crossing, or wilfully cause any obstruction in any thoroughfare:

7. Every person who shall lead or ride any horse or other animal, or draw or drive any cart or carriage, sledge, truck, or barrow, upon any footway or curbstone, or fasten any horse or other animal so that it can stand across or upon any footway:

8. Every person who shall roll or carry any cask, tub, hoop, or wheel, or any ladder, plank, pole, showboard, or placard, upon any footway[7], except for the purpose of loading or unloading any cart or carriage, or of crossing the footway:

9. Every person who, after being made acquainted with the regulations or directions which the commissioners of police shall have made for regulating the route of horses, carts, carriages, and persons for preventing obstructions during public processions and on other occasions herein-before specified, shall wilfully disregard or not conform himself thereunto:

10. Every person who, without the consent of the owner or occupier, shall affix any posting bill or other paper against or upon any building, wall, fence, or pale, or write upon, soil, deface, or mark any such building, wall, fence, or pale with chalk or paint, or in any other way whatsoever, or wilfully break, destroy, or damage any part of any such building, wall, fence, or pale, or any fixture or appendage thereunto, or any tree, shrub, or seat in any public walk park, or garden:

11. *Repealed.*

12. Every person who shall sell or distribute or offer for sale or distribution, or exhibit to public view, any profane, book, paper, print, drawing, painting or representation, or sing any profane, indecent, or obscene song or ballad, or use any profane, indecent or obscene language to the annoyance[8] of the inhabitants or passengers:

13. *Repealed.*

14. Every person except the guards and postmen belonging to her Majesty's Post Office in the performance of their duty, who shall blow any horn or use any other noisy instrument[9] for the purpose of calling persons together, or of announcing any show or entertainment, or for the purpose of hawking, selling, distributing, or collecting any article whatsoever, or of obtaining money or alms:

15. Every person who shall wantonly discharge any fire-arm or throw or discharge[10] any stone or other missile, to the damage or danger of any person, or make any bonfire, or throw or set fire to any firework:

16. Every person who shall wilfully and wantonly disturb any inhabitant by pulling or ringing any door-bell[11] or knocking at any door without lawful excuse, or who shall wilfully and unlawfully extinguish the light of any lamp:

17. Every person who shall fly any kite or play at any game to the annoyance of the inhabitants or passengers[12], or who shall make or use any slide upon ice or snow in any street or other thoroughfare, to the common danger of the passengers.

[Metropolitan Police Act 1839, s 54 as amended by Street Offences Act 1959, Criminal Justice Act 1967, Statute Law (Repeals) Act 1973, Criminal Law Act 1977, Sch 6, the Indecent Displays (Control) Act 1981, Sch, the Criminal Justice Act 1982, s 46, the Police and Criminal Evidence Act 1984, Sch 7 and the Public Order Act 1986, Sch 3.]

---

[1] There is no definition of "public place" in this Act. However, this section can be compared with the Town Police Clauses Act 1847, s 28, to which the definition of "public place" contained in the Public Health Amendment Act 1907, s 81, as amended (post) is expressly extended. Some of the offences created by the following subsections can, it is submitted, be committed on private property adjacent to public places and in view of persons thereon.

[2] To constitute an offence there must have been some annoyance in fact, or something necessarily calculated to be so (*Allen v Baldock* (1867) 31 JP 311). See also *Innes v Newman* [1894] 2 QB 292, 58 JP 543, where it was held, in respect of a prosecution under a byelaw, that as the act complained of was such as was calculated to annoy the inhabitants generally, it was sufficient to prove that one inhabitant was annoyed.

[3] It should be noted that there is no necessity for knowledge of the dog's ferocious nature to be proved.

[4] A similar provision appears in s 78 of the Highway Act 1835, ante.

[5] See also s 35 of the Offences Against the Person Act 1861, and s 28 of the London Hackney Carriages Act 1843.

[6] See note 1 to s 28 of the Town Police Clauses Act 1847, post.

[7] This subsection is wider in its application than similar provisions in s 72 of the Highway Act 1835, which is restricted to footpaths at the road side; see the words "thoroughfare or public place" in the opening sentence of this section.

[8] On a prosecution under s 54(12), where indecent or obscene language is alleged, it is sufficient to show that the words were calculated to annoy; proof of actual annoyance is not required (*Myers v Garrett* [1972] Crim LR 232). See also note 2 to s 54(1), supra.

[9] The Control of Pollution Act 1974, s 62 (see title PUBLIC HEALTH, post) prohibits the use of loudspeakers in streets otherwise than for certain specified purposes and between certain specified hours.

[10] There is a similar provision in the Explosives Act 1875, s 80, in relation to fireworks.

[11] See note 3, to the Town Police Clauses Act 1847, s 28, post.

[12] The playing of football or any game on a highway "to the annoyance of a user" is an offence against the Highways Act 1980, s 161, title HIGHWAYS, ante.

7.7696 58. **Indecent behaviour**[1] Every person who shall be guilty of any violent or indecent behaviour in any police station house, shall be liable to a penalty of not more than **level 1** on the standard scale for every such offence or may be committed, if the magistrate[2] before whom he shall be convicted shall think fit instead of inflicting on him any pecuniary penalty, [to a term of imprisonment not exceeding one month].

[Metropolitan Police Act 1839, s 58 as amended by the Penalties for Drunkenness Act 1962, the Criminal Justice Act 1967, Sch 7 and the Criminal Justice Act 1982, ss 38 and 46.]

---

1 The Criminal Justice Act 1967, s 91 in PART I: MAGISTRATES' COURTS, PROCEDURE, ante, has effect in place of this section where a person is guilty whilst drunk of disorderly behaviour (Criminal Justice Act 1967, s 91(2)).

2 Lay justices in the Inner London area have jurisdiction by virtue of the Justices of the Peace Act 1979, s 33, ante.

# Police Reform and Social Responsibility Act 2011

(2011 c 13)

## PART 3

## PARLIAMENT SQUARE ETC

### *Repeal of SOCPA 2005 provisions*

7.7697 141. **Demonstrations in vicinity of Parliament: repeal of SOCPA 2005 provisions**

(1) Sections 132 to 138 of the Serious Organised Crime and Police Act 2005 (which regulate demonstrations and use of loudspeakers in the vicinity of Parliament) are repealed.

(2) The public assemblies in relation to which section 14 of the Public Order Act 1986 applies, as a consequence of the repeal of section 132(6) of the Serious Organised Crime and Police Act 2005, include public assemblies which started, or were being organised, before this section comes into force.

[Police Reform and Social Responsibility Act 2011, s 141.]

### *Controls on activities in Parliament Square etc*

7.7698 142. **Controlled area of Parliament Square**[1] (1) For the purposes of this Part, the "controlled area of Parliament Square" means the area of land that is comprised in—

(*a*) the central garden of Parliament Square, and

(*b*) the footways that immediately adjoin the central garden of Parliament Square.

(2) In subsection (1)—

"the central garden of Parliament Square" means the site in Parliament Square on which the Minister of Works was authorised by the Parliament Square (Improvements) Act 1949 to lay out the garden referred to in that Act as "the new central garden";

"footway" has the same meaning as in the Highways Act 1980 (see section 329(1) of that Act).

[Police Reform and Social Responsibility Act 2011, s 142.]

---

1 An existing authorisation under s 135 of the Serious Organised Crime and Police Act 2005 did not make unlawful the decision of the authority to enforce Part 3 of this Act. The provisions of Part 3 are compatible with the European Convention on Human Rights as they are limited and proportionate: *R (Gallastegui) v Westminster City Council* [2012] EWHC 1123 (Admin); affd *R (on the application of Gallestegui) v Westminster City Council* [2013] EWCA Civ 28, [2013] 2 All ER 579, [2013] 1 WLR 2377.

7.7698A 142A. **Other controlled areas in vicinity of the Palace of Westminster**

7.7699 143. **Prohibited activities in controlled area of Parliament Square or in Palace of Westminster controlled area** (1) A constable or authorised officer who has reasonable grounds for believing that a person is doing, or is about to do, a prohibited activity may[1] direct the person—

(*a*) to cease doing that activity, or

(*b*) (as the case may be) not to start doing that activity.

(2) For the purposes of this Part, a "prohibited activity" is any of the following—

(*a*) operating any amplified noise equipment in the controlled area of Parliament Square or in the Palace of Westminster controlled area;

(*b*) erecting or keeping erected in the controlled area of Parliament Square—

(i) any tent, or

(ii) any other structure that is designed, or adapted, (solely or mainly) for the purpose of facilitating sleeping or staying in a place for any period;

(*c*) using any tent or other such structure in the controlled area of Parliament Square for the purpose of sleeping or staying in that area;

(*d*) placing or keeping in place in the controlled area of Parliament Square any sleeping equipment with a view to its use (whether or not by the person placing it or keeping it in place) for the purpose of sleeping overnight in that area;

(*e*) using any sleeping equipment in the controlled area of Parliament Square for the purpose of sleeping overnight in that area.

(3) But an activity is not to be treated as a "prohibited activity" within subsection (2) if it is done—

(*a*) for police, fire and rescue authority or ambulance purposes,

(*b*) by or on behalf of a relevant authority, or

(c) by a person so far as authorised under section 147 to do it (authorisation for operation of amplified noise equipment).

(4) In subsection (2)(a) "amplified noise equipment" means any device that is designed or adapted for amplifying sound, including (but not limited to)—

(a) loudspeakers, and

(b) loudhailers.

(5) In subsection (3)(b) "relevant authority" means any of the following—

(a) a Minister of the Crown or a government department,

(b) the Greater London Authority, or

(c) Westminster City Council.

(6) It is immaterial for the purposes of a prohibited activity—

(a) in the case of an activity within subsection (2)(b) or (c) of keeping a tent or similar structure erected or using a tent or similar structure, whether the tent or structure was first erected before or after the coming into force of this section;

(b) in the case of an activity within subsection (2)(d) or (e) of keeping in place any sleeping equipment or using any such equipment, whether the sleeping equipment was first placed before or after the coming into force of this section.

(7) In this section "sleeping equipment" means any sleeping bag, mattress or other similar item designed, or adapted, (solely or mainly) for the purpose of facilitating sleeping in a place.

(8) A person who fails without reasonable excuse to comply with a direction under subsection (1) commits an offence and is liable on summary conviction to a fine not exceeding level 5 on the standard scale.

[Police Reform and Social Responsibility Act 2011, s 143 as amended by the Anti-social Behaviour, Crime and Policing Act 2014, s 153.]

---

1 This creates a discretion not a duty and the discretion should be exercised so as to promote the policy and objectives of the 2011 Act. The discretion not to exercise the power must have been intended by Parliament to be exercised only in exceptional circumstances: *R (on the application of Gallestegui) v Westminster City Council* [2013] EWCA Civ 28, [2013] 2 All ER 579, [2013] 1 WLR 2377

7.7700 **144. Directions under section 143: further provision** (1) A direction requiring a person to cease doing a prohibited activity may include a direction that the person does not start doing that activity again after having ceased it.

(2) A direction requiring a person not to start doing a prohibited activity continues in force until—

(a) the end of such period beginning with the day on which the direction is given as may be specified by the constable or authorised officer giving the direction, or

(b) if no such period is specified, the end of the period of 90 days beginning with the day on which the direction is given.

(3) A period specified under subsection (2)(a) may not be longer than 90 days.

(4) A direction may be given to a person to cease operating, or not to start operating, any amplified noise equipment only if it appears to the constable or authorised officer giving the direction that the following condition is met.

(5) The condition is that the person is operating, or is about to operate, the equipment in such a manner as to produce sound that other persons in or in the vicinity of the controlled area of Parliament Square, or the Palace of Westminster controlled area, can hear or are likely to be able to hear.

(6) A direction—

(a) may be given orally,

(b) may be given to any person individually or to two or more persons together, and

(c) may be withdrawn or varied by the person who gave it.

(7) In this section—

"amplified noise equipment" has the meaning given by section 143(4);

"direction" means a direction given under section 143(1).

[Police Reform and Social Responsibility Act 2011, s 144 as amended by the Anti-social Behaviour, Crime and Policing Act 2014, s 153.]

7.7701 **145. Power to seize property** (1) A constable or authorised officer may seize and retain a prohibited item that is on any land in the controlled area of Parliament Square if it appears to that constable or officer that the item is being, or has been, used in connection with the commission of an offence under section 143 in that area.

(1A) A constable or authorised officer may seize and retain a prohibited item that is on any land in the Palace of Westminster controlled area if it appears to that constable or officer that the item is being, or has been, used in connection with the commission of an offence under section 143 in that area.

(2) A constable may seize and retain a prohibited item that is on any land outside of the controlled area of Parliament Square if it appears to the constable that the item has been used in connection with the commission of an offence under section 143 in that area.

(2A) A constable may seize and retain a prohibited item that is on any land outside of the Palace of Westminster controlled area if it appears to the constable that the item has been used in connection with the commission of an offence under section 143 in that area.

(3) A "prohibited item" is any item of a kind mentioned in section 143(2).

(4) A constable may use reasonable force, if necessary, in exercising a power of seizure under this section.

(5) An item seized under this section must be returned to the person from whom it was seized—

(*a*) no later than the end of the period of 28 days beginning with the day on which the item was seized, or

(*b*) if proceedings are commenced against the person for an offence under section 143 before the return of the item under paragraph (*a*), at the conclusion of those proceedings.

(6) If it is not possible to return an item under subsection (5) because the name or address of the person from whom it was seized is not known—

(*a*) the item may be returned to any other person appearing to have rights in the property who has come forward to claim it, or

(*b*) if there is no such person, the item may be disposed of or destroyed at any time after the end of the period of 90 days beginning with the day on which the item was seized.

(7) Subsections (5)(*b*) and (6) do not apply if a court makes an order under section 146(1)(*a*) for the forfeiture of the item.

(8) The references in this section to an item that is "on" any land include references to an item that is in the possession of a person who is on any such land.

[Police Reform and Social Responsibility Act 2011, s 145 as amended by the Anti-social Behaviour, Crime and Policing Act 2014, s 153.]

7.7702 146. **Power of court on conviction** (1) The court may do either or both of the following on the conviction of a person ("P") of an offence under section 143—

(*a*) make an order providing for the forfeiture of any item of a kind mentioned in subsection (2) of that section that was used in the commission of the offence;

(*b*) make such other order as the court considers appropriate for the purpose of preventing P from engaging in any prohibited activity in a relevant area.

(2) An order under subsection (1)(*b*) may (in particular) require P not to enter a relevant area for such period as may be specified in the order.

(2A) In this section "relevant area" means an area consisting of either or both of the following areas—

(*a*) the controlled area of Parliament Square, and

(*b*) the Palace of Westminster controlled area.

(3) Power of the court to make an order under this section is in addition to the court's power to impose a fine under section 143(8).

[Police Reform and Social Responsibility Act 2011, s 146 as amended by the Anti-social Behaviour, Crime and Policing Act 2014, s 153.]

7.7703 147. **Authorisation for operation of amplified noise equipment** (1) The responsible authority for any land in the controlled area of Parliament Square or the Palace of Westminster controlled area may authorise a person in accordance with this section to operate on that land (or any part of it) any amplified noise equipment (as defined by section 143(4)).

(2) An application for authorisation must be made to the responsible authority by or on behalf of the person (or persons) seeking the authorisation.

(3) The responsible authority may—

(*a*) determine the form in which, and the manner in which, an application is to be made;

(*b*) specify the information to be supplied in connection with an application;

(*c*) require a fee to be paid for determining an application.

(4) If an application is duly made to a responsible authority, the authority must—

(*a*) determine the application, and

(*b*) give notice in writing to the applicant of the authority's decision within the period of 21 days beginning with the day on which the authority receives the application.

(5) The notice must specify—

(*a*) the person (or persons) authorised (whether by name or description),

(*b*) the kind of amplified noise equipment to which the authorisation applies,

(*c*) the period to which the authorisation applies, and

(*d*) any conditions to which the authorisation is subject.

(6) The responsible authority may at any time—

(*a*) withdraw an authorisation given to a person under this section, or

(*b*) vary any condition to which an authorisation is subject.

(7) Variation under subsection (6)(*b*) includes—

(*a*) imposing a new condition,

(*b*) removing an existing condition, or

(*c*) altering any period to which a condition applies.

(8) The exercise of a power under subsection (6) to withdraw an authorisation or to vary a condition is effected by the responsible authority giving notice in writing to the applicant.

[Police Reform and Social Responsibility Act 2011, s 147 as amended by the Anti-social Behaviour, Crime and Policing Act 2014, s 153.]

7.7704 **148. Meaning of "authorised officer" and "responsible authority"** (1) This section applies for the purposes of this Part.

(2) "Authorised officer", in relation to any land in the controlled area of Parliament Square, or in relation to any land in the Palace of Westminster controlled area other than Royal Park land, means—

(*a*) an employee of the responsible authority for that land who is authorised in writing by the authority for the purposes of this Part, and

(*b*) any other person who, under arrangements made with the responsible authority (whether by that or any other person), is so authorised for the purposes of this Part.

(3) "Responsible authority", in relation to any land in the controlled area of Parliament Square, means—

(*a*) the Greater London Authority, for any land comprised in the central garden of Parliament Square (as defined by section 142(2)), and

(*b*) Westminster City Council, for any other land.

(4) "Responsible authority", in relation to any land in the Palace of Westminster controlled area, means—

(*a*) the Secretary of State, for any land comprised in Royal Park land;

(*b*) Westminster City Council, for any other land.

(5) In this section "Royal Park land" means any land of a description specified in Schedule 1 to the Royal Parks and Other Open Spaces Regulations 1997 (S.I. 1997/1639), as that Schedule has effect on the day on which the Anti-social Behaviour, Crime and Policing Act 2014 is passed

[Police Reform and Social Responsibility Act 2011, s 148 as amended by the Anti-social Behaviour, Crime and Policing Act 2014, s 153.]

**149.** *Byelaws not to be made in respect of prohibited activity within the meaning of this Part.*

## LICENSING

## Greater London Council (General Powers) Act 1978

(1978 c xiii)

### PART II

### PROVISIONS RELATING TO THE COUNCIL

*Licensing of public entertainments*

7.7705 **5. Licensing of entertainments booking offices** (1) No premises in a borough shall, on or after 1st October, 1978, be used as a booking office except under and in accordance with the terms of a licence (hereafter in this section referred to as a "booking office licence") granted by the borough council in pursuance of the provisions of this section.

(2) Subject to the next following subsection, the provisions of sub-paragraphs (2), (3) and (5) of paragraph 1, sub-paragraphs (1) and (2) of paragraph 2 and paragraphs 3, 6A, 6B, 7 to 10, 12, 12A, 12B, 12C and 17 to 20 of Schedule 12[1] to the Act of 1963 shall apply to a booking office licence as they apply in relation to a licence under paragraph 1 of that Schedule and as if the booking office licence had been granted under the said paragraph 1.

(3) For the purposes of the application of the provisions of the said Schedule 12, referred to in the foregoing subsection, to a booking office licence—

(*a*) for sub-paragraph (1) of paragraph 10 of the said Schedule there shall be substituted the following—

"(1) If any premises are used as a booking office, as defined in subsection (4) of section 5 (Licensing of entertainments booking offices) of the Greater London Council (General Powers) Act 1978, without a licence being held in respect thereof under the said section 5, then—

(*a*) any person concerned in the organisation or management of that booking office; and

(*b*) any other person who, knowing or having reasonable cause to suspect that those premises would be so used as a booking office—

(i) allowed the premises to be so used; or

(ii) let the premises, or otherwise made the premises available to any person by whom an offence in connection with that use of the premises has been committed;

shall be guilty of an offence.";

(*b*) in sub-paragraph (2) of the said paragraph 10, for the words "for any entertainment" there shall be substituted the words "as a booking office (as defined in subsection (4) of section 5 of the said Act of 1978)"; and

(*c*) in sub-paragraph (1) of paragraph 12 of the said Schedule 12, for the words "at which he has reason to believe that an entertainment to which either of those paragraphs applies is being given or is about to be given" there shall be substituted the words "which he has reason to believe are being used as a booking office (as defined in subsection (4) of section 5 of the said Act of 1978)" and for the word "entertainment", where it occurs for the second time, there shall be substituted the word "use".

(4)

(*a*) In this section "booking office" means any premises, not being premises exempted in accordance with paragraph (*b*) of this subsection or premises in use at the time in question for any of the following purposes, that is to say—
(i) public dancing or music or any other public entertainment of the like kind;
(ii) *repealed*
whose principal function at that time is to serve as premises at which members of the public may by the purchase of tickets or vouchers, or, on payment, by any other means, secure admission (whether or not on payment of a further charge) to any other premises (not being premises to which paragraph (*c*) of this subsection applies) used for any of the purposes mentioned in sub-paragraph (i) of this paragraph.

(*b*)
(i) If, in the opinion of the borough council, it is inappropriate that any premises or any class of premises should remain subject as booking offices to the provisions of this section, they may by resolution determine that as from a date to be fixed by the resolution those premises or that class of premises shall be exempted from such provisions.
(ii) If, in the opinion of the borough council, after the date fixed by a resolution passed under the foregoing sub-paragraph and having regard to any relevant circumstances, any premises or any class of premises exempted as booking offices from the provisions of this section by virtue of such a resolution should again become subject to the said provisions, they may by a further resolution determine that those premises or that class of premises shall again become subject as booking offices to the said provisions as from a date to be fixed by such further resolution.

(*c*) This paragraph applies (for the purposes of paragraph (*a*) of this subsection) to—
(i) the Theatre Royal Drury Lane, the Royal Covent Garden Opera House, the Theatre Royal Haymarket and the Royal Albert Hall;
(ii) premises which may be used for the performance of plays without a licence under the Theatres Act 1968 by virtue of any letters patent of the Crown; and
(iii) any other premises specified by resolution of the borough council from time to time for the purposes of this paragraph.

(5) In this section "borough" includes the City of London and "borough council" includes the Common Council.

[Greater London Council (General Powers) Act 1978, s 5 as amended by the Greater London Council (General Powers) Act 1984, s 4 and the Local Government Act 1985, Sch 8 and the Licensing Act 2003, Sch 6.]

---

1 Ante.

# London Local Authorities Act 1990

(1990 c vii)

## Part III

## Street Trading

7.7706 **21. Interpretation of Part III** (1) In this Part of this Act—

"grant", unless the context otherwise requires, includes renew and renewal, and cognate words shall be construed accordingly;

"ice cream trading" means the selling, exposing or offering for sale of goods consisting wholly or mainly of ice cream, frozen confectionery or other similar commodities from a vehicle;

"itinerant ice cream trading" means ice cream trading from a vehicle which goes from place to place remaining in any one location in the course of trading for periods of 15 minutes or less and not returning to that location or any other location in the same street on the same day;

"licence street" means a street designated under section 24 (Designation of licence streets) of this Act;

"receptacle" includes a vehicle or stall and any basket, bag, box, vessel, stand, easel, board, tray or thing which is used (whether or not constructed or adapted for such use) as a container for or for the display of any article or thing or equipment used in the provision of any service;

"street" includes—
(*a*) any road or footway;
(*b*) any other area, not being within permanently enclosed premises, within 7 metres of any road or footway, to which the public obtain access without payment—
(i) whether or not they need the consent of the owner or occupier; and
(ii) if they do, whether or not they have obtained it;
(*c*) any part of such road, footway or area;
(*d*) any part of any housing development provided or maintained by a local authority under Part II of the Housing Act 1985;

"street trading"[1] means subject to subsections (1ZA), (1) and (2) below—
(*a*) the selling or the exposure or offer for sale of any article (including a living thing); and
(*b*) the purchasing of or offering to purchase any ticket; and

(*c*) the supplying of or offering to supply any service,
in a street for gain or reward (whether or not the gain or reward accrues to the person actually carrying out the trading);

"street trading licence" means a licence granted under this Part of this Act and valid for the period specified therein being not less than six months and not more than three years;

"temporary licence" means a licence granted under this Part of this Act valid for a single day or for such period as may be specified in the licence not exceeding six months.

(1ZA) In this Part of this Act "street trading" shall also include the selling or exposure or offer for sale of any motor vehicle in the course of a business if the vehicle is—

(*a*) exposed or offered for sale on the internet; and

(*b*) kept on a street during the period when it is so exposed or offered for sale.

(1A) In determining whether activity amounts to street trading for the purposes of this Act, the fact that—

(*a*) a transaction was completed elsewhere than in a street in the case where the initial offer or display of the articles in question or the offer of services, as the case may be, took place in a street;

(*b*) either party to the transaction was not in a street at the time it was completed;

(*c*) the articles actually sold or services actually supplied, as the case may be, were different from those offered,

shall be disregarded.

(2) The following are not street trading for the purposes of this Part of this Act—

(*a*) trading by a person acting as a pedlar under the authority of a Pedlar's Certificate granted under the Pedlars Act 1871, if the trading is carried out only be means of visits from house to house;

(*b*) anything done in a market or fair the right to hold which was acquired by virtue of a grant (including a presumed grant) or acquired or established by virtue of any enactment or order;

(*c*) trading in a trunk road picnic area provided by the Secretary of State under section 112 of the Highways Act 1980;

(*d*) trading as a news-vendor provided that the only articles sold or exposed or offered for sale are current newspapers or periodicals and they are sold or exposed or offered for sale without a receptacle for them or, if with a receptacle for them such receptacle does not—

(i) exceed 1 metre in length or width or 2 metres in height; or

(ii) occupy a ground area exceeding 0.25 square metre; or

(iii) stand on the carriageway of a street; or

(iv) cause undue interference or inconvenience to persons using the street;

(*e*) selling articles or things to occupiers of premises adjoining any street, or offering or exposing them for sale from a vehicle which is used only for the regular delivery of milk or other perishable goods to those persons;

(*f*) *repealed*

(*g*) *repealed*

(*h*) the doing of anything authorised by regulations made under section 5 of the Police, Factories, etc (Miscellaneous Provisions) Act 1916 or by permit or order made under Part III of the Charities Act 1992 (c 41);*

(*i*) trading in a highway in relation to which a control order under section 7 of the Local Government (Miscellaneous Provisions) Act 1976 is in force, other than trading to which the control order does not apply; and

(*j*) the selling or the exposure or offer for sale of articles or the provision of services on private land adjacent to a shop provided that the selling or the exposure or offer for sale of the articles or the provision of the services—

(i) forms part of the business of the owner[2] of the shop or a person assessed for uniform business rate in respect of the shop; and

(ii) takes place during the period during which the shop is open to the public for business.

[London Local Authorities Act 1990, s 21 as amended by the London Local Authorities Act 1994, s 6, the London Local Authorities Act 2004, Sch 4 , the London Local Authorities Act 2007, s 38 and the London Local Authorities Act 2012, s 9.]

---

* **Substituted by the London Local Authorities Act 1996, s 26 from a date to be appointed.**

[1] Exposing goods for sale on a pavement outside a shop for payment within the shop is street trading for the purposes of this Act (*Wandsworth London Borough Council v Rosenthal* (1996) Times, 28 March).

[2] Prior to its amendment, this subsection referred to the "owner or occupier", and the phrase "owner or occupier" did not limit the person concerned to freeholder or possessor of the land; it was a question of fact and degree whether a person was the owner or occupier (*O'Gorman v Brent London Borough Council* (1993) 91 LGR 555).

7.7707 **22. Application of Part III** This Part of this Act applies to the borough of a participating council[1] as from the appointed day[2].

[London Local Authorities Act 1990, s 22.]

[1] The participating councils are listed in Sch 1 to the Act and include Inner and Outer London Boroughs. Subsections 23–33 of the Act make provision for the designation of licence streets, applications for licences, succession on death or retirement, conditions, revocation or variation, appeals, temporary licences, fees and charges, receptacles and containers.

[2] See the note to s 5 ante as to appointed day.

7.7708 **30. Part III appeals: refusal to grant a licence etc** (1) Any person aggrieved—

(*aa*) by the refusal of a borough council to renew a licence because they are not satisfied as mentioned in subsection (4)(*b*) of section 25 (Application for street trading licences) of this Act;

(*a*) by the refusal of a borough council to grant or renew a licence on any of the grounds mentioned in subsection (6)(*a*) to (*e*) of section 25 (Application for street trading licences); or

(*b*) by a decision of a borough council under subsection (7) of the said section 25 to grant him a licence either on terms mentioned in that subsection different from those on the licence which he previously held or different from those for which he applied; or

(*c*) by any further condition attached by a borough council under subsection (8) of section 27 (Conditions of street trading licences) of this Act in addition to the standard conditions; or

(*d*) by a decision of the borough council either—

(i) to vary the conditions of a licence under subsection (2) of section 28 (Revocation or variation of licences under Part III) of this Act; or

(ii) to revoke a licence under subsection (1) of the said section 28; or

(*e*) by a resolution of a borough council under section 37 (Ice cream trading) of this Act;

may appeal to a magistrates' court acting for the area in which the licence street is situated.

(2) An appeal under subsection (1) above may be brought—

(*a*) in the case of an appeal under paragraph (*aa*), (*a*), (*b*), (*c*) or (*d*) of that subsection, at any time before the expiration of the period of 21 days beginning with the date upon which notification in writing is given of the refusal or decision;

(*b*) in the case of an appeal under paragraph (*e*) of that subsection, at any time before the expiration of the period of 21 days beginning with the date of the second publication of the notice required by subsection (10) of section 24 (Designation of licence streets) as applied by the said section 37.

(3) A person desiring to appeal against such refusal or decision as is mentioned in subsection (1) above shall give a written notice to the magistrates' court and to the borough council specifying the refusal or decision against which he wishes to appeal and the grounds upon which such appeal is made.

(4) An appeal by either party against the decision of the magistrates' court under this section may be brought to the Crown Court.

(5) On an appeal to the magistrates' court or to the Crown Court under this section, the court may make such order as it thinks fit.

(6) subject to subsections (7) to (9) below, it shall be the duty of the borough council to give effect to the order of the magistrates' court or the Crown Court.

(7) A borough council need not give effect to the order of the magistrates' court until the time for bringing an appeal under subsection (4) above has expired and, if such an appeal is duly brought, until the determination or abandonment of the appeal.

(8) Where a licence holder applies for renewal of his licence, his existing licence shall remain valid—

(*a*) until the grant by the borough council of a new licence with the same conditions; or

(*b*) if the borough council refuse renewal of the licence or decide to grant a licence with conditions different from those of the existing licence and he has a right of appeal under this section, until the time for bringing an appeal has expired or where an appeal is duly brought, until the determination or abandonment of the appeal; or

(*c*) if he has no right of appeal under this section until the borough council either grant him a new licence with conditions different from those of the existing licence or notify him of their decision to refuse his application.

(9) Where—

(*a*) a borough council decide

(i) to vary the conditions of a licence under subsection (2) of the said section 28; or

(ii) to revoke a licence under subsection (1) of the said section 28; and

(*b*) a right of appeal is available to the licence holder under this section;

the variation or revocation shall not take effect until the time for bringing an appeal has expired or where an appeal is duly brought, until the determination or abandonment of the appeal.

(10) For the avoidance of doubt, it is hereby declared that an application under section 31 of the Senior Courts Act 1981 (application for judicial review) or under the Rules of the Supreme Court 1965 in respect of any matter which is or could be the subject of an appeal to the magistrates' court or to the Crown Court under this section shall not be treated as an appeal for the purposes of subsection (8) or (9) above.

(11) *Repealed.*
(12) *Repealed.*

[London Local Authorities Act 1990, s 30, as amended by the London Local Authorities Act 1994, s 6, the Constitutional Reform Act 2005, Sch 11 and the Deregulation Act 2015, s 91.]

7.7708A **30A. Other Part III appeals** (1) Any person aggrieved—

(*a*) by a resolution rescinding or varying a designating resolution;

(*b*) by a resolution under subsection (1)(*b*) of section 24 (Designation of licence streets) of this Act;

(*c*) by a standard condition prescribed by regulations under subsection (3) of section 27 (Conditions of street trading licences) of this Act; or

(*d*) by the amount of a fee or charge under section 32 (Fees and charges) of this Act;

may appeal to a magistrates' court acting for the area of the borough council which passed the resolution, prescribed the condition or determined the amount of the fee or charge (as the case may be).

(2) An appeal under subsection (1) may be brought—

(*a*) in the case of an appeal under paragraph (*a*) or (*b*) of that subsection, at any time before the expiration of the period of three months beginning with the date on which notice of the passing of the resolution is published for the second time in accordance with subsection (10) of section 24 (Designation of licence streets) of this Act;

(*b*) in the case of an appeal under paragraph (*c*) of that subsection, at any time before the expiration of the period of three months beginning with the date upon which the licence holders or a body or bodies representative of them were notified of the making of the regulations;

(*c*) in the case of an appeal under paragraph (d) of that subsection—

(i) if it relates to the amount of a fee payable under subsection (1) of section 32 (Fees and charges) of this Act, at any time before the expiration of the period of three months beginning with the date on which the fee payable is notified to the licence holders or a body or bodies representative of them;

(ii) if it relates to the amount of a charge under subsection (2) of section 32 (Fees and charges) of this Act, at any time before the expiration of the period of three months beginning with the date on which notice of the determination of the charge has been given to the licence holders or a body or bodies representative of them.

(3) A person desiring to appeal under subsection (1) shall give written notice to the magistrates' court and to the borough council specifying the matter about which the person is aggrieved and the grounds upon which the appeal is made.

(4) On an appeal to a magistrates' court under this section, the court may make such order as it thinks fit.

[London Local Authorities Act 1990, s 30A as inserted by the Deregulation Act 2015, s 91.]

7.7709 **34. Offences** Any person who without reasonable excuse—

(1) contravenes any of the conditions of a street trading licence or a temporary licence; or

(2) in connection with an application for a street trading licence or a temporary licence makes a statement which he knows to be false in a material particular; or

(3) resists or intentionally obstructs any authorised officer of a borough council in the execution of his duties under this Part of this Act; or

(4) fails on demand without reasonable excuse in the case of an individual licence holder to produce his licence bearing his photograph, and, in the case of an individual carrying on ice cream trading under a licence granted to a company incorporated under the Companies Acts or to a partnership, to produce the photograph required by subsection (2) of section 27 (Conditions of street trading licences) of this Act to an authorised officer of the borough council or to a constable;

shall be guilty of an offence and shall be liable on summary conviction to a fine not exceeding level 3 on the standard scale.

[London Local Authorities Act 1990, s 34 as amended by the London Local Authorities Act 1994, s 6 and the London Local Authorities Act 2007, s 42.]

7.7710 **36. Employment of assistants** Subject to the provisions of this section a person holding a street trading licence or a temporary licence may employ any other person to assist him in the conduct of street trading authorised by the licence but if any person employed by a licence holder during the temporary absence of the licence holder fails to comply with the conditions of the licence held by his employer such failure shall be deemed to be a failure by the licence holder.

[London Local Authorities Act 1990, s 36 as amended by the London Local Authorities Act 2007, s 43.]

7.7711 **37. Ice cream trading** (1) Nothing in this Part of this Act shall apply to itinerant ice cream trading in any street unless—

(*a*) that street is a licence street; or

(*b*) the street has been designated as a prohibited street under the following provisions of this section.

(2)–(4) *Designation of prohibited street.*

[London Local Authorities Act 1990, s 37 as amended by the London Local Authorities Act 1994, s 6.]

7.7712 **38. Unlicensed street trading** (1) A person who—

(*a*) is not the holder of a street trading licence or a temporary licence and who engages in street trading[1] in a borough whether or not from a stationary position; or

(*b*) is the holder of a street trading licence or a temporary licence and who, without the borough council's specific permission in writing engages in street trading[1] in a borough on a day or in a place not specified in that licence;

shall be guilty of an offence and shall be liable on summary conviction to a fine not exceeding **level 3** on the standard scale.

(2) In any proceedings for an offence under this section or for an offence of aiding, abetting, counselling or procuring the commission of an offence under this section where it is shown that—

(*a*) any article or thing was displayed (whether or not in or on any receptacle) in any street; or

(*b*) any receptacle or equipment used in the provision of any service was available in any street in such circumstances that a service was being offered;

the article, thing, receptacle or equipment concerned shall be presumed to have been exposed or offered for sale and the receptacle or equipment shall be deemed to have been used for the purposes for which a street trading licence was required unless it can be proved to the satisfaction of the court that the article or thing or receptacle or equipment was brought into that street for some purpose other than street trading[2].

(3) Where an offence under this section committed by a body corporate is proved to have been committed with the consent or connivance of, or to be attributable to any neglect on the part of, any director, manager, secretary or other similar officer of the body corporate, or any person who was purporting to act in any such capacity, he, as well as the body corporate, shall be guilty of the offence and liable to the same maximum penalty as the body corporate.

(4) Subject to section 38A (seizure of perishable items) of this Act if an authorised officer or a constable has reasonable grounds for suspecting that a person has committed an offence under this section he may seize—

(*a*) any article or thing being offered for sale, displayed or exposed for sale; or

(*b*) any other article or thing of a similar nature to that being offered or exposed for sale which is in the possession of or under the control of any person who is displaying an article or thing; or

(*c*) any receptacle or equipment being used by that person.

(4A) An authorised officer or constable may also seize, for examination purposes, any article or thing which he has reasonable cause to suspect may be an article or thing which is prohibited by a specifying resolution made under subsection (1)(*b*) of section 24 (Designation of licence streets) of this Act.

Unless the article or thing is required for evidential purposes it shall be returned as soon as possible to the person from whom it was seized.

(4B) An authorised officer shall produce his authority if required to do so by the person having control or possession of anything seized in pursuance of the powers in subsections (4) and (4A) above.

(4C)

(*a*) Subject to section 38B (motor vehicles) of this Act, the following provisions of this subsection shall have effect where any article or thing (including any receptacle or equipment) is seized under subsection (4) above or is seized and retained because it is required for evidential purposes under subsection (4A) above and references in those provisions to proceedings are to proceedings in respect of the alleged offence in relation to which the article or thing is seized.

(*b*) Subject to paragraph (*e*) below, following the conclusion of the proceedings the article or thing shall be returned to the person from whom it was seized unless—

(i) the court orders it to be forfeited under subsection (5) below; or

(ii) any award of costs to the council by the court, which may include removal, return and storage costs, have not been paid within 28 days of the making of the order.

(*ba*) Where after 28 days any costs awarded by the court to the council have not been paid to the council in full—

(i) the article or thing may be disposed of in any way the council thinks fit; and

(ii) any sum obtained by the council in excess of the costs awarded by the court shall be returned to the person to whom the article or thing belongs.

(*bb*) When any article or thing is disposed of by the council under this subsection the council shall have a duty to secure the best possible price which can reasonably be obtained for that article or thing.

(*c*) Subject to paragraph (*d*) below, where a receptacle seized under subsection (4) above is a motor vehicle used for ice cream trading, the borough council or the Commissioner of Police of the Metropolis (as the case may be) shall, within three days of the receipt of an application in writing by the owner or registered keeper of the vehicle, permit him to remove it.

(*d*) Paragraph (*c*) above shall not apply where—
(i) the owner or registered keeper of the vehicle has been convicted of an offence under this Part of this Act or under the City of Westminster Act 1999; or
(ii) the owner or registered keeper of the vehicle is being prosecuted for a previous alleged offence under this Part of this Act or the said Act of 1999; or
(iii) the vehicle has been used in the commission of such an offence or previous alleged offence;
if the offence or previous alleged offence was committed or is alleged to have been committed no more than three years before the seizure and (in the case of an alleged offence) the proceedings are continuing.

(*e*) If no proceedings are instituted before the expiration of a period of 28 days beginning with the date of seizure, or any proceedings instituted within that period are discontinued, at the expiration of that period or, as the case may be, on the discontinuance of the proceedings, the article or thing shall be returned to the person from whom it was seized unless it has not proved possible, after diligent enquiry, to identify that person or ascertain his address.

(*f*) paragraph (*g*) below applies where the article, thing, receptacle or equipment is not returned because—
(i) it has not proved possible to identify the person from whom it was seized or ascertain his address; or
(ii) the person from whom it was seized and the owner (if different) have disclaimed or refused to accept it.

(*g*) where this paragraph applies, the council may make a complaint to the magistrates' court for a disposal order under section 38C (disposal orders) of this Act (whether or not proceedings for an offence under this section have been commenced).

(5) Subject to subsection (6) below the court by or before which a person is convicted of an offence under this section or for an offence of aiding, abetting, counselling or procuring the commission of an offence under this section may order anything produced to the court[3], and shown to the satisfaction of the court to relate to the offence, to be forfeited and dealt with in such manner as the court may order.

(6) The court shall not order anything to be forfeited under subsection (5) above where a person claiming to be the owner of or otherwise interested in it applies to be heard by the court, unless an opportunity has been given to him to show cause why the order should not be made and in considering whether to make such an order a court shall have regard—
(i) to the value of the property; and
(ii) to the likely financial and other effects on the offender of the making of the order (taken together with any other order that the court contemplates making).

(6A) For the avoidance of doubt the court may order forfeiture notwithstanding that the value of the article, thing, receptacle or equipment exceeds the maximum penalties referred to in this section.

(7) An authorised officer shall produce his authority if required to do so by the person having care or control of anything seized in pursuance of the powers in subsection (4) above.

(8)
(*a*) This subsection shall have effect where—
(i) an article, thing or receptacle is seized under subsection (4) above; and
(ii)
(A) not less than six months have passed since the date of the seizure and no information has been laid against any person for an offence under this section in respect of the acts or circumstances which occasioned the seizure; or
(B) proceedings for such an offence have been brought and either the person charged has been acquitted (whether or not on appeal) and the time for appealing against or challenging the acquittal (where applicable) has expired without an appeal or challenge being brought, or the proceedings (including any appeal) have been withdrawn by, or have failed for want of prosecution by, the person by whom the original proceedings were brought.

(*b*) When this subsection has effect a person who has or at the time of seizure had a legal interest in the article, thing or receptacle seized may recover compensation from the borough council or (where it is seized by a constable) the Commissioner of Police of the Metropolis by civil action in the County Court in respect of any loss suffered by him as a result of the seizure and any such compensation shall not be included in the computation for calculating charges under section 22 (Fees and charges) of this Act.

(*c*) The court may not make an order for compensation under paragraph (*b*) above unless it is satisfied that seizure was not lawful under subsection (4) or (4A) above.

[London Local Authorities Act 1990, s 38 as amended by the London Local Authorities Act 1994, s 6, the London Local Authorities Act 2004, Sch 4 and the London Local Authorities 2007, Sch 4.]

[1] The term "street trading" is apt to cover the sale of one motor vehicle offered for sale in a street with a notice that it was for sale, the price and a telephone number: *Haringey London Borough Council v Michniewicz* [2004] TLR 354.

[2] The issue for the court is not whether the article was in the street entirely for a purpose unrelated to street trading but whether an article was "brought into that street for some purpose other than street trading" ie why was it in "that street" and nowhere else at the material time. Whilst there might be a duality of purpose, that does not mean that wherever that is so s 38(2) would not avail a defendant: *Onasanya v Newham London Borough Council* [2006] EWHC 1775 (Admin), [2006] 4 All ER 459 (defendant wrongly convicted where he had left a "for sale" sign and contact number in the window of his car when he was visiting his doctor).

[3] The items must be physically present or treated as being produced by virtue of being exhibited by a statement served under s 9 of the Criminal Justice Act 1967; but if there is a late objection to non-production in either of the aforementioned ways of the items it is open to the justices to adjourn for the items to be produced, or to make arrangements to view the items on some convenient occasion on the same or a future date (*R (on the application of London Borough of Islington) v Jordan* [2002] EWHC 2645 (Admin), 167 JP 1).

**7.7713 38A. Seizure of perishable items** (1) No item which is of a perishable nature (in this section referred to as a "perishable item") shall be seized under the provisions of subsection (4) of section 38 (unlicensed street trading) of this Act unless the authorised officer or constable gives a certificate under subsection (2) below to the person from whom the item is seized.

(2) Where a perishable item is seized under the said section 38, the person from whom it is seized must be given a certificate—

(*a*) stating the effect of subsection (4) below and subsection (6) of the said section 38;

(*b*) giving the address from which the item may be collected;

(*c*) informing the recipient that if he is not the owner of the item, then he should give the owner the information referred to in paragraphs (*a*) and (*b*) above.

(3) The council or the police shall store any perishable item seized under the said section 38 at an appropriate temperature.

(4) If the person from whom a perishable item was so seized fails to collect it within 48 hours of the seizure the council or the police may dispose of it.

(5) When any perishable item is disposed of by the council under subsection (4) above, the council shall have a duty to secure the best possible price which can reasonably be obtained for it.

(6) Paragraphs (*a*) to (*d*) of subsection (4C), and subsections (5) and (6) of the said section 38 shall apply to perishable items seized under that section only in cases where the item concerned has not been disposed of by the council at the conclusion of the proceedings in respect of the alleged offence in relation to which the item was seized.

(7) Paragraphs (*e*) and (*f*) of subsection (4C) of the said section 38 shall apply to perishable items seized under that section only in cases where the item concerned has not been disposed of by the council at the expiration of the period mentioned in the said paragraph (*e*); otherwise subsections (9) to (12) below shall apply.

(8) Subsection (8) of the said section 38 shall apply with the omission of paragraph (*c*) in respect of perishable items seized under that section only in cases where the item concerned has not been disposed of by the council by the time the circumstances mentioned in paragraph (*a*)(ii)(*a*) or (*b*) arise; otherwise subsections (9) to (12) below shall apply.

(9) Subsection (12) below shall have effect where the council have disposed of a perishable item under subsection (4) above and any of the following conditions apply.

(10) The first condition is that no proceedings in respect of the alleged offence in relation to which the item was seized are instituted before the expiration of a period of 28 days beginning with the date of seizure of the item, or any such proceedings instituted within that period are discontinued.

(11) The second condition is that—

(*a*) not less than six months have passed since the date of the seizure and no information has been laid against any person for an offence under the said section 38 in respect of the acts or circumstances which occasioned the seizure; or

(*b*) proceedings for such an offence have been brought and either the person charged has been acquitted (whether or not on appeal) and the time for appealing against or challenging the acquittal (where applicable) has expired without an appeal or challenge being brought, or the proceedings (including any appeal) have been withdrawn by, or have failed for want of prosecution by, the person by whom the original proceedings were brought.

(12) When this subsection has effect a person who has, or at the time of seizure had, a legal interest in the item seized may recover compensation from the borough council or (where it is seized by a constable) the Commissioner of Police of the Metropolis by civil action in the County Court in respect of any loss suffered by him as a result of the seizure and any such compensation shall not be included in the computation for calculating charges under section 32 (fees and charges) of this Act.

[London Local Authorities Act 1990, s 38A as inserted by the London Local Authorities 2007, s 45.]

**7.7714 38B. Motor vehicles** (1) Subsection (4) below applies where the following conditions are met.

(2) The first condition is that where, in ascertaining the identity of the person from whom a vehicle was seized under subsection (4) or (4A) of section 38 (unlicensed street trading) of this Act, a borough council has, before the expiry of 14 days from the date of the seizure, made a request to

the Secretary of State for the supply of relevant particulars.

(3) The second condition is that those particulars have not been supplied to the council before the date after which that council would, but for this section, have to return the vehicle in accordance with subsection (4C)(*e*) of that section.

(4) Where this subsection applies, the council must return the vehicle to its owner if—

(*a*) no proceedings are instituted in respect of the alleged offence in respect of which the vehicle was seized before the expiry of the period of 14 days beginning with the date on which the relevant particulars are supplied; or

(*b*) any such proceedings instituted within that period are discontinued,

at the expiry of that period or on the discontinuance of the proceedings, as the case may be.

(5) If the council seeks to return a vehicle in accordance with the said subsection (4C)(*e*) or subsection (4), but the person to whom the council seeks to return the vehicle cannot be found or disclaims or refuses to accept the vehicle, the council may make a complaint for a disposal order in respect of the vehicle under section 38C (disposal orders) of this Act.

(6) In this section, "relevant particulars" are particulars relating to the identity of the owner of the vehicle contained in the register of mechanically propelled vehicles maintained by the Secretary of State under the Vehicle Excise and Registration Act 1994 (c 22).

(7) The owner of a vehicle for the purposes of this section shall be taken to be the person by whom the vehicle is kept.

(8) In determining who was the owner of a motor vehicle at any time, it shall be presumed that the owner is the person in whose name the vehicle is at that time registered under the Vehicle Excise and Registration Act 1994.]

[London Local Authorities Act 1990, s 38B as inserted by the London Local Authorities 2007, s 46.]

7.7715 **38C. Disposal orders** (1) This section applies in respect of a complaint made by a borough council for a disposal order in respect of—

(*a*) an article or thing under subsection (4C)(*f*)(ii) of section 38 (unlicensed street trading) of this Act; or

(*b*) a motor vehicle under subsection (5) of section 38B (motor vehicles) of this Act,

and such articles, things and motor vehicles are together referred to as "seized items" in this section.

(2) In respect of a complaint to which this section applies, a magistrates' court may, if it is satisfied that the council has made reasonable efforts to identify the person from whom the seized item was seized or its owner, as the case may be, or has made reasonable efforts to return the seized item, it may make an order authorising the complainant council—

(*a*) to dispose of the seized item in question; and

(*b*) after payment out of any proceeds arising from the disposal of the expenses incurred in the seizure, storage and disposal, to apply the balance, if any, towards the costs of the council as mentioned in paragraphs (*a*) to (*d*) of subsection (2) of section 32 (fees and charges) of this Act.

(3) The court shall not make a disposal order under subsection (2) above where a person claiming to be the owner of or otherwise interested in the seized item in question applies to be heard by the court, unless an opportunity has been given to him to show cause why the order should not be made.

(4) Subsection (5) below applies where—

(*a*) a person appears before the court under subsection (3) above to show why the order should not be made; and

(*b*) the court makes an order under subsection (2) above authorising the council to dispose of the item; and

(*c*) the seized item in question is not of sufficient value to defray the expenses of seizing and storing it; and

(*d*) the court is satisfied that the person mentioned in paragraph (*a*) above was the owner of the seized item in question or was the person from whom it was seized, as the case may be.

(5) Where this section applies, the court may order that the person mentioned in subsection (4)(*a*) above pay the expenses, or the balance of the expenses, reasonably incurred by the council in seizing and storing the seized item in question.

(6) In considering whether to make an order under subsection (2) above a court shall have regard—

(*a*) to the value of the seized item;

(*b*) to the likely financial and other effects on the offender of the making of the order (taken together with any other order that the court contemplates making); and

(*c*) any other circumstances considered to be relevant.

(7) The court may make a disposal order under this section notwithstanding that the value of the seized item would exceed the maximum penalty for the offence in respect of which the seized item had originally been seized had the said offence been prosecuted to conviction.

(8) For the purposes of this section, "owner" in respect of a vehicle, has the same meaning as it has for the purposes of the said section 38B.

[London Local Authorities Act 1990, s 38C as inserted by the London Local Authorities 2007, s 47.]

7.7716 **39. Savings** (1) Nothing in this Part of this Act shall affect—

(*a*) section 13 of the Markets and Fairs Clauses Act 1847 (prohibition of sales elsewhere than in a market or in shops etc) as applied by any other Acts;

(*b*) section 56 of the Food Act 1984 (prohibition of certain sales during market hours);

(*c*) the sale or exposure or offer for sale by Transport for London or any or its subsidiaries (within the meaning of the Greater London Authority Act 1999) of refreshments at any shelter or other accommodation provided by either of them under section 65 (refreshment shelters etc) of the London Passenger Transport Act 1938.

(2) Nothing in this Part of this Act shall afford a defence to a charge in respect of any offence at common law or under an enactment other than this Part of this Act.

[London Local Authorities Act 1990, s 39, as amended by SI 2003/1615.]

# Traffic and Transport

## Port of London Act 1968

(1968 c 32)

7.7717 This Act makes provision for numerous offences relating to the operation of the Port of London. The penalties were substantially increased by the Port of London Act 1982 (c ix), Schedule 1. The 1982 Act also supplied a new s 199 to the 1968 Act which provides for traffic offences on dock roads and applies provisions in the (now) Road Traffic Regulation Act 1984 and the Road Traffic Act 1988 to those roads.

## London Local Authorities and Transport for London Act 2003

(2003 c iii)

### Part 1
### Preliminary

7.7718 **1. Citation and commencement** (1) This Act may be cited as the London Local Authorities and Transport for London Act 2003 and, except for—

section 4 (Penalty charges for road traffic contraventions);

section 5 (Contraventions of lorry ban order: supplementary);

section 7 (Disapplication of offences); and

section 16 (Vehicle crossings over footways and verges),

shall come into operation at the end of the period of two months beginning with the date on which it is passed.

(2) The said sections 4, 5, 7 and 16 shall come into operation on the appointed day.

(3) This Act and the London Local Authorities Acts 1990 to 2000 may be cited together as the London Local Authorities Acts 1990 to 2003.

[London Local Authorities and Transport for London Act 2003, s 1.]

7.7719 **2. Interpretation** (1) In this Act—

"the Act of 1984" means the Road Traffic Regulation Act 1984 (c 27);

"borough council" means London borough council and includes the Common Council of the City of London in its capacity as a local authority and "borough" and "council" shall be construed accordingly.

(2) Subject to paragraph 1(8) of Schedule 1 to this Act, the owner of a vehicle for the purposes of this Act, shall be taken to be the person by whom the vehicle is kept.

(3) Subject to the said paragraph 1(8), in determining, for the purposes of this Act, who was the owner of a vehicle at any time, it shall be presumed that the owner was the person in whose name the vehicle was at that time registered under the Vehicle Excise and Registration Act 1994 (c 22).

[London Local Authorities and Transport for London Act 2003, s 2.]

7.7720 **3. Appointed day** (1) In subsection (2) of section 1 (Citation and commencement) of this Act "the appointed day" means such day as may be fixed—

(*a*) in relation to a borough by resolution of the borough council; or

(*b*) in relation to a GLA road or a GLA side road by a decision of Transport for London,

subject to and in accordance with the provisions of this section.

(2) Different days may be fixed under this section for the purpose of the application of different provisions of this Act to a borough.

(3) Different days may be fixed under this section for the purpose of the application of the provisions of this Act to different GLA roads or GLA side roads.

(4) But no day fixed under this section may be before the end of the period of two months beginning with the date on which this Act is passed.

(5) The borough council or Transport for London shall cause to be published in a local newspaper circulating in their area and in the London Gazette notice—

(*a*) of the passing of any such resolution or taking of any such decision and of a day fixed thereby; and

(*b*) the general effect of the provisions of this Act coming into operation as from that day, and the day so fixed shall not be earlier than the expiration of three months from the publication of the said notice.

(6) Either a photostatic or other reproduction certified by the officer appointed for that purpose by the borough council or by Transport for London to be a reproduction of a page or part of a page of any such newspaper or the London Gazette bearing the date of its publication and containing any such notice shall be evidence of the publication of the notice, and of the date of publication.

(7) In subsection (5) above, "their area" in relation to Transport for London means the area of any borough council in which the GLA road or GLA side road to which the resolution or decision relates is situated.

[London Local Authorities and Transport for London Act 2003, s 3.]

## PART 2
## ROAD TRAFFIC AND HIGHWAYS

*Penalty charges*

7.7721 **4. Penalty charges for road traffic contraventions** (1) This section applies where—

*(a)* in relation to a GLA road or GLA side road, Transport for London or, subject to subsection (3) below, the relevant borough council; or

*(b)* in relation to any other road in the area of a borough council, the relevant borough council or, subject to subsection (4) below, Transport for London,

have reason to believe (whether or not on the basis of information provided by a camera or other device) that a penalty charge is payable under this section with respect to a motor vehicle.

(2) Transport for London or, as the case may be, the relevant borough council may serve a penalty charge notice—

*(a)* in relation to a penalty charge payable by virtue of subsection (5) below, on the person appearing to them to be the owner of the vehicle; and

*(b)* in relation to a penalty charge payable by virtue of subsection (7) below, on either or both of the following—

(i) the person appearing to them to be the operator of the vehicle; and

(ii) the person appearing to them to be the person who was in control of the vehicle at the time of the contravention.

(3) The relevant borough council shall not exercise the power exercisable by virtue of subsection (1)*(a)* above unless they have obtained the consent in writing of Transport for London.

(4) Transport for London shall not exercise the power exercisable by virtue of subsection (1)*(b)* above unless they have obtained the consent in writing of the relevant borough council.

(5) Subject to subsection (6) below, for the purposes of this section, a penalty charge is payable with respect to a motor vehicle by the owner of the vehicle if the person driving or propelling the vehicle—

*(a)* acts in contravention of a prescribed order; or

*(b)* fails to comply with an indication given by a scheduled section 36 traffic sign.

(6) No penalty charge shall be payable under subsection (5)*(a)* above where—

*(a)* the person acting in contravention of the prescribed order also fails to comply with an indication given by a scheduled section 36 traffic sign; or

*(b)* the contravention of the prescribed order would also give rise to a liability to pay a penalty charge under section 77 of the Road Traffic Act 1991 (c 40).

(7) For the purposes of this section, a penalty charge is payable with respect to a vehicle by—

*(a)* the operator of the vehicle; and

*(b)* the person in control of the vehicle,

if the person in control of the vehicle acts in contravention of the lorry ban order.

(8) A penalty charge notice under this section must—

*(a)* state—

(i) the grounds on which the council or, as the case may be, Transport for London believe that the penalty charge is payable with respect to the vehicle;

(ii) the amount of the penalty charge which is payable;

(iii) that the penalty charge must be paid before the end of the period of 28 days beginning with the date of the notice;

(iv) that if the penalty charge is paid before the end of the period of 14 days beginning with the date of the notice, the amount of the penalty charge will be reduced by the specified proportion;

(v) that, if the penalty charge is not paid before the end of the 28 day period, an increased charge may be payable;

(vi) the amount of the increased charge;

(vii) the address to which payment of the penalty charge must be sent; and

(viii) that the person on whom the notice is served may be entitled to make representations under paragraph 1 of Schedule 1 to this Act; and

*(b)* specify the form in which any such representations are to be made.

(9) The Secretary of State may by regulations prescribe additional matters which must be dealt

with in any penalty charge notice.

(10) In subsection (8)(*a*)(iv) above, "specified proportion" means such proportion, applicable in all cases, as may be determined for the purposes of this section by the borough councils and Transport for London acting through the Joint Committee.

(11) Schedule 1 to this Act shall have effect with respect to representations against penalty charge notices, and other matters supplementary to the provisions of this section.

(12) Subject to subsection (13) below, sections 74 and 74A of the Road Traffic Act 1991 (c 40) shall apply in relation to the levels of penalty charges under this section as they apply in relation to the levels of (among other charges) penalty charges under Part II of that Act.

(13) Before setting the level of any charges under the said section 74 as applied by subsection (12) above, the borough councils and Transport for London shall consult such bodies as in their opinion are sufficiently representative of such road users as would be affected by the imposition of such charges.

(14) No provision in this section shall apply to any vehicle on an occasion when it is being used for fire brigade, ambulance or police purposes.

(15) Schedule 2 to this Act shall have effect with respect to financial provisions relating to the provisions of this section.

(16) In this section—

"Joint Committee" means the Joint Committee established under section 73 of the Road Traffic Act 1991;

"motor vehicle" means a mechanically propelled vehicle intended or adapted for use on roads;

"prescribed order" means an order under section 6 or 9 of the Act of 1984 which makes provision for a relevant traffic control;

"relevant traffic control" means any requirement, restriction or prohibition (other than a requirement, restriction or prohibition under the lorry ban order) which is or may be conveyed by a scheduled traffic sign;

"road" has the same meaning as in the Act of 1984;

"scheduled section 36 traffic sign" means—

(*a*) a scheduled traffic sign of a type to which section 36 (Drivers to comply with traffic signs) of the Road Traffic Act 1988 (c 52) applies by virtue of regulations made under section 64(5) of the Act of 1984; but

(*b*) does not include a traffic sign which indicates any prohibition or restriction imposed by the lorry ban order;

"scheduled traffic sign" means a traffic sign of a type described in Schedule 3 to this Act;

"traffic sign" has the meaning given by section 64(1) of the Act of 1984.

(17) In this section and section 5 (Contraventions of lorry ban order: supplementary) of this Act—

"driver's notice" means a penalty charge notice served under subsection (2)(*b*)(ii) above on the person appearing to have been the person in control of the vehicle at the time of the alleged contravention of the lorry ban order;

"the lorry ban order" means the Greater London (Restriction of Goods Vehicles) Traffic Order 1985 made by the Greater London Council under section 6 of the Act of 1984, as amended, replaced or substituted by any subsequent order;

"operator of a vehicle" means the holder of any operator's licence in respect of that vehicle under section 2 of the Goods Vehicles (Licensing of Operators) Act 1995 (c 23);

"operator's notice" means a penalty charge notice served under subsection (2)(*b*)(i) above on the person appearing to be the operator of a vehicle;

"relevant borough council" means the borough council in whose area the alleged contravention or failure occurred.

(18) In determining, for the purposes of any provision of this Act, whether a penalty charge has been paid before the end of a particular period, it shall be taken to be paid when it is received by the council concerned, or as the case may be, Transport for London.

(19) The Secretary of State may, by regulations, amend Schedule 3 to this Act by—

(*a*) adding any traffic signs to the list of traffic signs in the Schedule; or

(*b*) making any other amendments to the Schedule as may be necessary as a consequence of any amendment, replacement or substitution of the Traffic Signs Regulations and General Directions 2002 (SI 2002/3113).* **

[London Local Authorities and Transport for London Act 2003, s 4, as amended by the London Local Authorities and Transport for London Act 2008, s 27.]

* **Repealed by the Traffic Management Act 2004, s 98, Sch 12, Pt 1, from a date to be appointed.**

** **Amended for a transitional period only beginning 31 March 2008 by SI 2007/2053 (itself amended by SI 2008/757).**

7.7722 **5. Contraventions of lorry ban order: supplementary** (1) An operator's notice shall state that before the end of the period of 14 days beginning with the date of the notice, the operator of the vehicle must provide the relevant borough council, or as the case may be, Transport for London, with the name and address of the person who was in control of the vehicle when the alleged contravention of the lorry ban order took place.

(2) Any person who in response to a requirement stated in a penalty charge notice by virtue of subsection (1) above fails to comply with the requirement shall be guilty of an offence unless he shows to the satisfaction of the court that—

(*a*) he was not the operator of the vehicle at the time the alleged contravention of the lorry ban order took place; or

(*b*) he did not know, and could not with reasonable diligence have ascertained, who was the person in control of the vehicle.

(3) Any person who in response to a requirement stated in a penalty charge notice by virtue of subsection (1) above gives information which is false in a material particular and does so recklessly or knowing it to be false in that particular shall be guilty of an offence.

(4) Any person guilty of an offence under subsection (2) or (3) above shall be liable on summary conviction—

(*a*) in the case of subsection (2) to a fine not exceeding level 3 on the standard scale; and

(*b*) in the case of subsection (3) to a fine not exceeding level 5 on the standard scale.

(5) In the case where an operator's notice is served on the person appearing to be the operator of the vehicle, the provisions of this Act mentioned below shall have effect as follows—

(*a*) for paragraph 1(4)(*a*) of Schedule 1 there shall be substituted—

"(*a*) that the recipient was not the operator of the vehicle at the time the alleged contravention of the order took place;";

(*b*) paragraph 1(4)(*c*) and (*d*), (5) and (6) of Schedule 1 shall be omitted; and

(*c*) after paragraph 1(4) of Schedule 1 the following sub-paragraph shall be inserted—

"(4A) Where the ground mentioned in sub-paragraph (4)(*a*) above is relied on in any representations made under this paragraph, those representations must include a statement of the name and address of the operator of the vehicle at the time of the alleged contravention or failure to comply (if that information is in his possession).".

(6) In the case where a driver's notice is served on the person appearing to have been in control of the vehicle at the time of the alleged contravention, the provisions of this Act mentioned below shall have effect as follows—

(*a*) for paragraph 1(4)(*a*) of Schedule 1 there shall be substituted—

"(*a*) that the recipient was not the person in control of the vehicle at the time the alleged contravention of the lorry ban order took place;";

(*b*) paragraph 1(4)(*c*) and (*d*), (5) and (6) of Schedule 1 shall be omitted; and

(*c*) after paragraph 1(4) of Schedule 1 the following sub-paragraph shall be inserted—

"(4A) Where the ground mentioned in sub-paragraph (4)(*a*) above is relied on in any representations made under this paragraph, those representations must include a statement of the name and address of the person in control of the vehicle at the time of the alleged contravention or failure to comply (if that information is in his possession).".

(7) In the case where, under paragraph 1(4) of Schedule 1 to this Act as so applied and having effect in accordance with subsections (5) or (6) above the relevant borough council or as the case may be Transport for London is provided with the name and address of—

(*a*) the operator of the vehicle; or

(*b*) the person who was in control of the vehicle at the time of the alleged contravention of the lorry ban order,

they may serve a fresh penalty charge notice in accordance with paragraph 2(2) of that Schedule on either of those persons, or both.*

[London Local Authorities and Transport for London Act 2003, s 5.]

* **Repealed by the Traffic Management Act 2004, s 98, Sch 12, Pt 1, from a date to be appointed.**

7.7723 **6. Limitation on service of penalty charge notice** (1) Subject to the provisions of this section, no penalty charge notice may be served under this Act after the expiry of the period of 28 days beginning with the date on which the alleged contravention or failure to comply occurred.

(2) Subsection (2A) below applies where—

(*a*) a penalty charge notice has been cancelled under paragraph 2 of Schedule 1 to this Act; or

(*b*) a penalty charge notice has been cancelled in compliance with a direction given by a traffic adjudicator under paragraph 4(2) of the said Schedule; or

(*c*) a penalty charge notice is deemed to have been cancelled under paragraph 7(8)(*c*) of the said Schedule (deemed cancellation where a statutory declaration under paragraph 7(2)(*a*) of that Schedule is served under paragraph 7(1)(*c*)),

(*d*) payment of the penalty charge has been made or has purportedly been made before the expiry of the period mentioned in subsection (1) above but the payment or purported payment is subsequently cancelled or withdrawn.

(2A) Subject to subsection (3) below, the borough council or Transport for London, as the case may be, may not serve a fresh penalty charge notice after the expiry of the period of 28 days from—

(*a*) the date of the cancellation of the penalty charge notice; or

(*b*) in a case falling within subsection (2)(*c*) above, the date on which the council or body are served with notice under paragraph 7(8)(*d*) of the said Schedule; or

(*c*) in a case falling within subsection (2)(*d*) above, the date on which the council or body received notification that the payment or purported payment had been cancelled or withdrawn.

(3) Subsection (6) below applies where the following conditions are met.

(4) The first condition is that where a borough council or Transport for London, as the case may be, has before the expiry of 14 days from—

(*a*) the date on which the alleged contravention or failure to comply occurred; or

(*b*) the date of the cancellation of the penalty charge notice in the case where a penalty charge notice has been cancelled—

(i) under paragraph 2 of the said Schedule; or

(ii) in compliance with a direction given by a traffic adjudicator under paragraph 4(2) of the said Schedule; or

(*c*) the date on which the borough council or Transport for London, as the case may be, are served with notice under paragraph 7(8)(*d*) of the said Schedule where the penalty charge notice is deemed to have been cancelled under paragraph 7(8)(*c*), or

(*d*) the date on which the council or body receives a notification that the payment or purported payment has been cancelled or withdrawn in the circumstances mentioned in subsection (2)(*d*) above,

made a request to the Secretary of State for the supply of relevant particulars.

(5) The second condition is that those particulars have not been supplied to the borough council or Transport for London, as the case may be, before the date after which that council or body would not be entitled to serve a penalty charge notice or a fresh penalty charge notice by virtue of subsection (1) or (2A) above.

(6) Where this subsection applies, the borough council or Transport for London, as the case may be, shall continue to be entitled to serve a penalty charge notice or a fresh penalty charge notice for a further period of 6 months beginning with the date mentioned in subsection (5) above.

(7) In this section, "relevant particulars" are particulars relating to the identity of the owner of the vehicle contained in the register of mechanically propelled vehicles maintained by the Secretary of State under the Vehicle Excise and Registration Act 1994 (c 22).*

[London Local Authorities and Transport for London Act 2003, s 6, as amended by the London Local Authorities and Transport for London Act 2008, s 7.]

* **Repealed by the Traffic Management Act 2004, s 98, Sch 12, Pt 1, from a date to be appointed.**

7.7724 **7. Disapplication of offences** (1) This section applies to the following roads—

(*a*) GLA roads and GLA side roads; and

(*b*) any other road in the area of a borough council.

(2) Section 8 of the Act of 1984 shall apply in respect of a road to which this section applies as if after subsection (1A), the following subsection were inserted—

"(1B) Subsection (1) above does not apply in relation to any person who acts in contravention of or fails to comply with—

(*a*) an order under section 6 of this Act; or

(*b*) the lorry ban order within the meaning of section 4 of the London Local Authorities and Transport for London Act 2003 (penalty charges for road traffic contraventions),

if as a result a penalty charge is payable under subsection (5) or, as the case may be, subsection (7) of section 4 of that Act.".

(3) Section 11 of the Act of 1984 shall apply in respect of a road to which this section applies as if after subsection (2), the following subsection were inserted—

"(2A) This section does not apply in relation to any person who acts in contravention of or fails to comply with an experimental traffic order if as a result a penalty charge is payable under section 4(5) of the London Local Authorities and Transport for London Act 2003 (penalty charges for road traffic contraventions).".

(4) Section 36 of the Road Traffic Act 1988 (c 52) shall apply in respect of a road to which this section applies as if after subsection (1), the following subsection were inserted—

"(1A) Subsection (1) above does not apply in relation to any such person who fails to comply with the indication given by the sign if as a result a penalty charge is payable under section 4(5) of the London Local Authorities and Transport for London Act 2003 (penalty charges for road traffic contraventions).".*

[London Local Authorities and Transport for London Act 2003, s 7.]

* **Repealed by the Traffic Management Act 2004, s 98, Sch 12, Pt 1, from a date to be appointed.**

*Fixed penalties*

7.7725 **8. Fixed penalty offences** (1) Where on any occasion an authorised officer of a borough council or Transport for London finds a person who he has reason to believe has on that occasion committed an offence under any of the enactments—

(*a*) mentioned in columns (1) and (2) of the table set out in Schedule 4 to this Act; and

(*b*) described in column (3) of that table;

the officer may give that person a notice offering him the opportunity of discharging any liability to conviction for that offence by payment of a fixed penalty.

(2) The powers of an authorised officer of a borough council under subsection (1) above may be exercised only in relation to offences alleged to have been committed in respect of a highway in

respect of which the council is highway authority.

(3) The powers of an authorised officer of Transport for London under subsection (1) above may be exercised only in relation to offences alleged to have been committed in respect of a GLA road or a GLA side road.

(4) Sections 9 (Fixed penalty notices), 10 (Levels of fixed penalties) and 11 (Fixed penalties: reserve powers of Secretary of State) of this Act shall apply in respect of fixed penalty notices under this section.

(5) Schedule 2 to this Act shall have effect with respect to financial provisions relating to the administration and enforcement of this section and sections 9 to 11 (Fixed penalties) of this Act.

(6) The Secretary of State may, by regulations, amend Schedule 4 to this Act by the addition of further offences to the list of offences therein described.

[London Local Authorities and Transport for London Act 2003, s 8.]

7.7726 **9. Fixed penalty notices** (1) The provisions of this section shall have effect in relation to notices ("fixed penalty notices") which may be given under section 8 (Fixed penalty offences) of this Act.

(2) Where a person is given a fixed penalty notice in respect of an offence—

(*a*) no proceedings shall be instituted for that offence before the expiration of 28 days following the date of the notice; and

(*b*) he shall not be convicted of that offence if he pays the fixed penalty before the expiration of that period.

(3) A fixed penalty notice under this section shall give such particulars of the circumstances alleged to constitute the offence as are necessary for giving reasonable information of the offence and shall state—

(*a*) the period during which, by virtue of subsection (2) above, proceedings will not be taken for the offence;

(*b*) the amount of the fixed penalty;

(*ba*) that if the fixed penalty is paid before the end of the period of 14 days beginning with the date of the notice, the amount of the fixed penalty will be reduced by the specified proportion; and

(*c*) the name of the person to whom and the address at which the fixed penalty may be paid; and, without prejudice to payment by any other method, payment of the fixed penalty may be made by pre-paying and posting to that person at that address a letter containing the amount of the penalty (in cash or otherwise).

(4) Where a letter is sent in accordance with subsection (3) above, payment shall be regarded as having been made at the time at which that letter would be delivered in the ordinary course of post.

(5) The form of notices under this section shall be such as the Secretary of State may by regulations prescribe.

(6) The fixed penalty payable in pursuance of a fixed penalty notice under this section shall be paid to the borough council or Transport for London, as the case may be.

(7) In any proceedings a certificate which—

(*a*) purports to be signed by or on behalf of the chief finance officer of the council, or as the case may be, Transport for London; and

(*b*) states that payment of a fixed penalty was or was not received by a date specified in the certificate,

shall be evidence of the facts stated.

(8) In this section—

(*a*) "chief finance officer" in relation to a borough council or Transport for London means the person having responsibility for the financial affairs of the council or Transport for London, as the case may be;

(*b*) "specified proportion" means such proportion, applicable in all cases, as may be determined for the purposes of this section by the borough councils acting through the Joint Committee as defined in section 4(16) of this Act.

[London Local Authorities and Transport for London Act 2003, s 9, as amended by the London Local Authorities and Transport for London Act 2008, s 26.]

7.7727 **10. Levels of fixed penalties**

7.7728 **11. Fixed penalties: reserve powers of Secretary of State**

*Parking*

7.7729 **13. False applications for parking authorisations** (1) Insofar as subsection (2) of section 115 of the Act of 1984 (mishandling of parking documents and related offences) relates to any authorisation which may be issued by a borough council or by Transport for London—

(*a*) proceedings for an offence under that section may be brought within a period of six months from the date on which evidence sufficient in the opinion of the prosecutor to warrant the proceedings came to his knowledge, but

(*b*) no such proceedings shall be brought by virtue of this section more than three years after the commission of the offence.

(2) For the purposes of subsection (1) above a certificate signed by or on behalf of the prosecutor and stating the date on which evidence such as is mentioned in that subsection came to

his knowledge, shall be conclusive evidence of that fact; and a certificate purporting to be so signed shall be deemed to be so signed unless the contrary is proved.

[London Local Authorities and Transport for London Act 2003, s 13.]

*Vehicle Crossings*

7.7730 **16. Vehicle crossings over footways and verges**

*Removal notices*

7.7731 **17. Removal of things deposited on the highway** (1) This section applies in respect of any part of—

(*a*) any highway for which Transport for London are the highway authority; and

(*b*) any highway for which a borough council are the highway authority.

(2) If the highway authority are satisfied that—

(*a*) things are deposited unlawfully and persistently on any part of the highway to which this section applies; and

(*b*) the depositing of the things is caused by persons having control of or an interest in a business carried on in premises in the vicinity of the part of the highway concerned,

the highway authority may serve a notice under this subsection ("a subsection (2) removal notice") on any person having control of or an interest in the relevant business.

(3) A subsection (2) removal notice shall—

(*a*) state the date on which it shall come into effect (which shall be no sooner than the date on which the period of 7 days beginning with the date of service of the notice expires);

(*b*) state the date on which it shall expire (which shall be no later than the date on which the period of 28 days beginning with the date on which it comes into effect expires);

(*c*) give a description of the part of the highway to which the notice relates;

(*d*) state that in the period during which the notice has effect, the highway authority may without further notice remove any thing deposited unlawfully on the part of the highway to which the notice relates;

(*e*) state the effect of subsections (5) and (12) below.

(4) Where a subsection (2) removal notice is served under subsection (2) above, a copy of the notice shall be affixed by the highway authority to a conspicuous place in the vicinity of the part of the highway to which the notice relates.

(5) If any thing is deposited unlawfully on any part of the highway to which a subsection (2) removal notice relates, the highway authority may—

(*a*) remove the thing forthwith; and

(*b*) no sooner than the relevant date, dispose of the thing.

(6) If a highway authority remove a thing under section 149(2) of the Highways Act 1980 (c 66) (which makes provision about things deposited on the highway so as to cause a danger), instead of proceeding under subsection (3) of that section, they may proceed in accordance with subsection (7) below.

(7) No later than 24 hours after the removal of the thing under the said section 149(2), the highway authority shall issue a notice ("a subsection (7) removal notice") and proceed in the manner described in subsection (9) below.

(8) A subsection (7) removal notice shall—

(*a*) give a description of the thing removed;

(*b*) state the effect of subsections (10) and (12) below.

(9) Where a subsection (7) removal notice is issued, the notice or a copy of the notice shall be affixed by the highway authority to a conspicuous place in the vicinity of the part of the highway from which the thing was removed.

(10) A highway authority may, no sooner than the relevant date, dispose of any thing which they have removed and in respect of which a subsection (7) removal notice has been issued.

(11) Any person who without reasonable excuse removes, alters or damages a notice affixed to any place under subsection (4) or (9) above shall be guilty of an offence and liable on summary conviction to a fine not exceeding level 3 on the standard scale.

(12) The authority by whom a thing is removed in pursuance of this section may recover from the person by whom it was deposited on the highway, or from any person claiming to be entitled to it, any expenses reasonably incurred by the authority in removing, storing or disposing of it.

(13) After payment out of any proceeds arising from the disposal of the thing of the expenses incurred in the removal, storage and disposal of the thing, the highway authority may apply the balance, if any, of the proceeds to the maintenance of the highways maintainable at the public expense by them.

(14) If the thing in question is not of sufficient value to defray the expenses of removing, storing and disposing of it, the highway authority may recover from the person who deposited it on the highway the expenses, or the balance of the expenses, reasonably incurred by them in removing, storing and disposing of it.

(15) If, after a thing has been disposed of by a highway authority pursuant to this section, a person claims to have been the owner of the thing at the time when it was removed and the conditions specified in subsection (16) below are fulfilled, there shall be payable to him by the

highway authority a sum calculated in accordance with subsection (17) below. (16) The conditions are that—

(*a*) the person claiming satisfies the highway authority that he was the owner of the thing at the time it was removed; and

(*b*) the claim is made before the expiry of the period of five months beginning with the date on which the thing was removed.

(17) The sum payable under subsection (15) above shall be calculated by deducting from the proceeds of sale the charges reasonably incurred by the highway authority for the removing, storing and disposing of the thing.

(18) In subsections (5) and (10) above, the "relevant date" in respect of a thing is the date on which expires the period of 14 days beginning with the date on which the thing was removed by the highway authority.

(19) For the purposes of this section and section 18 (Removal notices: appeals) of this Act—

(*a*) "the relevant business" means the business referred to in subsection (2) above; and

(*b*) a person having an interest in a relevant business includes a person who—

(i) owns the business; or

(ii) manages the business; or

(iii) employs any person to manage the business; or

(iv) is involved in the conduct of the business.

[London Local Authorities and Transport for London Act 2003, s 17, as amended by the London Local Authorities and Transport for London Act 2008, s 27.]

7.7732 **18. Removal notices: appeals**

7.7733 **19. Service of removal notices**

## PART 3
## SUPPLEMENTARY

7.7734 **20. Disclosure of information**

7.7735 **21. Authorised officers**

7.7736 **22. Obstruction of authorised officer** Any person who intentionally obstructs any authorised officer acting in the exercise of his powers under this Act shall be guilty of an offence and liable on summary conviction to a fine not exceeding level 3 on the standard scale.

[London Local Authorities and Transport for London Act 2003, s 22.]

7.7737 **23. Provision of information to authorised officer of Transport for London** (1) This section applies where an authorised officer of Transport for London has reasonable grounds for suspecting that any offence in respect of which that body may prosecute legal proceedings has been committed or attempted, or is being committed or attempted.

(2) If, on being requested by the authorised officer to furnish his name and address for service of a summons or fixed penalty notice the relevant person—

(*a*) fails to furnish a name; or

(*b*) furnishes a false name; or

(*c*) furnishes a false address,

the relevant person shall, unless the authorised officer failed to produce his authorisation on making the request, be guilty of an offence punishable on summary conviction by a fine not exceeding level 5 on the standard scale.

(3) In this section "the relevant person" means any person who the authorised officer has reasonable grounds to suspect of having committed or having attempted to commit the offence or being in the course of committing or attempting to commit it.

[London Local Authorities and Transport for London Act 2003, s 23.]

7.7738 **24. Defence of due diligence** (1) In proceedings for an offence under this Act it shall be a defence for the person charged to prove that he took all reasonable precautions and exercised all due diligence to avoid the commission of the offence.

(2) If in any case the defence provided under subsection (1) above involves the allegation that the commission of the offence was due to the act or default of another person, the person charged shall not, without leave of the court, be entitled to rely on that defence unless, no later than 7 clear days before the hearing, he has served on the prosecutor a notice in writing giving such information as was then in his possession identifying or assisting in the identification of that other person.

[London Local Authorities and Transport for London Act 2003, s 24.]

7.7739 **25. Liability of directors, etc** (1) Where an offence under this Act committed by a body corporate is proved to have been committed with the consent or connivance of, or to be attributable to any neglect on the part of, a director, manager, secretary or other similar officer of the body corporate or any person who was purporting to act in any such capacity, he, as well as the body corporate, shall be guilty of the offence.

(2) Where the affairs of the body corporate are managed by its members, subsection (1) above shall apply to the acts and defaults of a member in connection with his functions of management as if he were a director of the body corporate.

[London Local Authorities and Transport for London Act 2003, s 25.]

7.7740 **26. Regulations**

SCHEDULE 1

PENALTY CHARGE NOTICES ETC UNDER SECTION 4 (PENALTY CHARGES FOR ROAD TRAFFIC CONTRAVENTIONS) OF THIS ACT

Section 4

*Representations against penalty charge notice*

7.7741 **1.** (1) Where it appears to a person on whom a penalty charge notice has been served under section 4 (Penalty charges for road traffic contraventions) of this Act (in this Schedule referred to as "the recipient") that one or other of the grounds mentioned in sub-paragraph (4) below is satisfied, he may make representations to that effect to the enforcing authority.

(2) Any representations under this paragraph must be made in such form as may be specified by the enforcing authority, acting through the Joint Committee (within the meaning of subsection (16) of the said section 4).

(3) The enforcing authority may disregard any such representations which are received by them after the end of the period of 28 days beginning with the date on which the penalty charge notice in question was served.

(4) The grounds referred to in sub-paragraph (1) above are—

(*a*) that the recipient—
  (i) never was the owner of the vehicle in question;
  (ii) had ceased to be its owner before the date on which the penalty charge was alleged to have become payable; or
  (iii) became its owner after that date;

(*b*) that there was no—
  (i) contravention of a prescribed order; or
  (ii) failure to comply with an indication; or
  (iii) contravention of the lorry ban order,

under subsection (5) or (7) of the said section 4 as the case may be;

(*c*) that at the time the alleged contravention or failure took place the person who was in control of the vehicle was in control of the vehicle without the consent of the owner;

(*d*) that the recipient is a vehicle-hire firm and—
  (i) the vehicle in question was at the material time hired from that firm under a vehicle hiring agreement; and
  (ii) the person hiring it had signed a statement of liability acknowledging his liability in respect of any penalty charge notice issued in respect of the vehicle during the currency of the hiring agreement; or

(*e*) that the penalty charge exceeded the amount applicable in the circumstances of the case.

(5) Where the ground mentioned in sub-paragraph (4)(*a*)(ii) above is relied on in any representations made under this paragraph, those representations must include a statement of the name and address of the person to whom the vehicle was disposed of by the person making the representations (if that information is in his possession).

(6) Where the ground mentioned in sub-paragraph (4)(*a*)(iii) above is relied on in any representations made under this paragraph, those representations must include a statement of the name and address of the person from whom the vehicle was acquired by the person making the representations (if that information is in his possession).

(7) It shall be the duty of the enforcing authority to whom representations are duly made under this paragraph—

(*a*) to consider them and any supporting evidence which the person making them provides; and

(*b*) to serve on that person notice of their decision as to whether they accept that the ground in question has been established.

(8) Where the ground that is accepted is that mentioned in sub-paragraph (4)(*d*) above, the person hiring the vehicle shall be deemed to be its owner for the purposes of this Act.

(9) In this paragraph, "vehicle hiring agreement" and "vehicle-hire firm" have the same meanings as in section 66 of the Road Traffic Offenders Act 1988 (c 53) (Hired vehicles).

*Cancellation of penalty charge notice*

**2.** (1) Where representations are made under paragraph 1 above and the enforcing authority accept that the ground in question has been established they shall—

(*a*) cancel the penalty charge notice; and

(*b*) state in the notice served under sub-paragraph (7) of paragraph 1 above that the penalty charge notice has been cancelled.

(2) The cancellation of a penalty charge notice under this paragraph shall not be taken to prevent the enforcing authority serving a fresh penalty charge notice on another person.

*Rejection of representations against penalty charge notice*

**3.** Where any representations are made under paragraph 1 above but the enforcing authority do not accept that a ground has been established, the notice served under sub-paragraph (7) of the said paragraph 1 (in this Schedule referred to as "the notice of rejection") must—

(*a*) state that a charge certificate may be served under paragraph 5 below unless before the end of the period of 28 days beginning with the date of service of the notice of rejection—
  (i) the penalty charge is paid; or
  (ii) the person on whom the notice is served appeals to a traffic adjudicator against the penalty charge; and

(*b*) describe in general terms the form and manner in which such an appeal must be made,

and may contain such other information as the enforcing authority consider appropriate.

*Adjudication by traffic adjudicator*

4. (1) Where an enforcing authority serve a notice of rejection, the person who made the representations under paragraph 1 above in respect of which that notice was served may, before—

(*a*) the end of the period of 28 days beginning with the date of service of that notice; or

(*b*) such longer period as a traffic adjudicator may allow,

appeal to a traffic adjudicator against the decision of the enforcing authority.

(2) On an appeal under this paragraph, the traffic adjudicator shall consider the representations in question and any additional representations which are made by the appellant on any of the grounds mentioned in paragraph 1(4) above and may give the enforcing authority such directions as he considers appropriate.

(3) It shall be the duty of the enforcing authority to whom a direction is given under sub-paragraph (2) above to comply with it forthwith.

*Charge certificates*

5. (1) Where a penalty charge notice is served on any person and the penalty charge to which it relates is not paid before the end of the relevant period, the enforcing authority may serve on that person a statement (in this paragraph referred to as a "charge certificate") to the effect that the penalty charge in question is increased by 50 per cent.

(2) The relevant period, in relation to a penalty charge notice is the period of 28 days beginning—

(*a*) where no representations are made under paragraph 1 above, with the date on which the penalty charge notice is served;

(*b*) where such representations are made and a notice of rejection is served by the enforcing authority and no appeal against the notice of rejection is made with the date on which the period within which an appeal could have been made expires; or

(*c*) where there has been an unsuccessful appeal against a notice of rejection, with the date on which notice of the adjudicator's decision is served on the appellant.

(3) Where an appeal against a notice of rejection is made but is withdrawn before the decision of the adjudicator is made the relevant period in relation to a penalty charge notice is the period of 14 days beginning with the date on which the appeal is withdrawn.

*Enforcement of charge certificate*

6. (1) Where a charge certificate has been served on any person and the increased penalty charge provided for in the certificate is not paid before the end of the period of 14 days beginning with the date on which the certificate is served, the enforcing authority may, if a county court so orders, recover the increased charge as if it were payable under a county court order.

(2) Any notice of any county court order made under this paragraph and being served on any person shall be accompanied by a copy of the penalty charge notice to which the penalty charge relates.

(3) Section 78 of the Road Traffic Act 1991 (c 40) (which makes provision for the recovery of sums that are payable under or by virtue of any provision of Part II of that Act and are recoverable as if they were payable under a county court order) shall have effect as though an increased penalty charge recoverable under sub-paragraph (1) above were a Part II debt for the purposes of that section.

*Invalid notices*

7. (1) This paragraph applies where—

(*a*) a county court makes an order under paragraph 6 above;

(*b*) the person against whom it is made makes a statutory declaration complying with sub-paragraph (2) below; and

(*c*) that declaration is, before the end of the period of 21 days beginning with the date on which notice of the county court's order is served on him, served on the county court which made the order.

(2) The statutory declaration must state that the person making it—

(*a*) did not receive the penalty charge notice in question;

(*b*) made representations to the enforcing authority under paragraph 1 above but did not receive a notice of rejection from that authority; or

(*c*) appealed to a traffic adjudicator under paragraph 4 above against the rejection by that authority of representations made by him under paragraph 1 above but had no response to the appeal.

(3) A statutory declaration under this paragraph is invalid and sub-paragraph (8) below shall not apply in relation to the declaration if one or more of the following grounds is met—

(*a*) the person who made the declaration claims that more than one of the grounds mentioned in sub-paragraph (2) above is met;

(*b*) the declaration is not signed by any person purporting to make it;

(*c*) the declaration is not signed by or does not contain an address for a person purporting to be a witness to the signature of the person making it.

(4) The Secretary of State may by regulations amend sub-paragraph (3) above by the addition of further grounds for a statutory declaration to be invalid.

(5) Sub-paragraph (7) below applies where it appears to a district judge, on the application of a person on whom a charge certificate has been served, that it would be unreasonable in the circumstances of his case to insist on him serving his statutory declaration within the period of 21 days allowed for by sub-paragraph (1) above.

(6) In considering an application under sub-paragraph (5) above the district judge must take into consideration any representations made by the enforcing authority before the expiry of the period of 14 days beginning on the date on which copies of the application and the statutory declaration are served by the court on the enforcing authority.

(7) Where this sub-paragraph applies, the district judge may allow such longer period for service of the statutory declaration as he considers appropriate.

(8) Subject to sub-paragraphs (3) above and (10) below, where a statutory declaration is served under sub-paragraph (1)(*c*) above—

(*a*) the order of the court shall be deemed to have been revoked;

(*b*) the charge certificate shall be deemed to have been cancelled;

(*c*) in the case of a statutory declaration under sub-paragraph (2)(*a*) above, the penalty charge notice to which the charge certificate relates shall be deemed to have been cancelled; and (*d*) the district judge shall serve written notice of the effect of service of the statutory declaration on the person making it and on the enforcing authority.

(9) Service of a declaration under sub-paragraph (2)(*a*) above shall not prevent the enforcing authority serving a fresh penalty charge notice but if, when it was served, the relevant order under paragraph 6 was accompanied by a copy of the penalty charge notice to which the charge certificate relates, a fresh penalty charge notice in the same terms shall be deemed to have been served on the person making the declaration on the same day as the declaration was served.

(10) Where—

(*a*) sub-paragraph (7) above applies; and

(*b*) the order of the court is deemed to have been revoked under sub-paragraph (8) above,

the enforcing authority concerned shall not be liable to pay the person making the declaration any sums other than the increased charge which was payable under the county court order.

(11) Where a declaration has been served under sub-paragraph (2)(*b*) or (*c*) above, the enforcing authority shall refer the case to the traffic adjudicator who may give such direction as he considers appropriate.

*Offence of giving false information*

**8.** (1) A person who, in response to a penalty charge notice served under section 4 (Penalty charges for road traffic contraventions) of this Act makes any representation under paragraph 1 or 4 above which is false in a material particular and does so recklessly or knowing it to be false in that particular is guilty of an offence.

(2) Any person guilty of such an offence shall be liable on summary conviction to a fine not exceeding level 5 on the standard scale.

*Service by post*

**9.** Any charge certificate, or notice under section 4 (Penalty charges for road traffic contraventions) of this Act or this Schedule—

(*a*) may be served by post; and

(*b*) where the person on whom it is to be served is a body corporate, is duly served if it is sent by post to the secretary or clerk of that body.

*Traffic Adjudicators*

**10.** (1) Functions of traffic adjudicators under this Schedule shall be discharged by the persons who are appointed as parking adjudicators under section 73 of the Road Traffic Act 1991 (c 40).

(2) Regulations under section 73(11) of the said Act of 1991 (provision as to procedure to be followed in relation to proceedings before parking adjudicators) may make provision with respect to proceedings before parking adjudicators when exercising the functions of traffic adjudicators under this Schedule; and any regulations under that subsection in force at the coming into operation of section 4 (Penalty charges for road traffic contraventions) of this Act shall, with any necessary modifications, apply in relation to such proceedings.

(3) The references to a parking adjudicator or parking adjudicators in section 73(13) to (15) and (17) and (18) of the said Act of 1991 shall include references to a parking adjudicator or parking adjudicators exercising the functions of traffic adjudicators under this Schedule but section 73(15) of that Act shall not apply to a penalty charge under the said section 4 which remains payable following an adjudication under this Schedule.

*Interpretation*

**11.** In this Schedule "the enforcing authority", in relation to any penalty charge notice or charge certificate, means—

(*a*) where the notice was served by a borough council, or the certificate relates to a notice so served, that council;

(*b*) where the notice was served by Transport for London, or the certificate relates to a notice so served, Transport for London.* **

* **Repealed by the Traffic Management Act 2004, s 98, Sch 12, Pt 1, from a date to be appointed.**

** **Amended for a transitional period only beginning 31 March 2008 by SI 2007/2053 (itself amended by SI 2008/757).**

## SCHEDULE 2

Financial Provisions Relating to Sections 4 (Penalty Charges for Road Traffic Contraventions) and* 8 to 11 (Fixed Penalties) of this Act

* **Words repealed by the Traffic Management Act 2004, s 98, Sch 12, Pt 1, from a date to be appointed.**

## SCHEDULE 3

Scheduled Traffic Signs for the Purposes of Section 4 (Penalty Charges for Road Traffic Contraventions) of this Act*

* **Schedule repealed by the Traffic Management Act 2004, s 98, Sch 12, Pt 1, from a date to be appointed.**

SCHEDULE 4
Offences in Respect of which Fixed Penalty Notices may be Served under Section 8 (Fixed Penalty Offences) of this Act

7.7742

*(Amended by the Transport for London Act 2008, s 35.)* Section 8

| | (1) *Act* | (2) *Section* | (3) *Description of Offence* |
|---|---|---|---|
| 1 | Highways Act 1980 (c 66) | 132(1) | Painting or otherwise inscribing or affixing picture etc upon the surface of a highway or upon a tree, structure or works on or in a highway |
| 2 | | 137(1) | Wilful obstruction of highway |
| 3 | | 138 | Erecting a building, fence or hedge on highway |
| 4 | | 139(3) | Depositing builder's skip on highway without permission |
| 5 | | 139(4)(*a*) | Failure to secure lighting or other marking of builder's skip |
| 6 | | 139(4)(*b*) | Failure to secure marking of builder's skip with name and address |
| 7 | | 139(4)(*c*) | Failure to secure removal of builder's skip |
| 8 | | 139(4)(*d*) | Failure to comply with conditions of permission |
| 9 | | 140(3) | Failure to remove or reposition builder's skip |
| 10 | | 141(3) | Failure to comply with notice requiring removal of tree or shrub |
| 11 | | 147A(2) | Using of stall etc for road side sales in certain circumstances |
| 12 | | 148(*a*) | Depositing material etc on a made-up carriageway |
| 13 | | 148(*b*) | Depositing material etc within 15 feet from centre of made-up carriageway |
| 14 | | 148(*c*) | Depositing anything on highway to the interruption of user |
| 15 | | 148(*d*) | Pitching of booths, stalls or stands or encamping on highway |
| 16 | | 151(3) | Failure to comply with notice requiring works to prevent soil or refuse escaping onto street or into sewer |
| 17 | | 152(4) | Failure to comply with notice requiring removal of projection from buildings |
| 18 | | 153(5) | Failure to comply with notice requiring alteration of door, gate or bar opening outwards onto street |
| 19 | | 155(2) | Keeping of animals straying or lying on side of highway |
| 20 | | 161(1) | Depositing things on highway which cause injury or danger |
| 21 | | 169(5) | Erecting scaffolding or other structure without licence or failing to comply with terms of licence or perform duty under subsection (4) |
| 22 | Transport for London Act 2008 (c i) | 35(3) | Failure to comply with notice requiring works to prevent soil or refuse escaping onto street or into sewer |

# Transport for London Act 2008

(2008 c 1)

## PART 1
## PRELIMINARY

7.7743 **1. Citation and commencement** *This Act came into force on 22 July 2008 except ss 17–21, 23–25, 27 and Schs 1 and 2 which have effect from a date appointed by TfL.*

## PART 2
## ROAD USER CHARGING

7.7743A **4. Interpretation of Part 2** Expressions used in this Part and in Schedule 23 to the 1999 Act have the same meaning in this Part as in that Schedule.

[Transport for London Act 2008, s 4.]

7.7744 **5. Contravention of requirement of TfL scheme** (1) Subject to subsection (2), a TfL scheme may provide that any person who, without reasonable excuse, contravenes or fails to comply with any specified requirement of the scheme shall be liable on summary conviction to a fine for each offence not exceeding level 2 on the standard scale or not exceeding a lesser amount; but such a provision—

(*a*) shall not have effect unless and until it has been approved by the Secretary of State, and

(*b*) shall not apply in relation to anything done before the provision comes into effect.

(2) Subsection (1) shall not authorise the creation of an offence which consists only of—

(*a*) a failure to pay a charge or penalty charge imposed by a TfL scheme, or

(*b*) any other contravention or failure to comply with a requirement of a TfL scheme for which a penalty charge imposed by or under regulations made under paragraph 12 of Schedule 23 to the 1999 Act is payable.

(3) Nothing in this section shall affect the operation of section 8 (failure to notify changes in eligibility for exemptions etc) or paragraph 25 or 27 of Schedule 23 to the 1999 Act (specific offences relating to road user charging).

[Transport for London Act 2008, s 5.]

7.7745 **6. Extension of power to include enforcement provisions in TfL scheme** (1) Notwithstanding paragraph 31 of Schedule 23 to the 1999 Act, a TfL scheme may authorise—

(*a*) the examination, for any purpose relating to or connected with a TfL scheme, of a motor vehicle found in a charging area, or

(*b*) the fitting of an immobilisation device to, or the removal of, a motor vehicle found in such an area,

at a time at which the vehicle is on a public off-street parking place as well as at a time at which the vehicle is on a road.

(2) The powers conferred by the Charges and Penalty Charges Regulations on TfL, or for a TfL scheme to make provision for TfL, to examine, enter, immobilise or remove any vehicle which is on a road are also exercisable in respect of any vehicle which is on a public off-street parking place.

(3) Accordingly, the Charges and Penalty Charges Regulations, so far as they relate to TfL or a TfL scheme, shall have effect as if—

(*a*) the reference in regulation 8(1) to a vehicle which is on a road included a reference to a vehicle which is on a public off-street parking place;

(*b*) the references in regulations 10(1) and 12(1) to a vehicle which is stationary on a road in a charging area included references to a vehicle which is stationary on a public off-street parking place in a charging area;

(*c*) the references in regulations 10(1)(*a*) and 12(1)(*a*) to "that road" were references to a road in a charging area; and

(*d*) the reference in regulation 10(2)(*b*) to "another place on that road or another road" were a reference to another place on a road.

(4) TfL may not enter a public off-street parking place for the purpose of exercising any powers conferred on TfL by the Charges and Penalty Charges Regulations, or a TfL scheme, by virtue of this section to examine, enter, immobilise or remove any vehicle there without obtaining the prior consent of the operator.

(5) For the purposes of subsection (4) an operator's consent may be given to enter a public off-street parking place—

(*a*) on a specific occasion; or

(*b*) generally.

(6) An operator's consent required under subsection (4) is not to be unreasonably withheld but may be given subject to any reasonable conditions.

(7) Without prejudice to the generality of subsection (6), it is reasonable for consent to be given subject to conditions requiring TfL to reimburse the operator in respect of any loss of revenue, damage or other liability sustained as a result of the immobilisation or removal of any vehicle by TfL or the taking by TfL of any other action by virtue of this section.

(8) The owner, keeper or driver of a vehicle in a public off-street parking place which is immobilised or removed in accordance with the Charges and Penalty Charges Regulations, as they have effect in accordance with this section, shall not be required by the operator to pay any car parking charges or penalty additional to those already paid, or due to be paid, to the operator at the time that the vehicle was immobilised or removed.

(9) Where the powers conferred by the Charges and Penalty Charges Regulations are exercised pursuant to this section the notice required by regulation 10(3) shall summarise the effects of subsection (8).

(10) Unless the operator and TfL agree otherwise, TfL shall (whether or not conditions are imposed under subsection (6)) reimburse the operator in respect of any losses sustained as a result

of the operation of subsection (8).

(11) Consent to enter a public off-street parking place on a specific occasion shall be deemed to have been given unconditionally for the purposes of subsection (4) if—

(*a*) TfL has served a notice on the operator asking for consent to enter on that occasion and summarising the effect of subsections (8) and (10); and

(*b*) the operator fails within 14 days of the service of the notice to give TfL notice of his consent (whether or not subject to conditions) or his refusal to give it.

(12) At least 7 days before entering a public off-street parking place in accordance with subsection (11) TfL shall take reasonable steps to ascertain whether the operator has received the notice served under subsection (11)(*a*).

(13) Any question whether consent is unreasonably withheld or is given subject to reasonable conditions shall be referred to and determined by an arbitrator to be appointed, in default of agreement, by the President of the Chartered Institute of Arbitrators.

(14) In this section—

(*a*) "the Charges and Penalty Charges Regulations" means the Road User Charging (Charges and Penalty Charges) (London) Regulations 2001 (SI 2001/2285);

(*b*) "public off-street parking place" means a place, whether above or below ground and whether or not consisting of or including buildings, where off-street parking accommodation is made available by a local authority or any other person to the public (whether or not for payment); and

(*c*) any reference to the operator of such a parking place is a reference to the local authority or other person making such parking accommodation at the parking place so available.

[Transport for London Act 2008, s 6.]

**7.7745A 7. Power to suspend TfL scheme**

**7.7746 8. Failure to notify changes in eligibility for exemptions etc** (1) This section applies where a TfL scheme—

(*a*) makes provision for the maintenance of a register of non-chargeable, reduced rate and qualifying person's motor vehicles for the purposes of provisions in the scheme relating to—

(i) exemptions from charge,

(ii) the application of reduced rates of charge, or

(iii) the imposition of limits on the charges payable,

in the case of any particular class of motor vehicles or descriptions of persons; and

(*b*) requires the registered keeper of the motor vehicle or qualifying person in relation to whom particulars of the vehicle are entered on the register to notify TfL if the vehicle has ceased to be a non-chargeable vehicle, a reduced rate vehicle or a qualifying person's vehicle for the purposes of those provisions.

(2) In subsection (1) "qualifying person", in relation to a TfL scheme, means a person who qualifies for an exemption from charge, a reduced rate of charge or a limit on the charge payable.

(3) Where this section applies, any person who, without reasonable excuse, fails to comply with the requirement referred to in subsection (1)(*b*) is guilty of an offence and liable on summary conviction to a fine not exceeding level 2 on the standard scale.

(4) This section shall not apply in relation to anything done before this section comes into force.

[Transport for London Act 2008, s 8.]

## Part 3

## London Cabs and Private Hire Vehicles

*London cabs: general provisions*

**7.7747 9. Power to designate directional taxi ranks** (1) TfL may by London cab order designate any standing for hackney carriages appointed under section 4 of the London Hackney Carriages Act 1850 (c 7) to be a directional taxi rank—

(*a*) at all times; or

(*b*) for such times of the day, days or other periods as may be specified in the order.

(2) Where TfL designates a directional taxi rank, TfL shall cause a sign to be displayed at the rank clearly indicating—

(*a*) the direction or directions in which the drivers of vehicles plying for hire at that rank are required to travel if so requested by any person wishing to hire the vehicle in question; and

(*b*) the times, days or other periods for which the rank is designated to be a directional taxi rank.

(3) Notwithstanding section 35 of the London Hackney Carriage Act 1831 (c 22) and section 17 of the London Hackney Carriage Act 1853 (c 33), the driver of a hackney carriage plying for hire at a directional taxi rank may refuse to drive his vehicle in a direction which is not the specified direction or, where more than one direction is specified, which is not one of the specified directions.

(4) Where it appears to TfL to be desirable or expedient TfL may suspend the operation of a

designation under this section for such period or periods as TfL thinks fit.

(5) In this section—

"directional taxi rank" means a standing for hackney carriages whose drivers are plying for hire only for journeys in a specified direction or in one of several specified directions;

"London cab order" means an order made under section 9 of the Metropolitan Public Carriage Act 1869 (c 115); and

"specified direction", in relation to a directional taxi rank, means the direction (or any of the directions) specified in the designation relating to that rank.

[Transport for London Act 2008, s 9.]

7.7748 **10. Power to designate rest ranks** (1) TfL may by London cab order designate any standing (or part of a standing) for hackney carriages appointed under section 4 of the London Hackney Carriages Act 1850 (c 7) to be a rest rank—

(*a*) at all times; or

(*b*) for such times of the day, days or other periods as may be specified in the order.

(2) TfL may by London cab order prescribe the maximum length of time during which a hackney carriage may stand at a rest rank; and different maximum lengths of time may be prescribed—

(*a*) for different rest ranks; or

(*b*) for different times of the day, days or other periods.

(3) Where TfL designates a rest rank, TfL shall cause a sign to be displayed at the rank clearly indicating that the rank (or the relevant part of it) is a rest rank.

(4) Notwithstanding section 35 of the London Hackney Carriage Act 1831 (c 22) and section 17 of the London Hackney Carriage Act 1853 (c 33), the driver of a hackney carriage which is standing at a rest rank shall not be deemed to be plying for hire and, accordingly, may not be compelled to drive his vehicle to any place by any person wishing to hire it.

(5) Where it appears to TfL to be desirable or expedient TfL may suspend the operation of a designation under this section for such period or periods as TfL thinks fit.

(6) In this section "London cab order" means an order made under section 9 of the Metropolitan Public Carriage Act 1869 (c 115).

[Transport for London Act 2008, s 10.]

7.7749 **15. Fares for journeys ending outside London** (1) *Amends the London Cab and Stage Carriage Act 1907, s 1.*

(2) Nothing in this section shall affect the operation of section 35 of the London Hackney Carriage Act 1831 (c 22), sections 7 and 17 of the London Hackney Carriage Act 1853 (c 33) or any other enactment which makes provision as regards the obligation of drivers of hackney carriages to drive their vehicles on certain journeys if so requested by persons wishing to hire them.

[Transport for London Act 2008, s 15.]

*London cabs and private hire vehicles: fixed penalties*

7.7750 **17. Fixed penalty cab and private hire vehicle offences** (1) Where on any occasion an authorised officer finds a person who he has reason to believe has on that occasion committed an offence under any of the enactments—

(*a*) specified in columns (1) and (2) of the table set out in Schedule 1 to this Act; and

(*b*) described in column (3) of that table;

the authorised officer may give that person a notice offering him the opportunity of discharging any liability to conviction for that offence by payment of a fixed penalty.

(2) Sections 18 to 21 (fixed penalties) shall apply in respect of fixed penalty notices under this section.

(3) Schedule 2 to this Act shall have effect with respect to financial provisions relating to the administration and enforcement of this section and sections 18 to 21 (fixed penalties).

(4) In subsection (1) "authorised officer" means a person authorised in writing by TfL for the purposes of sections 17 to 21 of this Act.

[Transport for London Act 2008, s 17.]

7.7751 **18. Power to amend Schedule 1** (1) The Secretary of State may, after consulting—

(*a*) the Mayor,

(*b*) the Greater London Assembly,

(*c*) TfL,

(*d*) every London borough council,

(*e*) the Common Council of the City of London, and

(*f*) such bodies or persons as appear to him to be representative of persons who would be affected by the proposed regulations,

by regulations, amend Schedule 1 to this Act by adding a relevant offence to, or removing a relevant offence from, the offences for the time being mentioned in the table set out in that Schedule.

(2) In subsection (1) "relevant offence" means an offence under an enactment regulating hackney carriages or private hire vehicles in London or the drivers, proprietors or operators of such carriages or vehicles.

[Transport for London Act 2008, s 18.]

7.7752 **19. Fixed penalty notices** (1) The provisions of this section shall have effect in relation to notices ("fixed penalty notices") which may be given under section 17 (fixed penalty cab and private hire vehicle offences).

(2) Where a person is given a fixed penalty notice in respect of an offence—

(*a*) no proceedings shall be instituted for that offence before the expiration of 28 days following the date of the notice;

(*b*) he shall not be convicted of that offence if he pays the fixed penalty before the expiration of that period; and

(*c*) in the case of an offence in respect of which (but for this paragraph) section 38 of the London Hackney Carriages Act 1843 (c 86) (which as amended by section 14 (time limit for making complaints) requires complaints for certain offences to be made within 28 days) applies, proceedings may (notwithstanding that section) be instituted for that offence until the expiration of 42 days following the date of the notice.

(3) A fixed penalty notice under this section shall give such particulars of the circumstances alleged to constitute the offence as are necessary for giving reasonable information of the offence and shall state—

(*a*) the period during which, by virtue of subsection (2), proceedings will not be taken for the offence;

(*b*) the amount of the fixed penalty;

(*c*) the name of the person to whom and the address at which the fixed penalty may be paid; and

(*d*) the consequences of not making any payment within the period for payment;

and, without prejudice to payment by any other method, payment of the fixed penalty may be made by pre-paying and posting to that person at that address a letter containing the amount of the penalty (in cash or otherwise).

(4) Where a letter is sent in accordance with subsection (3) payment shall be regarded as having been made at the time at which that letter would be delivered in the ordinary course of post.

(5) The form of notices under this section shall be such as the Secretary of State may by regulations prescribe.

(6) The fixed penalty payable in pursuance of a fixed penalty notice under this section shall be paid to TfL.

(7) In any proceedings a certificate which—

(*a*) purports to be signed by or on behalf of the chief finance officer of TfL; and

(*b*) states that payment of a fixed penalty was or was not received by a date specified in the certificate,

shall be evidence of the facts stated.

[Transport for London Act 2008, s 19.]

7.7753 **20. Levels of fixed penalties** (1) It shall be the duty of TfL to set the levels of fixed penalties payable to TfL.

(2) Different levels may be set for different cases or classes of case.

(3) In setting the level of fixed penalty under subsection (1) TfL shall take into account the maximum fine for the particular fixed penalty offence in question and may take account of—

(*a*) any reasonable costs or expected costs incurred or to be incurred in connection with the administration of the provisions of the enactment under which the particular fixed penalty offence is created; and

(*b*) the cost or expected cost of enforcing the provisions of the relevant enactment.

(4) Levels of fixed penalties set by TfL in accordance with this section may only come into force in accordance with section 21 (fixed penalties: reserve powers of Secretary of State).

(5) TfL shall publish, in such manner as the Mayor may determine, the levels of fixed penalties which have been set by TfL in accordance with this section.

[Transport for London Act 2008, s 20.]

7.7754 **21. Fixed penalties: reserve powers of Secretary of State** (1) Where TfL sets any levels of fixed penalties under subsection (1) of section 20 (levels of fixed penalties), TfL shall notify the Secretary of State of the levels of fixed penalties so set.

(2) Where notification of any levels of fixed penalties is required to be given under subsection (1), the levels of fixed penalties shall not come into force until after the expiration of—

(*a*) the period of one month beginning with the day on which the notification is given; or

(*b*) such shorter period as the Secretary of State may allow.

(3) If, before the expiration of that period, the Secretary of State gives notice to TfL that he objects to the levels of fixed penalties on the grounds that some or all of them are or may be excessive, those levels of fixed penalties shall not come into force unless and until the objection has been withdrawn.

(4) If, at any time before the levels of fixed penalties required to be notified under subsection (1) to the Secretary of State have come into force, the Secretary of State considers that some or all of them are excessive, he may make regulations setting the levels of fixed penalties.

(5) Levels of fixed penalties set under subsection (4) must be no higher than those notified

under subsection (1).

(6) Where the Secretary of State makes any such regulations TfL must not set any further fixed penalties under subsection (1) until after the expiration of the period of 12 months beginning with the day on which the regulations are made.

[Transport for London Act 2008, s 21.]

7.7755 **22. Regulations** Any power to make regulations under section 18, 19 or 21—

(*a*) includes power to make provision in respect of such cases only as may be specified in the regulations and to make different provision for different circumstances, and

(*b*) shall be exercised by statutory instrument subject to annulment in pursuance of a resolution of either House of Parliament.

[Transport for London Act 2008, s 22.]

*Private hire vehicles*

7.7756 **23. Production of London PHV driver's badge** (1) In section 14(3) of the 1998 Act (obligation of driver of London private hire vehicle to wear badge) before "wear the badge in such position and manner as to be plainly and distinctly visible" insert "(*a*)" and after those words insert—

"and—

(*b*) at the request of any person, produce the badge for inspection.".

(2) In section 14(4) of the 1998 Act (power of TfL to exempt a driver from a requirement to wear his badge) for "subsection (3)" insert "subsection (3)(*a*)".[1]

[Transport for London Act 2008, s 23.]

---

[1] The wording above has been reproduced in accordance with the Queen's Printers' Copy. It is understood that there is a drafting error in para (2) and that the word "insert" should actually read "substitute".

7.7757 **24. Return of licences etc on suspension or revocation** (1) Section 22 of the 1998 Act (return of licences etc) shall be amended as follows.

(2) In subsection (1), at the beginning insert "Without prejudice to subsection (1A),".

(3) After subsection (1) insert—

"(1A) Where the suspension or revocation of a London PHV operator's licence has immediate effect by virtue of section 17(2), the holder of the licence shall, at the request of a constable or authorised officer, forthwith return the licence to the constable or officer.".

(4) In subsection (2)—

(*a*) at the beginning insert "Without prejudice to subsection (2A),";

(*b*) for "the plate or disc" substitute "every plate or disc"; and

(*c*) after "section 10" insert "or any regulations made under this Act".

(5) After subsection (2) insert—

"(2A) Where the suspension or revocation of a London PHV licence has immediate effect by virtue of section 9(3) or 17(2), the owner of the vehicle to which the licence relates shall, at the request of a constable or authorised officer, forthwith return to the constable or officer the licence and every plate or disc which was issued for the vehicle under section 10 or any regulations made under this Act.".

(6) In subsection (3), at the beginning insert "Without prejudice to subsection (3A),".

(7) After subsection (3) insert—

"(3A) Where the suspension or revocation of a London PHV driver's licence has immediate effect by virtue of section 17(2), the holder of the licence shall, at the request of a constable or authorised officer, forthwith return his driver's badge to the constable or officer.".

(8) In subsection (4)—

(*a*) at the beginning insert "Without prejudice to subsections (1A), (2A) and (3A),"; and

(*b*) in paragraph (*a*), for "the disc or plate" substitute "every disc or plate" and after "section 10" insert "or any regulations made under this Act".

(9) In subsection (7), for "the plate or disc" substitute "every disc or plate".

[Transport for London Act 2008, s 24.]

7.7758 **25. Obligation of London operators to keep records** In section 4(3) of the 1998 Act (records to be kept by London operators), for paragraph (*d*) substitute—

"(*d*) keep at the specified operating centre or, where more than one operating centre is specified, at one of the operating centres such records as may be prescribed of particulars of the private hire vehicles and drivers which are available to him for carrying out bookings accepted by him at that or, as the case may be, each centre;

(*da*) where more than one operating centre is specified—

(i) give notice to the licensing authority, and

(ii) display at each specified operating centre a notice,

stating the address of the operating centre at which the records are kept under paragraph (*d*);".

[Transport for London Act 2008, s 25.]

## Part 5
## Street Management

7.7759 **34. Power to erect flag poles etc on GLA roads** (1) Subject to subsection (2), TfL may—

(*a*) erect flagpoles, pylons and other structures on any GLA road for the purpose of displaying decorations;

(*b*) make slots in any GLA road for the purpose of erecting the structures, and

(*c*) remove any structure erected or slot made by TfL in pursuance of paragraph (*a*) or (*b*);

and any structures or slots which may be erected or made by virtue of this subsection are hereafter in this section referred to as "relevant works".

(2) TfL is not entitled to exercise the powers conferred on it by subsection (1) in respect of so much of a GLA road as—

(*a*) is carried by a bridge which a body other than TfL has a duty to maintain; or

(*b*) forms part of the approaches to such a bridge and is supported or protected by works or materials which a body other than TfL has a duty to maintain,

except with the consent in writing of that body.

(3) A body may give their consent in pursuance of subsection (2) on such terms as they think fit (including in particular, without prejudice to the generality of the preceding provisions of this subsection, terms providing for the body to remove any of the relevant works and reinstate the bridge or its approaches and to recover the reasonable cost of doing so from TfL).

(4) TfL shall not exercise any power conferred on it by subsection (1) in relation to a GLA road unless TfL has first obtained the consent of any local authority for the areas in which TfL proposes to exercise the power.

(5) If TfL erects or makes relevant works by virtue of the preceding provisions of this section TfL shall—

(*a*) ensure that the works are erected or made so as to obstruct the GLA road in question as little as is reasonably possible, so as not to obscure or conflict with traffic signs connected with the GLA road and so as to interfere as little as is reasonably possible with the enjoyment of premises adjacent to the GLA road and with, and with access to, any apparatus in or on the GLA road which belongs to or is used or maintained by statutory undertakers; and

(*b*) ensure that while the works are retained they are properly maintained and, so far as it is necessary to light them to avoid danger to users of the GLA road, are properly lit.

(6) A person who without lawful authority interferes with or removes any relevant works is guilty of an offence and liable on summary conviction to a fine not exceeding level 3 on the standard scale.

(7) In this section—

"bridge" includes a structure which carries a GLA road superimposed over a cutting; and

"statutory undertakers" means any of the following, namely, any body which is a statutory undertaker within the meaning provided by section 329(1) of the 1980 Act, any universal service provider in connection with the provision of a universal postal service, any licensee under a street works licence and the operator of an electronic communications code network or a driver information system.

(8) Nothing in this section shall affect the operation of section 144 of the 1980 Act.

[Transport for London Act 2008, s 34.]

7.7760 **35. Prevention of soil etc being washed on to GLA roads** (1) Subject to subsections (5) and (6), TfL may, by notice to the owner or occupier of any land adjoining a GLA road, require him, within 28 days from the date of service of the notice, to execute such works as will prevent soil or refuse from that land from falling, or being washed or carried, on to the GLA road or into any sewer or gully in it in such quantities as to obstruct the GLA road or choke the sewer or gully.

(2) A person aggrieved by a requirement under this section may appeal to a magistrate's court.

(3) Subject to any order made on appeal, if a person on whom a notice is served under this section fails to comply with it within the period specified in subsection (1), he is guilty of an offence and liable on summary conviction to a fine not exceeding level 3 on the standard scale; and if the offence is continued after conviction, he is guilty of a further offence and liable to a fine not exceeding £50 for each day on which the offence is so continued.

(4) Section 311 of the 1980 Act shall apply to any offence under subsection (3) as it applies to an offence under section 151(3) of that Act.

(5) Before serving a notice under subsection (1) TfL shall give not less than 7 days notice to the local authority, or each local authority, in whose area the GLA road is situated.

(6) A notice served under subsection (1) shall not have effect in any case where—

(*a*) a notice has been served under section 151 of the 1980 Act on the same person and in respect of the same land, and

(*b*) the works required by that notice will, if carried out, prevent the soil or refuse in question from obstructing the GLA road or choking the sewer or gully.

(7) At the end of Schedule 4 to the London Local Authorities and Transport for London Act 2003 (c iii) (offences in respect of which fixed penalty notices may be served) insert—

| | | | |
|---|---|---|---|
| 22 | Transport for London Act 2008 (c i) | 35(3) | Failure to comply with notice requiring works to prevent soil or refuse escaping onto street or into sewer. |

(8) Nothing in this section shall affect the operation of section 151 of the 1980 Act.
[Transport for London Act 2008, s 35.]

7.7761 **36. Dangerous land adjoining GLA roads** (1) Subject to subsections (4) to (6), if, in or on any land adjoining a GLA road there is an unfenced or inadequately fenced source of danger to persons using the GLA road, TfL may, by notice to the owner or occupier of that land, require him within such time as may be specified in the notice to execute such works of repair, protection, removal or enclosure as will obviate the danger.

(2) A person aggrieved by a requirement under subsection (1) may appeal to a magistrate's court.

(3) Subject to any order made on appeal, if a person on whom a notice is served under this section fails to comply with the notice within the time specified in it, TfL may execute such works as are necessary to comply with the notice and may recover the expenses reasonably incurred by it in so doing from that person.

(4) Subject to subsection (5), before serving a notice under subsection (1) TfL shall give not less than 7 days notice to the local authority, or each local authority, in whose area the GLA road is situated.

(5) Where a notice is served under subsection (1) in the case of emergency, TfL shall not be required to give prior notice to the local authority under subsection (4) but shall notify the authority at the same time as, or as soon as reasonably practicable after, the service of the first mentioned notice.

(6) A notice served under subsection (1) shall not have effect in any case where—

(*a*) a notice has been served under section 165 of the 1980 Act on the same person and in respect of the same land, and

(*b*) the works required by that notice will, if carried out, obviate the danger in question.

(7) Nothing in this section shall affect the operation of section 165 of the 1980 Act.
[Transport for London Act 2008, s 36.]

7.7762 **38. Powers relating to retaining walls near GLA roads** (1) This section applies to any length of a retaining wall, being a length—

(*a*) any cross-section of which is wholly or partly within 3.66 metres of a GLA road; and

(*b*) which is at any point of greater height than 1.37 metres above the level of the ground at the boundary of the GLA road nearest that point;

but does not apply to any length of a retaining wall erected on land belonging to any transport undertakers so long as that land is used by them primarily for the purpose of their undertaking or to any length of a retaining wall for the maintenance of which a highway authority are responsible.

(2) Subject to subsections (6) to (8), if a length of retaining wall to which this section applies is in such condition (whether for want of repair or some other reason) as to be liable to endanger persons using the GLA road, TfL may, by notice served on the owner or occupier of the land on which that length of wall is, require him to execute such works as will obviate the danger.

(3) Subsections (2) to (7) of section 290 of the Public Health Act 1936 (c 49) (appeals against, and the enforcement of, certain notices under that Act) apply to any notice served under subsection (2) as they apply to such notices as are mentioned in subsection (1) of that section, but subject to the following modifications—

(*a*) references to the local authority are to be construed as including references to TfL;

(*b*) for paragraph (*f*) of subsection (3) there is substituted the following paragraph—

"(*f*) that some other person ought to contribute towards the expense of executing any works required by the notice".

(4) Sections 300 to 302 of the Public Health Act 1936 (supplementary provisions relating to appeals under the said section 290) apply, with the necessary modifications, to appeals brought by virtue of subsection (3).

(5) In this section "retaining wall" means a wall, not forming part of a permanent building, which serves, or is intended to serve, as a support for earth or other material on one side only.

(6) Subject to subsection (7), before serving a notice under subsection (2) TfL shall give not less than 7 days notice to the local authority, or each local authority, in whose area the GLA road is situated.

(7) Where a notice is served under subsection (2) in the case of emergency, TfL shall not be required to give prior notice to the local authority under subsection (6) but shall notify the local authority at the same time as, or as soon as reasonably practicable after, the service of the first mentioned notice.

(8) A notice served under subsection (2) shall not have effect in any case where—

(*a*) a notice has been served under section 167 of the 1980 Act on the same person and in respect of the same land, and

(*b*) the works required by that notice will, if carried out, obviate the danger in question.

(9) Nothing in this section shall affect the operation of section 167 of the 1980 Act.
[Transport for London Act 2008, s 38.]

SCHEDULE 1
Offences in Respect of Which Fixed Penalty Notices may be Served Under Section 17 (Fixed Penalty Cab and Private Hire Vehicle Offences) of This Act Section 17(1)

**7.7763**

| (1) *Act/Instrument* | (2) *Enactment* | (3) *Description of offence* |
|---|---|---|
| London Hackney Carriages Act 1843 (c 86) | Section 17 | Failure to wear, or to produce, badge. |
| London Cab Order 1934 (SR&O/1346) | Article 28 | Failure to produce copy of licence. |
| | Article 31(1)(ii) | Plying outside licensed area. |
| | Article 33(1) | Carrying excess passengers. |
| Regulations for Enforcing Order at Cab Standings in the Metropolitan Police District made on 11th October 1963 | Regulation (1) | Failure to attend cab at cab standing. |

## Hackney carriages and private hire vehicles

# London Hackney Carriage Act 1831

(1 & 2 Will 4 c 22)

**7.7764 35.** Hackney carriage standing in a street or place and not already hired shall be deemed to be plying for hire; driver refusing hire and unable to adduce evidence to court of hiring shall forfeit a sum not exceeding **level 1** on the standard scale[1].

[London Hackney Carriage Act 1831, s 35, as amended by the Statute Law Revision (No 2) Act 1888, the Criminal Justice Act 1967, Sch 3 and the Criminal Justice Act 1982, ss 38 and 46—summarised.]

1 This section, for the purpose of hiring of taxis at separate fares under ss 10 and 11 of the Transport Act 1985, has been disapplied by the Licensed Taxis (Hiring at Separate Fares) (London) Order 1986, SI 1986/1387.

**7.7765 36.** Compensation to be made to drivers improperly summoned for refusing to carry any person.

[London Hackney Carriage Act 1831, s 36, as amended by the Statute Law Revision (No 2) Act 1888, and the Statute Law (Repeals) Act 1976—summarised.]

**7.7766 41. Persons refusing to pay the driver his fare, or in injuring his carriage, to be liable to make compensation, or to be committed to prison** If any person shall refuse or omit to pay the driver of any hackney carriage the sum justly due to him for the hire of such hackney carriage, or if any person shall deface or in any manner injure any such hackney carriage it shall be lawful for any justice of the peace, upon complaint thereof made to him, to grant a summons, or if it shall appear to him necessary, a warrant, for bringing before him or any other justice such defaulter or defender, and upon proof of the facts made upon oath before any such justice, to award reasonable satisfaction to the party so complaining for his fare or for his damages and costs, and also a reasonable compensation for his loss of time in attending to make and establish such complaint.

[London Hackney Carriage Act 1831, s 41 as amended by the Statute Law (Repeals) Act 1976.]

**7.7767 47.** Driver may demand deposit when required to wait with carriage—penalty on such driver refusing to wait, or to account for the deposit, etc **level 1** on the standard scale.

[London Hackney Carriage Act 1831, s 47 as amended by the Statute Law Revision Act 1974, the Statute Law Revision (No 2) Act 1888, the Criminal Law Act 1977, s 31 and the Criminal Justice Act 1982, s 46—summarised.]

**7.7768 56. Penalty on proprietors or drivers misbehaving** If the proprietor or driver of any hackney carriage, or any other person having the care thereof, shall, by intoxication, or by wanton and furious driving or by any other wilful misconduct, injure or endanger any person in his life, limbs or property, or if any such proprietor or driver shall make use of any abusive or insulting language, or be guilty of other rude behaviour to or towards any person whatever, or shall assault or obstruct any officer of police, constable, watchman, or patrole, in the execution of his duty, every such proprietor, driver or other person so offending in any of the several cases aforesaid, shall forfeit a sum not exceeding **level 1** on the standard scale[1].

[London Hackney Carriage Act 1831, s 56 as amended by the Summary Jurisdiction Act 1884, s 4, the Statute Law Revision (No 2) Act 1888, the Statute Law (Repeals) Act 1976, the Criminal Law Act 1977, s 31, the Criminal Justice Act 1982, s 46 and the Statute Law (Repeals) Act 2004.]

1 The wording of the section has been slightly edited to accord with modern circumstances. A conviction under this section can lead to the proprietor's licence being revoked.

# London Hackney Carriages Act 1843[1]

(6 & 7 Vict c 86)

7.7769 **10. Lending etc licence or badge** Any person transferring or lending a licence or permitting another person to use or wear a badge, or proprietor knowingly suffering unlicensed person to act as driver: penalty not exceeding **level 3** on the standard scale.

[London Hackney Carriages Act 1843, s 10 as amended by the Statute Law Revision Act 1874 (No 2), the Statute Law Revision Act 1891, the Criminal Justice Act 1967, Sch 3, the Statute Law (Repeals) Act 1976, the Criminal Justice Act 1982, ss 35, 38 and 46, the Statute Law (Repeals) Act 1993, Sch 1 and the Transport for London Act 2008, s 11—summarised.]

---

[1] A hackney carriage is defined for the purposes of these Acts by the Metropolitan Public Carriage Act 1869, s 4, as meaning any carriage for the conveyance of passengers which plies for hire (within the Metropolitan Police District or the City of London) and is not a stage carriage. A motor vehicle is included within the definition (Road Traffic Act 1988, s 191).

This Act, to the extent that it is part of the taxi code, except ss 3 and 33, shall apply to the use of taxis to provide local services under a special licence under s 12 of the Transport Act 1985 (Local Services (Operation by Taxis) (London) Regulations 1986, SI 1986/566).

7.7770 **14. Persons applying for licences to sign a requisition for the same, etc—Penalty on applicants or referees making false representations** Before any such licence shall be granted, a requisition for the same, in such form as Transport for London shall from time to time appoint for that purpose, shall be made and signed by the person by whom such licence shall be required; and in every such requisition all such particulars as Transport for London shall require shall be truly set forth; and every person applying for or attempting to procure any such licence who shall make or cause to be made any false representation in regard to any of the said particulars, or who shall not truly answer all questions which shall be demanded of him in relation to such application for a licence, and also every person to whom reference shall be made who shall, in regard to such application, wilfully and knowingly make any misrepresentation, shall forfeit for every such offence the sum of **level 3** on the standard scale; and it shall be lawful for Transport for London to proceed for recovering of such penalty before any magistrate at any time within one calendar month after the commission of the offence, or during the currency of the licence so improperly obtained.

[London Hackney Carriages Act 1843, s 14, as amended by the Statute Law Revision Act 1891, the Criminal Justice Act 1967, Sch 3, the Forgery and Counterfeiting Act 1981, Sch, the Criminal Justice Act 1982, ss 38 and 46 and the Greater London Authority Act 1999, Sch 20.]

7.7771 **17. Badges to be worn by drivers, etc** Every licensed driver shall at all times during his employment, and when he shall be required to attend before any justice of the peace, wear his badge conspicuously upon his breast, in such manner that the whole of the writing thereon shall be distinctly legible; and every driver who shall act as such, or who shall attend when required before any justice of the peace, without wearing such badge in manner aforesaid, or who, when thereunto required, shall refuse to produce such badge for inspection, or to permit any person to note the writing thereon, shall for every such offence forfeit a sum not exceeding level 1 on the standard scale.

[London Hackney Carriages Act 1843, s 17 as amended by the Statute Law Revision Act 1874 (No 2), the Statute Law Revision Act 1891, the Criminal Justice Act 1967, Sch 3, the Statute Law (Repeals) Act 1976, the Criminal Justice Act 1982, ss 38 and 46 and the Transport for London Act 2008, s 11.]

7.7772 **18. Licences and badges to be delivered up on the discontinuance of licences** Wilful neglect to deliver up within 3 days, or use or wear false badge for purposes of deception; maximum fine **level 1** on the standard scale; limitation period 12 months from expiry of licence.

[London Hackney Carriages Act 1843, s 18 as amended by the Statute Law Revision Act 1891, the Criminal Law Act 1977, s 31, the Criminal Justice Act 1982, s 46, the Transport for London Act 2008, s 11 and the Immigration Act 2016, Sch 5—summarised.]

7.7773 **19. New badges to be delivered instead of defaced or lost badges** Every person licensed under the authority of this Act who shall use or wear the badge granted to him after the writing thereon shall be obliterated, defaced or obscured so that the same shall not be distinctly legible, shall for every such offence forfeit the sum of **level 1** on the standard scale.

[London Hackney Carriages Act 1843, s 19 as amended by the Statute Law Revision Act 1891, the Criminal Law Act 1977, s 31 and the Criminal Justice Act 1982, s 46 and the Transport for London Act 2008, s 11—summarised.]

7.7774 **25. Licences may be revoked or suspended** It shall be lawful for any justice of the peace before whom any driver shall be convicted of any offence, whether under this Act or any other Act, if such justice in his discretion shall think fit, to revoke the licence of such driver, and also any other licence he shall hold under the provisions of this Act, or to suspend the same for such time as the justice shall think proper, and for that purpose to require the proprietor (*or*) driver in whose possession such licence and the badge thereunto belonging shall then be to deliver up the same; and every proprietor, (*or*) driver who, being so required, shall refuse or neglect to deliver up such licence and any such ticket, or either of them, shall forfeit[1] so often as he shall be so required and refuse or neglect as aforesaid the sum of **level 1** on the standard scale; and the justice shall forthwith send such licence and badge to Transport for London, who shall cancel such licence if it has been revoked by the justice, or, if it has been suspended shall, at the end of the time for which it shall have been suspended, re-deliver such licence with the badge, to the person to whom it was granted.

A magistrates' court that makes an order revoking or suspending any licence under this section may, if the court thinks fit, suspend the effect of the order pending an appeal against the order.

[London Hackney Carriages Act 1843, s 25 as amended by the Statute Law Revision Act 1874 (No 2), the Statute Law Revision Act 1891, the Statute Law (Repeals) Act 1976, the Criminal Law Act 1977, s 31, the Criminal Justice Act 1982, s 46, the Transport Act 1985, Sch 7, the Greater London Authority Act 1999, Sch 20 and the Transport for London Act 2008, s 11.]

[1] Penalty recoverable on summary conviction.

7.7775 **27. No person to act as driver etc of any carriage without the consent of the proprietor** The person and any driver suffering him to act liable to fine not exceeding **level 1** on the standard scale; driver not revealing name, address and (any) licence number of person he has allowed to act as driver is liable therefor to further penalty not exceeding **level 1** on the standard scale; police constable may take charge of carriage.

[London Hackney Carriages Act 1843, s 27 as amended by the Statute Law Revision Act (No 2), the Statute Law Revision Act 1891, the Statute Law (Repeals) Act 1976, the Criminal Law Act 1977, s 31, the Criminal Justice Act 1982, s 46 and the Police and Criminal Evidence Act 1984, Sch 6 and the Transport for London Act 2008, s 11—summarised.]

7.7776 **28. Punishment for furious driving, and wilful misbehaviour—Compensation[1] for injury, etc Proprietor paying compensation may recover from driver, etc.**—Every driver of a hackney carriage, who shall be guilty of wanton or furious driving, or who by carelessness or wilful misbehaviour shall cause any hurt or damage to any person or property being in any street or highway, and also every driver, who during his employment shall be drunk, or shall make use of any insulting or abusive language, or shall be guilty of any insulting gesture or any misbehaviour, shall for every such offence forfeit the sum of **level 1** on the standard scale; or it shall be lawful for the justice before whom such complaint shall be brought, <u>if in his discretion he shall think proper, instead of inflicting such penalty, forthwith to commit the offender to prison for any period not exceeding **two calendar months**.</u>*

[London Hackney Carriages Act 1843, s 28 as amended by the Statute Law Revision Act 1872 (No 2), the Statute Law Revision Act 1891, the Statute Law (Repeals) Act 1976, the Criminal Law Act 1977, s 31, the Criminal Justice Act 1982, s 46 and the Statute Law (Repeals) Act 1993, Sch 1.]

[1] The provision relating to compensation was repealed by the Statute Law (Repeals) Act 1993, Sch 1.
* **Words repealed by the Criminal Justice Act 2003, Sch 37 from a date to be appointed.**

7.7777 **33.** Penalty on drivers for loitering or causing any obstruction etc[1].—Every driver of a hackney carriage who shall ply for hire elsewhere than at some standing or place appointed for that purpose, or who by loitering or by any wilful misbehaviour shall cause any obstruction in or upon any public street, road or place, and every driver of a hackney carriage, whether hired or unhired, allowing any person beside himself, not being the hirer or a person employed by such hirer, to ride on the driving box, shall for every such offence forfeit a sum not exceeding **level 1** on the standard scale.

[London Hackney Carriages Act 1843, s 33 as amended by the Statute Law Revision Act 1891, the Criminal Justice Act 1967, Sch 3, the Statute Law (Repeals) Act 1976 and the Criminal Justice Act 1982, ss 38 and 46.]

[1] As to disapplication of this section to a taxi being used for local services under a special licence, see note 1 to s 10, ante.

7.7778 **38. Complaints to be made within 28 days** All complaints under the provisions of the London Hackney Carriage Act 1831, or of this Act, or of the orders and regulations made in pursuance of either of them, shall be made within 28 days next after the day on which the cause of complaint shall have arisen.

[London Hackney Carriages Act 1843, s 38 as amended by the Statute Law Revision Act 1891, the Statute Law (Repeals) Act 1976 and the Transport for London Act 2008, s 14.]

## London Hackney Carriages Act 1850

(13 & 14 Vict c 7)

7.7779 This Act is to be construed as one with the 1843 Act and the 1853 Act. Section 4 enables Transport for London to appoint standings for hackney carriages and to make regulations therefor. Breach of regulations is punishable under s 19 of the London Hackney Carriage Act 1853.

## London Hackney Carriage Act 1853

(16 & 17 Vict c 33)

7.7780 **17. Drivers liable to penalties for certain offences[1]** The driver of any hackney carriage who shall commit any of the following offences within the limits of this Act, shall be liable to a penalty not exceeding **level 3** on the standard scale for each offence:

(1) Every driver of a hackney carriage[2] who shall demand or take more than the proper fare[3], or who shall refuse to admit and carry in his carriage the number of persons painted or marked on such carriage or specified in the certificate granted by Transport for London in respect of such carriage, or who shall refuse to carry by his carriage a reasonable quantity of luggage for any person hiring or intending to hire such carriage:

(2) Every driver of a hackney carriage who shall refuse to drive such carriage to any place within the limits of the Act, not exceeding six miles[4] to which he shall be required to drive any person hiring or intending to hire such carriage, or who shall refuse to drive any such carriage for any time

not exceeding one hour, if so required by any person hiring or intending to hire such carriage, or who shall not drive the same at a reasonable and proper speed, not less than six miles an hour, except in cases of unavoidable delay, or when required by the hirer thereof to drive at any slower pace:

(3) Every driver of a hackney carriage who shall ply for hire with any carriage or horse which shall be at the time unfit for public use.

[London Hackney Carriage Act 1853, s 17 as amended by the Summary Jurisdiction Act 1884, the Statute Law Revision Act 1892, the Criminal Justice Act 1967, Sch 3, the Statute Law (Repeals) Act 1973, the Statute Law (Repeals) Act 1976, the Criminal Justice Act 1982, ss 39, 46 and Sch 3 and the Greater London Authority Act 1999, Sch 20.]

---

[1] This section, to the extent that it is part of the taxi code, has been disapplied as regards the use of a taxi to provide local services under a special licence under s 12 of the Transport Act 1985 (Local Services (Operation by Taxis) (London) Regulations 1986, SI 1986/566). Moreover, for the purpose of hiring of taxis at separate fares under ss 10 and 11 of the Transport Act 1985, the provisions of this section relating to obligatory hirings, the number of persons to be carried at the instance of the hirer, and the carriage of luggage have been disapplied by the Licensed Taxis (Hiring of Separate Fares) (London) Order 1986, SI 1986/1387.

[2] A vehicle licensed and commonly used as a hackney carriage which plies for hire within s 4 of the Metropolitan Public Carriage Act 1869 cannot be divested of the attribute of a hackney carriage (*Bassam v Green* [1981] RTR 362).

[3] A driver demands or takes more than the proper fare if he either asks for an excessive fare or asks for the proper fare and in addition for some supplemental payment which is not a fare (*Bassam v Green* [1981] RTR 362).

[4] Now twenty miles (London Cab Order 1972, SI 1972 No 1074). A taxi driver commits no offence by refusing to stop when hailed (*Hunt v Morgan* [1949] 1 KB 233, [1948] 2 All ER 1065). The driver must observe the general law despite the requirements of this section (*Levinson v Powell* [1967] 3 All ER 796, 132 JP 10).

# Metropolitan Public Carriage Act 1869[1]

(32 & 33 Vict c 115)

7.7781 **6.** *Grant of hackney carriage licences.*

---

[1] This Act, to the extent that it is part of the taxi code, except ss 2, 9, and 10, shall apply to the use of a taxi to provide local services under a special licence under s 12 of the Transport Act 1985 (Local Services (Operation by Taxis) (London) Regulations 1986, SI 1986/566).

7.7782 **7. Penalty on use of unlicensed carriage** If any unlicensed hackney carriage plies for hire[1], the owner of such carriage shall be liable to a penalty not exceeding **level 4** on the standard scale. And if any unlicensed hackney carriage is found on any stand within the limits of this Act[2], the owner of such carriage shall be liable to a penalty not exceeding **level 4** on the standard scale. The driver also shall in every such case be liable to a like penalty unless he proves that he was ignorant of the fact of the carriage being an unlicensed carriage.

Any hackney carriage plying for hire, and any hackney carriage found on any stand without having such distinguishing mark, or being otherwise distinguished in such manner as may for the time being be prescribed shall be deemed to be an unlicensed carriage.

[Metropolitan Public Carriage Act 1869, s 7 as amended by the Criminal Justice Act 1967, Sch 3, the Statute Law (Repeals) Act 1976, Sch 1, the Criminal Justice Act 1982, ss 35, 39, 46 and Sch 3 and the Greater London Authority Act 1999, Schs 20 and 34.]

---

[1] As to "plying for hire" see note to the Town Police Clauses Act 1847, s 38, in title TOWNS IMPROVEMENT: TOWN POLICE, post.

[2] The Metropolitan Police District and the City of London (Town Police Clauses Act 1847, s 2).

7.7783 **8. Hackney carriage to be driven by licensed drivers** (1) Transport for London shall have the function of licensing persons to be drivers of hackney carriages.

(2) No hackney carriage shall ply for hire within the limits of this Act unless under the charge of a driver having a licence under this section from Transport for London.

(3) If any hackney carriage plies for hire in contravention of this section—

(*a*) the person driving the carriage, and

(*b*) the owner of the carriage, unless he proves that the driver acted without his privity or consent,

shall each be liable to a penalty not exceeding level 3 on the standard scale.

(4) Transport for London may send to the Commissioner of Police of the Metropolis or the Commissioner of Police for the City of London—

(*a*) details of a person to whom Transport for London is considering granting a licence under this section, and

(*b*) a request for the Commissioner's observations;

and the Commissioner shall respond to the request.

(5) A licence under this section may—

(*a*) be granted on such conditions,

(*b*) be in such form,

(*c*) be subject to revocation or suspension in such event, and

(*d*) generally be dealt with in such manner,

as may be prescribed.

(6) Subsection (5) of this section is subject to the following provisions of this section.

(7) Subject to section 8A, a licence under this section shall, if not revoked or suspended, be in

force for three years.

(8) A fee of such amount (if any) as Transport for London may determine shall be paid to Transport for London—

(*a*) by any applicant for a licence under this section, on making the application for the licence;

(*b*) by any applicant for the taking or re-taking of any test or examination, or any part of a test or examination, with respect to any matter of fitness, on making the application for the taking or re-taking of the test, examination or part; and

(*c*) by any person granted a licence under this section, on the grant of the licence.

(9) In paragraph (*b*) of subsection (8) of this section "matter of fitness" means—

(*a*) any matter as respects which Transport for London must be satisfied before granting a licence under this section; or

(*b*) any matter such that, if Transport for London is not satisfied with respect to the matter, they may refuse to grant a licence under this section.

(10) Different amounts may be determined under subsection (8) of this section for different purposes or different cases.

(11) Transport for London may remit or refund the whole or part of a fee under subsection (8) of this section.

[Metropolitan Public Carriage Act 1869, s 8 as substituted by the Greater London Authority Act 1999, Sch 20 and amended by the Immigration Act 2016, Sch 5.]

**7.7783A 8A. Drivers' licences for persons subject to immigration control**

(1) Subsection (2) applies if—

(a) a licence under section 8 is to be granted to a person who has been granted leave to enter or remain in the United Kingdom for a limited period ("the leave period"),

(b) the person's leave has not been extended by virtue of section 3C of the Immigration Act 1971 (continuation of leave pending variation decision), and

(c) apart from subsection (2), the period for which the licence would have been in force would have ended after the end of the leave period.

(2) Transport for London must grant the licence for a period which ends at or before the end of the leave period.

(3) Subsection (4) applies if—

(a) a licence under section 8 is to be granted to a person who has been granted leave to enter or remain in the United Kingdom for a limited period, and

(b) the person's leave has been extended by virtue of section 3C of the Immigration Act 1971 (continuation of leave pending variation decision).

(4) Transport for London must grant the licence for a period that does not exceed six months.

(5) A licence under section 8 ceases to be in force if the person to whom it was granted becomes disqualified by reason of the person's immigration status from driving a hackney carriage.

(6) If a licence granted in accordance with subsection (2) or (4) expires, the person to whom it was granted must, within the period of 7 days beginning with the day after that on which it expired, return to Transport for London—

(a) the licence,

(b) the person's copy of the licence (if any), and

(c) the person's driver's badge.

(7) If subsection (5) applies to a licence, the person to whom it was granted must, within the period of 7 days beginning with the day after the day on which the person first became disqualified, return to Transport for London—

(a) the licence,

(b) the person's copy of the licence (if any), and

(c) the person's driver's badge.

(8) A person who, without reasonable excuse, contravenes subsection (6) or (7) is guilty of an offence and liable on summary conviction—

(a) to a fine not exceeding level 3 on the standard scale, and

(b) in the case of a continuing offence, to a fine not exceeding ten pounds for each day during which an offence continues after conviction.

(9) The Secretary of State may by regulations made by statutory instrument amend the amount for the time being specified in subsection (8)(b).

(10) Regulations under subsection (9) may make transitional, transitory or saving provision.

(11) A statutory instrument containing regulations under subsection (9) may not be made unless a draft of the instrument has been laid before, and approved by a resolution of, each House of Parliament.

(12) For the purposes of this section a person is disqualified by reason of the person's immigration status from driving a hackney carriage if the person is subject to immigration control and—

(a) the person has not been granted leave to enter or remain in the United Kingdom, or

(b) the person's leave to enter or remain in the United Kingdom—

(i) is invalid,

(ii) has ceased to have effect (whether by reason of curtailment, revocation, cancellation, passage of time or otherwise), or

(iii) is subject to a condition preventing the person from driving a hackney carriage.

(13) Where a person is on immigration bail within the meaning of Part 1 of Schedule 10 to the Immigration Act 2016—

(a) the person is to be treated for the purposes of this section as if the person had been granted leave to enter the United Kingdom, but

(b) any condition as to the person's work in the United Kingdom to which the person's immigration bail is subject is to be treated for those purposes as a condition of leave.

(14) For the purposes of this section a person is subject to immigration control if under the Immigration Act 1971 the person requires leave to enter or remain in the United Kingdom.

[Metropolitan Public Carriage Act 1869, s 8A as inserted by the Immigration Act 2016, Sch 5.]

**7.7784 9.** *Regulations as to hackney and stage carriages*[1].

[1] Various London Cab Orders have been made: see SR & O 1934 No 1346, amended by SI 1955/1853, SI 1962/289, SI 1971/333, SI 1974/601, SI 1980/588, SI 1983/653, SI 1986/857, SI 1987/999, SI 1988/996, SI 1990/1075 and 2003, SI 1992/1169, SI 1993/1093, SI 1994/1087, SI 1995/837 and 1181, SI 1996/960 and 1176, SI 1997/1116, SI 1998/1043, SI 1999/1117 and 3250 and SI 2000/1276. Penalty for contravention is fine not exceeding £20.

# London Cab Act 1896

(59 & 60 Vict c 27)

**7.7785 1. Penalties for defrauding cabmen** If any person commits any of the following offences with respect to a cab[1] namely:

(*a*) hires a cab[1] knowing or having reason to believe that he cannot pay the lawful fare, or with intent to avoid payment of the lawful fare; or

(*b*) fraudulently endeavours to avoid payment of a fare lawfully due from him; or

(*c*) having failed or refused to pay a fare lawfully due from him, either refuses to give to the driver an address at which he can be found, or, with intent to deceive, gives a false address,

he shall be liable on summary conviction to pay, in addition to the fare, a fine not exceeding level 1 on the standard scale, or in the discretion of the court, to be imprisoned for a term not exceeding fourteen days; and the whole or any part of any fine imposed may be applied in compensation to the driver.

[London Cab Act 1896, s 1, as amended by the Criminal Justice Act 1967, Sch 3 and the Criminal Justice Act 1982, ss 38 and 46.]

[1] A "cab" means a hackney carriage within the meaning of the Metropolitan Public Carriage Act 1869.

# Transport Act 1985

(1985 c 67)

**7.7786 17. London taxi and taxi driver licensing: appeals**

(1) In this section—

"licence" means a licence under section 6 of the Metropolitan Public Carriage Act 1869 (taxi licences) or under section 8 of that Act (taxi driver licences); and

"licensing authority" means the person empowered to grant a licence. (2) Where the licensing authority has refused to grant, or has suspended or revoked, a licence the applicant for, or (as the case may be) holder of, the licence may, before the expiry of the designated period—

(*a*) require the authority to reconsider his decision; or

(*b*) appeal to a magistrates' court.

(3) Any call for a reconsideration under subsection (2) above must be made to the licensing authority in writing.

(4) On any reconsideration under this section the person calling for the decision to be reconsidered shall be entitled to be heard either in person or by his representative.

(5) If the person calling for a decision to be reconsidered under this section is dissatisfied with the decision of the licensing authority on reconsideration, he may, before the expiry of the designated period, appeal to a magistrates' court.

(6) On any appeal to it under this section, the court may make such order as it thinks fit; and any order which it makes shall be binding on the licensing authority.

(7) Where a person holds a licence which is in force when he applies for a new licence in substitution for it, the existing licence shall continue in force until the application for the new licence, or any appeal under this section in relation to that application, is disposed of, but without prejudice to the exercise in the meantime of any power of the licensing authority to revoke the existing licence.

(8) For the purposes of subsection (7) above, where the licensing authority refuses to grant the new licence the application shall not be treated as disposed of—

(*a*) where no call for a reconsideration of the authority's decision is made under subsection (2) above, until the expiry of the designated period;

(*b*) where such a reconsideration is called for, until the expiry of the designated period which begins by reference to the decision of the authority on reconsideration.

(9) Where the licensing authority suspends or revokes a licence, or confirms a decision to do so, he may, if the holder of the licence so requests, direct that his decision shall not have effect until the expiry of the designated period.

(10) In this section

"designated period" means such period as may be specified for the purpose by London cab order;

"London cab order" means an order made by Transport for London.

(11) Any power to make a London cab order under this section includes power to vary or revoke a previous such order.

[Transport Act 1985, s 17 as amended by the Greater London Authority Act 1999, Sch 21and the Courts Act 2003, Sch 8.]

## Private Hire Vehicles (London) Act 1998[1]

(1998 c 34)

*Introductory*

7.7787 **1. Meaning of "private hire vehicle", "operator" and related expressions** (1) In this Act—

(*a*) "private hire vehicle" means a vehicle constructed or adapted to seat fewer than nine passengers which is made available with a driver for hire for the purpose of carrying passengers, other than a licensed taxi or a public service vehicle[2];

(*b*) "operator" means a person who makes provision for the invitation or acceptance of, or who accepts, private hire bookings; and

(*c*) "operate", in relation to a private hire vehicle, means to make provision for the invitation or acceptance of, or to accept, private hire bookings in relation to the vehicle.

(2) Any reference in this Act to a vehicle being "used as a private hire vehicle" is a reference to a private hire vehicle which—

(*a*) is in use in connection with a hiring for the purpose of carrying one or more passengers; or

(*b*) is immediately available to an operator to carry out a private hire booking.

(3) Any reference in this Act to the operator of a vehicle which is being used as a private hire vehicle is a reference to the operator who accepted the booking for the hiring or to whom the vehicle is immediately available, as the case may be.

(4) In this Act "private hire booking" means a booking for the hire of a private hire vehicle for the purpose of carrying one or more passengers (including a booking to carry out as sub-contractor a private hire booking accepted by another operator).

(5) In this Act "operating centre" means premises at which private hire bookings are accepted by an operator.

[Private Hire Vehicles (London) Act 1998, s 1 as amended by the Road Safety Act 2006, Sch 7 and the Immigration Act 2016, Sch 5.]

---

[1] This Act is to be brought into force in accordance with orders made under s 40. At the date of going to press, the Private Hire Vehicles (London) Act 1998 (Commencement No 1) Order 2000, SI 2000/3144; the (No 2) Order 2003, SI 2003/580; and the (No 3) Order 2004, SI 2004/241 had been made.

[2] For savings in respect of vehicles used for funerals and weddings, see s 29, post.

*Regulation of private hire vehicle operators in London*

7.7788 **2. Requirement for London operator's licence** (1) No person shall in London make provision for the invitation or acceptance of, or accept, private hire bookings unless he is the holder of a private hire vehicle operator's licence for London (in this Act referred to as a "London PHV operator's licence").

(2) A person who makes provision for the invitation or acceptance of private hire bookings, or who accepts such a booking, in contravention of this section is guilty of an offence and liable on summary conviction to a fine not exceeding level 4 on the standard scale.

[Private Hire Vehicles (London) Act 1998, s 2.]

7.7789 **3. London operator's licences** (1) Any person may apply to the licensing authority for a London PHV operator's licence.

(2) An application under this section shall state the address of any premises in London which the applicant proposes to use as an operating centre.

(3) The licensing authority shall grant a London PHV operator's licence to the applicant if the authority is satisfied that—

(*a*) the applicant is a fit and proper person to hold a London PHV operator's licence;

(*aa*) if the applicant is an individual, the applicant is not disqualified by reason of the applicant's immigration status from operating a private hire vehicle; and

(*b*) any further requirements that may be prescribed (which may include requirements relating to operating centres) are met.

(3A) In determining for the purposes of subsection (3) whether an applicant is disqualified by reason of the applicant's immigration status from operating a private hire vehicle, the licensing authority must have regard to any guidance issued by the Secretary of State.

(4) A London PHV operator's licence shall be granted subject to such conditions as may be

prescribed[1] and such other conditions as the licensing authority may think fit.

(5) Subject to section 3A, a London PHV operator's licence shall be granted for five years or such shorter period as the licensing authority may consider appropriate in the circumstances of the case.

(6) A London PHV operator's licence shall—

(*a*) specify the address of any premises in London which the holder of the licence may use as an operating centre;

(*b*) be in such form and contain such particulars as the licensing authority may think fit.

(7) An applicant for a London PHV operator's licence may appeal[2] to a magistrates' court against—

(*a*) a decision not to grant such a licence;

(*b*) a decision not to specify an address proposed in the application as an operating centre; or

(*c*) any condition (other than a prescribed condition) to which the licence is subject.

[Private Hire Vehicles (London) Act 1998, s 3 as amended by the Greater London Authority Act 1999, Sch 21 and the Immigration Act 2016, Sch 5.]

---

1 See the Private Hire Vehicles (London) (Operators' Licences) Regulations 2000, SI 2000/3146.

2 For provisions relating to appeals, see ss 25–26, post and the Magistrates' Courts Rules 1991, r 34 in PART 1 MAGISTRATES COURT PROCEDURE, ante.

**7.7789A 3A. London PHV operator's licences for persons subject to immigration control**

(1) Subsection (2) applies if—

(a) a London PHV operator's licence is to be granted to a person who has been granted leave to enter or remain in the United Kingdom for a limited period ("the leave period");

(b) the person's leave has not been extended by virtue of section 3C of the Immigration Act 1971 (continuation of leave pending variation decision); and

(c) apart from subsection (2), the period for which the licence would have been granted would have ended after the end of the leave period.

(2) The licence must be granted for a period which ends at or before the end of the leave period.

(3) Subsection (4) applies if—

(a) a London PHV operator's licence is to be granted to a person who has been granted leave to enter or remain in the United Kingdom for a limited period; and

(b) the person's leave has been extended by virtue of section 3C of the Immigration Act 1971 (continuation of leave pending variation decision).

(4) The licence must be granted for a period which does not exceed six months.

(5) A London PHV operator's licence ceases to be in force if the person to whom it was granted becomes disqualified by reason of the person's immigration status from operating a private hire vehicle.

(6) If subsection (5) applies to a licence, the person to whom it was granted must, within the period of 7 days beginning with the day after the day on which the person first became disqualified, return it to the licensing authority.

(7) A person who, without reasonable excuse, contravenes subsection (6) is guilty of an offence and liable on summary conviction—

(a) to a fine not exceeding level 3 on the standard scale; and

(b) in the case of a continuing offence, to a fine not exceeding ten pounds for each day during which an offence continues after conviction.

(8) The Secretary of State may by regulations amend the amount for the time being specified in subsection (7)(b).

[Private Hire Vehicles (London) Act 1998, s 3A as inserted by the Immigration Act 2016, Sch 5.]

**7.7790 4. Obligations of London operators** (1) The holder of a London PHV operator's licence (in this Act referred to as a "London PHV operator") shall not in London accept a private hire booking other than at an operating centre specified in his licence.

(2) A London PHV operator shall secure that any vehicle which is provided by him for carrying out a private hire booking accepted by him in London is—

(*a*) a vehicle for which a London PHV licence is in force driven by a person holding a London PHV driver's licence; or

(*b*) a London cab driven by a person holding a London cab driver's licence.

(3) A London PHV operator shall—

(*a*) display a copy of his licence at each operating centre specified in the licence;

(*b*) keep at each specified operating centre a record in the prescribed[1] form of the private hire bookings accepted by him there;

(*c*) before the commencement of each journey booked at a specified operating centre, enter in the record kept under paragraph (*b*) the prescribed[1] particulars of the booking;

(*d*) keep at each specified operating centre such records as may be prescribed[1] of particulars of the private hire vehicles and drivers which are available to him for carrying out bookings accepted by him at that centre;*

(*e*) at the request of a constable or authorised officer, produce for inspection any record required by this section to be kept.

(4) If a London PHV operator ceases to use an operating centre specified in his licence he shall preserve any record he was required by this section to keep there for such period as may be prescribed[1].

(5) A London PHV operator who contravenes any provision of this section is guilty of an offence and liable on summary conviction to a fine not exceeding **level 3** on the standard scale.

(6) It is a defence[2] in proceedings for an offence under this section for an operator to show that he exercised all due diligence to avoid committing such an offence.

[Private Hire Vehicles (London) Act 1998, s 4.]

* **Substituted by the Transport for London Act 2008, s 25 from a date to be appointed.**

[1] See the Private Hire Vehicles (London) (Operators' Licences) Regulations 2000, SI 2000/3146.

[2] An accused who raises this defence is not required to establish it beyond reasonable doubt, but on the balance of probabilities: see *R v Carr-Briant* [1943] KB 607, [1943] 2 All ER 156, 107 JP 167.

7.7791 **5. Hirings accepted on behalf of another operator** (1) A London PHV operator ("the first operator") who has in London accepted a private hire booking may not arrange for another operator to provide a vehicle to carry out that booking as sub-contractor unless—

(*a*) the other operator is a London PHV operator and the sub-contracted booking is accepted at an operating centre in London;

(*b*) the other operator is licensed under section 55 of the Local Government (Miscellaneous Provisions) Act 1976 (in this Act referred to as "the 1976 Act") by the council of a district and the sub-contracted booking is accepted in that district; or

(*c*) the other operator accepts the sub-contracted booking in Scotland.

(2) A London PHV operator who contravenes subsection (1) is guilty of an offence and liable on summary conviction to a fine not exceeding **level 3** on the standard scale.

(3) It is a defence[1] in proceedings for an offence under this section for an operator to show that he exercised all due diligence to avoid committing such an offence.

(4) It is immaterial for the purposes of subsection (1) whether or not sub-contracting is permitted by the contract between the first operator and the person who made the booking.

(5) For the avoidance of doubt (and subject to any relevant contract terms), a contract of hire between a person who made a private hire booking at an operating centre in London and the London PHV operator who accepted the booking remains in force despite the making of arrangements by that operator for another contractor to provide a vehicle to carry out that booking as sub-contractor.

[Private Hire Vehicles (London) Act 1998, s 5.]

[1] An accused who raises this defence is not required to establish it beyond reasonable doubt, but on the balance of probabilities: see *R v Carr-Briant* [1943] KB 607, [1943] 2 All ER 156, 107 JP 167.

*Regulation of private hire vehicles in London*

7.7792 **6. Requirement for private hire vehicle licence** (1) A vehicle shall not be used as a private hire vehicle on a road in London unless a private hire vehicle licence is in force for that vehicle.

(2) The driver and operator of a vehicle used in contravention of this section are each guilty of an offence.

(3) The owner[1] of a vehicle who permits it to be used in contravention of this section is guilty of an offence.

(4) It is a defence[2] in proceedings for an offence under subsection (2) for the driver or operator to show that he exercised all due diligence to prevent the vehicle being used in contravention of this section.

(5) A person guilty of an offence under this section is liable on summary conviction to a fine not exceeding **level 4** on the standard scale.

(6) In this section "private hire vehicle licence" means—

(*a*) except where paragraph (*b*) or (*c*) applies, a London PHV licence;

(*b*) if the vehicle is in use for the purposes of a hiring the booking for which was accepted outside London in a controlled district, a licence under section 48 of the 1976 Act issued by the council for that district; and

(*c*) if the vehicle is in use for the purposes of a hiring the booking for which was accepted in Scotland, a licence under section 10 of the Civic Government (Scotland) Act 1982 (in this Act referred to as "the 1982 Act"),

and for the purposes of paragraph (*b*) or (*c*) it is immaterial that the booking in question is a sub-contracted booking.

(7) This section does not apply to a vehicle used for the purposes of a hiring for a journey beginning outside London in an area of England and Wales which is not a controlled district.

[Private Hire Vehicles (London) Act 1998, s 6.]

[1] For "owner" see s 35, post.

[2] An accused who raises this defence is not required to establish it beyond reasonable doubt, but on the balance of probabilities: see *R v Carr-Briant* [1943] KB 607, [1943] 2 All ER 156, 107 JP 167.

7.7793 **7. London PHV licences** (1) The owner[1] of any vehicle constructed or adapted to seat fewer than nine passengers may apply to the licensing authority for a private hire vehicle licence for London (in this Act referred to as a "London PHV licence") for that vehicle.

(2) The licensing authority shall grant a London PHV licence for a vehicle if the authority is satisfied—

(*a*) that the vehicle—

(i) is suitable in type, size and design for use as a private hire vehicle;

(ii) is safe, comfortable and in a suitable mechanical condition for that use; and

(iii) is not of such design and appearance as would lead any person to believe that the vehicle is a London cab;

(*b*) that there is in force in relation to the use of the vehicle a policy of insurance or such security as complies with the requirements of Part VI of the Road Traffic Act 1988; and

(*c*) that any further requirements that may be prescribed are met.

(3) A London PHV licence may not be granted in respect of more than one vehicle.

(4) A London PHV licence shall be granted subject to such conditions as may be prescribed and such other conditions as the licensing authority may think fit.

(5) A London PHV licence shall be in such form and shall contain such particulars as the licensing authority may think fit.

(6) A London PHV licence shall be granted for one year or for such shorter period as the licensing authority may consider appropriate in the circumstances of the case.

(7) An applicant for a London PHV licence may appeal[2] to a magistrates' court against a decision not to grant such a licence or against any condition (other than a prescribed condition) to which the licence is subject.

[Private Hire Vehicles (London) Act 1998, s 7 as amended by the Greater London Authority Act 1999, Sch 21.]

1 For "owner" see s 35, post.

2 For provisions relating to appeals see ss 25–26, post and the Magistrates' Court Rules 1981, r 34 in PART 1: MAGISTRATES' COURTS PROCEDURE ante.

7.7794 **8. Obligations of owners of licensed vehicles** (1) This section applies to the owner of any vehicle to which a London PHV licence relates.

(2) The owner[1] shall present the vehicle for inspection and testing by or on behalf of the licensing authority within such period and at such place as the authority may by notice reasonably require.

The vehicle shall not be required to be presented under this subsection on more than three separate occasions during any one period of 12 months.

(3) The owner shall (without prejudice to section 170 of the Road Traffic Act 1988) report any accident to the vehicle materially affecting—

(*a*) the safety, performance or appearance of the vehicle, or

(*b*) the comfort or convenience of persons carried in the vehicle,

to the licensing authority as soon as reasonably practical and in any case within 72 hours of the accident occurring.

(4) If the ownership of the vehicle changes, the person who was previously the owner shall within 14 days of the change give notice to the licensing authority of that fact and the name and address of the new owner.

(5) A person who, without reasonable excuse, contravenes any provision of this section is guilty of an offence and liable on summary conviction to a fine not exceeding **level 3** on the standard scale.

[Private Hire Vehicles (London) Act 1998, s 8 as amended by the Greater London Authority Act 1999, Sch 21.]

1 For "owner" see s 35, post.

7.7795 **9. Fitness of licensed vehicles** (1) A constable or authorised officer has power at all reasonable times to inspect and test, for the purpose of ascertaining its fitness, any vehicle to which a London PHV licence relates.

(2) If a constable or authorised officer is not satisfied as to the fitness of such a vehicle he may by notice to the owner of the vehicle—

(*a*) require the owner[1] to make the vehicle available for further inspection and testing at such reasonable time and place as may be specified in the notice; and

(*b*) if he thinks fit, suspend the London PHV licence relating to that vehicle until such time as a constable or authorised officer is satisfied as to the fitness of the vehicle.

(3) A notice under subsection (2)(*b*) shall state the grounds on which the licence is being suspended and the suspension shall take effect on the day on which it is served on the owner.

(4) A licence suspended under subsection (2)(*b*) shall remain suspended until such time as a constable or authorised officer by notice to the owner directs that the licence is again in force.

(5) If a licence remains suspended at the end of the period of two months beginning with the day on which a notice under subsection (2)(*b*) was served on the owner of the vehicle—

(*a*) a constable or authorised officer may by notice to the owner direct that the licence is revoked; and

(*b*) the revocation shall take effect at the end of the period of 21 days beginning with the day on which the owner is served with that notice.

(6) An owner[1] may appeal[2] against a notice under subsection (2)(*b*) or (5) to a magistrates' court.

[Private Hire Vehicles (London) Act 1998, s 9.]

[1] For "owner" see s 35, post.

[2] For provisions relating to appeals see ss 25–26, post and the Magistrates' Court Rules 1981, r 34 in PART 1: MAGISTRATES' COURTS PROCEDURE ante.

7.7796 **10. Identification of licensed vehicles** (1) The licensing authority shall issue a disc or plate for each vehicle to which a London PHV licence relates which identifies that vehicle as a vehicle for which such a licence is in force.

(2) No vehicle to which a London PHV licence relates shall be used as a private hire vehicle on a road in London unless the disc or plate issued under this section is exhibited on the vehicle in such manner as may be prescribed.

(3) The licensing authority may by notice exempt a vehicle from the requirement under subsection (2) when it is being used to provide a service specified in the notice if the authority considers it inappropriate (having regard to that service) to require the disc or plate in question to be exhibited.

(4) The driver and operator of a vehicle used in contravention of subsection (2) are each guilty of an offence.

(5) The owner[1] of a vehicle who permits it to be used in contravention of subsection (2) is guilty of an offence.

(6) It is a defence[2] in proceedings for an offence under subsection (4) for the driver or operator to show that he exercised all due diligence to prevent the vehicle being used in contravention of subsection (2).

(7) A person guilty of an offence under this section is liable on summary conviction to a fine not exceeding **level 3** on the standard scale.

[Private Hire Vehicles (London) Act 1998, s 10 as amended by the Greater London Authority Act 1999, Sch 21.]

[1] For "owner" see s 35, post.

[2] An accused who raises this defence is not required to establish it beyond reasonable doubt, but on the balance of probabilities: see *R v Carr-Briant* [1943] KB 607, [1943] 2 All ER 156, 107 JP 167.

7.7797 **11. Prohibition of taximeters** (1) No vehicle to which a London PHV licence relates shall be equipped with a taximeter.

(2) If such a vehicle is equipped with a taximeter, the owner[1] of that vehicle is guilty of an offence and liable on summary conviction to a fine not exceeding **level 3** on the standard scale.

(3) In this section "taximeter" means a device for calculating the fare to be charged in respect of any journey by reference to the distance travelled or time elapsed since the start of the journey (or a combination of both).

[Private Hire Vehicles (London) Act 1998, s 11.]

[1] For "owner" see s 35, post.

*Regulation of drivers of private hire vehicles in London*

7.7798 **12. Requirement for private hire vehicle driver's licence** (1) No vehicle shall be used as a private hire vehicle on a road in London unless the driver holds a private hire vehicle driver's licence.

(2) The driver and operator of a vehicle used in contravention of this section are each guilty of an offence.

(3) The owner[1] of a vehicle who permits it to be used in contravention of this section is guilty of an offence.

(4) It is a defence[2] in proceedings against the operator of a vehicle for an offence under subsection (2) for the operator to show that he exercised all due diligence to prevent the vehicle being used in contravention of this section.

(5) A person guilty of an offence under this section is liable on summary conviction to a fine not exceeding **level 4** on the standard scale.

(6) In this section "private hire vehicle driver's licence" means—

(*a*) except where paragraph (*b*) or (*c*) applies, a London PHV driver's licence;

(*b*) if the vehicle is in use for the purposes of a hiring the booking for which was accepted outside London in a controlled district in England and Wales, a licence under section 51 of the 1976 Act issued by the council for that district; and

(*c*) if the vehicle is in use for a hiring the booking for which was accepted in Scotland, a licence under section 13 of the 1982 Act,

and for the purposes of paragraph (*b*) or (*c*) it is immaterial that the booking in question is a sub-contracted booking.

(7) This section does not apply to the use of a vehicle for the purposes of a hiring for a journey beginning outside London in an area of England and Wales which is not a controlled district.

[Private Hire Vehicles (London) Act 1998, s 12.]

[1] For "owner" see s 35, post.

[2] An accused who raises this defence is not required to establish it beyond reasonable doubt, but on the balance of probabilities: see *R v Carr-Briant* [1943] KB 607, [1943] 2 All ER 156, 107 JP 167.

7.7799 **13. London PHV driver's licences** (1) Any person may apply to the licensing authority for a private hire vehicle driver's licence for London (in this Act referred to as a "London

PHV driver's licence").

(2) The licensing authority shall grant a London PHV driver's licence to an applicant if the authority is satisfied that—

(*a*) the applicant has attained the age of 21, is (and has for at least three years been) authorised to drive a motor car and is a fit and proper person to hold a London PHV driver's licence;

(*aa*) the applicant is not disqualified by reason of the applicant's immigration status from driving a private hire vehicle; and

(*b*) the requirement mentioned in subsection (3), and any further requirements prescribed by the licensing authority, are met.

(2A) In determining for the purposes of subsection (2) whether an applicant is disqualified by reason of the applicant's immigration status from driving a private hire vehicle, the licensing authority must have regard to any guidance issued by the Secretary of State.

(3) The licensing authority shall require applicants to show to the authority's satisfaction (whether by taking a test or otherwise) that they possess a level—

(*a*) of knowledge of London or parts of London; and

(*b*) of general topographical skills,

which appears to the authority to be appropriate.

The licensing authority may impose different requirements in relation to different applicants.

(4) The licensing authority may send a copy of an application to the Commissioner of Police of the Metropolis or the Commissioner of Police for the City of London with a request for the Commissioner's observations; and the Commissioner shall respond to the request.

(5) A London PHV driver's licence—

(*a*) may be granted subject to such conditions as the licensing authority may think fit;

(*b*) shall be in such form and shall contain such particulars as the licensing authority may think fit; and

(*c*) subject to section 13A, shall be granted for three years or for such shorter period as the Secretary of State may consider appropriate in the circumstances of the particular case.

(6) An applicant may appeal[1] to a magistrates' court against a decision not to grant a London PHV driver's licence or against any condition to which such a licence is subject.

(7) For the purposes of subsection (2), a person is authorised to drive a motor car if—

(*a*) he holds a licence granted under Part III of the Road Traffic Act 1988 (other than a provisional licence) authorising him to drive a motor car; or

(*b*) he is authorised by virtue of section 99A(1) or 109(1) of that Act (Community licences and Northern Ireland licences) to drive a motor car in Great Britain.

[Private Hire Vehicles (London) Act 1998, s 13 as amended by the Greater London Authority Act 1999, Sch 21 and the Immigration Act 2016, Sch 5.]

---

1 For provisions relating to appeals see ss 25–26, post and the Magistrates' Court Rules 1981, r 34 in PART 1: MAGISTRATES' COURTS PROCEDURE ante.

**7.7799A 13A. London PHV driver's licences for persons subject to immigration control**

(1) Subsection (2) applies if—

(a) a London PHV driver's licence is to be granted to a person who has been granted leave to enter or remain in the United Kingdom for a limited period ("the leave period");

(b) the person's leave has not been extended by virtue of section 3C of the Immigration Act 1971 (continuation of leave pending variation decision); and

(c) apart from subsection (2), the period for which the licence would have been granted would have ended after the end of the leave period.

(2) The licence must be granted for a period which ends at or before the end of the leave period.

(3) Subsection (4) applies if—

(a) a London PHV driver's licence is to be granted to a person who has been granted leave to enter or remain in the United Kingdom for a limited period; and

(b) the person's leave has been extended by virtue of section 3C of the Immigration Act 1971 (continuation of leave pending variation decision).

(4) The licence must be granted for a period which does not exceed six months.

(5) A London PHV driver's licence ceases to be in force if the person to whom it was granted becomes disqualified by reason of the person's immigration status from driving a private hire vehicle.

(6) If subsection (5) applies to a licence, the person to whom it was granted must, within the period of 7 days beginning with the day after the day on which the person first became disqualified, return the licence and the person's driver's badge to the licensing authority.

(7) A person who, without reasonable excuse, contravenes subsection (6) is guilty of an offence and liable on summary conviction—

(a) to a fine not exceeding level 3 on the standard scale; and

(b) in the case of a continuing offence, to a fine not exceeding ten pounds for each day during which an offence continues after conviction.

(8) The Secretary of State may by regulations amend the amount for the time being specified in subsection (7)(b).

[Private Hire Vehicles (London) Act 1998, s 13A as inserted by the Immigration Act 2016, Sch 5.]

7.7800 **14. Issue of driver's badges** (1) The licensing authority shall issue a badge to each person to whom the authority has granted a London PHV driver's licence.

(2) The licensing authority may prescribe the form of badges issued under this section.

(3) A person issued with such a badge shall, when he is the driver of a vehicle being used as a private hire vehicle, wear the badge in such position and manner as to be plainly and distinctly visible.

(4) The licensing authority may by notice exempt a person from the requirement under subsection (3), when he is the driver of a vehicle being used to provide a service specified in the notice if the authority considers it inappropriate (having regard to that service) to require the badge to be worn.

(5) Any person who without reasonable excuse contravenes subsection (3) is guilty of an offence and liable on summary conviction to a fine not exceeding **level 3** on the standard scale.*

[Private Hire Vehicles (London) Act 1998, s 14 as amended by the Greater London Authority Act 1999, Sch 21.]

* **Amended by the Transport for London Act 2008, s 23 from a date to be appointed.**

*Licences: general provisions*

7.7801 **15. Applications for licences** (1) An application for the grant of a licence under this Act shall be made in such form, and include such declarations and information, as the licensing authority may require.

(2) The licensing authority may require an applicant to furnish such further information as the authority may consider necessary for dealing with the application.

(3) The information which an applicant for a London PHV operator's licence may be required to furnish includes in particular information about—

(*a*) any premises in London which he proposes to use as an operating centre;

(*b*) any convictions recorded against him;

(*c*) any business activities he has carried on before making the application;

(*d*) if the applicant is or has been a director or secretary of a company, that company;

(*e*) if the applicant is a company, information about the directors or secretary of that company;

(*f*) if the applicant proposes to act as an operator in partnership with any other person, information about that person.

(4) An applicant for a London PHV driver's licence may be required by the licensing authority—

(*a*) to produce a certificate signed by a registered medical practitioner to the effect that—

(i) he is physically fit to be the driver of a private hire vehicle; and

(ii) if any specific requirements of physical fitness have been prescribed for persons holding London PHV licences, that he meets those requirements; and

(*b*) whether or not such a certificate has been produced, to submit to examination by a registered medical practitioner selected by the licensing authority as to his physical fitness to be the driver of such a vehicle.

(5) The provisions of this Act apply to the renewal of a licence as they apply to the grant of a licence.

[Private Hire Vehicles (London) Act 1998, s 15 as amended by the Greater London Authority Act 1999, Sch 21.]

7.7802 **16. Power to suspend or revoke licences** (1) The licensing authority may suspend or revoke a licence under this Act for any reasonable cause including (without prejudice to the generality of this subsection) any ground mentioned below.

(2) A London PHV operator's licence may be suspended or revoked where—

(*a*) the licensing authority is no longer satisfied that the licence holder is fit to hold such a licence;

(*aa*) the licence holder has, since the grant of the licence, been convicted of an immigration offence or required to pay an immigration penalty; or

(*b*) the licence holder has failed to comply with any condition of the licence or any other obligation imposed on him by or under this Act.

(2A) Subsection (2)(aa) does not apply if—

(a) in a case where the licence holder has been convicted of an immigration offence, the conviction is a spent conviction within the meaning of the Rehabilitation of Offenders Act 1974, or

(b) in a case where the licence holder has been required to pay an immigration penalty—

(i) more than three years have elapsed since the date on which the penalty was imposed, and

(ii) the amount of the penalty has been paid in full.

(3) A London PHV licence may be suspended or revoked where—

(*a*) the Secretary of State is no longer satisfied that the vehicle to which it relates is fit for use as a private hire vehicle; or

(*b*) the owner has failed to comply with any condition of the licence or any other obligation imposed on him by or under this Act.

(4) A London PHV driver's licence may be suspended or revoked where—

(*a*) the licence holder has, since the grant of the licence, been convicted of an offence involving dishonesty, indecency or violence;

(*aa*) the licence holder has, since the grant of the licence, been convicted of an immigration offence or required to pay an immigration penalty;

(*b*) the licensing authority is for any other reason no longer satisfied that the licence holder is fit to hold such a licence; or

(*c*) the licence holder has failed to comply with any condition of the licence or any other obligation imposed on him by or under this Act.

(5) Subsection (4)(aa) does not apply if—

(a) in a case where the licence holder has been convicted of an immigration offence, the conviction is a spent conviction within the meaning of the Rehabilitation of Offenders Act 1974, or

(b) in a case where the licence holder has been required to pay an immigration penalty—

(i) more than three years have elapsed since the date on which the penalty was imposed, and

(ii) the amount of the penalty has been paid in full.

[Private Hire Vehicles (London) Act 1998, s 16 as amended by the Greater London Authority Act 1999, Sch 21 and the Immigration Act 2016, Sch 5.]

7.7803 **17. Suspension and revocation under section 16: procedure** (1) Where the licensing authority has decided to suspend or revoke a licence under section 16—

(*a*) the authority shall give notice of the decision and the grounds for the decision to the licence holder or, in the case of a London PHV licence, the owner of the vehicle to which the licence relates; and

(*b*) the suspension or revocation takes effect at the end of the period of 21 days beginning with the day on which that notice is served on the licence holder or the owner.

(2) If the licensing authority is of the opinion that the interests of public safety require the suspension or revocation of a licence to have immediate effect, and the authority includes a statement of that opinion and the reasons for it in the notice of suspension or revocation, the suspension or revocation takes effect when the notice is served on the licence holder or vehicle owner (as the case may be).

(3) A licence suspended under this section shall remain suspended until such time as the licensing authority by notice directs that the licence is again in force.

(4) The holder of a London PHV operator's or driver's licence, or the owner of a vehicle to which a PHV licence relates, may appeal[1] to a magistrates' court against a decision under section 16 to suspend or revoke that licence.

[Private Hire Vehicles (London) Act 1998, s 17 as amended by the Greater London Authority Act 1999, Sch 21.]

---

1 For provisions relating to appeals see ss 25–26, post and the Magistrates' Court Rules 1981, r 34 in PART 1: MAGISTRATES' COURTS PROCEDURE ante.

7.7804 **18. Variation of operator's licence at the request of the operator** (1) The licensing authority may, on the application of a London PHV operator, vary his licence by adding a reference to a new operating centre or removing an existing reference to an operating centre.

(2) An application for the variation of a licence under this section shall be made in such form, and include such declarations and information, as the licensing authority may require.

(3) The licensing authority may require an applicant to furnish such further information as he may consider necessary for dealing with the application.

(4) The licensing authority shall not add a reference to a new operating centre unless the authority is satisfied that the premises in question meet any requirements prescribed under section 3(3)(*b*).

(5) An applicant for the variation of a London PHV operator's licence under this section may appeal[1] to a magistrates' court against a decision not to add a new operating centre to the licence.

[Private Hire Vehicles (London) Act 1998, s 18 as amended by the Greater London Authority Act 1999, Sch 21.]

---

1 For provisions relating to appeals see ss 25–26, post and the Magistrates' Court Rules 1981, r 34 in PART 1: MAGISTRATES' COURTS PROCEDURE ante.

7.7805 **19. Variation of operator's licence by the licensing authority** (1) The licensing authority may—

(*a*) suspend the operation of a London PHV operator's licence so far as relating to any operating centre specified in the licence; or

(*b*) vary such a licence by removing a reference to an operating centre previously specified in the licence,

if the authority is no longer satisfied that the operating centre in question meets any requirements prescribed under section 3(3)(*b*) or for any other reasonable cause.

(2) Where the licensing authority has decided to suspend the operation of a licence as mentioned in subsection (1)(*a*) or vary a licence as mentioned in subsection (1)(*b*)—

(*a*) the authority shall give notice of the decision and the grounds for it to the licence holder; and

(*b*) the decision shall take effect at the end of the period of 21 days beginning with the day on which the licence holder is served with that notice.

(3) If the licensing authority is of the opinion that the interests of public safety require his decision to have immediate effect, and the authority includes a statement of that opinion and the reasons for it in the notice, the authority's decision shall take effect when the notice is served on the licence holder.

(4) If a licence is suspended in relation to an operating centre, the premises in question shall not be regarded for the purposes of this Act as premises at which the licence holder is authorised to accept private hire bookings, until such time as the licensing authority by notice states that the licence is no longer suspended in relation to those premises.

(5) The holder of a London PHV operator's licence may appeal[1] to a magistrates' court against a decision under subsection (1).

[Private Hire Vehicles (London) Act 1998, s 19 as amended by the Greater London Authority Act 1999, Sch 21.]

---

1 For provisions relating to appeals see ss 25–26, post and the Magistrates' Court Rules 1981, r 34 in PART 1: MAGISTRATES' COURTS PROCEDURE ante.

7.7806 **20. Fees for grant of licences, etc**

7.7807 **21. Production of documents** (1) The holder of a London PHV operator's licence or a London PHV driver's licence shall at the request of a constable or authorised officer produce his licence for inspection.

(2) The owner[1] of a vehicle to which a London PHV licence relates shall at the request of a constable or authorised officer produce for inspection—

(*a*) the London PHV licence for that vehicle;

(*b*) the certificate of the policy of insurance or security required in respect of the vehicle by Part VI of the Road Traffic Act 1988.

(3) A document required to be produced under this section shall be produced either forthwith or—

(*a*) if the request is made by a constable, at any police station within London nominated by the licence holder or vehicle owner when the request is made, or

(*b*) if the request is made by an authorised officer, at such place as the officer may reasonably require,

before the end of the period of 6 days beginning with the day on which the request is made.

(4) A person who without reasonable excuse contravenes this section is guilty of an offence and liable on summary conviction to a fine not exceeding **level 3** on the standard scale.

[Private Hire Vehicles (London) Act 1998, s 21.]

---

1 For "owner" see s 35, post.

7.7808 **22. Return of licences, etc** (1) The holder of a London PHV operator's licence shall return the licence to the licensing authority after the expiry or revocation of that licence, within the period of 7 days after the day on which the licence expires or the revocation takes effect.

(2) The owner[1] of a vehicle to which a London PHV licence relates shall return the licence and the plate or disc which was issued for the vehicle under section 10 to the licensing authority after the expiry or revocation of that licence within the period of 7 days after the day on which the licence expires or the revocation takes effect.

(3) The holder of a London PHV driver's licence shall return the licence and his driver's badge to the licensing authority after the expiry or revocation of that licence, within the period of 7 days after the day on which the licence expires or the revocation takes effect.

(4) On the suspension of a licence under this Act, the licensing authority, a constable or an authorised officer may by notice direct the holder of the licence, or the owner of the vehicle, to return the licence to the authority, constable or officer (as the case may be) within the period of 7 days after the day on which the notice is served on that person.

A direction under this subsection may also direct—

(*a*) the return by the vehicle owner of the disc or plate which was issued for the vehicle under section 10 (in the case of a London PHV licence); or

(*b*) the return by the licence holder of the driver's badge (in the case of a London PHV driver's licence).

(5) A person who without reasonable excuse fails to comply with any requirement or direction under this section to return a licence, disc, plate or badge is guilty of an offence.

(6) A person guilty of an offence under this section is liable on summary conviction—

(*a*) to a fine not exceeding **level 3** on the standard scale; and

(*b*) in the case of a continuing offence, to a fine not exceeding **ten pounds for each day** during which an offence continues after conviction.

(7) A constable or authorised officer is entitled to remove and retain the plate or disc from a vehicle to which an expired, suspended or revoked London PHV licence relates following—

(*a*) a failure to comply with subsection (2) or a direction under subsection (4);

(*b*) a suspension or revocation of the licence which has immediate effect by virtue of section 9(3) or 17(2).*

[Private Hire Vehicles (London) Act 1998, s 22 as amended by the Greater London Authority Act 1999, Sch 21.]

* **Amended by the Transport for London Act 2008, s 24 from a date to be appointed.**
1 For "owner" see s 35, post.

7.7809 **23. Register of licences**

7.7810 **24. Delegation of functions by the Secretary of State**

7.7811 **25. Appeals** (1) This section applies to any appeal which lies under this Act to a magistrates' court against a decision of the licensing authority, a constable or an authorised officer in relation to, or to an application for, a licence under this Act.

(2) If the licensing authority has exercised the power to delegate functions under section 24, such an appeal shall be heard by a magistrates' court.

(3) Any such appeal shall be by way of complaint for an order and the Magistrates' Courts Act 1980 shall apply to the proceedings.

(4) The time within which a person may bring such an appeal is 21 days from the date on which notice of the decision appealed against is served on him.

(5) In the case of a decision where an appeal lies, the notice of the decision shall state the right of appeal to a magistrates' court and the time within which an appeal may be brought.

(6) An appeal against any decision of a magistrates' court in pursuance of an appeal to which this section applies shall lie to the Crown Court at the instance of any party to the proceedings in the magistrates' court.

(7) Where on appeal a court varies or reverses any decision of the licensing authority, a constable or an authorised officer, the order of the court shall be given effect to by the licensing authority or, as the case may be, a constable or authorised officer.

(8) On an appeal under this Act to the magistrates' court or the Crown Court, the court is not entitled to entertain any question as to whether—

(a) a person should be, or should have been, granted leave to enter or remain in the United Kingdom; or

(b) a person has, after the date of the decision being appealed against, been granted leave to enter or remain in the United Kingdom.

[Private Hire Vehicles (London) Act 1998, s 25 as amended by the Greater London Authority Act 1999, Sch 21, SI 2005/886 and the Immigration Act 2016, Sch 5.]

7.7812 **26. Effect of appeal on decision appealed against** (1) If any decision of the licensing authority against which a right of appeal is conferred by this Act—

(*a*) involves the execution of any work or the taking of any action;

(*b*) makes it unlawful for any person to carry on a business which he was lawfully carrying on at the time of the decision,

the decision shall not take effect until the time for appealing has expired or (where an appeal is brought) until the appeal is disposed of or withdrawn.

(2) This section does not apply in relation to a decision to suspend, vary or revoke a licence if the notice of suspension, variation or revocation directs that, in the interests of public safety, the decision is to have immediate effect.

[Private Hire Vehicles (London) Act 1998, s 26 as amended by the Greater London Authority Act 1999, Sch 21.]

7.7813 **27. Obstruction of authorised officers etc** (1) A person who wilfully obstructs a constable or authorised officer acting in pursuance of this Act is guilty of an offence and liable on summary conviction to a fine not exceeding **level 3** on the standard scale.

(2) A person who, without reasonable excuse—

(*a*) fails to comply with any requirement properly made to such person by a constable or authorised officer acting in pursuance of this Act; or

(*b*) fails to give a constable or authorised officer acting in pursuance of this Act any other assistance or information which he may reasonably require of such person for the purpose of performing his functions under this Act,

is guilty of an offence and liable on summary conviction to a fine not exceeding level 3 on the standard scale.

(3) A person who makes any statement which he knows to be false in giving any information to an authorised officer or constable acting in pursuance of this Act is guilty of an offence and liable on summary conviction to a fine not exceeding **level 5** on the standard scale.

[Private Hire Vehicles (London) Act 1998, s 27.]

7.7814 **28. Penalty for false statements** A person who knowingly or recklessly makes a statement or furnishes information which is false or misleading in any material particular for the purpose of procuring the grant or renewal of a licence under this Act, or the variation of an operator's licence under section 18, is guilty of an offence and liable on summary conviction to a fine not exceeding **level 5** on the standard scale.

[Private Hire Vehicles (London) Act 1998, s 28.]

7.7815 **29. Saving for vehicles used for funerals and weddings** Nothing in this Act applies to any vehicle whose use as a private hire vehicle is limited to use in connection with funerals or weddings.

[Private Hire Vehicles (London) Act 1998, s 29.]

*Further controls*

7.7816 **30. Prohibition of certain signs, notices etc** (1) The licensing authority may make regulations prohibiting the display in London on or from vehicles (other than licensed taxis and public service vehicles) of any sign, notice or other feature of a description specified in the regulations.

(2) Before making the regulations the licensing authority shall consult such bodies appearing to the authority to represent the London cab trade and the private hire vehicle trade in London as the authority considers appropriate.

(3) Any person who—

(*a*) drives a vehicle in respect of which a prohibition imposed by regulations under this section is contravened; or

(*b*) causes or permits such a prohibition to be contravened in respect of any vehicle,

is guilty of an offence and liable on summary conviction to a fine not exceeding level 4 on the standard scale.

[Private Hire Vehicles (London) Act 1998, s 30 as amended by the Greater London Authority Act 1999, Sch 21.]

7.7817 **31. Prohibition of certain advertisements** (1) This section applies to any advertisement—

(*a*) indicating that vehicles can be hired on application to a specified address in London;

(*b*) indicating that vehicles can be hired by telephone on a telephone number being the number of premises in London; or

(*c*) on or near any premises in London, indicating that vehicles can be hired at those premises.

(2) No such advertisement shall include—

(*a*) any of the following words, namely "taxi", "taxis", "cab" or "cabs", or

(*b*) any word so closely resembling any of those words as to be likely to be mistaken for it,

(whether alone or as part of another word), unless the vehicles offered for hire are London cabs.

(3) An advertisement which includes the word "minicab", "mini-cab" or "mini cab" (whether in the singular or plural) does not by reason only of that fact contravene this section.

(4) Any person who issues, or causes to be issued, an advertisement which contravenes this section is guilty of an offence and liable on summary conviction to a fine not exceeding **level 4** on the standard scale.

(5) It is a defence for a person charged with an offence under this section to prove[1] that—

(*a*) he is a person whose business it is to publish or arrange for the publication of advertisements;

(*b*) he received the advertisement in question for publication in the ordinary course of business; and

(*c*) he did not know and had no reason to suspect that its publication would amount to an offence under this section.

(6) In this section—

"advertisement" includes every form of advertising (whatever the medium) and references to the issue of an advertisement shall be construed accordingly;

"telephone number" includes any number used for the purposes of communicating with another by electronic means; and "telephone" shall be construed accordingly.

[Private Hire Vehicles (London) Act 1998, s 31.]

1 An accused who raises this defence is not required to establish it beyond reasonable doubt, but on the balance of probabilities: see *R v Carr-Briant* [1943] KB 607, [1943] 2 All ER 156, 107 JP 167.

*Miscellaneous and supplementary*

7.7818 **32. Regulations[1]**

1 See the Private Hire Vehicles (London) (Operators' Licences) Regulations 2000, SI 2000/3146.

7.7819 **33. Offences due to fault of other person** (1) Where an offence by any person under this Act is due to the act or default of another person, then (whether proceedings are taken against the first mentioned person or not) that other person is guilty of the offence and is liable to be proceeded against and punished accordingly.

(2) Where an offence under this Act committed by a body corporate is proved to have been committed with the consent or connivance of, or attributable to any neglect on the part of, any director, manager, secretary or other similar officer of the body corporate (or any person purporting to act in that capacity), he as well as the body corporate is guilty of the offence is liable to be proceeded against and punished accordingly.

[Private Hire Vehicles (London) Act 1998, s 33.]

7.7820 **34. Service of notices** (1) Any notice authorised or required under this Act to be given to any person may be served by post.

(2) For the purposes of section 7 of the Interpretation Act 1978 any such notice is properly addressed to a London PHV operator if it is addressed to him at any operating centre of his in London.

(3) Any notice authorised or required under this Act to be given to the owner of a vehicle shall

be deemed to have been effectively given if it is given to the person who is for the time being notified to the licensing authority for the purposes of this Act as the owner of the vehicle (or, if more than one person is currently notified as the owner, if it is given to any of them).

[Private Hire Vehicles (London) Act 1998, s 34 as amended by the Greater London Authority Act 1999, Sch 21.]

7.7821 **35. References to the owner of a vehicle** (1) For the purposes of this Act the owner of a vehicle shall be taken to be the person by whom it is kept.

(2) In determining, in the course of any proceedings for an offence under this Act, who was the owner of a vehicle at any time it shall be presumed that the owner was the person who was the registered keeper of the vehicle at that time.

(3) Notwithstanding that presumption—

(*a*) it is open to the defence to show that the person who was the registered keeper of a vehicle at any particular time was not the person by whom the vehicle was kept at that time; and

(*b*) it is open to the prosecution to prove that the vehicle was kept at that time by some person other than the registered keeper.

(4) In this section "registered keeper", in relation to a vehicle, means the person in whose name the vehicle was registered under the Vehicle Excise and Registration Act 1994[1].

[Private Hire Vehicles (London) Act 1998, s 35.]

1 In PART IV: ROAD TRAFFIC, ante.

7.7821A **35A. Persons disqualified by reason of immigration status** (1) For the purposes of this Act a person is disqualified by reason of the person's immigration status from carrying on a licensable activity if the person is subject to immigration control and—

(a) the person has not been granted leave to enter or remain in the United Kingdom; or

(b) the person's leave to enter or remain in the United Kingdom—

(i) is invalid;

(ii) has ceased to have effect (whether by reason of curtailment, revocation, cancellation, passage of time or otherwise); or

(iii) is subject to a condition preventing the person from carrying on the licensable activity.

(2) Where a person is on immigration bail within the meaning of Part 1 of Schedule 10 to the Immigration Act 2016—

(a) the person is to be treated for the purposes of this Act as if the person had been granted leave to enter the United Kingdom; but

(b) any condition as to the person's work in the United Kingdom to which the person's immigration bail is subject is to be treated for those purposes as a condition of leave.

(3) For the purposes of this section a person is subject to immigration control if under the Immigration Act 1971 the person requires leave to enter or remain in the United Kingdom.

(4) For the purposes of this section a person carries on a licensable activity if the person—

(a) operates a private hire vehicle; or

(b) drives a private hire vehicle.

[Private Hire Vehicles (London) Act 1998, s 35A as inserted by the Immigration Act 2016, Sch 5.]

7.7821B **35B. Immigration offences and immigration penalties** (1) In this Act "immigration offence" means—

(a) an offence under any of the Immigration Acts;

(b) an offence under section 1 of the Criminal Attempts Act 1981 of attempting to commit an offence within paragraph (a); or

(c) an offence under section 1 of the Criminal Law Act 1977 of conspiracy to commit an offence within paragraph (a).

(2) In this Act "immigration penalty" means a penalty under—

(a) section 15 of the Immigration, Asylum and Nationality Act 2006 ("the 2006 Act"), or

(b) section 23 of the Immigration Act 2014 ("the 2014 Act").

(3) For the purposes of this Act a person to whom a penalty notice under section 15 of the 2006 Act has been given is not to be treated as having been required to pay an immigration penalty if—

(a) the person is excused payment by virtue of section 15(3) of that Act; or

(b) the penalty is cancelled by virtue of section 16 or 17 of that Act.

(4) For the purposes of this Act a person to whom a penalty notice under section 15 of the 2006 Act has been given is not to be treated as having been required to pay an immigration penalty until such time as—

(a) the period for giving a notice of objection under section 16 of that Act has expired and the Secretary of State has considered any notice given within that period; and

(b) if a notice of objection was given within that period, the period for appealing under section 17 of that Act has expired and any appeal brought within that period has been finally determined, abandoned or withdrawn.

(5) For the purposes of this Act a person to whom a penalty notice under section 23 of the 2014 Act has been given is not to be treated as having been required to pay an immigration penalty if—

(a) the person is excused payment by virtue of section 24 of that Act; or

(b) the penalty is cancelled by virtue of section 29 or 30 of that Act.

(6) For the purposes of this Act a person to whom a penalty notice under section 23 of the 2014 Act has been given is not to be treated as having been required to pay an immigration penalty until such time as—

(a) the period for giving a notice of objection under section 29 of that Act has expired and the Secretary of State has considered any notice given within that period; and

(b) if a notice of objection was given within that period, the period for appealing under section 30 of that Act has expired and any appeal brought within that period has been finally determined, abandoned or withdrawn.

[Private Hire Vehicles (London) Act 1998, s 35B as inserted by the Immigration Act 2016, Sch 5.]

7.7822 **36. Interpretation** In this Act, unless the context otherwise requires—

"authorised officer" means an officer authorised in writing by the licensing authority for the purposes of this Act;

"controlled district" means an area for which Part II of the 1976 Act is in force by virtue of—

(*a*) a resolution passed by a district council under section 45 of that Act;

(*b*) section 255(4) of the Greater London Authority Act 1999;

"driver's badge" means the badge issued to the holder of a London PHV driver's licence;

"hackney carriage" means a vehicle licensed under section 37 of the Town Police Clauses Act 1847 or any similar enactment;

"licensed taxi" means a hackney carriage, a London cab or a taxi licensed under Part II of the 1982 Act;

"the licensing authority" means Transport for London;

"London" means the area consisting of the metropolitan police district and the City of London (including the Temples);

"London cab" means a vehicle licensed under section 6 of the Metropolitan Public Carriage Act 1869;

"London PHV driver's licence" means a licence under section 13;

"London PHV licence" means a licence under section 7;

"London PHV operator" has the meaning given in section 4(1);

"London PHV operator's licence" means a licence under section 2;

"notice" means notice in writing;

"operate" has the meaning given in section 1(1);

"operating centre" has the meaning given in section 1(5);

"operator" has the meaning given in section 1(1);

"prescribed" means prescribed in regulations under section 32(1);

"private hire vehicle" has the meaning given in section 1(1);

"public service vehicle" has the same meaning as in the Public Passenger Vehicles Act 1981,

"road" means any length of highway or of any other road to which the public has access (including bridges over which a road passes);

"the 1976 Act" means the Local Government (Miscellaneous Provisions) Act 1976;

"the 1982 Act" means the Civic Government (Scotland) Act 1982; and

"vehicle" means a mechanically propelled vehicle (other than a tramcar) intended or adapted for use on roads.

[Private Hire Vehicles (London) Act 1998, s 36 as amended by the Greater London Authority Act 1999, Sch 21 and the Immigration Act 2016, Sch 5.]

7.7823 **37. Power to make transitional etc provisions** (1) The Secretary of State may by regulations[1] make such transitional provisions and such savings as he considers necessary or expedient in preparation for, in connection with, or in consequence of—

(*a*) the coming into force of any provision of this Act; or

(*b*) the operation of any enactment repealed or amended by a provision of this Act during any period when the repeal or amendment is not wholly in force.

(2) Regulations under this section may modify any enactment contained in this or in any other Act.

(3) Before making regulations under this section the Secretary of State shall consult the licensing authority.

[Private Hire Vehicles (London) Act 1998, s 37 as amended by the Greater London Authority Act 1999, Sch 21.]

---

1 See the Private Hire Vehicles (London) (Operators' Licences) Regulations 2000, SI 2000/3146. See also the Private Hire Vehicles (London) (Transitional and Saving Provisions) Regulations 2003, SI 2003/655 amended by SI 2003/3028 amended by SI 2006/584 and the Private Hire Vehicles (London) (Transitional Provisional) Regulations 2004, SI 2004/242 amended by SI 2997/3453.

7.7824 **39. Consequential amendments and repeals**

7.7825 **40. Short title, commencement and extent**

## MISCELLANEOUS

## Metropolitan Police Courts Act 1839

(1839 c 71)

7.7826 **27. Power to order goods stolen or fraudulently obtained, and in possession of a broker or other dealer in second-hand property, to be delivered up to owner** If any goods shall be stolen or unlawfully obtained from any person, or, being lawfully obtained, shall be unlawfully deposited, sold, or exchanged, and complaint shall be made thereof to any of the said magistrates, and that such goods are in the possession of any broker, dealer in marine stores, or other dealer in second-hand property within the metropolitan police district, it shall be lawful for such magistrate to issue a summons or warrant for the appearance of such broker or dealer, and for the production of the goods, and to order such goods to be delivered up to the owner thereof, either without any payment, or upon payment of such sum and at such a time as the magistrate shall think fit; and every broker or dealer who, being so ordered, shall refuse or neglect to deliver up the goods, or who shall dispose of or make away with the same after notice that such goods were stolen or unlawfully obtained as aforesaid, shall forfeit to the owner of the goods the full value thereof, to be determined by the magistrate: Provided always, that no such order shall bar any such broker or dealer from recovering possession of such goods by suit or action at law from the person into whose possession they may come by virtue of the magistrate's order, so that such action be commenced within six calendar months next after such order shall be made.

[Metropolitan Police Courts Act 1839, s 27.]

7.7827 **28. Power to order restoration of property unlawfully pawned, etc** It shall be lawful for any magistrate to order that any goods unlawfully exchanged, which shall be brought before him, and the ownership of which shall be established to the satisfaction of such magistrate, shall be delivered up to the owner by the party with whom they were so unlawfully exchanged, either without compensation, or with such compensation to the party in question as the magistrate may think fit.

[Metropolitan Police Courts Act 1839, s 28.]

## Greater London Council (General Powers) Act 1981

(1981 c xvii)

### PART I[1]

### PRELIMINARY

7.7829 **1. Short title** This Act may be cited as the Greater London Council (General Powers) Act 1981.

[Greater London Council (General Powers) Act 1981, s 1.]

1 Part I contains ss 1, 2.

7.7830 **2. Interpretation** In this Act, except as otherwise expressly provided or unless the context otherwise requires—

"the Act of 1936" means the Public Health Act 1936;

"borough council" means London borough council and includes the Common Council of the City of London; and "borough" shall be construed accordingly;

"the Council" means the Greater London Council;

"daily fine" means a fine for each day on which an offence is continued after conviction thereof.

[Greater London Council (General Powers) Act 1981, s 2.]

### PART IV[1]

### PROVISIONS RELATING TO CONTROL BY BOROUGH COUNCILS OF OVERCROWDING IN CERTAIN HOSTELS

7.7831 **8. Meaning of "hostel"** In this Part of this Act "hostel" means any premises in which there is provided on payment sleeping accommodation, whether with or without the provision of board or facilities for the preparation of food, in one or more common dormitories or other sleeping areas, if in any one of those areas four or more persons, not all being members of the same family or of the same household, are accommodated at the same time.

[Greater London Council (General Powers) Act 1981, s 8.]

1 Part IV contains ss 8–16.

7.7832 **9. Overcrowding in hostels** (1) If on or after 1 January 1982 it appears to a borough council that premises in the borough are being used as a hostel and that excessive numbers of persons are being accommodated in the premises having regard to any of the following matters, that is to say:

(*a*) the size and condition of the rooms available;

(*b*) the adequacy of the means of lighting, heating, sanitation, ventilation or (where appropriate) food storage or preparation provided in the premises;

(*c*) the adequacy of the personal washing facilities so provided; the borough council may serve on the occupier of the premises or on any person having the control and management thereof, or on both, a notice—

(i) stating, in relation to any room on the premises, or to any part of the premises not being a room, the maximum number of persons (if any) by whom it may be occupied as sleeping accommodation at any one time, or, as the case may be, that it shall not be occupied as aforesaid; and

(ii) informing him of the effect of section 12 (Part IV penalties) of this Act:

Provided that a notice under this subsection shall not apply limits in relation to the number of persons who may occupy any room on the premises, or any part of the premises not being a room, which are more onerous than any limits for the time being applied to the premises by a registration scheme a licence under Part 2 of the Housing Act 2004 or an overcrowding notice under section 134 of that Act.

(2) For the purposes of the foregoing subsection a notice may, in relation to any room, prescribe special maxima applicable in any case where some or all of the persons occupying the room are under such age as may be specified in the notice.

(3) A notice served under this section shall, if no appeal is brought under section 10 (Part IV appeals) of this Act, become operative in relation to the premises to which it relates on the expiration of twenty-one days from the date of service of the notice and shall be final and conclusive as to any matters which could have been raised on such an appeal, and any such notice against which an appeal is brought shall, if and so far as it is confirmed by the court, or if the appeal is withdrawn, become operative as from the date of the determination of the appeal, or of the withdrawal thereof, as the case may be.

[Greater London Council (General Powers) Act 1981, s 9 as amended by the Housing (Consequential Provisions) Act 1985, Sch 2 and the Housing Act 2004, Sch 15.]

7.7833 10. **Part IV appeals** Any person aggrieved by a notice under section 9 (Overcrowding in hostels) of this Act may, within twenty-one days after the service of the notice, appeal to a magistrates' court, and on any such appeal the court may make such order either confirming or quashing or varying the notice as the court thinks fit.

[Greater London Council (General Powers) Act 1981, s 10.]

7.7834 11. **Exhibition of notice** Any person occupying or having the control and management of premises in respect of which a notice under section 9 (Overcrowding in hostels) of this Act has become operative shall keep exhibited in a suitable place, to be specified in the notice, in the premises to which the notice relates a copy of the notice in the form in which it has come into effect, and if without reasonable excuse he fails to do so he shall be guilty of an offence and liable on summary conviction to a fine not exceeding **level 2** on the standard scale and to a daily fine not exceeding **£5**.

[Greater London Council (General Powers) Act 1981, s 11 as amended by the Criminal Justice Act 1982, s 46.]

7.7835 12. **Part IV penalties** (1) Any person who, while a notice is operative in pursuance of the provisions of this Part of this Act, knowingly causes or permits any room or other part of the premises to which the notice relates to be occupied as sleeping accommodation otherwise than in accordance with the notice shall be guilty of an offence:

Provided that a person shall not be convicted of an offence under this section where the facts which would otherwise have given rise to such an offence are, so far as is relevant, the same as the facts giving rise to an offence for which that person has been convicted under section 355(2) or 358(4) of the Housing Act 1985.

(2) Any person committing an offence under this section shall be liable on summary conviction to a fine not exceeding **level 4** on the standard scale.

[Greater London Council (General Powers) Act 1981, s 12 as amended by the Criminal Justice Act 1982, s 46 and the Housing (Consequential Provisions) Act 1985, Sch 2.]

7.7836 13. **Withdrawal of notice** Where a borough council have served a notice under section 9 (Overcrowding in hostels) of this Act in respect of any premises, they may at any time withdraw the notice, without prejudice to anything done in pursuance thereof or to the service of another notice, or, if there is any material change of circumstances, they may substitute for the notice a further notice under the said section 9.

[Greater London Council (General Powers) Act 1981, s 13.]

7.7837 14. **Powers of entry for inspection, etc** (1) An authorised officer of a borough council (on producing, if so required, some duly authenticated document showing his authority) may enter upon, inspect and examine any premises used, or which he has reasonable cause to believe are used, or intended to be used, as a hostel and may do all such things as are reasonably necessary for the purpose—

(*a*) of ascertaining whether or not circumstances exist which would authorise the borough council to take any action under this Part of this Act;

(*b*) of preparing a notice under subsection (1) of section 9 (Overcrowding in hostels) of this Act; or

(*c*) of ascertaining whether there is, or has been any contravention of the provisions of this

Part of this Act.

(2) Any person who intentionally obstructs any person acting in the exercise of his powers under this section shall be guilty of an offence and liable on summary conviction to a fine not exceeding **level 3** on the standard scale.

(3) The provisions of subsections (2), (3) and (4) of section 287 (which confers powers to enter on premises) of the Act of 1936 shall apply in respect of entry into any premises for the purposes of this section as they apply to entry into premises for the purposes of subsection (1) of that section.

[Greater London Council (General Powers) Act 1981, s 14 as amended by the Criminal Justice Act 1982, s 46.]

7.7838 **15. Evidence in legal proceedings** If in any proceedings under this Part of this Act it is alleged that persons occupying any premises or part thereof are members of the same family or of the same household, the burden of proving that allegation shall rest upon the person by whom it is made.

[Greater London Council (General Powers) Act 1981, s 15.]

7.7839 **16. Exemption for certain premises** Nothing in this Part of this Act shall apply to any premises used as a hostel being premises—

(*a*) occupied, used or managed by the Crown, by the Common Council of the City of London or by an authority or body established by or under any enactment or operating under Royal Charter;

(*b*) (not being premises referred to in the foregoing paragraph) occupied, used or managed by a school within the meaning of the Education Act 1996, by a university established by any enactment or operating under Royal Charter or by any college, school or similar institution forming part of, or connected with, such a university;

(*c*) occupied, used or managed by a polytechnic designated by the Secretary of State;

(*d*) (not being premises referred to in paragraph (*a*) or (*b*) above) occupied, used or managed by any college, school or similar institution assisted by a local education authority;

(*e*) *repealed*;

(*f*) used as a hospital by virtue of any enactment or under Royal Charter;

(*g*) used as a nursing home or a mental nursing home as defined in the Nursing Homes Act 1975;

(*gg*) used as a children's home as defined in section 63 of the Children Act 1989;

(*h*) used as a voluntary home as defined in section 60 of the Children Act 1989 and which—

(i) are registered under section 60;

(ii) are an assisted community home within the meaning of section 53 of that Act;

(*i*) liable to be inspected under section 67 of the Children Act 1989;

(*j*) *repealed*;

(*k*) occupied, used or managed by any person who is in receipt of a grant by virtue of regulations made under section 485 of the Education Act 1996;

(*l*) occupied, used or managed by a registered social landlord within the meaning of the Housing Act 1985 (see section 5(4) and (5) of that Act);

(*m*) occupied, used or managed, for the purposes specified in paragraph 4 of Schedule 5 to the Supplementary Benefits Act 1976, by a voluntary organisation which is in receipt of contributions from the Secretary of State under the said paragraph 4;

(*n*) approved by the Secretary of State under section 49(1) of the Powers of Criminal Courts Act 1973; or

(*o*) occupied, used or managed by any society or individual in receipt of a payment in respect of those premises under section 51(3)(*f*) of the said Act of 1973.

[Greater London Council (General Powers) Act 1981, s 16 as amended by the Housing (Consequential Provisions) Act 1985, Sch 2, the Children Act 1989, Sch 13, the Education Act 1996, Sch. 37, SI 1996/2325 and SI 1997/221 and the Care Standards Act 2000, s 116.]

## PART V[1]

### FURTHER PROVISIONS RELATING TO BOROUGH COUNCILS

7.7840 **18. Stopping up of streets** (1) Subject to the provisions of this section, if it appears to a magistrates' court, after a view, if the court thinks fit, by any two or more of the justices composing the court, that a street in a borough (other than the City of London or the Royal Borough of Kensington and Chelsea) or any part thereof (not being—

(*a*) a trunk road;

(*b*) a special road;

(*c*) a metropolitan road;

(*d*) a street forming part of the route of a stage carriage or express carriage service; or

(*e*) except with the consent of the British Railways Board, a street belonging to that board);

in respect of which a borough council have made an application to the court under this section—

(i) is temporarily not required to afford either vehicular access or both vehicular and pedestrian access to any premises or to secure the expeditious, convenient and safe movement of, as the case may be, either vehicular traffic or both vehicular traffic and foot passengers; and

(ii) is being used for the unauthorised deposit of refuse;

the court may by order authorise the borough council to stop up the street or that part thereof either to vehicular traffic or to both vehicular traffic and foot passengers, as the case may be, for such period not exceeding two years as may be specified in the order.

(2) Not later than twenty-eight days before the day on which the application is heard the borough council shall—

(*a*) cause a copy of a notice stating their intention to apply for the order, specifying the time and place at which the application is to be made and the terms of the order applied for (embodying a plan showing what will be the effect thereof) to be displayed in a prominent position at the ends of the street or part thereof in respect of which the application is to be made and shall serve a copy of that notice on the Council; and

(*b*) publish in a local newspaper circulating in the borough a copy of the said notice except that there may be substituted for the plan a statement of a place in the borough where the plan may be inspected free of charge at all reasonable hours; and

(*c*) deliver a copy of the said notice together with a copy of the plan to each owner and occupier of land adjoining the street or part thereof in respect of which the application is to be made; and

(*d*) deliver a copy of the said notice together with a copy of the plan to the Commissioner of Police of the Metropolis and to the Chief Officer of the London Ambulance Service.

(3) Before implementing an order for stopping up a street or part thereof under this section, the borough council shall serve a copy of the order on the Council, on any statutory undertaker affected and on any universal service provider (within the meaning of the Postal Services Act 2000) who provides a universal postal service (within the meaning of that Act) in an area which includes the street or part thereof to which the order applies.

(4) At any time when an order under this section is in force application may be made to a magistrates' court by the borough council or the Council, if they consider that the street or part thereof is required to secure the expeditious, convenient and safe movement of vehicular traffic or foot passengers, or by any person who wishes to use the street or part thereof to afford vehicular or pedestrian access to any premises, for the order to be rescinded or modified, and if it appears to the court that the street or part thereof is required to afford vehicular or pedestrian access to any premises or to secure the expeditious, convenient and safe movement of vehicular traffic or foot passengers the court shall by order rescind or modify the order made under this section.

(5) On the hearing of an application under this section the borough council, the Council, the applicant, any person who uses the street and any other person who would be aggrieved by the making of the order the subject of the application shall have a right to be heard.

(6) The provisions of section 41 (which imposes duties as to the maintenance of certain highways) of the Highways Act 1980 shall not apply in respect of any street or to any part thereof while that street or that part thereof, as the case may be, is stopped up to both vehicular traffic and foot passengers pursuant to an order of the court under subsection (1) of this section.

(7) Part II of Schedule 12 to the said Act of 1980 shall apply where—

(*a*) in pursuance of an order under this section a street or part of a street is stopped up to traffic; and

(*b*) immediately before the order is made there is in, upon, over, along or across the street any apparatus belonging to or used by any statutory undertakers for the purpose of their undertaking;

as if in that Schedule references to section 116 (which relates to the stopping up or diversion of highways) of the said Act of 1980 were references to this section.

(8) Where any street or part of a street is stopped up either to vehicular traffic or to both vehicular traffic and foot passengers under this section, the borough council shall afford vehicular access thereto to the British Railways Board, any universal service provider (within the meaning of the Postal Services Act 2000) who requires such access in connection with the provision of a universal postal service (within the meaning of that Act) and, without prejudice to paragraphs 18 and 19 of Part III of Schedule 9 to the London Government Act 1963, the Thames Water Authority.

(9) *Consequential provisions relating to the Post Office.*

(10) In this section the expression "telegraphic line" has the same meaning as in the Telegraph Act 1878.

[Greater London Council (General Powers) Act 1981, s 18 as amended by SI 2001/648.]

1 Part V contains ss 17–19.

7.7841 **19. Acupuncturists, tattooists and cosmetic piercers** (1) As from the appointed day in any borough a person shall not in that borough carry on the practice of acupuncture or the business of tattooing or cosmetic piercing unless he is registered by the borough council in respect of that practice or business under this section; and he shall not carry on any such practice or business on premises occupied by him unless the premises are so registered.

(2) Subject to subsection (9)(*b*) of this section, on application for registration under this section the borough council shall register the applicant and, if the application specifies premises,

those premises, and shall issue to the applicant a certificate of registration.

(3) The person making an application under this section shall when making the same pay to the borough council such amount as may be determined from time to time by resolution of the borough council as being appropriate and as may be sufficient in the aggregate to cover in whole or in part—

(*a*) the reasonable cost of carrying out inspections of premises for the purpose of determining whether any byelaws made under this section are being complied with; and

(*b*) any reasonable administrative or other cost incurred by the borough council in connection with the registration of persons or premises under this section.

(4) The borough council may make byelaws for the purpose of securing—

(*a*) the cleanliness of premises required to be registered under this section and the sterilising, so far as is appropriate, of the instruments, towels, materials and equipment used in connection with the practice or business;

(*b*) the cleanliness of persons engaged in such practice or business in regard to both themselves and their clothing; and

(*c*) that books, cards or forms are kept by persons registered under this section recording their activities in connection with the practice or business in respect of which they are so registered and that appropriate entries are made in such books, cards or forms;

and different provisions may be made by such byelaws as respects the different kinds of practice or business to which this section applies.

(5) Nothing in this section shall extend to the practice of acupuncture or the business of tattooing or cosmetic piercing by or under the supervision of a registered medical practitioner or to the practice of acupuncture by a dentist registered under the Dentists Act [1984] or to premises on which the practice of acupuncture or the business of tattooing or cosmetic piercing, as the case may be, is carried on by or under the supervision of a registered medical practitioner or on which the practice of acupuncture is carried on by or under the supervision of a dentist registered as aforesaid.

(6) Any person who without reasonable excuse contravenes subsection (1) above shall be guilty of an offence and liable on summary conviction to a fine not exceeding **level 3** on the standard scale.

(7) Any person who contravenes any byelaw made under subsection (4) above shall be guilty of an offence and liable on summary conviction to a fine not exceeding **level 2** on the standard scale and, if he is registered under this section, the court by which he is convicted may, instead of, or in addition to, imposing a fine, order the suspension or cancellation of his registration and of the registration of the premises in which the offence was committed if they are occupied by him.

(8) A court ordering the suspension or cancellation of registration under subsection (7) above may suspend the operation of the order until the expiration of the period prescribed under section 14 (which confers powers to make Crown Court rules) of the Courts Act 1971 for giving notice of appeal to the Crown Court:

Provided that if notice of appeal is given within the said period an order made under this subsection shall be suspended until the appeal is finally determined or abandoned.

(9) Where the registration of any person is cancelled by order of a court under subsection (7) above—

(*a*) he shall within seven days deliver up to the borough council the cancelled certificate of registration, and if without reasonable excuse he fails to do so, he shall be guilty of an offence and liable on summary conviction to a fine not exceeding **level 2** on the standard scale and to a daily fine not exceeding **£5;** and

(*b*) he shall not again be registered by a borough council under this section in respect of the practice or business in question except in pursuance of a further order of a magistrates' court made on his application.

(10) The occupier of premises registered under this section shall keep a copy of any byelaw made relating to his practice of acupuncture or business of tattooing or cosmetic piercing, as the case may be, and of the certificate of registration of the premises issued under this section prominently displayed in the premises; and if without reasonable excuse he fails to do so he shall be guilty of an offence and liable on summary conviction to a fine not exceeding **level 2** on the standard scale and to a daily fine not exceeding **£5**.

(11)

(*a*) Section 287 (which confers powers to enter on premises) of the Act of 1936 shall have effect as if references therein to that Act included a reference to this section.

(*b*) Any person who intentionally obstructs any person acting in the exercise of his powers under this subsection shall be guilty of an offence and liable on summary conviction to a fine not exceeding **level 3** on the standard scale.

(12) In this section "premises" includes a stall and "cosmetic piercing" means the piercing of any part of the body for cosmetic purposes.

(13)

(*a*) In this section "the appointed day" means such day as may be fixed in relation to a borough by resolution of the borough council, subject to and in accordance with the provisions of this subsection.

(*b*) The borough council shall cause to be published in one or more local newspapers circulating in the borough notice—

(i) of the passing of any such resolution and of the day fixed thereby;

(ii) of the general effect of the provisions of this section coming into operation as from that day;

and the day so fixed shall not be earlier than the expiration of twenty-eight days from the date of first publication of the said notice.

(*c*) Either a photostatic or other reproduction certified by the proper officer of the borough to be a true reproduction of a page, or part of a page, of any such newspaper being a page or part bearing the date of its publication and containing any such notice shall be evidence of the publication of the notice and of the date of publication.

(*d*) Different appointed days may be fixed for the different kinds of practice or business to which this section applies.*

[Greater London Council (General Powers) Act 1981, s 19 as amended by the Criminal Justice Act 1982, s 46.]

* **Repealed with savings by the London Local Authorities Act 1991, ss 16, 17, Schedule, as from days to be appointed by individual borough councils in accordance with s 3 thereof.**

## PART VI[1]

### MISCELLANEOUS AND SUPPLEMENTAL

7.7842 **20. Application of Shops Act 1950 to exhibition and conference premises**

(1) Sections 1, 2, 8 and 47 of the Shops Act 1950 shall not apply to—

(*a*) a shop to which this section applies at any of the scheduled premises during the course of an exhibition, trade fair or conference at those premises and in the period when works or facilities in respect of that exhibition, trade fair or conference are being provided or removed; and

(*b*) a stand provided at any of the scheduled premises, whether in a building or in the open, while used for the purposes, and as part, of an exhibition, trade fair or conference at any of the scheduled premises.

(2) A shop to which this section applies is a permanent shop used for the carrying on of any retail trade or business and forming part of any of the scheduled premises if that shop is being used for the purposes of, or in connection with, an exhibition, trade fair or conference at those premises and is being used, as the case may be, either—

(*a*) as part of that exhibition, trade fair or conference; or

(*b*) for the serving of persons engaged in the provision or removal of works or facilities in respect of that exhibition, trade fair or conference.

(3) In this section—

"the scheduled premises" means the premises described in Schedule 3 to this Act; and

"stand" includes any platform, structure, space or other area.

[Greater London Council (General Powers) Act 1981, s 20.]

[1] Part VI contains ss 20–23.

7.7843 **21. Liability of directors, etc** Where an offence under Part IV or section 19 (Acupuncturists, tattooists and cosmetic piercers) of this Act, or against any byelaw made under the said section 19 committed by a body corporate is proved to have been committed with the consent or connivance of, or to be attributable to any neglect on the part of, a director, manager, secretary or other similar officer of the body corporate or any person who was purporting to act in any such capacity, he, as well as the body corporate, shall be guilty of that offence.

[Greater London Council (General Powers) Act 1981, s 21.]

## SCHEDULE 3

### PREMISES IN GREATER LONDON IN RESPECT OF WHICH CERTAIN PROVISIONS OF THE SHOPS ACT 1950 SHALL NOT APPLY DURING EXHIBITIONS, TRADE FAIRS AND CONFERENCES

Section 20

7.7844

*(Amended by the Greater London Council (General Powers) Act 1983, s 7.)*

1. Alexandra Palace, Wood Green, London N22.
2. Barbican Centre for Arts and Conferences and North Barbican Exhibition Halls, London EC2.
3. Earl's Court, Warwick Road, London SW5.
4. Olympia, Blythe Road and Hammersmith Road, London W14.
5. Royal Festival Hall, South Bank, London SE1.
6. Wembley Conference Centre and Wembley Arena, Wembley, Middlesex.
7. Premises, forming part of the World Trade Centre, known as International House, St. Katherine's Way, London E1 and Europe House, and Ivory House, East Smithfield, London E1.

# Greater London Council (General Powers) Act 1982

(1982 c i)

## PART I

### PRELIMINARY

7.7845 **2. Interpretation** In this Act, except as otherwise expressly provided or unless the context otherwise requires—

"the Act of 1972" means the Greater London Council (General Powers) Act 1972;

"borough council" means London borough council and includes the Common Council of the City of London, and "borough" shall be construed accordingly;
"the Council" means the Greater London Council;
"the Kensington and Chelsea Council" means the council of the Royal Borough of Kensington and Chelsea; and
"local authority" means the Council or a borough council.

[Greater London Council (General Powers) Act 1982, s 2.]

### PART II

### PROVISIONS RELATING TO THE COUNCIL AND TO BOROUGH COUNCILS

7.7846 **4. Removal of vehicles illegally parked on housing estates** (1) The powers of a local authority under section 23(1) of the Housing Act 1985 (byelaws for regulation of authority's houses) as extended by section 7 (Byelaws as to parking, etc, on housing estates) of the Greater London Council (General Powers) Act 1975, to make byelaws prohibiting or regulating the parking or use of vehicles on any land held by them for the purposes of Part II of the Housing Act of 1985, not being a highway, shall include power to make byelaws with respect to—

(*a*) the removal from any place on such land (whether to any other such place or to some other place) of any vehicle left there in contravention of the byelaws;
(*b*) the safe custody of any such vehicle so removed;
(*c*) the taking of such steps as are reasonable to find a person appearing to them to be the owner of the vehicle;
(*d*) following the taking of such steps, the disposal (which may include the destruction in the case of a vehicle which in the opinion of the local authority is in such a condition that it ought to be destroyed) of any such vehicle which appears to the local authority to be abandoned in such circumstances as may be prescribed in the byelaws;
(*e*) the imposition of charges for such removal, safe custody or disposal and the recovery of those charges from any person responsible; and
(*f*) the payment to the owner of the vehicle of the balance, if any, of the proceeds of such disposal after deduction of the charges imposed in respect of such removal, safe custody and disposal.

(2) While a vehicle is in the custody of a local authority in pursuance of byelaws made under section 23(1) of the Housing Act 1985, other than a vehicle which in their opinion is in such a condition that it ought to be destroyed, it shall be their duty to take such steps as are reasonably necessary for the safe custody of the vehicle.

(3) In this section—
"person responsible" in relation to a vehicle means—
(*a*) the owner of the vehicle at the time when it was put in the place from which it was removed, unless he shows that he was not concerned in, and did not know of, its being there;
(*b*) any person by whom it was put in the place aforesaid; and
"vehicle" has the same meaning as in section 17 of the Act of 1972.

[Greater London Council (General Powers) Act 1982, s 4 as amended by the Housing (Consequential Provisions) Act 1985, Sch 2.]

## Greater London Council (General Powers) Act 1984

(1984 c xxvii)

### PART I[1]

### PRELIMINARY

7.7847 **2. Interpretation** In this Act, except as otherwise expressly provided or unless the context otherwise requires—
"the Act of 1963" means the London Government Act 1963;
"the Act of 1968" means the Greater London Council (General Powers) Act 1968;
"the Act of 1971" means the Town and Country Planning Act 1971;
"borough council" means London borough council and includes the Common Council of the City of London; and "borough" shall be construed accordingly; and
"the Council" means the Greater London Council.

[Greater London Council (General Powers) Act 1984, s 2.]

1 Part I contains ss 1, 2.

### PART IV[1]

### PROVISIONS RELATING TO THE REGISTRATION BY BOROUGH COUNCILS OF CERTAIN SLEEPING ACCOMMODATION

7.7848 **7. Repeal of Part II of Kensington and Chelsea Act 1972** Part II (Registration of sleeping accommodation) of the Kensington and Chelsea Corporation Act 1972 (hereafter in this Part of this Act referred to as "the Act of 1972") shall cease to have effect.

[Greater London Council (General Powers) Act 1984, s 7.]

1 Part IV contains ss 7–18.

7.7849 **8. Appointed day** (1) Subject to subsection (5) of this section and except in the Royal Borough of Kensington and Chelsea, in this Part of this Act "the appointed day" means such day as may be fixed in relation to a borough or to any part thereof by resolution of the borough council, subject to and in accordance with the provisions of this section.

(2) Subject and except as aforesaid, different days may be fixed under this section for the purpose of the application of this Part of this Act to different parts of a borough.

(3) Subject and except as aforesaid, the borough council shall cause to be published in a local newspaper circulating in the borough notice—

(*a*) of the passing of any such resolution and of the day fixed thereby;

(*b*) of the general effect of the provisions of this Part of this Act coming into operation as from that day; and

(*c*) (if the resolution relates to part of a borough) of the part of the borough to which the resolution relates;

and the day so fixed shall not be earlier than the expiration of three months from the publication of the said notice.

(4) Either a photostatic or other reproduction certified by the officer appointed for that purpose by the borough council to be a true reproduction of a page or part of a page of any such newspaper bearing the date of its publication and containing any such notice shall be evidence of the publication of the notice, and of the date of publication.

(5) This Part of this Act shall come into force in the Royal Borough of Kensington and Chelsea on the date of enactment of this Act and accordingly in this Part of this Act "the appointed day", in relation to the Royal Borough, means the said date of enactment.

[Greater London Council (General Powers) Act 1984, s 8.]

7.7850 **9. Meaning of "specified purpose"** In this Part of this Act, "specified purpose" means—

(*a*) the provision of sleeping accommodation in a building or any part thereof for payment in circumstances where the relationship of landlord and tenant is not thereby created; or

(*b*) the provision of sleeping accommodation in a building or any part thereof for payment in circumstances where the relationship of landlord and tenant is thereby created, but where the total duration of the letting creating such relationship is, or is expected to be, less than ninety consecutive days;

but does not include the provision of sleeping accommodation in a building, or any part thereof, for payment—

(i) for less than three persons; or

(ii) where that building or part of a building is occupied as the only or main residence of a person who is entitled to make application for registration in accordance with section 13 (Applications for registration) of this Act.

[Greater London Council (General Powers) Act 1984, s 9.]

7.7851 **10. Buildings to which Part IV of Act applies** (1) Subject to the following subsection, the buildings to which this Part of this Act applies are buildings which are, or are proposed to be, used for a specified purpose.

(2) Nothing in this Part of this Act shall apply to a building being a building—

(*a*) occupied, used or managed by the Common Council of the City of London or by a local authority established by or under the London Government Act 1963;

(*b*) used as a hospital as defined in section 275 of the National Health Service Act 2006 or section 145(1) of the Mental Health Act 1983;

(*c*) used as a care home, or an independent hospital, within the meaning of the Care Standards Act 2000;

(*d*) used as a children's home within the meaning of the Care Standards Act 2000 which is a home in respect of which a person is registered under Part II of that Act;

(*e*) liable to be inspected under section 67 of the Children Act 1989;

(*f*) *repealed*

(*g*) occupied, used or managed by any person who is in receipt of a grant by virtue of regulations made under section 485 of the Education Act 1996;

(*h*) occupied, used or managed by a registered social landlord within the meaning of the Housing Act 1985 (see section 5(4) and (5) of that Act);

(*i*) occupied, used or managed, for the purposes specified in paragraph 4 of Schedule 5 to the Supplementary Benefits Act 1976, by a voluntary organisation which is in receipt of contributions from the Secretary of State under the said paragraph 4;

(*j*) approved by the Secretary of State under section 49(1) of the Powers of Criminal Courts Act 1973;

(*k*) occupied, used or managed by any society or individual in receipt of a payment in respect of those premises under section 51(3)(*f*) of the said Act of 1973;

(*l*) *repealed*

(*m*) *repealed*

(*n*) held upon trust and used by an almshouse charity, being an institution within the meaning of the Charities Act 2011, whose charitable purposes are for the reception or relief of poor persons and which is prevented by its trusts from granting tenancies of properties occupied for its purposes; or

(*o*) occupied, used or managed by a polytechnic designated by the Secretary of State.

[Greater London Council (General Powers) Act 1984, s 10 as amended by the Housing (Consequential Provisions) Act 1985, Sch 2, the Charities Act 1993, Sch 6, the Education Act 1996, Sch 37, SI 1997/221, the Childrens Act 1989, Sch 13, the Care Standards Act 2000, Sch 4, the National Health Service (Consequential Provisions) Act 2006, Sch 1 and the Charities Act 2011, Sch 7.]

7.7852 **11. Obligation to compile register** On and after the appointed day in any borough or part thereof, the borough council shall, subject to the provisions of section 15 (Refusal of registration) of this Act, compile and maintain a register, comprising a list of the buildings to which this Part of this Act applies in the borough or part thereof:

Provided that, subject to section 14 (Saving for buildings in Kensington and Chelsea) of this Act, the borough council shall not include in the register a building other than one in respect of which an application has been made under section 13 (Applications for registration) of this Act.

[Greater London Council (General Powers) Act 1984, s 11.]

7.7853 **12. Period of registration** Subject to section 14 (Saving for buildings in Kensington and Chelsea) of this Act, registration of a building under this Part of this Act shall remain in force for such period (to be stated on the register), being not less than three years, as the borough council may determine.

[Greater London Council (General Powers) Act 1984, s 12.]

7.7854 **13. Applications for registration** (1) Application for registration or re-registration of a building under this Part of this Act may be made by any person who, by virtue of an estate or interest therein held by him, is entitled to possession thereof or who is concerned in the management of the building.

(2) An application for registration of a building under this Part of this Act shall state—

(*a*) the name and address of the applicant;

(*b*) the address of the building;

(*c*) the existing use of the building; and

(*d*) the name and address of any other persons known to the applicant to be the owners of the building or having such an interest as is mentioned in the foregoing subsection.

[Greater London Council (General Powers) Act 1984, s 13.]

7.7855 **14. Saving for buildings in Kensington and Chelsea** (1) A building to which this Part of this Act applies in the Royal Borough of Kensington and Chelsea which, immediately before the enactment of this Act, was registered under Part II (Registration of sleeping accommodation) of the Act of 1972 shall be deemed to be registered under this Part of this Act on the appointed day and notwithstanding section 15 (Refusal of registration) of this Act, the Royal Borough shall forthwith include the said building in the register compiled and maintained under section 11 (Obligation to compile register) of this Act.

(2) Notwithstanding section 12 (Period of registration) of this Act, a building referred to in the foregoing subsection shall be registered by the council of the Royal Borough—

(*a*) for a period being the unexpired balance of the period for which the building was immediately before the enactment of this Act registered under Part II of the Act of 1972; and

(*b*) otherwise on the terms and conditions, if any, on which it was so registered under the said Part II.

(3) Subsection (4) below shall have effect where an application in respect of a building to which this Part of this Act applies in the Royal Borough of Kensington and Chelsea has been made under section 7 (Applications for registration) of the Act of 1972 before the commencement of this Act and—

(*a*) the Royal Borough have neither registered nor refused to register the building in response to the application; or

(*b*) they have refused to register the building and either notice of appeal against refusal has been given under section 9 (Appeals under Part II of Act) of the Act of 1972, or the time for giving notice of appeal under that section has not expired.

(4) In any case falling within subsection (3) above the application shall be deemed to have been made in pursuance of section 13 (Applications for registration) of this Act, and where the case falls within subsection (3)(*b*)—

(*a*) if notice of appeal as been given, it shall be treated as having been given under section 16 (Appeals under Part IV of Act) of this Act;

(*b*) if no notice of appeal has been given, the period of 28 days referred to in that section shall be deemed to have begun on the day on which refusal of registration under the Act of 1972 was notified.

[Greater London Council (General Powers) Act 1984, s 14.]

7.7856 **15. Refusal of registration** (1) A borough council may refuse to register a building under this Part of this Act on the grounds of—

(*a*) loss of residential accommodation; or

(*b*) the use or proposed use being inappropriate to the area:

Provided that a borough council may not refuse to register—

(i) a building (other than a building in the Royal Borough of Kensington and Chelsea) which, immediately before the appointed day, is being used for a specified purpose; or

(ii) a building in respect of which there is in force immediately before the appointed day a justices' on-licence and the use of which for a specified purpose would not be in contravention of the provisions of the Act of 1971; or

(iii) a building the use of which for a specified purpose is in accordance with the terms of a current valid planning permission; or

(iv) a building already registered under this Part of this Act and in respect of which the application is for re-registration under section 13 (Applications for registration) of this Act at the expiry of a period of registration; or

(v) a building—

(*a*) in respect of which there is in force immediately before the appointed day a premises licence under the Licensing Act 2003 authorising the supply of alcohol (within the meaning of section 14 of that Act) for consumption on the premises, and

(*b*) the use of which for a specified purpose would not contravene the Town and Country Planning Act 1990.

(2) If the borough council do not notify the applicant of their refusal by serving a notice (together with a statement of the grounds of such refusal) on the applicant at his address as given in his application within 60 days of its receipt by the borough council or within such longer period as may be agreed between the borough council and the applicant they shall not be entitled to refuse registration of the building in respect of which the application was made and they shall forthwith register the building under this Part of this Act.

[Greater London Council (General Powers) Act 1984, s 15 as amended by the Licensing Act 2003, Sch 6.]

7.7857 **16. Appeals under Part IV of Act** (1) Any person aggrieved by the refusal of a borough council to register a building under this Part of this Act may appeal within 28 days of notification of such refusal to the Secretary of State by notice in writing.

(2) On an appeal to the Secretary of State under this section he may either confirm or reverse the decision of the borough council as he thinks fit and if he reverses the decision of the borough council they shall forthwith register the building.

(3) The Secretary of State may cause such local inquiries to be held as he may consider necessary for the purpose of this section.

(4) Subsections (2) to (5) of section 250 of the Local Government Act 1972 shall apply in relation to any such inquiry.

(5) Where a borough council have refused to register a building under this Part of this Act a person who up to the time of the refusal was lawfully using that building for any purpose may use that building for that purpose until the time for appealing has expired or, if an appeal is lodged, until the appeal is disposed of or withdrawn or fails for want of prosecution.

[Greater London Council (General Powers) Act 1984, s 16.]

7.7858 **17. Prohibition on providing unregistered accommodation** (1) On and after the appointed day, no person who, by virtue of an estate or interest held by him in a building to which this Part of this Act applies, is entitled to possession thereof or who is concerned in the management of that building, shall use that building for a specified purpose unless the building is registered under this Part of this Act.

(2) No person who, by virtue of an estate or interest held by him in a building in the Royal Borough of Kensington and Chelsea to which this Part of this Act applies and which, before the enactment of this Act, had been registered by the council of the Royal Borough under Part II (Registration of sleeping accommodation) of the Act of 1972 in the circumstances referred to in, and had been the subject of a notification under, section 8(3) of that Act, is entitled to possession of that building or who is concerned in the management thereof shall use the building in contravention of the notification given under the said section 8(3).

(3) Any person who knowingly contravenes the provisions of subsection (1) or (2) of this section shall be guilty of an offence and shall be liable on summary conviction to a fine not exceeding level 4 on the standard scale.

(4) It shall be lawful for any person who—

(*a*) immediately before the appointed day was using any building (other than a building in the Royal Borough of Kensington and Chelsea) for a specified purpose; and

(*b*) had before the appointed day duly applied for registration under this Part of this Act;

to continue to use that building for that purpose until he is informed of the decision with regard to his application and, if the decision is adverse, during such further time as is provided under section 16 (Appeals under Part IV of Act) of this Act.

(5)

(*a*) Where an offence under this section committed by a body corporate is proved to have been committed with the consent or connivance of, or to be attributable to any neglect on the part of, any director, manager, secretary or other similar officer of the body corporate, or any person who was purporting to act in any such capacity, he, as well as the body corporate, shall be guilty of that offence.

(*b*) Where the affairs of a body corporate are managed by its members the foregoing paragraph shall apply to acts and defaults of a member in connection with his functions of management as if he were a director of the body corporate.

[Greater London Council (General Powers) Act 1984, s 17.]

**7.7859 18. Application of Development of Tourism Act 1969 and other Acts** Nothing in this Part of this Act shall exempt any person from the provisions of any enactment, including the Development of Tourism Act 1969 or any regulations or orders made thereunder.

[Greater London Council (General Powers) Act 1984, s 18.]

## PART VI[1]

### PROVISIONS RELATING TO THE SALE OF GOODS BY COMPETITIVE BIDDING

**7.7860 23. Commencement** This Part of this Act shall come into operation at the expiration of two months beginning with the date on which it is passed.

[Greater London Council (General Powers) Act 1984, s 23.]

---

[1] Part VI contains ss 23–35.

**7.7861 24. Interpretation and application** In this Part of this Act unless the context otherwise requires—

"the Act of 1936" means the Public Health Act 1936;

"contravention" includes a failure to comply and "contravene" shall be construed accordingly;

"premises" includes land;

"prescribed articles" means any plate, plated articles, linen, china, glass, books, prints, furniture, jewellery, articles of household or personal use or ornament or any musical or scientific instrument or apparatus;

"sale of goods by way of competitive bidding" means any sale of prescribed articles at which the persons present, or some of them, are invited to buy articles by way of competitive bidding, references to selling goods by way of competitive bidding shall be construed accordingly and "competitive bidding" includes any mode of sale whereby prospective purchasers may be enabled to compete for the purchase of articles, whether by way of increasing bids or by the offer of articles to be bid for at successively decreasing prices or otherwise;

"stall" includes any stand, marquee, tent, vehicle (whether mobile or not), site or pitch from which prescribed articles are sold.

[Greater London Council (General Powers) Act 1984, s 24.]

---

[1] Part IV contains ss 23–35.

**7.7862 25. Prohibition of unregistered premises and stalls** (1) Subject to the provisions of section 30 (Exemptions) of this Act, it is an offence to sell or permit the sale of goods by way of competitive bidding—

(*a*) on premises in a borough which are not registered under this Part of this Act;

(*b*) on premises in a borough which are so registered, but in breach of a condition upon which they are so registered;

(*c*) from a stall in a borough which is not registered under this Part of this Act with the borough council;

(*d*) from a stall in a borough which is so registered, but in breach of a condition upon which it is registered.

(2) A person is not guilty of an offence under subsection (1)(*a*) or (*c*) above—

(*a*) by virtue of section 44 of the Magistrates' Courts Act 1980 (aiders and abettors); or

(*b*) consisting of permitting a sale;

unless at the time of the offence he knows that the premises or stall are not registered under this Part of this Act.

(3) A person is not guilty of an offence under subsection (1)(*b*) or (*d*) above if he took all reasonable precautions and exercised all due diligence to avoid the commission of the offence.

(4) If in any case the defence provided under subsection (3) above involves the allegation that the commission of the offence was due to the act or default of another person, the person charged shall not, without leave of the court, be entitled to rely on that defence unless, within a period ending 7 clear days before the hearing, he has served on the prosecutor a notice in writing giving such information as was then in his possession, identifying, or assisting in the identification of that other person.

[Greater London Council (General Powers) Act 1984, s 25.]

**7.7863 26. Application for registration** (1) Application for registration of premises or a stall under this Part of this Act shall be made to the borough council of the borough in which the premises are situated or in which the stall is or is proposed to be situated, in the case of premises, by the occupier of, or a person proposing to occupy, the premises or, in the case of a stall, the proprietor of, or a person proposing to become the proprietor of, the stall, stating—

(*a*) the name and address of the applicant;

(*b*) the address or situation of the premises or stall to which the application relates; and (*c*) such other information regarding the premises or stall, the persons concerned or intended to be concerned in the conduct or management of any sale of goods by way of competitive bidding thereon or therefrom, and the manner in which the premises or stall are to be used as the borough council may reasonably require.

(2) With his application for registration under this Part of this Act the applicant shall pay such reasonable fee as the borough council may by resolution prescribe which shall be sufficient in the aggregate taking one year with another to cover the costs of—

(*a*) carrying out inspections of premises or stalls for the purpose of determining whether they should be registered or exempted from registration under this Part of this Act; and

(*b*) reasonable administrative or other expenses in connection with the consideration by the borough council of applications for registration or exemption from registration.

(3) If any person knowingly or recklessly makes a false statement or omits any material particular in giving information under this section he is guilty of an offence.

[Greater London Council (General Powers) Act 1984, s 26.]

7.7864 27. **Penalties** A person guilty of an offence under either of the last two foregoing sections of this Act is liable on summary conviction to a fine not exceeding level 5 on the standard scale.

[Greater London Council (General Powers) Act 1984, s 27.]

7.7865 30. **Exemptions** (1) Notwithstanding anything in section 25 (Prohibition of unregistered premises and stalls) of this Act sales by way of competitive bidding of the under-mentioned classes may be conducted on premises or from stalls which are not registered under this Act, that is to say—

(*a*) any sale of goods by way of competitive bidding so long as no substantial part of the prescribed articles was brought onto the premises or stall for the purposes of the sale;

(*b*) any sale for the purpose of assisting the funds of any voluntary organisation if the whole, or substantially the whole, of the proceeds of sale are devoted to the funds of the organisation;

(*c*) any sale of goods by way of competitive bidding conducted or managed by a person who has provided such relevant information and paid such fees as the borough council of the borough in which the sale is to take place may reasonably require by virtue of subsection (2) of section 26 (Application for registration) of this Act and to whom the borough council has granted a certificate of exemption from the registration requirements of this Part of this Act;

but the exemption provided by paragraph (*a*) above shall not be available where a sale by way of competitive bidding has taken place on those premises or from that stall within the preceding six months.

(2) In this section "voluntary organisation" means a body the activities of which are carried on otherwise than for profit, but does not include any public or local authority.

[Greater London Council (General Powers) Act 1984, s 30.]

7.7866 31. **Powers of entry, inspection and examination** (1) An authorised officer of a borough council on producing if so required a duly authenticated document showing his authority, or any constable may at all reasonable times enter upon, inspect and examine any premises or stall which he has reasonable cause to believe is used, or is intended to be used, for the sale of goods by competitive bidding, and may do all such things as are reasonably necessary for the purpose of ascertaining—

(*a*) whether there is, or has been, in or in connection with the premises or stall, a contravention of the provisions of this Part of this Act or any condition imposed under this Part of this Act; or

(*b*) whether or not circumstances exist which would authorise the borough council to take action under this Part of this Act.

(2) The powers of this section may be exercised in respect of a dwelling-house believed to be used for the sale of goods by competitive bidding and which is not registered under this Part of this Act only on the grant of a warrant by a justice of the peace.

(3)

(*a*) A justice may grant a warrant under this section only if he is satisfied either—

(i) that notice of intention to apply for a warrant has been given to the occupier of the premises or stall; or

(ii) that the case is one of urgency or the occupier is temporarily absent, or that the giving of notice of intention to apply for a warrant would defeat the object of entry.

(*b*) A warrant under this section shall authorise entry, if need be, by force, but shall cease to have effect at the expiration of a period of 7 days beginning with the day on which it is granted.

[Greater London Council (General Powers) Act 1984, s 31.]

7.7867 32. **Restriction on right to prosecute** The written consent of the Director of Public Prosecutions is needed for the laying of an information of an offence created by or under this Part of this Act other than the laying of such an information by the borough council or a constable.

[Greater London Council (General Powers) Act 1984, s 32.]

7.7868 **33. Liability of directors, etc** (1) Where an offence under this Part of this Act, committed by a body corporate is proved to have been committed with the consent or connivance of, or to be attributable to any neglect on the part of, a director, manager, secretary or other similar officer of the body corporate or any person who was purporting to act in any such capacity, he, as well as the body corporate, shall be guilty of the offence.

(2) Where the affairs of a body corporate are managed by its members, subsection (1) above shall apply to the acts and defaults of a member in connection with his functions of management as if he were a director of the body corporate.

[Greater London Council (General Powers) Act 1984, s 33.]

7.7869 **34. Obstruction** (1) Any person who knowingly obstructs any person acting in pursuance of this Part of this Act or of any warrant made or issued thereunder or without reasonable cause fails to give such a person so acting any assistance or information which he may reasonably require of him for the purpose of the performance of his functions under this Part of this Act shall be guilty of an offence.

(2) If any person in giving such information as is mentioned in the preceding subsection makes any statement which he knows to be false he shall be guilty of an offence.

(3) Nothing in this section shall be construed as requiring a person to answer any question or give any information if to do so might incriminate him.

(4) A person guilty of an offence under this section shall be liable on summary conviction to a fine not exceeding level 5 on the standard scale.

[Greater London Council (General Powers) Act 1984, s 34.]

## PART VII[1]

## OTHER PROVISIONS RELATING TO BOROUGH COUNCILS

7.7870 **37. Removal of occupants of dangerous buildings in outer London** (1) If it appears to an outer London borough council that any building in the borough is in such a condition as to be dangerous to its occupants, that council may apply to a magistrates' court and the court may make an order directing that any occupants of the building be removed therefrom by a constable.

(2)

(*a*) Where a magistrates' court has made an order under the foregoing subsection it shall not be lawful for the building to be occupied unless the dangerous state thereof has been remedied to the satisfaction of the outer London borough council or a magistrates' court has revoked the order.

(*b*) Any person who, knowing that an order has been made by a magistrates' court under the foregoing subsection in respect of a building, occupies that building in contravention of this subsection or permits it to be so occupied, shall be liable on summary conviction to a fine not exceeding **level 5** on the standard scale.

(3) In this section—

"building" includes any structure or erection and any part of a building as so defined; and

"outer London borough council" means the council of an outer London borough.

[Greater London Council (General Powers) Act 1984, s 37.]

---

1 Part VII contains ss 36–41.

7.7871 **38. Removal of occupants of buildings in vicinity of dangerous structures, etc**

(1)

(*a*) This section applies where—

(i) in an inner London borough or the City of London, the district surveyor, or any surveyor required to make a survey under section 61 of the London Building Acts (Amendment) Act 1939, has certified under section 62 of that Act that a structure is in a dangerous state; or

(ii) in an outer London borough, it appears to the council of that borough that any building is in such a condition, or is used to carry such loads, as to be dangerous.

(*b*) In this subsection "structure" has the meaning assigned to it in section 60 of the said Act of 1939.

(2) Where this section applies and it appears to a borough council that the occupants of any building are in danger by reason of—

(*a*) the proximity of that building to any such structure or building as is referred to in the foregoing subsection; or

(*b*) any works being carried out, or proposed to be carried out, to any such structure or building as aforesaid for the purpose of remedying its dangerous state or condition;

the borough council may apply to a magistrates' court and the court may make an order directing that any occupants of the first-mentioned building be removed therefrom by a constable.

(3)

(*a*) Before applying to a magistrates' court for an order under the last foregoing subsection, a borough council shall give notice of the application to the occupants of the building in respect of which the application is made.

(*b*) Notwithstanding subsection (9) of that section, section 233 (which relates to the service of notices by local authorities) of the Local Government Act 1972 shall apply to the giving of notice under this subsection other than by the Common Council of the City of London.

(4)

(*a*) Where a magistrates' court has made an order under subsection (2) of this section it shall not be lawful for the building in respect of which the order was made to be occupied unless the danger has been removed, or the works have been completed, as the case may be, to the satisfaction of the borough council or a magistrates' court has revoked the order.

(*b*) Any person who, knowing that an order has been made by a magistrates' court under subsection (2) of this section in respect of a building, occupies that building in contravention of this subsection or permits it to be so occupied, shall be liable on summary conviction to a fine not exceeding **level 5** on the standard scale.

(5) An application may be made under subsection (2) of this section, and a magistrates' court may make an order under that subsection, in respect of a building in the proximity of such a structure as is referred to in sub-paragraph (*a*)(i) of subsection (1) of this section, or where the works described in paragraph (*b*) of the said subsection (2) are being carried out, or are proposed to be carried out, to such a structure, notwithstanding that the owner of the structure has served on the borough council a written requirement under section 63 of the said Act of 1939.

(6) In this section, "building" includes any structure or erection and any part of a building as so defined.

[Greater London Council (General Powers) Act 1984, s 38.]

7.7872 **39. Occupants removed from buildings to have priority housing need** For the purposes of Part VII of the Housing Act 1996 (homelessness) a person who resides in any building in respect of which an order has been made by a magistrates' court under section 37 (Removal of occupants of dangerous buildings in outer London) or section 38 (Removal of occupants of buildings in vicinity of dangerous structures, etc) of this Act shall be treated as if he were homeless or threatened with homelessness as a result of an emergency such as flood, fire or other disaster.

[Greater London Council (General Powers) Act 1984, s 39 as amended by the Housing (Consequential Provisions) Act 1985, Sch 2 and the Housing Act 1996, Sch 17.]

## London Local Authorities Act 1994

(1994 c xii)

7.7873 **1. Short title and commencement** This Act may be cited as the London Local Authorities Act 1994 and except section 5 (Night café licensing) of this Act shall come into operation at the end of the period of two months beginning with the date on which it is passed[1].

[London Local Authorities Act 1994, s 1.]

1 This Act was passed on 21 July 1994.

7.7874 **2. Interpretation** In this Act, except as otherwise expressly provided or unless the context otherwise requires—

"the Act of 1990" means the London Local Authorities Act 1990;

"borough council" means London borough council but does not include the Common Council of the City of London; and "borough" shall be construed accordingly.

[London Local Authorities Act 1994, s 2 as amended by the London Local Authorities Act 2004, Sch 4.]

7.7875 **3. Appointed day** (1) In this Act "the appointed day" means such day as may be fixed in relation to a borough by resolution of the borough council, subject to and in accordance with the provisions of this section.

(2) Different days may be fixed under this section for the purpose of the application of different provisions of this Act to a borough.

(3) The borough council shall cause to be published in a local newspaper circulating in the borough notice—

(*a*) of the passing of any such resolution and of the day fixed thereby; and

(*b*) of the general effect of the provisions of this Act coming into operation as from that day;

and the day so fixed shall not be earlier than the expiration of three months from the publication of the said notice.

(4) Either a photostatic or other reproduction certified by the officer appointed for that purpose by the borough council to be a true reproduction of a page or part of a page of any such newspaper bearing the date of its publication and containing any such notice shall be evidence of the publication of the notice, and of the date of publication.

[London Local Authorities Act 1994, s 3.]

7.7876 **10. Liability of directors, etc** (1) Where an offence under this Act committed by a body corporate is proved to have been committed with the consent or connivance of, or to be attributable to any neglect on the part of, a director, manager, secretary or other similar officer of the body corporate or any person who was purporting to act in any such capacity, he, as well as the body corporate, shall be guilty of the offence.

(2) Where the affairs of a body corporate are managed by its members, subsection (1) above shall apply to the acts and defaults of a member in connection with his functions of management as if he were a director of the body corporate.

[London Local Authorities Act 1994, s 10.]

# London Local Authorities Act 1995

(1995 c x)

## PART I[1]

## PRELIMINARY

7.7877 **1. Citation and commencement** (1) This Act may be cited as the London Local Authorities Act 1995.

(2) The London Local Authorities Act 1990, the London Local Authorities (No. 2) Act 1990, the London Local Authorities Act 1991, the London Local Authorities Act 1994 and this Act may together be cited as the London Local Authorities Acts 1990 to 1995.

(3) This Act, except Part V (Registration of door supervisors) and, save as otherwise provided by section 15 (Application of Part IV), Part IV (Near beer licensing) shall come into operation at the end of the period of two months beginning with the date on which it is passed.

[London Local Authorities Act 1995, s 1.]

1 Part I contains ss 1–3.

7.7878 **2. Interpretation** In this Act, except as otherwise expressly provided or unless the context otherwise requires—

"the Act of 1984" means the Road Traffic Regulation Act 1984;

"the Act of 1990" means the Town and Country Planning Act 1990;

"the Act of 1991" means the Road Traffic Act 1991;

"authorised officer" means an officer of a participating council authorised by the council in writing to act in relation to the relevant provision of this Act;

"the Commissioner" means the Commissioner of Police of the Metropolis or, in the City of London, the Commissioner of the City Police;

"the fire and rescue authority", in relation to premises, means—

(*a*) where the Regulatory Reform (Fire Safety) Order 2005 applies to the premises, the enforcing authority within the meaning given by article 25 of that Order; or

(*b*) in any other case, the London Fire and Emergency Planning Authority;

"participating council" means the common council of the City of London and the council of any London borough; and "borough" and "council" shall be construed accordingly;

"penalty charge" has the same meaning as in section 66 of the Act of 1991;

"road" has the same meaning as in section 142(1) of the Act of 1984;

"special enforcement area" means a special enforcement area designated by order of the Secretary of State under Schedule 10 of the Traffic Management Act 2004;

"traffic sign" has the same meaning as in section 64(1) of the Act of 1984.

[London Local Authorities Act 1995, s 2 as amended by the London Local Authorities Act 1996, s 27, the Greater London Authority Act 1999, Sch 21, SI 2005/1541 and the Traffic Management Act 2004, Sch 11.]

7.7879 **3. Appointed day** (1) In this Act "the appointed day" means such day as may be fixed in relation to a borough by resolution of the borough council, subject to and in accordance with the provisions of this section.

(2) Different days may be fixed under this section for the purpose of the application of different provisions of this Act to a borough.

(3) The borough council shall cause to be published in a local newspaper circulating in the borough notice—

(*a*) of the passing of any such resolution and of a day fixed thereby; and

(*b*) of the general effect of the provisions of this Act coming into operation as from that day;

and the day so fixed shall not be earlier than the expiration of three months from the publication of the said notice.

(4) Either a photostatic or other reproduction certified by the officer appointed for that purpose by the borough council to be a true reproduction of a page or part of a page of any such newspaper bearing the date of its publication and containing any such notice shall be evidence of the publication of the notice, and of the date of publication.

[London Local Authorities Act 1995, s 3.]

## PART IV[1]

## NEAR BEER LICENSING

7.7880 **14. Interpretation of Part IV** In this Part of this Act—

"the Act of 1964" means the Licensing Act 1964;

"near beer premises" means any premises, vehicle, vessel or stall used for a business which—

(*a*) consists to a significant degree in—

(i) the sale to customers for consumption on the premises of liquid refreshments which include in their trade description any of the following words:—beer, lager, pils, shandy, cider, wine, champagne, cocktail, sherry, gin, brandy, whisky, vodka or other words which imply that the liquid refreshment contains or can reasonably be expected to contain alcohol; or

(ii) the sale to customers for consumption on the premises of liquid refreshments which consist of any beverage commonly expected to contain alcohol or calculated to represent any alcoholic beverage; and

(*b*) offers, expressly or by implication, whether on payment of a fee or not, either or both of the following:—

(i) the provision of companions for customers on the premises; or

(ii) the provision of live entertainment on the premises;

but does not include any such premises in which the sale to customers for consumption of alcohol is not a licensable activity under or by virtue of section 173 of the Licensing Act 2003 or in respect of which there is in force—

(A) a premises licence under Part 3 of that Act which authorises the supply of alcohol (within the meaning of section 14 of that Act) for consumption on the premises;

(B) a licence granted by the council under section 21 (Licensing of public exhibitions, etc.) of the Greater London Council (General Powers) Act 1966 or a premises licence granted under Part 3 of the Licensing Act 2003 which authorises the provision of any form of regulated entertainment (within the meaning of Schedule 1 to that Act);

(C) repealed;

(D) repealed;

(E) repealed;

(F) a temporary event notice under the Licensing Act 2003, by virtue of which the premises may be used for the supply of alcohol (within the meaning of section 14 of that Act);

during the hours permitted by such licence or notice:

Provided that the premises are in use wholly or mainly and bona fide for the purpose authorised by such licence or notice; and

does not include premises in respect of which a casino premises licence, bingo premises licence, adult gaming centre premises licence, family entertainment centre premises licence or betting premises licence under Part 8, or a family entertainment centre gaming permit under section 247, of the Gambling Act 2005 has effect;

"occupier" in relation to any premises means an occupier who is—

(*a*) the freeholder; or

(*b*) a lessee; or

(*c*) a tenant holding a tenancy of at least one year in duration.*

[London Local Authorities Act 1995, s 14 as amended by the Licensing Act 2003, Sch 6 and the Gambling Act 2005, Sch 16.]

---

* **Repealed by the London Local Authorities Act 2007, s 35. In force in relation to the City of Westminster (19 September 2007), the London Borough of Newham (1 January 2008); the London Borough of Bexley (1 April 2008); and to be appointed for remaining purposes.**

[1] Part IV contains ss 14–28.

7.7881 **15. Application of Part IV** This Part of this Act applies to the City of Westminster as from the date of commencement and to the boroughs of all other participating councils as from the appointed day.*

[London Local Authorities Act 1995, s 15.]

---

* **Repealed by the London Local Authorities Act 2007, s 35. In force in relation to the City of Westminster (19 September 2007); the London Borough of Newham (1 January 2008); the London Borough of Bexley (1 April 2008); and to be appointed for remaining purposes.**

7.7882 **16. Licensing** (1) No premises shall be used in the borough as near beer premises except under and in accordance with a near beer licence granted under this section by the council.

(2) The council may grant to an applicant and from time to time, renew or transfer a near beer licence on such terms and conditions and subject to such restrictions as may be specified.

(3) Without prejudice to the generality of subsection (2) above, such conditions may relate to—

(*a*) the maintenance of public order and safety;

(*b*) the hours of opening and closing the premises for use as near beer premises to ensure that nuisance is not likely to be caused to residents in the neighbourhood;

(*c*) the display of advertisements on or near the near beer premises and the prohibition of touting in any form;

(*d*) the display of prices of goods and services offered on the premises;

(*e*) the number of persons who may be allowed to be on the premises at any time;

(*f*) the taking of proper precautions against fire, and the maintenance in proper order of means of escape in case of fire, fire-fighting equipment and means of lighting, sanitation and ventilation of the premises;

(*g*) the maintenance in safe condition of means of heating the premises.

(3A) No term, condition or restriction is to be imposed under subsection (2) above in so far as it relates to any matter in relation to which requirements or prohibitions are or could be imposed by or under the Regulatory Reform (Fire Safety) Order 2005 in respect of the premises.

(4) Provided it has not been cancelled or revoked the near beer licence shall remain in force for 18 months or such shorter period specified in the near beer licence as the council may think fit.*

[London Local Authorities Act 1995, s 16 as amended by SI 2005/1541.]

* **Repealed by the London Local Authorities Act 2007, s 35. In force in relation to the City of Westminster (19 September 2007), the London Borough of Newham (1 January 2008); the London Borough of Bexley (1 April 2008); and to be appointed for remaining purposes.**

7.7883 **17. Applications under Part IV** (1) The occupier of premises in the borough may apply for the grant, renewal or transfer of a near beer licence, and shall not later than the day the application is made send a copy to the Commissioner and a copy to the fire and rescue authority and, subject to subsection (2) below, no such application shall be considered by the council unless the applicant complies with this subsection.

(2) The council may in such cases as they think fit, after consulting with the Commissioner and the fire and rescue authority, consider an application for the grant, renewal or transfer of a near beer licence notwithstanding that the applicant has failed to comply with subsection (1) above.

(3) In considering any application for the grant, renewal or transfer of a near beer licence the council shall have regard to any observations submitted to them by the Commissioner or by the fire and rescue authority within 28 days of the making of the application and may have regard to any observations submitted by him or them thereafter.

(4) An applicant for the grant, renewal, transfer or variation of a near beer licence shall furnish such particulars and give such other notices, including the public advertisement of the application, as the council may by regulation prescribe.

(5) Regulations under subsection (4) above may, inter alia, prescribe the procedure for determining applications.

(6) An applicant for the grant, renewal or transfer of a near beer licence shall pay a reasonable fee determined by the council.

(7) Where, before the date of expiry of a near beer licence, an application has been made for its renewal or transfer, the near beer licence shall be deemed to remain in force, or as the case may require, to have effect with any necessary modifications until the determination of the application by the council or the withdrawal of the application.*

[London Local Authorities Act 1995, s 17 as amended by the Fire and Rescue Services Act 2004, Sch 1.]

* **Repealed by the London Local Authorities Act 2007, s 35. In force in relation to the City of Westminster (19 September 2007); the London Borough of Newham (1 January 2008); the London Borough of Bexley (1 April 2008); and to be appointed for remaining purposes.**

7.7884 **17A. Renewal and transfer of licence: supplementary** (1) The following provisions of this section shall have effect as respects cases where, before the date of expiry of a licence an application for renewal of the licence has been made ("a renewal case") or an application for transfer of the licence has been made ("a transfer case").

(2) If the application is not determined before the prospective expiry date, the licence shall not be deemed to remain in force under subsection (7) or (8) of section 17 (Applications) of this Act, after that date and the application shall be deemed to be withdrawn on that date, unless before then the applicant pays the council a continuation fee.

(3) Where a continuation fee is paid in pursuance of subsection (2) above in a renewal case, the applicant's application for renewal shall be deemed to be an application for renewal for a period of twelve months starting on the day following the prospective expiry date.

(4) Where a continuation fee is paid in pursuance of subsection (2) above in a transfer case—

(*a*) the applicant shall be deemed to have made an application for the renewal of the licence for a period of twelve months starting on the day following the prospective expiry date;

(*b*) the Council shall determine the application for transfer and deemed application for renewal together; and

(*c*) in the following provisions of this section, references to "the application" in a transfer case are references to the application for transfer and the application for renewal.

(5) If the application is not determined before the date of the expiry of the renewal period under subsection (3) or (4) above, as the case may be, the licence shall not be deemed to remain in force under subsection (7) or (8) of the said section 17, as the case may be, after that date, and the application shall be deemed to be withdrawn on that date, unless before then the applicant pays the council a further continuation fee.

(6) Where a further continuation fee is paid in pursuance of subsection (5) above then—

(*a*) in a renewal case, the applicant's application for renewal shall be deemed to be an application for renewal for a period starting on the day following the date of the expiry of the renewal period under subsection (3) above; and (*b*) in a transfer case, the applicant's application so far as it is a deemed application for renewal shall be deemed to be an application for renewal for a period starting on the day following the date of the expiry of the renewal period under subsection (4) above.

(7) A deemed application for renewal under subsection (6) shall be for a period expiring—

(*a*) where the application is withdrawn, on the date of withdrawal;

(*b*) where the application is refused, on the date of the refusal;

(*c*) where the application is granted, on one or other of the following:—

(i) the date twelve months after the beginning of the period; or

(ii) such other date as may be specified by the Council when allowing the application.

(8) In this section—

"the prospective expiry date" means—

(*a*) in a transfer case, the date on which the licence would have expired if the application for transfer had not been made; and

(*b*) in a renewal case, the date of the expiry of the period in respect of which the application for renewal of the licence was made;

"a continuation fee" is a fee of the same amount as the fee payable in respect of an application for renewal of a licence.*

[London Local Authorities Act 1995, s 17A as inserted by the London Local Authorities Act 2000, s 29.]

* **Repealed by the London Local Authorities Act 2007, s 35. In force in relation to the City of Westminster (19 September 2007); the London Borough of Newham (1 January 2008); the London Borough of Bexley (1 April 2008); and to be appointed for remaining purposes.**

7.7885 **18. Refusal of licence** (1) The council may refuse to grant, renew or transfer a near beer licence on any of the following grounds:—

(*a*) the premises are not structurally suitable for the purpose;

(*b*) there is a likelihood of nuisance being caused by reason of the conduct, management or situation of the premises or the character of the relevant locality or the use to which any premises in the vicinity are put;

(*c*) the persons concerned or intended to be concerned in the conduct or management of the premises as a near beer establishment could be reasonably regarded as not being fit and proper persons to hold such a licence;

(*d*) the premises are not provided with satisfactory means of lighting, sanitation and ventilation;

(*e*) the means of heating the premises are not safe;

(*f*) where the Regulatory Reform (Fire Safety) Order 2005 applies to the premises, that Order or any regulations made under it are not being complied with in respect of the premises;

(*g*) where the Regulatory Reform (Fire Safety) Order 2005 does not apply to the premises—

(i) proper precautions against fire on the premises are not being taken;

(ii) satisfactory means of escape in case of fire and suitable fire-fighting appliances are not provided on the premises; or

(*h*) the applicant has failed to comply with the requirements of subsection (4) or (6) of section 17 (Applications under Part IV) of this Act.

(2) The council shall not refuse an application without giving the applicant an opportunity to appear before the committee or sub-committee determining the application.

(3) The council may not delegate to an officer their function of refusing an application under this Part of this Act.

(4) Where the council refuse to grant, renew or transfer a licence, they shall, if required to do so by the applicant or holder of the licence, give him a statement in writing of the reasons for their decision within 7 days of his requiring them to do so.*

[London Local Authorities Act 1995, s 18 as amended by SI 2005/1541.]

* **Repealed by the London Local Authorities Act 2007, s 35. In force in relation to the City of Westminster (19 September 2007); the London Borough of Newham (1 January 2008); the London Borough of Bexley (1 April 2008); and to be appointed for remaining purposes.**

7.7886 **19. Transmission and cancellation of near beer licences** (1) In the event of the death of the holder of a near beer licence, the person carrying on at the place in respect of which the near beer licence was granted the function to which the near beer licence relates shall be deemed to be the holder of the near beer licence unless and until the near beer licence is transferred to some other person.

(2) The council may, at the written request of the holder of a near beer licence, cancel the near beer licence.*

[London Local Authorities Act 1995, s 19.]

* **Repealed by the London Local Authorities Act 2007, s 35. In force in relation to the City of Westminster (19 September 2007); the London Borough of Newham (1 January 2008); the London Borough of Bexley (1 April 2008); and to be appointed for remaining purposes.**

7.7887 **20. Power to prescribe standard terms, conditions and restrictions under Part IV**

(1) The council may make regulations prescribing standard conditions applicable to all, or any class of near beer licences, that is to say terms, conditions and restrictions on or subject to which such near beer licences, or near beer licences of that class are in general to be granted, renewed or transferred by them.

(1A) No standard condition that is applicable to premises to which the Regulatory Reform (Fire Safety) Order 2005 applies may be prescribed by regulation under subsection (1) above in so far as it relates to any matter in relation to which requirements or prohibitions are or could be imposed by or under that Order.

(2) Where the council have made regulations under this section, every such near beer licence granted, renewed or transferred by them shall be deemed to have been so granted, renewed or transferred subject to any standard conditions applicable to it unless those standard conditions have been expressly excluded or amended.*

[London Local Authorities Act 1995, s 20 as amended by SI 2005/1541.]

* **Repealed by the London Local Authorities Act 2007, s 35. In force in relation to the City of Westminster (19 September 2007); the London Borough of Newham (1 January 2008); the London Borough of Bexley (1 April 2008); and to be appointed for remaining purposes.**

7.7888 **21. Provisional grant of near beer licences** (1) Where application is made to the council for the grant of a near beer licence in respect of premises which are to be, or are in the course of being constructed, extended or altered or improved and the council are satisfied that the premises would if completed in accordance with plans or proposals deposited in pursuance of the requirements of the council be such that they would grant the near beer licence, the council may grant the near beer licence subject to a condition that it shall be of no effect until confirmed by them.

(2) The council shall, on application being made for the appropriate variation of the near beer licence, confirm any near beer licence granted by virtue of subsection (1) above if and when they are satisfied that the premises have been completed in accordance with the plans or proposals referred to in the said subsection (1) or in accordance with those plans or proposals as modified with the approval of the council.*

[London Local Authorities Act 1995, s 21.]

* **Repealed by the London Local Authorities Act 2007, s 35. In force in relation to the City of Westminster (19 September 2007); the London Borough of Newham (1 January 2008); the London Borough of Bexley (1 April 2008); and to be appointed for remaining purposes.**

7.7889 **22. Variation of near beer licences** (1) The holder of a near beer licence may at any time apply to the council for a variation in the terms, conditions or restrictions on or subject to which the near beer licence is held.

(2) The person making an application for such a variation of licence shall on making the application pay to the council such reasonable fee as the council may fix.

(3) The council may, subject to subsection (4) below—

(*a*) make the variation specified in the application;

(*b*) make that variation together with such further variation consequent thereon as the council may determine; or

(*c*) refuse the application:

Provided that no variation relating to fire safety conditions shall be made under this section before the fire and rescue authority have been consulted.

(4) No term, condition or restriction may be varied under this section in so far as the effect of the variation would be that the term, condition or restriction as varied would relate to any matter in relation to which requirements or prohibitions are or could be imposed by or under the Regulatory Reform (Fire Safety) Order 2005.*

[London Local Authorities Act 1995, s 22 as amended by the Fire and Rescue Services Act 2004, Sch 1 and SI 2005/1541.]

* **Repealed by the London Local Authorities Act 2007, s 35. In force in relation to the City of Westminster (19 September 2007); the London Borough of Newham (1 January 2008); the London Borough of Bexley (1 April 2008); and to be appointed for remaining purposes.**

7.7890 **23. Appeals under Part IV** (1) Any of the following persons, that is to say:—

(*a*) an applicant for the grant, renewal or transfer of a near beer licence whose application is refused;

(*b*) an applicant for the grant, renewal or transfer of a near beer licence who is aggrieved by any term, condition or restriction on or subject to which the near beer licence is granted, renewed or transferred;

(*c*) an applicant for the variation of the terms, conditions or restrictions on or subject to which a near beer licence is held whose application is refused;

(*d*) an applicant for the variation of the terms, conditions or restrictions on or subject to which a near beer licence is held who is aggrieved by any term, condition or restriction contained in a further variation made consequent on the variation applied for;

(*e*) a holder of any such near beer licence whose near beer licence is revoked under section 24 (Enforcement under Part IV) of this Act;

may at any time before the expiration of the period of 21 days beginning with the relevant date appeal to the magistrates' court acting for the petty sessions area in which the premises are situated by way of complaint for an order.

(2) In this section "the relevant date" means the date on which the person in question is notified in writing of the refusal of his application, the imposition of the terms, conditions or restrictions by which he is aggrieved or the revocation of his near beer licence, as the case may be.

(3) An appeal by either party against the decision of the magistrates' court under this section may be brought to the Crown Court.

(4) On an appeal to the magistrates' court or to the Crown Court under this section the court may make such order as it thinks fit and it shall be the duty of the council to give effect to such order.

(5) Where any near beer licence is revoked under the said section 24 of this Act or an application for the renewal of such a near beer licence is refused, the near beer licence shall be deemed to remain in force—

(*a*) until the time for bringing an appeal under this section has expired and, if such an appeal is duly brought, until the determination or abandonment of the appeal; and

(*b*) where an appeal relating to the refusal of an application for such a renewal is successful until the licence is renewed by the council.

(6) Where any near beer licence is renewed under section 16 (Licensing) of this Act and the council specify any term, condition or restriction which was not previously specified in relation to that licence, the near beer licence shall be deemed to be free of it until the time for bringing an appeal under this section has expired and, if such an appeal is duly brought, until the determination or abandonment of the appeal.

(7) Where the holder of a licence makes an application under section 22 (Variation of near beer licences) of this Act and the council make the variation applied for together with a further variation, then the licence shall continue as it was before the application—

(*a*) until the time for bringing an appeal under this section against any term, condition or restriction contained in the further variation has expired; and

(*b*) where any such appeal is brought, until the determination or abandonment of the appeal.*

[London Local Authorities Act 1995, s 23.]

---

*** Repealed by the London Local Authorities Act 2007, s 35. In force in relation to the City of Westminster (19 September 2007); the London Borough of Newham (1 January 2008); the London Borough of Bexley (1 April 2008); and to be appointed for remaining purposes.**

**7.7891 23A. Appeals: supplementary provisions** (1) The following provisions of this section shall have effect as respects cases where an appeal under section 23 (Appeals under Part IV) of this Act is brought, within the period for doing so, against the revocation of a licence ("a revocation case") or against the refusal of an application for renewal of a licence ("a refusal case").

(2) If the appeal is not determined before the prospective expiry date, the licence shall not be deemed to remain in force under subsection (5) of the said section 23 after that date, and the appeal shall be deemed to be abandoned on that date, unless before then—

(*a*) in a revocation case, the appellant makes an application for the renewal of the licence for a period of twelve months starting on the day following the prospective expiry date;

(*b*) in a refusal case the appellant pays the council a continuation fee.

(3) Where a continuation fee is paid in pursuance of subsection (2)(*b*) above, the appellant's refused application for renewal shall be deemed to be an application for renewal for a period of twelve months starting on the day following the prospective expiry date.

(4) If the appeal is not determined before the date of the expiry of the renewal period under subsection (2)(*a*) or (3) above, as the case may be, the licence shall not be deemed to remain in force under subsection (5) of the said section 23 after that date, and the appeal shall be deemed to be abandoned on that date, unless before then the appellant pays the council a continuation fee or, as the case may be, a further continuation fee.

(5) Where a continuation fee or a further continuation fee is paid in pursuance of subsection (4) above, the appellant's application for renewal or, as the case may be, refused application for renewal shall be deemed to be an application for renewal for a period starting on the day following the date of the expiry of the renewal period under subsection (2)(*a*) above or, as the case may be, subsection (3) above.

(6) A deemed application for renewal under subsection (5) shall be for a period expiring—

(*a*) where the appeal is withdrawn, on the date of withdrawal;

(*b*) where the appeal is unsuccessful—

(i) if a further appeal is available but is not made within the period for doing so, on the date of the expiry of that period;

(ii) if no further appeal is available, on the date of the decision of the court;

(*c*) where the appeal is successful, on the day before the date of the next anniversary of the beginning of the period; provided that where the period, at the time of the decision of the court, has been running for more than twelve months, the court may specify an earlier date.

(7) In this section—

"the prospective expiry date" means—

(*a*) in a revocation case, the date on which the licence would have expired if it had not been revoked; and

(*b*) in a refusal case, the date of the expiry of the period in respect of which the refused application for renewal of the licence was made;

"a continuation fee" is a fee of the same amount as the fee payable in respect of an application for renewal of a licence.*

[London Local Authorities Act 1995, s 23A as inserted by the London Local Authorities Act 2000, s 29.]

* **Repealed by the London Local Authorities Act 2007, s 35. In force in relation to the City of Westminster (19 September 2007); the London Borough of Newham (1 January 2008); the London Borough of Bexley (1 April 2008); and to be appointed for remaining purposes.**

7.7892 **24. Enforcement under Part IV** (1) If any occupier or other person concerned in the conduct or management of premises in the borough which are not currently licensed by the council under this Part of this Act—

(*a*) uses them as near beer premises; or

(*b*) permits them to be so used knowing or having reasonable cause to suspect that they are not currently so licensed;

he shall be guilty of an offence and shall be liable on summary conviction to a fine not exceeding **level 5** on the standard scale or to imprisonment for a term not exceeding **three months*** or to both.

(2) If any premises in respect of which a near beer licence is in force are used as near beer premises otherwise than in accordance with the terms, conditions or restrictions on or subject to which the near beer licence is held then the holder of the licence or other person concerned in the conduct or management of the premises shall be guilty of an offence and liable on summary conviction to a fine not exceeding level 5 on the standard scale.

(3) Subject to section 23 (Appeals under Part IV) of this Act, the council may revoke a near beer licence if its holder is convicted of an offence under subsection (2) above.**

[London Local Authorities Act 1995, s 24.]

* **Words substituted by the Criminal Justice Act 2003, Sch 26, from a date to be appointed.**

** **Repealed by the London Local Authorities Act 2007, s 35. In force in relation to the City of Westminster (19 September 2007); the London Borough of Newham (1 January 2008); the London Borough of Bexley (1 April 2008); and to be appointed for remaining purposes.**

7.7893 **25. Powers of entry under Part IV** (1) Any authorised officer (on production, if so required, of a duly authenticated document of his authority) or any police officer may at all reasonable times enter upon, inspect and examine any premises used, or which he has reasonable cause to believe are—

(*a*) used or intended to be used as a near beer premises either without the requisite near beer licence; or

(*b*) used in contravention of the terms, conditions or restrictions on or subject to which a near beer licence is granted;

and may do all things reasonably necessary for the purpose of ascertaining whether an offence has been committed.

(2) Subsections (2), (3) and (4) of section 287 of the Public Health Act 1936 shall apply in respect of entry to premises for the purposes of subsection (1) above as they apply to entry to premises for the purposes of subsection (1) of that section.

(3) An officer of the fire and rescue authority authorised by the fire and rescue authority in writing to act in relation to this Part of this Act may at all reasonable times enter upon, inspect and examine premises which are licensed under this Part of this Act to ascertain whether conditions attached to the licence by virtue of section 16(3)(*f*) (Licensing) of this Act are being complied with.

(4) Any person who intentionally obstructs any person acting in the exercise of his powers under this section shall be guilty of an offence and shall be liable on summary conviction to a fine not exceeding level 3 on the standard scale.*

[London Local Authorities Act 1995, s 25 as amended by the Fire and Rescue Services Act 2004, Sch 1.]

* **Repealed by the London Local Authorities Act 2007, s 35. In force in relation to the City of Westminster (19 September 2007); the London Borough of Newham (1 January 2008); the London Borough of Bexley (1 April 2008); and to be appointed for remaining purposes.**

7.7894 **26. Seizure** (1) Any police officer who enters any premises by virtue of the powers contained in subsection (1) of section 25 (Powers of entry under Part IV) of this Act or any authorised officer who enters any premises under the authority of a warrant granted under subsection (2) of the said section 25 of this Act may seize and remove any apparatus or equipment or other thing whatsoever found on the premises which he has reasonable cause to believe may be liable to be forfeited under section 143 of the Powers of Criminal Courts (Sentencing) Act 2000.

(2)

(*a*) The following provisions of this subsection shall have effect where any apparatus or equipment or any other thing is seized under subsection (1) above and references in those provisions to proceedings are to proceedings in respect of the alleged offence in relation to which the article or thing is seized.

(*b*) Subject to paragraphs (*c*) and (*d*) below, at the conclusion of the proceedings the apparatus, equipment or thing shall be returned to the premises from which it was seized unless the court orders it to be forfeited under any enactment.

(*c*) If no proceedings are instituted before the expiration of a period of 28 days beginning with the date of seizure, or any proceedings instituted within that period are discontinued, at the expiration of that period or, as the case may be, on the discontinuance of the proceedings, the apparatus, equipment or thing shall, subject to paragraph (*d*) below, be returned to the premises from which it was seized.

(*d*) Where, at the time at which any apparatus, equipment or thing falls to be returned under paragraph (*b*) or (*c*) above, the premises from which it was seized have ceased to be occupied or the occupier of the premises appears to the council to be different from the person who occupied the premises at the time of seizure the council may, instead of returning it to the premises apply to a magistrates' court for an order as to the manner in which it should be dealt with.*

[London Local Authorities Act 1995, s 26 as amended by the Powers of Criminal Courts (Sentencing) Act 2000, Sch 9.]

* **Repealed by the London Local Authorities Act 2007, s 35. In force in relation to the City of Westminster (19 September 2007); the London Borough of Newham (1 January 2008); the London Borough of Bexley (1 April 2008); and to be appointed for remaining purposes.**

7.7895 **27. Application to existing premises** Where near beer premises exist on the date this Part of this Act comes into force in the borough in which the near beer premises are situated and application for a near beer licence is made in respect of those premises within four weeks of that date those premises may lawfully continue to be used as near beer premises until the determination or withdrawal of that application and if an appeal is lodged until the determination or abandonment of the appeal.*

[London Local Authorities Act 1995, s 27.]

* **Repealed by the London Local Authorities Act 2007, s 35. In force in relation to the City of Westminster (19 September 2007); the London Borough of Newham (1 January 2008); the London Borough of Bexley (1 April 2008); and to be appointed for remaining purposes.**

## PART VI[1]
## MISCELLANEOUS

7.7896 **48. Offences by bodies corporate** (1) Where an offence under this Act committed by a body corporate is proved to have been committed with the consent or connivance of, or to be attributable to any neglect on the part of, any director, manager, secretary or other similar officer of the body corporate or any person who was purporting to act in any such capacity, he, as well as the body corporate, shall be guilty of that offence and shall be liable to be proceeded against and punished accordingly.

(2) Where the affairs of a body corporate are managed by its members subsection (1) above shall apply to the acts and defaults of a member in connection with his function of management as if he were a director of the body corporate.

[London Local Authorities Act 1995, s 48.]

1 Part VI contains ss 44–48.

# London Local Authorities Act 1996

(1996 c ix)

## PART I[1]
## PRELIMINARY

7.7897 **1. Citation and commencement** (1) This Act may be cited as the London Local Authorities Act 1996 and except where otherwise provided shall come into operation at the end of the period of two months beginning with the date on which it is passed[2].

(2) The London Local Authorities Act 1990, the London Local Authorities (No. 2) Act 1990, the London Local Authorities Act 1991, the London Local Authorities Act 1994, the London Local Authorities Act 1995 and this Act may together be cited as the London Local Authorities Acts 1990 to 1996.

[London Local Authorities Act 1996, s 1.]

1 Part I comprises ss 1 and 2.
2 This Act was passed on 17 October 1996.

7.7898 **2. Interpretation** In this Act, except as otherwise expressly provided or unless the context otherwise requires—

"borough council" means London borough council and includes the Common Council of the City of London; and "borough" and "council" shall be construed accordingly;

"Transport for London" means the body established by section 154 of the Greater London Authority Act 1999.

[London Local Authorities Act 1996, s 2 as amended by SI 2001/690 and the London Local Authorities Act 2004, Sch 4.]

## Part II[1]
## Bus lanes

7.7899 **3–9.** *Penalty charges for offences in relation to bus lanes.*

[1] Part II comprises ss 3–9.

## Part III[1]
## Occasional sales

7.7900 **10. Meaning of occasional sale** In this Part of this Act "occasional sale" means a concourse of buyers and sellers of articles held otherwise than on a highway or in a building (except a car park) and comprising not less than five stalls, stands, vehicles (whether movable or not) or pitches from which articles are sold, but does not include—

(*a*) a market or fair the right to hold which was acquired by virtue of a grant (including a presumed grant) or acquired or established by statute;

(*b*) a sale by auction of farm livestock or deadstock;

(*c*) sales of a class which from time to time is by resolution of the borough council excluded from the operation of this Part of this Act;

(*d*) a market held in accordance with a planning permission granted under section 58(1)(*b*) of the Town and Country Planning Act 1990 (which provides for the granting of planning permission) or under a similar provision of a predecessor to that Act; or

(*e*) a market the holding of which commenced before 1st July 1948 and has continued without extinguishment.

[London Local Authorities Act 1996, s 10.]

[1] Part III comprises ss 10–19.

7.7901 **11. Application of Part III** (1) This Part of this Act applies to a borough as from such day as may be fixed in relation to that borough by resolution of the borough council, subject to and in accordance with the provisions of this section.

(2) The borough council shall cause to be published in a local newspaper circulating in the borough notice—

(*a*) of the passing of any such resolution and of a day fixed thereby; and

(*b*) of the general effect of the provisions of this Part of this Act;

and the day so fixed shall not be earlier than the expiration of three months from the publication of the said notice.

(3) Either a photostatic or other reproduction certified by the officer appointed for that purpose by the borough council to be a true reproduction of a page or part of a page of any such newspaper bearing the date of its publication and containing any such notice shall be evidence of the publication of the notice, and of the date of publication.

[London Local Authorities Act 1996, s 11.]

7.7902 **12. Licensing of occasional sales** (1) Subject to the provisions of this Part of this Act it shall be unlawful for any person to hold an occasional sale within a borough unless that person is authorised to do so by a licence under this Part of this Act.

(2) No licence under this Part of this Act is required if the proceeds of the occasional sale are to be applied solely or principally for charitable, social, sporting, religious or political purposes.

(3) A person holds an occasional sale for the purposes of this Part of this Act if—

(*a*) he receives or is entitled to receive payment for any space or pitch hired or let on the site of the sale to persons wishing to trade at the sale; or

(*b*) as a person promoting the sale, or as the agent, licensee or assignee of a person promoting the sale, he receives or is entitled to receive payment from persons trading at the sale for goods sold or services rendered to persons attending the sale.

[London Local Authorities Act 1996, s 12.]

7.7903 **13. Application for licence** (1) An application for a licence under this Part of this Act shall be made in writing to the borough council, not later than 42 days before the date on which the occasional sale is to be held:

Provided that nothing in this section shall prevent a borough council from granting a licence, notwithstanding that application has been made at a later date than aforesaid if they consider it reasonable in the circumstances so to do.

(2)–(3) Information to be specified and fees.

[London Local Authorities Act 1996, s 13.]

7.7904 **14. Grant of licence** (1) The borough council may grant a licence under this Part of this Act and in granting a licence may impose reasonable conditions relating to—

(*a*) the time of commencement of the occasional sale;

(*b*) the duration of the occasional sale;

(*c*) the arrangements to be made for accommodating the vehicles of persons attending the occasional sale;

(*d*) the arrangements to be made for controlling road congestion, litter and noise caused by the occasional sale;

(*e*) a requirement that the names and addresses of persons selling articles at the occasional sale are publicly displayed.

(2) If the borough council have not refused to grant a licence within 21 days of the receipt by them of an application duly made for a licence under subsection (1) of section 13 (Application for licence) of this Act, they shall be deemed to have granted a licence for an occasional sale in accordance with the details specified in the application.

(3) The borough council shall grant an application for a licence under this Part of this Act unless they consider that the application ought to be refused on one or more of the grounds specified in subsection (4) below.

(4) The borough council may refuse an application on any of the following grounds—

(*a*) that inadequate arrangements have been proposed for accommodating the vehicles of persons attending the occasional sale;

(*b*) that inadequate arrangements have been proposed for controlling road congestion, litter or noise caused by the occasional sale; or

(*c*) that the applicant has been granted a licence by any borough council for an occasional sale within three years before the date of the application and failed to comply with conditions imposed in relation to that licence.

[London Local Authorities Act 1996, s 14.]

7.7905 **15. Part III appeals** (1) If the borough council refuse to grant a licence under this Part of this Act they shall notify the applicant in writing—

(*a*) of their decision and of the ground or grounds for such refusal; and

(*b*) of his rights of appeal specified in this section.

(2) Any person aggrieved—

(*a*) by the refusal of a borough council to grant a licence; or

(*b*) by a condition imposed by a borough council under subsection (1) of section 14 (Grant of licence) of this Act;

may appeal[1] to a magistrates' court acting for the area in which the proposed occasional sale is to be held.

(3) A person desiring to appeal against such refusal or condition shall give a written notice to the magistrates' court and to the borough council specifying the refusal or condition against which he wishes to appeal and the grounds upon which such appeal is made.

(4) On an appeal to the magistrates' court under this section, the court may make such order as it thinks fit and it shall be the duty of the borough council to give effect to the order.

[London Local Authorities Act 1996, s 15.]

1 An appeal shall be brought by way of complaint; see the Magistrates' Courts Rules 1981, r 34 in PART I: MAGISTRATES' COURTS, PROCEDURE, ante.

7.7906 **17. Powers of entry** An authorised officer on producing if so required a duly authenticated document showing his authority, or any constable, may enter and inspect any premises if he has reasonable cause to believe that they are being, have been or are intended to be, used for or in connection with an occasional sale for the purpose of ascertaining whether there is or has been or is intended to be a contravention of this Part of this Act in, or in connection with, the premises.

[London Local Authorities Act 1996, s 17.]

7.7907 **18. Enforcement** (1) Any person who contravenes section 12 (Licensing of occasional sales) of this Act shall be guilty of an offence and liable on summary conviction to a fine not exceeding **level 4** on the standard scale.

(2) Any person who contravenes a condition imposed under section 14 (Grant of licence) of this Act shall be guilty of an offence and liable on summary conviction to a fine not exceeding **level 3** on the standard scale.

(3) Repealed.

[London Local Authorities Act 1996, s 18 as amended by SI 2008/1277.]

7.7908 **19. Restriction on right to prosecute** The written consent of the Director of Public Prosecutions is needed for the laying of an information of an offence created by this Part of this Act by any person other than an authorised officer or a constable.

[London Local Authorities Act 1996, s 19.]

## PART V[1]
## MISCELLANEOUS

7.7909 **24. Application of Environmental Protection Act 1990** The Environmental Protection Act 1990 shall have effect in a borough as though—

(1) in section 79 (which relates to statutory nuisances and inspections therefor)—

(*a*) in subsection (1), after paragraph (*ga*) there were inserted the following paragraph—

"(*gb*) smoke, fumes or gases emitted from any vehicle, machinery or equipment on a street so as to be prejudicial to health or a nuisance other than from any vehicle, machinery or equipment being used for fire brigade purposes;";

(*b*) after subsection (6A) there were inserted the following subsection—

"(6B) Subsection (1) (*gb*) above does not apply in relation to smoke, fumes or gases emitted from the exhaust system of a vehicle."; and

(*c*) in subsection (7), after the definition of "street" there were inserted—

" 'vehicle' means a mechanically propelled vehicle intended or adapted for use on roads, whether or not it is in a fit state for such use, and includes any trailer intended or adapted for use as an attachment to such a vehicle, any chassis or body, with or without wheels, appearing to have formed part of such a vehicle or trailer and anything attached to such a vehicle or trailer;";

(2) in section 80A (1), after "section 79 (1) (*ga*)" there were inserted "or (*gb*)".

[London Local Authorities Act 1996, s 24.]

[1] Part V comprises ss 24–31.

**7.7910 28. Obstruction of authorised officer** (1) Any person who—

(*a*) internationally obstructs any authorised officer acting in the exercise of his powers under this Act; or

(*b*) without reasonable cause fails to give any authorised officer any assistance or information which the officer may reasonably require of him for the purposes of the exercise of the officer's functions under the provision of this Act;

shall be guilty of an offence and liable on summary conviction to a fine not exceeding **level 3** on the standard scale.

(2) Subsection (1)(*b*) above applies in relation to a constable as it applies in relation to an authorised officer.

(3) A person shall be guilty of an offence if, in giving any information which is required of him by virtue of subsection (1)(*b*) above—

(*a*) he can make any statement which he knows is false in a material particular; or

(*b*) he recklessly makes a statement which is false in a material particular.

(4) A person guilty of an offence under subsection (3) above shall be liable on summary conviction to a fine not exceeding **level 5** on the standard scale.

[London Local Authorities Act 1996, s 28.]

**7.7911 29. Defence of due diligence** (1) In proceedings for an offence under this Act it shall be a defence for the person charged to prove that he took all reasonable precautions and exercised all due diligence to avoid the commission of the offence.

(2) If in any case the defence provided under subsection (1) above involves the allegation that the commission of the offence was due to the act or default of another person, the person charged shall not, without leave of the court, be entitled to rely on that defence unless, no later than 7 clear days before the hearing, he has served on the prosecutor a notice in writing giving such information as was then in his possession identifying or assisting in the identification of that other person.

[London Local Authorities Act 1996, s 29.]

**7.7912 30. Liability of directors, etc** (1) Where an offence under this Act committed by a body corporate is provided to have been committed with the consent or connivance of, or to be attributable to any neglect on the part of, a director, manager, secretary or other similar officer of the body corporate or any person who was purporting to act in any such capacity, he, as well as the body corporate, shall be guilty of the offence.

(2) Where the affairs of the body corporate are managed by its members, subsection (1) above shall apply to the acts and defaults of a member in connection with his functions of management as if he were a director of the body corporate.

[London Local Authorities Act 1996, s 30.]

**7.7913 31.** Regulations.

## SCHEDULE 1

ENFORCEMENT NOTICES, ETC. UNDER PART II (BUS LANES) OF THIS ACT[1]

[1] Schedule 1 provides that where a penalty charge has been issued under s 4 of the Act but is not paid within 28 days, the enforcing authority may serve an enforcement notice on the owner or person in charge of the vehicle. Representations may be made against the charge or notice on grounds prescribed in para 4 which inter alia provides that where it is maintained that the recipient was not in charge of the vehicle, he must include a statement of the name and address of the person whom he believed to be in charge at the material time. Failure to comply is a summary offence punishable by a fine not exceeding **level 3** unless he shows that he did not know, and could not with reasonable diligence have ascertained, who was the driver.

It is also a summary offence under paragraph 11 punishable by a fine not exceeding **level 5** for a person to make any representation to a council or traffic adjudicator under paragraph 2 or 6 which is false in a material particular and who does so recklessly or knowing it to be false in that particular.

# Greater London Authority Act 1999[1]

(1999 c 29)

PART II[2]

GENERAL FUNCTIONS AND PROCEDURE

*General functions of the Assembly*

7.7914 **59. Review and investigation** (1) The Assembly shall keep under review the exercise by the Mayor of the statutory functions exercisable by him.

(2) For the purposes of subsection (1) above, the powers of the Assembly include in particular power to investigate, and prepare reports about—

(*a*) any actions and decisions of the Mayor,

(*b*) any actions and decisions of any member of staff of the Authority,

(*c*) matters relating to the principal purposes of the Authority,

(*d*) matters in relation to which statutory functions are exercisable by the Mayor, or

(*e*) any other matters which the Assembly considers to be of importance to Greater London.

[Greater London Authority Act 1999, s 59.]

---

[1] The Greater London Authority Act 1999 establishes and makes provision about the Greater London Authority, the Mayor of London and the London Assembly. The Act makes provision in relation to London borough councils and the common council of the city of London with respect to matters consequential on the establishment of the Greater London Authority. The Act also makes provision with respect to the functioning of other local authorities and statutory bodies exercising functions in Greater London including provision about transport and road traffic.

The Act contains a number of penal provisions, but only those that are thought likely to be of relevance to the work of the magistrates' courts in Greater London are set out in this work.

The Act is to be brought into force in accordance with s 425. At the date of going to press, the following Greater London Authority Act 1999 commencement orders had been made: Commencement (No 1) Order 1999, SI 1999/3271; Commencement (No 2) Order 1999, SI 1999/3376; Commencement (No 3) Order 1999, SI 1999/3434; Commencement (No 4) Order 1999, SI 2000/801; Commencement (No 5) Order 2000, SI 2000/1094; Commencement (No 6) Order 2000, SI 2000/1095; Commencement (No 7) Order SI 2000/1648; Commencement (No 8) Order 2000 SI 2000/3145; Commencement (No 9) Order 2000, SI 2000/3379; Commencement (No 10) Order 2001, SI 2001/3603; and Commencement (No 11) Order 2003, SI 2003/1920.

[2] Part II comprises ss 30 to 80.

*Attendance of witnesses and production of documents*

7.7915 **61. Power to require attendance at Assembly meetings** (1) Subject to section 63 below, the Assembly may require any person to whom subsection (2), (3), (4) or (5) below applies—

(*a*) to attend proceedings of the Assembly for the purpose of giving evidence, or

(*b*) to produce to the Assembly documents in his possession or under his control.

(2) This subsection applies to—

(*a*) any person who is a member of staff of the Authority, or of any functional body, to whom sections 1, 2 and 3A of the Local Government and Housing Act 1989 apply,

(*b*) any person who is the chairman of, or a member of, any functional body, and

(*c*) any person who has within the 8 years prior to the date of the requirement to be imposed under subsection (1) above been the chairman of, or a member of, any functional body.

(3) This subsection applies to—

(*a*) any person who has within the 8 years prior to the date of the requirement to be imposed under subsection (1) above had a contractual relationship with the Authority, and

(*b*) any person who is a member of, or a member of staff of, a body which has within the 8 years prior to the date of the requirement to be imposed under subsection (1) above had such a relationship.

(4) This subsection applies to—

(*a*) any person who has within the 8 years prior to the date of the requirement to be imposed under subsection (1) above received a grant from the Authority, and

(*b*) any person who is a member of, or a member of staff of, a body which has within the 8 years prior to the date of the requirement to be imposed under subsection (1) above received such a grant.

(5) This subsection applies to—

(*a*) any person who is an Assembly member,

(*b*) any person who has within the 8 years prior to the date of the requirement to be imposed under subsection (1) above been an Assembly member, and

(*c*) any person who has within the 8 years prior to the date of the requirement to be imposed under subsection (1) above been the Mayor.

(6) A requirement imposed under subsection (1) above on a person falling within subsection (2) above—

(*a*) if imposed under paragraph (*a*) of subsection (1) above, is to attend to give evidence in connection with matters in relation to which statutory functions are exercisable by the Authority or any functional body, and

(b) if imposed under paragraph (b) of subsection (1) above, is to produce documents which relate to those matters.

(7) A requirement imposed under subsection (1) above on a person falling within subsection (3) above—

(a) if imposed under paragraph (a) of subsection (1) above, is to attend to give evidence in connection with the contractual relationship with the Authority, and

(b) if imposed under paragraph (b) of subsection (1) above, is to produce documents which relate to that contractual relationship.

(8) A requirement imposed under subsection (1) above on a person falling within subsection (4) above—

(a) if imposed under paragraph (a) of subsection (1) above, is to attend to give evidence in connection with the grant received from the Authority, and

(b) if imposed under paragraph (b) of subsection (1) above, is to produce documents which relate to that grant.

(9) A requirement imposed under subsection (1) above on a person falling within subsection (5) above—

(a) if imposed under paragraph (a) of subsection (1) above, is to attend to give evidence in connection with the exercise by the person attending of the functions of the Authority, and

(b) if imposed under paragraph (b) of subsection (1) above, is to produce documents which relate to the exercise of those functions by that person.

(10) Nothing in this section shall require a person appointed under section 67(1) or (2), 72(1), 73(1) or 127A(1) below to—

(a) give any evidence, or

(b) produce any documents,

which disclose advice given by that person to the Mayor.

(11) Nothing in this section shall require a person who is—

(a) a member of a functional body, or

(b) a member of staff of a functional body,

to give any evidence, or produce any document, which discloses advice given to the Mayor by that person or, except as provided by subsection (12) below, by that functional body.

(12) Subsection (11) above does not relieve a person from a requirement to give any evidence, or produce any document, which discloses advice given to the Mayor by—

(a) *repealed*

(b) the London Fire and Emergency Planning Authority,

if or to the extent that the advice falls within subsection (13) below.

(13) Advice given to the Mayor by a functional body falls within this subsection if it has been disclosed—

(a) at a meeting of, or of a committee or sub-committee of, the functional body at a time when the meeting was open to members of the public by virtue of Part VA of the Local Government Act 1972 (access to meetings and documents); or

(b) in a document which has been open to inspection by members of the public by virtue of that Part of that Act.

(14) For the purposes of this section and sections 62 to 65 below—

(a) "document" means anything in which information is recorded in any form (and references to producing a document are to the production of the information in it in a visible and legible form, including the production of a copy of the document or an extract of the relevant part of the document),

(b) any reference to a member of staff of a body includes a reference to an officer or employee of that body, and

(c) any reference to proceedings is a reference to proceedings at a meeting.

[Greater London Authority Act 1999, s 61 as amended by the Local Government and Public Involvement in Health Act 2007, s 203, the Greater London Authority Act 2007, s 5 and the Police Reform and Social Responsibility Act 2011, Sch 16.]

7.7916 **62. Procedure for requiring attendance** (1) The powers of the Assembly under section 61(1) above may be exercised by and for the purposes of an ordinary committee of the Assembly, if the committee is expressly authorised to exercise those powers by the standing orders or by the Assembly, but may not be exercised by any individual Assembly member or by any member of staff of the Authority.

(2) Except in the case of a committee which is authorised by standing orders to exercise the powers of the Assembly under section 61(1) above, section 54 above shall not apply in relation to—

(a) the Assembly's function of deciding to exercise its powers under section 61(1) above; or

(b) the Assembly's function under subsection (1) above of authorising a committee to exercise those powers.

(3) In order to impose a requirement on a person under section 61(1) above the head of the Authority's paid service must give him notice specifying—

(a) the time and place at which he is to attend and the matters about which he is to be required to give evidence, or (*b*) the documents, or types of documents, which he is to produce, the date by which he is to produce them and the matters to which the document or documents relate.

(4) Where a requirement under section 61(1) above is imposed on a person to attend proceedings or produce documents on behalf of a body, the notice required to be given to him under subsection (3) above must also specify that body.

(5) A notice required by subsection (3) above to be given to a person must be given at least two weeks before the day on which the proceedings are to take place, or by which the documents are to be produced, unless he waives this right.

(6) A notice required by subsection (3) above to be given to a person shall be taken to have been given to him if it is sent by registered post or the recorded delivery service and—

(*a*) if he is a member of staff of the Authority or the chairman of, a member of, or a member of staff of a functional body, it is sent to his normal place of work,

(*b*) if he is a person required to attend proceedings or produce documents on behalf of a body, it is sent to the registered or principal office of the body,

(*c*) if he is any other individual, it is sent to his usual or last known address, or

(*d*) in the case of any person, where that person has given an address for service of the notice, it is sent to that address.

[Greater London Authority Act 1999, s 62.]

7.7917 **63. Restriction of information** The Secretary of State may by order—

(*a*) prescribe categories of information which a person who is required under subsection (1)(*a*) of section 61 above to attend proceedings of the Assembly may refuse to give, or

(*b*) prescribe categories of documents which a person who is required under subsection (1)(*b*) of that section to produce documents may refuse to produce.

[Greater London Authority Act 1999, s 63.]

7.7918 **64. Failure to attend proceedings etc** (1) A person to whom a notice under section 62(3) above has been given is guilty of an offence if he—

(*a*) refuses or fails, without reasonable excuse, to attend proceedings as required by the notice,

(*b*) refuses to answer any question which is properly put to him when attending any proceedings as required by the notice,

(*c*) refuses or fails, without reasonable excuse, to produce any document required by the notice to be produced by him, or

(*d*) intentionally alters, suppresses, conceals or destroys any document required by the notice to be produced by him.

(2) A person guilty of an offence under subsection (1) above is liable on summary conviction to—

(*a*) a fine not exceeding **level 5** on the standard scale, or

(*b*) imprisonment for a term not exceeding **three months***.

(3) A person is not obliged by section 61 above to answer any question or produce any document which he would be entitled to refuse to answer or produce in or for the purposes of proceedings in a court in England and Wales.

[Greater London Authority Act 1999, s 64.]

---

* **Words substituted by the Criminal Justice Act 2003, Sch 26 from a date to be appointed.**

7.7919 **65. Proceedings under section 61(1): openness** (1) In its application by virtue of section 58 above, Part VA of the Local Government Act 1972 (access to meetings and documents of certain authorities, committees and sub-committees), so far as relating to any proceedings under section 61(1) above ("the evidentiary proceedings"), shall have effect with the following additional modifications.

(2) In section 100B (access to agenda and connected reports) any reference to a report for a meeting includes a reference to any document (other than the agenda) supplied before, and for the purposes of, the evidentiary proceedings (a "relevant document").

(3) If a report or relevant document is supplied less than three clear days before the evidentiary proceedings, copies of the report or document shall be open to inspection by the public under subsection (1) of that section from the time such copies are available to Assembly members, notwithstanding anything in subsection (3) of section 100B.

(4) In section 100C (inspection of minutes and other documents after meetings)—

(*a*) any reference to the minutes of a meeting shall be taken to include a reference to a transcript or other record of evidence given in the course of the evidentiary proceedings; and

(*b*) any reference to a report for the meeting includes a reference to a relevant document.

(5) In section 100D (inspection of background papers) any reference in subsections (1) to (4) to background papers for a report (or part of a report) shall be taken as a reference to any additional documents supplied by a witness.

(6) In this section, "additional documents supplied by a witness" means documents supplied, whether before, during or after the evidentiary proceedings,—

(*a*) by a person attending to give evidence at the proceedings, and

(*b*) for the use of Assembly members in connection with the proceedings, but does not include any document which is a relevant document.

(7) In section 100F (additional rights of access for members) subsections (2) to (4) shall not have effect in relation to documents which contain material relating to any business to be transacted at the evidentiary proceedings.

(8) In section 100H (supplemental provisions and offences) in subsection (6), in the definition of "accessible documents"—

(*a*) the reference in paragraph (*d*) to a report for the meeting includes a reference to a relevant document; and

(*b*) the reference in paragraph (*e*) to background papers for a report for a meeting shall be taken as a reference to any additional documents supplied by a witness.

[Greater London Authority Act 1999, s 65.]

## PART IV[1]
## TRANSPORT

### CHAPTER IX[2]
### PENALTY FARES

7.7920 **245. Penalty fares** Schedule 17[3] to this Act shall have effect for the purpose of providing for the payment of penalty fares in the circumstances set out in that Schedule.

[Greater London Authority Act 1999, s 245.]

1 Part IV comprises ss 141–303.
2 Chapter IX comprises s 245.
3 See, post.

### CHAPTER XI[1]
### HACKNEY CARRIAGES AND PRIVATE HIRE VEHICLES

7.7921 **253. Hackney carriages** Schedule 20[2] to this Act (which makes provision about hackney carriages) shall have effect.

[Greater London Authority Act 1999, s 253.]

1 Chapter XI comprises ss 253–255.
2 See, post.

7.7922 **254. The Private Hire Vehicles (London) Act 1998** (1) Except as provided by the following provisions of this section, the functions of the Secretary of State under the Private Hire Vehicles (London) Act 1998[1] are transferred by this subsection to Transport for London.

(2) Subsection (1) above does not apply to any functions of the Secretary of State under section 37, 38 or 40 of that Act (transitional provisions, financial provisions and commencement etc).

(3) Schedule 21[2] to this Act (which makes amendments to the Private Hire Vehicles (London) Act 1998 in consequence of subsections (1) and (2) above) shall have effect.

(4) Any regulations made, licence issued, authorisation granted, or other thing done under the Private Hire Vehicles (London) Act 1998, other than section 37, 38 or 40, by or in relation to the Secretary of State before the coming into force of this section shall have effect as from the coming into force of this section as made, issued, granted or done by or in relation to Transport for London.

[Greater London Authority Act 1999, s 254.]

1 See, ante.
2 Schedule 21 is not set out in this work.

7.7923 **255. Provisions consequent on alteration of metropolitan police district**

(1) Where, by virtue of the coming into force of section 323 below, the whole or any part of the area of a district council ceases to be within the metropolitan police district, the following provisions of this section shall have effect[1].

(2) The provisions of the Town Police Clauses Act 1847[2] with respect to hackney carriages, as incorporated in the Public Health Act 1875, shall apply throughout the council's area.

(3) The council's area shall constitute a single licensing area for the purposes of those provisions, without the passing of any resolution under Part II of Schedule 14 to the Local Government Act 1972 (extension resolutions).

(4) The provisions of Part II of the Local Government (Miscellaneous Provisions) Act 1976[3] (hackney carriages and private hire vehicles) shall also apply throughout the council's area, without the passing of any resolution under section 45 of that Act (application of Part II).

(5) Where an order is made under section 425 below bringing section 323 below into force, the provision that may be made by virtue of section 420 or 425 below includes provision enabling or facilitating—

(*a*) the making of byelaws,

(*b*) the issuing of licences, discs or plates, and

(*c*) the establishment and operation of a licensing system,

in relation to hackney carriages or private hire vehicles by a district council falling within subsection (1) above in preparation for the coming into force of this section.

(6) The provision that may be made by virtue of subsection (5) above includes provision for the

application of any enactment with or without modification.

(7) Subsections (5) and (6) above are without prejudice to the provision that may be made by virtue of sections 420 and 425 below.

[Greater London Authority Act 1999, s 255.]

---

[1] See also the Greater London Authority Act 1999 (Hackney Carriages and Private Hire Vehicles) (Transitional and Consequential Provisions) Order 2000, SI 2000/412.

[2] See title, TOWNS IMPROVEMENT; TOWN POLICE, post.

[3] See title LOCAL GOVERNMENT, ante.

## SCHEDULE 17

### PENALTY FARES

Section 245

*(Amended by the Transport for London Act 2008, s 28)*

*Introductory*

7.7924 **1.** (1) In this Schedule unless the context otherwise requires—

"authorised person" means, in relation to any purpose, a person authorised for that purpose by Transport for London or by the person providing the service;

"compulsory ticket area" means that part of a station which, under the byelaws of the person providing a train service to which this Schedule applies, passengers are not permitted to enter without a fare ticket, general travel authority or platform ticket;

"fare ticket" means a ticket (including one issued by a third person) showing payment of a fare and authorising the person in respect of whom it is issued to make a single journey covered by that fare on a local service or train service to which this Schedule applies, or to make that journey and a return journey (whether or not it also authorises him to make a journey on a service provided by a third person);

"general travel authority" means any permit (including one issued by a third person), other than a fare ticket, authorising the person in respect of whom it is issued to travel on a local service or train service to which this Schedule applies (whether or not it also authorises him to travel on a service provided by a third person);

"penalty fare" means a penalty fare payable pursuant to paragraph 3 or 4 below;

"the penalty fare provisions" means paragraphs 3 to 8 below;

"person providing the service" means the operator of the service, except that, in the case of a service provided in pursuance of an agreement entered into by Transport for London under section 156(2) or (3)(*a*) of this Act or in pursuance of a transport subsidiary's agreement, means Transport for London;

"platform ticket" means a ticket authorising a person to enter a compulsory ticket area but not to make a journey;

"station" means a station serving a train service to which this Schedule applies;

"third person" means a person other than one referred to in paragraph 2(1)(*a*) or (*b*) below; and

"train service" means a service for the carriage of passengers by rail.

(2) Subject to sub-paragraph (3) below, a person is travelling on a train service to which this Schedule applies at any time when he is on a train forming part of that service or is in a compulsory ticket area.

(3) A person at a station is not to be taken as travelling by reason only of being in a compulsory ticket area or boarding a train at that station if he has entered that area or boards that train otherwise than for the purpose of making a journey and produces, if required to do so by an authorised person, a valid platform ticket.

(4) Any reference in this Schedule to a person producing a fare ticket or general travel authority on being required to do so by an authorised person is a reference to producing, when so required, a fare ticket or general travel authority which, either by itself or together with any other fare ticket or general travel authority produced by that person at the same time, is valid for the journey he has made.

(5) For the purposes of sub-paragraph (4) above—

(*a*) a person who has entered a compulsory ticket area otherwise than by transferring from a train service provided by a third person but has not boarded a train shall be taken to have made a journey for which the minimum fare is payable; and

(*b*) a person who is on a train shall be taken to have made a journey ending at the next station at which the train is scheduled to stop.

(6) In sub-paragraph (5) above "minimum fare" means the minimum fare for which a journey from the station in question could validly be made by the person in question.

(7) For the purposes of this Schedule a person is to be taken as transferring from a service provided by a third person to a service to which this Schedule applies if, but only if, having travelled on a train forming part of the former service, he—

(*a*) goes from that train into a compulsory ticket area and finishes his journey at the station of which that area forms part; or

(*b*) goes from that train into a compulsory ticket area and from that area boards a train forming part of a service to which this Schedule applies.

(8) For the purposes of sub-paragraph (7)(*b*) above, in a case where the transfer takes place at a station controlled by a third person, "compulsory ticket area" means such area at that station as corresponds with a compulsory ticket area within the meaning of this Schedule.

*Operation of this Schedule*

**2.** (1) This Schedule applies to any local service or train service provided—

(*a*) by Transport for London or any of its subsidiaries; or

(*b*) by any other person in pursuance of an agreement entered into by Transport for London under section 156(2) or (3)(*a*) of this Act, or in pursuance of a transport subsidiary's agreement, which provides that this Schedule is to apply to services provided in pursuance of that agreement.

(2) References in the following provisions of this Schedule to a local service or to a train service are, unless

the context otherwise requires, references to a local service or a train service to which this Schedule applies.

(3) The penalty fare provisions have effect in relation to travel on any local service or train service or any part of such a service if an order under sub-paragraph (4) below is for the time being in force in respect of such service or part of a service.

(4) The Mayor may by order provide that the penalty fare provisions shall have effect, as from such day as may be specified in the order, with respect to any local service or train service or any part of any local service or train service, and different days may be specified in any such order with respect to different services or different parts of any service.

(5) The revocation by the Mayor of an order made under sub-paragraph (4) above shall be without prejudice to the power of the Mayor to make further orders under that sub-paragraph as respects any service or part of a service dealt with by the order.

(6) Any activating order made by the Secretary of State under section 3(4) of the London Regional Transport (Penalty Fares) Act 1992 and in force immediately before the coming into force of sub-paragraph (4) above shall have effect as from the coming into force of that sub-paragraph as if it were an order made by the Mayor under that sub-paragraph.

(7) For the purposes of this Schedule a reference to an agreement entered into by Transport for London under section 156(2) or (3) of this Act includes a reference to an agreement—

(*a*) which was entered into by London Regional Transport under section 3(2) or (2A) of the London Regional Transport Act 1984, and

(*b*) which by virtue of section 300 or 415 of this Act has effect as if made by Transport for London.

*Penalty fares on local services*

**3.** (1) If a person travelling on a ticket bus service who has had a reasonable opportunity to obtain a fare ticket for a journey on that service fails to produce a fare ticket or a general travel authority on being required to do so by an authorised person, he shall be liable to pay a penalty fare if required to do so by an authorised person.

(2) If a person travels on a non-ticket bus service without paying the fare properly payable for a journey on that service and, while so travelling, fails to produce a general travel authority on being required to do so by an authorised person, he shall be liable to pay a penalty fare if required to do so by an authorised person.

(3) In this paragraph a "ticket bus service" means a local service on which fare tickets are issued in return for fares paid by persons travelling on that service, and a "non-ticket bus service" means a local service on which fare tickets are not so issued.

*Penalty fares on trains*

**4.** (1) Subject to sub-paragraph (2) below, if a person travelling on a train service fails to produce a fare ticket or a general travel authority on being required to do so by an authorised person, he shall be liable to pay a penalty fare if required to do so by an authorised person.

(2) Subject to sub-paragraph (3) below, a person shall not be liable to pay a penalty fare under this paragraph if at the time when and the station where he started to travel on the train service there were no facilities available for the sale of the necessary fare ticket for his journey.

(3) A person who starts to travel on a train service by transferring to that service from a train service provided by a third person shall not be liable to pay a penalty fare under this paragraph if—

(*a*) on being required to produce a fare ticket or general travel authority he produces a valid deferred fare authority issued by that person; or

(*b*) at the time when and the station where he started to travel on the train service provided by that person there were no facilities for either the sale of the necessary fare ticket for his journey or the sale of deferred fare authorities.

(4) Without prejudice to sub-paragraphs (2) or (3) above, a person shall not be liable to pay a penalty fare under this paragraph if at the time when and the station where his journey began—

(*a*) there was displayed a notice (however expressed) indicating that it was permissible for passengers beginning a journey at that station at that time to do so without having a fare ticket or a general travel authority or (in the case of a station controlled by a third person) a deferred fare authority; or

(*b*) a person in the uniform of the person controlling that station gave permission to the same effect.

(5) In sub-paragraph (3) above, "deferred fare authority" means a ticket or other document described as such on its face; and a deferred fare authority is valid for the purposes of that paragraph if it authorises a person in possession of it to start a journey at the time when and the station where the person producing it started his journey.

(6) Sub-paragraphs (7) and (8) below have effect with respect to the burden of proof in any action for the recovery of a penalty fare under this paragraph, so far as concerns the question whether the facts of the case fall within sub-paragraphs (2), (3)(*b*) or (4) above.

(7) In any case where the defendant has provided the plaintiff with a relevant statement in due time it shall be for the plaintiff to show that the facts of the case do not fall within sub-paragraph (2), (3)(*b*) or (4) above and in any other case it shall be for the defendant to show that the facts of the case fall within any of those provisions.

(8) For the purposes of sub-paragraph (7) above—

(*a*) a relevant statement is a statement giving an explanation of the defendant's failure to produce a fare ticket, general travel authority or (where relevant) deferred fare authority, together with any information as to his journey relevant to that explanation (including, in every case, an indication of the time when and the station where he started to travel on the train service and also, if he started so to travel when he transferred from a train service provided by a third person, the time when and the station where he started to travel on that service); and

(*b*) a statement is provided in due time if it is provided when the defendant is required to produce a fare ticket or general travel authority, or at any later time before the expiration of the period of 21 days beginning with the day following the day on which the journey is completed.

*Amount of penalty fare*

**5.** (1) Subject to sub-paragraph (2) below, a penalty fare shall be—

(*a*) in respect of any journey on a local service, £5;

(*b*) in respect of any train journey, £10;

and shall be payable to the person providing the service on which the requirement to pay the penalty fare is made before the expiration of the period of 21 days beginning with the day following the day on which the journey is completed.

(2) The Mayor may by order prescribe that the amount of the penalty fare in either or both of the cases set out in sub-paragraph (1) above shall be different (whether higher or lower).

(3) No order may be made by the Mayor under sub-paragraph (2) above unless he has consulted the Secretary of State and—

(*a*) such persons or bodies representative of local authorities,

(*b*) such persons or bodies representative of those who travel on local services and train services, and

(*c*) such other persons or bodies,

as the Mayor considers it appropriate to consult.*

* **Amended by the Transport for London Act 2008, s 27 from a date to be appointed.**

*Documents in connection with penalty fare requirement*

6. (1) An authorised person who requires a person (referred to below as "the passenger") to pay a penalty fare shall give him either a receipt for the payment of the amount of the penalty (where the passenger makes that payment to the authorised person) or a notice stating that the requirement has been made.

(2) A receipt or notice given under sub-paragraph (1) above shall specify the passenger's destination on the local service or train service on which he is travelling when required to pay the penalty fare, and shall operate as an authority to him to complete his journey to or at that destination.

(3) For the purposes of sub-paragraph (2) above, the passenger's destination shall (unless he is at that destination or only one destination is possible in the circumstances) be taken to be the destination stated by the passenger or, in default of any statement by him for that purpose, such destination as may be specified by the authorised person.

*Supplementary provision*

7. (1) A person shall, if required to do so by an authorised person, give his name and address to him if—

(*a*) he is required by the authorised person to pay a penalty fare, or

(*b*) he would be liable to pay a penalty fare if so required by the authorised person.

(2) A person failing to give his name and address when required to do so under sub-paragraph (1) above shall be guilty of an offence and liable on summary conviction to a fine not exceeding level 2 on the standard scale.

(3) Transport for London shall secure that the requirements of sub-paragraph (4) or, as the case may be, (5) below with respect to warning notices are met in the case of a local service or train service in relation to travel on which the penalty fare provisions have effect.

(4) In the case of a local service, a warning notice meeting the requirements of sub-paragraphs (6) and (7) below shall be posted in every vehicle used in providing that service or, where any such vehicle has more than one deck, on each deck of that vehicle, in such a position as to be readily visible to persons travelling on the vehicle.

(5) In the case of a train service, a warning notice meeting the requirements of sub-paragraphs (6) and (7) below shall be posted—

(*a*) at every station at which persons may start to travel on that service, in such a position as to be readily visible to prospective passengers; and

(*b*) in every carriage of every train used in providing that service in such a position as to be readily visible to passengers travelling in the carriage.

(6) A warning notice posted pursuant to sub-paragraph (4) or (5) above shall (however expressed) indicate the circumstances (as provided in paragraph 3(1) or (2) above or, as the case may be, paragraph 4(1) above) in which persons travelling on the service in question may be liable to pay a penalty fare.

(7) Every warning notice posted in pursuance of this paragraph shall state the amount of the relevant penalty fare.

(8) Where an authorised person requires any person to do anything pursuant to any provision of this Schedule he shall, if so requested by the person concerned, produce to that person a duly authenticated document showing his authority.

(9) A requirement by an authorised person shall be of no effect if, as respects that requirement, he fails to comply with sub-paragraph (8) above.

*Exclusion of double liability*

8. (1) Where a person has become liable under paragraph 3 or 4 above to pay a penalty fare in respect of any journey on a local service or any train journey (referred to below as "the relevant journey"), no proceedings may be brought against him for any of the offences specified in sub-paragraph (3) below before the end of the period mentioned in paragraph 5(1) above.

(2) No proceedings may be brought after the end of that period if—

(*a*) before the end of that period, the person who has become liable to pay the penalty fare has paid it to the person providing the service on which the requirement to pay it was made; or

(*b*) an action has been brought against the person who has become liable to pay the penalty fare for the recovery of that fare.

(3) The offences mentioned in sub-paragraph (1) above are—

(*a*) any offence under section 5(3)(*a*) or (*b*) of the Regulation of Railways Act 1889 (travelling without paying the correct fare with intent to avoid payment) arising from the relevant journey;

(*b*) any offence under byelaws made under section 67 of the Transport Act 1962 or paragraph 26 of Schedule 11 to this Act (byelaws for railways, etc) involving a failure to obtain or produce a fare ticket or general travel authority for the relevant journey; and

(*c*) any offence under section 25(3) of the Public Passenger Vehicles Act 1981 of contravening or failing to comply with any provision of regulations for the time being having effect by virtue of that section by failing to pay the fare properly payable for the relevant journey or any part of it.

(4) If proceedings are brought in contravention of this paragraph the person who has become liable to pay the penalty fare shall cease to be liable to pay it, but where that person has paid that fare, the person to whom it is paid shall be liable to repay to that person the amount of that fare.

*Power to apply Schedule to certain other train services*

**9.** (1) This paragraph applies to any services for the carriage of passengers by railway which do not fall within paragraph 2(1) above but which—

(*a*) are provided wholly within Greater London; and

(*b*) are services, or services of a class or description, designated in an order made by the Secretary of State as services in relation to which this paragraph is to apply;

and in the following provisions of this paragraph any such services are referred to as "qualifying train services".

(2) The Mayor may, on the application of a person who provides qualifying train services, by order provide that this Schedule shall apply, from such date and with such modifications as may be specified in the order, to qualifying train services provided by that person.

(3) The power to make an order under sub-paragraph (2) above includes power, exercisable in the same manner and subject to the same conditions and limitations, to revoke, amend or re-enact any such order.

(4) Without prejudice to sub-paragraph (3) above, an order under sub-paragraph (2) above may specify circumstances in which the order shall cease to have effect before the expiry of any period specified in such an order.

(5) An order under sub-paragraph (2) above, and any order revoking, amending or re-enacting such an order, may contain such incidental, supplemental, consequential or transitional provision as may appear to the Mayor to be necessary or expedient.

(6) Where a person makes an application for an order under sub-paragraph (2) above, or for an order revoking, amending or re-enacting such an order, the Mayor may recover from that person payments in respect of the administrative costs reasonably incurred in connection with—

(*a*) the application, and

(*b*) if an order is made as a result of the application, the making of the order,

not exceeding £5,000 in the aggregate.

(7) The Mayor shall secure that any order under sub-paragraph (2) above, and any order revoking, amending or re-enacting any such order, is printed and published.

(8) A fee may be charged for the sale of an order printed and published under sub-paragraph (7) above.

(9) Where any services become qualifying services by virtue of an order under sub-paragraph (1)(*b*) above, any order which—

(*a*) is contained in a statutory instrument made by the Secretary of State,

(*b*) makes provision for or in connection with the imposition of penalty fares on passengers travelling on those services, and

(*c*) is in force immediately before this paragraph begins to apply to the services by virtue of the order under sub-paragraph (1)(*b*) above,

may, so far as relating to those services, be revoked under this paragraph as if it were an order under sub-paragraph (2) above.

(10) This paragraph applies in relation to a tramway as it applies in relation to a railway.

(11) In this paragraph "railway" and "tramway" have the meaning given by section 67(1) of the Transport and Works Act 1992.

*Appeals*

**10.** (1) If requested to do so by the Mayor, the Secretary of State shall by regulations make provision enabling a person required to pay a penalty fare to appeal against that requirement.

(2) Regulations under this paragraph may include provision—

(*a*) for appeals to be heard and determined by independent adjudicators,

(*b*) for the appointment of such adjudicators,

(*c*) for requiring Transport for London to reconsider, before an appeal is determined, whether the appellant should be required to pay the penalty fare, and

(*d*) for the adjudicator's directions in relation to an appeal to be binding upon Transport for London and the appellant.

**11.** *Repeal of London Regional Transport (Penalty Fares) Act 1992.*

## SCHEDULE 20

HACKNEY CARRIAGES — Section 253

*(Amended by the Statute Law (Repeals) Act 2004.)*

## PART I

## TRANSFERS OF FUNCTIONS AND AMENDMENTS

*The London Hackney Carriages Act 1843*[1]

7.7935 **1.** (1) All the jurisdiction, powers, authorities, privileges, interests and duties which, immediately before the coming into force of this paragraph, were vested in or exercisable by the Commissioners of Police of the Metropolis by virtue of section 2 of the London Hackney Carriages Act 1850 (transfer of functions of registrar of metropolitan public carriages to Commissioners of Police of the Metropolis) are transferred to and vested in Transport for London by this sub-paragraph.

(2) The London Hackney Carriages Act 1843 shall accordingly be amended as follows.

(3) For "the registrar" and "the said registrar", wherever occurring, there shall be substituted "Transport for London".

(4) In section 18 (licences and tickets to be delivered up on discontinuance of licence) for "him" there shall be substituted "Transport for London".

(5) In section 19 (new tickets to be delivered instead of defaced or lost tickets) for "for the use of Her Majesty" there shall be substituted "to Transport for London".

**2–8.** *Amendment of other enactments relating to Hackney carriages*[1]

---

[1] These amendments have been incorporated into the relevant enactments contained in this work.

## Part II

## Transitional Provisions

*Saving*

**9.** This Part of this Schedule is without prejudice to the provision that may be made under any power conferred on a Minister of the Crown by this Act to make subordinate legislation, within the meaning of the Interpretation Act 1978.

*The London Hackney Carriages Act 1843*

**10.** (1) Any licence to act as driver of hackney carriages—

(*a*) which was issued under section 8 of the London Hackney Carriages Act 1843 by or on behalf of the Commissioner of Police of the Metropolis, and

(*b*) which is in force immediately before the coming into force of paragraph 1 above,

shall have effect as from the coming into force of that paragraph as if it had been issued by Transport for London.

(2) Any metal ticket—

(*a*) which was issued under that section by or on behalf of the Commissioner of Police of the Metropolis, and

(*b*) which is in force immediately before the coming into force of paragraph 1 above,

shall have effect as from the coming into force of that paragraph as if it had been issued by Transport for London.

*The London Hackney Carriages Act 1850*

**11.** Any regulations made or other thing done under section 4 of the London Hackney Carriages Act 1850 by or on behalf of a Commissioner of Police of the Metropolis and in force or otherwise having effect immediately before the coming into force of paragraph 2 above shall have effect as from the coming into force of that paragraph as if made or done by or, in the case of a signature, by a person authorised for the purpose by, Transport for London.

*The London Hackney Carriage Act 1853*

**12.** Any notice given under section 2 of the London Hackney Carriage Act 1853 and having effect immediately before the coming into force of sub-paragraph (2) of paragraph 3 above shall have effect as from the coming into force of that sub-paragraph as a notice given by Transport for London.

**13.** Repealed.

*The Metropolitan Public Carriage Act 1869*

**14.** (1) Any order—

(*a*) made by or on behalf of the Secretary of State under or by virtue of any enactment contained in the Metropolitan Public Carriage Act 1869, and

(*b*) in force immediately before the coming into force of any provision of paragraph 7 above in relation to that enactment,

shall, to the extent that the provision made by the order could be made by Transport for London, have effect as from the coming into force of that provision in relation to that enactment as a London cab order, but with the substitution for references to the Secretary of State of references to Transport for London.

(2) Any licence granted under section 6 or 8 of that Act and in force immediately before the coming into force of sub-paragraph (3) or (5) of paragraph 5 above in relation to that section shall have effect as from the coming into force of that sub-paragraph in relation to that section as a licence granted under that section by Transport for London.

(3) Any suspension or revocation of a licence under section 6 or 8 of that Act having effect immediately before the coming into force of sub-paragraph (3) or (5) of paragraph 5 above shall have effect as from the coming into force of that sub-paragraph in relation to that section as the suspension or revocation of the licence by Transport for London.

(4) Any appointment made under section 12 of that Act by the Secretary of State and in force immediately before the coming into force of sub-paragraph (9) of paragraph 5 above shall have effect as from the coming into force of that sub-paragraph as an appointment made by Transport for London.

*The London Cab and Stage Carriage Act 1907*

**15.** (1) Any regulations made by the Secretary of State by order by virtue of section 1 of the London Cab and Stage Carriage Act 1907 and in force immediately before the coming into force of sub-paragraph (2) of paragraph 6 above shall have effect as from the coming into force of that paragraph as regulations made by London cab order by virtue of that section.

(2) Any sum for the time being allowed by the Secretary of State under subsection (1) of section 2 of that Act immediately before the coming into force of paragraph (*a*) of sub-paragraph (4) of paragraph 6 above shall have effect as from the coming into force of that paragraph as the sum for the time being allowed under that subsection by Transport for London until such time as Transport for London allow a different sum.

(3) Any order made by the Secretary of State under section 2 of that Act and in force immediately before the coming into force of paragraph (*b*) of sub-paragraph (4) of paragraph 6 above shall have effect as from the coming into force of that paragraph as a London cab order.

(4) Any approval given by or on behalf of the Secretary of State for the purposes of the definition of "taximeter" in section 6(1) of that Act and in force immediately before the coming into force of the amendment made by paragraph (*b*) of sub-paragraph (5) of paragraph 6 above shall have effect as from the coming into force of that amendment as an approval given by Transport for London.

*The London Cab Act 1968*

**16.** (1) Any order made by the Secretary of State under section 2 of the London Cab Act 1968 and in force immediately before the coming into force of paragraph (*a*) of sub-paragraph (4) of paragraph 7 above shall have effect as from the coming into force of that paragraph as a London cab order.

(2) Any order made by the Secretary of State under section 4A of that Act and in force immediately before the coming into force of paragraph (*a*) of sub-paragraph (5) of paragraph 7 above shall have effect as a London cab order as from the coming into force of that paragraph.

*The Transport Act 1985*

**17.** (1) Any scheme made under section 10 of the Transport Act 1985 by the Secretary of State and in force immediately before the coming into force of paragraph (*a*) of sub-paragraph (2) of paragraph 8 above shall have effect as from the coming into force of that paragraph as a scheme made by Transport for London.

(2) Any regulations prescribing a period for the purposes of a provision of that Act specified in paragraph (*a*) of sub-paragraph (3) of paragraph 8 above and in force immediately before the coming into force of that paragraph shall, until such time as a period is specified by London cab order for the purposes of that provision, continue in force and have effect as if the period so prescribed were the period specified for the purposes of that provision by London cab order.

# London Local Authorities Act 2000

(2000 c vii)

## Part I[1]
## Preliminary

7.7937 **1. Citation and commencement** (1) This Act may be cited as the London Local Authorities Act 2000 and except where otherwise provided shall come into force at the end of the period of two months beginning with the date on which it is passed.

(2) The London Local Authorities Acts 1990 to 1996 and this Act may together be cited as the London Local Authorities Acts 1990 to 2000.

[London Local Authorities Act 2000, s 1.]

[1] Part I contains ss 1–2.

7.7938 **2. Interpretation** In this Act, except as otherwise expressly provided or unless the context otherwise requires—

"functions" includes powers and duties;

"participating council" means the common council in its capacity as a local authority and the council of any London borough; and "borough", "City" and "council" shall be construed accordingly.

[London Local Authorities Act 2000, s 2 as amended by the London Local Authorities Act 2004, s 27 and Sch 5.]

## Part II[1]
## Parking

[1] Part II contains ss 3–16.

## Part III[1]
## Public Health

7.7939 **17. Interpretation of Part III** (1) In this Part of this Act—

"the Act of 1936" means the Public Health Act 1936[2];

"the Act of 1990" means the Environmental Protection Act 1990[2];

"cleansing notice" means a notice served under subsection (1) of section 19 (Cleansing relevant land of litter and refuse) of this Act;

"relevant land" means any street in the area of a participating council together with any land which is in the open air and is adjacent to such a street otherwise than land comprised in a highway but does not include—

(*a*) any land which a person has a duty to ensure is, so far as is practicable, kept clear of litter and refuse by virtue of section 89 of the Act of 1990; or

(*b*) any canal or inland navigation belonging to or under the control of the British Waterways Board, or any works, lands or premises belonging to or under the control of the British Waterways Board and held or used by them in connection with such canal or inland navigation;

"relevant premises" means—

(*a*) premises which front or abut on relevant land; and

(*b*) premises which are served by the relevant land as a means of access; and

(*c*) where any such premises as are mentioned in paragraph (*a*) above form part of a building in which other premises are situated, those other premises;

"street" has the same meaning as in section 343 (Interpretation) of the Act of 1936 but does not include a highway;

"waste control enactments" means—

(*a*) the following sections of the Act of 1990:—

(i) section 45 (Collection of controlled waste); and

(ii) section 46 (Receptacles for household waste); and

(iii) section 47 (Receptacles for commercial or industrial waste); and

(*b*) section 19 (Cleansing relevant land of litter and refuse) of this Act.

(2) The definitions in section 75 of the Act of 1990 shall apply for the purposes of this Part of this Act.

[London Local Authorities Act 2000, s 17.]

[1] Part III contains ss 17–21.

[2] In this Part, title Public Health, post.

7.7940 **18. Enforcement of waste control enactments** The following sections of the Control of Pollution Act 1974[1] shall have effect as if references therein to that Act included references to the waste control enactments—

(*a*) section 91 (Rights of entry and inspection, etc); and

(*b*) section 92 (Provisions supplementary to s 91).

[London Local Authorities Act 2000, s 18.]

---

[1] In this PART, title PUBLIC HEALTH, post.

7.7941 **19. Cleansing relevant land of litter and refuse** (1) A participating council may by notice specify the standards and frequency at which relevant land requires to be swept and cleansed so as to keep it reasonably clear of litter and refuse and shall serve a copy of such notice on the owner of the relevant land or the owner or occupier of any relevant premises.

(2) If, at any time after the expiration of 42 days from the service of the cleansing notice, the council determine that the relevant land is not being swept and cleansed in accordance with the notice then the council shall give notice of this determination to the person on whom the cleansing notice was served and may cause the relevant land to be swept and cleansed.

(3) At any time the council may decide to revoke any cleansing notice or any determination made under subsection (2) above and shall give notice of any such decision to the person who was served with the cleansing notice or the determination, as the case may be and may serve a fresh cleansing notice or make a fresh determination as the case may be.

(4) A person served with a cleansing notice or a notice under subsection (2) above may appeal to a magistrates' court on any of the following grounds which are appropriate in the circumstances of the particular case:—

(*a*) that the notice or requirement under the notice is not justified by the terms of this section;

(*b*) that there has been some informality, defect or error in, or in connection with, the notice;

(*c*) that the standards and frequency at which the sweeping and cleansing is to be carried out are unreasonable;

(*d*) that it would have been equitable for the notice to have been served on the occupier of the premises in question instead of on the owner, or on the owner instead of on the occupier;

(*e*) where the sweeping and cleansing is for the common benefit of the premises in question and other premises, that some other person, being the owner or occupier of premises to be benefited, ought to contribute towards the expenses of executing any works required.

(5) If and in so far as an appeal under this section is based on the ground of some informality, defect or error in or in connection with the notice, the court shall dismiss the appeal, if it is satisfied that the informality, defect or error was not a material one.

(6) Where the grounds upon which an appeal under this section is brought include a ground specified in paragraph (*d*) or paragraph (*e*) of subsection (4) above, the appellant shall serve a copy of his notice of appeal on each other person referred to, and in the case of any appeal under this section may serve a copy of his notice of appeal on any other person having an estate or interest in the premises in question, and on the hearing of the appeal the court may make such order as it thinks fit with respect to the person by whom any sweeping and cleansing is to be carried out and the contribution to be made by any other person towards the cost of the work, or as to the proportions in which any expenses which may become recoverable by the council are to be borne by the appellant and such other person.

In exercising its powers under this subsection, the court shall have regard—

(*a*) as between an owner and an occupier, to the terms and conditions whether contractual or statutory, of the tenancy and to the nature of the works required; and

(*b*) in any case, to the degree of benefit to be derived by the different persons concerned.

(7) Subject to such right of appeal as aforesaid, where the council causes land to be swept and cleansed under subsection (2) above, they may recover from the person on whom the cleansing notice was served the expenses reasonably incurred by them in so doing.

(8) In proceedings by the council for the recovery of any expenses under subsection (7) above, it shall not be open to the defendant to raise any question which he could have raised on an appeal under this section.

(9) Sections 275, 283(1), 285, 289 and 300 of the Act of 1936 shall apply to a cleansing notice.

(10) Sections 278, 283(1), 285, 291 and 300 of the Act of 1936 shall apply to a notice under subsection (2) above.

(11) The sections of the Act of 1936 mentioned in subsections (9) and (10) above shall apply to notices served under this section as if—

(*a*) references therein to that Act included references to this section; and

(*b*) references therein to the execution of works included references to the carrying out of sweeping and cleansing and cognate terms shall be construed accordingly.

(12) Section 291 of the Act of 1936 shall apply to notices served under subsection (2) above as if references to the owner of the premises in respect of which the expenses were incurred included references to the person on whom the cleansing notice was served.

[London Local Authorities Act 2000, s 19 as amended by SI 2005/886.]

**7.7942 20. Collection and disposal of waste** Where a cleansing notice is served in respect of relevant land—

(*a*) if the land is swept and cleansed in accordance with the notice any resulting litter or refuse left for removal shall be treated as commercial waste; and

(*b*) if the land is swept and cleansed by the council in pursuance of subsection (2) of section 19 (Cleansing relevant land of litter and refuse) of this Act any such litter or refuse shall be treated as household waste.

[London Local Authorities Act 2000, s 20.]

**7.7943 21. Offence of leaving litter** Section 87 of the Act of 1990 (which provides for an offence of leaving litter) shall apply to any relevant land in respect of which a cleansing notice has been served in so far as that land does not constitute a public open place for the purposes of the said section 87.

[London Local Authorities Act 2000, s 21.]

## PART IV[1]
## LICENSING

**7.7944 27–28. *Special Treatment Premises***

1 Part IV contains ss 27–31.

**7.7945 29. Near beer premises** (1) Part IV (Near Beer Licensing) of the London Local Authorities Act 1995 applies in the area of a participating council in accordance with the following subsections.

(2) In section 14 (Interpretation of Part IV)—

(*a*) in the definition of "near beer premises" paragraph (*a*) is replaced by the following paragraph:—

"(*a*) consists in or includes the sale to customers for consumption on the premises of refreshments; and"

(*b*) the definition of "occupier" is left out.

(3) In section 17 (Applications under Part IV)—

(*a*) in subsection (1) the words from the beginning to "and shall" are replaced by "An applicant for the grant, renewal or transfer of a near beer licence shall";

(*b*) in subsection (7)—

(i) at the beginning, the words "Subject to section 17A (Renewal and transfer of licence: supplementary) of this Act," are inserted;

(ii) the words "or transfer" and the words from "or as the case may require, to have effect with any necessary modifications" are left out;

(*c*) at the end the following subsections are inserted:—

"(8) Subject to section 17A (Renewal and transfer of licence: supplementary) of this Act, where, before the date of expiry of a near beer licence, an application has been made for the transfer of that licence, the licence shall be deemed to remain in force (with any necessary modifications) notwithstanding that the date of expiry of the licence has passed, until the determination of the application by the council or the withdrawal of the application.

(9) Where an applicant for the transfer of a near beer licence is carrying on the functions to which the licence relates, "any necessary modifications" where those words appear in subsection (8) above, means the substitution for the name of the licence holder of the name of the applicant for the transfer of the licence and any other necessary modifications.".

(4) After the said section 17, the following section is inserted:—

**"17A Renewal and transfer of licence: supplementary** (1) The following provisions of this section shall have effect as respects cases where, before the date of expiry of a licence an application for renewal of the licence has been made ("a renewal case") or an application for transfer of the licence has been made ("a transfer case").

(2) If the application is not determined before the prospective expiry date, the licence shall not be deemed to remain in force under subsection (7) or (8) of section 17 (Applications) of this Act, after that date and the application shall be deemed to be withdrawn on that date, unless before then the applicant pays the council a continuation fee.

(3) Where a continuation fee is paid in pursuance of subsection (2) above in a renewal case, the applicant's application for renewal shall be deemed to be an application for renewal for a period of twelve months starting on the day following the prospective expiry date.

(4) Where a continuation fee is paid in pursuance of subsection (2) above in a transfer case—

(*a*) the applicant shall be deemed to have made an application for the renewal of the licence for a period of twelve months starting on the day following the prospective expiry date;

(*b*) the Council shall determine the application for transfer and deemed application for renewal together; and

(*c*) in the following provisions of this section, references to "the application" in a transfer case are references to the application for transfer and the application for renewal.

(5) If the application is not determined before the date of the expiry of the renewal period under

subsection (3) or (4) above, as the case may be, the licence shall not be deemed to remain in force under subsection (7) or (8) of the said section 17, as the case may be, after that date, and the application shall be deemed to be withdrawn on that date, unless before then the applicant pays the council a further continuation fee.

(6) Where a further continuation fee is paid in pursuance of subsection (5) above then—

(*a*) in a renewal case, the applicant's application for renewal shall be deemed to be an application for renewal for a period starting on the day following the date of the expiry of the renewal period under subsection (3) above; and

(*b*) in a transfer case, the applicant's application so far as it is a deemed application for renewal shall be deemed to be an application for renewal for a period starting on the day following the date of the expiry of the renewal period under subsection (4) above.

(7) A deemed application for renewal under subsection (6) shall be for a period expiring—

(*a*) where the application is withdrawn, on the date of withdrawal;

(*b*) where the application is refused, on the date of the refusal;

(*c*) where the application is granted, on one or other of the following:—

(i) the date twelve months after the beginning of the period; or

(ii) such other date as may be specified by the Council when allowing the application.

(8) In this section—

"the prospective expiry date" means—

(*a*) in a transfer case, the date on which the licence would have expired if the application for transfer had not been made; and

(*b*) in a renewal case, the date of the expiry of the period in respect of which the application for renewal of the licence was made;

"a continuation fee" is a fee of the same amount as the fee payable in respect of an application for renewal of a licence.".

(5) In section 23 (Appeals under Part IV) at the beginning of subsection (5) the words "Subject to section 23A below" are inserted.

(6) After the said section 23, the following section is inserted:—

"**23A Appeals: supplementary provisions** (1) The following provisions of this section shall have effect as respects cases where an appeal under section 23 (Appeals under Part IV) of this Act is brought, within the period for doing so, against the revocation of a licence ("a revocation case") or against the refusal of an application for renewal of a licence ("a refusal case").

(2) If the appeal is not determined before the prospective expiry date, the licence shall not be deemed to remain in force under subsection (5) of the said section 23 after that date, and the appeal shall be deemed to be abandoned on that date, unless before then—

(*a*) in a revocation case, the appellant makes an application for the renewal of the licence for a period of twelve months starting on the day following the prospective expiry date;

(*b*) in a refusal case the appellant pays the council a continuation fee.

(3) Where a continuation fee is paid in pursuance of subsection (2)(*b*) above, the appellant's refused application for renewal shall be deemed to be an application for renewal for a period of twelve months starting on the day following the prospective expiry date.

(4) If the appeal is not determined before the date of the expiry of the renewal period under subsection (2)(*a*) or (3) above, as the case may be, the licence shall not be deemed to remain in force under subsection (5) of the said section 23 after that date, and the appeal shall be deemed to be abandoned on that date, unless before then the appellant pays the council a continuation fee or, as the case may be, a further continuation fee.

(5) Where a continuation fee or a further continuation fee is paid in pursuance of subsection (4) above, the appellant's application for renewal or, as the case may be, refused application for renewal shall be deemed to be an application for renewal for a period starting on the day following the date of the expiry of the renewal period under subsection (2)(*a*) above or, as the case may be, subsection (3) above.

(6) A deemed application for renewal under subsection (5) shall be for a period expiring—

(*a*) where the appeal is withdrawn, on the date of withdrawal;

(*b*) where the appeal is unsuccessful—

(i) if a further appeal is available but is not made within the period for doing so, on the date of the expiry of that period;

(ii) if no further appeal is available, on the date of the decision of the court;

(*c*) where the appeal is successful, on the day before the date of the next anniversary of the beginning of the period; provided that where the period, at the time of the decision of the court, has been running for more than twelve months, the court may specify an earlier date.

(7) In this section—

"the prospective expiry date" means—

(*a*) in a revocation case, the date on which the licence would have expired if it had not been revoked; and

(*b*) in a refusal case, the date of the expiry of the period in respect of which the refused application for renewal of the licence was made;

"a continuation fee" is a fee of the same amount as the fee payable in respect of an application for renewal of a licence.".

(7) In subsection (2) of section 24 (Enforcement under Part IV) after the words "holder of the licence" the words ", an applicant for the transfer of a near beer licence where he is carrying out the functions to which the licence relates" are inserted.

[London Local Authorities Act 2000, s 29.]

7.7946 **30. Door supervisors** In its application to the area of a participating council, section 29 (Interpretation of Part V) of the London Local Authorities Act 1995 is amended as follows—

(*a*) in paragraph (*c*) of the definition of "licensed premises" the words "or licensed" are left out;

(*b*) in the definition of "door supervisor"—

(i) before the words "to maintain order" the words "any person employed" are inserted; and

(ii) at the end the words "but, in respect of premises in respect of which there is in force for the time being a justices' on-licence within the meaning of section 1(2) of the Licensing Act 1964 does not include the holder of that licence" are inserted.

[London Local Authorities Act 2000, s 30.]

7.7947 **31. Fees in relation to distribution of free literature** Subsection (6) of section 4 (Distribution of free literature) of the London Local Authorities Act 1994 is amended in its application to the area of a participating council other than the City by the substitution of the words "in whole or in part the reasonable administrative or other costs in connection with their functions under this section" for the words "the expense of the borough council in dealing with applications for such consents".

[London Local Authorities Act 2000, s 31.]

## Part V[1]
## Licensing of Buskers

7.7948 **32. Interpretation of Part V** In this Part of this Act—

"busking" means the provision of entertainment in a street[2] but does not include the provision of entertainment—

(*a*) of a class which from time to time is by resolution of a participating council excluded from the operation of this Part of this Act;

(*b*) under and in accordance with a premises licence under Part 3 of the Licensing Act 2003, or a temporary event notice having effect under Part 5 of that Act, which authorises the provision of regulated entertainment (within paragraph 2(1)(*e*) to (*h*) or 3(2) of Schedule 1 to that Act (music and dancing));

(*c*) which is authorised specifically to take place in a street under any other enactment; or

(*d*) consisting of music performed as an incident of a religious meeting, procession or service;

and "busk" and "busks" shall be construed accordingly;

"licence" means a licence under section 35 (Power to license) of this Act and "licensed" shall be construed accordingly;

"street" includes—

(*a*) any street or way to which the public commonly have access, whether or not as of right;

(*b*) any place, not being within permanently enclosed premises, within 7 metres of any such street or way, to which the public commonly have access;

(*c*) any area in the open air to which the public commonly have access;

(*d*) any street, way or open area within any housing development provided or maintained by a local authority under Part II of the Housing Act 1985;

but does not include any land in respect of which there are byelaws in force which regulate the provision of entertainment and which are made by London Transport Executive or London Regional Transport.

[London Local Authorities Act 2000, s 32 as amended by the Licensing Act 2003, Sch 6.]

---

1 Part V contains ss 32–44.

2 Given the nature of street entertainment it is impossible to come up with an absolute definition; the art would evolve so any definition had to be sufficiently flexible to cover that development; while busking engages art 10 it is not the most important right of freedom of expression and limiting it to prevent obstruction of the highway or the creation of a nuisance is an acceptable interference with art 10 rights: *Keep Streets Alive Campaign Ltd v Camden LBC* [2014] EWHC 67 (Admin), [2014] BLGR 286.

7.7949 **33. Application of Part V** (1) This Part of this Act applies in the area of a participating council as from such day as may be fixed in relation to that council by resolution, and the council may apply this Part to all their area or to any part identified in the resolution and notice under this section.

(2) The council shall not pass a resolution under this section in respect of any part of their area unless they have reason to believe that there has been, is being or is likely to be caused, as a result of busking—

(*a*) undue interference with or inconvenience to or risk to safety of persons using a street in that part of their area or other streets within the vicinity of that street; or

(*b*) nuisance to the occupiers of property in or in the vicinity of a street in that part of their area.

(3) The council shall cause to be published in a local newspaper circulating in the borough or the City notice—

(*a*) of the passing of any such resolution and of a day fixed thereby; and

(*b*) of the general effect of the provisions of this Act coming into operation as from that day;

and the day so fixed shall not be earlier than the expiration of three months from the publication of the said notice.

(4) Either a photostatic or other reproduction certified by the officer appointed for that purpose by the council to be a true reproduction of a page or part of a page of any such newspaper bearing the date of its publication and containing any such notice shall be evidence of the publication of the notice, and of the date of publication.

[London Local Authorities Act 2000, s 33.]

7.7950 **34. Designation of licence streets** If a participating council consider that busking should be licensed in their area they may pass any of the following resolutions:—

(*a*) a resolution (in this Part of this Act referred to as a "designating resolution") designating any street or part of a street within the borough or the City as a "licence street";

(*b*) a resolution prescribing in relation to any licence street or any part of a licence street any hours during which busking may take place;

and may by subsequent resolution rescind or vary any such resolution.

[London Local Authorities Act 2000, s 34.]

7.7951 **35. Power to license** (1) The council may license an applicant for one or more days or such period as may be specified in the licence on such terms and conditions and subject to such restrictions as may be so specified.

(2) Without prejudice to the generality of subsection (1) above, such conditions may relate to—

(*a*) the area in which busking may take place;

(*b*) the hours during which busking may take place;

(*c*) the prevention of obstruction to persons using the street; or

(*d*) the prevention of nuisance to the occupiers of nearby property.

[London Local Authorities Act 2000, s 35.]

7.7952 **36. Applicants under Part V** (1) An applicant for the grant of a licence shall provide such information as the council may by regulation prescribe.

(2) Regulations under subsection (1) above may, inter alia, prescribe the procedure for determining applications.

(3) An applicant for a licence shall pay such fee determined by the council as may be sufficient to cover in whole or in part the reasonable administrative or other costs incurred in connection with their functions under this Part of this Act.

[London Local Authorities Act 2000, s 36.]

7.7953 **37. Refusal of licence** (1) The council may refuse to grant a licence on any of the following grounds:—

(*a*) that the applicant could be reasonably regarded as not being a fit and proper person to hold a licence;

(*b*) that there is not enough space in the street in respect of which the application is made for busking to take place without causing undue interference with, or inconvenience to, or risk to the safety of persons using the street, or other streets within the vicinity of the street;

(*c*) that there is a likelihood of nuisance being caused to the occupiers of premises in or in the vicinity of the street in respect of which the application is made.

(2) The council shall refuse to grant a licence in respect of an application which relates to any street other than a licence street.

[London Local Authorities Act 2000, s 37.]

7.7954 **38. Cancellation of licence** The council may, at the written request of the holder of a licence, cancel that licence.

[London Local Authorities Act 2000, s 38.]

7.7955 **39. Revocation of licence** The council may revoke a licence on any of the following grounds:—

(*a*) that there has been a breach of the conditions of the licence;

(*b*) that undue interference with, or inconvenience to, or risk to the safety of persons using the street, or other streets within the vicinity of the street, has been caused as a result of the busking;

(*c*) that nuisance has been caused as a result of the busking to occupiers of property in or in the vicinity of the street in respect of which the licence was granted.

[London Local Authorities Act 2000, s 39.]

**7.7956 40. Power to prescribe standard terms, conditions and restrictions under Part V**

(1) The council may make regulations prescribing standard conditions applicable to all licences.

(2) Where the council have made regulations under this section, every licence granted by them shall be deemed to have been so granted subject to the standard conditions except so far as they are expressly excluded or amended in any particular case.

(3) Without prejudice to the generality of subsection (1) above, the standard conditions applied shall include a condition requiring the licence holder to carry his licence with him when busking.

[London Local Authorities Act 2000, s 40.]

**7.7957 41. Appeals under Part V** (1) Any of the following persons, that is to say:—

(*a*) an applicant for the grant of a licence whose application is refused;

(*b*) a licence holder who is aggrieved by any term, condition or restriction on or subject to which the licence is held; or

(*c*) a licence holder whose licence has been revoked;

may at any time before the expiration of the period of 21 days beginning with the relevant date appeal to the magistrates' court acting for the area in which the licence street is situated by way of complaint for an order.

(2) In subsection (1) above "the relevant date" means either the date on which the person in question or his representative is informed in writing of the refusal of his application, the imposition of the terms, conditions or restrictions by which he is aggrieved or the revocation of his registration, as the case may be, or 7 days after the date when such notification was posted to him by first class pre-paid letter, whichever is the earlier.

(3) An appeal by either party against the decision of the magistrates' court under this section may be made to the Crown Court.

(4) On an appeal to the magistrates' court or to the Crown Court under this section the court may make such order as it thinks fit in relation to the matter which is the subject of the appeal and it shall be the duty of the council to give effect to such order.

[London Local Authorities Act 2000, s 41.]

**7.7958 42. Enforcement under Part V** Any person who—

(*a*) busks in any street to which this Part of this Act applies without the authority of a licence; or

(*b*) is concerned with the organisation or management of busking which is not authorised by a licence; or

(*c*) contravenes any condition of his licence; or

(*d*) in connection with his application for a licence makes a statement which he knows to be false in a material particular;

shall be guilty of an offence and shall be liable on summary conviction to a fine not exceeding level 3 on the standard scale.

[London Local Authorities Act 2000, s 42.]

**7.7959 43. Seizure under Part V** (1) An authorised officer or a constable who has reasonable cause to believe that busking is taking place or is about to take place without a licence or in breach of the terms and conditions of a licence or in a street which is not a licence street to which this Part of this Act applies may require that busking either cease or not take place.

(2) Subject to subsection (3) below if the busking continues or takes place despite the requirement under subsection (1) above the authorised officer or constable may seize and remove any apparatus or equipment used in connection with the busking which may be required to be used in evidence in respect of an offence under section 42 (Enforcement under Part V) of this Act.

(3) An authorised officer or constable shall not seize any apparatus or equipment in pursuance of the powers in subsection (2) above unless the person busking fails to produce, in pursuance of a request by the constable or authorised officer, a licence authorising the busking.

(4) Before exercising any power under this section, an authorised officer shall, if requested to do so by the person busking, produce his authority.

(5)

(*a*) The following provisions of this subsection shall have effect where any apparatus or equipment or any other thing is seized by an authorised officer under subsection (2) above and reference in those provisions to proceedings are to proceedings in respect of the alleged offence in relation to which the apparatus or equipment is seized.

(*b*) Subject to paragraph (*c*) below, after the conclusion of the proceedings, the apparatus or equipment shall be returned to the person from whom it was seized unless—

(i) the court orders it to be forfeited under any enactment;

(ii) any costs awarded to the council by the court, have not been paid within 28 days of the making of the order.

(*c*) Where after 28 days any costs awarded by the court to the council have not been paid to the council in full, the apparatus or equipment may be disposed of in any way the council thinks fit and any sum obtained by the council in excess of the costs awarded by the court shall be returned to the person to whom the apparatus or equipment belongs and when any apparatus or equipment is disposed of by the council under this subsection the council shall have a duty to secure the best possible price which can reasonably be obtained for that apparatus or equipment.

(*d*) If no proceedings are instituted before the expiration of a period of 28 days beginning with the date of seizure, or any proceedings instituted within that period are discontinued, at the expiration of that period or, as the case may be, on the discontinuance of the proceedings, the apparatus or equipment shall, subject to paragraph (*e*) below, be returned to the person from whom it was seized unless it has not proved possible, after diligent enquiry, to identify that person and ascertain his address.

(*e*) Where the apparatus or equipment is not returned because it has not proved possible to identify the person from whom it was seized and ascertain his address, the council (whether the article or thing was seized by an authorised officer or a constable) may apply to a magistrates' court for an order as to the manner in which it should be dealt with.

(6) In this section "authorised officer" includes a person employed by any contractor of the council with whom the council has contracted for the purposes of this section where that person has been authorised in writing by that contractor to act in relation to this section.

(7)

(*a*) This subsection shall have effect where apparatus or equipment is seized under subsection (2) above and either—

(i) not less than six months have passed since the date of the seizure and no information has been laid against any person for an offence under this section in respect of the act or circumstances which occasioned the seizure; or

(ii) proceedings for such an offence have been brought and either the person charged has been acquitted (whether or not on appeal) and the time for appealing against or challenging the acquittal (where applicable) has expired without an appeal or challenge being brought, or the proceedings (including any appeal) have been withdrawn by, or have failed for want of prosecution by, the person by whom the original proceedings were brought.

(*b*) When this subsection has effect a person who has or at the time of seizure had a legal interest in the apparatus or equipment seized may recover compensation from the council or (where it is seized by a constable) the Commissioner by civil action in the County Court in respect of any loss suffered by him as a result of the seizure.

(*c*) The court may only make an order for compensation under paragraph (*b*) above if satisfied that seizure was not lawful under subsection (2) above.

[London Local Authorities Act 2000, s 43.]

**44. *Resolutions under Part V***

### PART VI[1]
### MISCELLANEOUS

1 Part VI contains ss 45–52.

## London Local Authorities Act 2004
(2004 c i)

### PART 1
### PRELIMINARY

7.7960 **1. Citation and commencement** (1) This Act may be cited as the London Local Authorities Act 2004 and shall come into operation at the end of the period of two months beginning with the date on which it is passed.

(2) This Act and the London Local Authorities Acts 1990 to 2003 may be cited together as the London Local Authorities Acts 1990 to 2004.

[London Local Authorities Act 2004, s 1.]

7.7961 **2. Interpretation** In this Act—

"the 1978 Act" means the Refuse Disposal (Amenity) Act 1978 (c 3);

"borough council" means London borough council and includes the Common Council of the City of London in its capacity as a local authority and "borough" and "council" shall be construed accordingly;

"operational land" has the same meaning as in the Town and Country Planning Act 1990 (c 8).

[London Local Authorities Act 2004, s 2.]

### PART 2
### ABANDONED VEHICLES

7.7962 **4. Recovery of expenses connected with removed vehicles** Section 5 (Recovery of expenses connected with removed vehicles) of the 1978 Act shall have effect in the area of a borough council as if—

(*a*) for paragraphs (*a*) to (*c*) of subsection (1) there were substituted "charges in respect of the removal, storage and disposal of the vehicle"; and (*b*) after that subsection there were inserted—

"(1A) The level of charges made by the appropriate authority for the removal, storage and disposal of vehicles under this section shall be the same as the level of charges set by London authorities for the removal, storage and disposal of vehicles under section 74 (Fixing of certain parking and other charges for London) of the Road Traffic Act 1991.".

[London Local Authorities Act 2004, s 4.]

7.7963 **5. Meaning of "owner" under the 1978 Act** (1) Section 11 (Interpretation) of the 1978 Act shall have effect in the area of a borough council as if after subsection (2) the following subsection were inserted—

"(2A) References in this Part of this Act to the "owner" of a vehicle at a particular time are to the person by whom it was then kept and the registered keeper at a particular time shall be taken, unless the contrary is shown, to be the person by whom the vehicle was kept at that time.".

(2) In section 11 of the 1978 Act the definition of "owner" shall cease to have effect in the area of a borough council.

[London Local Authorities Act 2004, s 5.]

7.7964 **6. Powers of entry** (1) This section applies where a vehicle is to be or has been removed from a road by a borough council under section 3 (Removal of abandoned vehicles) of the 1978 Act.

(2) An authorised officer may, at any time before the vehicle is lawfully removed from the custody of the council or is disposed of by the council under section 4 (Disposal of abandoned vehicles) of the 1978 Act, enter the vehicle for the purpose of—

(*a*) removing anything from it in the interests of the safety of persons or property; or

(*b*) preventing damage to or loss of the vehicle or any of its contents.

(3) Subject to subsections (4) and (5) below, the council shall retain and keep safe anything removed under subsection (2) above and shall deliver it to any person claiming it who satisfies the council that he is the owner of it or of the vehicle in question.

(4) The council may, in such manner as they think fit and at any time, dispose of any perishable item removed under subsection (2) above.

(5) Where the vehicle from which anything is removed under subsection (2) above is disposed of under the said section 4 the council may—

(*a*) no sooner than the date on which the period of 14 days beginning with the date on which the vehicle was removed expires; and

(*b*) in any manner they think fit,

dispose of the thing removed if it has not been claimed by any person who satisfies the council that he is its owner.

(6) If any person, no later than the date on which the period of five months beginning with the date on which the vehicle was removed expires satisfies the council that they were, at the time the vehicle was removed, the owner of anything disposed of under subsection (4) or (5) above, the council shall pay to that person the proceeds (if any) obtained on the disposal of the thing.

[London Local Authorities Act 2004, s 6.]

7.7965 **7. Disclosure of information** (1) Any person who, apart from this section, would not have power to disclose information obtained in identifying the owner of a vehicle under section 4 (Disposal of abandoned vehicles) of the 1978 Act (in the application of that section in the area of a borough council) to—

(*a*) a borough council;

(*b*) Transport for London; or

(*c*) a person acting on behalf of a borough council or Transport for London,

shall have power to do so in any case where the disclosure is necessary for the purposes of enforcing any provision of the enactments specified in subsection (2) below.

(2) The enactments are—

(*a*) sections 3 to 5 (Abandoned vehicles) of the 1978 Act;

(*b*) Part II (Traffic in London) of the Road Traffic Act 1991 (c 40);

(*c*) Part II (Bus lanes) of the London Local Authorities Act 1996 (c ix); and

(*d*) sections 4 (Penalty charges for road traffic contraventions) and 5 (Contraventions of lorry ban order: supplementary) of the London Local Authorities and Transport for London Act 2003 (c iii).

[London Local Authorities Act 2004, s 7.]

## Part 3

## Public Health and the Environment

7.7966 **9. Nuisance from birds** (1) If in the opinion of a borough council the habitual nesting, roosting or alighting of birds on any part of a building or structure (including a bridge) fronting upon, crossing or overhanging a highway in the area of the council is a source of nuisance to pedestrians using that highway, the council may serve a notice under this section upon the owner or occupier of the building or structure.

This subsection is subject to the provisions of the Wildlife and Countryside Act 1981 (c 69) and to subsection (4) below.

(2) If after reasonable enquiry the council have been unable to ascertain the name and address

of the owner or occupier, they may affix a notice to the building or structure.

(3) A notice under this section is a notice requiring, within such reasonable time (not being less than 28 days) as may be specified in the notice, the owner or occupier of the building or structure to take measures for the purpose of preventing or minimising the habitual nesting, roosting or alighting of birds on the part of the building or structure concerned and the council may specify such measures in the notice.

(4) The measures which may be specified in a notice under this section may include the erection of baffles, nets or wires or the laying of gel on the building or structure or other measures of a like nature but shall not include any method prohibited by the said Act of 1981.

(5) The sections of the Public Health Act 1936 (c 49) mentioned in Schedule 1 to this Act shall have effect as if references therein to that Act included references to this section.

(6) This section shall have effect as if it were an Act or order to which section 42 of the Local Government (Miscellaneous Provisions) Act 1976 (c 57) (which makes provision for certain local Acts and orders to be subject to the planning enactments) applies.

(7) Subsections (8) to (10) below apply where a borough council serve a notice under this section on—

(*a*) the British Railways Board, in respect of any bridge owned by the Board; or

(*b*) any protected party in respect of its operational land,

and the notice specifies measures to be taken for the purpose mentioned in subsection (3) above.

(8) The party on whom a notice under this section is served may, within a period of 28 days beginning with the day on which the notice is served, serve a counter-notice on the borough council specifying alternative measures which will in their reasonable opinion have the effect of preventing or minimising the habitual nesting, roosting or alighting of birds on the part of the building or structure concerned to the same or greater extent than the measures specified in the notice.

(9) Where a counter-notice is served under subsection (8) above, the notice served under subsection (1) above shall be deemed to specify the alternative measures specified in the counter-notice and shall be deemed to have been served on the date the counter-notice was served.

(10) Where a counter-notice is served under subsection (8) above and, before the expiry of the period of 28 days beginning with the date on which the counter-notice is served, the council serves a further notice requiring further measures to be taken, the protected party shall comply with the further notice within such period as may be specified in the further notice.

(11) The measures specified in any such further notice shall complement the measures specified in the counter-notice to which it relates.

(12) The period within which—

(*a*) an owner or occupier must comply with the requirements of a notice served under subsection (1) above; or

(*b*) a protected party must comply with the requirements of—

(i) a counter-notice served under subsection (8) above; or

(ii) a further notice under subsection (10) above,

may be extended with the agreement of the council.

(13) In this section "protected party" means—

(*a*) Network Rail Infrastructure Limited;

(*b*) Transport for London;

(*c*) the British Waterways Board;

(*d*) the Port of London Authority,

and their subsidiaries (within the meaning given by section 1159 of the Companies Act 2006), servants, agents and contractors.

[London Local Authorities Act 2004, s 9 as amended by SI 2009/1941.]

7.7967 **10. Dangerous structures and demolitions** (1) Section 81(1)(*b*) (Local Authority's power to serve notice about demolition) of the Act of 1984 shall have effect in the area of a borough council as if—

(*a*) for the reference to an order made under section 77 (Dangerous building) of the Act of 1984 there were substituted a reference to an order made under section 64 (Proceedings to enforce compliance with notice) of the Act of 1939; and

(*b*) for the reference to a notice given under section 79 (Ruinous and dilapidated buildings and neglected sites) of the Act of 1984 there were substituted a reference to an order under section 69 (Removal of dilapidated and neglected structures) of the Act of 1939.

(2) Section 45 of the London Local Authorities Act 2000 (c vii) is amended as follows—

(*a*) in subsection (4), after "dangerous buildings)" the words ", section 78 (Dangerous building – emergency measures)" are inserted;

(*b*) in subsection (5), the figures "77 to 80, 82, 83" are replaced by the figures "77 to 79"; and

(*c*) in subsection (6), in the definition of "the London Building Acts", the words "as amended" to the end are omitted.

(3) A borough council may recover from a person on whom a notice is served under section 81 of the Act of 1984 any expenses reasonably incurred by them under that section, in addition to any

expenses recoverable under section 99 of that Act.

(4) Sections 107 to 110 of the Act of 1984 shall apply in respect of expenses recoverable under subsection (3) above as they apply in respect of expenses to which those sections apply.

(5) In its application under subsection (4) above, for the reference in the said section 107 to the person who is the owner of the premises at the date on which the works were completed there shall be substituted a reference to the person on whom the notice under the said section 81 was served.

(6) In this section—

"the Act of 1939" means the London Building Acts (Amendment) Act 1939 (c xcvii);

"the Act of 1984" means the Building Act 1984 (c 55).

[London Local Authorities Act 2004, s 10.]

7.7968 **22. Soliciting for custom** (1) Subject to the following provisions of this section, it is an offence in the area of a borough council to solicit persons, or to permit the soliciting of persons, to attend premises—

(*a*) if the impression is given, by the soliciting, that licensable activities, within the meaning of section 1 of the Licensing Act 2003 (c 17), are carried on or from the premises;

(*b*) which are a sex establishment within the meaning of Schedule 3 to the Local Government (Miscellaneous Provisions) Act 1982 (c 30) (if that Schedule has effect in the borough).

(2) A person guilty of an offence under this section shall be liable on summary conviction to a fine not exceeding level 4 on the standard scale.

(2A) It shall be a defence in any proceedings for an offence under subsection (1)(*a*) if the premises concerned were licensed under Part 3 of the Licensing Act 2003 (c 17) at the time of the alleged offence.

(2B) It shall be a defence in any proceedings for an offence under subsection (1)(*b*) if, at the time of the alleged offence—

(*a*) the premises concerned were subject to a licence for a sexual entertainment venue under Schedule 3 to the Local Government (Miscellaneous Provisions) Act 1982,

(*b*) a waiver under paragraph 7 of that Schedule from the requirement for such a licence was in force, or

(*c*) article 6(1) of the Policing and Crime Act 2009 (Commencement No 1 and Transitional and Saving Provisions) (England) Order 2010 applied to the premises.

(3) This section shall not apply in respect of the operational land of a person authorised by any enactment to carry on any railway, light railway or tramway undertaking.

(4) *Repealed.*

[London Local Authorities Act 2004, s 22 as amended by the London Local Authorities Act 2007, s 72 and SI 2010/723.]

7.7969 **26. Provision of information to authorised officer** (1) This section applies where an authorised officer of a borough council has reasonable grounds for suspecting that any offence in respect of which the council may prosecute legal proceedings has been committed or attempted, or is being committed or attempted.

(2) If, on being requested by the authorised officer to furnish his name and address for service of a summons or fixed penalty notice, the relevant person

(*a*) fails to furnish a name; or

(*b*) furnishes a false name; or

(*c*) furnishes a false address,

the relevant person shall, unless the authorised officer failed to produce his authorisation on making the request, be guilty of an offence punishable on summary conviction by a fine not exceeding level 5 on the standard scale.

(3) In this section "the relevant person" means any person whom the authorised officer has reasonable grounds to suspect of having committed or having attempted to commit the offence or being in the course of committing or attempting to commit it.

(4) In this section "authorised officer" includes any person who is authorised in writing by a borough council to enforce any enactment which gives rise to a criminal offence.
No such person shall require any further authorisation under this Act for the purposes of this section.

[London Local Authorities Act 2004, s 26 as amended by the London Local Authorities Act 2007.]

## PART 6
## SUPPLEMENTAL

7.7970 **28. Authorised officers** (1) In this Act "authorised officer", in relation to a borough council, means—

(*a*) any employee of the council;

(*b*) any person by whom, in pursuance of arrangements made with the council, any functions under this Act fall to be discharged; or

(*c*) any employee of any such person,

who is authorised in writing by the council to act in relation to the relevant provision of this Act.

(2) In each of the scheduled Acts "authorised officer", in relation to a borough council, shall have the same meaning as in subsection (1) above save that—

(*a*) the reference to the relevant provision of this Act shall include a reference to the relevant provision of the Act as so mentioned; and

(*b*) where appropriate, the reference to the participating council includes a reference to the borough council under the Act so mentioned.

(3) The Environmental Protection Act 1990 (c 43) shall have effect in the area of a borough council as if—

(*a*) in subsection (10) of section 88, for the definition of "authorised officer" there were substituted the following definition—

""authorised officer" means—

(*a*) any employee of the litter authority;

(*b*) any person by whom, in pursuance of arrangements made with the litter authority, any functions under this Act fall to be discharged; or

(*c*) any employee of any such person,

who is authorised in writing by the litter authority to act in relation to the relevant provision of this Act.".

(4) The definition of "authorised officer" in section 2 of each of the scheduled Acts is hereby repealed.

(5) In this section the "scheduled Acts" means the Acts specified in Schedule 5 to this Act.

[London Local Authorities Act 2004, s 28.]

7.7971 **29. Obstruction of authorised officer** Any person who intentionally obstructs any authorised officer acting in the exercise of his powers under this Act shall be guilty of an offence and liable on summary conviction to a fine not exceeding level 3 the standard scale.

[London Local Authorities Act 2004, s 29.]

7.7972 **30. Defence of due diligence** (1) In proceedings for an offence under this Act it shall be a defence for the person charged to prove that he took all reasonable precautions and exercised all due diligence to avoid the commission of the offence.

(2) If in any case the defence provided under subsection (1) above involves the allegation that the commission of the offence was due to the act or default of another person, the person charged shall not, without leave of the court, be entitled to rely on that defence unless, no later than 7 clear days before the hearing, he has served on the prosecutor a notice in writing giving such information as was then in his possession identifying or assisting in the identification of that other person.

[London Local Authorities Act 2004, s 30.]

7.7973 **31. Liability of directors, etc** (1) Where an offence under this Act committed by a body corporate is proved to have been committed with the consent or connivance of, or to be attributable to any neglect on the part of, a director, manager, secretary or other similar officer of the body corporate or any person who was purporting to act in any such capacity, he, as well as the body corporate, shall be guilty of the offence.

(2) Where the affairs of the body corporate are managed by its members, subsection (1) above shall apply to the acts and defaults of a member in connection with his functions of management as if he were a director of the body corporate.

[London Local Authorities Act 2004, s 31.]

7.7974 **32. Regulations**

SCHEDULE 1

Sections of Public Health Act 1936 (c 49) Applied to Section 9 (Nuisance from Birds) of this Act

Section 9

7.7975

| *Section* | *Marginal Note* |
|---|---|
| 275 | Power of local authority to execute certain works on behalf of owners and occupiers. |
| 278 | Power of local authority to execute certain works on behalf of owners and occupiers. |
| 283(1) | Power of local authority to execute certain works on behalf of owners and occupiers. |
| 285 | Service of notices, etc. |
| 287 | Power to enter premises. |
| 289 | Power to require occupier to permit works to be executed by owner. |
| 290 | Provisions as to appeals against, and enforcement of, notices requiring execution of works. |
| 291 | Certain expenses recoverable from owners to be a charge on the premises: power to order payment by instalments. |
| 297 | Continuing offences and penalties. |
| 300 | Appeals and applications to courts of summary jurisdiction. |
| 341 | Power to apply provisions of Act to Crown property. |

SCHEDULE 5

Enactments in which Definition of Authorised Officer is Repealed — Section 28

**7.7976** The London Local Authorities Act 1990 (c vii)
The London Local Authorities Act 1991 (c xiii)
The London Local Authorities Act 1994 (c xii)
The London Local Authorities Act 1995 (c x)
The City of Westminster Act 1996 (c vii)
The London Local Authorities Act 1996 (c ix)
The City of Westminster Act 1999 (c i)
The London Local Authorities Act 2000 (c vii)

# London Olympic Games and Paralympic Games Act 2006[1]

(2006 c 12)

*Advertising*

**19–20.** Regulations[2] to be made by the Secretary of State about advertising in the vicinity of London Olympic events.

[1] This Act is to be brought into force in accordance with the provisions of s 40, post.

[2] The London Olympic Games and Paralympic Games (Advertising and Trading) (England) Regulations 2011, SI 2011/2898 and the London Olympic Games and Paralympic Games (Advertising and Trading) (Wales) Regulations 2012, SI 2012/60 have been made.

**7.7977 21. Offence** (1) A person commits an offence if he contravenes regulations under section 19.

(2) It shall be a defence for a person charged with an offence under subsection (1) to prove that the contravention of the regulations occurred—

(*a*) without his knowledge, or

(*b*) despite his taking all reasonable steps to prevent it from occurring or (where he became aware of it after its commencement) from continuing.

(3) A person guilty of an offence under subsection (1) shall be liable—

(*a*) on conviction on indictment, to a fine, or

(*b*) on summary conviction, to a fine not exceeding £20,000.

(4) *Repealed.*

[London Olympic Games and Paralympic Games Act 2006, s 21 as amended by the Police Reform and Social Responsibility Act 2011, Sch 16 and the London Olympic Games and Paralympic Games (Amendment) Act 2011, s 1.]

**7.7978 22. Enforcement: power of entry** (1) A constable officer may—

(*a*) enter land or premises on which they reasonably believe a contravention of regulations under section 19 is occurring (whether by reason of advertising on that land or premises or by the use of that land or premises to cause an advertisement to appear elsewhere);

(*b*) remove, destroy, conceal or erase any infringing article;

(*c*) when entering land under paragraph (*a*), be accompanied by one or more persons for the purpose of taking action under paragraph (*b*);

(*d*) use, or authorise the use of, reasonable force for the purpose of taking action under this subsection.

(2) The power to enter land or premises may be exercised only at a time that a constable thinks reasonable having regard to the nature and circumstances of the contravention of regulations under section 19.

(3) Before entering land or premises a constable must take reasonable steps to—

(*a*) establish the identity of an owner, occupier or person responsible for the management of the land or premises or of any infringing article on the land or premises, and

(*b*) give any owner, occupier or responsible person identified under paragraph (*a*) such opportunity as seems reasonable to the constable in the circumstances of the case to end the contravention of the regulations (whether by removing, destroying or concealing any infringing article or otherwise).

(4) The power to enter premises may be exercised in relation to a dwelling only in accordance with a warrant issued by a justice of the peace; and a justice of the peace may issue a warrant only if satisfied on the application of a constablethat—

(*a*) there are reasonable grounds to believe a contravention of regulations under section 19 is occurring in the dwelling or on land that can reasonably be entered only through the dwelling,

(*b*) the constable has complied with subsection (3),

(*c*) the constable has taken reasonable steps to give notice to persons likely to be interested of his intention to apply for a warrant, and

(*d*) that it is reasonable in the circumstances of the case to issue a warrant.

(5) The power to remove an article may be exercised only if the constable thinks it necessary for the purpose of—

(*a*) ending the contravention of regulations under section 19,

(*b*) preventing a future contravention of the regulations, or (*c*) enabling the article to be used as evidence in proceedings for an offence under section 21.

(*d*) *repealed.*

(6) *Repealed.*

(7) Having exercised a power under this section a constable—

(*a*) shall take reasonable steps to leave the land or premises secure, and

(*b*) shall comply with any provision of regulations under section 19 about informing specified persons of what the constable has done.

(8) Regulations under section 19 shall include provision enabling a person whose property is damaged in the course of the exercise or purported exercise of a power under this section (other than a person responsible for a contravention of the regulations or for the management of an infringing article) to obtain compensation from a local policing body or a police authority; and the regulations may, in particular, include provision—

(*a*) conferring jurisdiction on a court or tribunal;

(*b*) about appeals.

(9) A local policing body or a police authority may recover from a person responsible for the contravention of the regulations, as if it were a debt, the reasonable costs of taking action under this section.

(10) In this section—

"infringing article" means—

(*a*) an advertisement which contravenes regulations under section 19, and

(*b*) any other thing, or an animal that constitutes a contravention of regulations under section 19 or is being used in connection with a contravention of the regulations.

[London Olympic Games and Paralympic Games Act 2006, s 22 as amended by the Police Reform and Social Responsibility Act 2011, Sch 16, the London Olympic Games and Paralympic Games (Amendment) Act 2011, s 1 and SI 2014/3184.]

**25–26.** Regulations to be made by the Secretary of State or the Paymaster General about trading in the vicinity of London Olympic events.

7.7980 **27. Offence** (1) A person commits an offence if he contravenes regulations under section 25.

(2) A person guilty of an offence under subsection (1) shall be liable—

(*a*) on conviction on indictment, to a fine, or

(*b*) on summary conviction, to a fine not exceeding £20,000.

[London Olympic Games and Paralympic Games Act 2006, s 27.]

7.7981 **28. Enforcement: power of entry** (1) A constable may—

(*a*) enter land or premises on which they reasonably believe a contravention of regulations under section 25 is occurring;

(*b*) remove any infringing article;

(*c*) when entering land under paragraph (*a*), be accompanied by one or more persons for the purpose of taking action under paragraph (*b*);

(*d*) use, or authorise the use of, reasonable force for the purpose of taking action under this subsection.

(2) The power to remove an article may be exercised only if the constable thinks it necessary for the purpose of—

(*a*) ending the contravention of regulations under section 25,

(*b*) preventing a future contravention of the regulations, or

(*c*) enabling the article to be used as evidence in proceedings for an offence under section 27

(*d*) *repealed.*

(3) *Repealed.*

(4) *Repealed.*

(5) Having exercised a power under this section a constable—

(*a*) shall take reasonable steps to leave the land or premises secure, and

(*b*) shall comply with any provision of regulations under section 25 about informing specified persons of what the constable has done.

(6) Regulations[1] under section 25 shall include provision enabling a person whose property is damaged in the course of the exercise or purported exercise of a power under this section (other than a person responsible for a contravention of the regulations) to obtain compensation from a local policing body or a police authority; and the regulations may, in particular, include provision—

(*a*) conferring jurisdiction on a court or tribunal;

(*b*) about appeals.

(7) A local policing body or a police authority may recover from a person responsible for the contravention of regulations under section 25, as if it were a debt, the reasonable costs of taking action under this section.

(8) In this section—

"infringing article" means—

(*a*) an article or animal that is being offered for trade in contravention of regulations under section 25 or is otherwise being used in connection with a contravention of the regulations, and

(*b*) anything (other than a vehicle) containing an article or animal to which paragraph (*a*) applies.

[London Olympic Games and Paralympic Games Act 2006, s 28 as amended by the Police Reform and Social Responsibility Act 2011, Sch 16, the London Olympic Games and Paralympic Games (Amendment) Act 2011, s 1 and SI 2014/3184.]

---

[1] See the London Olympic Games and Paralympic Games (Advertising and Trading) (England) Regulations 2011, SI 2011/2898 and the London Olympic Games and Paralympic Games (Advertising and Trading) (Wales) Regulations 2012, SI 2012/60.

7.7983 **31. Sale of tickets** (1) A person commits an offence if he sells an Olympic ticket—

(*a*) in a public place or in the course of a business, and

(*b*) otherwise than in accordance with a written authorisation issued by the London Organising Committee.

(2) For the purposes of subsection (1)—

(*a*) "Olympic ticket" means anything which is or purports to be a ticket for one or more London Olympic events,

(*b*) a reference to selling a ticket includes a reference to—

(i) offering to sell a ticket,

(ii) exposing a ticket for sale,

(iii) advertising that a ticket is available for purchase, and

(iv) giving, or offering to give, a ticket to a person who pays or agrees to pay for some other goods or services, and

(*c*) a person shall (without prejudice to the generality of subsection (1)(*a*)) be treated as acting in the course of a business if he does anything as a result of which he makes a profit or aims to make a profit.

(3) A person does not commit an offence under subsection (1) by advertising that a ticket is available for purchase if—

(*a*) the sale of the ticket if purchased would be in the course of a business only by reason of subsection (2)(*c*), and

(*b*) the person does not know, and could not reasonably be expected to discover, that subsection (2)(*c*) would apply to the sale.

(4) A person does not commit an offence under subsection (1) (whether actual or inchoate) only by virtue of making facilities available in connection with electronic communication or the storage of electronic data.

(5) Where a person who provides services for electronic communication or for the storage of electronic data discovers that they are being used in connection with the commission of an offence under subsection (1), the defence in subsection (4) does not apply in respect of continued provision of the services after the shortest time reasonably required to withdraw them.

(6) A person guilty of an offence under subsection (1) shall be liable on summary conviction to a fine not exceeding £20,000.

(7) Section 32(2)(*b*) of the Police and Criminal Evidence Act 1984 (c 60) (power to search premises) shall, in its application to the offence under subsection (1) above, permit the searching of a vehicle which a constable reasonably thinks was used in connection with the offence.

(8) Subsection (9) applies where a person in Scotland is arrested in connection with the commission of an offence under subsection (1).

(9) For the purposes of recovering evidence relating to the offence, a constable in Scotland may without warrant enter and search—

(*a*) premises in which the person was when arrested or immediately before he was arrested, and

(*b*) a vehicle which the constable reasonably believes is being used or was used in connection with the offence.

(10) Subsection (9) is without prejudice to any power of entry or search which is otherwise exercisable by a constable in Scotland.

(11) The London Organising Committee shall make arrangements for the grant of authorisations under subsection (1)(*b*); and the arrangements may, in particular—

(*a*) make provision about charges;

(*b*) enable the Committee to exercise unfettered discretion.

(12) In this section a reference to a London Olympic event includes a reference to an event held by way of a pre-Olympic event in accordance with arrangements made by the London Organising Committee in pursuance of paragraph 7 of the Bye-Law to Rule 49 of the Olympic Charter.

[London Olympic Games and Paralympic Games Act 2006, s 31 as amended by the London Olympic Games and Paralympic Games (Amendment) Act 2011, s 3.]

*Miscellaneous*

7.7984 **40. Commencement and duration** (1) The following provisions of this Act shall come into force on Royal Assent—

(a) section 1,
(b) sections 3 to 5 and Schedule 1,
(c) section 32 and paragraphs 1 to 11 of Schedule 3,
(d) section 33 and Schedule 4,
(e) sections 34 and 35(1) and (2),
(f) section 36(3)(a) and (d),
(g) section 37, and
(h) section 38.

(2) The other preceding provisions of this Act (including paragraphs 12 to 14 of Schedule 3) shall come into force in accordance with provision made by order[1] of the Secretary of State or the Paymaster General.

(3) But the following provisions of this Act, so far as they extend to Scotland, shall come into force in accordance with provision made by order of the Scottish Ministers—
(a) sections 19 to 31, and
(b) section 39(2) and (3).

(4) An order under subsection (2) or (3)—
(a) may make provision generally or only for specified purposes,
(b) may make different provision for different purposes,
(c) may include transitional or incidental provision, and
(d) shall be made by statutory instrument.

(5) Despite subsection (1)(c), for the purposes of criminal proceedings under a provision of the Olympic Symbol etc (Protection) Act 1995 (c 32) in respect of anything done before the end of the period of two months beginning with the date on which this Act receives Royal Assent, no account shall be taken of any amendment made of that Act by Schedule 3 to this Act.

(6) Sections 10 to 18 (including any power to make orders or give directions) shall cease to have effect at the end of the London Olympics period.

(7) Paragraph 14 of Schedule 3, which inserts new sections 12A and 12B into the Olympic Symbol etc (Protection) Act 1995, shall have effect in relation to things arriving in the United Kingdom during the period—
(a) beginning with the day specified under subsection (2) above for the commencement of paragraph 14 of Schedule 3, and
(b) ending with 31st December 2012.

(8) Section 33 and Schedule 4 shall cease to have effect at the end of 31st December 2012.

(9) In respect of section 36(3)—
(a) paragraph (a) shall have effect in relation to compulsory purchase orders made on or after 1st October 2005,
(b) an order bringing paragraph (b) into force on a date ("the commencement date")—
(i) may provide for paragraph (b) to have effect in relation to purchases (whether compulsory or voluntary) completed before, on or after the commencement date, but
(ii) must include provision modifying section 295 of the Housing Act 1985 in its application by virtue of section 36(3)(b) so that extinguishment of rights and easements takes effect, in the case of a purchase completed before the commencement date, on the commencement date,
(c) an order bringing paragraph (c) into force on a date ("the commencement date")—
(i) may provide for paragraph (c) to have effect in relation to purchases (whether compulsory or voluntary) completed on or after 1st October 2005, but
(ii) shall not affect the lawfulness of anything done before the commencement date, and
(d) paragraph (d) shall be treated as having taken effect on 1st October 2005.

[London Olympic Games and Paralympic Games Act 2006, s 40 as amended by SI 2007/2129.]

---

[1] The following commencement orders has been made: (No 1) SI 2006/1118 which brought into force on 30 May 2006 ss 2, 6 to 12, 17 to 31, 35(3) to (5), 36(1), (2), (3)(b) and (c), (4) and (5), 39(2) and (3) and Sch 2; (No 2) SI 2007/1064 on 2 April 2007, Sch 2 paras 12, 13 (Part), 14; (No 3) SI 2009/2577 ss 13–16 (5 October 2009).

**7.7984A 41. Extent and application**

**7.7984B 42. Short title**

# London Local Authorities Act 2007

(2007 c ii)

## Part 1

### Preliminary

7.7985 1. **Citation and commencement** (1) This Act may be cited as the London Local Authorities Act 2007.

(2) This Act and the London Local Authorities Acts 1990 to 2004 may be cited together as the

London Local Authorities Acts 1990 to 2007.

(3) This Act, except—

(*a*) subsections (2) to (7) of section 33 (hostess bars) (as it applies otherwise than as regards the City of Westminster),

(*b*) section 73 (charges for pipe subways), and

(*c*) section 75 (mail forwarding businesses),

shall come into operation at the end of the period of two months beginning with the date on which it is passed.

(4) Subsections (2) to (7) of the said section 33 shall come into operation in accordance with subsection (1) of that section.

(5) Section 73 and section 75 of this Act shall come into operation on the appointed day.

[London Local Authorities Act 2007, s 1.]

7.7986 **2. General interpretation** In this Act, except where the context otherwise requires—

"authorised officer", in relation to a borough council, means—

(*a*) any employee of the council;

(*b*) any other person by whom, in pursuance of arrangements made with the council, any functions under this Act fall to be discharged; or

(*c*) any employee of any such person,

who is authorised in writing by the council to act in relation to the relevant provision of this Act;

"borough council" means London borough council and includes the Common Council of the City of London in its capacity as a local authority and "borough" and "council" shall be construed accordingly.

[London Local Authorities Act 2007, s 2.]

## PART 2
## PUBLIC HEALTH AND THE ENVIRONMENT

*Interpretation*

7.7987 **4. Interpretation of Part 2** In this Part of this Act—

"the 1978 Act" means the Refuse Disposal (Amenity) Act 1978 (c 3);

"the 1990 Act" means the Environmental Protection Act 1990 (c 43);

"an advertising offence" means an offence—

(*a*) under section 132 of the Highways Act 1980 (c 66) (unauthorised marks on highways);

(*b*) under section 224(3) of the Planning Act (enforcement of control as to advertisements);

(*c*) under subsection (4) of section 5 (portable advertisements, etc) of this Act; or

(*d*) of aiding, abetting, counselling or procuring the commission of an offence mentioned in paragraphs (*a*) to (*c*) above,

committed after the day on which section 13 (advertising: seizure) of this Act comes into effect;

"fly posting offence" means an offence—

(*a*) under section 224(3) of the Planning Act;

(*b*) committed in Greater London by a person who is deemed to display an advertisement for the purposes of that subsection by virtue of section 224(4)(*b*) of the Planning Act; and

(*c*) which relates to an advertisement affixed to any surface without the authorisation of the owner of that surface;

"the Planning Act" means the Town and Country Planning Act 1990 (c 8);

"the Police Commissioner" means the Commissioner of Police of the Metropolis or, in the City of London, the Commissioner of Police for the City of London;

"relevant object" means—

(*a*) any advertisement (whether displayed or not);

(*b*) any vehicle (including its fuel); or

(*c*) any equipment or materials which may be used for the purpose of fixing advertisements to surfaces or placing advertisements on surfaces;

"shroud advertisement" means an advertisement—

(*a*) which is made of a flexible material;

(*b*) which is not affixed to any hoarding or similar structure used, or designed or adapted for use, for the display of advertisements; and

(*c*) which is attached to a building or to scaffolding;

"shroud advertisement offence" means an offence—

(*a*) under section 224(3) of the Planning Act;

(*b*) committed in Greater London by a person who is deemed to display an advertisement for the purposes of that subsection by virtue of section 224(3)(*b*) of the Planning Act; and

(*c*) which is committed in respect of the display of a shroud advertisement.

[London Local Authorities Act 2007, s 4.]

*Advertising*

7.7988 5. **Portable advertisements, etc** (1) No portable advertisement may be displayed within a designated area, except in accordance with subsection (2) below.

(2) The display of an advertisement—

(*a*) for which express consent has been given; or

(*b*) for which deemed consent has been given,

is in accordance with this subsection.(3)

(3) Subsection (1) above is without prejudice to any prohibition or restriction on the display of a portable advertisement contained in advertising regulations or any other enactment or rule of law relating to the display of advertisements.

(4) Any person who—

(*a*) displays a portable advertisement in contravention of subsection (1) above; or

(*b*) causes or permits any person so to do,

shall be guilty of an offence and liable on summary conviction to a fine not exceeding level 4 on the standard scale.

(5) Without prejudice to the generality of subsection (4) above, a person shall be deemed to display a portable advertisement for the purposes of that subsection if the advertisement gives publicity to his goods, trade, business or other concerns.

(6) A person shall not be guilty of an offence under subsection (4) above by reason only of his goods, trade, business or other concerns being given publicity by the portable advertisement if he proves any of the matters specified in subsection (7) below.

(7) The matters are—

(*a*) that the portable advertisement was displayed without his knowledge; or

(*b*) that he took all reasonable steps and exercised all due diligence to prevent the display; or

(*c*) that the advertisement was displayed on an item used wholly or mainly for purposes other than advertising.

(8) The reference in subsection (4) above to a person who displays a portable advertisement in contravention of subsection (1) above shall be deemed to include a reference to a person who displays a portable advertisement on or from land within 7 metres of any street or way designated under subsection (1)(*c*) of section 6 (advertisements: designation of areas) of this Act and who is not—

(*a*) the owner of that land;

(*b*) the person liable to be assessed to the uniform business rate in respect of that land; or

(*c*) on that land with the consent in writing of either of the persons mentioned in paragraphs (*a*) and (*b*) above.

(9) In any proceedings for an offence under this section, it shall be presumed, unless the contrary is shown, that the area in which the alleged offence took place was designated in accordance with the said section 6.

(10) In this section—

"advertising regulations" means regulations made under section 220 of the Planning Act (regulations controlling display of advertisements);

"designated area" means an area designated in accordance with the said section 6; the

"display" of an advertisement means (subject to subsection (11) below) the display of the advertisement in the course of a business by means of an individual or individuals holding or carrying it or otherwise having control of it in person at the place where it is located;

"express consent" and "deemed consent" mean express consent and deemed consent for the purposes of any advertising regulations;

"portable advertisement" means any thing which is capable of being held or carried and which is an advertisement as defined in section 336(1) of the Planning Act but as if for "wholly or partly" there were substituted "wholly or mainly".

(11) A portable advertisement shall, for the purposes of this section, be deemed to be displayed as a portable advertisement notwithstanding that it is placed upon, leant against or attached to apparatus, street furniture or any other structure or object situated—

(*a*) in a designated area; or

(*b*) on any land within 7 metres of any street or way designated under subsection (1)(*c*) of the said section 6.

[London Local Authorities Act 2007, s 5.]

7.7989 6. **Advertisements: designation of areas** (1) A borough council may designate, in accordance with the following provisions of this section, areas comprising any of the following places or any part of such places in the borough as designated areas to which this section applies—

(*a*) a public off-street car park;

(*b*) a recreation ground, garden, park, pleasure ground or open place under the management or control of a borough council;

(*c*) a street or way to which the public commonly have access, whether or not as of right.

(2) The council shall exercise their powers under this section only in the interests of amenity and public safety, taking account of any material factors, and in particular—

(*a*) in the case of amenity—

(i) the general characteristics of the locality, including the presence of any features of historic, architectural, cultural or similar interest;

(ii) the desirability of preserving or enhancing the character or appearance of a conservation area, where appropriate,

disregarding, if they think fit, any advertisement being displayed there;

(*b*) in the case of public safety—

(i) the safety of any person who may use any road, railway, dock, harbour or aerodrome;

(ii) whether any display of advertisements is likely to obscure, or hinder the ready interpretation of, any road traffic sign, railway signal or aid to navigation by water or air.

(3) Before designating any area under this section, the council shall publish, or cause to be published, in at least one newspaper circulating in the locality, and on the same or a subsequent date in the London Gazette, a notice that such a proposal has been made, naming a place or places in the locality where a map or maps defining the area concerned may be inspected at all reasonable hours.

(4) Any notice under subsection (3) above shall state that any objection to the proposal may be made to the proper officer of the borough council in writing within such period (not being less than 21 days from the date when the notice was published) as is specified in the notice.

(5) The council shall not designate an area under this section until after the expiry of the specified period.

(6) In determining whether to designate an area under this section, the council—

(*a*) shall take into account any objections made in accordance with subsection (4) above;

(*b*) may modify the proposal if—

(i) they have notified, in writing, any person who has made an objection or representation to them of their intention and their reasons for it and has given them a reasonable opportunity to respond; and

(ii) the intended modification does not extend the area of land specified in the proposal.

(7) Where the council designates an area under this section, they shall notify any person who has made an objection in accordance with subsection (4) above.

(8) Notice of the designation of a particular area shall be published by the council in at least one newspaper circulating in the locality and on the same or a subsequent date in the London Gazette, and such notice shall—

(*a*) contain a full statement of the effect of the designation;

(*b*) name a place or places in the locality where a copy of the designation and of a map defining the area concerned may be seen at all reasonable hours; and

(*c*) specify a date when the designation shall come into force, being at least 14 and not more than 28 days after the publication of the notice in the London Gazette.

(9) A designation shall come into force on the date specified in the notice given under subsection (8) above.

(10) In this section, "conservation area" means a conservation area designated under section 69 of the Planning (Listed Buildings and Conservation Areas) Act 1990 (c 9) (designation of conservation areas).

[London Local Authorities Act 2007, s 6.]

7.7990 **8. Automatic minimum fine on third conviction for fly posting or shroud advertisement offence** (1) Where a person is convicted of a fly posting or shroud advertisement offence committed in Greater London, the court by which he is convicted shall, if the circumstances specified in subsection (4) below are present, impose a fine, the level of which shall be a minimum of level 4 on the standard scale and a maximum of £20,000.

(2) Subsection (1) above shall not apply where the court is of the opinion that there are particular circumstances which—

(*a*) relate to any of the offences or to the offender; and

(*b*) would make it unjust to do so in all the circumstances.

(3) Section 224(3) of the Planning Act, insofar as it makes provision for the punishment of offenders, shall not apply where subsection (1) above applies.

(4) The circumstances mentioned in subsection (1) above are that, during the five years ending with the date of the conviction, the person has been convicted of, in total, no fewer than three fly posting or shroud advertisement offences, providing that the conditions in subsections (5), (6) and (7) below are satisfied.

(5) The first condition is that the first of the three convictions was in respect of an offence which was committed after the date on which this section came into force.

(6) The second condition is that the second of the three convictions was in respect of an offence which was committed after the date of the first conviction.

(7) The third condition is that the third of the three convictions was in respect of an offence which was committed after the date of the second conviction.

(8) The Powers of Criminal Courts (Sentencing) Act 2000 (c 6) shall apply in Greater London as if in section 112(1)(*a*) (appeals where previous convictions set aside), after "or 111 above" the words "or under section 8(1) of the London Local Authorities Act 2007 (c ii) (automatic minimum fine on third conviction for fly posting or shroud advertisement offence)" were inserted.

[London Local Authorities Act 2007, s 8.]

7.7991 **9. Certificates of conviction for purposes of section 8** (1) Where—

(*a*) on any date after section 8 (automatic minimum fine on third conviction for fly posting or shroud advertisement offence) of this Act came into force a person is convicted of a fly posting or shroud advertisement offence; and

(*b*) the court by or before which he is so convicted states in open court that he has been convicted of such an offence on that date; and

(*c*) that court subsequently certifies that fact,

the certificate shall be evidence, for the purposes of the said section 8, that he was convicted of such an offence on that date.

(2) Where—

(*a*) on any date after the said section 8 came into force a person is convicted of a fly posting or shroud advertisement offence; and

(*b*) the court by or before which he is so convicted states in open court that the offence was committed on a particular day or over, or at some time during, a particular period; and

(*c*) that court subsequently certifies that fact,

the certificate shall be evidence, for the purposes of the said section 8, that the offence was committed on that day or over, or at some time during, that period.

[London Local Authorities Act 2007, s 9.]

7.7992 **10. Determination of day when offence committed** Where an offence is found to have been committed over a period of two or more days, or at some time during a period of two or more days, it shall be taken for the purposes of section 8 (automatic minimum fine on third conviction for fly posting or shroud advertisement offence) of this Act to have been committed on the last of those days.

[London Local Authorities Act 2007, s 10.]

*Advertising: seizure and forfeiture*

7.7993 **13. Advertising: seizure** (1) If an authorised officer or a constable has reasonable grounds for suspecting that a person has committed an advertising offence in Greater London and the conditions of subsection (2) below apply, the authorised officer or constable may seize any relevant object if the relevant object is in the possession of or under the control of that person at the time of the alleged offence.

(2) The conditions are that the relevant object—

(*a*) may be required to be used in evidence in any proceedings in respect of the suspected offence; or

(*b*) may be the subject of forfeiture under section 16 (forfeiture of seized items) of this Act.

(3) An authorised officer shall produce his authority if required to do so by the person having possession or control of any relevant object seized in pursuance of the powers in subsection (1) above.

(4) An authorised officer or a constable shall, forthwith after seizing any relevant object under subsection (1) above, give to the person from whom the object was seized a certificate containing the following information—

(*a*) the name and address of the person who the authorised officer or constable suspects has committed the suspected offence;

(*b*) if different from the name and address of the person mentioned in paragraph (*a*) above, the name and address of the owner of the relevant object;

(*c*) the type of object seized (including, in the case of a vehicle, its make and registration mark); and

(*d*) information about subsection (2) of the said section 16.

(5) If an authorised officer or constable—

(*a*) is unable, after reasonable inquiry of the person who he suspects has committed the suspected offence, to ascertain the name or address of—

(i) that person; or

(ii) the owner of the relevant object; or

(*b*) has reasonable cause to suspect that a name or address provided to him is incorrect,

he need not comply with paragraph (*a*) or (*b*), as the case may be, of subsection (4) above.

(6) The owner of a vehicle for the purposes of this section, shall be taken to be the person by whom the vehicle is kept.

(7) In determining, for the purposes of this section, who was the owner of a vehicle at any time, it shall be presumed that the owner was the person in whose name the vehicle was at that time registered under the Vehicle Excise and Registration Act 1994 (c 22).

[London Local Authorities Act 2007, s 13.]

7.7994 **14. Return and disposal of seized items** (1) The following provisions of this section shall have effect where any relevant object is seized under subsection (1) of section 13 (advertising: seizure) of this Act and references in those provisions to proceedings are to proceedings in respect of the alleged offence in relation to which the relevant object is seized.

(2) Subject to subsections (3) to (6) below, following the conclusion of the proceedings the relevant object shall be returned to the person from whom it was seized unless—

(*a*) the court orders it to be forfeited under section 16 (forfeiture of seized items) of this Act; or

(*b*) any award of costs to the council by the court, which may include removal, return and storage costs, have not been paid within 28 days of the making of the order.

(3) If—

(*a*) at the end of the period of 56 days beginning with the date of seizure—

(i) no proceedings have been instituted; or

(ii) any proceedings instituted within that period have been discontinued; or

(*b*) at any time after the end of that period any such proceedings are discontinued,

the relevant object shall, at the appropriate time, be returned to the person from whom it was seized unless it has not proved possible, after diligent enquiry, to identify that person and ascertain his address.

(4) In subsection (3) above, "the appropriate time" means—

(*a*) in the case of paragraph (*a*), the end of the period of 56 days mentioned in that paragraph;

(*b*) in the case of paragraph (*b*), the time when proceedings are discontinued.

(5) Where the relevant object is not returned because it has not proved possible to identify the person from whom it was seized and ascertain his address or because the person from whom it was seized or the owner has disclaimed or refused to accept it—

(*a*) a magistrates' court may make an order as to the manner in which it should be dealt with (in the case where proceedings for an offence under this section have been commenced in relation to the article or thing); or

(*b*) the council or the Police Commissioner may make a complaint to the magistrates' court for a disposal order under section 15 (disposal orders) of this Act (whether or not such proceedings have been commenced).

(6) Where after 28 days any costs awarded by the court to the council have not been paid to the council in full—

(*a*) the relevant object may be disposed of in any way the council thinks fit; and

(*b*) any sum obtained by the council in excess of the costs awarded by the court shall be returned to the person to whom the relevant object belongs.

(7) When any relevant object is disposed of by the council under subsection (6) above the council shall have a duty to secure the best possible price which can reasonably be obtained for it.

[London Local Authorities Act 2007, s 14.]

**7.7995 15. Disposal orders** (1) This section applies in respect of a complaint made by a borough council or the Police Commissioner for a disposal order in respect of a relevant object under subsection (5) of section 14 (return and disposal of seized items) of this Act.

(2) In the case of a relevant object which the council or the Police Commissioner has attempted to return to the person who the council believes is the person from whom it was seized or is its owner, and that person disclaimed or refused to accept it, a copy of the complaint shall be served on that person.

(3) In respect of a complaint to which this section applies, a magistrates' court may, if it is satisfied that the council or the Police Commissioner has made reasonable efforts to identify the person from whom the relevant object was seized or its owner, as the case may be, or has made reasonable efforts to return the relevant object it may make an order authorising the complainant council or the Police Commissioner—

(*a*) to dispose of the relevant object in question; and

(*b*) after payment out of any proceeds arising from the disposal of the expenses incurred in the seizure, storage and disposal, to retain the balance, if any.

(4) In the case where a copy of a complaint has been served under subsection (2) above, if the relevant object in question is not of sufficient value to defray the expenses of seizing and storing it, the magistrates' court may order that the recipient of the copy of the complaint pay the expenses, or the balance of the expenses, reasonably incurred by the council or the Police Commissioner in seizing and storing it, if it is satisfied that the recipient was the owner of the relevant object in question or was the person from whom it was seized, as the case may be.

(5) For the purposes of this section, "owner" in respect of a vehicle, has the same meaning as it has for the purposes of section 13 (advertising: seizure) of this Act.

[London Local Authorities Act 2007, s 15.]

**7.7996 16. Forfeiture of seized items** (1) Subject to subsection (2) below, the court by or before which a person is convicted of an advertising offence may order any relevant object which the court is satisfied relates to the offence to be forfeited and dealt with in such a manner as the court may order.

(2) The court shall not order a relevant object to be forfeited under subsection (1) above where a person claiming to be the owner of or otherwise interested in it applies to be heard by the court, unless an opportunity has been given to the owner or person interested in the object to show cause

why the order should not be made.

(3) In considering whether to make an order under subsection (1) above a court shall have regard—

(*a*) to the value of the object; and

(*b*) to the likely financial and other effects on—

(i) the offender; or

(ii) the owner of the object,

of the making of the order (taken together with any other order that the court contemplates making).

[London Local Authorities Act 2007, s 16.]

7.7997 **17. Compensation where seizure unlawful** (1) Subsection (2) below shall have effect where—

(*a*) any relevant object is seized under subsection (1) of section 13 (advertising: seizure) of this Act; and

(*b*) any of the following applies—

(i) not less than six months have passed since the date of the seizure and no information has been laid against any person for an advertising offence in respect of the act or circumstances which occasioned the seizure;

(ii) proceedings for an advertising offence have been brought and the person charged has been acquitted (whether or not on appeal) and the time for appealing against or challenging the acquittal (where applicable) has expired without an appeal or challenge being brought;

(iii) proceedings for an advertising offence have been brought and the proceedings (including any appeal) have been withdrawn by, or have failed for want of prosecution by, the person by whom the original proceedings were brought.

(2) Where this subsection has effect a person who has or at the time of seizure had a legal interest in the object seized may recover compensation from the council or (where it is seized by a constable) the Police Commissioner by civil action in the county court in respect of any loss suffered by him as a result of the seizure.

(3) The court may only make an order for compensation under subsection (2) above if satisfied that seizure was not lawful under the said section 13.

[London Local Authorities Act 2007, s 17.]

7.7998 **26. Civic amenity sites** (1) A borough council may require proof from a person depositing, intending to deposit or attempting to deposit refuse or waste at an amenity site that the person is resident in the area of the council or in the area of an adjoining local authority (such proof to be in such reasonable form as the council may specify).

(2) Any person who fails to prove to the council's reasonable satisfaction that he is resident in an area in accordance with a requirement under subsection (1) above may be the subject of a requirement under subsection (4) below.

(3) If a council—

(*a*) are satisfied that a person is depositing, intending to deposit or attempting to deposit at an amenity site refuse which is refuse falling to be disposed of in the course of a business; or

(*b*) are satisfied that refuse or waste is being or has been deposited at an amenity site in contravention of any requirements made by them relating to the receptacles to be used for the deposit of refuse or waste,

the person depositing, intending to deposit or attempting to deposit the refuse or waste may be the subject of a requirement under subsection (4) below.

(4) A requirement under this subsection is a requirement—

(*a*) not to enter the site;

(*b*) not to deposit waste or refuse at the site;

(*c*) to discontinue depositing waste or refuse at the site; or

(*d*) to retrieve any waste or refuse which has been deposited at the site and—

(i) remove it from the site; or

(ii) (in the case of waste or refuse which was placed in an incorrect receptacle) either place it in the correct receptacle or remove it from the site.

(5) Any person who without reasonable excuse fails to comply with a requirement under subsection (4) above shall be guilty of an offence and liable on summary conviction—

(*a*) in the case of an offence arising from an alleged failure to comply with a requirement under the said subsection (4) which was made as a result of the relevant authority being satisfied under subsection (3)(*b*) above, to a fine not exceeding level 1 on the standard scale;

(*b*) in any other case to a fine not exceeding level 3 on the standard scale.

(6) Any person who, in response to a requirement to show proof in accordance with subsection (1) above gives information which is false in a material particular and does so recklessly or knowing it to be false in that particular, shall be guilty of an offence and liable on summary conviction to a fine not exceeding level 5 on the standard scale.

(7) In any proceedings for an offence under subsection (5) above, it shall be a defence—

(*a*) (in the case of an alleged failure to comply with a requirement under subsection (4) above which was made as a result of the council not being satisfied under subsection (2) above), that the council's requirements relating to the proof required by them were not made clear by the provision of signs at or near to the entrance to the amenity site;

(*b*) (in the case of an alleged failure to comply with a requirement under subsection (4) above which was made as a result of the relevant authority being satisfied under subsection (3)(*b*)), that the council's requirements relating to the receptacles to be used for the deposit of refuse or waste were not made clear by the provision of signs at the amenity site.

(8) This subsection applies where a council have reasonable cause to believe that an offence under this section has been committed in their area by a person (in this section referred to as the "person responsible") who was—

(*a*) the driver of a vehicle in the amenity site;

(*b*) in charge of a vehicle in the amenity site;

(*c*) otherwise brought to the amenity site in a vehicle.

(9) Where subsection (8) above applies, the council may by notice in writing, specifying the offence and the provision of this section to which the notice relates, require—

(*a*) the registered keeper of the vehicle to give them such information as they may require as to the identity of the person responsible;

(*b*) any other person to give them any information which it is in that person's power to give and which may lead to the identification of the person responsible.

(10) A person shall be guilty of an offence if he fails to comply with a requirement of a notice under subsection (9) above or knowingly or recklessly gives false information in relation to the notice.

(11) In any proceedings for failing to comply with such a requirement brought against the registered keeper of the vehicle it shall be a defence if he shows to the satisfaction of the court that he did not know and could not with reasonable diligence have ascertained who was the person responsible.

(12) A person guilty of an offence under subsection (10) above shall be liable on summary conviction to a fine not exceeding level 3 on the standard scale.

(13) Where on summary trial of an information for an offence referred to in subsection (10) above—

(*a*) it is proved to the satisfaction of the court, on oath or in manner prescribed by rules made under section 144 of the Magistrates' Courts Act 1980 (c 43), that a requirement under subsection (9) above to give information as to the identity of the person responsible on the particular occasion to which the information relates has been served on the accused; and

(*b*) a written statement that the accused was the person responsible on that occasion is produced to the court; and

(*c*) the statement purports to be signed by the accused,

the court may accept that statement as evidence that the accused was the person responsible.

(14) In this section—

(*a*) an "amenity site" means a place provided by a council in compliance with a duty to provide places where refuse may be deposited, by virtue of section 1 of the 1978 Act;

(*b*) "local authority" means a borough council, a district council, or (in the case of a county in which there are no district councils) a county council;

(*c*) "registered keeper" in respect of a vehicle at any time means the person in whose name the vehicle was at that time registered under the Vehicle Excise and Registration Act 1994 (c 22).

[London Local Authorities Act 2007, s 26.]

*Abandoned and nuisance vehicles*

7.7999 **28. Disposal of removed vehicles** (1) Section 4 (disposal of abandoned vehicles) of the 1978 Act shall have effect in the area of a borough council in accordance with this section.

(2) For subsection (5), there is substituted—

"(5) The local authority shall permit a person to remove a vehicle from their custody before it is disposed of by the local authority in pursuance of this section, if that person—

(*a*) satisfies the authority that—
 (i) he is its owner; and
 (ii) either of subsections (5A) or (5B) below applies; and
 (iii) he is insured to drive the vehicle; and

(*b*) gives a bond in the prescribed sum to the authority in the case—
 (i) where no current licence is displayed on the vehicle; or
 (ii) where no test certificate is shown to the authority, in the case where section 47 of the Road Traffic Act 1988 (c 52) (obligatory test certificates) applies to the vehicle; and

(*c*) pays to the authority such sums in respect of its removal and storage as may be prescribed.

(5A) This subsection applies if the person in question has not been offered the opportunity to pay a fixed penalty under section 2A above.

(5B) This subsection applies if the person in question has been offered the opportunity to pay a fixed penalty under section 2A above and—

(*a*) he has paid it; or

(*b*) he has not paid it and the period mentioned in section 2A(2)(*a*) above has not expired; or

(*c*) he has not paid it and the period within which proceedings may be instituted for the offence in question has expired and no such proceedings have been issued;

(*d*) he has not paid it and proceedings for the offence have been instituted but not determined.

(5C) A bond under subsection (5)(*b*) above shall be repaid by the authority to the person who gave it once the authority is satisfied that a current licence has been obtained and can be displayed on the vehicle, or a test certificate has been issued in respect of the vehicle, as the case may be.

(5D) In subsection (5)(*b*) "prescribed sum" means such sum as may be prescribed by a joint committee established under section 101(5) of the Local Government Act 1972 (c 70) and consisting of at least one representative from each London borough council.".

[London Local Authorities Act 2007, s 28.]

*Enforcement action zones*

**7.8000 29–31.** A borough council (or two or more borough councils acting jointly) may designate an area of land in which, in their opinion, it is expedient that enhanced environmental crime enforcement action should be enabled. Schedule 2 makes provision for offences.

## Part 3
## Licensing

### Chapter 1
### Hostess Bars and Near Beer Premises

**7.8001 33. Hostess bars** (1) This section shall come into operation—

(*a*) at the end of the period of two months beginning with the date on which this Act is passed, as regards the City of Westminster;

(*b*) as from the appointed day as regards any other borough, where the borough council have resolved under section 2 of the Local Government (Miscellaneous Provisions) Act 1982 or paragraph 2(2) of Schedule 3 to the Policing and Crime Act 2009 that Schedule 3 to the Act of 1982 as amended by section 27 of the Act of 2009 is to apply to their area.

(2) The said Schedule 3 shall apply in the area of the borough as follows.

(3) In paragraph 2, after the words "sex cinema" the words ", a hostess bar" are inserted.

(4) *Repealed.*

(5) After paragraph 3, the following paragraph is inserted—

*"Meaning of "hostess bar"*

**3B** (1) Subject to sub-paragraph (2) below, in this Schedule "hostess bar" means—

(*a*) any premises used for a business which consists, whether in whole or in part, of the offering, expressly or by implication, whether on payment of a fee or not, of the provision of companions for customers on the premises; or

(*b*) any premises in respect of which any impression, by whatever means, is given to customers, or potential customers, that a performance, entertainment, service, exhibition or other experience of a sexual nature is available on the said premises; or

(*c*) any premises in respect of which any impression, by whatever means, is given to customers, or potential customers, that alcoholic refreshments are available on the said premises despite the premises not being the subject of a premises licence or a club certificate under the 2003 Act.

(2) The following premises are not hostess bars for the purposes of this paragraph, namely—

(*a*) premises in which the sale to customers for consumption of alcohol is not a licensable activity under or by virtue of the 2003 Act;

(*b*) premises in respect of which there is in force—

(i) a licence granted by the council under section 21 (licensing of public exhibitions, etc) of the Greater London Council (General Powers) Act 1966 (c xxviii);

(ii) a premises licence granted under Part 3 of the 2003 Act;

(iii) a club premises certificate granted under Part 4 of the 2003 Act;

(iv) a temporary event notice given under the 2003 Act, by virtue of which the premises may be used for the supply of alcohol (within the meaning of section 14 of that Act);

(v) a licence under Part II of the Gaming Act 1968 (c 65),

(3) Sub-paragraph (2)(*b*) applies—

(*a*) only during the hours permitted by the licence or notice there mentioned, and
(*b*) only if provided that the premises are in use wholly or mainly and bona fide for the purpose authorised by the licence, notice or certificate.

(4) In sub-paragraph (1) above, "premises" includes any vehicle, vessel or stall.

(5) In this paragraph, "the 2003 Act" means the Licensing Act 2003 (c 17).".

(6) In paragraphs 13(2)(*a*) and (*b*) after the words "sex cinemas" there shall be inserted the words ", hostess bars".

(7) *Repealed.*

[London Local Authorities Act 2007, s 33 as amended by SI 2010/723.]

**7.8002 34. Application to existing premises** (1) This section applies to premises falling within paragraph 3B of Schedule 3 to the Local Government (Miscellaneous Provisions) Act 1982 (c 30), inserted by section 33 (hostess bars) of this Act, which exist on the date on which that section comes into force in the borough in which they are situated.

(2) Until the period of four weeks commencing with that date has expired, paragraph 6(1) of that Schedule shall not apply to those premises by reason that they fall within the said paragraph 3B.

(3) If an application for a licence under that Schedule is made in respect of those premises during that period, they may lawfully continue to be used for the purposes mentioned in the said paragraph 3B until the determination or withdrawal of that application, and if an appeal is lodged until the determination or abandonment of the appeal.

[London Local Authorities Act 2007, s 34.]

**7.8003 35. Near beer premises** On the day that section 33 (hostess bars) of this Act comes into force in a borough, Part IV (near beer premises) of the London Local Authorities Act 1995 (c x) shall cease to have effect as respects that borough.

[London Local Authorities Act 2007, s 35.]

## Chapter 2
## Street Trading
### *Introductory*

**7.8004 36. Interpretation of Chapter 2** In this Chapter—

"the Act of 1990" means the London Local Authorities Act 1990 (c vii);

"the Act of 1999" means the City of Westminster Act 1999 (c i).

[London Local Authorities Act 2007, s 36.]

### *Street trading on certain bridges*

**7.8005 37. Bridges in the City of Westminster and London Borough of Lambeth**

(1) The city council and the borough council may enter into agreements to secure that—
(*a*) Part III (street trading) of the Act of 1990; or
(*b*) the Act of 1999,
shall apply as respects the whole or part of any relevant bridge.

(2) If an agreement is made under subsection (1) above, the Act of 1999 or Part III of the Act of 1990, as the case may be, shall apply to the part of the relevant bridge in question as though it was within the area of the city or, as the case may be, the borough.

(3) Without prejudice to the generality of subsection (2) above, proceedings in relation to an alleged offence of unlicensed street trading on a relevant bridge shall be commenced in the magistrates' court for the relevant petty sessions area.

(4) Either council may rescind any agreement under subsection (1) above by giving three months' written notice to the other.

(5) Where, immediately before the date on which an agreement under this section comes into effect or is rescinded (the "relevant date")—
(*a*) a street trading licence is held under Part III of the Act of 1990 or the Act of 1999, as the case may be, in respect of an area which is the subject of the agreement;
(*b*) any proceedings in respect of an offence under Part III of the Act of 1990 or under the Act of 1999, as the case may be, had been commenced; and
(*c*) by that agreement—
(i) the Act of 1999 applies to the area instead of Part III of the Act of 1990; or
(ii) Part III of the Act of 1990 applies to the area instead of the Act of 1999,
subsection (6) or (7) below shall apply, as appropriate.

(6) In the circumstances mentioned in subsection (5)(*a*) above, the licence in question shall continue in force subject to the same conditions as though it had been issued under whichever of Part III of the Act of 1990 or the Act of 1999 applies after the relevant date.

(7) In the circumstances mentioned in subsection (5)(*b*) above, the proceedings in question shall continue until their conclusion under whichever of Part III of the Act of 1990 or the Act of 1999 applied before the relevant date, notwithstanding that Part III of the Act of 1990 or the Act of 1999 no longer applies to the part of the bridge in question.

(8) In this section—

"the borough" means the borough of Lambeth and "borough council" shall be construed accordingly;

"the city" means the City of Westminster and "city council" shall be construed accordingly;

"relevant bridge" means—

(*a*) Westminster Bridge, the Hungerford Footbridges, Lambeth Bridge and Vauxhall Bridge; and

(*b*) any other bridge carrying a street across the river Thames constructed after the date on which this Act was passed, if part of the bridge is in the city and part in the borough; and

(*c*) the approaches to any such bridge;

"relevant petty sessions area" means—

(*a*) a petty sessions area, the whole or part of which is in the city, if the effect of an agreement under this section is to apply the Act of 1999 to the bridge;

(*b*) a petty sessions area, the whole or part of which is in the borough, if the effect of an agreement under this section is to apply Part III of the Act of 1990 to the bridge;

"street" means any street to which Part III of the Act of 1990 or the Act of 1999 applies, as the case may be.

[London Local Authorities Act 2007, s 37.]

## PART 5
## MISCELLANEOUS

7.8006 **70. Display of certain video recordings** (1) This section applies to a video work in respect of which a classification certificate has been issued stating that no video recording containing that work is to be supplied other than in a licensed sex shop.

(2) A person who at any place in a borough other than in a sex shop for which a licence is in force under Schedule 3 to the Local Government (Miscellaneous Provisions) Act 1982 (c 30) displays in the course of a business—

(*a*) a video recording containing a video work to which this section applies; or

(*b*) any packaging indicating that it contains such a video recording,

is guilty of an offence unless he is displaying the video recording or packaging for the purpose only of a supply which, if it took place, would be an exempted supply by virtue of section 12(6) of the 1984 Act.

(3) It is a defence to a charge of committing an offence under subsection (2) above to prove—

(*a*) that the accused neither knew nor had reasonable grounds to believe that the classification certificate contained the statement concerned;

(*b*) that the accused believed on reasonable grounds that the place concerned was a sex shop for which a licence was in force under the said Schedule 3;

(*c*) that the accused believed on reasonable grounds that were the video recording to have been supplied or offered for supply by him in the place concerned the supply would if it had taken place been, an exempted supply by virtue of section 3(4) or 12(6) of the 1984 Act.

(4) A person guilty of an offence under subsection (2) above shall be liable, on summary conviction, to imprisonment for a term not exceeding six months or a fine not exceeding level 5 on the standard scale or both.

(5) In this section—

"the 1984 Act" means the Video Recordings Act 1984 (c. 39);

"classification certificate", "video recording" and "video work" have the same meanings ascribed to them by the 1984 Act.

[London Local Authorities Act 2007, s 70.]

7.8007 **71. Temporary sleeping accommodation: powers of entry, search and seizure** (1) An authorised officer may, at all reasonable hours and on production, if required, of his credentials, exercise the following powers, that is to say—

(*a*) he may, for the purpose of ascertaining whether a relevant offence has been committed, inspect any relevant items and enter any premises other than premises used only as a dwelling;

(*b*) if he has reasonable cause to suspect that a relevant offence has been committed, he may, for the purpose of ascertaining whether it has been committed, require any person carrying on a trade or business or employed in connection with a trade or business to produce any books or documents relating to the trade or business and may take copies of, or of any entry in, any such book or document;

(*c*) if he has reasonable cause to believe that a relevant offence has been committed, he may seize and detain any relevant items or documents for the purpose of ascertaining, by testing or otherwise, whether the offence has been committed;

(*d*) he may seize and detain any relevant items or documents which he has reason to believe may be required as evidence in proceedings for a relevant offence;

(*e*) he may, for the purpose of exercising his powers under this subsection to seize relevant items or documents, but only if and to the extent that it is reasonably necessary in order to obtain evidence in proceedings for a relevant offence, break open any container and, if that person does not comply with the requirement, he may do so himself.

(2) An officer seizing any relevant items or documents in the exercise of his powers under this section shall inform the person from whom they are seized.

(3) If a justice of the peace, on sworn information in writing—

(*a*) is satisfied that there is reasonable ground to believe either—

(i) that any relevant items, books or documents which a duly authorised officer has power under this section to inspect are on any premises and that their inspection is likely to disclose evidence of the commission of a relevant offence; or

(ii) that any relevant offence has been, is being or is about to be committed on any premises; and

(*b*) is also satisfied either—

(i) that admission to the premises has been or is likely to be refused and that notice of intention to apply for a warrant under this subsection has been given to the occupier; or

(ii) that an application for admission, or the giving of such a notice, would defeat the object of the entry or that the premises are unoccupied or that the occupier is temporarily absent and it might defeat the object of the entry to await his return,

the justice may by warrant under his hand, which shall continue in force for a period of one month, authorise an authorised officer to enter the premises, if need be by force.

(4) An officer entering any premises by virtue of this section may take with him such other persons and such equipment as may appear to him necessary; and on leaving any premises which he has entered by virtue of a warrant under the preceding subsection he shall, if the premises are unoccupied or the occupier is temporarily absent, leave them as effectively secured against trespassers as he found them.

(5) If any person who is not an authorised officer purports to act as such under this section he shall be guilty of an offence liable on summary conviction to a fine not exceeding level 3 on the standard scale.

(6) Nothing in this section shall be taken to compel the production by a solicitor of a document containing a privileged communication made by or to him in that capacity or to authorise the taking of possession of any such document which is in his possession.

(7) In this section—

"relevant enforcement notice" means an enforcement notice issued under section 172 of the Town and Country Planning Act 1990 (c. 8) (issue of enforcement notice) in respect of a material change of use of the type described in section 25 (provision of temporary sleeping accommodation to constitute material change of use) of the Greater London Council (General Powers) Act 1973 (c. xxx);

"relevant items" means computers, software and other items which may be used to store or record information;

"relevant offence" means an offence under section 179 of the Town and Country Planning Act 1990 in relation to a relevant enforcement notice.

[London Local Authorities Act 2007, s 71.]

**7.8008** **75. Mail forwarding businesses** (1) On and after the appointed day, a person shall not in the area of a borough council carry on a mail forwarding business, whether alone or in conjunction with any other business when he is not registered by the council under this section.

(2) On application for registration under this section the council shall register the applicant and issue to the applicant a certificate of registration on which there shall appear a registration number.

(3) An application for registration under this section shall be made in writing to the council and the applicant shall in the application state—

(*a*) his name and private address or, if the application is made by or on behalf of a body corporate or partnership, the registered or principal office of such body or partnership as the case may be; and

(*b*) the address of each place in the borough which is occupied by the applicant for the purposes of the business.

(4) Where there is any alteration in the particulars mentioned in subsection (3)(*a*) or (*b*) above, the person registered shall within 14 days notify the council of the fact, and the council shall thereupon amend their register.

(5) A council may charge a reasonable fee for a registration under this section, calculated by reference to the cost of dealing with applications for such registration.

(6) A person who carries on a mail forwarding business shall keep a record of the following particulars—

(*a*) the full name, address and telephone number of every person for whom any post is received, or who has requested that postal packets received may be held or forwarded to that person;

(*b*) the nature of the business (if any) carried out by that person;

(*c*) any instructions that may have been received as to the delivery or forwarding of postal packets;

(*d*) in the case of every postal packet forwarded, the name and address of the person to whom it is forwarded (if different from the name and address mentioned in paragraph (*a*) above);

(*e*) copies of the originals of two documents of a type approved by the council for the purposes of identifying the persons and verifying the address mentioned in paragraph (*a*) above.

(7) In subsection (6)(*a*) above, the name and address to be kept must not be the name and address of another mail forwarding business and is—

(*a*) in the case of an individual, his private address;

(*b*) in the case of a body corporate or partnership—

(i) the registered or principal address of such body or partnership, as the case may be; and

(ii) the names and private addresses of the directors, partners or another person directly or indirectly responsible for the management of the body or partnership; and

(iii) the address of the principal place of business of the body or partnership, if different from any of the addresses mentioned in paragraphs (i) and (ii) above.

(8) The records kept under this section by a person carrying on a mail forwarding business, shall, in respect of a person by whom he is requested to hold or forward postal packets, be kept for a period of at least a year after the end of the arrangement under which that request was made, and must be kept at all reasonable times open to inspection by any police constable and any authorised officer.

(9) If any person—

(*a*) without reasonable excuse contravenes or fails to comply with any of the provisions of this section; or

(*b*) furnishes any false information—

(i) in making an application for registration under this section or notifying the council of any alteration in the particulars mentioned in subsection (3)(*a*) or (*b*) above; or

(ii) to a mail forwarding business which the business requires in order to comply with subsection (6) above; or

(*c*) without reasonable excuse, makes a false entry in the record kept under subsection (6) above,

he shall be guilty of an offence.

(10) A person guilty of an offence under subsection (9) above shall be liable on summary conviction to a fine not exceeding level 5 on the standard scale.

(11) Nothing in subsection (1) or (6) above shall apply to—

(a) a postal operator providing a service within the scope of the universal postal service (within the meaning of Part 3 of the Postal Services Act 2011), or

(b) a Post Office company (within the meaning of Part 1 of that Act).

(12) Section 28 of the Trade Descriptions Act 1968 (c 29) (power to enter premises and seize goods and documents) applies in relation to the enforcement of this section by a borough council as in relation to the enforcement of that Act by a weights and measures authority.

(13) In this section—

"mail forwarding business" means the business, carried out for reward, of making available to a person a postal address to which postal packets may be sent, and doing either or both of the following-

(*a*) holding postal packets so sent for collection by that person or his agent;

(*b*) forwarding, by whatever means, postal packets so sent to that person;

"postal packet" has the same meaning given to it by section 125 of the Postal Services Act 2000 (interpretation).

(14) For the purposes of this section, a person carries on a mail forwarding business in the area of a borough council if, in respect of that mail forwarding business, the postal address made available and to which postal packets may be sent is in the area of the council.

(15) Subsections (16) and (17) below apply to any person who carries on a mail forwarding business in a borough on the date on which this section comes into force in that borough.

(16) Until the period of four weeks commencing with that date has expired, subsections (1) and (6) above shall not apply to the person in question.

(17) If an application for registration under this section is made in respect of the mail forwarding business during that period, the person in question—

(*a*) may lawfully continue to carry on the business as a mail forwarding business; and

(*b*) need not comply with the requirements of subsection (6) above,

until the council issues a certificate under subsection (2) above or the application is withdrawn.

[London Local Authorities Act 2007, s 75 as amended by the Postal Services Act 2011, Sch 12.]

## PART 6
## SUPPLEMENTAL

7.8009 **79. Obstruction of authorised officer** Any person who intentionally obstructs any authorised officer acting in the exercise of his powers under this Act shall be guilty of an offence and liable on summary conviction to a fine not exceeding level 3 on the standard scale.

[London Local Authorities Act 2007, s 79.]

7.8010 **80. Proof of resolution** In any proceedings which require proof of the passing of a resolution under this Act it shall be presumed, unless the contrary is proved, that the said resolution was duly passed and that any requirements relating to the passing of the resolution and the giving of any notices or information before or after the passing of the resolution were properly complied with.

[London Local Authorities Act 2007, s 80.]

7.8011 **81. Liability of directors, etc** (1) Where an offence under this Act committed by a body corporate is proved to have been committed with the consent or connivance of, or to be attributable to any neglect on the part of, a director, manager, secretary or other similar officer of the body corporate or any person who was purporting to act in any such capacity, he, as well as the body corporate, shall be guilty of the offence.

(2) Where the affairs of the body corporate are managed by its members, subsection (1) above shall apply to the acts and defaults of a member in connection with his functions of management as if he were a director of the body corporate.

[London Local Authorities Act 2007, s 81.]

**82. Regulations**

SCHEDULE 2

Modification of Enactments in Enforcement Action Zone — Section 31

PART 1

MODIFICATION OF ENACTMENTS WITHIN ENFORCEMENT ACTION ZONE

7.8012

| *Enactment* | *Modification* |
|---|---|
| 1 Section 224(3) Town and Country Planning Act 1990 (c 8) (displaying advertisements in contravention of regulations) | For "level 4" substitute "level 5" where it appears in both places |
| 2 Section 87 Environmental Protection Act 1990 (c 43) (offence of leaving litter) | For "level 4" substitute "level 5" |
| 3 Section 4(3) Noise Act 1996 (c 37) (offence where noise exceeds permitted level after service of notice) | For "level 3" substitute "level 5" |

PART 2

MODIFICATION OF ENACTMENTS: GENERAL

| *Enactment* | *Modification* |
|---|---|
| 4 Section 88 Environmental Protection Act 1990 (fixed penalty notices for leaving litter) | After subsection (7) insert—<br>"(7A) The Secretary of State may, when making an order under subsection (7) above, substitute different penalties as regards enforcement action zones designated under section 29 (enforcement action zones) of the London Local Authorities Act 2007 (c ii)." |
| 5 Section 9 Noise Act 1996 (supplementary provisions about fixed penalties for noise offences) | After subsection (3) insert—<br>"(3A) The Secretary of State may, when making an order under subsection (3) above, substitute different penalties as regards enforcement action zones designated under section 29 (enforcement action zones) of the London Local Authorities Act 2007 (c ii)." |

# London Local Authorities Act 2012

(2012 c ii)

PART 1

PRELIMINARY

7.8013 **1 Citation and commencement** (1) This Act may be cited as the London Local Authorities Act 2012.

(2) This Act and the London Local Authorities Acts 1990 to 2007 may be cited together as the London Local Authorities Acts 1990 to 2012.

(3) This Act shall come into operation at the end of the period of two months beginning with the date on which it is passed but sections 11 (minor and consequential amendments) and 12 (Keeling Schedule) and Schedules 1 and 2 shall be deemed to have come into operation immediately after the other provisions of this Act.

[London Local Authorities Act 2012, s 1.]

7.8014 **2 General interpretation** In this Act—

"the Act of 2007" means the London Local Authorities Act 2007;

"authorised officer", in relation to a borough council, means—

(*a*) any employee of the council;

(*b*) any other person by whom, in pursuance of arrangements made with the council, any functions under this Act fall to be discharged; or

(*c*) any employee of any such person,

who is authorised in writing by the council to act in relation to the relevant provision of this Act;

"borough council" means London borough council and includes the Common Council of the City of London in its capacity as a local authority and "borough" and "council" shall be construed accordingly.

[London Local Authorities Act 2012, s 2.]

## Part 2

## Penalty Charges

7.8015 **3 Powers exercisable by police civilians and accredited persons** (1) Where a designation under section 38 of the Police Reform Act 2002 applies paragraph 1 of Schedule 4 to that Act (community support officers' powers to issue fixed penalty notices) to any person, that person shall have the power of a borough council to serve a penalty charge notice under section 61(2) of the Act of 2007 (penalty charges) where he has reason to believe that a penalty charge is payable by the person being served to the borough council by virtue of a penalty charge provision within the meaning of section 61(7) of that Act.

(2) An accredited person within the meaning of section 47 of the Police Reform Act 2002 whose accreditation specifies that this subsection applies to him shall have the power of a borough council to serve a penalty charge notice under section 61(2) of the Act of 2007 (penalty charges) where he has reason to believe that a penalty charge is payable by the person being served to the borough council by virtue of a penalty charge provision within the meaning of section 61(7) of that Act.

(3) An accreditation may only specify that subsection (2) applies to an accredited person if that person's accreditation also specifies that paragraph 1 of Schedule 5 to the Police Reform Act 2002 (accredited person's powers to issue fixed penalty notices) applies to him.

[London Local Authorities Act 2012, s 3.]

7.8016 **4 Power to require name and address** (1) If a borough council or a community support officer proposes to serve on a person a penalty charge notice under section 61(2) of the Act of 2007 (penalty charges), the council or community support officer may require the person to give him his name and address.

(2) Where a requirement of the borough council under subsection (1) is made in person then—

(*a*) it must be made by an authorised officer of the council; and

(*b*) the authorised officer must, if required to do so, show proof of his authorisation.

(3) A person commits an offence if—

(*a*) he fails to give his name and address when required to do so under subsection (1); or

(*b*) he gives a false or inaccurate name or address in response to a requirement under that subsection.

(4) A person guilty of an offence under subsection (3) is liable on summary conviction to a fine not exceeding level 3 on the standard scale.

[London Local Authorities Act 2012, s 4.]

## Part 3

## Public Health, Environmental Protection and Highways

7.8017 **5 Street litter control notices** Section 94(1)(*a*) of the Environmental Protection Act 1990 (street litter: supplementary provisions) shall apply in Greater London as though for "commercial or retail premises" there were substituted "premises other than dwellings".

[London Local Authorities Act 2012, s 5.]

7.8018 **6 Use of turnstiles at public toilets** Section 1 of the Public Lavatories (Turnstiles) Act 1963 (abolition of turnstiles) shall not apply in respect of a public lavatory or public sanitary convenience controlled or managed by a borough council.

[London Local Authorities Act 2012, s 6.]

7.8019 **7 Charges for permitting the use of objects, etc on the highway** (1) In relation to a relevant permission, "the standard amount" in section 115F(2) of the 1980 Act (power to impose conditions on permissions for execution of works and use of objects, etc on the highway) means such amount as may be sufficient in the aggregate taking one year with another to cover the reasonable costs of a borough council, not otherwise recovered, of—

(*a*) the cleansing of streets in which permitted activities take place so far as that cleansing is attributable to permitted activities; and (*b*) any reasonable administrative or other costs incurred in connection with the administration of Part VIIA of the 1980 Act (provision of amenities on certain highways) in relation to relevant permissions; and

(*c*) the cost of enforcing—

(i) the provisions of Part VIIA of the 1980 Act so far as it relates to permitted activities;

(ii) section 130 of the 1980 Act (protection of public rights) in relation to activities which are capable of being authorised by a relevant permission but are not;

(iii) the law in relation to obstruction of the highway in relation to activities which are capable of being authorised by a relevant permission but are not.

(2) Section 115F(3) of the 1980 Act shall not apply in the area of a borough council in relation to a relevant permission.

(3) In this section—

"the 1980 Act" means the Highways Act 1980;

"permitted activities" means activities carried out under the authority of a relevant permission;

"relevant permission" means a permission granted by a borough council under section 115E(1)(*b*)(i) of the 1980 Act (permission to use objects, etc on, in or over the highway resulting in the production of income).

[London Local Authorities Act 2012, s 7.]

# London Local Authorities and Transport for London Act 2013

(2013 c v)

## Part 3

## Builders' Skips

7.8020 **7. Interpretation of Part 3** In this Part—

"the 2007 Act" means the London Local Authorities Act 2007;

"builder's skip" has the same meaning as in section 139(11) of the 1980 Act;

"immobilisation device" means any device or appliance designed or adapted to be fixed to a builder's skip for the purpose of preventing it from being moved;

"owner" in relation to a builder's skip, is to be construed in accordance with section 139(11) of the 1980 Act.

[London Local Authorities and Transport for London Act 2013, s 7.]

7.8021 **8. Identifying the "owner" of a builder's skip** (1) A relevant highway authority may, for the purposes of identifying who is responsible for paying a penalty charge for the purposes of section 61 of the 2007 Act as applied by virtue of section 9, require the relevant person to provide them with the name and address of the owner of the builder's skip.

(2) In subsection (1), the "relevant person" is—

(*a*) if a permission was given to a person in respect of the skip in question under section 139(1) of the 1980 Act and the penalty charge became payable during the period of the permission, that person;

(*b*) if different from the person mentioned in paragraph (*a*) (if there is such a person), the person who the relevant highway authority have reason to believe—

(i) in the case of a builder's skip that is the subject of a hiring agreement for a hire of not less than one month, the person from whom the skip was hired; and

(ii) in the case of a builder's skip that is the subject of a hire purchase agreement, the bailor under that agreement.

(3) The person identified by the relevant person shall be an individual, a body corporate, an unincorporated association or other body that is capable of being sued.

(4) A requirement under this section shall specify the period within which it must be complied with, which must be a period no shorter than 14 working days beginning with the date on which the request was made.

(5) A person on whom a requirement is imposed under this section commits an offence if—

(*a*) without reasonable excuse he fails to comply within the period specified in accordance with subsection (4);

(*b*) in responding to the requirement he gives information that he knows is false in a material particular.

(6) A person convicted of an offence under subsection (5) is liable on summary conviction—

(*a*) in the case of an offence under paragraph (*a*) to a fine not exceeding level 3 on the standard scale;

(*b*) in the case of an offence under paragraph (*b*) to a fine not exceeding level 5 on the standard scale.

[London Local Authorities and Transport for London Act 2013, s 8.]

7.8022 **9. Builders' skips: penalty charge provisions** (1) This section is a penalty charge provision for the purposes of section 61 of the 2007 Act (penalty charges).

(2) Part 4 of the 2007 Act shall have effect so far as that Part applies by virtue of this section being designated as a penalty charge provision as mentioned in subsection (1) as if for references to a borough council there were substituted references to a relevant highway authority

within the meaning of this Act.

(3) A penalty charge is payable to a relevant highway authority for the purposes of the said section 61 if—

(*a*) a builder's skip is deposited on a highway without a permission granted under section 139 of the 1980 Act (control of builders' skips);

(*b*) a builder's skip has been deposited on a highway in accordance with a permission granted under the said section 139 but the owner of the skip does not secure that—

(i) the skip is properly lighted during the hours of darkness;

(ii) the skip is marked or lighted in accordance with regulations made under the said section 139 requiring builders' skips to be so marked or lighted;

(iii) the skip is clearly and indelibly marked with the owner's name and with his telephone number or address;

(iv) the skip is removed as soon as practicable after it has been filled;

(v) each of the conditions subject to which the permission was granted is complied with;

(*c*) the owner of a builder's skip who, under subsection (2) of section 140 of the 1980 Act (removal of builders' skips), is required to remove or reposition the skip or cause it to be removed or repositioned has failed to comply with the requirement as soon as is practicable.

(4) For the purposes of the said section 61 of the 2007 Act as it applies in respect of penalty charges payable under that section by virtue of subsection (3), a penalty charge is payable to a relevant highway authority by the owner of the builder's skip in respect of which the contravention of the relevant provision in question is alleged to have occurred.

(5) The owner of the builder's skip is the appropriate recipient for the purposes of the said section 61.

(6) For the purposes of section 62(1) of the 2007 Act (representations and appeals) the grounds on which representations may be made against a penalty charge notice arising from a penalty charge payable by virtue of this section are—

(*a*) that the recipient—

(i) never was the owner of the builder's skip in question;

(ii) had ceased to be the owner before the date on which the penalty charge was alleged to have become payable;

(iii) became the owner after that date;

(*b*) that there was no contravention of the relevant provision in question and in respect of which the penalty charge notice was issued;

(*c*) that the penalty charge exceeded the amount applicable in the circumstances of the case;

(*d*) that the contravention of the relevant provision in question was due to the act or default of another person and that he took all precautions and exercised all due diligence to avoid the contravention by himself or another person under his control.

(7) Where any of the grounds mentioned in subsection (6)(*a*) is relied on in any representations made under the said section 62(1), those representations must include a statement of the name and address of the owner (if that information is in the recipient's possession).

(8) Where the ground mentioned in subsection (6)(*d*) is relied on in any representations made under the said section 62(1), the relevant highway authority may disregard the representations unless, before the representations are considered, the person making the representations has served on the relevant highway authority a notice in writing giving such information identifying or assisting in the identification of that other person as was then in his possession.

(9) Subsections (3) to (7) of section 139 and subsection (3) of section 140 of the 1980 Act (offences related to builders' skips) cease to have effect in Greater London.

(10) Section 140(9) of the 1980 Act in its application to Greater London, is amended by the substitution for "guilty of an offence under section 139(4) above of failing" of the words "liable to pay a penalty charge under section 9 of the London Local Authorities and Transport for London Act 2013 in relation to the failure".

(11) The entries numbered 4 to 9 in the table contained in Schedule 4 to the London Local Authorities and Transport for London Act 2003 are repealed.

[London Local Authorities and Transport for London Act 2013, s 9.]

7.8023 **10. Builders' skips: requirements as to lighting and guarding** Conditions of the type referred to in section 139(2)(*e*) of the 1980 Act to which a permission under section 139 of the 1980 Act may be made subject, may include conditions that builders' skips have a light or lights or a guard or system of guarding that is or are an integral part of the skip.

[London Local Authorities and Transport for London Act 2013, s 10.]

7.8024 **11. Builders' skips: provision of lighting and covering by highway authority**

(1) Subsection (2) applies if a builder's skip is found by a relevant highway authority to be deposited on a highway in Greater London and the skip—

(*a*) is not lighted or covered in accordance with the conditions of a permission under section 139 of the 1980 Act;

(*b*) was deposited without a permission under that section having been obtained; or (*c*) is not properly lighted during the hours of darkness (or is not marked in accordance with regulations made under section 139(4)(*a*) of the 1980 Act).

(2) Where this section applies, the relevant highway authority in question may themselves light, cover or mark the skip or cause it to be lighted, covered or marked.

(3) Any expenses reasonably incurred by a relevant highway authority in the lighting, covering or marking of a skip under subsection (2) may be recovered from the owner of the skip in any court of competent jurisdiction or summarily as a civil debt.

(4) The owner of a skip is not liable to pay a penalty charge under section 9 in relation to a failure to secure that a condition or requirement relating to the lighting, covering or marking of the skip was complied with if the failure resulted from the lighting, covering or marking of the skip under subsection (2).

[London Local Authorities and Transport for London Act 2013, s 11.]

7.8025 12. **Builders' skips: immobilisation devices** (1) Where a penalty charge notice has been served in accordance with section 61 of the 2007 Act in relation to a penalty charge payable under section 9(3), an authorised officer of the relevant highway authority or a person acting under his direction may fix an immobilisation device to the builder's skip concerned while it remains in the place where it was found.

(2) On any occasion when an immobilisation device is fixed to a skip in accordance with this section, the person fixing the device shall also fix to the skip a notice—

(*a*) indicating that such a device has been fixed to the skip and warning that no attempt should be made to move it until it has been released from that device;

(*b*) specifying the steps to be taken in order to secure its release; and

(*c*) warning that unlawful removal of an immobilisation device is an offence.

(3) A notice fixed to a skip in accordance with this section shall not be removed or interfered with except by or under the authority of—

(*a*) the owner of the skip; or

(*b*) the relevant highway authority.

(4) A person contravening subsection (3) shall be guilty of an offence and liable on summary conviction to a fine not exceeding level 2 on the standard scale.

(5) Any person who, without being authorised to do so in accordance with this section, removes or attempts to remove an immobilisation device fixed to a skip in accordance with this section shall be guilty of an offence and shall be liable on summary conviction to a fine not exceeding level 3 on the standard scale.

[London Local Authorities and Transport for London Act 2013, s 12.]

7.8026 13. **Release of immobilised skips** (1) A skip to which an immobilisation device has been fixed in accordance with section 12 may only be released from that device by or under the direction of a person authorised by the relevant highway authority to give such a direction.

(2) Subject to subsection (1), such a skip shall be released from the device on payment in any manner specified in the notice fixed to the skip under section 12(2) of—

(*a*) the penalty charge payable in respect of the contravention inquestion; and

(*b*) such charge in respect of the release as may be prescribed by a joint committee.

(3) Section 66(2), (4) and (5) (levels of penalty charge) and section 67 (penalty charges: reserve powers of Secretary of State) of the 2007 Act shall apply in relation to the levels of charge prescribed by a joint committee under subsection (2) as they apply in relation to the levels of penalty charges set by borough councils under section 66(1) of that Act.

[London Local Authorities and Transport for London Act 2013, s 13.]

7.8027 14. **Appeals in relation to immobilisation** (1) If the owner of a skip makes representations under section 62(1) of the 2007 Act to a relevant highway authority in an immobilisation case, and the relevant highway authority accepts that a ground specified in section 9(6) applies, it shall, when it serves notice that it accepts that ground, refund (in addition to a sum representing the penalty charge paid) a sum representing the amount of any charge paid under section 13(2)(*b*).

(2) If the owner of a skip appeals to an adjudicator under section 62 of the 2007 Act (or regulations made under that section) in an immobilisation case, and the adjudicator accepts that a ground specified in section 9(6) applies the adjudicator shall direct the relevant highway authority to refund (in addition to a sum representing the penalty charge paid) a sum representing the amount of any charge paid under section 13(2)(*b*).

(3) It shall be the duty of a relevant highway authority to which a direction is given under subsection (2) to comply with it forthwith.

(4) In this section an "immobilisation case" means a case where a penalty charge notice has been served in accordance with section 61 of the 2007 Act in relation to a penalty charge payable under section 9(3) and an immobilisation device has been fixed to the skip under section 12.

[London Local Authorities and Transport for London Act 2013, s 14.]

## Part 4
## Road Traffic

7.8028 15. **Gated roads** (1) Any person who opens, closes or otherwise operates or interferes with a relevant barrier without lawful excuse shall be guilty of an offence and liable, on summary conviction, to a fine not exceeding level 3 on the standard scale.

(2) In subsection (1) a "relevant barrier" means any barrier lawfully placed in, on or over a highway by or on behalf of a traffic authority in London for the purpose of preventing or restricting the passage of vehicles or any class of vehicles into, out of or along a highway.

[London Local Authorities and Transport for London Act 2013, s 15.]

## Part 5
## Charging Points for Electric Vehicles

7.8029 **16. Charging points for electric vehicles** (1) A London authority may provide and operate charging apparatus for electrically powered motor vehicles—

(*a*) in any public off-street car park under the management and control of the authority;

(*b*) on any highway for which they are responsible as highway authority.

(2) A London authority may grant a person permission to provide or operate charging apparatus for electrically powered motor vehicles—

(*a*) in any public off-street car park under the management and control of the authority;

(*b*) on any highway for which they are responsible as highway authority.

(3) For the purposes of this Part, a person to whom permission is granted under subsection (2) is referred to as an "authorised person".

(4) Section 115D of the 1980 Act (limit on powers to provide amenities on the highway) shall apply in relation to the exercise of the powers under this section by a London authority as it applies in relation to the exercise of powers under sections 115B and 115C of that Act by a council.

(5) No charging apparatus may be provided on a local Act walkway unless walkway consent has been obtained first.

(6) Subject to subsection (7), a London authority may grant a permission under subsection (2) upon such conditions as they think fit, including conditions requiring the payment to the authority of such reasonable charges as they may determine.

(7) Nothing in this section—

(*a*) is to be taken as authorising the creation of a nuisance or of a danger to users of a highway or a public off-street car park; or

(*b*) (in relation to permissions granted under subsection (2)) is to be taken as imposing on a London authority by whom a permission has been granted any liability for injury, damage or loss resulting from the presence on a highway or public off-street car park of the charging apparatus to which the permission relates; or

(*c*) is to be taken as imposing on a London authority any liability for injury, damage or loss resulting from the presence on a highway or public offstreet car park of a connecting cable; or

(*d*) shall prejudice the right of a London authority to require an indemnity against any claim in respect of injury, damage or loss arising out of the grant of a permission granted under subsection (2),

but paragraph (*d*) is not to be taken as requiring any person to indemnify a London authority against any claim in respect of injury, damage or loss which is attributable to the negligence of the London authority.

(8) For the purposes of determining, in any proceedings in a court of civil jurisdiction, who is liable for injury, damage or loss resulting from the presence on a highway or public off-street car park of a connecting cable at or near charging apparatus provided under this section, it shall be presumed that the person in charge of the relevant vehicle at the relevant time had responsibility for and control of the cable.

(9) In subsection (8)—

"the relevant vehicle" means the vehicle in respect of which the connecting cable was about to be, was being or had been used for charging;

"the relevant time" means the time when the liability arose.

(10) This section is without prejudice to section 162 of the 1980 Act (penalty for placing rope, etc across highway).

(11) In this section—

"charging apparatus" includes any fixed equipment but excludes any connecting cable or wire which is not provided by the authority;

"connecting cable" means any cable or wire, whether provided by the authority or otherwise, used to connect the charging apparatus to a vehicle and that is not permanently attached to the charging apparatus;

"local Act walkway" and "walkway consent" have the same meanings as in section 115A of the 1980 Act;

"operate" in relation to charging apparatus for electronically powered motor vehicles includes supply or sell electricity by means of such charging apparatus;

"public off-street carpark" means a place, whether above or below ground and whether or not consisting of or including buildings, where off-street parking accommodation is made available to the public, whether or not for payment.

[London Local Authorities and Transport for London Act 2013, s 16.]

7.8030 **19. Offence of unlawful use of charging point** (1) A person shall be guilty of an offence and liable on summary conviction to a fine not exceeding level 3 on the standard scale if he uses charging apparatus in contravention of a sign displayed on the apparatus which indicates that—

(*a*) the apparatus is not to be used for any purpose other than charging a vehicle; and

(*b*) it is an offence to so use the apparatus.

(2) A person is not guilty of an offence under subsection (1) if—

(*a*) he had the permission of the person who operated the charging apparatus at the time to use the charging apparatus for the purpose in question; or

(*b*) he had reasonable cause to believe he had such permission; or

(*c*) at the time there was on the charging apparatus an indication given by the person who operated the charging apparatus that it could be used for the purpose for which it was used.

[London Local Authorities and Transport for London Act 2013, s 19.]

# MALICIOUS COMMUNICATIONS

## Malicious Communications Act 1988

(1988 c 27)

7.8031 **1. Offence of sending letters etc with intent to cause distress or anxiety** (1) Any person who sends to another person—

(*a*) a letter, electronic communication or article of any description which conveys—

(i) a message which is indecent or grossly offensive[1];

(ii) a threat; or

(iii) information which is false and known or believed to be false by the sender; or

(*b*) any article or electronic communication which is, in whole or part, of an indecent or grossly offensive nature,

is guilty of an offence if his purpose, or one of his purposes, in sending it is that it should, so far as falling within paragraph (*a*) or (*b*) above, cause distress or anxiety to the recipient or to any other person to whom he intends that it or its contents or nature should be communicated.

(2) A person is not guilty of an offence by virtue of subsection (1)(*a*)(ii) above if he shows—

(*a*) that the threat was used to reinforce a demand made by him on reasonable grounds; and

(*b*) that he believed, and had reasonable grounds for believing, that the use of the threat was a proper means of reinforcing the demand.

(2A) In this section "electronic communication" includes—

(*a*) any oral or other communication by means of an electronic communications network and

(*b*) any communication (however sent) that is in electronic form.

(3) In this section references to sending include references to delivering or transmitting and to causing to be sent, delivered or transmitted and "sender" shall be construed accordingly.

(4) A person guilty of an offence under this section is liable—

(*a*) on conviction on indictment to imprisonment for a term not exceeding two years or a fine (or both);

(*b*) on summary conviction to imprisonment for a term not exceeding 12 months or a fine (or both).

(5) In relation to an offence committed before section 154(1) of the Criminal Justice Act 2003 comes into force, the reference in subsection (4)(*b*) to 12 months is to be read as a reference to six months.

(6) In relation to an offence committed before section 85 of the Legal Aid Sentencing and Punishment of Offenders Act 2012 comes into force, the reference in subsection (4)(*b*) to a fine is to be read as a reference to a fine not exceeding the statutory maximum.

[Malicious Communications Act 1988, s 1 as amended by the Criminal Justice and Police Act 2001, s 43, the Communications Act 2003, Sch 17 and the Criminal Justice and Courts Act 2015, s 32.]

---

[1] The meaning of this term and its compatibility with ECHR were considered in *Connolly v DPP* [2007] EWHC 237 (Admin), [2007] 2 All ER 1012, [2008] 1 WLR 276, [2007] Cr App Rep 43, [2007] Crim LR 729, where an anti-abortion campaigner had sent close up colour photographs of aborted foetuses to a number of pharmacists that stocked the morning after pill. It was held (upholding the conviction) that the fact that a communication was political or educational in nature had no bearing on whether it was indecent or grossly offensive, although a person who sent an indecent or grossly offensive communication for a political or educational purpose would not be guilty of the offence unless it were proved that his purpose was also to cause distress and anxiety. Section 1 of the 1988 Act could be interpreted in a way that was compatible with arts 9 and 10 of ECHR by giving a heightened meaning to "grossly offensive" and "indecent" or by reading in a provision to the effect that the section would not apply where to create an offence would be in breach of a person's convention rights. In the instant case the interference with the defendant's arts 9 and 10 rights derived from the 1988 Act was sufficiently precise and foreseeable to meet the requirement that it be prescribed by law. Section 1 of the 1988 Act furthered the protection of the rights of others and the interference with the defendant's rights was proportionate and necessary in a democratic society.

# MEDICINE AND PHARMACY

**Contents**



## European Communities Act 1972: regulations

**7.8032** Within the scope of the title Medicines and Pharmacy would logically fall the subject matter of a number of regulations made under the very wide enabling power provided in s 2(2) of the European Communities Act 1972. Where such regulations create offences they are noted below in chronological order:

- Medicines (Administration of Radioactive Substances) Regulations 1978, SI 1978/1066 amended by SI 1995/2147, SI 2005/2754, SI 2006/2407 and SI 2006/2806;
- Ionising Radiation (Medical Exposure) Regulations 2000, SI 2000/1059 amended by SI 2004/1031, SI 2006/2523, SI 2007/1898 and SI 2011/1567;
- Medicines for Human Use (Clinical Trials) Regulations 2004, SI 2004/1031 amended by SI 2004/3224, SI 2005/2759, SI 2006/1928 and 2984, SI 2007/289 and 3101, SI 2008/941, SI 2009/1164, SI 2010/231, 551 and 1882, SI 2011/2581, SI 2012/504, 1479 and 1916, SI 2013/325 and 1855, SI 2015/137 and SI 2016/190 and 696;
- Controlled Drugs (Drug Precursors) (Intra-Community Trade) Regulations 2008, SI 2008/295 amended by SI 2010/231;
- Controlled Drugs (Drug Precursors) (Community External Trade) Regulations 2008, SI 2008/296;
- Human Medicines Regulations 2012, SI 2012/1916 amended by SI 2013/325, 1855 2593, SI 2014/490 and 1878, SI 2015/323, 903 and 1503 and SI 2016/186, 190 and 645;
- Veterinary Medicines Regulations 2013, SI 2013/2033 amended by SI 2014/599.

## Cancer Act 1939

(2 & 3 Geo 6 c 13)

**7.8033** **4. Prohibition of certain advertisements** (1) No person shall take any part in the publication of any advertisement[1]—

(*a*) containing an offer to treat any person for cancer, or to prescribe any remedy therefor, or to give any advice in connection with the treatment thereof; or

(*b*) *repealed.*

(2) If any person contravenes[2] any of the provisions of the foregoing subsection, he shall be liable to summary conviction, in the case of a first conviction, to a fine not exceeding **level 3** on the standard scale or to imprisonment for a term not exceeding **three months**, or to both such a fine and such imprisonment.*

(3) *Repealed.*

(4) In any proceedings for a contravention of subsection (1) of this section, it shall be a defence for the person charged to prove—

(*a*) that the advertisement to which the proceedings relate was published only so far as was reasonably necessary to bring it to the notice of persons of the following classes or of one or some of them, that is to say—

(i) members of either House of Parliament or of a local authority or of the governing body of a voluntary hospital[3];

(ii) *repealed;*
(iii) registered medical practitioners;
(iv) registered nurses;
(v) registered pharmacists and persons lawfully conducting a retail pharmacy business in accordance with s 69 of the Medicines Act 1968;
(vi) persons undergoing training with a view to becoming registered medical practitioners, registered nurses or pharmacists;
(vii) *repealed;*

(*b*) that the said advertisement was published only in a publication of a technical character intended for circulation mainly amongst persons of the classes mentioned in the last preceding paragraph or one or some of those classes; or

(*c*) that the said advertisement was published in such circumstances that he did not know and had no reason to believe that he was taking part in the publication thereof.

(5) Nothing in this section shall apply in respect of any advertisement published by a local authority or by the governing body of a voluntary hospital or by any person acting with the sanction of the Minister.

(6) *Repealed.*

(7) Each of the following may institute proceedings under this section—

(*a*) a county council in England;
(*b*) a non-metropolitan district council for an area in England for which there is no county council;
(*c*) a London borough council;
(*d*) the Common Council of the City of London; or
(*e*) a county council or county borough council in Wales.

(8) In this section the expression "advertisement" includes any notice, circular, label, wrapper or other document, and any announcement made orally or by any means of producing or transmitting sounds.

[Cancer Act 1939, s 4 as amended by the Medicines Act 1968, Schs 5 and 6, the Criminal Justice Act 1982, ss 35, 38 and 46, the Statute Law (Repeals) Act 1986, Sch 1 and SI 2008/2840.]

---

* **Words repealed by the Criminal Justice Act 2003, Sch 37 from a date to be appointed.**

1 "Advertisement" includes any notice, circular, label, wrapper or other document and any announcement made orally or by any means of producing or transmitting sounds (sub-s (8)).

2 A prosecution under this section shall not be instituted in England or Wales without the consent of the Attorney-General (sub-s (6)). Subject thereto, it shall be the duty of the council of every county and county borough to institute the proceedings (sub-s (7)).

3 "Hospital" includes a clinic, dispensary or other institution for the reception of the sick, whether as in-patients or out-patients (s 5(1)).

# Medicines Act 1968

(1968 c 67)

## Part I

## Medicines Commission

7.8034 *Part I of the Act (ss 1 to 5) establishes the Commission on Human Medicines to act with respect to medicinal products.*

## Part II

## Licences and Certificates Relating to Medicinal Products

### *General provisions and exemptions*

7.8035 7. **General provisions as to dealing with medicinal products** (1) The following provisions of this section have effect subject to—

(*a*) any exemption conferred by or under this Part of this Act[1];
(*b*) *repealed*
(*c*) the provisions of section 48[2] of this Act.

(2) Except in accordance with a licence granted[3] for the purposes of this section (in this Act referred to as a "product licence") no person shall[4], in the course of a business carried on by him, and in circumstances to which this subsection applies—

(*a*) sell, supply or export any medicinal product, or
(*b*) procure the sale, supply or exportation of any medicinal product, or
(*c*) procure the manufacture or assembly of any medicinal product for sale, supply or exportation.

(2A) *Repealed.*

(2B) *Repealed.*

(3) No person shall import any medicinal product except in accordance with a product licence.

(3A) The restrictions imposed by subsections (2) and (3) of this section shall not apply where the medicinal product concerned is an investigational medicinal product within the meaning of the Clinical Trials Regulations.

(3B) The restrictions imposed by subsections (2) and (3) of this section shall not apply where the medicinal product concerned is a homoeopathic medicinal product to which the 2001 Directive applies and which fulfils the conditions laid down in Article 14(1) of that Directive.

(4) In relation to an imported medicinal product, subsection (2) of this section applies to circumstances in which the person selling, supplying or exporting the medicinal product in question, or procuring the sale, supply or exportation or the manufacture or assembly for sale, supply or exportation of that product, has himself imported the product or procured its importation.

(5) In relation to any medicinal product which has not been imported, subsection (2) of this section applies to any circumstances in which the person selling, supplying or exporting the medicinal product in question, or procuring the sale, supply or exporting or the manufacture or assembly for sale, supply or exportation of that product,

(*a*) is responsible for the composition of the product, or

(*b*) if that product is a proprietary medicinal product or an industrially produced medicinal product is responsible for the placing of the product on the market in the United Kingdom.

(6) For the purposes of subsection (5) of this section a person shall be taken to be responsible for the composition of a medicinal product if (but only if) in the course of a business carried on by him—

(*a*) he procures the manufacture of the product to his order by another person, where the order specifies, or incorporates by reference to some other document, particulars of the composition of the product ordered, whether those particulars amount to a complete specification or not, or

(*b*) he manufactures the product otherwise than in pursuance of an order which fulfils the conditions specified in the preceding paragraph.

(6A) Subsection (5)(*b*) of this section shall not apply if the product is—

(*a*) *repealed*

(*b*) a radiopharmaceutical in which the radionuclide is in the form of a sealed source

(*c*) *repealed.*

(6B) *Repealed.*

(7) In this section—

"homoeopathic medicinal product" means any medicinal product (which may contain a number of principles) prepared from substances called homoeopathic stocks in accordance with a homoeopathic manufacturing procedure described by the European Pharmacopoeia or, in the absence thereof, by any pharmacopoeia used officially in a member State;

"proprietary medicinal product" means a ready-prepared medicinal product placed on the market in the United Kingdom under a special name and in a special pack;

"radiopharmaceutical" means a ready-prepared medicinal product which, when ready for use, contains one or more radionuclides included for a medicinal purpose.

[Medicines Act 1968, s 7 as amended by SI 1977/1050, SI 1983/1724, SI 1992/604, SI 1994/276, SI 2004/1031, SI 2005/50, SI 2005/2753 and SI 2006/2407.]

---

1 Sections 9–14 contain exemptions for doctors, dentists, veterinary surgeons and practitioners, pharmacists, nurses and midwives, herbal remedies, imports, and re-exports; s 16 contains transitional exemptions. A number of orders have been made giving exemption either from s 7 alone, or from some or all of Part II; the following include exemption from s 7:

the Medicines (Importation of Medicinal Products for Re-Exportation) Order 1971, SI 1971/1326 amended by SI 1977/640 and SI 2005/2745;

the Medicines (Exemption from Licences) (Food and Cosmetics) Order 1971, SI 1971/1410 amended by SI 1973/2079;

the Medicines (Exemption from Licences) (Special and Transitional Cases) Order 1971, SI 1971/1450 amended by SI 1972/1200, SI 1978/1139, SI 1979/1585, SI 1989/1184, SI 1989/2323 and SI 2005/2745;

the Medicines (Exemption from Licences) (Special Cases and Miscellaneous Provisions) Order 1972, SI 1972/1200 amended by SI 1974/498, SI 1978/1139, SI 1979/1585, SI 1989/2323,SI 2004/1031 and SI 2005/2745;

the Medicines (Exemption from Licences) (Emergency Importation) Order 1974, SI 1974/316 amended by SI 2005/2745;

the Medicines (Exemption from Licences) (Ingredients) Order 1974, SI 1974/1150 amended by SI 2005/2745;

the Medicines (Exemption from Licences) (Importation) Order 1984, SI 1984/763;

the Medicines (Exemption from Licences) (Intermediate Medicated Feeding Stuffs) Order 1990, SI 1990/567;

the Medicines (Exemption from Licensing) (Radiopharmaceuticals) Order 1992, SI 1992/2844.

2 Section 48 provides for the postponement of restrictions in relation to exports.

3 The licensing authority is the body of Ministers for health and agriculture for England, Scotland and Northern Ireland as specified in s 1(1) of the Act (s 6). Sections 18–30 and Sch 2 of the Act deal with the procedure, etc on an application for a licence, and s 107 states the validity of decisions and the right to apply to the High Court for a decision to be quashed.

4 These restrictions do not apply to anything done before the "first appointed day", being a day to be appointed by order: s 16(1).

*Supplementary provisions*

7.8037 **43. Extension of s 7 to certain special circumstances**

PART III

FURTHER PROVISIONS RELATING TO DEALINGS WITH MEDICINAL PRODUCTS

*Additional provisions*

7.8046 **58. Medicinal products on prescription only** (1) The Ministers may by order[1] specify descriptions or classes of medicinal products[2] for the purposes of this section; and, in relation to any description or class so specified, the order shall state which of the following, that is to say—

(*a*) doctors,

(*b*) dentists, and

(*c*) veterinary surgeons and veterinary practitioners,

(*d*) registered nurses or midwives who are of such a description and comply with such conditions as may be specified in the order, and

(*e*) other persons who are of such a description and comply with such conditions as may be specified in the order.

are to be appropriate practitioners for the purposes of this section.

(1A) *Repealed.*

(1ZA) Paragraphs (*a*) and (*g*) of subsection (1A) do not apply to persons in so far as they are registered as members of the social work profession in England or social care workers in England (each of those expressions having the same meaning as in section 60 of the Health Act 1999).

(1B) *Repealed.*

(2) *Repealed.*

(3) *Repealed.*

(4) Without prejudice to the last preceding subsection, any order[1] made by the Ministers for the purposes of this section may provide—

(*a*) that regulation 214(1) or (2) of the 2012 Regulations shall have effect subject to such exemptions as may be specified in the order or, in the case of an appropriate practitioner, other than a doctor or dentist, such modifications as may be so specified;

(*b*) that, for the purpose of regulation 214(1) of the 2012 Regulations, a medicinal product shall not be taken to be sold or supplied in accordance with a prescription given by an appropriate practitioner unless such conditions as are prescribed by the order are fulfilled.

(4A) An order under this section may provide, in relation to an appropriate practitioner, other than a doctor or dentist], that such a person may—

(*a*) give a prescription for a medicinal product falling within a description or class specified in the order;

(*b*) administer any such medicinal product; or

(*c*) give directions for the administration of any such medicinal product,

only where he complies with such conditions as may be specified in the order in respect of the cases or circumstances in which he may do so.

(4B) An order under this section may provide, in relation to a condition specified by virtue of subsection (4A), for the condition to have effect subject to such exemptions as may be specified in the order.

(4C) Where a condition is specified by virtue of subsection (4A), any prescription or direction given by a person in contravention of the condition is not (subject to such exemptions or modifications as may be specified in the order by virtue of subsection (4)(*a*) of this section) given by an appropriate practitioner for the purposes of regulation 214(1) or (2) of the 2012 Regulations.

(5) Any exemption conferred or modification made by an order in accordance with subsection (4)(*a*) or (4B) of this section may be conferred or made subject to such conditions or limitations as may be specified in the order.

(6) Before making an order under this section the Ministers shall consult the appropriate committee.

[Medicines Act 1968, s 58 as amended by the Medicinal Products: Prescription by Nurses etc Act 1994, s 1, the Health and Social Care Act 2001, s 63, SI 2002/253, SI 2003/1590, SI 2005/1094, SI 2006/2407 and Health and Social Care Act 2012.]

---

[1] See the Prescription Only Medicines (Human Use) Order 1997, SI 1997/1830 amended by SI 1997/2044, SI 1998/108, 1178 and 2081, SI 1999/1044 and 3463, SI 2000/1917, 2899 and 3231, SI 2001/2777 and 3942, SI 2002/549 and 2469, SI 2003/696 and 2915, SI 2004/2, 1031, 1189, 1771 and 2693, SI 2005/765, 848, 1507, 2759 and 3324, SI 2006/915 and 2807, SI 2007/289, SI 2008/464 and 1161, SI 2009/1165 and 3062, SI 2010/231, 1136, 1881 and 2998, SI 2011/1327 and 2581 and SI 2012/1479 and 1916; Medicines for Human Use (Prescribing) Order 2005, SI 2005/765 amended by SI 2005/1507, SI 2007/289, 2178 and 3101, SI 2010/231, SI 2011/2581 and SI 2012/1479.

[2] Sections 58A and 58B lay down the criteria to be applied in specifying which products are to be supplied on prescription only, s 59 contains special provisions relating to new products, and ss 60–62 give power to control sale or supply by regulations or order. The following orders have been made under s 62: Medicines (Bal Jivan Chamcho Prohibition) (No 2) Order 1977, SI 1977/670 amended by SI 1990/2487, SI 2008/548, SI 2010/231 and SI 2012/1809; Medicines (Prohibition of Non Medical Anti-Microbial Substances) Order 1977, SI 1977/2131, amended by SI 1990/2487, SI 1992/2684 and SI 2005/2745; Medicines (Chloroform Prohibition) Order 1979, 1979/382 amended by SI

1980/263 and SI 1989/1184; Medicines (Phenacetin Prohibition) Order 1979, SI 1979/1181; Medicine (Carbadox, Prohibition) Order 1986 SI 1986/1368; Medicines (Aristolochia and Mu Tong etc) (Prohibition) Order 2001, SI 2001/1841 amended by SI 2005/2750 and SI 2008/548 and SI 2012/1809 and 1916; Medicines for Human Use (Kava-kava) (Prohibition) Order 2002, SI 2002/3170 amended by SI 2005/2750, SI 2008/548 and SI 2012/1809 and 1916; Medicines for Human Use (Prohibition) (Senecio and Miscellaneous Amendments) Order 2008, SI 2008/548 amended by SI 2012/1809 and 1916.

7.8047 **63. Adulteration of medicinal products** No person shall—

(*a*) add any substance to, or abstract[1] any substance from, a medicinal product so as to affect injuriously the composition of the product, with intent that the product shall be sold or supplied in that state, or

(*b*) sell or supply, or offer or expose for sale or supply, or have in his possession for the purpose of sale or supply, any medicinal product whose composition has been injuriously affected by the addition or abstraction of any substance.

[Medicines Act 1968, s 63.]

1 The dilution of a substance so as to reduce the percentage of an ingredient is not abstraction (*Dearden v Whiteley* (1916) 80 JP 215).

7.8048 **64. Protection of purchasers of medicinal products** (1) No person shall, to the prejudice of the purchaser, sell any medicinal product which is not of the nature or quality demanded by the purchaser.

(2) For the purposes of this section the sale of a medicinal product shall not be taken to be otherwise than to the prejudice of the purchaser by reason only that the purchaser buys the product for the purpose of analysis or examination.

(3) Subsection (1) of this section shall not be taken to be contravened by reason only that a medicinal product contains some extraneous matter, if it is proved that the presence of that matter was an inevitable consequence of the process of manufacture of the product.

(4) Subsection (1) of this section shall not be taken to be contravened by reason only that a substance has been added to, or abstracted from, the medicinal product, if it is proved that—

(*a*) the addition or abstraction was not carried out fraudulently, and did not injuriously affect the composition of the product, and

(*b*) the product was sold having attached to it, or to a container or package in which it was sold, a conspicuous notice of adequate size and legibly printed, specifying the substance added or abstracted.

(5) Where a medicinal product is sold or supplied in pursuance of a prescription given by an appropriate practitioner, the preceding provisions of this section shall have effect as if—

(*a*) in those provisions any reference to sale included a reference to supply and (except as provided by the following paragraph) any reference to the purchaser included a reference to the person (if any) for whom the product was prescribed by the practitioner, and

(*b*) in subsection (1) of this section, for the words "demanded by the purchaser", there were substituted the words "specified in the prescription".

[Medicines Act 1968, s 64 as amended by SI 2012/1916.]

*Offences, and provision for disqualification*

7.8051 **67. Offences under Part III** (1) The following provisions of this section shall have effect subject to sections 121 and 122 of this Act[1].

(1A) Any person who gives a prescription or directions or administers a medicinal product in contravention of a condition imposed by an order under section 58 of this Act by virtue of subsection (4A) of that section shall be guilty of an offence.

(1B) Any person who—

(*a*) is an appropriate practitioner within the meaning of regulation 214 of the 2012 Regulations; and

(*b*) gives a prescription or directions in respect of a medicinal product of a description or class in relation to which he is not an appropriate practitioner,

shall be guilty of an offence.

(2) Any person who contravenes any of the following provisions of this Part of this Act, that is to say, sections 63 and 64, or who contravenes section 61 or any order[2] made under section 62 of this Act, shall be guilty of an offence.

(3) Where a medicinal product is sold, supplied or imported in contravention of an order made under section 62 of this Act, any person who, otherwise than for the purpose of performing or exercising a duty or power imposed or conferred by or under this Act or any other enactment, is in possession of the medicinal product, knowing or having reasonable cause to suspect that it was sold, supplied or imported in contravention of the order, shall be guilty of an offence.

(3A) *Repealed.*

(4) Any person guilty of an offence under subsection (1A), (1B), (2), (3) of this section shall be liable[3]—

(*a*) on summary conviction, to a fine not exceeding **the prescribed sum**;

(*b*) on conviction on indictment, to a **fine** or to imprisonment for a term not exceeding **two years** or to **both**.

(5) *Repealed*
(6) *Repealed.*

[Medicines Act 1968, s 67 as amended by the Criminal Law Act 1977, ss 28 and 31, the Magistrates' Courts Act 1980, s 32, the Criminal Justice Act 1982, ss 38 and 46, the Health and Social Care Act 2001, s 63 and SI 2005/2789 and SI 2012/1916.]

---

1 These sections deal with the liability of another person and the defence of warranty.
2 For orders made under s 62, see note to s 58, ante.
3 For procedure in respect of this offence, triable either way, see the Magistrates' Courts Act 1980, ss 17A–21 in PART I: MAGISTRATES' COURTS, PROCEDURE.

## PART IV
## PHARMACIES

### *Provisions as to use of certain titles, descriptions and emblems*

7.8053 78. **Restrictions on use of titles, descriptions and emblems** (1) The provisions of this section shall have effect subject to section 79[1] of this Act.

(2) No person shall—

(*a*) take or use any of the following titles, that is to say, chemist and druggist, druggist, dispensing chemist, and dispensing druggist, or

(*b*) take or use the title of chemist in connection with the sale of any goods by retail or the supply of any goods in circumstances corresponding to retail sale[2],

unless the conditions specified in the next following subsection are fulfilled.

(3) Those conditions are—

(*a*) in the case of an individual, that he is a person lawfully conducting a retail pharmacy business[3] (either alone or as a member of a partnership) and that he does not take or use the title in question in connection with any premises at which any goods are sold by retail, or are supplied in circumstances corresponding to retail sale, unless these premises are a registered pharmacy, and

(*b*) in the case of a body corporate, that the body is a person lawfully conducting a retail pharmacy business and that the title in question is not taken or used by that body in connection with any premises at which any goods are sold by retail, or are supplied in circumstances corresponding to retail sale, unless those premises are a registered pharmacy, and that the pharmacist who, in relation to that business, is such a superintendent as is referred to in section 71(1) of this Act is a member of the board of the body corporate.

(4) No person shall, in connection with a business carried on by him which consists of or includes the retail sale of any goods, or the supply of any goods in circumstances corresponding to retail sale, use the description "pharmacy" except in respect of a registered pharmacy or in respect of the pharmaceutical department of a hospital or a health centre.

(5) A person who is not registered in the register of pharmaceutical chemists for Northern Ireland or in the register of visiting pharmaceutical chemists from a relevant European State made out and maintained under Articles 6 and 9 of the Pharmacy (Northern Ireland) Order 1976 may not—

(*a*) take or use the title pharmaceutical chemist, pharmaceutist, pharmacist, member of the Pharmaceutical Society of Northern Ireland or Fellow of the Pharmaceutical Society of Northern Ireland; or

(*b*) take or use any of the titles mentioned in paragraph (*a*) in connection with a business carried on (whether by him or by some other person) at any premises which consists of or includes the retail sale of any goods, or the supply of any goods in circumstances corresponding to retail sale, unless those premises are a registered pharmacy or a hospital or health centre.

(5A) A person who is not registered as a pharmacist in Part 1 or 4 of the register maintained under article 19 of the Pharmacy Order 2010 may not take or use the title pharmacist or fferyllydd (its equivalent in the Welsh language) in connection with a business carried on (whether by him or by some other person) at any premises which consists of or includes the retail sale of any goods, or the supply of any goods in circumstances corresponding to retail sale, unless those premises are a registered pharmacy or a hospital or health centre.

(5B) Subsection (5) extends to Northern Ireland only; and subsection (5A) does not extend there.

(6) No person shall, in connection with any business, use any title, description or emblem likely to suggest—

(*a*) that he possesses any qualification with respect to the sale, manufacture or assembly of medicinal products which he does not in fact possess, or

(*b*) that any person employed in the business possesses any such qualification which that person does not in fact possess.

(7) For the purposes of the last preceding subsection the use of the description "pharmacy", in connection with a business carried on at any premises, shall be taken to be likely to suggest that the person carrying on the business (where that person is not a body corporate) is a pharmacist and that any other person, who is in charge of the business at those premises (so far as concerns the retail sale of medicinal products or the supply of such products in circumstances corresponding to retail sale)

is also a pharmacist.

(8) Where a person is lawfully conducting a retail pharmacy business as being a representative of a pharmacist in the circumstances specified in section 69(1)(*e*) of this Act, subsections (5) to (7) of this section shall not have effect so as to prevent the representative from taking or using, in connection with that business, any title, description or emblem which the pharmacist himself could have used in accordance with those subsections.

[Medicines Act 1968, s 78 amended by the Statute Law (Repeals) Act 1993, Sch 1, SI 2007/289, the Health Act 2006, s 27 and SI 2010/231.]

1 Section 79 gives the Minister power to modify or extend the restrictions under s 78.

2 A business name on a shop sign incorporating the word "chemist" was held not to be conclusive if there is another notice displayed denying that a qualified chemist is in charge of the shop under a previous enactment, see *Denerley v Spink* [1947] KB 768, [1947] 1 All ER 835, 111 JP 318; this case would seem to apply to this provision, provided the premises were a registered pharmacy.

3 Under provisions contained in ss 69–76 every retail pharmacy business, as defined in s 132(1), must be registered; and ss 80–83 contain provisions whereby the "Statutory Committee" of the Pharmaceutical Society may direct disqualification and removal from the register.

7.8054 **84. Offences under Part IV** (A1) A person who fails to comply with either of the following shall be guilty of an offence and liable on summary conviction to a fine not exceeding level 3 on the standard scale—

(*a*) subsection (4) of section 72A of this Act (which requires the making of entries in a record relating to the responsible pharmacist),

(*b*) subsection (5) of that section (which requires the keeping and preservation of the record).

(1) Any person who contravenes section 77 of this Act shall be guilty of an offence and liable on summary conviction to a fine not exceeding **level 3** on the standard scale.

(2) Any person who contravenes section 78 of this Act or who contravenes any regulations made under section 79(2) of this Act shall be guilty of an offence and liable on summary conviction to a fine not exceeding **level 3** on the standard scale.

[Medicines Act 1968, s 84 as amended by the Criminal Justice Act 1982, ss 38 and 46 and the Health Act 2006, s 30.]

7.8055 **84A. Rules by the General Pharmaceutical Council]** (1) The General Pharmaceutical Council may make such provision as it considers appropriate in rules for any purpose for which rules are authorised or required to be made by it under Part 4 of this Act.

(2) Article 66 of the Pharmacy Order 2010 (rules) applies to the making of rules by the General Pharmaceutical Council under Part 4 of this Act as it applies to the making of rules by the General Pharmaceutical Council under Part 3 of that Order (registered pharmacies: standards in retail pharmacies).

[Medicines Act 1968, s 84A as inserted by SI 2010/231.]

## PART V

## CONTAINERS, PACKAGES AND IDENTIFICATION OF MEDICINAL PRODUCTS

7.8056 **85. Labelling and marking of containers and packages** (1) The Ministers may make regulations[1] imposing such requirements as, for any of the purposes specified in subsection (2) of this section, they consider necessary or expedient with respect to any of the following matters, that is to say—

(*a*) the labelling of containers of medicinal products;

(*b*) the labelling of packages of medicinal products;

(*c*) the display of distinctive marks on containers and packages of medicinal products.

(2) The purposes referred to in the preceding subsection are—

(*a*) securing that medicinal products are correctly described and readily identifiable;

(*b*) securing that any appropriate warning or other appropriate information or instruction is given, and that false or misleading information is not given, with respect to medicinal products;

(*c*) promoting safety in relation to medicinal products.

(3) No person shall, in the course of a business carried on by him, sell or supply, or have in his possession for the purpose of sale or supply, any medicinal product in such circumstances as to contravene any requirements imposed by regulations under this section which are applicable to that product.

(4) In so far as any such requirements relate to the labelling or marking of containers of medicinal products, a person who, in the course of a business carried on by him, sells or supplies a medicinal product to which the requirements are applicable without its being enclosed in a container shall, except in so far as the regulations otherwise provide, be taken to contravene those requirements as if he had sold or supplied it in a container not complying with those requirements.

(5) Without prejudice to the preceding provisions of this section, no person shall, in the course of a business carried on by him[2], sell or supply, or have in his possession for the purpose of sale or supply, a medicinal product of any description in a container or package which is labelled or marked in such a way that the container or package—

(*a*) falsely describes the product, or

(*b*) is likely to mislead as to the nature or quality of the product or as to the uses or effects of medicinal products of that description.

[Medicines Act 1968, s 85 as amended by SI 2006/2407.]

[1] The Medicines (Labelling) Regulations 1976, SI 1976/1726, as amended by SI 1977/996 and 2168, SI 1978/41, SI 1981/1791, SI 1983/1729, SI 1985/1558 and 2008, SI 1992/3273, SI 1994/104 and 3142, SI 1996/2194, SI 2002/236, SI 2004/1031 and SI 2005/2745 and 2753 have been made; the penalty for contravention of the Regulations is the same as that set out in s 91(2), post. See also the Medicines (Contact Lens Fluids and Other Substances) (Labelling) Regulations 1979, SI 1979/1759, amended by SI 1981/1689.

[2] This section is aimed at ensuring that the person "carrying on the business" will label and mark medicinal products correctly. Where a locum self-employed pharmacist was working for a supermarket pharmacy, the business being carried on at the relevant time, in the course of which the medicines were supplied, was that of the supermarket. The person who is carrying on the business for the purposes of this section is the employer, not the "employee" and the extended definition in s 132(1) was to preclude, in different circumstances, a defence by a professional person that he was carrying on a profession and not a business (*R v Lee* [2010] EWCA Crim 1404, [2011] 1 WLR 418, [2010] 2 Cr App R 26).

7.8057 **86. Leaflets** (1) The Ministers may make regulations[1] imposing such requirements as, for any of the purposes specified in section 85(2) of this Act, they consider necessary or expedient with respect to leaflets relating to medicinal products which are supplied, or are intended to be supplied, with the products, whether by being enclosed in containers or packages of the product or otherwise.

(2) No person shall, in the course of a business carried on by him, supply with any medicinal product, or have in his possession for the purpose of so supplying, a leaflet which contravenes any requirements imposed by regulations under this section which are applicable to that leaflet.

(3) Without prejudice to the preceding provisions of this section, no person shall, in the course of a business carried on by him, supply with a medicinal product of any description, or have in his possession for the purpose of so supplying, a leaflet which—

(*a*) falsely describes the product, or

(*b*) is likely to mislead as to the nature or quality of the product or as to the uses or effects of medicinal products of that description.

(4) No person shall, in the course of a business carried on by him supply a product to which the 2001 Directive applies, unless—

(*a*) a leaflet enclosed in, or supplied with, the container or package of the product, or

(*b*) the container or package itself,

contains the particulars which a leaflet relating to the product is required by regulations under subsection (1) of this section to contain, and does so in the manner required by such regulations.

[Medicines Act 1968, s 86 as amended by SI 1994/276, SI 2002/236 and SI 2006/2407.]

[1] See note 1 to s 85, ante. The Medicines (Leaflets) Regulations 1977, SI 1977/1055 amended by SI 1992/3274, SI 1994/104 and SI 2005/2753 and the Medicines (Leaflets for Veterinary Drugs) Regulations 1983, SI 1983/1727, amended by SI 1985/2008, have also been made under s 86(1).

7.8058 **87. Requirements as to containers** (1) The Ministers may make regulations[1] prohibiting the sale or supply of medicinal products otherwise than in containers which comply with such requirements as the Ministers consider necessary or expedient for any of the purposes specified in section 85(2) of this Act, or for the purpose of preserving the quality of the products, and in particular, may by the regulations require such containers to be of such strength, to be made of such materials, and to be of shapes or patterns, as may be prescribed.

(2) No person shall, in the course of a business carried on by him, sell or supply, or have in his possession for the purpose of sale or supply, any medicinal product in such circumstances as to contravene any requirements imposed by regulations under this section which are applicable to that product.

(3) The purposes mentioned in subsection (1) are—

(*a*) securing that medicinal products are correctly described and readily identifiable;

(*b*) securing that any appropriate warning or other appropriate instruction or information is given, and that false or misleading information is not given, with respect to medicinal products;

(*c*) promoting safety in relation to medicinal products.

[Medicines Act 1968, s 87 as amended by SI 2006/2407 and SI 2012/1916.]

[1] See the Human Use Medicines Regulations 2012, SI 2012/1916 listed in the European Communities Act 1972 regulations, ante.

7.8059 **88. Distinctive colours, shapes and markings of medicinal products** (1) Regulations[1] made by the Ministers may impose such requirements as, for any of the purposes specified in section 87(3) of this Act, the Ministers consider necessary or expedient with respect to any one or more of the following matters, that is to say—

(*a*) the colour of the products;

(*b*) the shape of the products; and

(*c*) distinctive marks to be displayed on the products.

(2) Regulations[1] made under this section may provide that medicinal products of any such description, or falling within any such class, as may be specified in the regulations shall not except in such circumstances (if any) as may be so specified, be of any such colour or shape, or display any such mark, as may be so specified.

(3) No person shall, in the course of a business carried on by him, sell or supply, or have in his

possession for the purpose of sale or supply, any medicinal product which contravenes any requirements imposed by regulations under this section.

[Medicines Act 1968, s 88 as amended by SI 2006/2407 and SI 2012/1916.]

---

[1] See the Human Use Medicines Regulations 2012, SI 2012/1916 listed in the European Communities Act 1972 regulations, ante.

**7.8061 91. Offences under Part V, and supplementary provisions** (1) *Repealed.*

(2) Any regulations made under this Part of this Act may provide that any person who contravenes the regulations, or who contravenes the provisions of section 87(2) of this Act, shall be guilty of an offence and—

(*a*) shall be liable on summary conviction to a fine not exceeding **the prescribed sum**; or such lesser sum as may be specified in the regulations, and

(*b*) if the regulations so provide, shall be liable on conviction on indictment to a fine or to imprisonment for a term not exceeding **two years** or to both.

(3) Without prejudice to the application of section 129(5) of this Act, any power to make regulations conferred by section 87 of this Act may be exercised so as to impose requirements either in relation to medicinal products generally or in relation to medicinal products of a particular description, or falling within a particular class, specified in the regulations.

(4) In this Part of this Act "requirements" includes restrictions.

[Medicines Act 1968, s 91 as amended by the Criminal Law Act 1977, s 28, the Magistrates' Courts Act 1980, s 32 and SI 2006/2407 and SI 2012/1916.]

## PART VII

*British Pharmacopoeia and other publications*

**7.8068 99–103.** *Relates to the British Pharmacopoeia and other publications*

## PART VIII

### MISCELLANEOUS AND SUPPLEMENTARY PROVISIONS

**7.8069 104–106.** *Power to apply Act by order[1] to other substances and to activities other than carrying on a business.*

---

[1] See the Medicines (Cyanogenetic Substances) Order 1984, SI 1984/187 amended by SI 2006/2407.

**7.8070 108. Enforcement in England and Wales** (1) Subject to the provisions of subsection (6C) of this section,it shall be the duty of the appropriate Minister to enforce in England and Wales, or to secure the enforcement in England and Wales of, the provisions of this Act and any regulations and orders made under it.

(2) For the purposes of performing that duty in relation to—

(*a*) the provisions of any order made under paragraph (*a*) of section 62(1) of this Act and of section 63(*b*), section 64 and sections 87(2) and 88(3) of this Act, in the application of any of those provisions to the retail sale, offer or exposure for retail sale, or possession for the purpose of retail sale, of medicinal products and to the supply, offer or exposure for supply, or possession for the purpose of supply, of medicinal products in circumstances corresponding to retail sale;

(*b*) *repealed;*

(*c*) *repealed;*

the appropriate Minister shall, in respect of each area for which there is a drugs authority, make arrangements or give directions whereby the General Pharmaceutical Council, or the drugs authority for that area, or both the Council and that authority, to such extent as, in the case of that Council or authority, the arrangements or directions may provide, shall have power concurrently with the appropriate Minister, or shall be under a duty concurrently with him, to enforce the provisions specified in paragraph (*a*) of this subsection, in their application as mentioned in that paragraph.

(3) *Repealed.*

(4) *Repealed.*

(5) *Repealed.*

(6) The General Pharmaceutical Society shall be under a duty, concurrently with the appropriate Minister—

(*a*) *repealed;*

(*b*) to enforce the provisions of any regulations made under section 60 of this Act in their application to premises in England and Wales at which medicinal products are sold by retail or are supplied in circumstances corresponding to retail sale; and

(*c*) to enforce the provisions of section 78 of this Act, and of any regulations made under section 79(2) of this Act, in their application to England and Wales.

(6A) The General Pharmaceutical Society shall be under a duty, concurrently with the appropriate Minister, to enforce the provisions of subsections (4) and (5) of section 72A of this Act in their application to England and Wales.

(6B) The General Pharmaceutical Society shall be under a duty to enforce the other provisions of section 72A of this Act, and any regulations made under them, in their application to England

and Wales.

(6C) The appropriate Minister shall be under no duty to enforce those other provisions, or any regulations made under them, in their application to England and Wales.

(6D) Notwithstanding subsection (6C) of this section the appropriate Minister is to be treated for the purposes of sections 111 to 114 of this Act—

(*a*) as empowered by this section to enforce those other provisions, or any regulations made under them, in their application to England and Wales, and

(*b*) to that extent as an enforcement authority in relation to those other provisions or those regulations in their application to England and Wales.

(7) *Repealed.*

(8) *Repealed.*

(9) Notwithstanding anything in subsections (2) to (6D) of this section, no duty or power conferred or imposed by or under any of those subsections shall be performed or be exercisable in relation to—

(*a*) any hospital (except in relation to so much of the hospital premises as is a registered pharmacy), or

(*b*) so much of any premises as is used by a practitioner for carrying on his practice, or

(*c*) so much of any premises (not falling within either of the preceding paragraphs) as is used for veterinary medicine or veterinary surgery for the purposes of any institution.

(10) If the appropriate Minister is satisfied, after making such inquiry as he thinks fit, that the General Pharmaceutical Council has in relation to any matter failed to perform a duty imposed on it by subsections (6A) or (6B) to enforce any provisions mentioned in those subsections], and that the public interest requires that the provisions in question should be enforced in relation to it, he may determine that he will himself enforce those provisions in relation to that matter.

(11) In this section "the appropriate Minister"—

(*a*) *repealed*

(*b*) means the Secretary of State.[1].

(12) In this section "drugs authority" means—

(*a*) in relation to an area in England other than the City of London, the council of a non-metropolitan county, metropolitan district or London borough;

(*b*) in relation to the City of London (including the Inner Temple and the Middle Temple), the Common Council of the City of London; and

(*c*) in relation to an area in Wales, the council of a county or county borough.

[Medicines Act 1968, s 108 as amended by SI 1968/1699, the Local Government Act 1972, Sch 30, the Animal Health and Welfare Act 1984, Sch 1, SI 1988/1955, the Food Safety Act 1990, Sch 3, the Local Government (Wales) Act 1994, Sch 16, SI 2006/2407, the Health Act 2006, s 31 and SI 2012/1916.]

---

[1] Now the Secretary of State for Health, see the Transfer of Functions (Medicines and Poisons) Order 1999, SI 1999/3142.

**7.8071 111. Rights of entry** (1) Subject to the following provisions of this section, any person duly authorised in writing by an enforcement authority shall, on production, if required, of his credentials, have a right at any reasonable time to enter any premises—

(*a*) for the purpose of ascertaining whether there is or has been, on or in connection with those premises, any contravention of any provisions of this Act or of any regulations or order made under this Act which, by or under any provisions of sections 108 to 110 of this Act, that authority is required or empowered to enforce,

(*aa*) for the purpose specified in the third sub-paragraph of Article 111(1) of the 2001 Directive, or

(*b*) generally for the purposes of the performance by the authority of their functions under this Act or under any such regulations or order.

(2) Any person duly authorised in writing by an enforcement authority shall, on production, if required, of his credentials, have a right at any reasonable time—

(*a*) *repealed;*

(*b*) to enter any vehicle other than a hover vehicle, any stall or place other than premises, or any home-going ship, for any purpose for which under subsection (1) of this section, the person so authorised would have a right to enter any premises.

(3) *Repealed.*

(4) Admission to any premises used only as a private dwelling-house shall not be demanded as of right by virtue of the preceding provisions of this section unless twenty-four hours' notice of the intended entry has been given to the occupier.

(5) If a justice of the peace, on sworn information in writing, is satisfied that there are reasonable grounds for entering any premises for any purposes for which a person authorised by an enforcement authority has a right to enter them in accordance with the preceding provisions of this section, and is also satisfied—

(*a*) that admission to the premises has been refused, or that a refusal is apprehended, and (in either case) that notice of the intention to apply for a warrant has been given to the occupier, or

(*b*) that an application for admission, or the giving of such a notice, would defeat the object of the entry, or (*c*) that the case is one of urgency, or

(*d*) that the premises are unoccupied or the occupier is temporarily absent,

the justice may by warrant under his hand authorise the enforcement authority, or any person duly authorised by them, to enter the premises, if need be by force.

(6) The last preceding subsection shall have effect in relation to entering any ship, vehicle, stall or place which may be entered under subsection (2) of this section as it has effect in relation to entering any premises, as if in the last preceding subsection any reference to the occupier were a reference to the master or other person in charge of the ship, vehicle, stall or place.

(7) Any warrant granted under this section shall continue in force for a period of one month.

(8) In this section "home-going-ship" means a ship plying exclusively in inland waters or engaged exclusively in coastal voyages; and for the purposes of this subsection "inland waters" means any canal, river, lake, loch, navigation or estuary and "coastal voyage" means a voyage which starts and ends in the United Kingdom and does not involve calling at any place outside the United Kingdom.

(9) *Scotland.*

[Medicines Act 1968, s 111 as amended by SI 2005/2789 and SI 2012/1916.]

7.8072 **112. Power to inspect, take samples and seize goods and documents** (1) For the purpose of ascertaining whether there is or has been a contravention of this Act or of any regulations or order made thereunder which, by or under any provisions of sections 108 to 110 of this Act an enforcement authority is required or empowered to enforce, any person duly authorised in writing by that authority shall have a right to inspect—

(*a*) any substance or article appearing to him to be a medicinal product;

(*b*) any article appearing to him to be a container or package used or intended to be used to contain any medicinal product or to be a label or leaflet used or intended to be used in connection with a medicinal product; or

(*c*) any plant or equipment appearing to him to be used or intended to be used in connection with the manufacture or assembly of medicinal products, and any process of manufacture or assembly of any medicinal products and the means employed, at any stage in the processes of manufacture or assembly, for testing the materials after they have been subjected to those processes.

(2) Where for the purpose specified in the preceding subsection a person authorised as mentioned in that subsection requires a sample of any substance or article appearing to him to be—

(*a*) a medicinal product sold or supplied or intended to be sold or supplied, or

(*b*) a substance or article used or intended to be used in the manufacture of a medicinal product,

he shall (if he does not obtain the sample by purchase) have a right to take a sample of that substance or article.

(3) For the purpose specified in subsection (1) of this section, any person authorised as mentioned in that subsection shall have a right—

(*a*) to require any person carrying on a business which consists of or includes the manufacture, assembly, sale or supply of medicinal products, and any person employed in connection with such a business, to produce any books or documents relating to the business which are in his possession or under his control;

(*b*) to take copies of, or of any entry in, any book or document produced in pursuance of the preceding paragraph.

(4) Any person so authorised shall have a right to seize and detain any substance or article which he has reasonable cause to believe to be a substance or article in relation to which, or by means of which, an offence under this Act is being or has been committed, and any document which he has reasonable cause to believe to be a document which may be required as evidence in proceedings under this Act.

(5) For the purpose of exercising any such right as is specified in subsection (4) of this section the person having that right may, so far as is reasonably necessary in order to secure that the provisions of this Act and any regulations or order made thereunder are duly observed, require any person having authority to do so to break open any container or package or open any vending machine, or to permit him to do so.

(6) Where a person seizes any substance or article (including any document) in the exercise of such a right as is specified in subsection (4) of this section, he shall inform the person from whom it is seized, and, in the case of anything seized from a vending machine, the person whose name and address are stated on the machine as being those of the owner of the machine, or, if no name and address are so stated, the occupier of the premises on which the machine stands or to which it is affixed.

(7) Without prejudice to the preceding provisions of this section, any person duly authorised in writing by the licensing authority shall have the rights conferred by those provisions in relation to things belonging to, or any business carried on by, an applicant for a licence or certificate under Part II of this Act, and may exercise those rights for the purpose of verifying any statement contained in the application for the licence or certificate; and, where by virtue of this subsection a person exercises any such right as is specified in subsection (4) of this section, he shall be subject to

the duty imposed by subsection (6) of this section.

(8) Notwithstanding anything in the preceding provisions of this section, where a person claiming to exercise a right by virtue of this section is required to produce his credentials, the right shall not be exercisable by him except on production of those credentials.

(9) The provisions of Schedule 3 to this Act shall have effect with respect to samples obtained on behalf of enforcement authorities for the purposes of this Act.

[Medicines Act 1968, s 112.]

7.8073 **113. Application of sampling procedure to substance or article seized under s 112**

(1) The provisions of this section shall have effect where a person (in this section referred to as an "authorised officer") seizes a substance or article (other than a document) in the exercise of such a right as is specified in subsection (4) of section 112 of this Act.

(2) If any person who in accordance with subsection (6) of that section is entitled to be informed of the seizure so requests, either at the time of the seizure or at any subsequent time, not being later than twenty-one days after he is informed of the seizure, then, subject to the next following subsection, the authorised officer shall either—

(*a*) set aside a sample of the substance or article seized, or

(*b*) treat that substance or article as a sample,

whichever he considers more appropriate having regard to the nature of that substance or article.

(3) An authorised officer shall not be required by virtue of subsection (2) of this section to set aside a sample, or to treat a substance or article as a sample, if the nature of the substance or article is such that it is not reasonably practical to do either of those things.

(4) Where in accordance with subsection (2) of this section an authorised officer sets aside a sample, or treats a substance or article as a sample, he shall divide it into three parts, each part to be marked and sealed or fastened up in such manner as its nature will permit, and shall supply one part of it to the person who made the request under subsection (2) of this section.

(5) Paragraphs 10, 11 and 12 and paragraphs 15 to 27 of Schedule 3 to this Act shall have effect in relation to a sample set aside, or a substance or article treated as a sample, in accordance with subsection (2) of this section as they have effect in relation to a sample obtained as mentioned in paragraph 1 of that Schedule, but as if in those paragraphs—

(*a*) any reference to a sampling officer were a reference to an authorised officer;

(*b*) any reference to a sample included a reference to a substance or article treated as a sample;

(*c*) any reference to the preceding provisions of that Schedule were a reference to the preceding provisions of this section; and

(*d*) any reference to the relevant enforcement authority were a reference to the authority by whom the authorised officer is authorised for the purposes of section 112 of this Act,

and as if in paragraph 24(1) of that Schedule the reference to a substance or article obtained as mentioned in paragraph 1 of that Schedule were a reference to a substance or article of which a sample has been set aside, or which has been treated as a sample, in accordance with subsection (2) of this section.

[Medicines Act 1968, s 113 amended by SI 2012/1916.]

7.8074 **114. Supplementary provisions as to rights of entry and related rights** (1) Any person entering any property (that is to say, any premises, ship, vehicle, stall or place) by virtue of section 111 of this Act (whether in pursuance of a warrant or not) may take with him such other persons and such equipment as may appear to him to be necessary; and on leaving any such property which he has entered in pursuance of a warrant under that section he shall, if the property is unoccupied or the occupier (or, in the case of a ship, vehicle, stall or place, the master or other person in charge of it) is temporarily absent, leave it as effectively secured against trespass as he found it.

(2) Any person who—

(*a*) wilfully obstructs a person acting in pursuance of this Act and duly authorised so to act by an enforcement authority, or

(*b*) wilfully fails to comply with any requirement properly made to him by a person so acting under section 112 of this Act, or

(*c*) without reasonable cause fails to give to a person so acting any other assistance or information which that person may reasonably require of him for the purpose of the performance of his functions under this Act,

shall be guilty of an offence and shall be liable on summary conviction to a fine not exceeding **level 3** on the standard scale.

(3) If any person, in giving any such information as is mentioned in subsection (2)(*c*) of this section, makes any statement which he knows to be false, he shall be guilty of an offence and shall be liable[1]—

(*a*) on summary conviction, to a fine not exceeding **the prescribed sum**;

(*b*) on conviction on indictment, to a **fine** or to imprisonment for a term not exceeding **two years** or to **both**.

(4) Nothing in this section shall be construed as requiring a person to answer any question or give any information if to do so might incriminate that person or (where that person is married or a civil partner) the spouse or civil partner of that person.

[Medicines Act 1968, s 114 as amended by the Criminal Law Act 1977, s 28, the Magistrates' Courts Act 1980, s 32, the Criminal Justice Act 1982, ss 38 and 46 and the Civil Partnership Act 2004, Sch 27 and SI 2012/1916.]

[1] For procedure in respect of this offence, triable either way, see Magistrates' Courts Act 1980, ss 17A–21 in PART I: MAGISTRATES' COURTS, PROCEDURE.

7.8077 **118. Restrictions on disclosure of information** (1) If any person discloses to any other person—

(*a*) any information with respect to any manufacturing process or trade secret obtained by him in premises which he has entered by virtue of section 111 of this Act, or

(*b*) any information obtained by or furnished to him in pursuance of this Act,

he shall, unless the disclosure was made in the performance of his duty, be guilty of an offence.

(1A) Subsection (1) of this section does not apply if—

(*a*) the person making the disclosure referred to in that section is, or is acting on behalf of a person who is, a public authority for the purposes of the Freedom of Information Act 2000, and

(*b*) the information is not held by the authority on behalf of another person.

(2) Any person guilty of an offence under this section shall be liable[1]—

(*a*) on summary conviction, to a fine not exceeding **the prescribed sum**;

(*b*) on conviction on indictment, to a **fine** or to imprisonment for a term not exceeding **two years** or to **both**.

[Medicines Act 1968, s 118 as amended by the Criminal Law Act 1977, s 28, the Magistrates' Courts Act 1980, s 32 and SI 2004/3363.]

[1] For procedure in respect of this offence, triable either way, see Magistrates' Courts Act 1980, ss 17A–21 in PART I: MAGISTRATES' COURTS, PROCEDURE.

7.8078 **121. Contravention due to default of other person** (1) Where a contravention by any person of any provision to which this section applies constitutes an offence under this Act, and is due to an act or default of another person, then, whether proceedings are taken against the first-mentioned person or not, that other person may be charged with and convicted of that offence, and shall be liable on conviction to the same punishment as might have been imposed on the first-mentioned person if he had been convicted of the offence.

(2) Where a person who is charged with an offence under this Act in respect of a contravention of a provision to which this section applies proves to the satisfaction of the court—

(*a*) that he exercised all due diligence to secure that the provision in question would not be contravened, and

(*b*) that the contravention was due to the act or default of another person,

the first-mentioned person shall, subject to the next following subsection be acquitted of the offence.

(3) A person shall not, without the leave of the court, be entitled to rely on the defence provided by subsection (2) of this section unless, not later than seven clear days before the date of the hearing, he has served on the prosecutor a notice in writing giving such information identifying, or assisting in the identification of, the other person in question as was then in his possession.

(4) This section applies to the following provisions, that is to say, sections 63, 64, 87 and 88, and the provisions of any regulations made under any of those sections.

[Medicines Act 1968, s 121 as amended by SI 2006/2407 and SI 2012/1916.]

7.8079 **122. Warranty as defence** (1) Subject to the following provisions of this section, in any proceedings for an offence under this Act in respect of a contravention of a provision to which this section applies, it shall be a defence for the defendant to prove—

(*a*) that he purchased the substance or article to which the contravention relates in the United Kingdom as being a substance or article which could be lawfully sold, supplied, or offered or exposed for sale, or could be lawfully sold, supplied, or offered or exposed for sale under the name or description or for the purpose under or for which he sold, supplied, or offered or exposed it for sale, and with a written warranty to that effect;

(*b*) that at the time of the commission of the alleged offence he had no reason to believe that it was otherwise; and

(*c*) that the substance or article was then in the same state as when he purchased it.

(2) This section applies to the following provisions, that is to say, section 63(*b*), sections 63(*b*), 64, 87 and 88 and the provisions of any regulations made under any of those sections.

(3) A warranty shall not be a defence by virtue of this section unless the defendant has, not later than three clear days before the date of the hearing, sent to the prosecutor a copy of the warranty with a notice stating that he intends to rely on it and specifying the name and address of the person from whom he received it, and has also sent a like notice to that person.

(4) Where the defendant is a servant of the person who purchased the substance or article under the warranty, he shall be entitled to rely on the provisions of this section in the same way as his employer would have been entitled to do if he had been the defendant.

(5) The person by whom the warranty is alleged to have been given shall be entitled to appear at the hearing and to give evidence, and the court may, if it thinks fit, adjourn the hearing to enable him to do so.

(6) For the purposes of this section a name or description entered in an invoice shall be deemed

to be a written warranty that the article or substance to which the name or description applies can be sold, supplied, or offered or exposed for sale under that name or description by any person without contravening any provision to which this section applies.

(7) *Scotland.*

[Medicines Act 1968, s 122 as amended by SI 2006/2407 and SI 2012/1916.]

7.8080 **123. Offences in relation to warranties and certificates of analysis** (1) If a defendant in any such proceedings as are mentioned in section 122(1) of this Act wilfully applies to any substance or article—

(*a*) a warranty given in relation to a different substance or article, or

(*b*) a certificate issued under paragraph 19 of Schedule 3 to this Act, which related to a sample of a different substance or article,

he shall be guilty of an offence.

(2) A person who, in respect of any substance or article sold by him in respect of which a warranty might be pleaded under section 122 of this Act, gives to the purchaser a false warranty in writing shall be guilty of an offence, unless he proves that when he gave the warranty he had reason to believe that the statement or description contained in it was accurate.

(3) Where the defendant in any such proceedings as are mentioned in section 122(1) of this Act relies successfully on a warranty given to him or to his employer, any proceedings for an offence under subsection (2) of this section in respect of the warranty may, at the option of the prosecutor, be taken either before a court having jurisdiction in the place where a sample of the substance or article to which the warranty relates was procured, or before a court having jurisdiction in the place where the warranty was given.

(4) Any person guilty of an offence under this section shall be liable[1]—

(*a*) on summary conviction, to a fine not exceeding **the prescribed sum**;

(*b*) on conviction on indictment, to a **fine** or to imprisonment for a term not exceeding **two years** or to **both**.

[Medicines Act 1968, s 123 as amended by the Criminal Law Act 1977, s 28 and the Magistrates' Courts Act 1980, s 32 and SI 2012/1916.]

[1] For procedure in respect of this offence, triable either way, see the Magistrates' Courts Act 1980, ss 17A–21 in PART I: MAGISTRATES' COURTS, PROCEDURE.

7.8081 **124. Offences by bodies corporate** (1) Where an offence under this Act which is committed by a body corporate is proved to have been committed with the consent and connivance of, or to be attributable to any neglect on the part of, any director, manager, secretary or other similar officer of the body corporate, or any person who was purporting to act in any such capacity, he as well as the body corporate shall be guilty of that offence and shall be liable to be proceeded against and punished accordingly.

(2) In relation to a body corporate carrying on a retail pharmacy business as mentioned in subsection (1) of section 71 of this Act, the preceding subsection shall have effect in relation to a person who (not being such an officer of the body corporate as is mentioned in the preceding subsection)—

(*a*) is the superintendent referred to in subsection (1) of that section, or

(*b*) at any premises where the business is carried on, is the pharmacist referred to in subsection (4)(*b*) of that section who acts under the directions of the superintendent,

as if he were such an officer of the body corporate as is mentioned in the preceding subsection.

(3) In this section "director", in relation to a body corporate established by or under any enactment for the purpose of carrying on under national ownership any industry or part of an industry or undertaking, being a body corporate whose affairs are managed by its members, means a member of that body corporate.

[Medicines Act 1968, s 124 as amended by the Health Act 2006, s 28.]

7.8082 **125. Prosecutions** (1) Notwithstanding anything in section 127(1) of the Magistrates' Courts Act 1980, a magistrates' court in England or Wales may try an information for an offence under this Act if the information was laid at any time within twelve months from the commission of the offence.

(2) *Scotland.*

(3) *Northern Ireland.*

(4) Neither the General Pharmaceutical Society nor any other body referred to in subsection (2) of section 108 of this Act shall institute proceedings for an offence under this Act in respect of a contravention of a provision which, by virtue of that subsection, the Council or body have a power or duty to enforce, unless they have given to the appropriate Minister not less than twenty-eight days' notice of their intention to institute proceedings, together with a summary of the facts upon which the charges are founded.

(5) For the purposes of subsection (4) of this section the appropriate Minister, in relation to a contravention of any provision, is the Minister who in accordance with section 108 of this Act had a concurrent duty to enforce that provision.

(6) A health authority (as defined by section 110 of this Act) shall not prosecute for an offence under this Act in respect of a contravention of any provision which, by virtue of subsection (2) of that section, the authority have a power or duty to enforce, unless the authority have given to the

Minister of Health and Social Services for Northern Ireland not less than twenty-eight days' notice of their intentions to begin the prosecution, together with a summary of the facts upon which the charges are founded.

(7) A certificate of the Minister who is the appropriate Minister for the purposes of subsection (4) of this section that the requirements of that subsection have been complied with in relation to any proceedings, and a certificate of the Minister of Health and Social Services for Northern Ireland that the requirements of subsection (6) of this section have been complied with in relation to any prosecution, shall be conclusive evidence that those requirements have been so complied with; and any document purporting to be such a certificate and to be signed by or on behalf of that Minister shall be presumed to be such a certificate unless the contrary is proved.

[Medicines Act 1968, s 125 as amended by the Magistrates' Courts Act 1980, Sch 7 and SI 2006/2407 and SI 2012/1916.]

**7.8083 126. Presumptions** (1) For the purposes of any proceedings under this Act for an offence consisting of—

(*a*) *repealed*

(*b*) offering a medicinal product for sale by retail in contravention of section 52 or section 53 of this Act, or

(*c*) offering a medicinal product for sale in contravention of section 63(*b*) of this Act,

where it is proved that the medicinal product in question was found on a vehicle from which medicinal products are sold, it shall be presumed, unless the contrary is proved, that the person in charge of the vehicle offered that medicinal product for sale and, in a case falling within paragraph (*b*) of this subsection, that he offered it for sale by retail.

(2) For the purposes of any proceedings under this Act for an offence consisting of a contravention of so much of any provision to which this subsection applies as relates to a person's having any medicinal product in his possession for the purpose of sale or supply, where it is proved that the medicinal product in question was found on premises at which the person charged with the offence carries on a business consisting of or including the sale or supply of medicinal products, it shall be presumed, unless the contrary is proved, that he had that medicinal product in his possession for the purpose of sale or supply.

(3) Subsection (2) of this section applies to the following provisions of this Act, that is to say, section 63(*b*), subsections (3) and (5) of section 85, subsection (2) of section 87 and subsection (3) of section 88.

(4) For the purposes of any proceedings under this Act for an offence consisting of a contravention of subsection (2) or subsection (3) of section 86 of this Act, where it is proved that the leaflet in question was found on premises at which the person charged with the offence carries on a business consisting of or including the sale or supply of medicinal products, it shall be presumed, unless the contrary is proved, that he had the leaflet in his possession for the purpose of supplying it with a medicinal product.

[Medicines Act 1968, s 126 as amended by SI 2006/2407.]

**7.8084 127. Service of documents** Any notice or other document required or authorised by any provision of this Act to be served on any person, or to be given or sent to any person, may be served, given or sent—

(*a*) by delivering it to him; or

(*b*) by sending it by post[1] to him at his usual or last-known residence or place of business in the United Kingdom; or

(*c*) in the case of a body corporate, by delivering it to the secretary or clerk of the body corporate at its registered or principal office or sending it by post[1] to the secretary or clerk of that body corporate at that office.

[Medicines Act 1968, s 127.]

1 See presumption of due delivery in s 7 of the Interpretation Act 1978, in PART II: EVIDENCE, ante.

**7.8085 129. General power to make orders and regulations**

**7.8086 130. Meaning of "medicinal product" and related expressions** (1) In this Act, "medicinal product" has the meaning given by regulation 2 of the 2012 Regulations.

(2) *Repealed.*

(3) *Repealed.*

(3A) *Repealed.*

(3B) *Repealed.*

(3C) *Repealed.*

(4) *Repealed.*

(5) *Repealed.*

(5A) *Repealed.*

(5B) *Repealed.*

(6) *Repealed.*

(7) *Repealed.*

(8) *Repealed.*

(9) In this Act "administer" means administer to a human being, whether orally, by injection or by introduction into the body in any other way, or by external application, whether by direct contact

with the body or not; and any reference in this Act to administering a substance or article is a reference to administering it either in its existing state or after it has been dissolved or dispersed in, or diluted or mixed with, some other substance used as a vehicle.

(10) *Repealed.*

[Medicines Act 1968, s 130 as amended by the Animal Health and Welfare Act 1984, s 13 and Schs 1 and 2, SI 1994/3119, SI 2005/50, SI 2006/2407 and SI 2012/1916.]

7.8087 **131. Meaning of "wholesale dealing", "retail sale" and related expressions** (1) In this Act any reference to selling anything by way of wholesale dealing is a reference to selling it to a person as being a person who buys it for one or more of the purposes specified in subsection (2) of this section, except that it does not include any such sale by the person who manufactured it.

(2) The purposes referred to in the preceding subsection, in relation to a person to whom anything is sold, are the purposes of—

(*a*) selling or supplying it, or

(*b*) administering it or causing it to be administered to one or more human beings,

in the course of a business carried on by that person.

(3) In this Act any reference to selling by retail, or to retail sale, is a reference to selling a substance or article to a person as being a person who buys it otherwise than for a purpose specified in subsection (2) of this section.

(4) In this Act any reference to supplying anything in circumstances corresponding to retail sale is a reference to supplying it, otherwise than by way of sale, to a person as being a person who receives it for a purpose other than that of—

(*a*) selling or supplying it, or

(*b*) administering it or causing it to be administered to one or more human beings,

in the course of a business carried on by that person.

(5) For the purposes of this section the provision of services by or on behalf of the Minister of Health, the Secretary of State or the Ministry of Health and Social Services for Northern Ireland under the National Health Service Act 2006, the National Health Service (Wales) Act 2006, the National Health Service (Scotland) Act 1978, the Health and Personal Social Services (Northern Ireland) Order 1972 or the Health and Social Care (Reform) Act (Northern Ireland) 2009 shall be treated as the carrying on of a business by that Minister, the Secretary of State or that Ministry, as the case may be.

[Medicines Act 1968, s 131 as amended by the National Health Service Reorganisation Act 1973, Sch 4, the National Health Service Act 1977, Sch 15, the National Health Service (Scotland) Act 1978, Sch 16 and National Health Service (Consequential Provisions) Act 2006, Sch 1 and SI 2012/1916.]

7.8088 **132. General interpretation provisions** (1) In this Act—

(*a*) unless the context otherwise requires, any expression defined by any provision of the 2012 Regulations, and not defined in this Act, has the same meaning as it has for the purposes of those Regulations; and

(*b*) "the 2012 Regulations" means the Human Medicines Regulations 2012.

(2) *Repealed.*

(3) *Repealed.*

(4) Any reference in this Act to the holder of a certificate shall be construed as a reference to the holder of a certificate which is for the time being in force.

(5) *Repealed.*

(6) Except in so far as the context otherwise requires, any reference in this Act to an enactment shall be construed as a reference to that enactment as amended or extended by or under any other enactment, including this Act.

[Medicines Act 1968, s 132, as amended by the Local Government Act 1972, s 198, the Dentists Act 1984, Sch 5, the Food Act 1984, Sch 10, the Animal Health and Welfare Act 1984, s 13, the Food Safety Act 1990, Schs 3 and 5, the Medicines Act 1968 (Amendment) (No 2) Regulations 1992, SI 1992/3271, SI 1996/1496, SI 2002/236, SI 2003/2321, SI 2004/1031, SI 2005/1094, SI 2005/2754, SI 2005/2789, SI 2006/2407, the National Health Service (Consequential Provisions) Act 2006, Sch 1, SI 2007/289, SI 2007/3101 and SI 2010/231 and SI 2012/1916.]

7.8089 **133. General provisions as to operation of Act** (1) The provisions of this Act, and of any regulations or orders made under it, shall operate cumulatively; and any exemption or exception from any of those provisions shall not be construed as conferring any exemption or exception in relation to any other of those provisions.

(2) Except in so far as this Act otherwise expressly provides, and subject to the provisions of section 33 of the Interpretation Act 1889[1] (which relates to offences under two or more laws), the provisions of this Act shall not be construed as—

(*a*) conferring a right of action in any civil proceedings (other than proceedings for the recovery of a fine) in respect of any contravention of this Act or of any regulations or orders made under this Act, or

(*b*) affecting any restriction imposed by or under any other enactment, whether contained in a public general Act or in a local or private Act, or

(*c*) derogating from any right of action or other remedy (whether civil or criminal) in proceedings instituted otherwise than under this Act.

(3) No exemption conferred by or under any provision of this Act shall be construed as derogating from any exemption or immunity of the Crown.

[Medicines Act 1968, s 133.]

---

[1] Now s 18 of the Interpretation Act 1978 in PART II: EVIDENCE, ante.

## SCHEDULE 3

SAMPLING Sections 112 and 115

*(As amended by the Food Act 1984, Sch 10 and the Food Safety Act 1990, Sch 3, SI 1994/3144 and SI 2006/2407.)*

*Introductory*

7.8090 **1.** (1) The provisions of this Schedule shall have effect where a person authorised in that behalf by an enforcement authority (in this Schedule referred to as a "sampling officer") obtains a sample of any substance or article—

(*a*) for the purpose of ascertaining whether there is or has been, in connection with that substance or article, any contravention of any provisions of this Act or of any regulations or order made thereunder which, by or under any provisions of sections 108 to 110 of this Act, that authority (in this Schedule referred to as "the relevant enforcement authority") is required or empowered to enforce, or

(*b*) otherwise for any purpose connected with the performance by that authority of their functions under this Act or under any such regulations or order,

and the sampling officer obtains the sample by purchase or in the exercise of any power conferred by section 112 of this Act.

(2) In this Schedule "public analyst", except in relation to Northern Ireland, has the meaning assigned to it by section 27 of the Food Safety Act 1990, and in relation to Northern Ireland has the meaning assigned to it by section 31 of the Food and Drugs Act (Northern Ireland) 1958.

*Division of sample*

**2.** The sampling officer shall forthwith divide the sample into three parts, each part to be marked and sealed or fastened up in such manner as its nature will permit.

**3.** If the sample was purchased by the sampling officer, otherwise than from an automatic machine, he shall supply one part of the sample to the seller.

**4.** If the sampling officer obtained the sample from an automatic machine, then—

(*a*) if a person's name, and an address in the United Kingdom, are stated on the machine as being the name and address of the owner of the machine, the sampling officer shall supply one part of the sample to that person;

(*b*) in any other case, the sampling officer shall supply one part of the sample to the occupier of the premises on which the machine stands or to which it is affixed.

**5.** *Repealed.*

**6.** *Repealed.*

**7.** *Repealed.*

**8.** In any case not falling within any of paragraphs 3 or 4 of this Schedule the sampling officer shall supply one part of the sample to the person appearing to him to be the owner of the substance or article from which the sample was taken.

**9.** In every case falling within any of paragraphs 3, 4 or 8 of this Schedule the sampling officer shall inform the person to whom the part of the sample in question is supplied that the sample has been obtained for the purpose of analysis or other appropriate examination.

**10.** Of the remaining parts of the sample into which the sample is divided in accordance with paragraph 2 of this Schedule, the sampling officer, unless he decides not to submit the sample for analysis or other appropriate examination, shall—

(*a*) retain one part for future comparison, and

(*b*) submit the other part for analysis or examination in accordance with the following provisions of this Schedule.

**11.** Where a sample consists of substances or articles enclosed in unopened containers, and it appears to the sampling officer that to open the containers and divide the contents into parts—

(*a*) is not reasonably practicable, or

(*b*) might affect the composition or impede the proper analysis or other examination of the contents,

the sampling officer may divide the sample into parts by dividing the containers into three lots without opening them.

**12.** Section 127 of this Act shall have effect in relation to supplying any part of a sample in pursuance of the preceding paragraphs as it has effect in relation to the service of a document.

**13.** If after reasonable inquiry the sampling officer is unable to ascertain the name of a person to whom, or the address at which, a part of a sample ought to be supplied in pursuance of the preceding paragraphs, he may retain that part of the sample instead of supplying it.

*Notice to person named on container*

**14.** (1) Where it appears to the sampling officer that a substance or article of which he has obtained a sample was manufactured or assembled by a person whose name and address in the United Kingdom are stated on its container, and who is not a person to whom a part of the sample is required to be supplied under the preceding provisions of this Schedule, the sampling officer, unless he decides not to submit the sample for analysis or other appropriate examination, shall serve notice on that person—

(*a*) stating that the sample has been obtained by the sampling officer, and

(*b*) specifying the person from whom the sampling officer purchased it, or, if he obtained it otherwise than by purchase, the place from which he obtained it.

(2) The notice required to be served under the preceding sub-paragraph shall be served before the end of the period of three days beginning with the day on which the sample was obtained.

*Analysis or other examination of sample*

**15.** If the sampling officer decides to submit the sample for analysis or other appropriate examination, he shall—

(*a*) submit it for analysis to the public analyst for the area in which the sample was obtained, or, if for the time being there is no public analyst for that area, then to the public analyst for some other area, or

(*b*) submit it for other appropriate examination to the person having the management or control of any laboratory available for the purpose in accordance with any arrangements made in that behalf by the relevant enforcement authority.

**16.** Where the relevant enforcement authority is a Minister or the Pharmaceutical Society, and the sampling officer decides to have the sample analysed, he may (instead of submitting it to a public analyst) submit it for analysis to the person having the management or control of any laboratory available for the purpose in accordance with any arrangements made in that behalf by the relevant enforcement authority.

**17.** Any such arrangements as are mentioned in paragraph 15(*b*) or paragraph 16 of this Schedule—

(*a*) *repealed*

(*b*) if they are made by an enforcement authority in England and Wales other than the Secretary of State, shall be arrangements approved by the Secretary of State;

(*c*) if they are made by an enforcement authority in Scotland other than the Secretary of State, shall be arrangements approved by the Secretary of State;

and any such arrangements as are mentioned in paragraph 15(*b*) of this Schedule, if made by the Pharmaceutical Society of Northern Ireland in Northern Ireland, shall be arrangements approved by the Minister for Health, Social Services and Public Safety.

**18.** (1) Subject to the following sub-paragraph, the person to whom the sample is submitted under paragraph 15 or paragraph 16 of this Schedule shall analyse or examine the sample (as the case may be), or cause the sample to be analysed or examined by some other person under his direction, as soon as practicable.

(2) If the person to whom the sample is so submitted is a public analyst, and that analyst determines that for any reason an effective analysis of the sample cannot be performed by him or under his direction, he shall send it to the public analyst for some other area, and that other public analyst shall as soon as practicable analyse the sample or cause it to be analysed by some other person under his direction.

**19.** (1) A public analyst who has analysed a sample submitted to him under the preceding provisions of this Schedule, or who has caused such a sample to be analysed by some other person under his direction, shall issue and send to the sampling officer a certificate specifying the result of the analysis.

(2) A person having the management or control of a laboratory in which a sample submitted to him under the preceding provisions of this Schedule has been analysed or examined, or a person appointed by him for the purpose, shall issue and send to the sampling officer a certificate specifying the result of the analysis or examination.

(3) Any certificate issued under this paragraph shall be in a form prescribed by the Ministers and shall be signed by the person who issues the certificate.

**20.** (1) Any person to whom, in accordance with paragraphs 2 to 8 of this Schedule, a part of the sample is required to be supplied shall, on payment of the prescribed fee to the relevant enforcement authority, be entitled to be supplied with a copy of any certificate as to the result of an analysis or examination which is sent to the sampling officer under paragraph 19 of this Schedule.

(2) Any regulations prescribing a fee for the purposes of this paragraph shall be made by the Ministers.

*Provisions as to evidence*

**21.** In any proceedings for an offence under this Act a document produced by one of the parties to the proceedings and purporting to be a certificate issued under paragraph 19 of this Schedule shall be sufficient evidence of the facts stated in the document, unless the other party requires that the person who issued the certificate shall be called as a witness; and, in any proceedings in Scotland, if that person is called as a witness, his evidence shall be sufficient evidence of those facts.

**22.** In any proceedings for an offence under this Act a document produced by one of the parties to the proceedings, which has been supplied to him by the other party as being a copy of such a certificate, shall be sufficient evidence of the facts stated in the document.

**23.** (1) If in any such proceedings before a magistrates' court a defendant intends to produce such a certificate, or to require that the person by whom such a certificate was issued shall be called as a witness, a notice of his intention, and (where he intends to produce such a certificate) a copy of the certificate, shall be given to the other party at least three clear days before the day on which the summons is returnable.

(2) If the preceding sub-paragraph is not complied with, the court may, if it thinks fit, adjourn the hearing on such terms as it thinks proper.

(3), (4) *Scotland.*

*Analysis under direction of court*

**24.** (1) In any proceedings for an offence under this Act, where the proceedings relate to a substance or article of which a sample has been obtained as mentioned in paragraph 1 of this Schedule, the part of the sample retained in pursuance of paragraph 10(*a*) of this Schedule shall be produced as evidence; and the court—

(*a*) at the request of either party to the proceedings shall, and

(*b*) in the absence of any such request may if it thinks fit,

cause that part of the sample to be sent for analysis to the Government Chemist (or, in Northern Ireland, the Government Chemist for Northern Ireland) or to be sent for other appropriate examination to the person having the management or control of a laboratory specified by the court.

(2) If, in a case where an appeal is brought, no action has been taken under the preceding sub-paragraph, the provisions of that sub-paragraph shall have effect in relation to the court by which the appeal is heard.

(3) A person to whom a part of a sample is sent under this paragraph for analysis or other examination shall analyse or examine it, or cause it to be analysed or examined on his behalf, and shall transmit to the court a certificate specifying the result of the analysis or examination.

(4) Any such certificate shall be signed by that person, or signed on his behalf by the person who made the analysis or examination or a person under whose direction it was made.

(5) Any such certificate shall be evidence (and, in Scotland, shall be sufficient evidence) of the facts stated in the certificate unless any party to the proceedings requires that the person by whom it was signed shall be called as a witness; and, in any proceedings in Scotland, if that person is called as a witness, his evidence shall be sufficient evidence of those facts.

**25.** The costs of any analysis or examination under paragraph 24 of this Schedule shall be paid by the prosecutor or the defendant (or, in Scotland, the accused) as the court may order.

*Proof by written statement*

**26.** In relation to England and Wales section 9 of the Criminal Justice Act 1967, and in relation to Northern Ireland any corresponding enactments which may be passed by the Parliament of Northern Ireland, shall not have effect with respect to any document produced as mentioned in paragraph 21 or paragraph 22 of this Schedule or with respect to any certificate transmitted to a court under paragraph 24 of this Schedule.

*Power to modify sampling provisions*

**27.** The Ministers may by order provide that, in relation to substances or articles of any such description as may be specified in the order, the preceding provisions of this Schedule shall have effect subject to such exceptions and modifications as may be specified in the order.

*Payment for sample taken under compulsory powers*

**28.** (1) Where a sampling officer takes a sample in the exercise of any power conferred by section 112 of this Act he shall, if payment is demanded, pay the value of the sample to the person to whom a part of the sample is required under paragraph 5, paragraph 7 or paragraph 8 of this Schedule (as the case may be) to be supplied.

(2) In default of agreement between the sampling officer and the person mentioned in the preceding sub-paragraph, the value of the sample shall be determined by the arbitration of a single arbitrator appointed by the sampling officer and the other person in question or, if they are unable to agree on the appointment of an arbitrator, shall be determined by the county court for the district (or, in Northern Ireland, the division) in which the sample was taken.

(2A) For the purposes of this paragraph, England and Wales is to be treated as the district of the county court in England and Wales.

(3) *Scotland.*

*Application of s 64 to samples*

**29.** Where a medicinal product is taken as a sample by a sampling officer in the exercise of any power conferred by section 112 of this Act, the provisions of subsections (1) to (4) of section 64 of this Act shall have effect as if the taking of the product as a sample were a sale of it to the sampling officer by the person from whom it is taken; and, if the product was prepared in pursuance of a prescription given by a practitioner, those provisions shall so have effect as if, in subsection (1) of that section, for the words "demanded by the purchaser", there were substituted the words "specified in the prescription".

# Misuse of Drugs Act 1971[1]

(1971 c 38)

## 7.8100 1. Advisory Council on the Misuse of Drugs

[1] This Act, together with Orders made thereunder, regulates all matters concerning the use and abuse of controlled drugs. Only those parts of the Act which relate to proceedings in criminal courts are included in this work.

*Controlled drugs and their classification*

**7.8101 2. Controlled drugs and their classification for purposes of this Act** (1) In this Act—

(*a*) the expression "controlled drug" means any substance[1] or product for the time being specified—
  (i) in Part I, II, or III of Schedule 2, or
  (ii) in a temporary class drug order as a drug subject to temporary control (but this is subject to section 2A(6));

(*b*) the expressions "Class A drug", "Class B drug" and "Class C drug" mean any of the substances and products for the time being specified respectively in Part I, Part II and Part III of that Schedule; and

(*c*) the expression "temporary class drug" means any substance or product which is for the time being a controlled drug by virtue of a temporary class drug order;

and the provisions of Part IV of that Schedule shall have effect with respect to the meanings of expressions used in that Schedule.

(2) Her Majesty may by Order in Council make such amendments in Schedule 2 to this Act as may be requisite for the purpose of adding any substance or product to, or removing any substance or product from, any of Parts I to III of that Schedule, including amendments for securing that no substance or product is for the time being specified in a particular one of those Parts or for inserting any substance or product into any of those Parts in which no substance or product is for the time being specified.

(3) An Order in Council under this section may amend Part IV of Schedule 2 to this Act, and may do so whether or not it amends any other Part of that Schedule.

(4) An Order in Council under this section may be varied or revoked by a subsequent Order in Council thereunder.

(5) No recommendation shall be made to Her Majesty in Council to make an Order under this section unless a draft of the Order has been laid before Parliament and approved by a resolution of each House of Parliament; and the Secretary of State shall not lay a draft of such an Order before Parliament except after consultation with or on the recommendation of the Advisory Council.[2]

[Misuse of Drugs Act 1971, s 2 as amended by the Police Reform and Social Responsibility Act 2011, Sch 17.]

[1] "Substance" has a wider meaning than "product". Any kind of matter comes within the meaning of substance, whereas product envisages the result of some kind of process (*R v Greensmith* [1983] 3 All ER 444, [1983] 1 WLR 1124, 147 JP 730, CA).

[2] The following Misuse of Drugs Act 1971 (Temporary Class Drug) Orders have been made: SI 2012/980 (5 April 2012).

7.8102 **2A. Temporary class drug orders** *Secretary of State may make a "temporary class drug order" specifying any substance or product as a drug subject to temporary control provided the substance or product is not a Class A drug, a Class B drug or a Class C drug and the Secretary of State has consulted the Advisory Council and has determined that the order should be made, or has received a recommendation from the Council that the order should be made.*[1]

[1] A number of Misuse of Drugs Act 1971 (Temporary Class Drug) Orders have been made. These specify drugs to which the provisions of the Misuse of Drugs Regulations 2001 are to apply as if they were specified as controlled drugs to which Schedule 1 to the Misuse of Drugs Regulations 2001 applied. The specified drugs and related substances will cease to be subject to temporary control after the expiry of one year or, if earlier, upon the coming into force of an Order in Council under s 2(2) of the Act. Previous orders made are: SI 2012/980; SI 2013/1294; SI 2015/1027, 1396 and 1929.
Current orders are the Misuse of Drugs Act 1971 (Temporary Class Drug) Order 2016, SI 2016/650 and the Misuse of Drugs Act 1971 (Temporary Class Drug) (No 2) Order 2016, SI 2016/1126.

7.8103 **2B. Orders under section 2A: role of Advisory Council etc**

*Restrictions relating to controlled drugs etc*

7.8104 **3. Restriction of importation and exportation of controlled drugs** (1) Subject to subsection (2) below—

(*a*) the importation of a controlled drug[1]; and

(*b*) the exportation of a controlled[1] drug,

are hereby prohibited[2].

(2) Subsection (1) above does not apply—

(*a*) to the importation or exportation of a controlled drug which is for the time being excepted from paragraph (*a*) or, as the case may be, paragraph (*b*) of subsection (1) above by regulations under section 7 of this Act or by provision made in a temporary class drug order by virtue of section 7A; or

(*b*) to the importation or exportation of a controlled drug under and in accordance with the terms of a licence[3] issued by the Secretary of State and in compliance with any conditions attached thereto.

[Misuse of Drugs Act 1971, s 3 as amended by the Police Reform and Social Responsibility Act 2011, Sch 17.]

[1] See s 2, ante.

[2] These are offences punishable under the Customs and Excise Management Act 1979; see s 50 (improper importation), s 68 (improper exportation), and s 170 (fraudulent evasion of a prohibition or restriction affecting goods); also s 147 for time limit on prosecution.

[3] It is the defendant's responsibility to prove (on a balance of probabilities (*R v Oliver* [1944] KB 68, [1943] 2 All ER 800, 108 JP 30)) that he has a licence; *R v Ewens* [1967] 1 QB 322, [1966] 2 All ER 470. See also the Magistrates' Courts Act 1980, s 101, ante, for onus of proving exceptions, etc.

7.8105 **4. Restriction of production and supply of controlled drugs** (1) Subject to any regulations[1] under section 7 of this Act, or any provision made in a temporary class drug order by virtue of section 7A, for the time being in force, it shall not be lawful for a person—

(*a*) to produce[2] a controlled drug[3]; or

(*b*) to supply[2] or offer[4] to supply a controlled drug to another.

(2) Subject to section 28 of this Act[5], it is an offence[6] for a person—

(*a*) to produce[2] a controlled drug in contravention of subsection (1) above; or

(*b*) to be concerned in[7] the production[2] of such a drug in contravention of that subsection by another.

(3) Subject to section 28 of this Act[5], it is an offence[6] for a person—

(*a*) to supply[8] or offer to supply a controlled drug to another[9] in contravention of subsection (1) above; or

(*b*) to be concerned in[7] the supplying[8] of such a drug to another in contravention of that subsection; or

(*c*) to be concerned in[7] the making to another in contravention of that subsection of an offer to supply[5] such a drug.

[Misuse of Drugs Act 1971, s 4 as amended by the Police Reform and Social Responsibility Act 2011, Sch 17.]

[1] For exceptions to the restriction in this section, see the Misuse of Drugs Regulations 2001, post.

[2] See s 37(1), post, for definition of the terms "produce" and "supplying". See further the cases referred to in the footnote to "supply" in s 5(3), post.

[3] In *R v Harris* (1979) 69 Cr App Rep 122, it was held that co-defendants who had acquainted themselves with the proper process to produce amphetamine and had entered into an agreement to produce such a drug were properly convicted of conspiracy to produce a controlled drug, notwithstanding that the attempt failed because one ingredient was wrong and a further knowledge of the process was required; *DPP v Nock and DPP v Alsford* [1980] AC 979, [1978] 2 All ER 654, 67 Cr App Rep 116, HL, distinguished. There must be established some identifiable participation in the process of producing a controlled drug before a person can be convicted (*R v Farr* [1982] Crim LR 745, CA).

[4] It is an offence to *offer* to supply a controlled drug even though the substance in the defendant's possession is *not* such a drug (*aliter* if the offence charged is supplying) (*Haggard v Mason* [1976] 1 All ER 337, 140 JP 198). Cf *Mieras v Rees* (1975) 139 JP 549 (alleged attempt under s 19, post.) The offence is complete when the offer to supply a controlled drug is made, regardless of whether the offerer intends to carry the offer into effect by actually supplying the drug (*R v Goddard* [1992] Crim LR 588). Whether the words spoken and the circumstances in which they were uttered amounted to an offer is a question of fact having regard to the effect of the words and any relevant circumstances apparent to the offeree. An

offer once made cannot be withdrawn, any attempt to withdraw may only be relevant to the issue whether there was an offer in the first place. There is no need for the offer to meet the specificity as to date and time of delivery of the civil law and it does not matter whether the offeror or the offeree took the initiative (*R v Prior* [2004] EWCA Crim 1147, [2004] Crim LR 849).

5 Section 28 relates to the availability of the defence of lack of knowledge.

6 For method of trial, penalty, etc see s 25 and Sch 4, post. Anything shown to relate to the offence may be forfeited (see s 27, post). An information may be laid at any time within twelve months from the commission of the offence (see s 25(4), post). On a plea of guilty the prosecution is not bound to call scientific evidence to prove the nature of the drug: *R v Wells* [1976] Crim LR 518.

7 This is designed to provide a means of proceeding against the "trafficker", and individuals who have connived rather than contrived, and so have escaped prosecution for aiding and abetting the commission of an offence; for example someone assisting in the injection of a drug into someone else. It is also sufficient to involve people who may be at some distance from the actual making of the offer (*R v Blake* (1979) 68 Cr App Rep 1). To prove an offence under subs (3)(*b*) or (*c*), the prosecution has to prove (1) the supply of a drug to another or, as the case may be, the making of an offer to supply a drug to another in contravention of s 4(1); (2) participation by the defendant in an enterprise involving such supply, or as the case may be, such offer to supply; and (3) knowledge by the defendant of the nature of the enterprise, ie that it involved supply of a drug or, as the case may be, offering to supply a drug (*R v Hughes* (1985) 81 Cr App Rep 344).

The offence under s 4(3)(*b*) does not require an actual supply to another; it includes a transaction which is the process of supply where there would in due course be delivery to another person: *R v Martin and Brimecome* [2014] EWCA Crim 1940.

8 See s 37(1), post, for definition of the term "supplying". The word "supply" in s 4(3)(*a*) implies an act designed to benefit the recipient and does not cover the deposit of a controlled drug with another for safe keeping (*R v Dempsey* (1985) 82 Cr App Rep 291, 150 JP 213). "Supply" is a broad term which refers to the entire process of supply; it is not confined to the expressions "actual delivery" or "past supply": *R v Martin* [2014] EWCA Crim 1940, [2015] 1 WLR 588, [2015] 1 Cr App Rep 132.

9 The "another" cannot be someone who is also charged in the indictment (*R v Adepoju* [1988] Crim LR 378, CA).

**7.8106 4A. Aggravation of offence of supply of controlled drug** (1) This section applies if—

(*a*) a court is considering the seriousness of an offence under section 4(3) of this Act, and

(*b*) at the time the offence was committed the offender had attained the age of 18.

(2) If either of the following conditions is met the court—

(*a*) must treat the fact that the condition is met as an aggravating factor (that is to say, a factor that increases the seriousness of the offence), and

(*b*) must state in open court that the offence is so aggravated.

(3) The first condition is that the offence was committed on or in the vicinity of school premises at a relevant time.

(4) The second condition is that in connection with the commission of the offence the offender used a courier who, at the time the offence was committed, was under the age of 18.

(5) In subsection (3), a relevant time is—

(*a*) any time when the school premises are in use by persons under the age of 18;

(*b*) one hour before the start and one hour after the end of any such time.

(6) For the purposes of subsection (4), a person uses a courier in connection with an offence under section 4(3) of this Act if he causes or permits another person (the courier)—

(*a*) to deliver a controlled drug to a third person, or

(*b*) to deliver a drug related consideration to himself or a third person.

(7) For the purposes of subsection (6), a drug related consideration is a consideration of any description which—

(*a*) is obtained in connection with the supply of a controlled drug, or

(*b*) is intended to be used in connection with obtaining a controlled drug.

(8) In this section—

"school premises" means land used for the purposes of a school excluding any land occupied solely as a dwelling by a person employed at the school; and

"school" has the same meaning—

(*a*) in England and Wales, as in section 4 of the Education Act 1996;

(*b*) *Scotland;*

(*c*) *Northern Ireland, as in Article 2(2) of the Education and Libraries (Northern Ireland) Order 1986.*

[Misuse of Drugs Act 1971, s 4A as inserted by the Drugs Act 2005, s 1.]

**7.8107 5. Restriction of possession of controlled drugs** (1) Subject to any regulations[1] under section 7 of this Act for the time being in force, it shall not be lawful for a person to have a controlled drug in his possession[2].

(2) Subject to section 28 of this Act[3] and to subsection (4) below, it is an offence[4] for a person to have a controlled drug[5] in his possession[2] in contravention of subsection (1) above.

(2A) Subsections (1) and (2) do not apply in relation to a temporary class drug.

(3) Subject to section 28 of this Act[3], it is an offence[4] for a person to have a controlled drug[6] in his possession[2], whether lawfully or not, with intent[7] to supply[8] it to another in contravention of section 4(1) of this Act.

(4) In any proceedings for an offence under subsection (2) above in which it is proved that the accused had a controlled drug in his possession[2], it shall be a defence for him to prove—

(*a*) that, knowing or suspecting it to be a controlled drug, he took possession of it for the purpose of preventing another from committing or continuing to commit an offence in connection with that drug and that as soon as possible after taking possession of it he took all such steps as were reasonably open to him to destroy[9] the drug or to deliver it into the custody of a person lawfully entitled to take custody of it; or

(*b*) that, knowing or suspecting it to be a controlled drug, he took possession of it for the purpose of delivering it into the custody of a person lawfully entitled to take custody of it and that as soon as possible after taking possession of it he took all such steps as were reasonably open to him to deliver it into the custody of such a person.

(4A)–(4C) *Repealed.*

(5) *Repealed.*

(6) Nothing in subsection (4) above shall prejudice any defence which it is open to a person charged with an offence under this section to raise apart from that subsection.

[Misuse of Drugs Act 1971, s 5 as amended by the Criminal Attempts Act 1981, Sch, the Policing and Crime Act 2009, Schs 7 and 8 and the Police Reform and Social Responsibility Act 2011, Sch 17.]

---

[1] The Misuse of Drugs Regulations 2001, post, set out the persons authorised to supply and possess various classes of controlled drugs (see in particular reg 10 thereof) and except specified drugs from the prohibition on the possession of controlled drugs (see reg 4 thereof).

[2] The Act does not contain a definition of "possession" but the nature of possession has received extensive consideration in case law, in particular by the House of Lords in *R v Lambert* [2001] UKHL 37, [2002] 2 AC 545, [2001] 3 All ER 577, [2001] 3 WLR 206.

**Possession** embraces both a factual and a mental element.

***Control*** The factual element is control. Section 37(3) provides that for the purposes of the Act the things which a person has in his possession shall be taken to include any thing subject to his control which is in the custody of another.

In *R v Wright* (1975) 119 Sol Jo 825 (following *Warner v Metropolitan Police Comr* [1969] 2 AC 256, [1968] 2 All ER 356, HL) a distinction was made between mere physical custody of an object, and its possession for the commission of an offence. The defendant was given a container and told to throw it away, which he did instantly: he could not be convicted although he suspected it might contain drugs. A person having given directions to a supplier following which he receives a parcel containing a drug through his letter-box, becomes the possessor of the drug once the parcel is put through the letter-box (*R v Peaston* [1979] Crim LR 183).

If a person smokes cannabis resin he must have cannabis resin in his possession at the time of smoking (*Chief Constable of Cheshire Constabulary v Hunt* (1983) 147 JP 567). Once a controlled drug has been consumed and has changed in character, the consumer could not then be said to be "in possession" of it, though it might be evidence of possession immediately before he consumed it (*Hambleton v Callinan* [1968] 2 QB 427, [1968] 2 All ER 943, 132 JP 461.

Possession does not depend on the powers of memory of the alleged possessor and does not come and go as memory revives or fades; accordingly, a defendant who placed a drug knowing it was cannabis in his wallet was held to be in possession of it even though his memory of its presence had faded (*R v Martindale* [1986] 3 All ER 25, [1986] 1 WLR 1042, CA).

***Mental element*** The mental element in offences contrary to s 5 was exhaustively considered by the House of Lords in *R v Lambert*, supra from which the following propositions are derived.

The prosecution must prove:

(a) the defendant was in possession of something;

(b) the defendant knew he was in possession of that something; and

(c) the thing which the defendant possessed was a controlled drug.

*Lack of knowledge* The prosecution is not required to prove that the defendant knew that the thing which he possessed was a controlled drug but if the prosecution have adduced sufficient evidence to prove (*a*)–(*c*), s 28(2), (3) post, stipulates the way in which lack of knowledge etc can be a defence in proceedings. To bring himself within the provisions of s 28 (2), (3) the defendant must satisfy an evidential burden of adducing evidence which is sufficient to raise the issue of knowledge. If sufficient evidence is adduced to raise the issue, it will be for the prosecution to show beyond reasonable doubt that the defence is not made out by the evidence.

Quantity is of importance in two respects when determining whether or not an accused person has a controlled drug in his possession. First, is the quantity sufficient to enable a court to find as a matter of fact that it amounts to something? If it is visible, tangible and measurable, it is certainly something. The question is one of fact for the commonsense of the tribunal. Secondly, quantity may be relevant to the issue of knowledge. If the quantity in custody or control is minute, the question arises – was it so minute that it cannot be proved that the accuse knew he had it? If knowledge cannot be proved, possession is not established (*R v Boyeson* [1982] AC 768, [1982] 2 All ER 161, 146 JP 217, HL). See also *R v Colyer* [1974] Crim LR 243 (minute quantity) and *R v Ashton Rickardt* [1977] Crim LR 424. As to aggregating several amounts of a drug, see *R v Bayliss and Oliver* [1978] Crim LR 361. As to conviction for possessing a lesser amount than charged, see *R v Peevey* (1973) 579 Cr App Rep 554.

Mere presence in the same vehicle as cannabis, even if someone had said there was cannabis in the car, is not sufficient to prove possession (*R v Strong and R v Berry* [1989] 10 LS Gaz R 41, CA).

Once the prosecution prove that the defendant had control of a box which he was delivering on his motor cycle and knew it contained something, which was in fact the drug alleged, he has the onus of bringing himself within the provisions of s 28(3); see *R v McNamara* (1988) 87 Cr App Rep 246, 152 JP 390 approved in *R v Lambert*, supra.

***Controlled drug*** Where an experienced drug user admits possession of a substance which he himself identifies as a controlled drug, that admission and identification are sufficient to provide *prima facie* evidence of the nature of the substance and of unlawful possession of a controlled drug; see *R v Chatwood* [1980] 1 All ER 467, [1980] 1 WLR 874. It is important that the prosecution should prove possession of the drug as charged; see *Muir v Smith* [1978] Crim LR 293 where the prosecution failed as it could not be ascertained whether the substance was cannabis or herbal cannabis.

[3] Section 28 relates to the availability of the defence of lack of knowledge.

[4] For prosecution and punishment of offences, see s 25 and Sch 4, post. The defence of necessity is unavailable to this offence where the defendant's case is that he possessed the drug for the purpose of alleviating pain following a road traffic accident; nor can it be argued that, by forcing him to break the criminal law or to continue to suffer inhuman or degrading treatment, the State is in breach of art 3 where the State bore no responsibility for the causes of that condition: *R v Altham* [2006] EWCA Crim 7, [2006] 1 WLR 3287, [2006] 2 Cr App R 8, [2006] Crim LR 633. See further *R v Quayle* [2005] EWCA Crim 1415, [2005] 1 WLR 3642, [2005] 2 Cr App R 34, where, on similar facts, submissions based on art 8 similarly failed.

[5] The burden is on the prosecution to prove not only that the substance was a controlled drug within the meaning of the Act, but also that it was not in a form permitted by the Misuse of Drugs Regulations 1985, reg 4 and Sch 5, post (*R v Hunt* [1987] AC 352, [1987] 1 All ER 1). Prosecuting authorities must heed the observations in *R v Hunt, supra*, as to the desirability of clarity in the terms of the analyst's certificate (*R v Jones* (1997) 161 JP 597, [1998] Crim LR 56). As to raising objection to the admissibility of evidence of analysis during a trial, see *A-G for the Cayman Islands v Roberts* [2002] UKPC 18, [2002] 2 Cr App Rep 388.

[6] The prosecution only has to establish that the accused was in possession of the controlled drug as charged with the

necessary intent; the accused will not be able to avail himself of the defences in s 28(2) or 28(3)(*b*)(ii) where he believed the substance to be a different drug from that alleged by the prosecution as it is not necessary for the prosecution to prove which controlled drug it was in order to obtain a conviction. The only purpose of specifying the class of drug in the particulars of the offence is that that factor affects the sentence which can be passed on conviction (*R v Leeson* [2000] 1 Cr App Rep 233, 164 JP 224, [2000] Crim LR 195).

7 The defendant must intend to supply what is in possession. Where there was no suggestion that the appellant intended to supply the immature plants of which he was in possession at the material time, it was not sufficient that he intended to grow the plants to maturity and then to harvest a crop from them and then to supply the harvested crop, or some of it, to others: *R v Wright* [2011] EWCA Crim 1180, [2011] 2 Cr App R 15.

8 "Supply" covers a wide range of transactions, of which a feature common to all of those transactions is a transfer of physical control of a drug from one person to another (*R v Delgado* [1984] 1 All ER 449, [1984] 1 WLR 89, 148 JP 431, CA); but the transfer must be for the purposes of the transferee (*R v Maginnis* [1987] AC 303, [1987] 1 All ER 907). Where a defendant intends to supply drugs to a courier, even a commercial courier, for eventual supply to a person outside the jurisdiction, there is no contravention of s 4(1) (ante) since there is no intention to supply for the purposes of the transferee (the courier) and the offence does not have extraterritorial effect: *R v Hussain (Shabbir)* [2010] EWCA Crim 970 , [2011] QB, [2010] 2 WLR 808, [2010] 2 Cr App R 11.

A person in unlawful possession of a controlled drug which has been deposited with him for safe keeping has the intent to supply that drug to another if his intention is to return the drug to the person who deposited it with him (*R v Maginnis*, supra). Evidence of large amounts of money in the possession of the defendant or an extravagant life style *prima facie* explicable only if derived from drug dealing is admissible in cases of possession of drugs with intent to supply if it is of probative significance to an issue in the case (*R v Morris* [1995] 2 Cr App Rep 69, 159 JP 1 and see *R v Lucas* [1995] Crim LR 400, CA). Moreover, the finding of money, whether in the home of the defendant or perhaps, more cogently, in the possession of the defendant when away from his home, and in conjunction with a substantial quantity of drugs, is capable of being relevant to the issue of whether there is proved an intent to supply (*R v Grant* [1996] 1 Cr App Rep 73).

9 The act of destruction must be that of the defendant and relying on the forces of nature ultimately to destroy the drugs by burying the drugs them in the ground is not sufficient (*R v Murphy* [2002] EWCA Crim 1587, [2003] 1 Cr App Rep 276, [2002] Crim LR 819).

**7.8108 6. Restriction of cultivation of cannabis plant** (1) Subject to any regulations under section 7 of this Act for the time being in force, it shall not be lawful for a person to cultivate any plant of the genus *Cannabis*[1].

(2) Subject to section 28 of this Act[2], it is an offence[3] to cultivate any such plant in contravention of subsection (1) above.

[Misuse of Drugs Act 1971, s 6.]

---

1 See s 37, post, for definition and reg 12 of the Misuse of Drugs Regulations 2001, post.

2 See note 3 to s 5, ante.

3 See note 5 to s 4, ante.

**7.8109 7. Authorisation of activities otherwise unlawful** (1) The Secretary of State may by regulations[1]—

(*a*) except from section 3(1)(*a*) or (*b*), 4(1)(*a*) or (*b*) or 5(1) of this Act such controlled drugs as may be specified in the regulations; and

(*b*) make such other provision as he thinks fit for the purpose of making it lawful for persons to do things which under any of the following provisions of this Act, that is to say sections 4(1), 5(1) and 6(1), it would otherwise be unlawful for them to do.

(2) Without prejudice to the generality of paragraph (*b*) of subsection (1) above, regulations under that subsection authorising the doing of any such thing as is mentioned in that paragraph may in particular provide for the doing of that thing to be lawful—

(*a*) if it is done under and in accordance with the terms of a licence or other authority issued by the Secretary of State and in compliance with any conditions attached thereto; or

(*b*) if it is done in compliance with such conditions as may be prescribed.

(3) Subject to subsection (4) below, the Secretary of State shall so exercise his power to make regulations under subsection (1) above as to secure—

(*a*) that it is not unlawful under section 4(1) of this Act for a doctor, dentist, veterinary practitioner or veterinary surgeon[2], acting in his capacity as such, to prescribe, administer, manufacture, compound or supply a controlled drug, or for a pharmacist or a person lawfully conducting a retail pharmacy business[3], acting in either case in his capacity as such, to manufacture, compound or supply a controlled drug; and

(*b*) that it is not unlawful under section 5(1) of this Act for a doctor, dentist, veterinary practitioner, veterinary surgeon[2], pharmacist or person lawfully conducting a retail pharmacy business[3] to have a controlled drug in his possession for the purpose of acting in his capacity as such.

(4) If in the case of any controlled drug the Secretary of State is of the opinion that it is in the public interest—

(*a*) for production, supply and possession of that drug to be either wholly unlawful or unlawful except for purposes of research or other special purposes; or

(*b*) for it to be unlawful for practitioners, pharmacists and persons lawfully conducting retail pharmacy businesses to do in relation to that drug any of the things mentioned in subsection (3) above except under a licence or other authority issued by the Secretary of State,

he may by order designate that drug as a drug to which this subsection applies[4]; and while there is in force an order under this subsection designating a controlled drug as one to which this subsection applies, subsection (3) above shall not apply as regards that drug.

(5) Any order under subsection (4) above may be varied or revoked by a subsequent

order thereunder.

(6) The power to make orders under subsection (4) above shall be exercisable by statutory instrument, which shall be subject to annulment in pursuance of a resolution of either House of Parliament.

(7) The Secretary of State shall not make any order under subsection (4) above except after consultation with or on the recommendation of the Advisory Council.

(8) References in this section to a person's "doing" things include references to his having things in his possession.

(9) *Northern Ireland.*

(10) In this section a reference to "controlled drugs" does not include a reference to temporary class drugs (see instead section 7A).

[Misuse of Drugs Act 1971, s 7 as amended by the Police Reform and Social Responsibility Act 2011, Sch 17.]

---

[1] The Misuse of Drugs Regulations 2001, have been made, in this title, post. The following instruments have also been made: Misuse of Drugs (Designation) (Amendment) (England, Wales and Scotland) Order 2012, SI 2012/276 which was not published and was revoked before it came into effect by SI 2012/384 and the Misuse of Drugs (Amendment) (England, Wales and Scotland) Regulations 2012, SI 2012/277 which were not published and were revoked before they came into effect by SI 2012/385.

[2] For meaning of "doctor", "dentist", "veterinary practitioner" and "veterinary surgeon", see s 37(1), post.

[3] For meaning of a "person lawfully conducting a retail pharmacy business", see s 37(1), post.

[4] The Misuse of Drugs (Designation) (England, Wales and Scotland) Order 2015, SI 2015/704 amended by SI 2016/1124 has been made.

**7.8110 7A. Temporary class drug orders: power to make further provision**

*Miscellaneous offences involving controlled drugs etc*

**7.8111 8. Occupiers etc of premises to be punishable for permitting certain activities to take place there** A person commits an offence[1] if, being the occupier[2] or concerned in the management of any premises[3], he knowingly[4] permits[5] or suffers any of the following activities to take place on those premises, that is to say—

(*a*) producing or attempting to produce a controlled drug in contravention of section 4(1) of this Act;

(*b*) supplying or attempting to supply a controlled drug to another in contravention of section 4(1) of this Act, or offering to supply a controlled drug to another in contravention of section 4[6];

(*c*) preparing opium for smoking;

(*d*) smoking[7] cannabis[8], cannabis resin[8] or prepared opium[8].*

[Misuse of Drugs Act 1971, s 8.]

---

* **Para (*d*) substituted by the Criminal Justice and Police Act 2001, s 38 from a date to be appointed.**

[1] See note 5 to s 4, ante. For possible duplicity in informations under this section, see *Ware v Fox, Fox v Dingley* [1967] 1 All ER 100, 131 JP 113 (a case under the repealed Dangerous Drugs Act 1965).

[2] "Occupier" includes anyone in occupation of premises whose degree of occupation was such that he could exclude anyone likely to commit an offence under the Act (*R v Tao* [1977] QB 141, [1976] 3 All ER 65, 140 JP 596). The fact that one person can be identified as an occupier, even if enjoying a legal title or tenancy, does not preclude the application of that description to another person (*R v Coid* [1998] Crim LR 199).

[3] If a person is exercising control over premises, running them or managing them, the fact that he is not lawfully in possession of them is irrelevant (*R v Josephs and R v Christie* (1977) 65 Cr App Rep 253.

[4] That is, with *mens rea*; suspicion by itself is not enough to constitute permission (*R v Thomas* (1976) 63 Cr App Rep 65, [1976] Crim LR 517). On a charge of permitting premises to be used for supplying a controlled drug, it is not necessary for the Crown to prove more than knowledge of the supply of a controlled drug, even where the particular drug is specified in the charge (*R v Bett* [1999] 1 All ER 600, [1999] 1 Cr App Rep 361, 163 JP 65).

[5] To establish the offence of permitting under s 8(*b*) the prosecution must prove: (i) knowledge, actual or by closing eyes to the obvious, that dealing in controlled drugs is taking place; and (ii) unwillingness to prevent it, which can be inferred from failure to take steps readily available to prevent it. A defendant's belief that the steps he has taken are reasonable is irrelevant; it is not for a defendant to judge his own conduct: *R v Brock* [2001] 1WLR 1159, 165 JP 331, CA.

[6] See note 4 to s 4, ante.

[7] The commission of this offence requires the actual smoking of cannabis; mere tentative permission to smoke cannabis is insufficient (*R v Auguste* [2003] EWCA Crim 3929, [2004] 1WLR 917, [2004] 4 All ER 373, [2004] 2 Cr App Rep 173 (*d*)).

[8] For definition, see s 37, post.

**7.8112 9. Prohibition of certain activities etc relating to opium** Subject to section 28 of this Act[1], it is an offence[2] for a person—

(*a*) to smoke or otherwise use prepared opium[3]; or

(*b*) to frequent a place used for the purpose of opium smoking; or

(*c*) to have in his possession—

(i) any pipes or other utensils made or adapted for use in connection with the smoking of opium, being pipes or utensils which have been used by him or with his knowledge and permission in that connection or which he intends to use or permit others to use in that connection; or

(ii) any utensils which have been used by him or with his knowledge and permission in connection with the preparation of opium for smoking.

[Misuse of Drugs Act 1971, s 9.]

1 See note 5 to s 4, ante.
2 See note 4 to s 4, ante.
3 For definition, see s 37, post.

7.8113 **9A. Prohibition of supply etc, of articles for administering or preparing controlled drugs** (1) A person who supplies or offers to supply any article which may be used or adapted to be used (whether by itself or in combination with another article or other articles) in the administration by any person of a controlled drug to himself or another, believing that the article (or the article as adapted) is to be so used in circumstances where the administration is unlawful, is guilty of an offence.

(2) It is not an offence under subsection (1) above to supply or offer to supply a hypodermic syringe, or any part of one.

(3) A person who supplies or offers to supply any article which may be used to prepare a controlled drug for administration by any person to himself or another believing that the article is to be used in circumstances where the administration is unlawful is guilty of an offence.

(4) For the purposes of this section, any administration of a controlled drug is unlawful except—

(*a*) the administration by any person of a controlled drug to another in circumstances where the administration of the drug is not unlawful under section 4(1) of this Act,

(*b*) the administration by any person of a controlled drug, other than a temporary class drug, to himself in circumstances where having the controlled drug in his possession is not unlawful under section 5(1) of this Act, or

(*c*) the administration by any person of a temporary class drug to himself in circumstances where having the drug in his possession is to be treated as excepted possession for the purposes of this Act (see section 7A(2)(*c*)).

(5) In this section, references to administration by any person of a controlled drug to himself include a reference to his administering it to himself with the assistance of another.

[Misuse of Drugs Act 1971, s 9A as inserted by the Drug Trafficking Offences Act 1986, s 34 and amended by the Police Reform and Social Responsibility Act 2011, Sch 17.]

*Powers of Secretary of State for preventing misuse of controlled drugs*

7.8114 **10. Power to make regulations for preventing misuse of controlled drugs** (1) Subject to the provisions of this Act, the Secretary of State may by regulations make such provision as appears to him necessary or expedient for preventing the misuse of controlled drugs[1].

(2) Without prejudice to the generality of subsection (1) above, regulations under this section may in particular make provision—

(*a*) for requiring precautions to be taken for the safe custody of controlled drugs[2];

(*b*) for imposing requirements as to the documentation of transactions involving controlled drugs, and for requiring copies of documents relating to such transactions to be furnished to the prescribed authority;

(*c*) for requiring the keeping of records and the furnishing of information with respect to controlled drugs in such circumstances and in such manner as may be prescribed;

(*d*) for the inspection of any precautions taken or records kept in pursuance of regulations under this section;

(*e*) as to the packaging and labelling of controlled drugs;

(*f*) for regulating the transport of controlled drugs and the methods used for destroying or otherwise disposing of such drugs when no longer required;

(*g*) for regulating the issue of prescriptions containing controlled drugs and the supply of controlled drugs on prescriptions, and for requiring persons issuing or dispensing prescriptions containing such drugs to furnish to the prescribed authority such information relating to those prescriptions as may be prescribed;

(*h*) for requiring any doctor who attends a person who he considers, or has reasonable grounds to suspect, is addicted (within the meaning of the regulations) to controlled drugs of any description to furnish to the prescribed authority such particulars with respect to that person as may be prescribed;

(*i*) for prohibiting any doctor from administering, supplying and authorising the administration and supply to persons so addicted and from prescribing for such persons, such controlled drugs as may be prescribed, except under and in accordance with the terms of a licence issued by the Secretary of State in pursuance of the regulations

(3) In this section a reference to "controlled drugs" does not include a reference to temporary class drugs (see instead section 7A).

[Misuse of Drugs Act 1971, s 10 as amended by the Police Reform and Social Responsibility Act 2011, Sch 17.]

1 The following have been made; the Misuse of Drugs (Safe Custody) Regulations 1973, SI 1973/798 amended by SI 1974/1449, SI 1975/294, SI 1984/1146, SI 1985/2067, SI 1986/2332, SI 1999/1403, SI 2007/2154, SI 2011/2085 and 2581 and SI 2014/1275, the Misuse of Drugs (Supply to Addicts) Regulations 1997, SI 1997/1001 amended by SI 2005/2864 and SI 2012/2404 and the Misuse of Drugs Regulations 2001, this title, post.

2 The Misuse of Drugs (Safe Custody) Regulations 1973, SI 1973/798 amended by SI 1974/1449, SI 1975/294, SI 1984/1146, SI 1985/2067, SI 1986/2332, SI 1999/1403, SI 2007/2154, SI 2011/2085 and 2581 and SI 2014/1275 have

been made. Regulation 5(1) which requires drugs to be kept "in a locked receptacle" would not be complied with by leaving them in an unlocked case in a locked motor car (*Kameswara Rao v Wyles* [1949] 2 All ER 685, 113 JP 516).

7.8115 **11. Power to direct special precautions for safe custody of controlled drugs to be taken at certain premises** (1) Without prejudice to any requirement imposed by regulations made in pursuance of section 10(2)(*a*) of this Act or by provision made in a temporary class drug order by virtue of section 7A that is of a corresponding description to such regulations, the Secretary of State may by notice in writing served on the occupier of any premises on which controlled drugs are or are proposed to be kept give directions as to the taking of precautions or further precautions for the safe custody of any controlled drugs of a description in the notice which are kept on those premises.

(2) It is an offence[1] to contravene any directions given under subsection (1) above.

[Misuse of Drugs Act 1971, s 11 as amended by the Police Reform and Social Responsibility Act 2011, Sch 17.]

1 See note 5 to s 4, ante.

7.8116 **12. Directions prohibiting prescribing, supply etc of controlled drugs by practitioners etc convicted of certain offences** (1) Where a person who is a practitioner or pharmacist[1] has after the coming into operation of this subsection been convicted—

(*a*) of an offence[2] under this Act or under the Dangerous Drugs Act 1965 or any enactment repealed by that Act; or

(*b*) of an offence under sections 45, 56 or 304 of the Customs and Excise Act 1952 or under sections 50, 68 or 170 of the Customs and Excise Management Act 1979 in connection with a prohibition of or restriction on importation or exportation of a controlled drug having effect by virtue of section 3 of this Act or which had effect by virtue of any provision contained in or repealed by the Dangerous Drugs Act 1965,

(*c*) of an offence under section 12 or 13 of the Criminal Justice (International Co-operation) Act 1990;

the Secretary of State may give a direction under subsection (2) below in respect of that person.

(2) A direction under this subsection in respect of a person shall—

(*a*) if that person is a practitioner, be a direction prohibiting him from having in his possession, prescribing, administering, manufacturing, compounding and supplying and from authorising the administration and supply of such controlled drugs as may be specified in the direction;

(*b*) if that person is a pharmacist, be a direction prohibiting him from having in his possession, manufacturing, compounding and supplying and from supervising and controlling the manufacture, compounding and supply of such controlled drugs as may be specified in the direction.

(3) The Secretary of State may at any time give a direction cancelling or suspending any direction given by him under subsection (2) above, or cancelling any direction of his under this subsection by which a direction so given is suspended.

(4) The Secretary of State shall cause a copy of any direction given by him under this section to be served on the person to whom it applies, and shall cause notice of any such direction to be published in the London, Edinburgh and Belfast Gazettes.

(5) A direction under this section shall take effect when a copy of it is served on the person to whom it applies.

(6) It is an offence[3] to contravene a direction given under subsection (2) above.

(7) *Amends s 80 of the Medicines Act 1968.*

[Misuse of Drugs Act 1971, s 12 as amended by the Customs and Excise Management Act 1979, Sch 4 and the Criminal Justice (International Co-operation) Act 1990, s 23.]

1 For meaning of "practitioner", see s 37(1) of this Act, and for meaning of "pharmacist" see s 132(1) of the Medicines Act 1968.

2 This includes an offence under s 1 of the Criminal Attempts Act 1981 of attempting to commit an offence under the Misuse of Drugs Act 1971 (Criminal Attempts Act 1981, s 7 (3)).

3 See note 5 to s 4, ante.

7.8117 **13. Directions prohibiting prescribing, supply etc of controlled drugs by practitioners in other cases** (1) In the event of a contravention by a doctor of regulations made in pursuance of paragraph (*h*) or (*i*) of section 10(2) of this Act or of corresponding provision made in a temporary class drug order, or of the terms of a licence issued under regulations made in pursuance of the said paragraph (*i*) or of any such corresponding provision, the Secretary of State may, subject to and in accordance with section 14[1] of this Act, give a direction in respect of the doctor concerned prohibiting him from prescribing, administering and supplying and from authorising the administration and supply of such controlled drugs as may be specified in the direction.

(1A) For the purposes of subsection (1), provision made in a temporary class drug order is "corresponding provision" if it—

(*a*) is made by virtue of section 7A(2)(*d*), and

(*b*) is of a corresponding description to regulations made in pursuance of section 10(2)(*h*) or (as the case may be) 10(2)(i)

(2) If the Secretary of State is of the opinion that a practitioner is or has after the coming into operation of this subsection been prescribing, administering or supplying or authorising the

administration or supply of any controlled drugs in an irresponsible manner, the Secretary of State may, subject to and in accordance with section 14 or 15 of this Act, give a direction in respect of the practitioner concerned prohibiting him from prescribing, administering and supplying and from authorising administration and supply of such controlled drugs as may be specified in the direction.

(3) A contravention[2] such as is mentioned in subsection (1) above does not as such constitute an offence, but it is an offence[3] to contravene a direction given under subsection (1) or (2) above.

[Misuse of Drugs Act 1971, s 13 as amended by the Police Reform and Social Responsibility Act 2011, Sch 17.]

---

[1] Section 14 provides for the investigation of an alleged contravention, by a tribunal set up in accordance with s 16 and Sch 3 to this Act. It is following such investigation that the Secretary of State may give a direction, contravention of which will be an offence by virtue of sub-s (3) of this section.

[2] "Contravention" includes failure to comply (s 37(1)).

[3] See note 5 to s 4, ante.

7.8118 **17. Power to obtain information from doctors, pharmacists etc in certain circumstances** (1) If it appears to the Secretary of State that there exists in any area in Great Britain a social problem caused by the extensive misuse of dangerous or otherwise harmful drugs in that area, he may by notice in writing served on any doctor or pharmacist practising in the vicinity of that area, or on any person carrying on a retail pharmacy business within the meaning of the Medicines Act 1968 at any premises situated in or in the vicinity of that area, require him to furnish to the Secretary of State, with respect to any such drugs specified in the notices and as regards any period so specified, such particulars as may be so specified relating to the quantities in which and the number and frequency of the occasions on which those drugs—

(*a*) in the case of a doctor, were prescribed, administered or supplied by him;

(*b*) in the case of a pharmacist, were supplied by him; or

(*c*) in the case of a person carrying on a retail pharmacy business, were supplied in the course of that business at any premises so situated which may be specified in the notice.

(2) A notice under this section may require any such particulars to be furnished in such manner and within such time as may be specified in the notice and, if served on a pharmacist or person carrying on a retail pharmacy business, may require him to furnish the names and addresses of doctors on whose prescriptions any dangerous or otherwise harmful drugs to which the notice relates were supplied, but shall not require any person to furnish any particulars relating to the identity of any person for or to whom any such drug has been prescribed, administered or supplied.

(3) A person commits an offence[1] if without reasonable excuse (proof of which shall lie on him) he fails to comply with any requirement to which he is subject by virtue of subsection (1) above.

(4) A person commits an offence[1] if in purported compliance with a requirement imposed under this section he gives any information which he knows to be false in a material particular or recklessly gives any information which is so false.

(5) *Northern Ireland.*

[Misuse of Drugs Act 1971, s 17.]

---

[1] See note 5 to s 4, ante.

*Miscellaneous offences and powers*

7.8119 **18. Miscellaneous offences** (1) It is an offence[1] for a person to contravene any regulations made under this Act other than regulations made in pursuance of section 10(2)(*h*) or (*i*).

(2) It is an offence[1] for a person to contravene a condition or other term of a licence issued under section 3 of this Act or of a licence or other authority issued under regulations made under this Act, not being a licence issued under regulations made in pursuance of section 10(2)(*i*).

(3) A person commits an offence[1] if, in purported compliance with any obligation to give information to which he is subject under or by virtue of regulations made under this Act, he gives any information which he knows to be false in a material particular or recklessly gives any information which is so false.

(4) A person commits an offence[1] if, for the purpose of obtaining, whether for himself or another, the issue or renewal of a licence or other authority under this Act or under any regulations made under this Act, he—

(*a*) makes any statement or gives any information which he knows to be false in a material particular or recklessly gives any information which is so false; or

(*b*) produces or otherwise makes use of any book, record or other document which to his knowledge contains any statement or information which he knows to be false in a material particular.

(5) In this section (and in references in Schedule 4 that refer to this section), any reference to regulations made under this Act is to be taken as including a reference to provision made in a temporary class drug order by virtue of section 7A.

(6) For this purpose, a reference in subsection (1) or (2) to regulations made in pursuance of section 10(2)(*h*) or (i) is a reference to any provision of a temporary class drug order which—

(*a*) is made by virtue of section 7A(2)(*d*), and

(*b*) is of a corresponding description to regulations made in pursuance of section 10(2)(*h*) or (as the case may be) (i).

[Misuse of Drugs Act 1971, s 18 as amended by the Police Reform and Social Responsibility Act 2011, Sch 17.]

---

[1] See note 5 to s 4, ante.

7.8120 **19. Attempts etc to commit offences** It is an offence[1] for a person to incite another to commit an offence under any other provision of this Act[2].

[Misuse of Drugs Act 1971, s 19 as amended by the Criminal Attempts Act 1981, Sch and the Serious Crime Act 2007, Sch 6]

1 The method of trial and penalty for an offence under this section depends on the nature of the substantive offence. See s 25(3), post. Anything shown to relate to the offence may be forfeited. See s 27, post.

2 The Criminal Attempts Act 1981 is directed to the law of attempt and conspiracy and does not amend the law of incitement so that s 19 refers not only to the offences under s 18 but also to offences elsewhere in the 1971 Act (*R v Marlow* [1997] Crim LR 897, CA.)

7.8121 **20. Assisting in or inducing commission outside United Kingdom of offence punishable under a corresponding law** A person commits an offence[1] if in the United Kingdom he assists in or induces the commission in any place outside the United Kingdom[2] of an offence punishable under the provisions of a corresponding law[3] in force in that place.

[Misuse of Drugs Act 1971, s 20.]

1 See note 5 to s 4, ante.

2 This section repeats in a modified form, provisions in earlier legislation to deal with a person in this country who organises the smuggling of drugs, for instance from the Continent to the United States of America, but does not himself handle any of the drugs in this country. For power of search, see s 23(3). For a conviction, see *R v Yasukichi Miyagawa* [1924] 1 KB 614, 88 JP 44. The words "assist in the commission of an offence" are not to be narrowly construed; see *R v Vickers* [1975] 2 All ER 945, 139 JP 623 and *R v Evans* [1977] 1 All ER 228, 141 JP 141. The offence outside the UK must be committed: the provision will not apply where a yacht carrying cannabis from Spain to Holland is arrested in the UK (*R v Panayi and Karte* (1987) 86 Cr App Rep 261, [1987] Crim LR 764, CA); subsequent proceedings [1989] 1 WLR 187, CA.

3 For meaning of "corresponding law", see s 36, post.

7.8122 **21. Offences by corporations** Where any offence under this Act or Part II of the Criminal Justice (International Co-operation) Act 1990 committed by a body corporate is proved to have been committed with the consent or connivance of, to be attributable to any neglect on the part of, any director, manager, secretary or other similar officer of the body corporate, or any person purporting to act in any such capacity, he as well as the body corporate shall be guilty of that offence and shall be liable to be proceeded against accordingly.

[Misuse of Drugs Act 1971, s 21 as amended by the Criminal Justice (International Co-operation) Act 1990, s 23, the Drug Trafficking Act 1994, Sch 1 and the Proceeds of Crime Act 2002, s 457.]

7.8123 **22. Further powers to make regulations** (1) The Secretary of State may by regulations[1] make provision—

(*a*) for excluding in such cases as may be prescribed—
  (i) the application of any provision of this Act which creates an offence; or
  (ii) the application of any of the following provisions of the Customs and Excise Management Act 1979, that is to say, sections 50(1) to (4), 68(2) and (3) and 170, in so far as they apply in relation to a prohibition or restriction of importation or exportation having effect by virtue of section 3 of this Act;

(*b*) for applying any of the provisions of sections 14 to 16 of this Act and Schedule 3 thereto, with such modifications (if any) as may be prescribed—
  (i) in relation to any proposal by the Secretary of State to give a direction under section 12(2) of this Act; or
  (ii) for such purposes of regulations under this Act as may be prescribed;

(*c*) for the application of any of the provisions of this Act or regulations or orders thereunder to servants or agents of the Crown, subject to such exceptions, adaptations and modifications as may be prescribed.

(2) The power to make regulations under this section does not apply in relation to temporary class drugs (see instead section 7A).

[Misuse of Drugs Act 1971, s 22 as amended by the Customs and Excise Management Act 1979, Sch 4 and the Police Reform and Social Responsibility Act 2011, Sch 17.]

1 The Misuse of Drugs (Supply to Addicts) Regulations 1997, SI 1997/1001 amended by SI 2005/2864 and SI 2012/2404 and the Misuse of Drugs 2001, in this title, post, have been made.

*Law enforcement and punishment of offences*

7.8124 **23. Powers to search and obtain evidence** A constable or other person authorised in that behalf by a general or special order of the Secretary of State (or in Northern Ireland either of the Secretary of State or the Ministry of Home Affairs for Northern Ireland) shall, for the purposes of the execution of this Act, have power to enter the premises of a person carrying on business as a producer or supplier of any controlled drugs[1] and to demand the production of, and to inspect[2] any books or documents relating to dealings in any such drugs and to inspect any stocks of any such drugs.

(2) If a constable has reasonable grounds to suspect that any person is in possession of a controlled drug in contravention of this Act or of any regulations or orders made thereunder, the constable may—

(*a*) search that person, and detain him for the purpose of searching him;

(*b*) search any vehicle or vessel in which the constable suspects that the drug may be found, and for that purpose require the person in control of the vehicle or vessel to stop it;

(*c*) seize and detain, for the purposes of proceedings under this Act, anything found in the course of the search which appears to the constable to be evidence of an offence under this Act.

In this subsection "vessel" includes a hovercraft within the meaning of the Hovercraft Act 1968; and nothing in this subsection shall prejudice any power of search or any power to seize or detain property which is exercisable by a constable apart from this subsection.

(3) If a justice of the peace (or in Scotland a justice of the peace, a magistrate or a sheriff) is satisfied by information on oath that there is reasonable ground for suspecting—

(*a*) that any controlled drugs are, in contravention of this Act or of any regulations or orders made thereunder, in the possession of a person on any premises; or

(*b*) that a document directly or indirectly relating to, or connected with, a transaction or dealing which was, or an intended transaction or dealing which would if carried out be, an offence under this Act, or in the case of a transaction or dealing carried out or intended to be carried out in a place outside the United Kingdom, an offence against the provisions of a corresponding law in force in that place, is in the possession of a person on any premises,

he may grant a warrant[3] authorising any constable at any time or times within one month from the date of the warrant, to enter, if need by force, the premises named in the warrant, and to search the premises and any persons found therein[4] and, if there is reasonable ground for suspecting that an offence under this Act has been committed in relation to any controlled drugs found on the premises or in the possession of any such persons, or that a document so found is such a document as is mentioned in paragraph (*b*) above, to seize and detain those drugs or that document, as the case may be.

(3A) The powers conferred by subsection (1) above shall be exercisable also for the purposes of the execution of Part II of the Criminal Justice (International Co-operation) Act 1990 and subsection (3) above (excluding paragraph (*a*)) shall apply also to offences under section 12 or 13 of that Act of 1990, taking references in those provisions to controlled drugs as references to scheduled substances within the meaning of that Part.

(4) A person commits an offence[5] if he—

(*a*) intentionally obstructs[6] a person in the exercise of his powers under this section; or

(*b*) conceals from a person acting in the exercise of his powers under subsection (1) above any such books, documents, stocks or drugs as are mentioned in that subsection; or

(*c*) without reasonable excuse (proof of which shall lie on him) fails to produce any such books or documents as are so mentioned where their production is demanded by a person in the exercise of his powers under that subsection.

(5) *Repealed.*

[Misuse of Drugs Act 1971, s 23 as amended by the Criminal Justice (International Co-operation) Act 1990, s 23, the Drug Trafficking Act 1994, Sch 1, the Proceeds of Crime Act 2002, s 457, the Policing and Crime Act 2009, s 111 and Sch 8 and the Police Reform and Social Responsibility Act 2011, Sch 17.]

---

1 The power to enter and search premises is also exercisable for the purposes of arts 6 and 7 of Council Regulation (EC) No. 111/2005: the Community Drugs (Drug Precursors) (Community External Trade) Regulations 2008, SI 2008/296.

2 This includes the right to take notes of the entries therein. Cf *Hart v Cohen and Van der Laan* (1902) 4 F 445.

3 The warrant will authorise entry only to the premises described in the warrant, see *R v Atkinson* [1976] Crim LR 307 (wrong flat number applied for and stated in warrant), though misspellings or trivial errors will not necessarily invalidate the warrant.

4 Where a warrant provides for a search of premises and persons therein, the police may detain a person in one room while they search another room (*DPP v Meaden* [2003] EWHC 3005 (Admin), [2004] 4 All ER 75, [2004] 1 WLR 945, [2004] Crim LR 587).

5 See note 5 to s 4, ante.

6 In *James v DPP* [2012] EWHC 1317 (Admin), 176 JP 346, 176 CL&J 291 two officers in uniform gave reasons for requiring a search under s 23 and the defendant submitted to a pat down search, but had drugs in his mouth which he did his best to conceal and then swallow. One of the officers put his hand on the defendant's throat and subsequently applied force – found to be reasonable – when the defendant tried to swallow the drugs. The argument was whether a "forcible search" for the purposes of para 3.2 of Code A of the Statutory Codes of Practice was in progress before the defendant's attempt to swallow the drugs (and was not justified under the conditions prescribed by that provision). The conviction was upheld. The search did not become "forcible" until force was applied to thwart the attempt to swallow the drugs, and at that point a forcible search was justified.

**7.8125 23A. Temporary class drugs: further power to search, seize and detain**

(1) Subsection (3) applies in any case where—

(*a*) a constable has reasonable grounds to suspect that a person ("P") is in possession of a temporary class drug, and

(*b*) it does not appear to the constable that a power under section 23(2) applies to the case.

(2) But if any provision has been made by virtue of section 7A(2)(*c*) (excepted possession) that applies to the temporary class drug in question, subsection (3) applies only if the constable has no reason to believe that P's possession of the drug is to be treated as excepted possession for the purposes of this Act.

(3) The constable may—

(*a*) search P, and detain P for the purposes of searching P;

(*b*) search any vehicle or vessel in which the constable suspects that the drug may be found, and for that purpose require the person in control of the vehicle or vessel to stop it

(c) seize and detain anything found in the course of the search which appears to the constable to be a temporary class drug or to be evidence of an offence under this Act.

In this subsection, "vessel" has the same meaning as in section 23(2).

(4) Subsection (5) applies if a constable reasonably believes that anything detained under subsection (3)(c) is a temporary class drug but is not evidence of any offence under this Act.

(5) The constable may dispose of the drug in such manner as the constable thinks appropriate.

(6) A person who intentionally obstructs a constable in the exercise of the constable's powers under subsection (3) commits an offence.

[Misuse of Drugs Act 1971, s 23A as inserted by the Police Reform and Social Responsibility Act 2011, Sch 17.]

7.8126 25. **Prosecution**[1] **and punishment of offences** (1) Schedule 4[2] to this Act shall have effect, in accordance with subsection (2) below, with respect to the way in which offences under this Act are punishable on conviction.

(2) In relation to an offence under a provision of this Act specified in the first column of the Schedule (the general nature of the offence being described in the second column)—

(a) the third column shows whether an offence is punishable on summary conviction or on indictment or in either way;

(b) the fourth, fifth and sixth columns show respectively the punishments which may be imposed on a person convicted of the offence in the way specified in relation thereto in the third column (that is to say, summarily or on indictment) according to whether the controlled drug in relation to which the offence was committed was a Class A drug, a Class B drug or a Class C drug[3]; and

(c) the seventh column shows the punishments which may be imposed on a person convicted of the offence in the way specified in relation thereto in the third column (that is to say, summarily or on indictment), whether or not the offence was committed in relation to a controlled drug and, if it was so committed, irrespective of whether the drug was a Class A drug, a Class B drug or a Class C drug[3];

and in the fourth, fifth, sixth and seventh columns a reference to a period gives the maximum term of imprisonment and a reference to a sum of money the maximum fine.

(2A) Subsection (2B) applies if an offence specified in the first column of Schedule 4 is committed in relation to a temporary class drug.

(2B) The punishments which may be imposed on a person convicted of the offence summarily or (as the case may be) on indictment in relation to the temporary class drug are the same as those which could be imposed had the person been convicted of the offence in that way in relation to a Class B drug (see the fifth column of Schedule 4).

(3) An offence under section 19 of this Act shall be punishable on summary conviction, on indictment or in either way according to whether, under Schedule 4 to this Act, the substantive offence is punishable on summary conviction, on indictment or in either way; and the punishments which may be imposed on a person convicted of an offence under that section are the same as those which, under that Schedule, may be imposed on a person convicted of the substantive offence. In this subsection "the substantive offence" means the offence under this Act to which the incitement mentioned in section 19 was directed.

(3A) The punishments which may be imposed on a person convicted of an offence under section 23A(6) are the same as those which, under Schedule 4, may be imposed on a person convicted of an offence under section 23(4).

(4) Notwithstanding anything in section 127(1) of the Magistrates' Courts Act 1980, a magistrates' court in England and Wales may try an information for an offence under this Act if the information was laid at any time within twelve months from the commission of the offence.

(5) *Scotland.*

(6) *Northern Ireland.*

[Misuse of Drugs Act 1971, s 25, as amended by the Magistrates' Courts Act 1980, Sch 7 and the Criminal Attempts Act 1981, Schedule and the Police Reform and Social Responsibility Act 2011, Sch 17.]

---

1 There is no provision similar to that in earlier legislation whereby proceedings on indictment either required the consent of the Attorney General or had to be instituted by the Director of Public Prosecutions. Parliament has however expressed the hope that prosecutors will not proceed by way of indictment where summary proceedings are adequate.

2 See post.

3 See Sch 2, post, and s 2, ante.

7.8127 27. **Forfeiture** (1) Subject to subsection (2) below, the court by or before which a person is convicted of an offence[1] under this Act or an offence falling within subsection (3) below or an offence to which section 1 of the Criminal Justice (Scotland) Act 1987 relates may order anything[2] shown to the satisfaction[3] of the court to relate to the offence, to be forfeited and either destroyed or dealt with[4] in such other manner as the court may order.

(2) The court shall not order anything to be forfeited under this section, where a person claiming to be the owner of or otherwise interested in it applies to be heard by the court, unless an opportunity has been given to him to show cause why the order should not be made.

(3) An offence falls within this subsection if it is an offence specified in—

(a) paragraph 1 of Schedule 2 to the Proceeds of Crime Act 2002 (drug trafficking offences), or

(b) so far as it relates to that paragraph, paragraph 10 of that Schedule.

[Misuse of Drugs Act 1971, s 27 as amended by the Criminal Justice Act 1988, s 70, the Criminal Justice (International Co-operation) Act 1990, Sch 4, the Drug Trafficking Act 1994, Sch 1 and the Proceeds of Crime Act 2002, s 456.]

---

1 The power of forfeiture applies only to property shown to be connected with the offence of which the offender is convicted; the proceeds of the sale of drugs, not the subject of the charge, which the offender had in his possession prior to his being searched cannot therefore be forfeited (*R v Llewellyn* [1985] Crim LR 750) and see *R v Simms* (1988) 9 Cr App Rep (S) 417, CA.

2 In *R v Beard* [1974] 1 WLR 1549, Caulfield J held that "anything" includes money but would not include a house; but cf *Haggard v Mason* [1976] 1 All ER 337, 140 JP 198. The power of forfeiture applies only to tangible things capable of being destroyed or dealt with in some other manner as the court thinks fit, and not to choses in action or other intangibles (*R v Cuthbertson* [1980] 2 All ER 401, 144 JP 366). Cash seized by the police and placed in a deposit account does not cease to be a tangible asset and still be the subject of a forfeiture order (*R v Marland and Jones* (1985) 82 Cr App Rep 134).

Where a motor vehicle is used as a means of transport on the journey in the course of which the defendant is arrested and on other trips to purchase drugs, the vehicle may be the subject of a forfeiture order (*R v Bowers* (1993) 15 Cr App Rep (S) 315, [1994] Crim LR 230, CA (forfeiture order upheld notwithstanding the fact that the motor vehicle had been purchased with money provided by the defendant's elderly mother and the vehicle was used to take his mother to visit his mentally handicapped brother)).

3 The court must make a proper investigation to ensure that the statutory requirements are fulfilled before making a forfeiture order. Where the court is minded to make such an order, it should first allow the offender to put before the court any material tending the show that the thing in question is not related to the offence (*R v Churcher* (1986) 8 Cr App Rep (S) 94).

4 Disposal of forfeited articles should not be carried out until the time for appeal has expired.

*Miscellaneous and supplementary provisions*

7.8128 28. **Proof of lack of knowledge etc to be a defence in proceedings for certain offences**[1] (1) This section applies to offences under any of the following provisions of this Act, that is to say section 4(2) and (3), section 5 (2) and (3), section 6(2) and section 9[2].

(2) Subject to subsection (3) below, in any proceedings for an offence to which this section applies it shall be a defence for the accused to prove[3] that he neither knew of nor suspected nor had reason to suspect the existence of some fact[4] alleged by the prosecution which it is necessary for the prosecution to prove if he is to be convicted of the offence charged.

(3) Where in any proceedings for an offence to which this section applies it is necessary, if the accused is to be convicted of the offence charged, for the prosecution to prove that some substance or product involved in the alleged offence was the controlled drug which the prosecution alleges it to have been, and it is proved that the substance or product in question was that controlled drug, the accused[5]—

(*a*) shall not be acquitted[6] of the offence charged by reason only of proving that he neither knew nor suspected nor had reason to suspect that the substance or product in question was the particular controlled drug alleged; but

(*b*) shall be acquitted thereof—

(i) if he proves[3] that he neither believed nor suspected nor had reason to suspect[7] that the substance or product in question was a controlled drug; or

(ii) if he proves[3] that he believed the substance or product in question to be a controlled drug, or a controlled drug of a description, such that, if it had in fact been that controlled drug or a controlled drug of that description, he would not at the material time have been committing any offence to which this section applies.

(4) Nothing in this section shall prejudice any defence which it is open to a person charged with an offence to which this section applies to raise apart from this section.

[Misuse of Drugs Act 1971, s 28.]

---

1 The presumption of innocence given effect in article of the European Convention of Human Rights, is not breached by this provision which places an evidential burden on the defendant (*R v Lambert* [2001] UKHL 37, [2002] 2 AC 545, [2001] 3 All ER 577, [2001] 3 WLR 206). Nor can s 28 be read down to provide a religious exemption. Article 9 is a qualified right. The prohibition on the possession and supply of a dangerous drug is necessary in a democratic society "for the protection of public order, health or morals or for the protection of the rights and freedoms of others": *R v Aziz* [2012] EWCA Crim 1063, [2012] Crim LR 801.

2 These offences are production and supply (s 4), possession (s 5), cultivation of the cannabis plant (s 6), smoking using prepared opium (s 9) and allied offences.

3 This places an evidential burden on the defendant to raise certain issues which amount to a defence and which the prosecution must disprove beyond a reasonable doubt. The words "to prove" in sub-ss (2) and (3) must be read as "to give sufficient evidence". The effect is that the burden of proof remains on the prosecution throughout. If sufficient evidence is adduced to raise the issue, it will be for the prosecution to show beyond reasonable doubt that the defence is not made out by the evidence. What the accused must do is put evidence before the court which, if believed, could be taken by a reasonable jury or magistrates' court to support his defence. (*R v Lambert* [2001] UKHL 37, [2002] 2 AC 545, [2001] 3 All ER 577, [2001] 3 WLR 206).

4 For example, that he possessed some substance. The onus remains on the prosecution to prove the defendant knew he had something which was in fact a dangerous drug; once this is proved, it is open for the defendant to try and raise the issue of lack of knowledge under s 28; see note 2 to s 5, ante.

5 Once the prosecution prove that the defendant had control of a box which he was delivering on his motor cycle and knew it contained something, which was in fact the drug alleged, he has the onus of bringing himself within the provisions of s 28(3); see *R v McNamara* (1988) 152 JP 390, 87 Cr App Rep 246, CA, followed in *R v Matrix* [1997] Crim LR 901, CA (possession of obscene video film depicting children.).

6 This does not prevent a court from taking into account, in deciding sentence, the defendant's genuine belief that the drug in question was a different controlled drug.

7 The words "neither knew nor suspected nor had reason to suspect" are not to be read as one when considering

whether self-induced intoxication could act as a defence. It was a factor to be considered, and could eliminate the knowledge or suspicion of the first two tests, being subjective. But the third test "reason to suspect" called for an objective appraisal (*R v Young* [1984] 2 All ER 164, [1984] 1 WLR 654, 148 JP 492).

7.8129 **29. Service of documents** (1) Any notice or other document required or authorised by any provisions of this Act to be served on any person may be served on him either by delivering it to him or by leaving it at his proper address or by sending it by post.

(2) Any notice or other document so required or authorised to be served on a body corporate shall be duly served if it is served on the secretary or clerk of that body.

(3) For the purposes of this section, and of section 26 of the Interpretation Act 1889[1] in its application to this section, the proper address of any person shall, in the case of the secretary or clerk of a body corporate, be that of the registered or principal office of that body, and in any other case shall be the last address of the person to be served which is known to the Secretary of State.

(4) Where any of the following documents, that is to say—

(*a*) a notice under section 11(1) or section 15(6) of this Act; or

(*b*) a copy of a direction given under section 12(2), section 13(1) or (2) or section 16(3) of this Act,

is served by sending it by registered post or by the recorded delivery service, service thereof shall be deemed to have been affected at the time when the letter containing it would be delivered in the ordinary course of post; and so much of section 26 of the Interpretation Act 1889[1] as relates to the time when service by post is deemed to have been effected shall not apply to such a document if it is served by so sending it.

[Misuse of Drugs Act 1971, s 29.]

1 Now s 7 of the Interpretation Act 1978.

7.8130 **31. General provisions as to regulations** (1) Regulations made by the Secretary of State under any provisions of this Act—

(*a*) may make different provision in relation to different controlled drugs, different classes of persons, different provisions of this Act or other different cases or circumstances; and

(*b*) may make the opinion, consent or approval of a prescribed authority or of any person authorised in a prescribed manner material for purposes of any provision of the regulations; and

(*c*) may contain such supplementary, incidental and transitional provisions as appear expedient to the Secretary of State.

(2) Any power of the Secretary of State to make regulations under this Act shall be exercisable by statutory instrument, which shall be subject to annulment in pursuance of a resolution of either House of Parliament.

(2A) *Repealed.*

(3) The Secretary of State shall not make any regulations under this Act except after consultation with the Advisory Council.

(4) *Northern Ireland.*

(4A) *Repealed.*

[Misuse of Drugs Act 1971, s 31 as amended by the Policing and Crime Act 2009, Schs 7 and 8.]

7.8131 **36. Meaning of "corresponding law", and evidence of certain matters by certificate** (1) In this Act the expression "corresponding law" means a law stated in a certificate purporting to be issued by or on behalf of the government of a country outside the United Kingdom to be a law providing for the control and regulation in that country of the production, supply, use, export and import of drugs and other substances in accordance with the provisions of the Single Convention on Narcotic Drugs signed at New York on 30th March 1961 or a law providing for the control and regulation in that country of the production, supply, use, export and import of dangerous or otherwise harmful drugs in pursuance of any treaty, convention or other agreement or arrangement to which the government of that country and Her Majesty's Government in the United Kingdom are for the time being parties.

(2) A statement in any such certificate as aforesaid to the effect that any facts constitute an offence against the law mentioned in the certificate shall be evidence, and in Scotland sufficient evidence, of the matters stated.

[Misuse of Drugs Act 1971, s 36.]

7.8132 **37. Interpretation** (1) In this Act, except in so far as the context otherwise requires, the following expressions have the meanings hereby assigned to them respectively, that is to say—

"the Advisory Council" means the Advisory Council on the Misuse of Drugs established under this Act;

"cannabis" (except in the expression "cannabis resin") means any plant of the genus *Cannabis* or any part of any such plant (by whatever name designated)[1] except that it does not include cannabis resin or any of the following products after separation from the rest of the plant, namely—

(*a*) mature stalk of any such plant,

(*b*) fibre produced from mature stalk of any such plant, and

(*c*) seed of any such plant[2];

"cannabis resin" means the separated resin, whether crude or purified, obtained from any plant of the genus *Cannabis*[3];

"contravention" includes failure to comply, and "contravene" has a corresponding meaning;
"controlled drug" has the meaning assigned by section 2 of this Act;
"corresponding law" has the meaning assigned by section 36(1) of this Act;
"dentist" means a person registered in the dentists' register under the Dentists Act 1984;
"doctor" means a registered medical practitioner within the meaning of Schedule 1 to the Interpretation Act 1978;
"enactment" includes an enactment of the Parliament of Northern Ireland;
"person lawfully conducting retail pharmacy business" means a person lawfully conducting such a business in accordance with section 69 of the Medicines Act 1968;
"pharmacist" has the same meaning as in the Medicines Act 1968;
"practitioner" (except in the expression "veterinary practitioner") means a doctor, dentist, veterinary practitioner or veterinary surgeon;
"prepared opium" means opium prepared for smoking and includes dross and any other residues remaining after opium has been smoked;
"prescribed" means prescribed by regulations made by the Secretary of State under this Act;
"produce", where the reference is to producing a controlled drug, means producing it by manufacture, cultivation or any other method[4], and "production" has a corresponding meaning;
"supplying" includes distributing[5];
"temporary class drug order" means an order made under section 2A(1);
"veterinary practitioner" means a person registered in the supplementary veterinary register kept under section 8 of the Veterinary Surgeons Act 1966;
"veterinary surgeon" means a person registered in the register of veterinary surgeons kept under section 2 of the Veterinary Surgeons Act 1966.

(2) References in this Act to misusing a drug are references to misusing it by taking it; and the reference in the foregoing provision to the taking of a drug is a reference to the taking of it by a human being by way of any form of self-administration, whether or not involving assistance by another.

(3) For the purposes of this Act the things which a person has in his possession shall be taken to include any thing subject to his control which is in the custody of another.

(4) Except in so far as the context otherwise requires, any reference in this Act to an enactment shall be construed as a reference to that enactment as amended or extended by or under any other enactment.

(5) *Repealed.*

[Misuse of Drugs Act 1971, s 37 as amended by SI 1976/1213, the Criminal Law Act 1977, s 52, the Medical Act 1983, Sch 5, the Dentists Act 1984, Sch 5, SI 1996/1496, the Statute Law (Repeals) Act 2004, SI 2007/3101 and the Police Reform and Social Responsibility Act 2011, Sch 17.]

---

1 Eg, hashish, gunjah, bhang, marijuana.

2 For consideration of the effect the amendment of this definition by s 52 of the Criminal Law Act 1977 has had, see *Taylor v Chief Constable of Kent* [1981] 1 WLR 606, 72 Cr App Rep 318.

3 Leaves and stalk which have been removed from a cannabis plant do not amount to "cannabis resin", since the separation contemplated by the section is a serious and deliberate removal of resin from the plant, see *R v Goodchild (No 2), A-G's Reference (No 1 of 1977)* [1978] 1 All ER 649, [1977] 1 WLR 1213, 65 Cr App Rep 165, CA. Compacted shakings or scrapings of part of a cannabis plant which on microscopic examination were seen to contain intact cannabis oil-bearing glandular trichomes nevertheless came within the definition of cannabis resin (*R v Janet Thomas* [1981] Crim LR 496.)

4 Conversion from one form of a drug to another can amount to production (*R v Russell* (1991) 94 Cr App Rep 351, CA). The preparation of plants so as to discard the parts which are not usable for the drug and to put together those which are amounts to "production" of cannabis (*R v Harris* [1996] 1 Cr App Rep 369, [1996] Crim LR 36, CA. Making an infusion of out of B-Caapi and Chacruna amounts to "producing" a controlled drug (DMT) by making a "preparation": *R v Aziz* [2012] EWCA Crim 1063, [2012] Crim LR 801. See further para 5 of Pt 1 (Class A) to Sch 2, post, which provides " . . . any preparation or other product containing a substance or product for the time being specified in any of the paragraphs 1 to 4 above [is a Class A controlled drug]".

5 A person who purchased drugs for himself and others could supply the drugs to the others (*Holmes v Chief Constable Merseyside Police* [1976] Crim LR 125), followed in *R v Buckley* (1979) 69 Cr App Rep 371).

## SCHEDULES

### SCHEDULE 1

CONSTITUTION OF ADVISORY COUNCIL ON THE MISUSE OF DRUGS

### SCHEDULE 2

CONTROLLED DRUGS[1]

Section 2

**7.8133**

*(As amended by SI 1973/771, SI 1975/421, SI 1977/1243, SI 1979/299, SI 1983/765, SI 1984/859, SI 1985/1995, SI 1986/2230, SI 1989/1340, SI 1990/2589, SI 1995/1966, SI 1996/1300, SI 1998/750, SI 2001/3932, SI 2003/1243 and 3201, the Drugs Act 2005, s 21, SI 2005/1650 and 3178, SI 2006/3331, SI 2008/3130, SI 2009/3209, SI 2010/1207 and 1833, SI 2011/744, SI 2012/1390, SI 2013/239, SI 2014/1106,1352 and 3271, SI 2015/215 and SI 2016/1109.)*

#### PART I

#### CLASS A DRUGS

1. The following substances and products, namely—
(*a*)

Acetorphine.
Alfentanil.
Allylprodine.
Alphacetylmethadol.
Alphameprodine.
Alphamethadol.
Alphaprodine.
Anileridine.
Benzethidine.
Benzylmorphine (3-benzylmorphine).
Betacetylmethadol.
Betameprodine.
Betamethadol.
Betaprodine.
Bezitramide.
Bufotenine.
Carfentanil
Clonitazene.
Coca leaf.
Cocaine.[2]
Desomorphine.
Dextromoramide.
Diamorphine.
Diampromide.
Diethylthiambutene.
Difenoxin (1-(3-cyano-3,3-diphenylpropyl) -4-phenylpiperidine-4-carboxylic acid)
Dihydrocodeinone *O*-carboxymethyloxime.
Dihydroetorphine.
Dihydromorphine.
Dimenoxadole.
Dimepheptanol.
Dimethylthiambutene.
Dioxaphetyl butyrate.
Diphenoxylate.
Dipipanone.
(Drotebanol (3,4-dimethoxy-17-methylmorphinan-6 beta, 14-diol).
Ecgonine, and any derivative of ecgonine which is convertible to ecgonine or to cocaine.
Ethylmethylthiambutene.
Eticyclidine
Etonitazene.
Etorphine.
Etoxeridine.
Etryptamine
Fentanyl.
Fungus (of any kind) which contains psilocin or an ester of psilocin.
Furethidine.
Hydrocodone.
Hydromorphinol.
Hydromorphone.
Hydroxypethidine.
Isomethadone.
Ketobemidone.
Levomethorphan.
Levomoramide.
Levophenacylmorphan.
Levorphanol.
Lofentanil.
Lysergamide.
Lysergide and other *N*-alkyl derivatives of lysergamide.
Mescaline.
Metazocine.
Methadone.
Methadyl acetate.
Methylamphetamine.
Methyldesorphine.
Methyldihydromorphine (6-methyldihydromorphine).
Metopon.
Morpheridine.
Morphine.
Morphine methobromide, morphine *N*-oxide and other pentavalent nitrogen morphine derivatives.
Myrophine.
Nicomorphine (3,6-dinicotinoyl-morphine).
Noracymethadol.
Norlevorphanol.
Normethadone.
Normorphine.
Norpipanone.
Opium, whether raw, prepared or medicinal.

Oxycodone.
Oxymorphone.
Pethidine.
Phenadoxone.
Phenampromide.
Phenazocine.
Phencyclidine.
Phenomorphan.
Phenoperidine.
Piminodine.
Piritramide.
Poppy-straw and concentrate of poppy-straw.
Proheptazine.
Properidine (1-methyl-4-phenyl-piperidine-4-carboxylic acid isopropyl ester).
Psilocin.
Racemethorphan.
Racemoramide.
Racemorphan.
Remifentanil.
Rolicyclidine.
Sufentanil.
Tapentadol.
Tenocylidine.
Thebacon.
Thebaine.
Tilidate.
Trimeperidine.
(6aR,9R)-4-acetyl-N,N-diethyl-7-methyl-4,6,6a,7,8,9-hexahydroindolo[4,3-fg]quinoline- 9-carboxamide (ALD-52).
4-Bromo-2,5-dimethoxy-alpha-methylphenethylamine
4-Cyano-2-dimethylamino-4, 4-diphenylbutane
4-Cyano-1-methyl-4-phenyl-piperidine.
1-Cyclohexyl-4-(1,2-diphenylethyl)piperazine (MT-45).
3,4-dichloro-N-[[1-(dimethylamino)cyclohexyl]methyl]benzamide (AH-7921)
(6aR,9R)-N,N-diethyl-7-allyl-4,6,6a,7,8,9-hexahydroindolo[4,3-fg]quinoline-9- carboxamide (AL-LAD);
(6aR,9R)-N,N-diethyl-7-ethyl-4,6,6a,7,8,9-hexahydroindolo[4,3-fg]quinoline-9- carboxamide (ETH-LAD);
(6aR,9R)-N,N-diethyl-7-propyl-4,6,6a,7,8,9-hexahydroindolo[4,3-fg]quinoline-9-carboxamide (PRO-LAD).
*N,N*-Diethyltryptamine.
2,4-dimethylazetidinyl{(6aR,9R)-7-methyl-4,6,6a,7,8,9-hexahydroindolo[4,3- fg]quinolin-9-yl}methanone (LSZ)
*N,N*-Dimethyltryptamine.
2,5-Dimethoxy-alpha,4-dimethylphenethylamine.
N-Hydroxy-tenamphetamine.
1-Methyl-4-phenylpiperidine-4-carboxylic acid.
2-Methyl-3-morpholino-1, 1-diphenylpropanecarboxylic acid.
4-Methyl-aminorex.
4-Methyl-5-(4-methylphenyl)-4,5-dihydrooxazol-2-amine (4,4'-DMAR).
4-Phenylpiperidine-4-carboxylic acid ethyl ester.

(*b*) any compound (not being a compound for the time being specified in subparagraph (a) above) structurally derived from tryptamine or from a ring-hydroxy tryptamine by modification in any of the following ways, that is to say—

(i) by substitution at the nitrogen atom of the sidechain to any extent with alkyl or alkenyl substituents, or by inclusion of the nitrogen atom of the side chain (and no other atoms of the side chain) in a cyclic structure;

(ii) by substitution at the carbon atom adjacent to the nitrogen atom of the side chain with alkyl or alkenyl substituents;

(iii) by substitution in the 6-membered ring to any extent with alkyl, alkoxy, haloalkyl, thioalkyl, alkylenedioxy, or halide substituents;

(iv) by substitution at the 2-position of the tryptamine ring system with an alkyl substituent;

(*ba*) the following phenethylamine derivatives, namely:—

Allyl(α-methyl-3,4-methylenedioxyphenethyl)amine
2-Amino-1-(2,5-dimethoxy-4-methylphenyl)ethanol
2-Amino-1-(3,4-dimethoxyphenyl)ethanol
Benzyl(α-methyl-3,4-methylenedioxyphenethyl)amine
4-Bromo-β,2,5-trimethoxyphenethylamine
*N*-(4-*sec*-Butylthio-2,5-dimethoxyphenethyl)hydroxylamine
Cyclopropylmethyl(α-methyl-3,4-methylenedioxyphenethyl)amine
2-(4,7-Dimethoxy-2,3-dihydro-1*H*-indan-5-yl)ethylamine
2-(4,7-Dimethoxy-2,3-dihydro-1*H*-indan-5-yl)-1-methylethylamine
2-(2,5-Dimethoxy-4-methylphenyl)cyclopropylamine
2-(1,4-Dimethoxy-2-naphthyl)ethylamine
2-(1,4-Dimethoxy-2-naphthyl)-1-methylethylamine
*N*-(2,5-Dimethoxy-4-propylthiophenethyl)hydroxylamine
2-(1,4-Dimethoxy-5,6,7,8-tetrahydro-2-naphthyl)ethylamine
2-(1,4-Dimethoxy-5,6,7,8-tetrahydro-2-naphthyl)-1-methylethylamine
α,α -Dimethyl-3,4-methylenedioxyphenethylamine

α,,α -Dimethyl-3,4-methylenedioxyphenethyl(methyl)amine
Dimethyl(α-methyl-3,4-methylenedioxyphenethyl)amine
*N*-(4-Ethylthio-2,5-dimethoxyphenethyl)hydroxylamine
4-Iodo-2,5-dimethoxy-α-methylphenethyl(dimethyl)amine
2-(1,4-Methano-5,8-dimethoxy-1,2,3,4-tetrahydro-6-naphthyl)ethylamine
2-(1,4-Methano-5,8-dimethoxy-1,2,3,4-tetrahydro-6-naphthyl)-1-methylethylamine
2-(5-Methoxy-2,2-dimethyl-2,3-dihydrobenzo[*b*]furan-6-yl)-1-methylethylamine
2-Methoxyethyl(*a*-methyl-3,4-methylenedioxyphenethyl)amine
2-(5-Methoxy-2-methyl-2,3-dihydrobenzo[*b*]furan-6-yl)-1-methylethylamine
β;-Methoxy-3,4-methylenedioxyphenethylamine
1-(3,4-Methylenedioxybenzyl)butyl(ethyl)amine
1-(3,4-Methylenedioxybenzyl)butyl(methyl)amine
2-(α-Methyl-3,4-methylenedioxyphenethylamino)ethanol
α-Methyl-3,4-methylenedioxyphenethyl(prop-2-ynyl)amine
*N*-Methyl-*N*-(α-methyl-3,4-methylenedioxyphenethyl)hydroxylamine
*O*-Methyl-*N*-(α-methyl-3,4-methylenedioxyphenethyl)hydroxylamine
α-Methyl-4-(methylthio)phenethylamine
β,3,4,5-Tetramethoxyphenethylamine
β,2,5-Trimethoxy-4-methylphenethylamine;

(*c*) any compound (not being methoxyphenamine or a compound for the time being specified in sub-paragraph (*a*) above) structurally derived from phenethylamine, an *N*-alkylphenethylamine, alpha-methylphenethylamine, an *N*-alkyl-alpha-methylphenethylamine, alpha -ethylphenethylamine, or an *N*-alkyl-alpha-ethylphenethylamine by substitution in the ring to any extent with alkyl, alkoxy, alkylene- dioxy or halide substituents, whether or not further substituted in the ring by one or more other univalent substituents.

(*d*) any compound (not being a compound for the time being specified in sub-paragraph (*a*) above) structurally derived from fentanyl by modification in any of the following ways, that is to say,
(i) by replacement of the phenyl portion of the phenethyl group by any heteromonocycle whether or not further substituted in the heterocycle;
(ii) by substitution in the phenethyl group with alkyl, alkenyl, alkoxy, hydroxy, halogeno, haloalkyl, amino or nitro groups;
(iii) by substitution in the piperidine ring with alkyl or alkenyl groups;
(iv) by substitution in the aniline ring with alkyl, alkoxy, alkylenedioxy, halogeno or haloalkyl groups;
(v) by substitution at the 4-position of the piperidine ring with any alkoxycarbonyl or alkoxyalkyl or acyloxy group;
(vi) by replacement of the *N*-propionyl group by another acyl group;

(*e*) any compound (not being a compound for the time being specified in sub-paragraph (*a*) above) structurally derived from pethidine by modification in any of the following ways, that is to say,
(i) by replacement of the 1-methyl group by an acyl, alkyl whether or not unsaturated, benzyl or phenethyl group, whether or not further substituted;
(ii) by substitution in the piperidine ring with alkyl or alkenyl groups or with a propano bridge, whether or not further substituted;
(iii) by substitution in the 4-phenyl ring with alkyl, alkoxy, aryloxy, halogeno or haloalkyl groups;
(iv) by replacement of the 4-ethoxycarbonyl by any other alkoxycarbonyl or any alkoxyalkyl or acyloxy group;
(v) by formation of an *N*-oxide or of a quaternary base.

(*f*) any compound (not being benzyl(?-methyl-3,4-methylenedioxyphenethyl)amine) structurally derived from mescaline, 4-bromo-2,5-dimethoxy-?-methylphenethylamine, 2,5-dimethoxy-?,4-dimethylphenethylamine, *N*-hydroxytenamphetamine, or a compound specified in sub-paragraph (*ba*) or (*c*) above, by substitution at the nitrogen atom of the amino group with a benzyl substituent, whether or not substituted in the phenyl ring of the benzyl group to any extent.

**2.** Any stereoisomeric form of a substance for the time being specified in paragraph 1 above not being dextromethorphan or dextrophan.

**3.** Any ester or ether of a substance for the time being specified in paragraph 1 or 2 above, not being a substance for the time being specified in Part II of this Schedule.

**4.** Any salt of a substance for the time being specified in any of paragraphs 1 to 3 above.

**5.** Any preparation[3] or other product containing a substance or product for the time being specified in any of paragraphs 1 to 4 above.

**6.** Any preparation designed for administration by injections which includes a substance or product for the time being specified in any of paragraphs 1 to 3 of Part II of this Schedule.

[1] Schedule 2 classifies drugs for penalties for misuse and not for regimes of control; for the latter classification see the Schedules to the Misuse of Drugs Regulations 1985, post. The offence of lawful possession of any controlled drug described in Sch 2 by its scientific name is not established by proof of possession of naturally occurring material of which the described drug is one of the constituents unseparated from the others. This is so whether or not the naturally occurring material is also included as another item in the list of controlled drugs (*DPP v Goodchild*) [1978] 2 All ER 161, [1978] 1 WLR 578, 142 JP 338, HL).

[2] "Cocaine" can be a natural substance or a substance resulting from a chemical transformation and the word "cocaine" in para 1 of Part I of the Schedule is a generic word which includes both direct extracts from the coca leaf and whatever results from a chemical transformation (*R v Greensmith* [1983] 3 All ER 444, [1983] 1 WLR 1124, and see *A-G for the Cayman Islands v Roberts* [2002] UKPC 18, [2002] 2 Cr App Rep 388).

[3] "Preparation" has its ordinary and natural meaning and is not intended to have a technical meaning; *R v Stevens* [1981] Crim LR 568 (mushrooms altered by the hand of man to become a powder containing psilocybin). In *R v Cunliffe* [1986] Crim LR 547, CA, it was held that the defendant who had picked and allowed to dry a quantity of psilocybin mushrooms (Mexican magic mushrooms) was in possession of a *preparation* containing psilocybin an ester of psilocin. Similarly, in *Hodder v DPP* [1990] Crim LR 261, psilocybin mushrooms which were picked, separated into packages and then frozen, were held to be a *preparation* containing psilocybin. However, it was observed (obiter) in *Jama v Senior Public Prosecutor, Gera, Germany* [2013] EWHC 3276 (Admin), [2014] 1 WLR 1843 that:

"38 The decision in *Hodder v Director of Public Prosecutions* does not sit comfortably with the observations of Lord Diplock in *R v Goodchild (No 2)* [1978] 1 WLR 578: see para 19 above. In any event, however, it does not seem to us that the that plants described in the warrant could properly be regarded as a "preparation or other product" containing cathinone, within paragraph 4 of Schedule II to the 1971 Act, so as to bring the importation, exportation and supply of the plants themselves within the scope of the offences in sections 3(1) and 4(1) of the Act. The warrant does not suggest that anything had been done to the that beyond picking it and bundling it up in parcels. To our minds it remained the natural plant, not a product within the meaning of the statute (per Richards LJ)."

## Part II
## Class B Drugs

1. The following substances and products, namely—

(*a*)

Acetyldihydrocodeine.
Amphetamine.
Cannabinol.
Cannabinol derivatives
Cannabis and cannabis resin
Codeine.
Dihydrocodeine.
Ethylmorphine (3-ethylmorphine).
Glutethimide
Ketamine.
Lefetamine
Lisdexamphetamine.
Mecloqualone.
Methaqualone.
Methcathinone
*a*-Methylphenethylhydroxylamine;
Methylphenidate.
Methylphenobarbitone.
Nicodine.
Nicodicodine (6-nicotinoyldihydrocodeine)
Norcodeine.
Pentazocine
Phenmetrazine.
Pholcodine
Propiram
Zipeprol
2-((Dimethylamino)methyl)-1-(3-hydroxyphenyl)cyclohexanol.

(*aa*) Any compound (not being bupropion, cathinone, diethylpropion, pyrovalerone or a compound for the time being specified in sub-paragraph (*a*) above) structurally derived from 2-amino-1-phenyl-1-propanone by modification in any of the following ways, that is to say,

(i) by substitution in the phenyl ring to any extent with alkyl, alkoxy, alkylenedioxy, haloalkyl or halide substituents, whether or not further substituted in the phenyl ring by one or more other univalent substituents;

(ii) by substitution at the 3-position with an alkyl substituent;

(iii) by substitution at the nitrogen atom with alkyl or dialkyl groups, or by inclusion of the nitrogen atom in a cyclic structure.

(*ab*) Any compound structurally derived from 2-aminopropan-1-one by substitution at the 1-position with any monocyclic, or fused-polycyclic ring system (not being a phenyl ring or alkylenedioxyphenyl ring system), whether or not the compound is further modified in any of the following ways, that is to say,

(i) by substitution in the ring system to any extent with alkyl, alkoxy, haloalkyl or halide substituents, whether or not further substituted in the ring system by one or more other univalent substituents;

(ii) by substitution at the 3-position with an alkyl substituent;

(iii) by substitution at the 2-amino nitrogen atom with alkyl or dialkyl groups, or by inclusion of the 2-amino nitrogen atom in a cyclic structure.

(*ac*) Any compound (not being pipradrol) structurally derived from piperidine, pyrrolidine, azepane, morpholine or pyridine by substitution at a ring carbon atom with a diphenylmethyl group, whether or not the compound is further modified in any of the following ways, that is to say,

(i) by substitution in any of the phenyl rings to any extent with alkyl, alkoxy, haloalkyl or halide groups;

(ii) by substitution at the methyl carbon atom with an alkyl, hydroxyalkyl or hydroxy group;

(iii) by substitution at the ring nitrogen atom with an alkyl, alkenyl, haloalkyl or hydroxyalkyl group.";

(*b*)

any 5, 5 distributed barbituric acid.

(*c*)

[2,3-Dihydro-5-methyl-3-(4-morpholinylmethyl)pyrrolo[1, 2, 3-de]-1,4-benzoxazin-6-yl]-1-naphthalenylmethanone.
3-Dimethylheptyl-11-hydroxyhexahydrocannabinol.
[9-Hydroxy-6-methyl-3-[5-phenylpentan-2-yl] oxy-5, 6, 6a, 7, 8, 9, 10, 10a-octahydrophenanthridin-1-yl] acetate.
9-(Hydroxymethyl)-6, 6-dimethyl-3-(2-methyloctan-2-yl)-6a, 7, 10, 10a-tetrahydrobenzo[c]-chromen-1-ol.
Nabilone.
Any compound structurally derived from 3-(1-naphthoyl)indole, 3-(2-naphthoyl) indole, 1H-indol-3-yl-(1-naphthyl)methane or 1H-indol-3-yl-(2-naphthyl)methane by substitution at the nitrogen atom of the indole ring by alkyl, haloalkyl, alkenyl, cyanoalkyl, hydroxyalkyl,

cycloalkylmethyl, cycloalkylethyl, (N-methylpiperidin-2-yl)methyl or 2-(4-morpholinyl)ethyl, whether or not further substituted in the indole ring to any extent and whether or not substituted in the naphthyl ring to any extent.

Any compound structurally derived from 3-(1-naphthoyl)pyrrole or 3-(2-naphthoyl)pyrrole by substitution at the nitrogen atom of the pyrrole ring by alkyl, haloalkyl, alkenyl, cyanoalkyl, hydroxyalkyl, cycloalkylmethyl, cycloalkylethyl, (N-methylpiperidin-2-yl)methyl or 2-(4-morpholinyl)ethyl, whether or not further substituted in the pyrrole ring to any extent and whether or not substituted in the naphthyl ring to any extent.

Any compound structurally derived from 1-(1-naphthylmethylene)indene or 1-(2-naphthylmethylene)indene by substitution at the 3-position of the indene ring by alkyl, haloalkyl, alkenyl, cyanoalkyl, hydroxyalkyl, cycloalkylmethyl, cycloalkylethyl, (N-methylpiperidin-2-yl)methyl or 2-(4-morpholinyl)ethyl, whether or not further substituted in the indene ring to any extent and whether or not substituted in the naphthyl ring to any extent.

Any compound structurally derived from 3-phenylacetylindole by substitution at the nitrogen atom of the indole ring by alkyl, haloalkyl, alkenyl, cyanoalkyl, hydroxyalkyl, cycloalkylmethyl, cycloalkylethyl, (N-methylpiperidin-2-yl)methyl or 2-(4-morpholinyl)ethyl, whether or not further substituted in the indole ring to any extent and whether or not substituted in the phenyl ring to any extent.

Any compound structurally derived from 2-(3-hydroxycyclohexyl)phenol by substitution at the 5-position of the phenolic ring by alkyl, alkenyl, cycloalkylmethyl, cycloalkylethyl or 2-(4-morpholinyl)ethyl, whether or not further substituted in the cyclohexyl ring to any extent.

Any compound structurally derived from 3-benzoylindole by substitution at the nitrogen atom of the indole ring by alkyl, haloalkyl, alkenyl, cyanoalkyl, hydroxyalkyl, cycloalkylmethyl, cycloalkylethyl, (N-methylpiperidin-2-yl)methyl or 2-(4-morpholinyl)ethyl, whether or not further substituted in the indole ring to any extent and whether or not substituted in the phenyl ring to any extent.

Any compound structurally derived from 3-(1-adamantoyl)indole or 3-(2-adamantoyl)indole by substitution at the nitrogen atom of the indole ring by alkyl, haloalkyl, alkenyl, cyanoalkyl, hydroxyalkyl, cycloalkylmethyl, cycloalkylethyl, (N-methylpiperidin-2-yl)methyl or 2-(4-morpholinyl)ethyl, whether or not further substituted in the indole ring to any extent and whether or not substituted in the adamantyl ring to any extent.

Any compound structurally derived from 3-(2,2,3,3-tetramethylcyclopropylcarbonyl)indole by substitution at the nitrogen atom of the indole ring by alkyl, haloalkyl, alkenyl, cyanoalkyl, hydroxyalkyl, cycloalkylmethyl, cycloalkylethyl, (N-methylpiperidin-2-yl)methyl or 2-(4-morpholinyl)ethyl, whether or not further substituted in the indole ring to any extent.

(*ca*) any compound (not being clonitazene, etonitazene, acemetacin, atorvastatin, bazedoxifene, indometacin, losartan, olmesartan, proglumetacin, telmisartan, viminol, zafirlukast or a compound for the time being specified in sub-paragraph (c) above) structurally related to 1-pentyl-3-(1-naphthoyl)indole (JWH-018), in that the four substructures, that is to say the indole ring, the pentyl substituent, the methanone linking group and the naphthyl ring, are linked together in a similar manner, whether or not any of the sub-structures have been modified, and whether or not substituted in any of the linked sub-structures with one or more univalent substituents and, where any of the sub-structures have been modified, the modifications of the sub-structures are limited to any of the following, that is to say—

(i) replacement of the indole ring with indane, indene, indazole, pyrrole, pyrazole, imidazole, benzimidazole, pyrrolo[2,3-b]pyridine, pyrrolo[3,2-c]pyridine or pyrazolo[3,4-b]pyridine;

(ii) replacement of the pentyl substituent with alkyl, alkenyl, benzyl, cycloalkylmethyl, cycloalkylethyl, (N-methylpiperidin-2-yl)methyl, 2-(4- morpholinyl)ethyl or (tetrahydropyran-4-yl)methyl;

(iii) replacement of the methanone linking group with an ethanone, carboxamide, carboxylate, methylene bridge or methine group;

(iv) replacement of the 1-naphthyl ring with 2-naphthyl, phenyl, benzyl, adamantyl, cycloalkyl, cycloalkylmethyl, cycloalkylethyl, bicyclo[2.2.1]heptanyl, 1,2,3,4- tetrahydronaphthyl, quinolinyl, isoquinolinyl, 1-amino-1-oxopropan-2-yl, 1-hydroxy-1-oxopropan-2-yl, piperidinyl, morpholinyl, pyrrolidinyl, tetrahydropyranyl or piperazinyl.

(*d*) 1-Phenylcyclohexylamine or any compound (not being ketamine, tiletamine or a compound for the time being specified in paragraph 1(*a*) of Part 1 of this Schedule) structurally derived from 1-phenylcyclohexylamine or 2-amino-2-phenylcyclohexanone by modification in any of the following ways, that is to say,

(i) by substitution at the nitrogen atom to any extent by alkyl, alkenyl or hydroxyalkyl groups, or replacement of the amino group with a 1-piperidyl, 1-pyrrolidyl or 1-azepyl group, whether or not the nitrogen containing ring is further substituted by one or more alkyl groups;

(ii) by substitution in the phenyl ring to any extent by amino, alkyl, hydroxy, alkoxy or halide substituents, whether or not further substituted in the phenyl ring to any extent;

(iii) by substitution in the cyclohexyl or cyclohexanone ring by one or more alkyl substituents;

(iv) by replacement of the phenyl ring with a thienyl ring;

(*e*) Any compound (not being a compound for the time being specified in paragraph 1(*ba*) of Part 1 of this Schedule) structurally derived from 1-benzofuran, 2,3-dihydro-1-benzofuran, 1H-indole, indoline, 1H-indene, or indane by substitution in the 6-membered ring with a 2-ethylamino substituent whether or not further substituted in the ring system to any extent with alkyl, alkoxy, halide or haloalkyl substituents and whether or not substituted in the ethylamino side-chain with one or more alkyl substituents.

**2.** Any stereoisomeric form of a substance for the time being specified in paragraph 1 of this Part of this Schedule.

**2A.** Any ester or ether of cannabinol or of a cannabinol derivative or of a substance for the time being specified in paragraph 1(*ac*), (*c*), (*ca*) or (*d*) of this Part of this Schedule.

**3.** Any salt of a substance for the time being specified in paragraph 1, 2 or 2A of this Part of this Schedule.

**4.** Any preparation or other product containing a substance or product for the time being specified in any of paragraphs 1 to 3 of this Part of this Schedule, but not being a preparation falling within paragraph 6 of Part I of this Schedule.

## Part III
## Class C Drugs

**1.** The following substances, namely—

(*a*)

Alprazolam
Amineptine
Aminorex
Benzphetamine.
Bromazepam
7-bromo-5-(2-chlorophenyl)-1,3-dihydro-2*H*-1,4-benzodiazepin-2-one.
Brotizolam
Buprenorphine
Camazepam
Cathine
Cathinone
Chlordiazepoxide
Chlorphentermine.
Clobazam
Clonazepam
Clorazepic acid
Clotiazepam
Cloxazolam
Delorazepam
Dextropropoxyphene
Diazepam
Diethylpropion
Estazolam
Ethchlorvynol
Ethinamate
Ethyl loflazepate
Fencamfamin
Fenethylline
Fenproporex
Fludiazepam
Flunitrazepam
Flurazepam
Gamma-butyrolactone
Halazepam
Haloxazolam
4-Hydroxy-n-butyric acid
Ketazolam
Khat
Loprazolam
Lorazepam
Lormetazepam
Mazindol
Medazepam
Mefenorex
Mephentermine.
Meprobamate
Mesocarb
Methyprylone
Midazolam
Nimetazepam
Nitrazepam
Nordazepam
Oxazepam
Oxazolam
Pemoline
Phendimetrazine.
Phentermine
Pinazepam
Prazepam
Pyrovalerone
Temazepam
Tetrazepam
Tramadol
Triazolam
*N*-Ethylamphetamine
Zaleplon
Zolpidem
Zopiclone

(*b*)

5α-Androstane-3,17-diol.
Androst-4-ene-3,17-diol.

1-Androstenediol.
1-Androstenedione.
4-Androstene-3, 17-dione.
5-Androstenedione.
5-Androstene-3, 17-diol.
Atamestane.
Bolandiol.
Bolasterone.
Bolazine.
Boldenone.
Boldione.
Bolenol.
Bolmantalate.
1,4-Butanediol.
Calusterone.
4-Chloromethandienone.
Clostebol.
Danazol.
Desoxymethyltestosterone.
Dienedione (estra-4, 9-diene-3,17-dione).
Drostanolone.
Enestebol.
Epitiostanol.
Ethyloestrenol.
Fluoxymesterone.
Formebolone.
Furazabol.
Gestrinone.
3-Hydroxy-5α-androstan-17-one.
Mebolazine.
Mepitiostane.
Mesabolone.
Mestanolone.
Mesterolone.
Methandienone.
Methandriol.
Methenolone.
Methyltestosterone.
Metribolone.
Mibolerone.
Nandrolone.
19-Norandrostenedione.
19-Nor-4-Androstene-3, 17-dione
19-Nor-5-Androstene-3, 17-diol
19-Norandrosterone.
Norboletone.
Norclostebol.
Norethandrolone.
19-Noretiocholanolone.
Oripavine.
Ovandrotone.
Oxabolone.
Oxandrolone.
Oxymesterone.
Oxymetholone.
Pipradrol.
Prasterone.
Propetandrol.
Prostanozol.
Quinbolone.
Roxibolone.
Silandrone.
Stanolone.
Stanozolol.
Stenbolone.
Testosterone.
Tetrahydrogestrinone.
Thiomesterone.
Trenbolone.

(*c*) any compound (not being Trilostane or a compound for the time being specified in sub-paragraph (*b*) above) structurally derived from 17-hydroxyandrostan-3-one or from 17-hydroxyestran-3-one by modification in any of the following ways, that is to say,

(i) by further substitution at position 17 by a methyl or ethyl group;

(ii) by substitution to any extent at one or more of positions 1, 2, 4, 6, 7, 9, 11 or 16, but at no other position;

(iii) by unsaturation in the carbocyclic ring system to any extent, provided that there are no more than two ethylenic bonds in any one carbocyclic ring;

(iv) by fusion of ring A with a heterocyclic system

(*ca*) 1-benzylpiperazine or any compound structurally derived from 1-benzylpiperazine or 1-phenylpiperazine by modification in any of the following ways—

(i) by substitution at the second nitrogen atom of the piperazine ring with alkyl, benzyl, haloalkyl or phenyl groups;

(ii) by substitution in the aromatic ring to any extent with alkyl, alkoxy, alkylenedioxy, halide or haloalkyl groups.

(*d*) any substances which is an ester or ether (or, where more than one hydroxyl function is available, both an ester and an ether) of a substance specified in sub-paragraph (*b*) or described in sub-paragraph (*c*) above;

(*e*) Chorionic Gonadotrophin (HCG).
Clenbuterol.
Non-human chorionic gonadotrophin
Somatotropin
Somatrem.
Somatropin.
Zeranol.
Zilpaterol.

**2.** Any stereoisomeric form of a substance for the time being specified in paragraph 1 of this Part of this Schedule not being phenylpropanolamine.

**3.** Any salt of a substance for the time being specified in paragraph 1 or 2 of this Part of this Schedule.

**4.** Any preparation or other product containing a substance for the time being specified in any of paragraphs 1 to 3 of this Part of this Schedule.

## Part IV

### Meaning of certain Expressions used in this Schedule

For the purposes of this Schedule the following expressions (which are not among those defined in section 37(1) of this Act) have the meanings hereby assigned to them respectively, that is to say—

"cannabinol derivatives" means the following substances, except where contained in cannabis or cannabis resin, namely tetrahydro derivatives of cannabinol and 3-alkyl homologues of cannabinol or of its tetrahydro derivatives;

"coca leaf" means the leaf of any plant of the genus *Erythroxylon* from whose leaves cocaine can be extracted either directly or by chemical transformation;

"concentrate of poppy-straw" means the material produced when poppy-straw has entered into a process for the concentration of its alkaloids;

"khat" means the leaves, stems or shoots of the plant of the species *Catha edulis*;

"medicinal opium" means raw opium which has undergone the process necessary to adapt it for medicinal use in accordance with the requirements of the British Pharmacopoeia, whether it is in the form of powder or is granulated or is in any other form, and whether it is or is not mixed with natural substances;

"opium poppy" means the plant of the species *Papaver somniferum* L;

"poppy straw" means all parts, except the seeds, of the opium poppy, after mowing;

"raw opium" includes powdered or granulated opium but does not include medicinal opium.

## SCHEDULE 3

### Tribunals Advisory Bodies and Professional Panels

## SCHEDULE 4

**7.8137**

*(Amended by the Criminal Law Act 1977, ss 27 and 28 and Schs 5 and 6, the Criminal Justice Act 1982, s 46, the Controlled Drugs (Penalties) Act 1985, s 1, the Drug Trafficking Offences Act 1986, s 34, the Criminal Justice Act 2003, Sch 28 and the Criminal Justice and Public Order Act 1994, Sch 8.)*

**Prosecution and Punishment of Offences**[1]

| Section creating Offence | General Nature of Offence | Mode of Prosecution | Punishment | | | |
|---|---|---|---|---|---|---|
| | | | Class A drug[2] involved | Class B drug[2] involved | Class C drug[2] involved | General |
| Section 4 (2) | Production, or being concerned in the production, of a controlled drug. | (*a*) Summary. | 6 months or the statutory maximum, or both. | 6 months or the statutory maximum, or both. | 3 months or £2,500, or both. | |
| | | (*b*) On indictment. | Life, or a fine, or both. | 14 years or a fine, or both. | 14 years or a fine, or both. | |
| Section 4(3) | Supplying or offering to supply a controlled drug or being concerned in the doing of either activity by another | (*a*) Summary. | 6 months or the statutory maximum, or both. | 6 months or the statutory maximum, or both. | 3 months or £2,500, or both. | |
| | | (*b*) On indictment. | Life or a fine, or both | 14 years or a fine, or both | 14 years or a fine, or both | |
| Section 5(2) | Having possession of a controlled drug. | (*a*) Summary. | 6 months or the statutory maximum, or both. | 3 months or £2,500, or both. | 3 months or £1,000 or both. | |
| | | (*b*) On indictment. | 7 years or a fine, or both. | 5 years or a fine, or both. | 2 years or a fine, or both. | |
| Section 5(3) | Having possession of a controlled drug with intent to supply it to another. | (*a*) Summary | 6 months or the statutory maximum, or both. | 6 months or the statutory maximum, or both. | 3 months or £2,500, or both. | |
| | | (*b*) On indictment | Life, or a fine, or both. | 14 years or a fine, or both. | 14 years or a fine, or both. | |
| Section 6(2) | Cultivation of a cannabis plant. | (*a*) Summary. | — | — | — | 6 months or the statutory maximum, or both |
| | | (*b*) On indictment. | — | — | — | 14 years or a fine, or both. |

[1] For procedure in respect of the offences which are triable either way, see the Magistrates' Courts Act 1980, ss 17A–21, in Part I, Magistrates' Courts, Procedure, ante.

[2] See Sch 2, ante. The penalties expressed in money rather than levels, were specifically altered by Sch 5 to the Criminal Law Act 1977 to these amounts. The "standard scale" introduced by the Criminal Justice Act 1982 applies by s 46 thereof to summary offences only, and not to offences triable either way, like these; nor, by virtue of s 32 of the Magistrates' Courts Act 1980 does the "prescribed sum" apply.

| Section creating Offence | General Nature of Offence | Mode of Prosecution | Punishment Class A drug[3] involved | Class B drug[3] involved | Class C drug[3] involved | General |
|---|---|---|---|---|---|---|
| Section 8 | Being the occupier, or concerned in the management, of premises and permitting or suffering certain activities to take place there. | (*a*) Summary. | 6 months or the statutory maximum, or both. | 6 months or the statutory maximum, or both. | 3 months or £2,500, or both. | . |
| | | (*b*) On indictment | 14 years or a fine, or both. | 14 years or a fine, or both. | 14 years or a fine, or both. | |
| Section 9 | Offences relating to opium. | (*a*) Summary. | — | — | — | 6 months or the statutory maximum, or both. |
| | | (*b*) On indictment | — | — | — | 14 years or a fine, or both. |
| Section 9A | Prohibition of supply etc of articles for administering or preparing controlled drugs. | Summary. | — | — | — | 6 months or level 5 on the standard scale, or both |
| Section 11(2) | Contravention of directions relating to safe custody of controlled drugs. | (*a*) Summary. | — | — | — | 6 months or the statutory maximum, or both. |
| | | (*b*) On indictment. | — | — | — | 2 years or a fine, or both. |
| Section 12(6) | Contravention of direction prohibiting practitioner etc. from possessing, supplying etc. controlled drugs. | (*a*) Summary | 6 months or the statutory maximum, or both. | 6 months or the statutory maximum, or both. | 3 months or £2,500, or both. | |
| | | (*b*) On indictment. | 14 years or a fine, or both. | 14 years or a fine, or both. | 14 years or a fine, or both. | |
| Section 13(3) | Contravention of direction prohibiting practitioner etc. from prescribing, supplying etc. controlled drugs. | (*a*) Summary | 6 months or the statutory maximum, or both. | 6 months or the statutory maximum, or both. | 3 months or £2,500, or both | |
| | | (*b*) On indictment. | 14 years or a fine, or both. | 14 years or a fine, or both. | 14 years or a fine, or both. | |
| Section 17(3) | Failure to comply with notice requiring information relating to prescribing, supply etc. of drugs. | Summary | — | — | — | **Level 3** on the standard scale. |

| Section creating Offence | General Nature of Offence | Mode of Prosecution | Punishment Class A drug[3] involved | Class B drug[3] involved | Class C drug[3] involved | General |
|---|---|---|---|---|---|---|
| Section 17(4) | Giving false information in purported compliance, supply etc. of drugs. | (*a*) Summary | — | — | — | 6 months or the statutory maximum, or both. |
| | | (*b*) On indictment. | — | — | — | 2 years or a fine, or both. |
| Section 18(1) | Contravention of regulating (other than regulations relating to addicts). | (*a*) Summary | — | — | — | 6 months or the statutory maximum, or both. |
| | | (*b*) On indictment. | — | — | — | 2 years or a fine, or both. |
| Section 18 (2) | Contravention of terms of licence or other authority (other than licence issued under regulations relating to addicts). | (*a*) Summary | — | — | — | 6 months or the statutory maximum, or both. |
| | | (*b*) On indictment. | — | — | — | 2 years or a fine, or both. |
| Section 18(3) | Giving false information in purported compliance with obligation to give information imposed under or by virtue of regulations. | (*a*) Summary | — | — | — | 6 months or the statutory maximum, or both. |
| | | (*b*) On indictment. | — | — | — | 2 years or a fine, or both. |
| Section 18(4) | Giving false information, or producing document etc., for purposes of obtaining issue or renewal of a licence or other authority. | (*a*) Summary. | — | — | — | 6 months or the statutory maximum, or both. |
| | | (*b*) On indictment. | — | — | — | 2 years or a fine, or both. |
| Section 20 | Assisting in or inducing commission outside United Kingdom of an offence punishable under a corresponding law. | (*a*) Summary. | — | — | — | 6 months or the statutory maximum, or both. |

| Section creating Offence | General Nature of Offence | Mode of Prosecution | Punishment | | | |
|---|---|---|---|---|---|---|
| | | | Class A drug[3] involved | Class B drug[3] involved | Class C drug[3] involved | General |
| | | (*b*) On indictment. | — | — | — | 14 years or a fine, or both. |
| Section 23(4) | Obstructing exercise of powers of search etc. or concealing books, drugs, etc. | (*a*) Summary. | — | — | — | 6 months or the statutory maximum, or both. |
| | | (*b*) On indictment. | — | — | — | 2 years or a fine, or both. |

[3] See Sch 2, ante.

# Poisons Act 1972

(1972 c 66)

7.8138 2. **Regulated substances and reportable substances** (1) This section defines some key terms used in this Act.

(2) "Regulated substance" means a regulated explosives precursor or regulated poison.

(3) Subject to subsection (4), a "regulated explosives precursor"—

(*a*) is a substance listed in Part 1 of Schedule 1A in a concentration higher than the limit set out for that substance in that Part, and

(*b*) includes a mixture or another substance in which a substance listed in that Part is present in a concentration higher than the relevant limit,

but, in each case, only if the substance or mixture is not excluded.

(4) For the purposes of section 3C however, and the meaning of "regulated substance" in or in relation to that section, a "regulated explosives precursor"—

(*c*) is a substance listed in Part 1 of Schedule 1A, and

(*d*) includes a mixture or another substance in which a substance listed in that Part is present, but, in each case, only if the substance or mixture is not excluded."

(5) A "regulated poison"—

(*a*) is a substance listed in Part 2 of Schedule 1A in a concentration higher than the limit (if any) set out for that substance in that Part, and

(*b*) includes a mixture or another substance in which a substance listed in that Part is present in a concentration higher than the relevant limit,

but, in each case, only if the substance or mixture is not excluded.

(6) "Reportable substance" means a reportable explosives precursor or a reportable poison.

(7) A "reportable explosives precursor"—

(*a*) is a substance listed in Part 3 of Schedule 1A, and

(*b*) includes a mixture or another substance in which a substance listed in that Part is present,

but, in each case, only if the substance or mixture is not excluded.

(8) A "reportable poison"—

(*a*) is a substance listed in Part 4 of Schedule 1A in a concentration higher than the limit (if any) set out for that substance in that Part, and

(*b*) includes a mixture or another substance in which a substance listed in that Part is present in a concentration higher than the relevant limit,

but, in each case, only if the substance or mixture is not excluded.

(9) For the purposes of this section, a substance or mixture is "excluded" if—

(*a*) it is medicinal, or

(*b*) it is contained in a specific object.

(10) A substance or mixture is "medicinal" if it is—

(*a*) a medicinal product as defined by regulation 2 of the Human Medicines Regulations 2012 (SI 2012/1916),

(*b*) an investigational medicinal product as defined by regulation 2 of the Medicines for Human Use (Clinical Trials) Regulations 2004 (SI 2004/1031),

(*c*) a substance to which Part 12 of the Human Medicines Regulations 2012 or Part 6 of the Medicines for Human Use (Clinical Trials) Regulations 2004 applies by virtue of an order under section 104 or 105 of the Medicines Act 1968 (whether applying subject to exceptions and modifications or not and, in the case of an order under section 104, whether the substance is referred to in the order as a substance or an article), or

(*d*) a veterinary medicinal product as defined by regulation 2 of the Veterinary Medicines Regulations 2013 (SI 2013/2033).

(11) A "specific object" is—

(*a*) an object that, during production, is given a special shape, surface or design that determines its function to a greater degree than does its chemical composition, or

(*b*) an article that contains explosive substances or an explosive mixture of substances designed to produce heat, light, sound, gas or smoke or a combination of such effects through self-sustained exothermic chemical reactions, including—

(i) pyrotechnic equipment falling within the scope of Council Directive 96/98/EC on marine equipment, and

(ii) percussion caps intended specifically for toys falling within the scope of Council Directive 88/378/EEC concerning the safety of toys.

(12) See also section 9B (which contains power to disapply requirements of this Act in specified circumstances).

[Poisons Act 1972, s 2 as substituted (together with s 2A for original s 2) by the Deregulation Act 2015, Sch 21.]

7.8138A 2A. **Power to amend Schedule 1A** (1) The Secretary of State may by regulations—

(*a*) amend Schedule 1A (whether to add, vary or remove a substance or concentration limit or make any other change), and

(*b*) amend section 2 in consequence of any amendment made under paragraph (*a*).

(2) The power in subsection (1) to add a concentration limit includes power to add a

concentration limit in any Part of Schedule 1A (whether for an explosives precursor or a poison).

(3) In determining the distribution of substances as between the various Parts of Schedule 1A, regard must be had to the desirability of restricting Parts 3 and 4 to substances that meet each of the following criteria—

(*a*) they are in common use, or are likely to come into common use, for purposes other than the treatment of human ailments, and

(*b*) it is reasonably necessary to include them in one of those Parts if members of the general public are to have adequate facilities for obtaining them."

[Poisons Act 1972, s 2A as substituted (together with s 2 for original s 2) by the Deregulation Act 2015, Sch 21.]

7.8139 **3. Activities prohibited without a licence** (1) A member of the general public commits an offence if he or she does anything listed in subsection (2) without having a licence, or a recognised non-GB licence, to do that thing with respect to that substance.

(2) The things are—

(*a*) importing a regulated substance,

(*b*) acquiring a regulated substance,

(*c*) possessing a regulated substance,

(*d*) using a regulated substance.

(3) For the purposes of this section—

(*a*) "acquiring" means taking into your possession, custody or control,

(*b*) "importing" means bringing into Great Britain from a country or territory outside the United Kingdom,

(*c*) "member of the general public" means an individual who is acting (alone or with others) for purposes not connected with his or her trade, business or profession or the performance by him or her of a public function,

(*d*) "possessing" means having in your possession, custody or control, and

(*e*) "using" includes processing, formulating, storing, treating or mixing, including in the production of an article.

(4) A member of the general public does not commit an offence under subsection (1) if the requirements of this section do not apply to his or her case by virtue of regulations made under section 9B.

(5) This section does not apply to the possession or use of a regulated substance at any time before 3 March 2016.

[Poisons Act 1972, s 3 as substituted (together with ss 3A–3C for original s 3) by the Deregulation Act 2015, Sch 21.]

7.8139A **3A. Supply of regulated substances** (1) A person commits an offence if the person supplies a regulated substance to a member of the general public without first verifying that the member of the general public has a licence, or a recognised non-GB licence, to acquire, possess and use that substance.

(2) In order to verify that someone has a licence or recognised non-GB licence, it is sufficient for these purposes to—

(*a*) inspect the person's licence, and

(*b*) inspect the form of identification specified in that licence.

(3) A person commits an offence if the person supplies a regulated substance to a member of the general public without first entering details of the transaction (or causing details of the transaction to be entered) in the licence, or recognised non-GB licence, of the member of the general public.

(4) A person commits an offence if the person supplies a regulated substance to a member of the general public without first ensuring that a warning label is affixed to the packaging in which the substance is supplied.

(5) A "warning label" is a label clearly indicating that it is an offence for members of the general public to acquire, possess or use the substance in question without a licence (or recognised non-GB licence).

(6) A person does not commit an offence under subsection (1), (3) or (4) if the requirements of that subsection do not apply to the person's case by virtue of regulations made under section 9B.

(7) Before 3 March 2016, subsections (1) and (5) have effect as if the references to possession and use of the substance were omitted.

(8) The Secretary of State may by regulations[1] make provision modifying this section so far as it applies to any supplies that involve despatch of the substance to Northern Ireland or export of it from the United Kingdom.

[Poisons Act 1972, s 3A as substituted (together with ss 3, 3B, 3C for original s 3) by the Deregulation Act 2015, Sch 21.]

1 The Control of Poisons and Explosives Precursors Regulations 2015, SI 2015/966 have been made.

7.8139B **3B. Supply of regulated poisons other than by pharmacists** (1) A person commits an offence if the person supplies a regulated poison to a member of the general public other than in the circumstances described in subsection (2).

(2) Those circumstances are—

(*a*) the person is lawfully conducting a retail pharmacy business,

(*b*) the supply is made on premises that are a registered pharmacy, and (*c*) the supply is made by or under the supervision of a pharmacist.

(3) A person commits an offence if the person supplies a regulated poison to a member of the general public without complying with the record-keeping requirements before delivering the poison.

(4) The record-keeping requirements are—

(*a*) the person must make an entry (or cause an entry to be made) in a record to be kept by the person for the purposes of this subsection stating—

(i) the date of the supply,

(ii) the name and address of the member of the general public,

(iii) the name and quantity of the regulated poison supplied, and

(iv) the purposes for which it is stated by the member of the general public to be required, and

(*b*) the person must ensure that the member of the general public signs the entry.

(5) A person does not commit an offence under subsection (1) or (3) if the requirements of that subsection do not apply to the person's case by virtue of regulations made under section 9B.

[Poisons Act 1972, s 3B as substituted (together with ss 3, 3A, 3C for original s 3) by the Deregulation Act 2015, Sch 21.]

**7.8139C 3C. Reporting of suspicious transactions, disappearances and thefts** (1) A supplier must report any relevant transaction that it makes or proposes to make if the supplier has reasonable grounds for believing the transaction to be suspicious.

(2) A "relevant transaction" is a transaction involving the supply of a regulated substance or a reportable substance to a customer, whether an end user or a customer higher up the supply chain and whether a business or a private customer.

(3) A relevant transaction is "suspicious" if there are reasonable grounds for suspecting that the substance in question—

(*a*) if it is a regulated explosives precursor or reportable explosives precursor, is intended for the illicit manufacture of explosives, or

(*b*) if it is a regulated poison or a reportable poison, is intended for any illicit use.

(3) A person commits an offence if the person supplies a regulated poison to a member of the general public without complying with the record-keeping requirements before delivering the poison.

(4) In deciding whether there are reasonable grounds for suspecting such a thing, regard must be had to all the circumstances of the case, including in particular where the prospective customer—

(*a*) appears unclear about the intended use of the substance,

(*b*) appears unfamiliar with the intended use of the substance or cannot explain it plausibly,

(*c*) intends to buy substances in quantities, combinations or concentrations uncommon for private use,

(*d*) is unwilling to provide proof of identity or place of residence, or

(*e*) insists on using unusual methods of payment, including large amounts of cash.

(5) A person carrying on a trade, business or profession that involves regulated substances or reportable substances must report the disappearance or theft of any such substances if the disappearance or theft—

(*a*) is from stocks in the person's possession, custody or control in Great Britain, and

(*b*) is significant.

(6) In deciding whether a disappearance or theft is significant, regard must be had to whether the amount involved is unusual in all the circumstances of the case.

(7) A duty under this section to "report" something is a duty to give notice of it to the Secretary of State in accordance with such requirements as may be specified by the Secretary of State by regulations made under this subsection.

(8) A person who fails to comply with subsection (1) or (5) commits an offence.

(9) A person does not commit an offence under subsection (8) if the requirements of subsection (1) or, as the case may be, (5) do not apply to the person's case by virtue of regulations made under section 9B.

[Poisons Act 1972, s 3C as substituted (together with ss 3, 3A, 3B for original s 3) by the Deregulation Act 2015, Sch 21.]

**7.8140 4A. Licences** (1) The Secretary of State may grant a licence to a person on application by that person in accordance with this section.

(2) The licence may permit the person to do one or more of the things listed in section 3(2) with respect to one or more of the regulated substances.

(3) The term for which a licence is granted must not exceed 3 years, but this does not affect—

(*a*) a person's right to apply for a further licence to take effect on expiry of that term, nor

(*b*) any power of the Secretary of State under the terms and conditions of the licence to vary, suspend or revoke the licence before expiry of that term.

(4) The Secretary of State may charge applicants a fee for processing applications for the grant or amendment of a licence or for the replacement of any lost, damaged or stolen licence.

(5) The amount of any fees to be charged under subsection (4) must be specified in regulations made under subsection (10), and the amount specified must not exceed the reasonable cost of

processing such applications.

(6) In deciding whether to grant or amend a licence with respect to a substance, the Secretary of State must have regard to all the circumstances of the case, including in particular—

(*a*) the use intended to be made of the substance,

(*b*) the availability of alternative substances that would achieve the same purpose,

(*c*) the proposed arrangements to ensure that the substance is kept securely,

(*d*) any danger to public safety or public order that may be caused by possession of the substance, and

(*e*) whether the applicant is a fit and proper person to possess the substance.

(7) But if there are reasonable grounds for doubting the legitimacy of the use intended to be made of the substance or the intentions of the user to use the substance for a legitimate purpose, the Secretary of State must in any event refuse the application so far as it relates to that substance.

(8) A licence may be granted or amended subject to such terms and conditions as may be specified in the licence.

(9) Examples of terms and conditions that may be specified include, for any substances with respect to which the licence is granted, terms and conditions about—

(*a*) storage,

(*b*) use,

(*c*) maximum quantities,

(*d*) maximum levels of concentration, and

(*e*) reporting of disappearances or thefts.

(10) he Secretary of State may by regulations[1] make provision about the procedure for applying for and determining applications for the grant or amendment of licences under this section, including provision as to—

(*a*) who may make an application,,

(*b*) the form and manner in which an application is to be made and any documents or evidence that must accompany it,,

(*c*) the amount and payment of any fees,

(*d*) the supply of any further information or document required to determine an application,

(*e*) notice and publication of any decision about an application, and

(*f*) the procedure for an internal review of any such decision.

[Poisons Act 1972, s 4A as inserted by the Deregulation Act 2015, Sch 21.]

---

1 The Control of Poisons and Explosives Precursors Regulations 2015, SI 2015/966 have been made.

**7.8140A 4B. Recognised non-GB licences** (1) The Secretary of State must publish a list from time to time of recognised member States (if there are any).

(2) A member State is "recognised" for these purposes if licences granted by the competent authority of that State in accordance with the Precursors Regulation are recognised in the United Kingdom under Article 7(6) of that Regulation.

(3) References in this Act to a "recognised non-GB licence" are to—

(*a*) a licence granted in accordance with the Precursors Regulation by the competent authority of a member State that is included in the list (or latest list) published under subsection (1), or

(*b*) a licence granted under relevant Northern Ireland legislation.

(4) "Relevant Northern Ireland legislation" means—

(*a*) regulations made under the Explosives Act (Northern Ireland) 1970 (c 10 (N.I.)) by virtue of the Explosives (Northern Ireland) Order 1972 (SI 1972/730 (N.I. 3)),

(*b*) any legislative instrument that implements the Precursors Regulation in Northern Ireland, and

(*c*) any legislative instrument that replaces or supersedes (with or without modification) anything falling within paragraph (*a*) or (*b*) or this paragraph.

(5) In this section—

(*a*) references to the Precursors Regulation are to Regulation (EU) No 98/2013 of the European Parliament and of the Council of 15 January 2013 on the marketing and use of explosives precursors, and

(*b*) references to a legislative instrument are to—

(i) an Act or instrument made under an Act, or

(ii) any Northern Ireland legislation or instrument made under Northern Ireland legislation.

[Poisons Act 1972, s 4B as inserted by the Deregulation Act 2015, Sch 21.]

**7.8141 7. Regulations about poisons and explosives precursors** *The Secretary of State may make provision by regulations[1] about the importation, supply, acquisition, possession or use of substances by or to any person or class of person; storage, transportation and labelling of substances; containers in which substances may be supplied; addition to substances of specified ingredients for the purpose of rendering them readily distinguishable as such; the compounding of substances, and the supply of substances on and in* *accordance with a prescription duly given by a doctor, a dentist, a veterinary surgeon or a veterinary practitioner, or; the period for which any records required to be kept for the purposes of this Act are to be preserved.*

[1] The Control of Poisons and Explosives Precursors Regulations 2015, SI 2015/966 have been made.

7.8142 **7A. Proof of lack of knowledge** (1) This section applies to the following offences—

(*a*) an offence under section 3(1),

(*b*) an offence under section 3A(1), (3) or (4),

(*c*) an offence under section 3B(1) or (3).

(2) In any proceedings for an offence to which this section applies, it is a defence for the accused to prove that the accused neither knew of nor suspected nor had reason to suspect the existence of some fact alleged by the prosecution that it is necessary for the prosecution to prove if the accused is to be convicted of the offence charged.

(3) This is subject to subsection (5).

(4) Subsection (5) applies where, in any proceedings for an offence to which this section applies—

(*a*) it is necessary, if the accused is to be convicted of the offence charged, for the prosecution to prove that some substance or mixture involved in the alleged offence was the regulated substance that the prosecution allege it to have been, and

(*b*) it is proved that the substance or mixture in question was that regulated substance.

(5) Where this subsection applies—

(*a*) the accused must not be acquitted of the offence charged by reason only of proving that the accused neither knew nor suspected nor had reason to suspect that the substance or mixture was the particular regulated substance alleged, but

(*b*) the accused must be acquitted of the offence charged if—

(i) the accused proves that the accused neither believed nor suspected nor had reason to suspect that the substance or mixture was a regulated substance, or

(ii) the accused proves that the accused believed the substance or mixture to be a regulated substance such that, if it had in fact been that regulated substance, the accused would not at the material time have been committing any offence to which this section applies..

(6) Nothing in this section affects any defence that it is open to a person accused of an offence to which this section applies to raise apart from this section.

[Poisons Act 1972, s 7A as inserted by the Deregulation Act 2015, Sch 21.]

7.8143 **8. Penalties** (1) A person guilty of an offence under section 3(1), 3A(1) or 3B(1) is liable—

(*a*) on conviction on indictment, to imprisonment for a term not exceeding 2 years or a fine (or both);

(*b*) on summary conviction—

(i) in England and Wales, to imprisonment for a term not exceeding 3 months or to a fine (or both),

(ii) in Scotland, to imprisonment for a term not exceeding 3 months or to a fine not exceeding the statutory maximum (or both).

(2) A person guilty of an offence under section 3A(3) or (4) is liable on summary conviction to a fine not exceeding level 2 on the standard scale.

(3) A person guilty of an offence under section 3B(3) is liable on summary conviction to a fine not exceeding level 4 on the standard scale.

(4) A person guilty of an offence under section 3C(8) is liable on summary conviction—

(*a*) in England and Wales, to imprisonment for a term not exceeding 3 months or to a fine (or both);

(*b*) in Scotland, to imprisonment for a term not exceeding 3 months or to a fine not exceeding level 5 on the standard scale (or both).

(5) A person guilty of an offence under section 7(4) is liable on summary conviction—

(*a*) to a fine not exceeding level 4 on the standard scale, and

(*b*) in the case of a continuing offence, to a further fine not exceeding one-tenth of level 4 on the standard scale for every day subsequent to the day on which the person is convicted of the offence during which the contravention or default continues.

(6) In the case of proceedings against a person for an offence under section 3A, 3B or 3C, or an offence under section 7(4) in connection with the supply of a regulated substance or a reportable substance, where the act in question was done by an employee—

(*a*) it is not a defence that the employee acted without the authority of the employer, and

(*b*) any material fact known to the employee is deemed to have been known to the employer.

(7) Notwithstanding any provision in any Act, or Act of the Scottish Parliament, prescribing the period within which summary proceedings may be commenced, proceedings for an offence under section 3A(3) or (4), 3B(3), 3C(8) or 7(4) may be commenced at any time—

(*a*) within the period of 12 months next after the date of commission of the offence, or (*b*) in the case of proceedings instituted by, or by the direction of, the Secretary of State, within the later to end of—

(i) that 12-month period, and

(ii) the period of 3 months next after the date on which evidence sufficient in the Secretary of State's opinion to justify a prosecution for the offence comes to the Secretary of State's knowledge.

(8) For the purposes of subsection (7)(*b*)(ii), a certificate purporting to be signed by the Secretary of State as to the date on which such evidence came to the Secretary of State's knowledge is to be conclusive evidence of that fact.

(9) A document purporting to be a certificate signed by a person specified in subsection (10) stating the result of an analysis made by that person is admissible in any proceedings under this Act as evidence of the matters stated in the certificate, but either party may require the person to be called as a witness.

(10) The persons are—

(*a*) a public analyst appointed under section 27 of the Food Safety Act 1990, or

(*b*) a person appointed by the Secretary of State to make analyses for the purposes of this Act.

(11) In the application of this section to Scotland, subsections (7) and (8) have effect as if the references to the Secretary of State were references to the Lord Advocate.

(12) In relation to an offence committed before section 85(1) of the Legal Aid, Sentencing and Punishment of Offenders Act 2012 comes into force—

(*a*) the reference in subsection (1)(b)(i) to a fine is to be read as a reference to a fine not exceeding the statutory maximum;

(*b*) the reference in subsection (4)(a) to a fine is to be read as a reference to a fine not exceeding level 5 on the standard scale.

[Poisons Act 1972, s 8 as substituted (together with s 8A for original s 8) by the Deregulation Act 2015, Sch 21]

7.8144 **8A. Offences by bodies corporate etc** (1) If an offence under this Act is committed by a body corporate and is proved to have been committed with the consent or connivance of, or to be attributable to any neglect on the part of—

(*a*) a director, manager, secretary or other similar officer of the body corporate, or

(*b*) any person who was purporting to act in any such capacity,

(2) The reference in subsection (1) to a director, in relation to a body corporate whose affairs are managed by its members, is a reference to a member of the body corporate.

(3) If an offence under this Act is committed by a Scottish partnership and is proved to have been committed with the consent or connivance of, or to be attributable to any neglect on the part of—

(*a*) a partner, or

(*b*) any person who was purporting to act in that capacity,

that person, as well as the partnership, is guilty of the offence and liable to be proceeded against and punished accordingly.

[Poisons Act 1972, s 8A as substituted (together with s 8 for original s 8) by the Deregulation Act 2015, Sch 21]

7.8145 **9. Inspection and enforcement** (1) *Repealed.*

(2) *Repealed.*

(3) *Repealed.*

(4) An inspector appointed by the General Pharmaceutical Council under article 8(1) of the Pharmacy Order 2010 may at all reasonable times—

(*a*) enter any registered pharmacy to ascertain whether an offence under section 3A, 3B, 3C or 7(4) has been committed by a pharmacist or a person carrying on a retail pharmacy business;

(*b*) enter any suspicious premises to ascertain whether either of the following offences has been committed—

(i) an offence under section 3B, or

(ii) an offence under section 7(4) in relation to contravention of any regulations that relate solely to regulated poisons.

(4A) "Suspicious premises" are premises in which the inspector has reasonable cause to suspect that an offence mentioned in subsection (4)(*b*) has been committed.

(4B) An inspector appointed by the General Pharmaceutical Council under article 8(1) of the Pharmacy Order 2010 may also make such examination and inquiry and do such other things (including the taking, on payment, of samples) as may be necessary for ascertaining any of the things mentioned in subsection (4)(*a*) and (*b*).

(5) *Repealed.*

(5A) *Repealed.*

(6) *Repealed.*

(7) *Repealed*

(8) If a person—

(*a*) wilfully delays or obstructs an inspector in the exercise of any powers under this section, or (*b*) refuses to allow any sample to be taken in accordance with the provisions of this section, or

(*c*) fails without reasonable excuse to give any information which he is duly required under this section to give,

he shall in respect of each offence be liable on summary conviction to a fine not exceeding **level 2** on the standard scale.

(9) Nothing in this section shall authorise any inspector to enter or inspect the premises, not being a shop, of a doctor, a dentist, a veterinary surgeon or a veterinary practitioner.

[Poisons Act 1972, s 9 as amended by the Criminal Law Act 1977, Sch 6, the Criminal Justice Act 1982, s 46, SI 2007/289, the Legal Services Act 2007, Sch 21, SI 2010/231 and the Deregulation Act 2015, Sch 21.]

**7.8145A 9A. Application of PACE powers** As regards England and Wales, sections 8, 17 and 18 of the Police and Criminal Evidence Act 1984 (powers of entry and search) apply in relation to an offence under section 3A(3) or (4), 3B(3), 3C(8) or 7(4) of this Act as in relation to an indictable offence.

[Poisons Act 1972, s 9A as inserted by the Deregulation Act 2015, Sch 21.]

**7.8145B 9B. Power to disapply requirements or exclusions in specified circumstances**

*The Secretary of State may by regulations[1] provide that some or all of the requirements or either or both of the exclusions of this Act do not apply in circumstances specified in the regulations.*

1 The Control of Poisons and Explosives Precursors Regulations 2015, SI 2015/966 have been made.

**7.8146 11. Interpretation** (1) *Repealed.*

(2) In this Act, unless the context otherwise requires, the following expressions have the following meanings, that is to say—

"dentist" means a person registered in the dentists register kept under the Dentists Act 1984;

"doctor" means a registered medical practitioner within the meaning of Schedule 1 to the Interpretation Act 1978;

"Great Britain" includes the territorial sea of the United Kingdom other than the part adjacent to Northern Ireland;

"licence" (other than in the expression "recognised non-GB licence" and in section 4B) means a licence granted under section 4A;

"local authority" means—

(*a*) in relation to England, the council of a county metropolitan district or London borough or the Common Council of the City of London,

(*aa*) in relation to Wales, the council of a county or county borough, and

(*b*) *Scotland*;

"member of the general public" has the meaning given in section 3;

"mixture" means a mixture or solution composed of two or more substances;

"person lawfully conducting a retail pharmacy business" shall be construed in accordance with section 69 of the Medicines Act 1968;

"pharmacist" means a person registered in Part 1 of the register maintained under article 19 of the Pharmacy Order 2010 (pharmacists other than visiting practitioners);

"recognised non-GB licence" has the meaning given in section 4B;

"regulated substance", "regulated explosives precursor" and "regulated poison" have the meanings given in section 2;

"reportable substance", "reportable explosives precursor" and "reportable poison" have the meanings given in section 2;

"registered pharmacy" has the meaning assigned to it by section 74 of the Medicines Act 1968;

"retail pharmacy business" has the meaning assigned to it by section 8 of the Human Medicines Regulations 2012 (SI 2012/1916);

"substance" means a chemical element and its compounds in the natural state or obtained by any manufacturing process—

(*a*) including any additive necessary to preserve its stability and any impurity deriving from the process used, but

(*b*) excluding any solvent that may be separated without affecting the stability of the substance or changing its composition;

"veterinary practitioner" means a person registered in the supplementary veterinary register kept under section 8 of the Veterinary Surgeons Act 1966;

"veterinary surgeon" means a person registered in the register of veterinary surgeons kept under section 2 of the Veterinary Surgeons Act 1966.

(3) In relation to a regulated substance or a reportable substance, any reference to the substance is a reference to the substance or the mixture, as the case may be.

(4) References in this Act to supplying something include any kind of supply or making available, whether in return for payment or free of charge.

[Poisons Act 1972, s 11 as amended by the Local Government Act 1972, Sch 29, the Medical Act 1983, Sch 5, the Dentists Act 1984, Sch 5, the Local Government Act 1985, Sch 8, the Local Government (Wales) Act 1994, Sch 16, SI 1996/1496, SI 2006/2407, SI 2007/289, SI 2007/3101, SI 2010/1621 and the Deregulation Act 2015, Sch 21.]

## 7.8147 13. Commencement and transitional provisions

SCHEDULE 1A

Regulated Substances and Reportable Substances

(*As inserted by the Deregulation Act 2015, Sch 21*)

### PART 1

REGULATED EXPLOSIVES PRECURSORS

**7.8147A**

| Name of substance and Chemical Abstracts Service Registry number (CAS RN) | Concentration limit (weight in weight) |
|---|---|
| Hydrogen peroxide (CAS RN 7722-84-1) | 12% w/w |
| Nitromethane (CAS RN 75-52-5) | 30% w/w |
| Nitric acid (CAS RN 7697-37-2) | 3% w/w |
| Potassium chlorate (CAS RN 3811-04-9) | 40% w/w |
| Potassium perchlorate (CAS RN 7778-74-7) | 40% w/w |
| Sodium chlorate (CAS RN 7775-09-9) | 40% w/w |
| Sodium perchlorate (CAS RN 7601-89-0) | 40% w/w |

### PART 2

REGULATED POISONS

| Name of substance and Chemical Abstracts Service Registry number (CAS RN) | Concentration limit (weight in weight) |
|---|---|
| Aluminium phosphide (CAS RN 20859-73-8) | — |
| Arsenic (CAS RN 7440-38-2); its compounds, other than those listed in Part 4 of this Schedule | — |
| Barium (CAS RN 7440-39-3), salts of, other than barium sulphate (CAS RN 7727-43-7) and the salts of barium listed in Part 4 of this Schedule) | — |
| Bromomethane (CAS RN 74-83-9) | — |
| Chloropicrin (CAS RN 76-06-2) | — |
| Fluoroacetic acid (CAS RN 144-49-0); its salts; fluoroacetamide | — |
| Hydrogen cyanide (CAS RN 74-90-8); metal cyanides, other than ferrocyanides and ferricyanides | — |
| Lead acetates (CAS RN 15347-57-6); compounds of lead with acids from fixed oils | — |
| Magnesium phosphide (CAS RN 12057-74-8) | — |
| Mercury (CAS RN 7439-97-6), compounds of, the following—nitrates of mercury; oxides of mercury; mercuric cyanide oxides; mercuric thio cyanate; ammonium mercuric chlorides; potassium mercuric iodides; organic compounds of mercury that contain a methyl ($CH_3$) group directly linked to the mercury atom | — |
| Oxalic acid (CAS RN 144-62-7) | 10% w/w |
| Phenols (phenol; phenolic isomers of the following—cresols, xylenols, monoethylphenols); compounds of phenols with a metal | 60% w/w of phenols or, for compounds of phenols with a metal, the equivalent of 60% w/w of phenols |
| Phosphorus, yellow (CAS RN 7223-14-0) | — |
| Strychnine (CAS RN 57-24-9); its salts; its quaternary compounds | — |
| Thallium (CAS RN 7440-28-0), salts of | — |

### PART 3

REPORTABLE EXPLOSIVES PRECURSORS

Hexamine (CAS RN 100-97-0)
Sulphuric acid (CAS RN 7664-93-9)
Acetone (CAS RN 67-64-1)
Potassium nitrate (CAS RN 7757-79-1)
Sodium nitrate (CAS RN 7631-99-4)
Calcium nitrate (CAS RN 10124-37-5)
Calcium ammonium nitrate (CAS RN 15245-12-2)
Ammonium nitrate (CAS RN 6484-52-2) in concentration of 16% by weight of nitrogen in relation to ammonium nitrate or higher

## PART 4
### Reportable poisons

| Name of substance and Chemical Abstracts Service Registry number (CAS RN) | Concentration limit (weight in weight or, where specified, total caustic alkalinity) |
|---|---|
| Aldicarb (CAS RN 116-06-3) | — |
| Alpha-chloralose (CAS RN 15879-93-3) | — |
| Ammonia (CAS RN 7664-41-7 and CAS RN 1336-21-6) | 10% w/w |
| Arsenic, compounds of, the following—calcium arsenites; copper acetoarsenite; copper arsenates; copper arsenites; lead arsenates | — |
| Barium, salts of, the following—barium carbonate; barium silicofluoride | — |
| Carbofuran (CAS RN 1563-66-2) | — |
| Cycloheximide (CAS RN 66-81-9) | — |
| Dinitrocresols (DNOC) (CAS RN 534-52-1); their compounds with a metal or a base | — |
| Dinoseb (CAS RN 88-85-7); its compounds with a metal or a base | — |
| Dinoterb (CAS RN 1420-07-1) | — |
| Drazoxolon; its salts | — |
| Endosulfan (CAS RN 115-29-7) | — |
| Endothal (CAS RN 145-73-3); its salts | — |
| Endrin (CAS RN 72-20-8) | — |
| Fentin (CAS RN 668-34-8), compounds of | — |
| Formaldehyde (CAS RN 50-00-0) | 5% w/w |
| Formic acid (CAS RN 64-18-6) | 25% w/w |
| Hydrochloric acid (CAS RN 7647-01-0) | 10% w/w |
| Hydrofluoric acid (CAS RN 7664-39-3); alkali metal bifluorides; ammonium bifluoride (CAS RN 1341-49-7); alkali metal fluorides; ammonium fluoride (CAS RN 12125-01-8); sodium silicofluoride (CAS RN 16893-85-9) | — |
| Mercuric chloride (CAS RN 7487-94-7); mercuric iodide; organic compounds of mercury except compounds that contain a methyl ($CH_3$) group directly linked to the mercury atom | — |
| Metallic oxalates | — |
| Methomyl (CAS RN 16752-77-5) | — |
| Nicotine (CAS RN 54-11-5); its salts; its quaternary compounds | — |
| Nitrobenzene (CAS RN 98-95-3) | 0.1% w/w |
| Oxamyl (CAS RN 23135-22-0) | — |
| Paraquat (CAS RN 4685-14-7), salts of | — |
| Phenols (as defined in Part 2 of this Schedule) in substances containing no more than 60%, weight in weight, of phenols; compounds of phenols with a metal in substances containing no more than the equivalent of 60%, weight in weight, of phenols | — |
| Phosphoric acid (CAS RN 7664-38-2) | — |
| Phosphorus compounds, the following—azinphos-methyl, chlorfenvinphos, demephion, demeton-S-methyl, demeton-S-methyl sulphone, dialifos, dichlorvos, dioxathion, disulfoton, fonofos, mecarbam, mephosfolan, methidathion, mevinphos, omethoate, oxydemeton-methyl, parathion, phenkapton, phorate, phosphamidon, pirimiphos-ethyl, quinalphos, thiometon, thionazin, triazophos, vamidothion | — |
| Potassium hydroxide (CAS RN 1310-58-3) | 17% of total caustic alkalinity |
| Sodium hydroxide (CAS RN 1310-73-2) | 12% of total caustic alkalinity |
| Sodium nitrite | — |
| Thiofanox (CAS RN 39196-18-4) | — |
| Zinc phosphide (CAS RN 1314-84-7) | — |

*Note: for circumstances where requirements of this Act do not apply to a specified substance or mixture, see regulations made under section 9B.*

[Poisons Act 1972, Sch 1A inserted by the Deregulation Act 2015, s 16.]

# Medical Act 1983[1]

(1983 c 54)

## Part II[2]

## Medical Education and Registration

*Persons qualifying in the United Kingdom and elsewhere in the European Union*

**7.8148 18. Visiting medical practitioners from relevant European States** Schedule 2A to this Act (visiting medical practitioners from relevant European States) shall have effect.

[Medical Act 1983, s 18 as substituted by SI 2007/3101.]

---

[1] This Act consolidates the Medical Acts 1956 to 1978. The Act provides for the continuance of the General Medical Council (referred to in the Act as "the General Council") and its constitution. The General Council is responsible for the registration of medical practitioners, and the Registrar of the General Council is required to keep two registers of medical practitioners registered under the Act containing the names of those registered and the qualifications they are entitled to have registered. The two registers are "the register of medical practitioners", consisting of four lists, namely *(a)* the principal list, *(b)* the overseas list, *(c)* the visiting overseas doctors list, and *(d)* the visiting EEA practitioners list, and "the register of medical practitioners with limited registration". Medical practitioners shall be registered as fully registered medical practitioners, or provisionally or with limited registration as provided in Parts II and III of the Act and in the appropriate list of the register (s 2). Recognition of primary European qualifications and entitlement to full registration is provided by amendments to the Act by the European Primary Medical Qualifications Regulations 1996, SI 1996/1591 amended by SI 2006/1914 and SI 2007/3101.

[2] Part II contains ss 3–18A.

## Part VI[1]

## Privileges of Registered Practitioners

**7.8149 48. Certificates invalid if not signed by fully registered practitioners who hold licences to practise** A certificate required by any enactment, whether passed before or after the commencement of this Act, from any physician, surgeon, licentiate in medicine and surgery or other medical practitioner[2] shall not be valid unless the person signing it is fully registered and holds a licence to practise.

[Medical Act 1983, s 48 as amended by SI 2002/3135.]

---

[1] Part VI contains ss 46–49.

[2] Reference in any enactment to a "registered medical practitioner" means a fully registered person within the meaning of the Medical Act 1983 (Interpretation Act 1978, Sch 1, in Part II: Evidence, ante).

**7.8150 49. Penalty for pretending to be registered[1]** (1) Any person who wilfully and falsely pretends to be or takes or uses the name or title of physician, doctor of medicine, licentiate in medicine and surgery, bachelor of medicine, surgeon, general practitioner or apothecary, or any name, title, addition or description implying that he is registered[2] under any provision of this Act, or that he is recognised by law as a physician or surgeon or licentiate in medicine and surgery or a practitioner in medicine or an apothecary, shall be liable on summary conviction to a fine not exceeding **level 5** on the standard scale.

(2) *Repealed.*

(3)–(4) *Scotland.*

[Medical Act 1983, s 49 as amended by the Statute Law (Repeals) Act 1993, Sch 1, SI 1996/1591 and SI 2007/3101.]

---

[1] Reference in any enactment to a "registered medical practitioner" means a fully registered person within the meaning of the Medical Act 1983 (Interpretation Act 1978, Sch 1, in Part II: Evidence, ante).

[2] The Registrar is required by s 34 of the Act to cause to be printed, published and sold, under the direction of the General Council, a publication called "the Medical Register", being a register of all persons appearing in the principal list in the register of medical practitioners, as existing on the 1st January in that year except those whose registration is suspended or subject to conditions. The General Council may also direct publication of "the Overseas Medical Register". A copy of either publication purporting to be printed and published in accordance with s 34 shall be evidence that the persons specified therein are registered fully or provisionally in the principal list or the overseas list in the register of medical practitioners, as appears from the publication; and the absence of the name of any person from such a copy shall be evidence that he is not registered under ss 3, 15, 19 or 21 of the Act (s 34).

**7.8151 49A. Penalty for pretending to hold a licence to practise** (1) If a person who does not hold a licence to practise—

*(a)* holds himself out as having such a licence; or

*(b)* engages in conduct calculated to suggest that he has such a licence,

shall be liable on summary conviction to a fine not exceeding **level 5** on the standard scale.

(2)–(3) *Scotland.*

[Medical Act 1983, s 49A as inserted by SI 2002/3135.]

## Part VII[1]

## Miscellaneous and General

**7.8152 54. Saving for certain occupations** Nothing in this Act shall prejudice or in any way affect the lawful occupation, trade, or business of chemists and druggists and dentists, or the rights, privileges or employment of duly licensed apothecaries in Northern Ireland, so far as the occupation, trade or business extends to selling, compounding or dispensing medicines.

[Medical Act 1983, s 54.]

[1] Part VII contains ss 50–57.

7.8153 55. **Interpretation**[1] (1) In this Act—

"fully registered person" means a person for the time being registered under section 3, 14A, 19, 19A, 21B, 27A or 27B above as a fully registered medical practitioner, or under Schedule 2A as a visiting medical practitioner from a relevant European State, and—

(*a*) so far as mentioned in subsection (3) of section 15 (including that subsection as applied by section 15A(4), 21 or 21C above, but not further, includes a person for the time being provisionally registered;

(*b*) *repealed*

and "fully registered" shall be construed accordingly;

"the General Council" means the General Medical Council;

"national", in relation to a relevant European State, has the same meaning as in the Community Treaties, but does not include a person who by virtue of Article 2 of Protocol No 3 (Channel Islands and Isle of Man) to the Treaty of Accession is not to benefit from Community provisions relating to the free movement of persons and services;

"provisionally registered" means provisionally registered under section 15, 15A, 21 or 21C above;

"the register" means the register of medical practitioners;

"the Registrar" has the meaning given by section 2(1) above but subject to sub-paragraph (3) of paragraph 16 of Schedule 1 to this Act;

"relevant European State" means an EEA State or Switzerland;

[Medical Act 1983, s 55(1) as amended by SI 1996/1591, SI 2000/3041, SI 2002/3135, SI 2006/1914, SI 2007/3101—abridged.]

[1] Only those definitions which are likely to be relevant to the work of magistrates' courts are included in this work.

# Dentists Act 1984[1]

(1984 c 24)

## PART III[2]

## THE DENTAL PROFESSION

*Use of titles and descriptions*

7.8154 26. **Use of titles and descriptions** (1) A registered[3] dentist shall by virtue of being registered be entitled to take and use the description of dentist, dental surgeon or dental practitioner.

(2) A registered dentist shall not take or use, or affix to or use in connection with his premises, any title or description reasonably calculated to suggest that he possesses any professional status or qualification other than a professional status or qualification which he in fact possesses and which is indicated by particulars entered in the register in respect of him.

(3) If the Council are of opinion that any branch of dentistry has become so distinctive that it would be for the convenience of the public or of the dental profession that registered dentists qualified to practise, or practising, in that branch of dentistry should use a distinctive title, they may by regulations prescribe appropriate titles and conditions under which they may be used; and the use of a prescribed title under the prescribed conditions shall not constitute a contravention of subsection (2) above.

(4) In the case of any prescribed title regulations under subsection (3) above may provide—

(*a*) for a list to be kept by the Council of the names of registered dentists who are qualified under such regulations to use that title; and

(*b*) for any registered dentist who is so qualified to be entitled to have his name entered in the list;

and where regulations so provide as aforesaid nothing in that subsection shall permit that title to be used by any such dentist unless his name has been entered in the list.

(4A) The Council may make regulations—

(*a*) prescribing a fee to be charged on the entry of a name in a list for the time being kept by them under subsection (4), or on the restoration of any entry to such a list;

(*b*) prescribing a fee to be charged in respect of the retention of the name of a person in such a list.

(4B) Regulations under subsection (4A) may in particular authorise the registrar—

(*a*) to refuse to make in or restore to a list for the time being kept by the Council under subsection (4) any entry until a fee prescribed by the regulations has been paid; and

(*b*) to erase from such a list the name of a person who, after such notices and warnings as may be prescribed by the regulations, fails to pay a fee prescribed by the regulations in respect of the retention of a person's name in that list.

(5) *Repealed.*

(6) Any person who contravenes subsection (2) above shall be liable on summary conviction to a fine not exceeding the **third level** on the standard scale.

(7) The Council shall from time to time publish any list for the time being kept by them under subsection (4).

[Dentists Act 1984, s 26 as amended by SI 2005/2011.]

[1] This Act consolidates the Dentists Acts 1957 to 1983 and was extensively amended by the Dentists Act 1984 (Amendment) Order 2005, SI 2005/2011. The Act provides for the continuance of the General Dental Council (referred to in the Act as "the Council") and its constitution. It shall be the general concern of the Council (*a*) to promote high standards of education at all its stages in all aspects of dentistry; and (*b*) to promote high standards of professional conduct, performance and practice among persons registered under this Act (s 1). The Council is responsible for the registration of dentists, and the Registrar is required to keep the register. Subject to the provisions of the Act, the following persons are entitled to be registered in the dentists register, namely (*a*) any person who is a graduate or licentiate in dentistry of a dental authority; (*b*) any person who is a national of a member State and holds an appropriate European diploma; and (*c*) any person who holds a recognised overseas diploma (s 15).

The European Primary and Specialist Dental Qualification Regulations 1998, SI 1998/811 amended by SI 2003/3148 and SI 2007/3101 implement European obligations relating to the training of dentists and specialist dentists contained in the Council Directive 78/678/EEC. Under the regulations the General Dental Council is specified as the competent authority for the United Kingdom in relation to specified functions under those Directives.

The Professional Conduct Committee of the Council has power to erase the name of a dentist from the register or direct suspension of his registration where it is satisfied that a registered dentist has been convicted in the UK of a criminal offence or has been convicted elsewhere of an offence which, if committed in England and Wales, would constitute a criminal offence, or has been guilty of serious professional misconduct (s 27). Where the fitness of a registered dentist to practise is judged by the Health Committee of the Council to be seriously impaired by reason of his physical or mental condition the Committee may direct that his registration be suspended or that his registration be made conditional on compliance with specified requirements (s 28).

[2] Part III contains ss 14–36.

[3] A certificate purporting to be signed by the registrar, certifying that a person— (*a*) is registered in the register, (*b*) is not registered in the register, (*c*) was registered in the register at a specified date or during a specified period, (*d*) was not registered in the register at a specified date or during a specified period, or (*e*) has never been registered in the register, shall be prima facie evidence in all courts of law of the facts stated in the certificate (s 14(6)).

*Insurance*

**7.8155 26A, 26B.** *Registered dentists to be covered by insurance. General Dentists Council to issue guidance as to the standards of conduct, performance and practice expected of registered dentists.*

*Visiting dentists from relevant European States*

**7.8156 36. Visiting dentists from relevant European States** Schedule 4[1] to this Act (which makes provision for persons established in dental practice in other relevant European States to render dental services during a visit to the United Kingdom) shall have effect.

[Dentists Act 1984, s 36 as amended by SI 1996/1496 and SI 2007/3101.]

[1] Not reproduced in this Manual.

## PART 3A[1]
## PROFESSIONS COMPLEMENTARY TO DENTISTRY

**7.8157 36A. Professions complementary to dentistry** (2) The Council may by regulations specify—

(*a*) a profession complementary to dentistry; or

(*b*) a class of members of a profession complementary to dentistry.

[Dentists Act 1984, s 36A(2) as inserted by SI 2005/2011.]

[1] Part 3A contains ss 36A–36Z4.

**7.8158 36K. Use of titles and descriptions** (1) A registered dental care professional shall not take or use, or affix to or use in connection with his premises—

(*a*) any description reasonably calculated to suggest that he possesses any professional status or qualification other than a professional status or qualification which he in fact possesses and which is indicated by particulars entered in the dental care professionals register in respect of him; or

(*b*) any title specified in regulations under section 36A(2) except the title or titles under which he is registered in the dental care professionals register.

(2) Any person who contravenes subsection (1) shall be liable on summary conviction to a fine not exceeding level 3 on the standard scale.

[Dentists Act 1984, s 36K as inserted by SI 2005/2011.]

## PART IV[1]
## RESTRICTIONS ON PRACTICE OF DENTISTRY AND ON CARRYING ON BUSINESS OF DENTISTRY

*The practice of dentistry*

**7.8159 37. Definition of practice of dentistry** (1) Subject to subsection (1A), for the purposes of this Act, the practice of dentistry shall be deemed to include the performance of any such operation and the giving of any such treatment, advice[2] or attendance[2] as is usually performed or given by dentists; and any person who performs any operation or gives any treatment, advice or attendance on or to any person as preparatory to or for the purpose of or in connection with the fitting, insertion or fixing of dentures, artificial teeth or other dental appliances shall be deemed to have practised dentistry within the meaning of this Act.

(1A) For the purposes of this Act, the practice of dentistry shall be deemed not to include the performance of any medical task by a person who—

(*a*) is qualified to carry out such a task; and

(*b*) is a member of a profession regulated by a regulatory body (other than the Council) listed in section 25(3) of the National Health Service Reform and Health Care Professions Act 2002.

(2) Dental work to which subsection (2A) or (2B) applies shall not be treated for the purposes of this Act as amounting to the practice of dentistry if it is undertaken under the direct personal supervision of—

(*a*) a registered dentist; or

(*b*) a registered dental care professional of a kind authorised in rules under this section to carry out such supervision.

(2A) This subsection applies to dental work if it is undertaken—

(*a*) by a person recognised by a dental authority as a student of dentistry or by a medical authority as a medical student; and

(*b*) as part of a course of instruction or training approved by that authority for students of that kind or as part of an examination so approved.

(2B) This subsection applies to dental work if it is undertaken by a person as part of—

(*a*) a course of instruction or training which he is following in order to qualify for registration in the dental care professionals register under a particular title or titles; or

(*b*) an examination which he must pass in order to satisfy the requirements for registration in that register under a particular title or titles.

(3) In this section "medical authority" means a body or combination of bodies included in the list maintained under section 4(1) of the Medical Act 1983 (qualifying examinations and primary United Kingdom qualifications) which is entitled to hold qualifying examinations for the purpose of granting one or more primary United Kingdom medical qualifications.

[Dentists Act 1984, s 37 as amended by SI 2002/3135, SI 2005/2011 and SI 2008/1774.]

---

1 Part IV contains ss 37–44.

2 "Advice" means advice in connection with the fitting of the mouth itself; not as to the supply of new teeth to an existing denture (*Twyford v Puntschart* [1947] 1 All ER 773, 111 JP 315). The construction of these expressions was considered in *Almy v Thomas* [1953] 2 All ER 1050, 117 JP 561.

7.8160 **38. Prohibition on practice of dentistry by laymen** (1) A person who is not a registered[1] dentist or a registered dental care professional shall not practise or hold himself out, whether directly or by implication, as practising or as being prepared to practise dentistry.

(2) Any person who acts in contravention of subsection (1) above shall be liable on summary conviction to a fine not exceeding the **fifth level** on the standard scale.

(3) Summary proceedings for an offence under this section may be brought within the period of six months beginning with the date on which evidence sufficient in the opinion of the prosecutor to warrant the proceedings came to his knowledge; but no such proceedings shall be brought by virtue of this subsection more than two years after the commission of the offence.

(4) For the purposes of subsection (3) above a certificate signed by or on behalf of the prosecutor and stating the date on which such evidence as is mentioned in that subsection came to his knowledge shall be conclusive evidence of that date, and any certificate purporting to be so signed shall be taken to have been so signed unless the contrary is proved.

[Dentists Act 1984, s 38 as amended by SI 2005/2011 and SI 2007/3101.]

---

1 See note 2 to s 26, ante.

7.8161 **39. Prohibition on use of practitioners' titles by laymen** (1) A person shall not take or use the title of dentist, dental surgeon or dental practitioner, either alone or in combination with any other word, unless he is a registered dentist.

(2) No person shall take or use any title or description implying that he is a registered dentist unless he is a registered dentist.

(2A) A person who is not a registered dental care professional shall not take or use any title specified in regulations under section 36A(2), either alone or in combination with any other word.

(2B) No person shall take or use any title or description implying that he is a registered dental care professional unless he is a registered dental care professional.

(3) Any person who acts in contravention of this section shall be liable on summary conviction to a fine not exceeding the **fifth level** on the standard scale.

[Dentists Act 1984, s 39 as amended by SI 2005/2011 and SI 2007/3101.]

*Restrictions on carrying on the business of dentistry*

7.8162 **40. Definition of business of dentistry** (1) For the purposes of this Act a person shall be treated as carrying on the business of dentistry if, and only if, he or a partnership of which he is a member receives payment for services rendered in the course of the practice of dentistry by him or by a partner of his, or by an employee of his or of all or any of the partners.

(2) Notwithstanding subsection (1) above, the receipt of payments—

(*a*) by an authority providing national health services, or

(*aa*) by a person providing primary dental services under a contract under section 100 of the National Health Service Act 2006 or an agreement under section 107of that Act, or under a contract under section 57 of the National Health Service (Wales) Act 2006 or an agreement under section 64 of that Act, or (*ab*) by a person (other than one falling within paragraph (*a*) above) providing personal dental services under section 17C of the National Health Service (Scotland) Act 1978, or

(*b*) by a person providing dental treatment for his employees without a view to profit, or

(*c*) by a person providing dental treatment without a view to profit under conditions approved by the Secretary of State or the Department of Health and Social Services for Northern Ireland,

shall not constitute the carrying on of the business of dentistry for the purposes of this Act.

[Dentists Act 1984, s 40 as amended by SI 1998/1546, the Health and Social Care (Community Health and Standards) Act 2003, Sch 11, the National Health Service (Consequential Provisions) Act 2006, Sch 1 and the Health and Social Care Act 2012, Sch 5.]

**7.8163 41. Restriction on individuals** (1) Subject to the provisions of this section, an individual who is not a registered dentist shall not carry on the business of dentistry unless—

(*a*) he was engaged in carrying on the business of dentistry on 21st July 1955; or

(*b*) he falls within a class of registered dental care professionals prescribed in rules under this section.

(1A) For the purposes of this section, an "authorised dental care professional" means an individual who falls within subsection (1)(*b*).

(1B) Any individual who contravenes this section shall be liable on summary conviction to a fine not exceeding level 5 on the standard scale.

(2) The exemption conferred by subsection (1)(*a*) on persons who were carrying on the business of dentistry on the date there mentioned shall not extend to any person who has at any time ceased to be a registered dentist in consequence of a Practice Committee giving a direction under section 27B or 27C or making an order under section 30(1) for the erasure of his name from the register, or for the suspension of his registration, following a relevant determination that his fitness to practise as a dentist is impaired.

(2A) For the purposes of subsection (2), a "relevant determination" that a person's fitness to practise is impaired is a determination which is based solely on one or more of the grounds mentioned in paragraph (*a*), (*d*), (*e*), (*f*) or (g) of subsection (2) of section 27 (misconduct etc).

(3) This section shall not operate to prevent a person from carrying on the business of dentistry during any period for which—

(*a*) his registration in the register is suspended by virtue of a direction given by a Practice Committee under section 27B or 27C, or an order made by a Practice Committee under section 30(1), following a determination, based solely on the ground mentioned in paragraph (*c*) of subsection (2) of section 27 (adverse physical or mental health), that his fitness to practise is impaired, or

(*b*) his registration in the dental care professionals register is suspended by virtue of a direction given by a Practice Committee under section 36P or 36Q, or an order made by a Practice Committee under section 36U(1), following a determination, based solely on the ground mentioned in paragraph (*c*) of subsection (2) of section 36N (adverse physical or mental health), that his fitness to practise is impaired,

and subsections (4) and (6) shall apply in relation to a person whose registration is so suspended as they apply in relation to a registered dentist or an authorised dental care professional.

(4) Where a registered dentist or authorised dental care professional who died after 3rd July 1956 was at his death carrying on a business or practice constituting the business of dentistry, this section shall not operate to prevent his personal representatives or his surviving spouse or his surviving civil partner or any of his children, or trustees on behalf of his surviving spouse or his surviving civil partner or any of his children, from carrying on the business of dentistry in continuance of that business or practice during the three years beginning with his death.

(5) Where a registered dentist who died before 4th July 1956 was at his death carrying on a business or practice constituting the business of dentistry, this section shall not operate to prevent his widow, or trustees on behalf of his widow, from carrying on the business of dentistry in continuance of that business or practice at any time during her life.

(6) Where a registered dentist or authorised dental care professional becomes bankrupt at a time when he is carrying on a business or practice constituting the business of dentistry, this section shall not operate to prevent his trustee in bankruptcy, or in Northern Ireland the official assignee, from carrying on the business of dentistry in continuance of that business or practice during the three years beginning with the bankruptcy.

(7) Rules made under subsection (1)(*b*) shall not be amended or revoked in such a way that any class of registered dental care professionals prescribed in those rules ceases thereafter to be prescribed.

[Dentists Act 1984, s 41 as amended by the Civil Partnership Act 2004, Sch 27 and SI 2005/2011.]

**7.8164 43. Directors of bodies corporate** (1) A body corporate commits an offence if it carries on the business of dentistry at a time when a majority of its directors are not persons who are either registered dentists or registered dental care professionals.

(2) Where a person is the subject of a decision erasing his name from, or suspending him from, a register kept by any of the regulatory bodies listed in section 25(3) of the National Health Service Reform and Health Care Professions Act 2002, that person commits an offence if he is a director of a body corporate carrying on the business of dentistry at any time when such an erasure or

suspension remains in effect.

(3) Any body corporate committing an offence under subsection (1), or any person committing an offence under subsection (2), shall be liable on summary conviction to a fine not exceeding level 5 on the standard scale.

[Dentists Act 1984, s 43 as substituted by SI 2005/2011.]

## PART VI[1]

## MISCELLANEOUS AND SUPPLEMENTARY

7.8165 **52. Regulations and other documents** (1) The Statutory Instruments Act 1946 shall apply to a statutory instrument containing regulations made by the Council under this Act in like manner as if the regulations had been made by a Minister of the Crown.

(1A) Any power to make regulations under this Act may be exercised—

(*a*) so as to make different provision with respect to different cases or different classes of case or different provision in respect of the same case or class of case for different purposes of this Act; and

(*b*) either in relation to all cases to which the power extends or in relation to all those cases subject to specified exceptions.

(1B) Any power to make regulations under this Act includes power to make any incidental, consequential, saving, transitional, transitory or supplementary provision which the Council consider necessary or expedient.

(2) Prima facie evidence of any document issued by the Council may be given in all legal proceedings by the production of a copy or extract purporting to be certified to be a true copy or extract by the registrar or some other officer of the Council authorised to give a certificate for the purposes of this subsection.

(3) No proof shall be required of the handwriting or official position or authority of any person certifying in pursuance of this section to the truth of any copy of, or extract from, any regulations or other document.

[Dentists Act 1984, s 52 as amended by SI 2005/2011.]

[1] Part VI contains ss 49–56.

7.8166 **53. Interpretation** (1) In this Act—

"competent authority" means any authority or body of a relevant European State designated by that State for the purposes of the Directive as competent to—

(*a*) receive or issue evidence of qualifications or other information or documents, or

(*b*) receive applications and take the decisions referred to in the Directive,

in connection with the practice of dentistry or a profession complementary to dentistry;

"the Council" means the General Dental Council;

"dental authority" shall be construed in accordance with section 3(4) above.

"diploma" means any diploma, degree, fellowship, membership, licence, authority to practise, letters testimonial, certificate or other status or document granted by any university, corporation, college or other body or by any department of, or persons acting under the authority of, the government of any country or place (whether within or without Her Majesty's dominions);

"the Directive" means Directive 2005/36/EC of the European Parliament and of the Council of 7th September 2005 on the recognition of professional qualifications (OJ No L255, 30.09.2005, p 22), and references in this Act to the Directive or to any provision of the Directive are references to the Directive, or to that provision of the Directive, as amended from time to time;

"exempt person", in relation to the profession of dentistry or in relation to a profession complementary to dentistry, means—

(*a*) a national of a relevant European State other than the United Kingdom;

(*b*) a national of the United Kingdom who is seeking access to, or is pursuing, the profession by virtue of an enforceable Community right; or

(*c*) a person who is not a national of a relevant European State but who is, by virtue of an enforceable Community right, entitled to be treated, for the purposes of access to and pursuit of the profession, no less favourably than a national of a relevant European State;

"the General Systems Regulations" means the European Communities (Recognition of Professional Qualifications) Regulations 2007 (SI 2007/2781);

"interim order" means—

(*a*) an interim suspension order under section 32(4)(*a*) or section 36V(4)(*a*); or

(*b*) an order for interim conditional registration under section 32(4)(*b*) or section 36V(4)(*b*);

"national", in relation to a relevant European State, means the same as in the Community Treaties, but does not include a person who by virtue of Article 2 of Protocol No 3 (Channel Islands and Isle of Man) to the Treaty of Accession is not to benefit from Community provisions relating to the free movement of persons and services;

"Practice Committee" shall be construed in accordance with section 2;

"profession complementary to dentistry" shall be construed in accordance with section 36A(1);

"recognised overseas diploma" has the meaning given by section 15(2) above.
"the register" means the dentists register;
"registered dental care professional" means a person for the time being registered in the dental care professionals register under a title or titles;
"registered dentist" means (subject to section 17(4) above) a person for the time being registered in the register;
"the registrar" means the person for the time being appointed under section 14(2) above;
"relevant European State" means an EEA State or Switzerland.

(2) In this Act references to the practice of dentistry shall be construed in accordance with section 37 above, and references to carrying on the business of dentistry shall be construed in accordance with section 40 above.

(2A) In this Act references to a body corporate's principal office mean, in the case of a body corporate registered outside the United Kingdom, that body's principal office within the United Kingdom.

(3) References in this Act to the provision, supervision or management of national health services are references to the provision, supervision or management of—

(*a*) services under—
  (i) section 2, 3, 92 or 107 of, or paragraphs 1 to 6 of Schedule 1 to, the National Health Service Act 2006, or section 2, 3, 50 or 64 of, or paragraphs 1 to 6 of Schedule 1 to, the National Health Service (Wales) Act 2006;
  (ii) section 17C, 36, 38 or 39 of the National Health Service (Scotland) Act 1978; or
  (iii) *Northern Ireland*; and

(*b*) services at health centres provided under the said sections 2, 3 or 36 or the said Article 5.

(4) *Repealed.*

[Dentists Act 1984, s 53, as amended by the Statute Law (Repeals) Act 1993, Sch 1, SI 1996/1496, the National Health Service (Primary Care) Act 1997, Sch 2, SI 2005/2011, the National Health Service (Consequential Provisions) Act 2006, Sch 1, SI 2007/3101 and SI 2009/1182.]

# Health and Medicines Act 1988

(1988 c 49)

*HIV testing kits and services*

7.8168 **23. HIV testing kits and services** (1) The Secretary of State may provide by regulations that a person—

(*a*) who sells or supplies to another on HIV testing kit or any component part of such a kit;
(*b*) who provides another with HIV testing services; or
(*c*) who advertises such kits or component parts or such services,

shall be guilty of an offence.

(2)–(3) *Further provisions about regulations.*

(4) If any person contravenes regulations under this section, he shall be liable—

(*a*) on summary conviction to a fine not exceeding **the statutory maximum**; and
(*b*) on conviction on indictment to a **fine** or to imprisonment for a term of not more than **two years**, or to **both**.

(5) Where an offence under this section which is committed by a body corporate is proved to have been committed with the consent or connivance of, or to be attributable to any neglect on the part of, any director, manager, secretary or other similar officer of the body corporate, or any person who was purporting to act in any such capacity, he as well as the body corporate shall be guilty of that offence and shall be liable to be proceeded against and punished accordingly.

(6) In this section—
"HIV" means Immunodeficiency Virus of any type;
"HIV testing kit" means a diagnostic kit the purpose of which is to detect the presence of HIV or HIV antibodies; and
"HIV testing services" means diagnostic services the purpose of which is to detect the presence of HIV or HIV antibodies in identifiable individuals.

[Health and Medicines Act 1988, s 23.]

# Opticians Act 1989

(1989 c 44)

## Part IV[1]

## Restrictions On Testing Of Sight, Fitting Of Contact Lenses, Sale And Supply Of Optical Appliances And Use Of Titles And Descriptions

7.8169 **24. Testing of sight** (1) Subject to the following provisions of this section, a person who is not a registered medical practitioner or registered optometrist[2] shall not test[2] the sight of another person.

(2) Subsection (1) above shall not apply to the testing of sight by a person recognised by a medical authority[2] as a medical student, if carried out as part of a course of instruction approved by

that authority for medical students or as part of an examination so approved.

(3) The Council[2] may by rules[3] exempt from subsection (1) above the testing of sight by persons training as optometrists[2], or any prescribed class of such persons, in such cases and subject to compliance with such conditions as may be prescribed by the rules.

(4) Any person who contravenes subsection (1) above shall be liable on summary conviction to a fine of an amount not exceeding **level 5** on the standard scale.

[Opticians Act 1989, s 24 as amended by SI 2005/848.]

---

1 Part IV contains ss 24–30.

2 Defined in s 36.

3 The General Optical Council (Testing of Sight by Persons Training as Ophthalmic Opticians Rules) Order of Council 1994, SI 1994/70 amended by SI 1999/2897 and SI 2007/3101 has been made.

7.8170 25. **Fitting of contact lenses** (1) Subject to the following provisions of this section a person who is not a registered medical practitioner, a registered optometrist or a registered dispensing optician must not fit a contact lens for an individual.

(1A) A registered medical practitioner, a registered optometrist, a registered dispensing optician or a person to whom, by virtue of subsection (2) or (3) below, subsection (1) above does not apply, must not fit a contact lens for an individual unless—

(*a*) where the duty to give an individual a signed written prescription under section 26(2) below arises, he has the particulars of such a prescription given to the individual within the period of two years ending on the date the fitting begins; and

(*b*) the fitting begins before any re-examination date specified in that prescription.

(2) Subsection (1) above shall not apply to the fitting of contact lenses by a person recognised by a medical authority as a medical student, if carried out as part of a course of instruction approved by that authority for medical students or as part of an examination so approved.

(3) The Council may by rules exempt from subsection (1) above the fitting of contact lenses by persons training as optometrists or dispensing opticians, or any prescribed class of such persons, in such cases and subject to compliance with such conditions as may be prescribed by the rules.

(4) Any person who contravenes subsection (1) or (1A) above shall be liable on summary conviction to a fine of an amount not exceeding **level 5** on the standard scale.

(5) A person to whom this subsection applies who fits a contact lens to an individual must—

(*a*) on completion of the fitting, provide the individual with a signed, written specification of each lens fitted sufficient to enable the lens to be replicated unless, having carried out the assessment referred to in subsection (9)(*a*) below, he is of the view that a contact lens is not appropriate; and

(*b*) provide the individual with instructions and information on the care, wearing, treatment, cleaning and maintenance of the lens.

(6) The obligation to provide a specification or instructions or information under subsection (5) above applies—

(*a*) if only one person took part in fitting a contact lens for the individual, to that person;

(*b*) if a series of persons took part in fitting a contact lens for an individual, to the last person to fit a lens.

(7) A specification issued in accordance with subsection (5) above must—

(*a*) state the period during which the specification remains valid and its expiry date; and

(*b*) in the case of a specification provided by a registered medical practitioner, contain such particulars as the Secretary of State may specify in regulations[1].

(8) A specification becomes invalid after its expiry date.

(9) For the purposes of this section and section 27(3A) below, "fitting" a contact lens means—

(*a*) assessing whether a contact lens meets the needs of the individual; and, where appropriate

(*b*) providing the individual with one or more contact lenses for use during a trial period,

and "fit" and "fitted" shall be construed accordingly.

(10) *Northern Ireland.*

[Opticians Act 1989, s 25 as amended by SI 2005/848.]

---

1 See the Contact Lens (Specification) and Miscellaneous Amendments Regulations 2005, SI 2005/1481 and the General Optical Council (Therapeutics and Contact Lens Specialties) Rules Order of Council 2008, SI 2008/1940.

7.8171 26. **26 Duties to be performed on sight testing** *Secretary of State may make Regulations.*

[Opticians Act 1989, s 26—summarised.]

7.8172 27. **Sale and supply of optical appliances** (1) A person shall not sell—

(*a*) any contact lens for use by any person who does not have a valid specification provided pursuant to section 25(5) above; or

(*b*) subject to the following provisions of this section, any optical appliance or zero powered contact lens unless the sale is effected by or under the supervision of a registered medical practitioner, a registered optometrist or a registered dispensing optician.

(2) Subsection (1) above shall not apply to any of the following sales—

(*a*) a sale for a person who has attained the age of sixteen of spectacles which have two single vision lenses of the same positive spherical power not exceeding 4 dioptres where the sale is wholly for the purpose of correcting, remedying or relieving presbyopia;

(*b*) a sale of an optical appliance intended for use as protection or cover for the eyes in sports if—

(i) neither lens fitted to the appliance has a positive or negative spherical power exceeding 8 dioptres;

(ii) the appliance is an appliance with a single vision lens or single visions lenses; and

(iii) the appliance falls within any category of appliance specified in an order made by the Privy Council for the purposes of this section; or

(*c*) a sale of a contact lens for a person who has attained the age of sixteen where the sale satisfies the requirements of subsection (3) below.

(3) Those requirements are that—

(*a*) the seller has—

(i) the original specification;

(ii) a copy of the original specification which he verifies with the person who provided it; or

(iii) an order from the purchaser, submitted either in writing or electronically, which contains the particulars of the specification of the person who intends to wear the contact lens ("the wearer"), and the seller verifies those particulars with the person who provided the specification;

(*b*) the seller is reasonably satisfied that the goods ordered are for use by the person named in the specification;

(*c*) the sale is made before the expiry date mentioned in the specification;

(*d*) the seller is, or is under the general direction of, a registered medical practitioner, a registered optometrist or a registered dispensing optician; and

(*e*) the wearer—

(i) is not, so far as the seller knows registered as sight-impaired or severely sight-impaired in a register kept by a local authority under section 77(1) of the Care Act 2014 or registered as blind or registered as partially sighted in a register compiled by a local authority under section 29(4)(*g*) of the National Assistance Act 1948 (welfare services);

(ii) *Scotland*; or

(iii) *Northern Ireland*.

(3A) In this section—

(*a*) "seller"—

(i) includes any person who supplies the optical appliance or, as the case may be, the zero powered contact lens whether or not payment is made to him for the supply; and

(ii) does not include a person who supplies the contact lens as part of the assessment process in the course of fitting the lenses to the individual; and

(*b*) lenses are to be taken to have the same positive spherical power if the difference between them is within the tolerances relating to the power of such lenses specified from time to time by the British Standard Specification.

(3B) The seller must make arrangements, except in such cases or classes of cases as may be prescribed in rules made by the Council, for the individual for whom the optical appliance or, as the case may be, the zero powered contact lens is supplied to receive aftercare in so far as, and for so long as, may be reasonable in his particular case.

(3C) The Council may by rules specify the arrangements which are to be made or may be made under subsection (3B) above.

(4) Subsection (1) above shall apply to the supply of an optical appliance or zero powered contact lens in the course of the practice or business of an optometrist or dispensing optician, whether by the person carrying on the practice or business or by a person employed by him, if the supply was effected in pursuance of arrangements made—

(*a*) with a Minister of the Crown or Government Department (including a Northern Ireland department); or

(*b*) with any body on whom functions are conferred by or by virtue of—

(i) the National Health Service Act 2006 or the National Health Service (Wales) Act 2006;

(ii) *Scotland*; or

(iii) *Northern Ireland*,

as it applies to the sale of an optical appliance or zero powered contact lens.

(5) Subsection (1) above shall not apply to the sale of an optical appliance or zero powered contact lens—

(*a*) to a registered medical practitioner, registered optometrist, registered dispensing optician or business registrant for the purposes of his practice or of his or its business;

(*b*) to a manufacturer of or dealer in optical appliances or zero powered contact lenses for the purposes of his business

(*c*) to any authority or person carrying on a hospital, clinic, nursing home or other institution providing medical or surgical treatment;

(*cc*) *Scotland*;

(*d*) to a Minister of the Crown or government department (including a Northern Ireland department);

(*e*) for the purpose of its export; or

(*f*) in accordance with an order under subsection (6) below.

(6) An order under this subsection is an order made by the Privy Council and specifying—

(*a*) optical appliances to which it applies; and

(*b*) conditions subject to which their sale is exempted from the requirements of subsection (1) above.

(7) Any such order relating to optical appliances consisting of or including one or more lenses shall specify, as a condition subject to which the sale of any such appliance is so exempted, the condition that the appliance must be in accordance with a written prescription which—

(*a*) has been given by a registered medical practitioner or registered optometrist following a testing of sight by him; and

(*b*) bears a date not more than such time as is specified in the order before the prescription is presented to the proposed seller of the appliance.

(8) An order under subsection (6) above may not specify as appliances to which it applies—

(*a*) contact lenses; or

(*b*) any optical appliance for a person under 16 years of age

(9) On any prosecution for selling an optical appliance or zero powered contact lens in contravention of subsection (1) above it shall be a defence for the defendant to prove—

(*a*) that he sold the appliance or lens as an antique or secondhand article; and

(*b*) that he did not know, and had no reason to believe, that the appliance was bought for the purpose of being used for correcting, remedying or relieving a defect of sight.

(10) A person who contravenes subsection (1) above shall be liable on summary conviction to a fine of an amount not exceeding **level 5** on the standard scale.

[Opticians Act 1989, s 27 as amended by the Regulation of Care (Scotland) Act 2001, s 79, the National Health Service and Community Care Act 1990, Sch 9, SI 2005/848, the National Health Service (Consequential Provisions) Act 2006, Sch 1 and SI 2015/914.]

7.8173 **28. Penalty for pretending to be registered etc** (1) Any individual—

(*a*) who takes or uses the title of ophthalmic optician or the title of optometrist when he is not a registered optometrist; or

(*b*) who takes or uses the title of dispensing optician when he is not a registered dispensing optician; or

(*c*) who takes or uses the title of registered optometrist when he is not a registered optometrist;

(*cc*) who holds himself out as being a student registrant when he is not registered in the register of those undertaking training as optometrists or dispensing opticians maintained under section 8A above;

(*ccc*) who holds himself out as having a specialty or proficiency which qualifies for entry in the appropriate register in accordance with rules made under section 10(1A) above but for whom no entry is extant;

(*d*) who takes or uses any name, title, addition or description falsely implying that he is registered in any of the registers; or

(*e*) who otherwise pretends that he is registered in any of the registers,

shall be liable on summary conviction to a fine of an amount not exceeding **level 5** on the standard scale.

(2) On any prosecution for an offence under subsection (1)(*d*) or (*e*) above, the taking or use of the title of optician by a person to whom this subsection applies is to be taken to imply that he is registered in one of the registers, but the implication may be rebutted if the defendant proves that he took or, as the case may be, used the title in circumstances where it would have been unreasonable for people to believe, in consequence of his taking or, as the case may be, use of it, that he was in fact registered in one of the registers.

(3) Subject to subsection (4) below, subsection (2) above applies to a person who carries on the business—

(*a*) of selling optical appliances; or

(*b*) of supplying optical appliances in pursuance of arrangements made as mentioned in section 27(4) above.

(4) Subsection (2) above does not apply to a person who sells or supplies only optical appliances or zero powered contact lenses or both as mentioned in section 27(5)(*a*) to (*e*) above.

(5) Any body corporate which—

(*a*) takes or uses the title of ophthalmic optician, the title of optometrist, the title of dispensing optician or the title of registered optician when it is not registered;

(*b*) takes or uses any name, title, addition or description falsely implying that it is registered;

(*c*) otherwise pretends that it is registered,

shall be liable on summary conviction to a fine of an amount not exceeding level 5 on the standard scale.

(6) On any prosecution for an offence under subsection (5)(*b*) or (*c*) above, the taking or using of the title of optician by a body corporate to which this subsection applies is to be taken to imply that it is registered, but the implication may be rebutted if the body corporate took or, as the case may be, used the title in circumstances where it would have been unreasonable for people to believe, in consequence of its taking or, as the case may be, use of it, that it was in fact registered.

(7) Subject to subsection (8) below, subsection (6) above applies to a body corporate which carries on the business—

(*a*) of selling optical appliances or zero powered contact lenses; or

(*b*) of supplying optical appliances or zero powered contact lenses in pursuance of arrangements made as mentioned in section 27(4) above.

(8) Subsection (6) above does not apply to a body corporate which sells or supplies optical appliances or zero powered contact lenses only as mentioned in section 27(5)(*a*) to (*e*) above.

(9) It is immaterial for the purposes of this section whether a title was used alone or in combination with any other words.

[Opticians Act 1989, s 28 as amended by SI 2005/848 and SI 2007/3101.]

7.8174 29. **Provision as to death or bankruptcy of registered optician** (1) Where a registered optometrist or registered dispensing optician dies at a time when he is carrying on business or is in practice as an optometrist or dispensing optician, then during the three years beginning with his death or such longer period as the Council may in any particular case allow, section 28 above shall not operate to prevent—

(*a*) his executors or administrators;

(*b*) his surviving spouse or his surviving civil partner;

(*c*) any of his children; or

(*d*) trustees on behalf of his surviving spouse or his surviving civil partner or any of his children,

from taking or using in relation to that business or practice, but in conjunction with the name in which he carried it on, any title which he was entitled to take or use immediately before his death.

(2) Where a registered optometrist or registered dispensing optician becomes bankrupt at a time when he is carrying on business or is in practice as an optometrist or dispensing optician, then, during the three years beginning with the bankruptcy, section 28 above shall not operate to prevent his trustee in bankruptcy from taking or using in relation to that business or practice, but in conjunction with the name in which he carried it on, any title which he was entitled to take or use immediately before the bankruptcy.

(2A) In subsections (1) and (2)—

"registered optometrist" does not include a person registered in the register maintained under section 8B(1)(*a*);

"registered dispensing optician" does not include a person registered in the register maintained under section 8B(1)(*b*).

(3) Where—

(*a*) a person by virtue of subsection (1) or (2) above takes or uses any title in relation to the business or practice—

(i) of a deceased optometrist or dispensing optician; or

(ii) of an optometrist or dispensing optician who has become bankrupt; and

(*b*) an offence under section 24, 25 or 27 above is committed in the course of that business or practice,

the Fitness to Practice Committee may, if they think* fit, direct that subsection (1) or (2) above shall cease to apply in relation to that business or practice.

(4) This Act shall have effect in relation to any case in which it is alleged that there has been a conviction of any such offence and to any direction under subsection (3) above as it has effect in relation to a case in which it is alleged that a registrant's fitness to practise or as the case may be a business registrant's fitness to carry on business as an optometrist or a dispensing optician or both, is impaired and the making of an order under Part 2A above.

(5) *Scotland.*

(6) *Northern Ireland.*

[Opticians Act 1989, s 29 as amended by the Civil Partnership Act 2004, Sch 27, SI 2005/848 and SI 2007/3101.]

* **Words substituted by the Health and Social Care Act 2008, Sch 7 from a date to be appointed.**

7.8175 30. **Offences by bodies corporate** (1) Where an offence under this Act which has been committed by a body corporate is proved to have been committed with the consent or connivance of, or to be attributable to any neglect on the part of, any responsible officer of the body corporate, he, as well as the body corporate, shall be deemed to be guilty of that offence and shall be liable to be proceeded against and punished accordingly.

(2) In subsection (1) above, "responsible officer" means any director, manager, secretary or

other similar officer of the body corporate, or of a branch or department of the body corporate, or any person purporting to act in any such capacity.

[Opticians Act 1989, s 30 as amended by SI 2005/848.]

7.8176 **30A. Legal proceedings** (1) Notwithstanding anything in any enactment, proceedings for an offence under this Part of this Act may be begun at any time within the period of six months beginning with the date on which evidence sufficient in the opinion of the Council to justify a prosecution for the offence comes to the Council's knowledge, or within a period of two years beginning with the date of the commission of the offence, whichever period first expires.

(2) In this section, "enactment" means—

(*a*) an Act of Parliament;

(*b*) an Act of the Scottish Parliament;

(*c*) any Northern Ireland legislation; or

(*d*) any instrument made under or having effect by virtue of an Act of Parliament, an Act of the Scottish Parliament or any Northern Ireland legislation.

[Opticians Act 1989, s 30A as inserted by SI 2005/848.]

## PART V[1]
## MISCELLANEOUS AND SUPPLEMENTARY

### *Supplementary*

7.8177 **36. Interpretation** (1) In this Act, unless the context otherwise requires—[2]

"approved training establishment"[3] means an establishment approved by the Council under section 12(7)(*a*) above;

"approved qualification" means any qualification approved by the Council under section 12(7)(*b*) above;

"body corporate" includes a limited liability partnership and, in Scotland, a partnership; and in relation to such partnerships, a reference to a director or other officer of a body corporate is a reference to a member;

"business registrant" means a body corporate registered in the register maintained by the Council under section 9 above;

"the Council" means the General Optical Council;

"dispensing optician" means a person engaged or proposing to engage in the fitting and supply of optical appliances;

"electronic communication" has the same meaning as in the Electronic Communications Act 2000;

"exempt person", in relation to the profession of optometrist or the profession of dispensing optician, means—

(*a*) a national of a relevant European State other than the United Kingdom;

(*b*) a national of the United Kingdom who is seeking access to, or is pursuing, the profession by virtue of an enforceable EU right; or

(*c*) a person who is not a national of a relevant European State but who is, by virtue of an enforceable Community right, entitled to be treated, for the purposes of access to and pursuit of the profession, no less favourably than a national of a relevant European State;

"financial penalty order" means an order under Part 2A above that a registrant shall pay to the Council a sum specified in the order;

"functions" includes powers and duties;

"General Systems Regulations" means the European Communities (Recognition of Professional Qualifications) Regulations 2007 (SI 2007/2781);

"Hearings Panel" means the panel of persons appointed under section 5D(1) above;

"individual registrant" means any person whose name is in a register maintained by the Council under section 7, 8A or 8B above;

"medical authority" means a body or combination of bodies included in the list maintained by the General Medical Council under section 4(1) of the Medical Act 1983;

"optometrist" means a person engaged or proposing to engage in the testing of sight (otherwise than as a registered medical practitioner or a person recognised by a medical authority as a medical student), whether or not he is also engaged or proposing to engage in the fitting and supply of optical appliances;

"optical appliance" means an appliance designed to correct, remedy or relieve a defect of sight;

"prescribed" means prescribed by rules under this Act;

"register" means, unless the context otherwise requires, any one of the following registers—

(*a*) the register of optometrists maintained under section 7 above;

(*b*) the register of dispensing opticians maintained under section 7 above;

(*c*) the registers of students maintained under section 8A above;

(*ca*) the registers of visiting optometrists from relevant European States and visiting dispensing opticians from relevant European States maintained under section 8B;

(*d*) the register of bodies corporate under section 9 above,

and, except in the expressions "registered medical practitioner", "registered dispensing optician" and "registered optometrist", "registered" and "registration" have corresponding meanings;

"registered dispensing optician" means a person whose name is in the register of dispensing opticians maintained under section 7 or in the register of visiting dispensing opticians from relevant European States maintained under section 8B;

"registered optometrist" means a person whose name is in the register of optometrists maintained under section 7 or in the register of visiting optometrists from relevant European States maintained under section 8B;

"registrant", except in the expressions "individual registrant", "business registrant" and "student registrant", means a person whose name is in the appropriate register;

"relevant European State" means an EEA State or Switzerland;

"student registrant" means a person whose name is in one of the registers maintained by the Council under section 8A above;

(2) References in this Act to testing sight are references to testing sight with the object of determining whether there is any and, if so, what defect of sight and of correcting, remedying or relieving any such defect of an anatomical or physiological nature by means of an optical appliance prescribed on the basis of the determination.

[Opticians Act 1989, s 36 as amended by SI 2005/848, SI 2007/3101, SI 2008/1774 and SI 2011/1043.]

---

1 Part V includes ss 31–38.

2 Only relevant definitions are printed here.

3 **Definition inserted by the Health and Social Care Act 2008, Sch 7 from a date to be appointed.**

# Criminal Justice (International Co-operation) Act 1990[1]

(1990 c 5)

## Part II[2]

## The Vienna Convention

*Substances useful for manufacture of controlled drugs*

**7.8178 12. Manufacture and supply of scheduled substances** (1) It is an offence for a person—

(*a*) to manufacture a scheduled substance; or

(*b*) to supply such a substance to another person,

knowing or suspecting that the substance is to be used in or for the unlawful production of a controlled drug.

(1A) A person does not commit an offence under subsection (1) above if he manufactures or, as the case may be, supplies the scheduled substance with the express consent of a constable.

(2) A person guilty of an offence under subsection (1) above is liable[3]—

(*a*) on summary conviction, to imprisonment for a term not exceeding **six months** or a fine not exceeding **the statutory maximum** or **both;**

(*b*) on conviction on indictment, to imprisonment for a term not exceeding **fourteen years** or a **fine** or **both**.

(3) In this section "a controlled drug" has the same meaning as in the Misuse of Drugs Act 1971 and "unlawful production of a controlled drug" means the production of such a drug which is unlawful by virtue of section 4(1)(*a*) of that Act.

(4) In this section and elsewhere in this Part of this Act "a scheduled substance" means a substance for the time being specified in Schedule 2 to this Act.

(5) Her Majesty may by Order in Council amend that Schedule (whether by addition, deletion or transfer from one Table to the other) but—

(*a*) no such Order shall add any substance to the Schedule unless—

(i) it appears to Her Majesty to be frequently used in or for the unlawful production of a controlled drug; or

(ii) it has been added to the Annex to the Vienna Convention under Article 12 of that Convention; and

(*b*) no such Order shall be made unless a draft of it has been laid before and approved by a resolution of each House of Parliament.

[Criminal Justice (International Co-operation) Act 1990, s 12 as amended by the Criminal Justice (International Co-operation) Act 1998, s 1.]

---

1 Part I of this Act (Criminal Proceedings and Investigations) is printed in Part I: Magistrates' Courts, Procedure, ante.

2 Part II contains ss 12–14.

3 For procedure in respect of an offence which is triable either way, see the Magistrates' Courts Act 1980, ss 17A–21, in Part I: Magistrates' Court, Procedure, ante.

**7.8179 13. Regulations about scheduled substances** (1) The Secretary of State may by regulations[1] make provision—

(*a*) imposing requirements as to the documentation of transactions involving scheduled substances;

(*b*) requiring the keeping of records and the furnishing of information with respect to such substances;

(*c*) for the inspection of records kept pursuant to the regulations;

(*d*) for the labelling of consignments of scheduled substances.

(2) Regulations made by virtue of subsection (1)(*b*) may, in particular, require—

(*a*) the notification of the proposed exportation of substances specified in Table I in Schedule 2 to this Act to such countries as may be specified in the regulations; and

(*b*) the production, in such circumstances as may be so specified, of evidence that the required notification has been given;

and for the purposes of section 68 of the Customs and Excise Management Act 1979 (offences relating to exportation of prohibited or restricted goods) any such substance shall be deemed to be exported contrary to a restriction for the time being in force with respect to it under this Act if it is exported without the requisite notification having been given.

(3) Regulations under this section may make different provision in relation to the substances specified in Table I and Table II in Schedule 2 to this Act respectively and in relation to different cases or circumstances.

(4) The power to make regulations under this section shall be exercisable by statutory instrument subject to annulment in pursuance of a resolution of either House of Parliament.

(5) Any person who fails to comply with any requirement imposed by the regulations or, in purported compliance with any such requirement, furnishes information which he knows to be false in a material particular or recklessly furnishes information which is false in a material particular is guilty of an offence and liable[2]—

(*a*) on summary conviction, to imprisonment for a term not exceeding **six months** or a fine not exceeding the **statutory maximum** or **both;**

(*b*) on conviction on indictment, to imprisonment for a term not exceeding **two years** or a **fine** or **both**.

(6) No information obtained pursuant to the regulations shall be disclosed except for the purposes of criminal proceedings or of proceedings under the provisions of the Criminal Justice (Scotland) Act 1987 relating to the confiscation of the proceeds of drug trafficking or corresponding provisions in force in Northern Ireland or of proceedings under Part 2, 3 or 4 of the Proceeds of Crime Act 2002.

[Criminal Justice (International Co-operation) Act 1990, s 13 as amended by the Drug Trafficking Act 1994, Sch 1, the Proceeds of Crime Act 2002, Sch 11.]

---

[1] See the Controlled Drugs (Drug Precursors) (Intra-Community Trade) Regulations 2008, SI 2008/295 amended by SI 2010/231 and the Community Drugs (Drug Precursors) (Community External Trade) Regulations 2008, SI 2008/296 made under the European Communities Act 1972, s 2(2).

[2] For procedure in respect of an offence which is triable either way, see the Magistrates' Courts Act 1980, ss 17A–21, in PART I: MAGISTRATES' COURTS, PROCEDURE, ante.

*Proceeds of drug trafficking*

7.8180 **15. Interest on sums unpaid under confiscation orders** (1) If any sum required to be paid by a person under a confiscation order is not paid when it is required to be paid (whether forthwith on the making of the order or at a time specified under section 396(1) of the Criminal Procedure (Scotland) Act 1975) that person shall be liable to pay interest on that sum for the period for which it remains unpaid and the amount of the interest shall for the purposes of enforcement be treated as part of the amount to be recovered from him under the confiscation order.

(2) The sheriff may, on the application of the prosecutor, increase the term of imprisonment or detention fixed in respect of the confiscation order under section 396(2) of the said Act of 1975 (imprisonment in default of payment) if the effect of subsection (1) above is to increase the maximum period applicable in relation to the order under section 407(1A) of the said Act of 1975.

(3) The rate of interest under subsection (1) above shall be the rate payable under a decree of the Court of Session.

[Criminal Justice (International Co-operation) Act 1990, s 15 as amended by the Drug Trafficking Act 1994, Schs 1 and 3 and the Criminal Justice (Scotland) Act 1995, Sch 6.]

*Offences at sea*

7.8181 **18. Offences on British ships** Anything which would constitute a drug trafficking offence if done on land in any part of the United Kingdom shall constitute that offence if done on a British ship.

[Criminal Justice (International Co-operation) Act 1990, s 18.]

7.8182 **19. Ships used for illicit traffic** (1) This section applies to a British ship, a ship registered in a state other than the United Kingdom which is a party to the Vienna Convention (a "Convention state") and a ship not registered[1] in any country or territory.

(2) A person is guilty of an offence if on a ship to which this section applies, wherever it may be, he—

(*a*) has a controlled drug in his possession; or

(*b*) is in any way knowingly concerned in the carrying or concealing of a controlled drug on the ship,

knowing or having reasonable grounds to suspect that the drug is intended to be imported or has been exported contrary to section 3(1) of the Misuse of Drugs Act 1971 or the law of any state other than the United Kingdom.

(3) A certificate purporting to be issued by or on behalf of the government of any state to the effect that the importation or export of a controlled drug is prohibited by the law of that state shall be evidence, and in Scotland sufficient evidence, of the matters stated.

(4) A person guilty of an offence under this section is liable[2]—

(*a*) in a case where the controlled drug is a Class A drug—

(i) on summary conviction, to imprisonment for a term not exceeding **six months** or a fine not exceeding **the statutory maximum** or **both**;

(ii) on conviction on indictment, to imprisonment for **life** or a **fine** or **both**;

(*b*) in a case where the controlled drug is a Class B drug or a temporary class drug—

(i) on summary conviction, to imprisonment for a term not exceeding **six months** or a fine not exceeding **the statutory maximum** or **both**;

(ii) on conviction on indictment, to imprisonment for a term not exceeding **fourteen years** or **fine** or **both**;

(*c*) in a case where the controlled drug is a Class C drug—

(i) on summary conviction, to imprisonment for a term not exceeding **three months** or a fine not exceeding **the statutory maximum** or **both**;

(ii) on conviction on indictment, to imprisonment for a term not exceeding **fourteen years** or a **fine** or **both**.

(5) In this section "a controlled drug" and the references to controlled drugs of a specified Class have the same meaning as in the said Act of 1971; and an offence under this section shall be included in the offences to which section 28 of that Act (defences) applies.

[Criminal Justice (International Co-operation) Act 1990, s 19 as amended by the Criminal Justice Act 2003, Sch 28 and the Police Reform and Social Responsibility Act 2011, Sch 17.]

---

1 Evidence of searches of US computer databases which contained documentation information on all United States documented vessels was held to be both admissible and sufficient to establish that the defendants' yacht was not registered as a vessel of the United States; accordingly, the judge was entitled to reach the conclusion that if the yacht was not so registered there was an overwhelming inference that she was not registered anywhere (*R v Dean* [1998] 2 Cr App Rep 171).

2 For procedure in respect of an offence which is triable either way, see the Magistrates' Courts Act 1980, ss 17A–21, in PART I: MAGISTRATES' COURTS, PROCEDURE, ante.

**7.8183 20. Enforcement powers** (1) The powers conferred on an enforcement officer by Schedule 3 to this Act shall be exercisable in relation to any ship to which section 18 or 19 above applies for the purpose of detecting and the taking of appropriate action in respect of the offences mentioned in those sections.

(2) Those powers shall not be exercised outside the landward limits of the territorial sea of the United Kingdom in relation to a ship registered in a Convention state except with the authority of the Commissioners of Customs and Excise; and they shall not give their authority unless that state has in relation to that ship—

(*a*) requested the assistance of the United Kingdom for the purpose mentioned in subsection (1) above; or

(*b*) authorised the United Kingdom to act for that purpose.

(3) In giving their authority pursuant to a request or authorisation from a Convention state the Commissioners of Customs and Excise shall impose such conditions or limitations on the exercise of the powers as may be necessary to give effect to any conditions or limitations imposed by that state.

(4) The Commissioners of Customs and Excise may, either of their own motion or in response to a request from a Convention state, authorise a Convention state to exercise, in relation to a British ship, powers corresponding to those conferred on enforcement officers by Schedule 3 to this Act but subject to such conditions or limitations, if any, as they may impose.

(5) Subsection (4) above is without prejudice to any agreement made, or which may be made, on behalf of the United Kingdom whereby the United Kingdom undertakes not to object to the exercise by any other state in relation to a British ship of powers corresponding to those conferred by that Schedule.

(6) The powers conferred by that Schedule shall not be exercised in the territorial sea of any state other than the United Kingdom without the authority of the Commissioners of Customs and Excise and they shall not give their authority unless that state has consented to the exercise of those powers.

[Criminal Justice (International Co-operation) Act 1990, s 20 as amended by the Criminal Justice Act 1993, s 23.]

**7.8184 21. Jurisdiction and prosecutions** (1) Proceedings under this Part of this Act or Schedule 3 in respect of an offence on a ship may be taken, and the offence may for all incidental purposes be treated as having been committed, in any place in the United Kingdom.

(2) No such proceedings shall be instituted—

(*a*) in England or Wales except by or with the consent of the Director of Public Prosecutions;

(*b*) *Northern Ireland.*

(3) Without prejudice to subsection (2) above no proceedings for an offence under section 19 above alleged to have been committed outside the landward limits of the territorial sea of the United Kingdom on a ship registered in a Convention state shall be instituted except in pursuance of the

exercise with the authority of the Commissioners of Customs and Excise of the powers conferred by Schedule 3 to this Act; and section 3 of the Territorial Waters Jurisdiction Act 1878 (consent of Secretary of State for certain prosecutions) shall not apply to those proceedings.

[Criminal Justice (International Co-operation) Act 1990, s 21 as amended by the Criminal Justice Act 1993, s 23, the Commissioners for Revenue and Customs Act 2005, Sch 4 and SI 2014/834.]

*Supplementary*

7.8185 **24. Interpretation of Part II** (1) In this Part of this Act—

"British ship" means a ship registered in the United Kingdom or a colony;

"Convention state" has the meaning given in section 19(1) above;

"scheduled substance" has the meaning given in section 12(4) above;

"ship" includes any vessel used in navigation;

"the territorial sea of the United Kingdom" includes the territorial sea adjacent to any of the Channel Islands, the Isle of Man or any colony;

"the Vienna Convention" means the United Nations Convention against Illicit Traffic in Narcotic Drugs and Psychotropic Substances which was signed in Vienna on 20th December 1988.

(2) Any expression used in this Part of this Act which is also used in the Drug Trafficking Act 1994 has the same meaning as in that Act.

(3) *Scotland.*

(4) If in any proceedings under this Part of this Act any question arises whether any country or territory is a state or is a party to the Vienna Convention, a certificate issued by or under the authority of the Secretary of State shall be conclusive evidence on that question.

[Criminal Justice (International Co-operation) Act 1990, s 24 as amended by the Drug Trafficking Act 1994, Sch 1.]

## Part IV[1]
## General

7.8186 **30. Expenses and receipts** (1) Any expenses incurred by the Secretary of State under this Act shall be defrayed out of money provided by Parliament.

(2)–(3) *Repealed.*

[Criminal Justice (International Co-operation) Act 1990, s 30 as amended by the Criminal Justice Act 1993, s 25 and the Drug Trafficking Act 1994, Sch 3.]

1 Part IV contains ss 30–32.

7.8187 **32. Short title, commencement and extent** (1) This Act may be cited as the Criminal Justice (International Co-operation) Act 1990.

(2) This Act shall come into force on such day as may be appointed by the Secretary of State by an order[1] made by statutory instrument and different days may be appointed for different provisions and different purposes and for different parts of the United Kingdom.

(3) This Act extends to Northern Ireland.

(4) Her Majesty may by Order in Council direct that the provisions of this Act and those provisions of the Drug Trafficking Act 1994 which re-enact provisions of this Act shall extend, with such exceptions and modifications as appear to Her Majesty to be appropriate, to any of the Channel Islands, the Isle of Man or any colony.

[Criminal Justice (International Co-operation) Act 1990, s 32 as amended by the Drug Trafficking Act 1994, Sch 1.]

1 The Criminal Justice (International Co-operation) Act 1980 (Commencement No 1) Order 1991, SI 1991/1072, and (Commencement No 2) Order 1991, SI 1991/2108, have been made.

## SCHEDULE 2
### Substances Useful for Manufacturing Controlled Drugs

Sections 12 and 13

7.8188

*(Amended by SI 1992/2873 and SI 2001/3933.)*

*Table I*

*N*-ACETYLANTHRANILIC ACID
EPHEDRINE
EROGOMETRINE
ERGOTAMINE
ISOSAFROLE
LYSERGIC ACID
3, 4-METHYLENE DIOXYPHENYL-2-PROPANONE
NOREPHEDRINE
1-PHENYL-2-PROPANONE
PIPERONAL
PSEUDOEPHEDRINE
SAFROLE

The salts of the substances listed in this Table whenever the existence of such salts is possible.

*Table II*

ACETIC ANHYDRIDE
ACETONE
ANTHRANILIC ACID
ETHYL ETHER
HYDROCHLORIC ACID
METHYL ETHYL KETONE (also referred to as 2- BUTANONE or M.E.K.)
PHENYLACETIC ACID
PIPERIDINE
POTASSIUM PERMANGANATE
SULPHURIC ACID
TOLUENE

The salts of the substances listed in this Table whenever the existence of such salts is possible.

## SCHEDULE 3

ENFORCEMENT POWERS IN RESPECT OF SHIPS — Section 20

*(Amended by the Criminal Justice Act 1993, s 23.)*

*Preliminary*

**7.8189** **1.** (1) In this Schedule "an enforcement officer"[1] means—
(*a*) a constable;
(*b*) an officer commissioned by the Commissioners of Customs and Excise under section 6(3) of the Customs and Excise Management Act 1979; and
(*c*) any other person of a description specified in an order[1] made for the purposes of this Schedule by the Secretary of State.

(2) The power to make an order under sub-paragraph (1)(*c*) above shall be exercisable by statutory instrument subject to annulment in pursuance of a resolution of either House of Parliament.

(3) In this Schedule "the ship" means the ship in relation to which the powers conferred by this Schedule are exercised.

1 The Criminal Justice (International Co-operation) Act 1990 (Enforcement Officers) Order 1992, SI 1992/77, has been made and provides that the following descriptions of persons, in addition to those specified in paras (*a*) and (*b*), shall be enforcement officers under this Schedule—
(*a*) commissioned officers of any of Her Majesty's ships;
(*b*) officers of the sea-fishery inspectorate of the Ministry of Agriculture, Fisheries and Food;
(*c*) officers of the fishery protection service of the Secretary of State for Scotland holding the rank of commander, first officer or second officer.

*Power to stop, board, divert and detain*

**2.** (1) An enforcement officer may stop the ship, board it and, if he thinks it necessary for the exercise of his functions, require it to be taken to a port in the United Kingdom and detain it there.

(2) Where an enforcement officer is exercising his powers with the authority of the Commissioners of Customs and Excise given under section 20(2) of this Act the officer may require the ship to be taken to a port in the Convention state in question or, if that state has so requested, in any other country or territory willing to receive it.

(3) For any of those purposes he may require the master or any member of the crew to take such action as may be necessary.

(4) If an enforcement officer detains a vessel he shall serve on the master a notice in writing stating that it is to be detained until the notice is withdrawn by the service on him of a further notice in writing signed by an enforcement officer.

*Power to search and obtain information*

**3.** (1) An enforcement officer may search the ship, anyone on it and anything on it including its cargo.

(2) An enforcement officer may require any person on the ship to give information concerning himself or anything on the ship.

(3) Without prejudice to the generality of those powers an enforcement officer may—
(*a*) open any containers;
(*b*) make tests and take samples of anything on the ship;
(*c*) require the production of documents, books or records relating to the ship or anything on it;
(*d*) make photographs or copies of anything whose production he has power to require.

*Powers in respect of suspected offence*

**4.** If an enforcement officer has reasonable grounds to suspect that an offence mentioned in section 18 or 19 of this Act has been committed on a ship to which that section applies he may—
(*a*) arrest without warrant anyone whom he has reasonable grounds for suspecting to be guilty of the offence; and
(*b*) seize and detain anything found on the ship which appears to him to be evidence of the offence.

*Assistants*

**5.** (1) An enforcement officer may take with him, to assist him in exercising his powers—
(*a*) any other persons; and

(*b*) any equipment or materials.

(2) A person whom an enforcement officer takes with him to assist him may perform any of the officer's functions but only under the officer's supervision.

*Use of reasonable force*

6. An enforcement officer may use reasonable force, if necessary, in the performance of his functions.

*Evidence of authority*

7. An enforcement officer shall, if required, produce evidence of his authority.

*Protection of officers*

8. An enforcement officer shall not be liable in any civil or criminal proceedings for anything done in the purported performance of his functions under this Schedule if the court is satisfied that the act was done in good faith and that there were reasonable grounds for doing it.

*Offences*

9. (1) A person is guilty of an offence if he—

(*a*) intentionally obstructs an enforcement officer in the performance of any of his functions under this Schedule;

(*b*) fails without reasonable excuse to comply with a requirement made by an enforcement officer in the performance of those functions; or

(*c*) in purporting to give information required by an officer for the performance of those functions—

(i) makes a statement which he knows to be false in a material particular or recklessly makes a statement which is false in a material particular; or

(ii) intentionally fails to disclose any material particular.

(2) A person guilty of an offence under this paragraph is liable on summary conviction to a fine not exceeding **level** 5 on the standard scale.

# Osteopaths Act 1993[1]

(1993 c 21)

*The General Council and its committees*

7.8198 1. **The General Osteopathic Council and its committees** (1) There shall be a body corporate to be known as the General Osteopathic Council (referred to in this Act as "the General Council").

(2) It shall be the duty of the General Council to develop and regulate the profession of osteopathy.

(3) The General Council shall have such other functions as are conferred on it by this Act.

(4) The General Council[2] shall be constituted as provided for by order of the Privy Council, subject to Part 1 of the Schedule (which relates to orders under this subsection and powers of the General Council), which shall have effect.[3]

(5) There shall be four committees of the General Council, to be known as—

(*a*) the Education Committee;

(*b*) the Investigating Committee;

(*c*) the Professional Conduct Committee; and

(*d*) the Health Committee.

(6) The four committees are referred to in this Act as "the statutory committees".

(7) Each of the statutory committees shall have the functions conferred on it by or under this Act.

(8) The General Council may establish such other committees as it considers appropriate in connection with the discharge of its functions.

(9) *Supplementary provisions as to committees.*

(10)–(12) *Repealed.*

[Osteopaths Act 1993, s 1 as amended by SI 2008/1774.]

---

[1] This Act establishes a body to be known as the General Osteopathic Council; provides for the regulation of the profession of osteopathy, including making provision as to the registration of osteopaths and as to their professional education and conduct.

For commencement provisions, see s 42, post.

[2] See also the General Osteopathic Council (Constitiution) Order 2009, SI 2009/263 amended by SI 2012/3006 made under this section and Sch.

[3] The General Osteopathic Council (Constitution) Order 2009, SI 2009/263 amended by SI 2012/3006 has been made.

7.8199 32. **Offences** (1) A person who (whether expressly or by implication) describes himself as an osteopath, osteopathic practitioner, osteopathic physician, osteopathist, osteotherapist, or any other kind of osteopath, is guilty of an offence unless he is a registered osteopath.

(2) A person who, without reasonable excuse, fails to comply with any requirement imposed by—

(*a*) the Professional Conduct Committee,

(*b*) the Health Committee, or

(*c*) an appeal tribunal hearing an appeal under section 30[1],

under rules made by virtue of section 26(2)(*h*)[2] or under any corresponding rules made by virtue of section 30(4) is guilty of an offence.

(3) A person guilty of an offence under this section shall be liable on summary conviction to a fine not exceeding **level five** on the standard scale.

[Osteopaths Act 1993, s 32.]

1 Section 30 provides for a right of appeal to an appeal tribunal against decisions of the Health Committee.

2 Section 26(2)(*h*) of the Act empowers the General Council to make rules as to the procedure to be followed by the Professional Conduct Committee or the Health Committee in considering any allegation under s 22 (consideration of allegations by the Professional Conduct Committee) or 23 (consideration of allegations by the Health Committee), and under s 26(2)(*h*) the rules shall, in particular, include provision empowering the Committee to require persons to attend and give evidence or to produce documents.

*Supplemental*

7.8200 **41. Interpretation**[1] In this Act—

"conditionally registered osteopath" means a person who is registered with conditional registration;

"fully registered osteopath" means a person who is registered with full registration;

"the General Council" means the General Osteopathic Council;

"the General Systems Regulations" means the European Communities (Recognition of Professional Qualifications) Regulations 2007 (SI 2007/2781);

"prescribed" means prescribed by rules made by the General Council;

"provisionally registered osteopath" means a person who is registered with provisional registration;

"recognised qualification" has the meaning given by section 14(1);

"the register" means the register of osteopaths maintained by the Registrar under section 2;

"registered" means registered in the register;

"registered address", in relation to a registered osteopath, means the address which is entered in the register;

"registered osteopath" means a person who is registered as a fully registered osteopath, as a conditionally registered osteopath, as a provisionally registered osteopath or as a temporarily registered osteopath;

"temporarily registered osteopath" means a person who is registered with temporary registration;

"training" includes continuing professional development;

"the Registrar" has the meaning given in section 2(2);

"the statutory committees" has the meaning given by section 1(6).

[Osteopaths Act 1993, s 41 as amended by SI 2007/3101 and SI 2008/1774.]

1 Only those definitions which are relevant to this work are printed here.

7.8201 **42. Short title, commencement, transitional provisions and extent** (1) This Act may be cited as the Osteopaths Act 1993.

(2) This Act shall come into force on such day as the Secretary of State may by order[1] appoint.

(3) The power conferred by subsection (2) shall be exercisable by statutory instrument.

(4) Different days may be appointed by an order under subsection (2) for different purposes and different provisions.

(5) Any order under subsection (2) may make such transitional provision as the Secretary of State considers appropriate.

(6)–(7) *Transitional provisions; extent.*

[Osteopaths Act 1993, s 42.]

1 At the date of going to press the following commencement orders have been made: Commencement (No 1 and Transitional Provision) Order 1997, SI 1997/34; Commencement (No 2) Order 1998, SI 1998/872; Commencement (No 3) Order 1998, SI 1998/1138; Commencement (No 4) Order 1999, SI 1999/1767; Commencement (No 5) Order 2000, SI 2000/217; Commencement (No 6 and Transitional Provisions) Order 2000, SI 2000/1065; Commencement (No 7) Order 2002, SI 2002/500.

## Chiropractors Act 1994[1]

(1994 c 17)

*The General Council and its committees*

7.8202 **1. The General Chiropractic Council and its committees** (1) There shall be a body corporate to be known as the General Chiropractic Council (referred to in this Act as "the General Council").

(2) It shall be the duty of the General Council to develop and regulate the profession of chiropractic.

(3) The General Council shall have such other functions as are conferred on it by this Act.

(4) The General Council[2] shall be constituted as provided for by order[3] of the Privy Council, subject to Part 1 of Schedule 1 (which relates to orders under this subsection and powers of the General Council), which shall have effect.

(5) There shall be four committees of the General Council, to be known as—

(*a*) the Education Committee;

(*b*) the Investigating Committee;

(*c*) the Professional Conduct Committee; and
(*d*) the Health Committee.

(6) The four committees are referred to in this Act as "the statutory committees".

(7) Each of the statutory committees shall have the functions conferred on it by or under this Act.

(8) The General Council may establish such other committees as it considers appropriate in connection with the discharge of its functions.

(9) *Supplementary provisions as to committees.*

(10)–(12) *Repealed.*

[Chiropractors Act 1994, s 1 as amended by SI 2008/1774.]

1 This Act establishes a body to be known as the General Chiropractic Council; provides for the regulation of the chiropractic profession, including making provision as to the registration of chiropractors and as to their professional education and conduct.

The Act is to be brought into force in accordance with s 44, post.

2 See also the General Chiropractic Council (Constitution) Order 2008, SI 2008/3047 amended by SI 2012/3006.

3 The General Chiropractic Council (Constitution) Order 2008, SI 2008/3047 amended by SI 2012/3006 has been made.

*Offences*

7.8203 32. **Offences** (1) A person who (whether expressly or by implication) describes himself as a chiropractor, chiropractic practitioner, chiropractitioner, chiropractic physician, or any other kind of chiropractor, is guilty of an offence unless he is a registered chiropractor.

(2) A person who, without reasonable excuse, fails to comply with any requirement imposed by—

(*a*) the Professional Conduct Committee,
(*b*) the Health Committee, or
(*c*) an appeal tribunal hearing an appeal under section 30[1],

under rules made by virtue of section 26(2)(*h*)[2] or under any corresponding rules made by virtue of section 30(4) is guilty of an offence.

(3) A person guilty of an offence under this section shall be liable on summary conviction to a fine not exceeding **level five** on the standard scale.

[Chiropractors Act 1994, s 32.]

1 Section 30 provides for a right of appeal to an appeal tribunal against decisions of the Health Committee. See the General Chiropractic Council (Health Appeal Tribunal) Rules Order 2000, SI 2000/3214.

2 Section 26(2)(*h*) of the Act empowers the General Council to make rules as to the procedure to be followed by the Professional Conduct Committee or the Health Committee in considering any allegation under s 22 (consideration of allegations by the Professional Conduct Committee) or 23 (consideration of allegations by the Health Committee), and under s 26(2)(*h*) the rules shall, in particular, include provision empowering the Committee to require persons to attend and give evidence or to produce documents. See the General Chiropractic Council (Professional Conduct Committee) Rules Order of Council 2000, SI 2000/3290 amended by SI 2005/2114 and SI 2007/1630. See also the General Chiropractic Council (Health Committee) Rules Order of Council 2000, SI 2000/3291 amended by SI 2006/1630 made under s 26.

*Supplemental*

7.8204 43. **Interpretation**[1] In this Act—

"conditionally registered chiropractor" means a person who is registered with conditional registration;

"fully registered chiropractor" means a person who is registered with full registration;

"the General Council" means the General Chiropractic Council;

"prescribed" means prescribed by rules made by the General Council;

"provisionally registered chiropractor" means a person who is registered with provisional registration;

"recognised qualification" has the meaning given by section 14(1);

"the register" means the register of chiropractors maintained by the Registrar under section 2;

"registered" means registered in the register;

"registered address" means the address which is entered in the register, in relation to the chiropractor in question, in accordance with the requirements of section 6(1) and does not include any other address which may be entered in the register, in relation to him, by virtue of rules made under section 6(2);

"registered chiropractor" means a person who is registered as a fully registered chiropractor, as a conditionally registered chiropractor, as a provisionally registered chiropractor or as a temporarily registered chiropractor;

"the Registrar" has the meaning given in section 2(2);

"temporarily registered chiropractor" means a person who is registered with temporary registration;

"training" includes continuing professional development;

"the statutory committees" has the meaning given by section 1(6).

[Chiropractors Act 1994, s 43 as amended by SI 2007/3101 and SI 2008/1774.]

1 Only those definitions which are relevant to this work are printed here.

7.8205 44. **Short title, commencement, transitional provisions and extent** (1) This Act may be cited as the Chiropractors Act 1994.

(2) Section 42 and Schedule 2 shall come into force on the passing of this Act.

(3) The other provisions of this Act shall come into force on such day as the Secretary of State may by order[1] appoint.

(4) The power conferred by subsection (3) shall be exercisable by statutory instrument.

(5) Different days may be appointed by an order under subsection (3) for different purposes and different provisions.

(6) Any order under subsection (3) may make such transitional provision as the Secretary of State considers appropriate.

(7)–(8) *Transitional provisions; extent.*

[Chiropractors Act 1994, s 44.]

---

1 At the date of going to press the following commencement orders had been made: the Chiropractors Act 1994 (Commencement No 1 and Transitional Provision) Order 1998, SI 1998/2031; the Chiropractors Act 1999 (Commencement No 2) Order 1999, SI 1999/1309; the Chiropractors Act 1999 (Commencement No 3) Order 1999, SI 1999/1496; the Chiropractors Act 1994 (Commencement No 4) Order 2000, SI 2000/2388; the Chiropractors Act 1994 (Commencement Order No 5 and Transitional Provision) Order 2001, SI 2001/2028; the Chiropractors Act 1994 (Commencement No 6) Order 2002, SI 2002/312; the Chiropractors Act 1994 (Commencement No 7) Order 2004, SI 2004/1521.

# Drug Trafficking Act 1994

(1994 c 37)

## PART IV[1]

## MISCELLANEOUS AND SUPPLEMENTAL

*Investigations into drug trafficking*

7.8206 **55. Order to make material available** (1) A constable may, for the purpose of an investigation into drug trafficking, apply[2] to a Circuit judge for an order under subsection (2) below in relation to particular material or material of a particular description.

(2) If on such an application the judge is satisfied that the conditions in subsection (4) below are fulfilled, he may make an order that the person who appears to him in possession of the material to which the application relates shall—

(*a*) produce it to a constable for him to take away, or

(*b*) give a constable access to it,

within such period as the order may specify.

This subsection has effect subject to section 59(11) of this Act.

(3) The period to be specified in an order under subsection (2) above shall be seven days unless it appears to the judge that a longer or shorter period would be appropriate in the particular circumstances of the application.

(4) The conditions referred to in subsection (2) above are—

(*a*) that there are reasonable grounds for suspecting that a specified person has carried on drug trafficking;

(*b*) that there are reasonable grounds for suspecting that the material to which the application relates—

(i) is likely to be of substantial value (whether by itself or together with other material) to the investigation for the purpose of which the application is made; and

(ii) does not consist of or include items subject to legal privilege or excluded material; and

(*c*) that there are reasonable grounds for believing that it is in the public interest, having regard—

(i) to the benefit likely to accrue to the investigation if the material is obtained, and

(ii) to the circumstances under which the person in possession of the material holds it,

that the material should be produced or that access to it should be given.

(5) Where the judge makes an order under subsection (2)(*b*) above in relation to material on any premises he may, on the application of a constable, order any person who appears to him to be entitled to grant entry to the premises to allow a constable to enter the premises to obtain access to the material.

(6) An application under subsection (1) or (5) above may be made ex parte to a judge in chambers.

(7) Provision may be made by Criminal Procedure Rules as to—

(*a*) the discharge and variation of orders under this section; and

(*b*) proceedings relating to such orders.

(8) An order of a Circuit judge under this section shall have effect as if it were an order of the Crown Court.

(9) Where the material to which an application under subsection (1) above relates consists of information contained in a computer—

(*a*) an order under subsection 2(*a*) above shall have effect as an order to produce the material in a form in which it can be taken away and in which it is visible and legible; and

(*b*) an order under subsection 2(*b*) above shall have effect as an order to give access to the material in a form in which it is visible and legible.

(10) An order under subsection (2) above—

(*a*) shall not confer any right to production of, or access to, items subject to legal privilege or excluded material;

(*b*) shall have effect notwithstanding any obligation as to secrecy or other restriction upon the disclosure of information imposed by statute or otherwise; and

(*c*) may be made in relation to material in the possession of an authorised government department;

and in this subsection "authorised government department" means a government department which is an authorised department for the purposes of the Crown Proceedings Act 1947.

[Drug Trafficking Act 1994, s 55 as amended by the Proceeds of Crime Act 2002, Sch 11 and the Courts Act 2003, Sch 8.]

---

1 Part IV contains ss 55–69.

2 An application under s 55 should be made ex p (*R v Central Criminal Court, ex p Francis & Francis* [1989] AC 346, [1988] 1 All ER 677, 87 Cr App Rep 104, DC); however, the recipient of an order has the opportunity to apply to discharge or vary the order before it takes effect (Criminal Procedure Rules, Part 33, in the *Key Materials*). The power to make an order is not limited to investigations in the UK, but the information must show that the intention is to assist a foreign law enforcement agency. Only exceptionally will the judge require undertakings from the applicant before making the order (*R v Crown Court at Southwark, ex p Customs and Excise Comrs* [1990] 1 QB 650, [1989] 3 All ER 673, DC). Application may be made for an order for the production of material solely or partly for the purpose of assisting an investigation by a law enforcement agency of another country into drug trafficking, as well as for the purpose of an investigation by UK customs officers. Nevertheless, if the application is made in order to assist an investigation by a foreign law enforcement agency this must be made clear on the face of the information in support of the application (*R v Crown Court at Southwark, ex p Customs and Excise Comrs* [1990] 1 QB 650, [1989] 3 All ER 673).

**7.8207 56. Authority for search** (1) A constable may, for the purpose of an investigation into drug trafficking, apply to a Circuit judge for a warrant under this section in relation to specified premises.

(2) On such application the judge may issue a warrant authorising a constable to enter and search the premises if the judge is satisfied—

(*a*) that an order made under section 55 of this Act in relation to material on the premises has not been complied with;

(*b*) that the conditions in subsection (3) below are fulfilled; or

(*c*) that the conditions in subsection (4) below are fulfilled.

(3) The conditions referred to in subsection (2)(*b*) above are—

(*a*) that there are reasonable grounds for suspecting that a specified person has carried on drug trafficking;

(*b*) that the conditions in subsection (4)(*b*) and (*c*) of section 55 of this Act are fulfilled in relation to any material on the premises; and

(*c*) that it would not be appropriate to make an order under that section in relation to the material because—

(i) it is not practicable to communicate with any person entitled to produce the material;

(ii) it is not practicable to communicate with any person entitled to grant access to the material or entitled to grant entry to the premises in which the material is situated; or

(iii) the investigation for the purpose of which the application is made might be seriously prejudiced unless a constable could secure immediate access to the material.

(4) The conditions referred to in subsection (2)(*c*) above are—

(*a*) that there are reasonable grounds for suspecting that a specified person has carried on drug trafficking;

(*b*) that there are reasonable grounds for suspecting that there is on the premises material relating to the specified person or to drug trafficking which is likely to be of substantial value (whether by itself or together with other material) to the investigation for the purpose of which the application is made, but that the material cannot at the time of the application be particularised; and

(*c*) that—

(i) it is not practicable to communicate with any person entitled to grant entry to the premises;

(ii) entry to the premises will not be granted unless a warrant is produced; or

(iii) the investigation for the purpose of which the application is made might be seriously prejudiced unless a constable arriving at the premises could secure immediate entry to them.

(5) Where a constable has entered premises in the execution of a warrant issued under this section, he may seize and retain any material, other than items subject to legal privilege and

excluded material, which is likely to be of substantial value (whether by itself or together with other material) to the investigation for the purpose of which the warrant was issued[1].

[Drug Trafficking Act 1994, s 56 as amended by the Proceeds of Crime Act 2002, Sch 11.]

1 The Criminal Justice and Police Act 2001, Part 2 (see PART 1, ante) conferred additional powers of seizure. Section 55 of that Act (obligation to return excluded and special procedure material) has effect, in relation to the power of seizure conferred by s 56(5), with the omission of every reference to special procedure material: the Criminal Justice and Police Act 2001, s 55(5).

**7.8208 57. Provisions supplementary to sections 55 and 56** (1) For the purposes of sections 21 and 22 of the Police and Criminal Evidence Act 1984 (access to, and copying and retention of, seized material)—

(*a*) an investigation into drug trafficking shall be treated as if it were an investigation of or in connection with an offence; and

(*b*) material produced in pursuance of an order under section 55(2)(*a*) of this Act shall be treated as if it were material seized by a constable.

(2) In sections 55 and 56 of this Act "excluded material", "items subject to legal privilege" and "premises" have the same meaning as in the 1984 Act.

[Drug Trafficking Act 1994, s 57.]

**7.8209 58. Offence of prejudicing investigation** (1) Where, in relation to an investigation into drug trafficking—

(*a*) an order under section 55 of this Act has been made or has been applied for and has not been refused, or

(*b*) a warrant under section 56 of this Act has been issued,

a person is guilty of an offence if, knowing or suspecting that the investigation is taking place, he makes any disclosure which is likely to prejudice the investigation.

(2) In proceedings against a person for an offence under this section, it is a defence to prove—

(*a*) that he did not know or suspect that the disclosure was likely to prejudice the investigation; or

(*b*) that he had lawful authority or reasonable excuse for making the disclosure.

(3) Nothing in subsection (1) above makes it an offence for a professional legal adviser to disclose any information or other matter—

(*a*) to, or to a representative of, a client of his in connection with the giving by the adviser of legal advice to the client; or

(*b*) to any person—

(i) in contemplation of, or in connection with, legal proceedings; and

(ii) for the purpose of those proceedings.

(4) Subsection (3) above does not apply in relation to any information or other matter which is disclosed with a view to furthering any criminal purpose.

(5) A person guilty of an offence under this section shall be liable[1]—

(*a*) on summary conviction, to imprisonment for a term not exceeding **six months** or to a fine not exceeding **the statutory maximum** or to **both**; and

(*b*) on conviction on indictment, to imprisonment for a term not exceeding **five years** or to a **fine** or to **both**.

[Drug Trafficking Act 1994, s 58.]

1 For procedure in respect of this offence which is triable either way, see the Magistrates' Courts Act 1980, ss 17A-21, in PART I: MAGISTRATES' COURTS, PROCEDURE, ante.

**7.8210 59. Disclosure of information held by government departments**

(1)–(10) *Repealed.*

(11) In the case of material in the possession of an authorised government department, an order under section 55(2) of this Act may require any officer of the department (whether named in the order or not) who may for the time being be in possession of the material concerned to comply with it, and such an order shall be served as if the proceedings were civil proceedings against the department.

(12) The person on whom such an order is served—

(*a*) shall take all reasonable steps to bring it to the attention of the officer concerned; and

(*b*) if the order is not brought to that officer's attention within the period specified in an order under section 55(2), shall report the reasons for the failure to the court;

and it shall also be the duty of any other officer of the department in receipt of the order to take such steps as are mentioned in paragraph (*a*) above.

(13) In this section "authorised government department" means a government department which is an authorised department for the purposes of the Crown Proceedings Act 1947.

[Drug Trafficking Act 1994, s 59 as amended by the Proceeds of Crime Act 2002, Sch 11.]

**7.8211 59A. Construction of sections 55 to 59** (1) This section has effect for the purposes of sections 55 to 59.

(2) A reference to constable includes a reference to a customs officer.

(3) A customs officer is a person commissioned by the Commissioners of Customs and Excise

under section 6(3) of the Customs and Excise Management Act 1979 (c 2).

(4) Drug trafficking means doing or being concerned in any of the following (whether in England and Wales or elsewhere)—

(*a*) producing or supplying a controlled drug where the production or supply contravenes section 4(1) of the Misuse of Drugs Act 1971 or a corresponding law,

(*b*) transporting or storing a controlled drug where possession of the drug contravenes section 5(1) of that Act or a corresponding law;

(*c*) importing or exporting a controlled drug where the importation or exportation is prohibited by section 3(1) of that Act or a corresponding law;

(*d*) manufacturing or supplying a scheduled substance within the meaning of section 12 of the Criminal Justice (International Co-operation) Act 1990 where the manufacture or supply is an offence under that section or would be such an offence if it took place in England and Wales;

(*e*) using any ship for illicit traffic in controlled drugs in circumstances which amount to the commission of an offence under section 19 of that Act.

(5) In this section "corresponding law" has the same meaning as in the Misuse of Drugs Act 1971.

[Drug Trafficking Act 1994, s 59A as inserted by the Proceeds of Crime Act 2002, s 456.]

*Prosecution of offences etc*

7.8212 **60. Revenue and Customs prosecutions** (1) Proceedings for a specified offence may be instituted by the Director of Public Prosecutions or by order of the Commissioners for Her Majesty's Revenue and Customs ("the Commissioners").

(2) Any proceedings for a specified offence which are instituted by order of the Commissioners shall be commenced in the name of an officer of Revenue and Customs.

(3) *Repealed.*

(4) Where the Commissioners investigate, or propose to investigate, any matter with a view to determining—

(*a*) whether there are grounds for believing that a specified offence has been committed, or

(*b*) whether a person should be prosecuted for a specified offence,

that matter shall be treated as an assigned matter within the meaning of the Customs and Excise Management Act 1979.

(5) Nothing in this section shall be taken—

(*a*) to prevent any person (including any officer) who has power to arrest, detain or prosecute any person for a specified offence from doing so; or

(*b*) to prevent a court from proceeding to deal with a person brought before it following his arrest by an officer for a specified offence, even though the proceedings have not been instituted in accordance with this section.

(6) In this section—

"specified offence" means—

(*a*) an offence under section 58 of this Act;*

(*b*) attempting to commit, conspiracy to commit or incitement to commit any such offence;

(*c*) *repealed.*

(6A) Proceedings for an offence are instituted—

(*a*) when a justice of the peace issues a summons or warrant under section 1 of the Magistrates' Courts Act 1980 (issue of summons to, or warrant for arrest of, accused) in respect of the offence;*

(*b*) when a person is charged with the offence after being taken into custody without a warrant;

(*c*) when a bill of indictment is preferred under section 2 of the Administration of Justice (Miscellaneous Provisions) Act 1933 in a case falling within paragraph (*b*) of subsection (2) of that section (preferment by direction of the criminal division of the Court of Appeal or by direction, or with the consent, of a High Court judge).

(6B) Where the application of subsection (6A) would result in there being more than one time for the institution of proceedings they must be taken to have been instituted at the earliest of those times.

(7) *Repealed.*

(8) *Repealed.*

[Drug Trafficking Act 1994, s 60 as amended by the Proceeds of Crime Act 2002, Sch 11, the Commissioners for Revenue and Customs Act 2005, Sch 4 and SI 2014/834.]

---

* **Amended by the Criminal Justice Act 2003, Sch 36 from a date to be appointed (and as so amended is subsequently amended by the Criminal Justice and Courts Act 2015, Sch 11.)**

7.8213 **61. Extension of certain offences to Crown servants and exemptions for regulators etc** (1) The Secretary of State may by regulations[1] provide that, in such circumstances as may be prescribed, section 58 of this Act shall apply to such persons in the public service of the Crown, or such categories of person in that service, as may be prescribed.

(2) *Repealed.*

(3) *Repealed.*
(4) *Repealed.*
(5) In this section—
"the Crown" includes the Crown in right of Her Majesty's Government in Northern Ireland; and
"prescribed" means prescribed by regulations made by the Secretary of State.
(6) Any power to make regulations under this section shall be exercisable by statutory instrument.
(7) Any such instrument shall be subject to annulment in pursuance of a resolution of either House of Parliament.

[Drug Trafficking Act 1994, s 61 as amended by the Proceeds of Crime Act 2002, Sch 11.]

---

1 The Drug Trafficking Offences Act 1986 (Crown Servants and Regulators etc) Regulations 1994, SI 1994/1757 amended by SI 2001/3649, have been made and have effect as if made under this Act by virtue of Sch 2.

*Interpretation of Act*

**7.8214 63. General interpretation** (1) *Repealed.*
(2) *Repealed.*
(3) Subject to section 66(2) and (6) of this Act—
(*a*) *repealed*;
(*b*) any reference in this Act to "drug trafficking" includes a reference to drug trafficking carried out before the commencement of this Act.

[Drug Trafficking Act 1994, s 63 as amended by the Proceeds of Crime Act 2002, Sch 11.]

*Supplemental*

**7.8215 65. Consequential amendments and modifications of other Acts** (1) The enactments mentioned in Schedule 1 to this Act shall have effect subject to the amendments there specified (being amendments consequential upon the provisions of this Act).
(2) In section 1(2)(*a*) of the Rehabilitation of Offenders Act 1974 (failure to pay fines etc not to prevent person becoming rehabilitated) the reference to a fine or other sum adjudged to be paid by or imposed on a conviction does not include a reference to an amount payable under a confiscation order.
(3) Section 281(4) of the Insolvency Act 1986 (discharge of bankrupt not to release him from liabilities in respect of fines, etc) shall have effect as if the reference to a fine included a reference to a confiscation order.
(4) Section 55(2) of the Bankruptcy (Scotland) Act 1985 (discharge of debtor not to release him from liabilities in respect of fines etc) shall have effect as if the reference to a fine included a reference to a confiscation order.

[Drug Trafficking Act 1994, s 65.]

**7.8216 66. Transitional provisions and savings** (1) The transitional provisions and savings set out in Schedule 2 to this Act shall have effect.
(2) Part I and section 59 of this Act shall not apply—
(*a*) in relation to any proceedings for, or in respect of, an offence if the person accused (or, as the case may be, convicted) of that offence was charged with the offence (whether by the laying of an information or otherwise) before the date on which this Act comes into force, or
(*b*) in relation to any proceedings not within paragraph (*a*) above instituted before that date,

and references in this subsection to proceedings include a reference to any order made by a court in the proceedings.
(3) Accordingly (and without prejudice to section 16 of the Interpretation Act 1978), the relevant enactments and any instrument made under any of those enactments shall continue to apply in relation to any proceedings within subsection (2)(*a*) or (*b*) above (and, in particular, in relation to any confiscation order, within the meaning of the Drug Trafficking Offences Act 1986, made in any such proceedings) as if this Act had not been passed.
(4) In subsection (3) above "the relevant enactments" are—
(*a*) the enactments reproduced in Part I and section 59 of this Act,
(*b*) any other enactment reproduced by this Act, so far as applicable in relation to any of the enactments reproduced in that Part or that section, and
(*c*) any enactment amended by this Act,

but do not include any enactment which, immediately before the date on which this Act comes into force, had not come into force.
(5) Subsection (2) above is without prejudice to section 4(7), 7(4), 26(3) or 29(7) of this Act.
(6) Nothing in section 19(3) or (4) of this Act shall apply to any proceedings—
(*a*) for an offence committed before the commencement of this Act; or
(*b*) for one or more offences, any one of which was so committed.

[Drug Trafficking Act 1994, s 66.]

**7.8217 67. Repeals etc** (1) The enactments mentioned in Schedule 3 to this Act are repealed to the extent specified in the third column of that Schedule.

(2) *Northern Ireland.*

[Drug Trafficking Act 1994, s 67.]

7.8218 **68. Extent** (1) Subject to the following provisions of this section, this Act extends to England and Wales only.

(2) The following provisions of this Act also extend to Scotland—

(*a*) *repealed;*

(*b*) *repealed;*

(*c*) *repealed;*

(*d*) section 59(11) to (13);

(*e*) this section;

(*f*) section 69;

(*g*) sections 63, 65(1), 66 and 67(1), so far as they relate to provisions which extend to Scotland; and

(*h*) Schedule 2.

(3) The following provisions of this Act also extend to Northern Ireland—

(*a*) *repealed;*

(*b*) this section;

(*c*) section 69;

(*d*) sections 63, 65(1), 66 and 67(1), so far as they relate to provisions which extend to Northern Ireland; and

(*e*) Schedule 2.

(4) Section 67(2) of this Act extends to Northern Ireland only.

(5) The modifications of other enactments specified in section 65(2) to (4) of this Act, and the amendments specified in Schedule 1 to this Act, have the same extent as the enactments to which they relate.

(6) Subject to subsection (7) below, the repeals contained in Schedule 3 to this Act have the same extent as the provisions to which they relate.

(7) The repeals of—

(*a*) sections 14 and 23A of the Criminal Justice (International Co-operation) Act 1990, and

(*b*) paragraph 5 of Schedule 4 to the Criminal Justice Act 1993,

extend to England and Wales only.

[Drug Trafficking Act 1994, s 68 as amended by the Proceeds of Crime Act 2002, Sch 11.]

# Health Act 1999

(1999 c 8)

*Supplementary*

7.8219 **62. Regulations and orders**[1]

[1] The Nursing and Midwifery Order 2001, SI 2002/253 amended by SI 2004/1947, SI 2007/3101, SI 2008/1485, SI 2009/1182, SI 2013/235, SI 2014/1887 and 3272 and SI 2016/1030 provides for the regulation of nurses and midwives and creates a regulatory body, the Nursing and Midwifery Council, which is required to set standards of education, training, conduct and performance and to put in place arrangements to ensure that they are met. Certain offences are created by arts 44 and 45 punishable on summary conviction by a fine not exceeding **level 3** on the standard scale. These are, principally, where a person falsely represents himself as being registered or having professional qualifications or uses a title to which he is not entitled; or, although not falling within the specified categories, attends a woman in childbirth. Transitional provisions are made by the Nursing and Midwifery Order 2001 (Transitional Provisions) Order 2002, SI 2002/1125 and the Nursing and Midwifery Order 2001 (Transitional Provisions) Order 2004, SI 2004/1762. A number of Orders of Council have been made under SI 2002/253 which regulate the professions of nursing and midwifery, the subject matter of which is outside the scope of this Manual.

The Health and Social Work Professions Order 2001, SI 2002/254 amended by SI 2004/1947, SI 2007/3101, SI 2009/1182, SI 2010/233, Health and Social Care Act 2012, s 213(4) and (6), SI 2012/1479 and 2672, SI 2013/235, SI 2014/1887 and SI 2016/1030 provides for the regulation of a number of health professions (arts therapists; chiropodists; clinical scientists; dietitians; medical laboratory technicians; occupational therapists; orthoptists; paramedics; physiotherapists; prosthetists and orthotists; radiographers; and speech, language therapists and dispensers of hearing aids) it creates a regulatory body, the Health Professions Council, which is required to set standards of education, training, conduct and performance and to put in place arrangements to ensure that they are met. Article 39 provides for certain actions to be offences punishable on summary conviction by a fine not exceeding **level 5** on the standard scale. These are, principally, where a person falsely represents himself as being registered or having professional qualifications or uses a title to which he is not entitled. Transitional provisions are made by the Health Professions Order 2001 (Transitional Provisions) Order 2002, SI 2002/1124. The Pharmacy Order 2010, SI 2010/231 has been made, in this title, post, which makes provision for the regulation of pharmacists and pharmacy technicians. Regulation of health professionals was reformed by the 1999 Act and in accordance with the proposals of the White Paper – *Trust, Assurance and Safety: the Regulation of Health Professionals in the 21st Century*. In particular the 2010 Order establishes a new regulator for pharmacy to separate this function from that of professional leadership. The Order sets out the general duties and structure of the General Pharmaceutical Council and implements in part Council Directive 2005/36/EC on the recognition of professional qualifications. Part 3 makes provision for the inspection of registered pharmacies by inspectors appointed by the Council to ensure compliance with standards by the Council. Inspectors have powers to enter, search and remove items from premises (arts 10 and 11); intentional obstruction is an offence (art 12). Failure to comply with standards may result in service of an improvement (art 13) non-compliance with which is an offence (art 14) with a right of appeal to a magistrates' court against an improvement notice (arts 16 and 17).

Summary offences are created in relation to the Register of Pharmacists including provision for time limits for institution of such proceedings (art 38).

**7.8220 63. Supplementary and consequential provision etc** *Secretary of State may by order[1] make supplementary, incidental or consequential provision.*

[1] The Health Authorities Act 1995 (Rectification of Transitional Arrangements) Order 2000, SI 2000/179 has been made.

*Final provisions*

**7.8221 67. Commencement** (1) The preceding provisions of this Act (including the Schedules) are to come into force on such day as the Secretary of State may by order[1] appoint.

(2) Different days may be appointed under this section for different purposes.

(3) Subsection (1) does not apply to the repeal of section 10 of the Professions Supplementary to Medicine Act 1960 (power to extend or restrict application of Act), which comes into force on 1st July 1999 or, if later, on the day on which this Act is passed.

(4) Subsection (1) does not apply to section 66, of which—

(*a*) subsections (1) and (3) to (6) come into force on the day on which this Act is passed,

(*b*) subsection (2) comes into force on 1st July 1999 or, if later, the day on which this Act is passed.

[Health Act 1999, s 67.]

[1] At the date of going to press the following commencement orders relating to England and Wales had been made: Health Act 1999 (Commencement No 1) Order 1999, SI 1999/2177, Health Act 1999 (Commencement No 2) Order 1999, SI 1999/2342, Health Act 1999 (Commencement No 3) Order 1999, SI 1999/2540, Health Act 1999 (Commencement No 4) Order 1999, SI 1999/90, Health Act 1999 (Commencement No 5) Order 1999, SI 1999/2793, the Health Act 1999 (Commencement No 8) Order 2000, SI 2000/779, and the Health Act 1999 (Commencement No 9) Order 2000, SI 2000/1041; Health Act 1999 (Commencement No 1) (Wales) Order 1999, SI 1999/3184; Health Act 1999 (Commencement No 3) (Wales) Order 2000, SI 2000/2991; Health Act 1999 (Commencement No 10) Order 2001, SI 2001/270; Health Act 1999 (Commencement No 11) Order 2001, SI 2001/1985; Health Act 1999 (Commencement No 12) Order 2002, SI 2002/1167; Health Act 1999 (Commencement No 13) Order 2003, SI 2003/1689; Health Act 1999 (Commencement No 14) Order 2004, SI 2004/289; Health Act 1999 (Commencement No 15) Order 2004, SI 2004/1859; Health Act 1999 (Commencement No 16) Order 2007, SI 2007/1179. All the provisions set out in this work were brought into force no later than 4 January 2000.

**7.8222 68. Extent** (1) Subject to the following provisions—

(*a*) *repealed,*

(*b*) *Scotland*, and

(*c*) this Part extends to Northern Ireland (as well as to England and Wales and Scotland).

(2) The amendment or repeal of an enactment, or a power to amend or repeal an enactment, which extends to any part of the United Kingdom extends also to that part.

(3) Sections 22 and 25 extend to Scotland and Northern Ireland.

(4) *Repealed.*

(5) The Secretary of State may by order provide that so much of this Act as extends to England and Wales is to apply to the Isles of Scilly with such modifications (if any) as are specified in the order; but otherwise this Act does not extend there.

[Health Act 1999, s 68 as amended by the National Health Service (Consequential Provisions) Act 2006, Sch 4.]

**7.8223 69. Short title** This Act may be cited as the Health Act 1999.

[Health Act 1999, s 69.]

# Human Tissue Act 2004[1]

(2004 c 30)

## Part 1[2]

## Removal, Storage and Use of Human Organs and Other Tissue for Scheduled Purposes

**7.8224 1. Authorisation of activities for scheduled purposes** (1) The following activities shall be lawful if done with appropriate consent—

(*a*) the storage of the body of a deceased person for use for a purpose specified in Schedule 1, other than anatomical examination;

(*b*) the use of the body of a deceased person for a purpose so specified, other than anatomical examination;

(*c*) the removal from the body of a deceased person, for use for a purpose specified in Schedule 1, of any relevant material of which the body consists or which it contains;

(*d*) the storage for use for a purpose specified in Part 1 of Schedule 1 of any relevant material which has come from a human body;

(*e*) the storage for use for a purpose specified in Part 2 of Schedule 1 of any relevant material which has come from the body of a deceased person;

(*f*) the use for a purpose specified in Part 1 of Schedule 1 of any relevant material which has come from a human body;

(*g*) the use for a purpose specified in Part 2 of Schedule 1 of any relevant material which has come from the body of a deceased person.

(1A) *Repealed.*

(2) The storage of the body of a deceased person for use for the purpose of anatomical examination shall be lawful if done—

(*a*) with appropriate consent, and

(*b*) after the signing of a certificate—

(i) under section 22(1) of the Births and Deaths Registration Act 1953 (c 20), or

(ii) under Article 25(2) of the Births and Deaths Registration (Northern Ireland) Order 1976 (SI 1976/1041 (NI 14)),

of the cause of death of the person.*

(3) The use of the body of a deceased person for the purpose of anatomical examination shall be lawful if done—

(*a*) with appropriate consent, and

(*b*) after the death of the person has been registered—

(i) under section 15 of the Births and Deaths Registration Act 1953, or

(ii) under Article 21 of the Births and Deaths Registration (Northern Ireland) Order 1976.

(4) Subsections (1) to (3) do not apply to an activity of a kind mentioned there if it is done in relation to—

(*a*) a body to which subsection (5) applies, or

(*b*) relevant material to which subsection (6) applies.

(5) This subsection applies to a body if—

(*a*) it has been imported, or

(*b*) it is the body of a person who died before the day on which this section comes into force and at least one hundred years have elapsed since the date of the person's death.

(6) This subsection applies to relevant material if—

(*a*) it has been imported,

(*b*) it has come from a body which has been imported, or

(*c*) it is material which has come from the body of a person who died before the day on which this section comes into force and at least one hundred years have elapsed since the date of the person's death.

(7) Subsection (1)(*d*) does not apply to the storage of relevant material for use for the purpose of research in connection with disorders, or the functioning, of the human body if—

(*a*) the material has come from the body of a living person, and

(*b*) the research falls within subsection (9).

(8) Subsection (1)(*f*) does not apply to the use of relevant material for the purpose of research in connection with disorders, or the functioning, of the human body if—

(*a*) the material has come from the body of a living person, and

(*b*) the research falls within subsection (9).

(9) Research falls within this subsection if—

(*a*) it is ethically approved in accordance with regulations[3] made by the Secretary of State, and

(*b*) it is to be, or is, carried out in circumstances such that the person carrying it out is not in possession, and not likely to come into possession, of information from which the person from whose body the material has come can be identified.

(9A) Subsection (1)(*f*) does not apply to the use of relevant material for the purpose of research where the use of the material requires consent under paragraph 6(1) or 12(1) of Schedule 3 to the Human Fertilisation and Embryology Act 1990 (use of human cells to create an embryo or a human admixed embryo) or would require such consent but for paragraphs 16 and 20 of that Schedule.

(9B) Subsection (1) does not apply in relation to—

(*a*) transplantation activities done in Wales; or

(*b*) transplantation activities done outside Wales in relation to relevant material that was removed from a human body in Wales.

(10) The following activities shall be lawful—

(*a*) the storage for use for a purpose specified in Part 2 of Schedule 1 of any relevant material which has come from the body of a living person;

(*b*) the use for such a purpose of any relevant material which has come from the body of a living person;

(*c*) an activity in relation to which subsection (4), (7), (8) or (9B)(*b*) has effect.

(10A) In the case of an activity in relation to which subsection (8) has effect, subsection (10)(*c*) is to be read subject to any requirements imposed by Schedule 3 to the Human Fertilisation and Embryology Act 1990 in relation to the activity.

(11) The Secretary of State may by order—

(*a*) vary or omit any of the purposes specified in Part 1 or 2 of Schedule 1, or

(*b*) add to the purposes specified in Part 1 or 2 of that Schedule.

(12) Nothing in this section applies to—

(*a*) the use of relevant material in connection with a device to which Directive 98/79/EC of the European Parliament and of the Council on *in vitro* diagnostic medical devices applies, where the use falls within the Directive, or

(*b*) the storage of relevant material for use falling within paragraph (*a*).

(13) In this section, the references to a body or material which has been imported do not include a body or material which has been imported after having been exported with a view to its subsequently being re-imported.

(14) In this section "transplantation activities" has the same meaning as in the Human Transplantation (Wales) Act 2013 (which makes provision in relation to consent for transplantation activities done in Wales).

[Human Tissue Act 2004, s 1 as amended by the Human Fertilisation and Embryology Act 2008, Sch 7, the Human Transplantation (Wales) Act 2013, s 16 and SI 2015/865.]

---

* **Sub-s (2) amended by the Coroners and Justice Act 2009, Sch 21 from a date to be appointed.**

1 The Act provides a legislative framework for body donation and the taking, storage and use of human organs and tissue, and makes consent the fundamental principle underpinning these activities.

The Act sets up an authority the aim of which is to rationalise such activities as transplantation and anatomical examination, and it will regulate other activities such as post mortem examinations and the storage of human material for education, training and research.

The Act is in 3 Parts and has 7 Schedules.

The following commencement orders have been made: Human Tissue Act 2004 (Commencement No 1) Order 2005, SI 2005/919; Human Tissue Act 2004 (Commencement No 2) Order 2005, SI 2005/2632; Human Tissue Act 2004 (Commencement No 3 and Transitional Provisions) Order 2005, SI 2005/2792; Human Tissue Act 2004 (Commencement No 4 and Transitional Provisions) Order 2006, SI 2006/404; and Human Tissue Act 2004 (Commencement No 5 and Transitional Provisions) Order 2006, SI 2006/1997. The Act is fully in force.

2 Part 1 contains ss 1–12.

3 The Human Tissue Act 2004 (Ethical Approval, Exceptions from Licensing and Supply of Information about Transplants) Regulations 2006, SI 2006/1260 amended by SI 2008/3067, SI 2012/1809 and SI 2014/1459 have been made.

**7.8225 2. "Appropriate consent": children** (1) This section makes provision for the interpretation of "appropriate consent" in section 1 in relation to an activity involving the body, or material from the body, of a person who is a child or has died a child ("the child concerned").

(2) Subject to subsection (3), where the child concerned is alive, "appropriate consent" means his consent.

(3) Where—

(*a*) the child concerned is alive,

(*b*) neither a decision of his to consent to the activity, nor a decision of his not to consent to it, is in force, and

(*c*) either he is not competent to deal with the issue of consent in relation to the activity or, though he is competent to deal with that issue, he fails to do so,

"appropriate consent" means the consent of a person who has parental responsibility for him.

(4) Where the child concerned has died and the activity is one to which subsection (5) applies, "appropriate consent" means his consent in writing.

(5) This subsection applies to an activity involving storage for use, or use, for the purpose of—

(*a*) public display, or

(*b*) where the subject-matter of the activity is not excepted material, anatomical examination.

(6) Consent in writing for the purposes of subsection (4) is only valid if—

(*a*) it is signed by the child concerned in the presence of at least one witness who attests the signature, or

(*b*) it is signed at the direction of the child concerned, in his presence and in the presence of at least one witness who attests the signature.

(7) Where the child concerned has died and the activity is not one to which subsection (5) applies, "appropriate consent" means—

(*a*) if a decision of his to consent to the activity, or a decision of his not to consent to it, was in force immediately before he died, his consent;

(*b*) if paragraph (*a*) does not apply—

(i) the consent of a person who had parental responsibility for him immediately before he died, or

(ii) where no person had parental responsibility for him immediately before he died, the consent of a person who stood in a qualifying relationship to him at that time.

[Human Tissue Act 2004, s 2.]

**7.8226 3. "Appropriate consent": adults** (1) This section makes provision for the interpretation of "appropriate consent" in section 1 in relation to an activity involving the body, or material from the body, of a person who is an adult or has died an adult ("the person concerned").

(2) Where the person concerned is alive, "appropriate consent" means his consent.

(3) Where the person concerned has died and the activity is one to which subsection (4) applies, "appropriate consent" means his consent in writing.

(4) This subsection applies to an activity involving storage for use, or use, for the purpose of—

(*a*) public display, or

(*b*) where the subject-matter of the activity is not excepted material, anatomical examination.

(5) Consent in writing for the purposes of subsection (3) is only valid if—

(*a*) it is signed by the person concerned in the presence of at least one witness who attests the signature,

(*b*) it is signed at the direction of the person concerned, in his presence and in the presence of at least one witness who attests the signature, or

(*c*) it is contained in a will of the person concerned made in accordance with the requirements of—

(i) section 9 of the Wills Act 1837 (c 26), or

(ii) Article 5 of the Wills and Administration Proceedings (Northern Ireland) Order 1994 (SI 1994/1899 (NI 13)).

(6) Where the person concerned has died and the activity is not one to which subsection (4) applies, "appropriate consent" means—

(*a*) if a decision of his to consent to the activity, or a decision of his not to consent to it, was in force immediately before he died, his consent;

(*b*) if—

(i) paragraph (*a*) does not apply, and

(ii) he has appointed a person or persons under section 4 to deal after his death with the issue of consent in relation to the activity,

consent given under the appointment;

(*c*) if neither paragraph (*a*) nor paragraph (*b*) applies, the consent of a person who stood in a qualifying relationship to him immediately before he died.

(7) Where the person concerned has appointed a person or persons under section 4 to deal after his death with the issue of consent in relation to the activity, the appointment shall be disregarded for the purposes of subsection (6) if no one is able to give consent under it.

(8) If it is not reasonably practicable to communicate with a person appointed under section 4 within the time available if consent in relation to the activity is to be acted on, he shall be treated for the purposes of subsection (7) as not able to give consent under the appointment in relation to it.

[Human Tissue Act 2004, s 3.]

7.8227 4. **Nominated representatives** (1) An adult may appoint one or more persons to represent him after his death in relation to consent for the purposes of section 1.

(2) An appointment under this section may be general or limited to consent in relation to such one or more activities as may be specified in the appointment.

(3) An appointment under this section may be made orally or in writing.

(4) An oral appointment under this section is only valid if made in the presence of at least two witnesses present at the same time.

(5) A written appointment under this section is only valid if—

(*a*) it is signed by the person making it in the presence of at least one witness who attests the signature,

(*b*) it is signed at the direction of the person making it, in his presence and in the presence of at least one witness who attests the signature, or

(*c*) it is contained in a will of the person making it, being a will which is made in accordance with the requirements of—

(i) section 9 of the Wills Act 1837 (c 26), or

(ii) Article 5 of the Wills and Administration Proceedings (Northern Ireland) Order 1994 (SI 1994/1899 (NI 13)).

(6) Where a person appoints two or more persons under this section in relation to the same activity, they shall be regarded as appointed to act jointly and severally unless the appointment provides that they are appointed to act jointly.

(7) An appointment under this section may be revoked at any time.

(8) Subsections (3) to (5) apply to the revocation of an appointment under this section as they apply to the making of such an appointment.

(9) A person appointed under this section may at any time renounce his appointment.

(10) A person may not act under an appointment under this section if—

(*a*) he is not an adult, or

(*b*) he is of a description prescribed for the purposes of this provision by regulations made by the Secretary of State.

(11) Where an adult has appointed a person under section 8 of the Human Transplantation (Wales) Act 2013 to represent the adult after death in relation to consent for one or more transplantation activities, the adult is to be treated as also having appointed the person under this section in relation to those activities.

[Human Tissue Act 2004, s 4 as amended by SI 2015/865.]

7.8228 5. **Prohibition of activities without consent etc** (1) A person commits an offence if, without appropriate consent, he does an activity to which subsection (1), (2) or (3) of section 1 applies, unless he reasonably believes—

(*a*) that he does the activity with appropriate consent, or

(*b*) that what he does is not an activity to which the subsection applies.

(2) A person commits an offence if—

(*a*) he falsely represents to a person whom he knows or believes is going to, or may, do an activity to which subsection (1), (2) or (3) of section 1 applies—
(i) that there is appropriate consent to the doing of the activity, or
(ii) that the activity is not one to which the subsection applies, and
(*b*) he knows that the representation is false or does not believe it to be true.

(3) Subject to subsection (4), a person commits an offence if, when he does an activity to which section 1(2) applies, neither of the following has been signed in relation to the cause of death of the person concerned—
(*a*) a certificate under section 22(1) of the Births and Deaths Registration Act 1953 (c 20), and
(*b*) a certificate under Article 25(2) of the Births and Deaths Registration (Northern Ireland) Order 1976 (SI 1976/1041 (NI 14)).

(4) Subsection (3) does not apply—
(*a*) where the person reasonably believes—
(i) that a certificate under either of those provisions has been signed in relation to the cause of death of the person concerned, or
(ii) that what he does is not an activity to which section 1(2) applies, or
(*b*) where the person comes into lawful possession of the body immediately after death and stores it prior to its removal to a place where anatomical examination is to take place.

(5) Subject to subsection (6), a person commits an offence if, when he does an activity to which section 1(3) applies, the death of the person concerned has not been registered under either of the following provisions—
(*a*) section 15 of the Births and Deaths Registration Act 1953, and
(*b*) Article 21 of the Births and Deaths Registration (Northern Ireland) Order 1976.

(6) Subsection (5) does not apply where the person reasonably believes—
(*a*) that the death of the person concerned has been registered under either of those provisions, or
(*b*) that what he does is not an activity to which section 1(3) applies.

(7) A person guilty of an offence under this section shall be liable—
(*a*) on summary conviction to a fine not exceeding the statutory maximum;
(*b*) on conviction on indictment—
(i) to imprisonment for a term not exceeding 3 years, or
(ii) to a fine, or
(iii) to both.

(8) In this section, "appropriate consent" has the same meaning as in section 1.*

[Human Tissue Act 2004, s 5.]

* **Amended by the Coroners and Justice Act 2009, Sch 21 from a date to be appointed.**

**7.8229 6. Activities involving material from adults who lack capacity to consent**

(1) Where—
(*a*) an activity of a kind mentioned in section 1(1)(*d*) or (*f*) involves material from the body of a person who—
(i) is an adult, and
(ii) lacks capacity to consent to the activity, and
(*b*) neither a decision of his to consent to the activity, nor a decision of his not to consent to it, is in force,

there shall for the purposes of this Part be deemed to be consent of his to the activity if it is done in circumstances of a kind specified by regulations[1] made by the Secretary of State.

(2) This section does not apply in relation to transplantation activities done in Wales.

(For provision in these circumstances see section 9 of the Human Transplantation (Wales) Act 2013).

[Human Tissue Act 2004, s 6 as amended by the Human Transplantation (Wales) Act 2013, s 16.]

1 The Human Tissue Act 2004 (Persons who Lack Capacity to Consent and Transplants) Regulations 2006, SI 2006/1659 have been made.

**7.8230 7. Powers to dispense with need for consent** (1) If the Authority is satisfied—
(*a*) that relevant material has come from the body of a living person,
(*b*) that it is not reasonably possible to trace the person from whose body the material has come ("the donor"),
(*c*) that it is desirable in the interests of another person (including a future person) that the material be used for the purpose of obtaining scientific or medical information about the donor, and
(*d*) that there is no reason to believe—
(i) that the donor has died,
(ii) that a decision of the donor to refuse to consent to the use of the material for that purpose is in force, or

(iii) that the donor lacks capacity to consent to the use of the material for that purpose,

it may direct that subsection (3) apply to the material for the benefit of the other person.

(2) If the Authority is satisfied—

(*a*) that relevant material has come from the body of a living person,

(*b*) that it is desirable in the interests of another person (including a future person) that the material be used for the purpose of obtaining scientific or medical information about the person from whose body the material has come ("the donor"),

(*c*) that reasonable efforts have been made to get the donor to decide whether to consent to the use of the material for that purpose,

(*d*) that there is no reason to believe—

(i) that the donor has died,

(ii) that a decision of the donor to refuse to consent to the use of the material for that purpose is in force, or

(iii) that the donor lacks capacity to consent to the use of the material for that purpose, and

(*e*) that the donor has been given notice of the application for the exercise of the power conferred by this subsection,

it may direct that subsection (3) apply to the material for the benefit of the other person.

(3) Where material is the subject of a direction under subsection (1) or (2), there shall for the purposes of this Part be deemed to be consent of the donor to the use of the material for the purpose of obtaining scientific or medical information about him which may be relevant to the person for whose benefit the direction is given.

(4) The Secretary of State may by regulations enable the High Court, in such circumstances as the regulations may provide, to make an order deeming there for the purposes of this Part to be appropriate consent to an activity consisting of—

(*a*) the storage of the body of a deceased person for use for the purpose of research in connection with disorders, or the functioning, of the human body,

(*b*) the use of the body of a deceased person for that purpose,

(*c*) the removal from the body of a deceased person, for use for that purpose, of any relevant material of which the body consists or which it contains,

(*d*) the storage for use for that purpose of any relevant material which has come from a human body, or

(*e*) the use for that purpose of any relevant material which has come from a human body.

[Human Tissue Act 2004, s 7.]

7.8231 **8. Restriction of activities in relation to donated material** (1) Subject to subsection (2), a person commits an offence if he—

(*a*) uses donated material for a purpose which is not a qualifying purpose, or

(*b*) stores donated material for use for a purpose which is not a qualifying purpose.

(2) Subsection (1) does not apply where the person reasonably believes that what he uses, or stores, is not donated material.

(3) A person guilty of an offence under this section shall be liable—

(*a*) on summary conviction to a fine not exceeding the statutory maximum;

(*b*) on conviction on indictment—

(i) to imprisonment for a term not exceeding 3 years, or

(ii) to a fine, or

(iii) to both.

(4) In subsection (1), references to a qualifying purpose are to—

(*a*) a purpose specified in Schedule 1,

(*b*) the purpose of medical diagnosis or treatment,

(*c*) the purpose of decent disposal, or

(*d*) a purpose specified in regulations made by the Secretary of State.

(5) In this section, references to donated material are to—

(*a*) the body of a deceased person, or

(*b*) relevant material which has come from a human body,

which is, or has been, the subject of donation.

(6) For the purposes of subsection (5), a body, or material, is the subject of donation if authority under section 1(1) to (3) or section 3(1) to (3) of the Human Transplantation (Wales) Act 2013 exists in relation to it.

[Human Tissue Act 2004, s 8 as amended by the Human Transplantation (Wales) Act 2013, s 16.]

7.8232 **9. Existing holdings** (1) In its application to the following activities, section 1(1) shall have effect with the omission of the words "if done with appropriate consent"—

(*a*) the storage of an existing holding for use for a purpose specified in Schedule 1;

(*b*) the use of an existing holding for a purpose so specified.

(2) Subsection (1) does not apply where the existing holding is a body, or separated part of a

body, in relation to which section 10(3) or (5) has effect.

(3) Section 5(1) and (2) shall have effect as if the activities mentioned in subsection (1) were not activities to which section 1(1) applies.

(4) In this section, "existing holding" means—

(*a*) the body of a deceased person, or

(*b*) relevant material which has come from a human body,

held, immediately before the day on which section 1(1) comes into force, for use for a purpose specified in Schedule 1.

[Human Tissue Act 2004, s 9.]

7.8233 **10. Existing anatomical specimens** (1) This section applies where a person dies during the three years immediately preceding the coming into force of section 1.

(2) Subsection (3) applies where—

(*a*) before section 1 comes into force, authority is given under section 4(2) or (3) of the Anatomy Act 1984 (c 14) for the person's body to be used for anatomical examination, and

(*b*) section 1 comes into force before anatomical examination of the person's body is concluded.

(3) During so much of the relevant period as falls after section 1 comes into force, that authority shall be treated for the purposes of section 1 as appropriate consent in relation to—

(*a*) the storage of the person's body, or separated parts of his body, for use for the purpose of anatomical examination, and

(*b*) the use of his body, or separated parts of his body, for that purpose.

(4) Subsection (5) applies where—

(*a*) before section 1 comes into force, authority is given under section 6(2) or (3) of the Anatomy Act 1984 for possession of parts (or any specified parts) of the person's body to be held after anatomical examination of his body is concluded, and

(*b*) anatomical examination of the person's body is concluded—

(i) after section 1 comes into force, but

(ii) before the end of the period of three years beginning with the date of the person's death.

(5) With effect from the conclusion of the anatomical examination of the person's body, that authority shall be treated for the purposes of section 1 as appropriate consent in relation to—

(*a*) the storage for use for a qualifying purpose of a part of the person's body which—

(i) is a part to which that authority relates, and

(ii) is such that the person cannot be recognised simply by examination of the part, and

(*b*) the use for a qualifying purpose of such a part of the person's body.

(6) Where for the purposes of section 1 there would not be appropriate consent in relation to an activity but for authority given under the Anatomy Act 1984 (c 14) being treated for those purposes as appropriate consent in relation to the activity, section 1(1) to (3) do not authorise the doing of the activity otherwise than in accordance with that authority.

(7) In subsection (3), "the relevant period", in relation to a person, means whichever is the shorter of—

(*a*) the period of three years beginning with the date of the person's death, and

(*b*) the period beginning with that date and ending when anatomical examination of the person's body is concluded.

(8) In subsection (5), "qualifying purpose" means a purpose specified in paragraph 6 or 9 of Schedule 1.

(9) The Secretary of State may by order amend subsection (8).

[Human Tissue Act 2004, s 10.]

7.8234 **11. Coroners** (1) Nothing in this Part applies to anything done for purposes of functions of a coroner or under the authority of a coroner.

(2) Where a person knows, or has reason to believe, that—

(*a*) the body of a deceased person, or

(*b*) relevant material which has come from the body of a deceased person,

is, or may be, required for purposes of functions of a coroner, he shall not act on authority under section 1 in relation to the body, or material, except with the consent of the coroner.

[Human Tissue Act 2004, s 11.]

7.8235 **12. Interpretation of Part 1** In this Part, "excepted material" means material which has—

(*a*) come from the body of a living person, or

(*b*) come from the body of a deceased person otherwise than in the course of use of the body for the purpose of anatomical examination.

[Human Tissue Act 2004, s 12.]

## Part 2[1]
## Regulation of Activities Involving Human Tissue

### *The Human Tissue Authority*

7.8236 **13. The Human Tissue Authority** (1) There shall be a body corporate to be known as the Human Tissue Authority (referred to in this Act as "the Authority").

(2) Schedule 2 (which makes further provision about the Authority) has effect.

[Human Tissue Act 2004, s 13.]

---

1 Part 2 contains ss 13–41. Part 2 creates a body corporate known as the Human Tissue Authority and a licensing regime to regulate: anatomical and post mortem examinations; the removal of material and organs from deceased bodies; the storage of anatomical specimens, bodies and relevant material; and the use for public display of deceased persons and material from the bodies of deceased persons.

7.8237 **14, 15.** *Remit and general functions of the Human Tissue Authority.*

### *Licensing*

7.8238 **16. Licence requirement** (1) No person shall do an activity to which this section applies otherwise than under the authority of a licence granted for the purposes of this section.

(2) This section applies to the following activities—

(*a*) the carrying-out of an anatomical examination;

(*b*) the making of a post-mortem examination;

(*c*) the removal from the body of a deceased person (otherwise than in the course of an activity mentioned in paragraph (*a*) or (*b*)) of relevant material of which the body consists or which it contains, for use for a scheduled purpose other than transplantation;

(*d*) the storage of an anatomical specimen;

(*e*) the storage (in any case not falling within paragraph (*d*)) of—

(i) the body of a deceased person, or

(ii) relevant material which has come from a human body,

for use for a scheduled purpose;

(*f*) the use, for the purpose of public display, of—

(i) the body of a deceased person, or

(ii) relevant material which has come from the body of a deceased person.

(2A) This section does not apply to the procurement, testing, processing, preservation, storage, distribution, import or export of tissue and cells intended for human application in so far as those activities are activities to which regulation 7(1) or (2) of the 2007 Regulations applies.

(2B) Expressions used in subsection (2A) and in the 2007 Regulations have the same meaning in that subsection as in those Regulations; and the reference to activities to which regulation 7(1) or (2) of those Regulations applies is to be read subject to regulation 2(3) of those Regulations.

(3) The Secretary of State may by regulations[1] specify circumstances in which storage of relevant material by a person who intends to use it for a scheduled purpose is excepted from subsection (2)(*e*)(ii).

(4) An activity is excluded from subsection (2) if—

(*a*) it relates to the body of a person who died before the day on which this section comes into force or to material which has come from the body of such a person, and

(*b*) at least one hundred years have elapsed since the date of the person's death.

(5) The Secretary of State may by regulations amend this section for the purpose of—

(*a*) adding to the activities to which this section applies,

(*b*) removing an activity from the activities to which this section applies, or

(*c*) altering the description of an activity to which this section applies.

(6) Schedule 3 (which makes provision about licences for the purposes of this section) has effect.

(7) In subsection (2)—

(*a*) references to storage do not include storage which is incidental to transportation, and

(*b*) "relevant material", in relation to use for the scheduled purpose of transplantation, does not include blood or anything derived from blood.

[Human Tissue Act 2004, s 16 as amended by SI 2007/1523.]

---

1 The Human Tissue Act 2004 (Ethical Approval, Exceptions from Licensing and Supply of Information about Transplants) Regulations 2006, SI 2006/1260 (for amending instruments, see the note to s 1, ante).

7.8239 **17. Persons to whom licence applies** The authority conferred by a licence extends to—

(*a*) the designated individual,

(*b*) any person who is designated as a person to whom the licence applies by a notice given to the Authority by the designated individual, and

(*c*) any person acting under the direction of—

(i) the designated individual, or

(ii) a person designated as mentioned in paragraph (*b*).

[Human Tissue Act 2004, s 17.]

7.8240 **18. Duty of the designated individual** It shall be the duty of the individual designated in a licence as the person under whose supervision the licensed activity is authorised to be carried on to secure—

(*a*) that the other persons to whom the licence applies are suitable persons to participate in the carrying-on of the licensed activity,

(*b*) that suitable practices are used in the course of carrying on that activity, and

(*c*) that the conditions of the licence are complied with.

[Human Tissue Act 2004, s 18.]

7.8241 **25. Breach of licence requirement** (1) A person who contravenes section 16(1) commits an offence, unless he reasonably believes—

(*a*) that what he does is not an activity to which section 16 applies, or

(*b*) that he acts under the authority of a licence.

(2) A person guilty of an offence under subsection (1) shall be liable—

(*a*) on summary conviction to a fine not exceeding the statutory maximum;

(*b*) on conviction on indictment—

(i) to imprisonment for a term not exceeding 3 years, or

(ii) to a fine, or

(iii) to both.

[Human Tissue Act 2004, s 25.]

*Anatomy*

7.8242 **30. Possession of anatomical specimens away from licensed premises** (1) Subject to subsections (2) to (6), a person commits an offence if—

(*a*) he has possession of an anatomical specimen, and

(*b*) the specimen is not on premises in respect of which an anatomy licence is in force.

(2) Subsection (1) does not apply where—

(*a*) the specimen has come from premises in respect of which a storage licence is in force, and

(*b*) the person—

(i) is authorised in writing by the designated individual to have possession of the specimen, and

(ii) has possession of the specimen only for a purpose for which he is so authorised to have possession of it.

(3) Subsection (1) does not apply where—

(*a*) the specimen is the body of a deceased person which is to be used for the purpose of anatomical examination,

(*b*) the person who has possession of the body has come into lawful possession of it immediately after the deceased's death, and

(*c*) he retains possession of the body prior to its removal to premises in respect of which an anatomy licence is in force.

(4) Subsection (1) does not apply where the person has possession of the specimen only for the purpose of transporting it to premises—

(*a*) in respect of which an anatomy licence is in force, or

(*b*) where the specimen is to be used for the purpose of education, training or research.

(5) Subsection (1) does not apply where the person has possession of the specimen for purposes of functions of, or under the authority of, a coroner.

(6) Subsection (1) does not apply where the person reasonably believes—

(*a*) that what he has possession of is not an anatomical specimen,

(*b*) that the specimen is on premises in respect of which an anatomy licence is in force, or

(*c*) that any of subsections (2) to (5) applies.

(7) A person guilty of an offence under subsection (1) shall be liable—

(*a*) on summary conviction to a fine not exceeding the statutory maximum;

(*b*) on conviction on indictment—

(i) to imprisonment for a term not exceeding 3 years, or

(ii) to a fine, or

(iii) to both.

(8) In this section—

"anatomy licence" means a licence authorising—

(*a*) the carrying-out of an anatomical examination, or

(*b*) the storage of anatomical specimens;

"storage licence" means a licence authorising the storage of anatomical specimens.

[Human Tissue Act 2004, s 30.]

7.8243 **31. Possession of former anatomical specimens away from licensed premises** (1) Subject to subsections (2) to (5), a person commits an offence if—

(*a*) he has possession of a former anatomical specimen, and

(*b*) the specimen is not on premises in respect of which a storage licence is in force.

(2) Subsection (1) does not apply where—

(*a*) the specimen has come from premises in respect of which a storage licence is in force, and

(*b*) the person—

(i) is authorised in writing by the designated individual to have possession of the specimen, and

(ii) has possession of the specimen only for a purpose for which he is so authorised to have possession of it.

(3) Subsection (1) does not apply where the person has possession of the specimen only for the purpose of transporting it to premises—

(*a*) in respect of which a storage licence is in force, or

(*b*) where the specimen is to be used for the purpose of education, training or research.

(4) Subsection (1) does not apply where the person has possession of the specimen—

(*a*) only for the purpose of its decent disposal, or

(*b*) for purposes of functions of, or under the authority of, a coroner.

(5) Subsection (1) does not apply where the person reasonably believes—

(*a*) that what he has possession of is not a former anatomical specimen,

(*b*) that the specimen is on premises in respect of which a storage licence is in force, or

(*c*) that any of subsections (2) to (4) applies.

(6) A person guilty of an offence under subsection (1) shall be liable—

(*a*) on summary conviction to a fine not exceeding the statutory maximum;

(*b*) on conviction on indictment—

(i) to imprisonment for a term not exceeding 3 years, or

(ii) to a fine, or

(iii) to both.

(7) In this section, "storage licence" means a licence authorising the storage, for use for a scheduled purpose, of relevant material which has come from a human body.

[Human Tissue Act 2004, s 31.]

*Trafficking*

**7.8244 32. Prohibition of commercial dealings in human material for transplantation**

(1) A person commits an offence if he—

(*a*) gives or receives a reward for the supply of, or for an offer to supply, any controlled material;

(*b*) seeks to find a person willing to supply any controlled material for reward;

(*c*) offers to supply any controlled material for reward;

(*d*) initiates or negotiates any arrangement involving the giving of a reward for the supply of, or for an offer to supply, any controlled material;

(*e*) takes part in the management or control of a body of persons corporate or unincorporate whose activities consist of or include the initiation or negotiation of such arrangements.

(2) Without prejudice to subsection (1)(*b*) and (*c*), a person commits an offence if he causes to be published or distributed, or knowingly publishes or distributes, an advertisement—

(*a*) inviting persons to supply, or offering to supply, any controlled material for reward, or

(*b*) indicating that the advertiser is willing to initiate or negotiate any such arrangement as is mentioned in subsection (1)(*d*).

(3) A person who engages in an activity to which subsection (1) or (2) applies does not commit an offence under that subsection if he is designated by the Authority as a person who may lawfully engage in the activity.

(3A) The Authority may not designate a person under subsection (3) if doing so could result in the United Kingdom being in breach of—

(*a*) Article 12 of Directive 2004/23/EC of the European Parliament and of the Council on setting standards of quality and safety for the donation, procurement, testing, processing, preservation, storage and distribution of human tissues and cells, or

(*b*) Article 13 of Directive 2010/53/EU of the European Parliament and of the Council on standards of quality and safety of human organs intended for transplantation.

(4) A person guilty of an offence under subsection (1) shall be liable—

(*a*) on summary conviction—

(i) to imprisonment for a term not exceeding 12 months, or

(ii) to a fine not exceeding the statutory maximum, or

(iii) to both;

(*b*) on conviction on indictment—

(i) to imprisonment for a term not exceeding 3 years, or

(ii) to a fine, or

(iii) to both.

(5) A person guilty of an offence under subsection (2) shall be liable on summary conviction—

(*a*) to imprisonment for a term not exceeding 51 weeks, or

(*b*) to a fine not exceeding level 5 on the standard scale, or

(*c*) to both.

(6) For the purposes of subsections (1) and (2), payment in money or money's worth to the holder of a licence shall be treated as not being a reward where—

(*a*) it is in consideration for transporting, removing, preparing, preserving or storing controlled material, and

(*b*) its receipt by the holder of the licence is not expressly prohibited by the terms of the licence.

(7) References in subsections (1) and (2) to reward, in relation to the supply of any controlled material, do not include payment in money or money's worth for defraying or reimbursing—

(*a*) any expenses incurred in, or in connection with, transporting, removing, preparing, preserving or storing the material,

(*b*) any liability incurred in respect of—

(i) expenses incurred by a third party in, or in connection with, any of the activities mentioned in paragraph (*a*), or

(ii) a payment in relation to which subsection (6) has effect, or

(*c*) any expenses or loss of earnings incurred by the person from whose body the material comes so far as reasonably and directly attributable to his supplying the material from his body.

(8) For the purposes of this section, controlled material is any material which—

(*a*) consists of or includes human cells,

(*b*) is, or is intended to be removed, from a human body,

(*c*) is intended to be used for the purpose of transplantation, and

(*d*) is not of a kind excepted under subsection (9).

(9) The following kinds of material are excepted—

(*a*) gametes,

(*b*) embryos, and

(*c*) material which is the subject of property because of an application of human skill.

(10) Where the body of a deceased person is intended to be used to provide material which—

(*a*) consists of or includes human cells, and

(*b*) is not of a kind excepted under subsection (9),

for use for the purpose of transplantation, the body shall be treated as controlled material for the purposes of this section.

(11) In this section—

"advertisement" includes any form of advertising whether to the public generally, to any section of the public or individually to selected persons;

"reward" means any description of financial or other material advantage.

[Human Tissue Act 2004, s 32 as amended by SI 2014/1459.]

*Transplants*

7.8245 **33. Restriction on transplants involving a live donor** (1) Subject to subsections (3) and (5), a person commits an offence if—

(*a*) he removes any transplantable material from the body of a living person intending that the material be used for the purpose of transplantation, and

(*b*) when he removes the material, he knows, or might reasonably be expected to know, that the person from whose body he removes the material is alive.

(2) Subject to subsections (3) and (5), a person commits an offence if—

(*a*) he uses for the purpose of transplantation any transplantable material which has come from the body of a living person, and

(*b*) when he does so, he knows, or might reasonably be expected to know, that the transplantable material has come from the body of a living person.

(3) The Secretary of State may by regulations provide that subsection (1) or (2) shall not apply in a case where—

(*a*) the Authority is satisfied—

(i) that no reward has been or is to be given in contravention of section 32, and

(ii) that such other conditions as are specified in the regulations are satisfied, and

(*b*) such other requirements as are specified in the regulations are complied with.

(4) Regulations under subsection (3) shall include provision for decisions of the Authority in relation to matters which fall to be decided by it under the regulations to be subject, in such circumstances as the regulations may provide, to reconsideration in accordance with such procedure as the regulations may provide.

(5) Where under subsection (3) an exception from subsection (1) or (2) is in force, a person does not commit an offence under that subsection if he reasonably believes that the exception

applies.

(6) A person guilty of an offence under this section is liable on summary conviction—

(*a*) to imprisonment for a term not exceeding 51 weeks, or

(*b*) to a fine not exceeding level 5 on the standard scale, or

(*c*) to both.

(7) In this section—

"reward" has the same meaning as in section 32;

"transplantable material" means material of a description specified by regulations made by the Secretary of State.

[Human Tissue Act 2004, s 33.]

7.8246 **34. Information about transplant operations** (1) The Secretary of State may make regulations[1] requiring such persons as may be specified in the regulations to supply to such authority as may be so specified such information as may be so specified with respect to transplants that have been or are proposed to be carried out using transplantable material removed from a human body.

(2) Any such authority shall keep a record of information supplied to it in pursuance of regulations under this section.

(3) A person commits an offence if—

(*a*) he fails without reasonable excuse to comply with regulations under this section, or

(*b*) in purported compliance with such regulations, he knowingly or recklessly supplies information which is false or misleading in a material respect.

(4) A person guilty of an offence under subsection (3)(*a*) is liable on summary conviction to a fine not exceeding level 3 on the standard scale.

(5) A person guilty of an offence under subsection (3)(*b*) is liable on summary conviction to a fine not exceeding level 5 on the standard scale.

(6) In this section, "transplantable material" has the same meaning as in section 33.

[Human Tissue Act 2004, s 34.]

1 The Human Tissue Act 2004 (Ethical Approval, Exceptions from Licensing and Supply of Information about Transplants) Regulations 2006, SI 2006/1260 (for amending instruments, see the note to s 1, ante).

*Exceptions*

7.8247 **39. Criminal justice purposes** (1) Subject to subsection (2), nothing in section 14(1) or 16(2) applies to anything done for purposes related to—

(*a*) the prevention or detection of crime, or

(*b*) the conduct of a prosecution.

(2) Subsection (1) does not except from section 14(1) or 16(2) the carrying-out of a post-mortem examination for purposes of functions of a coroner.

(3) The reference in subsection (2) to the carrying-out of a post-mortem examination does not include the removal of relevant material from the body of a deceased person, or from a part of the body of a deceased person, at the first place where the body or part is situated to be attended by a constable.

(4) For the purposes of subsection (1)(*a*), detecting crime shall be taken to include—

(*a*) establishing by whom, for what purpose, by what means and generally in what circumstances any crime was committed, and

(*b*) the apprehension of the person by whom any crime was committed;

and the reference in subsection (1)(*a*) to the detection of crime includes any detection outside the United Kingdom of any crime or suspected crime.

(5) In subsection (1)(*b*), the reference to a prosecution includes a prosecution brought in respect of any crime in a country or territory outside the United Kingdom.

(6) In this section, references to crime include a reference to any conduct which—

(*a*) constitutes one or more criminal offences (whether under the law of a part of the United Kingdom or of a country or territory outside the United Kingdom),

(*b*) is, or corresponds to, any conduct which, if it all took place in any one part of the United Kingdom, would constitute one or more criminal offences, or

(*c*) constitutes one or more service offences within the meaning of the Armed Forces Act 2006.

[Human Tissue Act 2004, s 39 as amended by the Armed Forces Act 2006, Sch 16.]

7.8248 **40. Religious relics** (1) This section applies—

(*a*) to the use of—

(i) the body of a deceased person, or

(ii) relevant material which has come from a human body,

for the purpose of public display at a place of public religious worship or at a place associated with such a place, and

(*b*) to the storage of—

(i) the body of a deceased person, or

(ii) relevant material which has come from a human body,

for use for the purpose mentioned in paragraph (*a*).

(2) An activity to which this section applies is excluded from sections 14(1) and 16(2) if there is a connection between—

(*a*) the body or material to which the activity relates, and

(*b*) the religious worship which takes place at the place of public religious worship concerned.

(3) For the purposes of this section, a place is associated with a place of public religious worship if it is used for purposes associated with the religious worship which takes place there.

[Human Tissue Act 2004, s 40.]

*Supplementary*

7.8249 **41. Interpretation of Part 2** (1) In this Part—

"the 2007 Regulations" means the Human Tissue (Quality and Safety for Human Application) Regulations 2007;

"anatomical specimen" means—

(*a*) the body of a deceased person to be used for the purpose of anatomical examination, or

(*b*) the body of a deceased person in the course of being used for the purpose of anatomical examination (including separated parts of such a body);

"appeals committee" has the meaning given by section 20(2);

"designated individual", in relation to a licence, means the individual designated in the licence as the person under whose supervision the licensed activity is authorised to be carried on;

"export" means export from England, Wales or Northern Ireland to a place outside England, Wales and Northern Ireland;

"import" means import into England, Wales or Northern Ireland from a place outside England, Wales and Northern Ireland;

"scheduled purpose" means a purpose specified in Schedule 1.

(2) In this Part, references to the carrying-out of an anatomical examination are to the carrying-out of a macroscopic examination by dissection for anatomical purposes of the body of a deceased person, and, where parts of the body of a deceased person are separated in the course of such an examination, include the carrying-out of a macroscopic examination by dissection of the parts for those purposes.

(3) In this Part, references to a person to whom a licence applies are to a person to whom the authority conferred by the licence extends (as provided by section 17).

[Human Tissue Act 2004, s 41 as amended by SI 2007/1523.]

## Part 3[1]

## Miscellaneous and General

*Miscellaneous*

7.8250 **42. Power of Human Tissue Authority to assist other public authorities**

7.8251 **43. Preservation for transplantation** (1) Where part of a body lying in a hospital, nursing home or other institution is or may be suitable for use for transplantation, it shall be lawful for the person having the control and management of the institution—

(*a*) to take steps for the purpose of preserving the part for use for transplantation, and

(*b*) to retain the body for that purpose.

(2) Authority under subsection (1)(*a*) shall only extend—

(*a*) to the taking of the minimum steps necessary for the purpose mentioned in that provision, and

(*b*) to the use of the least invasive procedure.

(3) Authority under subsection (1) ceases to apply once it has been established that consent making removal of the part for transplantation lawful has not been, and will not be, given.

(4) Authority under subsection (1) shall extend to any person authorised to act under the authority by—

(*a*) the person on whom the authority is conferred by that subsection, or

(*b*) a person authorised under this subsection to act under the authority.

(5) An activity done with authority under subsection (1) shall be treated—

(*a*) for the purposes of Part 1, as not being an activity to which section 1(1) applies;

(*b*) for the purposes of Part 2, as not being an activity to which section 16 applies.*

(6) In this section, "body" means the body of a deceased person.

(7 This section does not apply in relation to a part of a body lying in an institution in Wales. (For provision in these circumstances see section 13 of the Human Transplantation (Wales) Act 2013).

[Human Tissue Act 2004, s 43 as amended by the Human Transplantation (Wales) Act 2013, s 16.]

---

* **Sub-s (5A) inserted by the Coroners and Justice Act 2009, Sch 21 from a date to be appointed.**

1 Part 3 contains ss 42–61.

7.8252 **44. Surplus tissue** (1) It shall be lawful for material to which subsection (2) or (3) applies to be dealt with as waste.

(2) This subsection applies to any material which consists of or includes human cells and which has come from a person's body in the course of his—

(*a*) receiving medical treatment,

(*b*) undergoing diagnostic testing, or

(*c*) participating in research.

(3) This subsection applies to any relevant material which—

(*a*) has come from a human body, and

(*b*) ceases to be used, or stored for use, for a purpose specified in Schedule 1.

(4) This section shall not be read as making unlawful anything which is lawful apart from this section.

[Human Tissue Act 2004, s 44.]

7.8253 **45. Non-consensual analysis of DNA** (1) A person commits an offence if—

(*a*) he has any bodily material intending—

(i) that any human DNA in the material be analysed without qualifying consent, and

(ii) that the results of the analysis be used otherwise than for an excepted purpose,

(*b*) the material is not of a kind excepted under subsection (2), and

(*c*) he does not reasonably believe the material to be of a kind so excepted.

(2) Bodily material is excepted if—

(*a*) it is material which has come from the body of a person who died before the day on which this section comes into force and at least one hundred years have elapsed since the date of the person's death,

(*b*) it is an existing holding and the person who has it is not in possession, and not likely to come into possession, of information from which the individual from whose body the material has come can be identified, or

(*c*) it is an embryo outside the human body.

(3) A person guilty of an offence under this section—

(*a*) is liable on summary conviction to a fine not exceeding the statutory maximum;

(*b*) is liable on conviction on indictment—

(i) to imprisonment for a term not exceeding 3 years, or

(ii) to a fine, or

(iii) to both.

(4) Schedule 4 (which makes provision for the interpretation of "qualifying consent" and "use for an excepted purpose" in subsection (1)(*a*)) has effect.

(5) In this section (and Schedule 4)—

"bodily material" means material which—

(*a*) has come from a human body, and

(*b*) consists of or includes human cells;

"existing holding" means bodily material held immediately before the day on which this section comes into force.

[Human Tissue Act 2004, s 45.]

*General*

7.8254 **48. Powers of inspection, entry, search and seizure** Schedule 5 (which makes provision about powers of inspection, entry, search and seizure for the purposes of this Act) has effect.

[Human Tissue Act 2004, s 48.]

7.8255 **49. Offences by bodies corporate** (1) Where an offence under this Act is committed by a body corporate and is proved to have been committed with the consent or connivance of or to be attributable to any neglect on the part of—

(*a*) any director, manager, secretary or other similar officer of the body corporate, or

(*b*) any person who was purporting to act in any such capacity,

he (as well as the body corporate) commits the offence and shall be liable to be proceeded against and punished accordingly.

(2) Where the affairs of a body corporate are managed by its members, subsection (1) applies in relation to the acts and defaults of a member in connection with his functions of management as if he were a director of the body corporate.

(3) Where an offence under this Act is committed by a Scottish partnership and is proved to have been committed with the consent or connivance of a partner, or to be attributable to any neglect on the part of a partner, he (as well as the partnership) commits the offence and shall be liable to be proceeded against and punished accordingly.

(4) In subsection (3), "partner" includes a person purporting to act as a partner.

[Human Tissue Act 2004, s 49.]

7.8256 **50. Prosecutions** No proceedings for an offence under section 5, 32 or 33 shall be instituted—

(*a*) in England and Wales, except by or with the consent of the Director of Public Prosecutions;

(*b*) in Northern Ireland, except by or with the consent of the Director of Public Prosecutions for Northern Ireland.

[Human Tissue Act 2004, s 50.]

**7.8257 53. "Relevant material"** (1) In this Act, "relevant material" means material, other than gametes, which consists of or includes human cells.

(2) In this Act, references to relevant material from a human body do not include—

(*a*) embryos outside the human body, or

(*b*) hair and nail from the body of a living person.

[Human Tissue Act 2004, s 53.]

**7.8258 54. General interpretation** (1) In this Act—

"adult" means a person who has attained the age of 18 years;

"anatomical examination" means macroscopic examination by dissection for anatomical purposes;

"anatomical purposes" means purposes of teaching or studying, or researching into, the gross structure of the human body;

"the Authority" has the meaning given by section 13(1);

"child", except in the context of qualifying relationships, means a person who has not attained the age of 18 years;

"licence" means a licence under paragraph 1 of Schedule 3;

"licensed activity", in relation to a licence, means the activity which the licence authorises to be carried on;

"parental responsibility"—

(*a*) in relation to England and Wales, has the same meaning as in the Children Act 1989 (c 41), and

(*b*) in relation to Northern Ireland, has the same meaning as in the Children (Northern Ireland) Order 1995 (SI 1995/755 (NI 2));

"relevant Northern Ireland department" means the Department of Health, Social Services and Public Safety.

(2) In this Act—

(*a*) references to material from the body of a living person are to material from the body of a person alive at the point of separation, and

(*b*) references to material from the body of a deceased person are to material from the body of a person not alive at the point of separation.

(3) In this Act, references to transplantation are to transplantation to a human body and include transfusion.

(4) In this Act, references to decent disposal include, in relation to disposal of material which has come from a human body, disposal as waste.

(5) In this Act, references to public display, in relation to the body of a deceased person, do not include—

(*a*) display for the purpose of enabling people to pay their final respects to the deceased, or

(*b*) display which is incidental to the deceased's funeral.

(6) In this Act "embryo" and "gametes" have the same meaning as they have by virtue of section 1(1), (4) and (6) of the Human Fertilisation and Embryology Act 1990 in the other provisions of that Act (apart from section 4A).

(7) For the purposes of this Act, material shall not be regarded as from a human body if it is created outside the human body.

(8) For the purposes of this Act, except section 49, a person is another's partner if the two of them (whether of different sexes or the same sex) live as partners in an enduring family relationship.

(9) The following are qualifying relationships for the purposes of this Act, spouse, civil partner, partner, parent, child, brother, sister, grandparent, grandchild, child of a brother or sister, stepfather, stepmother, half-brother, half-sister and friend of long standing.

(10) The Secretary of State may by order amend subsection (9).

[Human Tissue Act 2004, s 54 as amended by SI 2005/3129 and the Human Fertilisation and Embryology Act 2008, Sch 7.]

**7.8259 58. Transition** (1) In relation to an offence committed before the commencement of section 154(1) of the Criminal Justice Act 2003 (c 44), the reference in section 32(4)(*a*)(i) to 12 months is to be read as a reference to 6 months.

(2) In relation to an offence committed before the commencement of section 281(5) of the Criminal Justice Act 2003, the reference in each of sections 32(5)(*a*) and 33(6)(*a*) to 51 weeks is to be read as a reference to 6 months.

(3) The Secretary of State may by order made by statutory instrument make in connection with the coming into force of any provision of this Act such transitional provision or savings as he considers necessary or expedient.

(4) The power under subsection (3) includes power to make different provision for different cases.

(5) Before making provision under subsection (3) in connection with the coming into force in England and Wales of any provision of this Act, except section 47, the Secretary of State shall

consult the Welsh Ministers.

(6) Before making provision under subsection (3) in connection with the coming into force in Northern Ireland of any provision of this Act, except section 47, the Secretary of State shall consult the relevant Northern Ireland department.

(7) Before making provision under subsection (3) in connection with the coming into force in Scotland of any provision of this Act, except section 47, the Secretary of State shall consult the Scottish Ministers.

[Human Tissue Act 2004, s 58 as amended by the Human Transplantation (Wales) Act 2013, s 16.]

7.8260 **59. Extent** (1) Subject to the following provisions, this Act extends to England and Wales and Northern Ireland only.

(2) Sections 58(1), (2) and (5) and 60(3) extend to England and Wales only.

(3) Sections 51(1) to (3), 58(6) and 60(4) extend to Northern Ireland only.

(4) *Scotland.*

(5) *Scotland.*

(6) Subject to subsection (5), any amendment made by this Act has the same extent as the enactment to which it relates.

(7) Subject to subsection (8), any repeal or revocation made by this Act has the same extent as the enactment or instrument to which it relates.

(8) Except as provided by subsection (9), the repeals of the following do not extend to Scotland—

(*a*) the Human Tissue Act 1961 (c 54),
(*b*) the Anatomy Act 1984 (c 14),
(*c*) the Corneal Tissue Act 1986 (c 18), and
(*d*) the Human Organ Transplants Act 1989 (c 31).

(9) The repeals of the following provisions do extend to Scotland—

(*a*) in section 1(4A)(*b*) of the Human Tissue Act 1961, the words ", Primary Care Trust";
(*b*) in section 1(10) of that Act—
  (i) paragraph (*a*) of the definition of "health authority",
  (ii) in the definition of "NHS trust", the words "the National Health Service and Community Care Act 1990 or", and
  (iii) the words after the definition of that expression;
(*c*) section 4(5) of the Anatomy Act 1984;
(*d*) in the Human Organ Transplants Act 1989—
  (i) in section 1, the words "in Great Britain", in the first and third places where they occur,
  (ii) in sections 2 and 3, the words "in Great Britain", in each place, and
  (iii) sections 5 and 6.

[Human Tissue Act 2004, s 59 as amended by SI 2012/1501.]

7.8261 **60. Commencement**[1] (1) The following provisions shall come into force on the day on which this Act is passed—

this section, and
sections 58(3) to (7), 59 and 61.

(2) The remaining provisions of this Act shall come into force on such day as the Secretary of State may appoint by order made by statutory instrument, and different days may be so appointed for different purposes.

(3) Before exercising the power under subsection (2) in relation to the coming into force in England and Wales of any provision of this Act, except section 47, the Secretary of State shall consult the Welsh Ministers.

(4) Before exercising the power under subsection (2) in relation to the coming into force in Northern Ireland of any provision of this Act, except section 47, the Secretary of State shall consult the relevant Northern Ireland department.

(5) Before exercising the power under subsection (2) in relation to the coming into force in Scotland of any provision of this Act, except section 47, the Secretary of State shall consult the Scottish Ministers.

(6) No day may be appointed under subsection (2) for the coming into force of section 5 or 8 which is earlier than the end of the period of three months beginning with the day on which the Authority first issues a code of practice dealing with the matters mentioned in section 26(2)(*h*) and (*i*).

(7) If the Authority first issues a code of practice dealing with one of the matters mentioned in subsection (6) before it first issues a code of practice dealing with the other, that subsection shall have effect as if the three month period were one beginning with the later of—

(*a*) the day on which the Authority first issues a code of practice dealing with the matter mentioned in section 26(2)(*h*), and
(*b*) the day on which the Authority first issues a code of practice dealing with the matter mentioned in section 26(2)(i).

[Human Tissue Act 2004, s 60 as amended by the Human Transplantation (Wales) Act 2013, s 16.]

[1] For details of commencement orders made see the note to the title of this Act, ante.

## SCHEDULE 1

### Scheduled Purposes

Section 1

### Part 1

### Purposes Requiring Consent: General

7.8262 1 Anatomical examination.

2 Determining the cause of death.

3 Establishing after a person's death the efficacy of any drug or other treatment administered to him.

4 Obtaining scientific or medical information about a living or deceased person which may be relevant to any other person (including a future person).

5 Public display.

6 Research in connection with disorders, or the functioning, of the human body.

7 Transplantation.

### Part 2

### Purposes Requiring Consent: Deceased Persons

8 Clinical audit.

9 Education or training relating to human health.

10 Performance assessment.

11 Public health monitoring.

12 Quality assurance.

## SCHEDULE 2

### The Human Tissue Authority

Section 13

*Instruments*

7.8263 **18.** A document purporting—

(*a*) to be duly executed under the seal of the Authority, or

(*b*) to be signed on its behalf,

shall be received in evidence and be taken, without further proof, to be so executed or signed unless the contrary is shown.

*Application of Statutory Instruments Act 1946*

**22.** The Statutory Instruments Act 1946 (c 36) shall apply to any power to make orders or regulations conferred by an Act on the Authority as if the Authority were a Minister of the Crown.

## SCHEDULE 3

### Licences for the Purposes of Section 16

Section 16

*(Amended by SI 2012/1501.)*

*Power to grant licence*

7.8264 **1.** The Authority may on application grant a licence for the purposes of section 16.

*Characteristics of licence*

**2.** (1) A licence shall not authorise the carrying-on of more than one activity to which section 16 applies.

(2) A licence shall—

(*a*) specify the premises where the licensed activity is authorised to be carried on, and

(*b*) designate an individual as the person under whose supervision the licensed activity is authorised to be carried on.

(3) A licence shall not authorise the licensed activity to be carried on—

(*a*) on premises at different places, or

(*b*) under the supervision of more than one individual.

(4) It shall be a condition of a licence—

(*a*) that the licensed activity shall be carried on only on the premises specified in the licence;

(*b*) that the licensed activity shall be carried on only under the supervision of the individual designated in the licence as the person under whose supervision it is authorised to be carried on;

(*c*) that such information about such matters relating to the carrying-on of the licensed activity as may be specified in directions shall be recorded in such form as may be so specified;

(*d*) that any record made for the purposes of the condition in paragraph (*c*) shall be kept until the end of such period as may be specified in directions;

(*e*) that there shall be provided to such person and at such intervals as may be specified in directions—

(i) such copies of, or extracts from, any record to which the condition in paragraph (*d*) relates, and

(ii) such other information,

as may be so specified;

(*f*) that there shall be paid to the Authority at such times as may be specified in directions sums of such amount as may be so specified in respect of its costs in connection with superintending compliance with the terms of licences.

(5) Directions for the purposes of sub-paragraph (4) may be given in relation to licences generally, licences of a particular description or a particular licence.

**3.** (1) This paragraph applies to a licence authorising the storage of anatomical specimens.

(2) It shall be a condition of a licence to which this paragraph applies that storage at the premises specified in the licence of the body of a deceased person for use for the purpose of anatomical examination shall not begin before that body's storage there for use for that purpose has been authorised in writing by—

(*a*) the designated individual, or

(*b*) an individual who has the Authority's permission to give such authorisation (see paragraph 12).

(3) It shall be a condition of a licence to which this paragraph applies that any anatomical specimen which is stored at the premises specified in the licence shall be released from storage at the premises only into the possession of a person who is authorised in writing by the designated individual to have the specimen in his possession.

(4) It shall be a condition of a licence to which this paragraph applies that the designated individual shall give authority for the purposes of the condition in sub-paragraph (3) only if he is satisfied—

(*a*) that the person to whom authority is given is a suitable person to have the specimen in his possession, and

(*b*) that that person intends to use the specimen only for the purpose of education, training or research.

(5) It shall be a condition of a licence to which this paragraph applies that any authority given for the purposes of the condition in sub-paragraph (3) shall specify—

(*a*) the person to whom the authority is given,

(*b*) the specimen to which the authority relates,

(*c*) the purpose for which the specimen may be used, and

(*d*) the duration of the authority.

(6) It shall be a condition of a licence to which this paragraph applies that the designated individual shall give such notice of any authorisation for the purposes of the condition in sub-paragraph (3) as may be specified in directions.

(7) It shall be a condition of a licence to which this paragraph applies that such information about authorisations for the purposes of the condition in sub-paragraph (3) as may be specified in directions shall be recorded in such form as may be so specified.

4. (1) This paragraph applies to a licence authorising the activity mentioned in section 16(2)(*e*).

(2) It shall be a condition of a licence to which this paragraph applies that any former anatomical specimen which is stored at the premises specified in the licence shall be released from storage at the premises only into the possession of a person who is authorised in writing by the designated individual to have the specimen in his possession.

(3) The condition in sub-paragraph (2) does not apply to the release from storage of a specimen for the purpose of its decent disposal.

(4) It shall be a condition of a licence to which this paragraph applies that the designated individual shall give authority for the purposes of the condition in sub-paragraph (2) only if he is satisfied—

(*a*) that the person to whom authority is given is a suitable person to have the specimen in his possession, and

(*b*) that that person intends to use the specimen only for the purpose of education, training or research.

(5) It shall be a condition of a licence to which this paragraph applies that any authority given for the purposes of the condition in sub-paragraph (2) shall specify—

(*a*) the person to whom the authority is given,

(*b*) the specimen to which the authority relates,

(*c*) the purpose for which the specimen may be used, and

(*d*) the duration of the authority.

(6) It shall be a condition of a licence to which this paragraph applies that the designated individual shall give such notice of any authorisation for the purposes of the condition in sub-paragraph (2) as may be specified in directions.

(7) It shall be a condition of a licence to which this paragraph applies that such information about authorisations for the purposes of the condition in sub-paragraph (2) as may be specified in directions shall be recorded in such form as may be so specified.

*Power to impose conditions*

5. The Authority may grant a licence subject to such further conditions as it thinks fit.

*Pre-conditions to grant of licence*

6. (1) The Authority may not grant a licence in pursuance of an application unless the following requirements are met.

(2) The proposed designated individual must—

(*a*) be the applicant for the licence, or

(*b*) consent to the application for the licence.

(3) The Authority must be satisfied that the proposed designated individual—

(*a*) is a suitable person to supervise the activity to be authorised by the licence, and

(*b*) will perform the duty under section 18.

(4) Where the applicant for the licence is not the proposed designated individual, the Authority must be satisfied that the applicant is a suitable person to be the holder of the licence.

(5) The Authority must be satisfied that the premises in respect of which the licence is to be granted are suitable for the activity to be authorised by the licence.

(6) A copy of the conditions to be imposed by the licence must have been shown to, and acknowledged in writing by—

(*a*) the applicant for the licence, and

(*b*) where different, the proposed designated individual.

(7) In this paragraph, references to the proposed designated individual are to the individual whom the application proposes the licence designate as the person under whose supervision the activity to be authorised by the licence is to be carried on.

*Power to revoke licence*

7. (1) The Authority may revoke a licence on application by—

(*a*) the holder of the licence, or

(*b*) the designated individual.

(2) The Authority may revoke a licence otherwise than on an application under sub-paragraph (1) if—

(*a*) it is satisfied that any information given for the purposes of the application for the licence was in any material respect false or misleading,

(*b*) it is satisfied that the designated individual has failed to discharge, or is unable because of incapacity to discharge, the duty under section 18,
(*c*) it ceases to be satisfied that the premises specified in the licence are suitable for the licensed activity,
(*d*) it ceases to be satisfied that the person to whom the licence is granted is a suitable person to be the holder of the licence,
(*e*) it ceases to be satisfied that the designated individual is a suitable person to supervise the licensed activity,
(*f*) the designated individual dies, or
(*g*) it is satisfied that there has been any other material change of circumstances since the licence was granted.

*Power to vary licence*

**8.** (1) The Authority may on application by the holder of a licence vary the licence so as to substitute another individual for the designated individual if—
(*a*) the application is made with the consent of the other individual, and
(*b*) the authority is satisfied that the other individual is a suitable person to supervise the licensed activity.
(2) The Authority may vary a licence on application by—
(*a*) the holder of the licence, or
(*b*) the designated individual.
(3) The Authority may vary a licence without an application under sub-paragraph (2) if it has power to revoke the licence under paragraph 7(2).
(4) The powers under sub-paragraphs (2) and (3) do not extend to making the kind of variation mentioned in sub-paragraph (1).
(5) The Authority may vary a licence without an application under sub-paragraph (2) by—
(*a*) removing or varying a condition of the licence, or
(*b*) adding a condition to the licence.
(6) The powers conferred by this paragraph do not extend to the conditions required by paragraphs 2(4), 3 and 4.

*Power to suspend licence*

**9.** (1) Where the Authority—
(*a*) has reasonable grounds to suspect that there are grounds for revoking a licence, and
(*b*) is of the opinion that the licence should immediately be suspended,
it may by notice suspend the licence for such period not exceeding three months as may be specified in the notice.
(2) The Authority may continue suspension under sub-paragraph (1) by giving a further notice under that sub-paragraph.
(3) Notice under sub-paragraph (1) shall be given to the designated individual or, where the designated individual has died or appears to the Authority to be unable because of incapacity to discharge the duty under section 18—
(*a*) to the holder of the licence, or
(*b*) to some other person to whom the licence applies.
(4) Subject to sub-paragraph (5), a licence shall be of no effect while a notice under sub-paragraph (1) is in force.
(5) An application may be made under paragraph 7(1) or 8(1) or (2) notwithstanding the fact that a notice under sub-paragraph (1) is in force.

*Procedure in relation to licensing decisions*

**10.** (1) Before making a decision—
(*a*) to refuse an application for the grant, revocation or variation of a licence, or
(*b*) to grant an application for a licence subject to a condition under paragraph 5,
the Authority shall give the applicant notice of the proposed decision and of the reasons for it.
(2) Before making a decision under paragraph 7(2) or 8(3) or (5), the Authority shall give notice of the proposed decision and of the reasons for it to—
(*a*) the holder of the licence, and
(*b*) where different, the designated individual.
(3) A person to whom notice under sub-paragraph (1) or (2) is given has the right to require the Authority to give him an opportunity to make representations of one of the following kinds about the proposed decision, namely—
(*a*) oral representations by him, or a person acting on his behalf;
(*b*) written representations by him.
(4) The right under sub-paragraph (3) is exercisable by giving the Authority notice of exercise of the right before the end of the period of 28 days beginning with the day on which the notice under sub-paragraph (1) or (2) was given.
(5) The Authority may by regulations make such additional provision about procedure in relation to the carrying-out of functions under this Schedule as it thinks fit.

*Notification of licensing decisions*

**11.** (1) In the case of a decision to grant a licence, the Authority shall give notice of the decision to—
(*a*) the applicant, and
(*b*) the person who is to be the designated individual.
(2) In the case of a decision to revoke a licence, the Authority shall give notice of the decision to—
(*a*) the holder of the licence, and
(*b*) the designated individual.
(3) In the case of a decision to vary a licence on an application under paragraph 8(1), the Authority shall give notice of the decision to—
(*a*) the holder of the licence, and
(*b*) the person who is to be the designated individual.
(4) In the case of any other decision to vary a licence, the Authority shall give notice of the decision to—
(*a*) the holder of the licence, and

(*b*) the designated individual.

(5) In the case of a decision to refuse an application for the grant, revocation or variation of a licence, the Authority shall give notice of the decision to the applicant.

(6) Subject to sub-paragraph (7), a notice under sub-paragraph (2), (4) or (5) shall include a statement of the reasons for the decision.

(7) In the case of a notice under sub-paragraph (2) or (4), the notice is not required to include a statement of the reasons for the decision if the decision is made on an application under paragraph 7(1) or 8(2).

*Permission for the purposes of the licence condition required by paragraph 3(2)*

**12.** (1) This paragraph applies to a licence authorising the storage of anatomical specimens.

(2) The reference to the Authority's permission in the condition of the licence required by paragraph 3(2) ("the authorisation condition") is to—

(*a*) permission granted by the Authority on an application made, in conjunction with the application for the licence, by—

(i) the applicant for the licence, or

(ii) the person who, within the meaning of paragraph 6, is the proposed designated individual, or

(*b*) permission granted by the Authority on application by—

(i) the holder of the licence, or

(ii) the designated individual.

(3) The Authority may grant permission to an individual for the purposes of the authorisation condition only if it is satisfied that the individual is a suitable person to give authorisation under that condition.

(4) The Authority may revoke permission granted to an individual for the purposes of the authorisation condition—

(*a*) on application by the individual, the designated individual or the holder of the licence, or

(*b*) if it ceases to be satisfied that the individual is a suitable person to give authorisation under that condition.

(5) Before refusing an application for the grant or revocation of permission, the Authority shall give the applicant notice of the proposed refusal and of the reasons for it.

(6) Before revoking permission under sub-paragraph (4)(*b*), the Authority shall give notice of the proposed revocation and of the reasons for it—

(*a*) to the individual concerned, and

(*b*) to the designated individual and, where different, the holder of the licence.

(7) Paragraph 10(3) and (4) shall apply in relation to notice under sub-paragraph (5) or (6) as to notice under paragraph 10(1).

(8) In the case of a decision to refuse an application for the grant or revocation of permission, the Authority shall give notice of the decision to the applicant.

(9) In the case of a decision to grant or revoke permission, the Authority shall give notice of the decision—

(*a*) to the individual concerned, and

(*b*) to the designated individual and, where different, the holder of the licence.

(10) Notice under sub-paragraph (8), and notice under sub-paragraph (9) of revocation under sub-paragraph (4)(*b*), shall include a statement of the reasons for the refusal or revocation.

(11) Where the Authority—

(*a*) has reasonable grounds to suspect that there are grounds for revoking permission granted to an individual for the purposes of the authorisation condition, and

(*b*) is of the opinion that the permission should immediately be suspended,

it may by notice suspend the permission for such period not exceeding three months as may be specified in the notice.

(12) The Authority may continue suspension under sub-paragraph (11) by giving a further notice under that sub-paragraph.

(13) Notice under sub-paragraph (11) shall be given to—

(*a*) the individual concerned, and

(*b*) the designated individual and, where different, the holder of the licence.

*Applications under this Schedule*

**13.** (1) The Authority may by regulations make provision about applications under this Schedule, Schedule 1 to the 2007 Regulations and Schedule 1 to the 2012 Regulations and may, in particular, make provision about—

(*a*) the form and content of such an application,

(*b*) the information to be supplied with such an application, and

(*c*) procedure in relation to the determination of such an application.

(2) An application under this Schedule shall be accompanied by such fee (if any) as the Authority may determine.

## SCHEDULE 4

### SECTION 45: SUPPLEMENTARY

Section 45

*(Amended by the Armed Forces Act 2006, Sch 16)*

### PART 1
### QUALIFYING CONSENT

*Introductory*

**7.8265** **1.** This Part of this Schedule makes provision for the interpretation of "qualifying consent" in section 45(1)(*a*)(i).

*Qualifying consent*

**2.** (1) In relation to analysis of DNA manufactured by the body of a person who is alive, "qualifying consent" means his consent, except where sub-paragraph (2) applies.

(2) Where—

(*a*) the person is a child,

(*b*) neither a decision of his to consent, nor a decision of his not to consent, is in force, and (*c*) either he is not competent to deal with the issue of consent or, though he is competent to deal with that issue, he fails to do so,

"qualifying consent" means the consent of a person who has parental responsibility for him.

(3) In relation to analysis of DNA manufactured by the body of a person who has died an adult, "qualifying consent" means—

(*a*) if a decision of his to consent, or a decision of his not to consent, was in force immediately before he died, his consent;

(*b*) if paragraph (*a*) does not apply, the consent of a person who stood in a qualifying relationship to him immediately before he died.

(4) In relation to analysis of DNA manufactured by the body of a person who has died a child, "qualifying consent" means—

(*a*) if a decision of his to consent, or a decision of his not to consent, was in force immediately before he died, his consent;

(*b*) if paragraph (*a*) does not apply—

(i) the consent of a person who had parental responsibility for him immediately before he died, or

(ii) where no person had parental responsibility for him immediately before he died, the consent of a person who stood in a qualifying relationship to him at that time.

## PART 2
## USE FOR AN EXCEPTED PURPOSE

*Introductory*

**4.** This Part of this Schedule makes provision for the interpretation of "use for an excepted purpose" in section 45(1)(*a*)(ii).

*Purposes of general application*

**5.** (1) Use of the results of an analysis of DNA for any of the following purposes is use for an excepted purpose—

(*a*) the medical diagnosis or treatment of the person whose body manufactured the DNA;

(*b*) purposes of functions of a coroner;

(*c*) purposes of functions of a procurator fiscal in connection with the investigation of deaths;

(*d*) the prevention or detection of crime;

(*e*) the conduct of a prosecution;

(*f*) purposes of national security;

(*g*) implementing an order or direction of a court or tribunal, including one outside the United Kingdom.

(2) For the purposes of sub-paragraph (1)(*d*), detecting crime shall be taken to include—

(*a*) establishing by whom, for what purpose, by what means and generally in what circumstances any crime was committed, and

(*b*) the apprehension of the person by whom any crime was committed;

and the reference in sub-paragraph (1)(*d*) to the detection of crime includes any detection outside the United Kingdom of any crime or suspected crime.

(3) In sub-paragraph (1)(*e*), the reference to a prosecution includes a prosecution brought in respect of a crime in a country or territory outside the United Kingdom.

(4) In this paragraph, a reference to a crime includes a reference to any conduct which—

(*a*) constitutes one or more criminal offences (whether under the law of a part of the United Kingdom or a country or territory outside the United Kingdom),

(*b*) is, or corresponds to, conduct which, if it all took place in any one part of the United Kingdom, would constitute one or more criminal offences, or

(*c*) constitutes one or more service offences within the meaning of the Armed Forces Act 2006.

(5) Sub-paragraph (1)(*g*) shall not be taken to confer any power to make orders or give directions.

*Purpose of research in connection with disorders, or functioning, of the human body*

**6.** (1) Use of the results of an analysis of DNA for the purpose of research in connection with disorders, or the functioning, of the human body is use for an excepted purpose if the bodily material concerned is the subject of an order under sub-paragraph (2).

(2) The Secretary of State may by regulations specify circumstances in which the High Court or the Court of Session may order that this paragraph apply to bodily material.

*Purposes relating to existing holdings*

**7.** Use of the results of an analysis of DNA for any of the following purposes is use for an excepted purpose if the bodily material concerned is an existing holding—

(*a*) clinical audit;

(*b*) determining the cause of death;

(*c*) education or training relating to human health;

(*d*) establishing after a person's death the efficacy of any drug or other treatment administered to him;

(*e*) obtaining scientific or medical information about a living or deceased person which may be relevant to any other person (including a future person);

(*f*) performance assessment;

(*g*) public health monitoring;

(*h*) quality assurance;

(*i*) research in connection with disorders, or the functioning, of the human body;

(*j*) transplantation.

*Purposes relating to material from body of a living person*

**8.** Use of the results of an analysis of DNA for any of the following purposes is use for an excepted purpose if the bodily material concerned is from the body of a living person—

(*a*) clinical audit;

(*b*) education or training relating to human health;

(*c*) performance assessment;
(*d*) public health monitoring;
(*e*) quality assurance.

**9.** (1) Use of the results of an analysis of DNA for the purpose of obtaining scientific or medical information about the person whose body manufactured the DNA is use for an excepted purpose if—
(*a*) the bodily material concerned is the subject of a direction under sub-paragraph (2) or (3) or an order under sub-paragraph (4) or (5), and
(*b*) the information may be relevant to the person for whose benefit the direction is given or order is made.

(2) If the Authority is satisfied—
(*a*) that bodily material has come from the body of a living person,
(*b*) that it is not reasonably possible to trace the person from whose body the material has come ("the donor"),
(*c*) that it is desirable in the interests of another person (including a future person) that DNA in the material be analysed for the purpose of obtaining scientific or medical information about the donor, and
(*d*) that there is no reason to believe—
(i) that the donor has died,
(ii) that a decision of the donor to refuse consent to the use of the material for that purpose is in force, or
(iii) that the donor lacks capacity to consent to the use of the material for that purpose,
it may direct that this paragraph apply to the material for the benefit of the other person.

(3) If the Authority is satisfied—
(*a*) that bodily material has come from the body of a living person,
(*b*) that it is desirable in the interests of another person (including a future person) that DNA in the material be analysed for the purpose of obtaining scientific or medical information about the person from whose body the material has come ("the donor"),
(*c*) that reasonable efforts have been made to get the donor to decide whether to consent to the use of the material for that purpose,
(*d*) that there is no reason to believe—
(i) that the donor has died,
(ii) that a decision of the donor to refuse to consent to the use of the material for that purpose is in force, or
(iii) that the donor lacks capacity to consent to the use of the material for that purpose, and
(*e*) that the donor has been given notice of the application for the exercise of the power conferred by this sub-paragraph,

it may direct that this paragraph apply to the material for the benefit of the other person.

(4) If the Court of Session is satisfied—
(*a*) that bodily material has come from the body of a living person,
(*b*) that it is not reasonably possible to trace the person from whose body the material has come ("the donor"),
(*c*) that it is desirable in the interests of another person (including a future person) that DNA in the material be analysed for the purpose of obtaining scientific or medical information about the donor, and
(*d*) that there is no reason to believe—
(i) that the donor has died,
(ii) that a decision of the donor to refuse consent to the use of the material for that purpose is in force, or
(iii) that the donor is an incapable adult within the meaning of the Adults with Incapacity (Scotland) Act 2000 (asp 4),

it may order that this paragraph apply to the material for the benefit of the other person.

(5) If the Court of Session is satisfied—
(*a*) that bodily material has come from the body of a living person,
(*b*) that it is desirable in the interests of another person (including a future person) that DNA in the material be analysed for the purpose of obtaining scientific or medical information about the person from whose body the material has come ("the donor"),
(*c*) that reasonable efforts have been made to get the donor to decide whether to consent to the use of the material for that purpose,
(*d*) that there is no reason to believe—
(i) that the donor has died,
(ii) that a decision of the donor to refuse to consent to the use of the material for that purpose is in force, or
(iii) that the donor is an incapable adult within the meaning of the Adults with Incapacity (Scotland) Act 2000, and
(*e*) that the donor has been given notice of the application for the exercise of the power conferred by this sub-paragraph,

it may order that this paragraph apply to the material for the benefit of the other person.

**10.** Use of the results of an analysis of DNA for the purpose of research in connection with disorders, or the functioning, of the human body is use for an excepted purpose if—
(*a*) the bodily material concerned is from the body of a living person,
(*b*) the research is ethically approved in accordance with regulations[1] made by the Secretary of State, and
(*c*) the analysis is to be carried out in circumstances such that the person carrying it out is not in possession, and not likely to come into possession, of information from which the individual from whose body the material has come can be identified.

---

[1] The Human Tissue Act 2004 (Ethical Approval, Exceptions from Licensing and Supply of Information about Transplants) Regulations 2006, SI 2006/1260 (for amending instruments, see the note to s 1, ante).

*Purpose authorised under section 1*

**11.** Use of the results of an analysis of DNA for a purpose specified in paragraph 7 is use for an excepted purpose if the use in England and Wales, or Northern Ireland, for that purpose of the bodily material concerned is authorised by section 1(1) or (10)(*c*).

*Purposes relating to DNA of adults who lack capacity to consent*

**12.** (1) Use of the results of an analysis of DNA for a purpose specified under sub-paragraph (2) is use for an excepted purpose if—

(*a*) the DNA has been manufactured by the body of a person who—

(i) has attained the age of 18 years and, under the law of England and Wales or Northern Ireland, lacks capacity to consent to analysis of the DNA, or

(ii) under the law of Scotland, is an adult with incapacity within the meaning of the Adults with Incapacity (Scotland) Act 2000 (asp 4), and

(*b*) neither a decision of his to consent to analysis of the DNA for that purpose, nor a decision of his not to consent to analysis of it for that purpose, is in force.

(2) The Secretary of State may by regulations specify for the purposes of this paragraph purposes for which DNA may be analysed.

## SCHEDULE 5

### POWERS OF INSPECTION, ENTRY, SEARCH AND SEIZURE

Section 48

(*As amended by the Human Transplantation (Wales) Act 2013, s 16.*)

*Inspection of statutory records*

**7.8266** **1.** (1) A duly authorised person may require a person to produce for inspection any records which he is required to keep by, or by virtue of, this Act.

(2) Where records which a person is so required to keep are stored in any electronic form, the power under sub-paragraph (1) includes power to require the records to be made available for inspection—

(*a*) in a visible and legible form, or

(*b*) in a form from which they can readily be produced in a visible and legible form.

(3) A duly authorised person may inspect and take copies of any records produced for inspection in pursuance of a requirement under this paragraph.

*Entry and inspection of licensed premises*

**2.** (1) A duly authorised person may at any reasonable time enter and inspect any premises in respect of which a licence is in force.

(2) The power in sub-paragraph (1) is exercisable for purposes of the Authority's functions in relation to licences.

*Entry and search in connection with suspected offence*

**3.** (1) If a justice of the peace is satisfied on sworn information or, in Northern Ireland, on a complaint on oath that there are reasonable grounds for believing—

(*a*) that an offence under Part 1 or 2 or under the Human Transplantation (Wales) Act 2013 is being, or has been, committed on any premises, and

(*b*) that any of the conditions in sub-paragraph (2) is met in relation to the premises,

he may by signed warrant authorise a duly authorised person to enter the premises, if need be by force, and search them.

(2) The conditions referred to are—

(*a*) that entry to the premises has been, or is likely to be, refused and notice of the intention to apply for a warrant under this paragraph has been given to the occupier;

(*b*) that the premises are unoccupied;

(*c*) that the occupier is temporarily absent;

(*d*) that an application for admission to the premises or the giving of notice of the intention to apply for a warrant under this paragraph would defeat the object of entry.

(3) A warrant under this paragraph shall continue in force until the end of the period of 31 days beginning with the day on which it is issued.

*Execution of warrants*

**4.** (1) Entry and search under a warrant under paragraph 3 is unlawful if any of sub-paragraphs (2) to (4) and (6) is not complied with.

(2) Entry and search shall be at a reasonable time unless the person executing the warrant thinks that the purpose of the search may be frustrated on an entry at a reasonable time.

(3) If the occupier of the premises to which the warrant relates is present when the person executing the warrant seeks to enter them, the person executing the warrant shall—

(*a*) produce the warrant to the occupier, and

(*b*) give him—

(i) a copy of the warrant, and

(ii) an appropriate statement.

(4) If the occupier of the premises to which the warrant relates is not present when the person executing the warrant seeks to enter them, but some other person is present who appears to the person executing the warrant to be in charge of the premises, the person executing the warrant shall—

(*a*) produce the warrant to that other person,

(*b*) give him—

(i) a copy of the warrant, and

(ii) an appropriate statement, and

(*c*) leave a copy of the warrant in a prominent place on the premises.

(5) In sub-paragraphs (3)(*b*)(ii) and (4)(*b*)(ii), the references to an appropriate statement are to a statement in writing containing such information relating to the powers of the person executing the warrant and the rights and obligations of the person to whom the statement is given as may be prescribed by regulations[1] made by the

Secretary of State.

(6) If the premises to which the warrant relates are unoccupied, the person executing the warrant shall leave a copy of it in a prominent place on the premises.

(7) Where the premises in relation to which a warrant under paragraph 3 is executed are unoccupied or the occupier is temporarily absent, the person executing the warrant shall, when leaving the premises, leave them as effectively secured as he found them.

---

[1] The Human Tissue Act 2004 (Powers of Entry and Search: Supply of Information) Regulations 2006, SI 2006/538 and the Human Tissue Act 2004 (Ethical Approval, Exceptions from Licensing and Supply of Information about Transplants) Regulations 2006, SI 2006/1260 (for amending instruments, see the note to s 1, ante).

*Seizure in the course of inspection or search*

**5.** (1) A duly authorised person entering and inspecting premises under paragraph 2 may seize anything on the premises which he has reasonable grounds to believe may be required for purposes of the Authority's functions relating to the grant, revocation, variation or suspension of licences.

(2) A duly authorised person entering and searching premises under a warrant under paragraph 3 may seize anything on the premises which he has reasonable grounds to believe may be required for the purpose of being used in evidence in any proceedings for an offence under Part 1 or 2 or under the Human Transplantation (Wales) Act 2013.

(3) Where a person has power under sub-paragraph (1) or (2) to seize anything, he may take such steps as appear to be necessary for preserving the thing or preventing interference with it.

(4) The power under sub-paragraph (1) or (2) includes power to retain anything seized in exercise of the power for so long as it may be required for the purpose for which it was seized.

(5) Where by virtue of sub-paragraph (1) or (2) a person seizes anything, he shall leave on the premises from which the thing was seized a statement giving particulars of what he has seized and stating that he has seized it.

*Powers: supplementary*

**6.** (1) Power under this Schedule to enter and inspect or search any premises includes power to take such other persons and equipment as the person exercising the power reasonably considers necessary.

(2) Power under this Schedule to inspect or search any premises includes, in particular—

(*a*) power to inspect any equipment found on the premises,

(*b*) power to inspect and take copies of any records found on the premises, and

(*c*) in the case of premises in respect of which a licence is in force, power to observe the carrying-on on the premises of the licensed activity.

(3) Any power under this Schedule to enter, inspect or search premises includes power to require any person to afford such facilities and assistance with respect to matters under that person's control as are necessary to enable the power of entry, inspection or search to be exercised.

**7.** (1) A person's right to exercise a power under this Schedule is subject to his producing evidence of his entitlement to exercise it, if required.

(2) As soon as reasonably practicable after having exercised a power under this Schedule to inspect or search premises, the duly authorised person shall—

(*a*) prepare a written report of the inspection or search, and

(*b*) if requested to do so by the appropriate person, give him a copy of the report.

(3) In sub-paragraph (2), the "appropriate person" means—

(*a*) in relation to premises in respect of which a licence is in force, the designated individual (as defined in section 41);

(*b*) in relation to any other premises, the occupier.

*Enforcement*

**8.** (1) A person commits an offence if—

(*a*) he fails without reasonable excuse to comply with a requirement under paragraph 1(1) or 6(3), or

(*b*) he intentionally obstructs the exercise of any right under this Schedule.

(2) A person guilty of an offence under this paragraph is liable on summary conviction to a fine not exceeding level 5 on the standard scale.

*Interpretation*

**9.** In this Schedule, "duly authorised person", in the context of any provision, means a person authorised by the Authority to act for the purposes of that provision.

# Drugs Act 2005[1]

(2005 c 17)

---

[1] This Act received the Royal Assent on 7 April 2005. The Act is in four parts:

Part 1 makes provision for the aggravated supply of controlled drugs, and proof of intention to supply a controlled drug.

Part 2 amends police powers in relation to drugs searches, testing for the presence of drugs and extended detention for suspected drug offenders.

Part 3 provides for assessment following testing for presence of Class A drugs.

Part 4 provides for intervention orders to accompany anti-social behaviour orders in certain cases.

The Act will be brought into force in accordance with commencement orders made under s 24. At the time of going to press the following commencement orders had been made: Drugs Act 2005 (Commencement No 1) Order 2005, SI 2005/1650; Drugs Act 2005 (Commencement No 2) Order 2005, SI 2005/2223; Drugs Act 2005 (Commencement No 3) Order 2005, SI 2005/3053; Drugs Act 2005 (Commencement No 4) Order 2006, SI 2006/2136; and Drugs Act 2005 (Commencement No 5) Order, SI 2007/562. The provisions reproduced below are in force.

## Part 2[1]

## Police Powers Relating to Drugs

## Part 3[2]

## Assessment of Misuse of Drugs

**7.8267 9. Initial assessment following testing for presence of Class A drugs** (1) This section applies if—

(*a*) a sample is taken under section 63B of PACE (testing for presence of Class A drug) from a person detained at a police station,

(*b*) an analysis of the sample reveals that a specified Class A drug may be present in the person's body,

(*c*) the age condition is met, and

(*d*) the notification condition is met.

(2) A police officer may, at any time before the person is released from detention at the police station, require him to attend an initial assessment and remain for its duration.

(3) An initial assessment is an appointment with a suitably qualified person (an "initial assessor")—

(*a*) for the purpose of establishing whether the person is dependent upon or has a propensity to misuse any specified Class A drug,

(*b*) if the initial assessor thinks that he has such a dependency or propensity, for the purpose of establishing whether he might benefit from further assessment, or from assistance or treatment (or both), in connection with the dependency or propensity, and

(*c*) if the initial assessor thinks that he might benefit from such assistance or treatment (or both), for the purpose of providing him with advice, including an explanation of the types of assistance or treatment (or both) which are available.

(4) The age condition is met if the person has attained the age of 18 or such different age as the Secretary of State may by order made by statutory instrument specify for the purposes of this section.

(5) In relation to a person ("A") who has attained the age of 18, the notification condition is met if—

(*a*) the relevant chief officer has been notified by the Secretary of State that arrangements for conducting initial assessments for persons who have attained the age of 18 have been made for persons from whom samples have been taken (under section 63B of PACE) at the police station in which A is detained, and

(*b*) the notice has not been withdrawn.

(6) In relation to a person ("C") who is of an age which is less than 18, the notification condition is met if—

(*a*) the relevant chief officer has been notified by the Secretary of State that arrangements for conducting initial assessments for persons of that age have been made for persons from whom samples have been taken (under section 63B of PACE) at the police station in which C is detained, and

(*b*) the notice has not been withdrawn.

(7) In subsections (5) and (6), "relevant chief officer" means the chief officer of police of the police force for the police area in which the police station is situated.

[Drugs Act 2005, s 9.]

---

1 Part 2 contains ss 3–8.

2 Part 3 contains ss 9–19.

**7.8268 10. Follow-up assessment** (1) This section applies if—

(*a*) a police officer requires a person to attend an initial assessment and remain for its duration under section 9(2),

(*b*) the age condition is met, and

(*c*) the notification condition is met.

(2) The police officer must, at the same time as he imposes the requirement under section 9(2)—

(*a*) require the person to attend a follow-up assessment and remain for its duration, and

(*b*) inform him that the requirement ceases to have effect if he is informed at the initial assessment that he is no longer required to attend the follow-up assessment.

(3) A follow-up assessment is an appointment with a suitably qualified person (a "follow-up assessor")—

(*a*) for any of the purposes of the initial assessment which were not fulfilled at the initial assessment, and

(*b*) if the follow-up assessor thinks it appropriate, for the purpose of drawing up a care plan.

(4) A care plan is a plan which sets out the nature of the assistance or treatment (or both) which may be most appropriate for the person in connection with any dependency upon, or any propensity

to misuse, a specified Class A drug which the follow-up assessor thinks that he has.

(5) The age condition is met if the person has attained the age of 18 or such different age as the Secretary of State may by order made by statutory instrument specify for the purposes of this section.

(6) In relation to a person ("A") who has attained the age of 18, the notification condition is met if—

(*a*) the relevant chief officer has been notified by the Secretary of State that arrangements for conducting follow-up assessments for persons who have attained the age of 18 have been made for persons from whom samples have been taken (under section 63B of PACE) at the police station in which A is detained, and

(*b*) the notice has not been withdrawn.

(7) In relation to a person ("C") who is of an age which is less than 18, the notification condition is met if—

(*a*) the relevant chief officer has been notified by the Secretary of State that arrangements for conducting follow-up assessments for persons of that age have been made for persons from whom samples have been taken (under section 63B of PACE) at the police station in which C is detained, and

(*b*) the notice has not been withdrawn.

(8) In subsections (6) and (7), "relevant chief officer" means the chief officer of police of the police force for the police area in which the police station is situated.

[Drugs Act 2005, s 10.]

7.8269 **11. Requirements under sections 9 and 10: supplemental** (1) This section applies if a person is required to attend an initial assessment and remain for its duration by virtue of section 9(2).

(2) A police officer must—

(*a*) inform the person of the time when, and the place at which, the initial assessment is to take place, and

(*b*) explain that this information will be confirmed in writing.

(3) A police officer must warn the person that he may be liable to prosecution if he fails without good cause to attend the initial assessment and remain for its duration.

(4) If the person is also required to attend a follow-up assessment and remain for its duration by virtue of section 10(2), a police officer must also warn the person that he may be liable to prosecution if he fails without good cause to attend the follow-up assessment and remain for its duration.

(5) A police officer must give the person notice in writing which—

(*a*) confirms that he is required to attend and remain for the duration of an initial assessment or both an initial assessment and a follow-up assessment (as the case may be),

(*b*) confirms the information given in pursuance of subsection (2), and

(*c*) repeats the warning given in pursuance of subsection (3) and any warning given in pursuance of subsection (4).

(6) The duties imposed by subsections (2) to (5) must be discharged before the person is released from detention at the police station.

(7) A record must be made, as part of the person's custody record, of—

(*a*) the requirement imposed on him by virtue of section 9(2),

(*b*) any requirement imposed on him by virtue of section 10(2),

(*c*) the information and explanation given to him in pursuance of subsection (2) above,

(*d*) the warning given to him in pursuance of subsection (3) above and any warning given to him in pursuance of subsection (4) above, and

(*e*) the notice given to him in pursuance of subsection (5) above.

(8) If a person is given a notice in pursuance of subsection (5), a police officer or a suitably qualified person may give the person a further notice in writing which—

(*a*) informs the person of any change to the time when, or to the place at which, the initial assessment is to take place, and

(*b*) repeats the warning given in pursuance of subsection (3) and any warning given in pursuance of subsection (4).

[Drugs Act 2005, s 11.]

7.8270 **12. Attendance at initial assessment** (1) This section applies if a person is required to attend an initial assessment and remain for its duration by virtue of section 9(2).

(2) The initial assessor must inform a police officer or a police support officer if the person—

(*a*) fails to attend the initial assessment at the specified time and place, or

(*b*) attends the assessment at the specified time and place but fails to remain for its duration.

(3) A person is guilty of an offence if without good cause—

(*a*) he fails to attend an initial assessment at the specified time and place, or

(*b*) he attends the assessment at the specified time and place but fails to remain for its duration.

(4) A person who is guilty of an offence under subsection (3) is liable on summary conviction to imprisonment for a term not exceeding 51 weeks, or to a fine not exceeding level 4 on the standard scale, or to both.

(5) If a person fails to attend an initial assessment at the specified time and place, any requirement imposed on him by virtue of section 10(2) ceases to have effect.

(6) In this section—

(*a*) the specified time, in relation to the person concerned, is the time specified in the notice given to him in pursuance of subsection (5) of section 11 or, if a further notice specifying a different time has been given to him in pursuance of subsection (8) of that section, the time specified in that notice, and

(*b*) the specified place, in relation to the person concerned, is the place specified in the notice given to him in pursuance of subsection (5) of section 11 or, if a further notice specifying a different place has been given to him in pursuance of subsection (8) of that section, the place specified in that notice.

(7) In relation to an offence committed before the commencement of section 281(5) of the Criminal Justice Act 2003 (c 44) (alteration of penalties for summary offences), the reference in subsection (4) to 51 weeks is to be read as a reference to 3 months.

[Drugs Act 2005, s 12.]

7.8271 **13. Arrangements for follow-up assessment** (1) This section applies if—

(*a*) a person attends an initial assessment in pursuance of section 9(2), and

(*b*) he is required to attend a follow-up assessment and remain for its duration by virtue of section 10(2).

(2) If the initial assessor thinks that a follow-up assessment is not appropriate, he must inform the person concerned that he is no longer required to attend the follow-up assessment.

(3) The requirement imposed by virtue of section 10(2) ceases to have effect if the person is informed as mentioned in subsection (2).

(4) If the initial assessor thinks that a follow-up assessment is appropriate, the assessor must—

(*a*) inform the person of the time when, and the place at which, the follow-up assessment is to take place, and

(*b*) explain that this information will be confirmed in writing.

(5) The assessor must also warn the person that, if he fails without good cause to attend the follow-up assessment and remain for its duration, he may be liable to prosecution.

(6) The initial assessor must also give the person notice in writing which—

(*a*) confirms that he is required to attend and remain for the duration of the follow-up assessment,

(*b*) confirms the information given in pursuance of subsection (4), and

(*c*) repeats the warning given in pursuance of subsection (5).

(7) The duties mentioned in subsections (2) and (4) to (6) must be discharged before the conclusion of the initial assessment.

(8) If a person is given a notice in pursuance of subsection (6), the initial assessor or another suitably qualified person may give the person a further notice in writing which—

(*a*) informs the person of any change to the time when, or to the place at which, the follow-up assessment is to take place, and

(*b*) repeats the warning mentioned in subsection (5).

[Drugs Act 2005, s 13.]

7.8272 **14. Attendance at follow-up assessment** (1) This section applies if a person is required to attend a follow-up assessment and remain for its duration by virtue of section 10(2).

(2) The follow-up assessor must inform a police officer or a police support officer if the person—

(*a*) fails to attend the follow-up assessment at the specified time and place, or

(*b*) attends the assessment at the specified time and place but fails to remain for its duration.

(3) A person is guilty of an offence if without good cause—

(*a*) he fails to attend a follow-up assessment at the specified time and place, or

(*b*) he attends the assessment at the specified time and place but fails to remain for its duration.

(4) A person who is guilty of an offence under subsection (3) is liable on summary conviction to imprisonment for a term not exceeding 51 weeks, or to a fine not exceeding level 4 on the standard scale, or to both.

(5) In this section—

(*a*) the specified time, in relation to the person concerned, is the time specified in the notice given to him in pursuance of subsection (6) of section 13 or, if a further notice specifying a different time has been given to him in pursuance of subsection (8) of that section, the time specified in that notice, and

(*b*) the specified place, in relation to the person concerned, is the place specified in the notice given to him in pursuance of subsection (6) of section 13 or, if a further notice specifying a different place has been given to him in pursuance of subsection (8) of that section, the place specified in that notice.

(6) In relation to an offence committed before the commencement of section 281(5) of the Criminal Justice Act 2003 (c 44) (alteration of penalties for summary offences), the reference in subsection (4) to 51 weeks is to be read as a reference to 3 months.

[Drugs Act 2005, s 14.]

7.8273 **15. Disclosure of information about assessments** (1) An initial assessor may disclose information obtained as a result of an initial assessment to any of the following—

(*a*) a person who is involved in the conduct of the assessment;

(*b*) a person who is or may be involved in the conduct of any follow-up assessment.

(2) A follow-up assessor may disclose information obtained as a result of a follow-up assessment to a person who is involved in the conduct of the assessment.

(3) Subject to subsections (1) and (2), information obtained as a result of an initial or a follow-up assessment may not be disclosed by any person without the written consent of the person to whom the assessment relates.

(4) Nothing in this section affects the operation of section 17(4).

[Drugs Act 2005, s 15.]

7.8274 **16. Samples submitted for further analysis** (1) A requirement imposed on a person by virtue of section 9(2) or 10(2) ceases to have effect if at any time before he has fully complied with the requirement—

(*a*) a police officer makes arrangements for a further analysis of the sample taken from him as mentioned in section 9(1)(*a*), and

(*b*) the analysis does not reveal that a specified Class A drug was present in the person's body.

(2) If a requirement ceases to have effect by virtue of subsection (1), a police officer must so inform the person concerned.

(3) Nothing in subsection (1) affects the validity of anything done in connection with the requirement before it ceases to have effect.

(4) If a person fails to attend an assessment which he is required to attend by virtue of section 9(2) or fails to remain for the duration of such an assessment but, at any time after his failure, the requirement ceases to have effect by virtue of subsection (1) above—

(*a*) no proceedings for an offence under section 12(3) may be brought against him, and

(*b*) if any such proceedings were commenced before the requirement ceased to have effect, those proceedings must be discontinued.

(5) If a person fails to attend an assessment which he is required to attend by virtue of section 10(2) or fails to remain for the duration of such an assessment but, at any time after his failure, the requirement ceases to have effect by virtue of subsection (1) above—

(*a*) no proceedings for an offence under section 14(3) may be brought against him, and

(*b*) if any such proceedings were commenced before the requirement ceased to have effect, those proceedings must be discontinued.

[Drugs Act 2005, s 16.]

7.8275 **17. Relationship with Bail Act 1976 etc** (1) A requirement imposed on a person by virtue of section 9(2) or 10(2) ceases to have effect if at any time before he has fully complied with the requirement—

(*a*) he is charged with the related offence, and

(*b*) a court imposes on him a condition of bail under section 3(6D) of the Bail Act 1976 (c 63) (duty to impose condition to undergo relevant assessment etc).

(2) For the purposes of section 3(6D) of the 1976 Act, a relevant assessment (within the meaning of that Act) is to be treated as having been carried out if—

(*a*) a person attends an initial assessment and remains for its duration, and

(*b*) the initial assessor is satisfied that the initial assessment fulfilled the purposes of a relevant assessment.

(3) For the purposes of paragraph 6B(2)(*b*) of Schedule 1 to the 1976 Act (exceptions to right to bail for drug users in certain areas), a person is to be treated as having undergone a relevant assessment (within the meaning of that Act) if—

(*a*) the person attends an initial assessment and remains for its duration, and

(*b*) the initial assessor is satisfied that the initial assessment fulfilled the purposes of a relevant assessment.

(4) An initial assessor may disclose information relating to an initial assessment for the purpose of enabling a court considering an application for bail by the person concerned to determine whether subsection (2) or (3) applies.

(5) Nothing in subsection (1) affects—

(*a*) the validity of anything done in connection with the requirement before it ceases to have effect, or

(*b*) any liability which the person may have for an offence under section 12(3) or 14(3) committed before the requirement ceases to have effect.

(6) In subsection (1), "the related offence" is the offence in respect of which the condition specified in subsection (1A) or (2) of section 63B of PACE is satisfied in relation to the taking of the sample mentioned in section 9(1)(*a*) of this Act.

[Drugs Act 2005, s 17.]

7.8276 **18. Orders under this Part and guidance** (1) A statutory instrument containing an order under section 9(4) or 10(5) must not be made unless a draft of the instrument has been laid before, and approved by a resolution of, each House of Parliament.

(2) Any such order may—

(*a*) make different provision for different police areas;

(*b*) make such provision as the Secretary of State considers appropriate in connection with requiring persons who have not attained the age of 18 to attend and remain for the duration of an initial assessment or a follow-up assessment (as the case may be), including provision amending this Part.

(3) In exercising any functions conferred by this Part, a police officer and a suitably qualified person must have regard to any guidance issued by the Secretary of State for the purposes of this Part.

[Drugs Act 2005, s 18.]

7.8277 **19. Interpretation** (1) This section applies for the purposes of this Part.

(2) "Class A drug" and "misuse" have the same meanings as in the Misuse of Drugs Act 1971 (c 38).

(3) "Specified", in relation to a Class A drug, has the same meaning as in Part 3 of the Criminal Justice and Court Services Act 2000 (c 43).

(4) "Initial assessment" and "initial assessor" must be construed in accordance with section 9(3).

(5) "Follow-up assessment" and "follow-up assessor" must be construed in accordance with section 10(3).

(6) "Suitably qualified person" means a person who has such qualifications or experience as are from time to time specified by the Secretary of State for the purposes of this Part.

(7) "Police support officer" means—

(*a*) persons appointed by a chief constable under paragraph 4 of Schedule 2 to the Police Reform and Social Responsibility Act 2011 (civilian staff of police forces outside London), and

(*b*) persons appointed by the Commissioner of Police of the Metropolis under paragraph 1 of Schedule 4 to that Act (civilian staff of metropolitan police force).

(8) "PACE" means the Police and Criminal Evidence Act 1984 (c 60).

[Drugs Act 2005, s 19 as amended by the Police Reform and Social Responsibility Act 2011, Sch 16.]

## PART 4[1]

## MISCELLANEOUS AND GENERAL

7.8278 **24. Short title, commencement and extent** (1) This Act may be cited as the Drugs Act 2005.

(2) This section and section 22 come into force on the day on which this Act is passed.

(3) Otherwise, this Act comes into force on such day as the Secretary of State may by order[2] made by statutory instrument appoint.

(4) Different days may be appointed for different purposes.

(5) An order under subsection (3) may make—

(*a*) any supplementary, incidental or consequential provision, and

(*b*) any transitory, transitional or saving provision,

as the Secretary of State considers necessary or expedient in connection with the order.

(6) Subject to subsection (7), this Act (except this section and sections 22 and 23) extends to England and Wales only.

(7) So far as it amends or repeals any enactment, this Act has the same extent as the enactment amended or repealed.

[Drugs Act 2005, s 24.]

---

1 Part 4 contains ss 20–24.

2 For details of commencement orders made, see the note to the title of this Act, ante.

# National Health Service Act 2006[1]

(2006 c 41)

## PART 9[2]

## CHARGING

*Recovery, etc*

7.8279 **191. Recovery of charges** (1) All charges[3] recoverable under this Act by—

(*a*) the Secretary of State,

(*b*) a local social services authority[4], or

(*c*) any body established under this Act,

may be recovered summarily as a civil debt[5] (but this does not affect any other method of recovery).

(2) If any person, for the purpose of evading the payment of any charge under this Act, or of reducing the amount of any such charge—

(*a*) knowingly makes any false statement or false representation, or

(*b*) produces or furnishes, or causes or knowingly allows to be produced or furnished, any document or information which he knows to be false in a material particular,

the charge or the balance of the charge, may be recovered from him by the person by whom the cost of the service in question was defrayed.

[National Health Service Act 2006, s 191.]

---

1 This Act came into force on 1 March 2007 (see the National Health Service (Consequential Provisions Act 2006) and consolidates various provisions relating to the National Health Service. For provision in Wales, see the National Health Service (Wales) Act 2006, Part 9, ss 121–141.

2 Part 9 comprises ss 172–194.

3 Various charges are payable under this Part of the Act.

4 "Local social services authority" means the council of a non-metropolitan county, of a county borough or of a metropolitan district or London borough, or the Common Council of the City of London (National Health Service Act 2006, s 275(1)).

5 For procedure for recovery of a civil debt summarily, see s 58 of the Magistrates' Courts Act 1980 in Part I: Magistrates' Courts, Procedure, ante.

7.8280 **192. Recovery of charges and payments in relation to goods and services**

(1) Where goods or services to which this section applies are provided and—

(*a*) any charge payable by any person under this Act in respect of the provision of the goods or services is reduced, remitted or repaid, but that person is not entitled to the reduction, remission or repayment, or

(*b*) any payment under this Act is made to, or for the benefit of, any person in respect of the cost of obtaining the goods or services, but that person is not entitled to, or to the benefit of, the payment,

the amount mentioned in subsection (2) is recoverable summarily as a civil debt from the person in question by the responsible authority.

(2) That amount—

(*a*) in a case within subsection (1)(*a*), is the amount of the charge or (where it has been reduced) reduction,

(*b*) in a case within subsection (1)(*b*), is the amount of the payment.

(3) Where two or more persons are liable under section 191(1) or this section to pay an amount in respect of the same charge or payment, those persons are jointly and severally liable.

(4) For the purposes of this section, the circumstances in which a person is treated as not entitled to a reduction, remission or repayment of a charge, or to (or to the benefit of) a payment, include in particular those in which it is received (wholly or partly)—

(*a*) on the ground that he or another is a person of a particular description, where the person in question is not of that description,

(*b*) on the ground that he or another holds a particular certificate, when the person in question does not hold such a certificate or does hold such a certificate but is not entitled to it,

(*c*) on the ground that he or another has made a particular statement, when the person in question has not made such a statement or the statement made by him is false.

(5) In this section and section 193, "responsible authority" means—

(*a*) in relation to the recovery of any charge under section 191(1) in respect of the provision of goods or services to which this section applies, the person by whom the charge is recoverable,

(*b*) in relation to the recovery by virtue of this section of the whole or part of the amount of any such charge, the person by whom the charge would have been recoverable,

(*c*) in a case within subsection (1)(*b*), the person who made the payment.

(6) But the Secretary of State may by directions provide for—

(*a*) the functions of any responsible authority of recovering any charges under this Act in respect of the provision of goods or services to which this section applies,

(*b*) the functions of any responsible authority under this section and section 193,

to be exercised on behalf of the authority by another health service body.

(7) This section applies to the following goods and services—

(*a*) dental treatment and appliances provided in pursuance of this Act,

(*b*) drugs and medicines provided in pursuance of this Act,

(*c*) sight tests,

(*d*) optical appliances,

(*e*) any other appliances provided in pursuance of this Act.

(8) "Health service body" means a body which is a health service body for the purposes of section 9.

[National Health Service Act 2006, s 192.]

7.8281 **193. Penalties relating to charges** (1) Regulations may provide that, where a person fails to pay—

(*a*) any amount recoverable from him under section 191(1) in respect of the provision of goods or services to which section 192 applies, or

(*b*) any amount recoverable from him under section 192,

a notice (referred to in this section as a penalty notice) may be served on the person by the responsible authority.

(2) A penalty notice is a notice requiring the person on whom it is served to pay the amount to the authority within a prescribed period, together with a charge (referred to in this section as a penalty charge) of an amount determined in accordance with the regulations.

(3) The regulations may not provide for the amount of the penalty charge to exceed whichever is the smaller of—

(*a*) £100,

(*b*) the amount referred to in subsection (1)(*a*) or (*b*) multiplied by 5.

(4) The Secretary of State may by order provide for subsection (3) to have effect as if, for the sum specified in paragraph (*a*) or the multiplier specified in paragraph (*b*) (including that sum or multiplier as substituted by a previous order), there were substituted a sum or multiplier specified in the order.

(5) Regulations may provide that, if a person fails to pay the amount he is required to pay under a penalty notice within the period in question, he must also pay to the responsible authority by way of penalty a further sum determined in accordance with the regulations.

(6) The further sum must not exceed 50 per cent of the amount of the penalty charge.

(7) Any sum payable under the regulations (including the amount referred to in subsection (1)(*a*) or (*b*)) may be recovered by the responsible authority summarily as a civil debt.

(8) But a person is not liable by virtue of a penalty notice—

(*a*) to pay at any time so much of any amount referred to in subsection (1)(*a*) or (*b*) for which he is jointly and severally liable with another as at that time has been paid, or ordered by a court to be paid, by that other, or

(*b*) to a penalty charge, or a further sum by way of penalty, if he shows that he did not act wrongfully, or with any lack of care, in respect of the charge or payment in question.

[National Health Service Act 2006, s 193.]

7.8282 **194. Offences relating to charges** (1) A person is guilty of an offence if he does any act mentioned in subsection (2) with a view to securing for himself or another—

(*a*) the evasion of the whole or part of any charge under this Act in respect of the provision of goods or services to which section 192 applies,

(*b*) the reduction, remission or repayment of any such charge, where he or the other is not entitled to the reduction, remission or repayment,

(*c*) a payment under this Act (whether to, or for the benefit of, himself or the other) in respect of the cost of obtaining such goods or services, where he or the other is not entitled to, or to the benefit of, the payment.

(2) The acts referred to in subsection (1) are—

(*a*) knowingly making, or causing or knowingly allowing another to make, a false statement or representation, or

(*b*) in the case of any document or information which he knows to be false in a material particular, producing or providing it or causing or knowingly allowing another to produce or provide it.

(3) A person guilty of an offence under this section is liable on summary conviction to a fine not exceeding level 4 on the standard scale.

(4) A person may conduct any proceedings under this section before a magistrates' court if he is authorised to do so by the Secretary of State.

(5) Proceedings for an offence under this section may be begun within—

(*a*) the period of three months beginning with the date on which evidence, sufficient in the opinion of the Secretary of State to justify a prosecution for the offence, comes to his knowledge, or

(*b*) the period of 12 months beginning with the commission of the offence.

(6) For the purposes of subsection (5), a certificate purporting to be signed by or on behalf of the Secretary of State as to the date on which such evidence as is mentioned in paragraph (*a*) of that subsection came to his knowledge, is conclusive evidence of that date.

(7) Where a person is convicted of an offence under this section in respect of any charge or payment under this Act, he is not liable in respect of the charge or payment to pay any penalty charge or further sum by way of penalty which would otherwise be recoverable from him under section 193.

(8) Where a person pays any penalty charge, or further charge by way of penalty, recoverable under section 193 in respect of any charge or payment under this Act, he must not be convicted of an offence under this section in respect of the charge or payment.

(9) Subsection (4) of section 192 applies for the purposes of this section as it applies for the purposes of that.

[National Health Service Act 2006, s 194 as amended by the Legal Services Act 2007, Sch 21.]

## PART 10[1]

## PROTECTION OF NHS FROM FRAUD AND OTHER UNLAWFUL ACTIVITIES

### *Preliminary*

7.8283 **195. Compulsory disclosure of documents** (1) This Part confers power to require the production of documents in connection with the exercise of the Secretary of State's counter fraud functions or security management functions in relation to the health service.

(2) The Secretary of State's "counter fraud functions" in relation to the health service means his power (by virtue of section 2) to take action for the purpose of preventing, detecting or investigating fraud, corruption or other unlawful activities carried out against or otherwise affecting—

(*a*) the health service, or

(*b*) the Secretary of State in relation to his responsibilities for the health service.

(3) The Secretary of State's "security management functions" in relation to the health service means his power (by virtue of section 2) to take action for the purpose of protecting and improving the security of—

(*a*) persons employed by the Secretary of State or an NHS body in the provision of services for the purposes of the health service ("NHS services") or in arranging for the provision of such services,

(*b*) health service providers and persons employed by them so far as they or persons so employed are engaged in any activity directly related to the provision of NHS services,

(*c*) NHS contractors and persons employed by them so far as they or persons so employed are engaged in any activity directly related to the provision of NHS services,

(*d*) persons not within paragraphs (*a*) to (*c*) who work in any capacity on premises used by the Secretary of State, an NHS body, a health service provider, or an NHS contractor, in connection with the provision of NHS services or with arranging for the provision of such services,

(*e*) persons on such premises—

(i) who are there for the purpose of receiving, or are receiving or have received, treatment or other services as patients, or

(ii) who are accompanying persons within sub-paragraph (i),

(*f*) property and information used or held by the Secretary of State, an NHS body, a health service provider, or an NHS contractor, in connection with the provision of NHS services or in arranging for the provision of such services.

(4) In this Part, the Secretary of State's counter fraud functions and security management functions in relation to the health service are collectively referred to as functions to which this Part applies.

(5) "Investigating" means investigating in relation to civil or criminal proceedings.

[National Health Service Act 2006, s 195 as amended by the Health and Social Care Act 2012, Sch 4.]

---

[1] Part 10 comprises ss 195–210. For provision in Wales, see the National Health Service (Wales) Act 2006, Part 10, ss 143–158.

7.8284 **196. Persons and bodies about which provision is made by this Part** (1) This section applies for the purposes of this Part.

(2) Subject to subsection (3), and any provision made under subsection (7), "NHS body" has the meaning given by section 275(1).

(3) In section 195(3), and in section 197(1) so far as having effect in relation to the Secretary of State's security management functions referred to in section 195(3), an "NHS body" means—

(*za*) the Board,

(*zb*) a clinical commissioning group,

(*a*) *repealed*

(*b*) a Special Health Authority, so far as performing functions in respect of England,

(*c*) *repealed*

(*d*) *repealed*

(*e*) an NHS foundation trust.

(4) A "health service provider" means any person (other than an NHS body) providing—

(*a*) primary medical services, primary dental services or pharmaceutical services under this Act or the National Health Service (Wales) Act 2006 (c 42),

(*b*) general ophthalmic services under that Act, or

(*c*) primary ophthalmic services.

(5) An "NHS contractor" means any person (other than an NHS body or a person within subsection (4)) providing services of any description under arrangements made with an NHS body.

(5A) A "public health service contractor" means any person providing services of any description under arrangements made in the exercise of the public health functions of the Secretary of State or a local authority.

(6) A "statutory health body" means any body (other than an NHS body, or a person within subsection (4) or (5)) established by or under an enactment and—

(*a*) providing services in connection with the provision of, or (*b*) exercising functions in relation to,

the health service in either England or Wales or both.

(7) The Secretary of State may by order—

(*a*) make such amendments of any of subsections (2) to (6) as he considers appropriate,

(*b*) make such consequential amendments of this Part as he considers appropriate.

[National Health Service Act 2006, s 196 as amended by the Health and Social Care Act 2012, Sch 4.]

*Production of documents*

7.8285 **197. Notice requiring production of documents** (1) This section applies if it appears to the Secretary of State that there are reasonable grounds for suspecting—

(*a*) that any documents containing information relevant to the exercise of any of his functions to which this Part applies are in the possession or under the control of any NHS body, statutory health body, health service provider, public health service contractor or NHS contractor ("the relevant organisation"), and

(*b*) that a person within subsection (3) is accountable for the documents.

(2) The Secretary of State may serve on that person a notice requiring him to produce the documents to an authorised officer.

(3) The persons within this subsection are—

(*a*) any member, officer or director of the relevant organisation,

(*b*) any other person who takes part in the management of the affairs of that organisation,

(*c*) any person employed by that organisation, and

(*d*) (in the case of a health service provider, public health service contractor or NHS contractor who is an individual) that individual.

(4) A notice under this section must specify or describe the documents to which it relates.

(5) Subject to subsections (6) and (7), the notice may require those documents to be produced—

(*a*) at or by such time as is specified in the notice, or at once, and

(*b*) at such place, and in such manner, as is so specified.

(6) When specifying a time at or by which the documents must be produced, the notice must not require them to be produced otherwise than at a reasonable hour.

(7) If the notice requires documents to be produced at once, it may only be served at a reasonable hour.

(8) An authorised officer may, by agreement with the person served with a notice within subsection (6) or (7), vary the notice so as to extend the time for compliance with it.

(9) Any notice under this section, and any variation of such a notice under subsection (8), must be in writing.

(10) An individual is "accountable" for any documents if he has either day-to-day, or an overall, responsibility for the custody or control of the documents.

[National Health Service Act 2006, s 197 as amended by the Health and Social Care Act 2012, Sch 4.]

7.8286 **198. Production of documents** (1) This section applies where a notice has been served under section 197.

(2) An authorised officer may—

(*a*) take away any documents produced in compliance with the notice,

(*b*) take copies of or extracts from any documents so produced,

(*c*) require the person producing any such documents to provide an explanation of any of them.

(3) If—

(*a*) the officer takes away any such document,

(*b*) the person producing it requests the officer to provide him with a copy of it, and

(*c*) the request appears to the officer to be reasonable in the circumstances,

the officer must, as soon as is reasonably practicable, provide that person with a copy of the document (in such form as the officer considers appropriate).

(4) Documents produced in compliance with a notice under section 197 may be retained for so long as the Secretary of State considers that it is necessary to retain them (rather than copies of them) in connection with the exercise of any of his functions to which this Part applies.

(5) If the Secretary of State has reasonable grounds for believing—

(*a*) that any such documents may have to be produced for the purposes of any legal proceedings, and

(*b*) that they might otherwise be unavailable for those purposes,

they may be retained until the proceedings are concluded.

(6) If a person who is required by a notice under section 197 to produce any documents does not produce the documents in compliance with the notice, an authorised officer may require that person to state, to the best of his knowledge and belief, where they are.

(7) A person is not bound to comply with any requirement imposed by a notice under section 197 or any requirement under subsection (6) unless evidence of authority is given—

(*a*) at the time when the notice is served, or

(*b*) at the time when the requirement is imposed under subsection (6).

(8) In addition, a person may not be required under section 197 or subsection (6) to produce any document or disclose any information which he would be entitled to refuse to produce or disclose in proceedings in the High Court on grounds of legal professional privilege.

[National Health Service Act 2006, s 198.]

**7.8286B 199. Delegation of functions** *Secretary of State may delegate his functions to a Special Health Authority or a senior officer of such an authority.*

**7.8286B 200. Code of practice relating to delegated functions** *Secretary of State may issue Code of Practice relating to the exercise of functions under ss 197 and 198.*

**7.8287 201. Disclosure of information** (1) This section applies to information which—

(*a*) is held by or on behalf of the Secretary of State, and

(*b*) was obtained by virtue of section 197 or 198.

(2) The information must not be disclosed except in accordance with subsection (3).

(3) A disclosure is made in accordance with this subsection if it is made—

(*a*) for the purposes of the exercise of any of the functions of the Secretary of State, the Board, a clinical commissioning group or a local authority in relation to the health service in England;

(*b*) for the purposes of the exercise of any of the Welsh Ministers' functions in relation to the health service in Wales,

(*c*) for the purposes of any civil proceedings brought in the exercise of any of the functions mentioned in paragraph (*a*) or (*b*),

(*d*) for the purposes of any criminal investigation or proceedings,

(*e*) for the purposes of any relevant disciplinary proceedings, or

(*f*) in accordance with an enactment or order of a court or tribunal.

(4) In subsection (3)—

"relevant disciplinary proceedings" means disciplinary proceedings conducted in relation to an individual by—

(*a*) an NHS body, statutory health body or health service provider, or

(*b*) any of the regulatory bodies mentioned in section 25(3) of the National Health Service Reform and Health Care Professions Act 2002 (c 17) (bodies within remit of the Professional Standards Authority for Health and Social Care).

(5) Where information to which this section applies is disclosed to any person in accordance with subsection (3), the information must not be used or further disclosed except—

(*a*) for a purpose connected with the functions, investigation or proceedings for the purposes of which it was so disclosed, or

(*b*) in accordance with an enactment or order of a court or tribunal.

(6) Information to which this section applies may be disclosed in accordance with subsection (3) despite any obligation of confidence that would otherwise prohibit or restrict the disclosure.

(7) This section does not prohibit any disclosure or use of information relating to a particular person if it is made with the consent of that person.

[National Health Service Act 2006, s 201 as amended by the Health and Social Care Act 2012, Sch 4.]

**7.8288 202. Protection of personal information disclosed for purposes of proceedings** (1) Information obtained from personal records produced in compliance with a notice under section 197 is "protected information" for the purposes of this section if—

(*a*) a person ("the discloser"), in accordance with section 201(3), discloses the information for the purposes of any proceedings, and

(*b*) either—

(i) the identity of the individual in question can be ascertained from the information itself, or

(ii) the discloser has reasonable cause to believe that it will be possible for a person who obtains the information as a direct or indirect consequence of the disclosure to ascertain the individual's identity from that information taken with other information obtained by virtue of section 197 or 198 and disclosed by or on behalf of the Secretary of State.

(2) The discloser must take all reasonable steps to ensure that, once disclosed by him in accordance with section 201(3), the protected information is not further disclosed to any person who is not someone to whom it is necessary to disclose the information for any purpose connected with the proceedings mentioned in subsection (1)(*a*).

(3) In subsection (2) the reference to further disclosure of the information does not include any such disclosure—

(*a*) by way of evidence in any proceedings, or

(*b*) in accordance with an enactment or order of a court or tribunal.

(4) The Secretary of State must make provision, whether in a code of practice issued under section 200 or otherwise, for requiring any person disclosing protected information in accordance with section 201(3) to ensure, by the use of a distinguishing mark or in some other way, that the

information is clearly identified as protected information for the purposes of this section.

(5) Information that appears to be protected information must not be disclosed by way of evidence in any proceedings unless—

(*a*) the whole of the proceedings are held in private, or

(*b*) in any other case, the information is disclosed in accordance with permission given by the court or tribunal on an application under subsection (6).

(6) If, on an application by a party to—

(*a*) proceedings before a court, or

(*b*) proceedings of any description before a tribunal that sits, or may sit, in public during the whole or part of proceedings of that description,

the court or tribunal is satisfied that it is in the interests of justice for any information that appears to be protected information to be disclosed by way of evidence in the proceedings, it may give permission for the information to be so disclosed, on such terms as it thinks fit.

(7) When determining such an application, the court or tribunal must consider whether, in the interests of protecting the identity of the individual to whom the information relates, the whole or part of the proceedings should be held in private.

(8) If the court or tribunal is satisfied that the whole or part of the proceedings should be held in private, it must give such directions, or take such other steps, as appear to it to be appropriate.

(9) In this section "proceedings" means—

(*a*) criminal or civil proceedings, or

(*b*) relevant disciplinary proceedings (as defined by section 201(4)).

[National Health Service Act 2006, s 202.]

7.8289 **203. Manner in which disclosure notice may be served** (1) This section provides for the manner in which a notice may be served under section 197.

(2) The notice may be served on a person by—

(*a*) delivering it to him,

(*b*) leaving it at his proper address,

(*c*) sending it by post to him at that address.

(3) For the purposes of this section and section 7 of the Interpretation Act 1978 (c 30) (service of documents by post) in its application to this section, the proper address of a person is his usual or last-known address (whether residential or otherwise), except that—

(*a*) in the case of a notice to be served on the secretary, clerk or similar officer of a body corporate, it is the address of the registered office of that body or its principal office in the United Kingdom,

(*b*) in the case of a notice to be served on a partner or a person having the control or management of a partnership business, it is the address of the principal office of the partnership in the United Kingdom, and

(*c*) in the case of a notice to be served on an officer of an unincorporated association (other than a partnership), it is the address of the principal office of the association in the United Kingdom.

[National Health Service Act 2006, s 203.]

*Offences under this Part*

7.8290 **204. Offences in connection with production of documents** (1) A person commits an offence if, without reasonable excuse, he fails to comply with any requirement imposed on him under section 197 or 198.

(2) A person guilty of an offence under subsection (1) is liable on summary conviction—

(*a*) to imprisonment for a term not exceeding 51 weeks, or

(*b*) to a fine not exceeding level 3 the standard scale,

or to both.

(3) If a person is convicted of an offence under subsection (1) in respect of a failure to produce a document and the failure continues after the date of his conviction, the person—

(*a*) commits a further offence, and

(*b*) is liable on summary conviction to a fine not exceeding 2% of level 3 on the standard scale for each day on which the failure so continues.

(4) A person commits an offence if, in purported compliance with any requirement imposed on him under section 198—

(*a*) he makes a statement which is false or misleading, and

(*b*) he either knows that it is false or misleading or is reckless as to whether it is false or misleading.

(5) "False or misleading" means false or misleading in a material particular.

(6) A person guilty of an offence under subsection (4) is liable[1]—

(*a*) on conviction on indictment, to imprisonment for a term not exceeding two years or to a fine, or to both,

(*b*) on summary conviction, to imprisonment for a term not exceeding 12 months or to a fine not exceeding the statutory maximum, or to both.

[National Health Service Act 2006, s 204.]

1 For procedure in respect of this offence, which is triable either way, see the Magistrates' Courts Act 1980, ss 17–21, in PART I: MAGISTRATES' COURTS, PROCEDURE, ante.

7.8291 **205. Offences relating to disclosure or use of information** (1) A person commits an offence if he fails to comply with section 201(2) or (5) or section 202(2).

(2) A person guilty of an offence under subsection (1) is liable[1]—

(*a*) on conviction on indictment, to imprisonment for a term not exceeding two years or to a fine, or to both,

(*b*) on summary conviction to imprisonment for a term not exceeding 51 weeks or to a fine not exceeding the statutory maximum, or to both.

(3) It is a defence for a person charged with an offence under subsection (1) in respect of a disclosure of information to prove that at the time of the alleged offence—

(*a*) any of the circumstances in subsection (4) applied, or

(*b*) he reasonably believed that they applied.

(4) The circumstances referred to in subsection (3) are—

(*a*) that the disclosure was lawful,

(*b*) that the information had already been lawfully made available to the public,

(*c*) that the disclosure was necessary or expedient for the purpose of protecting the welfare of any individual,

(*d*) that the disclosure was made in a form in which no person to whom the information relates is identified.

(5) Subsection (4)(*d*) is not satisfied if the identity of any such person can be ascertained either—

(*a*) from the information itself, or

(*b*) from that information taken with other information obtained by virtue of section 197 or 198 and disclosed by or on behalf of the Secretary of State.

[National Health Service Act 2006, s 205.]

1 For procedure in respect of this offence, which is triable either way, see the Magistrates' Courts Act 1980, ss 17–21, in PART I: MAGISTRATES' COURTS, PROCEDURE, ante.

7.8292 **206. Offences by bodies corporate etc** (1) If an offence committed by a body corporate is proved—

(*a*) to have been committed with the consent or connivance of an officer, or

(*b*) to be attributable to any neglect on his part,

the officer as well as the body corporate is guilty of the offence and liable to be proceeded against and punished accordingly.

(2) "Officer", in relation to the body corporate, means a director, manager, secretary or other similar officer of the body, or a person purporting to act in any such capacity.

(3) If the affairs of a body corporate are managed by its members, subsection (1) applies in relation to the acts and defaults of a member in connection with his functions of management as if he were a director of the body corporate.

(4) If an offence committed by a partnership is proved—

(*a*) to have been committed with the consent or connivance of a partner, or

(*b*) to be attributable to any neglect on his part,

the partner as well as the partnership is guilty of the offence and liable to be proceeded against and punished accordingly.

(5) "Partner" includes a person purporting to act as a partner.

(6) If an offence committed by an unincorporated association (other than a partnership) is proved—

(*a*) to have been committed with the consent or connivance of an officer of the association or a member of its governing body, or

(*b*) to be attributable to any neglect on the part of such an officer or member,

the officer or member as well as the association is guilty of the offence and liable to be proceeded against and punished accordingly.

(7) "Offence" means an offence under this Part.

[National Health Service Act 2006, s 206.]

7.8293 **207. Offences committed by partnerships and other unincorporated associations**

(1) Proceedings for an offence alleged to have been committed by a partnership must be brought in the name of the partnership (and not in that of any of the partners).

(2) Proceedings for an offence alleged to have been committed by an unincorporated association (other than a partnership) must be brought in the name of the association (and not in that of any of its members).

(3) Rules of court relating to the service of documents have effect as if the partnership or unincorporated association were a body corporate.

(4) In proceedings for an offence brought against a partnership or an unincorporated association, section 33 of the Criminal Justice Act 1925 (c 86) and Schedule 3 to the Magistrates' Courts Act 1980 (c 43) apply as they apply in relation to a body corporate.

(5) A fine imposed on a partnership on its conviction for an offence must be paid out of the

partnership assets.

(6) A fine imposed on an unincorporated association on its conviction for an offence must be paid out of the funds of the association.

(7) Subsections (1) and (2) do not affect any liability of a partner, officer or member under section 206(4) or (6).

(8) "Offence" means an offence under this Part.

[National Health Service Act 2006, s 207.]

7.8294 **208. Penalties for offences under this Part: transitional modification** (1) In relation to an offence committed before the commencement of section 154(1) of the Criminal Justice Act 2003 (c 44) (general limit on magistrates' courts power to impose imprisonment), the reference in section 204(6)(*b*) to a period of imprisonment of 12 months is a reference to a period of imprisonment of 6 months.

(2) In relation to an offence committed before the commencement of section 281(5) of the Criminal Justice Act 2003 (alteration of penalties for summary offences), the references in sections 204(2)(*a*) and 205(2)(*b*) to periods of imprisonment of 51 weeks are references to periods of imprisonment of 3 months.

[National Health Service Act 2006, s 208.]

*Supplementary*

7.8295 **209. Orders and regulations under this Part** (1) Any power under this Part to make an order or regulations is exercisable by statutory instrument.

(2) Subject to subsection (3) a statutory instrument made by virtue of this Part is subject to annulment in pursuance of a resolution of either House of Parliament.

(3) A statutory instrument containing an order under section 196(7) may not be made unless a draft of the instrument has been laid before, and approved by a resolution of, each House of Parliament.

(4) Any power under this Part to make an order or regulations—

(*a*) may make different provision for different cases or descriptions of case or different purposes or areas, and

(*b*) may make incidental, supplementary, consequential, transitory, transitional or saving provision.

[National Health Service Act 2006, s 209.]

7.8296 **210. Interpretation of this Part** (1) In this Part—

"authorised officer", in relation to any function, means (subject to subsection (5)) an officer of the Secretary of State authorised by him to act in exercise of the function,

"document" means anything in which information of any description is recorded,

"enactment" includes any provision of subordinate legislation (within the meaning of the Interpretation Act 1978 (c 30)), and references to enactments include enactments passed or made after the passing of this Act,

"employed" means employed whether under a contract of service or a contract for services or otherwise, and whether for remuneration or not,

"functions to which this Part applies" has the meaning given by section 195(4),

"health service provider", "public health service contractor" and "NHS contractor" have the meaning given by section 196,

"NHS body" must be construed in accordance with section 196,

"personal records" has the meaning given by section 12 of the Police and Criminal Evidence Act 1984 (c 60),

"statutory health body" has the meaning given by section 196.

(2) References in this Part to the provision of services—

(*a*) in relation to the Secretary of State, local authorities, statutory health bodies, health service providers, public health service contractors or NHS contractors, include references to the provision of goods or facilities, and

(*b*) include references to the provision of services (or goods or facilities) wherever that takes place.

(3) References in this Part to the health service are references to the health service in England.

(4) In relation to information recorded otherwise than in legible form, any reference in this Part to the production of documents is a reference to the production of a copy of the information in legible form.

(5) Where functions of the Secretary of State are exercisable by a Special Health Authority—

(*a*) references in this Part to authorised officers include officers of the Special Health Authority authorised by or on behalf of the Special Health Authority to act in exercise of the functions, and

(*b*) references in this Part to information held or disclosed by or on behalf of the Secretary of State include information held or disclosed by or on behalf of the Special Health Authority.

[National Health Service Act 2006, s 210 as amended by the Health and Social Care Act 2012, Sch 4.]

## PART 13[1]
## MISCELLANEOUS

7.8297 **249. Joint working with the prison service** (1) In exercising their respective functions, NHS bodies (on the one hand) and the prison service (on the other) must co-operate with one another with a view to improving the way in which those functions are exercised in relation to securing and maintaining the health of prisoners.

(2) The Secretary of State may by regulations make provision for or in connection with enabling prescribed NHS bodies (on the one hand) and the prison service (on the other) to enter into prescribed arrangements in relation to the exercise of—

(*a*) prescribed functions of the NHS bodies, and

(*b*) prescribed health-related functions of the prison service,

if the arrangements are likely to lead to an improvement in the way in which those functions are exercised in relation to securing and maintaining the health of prisoners.

(3) The arrangements which may be prescribed include arrangements—

(*a*) for or in connection with the establishment and maintenance of a fund—

(i) which is made up of contributions by one or more NHS bodies and by the prison service, and

(ii) out of which payments may be made towards expenditure incurred in the exercise of both prescribed functions of the NHS body or bodies and prescribed health-related functions of the prison service,

(*b*) for or in connection with the exercise by an NHS body on behalf of the prison service of prescribed health-related functions of the prison service in conjunction with the exercise by the NHS body of prescribed functions of the NHS body,

(*c*) for or in connection with the exercise by the prison service on behalf of an NHS body of prescribed functions of the NHS body in conjunction with the exercise by the prison service of prescribed health-related functions of the prison service,

(*d*) as to the provision of staff, goods or services in connection with any arrangements mentioned in paragraph (*a*), (*b*) or (*c*),

(*e*) as to the making of payments by the prison service to an NHS body in connection with any arrangements mentioned in paragraph (*b*),

(*f*) as to the making of payments by an NHS body to the prison service in connection with any arrangements mentioned in paragraph (*c*).

(4) Any arrangements made by virtue of this section do not affect the liability of NHS bodies, or of the prison service, for the exercise of any of their functions.

(4A) For the purposes of this section, each local authority (within the meaning of section 2B) is to be treated as an NHS body.

(5) "The prison service" means the Minister of the Crown exercising functions in relation to prisons (within the meaning of the Prison Act 1952 (c 52)); and "Minister of the Crown" has the same meaning as in the Ministers of the Crown Act 1975.

[National Health Service Act 2006, s 249 as amended by the Health and Social Care Act 2012, s 29.]

---

[1] Part 13 comprises ss 248–270. For provision in Wales corresponding to s 249, see the National Health Service (Wales) Act 2006, s 188.

7.8298 **259. Sale of medical practices** (1) It is unlawful to sell the goodwill of the medical practice of a person to whom any of subsections (2) to (4) applies, unless the person—

(*a*) no longer provides or performs the services mentioned, and

(*b*) has never carried on the practice in a relevant area.

(2) This subsection applies to a person who has at any time provided general medical services under arrangements made—

(*a*) with any Council, Committee or Authority under the National Health Service Act 1946 (c 81) or the National Health Service Reorganisation Act 1973 (c 32), or

(*b*) with any Primary Care Trust, Health Authority or Local Health Board under section 29 of the National Health Service Act 1977 (c 49).

(3) This subsection applies to a person who has at any time provided or performed personal medical services in accordance with section 28C of the National Health Service Act 1977 (prior to the coming into force of section 16CC of that Act).

(4) This subsection applies to a person who has at any time, in prescribed circumstances or, if regulations so provide, in all circumstances, provided or performed primary medical services—

(*a*) in accordance with section 28C arrangements (within the meaning given by section 28D of the National Health Service Act 1977),

(*b*) in accordance with arrangements under section 16CC(2)(*b*) of that Act,

(*c*) under a general medical services contract (within the meaning of section 28Q(2) of that Act),

(*d*) in accordance with section 92 arrangements or section 50 arrangements,

(*e*) in accordance with arrangements under section 83(2)(*b*) of this Act, or section 41(2)(*b*) of the National Health Service (Wales) Act 2006 (c 42), (*f*) under a general medical services contract or a Welsh general medical services contract.

(5) In this section—

"goodwill" includes any part of goodwill and, in relation to a person practising in partnership, means his share of the goodwill of the partnership practice,

"medical practice" includes any part of a medical practice,

"relevant area", in relation to any Council, Committee, Primary Care Trust, Local Health Board or Authority by arrangement or contract with whom a person has at any time provided or performed services, means the area, district or locality of that Council, Committee, Primary Care Trust, Local Health Board or Authority (at that time),

"section 50 arrangements" means arrangements for the provision of services made under section 50 of the National Health Service (Wales) Act 2006 (c 42), and

"Welsh general medical services contract" means a contract under section 42(2) of the National Health Service (Wales) Act 2006.

(6) Schedule 21[1] makes further provision in relation to this section.

[National Health Service Act 2006, s 259.]

---

1 Post.

7.8299 **260. Control of maximum price of medical supplies other than health service medicines** (1) The Secretary of State may by order provide for the control of maximum prices to be charged for any medical supplies, other than health service medicines, required for the purposes of this Act.

(2) The Secretary of State may by direction given with respect to any undertaking, or by order made with respect to any class or description of undertakings, require persons carrying on the undertaking or undertakings of that class or description—

(*a*) to keep such books, accounts and records relating to the undertaking as may be prescribed by the direction, the order or a notice served under the order,

(*b*) to furnish at such times, in such manner and in such form as may be so prescribed such estimates, returns or information relating to the undertaking as may be so prescribed.

(3) The power to make an order under this section includes power to provide for any incidental and supplementary provisions which the Secretary of State considers it expedient for the purposes of the order to provide.

(4) Schedule 22[1] makes further provision in relation to this section.

(5) In this section and Schedule 22—

"medical supplies" includes surgical, dental and optical materials and equipment, and

"undertaking" means any public utility undertaking or any undertaking by way of trade or business, which is concerned with medical supplies required for the purposes of this Act,

and "equipment" includes any machinery, apparatus or appliance, whether fixed or not, and any vehicle.

[National Health Service Act 2006, s 260.]

---

1 Post.

7.8300 **269. Special notices of births and deaths[1]** (1) The requirements of this section with respect to the notification of births and deaths are in addition to, and not in substitution for, the requirements of any Act relating to the registration of births and deaths.

(2) Each registrar of births and deaths must furnish, to the Primary Care Trust the area of which includes the whole or part of the registrar's sub-district, such particulars of each birth and death which occurred in the area of the Primary Care Trust as are entered in a register of births or deaths kept for that sub-district.

(3) Regulations may provide as to the manner in which and the times at which particulars must be furnished under subsection (2).

(4) In the case of each child born—

(*a*) the child's father, if at the time of the birth he is residing on the premises where the birth takes place, and

(*b*) any person in attendance upon the mother at the time of, or within six hours after, the birth,

must give notice of the birth to the Primary Care Trust for the area in which the birth takes place.

(5) Subsection (4) applies to any child which is born after the expiry of the twenty-fourth week of pregnancy whether alive or dead.

(6) Notice under subsection (4) must be given either—

(*a*) by posting within 36 hours after the birth a prepaid letter or postcard addressed to the Primary Care Trust at its offices and containing the required information, or

(*b*) by delivering within that period at the offices of the Primary Care Trust a written notice containing the required information.

(7) A Primary Care Trust must, upon application to it, supply without charge to any medical practitioner or midwife residing or practising within its area prepaid addressed envelopes together with the forms of notice.

(8) Any person who fails to give notice of a birth in accordance with subsection (4) is liable on summary conviction to a fine not exceeding level 1 on the standard scale, unless he satisfies the court that he believed, and had reasonable grounds for believing, that notice had been duly given by

some other person.

(9) Proceedings in respect of an offence under subsection (8) must not, without the Attorney-General's written consent, be taken by any person other than a party aggrieved or the Primary Care Trust concerned.

(10) A registrar of births and deaths must, for the purpose of obtaining information concerning births which have occurred in his sub-district, have access at all reasonable times to—

(a) notices of births received by a Primary Care Trust under this section, or

(b) any book in which those notices may be recorded.

[National Health Service Act 2006, s 269.]

[1] For corresponding provision in Wales, see the National Health Service (Wales) Act 2006, s 200.

## SCHEDULE 21

### Prohibition of Sale of Medical Practices

Section 259

*Prohibition, and certificate of the Secretary of State*

7.8301 1. (1) Any person who sells or buys the goodwill of a medical practice which it is unlawful to sell by virtue of section 259 is guilty of an offence and liable on conviction on indictment to a fine not exceeding—

(a) such amount as will in the court's opinion secure that he derives no benefit from the offence, and

(b) the further amount of £500,

or to imprisonment for a term not exceeding three months, or both.

(2) Any person proposing to be a party to a transaction or series of transactions which he considers might amount to a sale of the goodwill of a medical practice in contravention of section 259 may ask the Secretary of State for a certificate under this paragraph.

(3) The Secretary of State must—

(a) consider any such application, and

(b) if he is satisfied that the transaction or series of transactions does not involve the giving of valuable consideration in respect of the goodwill of such a medical practice, issue to the applicant a certificate to that effect.

(4) The certificate must—

(a) be in the prescribed form, and

(b) set out all material circumstances disclosed to the Secretary of State.

(5) Where any person is charged with an offence under this paragraph in respect of any transaction or series of transactions, it is a defence to prove that the transaction or series of transactions was certified by the Secretary of State under sub-paragraph (3).

(6) Any document purporting to be such a certificate is admissible in evidence and is deemed to be such a certificate unless the contrary is proved.

(7) The court may disregard such a certificate if it appears to the court that the applicant for the certificate—

(a) failed to disclose to the Secretary of State all the material circumstances, or

(b) made any misrepresentation with respect to the material circumstances.

(8) A prosecution for an offence under this paragraph may be instituted only by or with the consent of the Director of Public Prosecutions, and the Secretary of State must, at the request of the Director, furnish him with—

(a) a copy of any certificate issued by the Secretary of State under sub-paragraph (3), and

(b) copies of any documents produced to him in connection with the application for that certificate.

*Certain transactions deemed sale of goodwill*

2. (1) For the purposes of section 259 and paragraph 1, a disposal of premises previously used for the purposes of a medical practice is deemed to be a sale of the goodwill of a medical practice if—

(a) the person disposing of the premises did so knowing that another person ("A") intended to use them for the purposes of A's medical practice, and

(b) the consideration for the disposal substantially exceeded the consideration that might reasonably have been expected if the premises had not previously been used for the purposes of a medical practice.

(2) If a person disposes of any premises together with any other property, the court must, for the purposes of sub-paragraph (1), make such apportionment of the consideration as it considers just.

(3) For the purposes of sub-paragraphs (1) and (2)—

(a) "disposal" means any sale, letting or other form of disposal (whether by a single transaction or a series of transactions) and "disposes" and "disposing" must be read accordingly, and

(b) a person who procures the disposal of any premises must be treated as having disposed of them.

(4) Where in pursuance of any partnership agreement—

(a) any valuable consideration, other than the performance of services in the partnership business, is given by a partner or proposed partner as consideration for his being taken into partnership,

(b) any valuable consideration is given to a partner, on or in contemplation of his retirement or of his acceptance of a reduced share of the partnership profits, or to the personal representative of a partner on his death, not being a payment in respect of that partner's share in past earnings of the partnership or in any partnership assets or any other payment required to be made to him as the result of the final settlement of accounts, as between him and the other partners, in respect of past transactions of the partnership, or

(c) services are performed by any partner for a consideration substantially less than those services might reasonably have been expected to be worth having regard to the circumstances at the time when the agreement was made,

there is deemed for the purposes of section 259 and paragraph 1 to have been a sale of goodwill as specified in sub-paragraph (5).

(5) The sale of goodwill is the sale of the goodwill of the practice—

(a) of any partner to whom, or to whose personal representative, the consideration (or any part of it) is given or for whose benefit the services are performed,

(b) to the partner or each of the partners by or on whose behalf the consideration (or any part of it) was given or to the partner who performed the services.

(6) The sale is deemed for the purposes of section 259 and paragraph 1 to have been effected—

(*a*) in a case to which sub-paragraph (4)(*a*) or (*b*) applies, at the time when the consideration was given, or, if the consideration was not all given at the same time, at the time when the first part was given, or

(*b*) in a case to which sub-paragraph (4)(*c*) applies, at the time when the agreement was made.

(7) Sub-paragraph (8) applies if a person ("the assistant")—

(*a*) performs services on behalf of a person who carries on a medical practice (or as an employee of a person employing a practitioner who carries on a medical practice),

(*b*) receives substantially less remuneration for performing those services than might reasonably have been expected, having regard to the circumstances at the time when the remuneration was fixed, and

(*c*) subsequently succeeds, whether as a result of a partnership agreement or otherwise, to that practice.

(8) For the purposes of section 259 and paragraph 1, a sale of the goodwill of the practice is deemed to have taken place (at the time when the remuneration was fixed) unless it is proved that the remuneration was not fixed in contemplation of the assistant's succeeding to the practice.

(9) For the purposes of section 259 and paragraph 1, the goodwill of a medical practice is deemed to have been sold if sub-paragraph (10) or (11) applies.

(10) This sub-paragraph applies where a person carrying on the practice (or employing a practitioner who carries on a medical practice) agrees, for valuable consideration—

(*a*) to do or refrain from doing any act for the purpose of facilitating the succession of another to the practice, or

(*b*) to allow any act to be done for that purpose.

(11) This sub-paragraph applies where a person—

(*a*) gives valuable consideration to a person carrying on the practice (or employing a practitioner who carries on a medical practice), and

(*b*) succeeds, or has previously succeeded, to the practice.

(12) Sub-paragraph (9) does not apply if it is proved that no part of the consideration was given in respect of the goodwill.

(13) Sub-paragraph (9) does not apply to anything done—

(*a*) in relation to the acquisition of premises for the purposes of a medical practice,

(*b*) in pursuance of a partnership agreement, or

(*c*) in the performance of medical services by one person as an assistant to another.

*Consideration*

**3.** (1) In determining for the purposes of section 259 and this Schedule the consideration given in respect of any transaction, the court must—

(*a*) have regard to any other transaction appearing to the court to be associated with the first transaction,

(*b*) estimate the total consideration given in respect of both or all the transactions, and

(*c*) apportion the total between the transactions in such manner as the court considers just.

(2) For the purposes of section 259 and this Schedule consideration is deemed to be given to a person ("B") if—

(*a*) it is given to another person but with B's knowledge and consent, and

(*b*) it appears to the court that B has derived, or will derive, a substantial benefit from the giving of the consideration.

*Carried-over goodwill*

**4.** The fact that a person's medical practice was previously carried on by another person who at any time provided or performed services as specified in section 259 does not, by itself, make it unlawful under section 259 for the goodwill of his practice to be sold.

*Interpretation*

**5.** In section 259 and this Schedule, unless the context otherwise requires, references to a person include, in the case of an individual who has died, references to his personal representative.

## SCHEDULE 22

CONTROL OF MAXIMUM PRICES FOR MEDICAL SUPPLIES — Section 260

*Orders and directions*

**7.8302** **1.** (1) An order under section 260 may make such provision (including provision for requiring any person to furnish any information) as the Secretary of State considers necessary or expedient for facilitating the introduction or operation of a scheme of control—

(*a*) for which provision has been made under that section, or

(*b*) for which, in his opinion, it will or may be necessary or expedient that provision should be made.

(2) An order under section 260—

(*a*) may prohibit the doing of anything regulated by the order except under the authority of a licence granted by such authority or person as may be specified in the order, and

(*b*) may be made so as to apply either to persons or undertakings generally or to any particular person or undertaking or class of persons or undertakings, and so as to have effect either generally or in any particular area.

*Notices, authorisations and proof of documents*

**2.** (1) A notice to be served on any person for the purposes of section 260, or of any order or direction made or given under that section, is deemed to have been duly served on the person to whom it is directed if—

(*a*) it is delivered to him personally, or

(*b*) it is sent by registered post or the recorded delivery service addressed to him at his last or usual place of abode or place of business.

(2) Where under section 260 or this Schedule a person has power to authorise other persons to act under those provisions, the power may be exercised so as to confer the authority either on particular persons or on a

specified class of persons.

(3) Any permit, licence, permission or authorisation granted for the purposes of section 260 or this Schedule may be revoked at any time by the authority or person empowered to grant it.

(4) A document purporting to be duly executed under or by virtue of section 260 or this Schedule and signed by or on behalf of the person making it must be received in evidence and, unless the contrary is proved, taken to be so executed and signed.

*Territorial extent*

**3.** (1) Provisions in or having effect under section 260 or this Schedule which impose prohibitions, restrictions or obligations apply to—

(*a*) persons in the United Kingdom,

(*b*) persons on board any British ship or aircraft (other than an excepted ship or aircraft within the meaning of sub-paragraph (2)), and

(*c*) persons (wherever they are) who are ordinarily resident in the United Kingdom and are—

(i) British citizens,

(ii) British overseas territories citizens,

(iii) British Overseas citizens,

(iv) British subjects under the British Nationality Act 1981 (c 61),

(v) British Nationals (Overseas) (within the meaning of that Act), or

(vi) British protected persons (within the meaning of that Act).

(2) In sub-paragraph (1)—

"British aircraft" means an aircraft registered in—

(*a*) any part of Her Majesty's dominions,

(*b*) any country outside Her Majesty's dominions in which Her Majesty has jurisdiction,

(*c*) any country consisting partly of one or more colonies and partly of one or more countries mentioned in paragraph (*b*),

"excepted ship or aircraft" means a ship or aircraft registered in any country listed in Schedule 3 to the British Nationality Act 1981 or in any territory administered by the government of any such country, other than a ship or aircraft at the disposal of, or chartered by or on behalf of, Her Majesty's Government in the United Kingdom.

*False documents and false statements*

**4.** (1) A person must not, with intent to deceive—

(*a*) use any document issued for the purposes of section 260 or this Schedule or of any order made under that section,

(*b*) have in his possession any document so closely resembling a document mentioned in paragraph (*a*) as to be calculated to deceive, or

(*c*) produce, furnish, send or otherwise make use of for purposes connected with that section or this Schedule or any order or direction made or given under that section, any book, account, estimate, return, declaration or other document which is false in a material particular.

(2) A person must not, in furnishing any information for the purposes of section 260 or this Schedule or of any order made under that section—

(*a*) make a statement which he knows to be false in a material particular, or

(*b*) recklessly make a statement which is false in a material particular.

*Restrictions on disclosing information*

**5.** No person who obtains any information by virtue of section 260 or this Schedule may, otherwise than in connection with the execution of that section or this Schedule or of an order made under that section, disclose that information except—

(*a*) for the purposes of any criminal proceedings, or of a report of any criminal proceedings, or

(*b*) with permission granted by or on behalf of a Minister of the Crown.

**6.** Paragraph 5 does not apply if—

(*a*) the person who has obtained any such information as is referred to in that paragraph is, or is acting on behalf of a person who is, a public authority for the purposes of the Freedom of Information Act 2000 (c 36), and

(*b*) the information is not held by the public authority on behalf of another person.

*Offences by corporations*

**7.** (1) Where an offence under section 260 or this Schedule committed by a body corporate is proved—

(*a*) to have been committed with the consent or connivance of any director, manager, secretary of other similar officer of the body corporate, or a person purporting to act in any such capacity, or

(*b*) to be attributable to any neglect on the part of such a person,

that person, as well as the body corporate, is guilty of the offence and liable to be proceeded against and punished accordingly.

(2) "Director", in relation to a body corporate—

(*a*) established by or under any enactment for the purpose of carrying on under national ownership any industry or part of an industry or undertaking, and

(*b*) whose affairs are managed by its members,

means a member of that body corporate.

*Penalties*

**8.** (1) A person who contravenes or fails to comply with—

(*a*) an order made under section 260,

(*b*) a direction given or requirement imposed under that section, or

(*c*) a provision of this Schedule,

is guilty of an offence.

(2) Sub-paragraph (1) does not apply if the contravention or failure is an offence under paragraph 9(3) or

10(5).

(3) A person guilty of an offence under sub-paragraph (1) is—

(*a*) on summary conviction, liable to imprisonment for a term not exceeding twelve months or to a fine not exceeding the prescribed sum, or to both, or

(*b*) on conviction on indictment, liable to imprisonment for a term not exceeding two years or to a fine, or to both.

(4) Sub-paragraph (3) is subject to paragraph 11.

*Production of documents*

**9.** (1) For the purposes of—

(*a*) securing compliance with any order made or direction given under section 260 by or on behalf of the Secretary of State, or

(*b*) verifying any estimates, returns or information furnished to the Secretary of State in connection with section 260 or any order made or direction given under that section,

an officer of the Secretary of State duly authorised in that behalf has power, on producing (if required to do so) evidence of his authority, to require any person carrying on an undertaking or employed in connection with an undertaking to produce to that officer forthwith any documents relating to the undertaking which that officer may reasonably require for the purposes set out above.

(2) The power conferred by this paragraph to require any person to produce documents includes power—

(*a*) if the documents are produced, to take copies of them or extracts from them and to require that person, or where that person is a body corporate, any other person who is a present or past officer of, or is employed by, the body corporate, to provide an explanation of any of them,

(*b*) if the documents are not produced, to require the person who was required to produce them to state, to the best of his knowledge and belief, where they are.

(3) If any requirement to produce documents or provide an explanation or make a statement which is imposed by virtue of this paragraph is not complied with, the person on whom the requirement was so imposed is guilty of an offence and liable on summary conviction to a fine not exceeding level 3 on the standard scale.

(4) Sub-paragraph (3) is subject to paragraph 11.

(5) Where a person is charged with such an offence in respect of a requirement to produce any document, it is a defence to prove that it was not in his possession or under his control and that it was not reasonably practicable for him to comply with the requirement.

**10.** (1) A justice of the peace may issue a warrant under this paragraph if he is satisfied, on information on oath laid on the Secretary of State's behalf, that there are any reasonable grounds for suspecting that there are on any premises any documents—

(*a*) of which production has been required by virtue of paragraph 9, and

(*b*) which have not been produced in compliance with that requirement.

(2) A warrant so issued may authorise any constable, together with any other persons named in the warrant and any other constables to—

(*a*) enter the premises specified in the information (using such force as is reasonably necessary for the purpose), and

(*b*) search the premises and take possession of any documents appearing to be such documents as are mentioned above, or to take in relation to any documents so appearing any other steps which may appear necessary for preserving them and preventing interference with them.

(3) Each warrant issued under this paragraph continues in force until the end of the period of one month after the date on which it is issued.

(4) Any documents of which possession is taken under this paragraph may be retained—

(*a*) for a period of three months, or

(*b*) if within that period proceedings to which they are relevant are commenced for an offence under section 260 or this Schedule, until the conclusion of those proceedings.

(5) A person is guilty of an offence, and liable on summary conviction to a fine not exceeding level 3 on the standard scale, if he obstructs the exercise of—

(*a*) any right of entry or search conferred by virtue of a warrant under this paragraph, or

(*b*) any rights so conferred to take possession of any documents.

(6) Sub-paragraph (5) is subject to paragraph 11.

*Penalties for offences: transitional modification for England and Wales*

**11.** (1) In relation to an offence committed in England and Wales before the commencement of section 154(1) of the Criminal Justice Act 2003 (c 44) (general limit on magistrates' courts power to impose imprisonment) paragraph 8(3) has effect as if for "twelve months" there were substituted "three months".

(2) In relation to an offence committed in England and Wales before the commencement of section 280 of the Criminal Justice Act 2003 (alteration of penalties for specified summary offences) paragraphs 9(3) and 10(5) have effect as if "to imprisonment for a term not exceeding three months or" were inserted after "conviction".

## Mesothelioma Act 2014[1]

(2014 c 1)

7.8303 **1. Power to establish the scheme** (1) The Secretary of State may by regulations[2] establish a scheme called the Diffuse Mesothelioma Payment Scheme for making payments to—

(*a*) eligible people with diffuse mesothelioma, and

(*b*) eligible dependants of those who have died with diffuse mesothelioma.

(2) Later sections of this Act set out things that must be included in the scheme and some of the things that may be included.

[Mesothelioma Act 2014, s 1.]

---

1 For commencement, see s 19, post.

2 The Diffuse Mesothelioma Payment Scheme Regulations 2014, SI 2014/916 amended by SI 2014/917 and SI 2015/367 have been made.

**7.8304** **7.83047.8304** **2–4** *Eligibility*

**7.8305** **4–6** *Payments and procedure*

**7.8306** **7** *Scheme administration*

**7.8307** **8. Unauthorised disclosure of information: offence** (1) A person involved in the administration of the scheme must not, without lawful authority, disclose information which—

(*a*) was acquired in connection with the administration of the scheme, and

(*b*) relates to a particular person who is identified in the information or whose identity could be deduced from it.

(2) A disclosure is made with "lawful authority" only if—

(*a*) it is made for the purposes of the administration of the scheme,

(*b*) it is made for the purpose of preventing or detecting crime,

(*c*) it is made in accordance with any enactment or an order of a court or tribunal,

(*d*) it is made for the purposes of proceedings before a court or tribunal, or

(*e*) it is made with consent given by or on behalf of the person to whom the information relates or the person's personal representatives.

(3) A person who breaches subsection (1) commits an offence (for penalties, see section 9).

(4) It is a defence for a person charged with the offence under subsection (3) to prove that he or she reasonably believed—

(*a*) that the disclosure was made with lawful authority, or

(*b*) that someone had, with lawful authority, previously disclosed the information to the public.

(5) In this section "person involved in the administration of the scheme" means a person who is or has been—

(*a*) the scheme administrator,

(*b*) a person providing services to the scheme administrator, or

(*c*) an officer or employee of a person within paragraph (*a*) or (*b*).

[Mesothelioma Act 2014, s 8.]

**7.8308** **9. Unauthorised disclosure of information: penalties etc** (1) A person guilty of an offence under section 8 is liable on conviction on indictment to imprisonment for a term not exceeding two years or a fine or both.

**7.8309** (2) A person guilty of an offence under section 8 is liable—

(*a*) on summary conviction in England and Wales, to imprisonment for a term not exceeding 12 months or a fine;

(*b*) on summary conviction in Scotland, to imprisonment for a term not exceeding 12 months or a fine not exceeding the statutory maximum or both;

(*c*) on summary conviction in Northern Ireland, to imprisonment for a term not exceeding 6 months or a fine not exceeding the statutory maximum or both.

(3) The court by or before which a person is convicted of an offence under section 8 may order the destruction of a document containing the information disclosed in breach of that section or, if the information disclosed is held in some other form, may order its erasure.

(4) Where an offence under section 8 committed by a body corporate—

(*a*) is committed with the consent or connivance of an officer, or

(*b*) is attributable to neglect on the part of an officer,

the officer as well as the body corporate is guilty of the offence.

(5) Where an offence under section 8 committed by a Scottish partnership—

(*a*) is committed with the consent or connivance of a partner, or

(*b*) is attributable to neglect on the part of a partner,

the partner as well as the Scottish partnership is guilty of the offence.

(6) In this section—

"director", in relation to a body corporate whose affairs are managed by its members, means a member of the body corporate;

"officer", in relation to a body corporate, means—

(*a*) a director, manager, secretary or other similar officer of the body corporate, or

(*b*) a person purporting to act in any such a capacity;

"partner", in relation to a Scottish partnership, includes any person who was purporting to act as a partner in the partnership.

(7) In relation to an offence committed in England and Wales before section 154(1) of the Criminal Justice Act 2003 comes into force, the reference in subsection (2)(*a*) above to "12 months" is to be read as a reference to "6 months".

(8) In relation to an offence committed in England and Wales before section 85 of the Legal Aid, Sentencing and Punishment of Offenders Act 2012 comes into force, the reference in subsection (2)(*a*) above to a fine is to be read as a reference to a fine not exceeding the statutory maximum.

[Mesothelioma Act 2014, s 9.]

*General*

7.8310 **19. Commencement** (1) This Act comes into force on such day or days as the Secretary of State may by order appoint, subject as follows[1].

(2) This section and sections 20 and 21 come into force on the day on which this Act is passed.

(3) The Secretary of State may by order make transitional, transitory or saving provision in connection with the coming into force of any provision of this Act.

(4) An order under subsection (1) may appoint different days for different purposes.

(5) An order under this section is to be made by statutory instrument.

[Mesothelioma Act 2014, s 19.]

---

1 At the date of going to press the following commencement order had been made: (No 1) Order SI 2014/459 (s 7 on 4 March 2014; ss 1 to 6, 8 to 10, 11 and Sch 1, 12 and Sch 2, 14, 17 and 18 on 31 March 2014; s 13 on 1 September 2014).

7.8311 **20. Extent**

7.8312 **21. Short title**

# Psychoactive Substances Act 2016[1]

(2016 c 2)

*Introductory*

7.8312A **1. Overview** (1) This Act contains provision about psychoactive substances.

(2) Section 2 defines what is meant by a "psychoactive substance".

(3) Sections 4 to 10 contain provision about offences relating to psychoactive substances.

(4) Section 11 provides for exceptions to those offences.

(5) Sections 12 to 35 contain powers for dealing with prohibited activities in respect of psychoactive substances, in particular powers to give prohibition notices and make prohibition orders.

(6) Sections 36 to 54 contain enforcement powers.

[Psychoactive Substances Act 2016, s 1.]

---

1 Sections 59, 61-63 came into force come into force on 28 January 2016 (the day on which this Act was passed). The remaining provisions of this Act came into force on 26 May 2016 in accordance with the Psychoactive Substances Act 2016 (Commencement) Regulations 2016, SI 2016/553.

*Psychoactive Substances*

7.8312B **2. Meaning of "psychoactive substance" etc** (1) In this Act "psychoactive substance" means any substance which—

(*a*) is capable of producing a psychoactive effect in a person who consumes it, and

(*b*) is not an exempted substance (see section 3).

(2) For the purposes of this Act a substance produces a psychoactive effect in a person if, by stimulating or depressing the person's central nervous system, it affects the person's mental functioning or emotional state; and references to a substance's psychoactive effects are to be read accordingly.

(3) For the purposes of this Act a person consumes a substance if the person causes or allows the substance, or fumes given off by the substance, to enter the person's body in any way.

[Psychoactive Substances Act 2016, s 2.]

7.8312C **3. Exempted substances** (1) In this Act "exempted substance" means a substance listed in Schedule 1.

(2) The Secretary of State may by regulations amend Schedule 1 in order to—

(*a*) add or vary any description of substance;

(*b*) remove any description of substance added under paragraph (*a*).

(3) Before making any regulations under this section the Secretary of State must consult—

(*a*) the Advisory Council on the Misuse of Drugs, and

(b) such other persons as the Secretary of State considers appropriate.

(4) The power to make regulations under this section is exercisable by statutory instrument.

(5) A statutory instrument containing regulations under this section may not be made unless a draft of the instrument has been laid before, and approved by a resolution of, each House of Parliament.

[Psychoactive Substances Act 2016, s 3.]

*Offences*

7.8312D **4. Producing a psychoactive substance** (1) A person commits an offence[1] if—

(*a*) the person intentionally produces a psychoactive substance,

(*b*) the person knows or suspects that the substance is a psychoactive substance, and

(*c*) the person—

(i) intends to consume the psychoactive substance for its psychoactive effects, or

(ii) knows, or is reckless as to whether, the psychoactive substance is likely to be consumed by some other person for its psychoactive effects.

(2) This section is subject to section 11 (exceptions to offences).

[Psychoactive Substances Act 2016, s 4.]

[1] For penalty, see s 10(1), post. See also s 19 (Prohibition orders following conviction), post.

**7.8312E 5. Supplying, or offering to supply, a psychoactive substance** (1) A person commits an offence[1] if—

(*a*) the person intentionally supplies a substance to another person,

(*b*) the substance is a psychoactive substance,

(*c*) the person knows or suspects, or ought to know or suspect, that the substance is a psychoactive substance, and

(*d*) the person knows, or is reckless as to whether, the psychoactive substance is likely to be consumed by the person to whom it is supplied, or by some other person, for its psychoactive effects.

(2) A person ("P") commits an offence[1] if—

(*a*) P offers to supply a psychoactive substance to another person ("R"), and

(*b*) P knows or is reckless as to whether R, or some other person, would, if P supplied a substance to R in accordance with the offer, be likely to consume the substance for its psychoactive effects.

(3) For the purposes of subsection (2)(*b*), the reference to a substance's psychoactive effects includes a reference to the psychoactive effects which the substance would have if it were the substance which P had offered to supply to R.

(4) This section is subject to section 11 (exceptions to offences).

[Psychoactive Substances Act 2016, s 5.]

[1] For penalty, see s 10(1), post. See also s 19 (Prohibition orders following conviction), post.

**7.8312F 6. Aggravation of offence under section 5** (1) This section applies if—

(*a*) a court is considering the seriousness of an offence under section 5, and

(*b*) at the time the offence was committed the offender was aged 18 or over.

(2) If condition A, B or C is met the court—

(*a*) must treat the fact that the condition is met as an aggravating factor (that is to say, a factor that increases the seriousness of the offence), and

(*b*) must state in open court that the offence is so aggravated.

(3) Condition A is that the offence was committed on or in the vicinity of school premises at a relevant time.

(4) For the purposes of subsection (3) a "relevant time" is—

(*a*) any time when the school premises are in use by persons under the age of 18;

(*b*) one hour before the start and one hour after the end of any such time.

(5) In this section—

"school premises" means land used for the purposes of a school, other than any land occupied solely as a dwelling by a person employed at the school;

"school" has the same meaning—

(*a*) in England and Wales, as in section 4 of the Education Act 1996[1];

(*b*) in Scotland, as in section 135(1) of the Education (Scotland) Act 1980;

(*c*) in Northern Ireland, as in Article 2(2) of the Education and Libraries (Northern Ireland) Order 1986 (SI 1986/594 (NI 3)).

(6) Condition B is that in connection with the commission of the offence the offender used a courier who, at the time the offence was committed, was under the age of 18.

(7) For the purposes of subsection (6) a person ("P") uses a courier in connection with an offence under section 5 if P causes or permits another person (the courier)—

(*a*) to deliver a substance to a third person, or

(*b*) to deliver a drug-related consideration to P or a third person.

(8) A drug-related consideration is a consideration of any description which—

(*a*) is obtained in connection with the supply of a psychoactive substance, or

(*b*) is intended to be used in connection with obtaining a psychoactive substance.

(9) Condition C is that the offence was committed in a custodial institution.

(10) In this section—

"custodial institution" means any of the following—

(*a*) a prison;

(*b*) a young offender institution, secure training centre, secure college, young offenders institution, young offenders centre, juvenile justice centre or remand centre;

(*c*) a removal centre, a short-term holding facility or pre-departure accommodation;

(*d*) service custody premises;

"removal centre", "short-term holding facility" and "pre-departure accommodation" have the meaning given by section 147 of the Immigration and Asylum Act 1999;

"service custody premises" has the meaning given by section 300(7) of the Armed Forces Act 2006.

[Psychoactive Substances Act 2016, s 6.]

[1] In this PART, title EDUCATION, ante.

**7.8312G 7. Possession of psychoactive substance with intent to supply** (1) A person commits an offence[1] if—

(*a*) the person is in possession of a psychoactive substance,
(*b*) the person knows or suspects that the substance is a psychoactive substance, and
(*c*) the person intends to supply the psychoactive substance to another person for its consumption, whether by any person to whom it is supplied or by some other person, for its psychoactive effects.

(2) This section is subject to section 11 (exceptions to offences).

[Psychoactive Substances Act 2016, s 7.]

[1] For penalty, see s 10(1), post. See also s 19 (Prohibition orders following conviction), post.

**7.8312H 8. Importing or exporting a psychoactive substance** (1) A person commits an offence[1] if—

(*a*) the person intentionally imports a substance,
(*b*) the substance is a psychoactive substance,
(*c*) the person knows or suspects, or ought to know or suspect, that the substance is a psychoactive substance, and
(*d*) the person—
  (i) intends to consume the psychoactive substance for its psychoactive effects, or
  (ii) knows, or is reckless as to whether, the psychoactive substance is likely to be consumed by some other person for its psychoactive effects.

(2) A person commits an offence[1] if—

(*a*) the person intentionally exports a substance,
(*b*) the substance is a psychoactive substance,
(*c*) the person knows or suspects, or ought to know or suspect, that the substance is a psychoactive substance, and
(*d*) the person—
  (i) intends to consume the psychoactive substance for its psychoactive effects, or
  (ii) knows, or is reckless as to whether, the psychoactive substance is likely to be consumed by some other person for its psychoactive effects.

(3) In a case where a person imports or exports a controlled drug suspecting it to be a psychoactive substance, the person is to be treated for the purposes of this section as if the person had imported or exported a psychoactive substance suspecting it to be such a substance.

In this subsection "controlled drug" has the same meaning as in the Misuse of Drugs Act 1971.

(4) Section 5 of the Customs and Excise Management Act 1979 (time of importation, exportation, etc)[2] applies for the purposes of this section as it applies for the purposes of that Act.

(5) This section is subject to section 11 (exceptions to offences).

[Psychoactive Substances Act 2016, s 8.]

[1] For penalty, see s 10(1), post. See also s 19 (Prohibition orders following conviction), post.
[2] In this PART, title CUSTOMS AND EXCISE, ante.

**7.8312I 9. Possession of a psychoactive substance in a custodial institution** (1) A person commits an offence[1] if—

(a) the person is in possession of a psychoactive substance in a custodial institution,
(*b*) the person knows or suspects that the substance is a psychoactive substance, and
(*c*) the person intends to consume the psychoactive substance for its psychoactive effects.

(2) In this section "custodial institution" has the same meaning as in section 6.

(3) This section is subject to section 11 (exceptions to offences).

[Psychoactive Substances Act 2016, s 9.]

[1] For penalty, see s 10(1), post.

**7.8312J 10. Penalties** (1) A person guilty of an offence under any of sections 4 to 8 is liable—

(*a*) on summary conviction in England and Wales—
  (i) to imprisonment for a term not exceeding 12 months (or 6 months, if the offence was committed before the commencement of section 154(1) of the Criminal Justice Act 2003), or
  (ii) to a fine,
  or both;
(*b*) on summary conviction in Scotland—
  (i) to imprisonment for a term not exceeding 12 months, or
  (ii) to a fine not exceeding the statutory maximum,
  or both;
(*c*) on summary conviction in Northern Ireland—
  (i) to imprisonment for a term not exceeding 6 months, or
  (ii) to a fine not exceeding the statutory maximum,

or both;

(d) on conviction on indictment, to imprisonment for a term not exceeding 7 years or a fine, or both.

(2) A person guilty of an offence under section 9 is liable—

(*a*) on summary conviction in England and Wales—

(i) to imprisonment for a term not exceeding 12 months (or 6 months, if the offence was committed before the commencement of section 154(1) of the Criminal Justice Act 2003), or

(ii) to a fine,

or both;

(*b*) on summary conviction in Scotland—

(i) to imprisonment for a term not exceeding 12 months, or

(ii) to a fine not exceeding the statutory maximum,

or both;

(*c*) on summary conviction in Northern Ireland—

(i) to imprisonment for a term not exceeding 6 months, or

(ii) to a fine not exceeding the statutory maximum,

or both;

(*d*) on conviction on indictment, to imprisonment for a term not exceeding 2 years or a fine, or both.

[Psychoactive Substances Act 2016, s 10.]

**7.8312K 11. Exceptions to offences** (1) It is not an offence under this Act for a person to carry on any activity listed in subsection (3) if, in the circumstances in which it is carried on by that person, the activity is an exempted activity.

(2) In this section "exempted activity" means an activity listed in Schedule 2.

(3) The activities referred to in subsection (1) are—

(*a*) producing a psychoactive substance;

(*b*) supplying such a substance;

(*c*) offering to supply such a substance;

(*d*) possessing such a substance with intent to supply it;

(*e*) importing or exporting such a substance;

(*f*) possessing such a substance in a custodial institution (within the meaning of section 9).

(4) The Secretary of State may by regulations amend Schedule 2 in order to—

(*a*) add or vary any description of activity;

(*b*) remove any description of activity added under paragraph (a).

(5) Before making any regulations under this section the Secretary of State must consult—

(*a*) the Advisory Council on the Misuse of Drugs, and

(*b*) such other persons as the Secretary of State considers appropriate.

(6) The power to make regulations under this section is exercisable by statutory instrument.

(7) A statutory instrument containing regulations under this section may not be made unless a draft of the instrument has been laid before, and approved by a resolution of, each House of Parliament.

[Psychoactive Substances Act 2016, s 11.]

*Powers for Dealing with Prohibited Activities*

**7.8312L 12. Meaning of "prohibited activity"** (1) In this Act "prohibited activity" means any of the following activities—

(*a*) producing a psychoactive substance that is likely to be consumed by individuals for its psychoactive effects;

(*b*) supplying such a substance;

(*c*) offering to supply such a substance;

(*d*) importing such a substance;

(*e*) exporting such a substance;

(*f*) assisting or encouraging the carrying on of a prohibited activity listed in any of paragraphs (*a*) to (*e*).

(2) The carrying on by a person of an activity listed in any of paragraphs (*a*) to (*e*) of subsection (1) is not the carrying on of a prohibited activity if the carrying on of the activity by that person would not be an offence under this Act by virtue of section 11.

[Psychoactive Substances Act 2016, s 12.]

**7.8312M 13. Prohibition notices** (1) A senior officer or a local authority may give a prohibition notice to a person if conditions A and B are met.

(2) A prohibition notice is a notice that requires the person to whom it is given not to carry on any prohibited activity or a prohibited activity of a description specified in the notice.

(3) Condition A is that the senior officer or local authority reasonably believes that the person is carrying on, or is likely to carry on, a prohibited activity.

(4) Condition B is that the senior officer or local authority reasonably believes that it is necessary and proportionate to give the prohibition notice for the purpose of preventing the person

from carrying on any prohibited activity.

(5) A prohibition notice may not be given—

(*a*) in England and Wales or Northern Ireland, to an individual who is under the age of 10, or

(*b*) in Scotland, to an individual who is under the age of 12.

(6) A prohibition notice given to an individual who is under the age of 18—

(*a*) must specify the period for which it has effect, and

(*b*) may not have effect for more than 3 years.

(7) In this Act "senior officer" means—

(*a*) a constable of at least the rank of inspector;

(*b*) a designated NCA officer of grade 3 or above;

(*c*) a general customs official of at least the grade of higher officer.

[Psychoactive Substances Act 2016, s 13.]

**7.8312N 14. Premises notices** (1) A senior officer or a local authority may give a premises notice to a person if conditions A and B are met.

(2) A premises notice is a notice that requires the person to whom it is given to take all reasonable steps to prevent any prohibited activity, or a prohibited activity of a description specified in the notice, from being carried on at any premises specified in the notice that are owned, leased, occupied, controlled or operated by the person.

(3) Condition A is that—

(*a*) the senior officer or local authority reasonably believes that a prohibited activity is being, or is likely to be, carried on at particular premises, and

(*b*) the person owns, leases, occupies, controls or operates the premises.

(4) Condition B is that the senior officer or local authority reasonably believes that it is necessary and proportionate to give the premises notice for the purpose of preventing any prohibited activity from being carried on at any premises owned, leased, occupied, controlled or operated by the person.

(5) A premises notice may not be given to an individual who is under the age of 18.

(6) For the purposes of this section a person (other than a mortgagee not in possession) "owns" premises in England and Wales or Northern Ireland if—

(*a*) the person is entitled to dispose of the fee simple in the premises, whether in possession or reversion, or

(*b*) the person holds or is entitled to the rents and profits of the premises under a lease that (when granted) was for a term of not less than 3 years.

(7) For the meaning of "senior officer", see section 13(7).

[Psychoactive Substances Act 2016, s 14.]

**7.8312O 15. Prohibition notices and premises notices: supplementary** (1) This section applies to the giving of prohibition notices and premises notices.

(2) A notice must—

(*a*) set out the grounds for giving the notice;

(*b*) explain the possible consequences of not complying with the notice.

(3) A notice may be withdrawn by a notice to that effect given by—

(*a*) where the notice was given by a senior officer, that officer or another senior officer acting on behalf of the same person as that officer;

(*b*) where the notice was given by a local authority, that local authority.

(4) The withdrawal of a notice does not prevent the giving of a further notice to the same person.

(5) For the meaning of "senior officer", see section 13(7).

[Psychoactive Substances Act 2016, s 15.]

**7.8312P 16. Further provision about giving notices under sections 13 to 15** (1) This section applies to the giving of notices under sections 13 to 15.

(2) A notice takes effect when it is given.

(3) A notice may be given to a person by—

(*a*) handing it to the person,

(*b*) leaving it at the person's proper address,

(*c*) sending it by post to the person at that address, or

(*d*) subject to subsection (9), sending it to the person by electronic means.

(4) A notice to a body corporate may be given to the secretary or clerk of that body.

(5) A notice to a partnership may be given to a partner or a person who has the control or management of the partnership business.

(6) For the purposes of this section and of section 7 of the Interpretation Act 1978 (service of documents by post) in its application to this section, the proper address of a person is—

(*a*) in the case of a body corporate or its secretary or clerk, the address of the body's registered or principal office;

(*b*) in the case of a partnership, a partner or a person having the control or management of the partnership business, the address of the principal office of the partnership;

(*c*) in any other case, the person's last known address.

(7) For the purposes of subsection (6) the principal office of a company registered outside the United Kingdom, or of a partnership carrying on business outside the United Kingdom, is its principal office within the United Kingdom.

(8) If a person has specified an address in the United Kingdom, other than the person's proper address within the meaning of subsection (6), as the one at which the person or someone on the person's behalf will accept notices of the same description as a notice under section 13, 14 or 15 (as the case may be), that address is also treated for the purposes of this section and section 7 of the Interpretation Act 1978 as the person's proper address.

(9) A notice may be sent to a person by electronic means only if—

(*a*) the person has indicated that notices of the same description as a notice under section 13, 14 or 15 (as the case may be) may be given to the person by being sent to an electronic address and in an electronic form specified for that purpose, and

(*b*) the notice is sent to that address in that form.

(10) A notice sent to a person by electronic means is, unless the contrary is proved, to be treated as having been given at 9 am on the working day immediately following the day on which it was sent.

(11) In this section—

"electronic address" means any number or address used for the purposes of sending or receiving documents or information by electronic means;

"working day" means a day other than a Saturday, a Sunday, Christmas Day, Good Friday or a bank holiday under the Banking and Financial Dealings Act 1971 in any part of the United Kingdom.

[Psychoactive Substances Act 2016, s 16.]

**7.8312Q 17. Meaning of "prohibition order"** (1) In this Act a "prohibition order" means an order prohibiting the person against whom it is made from carrying on any prohibited activity or a prohibited activity of a description specified in the order.

(2) A prohibition order may be made—

(*a*) on application (see section 18), or

(*b*) following conviction of an offence under any of sections 4 to 8 or a related offence (see section 19).

(3) For the meaning of "prohibited activity", see section 12.

[Psychoactive Substances Act 2016, s 17.]

**7.8312R 18. Prohibition orders on application** (1) The appropriate court may make a prohibition order under this section against a person if—

(*a*) condition A or B is met, and

(*b*) condition C is met.

(2) Condition A is that the court is satisfied on the balance of probabilities that the person has failed to comply with a prohibition notice.

(3) Condition B is that, where no prohibition notice has been given (or one was given but has been withdrawn)—

(*a*) the court is satisfied on the balance of probabilities that the person is carrying on, or is likely to carry on, a prohibited activity, and

(*b*) the court considers that the person would fail to comply with a prohibition notice if given.

(4) Condition C is that the court considers it necessary and proportionate to make the prohibition order for the purpose of preventing the person from carrying on any prohibited activity.

(5) If a court makes a prohibition order under this section based on condition A having been met, the prohibition notice is to be treated as having been withdrawn.

(6) A prohibition order under this section may not be made—

(*a*) in England and Wales or Northern Ireland, against an individual who is under the age of 10, or

(*b*) in Scotland, against an individual who is under the age of 12.

(7) A prohibition order under this section made against an individual who is under the age of 18 at the time the order is made—

(*a*) must specify the period for which it has effect, and

(*b*) may not have effect for more than 3 years.

(8) A prohibition order under this section may be made only on an application made in accordance with section 21.

(9) In this section "the appropriate court" means—

(*a*) in relation to England and Wales—

(i) where the person in respect of whom the application is made is an individual who is under the age of 18, a youth court, and

(ii) in any other case, a magistrates' court;

(*b*) in relation to Scotland, the sheriff;

(*c*) in relation to Northern Ireland—

(i) where the person in respect of whom the application is made is an individual who is under the age of 18, a youth court, and

(ii) in any other case, a court of summary jurisdiction.

[Psychoactive Substances Act 2016, s 18.]

**7.8312S 19. Prohibition orders following conviction** (1) Where a court is dealing with a person who has been convicted of a relevant offence, the court may make a prohibition order under this section if the court considers it necessary and proportionate for the purpose of preventing the person from carrying on any prohibited activity.

(2) A prohibition order may not be made under this section except—

(*a*) in addition to a sentence imposed in respect of the offence concerned, or

(*b*) in addition to an order discharging the person conditionally or, in Scotland, discharging the person absolutely.

(3) If a court makes a prohibition order under this section, any prohibition notice that has previously been given to the person against whom the order is made is to be treated as having been withdrawn.

(4) A prohibition order under this section made against an individual who is under the age of 18 at the time the order is made—

(*a*) must specify the period for which it has effect, and

(*b*) may not have effect for more than 3 years.

(5) In this section "relevant offence" means—

(*a*) an offence under any of sections 4 to 8;

(*b*) an offence of attempting or conspiring to commit an offence under any of sections 4 to 8;

(*c*) an offence under Part 2 of the Serious Crime Act 2007 in relation to an offence under any of sections 4 to 8;

(*d*) an offence of inciting a person to commit an offence under any of sections 4 to 8;

(*e*) an offence of aiding, abetting, counselling or procuring the commission of an offence under any of sections 4 to 8.

[Psychoactive Substances Act 2016, s 19.]

**7.8312T 20. Premises orders** (1) The appropriate court may make a premises order against a person if—

(*a*) condition A or B is met, and

(*b*) condition C is met.

(2) A premises order is an order that requires the person against whom it is made to take all reasonable steps to prevent any prohibited activity, or a prohibited activity of a description specified in the order, from being carried on at any premises specified in the order that are owned, leased, occupied, controlled or operated by the person.

(3) Condition A is that the court is satisfied on the balance of probabilities that the person has failed to comply with a premises notice.

(4) Condition B is that, where no premises notice has been given (or one was given but has been withdrawn)—

(*a*) the court is satisfied on the balance of probabilities that a prohibited activity is being, or is likely to be, carried on at particular premises,

(*b*) the person owns, leases, occupies, controls or operates the premises, and

(*c*) the court considers that the person would fail to comply with a premises notice if given.

(5) Condition C is that the court considers it necessary and proportionate to make the premises order for the purpose of preventing any prohibited activity from being carried on at any premises owned, leased, occupied, controlled or operated by the person.

(6) If a court makes a premises order based on condition A having been met, the premises notice is to be treated as having been withdrawn.

(7) A premises order may not be made against an individual who is under the age of 18.

(8) A premises order may be made only on an application made in accordance with section 21.

(9) In this section the "appropriate court" means—

(*a*) in relation to England and Wales, a magistrates' court;

(*b*) in relation to Scotland, the sheriff;

(*c*) in relation to Northern Ireland, a court of summary jurisdiction.

(10) Subsection (6) of section 14 (when a person "owns" premises) applies for the purposes of this section as it applies for the purposes of that section.

[Psychoactive Substances Act 2016, s 20.]

**7.8312U 21. Applications for prohibition orders and premises orders** (1) An application for a prohibition order under section 18 or a premises order may be made—

(*a*) in England and Wales, by the chief officer of police for a police area,

(*b*) in Scotland, by the chief constable of the Police Service of Scotland,

(*c*) in Northern Ireland, by the chief constable of the Police Service of Northern Ireland,

(*d*) in England and Wales or Scotland, by the chief constable of the British Transport Police Force,

(*e*) by the Director General of the National Crime Agency,

(*f*) by the Secretary of State by whom general customs functions are exercisable, or

(*g*) by a local authority.

This is subject to subsection (2).

(2) Where an application is made based on a failure to comply with a prohibition notice or a premises notice (as the case may be), the application must be made—

*(a)* where the notice was given by a constable, by the chief officer of police or chief constable (as the case may be) of the police force of which the constable was a member when the notice was given;

*(b)* where the notice was given by a designated NCA officer, by the Director General of the National Crime Agency;

*(c)* where the notice was given by a general customs official, by the Secretary of State by whom general customs functions are exercisable;

*(d)* where the notice was given by a local authority, by that local authority.

(3) An application for a prohibition order under section 18 or a premises order is—

*(a)* in England and Wales, to be made by complaint;

*(b)* in Northern Ireland, to be made by complaint under Part 8 of the Magistrates' Courts (Northern Ireland) Order 1981 (SI 1981/1675 (NI 26)).

[Psychoactive Substances Act 2016, s 21.]

**7.8312V 22. Provision that may be made by prohibition orders and premises orders** (1) A court making a prohibition order or a premises order, or a court varying such an order under or by virtue of any of sections 28 to 31, may by the order impose any prohibitions, restrictions or requirements that the court considers appropriate (in addition to the prohibition referred to in section 17(1) or the requirement referred to in section 20(2) (as the case may be)).

(2) Subsections (3) to (6) contain examples of the type of provision that may be made under subsection (1), but they do not limit the type of provision that may be so made.

(3) The prohibitions, restrictions or requirements that may be imposed on a person by a prohibition order or a premises order include prohibitions or restrictions on, or requirements in relation to, the person's business dealings (including the conduct of the person's business over the internet).

(4) The requirements that may be imposed on a person by a prohibition order include a requirement to hand over for disposal an item belonging to the person that the court is satisfied—

*(a)* is a psychoactive substance, or

*(b)* has been, or is likely to be, used in the carrying on of a prohibited activity.

(5) An item that is handed over in compliance with a requirement imposed by virtue of subsection (4) may not be disposed of—

*(a)* before the end of the period within which an appeal may be made against the imposition of the requirement (ignoring any power to appeal out of time), or

*(b)* if such an appeal is made, before it is determined or otherwise dealt with.

(6) The prohibitions that may be imposed on a person by a prohibition order or a premises order include a prohibition prohibiting access to premises owned, occupied, leased, controlled or operated by the person for a specified period (an "access prohibition").

(7) The period specified under subsection (6) may not exceed 3 months (but see subsections (3) to (5) of section 28).

(8) An access prohibition may prohibit access—

*(a)* by all persons, or by all persons except those specified, or by all persons except those of a specified description;

*(b)* at all times, or at all times except those specified;

*(c)* in all circumstances, or in all circumstances except those specified.

(9) An access prohibition may—

*(a)* be made in respect of the whole or any part of the premises;

*(b)* include provision about access to a part of the building or structure of which the premises form part.

(10) In this section "specified" means specified in the prohibition order or the premises order (as the case may be).

(11) Subsection (6) of section 14 (when a person "owns" premises) applies for the purposes of subsection (6) of this section as it applies for the purposes of that section.

[Psychoactive Substances Act 2016, s 22.]

**7.8312W 23. Enforcement of access prohibitions** (1) An authorised person may—

*(a)* enter premises in respect of which an access prohibition is in effect (see section 22(6));

*(b)* do anything necessary to secure the premises against entry.

(2) In this section "authorised person"—

*(a)* in relation to an access prohibition imposed by a prohibition order under section 18, or a premises order, made on the application of the chief officer of police for a police area, the chief constable of the Police Service of Scotland, the chief constable of the Police Service of Northern Ireland or the chief constable of the British Transport Police Force, means a constable or a person authorised by the chief officer of police or the chief constable (as the case may be) who applied for the order;

*(b)* in relation to an access prohibition imposed by a prohibition order under section 18, or a premises order, made on the application of the Director General of the National Crime Agency, means a person authorised by the Director General;

(*c*) in relation to an access prohibition imposed by a prohibition order under section 18, or a premises order, made on the application of the Secretary of State by whom general customs functions are exercisable, means a general customs official or a person authorised by that Secretary of State;

(*d*) in relation to an access prohibition imposed by a prohibition order under section 18, or a premises order, made on the application of a local authority, means a person authorised by that local authority;

(*e*) in relation to an access prohibition imposed by a prohibition order under section 19, means a constable, a general customs official or a person authorised by a person listed in subsection (3).

(3) Those persons are—

(*a*) the chief officer of police for a police area, in the case of an order made in England and Wales;

(*b*) the chief constable of the Police Service of Scotland, in the case of an order made in Scotland;

(*c*) the chief constable of the Police Service of Northern Ireland, in the case of an order made in Northern Ireland;

(*d*) the chief constable of the British Transport Police Force, in the case of an order made in England and Wales or Scotland;

(*e*) the Director General of the National Crime Agency;

(*f*) the Secretary of State by whom general customs functions are exercisable.

(4) A person acting under subsection (1) may use reasonable force.

(5) A person seeking to enter premises under subsection (1) must, if required to do so by the occupier of the premises or, where the occupier is not present, by another person appearing to be in charge of the premises—

(*a*) give his or her name;

(*b*) if not a constable in uniform, produce documentary evidence that he or she is an authorised person.

(6) An authorised person may also enter premises in respect of which an access prohibition is in effect to carry out essential maintenance or repairs to the premises.

[Psychoactive Substances Act 2016, s 23.]

**7.8312X 24. Access prohibitions: reimbursement of costs** (1) A person listed in subsection (2) that incurs expenditure for the purpose of clearing, securing or maintaining premises in respect of which an access prohibition is in effect (see section 22(6)) may apply to the court for an order under this section.

(2) Those persons are—

(*a*) a local policing body;

(*b*) the Scottish Police Authority;

(*c*) the chief constable of the Police Service of Northern Ireland;

(*d*) the British Transport Police Authority;

(*e*) the Director General of the National Crime Agency;

(*f*) the Secretary of State by whom general customs functions are exercisable;

(*g*) a local authority.

(3) On an application under this section the court may make whatever order it considers appropriate for the reimbursement (in full or in part) by the person against whom the order imposing the access prohibition was made of the expenditure mentioned in subsection (1).

(4) An application for an order under this section may not be heard unless it is made before the end of the period of 3 months starting with the day on which the access prohibition ceases to have effect.

(5) An application under this section must be served on the person against whom the order imposing the access prohibition was made.

(6) In this section "the court" means—

(*a*) in a case where the prohibition order or the premises order imposing the access prohibition was made by a court in England and Wales or Northern Ireland, the court that made the order, except where paragraph (*b*) or (*c*) applies;

(*b*) where the court that made the order was the Court of Appeal, the Crown Court;

(*c*) where the court that made the order was a youth court but the person against whom the order was made is aged 18 or over at the time of the application, a magistrates' court or, in Northern Ireland, a court of summary jurisdiction;

(*d*) in a case where the prohibition order or the premises order imposing the access prohibition was made by a court in Scotland, the sheriff.

[Psychoactive Substances Act 2016, s 24.]

**7.8312Y 25. Access prohibitions: exemption from liability** (1) Neither an authorised person, nor the person under whose direction or control the authorised person acts, is to be liable in damages for anything done, or omitted to be done, by the authorised person in the exercise or purported exercise of a power under section 23.

(2) Subsection (1) does not apply to an act or omission shown to have been in bad faith.

(3) Subsection (1) does not apply so as to prevent an award of damages made in respect of an act or omission on the ground that the act or omission was unlawful by virtue of section 6(1) of the Human Rights Act 1998.

(4) This section does not affect any other exemption from liability (whether at common law or otherwise).

(5) In this section "authorised person" has the same meaning as in section 23.

[Psychoactive Substances Act 2016, s 25.]

**7.8312Z 26. Offence of failing to comply with a prohibition order or premises order**

(1) A person against whom a prohibition order or a premises order is made commits an offence by failing to comply with the order.

(2) A person guilty of an offence under this section is liable—

(*a*) on summary conviction in England and Wales—

(i) to imprisonment for a term not exceeding 12 months (or 6 months, if the offence was committed before the commencement of section 154(1) of the Criminal Justice Act 2003), or

(ii) to a fine,

or both;

(*b*) on summary conviction in Scotland—

(i) to imprisonment for a term not exceeding 12 months, or

(ii) to a fine not exceeding the statutory maximum,

or both;

(*c*) on summary conviction in Northern Ireland—

(i) to imprisonment for a term not exceeding 6 months, or

(ii) to a fine not exceeding the statutory maximum,

or both;

(*d*) on conviction on indictment, to imprisonment for a term not exceeding 2 years or a fine, or both.

(3) A person does not commit an offence under this section if—

(*a*) the person took all reasonable steps to comply with the order, or

(*b*) there is some other reasonable excuse for the failure to comply.

[Psychoactive Substances Act 2016, s 26.]

**7.8312ZA 27. Offence of failing to comply with an access prohibition, etc** (1) This section applies where a prohibition order or a premises order imposes an access prohibition (see section 22(6)).

(2) A person, other than the person against whom the order was made, who without reasonable excuse remains on or enters premises in contravention of the access prohibition commits an offence.

(3) A person who without reasonable excuse obstructs a person acting under section 23(1) commits an offence.

(4) A person guilty of an offence under subsection (2) or (3) is liable—

(*a*) on summary conviction in England and Wales, to either or both of the following—

(i) imprisonment for a term not exceeding 51 weeks (or 6 months, if the offence was committed before the commencement of section 281(5) of the Criminal Justice Act 2003);

(ii) a fine;

(*b*) on summary conviction in Scotland, to either or both of the following—

(i) imprisonment for a term not exceeding 12 months;

(ii) a fine not exceeding level 5 on the standard scale;

(*c*) on summary conviction in Northern Ireland, to either or both of the following—

(i) imprisonment for a term not exceeding 6 months;

(ii) a fine not exceeding level 5 on the standard scale.

[Psychoactive Substances Act 2016, s 27.]

**7.8312ZB 28. Variation and discharge on application** (1) The court may vary or discharge a prohibition order or a premises order on the application of—

(*a*) the person who applied for the order (if any),

(*b*) the person against whom the order was made, or

(*c*) any other person who is significantly adversely affected by the order.

(2) Where a prohibition order is made under section 19, the court may also vary or discharge the order on the application of—

(*a*) in the case of an order made in England and Wales, the chief officer of police for a police area or the chief constable of the British Transport Police Force;

(*b*) in the case of an order made in Scotland, the Lord Advocate or a procurator fiscal;

(*c*) in the case of an order made in Northern Ireland, the chief constable of the Police Service of Northern Ireland;

(*d*) in the case of an order made in England and Wales or Northern Ireland, the Director General of the National Crime Agency;

(*e*) in the case of an order made in England and Wales or Northern Ireland, the Secretary of State by whom general customs functions are exercisable.

(3) Subsection (4) applies where—

(*a*) a prohibition order or a premises order imposes an access prohibition (see section 22(6)), and

(*b*) an application for the variation of the order is made by the person who applied for the order, or by a person mentioned in subsection (2), before the expiry of the period for which the access prohibition has effect.

(4) Where this subsection applies, the court may vary the order by extending (or further extending) the period for which the access prohibition has effect.

(5) The period for which an access prohibition has effect may not be extended so that it has effect for more than 6 months.

(6) In this section "the court" means—

(*a*) the court that made the order, except where paragraph (*b*) or (*c*) applies;

(*b*) where—

(i) the order was made under section 19 on an appeal in relation to a person's conviction or sentence for an offence, or

(ii) the order was made by a court under that section against a person committed or remitted to that court for sentencing for an offence,

the court by or before which the person was convicted (but see subsection (7));

(*c*) where the court that made the order was a youth court but the person against whom the order was made is aged 18 or over at the time of the application, a magistrates' court or, in Northern Ireland, a court of summary jurisdiction.

(7) Where the person mentioned in subsection (6)(*b*)—

(*a*) was convicted by a youth court, but

(*b*) is aged 18 or over at the time of the application,

the reference in subsection (6)(*b*) to the court by or before which the person was convicted is to be read as a reference to a magistrates' court or, in Northern Ireland, a court of summary jurisdiction.

(8) An order that has been varied under this section remains an order of the court that first made it for the purposes of—

(*a*) section 24;

(*b*) any further application under this section.

[Psychoactive Substances Act 2016, s 28.]

**7.8312ZC 29. Variation following conviction** (1) This section applies where—

(*a*) a court is dealing with a person who has been convicted of a relevant offence and against whom a prohibition order or a premises order has previously been made, or

(*b*) a court is dealing with a person who has been convicted of an offence under section 26 of failing to comply with a prohibition order or a premises order.

(2) The court may vary the prohibition order or (as the case may be) the premises order.

(3) An order that has been varied under subsection (2) remains an order of the court that first made it for the purposes of sections 24 and 28.

(4) An order may not be varied under this section except—

(*a*) in addition to a sentence imposed in respect of the offence concerned, or

(*b*) in addition to an order discharging the person conditionally or, in Scotland, discharging the person absolutely.

(5) In this section "relevant offence" has the same meaning as in section 19.

[Psychoactive Substances Act 2016, s 29.]

**7.8312ZD 30. Appeals against making of prohibition orders and premises orders** (1) A person against whom a prohibition order under section 18 or a premises order is made by a court specified in the first column of the table may appeal against the making of the order to the court specified in the corresponding entry in the second column of the table—

| *Court that made order* | *Court to which appeal lies* |
|---|---|
| Youth court in England and Wales<br>Magistrates' court | Crown Court |
| Sheriff | Sheriff Appeal Court |
| Youth court in Northern Ireland<br>Court of summary jurisdiction | County Court |

(2) An appeal under subsection (1) against the making of an order must be made before the end of the period of 28 days starting with the date of the order.

(3) On an appeal under subsection (1) the court hearing the appeal may by order affirm, vary or revoke the order, and may also make such incidental or consequential orders as appear to it to be just.

(4) An order that has been affirmed or varied under subsection (3) remains an order of the court that first made it for the purposes of sections 24 and 28.

(5) A person against whom a prohibition order is made under section 19 may appeal against the

making of the order as if it were a sentence passed on the person for the offence referred to in section 19(1) (to the extent it would not otherwise be so appealable).

[Psychoactive Substances Act 2016, s 30.]

**7.8312ZE 31. Appeals about variation and discharge** (1) An appeal may be made against a decision under section 28 of a court specified in the first column of the table to the court specified in the corresponding entry in the second column of the table—

| *Court that made section 28 decision* | *Court to which appeal lies* |
| --- | --- |
| Youth court in England and Wales<br>Magistrates' court | Crown Court |
| Sheriff | High Court of Justiciary sitting as the Court of Criminal Appeal, in a case where the relevant order was made under section 19 and the person against whom it was made had been convicted in proceedings on indictment<br>Sheriff Appeal Court, in any other case |
| Youth court in Northern Ireland<br>Court of summary jurisdiction | County Court |
| Crown Court | Court of Appeal |
| High Court of Justiciary | High Court of Justiciary sitting as the Court of Criminal Appeal |

(2) The right of appeal under subsection (1) is exercisable by—

*(a)* the person against whom the relevant order was made, and

*(b)* any other person who is significantly adversely affected by that order.

(3) In subsections (1) and (2) the "relevant order" means the order that was the subject of the application under section 28.

(4) An appeal under subsection (1) against the making of a decision must be made before the end of the period of 28 days starting with the date of the decision.

(5) On an appeal under subsection (1) the court hearing the appeal may (to the extent it would not otherwise have power to do so) make such orders as may be necessary to give effect to its determination of the appeal, and may also make such incidental or consequential orders as appear to it to be just.

(6) A prohibition order or a premises order that has been varied by virtue of subsection (5) remains an order of the court that first made it for the purposes of sections 24 and 28.

(7) A person against whom a prohibition order or a premises order has been made may appeal against a variation of the order under section 29 as if the varied order were a sentence passed on the person for the offence referred to in section 29(1) (to the extent it would not otherwise be so appealable).

[Psychoactive Substances Act 2016, s 31.]

**7.8312ZF 32. Nature of proceedings under sections 19 and 29, etc** (1) Proceedings before a court arising by virtue of section 19 or 29 are civil proceedings (like court proceedings under section 18, 20 or 28).

(2) The standard of proof to be applied by the court in the proceedings is the balance of probabilities.

(3) The court is not restricted in the proceedings to considering evidence that would have been admissible in the criminal proceedings in which the person concerned was convicted.

(4) The court may adjourn any proceedings arising by virtue of section 19 or 29 even after sentencing the person concerned.

(5) An Act of Adjournal under section 305 of the Criminal Procedure (Scotland) Act 1995 (Acts of Adjournal) may be made in relation to proceedings before the High Court of Justiciary, the sheriff or the Sheriff Appeal Court—

*(a)* arising by virtue of section 19 or 29;

*(b)* under section 28, where the application relates to a prohibition order made under section 19;

*(c)* under section 30(5);

*(d)* under subsection (1) of section 31, where the relevant order (as defined in subsection (3) of that section) was made under section 19;

*(e)* under section 31(7).

(6) A prohibition order may be made or varied as mentioned in section 19(2)*(b)* or 29(4)*(b)* (as the case may be) in spite of anything in the following provisions (which relate to orders discharging a person conditionally or absolutely and their effect)—

*(a)* sections 12 and 14 of the Powers of Criminal Courts (Sentencing) Act 2000;

*(b)* sections 246 and 247 of the Criminal Procedure (Scotland) Act 1995;

(*c*) Articles 4 and 6 of the Criminal Justice (Northern Ireland) Order 1996 (SI 1996/3160 (NI 24)).

[Psychoactive Substances Act 2016, s 32.]

**7.8312ZG 33. Special measures for witnesses: England and Wales** (1) Chapter 1 of Part 2 of the Youth Justice and Criminal Evidence Act 1999 (special measures directions in the case of vulnerable and intimidated witnesses) applies to relevant proceedings under this Act as it applies to criminal proceedings, but with—

(*a*) the omission of the provisions of that Act mentioned in subsection (2) (which make provision only in the context of criminal proceedings), and

(*b*) any other necessary modifications.

(2) The provisions are—

(*a*) section 17(4) to (7);

(*b*) section 21(4C)(*e*);

(*c*) section 22A;

(*d*) section 32.

(3) Rules of court made under or for the purposes of Chapter 1 of Part 2 of that Act apply to relevant proceedings under this Act—

(*a*) to the extent provided by rules of court, and

(*b*) subject to any modifications provided by rules of court.

(4) Section 47 of that Act (restrictions on reporting special measures directions etc) applies with any necessary modifications—

(*a*) to a direction under section 19 of that Act as applied by this section;

(*b*) to a direction discharging or varying such a direction.

Sections 49 and 51 of that Act (offences) apply accordingly.

(5) In this section "relevant proceedings under this Act" means—

(*a*) proceedings in England and Wales under section 18, 20, 28, 30 or 31, and

(*b*) proceedings in England and Wales arising by virtue of section 19 or 29.

[Psychoactive Substances Act 2016, s 33.]

**7.8312ZH 34. Special measures for witnesses: Northern Ireland**

**7.8312ZI 35. Transfer of proceedings from youth court** (1) This section applies where—

(*a*) an individual against whom a prohibition order is sought reaches the age of 18 while proceedings before a youth court for the making of the order are ongoing;

(*b*) an individual against whom a prohibition order has been made reaches the age of 18 while proceedings before a youth court for the variation or discharge of the order are ongoing;

(*c*) an individual against whom a prohibition order imposing an access prohibition has been made reaches the age of 18 while proceedings before a youth court under section 24 are ongoing.

(2) Rules of court[1] may provide for the transfer of the proceedings from the youth court to—

(*a*) in England and Wales, a magistrates' court;

(*b*) in Northern Ireland, a court of summary jurisdiction.

(3) Rules of court[1] may prescribe circumstances in which the proceedings may or must remain in the youth court.

[Psychoactive Substances Act 2016, s 35.]

---

1 The Magistrates' Courts (Psychoactive Substances Act 2016) (Transfer of Proceedings) Rules 2016, SI 2016/546 have been made, in PART V STATUTORY INSTRUMENTS ON YOUTH COURTS, ante

*Powers of Entry, Search and Seizure*

**7.8312ZJ 36. Power to stop and search persons** (1) This section applies where a police or customs officer has reasonable grounds to suspect that a person has committed, or is likely to commit, an offence under any of sections 4 to 9 or section 26.

(2) The officer may—

(*a*) search the person for relevant evidence, and

(*b*) stop and detain the person for the purposes of the search.

(3) The powers conferred by this section may be exercised in any place to which the officer lawfully has access (whether or not it is a place to which the public has access).

(4) In this Act—

"police or customs officer" means—

(*a*) a constable,

(*b*) a general customs official, or

(*c*) a designated NCA officer authorised by the Director General of the National Crime Agency (whether generally or specifically) to exercise the powers of a police or customs officer under this Act;

"relevant evidence" means evidence that an offence has been committed under any of sections 4 to 9 or section 26.

[Psychoactive Substances Act 2016, s 36.]

**7.8312ZK 37. Power to enter and search vehicles** (1) This section applies where—

(*a*) a police or customs officer has reasonable grounds to suspect that there is relevant evidence in a vehicle, and

(*b*) the vehicle is not a dwelling.

(2) The officer may at any time—

(*a*) enter the vehicle and search it for relevant evidence;

(*b*) stop and detain the vehicle for the purposes of entering and searching it.

(3) Where—

(*a*) a police or customs officer has stopped a vehicle under this section, and

(*b*) the officer considers that it would be impracticable to search the vehicle in the place where it has stopped,

the officer may require the vehicle to be taken to such place as the officer directs to enable the vehicle to be searched.

(4) A police or customs officer may require—

(*a*) any person travelling in a vehicle, or

(*b*) the registered keeper of a vehicle,

to afford such facilities and assistance with respect to matters under that person's control as the officer considers would facilitate the exercise of any power conferred by this section.

(5) The powers conferred by this section may be exercised in any place to which the officer lawfully has access (whether or not it is a place to which the public has access).

(6) In this section "vehicle" does not include any vessel or aircraft.

(7) For provision conferring additional powers to enter and search vehicles, see section 39.

[Psychoactive Substances Act 2016, s 37.]

**7.8312ZL 38. Power to board and search vessels or aircraft** (1) This section applies where—

(*a*) a police or customs officer has reasonable grounds to believe that there is relevant evidence in or on any vessel or aircraft, and

(*b*) the vessel or aircraft is not a dwelling.

(2) The officer may at any time—

(*a*) board the vessel or aircraft, and

(*b*) search it for relevant evidence.

(3) For the purposes of exercising the power conferred by subsection (2), the officer may require a vessel or aircraft—

(*a*) to stop, or

(*b*) to do anything else that will facilitate the boarding of that or any other vessel or aircraft.

(4) A police or customs officer who has boarded a vessel or aircraft may, for the purposes of disembarking from the vessel or aircraft, require that or any other vessel or aircraft—

(*a*) to stop, or

(*b*) to do anything else that will enable the officer to disembark from the vessel or aircraft.

(5) A police or customs officer may require any person on board a vessel or aircraft to afford such facilities and assistance with respect to matters under that person's control as the officer considers would facilitate the exercise of any power conferred by this section.

(6) For provision conferring additional powers to enter and search vessels and aircraft, see section 39.

[Psychoactive Substances Act 2016, s 38.]

**7.8312M 39. Power to enter and search premises** (1) Where a justice is satisfied that the requirements in subsection (4) are met in relation to any premises, the justice may issue a warrant (a "search warrant") authorising a relevant enforcement officer—

(*a*) to enter the premises, and

(*b*) to search them for relevant evidence.

(2) A search warrant may be issued only on the application of—

(*a*) a relevant enforcement officer, in England and Wales or Northern Ireland;

(*b*) a relevant enforcement officer or a procurator fiscal, in Scotland.

(3) A search warrant may be either—

(*a*) a warrant that relates only to premises specified in the warrant (a "specific-premises warrant"), or

(*b*) in the case of a warrant issued in England and Wales or Northern Ireland, a warrant that relates to any premises occupied or controlled by a person specified in the warrant (an "all-premises warrant").

(4) The requirements of this subsection are met in relation to premises if there are reasonable grounds to suspect that—

(*a*) there are items on the premises that are relevant evidence, and

(*b*) in a case where the premises are specified in the application, any of the conditions in subsection (5) is met.

(5) The conditions referred to in subsection (4)(*b*) are—

(*a*) that it is not practicable to communicate with any person entitled to grant entry to the premises;

(*b*) that it is not practicable to communicate with any person entitled to grant access to the items;

(*c*) that entry to the premises is unlikely to be granted unless a warrant is produced;

(*d*) that the purpose of entry may be frustrated or seriously prejudiced unless a relevant enforcement officer arriving at the premises can secure immediate entry to them.

(6) In this Act "relevant enforcement officer" means—

(*a*) a police or customs officer (see section 36(4)), or

(*b*) an officer of a local authority.

[Psychoactive Substances Act 2016, s 39.]

**7.8312ZN 40. Further provision about search warrants** (1) An application for a search warrant may be made without notice being given to persons who might be affected by the warrant.

(2) The application must be supported—

(*a*) in England and Wales, by an information in writing;

(*b*) in Scotland, by evidence on oath;

(*c*) in Northern Ireland, by a complaint on oath.

(3) A person applying for a search warrant must answer on oath any question that the justice hearing the application asks the person.

In the case of an application made by a procurator fiscal, that requirement may be met by a relevant enforcement officer.

(4) A search warrant may be executed by any relevant enforcement officer.

(5) A search warrant may authorise persons to accompany any relevant enforcement officer who is executing it.

(6) A person authorised under subsection (5) to accompany a relevant enforcement officer may exercise any power conferred by sections 39 to 45 which the officer may exercise as a result of the warrant.

But the person may exercise such a power only in the company of, and under the supervision of, a relevant enforcement officer.

(7) Schedule 3 contains further provision about—

(*a*) applications for search warrants made in England and Wales or Northern Ireland, and

(*b*) search warrants issued in England and Wales or Northern Ireland.

(8) An entry on or search of premises under a search warrant issued in England and Wales or Northern Ireland is unlawful unless it complies with the provisions of Part 3 of that Schedule (execution of search warrants).

[Psychoactive Substances Act 2016, s 40.]

**7.8312ZO 41. Powers of examination, etc** (1) This section applies where a relevant enforcement officer is exercising a power of search conferred by section 37, 38 or 39 in relation to any premises.

(2) The officer may examine anything that is in or on the premises.

(3) The officer may carry out any measurement or test of anything which the officer has power under this section to examine.

(4) The power conferred by subsection (3) includes power to take a sample from any live plant.

(5) For the purpose of exercising—

(*a*) a power of search conferred by section 37, 38 or 39, or

(*b*) any power conferred by this section,

the officer may, so far as is reasonably necessary for that purpose, break open any container or other locked thing.

(6) The officer may require any person in or on the premises to afford such facilities and assistance with respect to matters under that person's control as the officer considers would facilitate the exercise of—

(*a*) a power of search conferred by section 37, 38 or 39, or

(*b*) any power conferred by this section.

(7) Nothing in this section confers any power to search a person.

[Psychoactive Substances Act 2016, s 41.]

**7.8312ZP 42. Power to require production of documents, etc** (1) This section applies where a relevant enforcement officer is exercising a power of search conferred by section 37, 38 or 39 in relation to any premises.

(2) The officer may require any person in or on the premises to produce any document or record that is in the person's possession or control.

(3) A reference in this section to the production of a document includes a reference to the production of—

(*a*) a hard copy of information recorded otherwise than in hard copy form, or

(*b*) information in a form from which a hard copy can be readily obtained.

(4) For the purposes of this section—

(*a*) information is recorded in hard copy form if it is recorded in a paper copy or similar form capable of being read (and references to hard copy have a corresponding meaning);

(*b*) information can be read only if—

(i) it can be read with the naked eye, or

(ii) to the extent that it consists of images (for example photographs, pictures, maps, plans or drawings), it can be seen with the naked eye.

[Psychoactive Substances Act 2016, s 42.]

**7.8312ZQ 43. Powers of seizure, etc** (1) A police or customs officer who is exercising the power of search conferred by section 36 may seize and detain anything found in the course of the search.

(2) This subsection applies where a relevant enforcement officer—

(*a*) is exercising a power of search conferred by section 37, 38 or 39 in relation to any premises, or

(*b*) is otherwise lawfully on premises.

(3) Where subsection (2) applies, the officer may—

(*a*) seize and detain or remove any item found on the premises;

(*b*) take copies of or extracts from any document or record found on the premises.

(4) A relevant enforcement officer to whom any document or record has been produced in accordance with a requirement imposed under section 42 may—

(*a*) seize and detain or remove that document or record;

(*b*) take copies of or extracts from that document or record.

In this subsection "document" includes anything falling within paragraph (a) or (b) of section 42(3).

(5) The powers under this section may only be exercised—

(*a*) for the purposes of determining whether an offence under any of sections 4 to 9 or section 26 has been committed, or

(*b*) in relation to an item which a relevant enforcement officer reasonably believes to be—

(i) relevant evidence, or

(ii) a psychoactive substance (whether or not it is relevant evidence).

(6) Nothing in this section confers power on a relevant enforcement officer to seize an item which is an excluded item (see section 44).

[Psychoactive Substances Act 2016, s 43.]

**7.8312ZR 44. Excluded items** (1) This section defines what is meant by "excluded items" for the purposes of section 43.

(2) In England and Wales "excluded items" means—

(*a*) items subject to legal privilege, within the meaning of the Police and Criminal Evidence Act 1984 (see section 10 of that Act);

(*b*) excluded material, within the meaning of that Act (see section 11 of that Act);

(*c*) special procedure material, within the meaning of that Act (see section 14 of that Act).

(3) In Scotland "excluded items" means items in respect of which a claim to confidentiality of communications could be maintained in legal proceedings.

(4) In Northern Ireland "excluded items" means—

(*a*) items subject to legal privilege, within the meaning of the Police and Criminal Evidence (Northern Ireland) Order 1989 (SI 1989/1341 (NI 12)) (see Article 12 of that Order);

(*b*) excluded material, within the meaning of that Order (see Article 13 of that Order);

(*c*) special procedure material, within the meaning of that Order (see Article 16 of that Order).

[Psychoactive Substances Act 2016, s 44.]

**7.8312ZS 45. Further provision about seizure under section 43** (1) Where—

(*a*) any items which a relevant enforcement officer wishes to seize and remove are in a container, and

(*b*) the officer reasonably considers that it would facilitate the seizure and removal of the items if they remained in the container for that purpose,

any power to seize and remove the items conferred by section 43 includes power to seize and remove the container.

(2) If a container is seized under this section, reasonable efforts must be made to return it to—

(*a*) the person from whom it was seized, or

(*b*) (if different) a person to whom it belongs.

(3) Subsection (2) does not apply—

(*a*) if the container appears to be of negligible value,

(*b*) if it is not practicable for the container to be returned, or

(*c*) while the container is or may be needed for use as evidence at a trial for an offence.

(4) If, in the opinion of a relevant enforcement officer, it is not for the time being practicable for the officer to seize and remove any item, the officer may require—

(*a*) the person from whom the item is being seized, or

(*b*) where the officer is exercising a power of search conferred by section 37, 38 or 39 in relation to any premises, any person in or on the premises,

to secure that the item is not removed or otherwise interfered with until such time as the officer may seize and remove it.

[Psychoactive Substances Act 2016, s 45.]

**7.8312ZT 46. Notices and records in relation to seized items** (1) This section applies where a relevant enforcement officer, or a person accompanying a relevant enforcement officer, seizes any item under section 43.

(2) When the item is seized, the officer must make reasonable efforts to give written notice to each of the following persons—

(*a*) in the case of an item seized from a person, the person from whom the item was seized;

(*b*) in the case of an item seized from premises, any person who appears to the officer to be the occupier of the premises or otherwise to be in charge of the premises;

(*c*) if the officer thinks that the item may belong to any person not falling within paragraph (*a*) or (*b*), that other person.

A person falling within any of paragraphs (*a*) to (*c*) is referred to in this section as an "affected person".

(3) If—

(*a*) the item is seized from premises, and

(*b*) at the time of the seizure it is not reasonably practicable to give a notice to any affected person,

the officer must leave a copy of the notice in a prominent place on the premises.

(4) The notice must—

(*a*) state what has been seized and the reason for its seizure;

(*b*) specify any offence which the officer believes has been committed;

(*c*) explain the effect of sections 49 to 51 and 53.

(5) The officer must make a record of what has been seized.

(6) If a person who appears to a relevant enforcement officer to be an affected person asks for a copy of that record, the officer must, within a reasonable time, provide a copy of that record to that person.

[Psychoactive Substances Act 2016, s 46.]

**7.8312ZU 47. Powers of entry, search and seizure: supplementary provision** (1) A relevant enforcement officer may use reasonable force, if necessary, for the purpose of exercising any power conferred by sections 36 to 45.

(2) A person authorised under section 40(5) to accompany a relevant enforcement officer may use reasonable force, if necessary, for the purpose of exercising any power conferred by sections 39 to 45.

(3) The powers conferred on a relevant enforcement officer by any of sections 36 to 45 do not affect any powers exercisable by the officer apart from that section.

[Psychoactive Substances Act 2016, s 47.]

**7.8312ZV 48. Offences in relation to enforcement officers** (1) A person commits an offence if, without reasonable excuse, the person intentionally obstructs a relevant enforcement officer in the performance of any of the officer's functions under sections 36 to 45.

(2) A person commits an offence if—

(*a*) the person fails without reasonable excuse to comply with a requirement reasonably made, or a direction reasonably given, by a relevant enforcement officer in the exercise of any power conferred by sections 37 to 45, or

(*b*) the person prevents any other person from complying with any such requirement or direction.

(3) In this section any reference to a relevant enforcement officer includes a reference to a person authorised under section 40(5) to accompany a relevant enforcement officer.

(4) A person who is guilty of an offence under this section is liable—

(*a*) on summary conviction in England and Wales, to either or both of the following—
  (i) imprisonment for a term not exceeding 51 weeks (or 6 months, if the offence was committed before the commencement of section 281(5) of the Criminal Justice Act 2003);
  (ii) a fine;

(*b*) on summary conviction in Scotland, to either or both of the following—
  (i) imprisonment for a term not exceeding 12 months;
  (ii) a fine not exceeding level 5 on the standard scale;

(*c*) on summary conviction in Northern Ireland, to either or both of the following—
  (i) imprisonment for a term not exceeding 6 months;
  (ii) a fine not exceeding level 5 on the standard scale.

[Psychoactive Substances Act 2016, s 48.]

*Retention and Disposal of Items*

**7.8312ZW 49. Retention of seized items** (1) This section applies to any item seized under section 43.

(2) The item may be retained so long as is necessary in all the circumstances and in particular—

(*a*) for use as evidence at a trial for an offence under this Act, or

(*b*) for forensic examination or for investigation in connection with an offence under this

Act.

(3) No item may be retained for either of the purposes mentioned in subsection (2) if a photograph or a copy would be sufficient for that purpose.

[Psychoactive Substances Act 2016, s 49.]

**7.8312ZX 50. Power of police, etc to dispose of seized psychoactive substances** (1) This section applies if—

(*a*) a police or customs officer has seized an item found during the course of a search under section 36, 37 or 38,

(*b*) the search was carried out in a place to which the officer lawfully had access without a warrant (whether issued under this Act or under any other enactment),

(*c*) the officer reasonably believes that the item—

(i) is a psychoactive substance which, if it had not been seized, was likely to be consumed by an individual for its psychoactive effects, but

(ii) is not evidence of any offence under this Act, and

(*d*) the officer has no reason to believe that, at the time of the seizure, the item was being used for the purposes of, or in connection with, an exempted activity carried on by a person entitled to the item.

(2) The officer may dispose of the item in whatever way the officer thinks is suitable.

(3) For the purposes of this section—

(*a*) an activity is an "exempted activity" in relation to a person if the carrying on of the activity by that person would not be an offence under this Act by virtue of section 11;

(*b*) the persons "entitled" to an item are—

(i) the person from whom it was seized;

(ii) (if different) any person to whom it belongs.

(4) In this section "enactment" includes—

(*a*) an enactment contained in subordinate legislation;

(*b*) an enactment contained in, or in an instrument made under, an Act of the Scottish Parliament;

(*c*) an enactment contained in, or in an instrument made under, a Measure or Act of the National Assembly for Wales;

(*d*) an enactment contained in, or in an instrument made under, Northern Ireland legislation.

[Psychoactive Substances Act 2016, s 50.]

**7.8312ZY 51. Forfeiture of seized items by court on application** (1) A relevant enforcement officer may apply to the appropriate court for the forfeiture of an item retained under section 49.

(2) Where an application for the forfeiture of an item is made under this section, the item is to be retained while proceedings on the application are in progress.

(3) If the court is satisfied that—

(*a*) the item is a psychoactive substance which, if it had not been seized, was likely to be consumed by an individual for its psychoactive effects, and

(*b*) at the time of its seizure, the item was not being used for the purposes of, or in connection with, an exempted activity (see subsection (12)) carried on by a person entitled to the item,

the court must order the forfeiture of the item.

(4) If the item is not a psychoactive substance, the court may order the forfeiture of the item if satisfied that it has been used in the commission of an offence under this Act.

(5) Where an order for forfeiture of an item is made under subsection (3) or (4), the item may be disposed of in whatever way the officer who applied for the order, or another relevant enforcement officer acting on behalf of the same person as that officer, thinks is suitable.

(6) But the item may not be disposed of under subsection (5)—

(*a*) before the end of the period within which an appeal under section 52 may be made against the order, or

(*b*) if such an appeal is made, before it is determined or otherwise dealt with.

(7) If either subsection (8) or (9) applies in relation to an item, the court must order the item to be returned to a person entitled to it.

(For provision enabling an application for an order under this subsection to be made, see section 53.)

(8) This subsection applies in relation to an item if the court is not satisfied that the item—

(*a*) is a psychoactive substance, or

(*b*) has been used in the commission of an offence under this Act.

(9) This subsection applies in relation to an item if—

(*a*) the item is a psychoactive substance, and

(*b*) the court is satisfied that—

(i) if the item had not been seized, it was not likely to be consumed by any individual for its psychoactive effects, or

(ii) at the time of its seizure, the item was being used for the purposes of, or in connection with, an exempted activity carried on by a person entitled to the item.

(10) Where an order for the return of an item is made under subsection (7), the item may nevertheless be retained—

(*a*) until the end of the period within which an appeal under section 52 may be made against the order, or

(*b*) if such an appeal is made, until the time when it is determined or otherwise dealt with.

But if it is decided before the end of the period mentioned in paragraph (*a*) that there is to be no appeal, the item must be returned as soon as possible after that decision is made.

(11) In this section "the appropriate court" means—

(*a*) in relation to England and Wales—

(i) where the person in respect of whom the application is made is an individual who is under the age of 18, a youth court, and

(ii) in any other case, a magistrates' court;

(*b*) in relation to Scotland, the sheriff;

(*c*) in relation to Northern Ireland—

(i) where the person in respect of whom the application is made is an individual who is under the age of 18, a youth court, and

(ii) in any other case, a court of summary jurisdiction.

(12) For the purposes of this section—

(*a*) an activity is an "exempted activity" in relation to a person if the carrying on of the activity by that person would not be an offence under this Act by virtue of section 11;

(*b*) the persons "entitled" to an item are—

(i) the person from whom it was seized;

(ii) (if different) any person to whom it belongs.

[Psychoactive Substances Act 2016, s 51.]

**7.8312ZZ 52. Appeal against decision under section 51** (1) Where an order has been made under section 51, each of the following persons may appeal against the order—

(*a*) any party to the proceedings in which the order was made;

(*b*) any other person entitled to the item to which the order relates.

(2) Where—

(*a*) a relevant enforcement officer brings an appeal under this section, and

(*b*) no person entitled to the item in question was a party to the original proceedings,

the officer must make reasonable efforts to give notice of the appeal to every person who the officer thinks is or may be entitled to the item.

(3) An appeal under this section is to—

(*a*) the Crown Court, in England and Wales;

(*b*) the Sheriff Appeal Court, in Scotland;

(*c*) a county court, in Northern Ireland.

(4) An appeal under this section against an order must be made before the end of the period of 28 days starting with the date of the order.

(5) Subject to subsections (6) and (7), the court hearing the appeal may make any order the court thinks appropriate.

(6) If an appeal against an order for the return of an item is allowed—

(*a*) the court must order the item to be forfeited, and

(*b*) subsections (5) and (6) of section 51 apply with the necessary adaptations.

(7) If an appeal against an order forfeiting an item is allowed—

(*a*) the court must order the item to be returned to a person entitled to it, and

(*b*) subsection (10) of section 51 applies with the necessary adaptations.

(8) The persons "entitled" to an item for the purposes of this section are—

(*a*) the person from whom it was seized;

(*b*) (if different) any person to whom it belongs.

[Psychoactive Substances Act 2016, s 52.]

**7.8312ZZA 53. Return of item to person entitled to it, or disposal if return impracticable**

(1) Where the retention of an item has been, but is no longer, authorised under this Act—

(*a*) the item must be returned to a person entitled to it (but see subsection (4));

(*b*) the appropriate court must, if asked to do so by a person entitled to the item, order it to be returned to that person.

(2) A person who claims to be entitled to an item retained under this Act may apply to the appropriate court for an order under subsection (1)(*b*) or section 51(7) (as appropriate).

(3) Where—

(*a*) a court makes an order under this Act requiring an item to be returned to a particular person, and

(*b*) reasonable efforts have been made, without success, to find that person, or it is for some other reason impracticable to return the item to that person, the order has effect as if it required the item to be returned to any person entitled to it.

(4) Where—

(*a*) an item is required by a provision of this Act, or an order made under this Act, to be returned to a person entitled to it, and

(*b*) reasonable efforts have been made, without success, to find a person entitled to the item, or it is for some other reason impracticable to return the item to a person entitled to it,

a relevant enforcement officer may dispose of the item in whatever way the officer thinks is suitable.

(5) In this section "the appropriate court" means—

(*a*) in relation to England and Wales—

(i) where the person making the application is an individual who is under the age of 18, a youth court, and

(ii) in any other case, a magistrates' court;

(*b*) in relation to Scotland, the sheriff;

(*c*) in relation to Northern Ireland—

(i) where the person making the application is an individual who is under the age of 18, a youth court, and

(ii) in any other case, a court of summary jurisdiction.

(6) The persons "entitled" to an item for the purposes of this section are—

(*a*) the person from whom it was seized;

(*b*) (if different) any person to whom it belongs.

[Psychoactive Substances Act 2016, s 53.]

7.8312ZZB **54. Forfeiture by court following conviction** (1) This section applies where a person is convicted of—

(*a*) an offence under any of sections 4 to 9 and 26, or

(*b*) an ancillary offence (see subsection (11)).

(2) In this section "the court" means—

(*a*) the court by or before which the person is convicted of the offence, except where paragraph (*b*) or (*c*) applies;

(*b*) if the person is committed to the Crown Court to be dealt with for that offence, the Crown Court;

(*c*) if the person is remitted to the High Court of Justiciary to be dealt with for that offence, the High Court of Justiciary.

(3) The court must make an order for the forfeiture of any psychoactive substance in respect of which the offence was committed.

(4) The court may also make an order for the forfeiture of any other item that was used in the commission of the offence.

(5) An order under subsection (3) or (4) is referred to in this section as a "forfeiture order".

(6) Before making a forfeiture order under subsection (4) in relation to any item, the court must give an opportunity to make representations to any person (in addition to the convicted person) who claims to be the owner of the item or otherwise to have an interest in it.

(7) A forfeiture order may not be made so as to come into force at any time before there is no further possibility (ignoring any power to appeal out of time) of the order being varied or set aside on appeal.

(8) Where the court makes a forfeiture order, it may also make such other provision as it considers to be necessary for giving effect to the forfeiture.

(9) That provision may, in particular, include provision relating to the retention, handling, destruction or other disposal of the item.

(10) Provision made by virtue of this section may be varied at any time by the court that made it.

(11) In this section "ancillary offence" means—

(*a*) an offence of attempting or conspiring to commit an offence under any of sections 4 to 9 and 26;

(*b*) an offence under Part 2 of the Serious Crime Act 2007 in relation to an offence under any of sections 4 to 9 and 26;

(*c*) an offence of inciting a person to commit an offence under any of sections 4 to 9 and 26;

(*d*) an offence of aiding, abetting, counselling or procuring the commission of an offence under any of sections 4 to 9 and 26.

[Psychoactive Substances Act 2016, s 54.]

*Supplementary and Final Provisions*

7.8312ZZC **55. Application of Customs and Excise Management Act 1979** (1) Section 164 of the Customs and Excise Management Act 1979 (power to search persons) applies in relation to a psychoactive substance as it applies in relation to an article with respect to the importation or exportation of which any prohibition or restriction is for the time being in force under or by virtue of any enactment.

(2) A psychoactive substance is liable to forfeiture under the Customs and Excise Management Act 1979 if—

(*a*) the psychoactive substance—

(i) is imported or exported, or

(ii) is entered for exportation or brought to any place in the United Kingdom for exportation,

(*b*) the psychoactive substance is likely to be consumed by any individual for its psychoactive effects, and

(*c*) the importation or (as the case may be) exportation of the psychoactive substance is not an exempted activity.

(3) For the purposes of subsection (2) the importation or exportation of a psychoactive substance is an "exempted activity" if it would not be an offence under this Act by virtue of section 11.

(4) Section 5 of the Customs and Excise Management Act 1979 (time of importation, exportation, etc) applies for the purposes of subsection (2) as it applies for the purposes of that Act.

[Psychoactive Substances Act 2016, s 55.]

**7.8312ZZD 56. Offences by directors, partners, etc** (1) Where an offence under this Act has been committed by a body corporate and it is proved that the offence—

(*a*) has been committed with the consent or connivance of a person falling within subsection (2), or

(*b*) is attributable to any neglect on the part of such a person,

that person (as well as the body corporate) is guilty of that offence and liable to be proceeded against and punished accordingly.

(2) The persons are—

(*a*) a director, manager, secretary or similar officer of the body corporate;

(*b*) any person who was purporting to act in such a capacity.

(3) Where the affairs of a body corporate are managed by its members, subsection (1) applies in relation to the acts and defaults of a member, in connection with that management, as if the member were a director of the body corporate.

(4) Where an offence under this Act has been committed by a Scottish firm and it is proved that the offence—

(*a*) has been committed with the consent or connivance of a partner in the firm or a person purporting to act as such a partner, or

(*b*) is attributable to any neglect on the part of such a person,

that person (as well as the firm) is guilty of that offence and liable to be proceeded against and punished accordingly.

[Psychoactive Substances Act 2016, s 56.]

**7.8312ZZE 57. Providers of information society services** Schedule 4 contains provision about the application of certain provisions of this Act in relation to persons providing information society services within the meaning of that Schedule.

[Psychoactive Substances Act 2016, s 57.]

**7.8312ZZF 58. Review** (1) Before the end of the period mentioned in subsection (2), the Secretary of State must—

(*a*) review the operation of this Act,

(*b*) prepare a report of the review, and

(*c*) lay a copy of the report before Parliament.

(2) The period referred to in subsection (1) is the period of 30 months beginning with the day on which sections 4 to 8 come into force.

[Psychoactive Substances Act 2016, s 58.]

**7.8312ZZG 59. Interpretation** (1) In this Act—

"access prohibition" has the meaning given by section 22(6);

"designated NCA officer" means a National Crime Agency officer designated under section 10 of the Crime and Courts Act 2013 as a person having either or both of the following—

(*a*) the powers and privileges of a constable;

(*b*) the powers of an officer of Revenue and Customs;

"exempted substance" has the meaning given by section 3;

"general customs function" has the meaning given by section 1(8) of the Borders, Citizenship and Immigration Act 2009;

"general customs official" means a person designated as a general customs official under section 3(1) of the Borders, Citizenship and Immigration Act 2009;

"item" includes any substance;

"justice" means—

(*a*) in England and Wales, a justice of the peace,

(*b*) in Scotland, a sheriff or a justice of the peace, and

(*c*) in Northern Ireland, a lay magistrate;

"local authority" means—

(*a*) in England, a county council, a district council, a London borough council, the Common Council of the City of London or the Council of the Isles of Scilly,

(*b*) in Wales, a county council or county borough council,

(*c*) in Scotland, a council constituted under section 2 of the Local Government etc (Scotland) Act 1994, and

(*d*) in Northern Ireland, a district council constituted under section 1 of the Local Government Act (Northern Ireland) 1972;

"police or customs officer" has the meaning given by section 36(4);

"premises" includes any place and, in particular, includes—

(*a*) any vehicle, vessel or aircraft;

(*b*) any offshore installation within the meaning given by section 1 of the Mineral Workings (Offshore Installations) Act 1971;

(*c*) any renewable energy installation within the meaning given by section 104 of the Energy Act 2004;

(*d*) any tent or movable structure;

"premises notice" is to be read in accordance with section 14;

"premises order" is to be read in accordance with section 20;

"prohibited activity" has the meaning given by section 12;

"prohibition notice" is to be read in accordance with section 13;

"prohibition order" is to be read in accordance with section 17;

"psychoactive effects", in relation to a substance, is to be read in accordance with section 2(2);

"psychoactive substance" has the meaning given by section 2(1);

"relevant enforcement officer" has the meaning given by section 39(6);

"relevant evidence" has the meaning given by section 36(4);

"search warrant" means a warrant under section 39;

"senior officer" has the meaning given by section 13(7);

"vessel" is to be read in accordance with subsection (4).

(2) In this Act—

(*a*) any reference to producing a substance is a reference to producing it by manufacture, cultivation or any other method;

(*b*) any reference to supplying a substance includes a reference to distributing it;

(*c*) any reference to consuming a substance is to be read in accordance with section 2(3).

(3) For the purposes of this Act the items which are in a person's possession include any items which are—

(*a*) subject to that person's control, but

(*b*) in the custody of another person.

(4) In this Act any reference to a vessel includes a reference to—

(*a*) any ship or boat or any other description of vessel used in navigation, and

(*b*) any hovercraft, submersible craft or other floating craft,

but does not include a reference to anything that permanently rests on, or is permanently attached to, the sea bed.

(5) Before the commencement of section 109 of the Courts Reform (Scotland) Act 2014 (abolition of appeal from a sheriff to the sheriff principal), any reference in this Act to the Sheriff Appeal Court, other than the reference in section 31(1) in relation to a prohibition order made under section 19, is to be read as a reference to the sheriff principal.

[Psychoactive Substances Act 2016, s 59.]

**7.8312ZZH 60. Consequential amendments** Schedule 5 (which contains consequential amendments) has effect.

[Psychoactive Substances Act 2016, s 60.]

**7.8312ZZI 61. Power to make further consequential amendments** (1) The Secretary of State may by regulations make provision that is consequential on any provision of this Act.

(2) The power to make regulations under this section—

(*a*) is exercisable by statutory instrument;

(*b*) includes power to make transitional, transitory or saving provision;

(*c*) may, in particular, be exercised by amending, repealing, revoking or otherwise modifying any provision made by or under primary legislation passed before this Act or in the same Session.

(3) A statutory instrument that contains (with or without other provision) regulations under this section that amend, repeal or revoke any provision of primary legislation may not be made unless a draft of the instrument has been laid before, and approved by a resolution of, each House of Parliament.

(4) Any other statutory instrument containing regulations under this section is subject to annulment in pursuance of a resolution of either House of Parliament.

(5) In this section "primary legislation" means—

(*a*) an Act of Parliament;

(*b*) an Act of the Scottish Parliament;
(*c*) a Measure or Act of the National Assembly for Wales;
(*d*) Northern Ireland legislation.
[Psychoactive Substances Act 2016, s 61.]

**7.8312ZZJ 62. Extent** (1) Except as provided by subsection (2), this Act extends to England and Wales, Scotland and Northern Ireland.
(2) Any amendment or repeal made by this Act has the same extent as the provision amended or repealed.
(3) The power under section 384(1) of the Armed Forces Act 2006 ("the 2006 Act") may be exercised so as to extend to any of the Channel Islands (with or without modifications) any amendment or repeal made by or under this Act of any part of the 2006 Act.
(4) The power under section 384(2) of the 2006 Act may be exercised so as to modify any provision of that Act as amended by or under this Act as it extends to the Isle of Man or a British overseas territory.
[Psychoactive Substances Act 2016, s 62.]

**7.8312ZZK 63. Commencement and short title** (1) The following provisions of this Act come into force on the day on which this Act is passed—
(*a*) sections 59, 61 and 62 and this section;
(*b*) any power to make regulations under this Act.
(2) The remaining provisions of this Act come into force in accordance with provision contained in regulations made by the Secretary of State.
(3) Regulations under subsection (2) may—
(*a*) make different provision for different purposes;
(*b*) make such transitory or transitional provision, or savings, as the Secretary of State considers necessary or expedient.
(4) This Act may be cited as the Psychoactive Substances Act 2016.
[Psychoactive Substances Act 2016, s 63.]

## SCHEDULE 1
### Exempted Substances
Section 3

**7.8312ZZL** *Controlled drugs*
**1.** Controlled drugs (within the meaning of the Misuse of Drugs Act 1971).
*Medicinal products*
**2.** Medicinal products.
In this paragraph "medicinal product" has the same meaning as in the Human Medicines Regulations 2012 (SI 2012/1916) (see regulation 2 of those Regulations).
*Alcohol*
**3.** Alcohol or alcoholic products.
In this paragraph—
"alcohol" means ethyl alcohol, and
"alcoholic product" means any product which—
(*a*) contains alcohol, and
(*b*) does not contain any psychoactive substance.
*Nicotine and tobacco products*
**4.** Nicotine.
**5.** Tobacco products.
In this paragraph "tobacco product" means—
(*a*) anything which is a tobacco product within the meaning of the Tobacco Products Duty Act 1979 (see section 1 of that Act), and
(*b*) any other product which—
(i) contains nicotine, and
(ii) does not contain any psychoactive substance.
*Caffeine*
**6.** Caffeine or caffeine products.
In this paragraph "caffeine product" means any product which—
(*a*) contains caffeine, and
(*b*) does not contain any psychoactive substance.
*Food*
**7.** Any substance which—
(*a*) is ordinarily consumed as food, and
(*b*) does not contain a prohibited ingredient.
In this paragraph—
"food" includes drink;
"prohibited ingredient", in relation to a substance, means any psychoactive substance—
(*a*) which is not naturally occurring in the substance, and
(*b*) the use of which in or on food is not authorised by an EU instrument.

## SCHEDULE 2
### Exempted Activities
Section 11

**7.8312ZZM** *Healthcare-related activities*
**1.** Any activity carried on by a person who is a health care professional and is acting in the course of his or her profession.
In this paragraph "health care professional" has the same meaning as in the Human Medicines Regulations 2012 (SI 2012/1916) (see regulation 8 of those Regulations).

2. Any activity carried on for the purpose of, or in connection with—

(*a*) the supply to, or the consumption by, any person of a substance prescribed for that person by a health care professional acting in the course of his or her profession, or

(*b*) the supply to, or the consumption by, any person of a substance in accordance with the directions of a health care professional acting in the course of his or her profession.

In this paragraph "health care professional" has the same meaning as in the Human Medicines Regulations 2012 (see regulation 8 of those Regulations).

3. Any activity carried on in respect of an active substance by a person who—

(*a*) is registered in accordance with regulation 45N of the Human Medicines Regulations 2012, or

(*b*) is exempt from any requirement to be so registered by virtue of regulation 45M(2) or (3) of those Regulations.

In this paragraph "active substance" has the same meaning as in the Human Medicines Regulations 2012 (see regulation 8 of those Regulations).

*Research*

4. Any activity carried on in the course of, or in connection with, approved scientific research.

In this paragraph—

"approved scientific research" means scientific research carried out by a person who has approval from a relevant ethics review body to carry out that research;

"relevant ethics review body" means—

(*a*) a research ethics committee recognised or established by the Health Research Authority under Chapter 2 of Part 3 of the Care Act 2014, or

(*b*) a body appointed by any of the following for the purpose of assessing the ethics of research involving individuals—

(i) the Secretary of State, the Scottish Ministers, the Welsh Ministers, or a Northern Ireland department;

(ii) a relevant NHS body;

(iii) a body that is a Research Council for the purposes of the Science and Technology Act 1965;

(iv) an institution that is a research institution for the purposes of Chapter 4A of Part 7 of the Income Tax (Earnings and Pensions) Act 2003 (see section 457 of that Act);

(v) a charity which has as its charitable purpose (or one of its charitable purposes) the advancement of health or the saving of lives;

"charity" means—

(*a*) a charity as defined by section 1(1) of the Charities Act 2011,

(*b*) a body entered in the Scottish Charity Register, or

(*c*) a charity as defined by section 1(1) of the Charities Act (Northern Ireland) 2008;

"relevant NHS body" means—

(*a*) an NHS trust or NHS foundation trust in England,

(*b*) an NHS trust or Local Health Board in Wales,

(*c*) a Health Board or Special Health Board constituted under section 2 of the National Health Service (Scotland) Act 1978,

(*d*) the Common Services Agency for the Scottish Health Service, or

(*e*) any of the health and social care bodies in Northern Ireland falling within paragraphs (*a*) to (*d*) of section 1(5) of the Health and Social Care (Reform) Act (Northern Ireland) 2009.

## SCHEDULE 3

Search Warrants: England and Wales and Northern Ireland

Section 40

### Part 1

### Application of this Schedule

7.8312ZZN 1. This Schedule applies to—

(*a*) applications for search warrants made in England and Wales or Northern Ireland, and

(*b*) search warrants issued in England and Wales or Northern Ireland.

### Part 2

### Search Warrants: Applications and Safeguards

*Applications for warrants*

2. (1) A person applying for a search warrant must—

(*a*) state that the application is made under section 39 of this Act;

(*b*) specify the matters set out in sub-paragraph (2) or (3) (as the case may be);

(*c*) state what are the grounds for suspecting that relevant evidence is on the premises;

(*d*) identify, so far as is possible, the offence to which the relevant evidence relates.

(2) If the person is applying for a specific-premises warrant, the person must specify each set of premises that it is desired to enter and search.

(3) If the person is applying for an all-premises warrant, the person must specify—

(*a*) as many of the sets of premises that it is desired to enter and search as it is reasonably practicable to specify;

(*b*) the person who is in occupation or control of those premises and any others that it is desired to enter and search;

(*c*) why it is necessary to search more premises than those specified under paragraph (*a*);

(*d*) why it is not reasonably practicable to specify all the premises that it is desired to enter and search.

(4) If the person is applying for a search warrant authorising entry and search on more than one occasion, the person must also state—

(*a*) the ground on which the person applies for such a warrant, and

(*b*) whether the person seeks a warrant authorising an unlimited number of entries, or (if not) the maximum number of entries desired.

(5) In this paragraph "specific-premises warrant" and "all-premises warrant" have the meaning given by

section 39(3).

*Safeguards in connection with power of entry conferred by warrant*

**3.** A search warrant authorises entry on one occasion only, unless it specifies that it authorises multiple entries.

**4.** (1) A search warrant must—

(*a*) specify the name of the person who applies for it;

(*b*) specify the date on which it is issued;

(*c*) state that the warrant is issued under section 39 of this Act;

(*d*) specify each set of premises to be searched, or (in the case of an all-premises warrant) the person who is in occupation or control of premises to be searched, together with any premises to be searched that are under the person's occupation or control and can be specified;

(*e*) identify, so far as is possible, the offence to which the relevant evidence suspected to be on the premises relates.

(2) In sub-paragraph (1)(*d*) "all-premises warrant" has the meaning given by section 39(3).

**5.** (1) Two copies must be made of a search warrant that specifies only one set of premises and does not authorise multiple entries.

(2) As many copies as are reasonably required may be made of any other kind of search warrant.

(3) The copies must be clearly certified as copies.

## Part 3

## Execution of Search Warrants

*Warrant to be executed within one month*

**6.** Entry and search under a search warrant must be within one month from the date of its issue.

*All-premises warrants*

**7.** (1) In the case of an all-premises warrant, premises that are not specified in the warrant may be entered and searched only if a relevant enforcement officer of the appropriate grade has authorised them to be entered.

(2) An authorisation under sub-paragraph (1) must be in writing.

(3) In this paragraph—

"all-premises warrant" has the meaning given by section 39(3);

"relevant enforcement officer of the appropriate grade" means—

(*a*) a senior officer (see section 13(7)), or

(*b*) in the case of a search warrant issued on the application of an officer of a local authority, a person designated by the local authority for the purposes of this paragraph.

*Search of premises more than once*

**8.** (1) Premises may be entered or searched for the second or any subsequent time under a search warrant authorising multiple entries only if a relevant enforcement officer of the appropriate grade has authorised that entry to the premises.

(2) An authorisation under sub-paragraph (1) must be in writing.

(3) In this paragraph "relevant enforcement officer of the appropriate grade" has the same meaning as in paragraph 7.

*Time of search*

**9.** Entry and search under a search warrant must be at a reasonable hour unless it appears to the relevant enforcement officer executing it that the purpose of a search may be frustrated on an entry at a reasonable hour.

*Evidence of authority etc*

**10.** (1) Where the occupier of premises to be entered and searched under a search warrant is present at the time when a relevant enforcement officer seeks to execute the warrant, the following requirements must be satisfied—

(*a*) the occupier must be told the officer's name;

(*b*) if not a constable in uniform, the officer must produce to the occupier documentary evidence that the officer is a relevant enforcement officer;

(*c*) the officer must produce the warrant to the occupier;

(*d*) the officer must supply the occupier with a copy of it.

(2) Where the occupier of premises to be entered and searched under a search warrant is not present at the time when a relevant enforcement officer seeks to execute the warrant—

(*a*) if some other person who appears to the officer to be in charge of the premises is present, sub-paragraph (1) has effect as if a reference to the occupier were a reference to that other person;

(*b*) if not, the officer must leave a copy of the warrant in a prominent place on the premises.

*Extent of search*

**11.** A search under a search warrant may only be a search to the extent required for the purpose for which the warrant was issued.

*Securing premises after entry*

**12.** A relevant enforcement officer who enters premises under a search warrant must take reasonable steps to ensure that when the officer leaves the premises they are as secure as they were before the officer entered.

*Return and retention of warrant*

**13.** (1) A search warrant must be returned to the appropriate person (see sub-paragraph (2))—

(*a*) when the warrant has been executed, or

(*b*) on or before the expiry of the period of one month from the date of its issue, if the warrant is—

(i) a specific-premises warrant that has not been executed,

(ii) an all-premises warrant, or

(iii) a warrant authorising multiple entries.

(2) The appropriate person is—

(*a*) in the case of a warrant issued in England and Wales, the designated officer for the local justice area in which the justice of the peace was acting when issuing the warrant;

(*b*) in the case of a warrant issued in Northern Ireland, the clerk of petty sessions for the petty sessions district in which the lay magistrate was acting when issuing the warrant.

(3) The appropriate person must retain a search warrant returned under sub-paragraph (1) for 12 months from the date of its return.

(4) If during that period the occupier of premises to which the search warrant relates asks to inspect it, the

occupier must be allowed to do so.

(5) In this paragraph "specific-premises warrant" and "all-premises warrant" have the meaning given by section 39(3).

## SCHEDULE 4
Providers of Information Society Services — Section 57

### PART 1
### OFFERING TO SUPPLY A PSYCHOACTIVE SUBSTANCE

**7.8312ZZO** *Domestic service providers: extension of liability*

**1.** (1) If—

(*a*) a service provider established in a particular part of the United Kingdom does anything in an EEA state other than the United Kingdom in the course of providing information society services, and

(*b*) the action, if done in that part of the United Kingdom, would constitute an offence under section 5(2),

the service provider is guilty in that part of the United Kingdom of such an offence.

(2) Nothing in this paragraph affects the operation of paragraphs 3 to 5.

*Non-UK service providers: restriction on institution of proceedings*

**2.** (1) Proceedings for an offence under section 5(2) may not be instituted against a non-UK service provider in respect of anything done in the course of the provision of information society services unless the derogation condition is met.

(2) The derogation condition is that taking proceedings—

(*a*) is necessary for the purposes of the public interest objective,

(*b*) relates to an information society service that prejudices that objective or presents a serious and grave risk of prejudice to that objective, and

(*c*) is proportionate to that objective.

(3) In this paragraph—

"non-UK service provider" means a service provider established in an EEA state other than the United Kingdom;

"the public interest objective" means the pursuit of public policy.

*Exceptions for mere conduits*

**3.** (1) A service provider does not commit an offence under section 5(2) by providing access to a communication network or by transmitting, in a communication network, information provided by a recipient of the service, if the service provider does not—

(*a*) initiate the transmission,

(*b*) select the recipient of the transmission, or

(*c*) select or modify the information contained in the transmission.

(2) For the purposes of sub-paragraph (1)—

(*a*) providing access to a communication network, and

(*b*) transmitting information in a communication network,

include the automatic, intermediate and transient storage of the information transmitted so far as the storage is solely for the purpose of carrying out the transmission in the network.

(3) Sub-paragraph (2) does not apply if the information is stored for longer than is reasonably necessary for the transmission.

*Exception for caching*

**4.** (1) A service provider does not commit an offence under section 5(2) by storing information provided by a recipient of the service for transmission in a communication network if the first and second conditions are met.

(2) The first condition is that the storage of the information—

(*a*) is automatic, intermediate and temporary, and

(*b*) is solely for the purpose of making more efficient the onward transmission of the information to other recipients of the service at their request.

(3) The second condition is that the service provider—

(*a*) does not modify the information,

(*b*) complies with any conditions attached to having access to the information, and

(*c*) if sub-paragraph (4) applies, promptly removes the information or disables access to it.

(4) This sub-paragraph applies if the service provider obtains actual knowledge that—

(*a*) the information at the initial source of the transmission has been removed from the network,

(*b*) access to it has been disabled, or

(*c*) a court or administrative authority has ordered the removal from the network of, or the disablement of access to, the information.

*Exception for hosting*

**5.** (1) A service provider does not commit an offence under section 5(2) by storing information provided by a recipient of the service if—

(*a*) the service provider had no actual knowledge when the information was provided that its provision constituted an offence under section 5(2), or

(*b*) on obtaining actual knowledge that the provision of the information constituted such an offence, the service provider promptly removed the information or disabled access to it.

(2) Sub-paragraph (1) does not apply if the recipient of the service is acting under the authority or control of the service provider.

### PART 2
### PROHIBITION NOTICES AND PROHIBITION ORDERS

*Domestic service providers: extension of liability*

**6.** (1) If—

(*a*) a service provider established in a particular part of the United Kingdom does anything in an EEA state other than the United Kingdom in the course of providing information society services, and

(*b*) the action, if done in that part of the United Kingdom, would constitute an offence under section 26,

the service provider is guilty in that part of the United Kingdom of such an offence.

(2) Nothing in this paragraph affects the operation of paragraph 8.

*Non-UK service providers: restriction on including terms in prohibition notice or order*

**7.** (1) This paragraph applies where—

(*a*) a person proposes to give a prohibition notice,

(*b*) a person makes an application for a prohibition order under section 18, or

(*c*) a person mentioned in subsection (1)(*a*) or (2) of section 28 makes an application under that section for the variation of a prohibition order.

(2) The prohibition notice or prohibition order may include terms which restrict the freedom of a non-UK service provider to provide information society services in relation to an EEA state only if conditions A and B are met.

(3) Condition A is that the relevant person considers that the terms—

(*a*) are necessary for the purposes of the public interest objective,

(*b*) relate to an information society service that prejudices that objective or presents a serious and grave risk of prejudice to that objective, and

(*c*) are proportionate to that objective.

(4) In sub-paragraph (3)—

"the relevant person" means—

(*a*) in relation to a prohibition notice, the person giving the notice;

(*b*) in relation to a prohibition order, the court making or varying the order;

"the public interest objective" means the pursuit of public policy.

(5) Condition B is that—

(*a*) the relevant enforcement authority has requested the EEA state in which the service provider is established to take measures which the authority considers to be of equivalent effect under the law of the EEA state to the terms and the EEA state has failed to take the measures, and

(*b*) the relevant enforcement authority has notified the Commission of the European Union and the EEA state of the relevant matters (see sub-paragraph (6)).

(6) The "relevant matters" are—

(*a*) in the case of a prohibition notice, the intention to give a prohibition notice containing the terms;

(*b*) in the case of a prohibition order, the intention to apply for—

(i) a prohibition order containing the terms, or

(ii) the variation of a prohibition order so that it contains the terms;

(*c*) in either of those cases, the terms.

(7) In the case of a prohibition order, it does not matter for the purposes of sub-paragraph (5) whether the request or notification is made before or after the making of the application referred to in sub-paragraph (6)(*b*).

(8) In this paragraph—

"non-UK service provider" means a service provider established in an EEA state other than the United Kingdom;

"the relevant enforcement authority" means—

(*a*) in the case of a prohibition notice to be given by a constable, the chief officer of police or chief constable (as the case may be) of the police force of which the constable is a member;

(*b*) in the case of a prohibition notice to be given by a designated NCA officer, the Director General of the National Crime Agency;

(*c*) in the case of a prohibition notice to be given by a general customs official, the Secretary of State by whom general customs functions are exercisable;

(*d*) in the case of a prohibition notice to be given by a local authority, that local authority;

(*e*) in the case of a prohibition order, the person applying for the order or for the variation of the order (as the case may be).

*Protections for service providers of intermediary services*

**8.** (1) A prohibition notice or prohibition order may not include terms which impose liabilities on service providers of intermediary services so far as the imposition of those liabilities would result in a contravention of Article 12, 13 or 14 of the E-Commerce Directive (various protections for service providers of intermediary services).

(2) A prohibition notice or prohibition order may not include terms which impose a general obligation on service providers of intermediary services covered by Article 12, 13 or 14 of the E-Commerce Directive—

(*a*) to monitor the information which they transmit or store when providing those services, or

(*b*) actively to seek facts or circumstances indicating illegal activity when providing those services.

**9.** (1) In paragraph 8 "intermediary services" means an information society service which consists in any of the following—

(*a*) the provision of access to a communication network or the transmission, in a communication network, of information provided by a recipient of the service;

(*b*) the transmission in a communication network of information which—

(i) is provided by a recipient of the service, and

(ii) is the subject of automatic, intermediate and temporary storage which is solely for the purpose of making more efficient the onward transmission of the information to other recipients of the service at their request;

(*c*) the storage of information provided by a recipient of the service.

(2) For the purposes of sub-paragraph (1)(*a*)—

(*a*) providing access to a communication network, and

(*b*) transmitting information in a communication network,

include the automatic, intermediate and transient storage of the information transmitted so far as the storage is solely for the purpose of carrying out the transmission in the network.

(3) Sub-paragraph (2) does not apply if the information is stored for longer than is reasonably necessary for the transmission.

## PART 3

## INTERPRETATION

**10.** In this Schedule—

"established", in relation to a service provider, is to be read in accordance with paragraph 11;

"information society services"—

(*a*) has the meaning given in Article 2(a) of the E-Commerce Directive (which refers to Article 1(2) of Directive 98/34/EC of the European Parliament and of the Council of 22 June 1998 laying down a procedure for the provision of information in the field of technical standards and regulations), and

(*b*) is summarised in recital 17 of the E-Commerce Directive as covering "any service normally provided for remuneration, at a distance, by means of electronic equipment for the processing (including digital compression) and storage of data, and at the individual request of a recipient of a service";

"recipient", in relation to a service, means a person who, for professional ends or otherwise, uses an information society service, in particular for the purposes of seeking information or making it accessible;

"service provider" means a person providing an information society service;

"the E-Commerce Directive" means Directive 2000/31/EC of the European Parliament and of the Council of 8 June 2000 on certain legal aspects of information society services, in particular electronic commerce, in the Internal Market (Directive on electronic commerce).

**11.** (1) A service provider is "established" in a particular part of the United Kingdom, or in a particular EEA state, if the service provider—

(*a*) effectively pursues an economic activity using a fixed establishment in that part of the United Kingdom, or that EEA state, for an indefinite period, and

(*b*) is a national of an EEA state or a company or firm mentioned in Article 54 of the Treaty on the Functioning of the European Union.

(2) The presence or use in a particular place of equipment or other technical means of providing an information society service does not, of itself, constitute the establishment of a service provider.

(3) Where it cannot be determined from which of a number of establishments a given information society service is provided, that service is to be regarded as provided from the establishment at the centre of the service provider's activities relating to that service.

## Misuse of Drugs Regulations 2001[1]

(SI 2001/3998 amended by SI 2003/1432, 1653 and 2429, SI 2004/1031 and 1771 and SI 2005/271, 1653, 2864 and 3372, SI 2006/986, 1450 and 2178, SI 2007/2154, SI 2009/3136, SI 2010/231, 1144 and 1799, SI 2011/448, 2085 and 2581, SI 2012/973, 1311, 1479 and 1916, SI 2013/176, 235 and 625 and SI 2014/1275, 1377, 2081, 3277, SI 2015/231 and 891 and SI 2016/1125)

**7.8313** 1. *Citation and commencement*

[1] Made by the Secretary of State in pursuance of ss 7, 10, 22 and 31 of the Misuse of Drugs Act 1971. Contravention of the regulations is made an offence by s 18(1) of the Misuse of Drugs Act 1971; such offences are triable either way: Sch 4 to the Act. For procedure in respect of an offence triable either way see ss 17A–22 to the Magistrates' Courts Act 1980 in PART I: MAGISTRATES' COURTS, PROCEDURE.

**7.8314** 2. *Interpretation* (1) In these Regulations, unless the context otherwise requires—

"the Act" means the Misuse of Drugs Act 1971;

"accountable officer" has the same meaning as in the Health Act 2006;

"authorised as a member of a group" means authorised by virtue of being a member of a class as respects which the Secretary of State has granted an authority under and for the purposes of regulation 8(3), 9(3) or 10(3) which is in force, and "his group authority", in relation to a person who is a member of such a class, means the authority so granted to that class;

"care home" in relation to—

(*a*) England and Wales has the same meaning as in the Care Standards Act 2000; and

(*b*) *Scotland*;

"care home service" has the same meaning as in the Public Services Reform (Scotland) Act 2010;

"clinical management plan" has the same meaning as in the Human Medicines Regulations 2012;

"the Common Services Agency for the health service" means the body established under section 10 of the National Health Service (Scotland) Act 1978;

"document" means anything in which information of any description is recorded (within the meaning of the Civil Evidence Act 1995);

"equivalent body" means a Local Health Board in Wales, a Health Board in Scotland or the Northern Ireland Central Services Agency for the Health and Social Services in Northern Ireland;

"exempt product" means a preparation or other product consisting of one or more component parts, any of which contains a controlled drug, where—

(*a*) the preparation or other product is not designed for administration of the controlled drug to a human being or animal;

(*b*) the controlled drug in any component part is packaged in such a form, or in combination with other active or inert substances in such a manner, that it cannot be recovered by readily applicable means or in a yield which constitutes a risk to health; and

(*c*) no one component part of the product or preparation contains more than one milligram of the controlled drug or one microgram in the case of lysergide or any other *N*-alkyl derivative of lysergamide;

"Health Board" means a board constituted under section 2 of the National Health Service (Scotland) Act 1978;

"health prescription" means a prescription issued by a doctor, a dentist, a nurse independent prescriber, a pharmacist independent prescriber or a supplementary prescriber under the National Health Service Act 1977, the National Health Service (Scotland) Act 1978, the Health and Personal Social Services (Northern Ireland) Order 1972 or the National Health Service (Isle of Man) Acts 1948 to 1979 (Acts of Tynwald) or upon a form issued by a local authority for use in connection with the health service of that authority;

"installation manager" and "offshore installation" have the same meanings as in the Mineral Workings (Offshore Installations) Act 1971;

"Local Health Board" means a Local Health Board established in accordance with section 16BA of the National Health Service Act 1977;

"master" and "seamen" have the same meanings as in the Merchant Shipping Act 1995;

"NHS Business Services Authority" means the special health authority established under Article 2 of the NHS Business Services Authority (Awdurdod Gwasanaethau Busnes y GIG) (Establishment and Constitution) Order 2005;

"the Northern Ireland Central Services Agency for the Health and Social Services" means the body established under Article 26 of the Health and Personal Social Services (Northern Ireland) Order 1972;

"nurse independent prescriber" has the same meaning as in the Human Medicines Regulations 2012, and such a person may only prescribe controlled drugs in accordance with regulation 6B;

"officer of customs and excise" means an officer within the meaning of the Customs and Excise Management Act 1979;

"operating department practitioner" means a person who is registered under the Health Professions Order 2001 as an operating department practitioner;

"organisation providing ambulance services" means one of the following health service organisations—

(*a*) an NHS trust or NHS foundation trust established under the National Health Service Act 2006 which has a function of providing ambulance services;

(*b*) an NHS trust established under the National Health Service (Wales) Act 2006 which has a function of providing ambulance services;

(*c*) the Scottish Ambulance Board;

"patient group direction" has the same meaning as in the Human Medicines Regulations 2012;

"pharmacist" has the same meaning as in the Human Medicines Regulations 2012;

"pharmacist independent prescriber" has the same meaning as in the Human Medicines Regulations 2012, and such a person may only prescribe controlled drugs in accordance with regulation 6B;

"prescriber identification number" means the number recorded against a person's name by the relevant National Health Service agency for the purposes of that person's private prescribing;

"prescription" means a prescription issued by a doctor for the medical treatment of a single individual, by a supplementary prescriber for the medical treatment of a single individual, by a nurse independent prescriber for the medical treatment of a single individual, by a pharmacist independent prescriber for the medical treatment of a single individual, by a dentist for the dental treatment of a single individual or by a veterinary surgeon or veterinary practitioner for the purposes of animal treatment;

"prison" has the same meaning as in section 4(9) of the Regulation of Investigatory Powers Act 2000;

"private prescribing" means issuing prescriptions other than health prescriptions, where the definition of "prescription" has effect as if the words "or by a veterinary surgeon or veterinary practitioner for the purposes of animal treatment" were omitted;

"professional registration number" means the number recorded against a person's name in the register of any body that licenses or regulates any profession of which that person is a member;

"professional register" means the register maintained by the Nursing and Midwifery Council under article 5 of the Nursing and Midwifery Order 2001;

"register" means either a bound book, which does not include any form of loose leaf register or card index, or a computerised system which is in accordance with best practice guidance endorsed by the Secretary of State under section 2 of the National Health Service Act 1977;

"registered chiropodist" has the same meaning as in the Human Medicines Regulations 2012;

"registered midwife" has the same meaning as in the Human Medicines Regulations 2012;

"registered nurse" has the same meaning as in the Human Medicines Regulations 2012;

"registered occupational therapist" has the same meaning as in the Human Medicines Regulations 2012;

"registered optometrist" has the same meaning as in the Human Medicines Regulations 2012;

"registered orthoptist" has the same meaning as in the Human Medicines Regulations 2012;

"registered orthotist and prosthetist" has the same meaning as in the Human Medicines Regulations 2012;

"registered paramedic" has the same meaning as in the Human Medicines Regulations 2012;

"registered pharmacy" has the same meaning as in the Human Medicines Regulations 2012;

"registered physiotherapist" has the same meaning as in the Human Medicines Regulations 2012;

"registered radiographer" has the same meaning as in the Human Medicines Regulations 2012;

"relevant National Health Service agency" means, for England and Wales, the NHS Business Services Authority; for Scotland, the Common Services Agency for the health service; and for Northern Ireland, the Northern Ireland Central Services Agency for the Health and Social Services;

"retail dealer" means a person lawfully conducting a retail pharmacy business or a pharmacist engaged in supplying drugs to the public at a health centre within the meaning of the Medicines Act 1968;

"specialist community public health nurse" means a registered nurse or midwife who is also registered in the Specialist Community Public Health Nurses' Part of the professional register and against whose name in that Part of the register there is an annotation that she has a qualification in health visiting;

"supplementary prescriber" has the same meaning as in the Human Medicines Regulations 2012;

"veterinary prescription" means a prescription issued by a veterinary surgeon or veterinary practitioner for the purposes of animal treatment;

"wholesale dealer" means a person who carries on the business of selling drugs to persons who buy to sell again.

(2) In these Regulations any reference to a regulation or schedule shall be construed as a reference to a regulation contained in these Regulations or, as the case may be, to a schedule to these Regulations, and any reference in a regulation or schedule to a paragraph shall be construed as a reference to a paragraph of that regulation or schedule.

(3) Nothing in these Regulations shall be construed as derogating from any power or immunity of the Crown, its servants or agents.

**7.8315** 3. *Specification of controlled drugs for purposes of Regulations* Schedules 1 to 5 shall have effect for the purpose of specifying the controlled drugs to which certain provisions of these Regulations apply.

**7.8316** 4. *Exceptions for drugs in Schedules 4 and 5 and poppy-straw* (1) Section 3(1) of the Act (which prohibits the importation and exportation of controlled drugs) shall not have effect in relation to the drugs specified in Schedule 5.

(2) The application of section 3(1) of the Act, in so far as it creates an offence, and the application of sections 50(1) to (4), 68(2) and (3) or 170 of the Customs and Excise Management Act 1979, in so far as they apply in relation to a prohibition or restriction on importation or exportation having effect by virtue of section 3 of the Act, are hereby excluded in the case of importation or exportation which is carried out in person for administration to that person of any drug specified in Part II of Schedule 4.

(3) Section 5(1) of the Act (which prohibits the possession of controlled drugs) shall not have effect in relation to—

(*a*) any drug specified in Part II of Schedule 4;

(*b*) the drugs specified in Schedule 5[1].

(4) Sections 4(1) (which prohibits the production and supply of controlled drugs) and 5(1) of the Act shall not have effect in relation to poppy-straw.

(5) Sections 3(1), 4(1) and 5(1) of the Act shall not have effect in relation to any exempt product.

[1] On a prosecution for unlawful possession of a controlled drug, contrary to s 5(2) of the Misuse of Drugs Act 1971, the burden is on the prosecution to prove that the controlled drug was not in a form permitted by Sch 5, post (*R v Hunt* [1987] AC 352, [1987] 1 All ER 1, 82 Cr App Rep 173).

**7.8317** 4A. *Exceptions for drugs in Schedule 1* (1) Section 5(1) of the Act (which prohibits the possession of controlled drugs) shall not have effect in relation to a fungus (of any kind) which contains psilocin or an ester of psilocin where that fungus—

(*a*) is growing uncultivated;

(*b*) is picked by a person already in lawful possession of it for the purpose of delivering it as soon as is reasonably practicable into the custody of a person lawfully entitled to take custody of it and it remains in that person's possession for and in accordance with that purpose;

(*c*) is picked for either of the purposes specified in paragraph (2) and is held for and in accordance with the purpose specified in paragraph (2)(*b*), either by the person who picked it or by another person; or

(*d*) is picked for the purpose specified in paragraph (2)(*b*) and is held for and in accordance with the purpose in paragraph (2)(*a*), either by the person who picked it or by another person.

(2) The purposes specified for the purposes of this paragraph are—

(*a*) the purpose of delivering the fungus as soon as is reasonably practicable into the custody of a person lawfully entitled to take custody of it; and

(*b*) the purpose of destroying the fungus as soon as is reasonably practicable.

**7.8318** 4B. *Exceptions for gamma-butyrolactone and 1,4-butanediol* (1) Gamma-butyrolactone and 1,4-butanediol are excepted from sections 3(1) (import and export), 4(1) (production and supply) and 5(1) (possession) of the Act save where a person imports, exports, produces, supplies or offers to supply either substance, or has either substance in his possession, knowing or believing that it will be used for the purpose of human ingestion whether by himself or another person other than as a flavouring in food.

(2) In this regulation references to gamma-butyrolactone include—

(*a*) any salt of gamma-butyrolactone; and

(*b*) any preparation or other product containing gamma-butyrolactone or a substance specified in sub-paragraph (*a*) of this paragraph.

(3) In this regulation references to 1,4-butanediol include—

(*a*) any substance which is an ester or ether or both an ester and ether of 1,4-butanediol;

(*b*) any salt of 1,4-butanediol or of a substance specified in sub-paragraph (*a*) of this paragraph; and

(*c*) any preparation or other product containing 1,4-butanediol or a substance specified in sub-paragraph (*a*) or (*b*) of this paragraph.

**7.8319** 5. *Licences to produce etc controlled drugs* Where any person is authorised by a licence of the Secretary of State issued under this regulation and for the time being in force to produce, supply, offer to supply or have in his possession any controlled drug, it shall not by virtue of section 4(1) or 5(1) of the Act be unlawful for that person to produce, supply, offer to supply or have in his possession that drug in accordance with the terms of the licence and in compliance with any conditions attached to the licence.

**7.8320** 6. *General authority to supply and possess* (1) Notwithstanding the provisions of section 4(1)(*b*) of the Act, any person who is lawfully in possession of a controlled drug may supply that drug to the person from whom he obtained it.

(2) Notwithstanding the provisions of section 4(1)(*b*) of the Act, any person who has in his possession a drug specified in Schedule 2, 3, 4 or 5 which has been supplied by or on the prescription of a practitioner, a registered nurse, a pharmacist independent prescriber, a physiotherapist independent prescriber, a chiropodist independent prescriber, a supplementary prescriber or a person specified in Schedule 8 acting in accordance with a patient group direction for the treatment of that person, or of a person whom he represents, may supply that drug to any doctor, dentist or pharmacist for the purpose of destruction.

(3) Notwithstanding the provisions of section 4(1)(*b*) of the Act, any person who is lawfully in possession of a drug specified in Schedule 2, 3, 4 or 5 which has been supplied by or on the prescription of a veterinary practitioner or veterinary surgeon for the treatment of animals may supply that drug to any veterinary practitioner, veterinary surgeon or pharmacist for the purpose of destruction.

(4) It shall not by virtue of section 4(1)(*b*) or 5(1) of the Act be unlawful for any person in respect of whom a licence has been granted and is in force under section 16(1) of the Wildlife and Countryside Act 1981 to supply, offer to supply or have in his possession any drug specified in Schedule 2 or 3 for the purposes for which that licence was granted.

(5) Notwithstanding the provisions of section 4(1)(*b*) of the Act, any of the persons specified in paragraph (7) may supply any controlled drug to any person who may lawfully have that drug in his possession.

(6) Notwithstanding the provisions of section 5(1) of the Act, any of the persons so specified may have any controlled drug in his possession.

(7) The persons referred to in paragraphs (5) and (6) are

(*a*) a constable when acting in the course of his duty as such;

(*b*) a person engaged in the business of a carrier when acting in the course of that business;

(*c*) a person engaged in the business of a postal operator (within the meaning of Part 3 of the Postal Services Act 2011 when acting in the course of that business;

(*d*) an officer of customs and excise when acting in the course of his duty as such;

(*e*) a person engaged in the work of any laboratory to which the drug has been sent for forensic examination when acting in the course of his duty as a person so engaged;

(*f*) a person engaged in conveying the drug to a person who may lawfully have that drug in his possession.

(8) Notwithstanding the provisions of section 4(1)(*b*) of the Act, a person lawfully conducting a retail pharmacy business may supply or offer to supply medicines containing phenobarbital or phenobarbital sodium provided that the medicine is supplied (or in the case of an offer to supply would be supplied) in accordance with conditions A to E of regulation 224 or 225 of the Human Medicines Regulations 2012.

**7.8321** 6A. *Supply of articles for administering or preparing controlled drugs* (1) Notwithstanding the provisions of section 9A(1) and (3) of the Act, any of the persons specified in paragraph (2) may, when acting in their capacity as such, supply or offer to supply the following articles—

(*a*) a swab;

(*b*) utensils for the preparation of a controlled drug;

(*c*) citric acid;

(*d*) a filter;

(*e*) ampoules of water for injection, only when supplied or offered for supply in accordance with the Medicines Act 1968 and of any instrument which is in force thereunder;

(*f*) ascorbic acid

(2) The persons referred to in paragraph (1) are—

(*a*) a practitioner;

(*b*) a pharmacist;

(*c*) a person employed or engaged in the lawful provision of drug treatment services;

(*d*) a supplementary prescriber acting under and in accordance with the terms of a clinical management plan; and

(*e*) a nurse independent prescriber".

(3) Despite the provisions of section 9A(1) and (3) of the Act, a person employed or engaged in

the lawful provision of drug treatment services may, when acting in that capacity, supply or offer to supply aluminium foil in the context of structured steps—

(*a*) to engage a patient in a drug treatment plan, or

(*b*) which form part of a patient's drug treatment plan.

(4) In this regulation "drug treatment plan" means a written plan, relating to the treatment of an individual patient, and agreed by the patient and the person employed in the lawful provision of drug treatment services.

**7.8322** *6B. Authority for Nurse Independent Prescribers and Pharmacist Independent Prescribers to prescribe* (1) Subject to paragraph (2) of this regulation, a nurse independent prescriber or a pharmacist independent prescriber may prescribe any controlled drug specified in Schedule 2, 3, 4 or 5.

(2) Neither a nurse independent prescriber nor a pharmacist independent prescriber may prescribe any of the following substances to a person he considers, or has reasonable grounds to suspect, is addicted to any controlled drug listed in the Schedule to the Misuse of Drugs (Supply to Addicts) Regulations 1997 save for the purpose of treating organic disease or injury:

(*a*) cocaine, any salt of cocaine, and any preparation or other product containing cocaine or any salt of cocaine;

(*b*) diamorphine, any salt of diamorphine, and any preparation or other product containing diamorphine or any salt of diamorphine;

(*c*) dipipanone, any salt of dipipanone, and any preparation or other product containing dipipanone or any salt of dipipanone.

(3) For the purposes of paragraph (2) a person is addicted to a controlled drug if, and only if, he has as a result of repeated administration become so dependent upon that controlled drug that he has an overpowering desire for the administration of it to be continued.

**7.8322A** *6C. Authority for Physiotherapist Independent Prescribers and Chiropodist Independent Prescribers to prescribe* (1) A registered physiotherapist independent prescriber may prescribe any of the following controlled drugs for the treatment of organic disease or injury provided that the controlled drug is prescribed to be administered by the specified method—

(*a*) Diazepam by oral administration

(*b*) Dihydrocodeine by oral administration

(*c*) Fentanyl by transdermal administration

(*d*) Lorazepam by oral administration

(*e*) Morphine by oral administration or by injection

(*f*) Oxycodone by oral administration

(*g*) Temazepam by oral administration.

(2) A registered chiropodist independent prescriber may prescribe any of the following controlled drugs for the treatment of organic disease or injury provided that the controlled drug is prescribed to be administered by the specified method—

(*a*) Diazepam by oral administration

(*b*) Dihydrocodeine by oral administration

(*c*) Lorazepam by oral administration

(*d*) Temazepam by oral administration.

**7.8323** *7. Administration of drugs in Schedules 2, 3, 4 and 5* (1) Any person may administer to another any drug specified in Schedule 5.

(2) A doctor or dentist may administer to a patient any drug specified in Schedule 2, 3 or 4.

(3) Any person other than a doctor or dentist may administer to a patient, in accordance with the directions of a doctor or dentist, any drug specified in Schedule 2, 3 or 4, and for these purposes the circumstances in which a person is to be regarded as administering in accordance with the directions of a doctor or dentist include where that person is acting in accordance with a patient group direction.

(4) Notwithstanding the provisions of paragraph (3), a nurse independent prescriber or a pharmacist independent prescriber may administer to a patient, without the directions of a doctor or dentist, any controlled drug which such nurse independent prescriber or such pharmacist independent prescriber respectively may prescribe under regulation 6B provided it is administered for a purpose for which it may be prescribed under that regulation.

(5) Notwithstanding the provisions of paragraph (3), any person may administer to a patient in accordance with the specific directions of a nurse independent prescriber or a pharmacist independent prescriber any controlled drug which such nurse independent prescriber or such pharmacist independent prescriber respectively may prescribe under regulation 6B provided it is administered for a purpose for which it may be prescribed under that regulation.

(6) Notwithstanding the provisions of paragraph (3), a supplementary prescriber acting under and in accordance with the terms of a clinical management plan may administer to a patient, without the directions of a doctor or dentist, any drug specified in Schedule 2, 3 or 4.

(7) Notwithstanding the provisions of paragraph (3), any person may administer to a patient, in accordance with the directions of a supplementary prescriber acting under and in accordance with the terms of a clinical management plan, any drug specified in Schedule 2, 3 or 4.

(8) Notwithstanding the provisions of paragraph (3), a registered physiotherapist independent prescriber or registered chiropodist independent prescriber may administer to a patient without the directions of a doctor or a dentist, any controlled drug which such registered physiotherapist independent prescriber or registered chiropodist independent prescriber respectively may prescribe under regulation 6C provided it is administered for a purpose for which it may be

prescribed under that regulation and by the method by which it was prescribed to be administered.

(9) Notwithstanding the provisions of paragraph (3), any person may administer to a patient, in accordance with the specific instructions of a registered physiotherapist independent prescriber or registered chiropodist independent prescriber, any controlled drug which such registered physiotherapist independent prescriber or registered chiropodist independent prescriber may prescribe under regulation 6C, provided it is administered for a purpose for which it may be prescribed under that regulation and by the method by which it was prescribed to be administered.

**7.8324** 8. *Production and supply of drugs in Schedules 2 and 5* (1) Notwithstanding the provisions of section 4(1)(*a*) of the Act—

(*a*) a practitioner or pharmacist, acting in his capacity as such, may manufacture or compound any drug specified in Schedule 2 or 5;

(*b*) a person lawfully conducting a retail pharmacy business and acting in his capacity as such may, at the registered pharmacy at which he carries on that business, manufacture or compound any drug specified in Schedule 2 or 5, and

(*c*) a nurse independent prescriber acting in her capacity as such, or a supplementary prescriber acting under and in accordance with the terms of a clinical management plan, may compound any drug specified in Schedule 2 or 5 for the purposes of administration in accordance with regulation 7;

(*d*) any person acting in accordance with the written directions of a doctor, a dentist, a nurse independent prescriber, a pharmacist independent prescriber, or a supplementary prescriber acting under and in accordance with the terms of a clinical management plan, may compound any drug specified in Schedule 2 or 5 for the purposes of administration in accordance with regulation 7".

(2) Notwithstanding the provisions of section 4(1)(*b*) of the Act, any of the following persons, that is to say—

(*a*) a practitioner;

(*b*) a pharmacist;

(*c*) a person lawfully conducting a retail pharmacy business;

(*d*) the person in charge or acting person in charge of a hospital or care home which is wholly or mainly maintained by a public authority out of public funds or by a charity or by voluntary subscriptions;

(*da*) the person in charge or acting person in charge of an organisation providing ambulance services;

(*e*) in the case of such a drug supplied to her by a person responsible for the dispensing and supply of medicines at a hospital, care home or prison, the senior registered nurse, acting senior registered nurse, or registered midwife, for the time being in charge of a ward, theatre or other department in the hospital, care home or prison;

(*ea*) in the case of such a drug supplied to him by a person responsible for the dispensing and supply of medicines at a hospital, an operating department practitioner practising in that hospital;

(*f*) a person who is in charge of a laboratory the recognised activities of which consist in, or include, the conduct of scientific education or research and which is attached to a university, university college or such a hospital as aforesaid or to any other institution approved for the purpose under this sub-paragraph by the Secretary of State;

(*g*) a public analyst appointed under section 27 of the Food Safety Act 1990;

(*h*) a sampling officer within the meaning of Schedule 3 to the Medicines Act 1968;

(*i*) a person employed or engaged in connection with a scheme for testing the quality or amount of the drugs, preparations and appliances supplied under the National Health Service Act 1977 or the National Health Service (Scotland) Act 1978 and the regulations made thereunder;

(*j*) a person authorised by the General Pharmaceutical Council for the purposes of section 108 or 109 of the Medicines Act 1968,

(*k*) a supplementary prescriber acting under and in accordance with the terms of a clinical management plan,

may, when acting in his capacity as such, supply or offer to supply any drug specified in Schedule 2 or 5 to any person who may lawfully have that drug in his possession, except that nothing in this paragraph authorises—

(i) the person in charge or acting person in charge of a hospital, organisation providing ambulance services or care home, having a pharmacist responsible for the dispensing and supply of medicines, to supply or offer to supply any drug;

(ii) a senior registered nurse, acting senior registered nurse or registered midwife for the time being in charge of a ward, theatre or other department to supply any drug otherwise than for administration to a patient in that ward, theatre or department in accordance with the directions of a doctor, dentist, supplementary prescriber acting under and in accordance with the terms of a clinical management plan or, subject to paragraph (2A), a nurse independent prescriber or a pharmacist independent prescriber; or

(iii) an operating department practitioner to supply any drug otherwise than for administration to a patient in a ward, theatre or other department in accordance with the directions of a doctor, dentist, supplementary prescriber acting under and in accordance with the terms of a clinical management plan or, subject to paragraph (2A), a nurse independent prescriber or a pharmacist independent prescriber

(iv) the person in charge or acting person in charge of an organisation providing ambulance services to supply any drugs other than directly to employees of the organisation for the immediate treatment of sick or injured persons.

(2A) The directions given by a nurse independent prescriber or a pharmacist independent prescriber referred to in paragraph (2)(*k*)(ii) and (iii) shall relate only to a controlled drug which such nurse independent prescriber or such pharmacist independent prescriber respectively may prescribe under regulation 6B and a purpose for which it may be prescribed under that regulation.

(3) Notwithstanding the provisions of section 4(1)(*b*) of the Act, a person who is authorised as a member of a group may, under and in accordance with the terms of his group authority and in compliance with any conditions attached thereto, supply or offer to supply any drug specified in Schedule 2 or 5 to any person who may lawfully have that drug in his possession.

(4) Notwithstanding the provisions of section 4(1)(*b*) of the Act, a person who is authorised by a written authority issued by the Secretary of State under and for the purposes of this paragraph and for the time being in force may, at the premises specified in that authority and in compliance with any conditions so specified, supply or offer to supply any drug specified in Schedule 5 to any person who may lawfully have that drug in his possession.

(5) Notwithstanding the provisions of section 4(1)(*b*) of the Act—

(*a*) the owner of a ship, or the master of a ship which does not carry a doctor among the seamen employed in it; or

(*b*) the installation manager of an offshore installation,

may supply or offer to supply any drug specified in Schedule 2 or 5—

(i) for the purpose of compliance with any of the provisions specified in paragraph (6), to any person on that ship or installation;

(ii) to any person who may lawfully supply that drug to him;

(iii) to any constable for the purpose of the destruction of that drug.

(6) The provisions referred to in paragraph (5) are any provision of, or of any instrument which is in force under—

(*a*) the Mineral Workings (Offshore Installations) Act 1971;

(*b*) the Health and Safety at Work etc Act 1974 or

(*c*) the Merchant Shipping Act 1995.

(7) Notwithstanding the provisions of section 4(1)(*b*) of the Act, a nurse independent prescriber may, when acting in her capacity as such, supply or offer to supply any controlled drug specified in Schedule 2 or 5 to any person who may lawfully have any of those drugs in his possession provided it is supplied or offered in circumstances where she may prescribe it under regulation 6B.

(8) Notwithstanding the provisions of section 4(1)(*b*) of the Act—

(*a*) a registered nurse or a pharmacist, when acting in her capacity as such, may supply or offer to supply, under and in accordance with the terms of a patient group direction, diamorphine or morphine where administration of such drugs is required for the immediate, necessary treatment of sick or injured persons;

(*b*) a registered nurse or a person specified in Schedule 8 may, when acting in their capacity as such, supply or offer to supply, under and in accordance with the terms of a patient group direction, any drug specified in Schedule 5 or ketamine to any person who may lawfully have that drug in his possession, except that this paragraph shall not have effect in the case of ketamine or any preparation of ketamine which is designed for administration by injection and which is to be used for the purpose of treating a person who is addicted to a drug.

(9) For the purposes of paragraph (8)(*b*) above, a person shall be regarded as being addicted to a drug if, and only if, he has as a result of repeated administration become so dependent upon the drug that he has an overpowering desire for the administration of it to be continued

**7.8325** 9. *Production and supply of drugs in Schedules 3 and 4* (1) Notwithstanding the provisions of section 4(1)(*a*) of the Act—

(*a*) a practitioner or pharmacist, acting in his capacity as such, may manufacture or compound any drug specified in Schedule 3 or 4;

(*b*) a person lawfully conducting a retail pharmacy business and acting in his capacity as such may, at the registered pharmacy at which he carries on that business, manufacture or compound any drug specified in Schedule 3 or 4;

(*c*) a person who is authorised by a written authority issued by the Secretary of State under and for the purposes of this sub-paragraph and for the time being in force may, at the premises specified in that authority and in compliance with any conditions so specified, produce any drug specified in Schedule 3 or 4;

(*d*) a nurse independent prescriber acting in her capacity as such, or a supplementary prescriber acting under and in accordance with the terms of a clinical management plan, may compound any drug specified in Schedule 3 or 4 for the purposes of administration in accordance with regulation 7;

(*e*) any person acting in accordance with the written directions of a doctor, a dentist, a nurse independent prescriber, a pharmacist independent prescriber, or a supplementary prescriber acting under and in accordance with the terms of a clinical management plan, may compound any drug specified in Schedule 3 or 4 for the purposes of administration in accordance with regulation 7.

(2) Notwithstanding the provisions of section 4(1)(*b*) of the Act, any of the following persons, that is to say—

(*a*) a practitioner;

(*b*) a pharmacist;

(*c*) a person lawfully conducting a retail pharmacy business;
(*d*) a person in charge of a laboratory the recognised activities of which consist in, or include, the conduct of scientific education or research;
(*e*) a public analyst appointed under section 27 of the Food Safety Act 1990;
(*f*) a sampling officer within the meaning of Schedule 3 to the Medicines Act 1968;
(*g*) a person employed or engaged in connection with a scheme for testing the quality or amount of the drugs, preparations and appliances supplied under the National Health Service Act 1977 or the National Health Service (Scotland) Act 1978 and the regulations made thereunder;
(*h*) a person authorised by the General Pharmaceutical Council for the purposes of section 108 or 109 of the Medicines Act 1968,
(*i*) a supplementary prescriber acting under and in accordance with the terms of a clinical management plan,

may, when acting in his capacity as such, supply or offer to supply any drug specified in Schedule 3 or 4 to any person who may lawfully have that drug in his possession.

(3) Notwithstanding the provisions of section 4(1)(*b*) of the Act—
(*a*) a person who is authorised as a member of a group, under and in accordance with the terms of his group authority and in compliance with any conditions attached thereto;
(*b*) the person in charge or acting person in charge of a hospital, organisation providing ambulance services or care home;
(*c*) in the case of such a drug supplied to her by a person responsible for the dispensing and supply of medicines at that hospital, care home or prison, the senior registered nurse, acting senior registered nurse or registered midwife, for the time being in charge of a ward, theatre or other department in the hospital, care home or prison;
(*d*) in the case of such a drug supplied to him by a person responsible for the dispensing and supply of medicines at a hospital, an operating department practitioner practising in that hospital;

may, when acting in his capacity as such, supply or offer to supply any drug specified in Schedule 3, or any drug specified in Schedule 4, to any person who may lawfully have that drug in his possession, except that nothing in this paragraph authorises—
(i) the person in charge or acting person in charge of a hospital, organisation providing ambulance services or care home, having a pharmacist responsible for the dispensing and supply of medicines, to supply or offer to supply any drug;
(ii) a senior registered nurse, acting senior registered nurse or registered midwife for the time being in charge of a ward, theatre or other department to supply any drug otherwise than for administration to a patient in that ward, theatre or department in accordance with the directions of a doctor, dentist, supplementary prescriber acting under and in accordance with the terms of a clinical management plan or, subject to paragraph (3A), a nurse independent prescriber or a pharmacist independent prescriber; or
(iii) an operating department practitioner to supply any drug otherwise than for administration to a patient in a ward, theatre or other department in accordance with the directions of a doctor, dentist, supplementary prescriber acting under and in accordance with the terms of a clinical management plan or, subject to paragraph (3A), a nurse independent prescriber or a pharmacist independent prescriber.
(iv) the person in charge or acting person in charge of an organisation providing ambulance services to supply any drugs other than directly to employees of the organisation for the immediate treatment of sick or injured persons.

(3A) The directions given by a nurse independent prescriber or a pharmacist independent prescriber referred to in paragraph (3)(*d*)(ii) and (iii) shall relate only to a controlled drug which such nurse independent prescriber or such pharmacist independent prescriber respectively may prescribe under regulation 6B and a purpose for which it may be prescribed under that regulation.

(4) Notwithstanding the provisions of section 4(1)(*b*) of the Act—
(*a*) a person who is authorised by a written authority issued by the Secretary of State under and for the purposes of this sub-paragraph and for the time being in force may, at the premises specified in that authority and in compliance with any conditions so specified, supply or offer to supply any drug specified in Schedule 3 or 4 to any person who may lawfully have that drug in his possession;
(*b*) a person who is authorised under paragraph (1)(*c*) may supply or offer to supply any drug which he may, by virtue of being so authorised, lawfully produce to any person who may lawfully have that drug in his possession.

(5) Notwithstanding the provisions of section 4(1)(*b*) of the Act—
(*a*) the owner of a ship, or the master of a ship which does not carry a doctor among the seamen employed in it;
(*b*) the installation manager of an offshore installation,

may supply or offer to supply any drug specified in Schedule 3, or any drug specified in Schedule 4—
(i) for the purpose of compliance with any of the provisions specified in regulation 8(6), to any person on that ship or installation; or
(ii) to any person who may lawfully supply that drug to him.

(6) Notwithstanding the provisions of section 4(1)(*b*) of the Act, a person in charge of a laboratory

may, when acting in his capacity as such, supply or offer to supply any drug specified in Schedule 3 which is required for use as a buffering agent in chemical analysis to any person who may lawfully have that drug in his possession.

(7) Notwithstanding the provisions of section 4(1)(*b*) of the Act, a nurse independent prescriber may, when acting in her capacity as such, supply or offer to supply any controlled drug specified in Schedule 3 or 4 to any person who may lawfully have any of those drugs in his possession provided it is supplied or offered in circumstances where she may prescribe it under regulation 6B.

(8) Notwithstanding the provisions of section 4(1)(*b*) of the Act, a registered nurse or a person specified in Schedule 8, when acting in their capacity as such, may supply or offer to supply, under and in accordance with the terms of a patient group direction, any drug specified in Schedule 4 or Midazolam to any person who may lawfully have that drug in his possession, except that this paragraph shall not have effect in the case of—

(*a*) the supply or offer to supply of any of the anabolic steroid drugs specified in Part II of Schedule 4; and

(*b*) any drug or preparation which is designed for administration by injection and which is to be used for the purpose of treating a person who is addicted to a drug;

(*c*) for the purposes of paragraph (*b*) above, a person shall be regarded as being addicted to a drug if, and only if, he has as a result of repeated administration become so dependent upon the drug that he has an overpowering desire for the administration of it to be continued.

**7.8326** *10. Possession of drugs in Schedules 2, 3 and 4* (1) Notwithstanding the provisions of section 5(1) of the Act—

(*a*) a person specified in one of sub-paragraphs (*a*) to (k) of regulation 8(2) may have in his possession any drug specified in Schedule 2;

(*b*) a person specified in one of sub-paragraphs (*a*) to (i) of regulation 9(2) may have in his possession any drug specified in Schedule 3 or 4;

(*c*) a person specified in regulation 9(3)(*b*) to (*d*) or (6) may have in his possession any drug specified in Schedule 3;

(*d*) a person specified in regulation 9(3)(*b*) to (*d*) may have in his possession any drug specified in Part I of Schedule 4;

(*e*) a person specified in regulation 8(7), regulation 8(8)(*a*), regulation 9(7) or regulation 9(8) may have in her possession any drug specified in those regulations in accordance with the conditions specified in those regulations,

for the purpose of acting in his capacity as such a person[1], except that nothing in this paragraph authorises—

(i) a person specified in sub-paragraph (*e*) or (*ea*) of regulation 8(2);

(ii) a person specified in sub-paragraph (*c*) or (*d*) of regulation 9(3); or

(iii) a person specified in regulation 9(6),

to have in his possession any drug other than such a drug as is mentioned in the paragraph or sub-paragraph in question specifying him.

(2) Notwithstanding the provisions of section 5(1) of the Act, a person may have in his possession any drug specified in Schedule 2, 3 or Part I of Schedule 4 for administration for medical, dental or veterinary purposes in accordance with the directions of a practitioner, a supplementary prescriber acting under and in accordance with the terms of a clinical management plan, a nurse independent prescriber or a pharmacist independent prescriber, except that this paragraph shall not have effect in the case of a person to whom the drug has been supplied by or on the prescription of a doctor, a supplementary prescriber, a nurse independent prescriber, a pharmacist independent prescriber or a person specified in Schedule 8 acting in accordance with a patient group direction if—

(*a*) that person was then being supplied with any controlled drug by or on the prescription of another doctor, another supplementary prescriber, another nurse independent prescriber, another pharmacist independent prescriber or another person specified in Schedule 8 acting in accordance with a patient group direction and failed to disclose that fact to the first mentioned doctor, supplementary prescriber, nurse independent prescriber, pharmacist independent prescriber or person specified in Schedule 8 acting in accordance with a patient group direction before the supply by him or on his prescription; or

(*b*) that or any other person on his behalf made a declaration or statement, which was false in any particular, for the purpose of obtaining the supply or prescription.

(3) Notwithstanding the provisions of section 5(1) of the Act, a person who is authorised as a member of a group may, under and in accordance with the terms of his group authority and in compliance with any conditions attached thereto, have any drug specified in Schedule 2, 3 or Part I of Schedule 4 in his possession.

(4) Notwithstanding the provisions of section 5(1) of the Act—

(*a*) a person who is authorised by a written authority issued by the Secretary of State under and for the purposes of this sub-paragraph and for the time being in force may, at the premises specified in that authority and in compliance with any conditions so specified, have in his possession any drug specified in Schedule 3 or 4;

(*b*) a person who is authorised under regulation 9(1)(*c*) may have in his possession any drug which he may, by virtue of being so authorised, lawfully produce;

(*c*) a person who is authorised under regulation 9(4)(*a*) may have in his possession any drug which he may, by virtue of being so authorised, lawfully supply or offer to supply.

(5) Notwithstanding the provisions of section 5(1) of the Act—

(*a*) any person may have in his possession any drug specified in Schedule 2, 3 or Part I of Schedule 4 for the purpose of compliance with any of the provisions specified in regulation 8(6);

(*b*) the master of a foreign ship which is in a port in Great Britain may have in his possession any drug specified in Schedule 2, 3 or Part I of Schedule 4 so far as necessary for the equipment of the ship.

(6) The foregoing provisions of this regulation are without prejudice to the provisions of regulation 4(3)(*a*).

---

[1] A doctor bona fide treating himself is acting in his capacity as a doctor although he himself is receiving the benefit of the drug (*R v Dunbar* [1982] 1 All ER 188, [1981] 1 WLR 1536, 74 Cr App Rep 88).

**7.8327** 11. *Exemption for midwives* (1) Notwithstanding the provisions of sections 4(1)(*b*) and 5(1) of the Act, a registered midwife who has, in accordance with the provisions of rules made under article 42 of the Order, notified to the local supervising authority her intention to practise may, subject to the provisions of this regulation—

(*a*) so far as necessary to her professional practice, have in her possession;

(*b*) so far as necessary as aforesaid, administer or supply; and

(*c*) surrender to the appropriate medical officer such stocks in her possession as are no longer required by her of,

any controlled drug which she may, under and in accordance with the provisions of the Medicines Act 1968 and of any instrument which is in force thereunder, lawfully administer.

(2) Nothing in paragraph (1) authorises a midwife to have in her possession any drug which has been obtained otherwise than on a midwife's supply order signed by the appropriate medical officer.

(3) In this regulation—

"appropriate medical officer" means—

(*a*) a doctor who is for the time being authorised in writing for the purposes of this regulation by the local supervising authority for the region or area in which the drug was, or is to be, obtained; or

(*b*) for the purposes of paragraph (2), a person appointed under and in accordance with article 43 of the Order by that authority to exercise supervision over registered midwives within their area, who is for the time being authorised as aforesaid;

"local supervising authority" has the meaning it is given by Schedule 4 of the Order;

"midwife's supply order" means an order in writing specifying the name and occupation of the midwife obtaining the drug, the name of the person to whom it is to be administered or supplied, the purpose for which it is required and the total quantity to be obtained;

"the Order" means the Nursing and Midwifery Order 2001.

**7.8328** 12. *Cultivation under licence of cannabis plant* Where any person is authorised by a licence of the Secretary of State issued under this regulation and for the time being in force to cultivate plants of the genus Cannabis, it shall not by virtue of section 6 of the Act be unlawful for that person to cultivate any such plant in accordance with the terms of the licence and in compliance with any conditions attached to the licence.

**7.8329** 13. *Approval of premises for cannabis smoking for research purposes* Section 8 of the Act (which makes it an offence for the occupier of premises to permit certain activities there) shall not have effect in relation to the smoking of cannabis or cannabis resin for the purposes of research on any premises for the time being approved for the purpose under this regulation by the Secretary of State.

**7.8330** 14. *Documents to be obtained by supplier of controlled drugs* (1) Where a person (hereafter in this paragraph referred to as "the supplier"), not being a practitioner, supplies a controlled drug otherwise than on a prescription, the supplier shall not deliver the drug to a person who—

(*a*) purports to be sent by or on behalf of the person to whom it is supplied (hereafter in this paragraph referred to as "the recipient"); and

(*b*) is not authorised by any provision of these Regulations other than the provisions of regulation 6(6) and (7)(*f*) to have that drug in his possession,

unless that person produces to the supplier a statement in writing signed by the recipient to the effect that he is empowered by the recipient to receive that drug on behalf of the recipient, and the supplier is reasonably satisfied that the document is a genuine document.

(2) Where a person (hereafter in this regulation referred to as "the supplier") supplies a controlled drug, otherwise than on a prescription or by way of administration, to any of the persons specified in paragraph (4), the supplier shall not deliver the drug—

(*a*) until he has obtained a requisition in writing which—

(i) is signed by the person to whom the drug is supplied (hereafter in this paragraph referred to as "the recipient");

(ii) states the name, address and profession or occupation of the recipient;

(iii) specifies the purpose for which the drug supplied is required and the total quantity to be supplied; and

(iv) where appropriate, satisfies the requirements of paragraph (5);

(*b*) unless he is reasonably satisfied that the signature is that of the person purporting to have signed the requisition and that that person is engaged in the profession or occupation specified in the requisition, except that where the recipient is a practitioner and he represents that he urgently requires a controlled drug for the purpose of his profession, the supplier may, if he is reasonably satisfied that the recipient so requires the drug and is, by reason of some emergency, unable before delivery to furnish to the supplier a requisition in writing duly signed, deliver the drug to the recipient on an undertaking by the recipient to furnish such a requisition within the twenty-four hours next following.

(3) A person who has given such an undertaking as aforesaid shall deliver to the person by whom the controlled drug was supplied a signed requisition in accordance with the undertaking.

(4) The persons referred to in paragraph (2) are—

(*a*) a practitioner;

(*b*) the person in charge or acting person in charge of a hospital, organisation providing ambulance services or care home;

(*c*) a person who is in charge of a laboratory;

(*d*) the owner of a ship, or the master of a ship which does not carry a doctor among the seamen employed in it;

(*e*) the master of a foreign ship in a port in Great Britain;

(*f*) the installation manager of an offshore installation;

(*g*) a supplementary prescriber;

(*h*) a nurse independent prescriber;

(*i*) a pharmacist independent prescriber.

(*j*) a person who holds a certificate of proficiency in ambulance paramedic skills issued by, or with the approval of, the Secretary of State, or a person who is a registered paramedic;

(5) A requisition furnished for the purposes of paragraph (2) shall—

(*a*) where furnished by the person in charge or acting person in charge of a hospital, organisation providing ambulance services or care home, be signed by a doctor or dentist employed or engaged in that hospital, organisation or care home;

(*b*) where furnished by the master of a foreign ship, contain a statement, signed by the proper officer of the port health authority, or, in Scotland, a health board competent person designated under section 3 of the Public Health etc (Scotland) Act 2008 by the health board by the Health Board, within whose jurisdiction the ship is, that the quantity of the drug to be supplied is the quantity necessary for the equipment of the ship.

(5A) Subject to paragraph (5B), on receipt of a requisition (other than a veterinary requisition) mentioned in paragraph (2), the supplier shall—

(*a*) mark on the requisition in ink or otherwise indelibly his name and address; and

(*b*) send the requisition to the relevant National Health Service agency in accordance with arrangements specified by that agency.

(5B) Paragraph (5A) shall not apply where the supplier is—

(*a*) a wholesale dealer; or

(*b*) a person responsible for the dispensing and supply of medicines at a hospital, organisation providing ambulance services, care home or prison.

(6) Where the person responsible for the dispensing and supply of medicines at any hospital, care home or prison supplies a controlled drug to an operating department practitioner, senior registered nurse, acting senior registered nurse, or registered midwife, for the time being in charge of any ward, theatre or department in that hospital, care home or prison (hereafter in this paragraph referred to as "the recipient") he shall—

(*a*) obtain a requisition in writing, signed by the recipient, which specifies the total quantity of the drug to be supplied; and

(*b*) mark the requisition in such manner as to show that it has been complied with,

and any requisition obtained for the purposes of this paragraph shall be retained in the dispensary at which the drug was supplied and a copy of the requisition or a note of it shall be retained or kept by the recipient.

(7) Nothing in this regulation shall have effect in relation to—

(*a*) the drugs specified in Schedules 4 and 5 or poppy-straw;

(*b*) any drug specified in Schedule 3 contained in or comprising a preparation which—

(i) is required for use as a buffering agent in chemical analysis;

(ii) has present in it both a substance specified in paragraph 1 or 2 of that Schedule and a salt of that substance; and

(iii) is pre-mixed in a kit;

(*c*) any exempt product;

(*d*) subject to paragraph (6) any drug which is required—

(i) for use in a prison; or

(ii) for use in a care home, which as its whole or main purpose provides palliative care for persons resident there who are suffering from a progressive disease in its final stages.

(8) In this regulation, "veterinary requisition" means a requisition which states, in accordance with paragraph (2)(ii), that the recipient is a veterinary surgeon or veterinary practitioner.

**7.8331** 15. *Form of prescriptions* (1) Subject to the provisions of this regulation, a person shall not issue a prescription containing a controlled drug other than a drug specified in Schedule 4 or 5 unless the prescription complies with the following requirements, that is to say, it shall—

(*a*) be written so as to be indelible, be dated and be signed by the person issuing it with his usual signature or be prescribed on an electronic prescription form;

(*aa*) except in the case of a health prescription or a veterinary prescription, be written on a prescription form provided by the National Health Service Commissioning Board or an equivalent body for the purposes of private prescribing unless prescribed on an electronic prescription form;

(*ab*) except in the case of a health prescription or a veterinary prescription, specify the prescriber identification number of the person issuing it;

(*b*) *revoked*;

(*c*) except in the case of a health prescription, specify the address of the person issuing it;

(*d*) if issued by a dentist, have the words "for dental treatment only" written on it and, if issued by a veterinary surgeon or a veterinary practitioner, have a declaration written on it that the controlled drug is prescribed for an animal or herd under his care;

(*e*) specify the name and address of the person for whose treatment it is issued or, if it is issued by a veterinary surgeon or veterinary practitioner, of the person to whom the controlled drug prescribed is to be delivered;

(*f*) specify the dose to be taken and—

(i) in the case of a prescription containing a controlled drug which is a preparation, the form and, where appropriate, the strength of the preparation, and either the total quantity (in both words and figures) of the preparation or the number (in both words and figures) of dosage units, as appropriate, to be supplied;

(ii) in any other case, the total quantity (in both words and figures) of the controlled drug to be supplied;

(*g*) in the case of a prescription for a total quantity intended to be supplied by instalments, contain a direction specifying the amount of the instalments of the total amount which may be supplied and the intervals to be observed when supplying.

(1A) *omitted.*

(1B) Nothing in this regulation prevents the issue of a prescription, other than a health prescription, which is not written on a prescription form provided by the National Health Service Commissioning Board or an equivalent body for the purposes of private prescribing, containing a controlled drug other than a drug specified in Schedule 4 or 5, where the person issuing the prescription believes on reasonable grounds that the drug will be supplied by a pharmacist in a hospital.

(2) *Revoked.*

(3) In the case of a prescription issued for the treatment of a patient in a hospital, care home or prison, it shall be a sufficient compliance with paragraph (1)(*e*) if the prescription is written on the patient's bed card or case sheet.

(4) In this regulation, "electronic prescription form" has the same meaning as in the National Health Service (Pharmaceutical and Local Pharmaceutical) Regulations 2013.

**7.8332** *16. Provisions as to supply on prescription* (1) Subject to paragraph (5), a person shall not supply a controlled drug other than a drug specified in Schedule 4 or 5 on a prescription—

(*a*) subject to paragraphs (1A) and (1C), unless the prescription complies with the provisions of regulation 15;

(*b*) unless the address specified in the prescription as the address of the person issuing it is an address within the United Kingdom;

(*c*) unless he either is acquainted with the signature of the person by whom it purports to be issued and has no reason to suppose that it is not genuine, or has taken reasonably sufficient steps to satisfy himself that it is genuine;

(*d*) before the appropriate date;

(*e*) subject to paragraph (4), later than twenty-eight days after the appropriate date.

(1A) A pharmacist may supply a controlled drug other than a drug specified in Schedule 4 or 5 if the prescription contains minor typographical errors or spelling mistakes or if it does not comply with the provisions of regulation 15 in the way specified in paragraph (1B), provided that—

(*a*) having exercised all due diligence, he is satisfied on reasonable grounds that the prescription is genuine;

(*b*) having exercised all due diligence, he is satisfied on reasonable grounds that he is supplying the drug in accordance with the intention of the person issuing the prescription;

(*c*) he amends the prescription in ink or otherwise indelibly to correct the minor typographical errors or spelling mistakes or so that the prescription complies with the requirements of regulation 15 as the case may be; and

(*d*) he marks the prescription so that the amendment he has made under sub-paragraph (*c*) is attributable to him.

(1B) The way specified in paragraph (1A) is that, in relation to regulation 15(1)(*f*), the total quantity of the preparation or of the controlled drug or the number of dosage units as the case may be is specified in either words or figures but not both.

(1C) A pharmacist may supply a controlled drug other than a drug specified in Schedule 4 or 5 on a prescription other than a health prescription in a hospital if it does not comply with regulation 15 in the ways specified in paragraph (1D).

(1D) The ways specified in paragraph (1C) are—

(*a*) the prescription is not written on a prescription form provided by the National Health Service Commissioning Board or an equivalent body for the purposes of private prescribing;

(*b*) the prescription does not specify the prescriber identification number of the person issuing it.

(2) Subject to paragraphs (3) and (4), a person supplying on prescription a controlled drug other than a drug specified in Schedule 4 or 5 shall, at the time of the supply, mark on the prescription the date on which the drug is supplied and, if it is a veterinary prescription, shall retain the prescription on the premises from which the drug was supplied.

(3) A person supplying temazepam on prescription in accordance with a prescription form of a kind specified in regulation 2A(1)(*a*)(i) of the National Health Service (Pharmaceutical Services) Regulations 1992 shall, at the time of the supply, enter on the form by electronic means the date on which the drug is supplied.

(4) In the case of a prescription containing a controlled drug other than a drug specified in Schedule 4 or 5, which contains a direction that specified instalments of the total amount may be supplied at stated intervals, the person supplying the drug shall not do so otherwise than in accordance with that direction, and—

(*a*) paragraph (1) shall have effect as if for the requirement contained in sub-paragraph (*e*) thereof there were substituted a requirement that the occasion on which the first instalment is supplied shall not be later than twenty-eight days after the appropriate date;

(*b*) paragraph (2) shall have effect as if for the words "at the time of the supply" there were substituted the words "on each occasion on which an instalment is supplied".

(5) A person shall not supply a controlled drug specified in Schedule 4 on a prescription later than twenty-eight days after the appropriate date.

(6) A person who is asked to supply on prescription a controlled drug specified in Schedule 2 must first ascertain whether the person collecting the drug is the patient, the patient's representative or a healthcare professional acting in his professional capacity on behalf of the patient; and—

(*a*) where that person is the patient or the patient's representative, he may—

(i) request evidence of that person's identity; and

(ii) refuse to supply the drug if he is not satisfied as to the identity of that person;

(*b*) where that person is a healthcare professional acting in his professional capacity on behalf of the patient, he—

(i) must obtain that person's name and address;

(ii) must, unless he is acquainted with that person, request evidence of that person's identity; but

(iii) may supply the drug even if he is not satisfied as to the identity of that person.

(7) In this regulation—

"appropriate date" means the later of the date on which it was signed by the person issuing it or the date indicated by him as being the date before which it shall not be supplied;

"healthcare professional" has the same meaning as in the National Health Service Act 1977;

"patient" means the person named in the prescription as the person to whom the drug is to be supplied;

"patient's representative" means a person sent by or on behalf of the patient (other than a healthcare representative acting in his professional capacity).

**7.8333** *17. Exemption for certain prescriptions* Nothing in regulations 15 and 16 shall have effect in relation to a prescription issued for the purposes of a scheme for testing the quality or amount of the drugs, preparations and appliances supplied under the National Health Service Act 1977 or the National Health Service (Scotland) Act 1978 and the regulations made thereunder or to any prescriptions issued for the purposes of the Medicines Act 1968 to a sampling officer within the meaning of that Act.

**7.8334** *18. Marking of bottles and other containers* (1) Subject to paragraph (2), no person shall supply a controlled drug otherwise than in a bottle, package or other container which is plainly marked—

(*a*) in the case of a controlled drug other than a preparation, with the amount of the drug contained therein;

(*b*) in the case of a controlled drug which is a preparation—

(i) made up into tablets, capsules or other dosage units, with the amount of each component (being a controlled drug) of the preparation in each dosage unit and the number of dosage units in the bottle, package or other container;

(ii) not made up as aforesaid, with the total amount of the preparation in the bottle, package or other container and the percentage of each of its components which is a controlled drug.

(2) Nothing in this regulation shall have effect in relation to—

(*a*) the drugs specified in Schedules 4 and 5 or poppy-straw;

(*b*) any drug specified in Schedule 3 contained in or comprising a preparation which—

(i) is required for use as a buffering agent in chemical analysis;

(ii) has present in it both a substance specified in paragraph 1 or 2 of that Schedule and a salt of that substance; and

(iii) is premixed in a kit;

(*c*) any exempt product;

(*d*) the supply of a controlled drug by or on the prescription of a practitioner, a supplementary prescriber, a nurse independent prescriber or a pharmacist independent prescriber;

(*e*) the supply of a controlled drug for administration in a clinical trial or a medicinal test on animals.

(3) In this regulation—

"clinical trial" has the same meaning as in the Medicines for Human Use (Clinical Trials) Regulations 2003;

"medicinal test on animals" has the same meaning as in the Medicines Act 1968.

**7.8335** *19. Record-keeping requirements in respect of drugs in Schedules 1 and 2* (1) Subject to paragraph (3) and regulation 21, every person authorised by or under regulation 5 or 8 to supply any drug specified in Schedule 1 or 2 shall comply with the following requirements, that is to say—

(*a*) he shall, in accordance with the provisions of this regulation and of regulation 20, keep a register and shall enter therein in chronological sequence subject to subparagraph (*f*), using the headings specified in subparagraphs (*d*) and (*e*), particulars of every quantity of a drug specified in Schedule 1 or 2 obtained by him and of every quantity of such a drug supplied (whether by way of administration or otherwise) by him whether to persons within or outside Great Britain;

(*b*) he shall use a separate register or separate part of the register for entries made in respect of each class of drugs, and each of the drugs specified in paragraphs 1 and 3 of Schedule 1 and paragraphs 1, 3 and 6 of Schedule 2 together with its salts and any preparation or other product containing it or any of its salts shall be treated as a separate class, so however that any stereoisomeric form of a drug or its salts shall be classed with that drug.

(*c*) in the case of drugs specified in Schedule 2, where the drug was supplied on prescription, he shall in addition enter into the register in the form specified in Part II of Schedule 6, whether the person who collected the drug was the patient, the patient's representative or a healthcare professional acting on behalf of the patient and—

(i) if the person who collected the drug was a healthcare professional acting on behalf of the patient, that person's name and address; or

(iii) if the person who collected the drug was the patient or the patient's representative, whether evidence of identity was requested of that person;

and whether evidence of identity was provided by the person collecting the drug.

(*d*) The headings in respect of entries made for drugs obtained are—

(i) Date supply received;

(ii) Name and address from whom received;

(iii) Quantity received.

(*e*) The headings in respect of entries made for drugs supplied are—

(i) Date supplied;

(ii) Name/Address of person or firm supplied;

(iii) Details of authority to possess—prescriber or licence holder's details;

(iv) Quantity supplied;

(v) Person collecting Schedule 2 controlled drug (patient/ patient's rep/ healthcare professional) and if healthcare professional, name and address;

(vi) Was proof of identity requested of patient/ patient's rep (Yes/No);

(vii) Was proof of identity of person collecting provided (Yes/No).

(*f*) The headings at subparagraph (*e*)(v) to (vii) apply only in respect of drugs specified in Schedule 2.

(2) Entries made in respect of drugs obtained and drugs supplied may be made on the same page or on separate pages in the register.

(2A) Subject to regulation 20(*e*), nothing in paragraph (1) shall prevent the use of a register to record additional information to that required or allowed under those provisions.

(3) The foregoing provisions of this regulation shall not have effect in relation to—

(*a*) in the case of a drug supplied to him for the purpose of destruction in pursuance of regulation 6(2) or (3), a practitioner or pharmacist;

(*b*) a person licensed under regulation 5 to supply any drug, where the licence so directs; or

(*c*) the senior registered nurse, acting senior registered nurse or registered midwife, for the time being in charge of a ward, theatre or other department in a hospital, care home or prison.

**7.8336** *20. Requirements as to registers* Any person required to keep a register under regulation 19 shall comply with the following requirements, that is to say—

(*a*) in the separate register or separate part of the register used for each class of drug, a separate page shall be used in respect of each strength and form of that drug and the head of each such page shall specify the class of the drug, its strength and form;

(*b*) every entry required to be made under regulation 19 in such a register shall be made on the day on which the drug is obtained or, as the case may be, on which the transaction in respect of the supply of the drug by the person required to make the entry takes place or, if that is not reasonably practicable, on the day next following that day;

(*c*) no cancellation, obliteration or alteration of any such entry shall be made, and a correction of such an entry shall be made only by way of marginal note or footnote which shall specify the date on which the correction is made;

(*d*) every such entry and every correction of such an entry shall be made in ink or otherwise so as to be indelible or shall be in a computerised form in which every such entry is attributable and capable of being audited and which is in accordance with best practice guidance endorsed by the Secretary of State under section 2 of the National Health Service Act 1977;

(*e*) such a register shall not be used for any purpose other than purposes related to these Regulations;

(*f*) a separate register shall be kept in respect of each premises at which the person required to keep the register carries on his business or occupation, but subject to that not more than one register shall be kept at one time in respect of each class of drugs in respect of which he is required to keep a separate register, so, however, that a separate register may, with the approval of the Secretary of State, be kept in respect of each department of the business carried on by him;

(*g*) every such register in which entries are currently being made shall be kept at the premises to which it relates and, where the register is in computerised form, be accessible from those premises.

**7.8337** *21. Record-keeping requirements in respect of drugs in Schedule 2 in particular cases*
(1) Where a drug specified in Schedule 2 is supplied in accordance with regulation 8(5)(*a*)(i) to any person on a ship, an entry in the official log book required to be kept under the Merchant Shipping Act 1995 or, in the case of a ship which is not required to carry such an official logbook, a report signed by the master of the ship, shall, notwithstanding anything in these Regulations, be a sufficient record of the supply if the entry or report specifies the drug supplied and, in the case of a report, it is delivered as soon as may be to a superintendent at a Marine Office established and maintained under the Merchant Shipping Act 1995.

(2) Where a drug specified in Schedule 2 is supplied in accordance with regulation 8(5)(*b*)(i) to a person on an offshore installation, an entry in the installation logbook required to be maintained under the Offshore Installations (Logbooks and Registration of Death) Regulations 1972 which specifies the drug supplied shall, notwithstanding anything in these Regulations, be a sufficient record of the supply.

(3) A midwife authorised by regulation 11(1) to have any drug specified in Schedule 2 in her possession shall—

(*a*) on each occasion on which she obtains a supply of such a drug, enter in a book kept by her and used solely for the purposes of this paragraph the date, the name and address of the person from whom the drug was obtained, the name of the person to whom it is to be administered or supplied, the amount obtained and the form in which it was obtained; and

(*b*) on administering or supplying such a drug to a patient, enter in the said book as soon as practicable the name and address of the patient, the name of the person to whom it was administered or supplied, the amount administered and the form in which it was administered.

**7.8338** *22. Record-keeping requirements in respect of drugs in Schedules 3 and 4* (1) Every person who is authorised under regulation 5 or 9(1)(*c*) to produce any drug specified in Schedule 3 or 4 shall make a record of each quantity of such a drug produced by him.

(2) Every person who is authorised by or under any provision of the Act to import or export any drug specified in Schedule 3 shall make a record of each quantity of such a drug imported or exported by him.

(3) Every person who is authorised under regulation 9(4) to supply any drug specified in Schedule 4 shall make a record of each quantity of such a drug imported or exported by him.

(4) Paragraph (2) shall not have effect in relation to a person licensed under the Act to import or export any drug where the licence so directs.

(5) Every person who is authorised by or under any provision of the Act to have in his possession or to destroy, or cause to be destroyed, the substance specified in paragraph 5 of Part 1 of Schedule 4 shall make a record of each quantity of such drug possessed or destroyed.

(6) Paragraph (5) shall not have effect in relation to—

(*a*) a patient to whom the substance specified in paragraph 5 of Part 1 of Schedule 4 has been prescribed;

(*b*) a constable when acting in the course of his duty as such;

(*c*) a person engaged in the business of a carrier when acting in the course of that business;

(*d*) a person engaged in the business of a postal operator (within the meaning of Part 3 of the Postal Services Act 2011) when acting in the course of that business;

(*e*) an officer of customs and excise when acting in the course of his duty as such;

(*f*) a person engaged in the work of any laboratory to which the substance specified in paragraph 5 of Part 1 of Schedule 4 has been sent for forensic examination when acting in the course of his duty as a person so engaged; and

(g) a person engaged in conveying the substance specified in paragraph 5 of Part 1 of Schedule 4 to a person who may lawfully have that substance in his possession.

**7.8339** *23. Preservation of registers, books and other documents* (1) All registers and books kept in pursuance of regulation 19 or 21(3) shall be preserved for a period of two years from the date on which the last entry therein is made.

(2) Every record made in pursuance of regulation 22 shall be preserved for a period of two years from the date on which the record was made.

(3) Every veterinary prescription on which a controlled drug is supplied in pursuance of these Regulations, and every prescription (other than a health prescription) on which a controlled drug specified in Schedules 4 or 5 is so supplied, shall be preserved for a period of two years from the date on which the last delivery under it was made.

(4) Every prescription (other than a health prescription or a veterinary prescription) on which a controlled drug other than a drug specified in Schedule 4 or 5 is supplied shall be sent to the relevant National Health Service agency in accordance with arrangements specified by that agency.

**7.8340** *24. Preservation of records relating to drugs in Schedules 3 and 5* (1) A producer of any drug specified in Schedule 3 or 5 and a wholesale dealer in any such drug shall keep every invoice or other like record issued in respect of each quantity of such a drug obtained by him and in respect of each quantity of such a drug supplied by him.

(2) A person who is authorised under regulation 9(4)(*a*) to supply any drug specified in Schedule 3 shall keep every invoice or other like record issued in respect of each quantity of such a drug obtained by him and in respect of each quantity of such a drug supplied by him.

(3) A retail dealer in any drug specified in Schedule 3, a person in charge or acting person in charge of a hospital, organisation providing ambulance services or care home and a person in charge of a laboratory shall keep every invoice or other like record issued in respect of each quantity of such a drug obtained by him and in respect of each quantity of such a drug supplied by him.

(4) A retail dealer in any drug specified in Schedule 5 shall keep every invoice or other like record issued in respect of each quantity of such a drug obtained by him.

(5) Every invoice or other record which is required by this regulation to be kept in respect of a drug specified in Schedule 3 shall contain information sufficient to identify the date of the transaction and the person by whom or to whom the drug was supplied.

(6) Every document kept in pursuance of this regulation (other than a health prescription) shall be preserved for a period of two years from the date on which it is issued, except that the keeping of a copy of the document made at any time during the said period of two years shall be treated for the purposes of this paragraph as if it were the keeping of the original document.

**7.8341** *24A. Preservation of records: supplementary* For the purposes of regulations 23 and 24(6), "preserved" means kept in its original form, or copied and kept in a computerised form which is in accordance with best practice guidance endorsed by the Secretary of State under section 2 of the National Health Service Act 1977.

**7.8342** *25. Exempt products* Nothing in regulations 19 to 24 shall have effect in relation to any exempt product.

**7.8343** *26. Furnishing of information with respect to controlled drugs* (1) The persons specified in paragraph (2) shall on demand made by the Secretary of State or by any person authorised in writing by the Secretary of State in that behalf—

(*a*) furnish such particulars as may be requested in respect of the producing, obtaining or supplying by him of any controlled drug or in respect of any stock of such drugs in his possession;

(*b*) for the purpose of confirming any such particulars, produce any stock of such drugs in his possession;

(*c*) produce any register, book or document required to be kept under these Regulations relating to any dealings in controlled drugs which is in his possession.

(1A) For the purposes of paragraph (1)(*c*), the Secretary of State or any person authorised in writing by the Secretary of State in that behalf may request that a register which is kept in computerised form be produced by sending a copy of it, in computerised or other form, to the appropriate person.

(2) The persons referred to in paragraph (1) are—

(*a*) any person authorised by or under these Regulations to produce any controlled drug;

(*b*) any person authorised by or under any provision of the Act to import or export any controlled drug;

(*c*) a wholesale dealer;

(*d*) a retail dealer;

(*e*) a practitioner;

(*f*) the person in charge or acting person in charge of a hospital, organisation providing ambulance services or care home;

(*g*) a person who is in charge of a laboratory;

(*h*) a person who is authorised under regulation 9(4)(*a*) to supply any controlled drug;

(*i*) a supplementary prescriber;

(*j*) a nurse independent prescriber.

(3) Nothing in this regulation shall require the furnishing of personal records which a person has acquired or created in the course of his profession or occupation and which he holds in confidence; and in this paragraph "personal records" means documentary and other records concerning an individual (whether living or dead) who can be identified from them and relating to his physical or mental health.

**7.8344** *27. Destruction of controlled drugs* (1) No person who is required by any provision of, or by any term or condition of a licence having effect under, these Regulations to keep records with respect to a drug specified in Schedule 1, 2, 3 or 4 shall destroy such a drug or cause such a drug to be destroyed except in the presence of and in accordance with any directions given by a person authorised (whether personally or as a member of a class) for the purposes of this paragraph by the Secretary of State or, subject to paragraph (1A), an accountable officer (hereafter in this regulation referred to as an "authorised person").

(1A) An accountable officer shall not be an authorised person.

(2) An authorised person may, for the purposes of analysis, take a sample of a drug specified in Schedule 1, 2, 3 or 4 which is to be destroyed.

(3) Where a drug specified in Schedule 1, 2, 3 or 4 is destroyed in pursuance of paragraph (1) by or at the instance of a person who is required by any provision of, or by any term or condition of a

licence having effect under, these Regulations to keep a record in respect of the obtaining or supply of that drug, that record shall include particulars of the date of destruction and the quantity destroyed and shall be signed by the authorised person in whose presence the drug is destroyed.
(4) Where the master or owner of a ship or installation manager of an offshore installation has in his possession a drug specified in Schedule 2 which he no longer requires, he shall not destroy the drug or cause it to be destroyed but shall dispose of it to a constable, or to a person who may lawfully supply that drug to him.
(5) Nothing in paragraph (1) or (3) shall apply to any person who is required to keep records only by virtue of regulation 22(2), (3) or (5) or 24(3).
(6) Nothing in paragraph (1) or (3) shall apply to the destruction of a drug which has been supplied to a practitioner or pharmacist for that purpose in pursuance of regulation 6(2) or (3).

**7.8345** *28. Revocations* (1) The regulations specified in Schedule 7 are hereby revoked.
(2) Notwithstanding paragraph (1), any register, record, book, prescription or other document required to be preserved under regulation 23 or 24 of the Misuse of Drugs Regulations 1985 shall be preserved for the same period of time as if these Regulations had not been made.
(3) In the case of a prescription issued before the coming into force of these Regulations, regulation 16(1) shall have effect as if—
(*a*) in the case of a prescription containing a controlled drug other than a drug to which the provisions of regulation 15 of the Misuse of Drugs Regulations 1985 applied at the time the prescription was issued, sub-paragraphs (*a*) and (*b*) of that paragraph were omitted; and
(*b*) in any other case, for the said sub-paragraphs (*a*) and (*b*) there were substituted the words "unless the prescription complies with the provisions of the Misuse of Drugs Regulations 1985 relating to prescriptions".

SCHEDULE 1
CONTROLLED DRUGS SUBJECT TO THE REQUIREMENTS
OF REGULATIONS 14, 15, 16, 18, 19, 20, 23, 26 AND 27[1]
Regulation 3

**7.8346** *1.* The following substances and products, namely –
(*a*)
Bufotenine
Cannabinol
Cannabinol derivatives not being dronabinol or its stereoisomers
Cannabis (not being the substance specified in paragraph 5 of Part 1 of Schedule 4) and cannabis resin
Cathinone
Coca leaf
Concentrate of poppy-straw
2,3-Dihydro-5-methyl-3-(4-morpholinylmethyl)pyrrolo[1, 2, 3-de]-1,4-benzoxazin-6-yl]-1-naphthalenyl methanone
3-Dimethylheptyl-11-hydroxyhexahydrocannabinol
Eticyclidine
Etryptamine
Fungus (of any kind) which contains psilocin or an ester of psilocin
9-Hydroxy-6-methyl-3-[5-phenylpentan-2-yl] oxy-5, 6, 6a, 7, 8, 9, 10, 10a-octahydrophenanthridin-1-yl acetate
9-(Hydroxymethyl)-6, 6-dimethyl-3-(2-methyloctan-2-yl)-6a, 7, 10, 10a-tetrahydrobenzo[c]chromen-1-ol
Khat
Lysergamide
Lysergide and other *N*-alkyl derivatives of lysergamide
Mescaline
Methcathinone
Psilocin
Raw opium
Rolicyclidine
Tenocyclidine
(6aR,9R)-4-acetyl-N,N-diethyl-7-methyl-4,6,6a,7,8,9-hexahydroindolo[4,3- fg]quinoline-9-carboxamide (ALD-52)
4-Bromo-2,5-dimethoxy-α-methylphenethylamine
1-Cyclohexyl-4-(1,2-diphenylethyl)piperazine (MT-45)
3,4-dichloro-N-[[1-(dimethylamino)cyclohexyl]methyl]benzamide (AH-7921)
(6aR,9R)-N,N-diethyl-7-allyl-4,6,6a,7,8,9-hexahydroindolo[4,3-fg]quinoline-9- carboxamide (AL-LAD)
(6aR,9R)-N,N-diethyl-7-ethyl-4,6,6a,7,8,9-hexahydroindolo[4,3-fg]quinoline-9- carboxamide (ETH-LAD)
(6aR,9R)-N,N-diethyl-7-propyl-4,6,6a,7,8,9-hexahydroindolo[4,3-fg]quinoline-9- carboxamide (PRO-LAD)";
*N*,*N*-Diethyltryptamine
*N*,*N*-Dimethyltryptamine
2-((Dimethylamino)methyl)-1-(3-hydroxyphenyl)cyclohexanol
2,4-dimethylazetidinyl{(6aR,9R)-7-methyl-4,6,6a,7,8,9-hexahydroindolo[4,3- fg]quinolin-9-yl}methanone (LSZ)
2,5-Dimethoxy-α,4-dimethylphenethylamine
*N*-Hydroxy-tenamphetamine
4-Methyl-aminorex
4-Methyl-5-(4-methylphenyl)-4,5-dihydrooxazol-2-amine (4,4′-DMAR)

(*b*) any compound (not being a compound for the time being specified in subparagraph (*a*) above) structurally derived from tryptamine or from a ring-hydroxy tryptamine by modification in any of the following ways, that is to say—

(i) by substitution at the nitrogen atom of the sidechain to any extent with alkyl or alkenyl substituents, or by inclusion of the nitrogen atom of the side chain (and no other atoms of the side chain) in a cyclic structure;

(ii) by substitution at the carbon atom adjacent to the nitrogen atom of the side chain with alkyl or alkenyl substituents;

(iii) by substitution in the 6-membered ring to any extent with alkyl, alkoxy, haloalkyl, thioalkyl, alkylenedioxy, or halide substituents;

(iv) by substitution at the 2-position of the tryptamine ring system with an alkyl substituent;

(*c*) the following phenethylamine derivatives, namely—

Allyl(α-methyl-3,4-methylenedioxyphenethyl)amine
2-Amino-1-(2,5-dimethoxy-4-methylphenyl)ethanol
2-Amino-1-(3,4-dimethoxyphenyl)ethanol
Benzyl(α-methyl-3,4-methylenedioxyphenethyl)amine
4-Bromo-α,2,5-trimethoxyphenethylamine
*N*-(4-*sec*-Butylthio-2,5-dimethoxyphenethyl)hydroxylamine
Cyclopropylmethyl(α-methyl-3,4-methylenedioxyphenethyl)amine
2-(4,7-Dimethoxy-2,3-dihydro-1*H*-indan-5-yl)ethylamine
2-(4,7-Dimethoxy-2,3-dihydro-1*H*-indan-5-yl)-1-methylethylamine
2-(2,5-Dimethoxy-4-methylphenyl)cyclopropylamine
2-(1,4-Dimethoxy-2-naphthyl)ethylamine
2-(1,4-Dimethoxy-2-naphthyl)-1-methylethylamine
*N*-(2,5-Dimethoxy-4-propylthiophenethyl)hydroxylamine
2-(1,4-Dimethoxy-5,6,7,8-tetrahydro-2-naphthyl)ethylamine
2-(1,4-Dimethoxy-5,6,7,8-tetrahydro-2-naphthyl)-1-methylethylamine
α,α-Dimethyl-3,4-methylenedioxyphenethylamine
α,α-Dimethyl-3,4-methylenedioxyphenethyl(methyl)amine
Dimethyl(α-methyl-3,4-methylenedioxyphenethyl)amine
*N*-(4-Ethylthio-2,5-dimethoxyphenethyl)hydroxylamine
4-Iodo-2,5-dimethoxy-α-methylphenethyl(dimethyl)amine
2-(1,4-Methano-5,8-dimethoxy-1,2,3,4-tetrahydro-6-naphthyl)ethylamine
2-(1,4-Methano-5,8-dimethoxy-1,2,3,4-tetrahydro-6-naphthyl)-1-methylethylamine
2-(5-Methoxy-2,2-dimethyl-2,3-dihydrobenzo[*b*]furan-6-yl)-1-methylethylamine
2-Methoxyethyl(α-methyl-3,4-methylenedioxyphenethyl)amine
2-(5-Methoxy-2-methyl-2,3-dihydrobenzo[*b*]furan-6-yl)-1-methylethylamine
β-Methoxy-3,4-methylenedioxyphenethylamine
1-(3,4-Methylenedioxybenzyl)butyl(ethyl)amine
1-(3,4-Methylenedioxybenzyl)butyl(methyl)amine
2-(α-Methyl-3,4-methylenedioxyphenethylamino)ethanol
α-Methyl-3,4-methylenedioxyphenethyl(prop-2-ynyl)amine
*N*-Methyl-*N*-(α-methyl-3,4-methylenedioxyphenethyl)hydroxylamine
*O*-Methyl-*N*-(α-methyl-3,4-methylenedioxyphenethyl)hydroxylamine
α-Methyl-4-(methylthio)phenethylamine
β,3,4,5-Tetramethoxyphenethylamine
β,2,5-Trimethoxy-4-methylphenethylamine

(*d*) any compound (not being methoxyphenamine or a compound for the time being specified in sub-paragraph (*a*) above) structurally derived from phenethylamine, an *N*-alkylphenethylamine, □-methylphenethylamine, an *N*-alkyl-□-methylphenethylamine, □-ethylphenethylamine, or an *N*-alkyl-□-ethylphenethylamine by substitution in the ring to any extent with alkyl, alkoxy, alkylenedioxy or halide substitutents, whether or not further substituted in the ring by one or more other univalent substituents;

(*e*) any compound (not being a compound for the time being specified in Schedule 2) structurally derived from fentanyl by modification in any of the following ways, that is to say -

(i) by replacement of the phenyl portion of the phenethyl group by any heteromonocycle whether or not further substituted in the heterocycle;

(ii) by substitution in the phenethyl group with alkyl, alkenyl, alkoxy, hydroxy, halogeno, haloalkyl, amino or nitro groups;

(iii) by substitution in the piperidine ring with alkyl or alkenyl groups;

(iv) by substitution in the aniline ring with alkyl, alkoxy, alkylenedioxy, halogeno or haloalkyl groups;

(v) by substitution at the 4-position of the piperidine ring with any alkoxycarbonyl or alkoxyalkyl or acyloxy group;

(vi) by replacement of the *N*-propionyl group by another acyl group;

(*f*) any compound (not being a compound for the time being specified in Schedule 2) structurally derived from pethidine by modification in any of the following ways, that is to say—

(i) by replacement of the l-methyl group by an acyl, alkyl whether or not unsaturated, benzyl or phenethyl group, whether or not further substituted;

(ii) by substitution in the piperidine ring with alkyl or alkenyl groups or with a propano bridge, whether or not further substituted;

(iii) by substitution in the 4-phenyl ring with alkyl, alkoxy, aryloxy, halogeno or haloalkyl groups;

(iv) by replacement of the 4-ethoxycarbonyl by any other alkoxycarbonyl or any alkoxyalkyl or acyloxy group;

(v) by formation of an *N*-oxide or of a quaternary base.

(*g*) 1-benzylpiperazine or any compound (not being a compound for the time being specified in Schedule 4) structurally derived from 1-benzylpiperazine or 1-phenylpiperazine by modification in any of the following ways—

(i) by substitution at the second nitrogen atom of the piperazine ring with alkyl, benzyl, haloalkyl or phenyl groups;

(ii) by substitution in the aromatic ring to any extent with alkyl, alkoxy, alkylenedioxy, halide or haloalkyl groups;

(*h*) Any compound structurally derived from 3–(1–naphthoyl)indole, 3-(2-naphthoyl)indole, 1H–indol–3–yl–(1–naphthyl)methane or 1H-indol-3-yl-(2-naphthyl)methane by substitution at the nitrogen atom of the indole ring by alkyl, haloalkyl, alkenyl, cyanoalkyl, hydroxyalkyl, cycloalkylmethyl, cycloalkylethyl, (N-methylpiperidin-2-yl)methyl or 2–(4–morpholinyl)ethyl, whether or not further substituted in the indole ring to any extent and whether or not substituted in the naphthyl ring to any extent.

(*i*) Any compound structurally derived from 3–(1–naphthoyl)pyrrole or 3-(2-naphthoyl)pyrrole by substitution at the nitrogen atom of the pyrrole ring by alkyl, haloalkyl, alkenyl, cyanoalkyl, hydroxyalkyl, cycloalkylmethyl, cycloalkylethyl, (N-methylpiperidin-2-yl)methyl or 2–(4–morpholinyl)ethyl, whether or not further substituted in the pyrrole ring to any extent and whether or not substituted in the naphthyl ring to any extent.

(*j*) Any compound structurally derived from 1–(1–naphthylmethylene)indene or 1-(2-naphthylmethylene)indene by substitution at the 3–position of the indene ring by alkyl, haloalkyl, alkenyl, cyanoalkyl, hydroxyalkyl, cycloalkylmethyl, cycloalkylethyl, (N-methylpiperidin-2-yl)methyl or 2–(4–morpholinyl)ethyl, whether or not further substituted in the indene ring to any extent and whether or not substituted in the naphthyl ring to any extent.

(*k*) Any compound structurally derived from 3–phenylacetylindole by substitution at the nitrogen atom of the indole ring by alkyl, haloalkyl, alkenyl, cyanoalkyl, hydroxyalkyl, cycloalkylmethyl, cycloalkylethyl, (N-methylpiperidin-2-yl)methyl or 2–(4–morpholinyl)ethyl, whether or not further substituted in the indole ring to any extent and whether or not substituted in the phenyl ring to any extent.

(*l*) Any compound structurally derived from 3–phenylacetylindole by substitution at the nitrogen atom of the indole ring by alkyl, haloalkyl, alkenyl, cyanoalkyl, hydroxyalkyl, cycloalkylmethyl, cycloalkylethyl, (N-methylpiperidin-2-yl)methyl or 2–(4–morpholinyl)ethyl, whether or not further substituted in the indole ring to any extent and whether or not substituted in the phenyl ring to any extent.

any compound structurally derived from 2-(3-hydroxycyclohexyl)phenol by substitution at the 5-position of the phenolic ring by alkyl, alkenyl, cycloalkylmethyl, cycloalkylethyl or 2-(4-morpholinyl)ethyl, whether or not further substituted in the cyclohexyl ring to any extent.

(*la*) Any compound structurally derived from 3-benzoylindole by substitution at the nitrogen atom of the indole ring by alkyl, haloalkyl, alkenyl, cyanoalkyl, hydroxyalkyl, cycloalkylmethyl, cycloalkylethyl, (N-methylpiperidin-2-yl)methyl or 2–(4–morpholinyl)ethyl, whether or not further substituted in the indole ring to any extent and whether or not substituted in the phenyl ring to any extent.

(*lb*) Any compound structurally derived from 3-(1-adamantoyl)indole or 3-(2-adamantoyl)indole by substitution at the nitrogen atom of the indole ring by alkyl, haloalkyl, alkenyl, cyanoalkyl, hydroxyalkyl, cycloalkylmethyl, cycloalkylethyl, (N-methylpiperidin-2-yl)methyl or 2–(4–morpholinyl)ethyl, whether or not further substituted in the indole ring to any extent and whether or not substituted in the adamantyl ring to any extent.

(*lc*) Any compound structurally derived from 3-(2,2,3,3-tetramethylcyclopropylcarbonyl)indole by substitution at the nitrogen atom of the indole ring by alkyl, haloalkyl, alkenyl, cyanoalkyl, hydroxyalkyl, cycloalkylmethyl, cycloalkylethyl, (N-methylpiperidin-2-yl)methyl or 2–(4–morpholinyl)ethyl, whether or not further substituted in the indole ring to any extent.

(*ld*) any compound (not being clonitazene, etonitazene, acemetacin, atorvastatin, bazedoxifene, indometacin, losartan, olmesartan, proglumetacin, telmisartan, viminol, zafirlukast or a compound for the time being specified in sub-paragraphs (h) to (lc) above) structurally related to 1-pentyl-3-(1-naphthoyl)indole (JWH-018), in that the four substructures, that is to say the indole ring, the pentyl substituent, the methanone linking group and the naphthyl ring, are linked together in a similar manner, whether or not any of the substructures have been modified, and whether or not substituted in any of the linked substructures with one or more univalent substituents and, where any of the sub-structures have been modified, the modifications of the sub-structures are limited to any of the following, that is to say—

(i) replacement of the indole ring with indane, indene, indazole, pyrrole, pyrazole, imidazole, benzimidazole, pyrrolo[2,3-b]pyridine, pyrrolo[3,2-c]pyridine or pyrazolo[3,4-b]pyridine;

(ii) replacement of the pentyl substituent with alkyl, alkenyl, benzyl, cycloalkylmethyl, cycloalkylethyl, (N-methylpiperidin-2-yl)methyl, 2-(4- morpholinyl)ethyl or (tetrahydropyran-4-yl)methyl;

(iii) replacement of the methanone linking group with an ethanone, carboxamide, carboxylate, methylene bridge or methine group;

(iv) replacement of the 1-naphthyl ring with 2-naphthyl, phenyl, benzyl, adamantyl, cycloalkyl, cycloalkylmethyl, cycloalkylethyl, bicyclo[2.2.1]heptanyl, 1,2,3,4- tetrahydronaphthyl, quinolinyl, isoquinolinyl, 1-amino-1-oxopropan-2-yl, 1-hydroxy-1-oxopropan-2-yl, piperidinyl, morpholinyl, pyrrolidinyl, tetrahydropyranyl or piperazinyl;

(*m*)

any compound (not being bupropion, diethylpropion, pyrovalerone or a compound for the time being specified in sub–paragraph (*a*) above) structurally derived from 2–amino–1–phenyl–1–propanone by modification in any of the following ways, that is to say—

(i) by substitution in the phenyl ring to any extent with alkyl, alkoxy, alkylenedioxy, haloalkyl or halide substituents, whether or not further substituted in the phenyl ring by one or more other univalent substituents;

(ii) by substitution at the 3–position with an alkyl substituent;

(iii) by substitution at the nitrogen atom with alkyl or dialkyl groups, or by inclusion of the nitrogen atom in a cyclic structure.

(*n*)

any compound structurally derived from 2–aminopropan–1–one by substitution at the 1-position with any monocyclic, or fused-polycyclic ring system (not being a phenyl ring or alkylenedioxyphenyl ring system), whether or not the compound is further modified in any of the following ways, that is to say—

(i) by substitution in the ring system to any extent with alkyl, alkoxy, haloalkyl or halide substituents, whether or not further substituted in the ring system by one or more other univalent substituents;

(ii) by substitution at the 3–position with an alkyl substituent;

(iii) by substitution at the 2-amino nitrogen atom with alkyl or dialkyl groups, or by inclusion of the 2-amino nitrogen atom in a cyclic structure.

(*o*) Any compound (not being pipradrol) structurally derived from piperidine, pyrrolidine, azepane, morpholine or pyridine by substitution at a ring carbon atom with a diphenylmethyl group, whether or not the compound is further modified in any of the following ways, that is to say,

(i) by substitution in any of the phenyl rings to any extent with alkyl, alkoxy, haloalkyl or halide groups;

(ii) by substitution at the methyl carbon atom with an alkyl, hydroxyalkyl or hydroxy group;

(iii) by substitution at the ring nitrogen atom with an alkyl, alkenyl, haloalkyl or hydroxyalkyl group.

(*p*) 1-Phenylcyclohexylamine or any compound (not being eticyclidine, ketamine, phencyclidine, rolicyclidine, tenocyclidine or tiletamine) structurally derived from 1-phenylcyclohexylamine or 2-amino-2-phenylcyclohexanone by modification in any of the following ways, that is to say,
(i) by substitution at the nitrogen atom to any extent by alkyl, alkenyl or hydroxyalkyl groups, or replacement of the amino group with a 1-piperidyl, 1-pyrrolidyl or 1-azepyl group, whether or not the nitrogen containing ring is further substituted by one or more alkyl groups;
(ii) by substitution in the phenyl ring to any extent by amino, alkyl, hydroxy, alkoxy or halide substituents, whether or not further substituted in the phenyl ring to any extent;
(iii) by substitution in the cyclohexyl or cyclohexanone ring by one or more alkyl substituents;
(iv) by replacement of the phenyl ring with a thienyl ring;

(*q*) Any compound (not being benzyl(α-methyl-3,4-methylenedioxyphenethyl)amine) structurally derived from mescaline, 4-bromo-2,5-dimethoxy-α- methylphenethylamine, 2,5-dimethoxy-α,4-dimethylphenethylamine, Nhydroxytenamphetamine, or a compound specified in sub-paragraph (c) or (d) above, by substitution at the nitrogen atom of the amino group with a benzyl substituent, whether or not substituted in the phenyl ring of the benzyl group to any extent;

(*r*) Any compound (not being a compound for the time being specified in subparagraph (c) above) structurally derived from 1-benzofuran, 2,3-dihydro-1- benzofuran, 1H-indole, indoline, 1H-indene, or indane by substitution in the 6- membered ring with a 2-ethylamino substituent whether or not further substituted in the ring system to any extent with alkyl, alkoxy, halide or haloalkyl substituents and whether or not substituted in the ethylamino side-chain with one or more alkyl substituents.

*2.* Any stereoisomeric form of a substance specified in paragraph 1.

*3.* Any ester or ether of a substance specified in paragraph 1 (not being 2-((dimethylamino)methyl)-1-(3-hydroxyphenyl)cyclohexanol) or paragraph 2.

*4.* Any salt of a substance specified in any of paragraphs 1 to 3.

*5.* Any preparation or other product containing a substance or product specified in any of paragraphs 1 to 4, not being a preparation specified in Schedule 5.

---

[1] These Schedules classify drugs for regime of control and not for penalties for misuse. For the latter classifications, see Sch 2 to the Misuse of Drugs Act 1971, ante.

## SCHEDULE 2

CONTROLLED DRUGS SUBJECT TO THE REQUIREMENTS OF REGULATIONS 14, 15, 16, 18, 19, 20, 21, 23, 26 AND 27[1]

Regulation 3

**7.8347** *1.* The following substances and products, namely—

Acetorphine
Alfentanil
Allylprodine
Alphacetylmethadol
Alphameprodine
Alphamethadol
Alphaprodine
Amineptine
Anileridine
Benzethidine
Benzylmorphine (3-benzylmorphine)
Betacetylmethadol
Betameprodine
Betamethadol
Betaprodine
Bezitramide
Carfentanil
Clonitazene
Cocaine
Desomorphine
Dextromoramide
Diamorphine
Diampromide
Diethylthiambutene
Difenoxin
Dihydrocodeinone *O*-carboxymethyloxime
Dihydroetorphine
Dihydromorphine
Dimenoxadole
Dimepheptanol
Dimethylthiambutene
Dioxaphetyl butyrate
Diphenoxylate
Dipipanone
Dronabinol
Drotebanol
Levorphanol
Lofentanil
Medicinal opium
Metazocine
Methadone
Methadyl acetate
Methyldesorphine
Methyldihydromorphine (6-methyldihydromorphine)
Metopon
Morpheridine
Morphine
Morphine methobromide, morphine N-oxide and other pentavalent nitrogen morphine derivatives
Myrophine
Nabilone
Nicomorphine
Noracymethadol
Norlevorphanol
Normethadone
Normorphine
Norpipanone
Oripavine
Oxycodone
Oxymorphone
Pethidine
Phenadoxone
Phenampromide
Phenazocine
Phencyclidine
Phenomorphan
Phenoperidine
Piminodine
Piritramide
Proheptazine
Properidine
Racemethorphan
Racemoramide

Ecgonine, and any derivative of ecgonine which is convertible to ecgonine or to cocaine
Ethylmethylthiambutene
Etonitazene
Etorphine
Etoxeridine
Fentanyl
Furethidine
Hydrocodone
Hydromorphinol
Hydromorphone
4-Hydroxy-n-butyric acid
Hydroxypethidine
Isomethadone
Ketobemidone
Levomethorphan
Levomoramide
Levophenacylmorphan
Racemorphan
Remifentanil
Sufentanil
Tapentadol
Thebacon
Thebaine
Tilidate
Trimeperidine
Zipeprol
4-Cyano-2-dimethylamino-4,4-diphenylbutane
4-Cyano-1-methyl-4-phenylpiperidine
2-Methyl-3-morpholino-1,1-diphenylpropane-carboxylic acid
□-Methylphenethylhydroxylamine
1-Methyl-4-phenylpiperidine-4-carboxylic acid
4-Phenylpiperidine-4-carboxylic acid ethyl ester
Lisdexamphetamine

*2.* Any stereoisomeric form of a substance specified in paragraph 1 not being dextromethorphan or dextrorphan.
*3.* Any ester or ether of a substance specified in paragraph 1 or 2, not being a substance specified in paragraph 6.
*4.* Any salt of a substance specified in any of paragraphs 1 to 3.
*5.* Any preparation or other product containing a substance or product specified in any of paragraphs 1 to 4, not being a preparation specified in Schedule 5.
*6.* The following substances and products, namely—

Acetyldihydrocodeine
Amphetamine
Codeine
Dextropropoxyphene
Dihydrocodeine
Ethylmorphine (3-ethylmorphine)
Fenethylline
Glutethimide
Lefetamine
Mecloqualone
Methaqualone
Methylamphetamine
Methylphenidate
Nicocodine
Nicodicodine (6-nicotinoyldihydrocodeine)
Norcodeine
Phenmetrazine
Pholcodine
Propiram
Quinalbarbitone

*7.* Any stereoisomeric form of a substance specified in paragraph 6.
*8.* Any salt of a substance specified in paragraph 6 or 7.
*9.* Any preparation or other product containing a substance or product specified in any of paragraphs 6 to 8, not being a preparation specified in Schedule 5.

[1] See note 1 to Sch 1 to these Regulations, ante.

## SCHEDULE 3

CONTROLLED DRUGS SUBJECT TO THE REQUIREMENTS OF REGULATIONS 14, 15, 16, 18, 22, 23, 24, 26 AND 27[1] Regulation 3

**7.8348** *1.* The following substances, namely—
(*a*)

Benzphetamine
7-bromo-5-(2-chlorophenyl)-1,3-dihydro-2H-1,4-benzodiazepin-2-one
Buprenorphine
Cathine
Chlorphentermine
Diethylpropion
Ethchlorvynol
Ethinamate
Flunitrazepam
Mazindol
Mephentermine
Meprobamate
Methylphenobarbitone
Methyprylone
Midazolam
Pentazocine
Phendimetrazine
Phentermine
Pipradrol
Temazepam
Tramadol

(*b*) any 5, 5 disubstituted barbituric acid not being quinalbarbitone.
*2.* Any stereoisomeric form of a substance specified in paragraph 1 or 3 not being phenylpropanolamine.
*3.* Any ester or ether of pipradrol.
*4.* Any salt of a substance specified in any of paragraphs 1 to 3.
*5.* Any preparation or other product containing a substance specified in any of paragraphs 1 to 4, not being a preparation specified in Schedule 5.

[1] See note 1 to Sch 1 to these Regulations, ante.

## SCHEDULE 4[1]

Regulation 3

### PART I CONTROLLED DRUGS SUBJECT TO THE REQUIREMENTS OF REGULATIONS 22, 23, 26 AND 27

**7.8349** *1.* The following substances and products, namely—

Alprazolam
Aminorex
Bromazepam
Brotizolam
Camazepam
Chlordiazepoxide
1-(3-chlorophenyl)piperazine
1-(3-chlorophenyl)-4-(3-chloropropyl)piperazine
Clobazam
Clonazepam
Clorazepic acid
Clotiazepam
Cloxazolam
Delorazepam
Diazepam
Estazolam
Ethyl loflazepate
Fencamfamin
Fenproporex
Fludiazepam
Flurazepam
Halazepam
Haloxazolam
Ketamine
Ketazolam
Loprazolam
Lorazepam
Lormetazepam
Medazepam
Mefenorex
Mesocarb
Nimetazepam
Nitrazepam
Nordazepam
Oxazepam
Oxazolam
Pemoline
Pinazepam
Prazepam
Pyrovalerone
Tetrazepam
Triazolam
*N*-Ethylamphetamine
Zolpidem
Zaleplon
Zopiclone

*2.* Any stereoisomeric form of a substance specified in paragraph 1.
*3.* Any salt of a substance specified in paragraph 1 or 2.
*4.* Any preparation or other product containing a substance or product specified in any of paragraphs 1 to 3, not being a preparation specified in Schedule 5.
*5.* A liquid formulation—
(*a*) containing a botanical extract of cannabis—
(i) with a concentration of not more than 30 milligrams of cannabidiol per millilitre, and not more than 30 milligrams of delta-9-tetrahydrocannabinol per millilitre, and
(ii) where the ratio of cannabidiol to delta-9-tetrahydrocannabinol is between 0.7 and 1.3,
(*b*) which is dispensed through a metered dose pump as a mucosal mouth spray, and
(*c*) which was approved for marketing by the Medicines and Healthcare Products Regulatory Agency on 16th June 2010(*b*).

### PART II CONTROLLED DRUGS EXCEPTED FROM THE PROHIBITION ON POSSESSION; EXCLUDED FROM THE APPLICATION OF OFFENCES ARISING FROM THE PROHIBITION ON IMPORTATION AND EXPORTATION WHEN CARRIED OUT IN PERSON FOR ADMINISTRATION TO THAT PERSON; AND SUBJECT TO THE REQUIREMENTS OF REGULATIONS 22, 23, 26 AND 27

*1.* The following substances, namely—

5α-Androstane-3,17-diol
Androst-4-ene-3,17-diol
1-Androstenediol
1-Androstenedione
4-Androstene-3, 17-dione
5-Androstenedione
5-Androstene-3, 17 diol
Atamestane
Bolandiol
Bolasterone
Bolazine
Boldenone
Boldione
Bolenol
Bolmantalate
Calusterone
4-Chloromethandienone
Clostebol
Danazol
Desoxymethyltestosterone
Dienedione (estra-4, 9-diene-3,17-dione)
Methandienone
Methandriol
Methenolone
Methyltestosterone
Metribolone
Mibolerone
Nandrolone
19-Norandrostenedione
19-Nor-4-Androstene-3, 17-dione
19-Nor-5-Androstene-3, 17-diol
19-Norandrosterone
Norboletone
Norclostebol
Norethandrolone
19-Noretiocholanolone
Ovandrotone
Oxabolone
Oxandrolone
Oxymesterone
Oxymetholone
Prasterone

Drostanolone
Enestebol
Epitiostanol
Ethyloestrenol
Fluoxymesterone
Formebolone
Furazabol
Gestrinone
3-Hydroxy-5α-androstan-17-one
Mebolazine
Mepitiostane
Mesabolone
Mestanolone
Mesterolone
Propetandrol
Prostanozol
Quinbolone
Roxibolone
Silandrone
Stanolone
Stanozolol
Stenbolone
Testosterone
Tetrahydrogestrinone
Thiomesterone
Trenbolone

2. Any compound (not being Trilostane or a compound for the time being specified in paragraph 1 of this Part of this Schedule) structurally derived from 17-hydroxyandrostan-3-one or from 17-hydroxyestran-3-one by modification in any of the following ways, that is to say -

(*a*) by further substitution at position 17 by a methyl or ethyl group;

(*b*) by substitution to any extent at one or more of positions 1, 2, 4, 6, 7, 9, 11 or 16, but at no other position;

(*c*) by unsaturation in the carbocyclic ring system to any extent, provided that there are no more than two ethylenic bonds in any one carbocyclic ring;

(*d*) by fusion of ring A with a heterocyclic system.

3. Any substance which is an ester or ether (or, where more than one hydroxyl function is available, both an ester and an ether) of a substance specified in paragraph 1 or described in paragraph 2 of this Part of this Schedule.

4. The following substances, namely—

Chorionic Gonadotrophin (HCG)
Clenbuterol
Non-human chorionic gonadotrophin
Somatotropin
Somatrem
Somatropin
Zeranol
Zilpaterol

5. Any stereoisomeric form of a substance specified or described in any of paragraphs 1 to 4 of this Part of this Schedule.

6. Any salt of a substance specified or described in any of paragraphs 1 to 5 of this Part of this Schedule.

7. Any preparation or other product containing a substance or product specified or described in any of paragraphs 1 to 6 of this Part of this Schedule, not being a preparation specified in Schedule 5.

[1] See note 1 to Sch 1 to these Regulations, ante.

## SCHEDULE 5

CONTROLLED DRUGS EXCEPTED[2] FROM THE PROHIBITION ON IMPORTATION, EXPORTATION AND POSSESSION AND SUBJECT TO THE REQUIREMENTS OF REGULATIONS 24 AND 26[1]

Regulation 3

7.8350 *1.* (1) Any preparation of one or more of the substances to which this paragraph applies, not being a preparation designed for administration by injection, when compounded with one or more other active or inert ingredients and containing a total of not more than 100 milligrams of the substance or substances (calculated as base) per dosage unit or with a total concentration of not more than 2.5% (calculated as base) in undivided preparations.

(2) The substances to which this paragraph applies are acetyldihydrocodeine, codeine, dihydrocodeine, ethylmorphine, nicocodine, nicodicodine (6-nicotinoyldihydrocodeine), norcodeine and pholcodine and their respective salts.

*2.* *Revoked.*

*3.* Any preparation of medicinal opium or of morphine containing (in either case) not more than 0.2% of morphine calculated as anhydrous morphine base, being a preparation compounded with one or more other active or inert ingredients in such a way that the opium or, as the case may be, the morphine cannot be recovered by readily applicable means or in a yield which would constitute a risk to health.

*4.* Any preparation of dextropropoxyphene, being a preparation designed for oral administration, containing not more than 135 milligrams of dextropropoxyphene (calculated as base) per dosage unit or with a total concentration of not more than 2.5% (calculated as base) in undivided preparations.

*5.* Any preparation of difenoxin containing, per dosage unit, not more than 0.5 milligrams of difenoxin and a quantity of atropine sulphate equivalent to at least 5% of the dose of difenoxin.

*6.* Any preparation of diphenoxylate containing, per dosage unit, not more than 2.5 milligrams of diphenoxylate calculated as base, and a quantity of atropine sulphate equivalent to at least 1% of the dose of diphenoxylate.

*7.* Any preparation of propiram containing, per dosage unit, not more than 100 milligrams of propiram calculated as base and compounded with at least the same amount (by weight) of methylcellulose.

*8.* Any powder of ipecacuanha and opium comprising—

10% opium, in powder,
10% ipecacuanha root, in powder, well mixed with
80% of any other powdered ingredient containing no controlled drug.

*9.* Any mixture containing one or more of the preparations specified in paragraphs 1 to 8, being a mixture of which none of the other ingredients is a controlled drug.

[1] See note 1 to Sch 1 to these Regulations, ante.

[2] Unlike the exceptions contained in these Regulations permitting possession of controlled drugs specified in Schs 2 and 3, ante, in the case of controlled drugs in Sch 5, by virtue of reg 4, ante, the general exception referred to here is not restricted to any particular class of person; see reg 4, ante, and *R v Hunt* [1986] QB 125, [1986] 1 All ER 184, 150 JP 83, CA.

SCHEDULE 7
REGULATIONS REVOKED Regulation 28

SCHEDULE 8 Regulations 6(2), 8(8), 9(8) and 10(2)

7.8351 *1.* Any of the following persons may supply or administer a specified controlled drug under a patient group direction, namely—

(*a*) a person who holds a certificate of proficiency in ambulance paramedic skills issued by, or with the approval of, the Secretary of State, or a person who is a registered paramedic;

(*b*) *revoked*;

(*c*) a registered midwife;

(*d*) a registered optometrist;

(*e*) a registered chiropodist;

(*f*) a registered orthoptist;

(*g*) a registered physiotherapist;

(*h*) a registered radiographer;]

(*i*) a registered occupational therapist;

(*j*) a registered orthotist and prosthetist;

(*k*) a pharmacist.

# Pharmacy Order 2010[1]

(SI 2010/231 amended by SI 2011/2159, SI 2012/1909, SI 2015/968 and SI 2016/1030)[2]

## PART 1 PRELIMINARY

7.8352 *1. Citation and commencement* (1) This Order may be cited as the Pharmacy Order 2010.

(2) The following provisions come into force on the day after the day on which this Order is made—

(*a*) this article;

(*b*) articles 2, 3, 4(1), (2), (3)(*b*), (5) and (8) and 7 and Schedule 1; and

(*c*) articles 65, 66, 69(1) to (4) and 70 and Schedules 5 and 6.

(3) Except as provided for by paragraph (2), the provisions of this Order which confer powers enabling rules or orders to be made, or which enable standards or requirements to be set by the Council, come into force on the making of this Order, but for the purpose only of the exercise of those powers.

(4) Rules under article 7(1) and (4) are not to come into force before the end of the period of two years beginning with the day on which this Order is made.

(5) Except as provided for by paragraphs (2) and (3), this Order comes into force on such day as the Privy Council may by order[3] appoint.

(6) Different days may be appointed by an order under paragraph (5) for different provisions or different purposes.

---

[1] Made by Her Majesty in exercise of the powers conferred by ss 60 and 62(4) and (4A) of, and Sch 3 to, the Health Act 1999 as read with para 1A of Sch 2 to the European Communities Act 1972.

[2] Other amendments have been made to provisions not included in this Manual by the Health and Social Care Act 2012 (Consequential Amendments – the Professional Standards Authority for Health and Social Care) Order 2012, SI 2012/2672, the Protection of Freedoms Act 2012 (Disclosure and Barring Service Transfer of Functions) Order 2012, SI 2012/3006 and the National Treatment Agency (Abolition), the Health and Social Care Act 2012 (Consequential, Transitional and Saving Provisions) Order 2013, SI 2013/235, the Cosmetic Products Enforcement Regulations 2013, SI 2013/1478, the Health Care and Associated Professions (Indemnity Arrangements) Order 2014, SI 2014/1887 and the European Union (Recognition of Professional Qualifications) Regulations 2015, SI 2015/2059 amended by SI 2016/696, 1030 and 1094.

[3] At the date which this volume states the law, the following orders had been made: the Pharmacy Order 2010 (Commencement No 1) Order of Council 2010, SI 2010/299 (bringing Sch 4, para 12(*b*) into force on 12 March 2010); and the Pharmacy Order 2010 (Commencement No 2) Order of Council 2010, SI 2010/1621 (bringing into force the remainder of the Order on 27 September 2010, subject to arts 24(6)–(10), 40(2) coming into force on 4 January 2011).

7.8353 *2. Extent* (1) Subject to paragraph (2), this Order extends to England and Wales and Scotland.

(2) The extent of any amendment, revocation, repeal or saving of any enactment set out in Schedules 4 and 6 is the same as that of the enactment amended, revoked, repealed or saved.

7.8354 *3. Interpretation* (1) In this Order—

"the 2007 Order" means the Pharmacists and Pharmacy Technicians Order 2007;

"annotation" means an annotation in the Register;

"assessment team" means an assessment team appointed under rules made under article 55;

"competent authority" means any authority or body of a relevant European State designated by that State for the purposes of the Directive as competent, in connection with practice as a pharmacist or pharmacy technician—

(*a*) to receive or issue evidence of qualifications or other information or documents; and

(*b*) to receive applications and take the decisions referred to in the Directive;

"controlled drugs" has the meaning given in section 2(1)(*a*) of the Misuse of Drugs Act 1971 (controlled drugs and their classification);

"the Council" means the General Pharmaceutical Council established by article 4;

"the Directive" means Directive 2005/36/EC of the European Parliament and of the Council of 7 September 2005 on the recognition of professional qualifications, and references in this Order to the Directive, or to any provision of the Directive, are references to the Directive, or to that provision, as amended from time to time;

"Directive 95/46/EC" means Directive 95/46/EC of the European Parliament and of the Council of 24th October 1995 on the protection of individuals with regard to the processing of personal data and on the free movement of such data, as amended from time to time;

"Directive 2002/58/EC" means Directive 2002/58/EC of the European Parliament and of the Council of 12th July 2002 concerning the processing of personal data and the protection of privacy in the electronic communications sector (Directive on privacy and electronic communications), as amended from time to time;

"electronic communication" has the meaning given in section 15(1) of the Electronic Communications Act 2000 (general interpretation);

"enactment" means an enactment contained in, or in an instrument made under—

(*a*) an Act of Parliament;

(*b*) an Act of the Scottish Parliament; or

(*c*) a measure or Act of the National Assembly for Wales;

"European mutual recognition area" means the territory of the EEA States and Switzerland;

"European professional card" has the meaning given in the Directive;

"exempt person" means—

(*a*) a national of a relevant European State other than the United Kingdom;

(*b*) a national of the United Kingdom who is seeking access to, or is pursuing, the profession of pharmacist or pharmacy technician by virtue of an enforceable Community right; or

(*c*) a person who is not a national of a relevant European State but who is, by virtue of an enforceable Community right, entitled to be treated, for the purposes of access to and pursuit of the profession of pharmacist or pharmacy technician, no less favourably than a national of a relevant European State;

"General Systems Regulations" means the European Union (Recognition of Professional Qualifications) Regulations 2015;

"IMI" means the Internal Market Information System, the online, secure messaging system developed by the European Commission;

"IMI file" means a secure personal account in the IMI that is created in relation to an applicant for a European professional card by means of an online tool provided by the European Commission;

"improvement notice" means a notice served on any person under article 13;

"individual assessor" means an individual assessor appointed under rules made under article 55;

"inspector" means an inspector appointed by the Council under article 8(1);

"medical device" has the meaning given in regulation 2(2) of the Medical Devices Regulations 2002;

"medicinal product" has the same meaning as it has in the Medicines Act 1968 by virtue of section 130 of that Act (meaning of "medicinal product" and related expressions);

"medicinal product on a general sale list" means a medicinal product of a description, or falling within a class, specified in an order which is for the time being in force under section 51 of the Medicines Act 1968 (general sale lists);

"the Pharmacy Acts" means the Pharmacy Act 1852, the Pharmacy Act 1868, the Pharmacy Act 1908, the Pharmacy and Poisons Act 1933 and the Pharmacy Act 1954;

"prescribed" means prescribed by rules made by the Council;

"professional traineeship" means a period of professional practice, carried out under supervision, that—

(a) constitutes a condition for access to the profession of pharmacist or pharmacy technician in the country in which it is carried out; and

(b) takes place during or after completion of a course of education leading to an educational qualification pursued for the purpose of entry to that profession;

"the Register" means the register established and maintained under article 19;

"registered pharmacist" means a person who is entered in Part 1 or 4 of the Register;

"registered pharmacy technician" means a person who is entered in Part 2 or 5 of the Register;

"registered pharmacy" means premises that are entered in Part 3 of the Register;

"registrant" means a registered pharmacist or a registered pharmacy technician;

"Registrar", except where used in the expression "Registrar General", is to be construed in accordance with article 18(1) and (6);

"Registrar General" means—

(*a*) the Registrar General for England and Wales appointed under section 1 of the Registration Service Act 1953 (Registrar General); or

(*b*) the Registrar General for Scotland appointed under section 1(1) of the Registration of Births, Deaths and Marriages (Scotland) Act 1965 (the Registrar General);

"regulatory body" means a regulatory body which has the function of authorising persons to practise as a member of a health or social care profession;

"relevant European State" means an EEA State or Switzerland;

"retail pharmacy business" has the meaning given in section 132 of the Medicines Act 1968 (general interpretation provisions);

"retail sale" is to be construed in accordance with section 131(3) of the Medicines Act 1968 (meaning of "wholesale dealing", "retail sale" and related expressions);

"the Society" means the Royal Pharmaceutical Society of Great Britain;

"statutory committees" means the Committees of the Council listed in article 4(6);

"superintendent pharmacist" means a pharmacist who is a superintendent for the purposes of section 71(1) of the Medicines Act 1968 (business carried on by body corporate); and

"supply in circumstances corresponding to retail sale" is to be construed in accordance with section 131(4) of the Medicines Act 1968;

"third country" means a country other than a relevant European State.

(2) For the purposes of this Order, a person practises as a pharmacist or a pharmacy technician if, whilst acting in the capacity of or purporting to be a pharmacist or a pharmacy technician, that person undertakes any work or gives any advice in relation to the preparation, assembly, dispensing, sale, supply or use of medicines, the science of medicines, the practice of pharmacy or the provision of healthcare.

(3) For the purposes of articles 34 and 35, "emergency" means an emergency of the type described in subsection (1)(*a*) of section 19 of the Civil Contingencies Act 2004 (meaning of "emergency"), read with subsection (2)(*a*) and (*b*) of that section.

## Part 3 Registered Pharmacies: Standards in Retail Pharmacies

**7.8355** 7. *Standards: general* (1) In the exercise of its functions under article 4(3)(*b*), the Council must make provision in rules about the standards that are to be met in connection with the carrying on of a retail pharmacy business at a registered pharmacy.

(2) Those standards may relate to requirements that are to be met—

(*a*) by the person carrying on the retail pharmacy business; or

(*b*) by a superintendent pharmacist.

(3) The standards may, in particular, relate to—

(*a*) record keeping;

(*b*) standard operating procedures;

(*c*) the training of staff;

(*d*) incident reporting mechanisms;

(*e*) arrangements for the obtaining, keeping, handling, use and security of medicinal products or medical devices;

(*f*) the conditions in which medicinal products (including controlled drugs) are to be stored;

(*g*) the condition of the premises (including the physical state, safety and security of the premises);

(*h*) the availability or condition of facilities or equipment at the premises used to carry out certain activities (including the conducting of clinical procedures (such as the taking of blood), the undertaking of consultations with patients and the carrying on of activities to which section 10 of the Medicines Act 1968 (exemptions for pharmacists) applies);

(*i*) the management of waste (including the adequate procedures for the safe destruction and disposal of medicinal products kept on the premises); and

(*j*) the use of the premises as a training establishment.

(4) The Council must also make provision in rules—

(*a*) requiring any person carrying on a retail pharmacy business to provide information to the Council;

(*b*) for such information to be provided—

(i) at the request of the Council, or

(ii) on such dates or at such intervals as the Council may determine, either generally or in relation to particular persons carrying on a retail pharmacy business or such persons of a particular description; and

(*c*)) in respect of—

(i) the form and manner in which such information is to be provided to the Council, and

(ii) the time within which such information is to be provided to the Council pursuant to a request under sub-paragraph (*b*)(i).

(5) Rules under paragraph (4) must, in particular, enable the Council to obtain the following information—

(*a*) details of the person carrying on the retail pharmacy business including—

(i) where the business is carried on by an individual, details of the home address in the Register of that individual,

(ii) where the business is carried on by a partnership, details of the address of the principal office of the partnership and of the names and home addresses of the partners in the partnership,

(iii) where the business is carried on by a body corporate, details of the address of the registered or principal office of the body corporate and of the names and home addresses of its directors;

(*b*) a list of all premises at which the retail pharmacy business is carried on;

(*c*) where medicinal products, other than medicinal products on a general sale list, are sold by retail at any premises at which a retail pharmacy business is carried on, or are supplied in circumstances corresponding to retail sale, and the retail pharmacy business is owned by a body corporate, the name of the superintendent pharmacist under whose management the business is carried on;

(*d*) details of the type or types of activities undertaken at the premises at which the retail pharmacy business is carried on; and

(*e*) details of any relevant offence or relevant investigation.

(6) For the purposes of paragraph (5)(*e*)—

(a) a relevant offence is—
(i) where the retail pharmacy business is carried on by an individual, a criminal offence with which that individual has been charged,
(ii) where the retail pharmacy business is carried on by a partnership, a criminal offence with which any partner in the partnership has been charged,
(iii) where the retail pharmacy business is carried on by a body corporate, a criminal offence with which the body corporate or any of its directors has been charged,
and a criminal offence is a relevant offence whether or not the charge has resulted in a caution or conviction;
(b) a relevant investigation is an investigation by a licensing, regulatory or other body into the conduct of—
(i) where the retail pharmacy business is carried on by an individual, that individual,
(ii) where the retail pharmacy business is carried on by a partnership, any partner in the partnership,
(iii) where the retail pharmacy business is carried on by a body corporate, that body corporate or any director of it,
and the reference to details of a relevant investigation includes details of the outcome of that investigation.

(7) Rules under paragraph (4) must also enable the provision to the Council of a statement which confirms that the standards that are provided for in rules made under paragraph (1) are met in connection with the carrying on of the retail pharmacy business at the registered pharmacies at which it is carried on and which is signed—
(a) where the retail pharmacy business is carried on by an individual, by that individual;
(b) where the retail pharmacy business is carried on by a partnership, by a partner in the partnership;
(c) where the retail pharmacy business is carried on by a body corporate, by a director of that body corporate.

**7.8356** 8. *The Inspectorate* (1) The Council must establish an inspectorate which is to consist of inspectors appointed by the Council under this paragraph.

(2) An inspector appointed by the Council under paragraph (1) has the following functions—
(a) in connection with the Council's functions under article 4(3)(*b*), to enforce such standards as may be provided for by rules under article 7(1);
(b) to assist the Council in its investigation of matters to which Part 6 of this Order applies;
(c) to secure compliance by registrants and by persons carrying on a retail pharmacy business at a registered pharmacy with the provisions of Parts 3 and 4 of the Medicines Act 1968 (which contain provisions about dealings with medicinal products and about pharmacies) in so far as they relate to the sale and supply of medicinal products;
(d) to secure compliance by registered pharmacists and persons carrying on a retail pharmacy business with the provisions of the Poisons Act 1972 and of regulations made under that Act;
(e) to enforce—
(i) article 38 of this Order, and
(ii) any other provisions of this Order and of rules made under this Order.

(3) An inspector is to hold and vacate office in accordance with the terms of the inspector's appointment.

(4) The Council may pay to an inspector such remuneration, pensions, allowances, expenses or gratuities, or make such contributions or payments towards provision for such pensions, allowances or gratuities, as it may reasonably determine.

**7.8357** 9. *Inspection and enforcement* (1) The Council must make provision in rules relating to—
(a) the intervals at which inspectors may conduct routine inspections of registered pharmacies; and
(b) the circumstances in which inspectors may conduct special inspections of, and other visits to, registered pharmacies.

(2) Rules under paragraph (1) are not to limit an inspector's power of entry under article 10.

**7.8358** 10. *Power of entry* (1) An inspector, on producing (if required)—
(a) evidence of the inspector's identity; and
(b) evidence of the inspector's appointment,
may, for the purposes of the exercise of a function conferred on the inspector by article 8(2)(*a*), (*b*) or (*e*) enter any registered pharmacy or other premises at any reasonable hour.

(2) In the case of any premises which are or form part of a private dwelling house, an inspector may enter the premises by virtue of paragraph (1) only if 24 hours notice of the intended entry has been given to the occupier.

(3) If a justice of the peace, on sworn information in writing from an inspector, is satisfied that entry to a registered pharmacy or other premises is required for the purposes of the exercise of a function conferred on the inspector by article 8(2)(*a*), (*b*) or (*e*) and is also satisfied that—
(a) admission has been refused, or a refusal is expected, and (in either case) that notice to apply for a warrant has been given to the occupier;
(b) asking for admission, or the giving of such notice, would defeat the object of entry;
(c) the case is one of urgency; or
(d) the premises are unoccupied or the occupier is temporarily absent,

the justice may by signed warrant authorise the inspector to enter the premises, if need be by reasonable force.

(4) A warrant issued by a justice of the peace under paragraph (3) is valid for the period of one month beginning with the day on which the warrant is issued.

(5) An inspector who is authorised to enter any premises by a warrant issued by a justice of the peace under paragraph (3) must, on entering the premises, produce the warrant to any person at the premises appearing to the inspector to be in charge of, or responsible for, the premises or, if the premises are unoccupied, leave a copy of the warrant at the premises.

(6) An inspector entering premises by virtue of this article—

(*a*) may be accompanied by a police constable or by such other persons as the inspector considers necessary;

(*b*) may bring into the premises such equipment as the inspector considers necessary.

(7) If an inspector enters any unoccupied premises by virtue of this article, the inspector must leave the premises as effectively secured against unauthorised entry as the premises were found.

(8) In the application of this article to Scotland, a reference to a justice of the peace includes a reference to the sheriff and to a magistrate.

**7.8359** 11. *Powers of an inspector* (1) An inspector may, upon entering any premises by virtue of article 10—

(*a*) inspect the premises and any plant, machinery or equipment at the premises;

(*b*) search the premises;

(*c*) inspect and remove from the premises any substance, article or product (whether or not appearing to the inspector to be a medicinal product);

(*d*) take and remove from the premises samples of any substance, article or product;

(*e*) carry out any examinations and tests and make any enquiries (including such enquiries of any person as the inspector considers it appropriate to make relating to the fitness to practise of a registrant who is or has been employed on the premises to provide pharmaceutical services);

(*f*) require any person holding or accountable for any documents or records (whether or not kept at the premises being inspected) to produce them for inspection at the premises.

(2) The power conferred by paragraph (1)(*f*) includes power to require any documents or records that are kept by means of a computer or other electronic device to be produced in a form in which they are legible and may be taken away.

(3) If an inspector requires documents or records to be produced for inspection by virtue of the power conferred by paragraph (1)(*f*), the inspector may—

(*a*) take copies of or extracts from such documents or records;

(*b*) take possession of the documents or records or of the computer or other electronic device in which the documents or records are stored and retain them for as long as the inspector considers necessary;

(*c*) require access to any computer or other electronic device or to any associated apparatus or material that is or has been used in connection with the documents or records and inspect and check the operation of the computer, electronic device, apparatus or material.

(4) The power conferred by paragraph (3)(*c*)) includes power to require any person having charge of, or otherwise concerned with the operation of, the computer, device, apparatus or material to afford such assistance as the inspector may reasonably require.

(5) An inspector also has power to do anything which is calculated to facilitate the discharge of the inspector's functions or which is incidental or conducive to the discharge of those functions.

**7.8360** 12. *Obstruction: offences* Any person who—

(*a*) intentionally obstructs an inspector exercising functions under article 10 or 11;

(*b*) without reasonable cause, fails to give an inspector exercising any functions under this Order any assistance or information that the inspector may reasonably require from that person for the performance of those functions;

(*c*) furnishes to an inspector exercising any functions under this Order any information that the person knows to be false or misleading; or

(*d*) fails to produce a document or record when required to do so by an inspector exercising any functions under this Order,

commits an offence and is liable, on summary conviction, to a fine not exceeding level 3 on the standard scale.

**7.8361** 13. *Improvement notices* (1) If an inspector has reasonable grounds for believing that there is—

(*a*) a failure in connection with the carrying on of a retail pharmacy business at a registered pharmacy entered in the Register under section 74A of the Medicines Act 1968 (registration or premises: Great Britain) to meet the standards that are provided for in rules made under article 7(1); or

(*b*) a failure to comply with conditions to which the entry of a registered pharmacy entered in the Register under section 74A of the Medicines Act 1968 is subject by virtue of section 74D(1) of that Act (conditional registration: Great Britain),

the inspector may serve a notice on the person carrying on the retail pharmacy business at the registered pharmacy (in this Order referred to as an "improvement notice").

(2) An improvement notice must—

(*a*) state the inspector's grounds for believing that there is a failure referred to in paragraph (1)(*a*) or (*b*);

(*b*) specify the measures that the person to whom the notice is addressed must take in order to rectify that failure;

(*c*) require that person to take those measures, or measures that the inspector agrees are at least equivalent to them, within the period specified in the notice which may not be less than 28 days beginning with the day on which the notice is served; and

(*d*) state—

(i) that there is a right of appeal to a magistrates' court or to the sheriff under article 16, and

(ii) the period within which such an appeal may be brought.

(3) An improvement notice is served by an inspector—

(*a*) on an individual—

(i) if it is delivered to that individual personally,

(ii) if it is left at that individual's proper address, or

(iii) if it is sent by first class post or otherwise delivered to that individual at that individual's proper address;

(*b*) on a partnership—

(i) if it is delivered personally to a partner in the partnership,

(ii) if it is delivered personally to a person having control or management of the partnership business, or

(iii) if it is sent by first class post or otherwise delivered to the partnership's proper address;

(*c*) on a body corporate—

(i) if it is delivered personally to the secretary or clerk of that body,

(ii) if it is sent by first class post or otherwise delivered to that body's proper address.

(4) For the purposes of paragraph (3), and of section 7 of the Interpretation Act 1978 (which defines "service by post") in its application to that paragraph, the proper address of a person is—

(*a*) in the case of an individual, to that individual's home address in the Register;

(*b*) in the case of a partnership, the address of the principal office of the partnership;

(*c*) in the case of a body corporate, the address of the registered or principal office of the body.

(5) An improvement notice is treated as having been served, where the notice is sent by post, at the time at which the notice would be delivered in the ordinary course of post or, where the notice has been left at an address, it is treated as having been served on the next working day following the day on which it was left at that address.

(6) The Council may make rules providing for an improvement notice which is required to be served on any person under this article to be served by an electronic communication.

(7) Rules under paragraph (6) must secure that—

(*a*) an improvement notice cannot be served by an electronic communication unless the person consents in writing to the receipt of notices from the Council by electronic communication and the communication is sent to the number or address specified by that person when giving consent;

(*b*) an electronic communication received outside of a person's normal business hours is to be taken to have been served on the next working day.

(8) In this article "working day" means a day which is not a Saturday or Sunday, Christmas Day, Good Friday or a day which is a bank holiday under the Banking and Financial Dealings Act 1971 in the part of Great Britain in which the premises to which the notice relates are located.

**7.8362** 14. *Non-compliance with improvement notices* (1) A person carrying on a retail pharmacy business at a registered pharmacy who fails to comply with the terms of an improvement notice served under article 13 commits an offence and is liable on summary conviction to a fine not exceeding level 5 on the standard scale.

(2) Where an inspector is reasonably satisfied that a person carrying on a retail pharmacy business at a registered pharmacy has failed to comply with the terms of an improvement notice served under article 13, the inspector must give notice of that fact in writing to the Registrar.

(3) The obligation imposed by paragraph (2) applies whether or not proceedings are to be brought against the person for an offence under paragraph (1).

(4) Upon receipt of a notice given under paragraph (2), the Registrar may—

(*a*) remove the entry of the registered pharmacy from the Register; or

(*b*) suspend that entry pending compliance by the person with such requirements or conditions as the Registrar considers it necessary to impose.

(5) Where under paragraph (4) the Registrar removes or suspends the entry of a registered pharmacy, the Registrar must send to the person carrying on the retail pharmacy business a statement in writing giving that person notice of the removal or suspension and the reasons for it and of the right of appeal to the Appeals Committee under article 40.

(6) The notice under paragraph (5) must be sent—

(*a*) where the retail pharmacy business is carried on by an individual, to that individual at that individual's home address in the Register;

(*b*) where the retail pharmacy business is carried on by a partnership, to that partnership at its principal office;

(*c*) where the retail pharmacy business is carried on by a body corporate, to that body corporate at its registered address or principal office.

(7) Proceedings for an offence under this article may be begun—

(*a*) in England and Wales, at any time within the period of 6 months beginning with the date on which evidence sufficient in the opinion of the Council to justify a prosecution came to the Council's knowledge;

(*b*) in Scotland, at any time within the period of 6 months beginning with the date on which evidence sufficient in the opinion of the prosecutor to justify a prosecution came to the prosecutor' knowledge;

but no proceedings may be begun after the expiry of the period of two years beginning with the date of the commission of the offence.

(8) For the purposes of paragraph (7), the date of the commission of the offence is the day after the day on which the period specified under paragraph (2)(*c*) of article 13 expires.

**7.8363** *15. Offences committed by partnerships* (1) Proceedings for an offence under article 14 alleged to have been committed by a partnership must be brought in the name of the partnership (and not in that of any of the partners).

(2) Rules of court relating to the service of documents are to have effect as if the partnership were a body corporate.

(3) In proceedings for an offence brought against a partnership, Schedule 3 to the Magistrates' Courts Act 1980 (corporations) applies as it applies in relation to a body corporate.

(4) A fine imposed on a partnership on its conviction for an offence is to be paid out of the assets of the partnership.

**7.8364** *16. Appeals against improvement notices* (1) Any person on whom an improvement notice is served may appeal to a magistrates' court or, in Scotland, to the sheriff.

(2) The procedure on appeal to a magistrates' court under paragraph (1) is by way of complaint, and the Magistrates' Courts Act 1980 applies to the proceedings.

(3) An appeal to the sheriff under paragraph (1) is by summary application.

(4) The period within which an appeal may be brought is 28 days beginning with the date on which the notice was served.

(5) The court may suspend an improvement notice pending the determination or abandonment of an appeal.

**7.8365** *17. Powers of a court on appeal* On an appeal against an improvement notice, the court may either cancel the notice or confirm it, with or without modification.

## Part 4 Registration

**7.8366** *38. Offences relating to the Register* (1) A person who makes a false representation as to being—

(*a*) entered in the Register as a pharmacist;

(*b*) entered in the Register as a pharmacy technician; or

(*c*) entered in any part of the Register with a particular annotation,

commits an offence.

(2) A person who—

(*a*) uses the title "pharmacist" or "fferyllydd" (its equivalent in the Welsh language) without being entered as a pharmacist in Part 1 or 4 of the Register;

(*b*) uses the title "pharmacy technician" or "technegydd fferylliaeth" (its equivalent in the Welsh language) without being entered as a pharmacy technician in Part 2 or 5 of the Register; or

(*c*) uses a title in respect of a particular annotation, which is a prescribed specialist title, where that person does not have an entry in any part of the Register with that particular annotation,

commits an offence.

(3) For the purposes of paragraph (2)(*c*), "prescribed specialist title" means—

(*a*) in the case of a pharmacist, a title for a pharmacist which the Council prescribes by rules as being a title that is only to be used by a registrant with a particular annotation; and

(*b*) in the case of a pharmacy technician, a title for a pharmacy technician which the Council prescribes by rules as being a title that is only to be used by a registrant with a particular annotation.

(4) A person who practises—

(*a*) as a pharmacist while not being entered as such in Part 1 or 4 of the Register; or

(*b*) as a pharmacy technician while not being entered as such in Part 2 or 5 of the Register,

commits an offence.

(5) A person who exhibits any notice or certificate which—

(*a*) purports to be a notice of entry issued under article 26 in respect of a pharmacist but which is not a notice of entry issued under that article in respect of a pharmacist;

(*b*) purports to be a certificate of registration issued under one of the Pharmacy Acts in respect of a pharmaceutical chemist but which is not a certificate of registration issued under one of those Acts in respect of a pharmaceutical chemist; or

(*c*) purports to be a certificate of registration issued under the 2007 Order in respect of a pharmacist but which is not a certificate of registration issued under that Order in respect of a pharmacist,

commits an offence.

(6) A person who exhibits any notice or certificate which—

(*a*) purports to be a notice of entry issued under article 26 in respect of a pharmacy technician but which is not a notice of entry issued under that article in respect of a pharmacy technician;

(*b*) purports to be a certificate of registration issued under the 2007 Order in respect of a pharmacy technician but which is not a certificate of registration issued under that Order in respect of a pharmacy technician,

commits an offence.

(7) A person who, for fraudulent purposes—

(*a*) uses or lends to, or allows to be used by, another person—

(i) a notice of entry or certificate of registration in respect of a pharmacist or a pharmaceutical chemist (whether issued under article 26 or one of the Pharmacy Acts or the 2007 Order), or

(ii) a notice of entry or certificate of registration in respect of a pharmacy technician issued under article 26 or the 2007 Order; or

(*b*) makes or possesses any document closely resembling such a notice or certificate,

commits an offence.

(8) Any person who commits an offence under paragraph (1), (2) or (4) is liable on summary conviction to a fine not exceeding level 5 on the standard scale.

(9) Any person who commits an offence under paragraph (5), (6) or (7) is liable on summary conviction to a fine not exceeding level 3 on the standard scale.

(10) Proceedings for an offence under this article may be begun—

(*a*) in England and Wales, at any time within the period of 6 months beginning with the date on which evidence sufficient in the opinion of the Council to justify a prosecution came to the Council's knowledge;

(*b*) in Scotland, at any time within the period of 6 months beginning with the date on which evidence sufficient in the opinion of the prosecutor to justify a prosecution came to the prosecutor's knowledge,

but no proceedings may be begun after the expiry of the period of two years beginning with the date of the commission of the offence.

## Misuse of Drugs Act 1971 (Temporary Class Drug) Order 2015[1]

(SI 2015/1027)

**7.8366A** 1. *Citation and commencement* This Order may be cited as the Misuse of Drugs Act 1971 (Temporary Class Drug) Order 2015 and comes into force on 10th April 2015.

[1] Made by the Secretary of State in exercise of the powers conferred by ss 2A(1) and (5), 7A(2), (3) and (6) and 31(1) of the Misuse of Drugs Act 1971.

2. *Drugs subject to temporary control* The substances and products listed in the Schedule to this Order are specified under section 2A(1) of the Misuse of Drugs Act 1971 as drugs subject to temporary control.

3. *Application of other instruments* (1) The Misuse of Drugs (Safe Custody) Regulations 1973 and the Misuse of Drugs (Safe Custody) (Northern Ireland) Regulations 1973 apply to the substances and products listed in the Schedule to this Order.

(2) The Misuse of Drugs Regulations 2001 apply to the substances and products listed in the Schedule to this Order as if those substances and products were specified in Schedule 1 to those Regulations.

(3) The Misuse of Drugs Regulations (Northern Ireland) 2002 apply to the substances and products listed in the Schedule to this Order as if those substances and products were specified in Schedule 1 to those Regulations.

SCHEDULE

Article 2

*1.* The following substances, namely—

3,4-Dichloromethylphenidate (3,4-DCMP)

Ethylphenidate

Isopropylphenidate (IPP or IPPD)

Methylnaphthidate (HDMP-28)

Propylphenidate

*2.* Any stereoisomeric form of a substance specified in paragraph 1.

*3.* Any preparation or other product containing a substance specified in paragraph 1 or 2.

# MENTAL HEALTH

**Contents**



## Mental Health Act 1983[1]

(1983 c 20)

### PART I[2]

### APPLICATION OF ACT

7.8367 **1. Application of Act: "mental disorder"** (1) The provisions of this Act shall have effect with respect to the reception, care and treatment of mentally disordered patients, the management of their property and other related matters.

(2) In this Act—

"mental disorder" means any disorder or disability of the mind; and

"mentally disordered" shall be construed accordingly;

and other expressions shall have the meanings assigned to them in section 145 below.

(2A) But a person with learning disability shall not be considered by reason of that disability to be—

(*a*) suffering from mental disorder for the purposes of the provisions mentioned in subsection (2B) below; or

(*b*) requiring treatment in hospital for mental disorder for the purposes of sections 17E and 50 to 53 below,

unless that disability is associated with abnormally aggressive or seriously irresponsible conduct on his part.

(2B) The provisions are—

(*a*) sections 3, 7, 17A, 20 and 20A below;

(*b*) sections 35 to 38, 45A, 47, 48 and 51 below; and

(*c*) section 72(1)(*b*) and (*c*) and (4) below.

(3) Dependence on alcohol or drugs is not considered to be a disorder or disability of the mind for the purposes of subsection (2) above.

(4) In subsection (2A) above, "learning disability" means a state of arrested or incomplete development of the mind which includes significant impairment of intelligence and social functioning.

[Mental Health Act 1983, s 1 as amended by the Mental Health Act 2007, ss 1–3.]

---

1. This Act consolidates the law relating to mentally disordered persons which was previously contained in the Mental Health Act 1959 as amended by the Mental Health (Amendment) Act 1982.

Parts I to VI, VIII and X of the Act are described in a Memorandum entitled, "The Mental Health Act 1983", published by the Department of Health and Social Security (HMSO 1983).

2. Part I contains s 1.

### PART II[1]

### COMPULSORY ADMISSION TO HOSPITAL AND GUARDIANSHIP

*Procedure for hospital admission*

7.8368 **2. Admission for assessment** (1) A patient may be admitted to a hospital and detained there for the period allowed by subsection (4) below in pursuance of an application (in this Act referred to as "an application for admission for assessment") made in accordance with subsections (2) and (3) below.

(2) An application for admission for assessment may be made in respect of a patient on the grounds that—

(*a*) he is suffering from mental disorder of a nature or degree which warrants the detention of the patient in a hospital for assessment (or for assessment followed by medical treatment) for at least a limited period; and

(*b*) he ought to be so detained in the interests of his own health or safety or with a view to the protection of other persons.

(3) An application for admission for assessment shall be founded on the written recommendations in the prescribed form of two registered medical practitioners, including in each case a statement that in the opinion of the practitioner the conditions set out in subsection (2) above are complied with.

(4) Subject to the provisions of section 29(4) below, a patient admitted to hospital in pursuance of an application for admission for assessment may be detained for a period not exceeding 28 days beginning with the day on which he is admitted, but shall not be detained after the expiration of that

period unless before it has expired he has become liable to be detained by virtue of a subsequent application, order or direction under the following provisions of this Act.

[Mental Health Act 1983, s 2.]

1 Part II contains ss 2–34.

7.8369 3. **Admission for treatment** (1) A patient may be admitted to a hospital and detained there for the period allowed by the following provisions of this Act in pursuance of an application (in this Act referred to as "an application for admission for treatment") made in accordance with this section.

(2) An application for admission for treatment may be made in respect of a patient on the grounds that—

(*a*) he is suffering from mental disorder of a nature or degree which makes it appropriate for him to receive medical treatment in a hospital; and

(*b*) *repealed*

(*c*) it is necessary for the health or safety of the patient or for the protection of other persons that he should receive such treatment and it cannot be provided unless he is detained under this section; and

(*d*) appropriate medical treatment is available for him.

(3) An application for admission for treatment shall be founded on the written recommendations in the prescribed form of two registered medical practitioners, including in each case a statement that in the opinion of the practitioner the conditions set out in subsection (2) above are complied with; and each such recommendation shall include—

(*a*) such particulars as may be prescribed of the grounds for that opinion so far as it relates to the conditions set out in paragraphs (*a*) and (*d*) of that subsection; and

(*b*) a statement of the reasons for that opinion so far as it relates to the conditions set out in paragraph (*c*) of that subsection, specifying whether other methods of dealing with the patient are available and, if so, why they are not appropriate.

(4) In this Act, references to appropriate medical treatment, in relation to a person suffering from mental disorder, are references to medical treatment which is appropriate in his case, taking into account the nature and degree of the mental disorder and all other circumstances of his case.

[Mental Health Act 1983, s 3 as amended by the Mental Health Act 2007, s 4, Schs 1 and 11.]

7.8370 4. **Admission for assessment in cases of emergency** (1) In any case of urgent necessity, an application for admission for assessment may be made in respect of a patient in accordance with the following provisions of this section, and any application so made is in this Act referred to as "an emergency application".

(2) An emergency application may be made either by an approved mental health professional or by the nearest relative of the patient; and every such application shall include a statement that it is of urgent necessity for the patient to be admitted and detained under section 2 above, and that compliance with the provisions of this Part of this Act relating to applications under that section would involve undesirable delay.

(3) An emergency application shall be sufficient in the first instance if founded on one of the medical recommendations required by section 2 above, given, if practicable, by a practitioner who has previous acquaintance with the patient and otherwise complying with the requirements of section 12 below so far as applicable to a single recommendation, and verifying the statement referred to in subsection (2) above.

(4) An emergency application shall cease to have effect on the expiration of a period of 72 hours from the time when the patient is admitted to the hospital unless—

(*a*) the second medical recommendation required by section 2 above is given and received by the managers within that period; and

(*b*) that recommendation and the recommendation referred to in subsection (3) above together comply with all the requirements of section 12 below (other than the requirement as to the time of signature of the second recommendation).

(5) In relation to an emergency application, section 11 below shall have effect as if in subsection (5) of that section for the words "the period of 14 days ending with the date of the application" there were substituted the words "the previous 24 hours".

[Mental Health Act 1983, s 4 as amended by the Mental Health Act 2007, Sch 2.]

7.8371 5. **Application in respect of patient already in hospital** (1) An application for the admission of a patient to a hospital may be made under this Part of this Act notwithstanding that the patient is already an in-patient in that hospital or, in the case of an application for admission for treatment, that the patient is for the time being liable to be detained in the hospital in pursuance of an application for admission for assessment; and where an application is so made the patient shall be treated for the purposes of this Part of this Act as if he had been admitted to the hospital at the time when that application was received by the managers.

(2) If, in the case of a patient who is an in-patient in a hospital, it appears to the registered medical practitioner or approved clinician in charge of the treatment of the patient that an application ought to be made under this Part of this Act for the admission of the patient to hospital,

he may furnish to the managers a report in writing to that effect; and in any such case the patient may be detained in the hospital for a period of 72 hours from the time when the report is so furnished.

(3) The registered medical practitioner or approved clinician in charge of the treatment of a patient in a hospital may nominate one (but not more than one) person to act for him under subsection (2) above in his absence.

(3A) For the purposes of subsection (3) above—

(*a*) the registered medical practitioner may nominate another registered medical practitioner, or an approved clinician, on the staff of the hospital; and

(*b*) the approved clinician may nominate another approved clinician, or a registered medical practitioner, on the staff of the hospital.

(4) If, in the case of a patient who is receiving treatment for mental disorder as an in-patient in a hospital, it appears to a nurse of the prescribed class—

(*a*) that the patient is suffering from mental disorder to such a degree that it is necessary for his health or safety or for the protection of others for him to be immediately restrained from leaving the hospital; and

(*b*) that it is not practicable to secure the immediate attendance of a practitioner or clinician the purpose of furnishing a report under subsection (2) above,

the nurse may record that fact in writing; and in that event the patient may be detained in the hospital for a period of six hours from the time when that fact is so recorded or until the earlier arrival at the place where the patient is detained of a practitioner or clinician having power to furnish a report under that subsection.

(5) A record made under subsection (4) above shall be delivered by the nurse (or by a person authorised by the nurse in that behalf) to the managers of the hospital as soon as possible after it is made; and where a record is made under that subsection the period mentioned in subsection (2) above shall begin at the time when it is made.

(6) The reference in subsection (1) above to an in-patient does not include an in-patient who is liable to be detained in pursuance of an application under this Part of this Act or a community patient and the references in subsections (2) and (4) above do not include an in-patient who is liable to be detained in a hospital under this Part of this Act or a community patient.

(7) In subsection (4) above "prescribed" means prescribed by an order[1] made by the Secretary of State.

[Mental Health Act 1983, s 5 as amended by the Mental Health Act 2007, s 9.]

---

1 The Mental Health (Nurses) (England) Order 2008, SI 2008/1207 and the Mental Health (Nurses) (Wales) Order 2008, SI 2008/2441 have been made.

7.8372 **6. Effect of application for admission** (1) An application for the admission of a patient to a hospital under this Part of this Act, duly completed in accordance with the provisions of this Part of this Act, shall be sufficient authority for the applicant, or any person authorised by the applicant, to take the patient and convey him to the hospital at any time within the following period, that is to say—

(*a*) in the case of an application other than an emergency application, the period of 14 days beginning with the date on which the patient was last examined by a registered medical practitioner before giving a medical recommendation for the purposes of the application;

(*b*) in the case of an emergency application, the period of 24 hours beginning at the time when the patient was examined by the practitioner giving the medical recommendation which is referred to in section 4(3) above, or at the time when the application is made, whichever is the earlier.

(2) Where a patient is admitted within the said period to the hospital specified in such an application as is mentioned in subsection (1) above, or, being within that hospital, is treated by virtue of section 5 above as if he had been so admitted, the application shall be sufficient authority for the managers to detain the patient in the hospital in accordance with the provisions of this Act.

(3) Any application for the admission of a patient under this Part of this Act which appears to be duly made and to be founded on the necessary medical recommendations may be acted upon without further proof of the signature or qualification of the person by whom the application or any such medical recommendation is made or given or of any matter of fact or opinion stated in it.

(4) Where a patient is admitted to a hospital in pursuance of an application for admission for treatment, any previous application under this Part of this Act by virtue of which he was liable to be detained in a hospital or subject to guardianship shall cease to have effect.

[Mental Health Act 1983, s 6.]

*Guardianship*

7.8373 **7. Application for guardianship** (1) A patient who has attained the age of 16 years may be received into guardianship, for the period allowed by the following provisions of this Act, in pursuance of an application (in this Act referred to as "a guardianship application") made in accordance with this section.

(2) A guardianship application may be made in respect of a patient on the grounds that—

(*a*) he is suffering from mental disorder of a nature or degree which warrants his reception into guardianship under this section; and (*b*) it is necessary in the interests of the welfare of the patient or for the protection of other persons that the patient should be so received.

(3) A guardianship application shall be founded on the written recommendations in the prescribed form of two registered medical practitioners, including in each case a statement that in the opinion of the practitioner the conditions set out in subsection (2) above are complied with; and each such recommendation shall include—

(*a*) such particulars as may be prescribed of the grounds for that opinion so far as it relates to the conditions set out in paragraph (*a*) of that subsection; and

(*b*) a statement of the reasons for that opinion so far as it relates to the conditions set out in paragraph (*b*) of that subsection.

(4) A guardianship application shall state the age of the patient or, if his exact age is not known to the applicant, shall state (if it be the fact) that the patient is believed to have attained the age of 16 years.

(5) The person named as guardian in a guardianship application may be either a local social services authority or any other person (including the applicant himself); but a guardianship application in which a person other than a local social services authority is named as guardian shall be of no effect unless it is accepted on behalf of that person by the local social services authority for the area in which he resides, and shall be accompanied by a statement in writing by that person that he is willing to act as guardian.

[Mental Health Act 1983, s 7 as amended by the Mental Health Act 2007, Schs 1 and 11.]

7.8374 **8. Effect of guardianship application, etc** (1) Where a guardianship application, duly made under the provisions of this Part of this Act and forwarded to the local social services authority within the period allowed by subsection (2) below is accepted by that authority, the application shall, subject to regulations made by the Secretary of State, confer on the authority or person named in the application as guardian, to the exclusion of any other person—

(*a*) the power to require the patient to reside at a place specified by the authority or person named as guardian;

(*b*) the power to require the patient to attend at places and times so specified for the purpose of medical treatment, occupation, education or training;

(*c*) the power to require access to the patient to be given, at any place where the patient is residing, to any registered medical practitioner, approved mental health professional or other person so specified.

(2) The period within which a guardianship application is required for the purposes of this section to be forwarded to the local social services authority is the period of 14 days beginning with the date on which the patient was last examined by a registered medical practitioner before giving a medical recommendation for the purposes of the application.

(3) A guardianship application which appears to be duly made and to be founded on the necessary medical recommendations may be acted upon without further proof of the signature or qualification of the person by whom the application or any such medical recommendation is made or given, or of any matter of fact or opinion stated in the application.

(4) If within the period of 14 days beginning with the day on which a guardianship application has been accepted by the local social services authority the application, or any medical recommendation given for the purposes of the application, is found to be in any respect incorrect or defective, the application or recommendation may, within that period and with the consent of that authority, be amended by the person by whom it was signed; and upon such amendment being made the application or recommendation shall have effect and shall be deemed to have had effect as if it had been originally made as so amended.

(5) Where a patient is received into guardianship in pursuance of a guardianship application, any previous application under this Part of this Act by virtue of which he was subject to guardianship or liable to be detained in a hospital shall cease to have effect.

[Mental Health Act 1983, s 8 as amended by the Mental Health Act 2007, Sch 2.]

7.8375 **9. Regulations as to guardianship** (1) Subject to the provisions of this Part of this Act, the Secretary of State may make regulations[1]—

(*a*) for regulating the exercise by the guardians of patients received into guardianship under this Part of this Act of their powers as such; and

(*b*) for imposing on such guardians, and upon local social services authorities in the case of patients under the guardianship of persons other than local social services authorities, such duties as he considers necessary or expedient in the interests of the patients.

(2) Regulations under this section may in particular make provision for requiring the patients to be visited, on such occasions or at such intervals as may be prescribed by the regulations, on behalf of such local social services authorities as may be so prescribed, and shall provide for the appointment, in the case of every patient subject to the guardianship of a person other than a local social services authority, of a registered medical practitioner to act as the nominated medical attendant of the patient.

[Mental Health Act 1983, s 9.]

---

[1] The Mental Health (Hospital, Guardianship and Treatment) (England) Regulations 2008, SI 2008/1184 amended by SI 2008/2560 and SI 2012/1118 and SI 2013/235 and the Mental Health (Hospital, Guardianship, Community Treatment and Consent to Treatment) (Wales) Regulations 2008, SI 2008/2439 amended by SI 2013/235 have been made.

**7.8376 10. Transfer of guardianship in case of death, incapacity, etc of guardian** (1) If any person (other than a local social services authority) who is the guardian of a patient received into guardianship under this Part of this Act—

(*a*) dies; or

(*b*) gives notice in writing to the local social services authority that he desires to relinquish the functions of guardian,

the guardianship of the patient shall thereupon vest in the local social services authority, but without prejudice to any power to transfer the patient into the guardianship of another person in pursuance of regulations under section 19 below.

(2) If any such person, not having given notice under subsection (1)(*b*) above, is incapacitated by illness or any other cause from performing the functions of guardian of the patient, those functions may, during his incapacity, be performed on his behalf by the local social services authority or by any other person approved for the purposes by that authority.

(3) If it appears to the county court, upon application made by an approved mental health professional acting on behalf of the local social services authority, that any person other than a local social services authority having the guardianship of a patient received into guardianship under this Part of this Act has performed his functions negligently or in a manner contrary to the interests of the welfare of the patient, the court may order that the guardianship of the patient be transferred to the local social services authority or to any other person approved for the purpose by that authority.

(4) Where the guardianship of a patient is transferred to a local social services authority or other person by or under this section, subsection (2)(*c*) of section 19 below shall apply as if the patient had been transferred into the guardianship of that authority or person in pursuance of regulations under that section.

(5) In this section "the local social services authority", in relation to a person (other than a local social services authority) who is the guardian of a patient, means the local social services authority for the area in which that person resides (or resided immediately before his death).

[Mental Health Act 1983, s 10 as amended by the Mental Health Act 2007, Sch 2.]

*General provisions as to applications and recommendations*

**7.8377 11. General provisions as to applications** (1) Subject to the provisions of this section, an application for admission for assessment, an application for admission for treatment and a guardianship application may be made either by the nearest relative of the patient or by an approved mental health professional; and every such application shall specify the qualification of the applicant to make the application.

(1A) No application mentioned in subsection (1) above shall be made by an approved mental health professional if the circumstances are such that there would be a potential conflict of interest for the purposes of regulations under section 12A below.

(2) Every application for admission shall be addressed to the managers of the hospital to which admission is sought and every guardianship application shall be forwarded to the local social services authority named in the application as guardian, or, as the case may be, to the local social services authority for the area in which the person so named resides.

(3) Before or within a reasonable time after an application for the admission of a patient for assessment is made by an approved mental health professional, that professional shall take such steps as are practicable to inform the person (if any) appearing to be the nearest relative of the patient that the application is to be or has been made and of the power of the nearest relative under section 23(2)(*a*) below.

(4) An approved mental health professional may not make an application for admission for treatment or a guardianship application in respect of a patient in either of the following cases—

(*a*) the nearest relative of the patient has notified that professional, or the local social services authority on whose behalf the professional is acting, that he objects to the application being made; or

(*b*) that professional has not consulted the person (if any) appearing to be the nearest relative of the patient, but the requirement to consult that person does not apply if it appears to the professional that in the circumstances such consultation is not reasonably practicable or would involve unreasonable delay.

(5) None of the applications mentioned in subsection (1) above shall be made by any person in respect of a patient unless that person has personally seen the patient within the period of 14 days ending with the date of the application.

(6) *Repealed.*

(7) Each of the applications mentioned in subsection (1) above shall be sufficient if the recommendations on which it is founded are given either as separate recommendations, each signed by a registered medical practitioner, or as a joint recommendation signed by two such practitioners.

[Mental Health Act 1983, s 11 as amended by the Mental Health Act 2007, s 22, Schs 2 and 11.]

**7.8378 12. General provisions as to medical recommendations** (1) The recommendations required for the purposes of an application for the admission of a patient under this Part of this Act or a guardianship application (in this Act referred to as "medical recommendations") shall be signed on or before the date of the application, and shall be given by practitioners who have personally examined the patient either together or separately, but where they have examined the patient separately not more than five days must have elapsed between the days on which the separate examinations took place[1].

(2) Of the medical recommendations given for the purposes of any such application, one shall be given by a practitioner approved for the purposes of this section by the Secretary of State as having special experience in the diagnosis or treatment of mental disorder; and unless that practitioner has previous acquaintance with the patient, the other such recommendation shall, if practicable, be given by a registered medical practitioner who has such previous acquaintance.

(2A) A registered medical practitioner who is an approved clinician shall be treated as also approved for the purposes of this section under subsection (2) above as having special experience as mentioned there.

(3) No medical recommendation shall be given for the purposes of an application mentioned in subsection (1) above if the circumstances are such that there would be a potential conflict of interest for the purposes of regulations under section 12A below.

[Mental Health Act 1983, s 12 as amended by the Mental Health Act 2007, ss 16, 22.]

1 Approvals granted by NHS trusts or NHS foundation trusts in accordance with ultra vires delegation to them by SHAs were retrospectively validated by the Mental Health (Approval Functions) Act 2012.

**12ZA–12ZC.** *Approval functions.*

7.8379 **12A. Conflicts of interest** The appropriate national authority may make regulations[1] as to the circumstances in which there would be a potential conflict of interest such that an approved mental health professional shall not make an application mentioned in section 11(1) above; a registered medical practitioner shall not give a recommendation for the purposes of an application mentioned in section 12(1) above.

1 The Mental Health (Conflicts of Interest) (England) Regulations 2008, SI 2008/1205 and the Mental Health (Conflicts of Interest) (Wales) Regulations 2008, SI 2008/2440 have been made.

7.8380 **13. Duty of approved mental health professionals to make applications for admission or guardianship** (1) If a local social services authority have reason to think that an application for admission to hospital or a guardianship application may need to be made in respect of a patient within their area, they shall make arrangements for an approved mental health professional to consider the patient's case on their behalf.

(1A) If that professional is—

(*a*) satisfied that such an application ought to be made in respect of the patient; and

(*b*) of the opinion, having regard to any wishes expressed by relatives of the patient or any other relevant circumstances, that it is necessary or proper for the application to be made by him,

he shall make the application.

(1B) Subsection (1C) below applies where—

(*a*) a local social services authority makes arrangements under subsection (1) above in respect of a patient;

(*b*) an application for admission for assessment is made under subsection (1A) above in respect of the patient;

(*c*) while the patient is liable to be detained in pursuance of that application, the authority have reason to think that an application for admission for treatment may need to be made in respect of the patient; and

(*d*) the patient is not within the area of the authority.

(1C) Where this subsection applies, subsection (1) above shall be construed as requiring the authority to make arrangements under that subsection in place of the authority mentioned there.

(2) Before making an application for the admission of a patient to hospital an approved mental health professional shall interview the patient in a suitable manner and satisfy himself that detention in a hospital is in all the circumstances of the case the most appropriate way of providing the care and medical treatment of which the patient stands in need.

(3) An application under subsection (1A) above may be made outside the area of the local social services authority on whose behalf the approved mental health professional is considering the patient's case.

(4) It shall be the duty of a local social services authority, if so required by the nearest relative of a patient residing in their area, to make arrangements under subsection (1) above for an approved mental health professional to consider the patient's case with a view to making an application for his admission to hospital; and if in any such case that professional decides not to make an application he shall inform the nearest relative of his reasons in writing.

(5) Nothing in this section shall be construed as authorising or requiring an application to be made by an approved mental health professional in contravention of the provisions of section 11(4) above or of regulations under section 12A above, or as restricting the power of a local social services authority to make arrangements with an approved mental health professional to consider a patient's case or of an approved mental health professional to make any application under this Act.

[Mental Health Act 1983, s 13 as amended by the Mental Health Act 2007, s 22 and Sch 2.]

7.8381 **14. Social reports** Where a patient is admitted to a hospital in pursuance of an application (other than an emergency application) made under this Part of this Act by his nearest relative, the managers of the hospital shall as soon as practicable give notice of that fact to the local social services authority for the area in which the patient resided immediately before his admission;

and that authority shall as soon as practicable arrange for an approved mental health professional to interview the patient and provide the managers with a report on his social circumstances.

[Mental Health Act 1983, s 14 as amended by the Children Act 2004, Sch 5 and the Mental Health Act 2007, Sch 2.]

7.8382 **15. Rectification of applications and recommendations** (1) If within the period of 14 days beginning with the day on which a patient has been admitted to a hospital in pursuance of an application for admission for assessment or for treatment the application, or any medical recommendation given for the purposes of the application, is found to be in any respect incorrect or defective, the application or recommendation may, within that period and with the consent of the managers of the hospital, be amended by the person by whom it was signed; and upon such amendment being made the application or recommendation shall have effect and shall be deemed to have had effect as if it had been originally made as so amended.

(2) Without prejudice to subsection (1) above, if within the period mentioned in that subsection it appears to the managers of the hospital that one of the two medical recommendations on which an application for the admission of a patient is founded is insufficient to warrant the detention of the patient in pursuance of the application, they may, within that period, give notice in writing to that effect to the applicant; and where any such notice is given in respect of a medical recommendation, that recommendation shall be disregarded, but the application shall be, and shall be deemed always to have been, sufficient if—

(*a*) a fresh medical recommendation complying with the relevant provisions of this Part of this Act (other than the provisions relating to the time of signature and the interval between examinations) is furnished to the managers within that period; and

(*b*) that recommendation, and the other recommendation on which the application is founded, together comply with those provisions.

(3) Where the medical recommendations upon which an application for admission is founded are, taken together, insufficient to warrant the detention of the patient in pursuance of the application, a notice under subsection (2) above may be given in respect of either of those recommendations.

(4) Nothing in this section shall be construed as authorising the giving of notice in respect of an application made as an emergency application, or the detention of a patient admitted in pursuance of such an application, after the period of 72 hours referred to in section 4(4) above, unless the conditions set out in paragraphs (*a*) and (*b*) of that section are complied with or would be complied with apart from any error or defect to which this section applies.

[Mental Health Act 1983, s 15 as amended by the Mental Health Act 2007, Sch 11.]

7.8383 **17. Leave of absence from hospital** (1) The responsible clinician may grant to any patient who is for the time being liable to be detained in a hospital under this Part of this Act leave to be absent from the hospital subject to such conditions (if any) as that clinician considers necessary in the interests of the patient or for the protection of other persons.

(2) Leave of absence may be granted to a patient under this section either indefinitely or on specified occasions or for any specified period; and where leave is so granted for a specified period, that period may be extended by further leave granted in the absence of the patient.

(2A) But longer-term leave may not be granted to a patient unless the responsible clinician first considers whether the patient should be dealt with under section 17A instead.

(2B) For these purposes, longer-term leave is granted to a patient if—

(*a*) leave of absence is granted to him under this section either indefinitely or for a specified period of more than seven consecutive days; or

(*b*) a specified period is extended under this section such that the total period for which leave of absence will have been granted to him under this section exceeds seven consecutive days.

(3) Where it appears to the responsible clinician that it is necessary so to do in the interests of the patient or for the protection of other persons, he may, upon granting leave of absence under this section, direct that the patient remain in custody during his absence; and where leave of absence is so granted the patient may be kept in the custody of any officer on the staff of the hospital, or of any other person authorised in writing by the managers of the hospital or, if the patient is required in accordance with conditions imposed on the grant of leave of absence to reside in another hospital, of any officer on the staff of that other hospital.

(4) In any case where a patient is absent from a hospital in pursuance of leave of absence granted under this section, and it appears to the responsible clinician that it is necessary so to do in the interests of the patient's health or safety or for the protection of other persons, that clinician may, subject to subsection (5) below, by notice in writing given to the patient or to the person for the time being in charge of the patient, revoke the leave of absence and recall the patient to the hospital.

(5) A patient to whom leave of absence is granted under this section shall not be recalled under subsection (4) above after he has ceased to be liable to be detained under this Part of this Act.

(6) Subsection (7) below applies to a person who is granted leave by or by virtue of a provision—

(*a*) in force in Scotland, Northern Ireland, any of the Channel Islands or the Isle of Man; and

(*b*) corresponding to subsection (1) above.

(7) For the purpose of giving effect to a direction or condition imposed by virtue of a provision

corresponding to subsection (3) above, the person may be conveyed to a place in, or kept in custody or detained at a place of safety in, England and Wales by a person authorised in that behalf by the direction or condition.

[Mental Health Act 1983, s 17, as amended by the Mental Health (Patients in the Community) Act 1995, s 3 and the Mental Health Act 2007, ss 9 and 39.]

7.8384 **17A–17G.** *Community treatment orders*

7.8385 **18. Return and readmission of patients absent without leave** (1) Where a patient who is for the time being liable to be detained under this Part of this Act in a hospital—

(*a*) absents himself from the hospital without leave granted under section 17 above; or

(*b*) fails to return to the hospital on any occasion on which, or at the expiration of any period for which, leave of absence was granted to him under that section, or upon being recalled under that section; or

(*c*) absents himself without permission from any place where he is required to reside in accordance with conditions imposed on the grant of leave of absence under that section,

he may, subject to the provisions of this section, be taken into custody and returned to the hospital or place by any approved mental health professional, by any officer on the staff of the hospital, by any constable, or by any person authorised in writing by the managers of the hospital.

(2) Where the place referred to in paragraph (*c*) of subsection (1) above is a hospital other than the one in which the patient is for the time being liable to be detained, the references in that subsection to an officer on the staff of the hospital and the managers of the hospital shall respectively include references to an officer on the staff of the first-mentioned hospital and the managers of that hospital.

(2A) Where a community patient is at any time absent from a hospital to which he is recalled under section 17E above, he may, subject to the provisions of this section, be taken into custody and returned to the hospital by any approved mental health professional, by any officer on the staff of the hospital, by any constable, or by any person authorised in writing by the responsible clinician or the managers of the hospital.

(3) Where a patient who is for the time being subject to guardianship under this Part of this Act absents himself without the leave of the guardian from the place at which he is required by the guardian to reside, he may, subject to the provisions of this section, be taken into custody and returned to that place by any officer on the staff of a local social services authority, by any constable, or by any person authorised in writing by the guardian or a local social services authority.

(4) patient shall not be taken into custody under this section after the later of—

(*a*) the end of the period of six months beginning with the first day of his absence without leave; and

(*b*) the end of the period for which (apart from section 21 below) he is liable to be detained or subject to guardianship or, in the case of a community patient, the community treatment order is in force.

(4A) In determining for the purposes of subsection (4)(*b*) above or any other provision of this Act whether a person who is or has been absent without leave is at any time liable to be detained or subject to guardianship, a report furnished under section 20 or 21B below before the first day of his absence without leave shall not be taken to have renewed the authority for his detention or guardianship unless the period of renewal began before that day.

(4B) Similarly, in determining for those purposes whether a community treatment order is at any time in force in respect of a person who is or has been absent without leave, a report furnished under section 20A or 21B below before the first day of his absence without leave shall not be taken to have extended the community treatment period unless the extension began before that day.

(5) A patient shall not be taken into custody under this section if the period for which he is liable to be detained is that specified in section 2(4), 4(4) or 5(2) or (4) above and that period has expired.

(6) In this Act "absent without leave" means absent from any hospital or other place and liable to be taken into custody and returned under this section, and related expressions shall be construed accordingly.

(7) In relation to a patient who has yet to comply with a requirement imposed by virtue of this Act to be in a hospital or place, references in this Act to his liability to be returned to the hospital or place shall include his liability to be taken to that hospital or place; and related expressions shall be construed accordingly.

[Mental Health Act 1983, s 18 as amended by the Mental Health (Patients in the Community) Act 1995, s 2 and the Mental Health Act 2007, Schs 2 and 3.]

7.8386 **19. Regulations as to transfer of patients** (1) In such circumstances and subject to such conditions as may be prescribed by regulations[1] made by the Secretary of State—

(*a*) a patient who is for the time being liable to be detained in a hospital by virtue of an application under this Part of this Act may be transferred to another hospital or into the guardianship of a local social services authority or of any person approved by such an authority;

(*b*) a patient who is for the time being subject to the guardianship of a local social services authority or other person by virtue of an application under this Part of this Act may be transferred into the guardianship of another local social services authority or person, or be transferred to a hospital.

(2) Where a patient is transferred in pursuance of regulations under this section, the provisions of this Part of this Act (including this subsection) shall apply to him as follows, that is to say—

(*a*) in the case of a patient who is liable to be detained in a hospital by virtue of an application for admission for assessment or for treatment and is transferred to another hospital, as if the application were an application for admission to that other hospital and as if the patient had been admitted to that other hospital at the time when he was originally admitted in pursuance of the application;

(*b*) in the case of a patient who is liable to be detained in a hospital by virtue of such an application and is transferred into guardianship, as if the application were a guardianship application duly accepted at the said time;

(*c*) in the case of a patient who is subject to guardianship by virtue of a guardianship application and is transferred into the guardianship of another authority or person, as if the application were for his reception into the guardianship of that authority or person and had been accepted at the time when it was originally accepted;

(*d*) in the case of a patient who is subject to guardianship by virtue of a guardianship application and is transferred to a hospital, as if the guardianship application were an application for admission to that hospital for treatment and as if the patient had been admitted to the hospital at the time when the application was originally accepted.

(3) Without prejudice to subsections (1) and (2) above, any patient who is for the time being liable to be detained under this Part of this Act in a hospital vested in the Secretary of State for the purposes of his functions under the National Health Service Act 2006, in a hospital vested in the Welsh Ministers for the purposes of their functions under the National Health Service (Wales) Act 2006, in any accommodation used under either of those Acts by the managers of such a hospital or in a hospital vested in a National Health Service trust, NHS foundation trust or Local Health Board, may at any time be removed to any other such hospital or accommodation which is managed by the managers of, or is vested in the National Health Service trust, NHS foundation trust or Local Health Board for, the first-mentioned hospital; and paragraph (*a*) of subsection (2) above shall apply in relation to a patient so removed as it applies in relation to a patient transferred in pursuance of regulations made under this section.

(4) Regulations[1] made under this section may make provision for regulating the conveyance to their destination of patients authorised to be transferred or removed in pursuance of the regulations or under subsection (3) above.

[Mental Health Act 1983, s 19 as amended by the National Health Service and Community Care Act 1990, s 66, Sch 9, SI 2000/90, the Health and Social Care (Community Health and Standards) Act 2003, Sch 4, the National Health Service (Consequential Provisions) Act 2006, Sch 1, the Mental Health Act 2007, s 46 and the Health and Social Care Act 2012, Sch 5.]

---

1 The Mental Health (Hospital, Guardianship and Treatment) (England) Regulations 2008, SI 2008/1184 amended by SI 2008/2560, SI 2012/1118 and SI 2013/235 and the Mental Health (Hospital, Guardianship Community Treatment and Consent to Treatment) (Wales) Regulations 2008, SI 2008/2439 amended by SI 2013/235 have been made.

**7.8387 19A. Regulations[1] as to assignment of responsibility for community patients**

(1) Responsibility for a community patient may be assigned to another hospital in such circumstances and subject to such conditions as may be prescribed by regulations made by the Secretary of State (if the responsible hospital is in England) or the Welsh Ministers (if that hospital is in Wales).

(2) If responsibility for a community patient is assigned to another hospital—

(*a*) the application for admission for treatment in respect of the patient shall have effect (subject to section 17D above) as if it had always specified that other hospital;

(*b*) the patient shall be treated as if he had been admitted to that other hospital at the time when he was originally admitted in pursuance of the application (and as if he had subsequently been discharged under section 17A above from there); and

(*c*) that other hospital shall become "the responsible hospital" in relation to the patient for the purposes of this Act.

[Mental Health Act 1983, s 19A as inserted by the Mental Health Act 2007, Sch 3.]

---

1 The Mental Health (Hospital, Guardianship and Treatment) (England) Regulations 2008, SI 2008/1184 amended by SI 2008/2560, SI 2012/1118 and SI 2013/235 and the Mental Health (Hospital, Guardianship Community Treatment and Consent to Treatment) (Wales) Regulations 2008, SI 2008/2439 amended by SI 2013/235 have been made.

*Duration of authority and discharge*

**7.8388 20. Duration of authority** (1) Subject to the following provisions of this Part of this Act, a patient admitted to hospital in pursuance of an application for admission for treatment, and a patient placed under guardianship in pursuance of a guardianship application, may be detained in a hospital or kept under guardianship for a period not exceeding six months beginning with the day on which he was so admitted, or the day on which the guardianship application was accepted, as the case may be, but shall not be so detained or kept for any longer period unless the authority for his detention or guardianship is renewed under this section.

(2) Authority for the detention or guardianship of a patient may, unless the patient has previously been discharged under section 23 below, be renewed—

(*a*) from the expiration of the period referred to in subsection (1) above, for a further period of six months;

(*b*) from the expiration of any period of renewal under paragraph (*a*) above, for a further period of one year,

and so on for periods of one year at a time.

(3) Within the period of two months ending on the day on which a patient who is liable to be detained in pursuance of an application for admission for treatment would cease under this section to be so liable in default of the renewal of the authority for his detention, it shall be the duty of the responsible clinician—

(*a*) to examine the patient; and

(*b*) if it appears to him that the conditions set out in subsection (4) below are satisfied, to furnish to the managers of the hospital where the patient is detained a report to that effect in the prescribed form;

and where such a report is furnished in respect of a patient the managers shall, unless they discharge the patient under section 23 below, cause him to be informed.

(4) The conditions referred to in subsection (3) above are that—

(*a*) the patient is suffering from mental disorder of a nature or degree which makes it appropriate for him to receive medical treatment in a hospital; and

(*b*) *repealed*

(*c*) it is necessary for the health or safety of the patient or for the protection of other persons that he should receive such treatment and that it cannot be provided unless he continues to be detained; and

(*d*) appropriate medical treatment is available for him.

(5) Before furnishing a report under subsection (3) above the responsible clinician shall consult one or more other persons who have been professionally concerned with the patient's medical treatment.

(5A) But the responsible clinician may not furnish a report under subsection (3) above unless a person—

(*a*) who has been professionally concerned with the patient's medical treatment; but

(*b*) who belongs to a profession other than that to which the responsible clinician belongs,

states in writing that he agrees that the conditions set out in subsection (4) above are satisfied.

(6) Within the period of two months ending with the day on which a patient who is subject to guardianship under this Part of this Act would cease under this section to be so liable in default of the renewal of the authority for his guardianship, it shall be the duty of the appropriate practitioner—

(*a*) to examine the patient; and

(*b*) if it appears to him that the conditions set out in subsection (7) below are satisfied, to furnish to the guardian and, where the guardian is a person other than a local social services authority, to the responsible local social services authority a report to that effect in the prescribed form;

and where such a report is furnished in respect of a patient, the local social services authority shall, unless they discharge the patient under section 23 below, cause him to be informed.

(7) The conditions referred to in subsection (6) above are that—

(*a*) the patient is suffering from mental disorder of a nature or degree which warrants his reception into guardianship; and

(*b*) it is necessary in the interests of the welfare of the patient or for the protection of other persons that the patient should remain under guardianship.

(8) Where a report is duly furnished under subsection (3) or (6) above, the authority for the detention or guardianship of the patient shall be thereby renewed for the period prescribed in that case by subsection (2) above.

(9) *Repealed.*

(10) *Repealed.*

[Mental Health Act 1983, s 20 as amended by the Mental Health Act 2007, ss 4, 9, Schs 1, 3 and 11.]

**7.8389 20A, 20B.** *Community Treatment Orders – duration and expiry*

**7.8390 21. Special provisions as to patients absent without leave** (1) Where a patient is absent without leave—

(*a*) on the day on which (apart from this section) he would cease to be liable to be detained or subject to guardianship under this Part of this Act or, in the case of a community patient, the community treatment order would cease to be in force; or

(*b*) within the period of one week ending with that day,

he shall not cease to be so liable or subject, or the order shall not cease to be in force, until the relevant time.

(2) For the purposes of subsection (1) above the relevant time—

(*a*) where the patient is taken into custody under section 18 above, is the end of the period of one week beginning with the day on which he is returned to the hospital or place where he ought to be;

(*b*) where the patient returns himself to the hospital or place where he ought to be within the period during which he can be taken into custody under section 18 above, is the end of the period of one week beginning with the day on which he so returns himself; and

(*c*) otherwise, is the end of the period during which he can be taken into custody under section 18 above.

(3) Where a patient is absent without leave on the day on which (apart from this section) the managers would be required under section 68 below to refer the patient's case to the appropriate tribunal, that requirement shall not apply unless and until—

(*a*) the patient is taken into custody under section 18 above and returned to the hospital where he ought to be; or

(*b*) the patient returns himself to the hospital where he ought to be within the period during which he can be taken into custody under section 18 above.]

(4) Where a community patient is absent without leave on the day on which (apart from this section) the 72-hour period mentioned in section 17F above would expire, that period shall not expire until the end of the period of 72 hours beginning with the time when—

(*a*) the patient is taken into custody under section 18 above and returned to the hospital where he ought to be; or

(*b*) the patient returns himself to the hospital where he ought to be within the period during which he can be taken into custody under section 18 above.

(5) Any reference in this section, or in sections 21A to 22 below, to the time when a community treatment order would cease, or would have ceased, to be in force shall be construed as a reference to the time when it would cease, or would have ceased, to be in force by reason only of the passage of time.

[Mental Health Act 1983, s 21 as substituted by the Mental Health (Patients in the Community) Act 1995, s 2 and amended by the Mental Health Act 2007, s 37 and Sch 3 and SI 2008/2833.]

**7.8391 21A. Patients who are taken into custody or return within 28 days** (1) This section applies where a patient who is absent without leave is taken into custody under section 18 above, or returns himself to the hospital or place where he ought to be, not later than the end of the period of 28 days beginning with the first day of his absence without leave.

(2) Where the period for which the patient is liable to be detained or subject to guardianship is extended by section 21 above, any examination and report to be made and furnished in respect of the patient under section 20(3) or (6) above may be made and furnished within the period as so extended.

(3) Where the authority for the detention or guardianship of the patient is renewed by virtue of subsection (2) above after the day on which (apart from section 21 above) that authority would have expired, the renewal shall take effect as from that day.

(4) In the case of a community patient, where the period for which the community treatment order is in force is extended by section 21 above, any examination and report to be made and furnished in respect of the patient under section 20A(4) above may be made and furnished within the period as so extended.

(5) Where the community treatment period is extended by virtue of subsection (4) above after the day on which (apart from section 21 above) the order would have ceased to be in force, the extension shall take effect as from that day.

[Mental Health Act 1983, s 21A as inserted by the Mental Health (Patients in the Community) Act 1995, s 2 and amended by the Mental Health Act 2007, Sch 3.]

**7.8392 21B. Patients who are taken into custody or return after more than 28 days** (1) This section applies where a patient who is absent without leave is taken into custody under section 18 above, or returns himself to the hospital or place where he ought to be, later than the end of the period of 28 days beginning with the first day of his absence without leave.

(2) It shall be the duty of the appropriate practitioner, within the period of one week beginning with the day on which the patient is returned or returns himself to the hospital or place where he ought to be (his "return day")—

(*a*) to examine the patient; and

(*b*) if it appears to him that the relevant conditions are satisfied, to furnish to the appropriate body a report to that effect in the prescribed form;

and where such a report is furnished in respect of the patient the appropriate body shall cause him to be informed.

(3) Where the patient is liable to be detained or is a community patient (as opposed to subject to guardianship), the appropriate practitioner shall, before furnishing a report under subsection (2) above, consult—

(*a*) one or more other persons who have been professionally concerned with the patient's medical treatment; and

(*b*) an approved mental health professional.

(4) Where—

(*a*) the patient would (apart from any renewal of the authority for his detention or guardianship on or after his return day) be liable to be detained or subject to guardianship after the end of the period of one week beginning with that day; or (*b*) in the case of a community patient, the community treatment order would (apart from any extension of the community treatment period on or after that day) be in force after the end of that period,

he shall cease to be so liable or subject, or the community treatment period shall be deemed to expire, at the end of that period unless a report is duly furnished in respect of him under subsection (2) above.

(4A) If, in the case of a community patient, the community treatment order is revoked under section 17F above during the period of one week beginning with his return day—

(*a*) subsections (2) and (4) above shall not apply; and

(*b*) any report already furnished in respect of him under subsection (2) above shall be of no effect.

(5) Where the patient would (apart from section 21 above) have ceased to be liable to be detained or subject to guardianship on or before the day on which a report is duly furnished in respect of him under subsection (2) above, the report shall renew the authority for his detention or guardianship for the period prescribed in that case by section 20(2) above.

(6) Where the authority for the detention or guardianship of the patient is renewed by virtue of subsection (5) above—

(*a*) the renewal shall take effect as from the day on which (apart from section 21 above and that subsection) the authority would have expired; and

(*b*) if (apart from this paragraph) the renewed authority would expire on or before the day on which the report is furnished, the report shall further renew the authority, as from the day on which it would expire, for the period prescribed in that case by section 20(2) above.

(6A) In the case of a community patient, where the community treatment order would (apart from section 21 above) have ceased to be in force on or before the day on which a report is duly furnished in respect of him under subsection (2) above, the report shall extend the community treatment period for the period prescribed in that case by section 20A(3) above.

(6B) Where the community treatment period is extended by virtue of subsection (6A) above—

(*a*) the extension shall take effect as from the day on which (apart from section 21 above and that subsection) the order would have ceased to be in force; and

(*b*) if (apart from this paragraph) the period as so extended would expire on or before the day on which the report is furnished, the report shall further extend that period, as from the day on which it would expire, for the period prescribed in that case by section 20A(3) above.

(7) Where the authority for the detention or guardianship of the patient would expire within the period of two months beginning with the day on which a report is duly furnished in respect of him under subsection (2) above, the report shall, if it so provides, have effect also as a report duly furnished under section 20(3) or (6) above; and the reference in this subsection to authority includes any authority renewed under subsection (5) above by the report.

(7A) In the case of a community patient, where the community treatment order would (taking account of any extension under subsection (6A) above) cease to be in force within the period of two months beginning with the day on which a report is duly furnished in respect of him under subsection (2) above, the report shall, if it so provides, have effect also as a report duly furnished under section 20A(4) above.

(8) *Repealed.*

(9) *Repealed.*

(10) In this section—

"the appropriate body" means—

(*a*) in relation to a patient who is liable to be detained in a hospital, the managers of the hospital;

(*b*) in relation to a patient who is subject to guardianship, the responsible local social services authority;

(*c*) in relation to a community patient, the managers of the responsible hospital; and

"the relevant conditions" means—

(*a*) in relation to a patient who is liable to be detained in a hospital, the conditions set out in subsection (4) of section 20 above;

(*b*) in relation to a patient who is subject to guardianship, the conditions set out in subsection (7) of that section;

(*c*) in relation to a community patient, the conditions set out in section 20A(6) above.

[Mental Health Act 1983, s 21B as inserted by the Mental Health (Patients in the Community) Act 1995, s 2 and amended by the Mental Health Act 2007, s 9, Schs 2, 3 and 11.]

7.8393 22. **Special provisions as to patients sentenced to imprisonment, etc** (1) If—

(*a*) a qualifying patient is detained in custody in pursuance of any sentence or order passed or made by a court in the United Kingdom (including an order committing or remanding him in custody); and

(*b*) he is so detained for a period exceeding, or for successive periods exceeding in the aggregate, six months,

the relevant application shall cease to have effect on expiry of that period.

(2) A patient is a qualifying patient for the purposes of this section if—

(*a*) he is liable to be detained by virtue of an application for admission for treatment;
(*b*) he is subject to guardianship by virtue of a guardianship application; or
(*c*) he is a community patient.

(3) "The relevant application", in relation to a qualifying patient, means—
(*a*) in the case of a patient who is subject to guardianship, the guardianship application in respect of him;
(*b*) in any other case, the application for admission for treatment in respect of him.

(4) The remaining subsections of this section shall apply if a qualifying patient is detained in custody as mentioned in subsection (1)(*a*) above but for a period not exceeding, or for successive periods not exceeding in the aggregate, six months.

(5) If apart from this subsection—
(*a*) the patient would have ceased to be liable to be detained or subject to guardianship by virtue of the relevant application on or before the day on which he is discharged from custody; or
(*b*) in the case of a community patient, the community treatment order would have ceased to be in force on or before that day,

he shall not cease and shall be deemed not to have ceased to be so liable or subject, or the order shall not cease and shall be deemed not to have ceased to be in force, until the end of that day.

(6) In any case (except as provided in subsection (8) below), sections 18, 21 and 21A above shall apply in relation to the patient as if he had absented himself without leave on that day.

(7) In its application by virtue of subsection (6) above section 18 above shall have effect as if—
(*a*) in subsection (4) for the words from "later of" to the end there were substituted "end of the period of 28 days beginning with the first day of his absence without leave"; and
(*b*) subsections (4A) and (4B) were omitted.

(8) In relation to a community patient who was not recalled to hospital under section 17E above at the time when his detention in custody began—
(*a*) section 18 above shall not apply; but
(*b*) sections 21 and 21A above shall apply as if he had absented himself without leave on the day on which he is discharged from custody and had returned himself as provided in those sections on the last day of the period of 28 days beginning with that day.

[Mental Health Act 1983, s 22 as substituted by the Mental Health Act 2007, Sch 3.]

7.8394 **23. Discharge of patients** (1) Subject to the provisions of this section and section 25 below, a patient who is for the time being liable to be detained or subject to guardianship under this Part of this Act shall cease to be so liable or subject if an order in writing discharging him absolutely from detention or guardianship is made in accordance with this section.

(1A) Subject to the provisions of this section and section 25 below, a community patient shall cease to be liable to recall under this Part of this Act, and the application for admission for treatment cease to have effect, if an order in writing discharging him from such liability is made in accordance with this section.

(1B) An order under subsection (1) or (1A) above shall be referred to in this Act as "an order for discharge".

(2) An order for discharge may be made in respect of a patient—
(*a*) where the patient is liable to be detained in a hospital in pursuance of an application for admission for assessment or for treatment by the responsible clinician, by the managers or by the nearest relative of the patient;
(*b*) where the patient is subject to guardianship, by the responsible clinician, by the responsible local social services authority or by the nearest relative of the patient;
(*c*) where the patient is a community patient, by the responsible clinician, by the managers of the responsible hospital or by the nearest relative of the patient.

(3) *Repealed.*

(3A) *Repealed.*

(4) The powers conferred by this section on any authority trust, board (other than a NHS foundation trust), board or body of persons may be exercised subject to subsection (3) below by any three or more members of that authority trust, board or body authorised by them in that behalf or by three or more members of a committee or sub-committee of that authority trust, board or body which has been authorised by them in that behalf.

(5) The reference in subsection (4) above to the members of an authority, trust, board or body or the members of a committee or sub-committee of an authority, trust, board or body,—
(*a*) in the case of a Local Health Board or Special Health Authority or a committee or sub-committee of a Local Health Board or Special Health Authority, is a reference only to the chairman of the authority or board and such members (of the authority, board, committee or sub-committee, as the case may be) as are not also officers of the authority or board within the meaning of the National Health Service Act 2006 or the National Health Service (Wales) Act 2006; and
(*b*) in the case of a National Health Service trust or a committee or sub-committee of such a trust, is a reference only to the chairman of the trust and such directors or (in the case of a committee or sub-committee) members as are not also employees of the trust.

(6) The powers conferred by this section on any NHS foundation trust may be exercised by any

three or more persons authorised by the board of the trust in that behalf each of whom is neither an executive director of the board nor an employee of the trust.

[Mental Health Act 1983, s 23 as amended by the National Health Service and Community Care Act 1990, s 66, Sch 9, the Health Authorities Act 1995 s 2, Sch 1, SI 2000/90, the Care Standards Act 2000, s 116, the Health and Social Care (Community Health and Standards) Act 2003, Sch 4, the National Health Service (Consequential Provisions) Act 2006, Sch 1, SI 2007/961, the Mental Health Act 2007, ss 9, 45 and Sch 3 and the Health and Social Care Act 2012, s 39, Sch 5.]

7.8395 **24. Visiting and examination of patients** (1) For the purpose of advising as to the exercise by the nearest relative of a patient who is liable to be detained or subject to guardianship under this Part of this Act, or who is a community patient, of any power to order his discharge, any registered medical practitioner or approved clinician authorised by or on behalf of the nearest relative of the patient may, at any reasonable time, visit the patient and examine him in private.

(2) Any registered medical practitioner or approved clinician authorised for the purposes of subsection (1) above to visit and examine a patient may require the production of and inspect any records relating to the detention or treatment of the patient in any hospital or to any after-care services provided for the patient under section 117 below.

(3) *Repealed.*

(4) *Repealed.*

[Mental Health Act 1983, s 24 as amended by the Registered Homes Act 1984, s 57, Sch 1, the Health Authorities Act 1995, s 2, Sch 1, the Mental Health (Patients in the Community) Act 1995, s 1, Sch 1, SI 2000/90, the Care Standards Act 2000, s 116, the Health and Social Care (Community Health and Standards) Act 2003, Sch 4, SI 2007/961, the Mental Health Act 2007, s 9 and Sch 3, SI 2010/813 and the Health and Social Care Act 2012, s 39.]

7.8396 **25. Restrictions on discharge by nearest relative** (1) An order for the discharge of a patient who is liable to be detained in a hospital shall not be made under section 23 above by his nearest relative except after giving not less than 72 hours' notice in writing to the managers of the hospital; and if, within 72 hours after such notice has been given, the responsible clinician furnishes to the managers a report certifying that in the opinion of that clinician the patient, if discharged, would be likely to act in a manner dangerous to other persons or to himself,—

(*a*) any order for the discharge of the patient made by that relative in pursuance of the notice shall be of no effect; and

(*b*) no further order for the discharge of the patient shall be made by that relative during the period of six months beginning with the date of the report.

(1A) Subsection (1) above shall apply to an order for the discharge of a community patient as it applies to an order for the discharge of a patient who is liable to be detained in a hospital, but with the reference to the managers of the hospital being read as a reference to the managers of the responsible hospital.

(2) In any case where a report under subsection (1) above is furnished in respect of a patient who is liable to be detained in pursuance of an application for admission for treatment, or in respect of a community patient, the managers shall cause the nearest relative of the patient to be informed.

[Mental Health Act 1983, s 25 as amended by the Mental Health Act 2007, s 9 and Sch 3.]

*Functions of relatives of patients*

7.8397 **26. Definition of "relative" and "nearest relative"** (1) In this Part of this Act "relative" means any of the following persons:—

(*a*) husband or wife or civil partner;

(*b*) son or daughter;

(*c*) father or mother;

(*d*) brother or sister;

(*e*) grandparent;

(*f*) grandchild;

(*g*) uncle or aunt;

(*h*) nephew or niece.

(2) In deducing relationships for the purposes of this section, any relationship of the half-blood shall be treated as a relationship of the whole blood, and an illegitimate person shall be treated as the legitimate child of

(*a*) his mother, and

(*b*) if his father has parental responsibility for him within the meaning of section 3 of the Children Act 1989, his father.

(3) In this Part of this Act, subject to the provisions of this section and to the following provisions of this Part of this Act, the "nearest relative" means the person first described in subsection (1) above who is for the time being surviving, relatives of the whole blood being preferred to relatives of the same description of the half-blood and the elder or eldest of two or more relatives described in any paragraph of that subsection being preferred to the other or others of those relatives, regardless of sex.

(4) Subject to the provisions of this section and to the following provisions of this Part of this Act, where the patient ordinarily resides with or is cared for by one or more of his relatives (or, if he is for the time being an in-patient in a hospital, he last ordinarily resided with or was cared for by one or more of his relatives) his nearest relative shall be determined—

(*a*) by giving preference to that relative or those relatives over the other or others; and (*b*) as between two or more such relatives, in accordance with subsection (3) above.

(5) Where the person who, under subsection (3) or (4) above, would be the nearest relative of a patient—

(*a*) in the case of a patient ordinarily resident in the United Kingdom, the Channel Islands or the Isle of Man, is not so resident; or

(*b*) is the husband or wife or civil partner of the patient, but is permanently separated from the patient, either by agreement or under an order of a court, or has deserted or has been deserted by the patient for a period which has come to an end; or

(*c*) is a person other than the husband, wife, civil partner, father or mother of the patient, and is for the time being under 18 years of age;

(*d*) *repealed.*

the nearest relative of the patient shall be ascertained as if that person were dead.

(6) In this section "husband", "wife" and "civil partner" include a person who is living with the patient as the patient's husband or wife or as if they were civil partners as the case may be (or, if the patient is for the time being an in-patient in a hospital, was so living until the patient was admitted), and has been or had been so living for a period of not less than six months; but a person shall not be treated by virtue of this subsection as the nearest relative of a married patient or a patient in a civil partnership unless the husband, wife or civil partner unless the husband or wife of the patient is disregarded by virtue of paragraph (*b*) of subsection (5) above.

(7) A person, other than a relative, with whom the patient ordinarily resides (or, if the patient is for the time being an in-patient in a hospital, last ordinarily resided before he was admitted), and with whom he has or had been ordinarily residing for a period of not less than five years, shall be treated for the purposes of this Part of this Act as if he were a relative but—

(*a*) shall be treated for the purposes of subsection (3) above as if mentioned last in subsection (1) above; and

(*b*) shall not be treated by virtue of this subsection as the nearest relative of a married patient or a patient in a civil partnership unless the husband, wife or civil partner unless the husband or wife of the patient is disregarded by virtue of paragraph (*b*) of subsection (5) above.

[Mental Health Act 1983, s 26 as amended by SI 1991/1881, the Children Act 1989, s 108, Schs 14 and 15 and the Mental Health Act 2007, s 26.]

7.8398 **27. Children and young persons in care** Where—

(*a*) a patient who is a child or young person is in the care of a local authority by virtue of a care order within the meaning of the Children Act 1989; or

(*b*) the rights and powers of a parent of a patient who is a child or young person are vested in a local authority by virtue of section 16 of the Social Work (Scotland) Act 1968,

the authority shall be deemed to be the nearest relative of the patient in preference to any person except the patient's husband or wife or civil partner (if any).

[Mental Health Act 1983, s 27 as substituted by the Children Act 1989, s 108, Sch 14 and amended by the Mental Health Act 2007, s 26.]

7.8399 **28. Nearest relative of minor under guardianship, etc** (1) Where—

(*a*) a guardian has been appointed for a person who has not attained the age of eighteen years; or

(*b*) a person is named in a child arrangements order (as defined by section 8 of the Children Act 1989) as a person with whom a person who has not attained the age of eighteen years is to live,

the guardian (or guardians, where there is more than one) or the person so named (or the persons so named, where there is more than one) shall, to the exclusion of any other person, be deemed to be his nearest relative.

(2) Subsection (5) of section 26 above shall apply in relation to a person who is, or who is one of the persons, deemed to be the nearest relative of a patient by virtue of this section as it applies in relation to a person who would be the nearest relative under subsection (3) of that section.

(3) In this section "guardian" includes a special guardian (within the meaning of the Children Act 1989), but does not include a guardian under this Part of this Act.

(4) In this section "court" includes a court in Scotland or Northern Ireland, and "enactment" includes an enactment of the Parliament of Northern Ireland, a Measure of the Northern Ireland Assembly and an Order in Council under Schedule 1 of the Northern Ireland Act 1974.

[Mental Health Act 1983, s 28 as amended by the Children Act 1989, s 108, Schs 13 and 14, the Adoption and Children Act 2002, Sch 3 and the Children and Families Act 2014, Sch 2.]

7.8400 **29. Appointment by court of acting nearest relative** (1) The county court may, upon application made in accordance with the provisions of this section in respect of a patient, by order direct that the functions of the nearest relative of the patient under this Part of this Act and sections 66 and 69 below shall, during the continuance in force of the order, be exercisable by the person specified in the order.

(1A) If the court decides to make an order on an application under subsection (1) above, the following rules have effect for the purposes of specifying a person in the order—

(*a*) if a person is nominated in the application to act as the patient's nearest relative and that person is, in the opinion of the court, a suitable person to act as such and is willing to do so, the court shall specify that person (or, if there are two or more such persons, such one of them as the court thinks fit);

(*b*) otherwise, the court shall specify such person as is, in its opinion, a suitable person to act as the patient's nearest relative and is willing to do so.

(2) An order under this section may be made on the application of—

(*za*) the patient;

(*a*) any relative of the patient;

(*b*) any other person with whom the patient is residing (or, if the patient is then an in-patient in a hospital, was last residing before he was admitted); or

(*c*) an approved mental health professional.

(3) An application for an order under this section may be made upon any of the following grounds, that is to say—

(*a*) that the patient has no nearest relative within the meaning of this Act, or that it is not reasonably practicable to ascertain whether he has such a relative, or who that relative is;

(*b*) that the nearest relative of the patient is incapable of acting as such by reason of mental disorder or other illness;

(*c*) that the nearest relative of the patient unreasonably objects to the making of an application for admission for treatment or a guardianship application in respect of the patient;

(*d*) that the nearest relative of the patient has exercised without due regard to the welfare of the patient or the interests of the public his power to discharge the patient under this Part of this Act, or is likely to do so; or

(*e*) that the nearest relative of the patient is otherwise not a suitable person to act as such.

(4) If, immediately before the expiration of the period for which a patient is liable to be detained by virtue of an application for admission for assessment, an application under this section, which is an application made on the ground specified in subsection (3)(*c*) or (*d*) above, is pending in respect of the patient, that period shall be extended—

(*a*) in any case, until the application under this section has been finally disposed of; and

(*b*) if an order is made in pursuance of the application under this section, for a further period of seven days;

and for the purposes of this subsection an application under this section shall be deemed to have been finally disposed of at the expiration of the time allowed for appealing from the decision of the court or, if notice of appeal has been given within that time, when the appeal has been heard or withdrawn, and "pending" shall be construed accordingly.

(5) An order made on the ground specified in subsection (3)(*a*), (*b*) or (*e*) above may specify a period for which it is to continue in force unless previously discharged under section 30 below

(6) While an order made under this section is in force, the provisions of this Part of this Act (other than this section and section 30 below) and sections 66, 69, 132(4) and 133 below shall apply in relation to the patient as if for any reference to the nearest relative of the patient there were substituted a reference to the person having the functions of that relative and (without prejudice to section 30 below) shall so apply notwithstanding that the person who was the patient's nearest relative when the order was made is no longer his nearest relative; but this subsection shall not apply to section 66 below in the case mentioned in paragraph (h) of subsection (1) of that section.

[Mental Health Act 1983, s 29 as amended by the Mental Health Act 2007, s 23 and Schs 2, 3 and 11.]

7.8401 **30. Discharge and variation of orders under s 29** (1) An order made under section 29 above in respect of a patient may be discharged by the county court upon application made—

(*a*) in any case, by the patient or the person having the functions of the nearest relative of the patient by virtue of the order;

(*b*) where the order was made on the ground specified in paragraph (*a*), (*b*) or (*e*) of section 29(3) above, or where the person who was the nearest relative of the patient when the order was made has ceased to be his nearest relative, on the application of the nearest relative of the patient.

(1A) But, in the case of an order made on the ground specified in paragraph (*e*) of section 29(3) above, an application may not be made under subsection (1)(*b*) above by the person who was the nearest relative of the patient when the order was made except with leave of the county court.

(2) An order made under section 29 above in respect of a patient may be varied by the county court, on the application of the patient or of the person having the functions of the nearest relative by virtue of the order or on the application of an approved mental health professional, by substituting another person for the person having those functions.

(2A) If the court decides to vary an order on an application under subsection (2) above, the following rules have effect for the purposes of substituting another person—

(*a*) if a person is nominated in the application to act as the patient's nearest relative and that person is, in the opinion of the court, a suitable person to act as such and is willing to do so, the court shall specify that person (or, if there are two or more such persons, such one of them as the court thinks fit);

(*b*) otherwise, the court shall specify such person as is, in its opinion, a suitable person to act as the patient's nearest relative and is willing to do so.

(3) If the person having the functions of the nearest relative of a patient by virtue of an order under section 29 above dies—

(*a*) subsections (1) and (2) above shall apply as if for any reference to that person there were substituted a reference to any relative of the patient, and

(*b*) until the order is discharged or varied under those provisions the functions of the nearest relative under this Part of this Act and sections 66 and 69 below shall not be exercisable by any person.

(4) An order made on the ground specified in paragraph (*c*) or (*d*) of section 29(3) above shall, unless previously discharged under subsection (1) above, cease to have effect as follows—

(*a*) if—

(i) on the date of the order the patient was liable to be detained or subject to guardianship by virtue of a relevant application, order or direction; or

(ii) he becomes so liable or subject within the period of three months beginning with that date; or

(iii) he was a community patient on the date of the order,

it shall cease to have effect when he is discharged under section 23 above or 72 below or the relevant application, order or direction otherwise ceases to have effect (except as a result of his being transferred in pursuance of regulations under section 19 above);

(*b*) otherwise, it shall cease to have effect at the end of the period of three months beginning with the date of the order.

(4A) In subsection (4) above, reference to a relevant application, order or direction is to any of the following—

(*a*) an application for admission for treatment;

(*b*) a guardianship application;

(*c*) an order or direction under Part 3 of this Act (other than under section 35, 36 or 38).

(4B) An order made on the ground specified in paragraph (*a*), (*b*) or (*e*) of section 29(3) above shall—

(*a*) if a period was specified under section 29(5) above, cease to have effect on expiry of that period, unless previously discharged under subsection (1) above;

(*b*) if no such period was specified, remain in force until it is discharged under subsection (1) above.

(5) The discharge or variation under this section of an order made under section 29 above shall not affect the validity of anything previously done in pursuance of the order.

[Mental Health Act 1983, s 30 as amended by the Mental Health Act 2007, s 24 and Schs 2 and 3.]

*Supplemental*

7.8402 **31. Procedure on applications to county court** Rules of court which relate to applications authorised by this Part of this Act to be made to the county court may make provision—

(*a*) for the hearing and determination of such applications otherwise than in open court;

(*b*) for the admission on the hearing of such applications of evidence of such descriptions as may be specified in the rules notwithstanding anything to the contrary in any enactment or rule of law relating to the admissibility of evidence;

(*c*) for the visiting and interviewing of patients in private by or under the directions of the court.

[Mental Health Act 1983, s 31 amended by the Crime and Courts Act 2013, Sch 9.]

7.8403 **32. Regulations for purposes of Part II** (1) The Secretary of State may make regulations[1] for prescribing anything which, under this Part of this Act, is required or authorised to be prescribed, and otherwise for carrying this Part of this Act into full effect.

(2) Regulations under this section may in particular make provision—

(*a*) for prescribing the form of any application, recommendation, report, order, notice or other document to be made or given under this Part of this Act;

(*b*) for prescribing the manner in which any such application, recommendation, report, order, notice or other document may be proved, and for regulating the service of any such application, report, order or notice;

(*c*) for requiring such bodies as may be prescribed by the regulations to keep such registers or other records as may be so prescribed in respect of patients liable to be detained or subject to guardianship under this Part of this Act or community patients, and to furnish or make available to those patients, and their relatives, such written statements of their rights and powers under this Act as may be so prescribed;

(*d*) for the determination in accordance with the regulations of the age of any person whose exact age cannot be ascertained by reference to the registers kept under the Births and Deaths Registration Act 1953; and

(e) for enabling the functions under this Part of this Act of the nearest relative of a patient to be performed, in such circumstances and subject to such conditions (if any) as may be prescribed by the regulations, by any person authorised in that behalf by that relative;

and for the purposes of this Part of this Act any application, report or notice the service of which is regulated under paragraph (b) above shall be deemed to have been received by or furnished to the authority or person to whom it is authorised or required to be furnished, addressed or given if it is duly served in accordance with the regulations.

(3) Without prejudice to subsections (1) and (2) above, but subject to section 23(4) and (6) above, regulations[1] under this section may determine the manner in which functions under this Part of this Act of the managers of hospitals, local social services authorities, Local Health Board, Special Health Authorities, Primary Care Trusts, National Health Service trusts or NHS foundation trusts are to be exercised, and such regulations may in particular specify the circumstances in which, and the conditions subject to which, any such functions may be performed by officers of or other persons acting on behalf of those managers, boards, authorities and trusts.

[Mental Health Act 1983, s 32 as amended by the National Health Service and Community Care Act 1990, s 66, Sch 9, the Health Authorities Act 1995, s 2, Sch 1, the Mental Health (Patients in the Community) Act 1995, s 1, Sch 1, SI 2000/90, the Health and Social Care (Community Health and Standards) Act 2003, Sch 4, SI 2007/961 and the Mental Health Act 2007, s 45 and Schs 3 and 11.]

---

1 The Mental Health (Hospital, Guardianship and Treatment) (England) Regulations 2008, SI 2008/1184 amended by SI 2008/2560, SI 2012/1118 and SI 2013/235 and the Mental Health (Hospital, Guardianship, Community Treatment and Consent to Treatment) (Wales) Regulations 2008, SI 2008/2439 amended by SI 2013/235 have been made.

7.8404 **33. Special provisions as to wards of court** (1) An application for the admission to hospital of a minor who is a ward of court may be made under this Part of this Act with the leave of the court; and section 11(4) above shall not apply in relation to an application so made.

(2) Where a minor who is a ward of court is liable to be detained in a hospital by virtue of an application for admission under this Part of this Act or is a community patient, any power exercisable under this Part of this Act or under section 66 below in relation to the patient by his nearest relative shall be exercisable by or with the leave of the court.

(3) Nothing in this Part of this Act shall be construed as authorising the making of a guardianship application in respect of a minor who is a ward of court, or the transfer into guardianship of any such minor.

(4) Where a community treatment order has been made in respect of a minor who is a ward of court, the provisions of this Part of this Act relating to community treatment orders and community patients have effect in relation to the minor subject to any order which the court makes in the exercise of its wardship jurisdiction; but this does not apply as regards any period when the minor is recalled to hospital under section 17E above.

[Mental Health Act 1983, s 33 as amended by the Mental Health (Patients in the Community) Act 1995, s 1, Sch 1 and the Mental Health Act 2007, Sch 3.]

7.8405 **34. Interpretation of Part II** (1) In this Part of this Act—

"the appropriate practitioner" means—

(a) in the case of a patient who is subject to the guardianship of a person other than a local social services authority, the nominated medical attendant of the patient; and

(b) in any other case, the responsible clinician;

"the nominated medical attendant", in relation to a patient who is subject to the guardianship of a person other than a local social services authority, means the person appointed in pursuance of regulations made under section 9(2) above to act as the medical attendant of the patient;

"registered establishment" means an establishment which would not, apart from subsection (2) below, be a hospital for the purposes of this Part and which—

(a) in England, is a hospital as defined by section 275 of the National Health Service Act 2006 that is used for the carrying on of a regulated activity, within the meaning of Part 1 of the Health and Social Care Act 2008, which relates to the assessment or medical treatment of mental disorder and in respect of which a person is registered under Chapter 2 of that Part; and

(b) in Wales, is an establishment in respect of which a person is registered under Part 2 of the Care Standards Act 2000 as an independent hospital in which treatment or nursing (or both) are provided for persons liable to be detained under this Act;

"the responsible clinician" means—

(a) in relation to a patient liable to be detained by virtue of an application for admission for assessment or an application for admission for treatment, or a community patient, the approved clinician with overall responsibility for the patient's case;

(b) in relation to a patient subject to guardianship, the approved clinician authorised by the responsible local social services authority to act (either generally or in any particular case or for any particular purpose) as the responsible clinician;

(1A) *Repealed.*

(2) Except where otherwise expressly provided, this Part of this Act applies in relation to a registered establishment, being a home in respect of which the particulars of registration are for the time being entered in the separate part of the register kept for the purposes of section 23(5)(b) of the

Registered Homes Act 1984, as it applies in relation to a hospital, and references in this Part of this Act to a hospital, and any reference in this Act to a hospital to which this Part of this Act applies, shall be construed accordingly.**

(3) In relation to a patient who is subject to guardianship in pursuance of a guardianship application, any reference in this Part of this Act to the responsible local social services authority is a reference—

(*a*) where the patient is subject to the guardianship of a local social services authority, to that authority;

(*b*) where the patient is subject to the guardianship of a person other than a local social services authority, to the local social services authority for the area in which that person resides.

[Mental Health Act 1983, s 34 as amended by the Registered Homes Act 1984, s 57, Sch 1, the Mental Health (Patients in the Community) Act 1995, s 1, Sch 1, the Care Standards Act 2000, s 116, the Mental Health Act 2007, s 9 and Sch 11 and SI 2010/813.]

## PART III[1]

## PATIENTS CONCERNED IN CRIMINAL PROCEEDINGS OR UNDER SENTENCE

### *Remands to hospital*

7.8406 **35. Remand to hospital for report on accused's mental condition**[2] (1) Subject to the provisions of this section, the Crown Court or a magistrates' court may remand[3] an accused person to a hospital specified by the court for a report on his mental condition[4].

(2) For the purposes of this section an accused person is—

(*a*) in relation to the Crown Court, any person who is awaiting trial before the court for an offence punishable with imprisonment or who has been arraigned before the court for such an offence and has not yet been sentenced or otherwise dealt with for the offence on which he has been arraigned;

(*b*) in relation to a magistrates' court, any person who has been convicted by the court of an offence punishable on summary conviction with imprisonment and any person charged with such an offence if the court is satisfied that he did the act or made the omission charged or he has consented to the exercise by the court of the powers conferred by this section.

(3) Subject to subsection (4) below, the powers conferred by this section may be exercised if—

(*a*) the court is satisfied, on the written or oral evidence of a registered medical practitioner, that there is reason to suspect that the accused person is suffering from mental disorder; and

(*b*) the court is of the opinion that it would be impracticable for a report on his mental condition to be made if he were remanded on bail;

but those powers shall not be exercised by the Crown Court in respect of a person who has been convicted before the court if the sentence for the offence of which he has been convicted is fixed by law.

(4) The court shall not remand an accused person to a hospital under this section unless satisfied, on the written or oral evidence of the approved clinician who would be responsible for making the report or of some other person representing the managers of the hospital, that arrangements have been made for his admission to that hospital and for his admission to it within the period of seven days beginning with the date of the remand; and if the court is so satisfied it may, pending his admission, give directions for his conveyance to and detention in a place of safety.

(5) Where a court has remanded an accused person under this section it may further remand him if it appears to the court, on the written or oral evidence of the approved clinician responsible for making the report, that a further remand is necessary for completing the assessment of the accused person's mental condition.

(6) The power of further remanding an accused person under this section may be exercised by the court without his being brought before the court if he is represented by an authorised person who is given an opportunity of being heard.

(7) An accused person shall not be remanded or further remanded under this section for more than 28 days at a time or for more than 12 weeks in all; and the court may at any time terminate the remand if it appears to the court that it is appropriate to do so.

(8) An accused person remanded to hospital under this section shall be entitled to obtain at his own expense an independent report on his mental condition from a registered medical practitioner or approved clinician chosen by him and to apply to the court on the basis of it for his remand to be terminated under subsection (7) above.

(9) Where an accused person is remanded under this section—

(*a*) a constable or any other person directed to do so by the court shall convey the accused person to the hospital specified by the court within the period mentioned in subsection (4) above; and

(*b*) the managers of the hospital shall admit him within that period and thereafter detain him in accordance with the provisions of this section.

(10) If an accused person absconds from a hospital to which he has been remanded under this section, or while being conveyed to or from that hospital, he may be arrested[5] without warrant by any constable and shall, after being arrested, be brought as soon as practicable before the court that

remanded him; and the court may thereupon terminate the remand and deal with him in any way in which it could have dealt with him if he had not been remanded under this section.

[Mental Health Act 1983, s 35 as amended by the Mental Health Act 2007, s 10 and Sch 1 and the Legal Services Act 2007, Sch 21.]

1 Part III contains ss 35–55.

2 The purpose of an order under s 35 is to inform a court about issues relevant to the defendant's fitness to plead and disposal; it does not permit an order to be made for the purpose of obtaining evidence relevant to an issue at trial, eg his capacity to form the specific intent required by the offence: *R (on the application of M) v Kingston Crown Court, Crown Prosecution Service (Interested Party)* [2014] EWHC 2710 (Admin), [2015] All ER 1026, [2016] 1 WLR 1685, [2015] 1 Cr App Rep 27, 178 JP 438.

3 A general power to remand on bail or in custody for medical examination is given under s 30 of the Magistrates' Courts Act 1980 in PART I: MAGISTRATES' COURTS, PROCEDURE, ante.

4 For contents of note to be sent to provider of report or information, see the Criminal Procedure Rules, r 28.8, and for information to be supplied on admission to hospital or guardianship, r 28.9, in the *Key Materials*.

5 This power of arrest is preserved by the Police and Criminal Evidence Act 1984, s 26 and Sch 2.

7.8407 **36. Remand of accused person to hospital for treatment** (1) Subject to the provisions of this section, the Crown Court may, instead of remanding an accused person in custody, remand him to a hospital specified by the court if satisfied, on the written or oral evidence of two registered medical practitioners[1], that—

(*a*) he is suffering from mental disorder of a nature or degree which makes it appropriate for him to be detained in a hospital for medical treatment; and

(*b*) appropriate medical treatment is available for him.

(2) For the purposes of this section an accused person is any person who is in custody awaiting trial before the Crown Court for an offence punishable with imprisonment (other than an offence the sentence for which is fixed by law) or who at any time before sentence is in custody in the course of a trial before that court for such an offence.

(3) The court shall not remand an accused person under this section to a hospital unless it is satisfied, on the written or oral evidence of the approved clinician who would have overall responsibility for his case or of some other person representing the managers of the hospital, that arrangements have been made for his admission to that hospital and for his admission to it within the period of seven days beginning with the date of the remand; and if the court is so satisfied it may, pending his admission, give directions for his conveyance to and detention in a place of safety.

(4) Where a court has remanded an accused person under this section it may further remand him if it appears to the court, on the written or oral evidence of the responsible clinician, that a further remand is warranted.

(5) The power of further remanding an accused person under this section may be exercised by the court without his being brought before the court if he is represented by an authorised person who is given an opportunity of being heard.

(6) An accused person shall not be remanded or further remanded under this section for more than 28 days at a time or for more than 12 weeks in all; and the court may at any time terminate the remand if it appears to the court that it is appropriate to do so.

(7) An accused person remanded to hospital under this section shall be entitled to obtain at his own expense an independent report on his mental condition from a registered medical practitioner or approved clinician chosen by him and to apply to the court on the basis of it for his remand to be terminated under subsection (6) above.

(8) Subsections (9) and (10) of section 35 above shall have effect in relation to a remand under this section as they have effect in relation to a remand under that section.

[Mental Health Act 1983, s 36 as amended by the Mental Health Act 2007, ss 5, 10 and Sch 1 and the Legal Services Act 2007, Sch 21.]

1 For contents of note to be sent to provider of report or information, see the Criminal Procedure Rules, r 28.8, and for information to be supplied on admission to hospital or guardianship, r 28.9, in the *Key Materials*.

*Hospital and guardianship orders*

7.8408 **37. Powers[1] of courts to order hospital admission or guardianship** (1) Where a person is convicted before the Crown Court of an offence punishable with imprisonment other than an offence the sentence for which is fixed by law, or is convicted by a magistrates' court[2] of an offence punishable on summary conviction with imprisonment, and the conditions mentioned in subsection (2) below are satisfied, the court may by order authorise his admission to and detention in such hospital as may be specified in the order or, as the case may be, place him under the guardianship of a local social services authority or of such other person approved by a local social services authority as may be so specified[3].

(1A) In the case of an offence the sentence for which would otherwise fall to be imposed—

(*za*) under section 1(2B) or 1A(5) of the Prevention of Crime Act 1953,

(*a*) under section 51A(2) of the Firearms Act 1968,

(*aa*) under section 139(6B), 139A(5B) or 139AA(7) of the Criminal Justice Act 1988,

(*b*) under section 110(2) or 111(2) of the Powers of Criminal Courts (Sentencing) Act 2000[4],

(*ba*) under section 224A of the Criminal Justice Act 2003,

(*c*) under any of sections 225 to 228* of the Criminal Justice Act 2003, or (*d*) under section 29(4) or (6) of the Violent Crime Reduction Act 2006 (minimum sentences in certain cases of using someone to mind a weapon),

nothing in those provisions shall prevent a court from making an order under subsection (1) above for the admission of the offender to a hospital.

(1B) References in subsection (1A) above to a sentence falling to be imposed under any of the provisions mentioned in that subsection are to be read in accordance with section 305(4) of the Criminal Justice Act 2003.

(2) The conditions referred to in subsection (1) above are that—

(*a*) the court is satisfied, on the written or oral evidence of two registered medical practitioners, that the offender is suffering from mental disorder and that either—

(i) the mental disorder[5] from which the offender is suffering is of a nature or degree which makes it appropriate for him to be detained in a hospital for medical treatment and, appropriate medical treatment is available for him; or

(ii) in the case of an offender who has attained the age of 16 years, the mental disorder is of a nature or degree which warrants his reception into guardianship under this Act; and

(*b*) the court is of the opinion, having regard to all the circumstances including the nature of the offence and the character and antecedents of the offender, and to the other available methods of dealing with him, that the most suitable method of disposing of the case is by means of an order under this section.

(3) Where a person is charged before a magistrates' court[6] with any act or omission as an offence and the court would have power, on convicting him of that offence, to make an order under subsection (1) above in his case, then, if the court is satisfied that the accused did the act or made the omission charged, the court may, if it thinks fit, make such an order without convicting[7] him.

(4) An order for the admission of an offender to a hospital (in this Act referred to as "a hospital order") shall not be made under this section unless the court is satisfied on the written or oral evidence of the approved clinician who would have overall responsibility for his case or of some other person representing the managers of the hospital that arrangements have been made for his admission to that hospital, and for his admission to it within the period of 28 days beginning with the date of the making of such an order; and the court may, pending his admission within that period, give such directions as it thinks fit for his conveyance to and detention in a place of safety[8].

(5) If within the said period of 28 days it appears to the Secretary of State that by reason of an emergency or other special circumstances it is not practicable for the patient to be received into the hospital specified in the order, he may give directions for the admission of the patient to such other hospital as appears to be appropriate instead of the hospital so specified; and where such directions are given—

(*a*) the Secretary of State shall cause the person having the custody of the patient to be informed, and

(*b*) the hospital order shall have effect as if the hospital specified in the directions were substituted for the hospital specified in the order.

(6) An order placing an offender under the guardianship of a local social services authority or of any other person (in this Act referred to as "a guardianship order") shall not be made under this section unless the court is satisfied that that authority or person is willing to receive the offender into guardianship.

(7) *Repealed.*

(8) Where an order is made under this section, the court shall not—

(*a*) pass sentence of imprisonment or impose a fine or make community order (within the meaning of Part 12 of the Criminal Justice Act 2003) or a youth rehabilitation order (within the meaning of Part 1 of the Criminal Justice and Immigration Act 2008) in respect of the offence,

(*b*) if the order under this section is a hospital order, make a referral order (within the meaning of the Powers of Criminal Courts (Sentencing) Act 2000) in respect of the offence, or

(*b*) make in respect of the offender an order under section 150 of that Act (binding over of parent or guardian),

but the court may make any other order which it has power to make apart from this section; and for the purposes of this subsection "sentence of imprisonment" includes any sentence or order for detention.

[Mental Health Act 1983, s 37 as amended by the Crime (Sentences) Act 1997, Schs 4 and 6, the Crime and Disorder Act 1998, Sch 8, Youth Justice and Criminal Evidence Act 1999, Sch 4, the Powers of Criminal Courts (Sentencing) Act 2000, Sch 9, the Criminal Justice Act 2003, Sch 32, the Violent Crime Reduction Act 2006, Schs 1 and 5, the Mental Health Act 2007, s 10 and Sch 1, the Criminal Justice and Immigration Act 2008, Schs 4 and 28, the Legal Aid, Sentencing and Punishment of Offenders Act 2012, Sch 26 and the Criminal Justice and Courts Act 2015, Sch 5.]

---

* **Words substituted by the Criminal Justice and Immigration Act 2008, Sch 26 from a date to be appointed.**

1 See PART III: SENTENCING, para 3.132 for guidance on the making of orders under s 37 and consideration of restriction orders under s 41.

2 For contents of note to be sent to provider of report or information, see the Criminal Procedure Rules, r 28.8, and for information to be supplied on admission to hospital or guardianship, r 28.9, in the *Key Materials*.

3 This power to specify a hospital includes power to specify a hospital unit (Crime (Sentences) Act 1997, s 47, in PART III: SENTENCING, ante).

4 See PART III: SENTENCING, ante.

5 For the meaning of "mental disorder", "severe mental impairment", "mental impairment" and "psychopathic disorder", see s 1, ante.

6 This includes a youth court (*R (on the application of P) v Barking Youth Court* [2002] EWHC 734 (Admin), [2002] 2 Cr App Rep 294, 166 JP 641, [2002] Crim LR 657.

7 It follows that as there is no requirement for a trial, the provisions of s 20 of the Magistrates' Courts Act 1980 (procedure where summary trial appears more suitable for an offence triable either way) do not apply. However, the circumstances in which it will be appropriate to exercise this power will be very rare and will usually require the consent of those acting for the accused if he is under a disability so that he cannot be tried (*R v Lincolnshire (Kesteven) Justices, ex p O'Connor* [1983] 1 All ER 901, [1983] 1 WLR 335). Magistrates may still proceed to act under sub-s (3) even where the defendant has elected to go for trial by jury (*R v Ramsgate Justices, ex p Kazmarek* (1984) 149 JP 16). However, a magistrates' court has no jurisdiction under s 37(3) to make an order under sub-s (1) in respect of a defendant who is charged with an offence that is triable only on indictment (*R v Chippenham Magistrates' Court, ex p Thompson* (1995) 160 JP 207). As regards s 4A of the Criminal Procedure (Insanity) Act 1964 which makes analogous provisions relating to trial on indictment, it has been held that there is no incompatibility between procedures for determining whether the defendant "did the act" and Article 6 of the European Convention on Human Rights. The criminal charge provisions of Article 6 do not apply as these proceedings cannot result in a conviction (*R v M* [2001] EWCA Crim 2024, [2002] 1 Cr App Rep 25) nor punishment (*Re H (Tyrone)* [2002] EWCA Crim 2988).

8 For meaning of "place of safety", see s 55(1), post.

7.8409 **38. Interim hospital orders** (1) Where a person is convicted before the Crown Court of an offence punishable with imprisonment (other than an offence the sentence for which is fixed by law) or is convicted by a magistrates' court of an offence punishable on summary conviction with imprisonment and the court before or by which he is convicted is satisfied, on the written or oral evidence of two registered medical practitioners—

(*a*) that the offender is suffering from mental disorder; and

(*b*) that there is reason to suppose that the mental disorder from which the offender is suffering is such that it may be appropriate for a hospital order to be made in his case,

the court may, before making a hospital order or dealing with him in some other way, make an order (in this Act referred to as "an interim hospital order") authorising his admission to such hospital as may be specified in the order and his detention there in accordance with this section[1].

(2) In the case of an offender who is subject to an interim hospital order the court may make a hospital order without his being brought before the court if he is represented by an authorised person who is given an opportunity of being heard.

(3) At least one of the registered medical practitioners whose evidence is taken into account under subsection (1) above shall be employed at the hospital which is to be specified in the order.

(4) An interim hospital order shall not be made for the admission of an offender to a hospital unless the court is satisfied, on the written or oral evidence of the approved clinician who would have overall responsibility for his case or of some other person representing the managers of the hospital, that arrangements have been made for his admission to that hospital and for his admission to it within the period of 28 days beginning with the date of the order; and if the court is so satisfied the court may, pending his admission, give directions for his conveyance to and detention in a place of safety.

(5) An interim hospital order—

(*a*) shall be in force for such period, not exceeding 12 weeks, as the court may specify when making the order; but

(*b*) may be renewed for further periods of not more than 28 days at a time if it appears to the court, on the written or oral evidence of the responsible clinician, that the continuation of the order is warranted;

but no such order shall continue in force for more than 12 months in all and the court shall terminate the order if it makes a hospital order in respect of the offender or decides after considering the written or oral evidence of the responsible clinician to deal with the offender in some other way.

(6) The power of renewing an interim hospital order may be exercised without the offender being brought before the court if he is represented by counsel or a solicitor and his counsel or solicitor is given an opportunity of being heard.

(7) If an offender absconds from a hospital in which he is detained in pursuance of an interim hospital order, or while being conveyed to or from such a hospital, he may be arrested[2] without warrant by a constable and shall, after being arrested, be brought as soon as practicable before the court that made the order; and the court may thereupon terminate the order and deal with him in any way in which it could have dealt with him if no such order had been made.

[Mental Health Act 1983, s 38 as amended by the Crime (Sentences) Act 1997, s 49, the Mental Health Act 2007, s 10 and Sch 1 and the Legal Services Act 2007, Sch 21.]

---

1 For contents of note to be sent to provider of report or information, see the Criminal Procedure Rules, r 28.8, and for information to be supplied on admission to hospital or guardianship, r 28.9, in the *Key Materials*.

2 This power of arrest is preserved by the Police and Criminal Evidence Act 1984, s 26 and Sch 2.

7.8410 **39. Information as to hospitals** (1) Where a court is minded to make a hospital order or interim hospital order in respect of any person it may request—

(*a*) the clinical commissioning group or Local Health Board for the area in which that person resides or last resided; or

(*b*) the National Health Service Commissioning Board or the National Assembly for Wales or any other clinical commissioning group or Local Health Board that appears to the court to be appropriate, to furnish[1] the court with such information as that clinical commissioning group or Local Health Board or the National Health Service Commissioning Board or the National Assembly for Wales have or can reasonably obtain with respect to the hospital or hospitals (if any) in their area or elsewhere at which arrangements could be made for the admission of that person in pursuance of the order, and that clinical commissioning group or Local Health Board or the National Health Service Commissioning Board or the National Assembly for Wales shall comply with any such request

(1ZA) A request under this section to the National Health Service Commissioning Board may relate only to services or facilities the provision of which the Board arranges.

(1A) In relation to a person who has not attained the age of 18 years, subsection (1) above shall have effect as if the reference to the making of a hospital order included a reference to a remand under section 35 or 36 above or the making of an order under section 44 below.

(1B) Where the person concerned has not attained the age of 18 years, the information which may be requested under subsection (1) above includes, in particular, information about the availability of accommodation or facilities designed so as to be specially suitable for patients who have not attained the age of 18 years.

(2) *Repealed.*

[Mental Health Act 1983, s 39 as amended by the Health Authorities Act 1995, Schs 1 and 3, the National Health Service Reform and Health Care Professions Act 2002, Sch 2, SI 2007/961, the Mental Health Act 2007, s 31 and the Health and Social Care Act 2012, Sch 5.]

---

[1] In cases where it is desired to make use of this provision, the Clerk to the Justices should contact the Regional Medical Officer for the Regional Health Authority covering the area from which the offender appears to come; see Home Office Circular No 69/1983, dated 19 August 1983.

7.8411 **39A. Information to facilitate guardianship orders** Where a court is minded to make a guardianship order in respect of any offender, it may request the local social services authority for the area in which the offender resides or last resided, or any other local social services authority that appears to the court to be appropriate—

(*a*) to inform the court whether it or any other person approved by it is willing to receive the offender into guardianship; and

(*b*) if so, to give such information as it reasonably can about how it or the other person could be expected to exercise in relation to the offender the powers conferred by section 40(2) below;

and that authority shall comply with any such request.

[Mental Health Act 1983, s 39A as inserted by the Criminal Justice Act 1991, s 27(1).]

7.8412 **40. Effect of hospital orders, guardianship orders and interim hospital orders**

(1) A hospital order shall be sufficient authority—

(*a*) for a constable, an approved mental health professional or any other person directed to do so by the court to convey the patient to the hospital specified in the order within a period of 28 days; and

(*b*) for the managers of the hospital to admit him at any time within that period and thereafter detain him in accordance with the provisions of this Act.

(2) A guardianship order shall confer on the authority or person named in the order as guardian the same powers as a guardianship application made and accepted under Part II[1] of this Act.

(3) Where an interim hospital order is made in respect of an offender—

(*a*) a constable or any other person directed to do so by the court shall convey the offender to the hospital specified in the order within the period mentioned in section 38(4) above; and

(*b*) the managers of the hospital shall admit him within that period and thereafter detain him in accordance with the provisions of section 38 above.

(4) A patient who is admitted to a hospital in pursuance of a hospital order, or placed under guardianship by a guardianship order, shall, subject to the provisions of this subsection, be treated for the purposes of the provisions of this Act mentioned in Part I of Schedule 1 to this Act as if he had been so admitted or placed on the date of the order in pursuance of an application for admission for treatment or a guardianship application, as the case may be, duly made under Part II[1] of this Act, but subject to any modifications of those provisions specified in that Part of that Schedule.

(5) Where a patient is admitted to a hospital in pursuance of a hospital order, or placed under guardianship by a guardianship order, any previous application, hospital order or guardianship order by virtue of which he was liable to be detained in a hospital or subject to guardianship shall cease to have effect; but if the first-mentioned order, or the conviction on which it was made, is quashed on appeal, this subsection shall not apply and section 22 above shall have effect as if during any period for which the patient was liable to be detained or subject to guardianship under the order, he had been detained in custody as mentioned in that section.

(6) Where—

(*a*) a patient admitted to a hospital in pursuance of a hospital order is absent without leave;

(*b*) a warrant to arrest him has been issued under section 72 of the Criminal Justice Act 1967;

(*c*) he is held pursuant to the warrant in any country or territory other than the United Kingdom, any of the Channel Islands and the Isle of Man,

he shall be treated as having been taken into custody under section 18 above on first being so held.

[Mental Health Act 1983, s 40 as amended by the Mental Health (Patients in the Community) Act 1995, s 2 and the Mental Health Act 2007, Sch 2.]

[1] The provisions of Pt II of the Act are not included in this work.

*Restriction orders*

7.8413 **41. Power[1] of higher courts to restrict discharge from hospital** (1) Where a hospital order is made in respect of an offender by the Crown Court, and it appears to the court, having regard to the nature of the offence, the antecedents of the offender and the risk of his committing further offences if set at large, that it is necessary for the protection of the public from serious harm so to do[2], the court may, subject to the provisions of this section, further order that the offender shall be subject to the special restrictions set out in this section; and an order under this section shall be known as "a restriction order".

(2) A restriction order shall not be made in the case of any person unless at least one of the registered medical practitioners whose evidence is taken into account by the court under section 37(2)(*a*) above has given evidence orally before the court[3].

(3) The special restrictions applicable to a patient in respect of whom a restriction order is in force are as follows—

(*a*) none of the provisions of Part II[4] of this Act relating to the duration, renewal and expiration of authority for the detention of patients shall apply, and the patient shall continue to be liable to be detained by virtue of the relevant hospital order until he is duly discharged under the said Part II[4] or absolutely discharged under section 42, 73, 74 or 75 below;

(*aa*) none of the provisions of Part II of this Act relating to community treatment orders and community patients shall apply;

(*b*) no application shall be made to the appropriate tribunal in respect of a patient under section 66 or 69(1) below;

(*c*) the following powers shall be exercisable only with the consent of the Secretary of State, namely—

(i) power to grant leave of absence to the patient under section 17 above;

(ii) power to transfer the patient in pursuance of regulations under section 19 above or in pursuance of subsection (3) of that section; and

(iii) power to order the discharge of the patient under section 23 above;

and if leave of absence is granted under the said section 17 power to recall the patient under that section shall vest in the Secretary of State as well as the responsible clinician; and

(*d*) the power of the Secretary of State to recall the patient under the said section 17 and power to take the patient into custody and return him under section 18 above may be exercised at any time;

and in relation to any such patient section 40(4) above shall have effect as if it referred to Part II of Schedule 1 to this Act instead of Part I of that Schedule.

(4) A hospital order shall not cease to have effect under section 40(5) above if a restriction order in respect of the patient is in force at the material time.

(5) Where a restriction order in respect of a patient ceases to have effect while the relevant hospital order continues in force, the provisions of section 40 above and Part I of Schedule 1 to this Act shall apply to the patient as if he had been admitted to the hospital in pursuance of a hospital order (without a restriction order) made on the date on which the restriction order ceased to have effect.

(6) While a person is subject to a restriction order the responsible clinician shall at such intervals (not exceeding one year) as the Secretary of State may direct examine and report to the Secretary of State on that person; and every report shall contain such particulars as the Secretary of State may require.

[Mental Health Act 1983, s 41 as amended by the Mental Health (Patients in the Community) Act 1995, Sch 1, the Crime (Sentences) Act 1997, s 49, the Mental Health Act 2007, s 10 and Sch 11 and SI 2008/2833.]

[1] The provisions of Pt II of the Act are not included in this work. See also *R v Birch* (1989) 90 Cr App Rep 78, where the principles applicable to the imposition of a restriction order were considered.

[2] Where two psychiatrists recommend a hospital order with a restriction order this is not a sufficient reason, without more, to follow that course:

> "51 It is important to emphasise that the judge must carefully consider all the evidence in each case and not, as some of the early cases have suggested, feel circumscribed by the psychiatric opinions. A judge must therefore consider, where the conditions in section 37(2)(a) are met, what is the appropriate disposal. In considering that wider question the matters to which a judge will invariably have to have regard to include (1) the extent to which the offender needs treatment for the mental disorder from which the offender suffers, (2) the extent to which the offending is attributable to the mental disorder, (3) the extent to which punishment is required and (4) the protection of the public including the regime for deciding release and the regime after release. There must always be sound reasons for departing from the usual course of imposing a penal sentence and the judge must set these out.
>
> 52 As to the fourth of the considerations to which we have referred, Lord Bingham of Cornhill, at para 23 of his judgment in *R v Drew* [2003] 1 WLR 1213, [2003] UKHL 25, which was decided prior to the

amendment of section 45A, accepted that there was force in the submission of the Secretary of State that where the medical criteria were met, judges had given less than adequate weight to the conditions governing release. He was, at that time, unpersuaded that a change in practice was desirable. In the light of the amendments to section 45A, the observations of Hughes LJ which we have referred at para 48(ii) and the general evidence before us, we consider that a judge when sentencing must now pay very careful attention to the different effect in each case of the conditions applicable to and after release. As is shown by the case of *R v Teasdale* [2012] MHLR 387 to which we have referred at para 48(iv), this consideration may be one matter leading to the imposition of a hospital order under section 37/41.

53 The fact that two psychiatrists are of the opinion that a hospital order with restrictions under section 37/41 is the right disposal is therefore never a reason on its own to make such an order. The judge must first consider all the relevant circumstances, including the four issues we have set out in the preceding paragraphs and then consider the alternatives in the order in which we set them out in the next paragraph", per Lord Thomas CJ in *Regina v Vowles (and others)* [2015] EWCA Crim 45, [2015] EWCA Civ 56, [2015] 1 WLR 5131."

Before a restriction order can be made there must be evidence which points to the likely fact that if the offender were released in the relatively near future he would constitute a danger to other members of the public (*R v Courtney* [1988] Crim LR 130). See also *R v Kearney* [2002] EWCA Crim 2772, [2003] 2 Cr App Rep (S) 85 (it is not part of the justification for a restriction order that it might help or add to the protection of the offender himself). It is not necessary, however, that the risk itself be serious or significant; thus, where, in relation to a defendant convicted of burglary, there was a risk that if confronted by a householder he might cause serious harm, because he suffered from a psychosis that was not controlled and his predilection for drugs and alcohol might well lead him to behave violently in such circumstances which could lead to the infliction of serious harm, the court was entitled to make a restriction order (*R v Golding* [2006] EWCA Crim 1965, [2007] 1 Cr App Rep (S) 486, [2007] Crim LR 170). See also *R v Chiles (Raymond)* [2012] EWCA Crim 196, [2012] MHLR 60, where it was held that the judge had been wrong to take into account the "fluctuating state" of the health service, but had nonetheless been right to make a restriction in respect of a defendant suffering from paranoid schizophrenia who had set fire to his house to escape noises in his head intending only to cause sufficient damage to require his relocation and not to destroy the building or endanger others (though life had in fact been endangered). This was a severe and enduring illness. The defendant had residual symptoms and only limited insight into his condition. Past behaviour was a good predictor of future behaviour and the existence of a moderate risk of future fire-setting was a real concern.

[3] The evidence cannot be received by telephone: *R v Clarke* [2015] EWCA Crim 2192, [2016] 1 Cr App R (S) 52.

[4] See PART III: SENTENCING, para 3.132 for guidance on the making of orders under s 37 and consideration of restriction orders under s 41.

**7.8414 42. Powers of Secretary of State in respect of patients subject to restriction orders**

(1) If the Secretary of State is satisfied that in the case of any patient a restriction order is no longer required for the protection of the public from serious harm, he may direct that the patient shall cease to be subject to the special restrictions set out in section 41(3) above; and where the Secretary of State so directs, the restriction order shall cease to have effect, and section 41(5) above shall apply accordingly.

(2) At any time while a restriction order is in force in respect of a patient, the Secretary of State may, if he thinks fit, by warrant discharge the patient from hospital, either absolutely or subject to conditions; and where a person is absolutely discharged under this subsection, he shall thereupon cease to be liable to be detained by virtue of the relevant hospital order, and the restriction order shall cease to have effect accordingly.

(3) The Secretary of State may at any time during the continuance in force of a restriction order in respect of a patient who has been conditionally discharged under subsection (2) above by warrant recall[1] the patient to such hospital as may be specified in the warrant.

(4) Where a patient is recalled as mentioned in subsection (3) above—

(*a*) if the hospital specified in the warrant is not the hospital from which the patient was conditionally discharged, the hospital order and the restriction order shall have effect as if the hospital specified in the warrant were substituted for the hospital specified in the hospital order;

(*b*) in any case, the patient shall be treated for the purposes of section 18 above as if he had absented himself without leave from the hospital specified in the warrant.

(5) If a restriction order in respect of a patient ceases to have effect after the patient has been conditionally discharged under this section, the patient shall, unless previously recalled under subsection (3) above, be deemed to be absolutely discharged on the date when the order ceases to have effect, and shall cease to be liable to be detained by virtue of the relevant hospital order accordingly.

(6) The Secretary of State may, if satisfied that the attendance at any place in Great Britain of a patient who is subject to a restriction order is desirable in the interests of justice or for the purposes of any public inquiry, direct him to be taken to that place; and where a patient is directed under this subsection to be taken to any place he shall, unless the Secretary of State otherwise directs, be kept in custody while being so taken, while at that place and while being taken back to the hospital in which he is liable to be detained.

[Mental Health Act 1983, s 42 as amended by the Mental Health Act 2007, Sch 11.]

---

[1] "Recall" may refer not only to a physical recall to hospital but also to the reinstatement of a regime of control under s 41 such as in respect of a patient previously discharged conditionally by a Mental Health Review Tribunal but subsequently readmitted under s 3 of the Act (*R v Secretary of State for the Home Department, ex p D* (1996) Times, 10 May, CA).

**7.8415 43. Power of magistrates' courts to commit for restriction order** (1) If in the case of a person of or over the age of 14 years who is convicted by a magistrates' court of an offence punishable on summary conviction with imprisonment[1]—

(*a*) the conditions which under section 37(1) above are required to be satisfied for the making of a hospital order are satisfied in respect of the offender; but (*b*) it appears to the court, having regard to the nature of the offence, the antecedents[2] of the offender and the risk of his committing further offences if set at large, that if a hospital order is made a restriction order should also be made[3],

the court may, instead of making a hospital order or dealing with him in any other manner, commit him in custody to the Crown Court[4] to be dealt with in respect of the offence[5].

(2) Where an offender is committed to the Crown Court under this section, the Crown Court shall inquire into the circumstances of the case and may—

(*a*) if that court would have power so to do under the foregoing provisions of this Part of this Act upon the conviction of the offender before that court of such an offence as is described in section 37(1) above, make a hospital order in his case, with or without a restriction order;

(*b*) if the court does not make such an order, deal with the offender in any other manner in which the magistrates' court might have dealt with him.

(3) The Crown Court shall have the same power to make orders under sections 35, 36 and 38 above in the case of a person committed to the court under this section as the Crown Court has under those sections in the case of an accused person within the meaning of section 35 or 36 above or of a person convicted before that court as mentioned in section 38 above.

(4) The powers of a magistrates' court under section 3 or 3B of the Powers of Criminal Courts (Sentencing) Act 2000 (which enable such a court to commit an offender to the Crown Court where the court is of the opinion, or it appears to the court, as mentioned in the section in question) shall also be exercisable by a magistrates' court where it is of that opinion (or it so appears to it) unless a hospital order is made in the offender's case with a restriction order

(5) *Repealed.*

[Mental Health Act 1983, s 43 as amended by the Powers of Criminal Courts (Sentencing) Act 2000, Sch 9 and the Criminal Justice Act 2003, Schs 3 and 37.]

1 This means, so punishable in the case of an adult. Statutory restrictions imposed on the imprisonment of young offenders have no application in construing this expression (s 54(2), post).

2 Under s 38 of the Magistrates' Courts Act 1980 before it was substituted by the Criminal Justice Act 1991, "antecedents" was not limited to previous convictions.

3 The provisions of this section supply the only means whereby a magistrates' court can secure that an order is made restricting an offender's discharge.

4 For selection of the most convenient location of the Crown Court, see the Directions of the Lord Chief Justice, paras 8 and 9, in PART I: MAGISTRATES' COURTS, PROCEDURE, ante.

5 See the Criminal Procedure Rules, r 28.10, in the *Key Materials*.

7.8416 **44. Committal to hospital under s 43** (1) Where an offender is committed under section 43(1) above and the magistrates' court by which he is committed is satisfied on written or oral evidence that arrangements have been made for the admission of the offender to a hospital in the event of an order being made under this section, the court may, instead of committing him in custody, by order direct him to be admitted to that hospital, specifying it, and to be detained there until the case is disposed of by the Crown Court, and may give such directions as it thinks fit for his production from the hospital to attend the Crown Court by which his case is to be dealt with[1].

(2) The evidence required by subsection (1) above shall be given by the approved clinician who would have overall responsibility for the offender's case or by some other person representing the managers of the hospital in question.*

(3) The power to give directions under section 37(4) above, section 37(5) above and section 40(1) above shall apply in relation to an order under this section as they apply in relation to a hospital order, but as if references to the period of 28 days mentioned in section 40(1) above were omitted; and subject as aforesaid an order under this section shall, until the offender's case is disposed of by the Crown Court, have the same effect as a hospital order together with a restriction order.

[Mental Health Act 1983, s 44 as amended by the Mental Health Act 2007, s 10 and Sch 11.]

1 For contents of note to be sent to provider of report or information, see the Criminal Procedure Rules, r 28.8, and for information to be supplied on admission to hospital or guardianship, r 28.9, in the *Key Materials*.

7.8417 **45. Appeals from magistrates' courts** (1) Where on the trial of an information charging a person with an offence a magistrates' court makes a hospital order or guardianship order in respect of him without convicting him, he shall have the same right of appeal against the order as if it had been made on his conviction[1]; and on any such appeal the Crown Court shall have the same powers as if the appeal had been against both conviction and sentence.

(2) An appeal by a child or young person with respect to whom any such order has been made, whether the appeal is against the order or against the finding upon which the order was made, may be brought by him or by his parent or guardian on his behalf.

[Mental Health Act 1983, s 45.]

1 See the Magistrates' Courts Act 1980, ss 108–114 and the Criminal Procedure Rules, Part 34, in the *Key Materials*.

*Hospital and limitation directions*

7.8418 **45A. Power of higher courts to direct hospital admission** (1) This section applies where, in the case of a person convicted before the Crown Court of an offence the sentence for which is not fixed by law—

(*a*) the conditions mentioned in subsection (2) below are fulfilled; and (*b*) the court considers making a hospital order in respect of him before deciding to impose a sentence of imprisonment ("the relevant sentence") in respect of the offence.

(2) The conditions referred to in subsection (1) above are that the court is satisfied, on the written or oral evidence of two registered medical practitioners—

(*a*) that the offender is suffering from mental disorder;

(*b*) that the mental disorder from which the offender is suffering is of a nature or degree which makes it appropriate for him to be detained in a hospital for medical treatment; and

(*c*) that appropriate medical treatment is available for him.

(3) The court may give both of the following directions, namely—

(*a*) a direction that, instead of being removed to and detained in a prison, the offender be removed to and detained in such hospital[1] as may be specified in the direction (in this Act referred to as a "hospital direction"); and

(*b*) a direction that the offender be subject to the special restrictions set out in section 41 above (in this Act referred to as a "limitation direction")[2] .

(4) A hospital direction and a limitation direction shall not be given in relation to an offender unless at least one of the medical practitioners whose evidence is taken into account by the court under subsection (2) above has given evidence orally before the court.

(5) A hospital direction and a limitation direction shall not be given in relation to an offender unless the court is satisfied on the written or oral evidence of the approved clinician who would have overall responsibility for his case, or of some other person representing the managers of the hospital that arrangements have been made—

(*a*) for his admission to that hospital; and

(*b*) for his admission to it within the period of 28 days beginning with the day of the giving of such directions;

and the court may, pending his admission within that period, give such directions as it thinks fit for his conveyance to and detention in a place of safety.

(6) If within the said period of 28 days it appears to the Secretary of State that by reason of an emergency or other special circumstances it is not practicable for the patient to be received into the hospital specified in the hospital direction, he may give instructions for the admission of the patient to such other hospital as appears to be appropriate instead of the hospital so specified.

(7) Where such instructions are given—

(*a*) the Secretary of State shall cause the person having the custody of the patient to be informed, and

(*b*) the hospital direction shall have effect as if the hospital specified in the instructions were substituted for the hospital specified in the hospital direction.

(8) Section 38(1) and (5) and section 39 above shall have effect as if any reference to the making of a hospital order included a reference to the giving of a hospital direction and a limitation direction.

(9) A hospital direction and a limitation direction given in relation to an offender shall have effect not only as regards the relevant sentence but also (so far as applicable) as regards any other sentence of imprisonment imposed on the same or a previous occasion.

(10) *Repealed.*

(11) *Repealed.*

[Mental Health Act 1983, s 45A as inserted by the Crime (Sentences) Act 1997, s 46 and amended by the Criminal Justice Act 2003, Schs 32 and 37 and the Mental Health Act 2007, ss 4, 10 and Sch 1.]

---

1 This power to specify a hospital includes power to specify a hospital unit (Crime (Sentences) Act 1997, s 47, in PART III: SENTENCING, ante).

2 Section 45A(3) in the restrictions under s 41, does not incorporate into the court's consideration those conditions set out at s 41(1) as a pre-requisite for making an order under s 45A: *R v Poole* [2014] EWCA Crim 1641, [2015] 1 Cr App R (S) 2.

7.8419 **45B. Effect of hospital and limitation directions** (1) A hospital direction and a limitation direction shall be sufficient authority—

(*a*) for a constable or any other person directed to do so by the court to convey the patient to the hospital specified in the hospital direction within a period of 28 days; and

(*b*) for the managers of the hospital to admit him at any time within that period and thereafter detain him in accordance with the provisions of this Act.

(2) With respect to any person—

(*a*) a hospital direction shall have effect as a transfer direction; and

(*b*) a limitation direction shall have effect as a restriction direction.

(3) While a person is subject to a hospital direction and a limitation direction the responsible clinician shall at such intervals (not exceeding one year) as the Secretary of State may direct examine and report to the Secretary of State on that person; and every report shall contain such particulars as the Secretary of State may require.

[Mental Health Act 1983, s 45B as inserted by the Crime (Sentences) Act 1997, s 46 and amended by the Mental Health Act 2007, ss 4, 10 and Sch 1.]

*Transfer to hospital of prisoners, etc*

7.8420 **47. Removal to hospital of persons serving sentences of imprisonment, etc** (1) If in the case of a person serving a sentence of imprisonment the Secretary of State is satisfied, by reports from at least two registered medical practitioners—

(*a*) that the said person is suffering from mental disorder; and

(*b*) that the mental disorder from which that person is suffering is of a nature or degree which makes it appropriate for him to be detained in a hospital for medical treatment; and

(*c*) that appropriate medical treatment is available for him;

the Secretary of State may, if he is of the opinion having regard to the public interest and all the circumstances that it is expedient so to do, by warrant direct that that person be removed to and detained in such hospital[1] as may be specified in the direction; and a direction under this section shall be known as "a transfer direction".

(2) A transfer direction shall cease to have effect at the expiration of the period of 14 days beginning with the date on which it is given unless within that period the person with respect to whom it was given has been received into the hospital specified in the direction.

(3) A transfer direction with respect to any person shall have the same effect as a hospital order made in his case.

(4) *Repealed.*

(5) References in this Part of this Act to a person serving a sentence[2] of imprisonment include references—

(*a*) to a person detained in pursuance of any sentence or order for detention made by a court in criminal proceedings or service disciplinary proceedings (other than an order made in consequence of a finding of insanity or unfitness to stand trial) or a sentence of service detention within the meaning of the Armed Forces Act 2006);

(*b*) to a person committed to custody under section 115(3) of the Magistrates' Courts Act 1980[3] (which relates to persons who fail to comply with an order to enter into recognisances to keep the peace or be of good behaviour); and

(*c*) to a person committed by a court to a prison or other institution to which the Prison Act 1952 applies in default of payment of any sum adjudged to be paid on his conviction.

(6) In subsection (5)(*a*) "service disciplinary proceedings" means proceedings in respect of a service offence within the meaning of the Armed Forces Act 2006.

[Mental Health Act 1983, s 47 as amended by the Crime (Sentences) Act 1997, s 49 and Sch 6, the Domestic Violence, Crime and Victims Act 2004, Sch 10, the Armed Forces Act 2006, Sch 16 and the Mental Health Act 2007, s 10 and Sch 1.]

1 This power to specify a hospital includes power to specify a hospital unit (Crime (Sentences) Act 1997, s 47, in PART III: SENTENCING, ante).

2 This shall not be construed as references to a person subject to an order of the Court of Appeal under ss 6 and 14 of the Criminal Appeal Act 1968.

3 See PART I: MAGISTRATES' COURTS, PROCEDURE, ante.

7.8421 **48. Removal to hospital of other prisoners** (1) If in the case of a person to whom this section applies the Secretary of State is satisfied by the same reports as are required for the purposes of section 47 above that—

(*a*) that person is suffering from mental disorder of a nature or degree which makes it appropriate for him to be detained in a hospital for medical treatment;

(*b*) he is in urgent need of such treatment; and

(*c*) appropriate medical treatment is available for him;

the Secretary of State shall have the same power of giving a transfer direction in respect of him under that section as if he were serving a sentence of imprisonment.

(2) This section applies to the following persons, that is to say—

(*a*) persons detained in a prison or remand centre*, not being persons serving a sentence of imprisonment or persons falling within the following paragraphs of this subsection;

(*b*) persons remanded in custody by a magistrates' court;

(*c*) civil prisoners, that is to say, persons committed by a court to prison for a limited term, who are not persons falling to be dealt with under section 47 above;

(*d*) persons detained under the Immigration Act 1971 or under section 62 of the Nationality, Immigration and Asylum Act 2002 (detention by the Secretary of State).

(3) Subsections (2) and (3) of section 47 above shall apply for the purposes of this section and of any transfer direction given by virtue of this section as they apply for the purposes of that section and of any transfer direction under that section.

[Mental Health Act 1983, s 48 as amended by the Nationality, Immigration and Asylum Act 2002, s 62, the Statute Law (Repeals) Act 2004 and the Mental Health Act 2007, s 5 and Sch 1.]

* **Words repealed by the Criminal Justice and Court Services Act 2000, Sch 7 from a date to be appointed.**

7.8422 **49. Restriction on discharge of prisoners removed to hospital** (1) Where a transfer direction is given in respect of any person, the Secretary of State, if he thinks fit, may by warrant further direct that that person shall be subject to the special restrictions set out in section 41 above; and where the Secretary of State gives a transfer direction in respect of any such person as is described in paragraph (*a*) or (*b*) of section 48(2) above, he shall also give a direction under this section applying those restrictions to him.

(2) A direction under this section shall have the same effect as a restriction order made under section 41 above and shall be known as "a restriction direction".

(3) While a person is subject to a restriction direction the responsible clinician shall at such intervals (not exceeding one year) as the Secretary of State may direct examine and report to the Secretary of State on that person; and every report shall contain such particulars as the Secretary of State may require.

[Mental Health Act 1983, s 49 as amended by the Mental Health Act 2007, s 10.]

7.8423 **50. Further provisions as to prisoners under sentence** (1) Where a transfer direction and a restriction direction have been given in respect of a person serving a sentence of imprisonment and before his release date the Secretary of State is notified by the responsible clinician, any other approved clinician or the appropriate tribunal that that person no longer requires treatment in hospital for mental disorder or that no effective treatment for his disorder can be given in the hospital to which he has been removed, the Secretary of State may—

(*a*) by warrant direct that he be remitted to any prison or other institution in which he might have been detained if he had not been removed to hospital, there to be dealt with as if he had not been so removed; or

(*b*) exercise any power of releasing him on licence or discharging him under supervision which could have been exercisable if he had been remitted to such a prison or institution as aforesaid,

and on his arrival in the prison or other institution or, as the case may be, his release or discharge as aforesaid, the transfer direction and the restriction direction shall cease to have effect.

(2) A restriction direction in the case of a person serving a sentence of imprisonment shall cease to have effect on the expiration of the sentence.

(3) Subject to subsection (4) below, references in this section to the expiration of a person's sentence are references to the expiration of the period during which he would have been liable to be detained in a prison or other institution if the transfer direction had not been given.

(4) For the purposes of section 49(2) of the Prison Act 1952 (which provides for discounting from the sentences of certain prisoners periods while they are unlawfully at large) a patient who, having been transferred in pursuance of a transfer direction from any such institution as is referred to in that section, is at large in circumstances in which he is liable to be taken into custody under any provision of this Act, shall be treated as unlawfully at large and absent from that institution.

(5) The preceding provisions of this section shall have effect as if—

(*a*) the reference in subsection (1) to a transfer direction and a restriction direction having been given in respect of a person serving a sentence of imprisonment included a reference to a hospital direction and a limitation direction having been given in respect of a person sentenced to imprisonment;

(*b*) the reference in subsection (2) to a restriction direction included a reference to a limitation direction; and

(*c*) references in subsections (3) and (4) to a transfer direction included references to a hospital direction.*

[Mental Health Act 1983, s 50 as amended by the Criminal Justice Act 1991, Sch 13 and the Crime (Sentences) Act 1997, Sch 4, the Criminal Justice Act 2003, s 294, the Mental Health Act 2007, s 11 and SI 2008/2833.]

---

* **Amended by the Criminal Justice and Courts Act 2015, Sch 3 from a date to be appointed.**

7.8424 **51. Further provisions as to detained persons** (1) This section has effect where a transfer direction has been given in respect of any such person as is described in paragraph (*a*) of section 48(2) above and that person is in this section referred to as "the detainee".

(2) The transfer direction shall cease to have effect when the detainee's case is disposed of by the court having jurisdiction to try or otherwise deal with him, but without prejudice to any power of that court to make a hospital order or other order under this Part of this Act in his case.

(3) If the Secretary of State is notified by the responsible clinician, any other approved clinician or the appropriate tribunal at any time before the detainee's case is disposed of by that court—

(*a*) that the detainee no longer requires treatment in hospital for mental disorder; or

(*b*) that no effective treatment for his disorder can be given at the hospital to which he has been removed,

the Secretary of State may by warrant direct that he be remitted to any place where he might have been detained if he had not been removed to hospital, there to be dealt with as if he had not been so removed, and on his arrival at the place to which he is so remitted the transfer direction shall cease to have effect.

(4) If (no direction having been given under subsection (3) above) the court having jurisdiction to try or otherwise deal with the detainee is satisfied on the written or oral evidence of the responsible clinician—

(*a*) that the detainee no longer requires treatment in hospital for mental disorder; or

(*b*) that no effective treatment for his disorder can be given at the hospital to which he has been removed, the court may order him to be remitted to any such place as is mentioned in subsection (3) above or, subject to section 25 of the Criminal Justice and Public Order Act 1994, released on bail and on his arrival at that place or, as the case may be, his release on bail the transfer direction shall cease to have effect.

(5) If (no direction or order having been given or made under subsection (3) or (4) above) it appears to the court having jurisdiction to try or otherwise deal with the detainee—

(*a*) that it is impracticable or inappropriate[1] to bring the detainee before the court; and

(*b*) that the conditions set out in subsection (6) below are satisfied,

the court may make a hospital order (with or without a restriction order) in his case in his absence and, in the case of a person awaiting trial, without convicting him.

(6) A hospital order may be made in respect of a person under subsection (5) above if the court—

(*a*) is satisfied, on the written or oral evidence of at least two registered medical practitioners, that

(i) the detainee is suffering from mental disorder of a nature or degree which makes it appropriate for the patient to be detained in a hospital for medical treatment; and

(ii) appropriate medical treatment is available for him;

(*b*) is of the opinion, after considering any depositions or other documents required to be sent to the proper officer of the court, that it is proper to make such an order.

(7) Where a person committed to the Crown Court to be dealt with under section 43 above is admitted to a hospital in pursuance of an order under section 44 above, subsections (5) and (6) above shall apply as if he were a person subject to a transfer direction.

[Mental Health Act 1983, s 51 as amended by the Criminal Justice and Public Order Act 1994, Sch 10, the Mental Health Act 2007, s 5, 11 and Sch 1 and SI 2008/2833.]

---

[1] Where the defendant is in the court building no question of impracticability for the purposes of s 51(5)(*a*) arises and "inappropriate" must be construed restrictively as to pass sentence, without convicting, is a drastic step; although it is not necessary to construe "inappropriate" as meaning "physically impossible" a high degree of disablement or physical disorder needs to be present: *R (on the application of Kenneally) v Crown Court at Snaresbrook* [2001] EWHC Admin 968, [2002] QB 1169, [2002] 2 WLR 1430.

7.8425 **52. Further provisions as to persons remanded by magistrates' courts** (1) This section has effect where a transfer direction has been given in respect of any such person as is described in paragraph (*b*) of section 48(2) above; and that person is in this section referred to as "the accused".

(2) Subject to subsection (5) below, the transfer direction shall cease to have effect on the expiration of the period of remand unless the accused is committed in custody to the Crown Court for trial or to be otherwise dealt with.

(3) Subject to subsection (4) below, the power of further remanding[1] the accused under section 128 of the Magistrates' Courts Act 1980 may be exercised by the court without his being brought before the court; and if the court further remands the accused in custody (whether or not he is brought before the court) the period of remand shall, for the purposes of this section, be deemed not to have expired.

(4) The court shall not under subsection (3) above further remand the accused in his absence unless he has appeared before the court within the previous six months.

(5) If the magistrates' court is satisfied, on the written or oral evidence of the responsible clinician—

(*a*) that the accused no longer requires treatment in hospital for mental disorder; or

(*b*) that no effective treatment for his disorder can be given in the hospital to which he has been removed,

the court may direct that the transfer direction shall cease to have effect notwithstanding that the period of remand has not expired or that the accused is committed to the Crown Court as mentioned in subsection (2) above.

(6) If the accused is committed to the Crown Court as mentioned in subsection (2) above and the transfer direction has not ceased to have effect under subsection (5) above, section 51 above shall apply as if the transfer direction given in his case were a direction given in respect of a person falling within that section.

(7) The magistrates' court may, in the absence of the accused, send him to the Crown Court for trial under section 51 or 51A of the Crime and Disorder Act 1998—

(*a*) the court is satisfied, on the written or oral evidence of the responsible clinician, that the accused is unfit to take part in the proceedings; and

(*b*) the accused is represented by an authorised person.

[Mental Health Act 1983, s 52 as amended by the Criminal Justice Act 2003, Sch 3, the Mental Health Act 2007, s 11 and the Legal Services Act 2007, Sch 21.]

---

[1] Notice of the further remand must be sent by the court to the managers of the hospital (Criminal Procedure Rules, r 14.4, in the *Key Materials*).

**7.8426 53. Further provisions as to civil prisoners and persons detained under the Immigration Acts** (1) Subject to subsection (2) below, a transfer direction given in respect of any such person as is described in paragraph (*c*) or (*d*) of section 48(2) above shall cease to have effect on the expiration of the period during which he would, but for his removal to hospital, be liable to be detained in the place from which he was removed.

(2) Where a transfer direction and a restriction direction have been given in respect of any such person as is mentioned in subsection (1) above, then, if the Secretary of State is notified by the responsible clinician, any other approved clinician or the appropriate tribunal at any time before the expiration of the period there mentioned—

(*a*) that that person no longer requires treatment in hospital for mental disorder; or

(*b*) that no effective treatment for his disorder can be given in the hospital to which he has been removed,

the Secretary of State may by warrant direct that he be remitted to any place where he might have been detained if he had not been removed to hospital, and on his arrival at the place to which he is so remitted the transfer direction and the restriction direction shall cease to have effect.

[Mental Health Act 1983, s 53 as amended by the Nationality, Immigration and Asylum Act 2002, s 62, the Mental Health Act 2007, s 11 and SI 2008/2833.]

*Supplemental*

**7.8427 54. Requirements as to medical evidence** (1) The registered medical practitioner whose evidence is taken into account under section 35(3)(*a*) above and at least one of the registered medical practitioners whose evidence is taken into account under sections 36(1), 37(2)(*a*), 38(1), 45A(2) and 51(6)(*a*) above and whose reports are taken into account under sections 47(1) and 48(1) above shall be a practitioner approved for the purposes of section 12 above by the Secretary of State as having special experience in the diagnosis or treatment of mental disorder[1].

(2) For the purposes of any provision of this Part of this Act under which a court may act on the written evidence of any person, a report in writing purporting to be signed by that person may, subject to the provisions of this section, be received in evidence without proof of the following—

(*a*) the signature of the person; or

(*b*) his having the requisite qualifications or approval or authority or being of the requisite description to give the report.

(2A) But the court may require the signatory of any such report to be called to give oral evidence.

(3) Where, in pursuance of a direction of the court, any such report is tendered in evidence otherwise than by or on behalf of the person who is the subject of the report, then—

(*a*) if that person is represented by an authorised person, a copy of the report shall be given to that authorised person;

(*b*) if that person is not so represented, the substance of the report shall be disclosed to him or, where he is a child or young person, to his parent or guardian if present in court; and

(*c*) except where the report relates only to arrangements for his admission to a hospital, that person may require the signatory of the report to be called to give oral evidence, and evidence to rebut the evidence contained in the report may be called by or on behalf of that person.

[Mental Health Act 1983, s 54 as amended by the Crime (Sentences) Act 1997, Sch 4, the Mental Health Act 2007, s 11 and the Legal Services Act 2007, Sch 21.]

1 For contents of note to be sent to provider of report or information, see the Criminal Procedure Rules, r 28.8, in the *Key Materials*.

**7.8428 54A. Reduction of period for making hospital orders** Secretary of State may by order reduce periods in ss 37(4), (5) and 38(4) and make consequential amendments.

[Mental Health Act 1983, s 54A as inserted by the Criminal Justice Act 1991, s 27(2)—summarised.]

**7.8429 55. Interpretation of Part III** (1) In this Part of this Act—

"authorised person" means a person who, for the purposes of the Legal Services Act 2007, is an authorised person in relation to an activity which constitutes the exercise of a right of audience (within the meaning of that Act);

"child" and "young person" have the same meaning as in the Children and Young Persons Act 1933[1];

"civil prisoner" has the meaning given to it by section 48(2)(*c*) above;

"guardian", in relation to a child or young person, has the same meaning as in the Children and Young Persons Act 1933[1];

"place of safety", in relation to a person who is not a child or young person, means any police station, prison or remand centre, or any hospital the managers of which are willing temporarily to receive him, and in relation to a child or young person has the same meaning as in the Children and Young Persons Act 1933[1];

"responsible clinician", in relation to a person liable to be detained in a hospital within the meaning of Part 2 of this Act, means the approved clinician with overall responsibility for the patient's case.

(2) Any reference in this Part of this Act to an offence punishable on summary conviction with imprisonment shall be construed without regard to any prohibition or restriction imposed by or

under any enactment relating to the imprisonment of young offenders.

(3) *Repealed.*

(4) Any reference to a hospital order, a guardianship order or a restriction order in section 40(2), (4) or (5), section 41(3) to (5), or section 42 above or section 69(1) below shall be construed as including a reference to any order or direction under this Part of this Act having the same effect as the first-mentioned order; and the exceptions and modifications set out in Schedule 1 to this Act in respect of the provisions of this Act described in that Schedule accordingly include those which are consequential on the provisions of this subsection.

(5) Section 34(2) above shall apply for the purposes of this Part of this Act as it applies for the purposes of Part II of this Act.

(6) References in this Part of this Act to persons serving a sentence of imprisonment shall be construed in accordance with section 47(5) above.

(7) Section 99[2] of the Children and Young Persons Act 1933 (which relates to the presumption and determination of age) shall apply for the purposes of this Part of this Act as it applies for the purposes of that Act.

[Mental Health Act 1983, s 55 as amended by the Mental Health Act 2007, s 11 and Sch 11 and the Legal Services Act 2007, Sch 21.]

---

[1] See s 107, thereof, in PART V: YOUTH COURTS, ante.

[2] See PART V: YOUTH COURTS, ante.

## PART VIII[1]

## MISCELLANEOUS FUNCTIONS OF LOCAL AUTHORITIES AND THE SECRETARY OF STATE

### *Approved mental health professionals*

7.8430 **114. Approval by local social services authority** *Local social services authority may, in accordance with regulations,[2] approve a person (other than a registered medical practitioner) to act as an approved mental health professional for the purposes of this Act.*

[Mental Health Act 1983, s 114 as substituted by the Mental Health Act 2007, s 18.]

---

[1] Part VIII contains ss 114–125.

[2] The Mental Health (Approval of Persons to be Approved Mental Health Professionals) (England) Regulations 2008, SI 2008/1206 amended by SI 2012/1479 and SI 2017/52 and the Mental Health (Approval of Persons to be Approved Mental Health Professionals) (Wales) Regulations 2008, SI 2008/2436 amended by SI 2012/1479 and SI 2017/52 have been made.

7.8431 **114A. Approval of courses etc for approved mental health professionals**

7.8432 **114ZA. Approval of courses: England**

7.8433 **115. Powers of entry and inspection** (1) An approved mental health professional may at all reasonable times enter and inspect any premises (other than a hospital) in which a mentally disordered patient is living, if he has reasonable cause to believe that the patient is not under proper care.

(2) The power under subsection (1) above shall be exercisable only after the professional has produced, if asked to do so, some duly authenticated document showing that he is an approved mental health professional.

[Mental Health Act 1983, s 115 as substituted by the Mental Health Act 2007, Sch 2.]

### *Visiting patients*

7.8434 **116. Welfare of certain hospital patients** (1) Where a patient to whom this section applies is admitted to a hospital, independent hospital or care home in England and Wales (whether for treatment for mental disorder or for any other reason) then, without prejudice to their duties in relation to the patient apart from the provisions of this section, the authority shall arrange for visits to be made to him on behalf of the authority, and shall take such other steps in relation to the patient while in the hospital, independent hospital or care home as would be expected to be taken by his parents.

(2) This section applies to—

(*a*) a child or young person—

(i) who is in the care of a local authority by virtue of a care order within the meaning of the Children Act 1989, or

(ii) in respect of whom the rights and powers of a parent are vested in a local authority by virtue of section 16 of the Social Work (Scotland) Act 1968.

(*b*) a person who is subject to the guardianship of a local social services authority under the provisions of this Act; or

(*c*) a person the functions of whose nearest relative under this Act are for the time being transferred to a local social services authority.

[Mental Health Act 1983, s 116 as amended by the Mental Health (Scotland) Act 1984, Sch 3, the Care Standards Act 2000, s 116, SI 2005/2078 and SSI 2005/465.]

*After-care*

7.8435 **117. After-care**

PART IX[1]

*Offences*

7.8436 **126. Forgery, false statements, etc** (1) Any person who without lawful authority or excuse has in his custody or under his control any document to which this subsection applies, which is, and which he knows or believes to be, false within the meaning of Part I of the Forgery and Counterfeiting Act 1981, shall be guilty of an offence.

(2) Any person who without lawful authority or excuse makes, or has in his custody or under his control, any document so closely resembling a document to which subsection (1) above applies as to be calculated to deceive shall be guilty of an offence.

(3) The documents to which subsection (1) above applies are any documents purporting to be—

(*a*) an application under Part II of this Act;

(*b*) a medical or other recommendation or report under this Act; and

(*c*) any other document required or authorised to be made for any of the purposes of this Act.

(4) Any person who—

(*a*) wilfully makes a false entry or statement in application, recommendation, report, record or other document required or authorised to be made for any of the purposes of this Act; or

(*b*) with intent to deceive, makes use of any such entry or statement which he knows to be false,

shall be guilty of an offence.

(5) Any person guilty of an offence under this section shall be liable[2]—

(*a*) on summary conviction, to imprisonment for a term not exceeding **six months** or to a fine not exceeding **the statutory maximum**, or to **both**;

(*b*) on conviction on indictment, to imprisonment for a term not exceeding **two years** or to a **fine** of any amount, or to **both**.

[Mental Health Act 1983, s 126 as amended by the Mental Health (Patients in the Community) Act 1995, Sch 1.]

1 Part IX contains ss 126–130.

2 For procedure in respect of this offence which is triable either way, see the Magistrates' Courts Act 1980, ss 17A–21, in PART I: MAGISTRATES' COURTS, PROCEDURE, ante.

7.8437 **127. Ill-treatment of patients** (1) It shall be an offence for any person who is an officer on the staff of or otherwise employed in, or who is one of the managers of, a hospital, an independent hospital or care home—

(*a*) to ill-treat or wilfully to neglect[1] a patient for the time being receiving treatment for mental disorder as an in-patient in that hospital or home; or

(*b*) to ill-treat or wilfully to neglect[1], on the premises of which the hospital or home forms part, a patient for the time being receiving such treatment there as an out-patient.

(2) It shall be an offence for any individual to ill-treat or wilfully to neglect[1] a mentally disordered patient who is for the time being subject to his guardianship under this Act or otherwise in his custody or care (whether by virtue of any legal or moral obligation or otherwise).

(2A) *Repealed.*

(3) Any person guilty of an offence under this section shall be liable[2]—

(*a*) on summary conviction, to imprisonment for a term not exceeding **six months** or to a fine not exceeding **the statutory maximum**, or to **both**;

(*b*) on conviction on indictment, to imprisonment for a term not exceeding **five years** or to a **fine** of any amount, or to **both**.

(4) No proceedings shall be instituted for an offence under this section except by or with the consent of the Director of Public Prosecutions.

[Mental Health Act 1983, s 127 as amended by the Mental Health (Patients in the Community) Act 1995, Sch 1, the Care Standards Act 2000, s 116 and the Mental Health Act 2007, s 42 and Sch 11.]

1 Ill-treatment and wilful neglect are not the same, although ill-treatment can cover most, if not all, forms of neglect. For ill-treatment it must be proved that there was deliberate conduct which could properly be described as ill-treatment whether or not it damaged or threatened to damage the victim's health, plus a guilty mind involving an appreciation or recklessness of inexcusable ill-treatment (*R v Newington* (1990) 91 Cr App Rep 247, [1990] Crim LR 593, CA).

2 For procedure in respect of this offence which is triable either way, see the Magistrates' Courts Act 1980, ss 17A–21, in PART I: MAGISTRATES' COURTS, PROCEDURE, ante.

7.8438 **129. Obstruction** (1) Any person who without reasonable cause—

(*a*) refuses to allow the inspection of any premises; or

(*b*) refuses to allow the visiting, interviewing or examination of any person by a person authorised in that behalf by or under this Act or to give access to any person to a person so authorised; or

(*c*) refuses to produce for the inspection of any person so authorised any document or record the production of which is duly required by him; or (*ca*) fails to comply with a request made under section 120C; or

(*d*) otherwise obstructs any such person in the exercise of his functions,

shall be guilty of an offence.

(2) Without prejudice to the generality of subsection (1) above, any person who insists on being present when required to withdraw by a person authorised by or under this Act to interview or examine a person in private shall be guilty of an offence.

(3) Any person guilty of an offence under this section shall be liable on summary conviction to imprisonment for a term not exceeding **three months** or* to a fine not exceeding **level 4** on the standard scale or to **both**.*

[Mental Health Act 1983, s 129 as amended by the Mental Health (Patients in the Community) Act 1995, Sch 1 and the Health and Social Care Act 2008, Sch 3.]

* **Words repealed by the Criminal Justice Act 2003, Sch 37 from a date to be appointed.**

7.8439 **130. Prosecutions by local authorities** A local social services authority may institute proceedings for any offence under this Part of this Act, but without prejudice to any provision this Part of this Act requiring the consent of the Director of Public Prosecutions for the institution of such proceedings[1].

[Mental Health Act 1983, s 130.]

1 This consent is required for the institution of proceedings under s 127, ante.

## Part X[1]

## Miscellaneous and Supplementary

1 Part X contains ss 131–149.

*Miscellaneous provisions*

7.8440 **130A–130D. Independent mental health advocates** *Arrangements in accordance with regulations[1] for appointment of mental health advocates to help qualifying patients.*

1 The Mental Health Act 1983 (Independent Mental Health Advocates) (England) Regulations 2008, SI 2008/3166 amended by SI 2009/2376 have been made.

7.8441 **131. Informal admission of patients[1]** (1) Nothing in this Act shall be construed as preventing a patient who requires treatment for mental disorder from being admitted to any hospital or registered establishment in pursuance of arrangements made in that behalf and without any application, order or direction rendering him liable to be detained under this Act, or from remaining in any hospital or registered establishment in pursuance of such arrangements after he has ceased to be so liable to be detained.

(2) Subsections (3) and (4) below apply in the case of a patient aged 16 or 17 years who has capacity to consent to the making of such arrangements as are mentioned in subsection (1) above.

(3) If the patient consents to the making of the arrangements, they may be made, carried out and determined on the basis of that consent even though there are one or more persons who have parental responsibility for him.

(4) If the patient does not consent to the making of the arrangements, they may not be made, carried out or determined on the basis of the consent of a person who has parental responsibility for him.

(5) In this section—

(*a*) the reference to a patient who has capacity is to be read in accordance with the Mental Capacity Act 2005; and

(*b*) "parental responsibility" has the same meaning as in the Children Act 1989.

[Mental Health Act 1983, s 131 as amended by the Children Act 1989, Sch 13, the Care Standards Act 2000, s 116 and the Mental Health Act 2007, s 43.]

1 Where a child is not competent (within the terms of *Gillick v West Norfolk and Wisbech Area Health Authority* [1986] AC 112, [1985] 3 All ER 402, HL, [1986] 1 FLR 224) and the child is in the care of the local authority that authority was in the same position as a parent and could use its powers under the Child Care Act 1980, s 10 to arrange voluntary admission (*R v Kirklees Metropolitan Borough Council, ex p C* [1993] 2 FCR 381, [1993] 2 FLR 187, CA).

7.8442 **131A. Accommodation, etc for children** (1) This section applies in respect of any patient who has not attained the age of 18 years and who—

(*a*) is liable to be detained in a hospital under this Act; or

(*b*) is admitted to, or remains in, a hospital in pursuance of such arrangements as are mentioned in section 131(1) above.

(2) The managers of the hospital shall ensure that the patient's environment in the hospital is suitable having regard to his age (subject to his needs).

(3) For the purpose of deciding how to fulfil the duty under subsection (2) above, the managers shall consult a person who appears to them to have knowledge or experience of cases involving patients who have not attained the age of 18 years which makes him suitable to be consulted.

(4) In this section, "hospital" includes a registered establishment.

[Mental Health Act 1983, s 131A as inserted by the Mental Health Act 2007, s 31.]

**7.8443 132–133.** *Duty of managers of hospitals to give information to detained patients and to community patients and to inform nearest relatives of discharge.*

**7.8444 134. Correspondence of patients** (1) A postal packet addressed to any person by a patient detained in a hospital under this Act and delivered by the patient for dispatch may be withheld from the postal operator concerned—

(*a*) if that person has requested that communications addressed to him by the patient should be withheld; or

(*b*) subject to subsection (3) below, if the hospital is one at which high security psychiatric services are provided and the managers of the hospital consider that the postal packet is likely—

(i) to cause distress to the person to whom it is addressed or to any other person (not being a person on the staff of the hospital); or

(ii) to cause danger to any person;

and any request for the purposes of paragraph (*a*) above shall be made by a notice in writing given to the managers of the hospital, or the approved clinician with overall responsibility for the patient's case.

(2) Subject to subsection (3) below, a postal packet addressed to a patient detained under this Act in a hospital at which high security psychiatric services are provided may be withheld from the patient if, in the opinion of the managers of the hospital, it is necessary to do so in the interests of the safety of the patient or for the protection of other persons.

(3) Subsections (1)(*b*) and (2) above do not apply to any postal packet addressed by a patient to, or sent to a patient by or on behalf of—

(*a*) any Minister of the Crown or the Scottish Ministers or Member of either House of Parliament or member of the Scottish Parliament or of the Northern Ireland Assembly;

(*aa*) any of the Welsh Ministers, the Counsel General to the Welsh Assembly Government or a member of the National Assembly for Wales;

(*b*) any judge or officer of the Court of Protection, any of the Court of Protection Visitors or any person asked by that Court for a report under section 49 of the Mental Capacity Act 2005 concerning the patient;

(*c*) the Parliamentary Commissioner for Administration, the Scottish Public Services Ombudsman, the Public Services Ombudsman for Wales, the Health Service Commissioner for England or a Local Commissioner within the meaning of Part III of the Local Government Act 1974;

(*ca*) the Care Quality Commission;

(*d*) the First-tier Tribunal or the Mental Health Review Tribunal for Wales;

(*e*) the National Health Service Commissioning Board, a clinical commissioning group, a Local Health Board or Special Health Authority, a local social services authority, a Community Health Council, a local probation board established under section 4 of the Criminal Justice and Court Services Act 2000 or a provider of probation services;

(*ea*) a provider of a patient advocacy and liaison service for the assistance of patients at the hospital and their families and carers;

(*eb*) a provider of independent advocacy services for the patient;

(*f*) the managers of the hospital in which the patient is detained;

(*g*) any legally qualified person instructed by the patient to act as his legal adviser; or

(*h*) the European Commission of Human Rights or the European Court of Human Rights.

and for the purposes of paragraph (*d*) above the reference to the First-tier Tribunal is a reference to that tribunal so far as it is acting for the purposes of any proceedings under this Act or paragraph 5(2) of the Schedule to the Repatriation of Prisoners Act 1984.

(3A) In subsection (3) above—

(*a*) "patient advocacy and liaison service" means a service of a description prescribed by regulations[1] made by the Secretary of State, and

(*b*) "independent advocacy services" means services provided under—

(i) arrangements under section 130A above;

(ii) arrangements under section 223A of the Local Government and Public Involvement in Health Act 2007 or section 187 of the National Health Service (Wales) Act 2006; or

(iii) arrangements of a description prescribed as mentioned in paragraph (*a*) above.

(4) The managers of a hospital may inspect and open any postal packet for the purposes of determining—

(*a*) whether it is one to which subsection (1) or (2) applies, and

(*b*) in the case of a postal packet to which subsection (1) or (2) above applies, whether or not it should be withheld under that subsection;

and the power to withhold a postal packet under either of those subsections includes power to withhold anything contained in it.

(5) Where a postal packet or anything contained in it is withheld under subsection (1) or (2) above the managers of the hospital shall record that fact in writing.

(6) Where a postal packet or anything contained in it is withheld under subsection (1)(*b*) or (2)

above the managers of the hospital shall within seven days give notice of that fact to the patient and, in the case of a packet withheld under subsection (2) above, to the person (if known) by whom the postal packet was sent; and any such notice shall be given in writing and shall contain a statement of the effect of section 134A(1) to (4).

(7) The functions of the managers of a hospital under this section shall be discharged on their behalf by a person on the staff of the hospital appointed by them for that purpose and different persons may be appointed to discharge different functions.

(8) The Secretary of State may make regulations[1] with respect to the exercise of the powers conferred by this section.

(9) In this section and section 134A "hospital" has the same meaning as in Part II of this Act and "postal operator" and "postal packet" have the same meaning as in Part 3 of the Postal Services Act 2011 (see section 27).

[Mental Health Act 1983, s 134 as amended by the Probation Service Act 1993, Sch 3, the Health Authorities Act 1995, Sch 1, the Government ofWales Act 1998, Sch 12, the Health Act 1999, Sch 4, SI 2000/90, the Postal Services Act 2000, Sch 8, the Criminal Justice and Court Services Act 2000, Sch 7, the Health and Social Care Act 2001, s 67(1), the National Health Service Reform and Health Care Professions Act 2002, s 19, SI 2002/2469, SI 2004/1823, the Public Services Ombudsman (Wales) Act 2005, Sch 6, the Mental Capacity Act 2005, Sch 6, the National Health Service (Consequential Provisions) Act 2006, Sch 1, SI 2007/961, SI 2007/1388, the Local Government and Public Involvement in Health Act 2007, Sch 18, the Mental Health Act 2007, s 30, SI 2008/912, SI 2008/2833, the Health and Social Care Act 2008, Sch 3, the Postal Services Act 2011, Sch 12, the Health and Social Care Act 2012, s 44 and Sch 5]

1 The Mental Health (Hospital, Guardianship and Treatment) (England) Regulations 2008, SI 2008/1184 amended by SI 2008/2560, SI 2012/1118 and SI 2013/235 have been made.

7.8445 **134A. Review of decisions to withhold correspondence** (1) The regulatory authority must review any decision to withhold a postal packet (or anything contained in it) under subsection (1)(*b*) or (2) of section 134 if an application for a review of the decision is made—

(*a*) in a case under subsection (1)(*b*) of that section, by the patient; or

(*b*) in a case under subsection (2) of that section, either by the patient or by the person by whom the postal packet was sent.

(2) An application under subsection (1) must be made within 6 months of receipt by the applicant of the notice referred to in section 134(6).

(3) On an application under subsection (1), the regulatory authority may direct that the postal packet (or anything contained in it) is not to be withheld.

(4) The managers of the hospital concerned must comply with any such direction.

(5) The Secretary of State may by regulations make provision in connection with the making to and determination by the Care Quality Commission of applications under subsection (1), including provision for the production to the Commission of any postal packet which is the subject of such an application.

(6) The Welsh Ministers may by regulations make provision in connection with the making to them of applications under subsection (1), including provision for the production to them of any postal packet which is the subject of such an application.

[Mental Health Act 1983, s 134A as inserted by the Health and Social Care Act 2008, Sch 3.]

7.8446 **135. Warrant to search for and remove patients** (1) If it appears to a justice of the peace, on information on oath laid by an approved mental health professional, that there is reasonable cause to suspect that a person believed to be suffering from mental disorder—

(*a*) has been, or is being, ill-treated, neglected or kept otherwise than under proper control, in any place within the jurisdiction of the justice, or

(*b*) being unable to care for himself, is living alone in any such place,

the justice may issue a warrant[1] authorising any constable to enter, if need be by force, any premises specified in the warrant in which that person is believed to be, and, if thought fit, to remove him to a place of safety with a view to the making of an application in respect of him under Part II of this Act, or of other arrangements for his treatment or care.

(2) If it appears to a justice of the peace, on information on oath laid by any constable or other person who is authorised by or under this Act or under article 8 of the Mental Health (Care and Treatment) Scotland) Act 2003 (Consequential Provisions) Order 2005 to take a patient to any place, or to take into custody or retake a patient who is liable under this Act or under the said article 8 to be so taken or retaken—

(*a*) that there is reasonable cause to believe that the patient is to be found on premises within the jurisdiction of the justice; and

(*b*) that admission to the premises has been refused or that a refusal of such admission is apprehended,

the justice may issue a warrant authorising any constable to enter the premises, if need be by force, and remove the patient.

(3) A patient who is removed to a place of safety in the execution of a warrant issued under this section may be detained there for a period not exceeding 72 hours.

(3A) A constable, an approved mental health professional or a person authorised by either of them for the purposes of this subsection may, before the end of the period of 72 hours mentioned in subsection (3) above, take a person detained in a place of safety under that subsection to one or more other places of safety.

(3B) A person taken to a place of safety under subsection (3A) above may be detained there for a period ending no later than the end of the period of 72 hours mentioned in subsection (3) above.

(4) In the execution of a warrant issued under subsection (1) above, a constable shall be accompanied by an approved mental health professional and by a registered medical practitioner, and in the execution of a warrant issued under subsection (2) above a constable may be accompanied—

(*a*) by a registered medical practitioner;

(*b*) by any person authorised by or under this Act or under article 8 of the Mental Health (Care and Treatment) Scotland) Act 2003 (Consequential Provisions) Order 2005 to take or retake the patient.

(5) It shall not be necessary in any information or warrant under subsection (1) above to name the patient concerned.

(6) In this section "place of safety" means residential accommodation provided by a local social services authority under Part 1 of the Care Act 2014 or Part III of the National Assistance Act 1948, a hospital as defined by this Act, a police station, an independent hospital or care home for mentally disordered persons or any other suitable place the occupier of which is willing temporarily to receive the patient.

[Mental Health Act 1983, s 135 as amended by the Police and Criminal Evidence Act 1984, Schs 6 and 7, the Mental Health (Scotland) Act 1984, Sch 3 and the National Health Service and Community Care Act 1990, Sch 10, the Care Standards Act 2000, s 116, SI 2005/2078, the Mental Health Act 2007, s 44 and Sch 2 and SI 2015/914.]

1 See precedent, in Part VIII: Precedents and Forms, post. It is not permissible to imply into s 135 of the Mental Health Act 1983 a power to insist that named professionals are there when the police officer executes the warrant, and the inclusion of such names in a warrant is surplusage and has no effect on its legality or its execution: *Ward v Metropolitan Police Comr* [2005] UKHL 32, [2006] 1 AC 23, [2005] 3 All ER 1013, [2005] 2 WLR 1114.

7.8447 **136. Mentally disordered persons found in public places** (1) If a constable finds in a place to which the public have access a person who appears to him to be suffering from mental disorder and to be in immediate need of care or control, the constable may, if he thinks it necessary to do so in the interests of that person or for the protection of other persons, remove[1] that person to a place of safety within the meaning of section 135 above.

(2) A person removed to a place of safety under this section may be detained there for a period not exceeding 72 hours[2] for the purpose of enabling him to be examined by a registered medical practitioner and to be interviewed by an approved mental health professional and of making any necessary arrangements for his treatment or care.

(3) A constable, an approved mental health professional or a person authorised by either of them for the purposes of this subsection may, before the end of the period of 72 hours mentioned in subsection (2) above, take a person detained in a place of safety under that subsection to one or more other places of safety.

(4) A person taken to a place of a safety under subsection (3) above may be detained there for a purpose mentioned in subsection (2) above for a period ending no later than the end of the period of 72 hours mentioned in that subsection.

[Mental Health Act 1983, s 136 as amended by the Mental Health Act 2007, s 44 and Sch 2.]

1 This power of removal is preserved by the Police and Criminal Evidence Act 1984, s 26 and Sch 2.

2 During this period, arrangements can be made for admission to hospital for observation and, if necessary treatment, in accordance with Pt II of the Act which is not detailed in this work.

7.8448 **137. Provisions as to custody, conveyance and detention** (1) Any person required or authorised by or by virtue of this Act to be conveyed to any place or to be kept in custody or detained in a place of safety or at any place to which he is taken under section 42(6) above shall, while being so conveyed, detained or kept, as the case may be, be deemed to be in legal custody[1].

(2) A constable or any other person required or authorised by or by virtue of this Act to take any person into custody, or to convey or detain any person shall, for the purposes of taking him into custody or conveying or detaining him, have all the powers, authorities, protection and privileges which a constable has within the area for which he acts as constable.

(3) In this section "convey" includes any other expression denoting removal from one place to another.

[Mental Health Act 1983, s 137.]

1 It will therefore be an offence to induce or knowingly assist such a person to escape (see s 128, ante).

7.8449 **138. Retaking of patients escaping from custody** (1) If any person who is in legal custody by virtue of section 137 above escapes, he may, subject to the provisions of this section, be retaken[1]—

(*a*) in any case, by the person who had his custody immediately before the escape, or by any constable or approved mental health professional;

(*b*) if at the time of the escape he was liable to be detained in a hospital within the meaning of Part II of this Act, or subject to guardianship under this Act, or a community patient who was recalled to hospital under section 17E above, by any other person who could take him into custody under section 18 above if he had absented himself without leave[2].

(2) A person to whom paragraph (*b*) of subsection (1) above applies shall not be retaken under this section after the expiration of the period within which he could be retaken under section 18

above if he had absented himself without leave on the day of the escape unless he is subject to a restriction order under Part III of this Act or an order or direction having the same effect as such an order; and subsection (4) of the said section 18 shall apply with the necessary modifications accordingly.

(3) A person who escapes while being taken to or detained in a place of safety under section 135 or 136 above shall not be retaken under this section after the expiration of the period of 72 hours beginning with the time when he escapes or the period during which he is liable to be so detained, whichever expires first.

(4) This section, so far as it relates to the escape of a person liable to be detained in a hospital within the meaning of Part II of this Act, shall apply in relation to a person who escapes—

(*a*) while being taken to or from such a hospital in pursuance of regulations under section 19 above, or of any order, direction or authorisation under Part III or VI of this Act (other than under section 35, 36, 38, 53, 83 or 85) or under section 123 above; or

(*b*) while being taken to or detained in a place of safety in pursuance of an order under Part III of this Act (other than under section 35, 36 or 38 above) pending his admission to such a hospital,

as if he were liable to be detained in that hospital and, if he had not previously been received in that hospital, as if he had been so received.

(5) In computing for the purposes of the power to give directions under section 37(4) above and for the purposes of sections 37(5) and 40(1) above the period of 28 days mentioned in those sections, no account shall be taken of any time during which the patient is at large and liable to be retaken by virtue of this section.

(6) Section 21[3] above shall, with any necessary modifications, apply in relation to a patient who is at large and liable to be retaken by virtue of this section as it applies in relation to a patient who is absent without leave and references in that section to section 18 above shall be construed accordingly.

[Mental Health Act 1983, s 138 as amended by the Mental Health Act 2007, Sch 2.]

---

1 This power to retake is preserved by the Police and Criminal Evidence Act 1984, s 26 and Sch 2.

2 For power of magistrate to issue a warrant in respect of a person liable to be retaken, see Criminal Justice Act 1967, s 72, in this PART: title PRISONS, post.

3 By this section if a patient is absent without leave at the time when he would otherwise cease to be liable to be detained or subject to guardianship under Pt II of the Act, this liability shall not cease, but the special provisions contained in this section shall apply.

7.8450 **139. Protection for acts done in pursuance of this Act[1]** (1) No person shall be liable, whether on the ground of want of jurisdiction or on any other ground, to any civil or criminal proceedings to which he would have been liable apart from this section in respect of any act purporting to be done in pursuance of this Act or any regulations or rules made under this Act, unless the act was done in bad faith or without reasonable care[2].

(2) No civil proceedings shall be brought against any person in any court in respect of any such act without the leave of the High Court; and no criminal proceedings shall be brought against any person in any court in respect of any such act except by or with the consent of the Director of Public Prosecutions.

(3) This section does not apply to proceedings for an offence under this Act, being proceedings which, under any other provision of this Act, can be instituted only by or with the consent of the Director of Public Prosecutions.

(4) This section does not apply to proceedings against the Secretary of State or against a Strategic Health Authority, Local Health Board, Special Health Authority or Primary Care Trust or against a National Health Service trust established under the National Health Service Act 2006 or the National Health Service (Wales) Act 2006 or NHS foundation trust.

(5) *Northern Ireland.*

[Mental Health Act 1983, s 139 as amended by the National Health Service and Community Care Act 1990, Sch 9, the Health Authorities Act 1995, Sch 1, SI 2000/90, SI 2002/2469, the Health and Social Care (Community Health and Standards) Act 2003, Sch 4, the Mental Capacity Act 2005, Sch 6, the National Health Service (Consequential Provisions) Act 2006, Sch 1 and SI 2007/961.]

---

1 For a consideration of the scope of this section, see *Pountney v Griffiths* [1975] 2 All ER 881, 139 JP 590.

2 See *Kynaston v Secretary of State for Home Affairs* (1981) 73 Cr App Rep 281, CA.

7.8451 **140. Notification of hospitals having arrangements for special cases** It shall be the duty of every Primary Care Trust and of every Local Health Board to give notice to every local social services authority for an area wholly or partly comprised within the area of the Primary Care Trust or Local Health Board's specifying the hospital or hospitals administered by or otherwise available to the Primary Care Trust or Local Health Board in which arrangements are from time to time in force—

(*a*) for the reception of patients in cases of special urgency;

(*b*) for the provision of accommodation or facilities designed so as to be specially suitable for patients who have not attained the age of 18 years.

[Mental Health Act 1983, s 140 as amended by the National Health Service and Community Care Act 1990, Sch 9, the Health Authorities Act 1995, Sch 1, SI 2007/961 and the Mental Health Act 2007, s 31.]

7.8452 **141. Members of Parliament suffering from mental illness** (1) Where a member of the House of Commons is authorised to be detained under a relevant enactment on the ground (however formulated) that he is suffering from mental disorder, it shall be the duty of the court, authority or person on whose order or application, and of any registered medical practitioner upon whose recommendation or certificate, the detention was authorised, and of the person in charge of the hospital or other place in which the member is authorised to be detained, to notify the Speaker of the House of Commons that the detention has been authorised.

(2)–(7) *Powers of the Speaker of the House of Commons.*

(8) *Scotland.*

*(9) This section to have effect with modifications in relation to members of the National Assembly for Wales.*

(10) *Northern Ireland.*

[Mental Health Act 1983, s 141 as amended by the Government of Wales Act 1998, Sch 12 and the Mental Health Act 2007, Sch 1.]

**7.8453 142A. Regulations as to approvals in relation to England and Wales** The Secretary of State jointly with the Welsh Ministers may by regulations make provision as to the circumstances in which—

(*a*) a practitioner approved for the purposes of section 12 above, or

(*b*) a person approved to act as an approved clinician for the purposes of this Act,

approved in relation to England is to be treated, by virtue of his approval, as approved in relation to Wales too, and vice versa.

[Mental Health Act 1983, s 142A as inserted by the Mental Health Act 2007, s 17.]

**7.8454 142B. Delegation of powers of managers of NHS foundation trusts** (1) The constitution of an NHS foundation trust may not provide for a function under this Act to be delegated otherwise than in accordance with provision made by or under this Act.

(2) Paragraph 15(3) of Schedule 7 to the National Health Service Act 2006 (which provides that the powers of a public benefit corporation may be delegated to a committee of directors or to an executive director) shall have effect subject to this section.

[Mental Health Act 1983, s 142B as inserted by the Mental Health Act 2007, s 45.]

*Supplemental*

**7.8455 143.** *General provisions as to regulations, orders and rules.*

**7.8456 144.** *Power to amend local Acts.*

**7.8457 145. Interpretation** (1) In this Act, unless the context otherwise requires—

"absent without leave" has the meaning given to it by section 18 above and related expressions shall be construed accordingly;

"application for admission for assessment" has the meaning given in section 2 above;

"application for admission for treatment" has the meaning given in section 3 above;

"the appropriate tribunal" has the meaning given by section 66(4) above;

"approved clinician" means a person approved by the Secretary of State or another person by virtue of section 12ZA or 12ZB above (in relation to England) or by the Welsh Ministers (in relation to Wales) to act as an approved clinician for the purposes of this Act;

"approved mental health professional" has the meaning given in section 114 above;

"care home" has the same meaning as in the Care Standards Act 2000;

"community patient" has the meaning given in section 17A above;

"community treatment order" and "the community treatment order" have the meanings given in section 17A above;

"the community treatment period" has the meaning given in section 20A above;

"high security psychiatric services" has the same meaning as in section 4 of the National Health Service Act 2006 or section 4 of the National Health Service (Wales) Act 2006,

"hospital" means—

(*a*) any health service hospital within the meaning of the National Health Service Act 2006 or the National Health Service (Wales) Act 2006; and

(*b*) any accommodation provided by a local authority and used as a hospital by or on behalf of the Secretary of State under that Act; and

(*c*) any hospital as defined by section 206 of the National Health Service (Wales) Act 2006 which is vested in a Local Health Board;

and "hospital within the meaning of Part II of this Act" has the meaning given in section 34 above;

"hospital direction" has the meaning given in section 45A(3)(*a*) above;

"hospital order" and "guardianship order" have the meanings respectively given in section 37 above;

"independent hospital"—

(*a*) in relation to England, means a hospital as defined by section 275 of the National Health Service Act 2006 that is not a health service hospital as defined by that section, and

(*b*) in relation to Wales, has the same meaning as in the Care Standards Act 2000;

"interim hospital order" has the meaning given in section 38 above;

"limitation direction" has the meaning given in section 45A(3)(*b*) above;

"Local Health Board" means a Local Health Board established under section 11 of the National Health Services (Wales) Act 2006;

"local social services authority" means a council which is a local authority for the purpose of the Local Authority Social Services Act 1970;

"the managers" means—

(*a*) in relation to a hospital vested in the Secretary of State for the purposes of his functions under the National Health Service Act 2006, or in the Welsh Ministers for the purposes of their functions under the National Health Service (Wales) Act 2006, and in relation to any accommodation provided by a local authority and used as a hospital by or on behalf of the Secretary of State under the National Health Service Act 2006, or of the Welsh Ministers under the National Health Service (Wales) Act 2006, the Secretary of State where the Secretary is responsible for the administration of the hospital or the Local Health Board or Special Health Authority responsible for the administration of the hospital;

(*b*) *repealed*;

(*bb*) in relation to a hospital vested in a Primary Care Trust or a National Health Service trust, the trust;

(*bc*) in relation to a hospital vested in an NHS foundation trust, the trust;

(*bd*) in relation to a hospital vested in a Local Health Board, the Board;

(*c*) in relation to a registered establishment—

(i) if the establishment is in England, the person or persons registered as a service provider under Chapter 2 of Part 1 of the Health and Social Care Act 2008 in respect of the regulated activity (within the meaning of that Part) relating to the assessment or medical treatment of mental disorder that is carried out in the establishment, and

(ii) if the establishment is in Wales, the person or persons registered in respect of the establishment under Part 2 of the Care Standards Act 2000;

and in this definition " hospital" means a hospital within the meaning of Part II of this Act;

"medical treatment" includes nursing, psychological intervention and specialist mental health habilitation, rehabilitation and care (but see also subsection (4) below);

"mental disorder" has the meaning given in section 1 above (subject to sections 86(4) and 141(6B));

"nearest relative", in relation to a patient, has the meaning given in Part II of this Act;

"patient" means a person suffering or appearing to be suffering from mental disorder;

"Primary Care Trust" means a Primary Care Trust established under section 18 of the National Health Service Act 2006;

"registered establishment" has the meaning given in section 34 above;

"the regulatory authority" means—

(*a*) in relation to England, the Care Quality Commission;

(*b*) in relation to Wales, the Welsh Ministers;

"the responsible hospital" has the meaning given in section 17A above;

"restriction direction" has the meaning given to it by section 49 above;

"restriction order" has the meaning given to it by section 41 above;

"Special Health Authority" means a Special Health Authority established under section 28 of the National Health Service Act 2006, or section 22 of the National Health Service (Wales) Act 2006;

"transfer direction" has the meaning given to it by section 47 above.

(1AA) Where high security psychiatric services and other services are provided at a hospital, the part of the hospital at which high security psychiatric services are provided and the other part shall be treated as separate hospitals for the purposes of this Act.

(1AB) References in this Act to appropriate medical treatment shall be construed in accordance with section 3(4) above.

(1AC) References in this Act to an approved mental health professional shall be construed as references to an approved mental health professional acting on behalf of a local social services authority, unless the context otherwise requires.

(1A) *Repealed.*

(2) *Repealed.*

(3) In relation to a person who is liable to be detained or subject to guardianship or a community patient by virtue of an order or direction under Part III of this Act (other than under section 35, 36 or 38), any reference in this Act to any enactment contained in Part II of this Act or in section 66 or 67 above shall be construed as a reference to that enactment as it applies to that person by virtue of Part III of this Act.

(4) Any reference in this Act to medical treatment, in relation to mental disorder, shall be construed as a reference to medical treatment the purpose of which is to alleviate, or prevent a worsening of, the disorder or one or more of its symptoms or manifestations.

[Mental Health Act 1983, s 145 as amended by the Registered Homes Act 1984, Sch 1, the National Health Service and Community Care Act 1990, Sch 9, the Statute Law (Repeals) Act 1993, Sch 1, the Mental Health (Amendment) Act 1994, s 1, the Health Authorities Act 1995, Sch 1, the Mental Health (Patients in the Community) Act 1995, Sch 1, the Crime (Sentences) Act 1997, Sch 4, the Health Act 1999, Schs 4 and 5, SI 2000/90, the Care Standards Act 2000, s 116, SI 2002/2469, the Health and Social Care (Community Health and Standards) Act 2003, Sch 4, the Mental Capacity Act

2005, Sch 6, the National Health Service (Consequential Provisions) Act 2006, Sch 1, SI 2007/961, the Mental Health Act 2007, ss 4, 14, 46 and Sch 1, SI 2008/2833, the Health and Social Care Act 2008, Sch 3, SI 2010/813 and the Health and Social Care Act 2012, Sch 5.]

7.8458 **146–147.** *Application to Scotland and Northern Ireland.*

7.8459 **148. Consequential and transitional provisions and repeals** (1) Schedule 4 (consequential amendments) and Schedule 5 (transitional and saving provisions) to this Act shall have effect but without prejudice to the operation of sections 15 to 17 of the Interpretation Act 1978 (which relate to the effect of repeals).

(2) Where any amendment in Schedule 4 to this Act affects an enactment amended by the Mental Health (Amendment) Act 1982 the amendment in Schedule 4 shall come into force immediately after the provision of the Act of 1982 amending that enactment.

(3) The enactments specified in Schedule 6 to this Act are hereby repealed to the extent mentioned in the third column of that Schedule.

[Mental Health Act 1983, s 148.]

7.8460 **149. Short title, commencement and application to Scilly Isles** (1) This Act may be cited as the Mental Health Act 1983.

(2) Subject to subsection (3) below and Schedule 5 to this Act, this Act shall come into force on 30th September 1983.

(3) *Repealed.*

(4) Section 130(4) of the National Health Service Act 1977 (which provides for the extension of that Act to the Isles of Scilly) shall have effect as if the references to that Act included references to this Act.

[Mental Health Act 1983, s 149 as amended by the Statute Law (Repeals) Act 2004.]

# Mental Capacity Act 2005[1]

(2005 c 9)

7.8461 **1. The principles** (1) The following principles apply for the purposes of this Act.

(2) A person must be assumed to have capacity unless it is established that he lacks capacity.

(3) A person is not to be treated as unable to make a decision unless all practicable steps to help him to do so have been taken without success.

(4) A person is not to be treated as unable to make a decision merely because he makes an unwise decision.

(5) An act done, or decision made, under this Act for or on behalf of a person who lacks capacity must be done, or made, in his best interests.

(6) Before the act is done, or the decision is made, regard must be had to whether the purpose for which it is needed can be as effectively achieved in a way that is less restrictive of the person's rights and freedom of action.

[Mental Capacity Act 2005, s 1.]

---

[1] This Act repeals the Enduring Powers of Attorney Act 1985 and makes new provision relating to persons who lack capacity; establishes a superior court of record called the Court of Protection and makes provision in connection with the Convention on the International Protection of Adults signed at the Hague on 13 January 2000. The Act is to be brought into force by commencement orders made under s 68. At the date of going to press the Commencement (No 1) Order 2006, SI 2006/2814 amended by SI 2006/3473; Commencement (No 1) (England and Wales) Order 2007, SI 2007/563; Commencement (Wales) Order 2007, SI 2007/856; Commencement (No 2) Order 2007, SI 2007/1897 had been made. Of the provisions reproduced here the following provisions had been brought into force: ss 1–4 (for purposes relating to the independent mental capacity advocate service) and s 44 on 1 April 2007; ss 1–4 (remaining purposes), 5 and 6 on 1 October 2007.

The determination of capacity under Part 1 of the 2005 Act is decision-specific. Some decisions, for example agreeing to marry or consenting to divorce, are status or act-specific. Some other decisions, for example whether P should have contact with a particular individual, may be person-specific. But all decisions, whatever their nature, fall to be evaluated within the straightforward and clear structure of ss 1 to 3 of the 2005 Act, which requires the court to have regard to "a matter" requiring "a decision". There is neither need nor justification for the plain words of the statute to be "embellished."…"The central provisions of the 2005 Act have been widely welcomed as an example of plain and clear statutory language. I would therefore deprecate any attempt to add any embellishment or gloss to the statutory wording unless to do so is plainly necessary": *York City Council v C* [2013] EWCA Civ 478, [2014] 2 WLR 1, per McFarlane LJ at paras [35] and [37].

As for the distinction between the general capacity to give or withhold consent to sexual relations, which is the necessary forward-looking focus of the Court of Protection, and the person-specific, time and place-specific, occasion when that capacity is actually deployed and consent is either given or withheld which is the focus of the criminal law, see *IM v LM (by her litigation friend, the Official Solicitor) (capacity to consent to sexual relations)* [2014] EWCA Civ 37, [2014] 3 WLR 409, [2014] 2 FCR 13.

7.8462 **2. People who lack capacity** (1) For the purposes of this Act, a person lacks capacity in relation to a matter if at the material time he is unable to make a decision for himself in relation to the matter because of an impairment of, or a disturbance in the functioning of, the mind or brain.

(2) It does not matter whether the impairment or disturbance is permanent or temporary.

(3) A lack of capacity cannot be established merely by reference to—

(*a*) a person's age or appearance, or

(*b*) a condition of his, or an aspect of his behaviour, which might lead others to make unjustified assumptions about his capacity.

(4) In proceedings under this Act or any other enactment, any question whether a person lacks capacity within the meaning of this Act must be decided on the balance of probabilities.

(5) No power which a person ("D") may exercise under this Act—

(a) in relation to a person who lacks capacity, or
(b) where D reasonably thinks that a person lacks capacity,

is exercisable in relation to a person under 16.

(6) Subsection (5) is subject to section 18(3).

[Mental Capacity Act 2005, s 2.]

7.8463 3. **Inability to make decisions** (1) For the purposes of section 2, a person is unable to make a decision for himself if he is unable—

(a) to understand the information relevant to the decision,
(b) to retain that information,
(c) to use or weigh that information as part of the process of making the decision, or
(d) to communicate his decision (whether by talking, using sign language or any other means).

(2) A person is not to be regarded as unable to understand the information relevant to a decision if he is able to understand an explanation of it given to him in a way that is appropriate to his circumstances (using simple language, visual aids or any other means).

(3) The fact that a person is able to retain the information relevant to a decision for a short period only does not prevent him from being regarded as able to make the decision.

(4) The information relevant to a decision includes information about the reasonably foreseeable consequences of—

(a) deciding one way or another, or
(b) failing to make the decision.

[Mental Capacity Act 2005, s 3.]

7.8464 4. **Best interests** (1) In determining for the purposes of this Act what is in a person's best interests, the person making the determination must not make it merely on the basis of—

(a) the person's age or appearance, or
(b) a condition of his, or an aspect of his behaviour, which might lead others to make unjustified assumptions about what might be in his best interests.

(2) The person making the determination must consider all the relevant circumstances and, in particular, take the following steps.

(3) He must consider—

(a) whether it is likely that the person will at some time have capacity in relation to the matter in question, and
(b) if it appears likely that he will, when that is likely to be.

(4) He must, so far as reasonably practicable, permit and encourage the person to participate, or to improve his ability to participate, as fully as possible in any act done for him and any decision affecting him.

(5) Where the determination relates to life-sustaining treatment he must not, in considering whether the treatment is in the best interests of the person concerned, be motivated by a desire to bring about his death.

(6) He must consider, so far as is reasonably ascertainable—

(a) the person's past and present wishes and feelings (and, in particular, any relevant written statement made by him when he had capacity),
(b) the beliefs and values that would be likely to influence his decision if he had capacity, and
(c) the other factors that he would be likely to consider if he were able to do so.

(7) He must take into account, if it is practicable and appropriate to consult them, the views of—

(a) anyone named by the person as someone to be consulted on the matter in question or on matters of that kind,
(b) anyone engaged in caring for the person or interested in his welfare,
(c) any donee of a lasting power of attorney granted by the person, and
(d) any deputy appointed for the person by the court,

as to what would be in the person's best interests and, in particular, as to the matters mentioned in subsection (6).

(8) The duties imposed by subsections (1) to (7) also apply in relation to the exercise of any powers which—

(a) are exercisable under a lasting power of attorney, or
(b) are exercisable by a person under this Act where he reasonably believes that another person lacks capacity.

(9) In the case of an act done, or a decision made, by a person other than the court, there is sufficient compliance with this section if (having complied with the requirements of subsections (1) to (7)) he reasonably believes that what he does or decides is in the best interests of the person concerned.

(10) "Life-sustaining treatment" means treatment which in the view of a person providing health care for the person concerned is necessary to sustain life.

(11) "Relevant circumstances" are those—

(*a*) of which the person making the determination is aware, and
(*b*) which it would be reasonable to regard as relevant.
[Mental Capacity Act 2005, s 4.]

7.8465 **4A. Restriction on deprivation of liberty** (1) This Act does not authorise any person ("D") to deprive any other person ("P") of his liberty.
(2) But that is subject to—
(*a*) the following provisions of this section, and
(*b*) section 4B.
(3) D may deprive P of his liberty if, by doing so, D is giving effect to a relevant decision of the court.
(4) A relevant decision of the court is a decision made by an order under section 16(2)(*a*) in relation to a matter concerning P's personal welfare.
(5) D may deprive P of his liberty if the deprivation is authorised by Schedule A1 (hospital and care home residents: deprivation of liberty).
[Mental Capacity Act 2005, s 4A as inserted by the Mental Health Act 2007, s 50.]

7.8466 **4B. Deprivation of liberty necessary for life-sustaining treatment etc** (1) If the following conditions are met, D is authorised to deprive P of his liberty while a decision as respects any relevant issue is sought from the court.
(2) The first condition is that there is a question about whether D is authorised to deprive P of his liberty under section 4A.
(3) The second condition is that the deprivation of liberty—
(*a*) is wholly or partly for the purpose of—
(i) giving P life-sustaining treatment, or
(ii) doing any vital act, or
(*b*) consists wholly or partly of—
(i) giving P life-sustaining treatment, or
(ii) doing any vital act.
(4) The third condition is that the deprivation of liberty is necessary in order to—
(*a*) give the life-sustaining treatment, or
(*b*) do the vital act.
(5) A vital act is any act which the person doing it reasonably believes to be necessary to prevent a serious deterioration in P's condition.
[Mental Capacity Act 2005, s 4B as inserted by the Mental Health Act 2007, s 50.]

7.8467 **5. Acts in connection with care or treatment** (1) If a person ("D") does an act in connection with the care or treatment of another person ("P"), the act is one to which this section applies if—
(*a*) before doing the act, D takes reasonable steps to establish whether P lacks capacity in relation to the matter in question, and
(*b*) when doing the act, D reasonably believes—
(i) that P lacks capacity in relation to the matter, and
(ii) that it will be in P's best interests for the act to be done.
(2) D does not incur any liability in relation to the act that he would not have incurred if P—
(*a*) had had capacity to consent in relation to the matter, and
(*b*) had consented to D's doing the act.
(3) Nothing in this section excludes a person's civil liability for loss or damage, or his criminal liability, resulting from his negligence in doing the act.
(4) Nothing in this section affects the operation of sections 24 to 26 (advance decisions to refuse treatment).
[Mental Capacity Act 2005, s 5.]

7.8468 **6. Section 5 acts: limitations** (1) If D does an act that is intended to restrain P, it is not an act to which section 5 applies unless two further conditions are satisfied.
(2) The first condition is that D reasonably believes that it is necessary to do the act in order to prevent harm to P.
(3) The second is that the act is a proportionate response to—
(*a*) the likelihood of P's suffering harm, and
(*b*) the seriousness of that harm.
(4) For the purposes of this section D restrains P if he—
(*a*) uses, or threatens to use, force to secure the doing of an act which P resists, or
(*b*) restricts P's liberty of movement, whether or not P resists.
(5) *Repealed.*
(6) Section 5 does not authorise a person to do an act which conflicts with a decision made, within the scope of his authority and in accordance with this Part, by—
(*a*) a donee of a lasting power of attorney granted by P, or
(*b*) a deputy appointed for P by the court.
(7) But nothing in subsection (6) stops a person—
(*a*) providing life-sustaining treatment, or

(*b*) doing any act which he reasonably believes to be necessary to prevent a serious deterioration in P's condition,

while a decision as respects any relevant issue is sought from the court.

[Mental Capacity Act 2005, s 6 as amended by the Mental Health Act 2007, Sch 11.]

7.8469 **44. Ill-treatment or neglect** (1) Subsection (2) applies if a person ("D")—

(*a*) has the care of a person ("P") who lacks, or whom D reasonably believes to lack, capacity,

(*b*) is the donee of a lasting power of attorney, or an enduring power of attorney (within the meaning of Schedule 4), created by P, or

(*c*) is a deputy[1] appointed by the court for P.

(2) D is guilty of an offence if he ill-treats or wilfully neglects [2] P.

(3) A person guilty of an offence under this section is liable[3]—

(*a*) on summary conviction, to imprisonment for a term not exceeding 12 months or a fine not exceeding the statutory maximum or both;

(*b*) on conviction on indictment, to imprisonment for a term not exceeding 5 years or a fine or both.

[Mental Capacity Act 2005, s 44.]

1 "Deputy" has the meaning given in s 16(2)(*b*) ie where a person lacks capacity in relation to a matter or matters concerning his personal welfare, or his property and affairs and the court may make the decision or decisions on his behalf in relation to the matter or matters, or appoint a person (a "deputy") to make decisions on P's behalf in relation to the matter or matters.

2 For procedure in respect of this offence which is triable either way, see the Magistrates' Courts Act 1980, ss 17A–21 in PART I: MAGISTRATES' COURTS, PROCEDURE, ante.

3 "Wilfully" means deliberately refraining from acting or refraining from acting because of not caring whether action was required or not, ie the test is subjective. Mere neglect is not enough. It must be "wilful" which means that something more was required than a duty and what a reasonable person would regard as a reckless breach of that duty: *R v Turbill* [2013] EWCA Crim 1422, [2014] 1 Cr App Rep 62, [2014] Crim LR 388.

# NUISANCES

## PUBLIC NUISANCES

**7.8470** A person is guilty of a public nuisance who does an unlawful act or fails to discharge a legal duty and thereby— (*a*) endangers the lives, safety, health, property or comfort of the public; or (*b*) obstructs the public in the exercise or enjoyment of any right that is common to all the subjects of Her Majesty[1]. The offence of public nuisance is sufficiently clear to enable a person, with appropriate legal advice if necessary, to regulate his behaviour and meets the certainty requirement of art 7 of the European Convention on Human Rights and also meets the requirements of arts 8 and 10. Unless there is good reason for doing otherwise, where the conduct falls within the definition of a statutory offence, it is ordinarily proper that conduct falling within that definition should be prosecuted for the statutory offence and not for a common law offence. Nor is it in the ordinary way a reason for resorting to the common law offence that the prosecutor is freed from mandatory time limits or restrictions on penalty. It must rather be assumed that Parliament imposed such restrictions. Accordingly, the circumstances in which, in future, there can properly be resort to the common law crime of public nuisance will be relatively rare[1]. Earlier authorities, cited below, must be read in the light of this approach. A nuisance which materially affects the reasonable comfort and convenience of persons within its sphere, may be a public nuisance (*A-G v PYA Quarries Ltd* [1957] 2 QB 169, [1957] 1 All ER 894, 121 JP 323). See also *R v Madden* [1973] 3 All ER 155. As injury is caused to separate individuals rather than to the community or a significant section of it, whatever other offence may have constituted, the crime of public nuisance does not extend to separate and individual telephone calls, however persistent and vexatious, or postal communications[2]. *A fortiori* a single act by a male on foot of soliciting a woman for the purposes of prostitution within a recognised area cannot amount to an offence of public nuisance[3]. An offensive trade, either from the noise or smell, carried on to the annoyance or discomfort of all persons in the neighbourhood, is a nuisance; so is every unauthorised obstruction of the highway to the annoyance of the public (see *R v Train* (1862) 2 B & S 640, 26 JP 469).

It is sufficient if the inconvenience result as an immediate consequence of the act, as the erection of a booth for rope-dancing, or exhibiting effigies in a shop window, so as to attract crowds, and thereby causing the footway to be obstructed. In *R v Graham and Burns* (1888) 4 TLR 212, CHARLES J, ruled that there is no right to hold public meetings in Trafalgar Square, or in any other public place, but that such places are "for people to pass along," a use which is directly in conflict with that for public meeting; and in *Ex p Lewis* (1888) 21 QBD 191, 52 JP 773, the Court of Appeal acquiesced in this ruling. Keeping ferocious animals without proper control is a public nuisance (3 Burn's Justice, 30th ed, 1032); and exposing a person in public having a contagious disease (see also Public Health (Control of Diseases) Act 1984 in title PUBLIC HEALTH, post). Prior to the Obscene Publications Act 1959, selling obscene prints or books was an indictable offence but by s 2(4) of that Act, a person publishing an obscene article (as therein defined) shall no longer be proceeded against at common law[4]. Exposing a horse in a fair which has the glanders, is an indictable offence. So is an indecent exposure of the person in a public omnibus, in the view of persons travelling therein (*R v Holmes* (1853) Dears CC 207, 17 JP 390); or on the roof of a back of a house, so as to be visible to the persons in the back premises of many other houses (*R v Thallman* (1863) Le & Ca 326, 27 JP 790); and it is not necessary that the exposure should be on a[5] public highway (id). It may be at a spot where the public are in the habit of trespassing without interference, although not a public place (*R v Wellard* (1884) 14 QBD 63, 49 JP 296). Showing and keeping a booth on Epsom Downs for an indecent performance to anyone desirous of seeing it were held to constitute a common law offence (*R v Saunders* (1875) 1 QBD 15). More than one person must at least have been able to see the act of indecency complained of, but actual disgust or annoyance on the part of an observer need not be proved (*R v Mayling* [1963] 2 QB 717, [1963] 1 All ER 687, 127 JP 269; *R v Lunderbech* [1991] Crim LR 784; *Rose v DPP* [2006] EWHC 852 (Admin), [2006] 1 WLR 2626, [2006] 2 Cr App R 29, 171 JP 57); and *R v Hamilton* [2007] EWCA Crim 2062, [2008] 1 All ER 1103, [2008] 2 WLR 107. See further the title OUTRAGING PUBLIC DECENCY in this PART, post.

Drawing a crowd of noisy and disorderly people close to a dwelling-house by music and fireworks is a nuisance which will be restrained by injunction (*Walker v Brewster* (1867) LR 5 Eq 25, 32 JP 87, and Treat. 115). Defendants, the manager and proprietors of a theatre, were held liable for obstruction to access to plaintiff's premises by reason of the assembling of a large crowd or queue in the street previously to opening of theatre (COZENS-HARDY MR and SWINFEN-EADY LJ; PHILLIMORE LJ *diss*) (*Lyons, Sons & Co v Gulliver* [1914] 1 Ch 631, 78 JP 98).

If the nuisance is stopped before the hearing an injunction may not be granted (*Barber v Penley* [1893] 2 Ch 447, 57 JP 562). But if an injunction would have been granted in the first instance, costs may be given (*Wagstaff v Edison Bell Phonograph Co* (1893) 10 TLR 80). CHITTY J, granted an *interim* injunction restraining two defendants, one of whom had a "merry-go-round", from playing organs at a place resorted to by excursionists, sixty yards from a dwelling-house. It was held that what each did might not amount to a nuisance in law, yet if the aggregate noise caused by the two did amount to a legal nuisance, the plaintiff was entitled to the protection of the court (*Lambton v Mellish, Lambton v Cox* [1894] 3 Ch 163, 58 JP 835). As to the nuisance created by a circus, see *Inchbald v Robinson, Inchbald v Barrington* (1869) 4 Ch App 388, 38 JP 484. See also *Phillips v Thomas* (1890) 62 LT 793, and *Bedford v Leeds Corpn* (1913) 77 JP 430. Similar nuisances may be dealt with summarily under bye-laws. A bye-law made under the Municipal Corpns Act 1882, provided that no person should to the annoyance or disturbance of residents or passengers keep or manage a shooting gallery, swing-boat, roundabout, or other like thing on any street or public place or on land adjoining or near to such street or public place, provided that the bye-law should not apply to any fair lawfully held. The Queen's Bench Division upheld the bye-law (*Teale v Harris* (1896) 60 JP 744). No length of time will legalise a public nuisance (*R v Cross* (1812) 3 Camp 224, and Treat. 36 JP 242). Collecting crowds round a shop by exhibiting attractive objects and thus creating an obstruction on the highway is an indictable nuisance (*R v Lewis* (1881) 72 LT Jo 117, Treat, 46 JP 20). Nothing short of absolute necessity will justify a person in obstructing the highway. An encroachment on or enclosure of a town or village green, also any erection thereon, or disturbance, or interference or occupation of the soil thereof, which is made otherwise than with a view to the better enjoyment of such town or village green, or recreation ground, is a public nuisance (Commons Act 1876, 39 & 40 Vict c 56, s 29). A gipsy encampment may in certain circumstances be a public nuisance, and an injunction will be granted against the owner of the land restraining him from allowing his land to be used for such a purpose (*A-G v Stone* (1895) 60 JP 168).

A defendant is guilty if he knew or ought to have known that as a result of his actions a public nuisance would be committed; actual knowledge need not be established[6]

**Procedure.**—Offences at common law of public nuisance are triable either way (Magistrates' Courts Act 1980, s 17 and Sch 1); for procedure see ibid, ss 17A–21 in PART I: MAGISTRATES' COURTS, PROCEDURE, ante. Punishable on summary conviction by imprisonment not exceeding **six months** and/or a fine not exceeding **the statutory maximum** (ibid, s 32). For other summary proceedings see the Environmental Protection Act 1990, ss 80 ff in this PART: title PUBLIC HEALTH, post.

[1] *R v Rimmington; R v Goldstein* [2005] UKHL 63, [2006] 1 AC 459, [2006] 2 All ER 257, [2006] 1 Cr App R 17.

[2] *R v Rimmington* [2005] UKHL 63, [2006] 1 AC 459, [2006] 2 All ER 257, [2006] 1 Cr App R 17 (sending 538 separate postal packages containing racially offensive material to members of the public).

[3] *DPP v Fearon* [2010] EWHC 340 (Admin), (2010) 174 JP 174.

[4] See this PART: title OBSCENE PUBLICATIONS, post.

[5] A urinal adjoining a public footway in a public park is a public place, so as to subject parties committing gross indecencies there to an indictment for a nuisance (*R v Harris* (1871) LR 1 CCR 282, 35 JP 185). Where the indecency consists of an exposure of person with intent to insult any female, see the Vagrancy Act 1824, s 4, title VAGRANTS, post.

[6] *R v Shorrock* [1993] 3 All ER 917, 98 Cr App R 67, approved in *R v Rimmington; R v Goldstein* [2005] UKHL 63, [2006] 1 AC 459, [2006] 2 All ER 257, [2006] 1 Cr App R 17 (in *Goldstein* conviction quashed for causing nuisance to the public by posting or causing to be posted to a friend, an envelope containing salt which leaked causing an anthrax scare at the sorting office as no evidence that it was foreseeable by him).

# OBSCENE PUBLICATIONS

**Contents**



## Children and Young Persons (Harmful Publications) Act 1955

(3 & 4 Eliz 2 c 28)

7.8471 **1. Works to which this Act applies** This Act applies to any book, magazine or other like work which is of a kind likely to fall into the hands of children or young persons[1] and consists wholly or mainly of stories told in pictures (with or without the addition of written matter), being stories portraying—

(*a*) the commission of crimes; or
(*b*) acts of violence or cruelty; or
(*c*) incidents of a repulsive or horrible nature;

in such a way that the work as a whole would tend to corrupt a child or young person into whose hands it might fall.

[Children and Young Persons (Harmful Publications) Act 1955, s 1.]

1 "Child" means a person under the age of fourteen years: "young person" means a person who has attained the age of fourteen years and is under the age of eighteen years (Children and Young Persons Act 1933, s 107, applied by the Children and Young Persons (Harmful Publications) Act 1955, s 5(2)).

7.8472 **2. Penalty for printing, publishing, selling, etc, works to which this Act applies**

(1) A person who prints, publishes, sells or lets on hire a work to which this Act applies, or has any such work in his possession for the purpose of selling it or letting it on hire, shall be guilty of an offence and liable, on summary conviction, to imprisonment for a term not exceeding **four months*** or to a fine not exceeding **level 3** on the standard scale or to both:

Provided that, in any proceedings taken under this subsection against a person in respect of selling or letting on hire a work or of having it in his possession for the purpose of selling it or letting it on hire, it shall be a defence for him to prove that he had not examined the contents of the work and had no reasonable cause to suspect that it was one to which this Act applies.

(2) A prosecution for an offence under this section shall not, in England or Wales, be instituted[1] except by, or with the consent of, the Attorney-General[2].

[Children and Young Persons (Harmful Publications) Act 1955, s 2 as amended by the Criminal Justice Act 1982, ss 38 and 46.]

* **Words substituted by the Criminal Justice Act 2003, Sch 26 from a date to be appointed.**

1 The prosecution is "instituted" on the laying of an information for a summons or a warrant (*Willace's Case* (1797) 1 East PC 186; *Brooks v Bagshaw* [1904] 2 KB 798, 68 JP 514).

2 Any function of the Attorney-General may be discharged by the Solicitor-General if (*a*) the office of Attorney-General is vacant; (*b*) he is unable to act owing to absence or illness; or (*c*) he authorises the Solicitor-General to act in any particular case (Law Officers Act 1944, s 1).

7.8473 **3. Power to search for, and dispose of, works to which this Act applies and articles for printing them** (1) Where, upon an information being laid before a justice of the peace that a person has, or is suspected of having, committed an offence under the last foregoing section with respect to a work (thereafter in this subsection referred to as "the relevant work"), the justice issues a summons directed to that person requiring him to answer to the information or issues a warrant to arrest that person, that or any other justice, if satisfied by written information[1] substantiated on oath that there is reasonable ground for suspecting that the said person has in his possession or under his control—

(*a*) any copies of the relevant work or any other work to which this Act applies; or
(*b*) any plate[2] prepared for the purpose of printing copies of the relevant work or any other work to which this Act applies or any photographic film prepared for that purpose;

may grant a search warrant authorising any constable to enter (if necessary by force) any premises specified in the warrant and any vehicle or stall used by the said person for the purposes of trade or business and to search the premises, vehicle or stall and seize any of the following things which the constable finds therein or thereon, that is to say:

(i) any copies of the relevant work and any copies of any other work which the constable has reasonable cause to believe to be one to which this Act applies; and
(ii) any plate[2] which the constable has reasonable cause to believe to have been prepared for the purpose of printing copies of any such work as is mentioned in paragraph (i) of this subsection and any photographic film[3] which he has reasonable cause to believe to have been prepared for that purpose.

(2) The court by or before which a person is convicted of an offence under the last foregoing section with respect to a work may order any copies of that work and any plate[2] prepared for the

purpose of printing copies of that work or photographic film[3] prepared for that purpose, being copies which have, or a plate or film which has, been found in his possession or under his control, to be forfeited:

Provided that an order made under this subsection by a magistrates' court or, on appeal from a magistrates' court, by a court of quarter sessions shall not take effect until the expiration of the ordinary time[4] within which an appeal in the matter of the proceedings in which the order was made may be lodged (whether by giving notice of appeal or applying for a case to be stated for the opinion of the High Court) or, where such an appeal is duly lodged, until the appeal is finally decided or abandoned.

(3) *Scotland.*

[Children and Young Persons (Harmful Publications) Act 1955, s 3 as amended by the Police and Criminal Evidence Act 1984, Sch 7.]

---

[1] Note that this "written information" may not be submitted except at the same time or after a prosecution has been "instituted" by the issue of a summons or a warrant for an offence under s 2, supra, and this may only be with the consent of the Attorney-General (see s 2, supra).

[2] "Plate" includes block, mould, matrix and stencil (s 5(2)).

[3] "Photographic film" includes photographic plate (s 5(2)).

[4] This will be 21 days in respect of an appeal to the Crown Court (Criminal Procedure Rules, Part 34) or an application for a case stated (Magistrates' Courts Act 1980, s 111).

7.8474 4. **Prohibition of importation of works to which this Act applies and articles for printing them** The importation of—

(*a*) any work to which this Act applies; and

(*b*) any plate prepared for the purpose of printing copies of any such work and any photographic film prepared for that purpose;

is hereby prohibited[1].

[Children and Young Persons (Harmful Publications) Act 1955, s 4.]

---

[1] Importation will be an offence under the Customs and Excise Management Act 1979; see ss 49(1)(*b*) and 50 thereof.

## Obscene Publications Act 1959[1]

(7 & 8 Eliz 2 c 66)

7.8475 1. **Test of obscenity** (1) For the purposes of this Act an article shall be deemed to be obscene if its effect or (where the article comprises two or more distinct items) the effect of any one of its items[2] is, if taken as a whole, such as to tend to deprave and corrupt[3] persons[4] who are likely, having regard to all relevant circumstances, to read, see or hear the matter contained or embodied in it[5].

(2) In this Act "article"[6] means any description of article containing or embodying matter to be read or looked at or both, any sound record, and any film or other record of a picture or pictures.

(3) For the purposes of this Act a person publishes[7] an article who—

(*a*) [8] distributes, circulates, sells, lets on hire, gives, or lends it, or who offers[9] it for sale or for letting on hire; or

(*b*) in the case of an article containing or embodying matter to be looked at or a record, shows, plays or projects it, or, where the matter is data stored electronically, transmits that data:

(4) For the purposes of this Act a person also publishes an article to the extent that any matter recorded on it is included by him in a programme included in a programme service[10].

(5) Where the inclusion of any matter in a programme so included would, if that matter were recorded matter, constitute the publication of an obscene article for the purposes of this Act by virtue of subsection (4) above, this Act shall have effect in relation to the inclusion of that matter in that programme as if it were recorded matter.

(6) In this section "programme" and "programme service" have the same meaning as in the Broadcasting Act 1990[10].

[Obscene Publications Act 1959, s 1 as amended by the Criminal Law Act 1977, s 53, the Broadcasting Act 1990, s 162 and Sch 21 and the Criminal Justice and Public Order Act 1994, Sch 9.]

---

[1] For the application of this Act to television and sound programmes, reference should be made to the Broadcasting Act 1990, Sch 15, title Telecommunications and Broadcasting, post.

[2] Where an article, such as a magazine, comprises a number of distinct items, the test has to be applied to the individual items and if it shows one item to be obscene that is enough to make the whole article obscene (*R v Anderson* [1972] 1 QB 304, [1971] 3 All ER 1152, 136 JP 97).

[3] The words "deprave and corrupt" refer to the effect on the mind, including the emotions, and it is not necessary that any physical (or "overt") sexual activity should result: see *DPP v Whyte* [1972] AC 849, [1972] 3 All ER 12, 136 JP 686; in which case Lord Wilberforce and Lord Cross also stated that the proposition that likely readers of the books, being addicts of that type of material whose morals were already in a state of depravity or corruption, were incapable of being further depraved or corrupted, was fallacious.

[4] The questions of publication and obscenity are not to be confused. Publication to an individual can give rise to an offence under s 2(1) of the Act. There is no contextual reason for 'persons' not to include the singular. Where the evidence does not go beyond transmission to one person it is necessary to consider whether the effect of the material (here internet chat) was such as to tend to deprave and corrupt that person: *R v S(G)* [2012] EWCA Crim 398, [2012] 1 WLR 3368, [2012] 2 Cr App Rep 154.

In relation to a book "persons" cannot mean all readers, nor any one reader, nor, necessarily, the majority of readers or the average reader: the question is whether the effect of the book is to tend to deprave and corrupt a significant proportion; what is a significant proportion being a matter for the jury (or magistrates) to decide: *R v Calder & Boyars Ltd*

[1968] 3 All ER 644, 133 JP 20; but it is not appropriate for justices to consider what is the largest category of "most likely" readers and then to exclude persons falling within other categories from consideration, for it does not follow that the latter are not also "likely" readers: see *DPP v Whyte*, supra. For consideration of the position where obscene articles are intended for publication outside the jurisdiction of the English courts, see *Gold Star Publications v DPP* [1981] 2 All ER 257, [1981] 1 WLR 732.

[5] The test for obscenity depends upon the publication itself and the intention of the publisher is irrelevant (*R v Shaw* [1961] 1 All ER 330). (This was a decision of the Court of Criminal Appeal, on which issue there was no appeal to the House of Lords in the later state of this prosecution.) Obscenity and its tendency to deprave and corrupt are not limited to matters of sex (*John Calder (Publications) Ltd v Powell* [1965] 1 All ER 159, 129 JP 136, concerning a book relating to drug taking). In *DPP v A & BC Chewing Gum Ltd* [1968] 1 QB 159, [1967] 2 All ER 504, 131 JP 373, a Divisional Court of the Queen's Bench Division remitted a case for rehearing on the ground that a magistrates' court had wrongly refused to hear evidence of a psychiatrist about the likely effect on the minds of children of cards (sold with chewing gum) alleged by the prosecution to be obscene; but in *R v Anderson*, supra, the Court of Appeal held that that case should be regarded as highly exceptional in that the alleged obscene matter was (*a*) directed at very young children, and (*b*) was itself of a somewhat unusual kind; normally the issue "obscene or no" must be tried by the jury (or magistrates) without the assistance of expert evidence on that issue. See also *R v Staniforth* [1975] Crim LR 291, and *DPP v Jordan* [1977] AC 699, [1976] 3 All ER 775.

Proceedings at common law are now considerably restricted by s 2(4) of the Obscene Publications Act 1959.

See also s 28 of the Town Police Clauses Act 1847, in this PART: title TOWNS IMPROVEMENT; TOWN POLICE, post; Children and Young Persons Act 1933 s 39 in PART V: YOUTH COURTS, ante; Judicial Proceedings (Regulation of Reports) Act 1926, title LIBEL, ante.

[6] A video cassette is an article within the meaning of s 1(2) (*A-G's Reference (No 5 of 1980)* [1980] 3 All ER 816). Expert evidence may be necessary to act as guidance where the effects of potentially corrupting material was outside the experience of the ordinary man or woman; *R v Skirving, R v Grossman* [1985] QB 819, [1985] 2 All ER 705 (book containing instructions and recipes on how to make best use of the drug cocaine).

[7] The act of developing and printing a photographic film depicting obscene acts, of which a print was then returned to the customer, is capable of constituting an act of publication within the meaning of s 1(3) (*R v Taylor* [1995] 1 Cr App Rep 131, 158 JP 317, [1994] Crim LR 527). To publish an article to an individual is within the meaning of the Act. By transmitting comments to another person in the context of Internet relay chat, the defendant is publishing those comments and it is an act of publication falling within s 1(3)(b). It is not necessary for the defendant to transmit the comments to more than one person before the act can be caught by the statute. The fact that the identity of the recipient is not known is also irrelevant. Nor cannot it be said that because there is only one recipient and only one likely reader of an article, the article is incapable of meeting the test of obscenity for the purposes of the Act: *R v Smith* [2012] EWCA Crim 398, [2012] 1 WLR 3368, [2012] 2 Cr App Rep 14.

[8] Forms of publication fall into three distinct groups: (*i*) "sells, lets on hire, gives or lends" means publication to an individual; (*ii*) "distributes, circulates" involves more than one person; (*iii*) a mere "offer for sale or letting on hire" constitutes publication: discussed by the Court of Criminal Appeal in *R v Barker* [1962] 1 All ER 748, [1962] 1 WLR 349, 126 JP 274. Whether the article will tend to deprave and corrupt may depend upon the persons to whom it is published (*R v Barker*, supra; *R v Clayton and Halsey* [1963] 1 QB 163, [1962] 3 All ER 500, 127 JP 7 (purchase made by police officers)). See now Obscene Publications Act 1964, post.

[9] Display in a shop window may be merely "an invitation to treat" and not "an offer for sale", *cf Fisher v Bell* [1961] 1 QB 394, [1960] 3 All ER 731, 125 JP 101; applied to this Act by the Queen's Bench Divisional Court in *Mella v Monahan* [1961] Crim LR 175. See now the Obscene Publications Act 1964, post.

[10] For the meaning of "programme" and "programme service", see ss 202 and 201 of the Broadcasting Act 1990, in this PART: title TELECOMMUNICATIONS AND BROADCASTING, post. For the application of the Obscene Publications Act 1959 to television and sound programmes, see the Broadcasting Act 1990, Sch 15, in this PART: title TELECOMMUNICATIONS AND BROADCASTING, post.

7.8476 2. **Prohibition on publication of obscene matter**[1] (1) Subject as hereinafter provided, any person who, whether for gain or not, publishes an obscene article or who has an obscene article for publication for gain (whether gain to himself or gain to another)[2] shall be liable[3]—

(*a*) on summary conviction to a fine not exceeding the prescribed sum or to imprisonment for a term not exceeding **six months**;

(*b*) on conviction on indictment to a **fine** or to imprisonment for a term not exceeding **five years** or **both**.

(2) *Repealed.*

(3) A prosecution for an offence against this section shall not be commenced more than two years after the commission of the offence.

(3A) Proceedings for an offence under this section shall not be instituted except by or with the consent of the Director of Public Prosecutions in any case where the article in question is a moving picture film of a width of not less than sixteen millimetres and the relevant publication or the only other publication which followed or could reasonably have been expected to follow from the relevant publication took place or (as the case may be) was to take place in the course of an exhibition of a film and in this subsection "the relevant publication" means—

(*a*) in the case of any proceedings under this section for publishing an obscene article, the publication in respect of which the defendant would be charged if the proceedings were brought; and

(*b*) in the case of any proceedings under this section for having an obscene article for publication for gain, the publication which, if the proceedings were brought, the defendant would be alleged to have had in contemplation.

(4) A person publishing an article shall not be proceeded against for an offence at common law consisting of the publication of any matter contained or embodied in the article where it is of the essence of the offence that the matter is obscene[4].

(4A) Without prejudice to subsection (4) above, a person shall not be proceeded against for an offence at common law—

(*a*) in respect of an exhibition of a film or anything said or done in the course of an exhibition of a film, where it is of the essence of the common law offence that the exhibition or, as the case may be, what was said or done was obscene, indecent, offensive, disgusting or injurious to morality; or

(*b*) in respect of an agreement to give an exhibition of a film or to cause anything to be said or done in the course of such an exhibition where the common law offence consists of conspiring to corrupt public morals or to do any act contrary to public morals or decency.

(5) A person shall not be convicted of an offence against this section if he proves[5] that he had not examined the article in respect of which he is charged and had no reasonable cause to suspect that it was such that his publication of it would make him liable to be convicted of an offence against this section.

(6) In any proceedings against a person under this section the question whether an article is obscene shall be determined without regard to any publication by another person unless it could reasonably have been expected that the publication by the other person would follow from publication by the person charged.

(7) In this section, "exhibition of a film" has the meaning given in paragraph 15 of Schedule 1 to the Licensing Act 2003.

[Obscene Publications Act 1959, s 2 as amended by the Obscene Publications Act 1964, s 1, the Criminal Law Act 1977, ss 28, 53 and Sch 13, the Cinematograph (Amendment) Act 1982, Sch 1, the Cinemas Act 1985, Sch 2, the Licensing Act 2003, Sch 6 and the Criminal Justice and Immigration Act 2008, s 71.]

1 For the application of the Act to television and sound programmes see the Broadcasting Act 1990, Sch 15 in this PART, title TELECOMMUNICATIONS AND BROADCASTING post.

2 The alternative offence was added by the Obscene Publications Act 1964, post, to which reference should be made, particularly with regard to modifications of sub-ss. (5) and (6) of this section.

3 For procedure in respect of an offence triable either way, see the Magistrates' Courts Act 1980, ss 17A–21, ante.

4 A prosecution for the common law offence of outraging public decency is not barred by s 2(4) (*R v Gibson* [1990] 2 QB 619, [1991] 1 All ER 439, 155 JP 126, CA).

5 If the defendant avails himself of this statutory defence, the onus of proof is on him (*Cant v Harley & Sons Ltd* [1938] 2 All ER 768); but less so than on the prosecution in proving a case beyond reasonable doubt and the onus may be discharged by evidence of probability (*R v Carr-Briant* [1943] KB 607, [1943] 2 All ER 156, 107 JP 167). Note also the special defence that the publication was for the public good created by s 4, post.

7.8477 **3. Powers of search and seizure** (1) If a justice of the peace is satisfied by information[1] on oath that there is reasonable ground for suspecting that, in any premises or on any stall or vehicle in that area, being premises or a stall or vehicle specified in the information, obscene articles are, or are from time to time, kept for publication[2] for gain, the justice may issue a warrant[1] under his hand empowering any constable to enter[3] (if need be by force) and search the premises, or to search the stall or vehicle, and to seize and remove any articles found therein or thereon which the constable has reason to believe to be obscene articles and to be kept for publication for gain.

(2) A warrant under the foregoing subsection shall, if any obscene articles are seized under the warrant, also empower the seizure and removal of any documents found in the premises or, as the case may be, on the stall or vehicle which relate to a trade or business carried on at the premises or from the stall or vehicle.

(3) Subject to subsection (3A) of this section, any articles seized under subsection (1) of this section shall be brought before a justice of the peace acting in the local justice area in which the articles were seized, who may thereupon issue a summons[4] to the occupier of the premises or, as the case may be, the user of the stall or vehicle to appear on a day specified in the summons before a magistrates' court[5] acting in that local justice area to show cause why the articles or any of them should not be forfeited; and if the court is satisfied[6], as respects any of the articles, that at the time when they were seized they were obscene articles[7] kept for publication for gain, the court shall order[8] those articles to be forfeited[9];

Provided that if the person summoned does not appear, the court shall not make an order unless service of the summons is proved[10].

Provided also that this subsection does not apply in relation to any article seized under subsection (1) of this section which is returned to the occupier of the premises or, as the case may be, to the user of the stall or vehicle in or on which it was found.

(3A) Without prejudice to the duty of a court to make an order for the forfeiture of an article where section 1(4) of the Obscene Publications Act 1964 applies (orders made on conviction), in a case where by virtue of subsection (3A) of section 2 of this Act proceedings under the said section 2 for having an article for publication for gain could not be instituted except by or with the consent of the Director of Public Prosecutions, no order for the forfeiture of the article shall be made under this section unless the warrant under which the article was seized was issued on an information laid by or on behalf of the Director of Public Prosecutions.

(4) In addition to the person summoned, any other person being the owner, author or maker of any of the articles brought before the court, or any other person through whose hands they had passed before being seized, shall be entitled[11] to appear before the court on the day specified in the summons to show cause why they should not be forfeited.

(5) Where an order is made under this section for the forfeiture of any articles, any person who appeared, or was entitled[12] to appear, to show cause against the making of the order may appeal to the Crown Court; and no such order shall take effect until the expiration of the period within which notice of appeal to the Crown Court may be given against the order[13], or, if before the expiration thereof notice of appeal is duly given or application is made for the statement of a case for the opinion of the High Court, until the final determination or abandonment of the proceedings on the

appeal or case.

(6) If as respects any articles brought before it the court does not order forfeiture, the court may if it thinks fit order the person on whose information the warrant for the seizure of the articles was issued to pay such costs as the court thinks reasonable to any person who has appeared before the court to show cause why those articles should not be forfeited; and costs ordered to be paid under this subsection shall be enforceable as a civil debt[14].

(7) For the purposes of this section the question whether an article is obscene shall be determined on the assumption that copies of it would be published in any manner likely having regard to the circumstances in which it was found, but in no other manner[15].

[Obscene Publications Act 1959, s 3 as amended by the Courts Act 1971, Schs 8 and 9, the Criminal Law Act 1977, s 53 and Sch 12, the Police and Criminal Evidence Act 1984, Sch 7 and the Courts Act 2003, Sch 8.]

---

[1] A warrant under this subsection shall not be issued except on an information laid by or on behalf of the Director of Public Prosecutions or by a constable (Criminal Justice Act 1967, s 25). As to television and sound programmes, see also the Broadcasting Act 1990, Sch 15, title TELECOMMUNICATIONS AND BROADCASTING, post.

[2] Section 2 of the Obscene Publications Act 1964, post, provides in effect, that photographic negatives kept for the reproduction of photographs therefrom are articles kept for publication, thereby overriding the contrary decision in *Straker v DPP* [1963] 1 QB 926, [1963] 1 All ER 697, 127 JP 260.

[3] The issue and execution of the warrant must be in conformity with the Police and Criminal Evidence Act 1984, ss 15 and 16, ante in PART I: MAGISTRATES' COURTS, PROCEDURE.

[4] The summons will be issued on the information previously made on oath upon which the warrant was found: it is unnecessary to have a fresh information as a preliminary to the issue of a summons. It has been said by the High Court *obiter* that the summons must be issued within a reasonable time after the execution of the warrant (*Cox v Stinton* [1951] 2 KB 1021, [1951] 2 All ER 637, 115 JP 490).

[5] The court need not necessarily consist of justices different from the justices who examined the articles before the summons was issued (*Morgan v Bowker* [1964] 1 QB 507, [1963] 1 All ER 691, 127 JP 264).

[6] The Queen's Bench Divisional Court has upheld a direction of a judge hearing an appeal from justices by which appellant and respondent were enabled either to agree or to submit representative items of each of three degrees of obscenity for the court to consider; it would however have preferred a division into categories of pornographic behaviour or sexual perversions (*R v Crown Court at Snaresbrook, ex p Metropolitan Police Comr* (1984) 148 JP 449.

[7] An English court is both competent and entitled to hold that articles are obscene, notwithstanding that they are intended for publication outside the jurisdiction of the English courts (*Gold Star Publications v DPP* [1981] 2 All ER 257, [1981] 1 WLR 732).

[8] The order that the articles shall be forfeited relates to the "whole" articles even if parts only are obscene: thus where illustrations on the inside covers of a book were obscene, the whole book, and not the covers only, are required to be forfeited (*Paget Publications Ltd v Watson* [1952] 1 All ER 1256, 116 JP 320). Note the special defence that the publication was for the public good created by s 4, post. If articles are seized under this section and a person is convicted of having them for publication for gain (s 2 (as amended) ante), the court on conviction shall order forfeiture (Obscene Publications Act 1964, s 1(4), post).

[9] Where an order had been made for forfeiture of some only of many articles seized, it was held that appeal by way of case stated was appropriate in respect of the articles not ordered to be forfeited: but the court expressed the hope that such a course would be taken only in extreme cases (*Burke v Copper* [1962] 2 All ER 14, [1962] 1 WLR 700, 126 JP 319).

[10] For service of summons, see for proof of service, see Criminal Procedure Rules, Part 4, in the *Key Materials*.

[11] There is no duty to issue separate summonses to persons so entitled although each of them is entitled to "show cause" separately: their knowledge of the proceedings will be obtained from the summons issued to the occupier of the premises or user of the stall or vehicle.

[12] Note that the right of appeal is not restricted to persons who appeared before the magistrates' court: appeal is available to all who are entitled to appear by virtue of sub-s (4), supra.

[13] This is 21 days: see the Criminal Procedure Rules, Part 34, in the *Key Materials*.

[14] See the Magistrates' Courts Act 1980, s 58, in PART I, ante.

[15] The court must hear evidence tendered by the defence of the circumstances in which the articles were found, eg the nature of the business carried on, the methods employed in it, and then determine whether the articles would tend to deprave or corrupt persons to whom publication would be so made (*Morgan v Bowker* [1964] 1 QB 507, [1963] 1 All ER 691, 127 JP 264).

7.8478 4. **Defence of public good**[1] (1) Subject to subsection (1A) of this section, a person shall not be convicted of an offence against section two of this Act, and an order for forfeiture shall not be made under the foregoing section, if it is proved that publication of the article in question is justified as being for the public good on the ground that it is in the interests of science, literature, art or learning[2], or of other objects of general concern[3].

(1A) Subsection (1) of this section shall not apply where the article in question is a moving picture film or soundtrack, but—

(*a*) a person shall not be convicted of an offence against section 2 of this Act in relation to any such film or soundtrack, and

(*b*) an order for forfeiture of any such film or soundtrack shall not be made under section 3 of this Act,

if it is proved that publication of the film or soundtrack is justified as being for the public good on the ground that it is in the interests of drama, opera, ballet or any other art, or of literature or learning.

(2) It is hereby declared that the evidence of experts as to the literary, artistic, scientific or other merits of an article may be admitted in any proceedings under this Act either to establish or to negative the said ground[4].

(3) In this section "moving picture soundtrack" means any sound record designed for playing with a moving picture film, whether incorporated with the film or not.

[Obscene Publications Act 1959, s 4 as amended by the Criminal Law Act 1977, s 53.]

---

[1] On a charge under s 2(1) the proper course is for the court to determine the issues (i) whether the article is obscene and (ii) whether it was published by the defendant, before considering whether the defendant has succeeded in establishing the defence under s 4(1) (*DPP v Jordan* [1977] AC 699, [1976] 3 All ER 775, 141 JP 13).

2 "Learning" means a product of scholarship: *A-G's Reference* (*No* 3 *of* 1977) [1978] 3 All ER 1166, [1978] 1 WLR 1123.

3 These other objects must be such as not only conduce to the public good but are of concern to members of the public in general. The words "other objects of general concern" fall within the same area as "science, literature, art or learning". Expert evidence, in support of a defence under s 4, that obscene material is of therapeutic benefit to persons with certain sexual tendencies is, accordingly, inadmissible (*DPP v Jordan*, supra.)

4 The court is not bound by the evidence of such experts even though it is not contradicted by counter-evidence (*John Calder (Publications) Ltd v Powell* [1965] 1 QB 509, [1965] 1 All ER 159, 129 JP 136). The onus is on the defence to make out this defence on the balance of probabilities, but the court may require the defence witnesses on this defence to be heard first and the prosecution witnesses in rebuttal (*R v Calder & Boyars Ltd* [1968] 3 All ER 644).

## Obscene Publications Act 1964

(1964 c 74)

**7.8479** The Obscene Publications Act 1964 amends s 2(1) of the Act of 1959, by creating the offence of *having* an obscene article for publication for gain (s 1(1)).

A person shall be deemed to have an article for publication for gain if with a view to such publication he has the article in his ownership, possession or control (s 1(2)).

By this amendment, a conviction may be obtained in circumstances where a prosecution for publishing would fail by reason of the decisions in *R v Clayton and Halsey*, and *Mella v Monahan*, ante[1].

In proceedings brought under this amendment, the following provisions apply in place of sub-ss (5) and (6) of s 2 of the Act of 1959—

(*a*) he shall not be convicted of that offence if he proves that he had not examined the article and had no reasonable cause to suspect that it was such that his having it would make him liable to be convicted of an offence against that section; and

(*b*) the question whether the article is obscene shall be determined by reference to such publication for gain of the article as in the circumstances may reasonably be inferred he had in contemplation and to any further publication that could reasonably be expected to follow from it, but not to any other publication (s 1(3)).

1 See notes 7 and 8 to s 1 of the Obscene Publications Act 1959.

[Obscene Publications Act 1964, s 1.]

**7.8480 2. Negatives, etc for production of obscene articles** (1) The Obscene Publications Act 1959 (as amended by this Act) shall apply in relation to anything which is intended to be used, either alone or as one of a set, for the reproduction or manufacture therefrom of articles containing or embodying matter to be read, looked at or listened to, as if it were an article containing or embodying that matter so far as that matter is to be derived from it or from the set.

(2) For the purposes of the Obscene Publications Act 1959 (as so amended) an article shall be deemed to be had or kept for publication if it is had or kept for the reproduction or manufacture therefrom of articles for publication; and the question whether an article so had or kept is obscene shall—

(*a*) for purposes of s 2 of the Act be determined in accordance with s 1(3)(*b*) above as if any reference there to publication of the article were a reference to publication of articles reproduced or manufactured from it; and

(*b*) for purposes of s 3 of the Act be determined on the assumption that articles reproduced or manufactured from it would be published in any manner likely having regard to the circumstances in which it was found, but in no other manner.

[Obscene Publications Act 1964, s 2.]

## Indecent Displays (Control) Act 1981

(1981 c 42)

**7.8481 1. Indecent displays** (1) If any indecent matter is publicly displayed the person making the display and any person causing or permitting the display to be made shall be guilty of an offence.

(2) Any matter which is displayed in or so as to be visible from any public place shall, for the purposes of this section, be deemed to be publicly displayed.

(3) In subsection (2) above, "public place", in relation to the display of any matter, means any place to which the public have or are permitted to have access (whether on payment or otherwise) while that matter is displayed except—

(*a*) a place to which the public are permitted to have access only on payment which is or includes payment for that display; or

(*b*) a shop or any part of a shop to which the public can only gain access by passing beyond an adequate warning notice;

but the exclusions contained in paragraphs (*a*) and (*b*) above shall only apply where persons under the age of 18 years are not permitted to enter while the display in question is continuing.

(4) Nothing in this section applies in relation to any matter—

(*a*) included by any person in a television broadcasting service or other television programme service (within the meaning of Part I of the Broadcasting Act 1990);

(*b*) included in the display of an art gallery or museum and visible only from within the gallery or museum; or

(*c*) displayed by or with the authority of, and visible only from within a building occupied by, the Crown or any local authority; or

(*d*) included in a performance of a play (within the meaning of paragraph 14(1) of Schedule 1 to the Licensing Act 2003) in England and Wales or of a play (within the meaning of the Theatres Act 1968) in Scotland;

(*e*) included in an exhibition of a film, within the meaning of paragraph 15 of Schedule 1 to the Licensing Act 2003, in England and Wales, or a film exhibition, as defined in the Cinemas Act 1985, in Scotland—

(i) given in a place which as regards that exhibition is required to be licensed under section 1 of that Act or by virtue only of section 5, 7 or 8 of that Act is not required to be so licensed; or

(ii) which is an exhibition to which section 6 of that Act applies given by an exempted organisation as defined in subsection (6) of that section.

(5) In this section "matter" includes anything capable of being displayed, except that it does not include an actual human body or any part thereof; and in determining for the purpose of this section whether any displayed matter is indecent—

(*a*) there shall be disregarded any part of that matter which is not exposed to view; and

(*b*) account may be taken of the effect of juxtaposing one thing with another.

(6) A warning notice shall not be adequate for the purposes of this section unless it complies with the following requirements—

(*a*) The warning notice must contain the following words, and no others—

"WARNING

Persons passing beyond this notice will find material on display which they may consider indecent No admittance to persons under 18 years of age."

(*b*) The word "WARNING" must appear as a heading.

(*c*) No pictures or other matter shall appear on the notice.

(*d*) The notice must be so situated that no one could reasonably gain access to the shop or part of the shop in question without being aware of the notice and it must be easily legible by any person gaining such access.

[Indecent Displays (Control) Act 1981, s 1 as amended by the Cinemas Act 1985, Sch 2, the Broadcasting Act 1990, Sch 20 and the Licensing Act 2003, Sch 6.]

7.8482 **2. Powers of arrest, seizure and entry** (1) *Repealed.*

(2) A constable may seize any article which he has reasonable grounds for believing to be or to contain indecent matter and to have been used in the commission of an offence under this Act.

(3) In England and Wales, a justice of the peace if satisfied on information on oath that there are reasonable grounds for suspecting that an offence under this Act has been or is being committed on any premises and, in Scotland, a sheriff or justice of the peace on being so satisfied on evidence on oath, may issue a warrant[1] authorising any constable to enter the premises specified in the information or, as the case may be, evidence (if need be by force) to seize any article which the constable has reasonable grounds for believing to be or to contain indecent matter and to have been used in the commission of an offence under this Act.

[Indecent Displays (Control) Act 1981, s 2 as amended by the Police and Criminal Evidence Act 1984, Sch 7.]

1 The issue and execution of this warrant must conform to the Police and Criminal Evidence Act 1984, ss 15 and 16 in PART I: MAGISTRATES' COURTS, PROCEDURE, ante.

7.8483 **3. Offences by corporations** (1) Where a body corporate is guilty of an offence under this Act and it is proved that the offence occurred with the consent or connivance of, or was attributable to any neglect on the part of, any director, manager, secretary or other officer of the body, or any person who was purporting to act in any such capacity he, as well as the body corporate, shall be deemed to be guilty of that offence and shall be liable to be proceeded against and punished accordingly.

(2) Where the affairs of a body corporate are managed by its members, subsection (1) shall apply in relation to the acts and defaults of a member in connection with his functions of management as if he were a director of the body corporate.

[Indecent Displays (Control) Act 1981, s 3.]

7.8484 **4. Penalties** (1) In England and Wales, any person guilty of an offence under this Act shall be liable[1]—

(*a*) on summary conviction, to a fine not exceeding **the statutory maximum**; or

(*b*) on conviction on indictment, to imprisonment for a term not exceeding **two years** or a **fine** or **both**.

(2) *Scotland.*

(3) *Repealed.*

[Indecent Displays (Control) Act 1981, s 4 as amended by the Statute Law (Repeals) Act 1993, Sch 1.]

1 For procedure in respect of a triable either way offence, see the Magistrates' Courts Act 1980, ss 17A–21, in PART I, ante.

# OFFENSIVE WEAPONS

**Contents**



## Prevention of Crime Act 1953

(1 & 2 Eliz 2 c 14)

7.8485 **1. Prohibition of the carrying of offensive weapons without lawful authority or reasonable excuse** (1) Any person who without lawful authority or reasonable excuse[1], the proof whereof shall lie on him, has with[2] him in any public place any offensive weapon[3] shall be guilty of an offence, and shall be liable[4]—

(*a*) on summary conviction, to imprisonment for a term not exceeding **six months** or a fine not exceeding **the prescribed sum**, or **both**;

(*b*) on conviction on indictment, to imprisonment for a term not exceeding **four years** or a **fine** or **both**.

(2) Where any person is convicted of an offence under subsection (1) of this section the court may make an order for the forfeiture[5] or disposal of any weapon in respect of which the offence was committed.

(2A) Subsection (2B) applies where—

(*a*) a person is convicted of an offence under subsection (1) committed after this subsection is commenced, and

(*b*) when the offence was committed, the person was aged 16 or over and had at least one relevant conviction (see section 1ZA).

(2B) Where this subsection applies, the court must impose an appropriate custodial sentence (with or without a fine) unless the court is of the opinion that there are particular circumstances which—

(*a*) relate to the offence, to the previous offence or to the offender, and

(*b*) would make it unjust to do so in all the circumstances.

(2C) In this section "appropriate custodial sentence" means—

(*a*) in the case of a person who is aged 18 or over when convicted, a sentence of imprisonment for a term of at least 6 months;

(*b*) in the case of a person who is aged at least 16 but under 18 when convicted, a detention and training order of at least 4 months.

(2D) In considering whether it is of the opinion mentioned in subsection (2B) in the case of a person aged 16 or 17, the court must have regard to its duty under section 44 of the Children and Young Persons Act 1933 (general considerations).

(2E) Where—

(*a*) an appropriate custodial sentence has been imposed on a person under subsection (2B), and

(*b*) a relevant conviction without which subsection (2B) would not have applied has been subsequently set aside on appeal,

notice of appeal against the sentence may be given at any time within 28 days from the date on which the conviction was set aside (despite anything in section 18 of the Criminal Appeal Act 1968 (initiating procedure)).

(2F) Where an offence is found to have been committed over a period of two or more days, or at some time during a period of two or more days, it shall be taken for the purposes of this section to have been committed on the last of those days.

(2G) In relation to times before the coming into force of paragraph 180 of Schedule 7 to the Criminal Justice and Court Services Act 2000, the reference in subsection (2C)(*a*) to a sentence of imprisonment, in relation to an offender aged under 21 at the time of conviction, is to be read as a reference to a sentence of detention in a young offender institution.

(3) Repealed.

(4) In this section "public place"[6] includes any highway and any other premises or place to which at the material time the public have or are permitted to have access, whether on payment or

otherwise[3]; and "offensive weapon" means any article made or adapted[7] for use for causing injury to the person, or intended[8] by the person having it with him for such use by him[9] or by some other person.

[Prevention of Crime Act 1953, s 1 as amended by the Criminal Justice Act 1967, Sch 3, the Criminal Law Act 1977, ss 28 and 32, the Police and Criminal Evidence Act 1984, Sch 7, the Public Order Act 1986, Sch 2, the Criminal Justice Act 1988, s 46 and the Offensive Weapons Act 1996, s 2.]

---

1 This saving is identified with the carrying of the weapon, not with the manner of its use (*R v Jura* [1954] 1 QB 503, [1954] 1 All ER 696, 118 JP 280). Apart therefrom, injury caused by the weapon is evidence that it was carried for that use: see sub-s (4), infra; but if an article (possessed lawfully or for good reason) is used offensively to cause injury, this does not necessarily prove the intent required (ie to use for causing injury) which the prosecution must show in respect of articles which are not offensive weapons per se (*R v Dayle* [1973] 3 All ER 1151, 138 JP 65). The prosecution must prove, in the case of an article which is not an offensive weapon per se, e.g. a domestic knife (or an ordinary sheath knife, *R v Williamson* [1978] Crim LR 229), that at the time and place alleged it was the defendant's intention to use it for causing injury (*R v Allamby* [1974] 3 All ER 126, 138 JP 659. In *Bates v Bulman* (1979) 68 Cr App Rep 21 it was held that, as the purport of the Act was to prevent the carrying of offensive weapons, an offence was not committed by a defendant who seized a clasp knife, which he had not been carrying, for instant use on his victim. See also *C v DPP* [2002] Crim LR 322, where a dog was released from its lead and the lead was then used violently against police officers; it was held that the evidence had not been capable of sustaining the justices' conclusion that the intent to cause injury, which made the lead an offensive weapon, had been formed prior to the occasion of its actual use. A cricket bat is not an article made or adapted for causing injury to the person, but a person was rightly convicted where he took the bat from his flat and used it in an affray outside. This was not the case of an article carried lawfully and then used in the heat of the moment; by the time he entered the street, a public place, there was ample evidence to infer that at that stage he had formed an intention to injure: *R v Tucker* [2016] EWCA Crim 13, 180 JP 225. A flick knife is an offensive weapon per se (*R v Simpson* [1983] 3 All ER 789, [1983] 1 WLR 1494, 48 JP 33, CA. See also *Ohlson v Hylton* [1975] Crim LR 292, *R v Giles* [1976] Crim LR 253 and *R v Veasey* [1999] Crim LR 158, CA). "Injury" includes intimidation of a sort which is capable of producing injury through the operation of shock (*Woodward v Koessler* [1958] 3 All ER 557, 123 JP 14, as explained in *R v Edmonds* [1963] 2 QB 142, [1963] 1 All ER 828, 127 JP 283). Self protection from imminent attack may be a reasonable excuse (*Evans v Hughes* [1972] 3 All ER 412, 136 JP 725; followed in *R v Archbold* [2007] EWCA Crim 2137, (2007) 171 JP 664, though the Court found "considerable force" in the submission that the necessity for self defence had been created by the appellant's own actions in leaving his house armed with a knife to seek out the complainant; however, the issue of lawful authority or reasonable excuse should still have been left to the jury) but not the carrying of a knife on the off chance of being attacked (*R v Peacock* [1973] Crim LR 639), nor to repel unlawful violence which the defendant had knowingly and deliberately brought about by creating a situation in which violence was liable to be inflicted (*Malnik v DPP* [1989] Crim LR 451). See also *Bradley v Moss* [1974] Crim LR 430, and *Pittard v Mahoney* [1977] Crim LR 169. Security guards at dance halls who each carried a truncheon "as a deterrent and as part of the uniform" had no reasonable excuse in law (*R v Spanner, Poulter, Ward* [1973] Crim LR 704).

Unlike self defence, reasonable excuse is not subjective; where reasonable excuse is claimed it is for the defendant to prove both belief and the reasonableness of the belief on the balance of probabilities. Thus, a defendant had no reasonable excuse where he was carrying an iron bar for his own protection following an incident, five minutes earlier, when the defendant had feared (with reasonable cause) that he would be attacked. The risk of imminent attack had passed and it was irrelevant that the defendant believed otherwise: *N v DPP* [2011] EWHC 1807, 175 JP 337. (It was stated, however, in *R v Clancy* [2012] EWCA Crim 8, 176 JP 111 that "Insofar as the defendant relies on his own perception of the facts, we do not understand the court in that case to have held that it is necessary as a matter of law for him to show that his belief is reasonable. That would involve imposing an unjustifiable limitation on the meaning of that expression. All the court was doing was pointing out that if the defendant cannot show that his belief was reasonable, that too is a matter to be taken into account and the tribunal of fact may find that the defence is not made out (per Moore-Bick LJ).")

In *Bryan v Mott* [1976] Crim LR 64 it was held that it was not a "reasonable excuse" to have an offensive weapon for the purpose of committing suicide.

2 The onus is on the prosecution to prove that the accused knowingly had the weapon with him (*R v Cugullere* [1961] 2 All ER 343, 125 JP 414), and, where two or more are jointly charged, that each knew of weapons that another had with him and that there was a common purpose (*R v Edmonds* [1963] 2 QB 142, [1963] 1 All ER 828, 127 JP 283). The fact that the accused forgot he had the weapon is not in itself a reasonable excuse (*R v McCalla* (1988) 152 JP 481, 87 Cr App Rep 372, CA). However, depending on the circumstances of a particular case, forgetfulness may be relevant to whether or not a defendant has a reasonable excuse for possession of an offensive weapon (*R v Glidewell* (1999) 163 JP 557, CA). Where matters go beyond mere forgetfulness, it would normally be for a jury to decide whether there was a reasonable excuse or not: *R v Tsap* [2008] EWCA Crim 2923, 173 JP 4. (In *McCalla* there was no defence to put to the jury where the defendant had himself introduced the weapon into the glove compartment and forgotten it; this was distinguished in *Glidewell* where it was for the jury to decide whether the defence was made out in circumstances where a passenger in a taxi had left the item, and the taxi driver forgot he had then put it in the glove compartment; and in *Tsap* where the acquisition was innocent but the defendant discovered later the true nature of the item and then put it in his back pocket of a jacket which was not used for several months). The question of "lawful authority or reasonable excuse" does not arise until the prosecutor has established that the accused had with him an "offensive weapon" as alternatively defined by s 1(4) of the Act (*R v Petrie* [1961] 1 All ER 466, 125 JP 198).

3 Defined in s 1(4), post. See also note to the definition of "public place" in s 139 of the Criminal Justice Act 1988 and note thereto, post.

4 For procedure in respect of an offence triable either way, see the Magistrates' Courts Act 1980, ss 17A–21, in PART I: MAGISTRATES' COURTS, PROCEDURE, ante.

5 For disposal of forfeited weapons, see the Magistrates' Courts Act 1980, s 140, in PART I: MAGISTRATES' COURTS, PROCEDURE, ante.

6 In *Knox v Anderton* (1983) 147 JP 340, [1983] Crim LR 114, the upper landing of a block of flats on a housing estate was held to be a public place.

7 A machete in a scabbard and "Black Widow" catapult (a powerful catapult made of 2 strong pieces of rubber tubing, a leather sling and a forearm rest) were held not to be made or adapted for use for causing injury to the person (*Southwell v Chadwick* (1987) 85 Cr App Rep 235). However:

> "22 What is the position of a petrol bomb? It is specifically made to be easily portable, for use in public disorder, easily lit and thrown so as to cause explosion with resulting injury and damage. The fact that an offensive weapon might be used for an innocent purpose, as Lord Lane CJ observed (in *R v Simpson (Calvin)* [1983] 1 WLR 1494) in relation to flick knives, is not to the point. Indeed, this case is a fortiori to that: it is difficult to see an innocent purpose to which a petrol bomb could be put. In the circumstances, we have come to the conclusion that a petrol bomb is offensive per se and we venture to the view that the public would be astonished if the courts did not consider that to be clear" (per Sir Brian Leveson P in *R v Akhtar* [2015] EWCA Crim 176, [2015] 1 WLR 3046, [2015] 2 Cr App Rep 81)."

A half a pool cue (stuffed down the defendant's trousers and carried for his own protection) was capable of being an offensive weapon by reason of it constituting an article "adapted for use for causing injury" (*R (on the application of Sills) v DPP* [2006] EWHC 3383 (Admin), 171 JP 201). A weapon which has all the characteristics of a flick-knife does not cease to be a flick-knife (and thereby an offensive weapon per se) because it also has a secondary function such as being a lighter (*R v Vasili* [2011] EWCA Crim 615, [2011] 2 Cr App R 5, 175 JP 185). Similarly, where a leather belt had a detachable buckle in the form of a knuckle duster, the buckle was made or designed to cause injury and, thus, was offensive per se, even though it also served the purpose of being a belt buckle: *Direction of Public Prosecutions v Christof* [2015] EWHC 4096 (Admin), [2016] 2 Cr App R 6 at 9. (However, the buckle also had two holes, one for the belt to fit to it and the other for the purpose of tightening the belt; therefore, the item might have been made so as to make the belt with the buckle a fashion item rather than for the purpose of causing injury, even though the buckle might have been put to that use when removed from the belt. Therefore the case was remitted for further consideration):

> "9. Some further guidance as to what may and may not be an offensive weapon is provided by para.1 of Sch.1 to the Criminal Justice Act 1988 (Offensive Weapons) Order 1988 (SI 1988/2019), which lists weapons deemed offensive for the purposes of s.141 of the 1988 Act which prohibit a person from manufacturing, selling, hiring or offering for sale or hire, et cetera, a weapon to which the section applies or having such items in possession for those purposes. Paragraph 1(a) identifies as the first in the list:
>
> "A knuckleduster, that is, a band of metal or other hard material worn on one or more fingers, and designed to cause injury, and any weapon incorporating a knuckleduster."' (per Mitting J.)

[8] "Recklessness" as to whether the article will cause injury is insufficient: *R v Byrne* [2003] EWCA Crim 3253, [2004] Crim LR 582.

[9] A flick knife as defined in s 1(1)(*a*) of the Restriction of Offensive Weapons Act 1959 is an offensive weapon per se (*Gibson v Wales* [1983] 1 All ER 869, [1983] 1 WLR 393, 76 Cr App Rep 60.

**7.8485A 1ZA. Offence under section 1: previous relevant convictions** (1) For the purposes of section 1, "relevant conviction" means—

(a) a conviction for an offence under—
  (i) section 1 or 1A of this Act, or
  (ii) section 139, 139A or 139AA of the Criminal Justice Act 1988,
  (a "relevant offence"), whenever committed,

(*b*) a conviction in Scotland, Northern Ireland or a member State other than the United Kingdom for a civilian offence, whenever committed, which would have constituted a relevant offence if committed in England and Wales at the time of that conviction,

(*c*) a conviction for an offence under section 42 of the Armed Forces Act 2006, whenever committed, in respect of which the corresponding offence under the law of England and Wales (within the meaning of that section) is a relevant offence,

(*d*) a conviction for an offence under section 70 of the Army Act 1955, section 70 of the Air Force Act 1955 or section 42 of the Naval Discipline Act 1957, whenever committed, in respect of which the corresponding civil offence (within the meaning of the Act in question) is a relevant offence, and

(*e*) a conviction for a member State service offence, whenever committed, which would have constituted a relevant offence if committed in England and Wales at the time of conviction.

(2) In this section—

"civilian offence" means an offence other than—
  (*a*) an offence under an enactment mentioned in subsection (1)(*c*) or (*d*), or
  (*b*) a member State service offence;

"conviction" includes—
  (*a*) in relation to an offence under section 42 of the Armed Forces Act 2006, anything which by virtue of section 376(1) and (2) of that Act is to be treated as a conviction and
  (*b*) in relation to an offence under section 42 of the Naval Discipline Act 1957 and a member State service offence, a finding of guilt in respect of the person;

"member State service offence" means an offence which was the subject of proceedings under the law of a member State, other than the United Kingdom, governing all or any of the naval, military or air forces of that State.

(3) For the purposes of subsection (1)(*c*) and (*d*), where the offence was committed by aiding, abetting, counselling or procuring, it must be assumed that the act aided, abetted, counselled or procured was done in England and Wales.

[Prevention of Crime Act 1953, s 1ZA as inserted by the Criminal Justice and Courts Act 2015, s 28.]

**7.8486 1A. Offence of threatening with offensive weapon in public** (1) A person is guilty of an offence if that person—

(*a*) has an offensive weapon with him or her in a public place,
(*b*) unlawfully and intentionally threatens another person with the weapon, and
(*c*) does so in such a way that there is an immediate risk of serious physical harm to that other person.

(2) For the purposes of this section physical harm is serious if it amounts to grievous bodily harm for the purposes of the Offences against the Person Act 1861.

(3) In this section "public place" and "offensive weapon" have the same meaning as in

section 1.

(4) A person guilty of an offence under this section is liable—

(*a*) on summary conviction, to imprisonment for a term not exceeding 12 months or to a fine not exceeding the statutory maximum, or to both;

(*b*) on conviction on indictment, to imprisonment for a term not exceeding 4 years or to a fine, or to both.

(5) Where a person aged 16 or over is convicted of an offence under this section, the court must impose an appropriate custodial sentence (with or without a fine) unless the court is of the opinion that there are particular circumstances which—

(*a*) relate to the offence or to the offender, and

(*b*) would make it unjust to do so in all the circumstances.

(6) In this section "appropriate custodial sentence" means—

(*a*) in the case of a person who is aged 18 or over when convicted, a sentence of imprisonment for a term of at least 6 months;

(*b*) in the case of a person who is aged at least 16 but under 18 when convicted, a detention and training order of at least 4 months.

(7) In considering whether it is of the opinion mentioned in subsection (5) in the case of a person aged under 18, the court must have regard to its duty under section 44 of the Children and Young Persons Act 1933.

(8) In relation to an offence committed before the commencement of section 154(1) of the Criminal Justice Act 2003, the reference in subsection (4)(*a*) to 12 months is to be read as a reference to 6 months.

(9) In relation to times before the coming into force of paragraph 180 of Schedule 7 to the Criminal Justice and Court Services Act 2000, the reference in subsection (6)(*a*) to a sentence of imprisonment, in relation to an offender aged under 21 at the time of conviction, is to be read as a reference to a sentence of detention in a young offender institution.

(10) If on a person's trial for an offence under this section (whether on indictment or not) the person is found not guilty of that offence but it is proved that the person committed an offence under section 1, the person may be convicted of the offence under that section.

[Prevention of Crime Act 1953, s 1A as inserted by the Legal Aid, Sentencing and Punishment of Offenders Act 2012, s 142.]

## Restriction of Offensive Weapons Act 1959

(7 & 8 Eliz 2 c 37)

7.8487 **1. Penalties for offences in connection with dangerous weapons** (1) Any person who manufactures, sells or hires or offers for sale or hire or exposes or has in his possession for the purpose of sale or hire[1] or lends or gives to any other person—

(*a*) any knife which has a blade which opens automatically by hand pressure applied to a button, spring or other device in or attached to the handle of the knife, sometimes known as a "flick knife" or "flick gun"; or

(*b*) any knife which has a blade which is released from the handle or sheath thereof by the force of gravity or the application of centrifugal force and which, when released, is locked in place by means of a button, spring, lever, or other device, sometimes known as a "gravity knife",

shall be guilty of an offence and shall be liable on summary conviction to imprisonment for a term not exceeding **six months** or to a fine not exceeding **level 5** on the standard scale or to **both** such imprisonment and fine.

(2) The importation of any such knife as is described in the foregoing subsection is hereby prohibited[2].

[Restriction of Offensive Weapons Act 1959, s 1 as amended by the Restriction of Offensive Weapons Act 1961, s 1, the Criminal Justice Act 1982, ss 35, 38 and 46 and the Criminal Justice Act 1988, s 46.]

1 The inclusion of these words by the Act of 1961, meets the decision in *Fisher v Bell* [1961] 1 QB 394, [1960] 3 All ER 781, 125 JP 101.

2 Non-compliance with this prohibition is an offence within s 170 of the Customs and Excise Management Act 1979, in this PART: title CUSTOMS AND EXCISE, ante.

## Biological Weapons Act 1974

(1974 c 6)

7.8488 **1. Restriction on development etc of certain biological agents and toxins and biological weapons** (1) No person shall develop, produce, stockpile, acquire or retain—

(*a*) any biological agent or toxin of a type and in a quantity that has no justification for prophylactic, protective or other peaceful purposes; or

(*b*) any weapon, equipment or means of delivery designed to use biological agents or toxins for hostile purposes or in armed conflict.

(1A) A person shall not—

(*a*) transfer any biological agent or toxin to another person or enter into an agreement to do so, or

(*b*) make arrangements under which another person transfers any biological agent or toxin or enters into an agreement with a third person to do so,

if the biological agent or toxin is likely to be kept or used (whether by the transferee or any other person) otherwise than for prophylactic, protective or other peaceful purposes and he knows or has reason to believe that that is the case.

(2) In this section—

"biological agent" means any microbial or other biological agent; and

"toxin" means any toxin, whatever its origin or method of production.

(3) Any person contravening this section shall be guilty of an offence and shall, on conviction on indictment, be liable to imprisonment for **life**.

[Biological Weapons Act 1974, s 1 as amended by the Anti-terrorism, Crime and Security Act 2001, s 43.]

7.8489 **1A. Extraterritorial application of section 1** (1) Section 1 applies to acts done outside the United Kingdom, but only if they are done by a United Kingdom person.

(2) Proceedings for an offence committed under section 1 outside the United Kingdom may be taken, and the offence may for incidental purposes be treated as having been committed, in any place in the United Kingdom.

(3) Her Majesty may by Order in Council extend the application of section 1, so far as it applies to acts done outside the United Kingdom, to bodies incorporated under the law of any of the Channel Islands, the Isle of Man or any colony.

(4) In this section "United Kingdom person" means a United Kingdom national, a Scottish partnership or a body incorporated under the law of a part of the United Kingdom.

(5) For this purpose a United Kingdom national is an individual who is—

(*a*) a British citizen, a British overseas territories citizen, a British National (Overseas) or a British Overseas citizen;

(*b*) a person who under the British Nationality Act 1981 (c 61) is a British subject; or

(*c*) a British protected person within the meaning of that Act.

(6) Nothing in this section affects any criminal liability arising otherwise than under this section.

[Biological Weapons Act 1974, s 1A as inserted by the Anti-terrorism, Crime and Security Act 2001, s 44 and amended by the British Overseas Territories Act 2002, s 2(3).]

7.8490 **1B. Revenue and Customs prosecutions** (1) Proceedings for a biological weapons offence may be instituted by the Director of Public Prosecutions or by order of the Commissioners for Her Majesty's Revenue and Customs if it appears to the Director or to the Commissioners that the offence has involved—

(*a*) the development or production outside the United Kingdom of any thing mentioned in section 1(1)(*a*) or (*b*) above;

(*b*) the movement of any such thing into or out of any country or territory;

(*c*) any proposal or attempt to do anything falling within paragraph (*a*) or (*b*) above.

(2) In this section "biological weapons offence" means an offence under section 1 of this Act or section 50 of the Anti-terrorism, Crime and Security Act 2001 (including an offence of aiding, abetting, counselling, procuring or inciting the commission of, or attempting or conspiring to commit, such an offence).

(3) Any proceedings for an offence which are instituted by order of the Commissioners under subsection (1) above shall be commenced in the name of an officer of Revenue and Customs, but may be continued by another officer.

(4) Where the Commissioners investigate, or propose to investigate, any matter with a view to determining—

(*a*) whether there are grounds for believing that a biological weapons offence has been committed, or

(*b*) whether a person should be prosecuted for such an offence,

that matter shall be treated as an assigned matter within the meaning of the Customs and Excise Management Act 1979.

(5) Nothing in this section affects any power of any person (including any officer) apart from this section.

(6) Repealed.

(7) This section does not apply to the institution of proceedings in Scotland.]

[Biological Weapons Act 1974, s 1B as inserted by the Anti-terrorism, Crime and Security Act 2001, s 45 and amended by the Commissioners for Revenue and Customs Act 2005, Sch 4 and SI 2014/834.]

7.8491 **2. Prosecution of offences** (1) Proceedings for an offence under section 1 above shall not be instituted—

(*a*) in England or Wales, except by or with the consent of the Attorney General; or

(*b*) *Northern Ireland.*

(2), (3) Repealed.

[Biological Weapons Act 1974, s 2 as amended by the Criminal Jurisdiction Act 1975, Sch 6.]

7.8492 **3. Offences by bodies corporate** Where an offence under section 1 of this Act which is committed by a body corporate is proved to have been committed with the consent and connivance of, or to be attributable to any negligence on the part of, any director, manager, secretary or other similar officer of the body corporate, or any person who was purporting to act in any such capacity, he as well as the body corporate shall be guilty of that offence and shall be liable to be proceeded against and punished accordingly.

[Biological Weapons Act 1974, s 3.]

7.8493 4. **Powers to search and obtain evidence** (1) If a justice of the peace is satisfied by information on oath, or in Scotland the sheriff or a magistrate or justice of the peace is satisfied by evidence on oath, that there is reasonable ground for suspecting that an offence under section 1 of this Act has been, or is about to be, committed, he may grant a search warrant[1] authorising a constable—

(*a*) to enter, at any time within three months from the date of the warrant, any premises or place named therein, if necessary by force, and to search the premises or place and every person found therein;

(*b*) to inspect any document found in the premises or place or in the possession of any person found therein, and to take copies of, or seize or detain any such document;

(*c*) to inspect, seize and detain any equipment so found; and

(*d*) to inspect, sample, seize and detain any substance so found.

(2) A warrant issued under subsection (1) above, authorising a constable to take the steps mentioned in that subsection, may also authorise any person named in the warrant to accompany the constable and assist him in taking any of those steps.

[Biological Weapons Act 1974, s 4 as amended by the Police and Criminal Evidence Act 1984, Sch 7 and the Serious Organised Crime and Police Act 2005, Sch 16.]

---

1 The issue and execution of this warrant must conform to the Police and Criminal Evidence Act 1984, ss 15 and 16 in PART I: MAGISTRATES' COURTS, PROCEDURE, ante.

# Crossbows Act 1987

(1987 c 32)

7.8494 1. **Sale and letting on hire** A person who sells or lets on hire a crossbow or a part of a crossbow to a person under the age of eighteen is guilty of an offence, unless he believes him to be eighteen years of age or older and has reasonable ground for the belief.

[Crossbows Act 1987, s 1 as amended by the Violent Crime Reduction Act 2006, s 4.]

7.8495 2. **Purchase and hiring** A person under the age of eighteen who buys or hires a crossbow or a part of a crossbow is guilty of an offence.

[Crossbows Act 1987, s 2 as amended by the Violent Crime Reduction Act 2006, s 4.]

7.8496 3. **Possession** A person under the age of eighteen who has with him—

(*a*) a crossbow which is capable of discharging a missile, or

(*b*) parts of a crossbow which together (and without any other parts) can be assembled to form a crossbow capable of discharging a missile,

is guilty of an offence, unless he is under the supervision of a person who is twenty-one years of age or older.

[Crossbows Act 1987, s 3 as amended by the Violent Crime Reduction Act 2006, s 4.]

7.8497 4. **Powers of search and seizure etc** (1) If a constable suspects with reasonable cause that a person is committing or has committed an offence under section 3, the constable may—

(*a*) search that person for a crossbow or part of a crossbow;

(*b*) search any vehicle, or anything in or on a vehicle, in or on which the constable suspects with reasonable cause there is a crossbow, or part of a crossbow, connected with the offence.

(2) A constable may detain a person or vehicle for the purpose of a search under subsection (1).

(3) A constable may seize and retain for the purpose of proceedings for an offence under this Act anything discovered by him in the course of a search under subsection (1) which appears to him to be a crossbow or part of a crossbow.

(4) For the purpose of exercising the powers conferred by this section a constable may enter any land other than a dwelling-house.

[Crossbows Act 1987, s 4.]

7.8498 5. **Exception** This Act does not apply to crossbows with a draw weight of less than 1.4 kilograms.

[Crossbows Act 1987, s 5.]

7.8499 6. **Punishments** (1) A person guilty of an offence under section 1 shall be liable, on summary conviction, to imprisonment for a term not exceeding **six months**, to a fine not exceeding **level 5** on the standard scale, or to **both**.

(2) A person guilty of an offence under section 2 or 3 shall be liable, on summary conviction, to a fine not exceeding **level 3** on the standard scale.

(3) The court by which a person is convicted of an offence under this Act may make such order as it thinks fit as to the forfeiture or disposal of any crossbow or part of a crossbow in respect of which the offence was committed.

[Crossbows Act 1987, s 6.]

# Criminal Justice Act 1988[1]

(1988 c 33)

## Part XI[2]

## Miscellaneous

*Articles with blades or points and offensive weapons*

7.8500 **139. Offence of having article with blade or point in public place** (1) Subject to subsections (4) and (5) below, any person who has an article to which this section applies with him[3] in a public place[4] shall be guilty of an offence[5].

(2) Subject to subsection (3) below, this section applies to any article which has a blade or is sharply pointed except a folding pocketknife[6].

(3) This section applies to a folding pocketknife if the cutting edge of its blade exceeds 3 inches.

(4) It shall be a defence for a person charged with an offence under this section to prove[7] that he had good reason[8] or lawful authority[9] for having the article with him in a public place.

(5) Without prejudice to the generality of subsection (4) above, it shall be a defence for a person charged with an offence under this section to prove that he had the article with him—

(*a*) for use at work[10];

(*b*) for religious reasons[11]; or

(*c*) as part of any national costume.

(6) A person guilty of an offence under subsection (1) shall be liable[12]

(*a*) on summary conviction, to imprisonment for a term not exceeding **six months** or a fine not exceeding the **statutory maximum**, or to **both**;

(*b*) on conviction on indictment, to imprisonment for a term not exceeding **four years**, or a **fine**, or **both**.

(6A) Subsection (6B) applies where—

(*a*) a person is convicted of an offence under subsection (1) by a court in England and Wales,

(*b*) the offence was committed after this subsection is commenced, and

(*c*) when the offence was committed, the person was aged 16 or over and had at least one relevant conviction (see section 139AZA).

(6B) Where this subsection applies, the court must impose an appropriate custodial sentence (with or without a fine) unless the court is of the opinion that there are particular circumstances which—

(*a*) relate to the offence, to the previous offence or to the offender, and

(*b*) would make it unjust to do so in all the circumstances.

(6C) In this section "appropriate custodial sentence" means—

(*a*) in the case of a person who is aged 18 or over when convicted, a sentence of imprisonment for a term of at least 6 months;

(*b*) in the case of a person who is aged at least 16 but under 18 when convicted, a detention and training order of at least 4 months.

(6D) In considering whether it is of the opinion mentioned in subsection (6B) in the case of a person aged 16 or 17, the court must have regard to its duty under section 44 of the Children and Young Persons Act 1933 (general considerations).

(6E) Where—

(*a*) an appropriate custodial sentence has been imposed on a person under subsection (6B), and

(*b*) a relevant conviction without which subsection (6B) would not have applied has been subsequently set aside on appeal,

notice of appeal against the sentence may be given at any time within 28 days from the date on which the conviction was set aside (despite anything in section 18 of the Criminal Appeal Act 1968 (initiating procedure)).

(6F) Where an offence is found to have been committed over a period of two or more days, or at some time during a period of two or more days, it shall be taken for the purposes of this section to have been committed on the last of those days.

(6G) In relation to times before the coming into force of paragraph 180 of Schedule 7 to the Criminal Justice and Court Services Act 2000, the reference in subsection (6C)(*a*) to a sentence of imprisonment, in relation to an offender aged under 21 at the time of conviction, is to be read as a reference to a sentence of detention in a young offender institution.

(7) In this section "public place" includes any place to which at the material time the public have or are permitted access, whether on payment or otherwise[13].

(8) This section shall not have effect in relation to anything done before it comes into force.

[Criminal Justice Act 1988, s 139 as amended by the Offensive Weapons Act 1996, s 3, the Violent Crime Reduction Act 2006, s 42, SI 2008/1216 and the Criminal Justice and Courts Act 2015, s 28.]

---

1 Sections 139–142 of the Criminal Justice Act 1988 which are printed here came into force on the 29 September 1988. For other provisions of the Criminal Justice Act 1988, see in particular Part I: Magistrates' Courts, Procedure, ante.

2 Part XI contains ss 133–167.

3 In *R v Henderson* [2016] EWCA Crim 965, [2016] 4 WLR 172, [2017] 1 Cr App R 4 the defendant was with his

family in a second floor flat when the police found his car keys while searching the premises. The car was in a communal car park at the rear of the flats. The police found a lock knife in the car boot. It was agreed that the car park was a public place, but the defendant submitted there was no case to answer as he did not have the lock knife "with him" for the purposes of s 139(1). The judge rejected this submission, but Court of Appeal allow the appeal against conviction. It was held:

> "18 In the present case it is to be noted that: (1) The defendant was not near his car, as the defendant was in *Smith v Vannet* 1998 SCCR 410. He was in a second floor flat a considerable distance away. (2) There was no evidence that the defendant had shortly left or was shortly to return to the car, as was the case in *R v Pawlicki* [1992] 1 WLR 827. (3) There was no evidence that the knife in the car was linked in any way to his presence in the flat on that day or at all, unlike in *R v Pawlicki*. (4) There was no evidence linking the knife to any ongoing or indeed any criminal enterprise, unlike in *R v Pawlicki*. (5) The facts are comparable to the case of *McVey v Friel* 1996 SCCR 768 in which the appeal was allowed.
>
> 19 In this case there was no close geographical, temporal or purposive link between the knife which was in a public place and the defendant who was in a private flat. Nor do we consider that it can be said that the knife was immediately available or readily accessible to the defendant.
>
> 20 In the light of the considerations set out above we conclude that the defendant did not in law have the knife 'with him'." (per Hamblen LJ)

[4] Whether the place is actually a public place is a question of fact; whether a place is capable of being a public place is a question of law (*R v Hanrahan* (2004) 168 JPN 947).

[5] For an offence to be proved the prosecution must establish that the accused knew that he was in possession of the article in question. Accordingly, a direction to a jury that a mere belief by the accused that the knife was somewhere in his van would suffice to establish the offence was held to be wrong because there was neither sufficient knowledge, nor sufficient control or proximity to the article for the offence to be established (*R v Daubney* (2000) 164 JP 519, CA).

[6] For a knife to be a folding pocket-knife within the meaning of this section, it must be readily and immediately foldable at all times, simply by the folding process. A lock-knife, which required a further process, namely activating a trigger mechanism to fold the blade back into the handle, was held not to be a folding pocket-knife (*Harris v DPP* [1993] 1 All ER 562); followed in *R v Deegan* [1998] Crim LR 562, [1998] 2 Cr App Rep 121. The section applies to articles which have a blade or are sharply pointed, falling into the same broad category as a knife or sharply pointed instrument; it does not apply to a screwdriver just because it has a blade (*R v Davis* [1998] Crim LR 564). It is unnecessary for the blade to be sharp; the words of the statute, namely "any article that has a blade" are unqualified and will, thus, include a blunt butter knife: *Brooker v DPP* [2005] EWHC Admin 1132, 169 JP 368.

[7] This reverse burden of proof does not conflict with art 6 of the Convention, since it is a proportionate measure and well within reasonable limits: *L v DPP* [2001] EWHC Admin 882, [2003] QB 137, [2002] 3 WLR 863, [2003] 2 WLR 693, [2002] 1 Cr App Rep 420, 166 JP 113, followed in *R v Matthews* [2003] EWCA Crim 813, [2003] 2 Cr App Rep 302. Once the prosecution has discharged the burden of proving the ingredients of the offence against s 139(1), the defendant is guilty unless he can discharge the burden imposed by s 139(4) of the Act; see *Godwin v DPP* (1993) 96 Cr App Rep 244.

[8] The words "good reason" are both very general words and ordinary works which Parliament must have intended would normally be applied and interpreted by a jury or other fact finding tribunal such as justices: *R v McAuley* [2009] EWCA Crim 2130, [2010] 1 Cr App Rep 148, 173 JP 585, [2010] Crim LR 336. A fear of attack can constitute a good reason and it therefore follows that the defendant's state of mind is not wholly irrelevant; if the court considers that defendant's view of the facts was wholly unreasonable, for example, because he was drunk or had taken drugs or was suffering from mental illness, it may be unlikely to conclude that the defence has been made out, but it is a matter ultimately for the court to determine: *R v Clancy* [2012] EWCA Crim 8, [2012] 1 WLR 2536, [2012] 2 Cr App Rep 71. In *Clancy* it was suggested that a trial judge might properly rule that facts were incapable of constituting to "good reason" if a finding that a good reason existed would be perverse (see para 20 of the judgment). It was held in *R v Asmeron* [2013] EWCA Crim 435, [2013] 1 WLR 3457, [2013] 2 Cr App R 19 that this must be treated as per incuriam because it was contrary to the decision of the House of Lords in *R v Wang* [2005] 1 WLR 661, to which the court in *Clancy* had not been referred:

> "The court can only rule that the explanation advanced by a defendant is incapable in law of amounting to a good reason or a reasonable excuse if it can properly be said, on the true construction of the Act, that it would be inconsistent with the essential nature and purpose of the offence for the defendant's explanation to be capable of amounting to a defence. *R v Kelleher* 147 SJLB 1395 is a good example. In the present case it could not be said that it would be contrary to the manifest purpose of the statute for the defendant's explanation to be regarded by the jury as a reasonable excuse" (per Toulson SCJ at para 22 of the judgment in *Asmeron*).

Forgetfulness is not sufficient to prevent the state of possession from continuing, but there may be circumstances in which forgetfulness can be relevant to the "good reason" defence: for instance, if the reason that the defendant forgot that a bladed instrument, usually used for his work, was in his possession was a relevant illness or was occasioned by medication for such an illness: *Bayliss v DPP* (2003) 167 JPN 103. See also: *R v McCalla* (1988) 87 Cr App Rep 372; (*DPP v Gregson* (1992) 157 JP 201). In *R v Jolie* [2003] EWCA Crim 1543, [2004] 1 Cr App Rep 44, (2003) 167 JP 313, [2003] Crim LR 730 it was affirmed that forgetfulness does not bring possession to an end; that forgetfulness cannot be a good reason, though it can be part of a good reason; and that the words "good reason" do not require a judicial gloss. As to when forgetfulness might assist a defendant the court gave the example (in para 16) of a parent who, having bought a kitchen knife and put in the glove compartment of a car out of reach of a child then forgot to retrieve it when he got home; it seemed to the court contrary to Parliament's intention that such a person would be committing an offence the next time he drove the vehicle on a public road. See also *Chahal v DPP* [2010] EWHC 439 (Admin), [2010] 2 Cr App R 5. The defendant was found in possession of a knife. He claimed he had used it at work, put it in his coat, forgotten about it and then, at the time of the offence, when he realised it was in his jacket he decided to return home. The justices accepted that the defendant used the knife at work, but found that the work was of a casual nature, that the defendant did not regularly need the knife for work and, therefore, he did not have a "good reason" for its possession at the relevant time. The appeal by way of case stated succeeded. The justices had been misled into thinking that the nature of the defendant's work deprived him of the statutory defence. The real question was whether the defendant had genuinely forgotten about the knife and at the time when his recollection was restored whether he continued to have "good reason" for possession of the knife.

A reason may be capable of being a good reason, but fail to amount to a good reason on the facts of the case (see *Mohammed v Chief Constable of South Yorkshire Police* [2002] EWHC 406 (Admin), [2002] All ER (D) 374 (Feb), where the defendant took a meat cleaver to sharpen it but had it in his possession for that purpose for longer than he needed to). It cannot be a good reason to possess a knife that you may wish to commit self harm with it at some time the following day (*R v Bown* [2003] EWCA Crim 1989, [2003] 33 LS Gaz R 27, 167 JP 429, [2004] Crim LR 67).

[9] The fact that a blade may be used for other functions than as a weapon does not mean it is not prima facie a blade for the purposes of the statute, and for a defendant to prove he had a lawful purpose for having the bladed article he would have to have a specific good reason for having it in his possession at that moment: *R v Giles* (2003) 167 JPN 103.

[10] Interpretation of the ordinary everyday use of "for use at work" is not a matter of law but it is for the justices to

decide for themselves what the phrase means in the context of the case. Therefore possession of a bladed article by an unemployed mechanic to do some repairs on his car that was parked in the road could come within this defence, see *R v Manning* [1998] Crim LR 198, CA.

[11] 10 The religious reasons must constitute the predominant, if not the only motivation for the accused being in possession of the bladed article in a public place; and it must also be shown that the religious reason specifically motivated the accused to have the article with him on the occasion in question: *R v Wang* [2003] EWCA Crim 3228, 168 JP 224.

[12] For procedure in respect of this offence which is triable either way, see the Magistrates' Courts Act 1980, ss 17A–21, in PART I: MAGISTRATES' COURTS, PROCEDURE, ante.

[13] "Public place" should not be construed so as to include land adjacent to areas where the public has access from which harm against which the section was designed to provide protection could be inflicted (*R v Roberts* [2003] EWCA Crim 2753, [2004] 1 WLR 181, 167 JP 675, [2004] Crim LR 141). See also the definition of "public place" in s 1 of the Prevention of Crime Act 1953 and note thereto, ante.

7.8501 **139A. Offence of having article with blade or point (or offensive weapon) on school premises** (1) Any person who has an article to which section 139 of this Act applies with him on school premises shall be guilty of an offence.

(2) Any person who has an offensive weapon within the meaning of section 1 of the Prevention of Crime Act 1953 with him on school premises shall be guilty of an offence.

(3) It shall be defence for a person charged with an offence under subsection (1) or (2) above to prove that he had good reason or lawful authority for having the article or weapon with him on the premises in question.

(4) Without prejudice to the generality of subsection (3) above, it shall be a defence for a person charged with an offence under subsection (1) or (2) above to prove that he had the article or weapon in question with him—

(*a*) for use at work,
(*b*) for educational purposes,
(*c*) for religious reasons, or
(*d*) as part of any national costume.

(5) A person guilty of an offence—

(*a*) under subsection (1) above shall be liable[1]—
  (i) on summary conviction to imprisonment for a term not exceeding **six months**, or a fine not exceeding the **statutory maximum**, or **both;**
  (ii) on conviction on indictment, to imprisonment for a term not exceeding **four years**, or a **fine**, or **both;**

(*b*) under subsection (2) above shall be liable—
  (i) on summary conviction to imprisonment for a term not exceeding **six months**, or a fine not exceeding the **statutory maximum**, or **both;**
  (ii) on conviction on indictment, to imprisonment for a term not exceeding **four years**, or a **fine**, or **both**.

(5A) Subsection (5B) applies where—

(*a*) a person is convicted of an offence under subsection (1) or (2) by a court in England and Wales,
(*b*) the offence was committed after this subsection is commenced, and
(*c*) when the offence was committed, the person was aged 16 or over and had at least one relevant conviction (see section 139AZA).

(5B) Where this subsection applies, the court must impose an appropriate custodial sentence (with or without a fine) unless the court is of the opinion that there are particular circumstances which—

(*a*) relate to the offence, to the previous offence or to the offender, and
(*b*) would make it unjust to do so in all the circumstances.

(5C) In this section "appropriate custodial sentence" means—

(*a*) in the case of a person who is aged 18 or over when convicted, a sentence of imprisonment for a term of at least 6 months;
(*b*) in the case of a person who is aged at least 16 but under 18 when convicted, a detention and training order of at least 4 months.

(5D) In considering whether it is of the opinion mentioned in subsection (5B) in the case of a person aged 16 or 17, the court must have regard to its duty under section 44 of the Children and Young Persons Act 1933 (general considerations).

(5E) Where—

(*a*) an appropriate custodial sentence has been imposed on a person under subsection (5B), and
(*b*) a relevant conviction without which subsection (5B) would not have applied has been subsequently set aside on appeal,

notice of appeal against the sentence may be given at any time within 28 days from the date on which the conviction was set aside (despite anything in section 18 of the Criminal Appeal Act 1968 (initiating procedure)).

(5F) Where an offence is found to have been committed over a period of two or more days, or at some time during a period of two or more days, it shall be taken for the purposes of this section to have been committed on the last of those days.

(5G) In relation to times before the coming into force of paragraph 180 of Schedule 7 to the

Criminal Justice and Court Services Act 2000, the reference in subsection (5C)(a) to a sentence of imprisonment, in relation to an offender aged under 21 at the time of conviction, is to be read as a reference to a sentence of detention in a young offender institution.

(6) A person guilty of an offence under subsection (1) shall be liable—

(*a*) on summary conviction, to imprisonment for a term not exceeding 12 months or to a fine not exceeding the statutory maximum, or to both;

(*b*) on conviction on indictment, to imprisonment for a term not exceeding 4 years, or to a fine, or to both.

(7) Northern Ireland.

[Criminal Justice Act 1988, s 139A as inserted by the Offensive Weapons Act 1996, s 4 and amended by the Education Act 1996, Sch 37, the Violent Crime Reduction Act 2006, s 42, SI 2008/1216 and the Criminal Justice and Courts Act 2015, s 28.]

---

1 For procedure in respect of this offence which is triable either way, see the Magistrates' Courts Act 1980, ss 17A–21, in PART I: MAGISTRATES' COURTS, PROCEDURE, ante.

**7.8501A 139AZA. Offences under sections 139 and 139A: previous relevant convictions**

(1) For the purposes of sections 139 and 139A, "relevant conviction" means—

(*a*) a conviction for an offence under—

(i) section 1 or 1A of the Prevention of Crime Act 1953, or

(ii) section 139, 139A or 139AA of this Act,

(a "relevant offence"), whenever committed,

(*b*) a conviction in Scotland, Northern Ireland or a member State other than the United Kingdom for a civilian offence, whenever committed, which would have constituted a relevant offence if committed in England and Wales at the time of that conviction,

(c) a conviction for an offence under section 42 of the Armed Forces Act 2006, whenever committed, in respect of which the corresponding offence under the law of England and Wales (within the meaning of that section) is a relevant offence,

(*d*) a conviction for an offence under section 70 of the Army Act 1955, section 70 of the Air Force Act 1955 or section 42 of the Naval Discipline Act 1957, whenever committed, in respect of which the corresponding civil offence (within the meaning of the Act in question) is a relevant offence, and

(*e*) a conviction for a member State service offence, whenever committed, which would have constituted a relevant offence if committed in England and Wales at the time of conviction.

(2) In this section—

"civilian offence" means an offence other than—

(*a*) an offence under an enactment mentioned in subsection (1)(*c*) or (*d*), or

(*b*) a member State service offence;

"conviction" includes—

(*a*) in relation to an offence under section 42 of the Armed Forces Act 2006, anything which by virtue of section 376(1) and (2) of that Act is to be treated as a conviction, and

(*b*) in relation to an offence under section 42 of the Naval Discipline Act 1957 and a member State service offence, a finding of guilt in respect of the person;

"member State service offence" means an offence which was the subject of proceedings under the law of a member State, other than the United Kingdom, governing all or any of the naval, military or air forces of that State.

(3) For the purposes of subsection (1)(*c*) and (*d*), where the offence was committed by aiding, abetting, counselling or procuring, it must be assumed that the act aided, abetted, counselled or procured was done in England and Wales.

[Criminal Justice Act 1988, s 139AZA as inserted by the Criminal Justice and Courts Act 2015, s 28.]

**7.8502 139AA. Offence of threatening with article with blade or point or offensive weapon** (1) A person is guilty of an offence if that person—

(*a*) has an article to which this section applies with him or her in a public place or on school premises,

(*b*) unlawfully and intentionally threatens another person with the article, and

(*c*) does so in such a way that there is an immediate risk of serious physical harm to that other person.

(2) In relation to a public place this section applies to an article to which section 139 applies.

(3) In relation to school premises this section applies to each of these—

(*a*) an article to which section 139 applies;

(*b*) an offensive weapon within the meaning of section 1 of the Prevention of Crime Act 1953.

(4) For the purposes of this section physical harm is serious if it amounts to grievous bodily harm for the purposes of the Offences against the Person Act 1861.

(5) In this section—

"public place" has the same meaning as in section 139;

"school premises" has the same meaning as in section 139A.

(6) A person guilty of an offence under this section is liable—

(*a*) on summary conviction, to imprisonment for a term not exceeding 12 months or to a fine not exceeding the statutory maximum, or to both;

(*b*) on conviction on indictment, to imprisonment for a term not exceeding 4 years or to a fine, or to both.

(7) Where a person aged 16 or over is convicted of an offence under this section, the court must impose an appropriate custodial sentence (with or without a fine) unless the court is of the opinion that there are particular circumstances which—

(*a*) relate to the offence or to the offender, and

(*b*) would make it unjust to do so in all the circumstances.

(8) In this section "appropriate custodial sentence" means—

(*a*) in the case of a person who is aged 18 or over when convicted, a sentence of imprisonment for a term of at least 6 months;

(*b*) in the case of a person who is aged at least 16 but under 18 when convicted, a detention and training order of at least 4 months.

(9) In considering whether it is of the opinion mentioned in subsection (7) in the case of a person aged under 18, the court must have regard to its duty under section 44 of the Children and Young Persons Act 1933.

(10) In relation to an offence committed before the commencement of section 154(1) of the Criminal Justice Act 2003, the reference in subsection (6)(*a*) to 12 months is to be read as a reference to 6 months.

(11) In relation to times before the coming into force of paragraph 180 of Schedule 7 to the Criminal Justice and Court Services Act 2000, the reference in subsection (8)(*a*) to a sentence of imprisonment, in relation to an offender aged under 21 at the time of conviction, is to be read as a reference to a sentence of detention in a young offender institution.

(12) If on a person's trial for an offence under this section (whether on indictment or not) the person is found not guilty of that offence but it is proved that the person committed an offence under section 139 or 139A, the person may be convicted of the offence under that section.

[Criminal Justice Act 1988, s 139AA as inserted by the Legal Aid, Sentencing and Punishment of Offenders Act 2012, s 142.]

7.8503 **139B. Power of entry to search for articles with a blade or point and offensive weapons** (1) A constable may enter school premises and search those premises and any person on those premises for—

(*a*) any article to which section 139 of this Act applies, or

(*b*) any offensive weapon within the meaning of section 1 of the Prevention of Crime Act 1953,

if he has reasonable grounds for suspecting that an offence under section 139A or 139AA of this Act is being, or has been, committed.

(2) If in the course of a search under this section a constable discovers an article or weapon which he has reasonable grounds for suspecting to be an article or weapon of a kind described in subsection (1) above, he may seize and retain it.

(3) The constable may use reasonable force, if necessary, in the exercise of the power of entry conferred by this section.

(4) *Northern Ireland.*

[Criminal Justice Act 1988, s 139B as inserted by the Offensive Weapons Act 1996, s 4 and amended by the Violent Crime Reduction Act 2006, Sch 2 and the Legal Aid, Sentencing and Punishment of Offenders Act 2012, Sch 26.]

7.8504 **141. Offensive weapons** (1) Any person who manufactures, sells or hires or offers for sale or hire, exposes or has in his possession for the purpose of sale or hire, or lends or gives to any other person, a weapon to which this section applies shall be guilty of an offence and liable—

(*a*) on summary conviction, to imprisonment for a term not exceeding 12 months or a fine not exceeding the statutory maximum, or to both;

(*b*) on conviction on indictment, to imprisonment for a term not exceeding 4 years, or to a fine, or to both.

(2) The Secretary of State may by order[1] made by statutory instrument direct that this section shall apply to any description of weapon specified in the order except—

(*a*) any weapon subject to the Firearms Act 1968; and

(*b*) crossbows.

(3) Repealed.

(4) The importation of a weapon to which this section applies is hereby prohibited.

(5) It shall be a defence for any person charged in respect of any conduct of his relating to a weapon to which this section applies—

(*a*) with an offence under subsection (1) above; or

(*b*) with an offence under section 50(2) or (3) of the Customs and Excise Management Act 1979 (improper importation),

to show that his conduct was only for the purposes of functions carried out on behalf of the Crown or of a visiting force.

(6) In this section the reference to the Crown includes the Crown in right of Her Majesty's Government in Northern Ireland; and

"visiting force" means any body, contingent or detachment of the forces of a country—

(*a*) mentioned in subsection (1)(*a*) of section 1 of the Visiting Forces Act 1952; or

(*b*) designated for the purposes of any provision of that Act by Order in Council under subsection (2) of that section,

which is present in the United Kingdom (including United Kingdom territorial waters) or in any place to which subsection (7) below applies on the invitation of Her Majesty's Government in the United Kingdom.

(7) This subsection applies to any place on, under or above an installation in a designated area within the meaning of section 1(7) of the Continental Shelf Act 1964 or any waters within 500 metres of such an installation.

(8) It shall be a defence for any person charged in respect of any conduct of his relating to a weapon to which this section applies—

(*a*) with an offence under subsection (1) above; or

(*b*) with an offence under section 50(2) or (3) of the Customs and Excise Management Act 1979,

to show that the conduct in question was only for the purposes of making the weapon available to a museum or gallery to which this subsection applies.

(9) If a person acting on behalf of a museum or gallery to which subsection (8) above applies is charged with hiring or lending a weapon to which this section applies, it shall be a defence for him to show that he had reasonable grounds for believing that the person to whom he lent or hired it would use it only for cultural, artistic or educational purposes.

(10) Subsection (8) above applies to a museum or gallery only if it does not distribute profits.

(11) In this section "museum or gallery" includes any institution which has as its purpose, or one of its purposes, the preservation, display and interpretation of material of historical, artistic or scientific interest and gives the public access to it.

(11A) It shall be a defence for a person charged in respect of conduct of his relating to a weapon to which this section applies—

(*a*) with an offence under subsection (1) above, or

(*b*) with an offence under section 50(2) or (3) of the Customs and Excise Management Act 1979,

to show that his conduct was for the purpose only of making the weapon in question available for one or more of the purposes specified in subsection (11B).

(11B) Those purposes are—

(*a*) the purposes of theatrical performances and of rehearsals for such performances;

(*b*) the production of films (within the meaning of Part 1 of the Copyright, Designs and Patents Act 1988 – see section 5B of that Act);

(*c*) the production of television programmes (within the meaning of the Communications Act 2003 – see section 405(1) of that Act).

(11C) For the purposes of this section a person shall be taken to have shown a matter specified in subsection (5), (8), (9) or (11A) if—

(*a*) sufficient evidence of that matter is adduced to raise an issue with respect to it; and

(*b*) the contrary is not proved beyond a reasonable doubt.

(11D) The Secretary of State may by order made by statutory instrument—

(*a*) provide for exceptions and exemptions from the offence under subsection (1) above or from the prohibition in subsection (4) above; and

(*b*) provide for it to be a defence in proceedings for such an offence, or for an offence under section 50(2) or (3) of the Customs and Excise Management Act 1979, to show the matters specified or described in the order.

(11E) A statutory instrument containing an order under this section shall not be made unless a draft of the instrument has been laid before Parliament and approved by a resolution of each House.

(12) This section shall not have effect in relation to anything done before it comes into force.

(13)–(17) *Northern Ireland.**

[Criminal Justice Act 1988, s 141 as amended by the Violent Crime Reduction Act 2006, Schs 2 and 5, SI 2008/1216 and SI 2010/976.]

---

* **Amended by the Policing and Crime Act 2009, Schs 7 and 8 from a date to be appointed.**

1 See the Criminal Justice Act 1988 (Offensive Weapons) Order 1988, post.

**7.8504A 141ZA. Application of section 141 to swords: further provision** *Scotland.*

**7.8505 141ZB. Importation of offensive weapons: prohibition**[1] (1) The importation of an offensive weapon is prohibited, subject to section 141ZC.

(2) In this section "offensive weapon" means a weapon of a description specified in an order made by the Secretary of State for the purposes of this subsection.

(3) The Secretary of State may not specify any of the following under subsection (2)—

(*a*) a weapon subject to the Firearms Act 1968;

(*b*) a crossbow.

(4) Orders under this section are to be made by statutory instrument.

(5) A statutory instrument containing an order under this section may not be made unless a draft of the instrument has been laid before and approved by a resolution of each House of Parliament.

(6) In the application of this section to Northern Ireland the reference in subsection (3) to the Firearms Act 1968 is to be construed as a reference to the Firearms (Northern Ireland) Order 2004.*

[Criminal Justice Act 1988, s 141ZB as inserted by the Policing and Crime Act 2009, s 102.]

---

* **Not yet in force.**

[1] Sections 141ZB, 141ZC AND 141ZD were inserted by the Policing and Crime Act 2009, s 102, sub-ss (2)–(4) of which provide:

"(2) Subsection (3) applies where in any proceedings—

(*a*) a person ("the defendant") is charged in respect of the same conduct with—

(i) an offence under any provision of the Customs and Excise Management Act 1979 by virtue of the prohibition on importation in section 141(4) of the Criminal Justice Act 1988 as it had effect before its repeal by this Act ("the old offence"), and

(ii) an offence under that provision of the 1979 Act by virtue of the prohibition on importation in section 141ZB(1) of the 1988 Act ("the new offence"),

(*b*) the only thing preventing the defendant from being found guilty of the new offence is the fact that it has not been proved beyond a reasonable doubt that the conduct took place after the commencement of this section, and

(*c*) the only thing preventing the defendant from being found guilty of the old offence is the fact that it has not been proved beyond a reasonable doubt that the conduct took place before the commencement of this section.

(3) For the purpose of determining the guilt of the defendant it is to be conclusively presumed that the conduct took place after the commencement of this section.

(4) A reference in subsection (2) to an offence includes a reference to—

(*a*) aiding, abetting, counselling or procuring the commission of the offence,

(*b*) conspiracy to commit the offence,

(*c*) an attempt to commit the offence,

(*d*) incitement to commit the offence, and

(*e*) an offence under Part 2 of the Serious Crime Act 2007 (encouraging or assisting crime) in relation to the offence."

7.8506 **141ZC. Prohibition on importation of offensive weapons: exceptions** (1) The importation of a weapon is not prohibited by section 141ZB if one of the following exceptions applies.

(2) Exception 1 is that the weapon is imported for the purposes only of functions carried out on behalf of—

(*a*) the Crown, or

(*b*) a visiting force.

(3) Exception 2 is that the weapon is imported for the purposes only of making it available to a museum or gallery which does not distribute profits.

(4) Exception 3 is that the weapon is imported for the purposes only of making it available for one or more of the following—

(*a*) theatrical performances;

(*b*) rehearsals of theatrical performances;

(*c*) the production of films;

(*d*) the production of television programmes.

(5) In subsection (4)—

"films" has the meaning given by section 5B of the Copyright, Designs and Patents Act 1988;

"television programmes" has the meaning given by section 405 of the Communications Act 2003.

(6) The Secretary of State may by order provide for further exceptions from the prohibition on importation of weapons under section 141ZB.

(7) Orders under this section are to be made by statutory instrument.

(8) A statutory instrument containing an order under this section may not be made unless a draft of the instrument has been laid before and approved by a resolution of each House of Parliament.

(9) Expressions used in this section and in section 141 have the same meaning in this section as in that section.*

[Criminal Justice Act 1988, s 141ZC as inserted by the Policing and Crime Act 2009, s 102.]

---

* **Not yet in force. See note to title of s 141ZB, ante.**

7.8507 **141ZD. Prohibition on importation of offensive weapons: burdens of proof**

(1) This section applies for the purposes of proceedings for an offence under the Customs and Excise Management Act 1979 relating to a weapon the importation of which is prohibited by section 141ZB above.

(2) An exception conferred by or under section 141ZC is to be taken not to apply unless sufficient evidence is adduced to raise an issue with respect to the exception.

(3) Where sufficient evidence is adduced to raise an issue with respect to an exception, it is to be taken to apply unless the contrary is proved beyond a reasonable doubt.*

[Criminal Justice Act 1988, s 141ZD as inserted by the Policing and Crime Act 2009, s 102.]

* **Not yet in force. See note to title of s 141ZB, ante.**

7.8508 **141A. Sale of knives and certain articles with blade or point to persons under sixteen*** (1) Any person who sells to a person under the age of eighteen years an article to which this section applies shall be guilty of an offence and liable on summary conviction to imprisonment for a term not exceeding **six months**, or a fine not exceeding **level 5** on the standard scale, or both.

(2) Subject to subsection (3) below, this section applies to—

(*a*) any knife[1], knife blade or razor blade,

(*b*) any axe, and

(*c*) any other article which has a blade or which is sharply pointed and which is made or adapted for use for causing injury to the person.

(3) This section does not apply to any article described in—

(*a*) section 1 of the Restriction of Offensive Weapons Act 1959,

(*b*) an order made under section 141(2) of this Act, or

(*c*) an order[2] made by the Secretary of State under this section.

(3A) Scotland.

(4) It shall be a defence for a person charged with an offence under subsection (1) above to prove that he took all reasonable precautions and exercised all due diligence to avoid the commission of the offence[3].

(5) The power to make an order under this section shall be exercisable by statutory instrument which shall be subject to annulment in pursuance of a resolution of either House of Parliament.*

[Criminal Justice Act 1988, s 141A as inserted by the Offensive Weapons Act 1996, s 6 and amended by the Violent Crime Reduction Act 2006, s 43.]

* **Reproduced as in force in England and Wales.**

1 "Knife" bears its ordinary dictionary meaning and, thus, includes a grapefruit knife: *R (on the application of the Royal Borough of Windsor and Maidenhead) v East Berkshire Justices* [2010] EWHC 3020 (Admin), 174 JP 621, [2011] 1 Cr App R 21.

2 The Criminal Justice Act 1988 (Offensive Weapons) (Exemption) Order 1996, SI 1996/3064, has been made.

3 The defence made available by the Act is couched in ordinary language and it will only rarely be necessary for a court to formulate the test in anything other than the language used in the statute. Applying a test based on a need to prove both negligence and a reprehensible state of mind before a finding of guilt can be made risks importing a mental element which is inappropriate: *Croydon London Borough Council v Pinch A Pound (UK) Ltd* [2010] EWHC 3283 (Admin), [2011] 1 WLR 1189.

7.8509 **142. Power of justice of the peace to authorise entry and search of premises for offensive weapons** (1) If on an application made by a constable a justice of the peace (including, in Scotland, the sheriff) is satisfied that there are reasonable grounds for believing—

(*a*) that there are on premises specified in the application—

(i) knives such as are mentioned in section 1(1) of the Restriction of Offensive Weapons Act 1959; or

(ii) weapons to which section 141 above applies; and

(*b*) that an offence under section 1 of the Restriction of Offensive Weapons Act 1959 or section 141 above has been or is being committed in relation to them; and

(*c*) that any of the conditions specified in subsection (3) below applies,

he may issue a warrant authorising a constable to enter and search the premises.

(2) A constable may seize and retain anything for which a search has been authorised under subsection (1) above.

(3) The conditions mentioned in subsection (1)(*c*)[1] above are—

(*a*) that it is not practicable to communicate with any person entitled to grant entry to the premises;

(*b*) that it is practicable to communicate with a person entitled to grant entry to the premises but it is not practicable to communicate with any person entitled to grant access to the knives or weapons to which the application relates;

(*c*) that entry to the premises will not be granted unless a warrant is produced;

(*d*) that the purpose of a search may be frustrated or seriously prejudiced unless a constable arriving at the premises can secure immediate entry to them.

(4) Northern Ireland,

[Criminal Justice Act 1988, s 142 as amended by the Police and Justice Act 2006, Sch 14.]

## Chemical Weapons Act 1996[1]

(1996 c 6)

*Introduction*

7.8510 **1. General interpretation** (1) Chemical weapons are—

(*a*) toxic chemicals and their precursors;

(*b*) munitions and other devices designed to cause death or harm through the toxic properties of toxic chemicals released by them;

(*c*) equipment designed for use in connection with munitions and devices falling within paragraph (*b*).

(2) Subsection (1) is subject to sections 2(2) and (3), 10(1) and 11(2) (by virtue of which an object is not a chemical weapon if the use or intended use is only for permitted purposes).

(3) Permitted purposes are—

(*a*) peaceful purposes;

(*b*) purposes related to protection against toxic chemicals;

(*c*) legitimate military purposes;

(*d*) purposes of enforcing the law.

(4) Legitimate military purposes except those which depend on the use of the toxic properties of chemicals as a method of warfare in circumstances where the main object is to cause death, permanent harm or temporary incapacity to humans or animals.

(5) A toxic chemical is a chemical which through its chemical action on life processes can cause death, permanent harm or temporary incapacity to humans or animals; and the origin, method of production and place of production are immaterial.

(6) A precursor is a chemical reactant which takes part at any stage in the production (by whatever method) of a toxic chemical.

(7) References to an object include references to a substance.

(8) The Convention is the Convention on the Prohibition of the Development, Production, Stockpiling and Use of Chemical Weapons and on their Destruction, signed at Paris on 13 January 1993.

(9) This section applies for the purposes of this Act.

[Chemical Weapons Act 1996, s 1.]

---

1 This Act promotes the control of chemical weapons and of certain toxic chemicals and precursors. The Act implements in the UK the Convention on the Prohibition of the Development, Production, Stockpiling and Use of Chemical Weapons and on their Destruction, which was signed in Paris on 13 January 1993. The Chemical Weapons Act 1996 was brought fully into force on 16 September 1996 by the Chemical Weapons Act 1996 (Commencement) Order 1996, SI 1996/2054.

*Chemical weapons*

7.8511 2. **Use etc of chemical weapons** (1) No person shall—

(*a*) use a chemical weapon;

(*b*) develop or produce a chemical weapon;

(*c*) have a chemical weapon in his possession;

(*d*) participate in the transfer of a chemical weapon;

(*e*) engage in military preparations, or in preparations of a military nature, intending to use a chemical weapon.

(2) For the purposes of subsection (1)(*a*) an object is not a chemical weapon if the person uses the object only for permitted purposes; and in deciding whether permitted purposes are intended the types and quantities of objects shall be taken into account.

(3) For the purposes of subsection (1)(*b*), (*c*), (*d*) or (*e*) an object is not a chemical weapon if the person does the act there mentioned with the intention that the object will be used only for permitted purposes; and in deciding whether permitted purposes are intended the types and quantities of objects shall be taken into account.

(4) For the purposes of subsection (1)(*d*) a person participates in the transfer of an object if—

(*a*) he acquires or disposes of the object or enters into a contract to acquire or dispose of it, or

(*b*) he makes arrangements under which another person acquires or disposes of the object or another person enters into a contract to acquire or dispose of it.

(5) For the purposes of subsection (4)—

(*a*) to acquire an object is to buy it, hire it, borrow it or accept it as a gift;

(*b*) to dispose of an object is to sell it, let it on hire, lend it or give it.

(6) In proceedings for an offence under section (1)(*a*), (*c*) or (*d*) relating to an object it is a defence for the accused to prove—

(*a*) that he neither knew nor suspected nor had reason to suspect that the object was a chemical weapon, or

(*b*) that he knew or suspected it to be a chemical weapon and as soon as reasonably practicable after he first so knew or suspected he took all reasonable steps to inform the Secretary of State or a constable of his knowledge or suspicion.

(7) Nothing in subsection (6) prejudices any defence which it is open to a person charged with an offence under this section to raise apart from that subsection.

(8) A person contravening this section is guilty of an offence and liable on conviction on indictment to imprisonment for life.

[Chemical Weapons Act 1996, s 2.]

7.8512 3. **Application of section 2** (1) Section 2 applies to acts done in the United Kingdom or elsewhere.

(2) So far as it applies to acts done outside the United Kingdom, section 2 applies to United Kingdom nationals, Scottish partnerships, and bodies incorporated under the law of any part of the

United Kingdom.

(3) Her Majesty may by Order[1] in Council extend the application of section 2, so far as it applies to acts done outside the United Kingdom, to bodies incorporated under the law of any of the Channel Islands, the Isle of Man or any colony.

(4) For the purposes of this section a United Kingdom national is an individual who is—

(*a*) British citizen, a British overseas territories citizen, a British National (Overseas) or a British Overseas citizen,

(*b*) a person who under the British Nationality Act 1981 is a British subject, or

(*c*) a British protected person within the meaning of that Act.

(5) Proceedings for an offence committed under section 2 outside the United Kingdom may be taken, and the offence may for incidental purposes be treated as having been committed, in any place in the United Kingdom.

[Chemical Weapons Act 1996, s 3 as amended by the British Overseas Territories Act 2002, s 2(3).]

---

1 The following Chemical Weapons Act 1996 Orders have been made: Jersey, SI 1998/2565; Isle of Man, SI 1998/2794; Guernsey, SI 2000/743.

7.8513 **4. Suspicious objects** (1) If—

(*a*) the Secretary of State has grounds to suspect that an object is a chemical weapon, and

(*b*) at least one person falls within subsection (2),

the Secretary of State may serve on any person falling within that subsection a copy of a notice falling within subsection (3).

(2) The person falling within this subsection are—

(*a*) any person who appears to the Secretary of State to have the object in his possession, and

(*b*) any person not falling within paragraph (*a*) and who appears to the Secretary of State to have an interest which the Secretary of State believes is materially affected by the notice.

(3) A notice falling within this subsection is a notice which—

(*a*) describes the object and states its location;

(*b*) states that the Secretary of State suspects that the object is a chemical weapon and gives the reasons for his suspicion;

(*c*) states that he is considering whether to secure its destruction under sections 5 to 7;

(*d*) states that any person may make representations that the object is not a chemical weapon;

(*e*) states that a person on whom the notice is served and who has the object in his possession must not relinquish possession before a date specified in the notice.

[Chemical Weapons Act 1996, s 4.]

7.8514 **5. Power to remove or immobilise objects** (1) If the Secretary of State has reasonable cause to believe that—

(*a*) an object is on premises to which the public has access or which are occupied by a person who consents to action being taken under this subsection, and

(*b*) the object is a chemical weapon,

the Secretary of State may authorise a person to enter the premises and to search them.

(2) If—

(*a*) a justice of the peace is satisfied on information on oath that there is reasonable cause to believe that an object is on premises (of whatever nature) and that it is a chemical weapon, or

(*b*) in Scotland a justice, within the meaning of section 307 of the Criminal Procedure (Scotland) Act 1995, is satisfied by evidence on oath as mentioned in paragraph (*a*),

he may issue a warrant in writing authorising a person acting under the authority of the Secretary of State to enter the premises, if necessary by force, at any time within one month from the time of the issue of the warrant and to search them.

(3) A person who acts under an authorisation given under subsection (1) or (2) may take with him such other persons and such equipment as appear to him to be necessary.

(4) If a person enters premises under an authorisation given under subsection (1) or (2) and the object is found there he may make the object safe and—

(*a*) he may seize and remove it if it is reasonably practicable to do so, or

(*b*) he may in any other case affix a warning to the object or to something in a conspicuous position near the object, stating that the object is not to be moved or interfered with before a date specified in the warning)

(5) For the purposes of subsection (4) an object is made safe if, without being destroyed, it is prevented from being an immediate danger (as where a fuse is neutralised or the object is smothered in foam).

(6) The powers conferred on an authorised person under this section shall only be exercisable, if the authorisation under subsection (1) or the warrant so provides, in the presence of a constable.

(7) This section applies whether or not any copy of a notice has been served under section 4.

[Chemical Weapons Act 1996, s 5.]

7.8515 **6. Power to destroy removed objects** (1) This section applies if an object is removed from premises under section 5, and for the purposes of this section—

(*a*) the first six-month period is the period of six months beginning with the day after the removal;

(*b*) the second six-month period is the period of six months beginning with the day after the first six-month period ends.

(2) If at any time in the second six-month period the Secretary of State decides that the object should be destroyed he may authorise a person to destroy it; but this is subject to subsection (3) to (5).

(3) If at any time in the first six-month period—

(*a*) any person appears to the Secretary of State to have had the object in his possession immediately before its removal, or

(*b*) any person not falling within paragraph (*a*) appears to the Secretary of State to have an interest which the Secretary of State believes would be materially affected by the object's destruction,

the Secretary of State must serve on such a person a copy of a notice falling within subsection (4).

(4) A notice falling within this subsection is a notice which—

(*a*) describes the object and states its location;

(*b*) states that the Secretary of State proposes to secure its destruction and gives the reasons for his proposal;

(*c*) states that the person on whom the copy of the notice is served may object to the Secretary of State's proposal;

(*d*) states than an objection (if made) must be made in writing to the Secretary of State before such date as is specified in the notice and must state why the object should not be destroyed.

(5) Before he reaches a decision under subsection (2) the Secretary of State must—

(*a*) allow any person on whom a copy of a notice has been served under subsection (3) time to respond, and

(*b*) take into account any objections to the object's proposed destruction (whether made in response to a notice or otherwise).

(6) If an object is removed from premises under section 5 and destroyed under this section the Secretary of State may recover from a responsible person any costs reasonably incurred by the Secretary of State in connection with the removal and destruction; and a responsible person is any person who had possession of the object immediately before its removal.

(7) If—

(*a*) an object is removed from premises under section 5,

(*b*) at the end of the second six-month period the Secretary of State has not authorised the destruction of the object, and

(*c*) a person had possession of the object immediately before its removal,

the Secretary of State must return the object to the person mentioned in paragraph (*c*) or, if there is more than one, to such of them as the Secretary of State thinks appropriate.

[Chemical Weapons Act 1996, s 6.]

7.8516 **7. Power to enter premises and destroy objects** (1) This section applies if a warning has been affixed under section 5, and for the purposes of this section—

(*a*) the first six-month period is the period of six months beginning with the day after the warning was affixed;

(*b*) the second six-month period is the period of six months beginning with the day after the first six-month period ends.

(2) If at any time in the second six-month period the Secretary of State decides that the object should be destroyed it may be destroyed as provided by subsections (6) to (9); but this is subject to subsection (3) to (5).

(3) If at any time in the first six-month period—

(*a*) any person appears to the Secretary of State to have had the object in his possession immediately before the warning was affixed, or

(*b*) any person not falling within paragraph (*a*) appears to the Secretary of State to have an interest which the Secretary of State believes would be materially affected by the object's destruction,

the Secretary of State must serve on such a person a copy of a notice falling within subsection (4).

(4) A notice falling within this subsection is a notice which—

(*a*) describes the object and states its location;

(*b*) states that the Secretary of State proposes to secure its destruction and gives the reasons for his proposal;

(*c*) states that the person on whom the copy of the notice is served may object to the Secretary of State's proposal;

(*d*) states that an objection (if made) must be made in writing to the Secretary of State before such date as is specified in the notice and must state why the object should not be destroyed.

(5) Before he reaches a decision under subsection (2) the Secretary of State must—

(*a*) allow any person on whom a copy of a notice has been served under subsection (3) time to respond, and

(*b*) take into account any objections to the object's proposed destruction (whether made in response to a notice or otherwise).

(6) If—

(*a*) at any time in the second six-month period the Secretary of State decides that the object should be destroyed, and

(*b*) the object is on premises to which the public has access or which are occupied by a person who consents to action being taken under this subsection,

the Secretary of State may authorise a person to enter the premises and to destroy the object if it is found there.

(7) If (whatever the nature of the premises concerned)—

(*a*) a justice of the peace is satisfied on information on oath that a warning has been affixed under section 5, and that the Secretary of State has decided at any time in the second six-month period that the object should be destroyed, or

(*b*) in Scotland a justice, within the meaning of section 307 of the Criminal Procedure (Scotland) Act 1995, is satisfied by evidence on oath as mentioned in paragraph (*a*),

he may issue a warrant in writing authorising a person acting under the authority of the Secretary of State to enter the premises, if necessary by force, at any time within one month from the time of the issue of the warrant and to destroy the object if it is found there.

(8) A person who acts under an authorisation given under subsection (6) or (7) may take with him such other persons and such equipment as appear to him to be necessary.

(9) The powers conferred on an authorised person under this section shall only be exercisable, if the authorisation under subsection (6) or the warrant so provides, in the presence of a constable.

(10) Where an object is destroyed under this section the Secretary of State may recover from a responsible person any costs reasonably incurred by the Secretary of State in connection with the destruction; and a responsible person is any person who had possession of the object immediately before the warning was affixed under section 5.

[Chemical Weapons Act 1996, s 7.]

7.8517 8. **Compensation for destruction** (1) This section applies if a person claims that—

(*a*) an object has been destroyed under section 6 or 7,

(*b*) he had an interest which was materially affected by the destruction and he sustained loss as a result, and

(*c*) no copy of a notice was served on him under the section concerned (whether or not one was served on any other person).

(2) If the person concerned makes an application under this section to the High Court or in Scotland the Court of Session, and the Court finds that his claim is justified, the Court may order the Secretary of State to pay to the applicant such amount (if any) by way of compensation as the Court considers just.

(3) If the Court believes that the object would have been destroyed even if a copy of a notice had been served on the applicant under the section concerned the Court must not order compensation to be paid under this section.

[Chemical Weapons Act 1996, s 8.]

7.8518 9. **Offences relating to destruction etc** (1) If—

(*a*) a copy of a notice is served on a person under section 4,

(*b*) the notice relates to an object in his possession at the time the copy is served,

(*c*) he relinquishes possession before the date specified under section 4(3)(*e*), and;

(*d*) he has no reasonable excuse for so relinquishing possession,

he is guilty of an offence.

(2) If a person wilfully obstructs a person in—

(*a*) entering or searching premises under an authorisation given under section 5(1) or (2) or 7(6) or (7),

(*b*) making an object safe, seizing or removing an object, or affixing a warning, under section 5(4),

(*c*) destroying an object under an authorisation given under section 6(2) or 7(6) or (7), or

(*d*) attempting to do anything mentioned in paragraphs (*a*) to (*c*), the person so obstructing is guilty of an offence.

(3) If—

(*a*) a warning is affixed under section 5(4),

(*b*) a person interferes with the warning, or moves or interferes with the object before the date specified in the warning, and

(*c*) he has no reasonable excuse for doing so,

he is guilty of an offence.

(4) A person guilty of an offence under any of the preceding provisions of this section is liable[1].

(*a*) on summary conviction, to a fine of an amount not exceeding **the statutory maximum;**

(*b*) on conviction on indictment, to a **fine**.

(5) A person who knowingly makes a false or misleading statement in response to a copy of a notice served under section 4, 6 or 7 is guilty of an offence and liable[1]—

(*a*) on summary conviction, to a fine of an amount not exceeding **the statutory maximum;**

(*b*) on conviction on indictment, to imprisonment for a term not exceeding **two years** or to a **fine** or to **both**.

[Chemical Weapons Act 1996, s 9.]

---

1 For procedure in respect of this offence which is triable either way, see the Magistrates' Courts Act 1980, ss 17A–21, in PART I: MAGISTRATES' COURTS PROCEDURE, ante.

7.8519 **10. Destruction etc. supplementary** (1) If an object is in the possession of a person who intends that it will be used only for permitted purposes, it is not a chemical weapon for the purposes of sections 4(1) and (3) and 5(1) and (2); and in deciding whether permitted purposes are intended the types and quantities of objects shall be taken into account.

(2) For the purposes of sections 4 to 9—

(*a*) to the extent that an object consists of a toxic chemical or precursor, it is destroyed if it is permanently prevented from being used other than for permitted purposes;

(*b*) to the extent that an object consists of a munition or other device designed to cause death or harm through toxic chemicals released by it, it is destroyed if it is permanently prevented from doing so;

(*c*) to the extent that an object consists of equipment designed for use in connection with a munition or other device, it is destroyed if it is permanently prevented from being so used.

(3) In sections 5 to 9 "premises" includes land (including buildings), moveable structures, vehicles, vessels, aircraft and hovercraft.

(4) Nothing in sections 4 to 7 affects any power arising otherwise than by virtue of those sections (such as a power to dispose of property in police possession in connection with the investigation of a suspected offence).

[Chemical Weapons Act 1996, s 10.]

*Premises for producing chemical weapons etc.*

7.8520 **11. Premises or equipment for producing chemical weapons** (1) No person shall—

(*a*) construct premises he intends to be used to produce chemical weapons;

(*b*) alter premises in circumstances where he intends that they will be used to produce chemical weapons;

(*c*) install or construct equipment he intends to be used to produce chemical weapons;

(*d*) alter equipment in circumstances where he intends that it will be used to produce chemical weapons;

(*e*) permit the construction on land he occupies of premises he intends to be used to produce chemical weapons;

(*f*) permit premises on land he occupies to be altered in circumstances where he intends that they will be used to produce chemical weapons;

(*g*) permit the installation or construction on land he occupies of equipment he intends to be used to produce chemical weapons;

(*h*) permit equipment on land he occupies to be altered in circumstances where he intends that it will be used to produce chemical weapons.

(2) For the purposes of subsection (1) an object is not a chemical weapon if the person intends that the object will be used only for permitted purposes; and in deciding whether permitted purposes are intended the types and quantities of objects shall be taken into account.

(3) A person contravening this section is guilty of an offence and liable on conviction on indictment to imprisonment for life.

[Chemical Weapons Act 1996, s 11.]

7.8521 **12. Suspicious equipment or buildings** (1) If—

(*a*) the Secretary of State has grounds to suspect that any equipment or building is a chemical weapons production facility, and

(*b*) at least one person falls within subsection (2),

the Secretary of State may serve on any person falling within that subsection a copy of a notice falling within subsection (3).

(2) The persons falling within this subsection are—

(*a*) any person who appears to the Secretary of State to occupy the land on which the equipment or building is situated,

(*b*) if the Secretary of State's suspicion relates to equipment, any person not falling within paragraph (*a*) and who appears to the Secretary of State to have the equipment in his possession, and (*c*) any person not falling within paragraph (*a*) or (*b*) and who appears to the Secretary of State to have an interest which the Secretary of State believes is materially affected by the notice.

(3) A notice falling within this subsection is a notice which—

(*a*) describes the equipment or building and states its location;

(*b*) states that the Secretary of State suspects that the equipment or building is a chemical weapons production facility and gives the reasons for his suspicion;

(*c*) states that he is considering whether to require the equipment or building to be destroyed or altered;

(*d*) states that any person may make representations that the equipment or building is not a chemical weapons production facility.

(4) If the notice relates to equipment it must state that a person on whom the notice is served and who has the equipment in his possession must not relinquish possession of, or alter or use, the equipment before a date specified in the notice.

[Chemical Weapons Act 1996, s 12.]

7.8522 13. **Notice requiring destruction or alteration** (1) If—

(*a*) the secretary of State has reasonable cause to believe that any equipment or building is a chemical weapons production facility, and

(*b*) at least one person falls within subsection (2),

the Secretary of State may serve on each person falling within that subsection a copy of a notice falling within subsection (3).

(2) The persons falling within this subsection are—

(*a*) any person who appears to the Secretary of State to occupy the land on which the equipment or building is situated,

(*b*) if the Secretary of State's belief relates to equipment, any person not falling within paragraph (*a*) and who appears to the Secretary of State to have the equipment in his possession, and

(*c*) any person not falling within paragraph (*a*) or (*b*) and who appears to the Secretary of State to have an interest which the Secretary of State believes would be materially affected by the destruction or alteration of the equipment or building.

(3) A notice falling within this subsection is a notice which—

(*a*) describes the equipment or building and states its location;

(*b*) states that the Secretary of State believes the equipment or building is a chemical weapons production facility;

(*c*) requires the equipment or building to be destroyed or altered (as the case may be) in a manner, and before a date, specified in the notice.

(4) If a notice under this section requires any equipment or building to be altered, a further notice under this section may—

(*a*) revoke the first notice, and

(*b*) require the equipment or building to be destroyed;

and the preceding provisions of this section shall apply to the further notice accordingly.

(5) This section applies whether or not any copy of a notice has been served under section 12.

[Chemical Weapons Act 1996, s 13.]

7.8523 14. **Power where notice not complied with** (1) For the purposes of this section the qualifying condition is that—

(*a*) a notice has been prepared under section 13,

(*b*) the provisions of section 13(1) to (3) have been complied with in relation to the notice,

(*c*) the notice has not been revoked, and

(*d*) any requirement set out in the notice has not been complied with.

(2) If—

(*a*) a justice of the peace is satisfied on information on oath that the qualifying condition is fulfilled, or

(*b*) *Scotland*,

he may issue a warrant in writing authorising a person acting under the authority of the Secretary of State to take remedial action under this section.

(3) If a person is authorised by a warrant to take remedial action under this section he may—

(*a*) enter the land on which the equipment or building is situated, if necessary by force;

(*b*) do whatever is required to secure that the equipment or building is destroyed or altered in a manner specified in the notice;

(*c*) take with him such other persons and such equipment as appear to him to be necessary to help him to exercise the powers mentioned in paragraphs (*a*) and (*b*).

(4) The powers conferred on an authorised person under this section shall only be exercisable, if the warrant so provides, in the presence of a constable.

(5) If anything is done in exercise of the powers mentioned in this section, the Secretary of State may recover from a responsible person any costs reasonably incurred by the Secretary of State in connection with the exercise of those powers; and a responsible person is—

(*a*) in the case of equipment, any person in possession of the equipment at the time the land is entered;

(*b*) in the case of a building, any person occupying the land at the time it is entered.

[Chemical Weapons Act 1996, s 14.]

**7.8524 15. Position where no notice can be served** (1) For the purposes of this section the qualifying condition is that—

(*a*) the Secretary of State has reasonable cause to believe that any equipment or building is a chemical weapons production facility,

(*b*) in the period of six months beginning with the day after he formed his belief it has not been possible to serve a copy of a notice under section 13 because of the circumstances mentioned in subsection (2), and

(*c*) the Secretary of State has drawn up proposals for the destruction or alteration of the equipment or building in a manner specified in the proposals.

(2) The circumstances are that—

(*a*) no person appeared to the Secretary of State to occupy the land on which the equipment or building is situated,

(*b*) if the Secretary of State's belief relates to equipment, no person appeared to the Secretary of State to have the equipment in his possession, and

(*c*) no person appeared to the Secretary of State to have an interest which the Secretary of State believed would be materially affected by the destruction or alteration of the equipment or building.

(3) If—

(*a*) a justice of the peace is satisfied on information on oath that the qualifying condition is fulfilled, or

(*b*) *Scotland*,

he may issue a warrant in writing authorising a person acting under the authority of the Secretary of State to take remedial action under this section.

(4) If a person is authorised by a warrant to take remedial action under this section he may—

(*a*) enter the land on which the equipment or building is situated, if necessary by force;

(*b*) do whatever is required to secure that the equipment or building is destroyed or altered in a manner specified in the proposals drawn up by the Secretary of State;

(*c*) take with him such other persons and such equipment as appear to him to be necessary to help him to exercise the powers mentioned in paragraphs (*a*) and (*b*).

(5) The powers conferred on an authorised person under this section shall only be exercisable, if the warrant so provides, in the presence of a constable.

(6) If anything is done in exercise of the powers mentioned in this section, the Secretary of State may recover from a responsible person any costs reasonably incurred by the Secretary of State in connection with the exercise of those powers; and a responsible person is—

(*a*) in the case of equipment, any person in possession of the equipment at the time the land is entered;

(*b*) in the case of a building, any person occupying the land at the time it is entered.

[Chemical Weapons Act 1996, s 15.]

**7.8525 16. Compensation for destruction or alteration** (1) This section applies if a person claims that—

(*a*) any equipment or building has been destroyed or altered in compliance with a notice falling within section 13(3) or has been destroyed or altered under section 14,

(*b*) he had an interest which was materially affected by the destruction or alteration and he sustained loss as a result, and

(*c*) no copy of a notice was served on him under section 13.

(2) This section also applies if a person claims that—

(*a*) any equipment or building has been destroyed or altered under section 15, and

(*b*) he had an interest which was materially affected by the destruction or alteration and he sustained loss as a result.

(3) If a person concerned makes an application under this section to the High Court or in Scotland the Court of Session, and the Court finds that his claim is justified, the Court may order the Secretary of State to pay to the applicant such amount (if any) by way of compensation as the Court considers just.

(4) If the Court believes that the equipment or building would have been destroyed or altered even if a copy of a notice had been served on the application under section 13 the Court must not order compensation to be paid under this section.

[Chemical Weapons Act 1996, s 16.]

**7.8526 17. Offences relating to destruction etc** (1) If—

(*a*) a copy of a notice is served on a person under section 12,

(*b*) the notice relates to equipment in his possession at the time the copy is served,

(*c*) he relinquishes possession of, or alters or uses, the equipment before the date specified under section 12(4), and

(*d*) he has no reasonable excuse for doing so,

he is guilty of an offence.

(2) If—

(*a*) a copy of a notice is served on a person under section 13,

(*b*) the notice relates to equipment in his possession at the time the copy is served or to a building situated on land he occupies at that time,

(*c*) any requirement set out in the notice is not fulfilled, and

(*d*) he has no reasonable excuse for the requirement not being fulfilled,

he is guilty of an offence.

(3) If a person wilfully obstructs—

(*a*) a person exercising, or attempting to exercise, the powers mentioned in section 14(3)(*a*) or (*b*) or 15(4)(*a*) or (*b*), or

(*b*) any other person taken with him as mentioned in section 14(3)(*c*) or 15(4)(*c*) and helping him, or attempting to help him, to exercise those powers,

the person so obstructing is guilty of an offence.

(4) A person guilty of an offence under any of the preceding provisions of this section is liable[1]

(*a*) on summary conviction, to a fine of an amount not exceeding **the statutory maximum;**

(*b*) on conviction on indictment, to a **fine.**

(5) A person who knowingly makes a false or misleading statement in response to a notice served under section 12 is guilty of an offence and liable[1]—

(*a*) on summary conviction, to a fine of an amount not exceeding **the statutory maximum;**

(*b*) on conviction on indictment, to imprisonment for a term not exceeding **two years** or to a **fine** or to **both**.

[Chemical Weapons Act 1996, s 17.]

---

[1] For procedure in respect of this offence which is triable either way, see the Magistrates' Courts Act 1980, ss 17A–21, in PART I: MAGISTRATES' COURTS, PROCEDURE, ante.

7.8527 **18. Destruction etc: supplementary** (1) In sections 12 to 15 "chemical weapons production facility" has the meaning given by the definition of that expression in the Convention, and for this purpose—

(*a*) expressions used in the definition in the Convention shall be construed in accordance with the Convention, and

(*b*) section 1 shall be ignored.

(2) For the purposes of sections 12 to 16 "destroyed" and "destruction", in relation to a building, mean demolished and demolition.

(3) Nothing in sections 12 to 15 affects any power arising otherwise than by virtue of those sections (such as a power to dispose of property in police possession in connection with the investigation of a suspected offence).

[Chemical Weapons Act 1996, s 18.]

*Chemicals for permitted purposes*

7.8528 **19. Restriction on use etc** (1) Subject to section 20 (which relates to licences) no person shall—

(*a*) use a Schedule 1 toxic chemical or precursor for a permitted purpose, or

(*b*) produce or have in his possession a Schedule 1 toxic chemical or precursor with the intention that it will be used for a permitted purpose.

(2) A Schedule 1 toxic chemical or precursor is a toxic chemical or precursor listed in Schedule 1 to the annex on chemicals to the Convention; and for ease of reference that Schedule is set out in the Schedule to this Act.

(3) A person contravening this section is guilty of an offence and liable[1]—

(*a*) on summary conviction, to a fine of an amount not exceeding **the statutory maximum;**

(*b*) on conviction on indictment, to a **fine**.

[Chemical Weapons Act 1996, s 19.]

---

[1] For procedure in respect of this offence which is triable either way, see the Magistrates' Courts Act 1980, ss 17A–21, in PART I: MAGISTRATES' COURTS, PROCEDURE, ante.

7.8529 **20. Licences** (1) Section 19 does not apply to anything done in accordance with the terms of a licence granted by the Secretary of State and having effect at the time it is done.

(2) The Secretary of State may—

(*a*) grant a licence in such circumstances and on such terms as he thinks fits;

(*b*) vary or revoke a licence by serving a notice to that effect on the person to whom the licence was granted.

(3) A variation or revocation shall take effect at such reasonable time as is specified in the notice served under subsection (2)(*b*).

(4) The Secretary of State may by order make provision with respect to appealing against a

refusal to grant, renew or vary a licence or against a variation or revocation of a licence.

(5) An order under subsection (4) shall be made by statutory instrument subject to annulment in pursuance of a resolution of either House of Parliament.

(6) A person who knowingly makes a false or misleading statement for the purpose of obtaining a licence or a renewal or variation of a licence, or of opposing a variation or revocation of a licence, is guilty of an offence and liable[1]—

(*a*) on summary conviction, to a fine of an amount not exceeding **the statutory maximum;**

(*b*) on conviction on indictment, to imprisonment for a term not exceeding **two years** or to a **fine** or to **both**.

[Chemical Weapons Act 1996, s 20.]

---

[1] For procedure in respect of this offence which is triable either way, see the Magistrates' Courts Act 1980, ss 17A–21, in PART I: MAGISTRATES' COURTS, PROCEDURE, ante.

*Information and records*

7.8530 21. **Information for purposes of Act** (1) If the Secretary of State has grounds to suspect that a person is committing or has committed an offence under this Act the Secretary of State may by notice served on the person require him to give in such form as is specified in the notice, and within such reasonable period as is so specified, such information as—

(*a*) the Secretary of State has reasonable cause to believe will help to establish whether the person is committing or has committed such an offence, and

(*b*) is specified in the notice.

(2) A person who without reasonable excuse fails to comply with a notice served on him under subsection (1) is guilty of an offence and liable[1]—

(*a*) on summary conviction, to a fine of an amount not exceeding **the statutory maximum;**

(*b*) on conviction on indictment, to a **fine**.

(3) A person on whom a notice is served under subsection (1) and who knowingly makes a false or misleading statement in response to it is guilty of an offence and liable[1]—

(*a*) a summary conviction, to a fine of an amount not exceeding the **statutory maximum**;

(*b*) on conviction on indictment, to imprisonment for a term not exceeding **two years** or to a **fine** or to **both**.

[Chemical Weapons Act 1996, s 21.]

---

[1] For procedure in respect of this offence which is triable either way, see the Magistrates' Courts Act 1980, ss 17A–21, in PART I: MAGISTRATES' COURTS, PROCEDURE, ante.

7.8531 22. **Information and records for purposes of Convention** (1) The Secretary of State may by notice served on any person require him to give in such form as is specified in the notice, and within such reasonable period as is so specified, such information as—

(*a*) the Secretary of State has reasonable cause to believe is or will be needed in connection with anything to be done for the purposes of the Convention, and

(*b*) is specified in the notice;

and the information required by a notice may relate to a state of affairs subsisting before the coming into force of this Act or of the Convention.

(2) The Secretary of State may by notice served on any person require him to keep such records as—

(*a*) the Secretary of State has reasonable cause to believe will facilitate the giving of information the person may at any time be required to give under subsection (1), and

(*b*) are specified in the notice.

(3) A person who without reasonable excuse fails to comply with a notice served on him under subsection (1) or (2) is guilty of an offence and liable[1]—

(*a*) on summary conviction, to a fine of an amount not exceeding **the statutory maximum;**

(*b*) on conviction on indictment, to a **fine**.

(4) A person on whom a notice is served under subsection (1) and who knowingly makes a false or misleading statement in response to it is guilty of an offence and liable[1]—

(*a*) on summary conviction, to a fine of an amount not exceeding **the statutory maximum;**

(*b*) on conviction on indictment, to imprisonment for a term not exceeding **two years** or to a **fine** or to **both**

[Chemical Weapons Act 1996, s 22.]

---

[1] For procedure in respect of this offence which is triable either way, see the Magistrates' Courts Act 1980, ss 17A–21, in PART I: MAGISTRATES' COURTS, PROCEDURE, ante.

7.8532 23. **Identifying persons who have information** (1) The Secretary of State may make regulations[1] requiring persons of any description specified in the regulations to inform him that they are of such a description.

(2) Any such description must be so framed that persons within it are persons on whom the

Secretary of State is likely to want to serve a notice under section 22.

(3) If regulations are made under this section the Secretary of State shall arrange for a statement of the fact that they have been made to be published in such manner as is likely to bring them to the attention of persons affected by them.

(4) A person who without reasonable excuse fails to comply with a requirement imposed by the regulations is guilty of an offence and liable[2]—

(*a*) on summary conviction, to a fine of an amount not exceeding **the statutory maximum;**

(*b*) on conviction on indictment, to a **fine.**

(5) A person who knowingly makes a false or misleading statement in response to a requirement imposed by the regulations is guilty of an offence and liable[1]—

(*a*) a summary conviction, to a fine of an amount not exceeding **the statutory maximum;**

(*b*) on conviction on indictment, to imprisonment for a term not exceeding **two years** or to a **fine** or to **both**.

(6) The regulations shall be made by statutory instrument subject to annulment in pursuance of a resolution of either House of Parliament.

[Chemical Weapons Act 1996, s 23.]

---

1 See the Chemical Weapons (Notification) Regulations 1996, SI 1996/2503 amended by SI 1996/2669, SI 2004/2406, SI 2007/3224, SI 2009/229 and SI 2016/992.

2 For procedure in respect of this offence which is triable either way, see the Magistrates' Courts Act 1980, ss 17A–21, in PART I: MAGISTRATES' COURTS, PROCEDURE, ante.

*Inspections under Convention*

7.8533 **24. Inspections: interpretation** For the purposes of sections 25 to 28—

(*a*) the verification annex is the annex on implementation and verification to the Convention;

(*b*) a routine inspection is an inspection conducted pursuant to Parts II to IX of that annex;

(*c*) a challenge inspection is an inspection conducted pursuant to Parts II and X of that annex;

(*d*) an assistance inspection is an inspection conducted pursuant to Parts II and XI of that annex;

(*e*) "in-country escort," "inspector", "inspection team" and "observer" have the meanings given by Part I of that annex.

[Chemical Weapons Act 1996, s 24.]

7.8534 **25. Rights of entry etc. for purposes of inspections** (1) If it is proposed to conduct a routine inspection, a challenge inspection or an assistance inspection in the United Kingdom, the Secretary of State may issue an authorisation under this section in respect of that inspection.

(2) An authorisation under this section shall—

(*a*) contain a description of the area (the specified area) in which the inspection is to be conducted,

(*b*) specify the type of inspection concerned,

(*c*) state the name of the members of the inspection team by whom the inspection is to be carried out, and

(*d*) in the case of a challenge inspection, state the name of any observer who may accompany the team.

(3) Such an authorisation shall have the effect of authorising the inspection team—

(*a*) to exercise within the specified area such rights of access, entry and unobstructed inspection as are conferred on them by the verification annex, and

(*b*) to do such other things within that area in connection with the inspection as they are entitled to do by virtue of the verification annex (including things concerning the maintenance, replacement or adjustment of any instrument or other object).

(4) such an authorisation shall in addition have the effect of—

(*a*) authorising an in-country escort to accompany the inspection team in accordance with the provisions of the verification annex, and

(*b*) authorising any constable to give such assistance as the in-country escort may request for the purpose of facilitating the conduct of the inspection in accordance with the verification annex;

and the name of the person in charge of the in-country escort shall be stated in the authorisation.

(5) An authorisation under this section in the case of a challenge inspection shall in addition have the effect of authorising the observer to exercise within the specified area such rights of access and entry as are conferred on him by the verification annex.

(6) Any constable giving assistance in accordance with subsection (4)(*b*) may use such reasonable force as he considers necessary for the purpose mentioned in that provision.

(7) The occupier of any premises—

(*a*) in relation to which it is proposed to exercise a right of entry in reliance on an authorisation under this section, or

(*b*) on which an inspection is being carried out in reliance on such an authorisation, or a person acting on behalf of the occupier of any such premises, shall be entitled to require a copy of the authorisation to be shown to him by a member of the in-country escort.

(8) The validity of any authorisation purporting to be issued under this section in respect of any inspection shall not be called in question in any court of law at any time before the conclusion of that inspection.

(9) Accordingly, where an authorisation purports to be issued under this section in respect of any inspection, no proceedings (of whatever nature) shall be brought at any time before the conclusion of the inspection if they would, if successful, have the effect of preventing, delaying or otherwise affecting the carrying out of the inspection.

(10) If in any proceedings any question arises whether a person at any time was or was not, in relation to any routine, challenge or assistance inspection, a member of the inspection team or a member of the in-country escort or the observer, a certificate issued by or under the authority of the Secretary of State stating any fact relating to that question shall be conclusive evidence of that fact.

(11) If an authorisation is issued under this section the Secretary of State may issue an amendment varying the specified area, and—

(*a*) from the time when the amendment is expressed to take effect this section shall apply as if the specified area were the area as varied;

(*b*) subsection (8) shall apply to the amendment as it applies to the authorisation;

(*c*) the Secretary of State may issue further amendments varying the specified area and in such a case paragraphs (*a*) and (*b*) shall apply.

[Chemical Weapons Act 1996, s 24.]

7.8535 26. **Offences in connection with inspections** (1) If an authorisation has been issued under section 25 in respect of any inspection, a person is guilty of an offence if he—

(*a*) refuses without reasonable excuse to comply with any request made by any constable or a member of the in-country escort for the purpose of facilitating the conduct of that inspection in accordance with the verification annex,

(*b*) interferes without reasonable excuse with any container, instrument or other object installed in the course of that inspection in accordance with the verification annex, or

(*c*) wilfully obstructs any member of the inspection team or of the in-country escort, or the observer, in the conduct of that inspection in accordance with the verification annex.

(2) Subsection (1)(*b*) applies to interference which occurs at any time while the container, instrument or other objects is retained in accordance with the verification annex.

(3) A person guilty of an offence under this section is liable[1]—

(*a*) on summary conviction, to a fine of an amount not exceeding **the statutory maximum;**

(*b*) on conviction on indictment, to a **fine.**

[Chemical Weapons Act 1996, s 26.]

---

[1] For procedure in respect of this offence which is triable either way, see the Magistrates' Courts Act 1980, ss 17A–21, in PART I: MAGISTRATES' COURTS, PROCEDURE, ante.

7.8536 27. **Privileges and immunities in connection with inspections** (1) Members of inspection teams and observers shall enjoy the same privileges and immunities as are enjoyed by diplomatic agents in accordance with the following provisions of the 1961 Articles, namely—

(*a*) Article 29

(*b*) paragraphs 1 and 2 of the Article 30,

(*c*) paragraphs 1, 2 and 3 of Article 31, and

(*d*) Article 34.

(2) Such persons shall, in addition, enjoy the same privileges as are enjoyed by diplomatic agents in accordance with paragraph 1(*b*) of Article 36 of the 1961 Articles, except in relation to articles the importing or exporting of which is prohibited by law or controlled by the enactments relating to quarantine.

(3) Samples and approved equipment carried by members of an inspection team shall be inviolable and exempt from customs duties.

(4) The privileges and immunities accorded to members of inspection teams and observers by virtue of this section shall be enjoyed by them at any time when they are in the United Kingdom—

(*a*) in connection with the carrying out there of a routine inspection, a challenge inspection or an assistance inspection, or

(*b*) while in transit to or from the territory of another party to the Convention in connection with the carrying out of such an inspection there.

(5) If—

(*a*) immunity from jurisdiction of a member of an inspection team is waived in accordance with the verification annex, and

(*b*) a notice made by the Secretary of State and informing the member of the waiver is delivered to him in person,

then, from the time the notice is so delivered, this section shall not have effect to confer that immunity on the member.

(6) If in any proceedings any question arises whether a person is or is not entitled to any privilege or immunity by virtue of this section, a certificate issued by or under the authority of the

Secretary of State stating any fact relating to that question shall be conclusive evidence of that fact.

(7) In this section—

"the 1961 Articles" means the Articles which are set out in Schedule 1 to the Diplomatic Privileges Act 1964 (Articles of Vienna Convention on Diplomatic Relations of 1961 having force of law in United Kingdom);

"approved equipment" and "samples" shall be construed in accordance with the verification annex;

"enactment" includes an enactment comprised in subordinate legislation (within the meaning of the Interpretation Act 1978.

[Chemical Weapons Act 1996, s 27.]

*Offences: miscellaneous*

7.8537 **29. Power to search and obtain evidence** (1) If—

(*a*) a justice of the peace is satisfied on information on oath that there is reasonable ground for suspecting that an offence under this Act is being, has been or is about to be committed on any premises or that evidence of the commission of such an offence is to be found there, or

(*b*) *Scotland,*

he may issue a warrant in writing authorising a person acting under the authority of the Secretary of State to enter the premises, if necessary by force, at any time within one month form the time of the issue of the warrant and to search them.

(2) A person who enters the premises under the authority of the warrant may—

(*a*) take with him such other persons and such equipment as appear to him to be necessary;

(*b*) inspect any document found on the premises which he has reasonable cause to believe may be required as evidence for the purposes of proceedings in respect of an offence under this Act;

(*c*) take copies of, or seize and remove, any such document;

(*d*) inspect, seize and remove any device or equipment found on the premises which he has reasonable cause to believe may be required as such evidence;

(*e*) inspect, sample, seize and remove any substance found on the premises which he has reasonable cause to believe may be required as such evidence;

(*f*) search or cause to be searched any person found on the premises whom he has reasonable cause to believe to be in possession of any document, device, equipment or substance;

but no woman or girl shall be searched except by a woman.

(3) The powers conferred by a warrant under this section shall only be exercisable, if the warrant so provides, in the presence of a constable.

[Chemical Weapons Act 1996, s 29.]

7.8538 **30. Forfeiture in case of conviction** (1) The court by or before which a person is convicted of an offence under this Act may order that anything shown to the court's satisfaction to relate to the offence shall be forfeited, and either destroyed or otherwise dealt with in such manner as the court may order.

(2) In particular, the court may order the thing to be dealt with as the Secretary of State may see fit; and in such a case the Secretary of State may direct that it be destroyed or otherwise dealt with.

(3) Where—

(*a*) the court proposes to order anything to be forfeited under this section, and

(*b*) a person claiming to have an interest in it applies to be heard by the court,

the court must not order it to be forfeited unless he has been given an opportunity to show cause why the order should not be made.

[Chemical Weapons Act 1996, s 30.]

7.8539 **30A. Revenue and Customs prosecutions** (1) Proceedings for a chemical weapons offence may be instituted by the Director of Public Prosecutions or by order of the Commissioners for Her Majesty's Revenue and Customs if it appears to the Director or to the Commissioners that the offence has involved—

(*a*) the development or production outside the United Kingdom of a chemical weapon;

(*b*) the movement of a chemical weapon into or out of any country or territory;

(*c*) any proposal or attempt to do anything falling within paragraph (*a*) or (*b*).

(2) In this section "chemical weapons offence" means an offence under section 2 above or section 50 of the Anti-terrorism, Crime and Security Act 2001 (including an offence of aiding, abetting, counselling, procuring or inciting the commission of, or attempting or conspiring to commit, such an offence).

(3) Any proceedings for an offence which are instituted by order of the Commissioners under subsection (1) above shall be commenced in the name of an officer of Revenue and Customs, but may be continued by another officer.

(4) Where the Commissioners investigate, or propose to investigate, any matter with a view to determining—

(*a*) whether there are grounds for believing that a chemical weapons offence has been committed, or (*b*) whether a person should be prosecuted for such an offence,

that matter shall be treated as an assigned matter within the meaning of the Customs and Excise Management Act 1979.

(5) Nothing in this section affects any power of any person (including any officer) apart from this section.

(6) Repealed.

(7) This section does not apply to the institution of proceedings in Scotland.]

[Chemical Weapons Act 1996, s 30A as inserted by the Anti-terrorism, Crime and Security Act 2001, s 46 and amended by the Commissioners for Revenue and Customs Act 2005, Sch 4 and SI 2014/834.]

7.8540 **31. Offences: other provisions** (1) Proceedings for an offence under section 2 or 11 shall not be instituted—

(*a*) in England and Wales, except by or with the consent of the Attorney General;

(*b*) in Northern Ireland, except by or with the consent of the Attorney General for Northern Ireland.*

(2) Proceedings for an offence under any provision of this Act other than section 2 or 11 shall not be instituted except by or with the consent of the Secretary of State; but the preceding provisions of this section do not apply to Scotland.

(3) Where an offence under this Act is committed by a body corporate and is proved to have been committed with the consent or connivance of, or to be attributable to any neglect on the part of—

(*a*) a director, manager, secretary or other similar officer of the body corporate, or

(*b*) any person who was purporting to act in any such capacity,

he as well as the body corporate shall be guilty of that offence and shall be liable to be proceeded against and punished accordingly.

(4) In subsection (3) "director", in relation to a body corporate whose affairs are managed by its members, means a member of the body corporate.

(5) Where an offence under this Act is committed by a Scottish partnership and is proved to have been committed with the consent or connivance of a partner, he as well as the partnership shall be guilty of that offence and shall be liable to be proceeded against and punished accordingly.

[Chemical Weapons Act 1996, s 31.]

* **Words substituted by the Justice (Northern Ireland) Act 2002, s 28 from a date to be appointed.**

*Other miscellaneous provisions*

7.8541 **32. Disclosure of information** (1) This section applies to information if—

(*a*) it was obtained under, or in connection with anything done under, this Act or the Convention, and

(*b*) it relates to a particular business or other activity carried on by any person.

(2) So long as the business or activity continues to be carried on the information shall not be disclosed except—

(*a*) with the consent of the person for the time being carrying on the business or activity,

(*b*) in connection with anything done for the purposes of the Convention,

(*c*) in connection with anything done for the purposes of this Act,

(*d*) in connection with the investigation of any criminal offence or for the purposes of any criminal proceedings,

(*e*) in connection with the enforcement of any restriction on imports or exports,

(*f*) in dealing with an emergency involving danger to the public,

(*g*) with a view to ensuring the security of the United Kingdom, or

(*h*) to the International Court of Justice for the purpose of enabling that Court do deal with any dispute referred to it under the Convention.

(3) The reference to this Act in subsection (2)(*c*) does not include a reference to section 33.

(4) A person who discloses information in contravention of this section is guilty of an offence and liable[1]—

(*a*) on summary conviction, to a fine of an amount not exceeding **the statutory maximum;**

(*b*) on conviction on indictment, to imprisonment for a term not exceeding **two years** or to a **fine** or to **both.**

(5) Where a person proposes to disclose information to which this section applies in circumstances where the disclosure would by virtue of paragraphs (*b*) to (h) or subsection (2) not contravene this section, he may disclose the information notwithstanding any obligation not to disclose it that would otherwise apply.

[Chemical Weapons Act 1996, s 32.]

1 For procedure in respect of this offence which is triable either way, see the Magistrates' Courts Act 1980, ss 17A–21, in PART I: MAGISTRATES' COURTS, PROCEDURE, ante.

7.8542 **34. Service of notices** A notice under any provision of this Act, or a copy of a notice under any such provision, may be served on a person—

(*a*) by delivering it to him in person,

(*b*) by sending it by post to him at his usual or last-known residence or place of business in the United Kingdom, or

(*c*) in the case of a body corporate, by delivering it to the secretary or clerk of the body corporate at its registered or principal office or sending it by post to the secretary or clerk of that body corporate at that office.

[Chemical Weapons Act 1996, s 34.]

7.8543 **36. Power to amend this Act** (1) The Secretary of State may by order make such additions to, omissions from or other modifications to this Act as he considers necessary or desirable to give effect to any amendment of the Convention made in pursuance of its provisions.

(2) The power to make an order under this section shall, if the order solely modifies the Schedule to this Act, be exercisable by statutory instrument subject to annulment in pursuance of a resolution of either House of Parliament.

(3) The power to make any other order under this section shall be exercisable by statutory instrument, and no such order shall be made unless a draft of it has been laid before and approved by resolution of each House of Parliament.

[Chemical Weapons Act 1996, s 36.]

7.8544 **37. The Crown** (1) Subject to the following provisions of this section, this Act binds the Crown.

(2) No contravention by the Crown of a provision made by or under this Act shall make the Crown criminally liable; but the High Court or in Scotland the Court of Session may, on the application of a person appearing to the Court to have an interest, declare unlawful any act or omission of the Crown which constitutes such a contravention.

(3) Notwithstanding subsection (2), the provisions made by or under this Act apply to persons in the public service of the Crown as they apply to other persons.

(4) Nothing in this section affects Her Majesty in her private capacity; and this subsection shall be construed as if section 38(3) of the Crown Proceedings Act 1947 (meaning of Her Majesty in her private capacity) were contained in this Act.

[Chemical Weapons Act 1996, s 37.]

*General*

7.8545 **39. Commencement, extent and citation** (1) This Act (except this section) shall come into force on such day as the Secretary of State may appoint by order[1] made by statutory instrument.

(2) It is hereby declared that this Act extends to Northern Ireland.

(3) Her Majesty may by Order in Council make provision for extending any of the provisions of this Act, with such exceptions, adaptations or modifications as may be specified in the Order[2], to any of the Channel Islands, the Isle of Man or any colony.

(4) This Act may be cited as the Chemical Weapons Act 1996.

[Chemical Weapons Act 1996, s 39.]

1 The Act is fully in force; see the note to the title of the Act, ante.

2 The following Chemical Weapons Act 1996 Orders have been made under this provision: Jersey, SI 1998/2565; Isle of Man, SI 1998/2794; Guernsey, SI 2000/743; Overseas Territories SI 2005/854 amended by SI 2011/2984.

## SCHEDULE

SCHEDULED TOXIC CHEMICALS AND PRECURSORS

7.8547

| **A TOXIC CHEMICALS:** | | **(CAS registry number)** |
|---|---|---|
| (1) | O-Alkyl (less than or equal to C10, incl cycloalkyl) alkyl (Me, Et, n-Pr or i-Pr)-phosphonofluoridates | |
| | eg Sarin: O-Isopropyl methylphosphonofluoridate | (107-44-8) |
| | Soman: O-Pinacolyl methylphosphonofluoridate | (96-64-0) |
| (2) | O-Alkyl (less than or equal to C10, incl cycloalkyl) N,N-dialkyl (Me, Et, n-Pr or i-Pr) phosphoramidocyanidates | |
| | eg Tabun: 0-Ethyl N,N-dimethyl phosphoramidocyanidate | (77-81-6) |
| (3) | O-Alkyl (H or less than or equal to C10, incl cycloalkyl) S-2-dailkyl (Me, Et, n-Pr or i-Pr)-aminoethyl alkyl (Me, Et, n-Pr or i-Pr) phosphonothiolates and corresponding alkylated or protonated salts | |
| | eg VX: 0-Ethyl S-2-diisopropylaminoethyl methyl phosphonothiolate | (50782-69-9) |
| (4) | Sulfur mustards: | |
| | 2-Chloroethylchloromethylsulfide | (2625-76-5) |
| | Mustard gas: Bis (2-chloroethyl) sulfide | (505-60-2) |
| | Bis (2-chloroethylthio) methane | (63869-13-6) |
| | Sesquimustard: 1,2-Bis (2-chloroethylthio) ethane | (3563-36-8) |
| | 1,3-Bis (2-chloroethylthio)-n-propane | (63905-10-2) |
| | 1,4-Bis (2-chloroethylthio)-n-butane | (142868-93-7) |

| A TOXIC CHEMICALS: | | (CAS registry number) |
|---|---|---|
| | 1,5-Bis (2-chloroethylthio)-n-pentane | (142868-94-8) |
| | Bis (2-chloroethylthiomethyl) ether | (63918-90-1) |
| | O-Mustard: Bis (2-chloroethylthioethy) ether | (63918-89-8) |
| (5) | Lewisites: | |
| | Lewisite 1: 2-Chlorovinyldichloroarsine | (541-25-3) |
| | Lewisite 2: Bis (2-chlorovinyl) chloroarsine | (40334-69-8) |
| | Lewisite 3: Tris (2-chlorovinyl) arsine | (40334-70-1) |
| (6) | Nitrogen mustards: | |
| | HN1: Bis (2-chloroethyl) ethylamine | (538-07-8) |
| | HN2: Bis (2-chloroethyl) methylamine | (51-75-2) |
| | HN3: Tris (2-chloroethyl) amine | (555-77-1) |
| (7) | Saxitoxin | (35523-89-8) |
| (8) | Ricin | (9009-86-3) |

| B PRECURSORS: | | |
|---|---|---|
| (9) | Alkyl (Me, Et, n-Pr or i-Pr) phosphonyldifluorides | |
| | eg DF: Methylphosphonyldifluoride | (676-99-3) |
| (10) | O-Alkyl (H or less than or equal to C10, incl cycloalkyl) O-2-dialkyl (Me, Et, n-Pr or i-Pr)-aminoethyl alkyl (Me, Et, n-Pr or i-Pr) phosphonites and corresponding alkylated or protonated salts | |
| | eg QL: O-Ethyl O-2 diisopropylaminoethyl methylphosphonite | (57856-11-8) |
| (11) | Chlorosarin: O-Isopropyl methylphosphonochloridate | (1445-76-7) |
| (12) | Chlorosoman: O-Pinacolyl methylphosphonochloridate | (7040-57-5) |

*Notes:*

**1.** This Schedule sets out Schedule 1 to the annex on chemicals to the Convention as corrected.

**2.** In this Schedule the reference to the CAS registry is to the chemical abstract service registry.

**3.** This Schedule must be read subject to the following proposition, which is based on a note in the Convention: where reference is made to groups of dialkylated chemicals, followed by a list of alkyl groups in parentheses, all chemicals possible by all possible combinations of alkyl groups listed in the parentheses must be taken to be listed in the Schedule.

# Knives Act 1997[1]

(1997 c 21)

*The offences*

7.8548 **1. Unlawful marketing of knives** (1) A person is guilty of an offence if he markets a knife in a way which—

(*a*) indicates, or suggests, that it is suitable for combat; or

(*b*) is otherwise likely to stimulate or encourage violent behaviour involving the use of the knife as a weapon.

(2) "Suitable for combat" and "violent behaviour" are defined in section 10.

(3) For the purposes of this Act, an indication or suggestion that a knife is suitable for combat may, in particular, be given or made by a name or description—

(*a*) applied to the knife;

(*b*) on the knife or on any packaging in which it is contained; or

(*c*) included in any advertisement which, expressly or by implication, relates to the knife.

(4) For the purposes of this Act, a person markets a knife if—

(*a*) he sells or hires it;

(*b*) he offers, or exposes, it for sale or hire; or

(*c*) he has it in his possession for the purpose of sale or hire.

(5) A person guilty of an offence under this section shall be liable[2]—

(*a*) on summary conviction, to imprisonment for a term not exceeding **12 months** or to a fine not exceeding the **statutory maximum**, or to **both**;

(*b*) on conviction on indictment to imprisonment for a term not exceeding **4 years** or to a **fine**, or to **both**.

[Knives Act 1997, s 1 as amended by SI 2008/1216.]

1 With the exception of s 11, the provisions of this Act have been brought into force by orders made under s 11: the Knives Act 1997 (Commencement) (No 1) Order 1997, SI 1997/1906, bringing into force sections 1 to 7, 9 and 10 on 1 September 1997, and the Knives Act 1997 (Commencement) (No 2) Order 1999, SI 1999/5, bringing into force s 8 on 1 March 1999.

2 For procedure in respect of this offence which is triable either way, see the Magistrates' Courts Act 1980, ss 17A-21, in PART I: MAGISTRATES' COURTS, PROCEDURE, ante.

7.8549 **2. Publications** (1) A person is guilty of an offence if he publishes any written, pictorial or other material in connection with the marketing of any knife and that material—

(*a*) indicates, or suggests, that the knife is suitable for combat; or

(*b*) is otherwise likely to stimulate or encourage violent behaviour involving the use of the knife as a weapon.

(2) A person guilty of an offence under this section shall be liable[1]—

(*a*) on summary conviction, to imprisonment for a term not exceeding **12 months** or to a fine not exceeding the **statutory maximum**, or to **both**;

(*b*) on conviction on indictment to imprisonment for a term not exceeding **4 years** or to a **fine**, or to **both**.

[Knives Act 1997, s 2 as amended by SI 2008/1216.]

1 For procedure in respect of this offence which is triable either way, see the Magistrates' Courts Act 1980, ss 17A–21, in PART I: MAGISTRATES' COURTS, PROCEDURE, ante.

*The defences*

7.8550 3. **Exempt trades** (1) It is a defence for a person charged with an offence under section 1 to prove[1] that—

(*a*) the knife was marketed—

(i) for use by the armed forces of any country;

(ii) as an antique or curio; or

(iii) as falling within such other category (if any) as may be prescribed;

(*b*) it was reasonable for the knife to be marketed in that way; and

(*c*) there were no reasonable grounds for suspecting that a person into whose possession the knife might come in consequence of the way in which it was marketed would use it for an unlawful purpose.

(2) It is a defence for a person charged with an offence under section 2 to prove that—

(*a*) the material was published in connection with marketing a knife—

(i) for use by the armed forces of any country;

(ii) as an antique or curio; or

(iii) as falling within such other category (if any) as may be prescribed;

(*b*) it was reasonable for the knife to be marketed in that way; and

(*c*) there were no reasonable grounds for suspecting that a person into whose possession the knife might come in consequence of the publishing of the material would use it for an unlawful purpose.

(3) In this section "prescribed" means prescribed by regulations made by the Secretary of State.

[Knives Act 1997, s 3.]

1 The standard of proof is on a preponderance of probabilities, less onerous than on the prosecution; *R v Carr-Briant* [1943] KB 607, [1943] 2 All ER 156, 107 JP 167, *R v Dunbar* [1958] 1 QB 1, [1957] 2 All ER 737, [1957] 3WLR 330.

7.8551 4. **Other defences** (1) It is a defence for a person charged with an offence under section 1 to prove[1] that he did not know or suspect, and had no reasonable grounds for suspecting, that the way in which the knife was marketed—

(*a*) amounted to an indication or suggestion that the knife was suitable for combat; or

(*b*) was likely to stimulate or encourage violent behaviour involving the use of the knife as a weapon.

(2) It is a defence for a person charged with an offence under section 2 to prove[1] that he did not know or suspect, and had no reasonable grounds for suspecting, that the material—

(*a*) amounted to an indication or suggestion that the knife was suitable for combat; or

(*b*) was likely to stimulate or encourage violent behaviour involving the use of the knife as a weapon.

(3) It is a defence for a person charged with an offence under section 1 or 2 to prove[1] that he took all reasonable precautions and exercised all due diligence to avoid committing the offence.

[Knives Act 1997, s 4.]

1 The standard of proof is on a preponderance of probabilities, less onerous than on the prosecution; *R v Carr-Briant* [1943] KB 607, [1943] 2 All ER 156, 107 JP 167, *R v Dunbar* [1958] 1 QB 1, [1957] 2 All ER 737, [1957] 3WLR 330.

*Supplementary powers*

7.8552 5. **Supplementary powers of entry, seizure and retention** (1) If, on an application made by a constable, a justice of the peace or sheriff is satisfied that there are reasonable grounds for suspecting—

(*a*) that a person ("the suspect") has committed an offence under section 1 in relation to knives of a particular description, and

(*b*) that knives of that description and in the suspect's possession or under his control are to be found on particular premises,

the justice or sheriff may issue a warrant authorising a constable to enter those premises, search for the knives and seize and remove any that he finds.

(2) If, on an application made by a constable, a justice of the peace or sheriff is satisfied that there are reasonable grounds for suspecting—

(*a*) that a person ("the suspect") has committed an offence under section 2 in relation to particular material, and

(*b*) that publications consisting of or containing that material and in the suspect's possession or under his control are to be found on particular premises,

the justice or sheriff may issue a warrant authorising a constable to enter those premises, search for the publications and seize and remove any that he finds.

(3) A constable, in the exercise of his powers under a warrant issued under this section, may if necessary use reasonable force.

(4) Any knives or publications which have been seized and removed by a constable under a warrant issued under this section may be retained until the conclusion of proceedings against the suspect[1].

(5) For the purposes of this section, proceedings in relation to a suspect are concluded if—

(*a*) he is found guilty and sentenced or otherwise dealt with for the offence;

(*b*) he is acquitted;

(*c*) proceedings for the offence are discontinued; or

(*d*) it is decided not to prosecute him.

(6) In this section "premises" includes any place and, in particular, any vehicle, vessel, aircraft or hovercraft and any tent or movable structure.

[Knives Act 1997, s 5.]

---

1 See the Criminal Justice and Police Act 2001, Part 2 (PART I, ante). These provisions confer, by ss 50 and 51, additional powers of seizure of property in relation to searches carried out under existing powers. However, s 57 (retention of seized items) does not authorise the retention of any property which could not be retained under the provisions listed in s 57(1), which include s 5(4) of the Knives Act 1997, if the property was seized under the new powers (ie those conferred by ss 50 and 51) in reliance on one of those powers (ie those conferred by the provisions listed in s 57(1)). Section 57(4) further provides that nothing in any of the provisions listed in s 57(1) authorises the retention of anything after an obligation to return it has arisen under Part 2.

7.8553 **6. Forfeiture of knives and publications** (1) If a person is convicted of an offence under section 1 in relation to a knife of a particular description, the court may make an order for forfeiture in respect of any knives of that description—

(*a*) seized under a warrant issued under section 5; or

(*b*) in the offender's possession or under his control at the relevant time.

(2) If a person is convicted of an offence under section 2 in relation to particular material, the court may make an order for forfeiture in respect of any publications consisting of or containing that material which—

(*a*) have been seized under warrant issued under section 5; or

(*b*) were in the offender's possession or under his control at the relevant time.

(3) The court may make an order under subsection (1) or (2)—

(*a*) whether or not it also deals with the offender in respect of the offence in any other way; and

(*b*) without regard to any restrictions on forfeiture in any enactment.

(4) In considering whether to make an order, the court must have regard—

(*a*) to the value of the property; and

(*b*) to the likely financial and other effects on the offender of the making of the order (taken together with any other order that the court contemplates making).

(5) In this section "relevant time"—

(*a*) in relation to a person convicted in England and Wales or Northern Ireland of an offence under section 1 or 2, means the time of his arrest for the offence or of the issue of a summons in respect of it;

(*b*) in relation to a person so convicted in Scotland, means the time of his arrest for the offence or of his being cited as an accused in respect of it.

[Knives Act 1997, s 6.]

7.8554 **7. Effect of a forfeiture order** (1) An order under section 6 (a "forfeiture order") operates to deprive the offender of his rights, if any, in the property to which it relates.

(2) The property to which a forfeiture order relates must be taken into the possession of the police (if it is not already in their possession).

(3) The court may, on an application made by a person who—

(*a*) claims property to which a forfeiture order applies, but

(*b*) is not the offender from whom it was forfeited,

make an order (a "recovery order") for delivery of the property to the applicant if it appears to the court that he owns it.

(4) An application to a sheriff must be made in such manner as may be prescribed by act of adjournal.

(5) No application may be made after the end of the period of 6 months beginning with the date on which the forfeiture order was made.

(6) No application may succeed unless the claimant satisfies the court—

(*a*) that he had not consented to the offender having possession of the property; or

(*b*) that he did not know, and had no reason to suspect, that the offence was likely to be committed.

(7) If a person has a right to recover property which is in the possession of another in pursuance of a recovery order, that right—

(a) is not affected by the making of the recovery order at any time before the end of the period of 6 months beginning with the date on which the order is made; but

(b) is lost at the end of that period.

(8) The Secretary of State may make regulations[1], in relation to property forfeited under this section, for disposing of the property and dealing with the proceeds in cases where—

(a) no application has been made before the end of the period of 6 months beginning with the date on which the forfeiture order was made; or

(b) no such application has succeeded.

(9) The regulations[1] may also provide for investing money and auditing accounts.

(10) In this section, "application" means an application under subsection (3).

[Knives Act 1997, s 7.]

---

1 The Knives (Forfeited Property) Regulations 1997 have been made, in this TITLE, post.

7.8555 **8. Powers to stop and search for knives or offensive weapons** Amendment of the Criminal Justice and Public Order Act 1994.

*Miscellaneous*

7.8556 **9. Offences by bodies corporate** (1) If an offence under this Act committed by a body corporate is proved—

(a) to have been committed with the consent or connivance of an officer, or

(b) to be attributable to any neglect on his part,

he as well as the body corporate is guilty of the offence and liable to be proceeded against and punished accordingly.

(2) In subsection (1) "officer", in relation to a body corporate, means a director, manager, secretary or other similar office of the body, or a person purporting to act in any such capacity.

(3) If the affairs of a body corporate are managed by its members, subsection (1) applies in relation to the acts and defaults of a member in connection with his functions of management as if he were a director of the body corporate.

(4) Scotland.

[Knives Act 1997, s 9.]

7.8557 **10. Interpretation** In this Act—

"the court" means—

(a) in relation to England and Wales or Northern Ireland, the Crown Court or a magistrates' court;

(b) in relation to Scotland, the sheriff;

"knife" means an instrument which has a blade or is sharply pointed;

"marketing" and related expressions are to be read with section 1(4);

"publication" includes a publication in electronic form and, in the case of a publication which is, or may be, produced from electronic data, any medium on which the data are stored;

"suitable for combat" means suitable for use as a weapon for inflicting injury on a person or causing a person to fear injury;

"violent behaviour" means an unlawful act inflicting injury on a person or causing a person to fear injury.

[Knives Act 1997, s 10.]

7.8558 **11. Short title, commencement, extent etc** (1) This Act may be cited as the Knives Act 1997.

(2) This section comes into force on the passing of this Act.

(3) The other provisions of this Act come into force on such date as may be appointed by order[1] made by the Secretary of State; but different dates may be appointed for different provisions and for different purposes.

(4)–(6) Regulations and orders.

(7) Extent

[Knives Act 1997, s 11.]

---

1 As to commencement orders which has been made at the date of going to press, see note 1 to the short title of this Act, ante.

## Landmines Act 1998[1]

(1998 c 33)

7.8559 The Landmines Act 1998 implements obligations under the Ottawa Convention[2] and promotes the control of anti-personnel landmines. The use, development or production, acquisition, possession or transfer of an anti personnel mine defined in s 1, is an offence punishable on indictment by imprisonment not exceeding **14 years** or a **fine** or **both** (s 2). Prohibitions may apply to conduct by UK nationals outside the UK (s 3). Provision is made for defences including possession etc for the purpose of developing techniques for mine detection, clearance and destruction or other lawful purposes as defined (s 4) and for certain international military operations (s 5) or where the accused proves lack of the requisite knowledge (s 6). The Secretary of State may take steps to secure the destruction of anti-personnel mines by serving a notice on a person suspected of having a prohibited object in his possession giving him the opportunity to make representations (s 7) and a justice may issue a warrant authorising entry within one month of issue to search premises (s 8) for prohibited objects which may subsequently be ordered by the Secretary of State to be destroyed (s 9). Various offences are created in relation to failure to comply with or frustrating the procedures for searching for and destroying prohibited items which are punishable on summary conviction by a fine not exceeding the **statutory maximum** or on indictment by a **fine** or (in the case of an offence of knowingly making a false or misleading statement in response to a notice served by the Secretary of State under ss 7, 9 or 10) a term of imprisonment not exceeding **2 years** (s 12).

Provision is made for rights of entry for fact finding missions under the Ottawa Convention (ss 13–16); information and records (s 17) including power for a justice to issue a search warrant where there are reasonable grounds for suspecting an offence under the Act is being, has been or is about to be committed on any premises or that evidence of the commission of such an offence is to be found there (s 18). Proceedings for an offence under section 2 may not be instituted except by or with the consent of the Attorney General (s 20) and in certain circumstances may be conducted by Revenue and Customs (s 21). On conviction of an offence under the Act, the court may order forfeiture of anything relating to the offence (s 22).

---

[1] This Act was brought fully into force on 1 March 1999 by the Landmines Act 1998 (Commencement) Order 1999, SI 1999/448. See also the Landmines Act 1998 (Guernsey) Order 2000, SI 2000/2769, the Landmines Act (Isle of Man) Order 2000, SI 2000/2770, the Landmines Act 1998 (Overseas Territories) Order 2001, SI 2001/3499 amended by SI 2011/2984 and the Landmines Act 1998 (Jersey) Order 2001, SI 2001/3930.

[2] Convention on the Prohibition of the Use, Stockpiling, Production and Transfer of Anti-Personnel Mines and on their Destruction, which was signed by the United Kingdom at Ottawa on 3 December 1997.

## Nuclear Explosions (Prohibition and Inspections) Act 1998

(1998 c 7)

**7.8560** This Act gives effect to certain provisions of the Comprehensive Nuclear-Test-Ban Treaty adopted in New York on 10 September 1996 and the Protocol to that treaty.

Except where carried out in the course of an armed conflict any person who knowingly causes a nuclear weapons test explosion or other nuclear explosion is guilty of an offence triable only on indictment and is liable on conviction to imprisonment for **life** (s 1) and the offence may be committed by a United Kingdom national outside the United Kingdom (s 2). Proceedings may only be commenced with the consent of the Attorney General (s 3). Inspection teams may conduct on-site inspections in accordance with the Treaty and the Secretary of State may issue an authorisation granting rights of access, entry and unobstructed inspection and may authorise the police to assist such inspection (ss 4–5). A person is guilty of an offence punishable on summary conviction by a fine not exceeding **the statutory maximum** or on indictment by a fine if he fails without reasonable excuse to comply with a request to facilitate such an inspection or wilfully obstructs a member of the inspection team (s 7). A justice who is satisfied there are reasonable grounds for suspecting that an offence under this Act has been, is or is about to be committed on any premises or that evidence of such an offence is to be found there may issue a warrant to enter, by force if necessary, and search the premises (s 10).

## Violent Crime Reduction Act 2006[1]

(2006 c 38)

### Part 2[2]

### Weapons Etc

*Dangerous weapons*

**7.8561 47. Power to search persons in attendance centres for weapons** (1) A member of staff of an attendance centre who has reasonable grounds for suspecting that a relevant person may have with him or in his possessions—

(*a*) an article to which section 139 of the Criminal Justice Act 1988 (c 33) applies (knives and blades etc), or

(*b*) an offensive weapon (within the meaning of the Prevention of Crime Act 1953 (c 14)),

may search the relevant person or his possessions for such articles and weapons.

(2) A search under this section may be carried out only where the member of staff and the

relevant person are on the premises of the attendance centre.

(3) A person may carry out a search under this section only if—

(*a*) he is the officer in charge of the attendance centre; or

(*b*) he has been authorised by the officer in charge to carry out the search.

(4) A person who carries out a search of a relevant person under this section—

(*a*) may not require the relevant person to remove any clothing other than outer clothing;

(*b*) must be of the same sex as the relevant person; and

(*c*) may carry out the search only in the presence of another member of staff who is also of the same sex as the relevant person.

(5) A relevant person's possessions may not be searched under this section except in his presence and in the presence of another member of staff.

(6) If, in the course of a search under this section, the person carrying out the search finds—

(*a*) anything which he has reasonable grounds for suspecting falls within subsection (1)(*a*) or (*b*), or

(*b*) any other thing which he has reasonable grounds for suspecting is evidence in relation to an offence,

he may seize and retain it.

(7) A person who exercises a power under this section may use such force as is reasonable in the circumstances for exercising that power.

(8) A person who seizes anything under subsection (6) must deliver it to a police constable as soon as reasonably practicable.

(9) The Police (Property) Act 1897 (c 30) (disposal of property in the possession of the police) shall apply to property which has come into the possession of a police constable under this section as it applies to property which has come into the possession of the police in the circumstances mentioned in that Act.

(10) An authorisation for the purposes of subsection (3)(*b*) may be given either in relation to a particular search or generally in relation to searches under this section or to a particular description of such searches.

(11) In this section—

"attendance centre" has the same meaning as in Part 12 of the Criminal Justice Act 2003 (c 44) (see section 221 of that Act);

"officer in charge", in relation to an attendance centre, means the member of staff for the time being in charge of that centre;

"outer clothing" means—

(*a*) any item of clothing that is being worn otherwise than wholly next to the skin or immediately over a garment being worn as underwear; or

(*b*) a hat, shoes, boots, gloves or a scarf;

"possessions", in relation to a person, includes any goods over which he has or appears to have control;

"relevant person", in relation to an attendance centre, means a person who is required to attend at that centre by virtue of—

(*a*) a relevant order (within the meaning of section 196 of the Criminal Justice Act 2003 (c 44)); or

(*b*) a youth rehabilitation order under Part 1 of the Criminal Justice and Immigration Act 2008.

(12) The powers conferred by this section are in addition to any powers exercisable by the member of staff of an attendance centre in question apart from this section and are not to be construed as restricting such powers.

[Violent Crime Reduction Act 2006, s 47 as amended by the Criminal Justice and Immigration Act 2008, Sch 4.]

---

[1] The Violent Crime Reduction Act 2006 is reproduced partly in PART I and partly in PART VIII of this Manual. For the provisions of the Act which are not printed in this Part, reference should be made to the following: ss 1–27, 59–63. Sch 5 in PART I: MAGISTRATES' COURTS, PROCEDURE, ante; ss 28, 29, 32, 35–39, 50, in the title FIREARMS, post; and ss 55, 56 in the title SEXUAL OFFENCES, in Part VIII, post.

This Act is brought into effect in accordance with s 66, and orders made thereunder. All the provisions here were in force by 1 October 2007 (except s 43(3)–(5) in force on 6 April 2008).

[2] Part 2 comprises ss 28–51.

## Criminal Justice Act 1988 (Offensive Weapons) Order 1988[1]

(SI 1988/2019 amended by SI 2002/1668, SI 2004/1271, SI 2008/973 and 2039 and SI 2016/803)

**7.8562** 1. *Citation and Commencement.*

---

[1] Made by the Secretary of State under s 141(2) of the Criminal Justice Act 1988. Revoked in relation to Scotland by SSI 2005/483.

2. The Schedule to this Order shall have effect.

SCHEDULE

Article 2

**7.8563** 1. Section 141 of the Criminal Justice Act 1988 (offensive weapons) shall apply to the following descriptions of weapons, other than weapons of those descriptions which are antiques for the purposes of this Schedule:

(*a*) a knuckleduster, that is, a band of metal or other hard material worn on one or more fingers, and designed to cause injury, and any weapon incorporating a knuckleduster;

(*b*) a swordstick, that is, a hollow walking-stick or cane containing a blade which may be used as a sword;

(*c*) the weapon sometimes known as a "handclaw", being a band of metal or other hard material from which a number of sharp spikes protrude, and worn around the hand;
(*d*) the weapon sometimes known as a "belt buckle knife", being a buckle which incorporates or conceals a knife;
(*e*) the weapon sometimes known as a "push dagger", being a knife the handle of which fits within a clenched fist and the blade of which protrudes from between two fingers;
(*f*) the weapon sometimes known as a "hollow kubatan", being a cylindrical container containing a number of sharp spikes;
(*g*) the weapon sometimes known as a "footclaw", being a bar of metal or other hard material from which a number of sharp spikes protrude, and worn strapped to the foot;
(*h*) the weapon sometimes known as a "shuriken", "shaken" or "death star", being a hard non-flexible plate having three or more sharp radiating points and designed to be thrown;
(*i*) the weapon sometimes known as a "balisong" or "butterfly knife", being a blade enclosed by its handle, which is designed to split down the middle, without the operation of a spring or other mechanical means, to reveal the blade;
(*j*) the weapon sometimes known as a "telescopic truncheon", being a truncheon which extends automatically by hand pressure applied to a button, spring or other device in or attached to its handle;
(*k*) the weapon sometimes known as a "blowpipe" or "blow gun", being a hollow tube out of which hard pellets or darts are shot by the use of breath;
(*l*) the weapon sometimes known as a "kusari gama", being a length of rope, cord, wire or chain fastened at one end to a sickle;
(*m*) the weapon sometimes known as a "kyoketsu shoge", being a length of rope, cord, wire or chain fastened at one end to a hooked knife;
(*n*) the weapon sometimes known as a "manrikgusari" or "kusari", being a length of rope, cord, wire or chain fastened at each end to a hard weight or hand grip;
(*o*) a disguised knife, that is any knife which has a concealed blade or concealed sharp point and is designed to appear to be an everyday object of a kind commonly carried on the person or in a handbag, briefcase, or other hand luggage (such as a comb, brush, writing instrument, cigarette lighter, key, lipstick or telephone);
(*p*) a stealth knife, that is a knife or spike, which has a blade, or sharp point, made from a material that is not readuily detectable by apparatus used for detecting metal and which is not designed for domestic use or for use in the processing, preparatn or consumption of food or as a toy;
(*q*) a straight, side-handled or friction-lock truncheon (sometimes known as a baton);
(*r*) a sword with a curved blade of 50 centimetres or over in length; and for the purposes of this sub-paragraph, the length of the blade shall be the straight line distance from the top of the handle to the tip of the blade;
(*s*) the weapon sometimes known as a "zombie knife", "zombie killer knife" or "zombie slayer knife", being a blade with—
(i) a cutting edge;
(ii) a serrated edge; and
(iii) images or words (whether on the blade or handle) that suggest that it is to be used for the purpose of violence.

*2.* For the purposes of this Schedule, a weapon is an antique if it was manufactured more than 100 years before the date of any offence alleged to have been committed in respect of that weapon under subsection (1) of the said section 141 or section 50(2) or (3) of the Customs and Excise Management Act 1979 (improper importation).

*3.* It shall be a defence for a person charged—
(*a*) with an offence under section 141(1) of the Criminal Justice Act 1988; or
(*b*) with an offence under section 50(2) or (3) of the Customs and Excise Management Act 1979,
in respect of any conduct of his relating to a weapon to which section 141 of the Criminal Justice Act 1988 applies by virtue of paragraph 1(*r*) to show that the weapon in question was made before 1954 or was made at any other time according to traditional methods of making swords by hand.

*4.* It shall be a defence for a person charged—
(*a*) with an offence under section 141(1) of the Criminal Justice Act 1988; or
(*b*) with an offence under section 50(2) or (3) of the Customs and Excise Management Act 1979,
in respect of any conduct of his relating to a weapon to which section 141 of the Criminal Justice Act 1988 applies by virtue of paragraph 1(*r*) to show that his conduct was for the purpose only of making the weapon available for the purposes of the organisation and holding of a permitted activity for which public liability insurance is held in relation to liabilities to third parties arising from or in connection with the organisation and holding of such an activity.

*5.* For the purposes of paragraph 4—
"historical re-enactment" means any presentation or other event held for the purpose of re-enacting an event from the past or of illustrating conduct from a particular time or period in the past;
"insurance" means a contract of insurance or other arrangement made for the purpose of indemnifying a person or persons named in the contract or under the arrangement;
"permitted activity" means an historical re-enactment or a sporting activity;
"sporting activity" means the practising of a sport which requires the use of a weapon described in paragraph 1(r);
"third parties" includes participants in, and spectators of, a permitted activity and members of the public.

*5A.* It shall be a defence for a person charged—
(*a*) with an offence under section 141(1) of the Criminal Justice Act 1988; or
(*b*) with an offence under section 50(2) or (3) of the Customs and Excise Management Act 1979,
in respect of any conduct of his relating to a weapon to which section 141 of the Criminal Justice Act 1988 applies by virtue of paragraph 1(r) to show that his conduct was for the purpose only of making the weapon available for the purposes of use in religious ceremonies.

*6.* For the purposes of paragraphs 3, 4 and 5A, a person shall be taken to have shown a matter specified in those paragraphs if—
(*a*) sufficient evidence of that matter is adduced to raise an issue with respect to it; and
(*b*) the contrary is not proved beyond a reasonable doubt.

## Knives (Forfeited Property) Regulations 1997[1]

(SI 1997/1907 amended by SI 2000/1549 and SI 2011/3058)

**7.8564** *1. Citation and commencement.*

[1] Made by the Secretary of State, in exercise of the powers conferred on him by s 7(8) and (9) of the Knives Act 1997.

**7.8564A**

*Interpretation*

*2.* In these Regulations,

"museum or similar institution" means any institution which has as its purpose, or one of its purposes, the preservation and display of material of historical, aesthetic or technical interest to which the public are given access.

"the relevant authority" means

(*a*) in relation to a police area in England and Wales, the local policing body (within the meaning of s 101(1) of the Police Act 1996);

(*b*) *revoked*

(*c*) *Scotland.*

"the 1997 Act" means the Knives Act 1997.

**7.8564B**

*Property to which Regulations apply*

*3.* (1) Subject to paragraph (2) below, these Regulations apply to property which is in the possession of the police by virtue of a forfeiture order under section 6 of the 1997 Act and in respect of which—

(*a*) no application under section 7(3) of the 1997 Act has been made before the end of the period of 6 months beginning with the date on which the forfeiture order was made; or

(*b*) no such application has succeeded.

(2) Where, within the period specified in paragraph (1) above, an application by a claimant of the property has been made under section 7(3) of the 1997 Act or the person upon whose conviction the court ordered the forfeiture of the property under section 6 of that Act has appealed against the conviction or sentence, these Regulations shall not apply to the property until that application or appeal has been determined.

**7.8564C**

*Disposal of property*

*4.* (1) Subject to paragraph (2) below, property to which these Regulations apply shall be destroyed.

(2) Where the relevant authority are satisfied that property to which these Regulations apply which would otherwise fall to be destroyed is of particular rarity, aesthetic quality or technical or historical interest, they may, instead of arranging for its destruction, give or sell it to a museum or similar institution.

(3) The proceeds of disposals under these Regulations (if any) shall be paid to the relevant authority and

(*a*) in relation to authorities in England and Wales shall be subject to the regulations governing the application of the proceeds of sale of property made under section 2 of the Police (Property) Act 1897; and

(*b*) in relation to authorities in Scotland shall vest in the relevant authority.

# OFFICIAL SECRETS

**Contents**



## Official Secrets Act 1911[1]

(1 & 2 Geo 5 c 28)

**7.8565 1. Penalties for spying** (1) If any person for any purpose[2] prejudicial to the safety or interests of the State—

(*a*) approaches, inspects, passes over, or is in the neighbourhood of, or enters any prohibited place[3] within the meaning of this Act, or

(*b*) makes any sketch, plan, model[4], or note which is calculated to be or might be or is intended to be directly or indirectly useful to an enemy[5]; or

(*c*) obtains, collects, records or publishes or communicates[6] to any other person any secret official code word or pass word, or any sketch, plan, model, article, or note, or other document or information which is calculated to be or might be or is intended to be directly or indirectly useful to an enemy,

shall be guilty of an offence[7].

(2) On a prosecution under this section it shall not be necessary to show that the accused person was guilty of any particular act tending to show a purpose prejudicial to the safety or interests of the State, and, notwithstanding that no such act is proved against him, he may be convicted if, from the circumstances of the case, or his conduct, or his known character as proved, it appears that his purpose was a purpose prejudicial to the safety or interests of the State; and if any sketch, plan, model, article, note, document, or information relating to or used in any prohibited place[8] within the meaning of this Act, or anything is such a place, or any secret official code word or pass word, is made, obtained, collected, recorded, published or communicated by any person other than a person acting under lawful authority, it shall be deemed to have been made, obtained, collected, recorded, published, or communicated for a purpose prejudicial to the safety or interests of the State unless the contrary is proved.

[Official Secrets Act 1911, s 1 as amended by the Official Secrets Act 1920, First and Second Schedules.]

1 The Official Secrets Acts 1911, 1920 and 1939 shall be construed as one (Official Secrets Act 1939, s 2(1)). The Official Secrets Acts apply to acts done by a diplomatic agent in respect of the archives of the diplomatic mission in which he is employed (*R v AB* [1941] 1 KB 454). The communication of classified information in the UK or elsewhere by any person now or in the past a member of or having dealings with any Euratom institution is an offence by s 11(2) of the European Communities Act 1972, construed with these Acts.

2 The purpose is not limited by the reference to "spying" in the marginal note (*R v Chandler* [1962] 2 All ER 314; affd sub nom *Chandler v DPP* [1964] AC 763, [1962] 3 All ER 142, HL, where the meanings of phrases used in this section were considered in detail). See also *R v Bettaney* [1985] Crim LR 104, CA.

3 See 1911 Act, s 3, post.

4 "Sketch" includes any photograph or other mode of representing any plan or thing; "model" includes design, pattern, and specimen; and "document" includes part of a document (1911 Act, s 12).

5 The word "enemy" does not necessarily mean someone with whom this country is at war, but a potential enemy (*R v Parrott* (1913) 8 Cr App Rep 186).

6 Expressions referring to communicating include any communicating, whether in whole or in part, and whether the sketch, plan, model, article, note, document, or information itself or the substance, effect or description thereof only to be communicated; and expressions referring to the communication of any sketch, plan, model, article, note or document include the transfer or transmission of the sketch, plan, model, article, note or document (1911 Act, s 12 as amended by the Official Secrets Act 1989, Sch 2). The communication is an offence, even if made without any corruption (*R v Crisp and Homewood* (1919) 83 JP 121).

7 "Offence" is substituted for "felony" to accord with the Criminal Law Act 1967, s 12(5). For punishment, see 1920 Act, s 8, post.

8 See 1911 Act, s 3, post.

**7.8566 3. Definition of prohibited place** For the purposes of this Act, the expression "prohibited place" means—

(*a*) any work of defence, arsenal, naval or air force establishment or station, factory, dockyard, mine, mine-field, camp, ship, or aircraft belonging to or occupied by or on behalf of Her Majesty, or any telegraph, telephone, wireless or signal station, or office so belonging[1] or occupied and any place belonging to or occupied by or on behalf of Her Majesty and used for the purpose of building, repairing, making, or storing any munitions of war, or any sketches, plans, models, or documents, relating thereto, or for the purpose of getting any metals, oil, or minerals of use in time of war, [substituted by Official Secrets Act 1920, First Schedule].

(*b*) any place not belonging to Her Majesty where any munitions of war or any sketches, models, plans or documents relating thereto, are being made, repaired, gotten, or stored under contract with, or with any person on behalf of, Her Majesty, or otherwise on behalf of Her Majesty; and (*c*) any place[2] belonging to or used for the purposes of Her Majesty which is for the time being declared by order[3] of a Secretary of State to be a prohibited place for the purposes of this section on the ground that information with respect thereto, or damage thereto, would be useful to an enemy; and

(*d*) any railway, road, way or channel, or other means of communication by land or water (including any works or structures being part thereof or connected therewith) or any place used for gas, water, electricity works or other works for the purposes of a public character, or any place where munitions of war, or any sketches, models, plans or documents relating thereto are being made, repaired, or stored otherwise than on behalf of Her Majesty, which is for the time being declared by order of a Secretary of State to be a prohibited place for the purposes of this section, on the ground that information with respect thereto, or the destruction or obstruction thereof, or interference therewith, would be useful to an enemy[4].

[Official Secrets Act 1911, s 3 as amended by the Official Secrets Act 1920, First Schedule.]

---

1 Any reference to a place belonging to Her Majesty includes a place belonging to any department of the Government of the United Kingdom or of any British possessions, whether the place is or is not actually vested in Her Majesty (1911 Act, s 12).

2 For application of this paragraph to any place belonging to or used for the purposes of the United Kingdom Atomic Energy Authority, see Atomic Energy Authority Act 1954, s 6(3). A place belonging to or used for the purposes of the Civil Aviation Authority shall be deemed to be a place belonging to Her Majesty (Civil Aviation Act 1982, s 18(2)).

3 Places have been prescribed by the Official Secrets (Prohibited Places) Order 1994, SI 1994/968.

4 See note to "enemy" in s 1(1)(*b*), ante.

7.8567 7. **Penalty for harbouring spies** If any person, knowingly harbours any person whom he knows, or has reasonable grounds for supposing, to be a person who is about to commit or who has committed an offence under this Act, or knowingly permits to meet or assemble in any premises in his occupation or under his control any such persons, or if any person having harboured any such person, or permitted to meet or assemble in any premises in his occupation or under his control any such persons, wilfully omits or refuses to disclose to a superintendent of police any information which it is in his power to give in relation to any such person he shall be guilty of a misdemeanour.

[Official Secrets Act 1911, s 7 as amended by the Official Secrets Act 1920, First and Second Schedules.]

7.8568 8. **Restriction on prosecution** A prosecution for an offence under this Act[1] shall not be instituted except by or with the consent of the Attorney-General[2].

[Official Secrets Act 1911, s 8 as amended by the Criminal Jurisdiction Act 1975, Sch 6.]

---

1 The expression "offence under this Act" includes any act, omission or other thing which is punishable under this Act (1911 Act, s 12).

2 The expression "Attorney-General" means the Attorney-General for England (1911 Act, s 12, amended by the Law Officers Act 1997, Schedule). Nothing in s 2 of the Administration of Justice (Miscellaneous Provisions) Act 1933, shall affect this provision (Administration of Justice (Miscellaneous Provisions) Act 1933, s 2(7)).

7.8569 9. **Search warrants** (1) If a justice of the peace is satisfied by information on oath that there is reasonable ground for suspecting that an offence under this Act[1] has been or is about to be committed, he may grant a search warrant authorising any constable to enter at any time any premises or place named in the warrant, if necessary by force, and to search the premises or place and every person found therein; and to seize any sketch, plan, model, article, note or document, or anything of a like nature or anything which is evidence of an offence under this Act[1] having been or being about to be committed, which he may find on the premises or place or on any such person, and with regard to or in connection with which he has reasonable ground for suspecting that an offence under this Act[1] has been or is about to be committed.

(2) Where it appears to a superintendent of police[2] that the case is one of great emergency and that in the interest of the State immediate action is necessary, he may by a written order under his name give to any constable the like authority as may be given by the warrant of a justice under this section.

[Official Secrets Act 1911, s 9 as amended by the Police and Criminal Evidence Act 1984, Sch 7.]

---

1 This includes provisions under the Official Secrets Act 1989 other than s 8(1), (4) or (5); Official Secrets Act 1989, s 11 (3); the Police and Criminal Evidence Act 1984, s 9(2) (exclusion of legal privilege items etc) and Sch 1, para 3(*b*) (access conditions for special procedure) apply to s 9(1) of the 1911 Act; Official Secrets Act 1989, s 11(3).

2 The expression "superintendent of police" includes any police officer of a like or superior rank and any person upon whom the powers of a superintendent of police are for the purposes of this Act conferred by a Secretary of State (1911 Act, s 12 as amended by 1920 Act, Sch 1).

## Official Secrets Act 1920

(1920 c 75)

7.8570 **1–4.** Unauthorised use of uniforms, falsification of reports, personation and false documents [s 1 amended by the Forgery and Counterfeiting Act 1981, Sch.] Communications with foreign agents to be evidence of commission of certain offences [s 2]. Interfering with officers of the police or members of Her Majesty's forces [s 3][1].

---

1 This section relates to such interference "in the vicinity of" any prohibited place. In *Adler v George* [1964] 2 QB 7, [1964] 1 All ER 628, 128 JP 251, it was held that these words extended to the place itself.

7.8571 6. **Duty of giving information as to commission of offences** (1) Where a chief officer of police[1] is satisfied that there is reasonable ground for suspecting that an offence under section one of the principal Act has been committed and for believing that any person is able to furnish information as to the offence or suspected offence, he may apply to a Secretary of State for permission to exercise the powers conferred by this subsection and, if such permission is granted, he may authorise a superintendent of police[2], or any police officer not below the rank of inspector, to require the person believed to be able to furnish information to give any information in his power relating to the offence or suspected offence[3], and, if so required and on tender of his reasonable expenses, to attend at such reasonable time and place as may be specified by the superintendent or other officer; and if a person required in pursuance of such an authorisation to give information, or to attend as aforesaid, fails to comply with any such requirement or knowingly gives false information, he shall be guilty of a misdemeanour.

(2) Where a chief officer of police has reasonable ground to believe that the case is one of great emergency and that in the interest of the State immediate action is necessary, he may exercise the powers conferred by the last foregoing subsection without applying for or being granted the permission of a Secretary of State, but if he does so shall forthwith report the circumstances to the Secretary of State.

[Official Secrets Act 1920, s 6 as substituted by the Official Secrets Act 1939, s 1.]

---

[1] "Chief officer of police" includes any other officer of police expressly authorised by a chief officer of police to act on his behalf for the purposes of this section when by reason of illness, absence, or other cause he is unable to do so (sub-s (3)). As to the meaning of "chief officer of police", see the Official Secrets Act 1920, s 11(3).

[2] See note to s 9 of the 1911 Act, supra.

[3] This extends to an unauthorised person having received confidential police information (*Lewis v Cattle* [1938] 2 KB 454, [1938] 3 All ER 368, 102 JP 239).

7.8572 **7. Attempts, incitement, etc** Any person who attempts to commit any offence under the principal Act of this Act, or solicits or incites or endeavours to persuade another person to commit an offence, or aids or abets and[1] does any act preparatory to the commission of an offence under the principal Act or this Act, shall be guilty of an offence[2], and on conviction shall be liable to the same punishment, and to be proceeded against in the same manner as if he had committed the offence.

[Official Secrets Act 1920, s 7.]

---

[1] The word "and" should be read as "or" to give an intelligible meaning to the succeeding phrase (*R v Oakes* [1959] 2 QB 350, [1959] 2 All ER 92, 123 JP 290).

[2] "Offence" is substituted for "felony or misdemeanour or summary offence" to accord with Criminal Law Act 1967, s 12(5).

7.8573 **8. Provision as to trial and punishment of offences** (1) Any person who is guilty of an offence[1] under the principal Act or this Act shall be liable to imprisonment for a term not exceeding **fourteen years**.

(2) Any person who is guilty of a misdemeanour under the principal Act or this Act shall be liable[2] on conviction on indictment to imprisonment, for a term not exceeding **two years**[3], or, on conviction under the [Magistrates' Courts Act 1980] to imprisonment, for a term not exceeding **three months** or to a fine not exceeding **the statutory maximum**, or to **both** such imprisonment and fine: Provided that no misdemeanour under the principal Act or this Act shall be dealt with summarily except with the consent of the Attorney-General[4].

(3) For the purposes of the trial of a person for an offence under the principal Act or this Act, the offence shall be deemed to have been committed either at the place in which the same was actually committed, or at any place in the United Kingdom in which the offender may be found.

(4) In addition and without prejudice to any powers which a court may possess to order the exclusion of the public from any proceedings if, in the course of proceedings before a court against any person for an offence under the principal Act or this Act or the proceedings on appeal, or in the course of the trial of a person for an offence[1] under the principal Act or this Act, application is made by the prosecution, on the ground that the publication of any evidence to be given or of any statement to be made in the course of the proceedings would be prejudicial to the national safety, that all or any portion of the public shall be excluded during any part of the hearing, the court may make an order to that effect, but the passing of the sentence shall in any case take place in public.

(5) Where the person guilty of an offence under the principal Act or this Act is a company or corporation, every director[5] and officer of the company or corporation shall be guilty of the like offence unless he proves that the act or omission constituting the offence took place without his knowledge or consent.

[Official Secrets Act 1920, s 8 as amended by the Criminal Law Act 1977, s 28.]

---

[1] "Offence" is substituted for "felony or misdemeanour or summary offence" to accord with the Criminal Law Act 1967, s 12(5).

[2] For procedure in respect of an offence triable either way, see the Magistrates' Courts Act 1980, ss 17A–21, in PART I: MAGISTRATES' COURTS, PROCEDURE, ante.

[3] Offences under this Act, which are not arrestable offences by virtue of the term of imprisonment for which a person may be sentenced in respect of them are arrestable offences by virtue of Sch 1A to the Police and Criminal Evidence Act 1984.

[4] See PART I: MAGISTRATES' COURTS, PROCEDURE, para 1.112 **Criminal prosecutions**, ante.

[5] See *Dean v Hiesler* [1942] 2 All ER 340, 106 JP 282.

# Official Secrets Act 1989[1]

(1989 c 6)

7.8574 **1. Security and intelligence** (1) A person who is or has been—

(*a*) a member of the security and intelligence services; or

(*b*) a person notified that he is subject to the provisions of this subsection,

is guilty of an offence[2] if without lawful authority he discloses any information, document or other article relating to security or intelligence which is or has been in his possession by virtue of his position as a member of any of those services or in the course of his work while the notification is or was in force.

(2) The reference in subsection (1) above to disclosing information relating to security or intelligence includes a reference to making any statement which purports to be a disclosure of such information or is intended to be taken by those to whom it is addressed as being such a disclosure.

(3) A person who is or has been a Crown servant or government contractor is guilty of an offence[2] if without lawful authority he makes a damaging disclosure of any information, document or other article relating to security or intelligence which is or has been in his possession by virtue of his position as such but otherwise than as mentioned in subsection (1) above.

(4) For the purposes of subsection (3) above a disclosure is damaging if—

(*a*) it causes damage to the work of, or of any part of, the security and intelligence services; or

(*b*) it is of information or a document or other article which is such that its unauthorised disclosure would be likely to cause such damage or which falls within a class or description of information, documents or articles the unauthorised disclosure of which would be likely to have that effect.

(5) It is a defence for a person charged with an offence under this section to prove that at the time of the alleged offence he did not know, and had no reasonable cause to believe, that the information, document or article in question related to security or intelligence or, in the case of an offence under subsection (3), that the disclosure would be damaging within the meaning of that subsection.

(6) Notification that a person is subject to subsection (1) above shall be effected by a notice in writing served on him by a Minister of the Crown; and such a notice may be served if, in the Minister's opinion, the work undertaken by the person in question is or includes work connected with the security and intelligence services and its nature is such that the interests of national security require that he should be subject to the provisions of that subsection.

(7) Subject to subsection (8) below, a notification for the purposes of subsection (1) above shall be in force for the period of five years beginning with the day on which it is served but may be renewed by further notices under subsection (6) above for periods of five years at a time.

(8) A notification for the purposes of subsection (1) above may at any time be revoked by a further notice in writing served by the Minister on the person concerned; and the Minister shall serve such a further notice as soon as, in his opinion, the work undertaken by that person ceases to be such as is mentioned in subsection (6) above.

(9) In this section "security or intelligence" means the work of, or in support of, the security and intelligence services or any part of them, and references to information relating to security or intelligence include references to information held or transmitted by those services or by persons in support of, or of any part of, them.

[Official Secrets Act 1989, s 1.]

---

1 The effect of this Act is to replace s 2 of the Official Secrets Act 1911 by provisions protecting more limited classes of official information.

2 For prosecution, trial and penalties, see ss 9–11 post. A defendant prosecuted under ss 1(1)(*a*) and 4(1) and (3)(*a*) of this Act is not entitled to put forward a defence of disclosure in the national interest or belief that such disclosure was in the national interest: *R v Shayler* [2002] UKHL 11, [2003] 1 AC 247, [2002] 2 All ER 477, [2002] 2 WLR 754.

7.8575 **2. Defence** (1) A person who is or has been a Crown servant or government contractor is guilty of an offence[1] if without lawful authority he makes a damaging disclosure of any information, document or other article relating to defence which is or has been in his possession by virtue of his position as such.

(2) For the purposes of subsection (1) above a disclosure is damaging if—

(*a*) it damages the capability of, or of any part of, the armed forces of the Crown to carry out their tasks or leads to loss of life or injury to members of those forces or serious damage to the equipment or installations of those forces; or

(*b*) otherwise than as mentioned in paragraph (*a*) above, it endangers the interests of the United Kingdom abroad, seriously obstructs the promotion or protection by the United Kingdom of those interests or endangers the safety of British citizens abroad; or

(*c*) it is of information or of a document or article which is such that its unauthorised disclosure would be likely to have any of those effects.

(3) It is a defence for a person charged with an offence under this section to prove[2] that at the time of the alleged offence he did not know, and had no reasonable cause to believe, that the information, document or article in question related to defence or that its disclosure would be damaging within the meaning of subsection (1) above.

(4) In this section "defence" means—

(*a*) the size, shape, organisation, logistics, order of battle, deployment, operations, state of readiness and training of the armed forces of the Crown;

(*b*) the weapons, stores or other equipment of those forces and the invention, development, production and operation of such equipment and research relating to it;

(*c*) defence policy and strategy and military planning and intelligence;

(*d*) plans and measures for the maintenance of essential supplies and services that are or would be needed in time of war.

[Official Secrets Act 1989, s 2.]

1 For prosecution, trial and penalties, see ss 9–11 post.

2 This imposes an evidential rather than a legal burden on the defendant (*R v Keogh* [2007] EWCA Crim 528, [2007] 3 All ER 789, [2007] 1 WLR 1500, [2007] 2 Cr App Rep 112).

7.8576 **3. International relations** (1) A person who is or has been a Crown servant or government contractor is guilty of an offence[1] if without lawful authority he makes a damaging disclosure of—

(*a*) any information, document or other article relating to international relations; or

(*b*) any confidential information, document or other article which was obtained from a State other than the United Kingdom or an international organisation,

being information or a document or article which is or has been in his possession by virtue of his position as a Crown servant or government contractor.

(2) For the purposes of subsection (1) above a disclosure is damaging if—

(*a*) it endangers the interests of the United Kingdom abroad, seriously obstructs the promotion or protection by the United Kingdom of those interests or endangers the safety of British citizens abroad; or

(*b*) it is of information or of a document or article which is such that its unauthorised disclosure would be likely to have any of those effects.

(3) In the case of information or a document or article within subsection (1)(*b*) above—

(*a*) the fact that it is confidential, or

(*b*) its nature or contents,

may be sufficient to establish for the purposes of subsection (2)(*b*) above that the information, document or article is such that its unauthorised disclosure would be likely to have any of the effects there mentioned.

(4) It is a defence for a person charged with an offence under this section to prove[2] that at the time of the alleged offence he did not know, and had no reasonable cause to believe, that the information, document or article in question was such as is mentioned in subsection (1) above or that its disclosure would be damaging within the meaning of that subsection.

(5) In this section "international relations" means the relations between States, between international organisations or between one or more States and one or more such organisations and includes any matter relating to a State other than the United Kingdom or to an international organisation which is capable of affecting the relations of the United Kingdom with another State or with an international organisation.

(6) For the purposes of this section any information, document or article obtained from a State or organisation is confidential at any time while the terms on which it was obtained require it to be held in confidence or while the circumstances in which it was obtained make it reasonable for the State or organisation to expect that it would be so held.

[Official Secrets Act 1989, s 3.]

1 For prosecution, trial and penalties, see ss 9–11 post.

2 This imposes an evidential rather than a legal burden on the defendant (*R v Keogh* [2007] EWCA Crim 528, [2007] 3 All ER 789, [2007] 1 WLR 1500, [2007] 2 Cr App Rep 112).

7.8577 **4. Crime and special investigation powers** (1) A person who is or has been a Crown servant or government contractor is guilty of an offence[1] if without lawful authority he discloses any information, document or other article to which this section applies and which is or has been in his possession by virtue of his position as such.

(2) This section applies to any information, document or other article—

(*a*) the disclosure of which—

(i) results in the commission of an offence; or

(ii) facilitates an escape from legal custody or the doing of any other act prejudicial to the safekeeping of persons in legal custody; or

(iii) impedes the prevention or detection of offences or the apprehension or prosecution of suspected offenders; or

(*b*) which is such that its unauthorised disclosure would be likely to have any of those effects.

(3) This section also applies to—

(*a*) any information obtained by reason of the interception of any communication in obedience to a warrant issued under section 2 of the Interception of Communications Act 1985 or under the authority of an interception warrant under section 5 of the Regulation of Investigatory Powers Act 2000, any information relating to the obtaining of information by reason of any such interception and any document or other article which is or has been used or held for use in, or has been obtained by reason of, any such interception; and

(*b*) any information obtained by reason of action authorised by a warrant issued under section 3 of the Security Service Act 1989 or under section 5 of the Intelligence Services Act 1994 or by an authorisation given under section 7 of that Act, any information relating to the obtaining of information by reason of any such action and any document or other article which is or has been used or held for use in, or has been obtained by reason of, any such action.

(4) It is a defence for a person charged with an offence under this section in respect of a disclosure falling within subsection (2)(*a*) above to prove that at the time of the alleged offence he did not know, and had no reasonable cause to believe, that the disclosure would have any of the effects there mentioned.

(5) It is a defence for a person charged with an offence under this section in respect of any other disclosure to prove that at the time of the alleged offence he did not know, and had no reasonable cause to believe, that the information, document or article in question was information or a document or article to which this section applies.

(6) In this section "legal custody" includes detention in pursuance of any enactment or any instrument made under an enactment.*

[Official Secrets Act 1989, s 4 as amended by the Intelligence Services Act 1994, Sch 4 and the Regulation of Investigatory Powers Act 2000, Sch 4.]

---

* **Amended by the Investigatory Powers Act 2016, Sch 10 from a date to be appointed.**

1 For prosecution, trial and penalties see ss 9–11 post. A defendant prosecuted under ss 1(1)(*a*) and 4(1) and (3)(*a*) of this Act is not entitled to put forward a defence of disclosure in the national interest or belief that such disclosure was in the national interest: *R v Shayler* [2002] UKHL 11, [2003] 1 AC 247, [2002] 2 All ER 477, [2002] 2 WLR 754.

7.8578 **5. Information resulting from unauthorised disclosures or entrusted in confidence** (1) Subsection (2) below applies where—

(*a*) any information, document or other article protected against disclosure by the foregoing provisions of this Act has come into a person's possession as a result of having been—

(i) disclosed (whether to him or another) by a Crown servant or government contractor without lawful authority; or

(ii) entrusted to him by a Crown servant or government contractor on terms requiring it to be held in confidence or in circumstances in which the Crown servant or government contractor could reasonably expect that it would be so held; or

(iii) disclosed (whether to him or another) without lawful authority by a person to whom it was entrusted as mentioned in sub-paragraph (ii) above; and

(*b*) the disclosure without lawful authority of the information, document or article by the person into whose possession it has come is not an offence under any of those provisions.

(2) Subject to subsections (3) and (4) below, the person into whose possession the information, document or article has come is guilty of an offence[1] if he discloses it without lawful authority knowing, or having reasonable cause to believe, that it is protected against disclosure by the foregoing provisions of this Act and that it has come into his possession as mentioned in subsection (1) above.

(3) In the case of information or a document or article protected against disclosure by sections 1 to 3 above, a person does not commit an offence under subsection (2) above unless—

(*a*) the disclosure by him is damaging; and

(*b*) he makes it knowing, or having reasonable cause to believe, that it would be damaging;

and the question whether a disclosure is damaging shall be determined for the purposes of this subsection as it would be in relation to a disclosure of that information, document or article by a Crown servant in contravention of section 1(3), 2(1) or 3(1) above.

(4) A person does not commit an offence under subsection (2) above in respect of information or a document or other article which has come into his possession as a result of having been disclosed—

(*a*) as mentioned in subsection (1)(*a*)(i) above by a government contractor; or

(*b*) as mentioned in subsection (1)(*a*)(iii) above,

unless that disclosure was by a British citizen or took place in the United Kingdom, in any of the Channel Islands or in the Isle of Man or a colony.

(5) For the purposes of this section information or a document or article is protected against disclosure by the foregoing provisions of this Act if—

(*a*) it relates to security or intelligence, defence or international relations within the meaning of section 1, 2 or 3 above or is such as is mentioned in section 3(1)(*b*) above; or

(*b*) it is information or a document or article to which section 4 above applies;

and information or a document or article is protected against disclosure by sections 1 to 3 above if it falls within paragraph (*a*) above.

(6) A person is guilty of an offence[1] if without lawful authority he discloses any information, document or other article which he knows, or has reasonable cause to believe, to have come into his possession as a result of a contravention of section 1 of the Official Secrets Act 1911.

[Official Secrets Act 1989, s 5.]

1 For prosecution, trial and penalties, see ss 9–11 post.

7.8579 **6. Information entrusted in confidence to other States or international organisations** (1) This section applies where—

(*a*) any information, document or other article which—

(i) relates to security or intelligence, defence or international relations; and

(ii) has been communicated in confidence by or on behalf of the United Kingdom to another State or to an international organisation,

has come into a person's possession as a result of having been disclosed (whether to him or another) without the authority of that State or organisation or, in the case of an organisation, of a member of it; and

(*b*) the disclosure without lawful authority of the information, document or article by the person into whose possession it has come is not an offence under any of the foregoing provisions of this Act.

(2) Subject to subsection (3) below, the person into whose possession the information, document or article has come is guilty of an offence[1] if he makes a damaging disclosure of it knowing, or having reasonable cause to believe, that it is such as is mentioned in subsection (1) above, that it has come into his possession as there mentioned and that its disclosure would be damaging.

(3) A person does not commit an offence under subsection (2) above if the information, document or article is disclosed by him with lawful authority or has previously been made available to the public with the authority of the State or organisation concerned or, in the case of an organisation, of a member of it.

(4) For the purposes of this section "security or intelligence", "defence" and "international relations" have the same meaning as in sections 1, 2 and 3 above and the question whether a disclosure is damaging shall be determined as it would be in relation to a disclosure of the information, document or article in question by a Crown servant in contravention of section 1(3), 2(1) and 3(1) above.

(5) For the purposes of this section information or a document or article is communicated in confidence if it is communicated on terms requiring it to be held in confidence or in circumstances in which the person communicating it could reasonably expect that it would be so held.

[Official Secrets Act 1989, s 6.]

1 For prosecution, trial and penalties, see ss 9–11 post.

7.8580 **7. Authorised disclosures** (1) For the purposes of this Act a disclosure by—

(*a*) a Crown servant; or

(*b*) a person, not being a Crown servant or government contractor, in whose case a notification for the purposes of section 1(1) above is in force,

is made with lawful authority if, and only if, it is made in accordance with his official duty.

(2) For the purposes of this Act a disclosure by a government contractor is made with lawful authority if, and only if, it is made—

(*a*) in accordance with an official authorisation; or

(*b*) for the purposes of the functions by virtue of which he is a government contractor and without contravening an official restriction.

(3) For the purposes of this Act a disclosure made by any other person is made with lawful authority if, and only if, it is made—

(*a*) to a Crown servant for the purposes of his functions as such; or

(*b*) in accordance with an official authorisation.

(4) It is a defence for a person charged with an offence under any of the foregoing provisions of this Act to prove that at the time of the alleged offence he believed that he had lawful authority to make the disclosure in question and had no reasonable cause to believe otherwise.

(5) In this section "official authorisation" and "official restriction" mean, subject to subsection (6) below, an authorisation or restriction duly given or imposed by a Crown servant or government contractor or by or on behalf of a prescribed[1] body or a body of a prescribed[1] class.

(6) In relation to section 6 above "official authorisation" includes an authorisation duly given by or on behalf of the State or organisation concerned or, in the case of an organisation, a member of it.

[Official Secrets Act 1989, s 7.]

1 The Official Secrets Act 1989 (Prescription) Order 1990, SI 1990/200, amended by SI 1993/847, SI 2003/1918, SI 2004/1823, SI 2006/362, SI 2007/2148, SI 2012/2900 and SI 2016/655 has been made; Sch 3 to the order lists the prescribed bodies.

7.8581 **8. Safeguarding of information** (1) Where a Crown servant or government contractor, by virtue of his position as such, has in his possession or under his control any document or other article which it would be an offence under any of the foregoing provisions of this Act for him to disclose without lawful authority he is guilty of an offence[1] if—

(*a*) being a Crown servant, he retains the document or article contrary to his official duty; or

(*b*) being a government contractor, he fails to comply with an official direction for the return or disposal of the document or article,

or if he fails to take such care to prevent the unauthorised disclosure of the document or article as a person in his position may reasonably be expected to take.

(2) It is a defence for a Crown servant charged with an offence under subsection (1)(*a*) above to prove that at the time of the alleged offence he believed that he was acting in accordance with his official duty and had no reasonable cause to believe otherwise.

(3) In subsections (1) and (2) above references to a Crown servant include any person, not being a Crown servant or government contractor, in whose case a notification for the purposes of section 1(1) above is in force.

(4) Where a person has in his possession or under his control any document or other article which it would be an offence under section 5 above for him to disclose without lawful authority, he is guilty of an offence[1] if—

(*a*) he fails to comply with an official direction for its return or disposal; or

(*b*) where he obtained it from a Crown servant or government contractor on terms requiring it to be held in confidence or in circumstances in which that servant or contractor could reasonably expect that it would be so held, he fails to take such care to prevent its unauthorised disclosure as a person in his position may reasonably be expected to take.

(5) Where a person has in his possession or under his control any document or other article which it would be an offence under section 6 above for him to disclose without lawful authority, he is guilty of an offence[1] if he fails to comply with an official direction for its return or disposal.

(6) A person is guilty of an offence[1] if he discloses any official information, document or other article which can be used for the purpose of obtaining access to any information, document of other article protected against disclosure by the foregoing provisions of this Act and the circumstances in which it is disclosed are such that it would be reasonable to expect that it might be used for that purpose without authority.

(7) For the purposes of subsection (6) above a person discloses information or a document or article which is official if—

(*a*) he has or has had it in his possession by virtue of his position as a Crown servant or government contractor; or

(*b*) he knows or has reasonable cause to believe that a Crown servant or government contractor has or has had it in his possession by virtue of his position as such.

(8) Subsection (5) of section 5 above applies for the purposes of subsection (6) above as it applies for the purposes of that section.

(9) In this section "official direction" means a direction duly given by a Crown servant or government contractor or by or on behalf of a prescribed[2] body or a body of a prescribed[2] class.

[Official Secrets Act 1989, s 8.]

---

[1] For prosecution, trial and penalties, see ss 9–11 post.

[2] The Official Secrets Act 1989 (Prescription) Order 1990, SI 1990/200. For amending instruments, see note to s 8, ante.

7.8582 **9. Prosecutions** (1) Subject to subsection (2) below, no prosecution for an offence under this Act shall be instituted in England and Wales or in Northern Ireland except by or with the consent of the Attorney General or, as the case may be, the Attorney General for Northern Ireland.

(2) Subsection (1) above does not apply to an offence in respect of any such information, document or article as is mentioned in section 4(2) above but no prosecution for such an offence shall be instituted in England and Wales or in Northern Ireland except by or with the consent of the Director of Public Prosecutions or, as the case may be, the Director of Public Prosecutions for Northern Ireland.

[Official Secrets Act 1989, s 9.]

7.8583 **10. Penalties** (1) A person guilty of an offence under any provision of this Act other than section 8(1), (4) or (5) shall be liable[1]—

(*a*) on conviction on indictment, to imprisonment for a term not exceeding **two years** or a **fine** or **both**;

(*b*) on summary conviction, to imprisonment for a term not exceeding **six months** or a fine not exceeding the **statutory maximum** or **both**.

(2) A person guilty of an offence under section 8(1), (4) or (5) above shall be liable on summary conviction to imprisonment for a term not exceeding **three months*** or a fine not exceeding **level 5** on the standard scale or both.

[Official Secrets Act 1989, s 10.]

---

* **"51 weeks" substituted by the Criminal Justice Act 2003, Sch 26, from a date to be appointed.**

[1] For procedure in respect of an offence triable either way, see the Magistrates' Courts Act 1980, ss 17A–21, in PART I: MAGISTRATES' COURTS, PROCEDURE, ante.

**7.8584 11. Arrest[1], search and trial** (1)–(3) *Application to Police and Criminal Evidence Act 1984, s 24(2); s 9(2) of, and para 3(b) of Sch 1 to, that Act to apply to s 9(1) of the Official Secrets Act 1911; Criminal Law Act (Northern Ireland) Act 1967, s 2.*

(4) Section 8(4) of the Official Secrets Act 1920 (exclusion of public from hearing on grounds of national safety) shall have effect as if references to offences under that Act included references to offences under any provision of this Act other than section 8(1), (4) or (5).

(5) Proceedings for an offence under this Act may be taken in any place in the United Kingdom.

[Official Secrets Act 1989, s 11.]

1 Offences under this Act, other than offences contrary to s 8(1), (4) or (5) are arrestable offences by virtue of Sch 1A to the Police and Criminal Evidence Act 1984.

**7.8585 12. "Crown servant" and "government contractor"** (1) In this Act "Crown servant" means—

(*a*) a Minister of the Crown;

(*aa*) a member of the Scottish Executive or a junior Scottish Minister;

(*ab*) the First Minister for Wales, a Welsh Minister appointed under section 48 of the Government of Wales Act 2006, the Counsel General to the Welsh Assembly Government or a Deputy Welsh Minister;

(*b*) *repealed.*

(*c*) any person employed in the civil service of the Crown, including Her Majesty's Diplomatic Service, Her Majesty's Overseas Civil Service, the civil service of Northern Ireland and the Northern Ireland Court Service;

(*d*) any member of the naval, military or air forces of the Crown, including any person employed by an association established for the purposes of Part XI of the Reserve Forces Act 1996;

(e) any constable and any other person employed or appointed in or for the purposes of any police force (including a police force within the meaning of the Police (Northern Ireland) Act 1998 or of the Serious Organised Crime Agency;

(*f*) any person who is a member or employee of a prescribed body or a body of a prescribed[1] class and either is prescribed[1] for the purposes of this paragraph or belongs to a prescribed[1] class of members or employees of any such body;

(*g*) any person who is the holder of a prescribed[2] office or who is an employee of such a holder and either is prescribed[2] for the purposes of this paragraph or belongs to a prescribed[2] class of such employees.

(2) In this Act "government contractor" means, subject to subsection (3) below, any person who is not a Crown servant but who provides, or is employed in the provision of, goods or services—

(*a*) for the purposes of any Minister or person mentioned in paragraph (*a*), (*ab*) or (*b*) of subsection (1) above, of any office-holder in the Scottish Administration, of any of the services, forces or bodies mentioned in that subsection or of the holder of any office prescribed under that subsection;

(*aa*) *repealed*; or

(*b*) under an agreement or arrangement certified by the Secretary of State as being one to which the government of a State other than the United Kingdom or an international organisation is a party or which is subordinate to, or made for the purposes of implementing, any such agreement or arrangement.

(3) Where an employee or class of employees of any body, or of any holder of an office, is prescribed by an order made for the purposes of subsection (1) above—

(*a*) any employee of that body, or of the holder of that office, who is not prescribed or is not within the prescribed class; and

(*b*) any person who does not provide, or is not employed in the provision of, goods or services for the purposes of the performance of those functions of the body or the holder of the office in connection with which the employee or prescribed class of employees is engaged,

shall not be a government contractor for the purposes of this Act.

(4) In this section "office-holder in the Scottish Administration" has the same meaning as in section 126(7)(*a*) of the Scotland Act 1998.

(4A) In this section the reference to a police force includes a reference to the Civil Nuclear Constabulary.

(5) This Act shall apply to the following as it applies to persons falling within the definition of Crown servant—

(*a*) the First Minister and deputy First Minister in Northern Ireland; and

(*b*) Northern Ireland Ministers and junior Ministers.

[Official Secrets Act 1989, s 12 as amended by the Reserve Forces Act 1996, Sch 10, the Police Act 1997, Sch 9, the Government of Wales Act 1998, Sch 12, the Scotland Act 1998, Sch 8, the Government of Wales 1998, Sch 12, the Northern Ireland Act 1998, Sch 13 and the Police (Northern Ireland) Act 1998, Sch 4, the Energy Act 2004, s 198, the Serious Organised Crime and Police Act 2005, Sch 4 and the Government of Wales Act 2006, Sch 10.]

1 See Sch 1 to the Official Secrets Act 1989 (Prescription) Order 1990, SI 1990/200. For amending instruments, see note to s 8, ante.

[2] See Sch 2 to the Official Secrets Act 1989 (Prescription) Order 1990, SI 1990/200. For amending instruments, see note to s 8, ante.

7.8586 **13. Other interpretation provisions** (1) In this Act—

"disclose" and "disclosure", in relation to a document or other article, include parting with possession of it;

"international organisation" means, subject to subsections (2) and (3) below, an organisation of which only States are members and includes a reference to any organ of such an organisation;

"prescribed" means prescribed by an order made by the Secretary of State;

"State" includes the government of a State and any organ of its government and references to a State other than the United Kingdom include references to any territory outside the United Kingdom.

(2) In section 12(2)(*b*) above the reference to an international organisation includes a reference to any such organisation whether or not one of which only States are members and includes a commercial organisation.

(3) In determining for the purposes of subsection (1) above whether only States are members of an organisation, any member which is itself an organisation of which only States are members, or which is an organ of such an organisation, shall be treated as a State.

[Official Secrets Act 1989, s 13.]

7.8587 **15. Acts done abroad and extent** (1) Any act—

(*a*) done by a British citizen or Crown servant; or

(*b*) done by any person in any of the Channel Islands or the Isle of Man or any colony,

shall, if it would be an offence by that person under any provision of this Act other than section 8(1), (4) or (5) when done by him in the United Kingdom, be an offence under that provision.

(2)–(3) *Northern Ireland, Channel Islands, Isle of Man, any colony.*

[Official Secrets Act 1989, s 15.]

# OUTRAGING PUBLIC DECENCY

**7.8588** This rare, surviving common law offence[1] is triable either way[2]. Its elements are:

(1) Committing an act of such a lewd, obscene or disgusting nature as to outrage public decency.

(2) In a public place[3] and capable of being seen by two or more persons who actually present, whether or not the act caused actual disgust or annoyance or was actually seen by anyone[4].

---

[1] Its continued existence was affirmed by the House of Lords in *R v Knuller (Publishing, Printing and Promotions) Ltd* [1973] AC 435.

[2] See para 1A of Sch 1 to the Magistrates' Courts Act 1980 in PART I: MAGISTRATES' COURTS, PROCEDURE, ante.

[3] See the authorities considered under public nuisance at para 7.8470, ante.

[4] *R v Hamilton* [2007] EWCA Crim 2062, [2008] 1 QB 224, [2008] 1 All ER 1103, [2008] 2 WLR 107 (where the defendant covertly filmed under the skirt of a girl in a supermarket), and the authorities referred to therein. See also *Rose v DPP* [2006] EWHC 852 (Admin), [2006] 1 WLR 2626, 171 JP 57, where the defendant was involved in a lewd act at night in the foyer of a bank to which there was customers were admitted to use an ATM. This was seen the following day when CCTV footage was reviewed, but there was no evidence that the act was capable of being viewed by two persons at the time it occurred, and the court doubted whether the offence could be committed by a subsequent, private viewing (see para 29 of the judgment).

In *Hamilton*, supra, the view was expressed that the act could be witnessed in ways other than seeing, such as by hearing (see para 34). See further *R v F* [2010] EWCA Crim 2243, 174 JP 582 (no grounds were found for overturning an acquittal where the agreed facts were, from the account of the only witness, that the defendant, who was masturbating in his car outside that witness's house, ceased doing so and covered himself whenever anybody else might have been able to see what he was doing).

# PEDLARS

## Pedlars Act 1871

(34 & 35 Vict c 96)

*Preliminary*

7.8589 1. *Short title.*

7.8590 3. **Interpretation** In this Act, if not inconsistent with the context, the following terms have the meanings herein-after respectively assigned to them; that is to say,—

The term "pedlar" means any hawker, pedlar[1], pretty chapman, tinker, caster of metals, or other person who, without any horse or other beast bearing or drawing burden[2], travels and trades on foot and goes from town to town or to other men's houses,[3], carrying to sell or exposing for sale[4] any goods, wares, or merchandise, or procuring orders for goods, wares, or merchandise immediately to be delivered:

[Pedlars Act 1871, s 3 as amended by the Statute Law Revision (No 2) Act 1893, the Police Act 1964, Sch 10, the Statute Law (Repeals) Act 1993, s 1 and SI 2009/2999.]

---

1 A person need not derive his entire living or even a substantial part of it from acting as pedlar for him to be a pedlar for the purposes of s 3 (*Murphy v Duke* [1985] QB 905, [1985] 2 All ER 274, [1985] 2 WLR 773.)

2 The view was expressed in *Jones v Bath and North East Somerset Council* [2012] EWHC 1361 (Admin), 176 JP 530, 176 CL&J 370 that the term 'without any horse or other beast bearing or drawing burden' should now be read as 'motor van or car'. 'In modern times someone who drives with his goods in his own van or car to a town or city to offer goods for sale is not acting as a pedlar. He is not acting as a pedlar because he is not travelling there on foot. The requirement that he conducts his activities on foot applies both to travel and trade' (per Mitting J at para 13).

3 Persons who travelled from town to town by conveyance and then walked from house to house were travelling on foot and were pedlars (*Sample v Hulme* [1956] 3 All ER 447n, 120 JP 564). A pedlar trades as he travels as distinct from someone who merely travels to trade; thus a street trader who sold Christmas paper from a portable stand in a street could not claim to be a pedlar (*Watson v Malloy* [1988] 3 All ER 459, [1989] 1 WLR 1026, 86 LGR 766, DC). However, to be a pedlar a person does not have to travel and trade simultaneously; he does not have to be in motion while trading. A pedlar is an itinerant or peripatetic seller who is travelling when not trading. The use of a stall or stand might indicate an intention to remain longer than is necessary to effect a sale to an individual but is not determinative of the issue whether a person is a pedlar or not and in determining the nature of a seller's trading practices and the nature of his conduct while stationary for the purpose of selling it is necessary to consider the length of time for which a person is in one place and what he does in that place. A person who stood in one place for an hour selling goods from a bag at his feet and attracting people's attention to come to him to buy was not acting as a pedlar (*Stevenage Borough Council v Wright* (1996) Times, 10 April).

4 Ladies making up wearing apparel and offering the same for sale on behalf of a charity do not come within the definition of pedlar (*Gregg v Smith* (1873) LR 8 QB 302, 42 LJMC 121). Selling within the meaning of this section is to include bartering or exchanging goods for other goods so that a person bartering needles and thread for rags, bones, etc. was held to be a hawker and pedlar, and to require a hawker's licence (*Druce v Gabb* (1858) 31 LTOS 98, & WR 479). A person soliciting orders for goods but having no goods with him and subsequently delivering the goods for which he had taken orders is not a person "carrying to sell" or "exposing for sale" within the definition of pedlar (*R v M'Knight* (1830) 10 B & C 734, 5 Man & Ry KB 644).

*Certificates to be obtained by Pedlars*

7.8591 4. **No one to act as a pedlar without certificate** No Person shall act as a pedlar without such certificate as in this Act mentioned, or in any district where he is not authorised by his certificate so to act.

Any person who—

(1) acts as a pedlar without having obtained a certificate under this Act authorising him so to act;

(2) *repealed*,

shall be liable to a penalty not exceeding **level 1** on the standard scale.

[Pedlars Act 1871, s 4 as amended by the Pedlars Act 1881, s 2, the Criminal Law Act 1977, s 31 and the Criminal Justice Act 1982, ss 38 and 46.]

7.8592 5. **Grant of Certificate** The following regulations shall made with respect to the grant of pedlar certificates:

1. Subject as in this Act mentioned, a pedlar's certificate shall be granted to any person by the chief officer of police for the police area in which the person applying for a certificate has, during one month previous to such application, resided, on such officer being satisfied that the applicant is above seventeen years of age, is a person of good character, and in good faith intends to carry on the trade of a pedlar:
2. An application for a pedlar's certificate shall be in the form specified in schedule two to this Act, or as near thereto as circumstances admit:
3. There shall be paid for a pedlar's certificate previously to the delivery thereof to the applicant a fee of £12.25[1]
4. A pedlar's certificate shall be in the form specified in schedule two to this Act, or as near thereto as circumstances admit;
5. A pedlar's certificate shall remain in force for one year from the date of the issue thereof, and no longer:

6. On the delivery up of the old certificate, or on sufficient evidence being produced to the satisfaction of the chief officer of police that the old certificate has been lost, that officer may, either at the expiration of the current year, or during the currency of any year grant a new certificate in the same manner as upon a first application for a pedlar's certificate. In Great Britain one of Her Majesty's Principal Secretaries of State, and in Ireland the Department for Social Development may by order provide for the expiration of all pedlars certificates at the same period of each year, and in doing so shall provide for the apportionment of the fees payable in respect of any such certificate.

[Pedlars Act 1871, s 5 as amended by the Police Act 1996, Sch 7 and SI 1999/663.]

---

1 Pedlar's Certificates (Variation of Fee) Order 1985, SI 1985/2027.

7.8593 6. **Effect of certificate** For the purpose of the Markets and Fairs Clauses Act 1874[1] and any Act incorporating the same, a certificate under this Act shall have the same effect, within the district[2] for which it is granted, as a hawker's licence, and the term "licensed hawker" in the first-mentioned Act shall be construed to include a pedlar holding such a certificate.

[Pedlars Act 1871, s 6 as amended by the Pedlars Act 1881, Schedule.]

---

1 A pedlar selling tollable articles, such as vegetables and fruit, within the limits of a market, is exempted from the penalty imposed by s 13 of that statute (*Howard v Lupton* (1875) LR 10 QB 598, 40 JP 7). But so long only as he acts as a pedlar within the definition of s 3 of the Pedlars Act 1871 (*Woolwich Local Board of Health v Gardiner* [1895] 2 QB 497, 59 JP 597, 659). See also *Lee v Wallocks*(1914) 78 JP 365.

2 "A pedlar's certificate granted under the Pedlars Act 1871 shall during the time for which it continues in force authorise the person to whom it is granted to act as a pedlar within any part of the United Kingdom." (Pedlars Act 1881, s 2).

7.8594 8. **Register of certificates to be kept in each area** There shall be kept in each police area a register of the certificates granted in such area under this Act, in such form and with such particulars as may from time to time be directed in Great Britain by one of Her Majesty's Principal Secretaries of State, and in Ireland by the Department for Social Development.
The entries in such register, and any copy of any such entries, certified by the chief officer of police to be a true copy, shall be evidence of the facts stated therein.

[Pedlars Act 1871, s 8 as amended by the Pedlars Act 1881, Sch, the Police Act 1996, Sch 7 and SI 1999/663.]

7.8595 9. **Forms of application to be kept at chief police office** Forms of applications for certificates shall be kept at every police office in every police area, and shall be given gratis to any person applying for the same; and all applications for certificates shall be delivered at the police office of the division or subdivision of the police area within which the applicant resides, and certificates, when duly signed by the chief officer of police, shall be issued at such office.

[Pedlars Act 1871, s 9 as amended by the Police Act 1996, Sch 7.]

7.8596 10. **Certificate not to be assigned** A person to whom a pedlar's certificate is granted under this Act shall not lend, transfer, or assign the same to any other person, and any person who lends, transfers, or assigns such certificate to any other person shall for each offence be liable to a penalty not exceeding **level 1** on the standard scale.

[Pedlars Act 1871, s 10 as amended by the Criminal Law Act 1977, s 41 and the Criminal Justice Act 1982, ss 38 and 46.]

7.8597 11. **Certificate not to be borrowed** No person shall borrow or make use of a pedlar's certificate granted to any other person, and any person who borrows or makes use of such certificate shall for each offence be liable to a penalty not exceeding **level 1** on the standard scale.

[Pedlars Act 1871, s 11 as amended by Criminal Law Act 1977, s 41 and the Criminal Justice Act 1982, ss 38 and 46.]

7.8598 12. **Penalty for forging certificate** Any person who commits any of the following offences; (that is to say,)

(1) Makes false representations with a view to obtain a pedlar's certificate under this Act;

(2)–(5) *Repealed,*

shall be liable to imprisonment for a term not exceeding **six months** or to a fine not exceeding **level 2** on the standard scale, or to **both** such imprisonment and fine.

[Pedlars Act 1871, s 12 as amended by the Pedlars Act 1881, Schedule, the Criminal Law Act 1977, s 41, the Forgery and Counterfeiting Act 1981, Schedule and the Criminal Justice Act 1982, ss 38 and 46.]

7.8599 14. **Convictions to be indorsed on certificate** If any pedlar is convicted of any offence under this Act, the court, before which he is convicted shall indorse or cause to be indorsed on his certificate a record of such conviction.
The indorsements made under this Act on a pedlar's certificate shall be evidence of the facts stated therein.

[Pedlars Act 1871, s 14.]

7.8600 15. **Appeal against refusal of certificate by chief officer of police** If the chief officer of police refuses to grant a certificate, the applicant may appeal to a court of summary jurisdiction having jurisdiction in the place where such grant was refused, in accordance with the following provisions:

1. The applicant shall, within one week after the refusal, give to the chief officer of police notice in writing of the appeal:

2. The appeal shall be heard at the sitting of the court which happens next after the expiration of the said week, but the court may, on the application of either party, adjourn the case:
3. The court shall hear and determine the matter of the appeal, and make such order thereon, with or without costs to either party, as to the court seems just:
4. An appeal under this Act to a court of summary jurisdiction in England or Ireland shall be deemed to be a matter on which that court has authority by law to make an order in pursuance of the Summary Jurisdiction Acts, and in Scotland the court may adjudicate on matters arising under this section, in accordance with the enactments relating to the exercise of their ordinary jurisdiction:
5 Any certificate granted in pursuance of an order of the court, shall have the same effect as if it had been originally granted by the chief officer of police.

[Pedlars Act 1871, s 15 as amended by the Pedlars Act 1881, s 2.]

**7.8601 16. Deprivation of pedlars of certificates by court**[1] Any court before which any pedlar is convicted for any offence, whether under this or any other Act, or otherwise, may, if he or they think fit, deprive such pedlar of his certificate; and any such court shall deprive such pedlar of his certificate; and any such court shall deprive such pedlar of his certificate if he is convicted of begging.

Any court of summary jurisdiction may summon a pedlar holding a certificate under this Act to appear before them, and if he fail to appear, or on appearance to satisfy the court that he is in good faith carrying on the business of a pedlar, shall deprive him of his certificate.

[Pedlars Act 1871, s 16.]

[1] The only way that a pedlar can be deprived of his certificate during its currency is under this section; the Act contains no provision for the police to seize, suspend or revoke a pedlar's certificate: *R (on the application of Jones) v Chief Constable of Cheshire Police* [2005] EWHC 2457 (Admin), 170 JP 1.

*Duties of Pedlars*

**7.8602 17. Pedlar to show certificate to certain persons on demand** Any pedlar shall at all times, on demand, produce and show his certificate to any of the following persons; (that is to say,)

1. Any justice of the peace; or
2. Any constable or officer of police; or
3. Any person to whom such pedlar offers his goods for sale; or
4. Any person in whose private grounds of premises such pedlar is found:

And any pedlar who refuses, on demand, to show his certificate to, and allow it to be read and a copy thereof to be taken by, any of the persons hereby authorised to demand it, shall or each offence be liable to a penalty not exceeding **level 1** on the standard scale.

[Pedlars Act 1871, s 17 as amended by the Criminal Law Act 1977, s 41 and the Criminal Justice Act 1982, ss 38 and 46.]

*Legal Proceedings*

**7.8603 20.** *Summary proceedings for offences, etc*[1].

[1] Superseded for practical purposes by the Magistrates' Courts Act 1980 and the Criminal Procedure Rules.

**7.8604 21. Application of fees** All fees received under this Act in England and Ireland shall be applied in manner in which penalties recoverable under this Act are applicable.

[Pedlars Act 1871, s 21.]

**7.8605 22. Deputy of chief officer of police** Any act or thing by this Act authorised to be done by the chief officer of police may be done by any police officer under his command authorised by him in that behalf, and the term "chief officer of police" in this Act includes in relation to any such act or thing, the police officer so authorised.

[Pedlars Act 1871, s 22.]

**7.8606 23. Certificate not required by commercial travellers, sellers of fish, or sellers in fairs** Nothing in this Act shall render it necessary for a certificate to be obtained by the following persons as such; (that is to say,)

1. Commercial travellers or other persons selling or seeking orders for goods, wares, or merchandise to or from persons who are dealers therein, and who buy to sell again, or selling or seeking orders for books as agents authorised in writing by the publishers of such books:
2. Sellers of vegetables[1], fish, fruit, or victuals:
3. Persons selling or exposing to sale goods, wares, or merchandise in any public mart, market, or fair legally established.

[Pedlars Act 1871, s 23.]

[1] In a case under the Prevention of Crimes Act tried at Chester Assizes, COLERIDGE J, held that lavender was a vegetable within this exemption (see 77 JP J0 610).

7.8607 **24. Reservation of powers of local authority** Nothing in this Act shall take away or diminish any of the powers vested in any local authority by any general or local Act in force in the district of such local authority.

[Pedlars Act 1871, s 24.]

# SCHEDULES

## SCHEDULE 2

Form A Section 5

### FORM OF APPLICATION FOR PEDLAR'S CERTIFICATE

7.8608 1. I, *A.B.* (*Christian and surname of applicant in full*) have during the last calendar month resided at . . . . . . . . . . . . in the parish of . . . . . . . . . . . . in the county of . . . . . . . . . . . .

2. I am by trade and occupation a (*here state trade and occupation of applicant, eg, that he is a hawker, pedlar, etc*)

3. I am . . . . . . . . . . . . years of age.

4. I apply for a certificate under the Pedlars Act 1871 authorizing me to act as a pedlar within the . . . . . . . . . . . . police area.

Dated this . . . . . . . . . . . . day of . . . . . . . . . . . .

(Signed) . . . . . . . . . . . . *A.B.* . . . . . . . . . . . . (*Here insert Christian and surname of applicant.*)

### FORM B

### FORM OF PEDLAR'S CERTIFICATE[1]

In pursuance of the Pedlars Act, 1871, I certify that *A.B.* (*name of applicant*) of . . . . . . . . . . . . in the county of . . . . . . . . . . . . aged . . . . . . . . . . . . years, is hereby authorized to act as a pedlar within the . . . . . . . . . . . . police area for a year from the date of this certificate. (*To be altered, if necessary, to correspond to any order of the Secretary of State or Department for Social Development as to time of expiration of licenses.*)

Certified this . . . . . . . . . . . . day of . . . . . . . . . . . . A.D. . . . . . . . . . . . .

. . . . . . . . . . . . (Signed)

(*Here insert name and description of the officer signing the certificate.*)

The certificate will expire on the . . . . . . . . . . . . day of . . . . . . . . . . . . A.D.

---

[1] Authorises the person to whom it is granted to act as a pedlar within any part of the United Kingdom (Pedlars Act 1881, s 2).

# PERJURY

## Perjury Act 1911

(1 & 2 Geo 5 c 6)

**7.8609 1. Perjury—Judicial proceedings**[1] (1) If any person[2] lawfully sworn as a witness or as an interpreter in a judicial proceeding wilfully[3] makes a statement material[4] in that proceeding, which he knows to be false or does not believe to be true, he shall be guilty of perjury, shall, on conviction thereof on indictment, be liable to penal servitude for a term not exceeding **seven years**,[5], or to imprisonment with or without hard labour for a term not exceeding two years, or to a fine or to both such penal servitude or imprisonment and fine.

(2) The expression "judicial proceedings" includes a proceeding before any court[6], tribunal[7], or person[8] having by law power to hear, receive, and examine evidence on oath.

(3) Where a statement made for the purposes of a judicial proceeding is not made before the tribunal itself, but is made on oath before a person authorised by law to administer an oath to the person who makes the statement, and to record or authenticate the statement, it shall, for the purpose of this section, be treated as having been made in a judicial proceeding.

(4) A statement made by a person lawfully sworn in England for the purposes of a judicial proceeding—

(*a*) in another part of Her Majesty's dominions; or

(*b*) in a British tribunal lawfully constituted in any place by sea or land outside Her Majesty's dominions; or

(*c*) in a tribunal of any foreign state,

shall, for the purposes of this section, be treated as a statement made in a judicial proceeding in England.

(5) Where, for the purposes of a judicial proceeding in England, a person is lawfully sworn under the authority of an Act of Parliament—

(*a*) in any other part of Her Majesty's dominions; or

(*b*) before a British tribunal or a British officer in a foreign country, or within the jurisdiction[9] of the Admiralty of England;

a statement made by such person so sworn as aforesaid (unless the Act of Parliament under which it was made otherwise specifically provides) shall be treated for the purposes of this section as having need made in the judicial proceeding in England for the purposes whereof it was made.

(6) The question whether a statement on which perjury is assigned was material is a question of law to be determined by the court of trial.

[Perjury Act 1911, s 1.]

---

1 A person who, in sworn evidence before the European Court, makes any statement which he knows to be false or does not believe to be true shall, whether he is a British subject or not, be guilty of an offence and may be proceeded against and punished as for an offence under s 1(1) of the Perjury Act 1911 (European Communities Act 1972, s 11(1)). The report by the European Court leading to a bill of indictment is not admissible before the court in England or Wales.

2 A person not a competent witness, but sworn by mistake, cannot be indicted for perjury (per HANNEN J, *R v Clegg* (1868) 19 LT 47).

3 "Wilfully" requires the prosecution to prove that the defendant who made the statement did so deliberately and not inadvertently or by mistake (*R v Millward* [1985] QB 519, [1985] 1 All ER 859, 149 JP 545, CA).

4 The question of materiality is one of law to be determined by the court of trial (s 1(6)). This subsection settles a point as to which some doubt attached. As to materiality, see *R v Philpotts* (1851) 3 Car & Kir 135; *R v Gibbon* (1862) Le & Ca 109; *R v Mullany* (1865) Le & Ca 593; *R v Shaw* (1865) Le & Ca 579, 29 JP 339; *R v Tyson* (1867) LR 1 CCR 107, 32 JP 53; *R v Smith* (1867) LR 1 CCR 110, 32 JP 405; *R v Alsop* (1869) 33 JP 485; *R v Hadfield* (1886) 51 JP 344; *R v Baker* [1895] 1 QB 797; *R v Hewitt* (1913) 9 Cr App Rep 192; *R v Wheeler* [1917] 1 KB 283, 81 JP 75.

The defendant's belief as to the materiality of the statement is irrelevant. The materiality of the statement is a matter which by virtue of s 1(6) is to be decided objectively by the judge (*R v Millward* [1985] QB 519, [1985] 1 All ER 859, 149 JP 545, CA).

5 Imprisonment with hard labour was abolished by the Criminal Justice Act 1948, s 1(2); the punishment is now imprisonment for a term not exceeding seven years or a fine or both; see the Criminal Justice Act 1948, s 1(1) and (2).

6 For consideration of the release, for the purposes of committal proceedings, of confidential papers in wardship proceedings in which perjury is alleged, see *Re H (a minor)* [1985] 3 All ER 1, [1985] 1 WLR 1164, CA.

7 Two special commissioners acting under the Income Tax Acts, constitute a tribunal (*R v Hood-Barrs* [1943] 1 KB 455, [1943] 1 All ER 665).

8 As to perjury on an inquisition held before a deputy coroner, see *R v Johnson* (1873) LR 2 CCR 15, 37 JP 181. A witness, summoned under s 27 of the Bankruptcy Act 1883, was sworn before a registrar in bankruptcy, and was examined by the solicitor for the official receiver in the presence of his own solicitor, but not in the presence of the registrar, who sat in an adjoining room:— *Held:* the examination was not taken before a court of competent jurisdiction, and a conviction for perjury was quashed (*R v Lloyd* (1887) 19 QBD 213, 52 JP 86). The power of justices to administer oaths is limited; they must be acting under authority at the time (*R v Shaw* (1911) 75 JP 191). A witness was properly convicted for giving false evidence on the hearing of a charge against a prisoner who had been apprehended on a warrant improperly issued (*R v Hughes* (1879) 4 QBD 614, 43 JP 556). Where perjury was committed in an affidavit filed in an action against a non-existent person, it was held that the affidavit had been sworn in a "judicial proceeding" (*R v Castiglione* (1912) 76 JP 351).

9 This will cover the case of depositions taken on oath on a British steamship on the high seas, or in a foreign port, for use at a trial in this country.

7.8610 **1A. False unsworn statements under Evidence (Proceedings in Other Jurisdictions) Act 1975** If any person, in giving any testimony (either orally or in writing) otherwise than on oath, where required to do so by an order under s 2 of the Evidence (Proceedings in Other Jurisdictions) Act 1975, makes a statement—

(*a*) which he knows to be false in a material particular; or

(*b*) which is false in a material particular and which he does not believe to be true,

he shall be guilty of an offence[1] and shall be liable on conviction on indictment to imprisonment for a term not exceeding **two years** or a **fine** or **both**.

[Perjury Act 1911, s 1A as inserted by the Evidence (Proceedings in Other Jurisdictions) Act 1975, Sch 1.]

1 Triable either way; see the Magistrates' Courts Act 1980, s 17 and Sch 1, also ss 17A–21 (procedure) and s 32 (penalty), in PART I: MAGISTRATES' COURTS, PROCEDURE, ante.

7.8611 **2. False statement on oath not in judicial proceeding** If any person—

(1) being required or authorised by law to make any statement on oath for any purpose, and being lawfully sworn (otherwise than in a judicial proceeding) wilfully makes a statement which is material for that purpose and which he knows to be false or does not believe to be true; or

(2) wilfully uses any false affidavit for the purposes of the Bills of Sale Act 1878, as amended by any subsequent enactment,

he shall be guilty of a misdemeanour, and, on conviction thereof on indictment, shall be liable to penal servitude for a term not exceeding **seven years** [1], or to imprisonment with or without hard labour, for a term not exceeding two years, or to a fine or to both such penal servitude or imprisonment and fine.[2]

[Perjury Act 1911, s 2.]

1 Imprisonment with hard labour was abolished by the Criminal Justice Act 1948, s 1(2); the punishment is now imprisonment for a term not exceeding seven years or a fine or both; see the Criminal Justice Act 1948, s 1(1) and (2).

2 Triable either way; see the Magistrates' Courts Act 1980, s 17 and Sch 1, also ss 17A–21 (procedure) and s 32 (penalty), in PART I: MAGISTRATES' COURTS, PROCEDURE, ante.

7.8612 **3. False statements, etc. with reference to marriage** (1) If any person—

(*a*) for the purpose of procuring a marriage, or a certificate or licence for marriage, knowingly and wilfully makes a false oath, or makes or signs a false[1] declaration, notice or certificate required under any Act of Parliament for the time being in force relating to marriage; or

(*b*) knowingly and wilfully makes, or knowingly and wilfully causes to be made, for the purpose of being inserted in any register of marriage or register of conversions, a false statement as to any particular required by law to be known and registered relating to any marriage or any civil partnership which is to be converted into a marriage]; or

(*c*) forbids the issue of any certificate or licence for marriage by falsely representing himself to be a person whose consent to the marriage is required by law knowing such representation to be false, or

(*d*) with respect to a declaration made under section 16(1A) or 27B(2) of the Marriage Act 1949—

(i) enters a caveat under subsection (2) of the said section 16, or

(ii) makes a statement mentioned in subsection (4) of the said section 27B,

which he knows to be false in a material particular,

he shall be guilty of a misdemeanour, and, on conviction thereof on indictment, shall be liable to penal servitude for a term not exceeding **seven years**,[1], or to imprisonment, with or without hard labour, for a term not exceeding two years, or to a **fine** or to **both** such penal servitude or imprisonment and fine and on summary conviction thereof shall be liable to a penalty not exceeding the prescribed sum[2].

(2) No prosecution for knowingly and wilfully making a false declaration for the purpose of procuring any marriage out of the district in which the parties or one of them dwell shall take place after the expiration of eighteen months form the solemnization of the marriage to which the declaration refers.

(3) In subsection (1)(*b*), "register of conversions" means the register of conversions of civil partnerships into marriages kept by the Registrar General in accordance with section 9 of the Marriage (Same Sex Couples) Act 2013 and regulations made under that section.

[Perjury Act 1911, s 3 as amended by the Criminal Justice Act 1925, s 28(1), the Criminal Justice Act 1967, Sch 3, Criminal Law Act 1977, s 28 and the Marriage (Prohibited Degrees of Relationship) Act 1986, s 4 and SI 2014/3168.]

1 Imprisonment with hard labour was abolished by the Criminal Justice Act 1948, s 1(2); the punishment is now imprisonment for a term not exceeding seven years or a fine or both; see the Criminal Justice Act 1948, s 1(1) and (2).

2 For procedure in respect of an offence triable either way, see the Magistrates' Courts Act 1980, ss 17A–21, in PART I: MAGISTRATES' COURTS, PROCEDURE, ante. Offences under ss 3 and 4 remain triable either way despite Sch 1, para 14 to the Magistrates' Courts Act 1980 because of the saving provision of s 17(2) of that Act.

7.8613 **4. False statements, etc, as to births or deaths** (1) If any[1] person—

(*a*) wilfully makes any false answer to any question put to him by any registrar of births or deaths relating to the particulars required to be registered concerning any birth or death, or, wilfully gives to any such registrar any false information concerning any birth or death or the cause of any death; or

(*b*) wilfully makes any false certificate or declaration under or for the purposes of any Act relating to the registration of births or deaths, or, knowing any such certificate or declaration to be false, uses the same as true or gives or sends the same as true to any person; or

(*c*) wilfully makes, gives or uses any false statement or declaration as to a child born alive as having been still-born, or as to the body of a deceased person or a still-born child in any coffin, or falsely pretends that any child born alive was still-born; or

(*d*) makes any false statement with intent to have the same inserted in any register of births or deaths:

he shall be guilty of a misdemeanour and shall be liable—

(i) on conviction thereof on indictment, to penal servitude for a term not exceeding **seven years,**[2], or to imprisonment, with or without hard labour, for a term not exceeding two years, or to a **fine** instead of either of the said punishments; and

(ii) on summary conviction thereof, to a penalty not exceeding the prescribed sum[3].*

(2) A prosecution on indictment for an offence against this section shall not be commenced more than three years after the commission of the offence.

[Perjury Act 1911, s 4 as amended by the Magistrates' Courts Act 1980, s 32.]

---

* **Subsection (1A) inserted by the Welfare Reform Act 2009, Sch 6 from a date to be appointed.**

1 The falsity of a statement by a woman that her husband is the father of her child may not be proved by regimental records disclosing that her husband was serving abroad when the child was conceived, for regimental records are not public documents (*Pettit v Lilley* [1946] 1 All ER 593, 110 JP 218).

2 Imprisonment with hard labour was abolished by the Criminal Justice Act 1948, s 1(2); the punishment is now imprisonment for a term not exceeding 7 years or a fine or both; see the Criminal Justice Act 1948, s 1(1) and (2).

3 For procedure in respect of an offence triable either way, see the Magistrates' Courts Act 1980, ss 17A–21, in PART I: MAGISTRATES' COURTS, PROCEDURE, ante. Offences under ss 3 and 4 remain triable either way despite Sch 1, para 14 to the Magistrates' Courts Act 1980 because of the saving provision of s 17(2) of that Act.

**7.8614 5. False statutory declarations, etc, without oath** If any person knowingly and wilfully[1] makes (otherwise than on oath) a statement[2] false in a material particular, and the statement is made—

(*a*) in a statutory[3] declaration; or

(*b*) in an abstract, account, balance, sheet, book, certificate[4], declaration, entry, estimate, inventory, notice, report, return, or other document which he is authorised or required to make, attest, or verify, by any public general Act of Parliament for the time being in force; or

(*c*) in any oral declaration or oral answer which he is required to make by, under, or in pursuance of any public general Act of Parliament for the time being in force,

he shall be guilty of a misdemeanour and shall be liable[5] on conviction thereof on indictment to imprisonment, with or without hard labour[6], for any term not exceeding **two years,** or to a **fine** or to **both** such imprisonment and fine.

[Perjury Act 1911, s 5.]

---

1 This means an intention to do a particular act proscribed with the knowledge of the material circumstances which render it an offence. There is no further requirement to establish some further or ulterior intention on the part of the accused (*R v Sood* [1998] 2 Cr App Rep 355, [1999] Crim LR 85, CA).

2 See s 16(3), post; *R v Bradbury, R v Edlin* [1921] 1 KB 562, 85 JP 128. False statements made with intent to defraud the Crown, but not coming within the scope of this section, may constitute a common law misdemeanour (*R v Hudson* [1956] 2 QB 252, [1956] 1 All ER 814, 120 JP 216).

3 Justices are competent to take these declarations by virtue of the Statutory Declarations Act 1835, s 18, in PART II: EVIDENCE, ante. A personal representative (defined by s 55(xi)) making a false statement in writing that he has not given or made an assent or conveyance of a legal estate shall be liable in like manner as if the statement had been contained in a statutory declaration (Administration of Estates Act 1925, s 36(6)). Making a false declaration for the purpose of receiving payment out of a grant in pursuance of the Appropriation Act 1946, for half-pay or Navy, Army, Air, or Civil non-effective services is a misdemeanour (Appropriation Act 1946, s 7(2)).

4 It is an offence for a person to give a certificate under an Act relating to the registration of births and deaths, and which can be used under such an Act, and it is not necessary for the prosecution to prove that the accused gave the certificate with the intention that it should be so used (*R v Ryan* (1914) 78 JP 192).

5 Triable either way: see the Magistrates' Courts Act 1980, s 17 and Sch 1, also ss 17A–21 (procedure) and s 32 (penalty) in PART I: MAGISTRATES' COURTS, PROCEDURE, ante.

6 Imprisonment with hard labour was abolished by the Criminal Justice Act 1948, s 1(2).

**7.8615 6. False declarations, etc to obtain registration, etc** If any person—

(*a*) procures or attempts to procure himself to be registered on any register[1] or roll kept under or in pursuance of any public general Act of Parliament for the time being in force of persons qualified by law to practise any vocation or calling; or

(*b*) procures or attempts to procure a certificate of the registration of any person on any such register or roll as aforesaid,

by wilfully making or producing or causing to be made or produced either verbally or in writing, any declaration, certificate, or representation which he knows to be false or fraudulent, he shall be guilty of a misdemeanour and shall be liable[2] on conviction thereof on indictment to imprisonment for any term not exceeding **twelve months,** or to a fine, or to both such imprisonment and fine.

[Perjury Act 1911, s 6.]

[1] This will apply to existing registers under the Medical Act 1983; the Dentists Act 1984; the Veterinary Surgeons Act 1966; the Pharmacy Act 1954; the Nurses, Midwives and Health Visitors Act 1997; and also to professional registers which may be established in the future.

[2] Triable either way; see the Magistrates' Courts Act 1980, s 17 and Sch 1, also ss 17A–21 (procedure) and s 32 (penalty) in PART I: MAGISTRATES' COURTS, PROCEDURE, ante.

7.8616 **7. Aiders, abettors, suborners, etc** (1) Every person who aids, abets, counsels, procures, or suborns another person to commit an offence against this Act shall be liable to be proceeded against, indicted, tried and punished as if he were a principal offender.

(2) Every person who incites another person to commit an offence against this Act shall be guilty of a misdemeanour, and, on conviction thereof on indictment, shall be liable[1] to imprisonment, or to a fine, or to both such imprisonment and fine.

[Perjury Act 1911, s 7 as amended by the Criminal Law Act 1967, s 7 and the Criminal Attempts Act 1981, Sch.]

[1] On conviction on indictment this offence is punishable by a term of imprisonment for not more than two years (Powers of Criminal Courts Act 1973, s 18(1)). Triable either way; see the Magistrates' Courts Act 1980, s 17 and Sch 1, also ss 17A–21 (procedure) and s 32 (penalty) in PART I: MAGISTRATES' COURTS, PROCEDURE, ante.

7.8617 **8. Venue** Where an offence against this Act or any offence punishable as perjury or as subornation of perjury under any other Act of Parliament is committed in any place either on sea or land outside the United Kingdom, the offender may be proceeded against, indicted, tried, and punished in England.

[Perjury Act 1911, s 8 as amended by the Criminal Law 1967, s 10 and Sch 3.]

7.8618 **12.** *Form of indictment*[1].

[1] As to preferring a bill of indictment under this section, see the Administration of Justice (Miscellaneous Provisions) Act 1933, s 2(2)(*b*).

Separate counts may be laid in the same indictment where the perjury has been repeated at different times and places, and the prisoner may be sentenced on each count for an aggregate term exceeding the maximum punishment which can be adjudged for one offence (*Castro v R* (1881) 6 App Cas 229, 45 JP 452). On prosecution for perjury, etc, alleged to have been committed on trial of an indictment, fact of former trial to be proved by production of certificate signed by clerk of court or other person having custody of records, or his deputy (s 14). On a trial for perjury in a summary proceeding before justices, either the information should be produced or some evidence given of the precise nature of the charge before the justices (*R v Carr* (1867) 31 JP 789).

7.8619 **13. Corroboration** A person shall not be liable to be convicted of[1] any offence against this Act, or of any offence declared by any other Act to be perjury or subornation of perjury, or to be punishable as perjury or subornation of perjury solely upon the evidence of one witness[2] as to the falsity of any statement alleged to be false.

[Perjury Act 1911, s 13.]

[1] It will be observed that this section applies not only to perjury and offences punishable as perjury, but also to false statements not on oath. The offence must be proved either by two witnesses, or by one witness and proof of other material and relevant facts in confirmation. See *R v Threlfall* (1914) 111 LT 168. A general direction by the Judge on the need of corroboration of the evidence of an accomplice is sufficient, without a direction as to this section (*R v Saldanha* (1920) 85 JP 47). The warning must be the strongest possible (*R v Atkinson* (1934) 24 Cr App Rep 123). See heading *Corroboration* in title EVIDENCE, PART II, ante.

[2] Evidence of a confession that a sworn statement was false is evidence of the statement's falsity (*R v Peach* [1990] 2 All ER 966, [1990] 1 WLR 976, CA). The corroborative evidence must be independent of the witness who requires corroboration; for example, another witness or a confession or other incriminating letter written by the defendant: *R v Cooper* [2010] EWCA Crim 979, [2010] 1 WLR 2390, (2010) 174 JP 265, [2010] 2 Cr App R 13, [2010] Crim LR 949.

7.8620 **14. Proof of certain proceedings on which perjury is assigned** On a prosecution—

(*a*) for perjury alleged to have been committed on the trial of an indictment for misdemeanour; or

(*b*) for procuring a suborning the commission of perjury on any such trial,

the fact of the former trial shall be sufficiently proved by the production of a certificate containing the substance and effect (omitting the formal parts) of the indictment and trial purporting to be signed by the clerk of the court, or other person having the custody of the records of the court where the indictment was tried, or by the deputy of that clerk or other person, without proof of the signature or official character of the clerk or person appearing to have signed the certificate.

[Perjury Act 1911, s 14 as amended by the Criminal Law Act 1967, s 10 and Sch 3.]

7.8621 **15. Interpretation** (1) For the purposes of this Act, the forms and ceremonies used in administering an oath are immaterial, if the court or person before whom the oath is taken has power to administer an oath for the purpose of verifying the statement in question, and if the oath has been administered in a form and with ceremonies which the person taking the oath has accepted without objection, or has declared to be binding on him.

(2) The expression "oath" includes "affirmation" and "declaration", and the expression "swear" includes "affirm" and "declare"; the expression "statutory declaration" means a declaration made by virtue of the Statutory Declaration Act 1835[1], or of any Act, Order in Council, rule or regulation applying or extending the provisions thereof.

[Perjury Act 1911, s 15 as amended by the Administration of Justice Act 1977, Sch 5.]

[1] See PART II: EVIDENCE, ante.

7.8622 **16. Savings** (1) Where the making of a false statement is not only an offence under this Act, but also by virtue of some other Act is a corrupt practice or subjects the offender to any forfeiture or disqualification or to any penalty other than imprisonment, or fine, the liability of the offender under this Act shall be in addition to and not in substitution for his liability under such other Act.

(2) Nothing in this Act shall apply to a statement made without oath by a child under the provisions of the Prevention of Cruelty to Children Act 1904, and the[1] Children Act 1908.

(3) Where the making of a false statement is by any other Act, whether passed before or after the commencement of this Act, made punishable on[2] summary conviction, proceedings may be taken either under such other Act or under this Act:

Provided that where such an offence is by any Act passed before the commencement of this Act, as originally enacted, made punishable[3] only on summary conviction, it shall remain only so punishable.

[Perjury Act 1911, s 16.]

---

1 See the Criminal Justice Act 1988, s 33A in Part III, ante, and the Children and Young Persons Act 1933, s 38, ante.

2 See note 4 to s 5, ante.

3 The Court of Criminal Appeal held that these words mean that the offence cannot, under any circumstances, be punished otherwise than on summary conviction, and therefore exclude an offence triable either way under what is now ss 17A-21 of the Magistrates' Courts Act 1980 (*R v Bradbury, R v Edlin* [1921] 1 KB 562, 85 JP 128).

# PERSONS, OFFENCES AGAINST

**Contents**



## Common assault and battery

**7.8623** Common assault and battery are separate statutory offences and a person guilty of either is liable to a fine not exceeding **level 5** on the standard scale, or to imprisonment for a term not exceeding **six months** or to **both**[1].

An assault is any intentional or reckless act which causes a person to apprehend immediate unlawful force or personal violence. A battery is any intentional or reckless infliction of unlawful force or personal violence. A battery therefore, often (but not always[2]) includes an assault. As a result, the term "assault" tends to be used in a broad sense to cover both assault and battery[3]. Nevertheless, a clear distinction should be made between the two offences, particularly when laying an information. An information alleging "assault and battery" is bad for duplicity and where there is actual as well as apprehended unlawful violence the appropriate wording in the information is "assault by beating"[4].

Common assault and battery are summary offences but either may, in certain circumstances, be included in an indictment[5] or committed to the Crown Court for trial[6].

Although assault and battery are discrete offences for the purposes of s 39 of the Criminal Justice Act 1988, the term "assault" encompasses the offence of battery for the purposes of s 40 of the Criminal Justice Act 1988 (the power to join in an indictment the summary offence of assault)[3].

1 Criminal Justice Act 1988, s 39, see this title, post.

2 See *R v Nelson* [2013] EWCA Crim 30, [2013] 1 WLR 2861, [2013] 1 Cr App R 30, 177 JP 105, [2013] Crim LR 689 (an ingredient of common assault is that the victim apprehended immediate unlawful violence but such apprehension is not required for assault by beating).

3 See *R v Lynsey* [1995] 3 All ER 654, [1995] 2 Cr App Rep 667, 159 JP 437, CA.

4 *DPP v Taylor and Little* [1992] 1 All ER 299, [1991] Crim LR 904, 155 JP 713.

5 Criminal Justice Act 1988, s 40; see Part I: Magistrates' Courts, Procedure, ante.

6 Criminal Justice Act 1988, s 41; see Part I: Magistrates' Courts, Procedure, ante.

## Apprehension or infliction of unlawful force or violence

7.8624 Common assault involves causing a person to apprehend immediate unlawful violence. Physical injury or contact is not necessary[1]. The emphasis is on the reaction of the victim. Actions meant as a joke may be an assault if the victim is sufficiently frightened[2]. Words or gestures alone, depending on the circumstances, may constitute an assault[3]. Where the making of a silent telephone call causes fear of immediate and unlawful violence, the caller will be guilty of an assault[3]. On the other hand words can negative actions which would otherwise be an assault[4]. The victim must perceive the unlawful violence as being "immediate" but this tends to be interpreted widely. So, where a man terrified a woman by staring at her through her window it was held that she apprehended some immediate violence even though he was outside[5]. It has also been held to be sufficient to prove a fear of violence at some time not excluding the immediate future[6].

The infliction of unlawful force or personal violence constitutes a battery. "Force" has been defined as the least touching of another person in anger[7] but it is recognised that a certain degree of physical contact is inevitable in everyday life[8]. Most batteries involve the direct infliction of force or violence but there are cases which illustrate that a battery may be committed indirectly[9]. The offence of battery may be committed even though there is no direct physical contact between the assailant and the victim, provided the direct application of force is established through the use of another person as a medium or through the use of a weapon as a medium[10].

Although an omission cannot constitute an assault[11], an assault occasioning actual bodily harm is committed where the injury is the natural result of what the assailant said and did, ie that it was something that could reasonably have been foreseen as the consequence[12], or as being "the result of" what was said and done[13]. The cause must be more than *de minimis* for which a convenient term is "a substantial cause"[14] although this may imply a larger meaning and reference to "more than a slight or trifling" link is a useful way to avoid the term "*de minimis*"[15]. Accordingly, where someone (by act or word or a combination of the two) creates a danger and thereby exposes another to a reasonably foreseeable risk of injury which materializes, there is an evidential basis for the *actus reus* of an assault occasioning actual bodily harm (it remains for the prosecution to prove an intention to assault or appropriate recklessness)[16]. Therefore a person who created a dangerous situation by depositing acid in a hand-face drying machine and took the risk of someone using the machine before he could get back and render it harmless was guilty of assault occasioning actual bodily harm[17] as was a suspect the subject of a body search who had given a dishonest assurance to a police officer about the contents of his pockets where the officer was injured by an exposed needle of a hypodermic syringe in his pocket[18].

1 *R v Mansfield Justices, ex p Sharkey* [1985] 1 All ER 193, 149 JP 129, [1985] Crim LR 148.
2 *Logdon v DPP* [1976] Crim LR 121.
3 *R v Ireland* [1997] 4 All ER 225, [1997] 3 WLR 534, 161 JP 569, HL.
4 *Tuberville v Savage* (1669) 1 Mod Rep 3.
5 *Smith v Chief Superintendent, Woking Police Station* [1983] Crim LR 323.
6 *R v Constanza* [1997] 2 Cr App Rep 492 (defendant sending threatening letters to victim who suffered psychological damage from fear of violence).
7 *Cole v Turner* (1704) 6 Mod Rep 149.
8 *Wilson v Pringle* [1987] QB 237.
9 *R v Martin* (1881) 8 QBD 54; *DPP v K (a minor)* [1990] 1 All ER 331, 154 JP 192, 91 Cr App Rep 23.
10 *Haystead v Chief Constable of Derbyshire* [2000] 3 All ER 890, 164 JP 396, [2000] 2 Cr App Rep 339, DC.
11 *Fagan v Metropolitan Police Comr* [1968] 3 All ER 442, 133 JP 16, 52 Cr App Rep 700; *DPP v K (a minor)* [1990] 1 All ER 331, 154 JP 192, 91 Cr App Rep 23.
12 *R v Roberts* (1971) 56 Cr App Rep 95, CA.
13 See *R v Notman* [1994] Crim LR 518, CA.
14 *R v Hennigan* [1971] 3 All ER 133, 55 Cr App Rep 262, 135 JP 504; *R v Notman* [1994] Crim LR 518, CA.
15 *R v Kimsey* [1996] Crim LR 35.
16 *R v Roberts* (1971) 56 Cr App R 95, [1972] Crim LR 27, CA, *DPP v K (a minor)* [1990] 1 All ER 331, 154 JP 192, 91 Cr App R 23, *DPP v Santa-Bermudez* [2004] EWHC 2908 (Admin), 168 JP 373, [2004] Crim LR 471.
17 *DPP v K (a minor)* [1990] 1 All ER 331, 154 JP 192, 91 Cr App Rep 23.
18 *DPP v Santa-Bermudez* [2004] EWHC 2908 (Admin), 168 JP 373, [2004] Crim LR 471.

## Intention or recklessness

7.8625 In order to constitute an assault or battery punishable by the criminal law, it must be established that the defendant acted intentionally or recklessly[1]. Where the case is put on the basis of a deliberate blow, the court can convict on the basis of recklessness provided it is satisfied that the defendant committed an unlawful act (eg flailing his arms ill-temperedly) and had the requisite foresight of harm[2]. *Cunningham* (ie subjective) recklessness must be proved, namely that the accused actually foresaw the particular kind of harm that might be done but nonetheless proceeded to take the risk of it[3].

1 *R v Venna* [1976] QB 421, [1975] 3 All ER 788, 140 JP 31.
2 *Katonis v Crown Prosecution Service* [2011] EWHC 1860 (Admin), (2011) 175 JP 396.
3 *R v Savage; R v Parmenter* [1991] 4 All ER 698, 155 JP 935, HL. See para 1.91 ff, **Criminal Responsibility, Guilty mind (mens rea)**; Part I: Magistrates' Courts, Procedure, ante.

## Consent

**7.8626** Generally speaking, in order to prove a charge of assault, the prosecution must establish that the victim did not consent to the defendant's actions. If the victim consented to the assault the defendant is not guilty unless the public interest requires otherwise. It has been held that it was not in the public interest for people to cause or to try to cause each other actual bodily harm and a fight between two persons would be unlawful, whether in public or private, if actual bodily harm was intended or caused[1]. Furthermore, convictions under ss 47 and 20 of the Offences against the Person Act 1861 were upheld in respect of members of a sado-masochistic group who inflicted pain on each other for mutual sexual pleasure because public policy required that society be protected against a cult of violence[2]. Less extreme cases must be considered on a case by case basis so that, for example, public policy did not require that consensual activity between husband and wife which involved burning the husband's initials on the wife's buttocks where there was no aggressive intent should attract criminal sanctions[3].

A teacher at a special needs school, who took his position aware of the risk of violence from children with behavioural problems, did not thereby impliedly consent to being assaulted; the principles which apply in cases involving contact sports (see infra) have no application to incidents within special institutions dealing with children with special needs[4].

Consent to sexual intercourse does not include consent to the risk of contracting a sexually transmitted disease. Thus, where a person, knowing that he is suffering a serious sexual disease, recklessly transmits it to another through consensual sexual intercourse he can be guilty of inflicting grievous bodily harm, contrary to s 20 of the Offences Against the Person Act 1861; the victim's consent to sexual intercourse is not, of itself, to be regarded as consent to the risk of consequent disease; but that if the victim does consent to such a risk that will provide a defence to a charge under s 20[5].

Nevertheless, in charges of common assault and battery, if the facts or the defence raise the issue of consent, the prosecution must prove the absence of consent[6], or if there was consent that it was given through ignorance[7] or fraudulent misrepresentation[8]. Fraud will only negative consent if it deceived the victim as to the identity of the person or the nature of the act[9]. The concept of the "identity of the person" is not extended to the qualifications or attributes of the defendant[10].

A blow struck in sport, and not likely or intended to cause bodily harm, is not an assault[11], nor is rough horseplay provided it is innocent of anger or intention to cause bodily harm[12]. However, an injury inflicted on an opponent by deliberately flouting the rules of the game may form the basis of a criminal prosecution[13]. Most organised sports have their own disciplinary procedures to uphold their rules and standards of play; criminal prosecutions should, therefore, be brought only in cases that are so grave as to be properly categorised as criminal[14]. If what occurs goes beyond what a player can reasonably be regarded as having accepted by taking part in the sport, this indicates that the conduct will not be covered by the defence of consent; on the other hand, the fact that the play is within the rules and practice of the game and does not go beyond them, will be a firm indication that what has happened is not criminal[14]. "Prize fights" have been held to amount to batteries. A mere exhibition of skill in sparring is not illegal; but if parties meet intending to fight until one gives in from exhaustion or injury received it is a prize-fight, whether the combatants fight in gloves or not[15].

As distinct from the civil law, the maxim ex turpi causa non oritur actio does not apply to criminal proceedings and the criminal law will act to prevent serious injury or death even when the persons subject to such injury or death consented to or willingly accepted the risk of actual injury or death. Accordingly, it was no defence to manslaughter that there was no duty of care to the victims who were illegal immigrants engaged in the same enterprise as the defendant lorry driver[16].

---

1 *A–G's Reference (No 6 of 1980)* [1981] QB 715, [1981] 2 All ER 1057.

2 *R v Brown* [2004] 1 AC 212, [1993] 2 All ER 75, 157 JP 337, HL.

3 *R v Wilson* [1996] 3 WLR 125, [1996] 2 Cr App Rep 241, [1996] Crim LR 573, CA.

4 *H v Crown Prosecution Service* [2010] EWHC 1374 (Admin), [2012] 1 QB 257, [2010] 4 All ER 264, [2012] 2 WLR 296.

5 *R v Dica* [2004] EWCA Crim 1103, [2004] QB 1257, [2004] 3 All ER 593, [2003] 3 WLR 213. However, their lordships made clear that they were not considering an allegation of deliberate infection or spreading HIV with intent to cause grievous bodily harm; and in such circumstances the principle in *Brown* (see infra) meant that the agreement of the participants would provide no defence to a charge under s 18 of the 1861 Act.

See also *R v Konzani* [2005] EWCA Crim 706, [2005] 2 Cr App R 14,, 169 JPN 227 in which it was affirmed that, for a complainant's consent to the risks of contracting the HIV virus to provide a defence, her consent had to be an informed consent and, in that regard, there was a critical distinction between taking a risk of the various, potentially adverse consequences of sexual intercourse, and giving an informed consent the risk of infection with a fatal disease. Moreover, a complainant could not give consent to something of which she was ignorant and, in such circumstances, silence was not consistent with honest or with a genuine behalf that there was informed consent.

See also *R v Golding* [2014] EWCA Crim 889, [2014] Crim LR 686, which confirmed that that the herpes virus might be added to the list of communicable diseases that are considered sufficiently serious to constitute really serious harm.

6 *R v May* [1912] 3 KB 572, 77 JP 31; *R v Donovan* [1934] 2 KB 498, 98 JP 409.

7 *R v Lock* (1872) LR 2 CCR 10.

8 *R v Rosinski* (1824) 1 Mood CC 19; *R v Williams* (1838) 8 C & P 286; *R v Bennett* (1866) 4 F & F 105.

9 *R v Williams* [1923] KB 340 rape where victim was fraudulently induced to consent to sexual intercourse in the belief that the defendant had to perform an operation to enable her to produce her voice properly).

10 *R v Richardson* [1998] 3 WLR 1292, [1998] 2 Cr App Rep 200, CA, [1999] Crim LR 62. But see *R v Tabassum* [2000] 2 Cr App Rep 328, [2000] Crim LR 686, CA (defendant examined breasts of his female victims who believed he was medically qualified and working for a hospital. Although they consented to the nature of the act, they did not consent to the quality of the act ie that it was done by a person without medical qualifications).

11 *R v Coney* (1882) 8 QBD 534, 46 JP 404.

[12] *R v Bruce* (1847) 2 Cox CC 262.
[13] *R v Billinghurst* [1978] Crim LR 553.
[14] *R v Barnes* [2004] EWCA Crim 3246, [2005] 2 All ER 113, [2005] 1 Cr App Rep 507, [2005] Crim LR 381 in which the following guidance was given. It must be borne in mind that in highly competitive sports conduct outside the rules could be expected to occur in the heat of the moment and even if conduct justified not only being penalised but also a warning or even a sending off it still might not reach the threshold level required for it to be criminal. The type of sport, the level at which it was played, the nature of the act, the degree of force used, the extent of the risk of injury and the state of mind of the defendant were all likely to be relevant in determining whether the defendant's actions went beyond the threshold and warranted criminal proceedings.
[15] *R v Orton* (1878) 43 JP 72; See Treatise on "Boxing Matches", 61 JP 802, where the various authorities are cited and discussed.
[16] *R v Wacker* [2002] EWCA Crim 1944, [2003] QB 1207, [2003] 4 All ER 295, [2003] 1 Cr App Rep 329.

## Moderate chastisement

**7.8627** *Parents may inflict moderate and reasonable chastisement on their children, but standards of reasonableness change over the years. The current state of the law is that, in considering the reasonableness or otherwise of the chastisement, regard should be paid to the nature and context of the defendant's behaviour, its duration, its physical and mental consequences in relation to the child, the age and personal characteristics of the child and the reasons given by the defendant for administering punishment*[1]*. Where a defence of reasonable chastisement might be available, it is for the prosecution to prove that the accused did more than inflict moderate and reasonable chastisement on the child*[2]*.*

*By virtue of the Education Act 1996, s 548*[3]*, the giving of corporal punishment to a child cannot be justified in proceedings on the ground that it was done in pursuance of a right exercisable by a member of staff at a school by virtue of his position. "Child" for this purpose means a child for whom education is provided at any school; or for whom education is provided, otherwise than at school, under any arrangements made by a local education authority; or for whom specified nursery education is provided otherwise than at school.*

Section 58 of the Children Act 2004, which came into force on 15 January 2005, removes the justification of battery on the ground that it constituted reasonable punishment where the prosecution is brought under ss 18, 20 and 47 of the Offences Against the Person Act 1861 or s 1 of the Children and Young Persons Act 1933.

[1] *R v H (assault of child: reasonable chastisement)* [2001] EWCA Crim 1024, [2001] 3 FCR 144, [2001 2 FLR 431, [2002] 1 Cr App Rep 59.
[2] *R v Smith* [1985] Crim LR 42.
[3] In this Part: title Education, ante.

## Self defence and reasonable force in the prevention of crime or the making of an arrest

**7.8628** The law on self defence and the use of force in the prevention of crime or making an arrest was placed on a statutory footing by s 76 of the Criminal Justice and Immigration Act 2008[1]. The purpose of the section was "to clarify the operation" of these defences[2], and it uses elements of case law to improve understanding of the practical application of these areas of the law.

Previous case law is summarised in the corresponding paragraph of the 2007 edition of this work.

[1] In Part I: Magistrates' Courts, Procedure, ante.
[2] Section 76(9) of the Criminal Justice and Immigration Act 2008.

## Mistake

**7.8629** If a person believed mistakenly that the victim was consenting or that a crime was being committed which he intended to prevent, he must be judged against the mistaken facts or circumstances as he believed them to be[1]. If the belief was in fact held, its unreasonableness in objective terms is irrelevant so far as guilt or innocence is concerned[2]. A genuine belief in facts which if true would justify self-defence is a defence to a crime of personal violence as negativing intent to act unlawfully[3]. However, it would appear that an honest and reasonable belief that a constable is acting outside his duty will not always constitute a defence[4]. Nevertheless, a defendant is not entitled to rely on a mistake of fact induced by self-intoxication[5].

[1] *R v Williams (Gladstone)* (1983) 78 Cr App Rep 276.
[2] *R v Kimber* [1983] 3 All ER 316, [1983] 1 WLR 1118.
[3] *Beckford v R* [1988] AC 130, [1987] 3 All ER 425, 85 Cr App Rep 378.
[4] *R v Fennel* [1971] 1 QB 428, [1970] 3 All ER 215, [1970] Crim LR 581, 134 JP 678; *R v Ball* (1989) 90 Cr App Rep 378, [1989] Crim LR 581.
[5] *Re O'Grady* [1987] QB 995, [1987] 3 All ER 420, 85 Cr App Rep 315. See also *R v Hatton* [2005] EWCA Crim 2951, [2006] 1 Cr App R 247.

## Aggravated assaults

**7.8630** Some assaults are regarded as being of a more serious nature and specific statutory provisions cater for these in the Offences against the Person Act 1861. The more common offences are wounding or causing grievous bodily harm with intent[1], wounding or inflicting grievous bodily harm[2], assault with intent to resist or prevent arrest[3] and assault occasioning actual bodily harm[4].

1 Offences against the Person Act 1861, s 18, post.
2 Offences against the Person Act 1861, s 20, post.
3 Offences against the Person Act 1861, s 38, post.
4 Offences against the Person Act 1861, s 47, post.

## Harassment

**7.8631** Conduct which is less than a threat of immediate unlawful violence may amount to harassment[1]. A person who pursues a course of conduct which amounts to harassment of another and who knows or ought to know that it amounts to such harassment is, with certain exceptions, guilty of an offence contrary to s 2 of the Protection from Harassment Act 1997[1]. He may also (in civil proceedings) be liable for damages and be made subject to an injunction. Breach of such an injunction is an offence triable either way (s 3). Further, a person whose conduct causes another to fear on at least two occasions, that violence will be used against him is guilty of an offence if he knows or ought to have known that his course of conduct will cause the other so to fear on each of those occasions (s 4). A court may, when sentencing or dealing with a person convicted of an offence under section 2 or 4, make a restraining order to protect the victim of any other person named in the order from further conduct amounting to harassment or which will cause a fear of violence (s 5).

1 Protection from Harassment Act 1997, s 7(2), is this Part, post. See also *Chambers and Edwards v DPP* [1995] Crim LR 896 and see also s 5 of the Public Order Act 1986, this Part: title Public Meetings and Public Order, post.

## Kidnapping

**7.8632** The common law offence of kidnapping is an attack on, and infringement of, the personal liberty of an individual. The offence contains four ingredients: the taking away of one person by another, by force or fraud, without the consent of the person so taken or carried away and without lawful excuse[1]. Force extends to the threat of force[2]. The offence of kidnapping is not completed where a defendant, by a fraudulent misrepresentation, induces another person to go, unaccompanied by the defendant, from one place to another; in such circumstances there is nothing that is capable of constituting a taking and carrying away or a deprivation of liberty[3]. The offence may be committed by a man against his wife[4] and where only a short distance is involved[5]. A father may be guilty of kidnapping his child[1] but in such cases it is the absence of the child's consent which is material. In the case of a very young child the absence of consent would be a necessary inference from its age, but in the case of an older child it is a question of fact for the jury whether the child concerned has sufficient understanding and intelligence to give its consent, and, if the jury considers that it has these qualities, it must then consider whether it has been proved that the child did give its consent[1]. The intent required is basic intent and self-induced intoxication is no defence[6].

The offence is punishable on indictment by a fine and imprisonment. See also the Child Abduction Act 1984, in Part V: Youth Courts, ante.

1 *R v D* [1984] AC 778, [1984] 2 All ER 449. See also *R v Cort* [2003] EWCA Crim 2149, [2004] QB 388, [2003] 3 WLR 1300, 167 JP 504, [2004] 1 Cr App Rep 199 (the defendant falsely stated to women waiting at a bus stop that their bus had broken down and offered them a lift; it was held that what they were consenting to was a lift and not being taken away by fraud and that their consent was vitiated by that fraudulently induced mistake). See, however, the decision in *R v Hendy-Freegard*, post.
2 *R v Archer* [2011] EWCA Crim 2252, [2012] Crim LR 292, [2011] 39 LS Gaz R 19.
3 *R v Hendy-Freegard* [2007] EWCA Crim 1236, [2008] QB 57, [2007] 2 Cr App Rep 343, [2007] Crim LR 986, in which it was observed that the vital element of deprivation of liberty was not considered in *Cort*, supra, and since there had been no suggestion that the defendant in *Cort* had intended to detain the women against their will, this requirement of the offence had not been made out.
4 *R v Reid* [1973] QB 299, [1972] 2 All ER 1350.
5 *R v Wellard* [1978] 3 All ER 161, [1978] 1 WLR 921, 67 Cr App Rep 364.
6 *R v Hutchins* [1988] Crim LR 379.

## False imprisonment

**7.8633** The common law offence of false imprisonment comprises unlawful detention, compulsion, restraint of personal liberty[1] but is not committed merely by preventing someone from proceeding along a particular way[2]. A parent may be guilty of false imprisonment of a child where the facts take the circumstances outside reasonable parental discipline[3]. It is well established that a genuine but mistaken belief can be relied upon as a defence to a criminal charge such as false imprisonment where the Crown have to prove that the defendant's conduct was unlawful[4].

1 See *Mee v Cruikshank* (1902) 86 LT 708, 66 JP 89, 20 Cox 210; *R v Linsberg and Leies* (1905) 69 JP 107.
2 *Bird v Jones* (1845) 7 QB 742, 15 LJQB 82, 10 JP 4.
3 See *R v Rahman* (1985) 120 Sol Jo 431, CA.

[4] *R v Faraj* [2007] EWCA Crim 1033, [2007] 2 Cr App Rep 322.

# Offences Against the Person Act 1861

(24 & 25 Vict c 100)

*Homicide*

7.8634 **4. Soliciting to commit murder** Whosoever shall solicit[1], encourage, persuade, or endeavour to persuade, or shall propose to any person[2], to murder any other person, whether he be a subject of Her Majesty or not, and whether he be within the Queen's Dominions or not, shall be guilty of an offence and being convicted thereof shall be liable to imprisonment for life.

[Offences Against the Person Act 1861, s 4 as amended by the Statute Law Revision Act 1892, and the Criminal Law Act 1977, s 5.]

[1] As to conspiracy to murder, see now ss 1–5 of the Criminal Law Act 1977, in title CONSPIRACY, ante. A person who solicits a pregnant woman to murder her child after its birth commits an offence, at all events if the child is born alive (*R v Shephard* [1919] 2 KB 125, 83 JP 131). The offence may be completed by the publication of an article in a newspaper not addressed to a particular individual (*R v Most* (1881) 7 QBD 244, 45 JP 696). But the offence is not complete unless there has been some actual communication between the accused and the person solicited, etc, though it is not necessary to show that the mind of the person solicited was affected thereby; proof of posting will suffice (*R v Krause* (1902) 66 JP 121). An indictment charging a person with encouraging persons unknown to murder the sovereigns and rulers of Europe was held good as a sufficiently well defined class was referred to by the words "sovereigns of Europe" (*R v Antonelli and Barberi* (1906) 70 JP 4). This offence can be committed by a person who solicits another to commit murder as a secondary as opposed to a principal (*R v Winter* (2007) Times, 20 December, CA).

[2] Where the soliciting, etc, is to commit murder abroad there is nothing in the wording of the Act, which did not lay down rules of jurisdiction, and no principle of international comity requiring the persons so solicited to be British subjects (*R v Abu Hamza* [2006] EWCA Crim 2918, [2007] 1 QB 659, [2007] 3 All ER 451, [2007] 2 WLR 226, [2007] 1 Cr App Rep 345).

7.8635 **5. Manslaughter** Whosoever shall be convicted of manslaughter[1] shall be liable, at the discretion of the court, to imprisonment for life.

[Offences Against the Person Act 1861, s 5.]

[1] Manslaughter is based mainly, though not exclusively, on the **absence of the intention to kill**, but with the presence of an element of unlawfulness which is the elusive factor (*Andrews v DPP* [1937] AC 576, [1937] 2 All ER 552, 101 JP 386, HL): in order to establish criminal liability the facts must be such that in the opinion of the jury the negligence of the accused went beyond a mere matter of compensation between subjects and showed such disregard for the life and safety of others as to amount to a crime against the State and conduct deserving punishment (*per* Lord HEWART CJ, in *R v Bateman* (1925) 89 JP 162). An accused is guilty of manslaughter if it is proved that he intentionally did an act which was unlawful and dangerous and that it inadvertently caused death; but it is unnecessary to prove that he knew the act was unlawful or dangerous (*DPP v Newbury* [1977] AC 500, [1976] 2 All ER 365, 140 JP 370, HL). Approval was given in the case of *R v Watson* [1989] 2 All ER 865, [1989] 1 WLR 684, 89 Cr App Rep 211, to manslaughter being defined as the offence committed when one person causes the death of another by an act which is unlawful and which is also dangerous, dangerous in the sense that it is an act which all sober and reasonable people would inevitably realise must subject the victim to the risk of some harm resulting whether the defendant realised that or not. A jury must be satisfied that the unlawful act was such that all reasonable people would be bound to recognise that it exposed the victim to the risk of harm (*R v Mahal* [1991] Crim LR 632, CA). The risk of harm to be recognised is not dangerous in the sense that it must be potentially lethal or even serious harm: it is dangerous for this purpose because of the risk of "some harm": *R v M* [2012] EWCA Crim 2293, [2013] 1 WLR 1083, [2013] 1 Cr App Rep 144, [2013] Crim LR 335. Where the victim died as the result of injuries sustained from jumping from a speeding car in which he was threatened with robbery, the considerations were whether it was reasonably foreseeable that some physical harm, albeit not serious, was likely to result from the threat of robbery, and whether the victim's response was within the range which might be expected (*R v Williams and Davis* [1992] Crim LR 198, CA).

The elements of "unlawful act" manslaughter were reviewed in *R v JF* [2015] EWCA Crim 351, [2015] 2 Cr App Rep 64, [2015] All ER (D) 117 (Mar).

As to dangerousness:

> "21 It has therefore been established since at least 1943 (as affirmed by the House of Lords for nearly 40 years) that in determining whether the act was dangerous, the test is objective. In applying that test the knowledge of the circumstances attributed to the bystander are the circumstances known to the defendant (see *R v Watson (Clarence)* (1989) 89 Cr App R 211)."

As to the mental element:

> "26 The judge gave two directions in relation to the state of mind of the appellants:
>
> i) the acts that constituted the crime in the present case were malicious damage to the building. The judge, as we have set out, directed the jury that they had to be sure that the appellants either intended that damage to the building or were subjectively reckless; and
>
> ii) the judge then went on to direct the jury on the basis that the prosecution had to prove that the defendant had, at the time he or she started the fire, foreseen or contemplated the possibility that some persons might be in the building.
>
> The first direction required the jury to have the mens rea applicable to the unlawful act—the malicious damage to the building—as established by *R v G* [2003] UKHL 50, [2004] 1 Cr App R 21 (p 237), [2004] 1 AC 1034, that was plainly sufficient in the light of *Lamb* and *Newbury*. The second direction went further than was required, as it stated the law more favourably to the appellants. It appears to have been derived from the decision of this court in *R v Bristow* [2013] EWCA Crim 1540, [2014] Crim. LR 457, [2013] All ER (D) 109 (Sep), where issues of joint enterprise were engaged. That decision does not require the gloss on the well-established law which the judge set out in the further direction given by him to the jury in the present case." (per Thomas LCJ)

The defendants were teenagers and the Court was invited to reconsider the objective nature of the test of dangerousness in the light of the decision in *R v G*. However, it was held that it was a matter for Parliament to determine whether the long-established law needed changing having regard to the Law Commission's recommendations (in the Law Commission Consultation Paper No 135 (1994), Involuntary Manslaughter) or whether this was an area of law that required further examination by the Law Commission.

Where the charge of manslaughter is based on an unlawful and dangerous act, it must be an **act directed at the victim** and likely to cause him immediate injury (*R v Dalby* [1982] 1 All ER 916, [1982] 1 WLR 425), but in that case the court was concerned with the quality of the act rather than the identity of the person at whom it was aimed. Therefore, it does not matter that the act has been aimed at some person other than the victim or that the death has not arisen due to some immediate impact on, or physical contact with, the victim since the primary question is one of causation; ie whether the defendant's act caused the victim's death (*R v Mitchell* [1983] QB 741, [1983] 2 All ER 427, 76 Cr App Rep 293, CA). Although it is possible to imagine factual scenarios in which two people could properly be regarded as acting together, in cases where the accused supplies the victim with drugs, the defendant will not be guilty where the victim is a fully-informed and responsible adult and had freely and voluntarily self administered himself with a fatal dose (*R v Kennedy (No 2)* [2007] UKHL 38, [2008] AC 269, [2007] 4 All ER 1083, [2008] 1 Cr App R 19). An armed person who fires at the police and holds a woman by force in front of him as a shield when the police might well fire shots at him in self-defence commits two such unlawful and dangerous acts (*R v Pagett* (1983) 76 Cr App Rep 279, CA). Common sense standards apply when considering the defence of self-defence, in deciding whether more force was used than was necessary in the circumstances; see *R v Shannon* [1980] Crim LR 438. The act which caused death and the necessary mental state do not have to coincide in point of time; the mens rea may be contained in an initial unlawful assault and the actus reus may be the eventual act causing death (*R v Le Brun* [1992] QB 61, [1991] 4 All ER 673, CA).

**Particular circumstances**—A person may be convicted of manslaughter after a summary conviction of an assault (*R v Morris* (1867) LR 1 CCR 90, 31 JP 516). Evidence that death was due to a combination of physical exertion and fright or strong emotion, caused by an illegal act of the accused, is sufficient to support a conviction for manslaughter without proof of actual violence (*per* Ridley, J, in *R v Hayward* (1908) 21 Cox, CC 692; see also *R v Reid* [1976] Crim LR 570—joint possession of revolver intended to frighten; contrast *R v Perman* [1996] 1 Cr App Rep 24 where the defendant believed the gun in possession of the co-accused was unloaded.): also if death was connected with the state of health (*status lymphaticus*) of the deceased (*R v Woods* (1921) 85 JP 272). Where a number of people participate in the commission of a dangerous act, all may be convicted; as where three men fired off cartridges at a board in private grounds, one of which killed a boy, all were equally guilty although it was not shown which shot caused the death (*R v Salmon* (1880) 6 QBD 79, 45 JP 270; and see *R v Baldessare* (1930) 144 LT 185; *R v Wesley Smith* [1963] 3 All ER 597, 128 JP 13). Any person, whether licensed or unlicensed, who deals with the life or health of another person is bound to use competent skill and sufficient attention: if the patient dies for the want of either, there is manslaughter (*R v Burdee* (1916) 86 LJKB 871). One act of carelessness by a doctor in preparing too strong a mixture for injection whereby the patient dies does not amount to manslaughter: the negligence to be imputed depends upon the probable, not the actual, result (*Akerele v R* [1943] AC 255, [1943] 1 All ER 367). The death of a sick child accelerated by the refusal of a parent to procure medical assistance, even though the refusal is due to religious scruples, may lead to a conviction for manslaughter (*R v Senior* [1899] 1 QB 283, 63 JP 8). Where the allegation is neglect of a duty assumed to care for an infirm person, a reckless disregard of the infirm person's health and welfare must be shown; mere inadvertence is not enough (*R v Stone, R v Dobinson* [1977] QB 354, [1977] 2 All ER 341, 141 JP 354). It is clear from *R v Stanley Smith* [1979] 3 All ER 605, [1979] 1 WLR 1445, that the test of the recklessness is subjective, that a deliberate decision has been taken to run the risk involved in not getting medical attention, and in all the circumstances that was a wholly unjustified risk to take.

**Involuntary manslaughter** has been held to involve the following ingredients: (1) the existence of a duty; (2) a breach of the duty causing death; (3) gross negligence justifying criminal conviction. Gross negligence might properly be found based upon any of the following states of mind: (*a*) indifference to an obvious risk of injury to health; (*b*) actual foresight of the risk coupled with the determination nevertheless to run it; (*c*) an appreciation of the risk coupled with an intention to avoid it but also coupled with such a high degree of negligence in the attempted avoidance as the jury considered justified a conviction; (*d*) inattention or failure to avert to a serious risk which went beyond "mere inadvertence" in respect of an obvious and important matter which the defendant's duty demanded he should address (*R v Prentice* [1993] 4 All ER 935, CA, *R v Sullman* [1994] QB 302, CA, *R v Adomako* [1995] 1 AC 171, [1994] 3 All ER 79, HL, *R v Holloway* [1994] QB 302, [1993] 4 All ER 935, CA). The maxim ex turpi causa non oritur actio does not apply to criminal proceedings to preclude a duty of care to participants involved in an unlawful activity, even when the persons subject to such injury or death, consented to or willingly accepted the risk of actual injury or death (*R v Wacker* [2002] EWCA Crim 1944, [2003] QB 1207, [2003] 4 All ER 295, [2003] 1 Cr App Rep 329). The ingredients of the offence of gross negligent manslaughter have sufficient certainty to meet the requirements of art 7 of the European Convention on Human Rights (*R v Misra and Srivastava* [2004] EWCA Crim 2375, [2005] 1 Cr App Rep 328, [2005] Crim LR 324).

**Procedure**—For requirement for consent of Attorney-General to institute proceedings in certain circumstances see note to the Homicide Act 1957, s 1, post. Manslaughter by the driver of a motor vehicle involves compulsory disqualification for holding a driving licence (Road Traffic Offenders Act 1988, Sch 2).

For the obligation placed on the clerk to the justices to notify the coroner, who is responsible for holding an inquest, of the making of a charge of murder, manslaughter or infanticide and of the result of the proceedings before the court, see the Coroners Act 1988, s 17, in this Part, title Coroners, ante.

A coroner's inquest is not to find a person guilty of manslaughter; Criminal Law Act 1977, s 56.

As to corporate manslaughter, see *R v P & O European Ferries (Dover) Ltd* [1991] Crim LR 695.

**7.8636 9.** *Murder or manslaughter abroad*[1].

**7.8637 10.** *Provision for the trial of murder and manslaughter where the death or cause of death only happens in England or Ireland*[1].

1 Sections 9 and 10 give English courts jurisdiction where acts were committed abroad.

*Letters threatening to murder*

**7.8638 16. Threats to kill** A person who without lawful excuse[1] makes to another a[2] threat, intending that that other would fear it would be carried out, to kill that other or a third person[3] shall be guilty of an offence[4] and liable on conviction on indictment to imprisonment for a term not exceeding **ten years**.

[Offences against the Person Act 1861, s 16 as substituted by the Criminal Law Act 1977, Sch 12.]

1 A lawful excuse can exist if a threat to kill is made for the prevention of crime or for self-defence, provided that it is reasonable in the circumstances to make such a threat; the onus is on the prosecution to prove that there was no lawful excuse for making the threat (*R v Cousins* [1982] QB 526, [1982] 2 All ER 115, CA).

2 An allegation must particularise only one threat; there is no offence of making multiple threats to kill (*R v Marchese* [2008] EWCA Crim 389, [2009] 1 WLR 992, [2008] 2 Cr App R 12, [2008] Crim LR 797).

3 A foetus in utero is not a person distinct from its mother and therefore a threat to cause the mother to have a miscarriage is not an offence under s 16; however a threat to kill a child after its birth when it was still a foetus is an offence under s 16 (*R v Tait* [1990] 1 QB 290, [1989] 3 All ER 682, CA).

4 Triable either way; see Magistrates' Courts Act 1980, s 17 and Sch 1, also ss 17A–21 (procedure) and s 32 (penalty) in Part I: Magistrates' Courts, Procedure, ante.

*Acts causing or tending to cause danger to Life or Bodily Harm*

7.8639 17. **Impeding a person endeavouring to save himself from shipwreck** Whosoever shall unlawfully and maliciously[1] prevent or impede any person, being on board of, or having quitted any ship or vessel which shall be in distress or wrecked, stranded, or cast on shore, in his endeavour to save his life, or shall unlawfully and maliciously prevent or impede any person in his endeavour to save the life of any such person as in this section first aforesaid shall be guilty of an offence and being convicted thereof shall be liable to imprisonment for life.

[Offences Against the Person Act 1861, s 17 as amended by the Statute Law Revision Act 1892, the Statute Law Revision (No 2) Act 1893 and the Criminal Law Act 1967, s 1.]

[1] For meaning of "maliciously", see para 1.91 **Criminal responsibility—Guilty mind (mens rea)** in PART I: MAGISTRATES' COURTS, PROCEDURE, ante.

7.8640 18. **Wounding with intent to do grievous bodily harm** Whosoever shall unlawfully and maliciously[1] by any means whatsoever, wound[2] or cause[3] any grievous bodily harm[4] to any person with intent[5] to do some grievous bodily harm to any person, or with intent to resist or prevent the lawful[6] apprehension or detainer of any person, shall be guilty of an offence and being convicted thereof shall be liable to imprisonment for **life**.

[Offences Against the Person Act 1861, s 18, as amended by the Statute Law Revision Act 1892, the Statute Law Revision (No 2) Act 1983, the Criminal Law Act 1967, s 1 and Sch 3.]

[1] For meaning of "maliciously", see para 1.91 **Criminal responsibility—Guilty mind (mens rea)** in PART I: MAGISTRATES' COURTS, PROCEDURE, ante.

[2] To constitute a "wound" there must be a break in the continuity of the whole skin; accordingly, an injury where there has merely been internal rupturing of blood vessels is not a "wound" (*C (a minor) v Eisenhower* [1984] QB 331, [1983] 3 All ER 230).

[3] The test of causation is an objective one, and separate from the accused's intention. To establish that the defendant caused the victim's injuries, the prosecution must prove that the defendant's conduct caused or materially contributed to those injuries, ie were they reasonably foreseeable as a consequence by a reasonable person in the defendant's shoes. It is not necessary for the reasonable man to be taken to be of the same age and sex as the defendant (*R v Marjoram* [2000] Crim LR 373, CA (defendant caused victim's injuries sustained when she jumped through a window when the defendant accompanied by a large number of people shouting abuse and kicking at her door forced open the door to her room)).

[4] To constitute grievous bodily harm, really serious bodily harm must be caused (*R v Metharam* [1961] 3 All ER 200, 125 JP 578; *DPP v Smith* [1961] AC 290, [1960] 3 All ER 161, 124 JP 473); "grievous" means no more and no less than "really serious", and there is no distinction between the phrases "serious bodily harm" and "really serious bodily harm"; see *R v Saunders* [1985] LS Gaz R 1005, CA. A modified interpretation applied in *R v Ashman* (1858) 1 F & F 88, identifying the expression with serious interference with health or comfort, is no longer appropriate. In *R v Bollom* [2003] EWCA Crim 2846, [2004] 2 Cr App Rep 50, the question arose as to whether the degree of a harm had to be considered with or without reference to the health or other particular factors relating to the person harmed (in this case a 17-month-old baby who had suffered extensive bruising and some abrasions). It was held that it was necessary to consider the injuries in their real context and there was no pre-condition to a finding that the injuries amounted to grievous bodily harm that the victim should require treatment or that the harm would have lasting consequences; however, where it is alleged that the injuries collectively, though not individually, amount to grievous bodily harm the court must be satisfied that they were inflicted in a single assault and not in a series of assaults. In *R v Golding* [2014] EWCA Crim 889, [2014] Crim LR 686 it was confirmed that the herpes virus might be added to the list of communicable diseases that are considered sufficiently serious to constitute really serious harm. (See the commentary in the Criminal Law Review for a discussion on this topic.)

[5] Where intent is an ingredient of the offence, there is no onus on the defendant to prove that the alleged act was accidental. A person may be taken to intend the consequence only of his intentional acts (*R v Davies* (1913) 29 TLR 350). Recklessness cannot amount to the specific intent required (*R v Belfon* [1976] 3 All ER 46, 140 JP 523). In determining this intention, the court is not bound to draw an inference by reason only of the result being a natural and probable consequence of the defendant's actions. It shall decide upon his intent by reference to all the evidence, drawing such inferences there-from as appear proper. See the Criminal Justice Act 1967, s 8, ante. The approved direction to a jury is "You must feel sure that the defendant intended to cause serious bodily harm to the victim. You can only decide what his intention was by considering all the relevant circumstances and in particular what he did and what he said about it" (*R v Purcell* (1986) 83 Cr App Rep 45, CA).

If any person fire a pistol into a group of people, not aiming at any one in particular, but intending generally to do grievous bodily harm, the offender may be indicted for shooting at the person with intent to do grievous bodily harm (*R v Fretwell* (1864) Le & Ca 443, 28 JP 344; see *R v Ward* (1872) LR 1 CCR 356, 36 JP 453).

Provocation does not alter the nature of the offence, but it is allowed for in the sentence (per Viscount SIMON in *Holmes v DPP* [1946] AC 588, [1946] 2 All ER 124; *R v Cunningham* [1959] 1 QB 288, [1958] 3 All ER 711, 123 JP 134). For form of charge where a blow misses and hits another person, see *R v Monger* [1973] Crim LR 301. Drunkenness as a defence has to be very extreme before it should influence the prosecution to accept a plea of guilty to a charge under s 20 instead (*R v Stubbs* (1988) 88 Cr App Rep 53, CA).

[6] If the apprehension would not have been lawful an indictment under this section cannot be sustained (*R v Marsden* (1868) LR 1 CCR 131, 32 JP 436).

7.8641 20. **Inflicting bodily injury, with or without weapon**[1] Whosoever shall unlawfully and maliciously[2] wound[3] or inflict any grievous bodily harm[3] upon any other person, either with or without any weapon or instrument shall be guilty of [an offence] and being convicted thereof shall be liable to imprisonment not exceeding **five years**[4].

[Offences Against the Person Act 1861, s 20 as amended by the Statute Law Revision Act 1892, the Criminal Justice Act 1948, s 1 and the Criminal Law Act 1967, s 1.]

[1] As to having in possession any firearm or imitation firearm at the time of committing or at the time of apprehension for offences under ss 20–22, 30, 32, 38, 47 and 56 of this Act, aiding and abetting or attempting to commit any ch offence, see the Firearms Act, 1968, s 17, and Sch 1, ante.

[2] For the meaning of "maliciously" see para 1.91 **Criminal responsibility—Guilty mind (mens rea)** in PART I: MAGISTRATES' COURTS, PROCEDURE, ante. It is neither limited to, nor does it indeed require, any ill will towards the persons injured. (*R v Savage, R v Parmenter* [1992] 1 AC 699, [1991] 4 All ER 698, HL).The word "maliciously" in this statute was satisfied by a malice which had a different object for the blow. L had a quarrel with C and aimed a blow at him, but

accidentally struck and wounded E. The CCR confirmed the conviction, and distinguished the case from *R v Pembliton* (1874) LR 2 CCR 119, 38 JP 454 (*R v Latimer* (1886) 17 QBD 359, 51 JP 184). B extinguished the gaslights on the staircase of a theatre, and placed a bar across the passage; the darkness caused a panic, and two persons were seriously injured. He was rightly convicted under this section; personal malice need not be proved (*R v Martin* (1881) 8 QBD 54, 46 JP 228). This case was followed in *R v Chapin* (1909) 74 JP 71. A's wife being frightened by his threats, tried to get out of a window to escape, and fell and broke her leg. The conviction was affirmed (*R v Halliday* (1890) 54 JP 312; followed in *R v Beech* (1912) 76 JP 287; and *R v Coleman* (1920) 84 JP 112). An intention to frighten is not a sufficient *mens rea* (*Flack v Hunt* [1980] Crim LR 44; *R v Sullivan* [1981] Crim LR 46).

In order to establish that a defendant has acted maliciously it has to be shown that, on the facts known to him at the time, he actually foresaw that some bodily harm, not necessarily amounting to grievous bodily harm or wounding, might occur: *R v Parmenter* and *R v Savage* [1992] AC 699, [1991] 4 All ER 698, HL. Accordingly, a defendant who believed his gun to be unloaded, when in fact it contained pellets, and fired at another person thereby causing injury, was held not to have acted maliciously (*W (a minor) v Dolbey* [1983] Crim LR 681); and see *R v Rainbird* [1989] Crim LR 505.

There is no requirement in crimes of malice or subjective recklessness that the risk of proscribed harm is one which must be "obvious and significant": *R v Brady* [2006] EWCA Crim 2413, [2007] Crim LR 564.

[3] See notes 2 and 4 to s 18, ante. An offence contrary to s 20 of this Act may be committed where no physical violence is applied directly or indirectly to the body of the victim, and in this context "grievous bodily harm" may include psychiatric injury (*R v Ireland* [1997] 4 All ER 225, [1997] 3 WLR 534, 161 JP 569, HL).

[4] Triable either way; see the Magistrates' Courts Act 1980, s 17 and Sch 1, also ss 17A–21 (procedure) and s 32 (penalty) in PART I: MAGISTRATES' COURTS, PROCEDURE, ante. See criticism by Lord GODDARD, CJ, of justices who permitted a charge under s 18 to be reduced to one under this section, at the request of both prosecution and defence, so as to empower them to deal with the case summarily (*R v Bodmin Justices, ex p McEwen* [1947] KB 321, [1947] 1 All ER 109, 111 JP 47).

7.8642 **21. Attempting to choke etc in order to commit indictable offence** Whosoever shall by any means whatsoever attempt to choke, suffocate, or strangle any other person, or shall by any means calculated to choke, suffocate, or strangle, attempt to render any other person insensible, unconscious, or incapable of resistance, with intent in any of such cases thereby to enable himself or any other person to commit or with intent in any of such cases thereby to assist any other person in committing any indictable offence shall be guilty of an [offence][1] and being convicted thereof shall be liable to imprisonment for **life**.

[Offences Against the Person Act 1861, s 21 as amended by the Statute Law Revision Act 1892, the Criminal Justice Act 1948, s 1 and the Criminal Law Act 1967, s 1.]

7.8643 **22. Using chloroform etc to commit indictable offence** Whosoever shall unlawfully apply or administer to or cause to be taken by, or attempt to apply or administer to, or attempt to cause to be administered to or taken by, any person, any chloroform, laudanum, or other stupefying or overpowering drug, matter, or thing, with intent in any of such cases thereby to enable himself or any other person to commit, or with intent in any of such cases thereby to assist any other person in committing any indictable offence shall be guilty of an offence and being convicted thereof shall be liable to imprisonment for **life** [1].

[Offences Against the Person Act 1861, s 22 as amended by the Statute Law Revision Act 1892, the Criminal Justice Act 1948, s 1 and the Criminal Law Act 1967, s 1.]

[1] Where firearms were involved, see note 1 to s 20, ante.

7.8644 **23. Maliciously administering poison etc so as to endanger life etc** Whosoever shall unlawfully and maliciously[1] administer to, or cause to be administered to, or taken by, any other person[2], any poison, or other destructive or noxious thing, so as thereby to endanger the life of such person, or so as thereby to inflict upon any such person any grievous bodily harm shall be guilty of an offence[3], and being convicted thereof shall be liable to imprisonment for any term not exceeding **ten years**.

[Offences Against the Person Act 1861, s 23 as amended by the Statute Law Revision Act 1892, the Criminal Justice Act 1948 s 1 and the Criminal Law Act 1967, s 1.]

[1] For meaning of "maliciously", see para 1.91 **Criminal responsibility—Guilty mind (mens rea)** in PART I: MAGISTRATES' COURTS, PROCEDURE, ante. For "administer" see note to s 24, post.

[2] An unborn child is not 'any other person'; *CP (A Child) v First-tier Tribunal (Criminal Injuries Compensation) (British Pregnancy Advisory Service/Birthrights and another intervening)* [2014] EWCA Civ 1554, [2015] 2 WLR 463, [2015] 1 Cr App Rep 246.

The consent of the person to the administration to him of a noxious substance for the purpose of committing suicide is no defence to a charge under this section (*R v McShane* (1977) 66 Cr App Rep 97).

[3] A person charged under this section may be convicted of an offence against s 24, infra (Offences Against the Person Act 1861, s 25).

7.8645 **24. Maliciously administering poison etc with intent to injure, aggrieve or annoy** Whosoever shall unlawfully and maliciously[1] administer[2] to, or cause to be administered to or taken by any other person, any poison or other destructive or noxious thing[3], with intent to injure[4], aggrieve, or annoy[5] such person shall be guilty of [an offence], and being convicted thereof shall be liable to imprisonment not exceeding **five years**.

[Offences Against the Person Act 1861, s 24 as amended by the Statute Law Revision Act 1892, the Statute Law Revision (No 2) Act 1893, the Criminal Justice Act 1948, s 1 and the Criminal Law Act 1967, s 1.]

[1] For meaning of "maliciously", see para 1.91 **Criminal responsibility—Guilty mind (mens rea)** in PART I: MAGISTRATES' COURTS, PROCEDURE, ante.

[2] "Administer" includes conduct which, not being the application of direct physical force to the victim, nevertheless brought the noxious thing into contract with the victim's body (*R v Gillard* (1988) 87 Cr App Rep 189). The substance of the section creates three distinct offences: (1) administering a noxious thing to any other person; (2) causing a noxious thing to be administered to any other person; and (3) causing a noxious thing to be taken by any other person. Offence (1) is committed where D administers the noxious thing directly to V, as by injecting V with the noxious thing, holding a glass containing the noxious thing to V's lips, or spraying the noxious thing in V's face. Offence (2) is typically committed where

D does not directly administer the noxious thing to V but causes an innocent third party TP to administer it to V. If D, knowing a syringe to be filled with poison instructs TP to inject V, TP believing the syringe to contain a legitimate therapeutic substance, D would commit this offence. Offence (3) covers the situation where the noxious thing is not administered to V but taken by him, provided D causes the noxious thing to be taken by V and V does not make a voluntary and informed decision to take it. If D puts a noxious thing in food which V is about to eat and V, ignorant of the presence of the noxious thing, eats it, D commits offence (3).

Subject to exceptions eg in the case of the young or in cases of duress, the criminal law generally assumes the existence of free will and generally, informed adults of sound mind are treated as autonomous beings able to make their own decisions how they will act. Thus D is not to be treated as causing V to act in a certain way if V makes a voluntary and informed decision to act in that way rather than another. Section 23 draws a very clear contrast between a noxious thing administered to another person and a noxious thing taken by another person. It cannot ordinarily be both. Where the noxious thing was "freely and voluntarily self-administered" by the deceased, he had a choice whether to inject himself or not and it was his act (*R v Kennedy (No 2)* [2007] UKHL 38, [2008] AC 269, [2007] 4 All ER 1083, [2008] 1 Cr App Rep 19).

[3] Administering to a woman a noxious drug (cantharides) with intent to excite sexual passion, in order that the prisoner might have connection with her, will be an offence under this section (*R v Wilkins* (1861) Le & Ca 89, 25 JP 773); but not if the quantity administered is incapable of producing any effect, for it is not in that form noxious (*R v Hennah* (1877) 41 JP 171). See also *R v Wood* [1975] Crim LR 236 (sleeping tablets). The concept of the "noxious thing" involves not only the quality or nature of the substance, but also the quantity administered or sought to be administered; "noxious" means something less in importance than, and different in quality from, poison or other destructive things (*R v Marcus* [1981] 2 All ER 833, [1981] 1 WLR 774, 145 JP 380, CA). See also the Sexual Offences Act 2003, s 61 (administering a substance with the intention of stupefying or overpowering a person to facilitate sexual activity) in thie PART: title SEXUAL OFFENCES, post.

[4] There must be an intent to injure in the sense of causing physical harm; see *R v Hill* (1986) 83 Cr App Rep 386, [1986] Crim LR 815.

[5] Although the administration of the poison with intent to annoy is only a misdemeanour, if the effects are such as to cause grievous bodily harm the offence will amount to felony (*Tully v Corrie* (1867) 17 LT 140).

**7.8646 26. Not providing apprentices etc with food etc whereby life endangered**

Whosoever being legally liable, either as a master or mistress, to provide for any apprentice or servant necessary food, clothing, or lodging, shall wilfully and without lawful excuse refuse or neglect to provide the same, or shall unlawfully and maliciously do or cause to be done any bodily harm to any such apprentice or servant, so that the life of such apprentice or servant shall be endangered or the health of such apprentice of servant shall have been or shall be likely to be permanently injured shall be guilty of an offence[1] and being convicted thereof shall be liable to imprisonment not exceeding **five years**.

[Offences Against the Person Act 1861, s 26 as amended by the Statute Law Revision Act 1892, the Statute Law Revision (No 2) Act 1893, the Criminal Justice Act 1948, s 1 and the Criminal Law Act 1967, s 1.]

[1] Triable either way; see the Magistrates' Courts Act 1980, s 17 and Sch 1, also ss 18–21 (procedure) and s 32 (penalty).

**7.8647 27. Exposing child whereby life is in danger** Whosoever shall unlawfully abandon[1] or expose any child, being under the age of two years, whereby the life of such child shall be endangered, or the health of such child shall have been or shall be likely to be permanently injured shall be guilty of an offence[2] and being convicted hereof shall be liable to imprisonment not exceeding **five years**.

[Offences Against the Person Act 1861, s 27 as amended by the Statute Law Revision Act 1892, the Statute Law Revision (No 2) Act 1893, the Criminal Justice Act 1948, s 1 and the Criminal Law Act 1967, s 1.]

[1] A father knowingly leaving his child for some hours outside his house, after it has been left there by his wife, with whom he was not living, is guilty of abandonment (*R v White* (1871) LR 1 CCR 331, 36 JP 134). See also *R v Falkingham* (1870) LR 1 CCR 222, 34 JP 149, Treat 35 JP 417. For general offence of abandoning a child, see the Children and Young Persons Act 1933, s 1 in PART V: YOUTH COURTS.

[2] Triable either way; see the Magistrates' Courts Act 1980, s 17 and Sch 1, also ss 17A–21 (procedure) and s 32 (penalty) in PART I: MAGISTRATES' COURTS, PROCEDURE, ante.

**7.8648 28. Causing bodily injury by gunpowder** Whosoever shall unlawfully and maliciously[1], by the explosion of gunpowder or other explosive substance, burn, maim, disfigure, disable, or do any grievous bodily harm to any person shall be guilty of an offence and being convicted thereof shall be liable to imprisonment for **life**.

[Offences Against the Person Act 1861, s 28 as amended by the Statute Law Revision Act 1892, the Statute Law Revision (No 2) Act 1893, the Criminal Justice Act 1948, s 1 and Sch 10, and the Criminal Law Act 1967, s 1.]

[1] For meaning of "maliciously", see para 1.91 **Criminal responsibility—Guilty mind (mens rea)** in PART I: MAGISTRATES' COURTS, PROCEDURE, ante.

**7.8649 29. Causing gunpowder to explode, sending explosive substance or throwing corrosive fluid with intent to do grievous bodily harm** Whosoever shall unlawfully and maliciously[1] cause any gunpowder or other explosive substance[2] to explode, or send or deliver to, or cause to be taken or received by, any person any explosive substance, or any other dangerous or noxious thing, or put or lay at any place, or cast or throw at or upon, or otherwise apply to any person, any corrosive fluid or any[3] destructive or explosive substance with intent in any of the cases aforesaid to burn, maim, disfigure, or disable[4] any person, or to do some grievous bodily harm, to any person, whether any bodily injury be effected or not[5] shall be guilty of [an offence] and being convicted thereof shall be liable to imprisonment for **life**.

[Offences Against the Person Act 1861, s 29 as amended by the Statute Law Revision Act 1892, the Statute Law Revision (No 2) Act 1893, the Criminal Justice Act 1948, s 1 and Sch 10 and the Criminal Law Act 1967, s 1.]

[1] For meaning of "maliciously", see para 1.91 **Criminal responsibility—Guilty mind (mens rea)** in PART I: MAGISTRATES' COURTS, PROCEDURE, ante.

[2] A petrol bomb is an explosive substance (*R v Howard* [1993] Crim LR 213).

[3] Boiling water was held to be "destructive *matter*" within s 5 of the repealed statute, 1 Vict c 85 (*R v Crawford* (1845) 2 Car & Kir 129), but HUDDLESTON, B, held at Liverpool Spring Assizes, 1887, it is not "destructive *substance*" within this statute (*R v Martin* (1877) 62 LT Jo 372).

[4] "Disable" must be given its ordinary wide meaning and should not be limited to permanent disablement (*R v James* (1979) 70 Cr App Rep 215).

[5] Where firearms were involved, see note 1 to s 20, ante.

**7.8650 30. Placing gunpowder near building with intent to do bodily injury** Whosoever shall unlawfully and maliciously[1] place or throw in, into, upon, against, or near any building, ship, or vessel, any gunpowder, or other explosive substance[2], with intent to do any bodily injury to any person, whether or not any explosion takes place, or whether or not any bodily injury be effected shall be guilty of [an offence] and being convicted thereof shall be liable to imprisonment not exceeding **fourteen years**.

[Offences against the Person Act 1861, s 30 as amended by the Statute Law Revision Acts 1892 and 1893, the Criminal Justice Act 1948 s 1 and Sch 10 and the Criminal Law Act 1967, s 1.]

[1] For meaning of "maliciously", see para 1.91 **Criminal responsibility—Guilty mind (mens rea)** in PART I: MAGISTRATES' COURTS, PROCEDURE, ante.

[2] For offence of possessing explosives etc and power to search for same see ss 64, 65, post.

**7.8651 31. Setting spring-guns, etc with intent to inflict grievous bodily harm** Whosoever shall set or place, or cause to be set or placed, any spring-gun, man-trap, or other engine calculated to destroy human life or inflict grievous bodily harm, with the intent[1] that the same or whereby the same may destroy or inflict grievous bodily harm upon a trespasser or other person coming in contact therewith, shall be guilty of an offence and being convicted thereof shall be liable to imprisonment not exceeding **five years**; and whosoever shall knowingly and wilfully permit any such spring-gun, man-trap, or other engine which may have been set or placed in any place then being in or afterwards coming into his possession or occupation by some other person to continue so set or placed, shall be deemed to have set and placed such gun, trap, or engine with such intent as aforesaid; provided that nothing in this section contained shall extend to make it illegal to set or place any gin or trap such as may have been or may usually be set or placed with the intent of destroying vermin; provided also that nothing in this section shall be deemed to make it unlawful to set or place, or cause to be set or placed, or to be continued set or placed, from sunset to sunrise, any spring-gun, man-trap, or other engine, which shall be set or placed, or caused or continued to be set or placed, in a dwelling-house for the protection thereof.

[Offences Against the Person Act 1861, s 31 as amended by the Statute Law Revision Act 1892, the Criminal Justice Act 1948, s 1 and the Criminal Law Act 1967, s 1.]

[1] This section does not include a trap to catch badgers (*R v Carpenter* (1932) 76 Sol Jo 422). Causing death by a spring-gun, etc, set in contravention of this section is manslaughter (*R v Heaton* (1896) 60 JP 508). The word "engine" means a mechanical contrivance (*R v Munks* [1964] 1 QB 304, [1963] 3 All ER 757, 128 JP 77). However, to determine whether a contraption is an "engine" for the purposes of s 31 the object, as well as the manner in which it can be activated, must be considered pragmatically to see whether, viewing it overall, it falls within the statutory language; in *R v Munks* the court did not intend to and could not redefine the statutory language by replacing the words "other engine" with "other mechanical contrivance" (*R v Cockburn* [2008] EWCA Crim 316, [2008] QB 882, [2008] 2 All ER 1153, [2008] 2 WLR 1274, [2008] 2 Cr App Rep 4).

**7.8652 35. Drivers injuring persons by furious driving** Whosoever, having the charge of any carriage or[1] vehicle, shall, by wanton[2] or furious[3] driving or racing, or other wilful misconduct, or by wilful neglect, do or cause to be done any bodily harm to any person whatsoever shall be guilty of an offence and being convicted thereof shall be liable to be imprisoned for any term not exceeding **two years**[4].

[Offences Against the Person Act 1861, s 35 as amended by the Criminal Justice Act 1948, s 1 and the Criminal Law Act 1967, s 1.]

[1] A person riding or racing a bicycle in a wanton or furious manner resulting in injuries to another person may be convicted under this section (*R v Parker* (1895) 59 JP 793). A comparable offence of dangerous cycling is punishable under the Road Traffic Act 1988, s 28, post.

[2] "Wanton" is not a term of art, and need not be defined to a jury (*R v Crowden* (1911) 6 Cr App Rep 190; and see *R v Ikosi* [1997] RTR 450, CA). The standard for manslaughter by negligence is not applicable (*R v Burdon* (1927) 20 Cr App Rep 80). A failure on the part of any person to observe any provision of the Highway Code, in PART VI: TRANSPORT, ante, may in any proceedings be relied upon by any party to the proceedings as tending to establish or to negative any liability which is in question in those proceedings (Road Traffic Act 1988, s 38, ante).

[3] It will be observed furious *riding* is altogether omitted; but see *Williams v Evans* (1876) 1 Ex D 277, 41 JP 151.

[4] As to sentencing for this offence see: *R v Lambert* [2008] EWCA Crim 2109, [2009] 1 Cr App R (S) 542; and *R v Darren Kevin Hall* [2009] EWCA Crim 2236, [2010] 1 Cr App R (S) 95.

*Assaults*

**7.8653 36. Assaulting clergymen, etc[1]** Whoever shall, by threats or force, obstruct or prevent or endeavour to obstruct or prevent, any clergyman or other minister in or from celebrating Divine service or otherwise officiating in any church, chapel, meeting house, or other place of Divine worship, or in or from the performance of his duty in the lawful burial of the dead in any churchyard or other burial place, or shall strike or offer any violence to, or shall, upon any civil process, or under pretence of executing any civil process, arrest any clergyman or other minister who is engaged in, or to the knowledge of the offender is about to engage in, any of the rites or duties in this section aforesaid, or who to the knowledge of the offender shall be going to perform the same or returning from the performance thereof, shall be guilty of a misdemeanour, and being convicted thereof shall be liable, at the discretion of the Court, to be imprisoned for any term not exceeding **two years**.

[Offences Against the Person Act 1861, s 36.]

1 Triable either way; see the Magistrates' Courts Act 1980, s 17 and Sch 1, also ss 17A–21 (procedure) and s 32 (penalty) in PART I: MAGISTRATES' COURTS, PROCEDURE, ante.

7.8654 **37. Assaulting magistrate, etc, on account of wreck** Whosoever shall assault and strike or wound any magistrate, officer, or other person whatsoever lawfully authorised, in or on account of the exercise of his duty in or concerning the preservation of any vessel in distress, or of any vessel, goods, or effects wrecked, stranded, or cast on shore, or lying under water, shall be guilty of a misdemeanour, and being convicted thereof shall be liable to be imprisoned for any term not exceeding **seven years**.

[Offences Against the Person Act 1861, s 37.]

7.8655 **38. Assault with intent to resist apprehension, etc[1]** Whosoever shall assault any person with intent to resist or prevent the lawful apprehension or detainer of himself or of any other person for any offence, shall be guilty of misdemeanour, and being convicted thereof shall be liable, at the discretion of the Court, to be imprisoned for any term not exceeding **two years** [2].

[Offences Against the Person Act 1861, s 38 as amended by the Police Act 1964, 10th Sch and Criminal Law Act 1967, 3rd Sch.]

1 Triable either way; see the Magistrates' Courts Act 1980, s 17 and Sch 1, also ss 17A–21 (procedure) and s 32 (penalty) in PART I: MAGISTRATES' COURTS, PROCEDURE, ante. Once the prosecution has established that the arrest was lawful the mens rea for this offence is an intention by the defendant to resist arrest accompanied by knowledge that the person assaulted, who might or might not be a police officer, was a person who was seeking to arrest him.

Honest belief by the defendant that the arrest was unlawful is irrelevant as the mens rea required is an intention to resist arrest accompanied by knowledge that the person assaulted who might or might not be a police officer, was a person who was seeking to arrest him (*R v Lee* [2001] 1 Cr App Rep 293, 165 JP 344, [2000] Crim LR 991, CA).

Where the persons arresting him were police officers, it is not necessary for the prosecution to establish that the defendant knew they were police officers; see *R v Brightling* [1991] Crim LR 364.

2 As to having in possession any firearm or imitation firearm at the time of, or at the time of his arrest for, this offence, see s 17 and Sch 1 of the Firearms Act 1968, post.

7.8656 **44. Certificate of dismissal** If the justices upon the hearing of any case of assault or battery upon the merits[1] where the information was preferred by or on behalf of the party aggrieved[2], shall deem the offence not to be proved or shall find the assault or battery to have been justified, or so trifling as not to merit any punishment, and shall accordingly dismiss the information, they shall forthwith make out a certificate[3] under their hands, stating the fact of such dismissal, and shall deliver such certificate to the party against whom the complaint was preferred.

[Offences Against the Person Act 1861, s 44 as amended by the Criminal Justice Act 1988, Schs 15 and 16.]

1 A certificate under this section of the dismissal by a magistrate of a charge of assault, can only be granted where there has been a hearing "upon the merits." ie the parties are present before the justices, and the case is argued and is decided upon the facts, or upon the law applicable to the facts. Where, therefore, a prosecutor gave notice to a person against whom he had obtained a summons for an assault, that he should not attend before the magistrate or offer evidence in support of the summons, and did not in fact attend or offer evidence, but the person charged attended and obtained from the magistrate a certificate of dismissal under the above section, there had not been a hearing upon the merits; the magistrate had no jurisdiction to grant the certificate; and the certificate was therefore no bar under s 45 to a subsequent action in the county court to recover damages in respect of the same assault: *Reed v Nutt (No 1)* (1890) 24 QBD 669, 54 JP 599. Where the defendant pleads guilty, there is no hearing on the merits so the justices cannot use this section. To take advantage of the section it may be that the proper course for the defendant will be for him to plead not guilty and then to open the door for the justices, having heard all the evidence, to make an order under s 44 if they think fit. Similarly, when a summons is dismissed for want of prosecution there is not a hearing on the merits. A disposal of the matter otherwise than after a thorough going into of the evidence by the justices is not to be regarded as being a disposal on the merits for the purposes of this section: *Ellis v Burton* [1975] 1 All ER 395, 139 JP 199.

2 The provisions of s 44 are confined to private prosecutions. When the CPS undertakes prosecutions, it does not do so on behalf of the party aggrieved; it is acting in the public interest: *Austen v CPS* [2016] EWHC 2247 (Admin).

3 The justices cannot refuse to grant this certificate, but it is not necessary to draw it up unless applied for (*Hancock v Somes* (1859) 8 Cox CC172, 120 E R 1108; 1 El & El 795), and the word "forthwith" means "forthwith upon application" (*Costar v Hetherington* (1859) 23 JP 663, 8 Cox CC 175, 120 ER 1111). The certificate will not prevent justices ordering the defendant to enter into a recognisance to keep the peace (*Ex p Davis* (1871) 35 JP 551, 24 LT 547).

7.8657 **45. Release[1]** If any person against whom any such complaint as is mentioned in section 44 of this Act shall have been preferred by or on behalf of the party aggrieved shall have obtained such a certificate, or having been convicted, shall have paid the whole amount adjudged to be paid, or shall have suffered the imprisonment, in every such case he shall be released[2] from all further or other proceedings, civil[3] or criminal, for the same cause[4].

[Offences Against the Person Act 1861, s 45 as amended by the Criminal Justice Act 1948, s 1 and the Criminal Justice *Act 1988, Sch 15.]*

1 Notwithstanding the provisions of this section, proceedings may be taken against the acquitted person for the offence of which he was acquitted where an order is made under s 54(3) of the Criminal Procedure and Investigations Act 1996 (acquittals tainted by intimidation etc), in PART I: MAGISTRATES' COURTS, PROCEDURE, ante (Criminal Procedure and Investigations Act 1996, s 57(1), in PART I: MAGISTRATES' COURTS, PROCEDURE, ante).

2 These words include all proceedings arising out of the same assault, whether taken by the informant or by any other person consequently aggrieved. A certificate of dismissal under s 44 supersedes the necessity for other proof, but if such

certificate is not produced, it will be for the defendant to prove by other evidence, not only that the former information was for the same matter with which he is charged a second time, but that it was dismissed upon the merits, and the decision was intended to be final. If this be done, the plea of autrefois acquit will, it is conceived, be available in like manner as in indictments (*R v Newbury Justices* (1851) 15 JP Jo 321). So conviction, with payment of the fine, is an answer to an action for injuries to business occasioned by the assault (*Masper v Brown* (1876) 1 CPD 97, 40 JP 265; *Solomon v Frinigan* (1866) 30 JP Jo 756; *Holden v King* (1876) 41 JP 25). The conviction of a servant or agent does not operate to release the person by whom he was employed (*Dyer v Munday* [1895] 1 QB 742, 59 JP 276). If there be neither a conviction nor a dismissal with a certificate thereof, but merely an order for the defendant to enter into a recognisance to keep the peace and pay the costs thereof, no release can be pleaded (*Hartley v Hindmarsh* (1866) LR 1 CP 553). But where a prisoner was convicted and discharged conditionally on giving security to be of good behaviour, under the repealed s 16 of the Summary Jurisdiction Act 1879, the giving the security for good behaviour places the defendant precisely in the same position as if punishment had actually been inflicted and suffered and entitled to the benefits of s 45 (*R v Miles* (1890) 24 QBD 423, 54 JP 549).

[3] If justices desire to give a defendant the protection afforded by this Act they should found their proceedings and judgment upon s 44, inasmuch as the common law defence to an indictment would be no defence to civil proceedings (*R v Miles*, supra).

[4] Although not strictly a plea of autrefois convict, because the defendant will not have previously been convicted of an offence in the form in which he is subsequently charged, at common law a conviction for an offence by a court of competent jurisdiction is a bar to all further proceedings based on the same facts: *Wemyss v Hopkins* (1875) LR 10 QB 378, 39 JP 549 (conviction by justices under the Highway Act, 5 & 6 Wm. 4, c. 50, s. 78, for an offence which, though charged as a mere offence against the Highway Act, amounted also to an assault in law bar to conviction upon the same facts of an assault under s. 42 of 24 & 25 Vict. c. 100); and see PART I: MAGISTRATES' COURTS, PROCEDURE, para 1.160) **Res judicata, estoppel, autrefois convict/acquit, functus officio** ante.

It is not always been found easy to apply the rule to the facts of particular cases and difficulties have arisen in the application of the rule most frequently in cases where a conviction or acquittal for a simple offence has been set up as a bar to a subsequent charge against the same person in a more aggravated form. The law is that where a criminal charge has been adjudicated upon by a court having jurisdiction to hear and determine it, that adjudication, whether it takes the form of an acquittal or conviction, is final as to the matter so adjudicated upon, and may be pleaded in bar to any subsequent prosecution for the same offence, whether with or without circumstances of aggravation, and whether such circumstances of aggravation consist of the offence having been committed with malicious or wicked intent, or by reason that the committal of the offence was followed by serious consequences.

Whilst a certificate will be a bar to an indictment for unlawfully wounding: *R v Elrington* (1861) 26 JP 117, a conviction for assault has been held to be a bar at common law, apart from the statute, to a subsequent indictment upon the same facts for unlawfully wounding, unlawfully inflicting grievous bodily harm, assault occasioning actual bodily harm, and common assault: *R v Miles* (1890) 24 QBD 423, 54 JP 549.

However, where a defendant was convicted for assault and sentenced to imprisonment and underwent the punishment and was afterwards convicted of manslaughter for same assault, it was held that the conviction for assault was no bar, as the subsequent indictment for manslaughter was not for the "same cause" as the assault: *R v Morris* (1867) LR 1 CCR 90, 31 JP 516, Treat 60 JP 18. So a conviction for a common assault could not be pleaded in bar to an indictment for rape, though possibly it might be for an assault with intent to commit rape: *R v Miles*, supra. The ground for this decision seems to be that the aggravating circumstances, unless coupled with the assault, amount to no crime. In *Masper v Brown*, supra, it was held that the "same cause" meant the same assault; but *R v Morris* does not seem to have been cited or referred to in that case.

**7.8658 47. Assault occasioning bodily harm** Whosoever shall be convicted upon an indictment of any assault[1] occasioning actual bodily harm[2] shall be liable[3] to be imprisoned for any term not exceeding **5 years**.

[Offences Against the Person Act 1861, s 47 as amended by the Statute Law Revision Act 1892, the Criminal Justice Act 1948, s 1 and the Criminal Justice Act 1988, Sch 16.]

---

[1] The mental element of assault is an intention to cause the victim to apprehend immediate and unlawful violence, or recklessness whether such apprehension be caused; proof is required of an assault which occasioned actual bodily harm; the prosecution are not obliged to prove that the defendant intended to cause some actual bodily harm or was reckless as to whether such harm would be caused (*R v Savage, R v Parmenter* [1992] 1 AC 699, [1991] 4 All ER 698, HL). For the offence of common assault see the Criminal Justice Act 1988, s 39, post.

[2] "Actual" means that the bodily harm should not be so trivial or trifling as to be effectively without significance. "Bodily" means "concerned with the body". "Harm" is not limited to "injury" but extends to "hurt" and "damage". "Actual bodily harm" is not limited to "harm to the skin, flesh and bones of the victim"; it applies to all parts of the body including the victim's organs, his nervous system and his brain but not excluding other parts of the body. Physical pain consequent on an assault is not a necessary ingredient of this offence.

Hair is an attribute and part of the human body, even if the hair above the surface of the scalp is no more than dead tissue. Therefore the cutting off a substantial part of the victims' hair in the course of an assault is capable of amounting to an assault which occasions actual bodily harm (*DPP v Smith* [2006] EWHC 94 (Admin), [2006] 2 All ER 16, [2006] 1 WLR 1571, [2006] 2 Cr App R 1, 170 JP 45).

Loss of consciousness falls within the meaning of "actual bodily harm" since it involves an injurious impairment of the victim's sensory functions and it is axiomatic that the harm is "actual" (*R (on the application of T) v DPP* [2003] EWHC 266 (Admin), [2003] Crim LR 622).

The phrase "actual bodily harm" is capable of including psychiatric injury. But it does not include mere emotions such as fear or distress or panic, nor does it include, as such, states of mind that are not themselves evidence of some identifiable clinical condition (*R v Chan-Fook* [1994] 2 All ER 552, [1994] 1 WLR 689, [1994] Crim LR 432). The making of a telephone call followed by silence, or a series of telephone calls is capable of amounting to an assault occasioning actual bodily harm if the calls make the victims apprehensive and cause them psychological damage (*R v Ireland* [1997] 4 All ER 225, [1997] 3 WLR 534, 161 JP 569 HL). The preceding and other authorities on psychiatric injury were considered by the Court of Appeal in *R v Dhaliwal* [2006] EWCA Crim 1139, [2006] 2 Cr App R 24, [2006] Crim LR 923 where it was held that there was binding authority to the effect that the ambit of "bodily harm" was restricted to recognisable psychiatric illness. By adhering to that principle the issue which had to be addressed could be clearly understood and those responsible for advising the parties could do so with an appropriate degree of certainty. Where the victim claims to have suffered physical pain as a result of the defendant's non-physical assault the court must have the benefit of psychiatric evidence as to whether such injury could be caused by the defendant's conduct (*R v Morris* [1998] 1 Cr App Rep 386).

[3] This offence is triable either way (Magistrates' Courts Act 1980, Sch 1). For procedure, see ibid, ss 17A–21, in PART I: MAGISTRATES' COURTS, PROCEDURE, ante.

*Bigamy*

7.8659 57. **Bigamy** Whosoever, being married[1], shall marry[2] any other person during the life of the former husband or wife, whether the second marriage shall have taken place in England or Ireland or[3] elsewhere shall be guilty of [an offence], and being convicted thereof shall be liable to imprisonment for any term not exceeding **seven years** [8];
Provided that nothing in this section contained shall extend to any second marriage contracted elsewhere than in England and Ireland by any other than a subject of Her Majesty[4], or to any person marrying a second time, whose husband or wife shall have been continually absent from such person for the space of seven years[5] then last past, and shall not have been known[6] by such person to be living within that time[7] or shall extend to any person who, at the time of such second marriage, shall have been divorced from the bond of the first marriage, or to any person whose former marriage shall have been declared void by the sentence of any court of competent jurisdiction.

[Offences Against the Person Act 1861, s 57 as amended by the Criminal Justice Act 1925, Sch 3, the Criminal Justice Act 1948, s 1 and the Criminal Law Act 1967, s 1 and Sch 3.]

---

1 W was convicted of bigamy in marrying B, he subsequently married C, and in her lifetime married D, and was again indicted for marrying D in the lifetime of C. For the defence the previous conviction was proved, and the judge ruled that it lay on the prisoner to prove that his first wife was alive when he married D and C. The CCR held that the onus of proof that the first wife was dead at the time of the marriage with C was on the prosecution, and quashed the conviction (*R v Willshire* (1881) 6 QBD 366, 45 JP 375). Where a prisoner charged with bigamy alleged that his first marriage was invalid on the ground that when he married, his first wife had a husband living, the Common Sergeant held that it was for the prisoner, after the prosecution had proved his two marriages, to prove that the first husband was alive at the time of his (the prisoner's) first marriage (*R v Thomson* (1905) 70 JP 6), or for the accused to prove as a defence that at the time of the second marriage he had reasonable cause to believe, and honestly believed, that his first marriage was void on the ground that the woman he then married was already married (*R v Dolman* [1949] 1 All ER 813); applied, *R v King* [1964] 1 QB 285, [1963] 3 All ER 561. The relevant time for determining whether a person was married within the meaning of s 57 is the time of the alleged bigamous marriage (*R v Sagoo* [1975] QB 885, [1975] 2 All ER 926, 139 JP 604, CA).

The first marriage must be strictly proved by production of the certificate of the registrar of marriages; an admission by the prisoner is insufficient (*R v Lindsay* (1902) 66 JP 505). The wife or husband of a person charged with bigamy may be called as a witness either for the prosecution or defence and without the consent of the person charged (Criminal Justice Administration Act 1914, s 28(3)), but as he or she at the trial may elect not to give evidence, it is advisable to call another witness to prove the first marriage.

2 When a married man went through the form of a marriage with his wife's niece, the offence was held to be bigamy, although such marriage would have been void as being within the prohibited degree of affinity (*R v Allen* (1872) LR 1 CCR 367, 36 JP 820). The validity of the second marriage is immaterial (*R v Robinson* [1938] 1 All ER 301). So also when a married man married a woman under a false Christian name, and there was no evidence whether the woman knew of the name being false, a conviction was affirmed (*R v Rea* (1872) LR 1 CCR 365, 36 JP 422).

Where a prisoner alleges that, at the time of his second marriage, he *bona fide* believed that his first marriage was invalid, he must prove that he had such a belief and circumstances justify it (*R v Thomson* (1905) 70 JP 6). This decision was followed in *R v Connatty* (1919) 83 JP 292 and applied by the Court of Criminal Appeal in *R v King* [1964] 1 QB 285, [1963] 3 All ER 561, *R v Wheat, infra*, distinguished, An erroneous, but *bona fide*, belief on reasonable grounds, that the accused had been divorced is no defence. Dictum in *R v Thomson, supra*, doubted (*R v Stocks* [1921] 2 KB 119, 85 JP 203).

3 The English courts have jurisdiction to try a British subject for bigamy where the bigamous marriage takes place in a foreign country (*R v Earl Russell* [1901] AC 446). In order to prove a foreign marriage (other than in civil cases (*Spivack v Spivack* (1930) 94 JP 91)), expert evidence—by a professional lawyer, or a person peritus virtute officii (*R v Moscovitch* (1927) 138 LT 183)—must be adduced, whether the prisoner relies on it for his defence or the Crown relies on it in a prosecution for bigamy (*R v Naguib* [1917] 1 KB 359, 81 JP 116); Scotland is a foreign country (*R v Povey* (1852) Dears CC 32, 16 JP 745). As to proof of irregular marriages in Scotland, see 172 LTN 246. An Irish marriage, celebrated prior to 1922, may be proved by certified copies of the register (Marriages (Ireland) Act 1844; Registration of Marriages (Ireland) Act 1863), but, if since 1922, it must be proved as a foreign marriage (*Todd v Todd* [1961] 2 All ER 881). A Colonial marriage should be proved by an expert in the law of the colony, unless celebrated according to the rites of the Church of England (*Perry v Perry* [1920] P 361). By Orders made under the Evidence (Foreign, Dominion and Colonial Documents) Act 1933 (amended by the Oaths and Evidence (Overseas Authorities and Countries) Act 1963, s 5), duly authenticated certificates of entries in public registers in Belgium, France and Australia may be admitted in evidence (see *Practice Direction* [1955] 2 All ER 465, [1955] 1 WLR 668, *Motture v Motture* [1955] 3 All ER 242n, [1955] 1 WLR 1066). Similar Orders in respect of other parts of the Commonwealth are listed in Halsbury's Statutory Instruments, Vol 7, Evidence.

4 It is not necessary to aver in the indictment that the prisoner is a subject of Her Majesty (*R v Audley* [1907] 1 KB 383, 71 JP 101).

5 The defence of seven years' absence of the lawful husband or wife continues to be available in relation to a third or subsequent "marriage" (*R v Taylor* [1950] 2 KB 368, [1950] 2 All ER 170).

6 *Bona fide* belief on reasonable grounds in the death of the husband or wife before the second marriage is a good defence although the seven years have not expired. This case was reserved for the consideration of all the judges (*R v Tolson* (1889) 23 QBD 168, 54 JP 4): and an honest and reasonable belief that at the time of the second ceremony the first marriage had been dissolved is a defence to bigamy (*R v Gould* [1968] 2 QB 65, [1968] 1 All ER 849, 132 JP 209).

7 The husband had not been heard of for seventeen years, but it was incumbent on the prosecution to prove that he was alive at the date of the second marriage, it being a question of fact (*R v Lumley* (1869) LR 1 CCR 196, 33 JP 326). The burden of proof as to the knowledge of the prisoner that his first wife was alive within seven years of the second marriage, where the parties had separated *by consent*, was in *R v Curgerwen* (1865) LR 1 CCR 1, 29 JP 820 (followed in *R v Lund* (1921) 16 Cr App Rep 31; and *R v Peake* (1922) 17 Cr App Rep 22), held to be on the prosecution. Cf *Parkinson v Parkinson* [1939] 3 All ER 108. Also when the absence is caused through wilful desertion and such absence is proved, it lies on the prosecution to show not merely that the person charged had the means of knowledge, but that he or she knew that the first wife or husband, as the case may be, was living (per Kennedy, J, *R v Faulkes* (1903) 19 TLR 250). But in *R v Jones* (1883) 11 QBD 118, 47 JP 535, where prisoner was married in 1865, and went through a ceremony of marriage with another woman in 1882, and there was no evidence how long the married parties lived together or when they last saw each other, it was held not necessary to prove affirmatively that at the time of the second marriage the prisoner knew his first wife was alive, and prisoner was rightly convicted.

8 Triable either way; see the Magistrates' Courts Act 1980, s 17 and Sch 1, also ss 17A–21 (procedure) and s 32 (penalty) in Part I: Magistrates' Courts, Procedure, ante. In *R v Crowhurst* [1979] Crim LR 399, the Court of Appeal held that sentences for bigamy must vary in accordance with the circumstances of the case; where there was deception of the innocent party, with some injury resulting, an immediate custodial sentence was necessary, the length depending on

the gravity of the injury inflicted. In other cases a non-custodial sentence might be appropriate. Justices' clerks have been asked by Home Office Circular Letter of 17th February 1981 to notify the General Register Office of all convictions in magistrates' courts of bigamy. Notification by way of a copy of the certificate of conviction or finding of guilt should be sent, together with, if available, the addresses of the defendant and the person with whom the bigamous marriage was contracted to the Marriage Section, General Register Office, St Catherine's House, 10 Kingsway, London, WC2B 6JP.

*Attempts to procure abortion*[1]

7.8660 **58. Administering drugs or using instruments to procure abortion** Every woman being with child who, with intent to procure her own[2] miscarriage, shall unlawfully administer to herself any poison or other noxious[3] thing[4], or shall unlawfully use any instrument or other means whatsoever with the like intent, and whosoever with intent[5] to procure the miscarriage[6] of any woman, whether she be or be not with child, shall unlawfully administer to her or cause to be taken by her any poison or other noxious thing[4], or shall unlawfully[7] use any instrument or other means whatsoever with the like intent[8] shall be guilty of an offence, and being convicted thereof shall be liable to imprisonment for life.

Offences Against the Person Act 1861, s 58 as amended by the Statute Law Revision Act 1892, the Statute Law Revision (No 2) Act 1893, the Criminal Justice Act 1948, s 1 and the Criminal Law Act 1967, s 1.

1 These sections should be read in conjunction with the Abortion Act 1967, post.

2 When the woman is charged it is necessary to show that she was actually with child, which is not necessary where another person is charged with the offence, but she may be charged with conspiring with others to commit the offence although not in fact pregnant (see *R v Whitchurch* (1890) 24 QBD 420, 54 JP 472). A person who consents to another using an instrument upon her with intent to procure miscarriage can be convicted of aiding and abetting the felony under the second part of the section, although there is no allegation in the indictment that the accused was "with child" at the time of the offence (*R v Sockett* (1908) 72 JP 428). A conviction may be affirmed, although there is no proof that the stuff given was noxious otherwise than from its effects (*R v Hollis* (1873) 37 JP 582).

3 The offence is complete if the thing is noxious "as administered", although innoxious if differently administered (*R v Cramp* (1880) 5 QBD 307, 44 JP 411). Taking a thing in the belief that it is capable of procuring abortion, though in fact it is not, is an attempt to commit the crime (*R v Brown* (1899) 63 JP 790). Inciting a woman to take the thing believing it to be capable of procuring abortion is inciting her to commit the offence, although the commission of the offence in the manner proposed is impossible (*id.*). Where the accused was indicted for attempting to administer noxious things to a pregnant woman, and for inciting her to attempt to administer to herself noxious things with intent to procure her own miscarriage, ROWLATT, J, directed the jury that the substantial question was whether the things were noxious in the sense of being abortives to the knowledge of the accused (*R v Osborn* (1919) 84 JP 63).

4 "Thing" must be some sort of object or instrument, rather than a surgical procedure; thus, where a defendant sought to trick a woman into having an abortion at a clinic no offence was committed under the section: *R v Ahmed* [2010] EWCA Crim 1949, [2011] QB 512, [2011] 2 WLR 197, [2011] Cr App R 1, [2011] Crim LR 158.

5 Evidence of the use of instruments with intent to procure abortion on previous occasions was admitted to prove a systematic course of conduct on the part of the prisoner, and the intent with which the prisoner used the instruments (*R v Bond* (1906) 2 KB 389, 70 JP 424). An accomplice's evidence of a previous operation (*R v Lovegrove* [1920] 3 KB 643, 85 JP 75), and also, on a charge of administering under this section, of the use of instruments on another occasion, has been admitted (*R v Starkie* [1922] 2 KB 275, 86 JP 74).

6 The "morning-after pill" is not an abortificiant and does not procure a miscarriage as it prevents fertilisation or implantation and the word "miscarriage" presupposes that the fertilized ovum has become implanted in the uterus (*R (Smeaton) v Secretary of State for Health* [2002] EWHC 610 (Admin), [2002] 2 FCR 193, [2002] 2 FLR 146).

7 If a doctor using his best judgment comes to the opinion that the continuance of the pregnancy will endanger the life of the mother or make her a physical or mental wreck, he is not only entitled, but it is his duty, to perform the operation, and the operation will not be unlawful. The onus is on the prosecution to prove the negative beyond reasonable doubt. The desire of the woman to be relieved of her pregnancy is no justification (charge of MACNAGHTEN, J, to the jury in *R v Bourne* [1939] 1 KB 687, [1938] 3 All ER 615).

8 Upon the trial for murder or manslaughter of any child or for infanticide or for abortion, the jury may find the accused guilty of child destruction (Infant Life (Preservation) Act 1929, s 2(2)).

7.8661 **59. Procuring drugs etc to cause abortion** Whosoever shall unlawfully supply or procure[1] any poison or other noxious thing, or any instrument or thing whatsoever, knowing that the same is intended[2] to be unlawfully used or employed with intent to procure the miscarriage[3] of any woman, whether she be or be not with child shall be guilty of [an offence], and being convicted thereof shall be liable to imprisonment not exceeding **five years**.

[Offences Against the Person Act 1861, s 59 as amended by the Statute Law Revision Act 1892, the Criminal Justice Act 1948 s 1 and the Criminal Law Act 1967, s 1.]

1 In this context, the word "procure" has its ordinary meaning of getting possession of something from another person (*R v Mills* [1963] 1 QB 522, [1963] 1 All ER 202, 127 JP 176).

2 It is not necessary that the woman herself whose miscarriage it is intended to procure should intend to use the drug, or that any other person than the one who procured the drug should intend it to be used for the purpose of procuring a miscarriage (*R v Hillman* (1863) Le & Ca 343, 27 JP 805).

3 See note to "miscarriage" in s 58, ante.

*Concealing the birth of a child*

7.8662 **60. Concealing the birth of a child** If any woman[1] shall be delivered of a child, every person who shall by any secret disposition of the dead body[2] of the said child, whether such child died before, at, or after its birth, endeavour to conceal the birth[3] thereof shall be guilty of [an offence and being convicted thereof shall be liable[4] to be imprisoned for any term not exceeding **two years**.

[Offences Against the Person Act 1861, s 60 as amended by the Criminal Justice Act 1948, s 1 and the Criminal Law Act 1967, s 1 and Schs 2 and 3.]

1 There is no authority to order surgical examination of a woman's person. An action was successfully brought upon such an order against a justice and two doctors (*Agnew v Jobson* (1877) 42 JP 424, Treat 434). But if the woman submit to the examination, although reluctantly, it must be shown that what was done was against her will, in the absence of evidence of force, violence, or coercion (*Latter v Braddell* (1881) 45 JP 520).

[2] The concealment must be from a desire to keep the world at large in ignorance of the birth, and not from a desire to escape individual anger (*R v Morris* (1848) 2 Cox CC 489). There must be a concealment of the fact of birth, and that concealment must be carried out by the secret disposition of the dead body (*R v Rosenberg* (1906) 70 JP 264). The place of concealment need not be intended as the final deposit. Placing the dead body between the bed and the mattress was held under the repealed statutes to be a sufficient disposition of the body (see *R v Goldthorpe* (1841) Car & M 335, and *R v Perry* (1855) Dears CC 471). Throwing the dead body over a wall into a field, such wall forming the boundary of the yard of a public-house, was held to be evidence of "secret disposition" (*R v Brown* (1870) LR 1 CCR 244, 34 JP 436, 22 LT 484). Although placing the dead body in an unlocked box is not of itself sufficient evidence of concealment, all the attendant circumstances may be taken into consideration (*R v Cook* (1870) 22 LT 216). Under the present statute any "secret disposition" is sufficient, and this section is so framed as to include every person who uses any endeavours to conceal the birth, and it is immaterial whether "there be any evidence against the mother or not". A woman who endeavours to conceal the birth by depositing the child, while alive, in a field, leaving the infant to die from exposure, cannot be convicted under this section, which relates to the secret disposition of the *dead* body of a child (*R v May* (1867) 31 JP 356).

[3] An indictment for endeavouring to conceal the birth failed for want of proof of the child's death (*R v Bell* (1874) Ir R 8 CL 542); also for insufficient evidence to identify the body found as the child of which the woman was said to have been delivered (*R v Williams* (1871) 11 Cox CC 684). The confession of the accused is sufficient evidence to convict for concealment of birth, although no dead body is found (per Ridley, J, *R v Kersey* (1908) 21 Cox CC 690).

[4] Triable either way; see Magistrates' Courts Act 1980, s 17 and Sch 1, also ss 17A–21 (procedure) and s 32 (penalty) in Part I: Magistrates' Courts, Procedure, ante.

*Making gunpowder to commit offences and searching for the same*

7.8663 **64. Making or having gunpowder etc with intent to commit offence** Whosoever shall knowingly have in his possession, or make or manufacture[1] any gunpowder, explosive substance, or any dangerous or noxious thing, or any machine, engine, instrument, or thing, with intent, by means thereof, to commit, or for the purpose of enabling any other person to commit, any offence mentioned in this Act[2] shall be guilty of an offence and on being convicted thereof shall be liable, at the discretion of the court, to be imprisoned for any term not exceeding **two years**.

[Offences Against the Person Act 1861, s 64 as amended by the Statute Law Revision (No 2) Act 1893, the Criminal Justice Act 1948, Sch 10, the Sexual Offences Act 1956, Sch 4 and the Criminal Law Act 1967, s 10 and Sch 2.]

[1] See also the Explosive Substances Act 1883, ss 3, 4, in this Part: title Health and Safety, ante.

[2] Section 65 empowers a justice to grant a search warrant for the purposes of s 64.

# Infant Life (Preservation) Act 1929

(19 & 20 Geo 5 c 34)

7.8664 **1. Punishment for child destruction[1]** (1) Subject as hereinafter in this subsection provided, any person who, with intent to destroy the life of a child capable of being born alive[2], by any wilful act causes a child to die before it has an existence independent of its mother, shall be guilty of child destruction and shall be liable on conviction thereof on indictment to imprisonment for **life:** Provided that no person shall be found guilty of an offence under this section unless it is proved that the act which caused the death of the child was not done in good faith for the purpose only of preserving the life of the mother[3].

(2) For the purposes of this Act, evidence that a woman had at any material time been pregnant for a period of twenty-eight weeks or more shall be *prima facie* proof that she was at that time pregnant of a child capable of being born alive.

[Infant Life (Preservation) Act 1929, s 1.]

[1] See also the Infanticide Act 1938, post, and the Offences Against the Person Act 1861 ss 58, 59 (abortion). On the trial of a person charged with murder or manslaughter of a child or with infanticide there may be a verdict of guilty of child destruction (Infant Life (Preservation) Act 1929 s 2(2), and on a trial for child destruction there may be a verdict of guilty under s 58 of the 1861 Act (Infant Life (Preservation) Act 1929, s 2(3)).

[2] A foetus of between 18 and 21 weeks which if delivered by hysterotomy would never be capable of breathing either naturally or artificially, is not a "child capable of being born alive"; abortion thereof would not constitute an offence under this section (*C v S* [1988] QB 135, [1987] 1 All ER 1230, [1987] 2 FLR 505, CA).

[3] See *R v Bourne* [1939] 1 KB 687, [1938] 3 All ER 615, noted to the Offences Against the Person Act 1861, s 58, ante.

# Infanticide Act 1938

(1 & 2 Geo 6 c 36)

7.8665 **1. Offence of infanticide** (1) Where a woman by any wilful[1] act or omission causes the death of her child being a child under the age of twelve months, but at the time of the act or omission the balance of her mind was disturbed by reason of her not having fully recovered from the effect of giving birth to the child or by reason of the effect of lactation consequent upon the birth of the child, then, if the circumstances were such that but for this Act the offence would have amounted to murder or manslaughter, she shall be guilty of infanticide[2], and may for such offence be dealt with and punished as if she had been guilty of the offence of manslaughter of the child.

(2) Where upon the trial of a woman for the murder of her child, being a child under the age of twelve months, the jury are of opinion that she by any wilful act or omission caused its death, but at the time of the act or omission the balance of her mind was disturbed by reason of her not having fully recovered from the effect of giving birth to the child or by reason of the effect of lactation consequent upon the birth of the child, then the jury may, if the circumstances were such that but for the provisions of this Act they might have returned a verdict of murder or manslaughter, return in lieu thereof a verdict of infanticide[1].

[Infanticide Act 1938, s 1(1), (2) as amended by the Coroners and Justice Act 2009, s 57.]

[1] It was stated obiter in *R v Gore* [2007] EWCA Crim 2789, [2008] Crim LR 388 that there was no requirement that all the ingredients of murder had to be proved before a defendant could be convicted of infanticide, contrary to s 1 of the Infanticide Act 1938; the opening words of s 1(1) expressly contain the mens rea of the offence and if an intention to kill or cause grievous bodily harm had to be proved the word "wilful" would be superfluous.

[2] On a trial of a person for infanticide there may be a verdict of child destruction; see the Infant Life (Preservation) Act 1929, s 2(2). A coroner's inquest is not to find a person guilty of infanticide; Criminal Law Act 1977, s 56. The Consent of the Attorney-General will be required to institute proceedings where the mother has previously been convicted of an offence committed in circumstances alleged to be connected with the death (Law Reform (Year and a Day Rule) Act 1996, s 2(2)(*b*) .

# Homicide Act 1957

(5 & 6 Eliz 2 c 11)

*Murder*[1]

7.8666 **1. Abolition of "constructive malice"** (1) Where a person kills another in the course of furtherance of some other offence, the killing shall not amount to murder unless done with the same malice aforethought (express or implied[2]) as is required for a killing to amount to murder when not done in the course or furtherance of another offence.

(2) For the purposes of the foregoing subsection, a killing done in the course or for the purpose of resisting an officer of justice, or of resisting or avoiding or preventing a lawful arrest, or of effecting or assisting an escape or rescue from legal custody, shall be treated as a killing in the course or furtherance of an offence.

[Homicide Act 1957, s 1.]

[1] **Murder** is an offence at common law, For manslaughter, see the Offences Against the Person Act 1861 s 5 ante.

Death may be proved by circumstantial evidence, although no body is found (*R v Onufrejczyk* [1955] 1 QB 388, [1955] 1 All ER 247). In charges of murder, the Crown must prove (*a*) death as a result of the voluntary act of the accused, and (*b*) malice of the accused; malice is a question for the jury, and, if the jury are satisfied with the prisoner's explanation, or, on a review of all the evidence, are left in reasonable doubt whether, even if his explanation is not accepted, the act was unintentional or provoked, the prisoner is entitled to be acquitted (*Woolmington v DPP* [1935] AC 462, HL; explained in *Mancini v DPP* [1942] AC 1, [1941] 3 All ER 272, HL). The defence of duress is not available to a person charged with murder whether as principal in the first degree (the actual killer) or as a principal in the second degree (the aider and abettor) (*R v Howe* [1987] AC 417, [1987] 1 All ER 771). Common sense standards apply when considering the defence of self-defence, in deciding whether more force was used than was necessary in the circumstances; see *R v Shannon* [1980] Crim LR 438 and *R Oatridge* [1992] Crim LR 205 (which also deals with mistaken belief). In order to reduce a charge of murder to manslaughter, it has to be shown that the provocative conduct relied on had suddenly and temporarily deprived the accused of the power of self-control (*R v Thornton* [1992] 1 All ER 306), 96 Cr App Rep 112).

Manslaughter may be committed where unlawful injury is deliberately inflicted either to a child in utero or to a mother carrying a child in utero. The fact that the death of the child is caused solely in consequence of injury to the mother rather than as a consequence of injury to the foetus does not negative any liability for manslaughter (*A-G's Reference (No 3 of 1994)* [1998] 1 Cr App Rep 91, [1997] Crim LR 829, HL).

If the injury caused by the accused causes death, it matters not that the victim might have survived had he not refused a blood transfusion; persons who use violence must take their victims as they find them (*R v Blaue* [1975] 3 All ER 446, 139 JP 841). Where supervening events occur which may have had some causative effect leading to the victim's death, the prosecution must prove that the injuries inflicted by the defendant were a significant cause of death (*R v Mellor* [1996] 2 Cr App Rep 245, [1996] Crim LR 743, CA).

**Intent:** Before an act can be murder, it must be "aimed at someone" and in addition must be committed with (1) intention to cause death or (2) intention to cause grievous bodily harm or (3) intention to expose someone to a known serious risk of death or grievous bodily harm resulting from acts committed deliberately and without lawful excuse. It does not matter whether the defendant desired those consequences or not, nor that the act and intention were aimed at someone other than the eventual victim. Without one of the three types of intention, however, the mere fact that the defendant acts in the knowledge that grievous bodily harm is likely, or highly likely to ensue is not by itself enough to constitute murder (*Hyam v DPP* [1975] AC 55, [1974] 2 All ER 41, 138 JP 374, HL). Knowledge or foresight of consequences is at best material from which the jury, properly directed, may infer intention when considering a crime of specific intent, such as murder (*R v Moloney* [1985] AC 905, [1985] 1 All ER 1025, 149 JP 369, HL; considered in *R v Hancock and R v Shankland*) [1986] AC 455, [1986] 1 All ER 641, 150 JP 33). For proof of criminal intent, see the Criminal Law Act 1967, s 8 in PART I: MAGISTRATES' COURTS, PROCEDURE, ante. A coroner's inquest is not to find a person guilty of murder; Criminal Law Act 1977, s 56. In the case of a joint enterprise, proof is necessary that the principal party intended to kill or do serious harm at the time he killed; the secondary party must be proved to have lent himself to a criminal enterprise involving the inflicting, if necessary, of serious harm or death or have had an express or tacit understanding with the principal party that such harm or death should, if necessary, be inflicted (*R v Slack* [1989] QB 775, [1989] 3 All ER 90, CA). See also *R v Roberts* [1993] 1 All ER 583, (1993) 96 Cr App Rep 291. As to withdrawal from a joint enterprise *R v Rook* [1993] 2 All ER 955.

**Procedure:** The former common law rule that for the purposes of offences involving death and of suicide, an act or omission was conclusively presumed not to have caused a person's death if more than a year and a day elapsed before he died has been abolished (Law Reform (Year and a Day Rule) Act 1996, s 1). Proceedings in respect of an allegation of *murder, manslaughter, infanticide* or any other offence of which one of the elements is causing a person's death or aiding, abetting, counselling or procuring a person's suicide where the injury alleged to have caused the death was sustained more than three years before the death occurred or the person has previously been convicted of an offence committed in circumstances alleged to be connected with the death, may only be instituted by or with the consent of the Attorney General (s 2).

For the obligation placed on the clerk to the justices to notify the coroner, who is responsible for holding an inquest, or the making of a charge of murder, manslaughter or infanticide and of the result of the proceedings before the court, see the Coroners Act 1988, s 17, in this PART, title CORONERS, ante. If it appears to the court from a written statement of means furnished by the accused that his means are such that he requires assistance in meeting the costs of legal representation, he must be granted representation on committal for trial for murder (Legal Aid Act 1988, s 21); and he may be granted representation (which may include representation by counsel) for the committal proceedings; see the Legal Aid in Criminal and Care Proceedings (General) Regulations 1989, regs 40, 44 and 48 in PART I: MAGISTRATES' COURTS, PROCEDURE, ante.

In *R v Vernege* [1982] 1 All ER 403, [1982] 1 WLR 293 the Court of Appeal stated that in committal proceedings for murder, a proper consideration for the magistrates to take into account when considering bail is that in his own interests the accused should be examined by a prison doctor so that the various relevant matters affecting his state of mind at the time of the offence may be considered by the doctor, and in particular the possibility of a defence of diminished responsibility.

[2] Implied malice will arise where the act of the accused which causes death is voluntary and done with intent to cause grievous bodily harm. A court is not bound to infer that a person intended or foresaw a result of his actions by reason only of its being a natural or probable consequence thereof, but shall decide whether he did intend or foresee that result from all the evidence, drawing from the evidence such inferences as appear to be proper: see the Criminal Justice Act 1967, s 8, ante.

7.8667 2. **Persons suffering from diminished responsibility** (1) A person ("D") who kills or is a party to the killing of another is not to be convicted of murder if D was suffering from an abnormality of mental functioning[1] which—

(*a*) arose from a recognised medical condition,

(*b*) substantially impaired[2] D's ability to do one or more of the things mentioned in subsection (1A), and

(*c*) provides an explanation for D's acts and omissions in doing or being a party to the killing.

(1A) Those things are—

(*a*) to understand the nature of D's conduct;

(*b*) to form a rational judgment;

(*c*) to exercise self-control.

(1B) For the purposes of subsection (1)(*c*), an abnormality of mental functioning provides an explanation for D's conduct if it causes, or is a significant contributory factor in causing, D to carry out that conduct.

(2) On a charge of murder, it shall be for the defence to prove[3] that the person charged is by virtue of this section not liable to be convicted of murder.

(3) A person who but for this section would be liable, whether as principal or as accessory, to be convicted of murder shall be liable instead to be convicted of manslaughter.

(4) The fact that one party to a killing is by virtue of this section not liable to be convicted of murder shall not affect the question whether the killing amounted to murder in the case of any other party to it.

[Homicide Act 1957, s 2 as amended by the Coroners and Justice Act 2009, s 52.]

---

[1] It is not appropriate to consider only partial or borderline insanity as amounting to diminished responsibility (*R v Seers* (1984) 149 JP 124, [1985] Crim LR 315, CA). For whether alcohol dependency syndrome gives rise to a defence of diminished responsibility, see *R v Wood* [2008] EWCA Crim 1305, [2008] 3 All ER 898, [2009] 1 WLR 496, [2008] 2 Cr App Rep 34, and for further guidance for juries, *R v Stewart* [2009] EWCA Crim 593, [2010] 1 All ER 260, [2009] 2 Cr App Rep 50, *R v Williams* [2013] EWCA Crim 2749, [2014] 1 Cr App Rep 325.

[2] The words "substantially impaired" in the new s 2(1)(*b*) do not provide a different test from that previously applied to "substantial impairment" in the original enactment: *R v Brown* [2011] EWCA Crim 2796, [2012] 2 Cr App Rep (S) 156, [2012] Crim LR 223.

As a matter simply of dictionary definition, "substantial" can mean more than trivial, or important or weighty. In the context of diminished responsibility, the authorities establish that the latter sense is the correct one:

"36 This use of the expression accords with principle. Diminished responsibility effects a radical alteration in the offence of which a defendant is convicted. The context is a homicide. By definition, before any question of diminished responsibility can arise, the homicide must have been done with murderous intent, to kill or to do grievous bodily harm, and without either provocation or self-defence. Whilst it is true that at one end of the scale of responsibility the sentence in a case of diminished responsibility may be severe, or indeed an indefinite life sentence owing to the risk which the defendant presents to the public, the difference between a conviction for murder and a conviction for manslaughter is of considerable importance both for the public and for those connected with the deceased. It is just that where a substantial impairment is demonstrated, the defendant is convicted of the lesser offence and not of murder. But it is appropriate, as it always has been, for the reduction to the lesser offence to be occasioned where there is a weighty reason for it and not merely a reason which just passes the trivial. . . .

39 The sense in which "substantially impaired" is used in relation to diminished responsibility is, for the reasons set out above, the second of the two senses. It is not synonymous with 'anything more than merely trivial impairment'.

40 It does not follow that it is either necessary or wise to attempt a re-definition of 'substantially' for the jury. First, in many cases the debate here addressed will simply not arise. There will be many cases where the suggested condition is such that, if the defendant was affected by it at the time, the impairment could only be substantial, and the issue is whether he was or was not so affected. Second, if the occasion for elucidation does arise, the judge's first task is to convey to the jury, by whatever form of words suits the case before it, that the statute uses an ordinary English word and that they must avoid substituting a different one for it. Third, however, various phrases have been used in the cases to convey the sense in which 'substantially' is understood in this context. The words used by the Court of Appeal in the second certified question in the present case ('significant and appreciable') are one way of putting it, providing that the word 'appreciable' is treated not as being synonymous with merely recognisable but rather with the connotation of being considerable. Other phrases used have been 'a serious degree of impairment' (*Seers*), 'not total impairment but substantial' (*Ramchurn*) or 'something far wrong' (*Galbraith*). These are acceptable ways of elucidating the sense of the statutory requirement but it is neither necessary nor appropriate for this court to mandate a particular form of words in substitution for the language used by Parliament. The jury must understand that 'substantially' involves a matter of degree, and that it is for it to use the collective good sense of its members to say whether the condition in the case it is trying reaches that level or not . . .

43 It follows that the questions certified by the Court of Appeal should be answered as follows:

(1) Ordinarily in a murder trial where diminished responsibility is in issue the judge need not direct the jury beyond the terms of the statute and should not attempt to define the meaning of 'substantially'. Experience has shown that the issue of its correct interpretation is unlikely to arise in many cases. The jury should normally be given to understand that the expression is an ordinary English word, that it imports a question of degree, and that whether in the case before it the impairment can properly be described as substantial is for it to resolve.

(2) If, however, the jury has been introduced to the question of whether any impairment beyond the merely trivial will suffice, or if it has been introduced to the concept of a spectrum between the greater than trivial

and the total, the judge should explain that whilst the impairment must indeed pass the merely trivial before it need be considered, it is not the law that any impairment beyond the trivial will suffice. The judge should likewise make this clear if a risk arises that the jury might misunderstand the import of the expression; whether this risk arises or not is a judgment to be arrived at by the trial judge who is charged with overseeing the dynamics of the trial. Diminished responsibility involves an impairment of one or more of the abilities listed in the statute to an extent which the jury judges to be substantial, and which it is satisfied significantly contributed to his committing the offence. Illustrative expressions of the sense of the word may be employed so long as the jury is given clearly to understand that no single synonym is to be substituted for the statutory word: see para 40 above." (per Lord Hughes JSC in *R v Golds* [2016] UKSC 61, [2016] 1 WLR 5231)

3 Section 2(2) does not require the defendant to disprove an element of the offence but to establish an exception or excuse; even if the reverse onus it imposes might impact on the presumption of innocence, it does not constitute an unwarranted infringement of art 6(2) of the ECHR: *R v Foye* [2013] EWCA Crim 475, (2013) 177 JP 449. It was held in *R v Dowds* [2012] EWCA Crim 281, [2012] 3 All ER 154, [2012] 1 WLR 2576 that, voluntary acute intoxication, from alcohol or from other substances, was not capable of founding the partial defence of diminished responsibility. The amendments made to s 2 by the Coroners and Justice Act 2009 had not been intended to reverse that well-established rule.

Where, however, there is uncontradicted medical evidence which makes out the defence of diminished responsibility, the judge should not leave a count of murder to go before the jury: *R v Brennan* [2014] EWCA Crim 2387, [2015] 1 Cr App Rep 161, [2015] Crim LR 290.

In *R v Golds*, supra, the following guidance was given:

"49 Given the answers of the psychiatrist in *Brennan* and the state of the evidence, it is clear that the Crown could not properly ask the jury to convict of murder unless it was to reject one or more parts of the expert evidence. Certainly a jury is not bound by the expert. In some cases, pre-planning, especially involving meticulous preparations, may indicate self-control which gives grounds for rejecting an opinion that self-control was substantially impaired. In others, there may be legitimate grounds for asking the jury to disagree about the level of impairment. In yet further cases, it may be perfectly proper to ask the jury to conclude that it was the drink or drugs which led to the killing, whilst the underlying mental condition was in the background. That is not by any means an exhaustive catalogue of questions which a jury may properly be invited to decide. However, as the Court of Appeal rightly held, if the jury is to be invited to reject the expert opinion, some rational basis for doing so must at least be suggested, and none had been at trial nor was on appeal. It is not open to the Crown in this kind of situation simply to invite the jury to convict of murder without suggesting why the expert evidence ought not to be accepted. In particular, it would not have been a proper basis for rejecting diminished responsibility that the circumstances of the killing had been particularly violent or sadistic. It is a well-known factor in such cases that such brutality may (understandably) be taken by a jury to point away from the partial defence; sometimes it may truly do so, but not infrequently it is the product of the mental disorder.

50 It may be agreed that the ordinary principles of *R v Galbraith* are capable of being applied in a trial where the sole issue is diminished responsibility. A court ought, however, to be cautious about doing so, and for several reasons. First, a murder trial is a particularly sensitive event. If the issue is diminished responsibility, a killing with murderous intent must, ex hypothesi, have been carried out. If a trial is contested, it is of considerable importance that the verdict be that of the jury. Second, the onus of proof in relation to diminished responsibility lies on the defendant, albeit on the balance of probabilities rather than to the ordinary criminal standard. The *Galbraith* process is generally a conclusion that no jury, properly directed, could be satisfied that the Crown has proved the relevant offence so that it is sure. In the context of diminished responsibility, murder can only be withdrawn from the jury if the judge is satisfied that no jury could fail to find that the defendant has proved it. Thirdly, a finding of diminished responsibility is not a single-issue matter; it requires the defendant to prove that the answer to each of the four questions set out in para 8 above is 'yes'. Whilst the effect of the changes in the law has certainly been to emphasise the importance of medical evidence, causation (question 4) is essentially a jury question. So, for the reasons explained above, is question 3: whether the impairment of relevant ability(ies) was substantial. That the judge may entertain little doubt about what he thinks the right verdict ought to be is not sufficient reason in this context, any more than in any other, for withdrawing from the jury issues which are properly theirs to decide.

51 Where, however, in a diminished responsibility trial the medical evidence supports the plea and is uncontradicted, the judge needs to ensure that the Crown explains the basis on which it is inviting the jury to reject that evidence. He needs to ensure that the basis advanced is one which the jury can properly adopt. If the facts of the case give rise to it, he needs to warn the jury that brutal killings may be the product of disordered minds and that planning, whilst it may be relevant to self-control, may well be consistent with disordered thinking. While he needs to make it clear to the jury that, if there is a proper basis for rejecting the expert evidence, the decision is theirs - that trial is by jury and not by expert - it will also ordinarily be wise to advise the jury against attempting to make themselves amateur psychiatrists, and that if there is undisputed expert evidence the jury will probably wish to accept it, unless there is some identified reason for not doing so. To this extent, the approach of the court in *Brennan* is to be endorsed." (per Lord Hughes SCJ)

7.8668 **4. Suicide pacts** (1) It shall be manslaughter, and shall not be murder, for a person acting in pursuance of a suicide pact between him and another to kill the other or be a party to the other being killed by a third person.

(2) Where it is shown that a person charged with the murder of another killed the other or was a party to his being killed, it shall be for the defence to prove that the person charged was acting in pursuance of a suicide pact between him and the other.

(3) For the purposes of this section "suicide pact" means a common agreement between two or more persons having for its object the death of all of them, whether or not each is to take his own life, but nothing done by a person who enters into a suicide pact shall be treated as done by him in pursuance of the pact unless it is done while he has the settled intention of dying in pursuance of the pact.

[Homicide Act 1957, s 4 as amended by Suicide Act 1961, s 3(2) and 2nd Sch.]

# Suicide Act 1961

(9 & 10 Eliz 2 c 60)

7.8669 **1. Suicide to cease to be a crime** The rule of law whereby it is a crime for a person to commit suicide is hereby abrogated.

[Suicide Act 1961, s 1.]

7.8670 **2. Criminal liability for complicity in another's suicide** (1) A person ("D") commits an offence if—

(*a*) D does an act capable of encouraging or assisting the suicide or attempted suicide of another person, and

(*b*) D's act was intended to encourage or assist suicide or an attempt at suicide.

(1A) The person referred to in subsection (1)(*a*) need not be a specific person (or class of persons) known to, or identified by, D.

(1B) D may commit an offence under this section whether or not a suicide, or an attempt at suicide, occurs.

(1C) An offence under this section is triable on indictment and a person convicted of such an offence is liable to imprisonment for a term not exceeding 14 years[1].

(2) If on the trial of an indictment for murder or manslaughter of a person it is proved that the deceased person committed suicide, and the accused committed an offence under subsection (1) in relation to that suicide, the jury may find the accused guilty of the offence under subsection (1).

(3) The enactments mentioned in the first column of the First Schedule to this Act shall have effect subject to the amendments provided for in the second column (which preserve in relation to offences under this section the previous operation of those enactments in relation to murder or manslaughter)[2].

(4) No proceedings shall be instituted for an offence under this section except by or with the consent of the Director of Public Prosecutions[3].

[Suicide Act 1961, s 2 as amended by the Criminal Jurisdiction Act 1975, Sch 6 and the Coroners and Justice Act 2009, s 59.]

---

1 It has yet to be resolved whether the offence under s 2(1) is committed where the suicide occurs outside England and Wales and in a jurisdiction where assisted suicide is legal, though if the assisting occurs within England and Wales it appears that the offence is prosecutable: see *R (Purdy) v DPP (Society for the Protection of Unborn Children intervening)* [2009] UKHL 45, [2010] 1 AC 345, [2009] 4 All ER 1147, [2009] 3 WLR 403 and the academic opinions referred to therein. For the obligation placed on the clerk to the justices to notify the coroner, who is responsible for holding an inquest where a death has occurred, of a charge under s 2(1) and of the result of the proceedings before the magistrates' court, see the Coroners Act 1988, 17.

2 The Supreme Court has declined to declare that the prohibitions on euthanasia and assisted suicide in this section are incompatible with article 8 of the Human Rights Convention. The purpose of the Code for Crown Prosecutors issued under s 10 of the Prosecution of Offences Act 1985, is not to enable those who wish to commit a crime to know in advance whether they will get away with it. It is to ensure that, as far as is possible in practice and appropriate in principle, the DPP's policy is publicly available so that everyone knows what it is, and can see whether it is being applied consistently : *R (Nicklinson) v Ministry of Justice* [2014] UKSC 38, [2015] AC 657,[2014] 3 All ER 843, [2014] 3 WLR 200.

3 The consent of the Attorney General will be required instead of that of the Director of Public Prosecutions in the circumstances prescribed in s 2 of the Law Reform (Year and a Day Rule) Act 1996, see note to the Homicide Act 1957, s 1, ante.

Section 2(4) does not give the Director power to give an undertaking that he will not prosecute an offence under s 2 yet to be committed; his discretion can only be exercised in respect of past events giving rise to a suspicion of the commission of an offence under the section (*R (on the application of Pretty) v DPP* [2001] UKHL 61, [2002] 1 AC 800, [2002] 1 All ER 1, [2002] 1 FCR 1).

The Supreme Court has declined to declare that the prohibitions on euthanasia and assisted suicide in this section are incompatible with article 8 of the Human Rights Convention. The purpose of the Code for Crown Prosecutors issued under s 10 of the Prosecution of Offences Act 1985, is not to enable those who wish to commit a crime to know in advance whether they will get away with it. It is to ensure that, as far as is possible in practice and appropriate in principle, the DPP's policy is publicly available so that everyone knows what it is, and can see whether it is being applied consistently: *R (Nicklinson) v Ministry of Justice* [2014] UKSC 38, [2015] AC 657, [2014] 3 All ER 843, [2014] 3 WLR 200.

7.8671 **2A. Acts capable of encouraging or assisting** (1) If D arranges for a person ("D2") to do an act that is capable of encouraging or assisting the suicide or attempted suicide of another person and D2 does that act, D is also to be treated for the purposes of this Act as having done it.

(2) Where the facts are such that an act is not capable of encouraging or assisting suicide or attempted suicide, for the purposes of this Act it is to be treated as so capable if the act would have been so capable had the facts been as D believed them to be at the time of the act or had subsequent events happened in the manner D believed they would happen (or both).

(3) A reference in this Act to a person ("P") doing an act that is capable of encouraging the suicide or attempted suicide of another person includes a reference to P doing so by threatening another person or otherwise putting pressure on another person to commit or attempt suicide.

[Suicide Act 1961, s 2A as inserted by the Coroners and Justice Act 2009, s 59.]

7.8672 **2B. Course of conduct** A reference in this Act to an act includes a reference to a course of conduct, and a reference to doing an act is to be read accordingly.

[Suicide Act 1961, s 2A as inserted by the Coroners and Justice Act 2009, s 59.]

## Abortion Act 1967

(1967 c 87)

7.8673 **1. Medical termination of pregnancy** (1) Subject to the provisions of this section, a person shall not be guilty of an offence under the law relating to abortion[1], when a pregnancy is terminated by a registered medical practitioner[2] if two registered medical practitioners are of the opinion, formed in good faith[3]—

(*a*) that the pregnancy has not exceeded its twenty-fourth week and that the continuance of the pregnancy would involve risk, greater than if the pregnancy were terminated, of injury to the physical or mental health of the pregnant woman or any existing children of her family; or

(*b*) that the termination is necessary to prevent grave permanent injury to the physical or mental health of the pregnant woman; or (*c*) that the continuance of the pregnancy would involve risk to the life of the pregnant woman, greater than if the pregnancy were terminated; or

(*d*) that there is a substantial risk that if the child were born it would suffer from such physical or mental abnormalities as to be seriously handicapped.

(2) In determining whether the continuance of a pregnancy would involve such risk of injury to health as is mentioned in paragraph (*a*) or (*b*) of subsection (1) of this section, account may be taken of the pregnant woman's actual or reasonably foreseeable environment.

(3) Except as provided by subsection (4) of this section, any treatment for the termination of pregnancy must be carried out in a hospital vested in the Secretary of State for the purposes of his functions under the National Health Service Act 2006 or the National Health Service (Scotland) Act 1978 or in a hospital vested in a Primary Care Trust or a National Health Service trust or an NHS foundation trust or in a place approved for the purposes of this section by the Secretary of State.

(3A) The power under subsection (3) of this section to approve a place includes power, in relation to treatment consisting primarily in the use of such medicines as may be specified in the approval and carried out in such manner as may be so specified, to approve a class of places.

(4) Subsection (3) of this section, and so much of subsection (1) as relates to the opinion of two registered medical practitioners, shall not apply to the termination of a pregnancy by a registered medical practitioner in a case where he is of the opinion, formed in good faith, that the termination is immediately necessary to save the life or to prevent grave permanent injury to the physical or mental health of the pregnant woman.

[Abortion Act 1967, s 1 as amended by the Health Services Act 1980, Sch 1, the National Health Service and Community Care Act 1990, Sch 9, the Human Fertilisation and Embryology Act 1990, s 37, SI 2000/90, the Health and Social Care (Community Health and Standards) Act 2003, Sch 4 and the National Health Service (Consequential Provisions) Act 2006, Sch 1.]

---

1 Ie, ss 58 and 50 of the Offences Against the Person Act 1861, ante, and any rule of law relating to the procurement of abortion (s 6).

2 A pregnancy is "terminated by a registered medical practitioner" when the treatment prescribed and initiated by that practitioner, who remains in charge of it throughout, is carried out in accordance with his directions by qualified nursing staff entrusted with its execution in accordance with accepted medical practice (*Royal College of Nursing v Department of Health and Social Security* [1982] AC 800, [1981] 1 All ER 545.

3 The question of good faith must be determined on the total evidence and not just on the views of medical experts (*R v John Smith* [1974] 1 All ER 376, 138 JP 175).

7.8674 **2. Notification** (1) The Minister of Health in respect of England and Wales, and the Secretary of State in respect of Scotland, shall by statutory instrument make regulations[1] to provide—

(*a*) for requiring any such opinion as is referred to in s 1 of this Act to be certified by the practitioners or practitioner concerned in such form and at such time as may be prescribed by the regulations, and for requiring the preservation and disposal of certificates made for the purposes of the regulations;

(*b*) for requiring any registered medical practitioner who terminates a pregnancy to give notice of the termination and such other information relating to the termination as may be so prescribed;

(*c*) for prohibiting the disclosure, except to such persons or for such purposes as may be so prescribed, of notices given or information furnished pursuant to the regulations.

(2) The information furnished in pursuance of regulations made by virtue of paragraph (*b*) of subsection (1) of this section shall be notified solely to the Chief Medical Officer of the Department of Health, or of the Welsh Office, or of the Scottish Administration.

(3) Any person who wilfully contravenes or wilfully fails to comply with the requirements of regulations under subsection (1) of this section shall be liable on summary conviction to a fine not exceeding **level 5** on the standard scale.

(4) Any statutory instrument made by virtue of this section shall be subject to annulment in pursuance of a resolution of either House of Parliament.

[Abortion Act 1967, s 2 as amended by the Criminal Law Act 1977, Sch 6, the Criminal Justice Act 1982, s 46, SI 1969/388, SI 1988/1843 and SI 1999/1042.]

---

1 See the Abortion Regulations 1991, post.

7.8675 **3. Application of Act to visiting forces, etc** (1) In relation to the termination of a pregnancy in a case where the following conditions are satisfied, that is to say—

(*a*) the treatment for termination of the pregnancy was carried out in a hospital controlled by the proper authorities of a body to which this section applies; and

(*b*) the pregnant woman had at the time of the treatment a relevant association with that body; and

(*c*) the treatment was carried out by a registered medical practitioner or a person who at the time of the treatment was a member of that body appointed as a medical practitioner for that body by the proper authorities of that body,

this Act shall have effect as if any reference in s 1 to a registered medical practitioner and to a hospital vested in the Secretary of State included respectively a reference to such a person as is mentioned in paragraph (*c*) of this subsection and to a hospital controlled as aforesaid, and as if s 2 were omitted.

(2) The bodies to which this section applies are any force which is a visiting force within the meaning of any of the provisions of Part I of the Visiting Forces Act 1952 and any headquarters within the meaning of the Schedule to the International Headquarters and Defence Organisations Act 1964[1]; and for the purposes of this section—

(*a*) a woman shall be treated as having a relevant association at any time with a body to which this section applies if at that time—

(i) in the case of such a force as aforesaid, she had a relevant association within the meaning of the said Part I with the force; and

(ii) in the case of such a headquarters as aforesaid, she was a member of the headquarters or a dependant within the meaning of the Schedule aforesaid of such a member; and

(*b*) any reference to a member of a body to which this section applies shall be construed—

(i) in the case of such a force as aforesaid, as a reference to a member of or of a civilian component of that force within the meaning of the said Part I; and

(ii) in the case of such a headquarters as aforesaid, as a reference to a member of that headquarters within the meaning of the Schedule aforesaid.

[Abortion Act 1967, s 3 as amended by the Health Services Act 1980, Sch 1.]

1 See title ARMED FORCES, ante.

7.8676 **4. Conscientious objection to participation in treatment** (1) Subject to subsection (2) of this section, no person shall be under any duty, whether by contract or by any statutory or other legal requirement, to participate in any treatment authorised by this Act[1] to which he has a conscientious objection:

Provided that in any legal proceedings the burden of proof of conscientious objection shall rest on the person claiming to rely on it.

(2) Nothing in subsection (1) of this section shall affect any duty to participants in treatment which is necessary to save the life or to prevent grave permanent injury to the physical or mental health of a pregnant woman.

(3) *Scotland*

1 This means the whole course of medical treatment bringing about the termination of the pregnancy. It begins with the administration of the drugs designed to induce labour and normally ends with the ending of the pregnancy by delivery of the foetus, placenta and membrane. It would also include the medical and nursing care which is connected with the process of undergoing labour and giving birth - the monitoring of the progress of labour, the administration of pain relief, the giving of advice and support to the patient who is going through it all, the delivery of the foetus, which may require the assistance of forceps or an episiotomy, or in some cases an emergency Caesarian section, and the disposal of the foetus, placenta and membrane. In some cases, there may be specific aftercare which is required as a result of the process of giving birth, such as the repair of an episiotomy. But the ordinary nursing and pastoral care of a patient who has just given birth does not require the authorisation of the 1967 Act: *Greater Glasgow Health Board v Doogan* [2014] UKSC 68, [2015] AC 640, [2015] 2 All ER 1, [2015] 2 WLR 126.

[Abortion Act 1967, s 4.]

7.8677 **5. Supplementary provisions** (1) No offence under the Infant Life (Preservation) Act 1929 shall be committed by a registered medical practitioner who terminates a pregnancy in accordance with the provisions of this Act.

(2) For the purposes of the law relating to abortion, anything done with intent to procure a woman's miscarriage (or, in the case of a woman carrying more than one foetus, her miscarriage of any foetus) is unlawfully done unless authorised by section 1 of this Act and, in the case of a woman carrying more than one foetus, anything done with intent to procure her miscarriage of any foetus is authorised by that section if—

(*a*) the ground for termination of the pregnancy specified in subsection (1)(*d*) of that section applies in relation to any foetus and the thing is done for the purpose of procuring the miscarriage of that foetus, or

(*b*) any of the other grounds for termination of the pregnancy specified in that section applies.

[Abortion Act 1967, s 5 as amended by the Human Fertilisation and Embryology Act 1990, s 37.]

## Tattooing of Minors Act 1969

(1969 c 24)

7.8678 **1. Prohibition of tattooing of minors** It shall be an offence to tattoo[1] a person under the age of eighteen except when the tattoo is performed for medical reasons by a qualified medical practitioner or by a person working under his direction, but it shall be a defence for a person charged to show that at the time the tattoo was performed he had reasonable cause to believe that the person tattooed was of or over the age of eighteen and did in fact so believe.

[Tattooing of Minors Act 1969, s 1.]

1 "Tattoo" means the insertion into the skin of any colouring material designed to leave a permanent mark (Tattooing of Minors Act, s 3).

7.8679 **2. Penalties** Any person committing such an offence shall be liable to a fine not exceeding **level 3** on the standard scale.

[Tattooing of Minors Act 1969, s 2 as amended by the Criminal Justice Act 1982, ss 35, 38 and 46.]

## Internationally Protected Persons Act 1978

(1978 c 17)

**7.8680** This Act[1] implements the Convention on the prevention and punishment of crimes against Internationally Protected Persons adopted by the United Nations General Assembly in 1973. The Act provides that if a person, whether a citizen of the United Kingdom and Colonies or not, outside the United Kingdom—

(*a*) does any act in relation to a protected person (defined to include a Head of State, a Head of Government and an official representative of a State) which if done in the United Kingdom would have made him guilty of murder, manslaughter, rape, assault occasioning actual bodily harm or causing injury, kidnapping, abduction[2], false imprisonment, or certain offences under the Offences against the Person Act 1861 or s 2 of the Explosive Substances Act 1883, or

(*b*) in connection with an attack on premises or a vehicle, ordinarily used by a protected person, does any act which if done in the United Kingdom would have made him guilty of an offence under s 2 of the Explosive Substances Act 1883, or s 1 of the Criminal Damage Act 1971,

he shall in any part of the United Kingdom be guilty of the offences aforesaid of which the Act would have made him guilty if he had done it there. A person shall similarly be guilty of attempting or aiding, abetting, counselling or procuring the commission of such an offence. A person who threatens to commit, or attempts to threaten or aids, abets, counsels or procures the making of such a threat to commit such an offence shall be liable on conviction on indictment to imprisonment for a term not exceeding **ten years** and not exceeding the term of imprisonment to which a person would be liable for the offence constituted by doing the act threatened at the place where the contravention occurs[3].

Proceedings for an offence which would not be an offence apart from the provisions of section 1 of the Act shall not be begun in England and Wales except by or with the consent of the Attorney General.

[Internationally Protected Persons Act 1978, s 1—summarised.]
[Internationally Protected Persons Act 1978, s 2—summarised.]

1 Provision is also made by the Suppression of Terrorism Act 1978, title Extradition etc, ante, for giving United Kingdom courts jurisdiction with respect to offences committed outside the United Kingdom but in a convention country, and in particular offence against a protected person.

2 This reference to "abduction" shall be construed as not including an offence under s 1 of the Child Abduction Act 1984 (Child Abduction Act 1984, s 11(3)).

3 By virtue of the Extradition (Internationally Protected Persons) Order 1979, SI 1979/453 amended by SI 1982/147, SI 1985/1990, SI 1986/2013, SI 1987/454 and 2042 and SI 1988/2244 offences against internationally protected persons which are mentioned in s 1 are made extraditable offences for the purposes of the Extradition Act 1989 in the case of foreign States which are parties to the Convention.

## Taking of Hostages Act 1982[1]

(1982 c 28)

**7.8681 1. Hostage taking** (1) A person, whatever his nationality, who, in the United Kingdom or elsewhere,—

(*a*) detains any other person ("the hostage"), and

(*b*) in order to compel a State, international governmental organisation or person to do or abstain from doing any act, threatens to kill, injure or continue to detain the hostage,

commits an offence.

(2) A person guilty of an offence under this Act shall be liable, on conviction on indictment, to imprisonment for **life**.

[Taking of Hostages Act 1982, s 1.]

1 This Act came into force on 26 November 1982. The Extradition (Taking of Hostages) Order 1985, SI 1985/751 amended by SI 1985/1992, SI 1986/2015, SI 1987/455 and 2044 and SI 1988/2246, applies the Extradition Act 1989 so as to make extraditable the offences described in this Act and attempts to commit such offences, in the case of States Parties to the International Convention against the Taking of Hostages.

***7.8682 2. Prosecution of offences*** *(1)* Proceedings for an offence under this Act shall not be instituted—

(*a*) in England and Wales, except by or with the consent of the Attorney General; and

(*b*) *Northern Ireland.*

(2) *Scotland.*

(3) *Northern Ireland.*

[Taking of Hostages Act, 1982, s 2.]

**7.8683 5.** Application to Channel Islands, Isle of Man, etc[1].

1 The Taking of Hostages Act 1982 (Overseas Territories) Order 1982, SI 1992/1540 amended by SI 1987/455 applies the Act to certain named territories. See also SI 1982/1533 (Jersey), SI 1982/1539 (Guernsey) and SI 1982/1839 (Isle of Man).

# Criminal Justice Act 1988[1]

(1988 c 33)

## PART V[2]

## JURISDICTION, IMPRISONMENT, FINES, ETC

*Jurisdiction*

7.8684 **39. Common assault and battery[3] to be summary offences[4]** Common assault and battery shall be summary offences and a person guilty of either of them shall be liable to a fine not exceeding **level 5** on the standard scale, to imprisonment for a term not exceeding **six months**, or to **both** [5].

[Criminal Justice Act 1988, s 39.]

---

1 For other provisions of the Criminal Justice Act 1988, see in particular PART I: MAGISTRATES' COURTS, PROCEDURE, ante.

2 Part V contains ss 37–40.

3 There are two offences, assault by threats and assault by beating (*DPP v Taylor, DPP v Little* [1992] QB 645, [1992] 1 All ER 299, 155 JP 713, DC). The threat of physical contact or the actual physical contact as the case may be, requires a mental element which is an intention, or recklessness causing another person to apprehend immediate and unlawful violence; see *R v Venna* [1976] QB 421, [1976] 3 All ER 788, CA.

4 An alternative verdict of guilty of common assault on an indictment charging assault occasioning actual bodily harm may not be brought unless the terms of s 40 of this Act (ante, PART I: MAGISTRATES' COURTS, PROCEDURE) are followed (*R v Mearns* [1991] 1 QB 82, [1990] 3 All ER 989, 154 JP 447).

5 Although it is not a necessary ingredient of an offence of common assault that the victim suffer injury, nevertheless the court should take into account, when considering the gravity of the offence and the appropriate sentence, the consequences to the victim. It is not necessary to prefer a more serious charge provided the court's sentencing powers are adequate to reflect the actual gravity of the offending (*R v Nottingham Crown Court, ex p DPP* [1996] 1 Cr App Rep (S) 283, [1995] Crim LR 902).

## PART XI[1]

## MISCELLANEOUS

*Torture*

7.8685 **134. Torture** (1) A public official or person acting in an official capacity, whatever his nationality, commits the offence of torture if in the United Kingdom or elsewhere he intentionally inflicts severe pain or suffering on another in the performance or purported performance of his official duties.

(2) A person not falling within subsection (1) above commits the offence of torture, whatever his nationality, if—

(*a*) in the United Kingdom or elsewhere he intentionally inflicts severe pain or suffering on another at the instigation or with the consent or acquiescence—

(i) of a public official; or

(ii) of a person acting in an official capacity; and

(*b*) the official or other person is performing or purporting to perform his official duties when he instigates the commission of the offence or consents to or acquiesces in it.

(3) It is immaterial whether the pain or suffering is physical or mental and whether it is caused by an act or an omission.

(4) It shall be a defence for a person charged with an offence under this section in respect of any conduct of his to prove that he had lawful authority, justification or excuse for that conduct.

(5) For the purposes of this section "lawful authority, justification or excuse" means—

(*a*) in relation to pain or suffering inflicted in the United Kingdom, lawful authority, justification or excuse under the law of the part of the United Kingdom where it was inflicted;

(*b*) in relation to pain or suffering inflicted outside the United Kingdom—

(i) if it was inflicted by a United Kingdom official acting under the law of the United Kingdom or by a person acting in an official capacity under that law, lawful authority, justification or excuse under that law;

(ii) if it was inflicted by a United Kingdom official acting under the law of any part of the United Kingdom or by a person acting in an official capacity under such law, lawful authority, justification or excuse under the law of the part of the United Kingdom under whose law he was acting; and

(iii) in any other case, lawful authority, justification or excuse under the law of the place where it was inflicted.

(6) A person who commits the offence of torture shall be liable on conviction on indictment to imprisonment for **life**.

[Criminal Justice Act 1988, s 134.]

---

1 Part XI contains ss 133–167.

7.8686 **135. Requirement of Attorney General's consent for prosecutions** Proceedings for an offence under section 134 above shall not be begun—

(*a*) in England and Wales, except by, or with the consent of, the Attorney General; or

(*b*) *Northern Ireland.*

[Criminal Justice Act 1988, s 135.]

**7.8687 138. Application to Channel Islands, Isle of Man and colonies** (1) Her Majesty may by Order[1] in Council make provision for extending sections 134 and 135 above, with such modifications and exceptions as may be specified in the Order, to any of the Channel Islands, the Isle of Man or any colony.

(2)–(3) *Repealed.*

[Criminal Justice Act 1988, s 138 as amended by the Extradition Act 1989, Sch 2.]

[1] See the Criminal Justice Act 1988 (Torture) (Overseas Territories) Order 1988, SI 1988/2242, amended by SI 1992/1715 and SI 2011/2984.

# United Nations Personnel Act 1997

(1997 c 13)

**7.8688 1. Attacks on UN workers** (1) If a person does outside the United Kingdom any act to or in relation to a UN worker which, if he had done it in any part of the United Kingdom, would have made him guilty of any of the offences mentioned in subsection (2), he shall in that part of the United Kingdom be guilty of that offence.

(2) The offences referred to in subsection (1) are—

(*a*) murder, manslaughter, culpable homicide, rape, assault causing injury, kidnapping, abduction and false imprisonment;

(*b*) an offence under section 18, 20, 21, 22, 23, 24, 28, 29, 30 or 47 of the Offences against the Person Act 1861; and

(*c*) an offence under section 2 of the Explosive Substances Act 1883.

[United Nations Personnel Act 1997, s 1.]

**7.8689 2. Attacks in connection with premises and vehicles** (1) If a person does outside the United Kingdom any act, in connection with an attack on relevant premises or on a vehicle ordinarily used by a UN worker which is made when a UN worker is on or in the premises or vehicle, which, if he had done it in any part of the United Kingdom, would have made him guilty of any of the offences mentioned in subsection (2), he shall in that part of the United Kingdom be guilty of that offence.

(2) The offences referred to in subsection (1) are—

(*a*) an offence under section 2 of the Explosive Substances Act 1883;

(*b*) an offence under section 1 of the Criminal Damage Act 1971;

(*c*) an offence under article 3 of the Criminal Damage (Northern Ireland) Order 1977; and

(*d*) wilful fire-raising.

(3) In this section—

"relevant premises" means premises at which a UN worker resides or is staying or which a UN worker uses for the purpose of carrying out his functions as such a worker; and

"vehicle" includes any means of conveyance.

[United Nations Personnel Act 1997, s 2.]

**7.8690 3. Threats of attacks on UN workers** (1) If a person in the United Kingdom or elsewhere contravenes subsection (2) he shall be guilty of an offence.

(2) A person contravenes this subsection if, in order to compel a person to do or abstain from doing any act, he—

(*a*) makes to a person a threat that any person will do an act which is—

(i) an offence mentioned in section 1(2) against a UN worker, or

(ii) an offence mentioned in subsection (2) of section 2 in connection with such an attack as is mentioned in subsection (1) of that section, and

(*b*) intends that the person to whom he makes the threat shall fear that it will be carried out.

(3) A person guilty of an offence under this section shall be liable on conviction on indictment to imprisonment for a term—

(*a*) not exceeding **ten years**, and

(*b*) not exceeding the term of imprisonment to which a person would be liable for the offence constituted by doing the act threatened at the place where the conviction occurs and at the time of the offence to which the conviction relates.

[United Nations Personnel Act 1997, s 3.]

**7.8691 4. Meaning of UN worker** (1) For the purposes of this Act a person is a UN worker, in relation to an alleged offence, if at the time of the alleged offence—

(*a*) he is engaged or deployed by the Secretary-General of the United Nations as a member of the military, police or civilian component of a UN operation,

(*b*) he is, in his capacity as an official or expert on mission of the United Nations, a specialised agency of the United Nations or the International Atomic Energy Agency, present in an area where a UN operation is being conducted,

(*c*) he is assigned, with the agreement of an organ of the United Nations, by the Government of any State or by an international governmental organisation to carry out activities in support of the fulfilment of the mandate of a UN operation, (*d*) he is engaged by the Secretary-General of the United Nations, a specialised agency or the International Atomic Energy Agency to carry out such activities, or

(*e*) he is deployed by a humanitarian non-governmental organisation or agency under an agreement with the Secretary-General of the United Nations, with a specialised agency or with the International Atomic Energy Agency to carry out such activities.

(2) Subject to subsections (3) and (3A), in this section "UN operation" means an operation—

(*a*) which is established, in accordance with the Charter of the United Nations, by an organ of the United Nations,

(*b*) which is conducted under the authority and control of the United Nations, and

(*c*) which—

(i) has as its purpose a purpose mentioned in subsection (2A), or

(ii) has, for the purposes of the Convention, been declared by the Security Council or the General Assembly of the United Nations to be an operation where there exists an exceptional risk to the safety of the participating personnel.

(2A) The purposes referred to in subsection (2)(*c*) (i) are—

(*a*) maintaining or restoring international peace and security;

(*b*) delivering humanitarian, political or development assistance in peacebuilding;

(*c*) delivering emergency humanitarian assistance.

(3) In this section "UN operation" does not include any operation—

(*a*) which is authorised by the Security Council of the United Nations as an enforcement action under Chapter VII of the Charter of the United Nations,

(*b*) in which UN workers are engaged as combatants against organised armed forces, and

(*c*) to which the law of international armed conflict applies.

(3A) In this section "UN operation" also does not include any operation in respect of which a declaration is made in accordance with Article II(3) of the Optional Protocol (opt-out for operation to deliver emergency humanitarian assistance in response to natural disaster).

(4) In this section—

"the Convention" means the Convention on the Safety of United Nations and Associated Personnel adopted by the General Assembly of the United Nations on 9 December 1994; and

"the Optional Protocol" means the Optional Protocol to the Convention adopted by the General Assembly of the United Nations on 8 December 2005;

"specialised agency" has the meaning assigned to it by Article 57 of the Charter of the United Nations.

(5) If, in any proceedings, a question arises as to whether—

(*a*) a person is or was a UN worker, or

(*b*) an operation is or was a UN operation,

a certificate issued by or under the authority of the Secretary of State and stating any fact relating to the question shall be conclusive evidence of that fact.*

[United Nations Personnel Act 1997, s 4 as amended by the Geneva Conventions and United Nations Personnel (Protocols) Act 2009, s 2.]

7.8692 5. **Provisions supplementary to sections 1 to 3** (1) Proceedings for an offence which (disregarding the provisions of the Internationally Protected Persons Act 1978, the Suppression of Terrorism Act 1978, the Nuclear Material (Offences) Act 1983 and the Terrorism Act 2000) would not be an offence apart from section 1, 2 or 3 above shall not be begun—

(*a*) in England and Wales, except by or with the consent of the Attorney General;

(*b*) *Northern Ireland.*

(2) Without prejudice to any jurisdiction exercisable apart from this subsection, every sheriff court in Scotland shall have jurisdiction to entertain proceedings for an offence which (disregarding the provisions of the Internationally Protected Persons Act 1978, the Suppression of Terrorism Act 1978, the Nuclear Material (Offences) Act 1983 and the Terrorism Act 2000) would not be an offence in Scotland apart from section 1, 2 or 3 above.

(3) A person is guilty of an offence under, or by virtue of, section 1, 2 or 3 regardless of his nationality.

(4) For the purposes of those sections, it is immaterial whether a person knows that another person is a UN worker.

[United Nations Personnel Act 1997, s 5 as amended by the Crime (International Co-operation) Act 2003, Sch 5.]

7.8693 7. *Consequential amendments.*

7.8694 8. **Interpretation** In this Act—

"act" includes omission; and

"UN worker" has the meaning given in section 4.

[United Nations Personnel Act 1997, s 8.]

7.8695 9. *Extent*[1].

---

1 The United Nations Personnel (Guernsey) Order 1998, SI 1998/1075 has been made under s 9(2). This act has been extended with modifications, to the Bailwick of Jersey by the United Nations Personnel (Jersey) Order 1998, SI 1998/1267 and to the Isle of Man by the United Nations Personnel (Isle of Man) Order 1998, SI 1998/1509 and the United Nations Personnel (Isle of Man) Order 2012, SI 2012/2594.

7.8696 10. *Short title and commencement.*

# Protection from Harassment Act 1997[1]

(1997 c 40)

*England and Wales*

7.8697 **1. Prohibition of harassment** (1) A person must not pursue a course of conduct[2]—

(a) which amounts to harassment[3] of another[4], and

(b) which he knows or ought to know amounts to harassment[3] of the other.

(1A) A person must not pursue a course of conduct—

(a) which involves harassment of two or more persons, and

(b) which he knows or ought to know involves harassment of those persons, and

(c) by which he intends to persuade any person (whether or not one of those mentioned above)—

(i) not to do something that he is entitled or required to do, or

(ii) to do something that he is not under any obligation to do.

(2) For the purposes of this section or section 2A(2)(c), the person whose course of conduct is in question ought to know that it amounts to or involves harassment[3] of another if a reasonable person[5] in possession of the same information would think the course of conduct amounted to or involved harassment[3] of the other.

(3) Subsection (1) or (1A) does not apply to a course of conduct if the person who pursued it shows[6]—

(a) that it was pursued for the purpose[7] of preventing or detecting crime,

(b) that it was pursued under any enactment or rule of law or to comply with any condition or requirement imposed by any person under any enactment, or

(c) that in the particular circumstances the pursuit of the course of conduct was reasonable[8].

[Protection from Harassment Act 1997, s 1 as amended by the Serious Organised Crime and Police Act 2005, s 125 and the Protection of Freedoms Act 2012, Sch 9.]

---

1 With the exception of ss 13–16, the provisions of this Act are to be brought into force by orders made under s 15. For commencement orders made at the time of going to press, see note to s 15, post.

2 A "course of conduct" must involve conduct on at least two occasions and "conduct" includes speech (s 7(1)(2), post). While proof of two incidents can be sufficient to constitute an offence, the fewer the occasions and the wider they are spread the less likely it will be that a finding of harassment can reasonably be made (*Lau v DPP* [2000] 1 FLR 799, [2000] Crim LR 580, DC). See also *R v Hills* [2001] 1 FLR 580, [2001] Crim LR 318, CA (2 incidents, 6 months apart, held to be separate with no appropriate or sensible causal connection that could justify the conclusion that they amounted to a course of conduct); and *Pratt v DPP* [2001] EWHC 483 (Admin), 165 JP 800 (where the 2 incidents, almost 3 months apart, did amount to a course of conduct, but the case was "borderline".) The court ought to be alert to this where the evidence of some of the incidents is accepted but not others (see for a trial on indictment: *R v Patel* [2004] EWCA Crim 3284, 169 JP 93, [2005] 1 FLR 803, [2005] Crim LR 649). The fact that the victim was informed of the course of conduct (the contents of 2 telephone calls to her employer) by a third party rather than by the defendant himself did not mean that no offence was committed once she had been so informed, even in circumstances where the defendant had asked that she should not be so informed, provided there was evidence on the basis of which the court could properly conclude that the defendant was pursuing a course of conduct which he knew or ought to have known amounted to harassment of the victim: *Kellett v DPP* [2001] EWHC Admin 107. Similarly, the fact that the victim initiated the series of telephone calls alleged to constitute the harassment is irrelevant: *James v DPP* [2009] EWHC 2925, [2010] Crim LR 580.

It has also been held that the fewer incidents there are in a course of conduct, the more severe each is likely to have to be to make out the offence: *Jones v DPP* [2010] EWHC 523 (Admin), [2011] 1 WLR 833, 174 JP 278.

There is nothing to prevent the prosecution from including within the course of conduct acts which are the subject of a separate charge, but this must be made clear at the outset so that any issues of fairness and duplicity can be dealt with: *Jones v DPP*, supra. See also, *R v Widdows* [2011] EWCA Crim 1500, 175 JP 345, [2011] 2 FLR 869, [2011] Crim LR 959 (in the circumstances it was inappropriate to join two allegations of rape).

A "course of conduct" may include acts that occurred more than six months before the date on which the information was laid; this does not violate s 127 of the Magistrates' Courts Act 1980 if the final event relied on occurred within the six-month limitation period: *DPP v Baker* [2004] EWHC Admin 2792, (2005) 169 JP 140.

3 References to harassing a person include alarming the person or causing the person distress (s 7(2), post). See also *Chambers and Edwards v DPP* [1995] Crim LR 896 decided under the Public Order Act 1986, this PART: title PUBLIC MEETINGS AND PUBLIC ORDER, post. The terms "course of conduct" and "amounts to harassment" are inter-related; what must be proved is conduct targeted at an individual which was calculated to cause alarm or distress to that person and was oppressive and unreasonable. Sporadic outbursts of temper and bad behaviour, with violence on both sides, in a volatile relationship interspersed with considerable periods of affectionate life, could not be described as "a course of conduct amounting to harassment": *R v Curtis* [2010] EWCA Crim 123, [2010] 3 All ER 849, [2010] 1 WLR 2770, [2010] Crim LR 638 (a decision under s 4, post, which held that the "course of conduct" there required was a course of conduct amounting to harassment under s 1) followed in *R v Widdows* [2011] EWCA Crim 1500, 175 JP 345 (charge under s 4 not normally appropriate for use as a means of criminalising conduct, not charged as violence, during incidents in a long and predominantly affectionate relationship in which both parties persisted and wanted to continue). In *R v Haque* [2011] EWCA Crim 1871, [2012] 1 Cr App R 5, [2011] Crim LR 962 the Court of Appeal (with reluctance) found it was bound to follow *Curtis* and *Widdows*. First, the court doubted whether the 'course of conduct' for the purposes of the s 4(1) offence had to be conduct amounting to harassment within the meaning of s 1. Secondly, the court noted that the title of the Act referred to both harassment and similar conduct. Thirdly, the court did not consider that the availability of a conviction under s 2 as an alternative to s 4 meant that that proof of the former was a prerequisite to proof of the latter. See the commentary on *Haque* in the Criminal Law Review at pp 961 and 962.

This Act is directed at the prevention of stalking, anti-social behaviour by neighbours and racial harassment and its ambit does not extend to an alleged aggressive conduct of litigation (*Tuppen v Microsoft Corpn Ltd* (2000) Times, 15 November, QBD).

What may begin as a legitimate act can turn into harassment within the meaning of s 1 by reason of persistence and manner of pursuit: *DPP v Hardy* [2008] EWHC 2874 (Admin), (2009) 173 JP (legitimate phone call followed by persistent calls for 1½ hours which made the complainant feel intimidated).

[4] Two or more complainants may be named in one charge under s 1 of the Protection from Harassment Act 1997; and, if the complainants were "a close knit definable group" and the acts complained of constitute pursuing a single course of conduct aimed at the group, there is no unfairness to the defendant and such a charge is not bad for duplicity merely because only one of the complainants was present on a particular occasion: *DPP v Dunn* [2001] 1 Cr App Rep 352, 165 JP 130, [2001] Crim LR 130, DC. (Cf the narrower interpretation of s 4, post.)

[5] The defendant's mental disorder (paranoid schizophrenia) was not to be considered as a relevant condition of the hypothetical reasonable man under s 1(2) or to be taken into account when assessing whether the defendant's conduct was reasonable under s 1(3)(*c*); both s 1(2) and s 1(3) involved objective tests and it did not assist to consider the law relating to duress or provocation since their aims were different: *R v Colohan* [2001] EWCA Crim 1251, [2001] Crim LR 845.

[6] The standard of proof is on a preponderance of probabilities, less onerous than on the prosecution; *R v Carr-Briant* [1943] KB 607, [1943] 2 All ER 156, 107 JP 167, *R v Dunbar* [1958] 1 QB 1, [1957] 2 All ER 737, [1957] 3 WLR 330.

[7] "Purpose" is not a wholly subjective test. The purpose does not have to be "reasonable" but it must be "rational":

"12 . . . A large proportion of those engaging in the kind of persistent and deliberate course of targeted oppression with which the Act is concerned will in the nature of things be obsessives and cranks, who will commonly believe themselves to be entitled to act as they do.

13 Section 1(3)(*a*), although it was no doubt drafted mainly with an eye to the prevention or detection of crime by public authorities, applies equally to private persons who take it upon themselves to enforce the criminal law. Within broad limits, the law recognises the right of private persons to do this, but vigilantism can easily and imperceptibly merge into unlawful harassment. Cases such as the present one, where the harassment is said to consist in repeated and oppressive attempts to detect crime are quite likely to involve conduct falling within the sub-category of harassment defined as "stalking" by section 2A (added by section 111(1) of the Protection of Freedoms Act 2012). This includes not just sexual stalking, but any persistent course of harassment that consists in repeatedly following a person, contacting or attempting to contact them, publishing material about them, monitoring their use of the internet, loitering in any place, or watching or spying on them: see section 2A(3). Conduct said to be directed to preventing crime is likely to be an even more significant category than conduct said to be directed to its detection. Recent cases before the courts illustrate the propensity of obsessives to engage in conduct which is oppressive enough to constitute harassment, in the genuine belief that they are preventing crime. These ranging from the more extreme wings of the animal rights movement to the lone schizophrenic vigilante whom (counsel for the appellant) submitted would be protected by section 1(3)(*a*). Those who claim to be acting for the purpose of either preventing or detecting crime may at a purely subjective level entertain views about what acts are crimes which have no relation to reality, let alone to the law. Private persons seeking to enforce the law are not amenable to judicial review, as the police are. Unless they commit some other offence or civil wrong, such as assault or criminal damage, the 1997 Act will be the only means of controlling their activities by law. It cannot be the case that the mere existence of a belief, however absurd, in the mind of the harasser that he is detecting or preventing a possibly non-existent crime, will justify him in persisting in a course of conduct which the law characterises as oppressive. Some control mechanism is required, even if it falls well short of requiring the alleged harasser to prove that his alleged purpose was objectively reasonable.

14 I do not doubt that in the context of section 1(3)(*a*) purpose is a subjective state of mind. But in my opinion, the necessary control mechanism is to be found in the concept of rationality, which Eady J touched on in *Howlett v Holding* [2006] EWHC 41and Moses LJ seems to have been reaching for in his judgment in the present case. Rationality is a familiar concept in public law. It has also in recent years played an increasingly significant role in the law relating to contractual discretions, where the law's object is also to limit the decision-maker to some relevant contractual purpose: see *Ludgate Insurance Co Ltd v Citibank NA* [1998] Lloyds Rep IR 221, para 35 and *Socimer International Bank Ltd v Standard Bank Ltd* [2008] Bus LR 1304, para 66. Rationality is not the same as reasonableness. Reasonableness is an external, objective standard applied to the outcome of a person's thoughts or intentions. The question is whether a notional hypothetically reasonable person in his position would have engaged in the relevant conduct for the purpose of preventing or detecting crime. A test of rationality, by comparison, applies a minimum objective standard to the relevant person's mental processes. It imports a requirement of good faith, a requirement that there should be some logical connection between the evidence and the ostensible reasons for the decision, and (which will usually amount to the same thing) an absence of arbitrariness, of capriciousness or of reasoning so outrageous in its defiance of logic as to be perverse. For the avoidance of doubt, I should make it clear that, since we are concerned with the alleged harasser's state of mind, I am not talking about the broader categories of *Wednesbury* unreasonableness (*Associated Provincial Picture Houses Ltd v Wednesbury Corporation* [1948] 1 KB 223), a legal construct referring to a decision lying beyond the furthest reaches of objective reasonableness.

15 Before an alleged harasser can be said to have had the purpose of preventing or detecting crime, he must have sufficiently applied his mind to the matter. He must have thought rationally about the material suggesting the possibility of criminality and formed the view that the conduct said to constitute harassment was appropriate for the purpose of preventing or detecting it. If he has done these things, then he has the relevant purpose. The court will not test his conclusions by reference to the view which a hypothetical reasonable man in his position would have formed. If, on the other hand, he has not engaged in these minimum mental processes necessary to acquire the relevant state of mind, but proceeds anyway on the footing that he is acting to prevent or detect crime, then he acts irrationally. In that case, two consequences will follow. The first is that the law will not regard him as having had the relevant purpose at all. He has simply not taken the necessary steps to form one. The second is that the causal connection which section 1(3)(*a*) posits between the purpose of the alleged harasser and the conduct constituting the harassment, will not exist. The effect of applying a test of rationality to the question of purpose is to enable the court to apply to private persons a test which would in any event apply to public authorities engaged in the prevention or detection of crime as a matter of public law. It is not a demanding test, and it is hard to imagine that Parliament can have intended anything less." (per Lord Sumption SCJ in *Hayes v Willoughby* [2013] UKSC 17, [2013] 2 All ER 405, [2013] 1 WLR 935, [2013] Cr App R 11)

[8] It is not reasonable to pursue a course of conduct which is in breach of a court injunction designed to prevent it (*DPP v Selvanayagam* (1999) Times, 23 June, DC).

7.8698 **2. Offence of harassment** (1) A person who pursues a course of conduct in breach of section 1(1) or (1A) is guilty of an offence[1].

(2) A person guilty of an offence under this section is liable on summary conviction to imprisonment for a term not exceeding **six months**, or a fine not exceeding **level 5** on the standard scale, or **both**.

(3) *Repealed.*

[Protection from Harassment Act 1997, s 2 as amended by the Police Reform Act 2002, s 107(2) and the Serious Organised Crime and Police Act 2005, s 125.]

[1] In addition to the notes to s 1, reference should also be made to s 7 and the notes thereto for the interpretation of relevant terms.

7.8699 **2A. Offence of stalking** (1) A person is guilty of an offence if—

(*a*) the person pursues a course of conduct in breach of section 1(1), and

(*b*) the course of conduct amounts to stalking.

(2) For the purposes of subsection (1)(*b*) (and section 4A(1)(*a*)) a person's course of conduct amounts to stalking of another person if—

(*a*) it amounts to harassment of that person,

(*b*) the acts or omissions involved are ones associated with stalking, and

(*c*) the person whose course of conduct it is knows or ought to know that the course of conduct amounts to harassment of the other person.

(3) The following are examples of acts or omissions which, in particular circumstances, are ones associated with stalking—

(*a*) following a person,

(*b*) contacting, or attempting to contact, a person by any means,

(*c*) publishing any statement or other material—

(i) relating or purporting to relate to a person, or

(ii) purporting to originate from a person,

(*d*) monitoring the use by a person of the internet, email or any other form of electronic communication,

(*e*) loitering in any place (whether public or private),

(*f*) interfering with any property in the possession of a person,

(*g*) watching or spying on a person.

(4) A person guilty of an offence under this section is liable on summary conviction to imprisonment for a term not exceeding 51 weeks, or a fine not exceeding level 5 on the standard scale, or both.

(5) In relation to an offence committed before the commencement of section 281(5) of the Criminal Justice Act 2003, the reference in subsection (4) to 51 weeks is to be read as a reference to six months.

(6) This section is without prejudice to the generality of section 2.

[Protection from Harassment Act 1997, s 2A as inserted by the Protection of Freedoms Act 2012, s 111.]

**7.8700 2B. Power of entry in relation to offence of stalking** (1) A justice of the peace may, on an application by a constable, issue a warrant authorising a constable to enter and search premises if the justice of the peace is satisfied that there are reasonable grounds for believing that—

(*a*) an offence under section 2A has been, or is being, committed,

(*b*) there is material on the premises which is likely to be of substantial value (whether by itself or together with other material) to the investigation of the offence,

(*c*) the material—

(i) is likely to be admissible in evidence at a trial for the offence, and

(ii) does not consist of, or include, items subject to legal privilege, excluded material or special procedure material (within the meanings given by sections 10, 11 and 14 of the Police and Criminal Evidence Act 1984), and

(*d*) either—

(i) entry to the premises will not be granted unless a warrant is produced, or

(ii) the purpose of a search may be frustrated or seriously prejudiced unless a constable arriving at the premises can secure immediate entry to them.

(2) A constable may seize and retain anything for which a search has been authorised under subsection (1).

(3) A constable may use reasonable force, if necessary, in the exercise of any power conferred by virtue of this section.

(4) In this section "premises" has the same meaning as in section 23 of the Police and Criminal Evidence Act 1984.

[Protection from Harassment Act 1997, s 2A as inserted by the Protection of Freedoms Act 2012, s 112.]

**7.8701 3. Civil remedy** (1) An actual or apprehended breach of section 1(1) may be the subject of a claim in civil proceedings by the person[1] who is or may be the victim of the course of conduct in question.

(2) On such a claim, damages may be awarded for (among other things) any anxiety caused by the harassment and any financial loss resulting from the harassment[2].

(3) Where—

(*a*) in such proceedings the High Court or a county court grants an injunction for the purpose of restraining the defendant from pursuing any conduct which amounts to harassment, and

(*b*) the plaintiff considers that the defendant has done anything which he is prohibited from doing by the injunction.

the plaintiff may apply for the issue of a warrant for the arrest of the defendant.

(4) An application under subsection (3) may be made—

(*a*) where the injunction was granted by the High Court, to a judge of that court, and

(*b*) where the injunction was granted by the county court, to a judge of that court.

(5) The judge to whom an application under subsection (3) is made may only issue a warrant if—

(*a*) the application is substantiated on oath, and

(*b*) the judge has reasonable grounds for believing that the defendant has done anything which he is prohibited from doing by the injunction.

(6) Where—

(*a*) the High Court or the county court grants an injunction for the purpose mentioned in subsection (3)(*a*), and

(*b*) without reasonable excuse the defendant does anything which he is prohibited from doing by the injunction,

he is guilty of an offence.

(7) Where a person is convicted of an offence under subsection (6) in respect of any conduct, that conduct is not punishable as a contempt of court.

(8) A person cannot be convicted of an offence under subsection (6) in respect of any conduct which has been punished as a contempt of court.

(9) A person guilty of an offence under subsection (6) is liable[3]—

(*a*) on conviction on indictment, to imprisonment for a term not exceeding **five years**, or a **fine**, or **both**, or

(*b*) on summary conviction, to imprisonment for a term not exceeding **six months**, or a fine not exceeding the **statutory maximum**, or **both**.

[Protection from Harassment Act 1997, s 3 as amended by the Serious Organised Crime and Police Act 2005, s 125 and the Crime and Courts Act 2013, Sch 9.]

---

[1] This does not include a company which cannot be the subject of harassment and cannot bring proceedings under the Act (*Daiichi UK Ltd v Stop Huntingdon Animal Cruelty*) [2003] EWHC 2337 (QB), [2004} 1 WLR 1503, (2003) Times, 22 October, QBD).

A claim may be brought by a person who was not the primary target of the harassment: see *Levi v Bates* [2015] EWCA Civ 206, [2015] 3 WLR 769, [2015] 2 Cr App Rep 276, post.

[2] For procedure in respect of this offence which is triable either way, see the Magistrates' Courts Act 1980, ss 17A–21, in PART I: MAGISTRATES' COURTS, PROCEDURE, ante.

[3] Foreseeability of the injury or loss is not an essential element in the cause of action (*Jones v Ruth* [2011] EWCA Civ 804, [2012] 1 All ER 490).

7.8702 **3A. Injunctions to protect persons from harassment within section 1(1A)** (1) This section applies where there is an actual or apprehended breach of section 1(1A) by any person ("the relevant person").

(2) In such a case—

(*a*) any person who is or may be a victim of the course of conduct in question, or

(*b*) any person who is or may be a person falling within section 1(1A)(*c*),

may apply to the High Court or a county court for an injunction restraining the relevant person from pursuing any conduct which amounts to harassment in relation to any person or persons mentioned or described in the injunction.

(3) Section 3(3) to (9) apply in relation to an injunction granted under subsection (2) above as they apply in relation to an injunction granted as mentioned in section 3(3)(*a*).

[Protection from Harassment Act 1997, s 3A as inserted by the Serious Organised Crime and Police Act 2005, s 125.]

7.8703 **4. Putting people in fear of violence** (1) A person whose course of conduct[1] causes another to fear, on at least two occasions, that violence will be used against him[2] is guilty of an offence if he knows or ought to know that his course of conduct will cause the other so to fear on each of those occasions.

(2) For the purposes of this section, the person whose course of conduct is in question ought to know that it will cause another to fear that violence will be used against him on any occasion if a reasonable person in possession of the same information would think the course of conduct would cause the other so to fear on that occasion.

(3) It is a defence for a person charged with an offence under this section to show[3] that—

(*a*) his course of conduct was pursued for the purpose of preventing or detecting crime.

(*b*) his course of conduct was pursued under any enactment or rule of law or to comply with any condition or requirement imposed by any person under any enactment, or

(*c*) the pursuit of his course of conduct was reasonable for the protection of himself or another or for the protection of his or another's property.

(4) A person guilty of an offence under this section is liable[4]—

(*a*) on conviction on indictment, to imprisonment for a term not exceeding **ten years**, or a **fine**, or **both**, or

(*b*) on summary conviction, to imprisonment for a term not exceeding **six months**, or a fine not exceeding the **statutory maximum**, or **both**.

(5) If on the trial on indictment of a person charged with an offence under this section the jury find him not guilty of the offence charged, they may find him guilty of an offence under section 2[5] or 2A.

(6) The Crown Court has the same powers and duties in relation to a person who is by virtue of subsection (5) convicted before it of an offence under section 2 or 2A as a magistrates' court would have on convicting him of the offence.

[Protection from Harassment Act 1997, s 4 as amended by the Protection of Freedoms Act 2012, Sch 9 and the Policing and Crime Act 2017, s 175.]

[1] It has been held that the 'course of conduct' under s 4 must be a course of conduct amounting to harassment under s 1: *R v Curtis* [2010] EWCA Crim 123, [2010] 3 All ER 849, [2010] WLR 2770, [2010] Crim L R 638; followed in *R v Widdows* [2011] EWCA Crim 1500, 175 JP 345. These decisions were followed, with reluctance, in *R v Haque* [2011] EWCA Crim 1871, [2012] 1 Cr App R 5, [2011] Crim LR 962 (see further the notes to s 2, supra). The result of this and the authorities referred to in the notes to s 7, post, is that a prosecution under s 4 requires, in addition to the elements expressly set out: (*a*) proof of harassment; (*b*) that the conduct was targeted at an individual; and (*c*) that it was calculated to produce the consequence of alarm or distress (see paras 70–72 of the judgment in *R v Haque*, supra).

[2] Where, in relation to one of the two occasions relied on by the prosecution, the evidence was that the defendant threatened to blow the victim's dogs' brains out and the victim was not asked whether she had been caused to fear violence to herself on that occasion, the court was entitled to convict; words or conduct ostensibly directed to something or someone other than the victim did not, because so directed, fall outside conduct that could support a conviction: *R v DPP* [2001] EWHC Admin 17, [2001] Crim LR 397, 165 JP 349. However, it is not possible to read "others" for "another" or "them" rather than "him" in s 4; although there can be cases where the requirements of s 4 are met in relation to 2 persons, the course of conduct must cause 1 complainant to fear, on at least two occasions, that violence will be used against him, as opposed to another: *Caurti v DPP* [2002] Crim LR 131.

[3] The standard of proof is on a preponderance of probabilities, less onerous than on the prosecution: *R v Carr-Briant* [1943] KB 607, [1943] 2 All ER 156, 107 JP 167, *R v Dunbar* [1958] 1 QB 1, [1957] 2 All ER 737, [1957] 3 WLR 330.

[4] For procedure in respect of this offence which is triable either way, see the Magistrates' Courts Act 1980, ss 17A–21, in PART I: MAGISTRATES' COURTS, PROCEDURE, ante.

[5] After accepting a submission of no case to answer on a count of an offence contrary to s 4, but ruling that there was sufficient evidence to convict of a s 2 offence, the judge does not have to invite the jury to enter a not guilty verdict at this stage and dismiss the count but is entitled to leave the count on the indictment and inform the them that as a matter of law it was not open to them to convict of the s 4 offence but that it would be open to them to convict of the statutory alternative: *R v Livesey* [2006] EWCA Crim 3344, [2007] 1 Cr App R 35, [2007] Crim LR 635.

7.8704 **4A. Stalking involving fear of violence or serious alarm or distress** (1) A person ("A") whose course of conduct—

(*a*) amounts to stalking, and

(*b*) either—

(i) causes another ("B") to fear, on at least two occasions, that violence will be used against B, or

(ii) causes B serious alarm or distress which has a substantial adverse effect on B's usual day-to-day activities,

is guilty of an offence if A knows or ought to know that A's course of conduct will cause B so to fear on each of those occasions or (as the case may be) will cause such alarm or distress[1].

(2) For the purposes of this section A ought to know that A's course of conduct will cause B to fear that violence will be used against B on any occasion if a reasonable person in possession of the same information would think the course of conduct would cause B so to fear on that occasion.

(3) For the purposes of this section A ought to know that A's course of conduct will cause B serious alarm or distress which has a substantial adverse effect on B's usual day-to-day activities if a reasonable person in possession of the same information would think the course of conduct would cause B such alarm or distress.

(4) It is a defence for A to show that—

(*a*) A's course of conduct was pursued for the purpose of preventing or detecting crime,

(*b*) A's course of conduct was pursued under any enactment or rule of law or to comply with any condition or requirement imposed by any person under any enactment, or

(*c*) the pursuit of A's course of conduct was reasonable for the protection of A or another or for the protection of A's or another's property.

(5) A person guilty of an offence under this section is liable—

(*a*) on conviction on indictment, to imprisonment for a term not exceeding ten years, or a fine, or both, or

(*b*) on summary conviction, to imprisonment for a term not exceeding twelve months, or a fine not exceeding the statutory maximum, or both.

(6) In relation to an offence committed before the commencement of section 154(1) of the Criminal Justice Act 2003, the reference in subsection (5)(*b*) to twelve months is to be read as a reference to six months.

(7) If on the trial on indictment of a person charged with an offence under this section the jury find the person not guilty of the offence charged, they may find the person guilty of an offence under section 2 or 2A.

(8) The Crown Court has the same powers and duties in relation to a person who is by virtue of subsection (7) convicted before it of an offence under section 2 or 2A as a magistrates' court would have on convicting the person of the offence.

(9) This section is without prejudice to the generality of section 4.

[Protection from Harassment Act 1997, s 4A as inserted by the Protection of Freedoms Act 2012, s 111 and amended by the Policing and Crime Act 2017, s 175.]

[1] The section is wide enough to look to incidents of violence in the future and not only to incidents giving rise to a fear of violence arising directly out of the incident in question. Nor is there any requirement for the fear to be of violence on a particular date or time in the future, or at a particular place or in a particular manner, or for there to be a specific threat of violence. It is sufficient where that fear of violence is of violence on a separate and later occasion, eg somebody saying "I'll come back and get you". Whether or not fear of violence is sufficient to satisfy the requirements of s 4A(1)(*b*)(i) is a question of fact and degree on the evidence. What is key is that the complainant has to fear on at least two occasions that there *will* (rather than *might*) be violence directed at him or her: *R v Qosja* [2016] EWCA Crim 1543, [2017] 1 WLR 311.

7.8705 5. **Restraining orders on conviction** (1) A court sentencing or otherwise dealing with a person ("the defendant") convicted of an offence may[1] (as well as sentencing him or dealing with him in any other way[2]) make an order under this section.

(2) The order may, for the purpose of protecting the victim or victims of the offence, or any other person[3] mentioned in the order, from conduct which—

(*a*) amounts to harassment, or

(*b*) will cause a fear of violence,

prohibit the defendant from doing anything described in the order[4].

(3) The order may have effect for a specified period or until further order[5].

(3A) In proceedings under this section both the prosecution and the defence may lead, as further evidence, any evidence that would be admissible in proceedings for an injunction under section 3.

(4) The prosecutor, the defendant or any other person mentioned in the order may apply to the court which made the order for it to be varied or discharged by a further order.

(4A) Any person mentioned in the order is entitled to be heard on the hearing of an application under subsection (4).

(5) If without reasonable excuse the defendant does anything which he is prohibited from doing by an order under this section, he is guilty of an offence[6].

(6) A person guilty of an offence under this section is liable—

(*a*) on conviction on indictment, to imprisonment for a term not exceeding **five years**, or a **fine**, or **both**, or

(*b*) on summary conviction, to imprisonment for a term not exceeding **six months**, or a fine not exceeding the **statutory maximum**, or **both**.

(7) A court dealing with a person for an offence under this section may vary or discharge the order in question by a further order.

[Protection from Harassment Act 1997, s 5 as amended by the Domestic Violence, Crime and Victims Act 2004, s 12 and Sch 10 and 11 and the Serious Organised Crime and Police Act 2005, s 125.]

---

1 A restraining order was set aside in *R v James (Andrew)* [2013] EWCA Crim 655,[2013] 2 Cr App Rep (S) 542. Though the defendant was convicted of assault occasioning actual bodily harm on his step-daughter, he was acquitted of sexually assaulting her and all the important matters in dispute in the trial had been resolved in the defendant's favour. There was a history of false accusations by the stepdaughter and there was a risk that a restraining order, far from mending affairs for the future, would give rise to the making of further false complaints.

2 Where the court could make an order on conviction, the procedure and admissibility of hearsay evidence is regulated by the Criminal Procedure Rules, Part 31, in the *Key Materials*.

3 An order under this section must identify by name those who are protected by it. Accordingly it was not sufficient to make an order in the terms not to "contact or communicate with any member of staff" of a hostel; the staff had to be referred to by name: *R v Mann* (2000) Times, 11 April, CA.

A restraining order that restricts access to the courts may not be a disproportionate interference with the defendant's rights under art 6 of the ECHR if there is a history of harassments includes pursuing oppressive or vexatious claims: *R (on the application of Waxman) v Crown Prosecution Service* [2012] EWHC 133 (Admin), 176 JP 121.

The interpretation of ordinary words in a court order is a question of fact; the criminal context is not a reason for giving a narrow or strained meaning to words which bear their ordinary meaning, and the application of that meaning to the facts is a matter for the fact-finding tribunal: *R v Evans* [2004] EWCA Crim 3102, 169 JP 129, [2005] 1 Cr App Rep 546, [2005] Crim LR 654 (parking a car so that it blocked in the van of somebody visiting the complainants' property was held to breach a restraining order that prohibited the defendant from "abusive action" towards the complainants). However, the term "person" includes a limited company and a restraining order can be made to protect such a company or a group of persons such as its employees provided they were sufficiently clearly defined: *R v Buxton* [2010] EWCA Crim 2923, [2011] 1 WLR 857, [2011] 2 Cr App R (S) 23, [2011] Crim LR 332.

4 As to geographical prohibitions, see *R v Richardson* [2013] EWCA Crim 1905, [2014] 2 Cr App R (S) 5. The offences were committed in the course of a campaign of harassment against the victim. The effect of the restraining order was to prohibit the appellant from returning to her home address, or visiting the home of her elderly mother, as both houses were situated within the exclusion zone. The information before the judge was that if the appellant received a custodial sentence of two years or more, she would lose the tenancy of her home, and would be re-housed in another area. The victim and her family had moved out of the area because of the appellant's harassment, but wished to move back. The prohibition was upheld. The judge had concluded that the prohibition was necessary, otherwise the appellant would continue her campaign of harassment. Though the order prevented the appellant from returning to the area to visit her mother, there was no reason why her mother could not visit her.

5 A restraining order made for a specific period can be varied as to its expiry date: *DPP v Hall* [2005] EWHC 2612 (Admin), [2006] 3 All ER 170, [2006] 1 WLR 1000, 170 JP 11.

6 An information couched in the form of a s 1 offence (ie it referred to a "course of conduct") and alleging this to be in breach of the terms of a restraining order, contrary to s 5(5) and (6), was held not to be bad for duplicity in *McCaskill v DPP* [2005] EWHC 3208 (Admin), 170 JP 301.

7.8706 5A. **Restraining orders on acquittal** (1) A court before which a person ("the defendant") is acquitted[1] of an offence may, if it considers it necessary to do so to protect a person from harassment by the defendant, make an order prohibiting the defendant from doing anything described in the order.

(2) Subsections (3) to (7) of section 5 apply to an order under this section as they apply to an order under that one.

(3) Where the Court of Appeal allow an appeal against conviction they may remit the case to the Crown Court to consider whether to proceed under this section.

(4) Where—

(*a*) the Crown Court allows an appeal against conviction, or

(*b*) a case is remitted to the Crown Court under subsection (3),

the reference in subsection (1) to a court before which a person is acquitted of an offence is to be read as referring to that court.

(5) A person made subject to an order under this section has the same right of appeal against the order as if—

(*a*) he had been convicted of the offence in question before the court which made the order, and

(*b*) the order had been made under section 5[2].

[Protection from Harassment Act 1997, s 5A as inserted by the Domestic Violence, Crime and Victims Act 2004, s 12.]

---

[1] A person found "not guilty by reason of insanity" in the Crown Court has been acquitted of the offence: *R v R* [2013] EWCA Crim 591, [2013] 2 Cr App R 12. (However, a restraining order cannot be made where an offender is found unfit to plead and a jury then determines under s 4A(2) of the Criminal Procedure (Insanity) Act 1964 that he did the act charged against him: *R v Chinegwundoh* [2015] EWCA Crim 109, [2015] 1 WLR 2818, [2015] 1 Cr App R 26,[2015] 1 Cr App R (S) 61). A restraining order under s 5A must identify the potential victim or victims which it seeks to protect; further, since the purpose of the order is to protect a person from harassment by an acquitted defendant, the court must first be satisfied that the defendant is likely to pursue a course of conduct which amounts to harassment within the meaning of s 1. Pursuit of a course of conduct requires intention: *R v Smith* [2012] EWCA Crim 2566, [2013] 2 All ER 804 (order not to travel on any domestic or international flight quashed).

The power to make a restraining on acquittal requires that the acquittal is lawful, which it is not if the court has dismissed a charge of its own motion and failed to apply the provisions of s 9 of the Magistrates' Courts Act 1980.

[2] The provisions of this section were considered by the Court of Appeal in *R v Major* [2010] EWCA Crim 3016, [2011] 1 Cr App R 25, [2011] 2 Cr App R (S) 26, [2011] Crim LR 328. The making of an order is not confined to uncontested facts nor is it to be used rarely as this provision is to deal with those cases where there is clear evidence that the victim needs protection but there is insufficient evidence to convict of the particular charges before the court. The victim need not have been blameless. The order may prohibit the defendant doing acts that were not the subject matter of the charge of which he was acquitted. It is sufficient to establish conduct that falls short of harassment but which may, if repeated, amount to harassment so making an order necessary. The provision addresses a future risk, an evidential basis being the conduct of the defendant which is to be established to the civil standard and which must be identified by the court. Additional evidence may be called in relation to future risk. Compliance with bail conditions is a consideration but not a ground for not making an order as a defendant's compliance may have been motivated by concerns about being remanded into custody.

See also *R (on the application of Gonzales) v Folkestone Magistrates' Court, Crown Prosecution Service Interested Party* [2010] EWHC 3528 (Admin), 175 JP 453(conviction of assault quashed, but restraining order maintained since it was clear on a balance of probabilities that the defendant had committed the offence). There must, however, be a factual basis for the order and the procedures prescribed by the Criminal Procedure Rules, Part 31 must be followed in cases where the prosecution has called no evidence: *R v Brough* [2011] EWCA Crim 2802, [2012] 2 Cr App Rep 30, [2012] Crim LR 228, [2012] 2 Cr App R 8. See also *R v Kapotra* [2011] EWCA Crim 1843, [2012] 1 Cr App Rep (S) 523, 175 JP 378. It is a fundamental principle that any person faced with the possible imposition of a restraining order should be given proper notice of what was sought, the evidential basis for the application, and be allowed a proper opportunity to address the evidence and make informed representations.

**7.8707 6. Limitation** *Amendment to section 11 of the Limitation Act 1980 (special time limit for actions in respect of personal injuries).*

**7.8708 7. Interpretation of this group of sections** (1) This section applies for the interpretation of sections 1 to 5A.

(2) References to harassing a person include alarming the person or causing the person distress.

(3) A "course of conduct" must involve—

(*a*) in the case of conduct in relation to a single person (section 1(1)), conduct on at least two occasions in relation to that person, or

(*b*) in the case of conduct in relation to two or more persons (section 1(1A)), conduct on at least one occasion in relation to each of those persons.

(3A) A person's conduct on any occasion shall be taken, if aided, abetted, counselled or procured by another—

(*a*) to be conduct on that occasion of the other (as well as conduct of the person whose conduct it is); and

(*b*) to be conduct in relation to which the other's knowledge and purpose, and what he ought to have known, are the same as they were in relation to what was contemplated or reasonably foreseeable at the time of the aiding, abetting, counselling or procuring.

(4) "Conduct" includes speech.

(5) References to a person, in the context of the harassment of a person, are references to a person who is an individual[1].

[Protection from Harassment Act 1997, s 7 amended by the Criminal Justice and Police Act 2001, s 44(1) and the Criminal Justice and Police Act 2001, s 44, the Domestic Violence, Crime and Victims Act 2004, Sch 10 and the Serious Organised Crime and Police Act 2005, s 125.]

---

[1] Per Lord Philips MR in *Thomas v News Group Newspapers Ltd* [2001] EWCA Civ 1233, [2002] EMLR 78:

> "[29] Section 7 of the 1997 Act does not purport to provide a comprehensive definition of harassment. There are many actions that foreseeably alarm or cause a person distress that could not possibly be described as harassment. It seems to me that section 7 is dealing with that element of the offence which is constituted by the effect of the conduct rather than with the types of conduct that produce that effect.
>
> [30] The Act does not attempt to define the type of conduct that is capable of constituting harassment. "Harassment" is, however, a word which has a meaning which is generally understood. It describes conduct targeted at an individual which is calculated to produce the consequences described in section 7 and which is oppressive and unreasonable. The practice of stalking is a prime example of such conduct."

See also *Majrowski v Guy's and St Thomas's NHS Trust* [2006] UKHL 34, [2006] 4 All ER 395, [2007] 1 AC 224, [2006] 3 WLR 125.

Many actions that cause alarm or distress will not amount to harassment; the conduct must also be oppressive. "Harassment" describes conduct targeted at an individual and calculated to produce the consequences described in s 7 and which is oppressive and unreasonable. In proceedings for breach of a non-molestation order, "harassment" cannot simply be equated with "causing alarm or distress". The danger of doing so is that not all conduct, even if unattractive, unreasonable and causing alarm or distress, will be of an order justifying the sanction of the criminal law. On a prosecution for breach of a non-molestation order the judge's direction ought to include a reference to the jury needing to be sure that the conduct was oppressive, not merely causing alarm or distress: *R v N* [2016] EWCA Crim 92, [2016] 2 Cr App R 10, 180 JP 252. 'The requirement of oppression . . . always and of course to be considered in context . . . serves as a yardstick, helping the law to draw a sensible line between the give and take of daily life and conduct which justifies the sanction of the criminal law' (per Gross LJ at para 32); see also *Crawford v Jenkins* [2014] EWCA Civ 1035, [2016] QB 231, [2015] 3 WLR 843.

The meaning of "targeted at an individual" (see para [30] of the judgment in the *Thomas* case quoted above) was considered in *Levi v Bates* [2015] EWCA Civ 206, [2015] 3 WLR 769, [2015] 2 Cr App Rep 276, a civil case where the a civil claim by the second claimant had been dismissed because, save for one occasion, the conduct in question had not been targeted against her but against the first claimant (her husband). This followed the decision by Simon J in *Dowson v Chief Constable of Northumbria Police* [2010] EWHC 2612 (QB), [2010] All ER (D) 191 (Oct) that the conduct must be targeted at the claimant.

The Court of Appeal allowed the second claimant's appeal:

"26 The critical question, for present purposes, is whether in transforming Lord Phillips' phrase 'targeted at an individual' to the phrase 'targeted at the claimant', Simon J went a step too far. In my judgment he did. He may easily be forgiven for doing so in a case which, like the Thomas case, disclosed no disconnect between those who were targeted, and those who suffered the consequences. *Trimingham* was the first case where that disconnect arose on the facts, and Tugendhat J was careful to leave open the question whether the person who was not the primary target, but who was harmed in the relevant sense by the publications, could complain of harassment. It was however a classic case where the publications consisted of journalism about matters of intense and legitimate public interest, so that the claimant's claim was dismissed mainly on art.10 grounds which did not require him to decide the question which arises on this appeal. This is, so far as I know, only the second case in which such a disconnect between the target and the victim has arisen. The question now has to be decided because, for the reasons given by the judge, art.10 rights to freedom of speech are not decisive.

27 There are two main reasons why I consider that it is not a requirement of the statutory tort of harassment that the claimant be the (or even a) target of the perpetrator's conduct. The first is that I do not consider that Lord Philips had that question in mind. The purpose of the passage in his judgment in the *Thomas* case which I have cited was not designed to identify who may complain of harassment, but rather to draw out of the well-known word 'harassment' the concept that it is targeted behaviour, by which I mean behaviour aimed at someone, rather than behaviour which merely causes alarm or distress without being aimed at anyone. Lord Phillips MR's immediate example was stalking, conduct which is plainly targeted at someone.

28 The value of targeting as a concept is that it excludes behaviour which, however alarming or distressing it may be, is not aimed or directed at anyone. For example, a person may drive his fast sports car on regular occasions through a neighbourhood in a way that causes foreseeable alarm and distress to pedestrians and parents of young children. It may amount to speeding, careless or dangerous driving, but it is not harassment because it is not targeted at anyone at all. The driver is merely selfishly enjoying himself.

29 My second reason for concluding that, provided that it is targeted at someone, the conduct complained of need not be targeted at the claimant, if he or she is foreseeably likely to be directly alarmed or distressed by it, is that I cannot conceive why Parliament should by implication rather than express words (for there are none) have deliberately excluded from the protection of the Act persons who are foreseeably alarmed and distressed by a course of conduct of the targeted type contemplated by the word harassment. The only express requirement is that the claimant be a victim of the relevant course of conduct: see s.3(1).

30 Lord Phillips MR's example of stalking is again in point. A stalker may typically target his or her conduct at a former sexual partner who has, by the time the objectionable course of conduct begins, formed a new partnership with someone else. The stalking may be as alarming and distressing to that new partner as it is to the target, or even more so. Of course, in many cases, the target may achieve practicable protection for his or her new partner by obtaining the requisite injunction in a civil harassment claim, but this is by no means inevitable. The target may be indifferent to the conduct complained of by the new partner, or may simply be averse to civil litigation. Why should the law make protection from harassment for the new partner dependent upon the target taking the requisite proceedings?

31 Nor do I regard the fact that harassment is criminal conduct a good reason for excluding the victim of collateral damage, however important its criminal character may be for the identification of the type or seriousness of the relevant conduct. That analysis can be carried out as between the perpetrator and the target. If it is serious enough to be properly regarded as criminal, then it seems to me that the victim of collateral damage from the same conduct ought to be able to sue for harm foreseeably caused by it.

32 (Counsel for the respondent) protested that to include the victims of collateral damage in this way would be to widen the class of potential claimants under the Act to an alarming and indeterminate degree, and would enable the partners or close family members of targets of harassment to bring claims merely by asserting alarm and distress felt by way of natural sympathy for their spouse, partner, child or other close relation. The judge made much the same point.

33 I agree that alarm or distress suffered out of nothing more than sympathy for the targeted victim of harassment is insufficient to found a claim under the Act. The claimant must be harassed by it, in the sense that the conduct complained of must have some direct effect upon the claimant (in terms of causing foreseeable harm, usually, but not limited to, alarm and distress). This is because s.3(1) of the Act confers a right to bring a civil claim upon persons who are or may be the victim of the course of conduct in question, and because s.1(1) requires that course of conduct to amount to harassment of another. My view that the harm to the claimant must be foreseeable arises from s.1(1)(b) because of the requirement that the perpetrator knows or ought to know that the relevant course of conduct amounts to harassment.

34 The result of that analysis is that the ability to bring a harassment claim extends beyond the targeted individual only to those other persons who are foreseeably, and directly, harmed by the course of targeted conduct of which complaint is made, to the extent that they can properly be described as victims of it" (per Briggs LJ).

*General*

*7.8709* **12. National security etc** (1) If the Secretary of State certifies that in his opinion anything done by a specified person on a specified occasion related to—

(*a*) national security,

(*b*) the economic well-being of the United Kingdom, or

(*c*) the prevention or detection of serious crime,

and was done on behalf of the Crown, the certificate is conclusive evidence that this Act does not apply to any conduct of that person on that occasion.

(2) In subsection (1), "specified" means specified in the certificate in question.

(3) A document purporting to be a certificate under subsection (1) is to be received in evidence and, unless the contrary is proved, be treated as being such a certificate.

[Protection from Harassment Act 1997, s 12.]

**7.8710 13.** *Northern Ireland.*

**7.8711 14.** *Extent.*

**7.8712 15. Commencement** (1) Sections 1, 2, 4, 5 and 7 to 12 are to come into force on such day as the Secretary of State may by order made by statutory instrument appoint[1].

(2) Sections 3 and 6 are to come into force on such day as the Lord Chancellor may by order made by statutory instrument appoint[1].

(3) Different days may be appointed under this section for different purposes.

[Protection from Harassment Act 1997, s 15.]

---

[1] Sections 13–16 came into force at Royal Assent on 21 March 1997; the remaining provisions except s 3(3)–(9) (injunctions) were brought into force on 16 June 1997 by the following commencement orders made under s 15: Commencement Order (No 1), SI 1997/1418 and Commencement Order (No 2), SI 1997/1498. Section 3(3)–(9) was brought into force on 1 September 1998 by Commencement Order (No 3), SI 1998/1902.

**7.8713 16.** *Short title.*

# Terrorism Act 2000

(2000 c 11)

## PART I[1]

## INTRODUCTORY

**7.8714 1. Terrorism: interpretation** (1) In this Act "terrorism" means the use or threat of action where—

(*a*) the action falls within subsection (2),

(*b*) the use or threat is designed to influence the government[2] or an international governmental organisation or to intimidate the public or a section of the public, and

(*c*) the use or threat is made for the purpose of advancing a political, religious, racial or ideological cause[3].

(2) Action falls within this subsection if it—

(*a*) involves serious violence against a person,

(*b*) involves serious damage to property,

(*c*) endangers a person's life, other than that of the person committing the action,

(*d*) creates a serious risk to the health or safety of the public or a section of the public, or

(*e*) is designed seriously to interfere with or seriously to disrupt an electronic system.

(3) The use or threat of action falling within subsection (2) which involves the use of firearms or explosives is terrorism whether or not subsection (1)(*b*) is satisfied.

(4) In this section—

(*a*) "action" includes action outside the United Kingdom,

(*b*) a reference to any person or to property is a reference to any person, or to property, wherever situated,

(*c*) a reference to the public includes a reference to the public of a country other than the United Kingdom, and

(*d*) "the government" means the government of the United Kingdom, of a Part of the United Kingdom or of a country other than the United Kingdom.

(5) In this Act a reference to action taken for the purposes of terrorism includes a reference to action taken for the benefit of a proscribed organisation.

[Terrorism Act 2000, s 1 as amended by the Terrorism Act 2006, s 34 and the Counter-Terrorism Act 2008, s 75.]

---

[1] Part I contains ss 1–2 and Sch 1. With the exception of ss 2(1)(*b*) and (2) and 118, Sch 1 and 128–131, the provisions of this Act are to be brought into force by orders made under 128. For orders made at the time of going to press, see note to s 128, post.

The Terrorism (United Nations Measures) Order 2006, SI 2006/2657, made under s 1 of the United Nations Act 1946, gives effect in the United Kingdom to Resolution 1373 (2001) adopted by the Security Council of the United Nations on 28 September 2001 relating to terrorism and resolution 1453(2002) adopted on 20 December 2002 relating to humanitarian exemptions. It also provides for enforcement of Regulation (EC) 2580/2001 on specific measures directed at certain persons and entities with a view to combating terrorism. These include the freezing of funds, financial assets and economic resources of such persons and ensuring that any funds, financial assets, economic resources and financial services are not made available to them. A breach of any requirement or prohibition imposed by the Order is a criminal offence.

[2] The term "government" is not limited to those countries which are governed by democratic or representative principles: *R v F* [2007] EWCA Crim 243, [2007] 1 QB 960, [2007] 2 All ER 193, [2007] 3 WLR 164, [2007] 2 Cr App Rep 20.

In *R v Gul* [2013] UKSC 64, [2014] AC 1260, [2014] 1 All ER 463 the appellant advanced three contentions: a) that the 2000 Act, like the 2006 Act, was intended, at least in part, to give effect to the UK's international treaty obligations, and the concept of terrorism in international law does not extend to military attacks by a non-state armed group against state, or inter-governmental organisation, armed forces in the context of a non-international armed conflict, and that this limitation should be implied into the definition in s 1 of the 2000 Act; b) that it would be wrong to read the 2000 or

2006 Acts as criminalising in this country an act abroad, unless that act would be regarded as criminal by international law norms; and c) that, as a matter of domestic law and quite apart from international law considerations, some qualifications must be read into the very wide words of s 1 of the 2000 Act.

The Court rejected the argument that the requirement of consent to prosecution was relevant to the interpretation of "terrorism". However:

> "[38] Despite the undesirable consequences of the combination of the very wide definition of "terrorism" and the provisions of section 117, it is difficult to see how the natural, very wide, meaning of the definition can properly be cut down by this court . . . the definition of "terrorism" was indeed intended to be very wide. Unless it is established that the natural meaning of the legislation conflicts with the European Convention for the Protection of Human Rights and Fundamental Freedoms (which is not suggested) or any other international obligation of the United Kingdom (which we consider in the next section of this judgment), our function is to interpret the meaning of the definition in its statutory, legal and practical context. We agree with the wide interpretation favoured by the prosecution: it accords with the natural meaning of the words used in section 1(1)(*b*) of the 2000 Act, and, while it gives the words a concerningly wide meaning, there are good reasons for it (per Lords Neuburger and Judge in their joint judgment)."

The contentions based on international law similarly failed. (In brief summary) there was no accepted norm in international law as to what constitutes "terrorism', and there was no requirement in international law to "read down" s 1. In international humanitarian law, it did not appear that insurgents in non-international armed conflicts enjoyed combatant immunity. There was no general understanding, to the effect that terrorism did not extend to acts of insurgents or freedom fighters against a government or inter-governmental organisation in non-international armed conflicts. There was no reason why the UK government could not go further than international treaty when it came to legislating:

> "56 The appellant's reliance on the fact that there are provisions of the 2000 and 2006 Acts which criminalise various activities as terrorist offences even if committed abroad, runs into similar problems. Even if it were the case that, because of the need to take into account the UK's international law obligations, the wide definition of terrorism had to be read down when it comes to construing those provisions, that would be of no assistance to a defendant such as the appellant, who is a UK citizen being prosecuted for offences allegedly committed in this country. There is no reason to read down the wide definition of terrorism in a case such as this. The present case does not involve a defendant who has committed acts, which are said to be offences, abroad: the activities said to be offences were committed in the UK—and by a UK citizen."

Their Lordships expressed, however, these concerns about the width of the definition of "terrorism":

> "62 While acknowledging that the issue is ultimately one for Parliament, we should record our view that the concerns and suggestions about the width of the statutory definition of terrorism which Mr Anderson has identified in his two reports merit serious consideration. Any legislative narrowing of the definition of "terrorism", with its concomitant reduction in the need for the exercise of discretion under section 117 of the 2000 Act, is to be welcomed, provided that it is consistent with the public protection to which the legislation is directed.
>
> 63 The second general point is that the wide definition of "terrorism" does not only give rise to concerns in relation to the very broad prosecutorial discretion bestowed by the 2000 and 2006 Acts, as discussed in paras 36–37 above. The two Acts also grant substantial intrusive powers to the police and to immigration officers, including stop and search, which depend on what appears to be a very broad discretion on their part. While the need to bestow wide, even intrusive, powers on the police and other officers in connection with terrorism is understandable, the fact that the powers are so unrestricted and the definition of "terrorism" is so wide means that such powers are probably of even more concern than the prosecutorial powers to which the Acts give rise.
>
> 64 Thus, under Schedule 7 to the 2000 Act, the power to stop, question and detain in port and at borders is left to the examining officer. The power is not subject to any controls. Indeed, the officer is not even required to have grounds for suspecting that the person concerned falls within section 40(1) of the 2000 Act (ie that he has "committed an offence", or he "is or has been concerned in the commission, preparation or instigation of acts of terrorism"), or even that any offence has been or may be committed, before commencing an examination to see whether the person falls within that subsection. On this appeal, we are not, of course, directly concerned with that issue in this case. But detention of the kind provided for in the Schedule represents the possibility of serious invasions of personal liberty."

[3] "Terrorism" as it is ordinarily understood is the attempt to advance some political or religious cause not by persuasion but by violence, the endangerment of life etc: *Oxford County Council v Oxfordshire City Council* [2006] UKHL 25; [[2006] 2 AC 674; [2006] 2 WLR 1235 at [82], per Lord Scott. Section 1(1) and (2) , when read together, define "terrorism" as: (i) the use or threat of action which (ii) "endangers a person's life, other than that of the person committing the action" where (iii) the use of threat is designed to influence the government or an international governmental organisation or to intimidate the public or a section of the public and (iv) the use or threat is made for the purpose of advancing a political, religious, racial or ideological cause. A literal interpretation of the definition of terrorism would be too broad. It would include activity that is entirely non-violent; is in pursuit of a legitimate and mainstream political cause; may "endanger life" by accident; and where the person may be "concerned" in such activity wholly accidentally or even without knowledge. Three categories of action are described in s 1(2). The first is action falling within s 1(2)(*a*) and (*b*). This is the only category which is defined exclusively by reference to the nature of the action itself. It is not an ordinary use of language to describe a person as being "involved" in violence or damage to property if he is not aware that he is being so involved or if what he does is accidental.

The second category is action falling within s 1(2)(*c*) and (*d*). This is defined by reference to the consequences of the action: endangering a person's life and creating a serious risk to health or safety. The third category is action falling within s 1(2)(*e*). This is action which is defined by reference to its aim: action which is designed seriously to interfere with or disrupt an electronic system.

The third category of action is defined by reference to the state of mind of the actor. The first category of action must also be considered as importing a mental element. On a literal interpretation, the second category could include acts which endanger a person's life even if the actor is not aware that they do. But such an interpretation would dispense with the need for a mental element in the second category, whereas it is required in the first and third categories. It is unlikely that Parliament would have intended to make such a distinction between the three categories. If Parliament had intended to provide that a person commits an act of terrorism where he unwittingly or accidentally does something which in fact endangers another person's life, it would have spelt this out clearly.

It does not follow that publication of material cannot amount to an act of terrorism. If (i) the material that is published endangers a person's life (other than that of the person committing the action) or creates a serious risk to the health or safety of the public or a section of the public; and (ii) the person publishing the material intends it to have that effect (or is reckless as to whether or not it has that effect), then the publication is an act of terrorism, provided, of course, that the conditions stated in s 1(1)(*b*) and (*c*) are satisfied. Where a blog argues (on religious or political grounds) against the vaccination of children, such a blogger would not be a terrorist even if his blog were judged to create a serious risk to public health, unless he intends his publication to create the risk (or is reckless as to whether his blog will have that effect): *R (Miranda) v Secretary of State for the Home Department* [2016] EWCA Civ 6, [2016] 1 WLR 1505, [2016] 1 Cr App R 26.

**7.8715 2. *Repeal of temporary legislation***

PART II[1]

PROSCRIBED ORGANISATIONS

*Procedure*

**7.8716 3. Proscription** (1) For the purposes of this Act an organisation is proscribed if—

(*a*) it is listed in Schedule 2, or

(*b*) it operates under the same name as an organisation listed in that Schedule.

(2) Subsection (1)(*b*) shall not apply in relation to an organisation listed in Schedule 2 if its entry is the subject of a note in that Schedule.

(3) The Secretary of State may by order[1]—

(*a*) add an organisation to Schedule 2;

(*b*) remove an organisation from that Schedule;

(*c*) amend that Schedule in some other way.

(4) The Secretary of State may exercise his power under subsection (3)(*a*) in respect of an organisation only if he believes that it is concerned in terrorism.

(5) For the purposes of subsection (4) an organisation is concerned in terrorism[2] if it—

(*a*) commits or participates in acts of terrorism,

(*b*) prepares for terrorism,

(*c*) promotes or encourages terrorism, or

(*d*) is otherwise concerned in terrorism.

(5A) The cases in which an organisation promotes or encourages terrorism for the purposes of subsection (5)(*c*) include any case in which activities of the organisation—

(*a*) include the unlawful glorification of the commission or preparation (whether in the past, in the future or generally) of acts of terrorism; or

(*b*) are carried out in a manner that ensures that the organisation is associated with statements containing any such glorification.

(5B) The glorification of any conduct is unlawful for the purposes of subsection (5A) if there are persons who may become aware of it who could reasonably be expected to infer that what is being glorified, is being glorified as—

(*a*) conduct that should be emulated in existing circumstances, or

(*b*) conduct that is illustrative of a type of conduct that should be so emulated.

(5C) In this section—

"glorification" includes any form of praise or celebration, and cognate expressions are to be construed accordingly;

"statement" includes a communication without words consisting of sounds or images or both.

(6) Where the Secretary of State believes—

(*a*) that an organisation listed in Schedule 2 is operating wholly or partly under a name that is not specified in that Schedule (whether as well as or instead of under the specified name), or

(*b*) that an organisation that is operating under a name that is not so specified is otherwise for all practical purposes the same as an organisation so listed,

he may, by order[3], provide that the name that is not specified in that Schedule is to be treated as another name for the listed organisation.

(7) Where an order under subsection (6) provides for a name to be treated as another name for an organisation, this Act shall have effect in relation to acts occurring while—

(*a*) the order is in force, and

(*b*) the organisation continues to be listed in Schedule 2,

as if the organisation were listed in that Schedule under the other name, as well as under the name specified in the Schedule.

(8) The Secretary of State may at any time by order revoke an order under subsection (6) or otherwise provide for a name specified in such an order to cease to be treated as a name for a particular organisation.

(9) Nothing in subsections (6) to (8) prevents any liability from being established in any proceedings by proof that an organisation is the same as an organisation listed in Schedule 2, even though it is or was operating under a name specified neither in Schedule 2 nor in an order under subsection (6).

[Terrorism Act 2000, s 3 as amended by the Terrorism Act 2006, ss 21 and 22.]

---

[1] The Prescribed Organisations (Name Change) Orders 2009, SI 2009/578, 2010, SI 2010/34; 2011/2688 , SI 2013/1795 and 2742 and SI 2014/1612 and 2210 have been made, the effect of which have been noted to Sch 2, post.

[2] For "concerned in terrorism", see *Lord Alton of Liverpool v Secretary of State for the Home Department* [2008] EWCA Civ 443, [2008] 1 WLR 2341, [2008] 2 Cr App R 31.

[3] Various orders have been made which are noted to Sch 2, post.

7.8717 4. ***Deproscription: application***

7.8718 5. **Deproscription: appeal**

7.8719 6. **Further appeal**

7.8720 7. **Appeal: effect on conviction, etc** (1) This section applies where—

(*a*) an appeal under section 5 has been allowed in respect of an organisation,

(*b*) an order has been made under section 3(3)(*b*) in respect of the organisation in accordance with an order of the Commission under section 5(4) (and, if the order was made in reliance on section 123(5), a resolution has been passed by each House of Parliament under section 123(5)(*b*)),

(*c*) a person has been convicted of an offence in respect of the organisation under any of sections 11 to 13, 15 to 19 and 56, and

(*d*) the activity to which the charge referred took place on or after the date of the refusal to deproscribe against which the appeal under section 5 was brought.

(1A) This section also applies where—

(*a*) an appeal under section 5 has been allowed in respect of a name treated as the name for an organisation,

(*b*) an order has been made under section 3(8) in respect of the name in accordance with an order of the Commission under section 5(4),

(*c*) a person has been convicted of an offence in respect of the organisation under any of sections 11 to 13, 15 to 19 and 56, and

(*d*) the activity to which the charge referred took place on or after the date of the refusal, against which the appeal under section 5 was brought, to provide for a name to cease to be treated as a name for the organisation.

(2) If the person mentioned in subsection (1)(*c*) or (1A)(*c*) was convicted on indictment—

(*a*) he may appeal against the conviction to the Court of Appeal, and

(*b*) the Court of Appeal shall allow the appeal.

(3) A person may appeal against a conviction by virtue of subsection (2) whether or not he has already appealed against the conviction.

(4) An appeal by virtue of subsection (2)—

(*a*) must be brought within the period of 28 days beginning with the date on which the order mentioned in subsection (1)(*b*) or (1A)(*b*) comes into force, and

(*b*) shall be treated as an appeal under section 1 of the Criminal Appeal Act 1968 (but does not require leave).

(5) If the person mentioned in subsection (1)(*c*) or (1A)(*c*) was convicted by a magistrates' court—

(*a*) he may appeal against the conviction to the Crown Court, and

(*b*) the Crown Court shall allow the appeal.

(6) A person may appeal against a conviction by virtue of subsection (5)—

(*a*) whether or not he pleaded guilty,

(*b*) whether or not he has already appealed against the conviction, and

(*c*) whether or not he has made an application in respect of the conviction under section 111 of the Magistrates' Courts Act 1980 (case stated).

(7) An appeal by virtue of subsection (5)—

(*a*) must be brought within the period of 21 days beginning with the date on which the order mentioned in subsection (1)(*b*) or (1A)(*b* comes into force, and

(*b*) shall be treated as an appeal under section 108(1)(*b*) of the Magistrates' Courts Act 1980[1].

(8) *Amends the Criminal Justice Act 1988, s 133.*

[Terrorism Act 2000, s 7 as amended by the Terrorism Act 2006, s 22.]

---

[1] PART I: MAGISTRATES' COURTS, PROCEDURE, ante.

7.8721 8. ***Scotland and Northern Ireland***

7.8722 9. ***Application of Human Rights Act 1998 to appeals before the Proscribed Organisations Appeals Commission***

7.8723 10. **Immunity** (1) The following shall not be admissible as evidence in proceedings for an offence under any of sections 11 to 13, 15 to 19 and 56—

(*a*) evidence of anything done in relation to an application to the Secretary of State under section 4,

(*b*) evidence of anything done in relation to proceedings before the Proscribed Organisations Appeal Commission under section 5 above or section 7(1) of the Human Rights Act 1998,

(*c*) evidence of anything done in relation to proceedings under section 6 (including that section as applied by section 9(2)), and

(*d*) any document submitted for the purposes of proceedings mentioned in any of paragraphs (*a*) to (*c*).

(2) But subsection (1) does not prevent evidence from being adduced on behalf of the accused.

[Terrorism Act 2000, s 10.]

*Offences*

7.8724 **11. Membership** (1) A person commits an offence if he belongs or professes to belong to a proscribed organisation[1].

(2) It is a defence for a person charged with an offence under subsection (1) to prove[2]—

(*a*) that the organisation was not proscribed on the last (or only) occasion on which he became a member or began to profess to be a member, and

(*b*) that he has not taken part in the activities of the organisation at any time while it was proscribed.

(3) A person guilty of an offence under this section shall be liable[3]—

(*a*) on conviction on indictment, to imprisonment for a term not exceeding ten years, to a fine or to both, or

(*b*) on summary conviction, to imprisonment for a term not exceeding six months, to a fine not exceeding the statutory maximum or to both.

(4) In subsection (2) "proscribed" means proscribed for the purposes of any of the following—

(*a*) this Act;

(*b*) the Northern Ireland (Emergency Provisions) Act 1996;

(*c*) the Northern Ireland (Emergency Provisions) Act 1991;

(*d*) the Prevention of Terrorism (Temporary Provisions) Act 1989;

(*e*) the Prevention of Terrorism (Temporary Provisions) Act 1984;

(*f*) the Northern Ireland (Emergency Provisions) Act 1978;

(*g*) the Prevention of Terrorism (Temporary Provisions) Act 1976;

(*h*) the Prevention of Terrorism (Temporary Provisions) Act 1974;

(*i*) the Northern Ireland (Emergency Provisions) Act 1973.

[Terrorism Act 2000, s 11.]

---

1 In *R v Hundal and R v Dhaliwal* [2004] EWCA Crim 389, [2004] 2 Cr App Rep 307 the question arose as to whether persons resident abroad and visiting and UK, who belonged to a foreign branch of an organisation proscribed in the UK but not where they were resident, and who had not participated in any of the activities of the organisation inside United Kingdom, were guilty of this offence. It was held that: (1) The court could take into count the joining of an organisation outside the jurisdiction and activities outside the jurisdiction to determine whether the person was a member of the proscribed organisation; (2) what is required is for there to be someone who is in this country, and therefore subject to its jurisdiction who at the time that he is in this country is a member of the proscribed organisation; (3) To establish that the person concerned is a member of the proscribed organisation, evidence can be given that the person joined the organisation from abroad or when abroad, but he would only be guilty of an offence when he was in this country. Either he would have to travel to this country in order to commit an offence after he became a member or he would already have had to be in this country and joined the local foreign branch of the proscribed organisation while in this country.

Their lordships further held that evidence of membership of a proscribed organisation obtained as a result of a compulsory search under Sch 7 could be used in a prosecution under s 11; following the decision in *R v Kearns* [2002] EWCA 748, [2002] 1 WLR 2815, 1 Cr App Rep 111 this was not in breach of art 6.

2 It was held in *A-G's Reference (No 4 of 2002)* [2004] UKHL 43, [2005] 1 AC 264, [2004] 1 All ER 1, [2004] 3 WLR 976 (reversing the decision of the Court of Appeal) that since s 11(2) impermissibly infringed the presumption of innocence, it was appropriate, pursuant to s 3 of the 1998 Act, to read down s 11(2) so as to impose on the defendant an evidential burden only, even though that was not Parliament's intention when enacting the subsection.

3 For procedure in respect of this offence which is triable either way, see the Magistrates' Courts Act 1980, ss 17A–21, in PART I: MAGISTRATES' COURTS, PROCEDURE, ante.

7.8725 **12. Support** (1) A person commits an offence if—

(*a*) he invites support for a proscribed organisation, and

(*b*) the support is not, or is not restricted to, the provision of money or other property (within the meaning of section 15).

(2) A person commits an offence if he arranges, manages or assists in arranging or managing a meeting which he knows is—

(*a*) to support a proscribed organisation,

(*b*) to further the activities of a proscribed organisation, or

(*c*) to be addressed by a person who belongs or professes to belong to a proscribed organisation.

(3) A person commits an offence if he addresses a meeting and the purpose of his address is to encourage support for a proscribed organisation or to further its activities.

(4) Where a person is charged with an offence under subsection (2)(*c*) in respect of a private meeting it is a defence for him to prove[1] that he had no reasonable cause to believe that the address mentioned in subsection (2)(*c*) would support a proscribed organisation or further its activities.

(5) In subsections (2) to (4)—

(*a*) "meeting" means a meeting of three or more persons, whether or not the public are admitted, and

(*b*) a meeting is private if the public are not admitted.

(6) A person guilty of an offence under this section shall be liable—

(*a*) on conviction on indictment, to imprisonment for a term not exceeding ten years, to a fine or to both, or

(*b*) on summary conviction, to imprisonment for a term not exceeding six months, to a fine not exceeding the statutory maximum or to both[2].

[Terrorism Act 2000, s 12.]

[1] For this defence, see s 118, post.
[2] For procedure in respect of this offence which is triable either way, see the Magistrates' Courts Act 1980, ss 17A–21, in PART I: MAGISTRATES' COURTS, PROCEDURE, ante

7.8726 **13. Uniform** (1) A person in a public place commits an offence if he—

(*a*) wears an item of clothing, or

(*b*) wears, carries or displays an article,

in such a way or in such circumstances as to arouse reasonable suspicion that he is a member or supporter of a proscribed organisation.

(2) A constable in Scotland may arrest a person without a warrant if he has reasonable grounds to suspect that the person is guilty of an offence under this section.

(3) A person guilty of an offence under this section shall be liable on summary conviction to—

(*a*) imprisonment for a term not exceeding six months,

(*b*) a fine not exceeding level 5 on the standard scale, or

(*c*) both.

[Terrorism Act 2000, s 13.]

## PART III[1]
## TERRORIST PROPERTY

### *Interpretation*

7.8727 **14. Terrorist property** (1) In this Act "terrorist property" means—

(*a*) money or other property which is likely to be used for the purposes of terrorism (including any resources of a proscribed organisation),

(*b*) proceeds of the commission of acts of terrorism, and

(*c*) proceeds of acts carried out for the purposes of terrorism.

(2) In subsection (1)—

(*a*) a reference to proceeds of an act includes a reference to any property which wholly or partly, and directly or indirectly, represents the proceeds of the act (including payments or other rewards in connection with its commission), and

(*b*) the reference to an organisation's resources includes a reference to any money or other property which is applied or made available, or is to be applied or made available, for use by the organisation.

[Terrorism Act 2000, s 14.]

[1] Part III contains ss 14–31 and Schs 3 and 4.

### *Offences*

7.8728 **15. Fund-raising** (1) A person commits an offence[1] if he—

(*a*) invites another to provide money or other property, and

(*b*) intends that it should be used, or has reasonable cause to suspect that it may be used, for the purposes of terrorism.

(2) A person commits an offence[1] if he—

(*a*) receives money or other property, and

(*b*) intends that it should be used, or has reasonable cause to suspect that it may be used, for the purposes of terrorism.

(3) A person commits an offence[1] if he—

(*a*) provides money or other property, and

(*b*) knows or has reasonable cause to suspect that it will or may be used for the purposes of terrorism.

(4) In this section a reference to the provision of money or other property is a reference to its being given, lent or otherwise made available, whether or not for consideration.

[Terrorism Act 2000, s 15.]

[1] For mode of trial and punishment, see s 22, post.

7.8729 **16. Use and possession** (1) A person commits an offence[1] if he uses money or other property for the purposes of terrorism.

(2) A person commits an offence[1] if he—

(*a*) possesses money or other property, and

(*b*) intends that it should be used, or has reasonable cause to suspect that it may be used, for the purposes of terrorism.

[Terrorism Act 2000, s 16.]

[1] For mode of trial and punishment, see s 22, post.

7.8730 **17. Funding arrangements** A person commits an offence[1] if—

(*a*) he enters into or becomes concerned in an arrangement as a result of which money or other property is made available or is to be made available to another, and (*b*) he knows or has reasonable cause to suspect that it will or may be used for the purposes of terrorism.

[Terrorism Act 2000, s 17.]

[1] For mode of trial and punishment, see s 22, post.

7.8731 **18. Money laundering** (1) A person commits an offence[1] if he enters into or becomes concerned in an arrangement which facilitates the retention or control by or on behalf of another person of terrorist property—

(*a*) by concealment,

(*b*) by removal from the jurisdiction,

(*c*) by transfer to nominees, or

(*d*) in any other way.

(2) It is a defence for a person charged with an offence under subsection (1) to prove[2] that he did not know and had no reasonable cause to suspect that the arrangement related to terrorist property.

[Terrorism Act 2000, s 18.]

[1] For mode of trial and punishment, see s 22, post.

[2] On the balance of probabilities, see *R v Carr-Briant* [1943] KB 607, [1943] 2 All ER 156, 107 JP 167.

7.8732 **19. Disclosure of information: duty** (1) This section applies where a person—

(*a*) believes or suspects that another person has committed an offence under any of sections 15 to 18, and

(*b*) bases his belief or suspicion on information which comes to his attention—

(i) in the course of a trade, profession or business, or

(ii) in the course of his employment (whether or not in the course of a trade, profession or business).

(1A) But this section does not apply if the information came to the person in the course of a business in the regulated sector.

(2) The person commits an offence[1] if he does not disclose to a constable as soon as is reasonably practicable—

(*a*) his belief or suspicion, and

(*b*) the information on which it is based.

(3) It is a defence for a person charged with an offence under subsection (2) to prove[2] that he had a reasonable excuse for not making the disclosure.

(4) Where—

(*a*) a person is in employment,

(*b*) his employer has established a procedure for the making of disclosures of the matters specified in subsection (2), and

(*c*) he is charged with an offence under that subsection,

it is a defence for him to prove[2] that he disclosed the matters specified in that subsection in accordance with the procedure.

(5) Subsection (2) does not require disclosure by a professional legal adviser of—

(*a*) information which he obtains in privileged circumstances, or

(*b*) a belief or suspicion based on information which he obtains in privileged circumstances.

(6) For the purpose of subsection (5) information is obtained by an adviser in privileged circumstances if it comes to him, otherwise than with a view to furthering a criminal purpose—

(*a*) from a client or a client's representative, in connection with the provision of legal advice by the adviser to the client,

(*b*) from a person seeking legal advice from the adviser, or from the person's representative, or

(*c*) from any person, for the purpose of actual or contemplated legal proceedings.

(7) For the purposes of subsection (1)(*a*) a person shall be treated as having committed an offence under one of sections 15 to 18 if—

(*a*) he has taken an action or been in possession of a thing, and

(*b*) he would have committed an offence under one of those sections if he had been in the United Kingdom at the time when he took the action or was in possession of the thing.

(7A) The reference to a business in the regulated sector must be construed in accordance with Schedule 3A.

(7B) The reference to a constable includes a reference to a National Crime Agency officer authorised for the purposes of this section by the Director General of that Agency.

(8) A person guilty of an offence under this section shall be liable[3]—

(*a*) on conviction on indictment, to imprisonment for a term not exceeding five years, to a fine or to both, or

(*b*) on summary conviction, to imprisonment for a term not exceeding six months, or to a fine not exceeding the statutory maximum or to both.

[Terrorism Act 2000, s 19 as amended by the Anti-terrorism, Crime and Security Act, 2001, Sch 2, the Serious Organised Crime And Police Act 2005, Sch 4, the Counter-Terrorism Act 2008, s 77 and the Crime and Courts Act 2013, Sch 8.]

1 For mode of trial and punishment, see s 22, post.

2 On the balance of probabilities, see *R v Carr-Briant* [1943] KB 607, [1943] 2 All ER 156, 107 JP 167.

3 For procedure in respect of this offence which is triable either way, see the Magistrates' Courts Act 1980, ss 17A–21, in PART I: MAGISTRATES' COURTS, PROCEDURE, ante.

7.8733 **20. Disclosure of information: permission** (1) A person may disclose to a constable—

(*a*) a suspicion or belief that any money or other property is terrorist property or is derived from terrorist property;

(*b*) any matter on which the suspicion or belief is based.

(2) A person may make a disclosure to a constable in the circumstances mentioned in section 19(1) and (2).

(3) Subsections (1) and (2) shall have effect notwithstanding any restriction on the disclosure of information imposed by statute or otherwise.

(4) Where—

(*a*) a person is in employment, and

(*b*) his employer has established a procedure for the making of disclosures of the kinds mentioned in subsection (1) and section 19(2),

subsections (1) and (2) shall have effect in relation to that person as if any reference to disclosure to a constable included a reference to disclosure in accordance with the procedure.

(5) References to a constable includes a reference to a National Crime Agency officer authorised for the purposes of this section by the Director General of that Agency.

[Terrorism Act 2000, s 20, as amended by the Anti-terrorism, Crime and Security Act 2001, Sch 2, the Serious Organised Crime And Police Act 2005, Sch 4 and the Crime and Courts Act 2013, Sch 8.]

7.8734 **21. Cooperation with police** (1) A person does not commit an offence under any of sections 15 to 18 if he is acting with the express consent of a constable.

(2) Subject to subsections (3) and (4), a person does not commit an offence under any of sections 15 to 18 by involvement in a transaction or arrangement relating to money or other property if he discloses to a constable—

(*a*) his suspicion or belief that the money or other property is terrorist property, and

(*b*) the information on which his suspicion or belief is based.

(3) Subsection (2) applies only where a person makes a disclosure—

(*a*) after he becomes concerned in the transaction concerned,

(*b*) on his own initiative, and

(*c*) as soon as is reasonably practicable.

(4) Subsection (2) does not apply to a person if—

(*a*) a constable forbids him to continue his involvement in the transaction or arrangement to which the disclosure relates, and

(*b*) he continues his involvement.

(5) It is a defence for a person charged with an offence under any of sections 15(2) and (3) and 16 to 18 to prove[1] that—

(*a*) he intended to make a disclosure of the kind mentioned in subsections (2) and (3), and

(*b*) there is reasonable excuse for his failure to do so.

(6) Where—

(*a*) a person is in employment, and

(*b*) his employer has established a procedure for the making of disclosures of the same kind as may be made to a constable under subsection (2),

this section shall have effect in relation to that person as if any reference to disclosure to a constable included a reference to disclosure in accordance with the procedure.

(7) A reference in this section to a transaction or arrangement relating to money or other property includes a reference to use or possession.

[Terrorism Act 2000, s 21.]

1 On the balance of probabilities, see *R v Carr-Briant* [1943] KB 607, [1943] 2 All ER 156, 107 JP 167.

7.8735 **21ZA. Arrangements with prior consent** (1) A person does not commit an offence under any of sections 15 to 18 by involvement in a transaction or an arrangement relating to money or other property if, before becoming involved, the person—

(*a*) discloses to an authorised officer the person's suspicion or belief that the money or other property is terrorist property and the information on which the suspicion or belief is based, and

(*b*) has the authorised officer's consent to becoming involved in the transaction or arrangement.

(2) A person is treated as having an authorised officer's consent if before the end of the notice period the person does not receive notice from an authorised officer that consent is refused.

(3) The notice period is the period of 7 working days starting with the first working day after the

person makes the disclosure.

(4) A working day is a day other than a Saturday, a Sunday, Christmas Day, Good Friday or a day that is a bank holiday under the Banking and Financial Dealings Act 1971 (c 80) in the part of the United Kingdom in which the person is when making the disclosure.

(5) In this section "authorised officer" means a National Crime Agency officer authorised for the purposes of this section by the Director General of that Agency.

(6) The reference in this section to a transaction or arrangement relating to money or other property includes a reference to use or possession.

[Terrorism Act 2000, s 21ZA as inserted by SI 2007/3398 and amended by the Crime and Courts Act 2013, Sch 8.]

**7.8736 21ZB. Disclosure after entering into arrangements** (1) A person does not commit an offence under any of sections 15 to 18 by involvement in a transaction or an arrangement relating to money or other property if, after becoming involved, the person discloses to an authorised officer—

(*a*) the person's suspicion or belief that the money or other property is terrorist property, and

(*b*) the information on which the suspicion or belief is based.

(2) This section applies only where—

(*a*) there is a reasonable excuse for the person's failure to make the disclosure before becoming involved in the transaction or arrangement, and

(*b*) the disclosure is made on the person's own initiative and as soon as it is reasonably practicable for the person to make it.

(3) This section does not apply to a person if—

(*a*) an authorised officer forbids the person to continue involvement in the transaction or arrangement to which the disclosure relates, and

(*b*) the person continues that involvement.

(4) In this section "authorised officer" means a National Crime Agency officer authorised for the purposes of this section by the Director General of that Agency.

(5) The reference in this section to a transaction or arrangement relating to money or other property includes a reference to use or possession.

[Terrorism Act 2000, s 21ZB as inserted by SI 2007/3398 and amended by the Crime and Courts Act 2013, Sch 8.]

**7.8737 21ZC. Reasonable excuse for failure to disclose** It is a defence for a person charged with an offence under any of sections 15 to 18 to prove that—

(*a*) the person intended to make a disclosure of the kind mentioned in section 21ZA or 21ZB, and

(*b*) there is a reasonable excuse for the person's failure to do so.

[Terrorism Act 2000, s 21ZC as inserted by SI 2007/3398.]

**7.8738 21A. Failure to disclose: regulated sector** (1) A person commits an offence if each of the following three conditions is satisfied.

(2) The first condition is that he—

(*a*) knows or suspects, or

(*b*) has reasonable grounds for knowing or suspecting,

that another person has committed or attempted to commit an offence under any of sections 15 to 18.

(3) The second condition is that the information or other matter—

(*a*) on which his knowledge or suspicion is based, or

(*b*) which gives reasonable grounds for such knowledge or suspicion,

came to him in the course of a business in the regulated sector.

(4) The third condition is that he does not disclose the information or other matter to a constable or a nominated officer as soon as is practicable after it comes to him.

(5) But a person does not commit an offence under this section if—

(*a*) he has a reasonable excuse for not disclosing the information or other matter;

(*b*) he is a professional legal adviser or relevant professional adviser and the information or other matter came to him in privileged circumstances; or

(*c*) subsection (5A) applies to him.

(5A) This subsection applies to a person if—

(*a*) the person is employed by, or is in partnership with, a professional legal adviser or relevant professional adviser to provide the adviser with assistance or support,

(*b*) the information or other matter comes to the person in connection with the provision of such assistance or support, and

(*c*) the information or other matter came to the adviser in privileged circumstances.

(6) In deciding whether a person committed an offence under this section the court must consider whether he followed any relevant guidance which was at the time concerned—

(*a*) issued by a supervisory authority or any other appropriate body,

(*b*) approved by the Treasury, and

(*c*) published in a manner it approved as appropriate in its opinion to bring the guidance to the attention of persons likely to be affected by it.

(7) A disclosure to a nominated officer is a disclosure which—

(*a*) is made to a person nominated by the alleged offender's employer to receive disclosures under this section, and

(*b*) is made in the course of the alleged offender's employment and in accordance with the procedure established by the employer for the purpose.

(8) Information or other matter comes to a professional legal adviser or relevant professional adviser in privileged circumstances if it is communicated or given to him—

(*a*) by (or by a representative of) a client of his in connection with the giving by the adviser of legal advice to the client,

(*b*) by (or by a representative of) a person seeking legal advice from the adviser, or

(*c*) by a person in connection with legal proceedings or contemplated legal proceedings.

(9) But subsection (8) does not apply to information or other matter which is communicated or given with a view to furthering a criminal purpose.

(10) Schedule 3A has effect for the purpose of determining what is—

(*a*) a business in the regulated sector;

(*b*) a supervisory authority.

(11) For the purposes of subsection (2) a person is to be taken to have committed an offence there mentioned if—

(*a*) he has taken an action or been in possession of a thing, and

(*b*) he would have committed the offence if he had been in the United Kingdom at the time when he took the action or was in possession of the thing.

(12) A person guilty of an offence under this section is liable—

(*a*) on conviction on indictment, to imprisonment for a term not exceeding five years or to a fine or to both;

(*b*) on summary conviction, to imprisonment for a term not exceeding six months or to a fine not exceeding the statutory maximum or to both.

(13) An appropriate body is any body which regulates or is representative of any trade, profession, business or employment carried on by the alleged offender.

(14) The reference to a constable includes a reference to a National Crime Agency officer authorised for the purposes of this section by the Director General of that Agency.

(15) In this section "relevant professional adviser" means an accountant, auditor or tax adviser who is a member of a professional body which is established for accountants, auditors or tax advisers (as the case may be) and which makes provision for—

(*a*) testing the competence of those seeking admission to membership of such a body as a condition for such admission; and

(*b*) imposing and maintaining professional and ethical standards for its members, as well as imposing sanctions for non-compliance with those standards.

[Terrorism Act 2000, s 21A as inserted by the Anti-terrorism, Crime and Security Act 2001, Sch 2 and amended by the Serious Organised Crime And Police Act 2005, Sch 4, SI 2007/3398 and the Crime and Courts Act 2013, Sch 8.]

7.8739 **21B. Protected disclosures** (1) A disclosure which satisfies the following three conditions is not to be taken to breach any restriction on the disclosure of information (however imposed).

(2) The first condition is that the information or other matter disclosed came to the person making the disclosure (the discloser) in the course of a business in the regulated sector.

(3) The second condition is that the information or other matter—

(*a*) causes the discloser to know or suspect, or

(*b*) gives him reasonable grounds for knowing or suspecting,

that another person has committed or attempted to commit an offence under any of sections 15 to 18.

(4) The third condition is that the disclosure is made to a constable or a nominated officer as soon as is practicable after the information or other matter comes to the discloser.

(5) A disclosure to a nominated officer is a disclosure which—

(*a*) is made to a person nominated by the discloser's employer to receive disclosures under this section, and

(*b*) is made in the course of the discloser's employment and in accordance with the procedure established by the employer for the purpose.

(6) The reference to a business in the regulated sector must be construed in accordance with Schedule 3A.

(7) The reference to a constable includes a reference to a National Crime Agency officer authorised for the purposes of this section by the Director General of that Agency.

[Terrorism Act 2000, s 21B as inserted by the Anti-terrorism, Crime and Security Act 2001, Sch 2 and amended by the Serious Organised Crime And Police Act 2005, Sch 4, SI 2007/3398 and the Crime and Courts Act 2013, Sch 8.]

7.8740 **21C. Disclosures the National Crime Agency** (1) Where a disclosure is made under a provision of this Part to a constable, the constable must disclose it in full as soon as practicable after it has been made to a National Crime Agency officer authorised for the purposes of that provision by the Director General of that Agency.

(2) Where a disclosure is made under section 21 (cooperation with police) to a constable, the

constable must disclose it in full as soon as practicable after it has been made to a National Crime Agency officer authorised for the purposes of this subsection by the Director General of that Agency.

[Terrorism Act 2000, s 21C as inserted by SI 2007/3398 and amended by the Crime and Courts Act 2013, Sch 8.]

7.8741 **21D. Tipping off: regulated sector** (1) A person commits an offence if—

(*a*) the person discloses any matter within subsection (2);

(*b*) the disclosure is likely to prejudice any investigation that might be conducted following the disclosure referred to in that subsection; and

(*c*) the information on which the disclosure is based came to the person in the course of a business in the regulated sector.

(2) The matters are that the person or another person has made a disclosure under a provision of this Part—

(*a*) to a constable,

(*b*) in accordance with a procedure established by that person's employer for the making of disclosures under that provision,

(*c*) to a nominated officer, or

(*d*) to a National Crime Agency officer authorised for the purposes of that provision by the Director General of that Agency,

of information that came to that person in the course of a business in the regulated sector.

(3) A person commits an offence if—

(*a*) the person discloses that an investigation into allegations that an offence under this Part has been committed is being contemplated or is being carried out;

(*b*) the disclosure is likely to prejudice that investigation; and

(*c*) the information on which the disclosure is based came to the person in the course of a business in the regulated sector.

(4) A person guilty of an offence under this section is liable—

(*a*) on summary conviction to imprisonment for a term not exceeding three months, or to a fine not exceeding level 5 on the standard scale, or to both;

(*b*) on conviction on indictment to imprisonment for a term not exceeding two years, or to a fine, or to both.

(5) This section is subject to—

(*a*) section 21E (disclosures within an undertaking or group etc),

(*b*) section 21F (other permitted disclosures between institutions etc), and

(*c*) section 21G (other permitted disclosures etc).

[Terrorism Act 2000, s 21D as inserted by SI 2007/3398 and amended by the Crime and Courts Act 2013, Sch 8.]

7.8742 **21E. Disclosures within an undertaking or group etc** (1) An employee, officer or partner of an undertaking does not commit an offence under section 21D if the disclosure is to an employee, officer or partner of the same undertaking.

(2) A person does not commit an offence under section 21D in respect of a disclosure by a credit institution or a financial institution if—

(*a*) the disclosure is to a credit institution or a financial institution,

(*b*) the institution to whom the disclosure is made is situated in an EEA State or in a country or territory imposing equivalent money laundering requirements, and

(*c*) both the institution making the disclosure and the institution to whom it is made belong to the same group.

(3) In subsection (2) "group" has the same meaning as in Directive 2002/87/EC of the European Parliament and of the Council of 16th December 2002 on the supplementary supervision of credit institutions, insurance undertakings and investment firms in a financial conglomerate.

(4) A professional legal adviser or a relevant professional adviser does not commit an offence under section 21D if—

(*a*) the disclosure is to a professional legal adviser or a relevant professional adviser,

(*b*) both the person making the disclosure and the person to whom it is made carry on business in an EEA state or in a country or territory imposing equivalent money laundering requirements, and

(*c*) those persons perform their professional activities within different undertakings that share common ownership, management or control.

[Terrorism Act 2000, s 21E as inserted by SI 2007/3398.]

7.8743 **21F. Other permitted disclosures between institutions etc** (1) This section applies to a disclosure—

(*a*) by a credit institution to another credit institution,

(*b*) by a financial institution to another financial institution,

(*c*) by a professional legal adviser to another professional legal adviser, or

(*d*) by a relevant professional adviser of a particular kind to another relevant professional adviser of the same kind.

(2) A person does not commit an offence under section 21D in respect of a disclosure to which this section applies if—

(*a*) the disclosure relates to—

(i) a client or former client of the institution or adviser making the disclosure and the institution or adviser to whom it is made,

(ii) a transaction involving them both, or

(iii) the provision of a service involving them both;

(*b*) the disclosure is for the purpose only of preventing an offence under this Part of this Act;

(*c*) the institution or adviser to whom the disclosure is made is situated in an EEA State or in a country or territory imposing equivalent money laundering requirements; and

(*d*) the institution or adviser making the disclosure and the institution or adviser to whom it is made are subject to equivalent duties of professional confidentiality and the protection of personal data (within the meaning of section 1 of the Data Protection Act 1998).

[Terrorism Act 2000, s 21F as inserted by SI 2007/3398.]

7.8744 **21G. Other permitted disclosures etc** (1) A person does not commit an offence under section 21D if the disclosure is—

(*a*) to the authority that is the supervisory authority for that person by virtue of the Money Laundering Regulations 2007 (SI 2007/2157); or

(*b*) for the purpose of—

(i) the detection, investigation or prosecution of a criminal offence (whether in the United Kingdom or elsewhere),

(ii) an investigation under the Proceeds of Crime Act 2002, or

(iii) the enforcement of any order of a court under that Act.

(2) A professional legal adviser or a relevant professional adviser does not commit an offence under section 21D if the disclosure—

(*a*) is to the adviser's client, and

(*b*) is made for the purpose of dissuading the client from engaging in conduct amounting to an offence.

(3) A person does not commit an offence under section 21D(1) if the person does not know or suspect that the disclosure is likely to have the effect mentioned in section 21D(1)(*b*).

(4) A person does not commit an offence under section 21D(3) if the person does not know or suspect that the disclosure is likely to have the effect mentioned in section 21D(3)(*b*).

[Terrorism Act 2000, s 21G as inserted by SI 2007/3398.]

7.8745 **21H. Interpretation of sections 21D to 21G** (1) The references in sections 21D to 21G—

(*a*) to a business in the regulated sector, and

(*b*) to a supervisory authority,

are to be construed in accordance with Schedule 3A.

(2) In those sections—

"credit institution" has the same meaning as in Schedule 3A;

"financial institution" means an undertaking that carries on a business in the regulated sector by virtue of any of paragraphs (*b*) to (i) of paragraph 1(1) of that Schedule.

(3) References in those sections to a disclosure by or to a credit institution or a financial institution include disclosure by or to an employee, officer or partner of the institution acting on its behalf.

(4) For the purposes of those sections a country or territory imposes "equivalent money laundering requirements" if it imposes requirements equivalent to those laid down in Directive 2005/60/EC of the European Parliament and of the Council of 26th October 2005 on the prevention of the use of the financial system for the purpose of money laundering and terrorist financing.

(5) In those sections "relevant professional adviser" means an accountant, auditor or tax adviser who is a member of a professional body which is established for accountants, auditors or tax advisers (as the case may be) and which makes provision for—

(*a*) testing the competence of those seeking admission to membership of such a body as a condition for such admission; and

(*b*) imposing and maintaining professional and ethical standards for its members, as well as imposing sanctions for non-compliance with those standards.

[Terrorism Act 2000, s 21H as inserted by SI 2007/3398.]

7.8746 **22. Penalties** A person guilty of an offence under any of sections 15 to 18 shall be liable[1]—

(*a*) on conviction on indictment, to imprisonment for a term not exceeding 14 years, to a *fine or to both, or*

(*b*) on summary conviction, to imprisonment for a term not exceeding six months, to a fine not exceeding the statutory maximum or to both.

[Terrorism Act 2000, s 22.]

---

1 For procedure in respect of this offence which is triable either way, see the Magistrates' Courts Act 1980, ss 17A–21, in PART I: MAGISTRATES' COURTS, PROCEDURE, ante.

7.8747 **22A. Meaning of "employment"** In sections 19 to 21B—

(*a*) "employment" means any employment (whether paid or unpaid) and includes—
  (i) work under a contract for services or as an office-holder,
  (ii) work experience provided pursuant to a training course or programme or in the course of training for employment, and
  (iii) voluntary work;

(*b*) "employer" has a corresponding meaning.

[Terrorism Act 2000, s 22A as inserted by the Counter-Terrorism Act 2008, s 77.]

7.8748 **23. Forfeiture: terrorist property offences** (1) The court by or before which a person is convicted of an offence under any of sections 15 to 18 may make a forfeiture order in accordance with the provisions of this section.

(2) Where a person is convicted of an offence under section 15(1) or (2) or 16, the court may order the forfeiture of any money or other property which, at the time of the offence, the person had in their possession or under their control and which—

(*a*) had been used for the purposes of terrorism, or

(*b*) they intended should be used, or had reasonable cause to suspect might be used, for those purposes.

(3) Where a person is convicted of an offence under section 15(3) the court may order the forfeiture of any money or other property which, at the time of the offence, the person had in their possession or under their control and which—

(*a*) had been used for the purposes of terrorism, or

(*b*) which, at that time, they knew or had reasonable cause to suspect would or might be used for those purposes.

(4) Where a person is convicted of an offence under section 17 or 18 the court may order the forfeiture of any money or other property which, at the time of the offence, the person had in their possession or under their control and which—

(*a*) had been used for the purposes of terrorism, or

(*b*) was, at that time, intended by them to be used for those purposes.

(5) Where a person is convicted of an offence under section 17 the court may order the forfeiture of the money or other property to which the arrangement in question related, and which—

(*a*) had been used for the purposes of terrorism, or

(*b*) at the time of the offence, the person knew or had reasonable cause to suspect would or might be used for those purposes.

(6) Where a person is convicted of an offence under section 18 the court may order the forfeiture of the money or other property to which the arrangement in question related.

(7) Where a person is convicted of an offence under any of sections 15 to 18, the court may order the forfeiture of any money or other property which wholly or partly, and directly or indirectly, is received by any person as a payment or other reward in connection with the commission of the offence.

[Terrorism Act 2000, s 23 as substituted by the Counter-Terrorism Act 2008, s 34.]

7.8749 **23A. Forfeiture: other terrorism offences and offences with a terrorist connection**

(1) The court by or before which a person is convicted of an offence to which this section applies may order the forfeiture of any money or other property in relation to which the following conditions are met—

(*a*) that it was, at the time of the offence, in the possession or control of the person convicted; and

(*b*) that—
  (i) it had been used for the purposes of terrorism,
  (ii) it was intended by that person that it should be used for the purposes of terrorism, or
  (iii) the court believes that it will be used for the purposes of terrorism unless forfeited.

(2) This section applies to an offence under—

(*a*) any of the following provisions of this Act—
section 54 (weapons training);
section 57, 58 or 58A (possessing things and collecting information for the purposes of terrorism);
section 59, 60 or 61 (inciting terrorism outside the United Kingdom);

(*b*) any of the following provisions of Part 1 of the Terrorism Act 2006 (c 11)—
section 2 (dissemination of terrorist publications);
section 5 (preparation of terrorist acts);
section 6 (training for terrorism);
sections 9 to 11 (offences involving radioactive devices or materials).

(3) This section applies to any ancillary offence (as defined in section 94 of the Counter-Terrorism Act 2008) in relation to an offence listed in subsection (2).

(4) This section also applies to an offence specified in Schedule 2 to the Counter-Terrorism Act 2008 (offences where terrorist connection to be considered) as to which—

(*a*) in England and Wales, the court dealing with the offence has determined, in accordance with section 30 of that Act, that the offence has a terrorist connection;

(*b*) *Scotland.*

(5) The Secretary of State may by order amend subsection (2).

(6) An order adding an offence to subsection (2) applies only in relation to offences committed after the order comes into force.

[Terrorism Act 2000, s 23A as inserted by the Counter-Terrorism Act 2008, s 35.]

7.8750 **23B. Forfeiture: supplementary provisions** (1) Before making an order under section 23 or 23A, a court must give an opportunity to be heard to any person, other than the convicted person, who claims to be the owner or otherwise interested in anything which can be forfeited under that section.

(2) In considering whether to make an order under section 23 or 23A in respect of any property, a court shall have regard to—

(*a*) the value of the property, and

(*b*) the likely financial and other effects on the convicted person of the making of the order (taken together with any other order that the court contemplates making).

(3) *Scotland.*

(4) Schedule 4 makes further provision in relation to forfeiture orders under section 23 or 23A.

[Terrorism Act 2000, s 23B as inserted by the Counter-Terrorism Act 2008, s 36.]

## PART IV[1]

## TERRORIST INVESTIGATIONS

### *Interpretation*

7.8751 **32. Terrorist investigation** In this Act "terrorist investigation" means an investigation of—

(*a*) the commission, preparation or instigation of acts of terrorism,

(*b*) an act which appears to have been done for the purposes of terrorism,

(*c*) the resources of a proscribed organisation,

(*d*) the possibility of making an order under section 3(3), or

(*e*) the commission, preparation or instigation of an offence under this Act or under Part 1 of the Terrorism Act 2006 other than an offence under section 1 or 2 of that Act.

[Terrorism Act 2000, s 32 as amended by the Terrorism Act 2006, s 37.]

---

1 Part IV contains ss 32–39 and Schs 5 and 6.

### *Cordons*

7.8752 **33. Cordoned areas** (1) An area is a cordoned area for the purposes of this Act if it is designated under this section.

(2) A designation may be made only if the person making it considers it expedient for the purposes of a terrorist investigation.

(3) If a designation is made orally, the person making it shall confirm it in writing as soon as is reasonably practicable.

(4) The person making a designation shall arrange for the demarcation of the cordoned area, so far as is reasonably practicable—

(*a*) by means of tape marked with the word "police", or

(*b*) in such other manner as a constable considers appropriate.

[Terrorism Act 2000, s 33.]

7.8753 **34. Power to designate** (1) Subject to subsections (1A), (1B) and (2) a designation under section 33 may only be made—

(*a*) where the area is outside Northern Ireland and is wholly or partly within a police area, by an officer for the police area who is of at least the rank of superintendent, and

(*b*) where the area is in Northern Ireland, by a member of the Royal Ulster Constabulary who is of at least the rank of superintendent.

(1A) A designation under section 33 may be made in relation to an area (outside Northern Ireland) which is in a place specified in section 31(1)(*a*) to (*f*) of the Railways and Transport Safety Act, by a member of the British Transport Police Force who is of at least the rank of superintendent.

(1B) A designation under section 33 may be made by a member of the Ministry of Defence Police who is of at least the rank of superintendent in relation to an area outside or in Northern Ireland—

(*a*) if it is a place to which subsection (2) of section 2 of the Ministry of Defence Police Act 1987 (c 4) applies,

(*b*) if a request has been made under paragraph (*a*), (*b*) or (*d*) of subsection (3A) of that section in relation to a terrorist investigation and it is a place where he has the powers and privileges of a constable by virtue of that subsection as a result of the request, or

(*c*) if a request has been made under paragraph (*c*) of that subsection in relation to a terrorist investigation and it is a place described in subsection 1A of this section.

(1C) But a designation under section 33 may not be made by—

(*a*) a member of the British Transport Police Force, or

(*b*) a member of the Ministry of Defence Police,

in any other case.

(2) A constable who is not of the rank required by subsection (1) may make a designation if he considers it necessary by reason of urgency.

(3) Where a constable makes a designation in reliance on subsection (2) he shall as soon as is reasonably practicable—

(*a*) make a written record of the time at which the designation was made, and

(*b*) ensure that a police officer of at least the rank of superintendent is informed.

(4) An officer who is informed of a designation in accordance with subsection (3)(*b*)—

(*a*) shall confirm the designation or cancel it with effect from such time as he may direct, and

(*b*) shall, if he cancels the designation, make a written record of the cancellation and the reason for it.

[Terrorism Act 2000, s 34 as amended by the Anti-terrorism, Crime and Security Act 2001, Sch 7 and SI 2004/1573.]

7.8754 **35. Duration** (1) A designation under section 33 has effect, subject to subsections (2) to (5), during the period—

(*a*) beginning at the time when it is made, and

(*b*) ending with a date or at a time specified in the designation.

(2) The date or time specified under subsection (1)(*b*) must not occur after the end of the period of 14 days beginning with the day on which the designation is made.

(3) The period during which a designation has effect may be extended in writing from time to time by—

(*a*) the person who made it, or

(*b*) a person who could have made it (otherwise than by virtue of section 34(2)).

(4) An extension shall specify the additional period during which the designation is to have effect.

(5) A designation shall not have effect after the end of the period of 28 days beginning with the day on which it is made.

[Terrorism Act 2000, s 35.]

7.8755 **36. Police powers** (1) A constable in uniform may—

(*a*) order a person in a cordoned area to leave it immediately;

(*b*) order a person immediately to leave premises which are wholly or partly in or adjacent to a cordoned area;

(*c*) order the driver or person in charge of a vehicle in a cordoned area to move it from the area immediately;

(*d*) arrange for the removal of a vehicle from a cordoned area;

(*e*) arrange for the movement of a vehicle within a cordoned area;

(*f*) prohibit or restrict access to a cordoned area by pedestrians or vehicles.

(2) A person commits an offence if he fails to comply with an order, prohibition or restriction imposed by virtue of subsection (1).

(3) It is a defence for a person charged with an offence under subsection (2) to prove[1] that he had a reasonable excuse for his failure.

(4) A person guilty of an offence under subsection (2) shall be liable on summary conviction to—

(*a*) imprisonment for a term not exceeding three months *,

(*b*) a fine not exceeding level 4 on the standard scale, or

(*c*) both.

[Terrorism Act 2000, s 36.]

* **Words substituted by the Criminal Justice Act 2003, Sch 26 from a date to be appointed.**

1 On the balance of probabilities, see *R v Carr-Briant* [1943] KB 607, [1943] 2 All ER 156, 107 JP 167.

*Information and evidence*

7.8756 **37. Powers** Schedule 5 (power to obtain information, etc) shall have effect.

[Terrorism Act 2000, s 37.]

7.8757 **38. Financial information** Schedule 6 (financial information) shall have effect.

[Terrorism Act 2000, s 38.]

7.8758 **38A. Account monitoring orders** Schedule 6A (account monitoring orders) shall have effect.

[Terrorism Act 2000, s 38A as inserted by the Anti-terrorism, Crime and Security Act 2001, Sch 2.]

7.8759 **38B. Information about acts of terrorism** (1) This section applies where a person has information which he knows or believes might be of material assistance—

(*a*) in preventing the commission by another person of an act of terrorism, or

(*b*) in securing the apprehension, prosecution or conviction of another person, in the United Kingdom, for an offence involving the commission, preparation or instigation of an act of terrorism.

(2) The person commits an offence if he does not disclose the information as soon as reasonably practicable in accordance with subsection (3).

(3) Disclosure is in accordance with this subsection if it is made—

(*a*) in England and Wales, to a constable,

(*b*) in Scotland, to a constable, or

(*c*) in Northern Ireland, to a constable or a member of Her Majesty's forces.

(4) It is a defence for a person charged with an offence under subsection (2) to prove that he had a reasonable excuse for not making the disclosure.

(5) A person guilty of an offence under this section shall be liable—

(*a*) on conviction on indictment, to imprisonment for a term not exceeding five years, or to a fine or to both, or

(*b*) on summary conviction, to imprisonment for a term not exceeding six months, or to a fine not exceeding the statutory maximum or to both.

(6) Proceedings for an offence under this section may be taken, and the offence may for the purposes of those proceedings be treated as having been committed, in any place where the person to be charged is or has at any time been since he first knew or believed that the information might be of material assistance as mentioned in subsection (1).

[Terrorism Act 2000, s 38B as inserted by the Anti-terrorism, Crime and Security Act 2001, Sch 2.]

**7.8760 39. Disclosure of information, etc** (1) Subsection (2) applies where a person knows or has reasonable cause to suspect that a constable is conducting or proposes to conduct a terrorist investigation.

(2) The person commits an offence if he—

(*a*) discloses to another anything which is likely to prejudice the investigation, or

(*b*) interferes with material which is likely to be relevant to the investigation.

(3) Subsection (4) applies where a person knows or has reasonable cause to suspect that a disclosure has been or will be made under any of sections 19 to 21B or 38B.

(4) The person commits an offence if he—

(*a*) discloses to another anything which is likely to prejudice an investigation resulting from the disclosure under that section, or

(*b*) interferes with material which is likely to be relevant to an investigation resulting from the disclosure under that section.

(5) It is a defence for a person charged with an offence under subsection (2) or (4) to prove[1]—

(*a*) that he did not know and had no reasonable cause to suspect that the disclosure or interference was likely to affect a terrorist investigation, or

(*b*) that he had a reasonable excuse for the disclosure or interference.

(6) Subsections (2) and (4) do not apply to a disclosure which is made by a professional legal adviser—

(*a*) to his client or to his client's representative in connection with the provision of legal advice by the adviser to the client and not with a view to furthering a criminal purpose, or

(*b*) to any person for the purpose of actual or contemplated legal proceedings and not with a view to furthering a criminal purpose.

(6A) Subsections (2) and (4) do not apply if—

(*a*) the disclosure is of a matter within section 21D(2) or (3)(*a*) (terrorist property: tipping off), and

(*b*) the information on which the disclosure is based came to the person in the course of a business in the regulated sector.

(7) A person guilty of an offence under this section shall be liable[2]—

(*a*) on conviction on indictment, to imprisonment for a term not exceeding five years, to a fine or to both, or

(*b*) on summary conviction, to imprisonment for a term not exceeding six months, to a fine not exceeding the statutory maximum or to both.

(8) For the purposes of this section—

(*a*) a reference to conducting a terrorist investigation includes a reference to taking part in the conduct of, or assisting, a terrorist investigation, and

(*b*) a person interferes with material if he falsifies it, conceals it, destroys it or disposes of it, or if he causes or permits another to do any of those things.

(9) The reference in subsection (6A) to a business in the regulated sector is to be construed in accordance with Schedule 3A.

[*Terrorism Act 2000*, s 39 as amended by the Anti-terrorism, Crime and Security Act 2001, s 117(1), (3) and SI 2007/3398.]

---

1 On the balance of probabilities, see *R v Carr-Briant* [1943] KB 607, [1943] 2 All ER 156, 107 JP 167 and for the defence under sub-s (5)(*a*) see s 118, post.

2 For procedure in respect of this offence which is triable either way, see the Magistrates' Courts Act 1980, ss 17A–21, in PART I: MAGISTRATES' COURTS, PROCEDURE, ante.

## PART V[1]

## COUNTER-TERRORIST POWERS

*Suspected terrorists etc*

7.8761 **40. Terrorist: interpretation** (1) In this Part "terrorist" means a person who—

(*a*) has committed an offence under any of sections 11, 12, 15 to 18, 54 and 56 to 63, or

(*b*) is or has been concerned in the commission, preparation or instigation of acts of terrorism.

(2) The reference in subsection (1)(*b*) to a person who has been concerned in the commission, preparation or instigation of acts of terrorism includes a reference to a person who has been, whether before or after the passing of this Act, concerned in the commission, preparation or instigation of acts of terrorism within the meaning given by section 1.

[Terrorism Act 2000, s 40.]

1 Part V contains ss 40–53 and Schs 7 and 8.

7.8762 **41. Arrest without warrant**[1] (1) A constable may arrest without a warrant a person whom he reasonably suspects to be a terrorist.

(2) Where a person is arrested under this section the provisions of Schedule 8 (detention: treatment, review and extension) shall apply.

(3) Subject to subsections (4) to (7), a person detained under this section shall (unless detained under any other power) be released not later than the end of the period of 48 hours beginning—

(*a*) with the time of his arrest under this section, or

(*b*) if he was being detained under Schedule 7 when he was arrested under this section, with the time when his examination under that Schedule began.

(4) If on a review of a person's detention under Part II of Schedule 8 the review officer does not authorise continued detention, the person shall (unless detained in accordance with subsection (5) or (6) or under any other power) be released.

(5) Where a police officer intends to make an application for a warrant under paragraph 29 of Schedule 8 extending a person's detention, the person may be detained pending the making of the application.

(6) Where an application has been made under paragraph 29 or 36 of Schedule 8 in respect of a person's detention, he may be detained pending the conclusion of proceedings on the application.

(7) Where an application under paragraph 29 or 36 of Schedule 8 is granted in respect of a person's detention, he may be detained, subject to paragraph 37 of that Schedule, during the period specified in the warrant.

(8) The refusal of an application in respect of a person's detention under paragraph 29 or 36 of Schedule 8 shall not prevent his continued detention in accordance with this section.

(9) A person who has the powers of a constable in one Part of the United Kingdom may exercise the power under subsection (1) in any Part of the United Kingdom.

[Terrorism Act 2000, s 41.]

1 For the exercise of police powers of detention etc. in respect of persons arrested under this section, see the Code of Practice for the Detention, Treatment and Questioning by Police Officers of Persons under section 41 of, and Schedule 8 to, the Terrorism Act 2000, Code of Practice H, in PART II EVIDENCE, ante.

7.8763 **42. Search of premises** (1) A justice of the peace may on the application of a constable issue a warrant in relation to specified premises if he is satisfied that there are reasonable grounds for suspecting that a person whom the constable reasonably suspects to be a person falling within section 40(1)(*b*) is to be found there.

(2) A warrant under this section shall authorise any constable to enter and search the specified premises for the purpose of arresting the person referred to in subsection (1) under section 41.

(3) *Scotland.*

[Terrorism Act 2000, s 42.]

7.8764 **43. Search of persons** (1) A constable may stop and search a person whom he reasonably suspects to be a terrorist to discover whether he has in his possession anything which may constitute evidence that he is a terrorist.

(2) A constable may search a person arrested under section 41 to discover whether he has in his possession anything which may constitute evidence that he is a terrorist.

(3) *Repealed.*

(4) A constable may seize and retain anything which he discovers in the course of a search of a person under subsection (1) or (2) and which he reasonably suspects may constitute evidence that the person is a terrorist.

(4A) Subsection (4B) applies if a constable, in exercising the power under subsection (1) to stop a person whom the constable reasonably suspects to be a terrorist, stops a vehicle (see section 116(2)).

(4B) The constable—

(*a*) may search the vehicle and anything in or on it to discover whether there is anything which may constitute evidence that the person concerned is a terrorist, and

(*b*) may seize and retain anything which the constable—

(i) discovers in the course of such a search, and

(ii) reasonably suspects may constitute evidence that the person is a terrorist.

(4C) Nothing in subsection (4B) confers a power to search any person but the power to search in that subsection is in addition to the power in subsection (1) to search a person whom the constable reasonably suspects to be a terrorist.

(5) A person who has the powers of a constable in one Part of the United Kingdom may exercise a power under this section in any Part of the United Kingdom.

[Terrorism Act 2000, s 43 as amended by the Protection of Freedoms Act 2012, s 60 and Sch 10.]

7.8765 **43A. Search of vehicles** (1) Subsection (2) applies if a constable reasonably suspects that a vehicle is being used for the purposes of terrorism.

(2) The constable may stop and search—

(*a*) the vehicle;

(*b*) the driver of the vehicle;

(*c*) a passenger in the vehicle;

(*d*) anything in or on the vehicle or carried by the driver or a passenger;

to discover whether there is anything which may constitute evidence that the vehicle is being used for the purposes of terrorism.

(3) A constable may seize and retain anything which the constable—

(*a*) discovers in the course of a search under this section, and

(*b*) reasonably suspects may constitute evidence that the vehicle is being used for the purposes of terrorism.

(4) A person who has the powers of a constable in one Part of the United Kingdom may exercise a power under this section in any Part of the United Kingdom.

(5) In this section "driver", in relation to an aircraft, hovercraft or vessel, means the captain, pilot or other person with control of the aircraft, hovercraft or vessel or any member of its crew and, in relation to a train, includes any member of its crew.

[Terrorism Act 2000, s 43A as inserted by the Protection of Freedoms Act 2012, s 60.]

7.8766 **44–47.** *By virtue of the Terrorism Act 2000 (Remedial) Order 2011, SI 2011/631 the Act is to have effect as if ss 44 to 47(7) (power to stop and search) were repealed. The 2011 Order is now revoked and these sections are also repealed by the Protection of Freedoms Act 2012, s 59 and Sch 10.*

*Powers to stop and search in specified locations*

7.8767 **47A. Searches in specified areas or places** (1) A senior police officer may give an authorisation under subsection (2) or (3) in relation to a specified area or place if the officer—

(*a*) reasonably suspects that an act of terrorism will take place; and

(*b*) reasonably considers that—

(i) the authorisation is necessary to prevent such an act;

(ii) the specified area or place is no greater than is necessary to prevent such an act; and

(iii) the duration of the authorisation is no longer than is necessary to prevent such an act.

(2) An authorisation under this subsection authorises any constable in uniform to stop a vehicle in the specified area or place and to search—

(*a*) the vehicle;

(*b*) the driver of the vehicle;

(*c*) a passenger in the vehicle;

(*d*) anything in or on the vehicle or carried by the driver or a passenger.

(3) An authorisation under this subsection authorises any constable in uniform to stop a pedestrian in the specified area or place and to search—

(*a*) the pedestrian;

(*b*) anything carried by the pedestrian.

(4) A constable in uniform may exercise the power conferred by an authorisation under subsection (2) or (3) only for the purpose of discovering whether there is anything which may constitute evidence that the vehicle concerned is being used for the purposes of terrorism or (as the case may be) that the person concerned is a person falling within section 40(1)(*b*).

(5) But the power conferred by such an authorisation may be exercised whether or not the constable reasonably suspects that there is such evidence.

(6) A constable may seize and retain anything which the constable—

(*a*) discovers in the course of a search under such an authorisation; and

(*b*) reasonably suspects may constitute evidence that the vehicle concerned is being used for the purposes of terrorism or (as the case may be) that the person concerned is a person falling within section 40(1)(*b*).

(7) Schedule 6B (which makes supplementary provision about authorisations under this section) has effect.

(8) In this section—

"driver" has the meaning given by section 43A(5);

"senior police officer" has the same meaning as in Schedule 6B (see paragraph 14(1) and (2) of that Schedule);

"specified" means specified in an authorisation.

[Terrorism Act 2000, s 47A as inserted by the Protection of Freedoms Act 2012, s 61.]

*Code of practice relating to sections 43, 43A and 47A*

7.8768 **47AA. Code of practice relating to sections 43, 43A and 47A**

7.8769 **47AB. Issuing of code**[1]

---

1. The Terrorism Act 2000 (Codes of Practice for the Exercise of Stop and Search Powers) Order 2012, SI 2012/1794 has been made which came into force on 10 July 2012. The associated Code is the code of practice entitled 'Code of Practice (England, Wales and Scotland) for the Exercise of Stop and Search Powers under Sections 43 and 43A of the Terrorism Act 2000, and the Authorisation and Exercise of Stop and Search Powers Relating to Section 47A of, and Schedule 6B to, the Terrorism Act 2000' laid before Parliament on 10 May 2012.

7.8770 **47AC. Alteration or replacement of code** (1) The Secretary of State—

(*a*) must keep the search powers code under review, and

(*b*) may prepare an alteration to the code or a replacement code.

(2) Before preparing an alteration or a replacement code, the Secretary of State must consult the Lord Advocate and such other persons as the Secretary of State considers appropriate.

(3) Section 47AB (other than subsection (4)) applies to an alteration or a replacement code prepared under this section as it applies to a code prepared under section 47AA.

(4) In this section "the search powers code" means the code of practice issued under section 47AB(2) (as altered or replaced from time to time).

[Terrorism Act 2000, s 47AC as inserted by the Protection of Freedoms Act 2012, s 62.]

7.8771 **47AD. Publication of code** (1) The Secretary of State must publish the code (and any replacement code) issued under section 47AB(2).

(2) The Secretary of State must publish—

(*a*) any alteration issued under section 47AB(2), or

(*b*) the code or replacement code as altered by it.

[Terrorism Act 2000, s 47AD as inserted by the Protection of Freedoms Act 2012, s 62.]

7.8772 **47AE. Effect of code** (1) A constable must have regard to the search powers code when exercising any powers to which the code relates.

(2) A failure on the part of a constable to act in accordance with any provision of the search powers code does not of itself make that person liable to criminal or civil proceedings.

(3) The search powers code is admissible in evidence in any such proceedings.

(4) A court or tribunal may, in particular, take into account a failure by a constable to have regard to the search powers code in determining a question in any such proceedings.

(5) The references in this section to a constable include, in relation to any functions exercisable by a person by virtue of paragraph 15 of Schedule 4 to the Police Reform Act 2002 or paragraph 16 of Schedule 2A to the Police (Northern Ireland) Act 2003 (search powers in specified areas or places for community support officers), references to that person.

(6) In this section "the search powers code" means the code of practice issued under section 47AB(2) (as altered or replaced from time to time).

[Terrorism Act 2000, s 47AE as inserted by the Protection of Freedoms Act 2012, s 62.]

*Parking*

7.8773 **48. Authorisations** (1) An authorisation under this section authorises any constable in uniform to prohibit or restrict the parking of vehicles on a road specified in the authorisation.

(2) An authorisation may be given only if the person giving it considers it expedient for the prevention of acts of terrorism.

(3) An authorisation may be given—

(*a*) where the road specified is outside Northern Ireland and is wholly or partly within a police area other than one mentioned in paragraphs (*b*) or (*c*), by a police officer for the area who is of at least the rank of assistant chief constable;

(*b*) where the road specified is wholly or partly in the metropolitan police district, by a police officer for the district who is of at least the rank of commander of the metropolitan police;

(*c*) where the road specified is wholly or partly in the City of London, by a police officer for the City who is of at least the rank of commander in the City of London police force;

(*d*) where the road specified is in Northern Ireland, by a member of the Royal Ulster Constabulary who is of at least the rank of assistant chief constable.

(4) If an authorisation is given orally, the person giving it shall confirm it in writing as soon as is reasonably practicable.

[Terrorism Act 2000, s 48.]

7.8774 **49. Exercise of power** (1) The power conferred by an authorisation under section 48 shall be exercised by placing a traffic sign on the road concerned.

(2) A constable exercising the power conferred by an authorisation under section 48 may suspend a parking place.

(3) Where a parking place is suspended under subsection (2), the suspension shall be treated as a restriction imposed by virtue of section 48—

(*a*) for the purposes of section 99 of the Road Traffic Regulation Act 1984 (removal of vehicles illegally parked, etc) and of any regulations in force under that section, and

(*b*) *Northern Ireland.*

[Terrorism Act 2000, s 49.]

7.8775 **50. Duration of authorisation** (1) An authorisation under section 48 has effect, subject to subsections (2) and (3), during the period specified in the authorisation.

(2) The period specified shall not exceed 28 days.

(3) An authorisation may be renewed in writing by the person who gave it or by a person who could have given it; and subsections (1) and (2) shall apply as if a new authorisation were given on each occasion on which the authorisation is renewed.

[Terrorism Act 2000, s 50.]

7.8776 **51. Offences** (1) A person commits an offence if he parks a vehicle in contravention of a prohibition or restriction imposed by virtue of section 48.

(2) A person commits an offence if—

(*a*) he is the driver or other person in charge of a vehicle which has been permitted to remain at rest in contravention of any prohibition or restriction imposed by virtue of section 48, and

(*b*) he fails to move the vehicle when ordered to do so by a constable in uniform.

(3) It is a defence for a person charged with an offence under this section to prove[1] that he had a reasonable excuse for the act or omission in question.

(4) Possession of a current disabled person's badge shall not itself constitute a reasonable excuse for the purposes of subsection (3).

(5) A person guilty of an offence under subsection (1) shall be liable on summary conviction to a fine not exceeding level 4 on the standard scale.

(6) A person guilty of an offence under subsection (2) shall be liable on summary conviction to—

(*a*) imprisonment for a term not exceeding three months *,

(*b*) a fine not exceeding level 4 on the standard scale, or

(*c*) both.

[Terrorism Act 2000, s 51.]

---

* **Words substituted by the Criminal Justice Act 2003, Sch 26 from a date to be appointed.**

1 On the balance of probabilities, see *R v Carr-Briant* [1943] KB 607, [1943] 2 All ER 156, 107 JP 167.

7.8777 **52. Interpretation** In sections 48 to 51—

"disabled person's badge" means a badge issued, or having effect as if issued, under any regulations for the time being in force under section 21 of the Chronically Sick and Disabled Persons Act 1970 (in relation to England and Wales and Scotland) or section 14 of the Chronically Sick and Disabled Persons (Northern Ireland) Act 1978 (in relation to Northern Ireland);

"driver" means, in relation to a vehicle which has been left on any road, the person who was driving it when it was left there;

"parking" means leaving a vehicle or permitting it to remain at rest;

"traffic sign" has the meaning given in section 142(1) of the Road Traffic Regulation Act 1984 (in relation to England and Wales and Scotland) and in Article 28 of the Road Traffic Regulation (Northern Ireland) Order 1997 (in relation to Northern Ireland);

"vehicle" has the same meaning as in section 99(5) of the Road Traffic Regulation Act 1984 (in relation to England and Wales and Scotland) and Article 47(4) of the Road Traffic Regulation (Northern Ireland) Order 1997 (in relation to Northern Ireland).

[Terrorism Act 2000, s 52.]

*Port and border controls*

7.8778 **53. Port and border controls** (1) Schedule 7 (port and border controls) shall have effect.

(2) The Secretary of State may by order repeal paragraph 16 of Schedule 7.

(3) The powers conferred by Schedule 7 shall be exercisable notwithstanding the rights conferred by section 1 of the Immigration Act 1971 (general principles regulating entry into and staying in the United Kingdom).

[Terrorism Act 2000, s 53.]

## PART VI[1]

## MISCELLANEOUS

*Terrorist offences*

*7.8779 54. Weapons training (1)* A person commits an offence if he provides instruction or training in the making or use of—

(*a*) firearms,

(*aa*) radioactive material or weapons designed or adapted for the discharge of any radioactive material,

(*b*) explosives, or

(*c*) chemical, biological or nuclear weapons.

(2) A person commits an offence if he receives instruction or training in the making or use of—

(*a*) firearms,

(*aa*) radioactive material or weapons designed or adapted for the discharge of any radioactive material

(*b*) explosives, or

(*c*) chemical, biological or nuclear weapons.

(3) A person commits an offence if he invites another to receive instruction or training and the receipt—

(*a*) would constitute an offence under subsection (2), or

(*b*) would constitute an offence under subsection (2) but for the fact that it is to take place outside the United Kingdom.

(4) For the purpose of subsections (1) and (3)—

(*a*) a reference to the provision of instruction includes a reference to making it available either generally or to one or more specific persons, and

(*b*) an invitation to receive instruction or training may be either general or addressed to one or more specific persons.

(5) It is a defence[2] for a person charged with an offence under this section in relation to instruction or training to prove that his action or involvement was wholly for a purpose other than assisting, preparing for or participating in terrorism.

(6) A person guilty of an offence under this section shall be liable[3]—

(*a*) on conviction on indictment, to imprisonment for life, to a fine or to both, or

(*b*) on summary conviction, to imprisonment for a term not exceeding six months, to a fine not exceeding the statutory maximum or to both.

(7) *Repealed.*

(8) *Repealed.*

(9) *Repealed.*

[Terrorism Act 2000, s 54 as amended by the Anti-terrorism, Crime and Security Act 2001, s 120, the Counter-Terrorism Act 2008, Schs 3 and 9 and the Criminal Justice and Courts Act 2015, s 1.]

1 Part VI contains ss 54–64.

2 For defences to this offence, see further s 118, post

3 For procedure in respect of this offence which is triable either way, see the Magistrates' Courts Act 1980, ss 17A–21, in PART I: MAGISTRATES' COURTS, PROCEDURE, ante.

**7.8780 55. Weapons training: interpretation** In section 54—

"biological weapon" means a biological agent or toxin (within the meaning of the Biological Weapons Act 1974) in a form capable of use for hostile purposes or anything to which section 1(1)(*b*) of that Act applies,

"chemical weapon" has the meaning given by section 1 of the Chemical Weapons Act 1996, and

"radioactive material" means radioactive material capable of endangering life or causing harm to human health.

[Terrorism Act 2000, s 55 as amended by the Anti-terrorism, Crime and Security Act 2001, s 120(2).]

**7.8781 56. Directing terrorist organisation** (1) A person commits an offence if he directs, at any level, the activities of an organisation which is concerned in the commission of acts of terrorism.

(2) A person guilty of an offence under this section is liable on conviction on indictment to imprisonment for life.

[Terrorism Act 2000, s 56.]

**7.8782 57. Possession for terrorist purposes*** (1) A person commits an offence if he possesses an article[1] in circumstances which give rise to a reasonable suspicion that his possession is for a purpose connected with the commission, preparation or instigation of an act of terrorism.

(2) It is a defence[2] for a person charged with an offence under this section to prove that his possession of the article was not for a purpose connected with the commission, preparation or instigation of an act of terrorism.

(3) In proceedings for an offence under this section, if it is proved that an article—

(*a*) was on any premises at the same time as the accused, or

(*b*) was on premises of which the accused was the occupier or which he habitually used otherwise than as a member of the public,

the court may assume that the accused possessed the article, unless he proves that he did not know of its presence on the premises or that he had no control over it.

(4) A person guilty of an offence under this section shall be liable[3]—

(*a*) on conviction on indictment, to imprisonment for a term not exceeding 15 years[4], to a fine or to both, or

(*b*) on summary conviction, to imprisonment for a term not exceeding six months, to a fine not exceeding the statutory maximum or to both.

[Terrorism Act 2000, s 57 as amended by the Terrorism Act 2006, s 13.]

* **As to the interpretation of ss 57 and 58 and their relationship to one another, see now *R v G; R v J*** [2009] UKHL 13, [2009] 2 All ER 409, [2009] 1 WLR 724.

[1] This may include documents or records as s 58 would not thereby be superfluous. This section deals with possessing articles for the purpose of terrorist acts and s 58 deals with collecting or holding information that is of a kind likely to be useful to those involved in acts of terrorism. Section 57 includes a specific intention, s 58 does not: *R v Rowe* [2007] EWCA Crim 635, [2007] QB 975, [2007] 3 All ER 36, [2007] 2 Cr App Rep 171 and see *R v M* [2007] EWCA Crim 970, [2007] 3 All ER 53, [2007] 2 Cr App Rep 239, [2008] Crim LR 1 at 80. The section should be interpreted as if it reads: "A person commits an offence if he possesses an article in circumstances which give rise to a reasonable suspicion that he intends it to be used for the purpose of the commission, preparation or instigation of an act of terrorism.": *R v Zafar* [2008] EWCA Crim 184, [2008] QB 810, [2008] 4 All ER 46, [2008] 2 Cr App Rep 8.

[2] For defences to this offence, see further s 118, post.

[3] For procedure in respect of this offence which is triable either way, see the Magistrates' Courts Act 1980, ss 17A–21, in PART I: MAGISTRATES' COURTS, PROCEDURE, ante.

[4] Words "15 years" substituted for original words "10 years" except in relation to offences committed before 13 April 2006.

7.8783 **58. Collection of information*** [1] (1) A person commits an offence if—

(*a*) he collects[2] or makes a record of information of a kind likely to be useful[3] to a person committing or preparing an act of terrorism, or

(*b*) he possesses a document or record containing information of that kind.

(2) In this section "record" includes a photographic or electronic record.

(3) It is a defence[4] for a person charged with an offence under this section to prove that he had a reasonable excuse[5] for his action or possession.

(4) A person guilty of an offence under this section shall be liable[6]—

(*a*) on conviction on indictment, to imprisonment for a term not exceeding 10 years, to a fine or to both, or

(*b*) on summary conviction, to imprisonment for a term not exceeding six months, to a fine not exceeding the statutory maximum or to both.

(5) *Repealed.*

(6) *Repealed.*

(7) *Repealed.*

[Terrorism Act 2000, s 58 as amended by the Counter-Terrorism Act 2008, Schs 3 and 9.]

---

* **As to the interpretation of ss 57 and 58 and their relationship to one another, see now *R v G; R v J*** [2009] UKHL 13, [2010] 1 AC 43, [2009] 2 All ER 409, [2009] 2 All ER 409. **As to the compatibility of s 58 with art 10 of the ECHR, see *R v Brown*** [2011] EWCA Crim 2751, [2012] 2 Cr App Rep (S) 39.

[1] For the relation of this section to s 57, see note to that section. A document or record will only fall within section 58 if it is of a kind that is likely to provide practical assistance to a person committing or preparing an act of terrorism. A document that simply encourages the commission of acts of terrorism does not fall with s 58: *R v K* [2008] EWCA Crim 185, [2008] QB 827, [2008] 3 All ER 526.

[2] The prosecution does not have to prove that the defendant had a terrorist purpose for collecting or recording the information: *R v G, R v J* [2009] UKHL 13, [2010] AC 43, [2009] 2 All ER 409, [2009] 2 WLR 724.

[3] A narrow interpretation should not be given to "information likely to be useful" etc. Provided a document containing the information is not one in everyday use by members of the public eg published timetables and maps, it will be a matter for magistrates or a jury to decide whether it contains such information: *R v Muhammed* [2010] EWCA Crim 227, [2010] 3 All ER 759.

[4] For defences to this offence, see further s 118, post.

[5] It cannot amount to a "reasonable excuse" in the context of this provision that the record originated as part of an effort to change an undemocratic or illegal regime; to hold otherwise would mean that the reasonable excuse for the conduct which constituted the crime might be found in the commission of the very crime prohibited by the statute and such circularity would bring an impossible incoherence into the statutory provisions: *R v F* [2007] EWCA Crim 243, [2007] 1 QB 960, [2007] 2 All ER 193, [2007] 3 WLR 164. In *R v AY* [2010] EWCA Crim 762, [2010] 1 WLR 2644, [2010] 2 Cr App R 15, [2010] Crim LR 882, however, *R v F* was distinguished as "a case concerned with what was unarguably offensive purpose and not with a contention that there was a purpose confined solely to lawful defence" (para 14). The defendant had downloaded: The Mujahideen Terrorist Handbook; The Mujahideen Explosives Handbook; a video of instructions on the making of a ball-bearing suicide vest; and a video of instructions on the making of improvised explosive devices. He sought to advance the defence of reasonable excuse contending, inter alia, that he had downloaded it at a time when he had believed on reasonable grounds that the Somali people, and in particular those associated with the Islamic Courts Union (ICU) in Somalia, had been the victims of the use of unlawful and disproportionate force and were in need of assistance by way of the use of armed force, and that he had considered that the information which he had downloaded could potentially be of use for the purpose of resisting the unlawful invasion and occupation. Then trial judge declined to rule that part of the defence could not in law give rise to the defence of reasonable excuse. The issue on the prosecution's appeal was whether an alleged intended use for the lawful defence of others, or to assist them to employ lawful self-defence, was or was not capable of amounting to reasonable excuse within s 58(3). It was held that since self-defence might be relevant in the case of an act which would be within the definition of an act of terrorism or in that of a terrorist offence, the proposed element of the defence could not be withdrawn only on the ground that it involved the proposition that the information might be used "in the field". See, however, the criticism of the decision in the commentary in the Criminal Law Review.

What the defendant must show is an objectively reasonable excuse for possessing something that Parliament has made it, prima facie, an offence for him to possess because of its potential utility to a terrorist; thus, mental illness cannot be a reasonable excuse if it would not have been reasonable for a mentally well person to collect or record the information: *R v G, R v J* [2009] UKHL 13, [2010] AC 43, [2009] 2 All ER 409, [2009] 2 WLR 724.

[6] For procedure in respect of this offence which is triable either way, see the Magistrates' Courts Act 1980, ss 17A–21, in PART I: MAGISTRATES' COURTS, PROCEDURE, ante.

7.8784 **58A. *Eliciting, publishing or communicating information about members of armed forces etc***

*Inciting terrorism overseas*

7.8785 **59. England and Wales** (1) A person commits an offence if—

(*a*) he incites another person to commit an act of terrorism wholly or partly outside the United Kingdom, and (*b*) the act would, if committed in England and Wales, constitute one of the offences listed in subsection (2).

(2) Those offences are—

(*a*) murder,

(*b*) an offence under section 18 of the Offences against the Person Act 1861 (wounding with intent),

(*c*) an offence under section 23 or 24 of that Act (poison),

(*d*) an offence under section 28 or 29 of that Act (explosions), and

(*e*) an offence under section 1(2) of the Criminal Damage Act 1971 (endangering life by damaging property).

(3) A person guilty of an offence under this section shall be liable to any penalty to which he would be liable on conviction of the offence listed in subsection (2) which corresponds to the act which he incites.

(4) For the purposes of subsection (1) it is immaterial whether or not the person incited is in the United Kingdom at the time of the incitement.

(5) Nothing in this section imposes criminal liability on any person acting on behalf of, or holding office under, the Crown.

[Terrorism Act 2000, s 59.]

**7.8786 60–61.** ***Northern Ireland and Scotland***

*Terrorist bombing and finance offences*

**7.8787 62. Terrorist bombing: jurisdiction** (1) If—

(*a*) a person does anything outside the United Kingdom as an act of terrorism or for the purposes of terrorism, and

(*b*) his action would have constituted the commission of one of the offences listed in subsection (2) if it had been done in the United Kingdom,

he shall be guilty of the offence.

(2) The offences referred to in subsection (1)(*b*) are—

(*a*) an offence under section 2, 3 or 5 of the Explosive Substances Act 1883 (causing explosions, etc),

(*b*) an offence under section 1 of the Biological Weapons Act 1974 (biological weapons), and

(*c*) an offence under section 2 of the Chemical Weapons Act 1996 (chemical weapons).

[Terrorism Act 2000, s 62.]

**7.8788 63. Terrorist finance: jurisdiction** (1) If—

(*a*) a person does anything outside the United Kingdom, and

(*b*) his action would have constituted the commission of an offence under any of sections 15 to 18 if it had been done in the United Kingdom,

he shall be guilty of the offence.

(2) For the purposes of subsection (1)(*b*), section 18(1)(*b*) shall be read as if for "the jurisdiction" there were substituted "a jurisdiction".

[Terrorism Act 2000, s 63.]

*Extra-territorial jurisdiction for other terrorist offences etc*

**7.8789 63A. Other terrorist offences under this Act: jurisdiction** (1) If—

(*a*) a United Kingdom national or a United Kingdom resident does anything outside the United Kingdom, and

(*b*) his action, if done in any part of the United Kingdom, would have constituted an offence under any of sections 56 to 61,

he shall be guilty in that part of the United Kingdom of the offence.

(2) For the purposes of this section and sections 63B and 63C a "United Kingdom national" means an individual who is—

(*a*) a British citizen, a British overseas territories citizen, a British National (Overseas) or a British Overseas citizen,

(*b*) a person who under the British Nationality Act 1981 is a British subject, or

(*c*) a British protected person within the meaning of that Act.

(3) For the purposes of this section and sections 63B and 63C a "United Kingdom resident" means an individual who is resident in the United Kingdom.

[Terrorism Act 2000, s 63A as inserted by the Crime (International Co-operation) Act 2003, s 52 and amended by the Terrorism Act 2006, Sch 3.]

**7.8790 63B. Terrorist attacks abroad by UK nationals or residents: jurisdiction** (1) If—

(*a*) a United Kingdom national or a United Kingdom resident does anything outside the United Kingdom as an act of terrorism or for the purposes of terrorism, and

(*b*) his action, if done in any part of the United Kingdom, would have constituted an offence listed in subsection (2), he shall be guilty in that part of the United Kingdom of the offence.

(2) These are the offences—

(*a*) murder, manslaughter, culpable homicide, rape, assault causing injury, assault to injury, kidnapping, abduction or false imprisonment,

(*b*) an offence under section 4, 16, 18, 20, 21, 22, 23, 24, 28, 29, 30 or 64 of the Offences against the Person Act 1861,

(*c*) an offence under any of sections 1 to 5 of the Forgery and Counterfeiting Act 1981,

(*d*) *Scotland,*

(*e*) an offence under section 1 or 2 of the Criminal Damage Act 1971,

(*f*) an offence under Article 3 or 4 of the Criminal Damage (Northern Ireland) Order 1977,

(*g*) malicious mischief,

(*h*) wilful fire-raising.

[Terrorism Act 2000, s 63B as inserted by the Crime (International Co-operation) Act 2003, s 52.]

7.8791 **63C. Terrorist attacks abroad on UK nationals, residents and diplomatic staff etc: jurisdiction** (1) If—

(*a*) a person does anything outside the United Kingdom as an act of terrorism or for the purposes of terrorism,

(*b*) his action is done to, or in relation to, a United Kingdom national, a United Kingdom resident or a protected person, and

(*c*) his action, if done in any part of the United Kingdom, would have constituted an offence listed in subsection (2),

he shall be guilty in that part of the United Kingdom of the offence.

(2) These are the offences—

(*a*) murder, manslaughter, culpable homicide, rape, assault causing injury, assault to injury, kidnapping, abduction or false imprisonment,

(*b*) an offence under section 4, 16, 18, 20, 21, 22, 23, 24, 28, 29, 30 or 64 of the Offences against the Person Act 1861,

(*c*) an offence under section 1, 2, 3, 4 or 5(1) or (3) of the Forgery and Counterfeiting Act 1981,

(*d*) *Scotland.*

(3) For the purposes of this section and section 63D a person is a protected person if—

(*a*) he is a member of a United Kingdom diplomatic mission within the meaning of Article 1(*b*) of the Vienna Convention on Diplomatic Relations signed in 1961 (as that Article has effect in the United Kingdom by virtue of section 2 of and Schedule 1 to the Diplomatic Privileges Act 1964),

(*b*) he is a member of a United Kingdom consular post within the meaning of Article 1(*g*) of the Vienna Convention on Consular Relations signed in 1963 (as that Article has effect in the United Kingdom by virtue of section 1 of and Schedule 1 to the Consular Relations Act 1968),

(*c*) he carries out any functions for the purposes of the European Medicines Agency, or

(*d*) he carries out any functions for the purposes of a body specified in an order made by the Secretary of State.

(4) The Secretary of State may specify a body under subsection (3)(*d*) only if—

(*a*) it is established by or under the Treaty establishing the European Community or the Treaty on European Union, and

(*b*) the principal place in which its functions are carried out is a place in the United Kingdom.

(5) If in any proceedings a question arises as to whether a person is or was a protected person, a certificate—

(*a*) issued by or under the authority of the Secretary of State, and

(*b*) stating any fact relating to the question,

is to be conclusive evidence of that fact.

[Terrorism Act 2000, s 63C as inserted by the Crime (International Co-operation) Act 2003, s 52 and amended by SI 2004/3224.]

7.8792 **63D. Terrorist attacks or threats abroad in connection with UK diplomatic premises etc: jurisdiction** (1) If—

(*a*) a person does anything outside the United Kingdom as an act of terrorism or for the purposes of terrorism,

(*b*) his action is done in connection with an attack on relevant premises or on a vehicle ordinarily used by a protected person,

(*c*) the attack is made when a protected person is on or in the premises or vehicle, and

(*d*) his action, if done in any part of the United Kingdom, would have constituted an offence listed in subsection (2),

he shall be guilty in that part of the United Kingdom of the offence.

(2) These are the offences—

(*a*) an offence under section 1 of the Criminal Damage Act 1971,
(*b*) an offence under Article 3 of the Criminal Damage (Northern Ireland) Order 1977,
(*c*) malicious mischief,
(*d*) wilful fire-raising.

(3) If—
(*a*) a person does anything outside the United Kingdom as an act of terrorism or for the purposes of terrorism,
(*b*) his action consists of a threat of an attack on relevant premises or on a vehicle ordinarily used by a protected person,
(*c*) the attack is threatened to be made when a protected person is, or is likely to be, on or in the premises or vehicle, and
(*d*) his action, if done in any part of the United Kingdom, would have constituted an offence listed in subsection (4),

he shall be guilty in that part of the United Kingdom of the offence.

(4) These are the offences—
(*a*) an offence under section 2 of the Criminal Damage Act 1971,
(*b*) an offence under Article 4 of the Criminal Damage (Northern Ireland) Order 1977,
(*c*) breach of the peace (in relation to Scotland only).

(5) "Relevant premises" means—
(*a*) premises at which a protected person resides or is staying, or
(*b*) premises which a protected person uses for the purpose of carrying out his functions as such a person.

[Terrorism Act 2000, s 63D as inserted by the Crime (International Co-operation) Act 2003, s 52.]

7.8793 **63E. Sections 63B to 63D: supplementary** (1) Proceedings for an offence which (disregarding the Acts listed in subsection (2)) would not be an offence apart from section 63B, 63C or 63D are not to be started—
(*a*) in England and Wales, except by or with the consent of the Attorney General,
(*b*) *Northern Ireland.*

(2) These are the Acts—
(*a*) the Internationally Protected Persons Act 1978,
(*b*) the Suppression of Terrorism Act 1978,
(*c*) the Nuclear Material (Offences) Act 1983,
(*d*) the United Nations Personnel Act 1997.

(3) For the purposes of sections 63C and 63D it is immaterial whether a person knows that another person is a United Kingdom national, a United Kingdom resident or a protected person.

(4) In relation to any time before the coming into force of section 27(1) of the Justice (Northern Ireland) Act 2002, the reference in subsection (1)(*b*) to the Advocate General for Northern Ireland is to be read as a reference to the Attorney General for Northern Ireland.

[Terrorism Act 2000, s 63E as inserted by the Crime (International Co-operation) Act 2003, s 52.]

## PART VIII[1]
## GENERAL

7.8794 **114. Police powers** (1) A power conferred by virtue of this Act on a constable—
(*a*) is additional to powers which he has at common law or by virtue of any other enactment, and
(*b*) shall not be taken to affect those powers.

(2) A constable may if necessary use reasonable force for the purpose of exercising a power conferred on him by virtue of this Act (apart from paragraphs 2 and 3 of Schedule 7).

(3) Where anything is seized by a constable under a power conferred by virtue of this Act, it may (unless the contrary intention appears) be retained for so long as is necessary in all the circumstances.

[Terrorism Act 2000, s 114.]

1 Part VIII contains ss 114–131 and Schs 14–16.

7.8795 **115. Officers' powers** Schedule 14 (which makes provision about the exercise of functions by authorised officers for the purposes of sections 25 to 31 and examining officers for the purposes of Schedule 7) shall have effect.

[Terrorism Act 2000, s 115.]

7.8796 **116. Powers to stop and search** (1) A power to search premises conferred by virtue of this Act shall be taken to include power to search a container.

(2) A power conferred by virtue of this Act to stop a person includes power to stop a vehicle (other than an aircraft which is airborne).

(3) A person commits an offence if he fails to stop a vehicle when required to do so by virtue of this section.

(4) A person guilty of an offence under subsection (3) shall be liable on summary conviction to—
(*a*) imprisonment for a term not exceeding six months,

(*b*) a fine not exceeding level 5 on the standard scale, or
(*c*) both.

[Terrorism Act 2000, s 116.]

7.8797 **117. Consent to prosecution** (1) This section applies to an offence under any provision of this Act other than an offence under—

(*a*) section 36,
(*b*) section 51,
(*c*) paragraph 18 of Schedule 7,
(*d*) paragraph 12 of Schedule 12, or
(*e*) Schedule 13.

(2) Proceedings for an offence to which this section applies—

(*a*) shall not be instituted in England and Wales without the consent of the Director of Public Prosecutions, and
(*b*) *Northern Ireland.*

(2A) But if it appears to the Director of Public Prosecutions or the Director of Public Prosecutions for Northern Ireland that an offence to which this section applies has been committed outside the United Kingdom or for a purpose wholly or partly connected with the affairs of a country other than the United Kingdom, his consent for the purposes of this section may be given only with the permission—

(*a*) in the case of the Director of Public Prosecutions, of the Attorney General; and
(*b*) *Northern Ireland.*

(2B) In relation to any time before the coming into force of section 27(1) of the Justice (Northern Ireland) Act 2002, the reference in subsection (2A) to the Advocate General for Northern Ireland is to be read as a reference to the Attorney General for Northern Ireland.

[Terrorism Act 2000, s 117 as amended by the Terrorism Act 2006, s 37 and the Counter-Terrorism Act 2008, s 29.]

7.8798 **118. Defences** (1) Subsection (2) applies where in accordance with a provision mentioned in subsection (5) it is a defence for a person charged with an offence to prove a particular matter.

(2) If the person adduces evidence which is sufficient to raise an issue with respect to the matter the court or jury shall assume that the defence is satisfied unless the prosecution proves beyond reasonable doubt that it is not.

(3) Subsection (4) applies where in accordance with a provision mentioned in subsection (5) a court—

(*a*) may make an assumption in relation to a person charged with an offence unless a particular matter is proved, or
(*b*) may accept a fact as sufficient evidence unless a particular matter is proved.

(4) If evidence is adduced which is sufficient to raise an issue with respect to the matter mentioned in subsection (3)(*a*) or (*b*) the court shall treat it as proved unless the prosecution disproves it beyond reasonable doubt.

(5) The provisions in respect of which subsections (2) and (4) apply are—

(*a*) sections 12(4), 39(5)(*a*), 54, 57, 58, 58A, 77 and 103 of this Act, and
(*b*) sections 13, 32 and 33 of the Northern Ireland (Emergency Provisions) Act 1996 (possession and information offences) as they have effect by virtue of Schedule 1 to this Act.

[Terrorism Act 2000, s 118 as amended by the Counter-Terrorism Act 2008, s 76.]

7.8799 **119. Crown servants, regulators, etc** (1) The Secretary of State may make regulations[1] providing for any of sections 15 to 23A and 39 to apply to persons in the public service of the Crown.

(2) The Secretary of State may make regulations providing for section 19 not to apply to persons who are in his opinion performing or connected with the performance of regulatory, supervisory, investigative or registration functions of a public nature.

(3) Regulations—

(*a*) may make different provision for different purposes,
(*b*) may make provision which is to apply only in specified circumstances, and
(*c*) may make provision which applies only to particular persons or to persons of a particular description.

[Terrorism Act 2000, s 119 as amended by the Counter-Terrorism Act 2008, Sch 3.]

---

[1] See the Terrorism Act 2000 (Crown Servants and Regulators) Regulations 2001, SI 2001/192 amended by SI 2003/3075, SI 2007/2157 and SI 2013/472.

7.8800 **120. Evidence** (1) A document which purports to be—

(*a*) a notice or direction given or order made by the Secretary of State for the purposes of a provision of this Act, and
(*b*) signed by him or on his behalf,

shall be received in evidence and shall, until the contrary is proved, be deemed to have been given or made by the Secretary of State.

(2) A document bearing a certificate which—

(*a*) purports to be signed by or on behalf of the Secretary of State, and

(*b*) states that the document is a true copy of a notice or direction given or order made by the Secretary of State for the purposes of a provision of this Act,

shall be evidence (or, in Scotland, sufficient evidence) of the document in legal proceedings.

(3) In subsections (1) and (2) a reference to an order does not include a reference to an order made by statutory instrument.

(4) The Documentary Evidence Act 1868 shall apply to an authorisation given in writing by the Secretary of State for the purposes of this Act as it applies to an order made by him.

[Terrorism Act 2000, s 120.]

**7.8801 120A. Supplementary powers of forfeiture** (1) A court by or before which a person is convicted of an offence under a provision mentioned in column 1 of the following table may order the forfeiture of any item mentioned in column 2 in relation to that offence.

| ***Offence*** | ***Items liable to forfeiture*** |
|---|---|
| Section 54 (weapons training) | Anything that the court considers to have been in the possession of the person for purposes connected with the offence. |
| Section 57 (possession for terrorist purposes) | Any article that is the subject matter of the offence. |
| Section 58 (collection of information) | Any document or record containing information of the kind mentioned in subsection (1)(*a*) of that section. |
| Section 58A (eliciting, publishing or communicating information about members of armed forces etc) | Any document or record containing information of the kind mentioned in subsection (1)(*a*) of that section. |

(2) Before making an order under this section, a court must give an opportunity to be heard to any person, other than the convicted person, who claims to be the owner or otherwise interested in anything which can be forfeited under this section.

(3) An order under this section does not come into force until there is no further possibility of it being varied, or set aside, on appeal (disregarding any power of a court to grant leave to appeal out of time).

(4) Where a court makes an order under this section, it may also make such other provision as appears to it to be necessary for giving effect to the forfeiture, including, in particular, provision relating to the retention, handling, disposal or destruction of what is forfeited.

(5) Provision made by virtue of subsection (4) may be varied at any time by the court that made it.

(6) The power of forfeiture under this section is in addition to any power of forfeiture under section 23A.

[Terrorism Act 2000, s 120A as substituted by the Counter-Terrorism Act 2008, s 38.]

**7.8802 121. Interpretation** In this Act—

"act" and "action" include omission,

"article" includes substance and any other thing,

"British Transport Police Force" means the constables appointed under section 53 of the British Transport Commission Act 1949 (c xxix),

"customs officer" means an officer of Revenue and Customs,

"dwelling" means a building or part of a building used as a dwelling, and a vehicle which is habitually stationary and which is used as a dwelling,

"explosive" means—

(*a*) an article or substance manufactured for the purpose of producing a practical effect by explosion,

(*b*) materials for making an article or substance within paragraph (*a*),

(*c*) anything used or intended to be used for causing or assisting in causing an explosion, and

(*d*) a part of anything within paragraph (*a*) or (*c*),

"firearm" includes an air gun or air pistol,

"immigration officer" means a person appointed as an immigration officer under paragraph 1 of Schedule 2 to the Immigration Act 1971,

"the Islands" means the Channel Islands and the Isle of Man,

"organisation" includes any association or combination of persons,

"premises", except in section 63D, includes any place and in particular includes—

(*a*) a vehicle,

(*b*) an offshore installation within the meaning given in section 44 of the Petroleum Act 1998, and

(*c*) a tent or moveable structure,

"property" includes property wherever situated and whether real or personal, heritable or moveable, and things in action and other intangible or incorporeal property, "public place" means a place to which members of the public have or are permitted to have access, whether or not for payment,

"road" has the same meaning as in the Road Traffic Act 1988 (in relation to England and Wales), the Roads (Scotland) Act 1984 (in relation to Scotland) and the Road Traffic Regulation (Northern Ireland) Order 1997 (in relation to Northern Ireland), and includes part of a road, and

"vehicle", except in sections 48 to 52 and Schedule 7, includes an aircraft, hovercraft, train or vessel.

[Terrorism Act 2000, s 121 as amended by the Anti-terrorism, Crime and Security Act 2001, Sch 7, the Crime International Co-operation Act 2003, Sch 5, SI 2004/1573 and the Commissioners for Revenue and Customs Act 2005, Sch 4.]

7.8803 **122. Index of defined expressions** In this Act the expressions listed below are defined by the provisions specified.

| *Expression* | *Interpretation provision* |
|---|---|
| Act | Section 121 |
| Action | Section 121 |
| Action taken for the purposes of terrorism | Section 1(5) |
| Article | Section 121 |
| British Transport Police Force | Section 121 |
| Cordoned area | Section 33 |
| Customs officer | Section 121 |
| Dwelling | Section 121 |
| Examining officer | Schedule 7, paragraph 1 |
| Explosive | Section 121 |
| Firearm | Section 121 |
| Immigration officer | Section 121 |
| The Islands | Section 121 |
| Organisation | Section 121 |
| Policed Premises | Section 121 |
| Premises | Section 121 |
| Property | Section 121 |
| Proscribed organisation | Section 3(1) |
| Public place | Section 121 |
| Road | Section 121 |
| Scheduled offence (in Part VII) | Section 65 |
| Terrorism | Section 1 |
| Terrorist (in Part V) | Section 40 |
| Terrorist investigation | Section 32 |
| Terrorist property | Section 14 |
| Vehicle | Section 121 |
| Vehicle (in sections 48 to 51) | Section 52 |

[Terrorism Act 2000, s 122, as amended by the Anti-terrorism, Crime and Security Act 2001, Sch 7.]

7.8804 **123. *Orders and regulations***

7.8805 **124. *Directions***

7.8806 **125. *Amendments and repeals***

7.8807 **126. *Report to Parliament***

7.8808 **127. *Money***

7.8809 **128. Commencement** The preceding provisions of this Act, apart from sections 2(1)(*b*) and (2) and 118 and Schedule 1, shall come into force in accordance with provision made by the Secretary of State by order[1].

[Terrorism Act 2000, s 128.]

[1] The whole of the Act has been brought into force by the following orders: Commencement (No 1) Order 2000, SI 2000/2800; Commencement (No 2) Order 2001, SI 2001/2944; Commencement (No 3) Order 2001, SI 2001/421.

**7.8810 129. *Transitional provisions***

**7.8811 130. *Extent***

**7.8812 131. *Short title***

## SCHEDULE 2

PROSCRIBED ORGANISATIONS

Section 3

*(As amended by SI 2001/1261, SI 2002/2724, SI 2005/2892, SI 2006/1919 and 2016, SI 2007/2184, SI 2008/1645 and 1931, SI 2010/611, SI 2011/108, SI 2012/1771 and 2937, SI 2013/1746 and 3172, SI 2014/927, 1624, 3189, SI 2015/55 and 959 and SI 2016/391, 770 and 1238)*

7.8813 The Irish Republican Army[1].
Cumann na mBan.
Fianna na hEireann.
The Red Hand Commando.
Saor Eire.
The Ulster Freedom Fighters.
The Ulster Volunteer Force.
The Irish National Liberation Army.
The Irish People's Liberation Organisation.
The Ulster Defence Association.
The Loyalist Volunteer Force.
The Continuity Army Council.
The Orange Volunteers.
The Red Hand Defenders.
Al-Qa'ida
Egyptian Islamic Jihad
Al-Gama'at al-Islamiya
Armed Islamic Group (Groupe Islamique Armée) (GIA)
Salafist Group for Call and Combat (Groupe Salafiste pour la Prédication et le Combat) (GSPC)
Babbar Khalsa
Harakat Mujahideen
Jaish e Mohammed
Lashkar e Tayyaba
Liberation Tigers of Tamil Eelam (LTTE)
The military wing of Hizballah, including the Jihad Council and all units reporting to it (including the Hizballah External Security Organisation).
Hamas-Izz al-Din al-Qassem Brigades
Palestinian Islamic Jihad—Shaqaqi
Abu Nidal Organisation
Islamic Army of Aden
Kurdistan Workers' Party (Partiya Karkeren Kurdistan) (PKK)
Revolutionary Peoples' Liberation Party—Front (Devrimci Halk Kurtulus Partisi-Cephesi) (DHKP-C)
Basque Homeland and Liberty (Euskadi ta Askatasuna) (ETA)
17 November Revolutionary Organisation (N17)
Abu Sayyaf Group
Asbat Al-Ansar
Islamic Movement of Uzbekistan
Jemaah Islamiyah
Al Ittihad Al Islamia
Ansar Al Islam
Ansar Al Sunna
Groupe Islamique Combattant Marocain
Harakat-ul-Jihad-ul-Islami
Harakat-ul-Jihad-ul-Islami (Bangladesh)
Harakat-ul-Mujahideen/Alami
Hezb-e Islami Gulbuddin
Islamic Jihad Union
Jamaat ul-Furquan
Jundallah
Khuddam ul-Islam
Lashkar-e Jhangvi
Libyan Islamic Fighting Group
Sipah-e Sahaba Pakistan
Al-Ghurabaa
The Saved Sect
Baluchistan Liberation Army
Teyrebaz Azadiye Kurdistan
Jammat-ul Mujahideen Bangladesh
Tehrik Nefaz-e Shari'at Muhammadi
Al Shabaab
Tehrik-e Taliban Pakistan
Indian Mujahideen
Ansarul Muslimina Fi Biladis Sudan (Vanguard for the protection of Muslims in Black Africa) (Ansaru)
Jama'atu Ahli Sunna Lidda Awati Wal Jihad (Boko Haram)
Minbar Ansar Deen (Ansar Al Sharia UK)
Imarat Kavkaz (Caucasus Emirate)
Ansar Bayt al-Maqdis (Ansar Jerusalem)
Al Murabitun

Ansar al Sharia—Tunisia
Islamic State of Iraq and the Levant (Islamic State of Iraq and al-Sham) (Dawat al Islamiya fi Iraq wa al Sham (DAISh))
Turkiye Halk Kurtulus Partisi-Cephesi (Turkish People's Liberation Party) (The Hasty Ones) (Mukavamet Suriye)
Kateeba al-Kawthar (Ajnad al-sham) (Junud ar-Rahman al Muhajireen)
Abdallah Azzam Brigades, including the Ziyad al-Jarrah Battalions
Popular Front for the Liberation of Palestine—General Command
Ansar al-Sharia-Benghazi (Partisans of Islamic Law)
Ajnad Misr (Soldiers of Egypt)
Jaysh al Khalifatu Islamiya (Army of the Islamic Caliphate) (Majahideen of the Caucasus and the Levant)
Jund Al-Aqsa (Soldiers of Al-Aqsa)
Jund al Khalifa–Algeria (Soldiers of the Caliphate in Algeria)
Jamaat ul-Ahrar
The Haqqani Network
Global Islamic Media Front (including GIMF Bangla Team (Ansarullah Bangla Team) (Ansar-al Islam))
Mujahedeen Indonesia Timur (East Indonesia Mujahedeen)
Turkestan Islamic Party (East Turkestan Islamic Party) (East Turkestan Islamic Movement) (East Turkestan Jihadist Movement) (Hizb al-Islami al-Turkistani)
Jamaah Anshorut Daulah
National Action

*Note*

The entry for The Orange Volunteers refers to the organisation which uses that name and in the name of which a statement described as a press release was published on 14th October 1998.
The entry for Jemaah Islamiyah refers to the organisation using that name that is based in south-east Asia, members of which were arrested by the Singapore authorities in December 2001 in connection with a plot to attack US and other Western targets in Singapore.
The names Kongra Gele Kurdistan and KADEK are to be treated as another name for the Kurdistan Workers' Party (Partiya Karkeren Kurdistan) (PKK).
Jama'at ud Da'wa is to be treated as another name for Lashkar e Tayyaba (SI 2009/578); each of the following names is to be treated as another name for both Al-Ghurabaa and The Saved Sect: Al Muhajiroun (ALM), Call to Submission, Islam4UK, Islamic Path, and London School of Sharia (SI 2010/34).
The name Muslims Against Crusades is to be treated as another name for both Al-Ghurabaa and The Saved Sect (SI 2011/2688).
Al-Nusrah Front and Jabhat al-Nusrah li-ahl al Sham are each to be treated as another name for Al-Qa'ida (SI 2013/1795)
Ahle Sunnat wal Jamaat is to be treated as another name for the organisation listed in that Schedule as Lashkar-e Jhangvi and Sipah-e Sahaba Pakistan (SI 2013/2742).
Need4Khilafah, the Shariah Project and Islamic Dawah Association are to be treated as another name for both Al Ghurabaa and The Saved Sect (SI 2014/1612).
Islamic State (Dawlat al Islamiya) is to be treated as another name for Islamic State of Iraq and the Levant (Islamic State of Iraq and al-Sham) (Dawat al Islamiya fi Iraq wa al Sham (DAISh) (SI 2014/2210).
Jabhat Fatah al-Sham is to be treated as another name for the organisation operating under the names Al-Qa'ida, al-Nusrah Front and Jabhat al-Nusrah li-ahl al Sham (SI 2016/1187).

---

1 This is an umbrella term capable of describing all manifestations or splinter groups (*R v Z* [2005] UKHL 35, [2005] 2 AC 645, [2005] 3 All ER 95, [2005] Crim LR 985).
The name Muslims Against Crusades is to be treated as another name for both Al-Ghurabaa and The Saved Sect.

## SCHEDULE 3A
### Regulated Sector and Supervisory Authorities

*(Amended by SI 2003/3076, the Pensions Act 2004, Sch 12, the Gambling Act 2005, Sch 16, SI 2006/2384, SI 2006/3221, SI 2007/207 and 3288, SI 2008/948, the Localism Act 2011, Sch 18, SI 2011/99, 1043 and 2701 and SI 2012/1534 and 2299.)*

## Part 1
### Regulated Sector
*Business in the Regulated Sector*

7.8814 1. (1) A business is in the regulated sector to the extent that it consists of—
(*a*) the acceptance by a credit institution of deposits or other repayable funds from the public, or the granting by a credit institution of credits for its own account;
(*b*) the carrying on of one or more of the activities listed in points 2 to 12, 14 and 15 of Annex 1 to the Banking Consolidation Directive by an undertaking other than—
(i) a credit institution; or
(ii) an undertaking whose only listed activity is trading for own account in one or more of the products listed in point 7 of Annex 1 to the Banking Consolidation Directive and which does not act on behalf of a customer (that is, a third party which is not a member of the same group as the undertaking);
(*c*) the carrying on of activities covered by the Life Assurance Consolidation Directive by an insurance company authorised in accordance with that Directive;
(*d*) the provision of investment services or the performance of investment activities by a person (other than a person falling within Article 2 of the Markets in Financial Instruments Directive) whose regular occupation or business is the provision to other persons of an investment service or the performance of an investment activity on a professional basis;
(*e*) the marketing or other offering of units or shares by a collective investment undertaking;
(*f*) the activities of an insurance intermediary as defined in Article 2(5) of the Insurance Mediation Directive, other than a tied insurance intermediary as mentioned in Article 2(7) of that Directive, in respect of contracts of long-term insurance within the meaning given by article 3(1) of, and Part II of Schedule 1 to, the Financial Services and Markets Act 2000 (Regulated Activities) Order 2001;

(*g*) the carrying on of any of the activities mentioned in paragraphs (*b*) to (*f*) by a branch located in an EEA State of a person referred to in those paragraphs (or of an equivalent person in any other State), wherever its head office is located;
(*h*) the activities of the National Savings Bank;
(*i*) any activity carried on for the purpose of raising money authorised to be raised under the National Loans Act 1968 under the auspices of the Director of Savings;
(*j*) the carrying on of statutory audit work within the meaning of section 1210 of the Companies Act 2006 (meaning of "statutory auditor" etc) by any firm or individual who is a statutory auditor within the meaning of Part 42 of that Act (statutory auditors);
(*k*) the activities of a person appointed to act as an insolvency practitioner within the meaning of section 388 of the Insolvency Act 1986 (meaning of "act as insolvency practitioner") or article 3 of the Insolvency (Northern Ireland) Order 1989;
(*l*) the provision to other persons of accountancy services by a firm or sole practitioner who by way of business provides such services to other persons;
(*m*) the provision of advice about the tax affairs of other persons by a firm or sole practitioner who by way of business provides advice about the tax affairs of other persons;
(*n*) the participation in financial or real property transactions concerning—
(i) the buying and selling of real property (or, in Scotland, heritable property) or business entities;
(ii) the managing of client money, securities or other assets;
(iii) the opening or management of bank, savings or securities accounts;
(iv) the organisation of contributions necessary for the creation, operation or management of companies; or
(v) the creation, operation or management of trusts, companies or similar structures,
by a firm or sole practitioner who by way of business provides legal or notarial services to other persons;
(*o*) the provision to other persons by way of business by a firm or sole practitioner of any of the services mentioned in sub-paragraph (4);
(*p*) the carrying on of estate agency work by a firm or a sole practitioner who carries on, or whose employees carry on, such work;
(*q*) the trading in goods (including dealing as an auctioneer) whenever a transaction involves the receipt of a payment or payments in cash of at least 15,000 euros in total, whether the transaction is executed in a single operation or in several operations which appear to be linked, by a firm or sole trader who by way of business trades in goods;
(*r*) operating a casino under a casino operating licence (within the meaning given by section 65(2) of the Gambling Act 2005 (nature of licence));
(*s*) the auctioning by an auction platform of two-day spot or five-day futures, within the meanings given by Article 3 of the Emission Allowance Auctioning Regulation;
(*t*) bidding directly, on behalf of clients, in auctions of emissions allowances in accordance with the Emission Allowance Auctioning Regulation.

(2) For the purposes of sub-paragraph (1)(*a*) and (*b*) "credit institution" means—
(*a*) a credit institution as defined in Article 4(1) of the Banking Consolidation Directive; or
(*b*) a branch (within the meaning of Article 4(3) of that Directive) located in an EEA state of an institution falling within paragraph (*a*) (or of an equivalent institution in any other State) wherever its head office is located.

(3) For the purposes of sub-paragraph (1)(*n*) a person participates in a transaction by assisting in the planning or execution of the transaction or otherwise acting for or on behalf of a client in the transaction.

(4) The services referred to in sub-paragraph (1)(*o*) are—
(*a*) forming companies or other legal persons;
(*b*) acting, or arranging for another person to act—
(i) as a director or secretary of a company;
(ii) as a partner of a partnership; or
(iii) in a similar position in relation to other legal persons;
(*c*) providing a registered office, business address, correspondence or administrative address or other related services for a company, partnership or any other legal person or arrangement;
(*d*) acting, or arranging for another person to act, as—
(i) a trustee of an express trust or similar legal arrangement; or
(ii) a nominee shareholder for a person other than a company whose securities are listed on a regulated market.

(5) For the purposes of sub-paragraph (4)(*d*) "regulated market"—
(*a*) in relation to any EEA State, has the meaning given by point 14 of Article 4(1) of the Markets in Financial Instruments Directive; and
(*b*) in relation to any other State, means a regulated financial market which subjects companies whose securities are admitted to trading to disclosure obligations which are contained in international standards and are equivalent to the specified disclosure obligations.

(6) For the purposes of sub-paragraph (5) "the specified disclosure obligations" means disclosure requirements consistent with—
(*a*) Article 6(1) to (4) of Directive 2003/6/EC of the European Parliament and of the Council of 28th January 2003 on insider dealing and market manipulation;
(*b*) Articles 3, 5, 7, 8, 10, 14 and 16 of Directive 2003/71/EC of the European Parliament and of the Council of 4th November 2003 on the prospectuses to be published when securities are offered to the public or admitted to trading;
(*c*) Articles 4 to 6, 14, 16 to 19 and 30 of Directive 2004/109/EC of the European Parliament and of the Council of 15th December 2004 relating to the harmonisation of transparency requirements in relation to information about issuers whose securities are admitted to trading on a regulated market; or
(*d*) EU legislation made under the provisions mentioned in paragraphs (*a*) to (*c*).

(6A) For the purposes of sub-paragraph (1)(*p*) "estate agency work" is to be read in accordance with section 1 of the Estate Agents Act 1979 (estate agency work), but for those purposes references in that section to disposing of or acquiring an interest in land are (despite anything in section 2 of that Act) to be taken to include references to disposing of or acquiring an estate or interest in land outside the United Kingdom where that estate or interest is capable of being owned or held as a separate interest.

(7) For the purposes of sub-paragraph (1)(*j*) and (*l*) to (*q*) "firm" means any entity, whether or not a legal person, that is not an individual and includes a body corporate and a partnership or other unincorporated association.

(8) For the purposes of sub-paragraph (1)(*q*) "cash" means notes, coins or travellers' cheques in any currency.

(9) For the purposes of sub-paragraph (1)(*s*) "auction platform" means a platform on which auctions of emissions allowances are held in accordance with the Emission Allowance Auctioning Regulation.

*Excluded Activities*

2. (1) A business is not in the regulated sector to the extent that it consists of—

(*a*) the issuing of withdrawable share capital within the limit set by section 6 of the Industrial and Provident Societies Act 1965 (maximum shareholding in society), or the acceptance of deposits from the public within the limit set by section 7(3) of that Act (carrying on of banking by societies), by a society registered under that Act;

(*b*) the issuing of withdrawable share capital within the limit set by section 6 of the Industrial and Provident Societies Act (Northern Ireland) 1969 (maximum shareholding in society), or the acceptance of deposits from the public within the limit set by section 7(3) of that Act (carrying on of banking by societies), by a society registered under that Act;

(*c*) the carrying on of any activity in respect of which a person who is (or falls within a class of persons) specified in any of paragraphs 2 to 23, 25 to 38 or 40 to 49 of the Schedule to the Financial Services and Markets Act 2000 (Exemption) Order 2001 is exempt;

(*d*) the exercise of the functions specified in section 45 of the Financial Services Act 1986 (miscellaneous exemptions) by a person who was an exempted person for the purposes of that section immediately before its repeal; or

(*e*) the engaging in financial activity which fulfils all of the conditions set out in paragraphs (*a*) to (*g*) of sub-paragraph (3) of this paragraph by a person whose main activity is that of a high value dealer.

(*f*) *repealed.*

(2) For the purposes of sub-paragraph (1)(*e*) a "high value dealer" means a person mentioned in paragraph 1(1)(*q*) when carrying on the activities mentioned in that paragraph.

(3) A business is not in the regulated sector to the extent that it consists of financial activity if—

(*a*) the person's total annual turnover in respect of the financial activity does not exceed £64,000;

(*b*) the financial activity is limited in relation to any customer to no more than one transaction exceeding 1,000 euros, whether the transaction is carried out in a single operation, or a series of operations which appear to be linked;

(*c*) the financial activity does not exceed 5% of the person's total annual turnover;

(*d*) the financial activity is ancillary to the person's main activity and directly related to that activity;

(*e*) the financial activity is not the transmission or remittance of money (or any representation of monetary value) by any means;

(*f*) the main activity of the person carrying on the financial activity is not an activity mentioned in paragraph 1(1)(*a*) to (*p*) or (*r*); and

(*g*) the financial activity is provided only to customers of the person's main activity and is not offered to the public.

(4) A business is not in the regulated sector if it is carried on by—

(*a*) the Auditor General for Scotland;

(*b*) the Auditor General for Wales;

(*c*) the Bank of England;

(*d*) the Comptroller and Auditor General;

(*e*) the Comptroller and Auditor General for Northern Ireland;

(*f*) the Official Solicitor to the Supreme Court, when acting as trustee in his official capacity; or

(*g*) the Treasury Solicitor.

*Interpretation*

3. (1) In this Part—

"the Banking Consolidation Directive" means directive 2006/48/EC of the European Parliament and of the Council of 14th June 2006 relating to the taking up and pursuit of the business of credit institutions as last amended by Directive 2009/111/EC;

"the Emission Allowance Auctioning Regulation" means Commission Regulation (EU) No. 1031/2010 of 12 November 2010 on the timing, administration and other aspects of auctioning of greenhouse gas emission allowances pursuant to Directive 2003/87/EC of the European Parliament and of the Council establishing a scheme for greenhouse gas emission allowances trading within the Community;

"the Insurance Mediation Directive" means directive 2002/92/EC of the European Parliament and of the Council of 9th December 2002 on insurance mediation;

"the Life Assurance Consolidation Directive" means directive 2002/83/EC of the European Parliament and of the Council of 5th November 2002 concerning life assurance; and

"the Markets in Financial Instruments Directive" means directive 2004/39/EC of the European Parliament and of the Council of 12th April 2004 on markets in financial instruments.

(2) In this Part references to amounts in euros include references to equivalent amounts in another currency.

(3) Terms used in this Part and in the Banking Consolidation Directive or the Markets in Financial Instruments Directive have the same meaning in this Part as in those Directives.

## Part 2
## Supervisory Authorities

4. (1) The following bodies are supervisory authorities—

(*a*) the Commissioners for Her Majesty's Revenue and Customs;

(*b*) the Department of Enterprise, Trade and Investment in Northern Ireland;

(*c*) the Financial Services Authority;
(*d*) the Gambling Commission;
(*e*) the Office of Fair Trading;
(*f*) the Secretary of State; and
(*g*) the professional bodies listed in sub-paragraph (2).

(2) The professional bodies referred to in sub-paragraph (1)(*g*) are—
(*a*) the Association of Accounting Technicians;
(*b*) the Association of Chartered Certified Accountants;
(*c*) the Association of International Accountants;
(*d*) the Association of Taxation Technicians;
(*e*) the Chartered Institute of Management Accountants;
(*f*) the Chartered Institute of Public Finance and Accountancy;
(*g*) the Chartered Institute of Taxation;
(*h*) the Council for Licensed Conveyancers;
(*i*) the Faculty of Advocates;
(*j*) the Faculty Office of the Archbishop of Canterbury;
(*k*) the General Council of the Bar;
(*l*) the General Council of the Bar of Northern Ireland;
(*m*) the Insolvency Practitioners Association;
(*n*) the Institute of Certified Bookkeepers;
(*o*) the Institute of Chartered Accountants in England and Wales;
(*p*) the Institute of Chartered Accountants in Ireland;
(*q*) the Institute of Chartered Accountants of Scotland;
(*r*) the Institute of Financial Accountants;
(*s*) the International Association of Book-keepers;
(*t*) the Law Society;
(*u*) the Law Society for Northern Ireland; and
(*v*) the Law Society of Scotland.

## Part 3
## Power To Amend

**5.** (1) The Treasury may by order[1] amend Part 1 or 2 of this Schedule.

(2) An order under sub-paragraph (1) must be made by statutory instrument subject to annulment in pursuance of a resolution of either House of Parliament.

[1] Orders are noted to the heading to this Schedule.

# SCHEDULE 4
## Forfeiture Orders

*(As amended by the Anti-terrorism, Crime and Security Act 2001, Sch 2, the Land Registration Act 2002, ss 133 and 135, the Courts Act 2003, Sch 8, the Constitutional Reform Act 2005, Sch 11 and the Counter-Terrorism Act 2008, Sch 3.)* Section 23

## Part I
## England and Wales
### *Interpretation*

7.8817 **1.** In this Part of this Schedule—

"forfeiture order" means an order made by a court in England and Wales under section 23 or 23A, and

"forfeited property" means the money or other property to which a forfeiture order applies.

"relevant offence" means—
(*a*) an offence under any of sections 15 to 18,
(*b*) an offence to which section 23A applies, or
(*c*) in relation to a restraint order, any offence specified in Schedule 2 to the Counter-Terrorism Act 2008 (offences where terrorist connection to be considered).

### *Implementation of forfeiture orders*

**2.** (1) Where a court in England and Wales makes a forfeiture order it may make such other provision as appears to it to be necessary for giving effect to the order, and in particular it may—
(*a*) require any of the forfeited property to be paid or handed over to the proper officer or to a constable designated for the purpose by the chief officer of police of a police force specified in the order;
(*b*) direct any of the forfeited property other than money or land to be sold or otherwise disposed of in such manner as the court may direct and the proceeds (if any) to be paid to the proper officer;
(*c*) appoint a receiver to take possession, subject to such conditions and exceptions as may be specified by the court, of any of the forfeited property, to realise it in such manner as the court may direct and to pay the proceeds to the proper officer;
(*d*) direct a specified part of any forfeited money, or of the proceeds of the sale, disposal or realisation of any forfeited property, to be paid by the proper officer to a specified person falling within section 23B(1).

(2) A forfeiture order shall not come into force until there is no further possibility of it being varied, or set aside, on appeal (disregarding any power of a court to grant leave to appeal out of time).

(3) In sub-paragraph (1)(*b*) and (*d*) a reference to the proceeds of the sale, disposal or realisation of property is a reference to the proceeds after deduction of the costs of sale, disposal or realisation.

(4) Section 140 of the Magistrates' Courts Act 1980 (disposal of non-pecuniary forfeitures) shall not apply.

**3.** (1) A receiver appointed under paragraph 2 shall be entitled to be paid his remuneration and expenses by the proper officer out of the proceeds of the property realised by the receiver and paid to the proper officer under paragraph 2(1)(*c*).

(2) If and so far as those proceeds are insufficient, the receiver shall be entitled to be paid his remuneration

and expenses by the prosecutor.

(3) A receiver appointed under paragraph 2 shall not be liable to any person in respect of any loss or damage resulting from action—

(*a*) which he takes in relation to property which is not forfeited property, but which he reasonably believes to be forfeited property,

(*b*) which he would be entitled to take if the property were forfeited property, and

(*c*) which he reasonably believes that he is entitled to take because of his belief that the property is forfeited property.

(4) Sub-paragraph (3) does not apply in so far as the loss or damage is caused by the receiver's negligence.

**4.** (1) In paragraphs 2 and 3 "the proper officer" means—

(*a*) where the forfeiture order is made by a magistrates' court, the designated officer for that court,

(*b*) where the forfeiture order is made by the Crown Court and the defendant was committed to the Crown Court by a magistrates' court, the designated officer for the magistrates' court, and

(*c*) where the forfeiture order is made by the Crown Court and the proceedings were instituted by a bill of indictment preferred by virtue of section 2(2)(*b*) of the Administration of Justice (Miscellaneous Provisions) Act 1933, the designated officer for the magistrates' court for the place where the trial took place.

(2) The proper officer shall issue a certificate in respect of a forfeiture order if an application is made by—

(*a*) the prosecutor in the proceedings in which the forfeiture order was made,

(*b*) the defendant in those proceedings, or

(*c*) a person whom the court heard under section 23B(1) before making the order.

(3) The certificate shall state the extent (if any) to which, at the date of the certificate, effect has been given to the forfeiture order.

*Application of proceeds to compensate victims*

**4A.** (1) Where a court makes a forfeiture order in a case where—

(*a*) the offender has been convicted of an offence that has resulted in a person suffering personal injury, loss or damage, or

(*b*) any such offence is taken into consideration by the court in determining sentence,

the court may also order that an amount not exceeding a sum specified by the court is to be paid to that person out of the proceeds of the forfeiture.

(2) For this purpose the proceeds of the forfeiture means the aggregate amount of—

(*a*) any forfeited money, and

(*b*) the proceeds of the sale, disposal or realisation of any forfeited property, after deduction of the costs of the sale, disposal or realisation,

reduced by the amount of any payment under paragraph 2(1)(*d*) or 3(1).

(3) The court may make an order under this paragraph only if it is satisfied that but for the inadequacy of the offender's means it would have made a compensation order under section 130 of the Powers of Criminal Courts (Sentencing) Act 2000 under which the offender would have been required to pay compensation of an amount not less than the specified amount.

*Restraint orders*

**5.** (1) The High Court may make a restraint order under this paragraph where—

(*a*) proceedings have been instituted in England and Wales for a relevant offence,

(*b*) the proceedings have not been concluded,

(*c*) an application for a restraint order is made to the High Court by the prosecutor, and

(*d*) a forfeiture order has been made, or it appears to the High Court that a forfeiture order may be made, in the proceedings for the offence.

(2) The High Court may also make a restraint order under this paragraph where—

(*a*) a criminal investigation has been started in England and Wales with regard to a relevant offence,

(*b*) an application for a restraint order is made to the High Court by the person who the High Court is satisfied will have the conduct of any proceedings for the offence, and

(*c*) it appears to the High Court that a forfeiture order may be made in any proceedings for the offence.

(3) A restraint order prohibits a person to whom notice of it is given, subject to any conditions and exceptions specified in the order, from dealing with property in respect of which a forfeiture order has been or could be made in any proceedings referred to in sub-paragraph (1) or (2).

(4) An application for a restraint order may be made to a judge in chambers without notice.

(5) In this paragraph a reference to dealing with property includes a reference to removing the property from Great Britain.

(6) In this paragraph "criminal investigation" means an investigation which police officers or other persons have a duty to conduct with a view to it being ascertained whether a person should be charged with an offence.

**6.** (1) A restraint order shall provide for notice of it to be given to any person affected by the order.

(2) A restraint order may be discharged or varied by the High Court on the application of a person affected by it.

(3) A restraint order made under paragraph 5(1) shall in particular be discharged on an application under sub-paragraph (2) if the proceedings for the offence have been concluded.

(4) A restraint order made under paragraph 5(2) shall in particular be discharged on an application under sub-paragraph (2)—

(*a*) if no proceedings in respect of relevant offences are instituted within such time as the High Court considers reasonable, and

(*b*) if all proceedings in respect of relevant offences have been concluded.

**7.** (1) A constable may seize any property subject to a restraint order for the purpose of preventing it from being removed from Great Britain.

(2) Property seized under this paragraph shall be dealt with in accordance with the High Court's directions.

**8.** (1) The Land Charges Act 1972 and the Land Registration Act 2002—

(*a*) shall apply in relation to restraint orders as they apply in relation to orders affecting land made by the court for the purpose of enforcing judgments or recognizances, except that no notice may be entered in the register of title under the Land Registration Act 2002 in respect of such orders, and

(*b*) shall apply in relation to applications for restraint orders as they apply in relation to other pending land actions.

(2) *Repealed.*

(3) *Repealed.*

**9.** (1) This paragraph applies where a restraint order is discharged under paragraph 6(4)(*a*).

(2) This paragraph also applies where a forfeiture order or a restraint order is made in or in relation to proceedings for a relevant offence which—

(*a*) do not result in conviction for a relevant offence,

(*b*) result in conviction for a relevant offence in respect of which the person convicted is subsequently pardoned by Her Majesty, or

(*c*) result in conviction for a relevant offence which is subsequently quashed.

(3) A person who had an interest in any property which was subject to the order may apply to the High Court for compensation.

(4) The High Court may order compensation to be paid to the applicant if satisfied—

(*a*) that there was a serious default on the part of a person concerned in the investigation or prosecution of the offence,

(*b*) that the person in default was or was acting as a member of a police force, or was a member of the Crown Prosecution Service or was acting on behalf of the Service,

(*c*) that the applicant has suffered loss in consequence of anything done in relation to the property by or in pursuance of the forfeiture order or restraint order, and

(*d*) that, having regard to all the circumstances, it is appropriate to order compensation to be paid.

(5) The High Court shall not order compensation to be paid where it appears to it that proceedings for the offence would have been instituted even if the serious default had not occurred.

(6) Compensation payable under this paragraph shall be paid—

(*a*) where the person in default was or was acting as a member of a police force, out of the police fund out of which the expenses of that police force are met, and

(*b*) where the person in default was a member of the Crown Prosecution Service, or was acting on behalf of the Service, by the Director of Public Prosecutions.

**10.** (1) This paragraph applies where—

(*a*) a forfeiture order or a restraint order is made in or in relation to proceedings for a relevant offence, and

(*b*) the proceedings result in a conviction which is subsequently quashed on an appeal under section 7(2) or (5).

(2) A person who had an interest in any property which was subject to the order may apply to the High Court for compensation.

(3) The High Court may order compensation to be paid to the applicant if satisfied—

(*a*) that the applicant has suffered loss in consequence of anything done in relation to the property by or in pursuance of the forfeiture order or restraint order, and

(*b*) that, having regard to all the circumstances, it is appropriate to order compensation to be paid.

(4) Compensation payable under this paragraph shall be paid by the Secretary of State.

*Proceedings for an offence: timing*

**11.** (1) For the purposes of this Part of this Schedule proceedings for an offence are instituted—

(*a*) when a justice of the peace issues a summons or warrant under section 1 of the Magistrates' Courts Act 1980 in respect of the offence;

(*b*) when a person is charged with the offence after being taken into custody without a warrant;

(*c*) when a bill of indictment charging a person with the offence is preferred by virtue of section 2(2)(*b*) of the Administration of Justice (Miscellaneous Provisions) Act 1933.

(2) Where the application of sub-paragraph (1) would result in there being more than one time for the institution of proceedings they shall be taken to be instituted at the earliest of those times.

(3) For the purposes of this Part of this Schedule proceedings are concluded—

(*a*) when a forfeiture order has been made in those proceedings and effect has been given to it in respect of all the forfeited property, or

(*b*) when no forfeiture order has been made in those proceedings and there is no further possibility of one being made as a result of an appeal (disregarding any power of a court to grant leave to appeal out of time).* **

* **Para 11 amended by the Criminal Justice Act 2003, Sch 36 from a date to be appointed.**

** **New paras 11A–11G inserted by the Crime (International Co-operation) Act 2003, Sch 4 from a date to be appointed.**

*Enforcement of orders made elsewhere in the British Islands*

**12.** In the following provisions of this Part of this Schedule—

"a Scottish order" means—

(*a*) an order made in Scotland under section 23 or 23A ("a Scottish forfeiture order"),

(*b*) an order made under paragraph 18 ("a Scottish restraint order"), or

(*c*) an order made under any other provision of Part II of this Schedule in relation to a Scottish forfeiture or restraint order;

"a Northern Ireland order" means—

(*a*) an order made in Northern Ireland under section 23 or 23A ("a Northern Ireland forfeiture order"),

(*b*) an order made under paragraph 33 ("a Northern Ireland restraint order"), or

(*c*) an order made under any other provision of Part III of this Schedule in relation to a Northern Ireland forfeiture or restraint order;

"an Islands order" means an order made in any of the Islands under a provision of the law of that Island corresponding to—

(*a*) section 23 or 23A ("an Islands forfeiture order"),

(*b*) paragraph 5 ("an Islands restraint order"), or

(*c*) any other provision of this Part of this Schedule.

**13.** (1) Subject to the provisions of this paragraph, a Scottish, Northern Ireland or Islands order shall have effect in the law of England and Wales.

(2) But such an order shall be enforced in England and Wales only in accordance with—

(*a*) the provisions of this paragraph, and

(*b*) any provision made by rules of court as to the manner in which, and the conditions subject to which, such orders are to be enforced there.

(3) On an application made to it in accordance with rules of court for registration of a Scottish, Northern Ireland or Islands order, the High Court shall direct that the order shall, in accordance with such rules, be registered in that court.

(4) Rules of court shall also make provision—

(*a*) for cancelling or varying the registration of a Scottish, Northern Ireland or Islands forfeiture order when effect has been given to it, whether in England and Wales or elsewhere, in respect of all or, as the case may be, part of the money or other property to which the order applies;

(*b*) for cancelling or varying the registration of a Scottish, Northern Ireland or Islands restraint order which has been discharged or varied by the court by which it was made.

(5) If a Scottish, Northern Ireland or Islands forfeiture order is registered under this paragraph the High Court shall have, in relation to that order, the same powers as a court has under paragraph 2(1) to give effect to a forfeiture order made by it and—

(*a*) paragraph 3 shall apply accordingly,

(*b*) any functions of the designated officer for a magistrates' court shall be exercised by the appropriate officer of the High Court, and

(*c*) after making any payment required by virtue of paragraph 2(1)(*d*) or 3, the balance of any sums received by the appropriate officer of the High Court by virtue of an order made under this sub-paragraph shall be paid by him to the Secretary of State.

(6) If a Scottish, Northern Ireland or Islands restraint order is registered under this paragraph—

(*a*) paragraphs 7 and 8 shall apply as they apply to a restraint order under paragraph 5, and

(*b*) the High Court shall have power to make an order under section 33 of the Senior Courts Act 1981 (extended power to order inspection of property, etc) in relation to proceedings brought or likely to be brought for a Scottish, Northern Ireland or Islands restraint order as if those proceedings had been brought or were likely to be brought in the High Court.

(7) In addition, if a Scottish, Northern Ireland or Islands order is registered under this paragraph—

(*a*) the High Court shall have, in relation to its enforcement, the same power as if the order had originally been made in the High Court,

(*b*) proceedings for or with respect to its enforcement may be taken as if the order had originally been made in the High Court, and

(*c*) proceedings for or with respect to contravention of such an order, whether before or after such registration, may be taken as if the order had originally been made in the High Court.

(8) The High Court may also make such orders or do otherwise as seems to it appropriate for the purpose of—

(*a*) assisting the achievement in England and Wales of the purposes of a Scottish, Northern Ireland or Islands order, or

(*b*) assisting a receiver or other person directed by a Scottish, Northern Ireland or Islands order to sell or otherwise dispose of property.

(9) The following documents shall be received in evidence in England and Wales without further proof—

(*a*) a document purporting to be a copy of a Scottish, Northern Ireland or Islands order and to be certified as such by a proper officer of the court by which it was made, and

(*b*) a document purporting to be a certificate for purposes corresponding to those of paragraph 4(2) and (3) and to be certified by a proper officer of the court concerned.

*Enforcement of orders made in designated countries*

**14.** (1) Her Majesty may by Order[1] in Council make provision for the purpose of enabling the enforcement in England and Wales of external orders.

(2) An "external order" means an order—

(*a*) which is made in a country or territory designated for the purposes of this paragraph by the Order in Council, and

(*b*) which makes relevant provision.

(3) "Relevant provision" means—

(*a*) provision for the forfeiture of terrorist property ("an external forfeiture order"), or

(*b*) provision prohibiting dealing with property which is subject to an external forfeiture order or in respect of which such an order could be made in proceedings which have been or are to be instituted in the designated country or territory ("an external restraint order").

(4) An Order in Council under this paragraph may, in particular, include provision—

(*a*) which, for the purpose of facilitating the enforcement of any external order that may be made, has effect at times before there is an external order to be enforced;

(*b*) for matters corresponding to those for which provision is made by, or can be made under, paragraph 13(1) to (8) in relation to the orders to which that paragraph applies;

(*c*) for the proof of any matter relevant for the purposes of anything falling to be done in pursuance of the Order in Council.

(5) An Order in Council under this paragraph may also make provision with respect to anything falling to be done on behalf of the United Kingdom in a designated country or territory in relation to proceedings in that country or territory for or in connection with the making of an external order.

(6) An Order in Council under this paragraph—

(*a*) may make different provision for different cases, and

(*b*) shall not be made unless a draft of it has been laid before and approved by resolution of each House of Parliament.

---

* **Amended by the Crime (International Co-operation) Act 2003, Sch 4 from a date to be appointed.**

1 The Terrorism Act 2000 (Enforcement of External Orders) Order 2001, SI 2001/3927 has been made.

## SCHEDULE 5

TERRORIST INVESTIGATIONS: INFORMATION Section 37

*(As amended by the Anti-terrorism, Crime and Security Act 2001, s 121(1), SI 2003/427 and the Terrorism Act 2006, s 26.)*

### PART I

### ENGLAND AND WALES AND NORTHERN IRELAND

*Searches*

**7.8818** **1.** (1) A constable may apply to a justice of the peace for the issue of a warrant under this paragraph for the purposes of a terrorist investigation.

(2) A warrant under this paragraph shall authorise any constable—

(*a*) to enter premises mentioned in sub-paragraph (2A),

(*b*) to search the premises and any person found there, and

(*c*) to seize and retain any relevant material which is found on a search under paragraph (*b*).

(2A) The premises referred to in sub-paragraph (2)(*a*) are—

(*a*) one or more sets of premises specified in the application (in which case the application is for a "specific premises warrant"); or

(*b*) any premises occupied or controlled by a person specified in the application, including such sets of premises as are so specified (in which case the application is for an "all premises warrant").

(3) For the purpose of sub-paragraph (2)(*c*) material is relevant if the constable has reasonable grounds for believing that—

(*a*) it is likely to be of substantial value, whether by itself or together with other material, to a terrorist investigation, and

(*b*) it must be seized in order to prevent it from being concealed, lost, damaged, altered or destroyed.

(4) A warrant under this paragraph shall not authorise—

(*a*) the seizure and retention of items subject to legal privilege, or

(*b*) a constable to require a person to remove any clothing in public except for headgear, footwear, an outer coat, a jacket or gloves.

(5) Subject to paragraph 2, a justice may grant an application under this paragraph if satisfied—

(*a*) that the warrant is sought for the purposes of a terrorist investigation,

(*b*) that there are reasonable grounds for believing that there is material on premises to which the application relates which is likely to be of substantial value, whether by itself or together with other material, to a terrorist investigation and which does not consist of or include excepted material (within the meaning of paragraph 4 below),

(*c*) that the issue of a warrant is likely to be necessary in the circumstances of the case, and

(*d*) in the case of an application for an all premises warrant, that it is not reasonably practicable to specify in the application all the premises which the person so specified occupies or controls and which might need to be searched.

**2.** (1) This paragraph applies where an application for a specific premises warrant is made under paragraph 1 and—

(*a*) the application is made by a police officer of at least the rank of superintendent,

(*b*) the application does not relate to residential premises, and

(*c*) the justice to whom the application is made is not satisfied of the matter referred to in paragraph 1(5)(*c*).

(2) The justice may grant the application if satisfied of the matters referred to in paragraph 1(5)(*a*) and (*b*).

(3) Where a warrant under paragraph 1 is issued by virtue of this paragraph, the powers under paragraph 1(2)(*a*) and (*b*) are exercisable only within the period of 24 hours beginning with the time when the warrant is issued.

(4) For the purpose of sub-paragraph (1) "residential premises" means any premises which the officer making the application has reasonable grounds for believing are used wholly or mainly as a dwelling.

**2A.** (1) This paragraph applies where an application for an all premises warrant is made under paragraph 1 and—

(*a*) the application is made by a police officer of at least the rank of superintendent, and

(*b*) the justice to whom the application is made is not satisfied of the matter referred to in paragraph 1(5)(*c*).

(2) The justice may grant the application if satisfied of the matters referred to in paragraph 1(5)(*a*), (*b*) and (*d*).

(3) Where a warrant under paragraph 1 is issued by virtue of this paragraph, the powers under paragraph 1(2)(*a*) and (*b*) are exercisable only—

(*a*) in respect of premises which are not residential premises, and

(*b*) within the period of 24 hours beginning with the time when the warrant is issued.

(4) For the purpose of sub-paragraph (3) "residential premises", in relation to a power under paragraph 1(2)(*a*) or (*b*), means any premises which the constable exercising the power has reasonable grounds for believing are used wholly or mainly as a dwelling.

**3.** (1) Subject to sub-paragraph (2), a police officer of at least the rank of superintendent may by a written authority signed by him authorise a search of specified premises which are wholly or partly within a cordoned area.

(2) A constable who is not of the rank required by sub-paragraph (1) may give an authorisation under this paragraph if he considers it necessary by reason of urgency.

(3) An authorisation under this paragraph shall authorise any constable—

(*a*) to enter the premises specified in the authority,

(*b*) to search the premises and any person found there, and

(*c*) to seize and retain any relevant material (within the meaning of paragraph 1(3)) which is found on a search under paragraph (*b*).

(4) The powers under sub-paragraph (3)(*a*) and (*b*) may be exercised—

(*a*) on one or more occasions, and

(*b*) at any time during the period when the designation of the cordoned area under section 33 has effect.

(5) An authorisation under this paragraph shall not authorise—

(*a*) the seizure and retention of items subject to legal privilege;

(*b*) a constable to require a person to remove any clothing in public except for headgear, footwear, an outer coat, a jacket or gloves.

(6) An authorisation under this paragraph shall not be given unless the person giving it has reasonable grounds for believing that there is material to be found on the premises which—

(*a*) is likely to be of substantial value, whether by itself or together with other material, to a terrorist investigation, and

(*b*) does not consist of or include excepted material.

(7) A person commits an offence if he wilfully obstructs a search under this paragraph.

(8) A person guilty of an offence under sub-paragraph (7) shall be liable on summary conviction to—

(*a*) imprisonment for a term not exceeding three months *,

(*b*) a fine not exceeding level 4 on the standard scale, or

(*c*) both.

*Excepted material*

**4.** In this Part—

(*a*) "excluded material" has the meaning given by section 11 of the Police and Criminal Evidence Act 1984,

(*b*) "items subject to legal privilege" has the meaning given by section 10 of that Act, and

(*c*) "special procedure material" has the meaning given by section 14 of that Act;

and material is "excepted material" if it falls within any of paragraphs (*a*) to (*c*).

*Excluded and special procedure material: production & access*

**5.** (1) A constable may apply to a Circuit judge** for an order under this paragraph for the purposes of a terrorist investigation.

(2) An application for an order shall relate to particular material, or material of a particular description, which consists of or includes excluded material or special procedure material.

(3) An order under this paragraph may require a specified person—

(*a*) to produce to a constable within a specified period for seizure and retention any material which he has in his possession, custody or power and to which the application relates;

(*b*) to give a constable access to any material of the kind mentioned in paragraph (*a*) within a specified period;

(*c*) to state to the best of his knowledge and belief the location of material to which the application relates if it is not in, and it will not come into, his possession, custody or power within the period specified under paragraph (*a*) or (*b*).

(4) For the purposes of this paragraph—

(*a*) an order may specify a person only if he appears to the Circuit judge** to have in his possession, custody or power any of the material to which the application relates, and

(*b*) a period specified in an order shall be the period of seven days beginning with the date of the order unless it appears to the judge that a different period would be appropriate in the particular circumstances of the application.

(5) Where a Circuit judge** makes an order under sub-paragraph (3)(*b*) in relation to material on any premises, he may, on the application of a constable, order any person who appears to the judge to be entitled to grant entry to the premises to allow any constable to enter the premises to obtain access to the material.

**6.** (1) A Circuit judge** may[1] grant an application under paragraph 5 if satisfied—

(*a*) that the material to which the application relates consists of or includes excluded material or special procedure material,

(*b*) that it does not include items subject to legal privilege, and

(*c*) that the conditions in sub-paragraphs (2) and (3) are satisfied in respect of that material.

(2) The first condition is that—

(*a*) the order is sought for the purposes of a terrorist investigation, and

(*b*) there are reasonable grounds for believing that the material is likely to be of substantial value, whether by itself or together with other material, to a terrorist investigation.

(3) The second condition is that there are reasonable grounds for believing that it is in the public interest that the material should be produced or that access to it should be given having regard—

(*a*) to the benefit likely to accrue to a terrorist investigation if the material is obtained, and

(*b*) to the circumstances under which the person concerned has any of the material in his possession, custody or power.

**7.** (1) An order under paragraph 5 may be made in relation to—

(*a*) material consisting of or including excluded or special procedure material which is expected to come into existence within the period of 28 days beginning with the date of the order;

(*b*) a person who the Circuit judge** thinks is likely to have any of the material to which the application relates in his possession, custody or power within that period.

(2) Where an order is made under paragraph 5 by virtue of this paragraph, paragraph 5(3) shall apply with the following modifications—

(*a*) the order shall require the specified person to notify a named constable as soon as is reasonably practicable after any material to which the application relates comes into his possession, custody or power,

(*b*) the reference in paragraph 5(3)(*a*) to material which the specified person has in his possession, custody or power shall be taken as a reference to the material referred to in paragraph (*a*) above which comes into his possession, custody or power, and

(*c*) the reference in paragraph 5(3)(*c*) to the specified period shall be taken as a reference to the period of 28 days beginning with the date of the order.

(3) Where an order is made under paragraph 5 by virtue of this paragraph, paragraph 5(4) shall not apply and the order—

(*a*) may only specify a person falling within sub-paragraph (1)(*b*), and

(*b*) shall specify the period of seven days beginning with the date of notification required under sub-paragraph (2)(*a*) unless it appears to the judge that a different period would be appropriate in the particular circumstances of the application.

**8.** (1) An order under paragraph 5—

(*a*) shall not confer any right to production of, or access to, items subject to legal privilege, and
(*b*) shall have effect notwithstanding any restriction on the disclosure of information imposed by statute or otherwise.

(2) Where the material to which an application under paragraph 5 relates consists of information contained in a computer—
(*a*) an order under paragraph 5(3)(*a*) shall have effect as an order to produce the material in a form in which it can be taken away and in which it is visible and legible, and
(*b*) an order under paragraph 5(3)(*b*) shall have effect as an order to give access to the material in a form in which it is visible and legible.

**9.** (1) An order under paragraph 5 may be made in relation to material in the possession, custody or power of a government department.

(2) Where an order is made by virtue of sub-paragraph (1)—
(*a*) it shall be served as if the proceedings were civil proceedings against the department, and
(*b*) it may require any officer of the department, whether named in the order or not, who may for the time being have in his possession, custody or power the material concerned, to comply with the order.

(3) In this paragraph "government department" means an authorised government department for the purposes of the Crown Proceedings Act 1947.

**10.** (1) An order of a Circuit judge** under paragraph 5 shall have effect as if it were an order of the Crown Court.

(2) Criminal Procedure Rules may make provision about proceedings relating to an order under paragraph 5.

(3) In particular, the rules may make provision about the variation or discharge of an order.

*Excluded or special procedure material: search*

**11.** (1) A constable may apply to a Circuit judge** for the issue of a warrant under this paragraph for the purposes of a terrorist investigation.

(2) A warrant under this paragraph shall authorise any constable—
(*a*) to enter premises mentioned in sub-paragraph (3A),
(*b*) to search the premises and any person found there, and
(*c*) to seize and retain any relevant material which is found on a search under paragraph (*b*).

(3) A warrant under this paragraph shall not authorise—
(*a*) the seizure and retention of items subject to legal privilege;
(*b*) a constable to require a person to remove any clothing in public except for headgear, footwear, an outer coat, a jacket or gloves.

(3A) The premises referred to in sub-paragraph (2)(*a*) are—
(*a*) one or more sets of premises specified in the application (in which case the application is for a "specific premises warrant"); or
(*b*) any premises occupied or controlled by a person specified in the application, including such sets of premises as are so specified (in which case the application is for an "all premises warrant").

(4) For the purpose of sub-paragraph (2)(*c*) material is relevant if the constable has reasonable grounds for believing that it is likely to be of substantial value, whether by itself or together with other material, to a terrorist investigation.

**12.** (1) A Circuit judge** may grant an application for a specific premises warrant under paragraph 11 if satisfied that an order made under paragraph 5 in relation to material on the premises specified in the application has not been complied with.

(2) A Circuit judge** may also grant an application for a specific premises warrant under paragraph 11 if satisfied that there are reasonable grounds for believing that—
(*a*) there is material on premises specified in the application which consists of or includes excluded material or special procedure material but does not include items subject to legal privilege, and
(*b*) the conditions in sub-paragraphs (3) and (4) are satisfied.

(2A) A Circuit judge or a District Judge (Magistrates' Courts) may grant an application for an all premises warrant under paragraph 11 if satisfied—
(*a*) that an order made under paragraph 5 has not been complied with, and
(*b*) that the person specified in the application is also specified in the order.

(2B) A Circuit judge or a District Judge (Magistrates' Courts) may also grant an application for an all premises warrant under paragraph 11 if satisfied that there are reasonable grounds for believing—
(*a*) that there is material on premises to which the application relates which consists of or includes excluded material or special procedure material but does not include items subject to legal privilege, and
(*b*) that the conditions in sub-paragraphs (3) and (4) are met.

(3) The first condition is that—
(*a*) the warrant is sought for the purposes of a terrorist investigation, and
(*b*) the material is likely to be of substantial value, whether by itself or together with other material, to a terrorist investigation.

(4) The second condition is that it is not appropriate to make an order under paragraph 5 in relation to the material because—
(*a*) it is not practicable to communicate with any person entitled to produce the material,
(*b*) it is not practicable to communicate with any person entitled to grant access to the material or entitled to grant entry to the premises on which the material is situated, or
(*c*) a terrorist investigation may be seriously prejudiced unless a constable can secure immediate access to the material.

*Explanations*

**13.** (1) A constable may apply to a Circuit judge** for an order under this paragraph requiring any person specified in the order to provide an explanation of any material—
(*a*) seized in pursuance of a warrant under paragraph 1 or 11, or
(*b*) produced or made available to a constable under paragraph 5.

(2) An order under this paragraph shall not require any person to disclose any information which he would be entitled to refuse to disclose on grounds of legal professional privilege in proceedings in the High Court.

(3) But a lawyer may be required to provide the name and address of his client.

(4) A statement by a person in response to a requirement imposed by an order under this paragraph—

(*a*) may be made orally or in writing, and

(*b*) may be used in evidence against him only on a prosecution for an offence under paragraph 14.

(5) Paragraph 10 shall apply to orders under this paragraph as it applies to orders under paragraph 5.

**14.** (1) A person commits an offence if, in purported compliance with an order under paragraph 13, he—

(*a*) makes a statement which he knows to be false or misleading in a material particular, or

(*b*) recklessly makes a statement which is false or misleading in a material particular.

(2) A person guilty of an offence under sub-paragraph (1) shall be liable—

(*a*) on conviction on indictment, to imprisonment for a term not exceeding two years, to a fine or to both, or

(*b*) on summary conviction, to imprisonment for a term not exceeding six months, to a fine not exceeding the statutory maximum or to both.

*Urgent cases*

**15.** (1) A police officer of at least the rank of superintendent may by a written order signed by him give to any constable the authority which may be given by a search warrant under paragraph 1 or 11.

(2) An order shall not be made under this paragraph unless the officer has reasonable grounds for believing—

(*a*) that the case is one of great emergency, and

(*b*) that immediate action is necessary.

(3) Where an order is made under this paragraph particulars of the case shall be notified as soon as is reasonably practicable to the Secretary of State.

(4) A person commits an offence if he wilfully obstructs a search under this paragraph.

(5) A person guilty of an offence under sub-paragraph (4) shall be liable on summary conviction to—

(*a*) imprisonment for a term not exceeding three months *,

(*b*) a fine not exceeding level 4 on the standard scale, or

(*c*) both.

**16.** (1) If a police officer of at least the rank of superintendent has reasonable grounds for believing that the case is one of great emergency he may by a written notice signed by him require any person specified in the notice to provide an explanation of any material seized in pursuance of an order under paragraph 15.

(2) Sub-paragraphs (2) to (4) of paragraph 13 and paragraph 14 shall apply to a notice under this paragraph as they apply to an order under paragraph 13.

(3) A person commits an offence if he fails to comply with a notice under this paragraph.

(4) It is a defence for a person charged with an offence under sub-paragraph (3) to show that he had a reasonable excuse for his failure.

(5) A person guilty of an offence under sub-paragraph (3) shall be liable on summary conviction to—

(*a*) imprisonment for a term not exceeding six months,

(*b*) a fine not exceeding level 5 on the standard scale, or

(*c*) both.

*Supplementary*

**17.** For the purposes of sections 21 and 22 of the Police and Criminal Evidence Act 1984 (seized material: access, copying and retention)—

(*a*) a terrorist investigation shall be treated as an investigation of or in connection with an offence, and

(*b*) material produced in pursuance of an order under paragraph 5 shall be treated as if it were material seized by a constable.

*Northern Ireland*

**18.** In the application of this Part to Northern Ireland—

(*a*) the reference in paragraph 4(*a*) to section 11 of the Police and Criminal Evidence Act 1984 shall be taken as a reference to Article 13 of the Police and Criminal Evidence (Northern Ireland) Order 1989,

(*b*) the reference in paragraph 4(*b*) to section 10 of that Act shall be taken as a reference to Article 12 of that Order,

(*c*) the reference in paragraph 4(*c*) to section 14 of that Act shall be taken as a reference to Article 16 of that Order,

(*d*) the references in paragraph 9(1) and (2) to "government department" shall be taken as including references to an authorised Northern Ireland department for the purposes of the Crown Proceedings Act 1947,

(*dd*) the reference in paragraph 10(2) to "Criminal Procedure Rules" shall be taken as a reference to Crown Court Rules,

(*e*) *repealed*

(*f*) the reference in paragraph 17 to sections 21 and 22 of the Police and Criminal Evidence Act 1984 shall be taken as a reference to Articles 23 and 24 of the Police and Criminal Evidence (Northern Ireland) Order 1989, and

(*g*) references to "a Circuit judge" shall be taken as references to a Crown Court judge.

**19–21.** *Repealed.*

---

* **Substituted by the Criminal Justice Act 2003, Sch 26 from a date to be appointed.**

** **Words inserted by the Courts Act 2003, Sch 4 from a date to be appointed.**

[1] As to the operation of art 10 of the ECHR in relation to an application for a production order under Sch 5 of the Terrorism Act 2000 against a journalist, and the factors to be taken into account when deciding whether a person should be required to disclose material under para 6 where to do so risks infringing his privilege against self-incrimination, see *R (on the application of Malik) v Manchester Crown Court* [2008] EWHC 1362 (Admin), [2008] 4 All ER 403.

SCHEDULE 6

FINANCIAL INFORMATION Section 38

*(As amended by SI 2000/2952, the Anti-terrorism, Crime and Security Act 2001, Sch 2, SI 2001/3649, the Courts Act 2003, Sch 8, SI 2004/3379, SI 2006/3221, SI 2006/3384 and SI 2011/99.)*

*Orders*

**7.8819** **1.** (1) Where an order has been made under this paragraph in relation to a terrorist investigation, a constable named in the order may require a financial institution to which the order applies to provide customer information for the purposes of the investigation.

(1A) The order may provide that it applies to—

(*a*) all financial institutions,

(*b*) a particular description, or particular descriptions, of financial institutions, or

(*c*) a particular financial institution or particular financial institutions.

(2) The information shall be provided—

(*a*) in such manner and within such time as the constable may specify, and

(*b*) notwithstanding any restriction on the disclosure of information imposed by statute or otherwise.

(3) An institution which fails to comply with a requirement under this paragraph shall be guilty of an offence.

(4) It is a defence for an institution charged with an offence under sub-paragraph (3) to prove—

(*a*) that the information required was not in the institution's possession, or

(*b*) that it was not reasonably practicable for the institution to comply with the requirement.

(5) An institution guilty of an offence under sub-paragraph (3) shall be liable on summary conviction to a fine not exceeding level 5 on the standard scale.

*Procedure*

**2.** An order under paragraph 1 may be made only on the application of—

(*a*) in England and Wales or Northern Ireland, a police officer of at least the rank of superintendent, or

(*b*) *Scotland.*

**3.** An order under paragraph 1 may be made only by—

(*a*) in England and Wales, a Circuit judge,*

(*b*) *Scotland*, or

(*c*) in Northern Ireland, a Crown Court judge.

---

* **Words inserted by the Courts Act 2003, Sch 4 from a date to be appointed.**

**4.** (1) Criminal Procedure Rules may make provision about the procedure for an application under paragraph 1.

(2) The High Court of Justiciary may, by Act of Adjournal, make provision about the procedure for an application under paragraph 1.

(3) Crown Court Rules may make provision about the procedure for an application under paragraph 1.

*Criteria for making order*

**5.** An order under paragraph 1 may be made only if the person making it is satisfied that—

(*a*) the order is sought for the purposes of a terrorist investigation,

(*b*) the tracing of terrorist property is desirable for the purposes of the investigation, and

(*c*) the order will enhance the effectiveness of the investigation.

*Financial institution*

**6.** (1) In this Schedule "financial institution" means—

(*a*) a person who has permission under Part 4 of the Financial Services and Markets Act 2000 to accept deposits,

(*b*) *repealed,*

(*c*) a credit union (within the meaning of the Credit Unions Act 1979 or the Credit Unions (Northern Ireland) Order 1985),

(*d*) a person carrying on a relevant regulated activity,

(*e*) the National Savings Bank,

(*f*) a person who carries out an activity for the purposes of raising money authorised to be raised under the National Loans Act 1968 under the auspices of the Director of National Savings,

(*g*) a European institution carrying on a home regulated activity (within the meaning of Directive 2006/48/EC of the European Parliament and of the Council of 14 June 2006 relating to the taking up and pursuit of the business of credit institutions as last amended by Directive 2009/111/EC),

(*h*) a person carrying out an activity specified in any of points 1 to 12, 14 and 15 of Annex 1 to that Directive,

(*ha*) an electronic money institution within the meaning of Directive 2009/110/EC of the European Parliament and of the Council of 16th September 2009 relating to the taking up, pursuit and prudential supervision of the business of electronic money institutions, and

(*i*) a person who carries on an insurance business in accordance with an authorisation pursuant to Article 4 or 51 of Directive 2002/83/EC of the European Parliament and of the Council of 5th November 2002 concerning life assurance.

(1A) For the purposes of sub-paragraph (1)(*d*), a relevant regulated activity means—

(*a*) dealing in investments as principal or as agent,

(*b*) arranging deals in investments,

(*ba*) operating a multilateral trading facility,

(*c*) managing investments,

(*d*) safeguarding and administering investments,

(*e*) sending dematerialised instructions,

(*f*) establishing etc collective investment schemes,

(*g*) advising on investments.

(1B) Sub-paragraphs (1)(*a*) and (1A) must be read with—

(*a*) section 22 of the Financial Services and Markets Act 2000;
(*b*) any relevant order under that section; and
(*c*) Schedule 2 to that Act.

(2) The Secretary of State may by order provide for a class of person—
(*a*) to be a financial institution for the purposes of this Schedule, or
(*b*) to cease to be a financial institution for the purposes of this Schedule.

(3) An institution which ceases to be a financial institution for the purposes of this Schedule (whether by virtue of sub-paragraph (2)(*b*) or otherwise) shall continue to be treated as a financial institution for the purposes of any requirement under paragraph 1 to provide customer information which relates to a time when the institution was a financial institution.

*Customer information*

7. (1) In this Schedule "customer information" means (subject to sub-paragraph (3))—
(*a*) information whether a business relationship exists or existed between a financial institution and a particular person ("a customer"),
(*b*) a customer's account number,
(*c*) a customer's full name,
(*d*) a customer's date of birth,
(*e*) a customer's address or former address,
(*f*) the date on which a business relationship between a financial institution and a customer begins or ends,
(*g*) any evidence of a customer's identity obtained by a financial institution in pursuance of or for the purposes of any legislation relating to money laundering, and
(*h*) the identity of a person sharing an account with a customer.

(2) For the purposes of this Schedule there is a business relationship between a financial institution and a person if (and only if)—
(*a*) there is an arrangement between them designed to facilitate the carrying out of frequent or regular transactions between them, and
(*b*) the total amount of payments to be made in the course of the arrangement is neither known nor capable of being ascertained when the arrangement is made.

(3) The Secretary of State may by order provide for a class of information—
(*a*) to be customer information for the purposes of this Schedule, or
(*b*) to cease to be customer information for the purposes of this Schedule.

*Offence by body corporate, etc*

8. (1) This paragraph applies where an offence under paragraph 1(3) is committed by an institution and it is proved that the offence—
(*a*) was committed with the consent or connivance of an officer of the institution, or
(*b*) was attributable to neglect on the part of an officer of the institution.

(2) The officer, as well as the institution, shall be guilty of the offence.

(3) Where an individual is convicted of an offence under paragraph 1(3) by virtue of this paragraph, he shall be liable on summary conviction to—
(*a*) imprisonment for a term not exceeding six months,
(*b*) a fine not exceeding level 5 on the standard scale, or
(*c*) both.

(4) In the case of an institution which is a body corporate, in this paragraph "officer" includes—
(*a*) a director, manager or secretary,
(*b*) a person purporting to act as a director, manager or secretary, and
(*c*) if the affairs of the body are managed by its members, a member.

(5) In the case of an institution which is a partnership, in this paragraph "officer" means a partner.

(6) In the case of an institution which is an unincorporated association (other than a partnership), in this paragraph "officer" means a person concerned in the management or control of the association.

*Self-incrimination*

9. (1) Customer information provided by a financial institution under this Schedule shall not be admissible in evidence in criminal proceedings against the institution or any of its officers or employees.

(2) Sub-paragraph (1) shall not apply in relation to proceedings for an offence under paragraph 1(3) (including proceedings brought by virtue of paragraph 8).

## SCHEDULE 6A
## ACCOUNT MONITORING ORDERS

*(As inserted by the Anti-terrorism, Crime and Security Act 2001, Sch 2.)*

*Introduction*

7.8820 1. (1) This paragraph applies for the purposes of this Schedule.

(2) A judge is—
(*a*) a Circuit judge *, in England and Wales;
(*b*) *Scotland*;
(*c*) a Crown Court judge, in Northern Ireland.

(3) The court is—
(*a*) the Crown Court, in England and Wales or Northern Ireland;
(*b*) *Scotland*.

(4) An appropriate officer is—
(*a*) a police officer, in England and Wales or Northern Ireland;
(*b*) *Scotland*.

(5) "Financial institution" has the same meaning as in Schedule 6.

---

* **Words substituted by the Courts Act 2003, Sch 4 from a date to be appointed.**

*Account monitoring orders*

2. (1) A judge may, on an application made to him by an appropriate officer, make an account monitoring order if he is satisfied that—

(*a*) the order is sought for the purposes of a terrorist investigation,

(*b*) the tracing of terrorist property is desirable for the purposes of the investigation, and

(*c*) the order will enhance the effectiveness of the investigation.

(2) The application for an account monitoring order must state that the order is sought against the financial institution specified in the application in relation to information which—

(*a*) relates to an account or accounts held at the institution by the person specified in the application (whether solely or jointly with another), and

(*b*) is of the description so specified.

(3) The application for an account monitoring order may specify information relating to—

(*a*) all accounts held by the person specified in the application for the order at the financial institution so specified,

(*b*) a particular description, or particular descriptions, of accounts so held, or

(*c*) a particular account, or particular accounts, so held.

(4) An account monitoring order is an order that the financial institution specified in the application for the order must—

(*a*) for the period specified in the order,

(*b*) in the manner so specified,

(*c*) at or by the time or times so specified, and

(*d*) at the place or places so specified,

provide information of the description specified in the application to an appropriate officer.

(5) The period stated in an account monitoring order must not exceed the period of 90 days beginning with the day on which the order is made.

*Applications*

3. (1) An application for an account monitoring order may be made ex parte to a judge in chambers.

(2) The description of information specified in an application for an account monitoring order may be varied by the person who made the application.

(3) If the application was made by a police officer, the description of information specified in it may be varied by a different police officer.

*Discharge or variation*

4. (1) An application to discharge or vary an account monitoring order may be made to the court by—

(*a*) the person who applied for the order;

(*b*) any person affected by the order.

(2) If the application for the account monitoring order was made by a police officer, an application to discharge or vary the order may be made by a different police officer.

(3) The court—

(*a*) may discharge the order;

(*b*) may vary the order.

*Rules of court*

5. (1) Rules of court may make provision as to the practice and procedure to be followed in connection with proceedings relating to account monitoring orders.

(2) *Scotland.*

*Effect of orders*

6. (1) In England and Wales and Northern Ireland, an account monitoring order has effect as if it were an order of the court.

(2) An account monitoring order has effect in spite of any restriction on the disclosure of information (however imposed).

*Statements*

7. (1) A statement made by a financial institution in response to an account monitoring order may not be used in evidence against it in criminal proceedings.

(2) But sub-paragraph (1) does not apply—

(*a*) in the case of proceedings for contempt of court;

(*b*) in the case of proceedings under section 23 where the financial institution has been convicted of an offence under any of sections 15 to 18;

(*c*) on a prosecution for an offence where, in giving evidence, the financial institution makes a statement inconsistent with the statement mentioned in sub-paragraph (1).

(3) A statement may not be used by virtue of sub-paragraph (2)(*c*) against a financial institution unless—

(*a*) evidence relating to it is adduced, or

(*b*) a question relating to it is asked,

by or on behalf of the financial institution in the proceedings arising out of the prosecution.

## SCHEDULE 6B

### Searches in Specified Areas or Places: Supplementary

*(As inserted by the Protection of Freedoms Act 2012, Sch 5.)*

*Extent of search powers: supplementary*

**7.8821** 1. A constable exercising the power conferred by an authorisation under section 47A may not require a person to remove any clothing in public except for headgear, footwear, an outer coat, a jacket or gloves.

2. (1) Sub-paragraph (2) applies if a constable proposes to search a person or vehicle by virtue of

section 47A(2) or (3).

(2) The constable may detain the person or vehicle for such time as is reasonably required to permit the search to be carried out at or near the place where the person or vehicle is stopped.

*Requirements as to writing*

**3.** A senior police officer who gives an authorisation under section 47A orally must confirm it in writing as soon as reasonably practicable.

**4.** (1) Where—

(*a*) a vehicle or pedestrian is stopped by virtue of section 47A(2) or (3), and

(*b*) the driver of the vehicle or the pedestrian applies for a written statement that the vehicle was stopped, or that the pedestrian was stopped, by virtue of section 47A(2) or (as the case may be) (3),

the written statement must be provided.

(2) An application under sub-paragraph (1) must be made within the period of 12 months beginning with the date on which the vehicle or pedestrian was stopped.

*Duration of authorisations*

**5.** (1) An authorisation under section 47A has effect during the period—

(*a*) beginning at the time when the authorisation is given, and

(*b*) ending with the specified date or at the specified time.

(2) This paragraph is subject as follows.

**6.** The specified date or time must not occur after the end of the period of 14 days beginning with the day on which the authorisation is given.

**7.** (1) The senior police officer who gives an authorisation must inform the Secretary of State of it as soon as reasonably practicable.

(2) An authorisation ceases to have effect at the end of the period of 48 hours beginning with the time when it is given unless it is confirmed by the Secretary of State before the end of that period.

(3) An authorisation ceasing to have effect by virtue of sub-paragraph (2) does not affect the lawfulness of anything done in reliance on it before the end of the period concerned.

(4) When confirming an authorisation, the Secretary of State may—

(*a*) substitute an earlier date or time for the specified date or time;

(*b*) substitute a more restricted area or place for the specified area or place.

**8.** The Secretary of State may cancel an authorisation with effect from a time identified by the Secretary of State.

**9.** (1) A senior police officer may—

(*a*) cancel an authorisation with effect from a time identified by the officer concerned;

(*b*) substitute an earlier date or time for the specified date or time;

(*c*) substitute a more restricted area or place for the specified area or place.

(2) Any such cancellation or substitution in relation to an authorisation confirmed by the Secretary of State under paragraph 7 does not require confirmation by the Secretary of State.

**10.** An authorisation given by a member of the Civil Nuclear Constabulary does not have effect except in relation to times when the specified area or place is a place where members of that Constabulary have the powers and privileges of a constable.

**11.** The existence, expiry or cancellation of an authorisation does not prevent the giving of a new authorisation.

*Specified areas or places*

**12.** (1) An authorisation given by a senior police officer who is not a member of the British Transport Police Force, the Ministry of Defence Police or the Civil Nuclear Constabulary may specify an area or place together with—

(*a*) the internal waters adjacent to that area or place; or

(*b*) a specified area of those internal waters.

(2) In sub-paragraph (1) "internal waters" means waters in the United Kingdom that are not comprised in any police area.

**13.** Where an authorisation specifies more than one area or place—

(*a*) the power of a senior police officer under paragraph 5(1)(*b*) to specify a date or time includes a power to specify different dates or times for different areas or places (and the other references in this Schedule to the specified date or time are to be read accordingly), and

(*b*) the power of the Secretary of State under paragraph 7(4)(*b*), and of a senior police officer under paragraph 9(1)(*c*), includes a power to remove areas or places from the authorisation.

*Interpretation*

**14.** (1) In this Schedule—

"driver" has the meaning given by section 43A(5);

"senior police officer" means—

(*a*) in relation to an authorisation where the specified area or place is the whole or part of a police area outside Northern Ireland, other than of a police area mentioned in paragraph (*b*) or (*c*), a police officer for the area who is of at least the rank of assistant chief constable;

(*b*) in relation to an authorisation where the specified area or place is the whole or part of the metropolitan police district, a police officer for the district who is of at least the rank of commander of the metropolitan police;

(*c*) in relation to an authorisation where the specified area or place is the whole or part of the City of London, a police officer for the City who is of at least the rank of commander in the City of London police force;

(*d*) in relation to an authorisation where the specified area or place is the whole or part of Northern Ireland, a member of the Police Service of Northern Ireland who is of at least the rank of assistant chief constable;

"specified" means specified in an authorisation.

(2) References in this Schedule to a senior police officer are to be read as including—

(*a*) in relation to an authorisation where the specified area or place is the whole or part of a police area outside Northern Ireland and is in a place described in section 34(1A), a member of the British Transport Police Force who is of at least the rank of assistant chief constable;

(*b*) in relation to an authorisation where the specified area or place is a place to which section 2(2) of the Ministry of Defence Police Act 1987 applies, a member of the Ministry of Defence Police who is of at least the rank of assistant chief constable;

(*c*) in relation to an authorisation where the specified area or place is a place in which members of the Civil Nuclear Constabulary have the powers and privileges of a constable, a member of that Constabulary who is of at least the rank of assistant chief constable;

but such references are not to be read as including a member of the British Transport Police Force, the Ministry of Defence Police or the Civil Nuclear Constabulary in any other case.

## SCHEDULE 7

### PORT AND BORDER CONTROLS

Section 53

*(As amended by the Anti-terrorism, Crime and Security Act 2001, ss 118(1), 119(1), the Terrorism Act 2006, s 29, SI 2011/1938 and the Anti-social Behaviour, Crime and Policing Act 2014, Sch 9.)*

*Interpretation*

**7.8822** **1.** (1) In this Schedule "examining officer" means any of the following—

(*a*) a constable,

(*b*) an immigration officer who is designated for the purpose of this Schedule by the Secretary of State, and

(*c*) a customs officer who is designated for the purpose of this Schedule by the Secretary of State and the Commissioners of Customs and Excise.

(2) In this Schedule—

"the border area" has the meaning given by paragraph 4,

"captain" means master of a ship or commander of an aircraft,

"port" includes an airport and a hoverport,

"ship" includes a hovercraft, and

"vehicle" includes a train.

(3) A place shall be treated as a port for the purposes of this Schedule in relation to a person if an examining officer believes that the person—

(*a*) has gone there for the purpose of embarking on a ship or aircraft, or

(*b*) has arrived there on disembarking from a ship or aircraft.

*Examining officers etc*

**1A.** (1) The Secretary of State must under paragraph 6 of Schedule 14 issue a code of practice about—

(*a*) training to be undertaken by constables, immigration officers and customs officers who are to act as examining officers or exercise other functions under this Schedule, and

(*b*) the procedure for making designations under paragraph 1(1)(*b*) and (*c*).

(2) In particular, the code must make provision for consultation with the relevant chief officer of police before designations are made under paragraph 1(1)(*b*) or (*c*).

(3) "Relevant chief officer of police" means—

(*a*) in England and Wales, the chief officer of police for the police area in which the persons designated would act as examining officers,

(*b*) in Scotland, the Chief Constable of the Police Service of Scotland, and

(*c*) in Northern Ireland, the Chief Constable of the Police Service of Northern Ireland.

*Power to stop, question and detain*[1]

**2.** (1) An examining officer may question a person to whom this paragraph applies for the purpose of determining whether he appears to be a person falling within section 40(1)(*b*).

(2) This paragraph applies to a person if—

(*a*) he is at a port or in the border area, and

(*b*) the examining officer believes that the person's presence at the port or in the area is connected with his entering or leaving Great Britain or Northern Ireland or his travelling by air within Great Britain or within Northern Ireland.

(3) This paragraph also applies to a person on a ship or aircraft which has arrived at any place in Great Britain or Northern Ireland (whether from within or outside Great Britain or Northern Ireland).

(4) An examining officer may exercise his powers under this paragraph whether or not he has grounds for suspecting that a person falls within section 40(1)(*b*).

---

[1] *Note: the authorities considered below pre-date a number of amendments made to Sch 7 by Sch 9 to the Anti-social, Crime and Policing Act 2014. These amendments were brought into force on 31 July 2014 by art 3 of the Anti-social Behaviour, Crime and Policing Act 2014 (Commencement No 4 and Transitional Provisions) Order 2014, SI 2014/1916. The commenced provisions: reduce the maximum period of examination to six hours; extend to individuals detained at a port the statutory right to have a person informed of their detention and to consult a solicitor privately; clarify that the right to consult a solicitor includes consultation in person; ensure access to legal advice for all individuals examined under Sch 7 for more than one hour; establish a statutory basis for undertaking strip searches of persons detailed under Sch 7; repeal the power to seek intimate samples during the course of a Sch 7 examination; provide that an examining officer may make and retain a copy of information obtained or found in the course of an examination; and introduce a requirement to keep under periodic review the need for continued detention of a person who is being detained under Sch 7 powers.* As to the breadth of these powers and their proper exercise, see *CC v Comr of Police of the Metropolis* [2011] EWHC 3316 (Admin), [2012] 2 All ER 1004, [2012] 1 WLR 1913:

> " . . . the language of section 40(1)(*b*) is wide enough to allow for examination not only of whether he appears to be a terrorist but also of the way in which or the act by which he so appears" (per Collins J at para 16). And 'There may come a point when the officer does consider that the examinee does not appear to be a terrorist, but his conclusion may not be shared by others and may, when what has emerged from the examination or any search is put together with other material which may, for example, be in the possession of the Security Service be shown to be wrong. Equally, further examination may show that the officer's view formed at a particular point was wrong. Again, in my view he must be able

to ask all questions that he reasonably believes to be needed to enable him or others to reach the necessary determination" (per Collins J at para 18).

Schedule 7 powers are not conferred to enable an arrest to be made. There may be a number of reasons why an officer may form a reasonable suspicion from his examination, but determine not to make an arrest, eg because the information giving rise to the suspicion cannot be relayed to the suspect or deployed in a court.

It was held in *Beghal v DPP* [2015] UKSC 49, [2016] AC 88, [2015] 3 WLR 344, [2015] 2 Cr App Rep 489 that questioning and search under compulsion under Sch 7 to the Terrorism Act 2000 constituted an interference with the private life of the person questioned, and thus to be justified under art 8.2 of the ECHR it had to be in accordance with the law and a proportionate means to a legitimate end. However, the principle of legality was satisfied since there were sufficient safeguards against the arbitrary use of the power. The power was also proportionate since it was rationally connected to the proper objective of the prevention and detection of terrorism, and the level of intrusion into the privacy of the individual was comparatively light and not beyond the reasonable expectations of those who travelled across the UK's international borders. The port questioning and associated powers represented a fair balance between the rights of the individual and the interests of the community at large. The power of detention, which accompanied the Sch 7 powers of questioning and search fell within the exception to the art 5 right to liberty provided by art 5.1(b), but it did not follow that the power of detention was automatically justified. Detention which was necessary to prevent a person being questioned from leaving during that process would be justified, but if the detention continued beyond what was necessary to complete the process it had to be justified by objectively demonstrated suspicion. Such a suspicion could arise in whole or in part from a refusal to co-operate after explanation of the purpose of the inquiry. By necessary implication, privilege against self-incrimination did not apply to compulsory questioning under Sch 7. There was no real and appreciable risk of a prosecution based upon this since this evidence would in practice be excluded under s 78 of PACE on art 6, fair trial, grounds. Port questioning and search under Sch 7 was not, however, part of a criminal investigation and therefore no question of breach of the right to a fair trial arose.

An examining officer is not required to have any 'grounds for suspecting that a person falls within section 40(1)(b)'. Nor does Sch 7 provide that an examining officer must be the one to determine whether the subject appears to fall within that subsection. It may well be someone else, to whom the results of the stop are referred. Although the potential reach of para 2(1) is very wide, there are important constraints on the use of the Sch 7 power. First, although the examining officer need not have grounds for suspecting that the subject falls within s 40(1)(*b*), the general law requires that the power be exercised upon some reasoned basis, proportionately and in good faith. Secondly, there is a limitation upon the meaning of terrorism given by reference to the mental or purposive elements prescribed by s 1(1)(*b*) ('designed to influence . . . or to intimidate') and 1(1)(*c*) ('for the purpose of advancing a political, religious, racial or ideological cause'). Thirdly, the power may only be used where the subject is 'at a port or in the border area' (Sch 7, para 2(2)(*a*)) intending (in the examining officer's belief) to enter or leave Great Britain or Northern Ireland (para 2(2)(*b*)). Fourthly, the examining officers' power of detention is limited to nine hours (Sch 7, para 6). The Sch 7 power is given in order to provide a reasonable but limited opportunity for the ascertainment of a possibility: the possibility that a traveller at a port may be involved ('concerned'—s 40(1)(*b*)), directly or indirectly, in any of a range of activities enumerated in s 1(2). If the possibility is established, the statute prescribes no particular consequence. What happens will depend, plainly, on the outcome of the Sch 7 examination including any searches where those have been carried out. There may be a prosecution for an offence under the Act, or indeed some other offence; materials in the subject's possession may be retained if the general law allows it; the subject may be released with no further action. The fact that the outcome of a Sch 7 examination is open-ended supports the submission that there is no principled distinction, for the purpose of a proper understanding of the power, between an interest in the person examined and an interest in what may be found in his possession.

The s 1 definition is capable of covering the publication or threatened publication [for the purpose of advancing a political, religious, racial or ideological cause] of stolen classified information which, if published, would reveal personal details of members of the armed forces or security and intelligence agencies, thereby endangering their lives, where that publication or threatened publication is designed to influence government policy on the activities of the security and intelligence agencies: ss 1(1)(*b*) and (*c*), and (2)(*c*): *R (on the application of Miranda) v Secretary of State for the Home Department* [2014] EWHC 255 (Admin), [2014] 3 All ER 447, [2014] 1 WLR 3140. However, the stop power conferred by para 2(1) of Sch 7 is incompatible with art 10 of the Convention in relation to journalistic material in that it is not subject to adequate safeguards against its arbitrary exercise. It will be for Parliament to provide such protection. The most obvious safeguard would be some form of judicial or other independent and impartial scrutiny conducted in such a way as to protect the confidentiality in the material: *R (Miranda) v Secretary of State for the Home Department* [2016] EWCA Civ 6, [2016] 1 WLR 1505, [2016] 1 Cr App R 26.

**3.** An examining officer may question a person who is in the border area for the purpose of determining whether his presence in the area is connected with his entering or leaving Northern Ireland.

**4.** (1) A place in Northern Ireland is within the border area for the purposes of paragraphs 2 and 3 if it is no more than one mile from the border between Northern Ireland and the Republic of Ireland.

(2) If a train goes from the Republic of Ireland to Northern Ireland, the first place in Northern Ireland at which it stops for the purpose of allowing passengers to leave is within the border area for the purposes of paragraphs 2 and 3.

**5.** A person who is questioned under paragraph 2 or 3 must—

(*a*) give the examining officer any information in his possession which the officer requests;

(*b*) give the examining officer on request either a valid passport which includes a photograph or another document which establishes his identity;

(*c*) declare whether he has with him documents of a kind specified by the examining officer;

(*d*) give the examining officer on request any document which he has with him and which is of a kind specified by the officer.

**6.** (1) For the purposes of exercising a power under paragraph 2 or 3 an examining officer may—

(*a*) stop a person or vehicle;

(*b*) detain a person.

(2) For the purpose of detaining a person under this paragraph, an examining officer may authorise the person's removal from a ship, aircraft or vehicle.

(3) Where a person is detained under this paragraph the provisions of Parts 1 and 1A of Schedule 8 (treatment and review of detention) shall apply.

(4) *Repealed.*

**6A.** (1) This paragraph applies where a person is questioned under paragraph 2 or 3.

(2) After the end of the 1 hour period, the person may not be questioned under either of those paragraphs unless the person is detained under paragraph 6.

(3) If the person is detained under paragraph 6 the person must be released not later than the end of the 6 hour period (unless detained under another power).

(4) In this paragraph—

"the 1 hour period" is the period of 1 hour beginning with the time the person is first questioned under paragraph 2 or 3;

"the 6 hour period" is the period of 6 hours beginning with that time.

*Searches*

7. For the purpose of satisfying himself whether there are any persons whom he may wish to question under paragraph 2 an examining officer may—

(*a*) search a ship or aircraft;

(*b*) search anything on a ship or aircraft;

(*c*) search anything which he reasonably believes has been, or is about to be, on a ship or aircraft.

8. (1) An examining officer who questions a person under paragraph 2 may, for the purpose of determining whether he falls within section 40(1)(*b*)—

(*a*) search the person;

(*b*) search anything which he has with him, or which belongs to him, and which is on a ship or aircraft;

(*c*) search anything which he has with him, or which belongs to him, and which the examining officer reasonably believes has been, or is about to be, on a ship or aircraft;

(*d*) search a ship or aircraft for anything falling within paragraph (*b*);

(*e*) search a vehicle which is on a ship or aircraft;

(*f*) search a vehicle which the examining officer reasonably believes has been, or is about to be, on a ship or aircraft.

(2) Where an examining officer questions a person in the border area under paragraph 2 he may (in addition to the matters specified in sub-paragraph (1)), for the purpose of determining whether the person falls within section 40(1)(*b*)—

(*a*) search a vehicle;

(*b*) search anything in or on a vehicle;

(*c*) search anything which he reasonably believes has been, or is about to be, in or on a vehicle.

(3) A search of a person under this paragraph must be carried out by someone of the same sex.

(4) An intimate search of a person may not be carried out under this paragraph.

(5) A strip search of a person may not be carried out under this paragraph unless—

(*a*) the person is detained under paragraph 6,

(*b*) the examining officer has reasonable grounds to suspect that the person is concealing something which may be evidence that the person falls within section 40(1)(*b*), and

(*c*) the search is authorised by a senior officer who has not been directly involved in questioning the person.

(6) "Senior officer" means—

(*a*) where the examining officer is a constable, a constable of a higher rank than the examining officer,

(*b*) where the examining officer is an immigration officer, an immigration officer of a higher grade than the examining officer, and

(*c*) where the examining officer is a customs officer, a customs officer of a higher grade than the examining officer.

(7) In this paragraph—

"intimate search" means a search which consists of a physical examination of a person's body orifices other than the mouth;

"strip search" means a search which is not an intimate search but involves the removal of an article of clothing which—

(*a*) is being worn wholly or partly on the trunk, and

(*b*) is being so worn either next to the skin or next to an article of underwear.

9. (1) An examining officer may examine goods to which this paragraph applies for the purpose of determining whether they have been used in the commission, preparation or instigation of acts of terrorism.

(2) This paragraph applies to—

(*a*) goods which have arrived in or are about to leave Great Britain or Northern Ireland on a ship or vehicle, and

(*b*) goods which have arrived at or are about to leave any place in Great Britain or Northern Ireland on an aircraft (whether the place they have come from or are going to is within or outside Great Britain or Northern Ireland).

(3) In this paragraph "goods" includes—

(*a*) property of any description, and

(*b*) containers.

(4) An examining officer may board a ship or aircraft or enter a vehicle for the purpose of determining whether to exercise his power under this paragraph.

10. (1) An examining officer may authorise a person to carry out on his behalf a search or examination under any of paragraphs 7 to 9.

(2) A person authorised under this paragraph shall be treated as an examining officer for the purposes of—

(*a*) paragraphs 9(4) and 11 of this Schedule, and

(*b*) paragraphs 2 and 3 of Schedule 14.

*Detention of property*

11. (1) This paragraph applies to anything which—

(*a*) is given to an examining officer in accordance with paragraph 5(*d*),

(*b*) is searched or found on a search under paragraph 8, or

(*c*) is examined under paragraph 9.

(2) An examining officer may detain the thing—

(*a*) for the purpose of examination, for a period not exceeding seven days beginning with the day on which the detention commences,

(*b*) while he believes that it may be needed for use as evidence in criminal proceedings, or

(*c*) while he believes that it may be needed in connection with a decision by the Secretary of State whether to make a deportation order under the Immigration Act 1971.

*Power to make and retain copies*

**11A.** (1) This paragraph applies where the examining officer is a constable.

(2) The examining officer may copy anything which—

(*a*) is given to the examining officer in accordance with paragraph 5,

(*b*) is searched or found on a search under paragraph 8, or

(*c*) is examined under paragraph 9.

(3) The copy may be retained—

(*a*) for so long as is necessary for the purpose of determining whether a person falls within section 40(1)(*b*),

(*b*) while the examining officer believes that it may be needed for use as evidence in criminal proceedings, or

(*c*) while the examining officer believes that it may be needed in connection with a decision by the Secretary of State whether to make a deportation order under the Immigration Act 1971.

*Designated ports*

**12.** (1) This paragraph applies to a journey—

(*a*) to Great Britain from the Republic of Ireland, Northern Ireland or any of the Islands,

(*b*) from Great Britain to any of those places,

(*c*) to Northern Ireland from Great Britain, the Republic of Ireland or any of the Islands, or

(*d*) from Northern Ireland to any of those places.

(2) Where a ship or aircraft is employed to carry passengers for reward on a journey to which this paragraph applies the owners or agents of the ship or aircraft shall not arrange for it to call at a port in Great Britain or Northern Ireland for the purpose of disembarking or embarking passengers unless—

(*a*) the port is a designated port, or

(*b*) an examining officer approves the arrangement.

(3) Where an aircraft is employed on a journey to which this paragraph applies otherwise than to carry passengers for reward, the captain of the aircraft shall not permit it to call at or leave a port in Great Britain or Northern Ireland unless—

(*a*) the port is a designated port, or

(*b*) he gives at least 12 hours' notice in writing to a constable for the police area in which the port is situated (or, where the port is in Northern Ireland, to a member of the Police Service of Northern Ireland).

(4) A designated port is a port which appears in the Table at the end of this Schedule.

(5) The Secretary of State may by order—

(*a*) add an entry to the Table;

(*b*) remove an entry from the Table.

*Embarkation and disembarkation*

**13.** (1) The Secretary of State may by notice in writing to the owners or agents of ships or aircraft—

(*a*) designate control areas in any port in the United Kingdom;

(*b*) specify conditions for or restrictions on the embarkation or disembarkation of passengers in a control area.

(2) Where owners or agents of a ship or aircraft receive notice under sub-paragraph (1) in relation to a port they shall take all reasonable steps to ensure, in respect of the ship or aircraft—

(*a*) that passengers do not embark or disembark at the port outside a control area, and

(*b*) that any specified conditions are met and any specified restrictions are complied with.

**14.** (1) The Secretary of State may by notice in writing to persons concerned with the management of a port in the United Kingdom ("the port managers")—

(*a*) designate control areas in the port;

(*b*) require the port managers to provide at their own expense specified facilities in a control area for the purposes of the embarkation or disembarkation of passengers or their examination under this Schedule;

(*c*) require conditions to be met and restrictions to be complied with in relation to the embarkation or disembarkation of passengers in a control area;

(*d*) require the port managers to display, in specified locations in control areas, notices containing specified information about the provisions of this Schedule in such form as may be specified.

(2) Where port managers receive notice under sub-paragraph (1) they shall take all reasonable steps to comply with any requirement set out in the notice.

**15.** (1) This paragraph applies to a ship employed to carry passengers for reward, or an aircraft, which—

(*a*) arrives in Great Britain from the Republic of Ireland, Northern Ireland or any of the Islands,

(*b*) arrives in Northern Ireland from Great Britain, the Republic of Ireland or any of the Islands,

(*c*) leaves Great Britain for the Republic of Ireland, Northern Ireland or any of the Islands, or

(*d*) leaves Northern Ireland for Great Britain, the Republic of Ireland or any of the Islands.

(2) The captain shall ensure—

(*a*) that passengers and members of the crew do not disembark at a port in Great Britain or Northern Ireland unless either they have been examined by an examining officer or they disembark in accordance with arrangements approved by an examining officer;

(*b*) that passengers and members of the crew do not embark at a port in Great Britain or Northern Ireland except in accordance with arrangements approved by an examining officer;

(*c*) where a person is to be examined under this Schedule on board the ship or aircraft, that he is presented for examination in an orderly manner.

(3) Where paragraph 27 of Schedule 2 to the Immigration Act 1971 (disembarkation requirements on arrival in the United Kingdom) applies, the requirements of sub-paragraph (2)(*a*) above are in addition to the requirements of paragraph 27 of that Schedule.

*Carding*

**16.** (1) The Secretary of State may by order[1] make provision requiring a person to whom this paragraph applies, if required to do so by an examining officer, to complete and produce to the officer a card containing such information in such form as the order may specify.

(2) An order under this paragraph may require the owners or agents of a ship or aircraft employed to carry passengers for reward to supply their passengers with cards in the form required by virtue of sub-paragraph (1).

(3) This paragraph applies to a person—

(*a*) who disembarks in Great Britain from a ship or aircraft which has come from the Republic of Ireland, Northern Ireland or any of the Islands,

(*b*) who disembarks in Northern Ireland from a ship or aircraft which has come from Great Britain, the Republic of Ireland, or any of the Islands,

(*c*) who embarks in Great Britain on a ship or aircraft which is going to the Republic of Ireland, Northern Ireland or any of the Islands, or

(*d*) who embarks in Northern Ireland on a ship or aircraft which is going to Great Britain, the Republic of Ireland, or any of the Islands.

---

[1] The Terrorism Act 2000 (Carding) Order 2001, SI 2001/426 has been made.

*Provision of passenger information*

**17.** (1) This paragraph applies to a ship or aircraft which—

(*a*) arrives or is expected to arrive in any place in the United Kingdom (whether from another place in the United Kingdom or from outside the United Kingdom), or

(*b*) leaves or is expected to leave the United Kingdom.

(2) If an examining officer gives the owners or agents of a ship or aircraft to which this paragraph applies a written request to provide specified information, the owners or agents shall comply with the request as soon as is reasonably practicable.

(3) A request to an owner or agent may relate—

(*a*) to a particular ship or aircraft,

(*b*) to all ships or aircraft of the owner or agent to which this paragraph applies, or

(*c*) to specified ships or aircraft.

(4) Information may be specified in a request only if it is of a kind which is prescribed by order[1] of the Secretary of State and which relates—

(*a*) to passengers,

(*b*) to crew,

(*c*) to vehicles belonging to passengers or crew, or

(*d*) to goods.

(5) A passenger or member of the crew on a ship or aircraft shall give the captain any information required for the purpose of enabling the owners or agents to comply with a request under this paragraph.

(6) Sub-paragraphs (2) and (5) shall not require the provision of information which is required to be provided under or by virtue of paragraph 27(2) or 27B of Schedule 2 to the Immigration Act 1971.

---

[1] See Sch 7 to the Terrorism Act 2000 (Information) Order 2002, SI 2002/1945.

*Offences*

**18.** (1) A person commits an offence if he—

(*a*) wilfully fails to comply with a duty imposed under or by virtue of this Schedule,

(*b*) wilfully contravenes a prohibition imposed under or by virtue of this Schedule, or

(*c*) wilfully obstructs, or seeks to frustrate, a search or examination under or by virtue of this Schedule.

(2) A person guilty of an offence under this paragraph shall be liable on summary conviction to—

(*a*) imprisonment for a term not exceeding three months *,

(*b*) a fine not exceeding level 4 on the standard scale, or

(*c*) both.

---

* **Words substituted by the Criminal Justice Act 2003, Sch 26 from a date to be appointed.**

TABLE

DESIGNATED PORTS

*Great Britain*

**7.8823**

| *Seaports* | *Airports* |
|---|---|
| Ardrossan | Aberdeen |
| Cairnryan | Biggin Hill |
| Campbeltown | Birmingham |
| Fishguard | Blackpool |
| Fleetwood | Bournemouth (Hurn) |
| Heysham | Bristol |
| Holyhead | Cambridge |
| Loch Ryan | Cardiff |
| Pembroke Dock | Carlisle |
| Plymouth | Coventry |
| Poole Harbour | East Midlands |
| Port of Liverpool | Edinburgh |
| Portsmouth Continental Ferry Port | Exeter |
| Southampton | Glasgow |
| Swansea | Gloucester/Cheltenham (Staverton) |
| Torquay | Humberside |

| *Seaports* | *Airports* |
|---|---|
| Troon | Leeds/Bradford |
| Weymouth | Liverpool |
| | London-City |
| | London-Gatwick |
| | London-Heathrow |
| | Luton |
| | Lydd |
| | Manchester |
| | Manston |
| | Newcastle |
| | Norwich |
| | Plymouth |
| | Prestwick |
| | Sheffield City |
| | Southampton |
| | Southend |
| | Stansted |
| | Teesside |

*Northern Ireland*

| *Seaports* | *Airports* |
|---|---|
| Ballycastle | Belfast City |
| Belfast | Belfast International |
| Larne | City of Derry |
| Port of Londonderry | |
| Warrenpoint | |

## SCHEDULE 8*
### Detention
Section 41 and Schedule 7, para 6

*(Amended by the Criminal Justice and Police Act 2001, ss 75 and 84(4), the Anti-terrorism, Crime and Security Act 2001, s 127(2), the Proceeds of Crime Act 2002, s 456, the Serious Organised Crime and Police Act 2005, Sch 7, the Terrorism Act 2006, ss 23 and 24, the Counter-Terrorism Act 2008, ss 17, 82, Schs 3 and 9, the Protection of Freedoms Act 2012, ss 57, 58, Sch 10, the Anti-social Behaviour, Crime and Policing Act 2014, s 146 and Schs 9, 11 and the Policing and Crime Act 2017, s 71.)*

*** Schedule amended by the Protection of Freedoms Act 2012, Schs 1, 9 and 10 and the Legal Aid, Sentencing and Punishment of Offenders Act 2012, Sch 24 from a date to be appointed.**

## Part I
## Treatment of Persons Detained under Section 41 or Schedule 7
*Place of detention*

7.8824 1. (1) The Secretary of State shall designate places at which persons may be detained under Schedule 7 or section 41.

(2) In this Schedule a reference to a police station includes a reference to any place which the Secretary of State has designated under sub-paragraph (1) as a place where a person may be detained under section 41.

(3) Where a person is detained under Schedule 7, he may be taken in the custody of an examining officer or of a person acting under an examining officer's authority to and from any place where his attendance is required for the purpose of—
- (*a*) his examination under that Schedule,
- (*b*) establishing his nationality or citizenship, or
- (*c*) making arrangements for his admission to a country or territory outside the United Kingdom.

(4) A constable who arrests a person under section 41 shall take him as soon as is reasonably practicable to the police station which the constable considers the most appropriate.

(5) In this Schedule "examining officer" has the meaning given in Schedule 7.

(6) Where a person is arrested in one Part of the United Kingdom and all or part of his detention takes place in another Part, the provisions of this Schedule which apply to detention in a particular Part of the United Kingdom apply in relation to him while he is detained in that Part.

*Identification*

2. (1) An authorised person may take any steps which are reasonably necessary for—
- (*a*) photographing the detained person,
- (*b*) measuring him, or
- (*c*) identifying him.

(2) In sub-paragraph (1) "authorised person" means any of the following—
- (*a*) a constable,
- (*b*) a prison officer,
- (*c*) a person authorised by the Secretary of State, and

(*d*) in the case of a person detained under Schedule 7, an examining officer.

(3) This paragraph does not confer the power to take—

(*a*) fingerprints, non-intimate samples or intimate samples (within the meaning given by paragraph 15 below), or

(*b*) relevant physical data or samples as mentioned in section 18 of the Criminal Procedure (Scotland) Act 1995 as applied by paragraph 20 below.

*Audio and video recording of interviews*

**3.** (1) The Secretary of State shall—

(*a*) issue a code of practice about the audio recording of interviews to which this paragraph applies, and

(*b*) make an order[1] requiring the audio recording of interviews to which this paragraph applies in accordance with any relevant code of practice under paragraph (*a*).

(2) The Secretary of State may make an order[2] requiring the video recording of—

(*a*) interviews to which this paragraph applies;

(*b*) interviews to which this paragraph applies which take place in a particular Part of the United Kingdom.

(3) An order under sub-paragraph (2) shall specify whether the video recording which it requires is to be silent or with sound.

(4) Where an order is made under sub-paragraph (2)—

(*a*) the Secretary of State shall issue a code of practice about the video recording of interviews to which the order applies, and

(*b*) the order shall require the interviews to be video recorded in accordance with any relevant code of practice under paragraph (*a*).

(5) Where the Secretary of State has made an order under sub-paragraph (2) requiring certain interviews to be video recorded with sound—

(*a*) he need not make an order under sub-paragraph (1)(*b*) in relation to those interviews, but

(*b*) he may do so.

(6) This paragraph applies to any interview by a constable of a person detained under Schedule 7 or section 41 if the interview takes place in a police station.

(7) A code of practice under this paragraph—

(*a*) may make provision in relation to a particular Part of the United Kingdom;

(*b*) may make different provision for different Parts of the United Kingdom.

---

[1] The Terrorism Act 2000 (Code of Practice on Audio Recording of Interviews) (No 2) Order 2001, SI 2001/189 requires interviews of persons detained under s 41 or Sch 7 which are conducted by a police constable at a police station, to be audio recorded in accordance with the audio code of practice.

[2] The Terrorism Act 2000 (Video Recording with Sound Interviews and Associated Code of Practice) Order 2012, SI 2012/1792 has been made which came into force on 10 July 2012. The associated Code is the code of practice entitled *Code of Practice for the Video Recording with Sound of Interviews of Persons Detained under Section 41 of, or Schedule 7 to, the Terrorism Act 2000 and Post Charge Questioning of Persons Authorised under Sections 22 or 23 of the Counter-Terrorism Act 2008* laid before Parliament in draft on 10 May 2012.

**4.** (1) This paragraph applies to a code of practice under paragraph 3.

(2) Where the Secretary of State proposes to issue a code of practice he shall—

(*a*) publish a draft,

(*b*) consider any representations made to him about the draft, and

(*c*) if he thinks it appropriate, modify the draft in the light of any representations made to him.

(3) The Secretary of State shall lay a draft of the code before Parliament.

(4) When the Secretary of State has laid a draft code before Parliament he may bring it into operation by order[1].

(5) The Secretary of State may revise a code and issue the revised code; and sub-paragraphs (2) to (4) shall apply to a revised code as they apply to an original code.

(6) The failure by a constable to observe a provision of a code shall not of itself make him liable to criminal or civil proceedings.

(7) A code—

(*a*) shall be admissible in evidence in criminal and civil proceedings, and

(*b*) shall be taken into account by a court or tribunal in any case in which it appears to the court or tribunal to be relevant.

---

[1] The 19 February 2001 was appointed by the Terrorism Act 2000 (Code of Practice on Audio Recording of Interviews) Order 2001, SI 2001/159.

*Status*

**5.** A detained person shall be deemed to be in legal custody throughout the period of his detention.

*Rights: England, Wales and Northern Ireland*

**6.** (1) Subject to paragraph 8, a person detained under Schedule 7 or section 41 at a place in England, Wales or Northern Ireland shall be entitled, if he so requests, to have one named person informed as soon as is reasonably practicable that he is being detained there.

(2) The person named must be—

(*a*) a friend of the detained person,

(*b*) a relative, or

(*c*) a person who is known to the detained person or who is likely to take an interest in his welfare.

(3) Where a detained person is transferred from one place to another, he shall be entitled to exercise the right under this paragraph in respect of the place to which he is transferred.

**7.** (1) Subject to paragraphs 8 and 9, a person detained under Schedule 7 or section 41[1] in England, Wales or Northern Ireland shall be entitled, if he so requests, to consult a solicitor as soon as is reasonably practicable, privately and at any time.

(2) Where a request is made under sub-paragraph (1), the request and the time at which it was made shall be recorded.

[1] The words "at a police station" formerly appeared after s 41, and it was held that para 7(1) did not apply to a person detained elsewhere. However, para 5 of Sch 14 to the Act requires an examining officer to perform his functions under the 2000 Act in accordance with any relevant code of practice in operation under para 6. Accordingly, a detainee (in the present case, at an airport) is entitled to consult a solicitor before being interviewed and that right can be exercised at any time during the period of detention and repeatedly. Where a solicitor attends in person he can be present during the interview, and a reasonable delay to await the arrival of a solicitor may be required. A detainee may not, however, exercise his right in such a way as to frustrate the proper purpose of the examination: *R (Elosta) v Comr of Police for the Metropolis* [2013] EWHC 3397 (Admin), [2014] 1 WLR 239, [2014] RTR 378.

**7A.** (1) This paragraph applies where a person detained under Schedule 7 requests to consult a solicitor.

(2) The examining officer may not question the detained person under paragraph 2 or 3 of Schedule 7 until the person has consulted a solicitor (or no longer wishes to do so).

(3) Sub-paragraph (2) does not apply if the examining officer reasonably believes that postponing the questioning until then would be likely to prejudice determination of the relevant matters.

(4) The powers given by paragraph 8 of Schedule 7 (search powers where a person is questioned under paragraph 2 of Schedule 7) may be used when questioning is postponed because of sub-paragraph (2).

(5) The detained person is entitled to consult a solicitor in person.

(6) Sub-paragraph (5) does not apply if the examining officer reasonably believes that the time it would take to consult a solicitor in person would be likely to prejudice determination of the relevant matters.

(7) In that case the examining officer may require any consultation to take place in another way.

(8) In this paragraph "the relevant matters" means the matters the examining officer seeks to determine under paragraph 2 or 3 of Schedule 7.

**8.** (1) Subject to sub-paragraph (2), a police officer of at least the rank of superintendent may authorise a delay—

(*a*) in informing the person named by a detained person under paragraph 6;

(*b*) in permitting a detained person to consult a solicitor under paragraph 7.

(2) But where a person is detained under section 41 he must be permitted to exercise his rights under paragraphs 6 and 7 before the end of the period mentioned in subsection (3) of that section.

(3) Subject to sub-paragraph (5), an officer may give an authorisation under sub-paragraph (1) only if he has reasonable grounds for believing—

(*a*) in the case of an authorisation under sub-paragraph (1)(*a*), that informing the named person of the detained person's detention will have any of the consequences specified in sub-paragraph (4), or

(*b*) in the case of an authorisation under sub-paragraph (1)(*b*), that the exercise of the right under paragraph 7 at the time when the detained person desires to exercise it will have any of the consequences specified in sub-paragraph (4).

(4) Those consequences are—

(*a*) interference with or harm to evidence of a serious offence,

(*b*) interference with or physical injury to any person,

(*c*) the alerting of persons who are suspected of having committed a serious offence but who have not been arrested for it,

(*d*) the hindering of the recovery of property obtained as a result of a serious offence or in respect of which a forfeiture order could be made under section 23 or 23A,

(*e*) interference with the gathering of information about the commission, preparation or instigation of acts of terrorism,

(*f*) the alerting of a person and thereby making it more difficult to prevent an act of terrorism, and

(*g*) the alerting of a person and thereby making it more difficult to secure a person's apprehension, prosecution or conviction in connection with the commission, preparation or instigation of an act of terrorism.

(5) An officer may also give an authorisation under sub-paragraph (1) if he has reasonable grounds for believing that—

(*a*) the detained person has benefited from his criminal conduct, and

(*b*) the recovery of the value of the property constituting the benefit will be hindered by—

(i) informing the named person of the detained person's detention (in the case of an authorisation under sub-paragraph (1)(*a*)), or

(ii) the exercise of the right under paragraph 7 (in the case of an authorisation under sub-paragraph (1)(*b*)).

(5A) For the purposes of sub-paragraph (5) the question whether a person has benefited from his criminal conduct is to be decided in accordance with Part 2 of the Proceeds of Crime Act 2002.

(6) If an authorisation under sub-paragraph (1) is given orally, the person giving it shall confirm it in writing as soon as is reasonably practicable.

(7) Where an authorisation under sub-paragraph (1) is given—

(*a*) the detained person shall be told the reason for the delay as soon as is reasonably practicable, and

(*b*) the reason shall be recorded as soon as is reasonably practicable.

(8) Where the reason for authorising delay ceases to subsist there may be no further delay in permitting the exercise of the right in the absence of a further authorisation under sub-paragraph (1).

(9) In this paragraph, references to a "serious offence" are (in relation to England and Wales) to an indictable offence, and (in relation to Northern Ireland) to a serious arrestable offence within the meaning of Article 87 of the Police and Criminal Evidence (Northern Ireland) Order 1989; but it also include—

(*a*) an offence under any of the provisions mentioned in section 40(1)(*a*) of this Act, and

(*b*) an attempt or conspiracy to commit an offence under any of the provisions mentioned in section 40(1)(*a*).

**9.** (1) A direction under this paragraph may provide that a detained person who wishes to exercise the right under paragraph 7 may consult a solicitor only in the sight and hearing of a qualified officer.

(2) A direction under this paragraph may be given—

(*a*) where the person is detained in England or Wales, by a police officer of at least the rank of Commander or Assistant Chief Constable, or

(*b*) where the person is detained in Northern Ireland, by a police officer of at least the rank of Assistant

Chief Constable.

(3) A direction under this paragraph may be given only if the officer giving it has reasonable grounds for believing—

(*a*) that, unless the direction is given, the exercise of the right by the detained person will have any of the consequences specified in paragraph 8(4), or

(*b*) that the detained person has benefited from his criminal conduct and that, unless the direction is given, the exercise of the right by the detained person will hinder the recovery of the value of the property constituting the benefit.

(4) In this paragraph "a qualified officer" means a police officer who—

(*a*) is of at least the rank of inspector,

(*b*) is of the uniformed branch of the force of which the officer giving the direction is a member, and

(*c*) in the opinion of the officer giving the direction, has no connection with the detained person's case.

(5) A direction under this paragraph shall cease to have effect once the reason for giving it ceases to subsist.

**10.** (1) This paragraph applies where a person is detained in England, Wales or Northern Ireland under Schedule 7 or section 41.

(2) Fingerprints may be taken from the detained person only if they are taken by a constable—

(*a*) with the appropriate consent given in writing, or

(*b*) without that consent under sub-paragraph (4).

(3) A non-intimate sample may be taken from the detained person only if it is taken by a constable—

(*a*) with the appropriate consent given in writing, or

(*b*) without that consent under sub-paragraph (4).

(4) Fingerprints or a non-intimate sample may be taken from the detained person without the appropriate consent only if—

(*a*) he is detained at a police station and a police officer of at least the rank of superintendent authorises the fingerprints or sample to be taken, or

(*b*) he has been convicted of a recordable offence and, where a non-intimate sample is to be taken, he was convicted of the offence on or after 10th April 1995 (or 29th July 1996 where the non-intimate sample is to be taken in Northern Ireland).

(5) An intimate sample may be taken from a person detained under section 41, but only if—

(*a*) he is detained at a police station,

(*b*) the appropriate consent is given in writing,

(*c*) a police officer of at least the rank of superintendent authorises the sample to be taken, and

(*d*) subject to paragraph 13(2) and (3), the sample is taken by a constable.

(6) Subject to sub-paragraph (6A) an officer may give an authorisation under sub-paragraph (4)(*a*) or (5)(*c*) only if—

(*a*) in the case of a person detained under section 41, the officer reasonably suspects that the person has been involved in an offence under any of the provisions mentioned in section 40(1)(*a*), and the officer reasonably believes that the fingerprints or sample will tend to confirm or disprove his involvement, or

(*b*) in any case in which an authorisation under that sub-paragraph may be given, the officer is satisfied that the taking of the fingerprints or sample from the person is necessary in order to assist in determining whether he falls within section 40(1)(*b*).

(6A) An officer may also give an authorisation under sub-paragraph (4)(*a*) for the taking of fingerprints if—

(*a*) he is satisfied that the fingerprints of the detained person will facilitate the ascertainment of that person's identity; and

(*b*) that person has refused to identify himself or the officer has reasonable grounds for suspecting that that person is not who he claims to be.

(6B) In this paragraph references to ascertaining a person's identity include references to showing that he is not a particular person.

(7) If an authorisation under sub-paragraph (4)(*a*) or (5)(*c*) is given orally, the person giving it shall confirm it in writing as soon as is reasonably practicable.

**11.** (1) Before fingerprints or a sample are taken from a person under paragraph 10, he shall be informed—

(*a*) that the fingerprints or sample may be used for the purposes of a relevant search (within the meaning given by paragraph 20A(6)) or for the purposes of section 63A(1) of the Police and Criminal Evidence Act 1984 and Article 63A(1) of the Police and Criminal Evidence (Northern Ireland) Order 1989 (checking of fingerprints and samples), and

(*b*) where the fingerprints or sample are to be taken under paragraph 10(2)(*a*), (3)(*a*) or (4)(*b*), of the reason for taking the fingerprints or sample.

(2) Before fingerprints or a sample are taken from a person upon an authorisation given under paragraph 10(4)(*a*) or (5)(*c*), he shall be informed—

(*a*) that the authorisation has been given,

(*b*) of the grounds upon which it has been given, and

(*c*) where relevant, of the nature of the offence in which it is suspected that he has been involved.

(3) After fingerprints or a sample are taken under paragraph 10, there shall be recorded as soon as is reasonably practicable any of the following which apply—

(*a*) the fact that the person has been informed in accordance with sub-paragraphs (1) and (2),

(*b*) the reason referred to in sub-paragraph (1)(*b*),

(*c*) the authorisation given under paragraph 10(4)(*a*) or (5)(*c*),

(*d*) the grounds upon which that authorisation has been given, and

(*e*) the fact that the appropriate consent has been given.

**12.** (1) This paragraph applies where—

(*a*) two or more non-intimate samples suitable for the same means of analysis have been taken from a person under paragraph 10,

(*b*) those samples have proved insufficient, and

(*c*) the person has been released from detention.

(2) An intimate sample may be taken from the person if—

(*a*) the appropriate consent is given in writing,

(*b*) a police officer of at least the rank of superintendent authorises the sample to be taken, and

(*c*) subject to paragraph 13(2) and (3), the sample is taken by a constable.

(3) Paragraphs 10(6) and (7) and 11 shall apply in relation to the taking of an intimate sample under this

paragraph; and a reference to a person detained under section 41 shall be taken as a reference to a person who was detained under section 41 when the non-intimate samples mentioned in sub-paragraph (1)(*a*) were taken.

**13.** (1) Where appropriate written consent to the taking of an intimate sample from a person under paragraph 10 or 12 is refused without good cause, in any proceedings against that person for an offence—

(*a*) the court, in determining whether to commit him for trial or whether there is a case to answer, may draw such inferences from the refusal as appear proper, and

(*b*) the court or jury, in determining whether that person is guilty of the offence charged, may draw such inferences from the refusal as appear proper.

(2) An intimate sample other than a sample of urine or a dental impression may be taken under paragraph 10 or 12 only by a registered medical practitioner acting on the authority of a constable.

(3) An intimate sample which is a dental impression may be taken under paragraph 10 or 12 only by a registered dentist acting on the authority of a constable.

(4) Where a sample of hair other than pubic hair is to be taken under paragraph 10 the sample may be taken either by cutting hairs or by plucking hairs with their roots so long as no more are plucked than the person taking the sample reasonably considers to be necessary for a sufficient sample.

**14.** *Repealed.*

**15.** (1) In the application of paragraphs 10 to 13 in relation to a person detained in England or Wales the following expressions shall have the meaning given by section 65 of the Police and Criminal Evidence Act 1984 (Part V definitions)—

(*a*) "appropriate consent",
(*b*) "fingerprints",
(*c*) "insufficient",
(*d*) "intimate sample",
(*e*) "non-intimate sample",
(*f*) "registered dentist", and
(*g*) "sufficient".

(1A) In the application of section 65(2A) of the Police and Criminal Evidence Act 1984 for the purposes of sub-paragraph (1) of this paragraph, the reference to the destruction of a sample under section 63R of that Act is a reference to the destruction of a sample under paragraph 20G of this Schedule.

(2) In the application of paragraphs 10 to 13 in relation to a person detained in Northern Ireland the expressions listed in sub-paragraph (1) shall have the meaning given by Article 53 of the Police and Criminal Evidence (Northern Ireland) Order 1989 (definitions).

(3) In paragraph 10 "recordable offence" shall have—

(*a*) in relation to a person detained in England or Wales, the meaning given by section 118(1) of the Police and Criminal Evidence Act 1984 (general interpretation), and

(*b*) in relation to a person detained in Northern Ireland, the meaning given by Article 2(2) of the Police and Criminal Evidence (Northern Ireland) Order 1989 (definitions).

**16–20.** *Scotland*

*Destruction and retention of fingerprints and samples etc: United Kingdom*

**20A.** (1) This paragraph applies to—

(*a*) fingerprints taken under paragraph 10,
(*b*) a DNA profile derived from a DNA sample taken under paragraph 10 or 12,
(*c*) relevant physical data taken or provided by virtue of paragraph 20, and
(*d*) a DNA profile derived from a DNA sample taken by virtue of paragraph 20.

(2) Fingerprints, relevant physical data and DNA profiles to which this paragraph applies ("paragraph 20A material") must be destroyed if it appears to the responsible chief officer of police that—

(*a*) the taking or providing of the material or, in the case of a DNA profile, the taking of the sample from which the DNA profile was derived, was unlawful, or

(*b*) the material was taken or provided, or (in the case of a DNA profile) was derived from a sample taken, from a person in connection with that person's arrest under section 41 and the arrest was unlawful or based on mistaken identity.

(3) In any other case, paragraph 20A material must be destroyed unless it is retained under any power conferred by paragraphs 20B to 20E.

(4) Paragraph 20A material which ceases to be retained under a power mentioned in sub-paragraph (3) may continue to be retained under any other such power which applies to it.

(5) Nothing in this paragraph prevents a relevant search, in relation to paragraph 20A material, from being carried out within such time as may reasonably be required for the search if the responsible chief officer of police considers the search to be desirable.

(6) For the purposes of sub-paragraph (5), "a relevant search" is a search carried out for the purpose of checking the material against—

(*a*) other fingerprints or samples taken under paragraph 10 or 12 or a DNA profile derived from such a sample,

(*b*) any of the relevant physical data, samples or information mentioned in section 19C(1) of the Criminal Procedure (Scotland) Act 1995,

(*c*) any of the relevant physical data, samples or information held by virtue of section 56 of the Criminal Justice (Scotland) Act 2003,

(*d*) material to which section 18 of the Counter-Terrorism Act 2008 applies,

(*e*) any of the fingerprints, data or samples obtained under paragraph 1 or 4 of Schedule 6 to the Terrorism Prevention and Investigation Measures Act 2011, or information derived from such samples,

(*f*) any of the fingerprints, samples and information mentioned in section 63A(1)(*a*) and (*b*) of the Police and Criminal Evidence Act 1984 (checking of fingerprints and samples), and

(*g*) any of the fingerprints, samples and information mentioned in Article 63A(1)(*a*) and (*b*) of the Police and Criminal Evidence (Northern Ireland) Order 1989 (checking of fingerprints and samples).

**20B.** (1) This paragraph applies to paragraph 20A material relating to a person who is detained under section 41.

(2) In the case of a person who has previously been convicted of a recordable offence (other than a single

exempt conviction), or an offence in Scotland which is punishable by imprisonment, or is so convicted before the end of the period within which the material may be retained by virtue of this paragraph, the material may be retained indefinitely.

(2A) In sub-paragraph (2)—

(*a*) the reference to a recordable offence includes an offence under the law of a country or territory outside the United Kingdom where the act constituting the offence would constitute—

(i) a recordable offence under the law of England and Wales if done there, or

(ii) a recordable offence under the law of Northern Ireland if done there,

(and, in the application of sub-paragraph (2) where a person has previously been convicted, this applies whether or not the act constituted such an offence when the person was convicted);

(b) the reference to an offence in Scotland which is punishable by imprisonment includes an offence under the law of a country or territory outside the United Kingdom where the act constituting the offence would constitute an offence under the law of Scotland which is punishable by imprisonment if done there (and, in the application of sub-paragraph (2) where a person has previously been convicted, this applies whether or not the act constituted such an offence when the person was convicted).

(3) In the case of a person who has no previous convictions, or only one exempt conviction, the material may be retained until the end of the retention period specified in sub-paragraph (4).

(4) The retention period is—

(*a*) in the case of fingerprints or relevant physical data, the period of 3 years beginning with the date on which the fingerprints or relevant physical data were taken or provided, and

(*b*) in the case of a DNA profile, the period of 3 years beginning with the date on which the DNA sample from which the profile was derived was taken (or, if the profile was derived from more than one DNA sample, the date on which the first of those samples was taken).

(5) The responsible chief officer of police or a specified chief officer of police may apply[1] to a relevant court for an order extending the retention period.

(6) An application for an order under sub-paragraph (5) must be made within the period of 3 months ending on the last day of the retention period.

(7) An order under sub-paragraph (5) may extend the retention period by a period which—

(*a*) begins with the date on which the material would otherwise be required to be destroyed under this paragraph, and

(*b*) ends with the end of the period of 2 years beginning with that date.

(8) The following persons may appeal to the relevant appeal court against an order under sub-paragraph (5), or a refusal to make such an order—

(*a*) the responsible chief officer of police;

(*b*) a specified chief officer of police;

(*c*) the person from whom the material was taken.

(9) In Scotland—

(*a*) an application for an order under sub-paragraph (5) is to be made by summary application;

(*b*) an appeal against an order under sub-paragraph (5), or a refusal to make such an order, must be made within 21 days of the relevant court's decision, and the relevant appeal court's decision on any such appeal is final.

(10) In this paragraph—

"relevant court" means—

(*a*) in England and Wales, a District Judge (Magistrates' Courts),

(*b*) in Scotland, the sheriff—

(i) in whose sheriffdom the person to whom the material relates resides,

(ii) in whose sheriffdom that person is believed by the applicant to be, or

(iii) to whose sheriffdom that person is believed by the applicant to be intending to come; and

(*c*) in Northern Ireland, a district judge (magistrates' court) in Northern Ireland;

"the relevant appeal court" means—

(*a*) in England and Wales, the Crown Court,

(*b*) in Scotland, the sheriff principal, and

(*c*) in Northern Ireland, the County Court in Northern Ireland;

"a specified chief officer of police" means—

(*a*) in England and Wales and Northern Ireland—

(i) the chief officer of the police force of the area in which the person from whom the material was taken resides, or

(ii) a chief officer of police who believes that the person is in, or is intending to come to, the chief officer's police area, and

(*b*) in Scotland—

(i) the chief constable of the police force in the area in which the person who provided the material, or from whom it was taken, resides, or

(ii) a chief constable who believes that the person is in, or is intending to come to, the area of the chief constable's police force.

---

1 For procedure, see the Criminal Procedure Rules, Part 47, Section 5 in the *Key Materials*.

**20C.** (1) This paragraph applies to paragraph 20A material relating to a person who is detained under Schedule 7.

(2) In the case of a person who has previously been convicted of a recordable offence (other than a single exempt conviction), or an offence in Scotland which is punishable by imprisonment, or is so convicted before the end of the period within which the material may be retained by virtue of this paragraph, the material may be retained indefinitely.

(2A) In sub-paragraph (2)—

(*a*) the reference to a recordable offence includes an offence under the law of a country or territory outside the United Kingdom where the act constituting the offence would constitute—

(i) a recordable offence under the law of England and Wales if done there, or

(ii) a recordable offence under the law of Northern Ireland if done there, (and, in the application of sub-paragraph (2) where a person has previously been convicted, this applies whether or not the act constituted such an offence when the person was convicted);

(*b*) the reference to an offence in Scotland which is punishable by imprisonment includes an offence under the law of a country or territory outside the United Kingdom where the act constituting the offence would constitute an offence under the law of Scotland which is punishable by imprisonment if done there (and, in the application of sub-paragraph (2) where a person has previously been convicted, this applies whether or not the act constituted such an offence when the person was convicted).

(3) In the case of a person who has no previous convictions, or only one exempt conviction, the material may be retained until the end of the retention period specified in sub-paragraph (4).

(4) The retention period is—

(*a*) in the case of fingerprints or relevant physical data, the period of 6 months beginning with the date on which the fingerprints or relevant physical data were taken or provided, and

(*b*) in the case of a DNA profile, the period of 6 months beginning with the date on which the DNA sample from which the profile was derived was taken (or, if the profile was derived from more than one DNA sample, the date on which the first of those samples was taken).

**20D.** (1) For the purposes of paragraphs 20B and 20C, a person is to be treated as having been convicted of an offence if—

(*a*) in relation to a recordable offence in England and Wales or Northern Ireland—

(i) the person has been given a caution in respect of the offence which, at the time of the caution, the person has admitted,

(ii) the person has been found not guilty of the offence by reason of insanity,

(iii) the person has been found to be under a disability and to have done the act charged in respect of the offence, or

(iv) the person has been warned or reprimanded under section 65 of the Crime and Disorder Act 1998 for the offence,

(*b*) the person, in relation to an offence in Scotland punishable by imprisonment, has accepted or has been deemed to accept—

(i) a conditional offer under section 302 of the Criminal Procedure (Scotland) Act 1995,

(ii) a compensation offer under section 302A of that Act,

(iii) a combined offer under section 302B of that Act, or

(iv) a work offer under section 303ZA of that Act,

(*c*) the person, in relation to an offence in Scotland punishable by imprisonment, has been acquitted on account of the person's insanity at the time of the offence or (as the case may be) by virtue of section 51A of the Criminal Procedure (Scotland) Act 1995,

(*d*) a finding in respect of the person has been made under section 55(2) of the Criminal Procedure (Scotland) Act 1995 in relation to an offence in Scotland punishable by imprisonment,

(*e*) the person, having been given a fixed penalty notice under section 129(1) of the Antisocial Behaviour etc (Scotland) Act 2004 in connection with an offence in Scotland punishable by imprisonment, has paid—

(i) the fixed penalty, or

(ii) (as the case may be) the sum which the person is liable to pay by virtue of section 131(5) of that Act, or

(*f*) the person, in relation to an offence in Scotland punishable by imprisonment, has been discharged absolutely by order under section 246(3) of the Criminal Procedure (Scotland) Act 1995.

(2) Paragraphs 20B and 20C and this paragraph, so far as they relate to persons convicted of an offence, have effect despite anything in the Rehabilitation of Offenders Act 1974.

(3) But a person is not to be treated as having been convicted of an offence if that conviction is a disregarded conviction or caution by virtue of section 92 of the Protection of Freedoms Act 2012.

(4) For the purposes of paragraphs 20B and 20C—

(*a*) a person has no previous convictions if the person has not previously been convicted—

(i) in England and Wales or Northern Ireland of a recordable offence, or

(ii) in Scotland of an offence which is punishable by imprisonment, and

(b) if the person has previously been convicted of a recordable offence in England and Wales or Northern Ireland, the conviction is exempt if it is in respect of a recordable offence, other than a qualifying offence, committed when the person was aged under 18.

(5) In sub-paragraph (4), "qualifying offence" has—

(*a*) in relation to a conviction in respect of a recordable offence committed in England and Wales, the meaning given by section 65A of the Police and Criminal Evidence Act 1984, and

(*b*) in relation to a conviction in respect of a recordable offence committed in Northern Ireland, the meaning given by Article 53A of the Police and Criminal Evidence (Northern Ireland) Order 1989 (SI 1989/1341 (NI 12)).

(5A) For the purposes of sub-paragraph (4)—

(*a*) a person is to be treated as having previously been convicted in England and Wales of a recordable offence if—

(i) the person has previously been convicted of an offence under the law of a country or territory outside the United Kingdom, and

(ii) the act constituting the offence would constitute a recordable offence under the law of England and Wales if done there (whether or not it constituted such an offence when the person was convicted);

(*b*) a person is to be treated as having previously been convicted in Northern Ireland of a recordable offence if—

(i) the person has previously been convicted of an offence under the law of a country or territory outside the United Kingdom, and

(ii) the act constituting the offence would constitute a recordable offence under the law of Northern Ireland if done there (whether or not it constituted such an offence when the person was convicted);

(*c*) a person is to be treated as having previously been convicted in Scotland of an offence which is punishable by imprisonment if—

(i) the person has previously been convicted of an offence under the law of a country or territory outside the United Kingdom, and

(ii) the act constituting the offence would constitute an offence punishable by imprisonment under the law of Scotland if done there (whether or not it constituted such an offence when the person was convicted);

(*d*) the reference in sub-paragraph (4)(*b*) to a qualifying offence includes a reference to an offence under the law of a country or territory outside the United Kingdom where the act constituting the offence would constitute a qualifying offence under the law of England and Wales if done there or (as the case may be) under the law of Northern Ireland if done there (whether or not it constituted such an offence when the person was convicted).

(5B) For the purposes of paragraphs 20B and 20C and this paragraph—

(*a*) offence, in relation to any country or territory outside the United Kingdom, includes an act punishable under the law of that country or territory, however it is described;

(*b*) a person has in particular been convicted of an offence under the law of a country or territory outside the United Kingdom if—

(i) a court exercising jurisdiction under the law of that country or territory has made in respect of such an offence a finding equivalent to a finding that the person is not guilty by reason of insanity, or

(ii) such a court has made in respect of such an offence a finding equivalent to a finding that the person is under a disability and did the act charged against the person in respect of the offence.

(6) If a person is convicted of more than one offence arising out of a single course of action, those convictions are to be treated as a single conviction for the purposes of calculating under paragraph 20B or 20C whether the person has been convicted of only one offence.

(7) Nothing in paragraph 20B or 20C prevents the start of a new retention period in relation to paragraph 20A material if a person is detained again under section 41 or (as the case may be) Schedule 7 when an existing retention period (whether or not extended) is still in force in relation to that material.

**20E.** (1) Paragraph 20A material may be retained for as long as a national security determination made by the responsible chief officer of police has effect in relation to it.

(2) A national security determination is made if the responsible chief officer of police determines that it is necessary for any paragraph 20A material to be retained for the purposes of national security.

(3) A national security determination—

(*a*) must be made in writing,

(*b*) has effect for a maximum of 2 years beginning with the date on which the determination is made, and

(*c*) may be renewed.

**20F.** (1) If fingerprints or relevant physical data are required by paragraph 20A to be destroyed, any copies of the fingerprints or relevant physical data held by a police force must also be destroyed.

(2) If a DNA profile is required by that paragraph to be destroyed, no copy may be retained by a police force except in a form which does not include information which identifies the person to whom the DNA profile relates.

**20G.** (1) This paragraph applies to—

(*a*) samples taken under paragraph 10 or 12, or

(*b*) samples taken by virtue of paragraph 20.

(2) Samples to which this paragraph applies must be destroyed if it appears to the responsible chief officer of police that—

(*a*) the taking of the sample was unlawful, or

(*b*) the sample was taken from a person in connection with that person's arrest under section 41 and the arrest was unlawful or based on mistaken identity.

(3) Subject to this, the rule in sub-paragraph (4) or (as the case may be) (5) applies.

(4) A DNA sample to which this paragraph applies must be destroyed—

(*a*) as soon as a DNA profile has been derived from the sample, or

(*b*) if sooner, before the end of the period of 6 months beginning with the date on which the sample was taken.

(5) Any other sample to which this paragraph applies must be destroyed before the end of the period of 6 months beginning with the date on which it was taken.

(6) The responsible chief officer of police may apply[1] to a relevant court for an order to retain a sample to which this paragraph applies beyond the date on which the sample would otherwise be required to be destroyed by virtue of sub-paragraph (4) or (5) if—

(*a*) the sample was taken from a person detained under section 41 in connection with the investigation of a qualifying offence, and

(*b*) the responsible chief officer of police considers that the condition in sub-paragraph (7) is met.

(7) The condition is that, having regard to the nature and complexity of other material that is evidence in relation to the offence, the sample is likely to be needed in any proceedings for the offence for the purposes of—

(*a*) disclosure to, or use by, a defendant, or

(*b*) responding to any challenge by a defendant in respect of the admissibility of material that is evidence on which the prosecution proposes to rely.

(8) An application under sub-paragraph (6) must be made before the date on which the sample would otherwise be required to be destroyed by virtue of sub-paragraph (4) or (5).

(9) If, on an application made by the responsible chief officer of police under sub-paragraph (6), the relevant court is satisfied that the condition in sub-paragraph (7) is met, it may make an order under this sub-paragraph which—

(*a*) allows the sample to be retained for a period of 12 months beginning with the date on which the sample would otherwise be required to be destroyed by virtue of sub-paragraph (4) or (5), and

(*b*) may be renewed (on one or more occasions) for a further period of not more than 12 months from the end of the period when the order would otherwise cease to have effect.

(10) An application for an order under sub-paragraph (9) (other than an application for renewal)—

(*a*) may be made without notice of the application having been given to the person from whom the sample was taken, and

(*b*) may be heard and determined in private in the absence of that person.

(11) In Scotland, an application for an order under sub-paragraph (9) (including an application for renewal)

is to be made by summary application.

(12) A sample retained by virtue of an order under sub-paragraph (9) must not be used other than for the purposes of any proceedings for the offence in connection with which the sample was taken.

(13) A sample that ceases to be retained by virtue of an order under sub-paragraph (9) must be destroyed.

(14) Nothing in this paragraph prevents a relevant search, in relation to samples to which this paragraph applies, from being carried out within such time as may reasonably be required for the search if the responsible chief officer of police considers the search to be desirable.

(15) In this paragraph—

"ancillary offence", in relation to an offence for the time being listed in section 41(1) of the Counter-Terrorism Act 2008, means—

(*a*) aiding, abetting, counselling or procuring the commission of the offence, or
(*b*) inciting, attempting or conspiring to commit the offence;

"qualifying offence"—

(*a*) in relation to the investigation of an offence committed in England and Wales, has the meaning given by section 65A of the Police and Criminal Evidence Act 1984,
(*b*) in relation to the investigation of an offence committed in Scotland, means a relevant offence, an offence for the time being listed in section 41(1) of the Counter-Terrorism Act 2008 or an ancillary offence to an offence so listed, and
(*c*) in relation to the investigation of an offence committed in Northern Ireland, has the meaning given by Article 53A of the Police and Criminal Evidence (Northern Ireland) Order 1989 (SI 1989/1341 (NI 12)).

"relevant court" means—

(*a*) in England and Wales, a District Judge (Magistrates' Courts),
(*b*) in Scotland, the sheriff—
  (i) in whose sheriffdom the person to whom the sample relates resides,
  (ii) in whose sheriffdom that person is believed by the responsible chief officer of police to be, or
  (iii) to whose sheriffdom that person is believed by the responsible chief officer of police to be intending to come; and
(*c*) in Northern Ireland, a district judge (magistrates' court) in Northern Ireland;

"relevant offence" has the same meaning as in section 19A of the Criminal Procedure (Scotland) Act 1995;

"a relevant search" has the meaning given by paragraph 20A(6).

[1] For procedure, see the Criminal Procedure Rules, Part 47 Section 5 in the *Key Materials*.

**20H.** (1) Any material to which paragraph 20A or 20G applies must not be used other than—

(*a*) in the interests of national security,
(*b*) for the purposes of a terrorist investigation,
(*c*) for purposes related to the prevention or detection of crime, the investigation of an offence or the conduct of a prosecution, or
(*d*) for purposes related to the identification of a deceased person or of the person to whom the material relates.

(2) Subject to sub-paragraph (1), a relevant search (within the meaning given by paragraph 20A(6)) may be carried out in relation to material to which paragraph 20A or 20G applies if the responsible chief officer of police considers the search to be desirable.

(3) Material which is required by paragraph 20A or 20G to be destroyed must not at any time after it is required to be destroyed be used—

(*a*) in evidence against the person to whom the material relates, or
(*b*) for the purposes of the investigation of any offence.

(4) In this paragraph—

(*a*) the reference to using material includes a reference to allowing any check to be made against it and to disclosing it to any person,
(*b*) the reference to crime includes a reference to any conduct which—
  (i) constitutes one or more criminal offences (whether under the law of a part of the United Kingdom or of a country or territory outside the United Kingdom), or
  (ii) is, or corresponds to, any conduct which, if it all took place in any one part of the United Kingdom, would constitute one or more criminal offences, and
(*c*) the references to an investigation and to a prosecution include references, respectively, to any investigation outside the United Kingdom of any crime or suspected crime and to a prosecution brought in respect of any crime in a country or territory outside the United Kingdom.

(5) Sub-paragraphs (1), (2) and (4) do not form part of the law of Scotland.

**20I.** Paragraphs 20A to 20F and 20H do not apply to paragraph 20A material relating to a person detained under section 41 which is, or may become, disclosable under—

(*a*) the Criminal Procedure and Investigations Act 1996, or
(*b*) a code of practice prepared under section 23 of that Act and in operation by virtue of an order under section 25 of that Act.

**20J.** In paragraphs 20A to 20I—

"DNA profile" means any information derived from a DNA sample;

"DNA sample" means any material that has come from a human body and consists of or includes human cells;

"fingerprints" has the meaning given by section 65(1) of the Police and Criminal Evidence Act 1984 (Part 5 definitions);

"paragraph 20A material" has the meaning given by paragraph 20A(2);

"police force" means any of the following—

(*a*) the metropolitan police force;
(*b*) a police force maintained under section 2 of the Police Act 1996 (police forces in England and Wales outside London);
(*c*) the City of London police force;
(*d*) any police force maintained under or by virtue of section 1 of the Police (Scotland) Act 1967;
(*e*) the Scottish Police Services Authority;

(*f*) the Police Service of Northern Ireland;
(*g*) the Police Service of Northern Ireland Reserve;
(*h*) the Ministry of Defence Police;
(*i*) the Royal Navy Police;
(*j*) the Royal Military Police;
(*k*) the Royal Air Force Police;
(*l*) the British Transport Police;

"recordable offence" has—

(*a*) in relation to a conviction in England and Wales, the meaning given by section 118(1) of the Police and Criminal Evidence Act 1984, and
(*b*) in relation to a conviction in Northern Ireland, the meaning given by Article 2(2) of the Police and Criminal Evidence (Northern Ireland) Order 1989;

"relevant physical data" has the meaning given by section 18(7A) of the Criminal Procedure (Scotland) Act 1995;

"responsible chief officer of police" means, in relation to fingerprints or samples taken in England or Wales, or a DNA profile derived from a sample so taken, the chief officer of police for the police area—

(*a*) in which the material concerned was taken, or
(*b*) in the case of a DNA profile, in which the sample from which the DNA profile was derived was taken;

"responsible chief officer of police" means, in relation to relevant physical data or samples taken or provided in Scotland, or a DNA profile derived from a sample so taken or provided, the chief constable of the police force for the area—

(*a*) in which the material concerned was taken or provided, or
(*b*) in the case of a DNA profile, in which the sample from which the DNA profile was derived was taken;

"responsible chief officer of police" means, in relation to fingerprints or samples taken in Northern Ireland, or a DNA profile derived from a sample so taken, the Chief Constable of the Police Service of Northern Ireland.

## Part 1A
## Review of Detention Under Schedule 7

**General requirements**

**20K.** (1) A person's detention under Schedule 7 must be periodically reviewed by a review officer.

(2) The first review must be carried out before the end of the period of one hour beginning with the person's detention under that Schedule.

(3) Subsequent reviews must be carried out at intervals of not more than two hours.

(4) The review officer may authorise a person's continued detention under Schedule 7 only if satisfied that it is necessary for the purposes of exercising a power under paragraph 2 or 3 of that Schedule.

(5) If on a review under this paragraph the review officer does not authorise a person's continued detention, the person must be released (unless detained under another power).

(6) In this Part of this Schedule "review officer" means a senior officer who has not been directly involved in questioning the detained person under paragraph 2 or 3 of Schedule 7.

(7) "Senior officer" means—

(*a*) where the examining officer is a constable, a constable of a higher rank than the examining officer,
(*b*) where the examining officer is an immigration officer, an immigration officer of a higher grade than the examining officer, and
(*c*) where the examining officer is a customs officer, a customs officer of a higher grade than the examining officer.

(8) The Secretary of State must under paragraph 6 of Schedule 14 issue a code of practice about reviews under this Part of this Schedule.

(9) The code of practice must include provision about training to be undertaken by persons who are to act as review officers.

**Representations**

**20L.** (1) Before determining whether to authorise a person's continued detention, a review officer must give either of the following persons an opportunity to make representations about the detention—

(*a*) the detained person, or
(*b*) a solicitor representing the detained person who is available at the time of the review.

(2) Representations may be oral or written.

(3) A review officer may refuse to hear oral representations from the detained person if the officer considers that the detained person is unfit to make representations because of the detained person's condition or behaviour.

**Rights**

**20M.** (1) Where a review officer authorises continued detention the officer must inform the detained person—

(*a*) of any of the detained person's rights under paragraphs 6 and 7 which have not yet been exercised, and
(*b*) if the exercise of any of those rights is being delayed in accordance with the provisions of paragraph 8, of the fact that it is being delayed.

(2) Where a review of a person's detention is being carried out at a time when the person's exercise of a right under paragraph 6 or 7 is being delayed—

(*a*) the review officer must consider whether the reason or reasons for which the delay was authorised continue to subsist, and
(*b*) if in the review officer's opinion the reason or reasons have ceased to subsist, the review officer must inform the officer who authorised the delay of that opinion (unless the review officer was that officer).

(3) In the application of this paragraph to Scotland, for the references to paragraphs 6, 7 and 8 substitute references to paragraph 16.

**Record**

**20N.** (1) A review officer carrying out a review must make a written record of the outcome of the review and of any of the following which apply—

(*a*) the fact that the officer is satisfied that continued detention is necessary for the purposes of exercising a power under paragraph 2 or 3 of Schedule 7,
(*b*) the fact that the detained person has been informed as required under paragraph 20M(1),
(*c*) the officer's conclusion on the matter considered under paragraph 20M(2)(*a*), and
(*d*) the fact that the officer has taken action under paragraph 20M(2)(*b*).

(2) The review officer must inform the detained person whether the officer is authorising continued detention, and if so that the officer is satisfied that continued detention is necessary for the purposes of exercising a power under paragraph 2 or 3 of Schedule 7.

(3) Sub-paragraph (2) does not apply where the detained person is—
(*a*) incapable of understanding what is said,
(*b*) violent or likely to become violent, or
(*c*) in urgent need of medical attention.

## Part II

## Review of Detention under Section 41

*Requirement*

**21.** (1) A person's detention shall be periodically reviewed by a review officer.

(2) The first review shall be carried out as soon as is reasonably practicable after the time of the person's arrest.

(3) Subsequent reviews shall, subject to paragraph 22, be carried out at intervals of not more than 12 hours.

(4) No review of a person's detention shall be carried out after a warrant extending his detention has been issued under Part III.

*Postponement*

**22.** (1) A review may be postponed if at the latest time at which it may be carried out in accordance with paragraph 21—
(*a*) the detained person is being questioned by a police officer and an officer is satisfied that an interruption of the questioning to carry out the review would prejudice the investigation in connection with which the person is being detained,
(*b*) no review officer is readily available, or
(*c*) it is not practicable for any other reason to carry out the review.

(2) Where a review is postponed it shall be carried out as soon as is reasonably practicable.

(3) For the purposes of ascertaining the time within which the next review is to be carried out, a postponed review shall be deemed to have been carried out at the latest time at which it could have been carried out in accordance with paragraph 21.

*Grounds for continued detention*

**23.** (1) A review officer may authorise a person's continued detention only if satisfied that it is necessary—
(*a*) to obtain relevant evidence whether by questioning him or otherwise,
(*b*) to preserve relevant evidence,
(*ba*) pending the result of an examination or analysis of any relevant evidence or of anything the examination or analysis of which is to be or is being carried out with a view to obtaining relevant evidence,
(*c*) pending a decision whether to apply to the Secretary of State for a deportation notice to be served on the detained person,
(*d*) pending the making of an application to the Secretary of State for a deportation notice to be served on the detained person,
(*e*) pending consideration by the Secretary of State whether to serve a deportation notice on the detained person, or
(*f*) pending a decision whether the detained person should be charged with an offence.

(2) The review officer shall not authorise continued detention by virtue of sub-paragraph (1)(*a*) or (*b*) unless he is satisfied that the investigation in connection with which the person is detained is being conducted diligently and expeditiously.

(3) The review officer shall not authorise continued detention by virtue of sub-paragraph (1)(*c*) to (*f*) unless he is satisfied that the process pending the completion of which detention is necessary is being conducted diligently and expeditiously.

(4) In this paragraph "relevant evidence" means evidence which—
(*a*) relates to the commission by the detained person of an offence under any of the provisions mentioned in section 40(1)(*a*), or
(*b*) indicates that the detained person falls within section 40(1)(*b*).

(5) In sub-paragraph (1) "deportation notice" means notice of a decision to make a deportation order under the Immigration Act 1971.

*Review officer*

**24.** (1) The review officer shall be an officer who has not been directly involved in the investigation in connection with which the person is detained.

(2) In the case of a review carried out within the period of 24 hours beginning with the time of arrest, the review officer shall be an officer of at least the rank of inspector.

(3) In the case of any other review, the review officer shall be an officer of at least the rank of superintendent.

**25.** (1) This paragraph applies where—
(*a*) the review officer is of a rank lower than superintendent,
(*b*) an officer of higher rank than the review officer gives directions relating to the detained person, and
(*c*) those directions are at variance with the performance by the review officer of a duty imposed on him under this Schedule.

(2) The review officer shall refer the matter at once to an officer of at least the rank of superintendent.

*Representations*

**26.** (1) Before determining whether to authorise a person's continued detention, a review officer shall give either of the following persons an opportunity to make representations about the detention—

(*a*) the detained person, or

(*b*) a solicitor representing him who is available at the time of the review.

(2) Representations may be oral or written.

(3) A review officer may refuse to hear oral representations from the detained person if he considers that he is unfit to make representations because of his condition or behaviour.

*Rights*

**27.** (1) Where a review officer authorises continued detention he shall inform the detained person—

(*a*) of any of his rights under paragraphs 6 and 7 which he has not yet exercised, and

(*b*) if the exercise of any of his rights under either of those paragraphs is being delayed in accordance with the provisions of paragraph 8, of the fact that it is being so delayed.

(2) Where a review of a person's detention is being carried out at a time when his exercise of a right under either of those paragraphs is being delayed—

(*a*) the review officer shall consider whether the reason or reasons for which the delay was authorised continue to subsist, and

(*b*) if in his opinion the reason or reasons have ceased to subsist, he shall inform the officer who authorised the delay of his opinion (unless he was that officer).

(3) *Scotland.*

(4) The following provisions (requirement to bring an accused person before the court after his arrest) shall not apply to a person detained under section 41—

(*a*) section 135(3) of the Criminal Procedure (Scotland) Act 1995, and

(*b*) Article 8(1) of the Criminal Justice (Children) (Northern Ireland) Order 1998.

(5) Section 22(1) of the Criminal Procedure (Scotland) Act 1995 (interim liberation by officer in charge of police station) shall not apply to a person detained under section 41.

*Record*

**28.** (1) A review officer carrying out a review shall make a written record of the outcome of the review and of any of the following which apply—

(*a*) the grounds upon which continued detention is authorised,

(*b*) the reason for postponement of the review,

(*c*) the fact that the detained person has been informed as required under paragraph 27(1),

(*d*) the officer's conclusion on the matter considered under paragraph 27(2)(*a*),

(*e*) the fact that he has taken action under paragraph 27(2)(*b*), and

(*f*) the fact that the detained person is being detained by virtue of section 41(5) or (6).

(2) The review officer shall—

(*a*) make the record in the presence of the detained person, and

(*b*) inform him at that time whether the review officer is authorising continued detention, and if he is, of his grounds.

(3) Sub-paragraph (2) shall not apply where, at the time when the record is made, the detained person is—

(*a*) incapable of understanding what is said to him,

(*b*) violent or likely to become violent, or

(*c*) in urgent need of medical attention.

## PART III

## EXTENSION OF DETENTION UNDER SECTION 41

*Warrants of further detention*

**29.** (1) Each of the following—

(*a*) in England and Wales, a Crown Prosecutor,

(*b*) in Scotland, the Lord Advocate or a procurator fiscal,

(*c*) in Northern Ireland, the Director of Public Prosecutions for Northern Ireland,

(*d*) in any part of the United Kingdom, a police officer of at least the rank of superintendent,

may apply to a judicial authority for the issue of a warrant of further detention under this Part.

(2) A warrant of further detention—

(*a*) shall authorise the further detention under section 41 of a specified person for a specified period, and

(*b*) shall state the time at which it is issued.

(3) Subject to sub-paragraph (3A) and paragraph 36, the specified period in relation to a person shall be the period of seven days beginning—

(*a*) with the time of his arrest under section 41, or

(*b*) if he was being detained under Schedule 7 when he was arrested under section 41, with the time when his examination under that Schedule began.

(3A) A judicial authority may issue a warrant of further detention in relation to a person which specifies a shorter period as the period for which that person's further detention is authorised if—

(*a*) the application for the warrant is an application for a warrant specifying a shorter period; or

(*b*) the judicial authority is satisfied that there are circumstances that would make it inappropriate for the specified period to be as long as the period of seven days mentioned in sub-paragraph (3).

(4) In this Part "judicial authority" means—

(*a*) in England and Wales, a District Judge (Magistrates' Courts) who is designated for the purpose of this Part by the Lord Chief Justice of England and Wales,

(*b*) in Scotland, the sheriff, and

(*c*) in Northern Ireland, a county court judge, or a resident magistrate who is designated for the purpose of this Part by the Lord Chief Justice of Northern Ireland.

(5) The Lord Chief Justice may nominate a judicial office holder (as defined in section 109(4) of the Constitutional Reform Act 2005) to exercise his functions under sub-paragraph (4)(*a*).

(6) The Lord Chief Justice of Northern Ireland may nominate any of the following to exercise his functions under sub-paragraph (4)(*c*)—

(*a*) the holder of one of the offices listed in Schedule 1 to the Justice (Northern Ireland) Act 2002;
(*b*) a Lord Justice of Appeal (as defined in section 88 of that Act).

*Time limit*

**30.** (1) An application for a warrant shall be made—
(*a*) during the period mentioned in section 41(3), or
(*b*) within six hours of the end of that period.

(2) The judicial authority hearing an application made by virtue of sub-paragraph (1)(*b*) shall dismiss the application if he considers that it would have been reasonably practicable to make it during the period mentioned in section 41(3).

(3) For the purposes of this Schedule, an application for a warrant is made when written or oral notice of an intention to make the application is given to a judicial authority.

*Notice*

**31.** An application for a warrant may not be heard unless the person to whom it relates has been given a notice stating—
(*a*) that the application has been made,
(*b*) the time at which the application was made,
(*c*) the time at which it is to be heard, and
(*d*) the grounds upon which further detention is sought.

*Grounds for extension*

**32.** (1) A judicial authority may issue a warrant of further detention only if satisfied that—
(*a*) there are reasonable grounds for believing that the further detention of the person to whom the application relates is necessary as mentioned in sub-paragraph (1A), and
(*b*) the investigation in connection with which the person is detained is being conducted diligently and expeditiously.

(1A) The further detention of a person is necessary as mentioned in this sub-paragraph if it is necessary—
(*a*) to obtain relevant evidence whether by questioning him or otherwise;
(*b*) to preserve relevant evidence; or
(*c*) pending the result of an examination or analysis of any relevant evidence or of anything the examination or analysis of which is to be or is being carried out with a view to obtaining relevant evidence.

(2) In this paragraph "relevant evidence" means, in relation to the person to whom the application relates, evidence which—
(*a*) relates to his commission of an offence under any of the provisions mentioned in section 40(1)(*a*), or
(*b*) indicates that he is a person falling within section 40(1)(*b*).

*Representation*

**33.** (1) The person to whom an application relates shall—
(*a*) be given an opportunity to make oral or written representations to the judicial authority about the application, and
(*b*) subject to sub-paragraph (3), be entitled to be legally represented at the hearing.

(2) A judicial authority shall adjourn the hearing of an application to enable the person to whom the application relates to obtain legal representation where—
(*a*) he is not legally represented,
(*b*) he is entitled to be legally represented, and
(*c*) he wishes to be so represented.

(3) A judicial authority may exclude[1] any of the following persons from any part of the hearing—
(*a*) the person to whom the application relates;
(*b*) anyone representing him.

(4) A judicial authority may, after giving an opportunity for representations to be made by or on behalf of the applicant and the person to whom the application relates, direct—
(*a*) that the hearing of the application must be conducted, and
(*b*) that all representations by or on behalf of a person for the purposes of the hearing must be made,

by such means (whether a live television link or other means) falling within sub-paragraph (5) as may be specified in the direction and not in the presence (apart from by those means) of the applicant, of the person to whom the application relates or of any legal representative of that person.

(5) A means of conducting the hearing and of making representations falls within this sub-paragraph if it allows the person to whom the application relates and any legal representative of his (without being present at the hearing and to the extent that they are not excluded from it under sub-paragraph (3))—
(*a*) to see and hear the judicial authority and the making of representations to it by other persons; and
(*b*) to be seen and heard by the judicial authority.

(6) If the person to whom the application relates wishes to make representations about whether a direction should be given under sub-paragraph (4), he must do so by using the facilities that will be used if the judicial authority decides to give a direction under that sub-paragraph.

(7) Sub-paragraph (2) applies to the hearing of representations about whether a direction should be given under sub-paragraph (4) in the case of any application as it applies to a hearing of the application.

(8) A judicial authority shall not give a direction under sub-paragraph (4) unless—
(*a*) it has been notified by the Secretary of State that facilities are available at the place where the person to whom the application relates is held for the judicial authority to conduct a hearing by means falling within sub-paragraph (5); and
(*b*) that notification has not been withdrawn.

(9) If in a case where it has power to do so a judicial authority decides not to give a direction under sub-paragraph (4), it shall state its reasons for not giving it.

---

[1] For example, where the judge wishes to explore with the police the topics and questions on which they wish to question the accused further. "Exclude" includes the power not to disclose what took place during the period of exclusion: *Ward v Police Service of Northern Ireland* [2007] UKHL 50, [2008] 1 All ER 517.

*Information*

**34.** (1) The person who has made an application for a warrant may apply to the judicial authority for an order that specified information upon which he intends to rely be withheld from—

(*a*) the person to whom the application relates, and

(*b*) anyone representing him.

(2) Subject to sub-paragraph (3), a judicial authority may make an order under sub-paragraph (1) in relation to specified information only if satisfied that there are reasonable grounds for believing that if the information were disclosed—

(*a*) evidence of an offence under any of the provisions mentioned in section 40(1)(*a*) would be interfered with or harmed,

(*b*) the recovery of property obtained as a result of an offence under any of those provisions would be hindered,

(*c*) the recovery of property in respect of which a forfeiture order could be made under section 23 or 23A would be hindered,

(*d*) the apprehension, prosecution or conviction of a person who is suspected of falling within section 40(1)(*a*) or (*b*) would be made more difficult as a result of his being alerted,

(*e*) the prevention of an act of terrorism would be made more difficult as a result of a person being alerted,

(*f*) the gathering of information about the commission, preparation or instigation of an act of terrorism would be interfered with, or

(*g*) a person would be interfered with or physically injured.

(3) A judicial authority may also make an order under sub-paragraph (1) in relation to specified information if satisfied that there are reasonable grounds for believing that—

(*a*) the detained person has benefited from his criminal conduct, and

(*b*) the recovery of the value of the property constituting the benefit would be hindered if the information were disclosed.

(3A) For the purposes of sub-paragraph (3) the question whether a person has benefited from his criminal conduct is to be decided in accordance with Part 2 or 3 of the Proceeds of Crime Act 2002.

(4) The judicial authority shall direct that the following be excluded from the hearing of the application under this paragraph—

(*a*) the person to whom the application for a warrant relates, and

(*b*) anyone representing him.

*Adjournments*

**35.** (1) A judicial authority may adjourn the hearing of an application for a warrant only if the hearing is adjourned to a date before the expiry of the period mentioned in section 41(3).

(2) This paragraph shall not apply to an adjournment under paragraph 33(2).

*Extensions of warrants*

**36.** (1) Each of the following—

(*a*) in England and Wales, a Crown Prosecutor,

(*b*) in Scotland, the Lord Advocate or a procurator fiscal,

(*c*) in Northern Ireland, the Director of Public Prosecutions for Northern Ireland,

(*d*) in any part of the United Kingdom, a police officer of at least the rank of superintendent,

may apply for the extension or further extension of the period specified in a warrant of further detention.

(1A) The person to whom an application under sub-paragraph (1) may be made is—

(*a*) in the case of an application falling within sub-paragraph (1B), a judicial authority; and

(*b*) in any other case, a senior judge.

(1B) *Repealed.*

(2) Where the period specified is extended, the warrant shall be endorsed with a note stating the new specified period.

(3) Subject to sub-paragraph (3AA), the period by which the specified period is extended or further extended shall be the period which—

(*a*) begins with the time specified in sub-paragraph (3A); and

(*b*) ends with whichever is the earlier of—

(i) the end of the period of seven days beginning with that time; and

(ii) the end of the period of 14 days beginning with the relevant time.

(3A) The time referred to in sub-paragraph (3)(*a*) is—

(*a*) in the case of a warrant specifying a period which has not previously been extended under this paragraph, the end of the period specified in the warrant, and

(*b*) in any other case, the end of the period for which the period specified in the warrant was last extended under this paragraph.

(3AA) A judicial authority may extend or further extend the period specified in a warrant by a shorter period than is required by sub-paragraph (3) if—

(*a*) the application for the extension is an application for an extension by a period that is shorter than is so required; or

(*b*) the judicial authority is satisfied that there are circumstances that would make it inappropriate for the period of the extension to be as long as the period so required.

(3B) In this paragraph "the relevant time", in relation to a person, means—

(*a*) the time of his arrest under section 41, or

(*b*) if he was being detained under Schedule 7 when he was arrested under section 41, the time when his examination under that Schedule began.

(4) Paragraphs 30(3) and 31 to 34 shall apply to an application under this paragraph as they apply to an application for a warrant of further detention.

(5) A judicial authority may adjourn the hearing of an application under sub-paragraph (1) only if the hearing is adjourned to a date before the expiry of the period specified in the warrant.

(6) Sub-paragraph (5) shall not apply to an adjournment under paragraph 33(2).

(7) *Repealed.*

*Detention—conditions*

**37.** (1) This paragraph applies where—

(*a*) a person ("the detained person") is detained by virtue of a warrant issued under this Part of this Schedule; and

(*b*) his detention is not authorised by virtue of section 41(5) or (6) or otherwise apart from the warrant.

(2) If it at any time appears to the police officer or other person in charge of the detained person's case that any of the matters mentioned in paragraph 32(1)(*a*) and (*b*) on which the judicial authority last authorised his further detention no longer apply, he must—

(*a*) if he has custody of the detained person, release him immediately; and

(*b*) if he does not, immediately inform the person who does have custody of the detained person that those matters no longer apply in the detained person's case.

(3) A person with custody of the detained person who is informed in accordance with this paragraph that those matters no longer apply in his case must release that person immediately.

## Part 4

## Emergency Power when Parliament Dissolved etc for Temporary Extension of Maximum Period for Detention Under Section 41

**38.** (1) The Secretary of State may make a temporary extension order if—

(*a*) either—

(i) Parliament is dissolved, or

(ii) Parliament has met after a dissolution but the first Queen's Speech of the Parliament has not yet taken place, and

(*b*) the Secretary of State considers that it is necessary by reason of urgency to make such an order.

(2) A temporary extension order is an order which provides, in relation to the period of three months beginning with the coming into force of the order, for paragraphs 36 and 37 to be read as if—

(*a*) in paragraph 36(3)(*b*) (ii) for "14 days" there were substituted "28 days", and

(*b*) the other modifications in sub-paragraphs (3) and (4) were made.

(3) The other modifications of paragraph 36 are—

(*a*) the insertion at the beginning of sub-paragraph (1) of "Subject to sub-paragraphs (1ZA) to (1ZI),",

(*b*) the insertion, after sub-paragraph (1), of—

"(1ZA) Sub-paragraph (1ZB) applies in relation to any proposed application under sub-paragraph (1) for the further extension of the period specified in a warrant of further detention where the grant (otherwise than in accordance with sub-paragraph (3AA)(*b*)) of the application would extend the specified period to a time that is more than 14 days after the relevant time.

(1ZB) No person may make such an application—

(*a*) in England and Wales, without the consent of the Director of Public Prosecutions,

(*b*) in Scotland, without the consent of the Lord Advocate, and

(*c*) in Northern Ireland, without the consent of the Director of Public Prosecutions for Northern Ireland,

unless the person making the application is the person whose consent is required.

(1ZC) The Director of Public Prosecutions must exercise personally any function under sub-paragraph (1ZB) of giving consent.

(1ZD) The only exception is if—

(*a*) the Director is unavailable, and

(*b*) there is another person who is designated in writing by the Director acting personally as the person who is authorised to exercise any such function when the Director is unavailable.

(1ZE) In that case—

(*a*) the other person may exercise the function but must do so personally, and

(*b*) the Director acting personally—

(i) must review the exercise of the function as soon as practicable, and

(ii) may revoke any consent given.

(1ZF) Where the consent is so revoked after an application has been made or extension granted, the application is to be dismissed or (as the case may be) the extension is to be revoked.

(1ZG) Sub-paragraphs (1ZC) to (1ZF) apply instead of any other provisions which would otherwise have enabled any function of the Director of Public Prosecutions under sub-paragraph (1ZB) of giving consent to be exercised by a person other than the Director.

(1ZH) The Director of Public Prosecutions for Northern Ireland must exercise personally any function under sub-paragraph (1ZB) of giving consent unless the function is exercised personally by the Deputy Director of Public Prosecutions for Northern Ireland by virtue of section 30(4) or (7) of the Justice (Northern Ireland) Act 2002 (powers of Deputy Director to exercise functions of Director).

(1ZI) Sub-paragraph (1ZH) applies instead of section 36 of the Act of 2002 (delegation of the functions of the Director of Public Prosecutions for Northern Ireland to persons other than the Deputy Director) in relation to the functions of the Director of Public Prosecutions for Northern Ireland and the Deputy Director of Public Prosecutions for Northern Ireland under, or (as the case may be) by virtue of, sub-paragraph (1ZB) above of giving consent.",

(*c*) the substitution, for "a judicial authority" in sub-paragraph (1A), of "—

"(*a*) in the case of an application falling within sub-paragraph (1B), a judicial authority; and

(*b*) in any other case, a senior judge",

(*d*) the insertion, after sub-paragraph (1A), of—

"(1B) An application for the extension or further extension of a period falls within this sub-paragraph if—

(*a*) the grant of the application otherwise than in accordance with sub-paragraph (3AA)(*b*) would extend that period to a time that is no more than 14 days after the relevant time; and

(*b*) no application has previously been made to a senior judge in respect of that period.",

(*e*) the insertion, after "judicial authority" in both places in sub-paragraph (3AA) where it appears, of "or senior judge",

(*f*) the insertion, after "detention" in sub-paragraph (4), of

"but, in relation to an application made by virtue of sub-paragraph (1A)(*b*) to a senior judge, as if—

(*a*) references to a judicial authority were references to a senior judge; and

(*b*) references to the judicial authority in question were references to the senior judge in question",

(*g*) the insertion, after "judicial authority" in sub-paragraph (5), of "or senior judge", and

(*h*) the insertion, after sub-paragraph (6), of—
"(7) In this paragraph and paragraph 37 "senior judge" means a judge of the High Court or of the High Court of Justiciary."
(4) The modification of paragraph 37 is the insertion, in sub-paragraph (2), after "judicial authority", of "or senior judge".
(5) A temporary extension order applies, except so far as it provides otherwise, to any person who is being detained under section 41 when the order comes into force (as well as any person who is subsequently detained under that section).
(6) The Secretary of State may by order revoke a temporary extension order if the Secretary of State considers it appropriate to do so (whether or not the conditions mentioned in paragraphs (*a*) and (*b*) of sub-paragraph (1) are met).
(7) Sub-paragraph (8) applies if—
(*a*) any of the following events occurs—
(i) the revocation without replacement of a temporary extension order,
(ii) the expiry of the period of three months mentioned in sub-paragraph (2) in relation to such an order,
(iii) the ceasing to have effect of such an order by virtue of section 123(6B) and (6C), and
(*b*) at that time—
(i) a person is being detained by virtue of a further extension under paragraph 36,
(ii) the person's further detention was authorised by virtue of the temporary extension order concerned (before its revocation, expiry or ceasing to have effect) for a period ending more than 14 days after the relevant time (within the meaning given by paragraph 36(3B)),
(iii) that 14 days has expired, and
(iv) the person's detention is not otherwise authorised by law.
(8) The person with custody of that individual must release the individual immediately.
(9) Subject to sub-paragraphs (7) and (8), the fact that—
(*a*) a temporary extension order is revoked,
(*b*) the period of three months mentioned in sub-paragraph (2) has expired in relation to such an order, or
(*c*) such an order ceases to have effect by virtue of section 123(6B) and (6C),
is without prejudice to anything previously done by virtue of the order or to the making of a new order.

## SCHEDULE 8A
### Offence under Section 58A: Supplementary Provisions

*(As inserted by the Counter-Terrorism Act 2008, s 76, Sch 8.)*

*Introduction*

7.8827 **1.** (1) This Schedule makes supplementary provision relating to the offence in section 58A (eliciting, publishing or communicating information about members of the armed forces etc).
(2) The purpose of this Schedule is to comply with Directive 2000/31/EC of the European Parliament and of the Council of 8 June 2000 on certain legal aspects of information society services, in particular electronic commerce, in the Internal Market ("the E-Commerce Directive").

*Domestic service providers: extension of liability*

**2.** (1) This paragraph applies where a service provider is established in the United Kingdom (a "domestic service provider").
(2) Section 58A applies to a domestic service provider who—
(*a*) commits any of the acts specified in subsection (1) of that section in an EEA state other than the United Kingdom, and
(*b*) does so in the course of providing information society services,
as it applies to a person who commits such an act in the United Kingdom.
(3) In such a case—
(*a*) proceedings for the offence may be taken at any place in the United Kingdom, and
(*b*) the offence may for all incidental purposes be treated as having been committed at any such place.

*Non-UK service providers: restriction on proceedings*

**3.** (1) This paragraph applies where a service provider is established in an EEA state other than the United Kingdom (a "non-UK service provider").
(2) Proceedings for an offence under section 58A must not be brought against a non-UK service provider in respect of anything done in the course of the provision of information society services unless the following conditions are met.
(3) The conditions are—
(*a*) that the bringing of proceedings is necessary for one of the following reasons—
(i) public policy,
(ii) public security, including the safeguarding of national security and defence;
(*b*) that the proceedings are brought against an information society service that prejudices the objectives referred to in paragraph (*a*) or presents a serious and grave risk of prejudice to those objectives;
(*c*) that the bringing of the proceedings is proportionate to those objectives.

*Exceptions for mere conduits*

**4.** (1) A service provider is not guilty of an offence under section 58A in respect of anything done in the course of providing so much of an information society service as consists in—
(*a*) the provision of access to a communication network, or
(*b*) the transmission in a communication network of information provided by a recipient of the service,
if the following condition is satisfied.
(2) The condition is that the service provider does not—
(*a*) initiate the transmission,
(*b*) select the recipient of the transmission, or

(*c*) select or modify the information contained in the transmission.

(3) For the purposes of sub-paragraph (1)—

(*a*) the provision of access to a communication network, and

(*b*) the transmission of information in a communication network,

includes the automatic, intermediate and transient storage of the information transmitted so far as the storage is solely for the purpose of carrying out the transmission in the network.

(4) Sub-paragraph (3) does not apply if the information is stored for longer than is reasonably necessary for the transmission.

*Exception for caching*

**5.** (1) This paragraph applies where an information society service consists in the transmission in a communication network of information provided by a recipient of the service.

(2) The service provider is not guilty of an offence under section 58A in respect of the automatic, intermediate and temporary storage of information so provided, if—

(*a*) the storage of the information is solely for the purpose of making more efficient the onward transmission of the information to other recipients of the service at their request, and

(*b*) the following conditions are satisfied.

(3) The first condition is that the service provider does not modify the information.

(4) The second condition is that the service provider complies with any conditions attached to having access to the information.

(5) The third condition is that if the service provider obtains actual knowledge that—

(*a*) the information at the initial source of the transmission has been removed from the network,

(*b*) access to it has been disabled, or

(*c*) a court or administrative authority has ordered the removal from the network of, or the disablement of access to, the information,

the service provider expeditiously removes the information or disables access to it.

*Exception for hosting*

**6.** (1) A service provider is not guilty of an offence under section 58A in respect of anything done in the course of providing so much of an information society service as consists in the storage of information provided by a recipient of the service, if the condition is met.

(2) The condition is that—

(*a*) the service provider had no actual knowledge when the information was provided that it contained offending material, or

(*b*) on obtaining actual knowledge that the information contained offending material, the service provider expeditiously removed the information or disabled access to it.

(3) "Offending material" means information about a person who is or has been—

(*a*) a member of Her Majesty's forces,

(*b*) a member of any of the intelligence services, or

(*c*) a constable,

which is of a kind likely to be useful to a person committing or preparing an act of terrorism.

(4) This paragraph does not apply if the recipient of the service is acting under the authority or control of the service provider.

(5) In this paragraph "the intelligence services" means the Security Service, the Secret Intelligence Service and GCHQ (within the meaning of section 3 of the Intelligence Services Act 1994 (c 13)).

*Interpretation*

**7.** (1) In this Schedule—

"information society services"—

(*a*) has the meaning given in Article 2(*a*) of the E-Commerce Directive (which refers to Article 1(2) of Directive 98/34/EC of the European Parliament and of the Council of 22 June 1998 laying down a procedure for the provision of information in the field of technical standards and regulations), and

(*b*) is summarised in recital 17 of the E-Commerce Directive as covering "any service normally provided for remuneration, at a distance, by means of electronic equipment for the processing (including digital compression) and storage of data, and at the individual request of a recipient of a service";

"recipient", in relation to a service, means any person who, for professional ends or otherwise, uses an information society service, in particular for the purposes of seeking information or making it accessible;

"service provider" means a person providing an information society service.

(2) For the purposes of this Schedule whether a service provider is established in the United Kingdom, or in some other EEA state, shall be determined in accordance with the following provisions—

(*a*) a service provider is established in the United Kingdom, or in a particular EEA state, if the service provider—

(i) effectively pursues an economic activity using a fixed establishment in the United Kingdom, or that EEA state, for an indefinite period, and

(ii) is a national of an EEA state or a company or firm mentioned in Article 48 of the EEC Treaty;

(*b*) the presence or use in a particular place of equipment or other technical means of providing an information society service does not, of itself, constitute the establishment of a service provider;

(*c*) where it cannot be determined from which of a number of establishments a given information society service is provided, that service is to be regarded as provided from the establishment at the centre of the service provider's activities relating to that service.

SCHEDULE 14

Exercise of Officers' Powers

Section 115

*(Amended by the Anti-terrorism, Crime and Security Act 2001, s 2, the Serious Organised Crime and Police Act 2005, Sch 4, the Crime and Courts Act 2013, Sch 8 and the Anti-social Behaviour, Crime and Policing Act 2014, Sch 9.)*

*General*

7.8828 1. In this Schedule an "officer" (subject to paragraph 6A) means—
(*a*) an authorised officer within the meaning given by the terrorist cash provisions, and
(*b*) an examining officer within the meaning of Schedule 7

and "the terrorist cash provisions" means Schedule 1 to the Anti-terrorism, Crime and Security Act 2001.

**2.** An officer may enter a vehicle (within the meaning of section 121) for the purpose of exercising any of the functions conferred on him by virtue of this Act or the terrorist cash provisions.

**3.** An officer may if necessary use reasonable force for the purpose of exercising a power conferred on him by virtue of this Act (apart from paragraphs 2 and 3 of Schedule 7) or the terrorist cash provisions.

*Information*

**4.** (1) Information acquired by an officer may be supplied—
(*a*) to the Secretary of State for use in relation to immigration;
(*b*) to the Commissioners of Customs and Excise or a customs officer;
(*c*) to a constable;
(*d*) to the National Crime Agency;
(*e*) to a person specified by order of the Secretary of State for use of a kind specified in the order.

(2) Information acquired by a customs officer or an immigration officer may be supplied to an examining officer within the meaning of Schedule 7.

*Code of practice*[1]

**5.** An officer shall perform functions conferred on him by virtue of this Act or the terrorist cash provisions in accordance with any relevant code of practice in operation under paragraph 6.

1 As to detained persons and the right to legal advice, see the note to para 7(1) of Sch 7, ante. However, because para 5 of Sch 14 to the Act requires an examining officer to perform his functions under the 2000 Act in accordance with any relevant code of practice in operation under para 6, a detainee (in the present case, at an airport) is entitled to consult a solicitor before being interviewed and that right can be exercised at any time during the period of detention and repeatedly. Where a solicitor attends in person he can be present during the interview, and a reasonable delay to await the arrival of a solicitor may be required. A detainee may not, however, exercise his right in such a way as to frustrate the proper purpose of the examination: *R (Elosta) v Comr of Police for the Metropolis* [2013] EWHC 3397 (Admin), [2014] 1 WLR 239, [2014] RTR 378.

**6.** (1) The Secretary of State shall issue codes of practice[1] about the exercise by officers of functions conferred on them by virtue of this Act or the terrorist cash provisions.

(2) The failure by an officer to observe a provision of a code shall not of itself make him liable to criminal or civil proceedings.

(3) A code—
(*a*) shall be admissible in evidence in criminal and civil proceedings, and
(*b*) shall be taken into account by a court or tribunal in any case in which it appears to the court or tribunal to be relevant.

(4) The Secretary of State may revise a code and issue the revised code.

**6A.** In paragraphs 5 and 6, "officer" includes a constable, immigration officer or customs officer who—
(*a*) has functions under Schedule 7, or
(*b*) has functions under Schedule 8 in relation to a person detained under Schedule 7,

otherwise than as an examining officer.

**7.** (1) Before issuing a code of practice the Secretary of State shall—
(*a*) publish a draft code,
(*b*) consider any representations made to him about the draft, and
(*c*) if he thinks it appropriate, modify the draft in the light of any representations made to him.

(2) The Secretary of State shall lay a draft of the code before Parliament.

(3) When the Secretary of State has laid a draft code before Parliament he may bring it into operation by order[1].

(4) This paragraph has effect in relation to the issue of a revised code as it has effect in relation to the first issue of a code.

1 By the Terrorism Act 2000 (Code of Practice for Examining Officers and Review Officers) Order 2015, SI 2015/906 the code of practice entitled "Code of Practice for Examining Officers and Review Officers under Schedule 7 to the Terrorism Act 2000" and laid before Parliament in draft on 27 February 2015 came into operation on 25 March 2015.

# Anti-terrorism, Crime and Security Act 2001[1]

(2001 c 24)

## Part 1[2]

## Terrorist Property

7.8829 **1. Forfeiture of terrorist cash** (1) Schedule 1 (which makes provision for enabling cash which—
(*a*) is intended to be used for the purposes of terrorism,
(*b*) consists of resources of an organisation which is a proscribed organisation, or
(*c*) is, or represents, property obtained through terrorism,

to be forfeited in civil proceedings before a magistrates' court or (in Scotland) the sheriff) is to have effect.

(2) The powers conferred by Schedule 1 are exercisable in relation to any cash whether or not any proceedings have been brought for an offence in connection with the cash.

(3) Expressions used in this section have the same meaning as in Schedule 1.

(4) Sections 24 to 31 of the Terrorism Act 2000 (c 11) (seizure of terrorist cash) are to cease to

have effect.

(5) An order under section 127 bringing Schedule 1 into force may make any modifications of any code of practice then in operation under Schedule 14 to the Terrorism Act 2000 (exercise of officers' powers) which the Secretary of State thinks necessary or expedient.

[Anti-terrorism, Crime and Security Act 2001, s 1.]

---

[1] This Act was passed in response to the terrorist attack on New York on 11 September 2001. The Act amends the Terrorism Act 2000; makes further provision about terrorism and security; makes provision about immigration and asylum; amends or extends the criminal law and powers for preventing crime and enforcing that law; makes provision about the control of pathogens and toxins; provides for the retention of communications data; provides for the implementation of Title VI of the Treaty on European Union; and provides for certain connected purposes.

Part 1 of the Act, together with Sch 1, makes provision for the forfeiture of terrorist cash; Part 2 is concerned with freezing orders; Part 3 is concerned with the disclosure of information; Part 4 is concerned with immigration and asylum; Part 5 is concerned with race and religion; Part 6 is concerned with weapons of mass destruction; Part 7 is concerned with the security of pathogens and toxins; Part 8 is concerned with the security of the nuclear industry; Part 9 is concerned with aviation security; Part 10 is concerned with police powers; Part 11 is concerned with the retention of communications data; Part 12 is concerned with bribery and corruption; Part 13 makes miscellaneous provisions; Part 14 contains supplemental provisions.

As to commencement, see s 127, post. The majority of the Act's provisions came into force on, or soon, the date the Act received the Royal Assent. As to the remaining provisions, the following commencement orders have been made: Anti-terrorism, Crime and Security Act 2001 (Commencement No 1 and Consequential Provisions) Order 2001, SI 2001/4019; Anti-terrorism, Crime and Security Act 2001 (Commencement No 2) (Scotland) Order 2001, SI 2001/4014; Anti-terrorism, Crime and Security Act 2001 (Commencement No 3) Order 2001, SI 2002/228; Anti-terrorism, Crime and Security Act 2001 (Commencement No 4 and Consequential Provisions) Order 2001, SI 2002/1279; and the Anti-terrorism, Crime and Security Act 2001 (Commencement No 5 and Consequential Provisions) Order 2001, SI 2002/1558.

[2] Part 1 contains ss 1–3.

## PART 2[1]

## FREEZING ORDERS

### *Orders*

**4. Power to make order** *Treasury may make order by statutory instrument.*

---

[1] Part 2 contains ss 4–16.

7.8830 **5. Contents of order** (1) A freezing order is an order which prohibits persons from making funds available to or for the benefit of a person or persons specified in the order.

(2) The order must provide that these are the persons who are prohibited—

(*a*) all persons in the United Kingdom, and

(*b*) all persons elsewhere who are nationals of the United Kingdom or are bodies incorporated under the law of any part of the United Kingdom or are Scottish partnerships.

(3) The order may specify the following (and only the following) as the person or persons to whom or for whose benefit funds are not to be made available—

(*a*) the person or persons reasonably believed by the Treasury to have taken or to be likely to take the action referred to in section 4;

(*b*) any person the Treasury reasonably believe has provided or is likely to provide assistance (directly or indirectly) to that person or any of those persons.

(4) A person may be specified under subsection (3) by—

(*a*) being named in the order, or

(*b*) falling within a description of persons set out in the order.

(5) The description must be such that a reasonable person would know whether he fell within it.

(6) Funds are financial assets and economic benefits of any kind.

[Anti-terrorism, Crime and Security Act 2001, s 5.]

7.8831 **6. Contents: further provisions** Schedule 3 contains further provisions about the contents of freezing orders.

[Anti-terrorism, Crime and Security Act 2001, s 6.]

7.8832 **7. Review of order** The Treasury must keep a freezing order under review.

[Anti-terrorism, Crime and Security Act 2001, s 7.]

7.8833 **8. Duration of order** A freezing order ceases to have effect at the end of the period of 2 years starting with the day on which it is made.

[Anti-terrorism, Crime and Security Act 2001, s 8.]

### *Interpretation*

7.8834 **9. Nationals and residents** (1) A national of the United Kingdom is an individual who is—

(*a*) a British citizen, a British overseas territories citizen, a British National (Overseas) or a British Overseas citizen,

(*b*) a person who under the British Nationality Act 1981 (c 61) is a British subject, or

(*c*) a British protected person within the meaning of that Act.

(2) A resident of the United Kingdom is—

(*a*) an individual who is ordinarily resident in the United Kingdom,

(*b*) a body incorporated under the law of any part of the United Kingdom, or
(*c*) a Scottish partnership.

(3) A resident of a country or territory outside the United Kingdom is—
(*a*) an individual who is ordinarily resident in such a country or territory, or
(*b*) a body incorporated under the law of such a country or territory.

(4) For the purposes of subsection (3)(*b*) a branch situated in a country or territory outside the United Kingdom of—
(*a*) a body incorporated under the law of any part of the United Kingdom, or
(*b*) a Scottish partnership,

is to be treated as a body incorporated under the law of the country or territory where the branch is situated.

(5) This section applies for the purposes of this Part.

[Anti-terrorism, Crime and Security Act 2001, s 9 as amended by the British Overseas Territories Act 2002, s 2(3).]

*Orders: procedure etc*

**10–14.** *Procedure for making freezing orders, amending orders, revoking orders and supplementary provisions as to orders.*

*Miscellaneous*

**15–16.** *The Crown and repeals.*

PART 3[1]

DISCLOSURE OF INFORMATION

7.8835 **17. Extension of existing disclosure powers** (1) This section applies to the provisions listed in Schedule 4, so far as they authorise the disclosure of information.

(2) Each of the provisions to which this section applies shall have effect, in relation to the disclosure of information by or on behalf of a public authority, as if the purposes for which the disclosure of information is authorised by that provision included each of the following—
(*a*) the purposes of any criminal investigation whatever which is being or may be carried out, whether in the United Kingdom or elsewhere;
(*b*) the purposes of any criminal proceedings whatever which have been or may be initiated, whether in the United Kingdom or elsewhere;
(*c*) the purposes of the initiation or bringing to an end of any such investigation or proceedings;
(*d*) the purpose of facilitating a determination of whether any such investigation or proceedings should be initiated or brought to an end.

(3) The Treasury may by order made by statutory instrument add any provision contained in any subordinate legislation to the provisions to which this section applies.

(4) The Treasury shall not make an order under subsection (3) unless a draft of it has been laid before Parliament and approved by a resolution of each House.

(5) No disclosure of information shall be made by virtue of this section unless the public authority by which the disclosure is made is satisfied that the making of the disclosure is proportionate to what is sought to be achieved by it.

(6) Nothing in this section shall be taken to prejudice any power to disclose information which exists apart from this section.

(7) The information that may be disclosed by virtue of this section includes information obtained before the commencement of this section.

[Anti-terrorism, Crime and Security Act 2001, s 17.]

1 Part 3 contains ss 17–20.

7.8836 **18. Restriction on disclosure of information for overseas purposes** (1) Subject to subsections (2) and (3), the Secretary of State may give a direction which—
(*a*) specifies any overseas proceedings or any description of overseas proceedings; and
(*b*) prohibits the making of any relevant disclosure for the purposes of those proceedings or, as the case may be, of proceedings of that description.

(2) In subsection (1) the reference, in relation to a direction, to a relevant disclosure is a reference to a disclosure authorised by any of the provisions to which section 17 applies which—
(*a*) is made for a purpose mentioned in subsection (2)(*a*) to (*d*) of that section; and
(*b*) is a disclosure of any such information as is described in the direction.

(3) The Secretary of State shall not give a direction under this section unless it appears to him that the overseas proceedings in question, or that overseas proceedings of the description in question, relate or would relate—
(*a*) to a matter in respect of which it would be more appropriate for any jurisdiction or investigation to be exercised or carried out by a court or other authority of the United Kingdom, or of a particular part of the United Kingdom;
(*b*) to a matter in respect of which it would be more appropriate for any jurisdiction or investigation to be exercised or carried out by a court or other authority of a third country; or

(*c*) to a matter that would fall within paragraph (*a*) or (*b*)—
(i) if it were appropriate for there to be any exercise of jurisdiction or investigation at all; and
(ii) if (where one does not exist) a court or other authority with the necessary jurisdiction or functions existed in the United Kingdom, in the part of the United Kingdom in question or, as the case may be, in the third country in question.

(4) A direction under this section shall not have the effect of prohibiting—
(*a*) the making of any disclosure by a Minister of the Crown or by the Treasury; or
(*b*) the making of any disclosure in pursuance of a Community obligation.

(5) A direction under this section—
(*a*) may prohibit the making of disclosures absolutely or in such cases, or subject to such conditions as to consent or otherwise, as may be specified in it; and
(*b*) must be published or otherwise issued by the Secretary of State in such manner as he considers appropriate for bringing it to the attention of persons likely to be affected by it.

(6) A person who, knowing of any direction under this section, discloses any information in contravention of that direction shall be guilty of an offence and liable—
(*a*) on conviction on indictment, to imprisonment for a term not exceeding two years or to a fine or to both;
(*b*) on summary conviction, to imprisonment for a term not exceeding three months or to a fine not exceeding the statutory maximum or to both[1].

(7) The following are overseas proceedings for the purposes of this section—
(*a*) criminal proceedings which are taking place, or will or may take place, in a country or territory outside the United Kingdom;
(*b*) a criminal investigation which is being, or will or may be, conducted by an authority of any such country or territory.

(8) References in this section, in relation to any proceedings or investigation, to a third country are references to any country or territory outside the United Kingdom which is not the country or territory where the proceedings are taking place, or will or may take place or, as the case may be, is not the country or territory of the authority which is conducting the investigation, or which will or may conduct it.

(9) In this section "court" includes a tribunal of any description.

[Anti-terrorism, Crime and Security Act 2001, s 18.]

---

1 For procedure in respect of this offence, which is triable either way, see the Magistrates' Courts Act 1980, ss 17A–21, in PART 1: MAGISTRATES' COURTS, PROCEDURE, ante.

7.8837 **19. Disclosure of information held by revenue departments** (1) This section applies to information which is held by or on behalf of the Commissioners of Inland Revenue or by or on behalf of the Commissioners of Customs and Excise, including information obtained before the coming into force of this section.

(2) No obligation of secrecy imposed by statute or otherwise prevents the disclosure, in accordance with the following provisions of this section, of information to which this section applies if the disclosure is made—
(*a*) *repealed*;
(*b*) for the purposes of any criminal investigation whatever which is being or may be carried out, whether in the United Kingdom or elsewhere;
(*c*) for the purposes of any criminal proceedings whatever which have been or may be initiated, whether in the United Kingdom or elsewhere;
(*d*) for the purposes of the initiation or bringing to an end of any such investigation or proceedings; or
(*e*) for the purpose of facilitating a determination of whether any such investigation or proceedings should be initiated or brought to an end.

(3) No disclosure of information to which this section applies shall be made by virtue of this section unless the person by whom the disclosure is made is satisfied that the making of the disclosure is proportionate to what is sought to be achieved by it.

(4) Information to which this section applies shall not be disclosed by virtue of this section except by the Commissioners by or on whose behalf it is held or with their authority.

(5) Information obtained by means of a disclosure authorised by subsection (2) shall not be further disclosed except—
(*a*) for a purpose mentioned in that subsection; and
(*b*) with the consent of the Commissioners by whom or with whose authority it was initially disclosed;

and information so obtained otherwise than by or on behalf of any of the intelligence services shall not be further disclosed (with or without such consent) to any of those services, or to any person acting on behalf of any of those services, except for a purpose mentioned in paragraphs (*b*) to (*e*) of that subsection.

(6) A consent for the purposes of subsection (5) may be given either in relation to a particular disclosure or in relation to disclosures made in such circumstances as may be specified or described in the consent.

(7) Nothing in this section authorises the making of any disclosure which is prohibited by any provision of the Data Protection Act 1998 (c 29).

(8) References in this section to information which is held on behalf of the Commissioners of Inland Revenue or of the Commissioners of Customs and Excise include references to information which—

(*a*) is held by a person who provides services to the Commissioners of Inland Revenue or, as the case may be, to the Commissioners of Customs and Excise; and

(*b*) is held by that person in connection with the provision of those services.

(9) In this section "intelligence service" has the same meaning as in the Regulation of Investigatory Powers Act 2000 (c 23).

(10) Nothing in this section shall be taken to prejudice any power to disclose information which exists apart from this section.

[Anti-terrorism, Crime and Security Act 2001, s 19 as amended by the Counter-Terrorism Act 2008, Sch 9.]

**7.8838 20. Interpretation of Part 3** (1) In this Part—

"criminal investigation" means an investigation of any criminal conduct, including an investigation of alleged or suspected criminal conduct and an investigation of whether criminal conduct has taken place;

"information" includes—

(*a*) documents; and

(*b*) in relation to a disclosure authorised by a provision to which section 17 applies, anything that falls to be treated as information for the purposes of that provision;

"public authority" has the same meaning as in section 6 of the Human Rights Act 1998 (c 42); and

"subordinate legislation" has the same meaning as in the Interpretation Act 1978 (c 30).

(2) Proceedings outside the United Kingdom shall not be taken to be criminal proceedings for the purposes of this Part unless the conduct with which the defendant in those proceedings is charged is criminal conduct or conduct which, to a substantial extent, consists of criminal conduct.

(3) In this section—

"conduct" includes acts, omissions and statements; and

"criminal conduct" means any conduct which—

(*a*) constitutes one or more criminal offences under the law of a part of the United Kingdom; or

(*b*) is, or corresponds to, conduct which, if it all took place in a particular part of the United Kingdom, would constitute one or more offences under the law of that part of the United Kingdom.

[Anti-terrorism, Crime and Security Act 2001, s 20.]

## PART 6[1]

## WEAPONS OF MASS DESTRUCTION[2]

[1] Part 6 contains ss 43–50.

[2] Sections 43–46 amend the Biological Weapons Act 1974 and the Chemical Weapons Act 1996.

### *Nuclear weapons*

**7.8839 47. Use etc of nuclear weapons** (1) A person who—

(*a*) knowingly causes a nuclear weapon explosion;

(*b*) develops or produces, or participates in the development or production of, a nuclear weapon;

(*c*) has a nuclear weapon in his possession;

(*d*) participates in the transfer of a nuclear weapon; or

(*e*) engages in military preparations, or in preparations of a military nature, intending to use, or threaten to use, a nuclear weapon, is guilty of an offence.

(2) Subsection (1) has effect subject to the exceptions and defences in sections 48 and 49.

(3) For the purposes of subsection (1)(*b*) a person participates in the development or production of a nuclear weapon if he does any act which—

(*a*) facilitates the development by another of the capability to produce or use a nuclear weapon, or

(*b*) facilitates the making by another of a nuclear weapon,

knowing or having reason to believe that his act has (or will have) that effect.

(4) For the purposes of subsection (1)(*d*) a person participates in the transfer of a nuclear weapon if—

(*a*) he buys or otherwise acquires it or agrees with another to do so;

(*b*) he sells or otherwise disposes of it or agrees with another to do so; or

(*c*) he makes arrangements under which another person either acquires or disposes of it or agrees with a third person to do so.

(5) A person guilty of an offence under this section is liable on conviction on indictment to imprisonment for life.

(6) In this section "nuclear weapon" includes a nuclear explosive device that is not intended for use as a weapon.

(7) This section applies to acts done outside the United Kingdom, but only if they are done by a United Kingdom person.

(8) Nothing in subsection (7) affects any criminal liability arising otherwise than under that subsection.

(9) Paragraph (*a*) of subsection (1) shall cease to have effect on the coming into force of the Nuclear Explosions (Prohibition and Inspections) Act 1998 (c 7).

[Anti-terrorism, Crime and Security Act 2001, s 47.]

7.8840 **48. Exceptions** (1) Nothing in section 47 applies—

(*a*) to an act which is authorised under subsection (2); or

(*b*) to an act done in the course of an armed conflict.

(2) The Secretary of State may—

(*a*) authorise any act which would otherwise contravene section 47 in such manner and on such terms as he thinks fit; and

(*b*) withdraw or vary any authorisation given under this subsection.

(3) Any question arising in proceedings for an offence under section 47 as to whether anything was done in the course of an armed conflict shall be determined by the Secretary of State.

(4) A certificate purporting to set out any such determination and to be signed by the Secretary of State shall be received in evidence in any such proceedings and shall be presumed to be so signed unless the contrary is shown.

[Anti-terrorism, Crime and Security Act 2001, s 48.]

7.8841 **49. Defences** (1) In proceedings for an offence under section 47(1)(*c*) or (*d*) relating to an object it is a defence for the accused to show that he did not know and had no reason to believe that the object was a nuclear weapon.

(2) But he shall be taken to have shown that fact if—

(*a*) sufficient evidence is adduced to raise an issue with respect to it; and

(*b*) the contrary is not proved by the prosecution beyond reasonable doubt.

(3) In proceedings for such an offence it is also a defence for the accused to show that he knew or believed that the object was a nuclear weapon but, as soon as reasonably practicable after he first knew or believed that fact, he took all reasonable steps to inform the Secretary of State or a constable of his knowledge or belief.

[Anti-terrorism, Crime and Security Act 2001, s 49.]

*Assisting or inducing weapons-related acts overseas*

7.8842 **50. Assisting or inducing certain weapons-related acts overseas** (1) A person who aids, abets, counsels or procures, or incites, a person who is not a United Kingdom person to do a relevant act outside the United Kingdom is guilty of an offence.

(2) For this purpose a relevant act is an act that, if done by a United Kingdom person, would contravene any of the following provisions—

(*a*) section 1 of the Biological Weapons Act 1974 (offences relating to biological agents and toxins);

(*b*) section 2 of the Chemical Weapons Act 1996 (offences relating to chemical weapons); or

(*c*) section 47 above (offences relating to nuclear weapons).

(3) Nothing in this section applies to an act mentioned in subsection (1) which—

(*a*) relates to a relevant act which would contravene section 47; and

(*b*) is authorised by the Secretary of State;

and section 48(2) applies for the purpose of authorising acts that would otherwise constitute an offence under this section.

(4) A person accused of an offence under this section in relation to a relevant act which would contravene a provision mentioned in subsection (2) may raise any defence which would be open to a person accused of the corresponding offence ancillary to an offence under that provision.

(5) A person convicted of an offence under this section is liable on conviction on indictment to imprisonment for life.

(6) This section applies to acts done outside the United Kingdom, but only if they are done by a United Kingdom person.

(7) Nothing in this section prejudices any criminal liability existing apart from this section.

[Anti-terrorism, Crime and Security Act 2001, s 50.]

*Supplemental provisions relating to sections 47 and 50*

7.8843 **51. Extraterritorial application** (1) Proceedings for an offence committed under section 47 or 50 outside the United Kingdom may be taken, and the offence may for incidental purposes be treated as having been committed, in any part of the United Kingdom.

(2) Her Majesty may by Order in Council extend the application of section 47 or 50, so far as it applies to acts done outside the United Kingdom, to bodies incorporated under the law of any of the Channel Islands, the Isle of Man or any colony.

[Anti-terrorism, Crime and Security Act 2001, s 51.]

7.8844 **52. Powers of entry** (1) If—

(*a*) a justice of the peace is satisfied on information on oath that there are reasonable grounds for suspecting that evidence of the commission of an offence under section 47 or 50 is to be found on any premises; or

(*b*) *Scotland,*

he may issue a warrant authorising an authorised officer to enter the premises, if necessary by force, at any time within one month from the time of the issue of the warrant and to search them.

(2) The powers of a person who enters the premises under the authority of the warrant include power—

(*a*) to take with him such other persons and such equipment as appear to him to be necessary;

(*b*) to inspect, seize and retain any substance, equipment or document found on the premises;

(*c*) to require any document or other information which is held in electronic form and is accessible from the premises to be produced in a form—

(i) in which he can read and copy it; or

(ii) from which it can readily be produced in a form in which he can read and copy it;

(*d*) to copy any document which he has reasonable cause to believe may be required as evidence for the purposes of proceedings in respect of an offence under section 47 or 50.

(3) A constable who enters premises under the authority of a warrant or by virtue of subsection (2)(*a*) may—

(*a*) give such assistance as an authorised officer may request for the purpose of facilitating the exercise of any power under this section; and

(*b*) search or cause to be searched any person on the premises who the constable has reasonable cause to believe may have in his possession any document or other thing which may be required as evidence for the purposes of proceedings in respect of an offence under section 47 or 50.

(4) No constable shall search a person of the opposite sex.

(5) The powers conferred by a warrant under this section shall only be exercisable, if the warrant so provides, in the presence of a constable.

(6) A person who—

(*a*) wilfully obstructs an authorised officer in the exercise of a power conferred by a warrant under this section; or

(*b*) fails without reasonable excuse to comply with a reasonable request made by an authorised officer or a constable for the purpose of facilitating the exercise of such a power,

is guilty of an offence.

(7) A person guilty of an offence under subsection (6) is liable—

(*a*) on summary conviction, to a fine not exceeding the statutory maximum; and

(*b*) on conviction on indictment, to imprisonment for a term not exceeding two years or a fine (or both)[1].

(8) In this section "authorised officer" means an authorised officer of the Secretary of State.

[Anti-terrorism, Crime and Security Act 2001, s 52.]

---

1 For procedure in respect of this offence, which is triable either way, see the Magistrates' Courts Act 1980, ss 17A–21, in PART I: MAGISTRATES' COURTS, PROCEDURE, ante.

7.8845 **53. Revenue and Customs prosecutions** (1) Proceedings for a nuclear weapons offence may be instituted by the Director of Public Prosecutions or by order of the Commissioners for Her Majesty's Revenue and Customs if it appears to the Director or to the Commissioners that the offence has involved—

(*a*) the development or production outside the United Kingdom of a nuclear weapon;

(*b*) the movement of a nuclear weapon into or out of any country or territory;

(*c*) any proposal or attempt to do anything falling within paragraph (*a*) or (*b*).

(2) In this section "nuclear weapons offence" means an offence under section 47 or 50 (including an offence of aiding, abetting, counselling, procuring or inciting the commission of, or attempting or conspiring to commit, such an offence).

(3) Any proceedings for an offence which are instituted by order of the Commissioners under subsection (1) shall be commenced in the name of an officer of Revenue and Customs, but may be continued by another officer.

(4) Where the Commissioners investigate, or propose to investigate, any matter with a view to determining—

(*a*) whether there are grounds for believing that a nuclear weapons offence has been committed, or

(*b*) whether a person should be prosecuted for such an offence,

that matter shall be treated as an assigned matter within the meaning of the Customs and Excise Management Act 1979 (c 2).

(5) Nothing in this section affects any powers of any person (including any officer) apart from this section.

(6) *Repealed.*

(7) This section does not apply to the institution of proceedings in Scotland.

[Anti-terrorism, Crime and Security Act 2001, s 53 as amended by the Commissioners for Revenue and Customs Act 2005, Sch 4 and SI 2014/834.]

7.8846 **54. Offences** (1) A person who knowingly or recklessly makes a false or misleading statement for the purpose of obtaining (or opposing the variation or withdrawal of) authorisation for the purposes of section 47 or 50 is guilty of an offence.

(2) A person guilty of an offence under subsection (1) is liable—

(*a*) on summary conviction, to a fine of an amount not exceeding the statutory maximum;

(*b*) on conviction on indictment, to imprisonment for a term not exceeding two years or a fine (or both)[1].

(3) Where an offence under section 47, 50 or subsection (1) above committed by a body corporate is proved to have been committed with the consent or connivance of, or to be attributable to any neglect on the part of—

(*a*) a director, manager, secretary or other similar officer of the body corporate; or

(*b*) any person who was purporting to act in any such capacity,

he as well as the body corporate shall be guilty of that offence and shall be liable to be proceeded against and punished accordingly.

(4) In subsection (3) "director", in relation to a body corporate whose affairs are managed by its members, means a member of the body corporate.

[Anti-terrorism, Crime and Security Act 2001, s 54.]

1 For procedure in respect of this offence, which is triable either way, see the Magistrates' Courts Act 1980, ss 17A–21, in PART I: MAGISTRATES' COURTS, PROCEDURE, ante.

7.8847 **55. Consent to prosecutions** Proceedings for an offence under section 47 or 50 shall not be instituted—

(*a*) in England and Wales, except by or with the consent of the Attorney General;

(*b*) in Northern Ireland, except by or with the consent of the Advocate General for Northern Ireland.

[Anti-terrorism, Crime and Security Act 2001, s 55 as amended by the Justice (Northern Ireland) Act 2002, s 28.]

7.8848 **56. Interpretation of Part 6** (1) In this Part "United Kingdom person" means a United Kingdom national, a Scottish partnership or a body incorporated under the law of a part of the United Kingdom.

(2) For this purpose a United Kingdom national is an individual who is—

(*a*) a British citizen, a British overseas territories citizen, a British National (Overseas) or a British Overseas citizen;

(*b*) a person who under the British Nationality Act 1981 (c 61) is a British subject; or

(*c*) a British protected person within the meaning of that Act.

[Anti-terrorism, Crime and Security Act 2001, s 56 as amended by the British Overseas Territories Act 2002, s 2(3).]

*Extension of Part 6 to dependencies*

7.8849 **57. Power to extend Part 6 to dependencies** Her Majesty may by Order in Council[1] direct that any of the provisions of this Part shall extend, with such exceptions and modifications as appear to Her Majesty to be appropriate, to any of the Channel Islands, the Isle of Man or to any British overseas territory.

[Anti-terrorism, Crime and Security Act 2001, s 57.]

1 The Chemical Weapons (Overseas Territories) Order 2005, SI 2005/854 amended by SI 2011/2984 has been made.

PART 8[1]

SECURITY OF NUCLEAR INDUSTRY

7.8850 **77. Regulation of security of civil nuclear industry** *Secretary of State may make regulations for the purpose of ensuring the security of nuclear sites etc[1].*

1 The Nuclear Industries Security Regulations 2003, SI 2003/403 amended by SI 2006/2815, SI 2007/3224 and SI 2009/229, SI 2013/190 and SI 2014/469 and 526, have been made. Reference should also be made to the Energy Act 2013 (Office for Nuclear Regulation) (Consequential Amendments, Transitional Provisions and Savings) Order 2014, SI 2014/469 which provides that in relation to an offence which is committed before s 85(1) of the Legal Aid, Sentencing and Punishment of Offenders Act 2012 (removal of limit on certain fines on conviction by magistrates' court) came into force, the first reference in s 77(3)(*a*)(ii) of this Act is to be treated as a reference to a fine not exceeding £20,000.

7.8851 **79. Prohibition of disclosures relating to nuclear security** (1) A person is guilty of an offence if he discloses any information or thing the disclosure of which might prejudice the security of any nuclear site or of any nuclear material—

(*a*) with the intention of prejudicing that security; or

(*b*) being reckless as to whether the disclosure might prejudice that security.

(2) The reference in subsection (1) to nuclear material is a reference to—

(*a*) nuclear material which is being held on any nuclear site, or

(*b*) nuclear material anywhere in the world which is being transported to or from a nuclear site or carried on board a British ship,

(including nuclear material which is expected to be so held, transported or carried).

(3) A person guilty of an offence under subsection (1) is liable—

(*a*) on conviction on indictment, to imprisonment for a term not exceeding seven years or a fine (or both); and

(*b*) on summary conviction, to imprisonment for a term not exceeding six months or a fine not exceeding the statutory maximum (or both)[1].

(4) In this section—

"British ship" means a ship (including a ship belonging to Her Majesty) which is registered in the United Kingdom;

"disclose" and "disclosure", in relation to a thing, include parting with possession of it;

"nuclear material" has the same meaning as in Chapter 3 of Part 1 of the Energy Act 2004; and

"nuclear site" means a site in the United Kingdom (including a site occupied by or on behalf of the Crown) which is (or is expected to be) used for any purpose mentioned in section 1(1) of the Nuclear Installations Act 1965 (c 57).

(5) This section applies to acts done outside the United Kingdom, but only if they are done by a United Kingdom person.

(6) Proceedings for an offence committed outside the United Kingdom may be taken, and the offence may for incidental purposes be treated as having been committed, in any place in the United Kingdom.

(7) Nothing in subsection (5) affects any criminal liability arising otherwise than under that subsection.

[Anti-terrorism, Crime and Security Act 2001, s 79 as amended by the Energy Act 2004, Sch 14.]

---

1 For procedure in respect of this offence, which is triable either way, see the Magistrates' Courts Act 1980, ss 17A–21, in PART I: MAGISTRATES' COURTS, PROCEDURE, ante.

7.8852 **80. Prohibition of disclosures of uranium enrichment technology** (1) This section applies to—

(*a*) any information about the enrichment of uranium; or

(*b*) any information or thing which is, or is likely to be, used in connection with the enrichment of uranium;

and for this purpose "the enrichment of uranium" means any treatment of uranium that increases the proportion of the isotope 235 contained in the uranium.

(2) The Secretary of State may make regulations[1] prohibiting the disclosure of information or things to which this section applies.

(3) A person who contravenes a prohibition is guilty of an offence and liable—

(*a*) on conviction on indictment, to imprisonment for a term not exceeding seven years or a fine (or both); and

(*b*) on summary conviction, to imprisonment for a term not exceeding six months or a fine not exceeding the statutory maximum (or both)[2].

(4) The regulations may, in particular, provide for—

(*a*) a prohibition to apply, or not to apply—

(i) to such information or things; and

(ii) in such cases or circumstances,

as may be prescribed;

(*b*) the authorisation by the Secretary of State of disclosures that would otherwise be prohibited; and

(*c*) defences to an offence under subsection (3) relating to any prohibition.

(5) The regulations may—

(*a*) provide for any prohibition to apply to acts done outside the United Kingdom by United Kingdom persons;

(*b*) make different provision for different purposes; and

(*c*) make such incidental, supplementary and transitional provision as the Secretary of State thinks fit.

(6) The power to make the regulations is exercisable by statutory instrument.

(7) The regulations shall not be made unless a draft of the regulations has been laid before and approved by each House of Parliament.

(8) In this section—

"disclosure", in relation to a thing, includes parting with possession of it;

"information" includes software; and

"prescribed" means specified or described in the regulations.

[Anti-terrorism, Crime and Security Act 2001, s 80.]

---

1 The Uranium Enrichment Technology (Prohibition on Disclosure) Regulations 2004, SI 2004/1818 amended by SI 2014/469 have been made.

2 For procedure in respect of this offence, which is triable either way, see the Magistrates' Courts Act 1980, ss 17A–21, in PART I: MAGISTRATES' COURTS, PROCEDURE, ante.

7.8853 **80A. Extension of Official Secrets Acts to certain places** (1) A place to which subsection (2) applies is deemed to be a place belonging to or used for the purposes of Her Majesty for the purposes of section 3(*c*) of the Official Secrets Act 1911 (c 28) (power of Secretary of State to declare a place belonging to or used for the purposes of Her Majesty a prohibited place).

(2) This subsection applies to a place if—

(*a*) equipment or software which is designed or adapted for use in, or in connection with, the enrichment of uranium (or which is not so designed or adapted but is likely to be of exceptional use in that connection) is held at the place, or

(*b*) information relating to, or capable of use in connection with, the enrichment of uranium is held at the place.

(3) In this section—

"enrichment of uranium" means a treatment of uranium which increases the proportion of isotope 235 contained in the uranium, and

"equipment" includes equipment which has not yet been assembled and a component of equipment.

[Anti-terrorism, Crime and Security Act 2001, s 80A as inserted by the Energy Act 2008, s 101.]

7.8854 **81. Part 8: supplementary** (1) Proceedings for an offence under section 79 or 80 shall not be instituted—

(*a*) in England and Wales, except by or with the consent of the Attorney General; or

(*b*) in Northern Ireland, except by or with the consent of the Advocate General for Northern Ireland.

(2) In this Part "United Kingdom person" means a United Kingdom national, a Scottish partnership or a body incorporated under the law of any part of the United Kingdom.

(3) For this purpose a United Kingdom national is an individual who is—

(*a*) a British citizen, a British overseas territories citizen, a British National (Overseas) or a British Overseas citizen;

(*b*) a person who under the British Nationality Act 1981 (c 61) is a British subject; or

(*c*) a British protected person within the meaning of that Act.

[Anti-terrorism, Crime and Security Act 2001, s 81 as amended by the British Overseas Territories Act 2002, s 2(3) and the Justice (Northern Ireland) Act 2002, s 28.]

## PART 9[1]

## AVIATION SECURITY[2]

7.8855 **88. Extent outside United Kingdom** (1) The powers in section 108(1) and (2) of the Civil Aviation Act 1982 (c 16) (extension outside United Kingdom) apply to provisions of this Part which amend that Act.

(2) The powers in section 39(3) of the Aviation Security Act 1982 (extension outside United Kingdom) apply to provisions of this Part which amend that Act.

[Anti-terrorism, Crime and Security Act 2001, s 88.]

---

1 Part 9 contains ss 82–88.

2 Sections 82–87 amend or add provisions to the Police and Criminal Evidence Act 1984 (new arrest without warrant powers) and the Civil Aviation Act 1982 (increased penalty for trespass on aerodrome) and the Aviation Security Act 1982 (approved providers of aviation security services; detention of aircraft; and offence relating to air cargo agent documents). Section 88 provides that the jurisdiction extending powers contained in s 108(1) and (2) of the Civil Aviation Act 1982 and s 39(3) of the Aviation Security Act 1982 apply to the provisions of Part 9 of the Anti-terrorism, Crime and Security Act 2001 that amend those Acts.

## PART 10[1]

## POLICE POWERS[2]

### *MoD and transport police*

7.8856 **100. Jurisdiction of transport police** (1) Where a member of the British Transport Police Force has been requested by a constable of—

(*a*) the police force for any police area,

(*b*) the Ministry of Defence Police, or

(*c*) the Civil Nuclear Constabulary,

("the requesting force") to assist him in the execution of his duties in relation to a particular incident, investigation or operation, members of the British Transport Police Force have for the purposes of that incident, investigation or operation the same powers and privileges as constables of the requesting force.

(2) Members of the British Transport Police Force have in any police area the same powers and privileges as constables of the police force for that police area—

(*a*) in relation to persons whom they suspect on reasonable grounds of having committed, being in the course of committing or being about to commit an offence, or

(*b*) if they believe on reasonable grounds that they need those powers and privileges in order to save life or to prevent or minimise personal injury or damage to property.

(3) But members of the British Transport Police Force have powers and privileges by virtue of subsection (2) only if—

(*a*) *repealed*;

(*b*) they believe on reasonable grounds that a power of a constable which they would not have apart from that subsection ought to be exercised and that, if it cannot be exercised until they secure the attendance of or a request under subsection (1) by a constable who has it, the purpose for which they believe it ought to be exercised will be frustrated or seriously prejudiced.

(4) In this section—

"British Transport Police Force" means the constables appointed under section 53 of the British Transport Commission Act 1949 (c xxix)

[Anti-terrorism, Crime and Security Act 2001, s 100 as amended by the Energy Act 2004, Sch 14 and the Infrastructure Act 2015, s 22.]

---

1 Part 10 contains ss 89–101.

2 Part 10 amends Sch 8 to the Terrorism Act 2000 (fingerprinting, etc); the Police and Criminal Evidence Act 1984 (as to searches and examination to establish identity and photographing of suspects); the Criminal Justice and Public Order Act 1994 (powers to require removal of disguises); and the Ministry of Defence Police Act 1987 (as to the jurisdiction of MoD police and the provision of assistance to other forces).

7.8857 **101. Further provisions about transport police and MoD police** Schedule 7 contains amendments relating to the British Transport Police Force and the Ministry of Defence Police.

[Anti-terrorism, Crime and Security Act 2001, s 101.]

## Part 11[1]

## Retention of Communications Data[2]

7.8858 **102. Codes and agreements about the retention of communications data** (5) A code of practice or agreement under this section which is for the time being in force shall be admissible in evidence in any legal proceedings in which the question arises whether or not the retention of any communications data is justified on the grounds that a failure to retain the data would be likely to prejudice national security, the prevention or detection of crime or the prosecution of offenders.*

[Anti-terrorism, Crime and Security Act 2001, s 102.]

---

* **Repealed by the Investigatory Powers Act 2016, Sch 10 from a date to be appointed.**

1 Part 11 contains ss 102–107. Part 11 is repealed by the Investigatory Powers Act 2016, Sch 10 from a date to be appointed.

2 Part 11 requires the Security of State, following publication of a draft before which he must consult the Information Commissioner and affected communications providers, to issue a code of practice relating to the retention by communications providers of communications data obtained by or held by them. The code shall be brought into force by an order made by statutory instrument, a draft of which must be approved by resolution of each House of Parliament. The code may be revised from time to time, subject to the procedures stated above. The draft code of practice entitled "Voluntary Retention of Communications Data under Part 11: Anti-terrorism, Crime and Security Act 2001—Voluntary Code of Practice", laid before each House of Parliament on 11 September 2003 came into force on 5 December 2003 by the Retention of Communications Data (Code of Practice) Order 2003, SI 2003/3175.

The Security of State may also enter into agreements with communications providers as to the practices the latter are to follow in relation to the retention of communications data obtained by or held by them.

The Secretary of State may also by order made by statutory instrument (subject to the same Parliamentary approval) authorize himself to give directions about the retention of communications data. Before giving such directions the Secretary of State must consult affected communications providers. The duty of communications providers to comply with directions is enforceable by civil proceedings. The period within which the Secretary of State may give such directions has been extended for two years commencing on 14 December 2003 by the Retention of Communications Data (Extension of Initial Period) Order 2003, SI 2003/3173 and extended for a further two years commencing on 14 December 2005 by the Retention of Communications Data (Further Extension of Initial Period) Order 2005, SI 2005/3335.

7.8859 **107. Interpretation of Part 11** (1) In this Part—

"communications data" has the same meaning as in Chapter 2 of Part 1 of the Regulation of Investigatory Powers Act 2000 (c 23);

"communications provider" means a person who provides a postal service or a telecommunications service;

"legal proceedings", "postal service" and "telecommunications service" each has the same meaning as in that Act;

and any reference in this Part to the prevention or detection of crime shall be construed as if contained in Chapter 2 of Part 1 of that Act.

(2) References in this Part, in relation to any code of practice, agreement or direction, to the retention by a communications provider of any communications data include references to the retention of any data obtained by that provider before the time when the code was issued, the agreement made or the direction given, and to data already held by that provider at that time.*

[Anti-terrorism, Crime and Security Act 2001, s 107.]

* **Repealed by the Investigatory Powers Act 2016, Sch 10 from a date to be appointed.**

## PART 12[1]
## BRIBERY AND CORRUPTION [2]

[1] Part 12 contains ss 108–110

[2] Part 12 amends the common law offence of bribery by making it immaterial whether the briber or recipient of the bribe has any functions connected with or carried out in the UK. Similar amendments are made to the offences under s 1 of the Prevention of Corruption Act 1906; s 7 of the Public Bodies Corrupt Practices Act 1889; and s 4(2) of the Prevention of Corruption Act 1916.

Part 12 also makes the offences listed above (save the last) extra-territorial when committed by a UK national (as defined). Prior to the coming into force of these provisions it was an offence under s 1 of the Prevention of Corruption Act 1906 to corrupt an agent of a foreign principal or a foreign body; unlike the Public Bodies Corrupt Practices Act 1889 the 1906 Act contained no wording limiting the terms 'agent' or 'principal' to UK persons: *R v AIL (a company)* [2016] EWCA Crim 2, [2016] 2 WLR 1287.

## PART 13[1]
## MISCELLANEOUS

*Dangerous substances*

7.8860 **113. Use of noxious substances or things to cause harm and intimidate** (1) A person who takes any action which—

(*a*) involves the use of a noxious substance or other noxious thing;
(*b*) has or is likely to have an effect falling within subsection (2); and
(*c*) is designed to influence the government or an international governmental organisation or to intimidate the public or a section of the public,

is guilty of an offence.

(2) Action has an effect falling within this subsection if it—

(*a*) causes serious violence against a person anywhere in the world;
(*b*) causes serious damage to real or personal property anywhere in the world;
(*c*) endangers human life or creates a serious risk to the health or safety of the public or a section of the public; or
(*d*) induces in members of the public the fear that the action is likely to endanger their lives or create a serious risk to their health or safety;

but any effect on the person taking the action is to be disregarded.

(3) A person who—

(*a*) makes a threat that he or another will take any action which constitutes an offence under subsection (1); and
(*b*) intends thereby to induce in a person anywhere in the world the fear that the threat is likely to be carried out,

is guilty of an offence.

(4) A person guilty of an offence under this section is liable—

(*a*) on summary conviction, to imprisonment for a term not exceeding six months or a fine not exceeding the statutory maximum (or both); and
(*b*) on conviction on indictment, to imprisonment for a term not exceeding fourteen years or a fine (or both)[1].

(5) In this section—

"the government" means the government of the United Kingdom, of a part of the United Kingdom or of a country other than the United Kingdom; and
"the public" includes the public of a country other than the United Kingdom.

[Anti-terrorism, Crime and Security Act 2001, s 113 as amended by the Terrorism Act 2006, s 34(*b*).]

[1] For procedure in respect of this offence, which is triable either way, see the Magistrates' Courts Act 1980, ss 17A–21, in PART I: MAGISTRATES' COURTS, PROCEDURE, ante.

7.8861 **113A. Application of section 113** (1) Section 113 applies to conduct done—

(*a*) in the United Kingdom; or
(*b*) outside the United Kingdom which satisfies the following two conditions.

(2) The first condition is that the conduct is done for the purpose of advancing a political, religious, racial or ideological cause.

(3) The second condition is that the conduct is—

(*a*) by a United Kingdom national or a United Kingdom resident;
(*b*) by any person done to, or in relation to, a United Kingdom national, a United Kingdom resident or a protected person; or
(*c*) by any person done in circumstances which fall within section 63D(1)(*b*) and (*c*) or (3)(*b*) and (*c*) of the Terrorism Act 2000.

(4) The following expressions have the same meaning as they have for the purposes of sections 63C and 63D of that Act—

(*a*) "United Kingdom national";
(*b*) "United Kingdom resident";

(*c*) "protected person".

(5) For the purposes of this section it is immaterial whether a person knows that another is a United Kingdom national, a United Kingdom resident or a protected person.

[Anti-terrorism, Crime and Security Act 2001, s 113A as inserted by the Criminal Justice (International Co-operation) Act 2003, s 53 and amended by the Counter-Terrorism Act 2008, s 75.]

**7.8862 113B. Consent to prosecution for offence under section 113** (1) Proceedings for an offence committed under section 113 outside the United Kingdom are not to be started—

(*a*) in England and Wales, except by or with the consent of the Attorney General;

(*b*) in Northern Ireland, except by or with the consent of the Advocate General for Northern Ireland.

(2) Proceedings for an offence committed under section 113 outside the United Kingdom may be taken, and the offence may for incidental purposes be treated as having been committed, in any part of the United Kingdom.

(3) In relation to any time before the coming into force of section 27(1) of the Justice (Northern Ireland) Act 2002, the reference in subsection (1)(*b*) to the Advocate General for Northern Ireland is to be read as a reference to the Attorney General for Northern Ireland.

[Anti-terrorism, Crime and Security Act 2001, s 113B as inserted by the Criminal Justice (International Co-operation) Act 2003, s 53.]

**7.8863 114. Hoaxes involving noxious substances or things** (1) A person is guilty of an offence if he—

(*a*) places any substance or other thing in any place; or

(*b*) sends any substance or other thing from one place to another (by post, rail or any other means whatever);

with the intention of inducing in a person anywhere in the world a belief that it is likely to be (or contain) a noxious substance or other noxious thing and thereby endanger human life or create a serious risk to human health.

(2) A person is guilty of an offence if he communicates any information which he knows or believes to be false with the intention of inducing in a person anywhere in the world a belief that a noxious substance or other noxious thing is likely to be present (whether at the time the information is communicated or later) in any place and thereby endanger human life or create a serious risk to human health.

(3) A person guilty of an offence under this section is liable—

(*a*) on summary conviction, to imprisonment for a term not exceeding six months or a fine not exceeding the statutory maximum (or both); and

(*b*) on conviction on indictment, to imprisonment for a term not exceeding seven years or a fine (or both)[1].

[Anti-terrorism, Crime and Security Act 2001, s 114.]

1 For procedure in respect of this offence, which is triable either way, see the Magistrates' Courts Act 1980, ss 17A–21, in PART I: MAGISTRATES' COURTS, PROCEDURE, ante.

**7.8864 115. Sections 113 and 114: supplementary** (1) For the purposes of sections 113 and 114 "substance" includes any biological agent and any other natural or artificial substance (whatever its form, origin or method of production).

(2) For a person to be guilty of an offence under section 113(3) or 114 it is not necessary for him to have any particular person in mind as the person in whom he intends to induce the belief in question.

[Anti-terrorism, Crime and Security Act 2001, s 115.]

## PART 14[1]

### SUPPLEMENTAL

**7.8865 127. Commencement[2]** (1) Except as provided in subsections (2) to (4), this Act comes into force on such day as the Secretary of State may appoint by order.

(2) The following provisions come into force on the day on which this Act is passed—

(*a*) Parts 2 to 6,

(*b*) Part 8, except section 78,

(*c*) Part 9, except sections 84 and 87,

(*d*) sections 89 to 97,

(*e*) *sections 98 to 100*, except so far as they extend to Scotland,

(*f*) section 101 and Schedule 7, except so far as they relate to the entries in respect of the Police (Scotland) Act 1967,

(*g*) Part 11,

(*h*) Part 13, except section 121,

(i) this Part, except section 125 and Schedule 8 so far as they relate to the entries—

(i) in Part 1 of Schedule 8,

(ii) in Part 5 of Schedule 8, in respect of the Nuclear Installations Act 1965,

(iii) in Part 6 of Schedule 8, in respect of the British Transport Commission Act 1962 and the Ministry of Defence Police Act 1987, so far as those entries extend to Scotland,

(iv) in Part 7 of Schedule 8, in respect of Schedule 5 to the Terrorism Act 2000.

(3) The following provisions come into force at the end of the period of two months beginning with the day on which this Act is passed—

(*a*) section 84,

(*b*) section 87.

(4) The following provisions come into force on such day as the Secretary of State and the Scottish Ministers, acting jointly, may appoint by order—

(*a*) sections 98 to 100, so far as they extend to Scotland,

(*b*) section 101 and Schedule 7, so far as they relate to the entries in respect of the Police (Scotland) Act 1967, and

(*c*) section 125 and Schedule 8, so far as they relate to the entries in Part 6 of Schedule 8 in respect of the British Transport Commission Act 1962 and the Ministry of Defence Police Act 1987, so far as those entries extend to Scotland.

(5) Different days may be appointed for different provisions and for different purposes.

(6) An order under this section—

(*a*) must be made by statutory instrument, and

(*b*) may contain incidental, supplemental, consequential or transitional provision.

[Anti-terrorism, Crime and Security Act 2001, s 127.]

1 Part 14 contains 124–129.

2 For details of commencement orders made, see the note to the title of this Act, ante.

7.8866 **128. Extent** (1) The following provisions do not extend to Scotland—

(*a*) Part 5,

(*b*) Part 12,

(*c*) in Part 6 of Schedule 8, the repeals in the Criminal Justice and Police Order Act 1994 and in the Crime and Disorder Act 1998.

(2) The following provisions do not extend to Northern Ireland—

(*a*) section 76,

(*b*) section 100.

(3) Except as provided in subsections (1) and (2), an amendment, repeal or revocation in this Act has the same extent as the enactment amended, repealed or revoked.

[Anti-terrorism, Crime and Security Act 2001, s 128.]

7.8867 **129. Short title** This Act may be cited as the Anti-terrorism, Crime and Security Act 2001.

[Anti-terrorism, Crime and Security Act 2001, s 129.]

## SCHEDULE 1
### Forfeiture of Terrorist Cash

*(Amended by the Criminal Justice Act 2003, s 331, the Terrorism Act 2006, s 35, the Armed Forces Act 2006, Sch 16 and the Counter-Terrorism Act 2008, ss 83 and 84.)*

### Part 1
### Introductory

7.8868 **1. Terrorist cash** (1) This Schedule applies to cash ("terrorist cash") which—

(*a*) is within subsection (1)(*a*) or (*b*) of section 1, or

(*b*) is property earmarked as terrorist property.

(2) "Cash" means—

(*a*) coins and notes in any currency,

(*b*) postal orders,

(*c*) cheques of any kind, including travellers' cheques,

(*d*) bankers' drafts,

(*e*) bearer bonds and bearer shares,

found at any place in the United Kingdom.

(3) Cash also includes any kind of monetary instrument which is found at any place in the United Kingdom, if the instrument is specified by the Secretary of State by order.

(4) The power to make an order under sub-paragraph (3) is exercisable by statutory instrument, which is subject to annulment in pursuance of a resolution of either House of Parliament.

### Part 2
### Seizure and Detention

**2. Seizure of cash** (1) An authorised officer may seize any cash if he has reasonable grounds for suspecting that it is terrorist cash.

(2) An authorised officer may also seize cash part of which he has reasonable grounds for suspecting to be terrorist cash if it is not reasonably practicable to seize only that part.

**3. Detention of seized cash** (1) While the authorised officer continues to have reasonable grounds for his suspicion, cash seized under this Schedule may be detained initially for a period of 48 hours.

(1A) In determining the period of 48 hours specified in sub-paragraph (1) there shall be disregarded—

(*a*) any Saturday or Sunday;

(*b*) Christmas Day;

(*c*) Good Friday;

(*d*) any day that is a bank holiday under the Banking and Financial Dealings Act 1971 in the part of the United Kingdom in which the cash is seized;

(*e*) any day prescribed under section 8(2) of the Criminal Procedure (Scotland) Act 1995 as a court holiday in the sheriff court district in which the cash is seized.

(2) The period for which the cash or any part of it may be detained may be extended by an order made by a magistrates' court or (in Scotland) the sheriff; but the order may not authorise the detention of any of the cash—

(*a*) beyond the end of the period of three months beginning with the date of the order, and

(*b*) in the case of any further order under this paragraph, beyond the end of the period of two years beginning with the date of the first order.

(3) A justice of the peace may also exercise the power of a magistrates' court to make the first order under sub-paragraph (2) extending the period.

(3A) An application to a justice of the peace or the sheriff for an order under sub-paragraph (2) making the first extension of the period—

(*a*) may be made and heard without notice of the application or hearing having been given to any of the persons affected by the application or to the legal representative of such a person, and

(*b*) may be heard and determined in private in the absence of persons so affected and of their legal representatives.[1]

(4) An order under sub-paragraph (2) must provide for notice to be given to persons affected by it.

(5) An application for an order under sub-paragraph (2)—

(*a*) in relation to England and Wales and Northern Ireland, may be made by the Commissioners of Customs and Excise or an authorised officer,

(*b*) *Scotland*,

and the court, sheriff or justice may make the order if satisfied, in relation to any cash to be further detained, that one of the following conditions is met.

(6) The first condition is that there are reasonable grounds for suspecting that the cash is intended to be used for the purposes of terrorism and that either—

(*a*) its continued detention is justified while its intended use is further investigated or consideration is given to bringing (in the United Kingdom or elsewhere) proceedings against any person for an offence with which the cash is connected, or

(*b*) proceedings against any person for an offence with which the cash is connected have been started and have not been concluded.

(7) The second condition is that there are reasonable grounds for suspecting that the cash consists of resources of an organisation which is a proscribed organisation and that either—

(*a*) its continued detention is justified while investigation is made into whether or not it consists of such resources or consideration is given to bringing (in the United Kingdom or elsewhere) proceedings against any person for an offence with which the cash is connected, or

(*b*) proceedings against any person for an offence with which the cash is connected have been started and have not been concluded.

(8) The third condition is that there are reasonable grounds for suspecting that the cash is property earmarked as terrorist property and that either—

(*a*) its continued detention is justified while its derivation is further investigated or consideration is given to bringing (in the United Kingdom or elsewhere) proceedings against any person for an offence with which the cash is connected, or

(*b*) proceedings against any person for an offence with which the cash is connected have been started and have not been concluded.

---

[1] Sub-para (3A) applies to applications made after 13 April 2006.

**4. Payment of detained cash into an account** (1) If cash is detained under this Schedule for more than 48 hours (determined in accordance with paragraph 3(1A)), it is to be held in an interest-bearing account and the interest accruing on it is to be added to it on its forfeiture or release.

(2) In the case of cash seized under paragraph 2(2), the authorised officer must, on paying it into the account, release so much of the cash then held in the account as is not attributable to terrorist cash.

(3) Sub-paragraph (1) does not apply if the cash is required as evidence of an offence or evidence in proceedings under this Schedule.

**5. Release of detained cash** (1) This paragraph applies while any cash is detained under this Schedule.

(2) A magistrates' court or (in Scotland) the sheriff may direct the release of the whole or any part of the cash if satisfied, on an application by the person from whom it was seized, that the conditions in paragraph 3 for the detention of cash are no longer met in relation to the cash to be released.

(3) A authorised officer or (in Scotland) a procurator fiscal may, after notifying the magistrates' court, sheriff or justice under whose order cash is being detained, release the whole or any part of it if satisfied that the detention of the cash to be released is no longer justified.

(4) But cash is not to be released—

(*a*) if an application for its forfeiture under paragraph 6, or for its release under paragraph 9, is made, until any proceedings in pursuance of the application (including any proceedings on appeal) are concluded,

(*b*) if (in the United Kingdom or elsewhere) proceedings are started against any person for an offence with which the cash is connected, until the proceedings are concluded.

## PART 3
## FORFEITURE

**6. Forfeiture** (1) While cash is detained under this Schedule, an application for the forfeiture of the whole or any part of it may be made—

(*a*) to a magistrates' court by the Commissioners of Customs and Excise or an authorised officer,

(*b*) *Scotland.*

(2) The court or sheriff may order the forfeiture of the cash or any part of it if satisfied that the cash or part is terrorist cash.

(3) In the case of property earmarked as terrorist property which belongs to joint tenants one of whom is an excepted joint owner, the order may not apply to so much of it as the court or sheriff thinks is attributable to the excepted joint owner's share.

(4) An excepted joint owner is a joint tenant who obtained the property in circumstances in which it would

not (as against him) be earmarked; and references to his share of the earmarked property are to so much of the property as would have been his if the joint tenancy had been severed.

**7. Appeal against decision in forfeiture proceedings** (1) A party to proceedings for an order under paragraph 6 ("a forfeiture order") who is aggrieved by a forfeiture order made in the proceedings or by the decision of the court or sheriff not to make a forfeiture order may appeal—

(*a*) in England and Wales, to the Crown Court;

(*b*) *Scotland,*

(*c*) *Northern Ireland.*

(2) The appeal must be brought before the end of the period of 30 days beginning with the date on which the order is made or, as the case may be, the decision is given.

This is subject to paragraph 7A (extended time for appealing in certain cases of deproscription).

(3) The court or sheriff principal hearing the appeal may make any order that appears to the court or sheriff principal to be appropriate.

(4) If an appeal against a forfeiture order is upheld, the court or sheriff principal may order the release of the cash.

**7A. Extended time for appealing in certain cases where deproscription order made** (1) This paragraph applies where—

(*a*) a successful application for a forfeiture order relies (wholly or partly) on the fact that an organisation is proscribed,

(*b*) an application under section 4 of the Terrorism Act 2000 for a deproscription order in respect of the organisation is refused by the Secretary of State,

(*c*) the forfeited cash is seized under this Schedule on or after the date of the refusal of that application,

(*d*) an appeal against that refusal is allowed under section 5 of that Act,

(*e*) a deproscription order is made accordingly, and

(*f*) if the order is made in reliance on section 123(5) of that Act, a resolution is passed by each House of Parliament under section 123(5)(*b*).

(2) Where this paragraph applies, an appeal under paragraph 7 above against the forfeiture order may be brought at any time before the end of the period of 30 days beginning with the date on which the deproscription order comes into force.

(3) In this paragraph a "deproscription order" means an order under section 3(3)(*b*) or (8) of the Terrorism Act 2000.

**8. Application of forfeited cash** (1) Cash forfeited under this Schedule, and any accrued interest on it—

(*a*) if forfeited by a magistrates' court in England and Wales or Northern Ireland, is to be paid into the Consolidated Fund,

(*b*) *Scotland.*

(2) But it is not to be paid in—

(*a*) before the end of the period within which an appeal under paragraph 7 may be made, or

(*b*) if a person appeals under that paragraph, before the appeal is determined or otherwise disposed of.

## PART 4

## MISCELLANEOUS

**9. Victims** (1) A person who claims that any cash detained under this Schedule, or any part of it, belongs to him may apply to a magistrates' court or (in Scotland) the sheriff for the cash or part to be released to him.

(2) The application may be made in the course of proceedings under paragraph 3 or 6 or at any other time.

(3) If it appears to the court or sheriff concerned that—

(*a*) the applicant was deprived of the cash claimed, or of property which it represents, by criminal conduct,

(*b*) the property he was deprived of was not, immediately before he was deprived of it, property obtained by or in return for criminal conduct and nor did it then represent such property, and

(*c*) the cash claimed belongs to him,

the court or sheriff may order the cash to be released to the applicant.

**10. Compensation** (1) If no forfeiture order is made in respect of any cash detained under this Schedule, the person to whom the cash belongs or from whom it was seized may make an application to the magistrates' court or (in Scotland) the sheriff for compensation.

(2) If, for any period after the initial detention of the cash for 48 hours (determined in accordance with paragraph 3(1A)), the cash was not held in an interest-bearing account while detained, the court or sheriff may order an amount of compensation to be paid to the applicant.

(3) The amount of compensation to be paid under sub-paragraph (2) is the amount the court or sheriff thinks would have been earned in interest in the period in question if the cash had been held in an interest-bearing account.

(4) If the court or sheriff is satisfied that, taking account of any interest to be paid under this Schedule or any amount to be paid under sub-paragraph (2), the applicant has suffered loss as a result of the detention of the cash and that the circumstances are exceptional, the court or sheriff may order compensation (or additional compensation) to be paid to him.

(5) The amount of compensation to be paid under sub-paragraph (4) is the amount the court or sheriff thinks reasonable, having regard to the loss suffered and any other relevant circumstances.

(6) If the cash was seized by a customs officer, the compensation is to be paid by the Commissioners of Customs and Excise.

(7) If the cash was seized by a constable, the compensation is to be paid as follows—

(*a*) in the case of a constable of a police force in England and Wales, it is to be paid out of the police fund from which the expenses of the police force are met,

(*b*) *Scotland,*

(*c*) *Northern Ireland.*

(8) If the cash was seized by an immigration officer, the compensation is to be paid by the Secretary of State.

(9) If a forfeiture order is made in respect only of a part of any cash detained under this Schedule, this paragraph has effect in relation to the other part.

(10) This paragraph does not apply if the court or sheriff makes an order under paragraph 9.

## PART 5
## PROPERTY EARMARKED AS TERRORIST PROPERTY

**11. Property obtained through terrorism** (1) A person obtains property through terrorism if he obtains property by or in return for acts of terrorism, or acts carried out for the purposes of terrorism.

(2) In deciding whether any property was obtained through terrorism—

(*a*) it is immaterial whether or not any money, goods or services were provided in order to put the person in question in a position to carry out the acts,

(*b*) it is not necessary to show that the act was of a particular kind if it is shown that the property was obtained through acts of one of a number of kinds, each of which would have been an act of terrorism, or an act carried out for the purposes of terrorism.

**12. Property earmarked as terrorist property** (1) Property obtained through terrorism is earmarked as terrorist property.

(2) But if property obtained through terrorism has been disposed of (since it was so obtained), it is earmarked as terrorist property only if it is held by a person into whose hands it may be followed.

(3) Earmarked property obtained through terrorism may be followed into the hands of a person obtaining it on a disposal by—

(*a*) the person who obtained the property through terrorism, or

(*b*) a person into whose hands it may (by virtue of this sub-paragraph) be followed.

**13. Tracing property** (1) Where property obtained through terrorism ("the original property") is or has been earmarked as terrorist property, property which represents the original property is also earmarked.

(2) If a person enters into a transaction by which—

(*a*) he disposes of earmarked property, whether the original property or property which (by virtue of this Part) represents the original property, and

(*b*) he obtains other property in place of it,

the other property represents the original property.

(3) If a person disposes of earmarked property which represents the original property, the property may be followed into the hands of the person who obtains it (and it continues to represent the original property).

**14. Mixing property** (1) Sub-paragraph (2) applies if a person's property which is earmarked as terrorist property is mixed with other property (whether his property or another's).

(2) The portion of the mixed property which is attributable to the property earmarked as terrorist property represents the property obtained through terrorism.

(3) Property earmarked as terrorist property is mixed with other property if (for example) it is used—

(*a*) to increase funds held in a bank account,

(*b*) in part payment for the acquisition of an asset,

(*c*) for the restoration or improvement of land,

(*d*) by a person holding a leasehold interest in the property to acquire the freehold.

**15. Accruing profits** (1) This paragraph applies where a person who has property earmarked as terrorist property obtains further property consisting of profits accruing in respect of the earmarked property.

(2) The further property is to be treated as representing the property obtained through terrorism.

**16. General exceptions** (1) If—

(*a*) a person disposes of property earmarked as terrorist property, and

(*b*) the person who obtains it on the disposal does so in good faith, for value and without notice that it was earmarked,

the property may not be followed into that person's hands and, accordingly, it ceases to be earmarked.

(2) If—

(*a*) in pursuance of a judgment in civil proceedings (whether in the United Kingdom or elsewhere), the defendant makes a payment to the claimant or the claimant otherwise obtains property from the defendant,

(*b*) the claimant's claim is based on the defendant's criminal conduct, and

(*c*) apart from this sub-paragraph, the sum received, or the property obtained, by the claimant would be earmarked as terrorist property,

the property ceases to be earmarked.

In relation to Scotland, "claimant" and "defendant" are to be read as "pursuer" and "defender"; and, in relation to Northern Ireland, "claimant" is to be read as "plaintiff".

(3) If—

(*a*) a payment is made to a person in pursuance of a compensation order under Article 14 of the Criminal Justice (Northern Ireland) Order 1994 (SI 1994/2795 (NI 15)), section 249 of the Criminal Procedure (Scotland) Act 1995 (c 46) or section 130 of the Powers of Criminal Courts (Sentencing) Act 2000 (c 6) or in pursuance of a service compensation order under the Armed Forces Act 2006, and

(*b*) apart from this sub-paragraph, the sum received would be earmarked as terrorist property,

the property ceases to be earmarked.

(4) If—

(*a*) a payment is made to a person in pursuance of a restitution order under section 27 of the Theft Act (Northern Ireland) 1969 (c 16 (NI)) or section 148(2) of the Powers of Criminal Courts (Sentencing) Act 2000 or a person otherwise obtains any property in pursuance of such an order, and

(*b*) apart from this sub-paragraph, the sum received, or the property obtained, would be earmarked as terrorist property,

the property ceases to be earmarked.

(5) If—

(*a*) in pursuance of an order made by the court under section 382(3) or 383(5) of the Financial Services and Markets Act 2000 (c 8) (restitution orders), an amount is paid to or distributed among any persons in accordance with the court's directions, and

(*b*) apart from this sub-paragraph, the sum received by them would be earmarked as terrorist property,

the property ceases to be earmarked.

(6) If—

(*a*) in pursuance of a requirement of the Financial Services Authority under section 384(5) of the Financial Services and Markets Act 2000 (c 8) (power of authority to require restitution), an amount is paid to or distributed among any persons, and

(*b*) apart from this sub-paragraph, the sum received by them would be earmarked as terrorist property,

the property ceases to be earmarked.

(7) Where—

(*a*) a person enters into a transaction to which paragraph 13(2) applies, and

(*b*) the disposal is one to which sub-paragraph (1) applies,

this paragraph does not affect the question whether (by virtue of paragraph 13(2)) any property obtained on the transaction in place of the property disposed of is earmarked.

## Part 6

## Interpretation

**17. Property** (1) Property is all property wherever situated and includes—

(*a*) money,

(*b*) all forms of property, real or personal, heritable or moveable,

(*c*) things in action and other intangible or incorporeal property.

(2) Any reference to a person's property (whether expressed as a reference to the property he holds or otherwise) is to be read as follows.

(3) In relation to land, it is a reference to any interest which he holds in the land.

(4) In relation to property other than land, it is a reference—

(*a*) to the property (if it belongs to him), or

(*b*) to any other interest which he holds in the property.

**18. Obtaining and disposing of property** (1) References to a person disposing of his property include a reference—

(*a*) to his disposing of a part of it, or

(*b*) to his granting an interest in it,

(or to both); and references to the property disposed of are to any property obtained on the disposal.

(2) If a person grants an interest in property of his which is earmarked as terrorist property, the question whether the interest is also earmarked is to be determined in the same manner as it is on any other disposal of earmarked property.

(3) A person who makes a payment to another is to be treated as making a disposal of his property to the other, whatever form the payment takes.

(4) Where a person's property passes to another under a will or intestacy or by operation of law, it is to be treated as disposed of by him to the other.

(5) A person is only to be treated as having obtained his property for value in a case where he gave unexecuted consideration if the consideration has become executed consideration.

**19. General interpretation** (1) In this Schedule—

"authorised officer" means a constable, a customs officer or an immigration officer,

"cash" has the meaning given by paragraph 1,

"constable", in relation to Northern Ireland, means a police officer within the meaning of the Police (Northern Ireland) Act 2000 (c 32),

"criminal conduct" means conduct which constitutes an offence in any part of the United Kingdom, or would constitute an offence in any part of the United Kingdom if it occurred there,

"customs officer" means an officer commissioned by the Commissioners of Customs and Excise under section 6(3) of the Customs and Excise Management Act 1979 (c 2),

"forfeiture order" has the meaning given by paragraph 7,

"immigration officer" means a person appointed as an immigration officer under paragraph 1 of Schedule 2 to the Immigration Act 1971 (c 77),

"interest", in relation to land—

(*a*) in the case of land in England and Wales or Northern Ireland, means any legal estate and any equitable interest or power,

(*b*) *Scotland,*

"interest", in relation to property other than land, includes any right (including a right to possession of the property),

"part", in relation to property, includes a portion,

"property obtained through terrorism" has the meaning given by paragraph 11,

"property earmarked as terrorist property" is to be read in accordance with Part 5,

"proscribed organisation" has the same meaning as in the Terrorism Act 2000 (c 11),

"terrorism" has the same meaning as in the Terrorism Act 2000,

"terrorist cash" has the meaning given by paragraph 1,

"value" means market value.

(2) Paragraphs 17 and 18 and the following provisions apply for the purposes of this Schedule.

(3) For the purpose of deciding whether or not property was earmarked as terrorist property at any time (including times before commencement), it is to be assumed that this Schedule was in force at that and any other relevant time.

(4) References to anything done or intended to be done for the purposes of terrorism include anything done or intended to be done for the benefit of a proscribed organisation.

(5) An organisation's resources include any cash which is applied or made available, or is to be applied or made available, for use by the organisation.

(6) Proceedings against any person for an offence are concluded when—

(*a*) the person is convicted or acquitted,

(*b*) the prosecution is discontinued or, in Scotland, the trial diet is deserted simpliciter, or

(*c*) the jury is discharged without a finding otherwise than in circumstances where the proceedings are continued without a jury.

SCHEDULE 3
FREEZING ORDERS

Section 6

*(As amended by the Counter-Terrorism Act 2008, s 70 and the Policing and Crime Act 2017, s 145)*

7.8874 **1. Interpretation** References in this Schedule to a person specified in a freezing order as a person to whom or for whose benefit funds are not to be made available are to be read in accordance with section 5(4).

**2. Funds** A freezing order may include provision that funds include gold, cash, deposits, securities (such as stocks, shares and debentures) and such other matters as the order may specify.

**3. Making funds available** (1) A freezing order must include provision as to the meaning (in relation to funds) of making available to or for the benefit of a person.

(2) In particular, an order may provide that the expression includes—

(*a*) allowing a person to withdraw from an account;
(*b*) honouring a cheque payable to a person;
(*c*) crediting a person's account with interest;
(*d*) releasing documents of title (such as share certificates) held on a person's behalf;
(*e*) making available the proceeds of realisation of a person's property;
(*f*) making a payment to or for a person's benefit (for instance, under a contract or as a gift or under any enactment such as the enactments relating to social security);
(*g*) such other acts as the order may specify.

**4. Licences** (1) A freezing order must include—

(*a*) provision for the granting of licences authorising funds to be made available;
(*b*) provision that a prohibition under the order is not to apply if funds are made available in accordance with a licence.

(2) In particular, an order may provide—

(*a*) that a licence may be granted generally or to a specified person or persons or description of persons;
(*b*) that a licence may authorise funds to be made available to or for the benefit of persons generally or a specified person or persons or description of persons;
(*c*) that a licence may authorise funds to be made available generally or for specified purposes;
(*d*) that a licence may be granted in relation to funds generally or to funds of a specified description;
(*e*) for a licence to be granted in pursuance of an application or without an application being made;
(*f*) for the form and manner in which applications for licences are to be made;
(*g*) for licences to be granted by the Treasury or a person authorised by the Treasury;
(*h*) for the form in which licences are to be granted;
(i) for licences to be granted subject to conditions;
(*j*) for licences to be of a defined or indefinite duration;
(*k*) for the charging of a fee to cover the administrative costs of granting a licence;
(*l*) for the variation and revocation of licences.

**5. Information and documents** (1) A freezing order may include provision that a person—

(*a*) must provide information if required to do so and it is reasonably needed for the purpose of ascertaining whether an offence under the order has been committed;
(*b*) must produce a document if required to do so and it is reasonably needed for that purpose.

(2) In particular, an order may include—

(*a*) provision that a requirement to provide information or to produce a document may be made by the Treasury or a person authorised by the Treasury;
(*b*) provision that information must be provided, and a document must be produced, within a reasonable period specified in the order and at a place specified by the person requiring it;
(*c*) provision that the provision of information is not to be taken to breach any restriction on the disclosure of information (however imposed);
(*d*) provision restricting the use to which information or a document may be put and the circumstances in which it may be disclosed;
(*e*) provision that a requirement to provide information or produce a document does not apply to privileged information or a privileged document;
(*f*) provision that information is privileged if the person would be entitled to refuse to provide it on grounds of legal professional privilege in proceedings in the High Court or (in Scotland) on grounds of confidentiality of communications in proceedings in the Court of Session;
(*g*) provision that a document is privileged if the person would be entitled to refuse to produce it on grounds of legal professional privilege in proceedings in the High Court or (in Scotland) on grounds of confidentiality of communications in proceedings in the Court of Session;
(*h*) provision that information or a document held with the intention of furthering a criminal purpose is not privileged.

**6. Disclosure of information** (1) A freezing order may include provision requiring a person to disclose information as mentioned below if the following three conditions are satisfied.

(2) The first condition is that the person required to disclose is specified or falls within a description specified in the order.

(3) The second condition is that the person required to disclose knows or suspects, or has grounds for knowing or suspecting, that a person specified in the freezing order as a person to whom or for whose benefit funds are not to be made available—

(*a*) is a customer of his or has been a customer of his at any time since the freezing order came into force, or
(*b*) is a person with whom he has dealings in the course of his business or has had such dealings at any time since the freezing order came into force.

(4) The third condition is that the information—

(*a*) on which the knowledge or suspicion of the person required to disclose is based, or
(*b*) which gives grounds for his knowledge or suspicion,

came to him in the course of a business in the regulated sector.

(5) The freezing order may require the person required to disclose to make a disclosure to the Treasury of that information as soon as is practicable after it comes to him.

(6) The freezing order may include—

(*a*) provision that Schedule 3A to the Terrorism Act 2000 (c 11) is to have effect for the purpose of determining what is a business in the regulated sector;

(*b*) provision that the disclosure of information is not to be taken to breach any restriction on the disclosure of information (however imposed);

(*c*) provision restricting the use to which information may be put and the circumstances in which it may be disclosed by the Treasury;

(*d*) provision that the requirement to disclose information does not apply to privileged information;

(*e*) provision that information is privileged if the person would be entitled to refuse to disclose it on grounds of legal professional privilege in proceedings in the High Court or (in Scotland) on grounds of confidentiality of communications in proceedings in the Court of Session;

(*f*) provision that information held with the intention of furthering a criminal purpose is not privileged.

**7. Offences** (1) A freezing order may include any of the provisions set out in this paragraph.

(2) A person commits an offence if he fails to comply with a prohibition imposed by the order.

(3) A person commits an offence if he engages in an activity knowing or intending that it will enable or facilitate the commission by another person of an offence under a provision included under sub-paragraph (2).

(4) A person commits an offence if—

(*a*) he fails without reasonable excuse to provide information, or to produce a document, in response to a requirement made under the order;

(*b*) he provides information, or produces a document, which he knows is false in a material particular in response to such a requirement or with a view to obtaining a licence under the order;

(*c*) he recklessly provides information, or produces a document, which is false in a material particular in response to such a requirement or with a view to obtaining a licence under the order;

(*d*) he fails without reasonable excuse to disclose information as required by a provision included under paragraph 6.

(5) A person does not commit an offence under a provision included under sub-paragraph (2) or (3) if he proves that he did not know and had no reason to suppose that the person to whom or for whose benefit funds were made available, or were to be made available, was the person (or one of the persons) specified in the freezing order as a person to whom or for whose benefit funds are not to be made available.

(6) A person guilty of an offence under a provision included under sub-paragraph (2) or (3) is liable—

(a) on summary conviction—

(i) in England and Wales, to imprisonment for a term not exceeding 12 months (or, in relation to offences committed before section 154(1) of the Criminal Justice Act 2003 comes into force, 6 months) or to a fine, or to both;

(ii) in Scotland, to imprisonment for a term not exceeding 12 months, or to a fine not exceeding the statutory maximum, or to both;

(iii) in Northern Ireland, to imprisonment for a term not exceeding 6 months, or to a fine not exceeding the statutory maximum, or to both;

(b) on conviction on indictment, to imprisonment for a term not exceeding 7 years or to a fine, or to both.

(7) A person guilty of an offence under a provision included under sub-paragraph (4) is liable—

(a) on summary conviction—

(i) in England and Wales, to imprisonment for a term not exceeding 12 months (or, in relation to offences committed before section 154(1) of the Criminal Justice Act 2003 comes into force, 6 months) or to a fine, or to both;

(ii) in Scotland, to imprisonment for a term not exceeding 12 months, or to a fine not exceeding the statutory maximum, or to both;

(iii) in Northern Ireland, to imprisonment for a term not exceeding 6 months, or to a fine not exceeding the statutory maximum, or to both;

(b) on conviction on indictment, to imprisonment for a term not exceeding 2 years or to a fine, or to both.

**8. Offences: procedure** (1) A freezing order may include any of the provisions set out in this paragraph.

(2) Proceedings for an offence under the order are not to be instituted in England and Wales except by or with the consent of the Treasury or the Director of Public Prosecutions.

(3) Proceedings for an offence under the order are not to be instituted in Northern Ireland except by or with the consent of the Treasury or the Director of Public Prosecutions for Northern Ireland.

(4) Despite anything in section 127(1) of the Magistrates' Courts Act 1980 (c 43) (information to be laid within 6 months of offence) an information relating to an offence under the order which is triable by a magistrates' court in England and Wales may be so tried if it is laid at any time in the period of one year starting with the date of the commission of the offence.

(5) *Scotland.*

(6) *Northern Ireland.*

**9. Offences by bodies corporate etc** (1) A freezing order may include any of the provisions set out in this paragraph.

(2) If an offence under the order—

(*a*) is committed by a body corporate, and

(*b*) is proved to have been committed with the consent or connivance of an officer, or to be attributable to any neglect on his part,

he as well as the body corporate is guilty of the offence and liable to be proceeded against and punished accordingly.

(3) These are officers of a body corporate—

(*a*) a director, manager, secretary or other similar officer of the body;

(*b*) any person purporting to act in any such capacity.

(4) If the affairs of a body corporate are managed by its members sub-paragraph (2) applies in relation to the acts and defaults of a member in connection with his functions of management as if he were an officer of the body.

(5) If an offence under the order—

(*a*) is committed by a Scottish partnership, and

(*b*) is proved to have been committed with the consent or connivance of a partner, or to be attributable to any neglect on his part,

he as well as the partnership is guilty of the offence and liable to be proceeded against and punished accordingly.

**10. Compensation** (1) A freezing order may include provision for the award of compensation to or on behalf of a person on the grounds that he has suffered loss as a result of—

(*a*) the order;
(*b*) the fact that a licence has not been granted under the order;
(*c*) the fact that a licence under the order has been granted on particular terms rather than others;
(*d*) the fact that a licence under the order has been varied or revoked.

(2) In particular, the order may include—

(*a*) provision about the person who may make a claim for an award;
(*b*) provision about the person to whom a claim for an award is to be made (which may be provision that it is to be made to the High Court or, in Scotland, the Court of Session);
(*c*) provision about the procedure for making and deciding a claim;
(*d*) provision that no compensation is to be awarded unless the claimant has behaved reasonably (which may include provision requiring him to mitigate his loss, for instance by applying for a licence);
(*e*) provision that compensation must be awarded in specified circumstances or may be awarded in specified circumstances (which may include provision that the circumstances involve negligence or other fault);
(*f*) provision about the amount that may be awarded;
(*g*) provision about who is to pay any compensation awarded (which may include provision that it is to be paid or reimbursed by the Treasury);
(*h*) provision about how compensation is to be paid (which may include provision for payment to a person other than the claimant).

**11. Treasury's duty to give reasons** (1) A freezing order must include provision that if—

(*a*) a person is specified in the order as a person to whom or for whose benefit funds are not to be made available, and
(*b*) he makes a written request to the Treasury to give him the reason why he is so specified,

as soon as is practicable the Treasury must give the person the reason in writing.

(2) Sub-paragraph (1) does not apply if, or to the extent that, particulars of the reason would not be required to be disclosed to the applicant in proceedings to set aside the freezing order.

---

[1] For procedure in respect of this offence, which is triable either way, see the Magistrates' Courts Act 1980, ss 17A–21, in PART I: MAGISTRATES' COURTS, PROCEDURE, ante.

SCHEDULE 4

EXTENSION OF EXISTING DISCLOSURE POWERS — Section 17

*(Amended by the Enterprise Act 2002, Sch 26, the Communications Act 2003, Sch 19, the Health and Social Care (Community Health and Standards) Act 2003, Sch 4, the Companies (Audit, Investigations and Community Enterprise) Act 2002, Sch 2, the National Health Service (Consequential Provisions) Act 2006, Sch 1, the Equality Act 2006, Schs 3 and 4, SI 2009/1941, the Legal Aid, Sentencing and Punishment of Offenders Act 2012, Sch 5, the Postal Services Act 2011, s 91(1), (2), Sch 12 and the Legal Aid, Sentencing and Punishment of Offenders Act 2012, Sch 5.)*

PART 1

ENACTMENTS TO WHICH SECTION 17 APPLIES

7.8875 **1. Agricultural Marketing Act 1958 (c 47)** Section 47(2) of the Agricultural Marketing Act 1958.

**2. Harbours Act 1964 (c 40)** Section 46(1) of the Harbours Act 1964.

**3. Cereals Marketing Act 1965 (c 14)** Section 17(2) of the Cereals Marketing Act 1965.

**4. Agriculture Act 1967 (c 22)** Section 24(1) of the Agriculture Act 1967.

5. *Repealed.*

**6. Sea Fish Industry Act 1970 (c 11)** Section 14(2) of the Sea Fish Industry Act 1970.

**7. National Savings Bank Act 1971 (c 29)** Section 12(2) of the National Savings Bank Act 1971.

**8. Employment Agencies Act 1973 (c 35)** Section 9(4) of the Employment Agencies Act 1973.

9–11. *Repealed.*

**12. Health and Safety at Work etc Act 1974 (c 37)** Section 28(7) of the Health and Safety at Work etc Act 1974.

13, 14. *Repealed.*

**15. Energy Act 1976 (c 76)** Paragraph 7 of Schedule 2 to the Energy Act 1976.

16, 17. *Repealed.*

**18. Public Passenger Vehicles Act 1981 (c 14)** Section 54(8) of the Public Passenger Vehicles Act 1981.

**19. Fisheries Act 1981 (c 29)** Section 12(2) of the Fisheries Act 1981.

**20. Merchant Shipping (Liner Conferences) Act 1982 (c 37)** Section 10(2) of the Merchant Shipping (Liner Conferences) Act 1982.

**21. Civil Aviation Act 1982 (c 16)** Section 23(4) of the Civil Aviation Act 1982.

**22. Diseases of Fish Act 1983 (c 30)** Section 9(1) of the Diseases of Fish Act 1983.

**23. Telecommunications Act 1984 (c 12)** Section 101(2) of the Telecommunications Act 1984.

**24. Companies Act 1985 (c 6)** Section 449 of the Companies Act 1985.

**25. Airports Act 1986 (c 31)** Section 74(2) of the Airports Act 1986.

26. *Scotland.*

27. *Repealed.*

**28. Companies Act 1989 (c 40)** Section 87(1) of the Companies Act 1989.

29, 30. *Repealed.*

**31. Water Industry Act 1991 (c 56)** Section 206(3) of the Water Industry Act 1991.

**32. Water Resources Act 1991 (c 57)** Section 204(2) of the Water Resources Act 1991.

33. *Repealed.*

**34. Railways Act 1993 (c 43)** Section 145(2) of the Railways Act 1993.

**35. Coal Industry Act 1994 (c 21)** Section 59(2) of the Coal Industry Act 1994.

**36. Shipping and Trading Interests (Protection) Act 1995 (c 22)** Section 3(4) of the Shipping and Trading Interests (Protection) Act 1995.

37. *Repealed.*

**38. Goods Vehicles (Licensing of Operators) Act 1995 (c 23)** Section 35(4) of the Goods Vehicles (Licensing of Operators) Act 1995.

**39. Chemical Weapons Act 1996 (c 6)** Section 32(2) of the Chemical Weapons Act 1996.
**40. Bank of England Act 1998 (c 11)** (1) Paragraph 5 of Schedule 7 to the Bank of England Act 1998.
(2) Paragraph 2 of Schedule 8 to that Act.
**41. Audit Commission Act 1998 (c 18)** Section 49(1) of the Audit Commission Act 1998.
**42. Data Protection Act 1998 (c 29)** Section 59(1) of the Data Protection Act 1998.
**43.** *Northern Ireland.*
**44. Landmines Act 1998 (c 33)** Section 19(2) of the Landmines Act 1998.
**45, 46.** *Repealed.*
**47.** *Repealed.*
**48. Nuclear Safeguards Act 2000 (c 5)** Section 6(2) of the Nuclear Safeguards Act 2000.
**49. Finance Act 2000 (c 21)** Paragraph 34(3) of Schedule 22 to the Finance Act 2000.
**50. Local Government Act 2000 (c 22)** Section 63(1) of the Local Government Act 2000.
**51. Postal Services Act 2000 (c 26)** Paragraph 3(1) of Schedule 7 to the Postal Services Act 2000.
**52. Utilities Act 2000 (c 27)** Section 105(4) of the Utilities Act 2000.
**53. Transport Act 2000 (c 38)** (1) Section 143(5)(*b*) of the Transport Act 2000.
(2) Paragraph 13(3) of Schedule 10 to that Act.
**53A.** Paragraph 8(1) of Schedule 10 to the National Health Service Act 2006.*
**53B. Equality Act 2006** Section 6 of the Equality Act 2006.
**53C.** Paragraph 5 of Schedule 22 to the National Health Service Act 2006.
**53D.** Section 56(2) of the Postal Services Act 2011.
**53E.** Sections 34(2) and 35 of the Legal Aid, Sentencing and Punishment of Offenders Act 2012.

# Female Genital Mutilation Act 2003[1]

(2003 c 31)

**7.8876 1. Offence of female genital mutilation** (1) A person is guilty of an offence if he excises, infibulates or otherwise mutilates the whole or any part of a girl's labia majora, labia minora or clitoris.

(2) But no offence is committed by an approved person who performs—

(*a*) a surgical operation on a girl which is necessary for her physical or mental health, or

(*b*) a surgical operation on a girl who is in any stage of labour, or has just given birth, for purposes connected with the labour or birth.

(3) The following are approved persons—

(*a*) in relation to an operation falling within subsection (2)(*a*), a registered medical practitioner,

(*b*) in relation to an operation falling within subsection (2)(*b*), a registered medical practitioner, a registered midwife or a person undergoing a course of training with a view to becoming such a practitioner or midwife.

(4) There is also no offence committed by a person who—

(*a*) performs a surgical operation falling within subsection (2)(*a*) or (*b*) outside the United Kingdom, and

(*b*) in relation to such an operation exercises functions corresponding to those of an approved person.

(5) For the purpose of determining whether an operation is necessary for the mental health of a girl it is immaterial whether she or any other person believes that the operation is required as a matter of custom or ritual.

[Female Genital Mutilation Act 2003, s 1.]

1 This Act restates in amended form the law relating to female genital mutilation. The whole of the Act came into force on 3 March 2004 (see the Female Genital Mutilation Act 2003 (Commencement) Order 2004, SI 2004/286)

**7.8877 2. Offence of assisting a girl to mutilate her own genitalia** A person is guilty of an offence if he aids, abets, counsels or procures a girl to excise, infibulate or otherwise mutilate the whole or any part of her own labia majora, labia minora or clitoris.

[Female Genital Mutilation Act 2003, s 2.]

**7.8878 3. Offence of assisting a non-UK person to mutilate overseas a girl's genitalia** (1) A person is guilty of an offence if he aids, abets, counsels or procures a person who is not a United Kingdom national or United Kingdom resident to do a relevant act of female genital mutilation outside the United Kingdom.

(2) An act is a relevant act of female genital mutilation if—

(*a*) it is done in relation to a United Kingdom national or United Kingdom resident, and

(*b*) it would, if done by such a person, constitute an offence under section 1.

(3) But no offence is committed if the relevant act of female genital mutilation—

(*a*) is a surgical operation falling within section 1(2)(*a*) or (*b*), and

(*b*) is performed by a person who, in relation to such an operation, is an approved person or exercises functions corresponding to those of an approved person.

[Female Genital Mutilation Act 2003, s 3 as amended by the Serious Crime Act 2015, s 70.]

**7.8878A 3A. Offence of failing to protect girl from risk of genital mutilation** (1) If a genital mutilation offence is committed against a girl under the age of 16, each person who is responsible for the girl at the relevant time is guilty of an offence.

This is subject to subsection (5).

(2) For the purposes of this section a person is "responsible" for a girl in the following two cases.

(3) The first case is where the person—

(*a*) has parental responsibility for the girl, and
(*b*) has frequent contact with her.
(4) The second case is where the person—
(*a*) is aged 18 or over, and
(*b*) has assumed (and not relinquished) responsibility for caring for the girl in the manner of a parent.
(5) It is a defence for the defendant to show that—
(*a*) at the relevant time, the defendant did not think that there was a significant risk of a genital mutilation offence being committed against the girl, and could not reasonably have been expected to be aware that there was any such risk, or
(*b*) the defendant took such steps as he or she could reasonably have been expected to take to protect the girl from being the victim of a genital mutilation offence.
(6) A person is taken to have shown the fact mentioned in subsection (5)(*a*) or (*b*) if—
(*a*) sufficient evidence of the fact is adduced to raise an issue with respect to it, and
(*b*) the contrary is not proved beyond reasonable doubt.
(7) For the purposes of subsection (3)(*b*), where a person has frequent contact with a girl which is interrupted by her going to stay somewhere temporarily, that contact is treated as continuing during her stay there.
(8) In this section—
"genital mutilation offence" means an offence under section 1, 2 or 3 (and for the purposes of subsection (1) the prosecution does not have to prove which section it is);
"parental responsibility"—
(*a*) in England Wales, has the same meaning as in the Children Act 1989;
(*b*) in Northern Ireland, has the same meaning as in the Children (Northern Ireland) Order 1995 (SI 1995/755 (NI 2));
"the relevant time" means the time when the mutilation takes place.
[Female Genital Mutilation Act 2003, s 3A as inserted by the Serious Crime Act 2015, s 72.]

**7.8879 4. Extension of sections 1 to 3A to extra-territorial acts or omissions**
(1) Sections 1 to 3 extend to any act done outside the United Kingdom by a United Kingdom national or United Kingdom resident.
(1A) An offence under section 3A can be committed wholly or partly outside the United Kingdom by a person who is a United Kingdom national or a United Kingdom resident.
(2) If an offence under this Act is committed outside the United Kingdom—
(*a*) proceedings may be taken, and
(*b*) the offence may for incidental purposes be treated as having been committed,
in any place in England and Wales or Northern Ireland.
[Female Genital Mutilation Act 2003, s 4 as amended by the Serious Crime Act 2015, ss 70, 72.]

**8.8879A 4A. Anonymity of victims** Schedule 1 provides for the anonymity of persons against whom a female genital mutilation offence (as defined in that Schedule) is alleged to have been committed.
[Female Genital Mutilation Act 2003, s 4A as inserted by the Serious Crime Act 2015, s 71.]

**7.8880 5. Penalties for offences** (1) A person guilty of an offence under section 1, 2 or 3 is liable—
(*a*) on conviction on indictment[1], to imprisonment for a term not exceeding 14 years or a fine (or both),
(*b*) on summary conviction, to imprisonment for a term not exceeding six months or a fine not exceeding the statutory maximum (or both).
(2) A person guilty of an offence under section 3A is liable—
(*a*) on conviction on indictment, to imprisonment for a term not exceeding seven years or a fine (or both),
(*b*) on summary conviction in England and Wales, to imprisonment for a term not exceeding 12 months or a fine (or both),
(*c*) on summary conviction in Northern Ireland, to imprisonment for a term not exceeding 6 months or a fine not exceeding the statutory maximum (or both).
[Female Genital Mutilation Act 2003, s 5 as amended by the Serious Crime Act 2015, s 72.]

1 For procedure in respect of offences triable either way see the Magistrates' Courts' Act 1980, s 17A–21 in PART *I*: MAGISTRATES' COURTS, PROCEDURE, ante.

**7.8880A 5A. Female genital mutilation protection orders** (1) Schedule 2 provides for the making of female genital mutilation protection orders.
(2) In that Schedule—
(*a*) Part 1 makes provision about powers of courts in England and Wales to make female genital mutilation protection orders;
(*b*) Part 2 makes provision about powers of courts in Northern Ireland to make such orders.
[Female Genital Mutilation Act 2003, s 5A as inserted by the Serious Crime Act 2015, s 73.]

**7.8880B 5B. Duty to notify police of female genital mutilation** (1) A person who works in a regulated profession in England and Wales must make a notification under this section (an "FGM notification") if, in the course of his or her work in the profession, the person discovers that an act of female genital mutilation appears to have been carried out on a girl who is aged under 18.

(2) For the purposes of this section—

(*a*) a person works in a "regulated profession" if the person is—

(i) a healthcare professional,

(ii) a teacher, or

(iii) a social care worker in Wales;

(*b*) a person "discovers" that an act of female genital mutilation appears to have been carried out on a girl in either of the following two cases.

(3) The first case is where the girl informs the person that an act of female genital mutilation (however described) has been carried out on her.

(4) The second case is where—

(*a*) the person observes physical signs on the girl appearing to show that an act of female genital mutilation has been carried out on her, and

(*b*) the person has no reason to believe that the act was, or was part of, a surgical operation within section 1(2)(*a*) or (*b*).

(5) An FGM notification—

(*a*) is to be made to the chief officer of police for the area in which the girl resides;

(*b*) must identify the girl and explain why the notification is made;

(*c*) must be made before the end of one month from the time when the person making the notification first discovers that an act of female genital mutilation appears to have been carried out on the girl;

(*d*) may be made orally or in writing.

(6) The duty of a person working in a particular regulated profession to make an FGM notification does not apply if the person has reason to believe that another person working in that profession has previously made an FGM notification in connection with the same act of female genital mutilation.

For this purpose, all persons falling within subsection (2)(*a*)(i) are to be treated as working in the same regulated profession.

(7) A disclosure made in an FGM notification does not breach—

(*a*) any obligation of confidence owed by the person making the disclosure, or

(*b*) any other restriction on the disclosure of information.

(8) The Secretary of State may by regulations amend this section for the purpose of adding, removing or otherwise altering the descriptions of persons regarded as working in a "regulated profession" for the purposes of this section.

(9) The power to make regulations under this section—

(*a*) is exercisable by statutory instrument;

(*b*) includes power to make consequential, transitional, transitory or saving provision.

(10) A statutory instrument containing regulations under this section is not to be made unless a draft of the instrument has been laid before, and approved by a resolution of, each House of Parliament.

(11) In this section—

"act of female genital mutilation" means an act of a kind mentioned in section 1(1);

"healthcare professional" means a person registered with any of the regulatory bodies mentioned in section 25(3) of the National Health Service Reform and Health Care Professions Act 2002 (bodies within remit of the Professional Standards Authority for Health and Social Care);

"registered", in relation to a regulatory body, means registered in a register that the body maintains by virtue of any enactment;

"social care worker" means a person registered in a register maintained by the Care Council for Wales under section 56 of the Care Standards Act 2000;

"teacher" means—

(*a*) in relation to England, a person within section 141A(1) of the Education Act 2002 (persons employed or engaged to carry out teaching work at schools and other institutions in England);

(*b*) in relation to Wales, a person who falls within a category listed in the table in paragraph 1 of Schedule 2 to the Education (Wales) Act 2014 (anaw 5) (categories of registration for purposes of Part 2 of that Act) or any other person employed or engaged as a teacher at a school (within the meaning of the Education Act 1996) in Wales.

(12) For the purposes of the definition of "healthcare professional", the following provisions of section 25 of the National Health Service Reform and Health Care Professions Act 2002 are to be ignored—

(*a*) paragraph (*g*) of subsection (3);

(*b*) subsection (3A).

[Female Genital Mutilation Act 2003, s 5B as inserted by the Serious Crime Act 2015, s 74.]

**7.8880C 5C. Guidance** (1) The Secretary of State may issue guidance to whatever persons in England and Wales the Secretary of State considers appropriate about—

(*a*) the effect of any provision of this Act, or

(*b*) other matters relating to female genital mutilation.

(2) A person exercising public functions to whom guidance is given under this section must have regard to it in the exercise of those functions.

(3) Nothing in this section permits the Secretary of State to give guidance to any court or tribunal.

(4) Before issuing guidance under this section the Secretary of State must consult—

(*a*) the Welsh Ministers so far as the guidance is to a body exercising devolved Welsh functions;

(*b*) any person whom the Secretary of State considers appropriate.

(5) A body is exercising "devolved Welsh functions" if its functions are exercisable only in or as regards Wales and are wholly or mainly functions relating to—

(*a*) a matter in respect of which functions are exercisable by the Welsh Ministers, the First Minister for Wales or the Counsel General to the Welsh Government, or

(*b*) a matter within the legislative competence of the National Assembly for Wales.

(6) The Secretary of State may from time to time revise any guidance issued under this section.

(7) Subsections (2) and (3) have effect in relation to any revised guidance.

(8) Subsection (4) has effect in relation to any revised guidance unless the Secretary of State considers the proposed revisions of the guidance are insubstantial.

(9) The Secretary of State must publish the current version of any guidance issued under this section.

[Female Genital Mutilation Act 2003, s 5C as inserted by the Serious Crime Act 2015, s 75.]

**7.8881 6. Definitions** (1) Girl includes woman.

(2) A United Kingdom national is an individual who is—

(*a*) a British citizen, a British overseas territories citizen, a British National (Overseas) or a British Overseas citizen,

(*b*) a person who under the British Nationality Act 1981 (c 61) is a British subject, or

(*c*) a British protected person within the meaning of that Act.

(3) A United Kingdom resident is an individual who is habitually resident in the United Kingdom.

(4) This section has effect for the purposes of this Act.

[Female Genital Mutilation Act 2003, s 6 as amended by the Serious Crime Act 2015, s 70.]

**7.8882 7. Consequential provision** (1) The Prohibition of Female Circumcision Act 1985 (c 38) ceases to have effect.

(2) *Amends the Visiting Forces Act 1952, Schedule.*

[Female Genital Mutilation Act 2003, s 7.]

**7.8883 8. Short title, commencement, extent and general saving** (1) This Act may be cited as the Female Genital Mutilation Act 2003.

(2) This Act comes into force on such day as the Secretary of State may by order made by statutory instrument appoint.

(3) An order under subsection (2) may include transitional or saving provisions.

(4) This Act does not extend to Scotland and sections 5B and 5C do not extend to Northern Ireland.

(5) Nothing in this Act affects any criminal liability arising apart from this Act.

[Female Genital Mutilation Act 2003, s 8 as amended by the Serious Crime Act 2015, Sch 4.]

## SCHEDULE 1
Anonymity of Victims

(*As inserted by the Serious Crime Act 2015, s 71*)

***Prohibition on the identification of victims in publications***

1. (1) This paragraph applies where an allegation has been made that a female genital mutilation offence has been committed against a person.

(2) No matter likely to lead members of the public to identify the person, as the person against whom the offence is alleged to have been committed, may be included in any publication during the person's lifetime.

(3) For the purposes of this Schedule, any consent of the person to an act giving rise to the alleged offence is not to be taken as preventing that person from being regarded as a person against whom the alleged offence was committed.

(4) In any criminal proceedings before a court, the court may direct that the restriction imposed by sub-paragraph (2) is not to apply (whether at all in England and Wales and Northern Ireland, or to the extent specified in the direction) if the court is satisfied that either of the following conditions is met.

(5) The first condition is that the conduct of a person's defence at a trial of a female genital mutilation offence would be substantially prejudiced if the direction was not given.

(6) The second condition is that—

(*a*) the effect of sub-paragraph (2) is to impose a substantial and unreasonable restriction on the reporting of the proceedings, and

(*b*) it is in the public interest to remove or relax the restriction.

(7) A direction under sub-paragraph (4) does not affect the operation of sub-paragraph (2) at any time

before the direction is given.

(8) In this paragraph "the court" means—

(*a*) in England and Wales, a magistrates' court or the Crown Court;

(*b*) in Northern Ireland, a magistrates' court, a county court or the Crown Court.

***Penalty for breaching prohibition imposed by paragraph 1(2)***

**2.** (1) If anything is included in a publication in contravention of the prohibition imposed by paragraph 1(2), each of the persons responsible for the publication is guilty of an offence.

(2) A person guilty of an offence under this paragraph is liable—

(*a*) on summary conviction in England and Wales, to a fine;

(*b*) on summary conviction in Northern Ireland, to a fine not exceeding level 5 on the standard scale.

(3) The persons responsible for a publication are as follows—

| *Type of publication* | *Persons responsible* |
|---|---|
| Newspaper or other periodical | Any person who is a proprietor, editor or publisher of the newspaper or periodical. |
| Relevant programme | Any person who—<br>(*a*) is a body corporate engaged in providing the programme service in which the programme is included, or<br>(*b*) has functions in relation to the programme corresponding to those of an editor of a newspaper. |
| Any other kind of publication | Any person who publishes the publication. |

(4) If an offence under this paragraph is proved to have been committed with the consent or connivance of, or to be attributable to any neglect on the part of—

(*a*) a senior officer of a body corporate, or

(*b*) a person purporting to act in such a capacity,

the senior officer or person (as well as the body corporate) is guilty of the offence and liable to be proceeded against and punished accordingly.

(5) "Senior officer", in relation to a body corporate, means a director, manager, secretary or other similar officer of the body corporate; and for this purpose "director", in relation to a body corporate whose affairs are managed by its members, means a member of the body corporate.

(6) Proceedings for an offence under this paragraph—

(*a*) if alleged to have been committed in England and Wales, may not be instituted except by, or with the consent of, the Attorney General;

(*b*) if alleged to have been committed in Northern Ireland, may not be instituted except by, or with the consent of, the Director of Public Prosecutions for Northern Ireland.

***Offence under paragraph 2: defences***

**3.** (1) This paragraph applies where a person ("the defendant") is charged with an offence under paragraph 2 as a result of the inclusion of any matter in a publication.

(2) It is a defence for the defendant to prove that at the time of the alleged offence, the defendant was not aware, and did not suspect or have reason to suspect, that—

(*a*) the publication included the matter in question, or

(*b*) the allegation in question had been made.

(3) It is a defence for the defendant to prove that the publication in which the matter appeared was one in respect of which the victim had given written consent to the appearance of matter of that description.

(4) The defence in sub-paragraph (3) is not available if—

(*a*) the victim was under the age of 16 at the time when her consent was given, or

(*b*) a person interfered unreasonably with the peace and comfort of the victim with a view to obtaining her consent.

(5) In this paragraph "the victim" means the person against whom the female genital mutilation offence in question is alleged to have been committed.

***Special rules for providers of information society services***

**4.** (1) Paragraph 2 applies to a domestic service provider who, in the course of providing information society services, publishes prohibited matter in an EEA state other than the United Kingdom (as well as to a person, of any description, who publishes prohibited matter in England and Wales or Northern Ireland).

(2) Proceedings for an offence under paragraph 2, as it applies to a domestic service provider by virtue of sub-paragraph (1), may be taken at any place in England and Wales or Northern Ireland.

(3) Nothing in this paragraph affects the operation of any of paragraphs 6 to 8.

**5.** (1) Proceedings for an offence under paragraph 2 may not be taken against a non-UK service provider in respect of anything done in the course of the provision of information society services unless the derogation condition is met.

(2) The derogation condition is that taking proceedings—

(*a*) is necessary for the purposes of the public interest objective,

(*b*) relates to an information society service that prejudices that objective or presents a serious and grave risk of prejudice to that objective, and

(*c*) is proportionate to that objective.

(3) "The public interest objective" means the pursuit of public policy.

**6.** (1) A service provider does not commit an offence under paragraph 2 by providing access to a communication network or by transmitting, in a communication network, information provided by a recipient of the service, if the service provider does not—

(*a*) initiate the transmission,

(*b*) select the recipient of the transmission, or

(*c*) select or modify the information contained in the transmission.

(2) For the purposes of sub-paragraph (1)—

(*a*) providing access to a communication network, and

(*b*) transmitting information in a communication network,

include the automatic, intermediate and transient storage of the information transmitted so far as the storage is solely for the purpose of carrying out the transmission in the network.

(3) Sub-paragraph (2) does not apply if the information is stored for longer than is reasonably necessary for the transmission.

7. (1) A service provider does not commit an offence under paragraph 2 by storing information provided by a recipient of the service for transmission in a communication network if the first and second conditions are met.

(2) The first condition is that the storage of the information—

(*a*) is automatic, intermediate and temporary, and

(*b*) is solely for the purpose of making more efficient the onward transmission of the information to other recipients of the service at their request.

(3) The second condition is that the service provider—

(*a*) does not modify the information,

(*b*) complies with any conditions attached to having access to the information, and

(*c*) if sub-paragraph (4) applies, promptly removes the information or disables access to it.

(4) This sub-paragraph applies if the service provider obtains actual knowledge that—

(*a*) the information at the initial source of the transmission has been removed from the network,

(*b*) access to it has been disabled, or

(*c*) a court or administrative authority has ordered the removal from the network of, or the disablement of access to, the information.

**8.** (1) A service provider does not commit an offence under paragraph 2 by storing information provided by a recipient of the service if—

(*a*) the service provider had no actual knowledge when the information was provided that it was, or contained, a prohibited publication, or

(*b*) on obtaining actual knowledge that the information was, or contained, a prohibited publication, the service provider promptly removed the information or disabled access to it.

(2) Sub-paragraph (1) does not apply if the recipient of the service is acting under the authority or control of the service provider.

### *Interpretation*

**9.** (1) In this Schedule—

"domestic service provider" means a service provider established in England and Wales or Northern Ireland;

"the E-Commerce Directive" means Directive 2000/31/EC of the European Parliament and of the Council of 8 June 2000 on certain legal aspects of information society services, in particular electronic commerce, in the Internal Market (Directive on electronic commerce);

"female genital mutilation offence" means—

(*a*) an offence under section 1, 2, 3 or 3A;

(*b*) an offence of attempt or conspiracy to commit any such offence;

(*c*) an offence under Part 2 of the Serious Crime Act 2007 (encouraging or assisting crime) in relation to any such offence;

"information society services"—

(*a*) has the meaning given in Article 2(a) of the E-Commerce Directive (which refers to Article 1(2) of Directive 98/34/EC of the European Parliament and of the Council of 22 June 1998 laying down a procedure for the provision of information in the field of technical standards and regulations), and

(*b*) is summarised in recital 17 of the E-Commerce Directive as covering "any service normally provided for remuneration, at a distance, by means of electronic equipment for the processing (including digital compression) and storage of data, and at the individual request of a recipient of a service";

"non-UK service provider" means a service provider established in an EEA state other than the United Kingdom;

"programme service" has the same meaning as in the Broadcasting Act 1990 (see section 201(1) of that Act);

"prohibited material" means any material the publication of which contravenes paragraph 1(2);

"publication" includes any speech, writing, relevant programme or other communication (in whatever form) which is addressed to, or is accessible by, the public at large or any section of the public;

"recipient", in relation to a service, means a person who, for professional ends or otherwise, uses an information society service, in particular for the purposes of seeking information or making it accessible;

"relevant programme" means a programme included in a programme service;

"service provider" means a person providing an information society service.

(2) For the purposes of the definition of "publication" in sub-paragraph (1)—

(*a*) an indictment or other document prepared for use in particular legal proceedings is not to be taken as coming within the definition;

(*b*) every relevant programme is to be taken as addressed to the public at large or to a section of the public.

(3) For the purposes of the definitions of "domestic service provider" and "non-UK service provider" in sub-paragraph (1)—

(*a*) a service provider is established in a particular part of the United Kingdom, or in a particular EEA state, if the service provider—

(i) effectively pursues an economic activity using a fixed establishment in that part of the United Kingdom, or that EEA state, for an indefinite period, and

(ii) is a national of an EEA state or a company or firm mentioned in Article 54 of the Treaty on the Functioning of the European Union;

(*b*) the presence or use in a particular place of equipment or other technical means of providing an information society service does not, of itself, constitute the establishment of a service provider;

(*c*) where it cannot be determined from which of a number of establishments a given information society service is provided, that service is to be regarded as provided from the establishment at the centre of the service provider's activities relating to that service.

## SCHEDULE 2

Female Genital Mutilation Protection Orders

(*As inserted by the Serious Crime Act 2015, s 73*)

## PART 1

## ENGLAND AND WALES

**Power to make FGM protection order**

1. (1) The court in England and Wales may make an order (an "FGM protection order") for the purposes of—

(*a*) protecting a girl against the commission of a genital mutilation offence, or

(*b*) protecting a girl against whom any such offence has been committed.

(2) In deciding whether to exercise its powers under this paragraph and, if so, in what manner, the court must have regard to all the circumstances, including the need to secure the health, safety and well-being of the girl to be protected.

(3) An FGM protection order may contain—

(*a*) such prohibitions, restrictions or requirements, and

(*b*) such other terms,

as the court considers appropriate for the purposes of the order.

(4) The terms of an FGM protection order may, in particular, relate to—

(*a*) conduct outside England and Wales as well as (or instead of) conduct within England and Wales;

(*b*) respondents who are, or may become, involved in other respects as well as (or instead of) respondents who commit or attempt to commit, or may commit or attempt to commit, a genital mutilation offence against a girl;

(*c*) other persons who are, or may become, involved in other respects as well as respondents of any kind.

(5) For the purposes of sub-paragraph (4) examples of involvement in other respects are—

(*a*) aiding, abetting, counselling, procuring, encouraging or assisting another person to commit, or attempt to commit, a genital mutilation offence against a girl;

(*b*) conspiring to commit, or to attempt to commit, such an offence.

(6) An FGM protection order may be made for a specified period or until varied or discharged (see paragraph 6).

**Applications and other occasions for making orders**

2. (1) The court may make an FGM protection order—

(*a*) on an application being made to it, or

(*b*) without an application being made to it but in the circumstances mentioned in sub-paragraph (6).

(2) An application may be made by—

(*a*) the girl who is to be protected by the order, or

(*b*) a relevant third party.

(3) An application may be made by any other person with the leave of the court.

(4) In deciding whether to grant leave, the court must have regard to all the circumstances including—

(*a*) the applicant's connection with the girl to be protected;

(*b*) the applicant's knowledge of the circumstances of the girl.

(5) An application under this paragraph may be made in other family proceedings or without any other family proceedings being instituted.

(6) The circumstances in which the court may make an order without an application being made are where—

(*a*) any other family proceedings are before the court ("the current proceedings"),

(*b*) the court considers that an FGM protection order should be made to protect a girl (whether or not a party to the proceedings), and

(*c*) a person who would be a respondent to any proceedings for an FGM protection order is a party to the current proceedings.

(7) In this paragraph—

"family proceedings" has the same meaning as in Part 4 of the Family Law Act 1996 (see section 63(1) and (2) of that Act), but also includes—

(*a*) proceedings under the inherent jurisdiction of the High Court in relation to adults,

(*b*) proceedings in which the court has made an emergency protection order under section 44 of the Children Act 1989 which includes an exclusion requirement (as defined in sec tion 44A(3) of that Act), and

(*c*) proceedings in which the court has made an order under section 50 of the Children Act 1989 (recovery of abducted children etc);

"relevant third party" means a person specified, or falling within a description of persons specified, by regulations[1] made by the Lord Chancellor (and such regulations may, in particular, specify the Secretary of State).

(8) Regulations under sub-paragraph (7) are to be made by statutory instrument, and any such instrument is subject to annulment in pursuance of a resolution of either House of Parliament.

---

[1] The Female Genital Mutilation Order (Relevant Third Party) Regulations 2015, SI 2015/1422 have been made which specify local authorities as a 'relevant third party'.

**Power to make order in criminal proceedings**

3. The court before which there are criminal proceedings in England and Wales for a genital mutilation offence may make an FGM protection order (without an application being made to it) if—

(*a*) the court considers that an FGM protection order should be made to protect a girl (whether or not the victim of the offence in relation to the criminal proceedings), and

(*b*) a person who would be a respondent to any proceedings for an FGM protection order is a defendant in the criminal proceedings.

**Offence of breaching order**

**4.** (1) A person who without reasonable excuse does anything that the person is prohibited from doing by an FGM protection order is guilty of an offence.

(2) In the case of an FGM protection order made by virtue of paragraph 5(1), a person can be guilty of an offence under this paragraph only in respect of conduct engaged in at a time when the person was aware of the existence of the order.

(3) Where a person is convicted of an offence under this paragraph in respect of any conduct, the conduct is not punishable as a contempt of court.

(4) A person cannot be convicted of an offence under this paragraph in respect of any conduct which has been punished as a contempt of court.

(5) A person guilty of an offence under this paragraph is liable—

(*a*) on conviction on indictment, to imprisonment for a term not exceeding five years, or a fine, or both;

(*b*) on summary conviction, to imprisonment for a term not exceeding 12 months, or a fine, or both.

(6) A reference in any enactment to proceedings under this Part of this Schedule, or to an order under this Part of this Schedule, does not include a reference to proceedings for an offence under this paragraph or to an order made in proceedings for such an offence.

(7) "Enactment" includes an enactment contained in subordinate legislation within the meaning of the Interpretation Act 1978.

**Ex parte orders**

**5.** (1) The court may, in any case where it is just and convenient to do so, make an FGM protection order even though the respondent has not been given such notice of the proceedings as would otherwise be required by rules of court.

(2) In deciding whether to exercise its powers under sub-paragraph (1), the court must have regard to all the circumstances including—

(*a*) the risk to the girl, or to another person, of becoming a victim of a genital mutilation offence if the order is not made immediately,

(*b*) whether it is likely that an applicant will be deterred or prevented from pursuing an application if an order is not made immediately, and

(*c*) whether there is reason to believe that—

(i) the respondent is aware of the proceedings but is deliberately evading service, and

(ii) the delay involved in effecting substituted service will cause serious prejudice to the girl to be protected or (if different) an applicant.

(3) The court must give the respondent an opportunity to make representations about an order made by virtue of sub-paragraph (1).

(4) The opportunity must be—

(*a*) as soon as just and convenient, and

(*b*) at a hearing of which notice has been given to all the parties in accordance with rules of court.

**Variation and discharge of orders**

**6.** (1) The court may vary or discharge an FGM protection order on an application by—

(*a*) any party to the proceedings for the order,

(*b*) the girl being protected by the order (if not a party to the proceedings for the order), or

(*c*) any person affected by the order.

(2) In the case of an order made in criminal proceedings under paragraph 3, the reference in sub-paragraph (1)(*a*) to a party to the proceedings for the order is to be read as a reference to the prosecution and the defendant.

(3) In addition, the court may vary or discharge an FGM protection order made by virtue of paragraph 2(1)(*b*) or 3 even though no application under sub-paragraph (1) above has been made to the court.

(4) Paragraph 5 applies to a variation of an FGM protection order as it applies to the making of such an order (and references in that paragraph to the making of an FGM protection order are to be read accordingly).

**Arrest under warrant**

**7.** (1) An interested party may apply to the relevant judge for the issue of a warrant for the arrest of a person if the interested party considers that the person has failed to comply with an FGM protection order or is otherwise in contempt of court in relation to such an order.

(2) The relevant judge must not issue a warrant on an application under sub-paragraph (1) unless—

(*a*) the application is substantiated on oath, and

(*b*) the relevant judge has reasonable grounds for believing that the person to be arrested has failed to comply with the order or is otherwise in contempt of court in relation to the order.

(3) In this paragraph "interested party", in relation to an FGM protection order, means—

(*a*) the girl being protected by the order,

(*b*) (if a different person) the person who applied for the order, or

(*c*) any other person;

but no application may be made under sub-paragraph (1) by a person falling within paragraph (*c*) without leave of the relevant judge.

**Remand: general**

**8.** (1) The court before which an arrested person is brought by virtue of a warrant under paragraph 7 may, if the matter is not then disposed of immediately, remand the person concerned.

(2) Paragraphs 9 to 14 contain further provision about the powers of a court to remand under this paragraph.

(3) Sub-paragraph (4) applies if a person remanded under this paragraph is granted bail under paragraphs 10 to 14.

(4) The person may be required by the relevant judge to comply, before release on bail or later, with such requirements as appear to the judge to be necessary to secure that the person does not interfere with witnesses or otherwise obstruct the course of justice.

**Remand: medical examination and report**

**9.** (1) Any power to remand a person under paragraph 8(1) may be exercised for the purpose of enabling a medical examination and report to be made if the relevant judge has reason to consider that a medical report will be required.

(2) If such a power is so exercised, the adjournment must not be for more than four weeks at a time unless the relevant judge remands the accused in custody.

(3) If the relevant judge remands the accused in custody, the adjournment must not be for more than three

weeks at a time.

(4) Sub-paragraph (5) applies if there is reason to suspect that a person who has been arrested under a warrant issued on an application under paragraph 7(1) is suffering from mental disorder within the meaning of the Mental Health Act 1983.

(5) The relevant judge has the same power to make an order under section 35 of the Mental Health Act 1983 (remand for report on accused's mental condition) as the Crown Court has under section 35 of that Act in the case of an accused person within the meaning of that section.

**Remand: further provision**

**10.** (1) Where a court has power to remand a person under paragraph 8, the court may remand the person in custody or on bail.

(2) If remanded in custody, the person is to be committed to custody to be brought before the court—

(*a*) at the end of the period of remand, or

(*b*) at such earlier time as the court may require.

(3) The court may remand a person on bail—

(*a*) by taking from the person a recognizance (with or without sureties) conditioned as provided in paragraph 11, or

(*b*) by fixing the amount of the recognizances with a view to their being taken subsequently in accordance with paragraph 14 and, in the meantime, committing the person to custody as mentioned in sub-paragraph (2) above.

(4) Where a person is brought before the court after remand the court may further remand the person.

(5) In this paragraph and in paragraphs 11 to 14, references to "the court" includes a reference to a judge of the court or, in the case of proceedings in a magistrates' court, a justice of the peace.

**11.** (1) Where a person is remanded on bail, the court may direct that the person's recognizance be conditioned for his or her appearance—

(*a*) before the court at the end of the period of remand, or

(*b*) at every time and place to which during the course of the proceedings the hearing may from time to time be adjourned.

(2) Where a recognizance is conditioned for a person's appearance as mentioned in sub-paragraph (1), the fixing of any time for the person next to appear is to be treated as a remand.

(3) Nothing in this paragraph deprives the court of power at any subsequent hearing to remand a person afresh.

**12.** (1) The court may not remand a person for a period exceeding 8 clear days unless—

(*a*) the court adjourns a case under paragraph 9(1), or

(*b*) the person is remanded on bail and both that person and the other party to the proceedings (or, in the case of criminal proceedings, the prosecution) consent.

(2) If sub-paragraph (1)(*a*) applies, the person may be remanded for the period of the adjournment.

(3) Where the court has power to remand a person in custody, the person may be committed to the custody of a constable if the remand is for a period not exceeding 3 clear days.

**13.** (1) If the court is satisfied that a person who has been remanded is unable by reason of illness or accident to appear before the court at the end of the period of remand, the court may further remand the person in his or her absence.

(2) The power in sub-paragraph (1) may, in the case of a person who was remanded on bail, be exercised by enlarging the person's recognizance and those of any sureties to a later time.

(3) Where a person remanded on bail is bound to appear before the court at any time and the court has no power to remand the person under sub-paragraph (1), the court may, in the person's absence, enlarge the person's recognizance and those of any sureties for the person to a later time.

(4) The enlargement of a person's recognizance is to be treated as a further remand.

(5) Paragraph 12(1) (limit of remand) does not apply to the exercise of the powers conferred by this paragraph.

**14.** (1) This paragraph applies where under paragraph 10(3)(*b*) the court fixes the amount in which the principal and the sureties (if any) are to be bound.

(2) The recognizance may afterwards be taken by a person prescribed by rules of court (with the same consequences as if it had been entered into before the court).

**Contempt proceedings**

**15.** The powers of the court in relation to contempt of court arising out of a person's failure to comply with an FGM protection order, or otherwise in connection with such an order, may be exercised by the relevant judge.

**Other protection or assistance against female genital mutilation**

**16.** (1) Nothing in this Part of this Schedule affects any other protection or assistance available to a girl who is or may become the victim of a genital mutilation offence.

(2) In particular, it does not affect—

(*a*) the inherent jurisdiction of the High Court;

(*b*) any criminal liability;

(*c*) any civil remedies under the Protection from Harassment Act 1997;

(*d*) any right to an occupation order or a non-molestation order under Part 4 of the Family Law Act 1996;

(*e*) any right to a forced marriage protection order under Part 4A of that Act;

(*f*) any protection or assistance under the Children Act 1989;

(*g*) any claim in tort.

**Interpretation**

**17.** (1) In this Part of this Schedule—

"the court", except as provided in sub-paragraph (2), means the High Court, or the family court, in England and Wales;

"FGM protection order" means an order under paragraph 1;

"genital mutilation offence" means an offence under section 1, 2 or 3;

"the relevant judge", in relation to an FGM protection order, means—

(*a*) where the order was made by the High Court, a judge of that court;

(*b*) where the order was made by the family court, a judge of that court;

(*c*) where the order was made by a court in criminal proceedings under paragraph 3—

(i) a judge of that court, or

(ii) a judge of the High Court or of the family court.

(2) Where the power to make an FGM protection order is exercisable by a court in criminal proceedings under paragraph 3, references in this Part of this Schedule to "the court" (other than in paragraph 2) are to be read as references to that court.

(3) In paragraph (*c*)(i) of the definition of "relevant judge" in sub-paragraph (1), the reference to a judge of the court that made the order includes, in the case of criminal proceedings in a magistrates' court, a reference to a justice of the peace.

PART 2

NORTHERN IRELAND

**Power to make FGM protection order**

# Terrorism Act 2006[1]

(2006 c 11)

## PART 1

## OFFENCES

*Encouragement etc of terrorism*

7.8884 **1. Encouragement of terrorism** (1) This section applies to a statement that is likely to be understood by some or all of the members of the public to whom it is published as a direct or indirect encouragement or other inducement to them to the commission, preparation or instigation of acts of terrorism or Convention offences.

(2) A person commits an offence if—

(*a*) he publishes a statement to which this section applies or causes another to publish such a statement; and

(*b*) at the time he publishes it or causes it to be published, he—

(i) intends members of the public to be directly or indirectly encouraged or otherwise induced by the statement to commit, prepare or instigate acts of terrorism or Convention offences; or

(ii) is reckless as to whether members of the public will be directly or indirectly encouraged or otherwise induced by the statement to commit, prepare or instigate such acts or offences.

(3) For the purposes of this section, the statements that are likely to be understood by members of the public as indirectly encouraging the commission or preparation of acts of terrorism or Convention offences include every statement which—

(*a*) glorifies the commission or preparation (whether in the past, in the future or generally) of such acts or offences; and

(*b*) is a statement from which those members of the public could reasonably be expected to infer that what is being glorified is being glorified as conduct that should be emulated by them in existing circumstances.

(4) For the purposes of this section the questions how a statement is likely to be understood and what members of the public could reasonably be expected to infer from it must be determined having regard both—

(*a*) to the contents of the statement as a whole; and

(*b*) to the circumstances and manner of its publication.

(5) It is irrelevant for the purposes of subsections (1) to (3)—

(*a*) whether anything mentioned in those subsections relates to the commission, preparation or instigation of one or more particular acts of terrorism or Convention offences, of acts of terrorism or Convention offences of a particular description or of acts of terrorism or Convention offences generally; and,

(*b*) whether any person is in fact encouraged or induced by the statement to commit, prepare or instigate any such act or offence.

(6) In proceedings for an offence under this section against a person in whose case it is not proved that he intended the statement directly or indirectly to encourage or otherwise induce the commission, preparation or instigation of acts of terrorism or Convention offences, it is a defence for him to show—

(*a*) that the statement neither expressed his views nor had his endorsement (whether by virtue of section 3 or otherwise); and

(*b*) that it was clear, in all the circumstances of the statement's publication, that it did not express his views and (apart from the possibility of his having been given and failed to comply with a notice under subsection (3) of that section) did not have his endorsement.

(7) A person guilty of an offence under this section shall be liable—

(*a*) on conviction on indictment, to imprisonment for a term not exceeding 7 years or to a fine, or to both;

(*b*) on summary conviction in England and Wales, to imprisonment for a term not exceeding 12 months or to a fine not exceeding the statutory maximum, or to both;

(*c*) *Scotland, Northern Ireland.*

(8) In relation to an offence committed before the commencement of section 154(1) of the Criminal Justice Act 2003 (c 44), the reference in subsection (7)(*b*) to 12 months is to be read as a reference to 6 months.

[Terrorism Act 2006, s 1.]

[1] This Act, except s 39, is to be brought into force in accordance with orders made under s 39, post. At the date of press, the following orders had been made: (Commencement No 1) SI 2006/1013 which brought into force on 13 April 2006 ss 1 to 22, Sch 1; ss 26 to 36, Sch 2; ss 37(1) to (4) and 38; s 37(5) all of the entries in Sch 3 except those relating to paragraph 36(1) of Schedule 8 to the Terrorism Act 2000 and s 306(2) and (3) of the Criminal Justice Act 2003; (No 2) SI 2006/1936 which brought into force on 25 July 2006 ss 23 to 25; s 37(5) to the extent that it has not already been brought into force; Sch 3 relating to para 36(1) of Sch 8 to the Terrorism Act 2000 and s 306(2) and (3) of the Criminal Justice Act 2003.

The Electronic Commerce Directive (Terrorism Act 2006) Regulations 2007, SI 2007/1550 amended by SI 2012/1809 have been made which give effect to Directive 2000/31/EC. Offences in ss 1 and 2 of the Terrorism Act apply to UK established ISS providers where they provide information society services in EEA states other than the UK. Sections 3 and 4 of the Terrorism Act 2006 also apply in such a case. Regulation 3 does not apply where s 17 of the Terrorism Act 2006 (commission of offences abroad) already applies. By reg 4 service providers who are established in an EEA state other than the UK can only be prosecuted for an offence under ss 1 or 2 of the Terrorism Act, or given a notice under s 3, where the conditions laid down in Article 3(4) of the Directive are satisfied. Regulations 5 to 7 create exceptions from liability for the offences under ss 1 and 2 of the Terrorism Act 2006 for intermediary ISS providers when they provide mere conduit, caching or hosting services in the circumstances specified by Articles 12 to 14 of the Directive.

**7.8885 2. Dissemination of terrorist publications**[1] (1) A person commits an offence if he engages in conduct falling within subsection (2) and, at the time he does so—

(*a*) he intends an effect of his conduct to be a direct or indirect encouragement or other inducement to the commission, preparation or instigation of acts of terrorism;

(*b*) he intends an effect of his conduct to be the provision of assistance in the commission or preparation of such acts; or

(*c*) he is reckless as to whether his conduct has an effect mentioned in paragraph (*a*) or (*b*).

(2) For the purposes of this section a person engages in conduct falling within this subsection if he—

(*a*) distributes or circulates a terrorist publication;

(*b*) gives, sells or lends such a publication;

(*c*) offers such a publication for sale or loan;

(*d*) provides a service to others that enables them to obtain, read, listen to or look at such a publication, or to acquire it by means of a gift, sale or loan;

(*e*) transmits the contents of such a publication electronically; or

(*f*) has such a publication in his possession with a view to its becoming the subject of conduct falling within any of paragraphs (*a*) to (*e*).

(3) For the purposes of this section a publication is a terrorist publication, in relation to conduct falling within subsection (2), if matter contained in it is likely—

(*a*) to be understood, by some or all of the persons to whom it is or may become available as a consequence of that conduct, as a direct or indirect encouragement or other inducement to them to the commission, preparation or instigation of acts of terrorism[2]; or

(*b*) to be useful in the commission or preparation of such acts and to be understood, by some or all of those persons, as contained in the publication, or made available to them, wholly or mainly for the purpose of being so useful to them.

(4) For the purposes of this section matter that is likely to be understood by a person as indirectly encouraging the commission or preparation of acts of terrorism includes any matter which—

(*a*) glorifies the commission or preparation (whether in the past, in the future or generally) of such acts; and

(*b*) is matter from which that person could reasonably be expected to infer that what is being glorified is being glorified as conduct that should be emulated by him in existing circumstances.

(5) For the purposes of this section the question whether a publication is a terrorist publication in relation to particular conduct must be determined—

(*a*) as at the time of that conduct; and

(*b*) having regard both to the contents of the publication as a whole and to the circumstances in which that conduct occurs.

(6) In subsection (1) references to the effect of a person's conduct in relation to a terrorist publication include references to an effect of the publication on one or more persons to whom it is or may become available as a consequence of that conduct.

(7) It is irrelevant for the purposes of this section whether anything mentioned in subsections (1) to (4) is in relation to the commission, preparation or instigation of one or more particular acts of terrorism, of acts of terrorism of a particular description or of acts of terrorism generally.

(8) For the purposes of this section it is also irrelevant, in relation to matter contained in any article whether any person—

(*a*) is in fact encouraged or induced by that matter to commit, prepare or instigate acts of terrorism; or (*b*) in fact makes use of it in the commission or preparation of such acts.

(9) In proceedings for an offence under this section against a person in respect of conduct to which subsection (10) applies, it is a defence for him to show—

(*a*) that the matter by reference to which the publication in question was a terrorist publication neither expressed his views nor had his endorsement (whether by virtue of section 3 or otherwise); and

(*b*) that it was clear, in all the circumstances of the conduct, that that matter did not express his views and (apart from the possibility of his having been given and failed to comply with a notice under subsection (3) of that section) did not have his endorsement.

(10) This subsection applies to the conduct of a person to the extent that—

(*a*) the publication to which his conduct related contained matter by reference to which it was a terrorist publication by virtue of subsection (3)(*a*); and

(*b*) that person is not proved to have engaged in that conduct with the intention specified in subsection (1)(*a*).

(11) A person guilty of an offence under this section shall be liable—

(*a*) on conviction on indictment, to imprisonment for a term not exceeding 7 years or to a fine, or to both;

(*b*) on summary conviction in England and Wales, to imprisonment for a term not exceeding 12 months or to a fine not exceeding the statutory maximum, or to both[3];

(*c*) *Scotland, Northern Ireland.*

(12) In relation to an offence committed before the commencement of section 154(1) of the Criminal Justice Act 2003 (c 44), the reference in subsection (11)(*b*) to 12 months is to be read as a reference to 6 months.

(13) In this section—

"lend" includes let on hire, and "loan" is to be construed accordingly;

"publication" means an article or record of any description that contains any of the following, or any combination of them—

(*a*) matter to be read;
(*b*) matter to be listened to;
(*c*) matter to be looked at or watched.

[Terrorism Act 2006, s 2.]

---

1 An act of circulation cannot be saved by reference to the principle of freedom of speech: *R v Brown* [2011] EWCA Crim 2751, [2012] 2 Cr App Rep (S) 39.

2 In *R v Faraz* [2012] EWCA Crim 2820, [2013] 1 Cr App R 29 the defendant had managed an Islamic bookshop and was charged relating to books, etc, which allegedly supported the case for militant Islam. His defence was that the materials did not encourage acts of terrorism, but encouraged only intelligent discussion of religious and political theory. The prosecution was allowed to adduce evidence that named terrorist offenders had possessed similar or identical materials and, at that date, similar or identical material had been found in 26% of police terrorist investigations. Quashing the convictions, the Court of Appeal held that the evidence of possession by known terrorists was admissible, if at all, for the very limited purpose of demonstrating that the readership included those prepared to commit terrorist acts. It was not admissible to prove the fact that people had been so encouraged. While it was powerfully tempting to conclude that terrorists would not possess such material unless it encouraged them, such a conclusion was speculative, unfair and prejudicial. The statistic had added another prejudicial dimension and had had no probative value.

3 The Court of Appeal gave sentencing guidance for this offence in *R v Abdul Rahman and Bilal Mohammed* [2008] EWCA Crim 1465, [2008] Crim LR 906. Matters other than quality and quantity are not of minor importance only; sub-ss (7) and (8) are concerned with the ingredients of the offence, not seriousness. Whether the defendant intended dissemination of terrorist publications to encourage the commission, preparation or instigation of acts of terrorism, or was merely reckless as to such consequences, was likely to be significant when assessing culpability; and the volume and content of the material disseminated would be relevant to the harm caused, intended or foreseen.

**7.8886 3. Application of ss 1 and 2 to internet activity etc** (1) This section applies for the purposes of sections 1 and 2 in relation to cases where—

(*a*) a statement is published or caused to be published in the course of, or in connection with, the provision or use of a service provided electronically; or

(*b*) conduct falling within section 2(2) was in the course of, or in connection with, the provision or use of such a service.

(2) The cases in which the statement, or the article or record to which the conduct relates, is to be regarded as having the endorsement of a person ("the relevant person") at any time include a case in which—

(*a*) a constable has given him a notice under subsection (3);

(*b*) that time falls more than 2 working days after the day on which the notice was given; and

(*c*) the relevant person has failed, without reasonable excuse, to comply with the notice.

(3) A notice under this subsection is a notice which—

(*a*) declares that, in the opinion of the constable giving it, the statement or the article or record is unlawfully terrorism-related;

(*b*) requires the relevant person to secure that the statement or the article or record, so far as it is so related, is not available to the public or is modified so as no longer to be so related;

(*c*) warns the relevant person that a failure to comply with the notice within 2 working days will result in the statement, or the article or record, being regarded as having his endorsement; and

(*d*) explains how, under subsection (4), he may become liable by virtue of the notice if the statement, or the article or record, becomes available to the public after he has complied with the notice.

(4) Where—

(*a*) a notice under subsection (3) has been given to the relevant person in respect of a statement, or an article or record, and he has complied with it, but

(*b*) he subsequently publishes or causes to be published a statement which is, or is for all practical purposes, the same or to the same effect as the statement to which the notice related, or to matter contained in the article or record to which it related, (a "repeat statement");

the requirements of subsection (2)(*a*) to (*c*) shall be regarded as satisfied in the case of the repeat statement in relation to the times of its subsequent publication by the relevant person.

(5) In proceedings against a person for an offence under section 1 or 2 the requirements of subsection (2)(*a*) to (*c*) are not, in his case, to be regarded as satisfied in relation to any time by virtue of subsection (4) if he shows that he—

(*a*) has, before that time, taken every step he reasonably could to prevent a repeat statement from becoming available to the public and to ascertain whether it does; and

(*b*) was, at that time, a person to whom subsection (6) applied.

(6) This subsection applies to a person at any time when he—

(*a*) is not aware of the publication of the repeat statement; or

(*b*) having become aware of its publication, has taken every step that he reasonably could to secure that it either ceased to be available to the public or was modified as mentioned in subsection (3)(*b*).

(7) For the purposes of this section a statement or an article or record is unlawfully terrorism-related if it constitutes, or if matter contained in the article or record constitutes—

(*a*) something that is likely to be understood, by any one or more of the persons to whom it has or may become available, as a direct or indirect encouragement or other inducement to the commission, preparation or instigation of acts of terrorism or Convention offences; or

(*b*) information which—

(i) is likely to be useful to any one or more of those persons in the commission or preparation of such acts; and

(ii) is in a form or context in which it is likely to be understood by any one or more of those persons as being wholly or mainly for the purpose of being so useful.

(8) The reference in subsection (7) to something that is likely to be understood as an indirect encouragement to the commission or preparation of acts of terrorism or Convention offences includes anything which is likely to be understood as—

(*a*) the glorification of the commission or preparation (whether in the past, in the future or generally) of such acts or such offences; and

(*b*) a suggestion that what is being glorified is being glorified as conduct that should be emulated in existing circumstances.

(9) In this section "working day" means any day other than—

(*a*) a Saturday or a Sunday;

(*b*) Christmas Day or Good Friday; or

(*c*) a day which is a bank holiday under the Banking and Financial Dealings Act 1971 (c 80) in any part of the United Kingdom.

[Terrorism Act 2006, s 3.]

**7.8887 4. Giving of notices under s 3** (1) Except in a case to which any of subsections (2) to (4) applies, a notice under section 3(3) may be given to a person only—

(*a*) by delivering it to him in person; or

(*b*) by sending it to him, by means of a postal service providing for delivery to be recorded, at his last known address.

(2) Such a notice may be given to a body corporate only—

(*a*) by delivering it to the secretary of that body in person; or

(*b*) by sending it to the appropriate person, by means of a postal service providing for delivery to be recorded, at the address of the registered or principal office of the body.

(3) Such a notice may be given to a firm only—

(*a*) by delivering it to a partner of the firm in person;

(*b*) by so delivering it to a person having the control or management of the partnership business; or

(*c*) by sending it to the appropriate person, by means of a postal service providing for delivery to be recorded, at the address of the principal office of the partnership.

(4) Such a notice may be given to an unincorporated body or association only—

(*a*) by delivering it to a member of its governing body in person; or (*b*) by sending it to the appropriate person, by means of a postal service providing for delivery to be recorded, at the address of the principal office of the body or association.

(5) In the case of—

(*a*) a company registered outside the United Kingdom,

(*b*) a firm carrying on business outside the United Kingdom, or

(*c*) an unincorporated body or association with offices outside the United Kingdom,

the references in this section to its principal office include references to its principal office within the United Kingdom (if any).

(6) In this section "the appropriate person" means—

(*a*) in the case of a body corporate, the body itself or its secretary;

(*b*) in the case of a firm, the firm itself or a partner of the firm or a person having the control or management of the partnership business; and

(*c*) in the case of an unincorporated body or association, the body or association itself or a member of its governing body.

(7) For the purposes of section 3 the time at which a notice under subsection (3) of that section is to be regarded as given is—

(*a*) where it is delivered to a person, the time at which it is so delivered; and

(*b*) where it is sent by a postal service providing for delivery to be recorded, the time recorded as the time of its delivery.

(8) In this section "secretary", in relation to a body corporate, means the secretary or other equivalent officer of the body.

[Terrorism Act 2006, s 4.]

*Preparation of terrorist acts and terrorist training*

**7.8888** 5. **Preparation of terrorist acts** (1) A person commits an offence if, with the intention of—

(*a*) committing acts of terrorism, or

(*b*) assisting another to commit such acts,

he engages in any conduct in preparation for giving effect to his intention.

(2) It is irrelevant for the purposes of subsection (1) whether the intention and preparations relate to one or more particular acts of terrorism, acts of terrorism of a particular description or acts of terrorism generally.

(3) A person guilty of an offence under this section shall be liable, on conviction on indictment, to imprisonment for life.

[Terrorism Act 2006, s 5.]

**7.8889** 6. **Training for terrorism** (1) A person commits an offence if—

(*a*) he provides instruction or training in any of the skills mentioned in subsection (3); and

(*b*) at the time he provides the instruction or training, he knows that a person receiving it intends to use the skills in which he is being instructed or trained—

(i) for or in connection with the commission or preparation of acts of terrorism or Convention offences; or

(ii) for assisting the commission or preparation by others of such acts or offences.

(2) A person commits an offence if—

(*a*) he receives instruction or training in any of the skills mentioned in subsection (3); and

(*b*) at the time of the instruction or training, he intends to use the skills in which he is being instructed or trained—

(i) for or in connection with the commission or preparation of acts of terrorism or Convention offences; or

(ii) for assisting the commission or preparation by others of such acts or offences.

(3) The skills are—

(*a*) the making, handling or use of a noxious substance, or of substances of a description of such substances;

(*b*) the use of any method or technique for doing anything else that is capable of being done for the purposes of terrorism, in connection with the commission or preparation of an act of terrorism or Convention offence or in connection with assisting the commission or preparation by another of such an act or offence; and

(*c*) the design or adaptation for the purposes of terrorism, or in connection with the commission or preparation of an act of terrorism or Convention offence, of any method or technique for doing anything.

(4) It is irrelevant for the purposes of subsections (1) and (2)—

(*a*) whether any instruction or training that is provided is provided to one or more particular persons or generally;

(*b*) whether the acts or offences in relation to which a person intends to use skills in which he is instructed or trained consist of one or more particular acts of terrorism or Convention offences, acts of terrorism or Convention offences of a particular description or acts of terrorism or Convention offences generally; and (*c*) whether assistance that a person intends to provide to others is intended to be provided to one or more particular persons or to one or more persons whose identities are not yet known.

(5) A person guilty of an offence under this section shall be liable—

(*a*) on conviction on indictment, to imprisonment for life or to a fine, or to both;

(*b*) on summary conviction in England and Wales, to imprisonment for a term not exceeding 12 months or to a fine not exceeding the statutory maximum, or to both;

(*c*) *Scotland, Northern Ireland.*

(6) In relation to an offence committed before the commencement of section 154(1) of the Criminal Justice Act 2003 (c 44), the reference in subsection (5)(*b*) to 12 months is to be read as a reference to 6 months.

(7) In this section—

"noxious substance" means—

(*a*) a dangerous substance within the meaning of Part 7 of the Anti-terrorism, Crime and Security Act 2001 (c 24); or

(*b*) any other substance which is hazardous or noxious or which may be or become hazardous or noxious only in certain circumstances;

"substance" includes any natural or artificial substance (whatever its origin or method of production and whether in solid or liquid form or in the form of a gas or vapour) and any mixture of substances.

[Terrorism Act 2006, s 6 as amended by the Criminal Justice and Courts Act 2015, s 1.]

**7.8890 7. Powers of forfeiture in respect of offences under s 6** (1) A court before which a person is convicted of an offence under section 6 may order the forfeiture of anything the court considers to have been in the person's possession for purposes connected with the offence.

(2) Before making an order under subsection (1) in relation to anything the court must give an opportunity of being heard to any person (in addition to the convicted person) who claims to be the owner of that thing or otherwise to have an interest in it.

(3) An order under subsection (1) may not be made so as to come into force at any time before there is no further possibility (disregarding any power to grant permission for the bringing of an appeal out of time) of the order's being varied or set aside on appeal.

(4) Where a court makes an order under subsection (1), it may also make such other provision as appears to it to be necessary for giving effect to the forfeiture.

(5) That provision may include, in particular, provision relating to the retention, handling, destruction or other disposal of what is forfeited.

(6) Provision made by virtue of this section may be varied at any time by the court that made it.

(7) The power of forfeiture under this section is in addition to any power of forfeiture under section 23A of the Terrorism Act 2000.

[Terrorism Act 2006, s 7 as amended by the Counter-Terrorism Act 2008, s 38.]

**7.8891 8. Attendance at a place used for terrorist training** (1) A person commits an offence if—

(*a*) he attends at any place, whether in the United Kingdom or elsewhere;

(*b*) while he is at that place, instruction or training of the type mentioned in section 6(1) of this Act or section 54(1) of the Terrorism Act 2000 (c 11) (weapons training) is provided there;

(*c*) that instruction or training is provided there wholly or partly for purposes connected with the commission or preparation of acts of terrorism or Convention offences; and

(*d*) the requirements of subsection (2) are satisfied in relation to that person.

(2) The requirements of this subsection are satisfied in relation to a person if—

(*a*) he knows or believes that instruction or training is being provided there wholly or partly for purposes connected with the commission or preparation of acts of terrorism or Convention offences; or

(*b*) a person attending at that place throughout the period of that person's attendance could not reasonably have failed to understand that instruction or training was being provided there wholly or partly for such purposes.

(3) It is immaterial for the purposes of this section—

(*a*) whether the person concerned receives the instruction or training himself; and

(*b*) whether the instruction or training is provided for purposes connected with one or more particular acts of terrorism or Convention offences, acts of terrorism or Convention offences of a particular description or acts of terrorism or Convention offences generally.

(4) A person guilty of an offence under this section shall be liable—

(*a*) on conviction on indictment, to imprisonment for a term not exceeding 10 years or to a fine, or to both;

(*b*) on summary conviction in England and Wales, to imprisonment for a term not exceeding 12 months or to a fine not exceeding the statutory maximum, or to both;

(*c*) *Scotland, Northern Ireland.*

(5) In relation to an offence committed before the commencement of section 154(1) of the Criminal Justice Act 2003 (c 44), the reference in subsection (4)(*b*) to 12 months is to be read as a

reference to 6 months.

(6) References in this section to instruction or training being provided include references to its being made available.

[Terrorism Act 2006, s 8.]

*Offences involving radioactive devices and materials and nuclear facilities and sites*

7.8892 **9. Making and possession of devices or materials** (1) A person commits an offence if—

(*a*) he makes or has in his possession a radioactive device, or

(*b*) he has in his possession radioactive material,

with the intention of using the device or material in the course of or in connection with the commission or preparation of an act of terrorism or for the purposes of terrorism, or of making it available to be so used.

(2) It is irrelevant for the purposes of subsection (1) whether the act of terrorism to which an intention relates is a particular act of terrorism, an act of terrorism of a particular description or an act of terrorism generally.

(3) A person guilty of an offence under this section shall be liable, on conviction on indictment, to imprisonment for life.

(4) In this section—

"radioactive device" means—

(*a*) a nuclear weapon or other nuclear explosive device;

(*b*) a radioactive material dispersal device;

(*c*) a radiation-emitting device;

"radioactive material" means nuclear material or any other radioactive substance which—

(*a*) contains nuclides that undergo spontaneous disintegration in a process accompanied by the emission of one or more types of ionising radiation, such as alpha radiation, beta radiation, neutron particles or gamma rays; and

(*b*) is capable, owing to its radiological or fissile properties, of—

(i) causing serious bodily injury to a person;

(ii) causing serious damage to property;

(iii) endangering a person's life; or

(iv) creating a serious risk to the health or safety of the public.

(5) In subsection (4)—

"device" includes any of the following, whether or not fixed to land, namely, machinery, equipment, appliances, tanks, containers, pipes and conduits;

"nuclear material" has the same meaning as in the Nuclear Material (Offences) Act 1983 (c 18) (see section 6 of that Act).

[Terrorism Act 2006, s 9.]

7.8893 **10. Misuse of devices or material and misuse and damage of facilities** (1) A person commits an offence if he uses—

(*a*) a radioactive device, or

(*b*) radioactive material,

in the course of or in connection with the commission of an act of terrorism or for the purposes of terrorism.

(2) A person commits an offence if, in the course of or in connection with the commission of an act of terrorism or for the purposes of terrorism, he uses or damages a nuclear facility in a manner which—

(*a*) causes a release of radioactive material; or

(*b*) creates or increases a risk that such material will be released.

(3) A person guilty of an offence under this section shall be liable, on conviction on indictment, to imprisonment for life.

(4) In this section—

"nuclear facility" means—

(*a*) a nuclear reactor, including a reactor installed in or on any transportation device for use as an energy source in order to propel it or for any other purpose; or

(*b*) a plant or conveyance being used for the production, storage, processing or transport of radioactive material;

"radioactive device" and "radioactive material" have the same meanings as in section 9.

(5) In subsection (4)—

"nuclear reactor" has the same meaning as in the Nuclear Installations Act 1965 (c 57) (see section 26 of that Act);

"transportation device" means any vehicle or any space object (within the meaning of the Outer Space Act 1986 (c 38)).

[Terrorism Act 2006, s 10.]

7.8894 **11. Terrorist threats relating to devices, materials or facilities** (1) A person commits an offence if, in the course of or in connection with the commission of an act of terrorism or for the purposes of terrorism—

(*a*) he makes a demand—

(i) for the supply to himself or to another of a radioactive device or of radioactive material;
(ii) for a nuclear facility to be made available to himself or to another; or
(iii) for access to such a facility to be given to himself or to another;

(*b*) he supports the demand with a threat that he or another will take action if the demand is not met; and

(*c*) the circumstances and manner of the threat are such that it is reasonable for the person to whom it is made to assume that there is real risk that the threat will be carried out if the demand is not met.

(2) A person also commits an offence if—

(*a*) he makes a threat falling within subsection (3) in the course of or in connection with the commission of an act of terrorism or for the purposes of terrorism; and

(*b*) the circumstances and manner of the threat are such that it is reasonable for the person to whom it is made to assume that there is real risk that the threat will be carried out, or would be carried out if demands made in association with the threat are not met.

(3) A threat falls within this subsection if it is—

(*a*) a threat to use radioactive material;

(*b*) a threat to use a radioactive device; or

(*c*) a threat to use or damage a nuclear facility in a manner that releases radioactive material or creates or increases a risk that such material will be released.

(4) A person guilty of an offence under this section shall be liable, on conviction on indictment, to imprisonment for life.

(5) In this section—

"nuclear facility" has the same meaning as in section 10;

"radioactive device" and "radioactive material" have the same meanings as in section 9.

[Terrorism Act 2006, s 11.]

7.8895 **11A. Forfeiture of devices, materials or facilities** (1) A court by or before which a person is convicted of an offence under section 9 or 10 may order the forfeiture of any radioactive device or radioactive material, or any nuclear facility, made or used in committing the offence.

(2) A court by or before which a person is convicted of an offence under section 11 may order the forfeiture of any radioactive device or radioactive material, or any nuclear facility, which is the subject of—

(*a*) a demand under subsection (1) of that section, or

(*b*) a threat falling within subsection (3) of that section.

(3) Before making an order under this section, a court must give an opportunity to be heard to any person, other than the convicted person, who claims to be the owner or otherwise interested in anything which can be forfeited under this section.

(4) An order under this section does not come into force until there is no further possibility of it being varied, or set aside, on appeal (disregarding any power of a court to grant leave to appeal out of time).

(5) Where a court makes an order under this section, it may also make such other provision as appears to it to be necessary for giving effect to the forfeiture, including, in particular, provision relating to the retention, handling, disposal or destruction of what is forfeited.

(6) Provision made by virtue of subsection (5) may be varied at any time by the court that made it.

(7) The power of forfeiture under this section is in addition to any power of forfeiture under section 23A of the Terrorism Act 2000.

[Terrorism Act 2006, s 11A as inserted by the Counter-Terrorism Act 2008, s 38.]

*Incidental provisions about offences*

7.8896 **17. Commission of offences abroad** (1) If—

(*a*) a person does anything outside the United Kingdom, and

(*b*) his action, if done in a part of the United Kingdom, would constitute an offence falling within subsection (2),

he shall be guilty in that part of the United Kingdom of the offence.

(2) The offences falling within this subsection are—

(*a*) an offence under section 1 of this Act so far as it is committed in relation to any statement in relation to which that section has effect by reason of its relevance to the commission, preparation or instigation of one or more Convention offences;

(*b*) an offence under section 5 or 6 or any of sections 8 to 11 of this Act;

(*c*) an offence under section 11(1) of the Terrorism Act 2000 (c 11) (membership of proscribed organisations);

(*d*) an offence under section 54 of that Act (weapons training);

(*e*) conspiracy to commit an offence falling within this subsection;

(*f*) inciting a person to commit such an offence;

(*g*) attempting to commit such an offence;

(*h*) aiding, abetting, counselling or procuring the commission of such an offence.

(3) Subsection (1) applies irrespective of whether the person is a British citizen or, in the case of

a company, a company incorporated in a part of the United Kingdom.

(4) In the case of an offence falling within subsection (2) which is committed wholly or partly outside the United Kingdom—

(*a*) proceedings for the offence may be taken at any place in the United Kingdom; and

(*b*) the offence may for all incidental purposes be treated as having been committed at any such place.

(5) In section 3(1)(*a*) and (*b*) of the Explosive Substances Act 1883 (c 3) (offences committed in preparation for use of explosives with intent to endanger life or property in the United Kingdom or the Republic of Ireland), in each place, for "the Republic of Ireland" substitute "elsewhere".

(6) Subsection (5) does not extend to Scotland except in relation to—

(*a*) the doing of an act as an act of terrorism or for the purposes of terrorism; or

(*b*) the possession or control of a substance for the purposes of terrorism.

[Terrorism Act 2006, s 17 as amended by the Serious Crime Act 2015, s 81, Sch 4.]

7.8897 **18. Liability of company directors etc** (1) Where an offence under this Part is committed by a body corporate and is proved to have been committed with the consent or connivance of—

(*a*) a director, manager, secretary or other similar officer of the body corporate, or

(*b*) a person who was purporting to act in any such capacity,

he (as well as the body corporate) is guilty of that offence and shall be liable to be proceeded against and punished accordingly.

(2) Where an offence under this Part—

(*a*) is committed by a Scottish firm, and

(*b*) is proved to have been committed with the consent or connivance of a partner of the firm,

he (as well as the firm) is guilty of that offence and shall be liable to be proceeded against and punished accordingly.

(3) In this section "director", in relation to a body corporate whose affairs are managed by its members, means a member of the body corporate.

[Terrorism Act 2006, s 18.]

7.8898 **19. Consents to prosecutions** (1) Proceedings for an offence under this Part—

(*a*) may be instituted in England and Wales only with the consent of the Director of Public Prosecutions; and

(*b*) may be instituted in Northern Ireland only with the consent of the Director of Public Prosecutions for Northern Ireland.

(2) But if it appears to the Director of Public Prosecutions or the Director of Public Prosecutions for Northern Ireland that an offence under this Part has been committed outside the United Kingdom or for a purpose wholly or partly connected with the affairs of a country other than the United Kingdom, his consent for the purposes of this section may be given only with the permission—

(*a*) in the case of the Director of Public Prosecutions, of the Attorney General; and

(*b*) in the case of the Director of Public Prosecutions for Northern Ireland, of the Advocate General for Northern Ireland.

(3) In relation to any time before the coming into force of section 27(1) of the Justice (Northern Ireland) Act 2002 (c 26), the reference in subsection (2)(*b*) to the Advocate General for Northern Ireland is to be read as a reference to the Attorney General for Northern Ireland.

[Terrorism Act 2006, s 19 as amended by the Counter-Terrorism Act 2008, s 29.]

*Interpretation of Part 1*

7.8899 **20. Interpretation of Part 1** (1) Expressions used in this Part and in the Terrorism Act 2000 (c 11) have the same meanings in this Part as in that Act.

(2) In this Part—

"act of terrorism" includes anything constituting an action taken for the purposes of terrorism, within the meaning of the Terrorism Act 2000 (see section 1(5) of that Act);

"article" includes anything for storing data;

"Convention offence" means an offence listed in Schedule 1 or an equivalent offence under the law of a country or territory outside the United Kingdom;

"glorification" includes any form of praise or celebration, and cognate expressions are to be construed accordingly;

"public" is to be construed in accordance with subsection (3);

"publish" and cognate expressions are to be construed in accordance with subsection (4);

"record" means a record so far as not comprised in an article, including a temporary record created electronically and existing solely in the course of, and for the purposes of, the transmission of the whole or a part of its contents;

"statement" is to be construed in accordance with subsection (6).

(3) In this Part references to the public—

(*a*) are references to the public of any part of the United Kingdom or of a country or territory outside the United Kingdom, or any section of the public; and (*b*) except in section 9(4), also include references to a meeting or other group of persons which is open to the public (whether unconditionally or on the making of a payment or the satisfaction of other conditions).

(4) In this Part references to a person's publishing a statement are references to—

(*a*) his publishing it in any manner to the public;

(*b*) his providing electronically any service by means of which the public have access to the statement; or

(*c*) his using a service provided to him electronically by another so as to enable or to facilitate access by the public to the statement;

but this subsection does not apply to the references to a publication in section 2.

(5) In this Part references to providing a service include references to making a facility available; and references to a service provided to a person are to be construed accordingly.

(6) In this Part references to a statement are references to a communication of any description, including a communication without words consisting of sounds or images or both.

(7) In this Part references to conduct that should be emulated in existing circumstances include references to conduct that is illustrative of a type of conduct that should be so emulated.

(8) In this Part references to what is contained in an article or record include references—

(*a*) to anything that is embodied or stored in or on it; and

(*b*) to anything that may be reproduced from it using apparatus designed or adapted for the purpose.

(9) The Secretary of State may by order made by statutory instrument—

(*a*) modify Schedule 1 so as to add an offence to the offences listed in that Schedule;

(*b*) modify that Schedule so as to remove an offence from the offences so listed;

(*c*) make supplemental, incidental, consequential or transitional provision in connection with the addition or removal of an offence.

(10) An order under subsection (9) may add an offence in or as regards Scotland to the offences listed in Schedule 1 to the extent only that a provision creating the offence would be outside the legislative competence of the Scottish Parliament.

(11) The Secretary of State must not make an order containing (with or without other provision) any provision authorised by subsection (9) unless a draft of the order has been laid before Parliament and approved by a resolution of each House.

[Terrorism Act 2006, s 20.]

## PART 2
## MISCELLANEOUS PROVISIONS

*Searches etc*

7.8900 **28. Search, seizure and forfeiture of terrorist publications** (1) If a justice of the peace is satisfied that there are reasonable grounds for suspecting that articles to which this section applies are likely to be found on any premises, he may issue a warrant authorising a constable—

(*a*) to enter and search the premises; and

(*b*) to seize anything found there which the constable has reason to believe is such an article.

(2) This section applies to an article if—

(*a*) it is likely to be the subject of conduct falling within subsection (2)(*a*) to (*e*) of section 2; and

(*b*) it would fall for the purposes of that section to be treated, in the context of the conduct to which it is likely to be subject, as a terrorist publication.

(3) A person exercising a power conferred by a warrant under this section may use such force as is reasonable in the circumstances for exercising that power.

(4) An article seized under the authority of a warrant issued under this section—

(*a*) may be removed by a constable to such place as he thinks fit; and

(*b*) must be retained there in the custody of a constable until returned or otherwise disposed of in accordance with this Act.

(5) An article to which this section applies which is seized under the authority of a warrant issued under this section on an information laid by or on behalf of the Director of Public Prosecutions or the Director of Public Prosecutions for Northern Ireland—

(*a*) shall be liable to forfeiture; and

(*b*) if forfeited, may be destroyed or otherwise disposed of by a constable in whatever manner he thinks fit.

(6) *Amends the Criminal Justice and Police Act 2001, Sch 1.*

(7) Nothing in—

(*a*) the Police (Property) Act 1897 (c 30) (property seized in the investigation of an offence), or

(*b*) section 31 of the Police (Northern Ireland) Act 1998 (c 32) (which makes similar provision in Northern Ireland), applies to an article seized under the authority of a warrant under this section.

(8) Schedule 2 (which makes provision about the forfeiture of articles to which this section applies) has effect.

(9) In this section—

"article" has the same meaning as in Part 1 of this Act;

"forfeited" means treated or condemned as forfeited under Schedule 2, and "forfeiture" is to be construed accordingly;

"premises" has the same meaning as in the Police and Criminal Evidence Act 1984 (c 60) (see section 23 of that Act).

(10) *Scotland.*

[Terrorism Act 2006, s 28.]

## PART 3
## SUPPLEMENTAL PROVISIONS

**7.8900A 36. Review of terrorism legislation**

**7.8900B 37. Consequential amendments and repeals**

**7.8900C 38. Expenses**

**7.8904 39. Short title, commencement and extent** (1) This Act may be cited as the Terrorism Act 2006.

(2) This Act (apart from this section) shall come into force on such day as the Secretary of State may by order made by statutory instrument appoint.

(3) An order made under subsection (2) may make different provision for different purposes.

(4) Subject to section 17(6), an amendment or repeal by this Act of another enactment has the same extent as the enactment amended or repealed.

(5) Subject to section 17(6) and to subsection (4) of this section, this Act extends to the whole of the United Kingdom.

(6) Her Majesty may by Order in Council direct that any provisions of this Act shall extend, with such modifications as appear to Her Majesty to be appropriate, to any of the Channel Islands or the Isle of Man.

(7) In subsection (6) "modification" includes omissions, additions and alterations.

[Terrorism Act 2006, s 39.]

## SCHEDULE 1
### Convention Offences

*(As amended by the Criminal Justice and Immigration Act 2008, Sch 26)* Section 20

*Explosives offences*

**7.8906** **1.** (1) Subject to sub-paragraph (3), an offence under any of sections 28 to 30 of the Offences against the Person Act 1861 (c 100) (causing injury by explosions, causing explosions and handling or placing explosives).

(2) Subject to sub-paragraph (3), an offence under any of the following provisions of the Explosive Substances Act 1883 (c 3)—

(*a*) section 2 (causing an explosion likely to endanger life);
(*b*) section 3 (preparation of explosions);
(*c*) section 5 (ancillary offences).

(3) *Scotland.*

*Biological weapons*

**2.** An offence under section 1 of the Biological Weapons Act 1974 (c 6) (development etc of biological weapons).

*Offences against internationally protected persons*

**3.** (1) Subject to sub-paragraph (4), an offence mentioned in section 1(1)(*a*) of the Internationally Protected Persons Act 1978 (c 17) (attacks against protected persons committed outside the United Kingdom) which is committed (whether in the United Kingdom or elsewhere) in relation to a protected person.

(2) Subject to sub-paragraph (4), an offence mentioned in section 1(1)(*b*) of that Act (attacks on relevant premises etc) which is committed (whether in the United Kingdom or elsewhere) in connection with an attack—

(*a*) on relevant premises or on a vehicle ordinarily used by a protected person, and
(*b*) at a time when a protected person is in or on the premises or vehicle.

(3) Subject to sub-paragraph (4), an offence under section 1(3) of that Act (threats etc in relation to protected persons).

(4) *Scotland.*

(5) Expressions used in this paragraph and section 1 of that Act have the same meanings in this paragraph as in that section.

*Hostage-taking*

**4.** An offence under section 1 of the Taking of Hostages Act 1982 (c 28) (hostage-taking).

*Hijacking and other offences against aircraft*

**5.** Offences under any of the following provisions of the Aviation Security Act 1982 (c 36)—

(*a*) section 1 (hijacking);
(*b*) section 2 (destroying, damaging or endangering safety of aircraft);

(*c*) section 3 (other acts endangering or likely to endanger safety of aircraft);
(*d*) section 6(2) (ancillary offences).

*Offences involving nuclear material or nuclear facilities*

**6.** (1) An offence mentioned in section 1(1)(*a*) to (*d*) of the Nuclear Material (Offences) Act 1983 (c 18) (offences in relation to nuclear material committed outside the United Kingdom) which is committed (whether in the United Kingdom or elsewhere) in relation to or by means of nuclear material.

(2) An offence mentioned in section 1(1)(*a*) or (*b*) of that Act where the act making the person guilty of the offence (whether done in the United Kingdom or elsewhere)—
(*a*) is directed at a nuclear facility or interferes with the operation of such a facility, and
(*b*) causes death, injury or damage resulting from the emission of ionising radiation or the release of radioactive material.

(3) An offence under any of the following provisions of that Act—
(*a*) section 1B (offences relating to damage to environment);
(*b*) section 1C (offences of importing or exporting etc nuclear material: extended jurisdiction);
(*c*) section 2 (offences involving preparatory acts and threats).

(4) Expressions used in this paragraph and that Act have the same meanings in this paragraph as in that Act.

**6A.** (1) Any of the following offences under the Customs and Excise Management Act 1979—
(*a*) an offence under section 50(2) or (3) (improper importation of goods) in connection with a prohibition or restriction relating to the importation of nuclear material;
(*b*) an offence under section 68(2) (exportation of prohibited or restricted goods) in connection with a prohibition or restriction relating to the exportation or shipment as stores of nuclear material;
(*c*) an offence under section 170(1) or (2) (fraudulent evasion of duty etc) in connection with a prohibition or restriction relating to the importation, exportation or shipment as stores of nuclear material.

(2) In this paragraph "nuclear material" has the same meaning as in the Nuclear Material (Offences) Act 1983 (see section 6 of that Act).

*Offences under the Aviation and Maritime Security Act 1990 (c 31)*

**7.** Offences under any of the following provisions of the Aviation and Maritime Security Act 1990—
(*a*) section 1 (endangering safety at aerodromes);
(*b*) section 9 (hijacking of ships);
(*c*) section 10 (seizing or exercising control of fixed platforms);
(*d*) section 11 (destroying ships or fixed platforms or endangering their safety);
(*e*) section 12 (other acts endangering or likely to endanger safe navigation);
(*f*) section 13 (offences involving threats relating to ships or fixed platforms);
(*g*) section 14 (ancillary offences).

*Offences involving chemical weapons*

**8.** An offence under section 2 of the Chemical Weapons Act 1996 (c 6) (use, development etc of chemical weapons).

*Terrorist funds*

**9.** An offence under any of the following provisions of the Terrorism Act 2000 (c 11)—
(*a*) section 15 (terrorist fund-raising);
(*b*) section 16 (use or possession of terrorist funds);
(*c*) section 17 (funding arrangements for terrorism);
(*d*) section 18 (money laundering of terrorist funds).

*Directing terrorist organisations*

**10.** An offence under section 56 of the Terrorism Act 2000 (directing a terrorist organisation).

*Offences involving nuclear weapons*

**11.** An offence under section 47 of the Anti-terrorism, Crime and Security Act 2001 (c 24) (use, development etc of nuclear weapons).

*Conspiracy etc*

**12.** Any of the following offences—
(*a*) conspiracy to commit a Convention offence;
(*b*) inciting the commission of a Convention offence;
(*c*) attempting to commit a Convention offence;
(*d*) aiding, abetting, counselling or procuring the commission of a Convention offence.

## SCHEDULE 2

### Seizure and Forfeiture of Terrorist Publications

Section 28

*Application of Schedule*

**7.8909** **1.** This Schedule applies where an article—
(*a*) has been seized under the authority of a warrant under section 28; and
(*b*) is being retained in the custody of a constable ("the relevant constable").

*Notice of seizure*

**2.** (1) The relevant constable must give notice of the article's seizure to—
(*a*) every person whom he believes to have been the owner of the article, or one of its owners, at the time of the seizure; and
(*b*) if there is no such person or it is not reasonably practicable to give him notice, every person whom the relevant constable believes to have been an occupier at that time of the premises where the article was seized.

(2) The notice must set out what has been seized and the grounds for the seizure.

(3) The notice may be given to a person only by—

(*a*) delivering it to him personally;

(*b*) addressing it to him and leaving it for him at the appropriate address; or

(*c*) addressing it to him and sending it to him at that address by post.

(4) But where it is not practicable to give a notice in accordance with sub-paragraph (3), a notice given by virtue of sub-paragraph (1)(*b*) to the occupier of the premises where the article was seized may be given by—

(*a*) addressing it to "the occupier" of those premises, without naming him; and

(*b*) leaving it for him at those premises or sending it to him at those premises by post.

(5) An article may be treated or condemned as forfeited under this Schedule only if—

(*a*) the requirements of this paragraph have been complied with in the case of that article; or

(*b*) it was not reasonably practicable for them to be complied with.

(6) In this paragraph "the appropriate address", in relation to a person, means—

(*a*) in the case of a body corporate, its registered or principal office in the United Kingdom;

(*b*) in the case of a firm, the principal office of the partnership;

(*c*) in the case of an unincorporated body or association, the principal office of the body or association; and

(*d*) in any other case, his usual or last known place of residence in the United Kingdom or his last known place of business in the United Kingdom.

(7) In the case of—

(*a*) a company registered outside the United Kingdom,

(*b*) a firm carrying on business outside the United Kingdom, or

(*c*) an unincorporated body or association with offices outside the United Kingdom,

the references in this paragraph to its principal office include references to its principal office within the United Kingdom (if any).

*Notice of claim*

**3.** (1) A person claiming that the seized article is not liable to forfeiture may give notice of his claim to a constable at any police station in the police area in which the premises where the seizure took place are located.

(2) Oral notice is not sufficient for these purposes.

**4.** (1) A notice of claim may not be given more than one month after—

(*a*) the day of the giving of the notice of seizure; or

(*b*) if no such notice has been given, the day of the seizure.

(2) A notice of claim must specify—

(*a*) the name and address of the claimant; and

(*b*) in the case of a claimant who is outside the United Kingdom, the name and address of a solicitor in the United Kingdom who is authorised to accept service, and to act, on behalf of the claimant.

(3) Service upon a solicitor so specified is to be taken to be service on the claimant for the purposes of any proceedings by virtue of this Schedule.

(4) In a case in which notice of the seizure was given to different persons on different days, the reference in this paragraph to the day on which that notice was given is a reference—

(*a*) in relation to a person to whom notice of the seizure was given, to the day on which that notice was given to that person; and

(*b*) in relation to any other person, to the day on which notice of the seizure was given to the last person to be given such a notice.

*Automatic forfeiture in a case where no claim is made*

**5.** The article is to be treated as forfeited if, by the end of the period for the giving of a notice of claim in respect of it—

(*a*) no such notice has been given; or

(*b*) the requirements of paragraphs 3 and 4 have not been complied with in relation to the only notice or notices of claim that have been given.

*Forfeiture by the court in other cases*

**6.** (1) Where a notice of claim in respect of an article is duly given in accordance with paragraphs 3 and 4, the relevant constable must decide whether to take proceedings to ask the court to condemn the article as forfeited.

(2) The decision whether to take such proceedings must be made as soon as reasonably practicable after the giving of the notice of claim.

(3) If the relevant constable takes such proceedings and the court—

(*a*) finds that the article was liable to forfeiture at the time of its seizure, and

(*b*) is not satisfied that its forfeiture would be inappropriate,

the court must condemn the article as forfeited.

(4) If that constable takes such proceedings and the court—

(*a*) finds that the article was not liable to forfeiture at the time of its seizure, or

(*b*) is satisfied that its forfeiture would be inappropriate,

the court must order the return of the article to the person who appears to the court to be entitled to it.

(5) If the relevant constable decides not to take proceedings for condemnation in a case in which a notice of claim has been given, he must return the article to the person who appears to him to be the owner of the article, or to one of the persons who appear to him to be owners of it.

(6) An article required to be returned in accordance with sub-paragraph (5) must be returned as soon as reasonably practicable after the decision not to take proceedings for condemnation.

*Forfeiture proceedings*

**7.** Proceedings by virtue of this Schedule are civil proceedings and may be instituted—

(*a*) in England or Wales, either in the High Court or in a magistrates' court;

(*b*), (*c*) *Scotland, Northern Ireland.*

**8.** Proceedings by virtue of this Schedule in—

(*a*) a magistrates' court in England or Wales,

(*b*), (*c*)*Scotland, Northern Ireland.* may be instituted in that court only if it has jurisdiction in relation to the place where the article to which they relate was seized.

**9.** (1) In proceedings by virtue of this Schedule that are instituted in England and Wales or Northern Ireland, the claimant or his solicitor must make his oath that, at the time of the seizure, the seized article was, or was to the best of his knowledge and belief, the property of the claimant.

(2) In any such proceedings instituted in the High Court—

(*a*) the court may require the claimant to give such security for the costs of the proceedings as may be determined by the court; and

(*b*) the claimant must comply with any such requirement.

(3) If a requirement of this paragraph is not complied with, the court must find against the claimant.

**10.** (1) In the case of proceedings by virtue of this Schedule that are instituted in a magistrates' court in England or Wales, either party may appeal against the decision of that court to the Crown Court.

(2) In the case of such proceedings that are instituted in a court of summary jurisdiction in Northern Ireland, either party may appeal against the decision of that court to the county court.

(3) This paragraph does not affect any right to require the statement of a case for the opinion of the High Court.

**11.** Where an appeal has been made (whether by case stated or otherwise) against the decision of the court in proceedings by virtue of this Schedule in relation to an article, the article is to be left in the custody of a constable pending the final determination of the matter.

*Effect of forfeiture*

**12.** Where an article is treated or condemned as forfeited under this Schedule, the forfeiture is to be treated as having taken effect as from the time of the seizure.

*Disposal of unclaimed property*

**13.** (1) This paragraph applies where the article seized under the authority of a warrant under section 28 is required to be returned to a person.

(2) If—

(*a*) the article is (without having been returned) still in the custody of a constable after the end of the period of 12 months beginning with the day after the requirement to return it arose, and

(*b*) it is not practicable to dispose of the article by returning it immediately to the person to whom it is required to be returned,

the constable may dispose of it in any manner he thinks fit.

*Provisions as to proof*

**14.** In proceedings arising out of the seizure of an article, the fact, form and manner of the seizure is to be taken, without further evidence and unless the contrary is shown, to have been as set forth in the process.

**15.** In proceedings, the condemnation by a court of an article as forfeited under this Schedule may be proved by the production of either—

(*a*) the order of condemnation; or

(*b*) a certified copy of the order purporting to be signed by an officer of the court by which the order was made.

*Special provisions as to certain claimants*

**16.** (1) This paragraph applies where, at the time of the seizure of the article, it was—

(*a*) the property of a body corporate;

(*b*) the property of two or more partners; or

(*c*) the property of more than five persons.

(2) The oath required by paragraph 9, and any other thing required by this Schedule or by rules of court to be done by an owner of the article, may be sworn or done by—

(*a*) a person falling within sub-paragraph (3); or

(*b*) a person authorised to act on behalf of a person so falling.

(3) The persons falling within this sub-paragraph are—

(*a*) where the owner is a body corporate, the secretary or some duly authorised officer of that body;

(*b*) where the owners are in partnership, any one or more of the owners;

(*c*) where there are more than five owners and they are not in partnership, any two or more of the owners acting on behalf of themselves and any of their co-owners who are not acting on their own behalf.

*Saving for owner's rights*

**17.** Neither the imposition of a requirement by virtue of this Schedule to return an article to a person nor the return of an article to a person in accordance with such a requirement affects—

(*a*) the rights in relation to that article of any other person; or

(*b*) the right of any other person to enforce his rights against the person to whom it is returned.

*Interpretation of Schedule*

**18.** In this Schedule—

"article" has the same meaning as in Part 1 of this Act;

"the court" is to be construed in accordance with paragraph 7.

SCHEDULE 3

Repeals

# Corporate Manslaughter and Corporate Homicide Act 2007[1]

(2007 c 19)

*Corporate manslaughter and corporate homicide*

**7.8911 1. The offence** (1) An organisation to which this section applies is guilty of an offence if the way in which its activities are managed or organised—

(*a*) causes a person's death, and

(*b*) amounts to a gross breach of a relevant duty of care owed by the organisation to the deceased.

(2) The organisations to which this section applies are—

(*a*) a corporation;

(*b*) a department or other body listed in Schedule 1;

(*c*) a police force;

(*d*) a partnership, or a trade union or employers' association, that is an employer.

(3) An organisation is guilty of an offence under this section only if the way in which its activities are managed or organised by its senior management is a substantial element in the breach referred to in subsection (1).

(4) For the purposes of this Act—

(*a*) "relevant duty of care" has the meaning given by section 2, read with sections 3 to 7;

(*b*) a breach of a duty of care by an organisation is a "gross" breach if the conduct alleged to amount to a breach of that duty falls far below what can reasonably be expected of the organisation in the circumstances;

(*c*) "senior management", in relation to an organisation, means the persons who play significant roles in—

(i) the making of decisions about how the whole or a substantial part of its activities are to be managed or organised, or

(ii) the actual managing or organising of the whole or a substantial part of those activities.

(5) The offence under this section is called—

(*a*) corporate manslaughter, in so far as it is an offence under the law of England and Wales or Northern Ireland;

(*b*) corporate homicide, in so far as it is an offence under the law of Scotland.

(6) An organisation that is guilty of corporate manslaughter or corporate homicide is liable on conviction on indictment to a fine.

(7) The offence of corporate homicide is indictable only in the High Court of Justiciary.

[Corporate Manslaughter and Corporate Homicide Act 2007, s 1.]

---

[1] This Act creates a new offence of corporate manslaughter and corporate homicide. In so doing it disapplies manslaughter by gross negligence from corporations and the other organisations that are listed.

In summary, the new offence arises where death is caused by "a gross breach of a relevant duty of care" and the management or organisation of the organisation's activities by its senior management formed a substantial element in that breach. The Act applies to the Crown and public bodies, though the "relevant duty of care" is modified in its application to some of them.

The Act is brought into force in accordance with s 27 and commencement orders made thereunder. The Corporate Manslaughter and Corporate Homicide Act 2007 (Commencement No 1) Order 2008, SI 2008/401 brought the remainder of the Act largely into force on 6 April 2008 and the Corporate Manslaughter and Corporate Homicide Act 2007 (Commencement No 2) Order 2010, SI 2010/276 brought s 10 into force on 15 February 2010.

*Relevant duty of care*

**7.8912 2. Meaning of "relevant duty of care"** (1) A "relevant duty of care", in relation to an organisation, means any of the following duties owed by it under the law of negligence—

(*a*) a duty owed to its employees or to other persons working for the organisation or performing services for it;

(*b*) a duty owed as occupier of premises;

(*c*) a duty owed in connection with—

(i) the supply by the organisation of goods or services (whether for consideration or not),

(ii) the carrying on by the organisation of any construction or maintenance operations,

(iii) the carrying on by the organisation of any other activity on a commercial basis, or

(iv) the use or keeping by the organisation of any plant, vehicle or other thing;

(*d*) a duty owed to a person who, by reason of being a person within subsection (2), is someone for whose safety the organisation is responsible.

(2) A person is within this subsection if—

(*a*) he is detained at a custodial institution or in a custody area at a court, a police station or customs premises;

(*aa*) he is detained in service custody premises;

(*b*) he is detained at a removal centre, a short-term holding facility or in pre-departure accommodation;

(*c*) he is being transported in a vehicle, or being held in any premises, in pursuance of prison escort arrangements or immigration escort arrangements;

(*d*) he is living in secure accommodation in which he has been placed;

(*e*) he is a detained patient.

(3) Subsection (1) is subject to sections 3 to 7.

(4) A reference in subsection (1) to a duty owed under the law of negligence includes a reference to a duty that would be owed under the law of negligence but for any statutory provision under which liability is imposed in place of liability under that law.

(5) For the purposes of this Act, whether a particular organisation owes a duty of care to a particular individual is a question of law.
The judge must make any findings of fact necessary to decide that question.

(6) For the purposes of this Act there is to be disregarded—

(*a*) any rule of the common law that has the effect of preventing a duty of care from being owed by one person to another by reason of the fact that they are jointly engaged in unlawful conduct;

(*b*) any such rule that has the effect of preventing a duty of care from being owed to a person by reason of his acceptance of a risk of harm.

(7) In this section—

"construction or maintenance operations" means operations of any of the following descriptions—

(*a*) construction, installation, alteration, extension, improvement, repair, maintenance, decoration, cleaning, demolition or dismantling of—

(i) any building or structure,

(ii) anything else that forms, or is to form, part of the land, or

(iii) any plant, vehicle or other thing;

(*b*) operations that form an integral part of, or are preparatory to, or are for rendering complete, any operations within paragraph (*a*);

"custodial institution" means a prison, a young offender institution, a secure training centre, a young offenders institution, a young offenders centre, a juvenile justice centre or a remand centre;

"customs premises" means premises wholly or partly occupied by persons designated under section 3 (general customs officials) or 11 (customs revenue officials) of the Borders, Citizenship and Immigration Act 2009;

"detained patient" means—

(*a*) a person who is detained in any premises under—

(i) Part 2 or 3 of the Mental Health Act 1983 (c 20) ("the 1983 Act"), or

(ii) Part 2 or 3 of the Mental Health (Northern Ireland) Order 1986 (SI 1986/595 (NI 4)) ("the 1986 Order");

(*b*) a person who (otherwise than by reason of being detained as mentioned in paragraph (*a*)) is deemed to be in legal custody by—

(i) section 137 of the 1983 Act,

(ii) Article 131 of the 1986 Order, or

(iii) article 11 of the Mental Health (Care and Treatment) (Scotland) Act 2003 (Consequential Provisions) Order 2005 (SI 2005/2078);

(*c*) a person who is detained in any premises, or is otherwise in custody, under the Mental Health (Care and Treatment) (Scotland) Act 2003 (asp 13) or Part 6 of the Criminal Procedure (Scotland) Act 1995 (c 46) or who is detained in a hospital under section 200 of that Act of 1995;

"immigration escort arrangements" means arrangements made under section 156 of the Immigration and Asylum Act 1999 (c 33);

"the law of negligence" includes—

(*a*) in relation to England and Wales, the Occupiers' Liability Act 1957 (c 31), the Defective Premises Act 1972 (c 35) and the Occupiers' Liability Act 1984 (c 3);

(*b*) *Scotland*;

(*c*) in relation to Northern Ireland, the Occupiers' Liability Act (Northern Ireland) 1957 (c 25), the Defective Premises (Northern Ireland) Order 1975 (SI 1975/1039 (NI 9)), the Occupiers' Liability (Northern Ireland) Order 1987 (SI 1987/1280 (NI 15)) and the Defective Premises (Landlord's Liability) Act (Northern Ireland) 2001 (c 10);

"prison escort arrangements" means arrangements made under section 80 of the Criminal Justice Act 1991 (c 53) or under section 102 or 118 of the Criminal Justice and Public Order Act 1994 (c 33);

"removal centre", "short-term holding facility" and "pre-departure accommodation" have the meaning given by section 147 of the Immigration and Asylum Act 1999;

"secure accommodation" means accommodation, not consisting of or forming part of a custodial institution, provided for the purpose of restricting the liberty of persons under the age of 18;

"service custody premises" has the meaning given by section 300(7) of the Armed Forces Act 2006.

[Corporate Manslaughter and Corporate Homicide Act 2007, s 2 as amended by SI 2011/1868 and the Immigration Act 2014, Sch 9.]

**7.8913 3. Public policy decisions, exclusively public functions and statutory inspections**

(1) Any duty of care owed by a public authority in respect of a decision as to matters of public policy (including in particular the allocation of public resources or the weighing of competing public interests) is not a "relevant duty of care".

(2) Any duty of care owed in respect of things done in the exercise of an exclusively public function is not a "relevant duty of care" unless it falls within section 2(1)(*a*), (*b*) or (*d*).

(3) Any duty of care owed by a public authority in respect of inspections carried out in the exercise of a statutory function is not a "relevant duty of care" unless it falls within section 2(1)(*a*) or (*b*).

(4) In this section—

"exclusively public function" means a function that falls within the prerogative of the Crown or is, by its nature, exercisable only with authority conferred—

(*a*) by the exercise of that prerogative, or

(*b*) by or under a statutory provision;

"statutory function" means a function conferred by or under a statutory provision.

[Corporate Manslaughter and Corporate Homicide Act 2007, s 3.]

**7.8914 4. Military activities** (1) Any duty of care owed by the Ministry of Defence in respect of—

(*a*) operations within subsection (2),

(*b*) activities carried on in preparation for, or directly in support of, such operations, or

(*c*) training of a hazardous nature, or training carried out in a hazardous way, which it is considered needs to be carried out, or carried out in that way, in order to improve or maintain the effectiveness of the armed forces with respect to such operations,

is not a "relevant duty of care".

(2) The operations within this subsection are operations, including peacekeeping operations and operations for dealing with terrorism, civil unrest or serious public disorder, in the course of which members of the armed forces come under attack or face the threat of attack or violent resistance.

(3) Any duty of care owed by the Ministry of Defence in respect of activities carried on by members of the special forces is not a "relevant duty of care".

(4) In this section "the special forces" means those units of the armed forces the maintenance of whose capabilities is the responsibility of the Director of Special Forces or which are for the time being subject to the operational command of that Director.

[Corporate Manslaughter and Corporate Homicide Act 2007, s 4.]

**7.8915 5. Policing and law enforcement** (1) Any duty of care owed by a public authority in respect of—

(*a*) operations within subsection (2),

(*b*) activities carried on in preparation for, or directly in support of, such operations, or

(*c*) training of a hazardous nature, or training carried out in a hazardous way, which it is considered needs to be carried out, or carried out in that way, in order to improve or maintain the effectiveness of officers or employees of the public authority with respect to such operations,

is not a "relevant duty of care".

(2) Operations are within this subsection if—

(*a*) they are operations for dealing with terrorism, civil unrest or serious disorder,

(*b*) they involve the carrying on of policing or law-enforcement activities, and

(*c*) officers or employees of the public authority in question come under attack, or face the threat of attack or violent resistance, in the course of the operations.

(3) Any duty of care owed by a public authority in respect of other policing or law-enforcement activities is not a "relevant duty of care" unless it falls within section 2(1)(*a*), (*b*) or (*d*).

(4) In this section "policing or law-enforcement activities" includes—

(*a*) activities carried on in the exercise of functions that are—

(i) functions of police forces, or

(ii) functions of the same or a similar nature exercisable by public authorities other than police forces;

(*b*) activities carried on in the exercise of functions of constables employed by a public authority;

(*c*) activities carried on in the exercise of functions exercisable under Chapter 4 of Part 2 of the Serious Organised Crime and Police Act 2005 (c 15) (protection of witnesses and other persons);

(*d*) activities carried on to enforce any provision contained in or made under the Immigration Acts.

[Corporate Manslaughter and Corporate Homicide Act 2007, s 5.]

7.8916 6. **Emergencies** (1) Any duty of care owed by an organisation within subsection (2) in respect of the way in which it responds to emergency circumstances is not a "relevant duty of care" unless it falls within section 2(1)(*a*) or (*b*).

(2) The organisations within this subsection are—

(*a*) a fire and rescue authority in England and Wales;

(*b*) a fire and rescue authority or joint fire and rescue board in Scotland;

(*c*) the Northern Ireland Fire and Rescue Service Board;

(*d*) any other organisation providing a service of responding to emergency circumstances either—

(i) in pursuance of arrangements made with an organisation within paragraph (*a*), (*b*) or (*c*), or

(ii) (if not in pursuance of such arrangements) otherwise than on a commercial basis;

(*e*) a relevant NHS body;

(*f*) an organisation providing ambulance services in pursuance of arrangements—

(i) made by, or at the request of, a relevant NHS body, or

(ii) made with the Secretary of State or with the Welsh Ministers;

(*g*) an organisation providing services for the transport of organs, blood, equipment or personnel in pursuance of arrangements of the kind mentioned in paragraph (*f*);

(*h*) an organisation providing a rescue service;

(*i*) the armed forces.

(3) For the purposes of subsection (1), the way in which an organisation responds to emergency circumstances does not include the way in which—

(*a*) medical treatment is carried out, or

(*b*) decisions within subsection (4) are made.

(4) The decisions within this subsection are decisions as to the carrying out of medical treatment, other than decisions as to the order in which persons are to be given such treatment.

(5) Any duty of care owed in respect of the carrying out, or attempted carrying out, of a rescue operation at sea in emergency circumstances is not a "relevant duty of care" unless it falls within section 2(1)(*a*) or (*b*).

(6) Any duty of care owed in respect of action taken—

(*a*) in order to comply with a direction under Schedule 3A to the Merchant Shipping Act 1995 (c 21) (safety directions), or

(*b*) by virtue of paragraph 4 of that Schedule (action in lieu of direction),

is not a "relevant duty of care" unless it falls within section 2(1)(*a*) or (*b*).

(7) In this section—

"emergency circumstances" means circumstances that are present or imminent and—

(*a*) are causing, or are likely to cause, serious harm or a worsening of such harm, or

(*b*) are likely to cause the death of a person;

"medical treatment" includes any treatment or procedure of a medical or similar nature;

"relevant NHS body" means—

(*a*) a Strategic Health Authority, Primary Care Trust, NHS trust, Special Health Authority or NHS foundation trust in England;

(*b*) a Local Health Board, NHS trust or Special Health Authority in Wales;

(*c*) a Health Board or Special Health Board in Scotland, or the Common Services Agency for the Scottish Health Service;

(*d*) a Health and Social Services trust or Health and Social Services Board in Northern Ireland;

"serious harm" means—

(*a*) serious injury to or the serious illness (including mental illness) of a person;

(*b*) serious harm to the environment (including the life and health of plants and animals);

(*c*) serious harm to any building or other property.

(8) A reference in this section to emergency circumstances includes a reference to circumstances that are believed to be emergency circumstances.

[Corporate Manslaughter and Corporate Homicide Act 2007, s 6.]

7.8917 7. **Child-protection and probation functions** (1) A duty of care to which this section applies is not a "relevant duty of care" unless it falls within section 2(1)(*a*), (*b*) or (*d*).

(2) This section applies to any duty of care that a local authority or other public authority owes in respect of the exercise by it of functions conferred by or under—

(*a*) Parts 4 and 5 of the Children Act 1989 (c 41),

(*b*) *Scotland,*

(*ba*) *Scotland*, or

(*c*) Parts 5 and 6 of the Children (Northern Ireland) Order 1995 (SI 1995/755 (NI 2)).

(3) This section also applies to any duty of care that a local probation board, a provider of probation services or other public authority owes in respect of the exercise by it of functions conferred by or under—

(*a*) Chapter 1 of Part 1 of the Criminal Justice and Court Services Act 2000 (c 43),

(*aa*) section 13 of the Offender Management Act 2007 (c 21),

(*b*) *Scotland*, or

(*c*) Article 4 of the Probation Board (Northern Ireland) Order 1982 (SI 1982/713 (NI 10)).

(4) This section also applies to any duty of care that a provider of probation services owes in respect of the carrying out by it of activities in pursuance of arrangements under section 3 of the Offender Management Act 2007.

[Corporate Manslaughter and Corporate Homicide Act 2007, s 7 as amended by SI 2008/912 and SI 2013/1465.]

*Gross breach*

7.8918 **8. Factors for jury** (1) This section applies where—

(*a*) it is established that an organisation owed a relevant duty of care to a person, and

(*b*) it falls to the jury to decide whether there was a gross breach of that duty.

(2) The jury must consider whether the evidence shows that the organisation failed to comply with any health and safety legislation that relates to the alleged breach, and if so—

(*a*) how serious that failure was;

(*b*) how much of a risk of death it posed.

(3) The jury may also—

(*a*) consider the extent to which the evidence shows that there were attitudes, policies, systems or accepted practices within the organisation that were likely to have encouraged any such failure as is mentioned in subsection (2), or to have produced tolerance of it;

(*b*) have regard to any health and safety guidance that relates to the alleged breach.

(4) This section does not prevent the jury from having regard to any other matters they consider relevant.

(5) In this section "health and safety guidance" means any code, guidance, manual or similar publication that is concerned with health and safety matters and is made or issued (under a statutory provision or otherwise) by an authority responsible for the enforcement of any health and safety legislation.

[Corporate Manslaughter and Corporate Homicide Act 2007, s 8.]

*Remedial orders and publicity orders*

7.8919 **9. Power to order breach etc to be remedied** (1) A court before which an organisation is convicted of corporate manslaughter or corporate homicide may make an order (a "remedial order") requiring the organisation to take specified steps to remedy—

(*a*) the breach mentioned in section 1(1) ("the relevant breach");

(*b*) any matter that appears to the court to have resulted from the relevant breach and to have been a cause of the death;

(*c*) any deficiency, as regards health and safety matters, in the organisation's policies, systems or practices of which the relevant breach appears to the court to be an indication.

(2) A remedial order may be made only on an application by the prosecution specifying the terms of the proposed order.

Any such order must be on such terms (whether those proposed or others) as the court considers appropriate having regard to any representations made, and any evidence adduced, in relation to that matter by the prosecution or on behalf of the organisation.

(3) Before making an application for a remedial order the prosecution must consult such enforcement authority or authorities as it considers appropriate having regard to the nature of the relevant breach.

(4) A remedial order—

(*a*) must specify a period within which the steps referred to in subsection (1) are to be taken;

(*b*) may require the organisation to supply to an enforcement authority consulted under subsection (3), within a specified period, evidence that those steps have been taken.

A period specified under this subsection may be extended or further extended by order of the court on an application made before the end of that period or extended period.

(5) An organisation that fails to comply with a remedial order is guilty of an offence, and liable on conviction on indictment to a fine.

[Corporate Manslaughter and Corporate Homicide Act 2007, s 9.]

7.8920 **10. Power to order conviction etc to be publicised** (1) A court before which an organisation is convicted of corporate manslaughter or corporate homicide may make an order (a "publicity order") requiring the organisation to publicise in a specified manner—

(*a*) the fact that it has been convicted of the offence;

(*b*) specified particulars of the offence;
(*c*) the amount of any fine imposed;
(*d*) the terms of any remedial order made.

(2) In deciding on the terms of a publicity order that it is proposing to make, the court must—
(*a*) ascertain the views of such enforcement authority or authorities (if any) as it considers appropriate, and
(*b*) have regard to any representations made by the prosecution or on behalf of the organisation.

(3) A publicity order—
(*a*) must specify a period within which the requirements referred to in subsection (1) are to be complied with;
(*b*) may require the organisation to supply to any enforcement authority whose views have been ascertained under subsection (2), within a specified period, evidence that those requirements have been complied with.

(4) An organisation that fails to comply with a publicity order is guilty of an offence, and liable on conviction on indictment to a fine.

[Corporate Manslaughter and Corporate Homicide Act 2007, s 10.]

*Application to particular categories of organisation*

7.8921 **11. Application to Crown bodies** (1) An organisation that is a servant or agent of the Crown is not immune from prosecution under this Act for that reason.

(2) For the purposes of this Act—
(*a*) a department or other body listed in Schedule 1, or
(*b*) a corporation that is a servant or agent of the Crown,
is to be treated as owing whatever duties of care it would owe if it were a corporation that was not a servant or agent of the Crown.

(3) For the purposes of section 2—
(*a*) a person who is—
(i) employed by or under the Crown for the purposes of a department or other body listed in Schedule 1, or
(ii) employed by a person whose staff constitute a body listed in that Schedule,
is to be treated as employed by that department or body;
(*b*) any premises occupied for the purposes of—
(i) a department or other body listed in Schedule 1, or
(ii) a person whose staff constitute a body listed in that Schedule,
are to be treated as occupied by that department or body.

(4) For the purposes of sections 2 to 7 anything done purportedly by a department or other body listed in Schedule 1, although in law by the Crown or by the holder of a particular office, is to be treated as done by the department or other body itself.

(5) Subsections (3)(*a*)(i), (3)(*b*)(i) and (4) apply in relation to a Northern Ireland department as they apply in relation to a department or other body listed in Schedule 1.

[Corporate Manslaughter and Corporate Homicide Act 2007, s 11.]

7.8922 **12. Application to armed forces** (1) In this Act "the armed forces" means any of the naval, military or air forces of the Crown raised under the law of the United Kingdom.

(2) For the purposes of section 2 a person who is a member of the armed forces is to be treated as employed by the Ministry of Defence.

(3) A reference in this Act to members of the armed forces includes a reference to—
(*a*) members of the reserve forces (within the meaning given by section 1(2) of the Reserve Forces Act 1996 (c 14)) when in service or undertaking training or duties;
(*b*) persons serving on Her Majesty's vessels (within the meaning given by section 132(1) of the Naval Discipline Act 1957 (c 53)).

[Corporate Manslaughter and Corporate Homicide Act 2007, s 12.]

7.8923 **13. Application to police forces** (1) In this Act "police force" means—
(*a*) a police force within the meaning of—
(i) the Police Act 1996 (c 16).
(ii) *repealed*;
(*aa*) Scotland;
(*b*) the Police Service of Northern Ireland;
(*c*) the Police Service of Northern Ireland Reserve;
(*d*) the British Transport Police Force;
(*e*) the Civil Nuclear Constabulary;
(*f*) the Ministry of Defence Police.

(2) For the purposes of this Act a police force is to be treated as owing whatever duties of care it would owe if it were a body corporate.

(3) For the purposes of section 2—
(*a*) a member of a police force is to be treated as employed by that force;

(*b*) a special constable appointed for a police area in England and Wales is to be treated as employed by the police force maintained by the local policing body for that area;

(*c*) a special constable appointed for a police force mentioned in paragraph (*d*) or (*f*) of subsection (1) is to be treated as employed by that force;

(*d*) a police cadet undergoing training with a view to becoming a member of a police force mentioned in paragraph (*a*), (*aa*) or (*d*) of subsection (1) is to be treated as employed by that force;

(*e*) a police trainee appointed under section 39 of the Police (Northern Ireland) Act 2000 (c 32) or a police cadet appointed under section 42 of that Act is to be treated as employed by the Police Service of Northern Ireland;

(*f*) a police reserve trainee appointed under section 40 of that Act is to be treated as employed by the Police Service of Northern Ireland Reserve;

(*g*) a member of a police force seconded to the National Crime Agency to serve as a National Crime Agency officer is to be treated as employed by that Agency.

(4) A reference in subsection (3) to a member of a police force is to be read, in the case of the Police Service of Scotland, as a reference to a constable of that Service.

(5) For the purposes of section 2 any premises occupied for the purposes of a police force are to be treated as occupied by that force.

(6) For the purposes of sections 2 to 7 anything that would be regarded as done by a police force if the force were a body corporate is to be so regarded.

(7) Where—

(*a*) by virtue of subsection (3) a person is treated for the purposes of section 2 as employed by a police force, and

(*b*) by virtue of any other statutory provision (whenever made) he is, or is treated as, employed by another organisation,

the person is to be treated for those purposes as employed by both the force and the other organisation.

[Corporate Manslaughter and Corporate Homicide Act 2007, s 13 as amended by the Police Reform and Social Responsibility Act 2011, Sch 16, SI 2013/602 and the Crime and Courts Act 2013, Sch 8.]

7.8924 14. **Application to partnerships** (1) For the purposes of this Act a partnership is to be treated as owing whatever duties of care it would owe if it were a body corporate.

(2) Proceedings for an offence under this Act alleged to have been committed by a partnership are to be brought in the name of the partnership (and not in that of any of its members).

(3) A fine imposed on a partnership on its conviction of an offence under this Act is to be paid out of the funds of the partnership.

(4) This section does not apply to a partnership that is a legal person under the law by which it is governed.

[Corporate Manslaughter and Corporate Homicide Act 2007, s 14.]

*Miscellaneous*

7.8925 15. **Procedure, evidence and sentencing** (1) Any statutory provision (whenever made) about criminal proceedings applies, subject to any prescribed adaptations or modifications, in relation to proceedings under this Act against—

(*a*) a department or other body listed in Schedule 1,

(*b*) a police force,

(*c*) a partnership,

(*d*) a trade union, or

(*e*) an employers' association that is not a corporation,

as it applies in relation to proceedings against a corporation.

(2) In this section—

"prescribed" means—

(*a*) in relation to proceedings under this Act in England and Wales, prescribed by an order made by the Secretary of State;

(*b*) in relation to proceedings under this Act in Northern Ireland, prescribed by an order made by the Department of Justice in Northern Ireland;

"provision about criminal proceedings" includes—

(*a*) provision about procedure in or in connection with criminal proceedings;

(*b*) provision about evidence in such proceedings;

(*c*) provision about sentencing, or otherwise dealing with, persons convicted of offences;

"statutory" means contained in, or in an instrument made under, any Act or any Northern Ireland legislation.

(3) A reference in this section to proceedings (except in the definition of "prescribed" in subsection (2)) is to proceedings in England and Wales or Northern Ireland.

(4) An order of the Secretary of State under this section is subject to negative resolution procedure.

[Corporate Manslaughter and Corporate Homicide Act 2007, s 15 as amended by SI 2010/976.]

7.8926 16. **Transfer of functions** (1) This section applies where—

(a) a person's death has occurred, or is alleged to have occurred, in connection with the carrying out of functions by a relevant public organisation, and

(b) subsequently there is a transfer of those functions, with the result that they are still carried out but no longer by that organisation.

(2) In this section "relevant public organisation" means—

(a) a department or other body listed in Schedule 1;

(b) a corporation that is a servant or agent of the Crown;

(c) a police force.

(3) Any proceedings instituted against a relevant public organisation after the transfer for an offence under this Act in respect of the person's death are to be instituted against—

(a) the relevant public organisation, if any, by which the functions mentioned in subsection (1) are currently carried out;

(b) if no such organisation currently carries out the functions, the relevant public organisation by which the functions were last carried out.

This is subject to subsection (4).

(4) If an order made by the Secretary of State so provides in relation to a particular transfer of functions, the proceedings referred to in subsection (3) may be instituted, or (if they have already been instituted) may be continued, against—

(a) the organisation mentioned in subsection (1), or

(b) such relevant public organisation (other than the one mentioned in subsection (1) or the one mentioned in subsection (3)(*a*) or (*b*)) as may be specified in the order.

(5) If the transfer occurs while proceedings for an offence under this Act in respect of the person's death are in progress against a relevant public organisation, the proceedings are to be continued against—

(a) the relevant public organisation, if any, by which the functions mentioned in subsection (1) are carried out as a result of the transfer;

(b) if as a result of the transfer no such organisation carries out the functions, the same organisation as before.

This is subject to subsection (6).

(6) If an order made by the Secretary of State so provides in relation to a particular transfer of functions, the proceedings referred to in subsection (5) may be continued against—

(a) the organisation mentioned in subsection (1), or

(b) such relevant public organisation (other than the one mentioned in subsection (1) or the one mentioned in subsection (5)(*a*) or (*b*)) as may be specified in the order.

(7) An order under subsection (4) or (6) is subject to negative resolution procedure.

[Corporate Manslaughter and Corporate Homicide Act 2007, s 16.]

7.8927 17. **DPP's consent required for proceedings** Proceedings for an offence of corporate manslaughter—

(a) may not be instituted in England and Wales without the consent of the Director of Public Prosecutions;

(b) may not be instituted in Northern Ireland without the consent of the Director of Public Prosecutions for Northern Ireland.

[Corporate Manslaughter and Corporate Homicide Act 2007, s 17.]

7.8928 18. **No individual liability** (1) An individual cannot be guilty of aiding, abetting, counselling or procuring the commission of an offence of corporate manslaughter.

(1A) An individual cannot be guilty of an offence under Part 2 of the Serious Crime Act 2007 (encouraging or assisting crime) by reference to an offence of corporate manslaughter.

(2) An individual cannot be guilty of aiding, abetting, counselling or procuring, or being art and part in, the commission of an offence of corporate homicide.

[Corporate Manslaughter and Corporate Homicide Act 2007, s 18 as amended by the Serious Crime Act 2007, s 62.]

7.8929 19. **Convictions under this Act and under health and safety legislation**

7.8930 20. **Abolition of liability of corporations for manslaughter at common law** The common law offence of manslaughter by gross negligence is abolished in its application to corporations, and in any application it has to other organisations to which section 1 applies.

[Corporate Manslaughter and Corporate Homicide Act 2007, s 20.]

*General and supplemental*

7.8931 21. **Power to extend section 1 to other organisations** (1) The Secretary of State may by order amend section 1 so as to extend the categories of organisation to which that section applies.

(2) An order under this section may make any amendment to this Act that is incidental or supplemental to, or consequential on, an amendment made by virtue of subsection (1).

(3) An order under this section is subject to affirmative resolution procedure.

[Corporate Manslaughter and Corporate Homicide Act 2007, s 21.]

7.8932 22. **Power to amend Schedule 1** (1) The Secretary of State may amend Schedule 1 by order.

(2) A statutory instrument containing an order under this section is subject to affirmative resolution procedure, unless the only amendments to Schedule 1 that it makes are amendments within subsection (3).

In that case the instrument is subject to negative resolution procedure.

(3) An amendment is within this subsection if—

(*a*) it is consequential on a department or other body listed in Schedule 1 changing its name,

(*b*) in the case of an amendment adding a department or other body to Schedule 1, it is consequential on the transfer to the department or other body of functions all of which were previously exercisable by one or more organisations to which section 1 applies, or

(*c*) in the case of an amendment removing a department or other body from Schedule 1, it is consequential on—

(i) the abolition of the department or other body, or

(ii) the transfer of all the functions of the department or other body to one or more organisations to which section 1 applies.

[Corporate Manslaughter and Corporate Homicide Act 2007, s 22.]

7.8933 **23. Power to extend section 2(2)** (1) The Secretary of State may by order amend section 2(2) to make it include any category of person (not already included) who—

(*a*) is required by virtue of a statutory provision to remain or reside on particular premises, or

(*b*) is otherwise subject to a restriction of his liberty.

(2) An order under this section may make any amendment to this Act that is incidental or supplemental to, or consequential on, an amendment made by virtue of subsection (1).

(3) An order under this section is subject to affirmative resolution procedure.

[Corporate Manslaughter and Corporate Homicide Act 2007, s 23.]

7.8934 **23A. Northern Ireland**

7.8935 **24. Orders** (1) A power of the Secretary of State to make an order under this Act is exercisable by statutory instrument.

(2) Where an order under this Act is subject to "negative resolution procedure" the statutory instrument containing the order is subject to annulment in pursuance of a resolution of either House of Parliament.

(3) Where an order under this Act is subject to "affirmative resolution procedure" the order may not be made unless a draft has been laid before, and approved by a resolution of, each House of Parliament.

(4) An order under this Act—

(*a*) may make different provision for different purposes;

(*b*) may make transitional or saving provision.

(5)–(10) *Northern Ireland.*

[Corporate Manslaughter and Corporate Homicide Act 2007, s 24 as amended by SI 2010/976.]

7.8936 **25. Interpretation** In this Act—

"armed forces" has the meaning given by section 12(1);

"corporation" does not include a corporation sole but includes any body corporate wherever incorporated;

"employee" means an individual who works under a contract of employment or apprenticeship (whether express or implied and, if express, whether oral or in writing), and related expressions are to be construed accordingly; see also sections 11(3)(*a*), 12(2) and 13(3) (which apply for the purposes of section 2);

"employers' association" has the meaning given by section 122 of the Trade Union and Labour Relations (Consolidation) Act 1992 (c 52) or Article 4 of the Industrial Relations (Northern Ireland) Order 1992 (SI 1992/807 (NI 5));

"enforcement authority" means an authority responsible for the enforcement of any health and safety legislation;

"health and safety legislation" means any statutory provision dealing with health and safety matters, including in particular provision contained in the Health and Safety at Work etc Act 1974 (c 37) or the Health and Safety at Work (Northern Ireland) Order 1978 (SI 1978/1039 (NI 9)) and provision dealing with health and safety matters contained in Part 3 of the Energy Act 2013 (nuclear regulation);

"member", in relation to the armed forces, is to be read in accordance with section 12(3);

"partnership" means—

(*a*) a partnership within the Partnership Act 1890 (c 39), or

(*b*) a limited partnership registered under the Limited Partnerships Act 1907 (c 24),

or a firm or entity of a similar character formed under the law of a country or territory outside the United Kingdom;

"police force" has the meaning given by section 13(1);

"premises" includes land, buildings and moveable structures;

"public authority" has the same meaning as in section 6 of the Human Rights Act 1998 (c 42) (disregarding subsections (3)(*a*) and (4) of that section);

"publicity order" means an order under section 10(1);
"remedial order" means an order under section 9(1);
"statutory provision", except in section 15, means provision contained in, or in an instrument made under, any Act, any Act of the Scottish Parliament or any Northern Ireland legislation;
"trade union" has the meaning given by section 1 of the Trade Union and Labour Relations (Consolidation) Act 1992 (c 52) or Article 3 of the Industrial Relations (Northern Ireland) Order 1992 (SI 1992/807 (NI 5)).

[Corporate Manslaughter and Corporate Homicide Act 2007, s 25 as amended by the Energy Act 2013, Sch 12.]

7.8937 **26. Minor and consequential amendments** Schedule 2 (minor and consequential amendments) has effect.

[Corporate Manslaughter and Corporate Homicide Act 2007, s 26.]

7.8938 **27. Commencement and savings** (1) The preceding provisions of this Act come into force in accordance with provision made by order by the Secretary of State (subject to subsection (1A)).

(1A) *Northern Ireland.*

(2) An order of the Secretary of State bringing into force paragraph (*d*) of section 2(1) is subject to affirmative resolution procedure.

(3) Section 1 does not apply in relation to anything done or omitted before the commencement of that section.

(4) Section 20 does not affect any liability, investigation, legal proceeding or penalty for or in respect of an offence committed wholly or partly before the commencement of that section.

(5) For the purposes of subsection (4) an offence is committed wholly or partly before the commencement of section 20 if any of the conduct or events alleged to constitute the offence occurred before that commencement.

[Corporate Manslaughter and Corporate Homicide Act 2007, s 27 as amended by SI 2010/976.]

7.8939 **28. Extent and territorial application** (1) Subject to subsection (2), this Act extends to England and Wales, Scotland and Northern Ireland.

(2) An amendment made by this Act extends to the same part or parts of the United Kingdom as the provision to which it relates.

(3) Section 1 applies if the harm resulting in death is sustained in the United Kingdom or—

(*a*) within the seaward limits of the territorial sea adjacent to the United Kingdom;
(*b*) on a ship registered under Part 2 of the Merchant Shipping Act 1995 (c 21);
(*c*) on a British-controlled aircraft as defined in section 92 of the Civil Aviation Act 1982 (c 16);
(*d*) on a British-controlled hovercraft within the meaning of that section as applied in relation to hovercraft by virtue of provision made under the Hovercraft Act 1968 (c 59);
(*e*) in any place to which an Order in Council under section 10(1) of the Petroleum Act 1998 (c 17) applies (criminal jurisdiction in relation to offshore activities).

(4) For the purposes of subsection (3)(*b*) to (*d*) harm sustained on a ship, aircraft or hovercraft includes harm sustained by a person who—

(*a*) is then no longer on board the ship, aircraft or hovercraft in consequence of the wrecking of it or of some other mishap affecting it or occurring on it, and
(*b*) sustains the harm in consequence of that event.

[Corporate Manslaughter and Corporate Homicide Act 2007, s 28.]

7.8940 **29. Short title** This Act may be cited as the Corporate Manslaughter and Corporate Homicide Act 2007.

[Corporate Manslaughter and Corporate Homicide Act 2007, s 29.]

# Counter-Terrorism Act 2008[1]

(2008 c 28)

## PART 1[2]

## POWERS TO GATHER AND SHARE INFORMATION

*Power to remove documents for examination*

7.8970 **1. Power to remove documents for examination** (1) This section applies to a search under any of the following provisions—

(*a*) section 43(1) of the Terrorism Act 2000 (c 11) (search of suspected terrorist);
(*b*) section 43(2) of that Act (search of person arrested under section 41 on suspicion of being a terrorist);
(*ba*) section 43(4B) of that Act (search of vehicle in relation to suspected terrorist);
(*bb*) section 43A of that Act (search of vehicle suspected of being used for the purposes of terrorism);
(*c*) paragraph 1, 3, 11, 15, 28 or 31 of Schedule 5 to that Act (terrorist investigations);
(*d*) section 52(1) or (3)(*b*) of the Anti-terrorism, Crime and Security Act 2001 (c 24) (search for evidence of commission of weapons-related offences);
(*e*) *repealed*

(*f*) section 28 of the Terrorism Act 2006 (c 11) (search for terrorist publications);

(*g*) paragraphs 6, 7, 8 or 10 of Schedule 5 to the Terrorism Prevention and Investigation Measures Act 2011.

(2) A constable who carries out a search to which this section applies may, for the purpose of ascertaining whether a document is one that may be seized, remove the document to another place for examination and retain it there until the examination is completed.

(3) Where a constable carrying out a search to which this section applies has power to remove a document by virtue of this section, and the document—

(*a*) consists of information that is stored in electronic form, and

(*b*) is accessible from the premises being searched,

the constable may require the document to be produced in a form in which it can be taken away, and in which it is visible and legible or from which it can readily be produced in a visible and legible form.

(4) A constable has the same powers of seizure in relation to a document removed under this section as the constable would have if it had not been removed (and if anything discovered on examination after removal had been discovered without it having been removed).

[Counter-Terrorism Act 2008, s 1, as amended by the Terrorism Prevention and Investigation Measures Act 2011, Sch 7 and the Protection of Freedoms Act 2012, Sch 9.]

---

[1] This Act amends the law relating to terrorism in a number of ways.

Part 1 (powers to gather and share information) contains provisions for new powers relating to the removal of documents for examination in the context of a search under existing terrorism legislation; provides a power for a constable to take fingerprints and samples from individuals subject to control orders; amends the law relating to the retention and use of fingerprints and DNA samples; and contains provisions on the disclosure of information to and by the intelligence services and their use of such information.

Part 2 (post-charge questioning of terrorist suspects) provides that terrorist suspects may be questioned after they have been charged. The questioning will be authorised by a judge and adverse inferences from the silence of the suspect may be drawn by a court in England and Wales or Northern Ireland.

Part 3 (prosecution and punishment of offences) provides for specified terrorism offences committed anywhere in the UK to be tried in any part of the UK. It also requires the Attorney General's or Advocate General for Northern Ireland's consent for prosecution of certain terrorism offences committed outside the UK. This Part also deals with sentences for terrorism cases tried under the general criminal law: the court is to treat a terrorist connection as an aggravating factor when considering sentence. It also extends the forfeiture regime that applies in terrorist cases.

Part 4 (notification requirements) makes provision about the notification of information to the police by certain individuals convicted of terrorism or terrorism-related offences. Under Sch 5, a court may, on application, impose a foreign travel restriction order on an individual subject to the notification requirements, restricting that person's overseas travel.

Part 5 (terrorist financing and money laundering) confers powers on the Treasury to direct persons operating in the financial sector to take certain actions in respect of transactions or business with persons in a country of money laundering, terrorist financing or proliferation concern.

Part 6 (financial restrictions proceedings) creates a statutory basis for a person affected by certain kinds of Treasury decision to apply to have the decision set aside. The Treasury decisions to which this part relates are those made under (i) the UN Terrorism Orders, (ii) Part 2 of the Anti-terrorism, Crime and Security Act 2001, or (iii) Sch 7 to this Act. It also provides for Rules of Court to make provision about such applications, in particular for the procedure which is to apply where the reason for the Treasury's decision (or part of it) cannot be disclosed to the applicant because disclosure would be contrary to the public interest (ie it involves "closed source material"). Part 6 is not reproduced in this work.

Part 7 (miscellaneous) amends the Regulation of Investigatory Powers Act 2000 to allow intercept material to be disclosed in exceptional circumstances to counsel to an inquiry held under the Inquiries Act 2005 (in addition to the inquiry panel); it also amends the definition of terrorism in s 1 of the Terrorism Act 2000 and various other pieces of terrorism legislation) by inserting a reference to a racial cause. This Part also creates an offence of eliciting, publishing or communicating information about members of the armed forces, members of the intelligence services or constables which is likely to be of use to terrorists; amends the offence of failing to disclose information about a suspected terrorist finance offence; includes some amendments to the control order system under the Prevention of Terrorism Act 2005; makes minor amendments to the provisions on pre-charge detention of terrorist suspects under the 2000 Act, and amendments to provisions on forfeiture of terrorist cash; and establishes a new scheme for the recovery of costs of policing at gas facilities.

Part 8 contains supplementary provisions.

Parts 5 and 6, ss 85–90 of Part 7 and Part 8 came into force on or the day after the Act was passed; the remaining provisions will be brought into force in accordance with commencement orders made under s 100. At the date at which this work states the law, the following commencement orders had been made: the Counter-Terrorism Act 2008 (Commencement No 1) Order 2008, SI 2008/3296, which brought into force ss 19–21; the Counter-Terrorism Act 2008 (Commencement No 2) Order 2009, SI 2009/58, which brought into force ss 29, 74–78, 82–84 and 99; the Counter-Terrorism Act 2008 (Commencement No 3) Order 2009, SI 2009/1256 which brought into force ss 28, 30–33 (with Sch 2), and 34–39 (with Sch 3); the Counter-Terrorism Act 2008 (Commencement No 4) Order 2009, SI 2009/1493 which brought into force ss 40–61 (with Schs 4, 5 & 6); the Counter-Terrorism Act 2008 (Commencement No 5) Order 2012, SI 2012/1121 which brought s 26 into force; the Counter-Terrorism Act 2008 (Commencement No 6) Order 2012, SI 2012/1724 which brought into force ss 22, 23 and 25; and the Counter-Terrorism Act 2008 (Commencement No 7) Order 2012, SI 2012/1966, which brought s 27 into force.

[2] PART 1 contains ss 1–21.

7.8971 **2. Offence of obstruction** (1) A person who wilfully obstructs a constable in the exercise of the power conferred by section 1 commits an offence.

(2) A person guilty of an offence under this section is liable on summary conviction—

(*a*) in England and Wales, to imprisonment for a term not exceeding 51 weeks or a fine not exceeding level 5 on the standard scale, or both;

(*b*) in Scotland, to imprisonment for a term not exceeding twelve months or a fine not exceeding level 5 on the standard scale, or both;

(*c*) in Northern Ireland, to imprisonment for a term not exceeding six months or a fine not exceeding level 5 on the standard scale, or both.

(3) In subsection (2)(*a*) as it applies in relation to an offence committed before section 281(5) of the Criminal Justice Act 2003 (c 44) comes into force, for "51 weeks" substitute "six months".

[Counter-Terrorism Act 2008, s 2.]

7.8973 **3. Items subject to legal privilege** (1) Section 1 does not authorise a constable to remove a document if the constable has reasonable cause to believe—

(*a*) it is an item subject to legal privilege, or

(*b*) it has an item subject to legal privilege comprised in it.

(2) Subsection (1)(*b*) does not prevent the removal of a document if it is not reasonably practicable for the item subject to legal privilege to be separated from the rest of the document without prejudicing any use of the rest of the document that would be lawful if it were subsequently seized.

(3) If, after a document has been removed under section 1, it is discovered that—

(*a*) it is an item subject to legal privilege, or

(*b*) it has an item subject to legal privilege comprised in it,

the document must be returned forthwith.

(4) Subsection (3)(*b*) does not require the return of a document if it is not reasonably practicable for the item subject to legal privilege to be separated from the rest of the document without prejudicing any use of the rest of the document that would be lawful if it were subsequently seized.

(5) Where an item subject to legal privilege is removed under subsection (2) or retained under subsection (4), it must not be examined or put to any other use except to the extent necessary for facilitating the examination of the rest of the document.

(6) For the purposes of this section "item subject to legal privilege"—

(*a*) in England and Wales, has the same meaning as in the Police and Criminal Evidence Act 1984 (c 60);

(*b*) in Scotland, has the meaning given by section 412 of the Proceeds of Crime Act 2002 (c 29);

(*c*) in Northern Ireland, has the same meaning as in the Police and Criminal Evidence (Northern Ireland) Order 1989 (SI 1989/1341 (NI 12)).

[Counter-Terrorism Act 2008, s 3.]

7.8975 **4. Record of removal** (1) A constable who removes a document under section 1 must make a written record of the removal.

(2) The record must be made as soon as is reasonably practicable and in any event within the period of 24 hours beginning with the time when the document was removed.

(3) The record must—

(*a*) describe the document,

(*b*) specify the object of the removal,

(*c*) where the document was found in the course of a search of a person, state the person's name (if known),

(*d*) where the document was found in the course of a search of any premises, state the address of the premises where the document was found,

(*e*) where the document was found in the course of a search of any premises, state the name (if known) of—

(i) any person who, when the record is made, appears to the constable to have been the occupier of the premises when the document was found, and

(ii) any person who, when the record is made, appears to the constable to have had custody or control of the document when it was found, and

(*f*) state the date and time when the document was removed.

(4) If, in a case where the document was found in the course of a search of a person, the constable does not know the person's name, the record must include a description of the person.

(5) If, in a case where the document was found in the course of a search of any premises, the constable does not know the name of a person mentioned in subsection (3)(*e*) but is able to provide a description of that person, the record must include such a description.

(6) The record must identify the constable by reference to the constable's police number.

(7) The following are entitled, on a request made to the constable, to a copy of the record made under this section—

(*a*) where the document was found in the course of a search of a person, that person; and

(*b*) where the document was found in the course of a search of any premises—

(i) the occupier of the premises when it was found, and

(ii) any person who had custody or control of the document when it was found.

(8) The constable must provide the copy within a reasonable time from the making of the request.

(9) If, in England and Wales or Northern Ireland, the document is found in the course of a search under a warrant, the constable must make an endorsement on the warrant stating that the document has been removed under section 1.

(10) In the application of this section in relation to the search of a vehicle, the reference to the address of the premises is to the location of the vehicle together with its registration number (if any).

[Counter-Terrorism Act 2008, s 4.]

7.8977 **5. Retention of documents** (1) A document may not be retained by virtue of section 1 for more than 48 hours without further authorisation.

(2) A constable of at least the rank of chief inspector may authorise the retention of the document for a further period or periods if satisfied that—

(*a*) the examination of the document is being carried out expeditiously, and

(*b*) it is necessary to continue the examination for the purpose of ascertaining whether the document is one that may be seized.

(3) This does not permit the retention of a document after the end of the period of 96 hours beginning with the time when it was removed for examination.

[Counter-Terrorism Act 2008, s 5.]

7.8979 **6. Access to documents** (1) Where—

(*a*) a document is retained by virtue of section 5, and

(*b*) a request for access to the document is made to the officer in charge of the investigation by a person within subsection (3),

the officer must grant that person access to the document, under the supervision of a constable, subject to subsection (4).

(2) Where—

(*a*) a document is retained by virtue of section 5, and

(*b*) a request for a copy of the document is made to the officer in charge of the investigation by a person within subsection (3),

that person must be provided with a copy of the document within a reasonable time from the making of the request, subject to subsection (4).

(3) The persons entitled to make a request under subsection (1) or (2) are—

(*a*) where the document was found in the course of a search of a person, that person,

(*b*) where the document was found in the course of a search of any premises—

(i) the occupier of the premises when it was found, and

(ii) any person who had custody or control of the document when it was found, and

(*c*) a person acting on behalf of a person within paragraph (*a*) or (*b*).

(4) The officer in charge of the investigation may refuse access to the document, or (as the case may be) refuse to provide a copy of it, if the officer has reasonable grounds for believing that to do so—

(*a*) would prejudice any investigation for the purposes of which—

(i) the original search was carried out, or

(ii) the document was removed or is being retained,

(*b*) would prejudice the investigation of any offence,

(*c*) would prejudice any criminal proceedings that may be brought as the result of an investigation within paragraph (*a*) or (*b*), or

(*d*) would facilitate the commission of an offence.

(5) In this section—

"the officer in charge of the investigation" means the officer in charge of the investigation for the purposes of which the document is being retained; and

"the original search" means the search in the course of which the document was removed.

[Counter-Terrorism Act 2008, s 6.]

7.8981 **7. Photographing and copying of documents** (1) Where a document is removed under section 1 it must not be photographed or copied, except that—

(*a*) a document may be copied for the purpose of providing a copy in response to a request under section 6(2), and

(*b*) a document consisting of information stored in electronic form may be copied for the purpose of producing it in a visible and legible form.

(2) Where the original document is returned, any copy under subsection (1)(*b*) must—

(*a*) in the case of a copy in electronic form, be destroyed or made inaccessible as soon as is reasonably practicable, and

(*b*) in any other case, be returned at the same time as the original document is returned.

(3) The following are entitled, on a request made to the relevant chief officer of police, to a certificate that subsection (2) has been complied with—

(*a*) where the document was found in the course of a search of a person, that person;

(*b*) where the document was found in the course of a search of any premises—

(i) the occupier of the premises when it was found, and

(ii) any person who had custody or control of the document when it was found.

(4) The certificate must be issued by the relevant chief officer of police, or a person authorised by or on behalf of that chief officer, not later than the end of the period of three months beginning with the day on which the request is made.

(5) For this purpose the relevant chief officer of police is—

(*a*) where the search was carried out in England or Wales, the chief officer of police in whose area the search was carried out;

(*b*) where the search was carried out in Scotland, the chief constable of the Police Service of Scotland;

(*c*) where the search was carried out in Northern Ireland, the Chief Constable of the Police Service of Northern Ireland.

[Counter-Terrorism Act 2008, s 7 amended by SI 2013/602.]

7.8983 8. **Return of documents** (1) Where a document removed under section 1 is required to be returned, it must be returned—

(*a*) where the document was found in the course of a search of a person, to that person;

(*b*) where the document was found in the course of a search of any premises, to the occupier of the premises when it was found.

(2) Subsection (1) does not apply where a person who is required to return the document is satisfied that another person has a better right to it; and in such a case it must be returned—

(*a*) to that other person, or

(*b*) to whoever appears to the person required to return the document to have the best right to it.

(3) Where different persons claim to be entitled to the return of the document, it may be retained for as long as is reasonably necessary for the determination of the person to whom it must be returned.

(4) This section also applies in relation to a copy of a document that is required to be returned at the same time as the original; and in such a case references to the document in paragraphs (*a*) and (*b*) of subsection (1) are to the original.

[Counter-Terrorism Act 2008, s 8.]

7.8985 9. **Power to remove documents: supplementary provisions** (1) In sections 1 to 8 "document" includes any record and, in particular, includes information stored in electronic form.

(2) In the application of those sections to a search under 52(1) of the Anti-terrorism, Crime and Security Act 2001 (c 24), for references to a constable substitute references to an authorised officer within the meaning of that section.

(3) In the application of those sections in relation to the search of a vehicle references to the occupier of the premises are to the person in charge of the vehicle.

[Counter-Terrorism Act 2008, s 9.]

*Retention and use of fingerprints and samples*

7.8987 14. **Material subject to the Police and Criminal Evidence Act 1984** (1) The Police and Criminal Evidence Act 1984 (c 60) is amended as follows.

(2) In section 63A(1) (fingerprints, impressions of footwear and samples: what they may be checked against), for paragraphs (*a*) and (*b*) substitute—

"(*a*) other fingerprints, impressions of footwear or samples—

(i) to which the person seeking to check has access and which are held by or on behalf of any one or more relevant law-enforcement authorities or are held in connection with or as a result of an investigation of an offence, or

(ii) which are held by or on behalf of the Security Service or the Secret Intelligence Service;

(*b*) information derived from other samples—

(i) which is contained in records to which the person seeking to check has access and which are held as mentioned in paragraph (*a*)(i) above, or

(ii) which is held by or on behalf of the Security Service or the Secret Intelligence Service.".

(3) In section 63A(1ZA) (fingerprints from a person whose identity is unclear: what they may be checked against), for the words from "other fingerprints" to the end, substitute

"other fingerprints—

(*a*) to which the person seeking to check has access and which are held by or on behalf of any one or more relevant law-enforcement authorities or which are held in connection with or as a result of an investigation of an offence, or

(*b*) which are held by or on behalf of the Security Service or the Secret Intelligence Service.".

(4) *Repealed.*

(5) *Repealed.*

(6) *Repealed.*

[Counter-Terrorism Act 2008, s 14 as amended by the Protection of Freedoms Act 2012, Sch 10.]

7.8990 18. **Destruction of national security material not subject to existing statutory restrictions*** (1) This section applies to fingerprints, DNA samples and DNA profiles that—

(*a*) are held for the purposes of national security by a law enforcement authority under the law of England and Wales or Northern Ireland, and

(*b*) are not held subject to existing statutory restrictions.

(2) Material to which this section applies ("section 18 material") must be destroyed if it appears to the responsible officer that the condition in subsection (3) is not met.

(3) The condition is that the material has been—

(*a*) obtained by the law enforcement authority pursuant to an authorisation under Part 3 of the Police Act 1997 (authorisation of action in respect of property),

(*b*) obtained by the law enforcement authority in the course of surveillance, or use of a covert human intelligence source, authorised under Part 2 of the Regulation of Investigatory Powers Act 2000,

(*c*) supplied to the law enforcement authority by another law enforcement authority, or

(*d*) otherwise lawfully obtained or acquired by the law enforcement authority for any of the purposes mentioned in section 18D(1).

(4) In any other case, section 18 material must be destroyed unless it is retained by the law enforcement authority under any power conferred by section 18A or 18B, but this is subject to subsection (5).

(5) A DNA sample to which this section applies must be destroyed—

(*a*) as soon as a DNA profile has been derived from the sample, or

(*b*) if sooner, before the end of the period of 6 months beginning with the date on which it was taken.

(6) Section 18 material which ceases to be retained under a power mentioned in subsection (4) may continue to be retained under any other such power which applies to it.

(7) Nothing in this section prevents section 18 material from being checked against other fingerprints, DNA samples or DNA profiles held by a law enforcement authority within such time as may reasonably be required for the check, if the responsible officer considers the check to be desirable.

(8) For the purposes of subsection (1), the following are "existing statutory restrictions"—

(*a*) paragraph 18(2) of Schedule 2 to the Immigration Act 1971;

(*b*) sections 22, 63A and 63D to 63U of the Police and Criminal Evidence Act 1984 and any corresponding provision in an order under section 113 of that Act;

(*c*) Articles 24, 63A and 64 of the Police and Criminal Evidence (Northern Ireland) Order 1989 (SI 1989/1341 (NI 12));

(*d*) section 2(2) of the Security Service Act 1989;

(*e*) section 2(2) of the Intelligence Services Act 1994;

(*f*) paragraphs 20(3) and 20A to 20J of Schedule 8 to the Terrorism Act 2000;

(*g*) section 56 of the Criminal Justice and Police Act 2001;

(*h*) paragraph 8 of Schedule 4 to the International Criminal Court Act 2001;

(*i*) sections 73, 83, 87, 88 and 89 of the Armed Forces Act 2006 and any provision relating to the retention of material in an order made under section 74, 93 or 323 of that Act;

(*j*) paragraphs 5 to 14 of Schedule 6 to the Terrorism Prevention and Investigation Measures Act 2011.

[Counter-Terrorism Act 2008, s 18 as substituted by the Protection of Freedoms Act 2012, Sch 1.]

**7.8991 18A. Retention of material: general** (1) Section 18 material which is not a DNA sample and relates to a person who has no previous convictions or only one exempt conviction may be retained by the law enforcement authority until the end of the retention period specified in subsection (2), but this is subject to subsection (5).

(2) The retention period is—

(*a*) in the case of fingerprints, the period of 3 years beginning with the date on which the fingerprints were taken, and

(*b*) in the case of a DNA profile, the period of 3 years beginning with the date on which the DNA sample from which the profile was derived was taken (or, if the profile was derived from more than one DNA sample, the date on which the first of those samples was taken).

(3) Section 18 material which is not a DNA sample and relates to a person who has previously been convicted of a recordable offence (other than a single exempt conviction), or is so convicted before the material is required to be destroyed by virtue of this section, may be retained indefinitely.

(4) Section 18 material which is not a DNA sample may be retained indefinitely if—

(*a*) it is held by the law enforcement authority in a form which does not include information which identifies the person to whom the material relates, and

(*b*) the law enforcement authority does not know, and has never known, the identity of the person to whom the material relates.

(5) In a case where section 18 material is being retained by a law enforcement authority under subsection (4), if—

(*a*) the law enforcement authority comes to know the identity of the person to whom the material relates, and

(*b*) the material relates to a person who has no previous convictions or only one exempt conviction,

the material may be retained by the law enforcement authority until the end of the retention period specified in subsection (6).

(6) The retention period is the period of 3 years beginning with the date on which the identity of the person to whom the material relates comes to be known by the law enforcement authority.

[Counter-Terrorism Act 2008, s 18A as inserted by the Protection of Freedoms Act 2012, Sch 1.]

7.8992 **18B. Retention for purposes of national security** (1) Section 18 material which is not a DNA sample may be retained for as long as a national security determination made by the responsible officer has effect in relation to it.

(2) A national security determination is made if the responsible officer determines that it is necessary for any such section 18 material to be retained for the purposes of national security.

(3) A national security determination—

(*a*) must be made in writing,

(*b*) has effect for a maximum of 2 years beginning with the date on which the determination is made, and

(*c*) may be renewed.

[Counter-Terrorism Act 2008, s 18B as inserted by the Protection of Freedoms Act 2012, Sch 1.]

7.8993 **18C. Destruction of copies** (1) If fingerprints are required by section 18 to be destroyed, any copies of the fingerprints held by the law enforcement authority concerned must also be destroyed.

(2) If a DNA profile is required by that section to be destroyed, no copy may be retained by the law enforcement authority concerned except in a form which does not include information which identifies the person to whom the DNA profile relates.

[Counter-Terrorism Act 2008, s 18C as inserted by the Protection of Freedoms Act 2012, Sch 1.]

7.8994 **18D. Use of retained material** (1) Section 18 material must not be used other than—

(*a*) in the interests of national security,

(*b*) for the purposes of a terrorist investigation,

(*c*) for purposes related to the prevention or detection of crime, the investigation of an offence or the conduct of a prosecution, or

(*d*) for purposes related to the identification of a deceased person or of the person to whom the material relates.

(2) Subject to subsection (1), section 18 material may be checked against other fingerprints, DNA samples or DNA profiles held by a law enforcement authority or the Scottish Police Authority if the responsible officer considers the check to be desirable.

(3) Material which is required by section 18 to be destroyed must not at any time after it is required to be destroyed be used—

(*a*) in evidence against the person to whom the material relates, or

(*b*) for the purposes of the investigation of any offence.

(4) In this section—

(*a*) the reference to using material includes a reference to allowing any check to be made against it and to disclosing it to any person,

(*b*) the reference to crime includes a reference to any conduct which—

(i) constitutes one or more criminal offences (whether under the law of a part of the United Kingdom or of a country or territory outside the United Kingdom), or

(ii) is, or corresponds to, any conduct which, if it all took place in any one part of the United Kingdom, would constitute one or more criminal offences, and

(*c*) the references to an investigation and to a prosecution include references, respectively, to any investigation outside the United Kingdom of any crime or suspected crime and to a prosecution brought in respect of any crime in a country or territory outside the United Kingdom.

[Counter-Terrorism Act 2008, s 18D as inserted by the Protection of Freedoms Act 2012, Sch 1 and amended by the Anti-social Behaviour, Crime and Policing Act 2014, Sch 11.]

7.8995 **18E. Sections 18 to 18E: supplementary provisions** (1) In sections 18 to 18D and this section—

"DNA profile" means any information derived from a DNA sample;

"DNA sample" means any material that has come from a human body and consists of or includes human cells;

"fingerprints" means a record (in any form and produced by any method) of the skin pattern and other physical characteristics or features of a person's fingers or either of a person's palms;

"law enforcement authority" means—

(*a*) a police force,

(*b*) the National Crime Agency,

(*c*) the Commissioners for Her Majesty's Revenue and Customs, or

(*d*) a person formed or existing under the law of a country or territory outside the United Kingdom so far as exercising functions which—

(i) correspond to those of a police force, or

(ii) otherwise involve the investigation or prosecution of offences;

"police force" means any of the following—

(*a*) the metropolitan police force;

(*b*) a police force maintained under section 2 of the Police Act 1996 (police forces in England and Wales outside London);

(*c*) the City of London police force;

(*d*) the Police Service of Scotland;

(*e*) the Police Service of Northern Ireland;
(*f*) the Police Service of Northern Ireland Reserve;
(*g*) the Ministry of Defence Police;
(*h*) the Royal Navy Police;
(*i*) the Royal Military Police;
(*j*) the Royal Air Force Police;
(*k*) the British Transport Police;

"recordable offence" has—

(*a*) in relation to a conviction in England and Wales, the meaning given by section 118(1) of the Police and Criminal Evidence Act 1984, and
(*b*) in relation to a conviction in Northern Ireland, the meaning given by Article 2(2) of the Police and Criminal Evidence (Northern Ireland) Order 1989 (SI 1989/1341 (NI 12));

"the responsible officer" means—

(*a*) in relation to material obtained or acquired by a police force in England and Wales, the chief officer of the police force;
(*b*) in relation to material obtained or acquired by the Police Service of Northern Ireland or the Police Service of Northern Ireland Reserve, the Chief Constable of the Police Service of Northern Ireland;
(*c*) in relation to material obtained or acquired by the Ministry of Defence Police, the Chief Constable of the Ministry of Defence Police;
(*d*) in relation to material obtained or acquired by the Royal Navy Police, the Royal Military Police or the Royal Air Force Police, the Provost Marshal for the police force which obtained or acquired the material;
(*e*) in relation to material obtained or acquired by the British Transport Police, the Chief Constable of the British Transport Police;
(*f*) in relation to material obtained or acquired by the National Crime Agency, the Director General of the National Crime Agency;
(*g*) in relation to material obtained or acquired by the Commissioners for Her Majesty's Revenue and Customs, any of those Commissioners;
(*h*) in relation to any other material, such person as the Secretary of State may by order specify;

"section 18 material" has the meaning given by section 18(2);

"terrorist investigation" has the meaning given by section 32 of the Terrorism Act 2000.

(2) An order under subsection (1) is subject to negative resolution procedure.

(3) For the purposes of section 18A, a person is to be treated as having been convicted of an offence if the person—

(*a*) has been given a caution in respect of the offence which, at the time of the caution, the person has admitted,
(*b*) has been warned or reprimanded under section 65 of the Crime and Disorder Act 1998 for the offence,
(*c*) has been found not guilty of the offence by reason of insanity, or
(*d*) has been found to be under a disability and to have done the act charged in respect of the offence.

(4) Sections 18A and this section, so far as they relate to persons convicted of an offence, have effect despite anything in the Rehabilitation of Offenders Act 1974.

(5) But a person is not to be treated as having been convicted of an offence if that conviction is a disregarded conviction or caution by virtue of section 92 of the Protection of Freedoms Act 2012.

(6) For the purposes of section 18A—

(*a*) a person has no previous convictions if the person has not previously been convicted in England and Wales or Northern Ireland of a recordable offence, and
(*b*) if the person has been previously so convicted of a recordable offence, the conviction is exempt if it is in respect of a recordable offence, other than a qualifying offence, committed when the person was aged under 18.

(7) In subsection (6), "qualifying offence" has—

(*a*) in relation to a conviction in respect of a recordable offence committed in England and Wales, the meaning given by section 65A of the Police and Criminal Evidence Act 1984, and
(*b*) in relation to a conviction in respect of a recordable offence committed in Northern Ireland, the meaning given by Article 53A of the Police and Criminal Evidence (Northern Ireland) Order 1989 (SI 1989/1341 (NI 12)).

(8) If a person is convicted of more than one offence arising out of a single course of action, those convictions are to be treated as a single conviction for the purposes of calculating under section 18A whether the person has been convicted of only one offence.

[Counter-Terrorism Act 2008, s 18E as inserted by the Protection of Freedoms Act 2012, Sch 1 and amended by the Crime and Courts Act 2013, Sch 8 and the Anti-social Behaviour, Crime and Policing Act 2014, s 181(1), Sch 11.]

*Disclosure of information and the intelligence services*

7.8996 **19. Disclosure and the intelligence services** (1) A person may disclose information to any of the intelligence services for the purposes of the exercise by that service of any of its functions.

(2) Information obtained by any of the intelligence services in connection with the exercise of any of its functions may be used by that service in connection with the exercise of any of its other functions.

(3) Information obtained by the Security Service for the purposes of any of its functions may be disclosed by it—

(*a*) for the purpose of the proper discharge of its functions,

(*b*) for the purpose of the prevention or detection of serious crime, or

(*c*) for the purpose of any criminal proceedings.

(4) Information obtained by the Secret Intelligence Service for the purposes of any of its functions may be disclosed by it—

(*a*) for the purpose of the proper discharge of its functions,

(*b*) in the interests of national security,

(*c*) for the purpose of the prevention or detection of serious crime, or

(*d*) for the purpose of any criminal proceedings.

(5) Information obtained by GCHQ for the purposes of any of its functions may be disclosed by it—

(*a*) for the purpose of the proper discharge of its functions, or

(*b*) for the purpose of any criminal proceedings.

(6) A disclosure under this section does not breach—

(*a*) any obligation of confidence owed by the person making the disclosure, or

(*b*) any other restriction on the disclosure of information (however imposed).

(7) The provisions of this section are subject to section 20 (savings and other supplementary provisions).

[Counter-Terrorism Act 2008, s 19.]

7.8998 **20. Disclosure and the intelligence services: supplementary provisions** (1) The provisions of section 19 (disclosure and use of information) do not affect the duties with respect to the obtaining or disclosure of information imposed—

(*a*) on the Director-General of the Security Service, by section 2(2) of the Security Service Act 1989;

(*b*) on the Chief of the Intelligence Service, by section 2(2) of the Intelligence Services Act 1994;

(*c*) on the Director of GCHQ, by section 4(2) of that Act.

(2) Nothing in that section authorises a disclosure that—

(*a*) contravenes the Data Protection Act 1998 (c 29), or

(*b*) is prohibited by Part 1 of the Regulation of Investigatory Powers Act 2000 (c 23).

(3) The provisions of that section are without prejudice to any rule of law authorising the obtaining, use or disclosure of information by any of the intelligence services.

(4) Schedule 1 contains amendments consequential on that section.*

[Counter-Terrorism Act 2008, s 20.]

---

* **Amended by the Investigatory Powers Act 2016, Sch 10 from a date to be appointed.**

7.9000 **21. Disclosure and the intelligence services: interpretation** (1) In sections 19 and 20 "the intelligence services" means the Security Service, the Secret Intelligence Service and GCHQ.

(2) References in section 19 to the functions of those services are—

(*a*) in the case of the Security Service, to the functions specified in section 1(2) to (4) of the Security Service Act 1989 (c 5);

(*b*) in the case of the Secret Intelligence Service, to the functions specified in section 1(1)(*a*) and (*b*) of the Intelligence Services Act 1994 (c 13), exercised in accordance with section 1(2) of that Act;

(*c*) in the case of GCHQ—

(i) to the functions specified in section 3(1)(*a*) of that Act, exercised in accordance with section 3(2) of that Act, and

(ii) to the functions specified in section 3(1)(*b*) of that Act.

(3) In sections 19, 20 and this section "GCHQ" has the same meaning as in the Intelligence Services Act 1994 (see section 3(3) of that Act).

(4) Section 81(5) of the Regulation of Investigatory Powers Act 2000 (meaning of "prevention" and "detection"), so far as it relates to serious crime, applies for the purposes of section 19 as it applies for the purposes of the provisions of that Act not contained in Chapter 1 of Part 1.

[Counter-Terrorism Act 2008, s 21.]

## PART 2[1]

## POST-CHARGE QUESTIONING OF TERRORIST SUSPECTS

7.9002 **22. Post-charge questioning: England and Wales** (1) The following provisions apply in England and Wales.

(2) A judge of the Crown Court may authorise the questioning of a person about an offence—

(a) after the person has been charged with the offence or been officially informed that they may be prosecuted for it, or

(b) after the person has been sent for trial for the offence,

if the offence is a terrorism offence or it appears to the judge that the offence has a terrorist connection.

(3) The judge—

(a) must specify the period during which questioning is authorised, and

(b) may impose such conditions as appear to be necessary in the interests of justice, which may include conditions as to the place where the questioning is to be carried out.

(4) The period during which questioning is authorised—

(a) begins when questioning pursuant to the authorisation begins and runs continuously from that time (whether or not questioning continues), and

(b) must not exceed 48 hours.

This is without prejudice to any application for a further authorisation under this section.

(5) Where the person is in prison or otherwise lawfully detained, the judge may authorise the person's removal to another place and detention there for the purpose of being questioned.

(6) A judge must not authorise the questioning of a person under this section unless satisfied—

(a) that further questioning of the person is necessary in the interests of justice,

(b) that the investigation for the purposes of which the further questioning is proposed is being conducted diligently and expeditiously, and

(c) that what is authorised will not interfere unduly with the preparation of the person's defence to the charge in question or any other criminal charge.

(7) Codes of practice under section 66 of the Police and Criminal Evidence Act 1984 (c 60) must make provision about the questioning of a person by a constable in accordance with this section.

(8) Nothing in this section prevents codes of practice under that section making other provision for the questioning of a person by a constable about an offence—

(a) after the person has been charged with the offence or been officially informed that they may be prosecuted for it, or

(b) after the person has been sent for trial for the offence.

(9) *Amends section 34(1) of the Criminal Justice and Public Order Act 1994.*

(10) Nothing in section 36 or 37 of that Act (effect of accused's failure or refusal to account for certain matters) is to be read as excluding the operation of those sections in relation to a request made in the course of questioning under this section.

[Counter-Terrorism Act 2008, s 22.]

---

1 PART 2 contains ss 22–27.

7.9004 **25. Recording of interviews** (1) This section applies to any interview of a person by a constable under section 22, 23 or 24 (post-charge questioning).

(2) Any such interview must be video recorded, and the video recording must be with sound.

(3) The Secretary of State must issue a code of practice about the video recording of interviews to which this section applies.

(4) The interview and video recording must be conducted in accordance with that code of practice.

(5) A code of practice under this section—

(a) may make provision in relation to a particular part of the United Kingdom, and

(b) may make different provision for different parts of the United Kingdom.

[Counter-Terrorism Act 2008, s 25.]

7.9006 **26. Issue and revision of code of practice** (1) This section applies to the code of practice under section 25 (recording of interviews).

(2) The Secretary of State must—

(a) publish a draft of the proposed code, and

(b) consider any representations made about the draft,

and may modify the draft in the light of the representations made.

(3) The Secretary of State must lay a draft of the code before Parliament.

(4) After laying the draft code before Parliament the Secretary of State may bring it into operation by order[1].

(5) The order is subject to affirmative resolution procedure.

(6) The Secretary of State may revise a code and issue the revised code, and subsections (2) to (5) apply to a revised code as they apply to an original code.

(7) Failure to observe a provision of a code does not of itself render a constable liable to criminal or civil proceedings.

(8) A code—

(a) is admissible in evidence in criminal and civil proceedings, and

(b) shall be taken into account by a court or tribunal in any case in which it appears to the court or tribunal to be relevant.

[Counter-Terrorism Act 2008, s 26.]

[1] The Counter-Terrorism Act 2008 (Code of Practice for the Video Recording with Sound of Post-Charge Questioning) Order 2012, SI 2012/1793 has been made which came into force on 10 July 2012. The associated Code is the code of practice entitled *Code of Practice for the Video Recording with Sound of Interviews of Persons Detained under Section 41 of, or Schedule 7 to, the Terrorism Act 2000 and Post Charge Questioning of Persons Authorised under Sections 22 or 23 of the Counter-Terrorism Act 2008* laid before Parliament in draft on 10 May 2012.

7.9008 27. **Meaning of "terrorism offence"** (1) For the purposes of sections 22 to 24 (post-charge questioning) the following are terrorism offences—

(*a*) an offence under any of the following provisions of the Terrorism Act 2000 (c 11)—
sections 11 to 13 (offences relating to proscribed organisations),
sections 15 to 19, 21A and 21D (offences relating to terrorist property),
sections 38B and 39 (disclosure of and failure to disclose information about terrorism),
section 54 (weapons training),
sections 56 to 58A (directing terrorism, possessing things and collecting information for the purposes of terrorism),
sections 59 to 61 (inciting terrorism outside the United Kingdom),
paragraph 14 of Schedule 5 (order for explanation of material: false or misleading statements),
paragraph 1 of Schedule 6 (failure to provide customer information in connection with a terrorist investigation),
paragraph 18 of Schedule 7 (offences in connection with port and border controls);

(*b*) an offence in respect of which there is jurisdiction by virtue of any of sections 62 to 63D of that Act (extra-territorial jurisdiction in respect of certain offences committed outside the United Kingdom for the purposes of terrorism etc);

(*c*) an offence under section 113 of the Anti-Terrorism, Crime and Security Act 2001 (c 24) (use of noxious substances or things);

(*d*) an offence under any of the following provisions of Part 1 of the Terrorism Act 2006 (c 11)—
sections 1 and 2 (encouragement of terrorism),
sections 5, 6 and 8 (preparation and training for terrorism),
sections 9, 10 and 11 (offences relating to radioactive devices and material and nuclear facilities);

(*e*) an offence in respect of which there is jurisdiction by virtue of section 17 of that Act (extra-territorial jurisdiction in respect of certain offences committed outside the United Kingdom for the purposes of terrorism etc);

(*f*) an offence under paragraph 8 or 9 of Schedule 3 to the Justice and Security (Northern Ireland) Act 2007 (c 6) (offences in connection with searches for munitions and transmitters in Northern Ireland).

(2) Any ancillary offence in relation to an offence listed in subsection (1) is a terrorism offence for the purposes of sections 22 to 24.

(3) The Secretary of State may by order amend subsection (1).

(4) Any such order is subject to affirmative resolution procedure.

[Counter-Terrorism Act 2008, s 27.]

## PART 3[1]
## PROSECUTION AND PUNISHMENT OF TERRORIST OFFENCES

### *Jurisdiction*

7.9010 28. **Jurisdiction to try offences committed in the UK** (1) Where an offence to which this section applies is committed in the United Kingdom—

(*a*) proceedings for the offence may be taken at any place in the United Kingdom, and

(*b*) the offence may for all incidental purposes be treated as having been committed at any such place.

(2) The section applies to—

(*a*) an offence under any of the following provisions of the Terrorism Act 2000 (c 11)—
sections 11 to 13 (offences relating to proscribed organisations),
sections 15 to 19, 21A and 21D (offences relating to terrorist property),
sections 38B and 39 (disclosure of and failure to disclose information about terrorism),
section 47 (offences relating to stop and search powers),
section 51 (parking a vehicle in contravention of an authorisation or restriction),
section 54 (weapons training),
sections 56 to 58A (directing terrorism and possessing things or collecting information for the purposes of terrorism),
section 116 (failure to stop a vehicle when required to do so),
paragraph 1 of Schedule 6 (failure to provide customer information in connection with a terrorist investigation),
paragraph 18 of Schedule 7 (offences in connection with port and border controls);

(*b*) an offence under section 113 of the Anti-terrorism, Crime and Security Act 2001 (c 24) (use of noxious substances or things to cause harm and intimidate);

(*c*) an offence under any of the following provisions of the Terrorism Act 2006 (c 11)—

sections 1 and 2 (encouragement of terrorism),
sections 5, 6 and 8 (preparation and training for terrorism),
sections 9, 10 and 11 (offences relating to radioactive devices etc;

(*d*) an offence under any provision of Part 1 of the Terrorist Asset-Freezing etc Act 2010.

(3) The Secretary of State may by order amend subsection (2).

(4) Any such order is subject to affirmative resolution procedure.

(5) The power conferred by subsection (3) may be exercised so as to add offences to subsection (2) only if it appears to the Secretary of State necessary to do so for the purpose of dealing with terrorism.

(6) *Amends section 1 of the Justice and Security (Northern Ireland) Act 2007.*

[Counter-Terrorism Act 2008, s 28 as amended by the Terrorist Asset-Freezing etc Act 2010, s 35.]

---

1 PART 3 contains ss 28–39.

*Sentencing*

**7.9012 30. Sentences for offences with a terrorist connection: England and Wales**

(1) This section applies where a court in England and Wales is considering for the purposes of sentence the seriousness of an offence specified in Schedule 2 (offences where terrorist connection to be considered).

(2) If having regard to the material before it for the purposes of sentencing it appears to the court that the offence has or may have a terrorist connection, the court must determine whether that is the case.

(3) For that purpose the court may hear evidence, and must take account of any representations made by the prosecution and the defence, as in the case of any other matter relevant for the purposes of sentence.

(4) If the court determines that the offence has a terrorist connection, the court—

(*a*) must treat that fact as an aggravating factor, and

(*b*) must state in open court that the offence was so aggravated.

(5) In this section "sentence", in relation to an offence, includes any order made by a court when dealing with a person in respect of the offence.

(6) This section has effect in relation only to offences committed on or after the day it comes into force.

[Counter-Terrorism Act 2008, s 30.]

**7.9014 32. Sentences for offences with a terrorist connection: armed forces** (1) This section applies where a service court is considering for the purposes of sentence the seriousness of a service offence as respects which the corresponding civil offence is an offence specified in Schedule 2.

(2) If having regard to the material before it for the purposes of sentencing it appears to the court that the offence has or may have a terrorist connection, the court must determine whether that is the case.

(3) For that purpose the court may hear evidence, and must take account of any representations made by the prosecution and the defence, as in the case of any other matter relevant for the purposes of sentence.

(4) If the court determines that the offence has a terrorist connection, the court—

(*a*) must treat that fact as an aggravating factor, and

(*b*) must state in open court that the offence was so aggravated.

(5) This section has effect in relation only to offences committed on or after the day it comes into force.

[Counter-Terrorism Act 2008, s 32.]

**7.9016 33. Power to amend list of offences where terrorist connection to be considered**

(1) The Secretary of State may by order amend Schedule 2 (offences where terrorist connection to be considered).

(2) Any such order is subject to affirmative resolution procedure.

(3) An order adding an offence to that Schedule applies only in relation to offences committed after the order comes into force.

[Counter-Terrorism Act 2008, s 33.]

## PART 4[1]
## NOTIFICATION REQUIREMENTS

*Introductory*

**7.9018 40. Scheme of this Part** (1) This Part imposes notification requirements on persons dealt with in respect of certain offences—

(*a*) sections 41 to 43 specify the offences to which this Part applies;

(*b*) sections 44 to 46 make provision as to the sentences or orders triggering the notification requirements;

(*c*) sections 47 to 52 contain the notification requirements; and

(*d*) section 53 makes provision as to the period for which the requirements apply.

(2) This Part also provides for—

(*a*) orders applying the notification requirements to persons dealt with outside the United Kingdom for corresponding foreign offences (see section 57 and Schedule 4); and

(*b*) orders imposing restrictions on travel outside the United Kingdom on persons subject to the notification requirements (see section 58 and Schedule 5).

(3) Schedule 6 provides for the application of this Part to service offences and related matters.

[Counter-Terrorism Act 2008, s 40.]

---

[1] PART 4 contains ss 40–61. The whole of Part 4 is in force, together with Schs 4, 5 and 6: see SI 2009/1493.

*Offences to which this Part applies*

7.9020 **41. Offences to which this Part applies: terrorism offences** (1) This Part applies to—

(*a*) an offence under any of the following provisions of the Terrorism Act 2000 (c 11)—
section 11 or 12 (offences relating to proscribed organisations),
sections 15 to 18 (offences relating to terrorist property),
section 38B (failure to disclose information about acts of terrorism),
section 54 (weapons training),
sections 56 to 61 (directing terrorism, possessing things and collecting information for the purposes of terrorism and inciting terrorism outside the United Kingdom);

(*b*) an offence in respect of which there is jurisdiction by virtue of any of sections 62 to 63D of that Act (extra-territorial jurisdiction in respect of certain offences committed outside the United Kingdom for the purposes of terrorism etc);

(*c*) an offence under section 113 of the Anti-terrorism, Crime and Security Act 2001 (c 24) (use of noxious substances or things);

(*d*) an offence under any of the following provisions of Part 1 of the Terrorism Act 2006 (c 11)—
sections 1 and 2 (encouragement of terrorism),
sections 5, 6 and 8 (preparation and training for terrorism),
sections 9, 10 and 11 (offences relating to radioactive devices and material and nuclear facilities);

(*e*) an offence in respect of which there is jurisdiction by virtue of section 17 of that Act (extra-territorial jurisdiction in respect of certain offences committed outside the United Kingdom for the purposes of terrorism etc).

(2) This Part also applies to any ancillary offence in relation to an offence listed in subsection (1).

(3) The Secretary of State may by order amend subsection (1).

(4) Any such order is subject to affirmative resolution procedure.

(5) An order adding an offence applies only in relation to offences dealt with after the order comes into force.

(6) An order removing an offence has effect in relation to offences whenever dealt with, whether before or after the order comes into force.

(7) Where an offence is removed from the list, a person subject to the notification requirements by reason of that offence being listed (and who is not otherwise subject to those requirements) ceases to be subject to them when the order comes into force.

[Counter-Terrorism Act 2008, s 41.]

7.9022 **42. Offences to which this Part applies: offences having a terrorist connection** (1) This Part applies to—

(*a*) an offence as to which a court has determined under section 30 (sentences for offences with a terrorist connection: England and Wales) that the offence has a terrorist connection, and

(*b*) an offence in relation to which section 31 applies (sentences for offences with terrorist connection: Scotland).

(2) A person to whom the notification requirements apply by virtue of such a determination as is mentioned in subsection (1)(*a*) may appeal against it to the same court, and subject to the same conditions, as an appeal against sentence.

(3) If the determination is set aside on appeal, the notification requirements are treated as never having applied to that person in respect of the offence.

(4) Where an order is made under section 33 removing an offence from the list in Schedule 2, a person subject to the notification requirements by reason of that offence being so listed (and who is not otherwise subject to those requirements) ceases to be subject to them when the order comes into force.

[Counter-Terrorism Act 2008, s 42.]

7.9024 **43. Offences dealt with before commencement** (1) This Part applies to a person dealt with for an offence before the commencement of this Part only if—

(*a*) the offence is on the commencement of this Part within section 41(1) or (2) (offences to which this Part applies: terrorism offences), and

(*b*) immediately before the commencement of this Part the person—

(i) is imprisoned or detained in pursuance of the sentence passed or order made in respect of the offence,

(ii) would be so imprisoned or detained but for being unlawfully at large, absent without leave, on temporary leave or leave of absence, or on bail pending an appeal, or

(iii) is on licence, having served the custodial part of a sentence of imprisonment in respect of the offence.

(2) In relation to a person dealt with for an offence before the commencement of this Part—

(*a*) any reference in this Part to a sentence or order under a specified statutory provision includes a sentence or order under any corresponding earlier statutory provision;

(*b*) any reference in this Part to a person being or having been found to be under a disability and to have done the act charged against them in respect of an offence includes a reference to their being or having been found—

(i) unfit to be tried for the offence,

(ii) insane so that their trial for the offence cannot or could not proceed, or

(iii) unfit to be tried and to have done the act charged against them in respect of the offence.

[Counter-Terrorism Act 2008, s 43.]

*Persons to whom the notification requirements apply*

7.9026 **44. Persons to whom the notification requirements apply** The notification requirements apply to a person who—

(*a*) is aged 16 or over at the time of being dealt with for an offence to which this Part applies, and

(*b*) is made subject in respect of the offence to a sentence or order within section 45 (sentences or orders triggering notification requirements).

[Counter-Terrorism Act 2008, s 44.]

7.9028 **45. Sentences or orders triggering notification requirements** (1) The notification requirements apply to a person who in England and Wales—

(*a*) has been convicted of an offence to which this Part applies and sentenced in respect of the offence to—

(i) imprisonment or custody for life,

(ii) imprisonment or detention in a young offender institution for a term of 12 months or more,

(iii) imprisonment or detention in a young offender institution for public protection under section 225 of the Criminal Justice Act 2003 (c 44),

(iv) detention for life or for a period of 12 months or more under section 91 of the Powers of Criminal Courts (Sentencing) Act 2000 (c 6) (offenders under 18 convicted of certain serious offences),

(v) a detention and training order for a term of 12 months or more under section 100 of that Act (offenders under age of 18),

(vi) detention for public protection under section 226 of the Criminal Justice Act 2003 (serious offences committed by persons under 18), or

(vii) detention during Her Majesty's pleasure; or

(*b*) has been—

(i) convicted of an offence to which this Part applies carrying a maximum term of imprisonment of 12 months or more,

(ii) found not guilty by reason of insanity of such an offence, or

(iii) found to be under a disability and to have done the act charged against them in respect of such an offence,

and made subject in respect of the offence to a hospital order.

(2) *Scotland.*

(3) The notification requirements apply to a person who in Northern Ireland—

(*a*) has been convicted of an offence to which this Part applies and sentenced in respect of the offence to—

(i) imprisonment for life,

(ii) imprisonment or detention in a young offenders centre for a term of 12 months or more,

(iii) an indeterminate custodial sentence under Article 13 of the Criminal Justice (Northern Ireland) Order 2008 (SI 2008/1216 (NI 1)),

(iv) an extended custodial sentence under Article 14(5) of that Order (offenders under 21 convicted of certain offences),

(v) a juvenile justice centre order under Article 39 of the Criminal Justice (Children) (Northern Ireland) Order 1998 (SI 1998/1504 (NI 9)) for a period of 12 months or more,

(vi) detention during the pleasure of the Secretary of State under Article 45(1) of that Order (punishment of certain grave crimes committed by a child), or

(vii) detention under Article 45(2) of that Order for a period of 12 months or more (other serious offences committed by a child); or

(*b*) has been—
(i) convicted of an offence to which this Part applies carrying a maximum term of imprisonment of 12 months or more,
(ii) found not guilty by reason of insanity of such an offence, or
(iii) found to be unfit to be tried and to have done the act charged against them in respect of such an offence,

and made subject in respect of the offence to a hospital order.

(4) The references in this section to an offence carrying a maximum term of imprisonment of 12 months or more—

(*a*) are to an offence carrying such a maximum term in the case of a person who has attained the age of 21 (18 in relation to England and Wales), and
(*b*) include an offence carrying in the case of such a person a maximum term of life imprisonment and an offence for which in the case of such a person the sentence is fixed by law as life imprisonment.

(5) In relation to any time before the coming into force of section 61 of the Criminal Justice and Court Services Act 2000 (c 43) subsection (4)(*a*) above has effect with the omission of the words "(18 in relation to England and Wales)".

[Counter-Terrorism Act 2008, s 45.]

**7.9030 46. Power to amend specified terms or periods of imprisonment or detention**
(1) The Secretary of State may by order amend the provisions of section 45 referring to a specified term or period of imprisonment or detention.

(2) An order reducing a specified term or period has effect only in relation to persons dealt with after the order comes into force.

(3) Where an order increases a specified term or period—

(*a*) it has effect in relation to persons dealt with at any time, whether before or after the order comes into force, and
(*b*) a person who would not have been subject to the notification requirements if the order had been in force when the offence was dealt with (and who is not otherwise subject to those requirements) ceases to be subject to the requirements when the order comes into force.

(4) An order under this section is subject to affirmative resolution procedure.

[Counter-Terrorism Act 2008, s 46.]

*Notification requirements*[1]

**7.9032 47. Initial notification** (1) A person to whom the notification requirements apply must notify the following information to the police within the period of three days beginning with the day on which the person is dealt with in respect of the offence in question.

(2) The information required is—

(*a*) date of birth;
(*b*) national insurance number;
(*c*) name on the date on which the person was dealt with in respect of the offence (where the person used one or more other names on that date, each of those names);
(*d*) home address on that date;
(*e*) name on the date on which notification is made (where the person uses one or more other names on that date, each of those names);
(*f*) home address on the date on which notification is made;
(*g*) address of any other premises in the United Kingdom at which, at the time the notification is made, the person regularly resides or stays;
(*h*) any prescribed information.

(3) In subsection (2) "prescribed" means prescribed by regulations made by the Secretary of State.

Such regulations are subject to affirmative resolution procedure.

(4) In determining the period within which notification is to be made under this section, there shall be disregarded any time when the person is—

(*a*) remanded in or committed to custody by an order of a court,
(*b*) serving a sentence of imprisonment or detention,
(*c*) detained in a hospital, or
(*d*) detained under the Immigration Acts.

(5) This section does not apply to a person who—

(*a*) is subject to the notification requirements in respect of another offence (and does not cease to be so subject before the end of the period within which notification is to be made), and
(*b*) has complied with this section in respect of that offence.

(6) In the application of this section to a person dealt with for an offence before the commencement of this Part who, immediately before commencement—

(*a*) would be imprisoned or detained in respect of the offence but for being unlawfully at large, absent without leave, on temporary leave or leave of absence, or on bail pending an appeal, or (*b*) is on licence, having served the custodial part of a sentence of imprisonment in respect of the offence,

the reference in subsection (1) to the day on which the person is dealt with in respect of the offence shall be read as a reference to the commencement of this Part.

[Counter-Terrorism Act 2008, s 47.]

---

1 Given the relatively moderate intrusion caused by the interference with the private lives of convicted terrorists generally, and having particular regard to the interference with the private life of this claimant, the notification scheme is not disproportionate and the statute is compatible with art 8 of the Human Rights Act 1998: *R (Irfan) v Secretary of State for the Home Department* [2012] EWCA Civ 1471, [2013] QB 885, [2013] 2 WLR 1340.

7.9034 48. **Notification of changes** (1) A person to whom the notification requirements apply who uses a name that has not previously been notified to the police must notify the police of that name.

(2) If there is a change of the home address of a person to whom the notification requirements apply, the person must notify the police of the new home address.

(3) A person to whom the notification requirements apply who resides or stays at premises in the United Kingdom the address of which has previously not been notified to the police—

(*a*) for a period of 7 days, or

(*b*) for two or more periods, in any period of 12 months, that taken together amount to 7 days,

must notify the police of the address of those premises.

(4) A person to whom the notification requirements apply who is released—

(*a*) from custody pursuant to an order of a court,

(*b*) from imprisonment or detention pursuant to a sentence of a court,

(*c*) from detention in a hospital, or

(*d*) from detention under the Immigration Acts,

must notify the police of that fact.

This does not apply if the person is at the same time required to notify the police under section 47 (initial notification).

(5) A person who is required to notify information within section 47(2)(*h*) (prescribed information) must notify the police of the prescribed details of any prescribed changes in that information.

(6) In subsection (5) "prescribed" means prescribed by regulations made by the Secretary of State.

Such regulations are subject to affirmative resolution procedure.

(7) Notification under this section must be made before the end of the period of three days beginning with the day on which the event in question occurs.

Where subsection (3) applies that is the day with which the period referred to in paragraph (*a*) or (*b*) (as the case may be) ends.

(8) In determining the period within which notification is to be made under this section, there shall be disregarded any time when the person is—

(*a*) remanded in or committed to custody by an order of a court,

(*b*) serving a sentence of imprisonment or detention,

(*c*) detained in a hospital, or

(*d*) detained under the Immigration Acts.

(9) References in this section to previous notification are to previous notification by the person under section 47 (initial notification), this section, section 49 (periodic re-notification) or section 56 (notification on return after absence from UK).

(10) Notification under this section must be accompanied by re-notification of the other information mentioned in section 47(2).

[Counter-Terrorism Act 2008, s 48.]

7.9036 49. **Periodic re-notification** (1) A person to whom the notification requirements apply must, within the period of one year after last notifying the police in accordance with—

(*a*) section 47 (initial notification),

(*b*) section 48 (notification of change),

(*c*) this section, or

(*d*) section 56 (notification on return after absence from UK),

re-notify to the police the information mentioned in section 47(2).

(2) Subsection (1) does not apply if the period referred to in that subsection ends at a time when the person is—

(*a*) remanded in or committed to custody by an order of a court,

(*b*) serving a sentence of imprisonment or detention,

(*c*) detained in a hospital, or

(*d*) detained under the Immigration Acts.

(3) In that case section 48(4) and (10) (duty to notify of release and to re-notify other information) apply when the person is released.

[Counter-Terrorism Act 2008, s 49.]

7.9038 **50. Method of notification and related matters** (1) This section applies to notification under—

(*a*) section 47 (initial notification),

(*b*) section 48 (notification of change),

(*c*) section 49 (periodic re-notification), or

(*d*) section 56 (notification on return after absence from UK).

(2) Notification must be made by the person—

(*a*) attending at a police station in the person's local police area, and

(*b*) making an oral notification to a police officer or to a person authorised for the purpose by the officer in charge of the station.

(3) A person making a notification under section 48 (notification of change) in relation to premises referred to in subsection (3) of that section may make the notification at a police station that would fall within subsection (2)(*a*) above if the address of those premises were the person's home address.

(4) The notification must be acknowledged.

(5) The acknowledgement must be in writing, and in such form as the Secretary of State may direct.

(6) The person making the notification must, if requested to do so by the police officer or person to whom the notification is made, allow the officer or person to—

(*a*) take the person's fingerprints,

(*b*) photograph any part of the person, or

(*c*) do both these things,

for the purpose of verifying the person's identity.

(7) In the application of this section to Scotland, references to a police officer are to be read as references to a constable.

[Counter-Terrorism Act 2008, s 50.]

7.9040 **51. Meaning of "local police area"** (1) For the purposes of section 50(2) (method of notification) a person's "local police area" means—

(*a*) the police area in which the person's home address is situated;

(*b*) in the absence of a home address, the police area in which the home address last notified is situated;

(*c*) in the absence of a home address and of any such notification, the police area in which the court of trial was situated.

(2) In subsection (1)(*c*) "the court of trial" means—

(*a*) the court by or before which the conviction or finding was made by virtue of which the notification requirements apply to the person, or

(*b*) if that conviction or finding was one substituted on an appeal or reference, the court by or before which the proceedings were taken from which the appeal or reference was brought.

(3) This section and section 50(2) apply in relation to Northern Ireland as if Northern Ireland were a police area.

[Counter-Terrorism Act 2008, s 51.]

7.9042 **52. Travel outside the United Kingdom** (1) The Secretary of State may by regulations[1] make provision requiring a person to whom the notification requirements apply who leaves the United Kingdom—

(*a*) to notify the police of their departure before they leave, and

(*b*) to notify the police of their return if they subsequently return to the United Kingdom.

(2) Notification of departure must disclose—

(*a*) the date on which the person intends to leave the United Kingdom;

(*b*) the country (or, if there is more than one, the first country) to which the person will travel;

(*c*) the person's point of arrival (determined in accordance with the regulations) in that country;

(*d*) any other information required by the regulations.

(3) Notification of return must disclose such information as is required by the regulations about the person's return to the United Kingdom.

(4) Notification under this section must be given in accordance with the regulations.

(5) Regulations[1] under this section are subject to affirmative resolution procedure.

[Counter-Terrorism Act 2008, s 52.]

---

[1] The Counter-Terrorism Act 2008 (Foreign Travel Notification Requirements) Regulations 2009, SI 2009/2494 have been made.

*Period for which notification requirements apply*

7.9044 **53. Period for which notification requirements apply[1]** (1) The period for which the notification requirements apply is—

(*a*) 30 years in the case of a person who—

(i) is aged 18 or over at the time of conviction for the offence, and

(ii) receives in respect of the offence a sentence within subsection (2);

(*b*) 15 years in the case of a person who—

(i) is aged 18 or over at the time of conviction for the offence, and

(ii) receives in respect of the offence a sentence within subsection (3);

(*c*) 10 years in any other case.

(2) The sentences in respect of which a 30 year period applies are—

(*a*) in England and Wales—

(i) imprisonment or custody for life,

(ii) imprisonment or detention in a young offender institution for a term of 10 years or more,

(iii) imprisonment or detention in a young offender institution for public protection under section 225 of the Criminal Justice Act 2003 (c 44),

(iv) detention during Her Majesty's pleasure;

(*b*) *Scotland.*

(*c*) *Northern Ireland.*

(3) The sentences in respect of which a 15 year period applies are—

(*a*) in England and Wales, imprisonment or detention in a young offender institution for a term of 5 years or more but less than 10 years;

(*b*) in Scotland, imprisonment or detention in a young offenders institution for a term of 5 years or more but less than 10 years;

(*c*) in Northern Ireland—

(i) imprisonment for a term of 5 years or more but less than 10 years,

(ii) an extended custodial sentence for a term of 5 years or more but less than 10 years under Article 14(5) of the Criminal Justice (Northern Ireland) Order 2008 (SI 2008/1216 (NI 1)) (offenders under 21 convicted of certain offences).

(4) The period begins with the day on which the person is dealt with for the offence.

(5) If a person who is the subject of a finding within section 45(1)(*b*)(iii), (2)(*b*)(iii) or (3)(*b*)(iii) (finding of disability, etc) is subsequently tried for the offence, the period resulting from that finding ends—

(*a*) if the person is acquitted, at the conclusion of the trial;

(*b*) if the person is convicted, when the person is again dealt with in respect of the offence.

(6) For the purposes of determining the length of the period—

(*a*) a person who has been sentenced in respect of two or more offences to which this Part applies to consecutive terms of imprisonment is treated as if sentenced, in respect of each of the offences, to a term of imprisonment equal to the aggregate of the terms; and

(*b*) a person who has been sentenced in respect of two or more such offences to concurrent terms of imprisonment (X and Y) that overlap for a period (Z) is treated as if sentenced, in respect of each of the offences, to a term of imprisonment equal to X plus Y minus Z.

(7) In determining whether the period has expired, there shall be disregarded any period when the person was—

(*a*) remanded in or committed to custody by an order of a court,

(*b*) serving a sentence of imprisonment or detention,

(*c*) detained in a hospital, or

(*d*) detained under the Immigration Acts.

[Counter-Terrorism Act 2008, s 53.]

[1] Given the relatively moderate intrusion caused by the interference with the private lives of convicted terrorists generally, and having particular regard to the interference with the private life of this claimant, the notification scheme is not disproportionate and the statute is compatible with art 8 of the Human Rights Act 1998: *R (Irfan) v Secretary of State for the Home Department* [2012] EWCA Civ 1471, [2013] 2 WLR 1340.

*Offences in relation to notification*

7.9046 **54. Offences relating to notification** (1) A person commits an offence who—

(*a*) fails without reasonable excuse to comply with—

section 47 (initial notification),
section 48 (notification of changes),
section 49 (periodic re-notification),
section 50(6) (taking of fingerprints or photographs),
any regulations made under section 52(1) (travel outside United Kingdom), or
section 56 (notification on return after absence from UK); or

(*b*) notifies to the police in purported compliance with—

section 47 (initial notification),
section 48 (notification of changes),
section 49 (periodic re-notification),
any regulations made under section 52(1) (travel outside United Kingdom), or
section 56 (notification on return after absence from UK),
any information that the person knows to be false.

(2) A person guilty of an offence under this section is liable—

(*a*) on summary conviction, to imprisonment for a term not exceeding 12 months or a fine not exceeding the statutory maximum or both;

(*b*) on conviction on indictment, to imprisonment for a term not exceeding 5 years or a fine or both[1].

(3) In the application of subsection (2)(*a*)—

(*a*) in England and Wales, in relation to an offence committed before the commencement of section 154(1) of the Criminal Justice Act 2003 (c 44), or

(*b*) in Northern Ireland,

for "12 months" substitute "6 months".

(4) A person—

(*a*) commits an offence under subsection (1)(*a*) above on the day on which the person first fails without reasonable excuse to comply with—

section 47 (initial notification),
section 48 (notification of changes),
section 49 (periodic re-notification),
any regulations made under section 52(1) (travel outside United Kingdom), or
section 56 (notification on return after absence from UK), and

(*b*) continues to commit it throughout any period during which the failure continues.

But a person must not be prosecuted under subsection (1) more than once in respect of the same failure.

(5) Proceedings for an offence under this section may be commenced in any court having jurisdiction in any place where the person charged with the offence resides or is found.

[Counter-Terrorism Act 2008, s 54.]

---

1 For procedure in respect of offences triable either way, see ss 17A–21 of the Magistrates Courts Act 1980 in PART I: MAGISTRATES' COURTS PROCEDURE, ante.

7.9049 55. **Effect of absence abroad** (1) If a person to whom the notification requirements apply is absent from the United Kingdom for any period the following provisions apply.

(2) During the period of absence the period for which the notification requirements apply continues to run.

(3) The period of absence does not affect the obligation under section 47 (initial notification). This is subject to subsection (4).

(4) Section 47 does not apply if—

(*a*) the period of absence begins before the end of the period within which notification must be made under that section, and

(*b*) the person's absence results from the person's removal from the United Kingdom.

(5) Section 48 (notification of changes)—

(*a*) applies in relation to an event that occurs before the period of absence, but

(*b*) does not apply in relation to an event that occurs during the period of absence.

Paragraph (*a*) is subject to subsection (6).

(6) Section 48 does not apply in relation to an event that occurs before the period of absence if—

(*a*) the period of absence begins before the end of the period within which notification must be made under that section, and

(*b*) the person's absence results from the person's removal from the United Kingdom.

(7) Section 49 (periodic re-notification) does not apply if the period referred to in subsection (1) of that section ends during the period of absence.

(8) Section 53(7) (disregard of period of custody etc) applies in relation to the period of absence as if it referred to any period when the person was—

(*a*) remanded in or committed to custody by an order of a court outside the United Kingdom,

(*b*) serving a sentence of imprisonment or detention imposed by such a court,

(*c*) detained in a hospital pursuant to an order of such a court that is equivalent to a hospital order, or

(*d*) subject to a form of detention outside the United Kingdom that is equivalent to detention under the Immigration Acts.

(9) References in this section and section 56 to a person's removal from the United Kingdom include—

(*a*) the person's removal from the United Kingdom in accordance with the Immigration Acts,

(*b*) the person's extradition from the United Kingdom, or

(*c*) the person's transfer from the United Kingdom to another country pursuant to a warrant under section 1 of the Repatriation of Prisoners Act 1984 (c 47).

[Counter-Terrorism Act 2008, s 55.]

7.9051 56. **Notification on return after absence from UK** (1) This section applies if, before the end of the period for which the notification requirements apply, a person to whom the requirements apply returns to the United Kingdom after a period of absence and—

(*a*) the person was not required to make a notification under section 47 (initial notification),

(*b*) there has been a change to any of the information last notified to the police in accordance with—

(i) section 47,

(ii) section 48 (notification of changes),

(iii) section 49 (periodic re-notification), or

(iv) this section, or

(*c*) the period referred to in section 49(1) (period after which re-notification required) ended during the period of absence.

(2) The person must notify or (as the case may be) re-notify to the police the information mentioned in section 47(2) within the period of three days beginning with the day of return.

(3) In determining the period within which notification is to be made under this section, there shall be disregarded any time when the person is—

(*a*) remanded in or committed to custody by an order of a court,

(*b*) serving a sentence of imprisonment or detention,

(*c*) detained in a hospital, or

(*d*) detained under the Immigration Acts.

(4) This section does not apply if—

(*a*) the person subsequently leaves the United Kingdom,

(*b*) the period of absence begins before the end of the period within which notification must be made under this section, and

(*c*) the person's absence results from the person's removal from the United Kingdom.

(5) The obligation under this section does not affect any obligation to notify information under section 52(3) (regulations requiring notification of return etc).

[Counter-Terrorism Act 2008, s 56.]

*Supplementary provisions*

7.9053 **57. Notification orders** Schedule 4 makes provision for notification orders applying the notification requirements of this Part to persons who have been dealt with outside the United Kingdom in respect of a corresponding foreign offence.

[Counter-Terrorism Act 2008, s 57.]

7.9055 **58. Foreign travel restriction orders** Schedule 5 makes provision for foreign travel restriction orders prohibiting persons to whom the notification requirements apply from—

(*a*) travelling to a country outside the United Kingdom named or described in the order,

(*b*) travelling to any country outside the United Kingdom other than a country named or described in the order, or

(*c*) travelling to any country outside the United Kingdom.

[Counter-Terrorism Act 2008, s 58.]

7.9057 **59. Application of Part to service offences and related matters** Schedule 6 makes provision for the application of this Part to service offences and related matters.

[Counter-Terrorism Act 2008, s 59.]

7.9059 **60. Minor definitions for Part 4** In this Part—

"country" includes a territory;

"detained in a hospital" means detained in a hospital under—

(*a*) Part 3 of the Mental Health Act 1983 (c 20),

(*b*) Part 6 of the Criminal Procedure (Scotland) Act 1995 (c 46) or the Mental Health (Care and Treatment) (Scotland) Act 2003 (asp 13), or

(*c*) Part 3 of the Mental Health (Northern Ireland) Order (SI 1986/595 (NI 4));

"home address" means, in relation to a person—

(*a*) the address of the person's sole or main residence in the United Kingdom, or

(*b*) where the person has no such residence, the address or location of a place in the United Kingdom where the person can regularly be found and, if there is more than one such place, such one of those places as the person may select;

"hospital order" means—

(*a*) a hospital order within the meaning of the Mental Health Act 1983,

(*b*) an order under Part 6 of the Criminal Procedure (Scotland) Act 1995, or

(*c*) a hospital order within the meaning of the Mental Health (Northern Ireland) Order 1986 (SI 1986/595 (NI 4));

"passport" means—

(*a*) a United Kingdom passport within the meaning of the Immigration Act 1971 (c 77), or

(*b*) a passport issued by or on behalf of the authorities of a country outside the United Kingdom or by or on behalf of an international organisation,

and includes any document that can be used (in some or all circumstances) instead of a passport;

"photograph" includes any process by means of which an image may be produced;

"release" from imprisonment or detention includes release on licence but not temporary release.

[Counter-Terrorism Act 2008, s 60.]

7.9061 **61. References to a person being "dealt with" for an offence** (1) References in this Part to a person being dealt with for or in respect of an offence are to their being sentenced, or made subject to a hospital order, in respect of the offence.

References in this Part to an offence being dealt with are to a person being dealt with in respect of the offence.

(2) Subject to the following provisions of this section, references in this Part to the time at which a person is dealt with for an offence are to the time at which they are first dealt with—

(*a*) in England and Wales, by a magistrates' court or the Crown Court;

(*b*) in Scotland, by a sheriff or by the High Court of Justiciary;

(*c*) in Northern Ireland, by the county court.

This is referred to below as "the original decision".

(3) Where the original decision is varied (on appeal or otherwise), then—

(*a*) if the result is that the conditions for application of the notification requirements to a person in respect of an offence cease to be met (and paragraph (*c*) below does not apply), the notification requirements are treated as never having applied to that person in respect of that offence;

(*b*) if the result is that the conditions for application of the notification requirements to a person in respect of an offence are met where they were not previously met (and paragraph (*c*) below does not apply)—

(i) the person is treated as dealt with for the offence when the variation takes place, and

(ii) the notification requirements apply accordingly;

(*c*) if—

(i) a conviction of, or finding in relation to, a different offence is substituted, and

(ii) the conditions for application of the notification requirements were met in respect of the original offence and are also met in respect of the substituted offence,

the person is treated as if they had been dealt with for the substituted offence at the time of the original decision;

(*d*) if the sentence is varied so as to become one by virtue of which the notification requirements would apply for a different period, the period for which those requirements apply shall be determined as if the sentence as varied had been imposed at the time of the original decision;

(*e*) in any other case, the variation is disregarded.

(4) For the purposes of—

(*a*) section 41(5) (effect of order adding offence to list of terrorism offences),

(*b*) section 44(*a*) or paragraph 4(*a*) of Schedule 6 (persons subject to notification requirements: age when dealt with for offence),

(*c*) section 46(2) or paragraph 6(2) of Schedule 6 (effect of order reducing term or period triggering notification requirements),

(*d*) section 53(5)(*b*) or paragraph 7(5)(*b*) of Schedule 6 (period for which notification requirements apply: ending of period resulting from finding of disability etc where person subsequently tried), and

(*e*) paragraph 2(3) of Schedule 5 (conditions for making foreign travel restriction order: behaviour since offence dealt with),

a person is treated as dealt with at the time of the original decision and any subsequent variation of the decision is disregarded.

(5) For the purposes of—

(*a*) section 43(1) and (2) or paragraph 3(1) and (2) of Schedule 6 (application of Part to offences dealt with before commencement), and

(*b*) paragraph 2(4) of Schedule 5 (conditions for making foreign travel restriction order where offence dealt with before commencement),

a person is dealt with for an offence before the commencement of this Part if the time of the original decision falls before the commencement of this Part.

Where in such a case subsection (3) above applies for the purposes of any provision of this Part, that subsection has effect as if the provisions of this Part had been in force at all material times.

(6) In section 47(6) (adaptation of initial notification requirements in case of offence dealt with before commencement)—

(*a*) the reference in the opening words to an offence dealt with before the commencement of this Part is to an offence where the time of the original decision falls before the commencement of this Part, and

(*b*) the reference in the closing words to when the offence is dealt with has the same meaning as in subsection (1) of that section.

(7) References in this section to the variation of a decision include any proceedings by which the decision is altered, set aside or quashed, or in which a further decision is come to following the setting aside or quashing of the decision.

[Counter-Terrorism Act 2008, s 61.]

## PART 5
## TERRORIST FINANCING AND MONEY LAUNDERING

7.9063 **62. Terrorist financing and money laundering** Schedule 7 makes provision conferring powers on the Treasury to act against terrorist financing, money laundering and certain other activities.

[Counter-Terrorism Act 2008, s 62.]

## PART 8[1]
## SUPPLEMENTARY PROVISIONS

### *General definitions*

7.9066 **92. Meaning of "terrorism"** In this Act "terrorism" has the same meaning as in the Terrorism Act 2000 (c 11) (see section 1 of that Act).

[Counter-Terrorism Act 2008, s 92.]

1 PART 8 contains ss 92–98.

7.9067 **93. Meaning of offence having a "terrorist connection"** For the purposes of this Act an offence has a terrorist connection if the offence—

(*a*) is, or takes place in the course of, an act of terrorism, or

(*b*) is committed for the purposes of terrorism.

[Counter-Terrorism Act 2008, s 93.]

7.9069 **94. Meaning of "ancillary offence"** (1) In this Act "ancillary offence", in relation to an offence, means any of the following—

(*a*) aiding, abetting, counselling or procuring the commission of the offence (or, in Scotland, being art and part in the commission of the offence);

(*b*) an offence under Part 2 of the Serious Crime Act 2007 (c 27) (encouraging or assisting crime) in relation to the offence (or, in Scotland, inciting a person to commit the offence);

(*c*) attempting or conspiring to commit the offence.

(2) In subsection (1)(*b*) the reference to an offence under Part 2 of the Serious Crime Act 2007 includes, in relation to times before the commencement of that Part, an offence of incitement under the law of England and Wales or Northern Ireland.

[Counter-Terrorism Act 2008, s 94.]

7.9073 **95. Meaning of "service court" and "service offence"** (1) In this Act "service court" means the Court Martial, the Service Civilian Court or the Court Martial Appeal Court.

(2) Until the commencement of the relevant provisions of the Armed Forces Act 2006 (c 52), the following is substituted for subsection (1)—

"(1) In this Act "service court" means—

(*a*) a court-martial constituted under the Army Act 1955 (3 & 4 Eliz 2 c 18), the Air Force Act 1955 (3 & 4 Eliz 2 c 19) or the Naval Discipline Act 1957 (c 53);

(*b*) the Courts-Martial Appeal Court; or

(*c*) a Standing Civilian Court.".

(3) In this Act "service offence" means an offence under—

(*a*) section 42 of the Armed Forces Act 2006,

(*b*) section 70 of the Army Act 1955 or the Air Force Act 1955, or

(*c*) section 42 of the Naval Discipline Act 1957.

(4) References in this Act to the "corresponding civil offence" in relation to a service offence are—

(*a*) in relation to an offence under section 42 of the Armed Forces Act 2006, to the corresponding offence under the law of England and Wales within the meaning of that section;

(*b*) in relation to an offence under section 70 of the Army Act 1955 or the Air Force Act 1955, to the corresponding civil offence within the meaning of that Act;

(*c*) in relation to an offence under section 42 of the Naval Discipline Act 1957, to the civil offence within the meaning of that section.

(5) Section 48 of the Armed Forces Act 2006 (c 52) (supplementary provisions relating to ancillary service offences) applies for the purposes of subsection (4)(*a*) above as it applies for the purposes of the provisions of that Act referred to in subsection (3)(*b*) of that section.

[Counter-Terrorism Act 2008, s 95.]

### *Orders and regulations*

**96–98.** *Orders and regulations; financial provisions.*

## SCHEDULE 2
OFFENCES WHERE TERRORIST CONNECTION TO BE CONSIDERED

Sections 30, 31, 33, 35 and 42

*Common law offences*

**7.9074** Murder.
Manslaughter.
Culpable homicide.
Kidnapping.
Abduction.

*Statutory offences*

An offence under any of the following sections of the Offences against the Person Act 1861 (c 100)—
(*a*) section 4 (soliciting murder),
(*b*) section 23 (maliciously administering poison etc so as to endanger life or inflict grievous bodily harm),
(*c*) section 28 (causing bodily injury by explosives),
(*d*) section 29 (using explosives etc with intent to do grievous bodily harm),
(*e*) section 30 (placing explosives with intent to do bodily injury),
(*f*) section 64 (making or having gunpowder etc with intent to commit or enable any person to commit any felony mentioned in the Act).

An offence under any of the following sections of the Explosive Substances Act 1883 (c 3)—
(*a*) section 2 (causing explosion likely to endanger life or property),
(*b*) section 3 (attempt to cause explosion or making or keeping explosive with intent to endanger life or property),
(*c*) section 4 (making or possession of explosive under suspicious circumstances),
(*d*) section 5 (punishment of accessories).

An offence under section 1 of the Biological Weapons Act 1974 (c 6) (restriction on development etc of certain biological agents and toxins and of biological weapons).

An offence under section 1 of the Taking of Hostages Act 1982 (c 28) (hostage-taking).

An offence under any of the following sections of the Aviation Security Act 1982 (c 36)—
(*a*) section 1 (hijacking),
(*b*) section 2 (destroying, damaging or endangering safety of aircraft),
(*c*) section 3 (other acts endangering or likely to endanger safety of aircraft),
(*d*) section 4 (offences in relation to certain dangerous articles),
(*e*) section 6(2) (inducing or assisting commission of offence under section 1, 2 or 3 outside the United Kingdom).

An offence under any of the following sections of the Nuclear Material (Offences) Act 1983 (c 18)—
(*a*) section 1B (offences relating to damage to the environment),
(*b*) section 1C (offences of importing or exporting etc nuclear materials: extended jurisdiction),
(*c*) section 2 (offences involving preparatory acts and threats), so far as relating to an offence specified in this Schedule.

An offence under any of the following sections of the Aviation and Maritime Security Act 1990 (c 31)—
(*a*) section 1 (endangering safety at aerodromes),
(*b*) section 9 (hijacking of ships),
(*c*) section 10 (seizing or exercising control of fixed platforms),
(*d*) section 11 (destroying ships or fixed platforms or endangering their safety),
(*e*) section 14(4) (inducing or assisting the commission of an offence outside the United Kingdom), so far as relating to an offence under section 9 or 11 of that Act.

An offence under Part 2 of the Channel Tunnel (Security) Order 1994 (SI 1994/570) (offences against the safety of channel tunnel trains and the tunnel system).

An offence under any of the following sections of the Chemical Weapons Act 1996 (c 6)—
(*a*) section 2 (use etc of chemical weapons),
(*b*) section 11 (premises or equipment for producing chemical weapons).

An offence under any of the following sections of the Anti-Terrorism, Crime and Security Act 2001 (c 24)—
(*a*) section 47 (use etc of nuclear weapons),
(*b*) section 114 (hoaxes involving noxious substances or things).

*Ancillary offences*

Any ancillary offence in relation to an offence specified in this Schedule.

## SCHEDULE 4
NOTIFICATION ORDERS

Section 57

*Introductory*

**7.9076** **1.** A "notification order" is an order applying the notification requirements of this Part to a person who has been dealt with outside the United Kingdom in respect of a corresponding foreign offence.

*Corresponding foreign offences*

**2.** (1) A "corresponding foreign offence" means an act that—
(*a*) constituted an offence under the law in force in a country outside the United Kingdom, and
(*b*) corresponds to an offence to which this Part applies.

(2) For this purpose an act punishable under the law in force in a country outside the United Kingdom is regarded as constituting an offence under that law however it is described in that law.

(3) An act corresponds to an offence to which this Part applies if—
(*a*) it would have constituted an offence to which this Part applies by virtue of section 41 if it had been done in any part of the United Kingdom[1], or
(*b*) it was, or took place in the course of, an act of terrorism or was done for the purposes of terrorism.

(4) On an application for a notification order the condition in sub-paragraph (3)(*a*) or (*b*) is to be taken to be met unless—

(*a*) the defendant serves on the applicant, not later than rules of court may provide, a notice—
(i) stating that, on the facts as alleged with respect to the act concerned, the condition is not in the defendant's opinion met,
(ii) showing the defendant's grounds for that opinion, and
(iii) requiring the applicant to prove that the condition is met; or
(*b*) the court permits the defendant to require the applicant to prove that the condition is met without service of such a notice.

(5) In the application of this paragraph in Scotland, for "defendant" substitute "respondent".

*Conditions for making a notification order*

**3.** (1) The conditions for making a notification order in respect of a person are as follows.

(2) The first condition is that under the law in force in a country outside the United Kingdom—
(*a*) the person has been convicted of a corresponding foreign offence and has received in respect of the offence a sentence equivalent to a sentence mentioned in section 45(1)(*a*), (2)(*a*) or (3)(*a*), or
(*b*) a court exercising jurisdiction under that law has, in respect of a corresponding foreign offence—
(i) convicted the person or made a finding in relation to the person equivalent to a finding mentioned in section 45(1)(*b*)(ii) or (iii), (2)(*b*)(ii) or (iii) or (3)(*b*)(ii) or (iii) (finding of insanity or disability), and
(ii) made the person subject to an order equivalent to a hospital order.

(3) This condition is not met if there was a flagrant denial of the person's right to a fair trial.

(4) The second condition is that—
(*a*) the sentence was imposed or order made after the commencement of this Part, or
(*b*) the sentence was imposed or order made before the commencement of this Part and immediately before that time the person—
(i) was imprisoned or detained in pursuance of the sentence or order,
(ii) would have been so imprisoned or detained but for being unlawfully at large or otherwise unlawfully absent, lawfully absent on a temporary basis or on bail pending an appeal, or
(iii) had been released on licence, or was subject to an equivalent form of supervision, having served the whole or part of a sentence of imprisonment for the offence.

(5) The third condition is that the period for which the notification requirements would apply in respect of the offence (in accordance with section 53 as modified by paragraph 8(*e*)) has not expired.

(6) If on an application for a notification order it is proved that the conditions in sub-paragraphs (2), (4) and (5) are met, the court must make the order.

---

[1] In *Metropolitan Police Commissioner v Ahsan* [2015] EWHC 2354, [2016] 3 All ER 160, [2016] 1 WLR 654 it was contended that the requirement of para 2(3)(*a*) was not met if the offence could have been prosecuted in the UK because some or all of the acts constituting the offence occurred here. It was held:

> "(that) construction of the 2008 Act will not do. The context of the legislation is of terrorist offending, which can have an extra-territorial and cross-border character. Such offending may be an offence and be prosecuted in more than one jurisdiction. Parliament's intention must have been to encompass it. In my view the plain intention of Parliament is to ensure that those who commit serious terrorist offences, whether here or abroad, should be the subject of the notification requirements in the 2008 Act. That may be strained construction of para 2(3)(*a*) of Sch 4 to the Act but one giving effect to the Parliamentary intention: *Cutter v Eagle Star Insurance Co Ltd, Clarke v Kato* [1998] 4 All ER 417 at 427, [1998] 1 WLR 1647 at 1658 per Lord Clyde. Parliament must have intended that the notification requirements should apply to terrorist conduct committed here which results in a conviction in a foreign court, even if it could have been prosecuted here but was not." (per Cranston J)

*Application for notification order*

**4.** (1) In England and Wales an application for a notification order in respect of a person may only be made by a chief officer of police.

(2) An application may only be made if—
(*a*) the person resides in the chief officer's police area, or
(*b*) the chief officer believes that the person is in, or is intending to come to, that area.

(3) The application must be made to the High Court.

**5.** (1) In Scotland an application for a notification order in respect of a person may only be made by a chief constable.

(2) An application may only be made if—
(*a*) the person resides in the area of the chief constable's police force, or
(*b*) the chief constable believes that the person is in, or is intending to come to, that area.

(3) The application must be made to the Court of Session.

**6.** (1) In Northern Ireland an application for a notification order in respect of a person may only be made by the Chief Constable of the Police Service of Northern Ireland.

(2) An application may only be made if—
(*a*) the person resides in Northern Ireland, or
(*b*) the Chief Constable believes that the person is in, or is intending to come to, Northern Ireland.

(3) The application must be made to the High Court.

*Effect of notification order*

**7.** The effect of a notification order is that the notification requirements of this Part apply to the person in respect of whom it is made.

*Adaptation of provisions of this Part in relation to foreign proceedings*

**8.** The provisions of this Part have effect with the following adaptations in relation to foreign proceedings and cases where the notification requirements apply because a notification order has been made—
(*a*) in section 61(1) (references to dealing with an offence) for "being sentenced, or made subject to a hospital order" substitute "being made subject by the foreign court to a sentence or order within paragraph 3(2)(*a*) or (*b*) of Schedule 4";
(*b*) in section 61(2) (references to time when person dealt with for an offence) for paragraphs (*a*) to (*c*) substitute "by the foreign court of first instance";

(*c*) for the purposes of section 47 (initial notification) the period within which notification is to be made begins with the date of service of the notification order;
(*d*) in section 51 (meaning of "local police area") the reference in subsection (1)(*c*) to the court of trial shall be read as a reference to the court by which the notification order was made;
(*e*) in section 53 (period for which notification requirements apply) a reference to a sentence or order of any description is to be read as a reference to an equivalent sentence or order of the foreign court.

## SCHEDULE 5

### Foreign Travel Restriction Orders

Section 58

*Introductory*

7.9080 1. A foreign travel restriction order is an order prohibiting the person to whom it applies from doing whichever of the following is specified in the order—
(*a*) travelling to a country outside the United Kingdom named or described in the order;
(*b*) travelling to any country outside the United Kingdom other than a country named or described in the order;
(*c*) travelling to any country outside the United Kingdom.

*Conditions for making a foreign travel restriction order*

2. (1) The conditions for making a foreign travel restriction order in respect of a person are as follows.
(2) The first condition is that the notification requirements apply to the person.
(3) The second condition is that the person's behaviour since the person was dealt with for the offence by virtue of which those requirements apply makes it necessary for a foreign travel restriction order to be made to prevent the person from taking part in terrorism activity outside the United Kingdom.
(4) If the person was dealt with for the offence before the commencement of this Part, the condition in sub-paragraph (3) is not met unless the person has acted in that way since the commencement of this Part.
(5) If on an application for a foreign travel restriction order the court is satisfied that the conditions in sub-paragraphs (2) and (3) are met, it may make a foreign travel restriction order.

*Application for foreign travel restriction order*

3. (1) In England and Wales an application for a foreign travel restriction order in respect of a person may only be made by a chief officer of police.
(2) An application may only be made if—
(*a*) the person resides in the chief officer's police area, or
(*b*) the chief officer believes that the person is in, or is intending to come to, that area.
(3) The application must be made by complaint to a magistrates' court whose commission area includes any part of the chief officer's police area.
4. (1) In Scotland an application for a foreign travel restriction order in respect of a person may only be made by a chief constable.
(2) An application may only be made if—
(*a*) the person resides in the area of the chief constable's police force, or
(*b*) the chief constable believes that the person is in, or is intending to come to, that area.
(3) The application must be made by summary application to a sheriff within whose sheriffdom any part of the area of the chief constable's police force lies.
(4) A record of evidence is to be kept on any such summary application.
(5) Where the sheriff makes a foreign travel restriction order, the clerk of the court must give a copy of the order to the respondent or send a copy to the respondent by registered post or the recorded delivery service.
(6) An acknowledgement or certificate of delivery issued by the Post Office is sufficient evidence of the delivery of the copy on the day specified in the acknowledgement or certificate.
5. (1) In Northern Ireland an application for a foreign travel restriction order in respect of a person may only be made by the Chief Constable of the Police Service of Northern Ireland.
(2) An application may only be made if—
(*a*) the person resides in Northern Ireland, or
(*b*) the Chief Constable believes that the person is in, or is intending to come to, Northern Ireland.
(3) The application must be made by complaint under Part 8 of the Magistrates' Courts (Northern Ireland) Order 1981 (SI 1981/1675 (NI 26)) to a court of summary jurisdiction.

*Provisions of a foreign travel restriction order*

6. (1) A foreign travel restriction order may prohibit the person to whom it applies—
(*a*) from travelling to any country outside the United Kingdom named or described in the order; or
(*b*) from travelling to any country outside the United Kingdom other than a country named or described in the order; or
(*c*) from travelling to any country outside the United Kingdom.
(2) The order must only impose such prohibitions as are necessary for the purpose of preventing the person from taking part in terrorism activity outside the United Kingdom.
(3) A foreign travel restriction order containing a prohibition within sub-paragraph (1)(*c*) must require the person to whom it applies to surrender all that person's passports, at a police station specified in the order—
(*a*) on or before the date when the prohibition takes effect, or
(*b*) within a period specified in the order.
(4) Any passports surrendered must be returned as soon as reasonably practicable after the person ceases to be subject to a foreign travel restriction order containing such a prohibition.

*Duration of foreign travel restriction order*

7. (1) A foreign travel restriction order has effect for a fixed period of not more than 6 months.
(2) The period must be specified in the order.
(3) A foreign travel restriction order ceases to have effect if a court (whether the same or another court) makes another foreign travel restriction order in relation to the person to whom the earlier order applies.

*Variation, renewal or discharge of order*

**8.** (1) In England and Wales an application for an order varying, renewing or discharging a foreign travel restriction order may be made by—

(*a*) the person subject to the order;

(*b*) the chief officer of police on whose application the order was made;

(*c*) the chief officer of police for the area in which the person subject to the order resides; or

(*d*) a chief officer of police who believes that the person subject to the order is in, or is intending to come to, the officer's police area.

(2) The application must be made by complaint to—

(*a*) a magistrates' court for the same area as the court that made the order,

(*b*) a magistrates' court for the area in which the person subject to the order resides, or

(*c*) where the application is made by a chief officer of police, any magistrates' court whose commission area includes any part of that chief officer's police area.

(3) On an application under this paragraph the court may make such order varying, renewing or discharging the foreign travel restriction order as it considers appropriate.

(4) Before doing so it must hear the person making the application and (if they wish to be heard) the other persons mentioned in sub-paragraph (1).

**9.** (1) In Scotland an application for an order varying, renewing or discharging a foreign travel restriction order may be made by—

(*a*) the person subject to the order;

(*b*) the chief constable on whose application the order was made;

(*c*) the chief constable in the area of whose police force the person subject to the order resides; or

(*d*) a chief constable who believes that the person subject to the order is in, or is intending to come to, the area of that chief constable's police force.

(2) The application must be made by summary application—

(*a*) to the sheriff who made the order, or

(*b*) to a sheriff—

(i) within whose sheriffdom the person subject to the order resides, or

(ii) where the application is made by a chief constable, within whose sheriffdom any part of the area of the chief constable's police force lies.

(3) A record of evidence is to be kept on any summary application under this paragraph.

(4) On an application under this paragraph the sheriff may make such order varying, renewing or discharging the foreign travel restriction order as the sheriff considers appropriate.

(5) Before doing so the sheriff must hear the person making the application and (if they wish to be heard) the other persons mentioned in sub-paragraph (1).

**10.** (1) In Northern Ireland an application for an order varying, renewing or discharging a foreign travel restriction order may be made by—

(*a*) the person subject to the order; or

(*b*) the Chief Constable of the Police Service of Northern Ireland.

(2) The application must be made by complaint under Part 8 of the Magistrates' Courts (Northern Ireland) Order 1981 (SI 1981/1675 (NI 26)) to a court of summary jurisdiction for the petty sessions district which includes the area where the person subject to the order resides.

(3) On an application under this paragraph the court may make such order varying, renewing or discharging the foreign travel restriction order as it considers appropriate.

(4) It may do so only after hearing the person making the application and (if they wish to be heard) the other person mentioned in sub-paragraph (1).

*Provisions of renewed or varied order*

**11.** (1) A foreign travel restriction order may be renewed, or varied so as to impose additional prohibitions, but only if it is necessary to do so for the purpose of preventing the person subject to the order from taking part in terrorism activities outside the United Kingdom.

(2) Any renewed or varied order must contain only the prohibitions necessary for that purpose.

*Appeals*

**12.** (1) In England and Wales—

(*a*) a person against whom a foreign travel restriction order is made may appeal against the making of the order;

(*b*) a person subject to a foreign travel restriction order may appeal against—

(i) an order under paragraph 8 varying or renewing the order, or

(ii) a refusal to make an order under that paragraph varying or discharging the order.

(2) The appeal lies to the Crown Court.

(3) On an appeal under this paragraph the court may make—

(*a*) such orders as it considers necessary to give effect to its determination of the appeal, and

(*b*) such incidental and consequential orders as appear to it to be just.

**13.** (1) In Scotland an interlocutor of the sheriff granting or refusing a foreign travel restriction order, or an order under paragraph 9 (variation, renewal or discharge of foreign travel restriction order), is appealable.

(2) Where an appeal is taken against such an interlocutor, the interlocutor continues in effect pending disposal of the appeal.

**14.** (1) In Northern Ireland—

(*a*) a person against whom a foreign travel restriction order is made may appeal against the making of the order;

(*b*) a person subject to a foreign travel restriction order may appeal against—

(i) an order under paragraph 10 varying or renewing the order, or

(ii) a refusal to make an order under that paragraph varying or discharging the order.

(2) The appeal lies to the county court.

(3) On an appeal under this paragraph the court may make—

(*a*) such orders as it considers necessary to give effect to its determination of the appeal, and

(*b*) such incidental and consequential orders as appear to it to be just.

*Breach of foreign travel restriction order an offence*

**15.** (1) A person commits a offence who, without reasonable excuse—
(*a*) does anything they are prohibited from doing by a foreign travel restriction order, or
(*b*) fails to comply with a requirement imposed on them by such an order.
(2) A person guilty of an offence under this paragraph is liable—
(*a*) on summary conviction, to imprisonment for a term not exceeding 12 months or a fine not exceeding the statutory maximum or both;
(*b*) on conviction on indictment, to imprisonment for a term not exceeding 5 years or a fine or both.
(3) In the application of sub-paragraph (2)(*a*)—
(*a*) in England and Wales, in relation to an offence committed before the commencement of section 154(1) of the Criminal Justice Act 2003 (c 44), or
(*b*) in Northern Ireland,
for "12 months" substitute "6 months".
(4) Where a person is convicted of an offence under this paragraph, it is not open to the court by or before which they are convicted—
(*a*) in England and Wales or Northern Ireland, to make an order for conditional discharge in respect of the offence;
(*b*) in Scotland, to make a probation order in respect of the offence.

*Meaning of "terrorism activity"*

**16.** In this Schedule "terrorism activity" means anything that—
(*a*) if done in any part of the United Kingdom, would constitute an offence to which this Part applies by virtue of section 41, or
(*b*) is, or takes place in the course of, an act of terrorism or is for the purposes of terrorism.

## SCHEDULE 6

NOTIFICATION REQUIREMENTS: APPLICATION TO SERVICE OFFENCES — Section 59

*Service offences to which this Part applies: terrorism offences*

**7.9082** **1.** This Part applies to a service offence as respects which the corresponding civil offence is an offence within section 41(1) or (2) (offences to which this Part applies: terrorism offences).

*Service offences to which this Part applies: offences having a terrorist connection*

**2.** (1) This Part applies to a service offence as to which the service court dealing with the offence has determined in accordance with section 32 that the offence has a terrorist connection.
(2) A person to whom the notification requirements apply by virtue of such a determination may appeal against it to the same court, and subject to the same conditions, as an appeal against sentence.
(3) If the determination is set aside on appeal, the notification requirements are treated as never having applied to that person in respect of the offence.

*Service offences dealt with before commencement*

**3.** (1) This Part applies to a person dealt with for a service offence before the commencement of this Part only if—
(*a*) the corresponding civil offence is on the commencement of this Part within section 41(1) or (2) (offences to which this Part applies: terrorism offences), and
(*b*) immediately before the commencement of this Part the person—
(i) is imprisoned or detained in pursuance of the sentence or other order made in respect of the offence,
(ii) would be so imprisoned or detained but for being unlawfully at large, absent without leave, on temporary leave or leave of absence, or released from custody (or on bail) pending an appeal, or
(iii) is on licence having served the custodial part of a sentence of imprisonment in respect of the offence.
(2) In relation to a person dealt with for a service offence before the commencement of this Part, any reference in this Schedule to a sentence, order or finding under a specified statutory provision includes a sentence or order under any corresponding earlier statutory provision.

*Service offences: persons to whom notification requirements apply*

**4.** The notification requirements apply to a person who—
(*a*) is aged 16 or over at the time of being dealt with for a service offence to which this Part applies, and
(*b*) is made subject in respect of the offence to a sentence or order within paragraph 5 (sentences or orders triggering notification requirements).

*Service offences: sentences or orders triggering notification requirements*

**5.** (1) The notification requirements apply to a person who—
(*a*) has been convicted of a service offence to which this Part applies and sentenced in respect of the offence to—
(i) imprisonment or custody for life,
(ii) imprisonment or custodial order for a term of 12 months or more,
(iii) imprisonment or detention in a young offender institution for public protection under section 225 of the Criminal Justice Act 2003 (c 44),
(iv) detention for life or for a period of 12 months or more under section 71A(4) of the Army Act 1955 or the Air Force Act 1955, section 43A(4) of the Naval Discipline Act 1957 or section 209 of the Armed Forces Act 2006 (c 52),
(v) detention and training (and supervision) under section 211 of that Act, where the term of the order under that section is 12 months or more,
(vi) detention for public protection under section 226 of the Criminal Justice Act 2003, or
(vii) detention during Her Majesty's pleasure; or
(*b*) has been—

(i) convicted of a service offence to which this Part applies carrying a maximum term of imprisonment of 12 months or more,

(ii) found not guilty by reason of insanity of such an offence, or

(iii) found to be unfit to stand trial and to have done the act charged against them in respect of such an offence,

and made subject in respect of the offence to a hospital order.

(2) The reference in sub-paragraph (1)(*b*)(i) to an offence carrying a maximum term of imprisonment of 12 months or more—

(*a*) is to an offence carrying such a maximum term in the case of a person who has attained the age of 18 (or 21, as respects any time before the coming into force of section 61 of the Criminal Justice and Court Services Act 2000 (c 43)), and

(*b*) includes an offence carrying in the case of such a person a maximum term of life imprisonment and an offence for which in the case of such a person the sentence is fixed by law as life imprisonment.

*Service offences: power to amend specified terms or periods of imprisonment or detention*

**6.** (1) The Secretary of State may by order amend the provisions of paragraph 5 referring to a specified term or period of imprisonment or detention.

(2) An order reducing a specified term or period has effect only in relation to persons dealt with after the order comes into force.

(3) Where an order increases a specified term or period—

(*a*) it has effect in relation to persons dealt with at any time, whether before or after the order comes into force, and

(*b*) a person who would not have been subject to the notification requirements if the order had been in force when the offence was dealt with (and who is not otherwise subject to those requirements) ceases to be subject to the requirements when the order comes into force.

(4) An order under this paragraph is subject to affirmative resolution procedure.

*Service offences: period for which notification requirements apply*

**7.** (1) The period for which the notification requirements apply is—

(*a*) 30 years in the case of a person who—

(i) is aged 18 or over at the time of conviction for the service offence, and

(ii) receives in respect of the offence a sentence within sub-paragraph (2);

(*b*) 15 years in the case of a person who—

(i) is aged 18 or over at the time of conviction for the service offence, and

(ii) receives in respect of the offence a sentence within sub-paragraph (3);

(*c*) 10 years in any other case.

(2) The sentences where a 30 year period applies are—

(*a*) imprisonment or custody for life,

(*b*) imprisonment or a custodial order for a term of 10 years or more,

(*c*) imprisonment or detention in a young offender institution for public protection under section 225 of the Criminal Justice Act 2003 (c 44),

(*d*) detention during Her Majesty's pleasure.

(3) The sentences where a 15 year period applies are imprisonment or a custodial order for a term of 5 years or more but less than 10 years.

(4) The period begins with the day on which the person is dealt with for the offence.

(5) If a person who is the subject of a finding within paragraph 5(1)(*b*)(iii) (finding of unfitness to stand trial etc) is subsequently tried for the offence, the period resulting from that finding ends—

(*a*) if the person is acquitted, at the conclusion of the trial;

(*b*) if the person is convicted, when the person is again dealt with in respect of the offence.

(6) For the purposes of determining the length of the period—

(*a*) a person who has been sentenced in respect of two or more terrorism offences to consecutive terms of imprisonment is treated as if sentenced, in respect of each of the offences, to a term of imprisonment equal to the aggregate of the terms; and

(*b*) a person who has been sentenced in respect of two or more such offences to concurrent terms of imprisonment (X and Y) that overlap for a period (Z) is treated as if sentenced, in respect of each of the offences, to a term of imprisonment equal to X plus Y minus Z.

(7) In determining whether the period has expired, there shall be disregarded any period when the person was—

(*a*) remanded in or committed to custody by an order of a court,

(*b*) in service custody pursuant to a decision of a court or judge advocate (or an order of a commanding officer under section 110 of the Armed Forces Act 2006 (c 52)),

(*c*) serving a sentence of imprisonment or detention,

(*d*) detained in a hospital, or

(*e*) detained under the Immigration Acts.

(8) In sub-paragraph (7)(*b*)—

(*a*) "service custody" includes, in relation to times before the commencement of the relevant provisions of the Armed Forces Act 2006, military custody, air-force custody and naval custody;

(*b*) "judge advocate" includes, in relation to such times, judicial officer;

(*c*) the reference to section 110 of the Armed Forces Act 2006 includes, in relation to times before the commencement of that section, a reference to—

(i) section 75K of the Army Act 1955 (3 & 4 Eliz 2 c 18) or the Air Force Act 1955 (3 & 4 Eliz 2 c 19);

(ii) section 47L of the Naval Discipline Act 1957 (c 53).

*Modifications in relation to service offences etc*

**8.** (1) In the following provisions, references to a person committed to custody by an order of a court include a person in service custody pursuant to a decision of a court or judge advocate (or an order of a commanding officer under section 110 of the Armed Forces Act 2006)—

(*a*) section 47(4) (initial notification);

(*b*) section 48(8) (notification of changes);
(*c*) section 49(2) (periodic re-notification);
(*d*) section 53(7) (period for which requirements apply);
(*e*) section 56(3) (notification on return after absence from UK).

(2) In section 48(4) (notification on release from custody etc) the reference to custody pursuant to an order of a court includes service custody pursuant to a decision of a court or judge advocate (or an order of a commanding officer under section 110 of the Armed Forces Act 2006).

(3) Paragraph 7(8) (meaning of "service custody" and "judge advocate" etc) applies for the purposes of this paragraph.

**9.** In the application of section 47(6) (initial notification: person dealt with before commencement) in relation to a service offence, the reference to a person being on bail pending an appeal includes a person released from custody pending an appeal.

**10.** Where in relation to a service offence the court of trial (as defined by subsection (2) of section 51 (meaning of "local police area")) was situated outside the United Kingdom, that section has effect as if subsection (1)(*c*) were omitted.

**11.** References in this Part to a sentence of detention do not include—
(*a*) a sentence of service detention (as defined by section 374 of the Armed Forces Act 2006 (c 52)), or
(*b*) a corresponding sentence passed under (or by virtue of) the Army Act 1955 (3 & 4 Eliz 2 c 18), the Air Force Act 1955 (3 & 4 Eliz 2 c 19) or the Naval Discipline Act 1957 (c 53).

**12.** The following provisions do not apply in relation to service offences—
(*a*) section 43 (offences dealt with before commencement);
(*b*) section 45 (sentences or orders triggering notification requirements);
(*c*) section 53 (period for which requirements apply).

*Application of power to make transitional modifications etc*

**13.** An order[1] under subsection (4) of section 380 of the Armed Forces Act 2006 (power to make transitional modifications etc) which makes provision of the kind mentioned in subsection (6) of that section may provide for paragraph 5(1)(*a*) or paragraph 7(2) or (3) above to have effect with such modifications (relating to custodial punishments specified in the order) as are so specified.

---

[1] The Armed Forces Act 2006 (Transitional Provisions etc) Order 2009, SI 2009/1059 amended by SI 2012/2824 has been made.

## SCHEDULE 7

TERRORIST FINANCING AND MONEY LAUNDERING Section 62

*(As amended by the Terrorist Asset-Freezing etc Act 2010, ss 48–52, Schs 1, 2 and the Policing and Crime Act 2017, s 145)*

### PART 5

### ENFORCEMENT: INFORMATION POWERS

*Enforcement authorities and officers*

7.9084 **18.** (1) In this Schedule "enforcement authority" means—
(*a*) The Financial Conduct Authority ("the FCA"),
(*b*) the Commissioners for Her Majesty's Revenue and Customs ("HMRC"),
(*c*) *repelaed,*
(*d*) *repealed.*

(2) In this Part of this Schedule "enforcement officer" means—
(*a*) an officer of the FCA, including a member of the staff or an agent of the FCA,
(*b*) an officer of Revenue and Customs,
(*c*) *repelaed,*
(*d*) *repealed,* or
(*e*) a local enforcement officer.

(3) A "local enforcement officer" means—
(*a*) in Great Britain, an officer of a local weights and measures authority;
(*b*) in Northern Ireland, an officer of the Department of Enterprise, Trade and Investment in Northern Ireland ("DETINI") acting pursuant to arrangements made with the FCA for the purposes of this Schedule.

*Power to require information or documents*

**19.** (1) An enforcement officer may by notice to a relevant person require the person—
(*a*) to provide such information as may be specified in the notice, or
(*b*) to produce such documents as may be so specified.

(2) An officer may exercise powers under this paragraph only if the information or documents sought to be obtained as a result are reasonably required in connection with the exercise by the enforcement authority for whom the officer acts of its functions under this Schedule.

(3) Where an officer requires information to be provided or documents produced under this paragraph—
(*a*) the notice must set out the reasons why the officer requires the information to be provided or the documents produced, and
(*b*) the information must be provided or the documents produced—
(i) before the end of such reasonable period as may be specified in the notice; and
(ii) at such place as may be so specified.

(4) In relation to a document in electronic form the power to require production of it includes a power to require the production of a copy of it in legible form or in a form from which it can readily be produced in visible and legible form.

(5) An enforcement officer may take copies of, or make extracts from, any document produced under this paragraph.

(6) The production of a document does not affect any lien which a person has on the document.

*Entry, inspection without a warrant etc*

**20.** (1) Where an enforcement officer has reasonable cause to believe that any premises are being used by a relevant person in connection with the person's business activities, the officer may on producing evidence of authority at any reasonable time—

(*a*) enter the premises;
(*b*) inspect the premises;
(*c*) observe the carrying on of business activities by the relevant person;
(*d*) inspect any document found on the premises;
(*e*) require any person on the premises to provide an explanation of any document or to state where it may be found.

(2) An enforcement officer may take copies of, or make extracts from, any document found under sub-paragraph (1).

(3) An officer may exercise powers under this paragraph only if the information or document sought to be obtained as a result is reasonably required in connection with the exercise by the enforcement authority for whom the officer acts of its functions under this Schedule.

(4) In this paragraph "premises" means any premises other than premises used only as a dwelling.

*Entry to premises under warrant*

**21.** (1) A justice may issue a warrant under this paragraph if satisfied on information on oath given by an enforcement officer that there are reasonable grounds for believing that the first, second or third set of conditions is satisfied.

(2) The first set of conditions is—

(*a*) that there is on the premises specified in the warrant a document in relation to which a requirement could be imposed under paragraph 19(1)(*b*), and
(*b*) that if such a requirement were to be imposed—
  (i) it would not be complied with, or
  (ii) the document to which it relates would be removed, tampered with or destroyed.

(3) The second set of conditions is—

(*a*) that a person on whom a requirement has been imposed under paragraph 19(1)(*b*) has failed (wholly or in part) to comply with it, and
(*b*) that there is on the premises specified in the warrant a document that has been required to be produced.

(4) The third set of conditions is—

(*a*) that an enforcement officer has been obstructed in the exercise of a power under paragraph 20, and
(*b*) that there is on the premises specified in the warrant a document that could be inspected under paragraph 20(1)(*d*).

(5) A justice may issue a warrant under this paragraph if satisfied on information on oath given by an officer that there are reasonable grounds for suspecting that—

(*a*) an offence under this Schedule has been, is being or is about to be committed by a relevant person, and
(*b*) there is on the premises specified in the warrant a document relevant to whether that offence has been, or is being or is about to be committed.

(6) A warrant issued under this paragraph shall authorise an enforcement officer—

(*a*) to enter the premises specified in the warrant;
(*b*) to search the premises and take possession of anything appearing to be a document specified in the warrant or to take, in relation to any such document, any other steps which may appear to be necessary for preserving it or preventing interference with it;
(*c*) to take copies of, or extracts from, any document specified in the warrant;
(*d*) to require any person on the premises to provide an explanation of any document appearing to be of the kind specified in the warrant or to state where it may be found;
(*e*) to use such force as may reasonably be necessary.

(7) Where a warrant is issued by a justice under sub-paragraph (1) or (5) on the basis of information on oath given by an officer of the FSA, for "an enforcement officer" in sub-paragraph (6) substitute "a constable".

(8) In sub-paragraphs (1), (5) and (7), "justice" means—

(*a*) in relation to England and Wales, a justice of the peace;
(*b*) in relation to Scotland, a justice within the meaning of section 307 of the Criminal Procedure (Scotland) Act 1995 (c 46) (interpretation);
(*c*) in relation to Northern Ireland, a lay magistrate.

(9) In the application of this paragraph to Scotland, the references in sub-paragraphs (1), (5) and (7) to information on oath are to be read as references to evidence on oath.

*Restrictions on powers*

**22.** (1) This paragraph applies in relation to the powers conferred by—

(*a*) paragraph 19 (power to require information or documents),
(*b*) paragraph 20 (entry, inspection without warrant etc), or
(*c*) paragraph 21 (entry to premises under warrant).

(2) Those powers are not exercisable in relation to information or documents in respect of which a claim to legal professional privilege (in Scotland, to confidentiality of communications) could be maintained in legal proceedings.

(3) The exercise of those powers and the provision of information or production of documents under them is not otherwise subject to any restriction on the disclosure of information, whether imposed by statute or otherwise.

*Failure to comply with information requirement*

**23.** (1) If on an application made by—

(*a*) an enforcement authority, or
(*b*) a local weights and measures authority or DETINI pursuant to arrangements made with the OFT—
  (i) by or on behalf of the authority; or
  (ii) by DETINI,

it appears to the court that a person (the "information defaulter") has failed to do something that they were required to do under paragraph 19(1), the court may make an order under this paragraph.

(2) An order under this paragraph may require the information defaulter—

(*a*) to do the thing that they failed to do within such period as may be specified in the order;

(*b*) otherwise to take such steps to remedy the consequences of the failure as may be so specified.

(3) If the information defaulter is a body corporate, a partnership or an unincorporated body of persons that is not a partnership, the order may require any officer of the body corporate, partnership or body, who is (wholly or partly) responsible for the failure to meet such costs of the application as are specified in the order.

(4) In this paragraph "the court" means—

(*a*) in England and Wales and Northern Ireland, the High Court or the county court;

(*b*) in Scotland, the Court of Session or the sheriff court.

*Powers of local enforcement officers*

**24.** (1) A local enforcement officer may only exercise powers under this Part of this Schedule pursuant to arrangements made with the FCA—

(*a*) by or on behalf of the relevant local weights and measures authority, or

(*b*) by DETINI.

(2) Anything done or omitted to be done by, or in relation to, a local enforcement officer in the exercise or purported exercise of a power in this Part of this Schedule is treated for all purposes as if done or omitted to be done by, or in relation to, an officer of the FCA.

(3) Sub-paragraph (2) does not apply for the purposes of criminal proceedings brought against the local enforcement officer, the relevant local weights and measures authority, DETINI or the OFT, in respect of anything done or omitted to be done by the officer.

(4) A local enforcement officer must not disclose to any person other than the FCA and the relevant local weights and measures authority or, as the case may be, DETINI information obtained by the officer in the exercise of powers under this Part of this Schedule unless—

(*a*) the officer has the approval of the FCA to do so, or

(*b*) the officer is under a duty to make the disclosure.

(5) In this paragraph "the relevant local weights and measures authority", in relation to a local enforcement officer, means the authority of which the officer is an officer.

## Part 7

## Enforcement: Offences

*Offences: failure to comply with requirement imposed by direction*

**30.** (1) A person who fails to comply with a requirement imposed by a direction under this Schedule commits an offence, subject to the following provisions.

(2) No offence is committed if the person took all reasonable steps and exercised all due diligence to ensure that the requirement would be complied with.

(3) In deciding whether a person has committed an offence under this paragraph the court must consider whether the person followed any relevant guidance that was at the time—

(*a*) issued by a supervisory authority or any other appropriate body,

(*b*) approved by the Treasury, and

(*c*) published in a manner approved by the Treasury as suitable in their opinion to bring the guidance to the attention of persons likely to be affected by it.

(4) In sub-paragraph (3) "appropriate body" means a body that regulates or is representative of any trade, profession, business or employment carried on by the alleged offender.

(4A) In a case where a person is guilty of an offence under this paragraph by failing to comply with a requirement of a kind mentioned in paragraph 13, the person is liable—

(a) on summary conviction—

(i) in England and Wales, to imprisonment for a term not exceeding 12 months (or, in relation to offences committed before section 154(1) of the Criminal Justice Act 2003 comes into force, 6 months) or to a fine, or to both;

(ii) in Scotland, to imprisonment for a term not exceeding 12 months, or to a fine not exceeding the statutory maximum, or to both;

(iii) in Northern Ireland, to imprisonment for a term not exceeding 6 months, or to a fine not exceeding the statutory maximum, or to both;

(b) on conviction on indictment, to imprisonment for a term not exceeding 7 years or to a fine, or to both.

(5) In any other case, a person guilty of an offence under this paragraph is liable—

(*a*) on summary conviction, to a fine not exceeding the statutory maximum;

(*b*) on conviction on indictment, to imprisonment for a term not exceeding two years or a fine or both.

(6) A person who is convicted of an offence under this paragraph is not liable to a penalty under paragraph 25 in respect of the same failure.

*Offences: relevant person circumventing requirements*

**30A.** (1) A relevant person who intentionally participates in activities knowing that the object or effect of them is (whether directly or indirectly) to circumvent a requirement imposed by a direction under this Schedule commits an offence.

(1A) In a case where a person is guilty of an offence under this paragraph in relation to a requirement of a kind mentioned in paragraph 13, the person is liable—

(a) on summary conviction—

(i) in England and Wales, to imprisonment for a term not exceeding 12 months (or, in relation to offences committed before section 154(1) of the Criminal Justice Act 2003 comes into force, 6 months) or to a fine, or to both;

(ii) in Scotland, to imprisonment for a term not exceeding 12 months, or to a fine not exceeding the statutory maximum, or to both;

(iii) in Northern Ireland, to imprisonment for a term not exceeding 6 months, or to a fine not exceeding the statutory maximum, or to both;

(b) on conviction on indictment, to imprisonment for a term not exceeding 7 years or to a fine, or to both.

(2) In any other case, a person guilty of an offence under this paragraph is liable—

(*a*) on summary conviction, to a fine not exceeding the statutory maximum;
(*b*) on conviction on indictment, to imprisonment for a term not exceeding two years or a fine or both.

(3) A person who is convicted of an offence under this paragraph is not liable to a penalty under paragraph 25A in respect of participation in the same activities.

*Offences in connection with licences*

**31.** (1) A person commits an offence who for the purpose of obtaining a licence under paragraph 17—
(*a*) provides information that is false in a material respect or a document that is not what it purports to be, and
(*b*) knows that, or is reckless as to whether, the information is false or the document is not what it purports to be.

(2) A person guilty of an offence under this paragraph is liable—
(a) on summary conviction—
(i) in England and Wales, to imprisonment for a term not exceeding 12 months (or, in relation to offences committed before section 154(1) of the Criminal Justice Act 2003 comes into force, 6 months) or to a fine, or to both;
(ii) in Scotland, to imprisonment for a term not exceeding 12 months, or to a fine not exceeding the statutory maximum, or to both;
(iii) in Northern Ireland, to imprisonment for a term not exceeding 6 months, or to a fine not exceeding the statutory maximum, or to both;
(b) on conviction on indictment, to imprisonment for a term not exceeding 2 years or to a fine, or to both.

*Extra-territorial application of offences*

**32.** (1) An offence under this Schedule may be committed by a United Kingdom person by conduct wholly or partly outside the United Kingdom.

(2) Nothing in this paragraph affects any criminal liability arising otherwise than under this paragraph.

*Prosecution of offences*

**33.** (1) Proceedings for an offence under this Schedule may be instituted in England and Wales only by—
(*a*) the FCA;
(*b*) *repealed;*
(*c*) *repealed;*
(*d*) a local weights and measures authority; or
(*e*) the Director of Public Prosecutions.

(2) Proceedings for an offence under this Schedule may be instituted in Northern Ireland only by—
(*a*) the FCA;
(*b*) HMRC;
(*c*) *repealed;*
(*d*) DETINI; or
(*e*) the Director of Public Prosecutions for Northern Ireland.

(3) In section 168(4) of the Financial Services and Markets Act 2000 (c 8) (appointment of persons to carry out investigation), after paragraph (*b*) insert—

"(*ba*) a person may be guilty of an offence under Schedule 7 to the Counter-Terrorism Act 2008 (terrorist financing or money laundering);".

(4) In section 402(1) of that Act (power of FSA to institute proceedings), omit the "or" before paragraph (*b*) and after that paragraph insert—

"or
(*c*) Schedule 7 to the Counter-Terrorism Act 2008 (terrorist financing or money laundering).".

(5) HMRC may conduct a criminal investigation into any offence under this Schedule.

(6) In sub-paragraph (5) "criminal investigation" has the meaning given by section 35(5)(*b*) of the Commissioners for Revenue and Customs Act 2005 (c 11).

*Jurisdiction to try offences*

**34.** Where an offence under this Schedule is committed outside the United Kingdom—
(*a*) proceedings for the offence may be taken at any place in the United Kingdom, and
(*b*) the offence may for all incidental purposes be treated as having been committed at any such place.

*Time limit for summary proceedings*

**35.** (1) An information relating to an offence under this Schedule that is triable by a magistrates' court in England and Wales may be so tried if it is laid—
(*a*) at any time within three years after the commission of the offence, and
(*b*) within twelve months after the date on which evidence sufficient in the opinion of the prosecutor to justify the proceedings comes to the knowledge of the prosecutor.

(2) Summary proceedings in Scotland for an offence under this Schedule—
(*a*) must not be commenced after the expiration of three years from the commission of the offence;
(*b*) subject to that, may be commenced at any time within twelve months after the date on which evidence sufficient in the Lord Advocate's opinion to justify the proceedings came to the knowledge of the Lord Advocate.

Section 136(3) of the Criminal Procedure (Scotland) Act 1995 (c 46) (date when proceedings deemed to be commenced) applies for the purposes of this sub-paragraph as for the purposes of that section.

(3) A magistrates' court in Northern Ireland has jurisdiction to hear and determine a complaint charging the commission of a summary offence under this Schedule provided that the complaint is made—
(*a*) within three years from the time when the offence was committed, and
(*b*) within twelve months from the date on which evidence sufficient in the opinion of the prosecutor to justify the proceedings comes to the knowledge of the prosecutor.

(4) For the purposes of this paragraph a certificate of the prosecutor (or, in Scotland, the Lord Advocate) as to the date on which such evidence as is referred to above came to their notice is conclusive evidence.

*Liability of officers of bodies corporate etc*

**36.** (1) If an offence under this Schedule committed by a body corporate is shown—
(*a*) to have been committed with the consent or the connivance of an officer of the body corporate, or
(*b*) to be attributable to any neglect on the part of any such officer,
the officer as well as the body corporate is guilty of an offence and liable to be proceeded against and punished accordingly.

(2) If an offence under this Schedule committed by a partnership is shown—
(*a*) to have been committed with the consent or the connivance of a partner, or
(*b*) to be attributable to any neglect on the part of a partner,
the partner as well as the partnership is guilty of an offence and liable to be proceeded against and punished accordingly.

(3) If an offence under this Schedule committed by an unincorporated association (other than a partnership) is shown—
(*a*) to have been committed with the consent or the connivance of an officer of the association, or
(*b*) to be attributable to any neglect on the part of any such officer,
the officer as well as the association is guilty of an offence and liable to be proceeded against and punished accordingly.

(4) If the affairs of a body corporate are managed by its members, sub-paragraph (1) applies in relation to the acts and defaults of a member in connection with the member's functions of management as if the member were a director of the body.

(5) In this paragraph—
"officer"—
(*a*) in relation to a body corporate, means a director, manager, secretary, chief executive, member of the committee of management, or a person purporting to act in such a capacity, and
(*b*) in relation to an unincorporated association, means any officer of the association or any member of its governing body, or a person purporting to act in such capacity;
"partner" includes a person purporting to act as a partner.

*Proceedings against unincorporated bodies*

**37.** (1) Proceedings for an offence under this Schedule alleged to have been committed by a partnership or an unincorporated association must be brought in the name of the partnership or association (and not in that of its members).

(2) In proceedings for such an offence brought against a partnership or unincorporated association—
(*a*) section 33 of the Criminal Justice Act 1925 (c 86) (procedure on charge of offence against corporation) and Schedule 3 to the Magistrates' Courts Act 1980 (c 43) (corporations) apply as they do in relation to a body corporate;
(*b*) section 70 of the Criminal Procedure (Scotland) Act 1995 (c 46) (proceedings against bodies corporate) applies as it does in relation to a body corporate;
(*c*) section 18 of the Criminal Justice (Northern Ireland) Act 1945 (c 15 (NI)) (procedure on charge) and Schedule 4 to the Magistrates' Courts (Northern Ireland) Order 1981 (SI 1981/1675 (NI 26)) (corporations) apply as they do in relation to a body corporate.

(3) Rules of court relating to the service of documents have effect in relation to proceedings for an offence under this Schedule as if the partnership or association were a body corporate.

(4) A fine imposed on the partnership or association on its conviction of such an offence is to be paid out of the funds of the partnership or association.

# Terrorist Asset-Freezing etc Act 2010[1]

(2010 c 38)

## PART 1[2]
## TERRORIST ASSET-FREEZING

### CHAPTER 1[3]
### DESIGNATED PERSONS

*Introductory*

7.9085 **1. Meaning of "designated person"** In this Part "designated person" means—
(*a*) a person designated by the Treasury for the purposes of this Part, or
(*b*) a natural or legal person, group or entity included in the list provided for by Article 2(3) of Council Regulation (EC) No 2580/2001 of 27 December 2001 on specific restrictive measures directed against certain persons and entities with a view to combating terrorism.

[Terrorist Asset-Freezing etc Act 2010, s 1.]

---

1 The purpose of Part 1 of the Act is to give effect in the United Kingdom to resolution 1373 (2001) adopted by the Security Council of the United Nations on 28th September 2001 relating to terrorism and resolution 1452 (2002) adopted on 20th December 2002 relating to humanitarian exemptions. It also provides for enforcement of Regulation (EC) 2580/2001 on specific measures directed at certain persons and entities with a view to combating terrorism. The Act was passed in response to the decision in *Ahmed v HM Treasury* [2010] UKSC 2 concerning the vires of one of the Orders in Council which had made to implement resolution 1373. Part 1 came into effect on the day on which the Act received the Royal Assent.

The purpose of Part 2 of the Act is to amend Sch 7 to the Counter-Terrorism Act 2008. Schedule 7 provides the Treasury with powers by directions to impose financial restrictions in relation to persons connected with a country in response to money laundering, terrorist financing or the development or production of nuclear, radiological, biological or chemical weapons that poses a risk to the national interests of the United Kingdom, or where the Financial Action Task Force has advised that measures should be taken in relation to the country because of the risk of terrorist financing or money laundering activities. The amendments to the Sch 7 clarify the persons to whom a direction may be given, broaden the definition of persons in relation to whom restrictions may be applied, and introduce a prohibition on circumventing the requirements of a direction.

[2] Part 1 contains ss 1–40.

[3] Chapter 1 contains ss 1–10.

*Confidential information*

7.9086 **10. Confidential information** (1) Where the Treasury in accordance with section 3(4) or 7(4) inform only certain persons of a designation, they may specify that information contained in it is to be treated as confidential.

(2) A person ("P") who—

(*a*) is provided with information that is to be treated as confidential in accordance with subsection (1), or

(*b*) obtains such information,

must not, subject to subsection (3), disclose it if P knows, or has reasonable cause to suspect, that the information is to be treated as confidential.

(3) The prohibition in subsection (2) does not apply to any disclosure made by P with lawful authority.

(4) For this purpose information is disclosed with lawful authority only if and to the extent that—

(*a*) the disclosure is by, or is authorised by, the Treasury,

(*b*) the disclosure is by or with the consent of the designated person,

(*c*) the disclosure is necessary to give effect to a requirement imposed under or by virtue of this Part or any other enactment, or

(*d*) the disclosure is required, under rules of court, tribunal rules or a court or tribunal order, for the purposes of legal proceedings of any description.

(5) This section does not prevent the disclosure of information that is already, or has previously been, available to the public from other sources.

(6) A person who contravenes the prohibition in subsection (2) commits an offence.

(7) The High Court (in Scotland, the Court of Session) may, on the application of—

(*a*) the person who is the subject of the information, or

(*b*) the Treasury,

grant an injunction (in Scotland, an interdict) to prevent a breach of the prohibition in subsection (2).

[Terrorist Asset-Freezing etc Act 2010, s 10.]

## CHAPTER 2[1]
## PROHIBITIONS IN RELATION TO DESIGNATED PERSONS

*Prohibitions*

7.9088 **11. Freezing of funds and economic resources** (1) A person ("P") must not deal with funds[2] or economic resources owned, held or controlled by a designated person if P knows, or has reasonable cause to suspect, that P is dealing with such funds or economic resources[2].

(2) In subsection (1) "deal with" means—

(*a*) in relation to funds—

(i) use, alter, move, allow access to or transfer,

(ii) deal with the funds in any other way that would result in any change in volume, amount, location, ownership, possession, character or destination, or

(iii) make any other change that would enable use, including portfolio management;

(*b*) in relation to economic resources, exchange or use in exchange for funds, goods or services.

(3) Subsection (1) is subject to sections 16 and 17 (exceptions and licences).

(4) A person who contravenes the prohibition in subsection (1) commits an offence.

[Terrorist Asset-Freezing etc Act 2010, s 11.]

[1] Chapter 2 contains ss 11–18.

[2] Defined in s 39, post.

7.9090 **12. Making funds or financial services available to designated person** (1) A person ("P") must not make funds[1] or financial services[2] available (directly or indirectly) to a designated person if P knows, or has reasonable cause to suspect, that P is making the funds or financial services so available.

(2) Subsection (1) is subject to sections 16 and 17 (exceptions and licences).

(3) A person who contravenes the prohibition in subsection (1) commits an offence.

[Terrorist Asset-Freezing etc Act 2010, s 12.]

[1] Defined in s 39, post.

[2] Defined in s 40, post

7.9092 **13. Making funds or financial services available for benefit of designated person**

(1) A person ("P") must not make funds[1] or financial services[2] available to any person for the benefit of a designated person if P knows, or has reasonable cause to suspect, that P is making the

funds or financial services so available.

(2) For the purposes of this section—

(*a*) funds are made available for the benefit of a designated person only if that person thereby obtains, or is able to obtain, a significant financial benefit, and

(*b*) "financial benefit" includes the discharge of a financial obligation for which the designated person is wholly or partly responsible.

(3) Subsection (1) is subject to sections 16 and 17 (exceptions and licences).

(4) A person who contravenes the prohibition in subsection (1) commits an offence.

[Terrorist Asset-Freezing etc Act 2010, s 13.]

---

1 Defined in s 39, post.

2 Defined in s 40, post

7.9094 **14. Making economic resources available to designated person** (1) A person ("P") must not make economic resources[1] available (directly or indirectly) to a designated person if P knows, or has reasonable cause to suspect—

(*a*) that P is making the economic resources so available, and

(*b*) that the designated person would be likely to exchange the economic resources, or use them in exchange, for funds, goods or services.

(2) Subsection (1) is subject to section 17 (licences).

(3) A person who contravenes the prohibition in subsection (1) commits an offence.

[Terrorist Asset-Freezing etc Act 2010, s 14.]

---

1 Defined in s 39, post.

7.9096 **15. Making economic resources available for benefit of designated person** (1) A person ("P") must not make economic resources[1] available to any person for the benefit of a designated person if P knows, or has reasonable cause to suspect, that P is making the economic resources so available.

(2) For the purposes of this section—

(*a*) economic resources are made available for the benefit of a designated person only if that person thereby obtains, or is able to obtain, a significant financial benefit, and

(*b*) "financial benefit" includes the discharge of a financial obligation for which the designated person is wholly or partly responsible.

(3) Subsection (1) is subject to section 17 (licences).

(4) A person who contravenes the prohibition in subsection (1) commits an offence.

[Terrorist Asset-Freezing etc Act 2010, s 15.]

---

1 Defined in s 39, post.

*Exceptions and licences*

7.9098 **16. Exceptions** (1) The prohibitions in sections 11 to 13 are not contravened by a relevant institution crediting a frozen account with—

(*a*) interest or other earnings due on the account, or

(*b*) payments due under contracts, agreements or obligations that were concluded or arose before the account became a frozen account.

(2) The prohibitions in sections 12 and 13 on making funds available do not prevent a relevant institution from crediting a frozen account where it receives funds transferred to the account.

(3) The prohibition in section 13 is not contravened by the making of a payment which—

(*a*) is a benefit under or by virtue of an enactment relating to social security (irrespective of the name or nature of the benefit), and

(*b*) is made to a person who is not a designated person,

whether or not the payment is made in respect of a designated person.

(4) A relevant institution must inform the Treasury without delay if it credits a frozen account in accordance with subsection (1)(*b*) or (2).

(5) In this section "frozen account" means an account with a relevant institution which is held or controlled (directly or indirectly) by a designated person.

[Terrorist Asset-Freezing etc Act 2010, s 16.]

7.9100 **17. Licences** (1) The prohibitions in sections 11 to 15 do not apply to anything done under the authority of a licence granted by the Treasury.

(2) Where relevant such a licence also constitutes authorisation under Article 6 of Council Regulation (EC) No 2580/2001 of 27 December 2001 on specific restrictive measures directed against certain persons and entities with a view to combating terrorism.

(3) A licence must specify the acts authorised by it and may be—

(*a*) general or granted to a category of persons or to a particular person;

(*b*) subject to conditions;

(*c*) of indefinite duration or subject to an expiry date.

(4) The Treasury may vary or revoke a licence at any time.

(5) On the grant, variation or revocation of a licence, the Treasury must—

(*a*) in the case of a licence granted to a particular person, give written notice of the grant, variation or revocation to that person;

(*b*) in the case of a general licence or a licence granted to a category of persons, take such steps as the Treasury consider appropriate to publicise the grant, variation or revocation of the licence.

(6) A person commits an offence who, for the purpose of obtaining a licence, knowingly or recklessly—

(*a*) provides information that is false in a material respect, or

(*b*) provides or produces a document that is not what it purports to be.

(7) A person who purports to act under the authority of a licence but who fails to comply with any conditions included in the licence commits an offence.

[Terrorist Asset-Freezing etc Act 2010, s 17.]

*Circumventing prohibitions etc*

7.9102 **18. Circumventing prohibitions etc** A person commits an offence who intentionally participates in activities knowing that the object or effect of them is (whether directly or indirectly)—

(*a*) to circumvent any of the prohibitions in sections 11 to 15, or

(*b*) to enable or facilitate the contravention of any such prohibition.

[Terrorist Asset-Freezing etc Act 2010, s 18.]

## CHAPTER 3[1]
## INFORMATION

*Information for Treasury*

7.9104 **19. Reporting obligations of relevant institutions** (1) A relevant institution must inform the Treasury as soon as practicable if—

(*a*) it knows, or has reasonable cause to suspect, that a person—

(i) is a designated person, or

(ii) has committed an offence under any provision of Chapter 2 (prohibitions in relation to designated persons), and

(*b*) the information or other matter on which the knowledge or suspicion is based came to it in the course of carrying on its business.

(2) Where a relevant institution informs the Treasury under subsection (1), it must state—

(*a*) the information or other matter on which the knowledge or suspicion is based, and

(*b*) any information it holds about the person by which the person can be identified.

(3) Subsection (4) applies if—

(*a*) a relevant institution informs the Treasury under subsection (1) that it knows, or has reasonable cause to suspect, that a person is a designated person, and

(*b*) that person is a customer of the institution.

(4) The relevant institution must also state the nature and amount or quantity of any funds or economic resources held by it for the customer at the time when it first had the knowledge or suspicion.

(5) A relevant institution that fails to comply with any requirement of subsection (1), (2) or (4) commits an offence.

[Terrorist Asset-Freezing etc Act 2010, s 19.]

---

1 Chapter 3 contains ss 19–25.

7.9106 **20. Powers to request information** (1) The Treasury may request a designated person to provide information concerning—

(*a*) funds or economic resources owned, held or controlled by or on behalf of the designated person, or

(*b*) any disposal of such funds or economic resources.

(2) The Treasury may request a designated person to provide such information as the Treasury may reasonably require about expenditure—

(*a*) by or on behalf of the designated person, or

(*b*) for the benefit of the designated person.

(3) The power in subsection (1) or (2) is exercisable only where the Treasury believe that it is necessary for the purpose of monitoring compliance with or detecting evasion of this Part.

(4) The Treasury may request a person acting under a licence granted under section 17 to provide information concerning—

(*a*) funds or economic resources dealt with under the licence, or

(*b*) funds, economic resources or financial services made available under the licence.

(5) The Treasury may request any person in or resident in the United Kingdom to provide such information as the Treasury may reasonably require for the purpose of—

(*a*) establishing for the purposes of this Part—

(i) the nature and amount or quantity of any funds or economic resources owned, held or controlled by or on behalf of a designated person,

(ii) the nature and amount or quantity of any funds, economic resources or financial services made available directly or indirectly to, or for the benefit of, a designated person, or

(iii) the nature of any financial transactions entered into by a designated person,

(*b*) monitoring compliance with or detecting evasion of this Part, or

(*c*) obtaining evidence of the commission of an offence under this Part.

(6) The Treasury may specify the manner in which, and the period within which, information is to be provided.

(7) If no such period is specified, the information which has been requested must be provided within a reasonable time.

(8) A request may include a continuing obligation to keep the Treasury informed as circumstances change, or on such regular basis as the Treasury may specify.

(9) Information requested under this section may relate to any period of time during which a person is, or was, a designated person.

(10) Information requested under subsection (1)(*b*), (2) or (5)(*a*)(iii) may relate to any period of time before a person became a designated person (as well as, or instead of, any subsequent period of time).

[Terrorist Asset-Freezing etc Act 2010, s 20.]

7.9108 21. **Production of documents** (1) A request under section 20 may include a request to produce specified documents or documents of a specified description.

(2) Where the Treasury request that documents be produced, they may—

(*a*) take copies of or extracts from any document so produced,

(*b*) request any person producing a document to give an explanation of it, and

(*c*) where that person is a body corporate, partnership or unincorporated body other than a partnership, request any person who is—

(i) in the case of a partnership, a present or past partner or employee of the partnership,

(ii) in any other case, a present or past officer or employee of the body concerned,

to give such an explanation.

(3) Where the Treasury request a designated person or a person acting under a licence granted under section 17 to produce documents, that person must—

(*a*) take reasonable steps to obtain the documents (if not already in the person's possession or control);

(*b*) keep the documents under the person's possession or control (except for the purpose of providing them to the Treasury or as the Treasury may otherwise permit).

[Terrorist Asset-Freezing etc Act 2010, s 21.]

7.9110 22. **Failure to comply with request for information** (1) A person commits an offence who—

(*a*) without reasonable excuse refuses or fails within the time and in the manner specified (or, if no time has been specified, within a reasonable time) to comply with any request made under this Chapter,

(*b*) knowingly or recklessly gives any information, or produces any document, which is false in a material particular in response to such a request,

(*c*) with intent to evade the provisions of this Chapter, destroys, mutilates, defaces, conceals or removes any document, or

(*d*) otherwise intentionally obstructs the Treasury in the exercise of their powers under this Chapter.

(2) Where a person is convicted of an offence under this section, the court may make an order requiring that person, within such period as may be specified in the order, to comply with the request.

[Terrorist Asset-Freezing etc Act 2010, s 22.]

*Disclosure of information by Treasury*

7.9112 23. **General power to disclose information** (1) The Treasury may disclose any information obtained by them in exercise of their powers under this Part (including any document so obtained and any copy or extract made of any document so obtained)—

(*a*) to a police officer;

(*b*) to any person holding or acting in any office under or in the service of—

(i) the Crown in right of the Government of the United Kingdom,

(ii) the Crown in right of the Scottish Administration, the Northern Ireland Administration or the Welsh Assembly Government,

(iii) the States of Jersey, Guernsey or Alderney or the Chief Pleas of Sark,

(iv) the Government of the Isle of Man, or

(v) the Government of any British overseas territory;

(*c*) to any law officer of the Crown for Jersey, Guernsey or the Isle of Man;

(*d*) to the Scottish Legal Aid Board or the Northern Ireland Legal Services Commission;

(*e*) to the Financial Services Authority, the Jersey Financial Services Commission, the Guernsey Financial Services Commission, the Isle of Man Insurance and Pensions Authority and the Isle of Man Financial Supervision Commission;

(*f*) for the purpose of giving assistance or co-operation, pursuant to the relevant Security Council resolutions, to—

(i) any organ of the United Nations, or

(ii) any person in the service of the United Nations, the Council of the European Union, the European Commission or the Government of any country;

(*g*) with a view to instituting, or otherwise for the purposes of, any proceedings—

(i) in the United Kingdom, for an offence under this Part, or

(ii) in any of the Channel Islands, the Isle of Man or any British overseas territory, for an offence under a similar provision in any such jurisdiction; or

(*h*) with the consent of a person who, in their own right, is entitled to the information or to possession of the document, copy or extract, to any third party.

(2) In subsection (1)(*h*) "in their own right" means not merely in the capacity as a servant or agent of another person.

[Terrorist Asset-Freezing etc Act 2010, s 23 amended by the Legal Aid, Sentencing and Punishment of Offenders Act 2012, Sch 5.]

## Chapter 4[1]

## Supplementary Provisions

### *Offences*

**7.9114 32. Penalties** (1) A person guilty of an offence under section 11, 12, 13, 14, 15 or 18 is liable—

(*a*) on conviction on indictment, to imprisonment for a term not exceeding seven years or to a fine or to both;

(*b*) on summary conviction, to imprisonment for a term not exceeding the relevant maximum or to a fine not exceeding the statutory maximum or to both[2].

(2) A person guilty of an offence under section 10 or 17 is liable—

(*a*) on conviction on indictment, to imprisonment for a term not exceeding two years or to a fine or to both;

(*b*) on summary conviction, to imprisonment for a term not exceeding the relevant maximum or to a fine not exceeding the statutory maximum or to both[2].

(3) For the purposes of subsections (1)(*b*) and (2)(*b*) "the relevant maximum" is—

(*a*) in England and Wales, 12 months (or 6 months, if the offence was committed before the commencement of section 154(1) of the Criminal Justice Act 2003);

(*b*) in Scotland, 12 months;

(*c*) in Northern Ireland, 6 months.

(4) A person guilty of an offence under section 19(5) or 22 is liable on summary conviction to imprisonment for a term not exceeding the relevant maximum or to a fine not exceeding level 5 on the standard scale or to both.

(5) For the purposes of subsection (4) "the relevant maximum" is—

(*a*) in England and Wales, 51 weeks (or 6 months, if the offence was committed before the commencement of section 281(4) and (5) of the Criminal Justice Act 2003);

(*b*) in Scotland or Northern Ireland, 6 months.

[Terrorist Asset-Freezing etc Act 2010, s 32.]

---

[1] Chapter 4 contains ss 26–45.

[2] For procedure in respect of offences triable either way, see the Magistrates' Courts Act 1980, ss 17A–21, in Part I: Magistrates' Courts, Procedure, ante.

**7.9116 33. Extra-territorial application of offences** (1) An offence under this Part may be committed by conduct wholly or partly outside the United Kingdom by—

(*a*) a UK national, or

(*b*) a body incorporated or constituted under the law of any part of the United Kingdom.

(2) In subsection (1) "UK national" means—

(*a*) a British citizen, a British overseas territories citizen, a British National (Overseas) or a British Overseas citizen,

(*b*) a person who under the British Nationality Act 1981 is a British subject, or

(*c*) a British protected person within the meaning of that Act.

(3) Her Majesty may by Order in Council provide for this section to have effect as if the list of persons in subsection (1) included a body incorporated or constituted under the law of any territory named in the Order.

(4) An Order under subsection (3) may name—

(*a*) one or more of the Channel Islands,

(*b*) the Isle of Man, or

(*c*) one or more of the British overseas territories.

(5) In this section "conduct" includes acts and omissions.

(6) Nothing in this section affects any criminal liability arising otherwise than under this section.

[Terrorist Asset-Freezing etc Act 2010, s 33.]

7.9118 34. **Liability of officers of body corporate etc** (1) Where an offence under this Part committed by a body corporate—

(*a*) is committed with the consent or connivance of any director, manager, secretary or other similar officer of the body corporate, or any person who was purporting to act in any such capacity, or

(*b*) is attributable to any neglect on the part of any such person,

that person as well as the body corporate is guilty of the offence and is liable to be proceeded against and punished accordingly.

(2) In subsection (1) "director", in relation to a body corporate whose affairs are managed by its members, means a member of the body corporate.

(3) Subsection (1) also applies in relation to a body that is not a body corporate, with the substitution for the reference to a director of the body of a reference—

(*a*) in the case of a partnership, to a partner;

(*b*) in the case of an unincorporated body other than a partnership—

(i) where the body's affairs are managed by its members, to a member of the body;

(ii) in any other case, to a member of the governing body.

[Terrorist Asset-Freezing etc Act 2010, s 34.]

7.9120 35. **Jurisdiction to try offences** (1) Where an offence under this Part is committed outside the United Kingdom—

(*a*) proceedings for the offence may be taken at any place in the United Kingdom, and

(*b*) the offence may for all incidental purposes be treated as having been committed at any such place.

(2) In the application of subsection (1) to Scotland, any such proceedings against a person may be taken—

(*a*) in any sheriff court district in which the person is apprehended or is in custody, or

(*b*) in such sheriff court district as the Lord Advocate may determine.

(3) In subsection (2) "sheriff court district" is to be read in accordance with the Criminal Procedure (Scotland) Act 1995 (see section 307(1) of that Act).

(4) In section 28(2) of the Counter-Terrorism Act 2008 (jurisdiction to try offences committed in another part of the UK: offences to which the section applies), after paragraph (*c*) insert—

"(*d*) an offence under any provision of Part 1 of the Terrorist Asset-Freezing etc Act 2010."

[Terrorist Asset-Freezing etc Act 2010, s 35.]

7.9122 36. **Time limit for proceedings for summary offences** (1) In England and Wales an information relating to an offence under section 19(5) or 22 may be tried by a magistrates' court if it is laid—

(*a*) at any time within three years after the commission of the offence, and

(*b*) within twelve months after the date on which evidence sufficient in the opinion of the prosecutor to justify the proceedings comes to the knowledge of the prosecutor.

(2) *Scotland.*

(3) Northern Ireland.

(4) For the purposes of this section a certificate of the prosecutor (or, in Scotland, the Lord Advocate) as to the date on which such evidence as is referred to above came to their notice is conclusive evidence.

[Terrorist Asset-Freezing etc Act 2010, s 36.]

7.9124 37. **Consent to prosecution** (1) Proceedings for an offence under this Part (other than an offence under section 19(5) or 22) may not be instituted—

(*a*) in England and Wales, except by or with the consent of the Attorney General;

(*b*) in Northern Ireland, except by or with the consent of the Advocate General for Northern Ireland.

(2) Nothing in subsection (1) prevents—

(*a*) the arrest of a person in respect of an offence under this Part, or

(*b*) the remand in custody or on bail of a person charged with such an offence.

[Terrorist Asset-Freezing etc Act 2010, s 37.]

7.9126 38. **Procedure for offences by unincorporated bodies** (1) A fine imposed on an unincorporated body on its conviction of an offence under this Part must be paid out of the funds of the body.

(2) Subsections (3) to (6) apply if it is alleged that an offence under this Part has been committed by an unincorporated body (as opposed to by a member of the body).

(3) Proceedings in England and Wales or Northern Ireland for such an offence must be brought in the name of the body.

(4) For the purposes of such proceedings—

(*a*) any rules of court relating to the service of documents have effect as if the body were a body corporate, and

(*b*) the following provisions apply as they apply in relation to a body corporate—
(i) in England and Wales, section 33 of the Criminal Justice Act 1925 and Schedule 3 to the Magistrates' Courts Act 1980;
(ii) in Northern Ireland, section 18 of the Criminal Justice Act (Northern Ireland) 1945 and Article 166 of, and Schedule 4 to, the Magistrates' Courts (Northern Ireland) Order 1981 (SI 1981/1675 (N.I.26)).

(5) For the purposes of proceedings in Scotland for such an offence—
(*a*) any rules of court relating to the service of documents have effect as if the body were a body corporate, and
(*b*) in the case of proceedings on indictment, section 70 of the Criminal Procedure (Scotland) Act 1995 applies as it applies in relation to a body corporate.

(6) Subsection (5)(*b*) does not apply so far as the amendments made to section 70 of the Act of 1995 by section 66 of the Criminal Justice and Licensing (Scotland) Act 2010 (proceedings on indictment against organisations) are in force instead.

[Terrorist Asset-Freezing etc Act 2010, s 38.]

*Interpretation*

7.9128 **39. Meaning of "funds" and "economic resources"** (1) In this Part, "funds" means financial assets and benefits of every kind, including (but not limited to)—
(*a*) cash, cheques, claims on money, drafts, money orders and other payment instruments;
(*b*) deposits with relevant institutions or other persons, balances on accounts, debts and debt obligations;
(*c*) publicly and privately traded securities and debt instruments, including stocks and shares, certificates representing securities, bonds, notes, warrants, debentures and derivative products;
(*d*) interest, dividends and other income on or value accruing from or generated by assets;
(*e*) credit, rights of set-off, guarantees, performance bonds and other financial commitments;
(*f*) letters of credit, bills of lading and bills of sale;
(*g*) documents providing evidence of an interest in funds or financial resources;
(*h*) any other instrument of export financing.

(2) In this Part, "economic resources" means assets of every kind, whether tangible or intangible, movable or immovable, which are not funds but can be used to obtain funds, goods or services.

[Terrorist Asset-Freezing etc Act 2010, s 39.]

7.9130 **40. Meaning of "financial services"** (1) In this Part, "financial services" means any service of a financial nature, including (but not limited to)—
(*a*) insurance-related services consisting of—
(i) direct life assurance;
(ii) direct insurance other than life assurance;
(iii) reinsurance and retrocession;
(iv) insurance intermediation, such as brokerage and agency;
(v) services auxiliary to insurance, such as consultancy, actuarial, risk assessment and claim settlement services;
(*b*) banking and other financial services consisting of—
(i) accepting deposits and other repayable funds;
(ii) lending (including consumer credit, mortgage credit, factoring and financing of commercial transactions);
(iii) financial leasing;
(iv) payment and money transmission services (including credit, charge and debit cards, travellers' cheques and bankers' drafts);
(v) providing guarantees or commitments;
(vi) financial trading (as defined in subsection (2) below);
(vii) participating in issues of any kind of securities (including underwriting and placement as an agent, whether publicly or privately) and providing services related to such issues;
(viii) money brokering;
(ix) asset management, such as cash or portfolio management, all forms of collective investment management, pension fund management, custodial, depository and trust services;
(x) settlement and clearing services for financial assets (including securities, derivative products and other negotiable instruments);
(xi) providing or transferring financial information, and financial data processing or related software (but only by suppliers of other financial services);
(xii) providing advisory and other auxiliary financial services in respect of any activity listed in sub-paragraphs (i) to (xi) (including credit reference and analysis, investment and portfolio research and advice, advice on acquisitions and on

corporate restructuring and strategy).

(2) In subsection (1)(*b*)(vi), "financial trading" means trading for own account or for account of customers, whether on an investment exchange, in an over-the- counter market or otherwise, in—

(*a*) money market instruments (including cheques, bills and certificates of deposit);

(*b*) foreign exchange;

(*c*) derivative products (including futures and options);

(*d*) exchange rate and interest rate instruments (including products such as swaps and forward rate agreements);

(*e*) transferable securities;

(*f*) other negotiable instruments and financial assets (including bullion).

[Terrorist Asset-Freezing etc Act 2010, s 40.]

7.9132 **41. Meaning of "relevant institution"** (1) In this Part "relevant institution" means-

(*a*) a person that has permission under Part 4 of the Financial Services and Markets Act 2000 (permission to carry on regulated activity);

(*b*) an EEA firm of the kind mentioned in paragraph 5(*b*) of Schedule 3 to that Act that has permission under paragraph 15 of that Schedule (as a result of qualifying for authorisation under paragraph 12 of that Schedule) to accept deposits; or

(*c*) an undertaking that by way of business—

(i) operates a currency exchange office,

(ii) transmits money (or any representation of monetary value) by any means, or

(iii) cashes cheques that are made payable to customers.

(2) The definition of "relevant institution" in subsection (1) must be read with section 22 of the Financial Services and Markets Act 2000, any relevant order under that section and Schedule 2 to that Act (classes of regulated activities and categories of investment).

[Terrorist Asset-Freezing etc Act 2010, s 41.]

7.9134 **42. Interpretation: general** (1) In this Part—

"designated person" has the meaning given by section 1;

"document" includes information recorded in any form and, in relation to information recorded otherwise than in legible form, references to its production include producing a copy of the information in legible form;

"economic resources" has the meaning given by section 39(2);

"enactment" includes—

(*a*) an enactment comprised in subordinate legislation (within the meaning of the Interpretation Act 1978);

(*b*) an enactment comprised in, or in an instrument made under—

(i) an Act of the Scottish Parliament;

(ii) Northern Ireland legislation; or

(iii) a Measure or Act of the National Assembly for Wales;

"final designation" means a designation under section 2 (including any renewed such designation);

"financial services" has the meaning given by section 40;

"funds" has the meaning given by section 39(1);

"interim designation" means a designation under section 6;

"relevant institution" has the meaning given by section 41;

"the relevant Security Council resolutions" has the meaning given by subsection (2) below.

(2) For the purposes of this Part "the relevant Security Council resolutions" are—

(*a*) resolution 1373 (2001) adopted by the Security Council of the United Nations on 28th September 2001, and

(*b*) resolution 1452 (2002) adopted by the Security Council of the United Nations on 20th December 2002.

(3) The Treasury may by order amend subsection (2) so as to add further relevant Security Council resolutions or remove any that are superseded.

(4) Any such order must be made by statutory instrument subject to annulment in pursuance of a resolution of either House of Parliament.

[Terrorist Asset-Freezing etc Act 2010, s 42.]

*Miscellaneous*

7.9136 **43. Service of notices** (1) This section applies in relation to any notice to be given to a person by the Treasury under this Part.

(2) Any such notice may be given—

(*a*) by posting it to the person's last known address, or

(*b*) where the person is a body corporate, partnership or unincorporated body other than a partnership, by posting it to the registered or principal office of the body or partnership concerned.

(3) Where the Treasury do not have an address for the person, they must make arrangements for the notice to be given to the person at the first available opportunity.

[Terrorist Asset-Freezing etc Act 2010, s 43.]

7.9138 **44. Crown application** (1) This Part binds the Crown.

(2) No contravention by the Crown of a provision of this Part makes the Crown criminally liable.

(3) The High Court or, in Scotland, the Court of Session may, on the application of a person appearing to the court to have an interest, declare unlawful any act or omission of the Crown that constitutes a contravention of a provision of this Part.

(4) Nothing in this section affects Her Majesty in her private capacity.

(5) Subsection (4) is to be read as if section 38(3) of the Crown Proceedings Act 1947 (meaning of Her Majesty in her private capacity) were contained in this Part.

[Terrorist Asset-Freezing etc Act 2010, s 44.]

7.9140 **45. Consequential amendments, repeals and revocations** (1) Part 1 of Schedule 1 (which contains amendments consequential on this Part) has effect.

(2) Part 1 of Schedule 2 (which contains repeals and revocations consequential on this Part) has effect.

[Terrorist Asset-Freezing etc Act 2010, s 45.]

PART 3[1]

FINAL PROVISIONS

*Extent etc*

7.9142 **53. Extent** (1) Subject as follows, this Act extends to England and Wales, Scotland and Northern Ireland.

(2) Sections 54 and 56 (and this section and section 55 so far as relating to sections 54 and 56) also extend to the Channel Islands, the Isle of Man and the British overseas territories.

(3) The amendments made by section 28(1) (amendment of Senior Courts Act 1981) and paragraph 5 of Schedule 1 (amendment of civil procedure rules: England and Wales) extend to England and Wales only.

(4) The amendments made by paragraphs 1 to 4 of Schedule 1 (amendments of rules of the Court of Judicature (Northern Ireland)) extend to Northern Ireland only.

[Terrorist Asset-Freezing etc Act 2010, s 53.]

1 Part 3 contains ss 53–56.

7.9144 **54. Channel Islands, Isle of Man and British overseas territories** (1) Her Majesty may by Order in Council[1] provide for any of the provisions of Part 1 (including Part 1 of Schedules 1 and 2) to extend, with or without modifications, to any of the Channel Islands, the Isle of Man or any British overseas territory.

(2) Sections 1 and 3 of the Terrorist Asset-Freezing (Temporary Provisions) Act 2010, so far as they have effect as part of the law of Guernsey, Jersey, the Isle of Man and the territories listed in Schedule 1 to the Terrorism (United Nations Measures) (Overseas Territories) Order 2001 (SI 2001/3366), have effect as if the reference in section 1(1) of that Act to 31 December 2010 were a reference to 31 March 2011.

[Terrorist Asset-Freezing etc Act 2010, s 54.]

1 The Terrorist Asset-Freezing etc Act 2010 (Guernsey) Order 2011, SI 2011/1082 has been made.

*Commencement and short title*

7.9146 **55. Commencement** (1) Subject to subsection (2), Parts 1 and 2 (including Schedules 1 and 2) come into force on the day following that on which this Act is passed.

(2) Section 51 (and section 52, and Part 2 of Schedules 1 and 2, so far as relating to section 51) come into force on such day as the Treasury may by order[1] made by statutory instrument appoint.

(3) An order under subsection (2) may include such transitional, transitory or saving provision as the Treasury consider appropriate.

(4) This Part comes into force on the day on which this Act is passed.

[Terrorist Asset-Freezing etc Act 2010, s 55.]

1 The Terrorist Asset-Freezing etc. Act 2010 (Commencement) Order 2011, SI 2011/2835 has been made.

7.9148 **56. Short title** This Act may be cited as the Terrorist Asset-Freezing etc Act 2010.

[Terrorist Asset-Freezing etc Act 2010, s 56.]

# Terrorism Prevention and Investigation Measures Act 2011

(2011 c 23)

*This Act, which came fully into force on 15 December 2011, abolished control orders and repealed the Prevention of Terrorism Act 2005 (**s 1**). The Secretary of State may by notice (a "TPIM notice") impose specified terrorism prevention and investigation measures on an individual if certain conditions are met (**s 2**). These conditions relate to the Secretary of State having reasonable belief that the individual is, or has been, involved in terrorism-related activity (the "relevant activity"); that some or all of the relevant activity is new terrorism-related activity; the Secretary of State reasonably considers that it is necessary, for purposes connected with protecting members of the public from a risk of* *terrorism, for terrorism prevention and investigation measures to be imposed on the individual and that it is necessary, for purposes connected with preventing or restricting the individual's involvement in terrorism-related activity, for the specified terrorism prevention and investigation measures to be imposed on the individual; and the High Court gives the Secretary of State permission (provision is made for the Secretary of State to act without permission in urgent cases). On granting permission, the court will fix a directions hearing which the individual is given the opportunity to attend and thereafter a review hearing in relation to the imposition of measures on the individual. A TPIM extends for one year but may be renewed once by the Secretary of State for a further year* (**ss 3–9**). *The Secretary of State's TPIM powers were to expire at the end of five years beginning with the day on which this Act was passed unless extended by Order made under s 21. The Terrorism Prevention and Investigation Measures Act 2011 (Continuation) Order 2016, SI 2016/116 has been made which provides that the powers will continue in force until the end of 13 December 2021.*

7.9150 **23. Offence** (1) An individual is guilty of an offence if—

(*a*) a TPIM notice is in force in relation to the individual, and

(*b*) the individual contravenes, without reasonable excuse, any measure specified in the TPIM notice.

(2) If the individual has the permission of the Secretary of State by virtue of Schedule 1 for an act which would, without that permission, contravene such a measure, the individual contravenes that measure by virtue of that act if the act is not in accordance with the terms of the permission.

(3) An individual guilty of an offence under subsection (1) is liable—

(*a*) on conviction on indictment, to imprisonment for a term not exceeding 5 years or to a fine, or to both;

(*b*) on summary conviction in England and Wales, to imprisonment for a term not exceeding 12 months or to a fine not exceeding the statutory maximum, or to both;

(*c*) on summary conviction in Northern Ireland, to imprisonment for a term not exceeding 6 months or to a fine not exceeding the statutory maximum, or to both;

(*d*) on summary conviction in Scotland, to imprisonment for a term not exceeding 12 months or to a fine not exceeding the statutory maximum, or to both.

(4) In relation to an offence committed before the commencement of section 154(1) of the Criminal Justice Act 2003, the reference in subsection (3)(*b*) to 12 months is to be read as a reference to 6 months.

(5) Where an individual is convicted by or before a court of an offence under subsection (1), it is not open to that court to make in respect of the offence—

(*a*) an order under section 12(1)(*b*) of the Powers of Criminal Courts (Sentencing) Act 2000 (conditional discharge);

(*b*) an order under section 227A of the Criminal Procedure (Scotland) Act 1995 (community payback orders); or

(*c*) an order under Article 4(1)(*b*) of the Criminal Justice (Northern Ireland) Order 1996 (SI 1996/3160 (N.I. 24)) (conditional discharge in Northern Ireland).

[Terrorism Prevention and Investigation Measures Act 2011, s 23.]

7.9151 **24. Powers of entry etc** Schedule 5 (powers of entry, search, seizure and retention) has effect.

[Terrorism Prevention and Investigation Measures Act 2011, s 24.]

7.9152 **25. Fingerprints and samples** Schedule 6 (fingerprints and samples) has effect.

[Terrorism Prevention and Investigation Measures Act 2011, s 25.]

SCHEDULE 1

Terrorism Prevention and Investigation Measures

SCHEDULE 5

Powers of Entry, Search, Seizure and Retention

Section 24

**Introductory**

7.9153 1. This Schedule confers powers of entry, search, seizure and retention on constables in connection with the imposition of measures on individuals.

2. A power conferred on a constable by virtue of this Schedule—

(*a*) is additional to powers which the constable has at common law or by virtue of any other enactment, and

(*b*) is not to be taken as affecting those powers.

**3.** A constable may detain an individual for the purpose of carrying out a search of that individual under a power conferred by virtue of this Schedule.

**4.** A constable may use reasonable force, if necessary, for the purpose of exercising a power conferred on the constable by virtue of this Schedule.

**Entry and search for purposes of serving TPIM notice**

5. (1) For the purpose of serving a relevant notice on an individual, a constable may—

(*a*) enter any premises where the constable has reasonable grounds for believing the individual to be, and

(*b*) search those premises for that individual.

(2) A "relevant notice" means—

(*a*) a TPIM notice;

(*b*) a notice under section 5(2) extending a TPIM notice;

(*c*) a notice under section 12(1) varying a TPIM notice as mentioned in paragraph (*c*) of that subsection; or

(*d*) a notice under section 13(1) reviving a TPIM notice.

**Search of individual or premises at time of serving TPIM notice**

**6.** (1) This paragraph applies if a TPIM notice is being, or has just been, served on an individual.

(2) A constable may (without a warrant)—

(*a*) search the individual for the purpose mentioned in sub-paragraph (3);

(*b*) enter and search, for that purpose, any premises mentioned in sub-paragraph (4).

(3) The purpose is that of ascertaining whether there is anything on the individual, or (as the case may be) in the premises, that contravenes measures specified in the TPIM notice.

(4) The premises referred to in sub-paragraph (2)(*b*) are—

(*a*) the individual's place of residence;

(*b*) other premises to which the individual has power to grant access.

(5) A constable may seize anything that the constable finds in the course of a search carried out under a power conferred by this paragraph—

(*a*) for the purpose of ascertaining whether measures specified in the TPIM notice are being or are about to be contravened by the individual;

(*b*) for the purpose of securing compliance by the individual with measures specified in the TPIM notice;

(*c*) if the constable has reasonable grounds for suspecting that—

(i) the thing is or contains evidence in relation to an offence, and

(ii) it is necessary to seize it in order to prevent it being concealed, lost, damaged, altered or destroyed.

**Search of premises on suspicion of absconding**

**7.** (1) This paragraph applies if a constable reasonably suspects that an individual in respect of whom a TPIM notice is in force has absconded.

(2) The constable may (without a warrant) enter and search any premises mentioned in sub-paragraph (3)—

(*a*) for the purposes of determining whether the individual has absconded;

(*b*) if it appears that the individual has absconded, for anything that may assist in the pursuit and arrest of the individual.

(3) The premises referred to in sub-paragraph (2) are—

(*a*) the individual's place of residence;

(*b*) other premises to which the individual has power to grant access;

(*c*) any premises to which the individual had power to grant access and with which there is reason to believe that the individual is or was recently connected.

(4) A constable may seize anything that the constable finds in the course of a search carried out under a power conferred by this paragraph—

(*a*) if the constable reasonably believes that the thing will assist in the pursuit or arrest of the individual;

(*b*) if the constable has reasonable grounds for suspecting that—

(i) the thing is or contains evidence in relation to an offence, and

(ii) it is necessary to seize it in order to prevent it being concealed, lost, damaged, altered or destroyed.

**Search for compliance purposes**

**8.** (1) A constable may apply for the issue of a warrant under this paragraph for the purpose of determining whether an individual in respect of whom a TPIM notice is in force is complying with measures specified in the notice.

(2) A warrant under this paragraph may authorise a constable to do either or both of the following—

(*a*) to search the individual;

(*b*) to enter and search the individual's place of residence or any other premises that are specified in the warrant.

(3) An application for a warrant under this paragraph must be made to the appropriate judicial authority.

(4) The appropriate judicial authority may, on such an application, grant the warrant only if satisfied that the warrant is necessary for the purpose mentioned in sub-paragraph (1).

(5) A constable may seize anything that the constable finds in the course of a search carried out under a power conferred by a warrant issued under this paragraph—

(*a*) for the purpose of ascertaining whether any measure specified in the TPIM notice has been, is being, or is about to be, contravened by the individual;

(*b*) for the purpose of securing compliance by the individual with measures specified in the TPIM notice;

(*c*) if the constable has reasonable grounds for suspecting that—

(i) the thing is or contains evidence in relation to an offence, and

(ii) it is necessary to seize it in order to prevent it being concealed, lost, damaged, altered or destroyed.

(6) In this paragraph "appropriate judicial authority", in relation to a warrant, means—

(*a*) a justice of the peace, if the application for the warrant is made in England or Wales;

(*b*) the sheriff, if the application is made in Scotland;

(*c*) a lay magistrate, if the application is made in Northern Ireland.

**9.** (1) This paragraph applies in relation to a warrant issued in England, Wales or Northern Ireland under paragraph 8 so far as it authorises a constable to search an individual.

(2) In relation to warrants issued under that paragraph so far as authorising the entry and search of premises, see—

(*a*) sections 15 and 16 of the Police and Criminal Evidence Act 1984, in relation to warrants issued in England and Wales;

(*b*) Articles 17 and 18 of the Police and Criminal Evidence (Northern Ireland) Order 1989 (SI 1989/1341 (N.I. 12)), in relation to warrants issued in Northern Ireland.

(3) The constable applying for the warrant must—

(*a*) state the ground on which the application is made, and

(*b*) identify, so far as practicable, the articles to be sought.

(4) The application for the warrant is to be made without notice and—

(*a*) if made in England or Wales, supported by an information in writing;

(*b*) if made in Northern Ireland, supported by a complaint in writing and substantiated on oath.

(5) The constable must answer on oath any questions that the appropriate judicial authority (within the meaning of paragraph 8) hearing the application may ask of the constable.

(6) If the warrant is issued it authorises a search of the individual on one occasion only.

(7) The warrant must—

(*a*) specify the name of the constable applying for it, the date on which it is issued and the fact that it is issued under paragraph 8, and

(*b*) identify, so far as practicable, the articles to be sought.

(8) Two copies must be made of the warrant and clearly certified as copies.

(9) The warrant may be executed by any constable.

(10) The search under the warrant must be carried out within 28 days of its issue.

(11) The search must be carried out at a reasonable hour unless it appears to the constable executing the warrant that the purposes of the search may be frustrated if carried out then.

(12) The constable seeking to execute the warrant must, before carrying out the search—

(*a*) identify himself or herself to the individual,

(*b*) if not in uniform, produce documentary evidence that he or she is a constable to the individual,

(*c*) produce the warrant to the individual, and

(*d*) supply the individual with a copy of the warrant (which, in Northern Ireland, must be a certified copy).

(13) The constable executing the warrant must make an endorsement on it stating—

(*a*) whether anything sought was found in the course of the search, and

(*b*) whether anything was seized.

(14) When the warrant has been executed it must be returned to the designated officer.

(15) The designated officer must retain a warrant returned under sub-paragraph (14) for a period of 12 months from the time of its return and, if requested during that period, allow the individual to inspect it.

(16) The "designated officer" is—

(*a*) in relation to a warrant issued in England and Wales, the designated officer for the local justice area in which the justice of the peace who issued the warrant was acting when it was issued;

(*b*) in relation to a warrant issued in Northern Ireland, the clerk for the petty sessions district in which the lay magistrate who issued the warrant was acting when it was issued.

**Search of individual for public safety purposes**

**10.** (1) A constable may (without a warrant) search an individual in respect of whom a TPIM notice is in force for the purpose of ascertaining whether the individual is in possession of anything that could be used to threaten or harm any person.

(2) The power of a constable to search the individual under this paragraph may be exercised—

(*a*) following entry onto premises by virtue of this Act, or

(*b*) at any other time when the constable is in the presence of the individual.

(3) A constable may seize anything that the constable finds in the course of a search carried out under a power conferred by this paragraph—

(*a*) if the constable has reasonable grounds for suspecting that the thing may be used to threaten or harm any person;

(*b*) if the constable has reasonable grounds for suspecting that—

(i) the thing is or contains evidence in relation to an offence, and

(ii) it is necessary to seize it to prevent it being concealed, lost, damaged, altered or destroyed.

**Power to retain items**

**11.** (1) Anything that is seized under a power conferred by virtue of this Schedule may be—

(*a*) subjected to tests;

(*b*) retained for as long as is necessary in all the circumstances.

(2) In particular (and regardless of the ground on which the thing was seized)—

(*a*) if a constable has reasonable grounds for believing that the thing is or contains evidence in relation to an offence, it may be retained—

(i) for use as evidence at a trial for an offence, or

(ii) for forensic examination or for investigation in connection with an offence; and

(*b*) if a constable has reasonable grounds for believing that the thing has been obtained in consequence of the commission of an offence, it may be retained in order to establish its lawful owner.

(3) Nothing may be retained for either of the purposes mentioned in sub-paragraph (2)(*a*) if a photograph or copy would be sufficient for that purpose.

(4) Nothing in this paragraph or in paragraph 12 affects any power of a court to make an order under section 1 of the Police (Property) Act 1897.

**12.** (1) This paragraph applies if—

(*a*) a device is surrendered by virtue of a condition of the kind mentioned in paragraph 7(4)(*e*) of Schedule 1 (surrendering of electronic communication devices for inspection or modification purposes), and

(*b*) a constable has reasonable grounds for believing that the device is or contains evidence in relation to an offence.

(2) The device may be seized and retained for as long as is necessary in all the circumstances.

(3) In particular—

(*a*) the thing may be retained—

(i) for use as evidence at a trial for an offence, or

(ii) for forensic examination or for investigation in connection with an offence; and

(*b*) if a constable has reasonable grounds for believing that the device has been obtained in consequence of the commission of an offence, it may be retained in order to establish its lawful owner.

(4) Nothing may be retained for either of the purposes mentioned in sub-paragraph (3)(*a*) if a photograph or copy would be sufficient for that purpose.

# Counter-Terrorism and Security Act 2015[1]

2015 c 6

## PART 1

## TEMPORARY RESTRICTIONS ON TRAVEL

### CHAPTER 1

### POWERS TO SEIZE TRAVEL DOCUMENTS

7.9153A **1. Seizure of passports etc from persons suspected of involvement in terrorism**[2]

[3] (1) Schedule 1 makes provision for the seizure and temporary retention of travel documents where a person is suspected of intending to leave Great Britain or the United Kingdom in connection with terrorism-related activity.

[Counter-Terrorism and Security Act 2015, s 1.]

---

1 The seven Parts of the Act deal with: powers to seize travel documents and temporary exclusion from the UK; terrorism prevention and investigation measures; data retention; aviation shipping and rail; risk of being drawn into terrorism; amendments of or relating to the Terrorism Act 2000; and miscellaneous and general matters.

The Act received the Royal Assent on 12 February 2015. Most of its provisions came into effect immediately or the following day: see s 52. The only provisions which are to be brought into force by statutory instrument are those listed in s 52(3). All the provisions reproduced below are in force.

2 PART 1 contains ss 1–15.

3 Chapter 1 contains s 1.

### CHAPTER 2[1]

### TEMPORARY EXCLUSION FROM THE UNITED KINGDOM

*Imposition of temporary exclusion orders*

7.9153B **2. Temporary exclusion orders** (1) A "temporary exclusion order" is an order which requires an individual not to return to the United Kingdom unless—

(*a*) the return is in accordance with a permit to return issued by the Secretary of State before the individual began the return, or

(*b*) the return is the result of the individual's deportation to the United Kingdom.

(2) The Secretary of State may impose a temporary exclusion order on an individual if conditions A to E are met.

(3) Condition A is that the Secretary of State reasonably suspects that the individual is, or has been, involved in terrorism-related activity outside the United Kingdom[2].

(4) Condition B is that the Secretary of State reasonably considers that it is necessary, for purposes connected with protecting members of the public in the United Kingdom from a risk of terrorism, for a temporary exclusion order to be imposed on the individual.

(5) Condition C is that the Secretary of State reasonably considers that the individual is outside the United Kingdom.

(6) Condition D is that the individual has the right of abode in the United Kingdom.

(7) Condition E is that—

(*a*) the court gives the Secretary of State permission under section 3, or

(*b*) the Secretary of State reasonably considers that the urgency of the case requires a temporary exclusion order to be imposed without obtaining such permission.

(8) During the period that a temporary exclusion order is in force, the Secretary of State must keep under review whether condition B is met.

[Counter-Terrorism and Security Act 2015, s 2.]

---

1 Chapter 2 contains ss 2–14.

2 As to the meaning of 'involved in terrorism-related activity, see s 14(4)–(6), post.

7.9153C **3. Temporary exclusion orders: prior permission of the court** (1) This section applies if the Secretary of State—

(*a*) makes the relevant decisions in relation to an individual, and

(*b*) makes an application to the court for permission to impose a temporary exclusion order on the individual.

(2) The function of the court on the application is to determine whether the relevant decisions of the Secretary of State are obviously flawed.

(3) The court may consider the application—

(*a*) in the absence of the individual,

(*b*) without the individual having been notified of the application, and

(*c*) without the individual having been given an opportunity (if the individual was aware of the application) of making any representations to the court.

(4) But that does not limit the matters about which rules of court may be made.

(5) In determining the application, the court must apply the principles applicable on an application for judicial review.

(6) In a case where the court determines that any of the relevant decisions of the Secretary of State is obviously flawed, the court may not give permission under this section.

(7) In any other case, the court must give permission under this section.

(8) Schedule 2 makes provision for references to the court etc where temporary exclusion

orders are imposed in cases of urgency.

(9) Only the Secretary of State may appeal against a determination of the court under—

(*a*) this section, or

(*b*) Schedule 2;

and such an appeal may only be made on a question of law.

(10) In this section "the relevant decisions" means the decisions that the following conditions are met—

(*a*) condition A;

(*b*) condition B;

(*c*) condition C;

(*d*) condition D.

[Counter-Terrorism and Security Act 2015, s 3.]

**7.9153D 4. Temporary exclusion orders: supplementary provision** (1) The Secretary of State must give notice of the imposition of a temporary exclusion order to the individual on whom it is imposed (the "excluded individual").

(2) Notice of the imposition of a temporary exclusion order must include an explanation of the procedure for making an application under section 6 for a permit to return.

(3) A temporary exclusion order—

(*a*) comes into force when notice of its imposition is given; and

(*b*) is in force for the period of two years (unless revoked or otherwise brought to an end earlier).

(4) The Secretary of State may revoke a temporary exclusion order at any time.

(5) The Secretary of State must give notice of the revocation of a temporary exclusion order to the excluded individual.

(6) If a temporary exclusion order is revoked, it ceases to be in force when notice of its revocation is given.

(7) The validity of a temporary exclusion order is not affected by the excluded individual—

(*a*) returning to the United Kingdom, or

(*b*) departing from the United Kingdom.

(8) The imposition of a temporary exclusion order does not prevent a further temporary exclusion order from being imposed on the excluded individual (including in a case where an order ceases to be in force at the expiry of its two year duration).

(9) At the time when a temporary exclusion order comes into force, any British passport held by the excluded individual is invalidated.

(10) During the period when a temporary exclusion order is in force, the issue of a British passport to the excluded individual while he or she is outside the United Kingdom is not valid.

(11) In this section "British passport" means a passport, or other document which enables or facilitates travel from one state to another (except a permit to return), that has been—

(*a*) issued by or for Her Majesty's Government in the United Kingdom, and

(*b*) issued in respect of a person's status as a British citizen.

[Counter-Terrorism and Security Act 2015, s 4.]

*Permit to return*

**7.9153E 5. Permit to return** (1) A "permit to return" is a document giving an individual (who is subject to a temporary exclusion order) permission to return to the United Kingdom.

(2) The permission may be made subject to a requirement that the individual comply with conditions specified in the permit to return.

(3) The individual's failure to comply with a specified condition has the effect of invalidating the permit to return.

(4) A permit to return must state—

(*a*) the time at which, or period of time during which, the individual is permitted to arrive on return to the United Kingdom;

(*b*) the manner in which the individual is permitted to return to the United Kingdom; and

(*c*) the place where the individual is permitted to arrive on return to the United Kingdom.

(5) Provision made under subsection (4)(*a*) or (*c*) may, in particular, be framed by reference to the arrival in the United Kingdom of a specific flight, sailing or other transport service.

(6) Provision made under subsection (4)(*b*) may, in particular, state—

(*a*) a route,

(*b*) a method of transport,

(*c*) an airline, shipping line or other passenger carrier, or

(*d*) a flight, sailing or other transport service,

which the individual is permitted to use to return to the United Kingdom.

(7) The Secretary of State may not issue a permit to return except in accordance with section 6 or 7.

(8) It is for the Secretary of State to decide the terms of a permit to return (but this is subject to section 6(3)).

[Counter-Terrorism and Security Act 2015, s 5.]

**7.9153F 6. Issue of permit to return: application by individual** (1) If an individual applies to the Secretary of State for a permit to return, the Secretary of State must issue a permit within a reasonable period after the application is made.

(2) But the Secretary of State may refuse to issue the permit if—

(*a*) the Secretary of State requires the individual to attend an interview with a constable or immigration officer at a time and a place specified by the Secretary of State, and

(*b*) the individual fails to attend the interview.

(3) Where a permit to return is issued under this section, the relevant return time must fall within a reasonable period after the application is made.

(4) An application is not valid unless it is made in accordance with the procedure for applications specified by the Secretary of State.

(5) In this section—

"application" means an application made by an individual to the Secretary of State for a permit to return to be issued;

"relevant return time" means—

(*a*) the time at which the individual is permitted to arrive on return to the United Kingdom (in a case where the permit to return states such a time), or

(*b*) the start of the period of time during which the individual is permitted to arrive on return to the United Kingdom (in a case where the permit to return states such a period).

[Counter-Terrorism and Security Act 2015, s 6.]

**7.9153G 7. Issue of permit to return: deportation or urgent situation** (1) The Secretary of State must issue a permit to return to an individual if the Secretary of State considers that the individual is to be deported to the United Kingdom.

(2) The Secretary of State may issue a permit to return to an individual if—

(*a*) the Secretary of State considers that, because of the urgency of the situation, it is expedient to issue a permit to return even though no application has been made under section 6, and

(*b*) there is no duty to issue a permit to return under subsection (1).

(3) Subsection (1) or (2) applies whether or not any request has been made to issue the permit to return under that provision.

[Counter-Terrorism and Security Act 2015, s 7.]

**7.9153H 8. Permit to return: supplementary provision** (1) The Secretary of State may vary a permit to return.

(2) The Secretary of State may revoke a permit to return issued to an individual only if—

(*a*) the permit to return has been issued under section 6 and the individual asks the Secretary of State to revoke it;

(*b*) the permit to return has been issued under section 7(1) and the Secretary of State no longer considers that the individual is to be deported to the United Kingdom;

(*c*) the permit to return has been issued under section 7(2) and the Secretary of State no longer considers that, because of the urgency of the situation, the issue of the permit to return is expedient;

(*d*) the Secretary of State issues a subsequent permit to return to the individual; or

(*e*) the Secretary of State considers that the permit to return has been obtained by misrepresentation.

(3) The making of an application for a permit to return to be issued under section 6 (whether or not resulting in a permit to return being issued) does not prevent a subsequent application from being made.

(4) The issuing of a permit to return (whether or not resulting in the individual's return to the United Kingdom) does not prevent a subsequent permit to return from being issued (whether or not the earlier permit is still in force).

[Counter-Terrorism and Security Act 2015, s 8.]

*Obligations after return to the United Kingdom*

**7.9153I 9. Obligations after return to the United Kingdom** (1) The Secretary of State may, by notice, impose any or all of the permitted obligations on an individual who—

(*a*) is subject to a temporary exclusion order, and

(*b*) has returned to the United Kingdom.

(2) The "permitted obligations" are—

(*a*) any obligation of a kind that may be imposed (on an individual subject to a TPIM notice) under these provisions of Schedule 1 to the Terrorism Prevention and Investigation Measures Act 2011—

(i) paragraph 10 (reporting to police station);

(ii) paragraph 10A (attendance at appointments etc);

(*b*) an obligation to notify the police, in such manner as a notice under this section may require, of—

(i) the individual's place (or places) of residence, and

(ii) any change in the individual's place (or places) of residence.

(3) A notice under this section—

(*a*) comes into force when given to the individual; and

(*b*) is in force until the temporary exclusion order ends (unless the notice is revoked or otherwise brought to an end earlier).

(4) The Secretary of State may, by notice, vary or revoke any notice given under this section.

(5) The variation or revocation of a notice under this section takes effect when the notice of variation or revocation is given to the individual.

(6) The validity of a notice under this section is not affected by the individual—

(*a*) departing from the United Kingdom, or

(*b*) returning to the United Kingdom.

(7) The giving of any notice to an individual under this section does not prevent any further notice under this section from being given to that individual.

[Counter-Terrorism and Security Act 2015, s 9.]

*Offences and proceedings etc*

**7.9153J 10. Offences** (1) An individual subject to a temporary exclusion order is guilty of an offence if, without reasonable excuse, the individual returns to the United Kingdom in contravention of the restriction on return specified in the order.

(2) It is irrelevant for the purposes of subsection (1) whether or not the individual has a passport or other similar identity document.

(3) An individual subject to an obligation imposed under section 9 is guilty of an offence if, without reasonable excuse, the individual does not comply with the obligation.

(4) In a case where a relevant notice has not actually been given to an individual, the fact that the relevant notice is deemed to have been given to the individual under regulations under section 13 does not (of itself) prevent the individual from showing that lack of knowledge of the temporary exclusion order, or of the obligation imposed under section 9, was a reasonable excuse for the purposes of this section.

(5) An individual guilty of an offence under this section is liable—

(*a*) on conviction on indictment, to imprisonment for a term not exceeding 5 years or to a fine, or to both;

(*b*) on summary conviction in England and Wales, to imprisonment for a term not exceeding 12 months or to a fine, or to both[1];

(*c*) on summary conviction in Northern Ireland, to imprisonment for a term not exceeding 6 months or to a fine not exceeding the statutory maximum, or to both;

(*d*) on summary conviction in Scotland, to imprisonment for a term not exceeding 12 months or to a fine not exceeding the statutory maximum, or to both.

(6) Where an individual is convicted by or before a court of an offence under this section, it is not open to that court to make in respect of the offence—

(*a*) an order under section 12(1)(b) of the Powers of Criminal Courts (Sentencing) Act 2000 (conditional discharge);

(*b*) an order under section 227A of the Criminal Procedure (Scotland) Act 1995 (community pay-back orders); or

(*c*) an order under Article 4(1)(b) of the Criminal Justice (Northern Ireland) Order 1996 (SI 1996/3160 (N.I. 24)) (conditional discharge in Northern Ireland).

(7) In this section—

"relevant notice" means—

(*a*) notice of the imposition of a temporary exclusion order, or

(*b*) notice under section 9 imposing an obligation;

"restriction on return" means the requirement specified in a temporary exclusion order in accordance with section 2(1).

(8) In section 2 of the UK Borders Act 2007 (detention at ports), in subsection (1A), for "the individual is subject to a warrant for arrest" substitute

"the individual—

(*a*) may be liable to be detained by a constable under section 14 of the Criminal Procedure (Scotland) Act 1995 in respect of an offence under section 10(1) of the Counter-Terrorism and Security Act 2015, or

(*b*) is subject to a warrant for arrest."

[Counter-Terrorism and Security Act 2015, s 10.]

[1] For procedure in respect of offences triable either way see Magistrates' Courts Act 1980, s 17A–21, in PART 1: MAGISTRATES' COURTS, PROCEDURE, ante.

**7.9153K 11. Review of decisions relating to temporary exclusion orders** (1) This section applies where an individual who is subject to a temporary exclusion order is in the United Kingdom.

(2) The individual may apply to the court to review any of the following decisions of the Secretary of State—

(*a*) a decision that any of the following conditions was met in relation to the imposition of the temporary exclusion order—
(i) condition A;
(ii) condition B;
(iii) condition C;
(iv) condition D;
(*b*) a decision to impose the temporary exclusion order;
(*c*) a decision that condition B continues to be met;
(*d*) a decision to impose any of the permitted obligations on the individual by a notice under section 9.

(3) On a review under this section, the court must apply the principles applicable on an application for judicial review.

(4) On a review of a decision within subsection (2)(*a*) to (*c*), the court has the following powers (and only those powers)—
(*a*) power to quash the temporary exclusion order;
(*b*) power to give directions to the Secretary of State for, or in relation to, the revocation of the temporary exclusion order.

(5) If the court does not exercise either of its powers under subsection (4), the court must decide that the temporary exclusion order is to continue in force.

(6) On a review of a decision within subsection (2)(*d*), the court has the following powers (and only those powers)—
(*a*) power to quash the permitted obligation in question;
(*b*) if that is the only permitted obligation imposed by the notice under section 9, power to quash the notice;
(*c*) power to give directions to the Secretary of State for, or in relation to—
(i) the variation of the notice so far as it relates to that permitted obligation, or
(ii) if that is the only permitted obligation imposed by the notice, the revocation of the notice.

(7) If the court does not exercise any of its powers under subsection (6), the court must decide that the notice under section 9 is to continue in force.

(8) If the court exercises a power under subsection (6)(*a*) or (*c*)(i), the court must decide that the notice under section 9 is to continue in force subject to that exercise of that power.

(9) The power under this section to quash a temporary exclusion order, permitted obligation or notice under section 9 includes—
(*a*) in England and Wales or Northern Ireland, power to stay the quashing for a specified time, or pending an appeal or further appeal against the decision to quash; or
(*b*) in Scotland, power to determine that the quashing is of no effect for a specified time or pending such an appeal or further appeal.

(10) An appeal against a determination of the court on a review under this section may only be made on a question of law.

(11) For the purposes of this section, a failure by the Secretary of State to make a decision whether condition B continues to be met is to be treated as a decision that it continues to be met.

[Counter-Terrorism and Security Act 2015, s 11.]

**7.9153L 12. Temporary exclusion orders: proceedings and appeals against convictions**

(1) Schedule 3 makes provision about proceedings relating to temporary exclusion orders.

(2) Schedule 4 makes provision about appeals against convictions in cases where a temporary exclusion order, a notice under section 9 or a permitted obligation is quashed.

[Counter-Terrorism and Security Act 2015, s 12.]

*Supplementary*

**7.9153M 13. Regulations: giving of notices, legislation relating to passports** (1) The Secretary of State may by regulations[1] make provision about the giving of—
(*a*) notice under section 4, and
(*b*) notice under section 9.

(2) The regulations may, in particular, make provision about cases in which notice is to be deemed to have been given.

(3) The Secretary of State may make regulations providing for legislation relating to passports or other identity documents (whenever passed or made) to apply (with or without modifications) to permits to return.

(4) The power to make regulations under this section—
(*a*) is exercisable by statutory instrument;
(*b*) includes power to make transitional, transitory or saving provision.

(5) A statutory instrument containing regulations under this section is subject to annulment in pursuance of a resolution of either House of Parliament.

[Counter-Terrorism and Security Act 2015, s 13.]

---

1 The Temporary Exclusion Orders (Notices) Regulations 2015, SI 2015/438 have been made.

**7.9153N 14. Chapter 2: interpretation** (1) This section applies for the purposes of this

Chapter.

(2) These expressions have the meanings given—

"act" and "conduct" include omissions and statements;

"act of terrorism" includes anything constituting an action taken for the purposes of terrorism, within the meaning of the Terrorism Act 2000 (see section 1(5) of that Act);

"condition A", "condition B", "condition C", "condition D" or "condition E" means that condition as set out in section 2;

"court" means—

(*a*) in the case of proceedings relating to an individual whose principal place of residence is in Scotland, the Outer House of the Court of Session;

(*b*) in the case of proceedings relating to an individual whose principal place of residence is in Northern Ireland, the High Court in Northern Ireland;

(*c*) in any other case, the High Court in England and Wales;

"permit to return" has the meaning given in section 5;

"temporary exclusion order" has the meaning given in section 2;

"terrorism" has the same meaning as in the Terrorism Act 2000 (see section 1(1) to (4) of that Act).

(3) An individual is—

(*a*) subject to a temporary exclusion order if a temporary exclusion order is in force in relation to the individual; and

(*b*) subject to an obligation imposed under section 9 if an obligation is imposed on the individual by a notice in force under that section.

(4) Involvement in terrorism-related activity is any one or more of the following—

(*a*) the commission, preparation or instigation of acts of terrorism;

(*b*) conduct that facilitates the commission, preparation or instigation of such acts, or is intended to do so;

(*c*) conduct that gives encouragement to the commission, preparation or instigation of such acts, or is intended to do so;

(*d*) conduct that gives support or assistance to individuals who are known or believed by the individual concerned to be involved in conduct falling within paragraph (a).

It is immaterial whether the acts of terrorism in question are specific acts of terrorism or acts of terrorism in general.

(5) It is immaterial whether an individual's involvement in terrorism-related activity occurs before or after the coming into force of section 2.

(6) References to an individual's return to the United Kingdom include, in the case of an individual who has never been in the United Kingdom, a reference to the individual's coming to the United Kingdom for the first time.

(7) References to deportation include references to any other kind of expulsion.

[Counter-Terrorism and Security Act 2015, s 14.]

## PART 2

## TERRORISM PREVENTION AND INVESTIGATION MEASURES

PART 2 contains ss 16–20. These provisions make amendments to the Terrorism Prevention and Investigation Measures Act 2011.

## PART 3

## DATA RETENTION

PART 3 contains s 21, which made amendments to the Data Retention and Investigatory Powers Act 2014. It has been repealed by the Investigatory Powers Act 2016, Sch 10.

## PART 4

## AVIATION, SHIPPING AND RAIL

PART 4 contains ss 22–25. These provisions are not reproduced in this work.

## PART 5

## RISK OF BEING DRAWN INTO TERRORISM

PART 5 contains ss 26–41.

### CHAPTER 1

### PREVENTING PEOPLE BEING DRAWN INTO TERRORISM

Chapter 1 contains ss 26–35. These provisions are not reproduced in this work.

### CHAPTER 2[1]

### SUPPORT ETC FOR PEOPLE VULNERABLE TO BEING DRAWN INTO TERRORISM

7.9153P **36. Assessment and support: local panels** (1) Each local authority must ensure that a panel of persons is in place for its area—

(*a*) with the function of assessing the extent to which identified individuals are vulnerable to being drawn into terrorism, and (*b*) with the other functions mentioned in subsection (4).

(2) "Identified individual", in relation to a panel, means an individual who is referred to the panel by a chief officer of police for an assessment of the kind mentioned in subsection (1)(*a*).

(3) A chief officer of police may refer an individual to a panel only if there are reasonable grounds to believe that the individual is vulnerable to being drawn into terrorism.

(4) The functions of a panel referred to in subsection (1)(*b*) are—

(*a*) to prepare a plan in respect of identified individuals who the panel considers should be offered support for the purpose of reducing their vulnerability to being drawn into terrorism;

(*b*) if the necessary consent is given, to make arrangements for support to be provided to those individuals in accordance with their support plan;

(*c*) to keep under review the giving of support to an identified individual under a support plan;

(*d*) to revise a support plan, or withdraw support under a plan, if at any time the panel considers it appropriate;

(*e*) to carry out further assessments, after such periods as the panel considers appropriate, of an individual's vulnerability to being drawn into terrorism in cases where—

(i) the necessary consent is refused or withdrawn to the giving of support under a support plan, or

(ii) the panel has determined that support under a plan should be withdrawn;

(*f*) to prepare a further support plan in such cases if the panel considers it appropriate.

(5) A support plan must include the following information—

(*a*) how, when and by whom a request for the necessary consent is to be made;

(*b*) the nature of the support to be provided to the identified individual;

(*c*) the persons who are to be responsible for providing it;

(*d*) how and when such support is to be provided.

(6) Where in the carrying out of its functions under this section a panel determines that support should not be given to an individual under a support plan, the panel—

(*a*) must consider whether the individual ought to be referred to a provider of any health or social care services, and

(*b*) if so, must make such arrangements as the panel considers appropriate for the purpose of referring the individual.

(7) In exercising its functions under this section a panel must have regard to any guidance given by the Secretary of State about the exercise of those functions[2].

(8) Before issuing guidance under subsection (7) the Secretary of State must (whether before or after this Act is passed) consult—

(*a*) the Welsh Ministers so far as the guidance relates to panels in Wales;

(*b*) the Scottish Ministers so far as the guidance relates to panels in Scotland;

(*c*) any person whom the Secretary of State considers appropriate.

[Counter-Terrorism and Security Act 2015, s 36.]

1 Chapter 2 contains ss 36–41.

2 See *Protecting vulnerable people from being drawn into terrorism* HM Government (2015).

**7.9153Q 37. Membership and proceedings of panels** (1) The members of a panel must include—

(*a*) the responsible local authority;

(*b*) the chief officer of police for a police area the whole or any part of which is in the area of that authority.

(2) Each of those members must appoint a person to represent them on the panel; and the representative must be a person whom the member concerned considers to have the required skills and experience.

(3) Where more than one chief officer of police comes within subsection (1)(b), a person may represent more than one of the chief officers; but at any meeting of the panel at which an identified individual is to be discussed there must be a person present from the police force for the area in which the individual resides to act as the representative.

(4) A panel may also include such other persons as the responsible local authority considers appropriate (whether generally or in the case of a particular identified individual).

(5) The chair of a panel is the responsible local authority; but where more than one local authority is the responsible local authority, the authorities may determine that one (or more) of them is to be the chair.

(6) If a panel cannot reach a unanimous decision on a question arising before it, the question must be decided—

(*a*) according to the opinion of the majority of the panel, or

(*b*) if there is no majority opinion, by the chair.

(7) Subject to subsection (6), a panel may determine its own procedure.

[Counter-Terrorism and Security Act 2015, s 37.]

**7.9153R 38. Co-operation** (1) The partners of a panel must, so far as appropriate and reasonably practicable, act in co-operation with—

(*a*) the panel in the carrying out of its functions;

(*b*) the police in the carrying out of their functions in connection with section 36.

(2) The partners of a panel are the persons and bodies specified in Schedule 7.

(3) The duty of a partner of a panel to act in co-operation with the panel—

(*a*) includes the giving of information (subject to subsection (4));

(*b*) extends only so far as the co-operation is compatible with the exercise of the partner's functions under any other enactment or rule of law.

(4) Nothing in this section requires or authorises the making of—

(*a*) a disclosure that would contravene the Data Protection Act 1998;

(*b*) a disclosure of any sensitive information.

(5) "Sensitive information" means information—

(*a*) held by an intelligence service,

(*b*) obtained (directly or indirectly) from, or held on behalf of, an intelligence service,

(*c*) derived in whole or part from information obtained (directly or indirectly) from, or held on behalf of, an intelligence service, or

(*d*) relating to an intelligence service.

(6) In carrying out the duty imposed by subsection (1), partners of a panel must have regard to any guidance given by the Secretary of State about the carrying out of that duty[1].

(7) Before issuing guidance under subsection (6) the Secretary of State must (whether before or after this Act is passed) consult—

(*a*) the Welsh Ministers so far as the guidance relates to panels in Wales;

(*b*) the Scottish Ministers so far as the guidance relates to panels in Scotland;

(*c*) any person whom the Secretary of State considers appropriate.

(8) The reference in subsection (1)(*b*) to functions of the police in connection with section 36 includes, in particular, a chief officer's function of determining whether an individual should be referred to a panel for the carrying out of an assessment of the kind mentioned in subsection (1)(*a*) of that section.

[Counter-Terrorism and Security Act 2015, s 38.]

---

[1] See *Protecting vulnerable people from being drawn into terrorism* HM Government (2015).

**7.9153S 39. Power to amend Chapter 2** (1) The Secretary of State may by regulations made by statutory instrument amend—

(*a*) the definition of "local authority" in section 41;

(*b*) Schedule 7.

(2) The Secretary of State must consult the Welsh Ministers before making regulations under subsection (1) that—

(*a*) add a Welsh authority to Schedule 7, or

(*b*) amend or remove an entry in that Schedule relating to a Welsh authority.

(3) The Secretary of State must consult the Scottish Ministers before making regulations under subsection (1) that—

(*a*) add a description of authority in Scotland to the definition of "local authority",

(*b*) add a Scottish authority to Schedule 7, or

(*c*) amend or remove an entry in that Schedule relating to a Scottish authority.

(4) Regulations under this section may amend this Chapter so as to make consequential or supplemental provision.

(5) A statutory instrument containing regulations under this section may not be made unless a draft of the instrument has been laid before each House of Parliament and approved by a resolution of each House.

(6) Subsection (5) does not apply to a statutory instrument containing regulations that only make provision for—

(a) the omission of an entry in Schedule 7 where the body concerned has ceased to exist, or

(b) the variation of an entry in consequence of a change of name or transfer of functions.

(7) A statutory instrument that falls within subsection (6) is subject to annulment in pursuance of a resolution of either House of Parliament.

(8) In this section "Welsh authority" and "Scottish authority" have the same meaning as in Chapter 1.

[Counter-Terrorism and Security Act 2015, s 39.]

**7.9153T 40. Indemnification** (1) The Secretary of State may agree to indemnify a support provider against any costs and expenses that the provider reasonably incurs in connection with any decision or action taken by the provider in good faith in carrying out functions as a provider.

(2) The agreement may be made in whatever manner, and on whatever terms, the Secretary of State considers appropriate.

(3) In this section "support provider" means a person who provides support under a support plan.

[Counter-Terrorism and Security Act 2015, s 40.]

**7.9153U 41. Chapter 2: interpretation** (1) In this Chapter—

"health or social care services" means services relating to health or social care within the meaning given by section 9 of the Health and Social Care Act 2008;

"identified individual" has the meaning given in section 36(2);

"intelligence service" means—

(*a*) the Security Service,

(*b*) the Secret Intelligence Service,

(*c*) the Government Communications Headquarters, or

(*d*) any part of Her Majesty's forces, or of the Ministry of Defence, which engages in intelligence activities;

"local authority" means—

(*a*) a county council in England;

(*b*) a district council in England, other than a council for a district in a county for which there is a county council;

(*c*) a London Borough Council;

(*d*) the Common Council of the City of London in its capacity as a local authority;

(*e*) the Council of the Isles of Scilly;

(*f*) a county council or county borough council in Wales;

(*g*) a council constituted under section 2 of the Local Government etc (Scotland) Act 1994;

"the necessary consent", in relation to an identified individual, means—

(*a*) if the individual is aged 18 years or over, his or her consent;

(*b*) if the individual is aged under 18 years, the consent of his or her parent or guardian;

"panel" means a panel of persons in place under the duty imposed by section 36(1);

"responsible local authority", in relation to a panel, means the local authority responsible for ensuring that the panel is in place under the duty imposed by section 36(1);

"support plan" means a plan prepared by a panel in carrying out its functions mentioned in section 36(4)(*a*) or (*f*);

"terrorism" has the same meaning as in the Terrorism Act 2000 (see section 1(1) to (4) of that Act).

(2) For the purposes of the definition of "local authority" in subsection (1), the Inner Temple and the Middle Temple are to be taken as falling within the area of the Common Council of the City of London.

(3) Where two or more local authorities exercise their respective duties under section 36(1) by ensuring that a panel is in place for their combined area—

(*a*) a reference in this Chapter to the responsible local authority is to be read as a reference to the responsible local authorities for the panel;

(*b*) a reference in this Chapter to the authority's area is to be read as a reference to the combined area.

(4) References in this Chapter to a chief officer of police are to be read as including references to the chief constable of the Police Service of Scotland.

[Counter-Terrorism and Security Act 2015, s 41 as amended by SI 2015/928.]

## PART 6

## AMENDMENTS OF OR RELATING TO THE TERRORISM ACT 2000

PART 6 contains ss 42 and 43, which make amendments to the Terrorism Act 2000.

## PART 7[1]

## MISCELLANEOUS AND GENERAL

### *General*

7.9153V **48. Power to make consequential provision** (1) The Secretary of State may by regulations make provision that is consequential on any provision of this Act.

(2) The power to make regulations under this section—

(*a*) is exercisable by statutory instrument;

(*b*) includes power to make transitional, transitory or saving provision;

(*c*) may, in particular, be exercised by amending, repealing, revoking or otherwise modifying any provision made by or under primary legislation passed before this Act or in the same Session.

(3) Before making regulations under this section the Secretary of State must—

(*a*) if the regulations contain provision that would fall within the legislative competence of the Scottish Parliament if included in an Act of that Parliament, consult the Scottish Ministers;

(*b*) if the regulations contain provision that would fall within the legislative competence of the National Assembly for Wales if included in an Act of that Assembly, consult the Welsh Ministers;

(*c*) if the regulations contain provision that would fall within the legislative competence of the Northern Ireland Assembly if included in an Act of that Assembly, consult the

Department of Justice in Northern Ireland.

(4) A statutory instrument containing regulations under this section that amend, repeal or revoke anything in primary legislation (whether alone or with other provision) may be made only if a draft of the instrument has been laid before each House of Parliament and approved by a resolution of each House.

(5) Any other statutory instrument containing regulations under this section is subject to annulment in pursuance of a resolution of either House of Parliament.

(6) In this section "primary legislation" means—

(*a*) an Act of Parliament;

(*b*) an Act of the Scottish Parliament;

(*c*) a Measure or Act of the National Assembly for Wales;

(*d*) Northern Ireland legislation.

[Counter-Terrorism and Security Act 2015, s 48.]

---

[1] PART 7 contains ss 44–53.

**7.9153W 49. Transitional provision** (1) In relation to offences committed before section 154(1) of the Criminal Justice Act 2003 comes into force, the reference in section 10(5)(*b*) to 12 months is to be read as a reference to 6 months.

(2) In relation to offences committed before section 85(1) of the Legal Aid, Sentencing and Punishment of Offenders Act 2012 comes into force—

(*a*) the reference in section 10(5)(*b*) to a fine is to be read as a reference to a fine not exceeding the statutory maximum;

(*b*) paragraph 15(3)(*b*) of Schedule 1 has effect as if the words "in Scotland or Northern Ireland" were omitted.

(3) The amendments made by subsections (3) and (4) of section 17 apply only to things done and offences committed after that section comes into force.

(4) A reference to a calendar year in the following subsections does not include a year before 2016—

(*a*) subsection (3) of section 44;

(*b*) subsection (4C) of section 36 of the Terrorism Act 2006 (inserted by section 45(1) above);

(*c*) subsection (2) of section 31 of the Terrorist Asset-Freezing etc Act 2010 (substituted by section 45(2) above);

(*d*) subsection (2) of section 20 of the Terrorism Prevention and Investigation Measures Act 2011 (substituted by section 45(3) above).

[Counter-Terrorism and Security Act 2015, s 49.]

**7.9153X 51. Extent** (1) Part 5 extends to England and Wales and Scotland.

(2) The other provisions of this Act extend to England and Wales, Scotland and Northern Ireland.

(3) Her Majesty may by Order in Council direct that any of the provisions of Parts 1 and 4 are to extend, with whatever modifications appear to Her Majesty to be appropriate, to any of the Channel Islands or the Isle of Man.

(4) The power under section 39(6) of the Terrorism Act 2006 (extension to the Channel Islands or the Isle of Man) may be exercised in relation to any amendments made to that Act by this Act.

(5) The power under section 31(4) of the Terrorism Prevention and Investigation Measures Act 2011 (extension to the Isle of Man) may be exercised in relation to any amendments made to that Act by this Act.

(6) The power under section 39(3) of the Aviation Security Act 1982 (extension to the Channel Islands, Isle of Man etc) may be exercised in relation to any amendments made to that Act by this Act.

(7) The power under section 51(1) of the Aviation and Maritime Security Act 1990 (extension to the Channel Islands, Isle of Man etc) may be exercised in relation to any amendments made to that Act by this Act.

(8) The power under section 9(3) of the Special Immigration Appeals Commission Act 1997 (extension to the Channel Islands or the Isle of Man) may be exercised in relation to any amendments made to that Act by this Act.

[Counter-Terrorism and Security Act 2015, s 51.]

**7.9153Y 52. Commencement** (1) Chapter 1 of Part 1 comes into force on the day after the day on which this Act is passed.

(2) The following provisions come into force at the end of the period of two months beginning with the day on which this Act is passed—

(*a*) sections 36 to 38 and 40;

(*b*) sections 44 to 46.

(3) The following provisions come into force on whatever day or days the Secretary of State appoints by regulations made by statutory instrument—

(*a*) *repealed*

(*b*) section 22(10);

(*c*) paragraphs 12 to 14 of Schedule 5 and section 25 so far as relating to those paragraphs;

(*d*) sections 26 and 30, section 31(2) and (4) and sections 32 to 34.

(4) Regulations under subsection (3)—

(*a*) may make different provision for different purposes;

(*b*) may make transitory, transitional or saving provision.

(5) The other provisions of this Act come into force on the day on which this Act is passed.

[Counter-Terrorism and Security Act 2015, s 52 as amended by the Investigatory Powers Act 2016, Sch 10.]

**7.9153Z 53. Short title** This Act may be cited as the Counter-Terrorism and Security Act 2015.

[Counter–Terrorism and Security Act 2015, s 53.]

SCHEDULE 1

Seizure of Passports etc from Persons Suspected of Involvement in Terrorism Section 1

**Interpretation**

**7.9153ZA 1.** (1) The following definitions have effect for the purposes of this Schedule.

(2) "Immigration officer" means a person who is appointed as an immigration officer under paragraph 1 of Schedule 2 to the Immigration Act 1971.

(3) "Customs official" means a person who is designated as a general customs official under section 3(1) of the Borders, Citizenship and Immigration Act 2009 or as a customs revenue official under section 11(1) of that Act.

(4) "Qualified officer" means an immigration officer or customs official who is designated by the Secretary of State for the purposes of this Schedule.

(5) "Senior police officer" means a police officer of at least the rank of superintendent.

(6) "Travel document" means anything that is or appears to be—

(*a*) a passport, or

(*b*) a ticket or other document that permits a person to make a journey by any means from a place within Great Britain to a place outside Great Britain, or from a place within Northern Ireland to a place outside the United Kingdom.

(7) "Passport" means—

(*a*) a United Kingdom passport (within the meaning of the Immigration Act 1971),

(*b*) a passport issued by or on behalf of the authorities of a country or territory outside the United Kingdom, or by or on behalf of an international organisation, or

(*c*) a document that can be used (in some or all circumstances) instead of a passport.

(8) "Port" means—

(*a*) an airport,

(*b*) a sea port,

(*c*) a hoverport,

(*d*) a heliport,

(*e*) a railway station where passenger trains depart for, or arrive from, places outside the United Kingdom, or

(*f*) any other place at which a person is able, or attempting, to get on or off any craft, vessel or vehicle in connection with entering or leaving Great Britain or Northern Ireland.

(9) A place is "in the border area" if it is in Northern Ireland and is no more than one mile from the border between Northern Ireland and the Republic of Ireland.

(10) "Involvement in terrorism-related activity" is any one or more of the following—

(*a*) the commission, preparation or instigation of acts of terrorism;

(*b*) conduct that facilitates the commission, preparation or instigation of such acts, or is intended to do so;

(*c*) conduct that gives encouragement to the commission, preparation or instigation of such acts, or is intended to do so;

(*d*) conduct that gives support or assistance to individuals who are known or believed by the person concerned to be involved in conduct falling within paragraph (*a*).

It is immaterial whether the acts of terrorism in question are specific acts of terrorism or acts of terrorism in general.

(11) "Terrorism" and "terrorist" have the same meaning as in the Terrorism Act 2000 (see sections 1(1) to (4) and 40 of that Act).

(12) "Judicial authority" means—

(*a*) in England and Wales, a District Judge (Magistrates' Courts) who is—

(i) designated under paragraph 29(4)(*a*) of Schedule 8 to the Terrorism Act 2000, or

(ii) designated for the purposes of this Schedule by the Lord Chief Justice of England and Wales;

(*b*) in Scotland, the sheriff;

(*c*) in Northern Ireland, a county court judge, or a district judge (magistrates' courts) who is—

(i) designated under paragraph 29(4)(*c*) of Schedule 8 to the Terrorism Act 2000, or

(ii) designated for the purposes of this Schedule by the Lord Chief Justice of Northern Ireland.

(13) The Lord Chief Justice may nominate a judicial office holder (as defined in section 109(4) of the Constitutional Reform Act 2005) to exercise his or her functions under sub-paragraph (12)(*a*)(ii).

(14) The Lord Chief Justice of Northern Ireland may nominate any of the following to exercise his or her functions under sub-paragraph (12)(*c*)(ii)—

(*a*) the holder of one of the offices listed in Schedule 1 to the Justice (Northern Ireland) Act 2002;

(*b*) a Lord Justice of Appeal (as defined in section 88 of that Act).

(15) "The 14-day period" and "the 30-day period" have the meanings given by paragraphs 5(2) and 8(7) respectively.

**Powers of search and seizure etc**

**2.** (1) This paragraph applies in the case of a person at a port in Great Britain if a constable has reasonable grounds to suspect that the person—

(*a*) is there with the intention of leaving Great Britain for the purpose of involvement in terrorism-related activity outside the United Kingdom, or (*b*) has arrived in Great Britain with the intention of leaving it soon for that purpose.

(2) This paragraph applies in the case of a person at a port in Northern Ireland, or in the border area, if a constable has reasonable grounds to suspect that the person—

(*a*) is there with the intention of leaving the United Kingdom for the purpose of involvement in terrorism-related activity outside the United Kingdom, or

(*b*) has arrived in Northern Ireland with the intention of leaving the United Kingdom soon for that purpose.

(3) The constable may—

(*a*) exercise any of the powers in sub-paragraph (5) in the case of the person, or

(*b*) direct a qualified officer to do so.

(4) A qualified officer must (if able to do so) comply with any direction given by a constable under sub-paragraph (3)(*b*).

(5) The powers are—

(*a*) to require the person to hand over all travel documents in his or her possession to the constable or (as the case may be) the qualified officer;

(*b*) to search for travel documents relating to the person and to take possession of any that the constable or officer finds;

(*c*) to inspect any travel document relating to the person;

(*d*) to retain any travel document relating to the person that is lawfully in the possession of the constable or officer.

(6) The power in sub-paragraph (5)(*b*) is a power to search—

(*a*) the person;

(*b*) anything that the person has with him or her;

(*c*) any vehicle in which the officer believes the person to have been travelling or to be about to travel.

(7) A constable or qualified officer—

(*a*) may stop a person or vehicle for the purpose of exercising a power in sub-paragraph (5)(*a*) or (*b*);

(*b*) may if necessary use reasonable force for the purpose of exercising a power in sub-paragraph (5)(*a*) or (*b*);

(*c*) may authorise a person to carry out on the constable's or officer's behalf a search under sub-paragraph (5)(*b*).

(8) A constable or qualified officer exercising a power in sub-paragraph (5)(*a*) or (*b*) must tell the person that—

(*a*) the person is suspected of intending to leave Great Britain or (as the case may be) the United Kingdom for the purpose of involvement in terrorism-related activity outside the United Kingdom, and

(*b*) the constable or officer is therefore entitled under this Schedule to exercise the power.

(9) Where a travel document relating to the person is in the possession of an immigration officer or customs official (whether a qualified officer or not), the constable may direct the officer or official—

(*a*) to pass the document to a constable as soon as practicable, and

(*b*) in the meantime to retain it.

The officer or official must comply with any such direction.

**Travel documents in possession of immigration officers or customs officials**

3. (1) Where—

(*a*) a travel document lawfully comes into the possession of an immigration officer or customs official (whether a qualified officer or not) without a power under paragraph 2 being exercised, and

(*b*) as soon as possible after taking possession of the document, the officer or official asks a constable whether the constable wishes to give a direction under paragraph 2(9) in relation to the document,

the officer or official may retain the document until the constable tells him or her whether or not the constable wishes to give such a direction.

(2) A request under sub-paragraph (1) must be considered as soon as possible.

**Authorisation by senior police officer for retention of travel document**

4. (1) Where a travel document is in the possession of a constable or qualified officer as a result of the exercise of a power under paragraph 2, the relevant constable must as soon as possible either—

(*a*) seek authorisation from a senior police officer for the document to be retained, or

(*b*) ensure that the document is returned to the person to whom it relates.

"The relevant constable" means the constable by whom, or on whose direction, the power was exercised.

(2) The document may be retained while an application for authorisation is considered.

(3) A constable or qualified officer retaining a travel document under sub-paragraph (2) must tell the person to whom the document relates that—

(*a*) the person is suspected of intending to leave Great Britain or (as the case may be) the United Kingdom for the purpose of involvement in terrorism-related activity outside the United Kingdom, and

(*b*) the constable or officer is therefore entitled under this Schedule to retain the document while the matter is considered by a senior police officer.

This does not apply if the constable or qualified officer expects the application for authorisation to be dealt with immediately, or if sub-paragraph (4) has been complied with.

(4) An immigration officer or customs official to whom a direction is given under paragraph 2(9) must tell the person to whom the travel document in question relates that—

(*a*) the person is suspected of intending to leave Great Britain or (as the case may be) the United Kingdom for the purpose of involvement in terrorism-related activity outside the United Kingdom, and

(*b*) a constable is therefore entitled under this Schedule to retain the document while the matter is considered by a senior police officer.

This does not apply if the immigration officer or customs official expects the application for authorisation to be dealt with immediately.

(5) If an application for authorisation is granted—

(*a*) the travel document must be passed to a constable if it is not already in the possession of a constable, and (*b*) paragraph 5 applies.

(6) If an application for authorisation is refused, the travel document must be returned to the person as soon as possible.

(7) A senior police officer may grant an application for authorisation only if satisfied that there are reasonable grounds for the suspicion referred to in paragraph 2(1) or (2).

(8) An authorisation need not be in writing.

(9) Sub-paragraphs (1)(*b*) and (6) are subject to paragraph 7 and to any power or provision not in this Schedule under which the document may be lawfully retained or otherwise dealt with.

**Retention or return of documents seized**

**5.** (1) Where authorisation is given under paragraph 4 for a travel document relating to a person to be retained, it may continue to be retained—

(*a*) while the Secretary of State considers whether to cancel the person's passport,

(*b*) while consideration is given to charging the person with an offence,

(*c*) while consideration is given to making the person subject to any order or measure to be made or imposed by a court, or by the Secretary of State, for purposes connected with protecting members of the public from a risk of terrorism, or

(*d*) while steps are taken to carry out any of the actions mentioned in paragraphs (*a*) to (*c*).

(2) But a travel document may not be retained under this Schedule after the end of the period of 14 days beginning with the day after the document was taken ("the 14-day period"), unless that period is extended under paragraph 8 or 11(3).

(3) The travel document must be returned to the person as soon as possible—

(*a*) once the 14-day period (or the 14-day period as extended under paragraph 8 or 11(3)) expires;

(*b*) once the power in sub-paragraph (1) ceases to apply, if that happens earlier.

This is subject to paragraph 7 and to any power or provision not in this Schedule under which the document may be lawfully retained or otherwise dealt with.

(4) The constable to whom a travel document is passed under paragraph 2(9) or 4(5)(*a*), or who is in possession of it when authorisation is given under paragraph 4, must explain to the person the effect of sub-paragraphs (1) to (3).

(5) The constable must also tell the person, if he or she has not been told already under paragraph 2(8) or 4(3) or (4), that the person is suspected of intending to leave Great Britain or (as the case may be) the United Kingdom for the purpose of involvement in terrorism-related activity outside the United Kingdom.

**Review of retention of travel documents**

**6.** (1) This paragraph applies where—

(*a*) authorisation is given under paragraph 4 for a travel document relating to a person to be retained, and

(*b*) the document is still being retained by a constable at the end of the period of 72 hours beginning when the document was taken from the person ("the 72-hour period").

(2) A police officer who is—

(*a*) of at least the rank of chief superintendent, and

(*b*) of at least as high a rank as the senior police officer who gave the authorisation,

must carry out a review of whether the decision to give authorisation was flawed.

(3) The reviewing officer must—

(*a*) begin carrying out the review within the 72-hour period,

(*b*) complete the review as soon as possible, and

(*c*) communicate the findings of the review in writing to the relevant chief constable.

(4) The relevant chief constable must consider those findings and take whatever action seems appropriate.

(5) If a power under paragraph 2 was exercised in relation to the travel document by an immigration officer or customs official designated under paragraph 17, the reviewing officer must also communicate the findings of the review in writing to the Secretary of State.

(6) In this paragraph—

"reviewing officer" means the officer carrying out a review under this paragraph;

"relevant chief constable" means—

(*a*) (except where paragraph (*b*) or (*c*) applies) the chief officer of police under whose direction and control is the constable retaining the document;

(*b*) the chief constable of the Police Service of Scotland, if the constable retaining the document is under that chief constable's direction and control;

(*c*) the chief constable of the Police Service of Northern Ireland, if the constable retaining the document is under that chief constable's direction and control.

**Detention of document for criminal proceedings etc**

**7.** (1) A requirement under paragraph 4 or 5 to return a travel document in the possession of a constable or qualified officer does not apply while the constable or officer has power to detain it under sub-paragraph (2).

(2) The constable or qualified officer may detain the document—

(*a*) while the constable or officer believes that it may be needed for use as evidence in criminal proceedings, or

(*b*) while the constable or officer believes that it may be needed in connection with a decision by the Secretary of State whether to make a deportation order under the Immigration Act 1971.

**Extension of 14-day period by judicial authority**

**8.** (1) A senior police officer may apply to a judicial authority for an extension of the 14-day period.

(2) An application must be made before the end of the 14-day period.

(3) An application may be heard only if reasonable efforts have been made to give to the person to whom the application relates a notice stating—

(*a*) the time when the application was made;

(*b*) the time and place at which it is to be heard.

(4) On an application—

(*a*) the judicial authority must grant an extension if satisfied that the relevant persons have been acting diligently and expeditiously in relation to the matters and steps referred to in sub-paragraph (5);

(*b*) otherwise, the judicial authority must refuse to grant an extension.

(5) In sub-paragraph (4) "the relevant persons" means—

(*a*) the persons responsible for considering whichever of the matters referred to in paragraph 5(1)(*a*) to (*c*) are under consideration, and (*b*) the persons responsible for taking whichever of the steps referred to in paragraph 5(1)(*d*) are being taken or are intended to be taken.

(6) An extension must be for a further period ending no later than the end of the 30-day period.

(7) "The 30-day period" means the period of 30 days beginning with the day after the document in question was taken.

**9.** (1) The person to whom an application under paragraph 8 relates—

(*a*) must be given an opportunity to make oral or written representations to the judicial authority about the application;

(*b*) subject to sub-paragraph (3), is entitled to be legally represented at the hearing.

(2) A judicial authority must adjourn the hearing of an application to enable the person to whom the application relates to obtain legal representation where the person—

(*a*) is not legally represented,

(*b*) is entitled to be legally represented, and

(*c*) wishes to be legally represented.

(3) A judicial authority may exclude any of the following persons from any part of the hearing—

(*a*) the person to whom the application relates;

(*b*) anyone representing that person.

**10.** (1) A person who has made an application under paragraph 8 may apply to the judicial authority for an order that specified information upon which he or she intends to rely be withheld from—

(*a*) the person to whom the application relates, and

(*b*) anyone representing that person.

(2) A judicial authority may make an order under sub-paragraph (1) in relation to specified information only if satisfied that there are reasonable grounds for believing that if the information was disclosed—

(*a*) evidence of an offence under any of the provisions mentioned in section 40(1)(*a*) of the Terrorism Act 2000 would be interfered with or harmed,

(*b*) the recovery of property obtained as a result of an offence under any of those provisions would be hindered,

(*c*) the recovery of property in respect of which a forfeiture order could be made under section 23 or 23A of that Act would be hindered,

(*d*) the apprehension, prosecution or conviction of a person who is suspected of being a terrorist would be made more difficult as a result of the person being alerted,

(*e*) the prevention of an act of terrorism would be made more difficult as a result of a person being alerted,

(*f*) the gathering of information about the commission, preparation or instigation of an act of terrorism would be interfered with,

(*g*) a person would be interfered with or physically injured, or

(*h*) national security would be put at risk.

(3) The judicial authority must direct that the following be excluded from the hearing of an application under this paragraph—

(*a*) the person to whom the application under paragraph 8 relates;

(*b*) anyone representing that person.

**11.** (1) A judicial authority may adjourn the hearing of an application under paragraph 8 only if the hearing is adjourned to a date before the expiry of the 14-day period.

(2) Sub-paragraph (1) does not apply to an adjournment under paragraph 9(2).

(3) If an application is adjourned under paragraph 9(2) to a date after the expiry of the 14-day period, the judicial authority must extend the period until that date.

**12.** (1) If an extension is granted under paragraph 8 for a period ending before the end of the 30-day period, one further application may be made under that paragraph.

(2) Paragraphs 8 to 11 apply to a further application as if references to the 14-day period were references to that period as previously extended.

**Restriction on repeated use of powers**

**13.** (1) Where—

(*a*) a power under paragraph 4 or 5 to retain a document relating to a person is exercised, and

(*b*) powers under this Schedule have been exercised in the same person's case on two or more occasions in the previous 6 months,

this Schedule has effect with the following modifications.

(2) References to 14 days (in paragraph 5(2) and elsewhere) are to be read as references to 5 days.

(3) Paragraph 8 has effect as if the following were substituted for sub-paragraph (4)—

"(4) On an application, the judicial authority must grant an extension if satisfied that—

(*a*) the relevant persons have been acting diligently and expeditiously in relation to the matters and steps referred to in sub-paragraph (5), and

(*b*) there are exceptional circumstances justifying the further use of powers under this Schedule in relation to the same person.

Otherwise, the judicial authority must refuse to grant an extension."

**Persons unable to leave the United Kingdom**

**14.** (1) This paragraph applies where a person's travel documents are retained under this Schedule with the result that, for the period during which they are so retained ("the relevant period"), the person is unable to leave the United Kingdom.

(2) The Secretary of State may make whatever arrangements he or she thinks appropriate in relation to the person—

(*a*) during the relevant period;

(*b*) on the relevant period coming to an end.

(3) If at any time during the relevant period the person does not have leave to enter or remain in the United Kingdom, the person's presence in the United Kingdom at that time is nevertheless not unlawful for the purposes of the Immigration Act 1971.

**Offences**

**15.** (1) A person who is required under paragraph 2(5)(*a*) to hand over all travel documents in the person's possession commits an offence if he or she fails without reasonable excuse to do so.

(2) A person who intentionally obstructs, or seeks to frustrate, a search under paragraph 2 commits an

offence.

(3) A person guilty of an offence under this paragraph is liable on summary conviction—

(*a*) to imprisonment for a term not exceeding 6 months, or

(*b*) to a fine, which in Scotland or Northern Ireland may not exceed level 5 on the standard scale,

or to both.

**16.** A qualified officer exercising a power under paragraph 2 has the same powers of arrest without warrant as a constable in relation to an offence under paragraph 15.

**Accredited immigration officers and customs officials**

**17.** (1) For the purposes of this paragraph, a qualified officer is an "accredited" immigration officer or customs official if designated as such by the Secretary of State.

(2) Sub-paragraphs (1), (2) and (3)(*a*) of paragraph 2 apply to an accredited immigration officer or customs official as they apply to a constable.

(3) In paragraph 2(3)(*b*) and (4) "qualified officer" does not include an accredited immigration officer or customs official.

(4) In paragraphs 2(9) and 3 "immigration officer or customs official" does not include an accredited immigration officer or customs official.

(5) Paragraph 4(1) has effect, in relation to a travel document that is in the possession of an accredited immigration officer or customs official as a result of the exercise of a power under paragraph 2 by that officer or official, as if the reference to the relevant constable were a reference to that officer or official.

**Code of practice**

**18.** (1) The Secretary of State must issue a code of practice[1] with regard to the exercise of functions under this Schedule.

(2) The code of practice must in particular deal with the following matters—

(*a*) the procedure for making designations under paragraphs 1(4) and 17;

(*b*) training to be undertaken by persons who are to exercise powers under this Schedule;

(*c*) the exercise by constables, immigration officers and customs officials of functions conferred on them by virtue of this Schedule;

(*d*) information to be given to a person in whose case a power under this Schedule is exercised;

(*e*) how and when that information is to be given;

(*f*) reviews under paragraph 6.

(3) A constable, immigration officer or customs official must perform functions conferred on him or her by virtue of this Schedule in accordance with any relevant provision included in the code by virtue of sub-paragraph (2)(*c*) to (*e*).

(4) The failure by a constable, immigration officer or customs official to observe any such provision does not of itself make him or her liable to criminal or civil proceedings.

(5) The code of practice—

(*a*) is admissible in evidence in criminal and civil proceedings;

(*b*) is to be taken into account by a court or tribunal in any case in which it appears to the court or tribunal to be relevant.

**19.** (1) Before issuing the code of practice the Secretary of State must—

(*a*) publish it in draft,

(*b*) consider any representations made about the draft, and

(*c*) if the Secretary of State thinks it appropriate, modify the draft in the light of any representations made.

(2) The Secretary of State must lay a draft of the code before Parliament.

(3) Anything done before the day on which this Act is passed is as valid as if done on or after that day for the purposes of sub-paragraphs (1) and (2).

(4) Once the code has been laid in draft before Parliament the Secretary of State may bring it into operation by regulations[2] made by statutory instrument.

(5) The first regulations under sub-paragraph (4) cease to have effect at the end of the period of 40 days beginning with the day on which the Secretary of State makes the regulations, unless a resolution approving the regulations is passed by each House of Parliament during that period.

(6) A statutory instrument containing any subsequent regulations under sub-paragraph (4) may not be made unless a draft of the instrument has been laid before each House of Parliament and approved by a resolution of each House.

(7) If regulations cease to have effect under sub-paragraph (5)—

(*a*) the code of practice to which the regulations relate also ceases to have effect, but

(*b*) that does not affect anything previously done, or the power to make new regulations or to issue a new code.

(8) For the purposes of sub-paragraph (5), the period of 40 days is to be computed in accordance with section 7(1) of the Statutory Instruments Act 1946.

**20.** (1) The Secretary of State may revise the code of practice and issue the revised code.

(2) Paragraph 19 has effect in relation to the issue of a revised code as it has effect in relation to the first issue of the code.

---

[1] The Counter-Terrorism and Security Act 2015 (Code of Practice for Officers exercising functions under Schedule 1) Regulations 2015, SI 2015/217 have been made which brought into force on 13 February 2015 the Code of Practice for Officers exercising functions under Sch 1 to the Counter-Terrorism and Security Act 2015 laid before Parliament on 12 February 2015.

[2] See note to para 18, ante.

[Counter-Terrorism and Security Act 2015, Sch 1.]

## SCHEDULE 2

Urgent Temporary Exclusion Orders: Reference to the Court etc — Section 3

**Application**

7.9153ZB **1.** This Schedule applies if the Secretary of State—

(*a*) makes the urgent case decisions in relation to an individual, and

(*b*) imposes a temporary exclusion order on the individual.

**Statement of urgency**

2. The temporary exclusion order must include a statement that the Secretary of State reasonably considers that the urgency of the case requires the order to be imposed without obtaining the permission of the court under section 3.

**Reference to court**

3. (1) Immediately after giving notice of the imposition of the temporary exclusion order, the Secretary of State must refer to the court the imposition of the order on the individual.

(2) The function of the court on the reference is to consider whether the urgent case decisions were obviously flawed.

(3) The court's consideration of the reference must begin within the period of 7 days beginning with the day on which notice of the imposition of the temporary exclusion order is given to the individual.

(4) The court may consider the reference—

(*a*) in the absence of the individual,

(*b*) without the individual having been notified of the reference, and

(*c*) without the individual having been given an opportunity (if the individual was aware of the reference) of making any representations to the court.

(5) But that does not limit the matters about which rules of court may be made.

**Decision by court**

4. (1) In a case where the court determines that any of the relevant decisions of the Secretary of State is obviously flawed, the court must quash the temporary exclusion order.

(2) If sub-paragraph (1) does not apply, the court must confirm the temporary exclusion order.

(3) If the court determines that the decision of the Secretary of State that the urgency condition is met is obviously flawed, the court must make a declaration of that determination (whether it quashes or confirms the temporary exclusion order under the preceding provisions of this paragraph).

**Procedures on reference**

5. (1) In determining a reference under paragraph 3, the court must apply the principles applicable on an application for judicial review.

(2) The court must ensure that the individual is notified of the court's decision on a reference under paragraph 3.

**Interpretation**

6. (1) References in this Schedule to the urgency condition being met are references to condition E being met by virtue of section 2(7)(*b*) (urgency of the case requires a temporary exclusion order to be imposed without obtaining the permission of the court).

(2) In this Schedule "the urgent case decisions" means the relevant decisions and the decision that the urgency condition is met.

(3) In this Schedule "the relevant decisions" means the decisions that the following conditions are met—

(*a*) condition A;

(*b*) condition B;

(*c*) condition C;

(*d*) condition D.

[Counter–Terrorism and Security Act 2015, Sch 1.]

## SCHEDULE 3

### Temporary Exclusion Orders: Proceedings

Section 12

[Counter–Terrorism and Security Act 2015, Sch 3.]

## SCHEDULE 4

### Temporary Exclusion Orders: Appeals Against Convictions

Section 12

**Right of appeal**

7.9153ZC 1. (1) An individual who has been convicted of an offence under section 10(1) or (3) may appeal against the conviction if—

(*a*) a temporary exclusion order is quashed, and

(*b*) the individual could not have been convicted had the quashing occurred before the proceedings for the offence were brought.

(2) An individual who has been convicted of an offence under section 10(3) may appeal against the conviction if—

(*a*) a notice under section 9, or a permitted obligation imposed by such a notice, is quashed, and

(*b*) the individual could not have been convicted had the quashing occurred before the proceedings for the offence were brought.

**Court in which appeal to be made**

2. An appeal under this Schedule is to be made—

(*a*) in the case of a conviction on indictment in England and Wales or Northern Ireland, to the Court of Appeal;

(*b*) in the case of a conviction on indictment or summary conviction in Scotland, to the High Court of Justiciary;

(*c*) in the case of a summary conviction in England and Wales, to the Crown Court; or

(*d*) in the case of a summary conviction in Northern Ireland, to the county court.

**When the right of appeal arises**

3. (1) The right of appeal under this Schedule does not arise until there is no further possibility of an appeal against—

(*a*) the decision to quash the temporary exclusion order, notice or permitted obligation (as the case may be), or

(*b*) any decision on an appeal made against that decision.

(2) In determining whether there is no further possibility of an appeal against a decision of the kind mentioned in sub-paragraph (1), any power to extend the time for giving notice of application for leave to appeal, or for applying for leave to appeal, must be ignored.

**The appeal**

4. (1) On an appeal under this Schedule to any court, that court must allow the appeal and quash the

conviction.

(2) An appeal under this Schedule to the Court of Appeal against a conviction on indictment—

(*a*) may be brought irrespective of whether the appellant has previously appealed against the conviction;

(*b*) may not be brought after the end of the period of 28 days beginning with the day on which the right of appeal arises by virtue of paragraph 3; and

(*c*) is to be treated as an appeal under section 1 of the Criminal Appeal Act 1968 or, in Northern Ireland, under section 1 of the Criminal Appeal (Northern Ireland) Act 1980, but does not require leave in either case.

(3) An appeal under this Schedule to the High Court of Justiciary against a conviction on indictment—

(*a*) may be brought irrespective of whether the appellant has previously appealed against the conviction;

(*b*) may not be brought after the end of the period of 28 days beginning with the day on which the right of appeal arises by virtue of paragraph 3; and

(*c*) is to be treated as an appeal under section 106 of the Criminal Procedure (Scotland) Act 1995 for which leave has been granted.

(4) An appeal under this Schedule to the High Court of Justiciary against a summary conviction—

(*a*) may be brought irrespective of whether the appellant pleaded guilty;

(*b*) may be brought irrespective of whether the appellant has previously appealed against the conviction;

(*c*) may not be brought after the end of the period of two weeks beginning with the day on which the right of appeal arises by virtue of paragraph 3;

(*d*) is to be by note of appeal, which shall state the ground of appeal;

(*e*) is to be treated as an appeal for which leave has been granted under Part 10 of the Criminal Procedure (Scotland) Act 1995; and

(*f*) must be in accordance with such procedure as the High Court of Justiciary may, by Act of Adjournal, determine.

(5) An appeal under this Schedule to the Crown Court or to the county court in Northern Ireland against a summary conviction—

(*a*) may be brought irrespective of whether the appellant pleaded guilty;

(*b*) may be brought irrespective of whether the appellant has previously appealed against the conviction or made an application in respect of the conviction under section 111 of the Magistrates' Courts Act 1980 or Article 146 of the Magistrates' Courts (Northern Ireland) Order 1981 (SI 1981/1675 (N.I. 26)) (case stated);

(*c*) may not be brought after the end of the period of 21 days beginning with the day on which the right of appeal arises by virtue of paragraph 3; and

(*d*) is to be treated as an appeal under section 108(1)(*b*) of that Act or, in Northern Ireland, under Article 140(1)(*b*) of that Order.

[Counter-Terrorism and Security Act 2015, Sch 4.]

## Abortion Regulations 1991[1]

(SI 1991/499 amended by SI 2002/887, 2879 and 3135 and SI 2008/735 and 1338)

**7.9154** 1. *Citation and commencement.*

(2) These Regulations extend to England and Wales only.

1 Made by the Secretary of State for Health, in exercise of the powers conferred by s 2 of the Abortion Act 1967.

### *Interpretation*

**7.9155** 2. In these Regulations—

"the Act" means the Abortion Act 1967;

"the Chief Medical Officer for Wales" means the Chief Medical Officer to the Welsh Assembly Government;

"electronic communication" has the same meaning as in section 15 of the Electronic Communications Act 2000;

"practitioner" means a registered medical practitioner;

"solicitor" means a person who is qualified to act as a solicitor as provided by section 1 of the Solicitors Act 1974;

"the Statistics Board" means the Statistics Board established under section 1 of the Statistics and Registration Service Act 2007.

### *Certificate of opinion*

**7.9156** 3. (1) Any opinion to which section 1 of the Act refers shall be certified—

(*a*) in the case of a pregnancy terminated in accordance with section 1(1) of the Act, either—

(i) in the form set out in Part I of Schedule 1 to these Regulations; or

(ii) in a certificate signed and dated by both practitioners jointly or in separate certificates signed and dated by each practitioner stating:—

(*a*) the full name and address of each practitioner;

(*b*) the full name and address of the pregnant woman;

(*c*) whether or not each practitioner has seen or examined, or seen and examined, the pregnant woman; and

(*d*) that each practitioner is of the opinion formed in good faith that at least one and the same ground mentioned in paragraph (*a*) to (*d*) of section 1(1) of the Act is fulfilled.

(*b*) in the case of a pregnancy terminated in accordance with section 1(4) of the Act, either—

(i) in the form set out in Part II of Schedule 1 to these Regulations; or

(ii) in a certificate giving the full name and address of the practitioner and containing the full name and address of the pregnant woman and stating that the practitioner is of the opinion formed in good faith that one of the grounds mentioned in section 1(4) of the Act is fulfilled.

(2) Any certificate of an opinion referred to in section 1(1) of the Act shall be given before the commencement of the treatment for the termination of the pregnancy to which it relates.

(3) Any certificate of an opinion referred to in section 1(4) of the Act shall be given before the commencement of the treatment for the termination of the pregnancy to which it relates or, if that is not reasonably practicable, not later than 24 hours after such termination.

(4) Any such certificate as is referred to in paragraphs (2) and (3) of this regulation shall be preserved by the practitioner who terminated the pregnancy to which it relates for a period of not less than three years beginning with the date of the termination.

(5) A certificate which is no longer to be preserved shall be destroyed by the person in whose custody it then is.

*Notice of termination of pregnancy and information relating to the termination*

7.9157 *4.* (1) Any practitioner who terminates a pregnancy in England or Wales shall give to the appropriate Chief Medical Officer—

(*a*) notice of the termination, and

(*b*) such other information relating to the termination as is specified in Schedule 2 to these Regulations,

and shall do so by sending them to him within 14 days of the termination either in a sealed envelope or by an electronic communication transmitted by an electronic communications system used solely for the transfer of confidential information to him.

(2) The appropriate Chief Medical Officer is—

(*a*) where the pregnancy was terminated in England, the Chief Medical Officer of the Department of Health, Richmond House, 79 Whitehall, London SW1A 2NS; or

(*b*) where the pregnancy was terminated in Wales, the Chief Medical Officer for Wales, Welsh Assembly Government, Cathays Park, Cardiff CF1 3NQ.

*Restriction on disclosure of information*

7.9158 *5.* A notice given or any information furnished to a Chief Medical Officer in pursuance of these Regulations shall not be disclosed except that disclosure may be made—

(*a*) for the purposes of carrying out their duties—

(i) to an officer of the Department of Health authorised by the Chief Medical Officer of that Department, or to an officer of the Welsh Assembly Government authorised by the Chief Medical Officer for Wales, as the case may be, or

(ii) to the National Statistician duly appointed under section 5 of the Statistics and Registration Service Act 2007 or an employee of the Statistics Board (established under section 1 of that Act) authorised by the National Statistician

(ii) to the chairman of the Statistics Board or a member of the Statistics Board's staff who has been duly authorised by the chairman; or*

(iii) to an individual authorised by the Chief Medical Officer who is engaged in setting up, maintaining and supporting a computer system used for the purpose of recording, processing and holding such notice or information; or

(*b*) for the purposes of carrying out his duties in relation to offences against the Act or the law relating to abortion, to the Director of Public Prosecutions or a member of his staff authorised by him; or

(*c*) for the purposes of investigating whether an offence has been committed under the Act or the law relating to abortion, to a police officer not below the rank of superintendent or a person authorised by him; or

(*d*) pursuant to a court order, for the purposes of proceedings which have begun; or

(*e*) for the purposes of bona fide scientific research; or

(*f*) to the practitioner who terminated the pregnancy; or

(*g*) to a practitioner, with the consent in writing of the woman whose pregnancy was terminated; or

(*h*) when requested by the President of the General Medical Council for the purpose of investigating whether the fitness to practise of the practitioner is impaired, there has been serious professional misconduct by a practitioner, to the President of the General Medical Council or a member of its staff authorised by him.

(*i*) to the woman whose pregnancy was terminated, on her supplying to the Chief Medical Officer written details of her date of birth, the date and place of the termination and a copy of the certificate of registration of her birth certified as a true copy of the original by a solicitor or a practitioner.

* **Second para (*a*)(ii) applies in relation to Wales only.**

7.9159 *6. Revocations.*

## Counter-Terrorism and Security Act 2015 (Code of Practice for Officers exercising functions under Schedule 1) Regulations 2015[1]

(SI 2015/217)

7.9159A *1. Citation and commencement* These Regulations may be cited as the Counter-Terrorism and Security Act 2015 (Code of Practice for Officers exercising functions under Schedule 1) Regulations 2015 and come into force on the day after the day on which they were made.

---

[1] Made by the Secretary of State in exercise of the power conferred by para 19(3) of Sch 1 to the Counter-Terrorism and Security Act 2015.

*2. Code of Practice* The Code of Practice entitled, "Code of Practice for Officers exercising functions under Schedule 1 to the Counter-Terrorism and Security Act 2015 in connection with seizing and retaining travel documents" and laid before Parliament in draft on 12th February 2015 comes into operation on the day after the day on which these Regulations were made.

# PERVERTING JUSTICE

**7.9160** The common law offence of perverting, or attempting to pervert the course of justice, is triable only on indictment[1]. This offence has survived the statutory offences created by the Criminal Law Act 1967 of acting to impede the apprehension or prosecution of an offender (s 4) and of concealing offences or giving false information (s 5)[2].

It is committed where a person:

(a) acts or embarks on a course of conduct;
(b) which has a tendency to;
(c) is intended to pervert; and
(d) the course of public justice (where the course of public justice may be understood as the administration of public justice)[3].

A conspiracy within the meaning of s 1 of the Criminal Law Act 1977 to so pervert is an offence under that section[4]. The offence of attempting to pervert the course of justice is in itself a substantive common law offence, reference to the Criminal Attempts Act 1981 would therefore be wrong[5].

"To be punishable as conduct tending to pervert the course of justice, the conduct must be such as can be properly and seriously so described. 'Pervert' is a strong word (cf 'corrupt' and 'outrage' as explained in *Knuller* )[1973] AC 435[6]." Perverting the course of public justice is not a catch-all offence and caution is exercised in extending the ambit of the offence to new fact patterns[7]. Although there is no closed list of acts which may give rise to the offence art 7 of the ECHR requires any criminal offence to be clearly defined by law[8]. The scope of the offence of perverting the course of justice is sufficiently clear so as not be incompatible with art 7 of the Convention; the article permits the gradual clarification of the rules of criminal liability from case to case through judicial interpretation provided that the development is consistent with the essence of the offence and could have been foreseen[9]. The ECtHR has approved such a process of clarification[10].

The principles in regard to extending the ambit of the offence of perverting the course of justice to a novel situation may be summarised as:

(1) There is no closed list of acts which may give rise to the offence.
(2) That said, any expansion of the offence should only take place incrementally and with caution, reflecting both principles of common law reasoning and the requirements of Art 7 of the ECHR.
(3) Neither authority nor principle supports confining the requisite acts to those giving rise to some other independent criminal wrongdoing.
(4) If there is no such limitation generally, then there is no basis for importing such a restriction – *as a matter of law* – into the elements of the offence where it arises in the context of a breach of a restraint order[11].

It is only right to charge perverting the course of justice where there are seriously aggravating features such as wasted police time and where members of the public, have been detained[12]. The essence of the offence (in contrast to the offence of wasting police time) is not a risk of an innocent person being subjected to wrongful arrest, so that if the innocent person targeted was not alive at that time there could be no such risk; the essence is that a defendant has put in train the machinery of public justice which, if the matter were carried through in a way he wished or foresaw, would cause a risk to an innocent person, and if that person has in fact died it is a classic case of impossible attempt[13]. A breach of a restraint order made under the POCA is capable, without involving no illegality beyond the breach of the order itself, of constituting the offence of perverting the course of justice. Whether any particular breach of a restraint order does give rise to the offence of perverting the course of justice depends on the facts and circumstances of the individual case. In cases of breach of restraint orders, ordinarily the sanction of contempt of court will suffice; the offence of perverting the course of justice should only be charged where there are serious aggravating features[14].

The "course of justice" is distinct from the "ends of justice"; an intention to pervert the course of justice can exist even though the motive is to further the ends of justice[15]. A course of justice must have been embarked upon, and the defendant must be shown to have intended to interfere with the administration of justice[16]. It is not necessary for a police investigation to have commenced when the acts in question occurred[17]. It is sufficient for a conviction if the defendant intended to mislead a judicial tribunal in any or all of the possible judicial proceedings which might ensue[18].

In relation to witnesses, the fact that proceedings have not been commenced when the offence is alleged to have been committed does not make it impossible to describe a person at that time as a witness. The question whether a person is to be treated as a witness or not can only be answered by having regard to the proceedings contemplated. If a person has made a statement with a view to the provision of evidence in support of criminal proceedings, in that case such a person in relation to those proceedings is a witness, and it is a perversion of the course of justice to offer him an inducement to alter or withdraw the statement[19]. It is not the case that any interference with a witness is an attempt to pervert the course of justice. That would make a man guilty of this offence if he went privately to a witness who had made a false statement and by reasoned argument supported by material facts and documents tried to dissuade him from committing perjury and to persuade him to retract lies and tell the truth. However, the exercise of a legal right or the threat of exercising it, is an attempt to pervert the course of justice if one of the motives which activates the accused in making the threat is to intimidate the witness into altering or withdrawing evidence. It is not necessary for his threat to be empty or not bona fide[20]. In the great majority of cases of perverting the course of justice by interfering with a witness the actus reus will be accompanied by unlawful means such as threats, bribery or improper pressure. The use of unlawful means is not however an essential ingredient in the offence. In cases where the defendant might otherwise have a defence of lawful excuse, for example where his purpose is to persuade a false witness or a witness he believes to be false, not to commit perjury, he will nevertheless be liable if he employs unlawful means. "Unlawful means" in this context includes a threat to do an otherwise lawful act or to exercise a legal right. In all cases the prosecution must prove the necessary intent[21].

An act which is intended to assist, and does assist, a suspect to avoid arrest, is sufficient to constitute the offence of attempting to pervert or perverting the course of public justice, notwithstanding that the interference does not involve dishonest, corrupt or threatening conduct[22].

Inaction is not an act or a course of conduct[23]. Nor is driving home after an accident and not reporting it until the following day because the accused knew he would have been in difficulty with the breathalyser; the actus reus of the offence requires more than driving off and waiting for alcohol to dissipate from the body[24].

The prosecution must prove either an intent to pervert the course of justice or an intent to do something which, if achieved, would pervert the course of justice[25]. The offence should not be charged where the prosecution can only present its case on the alternative basis that the defendant must either have committed perjury or have given false information to the police[26].

---

1 *R v Vreones* [1891] 1 QB 360; *R v Grimes* [1968] 3 All ER 179; *R v Andrews* [1973] QB 422, [1973] 1 All ER 857 (witness of traffic accident offering in return for payment to give false evidence in court could be charged with incitement to commit the substantive offence of perverting the course of public justice).

2 *R v Panayiotou* [1973] 3 All ER 112, [1973] 1 WLR 1032.

3 *DPP v SK* [2016] EWHC 837 (Admin), [2017] Crim LR 226.

4 See this Part, title Conspiracy, ante.

5 See *R v Williams* [1991] Crim LR 205.

6 ; *DPP v Withers* [1975] AC 842, per Lord Simon of Glaisdale at 867.

7 *R v Selvage* and *R v Morgan* [1982] QB 372 per Watkins LJ.

8 *R v Clark* [2003] EWCA Crim 991, [2003] 2 Cr App Rep 63, [2003] Crim LR 558.

9 *R v Cotter* [2002] EWCA Crim 1033.

10 *SW v UK* (1995) Series A No 355B.

11 *R v Kenny* [2013] EWCA Crim 1.

12 *R v Sookoo* (2002) Times, 10 April, CA.

13 *R v Brown* [2004] EWCA Crim 744, [2004] Crim LR 665.

14 *R v Kenny* [2013] EWCA Crim 1, [2013] QB 896, [2013] 3 All ER 85, [2013] 3 WLR 59.

15 *A-G's Reference (No 1 of 2002)* [2002] EWCA Crim 2392, [2003] Crim LR 410.

16 *R v Selvage and R v Morgan* [1982] Crim LR 47.

17 *R v Rafique* [1993] 4 All ER 1, [1993] 3 WLR 617.

18 *R v Sinha* [1995] Crim LR 68.

19 *R v Panayiotou* [1973] 3 All ER 112, [1973] 1 WLR 1032.

20 *R v Kellett* [1976] QB 372, [1975] 3 All ER 468, CA.

21 *R v Toney* [1993] 2 All ER 409, [1993] Crim LR 397.

22 *R v Thomas* [1979] 1 All ER 577. See also, *R v Britton* [1973] RTR 502, [1973] Crim LR 375 (motorist who, having been required to take a breathalyser test, went into his own house, and before the breathalyser could be administered to him took a drink from a bottle of some alcoholic liquor, thereby, on well established authority, putting himself beyond the reach of the procedure leading to a conviction for driving with excess alcohol in the blood was rightly convicted of attempting to defeat the course of justice although it could not have been said that the act of taking additional alcoholic drink after his driving had ceased involved a dishonest, corrupt or threatening course of conduct on the part of the appellant).

23 *R v Headley* [1996] RTR 173 (defendant ignored summons in his name and allowed informations alleging contraventions of the Road Traffic Acts by his brother to be proved in his own name).

24 *R v Clark* [2003] EWCA Crim 991, [2003] 2 Cr App Rep 63, [2003] Crim LR 558.

25 *R v Lalani* [1999] 1 Cr App Rep 481, CA (juror communicating with defendant acquitted as no evidence adduced of her state of mind).

26 *Tsang Ping-nam v R* [1982] Crim LR 46.

# POLICE

**Contents**



**7.9161** This title is concerned with constables, being mainly police officers appointed under the Police Act 1996 and the Railways and Transport Safety Act 2003[1] and the Ministry of Defence Police Act 1987. The appointment and jurisdiction of constables[2] are dealt with by s 30 of the 1996 Act; their powers are largely defined by the Police and Criminal Evidence Act 1984 in Part I: Magistrates' Courts, Procedure, ante; see also "Investigation of Offences", paras 1.62 to 1.88, ante. Police complaints and discipline are provided for in Part 2, ss 9–29 of the Police Reform Act 2002 (not reproduced in this Manual), and ss 50 and 84 of the 1996 Act enables the making of discipline regulations; some current regulations are printed post.

The Crime and Courts Act 2013 created the National Crime Agency, the officers of which may be designated under s 10 as having the powers and privileges of a constable (Sch 5, Part 4) (and of an officer of Revenue and Customs and an immigration officer (Sch 5, Parts 5 and 6)). Assaults, obstruction etc. of such officers are offences under Sch 5, Part 7 to the 2013 Act. The relevant provisions of the 2013 Act are reproduced in Part I: Statutes on Procedure, ante.

1 Note however the following appointments of police for limited purposes: airport police (Civil Aviation Act 1982, s 57); fishery officers (Sea Fisheries Regulation Act 1966, s 10); harbour, docks or pier police (Harbours, Docks and Piers Clauses Act 1847, ss 79, 80); nominated special constables (Special Constables Act 1923, s 3, Emergency Laws (Miscellaneous Provisions) Act 1947, Sch 2, Atomic Energy Authority Act 1954, ss 6, 9, Sch 3, Atomic Energy Authority Act 1971, Sch, Atomic Energy Authority (Special Constables) Act 1976, Visiting Forces and International Headquarters (Application of Law) Order 1965 (SI 1965/1536), art 6); Port of London Police (Port of London Act 1968, s 154); university police (Universities Act 1825, s 1); water bailiffs (Salmon and Freshwater Fisheries Act 1975, s 36).

2 That is, a person holding the *office* of constable, and not just the rank: see Police Act 1996, s 29.

## Constables, execution of warrant of commitment

**7.9162** The person apprehended on a warrant issued in England or Wales may be conveyed either to the prison mentioned in the warrant, or to any other prison (Criminal Procedure Rules, r 13.3, in the *Key Materials*.

A warrant of commitment issued by a justice of the peace may be executed anywhere in England and Wales by any person to whom it is directed or by any constable acting within his police area[1]. A sentence of imprisonment imposed on an offender shall be treated as reduced by any period during which the offender was in police detention in connection with the offence for which the sentence was passed. Therefore, any period spent by an offender in police detention prior to his conveyance to prison will be treated as part of the term of imprisonment[2].

1 Magistrates' Courts Act 1980, s 125(2), in Part I: Magistrates' Courts, Procedure, ante.

2 See the Criminal Justice Act 1967, s 67, in Part I: Magistrates' Courts, Procedure, ante.

## Refusing to assist a constable

**7.9163** It is an indictable misdemeanour at common law punishable by fine or imprisonment or both to refuse to aid and assist a constable in the execution of his duty when duly called on to do so, if the person so called upon is physically capable of helping, and has no lawful excuse for refusing.

To support an indictment for refusing to aid in quelling a riot it was held that it was necessary to prove, first, that the constable saw a breach of the peace committed; secondly, that there was reasonable necessity for calling on the defendant for his assistance; and, thirdly, that the defendant refused without any physical impossibility or lawful excuse (*R v Brown* (1841) Car & M 314, Treat 34 JP 129). As to the indictment for refusing to assist, see *R v Sherlock* (1866) LR 1 CCR 20, 30 JP 85. A person assaulting the party charged to assist the constable may be punished for the assault (Police Act 1996, s 89); and if he rescues the prisoner, may be indicted for the rescue. Where a person is in custody of a private party, he should give notice to the rescuer of the cause for which he is in custody; where in that of a constable, the rescuer must take notice of it himself at his peril (6 JP 319).

## Police (Property) Act 1897

(60 & 61 Vict c 30)

7.9164 **1. Power to make orders with respect to property in possession of police**[1]

(1) Where any property has come into the possession of the police in connection with their investigation of a suspected offence, a court of summary jurisdiction may, on application either by an officer of police[2] or by a claimant of the property, make an order[3] for the delivery of the property to the person appearing to the magistrate or court to be the owner[4] thereof, or, if the owner cannot be ascertained, make such order with respect to the property as to the magistrate or court may seem meet.

(2) An order under this section shall not affect the right of any person to take within six months from the date of the order legal proceedings against any person in possession of property delivered by virtue of the order for the recovery of the property, but on the expiration of those six months the right shall cease.*

(3) *Repealed.*

[Police (Property) Act 1897, s 1 as amended by Theft Act 1968, the Criminal Justice Act 1972, s 58 and the Consumer Credit Act 1974, Sch 5 and the Statute Law (Repeals) Act 1989, Sch 1.]

---

* **Repealed in relation to Northern Ireland by the Police (Northern Ireland) Act 1998, Sch 6.**

1 See the Police (Property) Regulations 1997, in this title, post. Procedure is regulated by the Criminal Procedure Rules, rr 47.35-47.37 and 47.39 in the *Key Materials*. The rules now provide for an application in writing, determination at or without a hearing or in a person's absence, attendance by live link or telephone and for written representations.

The 1897 Act applies with modifications where property is in the possession of the police by virtue of a deprivation order made under s 143 of the Powers of Criminal Courts (Sentencing) Act 2000. These modification are made by s 144 of the PCC(S)A 2000 which is reproduced at para 3.275 in PART III SENTENCING, ante.

2 The police should apply for an order under this section before parting with the property. The plaintiff having lost a gig, the person in whose possession it was found was tried for larceny and acquitted. A police officer who handed it over to the person so acquitted was liable in trover to the plaintiff (*Winter v Bancks* (1901) 65 JP 468). For consideration of a successful claimant's title to property after the making of an order, see *Irving v National Provincial Bank Ltd* [1902] 2 QB 73, [1962] 1 All ER 157, 126 JP 76.

3 Prior to the Criminal Procedure Rules it had been held that proceedings were appropriately to be brought by way of complaint and there was power to award costs under s 64 of the MCA 1980 (*R v Uxbridge Justices, ex p Metropolitan Police Comr* [1981] QB 829, [1981] 3 All ER 129, 146 JP 42, CA; and in appropriate circumstances this included making an order for costs against the police (*Mercer v Oldham* [1984] Crim LR 232). However, where the chief constable had brought an application to determine to whom cash should be returned – the person from whom it was seized or the company that was the victim of that person's offending – and the court made an order in favour of the former, there was no power, having regard to the terms of s 64(1)(*b*) of the MCA 1980, to order the chief constable to pay that person's costs, since the complaint had not been dismissed; moreover, the order was wholly unreasonable: *R (on the application of the Chief Constable of Northamptonshire) v Daventry Justices* [2001] Admin 446). It would seem now to be settled that where proceedings are brought by way of written application in accordance with the rules, there is no power to order costs. Justices are to be discouraged from using the procedure of this Act in cases which involve a real issue of law or any real difficulty in determining whether a particular person is or is not the owner; see dicta in *Raymond Lyons & Co v Metropolitan Police Comr*, infra.

4 The innkeeper's lien attaches to stolen property received by an innkeeper from a guest as a security for payment of his bill. The meaning of "owner" was not decided (*Marsh v Police Comr* [1945] KB 43, [1944] 2 All ER 392, 109 JP 45). In *Raymond Lyons & Co Ltd v Metropolitan Police Comr* [1975] QB 321, [1975] 1 All ER 335, 139 JP 213 it was held that "owner" is to be given its ordinary popular meaning. A court may make an order in favour of an offender despite the property having passed under an illegal contract (*Chief Constable of West Midlands v White* (1992) 157 JP 222). Where police officers seized a stolen vehicle then in the possession of C, who was its registered keeper, but C, though aware that the car was stolen, was not prosecuted, and the police were unable to trace anybody with a better title to the vehicle than C, C was entitled to the return of the vehicle once the purposes of s 22 of PACE had been exhausted: *Costello v Chief Constable of Derbyshire Constabulary* [2001] EWCA Civ 381, [2001] 3 All ER 150, [2001] 1 WLR 1437.

*Costello* was not dealing with the 1897 Act; however, it was held in *R (on the application of Ian Carter) v Ipswich Magistrates' Court* [2002] EWHC 332 (Admin), [2002] All ER (D) 110 (Feb) that the same principles apply both to civil actions in the county court and to applications under the 1897 Act. If there is no defence to a civil action, the position is the same in a claim under this section: *Chief Constable of Merseyside Police v Owens* [2012] EWHC 1515 (Admin), 176 JP 688, 176 CL&J 353(where the court was prepared to assume, pace *Webb v Chief Constable of Merseyside Police* [2000] QB 427 , [2000] 1 All ER 209, CA, that a civil court or a magistrates' court could refuse to grant relief and refuse to order the return of property if on the facts it could be established that the return of property would indirectly encourage or assist a person in his criminal act).

Where claimants had paid for vehicles and, though they had been stolen, they had not been the thieves or been concerned in the thefts, those were significant facts and the justices had been wrong to order destruction of the vehicles on the grounds that they could never have become "legal", the significance of which, whatever it meant, was difficult to see where the court was endeavouring to determine ownership for the purposes of s 1 (*Haley v Chief Constable of Northamptonshire Police* [2002] EWHC 1492 (Admin), 166 JP 719).

7.9165 **2. Regulations with respect to unclaimed property** (1) A Secretary of State may make regulations[1] (limited by sub-s (2)) for the disposal of property which has come into the possession of the police under the circumstances mentioned in this Act in cases where the owner of the property has not been ascertained, and no order of a competent court has been made with respect thereto.

(2)–(2B) *Regulations.*

(3) Where the property is a perishable article or its custody involves unreasonable expense or inconvenience, it may be sold at any time, but the proceeds of sale shall not be disposed of until they have remained in the possession of the police for a year. In any other case the property shall not be

sold until it has remained in the possession of the police for a year.

(4) Regulations[1] may be made by the Secretary of State as to the investment of money and audit of accounts.*

[Police (Property) Act 1897, s 2 as amended by the Statute Law Repeals Act 1908, the Police Property Act 1997, s 1 and the Police Reform and Social Responsibility Act 2011, Sch 16.]

* **Repealed in relation to Northern Ireland by the Police (Northern Ireland) Act 1998, Sch 6.**

1 See the Police (Property) Regulations 1997, in this title, post.

7.9166 **2A.** ***Application to National Crime Agency***

## Police Pensions Act 1976[1]

(1976 c 35)

7.9167 **1.** Regulations[2] by the Secretary of State may make detailed provision for police pensions. They may enable pensions to be varied, suspended, terminated or forfeited or applied otherwise than by being paid to the persons to whom they were awarded [s 1—summarised.]

1 The Pension scheme under this Act has been superseded by a new scheme made under the Public Service Pensions Act 2013 and regulations made under s 1 thereof. Consequential amendments are made to a number of statutory provisions in relation to a member of an old scheme who transfers to the new scheme by the Police Pensions (Consequential Provisions) Regulations 2015, SI 2015/370. The new scheme regulations are the Police Pension Regulations 2015, SI 2015/445.

2 Section 12 provides savings for existing regulations, see the Police Pensions Regulations, SI 1971/232 as amended and SI 1973/428 as amended with supplementary provisions made by SI 1987/256 as amended; there are also transitional savings (by s 12(2)) for the provisions of ss 4(1) and (2) and 5(1) and (5) of the Police Pensions Act 1948 as amended by the Criminal Justice Act 1948, Sch 9 and the Superannuation Act 1972, s 15 and Sch 8 (forfeiture of pensions and appeals). The former provisions are the Police Pensions Regulations 1987, SI 1987/257 as amended by SI 1987/341 and 2215, SI 1988/1339, SI 1989/733, SI 1990/805, SI 1991/1517, 1992/1343 and 2349, SI 1994/641, SI 1996/867, SI 1997/2852, SI 1998/577, SI 2000/843 and 1549, SI 2001/3649 and 3888, SI 2002/2529 and 3202, SI 2003/27, 535 and 2716, SI 2004/1491, 1760 and 2354, SI 2005/1439, SI 2006/740 and 932, SI 2007/1932, SI 2008/1887, SI 2009/2060, SI 2010/431, SI 2011/3063, SI 2012/640, 2811, 2954 and 3057, SI 2013/487 and 2318, SI 2014/79, 381 and 3061 and SI 2015/2057. See also the Police Pensions (Purchase of Increased Benefits) Regulations 1987, SI 1987/2215 amended by SI 2004/2354, SI 2005/1439, SI 2008/1887, SI 2011/3063 and SI 2012/640; Police Pensions (Additional Voluntary Contributions) Regulations 1991, SI 1991/1304 amended by SI 2003/27, 535 and 2717, SI 2006/740, SI 2010/2235 and SI 2011/3063; and the Police Pensions (Part-time Service) Regulations 2005, SI 2005/1439 amended by SI 2006/932 and SI 2011/3063; Police (Injury Benefit) Regulations 2006, SI 2006/932 amended by SI 2007/1932, SI 2008/1887, SI 2009/2060, SI 2010/431, SI 2011/3063, SI 2015/2057 and SI 2017/21; Police Pensions Regulations 2006, SI 2006/3415 amended by SI 2007/1932, SI 2008/1887, SI 2009/2060, SI 2010/431, SI 2011/3063, SI 2012/640, 2811 and 3057, SI 2013/487 and 2318 and SI 2014/381.

7.9168 **10. Obtaining pension by self-inflicted injury etc** If any person obtains or attempts to obtain for himself or any other person any pension under any regulations made under section 1 above by maiming or injuring himself, or causing himself to be maimed or injured, or otherwise producing disease or infirmity, he shall be liable[1]—

(*a*) on conviction on indictment, to imprisonment for a term not exceeding **two years**; or

(*b*) on summary conviction, to imprisonment for a term not exceeding **three months** or to a fine not exceeding the **prescribed sum**.

[Police Pensions Act 1976, s 10 as amended by the Magistrates' Courts Act 1980, s 32.]

1 For procedure in respect of an offence triable either way, see the Magistrates' Courts Act 1980, ss 17A–21, ante.

SCHEDULE 1

PENSIONS UNDER REPEALED ENACTMENTS

7.9169 This Schedule makes provision for pensions excluded from the operation of regulations under this Act and the forfeiture of pensions under repealed enactments.

## Ministry of Defence Police Act 1987

(1987 c 4)

7.9170 **1. The Ministry of Defence Police** (1) There shall be a police force to be known as the Ministry of Defence Police and consisting—

(*a*) of persons nominated by the Secretary of State; and

(*b*) of persons who at the coming into force of this Act are special constables by virtue of appointment under section 3 of the Special Constables Act 1923 on the nomination of the Defence Council.

(2) A person nominated under subsection (1) above shall—

(*a*) in England and Wales be attested as a constable by making the declaration required of a member of a police force maintained under the Police Act 1996 before a justice of the peace;

(*b*)–(*c*) *Scotland; Northern Ireland.*

(3)–(6) *Power of the Secretary of State to appoint a chief constable for the Ministry of Defence Police; to suspend a member of the Police from duty; to appoint the Ministry of Defence Police Committee, and to make regulations*[1].

[Ministry of Defence Police Act 1987, s 1 as amended by the Police Act 1996, Sch 7, the Police Reform Act 2002, s 79 and SI 2013/602.]

[1] The following regulations have been made under this provision: Ministry of Defence Police (Committee) Regulations 2009, SI 2009/1609; Ministry of Defence Police Appeal Tribunals Regulations 2009, SI 2009/3070 amended by SI 2015/25 and SI 2017/84; Ministry of Defence Police (Conduct) Regulations 2015, SI 2015/25 amended by SI 2017/84.

7.9171 2. **Jurisdiction** (1) In any place in the United Kingdom to which subsection (2) below for the time being applies, members of the Ministry of Defence Police shall have the powers and privileges of constables.

(2) [1]The places to which this subsection applies are—

(*a*) land, vehicles, vessels, aircraft and hovercraft in the possession, under the control or used for the purposes of—

(i) the Secretary of State for Defence;

(ii) the Defence Council;

(iii) a headquarters or defence organisation; or

(iv) the service authorities of a visiting force;

(*b*) land, vehicles, vessels, aircraft and hovercraft which are—

(i) in the possession, under the control or used for the purposes of an ordnance company; and

(ii) used for the purpose of, or for purposes which include, the making or development of ordnance or otherwise for naval, military or air force purposes;

(*c*) land, vehicles, vessels, aircraft and hovercraft which are—

(i) in the possession, under the control or used for the purposes of a dockyard contractor; and

(ii) used for the purpose of, or for purposes which include, providing designated services or otherwise for naval, military or air force purposes;

(*d*) *repealed*; and

(*e*) land where the Secretary of State has agreed to provide the services of the Ministry of Defence Police under an agreement notice of which has been published in the appropriate Gazette.

(3) Members of the Ministry of Defence Police shall also have the powers and privileges of constables in any place in the United Kingdom to which subsection (2) above does not for the time being apply—

(*a*) in relation to Crown property[2], international defence property, ordnance property and dockyard property;

(*b*) in relation to persons—

(i) subject to the control of the Defence Council;

(ii) employed under or for the purposes of the Ministry of Defence or the Defence Council; or

(iii) in respect of whom the service courts and service authorities of any country may exercise powers by virtue of section 2 of the Visiting Forces Act 1952;

(*ba*) in connection with offences against persons within paragraph (*b*) above, with the incitement of such persons to commit offences and with offences under the Bribery Act 2010 in relation to such persons;

(*c*) in relation to matters connected with anything done under a contract entered into by the Secretary of State for Defence for the purposes of his Department or the Defence Council; and

(*d*) for the purpose of securing the unimpeded passage of any such property as is mentioned in paragraph (*a*) above.

(3A) Where a member of the Ministry of Defence Police has been requested by a constable of—

(*a*) the police force for any police area;

(*aa*) the Police Service of Scotland;

(*b*) the Police Service of Northern Ireland;

(*c*) the British Transport Police Force; or

(*d*) the Civil Nuclear Constabulary,

to assist him in the execution of his duties in relation to a particular incident, investigation or operation, members of the Ministry of Defence Police shall have the powers and privileges of constables for the purposes of that incident, investigation or operation but subject to subsection (3B) below.

(3B) Members of the Ministry of Defence Police have the powers and privileges of constables for the purposes of an incident, investigation or operation by virtue of subsection (3A) above—

(*a*) if the request was made under paragraph (*a*) of that subsection by a constable of the police force for a police area, only in that police area;

(*aa*) if it was made under paragraph (aa) of that subsection, only in Scotland;

(*b*) if it was made under paragraph (*b*) of that subsection, only in Northern Ireland;

(*c*) if it was made under paragraph (*c*) of that subsection, only to the extent that those powers and privileges would in the circumstances be exercisable for those purposes by a constable of the British Transport Police Force by virtue of subsection (1A) or, in Scotland, subsection (4) of section 53 of the British Transport Commission Act 1949 (c xxix); or

(*d*) if it was made under paragraph (*d*) of that subsection, only to the extent that those powers and privileges would in the circumstances be exercisable for those purposes by a constable of the Civil Nuclear Constabulary.

(3C) Members of the Ministry of Defence Police shall have in any police area the same powers and privileges as constables of the police force for that police area, in Scotland the same powers and privileges as constables of the Police Service of Scotland, and in Northern Ireland the same powers and privileges as constables of the Police Service of Northern Ireland—

(*a*) in relation to persons whom they suspect on reasonable grounds of having committed, being in the course of committing or being about to commit an offence; or

(*b*) if they believe on reasonable grounds that they need those powers and privileges in order to save life or to prevent or minimise personal injury.

(3D) But members of the Ministry of Defence Police have powers and privileges by virtue of subsection (3C) above only if—

(*a*) they are in uniform or have with them documentary evidence that they are members of the Ministry of Defence Police; and

(*b*) they believe on reasonable grounds that a power of a constable which they would not have apart from that subsection ought to be exercised and that, if it cannot be exercised until they secure the attendance of or a request under subsection (3A) above by a constable who has it, the purpose for which they believe it ought to be exercised will be frustrated or seriously prejudiced.

(4) Subsections (1) to (3D) above shall have effect in the territorial waters adjacent to the United Kingdom, but as if the references in those subsections to the powers and privileges of constables were references in those subsections to the powers and privileges of constables in the nearest part of the United Kingdom.

(5) In this section—

"appropriate Gazette" means—

(i) in relation to land in England or Wales, the London Gazette;

(ii) *Scotland*, and

(iii) *Northern Ireland*;

"British Transport Police Force" means the constables appointed under section 53 of the British Transport Commission Act 1949 (c xxix);

"Crown property" includes property in the possession or under the control of the Crown and property which has been unlawfully removed from its possession or control;

"designated services" means services designated under subsection (1) of section 1 of the Dockyard Services Act 1986;

"dockyard contractor" means a company which is a dockyard contractor as defined by subsection (13) of that section;

"dockyard property" means property which—

(*a*) belongs to a dockyard contractor, is in its possession or under its control or has been unlawfully removed from its possession or control; and

(*b*) is (or was immediately before its removal) used to any extent for the purpose of providing designated services or otherwise for naval, military or air force purposes;

"headquarters", "defence organisation" and "visiting force" mean respectively a headquarters, defence organisation or visiting force to which the Visiting Forces and International Headquarters (Application of Law) Order 1965, or any order replacing that order, applies;

"international defence property" means property which belongs to, is in the possession or under the control of or has been unlawfully removed from the possession or control of a headquarters, a defence organisation or the service authorities of a visiting force;

"ordnance company" means a company in which there is for the time being vested any property, right or liability which has at some time been the subject of a transfer by virtue of a provision made under section 1(1)(*a*) of the Ordnance Factories and Military Services Act 1984;

"ordnance property" means property which—

(*a*) belongs to an ordnance company, is in its possession or under its control or has been unlawfully removed from its possession or control; and

(*b*) is (or was immediately before its removal) used to any extent for the purpose of, or for purposes including, the making or development of ordnance or otherwise for naval, military or air force purposes;

"service authorities" means naval, military or air force authorities; and

"vessel" includes any ship or boat or any other description of vessel used in navigation.

[Ministry of Defence Police Act 1987, s 2 as amended by the Anti-terrorism, Crime and Security Act 2001, Sch 8, the Energy Act 2004, Schs 14 and 23, the Bribery Act 2010, Sch 1 and SI 2013/602.]

---

[1] The places to which subsection (2) applies shall also include land, vehicles, vessels, aircraft and hovercraft which are (*a*) in the possession, under the control or used for the purposes of a contractor within the meaning of the Atomic Weapons Establishment Act 1991, s 1(4); and (*b*) used for the purposes of, or for purposes which include, carrying on

designated activities within the meaning of s 1, Ministry of Defence Police Act 1987 (Atomic Weapons Establishment Act 1991, s 4(1)).

2 The reference in subsection (3) to Crown property includes a reference to property which (*a*) belongs to a contractor, within the meaning of s 1(4) of the Atomic Weapons Establishment Act 1991, is in its possession or under its control or has been unlawfully removed from its possession or control; and (*b*) is (or was immediately before its removal) used to any extent for the purpose of carrying on designated activities within the meaning of s 1, Ministry of Defence Police Act 1987 (Atomic Weapons Establishment Act 1991, s 4).

7.9172 **2A. Provision of assistance to other forces** (1) The Chief Constable of the Ministry of Defence Police may, on the application of the chief officer of any relevant force, provide constables or other assistance for the purpose of enabling that force to meet any special demand on its resources.

(2) Where a member of the Ministry of Defence Police is provided for the assistance of a relevant force under this section—

(*a*) he shall be under the direction and control of the chief officer of that force; and

(*b*) he shall have the same powers and privileges as a member of that force.

(3) Constables are not to be regarded as provided for the assistance of a relevant force under this section in a case where assistance is provided under section 2 above.

(4) In this section—

"British Transport Police Force" has the same meaning as in section 2 above;

"chief officer" means—

(*a*) the chief officer of the police force for any police area;

(*aa*) the chief constable of the Police Service of Scotland;

(*b*) the Chief Constable of the Police Service of Northern Ireland;

(*c*) the Chief Constable of the British Transport Police Force; or

(*d*) the Chief Constable of the Civil Nuclear Constabulary

"relevant force" means—

(*a*) the police force for any police area;

(*aa*) the Police Service of Scotland;

(*b*) the Police Service of Northern Ireland;

(*c*) the British Transport Police Force; or

(*d*) the Civil Nuclear Constabulary

[Ministry of Defence Police Act 1987, s 2A as inserted by the Anti-Terrorism, Crime and Security Act 2001, s 99 and amended by the Energy Act 2004, Schs 14 and 23 and SI 2013/602.]

7.9173 **2B. Constables serving with other forces** (1) This section applies where a member of the Ministry of Defence Police serves with a relevant force under arrangements made between the chief officer of that force and the chief constable of the Ministry of Defence Police.

(2) The member of the Ministry of Defence Police—

(*a*) shall be under the direction and control of the chief officer of the relevant force; and

(*b*) shall have the same powers and privileges as a member of that force.

(3) In this section—

"British Transport Police Force" has the same meaning as in section 2 above;

"chief officer" means—

(*a*) any chief officer of police of a police force for a police area in England and Wales;

(*aa*) the chief constable of the Police Service of Scotland;

(*b*) the chief constable of the Police Service of Northern Ireland;

(*c*) *repealed*;

(*d*) *repealed*;

(*e*) the chief constable of the British Transport Police Force; or

(*f*) the chief constable of the Civil Nuclear Constabulary;

"relevant force" means—

(*a*) any police force for a police area in England and Wales;

(*aa*) the Police Service of Scotland;

(*b*) the Police Service of Northern Ireland;

(*c*) *repealed*;

(*d*) *repealed*;

(*e*) the British Transport Police Force; or

(*f*) Civil Nuclear Constabulary.

[Ministry of Defence Police Act 1987, s 2B as inserted by the Police Reform Act 2002, s 78 and amended by the Energy Act 2004, Schs 14 and 23, the Serious Organised Crime and Police Act 2005, Sch 4 and SI 2013/602.]

7.9174 **2C. Constables serving with National Crime Agency** (1) A member of the Ministry of Defence Police serving with the National Crime Agency under arrangements to which subsection (2) applies shall—

(*a*) be under the direction and control of the Director General of the National Crime Agency, and

(*b*) continue to be a constable.

(2) This subsection applies to arrangements made between—

(*a*) the Director General of the National Crime Agency, and

(*b*) the chief constable of the Ministry of Defence Police.

[Ministry of Defence Police Act 1987, s 2C as inserted by the Serious Organised Crime and Police Act 2005, Sch 4 and amended by the Crime and Courts Act 2013, Sch 8.]

7.9175 **3–4A**[1]. *Defence Police Federation; representation at disciplinary hearings.*

[1] In exercise of the powers conferred by ss 3A and 4 the Ministry of Defence Police (Performance) Regulations 2012, SI 2012/808 amended by SI 2015/25 amended by SI 2017/84 have been made.

7.9176 **5. Impersonation etc** (1) Any person who with intent to deceive impersonates a member of the Ministry of Defence Police, or makes any statement or does any act calculated falsely to suggest that he is such a member, shall be guilty of an offence and liable on summary conviction to imprisonment for a term not exceeding **six months** or to a fine not exceeding **level 5** on the standard scale, or to both.

(2) Any person who, not being a member of the Ministry of Defence Police, wears any article of the uniform of the Ministry of Defence Police in circumstances where it gives him an appearance so nearly resembling that of a member as to be calculated to deceive shall be guilty of an offence and liable on summary conviction to a fine not exceeding **level 3** on the standard scale.

(3) Any person who, not being a member of the Ministry of Defence Police, has in his possession any article of uniform of the Ministry of Defence Police shall, unless he proves that he obtained possession of that article lawfully and has possession of it for a lawful purpose, be guilty of an offence and liable on summary conviction to a fine not exceeding **level 1** on the standard scale.

(4) In this section "article of uniform" means any article of uniform or any distinctive badge or mark or document of identification usually issued to members of the Ministry of Defence Police, or any thing having the appearance of such an article, badge, mark or document.

[Ministry of Defence Police Act 1987, s 5.]

7.9177 **6. Causing disaffection** Any person who causes, or attempts to cause, or does any act calculated to cause, disaffection amongst the members of the Ministry of Defence Police, or induces or attempts to induce, or does any act calculated to induce, any member of the Ministry of Defence Police to withhold his services or to commit breaches of discipline, shall be guilty of an offence and liable[1]—

(*a*) on summary conviction, to imprisonment for a term not exceeding **six months** or to a fine not exceeding the **statutory maximum**, or to **both**;

(*b*) on conviction on indictment, to imprisonment for a term not exceeding **two years** or to a **fine** or to **both**.

[Ministry of Defence Police Act 1987, s 6.]

[1] For procedure in respect of this offence which is triable either way, see the Magistrates' Courts Act 1980, ss 17A–21, in PART I: MAGISTRATES' COURTS, PROCEDURE, ante.

7.9178 **6A. Powers to make regulations** Any power of the Secretary of State under this Act to make regulations shall include power to make different provision for different purposes.

[Ministry of Defence Police Act 1987, s 6A as inserted by the Police Reform Act 2002, s 79.]

7.9179 **7–8.** *Consequential amendments and repeals; short title, commencement and extent.*

# Police Act 1996[1]

(1996 c 16)

## PART I[2]

## ORGANISATION OF POLICE FORCES

*Police areas and police forces*

7.9180 **1. Police areas** (1) England and Wales shall be divided into police areas.

(2) The police areas referred to in subsection (1) shall be—

(*a*) those listed in Schedule 1 (subject to any amendment made to the first column of that Schedule by regulations under section 31A or any amendment made to the second column, or to the first and second columns, by an order under section 32 below, section 58 of the Local Government Act 1972, or section 17 of the Local Government Act 1992 or Part 1 of the Local Government and Public Involvement in Health Act 2007),

(*b*) the metropolitan police district, and

(*c*) the City of London police area.

(3) References in Schedule 1 to any local government area are to that area as it is for the time being.

[Police Act 1996, s 1 as amended by the Greater London Authority Act 1999, Schs 27 and 34, the Local Government and Public Involvement in Health Act 2007, Sch 2 and the Policing and Crime Act 2017, s 124.]

[1] The Police Act 1996 shall come into force in accordance with the provisions of s 104, post. All the provisions reproduced here are in force.

[2] Part I comprises ss 1–35.

*Forces outside London*

7.9181 **2. Maintenance of police forces** (1) A police force shall be maintained for every police area for the time being listed in Schedule 1.

(2) For further provision about the maintenance of those police forces, see Chapter 1 of Part 1 of the Police Reform and Social Responsibility Act 2011.]

[Police Act 1996, s 2 as amended by the Police Reform and Social Responsibility Act 2011, Sch 16.]

7.9182 **5A. Maintenance of the metropolitan police force** (1) A police force shall be maintained for the metropolitan police district.

(2) For further provision about the maintenance of the metropolitan police force, see Chapter 2 of Part 1 of the Police Reform and Social Responsibility Act 2011.

[Police Act 1996, s 5A as inserted by the Greater London Authority Act 1999, s 310 and amended by the Police Reform and Social Responsibility Act 2011, Sch 16.]

*General provisions*

7.9183 **23–25.** ***Collaboration agreements, aid of one police force by another and provision of special services***

7.9184 **29. Attestation of constables**[1] Every member of a police force maintained for a police area and every special constable appointed for a police area shall, on appointment, be attested as a constable by making a declaration in the form set out in Schedule 4—

(*a*) *repealed*,

(*b*) before a justice of the peace having jurisdiction within the police area.

[Police Act 1996, s 29 as amended by the Greater London Authority Act 1999, Schs 27 and 34.]

---

[1] This section applies to a constable or special constable of the British Transport Police Force with the omission of the words in paragraph (*b*) "having jurisdiction within the police area" (Railways and Transport Safety Act 2003, ss 24 and 25).

7.9185 **30. Jurisdiction of constables** (1) A member of a police force shall have all the powers and privileges of a constable throughout England and Wales and the adjacent United Kingdom waters.

(2) A special constable shall have all the powers and privileges of a constable throughout England and Wales and the adjacent United Kingdom waters.[1]

(3) *Repealed.*

(3A) A member of the British Transport Police Force who is for the time being required by virtue of section 22A to serve with a police force maintained by a local policing body shall have all the powers and privileges of a member of that police force.

(3B) Where a member of the British Transport Police Force is for the time being under the direction and control of the chief officer of another police force by virtue of a collaboration agreement under section 22A, the member shall have all the powers and privileges of a member of that other force.

(3C) In subsection (3B), "police force" and "chief officer" have the meanings given by section 23I.

(4) *Repealed.*

(5) In this section—

"powers" includes powers under any enactment, whenever passed or made;

"United Kingdom waters" means the sea and other waters within the seaward limits of the territorial sea;

and this section, so far as it relates to powers under any enactment, makes them exercisable throughout the United Kingdom waters whether or not the enactment applies to those waters apart from this provision.

(6) This section is without prejudice to—

(*a*) sections 98 and 99 below[2]; and

(*b*) to any other enactment conferring powers on constables for particular purposes.

[Police Act 1996, s 30 as amended by the Anti-terrorism, Crime and Security Act 2001, Sch 7, the Police and Justice Act 2006, Schs 2 and 15, the Policing and Crime Act 2009, Sch 7 and the Police Reform and Social Responsibility Act 2011, Sch 16.]

---

[1] By ss 1 and 2 of the Metropolitan Police Act 1860 (as amended by the Defence (Transfer of Functions) (No 1) Order 1964) constables of the Metropolitan Police Force could be employed in HM yards (which by s 6 of the Air Force (Application of Enactments) (No 2) Order 1918, includes steam factory yards and aircraft factories) or at HM principal military or air force stations in England and Wales and within 15 miles of such yards or stations. Any two justices may appoint persons nominated by the Minister of Aviation to be special constables on any premises vested in the Minister or under his control (Civil Aviation Act 1982, s 57). Any two justices may appoint persons nominated by the Defence Council, who will exclusively control them with power to suspend their employment, to be special constables within the yards and stations and limits within which constables of the Metropolitan Police Force may by the Metropolitan Police Act 1860, both as originally enacted and as applied to the Air Force, be employed (Special Constables Act 1923, s 3 (as amended)). The Metropolitan Police Act 1860 is repealed by the Police Act 1964, Sch 10, but not so far as it is applied by the Special Constables Act 1923 (for transitional provisions and savings, see the Police Act 1996, Sch 8). The power conferred by s 8 of the 1923 Act shall extend to the appointment of persons so nominated to be special constables in, and within 15 miles of, any other premises in Great Britain which are for the time being in the possession or under the control of the Defence Council, the Secretary of State for Defence or the Minister of Aviation, or are for the time being used for or in connection with naval, military or air force purposes, and the said s 3 shall have effect accordingly (Emergency Laws (Miscellaneous Provisions) Act 1947, Sch 2, para 1 (as amended)). These powers are related to the property of service authorities of a visiting force and to persons subject to the service law of any such force by the Visiting Forces and International Headquarters (Application of Law) Order 1965, SI 1965/1536, art 6. The Order extends to the international headquarters and defence organisations specified therein. For application of these provisions to premises in the

possession or under the control of the United Kingdom Atomic Energy Authority, see the Atomic Energy Authority 1954, Sch 3. As to the effect of change in police authority areas, see the Transfer of Police Officers Order 1974, SI 1974/551.

2 These sections provide for cross border aid of one police force by another and for jurisdiction of metropolitan police officers on particular duties in Scotland or Northern Ireland. See note to the Magistrates' Courts Act 1980, s 125(2), in PART I: MAGISTRATES' COURTS, PROCEDURE, ante.

## PART II[1]

## CENTRAL SUPERVISION, DIRECTION AND FACILITIES

*Functions of Secretary of State*

7.9186 **36. General duty of Secretary of State** (1) The Secretary of State shall exercise his powers[2] under the provisions of this Act referred to in subsection (2) in such manner and to such extent as appears to him to be best calculated to promote the efficiency and effectiveness of the police.

(2) The provisions of this Act mentioned in subsection (1) are—

(*a*) Part I;

(*b*) this Part;

(*c*) Part III;

(*d*) in Chapter II of Part IV, sections 84 and 85 and Schedule 6; and

(*e*) in Part V, section 95.

[Police Act 1996, s 36 as amended by the Criminal Justice and Immigration Act 2008, Sch 22 and the Anti-social Behaviour, Crime and Policing Act 2014, Sch 11.]

1 Part II comprises ss 36–58.

2 These include in respect of police authorities, the setting of objectives, performance targets and directions to take remedial measures after an adverse inspection report, the submissions of reports, the setting of a minimum budget and the issue of a Code of Practice by the Secretary of State; in respect of Chief Constables their retirement in the interest of efficiency or effectiveness and the submission of reports; the provision of criminal statistics; the making of grants for police purposes.

**7.9187 50.** *Regulations for police forces[1].*

1 The following regulations have been made: Police (Promotion) Regulations 1996, SI 1996/1685 amended by SI 2002/767, SI 2003/2595, SI 2005/178, SI 2006/594 and 1442, SI 2008/273, SI 2013/1780, 2793 and SI 2015/453; Police Appeals Tribunal Rules 1999, SI 1999/818 amended by SI 2003/527 and 2597, SI 2006/594, SI 2008/2683 and SI 2011/3029; Police Regulations 2003, SI 2003/527 amended by SI 2003/2594, SI 2004/3216, SI 2005/2834, SI 2006/594, 1467, 2278 and 3449, SI 2007/1160 and 1162, SI 2008/2865, SI 2011/3026, SI 2012/192, 680, 1960, 2712, 3058, SI 2013/2318, SI 2014/2372, SI 2015/455 and SI 2016/798 and 1200; Police (Performance) Regulations 2012, SI 2012/2631 amended by SI 2014/2403; Police Conduct Regulations 2012, SI 2012/2632 amended by SI 2014/3347 and SI 2015/626.

**7.9188 51.** *Regulations for special constables[1].*

1 The Special Constables Regulations 1965, SI 1965/536 amended by SI 1968/899 (revoked), SI 1992/1526 (revoked) and 1641, SI 2002/3180 and SI 2004/645, SI 2006/2278, SI 2007/1162, SI 2012/1961 and SI 2015/461; Police (Performance) Regulations 2008, SI 2008/2862 amended by SI 2011/3027 have been made.

**7.9189 52.** *Regulations for police cadets[1].*

1 The Police Cadets Regulations 1979, SI 1979/1727 amended by SI 1982/350 and 1487, SI 1983/161, SI 1984/1633, SI 1985/131 and 686, SI 1987/1754, SI 1988/728, 1992/276 and SI 1993/2528 have been made.

**7.9190 53.** *Regulations as to standard of equipment.[1]*

**7.9190A 53A.** *Regulation of procedures and practices.*

**7.9190B 53B–53D.** *Police Senior Appointments Panel.*

1 The Police Act 1996 (Equipment) Regulations 2011, SI 2011/300 amended by SI 2014/395 have been made.

**7.9191 54–56.** *Inspectorate of Constabulary.*

**7.9192 57.** *Secretary of State may provide or contribute to common services to promote the efficiency or effectiveness of the police.*

## PART V[1]

## MISCELLANEOUS AND GENERAL

*Offences*

**7.9193 89. Assaults on constables[2]** (1) Any person who assaults a constable in the execution of his duty[3], or a person assisting a constable in the execution of his duty[4], shall be guilty of an offence and liable on summary conviction to imprisonment for a term not exceeding **six months** or to a fine not exceeding **level 5** on the standard scale, or to **both**.

(2) Any person who resists or wilfully[5] obstructs[6] a constable in the execution of his duty, or a person assisting a constable in the execution of his duty[7], shall be guilty of an offence[8] and liable on summary conviction to imprisonment for a term not exceeding **one month** * or to a fine not exceeding **level 3** on the standard scale, or to **both**.

(3) This section also applies to a constable who is a member of a police force maintained in Scotland or Northern Ireland when he is executing a warrant, or otherwise acting in England or

Wales, by virtue of any enactment conferring powers on him in England and Wales.

(4) In this section references to a person assisting a constable in the execution of his duty include references to any person who is neither a constable nor in the company of a constable but who—

(*a*) is a member of an international joint investigation team that is led by a member of a police force; and

(*b*) is carrying out his functions as a member of that team.

(5) In this section "international joint investigation team" means any investigation team formed in accordance with—

(*a*) any framework decision on joint investigation teams adopted under Article 34 of the Treaty on European Union;

(*b*) the Convention on Mutual Assistance in Criminal Matters between the Member States of the European Union, and the Protocol to that Convention, established in accordance with that Article of that Treaty; or

(*c*) any international agreement to which the United Kingdom is a party and which is specified for the purposes of this section in an order[9] made by the Secretary of State.

(6) A statutory instrument containing an order under subsection (5) shall be subject to annulment in pursuance of a resolution of either House of Parliament.

[Police Act 1996, s 89 as amended by the Police Reform Act 2002, s 104 and the Serious Organised Crime and Police Act 2005, Sch 4.]

---

* **"51 weeks" substituted by the Criminal Justice Act 2003, Sch 26 from a date to be appointed.**

1 Part V comprises ss 89–106.

2 Subsections (1) and (2) apply in relation to a constable of the British Transport Police (Railways and Transport Safety Act 2003, s 68).

The normal mental element of assault – intention or subjective recklessness – applies to this offence. In relation to recklessness, and the need to set out the facts or matters capable of supporting such a finding, see *Cooper v DPP* [2002] EWHC Admin 1878, [2203] Crim LR 116 and *D v DPP* [2005] EWHC 967 (Admin), [2005] Crim LR 962.

3 It is not always clear how far this duty extends. It is sufficient in the case of all peace officers to prove that they acted in that character, without producing their appointment (*Berryman v Wise* (1791) 4 Term Rep 366); and in *Butler v Ford* (1833) 1 Cr & M 662, the court held that proof of acting was sufficient, although the constable was appointed under a local Act. In order to substantiate an offence of assaulting a police officer in the execution of his duty by a person who had been arrested for obstruction of police officers when engaged in the arrest of a third party, it is necessary for the justices to find that the arrest of the third party was lawful, which it is not open to them to do if they are not told of the reason for the arrest: *Riley v DPP* (1989) 154 JP 453, 91 Cr App Rep 14; followed in *R (on the application of Odewale) v DPP* CO/1381/2000 where it was held that justices were not entitled to infer that a police officer was acting in the course of his duty in carrying out a search pursuant to s 18 of PACE from his bare, albeit unchallenged, assertion in evidence that he was carrying out such a search (*Riley v DPP* (1989) 154 JP 453, 91 Cr App Rep 14).

If a person is unlawfully arrested (due to lack of reasonable grounds for suspicion) that person cannot be guilty of resisting, not only the arresting officer, but also any officer that who comes to assist him to complete the arrest (unless he has used unreasonable force against the first officer); similarly, while a police officer is entitled to use reasonable force to prevent a breach of the peace, if the actual or threatened breach of the peace is indissolubly linked with the unlawful arrest of another and is not directed at anyone else, any officer seeking to prevent that interference or protest is not acting in the course of his duty any more than the arresting officer, though the position would be different if the breach of the peace were independent and free-standing: *Cumberbatch v Crown Prosecution Service; Ali v DPP* [2009] EWHC 3353 (Admin), 174 JP 149. There is a distinction, however, between an unlawful act and an act which is not unlawful but is intended to lead to an unlawful act. Thus, where a community support officer put out his hand to stop a person she intended (unlawfully) to detain to be searched from drugs by a police constable but did not make physical contact with that person, and that person pushed past the officer causing her to stumble, the officer was acting in the execution of her duty. It was irrelevant that within a short while she would not have been so acting: *D v DPP* [2010] EWHC 3400 (Admin), [2011] 1 WLR 882, applied in *Tester v DPP* [2015] EWHC 1353 (Admin), [2015] Crim LR 812. Where an officer's search of a person was unlawful (owing to non-compliance with the requirements of s 2 of PACE), a sufficient gap in time (a matter for the judgment of the court) may make a subsequent incident separate and distinct so that the officer is then acting in the execution of his duty: *Sobczak v DPP* [2012] EWHC 1319 (Admin), 176 JP 575, [2013] Crim LR 515, 176 CL & J 371.

As to the need to consider alternatives to arrest (the necessity condition) see s 24 of PACE 1984 in Part 1 Magistrates' Courts, Procedure, ante, and the notes thereto, in particular the decision in *Hayes v Chief Constable of Merseyside Police* [2011] EWCA Civ 911, [2012] 1 WLR 517, [2011] 2 Cr App R 30. What has to be shown is: (i) that the constable actually believed that arrest was necessary, and for a subs (5) reason; and (ii) that objectively that belief was reasonable.

As to what constitutes reasonable grounds to suspect the commission of an offence contrary to s 5 of the Public Order Act 1986, see *R (on the application of Reda) v DPP* [2011] EWHC 1550, 175 JP 329.

In *R v Forbes* (1865) 10 Cox CC 362, the defendant was convicted before the Recorder of London for assaulting two police officers who were in plain clothes, although the prisoner contended that he did not know the men were constables. This decision was approved by the Court of Criminal Appeal in *R v Maxwell and Clanchy* (1909) 73 JP 176 (see Treat 31 JP 225). It is not a defence to a charge of assault if the defendant honestly and mistakenly disbelieved the identity of an officer and believed that his actions were justified in self-defence, unless there were reasonable grounds for that belief (*Albert v Lavin* [1982] AC 546, [1981] 1 All ER 628, 145 JP 184, CA; affd [1982] AC 546, [1981] 3 All ER 878, 146 JP 78, HL). In *R v Mark* [1961] Crim LR 173, Maxwell Turner, J, ruled that if it were found as a fact that the defendant acted under a genuine belief, honestly and reasonably held, that the constable assaulted was committing a crime or breach of the peace this would be a good defence. In *R v Fennell* [1971] 1 QB 428, [1970] 3 All ER 215, 134 JP 678, the Court of Appeal reserved the question, whether an assault would be justifiable to release another person wrongfully arrested, but held that if the arrest is, in fact, lawful an assault is not justifiable even if it is honestly believed on reasonable grounds that the arrest was unlawful.

Where a constable is empowered at common law or by statute to search a person on reasonable suspicion, he acts when so doing in the execution of his duty, and an assault upon him is not excused by the fact that the search does not confirm the reasonable suspicion (*Willey v Peace* [1951] 1 KB 94, [1950] 2 All ER 724, 114 JP 502). A custody sergeant is entitled to remove obstructive or abusive persons from his custody suite and provided that, in the course of that, he uses no more force than is reasonable he is acting in the course of his duty (*R (on the application of Bucher) v DPP* [2003] EWHC 580 (Admin), CO/4484/2002, (2003) 167 JPN 182). Where, however, a constable took hold of a missing 14-year-old girl by her elbow and told her that she had to come with him, he had exceeded his duty; he should have told her that he had spoken to her father, her father wanted her home and he proposed to take her home (*C v DPP* [2003] All ER (D) 37 (Nov), 167 JPN 864).

A constable may only use force to the extent that this is permitted by common law or statute; by virtue of the Criminal Law Act 1967, s 3, an officer was entitled to use reasonable force (by pushing away) against a person who had made it clear by his words and actions that he intended to continue to obstruct that and another officer as they were attempting to take away two men who had been arrested following a public disturbance. Burnton LJ added that, in any event, the push had no bearing on the question whether the appellant's conduct before that time amounted to wilful obstruction. An unlawful push cannot retrospectively render conduct lawful, which was otherwise criminal (see para 14 of the judgment): *Metcalf v Crown Prosecution Service* [2015] EWHC 1091 (Admin), [2015] 2 Cr App Rep 349, 179 JP 288, [2015] Crim LR 722.

In *McCann v Crown Prosecution Service* [2015] EWHC 2461 (Admin), 179 JP 470, [2016] 1 Cr App R 6, [2016] Crim LR 59 in the course of an anti "fracking" protest, the defendant and other were seated in the middle of the road, locked together and thereby preventing lorries heading for the drilling site from passing. The local police inspector instructed the defendant and those locked with her to move. They refused on the ground, subsequently accepted to be correct, that the passageway was a private road with a public footpath. The inspector believed the road to be a public highway and the defendant was arrested for obstructing the highway. Shortly afterwards, the appellant was further arrested for obstructing a police officer, contrary to s 89(2) of the Police Act 1996 and this was the charge which proceeded to trial. It was submitted by the defence that even if the officer had been acting in good faith or that the error was reasonable, it did not make the request to move lawful and, consequently, the inspector was not acting in the execution of his duty. The district judge rejected this argument, holding that it mattered not that the officer had the wrong offence in mind because her belief, albeit mistaken, was reasonable, she acted in response to the same activity and the same mischief and the facts could have lent themselves to another offence (aggravated trespass). The defendant was convicted and appealed by way of case stated.

The appeal proceeded on two grounds only: whether the mistake of fact regarding the classification of the road was unreasonable so as to place the inspector outside the execution of her duty; and whether in the circumstances the inspector could not be acting within the execution of her duty on the basis that another offence, namely aggravated trespass, may have been committed. The respondent submitted that the essential question was whether the inspector was acting in the course of her duty in giving the direction to move, and that the focus of the appellant's on the reasonableness of the mistake and on powers of arrest was misplaced.

Following an extensive review of the authorities, Treacy LJ held:

> "27. In this case the inspector's request or direction to the appellant to move could not in the circumstances amount to anything which was prima facie any unlawful interference with the appellant's liberty or property. Indeed, it was accepted on behalf of the appellant that had the officer's direction been given in different terms, she might or would have moved. This is a clear indicator that the matter raised is one of form rather than of substance. The inspector's duty in this case was to secure the lawful passage of the vehicles across the land. Put differently, she reasonably perceived that her task was to prevent any person from committing crime by unlawfully obstructing their passing. Her plan was first to request the appellant and her associates to move and, if they did not, to arrest them for an offence under the Highways Act 1980 and to move them by force. By refusing to move when asked to do so, the appellant gave her reasonable grounds to suspect that she intended to continue to obstruct the highway wilfully. That same act of wilful obstruction would not only obstruct the highway but also the inspector in the execution of her duty to clear it. Accordingly, she could choose which offence to arrest for, and chose both. The issue is whether that plan was reasonable and lawful. There was nothing unlawful about asking the appellant to move and informing her that if she does not she will be committing a criminal offence. It would not, however, be reasonable for a police officer to do that unless she reasonably believed that it was true and was acting in good faith. The request carried an express or implied threat that an arrest would follow unless there was compliance. Whether that threat was reasonably made depended on whether any arrest would be lawful.
>
> 28. The question therefore arises as to whether the fact that the officer had the wrong offence in mind affects the position. I return to Lord Simonds' observations *in Christie v. Leachinsky* to the effect that it is not an essential condition of lawful arrest that the constable should formulate any charge at all, much less a charge which may ultimately be found in the indictment. What is required is that the arrested person be told what is the act for which he is being arrested. Lord Simonds said:
>
> > "This is I think, the fundamental principle, viz, that a man is entitled to know what, in the apt words of Lawrence LJ, are 'the facts which are said to constitute a crime on his part.'"
>
> 29. More recently in *Chapman v DPP* (1989) 89 Cr App R 190 [(1989) 153 JP 27], at p.197 Bingham LJ, as he then was, said:
>
> > "It is not of course to be expected that a police constable in the heat of an emergency, or while in hot pursuit of a suspected criminal, should always have in mind specific statutory provisions, or that he should mentally identify specific offences with technicality or precision. He must, in my judgment, reasonably suspect the existence of facts amounting to an arrestable offence of a kind which he has in mind."
>
> 30. That was a decision made in a context where at that time s.24(6) of the Police and Criminal Evidence Act 1984 required a constable to have reasonable grounds for suspecting that an arrestable offence had been committed before he could arrest without warrant. That particular provision has subsequently been amended, but the passage cited is consistent with what was said in *Christie v Leachinsky* about the absence of formality involved. Those authorities relate to the formalities of arrest, but it seems to me that there is no reason why similar principles should not apply to the directions of the officer in the phase immediately preceding arrest.
>
> 31. I therefore conclude that it was not necessary for the officer to have had the correct offence in mind at the time the direction to move was given. It was sufficient for the officer to have taken steps which reasonably appeared to her to be necessary for preventing crime. The fact that the officer in fact had an offence of which the appellant was not guilty in mind did not prevent her from taking steps which in the circumstances, as she believed them to be, reasonably appeared to her to be necessary for preventing crime.
>
> 32. In the light of the findings that the officer reasonably believed at the material time that the road was a public highway and that she had reasonable grounds to suspect that an offence was being committed, I would hold that the officer was acting within the execution of her duty..."

If a constable apprehends on reasonable grounds that a breach of the peace may be committed, he is not only entitled, but is under a duty, to take reasonable steps to prevent that breach occurring. Provided he honestly and reasonably forms the opinion that there is a real risk of a breach of the peace in the sense that it is in close proximity both in place and time, then the conditions exist for reasonable preventive action. Accordingly, where police officers stopped a convoy of striking miners whom they believed were intending to demonstrate and form a mass picket at one or more of four collieries in the area, it was held that the police officers acted reasonably and in the execution of their duty by preventing the striking miners from passing through the police cordon and, when they did attempt to force their way through the cordon, were justified in arresting them on the ground that if they proceeded it was feared a breach of the peace would occur at one of the collieries (*Moss v McLachlan* (1984) 149 JP 167, [1985] IRLR 76). Officers who have helped a youth leader eject persons from a youth club and who are subsequently assaulted, may be acting in the execution of their duty (*Coffin v Smith* (1980) 71 Cr App Rep 221). Where a police officer genuinely suspects on reasonable grounds that a breach of the peace is likely to occur inside private premises he is entitled to exercise his common law power to arrest for breach of the peace without a warrant (*McConnell v Chief Constable of the Greater Manchester Police* [1990] 1 All ER 423, [1990] 1 WLR 364, CA).

In *R (on the application of Laporte) v Chief Constable of Gloucestershire Constabulary* [2006] UKHL 55, [2007] 2 AC 105, [2007] 2 All ER 529, [2007] 2 WLR 46, persons travelling by coach to a demonstration were stopped, the coaches were prevented from proceeding and were forcibly returned and the protesters were detained on the coaches throughout the return journey. The question arose as to whether this police action, which was short of arrest, was legitimate. The House of Lords held that the common law entitled and bound all police officers and citizens alike to seek to prevent, by arrest or action short of arrest, any breach of the peace occurring in their presence, or which they reasonably believed was about to occur, but where no breach of the peace had yet occurred a reasonable apprehension of an imminent breach was required before any form of preventive action was permissible. The police could not, therefore, take whatever action short of arrest they reasonably judged to be reasonable to prevent a breach of the peace which was not sufficiently imminent to justify arrest. Since there had been no indication of any imminent breach of the peace when the coaches were intercepted and searched, and since the defendant had not considered that such a breach was then likely to occur, the action taken in preventing the claimant from continuing to the demonstration had been an interference with her right to demonstrate at a lawful assembly which was not prescribed by domestic law.

The test of the reasonableness of a constable's action is objective in the sense that it is for the court to decide not whether the view taken by the constable fell within the broad band of rational decisions but whether in the light of what he knew and perceived at the time the court is satisfied that it was reasonable to fear an imminent breach of the peace. Accordingly, although reasonableness of belief is a question for the court, it is to be evaluated without the qualifications of hindsight. The court must restrict itself to considering the reasonableness, in the context of the events, of the constable's assessment of the imminence of a breach of the peace; it is not for the court to form its own assessment of that imminence (*R (on the application of Moos) v Commissioner of Police for the Metropolis* [2012] EWCA Civ 12, [2012] All ER (D) 83 (Jan)). The next and critical question for the constable, and in turn for the court, is where the threat is coming from, because it is there that the preventative action must be directed. If there is no real threat, no question of intervention for breach of the peace arises. If the defendant is being so provocative that someone in the crowd, without behaving wholly unreasonably, might be moved to violence, the constable is entitled to ask him to stop and arrest him if he will not. If the threat of disorder or violence is coming from passers-by who are taking that opportunity to react so as to cause trouble, then it is they and not the defendant who should be asked to desist and arrested if they will not (*Redmond-Bate v DPP* (1999) 163 JP 789, [1999] Crim LR 998 – constable held not to be acting in the execution of his duty when he required three women preachers to stop preaching from the steps of a cathedral because some of those in the crowd that had gathered were showing hostility towards the preachers and he feared a breach of the peace).

Where a constable is given permission to enter premises, it is necessary to approach with common sense the terms of the licence given by the occupier. Thus, where a constable was asked to enter premises to remove the party's partner, the common sense terms of the constable's licence permitted him to speak to the partner to get his side of the story, and when the partner said to the constable 'Fuck off this is nothing to do with you' this could, but did not necessarily, amount to a request to leave the premises since other constructions, for example the mere use of abuse, were capable of being made: *Marsden v Crown Prosecution Service* [2014] EWHC 3359 (Admin), 178 JP 497.

When a constable enters private premises found insecure at night in order to protect private property therein, he is not acting in the execution of his duty (*Great Central Rly Co v Bates* [1921] 3 KB 578; as explained by Du Parcq, J, in *Davis v Lisle*, infra). Nor when he is assaulted after being requested by the occupier to leave his garage that he has entered without a warrant in order to make inquiries; but if the assault occurred when he is acting on a request to leave the premises or while he was where he was entitled to be by implied licence, eg, in the pathway leading to the door of the premises, an offence would be committed (*Davis v Lisle* [1936] 2 KB 434, [1936] 2 All ER 213, 100 JP 280; *Robson v Hallett* [1967] 2 QB 939, [1967] 2 All ER 407, 131 JP 333). A police officer is entitled to remain on premises to prevent a breach of the peace even though he is there as a trespasser. Where an officer visited a house and told one of the occupiers (D) that he had come to speak to a member of the household (S) and the officer was allowed entry by D, and the officer then told S that he was under arrest, the justices were entitled to conclude that D had given informed consent to the officer to enter; the officer had not acted covertly and, given the family's previous dealings with the police, it would have been obvious why the officer wanted to speak to S: *Hobson v Chief Constable of Cheshire Constabulary* [2003] EWHC 3011 (Admin), (2003) 168 JP 111. The officer is not obliged to nullify his trespass by leaving the premises before returning to deal with the breach of the peace (*Lamb v DPP* (1989) 154 JP 381). The activation of a burglar alarm in a police station gives a constable an implied authority to enter the premises to investigate the matter, and having entered as a licensee, a reasonable time must be allowed for investigation before the licence is revoked (*Kay v Hibbert* [1977] Crim LR 226). In *Great Central Rly Co v Bates*, supra, Atkin, LJ, said: "It appears to be very important that it should be established that nobody has a right to enter premises except strictly in accordance with authority." It is the duty of a constable to stop a breach of the peace and to take the necessary steps to prevent one that he reasonably apprehends is likely to take place. Accordingly, if he reasonably apprehends that a breach of the peace in the vicinity will be caused by the holding of a public meeting in a street, he is acting in the execution of his duty in requesting the promoter to desist and in taking all requisite steps to stop the meeting (*Duncan v Jones* [1936] 1 KB 218, 99 JP 399; See also *Thomas v Sawkins* [1935] 2 KB 249, [1935] All ER Rep 655, 99 JP 295; cf *Davies v Griffiths* [1937] 2 All ER 671, 101 JP 247). The Sessional Orders of the House of Commons requiring metropolitan police constables to prevent obstruction of streets leading to that House are binding on them, and therefore those constables are in the execution of their duty when taking steps to prevent that obstruction (*Pankhurst v Jarvis* (1910) 74 JP 64; *Despard v Wilcox* (1910) 74 JP 115). For officers acting in their duty to assist in dispersing public meetings, see *Laporte v Commissioner of Police of the Metropolis* [2014] EWHC 3574 (QB), [2015] 3 All ER 438, [2014] All ER (D) 11 (Nov) and the Public Meeting Act 1908 and notes thereto, in the title, PUBLIC MEETING AND PUBLIC ORDER, post.

Powers to stop and search, enter premises, arrest etc are now extensively defined by the Police and Criminal Evidence Act 1984. See generally paras 1.170 to para 1.190, ante, PART I: MAGISTRATES' COURTS, PROCEDURE. A court may in appropriate circumstances infer that an entry on private property was justified by a search warrant without seeing the warrant: *Sykes v Crown Prosecution Service (Manchester)* [2013] EWHC 3600 (Admin), [2014] Crim LR 542.

A person charged in the information with assaulting a constable in the execution of his duty cannot be convicted of a common assault on the hearing of such information (*R v Brickill* (1860) 28 JP 359); but a fresh information may be laid.

4 Where a constable, acting in the execution of his duty by questioning the defendant, goes outside his duty by catching hold of that person to detain him, the defence of justification of self-defence to an offence under this section will succeed if the defendant did not use unreasonable force to resist the detention (*Kenlin v Gardiner* [1967] 2 QB 510, [1966] 3 All ER 931, 131 JP 91). The fact that a defendant mistakenly believes he is being arrested when in fact he is not and the

restraint is unlawful, does not impact on his entitlement to resist such unlawful restraint (*R v McKoy* (2002) Times, 17 June, CA).

[5] A person wilfully obstructs a police constable in the execution of his duty if he deliberately does an act which, though not necessarily "aimed at" or "hostile to" the police, in fact prevents a constable from carrying out his duty or makes it more difficult for him to do so, and if he knows and intends (whether or not that is his predominant intention) that his conduct will have that effect; the motive with which the act is committed is irrelevant unless it constitutes a lawful excuse for the obstruction (*Lewis v Cox* [1985] QB 509, [1984] 3 All ER 672, 148 JP 601). It is immaterial that the defendant does not appreciate that his action amounted to obstruction (*Moore v Green* [1983] 1 All ER 663). A person cannot obstruct a police officer in the execution of his duty when he reasonably believes that he is not a police officer (*Ostler v Elliott* [1980] Crim LR 584).

[6] A person who simply gave drivers of motor cars notice of a "police trap" was held not guilty of obstruction under an enactment replaced by this subsection (*Bastable v Little* [1907] 1 KB 59, 71 JP 52). The obstruction, however, is not limited to physical obstruction, so where cars when warned of a police trap are being driven at an illegal speed, the person so warning may be convicted of obstruction (*Betts v Stevens* [1910] 1 KB 1, 73 JP 486; *Bastable v Little*, supra distinguished). But see *Green v Moore* [1982] 1 All ER 428, 146 JP 142, where the Divisional Court criticised the decision in *Bastable v Little*, supra, and expressed the view that it should be strictly confined to its own facts. In *Green v Moore*, supra, the court was unable to find any distinction between a warning given in order that the commission of a crime might be suspended whilst there is a danger of detection and one which is given in order that the commission of a crime may be postponed until after the danger of detection has passed. In *R (on the application of DPP) v Glendinning* [2005] EWHC Admin 2333, 169 JP 649, however, it was re-affirmed that a conviction for obstruction required evidence that there were vehicles that were speeding or were likely to speed at the location of the speed trap. A person's mere refusal to answer a constable's questions which, in the circumstances, he was not legally obliged to answer, is not caught by the section (*Rice v Connolly* [1966] 2 QB 414, [1966] 2 All ER 649, 130 JP 322), but in *Ricketts v Cox* (1981) 74 Cr App Rep 298, [1982] Crim LR 184, it was held that a defendant who was abusive, un-cooperative and positively hostile to police officers, using obscene language calculated to provoke and antagonise the officers, amounted to obstruction. Running off to avoid apprehension amounts to an act that is capable of constituting the wilful obstruction of a police officer: *Sekfall, Banamira and Ouham v DPP* [2006] EWHC 894 (Admin), 170 JP 393. While it is lawful for a third party to advise a suspect of his right not to answer questions put to him by a police officer, if the third party by his abusive, persistent and unruly behaviour, acts in a way that goes well beyond the exercise of his legal rights and prevents communication between the officer and the suspect, or makes it more difficult, he will be guilty of obstructing the police; see *Green v DPP* (1991) 155 JP 816, DC. In *Ingleton v Dibble* [1972] 1 QB 480, [1972] 1 All ER 275, 136 JP 155, it was held that there was a distinction between a refusal to act (as in *Rice v Connolly*, supra) and the doing of some positive act, and that it was not necessary to show, where the obstruction consists of a positive act, that it must be unlawful independently. It was held that the driver of a motor car who drank whisky after being asked to take a breath test with the object and effect of frustrating the procedure under ss 2 and 3 of the Road Safety Act 1967 was guilty of obstructing the police, and in *R v Britton* [1973] Crim LR 375 a similar action with a bottle of beer led to a conviction for the common law misdemeanour of attempting to defeat the due course of justice. A private citizen can never have a lawful excuse for interfering with an arrest by a police officer which is lawful (*Hills v Ellis* [1983] QB 680, [1983] 1 All ER 667).

A person who shouted, outside a public house, outside "permitted hours", that the police were waiting to enter, was rightly convicted (*Hinchliffe v Sheldon* [1955] 3 All ER 406, 120 JP 13). Failure to accord entry to police officers acting under s 4 of the Road Traffic Act 1988 may be a wilful obstruction (*Lunt v DPP* [1993] Crim LR 534). Persons waiting outside the residence of the Prime Minister to present a petition, and refusing to go away when requested by the police, were held rightly convicted under an enactment replaced by this subsection (*Despard v Wilcox* (1910) 74 JP 115; see also *Pankhurst v Jarvis* (1910) 74 JP 64); so also were persons acting as pickets in connection with a trade dispute who refused to move when requested by a police officer who was limiting the number of pickets to what was reasonable because of an anticipated breach of the peace (*Piddington v Bates, Robson v Ribton-Turner* [1960] 3 All ER 660). An offence was committed under this section where an excessive number of pickets carried on a circling manœuvre and obstructed the highway causing vehicles to stop, although there was no anticipated breach of the peace (*Tynan v Balmar* [1967] 1 QB 91, [1966] 2 All ER 133). Striking miners, intending to join a mass picket at a local colliery, who attempted to force their way through a police cordon which had been set up to prevent a breach of the peace occurring at one or more of four collieries, were held to have been properly convicted (*Moss v McLachlan* (1984) 149 JP 167, [1985] IRLR 76). A person shooting by "firing wide" is guilty of resisting or wilfully obstructing a constable in the execution of his duty (*R v Hufflett* (1919) 84 JP 24). A police officer can require other persons to break traffic regulations if it is reasonably necessary to protect life or property; refusal to comply is an obstruction (*Johnson v Phillips* [1975] 3 All ER 682, 140 JP 37). Where the police have removed the driver of a motor car, they have a duty to see that the vehicle is properly looked after; that might be done where the passenger shows the capacity and right to do so but not where he appears unfit. If the passenger then prevents the constable from taking the car he will be guilty of obstruction: *Liepens v Spearman* [1985] Crim LR 229.

[7] See note 2, ante.

[8] Unless one of the general arrest conditions under s 25 of the Police and Criminal Evidence Act 1984 applies, there is no statutory power of arrest for the offence of obstructing a police officer in the execution of his duties. While there is no common law power to arrest for obstruction per se, there is a common law power to arrest for such an obstruction where its nature was such that it actually caused, or was likely to cause, a breach of the peace, or was calculated to prevent the lawful arrest or detention of another (*Wershof v Metropolitan Police Comr* [1978] 3 All ER 540; *R v Redman* [1994] Crim LR 914). Note that s 25 of PACE has subsequently been repealed and s 24 has been amended to provide a general power of arrest where the offence and necessity grounds therein set out are satisfied.

[9] The following International Joint Investigation Teams (International Agreement) Orders have been made which have the effect that officials of a contributing party are regarded as officials of the hosting party for the purpose of any offences committed by or against them: 2004, SI 2004/1127 (Convention implementing the Schengen Agreement of 14 June 2004); 2009, SI 2009/3269 (Second Additional Protocol to the European Convention on Mutual Legal Assistance in Criminal Matters).

**7.9194 90. Impersonation, etc** (1) Any person who with intent to deceive impersonates a member of a police force[1] or special constable, or makes any statement or does any act calculated falsely to suggest that he is such a member or constable, shall be guilty of an offence and liable on summary conviction to imprisonment for a term not exceeding **six months** or to a fine not exceeding **level 5** on the standard scale, or to **both**.

(2) Any person who, not being a constable, wears any article of police uniform in circumstances where it gives him an appearance so nearly resembling that of a member of a police force[1] as to be calculated to deceive[2] shall be guilty of an offence and liable on summary conviction to a fine not exceeding **level 3** on the standard scale.

(3) Any person who, not being a member of a police force[1] or special constable, has in his possession any article of police uniform shall, unless he proves that he obtained possession of that article lawfully and has possession of it for a lawful purpose[3], be guilty of an offence and liable on

summary conviction to a fine not exceeding **level 1** on the standard scale.

(4) In this section—

(*a*) "article of police uniform" means any article of uniform or any distinctive badge or mark or document of identification usually issued to members of police forces or special constables, or anything having the appearance of such an article, badge, mark or document,

(*ab*) "member of a police force" includes a member of the staff of the National Policing Improvement Agency who is a constable, and

(*b*) "special constable" means a special constable appointed for a police area.

[Police Act 1996, s 90 as amended by the Anti-terrorism, Crime and Security Act 2001, Sch 7 and the Police and Justice Act 2006, Sch 1.]

1 This includes constables and special constables of the British Transport Police (Railways and Transport Safety Act 2003, s 68).

2 The words "calculated to deceive" mean "likely (or reasonably likely) to deceive" and do not involve that there should be an intention to deceive (*Turner v Shearer* [1973] 1 All ER 397, 137 JP 191).

3 Where a trader had possession of articles of police uniform for a commercial purpose, namely to sell them at a profit, the statutory defence did not require him to prove that he had taken steps to satisfy himself that his customers were buying the items from him for a lawful purpose. If he proved that he did not know or have reason to believe that the buyer had an illicit purpose, he had acted lawfully and succeeded in establishing the statutory defence: *Cooke v Director of Public Prosecutions* [2015] EWHC 2212 (Admin), 180 JP 27.

7.9195 **91. Causing disaffection** (1) Any person who causes, or attempts to cause, or does any act calculated to cause, disaffection amongst the members of any police force, or induces or attempts to induce, or does any act calculated to induce, any member of a police force to withhold his services, shall be guilty of an offence and liable[1]—

(*a*) on summary conviction, to imprisonment for a term not exceeding **six months** or to a fine not exceeding the **statutory maximum**, or to **both**;

(*b*) on conviction on indictment, to imprisonment for a term not exceeding **two years** or to a **fine**, or to **both**.

(2) This section applies in the case of—

(*a*) special constables appointed for a police area,

(*aa*) members of the staff of the National Policing Improvement Agency who are constables,

(*b*) members of the Civil Nuclear Constabulary, and

(*c*) members of the British Transport police force,

as it applies in the case of members of a police force.

(3) Liability under subsection (1) for any behaviour is in addition to any civil liability for that behaviour.

[Police Act 1996, s 91 as amended by the Anti-terrorism, Crime and Security Act 2001, Sch 7, the Energy Act 2004, s 68 and the Police and Justice Act 2006, Schs 1 and 14.]

1 For procedure in respect of an offence triable either way, see the Magistrates' Courts Act 1980, ss 17A–21, in PART I: MAGISTRATES' COURTS PROCEDURE, ante.

*Supplemental*

7.9196 **101. Interpretation** (1) Except where the context otherwise requires, in this Act—

"British Transport Police Force" means the constables appointed under section 53 of the British Transport Commission Act 1949 (c xxix);

"chief officer of police" means—

(*a*) In relation to a police force maintained under section 2, the chief constable,

(*b*) in relation to the metropolitan police force, the Commissioner of Police of the Metropolis, and

(*c*) in relation to the City of London police force, the Commissioner of Police for the City of London;

"City of London police area" means the City of London as defined for the purposes of the Acts relating to the City of London police force;

"Common Council" means the Common Council of the City of London in its capacity as police authority for the City of London police area;

"elected local policing body" means—

(*a*) a police and crime commissioner;

(*b*) the Mayor's Office for Policing and Crime;

"local policing body" means—

(*a*) a police and crime commissioner (in relation to a police area listed in Schedule 1);

(*b*) the Mayor's Office for Policing and Crime (in relation to the metropolitan police district);

(*c*) the Common Council (in relation to the City of London police area);

"Mayor's Office for Policing and Crime" means the body established under section 3 of the Police Reform and Social Responsibility Act 2011;

"metropolitan police district" means that district as defined in section 76 of the London Government Act 1963;

"national or international functions" means functions relating to—

(*a*) the protection of prominent persons or their residences,

(*b*) national security,

(*c*) counter-terrorism, or

(*d*) the provision of services for any other national or international purpose;

"the National Police Chiefs' Council" means the body called the National Police Chiefs' Council which was established in accordance with a collaboration agreement under section 22A above entered into on 1 April 2015;

"police and crime commissioner" means a body established under section 1 of the Police Reform and Social Responsibility Act 2011;

"police area" means a police area provided for by section 1;

"police force" means a force maintained by a local policing body;

"police fund" means—

(*a*) in relation to a police area for which there is an elected local policing body, the fund kept by that body under section 21 of the Police Reform and Social Responsibility Act 2011;

(*b*) *repealed*; and

(*c*) in relation to the City of London police force, the fund out of which the expenses of that force are paid.

(2) In this Act "police purposes", in relation to a police area, includes the purposes of—

(*a*) special constables appointed for that area,

(*b*) police cadets undergoing training with a view to becoming members of the police force maintained for that area, and

(*c*) civilians employed for the purposes of that force or of any such special constables or cadets.

(3) References in this Act to the staff of a police and crime commissioner, or to the staff of the Mayor's Office for Policing and Crime, have the same meaning as in the Police Reform and Social Responsibility Act 2011.

[Police Act 1996, s 101 as amended by the Greater Police Authority Act 1999, s 312 and Sch 34, the Anti-terrorism, Crime and Security Act 2001, Sch 7, the Police and Justice Act 2006, Sch 4, the Police Reform and Social Responsibility Act 2011, s 96 and the Policing and Crime Act 2017, Sch 14.]

**7.9197 102.** *Orders, rules and regulations.*

**7.9198 103.** *Consequential amendments, transitional provisions, repeals, etc.*

**7.9199 104. Commencement** (1) Except as provided by subsection (2), this Act shall come into force at the end of the period of three months beginning with the day on which it is passed.

(2) The following provisions of this Act—

section 50(3),

Part IV (including Schedules 5 and 6) other than section 88,

paragraphs 43, 45 and 46 of Schedule 7,

paragraph 12 of Schedule 8, and

Part II of Schedule 9,

shall come into force on such day as the Secretary of State may by order[1] appoint.

(3) An order under this section may appoint different days for different purposes or different areas.

(4) The power to make order under this section includes power to make such transitional provisions and savings as appear to the Secretary of State to be necessary or expedient.

(5) Where an order under this section contains provisions made by virtue of subsection (4), the statutory instrument containing that order shall be subject to annulment in pursuance of a resolution of either House of Parliament.

[Police Act 1996, s 104.]

---

[1] These remaining provisions of this Act were brought fully into force on 1 April 1999 by the Police Act 1996 (Commencement and Transitional Provisions) Order 1999, SI 1999/533.

**7.9200 105.** *Extent.*

**7.9201 106.** *Citation.*

## SCHEDULES

### SCHEDULE 4
FORM OF DECLARATION

Section 29

*(Substituted by the Police Reform Act 2002, s 83.)*

**7.9202** ["I . . . . . . . . . . . . of . . . . . . . . . . . . . do solemnly and sincerely declare and affirm that I will well and truly serve the Queen in the office of constable, with fairness, integrity, diligence and impartiality, upholding fundamental human rights and according equal respect to all people; and that I will, to the best of my power, cause the peace to be kept and preserved and prevent all offences against people and property; and that while I continue to hold the said office I will, to the best of my skill and knowledge, discharge all the duties thereof faithfully according to law."]

# Police Act 1997

(1997 c 50)

## PART III[1, 2]

## AUTHORISATIONS IN RESPECT OF PROPERTY

7.9203 This Part provides that no entry on or interference with property or with wireless telegraphy shall be unlawful if it is authorised in accordance with an authorisation having effect under this Part (s 92). An "authorising officer" ie a chief constable, a police commissioner, their military equivalents, the Director General of the National Crime Agency or a designated officer of the Agency, an officer designated by the Commissioners for Customs and Excise or the Chairman of the Office of Fair Trading may authorise such action as he may specify, where he believes that it is necessary for the action to be taken on the ground that it is likely to be of substantial value in the prevention or detection of serious crime, and what is sought to be achieved cannot reasonably be achieved by other means (s 93). In cases of urgency such powers may be exercised by the next officer in line of command (s 94 amended by the Crime and Disorder Act 1998, s 113 and Sch 10). Except in cases of urgency, authorisations must be in writing (s 95)[3].

Authorisations must be notified to Commissioners appointed by the Prime Minister under s 91 and must be approved by them where the authorisation relates to circumstances where the person who gives the authorisation believes that any of the property specified in the authorisation is used wholly or mainly as a dwelling or as a bedroom in a hotel or constitutes office premises; or the action authorised is likely to result in a person acquiring knowledge of matters subject to legal privilege, confidential personal information, or confidential journalistic material (ss 97–100)[4]. Provision is made for quashing an authorisation (s 103). Appeals may be made by authorising officers (ss 104–105).

1 This Act is to be brought into force in accordance with orders made under s 135. At the date of going to press the following commencement orders have been made: (No 1) SI 1997/1377; (No 2) SI 1997/1696; (No 3) SI 1997/1930; (No 4) SI 1997/2390; (No 5 and Transitional Provisions), SI 1998/354; (No 6) 1999, SI 1999/151; (No 7), SI 2001/1097; (No 8) (Scotland) SSI 2001/482; (No 9), SI 2002/413; (No 10) SI 2007/3342 (Northern Ireland); (No 11) SI 2008/692 (Northern Ireland); and (No 12) SI 2014/237 (England and Wales) SI 2014/237 (s 112 10 March 2014). Of the provisions reproduced in this Manual Pts I, II, III, IV and V, ss 134 (partly), 135–138 have been brought into force.

2 Part III comprises ss 91–108.

3 The Police Act 1997 (Notification of Authorisations, etc) Order 1998, SI 1998/3241 specifies the particulars to be included in an authorisation to interfere with property and a renewal or cancellation of such authorisation.

4 The Police Act 1997 (Authorisation of Action in Respect of Property) (Code of Practice) Order 1998, SI 1998/3240 has been made which makes provision for a Code of Practice applying to operations involving interference with property or wireless telegraphy carried out by the police, Customs and Excise, NCIS and NCS.

## PART V[1]

## CERTIFICATES OF CRIMINAL RECORDS, ETC.

7.9204 **112. Criminal conviction certificates** (1) DBS shall issue a criminal conviction certificate to any individual who—

(*a*) makes an application[2],

(*aa*) is aged 16 or over at the time of making the application, and

(*b*) pays any fee that is payable in relation to the application under regulations[2] made by the Secretary of State.

(2) A criminal conviction certificate is a certificate which—

(*a*) gives the prescribed details of every conviction or conditional caution of the applicant which is recorded in central records, or

(*b*) states that there are no such convictions and conditional cautions.

(3) In this section—

"central records" means such records of convictions and conditional cautions held for the use of police forces generally as may be prescribed;

"conditional caution" means a caution given under section 22 of the Criminal Justice Act 2003 (c 44) or section 66A of the Crime and Disorder Act 1998, other than one that is spent for the purposes of Schedule 2 to the Rehabilitation of Offenders Act 1974.

"conviction" means a conviction within the meaning of the Rehabilitation of Offenders Act 1974, other than a spent conviction.

(4) Where an applicant has received a criminal conviction certificate, DBS may refuse to issue another certificate to that applicant during such period as may be prescribed.

[Police Act 1997, s 112 as amended by the Criminal Justice Act 2003, Sch 35, the Criminal Justice and Immigration Act 2008, s 50, the Policing and Crime Act 2009, Sch 8, the Protection of Freedoms Act 2012, ss 80 and 84 and SI 2012/3006.]

1 Part V comprises ss 112–127.

2 The Police Act 1997 (Criminal Records) Regulations 2002 have been made, in this PART, post.

7.9205 **113A. Criminal record certificates** (1) DBS must issue a criminal record certificate to any individual who—

(*a*) makes an application,

(*aa*) is aged 16 or over at the time of making the application, and (*b*) pays in the prescribed[1] manner any prescribed[1] fee.

(2) The application must—

(*a*) be countersigned by a registered person, and

(*b*) be accompanied by a statement by the registered person that the certificate is required for the purposes of an exempted question.

(2A) But an application for a criminal record certificate need not be countersigned by a registered person if—

(*a*) the application is transmitted to DBS electronically by a registered person who satisfies conditions determined by DBS, and

(*b*) it is transmitted in accordance with requirements determined by DBS.

(3) A criminal record certificate is a certificate which—

(*a*) gives the prescribed[1] details of every relevant matter relating to the applicant which is recorded in central records, or

(*b*) states that there is no such matter.

(4) *Repealed.*

(5) DBS may treat an application under this section as an application under section 113B if—

(*a*) in its opinion the certificate is required for a purpose prescribed under subsection (2) of that section,

(*b*) the registered person provides it with the statement required by that subsection, and

(*c*) the applicant consents and pays to DBS the amount (if any) by which the fee payable in relation to an application under that section exceeds the fee paid in relation to the application under this section.

(6) In this section—

"central records" means such records of convictions and cautions held for the use of police forces generally as may be prescribed;

"exempted question" means a question which—

(*a*) so far as it applies to convictions, is a question in relation to which section 4(2)(*a*) or (*b*) of the Rehabilitation of Offenders Act 1974 (effect of rehabilitation) has been excluded by an order of the Secretary of State under section 4(4) of that Act; and

(*b*) so far as it applies to cautions, is a question to which paragraph 3(3) or (4) of Schedule 2 to that Act has been excluded by an order of the Secretary of State under paragraph 4 of that Schedule;

"relevant matter", in this section as it has effect in England and Wales, means—

(*a*)in relation to a person who has one conviction only—

(i) a conviction of an offence within subsection (6D);

(ii) a conviction in respect of which a custodial sentence or a sentence of service detention was imposed; or

(iii) a current conviction;

(*b*)in relation to any other person, any conviction;

(*c*)a caution given in respect of an offence within subsection (6D);

(*d*)a current caution.

(7) The Secretary of State may by order amend the definitions of "central records" and "relevant matter" in subsection (6).

(8) The power to make an order under subsection (7) is exercisable by statutory instrument, but no such order may be made unless a draft of the instrument containing the order is laid before and approved by resolution of each House of Parliament.

(9) For the purposes of this Part a person acts as the registered person in relation to an application for a criminal record certificate if the person—

(*a*) countersigns the application, or

(*b*) transmits the application to DBS under subsection (2A).

(10) *Repealed.*.

[Police Act 1997, s 113A as inserted by the Serious Organised Crime and Police Act 2005, s 163 and amended by the Safeguarding Vulnerable Groups Act 2006, Sch 9, the Criminal Justice and Immigration Act 2008, s 50, SI 2009/203, the Policing and Crime Act 2009, Sch 8, SI 2010/1146, the Protection of Freedoms Act 2012, s 80 and Schs 9, 10, SI 2012/3006 and SI 2013/1200.]

---

[1] See the Police Act (Criminal Records) Regulations 2002, in this title, post. Equivalent provision is made for applications in Guernsey by the Police Act 1997 (Criminal Records and Registration) (Guernsey Order 2009, SI 2009/3297 amended by SI 2010/2700 and SI 2011/718 and SI 2012/2107 and 2666 made under s 113 of this Act as extended by the Police Act 1997 (Criminal Records) (Guernsey) Order 2009, SI 2009/3215 amended by SI 2012/1762, the Police Act 1997 (Criminal Records and Registration) (Jersey) Regulations 2010, SI 2010/1087 amended by SI 2010/2701, SI 2011/717 and SI 2012/2108 and 2668 and the Police Act 1997 (Criminal Records and Registration) (Isle of Man) Regulations 2011, SI 2011/2296 amended by SI 2012/2109 and 2667.

**7.9206 113B. Enhanced criminal record certificates[1]** (1) DBS must issue an enhanced criminal record certificate to any individual who—

(*a*) makes an application,

(*aa*) is aged 16 or over at the time of making the application, and (*b*) pays in the prescribed[1] manner any prescribed[2] fee.

(2) The application must—

(*a*) be countersigned by a registered person, and

(*b*) be accompanied by a statement by the registered person that the certificate is required for the purposes of an exempted question asked for a prescribed[2] purpose.

(2A) But an application for an enhanced criminal record certificate need not be countersigned by a registered person if—

(*a*) the application is transmitted to DBS electronically by a registered person who satisfies conditions determined by DBS, and

(*b*) it is transmitted in accordance with requirements determined by DBS.

(3) An enhanced criminal record certificate is a certificate which—

(*a*) gives the prescribed details of every relevant matter relating to the applicant which is recorded in central records and any information provided in accordance with subsection (4), or

(*b*) states that there is no such matter or information.

(4) Before issuing an enhanced criminal record certificate DBS must request any relevant chief officer to provide any information which—

(*a*) the chief officer reasonably believes to be relevant[3] for the purpose described in the statement under subsection (2), and

(*b*) in the chief officer's opinion, ought to be included in the certificate.

(4A) In exercising functions under subsection (4) a relevant chief officer must have regard to any guidance for the time being published by the Secretary of State.

(5) *Repealed.*

(6) *Repealed.*

(7) DBS may treat an application under this section as an application under section 113A if in its opinion the certificate is not required for a purpose prescribed under subsection (2).

(8) If by virtue of subsection (7) DBS treats an application under this section as an application under section 113A, it must refund to the applicant the amount (if any) by which the fee paid in relation to the application under this section exceeds the fee payable in relation to an application under section 113A.

(9) In this section—

"central records", "exempted question", and "relevant matter" have the same meaning as in section 113A;

"relevant chief officer" means any chief officer of a police force who is identified by DBS for the purposes of making a request under subsection (4).

(10) For the purposes of this section references to a police force include any of the following—

(*a*) the Royal Navy Police;

(*b*) *repealed;*

(*c*) the Royal Military Police;

(*d*) the Royal Air Force Police;

(*e*) the Ministry of Defence Police;

(*f*) *repealed*

(*g*) *repealed*

(*h*) the British Transport Police;

(*i*) the Civil Nuclear Constabulary;

(*j*) the States of Jersey Police Force;

(*k*) the salaried police force of the Island of Guernsey;

(*l*) the Isle of Man Constabulary;

(*m*) a body with functions in any country or territory outside the British Islands which correspond to those of a police force in any part of the United Kingdom,

and any reference to the chief officer of a police force includes the person responsible for the direction of a body mentioned in this subsection.

(11) For the purposes of this section each of the following must be treated as if it were a police force—

(*a*) the Commissioners for Her Majesty's Revenue and Customs (and for this purpose a reference to the chief officer of a police force must be taken to be a reference to any one of the Commissioners);

(*b*) the National Crime Agency (and for this purpose a reference to the chief officer of a police force must be taken to be a reference to the Director General of the Agency);

(*c*) such other department or body as is prescribed (and regulations may prescribe in relation to the department or body the person to whom a reference to the chief officer is to be taken to be).

(12) For the purposes of this Part a person acts as the registered person in relation to an application for an enhanced criminal record certificate if the person—

(*a*) countersigns the application, or

(*b*) transmits the application to DBS under subsection (2A).

(13) *Repealed..*

[Police Act 1997, s 113B as inserted by the Serious Organised Crime and Police Act 2005, s 163 and amended by the Armed Forces Act 2006, Sch 16, the Safeguarding Vulnerable Groups Act 2006, Sch 9, SI 2009/203, the Policing and Crime Act 2009, Sch 8, SI 2010/1146, the Protection of Freedoms Act 2012, ss 79, 80, 82 and Schs 9, 10, SI 2012/3006 and the Crime and Courts Act 2013, Sch 8.]

---

[1] The Police Act 1997 (Criminal Records) Regulations 2009, SI 2009/460 provide:

"2. For the purposes of section 113B of the Police Act 1997 (enhanced criminal records)—
(*a*) the Criminal Records Bureau must be treated as if it were a police force;
(*b*) any reference to the chief officer of police, in relation to the Criminal Records Bureau, is to be taken to be the Chief Executive of the Criminal Records Bureau;
(*c*) the Scottish Crime and Drug Enforcement Agency must be treated as if it were a police force;
(*d*) any reference to the chief officer of police, in relation to the Scottish Crime and Drug Enforcement Agency, is to be taken to be the Director General of the Scottish Crime and Drug Enforcement Agency."

[2] See the Police Act (Criminal Records) Regulations 2002, in this title, post. For Guernsey and Jersey, see the note to s 113A, ante.

[3] In considering the predecessor of this provision (s 115(7) now repealed), there are competing rights between the social need to protect the vulnerable as against the right to respect for private life of the subject of the application under art 8 of the Human Rights Convention. Neither consideration has precedence over the other. Careful consideration is required in all cases where the disruption to the private life of anyone is judged to be as great, or more so, as the risk of non-disclosure to the vulnerable group. There is not a presumption for disclosure unless there is a good reason for not doing so. The issue is essentially one of proportionality (*R (L) v Metropolitan Police Comr* [2009] UKSC 3, [2010] 1 AC 410, [2010] 2 FCR 25, [2010] 1 FLR 643).

See further *R (T) v Chief Constable of Greater Manchester Police (Liberty and others intervening)*, *R (B) v Secretary of State for the Home Department (Same intervening)* [2014] UKSC 35, [2014] 4 All ER 159, [2014] 3 WLR 96. Note, however, before the Supreme Court heard these appeals the Rehabilitation of Offenders Act 1974 (Exceptions) Order 1975 (Amendment) (England and Wales) Order 2013 (SI 2013/1198) and the Police Act 1997 (Criminal Record Certificates: Relevant Matters) (Amendment) (England and Wales) Order 2013 (SI 2013/1200) had been made with a view to eliminating the identified incompatibilities and invalidities found by the Court of Appeal.

7.9207 **113BA. Suitability information relating to children** (1) In such cases as are prescribed[1], an enhanced criminal record certificate must also include suitability information relating to children.

(2) Suitability information relating to children is—

(*a*) whether the applicant is barred from regulated activity relating to children;

(*b*)–(*d*) *repealed*;

(*e*) whether the applicant is subject to a direction under section 167A of the Education Act 2002 (prohibition on participation in management of independent school).

(3) Expressions used in this section and in the 2006 Act have the same meaning in this section as in that Act, except that "prescribed" must be construed in accordance with section 125 of this Act.

(4) "The 2006 Act" means the Safeguarding Vulnerable Groups Act 2006.*

[Police Act 1997, s 113BA as inserted by the Safeguarding Vulnerable Groups Act 2006, Sch 9 and amended by the Education and Inspections Act 2006, s 170, the Policing and Crime Act 2009, s 81 and the Protection of Freedoms Act 2012, Schs 9 and 10.]

---

* **Amended by the Education and Skills Act 2008, Sch 1 from a date to be appointed.**

[1] See the Police Act 1997 (Criminal Records) Regulations 2002, in this title, post. For Guernsey and Jersey, see note to s 113B, ante. The Police Act 1997 (Criminal Records) (No 2) Regulations 2009, SI 2009/1882 amended by SI 2010/817, SI 2012/523 and SI 2013/2669 and reg 5 provides that the following are prescribed for the purposes of s 113BA of the 1997 Act:

"**Suitability information relating to children**

5. Cases in which an application for an enhanced criminal records certificate is made for the purposes of—
(a) considering the applicant's suitability to engage in any activity which is a regulated activity relating to children within the meaning of Part 1 of Schedule 4 to the Safeguarding Vulnerable Groups Act 2006;
(b) assessing the suitability of a person to have regular contact with children who is aged 16 or over and who lives in the same household as an individual who is having or who has had their suitability assessed for the purposes of engaging in a regulated activity relating to children, where that individual, and the person who lives in the same household, live on the premises where that regulated activity would normally take place;
(c) considering the suitability of a person for the purposes of registration for childcare, including assessing the suitability of a person to have regular contact with children who is—
(i) aged 16 or over and living on the premises at which childcare is being or is to be provided;
(ii) aged 16 or over and working, or who will be working, on the premises at which childcare is being or is to be provided at times when such childcare is being provided or is to be provided;
where that childcare is the provision of childminding or day care within the meaning of section 19 of the Children and Families (Wales) Measure 2010 or the provision of childcare within the meaning of section 18 of the Childcare Act 2006;
(d) placing children with foster parents in accordance with any provision of, or made by virtue of, the Children Act 1989 or the Children (Northern Ireland) Order 1995 or the exercise of any duty under or by virtue of section 67 of that Act or Article 108 of that Order (welfare of privately fostered children) including obtaining information in respect of any person who is—
(i) aged 16 or over and living in the same household as a person who is, or who wishes to be approved as, a foster parent within the meaning of section 53(7)(*a*) or (*b*) of the Safeguarding Vulnerable Groups Act 2006;
(ii) aged 16 or over and living in the same household as a person who fosters, or intends to foster, a child privately within the meaning of section 66(1) of the Children Act 1989 or who is otherwise a private foster parent within the meaning of section 53(7)(*c*) of the Safeguarding Vulnerable Groups Act 2006;
(e) a decision made by an adoption agency within the meaning of section 2 of the Adoption and Children Act 2002 as to a person's suitability to adopt a child, including obtaining information in respect of any person aged 18 years or over living in the same household as the prospective adopter;
(f) considering the applicant's suitability for any office or employment or other work in the Criminal Records Bureau;

(g) considering the applicant's suitability to obtain or hold a licence under section 46 of the Town Police Clauses Act 1847; section 8 of the Metropolitan Public Carriage Act 1869; section 9 of the Plymouth City Council Act 1975; section 51 of the Local Government (Miscellaneous Provisions) Act 1976; or section 13 of the Private Hire Vehicles (London) Act 1998."

Working with the Children (Exchange of Criminal Conviction Information) (England and Wales and Northern Ireland) Regulations 2013, SI 2013/2945 have been made under s 2 of the European Communities Act 1972 which require a chief officer of a police force to comply with EC Directive obligations to share information to combat the sexual abuse and sexual exploitation of children and child pornography and to request relevant information relating to disqualification from working with children from the Disclosure and Barring Service.

7.9208 **113BB. Suitability information relating to vulnerable adults** (1) In such cases as are prescribed[1], an enhanced criminal record certificate must also include suitability information relating to vulnerable adults.

(2) Suitability information relating to vulnerable adults is—

(*a*) whether the applicant is barred from regulated activity relating to vulnerable adults;

(*b*)–(*d*) *repealed*;

(3) Expressions used in this section and in the 2006 Act have the same meaning in this section as in that Act, except that "prescribed" must be construed in accordance with section 125 of this Act.

(4) "The 2006 Act" means the Safeguarding Vulnerable Groups Act 2006.

[Police Act 1997, s 113BB as inserted by the Safeguarding Vulnerable Groups Act 2006, Sch 9 and amended by the Policing and Crime Act 2009, s 81 and the Protection of Freedoms Act 2012, Schs 9 and 10.]

---

1 See the Police Act 1997 (Criminal Records) Regulations 2002, in this title, post. For Guernsey and Jersey, see note to s 113B, ante. The Police Act 1997 (Criminal Records) (No 2) Regulations 2009, SI 2009/1882 amended by SI 2010/817, SI 2012/523, reg 6 and SI 2013/2669 provides that the following are prescribed for the purposes of s 113BB of the 1997 Act:

"**6 Suitability information relating to vulnerable adults**
Cases in which an application for an enhanced criminal records certificate is made for the purposes of—

(a) considering the applicant's suitability to engage in any activity which is a regulated activity relating to vulnerable adults within the meaning of Part 2 of Schedule 4 to the Safeguarding Vulnerable Groups Act 2006;

(b) considering the applicant's suitability for any office or employment or other work in the Criminal Records Bureau;

(c) considering the applicant's suitability to obtain or hold a licence under section 46 of the Town Police Clauses Act 1847; section 8 of the Metropolitan Public Carriage Act 1869; section 9 of the Plymouth City Council Act 1975; section 51 of the Local Government (Miscellaneous Provisions) Act 1976; or section 13 of the Private Hire Vehicles (London) Act 1998."

7.9209 **113BC. Suitability information: power to amend** (1) The Secretary of State may by order made by statutory instrument—

(*a*) amend section 113BA for the purpose of altering the meaning of suitability information relating to children;

(*b*) amend section 113BB for the purpose of altering the meaning of suitability information relating to vulnerable adults;

(*c*) amend section 120AC(4)(*b*) in consequence of an order made under paragraph (*a*) or (*b*).

(2) Such an order is subject to annulment in pursuance of a resolution of either House of Parliament.

[Police Act 1997, s 113BC as inserted by the Safeguarding Vulnerable Groups Act 2006, Sch 9 and amended by the Protection of Freedoms Act 2012, Sch 9.]

**113CC. Suitability information: supplementary** *Scotland.*

7.9210 **113CD. Immigration information relevant to employment*** (1) This section applies where—

(*a*) an application for a certificate under section 112, 113A or 113B contains a request for information under this section,

(*b*) in the case of an application for a certificate under section 112, the application contains a statement that the information is sought for the purposes of employment with a person specified in the application, and

(*c*) the applicant pays in the prescribed manner any additional fee prescribed in respect of the application.

(2) The certificate must state—

(*a*) whether according to records held by the Secretary of State the applicant is subject to immigration control, or

(*b*) that records held by the Secretary of State do not show whether the applicant is subject to immigration control.

(3) If the records show that the applicant is subject to immigration control, the certificate must state—

(*a*) whether according to the records the applicant has been granted leave to enter or remain in the United Kingdom, or

(*b*) that the records do not show whether the applicant has been granted leave to enter or remain in the United Kingdom.

(4) If the records show that the applicant has been granted leave to enter or remain in the United Kingdom, the certificate must state—

(*a*) whether according to the records the applicant's leave to enter or remain in the United Kingdom is current, or

(*b*) that the records do not show whether the applicant's leave to enter or remain in the United Kingdom is current. (5) If the records show that the applicant has been granted leave to enter or remain in the United Kingdom and that it is current, the certificate must also state any conditions to which the leave to enter or remain is subject and which relate to the applicant's employment.

(6) A certificate under this section must contain such advice as the Secretary of State thinks appropriate about where to obtain further information about the matters mentioned in subsections (2) to (5).

(7) For the purposes of this section a person's leave to enter or remain in the United Kingdom is current unless—

(*a*) it is invalid, or

(*b*) it has ceased to have effect (whether by reason of curtailment, revocation, cancellation, passage of time or otherwise).

(8) For the purposes of this section a person is subject to immigration control if under the Immigration Act 1971 the person requires leave to enter or remain in the United Kingdom.

[Police Act 1997, s 113CD as inserted by the Policing and Crime Act 2009, s 94.]

* **Not yet in force.**

**7.9211 113E. Criminal record certificates: specified children's and adults' lists: urgent cases** (1) Subsection (2) applies to an application under section 113A or 113B if—

(*a*) it is accompanied by a children's suitability statement,

(*b*) the registered person requests an urgent preliminary response, and

(*c*) the applicant pays in the prescribed manner such additional fee as is prescribed in respect of the application.

(2) DBS must notify the registered person—

(*a*) if the applicant is not included in a specified children's list, of that fact;

(*b*) if the applicant is included in such a list, of the details prescribed for the purposes of section 113C(1)(*b*) above;

(*c*) if the applicant is not subject to a specified children's direction, of that fact;

(*d*) if the applicant is subject to such a direction, of the grounds on which the direction was given and the details prescribed for the purposes of section 113C(1)(*d*) above.

(3) Subsection (4) applies to an application under section 113A or 113B if—

(*a*) it is accompanied by an adults' suitability statement,

(*b*) the registered person requests an urgent preliminary response, and

(*c*) the applicant pays in the prescribed[1] manner such additional fee as is prescribed[1] in respect of the application.

(4) DBS must notify the registered person either—

(*a*) that the applicant is not included in a specified adults' list, or

(*b*) that a criminal record certificate or enhanced criminal record certificate will be issued in due course.

(5) In this section—

"criminal record certificate" has the same meaning as in section 113A;

"enhanced criminal record certificate" has the same meaning as in section 113B;

"children's suitability statement", "specified children's direction" and "specified children's list" have the same meaning as in section 113C;

"adults' suitability statement" and "specified adults' list" have the same meaning as in section 113D.*

[Police Act 1997, s 113E as inserted by the Serious Organised Crime and Police Act 2005, s 163 and amended by SI 2012/3006.]

* **Repealed in relation to England and Wales by the Safeguarding Vulnerable Groups Act 2006, Sch 10 from a date to be appointed.**

1 See the Police Act (Criminal Records) Regulations 2002, in this title, post. For Guernsey and Jersey, see note to s 113B, ante.

**7.9211A 114. Criminal record certificates: Crown employment**

**7.9211B 116. Enhanced criminal record certificates: judicial appointments and Crown employment**

**116A. Up-dating certificates**

**7.9212 117. Disputes about certificates and up-date information** (1) Where an applicant for a certificate under any of sections 112 to 116 believes that the information contained in the certificate is inaccurate he may make an application in writing to DBS for a new certificate.

(1A) Where any person other than the applicant believes that the information contained in a certificate under any of sections 112 to 116 is inaccurate, that person may make an application in writing to DBS for a decision as to whether or not the information is inaccurate.

(1B) Where a person believes that the wrong up-date information has been given under section 116A in relation to the person's certificate, the person may make an application in writing to DBS for corrected up-date information.

(2) DBS shall consider any application under this section; and where it is of the opinion that the information in the certificate is inaccurate it shall issue a new certificate or (as the case may be) corrected up-date information.

(2A) In this section—

"corrected up-date information", in relation to a certificate, means information which includes—

(*a*) information that the wrong up-date information was given in relation to the certificate on a particular date, and

(*b*) new up-date information in relation to the certificate,

"up-date information" has the same meaning as in section 116A.

(3), (4) *Scotland.*

[Police Act 1997, s 117 as amended by the Protection of Freedoms Act 2012, s 82 and Sch 9 and SI 2012/3006

7.9213 **117A. Other disputes about section 113B(4) information** (1) Subsection (2) applies if a person believes that information provided in accordance with section 113B(4) and included in a certificate under section 113B or 116—

(*a*) is not relevant for the purpose described in the statement under section 113B(2) or (as the case may be) 116(2), or

(*b*) ought not to be included in the certificate.

(2) The person may apply in writing to the independent monitor appointed under section 119B for a decision as to whether the information is information which falls within subsection (1)(*a*) or (*b*) above.

(3) The independent monitor, on receiving such an application, must ask such chief officer of a police force as the independent monitor considers appropriate to review whether the information concerned is information which—

(*a*) the chief officer reasonably believes to be relevant for the purpose described in the statement under section 113B(2) or (as the case may be) 116(2), and

(*b*) in the chief officer's opinion, ought to be included in the certificate.

(4) In exercising functions under subsection (3), the chief officer concerned must have regard to any guidance for the time being published under section 113B(4A).

(5) If, following a review under subsection (3), the independent monitor considers that any of the information concerned is information which falls within subsection (1)(*a*) or (*b*)—

(*a*) the independent monitor must inform DBS of that fact, and

(*b*) on being so informed, DBS must issue a new certificate.

(6) In issuing such a certificate, DBS must proceed as if the information which falls within subsection (1)(*a*) or (*b*) had not been provided under section 113B(4).

(7) In deciding for the purposes of this section whether information is information which falls within subsection (1)(*a*) or (*b*), the independent monitor must have regard to any guidance for the time being published under section 113B(4A).

(8) Subsections (10) and (11) of section 113B apply for the purposes of this section as they apply for the purposes of that section.

[Police Act 1997, s 117A as inserted by the Protection of Freedoms Act 2012, s 82 and amended by SI 2012/3006.]

7.9214 **118. Evidence of identity** *DBS may require evidence of identity including fingerprint.*

7.9215 **119. Sources of information** *Any person who holds records of convictions or cautions for the use of police forces generally shall make those records available to DBS.*

7.9216 **119B. Independent monitor** (1) There is to be an independent monitor for the purposes of this Part.

(2) The independent monitor is a person appointed by the Secretary of State—

(*a*) for such period, not exceeding three years, as the Secretary of State decides;

(*b*) on such terms as the Secretary of State decides.

(3) A person may be appointed for a further period or periods.

(4) The Secretary of State may terminate the appointment of the independent monitor before the end of the period mentioned in subsection (2)(*a*) by giving the monitor notice of the termination not less than three months before it is to take effect.

(5) The independent monitor must review—

(*a*) *repealed;*

(*b*) a sample of cases in which a certificate issued under section 113B has included information in pursuance of subsection (4)(*b*) of that section;

(*c*) a sample of cases in which the chief officer of a police force has decided that information must not be included in a certificate or report in pursuance of section 113B(4)(*b*);

(*ca*) a sample of cases in which the chief officer of a police force has decided that information should be disclosed or not disclosed to DBS for the purpose of the provision by DBS of up-date information under section 116A.

(*d*) *repealed;*

(*e*) *repealed.*

(6) The purpose of a review under subsection (5) is to ensure compliance with Article 8 of the European Convention of Human Rights.

(7) The independent monitor must in relation to each year make a report to the Secretary of State about the performance of police forces in exercising their functions under this Part.

(8) The independent monitor may make recommendations to the Secretary of State as to—

(*a*) any guidance issued by the Secretary of State or which the monitor thinks it would be appropriate for the Secretary of State to issue;

(*b*) any changes to any enactment which the monitor thinks may be appropriate.

(8A) The independent monitor has the functions conferred on the monitor by section 117A.

(9) The chief officer of a police force must provide to the independent monitor such information as the monitor reasonably requires in connection with the exercise of his functions under this section or section 117A.

[Police Act 1997, s 119B as inserted by the Safeguarding Vulnerable Groups Act 2006, s 28 and amended by the Protection of Freedoms Act 2012, Schs 9 and 10 and SI 2012/3006.]

**7.9217 120. Registered persons** (1) For the purposes of this Part a registered person is a person who is listed in a register to be maintained by DBS for the purposes of this Part.

(2)–(3) *Regulations.*

(4) A person applying for registration under this section must be—

(*a*) a body corporate or unincorporate,

(*b*) a person who is appointed to an office by virtue of any enactment and who, in the case of an individual, is aged 18 or over, or

(*c*) an individual aged 18 or over who employs others in the course of a business.

(5) A body applying for registration under this section must satisfy DBS that it—

(*a*) is likely to ask exempted questions, or

(*b*) is likely to act as the registered person in relation to applications under section 113A or 113B at the request of bodies or individuals asking exempted questions.

(6) A person, other than a body, applying for registration under this section must satisfy DBS that he is likely to ask exempted questions.

(7) In this section "exempted question" has the same meaning as in section 113A.

[Police Act 1997, s 120 as amended by the Serious Organised Crime and Police Act 2005, Sch 14 and SI 2009/203, the Protection of Freedoms Act 2012, s 80 and SI 2012/3006.]

**120ZA. Regulations about registration** *Regulations to make further provision about registration*[1].

---

[1] The Police Act 1997 (Criminal Records) (Registration) Regulations 2006, SI 2006/750 amended by SI 2009/203 and SI 2012/3006 have been made. For Guernsey, see note to s 113B, ante.

**7.9218 120A. Refusal and cancellation of registration on grounds related to disclosure**

(1) DBS may refuse to include a person in the register maintained for the purposes of this Part if it appears to it that the registration of that person is likely to make it possible for information to become available to an individual who, in DBS's opinion, is not a suitable person to have access to that information.

(2) DBS may remove a person from the register if it appears to DBS—

(*a*) that the registration of that person is likely to make it possible for information to become available to an individual who, in DBS's opinion, is not a suitable person to have access to that information; or

(*b*) that the registration of that person has resulted in information becoming known to such an individual.

(3) In determining for the purposes of this section whether an individual is a suitable person to have access to any information, DBS may have regard, in particular, to—

(*a*) any information relating to that person which concerns a relevant matter;

(*b*) any information relating to the person of a kind specified in subsection (3A); and

(*c*) any information provided to DBS under subsection (4).

(3A) The information is—

(*a*) whether the person is barred from regulated activity;

(*b*) *repealed*

(*c*) *repealed*

(*d*) whether the person is subject to a direction under section 167A of the Education Act 2002 (prohibition on participation in management of independent school).

(3B) *Repealed.*

(3C) *Repealed.*

(3D) Expressions used in subsection (3A) and in the Safeguarding Vulnerable Groups Act 2006 have the same meaning in that subsection as in that Act.

(4) It shall be the duty of the chief officer of any police force to comply, as soon as practicable after receiving it, with any request by DBS to provide DBS with information which—

(*a*) is available to the chief officer;

(*b*) relates to—

(i) an applicant for registration;

(ii) a registered person; or

(iii) an individual who is likely to have access to information in consequence of a particular applicant for registration, or a particular registered person, acting as the registered person in relation to applications under this Part;

and

(*c*) concerns a matter which DBS has notified to the chief officer to be a matter which, in the opinion of DBS, is relevant to the determination of the suitability of individuals for having access to the information that may be provided in consequence of a person acting as the registered person in relation to applications under this Part.

(5) In this section "relevant matter" has the same meaning as in section 113A.

(6) For the purposes of this section references to a police force include any body mentioned in subsections (10)(*a*) to (*i*) and (11) of section 113B and references to a chief officer must be construed accordingly.

(7) The Secretary of State may by order made by statutory instrument amend subsection (3A) for the purpose of altering the information specified in that subsection.

(8) Such an order is subject to annulment in pursuance of a resolution of either House of Parliament.

[Police Act 1997, s 120A as inserted by the Criminal Justice and Police Act 2001, s 134(1), and amended by the Criminal Justice Act 2003, s 336, the Serious Organised Crime and Police Act 2005, Sch 14, SI 2009/203, the Policing and Crime Act 2009, s 96, the Protection of Freedoms Act 2012, Schs 9 and 10 and SI 2012/3006.]

7.9219 **120AA. Refusal, cancellation or suspension of registration on other grounds**

(1) Regulations[1] may make provision enabling DBS in prescribed cases to refuse to register a person who, in the opinion of DBS, is likely to act as the registered person in relation to fewer applications under this Part in any period of twelve months than a prescribed minimum number.

(2) Subsection (3) applies where a registered person—

(*a*) is, in the opinion of DBS, no longer likely to wish to act as the registered person in relation to applications under this Part,

(*b*) has, in any period of twelve months during which he was registered, acted as the registered person in relation to fewer applications under this Part than the minimum number specified in respect of him by regulations under subsection (1), or

(*c*) has failed to comply with any condition of his registration.

(3) Subject to section 120AB, DBS may—

(*a*) suspend that person's registration for such period not exceeding 6 months as DBS thinks fit, or

(*b*) remove that person from the register.

(4) Subsection (6) applies if an application is made under section 120 by an individual who—

(*a*) has previously been a registered person; and

(*b*) has been removed from the register (otherwise than at that individual's own request).

(5) Subsection (6) also applies if an application is made under section 120 by a body corporate or unincorporate which—

(*a*) has previously been a registered person; and

(*b*) has been removed from the register (otherwise than at its own request).

(6) DBS may refuse the application.

[Police Act 1997, s 120AA as inserted by the Criminal Justice Act 2003, Sch 35 and amended by SI 2009/203, the Protection of Freedoms Act 2012, s 81 and SI 2012/3006.]

---

1 The Police Act 1997 (Criminal Records) (Registration) Regulations 2006, SI 2006/750 amended by SI 2009/203 and SI 2012/3006 have been made.

7.9220 **120AB. Procedure for cancellation or suspension under section 120AA**

(1) Before cancelling or suspending a person's registration by virtue of section 120AA, DBS must send him written notice of its intention to do so.

(2) Every such notice must—

(*a*) give DBS's reasons for proposing to cancel or suspend the registration, and

(*b*) inform the person concerned of his right under subsection (3) to make representations.

(3) A person who receives such a notice may, within 21 days of service, make representations in writing to DBS as to why the registration should not be cancelled or suspended.

(4) After considering such representations, DBS must give the registered person written notice—

(*a*) that at the end of a further period of six weeks beginning with the date of service, the person's registration will be cancelled or suspended, or

(*b*) that it does not propose to take any further action.

(5) If no representations are received within the period mentioned in subsection (3) DBS may cancel or suspend the person's registration at the end of the period mentioned in that subsection.

(6) Subsection (1) does not prevent DBS from imposing on the registered person a lesser sanction than that specified in the notice under that subsection.

(7) Any notice under this section that is required to be given in writing may be given by being transmitted electronically.

(8) This section does not apply where—

(*a*) DBS is satisfied, in the case of a registered person other than a body, that the person has died or is incapable, by reason of physical or mental impairment, of acting as the registered person in relation to applications under this Part, or

(*b*) the registered person has requested to be removed from the register.

(9) The Secretary of State may by regulations amend subsection (4)(*a*) by substituting for the period there specified, such other period as may be specified in the regulations.

[Police Act 1997, s 120AB as inserted by the Criminal Justice Act 2003, Sch 35 and amended by SI 2009/203 and SI 2012/3006.]

**7.9221 120AC. Registered persons: information on progress of an application** (1) DBS must, in response to a request from a person who is acting as the registered person in relation to an application under section 113A or 113B, inform that person whether or not a certificate has been issued in response to the application.

(2) Subsections (3) and (4) apply if, at the time a request is made under subsection (1), a certificate has been issued.

(3) In the case of a certificate under section 113A, if it was a certificate stating that there is no relevant matter recorded in central records, DBS may inform the person who made the request that the certificate was such a certificate.

(4) In the case of a certificate under section 113B, if it was a certificate—

(*a*) stating that there is no relevant matter recorded in central records and no information provided in accordance with subsection (4) of that section, and

(*b*) if section 113BA(1) or 113BB(1) applies to the certificate, containing no suitability information indicating that the person to whom the certificate is issued—

(i) is barred from regulated activity relating to children or to vulnerable adults, or

(ii) is subject to a direction under 128 of the Education and Skills Act 2008 or section 167A of the Education Act 2002,

DBS may inform the person who made the request that the certificate was such a certificate.

(5) If no certificate has been issued, DBS must inform the person who made the request of such other matters relating to the processing of the application as DBS considers appropriate.

(6) Subject to subsections (2) to (4), nothing in this section permits DBS to inform a person who is acting as the registered person in relation to an application under section 113A or 113B of the content of any certificate issued in response to the application.

(7) DBS may refuse a request under subsection (1) if it is made after the end of a prescribed period beginning with the day on which the certificate was issued.

(8) In this section—

"central records" and "relevant matter" have the same meaning as in section 113A,

"suitability information" means information required to be included in a certificate under section 113B by virtue of section 113BA or 113BB.

(9) Expressions in subsection (4)(*b*) and in the Safeguarding Vulnerable Groups Act 2006 have the same meaning in that paragraph as in that Act.

[Police Act 1997, s 120AC as inserted by the Protection of Freedoms Act 2012, s 79 and amended by SI 2012/3006.]

**7.9222 120AD. Registered persons: copies of certificates in certain circumstances**

(1) Subsection (2) applies if—

(*a*) DBS gives up-date information in relation to a criminal record certificate or enhanced criminal record certificate,

(*b*) the up-date information is advice to apply for a new certificate or (as the case may be) request another person to apply for such a certificate, and

(*c*) the person whose certificate it is in respect of which the up-date information is given applies for a new criminal record certificate or (as the case may be) enhanced criminal record certificate.

(2) DBS must, in response to a request made within the prescribed period by the person who is acting as the registered person in relation to the application, send to that person a copy of any certificate issued in response to the application if the registered person—

(*a*) has counter-signed the application or transmitted it to DBS under section 113A(2A) or 113B(2A),

(*b*) has informed DBS that the applicant for the new certificate has not, within such period as may be prescribed, sent a copy of it to a person of such description as may be prescribed, and

(*c*) no prescribed circumstances apply.

(3) The power under subsection (2)(*b*) to prescribe a description of person may be exercised to describe the registered person or any other person.

(4) In this section "up-date information" has the same meaning as in section 116A.

[Police Act 1997, s 120AD as inserted by the Protection of Freedoms Act 2012, s 79 and amended by SI 2012/3006.]

**122. Code of practice**

**7.9223 123. Offences: falsification, etc** (1) A person commits an offence if, with intent to deceive, he—

(*a*) makes a false certificate under this Part,

(*b*) alters a certificate under this Part,

(*c*) uses a certificate under this Part which relates to another person in a way which suggests that it relates to himself, or

(*d*) allows a certificate under this Part which relates to him to be used by another person in a way which suggests that it relates to that other person.

(2) A person commits an offence if he knowingly makes a false statement for the purpose of obtaining, or enabling another person to obtain, a certificate under this Part.

(3) A person who is guilty of an offence under this section shall be liable on summary conviction to imprisonment for a term not exceeding **six months** or to a fine not exceeding **level 5** on the standard scale, or to **both**.

[Police Act 1997, s 123.]

7.9224 **124. Offences: disclosure** (1) A member, officer or employee of a body registered under section 120 commits an offence if he discloses information provided following an application under section 113A or 113B unless he discloses it, in the course of his duties—

(*a*) to another member, officer or employee of the registered body,

(*b*) to a member, officer or employee of a body at the request of which the registered body acted as the registered person in relation to the application, or

(*c*) to an individual at whose request the registered body acted as the registered person in relation to the relevant application.

(2) When information is provided under section 113A or 113B following an application in relation to which the person who acted as the registered person did so at the request of a body which is not registered under section 120, a member, officer or employee of the body commits an offence if he discloses the information unless he discloses it, in the course of his duties, to another member, officer or employee of that body.

(3) Where information is provided under section 113A or 113B following an application in relation to which an individual acted as the registered person, or in relation to which the person who acted as the registered person did so at the request of an individual—

(*a*) the individual commits an offence if he discloses the information unless he discloses it to an employee of his for the purpose of the employee's duties, and

(*b*) an employee of the individual commits an offence if he discloses the information unless he discloses it, in the course of his duties, to another employee of the individual.

(4) Where information provided under section 113A or 113B is disclosed to a person and the disclosure—

(*a*) is an offence under this section, or

(*b*) would be an offence under this section but for subsection (6)(*a*), (*d*), (*e*) or (*f*),

the person to whom the information is disclosed commits an offence (subject to subsection (6)) if he discloses it to any other person.

(5) *Repealed.*

(6) Subsections (1) to (4) do not apply to a disclosure of information contained in a certificate under section 113A or 113B which is made—

(*a*) with a written consent of the applicant for the certificate, or

(*b*) to a government department, or

(*c*) to a person appointed to an office by virtue of any enactment, or

(*d*) in accordance with an obligation to provide information under or by virtue of any enactment, or

(*e*) for the purposes of answering an exempted question (within the meaning of section 113A) of a kind specified in regulations made by the Secretary of State, or

(*f*) for some other purpose specified in regulations made by the Secretary of State.

(7) A person who is guilty of an offence under this section shall be liable on summary conviction to imprisonment for a term not exceeding **six months** or to a fine not exceeding **level 3** on the standard scale, or to **both**.

[Police Act 1997, s 124 as amended by the Serious Organised Crime and Police Act 2005, Sch 4, SI 2009/203 and the Protection of Freedoms Act 2012, Schs 9 and 10.]

7.9225 **125.** *Regulations*

7.9225A **125B.** *Form of applications*

7.9226 **126. Interpretation of Part V** (1) In this Part—

"caution" means a caution given to a person in England and Wales or Northern Ireland in respect of an offence which, at the time when the caution is given, he has admitted;

"certificate" means any one or more documents issued in response to a particular application but does not include any documents issued in response to—

(*a*) a request under section 116A(1),

(*b*) an application as mentioned in section 116A(4)(*a*) or (5)(*a*), or

(*c*) a request under section 120AC or 120AD;

"chief officer" means—

(i) a chief officer of police of a police force in England and Wales.

(ii) a chief constable of a police force in Scotland, and

(iii) the Chief Constable of the Police Service of Northern Ireland;

"DBS" means the Disclosure and Barring Service established by section 87(1) of the Protection of Freedoms Act 2012;

"government department" includes a Northern Ireland department;

"Minister of the Crown" includes a Northern Ireland department;

"police authority" means—

(i) a police authority for an area in Scotland or a joint police board (within the meaning of the Police (Scotland) Act 1967), and

(ii) the Northern Ireland Policing Board;

"police force" means—

(i) a police force in Great Britain, and

(ii) the Police Service of Northern Ireland and the Police Service of Northern Ireland Reserve;

"prescribed" shall be construed in accordance with section 125(1).

(2) *Northern Ireland.*

(3)–(4) *Scotland.*

[Police Act 1997, s 126 as amended by the Police (Northern Ireland) Act 2000, Sch 6, the Serious Organised Crime and Police Act 2005, s 166, the Police Reform and Social Responsibility Act 2011, Sch 16, the Protection of Freedoms Act 2012, Sch 9 and SI 2012/3006.]

7.9227 **127. Saving: disclosure of information and records** Nothing in sections 112 to 119 shall be taken to prejudice any power which exists apart from this Act to disclose information or to make records available.

[Police Act 1997, s 127.]

## PART VII[1]
## GENERAL

7.9228 **134. Amendments and repeals**

[1] Part VII comprises ss 134–138.

7.9229 **135. Commencement**[1] (1) The preceding provisions of this Act shall come into force on such day as the Secretary of State may by order made by statutory instrument appoint.

(2)–(5) *Further provisions.*

[Police Act 1997, s 135.]

[1] For commencement orders made at the date of going to press, see the note to the short title to this Act, ante.

7.9230 **136. Police: co-operation and implementation**

7.9231 **137. Extent**

7.9232 **138. Short title**

# Police Reform Act 2002[1]

(2002 c 30)

## PART 2
## COMPLAINTS AND MISCONDUCT[2]

*The Independent Police Complaints Commission*

*Application of Part 2*

7.9233 This Part (ss 9–29) establishes an Independent Police Complaints Commission which consists of a Chairman appointed by the Queen and not less than 10 other members appointed by the Secretary of State (s 9). The functions of the Commission include handling complaints about the conduct of persons serving with the police and the recording of conduct which constitutes or involves the commission of a criminal offence or which justifies disciplinary proceedings and the manner in which such matters are investigated (s 11). The Commission must make a report to the Secretary of State at the end of each financial year (s 11).

[1] With the exception of s 100 and related amendments in Sch 8 which came into force on 24 July 2002, this Act is to be brought into force in accordance with commencement orders made under s 108. At the date of going to press the following commencement orders had been made: (No 1) SI 2002/2306; (No 2) SSI 2002/420 (Scotland); (No 3) SI 2002/2750; (No 4) SI 2003/808; (No 5) SI 2003/2593; (No 6) SI 2004/119; (No 7) SI 2004/636; (No 8) SI 2004/913; (No 9) SI 2004/1319; (No 10) SI 2004/3338. All the provisions reproduced here (including ss 38A-38C and 41A-41B) except s 45 are in force.

[2] Part 2 comprises ss 9–29 and Schs 2 and 3.

7.9234 **12. Complaints, matters and persons to which Part 2 applies** (1) In this Part references to a complaint are references (subject to the following provisions of this section) to any complaint about the conduct of a person serving with the police which is made (whether in writing or otherwise) by—

(*a*) a member of the public who claims to be the person in relation to whom the conduct took place;

(*b*) a member of the public not falling within paragraph (*a*) who claims to have been adversely affected by the conduct;

(*c*) a member of the public who claims to have witnessed the conduct;
(*d*) a person acting on behalf of a person falling within any of paragraphs (*a*) to (*c*).

(2) In this Part "conduct matter" means (subject to the following provisions of this section, section 28A and any regulations made under it, paragraph 2(4) of Schedule 3 and any regulations made by virtue of section 23(2)(*d*)) any matter which is not and has not been the subject of a complaint but in the case of which there is an indication (whether from the circumstances or otherwise) that a person serving with the police may have—
(*a*) committed a criminal offence; or
(*b*) behaved in a manner which would justify the bringing of disciplinary proceedings.

(2A) In this Part "death or serious injury matter" (or "DSI matter" for short) means (subject to section 28A and any regulations made under it) any circumstances (other than those which are or have been the subject of a complaint or which amount to a conduct matter)—
(*a*) in or in consequence of which a person has died or has sustained serious injury; and
(*b*) in relation to which the requirements of either subsection (2B) or subsection (2C) are satisfied.

(2B) The requirements of this subsection are that at the time of the death or serious injury the person—
(*a*) had been arrested by a person serving with the police and had not been released from that arrest; or
(*b*) was otherwise detained in the custody of a person serving with the police.

(2C) The requirements of this subsection are that—
(*a*) at or before the time of the death or serious injury the person had contact (of whatever kind, and whether direct or indirect) with a person serving with the police who was acting in the execution of his duties; and
(*b*) there is an indication that the contact may have caused (whether directly or indirectly) or contributed to the death or serious injury.

(2D) In subsection (2A) the reference to a person includes a person serving with the police, but in relation to such a person "contact" in subsection (2C) does not include contact that he has whilst acting in the execution of his duties.

(3) The complaints that are complaints for the purposes of this Part by virtue of subsection (1)(*b*) do not, except in a case falling within subsection (4), include any made by or on behalf of a person who claims to have been adversely affected as a consequence only of having seen or heard the conduct, or any of the alleged effects of the conduct.

(4) A case falls within this subsection if—
(*a*) it was only because the person in question was physically present, or sufficiently nearby, when the conduct took place or the effects occurred that he was able to see or hear the conduct or its effects; or
(*b*) the adverse effect is attributable to, or was aggravated by, the fact that the person in relation to whom the conduct took place was already known to the person claiming to have suffered the adverse effect.

(5) For the purposes of this section a person shall be taken to have witnessed conduct if, and only if—
(*a*) he acquired his knowledge of that conduct in a manner which would make him a competent witness capable of giving admissible evidence of that conduct in criminal proceedings; or
(*b*) he has in his possession or under his control anything which would in any such proceedings constitute admissible evidence of that conduct.

(6) For the purposes of this Part a person falling within subsection 1(*a*) to (*c*) to shall not be taken to have authorised another person to act on his behalf unless—
(*a*) that other person is for the time being designated for the purposes of this Part by the Commission as a person through whom complaints may be made, or he is of a description of persons so designated; or
(*b*) the other person has been given, and is able to produce, the written consent to his so acting of the person on whose behalf he acts.

(7) For the purposes of this Part, a person is serving with the police if—
(*a*) he is a member of a police force;
(*aa*) he is a civilian employee of a police force;
(*b*) he is an employee of the Common Council of the City of London who is under the direction and control of a chief officer; or
(*c*) he is a special constable who is under the direction and control of a chief officer.*

(8) The Secretary of State may make regulations[1] providing that, for the purposes of this Part and of any regulations made under this Part—
(*a*) a contractor,
(*b*) a sub-contractor of a contractor, or
(*c*) an employee of a contractor or a sub-contractor,

is to be treated as a person serving with the police.

(9) Regulations under subsection (8) may make modifications to this Part, and to any

regulations made under this Part, in its application to those persons.

(10) In subsection (8) "contractor" means a person who has entered into a contract with a local policing body or a chief officer to provide services to a chief officer.*

[Police Reform Act 2002, s 12 as amended by the Serious Organised Crime and Police Act 2005, Sch 12, the Police Reform and Social Responsibility Act 2011, Sch 16, the Police (Complaints and Conduct) Act 2012, s 2 and the Anti-social Behaviour, Crime and Policing Act 2014, s 135.]

* **Amended by the Policing and Crime Act 2017, s 14 from a date to be appointed.**

1 The Independent Police Complaints Commission (Complaints and Misconduct) (Contractors) Regulations 2015, SI 2015/431 have been made.

*Handling of complaints, conduct matters and DSI matters etc*

7.9235 **13. Handling of complaints, conduct matters and DSI matters etc** Schedule 3 (which makes provision for the handling of complaints, conduct matters and DSI matters and for the carrying out of investigations) shall have effect subject to section 14(1).*

[Police Reform Act 2002, s 13 as amended by the Serious Organised Crime and Police Act 2005, Sch 12.]

* **New s 13A inserted by the Policing and Crime Act 2017, s 13 from a date to be appointed.**

*Co-operation, assistance and information*

Sections 15–29 make provision for the co-operation of police forces with the Commission in the investigation of complaints and for funding of investigations, provision of information to the Commission, inspection of police premises and use of investigatory powers, and a duty to keep the complainant informed. The Commission may also issue guidance to police authorities and chief officers concerning the exercise of their functions under this Part and the Secretary of State may make regulations.*

* **Pts 2A, 2B (ss 29A–29N) inserted by the Policing and Crime Act 2017 from a date to be appointed.**

## PART 4
## POLICE POWERS ETC[1]

### CHAPTER 1
### EXERCISE OF POLICE POWERS ETC BY CIVILIANS[2]

7.9236 **38. Police powers for civilian staff** (1) The chief officer of police of any police force may designate a relevant employee as an officer of one or more of the descriptions specified in subsection (2).

(2) The description of officers are as follows—

(*a*) community support officer;
(*b*) investigating officer;
(*c*) detention officer;
(*d*) escort officer;
(*e*) *repealed.*

(3) *Repealed.*

(4) A chief officer of police shall not designate a person under this section unless he is satisfied that that person—

(*a*) is a suitable person to carry out the functions for the purposes of which he is designated;
(*b*) is capable of effectively carrying out those functions; and
(*c*) has received adequate training in the carrying out of those functions and in the exercise and performance of the powers and duties to be conferred or imposed on him by virtue of the designation.

(5) A person designated under this section shall have the powers and duties conferred or imposed on him by the designation.

(5A) A person designated under this section as a community support officer shall also have the standard powers and duties of a community support officer (see section 38A(2)).

(5B) The reference in subsection (4)(*c*) to the powers and duties to be conferred or imposed on a person by virtue of his designation, so far as it is a reference to the standard powers and duties of a community support officer, is a reference to the powers and duties that at the time of the person's designation are the standard powers and duties of a community support officer.

(6) Powers and duties may be conferred or imposed on a designated person by means only of the application to him by his designation of provisions of the applicable Part of Schedule 4 that are to apply to the designated person; and for this purpose the applicable Part of that Schedule is—

(*a*) in the case of a person designated as a community support officer, Part 1;
(*b*) in the case of a person designated as an investigating officer, Part 2;
(*c*) in the case of a person designated as a detention officer, Part 3; and
(*d*) in the case of a person designated as an escort officer, Part 4.
(*e*) *repealed.*

(6A) Subsection (6) has effect subject to subsections (5A) and (8).

(7) An relevant employee authorised or required to do anything by virtue of a designation under this section—

(*a*) shall not be authorised or required by virtue of that designation to engage in any conduct otherwise than in the course of that employment; and

(*b*) shall be so authorised or required subject to such restrictions and conditions (if any) as may be specified in his designation.

(8) Where any power exercisable by any person in reliance on his designation under this section is a power which, in the case of its exercise by a constable, includes or is supplemented by a power to use reasonable force, any person exercising that power in reliance on that designation shall have the same entitlement as a constable to use reasonable force.

(9) Where any power exercisable by any person in reliance on his designation under this section includes power to use force to enter any premises, that power shall not be exercisable by that person except—

(*a*) in the company, and under the supervision, of a constable; or

(*b*) for the purpose of saving life or limb or preventing serious damage to property.

(10) *Repealed.*

(11) In this section "relevant employee" means—

(*a*) in the case of—

(i) a police force maintained for a police area in accordance with section 2 of the Police Act 1996, or

(ii) the police force maintained for the metropolitan police district in accordance with section 5A of that Act,

a member of the civilian staff of that police force (within the meaning of Part 1 of the Police Reform and Social Responsibility Act 2011);

(*b*) in the case of any other police force, a person who—

(i) is employed by the police authority maintaining that force, and

(ii) is under the direction and control of the chief officer making a designation under subsection (1).*

[Police Reform Act 2002, s 38 as amended by the Serious Organised Crime and Police Act 2005, Sch 4, the Police and Justice Act 2006, s 7 and Sch 5, the Policing and Crime Act 2009, Schs 7 and 8 and the Police Reform and Social Responsibility Act 2011, Sch 16.]

---

* **Amended by the Policing and Crime Act 2017, ss 8, 38, Sch 1 from a date to be appointed.**

[1] Part 4 comprises ss 38–77 and Sch 4–6.

[2] Chapter 1 comprises ss 38–47 and Schs 4 and 5.

7.9237 **38A. Standard powers and duties of community support officers** (1) The Secretary of State may by order[1] provide for provisions of Part 1 of Schedule 4 to apply to every person who under section 38 is designated as a community support officer.

(2) The powers and duties conferred or imposed by the provisions for the time being applied under subsection (1) are to be known as the standard powers and duties of a community support officer.

(3) Before making an order under subsection (1), the Secretary of State shall consult with—

(*a*) such persons as appear to the Secretary of State to represent the views of police and crime commissioners;

(*ab*) the Mayor's Office for Policing and Crime;

(*ac*) the Common Council of the City of London; and

(*b*) the National Police Chiefs' Council.

(4) The Secretary of State shall not make an order containing (with or without any other provision) any provision authorised by subsection (1) unless a draft of that order has been laid before Parliament and approved by a resolution of each House.

(5) A provision of Part 1 of Schedule 4 may be applied to a person concurrently by an order under subsection (1) and a designation under section 38.

(6) If an order under subsection (1) confers or imposes additional powers and duties on a person who is under the direction and control of a chief officer of police of a police force, that chief officer must ensure that the person receives adequate training in the exercise and performance of the additional powers and duties.*

[Police Reform Act 2002, s 38A as inserted by the Police and Justice Act 2006, s 7 and amended by the Police Reform and Social Responsibility Act 2011, Sch 16 and the Policing and Crime Act 2017, Sch 14.]

---

* **Amended by the Policing and Crime Act 2017, s 38 from a date to be appointed.**

[1] The Police Reform Act 2002 (Standard Powers and Duties of Community Support Officers) Order 2007, SI 2007/3202 has been made, in this title, post.

7.9238 **38B. Police powers for civilian employees under collaboration agreements** (1) The chief officer of police of a police force (the "assisted force") may designate a person ("C") who—

(*a*) is a civilian employee of another police force (the "assisting force"),

(*b*) is designated under section 38 by the chief officer of police of the assisting police force (the "section 38 designation"), and (*c*) is permitted, under relevant police collaboration provision, to discharge powers and duties specified in that provision for the purposes of the assisted force.

(2) The designation under subsection (1) (the "collaboration designation") must designate C as an officer of one or more of the descriptions specified in section 38(2).

(3) The collaboration designation may designate C as an officer of a particular description specified in section 38(2) only if the section 38 designation designates C as an officer of that description.

(4) C shall have the powers and duties conferred or imposed on C by the collaboration designation.

(5) A power or duty may be conferred or imposed on C by the collaboration designation only if C is permitted, under the relevant police collaboration provision, to discharge that power or duty for the purposes of the assisted force.

(6) C shall not be authorised or required by virtue of the collaboration designation to engage in any conduct otherwise than in the course of discharging a power or duty conferred or imposed on C by the collaboration designation.

(7) The collaboration designation must specify the restrictions and conditions to which C is subject in the discharge of the powers and duties conferred or imposed by the collaboration designation.

(8) Those restrictions and conditions must include the restrictions and conditions specified in the relevant police collaboration provision.

(9) C is authorised or required to discharge any power or duty conferred or imposed by the collaboration designation subject to the restrictions and conditions specified in the collaboration designation.

(10) References in this section to the discharge of functions by civilian employees of the assisting force for the purposes of the assisted force have the same meaning as in section 23B of the Police Act 1996.

(11) In this section—

"civilian employee" has the meaning given by section 23I of the Police Act 1996;

"relevant police collaboration provision" means provision, contained in a collaboration agreement under section 22A of the Police Act 1996, which is of the kind referred to in section 23AA of that Act.*

[Police Reform Act 2002, s 38B as inserted by the Police Reform and Social Responsibility Act 2011, Sch 13.]

* **Amended by the Policing and Crime Act 2017, Sch 12 from a date to be appointed.**

**7.9239 38C. Designations under section 38B: supplementary provision** (1) The collaboration designation of C must be in accordance with the relevant police collaboration provision.

(2) Subsection (1) is in addition to section 38B(5) and (8).

(3) Subsections (8) and (9) of section 38 apply to any power exercisable by C in reliance on the collaboration designation as they apply to a power exercisable by a person in reliance on a designation under section 38.

(4) In exercising or performing any power or duty in reliance on the collaboration designation, C is to be taken—

(*a*) as exercising or performing that power or duty in reliance on that collaboration designation (and not in reliance on any designation under section 38); and

(*b*) accordingly, as not being a designated person (within the meaning of section 46(1)) by virtue of any designation under section 38.

(5) Expressions used in this section and section 38B have the same meanings in this section as in section 38B.

[Police Reform Act 2002, s 38C as inserted by the Police Reform and Social Responsibility Act 2011, Sch 13.]

**7.9240 39. Police powers for contracted-out staff** (1) This section applies if a local policing body has entered into a contract with a person ("the contractor") for the provision of services relating to the detention or escort of persons who have been arrested or are otherwise in custody.

(2) The chief officer of police of the police force maintained by that local policing body may designate any person who is an employee of the contractor as either or both of the following—

(*a*) a detention officer; or

(*b*) an escort officer.

(3) A person designated under this section shall have the powers and duties conferred or imposed on him by the designation.

(4) A chief officer of police shall not designate a person under this section unless he is satisfied that that person—

(*a*) is a suitable person to carry out the functions for the purposes of which he is designated;

(*b*) is capable of effectively carrying out those functions; and

(*c*) has received adequate training in the carrying out of those functions and in the exercise and performance of the powers and duties to be conferred on him by virtue of the designation.

(5) A chief officer of police shall not designate a person under this section unless he is satisfied that the contractor is a fit and proper person to supervise the carrying out of the functions for the purposes of which that person is designated.

(6) Powers and duties may be conferred or imposed on a designated person by means only of the application to him by his designation of provisions of the applicable Part of Schedule 4 that are to apply to the designated person; and for this purpose the applicable Part of that Schedule is—

(*a*) in the case of a person designated as a detention officer, Part 3; and

(*b*) in the case of a person designated as an escort officer, Part 4.

(7) An employee of the contractor authorised or required to do anything by virtue of a designation under this section—

(*a*) shall not be authorised or required by virtue of that designation to engage in any conduct otherwise than in the course of that employment; and

(*b*) shall be so authorised or required subject to such restrictions and conditions (if any) as may be specified in his designation.

(8) Where any power exercisable by any person in reliance on his designation under this section is a power which, in the case of its exercise by a constable, includes or is supplemented by a power to use reasonable force, any person exercising that power in reliance on that designation shall have the same entitlement as a constable to use reasonable force.

(9) *Repealed.*

(10) *Repealed.*

(11) *Repealed.*

(12) A designation under this section, unless it is previously withdrawn or ceases to have effect in accordance with subsection (13), shall remain in force for such period as may be specified in the designation; but it may be renewed at any time with effect from the time when it would otherwise expire.

(13) A designation under this section shall cease to have effect—

(*a*) if the designated person ceases to be an employee of the contractor; or

(*b*) if the contract between the local policing body and the contractor is terminated or expires.

[Police Reform Act 2002, s 39 as amended by the Police and Justice Act 2006, Sch 4 , the Police Reform and Social Responsibility Act 2011, Sch 16 and the Anti-social Behaviour, Crime and Policing Act 2014, Sch 11.]

7.9241 **40. Community safety accreditation schemes** (1) The chief officer of police of any police force may, if he considers that it is appropriate to do so for the purposes specified in subsection (3), establish and maintain a scheme ("a community safety accreditation scheme").

(2) A community safety accreditation scheme is a scheme for the exercise in the chief officer's police area by persons accredited by him under section 41 of the powers conferred by their accreditations under that section.

(3) Those purposes are—

(*a*) contributing to community safety and security; and

(*b*) in co-operation with the police force for the area, combatting crime and disorder, public nuisance and other forms of anti-social behaviour.

(4) Before establishing a community safety accreditation scheme for his police area, a chief officer of any police force (other than the Commissioner of Police of the Metropolis) must consult with—

(*a*) the local policing body maintaining that force, and

(*b*) every local authority any part of whose area lies within the police area.

(5) Before establishing a community safety accreditation scheme for the metropolitan police district, the Commissioner of Police of the Metropolis must consult with—

(*a*) the Mayor's Office for Policing and Crime;

(*b*) the Mayor of London; and

(*c*) every local authority any part of whose area lies within the metropolitan police district.

(6) In subsections (4)(*b*) and (5)(*c*) "local authority" means—

(*a*) in relation to England, a district council, a London borough council, the Common Council of the City of London or the Council of the Isles of Scilly; and

(*b*) in relation to Wales, a county council or a county borough council.

(7) Every police and crime plan under section 5 or 6 of the Police Reform and Social Responsibility Act 2011 which is issued after the commencement of this section, must set out—

(*a*) whether a community safety accreditation scheme is maintained for the police area in question;

(*b*) if not, whether there is any proposal to establish such a scheme for that area during the period to which the plan relates;

(*c*) particulars of any such proposal or of any proposal to modify during that period any community safety accreditation scheme that is already maintained for that area;

(*d*) the extent (if any) of any arrangements for provisions specified in Schedule 4 to be applied to designated persons employed by the local policing body; and

(*e*) the respects in which any community safety accreditation scheme that is maintained or proposed will be supplementing those arrangements during the period to which the plan relates.*

(8) A community safety accreditation scheme must contain provision for the making of arrangements with employers who—

(*a*) are carrying on business in the police area in question, or

(*b*) are carrying on business in relation to the whole or any part of that area or in relation to places situated within it,

for those employers to supervise the carrying out by their employees of the community safety functions for the purposes of which powers are conferred on those employees by means of accreditations under section 41.

(9) It shall be the duty of a chief officer of police who establishes and maintains a community safety accreditation scheme to ensure that the employers of the persons on whom powers are conferred by the grant of accreditations under section 41 have established and maintain satisfactory arrangements for handling complaints relating to the carrying out by those persons of the functions for the purposes of which the powers are conferred.

[Police Reform Act 2002, s 40 as amended by the Police Reform and Social Responsibility Act 2011, Sch 16.]

---

* **Subsection (7) repealed by the Police and Justice Act 2006, Sch 15 from a date to be appointed.**

7.9242 **41. Accreditation under community safety accreditation schemes** (1) This section applies where a chief officer of police has, for the purposes of a community safety accreditation scheme, entered into any arrangements with any employer for or with respect to the carrying out of community safety functions by employees of that employer.

(2) The chief officer of police may, on the making of an application for the purpose by such person and in such manner as he may require, grant accreditation under this section to any employee of the employer.

(3) Schedule 5 (which sets out the powers that may be conferred on accredited persons) shall have effect.

(4) A chief officer of police shall not grant accreditation to a person under this section unless he is satisfied—

(*a*) that that person's employer is a fit and proper person to supervise the carrying out of the functions for the purposes of which the accreditation is to be granted;

(*b*) that the person himself is a suitable person to exercise the powers that will be conferred on him by virtue of the accreditation;

(*c*) that that person is capable of effectively carrying out the functions for the purposes of which those powers are to be conferred on him; and

(*d*) that that person has received adequate training for the exercise of those powers.

(4A) A chief officer of police may not grant accreditation under this section to a weights and measures inspector.

(5) A chief officer of police may charge such fee as he considers appropriate for one or both of the following—

(*a*) considering an application for or for the renewal of an accreditation under this section;

(*b*) granting such an accreditation.

(6) A person authorised or required to do anything by virtue of an accreditation under this section—

(*a*) shall not be authorised or required by virtue of that accreditation to engage in any conduct otherwise than in the course of his employment by the employer with whom the chief officer of police has entered into the arrangements mentioned in subsection (1); and

(*b*) shall be so authorised or required subject to such other restrictions and conditions (if any) as may be specified in his accreditation.

(7) An accreditation under this section, unless it is previously withdrawn or ceases to have effect in accordance with subsection (8), shall remain in force for such period as may be specified in the accreditation; but it may be renewed at any time with effect from the time when it would otherwise expire.

(8) An accreditation under this section shall cease to have effect—

(*a*) if the accredited person ceases to be an employee of the person with whom the chief officer of police has entered into the arrangements mentioned in subsection (1); or

(*b*) if those arrangements are terminated or expire.

[Police Reform Act 2002, s 41 as amended by the Police and Justice Act 2006, Sch 14.]

7.9243 **41A. Accreditation of weights and measures inspectors** (1) The chief officer of police of any police force may, on the making of an application for the purpose by such person and in such manner as he may require, grant accreditation under this section to a weights and measures inspector.

(2) A weights and measures inspector to whom an accreditation under this section is granted by a chief officer of police may exercise the powers conferred by the accreditation in the chief officer's police area.

(3) Schedule 5A (which sets out the powers that may be conferred on inspectors accredited

under this section) shall have effect.

(4) A chief officer of police shall not grant accreditation to a weights and measures inspector under this section unless he is satisfied that—

(*a*) the inspector is a suitable person to exercise the powers that will be conferred on him by virtue of the accreditation; and

(*b*) the inspector has received adequate training for the exercise of those powers.

(5) A chief officer of police may charge such fee as he considers appropriate for one or both of the following—

(*a*) considering an application for or for the renewal of an accreditation under this section;

(*b*) granting an accreditation under this section.

(6) A weights and measures inspector authorised or required to do anything by virtue of an accreditation under this section—

(*a*) shall not be authorised or required by virtue of that accreditation to engage in any conduct otherwise than in the course of his duties as a weights and measures inspector; and

(*b*) shall be so authorised or required subject to such other restrictions and conditions (if any) as may be specified in his accreditation.

(7) An accreditation under this section, unless it is previously withdrawn or ceases to have effect in accordance with subsection (8), shall remain in force for such period as may be specified in the accreditation, but it may be renewed at any time with effect from the time when it would otherwise expire.

(8) An accreditation under this section shall cease to have effect if the accredited inspector ceases to hold office as a weights and measures inspector.

[Police Reform Act 2002, s 41A as inserted by the Police and Justice Act 2006, s 15.]

7.9244 **41B. Power to apply accreditation provisions** *Secretary of State may apply accreditation provisions to persons of a description specified by order.*

7.9245 **42. Supplementary provisions relating to designations and accreditations**

(A1) A person who exercises or performs any power or duty in relation to any person in reliance on his designation under section 38 as a community support officer, or who purports to do so, shall produce to that person evidence of his designation, if requested to do so.

(B1) A person who exercises or performs any non-standard power or non-standard duty in relation to any person in reliance on his designation under section 38 as a community support officer, or who purports to do so, shall produce to that person evidence that the power or duty has been conferred or imposed on him, if requested to do so.

(C1) For the purposes of subsection (B1), a power or duty is "non-standard" if it is not one of the standard powers and duties of a community support officer.

(1) A person who exercises or performs any power or duty in relation to any person in reliance on his designation under section 38, 38B or 39 or his accreditation under section 41 or 41A, or who purports to do so, shall produce that designation or accreditation to that person, if requested to do so.*

(1A) Subsection (1) does not apply to a person who exercises or performs any power or duty in reliance on his designation under section 38 as a community support officer, or who purports to do so.

(2) A power exercisable by any person in reliance on his designation by a chief officer of police under section 38 or 39 or his accreditation under section 41 shall, subject to subsection (2A), be exercisable only by a person wearing such uniform as may be—

(*a*) determined or approved for the purposes of this Chapter by the chief officer of police who granted the designation or accreditation; and

(*b*) identified or described in the designation or accreditation;

and, in the case of an accredited person, such a power shall be exercisable only if he is also wearing such badge as may be specified for the purposes of this subsection by the Secretary of State, and is wearing it in such manner, or in such place, as may be so specified.

(2ZA) A power exercisable by any person in reliance on a designation under section 38B by the chief officer of police of the assisted force shall, subject to subsection (2A), be exercisable only by a person wearing such uniform as may be—

(*a*) determined or approved for the purposes of this Chapter by the chief officer of police of the assisting police force; and

(*b*) identified or described in the designation.

In this subsection, "assisted force" and "assisting force" have the same meanings as in section 38B.

(2A) A police officer of or above the rank of inspector may direct a particular investigating officer not to wear a uniform for the purposes of a particular operation; and if he so directs, subsection (2) or (2ZA) shall not apply in relation to that investigating officer for the purposes of that operation.

(2B) In subsection (2A), "investigating officer" means a person designated as an investigating officer under section 38 (in relation to subsection (2)) or section 38B (in relation to subsection (2ZA)) by the chief officer of police of the same force as the officer giving the direction.

(3) A chief officer of police who has granted a designation or accreditation to any person under

section 38, 38B, 39 or 41 or an accreditation to any weights and measures inspector under section 41A may at any time, by notice to the designated or accredited person or the accredited inspector, modify or withdraw that designation or accreditation.

(4) *Repealed.*

(5) Where any person's designation under section 39 is modified or withdrawn, the chief officer giving notice of the modification or withdrawal shall send a copy of the notice to the contractor responsible for supervising that person in the carrying out of the functions for the purposes of which the designation was granted.

(6) Where any person's accreditation under section 41 is modified or withdrawn, the chief officer giving notice of the modification or withdrawal shall send a copy of the notice to the employer responsible for supervising that person in the carrying out of the functions for the purposes of which the accreditation was granted.

(6A) Where the accreditation of a weights and measures inspector under section 41A is modified or withdrawn, the chief officer giving notice of the modification or withdrawal shall send a copy of the notice to the local weights and measures authority by which the inspector was appointed.

(7) For the purposes of determining liability for the unlawful conduct of employees of a chief officer of police or local policing body, conduct by such an employee in reliance or purported reliance on a designation under section 38 shall be taken to be conduct in the course of his employment by the chief officer of police or local policing body; and, in the case of a tort, that chief officer or body shall fall to be treated as a joint tortfeasor accordingly.

(7A) For the purposes of determining liability for the unlawful conduct of a civilian employee of a police force (within the meaning of section 38B), conduct by such an employee in reliance or purported reliance on a designation under section 38B shall be taken to be conduct in the course of the employee's employment by the employer; and, in the case of a tort, that employer shall fall to be treated as a joint tortfeasor accordingly.

(8) *Repealed.*

(9) For the purposes of determining liability for the unlawful conduct of employees of a contractor (within the meaning of section 39), conduct by such an employee in reliance or purported reliance on a designation under that section shall be taken to be conduct in the course of his employment by that contractor; and, in the case of a tort, that contractor shall fall to be treated as a joint tortfeasor accordingly.

(10) For the purposes of determining liability for the unlawful conduct of employees of a person with whom a chief officer of police has entered into any arrangements for the purposes of a community safety accreditation scheme, conduct by such an employee in reliance or purported reliance on an accreditation under section 41 shall be taken to be conduct in the course of his employment by that employer; and, in the case of a tort, that employer shall fall to be treated as a joint tortfeasor accordingly.

(11) For the purposes of determining liability for the unlawful conduct of weights and measures inspectors, conduct by such an inspector in reliance or purported reliance on an accreditation under section 41A shall be taken to be conduct in the course of his duties as a weights and measures inspector; and, in the case of a tort, the local weights and measures authority by which he was appointed shall fall to be treated as a joint tortfeasor accordingly.**

[Police Reform Act 2002, s 42 as amended by the Serious Organised Crime and Police Act 2005, s 122 and Schs 4 and 17, the Police and Justice Act 2006, Schs 5 and 14 and the Police Reform and Social Responsibility Act 2011, Schs 13 and 16.]

---

* **Words substituted by the Criminal Justice Act 2003, Sch 26 from a date to be appointed. Amended by the Policing and Crime Act 2017, Sch 12 from a date to be appointed.**

7.9246 **43. Railway safety accreditation scheme** (1) The Secretary of State may make regulations[1] for the purpose of enabling the chief constable of the British Transport Police Force to establish and maintain a scheme ("a railway safety accreditation scheme").

(2) A railway safety accreditation scheme is a scheme for the exercise, within a place specified in section 21(1)(*a*) to (*f*) of the Railways and Transport Safety Act 2003 in England and Wales, by persons accredited by the chief constable of the British Transport Police Force under the scheme, of the powers conferred on those persons by their accreditation under that scheme.

(3)–(9) *Regulations*

(10) In this section—

"local authorities" means district councils, London borough councils, county councils in Wales, county borough councils and the Common Council of the City of London.

[Police Reform Act 2002, s 43 as amended by SI 2004/1573, the Police Reform and Social Responsibility Act 2011, Sch 16, the Legal Aid, Sentencing and Punishment of Offenders Act 2012, Sch 23 and the Policing and Crime Act 2017, Sch 14.]

---

1 The Railway Safety Accreditation Scheme Regulations 2004, SI 2004/915 amended by SI 2004/1573, SI 2012/2732 and SI 2013/903 have been made.

7.9247 **45.** ***Code of practice relating to chief officers' powers under Chapter 1**** 

---

* **Repealed by the Policing and Crime Act 2017, Sch 12 from a date to be appointed.**

7.9248 **46. Offences against designated and accredited persons etc** (1) Any person who assaults—

(*a*) a designated person in the execution of his duty,
(*b*) an accredited person in the execution of his duty,
(*ba*) an accredited inspector in the execution of his duty, or
(*c*) a person assisting a designated or accredited person or an accredited inspector in the execution of his duty,

is guilty of an offence and shall be liable, on summary conviction, to imprisonment for a term not exceeding six months or to a fine not exceeding level 5 on the standard scale, or to both.

(2) Any person who resists or wilfully obstructs—
(*a*) a designated person in the execution of his duty,
(*b*) an accredited person in the execution of his duty,
(*ba*) an accredited inspector in the execution of his duty, or
(*c*) a person assisting a designated or accredited person or an accredited inspector in the execution of his duty,

is guilty of an offence and shall be liable, on summary conviction, to imprisonment for a term not exceeding one month* or to a fine not exceeding level 3 on the standard scale, or to both.

(3) Any person who, with intent to deceive—
(*a*) impersonates a designated person, an accredited person or an accredited inspector,
(*b*) makes any statement or does any act calculated falsely to suggest that he is a designated person, that he is an accredited person or that he is an accredited inspector, or
(*c*) makes any statement or does any act calculated falsely to suggest that he has powers as a designated or accredited person or as an accredited inspector that exceed the powers he actually has,

is guilty of an offence and shall be liable, on summary conviction, to imprisonment for a term not exceeding six months or to a fine not exceeding level 5 on the standard scale, or to both.

(4) In this section references to the execution by a designated person, accredited person or accredited inspector of his duty are references to his exercising any power or performing any duty which is his by virtue of his designation or accreditation.

(5) References in this section to a designated person are to—
(*a*) a designated person within the meaning given by section 47(1), and
(*b*) a person in relation to whom a designation under section 38B is for the time being in force.

[Police Reform Act 2002, s 46 as amended by the Police and Justice Act 2006, Sch 14 and the Police Reform and Social Responsibility Act 2011, Sch 13.]

* **Words substituted by the Criminal Justice Act 2003, Sch 26 from a date to be appointed.**

7.9249 **47. Interpretation of Chapter 1** (1) In this Chapter—

"accredited inspector" means a weights and measures inspector in relation to whom an accreditation under section 41A is for the time being in force;

"accredited person" means a person in relation to whom an accreditation under section 41 is for the time being in force;

"community safety functions" means any functions the carrying out of which would be facilitated by the ability to exercise one or more of the powers mentioned in Schedule 5;

"conduct" includes omissions and statements;

"designated person" means a person in relation to whom a designation under section 38 or 39 is for the time being in force;

"weights and measures inspector" means an inspector of weights and measures appointed under section 72(1) of the Weights and Measures Act 1985

(2) In this Chapter—
(*a*) references to carrying on business include references to carrying out functions under any enactment; and
(*b*) references to the employees of a person carrying on business include references to persons holding office under a person, and references to employers shall be construed accordingly.

[Police Reform Act 2002, s 47 as amended by the Serious Organised Crime and Police Act 2005, Sch 4 and the Police and Justice Act 2006, Sch 14.]

## CHAPTER 2
## PROVISIONS MODIFYING AND SUPPLEMENTING POLICE POWERS[1]

*Power to require name and address*

7.9250 **50. Persons acting in an anti-social manner** (1) If a constable in uniform has reason to believe that a person has been acting, or is acting, in an anti-social manner, he may require that person to give his name and address to the constable.

(1A) In subsection (1) "anti-social behaviour" has the meaning given by section 2 of the Anti-social Behaviour, Crime and Policing Act 2014 (ignoring subsection (2) of that section).

(2) Any person who—
(*a*) fails to give his name and address when required to do so under subsection (1), or
(*b*) gives a false or inaccurate name or address in response to a requirement under that subsection,

is guilty of an offence and shall be liable, on summary conviction, to a fine not exceeding level 3 on the standard scale.*

[Police Reform Act 2002, s 50 as amended by the Anti-social Behaviour, Crime and Policing Act 2014, Sch 11.]

* **Amended by the Policing and Crime Act 2017, Sch 12 from a date to be appointed.**

1 Chapter 2 comprises ss 48–77 and Sch 6.

*Persons in police detention*

**7.9251 51. Independent custody visitors for places of detention** (1) Every local policing body shall—

(*a*) make arrangements for detainees to be visited by persons appointed under the arrangements ("independent custody visitors"); and

(*b*) keep those arrangements under review and from time to time revise them as they think fit.

(1A) Every local policing body must ensure—

(*a*) that the arrangements made by it require independent custody visitors to prepare and submit to it a report of any visit made under the arrangements to a suspected terrorist detainee, and

(*b*) that a copy of any report submitted under paragraph (*a*) is given to the person appointed under section 36(1) of the Terrorism Act 2006 (independent reviewer of terrorism legislation).

(2) The arrangements must secure that the persons appointed under the arrangements are independent of both—

(*a*) the local policing body; and

(*b*) the chief officer of police of the police force maintained by that body.

(3) The arrangements may confer on independent custody visitors such powers as the local policing body considers necessary to enable them to carry out their functions under the arrangements and may, in particular, confer on them powers—

(*a*) to require access to be given to each police station;

(*b*) to examine records relating to the detention of persons there;

(*ba*) in relation to suspected terrorist detainees, to listen to the audio recordings and view the video recordings (with or without sound) of interviews with those detainees which have taken place during their detention there and which were conducted by a constable;

(*c*) to meet detainees there for the purposes of a discussion about their treatment and conditions while detained; and

(*d*) to inspect the facilities there including in particular, cell accommodation, washing and toilet facilities and the facilities for the provision of food.

(3A) The arrangements may include provision for access to the whole or part of an audio or video recording of an interview of the kind mentioned in subsection (3)(*ba*) to be denied to independent custody visitors if—

(*a*) it appears to an officer of or above the rank of inspector that there are grounds for denying access at the time it is requested;

(*b*) the grounds are grounds specified for the purposes of paragraph (*a*) in the arrangements; and

(*c*) the procedural requirements imposed by the arrangements in relation to a denial of access to such recordings are complied with.

(3B) Grounds are not to be specified in any arrangements for the purposes of subsection (3A)(*a*) unless they are grounds for the time being set out for the purposes of this subsection in the code of practice issued by the Secretary of State under subsection (6).

(4) The arrangements may include provision for access to a detainee to be denied to independent custody visitors if—

(*a*) it appears to an officer of or above the rank of inspector that there are grounds for denying access at the time it is requested;

(*b*) the grounds are grounds specified for the purposes of paragraph (*a*) in the arrangements; and

(*c*) the procedural requirements imposed by the arrangements in relation to a denial of access are complied with.

(5) Grounds shall not be specified in any arrangements for the purposes of subsection (4)(*a*) unless they are grounds for the time being set out for the purposes of this subsection in the code of practice issued by the Secretary of State under subsection (6).

(6) The Secretary of State shall issue, and may from time to time revise, a code of practice as to the carrying out by local policing bodies and independent custody visitors of their functions under the arrangements.

(7) Before issuing or revising a code of practice under this section, the Secretary of State shall consult with—

(*a*) such persons as appear to the Secretary of State to represent the views of police and crime commissioners;

(*aa*) the Mayor's Office for Policing and Crime;
(*ab*) the Common Council of the City of London;
(*b*) the National Police Chiefs' Council; and
(*c*) such other persons as he thinks fit.

(8) The Secretary of State shall lay any code of practice issued by him under this section, and any revisions of any such code, before Parliament.

(9) Local policing bodies and independent custody visitors shall have regard to the code of practice for the time being in force under subsection (6) in the carrying out of their functions under the preceding provisions of this section.

(10) In this section—

"detainee", in relation to arrangements made under this section, means a person detained in a police station in the police area of the local policing body;

"suspected terrorist detainee" means a detainee detained under section 41 of the Terrorism Act 2000.

[Police Reform Act 2002, s 51 as amended by the Police and Justice Act 2006, Sch 4, the Coroners and Justice Act 2009, s 117, the Police Reform and Social Responsibility Act 2011, Sch 16 and the Policing and Crime Act 2017, Sch 14.]

*Seizure of motor vehicles*

7.9252 **59. Vehicles used in manner causing alarm, distress or annoyance** (1) Where a constable in uniform has reasonable grounds for believing that a motor vehicle is being used on any occasion in a manner which—

(*a*) contravenes section 3 or 34 of the Road Traffic Act 1988 (c 52) (careless and inconsiderate driving and prohibition of off-road driving), and
(*b*) is causing, or is likely to cause, alarm, distress or annoyance to members of the public,

he shall have the powers set out in subsection (3).

(2) A constable in uniform shall also have the powers set out in subsection (3) where he has reasonable grounds for believing that a motor vehicle has been used on any occasion in a manner falling within subsection (1).

(3) Those powers are—

(*a*) power, if the motor vehicle is moving, to order the person driving it to stop the vehicle;
(*b*) power to seize and remove the motor vehicle;
(*c*) power, for the purposes of exercising a power falling within paragraph (*a*) or (*b*), to enter any premises on which he has reasonable grounds for believing the motor vehicle to be;
(*d*) power to use reasonable force, if necessary, in the exercise of any power conferred by any of paragraphs to (*a*) to (*c*).

(4) A constable shall not seize a motor vehicle in the exercise of the powers conferred on him by this section unless—

(*a*) he has warned the person appearing to him to be the person whose use falls within subsection (1) that he will seize it, if that use continues or is repeated; and
(*b*) it appears to him that the use has continued or been repeated after the warning.

(5) Subsection (4) does not require a warning to be given by a constable on any occasion on which he would otherwise have the power to seize a motor vehicle under this section if—

(*a*) the circumstances make it impracticable for him to give the warning;
(*b*) the constable has already on that occasion given a warning under that subsection in respect of any use of that motor vehicle or of another motor vehicle by that person or any other person;
(*c*) the constable has reasonable grounds for believing that such a warning has been given on that occasion otherwise than by him; or
(*d*) the constable has reasonable grounds for believing that the person whose use of that motor vehicle on that occasion would justify the seizure is a person to whom a warning under that subsection has been given (whether or not by that constable or in respect the same vehicle or the same or a similar use) on a previous occasion in the previous twelve months.

(6) A person who fails to comply with an order under subsection (3)(*a*) is guilty of an offence and shall be liable, on summary conviction, to a fine not exceeding level 3 on the standard scale.

(7) Subsection (3)(*c*) does not authorise entry into a private dwelling house.

(8) The powers conferred on a constable by this section shall be exercisable only at a time when regulations under section 60 are in force.

(9) In this section—

"driving" has the same meaning as in the Road Traffic Act 1988 (c 52);

"motor vehicle" means any mechanically propelled vehicle, whether or not it is intended or adapted for use on roads; and

"private dwelling house" does not include any garage or other structure occupied with the dwelling house, or any land appurtenant to the dwelling house.

[Police Reform Act 2002, s 59.]

7.9253 **60. Retention etc of vehicles seized under section 59** (1) The Secretary of State may by regulations[1] make provision as to—

(*a*) the removal and retention of motor vehicles seized under section 59; and

(*b*) the release or disposal of such motor vehicles.

(2) *Regulations*

[Police Reform Act 2002, s 60.]

---

1. The Police (Retention and Disposal of Motor Vehicles) Regulations 2002, SI 2002/3049 amended by SI 2005/2702 and SI 2008/2096 have been made.

## PART 6

## MISCELLANEOUS[1]

*Appointment and attestation of police officers etc*

7.9254 **82. Nationality requirements applicable to police officers etc** *Subject to regulations, a person of any nationality can hold office as a constable.*

---

1. Part 6 comprises ss 82–104.

## PART 7

## SUPPLEMENTAL[1]

7.9255 **105. Powers of Secretary of State to make orders and regulations**

---

1. Part 7 comprises ss 105–108 and Schs 7 and 8.

7.9256 **106. General interpretation** In this Act—

"the 1984 Act" means the Police and Criminal Evidence Act 1984 (c 60);

"the 1996 Act" means the Police Act 1996 (c 16);

"the 1997 Act" means the Police Act 1997 (c 50);

"the British Transport Police Force" means the force of constables appointed under section 53 of the British Transport Commission Act 1949 (c xxix);

"modifications" includes omissions, alterations and additions, and cognate expressions shall be construed accordingly.

[Police Reform Act 2002, s 106 as amended by the Police and Justice Act 2006, Sch 4 and the Policing and Crime Act 2017, Sch 14.]

7.9257 **107. Consequential amendments and repeals**

7.9258 **108. Short title, commencement and extent** (1) This Act may be cited as the Police Reform Act 2002.

(2) This Act, except—

(*a*) the provisions specified in subsection (3) (which come into force on the day on which this Act is passed), and

(*b*) the provisions to which subsections (4) and (5) apply,

shall come into force on such day as the Secretary of State may by order[1] appoint; and different days may be appointed under this subsection for different purposes or different areas.

(3) The provisions coming into force on the day on which this Act is passed are—

(*a*) section 100, the entries in Schedule 8 relating to the Housing Act 1985 (c 68), the Housing Act 1988 (c 50), paragraphs 51 and 59 of Schedule 27 to the Greater London Authority Act 1999 (c 29) and paragraph 74 of Schedule 6 to the Criminal Justice and Police Act 2001 (c 16) and section 107(2) (so far as relating to those entries); and

(*b*) sections 105 and 106 and this section.

(4) The provisions of sections 97 and 98, so far as they relate to local government areas in Wales, shall come into force on such day as the National Assembly for Wales may by order made by statutory instrument appoint; and different days may be appointed under this subsection for different purposes or different areas.

(5) Sections 70 and 71, and sections 102 to 104 so far as they amend the Police (Scotland) Act 1967 (c 77), shall come into force on such day as the Scottish Ministers may by order appoint; and different days may be appointed under this subsection for different purposes or different areas.

(6) Subject to subsections (7) to (9), this Act extends to England and Wales only.

(7) This Act extends to the United Kingdom so far as it makes the following provision—

(*za*) the provision contained in paragraph 19F of Schedule 3 (and any interpretative or other supplementary provision as it has effect for the purposes of that provision);

(*a*) the provision contained in Part 5;

(*b*) the provision contained in section 82;

(*c*) *repealed*;

(*d*) the provision contained in section 103(6);

(*e*) *repealed*.

(8) Section 96 also extends to Northern Ireland.

(9) Subject to subsection (10), this Act, so far as it amends or repeals any enactment (other than one that extends to England and Wales only), has the same extent as the enactment amended or

repealed.

(10) The amendments and repeals made by this Act—

(*a*) in section 96 of the Road Traffic Regulation Act 1984 (c 27) (traffic wardens),

(*b*) in sections 103 and 183 of the Road Traffic Act 1988 (c 52) (driving while disqualified), and

(*c*) Part 3 of the Road Traffic Offenders Act 1988 (c 53) (fixed penalties),

do not extend to Scotland.

[Police Reform Act 2002, s 108 as amended by the Serious Organised Crime and Police Act 2005, Sch 2, the Police and Justice Act 2006, Sch 15 and the Police (Complaints and Conduct) Act 2012, s 1.]

[1] For commencement orders made under this provision see note to title of this Act, ante.

## SCHEDULES

### SCHEDULE 2
The Independent Police Complaints Commission — Section 9

### SCHEDULE 3
Handling of Complaints and Conduct Matters etc[1] — Section 13

*(Amended by the Serious Organised Crime and Police Act 2005, Schs 2 and 12, the Police and Justice Act 2006, Sch 1, the Criminal Justice and Immigration Act 2008, Schs 23 and 28, the Police Reform and Social Responsibility Act 2011, Schs 14 and 16, the Police (Complaints and Conduct) Act 2012, s 1, the Crime and Courts Act 2013, Sch 6 and the Anti-social Behaviour, Crime and Policing Act 2014, ss 136–139, Sch 11.)* *

* **Amended by the Investigatory Powers Act 2016 and the Policing and Crime Act 2017 from a date to be appointed.**

[1] Schedule 3 gives the IPCC ultimate control over the progress of an investigation and any consequential disciplinary and criminal proceedings. It sets out a regime for the holistic handling of police complaint matters from end to end. While there are intermediate stages in the handling of such matters, the process was not be treated as a number of self-contained steps that must be undertaken without regard to the overall statutory objective to deal with matters efficiently, effectively and with public confidence. The IPCC does not perform its function until the complaint has been resolved or concluded, and until this point a step can be reviewed if that is shown to be desirable and in the public interest: *R (Demetro) v Independent Police Complaints Commission, R (Commissioner of Police for the Metropolis) v Independent Police Complaints Commission* [2015] EWCA Civ 1248, [2016] PTSR 891 (IPCC entitled to re-open a strangling allegation after previously deciding there was no case to answer; it had not discharged all its functions and there had been compelling reasons to re-open the matter).

### PART 1
### HANDLING OF COMPLAINTS

*Duties to preserve evidence relating to complaints*

7.9259 1. (1) Where a complaint is made about the conduct of a chief officer, it shall be the duty of the local policing body maintaining his force to secure that all such steps as are appropriate for the purposes of Part 2 of this Act are taken, both initially and from time to time after that, for obtaining and preserving evidence relating to the conduct complained of.

(2) Where—

(*a*) a complaint is made to a chief officer about the conduct of a person under his direction and control, or

(*b*) a chief officer becomes aware that a complaint about the conduct of a person under his direction or control has been made to the Commission or to a local policing body,

the chief officer shall take all such steps as appear to him to be appropriate for the purposes of Part 2 of this Act for obtaining and preserving evidence relating to the conduct complained of.

(3) The chief officer's duty under sub-paragraph (2) must be performed as soon as practicable after the complaint is made or, as the case may be, he becomes aware of it.

(4) After that, he shall be under a duty, until he is satisfied that it is no longer necessary to do so, to continue to take the steps from time to time appearing to him to be appropriate for the purposes of Part 2 of this Act for obtaining and preserving evidence relating to the conduct complained of.

(5) It shall be the duty of a local policing body to comply with all such directions as may be given to it by the Commission in relation to the performance of its duty under sub-paragraph (1).

(6) It shall be the duty of a chief officer to take all such specific steps for obtaining or preserving evidence relating to any conduct that is the subject-matter of a complaint as he may be directed to take for the purposes of this paragraph by the local policing body maintaining his force or by the Commission.

*Initial handling and recording of complaints*

2. (1) Where a complaint is made to the Commission, it shall give notification of the complaint to the appropriate authority.

(1A) But the Commission need not give that notification if the Commission considers that there are exceptional circumstances that justify its not being given.

(2) Where a complaint is made to a local policing body, it shall—

(*a*) determine whether or not it is itself the appropriate authority; and

(*b*) if it determines that it is not, give notification of the complaint to the person who is.

(3) Where a complaint is made to a chief officer, he shall—

(*a*) determine whether or not he is himself the appropriate authority; and

(*b*) if he determines that he is not, give notification of the complaint to the person who is.

(4) *Repealed.*

(5) Where the Commission, a local policing body or a chief officer gives notification of a complaint under any of sub-paragraphs (1) to (3), the person who gave the notification shall notify the complainant—

(*a*) that the notification has been given and of what it contained.

(*b*) *repealed.*

(6) Where—

(*a*) a local policing body determines, in the case of any complaint made to the body, that it is itself the appropriate authority,

(*b*) a chief officer determines, in the case of any complaint made to that chief officer, that he is himself the appropriate authority, or

(*c*) a complaint is notified to a local policing body or chief officer under this paragraph,

the body or chief officer shall record the complaint.

(7) Nothing in this paragraph shall require the notification or recording by any person of any complaint about any conduct if—

(*a*) that person is satisfied that the subject-matter of the complaint has been, or is already being, dealt with by means of criminal or disciplinary proceedings against the person whose conduct it was; or

(*b*) the complaint has been withdrawn.

(8) Nothing in this paragraph shall require the recording by any person of any complaint about any conduct if that person considers that the complaint falls within a description of complaints specified in regulations made by the Secretary of State for the purposes of this paragraph.

*Failures to notify or record a complaint*

**3.** (1) This paragraph applies where anything which is or purports to be a complaint in relation to which paragraph (2) has effect is received by a local policing body or chief officer (whether in consequence of having been made directly or of a notification under that paragraph).

(2) If the local policing body or chief officer decides not to take action under paragraph (2) for notifying or recording the whole or any part of what has been received, the body or chief officer shall notify the complainant of the following matters—

(*a*) the decision to take no action and, if that decision relates to only part of what was received, the part in question;

(*b*) the grounds on which the decision was made; and

(*c*) that complainant's right to appeal against that decision under this paragraph.

(3) The complainant shall have a right of appeal to the Commission against any failure by the local policing body or chief officer to make a determination under paragraph 2 or to notify or record anything under that paragraph.

(3A) But the complainant has no right of appeal under sub-paragraph (3) in either of the following cases.

(3B) The first case is where, by virtue of paragraph 2(7), there is no requirement to record the complaint.

(3C) The second case is where—

(*a*) the complaint relates to a direction and control matter, and

(*b*) the appeal relates to a failure by a local policing body.

(4) On an appeal under this paragraph, the Commission shall—

(*a*) determine whether any action under paragraph 2 should have been taken in the case in question; and

(*b*) if the Commission finds in the complainant's favour, give such directions as the Commission considers appropriate to the local policing body or chief officer as to the action to be taken for making a determination, or for notifying or recording what was received;

and it shall be the duty of a local policing body or chief officer to comply with any directions given under paragraph (*b*).

(5) Directions under sub-paragraph (4)(*b*) may require action taken in pursuance of the directions to be treated as taken in accordance with any such provision of paragraph 2 as may be specified in the direction.

(6) The Commission—

(*a*) shall give notification both to the local policing body or, as the case may be, the chief officer and to the complainant of any determination made by it under this paragraph; and

(*b*) shall give notification to the complainant of any direction given by it under this paragraph to the local policing body or chief officer.

(7) The Secretary of State may by regulations[1] make provision—

(*a*) for the form and manner in which appeals under this paragraph are to be brought;

(*b*) for the period within which any such appeal must be brought; and

(*c*) for the procedure to be followed by the Commission when dealing with or disposing of any such appeal.

*Reference of complaints to the Commission*

**4.** (1) It shall be the duty of the appropriate authority to refer a complaint to the Commission if—

(*a*) the complaint is one alleging that the conduct complained of has resulted in death or serious injury;

(*b*) the complaint is of a description specified for the purposes of this sub-paragraph in regulations[1] made by the Secretary of State; or

(*c*) the Commission notifies the appropriate authority that it requires the complaint in question to be referred to the Commission for its consideration.

(2) In a case where there is no obligation under sub-paragraph (1) to make a reference, the appropriate authority may refer a complaint to the Commission if that authority considers that it would be appropriate to do so by reason of—

(*a*) the gravity of the subject-matter of the complaint; or

(*b*) any exceptional circumstances.

(3) In a case in which a reference under sub-paragraph (1) or (2) is neither made nor required to be made, a local policing body may refer a complaint to the Commission if—

(*a*) it is one in relation to which the chief officer of police of the police force maintained by that body is the appropriate authority; and

(*b*) the local policing body considers that it would be appropriate to do so reason of—

(i) the gravity of the subject-matter of the complaint; or

(ii) any exceptional circumstances.

(4) Where there is an obligation under this paragraph to refer a complaint to the Commission, it must be so referred within such period as may be provided for by regulations[1] made by the Secretary of State.

(5) Subject to sub-paragraph (7), the following powers—

(*a*) the power of the Commission by virtue of sub-paragraph (1)(*c*) to require a complaint to be referred to it, and

(*b*) the power of a local policing body or chief officer to refer a complaint to the Commission under sub-paragraph (2) or (3),

shall each be exercisable at any time irrespective of whether the complaint is already being investigated by any person or has already been considered by the Commission.

(6) A local policing body or chief officer which refers a complaint to the Commission under this paragraph shall give a notification of the making of the reference—

(*a*) to the complainant, and

(*b*) except in a case where it appears to that body or chief officer that to do so might prejudice a possible future investigation of the complaint, to the person complained against.

(7) A complaint that has already been referred to the Commission under this paragraph on a previous occasion—

(*a*) shall not be required to be referred again under this paragraph unless the Commission so directs; and

(*b*) shall not be referred in exercise of any power conferred by this paragraph unless the Commission consents.

(8) In a case where—

(*a*) a complaint relates to a direction and control matter, and

(*b*) there is no obligation under this paragraph for the appropriate authority to refer the complaint to the Commission,

the appropriate authority may refer the complaint to the Commission under this paragraph only if the Commission consents.

(8)

(*a*)

(*b*)

*Duties of Commission on references under paragraph 4*

5. (1) It shall be the duty of the Commission in the case of every complaint referred to it by a local policing body or chief officer, to determine whether or not it is necessary for the complaint to be investigated.

(2) Where the Commission determines under this paragraph that it is not necessary for a complaint to be investigated, it may, if it thinks fit, refer the complaint back to the appropriate authority to be dealt with by that authority in accordance with paragraph 6.

(3) Where the Commission refers a complaint back under sub-paragraph (2), it shall give a notification of the making of the reference back—

(*a*) to the complainant, and

(*b*) except in a case where it appears to the Commission that to do so might prejudice a possible future investigation of the complaint, to the person complained against.

*Handling of complaints by the appropriate authority*

**6.** (1) This paragraph applies where a complaint has been recorded by the appropriate authority.

(2) But this paragraph does not apply to a complaint if it is one that has been, or must be, referred to the Commission under paragraph 4, unless the complaint is for the time being—

(*a*) referred back to the authority under paragraph 5, or

(*b*) the subject of a determination under paragraph 15.

(3) Subject to paragraph 7, the appropriate authority shall determine whether or not the complaint is suitable for being subjected to local resolution.

(4) If the appropriate authority determines that the complaint is suitable for being subjected to local resolution, it shall make arrangements for it to be so subjected.

(5) If the appropriate authority determines that the complaint is not so suitable, it shall make arrangements for the complaint to be investigated by the authority on its own behalf.

(6) A determination that a complaint is suitable for being subjected to local resolution may not be made unless the following conditions are both met.

(7) The first condition is that the appropriate authority is satisfied that the conduct complained of (even if it were proved) would not justify the bringing of any criminal or disciplinary proceedings against the person whose conduct is complained of.

(8) The second condition is that the appropriate authority is satisfied that the conduct complained of (even if it were proved) would not involve the infringement of a person's rights under Article 2 or 3 of the Convention (within the meaning of the Human Rights Act 1998).

(9) In a case where this paragraph applies to a complaint by virtue of sub-paragraph (2)(*b*), a determination that the complaint is suitable for being subjected to local resolution may not be made unless the Commission approves the determination.

(10) No more than one application may be made to the Commission for the purposes of sub-paragraph (9) in respect of the same complaint.

(11) Sub-paragraph (9) (where applicable) is in addition to subparagraphs (6) to (8).

*Disapplication of requirements of Schedule*

7. (1) If, in a case in which paragraph (6) applies, the appropriate authority considers—

(*a*) that it should handle the complaint otherwise than in accordance with this Schedule or should take no action in relation to it, and

(*b*) that the complaint falls within a description of complaints specified in regulations made by the Secretary of State for the purposes of this paragraph,

the appropriate authority may handle the complaint in whatever manner (if any) that authority thinks fit.

(1A) But, in a case where paragraph 6 applies by virtue of paragraph 6(2)(*a*) or (*b*), the appropriate authority may not handle the complaint in whatever manner (if any) the authority thinks fit unless—

(*a*) the authority applies to the Commission, in accordance with the regulations, for permission to so handle the complaint, and

(*b*) the Commission gives permission.

(2) The appropriate authority shall notify the complainant—

(*a*) that the appropriate authority has decided to handle the complaint as permitted by sub-paragraph (1) (in a case where the appropriate authority is not required to apply for permission under sub-paragraph (1A) to so handle the complaint); or

(*b*) about the making of the application under sub-paragraph (1A) (in a case where the appropriate authority makes such an application).

(3) Where such an application is made to the Commission, it shall, in accordance with regulations[1] made by the Secretary of State—

(*a*) consider the application and determine whether to grant the permission applied for; and

(*b*) notify its decision to the appropriate authority and the complainant.

(4) Where an application is made under this paragraph in respect of any complaint, the appropriate authority shall not, while the application is being considered by the Commission, take any action in accordance with the provisions of this Schedule (other than under paragraph 1) in relation to that complaint.

(5) Where the complaint is to be handled in whatever manner (if any) the authority thinks fit (whether or not the Commission's permission is needed), the authority—

(*a*) shall not be required by virtue of any of the provisions of this Schedule (other than paragraph 1) to take any action in relation to the complaint; but

(*b*) may handle the complaint in whatever manner it thinks fit, or take no action in relation to the complaint, and for the purposes of handling the complaint may take any step that it could have taken, or would have been required to take, if it were not proceeding in accordance with this paragraph.

(6) Where the appropriate authority applies to the Commission under sub-paragraph (1A) and the Commission determines that no permission should be granted—

(*a*) it shall refer the matter back to the appropriate authority for the making of a determination under paragraph 6(3); and

(*b*) the authority shall then make that determination.

(7) No more than one application may be made to the Commission under this paragraph in respect of the same complaint.

(8) The complainant shall have a right of appeal to the relevant appeal body against any decision by the appropriate authority under this paragraph to handle the complaint otherwise than in accordance with this Schedule or to take no action in relation to it.

(9) But the complainant has no right of appeal in either of the following cases.

(10) The first case is where the appeal relates to a decision for which the Commission has given permission under this paragraph.

(11) The second case is where the complaint relates to a direction and control matter.

(12) On an appeal under this paragraph, subject to sub-paragraphs (13) and (14), the relevant appeal body shall—

(*a*) determine whether any decision taken by the appropriate authority under this paragraph should have been taken in the case in question; and (

(*b*) if the relevant appeal body finds in the complainant's favour, give such directions as the relevant appeal body thinks appropriate to the local policing body or chief officer as to the action to be taken for handling the complaint in accordance with this Schedule or handling it otherwise than in accordance with this Schedule;

and it shall be the duty of a local policing body or chief officer to comply with any directions given under paragraph (*b*).

(13) Sub-paragraph (12) does not apply in a case where a particular chief officer of police is—

(*a*) the person in respect of whose decision the appeal is made under this paragraph, and

(*b*) the relevant appeal body in relation to the appeal.

(14) In such a case—

(*a*) the appeal shall determine whether any decision taken by the appropriate authority under this paragraph should have been taken in the case in question; and

(*b*) if the appeal finds in the complainant's favour, the chief officer of police must take such action as the chief officer thinks appropriate for handling the complaint in accordance with this Schedule or handling it otherwise than in accordance with this Schedule.

*Local resolution of complaints*

**8.** (1) The arrangements made by the appropriate authority for subjecting any complaint to local resolution may include the appointment of a person who—

(*a*) is serving with the police, and

(*b*) is under the direction and control of the chief officer of police of the relevant force,

to secure the local resolution of the complaint.

(2) The Secretary of State may by regulations[1] make provision—

(*a*) for the different descriptions of procedures that are to be available for dealing with a complaint where it is decided it is to be subjected to local resolution;

(*b*) for requiring a person complained against in a case in which the complaint is subjected to local resolution to be given an opportunity of commenting, in such manner as may be provided for in the regulations, on the complaint;

(*c*) for requiring that, on the making of an application in accordance with the regulations, a record of the outcome of any procedure for the local resolution of any complaint is to be given to the complainant.

(3) A statement made by any person for the purposes of the local resolution of any complaint shall not be admissible in any subsequent criminal, civil or disciplinary proceedings except to the extent that it consists of an admission relating to a matter that has not been subjected to local resolution.

(4) If, after attempts have been made to resolve a complaint using local resolution, it appears to the appropriate authority—

(*a*) that the resolution of the complaint in that manner is impossible, or

(*b*) that the complaint is, for any other reason, not suitable for such resolution,

it shall make arrangements for the complaint to be investigated by that authority on its own behalf.

(5) The local resolution of any complaint shall be discontinued if—

(*a*) any arrangements are made under sub-paragraph (4);

(*b*) the Commission notifies the appropriate authority that it requires the complaint to be referred to the Commission under paragraph 4; or (*c*) the complaint is so referred otherwise than in pursuance of such a notification.

(6) A person who has participated in any attempt to resolve a complaint using local resolution shall be disqualified for appointment under any provision of this Schedule to investigate that complaint, or to assist with the carrying out of the investigation of that complaint.

*Appeals relating to complaints dealt with other than by investigation*

**8A.** (1) The complainant shall have a right of appeal to the relevant appeal body against the outcome of any complaint that is—

(*a*) subjected to local resolution, or

(*b*) handled otherwise than in accordance with this Schedule.

(2) But the complainant has no right of appeal if the complaint relates to a direction and control matter.

(3) On an appeal under this paragraph, subject to sub-paragraphs (4) and (5), the relevant appeal body shall—

(*a*) determine whether the outcome of the complaint is a proper outcome; and

(*b*) if the relevant appeal body finds in the complainant's favour, give such directions as the relevant appeal body thinks appropriate to the appropriate authority as to the action to be taken in relation to the complaint;

and it shall be the duty of the appropriate authority to comply with any directions given under paragraph (*b*).

(4) Sub-paragraph (3) does not apply in a case where a chief officer of police is the relevant appeal body in relation to the appeal.

(5) In such a case—

(*a*) the appeal shall determine whether the outcome of the complaint is a proper outcome; and

(*b*) if the appeal finds in the complainant's favour, the chief officer of police must take such action as the chief officer thinks appropriate in relation to the complaint.".

---

[1] The Police (Complaints and Misconduct) Regulations 2012, SI 2012/1204 have been made.

## PART 2

## HANDLING OF CONDUCT MATTERS

*Conduct matters arising in civil proceedings*

7.9260 **10.** (1) This paragraph applies where—

(*a*) a local policing body or chief officer has received notification (whether or not under this paragraph) that civil proceedings relating to any matter have been brought by a member of the public against that body or chief officer, or it otherwise appears to a local policing body or chief officer that such proceedings are likely to be so brought; and

(*b*) it appears to that body or chief officer (whether at the time of the notification or at any time subsequently) that those proceedings involve or would involve a conduct matter.

(2) The body or chief officer—

(*a*) shall consider whether it or, as the case may be, he is the appropriate authority in relation to the conduct matter in question; and

(*b*) if it or he is not, shall notify the person who is the appropriate authority about the proceedings, or the proposal to bring them, and about the circumstances that make it appear as mentioned in sub-paragraph (1)(*b*).

(3) Where a local policing body or chief officer determines for the purposes of this paragraph that it or, as the case may be, he is the appropriate authority in relation to any conduct matter, it or he shall determine whether the matter is one which it or he is required to refer to the Commission under paragraph 13 or is one which it would be appropriate to so refer.

(4) In a case where the appropriate authority determines that the matter is one which it or he is required to refer to the Commission under paragraph 13, or is one which it would be appropriate to so refer, it or he shall record the matter.

(4A) In any other case, the appropriate authority shall determine whether the matter falls within a description of matters specified in regulations made by the Secretary of State for the purposes of this sub-paragraph.

(4B) In a case where the appropriate authority determines that the matter does not fall within such a description, it or he shall record the matter.

(4C) In any other case, the appropriate authority may (but need not) record the matter.

(4D) In a case where the appropriate authority—

(*a*) records a matter under this paragraph, and

(*b*) is not required to refer the matter to the Commission under paragraph 13 and does not do so,

the appropriate authority may deal with the matter in such other manner (if any) as it or he may determine.

(5) Nothing in sub-paragraph (4) or (4B) shall require the appropriate authority to record any conduct matter if it is satisfied that the matter has been, or is already being, dealt with by means of criminal or disciplinary proceedings against the person to whose conduct the matter relates.

(6) For the purposes of this paragraph civil proceedings involve a conduct matter if—

(*a*) they relate to such a matter; or

(*b*) they are proceedings that relate to a matter in relation to which a conduct matter, or evidence of a conduct matter, is or may be relevant.

(7) The Secretary of State may by regulations provide for the times at which, or the periods within which, any requirement of this paragraph is to be complied with; and the period from which any such period is to run shall be such time as may be specified in those regulations or as may be determined in a manner set out in the regulations.

*Recording etc of conduct matters in other cases*

**11.** (1) This paragraph applies where—

(*a*) a conduct matter comes (otherwise than as mentioned in paragraph 10) to the attention of the local policing body or chief officer who is the appropriate authority in relation to that matter, and

(*b*) it appears to the appropriate authority that the conduct involved in that matter falls within sub-paragraph (2).

(2) Conduct falls within this sub-paragraph if (assuming it to have taken place)—

(*a*) it appears to have resulted in the death of any person or in serious injury to any person;

(*b*) a member of the public has been adversely affected by it; or

(*c*) it is of a description specified for the purposes of this sub-paragraph in regulations[1] made by the Secretary of State.

(3) The appropriate authority must determine whether the matter is one which it or he is required to refer to the Commission under paragraph 13, or is one which it would be appropriate to so refer.

(3A) In a case where the appropriate authority determines that the matter is one which it or he is required to refer to the Commission under paragraph 13, or is one which it would be appropriate to so refer, it or he shall record the matter.

(3B) In any other case, the appropriate authority shall determine whether the matter falls within a description of matters specified in regulations made by the Secretary of State for the purposes of this sub-paragraph.

(3C) In a case where the appropriate authority determines that the matter does not fall within such a description, it or he shall record the matter.

(3D) In any other case, the appropriate authority may (but need not) record the matter.

(3E) In a case where the appropriate authority—

(*a*) records a matter under this paragraph, and

(*b*) is not required to refer the matter to the Commission under paragraph 13 and does not do so,

the appropriate authority may deal with the matter in such other manner (if any) as it or he may determine.

(4) Nothing in sub-paragraph (3A) or (3C) shall require the appropriate authority to record any conduct matter if it is satisfied that the matter has been, or is already being, dealt with by means of criminal or disciplinary proceedings against the person to whose conduct the matter relates.

(5) If it appears to the Commission—

(*a*) that any matter that has come to its attention is a recordable conduct matter, but

(*b*) that that matter has not been recorded by the appropriate authority,

the Commission may direct the appropriate authority to record that matter; and it shall be the duty of that authority to comply with the direction.

*Duties to preserve evidence relating to conduct matters*

**12.** (1) Where a recordable conduct matter that relates to the conduct of a chief officer comes to the attention of the local policing body maintaining his force, it shall be the duty of that body to secure that all such steps as are appropriate for the purposes of Part 2 of this Act are taken, both initially and from time to time after that, for obtaining and preserving evidence relating to that matter.

(2) Where a chief officer becomes aware of any recordable conduct matter relating to the conduct of a person under his direction and control, it shall be his duty to take all such steps as appear to him to be appropriate for the purposes of Part 2 of this Act for obtaining and preserving evidence relating to that matter.

(3) The chief officer's duty under sub-paragraph (2) must be performed as soon as practicable after he becomes aware of the matter in question.

(4) After that, he shall be under a duty, until he is satisfied that it is no longer necessary to do so, to continue to take the steps from time to time appearing to him to be appropriate for the purposes of Part 2 of this Act for obtaining and preserving evidence relating to the matter.

(5) It shall be the duty of a local policing body to comply with all such directions as may be given to it by the Commission in relation to the performance of any duty imposed on it by virtue of sub-paragraph (1).

(6) It shall be the duty of the chief officer to take all such specific steps for obtaining or preserving evidence relating to any recordable conduct matter as he may be directed to take for the purposes of this paragraph by the local policing body maintaining his force or by the Commission.

*Reference of conduct matters to the Commission*

**13.** (1) It shall be the duty of a local policing body or a chief officer to refer a recordable conduct matter to the Commission if, in a case (whether or not falling within paragraph 10) in which the body or chief officer is the appropriate authority—

(*a*) that matter relates to any incident or circumstances in or in consequence of which any person has died or suffered serious injury;

(*b*) that matter is of a description specified for the purposes of this sub-paragraph in regulations made by the Secretary of State; or

(*c*) the Commission notifies the appropriate authority that it requires that matter to be referred to the Commission for its consideration.

(2) In any case where there is no obligation under sub-paragraph (1) to make a reference, the appropriate authority may refer a recordable conduct matter to the Commission if that authority considers that it would be appropriate to do so by reason of—

(*a*) the gravity of the matter; or

(*b*) any exceptional circumstances.

(3) In a case in which a reference under sub-paragraph (1) or (2) is neither made nor required to be made, a local policing body maintaining any police force may refer any recordable conduct matter to the Commission if—

(*a*) it is one in relation to which the chief officer of police of that force is the appropriate authority; and

(*b*) the local policing body considers that it would be appropriate to do so by reason of—

(i) the gravity of the matter; or

(ii) any exceptional circumstances.

(4) Where there is an obligation under this paragraph to refer any matter to the Commission, it must be so referred within such period as may be provided for by regulations[1] made by the Secretary of State.

(5) Subject to sub-paragraph (7), the following powers—

(*a*) the power of the Commission by virtue of sub-paragraph (1)(*c*) to require a matter to be referred to it, and

(*b*) the power of a local policing body or chief officer to refer any matter to the Commission under sub-paragraph (2) or (3),

shall each be exercisable at any time irrespective of whether the matter is already being investigated by any person or has already been considered by the Commission.

(6) Where—

(*a*) a local policing body or chief officer refers a matter to the Commission under this paragraph, and

(*b*) that body or chief officer does not consider that to do so might prejudice a possible future investigation of that matter,

that body or chief officer shall give a notification of the making of the reference to the person to whose conduct that matter relates.

(7) A matter that has already been referred to the Commission under this paragraph on a previous occasion—

(*a*) shall not be required to be referred again under this paragraph unless the Commission so directs; and

(*b*) shall not be referred in exercise of any power conferred by this paragraph unless the Commission consents.

*Duties of Commission on references under paragraph 13*

**14.** (1) It shall be the duty of the Commission, in the case of every recordable conduct matter referred to it by a local policing body or chief officer under paragraph 13, to determine whether or not it is necessary for the matter to be investigated.

(2) Where the Commission determines under this paragraph that it is not necessary for a recordable conduct matter to be investigated, it may if it thinks fit refer the matter back to the appropriate authority to be dealt with by that authority in such manner (if any) as that authority may determine.

(3) Where—

(*a*) the Commission refers a matter back to the appropriate authority under this paragraph, and

(*b*) the Commission does not consider that to do so might prejudice a possible future investigation of that matter,

the Commission shall give a notification of the making of the reference to the person to whose conduct that matter relates.

[1] The Police (Complaints and Misconduct) Regulations 2012, SI 2012/1204 have been made.

## PART 2A

## HANDLING OF DEATH AND SERIOUS INJURY (DSI) MATTERS

*Duty to record DSI matters*

**14A.** (1) Where a DSI matter comes to the attention of the local policing body or chief officer who is the appropriate authority in relation to that matter, it shall be the duty of the appropriate authority to record that matter.

(2) If it appears to the Commission—

(*a*) that any matter that has come to its attention is a DSI matter, but

(*b*) that that matter has not been recorded by the appropriate authority,

the Commission may direct the appropriate authority to record that matter; and it shall be the duty of that authority to comply with the direction.

*Duty to preserve evidence relating to DSI matters*

**14B.** (1) Where—

(*a*) a DSI matter comes to the attention of a local policing body, and

(*b*) the relevant officer in relation to that matter is the chief officer of the force maintained by that body,

it shall be the duty of that body to secure that all such steps as are appropriate for the purposes of Part 2 of this Act are taken, both initially and from time to time after that, for obtaining and preserving evidence relating to that matter.

(2) Where—

(*a*) a chief officer becomes aware of a DSI matter, and

(*b*) the relevant officer in relation to that matter is a person under his direction and control,

it shall be his duty to take all such steps as appear to him to be appropriate for the purposes of Part 2 of this Act for obtaining and preserving evidence relating to that matter.

(3) The chief officer's duty under sub-paragraph (2) must be performed as soon as practicable after he becomes aware of the matter in question.

(4) After that, he shall be under a duty, until he is satisfied that it is no longer necessary to do so, to continue to take the steps from time to time appearing to him to be appropriate for the purposes of Part 2 of this Act for obtaining and preserving evidence relating to the matter.

(5) It shall be the duty of a local policing body to comply with all such directions as may be given to it by the Commission in relation to the performance of any duty imposed on it by virtue of sub-paragraph (1).

(6) It shall be the duty of the chief officer to take all such specific steps for obtaining or preserving evidence relating to any DSI matter as he may be directed to take for the purposes of this paragraph by the local policing body maintaining his force or by the Commission.

*Reference of DSI matters to the Commission*

**14C.** (1) It shall be the duty of the appropriate authority to refer a DSI matter to the Commission.

(2) The appropriate authority must do so within such period as may be provided for by regulations made by the Secretary of State.

(3) A matter that has already been referred to the Commission under this paragraph on a previous occasion shall not be required to be referred again under this paragraph unless the Commission so directs.

*Duties of Commission on references under paragraph 14C*

**14D.** (1) It shall be the duty of the Commission, in the case of every DSI matter referred to it by a local policing body or a chief officer, to determine whether or not it is necessary for the matter to be investigated.

(2) Where the Commission determines under this paragraph that it is not necessary for a DSI matter to be investigated, it may if it thinks fit refer the matter back to the appropriate authority to be dealt with by that authority in such manner (if any) as that authority may determine.

## Part 3

## Investigations and Subsequent Proceedings

*Power of the Commission to determine the form of an investigation*

7.9261 **15.** (1) This paragraph applies where—

(*a*) a complaint, recordable conduct matter or DSI matter is referred to the Commission; and

(*b*) the Commission determines that it is necessary for the complaint or matter to be investigated.

(2) It shall be the duty of the Commission to determine the form which the investigation should take.

(3) In making a determination under sub-paragraph (2) the Commission shall have regard to the following factors—

(*a*) the seriousness of the case; and

(*b*) the public interest.

(4) The only forms which the investigation may take in accordance with a determination made under this paragraph are—

(*a*) an investigation by the appropriate authority on its own behalf;

(*b*) an investigation by that authority under the supervision of the Commission;

(*c*) an investigation by that authority under the management of the Commission;

(*d*) an investigation by the Commission.

(5) The Commission may at any time make a further determination under this paragraph to replace an earlier one.

(6) Where a determination under this paragraph replaces an earlier determination under this paragraph, or relates to a complaint or matter in relation to which the appropriate authority has already begun an investigation on its own behalf, the Commission may give—

(*a*) the appropriate authority, and

(*b*) any person previously appointed to carry out the investigation,

such directions as it considers appropriate for the purpose of giving effect to the new determination.

(7) It shall be the duty of a person to whom a direction is given under sub-paragraph (6) to comply with it.

(8) The Commission shall notify the appropriate authority of any determination that it makes under this paragraph in relation to a particular complaint, recordable conduct matter or DSI matter.

*Investigations by the appropriate authority on its own behalf*

**16.** (1) This paragraph applies if the appropriate authority is required by virtue of—

(*a*) any determination made by that authority under paragraph 6(3) (whether following the recording of a complaint or on a reference back under paragraph 5(2)) or under paragraph 8(4), or

(*b*) any determination made by the Commission under paragraph 15,

to make arrangements for a complaint, recordable conduct matter or DSI matter to be investigated by the appropriate authority on its own behalf.

(2) This paragraph also applies if—

(*a*) a determination falls to be made by that authority under paragraph 10(4D), or 11(3E) or 14(2) in relation to any recordable conduct matter or under paragraph 14D(2) in relation to any DSI matter; and

(*b*) the appropriate authority determine that it is necessary for the matter to be investigated by the authority on its own behalf.

(3) Subject to sub-paragraph (4) or (5), it shall be the duty of the appropriate authority to appoint—

(*a*) a person serving with the police (whether under the direction and control of the chief officer of police of the relevant force or of the chief officer of another force), or

(*b*) a National Crime Agency officer,

to investigate the complaint or matter.

(4) The person appointed under this paragraph to investigate any complaint or conduct matter—

(*a*) in the case of an investigation relating to any conduct of a chief officer, must not be a person under that chief officer's direction and control; and

(*b*) in the case of an investigation relating to any conduct of the Commissioner of Police of the Metropolis or of the Deputy Commissioner of Police of the Metropolis, must be the person nominated by the Secretary of State for appointment under this paragraph.

(5) The person appointed under this paragraph to investigate any DSI matter—

(*a*) in relation to which the relevant officer is a chief officer, must not be a person under that chief officer's direction and control;

(*b*) in relation to which the relevant officer is the Commissioner of Police of the Metropolis or the Deputy Commissioner of Police of the Metropolis, must be the person nominated by the Secretary of State for appointment under this paragraph.

*Investigations supervised by the Commission*

**17.** (1) This paragraph applies where the Commission has determined that it should supervise the investigation by the appropriate authority of any complaint, recordable conduct matter or DSI matter.

(2) On being given notice of that determination, the appropriate authority shall, if it has not already done so, appoint—

(*a*) a person serving with the police (whether under the direction and control of the chief officer of police of the relevant force or of the chief officer of another force), or

(*b*) a National Crime Agency officer,

to investigate the complaint or matter.

(3) The Commission may require that no appointment is made under sub-paragraph (2) unless it has given notice to the appropriate authority that it approves the person whom that authority proposes to appoint.

(4) Where a person has already been appointed to investigate the complaint or matter, or is selected under this sub-paragraph for appointment, and the Commission is not satisfied with that person, the Commission may require the appropriate authority, as soon as reasonably practicable after being required to do so—

(*a*) to select another person falling within sub-paragraph (2)(*a*), (*b*) or (*c*) to investigate the complaint or matter; and (*b*) to notify the Commission of the person selected.

(5) Where a selection made in pursuance of a requirement under sub-paragraph (4) has been notified to the Commission, the appropriate authority shall appoint that person to investigate the complaint or matter if, but only if, the Commission notifies the authority that it approves the appointment of that person.

(6) A person appointed under this paragraph to investigate any complaint or conduct matter—

(*a*) in the case of an investigation relating to any conduct of a chief officer, must not be a person under that chief officer's direction and control; and

(*b*) in the case of an investigation relating to any conduct of the Commissioner of Police of the Metropolis or of the Deputy Commissioner of Police of the Metropolis, must be the person nominated by the Secretary of State for appointment under this paragraph.

(6A) The person appointed under this paragraph to investigate any DSI matter—

(*a*) in relation to which the relevant officer is a chief officer, must not be a person under that chief officer's direction and control;

(*b*) in relation to which the relevant officer is the Commissioner of Police of the Metropolis or the Deputy Commissioner of Police of the Metropolis, must be the person nominated by the Secretary of State for appointment under this paragraph.

(7) The person appointed to investigate the complaint or matter shall comply with all such requirements in relation to the carrying out of that investigation as may, in accordance with regulations made for the purposes of this sub-paragraph by the Secretary of State, be imposed by the Commission in relation to that investigation.

*Investigations managed by the Commission*

**18.** (1) This paragraph applies where the Commission has determined that it should manage the investigation by the appropriate authority of any complaint, recordable conduct matter or DSI matter.

(2) Sub-paragraphs (2) to (6A) of paragraph 17 shall apply as they apply in the case of an investigation which the Commission has determined is one that it should supervise.

(3) The person appointed to investigate the complaint or matter shall, in relation to that investigation, be under the direction and control of the Commission.

*Investigations by the Commission itself*

**19.** (1) This paragraph applies where the Commission has determined that it should itself carry out the investigation of a complaint, recordable conduct matter or DSI matter.

(2) The Commission shall designate both—

(*a*) a member of the Commission's staff to take charge of the investigation on behalf of the Commission, and

(*b*) all such other members of the Commission's staff as are required by the Commission to assist him.

(3) The person designated under sub-paragraph (2) to be the person to take charge of an investigation relating to any conduct of the Commissioner of Police of the Metropolis or of the Deputy Commissioner of Police of the Metropolis must be the person nominated by the Secretary of State to be so designated under that sub-paragraph.

(3A) The person designated under sub-paragraph (2) to be the person to take charge of an investigation of a DSI matter in relation to which the relevant officer is the Commissioner of Police of the Metropolis or the Deputy Commissioner of Police of the Metropolis must be the person nominated by the Secretary of State to be so designated under that sub-paragraph.

(4) A member of the Commission's staff who—

(*a*) is designated under sub-paragraph (2) in relation to any investigation, but

(*b*) does not already, by virtue of section 97(8) of the 1996 Act, have all the powers and privileges of a constable throughout England and Wales and the adjacent United Kingdom waters,

shall, for the purposes of the carrying out of the investigation and all purposes connected with it, have all those powers and privileges throughout England and Wales and those waters.

(5) A member of the Commission's staff who is not a constable shall not, as a result of sub-paragraph (4), be treated as being in police service for the purposes of—

(*a*) section 280 of the Trade Union and Labour Relations (Consolidation) Act 1992 (c 52) (person in police service excluded from definitions of "worker" and "employee"); or

(*b*) section 200 of the Employment Rights Act 1996 (c 18) (certain provisions of that Act not to apply to persons in police service).

(6) The Secretary of State may by order provide that—

(*a*) such provisions of the 1984 Act relating to investigations of offences conducted by police officers as may be specified in the order, and

(*b*) such provisions of a code of practice under section 60, 60A or 66 of that Act as may be so specified,

shall apply subject to such modifications as may be so specified, to investigations of offences conducted by virtue of this paragraph by members of the Commission's staff designated under sub-paragraph (2).

(6A) An order under sub-paragraph (6) may, in particular, provide that where a provision applied by the order allows a power to be exercised only if an authorisation is given by a police officer of or above a particular rank, the authorisation may be given by a member of the Commission's staff of or above a specified grade.

(7) References in this paragraph to the powers and privileges of a constable—

(*a*) are references to any power or privilege conferred by or under any enactment (including one passed after the passing of this Act) on a constable;

(*aa*) a body required by section 26BA to enter into an agreement with the Commission, or

(*b*) shall have effect as if every such power were exercisable, and every such privilege existed, throughout England and Wales and the adjacent United Kingdom waters (whether or not that is the case apart from this sub-paragraph).

(8) In this paragraph "United Kingdom waters" means the sea and other waters within the seaward limits of the United Kingdom's territorial sea.

**19ZA–19ZD.** *Investigations by the Commission; power to serve information notice; failure to comply with information notice; appeals and sensitive information.*

*Special procedure where investigation relates to police officer or special constable*

**19A.** Paragraphs 19B to 19E apply to investigations of complaints or recordable conduct matters in cases where the person concerned (see paragraph 19B(11)) is a member of a police force or a special constable.

*Assessment of seriousness of conduct under investigation*

**19B.** (1) If, during the course of an investigation of a complaint, it appears to the person investigating that there is an indication that a person to whose conduct the investigation relates may have—

(*a*) committed a criminal offence, or

(*b*) behaved in a manner which would justify the bringing of disciplinary proceedings,

the person investigating must certify the investigation as one subject to special requirements.

(2) If the person investigating a complaint certifies the investigation as one subject to special requirements, the person must, as soon as is reasonably practicable after doing so, make a severity assessment in relation to the conduct of the person concerned to which the investigation relates.

(3) The person investigating a recordable conduct matter must make a severity assessment in relation to the conduct to which the investigation relates—

(*a*) as soon as is reasonably practicable after his appointment or designation, or

(*b*) in the case of a matter recorded in accordance with paragraph 21A(5) or 24B(2), as soon as is reasonably practicable after it is so recorded.

(4) For the purposes of this paragraph a "severity assessment", in relation to conduct, means an assessment as to—

(*a*) whether the conduct, if proved, would amount to misconduct or gross misconduct, and

(*b*) if the conduct were to become the subject of disciplinary proceedings, the form which those proceedings would be likely to take.

(5) An assessment under this paragraph may only be made after consultation with the appropriate authority.

(6) On completing an assessment under this paragraph, the person investigating the complaint or matter must give a notification to the person concerned that complies with sub-paragraph (7).

(7) The notification must—

(*a*) give the prescribed information about the results of the assessment;

(*b*) give the prescribed information about the effect of paragraph 19C and of regulations under paragraph 19D;

(*c*) set out the prescribed time limits for providing the person investigating the complaint or matter with relevant statements and relevant documents respectively for the purposes of paragraph 19C(2);

(*d*) give such other information as may be prescribed.

(8) Sub-paragraph (6) does not apply for so long as the person investigating the complaint or matter considers that giving the notification might prejudice—

(*a*) the investigation, or

(*b*) any other investigation (including, in particular, a criminal investigation).

(9) Where the person investigating a complaint or matter has made a severity assessment and considers it appropriate to do so, the person may revise the assessment.

(10) On revising a severity assessment, the person investigating the complaint or matter must notify the prescribed information about the revised assessment to the person concerned.

(11) In this paragraph and paragraphs 19C to 19E—

"the person concerned"—

(*a*) in relation to an investigation of a complaint, means the person in respect of whom it appears to the person investigating that there is the indication mentioned in paragraph 19B(1);

(*b*) in relation to an investigation of a recordable conduct matter, means the person to whose conduct the investigation relates;

"relevant document"—

(*a*) means a document relating to any complaint or matter under investigation, and

(*b*) includes such a document containing suggestions as to lines of inquiry to be pursued or witnesses to be interviewed;

"relevant statement" means an oral or written statement relating to any complaint or matter under investigation.

*Duty to consider submissions from person whose conduct is being investigated*

**19C.** (1) This paragraph applies to—

(*a*) an investigation of a complaint that has been certified under paragraph 19B(1) as one subject to special requirements, or

(*b*) an investigation of a recordable conduct matter.

(2) If before the expiry of the appropriate time limit notified in pursuance of paragraph 19B(7)(*c*)—

(*a*) the person concerned provides the person investigating the complaint or matter with a relevant statement or a relevant document, or

(*b*) any person of a prescribed description provides that person with a relevant document,

that person must consider the statement or document.

*Interview of person whose conduct is being investigated*

**19D.** (1) The Secretary of State may by regulations make provision as to the procedure to be followed in connection with any interview of the person concerned which is held during the course of an investigation within paragraph 19C(1)(*a*) or (*b*) by the person investigating the complaint or matter.

(2) Regulations under this paragraph may, in particular, make provision—

(*za*) requiring the person concerned to attend an interview,

(*a*) for determining how the time at which an interview is to be held is to be agreed or decided,

(*b*) about the information that must be provided to the person being interviewed,

(*c*) for enabling that person to be accompanied at the interview by a person of a prescribed description.

*Duty to provide certain information to appropriate authority*

**19E.** (1) This paragraph applies during the course of an investigation within paragraph 19C(1)(*a*) or (*b*).

(2) The person investigating the complaint or matter must supply the appropriate authority with such information in that person's possession as the authority may reasonably request for the purpose mentioned in sub-paragraph (3).

(3) That purpose is determining, in accordance with regulations under section 50 or 51 of the 1996 Act, whether the person concerned should be, or should remain, suspended—

(*a*) from office as constable, and
(*b*) where that person is a member of a police force, from membership of that force.

*Interview of persons serving with the police etc during certain investigations*

**19F.** (1) This paragraph applies to an investigation of a complaint, recordable conduct matter or DSI matter which—
(*a*) is carried out by the appropriate authority under the management of the Commission, or
(*b*) is carried out by the Commission itself.

(2) The Secretary of State may by regulations[1] make provision as to the procedure to be followed in connection with an interview which—
(*a*) is held with a serving officer during the course of the investigation by the person investigating the complaint or matter, and
(*b*) is not within paragraph 19D(1).

(3) Regulations[1] under sub-paragraph (2) may in particular make provision—
(*a*) requiring a serving officer to attend an interview,
(*b*) for determining how the time at which an interview is to be held is to be agreed or decided,
(*c*) about the information that must be provided to a serving officer being interviewed,
(*d*) for enabling a serving officer to be accompanied at the interview by a person of a prescribed description.

(4) "Serving officer" means a person who—
(*a*) is serving with the police, or
(*b*) is serving with an additional police body.

(5) A person is serving with an additional police body if the person is a member of, or is employed or otherwise engaged for the purposes of, that body (subject to sub-paragraph (6)).

(6) The Secretary of State may by regulations provide, in relation to an additional police body, that a person is serving with that body only if the person—
(*a*) is a member of, or is employed or otherwise engaged for the purposes of, that body, and
(*b*) is of a prescribed description.

(7) An "additional police body" means—
(*a*) a body of constables which is maintained by an authority other than a local policing body and is prescribed in regulations[1] made by the Secretary of State under this sub-paragraph, or
(*b*) a body required by section 26A or 26B to enter into an agreement with the Commission.

(8) The Secretary of State must obtain the consent of the Northern Ireland Assembly before making provision in regulations under this paragraph which would be within the legislative competence of the Northern Ireland Assembly.

(9) But consent under sub-paragraph (8) is not required in relation to a provision if—
(*a*) a Bill for an Act of the Northern Ireland Assembly containing the provision would require the consent of the Secretary of State under section 8 of the Northern Ireland Act 1998, and
(*b*) the provision does not affect, other than incidentally, a transferred matter (within the meaning of that Act).

(10) Nothing in this paragraph prevents or restricts the holding of interviews to which regulations under this paragraph do not apply during the course of any investigation under this Schedule.

---

[1] The Police (Complaints and Conduct) Regulations 2013, SI 2013/281 have been made.

*Restrictions on proceedings pending the conclusion of an investigation*

**20.** (1) No criminal or disciplinary proceedings shall be brought in relation to any matter which is the subject of an investigation in accordance with the provisions of this Schedule until—
(*a*) the appropriate authority has certified the case as a special case under paragraph 20B(3) or 20E(3), or]
(*b*) a report on that investigation has been submitted to the Commission or to the appropriate authority under paragraph 22 or 24A.

(2) Nothing in this paragraph shall prevent the bringing of criminal or disciplinary proceedings in respect of any conduct at any time after the discontinuance of the investigation in accordance with the provisions of this Schedule which relates to that conduct.

(3) The restrictions imposed by this paragraph in relation to the bringing of criminal proceedings shall not apply to the bringing of criminal proceedings by the Director of Public Prosecutions in any case in which it appears to him that there are exceptional circumstances which make it undesirable to delay the bringing of such proceedings.

*Accelerated procedure in special cases*

**20A.** (1) If, at any time before the completion of his investigation, the person investigating a complaint or recordable conduct matter believes that the appropriate authority would, on consideration of the matter, be likely to consider that the special conditions are satisfied, he shall proceed in accordance with the following provisions of this paragraph.

(2) If the person was appointed under paragraph 16, he shall submit to the appropriate authority—
(*a*) a statement of his belief and the grounds for it; and
(*b*) a written report on his investigation to that point;

and if he was appointed following a determination made by the Commission under paragraph 15 he shall send a copy of the statement and the report to the Commission.

(3) If the person was appointed under paragraph 17 or 18 or designated under paragraph 19, he shall submit to the appropriate authority—
(*a*) a statement of his belief and the grounds for it; and
(*b*) a written report on his investigation to that point;

and shall send a copy of the statement and the report to the Commission.

(4) A person submitting a report under this paragraph shall not be prevented by any obligation of secrecy imposed by any rule of law or otherwise from including all such matters in his report as he thinks fit.

(5) A statement and report may be submitted under this paragraph whether or not a previous statement and

report have been submitted; but a second or subsequent statement and report may be submitted only if the person submitting them has grounds to believe that the appropriate authority will reach a different determination under paragraph 20B(2) or 20E(2).

(6) After submitting a report under this paragraph, the person investigating the complaint or recordable conduct matter shall continue his investigation to such extent as he considers appropriate.

(7) The special conditions are that—

(*a*) there is sufficient evidence, in the form of written statements or other documents, to establish on the balance of probabilities that conduct to which the investigation relates constitutes gross misconduct;

(*c*) it is in the public interest for the person whose conduct it is to cease to be a member of a police force, or to be a special constable, without delay.

(8) *Repealed.*

(9) In paragraphs 20B to 20H "special report" means a report submitted under this paragraph.

*Investigations managed or carried out by Commission: action by appropriate authority*

**20B.** (1) This paragraph applies where—

(*a*) a statement and special report on an investigation carried out under the management of the Commission, or

(*b*) a statement and special report on an investigation carried out by a person designated by the Commission,

are submitted to the appropriate authority under paragraph 20A(3).

(2) The appropriate authority shall determine whether the special conditions are satisfied.

(3) If the appropriate authority determines that the special conditions are satisfied then, unless it considers that the circumstances are such as to make it inappropriate to do so, it shall—

(*a*) certify the case as a special case for the purposes of regulations under section 50(3) or 51(2A) of the 1996 Act; and

(*b*) take such steps as are required by those regulations in relation to a case so certified.

(5) *Repealed.*

(6) The appropriate authority shall notify the Commission of a certification under sub-paragraph (3).

(7) If the appropriate authority determines—

(*a*) that the special conditions are not satisfied, or

(*b*) that, although those conditions are satisfied, the circumstances are such as to make it inappropriate at present to bring disciplinary proceedings,

it shall submit to the Commission a memorandum under this sub-paragraph.

(8) The memorandum required to be submitted under sub-paragraph (7) is one which—

(*a*) notifies the Commission of its determination that those conditions are not satisfied or (as the case may be) that they are so satisfied but the circumstances are such as to make it inappropriate at present to bring disciplinary proceedings; and

(*b*) (in either case) sets out its reasons for so determining.

(9) In this paragraph "special conditions" has the meaning given by paragraph 20A(7).

*Investigations managed or carried out by Commission: action by Commission*

**20C.** (1) On receipt of a notification under paragraph 20B(6), the Commission shall give a notification—

(*a*) in the case of a complaint, to the complainant and to every person entitled to be kept properly informed in relation to the complaint under section 21; and

(*b*) in the case of a recordable conduct matter, to every person entitled to be kept properly informed in relation to that matter under that section.

(2) The notification required by sub-paragraph (1) is one setting out—

(*a*) the findings of the special report;

(*b*) the appropriate authority's determination under paragraph 20B(2); and

(*c*) the action that the appropriate authority is required to take as a consequence of that determination.

(3) Subsections (5) to (7) of section 20 shall have effect in relation to the duties imposed on the Commission by sub-paragraph (1) as they have effect in relation to the duties imposed on the Commission by that section.

(4) Except so far as may be otherwise provided by regulations made by virtue of sub-paragraph (3), the Commission shall be entitled (notwithstanding any obligation of secrecy imposed by any rule of law or otherwise) to discharge the duty to give a person mentioned in sub-paragraph (1) notification of the findings of the special report by sending that person a copy of that report.

**20D.** (1) On receipt of a memorandum under paragraph 20B(7), the Commission shall—

(*a*) consider the memorandum;

(*b*) determine, in the light of that consideration, whether or not to make a recommendation under paragraph 20H; and

(*c*) if it thinks fit to do so, make a recommendation under that paragraph.

(2) If the Commission determines not to make a recommendation under paragraph 20H, it shall notify the appropriate authority and the person investigating the complaint or matter of its determination.

*Other investigations: action by appropriate authority*

**20E.** (1) This paragraph applies where—

(*a*) a statement and a special report on an investigation carried out by an appropriate authority on its own behalf, or

(*b*) a statement and a special report on an investigation carried out under the supervision of the Commission,

are submitted to the appropriate authority under paragraph 20A(2) or (3).

(2) The appropriate authority shall determine whether the special conditions are satisfied.

(3) If the appropriate authority determines that the special conditions are satisfied then, unless it considers that the circumstances are such as to make it inappropriate to do so, it shall—

(*a*) certify the case as a special case for the purposes of regulations under section 50(3) or 51(2A) of the 1996 Act; and

(*b*) take such steps as are required by those regulations in relation to a case so certified.

(5) *Repealed.*

(6) Where the statement and report were required under paragraph 20A(2) to be copied to the Commission,

the appropriate authority shall notify the Commission of a certification under sub-paragraph (3).

(7) If the appropriate authority determines—

(*a*) that the special conditions are not satisfied, or

(*b*) that, although those conditions are satisfied, the circumstances are such as to make it inappropriate at present to bring disciplinary proceedings,

it shall notify the person investigating the complaint or matter of its determination.

(8) In this paragraph "special conditions" has the meaning given by paragraph 20A(7).

**20F.** (1) If the appropriate authority certifies a case under paragraph 20E(3), it shall give a notification—

(*a*) in the case of a complaint, to the complainant and to every person entitled to be kept properly informed in relation to the complaint under section 21; and

(*b*) in the case of a recordable conduct matter, to every person entitled to be kept properly informed in relation to that matter under that section.

(2) The notification required by sub-paragraph (1) is one setting out—

(*a*) the findings of the report;

(*b*) the authority's determination under paragraph 20E(2); and

(*c*) the action that the authority is required to take in consequence of that determination.

(3) Subsections (5) to (7) of section 20 shall have effect in relation to the duties imposed on the appropriate authority by sub-paragraph (1) as they have effect in relation to the duties imposed on the appropriate authority by that section.

(4) Except so far as may be otherwise provided by regulations made by virtue of sub-paragraph (3), the appropriate authority shall be entitled (notwithstanding any obligation of secrecy imposed by any rule of law or otherwise) to discharge the duty to give a person mentioned in sub-paragraph (1) notification of the findings of the special report by sending that person a copy of that report.

**20G.** *Repealed.*

*Special cases: recommendation or direction of Commission*

**20H.** (1) Where the appropriate authority has submitted, or is required to submit, a memorandum to the Commission under paragraph 20B(7), the Commission may make a recommendation to the appropriate authority that it should certify the case under paragraph 20B(3).

(2) If the Commission determines to make a recommendation under this paragraph, it shall give a notification—

(*a*) in the case of a complaint, to the complainant and to every person entitled to be kept properly informed in relation to the complaint under section 21; and

(*b*) in the case of a recordable conduct matter, to every person entitled to be kept properly informed in relation to that matter under that section.

(3) The notification required by sub-paragraph (2) is one setting out—

(*a*) the findings of the special report; and

(*b*) the Commission's recommendation under this paragraph.

(4) Subsections (5) to (7) of section 20 shall have effect in relation to the duties imposed on the Commission by sub-paragraph (2) as they have effect in relation to the duties imposed on the Commission by that section.

(5) Except so far as may be otherwise provided by regulations made by virtue of sub-paragraph (4), the Commission shall be entitled (notwithstanding any obligation of secrecy imposed by any rule of law or otherwise) to discharge the duty to give a person mentioned in sub-paragraph (2) notification of the findings of the special report by sending that person a copy of the report.

(6) It shall be the duty of the appropriate authority to notify the Commission whether it accepts the recommendation and (if it does) to certify the case and proceed accordingly.

(7) If, after the Commission has made a recommendation under this paragraph, the appropriate authority does not certify the case under paragraph 20B(3)—

(*a*) the Commission may direct the appropriate authority so to certify it; and

(*b*) it shall be the duty of the appropriate authority to comply with the direction and proceed accordingly.

(8) Where the Commission gives the appropriate authority a direction under this paragraph, it shall supply the appropriate authority with a statement of its reasons for doing so.

(9) The Commission may at any time withdraw a direction given under this paragraph.

(10) The appropriate authority shall keep the Commission informed of whatever action it takes in response to a recommendation or direction.

**20I.** (1) Where—

(*a*) the Commission makes a recommendation under paragraph 20H in the case of an investigation of a complaint, and

(*b*) the appropriate authority notifies the Commission that the recommendation has been accepted,

the Commission shall notify the complainant and every person entitled to be kept properly informed in relation to the complaint under section 21 of that fact and of the steps that have been, or are to be, taken by the appropriate authority to give effect to it.

(2) Where in the case of an investigation of a complaint the appropriate authority—

(*a*) notifies the Commission that it does not accept the recommendation made by the Commission under paragraph 20H, or

(*b*) fails to certify the case under paragraph 20B(3) and to proceed accordingly,

it shall be the duty of the Commission to determine what (if any) further steps to take under paragraph 20H.

(3) It shall be the duty of the Commission to notify the complainant and every person entitled to be kept properly informed in relation to the complaint under section 21—

(*a*) of any determination under sub-paragraph (2) not to take further steps under paragraph 20H; and

(*b*) where it determines under that sub-paragraph to take further steps under that paragraph, of the outcome of the taking of those steps.

*Power to discontinue an investigation*

**21.** (1) The Commission may by order require the discontinuance of the investigation of a complaint or matter if (whether on the application of the appropriate authority or otherwise) it appears to the Commission that—

(*a*) the complaint or matter is of a description specified in regulations made by the Secretary of State for the purposes of this paragraph, and (*b*) discontinuance of the investigation is within the Commission's power.

(1A) The appropriate authority that is investigating a complaint or matter may discontinue the investigation if it appears to that authority that—

(*a*) the complaint or matter is of a description specified in regulations made by the Secretary of State for the purposes of this paragraph, and

(*b*) discontinuance of the investigation is not within the Commission's power.

(1B) For the purposes of this paragraph—

(*a*) discontinuance of the investigation of a complaint is within the Commission's power if—

(i) the investigation is being undertaken by the appropriate authority on its own behalf and the complaint is one required to be referred to the Commission under paragraph 4; or

(ii) the investigation is under the supervision or management of the Commission;

(*b*) discontinuance of the investigation of a matter other than a complaint is within the Commission's power if the investigation is under the supervision or management of the Commission.

(2) The Commission shall not discontinue any investigation that is being carried out in accordance with paragraph 19 except in such cases as may be authorised by regulations made by the Secretary of State.

(3) Where the Commission makes an order under this paragraph or discontinues an investigation being carried out in accordance with paragraph 19, it shall give notification of the discontinuance—

(*a*) to the appropriate authority;

(*b*) to every person entitled to be kept properly informed in relation to the subject matter of the investigation under section 21; and

(*c*) in a case where the investigation that is discontinued is an investigation of a complaint, to the complainant.

(3A) Where the appropriate authority discontinues an investigation under sub-paragraph (1A), the appropriate authority shall give notification of the discontinuance—

(*a*) to every person entitled to be kept properly informed in relation to the investigation under section 21; and

(*b*) in a case where the investigation that is discontinued is an investigation of a complaint, to the complainant.

(4) Where an investigation of a complaint, recordable conduct matter or DSI matter is discontinued in accordance an order under sub-paragraph (1)—

(*a*) the Commission may give the appropriate authority directions to do any such things as it is authorised to direct by regulations made by the Secretary of State;

(*b*) the Commission may itself take any such steps of a description specified in regulations so made as it considers appropriate for purposes connected with the discontinuance of the investigation; and

(*c*) subject to the preceding paragraphs, neither the appropriate authority nor the Commission shall take any further action in accordance with the provisions of this Schedule in relation to that complaint or matter.

(5) The appropriate authority shall comply with any directions given to it under sub-paragraph (4).

(6) Where an investigation of a complaint, recordable conduct matter or DSI matter is discontinued in accordance with sub-paragraph (1A)—

(*a*) the appropriate authority may take any such steps of a description specified in regulations made by the Secretary of State as he or it considers appropriate for purposes connected with the discontinuance of the investigation; and

(*b*) subject to the preceding paragraphs, neither the appropriate authority nor the Commission shall take any further action in accordance with the provisions of this Schedule in relation to that complaint or matter.

(7) The complainant shall have a right of appeal to the relevant appeal body against any decision by the appropriate authority under subparagraph (1A) to discontinue the investigation of the complaint.

(8) But the complainant has no right of appeal if the complaint relates to a direction and control matter.

(9) On an appeal under this paragraph, subject to sub-paragraphs (10) and (11), the relevant appeal body shall—

(*a*) determine whether any decision taken by the appropriate authority under this paragraph should have been taken in the case in question; and

(*b*) if the relevant appeal body finds in the complainant's favour, give such directions as the relevant appeal body thinks appropriate to the local policing body or chief officer as to the action to be taken for investigating the complaint;

and it shall be the duty of a local policing body or chief officer to comply with any directions given under paragraph (*b*).

(10) Sub-paragraph (9) does not apply in a case where a particular chief officer of police is—

(*a*) the person in respect of whose decision an appeal is made under this paragraph, and

(*b*) the relevant appeal body in relation to the appeal.

(11) In such a case—

(*a*) the appeal shall determine whether any decision taken by the appropriate authority under this paragraph should have been taken in the case in question; and

(*b*) if the appeal finds in the complainant's favour, the chief officer of police must take such action as the chief officer thinks appropriate for investigating the complaint.

*Procedure where conduct matter is revealed during investigation of DSI matter*

**21A.** (1) If during the course of an investigation of a DSI matter it appears to a person appointed under paragraph 18 or designated under paragraph 19 that there is an indication that a person serving with the police ("the person whose conduct is in question") may have—

(*a*) committed a criminal offence, or

(*b*) behaved in a manner which would justify the bringing of disciplinary proceedings,

he shall make a submission to that effect to the Commission.

(2) If, after considering a submission under sub-paragraph (1), the Commission determines that there is such an indication, it shall—

(*a*) notify the appropriate authority in relation to the DSI matter and (if different) the appropriate authority in relation to the person whose conduct is in question of its determination; and (*b*) send to it (or each of them) a copy of the submission under sub-paragraph (1).

(3) If during the course of an investigation of a DSI matter it appears to a person appointed under paragraph 16 or 17 that there is an indication that a person serving with the police ("the person whose conduct is in question") may have—

(*a*) committed a criminal offence, or

(*b*) behaved in a manner which would justify the bringing of disciplinary proceedings,

he shall make a submission to that effect to the appropriate authority in relation to the DSI matter.

(4) If, after considering a submission under sub-paragraph (3), the appropriate authority determines that there is such an indication, it shall—

(*a*) if it is not the appropriate authority in relation to the person whose conduct is in question, notify that other authority of its determination and send to that authority a copy of the submission under sub-paragraph (3); and

(*b*) notify the Commission of its determination and send to it a copy of the submission under sub-paragraph (3).

(5) Where the appropriate authority in relation to the person whose conduct is in question—

(*a*) is notified of a determination by the Commission under sub-paragraph (2),

(*b*) (in a case where it is also the appropriate authority in relation to the DSI matter) makes a determination under sub-paragraph (4), or

(*c*) (in a case where it is not the appropriate authority in relation to the DSI matter) is notified by that other authority of a determination by it under sub-paragraph (4),

it shall record the matter under paragraph 11 as a conduct matter.

(6) Where a DSI matter is recorded under paragraph 11 as a conduct matter by virtue of sub-paragraph (5)—

(*a*) the person investigating the DSI matter shall (subject to any determination made by the Commission under paragraph 15(5)) continue the investigation as if appointed or designated to investigate the conduct matter, and

(*b*) the other provisions of this Schedule shall apply in relation to that matter accordingly.

*Final reports on investigations: complaints, conduct matters and certain DSI matters*

**22.** (1) This paragraph applies on the completion of an investigation of—

(*a*) a complaint, or

(*b*) a conduct matter,

(*c*) *repealed.*

(2) A person appointed under paragraph 16 shall submit a report on his investigation to the appropriate authority.

(3) A person appointed under paragraph 17 or 18 shall—

(*a*) submit a report on his investigation to the Commission; and

(*b*) send a copy of that report to the appropriate authority.

(4) In relation to a matter that was formerly a DSI matter but has been recorded as a conduct matter in pursuance of paragraph 21A(5), the references in sub-paragraphs (2) and (3) of this paragraph to the appropriate authority are references to—

(*a*) the appropriate authority in relation to the DSI matter; and

(*b*) (where different) the appropriate authority in relation to the person whose conduct is in question.

(5) A person designated under paragraph 19 as the person in charge of an investigation by the Commission itself shall submit a report on it to the Commission.

(6) A person submitting a report under this paragraph shall not be prevented by any obligation of secrecy imposed by any rule of law or otherwise from including all such matters in his report as he thinks fit.

(7) The Secretary of State may by regulations make provision requiring a report on an investigation within paragraph 19C(1)(*a*) or (*b*)—

(*a*) to include such matters as are specified in the regulations;

(*b*) to be accompanied by such documents or other items as are so specified.

(8) A person who has submitted a report under this paragraph on an investigation within paragraph 19C(1)(*a*) or (*b*) must supply the appropriate authority with such copies of further documents or other items in that person's possession as the authority may request.

(9) The appropriate authority may only make a request under sub-paragraph (8) in respect of a copy of a document or other item if the authority—

(*a*) considers that the document or item is of relevance to the investigation, and

(*b*) requires a copy of the document or the item for either or both of the purposes mentioned in sub-paragraph (10).

(10) Those purposes are—

(*a*) complying with any obligation under regulations under section 50(3) or 51(2A) of the 1996 Act which the authority has in relation to any person to whose conduct the investigation related;

(*b*) ensuring that any such person receives a fair hearing at any disciplinary proceedings in respect of any such conduct of his.

*Action by the Commission in response to an investigation report under paragraph 22*

**23.** (1) This paragraph applies where—

(*a*) a report on an investigation carried out under the management of the Commission is submitted to it under sub-paragraph (3) of paragraph 22; or

(*b*) a report on an investigation carried out by a person designated by the Commission is submitted to it under sub-paragraph (5) of that paragraph.

(2) On receipt of the report, the Commission—

(*a*) if it appears that the appropriate authority has not already been sent a copy of the report, shall send a copy of the report to that authority;

(*b*) shall determine whether the conditions set out in sub-paragraphs (2A) and (2B) are satisfied in respect of the report;

(*c*) if it determines that those conditions are so satisfied, shall notify the Director of Public Prosecutions of the determination and send him a copy of the report; and

(*d*) shall notify the appropriate authority and the persons mentioned in sub-paragraph (5) of its determination under paragraph (*b*) and of any action taken by it under paragraph (*c*).

(2A) The first condition is that the report indicates that a criminal offence may have been committed by a person to whose conduct the investigation related.

(2B) The second condition is that—

(*a*) the circumstances are such that, in the opinion of the Commission, it is appropriate for the matters dealt with in the report to be considered by the Director of Public Prosecutions, or

(*b*) any matters dealt with in the report fall within any prescribed category of matters.

(3) The Director of Public Prosecutions shall notify the Commission of any decision of his to take, or not to take, action in respect of the matters dealt with in any report a copy of which has been sent to him under sub-paragraph (2)(*c*).

(4) It shall be the duty of the Commission to notify the persons mentioned in sub-paragraph (5) if criminal proceedings are brought against any person by the Director of Public Prosecutions in respect of any matters dealt with in a report copied to him under sub-paragraph (2)(*c*).

(5) The persons are—

(*a*) in the case of a complaint, the complainant and every person entitled to be kept properly informed in relation to the complaint under section 21; and

(*b*) in the case of a recordable conduct matter, every person entitled to be kept properly informed in relation to that matter under that section.

(6) On receipt of the report, the Commission shall also notify the appropriate authority that it must—

(*a*) in accordance with regulations under section 50 or 51 of the 1996 Act, determine—

(i) whether any person to whose conduct the investigation related has a case to answer in respect of misconduct or gross misconduct or has no case to answer, and

(i *a*) whether or not any such person's performance is unsatisfactory, and

(ii) what action (if any) the authority is required to, or will in its discretion, take in respect of the matters dealt with in the report, and

(*b*) determine what other action (if any) the authority will in its discretion take in respect of those matters."

(7) On receipt of a notification under sub-paragraph (6) the appropriate authority shall make those determinations and submit a memorandum to the Commission which—

(*a*) sets out the determinations the authority has made, and

(*b*) if the appropriate authority has decided in relation to any person to whose conduct the investigation related that disciplinary proceedings should not be brought against that person, sets out its reasons for so deciding.

(8) On receipt of a memorandum under sub-paragraph (7), the Commission shall—

(*a*) consider the memorandum and whether the appropriate authority has made the determinations under sub-paragraph (6)(*a*) that the Commission considers appropriate in respect of the matters dealt with in the report;

(*b*) determine, in the light of its consideration of those matters, whether or not to make recommendations under paragraph 27; and

(*c*) make such recommendations (if any) under that paragraph as it thinks fit.

(9) On the making of a determination under sub-paragraph (8)(*b*) the Commission shall give a notification—

(*a*) in the case of a complaint, to the complainant and to every person entitled to be kept properly informed in relation to the complaint under section 21; and

(*b*) in the case of a recordable conduct matter, to every person entitled to be kept properly informed in relation to that matter under that section.

(10) The notification required by sub-paragraph (9) is one setting out—

(*a*) the findings of the report;

(*b*) the Commission's determination under sub-paragraph (8)(*b*); and

(*c*) the action which the appropriate authority is to be recommended to take as a consequence of the determination.

(11) Subsections (5) to (7) of section 20 shall have effect in relation to the duties imposed on the Commission by sub-paragraph (9) of this paragraph as they have effect in relation to the duties imposed on the Commission by that section.

(12) Except so far as may be otherwise provided by regulations made by virtue of sub-paragraph (11), the Commission shall be entitled (notwithstanding any obligation of secrecy imposed by any rule of law or otherwise) to discharge the duty to give a person mentioned in sub-paragraph (9) notification of the findings of the report by sending that person a copy of the report.

(13) In relation to a DSI matter in respect of which a determination has been made under paragraph 21A(2) or (4), the references in this paragraph to the appropriate authority are references to the appropriate authority in relation to the person whose conduct is in question.

*Action by the appropriate authority in response to an investigation report under paragraph 22*

**24.** (1) This paragraph applies where—

(*a*) a report of an investigation is submitted to the appropriate authority in accordance with paragraph 22(2); or

(*b*) a copy of a report on an investigation carried out under the supervision of the Commission is sent to the appropriate authority in accordance with paragraph 22(3).

(2) On receipt of the report or (as the case may be) of the copy, the appropriate authority—

(*a*) shall determine whether the conditions set out in sub-paragraphs (2A) and (2B) are satisfied in respect of the report;

(*b*) if it determines that those conditions are so satisfied, shall notify the Director of Public Prosecutions of the determination and send him a copy of the report; and

(*c*) shall notify the persons mentioned in sub-paragraph (5) of its determination under paragraph (*a*) and of any action taken by it under paragraph (*b*).

(2A) The first condition is that the report indicates that a criminal offence may have been committed by a person to whose conduct the investigation related.

(2B) The second condition is that—

(*a*) the circumstances are such that, in the opinion of the appropriate authority, it is appropriate for the matters dealt with in the report to be considered by the Director of Public Prosecutions, or

(*b*) any matters dealt with in the report fall within any prescribed category of matters.

(3) The Director of Public Prosecutions shall notify the appropriate authority of any decision of his to take, or not to take, action in respect of the matters dealt with in any report a copy of which has been sent to him under sub-paragraph (2).

(4) It shall be the duty of the appropriate authority to notify the persons mentioned in sub-paragraph (5) if criminal proceedings are brought against any person by the Director of Public Prosecutions in respect of any matters dealt with in a report copied to him under sub-paragraph (2)(*b*).

(5) The persons are—

(*a*) in the case of a complaint, the complainant and every person entitled to be kept properly informed in relation to the complaint under section 21; and

(*b*) in the case of a recordable conduct matter, every person entitled to be kept properly informed in relation to that matter under that section.

(5A) In the case of a report falling within sub-paragraph (1)(*b*) which relates to a recordable conduct matter, the appropriate authority shall also notify the Commission of its determination under sub-paragraph (2)(*a*).

(5B) On receipt of such a notification that the appropriate authority has determined that the conditions in sub-paragraphs (2A) and (2B) are not satisfied in respect of the report, the Commission—

(*a*) shall make its own determination as to whether those conditions are so satisfied, and

(*b*) if it determines that they are so satisfied, shall direct the appropriate authority to notify the Director of Public Prosecutions of the Commission's determination and to send the Director a copy of the report.

(5C) It shall be the duty of the appropriate authority to comply with any direction given to it under sub-paragraph (5B).

(6) On receipt of the report or (as the case may be) copy, the appropriate authority shall also—

(*a*) in accordance with regulations under section 50 or 51 of the 1996 Act, determine—

(i) whether any person to whose conduct the investigation related has a case to answer in respect of misconduct or gross misconduct or has no case to answer, and

(i *a*) whether or not any such person's performance is unsatisfactory, and

(ii) what action (if any) the authority is required to, or will in its discretion, take in respect of the matters dealt with in the report, and

(*b*) determine what other action (if any) the authority will in its discretion take in respect of those matters.

(7) On the making of the determinations under sub-paragraph (6) the appropriate authority shall give a notification—

(*a*) in the case of a complaint, to the complainant and to every person entitled to be kept properly informed in relation to the complaint under section 21; and

(*b*) in the case of a recordable conduct matter, to every person entitled to be kept properly informed in relation to that matter under that section.

(8) The notification required by sub-paragraph (7) is one setting out—

(*a*) the findings of the report;

(*b*) the determinations the authority has made under sub-paragraph (6); and

(*d*) the complainant's right of appeal under paragraph 25.

(9) Subsections (5) to (7) of section 20 shall have effect in relation to the duties imposed on the appropriate authority by sub-paragraph (7) of this paragraph as they have effect in relation to the duties imposed on the appropriate authority by that section.

(10) Except so far as may be otherwise provided by regulations made by virtue of sub-paragraph (9), the appropriate authority shall be entitled (notwithstanding any obligation of secrecy imposed by any rule of law or otherwise) to discharge the duty to give a person mentioned in sub-paragraph (7) notification of the findings of the report by sending that person a copy of the report.

(11) In relation to a DSI matter in respect of which a determination has been made under paragraph 21A(2) or (4), the references in this paragraph to the appropriate authority are references to the appropriate authority in relation to the person whose conduct is in question.

*Final reports on investigations: other DSI matters*

**24A.** (1) This paragraph applies on the completion of an investigation of a DSI matter in respect of which neither the Commission nor the appropriate authority has made a determination under paragraph 21A(2) or (4).

(2) The person investigating shall—

(*a*) submit a report on the investigation to the Commission; and

(*b*) send a copy of that report to the appropriate authority.

(3) A person submitting a report to the Commission under this paragraph shall not be prevented by any obligation of secrecy imposed by any rule of law or otherwise from including all such matters in his report as he thinks fit.

(4) On receipt of the report, the Commission shall determine whether the report indicates that a person serving with the police may have—

(*a*) committed a criminal offence, or

(*b*) behaved in a manner which would justify the bringing of disciplinary proceedings.

*Action by the Commission in response to an investigation report under paragraph 24A*

**24B.** (1) If the Commission determines under paragraph 24A(4) that the report indicates that a person serving with the police may have—

(*a*) committed a criminal offence, or

(*b*) behaved in a manner which would justify the bringing of disciplinary proceedings,

it shall notify the appropriate authority in relation to the person whose conduct is in question of its determination and, if it appears that that authority has not already been sent a copy of the report, send a copy of the report to that authority.

(2) Where the appropriate authority in relation to the person whose conduct is in question is notified of a determination by the Commission under sub-paragraph (1), it shall record the matter under paragraph 11 as a

conduct matter.

(3) Where a DSI matter is recorded under paragraph 11 as a conduct matter by virtue of sub-paragraph (2)—

(*a*) the person investigating the DSI matter shall (subject to any determination made by the Commission under paragraph 15(5)) investigate the conduct matter as if appointed or designated to do so, and

(*b*) the other provisions of this Schedule shall apply in relation to that matter accordingly.

**24C.** (1) This paragraph applies where the Commission determines under paragraph 24A(4) that there is no indication in the report that a person serving with the police may have—

(*a*) committed a criminal offence, or

(*b*) behaved in a manner which would justify the bringing of disciplinary proceedings.

(2) *Repealed.*

(3) The Commission may notify the appropriate authority that it must, in accordance with regulations under section 50 or 51 of the 1996 Act, determine—

(*a*) whether or not the performance of a person serving with the police is unsatisfactory, and

(*b*) what action (if any) the authority will take in respect of any such person's performance.

(4) On receipt of a notification under sub-paragraph (3) the appropriate authority shall make those determinations and submit a memorandum to the Commission setting out the determinations the authority has made.

(5) On receipt of a memorandum under sub-paragraph (4), the Commission shall—

(*a*) consider the memorandum and whether the appropriate authority has made the determinations under sub-paragraph (4) that the Commission considers appropriate;

(*b*) determine whether or not to make recommendations under paragraph 27;

(*c*) make such recommendations (if any) under that paragraph as it thinks fit.

*Appeals with respect to an investigation*

**25.** (1) This paragraph applies where a complaint has been subjected to—

(*a*) an investigation by the appropriate authority on its own behalf; or

(*b*) an investigation under the supervision of the Commission.

(2) The complainant shall have the following rights of appeal to the relevant appeal body—

(*a*) a right to appeal on the grounds that he has not been provided with adequate information—

(i) about the findings of the investigation; or

(ii) about any determination of the appropriate authority relating to the taking (or not taking) of action in respect of any matters dealt with in the report on the investigation;

(*b*) a right to appeal against the findings of the investigation;

(*ba*) a right of appeal against any determination by the appropriate authority that a person to whose conduct the investigation related has a case to answer in respect of misconduct or gross misconduct or has no case to answer or that such a person's performance is, or is not, unsatisfactory;

(*c*) a right of appeal against any determination by the appropriate authority relating to the taking (or not taking) of action in respect of any matters dealt with in the report; and

(*d*) a right of appeal against any determination by the appropriate authority under paragraph 24(2)(*a*) as a result of which it is not required to send the Director of Public Prosecutions a copy of the report;

and it shall be the duty of the relevant appeal body to notify the appropriate authority, every person entitled to be kept properly informed in relation to the complaint under section 21 and the person complained against of any appeal brought under this paragraph (except that the duty to notify the appropriate authority does not apply where that authority is the relevant appeal body).

(2ZA) But the complainant has no right of appeal if the complaint relates to a direction and control matter.

(2A) In sub-paragraph (2)—

(*a*) references to the findings of an investigation do not include a reference to findings on a report submitted under paragraph 20A; and

(*b*) references to the report of an investigation do not include a reference to a report submitted under that paragraph.

(3) On the bringing of an appeal under this paragraph, the Commission may require the appropriate authority to submit a memorandum to the Commission which—

(*za*) sets out whether the appropriate authority has determined that a person to whose conduct the investigation related has a case to answer in respect of misconduct or gross misconduct or has no case to answer;

(*zb*) sets out whether the appropriate authority has determined any such person's performance is, or is not, unsatisfactory;

(*a*) sets out what action (if any) the authority has determined that it is required to or will, in its discretion, take in respect of the matters dealt with in the report;

(*c*) if the appropriate authority has decided in relation to a person to whose conduct the investigation related that disciplinary proceedings should not be brought against that person, sets out its reasons for so deciding; and

(*d*) if the appropriate authority made a determination under paragraph 24(2)(*a*) as a result of which it is not required to send the Director of Public Prosecutions a copy of the report, sets out the reasons for that determination;

and it shall be the duty of the appropriate authority to comply with any requirement under this sub-paragraph.

(4) Where the Commission so requires on the bringing of any appeal under this paragraph in the case of an investigation by the appropriate authority on its own behalf, the appropriate authority shall provide the Commission with a copy of the report of the investigation.

(5) On an appeal under this paragraph, the relevant appeal body shall determine such of the following as it considers appropriate in the circumstances—

(*a*) whether the complainant has been provided with adequate information about the matters mentioned in sub-paragraph (2)(*a*);

(*b*) whether the findings of the investigation need to be reconsidered;

(*c*) whether the appropriate authority—

(i) has made such a determination as is mentioned in sub-paragraph (3)(*za*) or (*zb*) that the relevant appeal body considers to be appropriate in respect of the matters dealt with in the report, and

(ii) has determined that it is required to or will, in its discretion, take the action (if any) that the relevant appeal body considers to be so appropriate; and

(*d*) whether the conditions set out in paragraph 24(2A) and (2B) are satisfied in respect of the report.

(6) If, on an appeal under this paragraph, the relevant appeal body determines that the complainant has not been provided with adequate information about any matter,

(*a*) in a case where the Commission is the relevant appeal body, the Commission shall give the appropriate authority all such directions as the Commission considers appropriate for securing that the complainant is properly informed; and

(*b*) in a case where the appropriate authority is the relevant appeal body, that authority shall take such steps as it considers appropriate for securing that the complainant is properly informed.

(7) Nothing in sub-paragraph (6)(*a*) shall authorise the Commission to require the disclosure of any information the disclosure of which to the appellant has been or is capable of being withheld by virtue of regulations made under section 20(5).

(8) If, on an appeal under this paragraph, the Commission determines that the findings of the investigation need to be reconsidered in a case where the Commission is the relevant appeal body, it shall either—

(*a*) review those findings without an immediate further investigation; or

(*b*) direct that the complaint be re-investigated; and in a case where the appropriate authority is the relevant appeal body, that authority shall re-investigate the complaint.

(9) If, on an appeal under this paragraph, the relevant appeal body determines that the appropriate authority has not made a determination as to whether there is a case for a person to whose conduct the investigation related to answer that the relevant appeal body considers appropriate, or determines that the appropriate authority has not made a determination as to whether a person's performance is or is not unsatisfactory, or determines that the appropriate authority has not determined that it is required to or will, in its discretion, take the action in respect of the matters dealt with in the report that the relevant appeal body considers appropriate—

(*a*) sub-paragraph (9ZA) applies if the Commission is the relevant appeal body; or

(*b*) sub-paragraph (9ZB) applies if the chief officer of police is the relevant appeal body.

(9ZA) The Commission shall—

(*a*) determine, in the light of that determination, whether or not to make recommendations under paragraph 27; and

(*b*) make such recommendations (if any) under that paragraph as it thinks fit.

(9ZB) The chief officer of police shall take such action as the chief officer thinks appropriate in relation to the bringing of disciplinary proceedings in respect of the matters dealt with in the report.

(9ZC) If disciplinary proceedings are brought by virtue of sub-paragraph (9ZB), it shall be the duty of the appropriate authority to ensure that they are proceeded with to a proper conclusion

(9A) If, on an appeal under this paragraph, the relevant appeal body determines that the conditions set out paragraph 24(2A) and (2B) are satisfied in respect of the report, in a case where the Commission is the relevant appeal body it shall direct the appropriate authority to, or in a case where the appropriate authority is the relevant appeal body it shall—

(*a*) notify the Director of Public Prosecutions of the determination, and

(*b*) send the Director a copy of the report.

(10) The relevant appeal body shall give notification of any determination under this paragraph—

(*a*) to the appropriate authority (unless it is the relevant appeal body),

(*b*) to the complainant;

(*c*) to every person entitled to be kept properly informed in relation to the complaint under section 21; and

(*d*) except in a case where it appears to the relevant appeal body that to do so might prejudice any proposed review or re-investigation of the complaint, to the person complained against.

(11) In a case where the Commission is the relevant appeal body, it shall also give notification of any directions given to the appropriate authority under this paragraph—

(*a*) to the complainant;

(*b*) to every person entitled to be kept properly informed in relation to the complaint under section 21; and

(*c*) except in a case where it appears to the Commission that to do so might prejudice any proposed review or re-investigation of the complaint, to the person complained against.

(12) It shall be the duty of the appropriate authority to comply with any directions given to it under this paragraph.

(13) The Secretary of State may by regulations[1] make provision—

(*a*) for the form and manner in which appeals under this paragraph are to be brought;

(*b*) for the period within which any such appeal must be brought; and

(*c*) for the procedure to be followed by the relevant appeal body when dealing with or disposing of any such appeal.

*Reviews and re-investigations following an appeal*

**26.** (1) On a review under paragraph 25(8)(*a*) of the findings of an investigation the powers of the Commission shall be, according to its determination on that review, to do one or more of the following—

(*a*) to uphold the findings in whole or in part;

(*b*) to give the appropriate authority such directions—

(i) as to the carrying out by the appropriate authority of its own review of the findings,

(ii) as to the information to be provided to the complainant, and

(iii) generally as to the handling of the matter in future,

as the Commission thinks fit;

(*c*) to direct that the complaint be re-investigated.

(2) Where the Commission directs under paragraph 25 or sub-paragraph (1) that a complaint be re-investigated, it shall make a determination of the form that the re-investigation should take.

(3) Sub-paragraphs (3) to (7) of paragraph 15 shall apply in relation to a determination under sub-paragraph (2) as they apply in the case of a determination under that paragraph.

(4) The other provisions of this Schedule (including this paragraph) shall apply in relation to any re-investigation in pursuance of a direction under paragraph 25(8) or sub-paragraph (1) of this paragraph as they

apply in relation to any investigation in pursuance of a determination under paragraph 15.

(5) The Commission shall give notification of any determination made by it under this paragraph—

(*a*) to the appropriate authority;

(*b*) to the complainant;

(*c*) to every person entitled to be kept properly informed in relation to the complaint under section 21; and

(*d*) except in a case where it appears to the Commission that to do so might prejudice any proposed re-investigation of the complaint, to the person complained against.

(6) The Commission shall also give notification of any directions given to the appropriate authority under this paragraph—

(*a*) to the complainant;

(*b*) to every person entitled to be kept properly informed in relation to the complaint under section; and

(*c*) except in a case where it appears to the Commission that to do so might prejudice any proposed review or re-investigation of the complaint, to the person complained against.

*Duties with respect to disciplinary proceedings etc*

**27.** (1) This paragraph applies where, in the case of any investigation, the appropriate authority—

(*a*) has given, or is required to give, a notification under paragraph 24(7) of the action it is required to or will, in its discretion, take in relation to the matters dealt with in any report of the investigation; or

(*b*) has submitted, or is required to submit, a memorandum to the Commission under paragraph 23 or 25 setting out the action that it is required to or will, in its discretion, take in relation to those matters; or

(*c*) has submitted, or is required to submit, a memorandum to the Commission under paragraph 24C(4).

(2) Subject to paragraph 20 and to any recommendations or directions under the following provisions of this paragraph, it shall be the duty of the appropriate authority—

(*a*) to take the action which has been or is required to be notified or, as the case may be, which is or is required to be set out in the memorandum; and

(*b*) in a case where that action consists of or includes the bringing of disciplinary proceedings, to secure that those proceedings, once brought, are proceeded with to a proper conclusion.

(3) Where this paragraph applies by virtue of sub-paragraph (1)(*b*), the Commission may make a recommendation to the appropriate authority in respect of any person serving with the police—

(*za*) that the person has a case to answer in respect of misconduct or gross misconduct or has no case to answer in relation to his conduct to which the investigation related;

(*zb*) that the person's performance is, or is not, unsatisfactory;

(*a*) that disciplinary proceedings of the form specified in the recommendation are brought against that person in respect of his conduct, efficiency or effectiveness to which the investigation related;

(*b*) that any disciplinary proceedings brought against that person are modified so as to deal with such aspects of that conduct, efficiency or effectiveness as may be so specified;

and it shall be the duty of the appropriate authority to notify the Commission whether it accepts the recommendation and (if it does) to set out in the notification the steps that it is proposing to take to give effect to it.

(3A) Where this paragraph applies by virtue of sub-paragraph (1)(*c*), the Commission may make a recommendation to the appropriate authority—

(*a*) that the performance of a person serving with the police is, or is not, satisfactory;

(*b*) that action of the form specified in the recommendation is taken in respect of the person's performance;

and it shall be the duty of the appropriate authority to notify the Commission whether it accepts the recommendation and (if it does) to set out in the notification the steps that it is proposing to take to give effect to it.

(4) If, after the Commission has made a recommendation under this paragraph, the appropriate authority does not take steps to secure that full effect is given to the recommendation—

(*a*) the Commission may direct the appropriate authority to take steps for that purpose; and

(*b*) it shall be the duty of the appropriate authority to comply with the direction.

(5) A direction under sub-paragraph (4) may, to such extent as the Commission thinks fit, set out the steps to be taken by the appropriate authority in order to give effect to the recommendation.

(6) Where the Commission gives the appropriate authority a direction under this paragraph, it shall supply the appropriate authority with a statement of its reasons for doing so.

(7) Where disciplinary or other proceedings have been brought in accordance with a recommendation or direction under this paragraph, it shall be the duty of the authority to ensure that they are proceeded with to a proper conclusion.

(8) The Commission may at any time withdraw a direction given under this paragraph; and sub-paragraph (7) shall not impose any obligation in relation to any time after the withdrawal of the direction.

(9) The appropriate authority shall keep the Commission informed—

(*a*) in a case in which this paragraph applies by virtue of sub-paragraph (1)(*b*) or (*c*), of whatever action it takes in pursuance of its duty under sub-paragraph (2); and

(*b*) in every case of a recommendation or direction under this paragraph, of whatever action it takes in response to that recommendation or direction.

*Information for complainant about disciplinary recommendations*

**28.** (1) Where—

(*a*) the Commission makes recommendations under paragraph 27 in the case of an investigation of a complaint, and

(*b*) the appropriate authority notify the Commission that the recommendations have been accepted,

the Commission shall notify the complainant and every person entitled to be kept properly informed in relation to the complaint under section 21 of that fact and of the steps that have been, or are to be taken, by the appropriate authority to give effect to it.

(2) Where in the case of an investigation of a complaint the appropriate authority—

(*a*) notify the Commission that it does not (either in whole or in part) accept recommendations made by the Commission under paragraph 27, or (*b*) fails to take steps to give full effect to any such recommendations,

it shall be the duty of the Commission to determine what if any further steps to take under that paragraph.

(3) It shall be the duty of the Commission to notify the complainant and every person entitled to be kept properly informed in relation to the complaint under section 21—

(*a*) of any determination under sub-paragraph (2) not to take further steps under paragraph 27; and

(*b*) where they determine under that sub-paragraph to take further steps under that paragraph, of the outcome of the taking of those steps.

**28A . Recommendations by the Commission** (1) This paragraph applies where the Commission has received a report under—

(*a*) paragraph 22(3) (report on completion of investigation of complaint or conduct matter supervised or managed by Commission),

(*b*) paragraph 22(5) (report on completion of investigation of complaint or conduct matter by Commission itself ), or

(*c*) paragraph 24A(2) (report on completion of investigation of DSI matter that is not also conduct matter).

(2) This paragraph also applies where the Commission has made a determination on an appeal under—

(*a*) paragraph 8A (appeal relating to complaint dealt with other than by investigation), or

(*b*) paragraph 25 (appeal with respect to an investigation).

(3) The Commission may make a recommendation in relation to a matter dealt with in the report or appeal.

(4) A recommendation under this paragraph may be made to any person if it is made—

(*a*) following the receipt of a report relating to—

(i) a DSI matter,

(ii) a conduct matter of a type specified in regulations, or

(iii) a complaint of a type specified in regulations; or

(*b*) following a determination on an appeal relating to a complaint of a type specified in regulations.

(5) In any other case, a recommendation under this paragraph may be made only to—

(*a*) a person serving with the police, or

(*b*) a local policing body.

(6) Where the Commission makes a recommendation under this paragraph, it must also—

(*a*) publish the recommendation, and

(*b*) send a copy of it—

(i) in a case where the recommendation is made to a local policing body, to the chief officer of the police force maintained by that body;

(ii) in a case where the recommendation is made to a chief officer of a police force, to the local policing body that maintains the police force;

(iii) in a case where the recommendation is made to a contractor (within the meaning of section 12(10)), to the chief officer of a police force to whom the contractor is providing services, and the local policing body that maintains the police force;

(iv) in a case where the recommendation is made to a sub-contractor or an employee of a contractor, to the contractor and the persons to whom a copy must be sent under paragraph (iii);

(v) in a case where the recommendation is made to an employee of a sub-contractor, to the sub-contractor, the contractor and the persons to whom a copy must be sent under sub-paragraph (iii);

(vi) in any other case, to any person to whom the Commission thinks a copy should be sent.

(7) Nothing in this paragraph affects the power of the Commission to make recommendations or give advice under section 10(1)(*e*) (whether arising under this Schedule or otherwise).

**28B. Response to recommendation** (1) A person to whom a recommendation under paragraph 28A is made must provide to the Commission a response in writing stating—

(*a*) what action the person has taken or proposes to take in response to the recommendation, or

(*b*) why the person has not taken, or does not propose to take, any action in response.

(2) The person must provide the response to the Commission before the end of the period of 56 days beginning with the day on which the recommendation was made, unless sub-paragraph (3) applies.

(3) The Commission may extend the period of 56 days following an application received before the end of the period; and if the Commission grants an extension, the person must provide the response before the end of the extended period.

(4) But if proceedings for judicial review of the Commission's decision to make a recommendation are started during the period allowed by sub-paragraph (2) or (3), that period is extended by however many days the proceedings are in progress.

(5) On receiving a response, the Commission must, within the period of 21 days beginning with the day on which the Commission received it—

(*a*) publish the response, and

(*b*) send a copy of it to any person who was sent a copy of the recommendation under paragraph 28A(6)(*b*),

unless the person giving the response has made representations under sub-paragraph (6).

(6) The person giving the response may, at the time of providing it to the Commission, make representations to the Commission asserting that the requirements of publication and disclosure under sub-paragraph (5) should not apply to the response, or to particular parts of it.

(7) On receiving such representations, the Commission may decide—

(*a*) that the response should not be published, or that only parts of it should be published;

(*b*) that the response should not be disclosed, or that only parts of the response should be disclosed.

(8) Where, following a decision on representations, the Commission decides to publish or disclose a response (in whole or in part), it must do so only after the person giving the response has been informed of the Commission's decision, and—

(*a*) in a case where the Commission has decided to accept all of the representations, it must do so within the period of 21 days beginning with the day on which it received the response;

(*b*) in a case where the Commission has decided to reject any of the representations, it must do so—

(i) within the period of 21 days beginning with the day on which the person was informed of the Commission's decision on the representations, but

(ii) not before the end of the period of 7 days beginning with that day.

(9) But if proceedings for judicial review of the Commission's decision to reject a representation are started during the period of 7 days referred to in sub-paragraph (8)(*b*)(ii)—

(*a*) the Commission must not publish or disclose the response while the proceedings are in progress;

(*b*) if the court upholds the Commission's decision to reject a representation, the Commission must publish and disclose the response (in whole or in part, as appropriate) before the end of the period of 7 days beginning with the day on which the proceedings are no longer in progress.

(10) Where a local policing body or a chief officer makes a response under this paragraph, the body or officer must, at the time the Commission publishes the response, also publish the response (to the same extent as published by the Commission) and the recommendation under paragraph 28A.

(11) For the purposes of this paragraph—

(*a*) "disclosing" a response means sending a copy of it as mentioned in sub-paragraph (5)(*b*);

(*b*) the period during which judicial review proceedings are in progress includes any day on which an appeal is in progress or may be brought.

*Minor definitions*

**29.** In this Part of this Schedule—

"direction and control matter" means a matter that relates to the direction and control of a police force by—

(*a*) the chief officer of police of that force, or

(*b*) a person for the time being carrying out the functions of the chief officer of police of that force;

"gross misconduct" means a breach of the Standards of Professional Behaviour that is so serious as to justify dismissal;

"misconduct" means a breach of the Standards of Professional Behaviour;

"the person investigating", in relation to a complaint, recordable conduct matter or DSI matter, means the person appointed or designated to investigate that complaint or matter;

"prescribed" means prescribed by regulations made by the Secretary of State;

"the Standards of Professional Behaviour" means the standards so described in, and established by, regulations made by the Secretary of State.

---

[1] The Police (Complaints and Misconduct) Regulations 2012, SI 2012/1204 amended by SI 2014/2406 have been made.

*Appeals: the relevant appeal body*

**30.** (1) The relevant appeal body in relation to an appeal is—

(*a*) the Commission, in a case where the relevant complaint falls within a description of complaints specified in regulations made by the Secretary of State for the purposes of this paragraph; or

(*b*) the chief officer of police who is the appropriate authority in relation to the relevant complaint, in any other case.

(2) In this paragraph and paragraphs 31 and 32—

"appeal" means an appeal under paragraph 7(8), 8A, 21(7) or 25(2);

"relevant complaint", in relation to an appeal, means the complaint to which the appeal relates.

**31.** (1) This paragraph applies in a case where—

(*a*) an appeal is made to the Commission, and

(*b*) the appropriate authority is the relevant appeal body in relation to the appeal.

(2) The Commission must—

(*a*) forward the appeal to the appropriate authority; and

(*b*) notify the person who made the appeal—

(i) that the appropriate authority is the relevant appeal body; and

(ii) the appeal has been forwarded.

(3) The appeal is to be taken to have been—

(*a*) made to the appropriate authority, and

(*b*) so made at the time when it is forwarded to the appropriate authority.

**32.** (1) This paragraph applies in a case where—

(*a*) an appeal is made to the appropriate authority; and

(*b*) the Commission is the relevant appeal body in relation to the appeal.

(2) The appropriate authority must—

(*a*) forward the appeal to the Commission; and

(*b*) notify the person who made the appeal—

(i) that the Commission is the relevant appeal body; and

(ii) the appeal has been forwarded.

(3) The appeal is to be taken to have been—

(*a*) made to the Commission; and

(*b*) so made at the time when it is forwarded to the Commission.

## SCHEDULE 4

### Powers Exercisable by Police Civilians

Section 38

*(Amended by the Anti-social Behaviour Act 2003, s 93, the Criminal Justice Act 2003, Sch 1, the Serious Organised Crime and Police Act 2005, Sch 8, the Drugs Act 2005, s 5, the Clean Neighbourhoods and Environment Act 2005, ss 62 and Sch 3, the Violent Crime Reduction Act 2006, s 24, the Police and Justice Act 2006, Sch 5, the Education and Inspections Act 2006, s 108, the UK Borders Act 2007, s 47, the Local Government and Public Involvement in Health Act 2007, s 133, the Local Transport Act 2008, Sch 4, the Policing and Crime Act 2009, Schs 7 and 8, the Local Democracy, Economic Development and Construction Act 2009, Sch 6, the Coroners and Justice Act 2009, s 108, the Crime and Security Act 2010, ss 4, 6, the Police Reform and Social Responsibility Act 2011, Sch 16, the Legal Aid, Sentencing and Punishment of Offenders Act 2012, Sch 23, the Anti-social Behaviour, Crime and Policing Act 2014, ss 40, 53, 69, Schs 10, 11 and the Psychoactive Substances Act 2015, Sch 5.)*

## Part 1
## Community Support Officers[1]

*Powers to issue fixed penalty notices*

7.9262 1. (1) Where a designation applies this paragraph to any person, that person shall have the powers specified in sub-paragraph (2) in relation to any individual who he has reason to believe has committed a relevant fixed penalty offence at a place within the relevant police area.

(2) Those powers are the following powers so far as exercisable in respect of a relevant fixed penalty offence—

(*a*) the powers of a constable to give a penalty notice under Chapter 1 of Part 1 of the Criminal Justice and Police Act 2001 (c 16) (fixed penalty notices in respect of offences of disorder);

(*aa*) the power of a constable to give a penalty notice under section 444A of the Education Act 1996 (penalty notice in respect of failure to secure regular attendance at school of registered pupil);

(*ab*) the power of a constable to give a penalty notice under section 105 of the Education and Inspections Act 2006 (penalty notice in respect of presence of excluded pupil in public place);

(*ac*) the power of a constable to issue a fixed penalty notice under section 52 of the Anti-social Behaviour, Crime and Policing Act 2014 (fixed penalty notice in respect of failure to comply with community protection notice);

(*b*) the power of a constable in uniform to give a person a fixed penalty notice under section 54 of the Road Traffic Offenders Act 1988 (c 53) (fixed penalty notices) in respect of an offence listed in sub-paragraph (2B);

(*c*) *repealed*;

(*ca*) the power of an authorised officer of a local authority to give a notice under section 43(1) of the Anti-social Behaviour Act 2003 (penalty notices in respect of graffiti or fly-posting);

(*cb*) the power of an authorised officer of a borough council to give a notice under section 15 of the London Local Authorities Act 2004 in respect of an offence under section 38(1) of the London Local Authorities Act 1990 or section 27(1) of the City of Westminster Act 1999 (unlicensed street trading); and

(*d*) the power of an authorised officer of a litter authority to give a notice under section 88 of the Environmental Protection Act 1990 (c 43) (fixed penalty notices in respect of litter);

(*e*) *repealed*

(*f*) the power of a constable to issue a fixed penalty notice under section 68 of the Anti-social Behaviour, Crime and Policing Act 2014 (fixed penalty notice in respect of failure to comply with public spaces protection order).

(2A) The reference to the powers mentioned in sub-paragraph (2)(*a*) does not include those powers so far as they relate to an offence under the provisions in the following list—

section 1 of the Theft Act 1968,

section 87 of the Environmental Protection Act 1990.

(2B) The offences referred to in sub-paragraph (2)(*b*) are—

(*a*) an offence under section 72 of the Highway Act 1835 (riding on a footway) committed by cycling;

(*b*) an offence under section 5(1) or 8(1) of the Road Traffic Regulation Act 1984 involving a contravention of a prohibition or restriction that relates to—

(i) stopping, waiting or parking at or near a school entrance,

(ii) one-way traffic on a road, or

(iii) lanes or routes for use only by cycles, only by buses or only by cycles and buses;

(*c*) an offence under section 24 of the Road Traffic Act 1988 (more than one person on a one-person bicycle);

(*d*) an offence under section 35 of that Act (failing to comply with traffic directions) committed by the rider of a cycle;

(*e*) an offence under section 36 of that Act (failing to comply with traffic signs) committed by the rider of a cycle who fails to comply with the indication given by a red traffic light;

(*f*) an offence under section 42 of that Act of contravening or failing to comply with a construction or use requirement about—

(i) lighting equipment or reflectors for cycles,

(ii) the use on a road of a motor vehicle in a way that causes excessive noise,

(iii) stopping the action of a stationary vehicle's machinery,

(iv) the use of a vehicle's horn on a road while the vehicle is stationary or on a restricted road at night, or

(v) opening a vehicle's door on a road so as to injure or endanger a person;

(*g*) an offence under section 163 of that Act (failing to stop vehicle or cycle when required to do so by constable or traffic officer).

(2C) Before a chief officer of police makes a designation applying this paragraph to any person and specifying or describing an offence listed in sub-paragraph (2B)(*b*)(i), the officer shall consult every local authority any part of whose area lies within the officer's police area.

(2D) In paragraph (2C) "local authority" means—

(*a*) in relation to England, a district council, a London borough council, the Common Council of the City of London or the Council of the Isles of Scilly; and

(*b*) in relation to Wales, a county council or a county borough council.

(3) In this paragraph "relevant fixed penalty offence", in relation to a designated person, means an offence which—

(*a*) is an offence by reference to which a notice may be given to a person in exercise of any of the powers mentioned in sub-paragraph 1(2)(*a*) to (*e*); and

(*b*) is specified or described in a designation by which this paragraph is applied to the designated person as an offence which the designated person has been designated to enforce under this paragraph.

(3A) For the purposes of paragraph (*e*) of section 64A(1B) of the Police and Criminal Evidence Act 1984 (photographing of suspects in relation to fixed penalty offences) "relevant fixed penalty offence", in relation to a designated person, includes an offence under a relevant byelaw within the meaning of paragraph 1ZA(4) (and, accordingly, the reference in that paragraph (*e*) to paragraph 1 of this Schedule includes a reference to paragraph 1ZA of this Schedule).

(4) In its application to an offence which is an offence by reference to which a notice may be given to a person in exercise of the power mentioned in sub-paragraph (2)(*aa*) or (*ab*), sub-paragraph (1) shall have effect as if for the words from "who he has reason to believe" to the end there were substituted "in the relevant police area who he has reason to believe has committed a relevant fixed penalty offence".

(5) In this paragraph "cycle" has the same meaning as in the Road Traffic Act 1988 (see section 192(1) of that Act).

---

[1] The Police Reform Act 2002 (Standard Powers and Duties of Community Support Officers) Order 2007, SI 2007/3202 has been made, in this title, post.

**1ZA.** (1) This paragraph applies if a designation applies it to any person.

(2) Such a designation may specify that, in relation to that person, the application of sub-paragraph (3) is confined to one or more only (and not all) relevant byelaws, being in each case specified in the designation.

(3) Where that person has reason to believe that an individual has committed an offence against a relevant byelaw at a place within the relevant police area, he may exercise the power of an authorised officer of an authority to give a notice under section 237A of the Local Government Act 1972 (fixed penalty notices in relation to offences against certain byelaws).

(4) In this paragraph "relevant byelaw", in relation to a designated person, means a byelaw which—

(*a*) falls within sub-paragraph (5); and

(*b*) is specified or described in that person's designation as a byelaw he has been designated to enforce under this paragraph.

(5) A byelaw falls within this sub-paragraph if—

(*a*) it is a byelaw to which section 237A of the Local Government Act 1972 applies (fixed penalty notices in relation to offences against certain byelaws); and

(*b*) the chief officer of the police force for the relevant police area and the authority who made the byelaw have agreed to include it in a list of byelaws for the purposes of this sub-paragraph.

(6) A list under sub-paragraph (5)(*b*) must be published by the chief officer in such a way as to bring it to the attention of members of the public in localities where the byelaws in the list apply.

(7) The list may be amended from time to time by agreement between the chief officer and the authority, by adding byelaws to it or removing byelaws from it, and the amended list shall also be published by the chief officer as mentioned in sub-paragraph (6).

*Power to issue community protection notices*

**1ZB.** A person shall have the power of a constable to issue a community protection notice under section 43 of the Anti-social Behaviour, Crime and Policing Act 2014 if—

(*a*) a designation applies this paragraph to that person, and

(*b*) the conduct specified in the notice has (according to the notice) been taking place within the relevant police area.

*Power to require name and address*

**1A.** (1) This paragraph applies if a designation applies it to any person.

(2) A designation by which this paragraph is applied to a person may specify that the application of sub-paragraph (3) by that designation to that person is confined to one or more only (and not to all) relevant offences or relevant licensing offences, being in each case specified in the designation.

(3) Subject to sub-paragraph (4), where that person has reason to believe that another person has committed a relevant offence in the relevant police area, or a relevant licensing offence (whether or not in the relevant police area), he may require that other person to give him his name and address.

(4) The power to impose a requirement under sub-paragraph (3) in relation to an offence under a relevant byelaw is exercisable only in a place to which the byelaw relates.

(5) A person who fails to comply with a requirement under sub-paragraph (3) is guilty of an offence and shall be liable, on summary conviction, to a fine not exceeding level 3 on the standard scale.

(6) In its application to an offence which is an offence by reference to which a notice may be given to a person in exercise of the power mentioned in paragraph 1(2)(*aa*), sub-paragraph (3) of this paragraph shall have effect as if for the words "has committed a relevant offence in the relevant police area" there were substituted "in the relevant police area has committed a relevant offence".

(7) In this paragraph, "relevant offence", "relevant licensing offence" and "relevant byelaw" have the meaning given in paragraph 2 (reading accordingly the references to "this paragraph" in paragraph 2(6)).

*Power to detain etc*

**2.** (1) This paragraph applies if a designation applies it to any person.

(2) A designation may not apply this paragraph to any person unless a designation also applies paragraph 1A to him.

(3) Where, in a case in which a requirement under paragraph 1A(3) has been imposed on another person—

(*a*) that other person fails to comply with the requirement, or

(*b*) the person who imposed the requirement has reasonable grounds for suspecting that the other person has given him a name or address that is false or inaccurate,

the person who imposed the requirement may require the other person to wait with him, for a period not exceeding thirty minutes, for the arrival of a constable.

This sub-paragraph does not apply if the requirement was imposed in connection with a relevant licensing offence mentioned in paragraph (*a*), (*c*) or (*f*) of sub-paragraph (6A) believed to have been committed on licensed premises (within the meaning of the Licensing Act 2003).

(3A) Where—

(*a*) a designation applies this paragraph to any person ("the CSO"); and

(*b*) by virtue of a designation applying paragraph 1A to the CSO, the CSO has the power to impose a requirement under sub-paragraph (3) of that paragraph in relation to an offence under a relevant byelaw,

the CSO shall also have any power a constable has under the relevant byelaw to remove a person from a place.

(3B) Where a person to whom this paragraph applies ("the CSO") has reason to believe that another person is committing an offence under section 3 or 4 of the Vagrancy Act 1824, and requires him to stop doing whatever gives rise to that belief, the CSO may, if the other person fails to stop as required, require him to wait with the CSO, for a period not exceeding thirty minutes, for the arrival of a constable.

(4) A person who has been required under sub-paragraph (3) or (3B) to wait with a person to whom this paragraph is applied may, if requested to do so, elect that (instead of waiting) he will accompany the person imposing the requirement to a police station in the relevant police area.

(4A) If a person has imposed a requirement under sub-paragraph (3) or (3B) on another person ("P"), and P does not make an election under sub-paragraph (4), the person imposing the requirement shall, if a constable arrives within the thirty-minute period, be under a duty to remain with the constable and P until he has transferred control of P to the constable.

(4B) If, following an election under sub-paragraph (4), the person imposing the requirement under sub-paragraph (3) or (3B) ("the CSO") takes the person upon whom it is imposed ("P") to a police station, the CSO—

(*a*) shall be under a duty to remain at the police station until he has transferred control of P to the custody officer there;

(*b*) until he has so transferred control of P, shall be treated for all purposes as having P in his lawful custody; and

(*c*) for so long as he is at the police station, or in its immediate vicinity, in compliance with, or having complied with, his duty under paragraph (*a*), shall be under a duty to prevent P's escape and to assist in keeping P under control.

(5) A person who—

(*a*) *repealed*,

(*b*) makes off while subject to a requirement under sub-paragraph (3) or (3B), or

(*c*) makes off while accompanying a person to a police station in accordance with an election under sub-paragraph (4),

is guilty of an offence and shall be liable, on summary conviction, to a fine not exceeding level 3 on the standard scale.

(6) In this paragraph "relevant offence", in relation to a person to whom this paragraph applies, means any offence which is—

(*a*) a relevant fixed penalty offence for the purposes of the application of paragraph 1 to that person; or

(*aa*) an offence under section 39 of the Anti-social Behaviour, Crime and Policing Act 2014;

(*aza*) an offence under a relevant byelaw within the meaning of paragraph 1ZA(4); or

(*ab*) an offence committed in a specified park which by virtue of section 2 of the Parks Regulation (Amendment) Act 1926 is an offence against the Parks Regulation Act 1872; or

(*ac*) an offence under section 3 or 4 of the Vagrancy Act 1824; or

(*ad*) an offence under a relevant byelaw; or

(*b*) an offence the commission of which appears to that person to have caused—

(i) injury, alarm or distress to any other person; or

(ii) the loss of, or any damage to, any other person's property;

but a designation applying this paragraph to any person may provide that, for the purposes of this paragraph as applied to that person by that designation, an offence is not to be treated as a relevant offence by virtue of paragraph (*b*) unless it satisfies such other conditions as may be specified in the designation.

(6A) In this paragraph "relevant licensing offence" means an offence under any of the following provisions of the Licensing Act 2003—

(*a*) section 141 (otherwise than by virtue of subsection (2)(*c*) or (3) of that section);

(*b*) section 142;

(*c*) section 146(1);

(*d*) section 149(1)(*a*), (3)(*a*) or (4)(*a*);

(*e*) section 150(1);

(*f*) section 150(2) (otherwise than by virtue of subsection (3)(*b*) of that section);

(*g*) section 152(1) (excluding paragraph (*b*)).

(6B) In this paragraph "relevant byelaw" means a byelaw included in a list of byelaws which—

(*a*) have been made by a relevant body with authority to make byelaws for any place within the relevant police area; and

(*b*) the chief officer of the police force for the relevant police area and the relevant body have agreed to include in the list.

(6C) The list must be published by the chief officer in such a way as to bring it to the attention of members of the public in localities where the byelaws in the list apply.

(6D) A list of byelaws mentioned in sub-paragraph (6B) may be amended from time to time by agreement between the chief officer and the relevant body in question, by adding byelaws to it or removing byelaws from it, and the amended list shall also be published by the chief officer as mentioned in sub-paragraph (6C).

(6E) A relevant body for the purposes of sub-paragraph (6B) is—

(*a*) in England, a county council, a district council, a London borough council or a parish council; or in Wales, a county council, a county borough council or a community council;

(*b*) the Greater London Authority;

(*c*) Transport for London;

(*d*) an Integrated Transport Authority for an integrated transport area in England;

(*da*) a combined authority established under section 103 of the Local Democracy, Economic Development and Construction Act 2009;

(*e*) any body specified in an order made by the Secretary of State.

(6F) An order under sub-paragraph (6E)(*e*) may provide, in relation to any body specified in the order, that the agreement mentioned in sub-paragraph (6B)(*b*) and (6D) is to be made between the chief officer and the Secretary of State (rather than between the chief officer and the relevant body).

(7) *Repealed.*

(8) The application of any provision of this paragraph by paragraph 3(2), 3A(2), 7A(8) or 7C(2) has no effect unless a designation has applied this paragraph to the CSO in question.

*Powers to search individuals and to seize and retain items*

**2A.** (1) Where a designation applies this paragraph to any person, that person shall (subject to sub-paragraph (3)) have the powers mentioned in sub-paragraph (2) in relation to a person upon whom he has imposed a requirement to wait under paragraph 2(3) or (3B) (whether or not that person makes an election under paragraph 2(4)).

(2) Those powers are the same powers as a constable has under section 32 of the 1984 Act in relation to a person arrested at a place other than a police station—

(*a*) to search the arrested person if the constable has reasonable grounds for believing that the arrested person may present a danger to himself or others; and to seize and retain anything he finds on exercising that power, if the constable has reasonable grounds for believing that the person being searched might use it to cause physical injury to himself or to any other person;

(*b*) to search the arrested person for anything which he might use to assist him to escape from lawful custody; and to seize and retain anything he finds on exercising that power (other than an item subject to legal privilege) if the constable has reasonable grounds for believing that the person being searched might use it to assist him to escape from lawful custody.

(3) If in exercise of the power conferred by sub-paragraph (1) the person to whom this paragraph applies seizes and retains anything by virtue of sub-paragraph (2), he must—

(*a*) tell the person from whom it was seized where inquiries about its recovery may be made; and

(*b*) comply with a constable's instructions about what to do with it.

*General power of seizure*

**2B.** Where a designation applies this paragraph to any person—

(*a*) that person shall, when lawfully on any premises in the relevant police area, have the same powers as a constable under section 19 of the 1984 Act (general powers of seizure) to seize things;

(*b*) that person shall also have the powers of a constable to impose a requirement by virtue of subsection (4) of that section in relation to information accessible from such premises;

(*c*) subsection (6) of that section (protection for legally privileged material from seizure) shall have effect in relation to the seizure of anything by that person by virtue of sub-paragraph (*a*) as it has effect in relation to the seizure of anything by a constable;

(*d*) section 21(1) and (2) of that Act (provision of record of seizure) shall have effect in relation to the seizure of anything by that person in exercise of the power conferred on him by virtue of sub-paragraph (*a*) as if the references to a constable and to an officer included references to that person; and

(*e*) sections 21(3) to (8) and 22 of that Act (access, copying and retention) shall have effect in relation to anything seized by that person in exercise of that power or taken away by him following the imposition of a requirement by virtue of sub-paragraph (*b*)—

(i) as they have effect in relation to anything seized in exercise of the power conferred on a constable by section 19(2) or (3) of that Act or taken away by a constable following the imposition of a requirement by virtue of section 19(4) of that Act; and

(ii) as if the references to a constable in subsections (3), (4) and (5) of section 21 included references to a person to whom this paragraph applies.

*Power to require name and address of person acting in an anti-social manner*

**3.** (1) Where a designation applies this paragraph to any person, that person shall, in the relevant police area, have the powers of a constable in uniform under section 50 to require a person whom he has reason to believe to have been acting, or to be acting, in an anti-social manner (within the meaning of section 1 of the Crime and Disorder Act 1998 (c 37) (anti-social behaviour orders)) to give his name and address.

(2) Sub-paragraphs (3) to (5) of paragraph 2 apply in the case of a requirement imposed by virtue of sub-paragraph (1) as they apply in the case of a requirement under paragraph 1A(3).

*Power to require name and address: road traffic offences*

**3A.** (1) Where a designation applies this paragraph to any person, that person shall, in the relevant police area, have the powers of a constable—

(*a*) under subsection (1) of section 165 of the Road Traffic Act 1988 to require a person mentioned in paragraph (*c*) of that subsection who he has reasonable cause to believe has committed, in the relevant police area, an offence under subsection (1) or (2) of section 35 of that Act (including that section as extended by paragraphs 11B(4) and 12(2) of this Schedule) to give his name and address; and

(*b*) under section 169 of that Act to require a person committing an offence under section 37 of that Act (including that section as extended by paragraphs 11B(4) and 12(2) of this Schedule) to give his name and address.

(2) Sub-paragraphs (3) to (5) of paragraph 2 apply in the case of a requirement imposed by virtue of sub-paragraph (1) as they apply in the case of a requirement under paragraph 1A(3).

(3) The reference in section 169 of the Road Traffic Act 1988 to section 37 of that Act is to be taken to include a reference to that section as extended by paragraphs 11B(4) and 12(2) of this Schedule.

*Power to require name and address etc: charity collectors*

**3B.** Where a designation applies this paragraph to any person, that person shall, in the relevant police area, have the powers of a constable—

(*a*) under section 6 of the House to House Collections Act 1939 to require a person to give his name and address and to sign his name; and

(*b*) under regulations under section 4 of that Act to require a person to produce his certificate of authority.

*Power to use reasonable force to detain person*

**4.** (1) Sub-paragraph (3) applies where a designation—

(*a*) applies this paragraph to a person to whom any or all of paragraphs 1 to 3 are also applied; and (*b*) sets out matters in respect of which that person has the power conferred by this paragraph.

(2) The matters that may be set out in a designation as matters in respect of which a person has the power conferred by this paragraph shall be confined to—

(*a*) offences that are relevant penalty notice offences for the purposes of the application of paragraph 1 to the designated person;

(*b*) offences that are relevant offences or relevant licensing offences for the purposes of the application of paragraph 1A or 2 to the designated person; and

(*c*) behaviour that constitutes acting in an anti-social manner (within the meaning of section 1 of the Crime and Disorder Act 1998 (c 37) (anti-social behaviour orders)).

(3) In any case in which a person to whom this paragraph applies has imposed a requirement on any other person under paragraph 1A(3) or 3(1) in respect of anything appearing to him to be a matter set out in the designation, he may use reasonable force to prevent that other person from making off and to keep him under control while he is either—

(*a*) subject to a requirement imposed in that case by the designated person under sub-paragraph (3) of paragraph 2; or

(*b*) accompanying the designated person to a police station in accordance with an election made in that case under sub-paragraph (4) of that paragraph.

**4ZA.** Where a designation applies this paragraph to any person, that person may, if he has imposed a requirement on any person to wait with him under paragraph 2(3B) or by virtue of paragraph 7A(8) or 7C(2)(*a*), use reasonable force to prevent that other person from making off and to keep him under control while he is either—

(*a*) subject to that requirement; or

(*b*) accompanying the designated person to a police station in accordance with an election made under paragraph 2(4).

**4ZB.** Where a designation applies this paragraph to any person, that person, if he is complying with any duty under sub-paragraph (4A) or (4B) of paragraph 2, may use reasonable force to prevent P (as identified in those sub-paragraphs) from making off (or escaping) and to keep him under control.

*Power to disperse groups and remove young persons to their place of residence*

**4A.** Where a designation applies this paragraph to a person, that person has within the relevant police area the powers conferred on a constable by section 35 of the Anti-social Behaviour, Crime and Policing Act 2014.

**4AB.** (1) Where a designation applies this paragraph to a person, that person has within the relevant police area the powers conferred on a constable by section 37 of the Anti-social Behaviour, Crime and Policing Act 2014.

(2) A designation may not apply this paragraph to a person unless a designation also applies paragraph 4A to that person.

**4B.** *Repealed.*

*Power to remove truants and excluded pupils to designated premises etc*

**4C.** Where a designation applies this paragraph to any person, that person shall—

(*a*) as respects any area falling within the relevant police area and specified in a direction under section 16(2) of the Crime and Disorder Act 1998, but

(*b*) only during the period specified in the direction,

have the powers conferred on a constable by section 16(3) of that Act (power to remove truant found in specified area to designated premises or to the school from which truant is absent)*.

*Alcohol consumption in restricted areas*

**5.** Where a designation applies this paragraph to any person, that person shall, within the relevant police area, have the powers of a constable under section 63 of the Anti-social Behaviour, Crime and Policing Act 2014 (consumption of alcohol in breach of prohibition in public spaces protection order)—

(*a*) to impose a requirement under subsection (2) of that section; and

(*b*) to dispose under subsection (5) of that section of anything surrendered to the person;

and that section shall have effect in relation to the exercise of those powers by that person as if the references to a constable were references to that person.

*Power to serve closure notice for licensed premises persistently selling to children*

**5A.** Where a designation applies this paragraph to any person, that person shall have—

(*a*) within the relevant police area, and

(*b*) if it appears to him as mentioned in subsection (7) of section 169A of the Licensing Act 2003 (closure notices served on licensed premises persistently serving children),

the capacity of a constable under that subsection to be the person by whose delivery of a closure notice that notice is served.

*Confiscation of alcohol*

**6.** Where a designation applies this paragraph to any person, that person shall, within the relevant police area, have the powers of a constable under section 1 of the Confiscation of Alcohol (Young Persons) Act 1997 (c 33) (confiscation of intoxicating liquor)—

(*a*) to impose a requirement under subsection (1) or (1AA) of that section; and

(*b*) to dispose under subsection (2) of that section of anything surrendered to him;

and that section shall have effect in relation to the exercise of those powers by that person as if the references to a constable in subsections (1), (1AA) and (4) (but not the reference in subsection (1AB) (removal)) were references to that person.

*Confiscation of tobacco etc*

**7.** Where a designation applies this paragraph to any person, that person shall, within the relevant police area, have—

(*a*) the power to seize anything that a constable in uniform has a duty to seize under subsection (3) of section 7 of the Children and Young Persons Act 1933 (c 12) (seizure of tobacco etc from young persons); and

(*b*) the power to dispose of anything that a constable may dispose of under that subsection;

and the power to dispose of anything shall be a power to dispose of it in such manner as the local policing body may direct.

*Search and seizure powers: alcohol and tobacco*

**7A.** (1) Where a designation applies this paragraph to any person ("the CSO"), the CSO shall have the powers set out below.

(2) Where—

(*a*) in exercise of the powers referred to in paragraph 5 or 6 the CSO has imposed, under section 12(2) of the Criminal Justice and Police Act 2001 or under section 1 of the Confiscation of Alcohol (Young Persons) Act 1997, a requirement on a person to surrender alcohol or a container for alcohol;

(*b*) that person fails to comply with that requirement; and

(*c*) the CSO reasonably believes that the person has alcohol or a container for alcohol in his possession,

the CSO may search him for it.

(3) Where—

(*a*) in exercise of the powers referred to in paragraph 7 the CSO has sought to seize something which by virtue of that paragraph he has a power to seize;

(*b*) the person from whom he sought to seize it fails to surrender it; and

(*c*) the CSO reasonably believes that the person has it in his possession,

the CSO may search him for it.

(4) The power to search conferred by sub-paragraph (2) or (3)—

(*a*) is to do so only to the extent that is reasonably required for the purpose of discovering whatever the CSO is searching for; and

(*b*) does not authorise the CSO to require a person to remove any of his clothing in public other than an outer coat, jacket or gloves.

(5) A person who without reasonable excuse fails to consent to being searched is guilty of an offence and shall be liable, on summary conviction, to a fine not exceeding level 3 on the standard scale.

(6) A CSO who proposes to exercise the power to search a person under sub-paragraph (2) or (3) must inform him that failing without reasonable excuse to consent to being searched is an offence.

(7) If the person in question fails to consent to being searched, the CSO may require him to give the CSO his name and address.

(8) Sub-paragraph (3) of paragraph 2 applies in the case of a requirement imposed by virtue of sub-paragraph (7) as it applies in the case of a requirement under paragraph 1A(3); and sub-paragraphs (4) to (5) of paragraph 2 also apply accordingly.

(9) If on searching the person the CSO discovers what he is searching for, he may seize it and dispose of it.

*Powers to seize and detain: controlled drugs*

**7B.** (1) Where a designation applies this paragraph to any person ("the CSO"), the CSO shall, within the relevant police area, have the powers set out in sub-paragraphs (2) and (3).

(2) If the CSO—

(*a*) finds a controlled drug in a person's possession (whether or not the CSO finds it in the course of searching the person by virtue of any paragraph of this Part of this Schedule being applied to the CSO by a designation); and

(*b*) reasonably believes that it is unlawful for the person to be in possession of it,

the CSO may seize it and retain it.

(3) If the CSO—

(*a*) finds a controlled drug in a person's possession (as mentioned in sub-paragraph (2)); or

(*b*) reasonably believes that a person is in possession of a controlled drug,

and reasonably believes that it is unlawful for the person to be in possession of it, the CSO may require him to give the CSO his name and address.

(4) If in exercise of the power conferred by sub-paragraph (2) the CSO seizes and retains a controlled drug, he must—

(*a*) if the person from whom it was seized maintains that he was lawfully in possession of it, tell the person where inquiries about its recovery may be made; and

(*b*) comply with a constable's instructions about what to do with it.

(5) A person who fails to comply with a requirement under sub-paragraph (3) is guilty of an offence and shall be liable, on summary conviction, to a fine not exceeding level 3 on the standard scale.

(6) In this paragraph, "controlled drug" has the same meaning as in the Misuse of Drugs Act 1971.

**7C.** (1) Sub-paragraph (2) applies where a designation applies this paragraph to any person ("the CSO").

(2) If the CSO imposes a requirement on a person under paragraph 7B(3)—

(*a*) sub-paragraph (3) of paragraph 2 applies in the case of such a requirement as it applies in the case of a requirement under paragraph 1A(3); and

(*b*) sub-paragraphs (4) to (5) of paragraph 2 also apply accordingly.

*Park Trading offences*

**7D.** (1) This paragraph applies if—

(*a*) a designation applies it to any person ("the CSO"), and

(*b*) the CSO has under paragraph 2(3) required another person ("P") to wait with him for the arrival of a constable.

(2) If the CSO reasonably suspects that P has committed a park trading offence, the CSO may take possession of anything of a non-perishable nature which—

(*a*) P has in his possession or under his control, and

(*b*) the CSO reasonably believes to have been used in the commission of the offence.

(3) The CSO may retain possession of the thing in question for a period not exceeding 30 minutes unless P makes an election under paragraph 2(4), in which case the CSO may retain possession of the thing in question

until he is able to transfer control of it to a constable.

(4) In this paragraph "park trading offence" means an offence committed in a specified park which is a park trading offence for the purposes of the Royal Parks (Trading) Act 2000.

*Powers to seize and detain: psychoactive substances*

**7E.** (1) Where a designation applies this paragraph to any person ("the CSO"), the CSO shall, within the relevant police area, have the powers set out in sub-paragraphs (2) and (3).

(2) If the CSO—

(*a*) finds a psychoactive substance in a person's possession (whether or not the CSO finds it in the course of searching the person by virtue of any paragraph of this Part of this Schedule being applied to the CSO by a designation), and

(*b*) reasonably believes that it is unlawful for the person to be in possession of it,

the CSO may seize it and retain it.

(3) If the CSO—

(*a*) finds a psychoactive substance in a person's possession (as mentioned in sub-paragraph (2)), or

(*b*) reasonably believes that a person is in possession of a psychoactive substance,

and reasonably believes that it is unlawful for the person to be in possession of it, the CSO may require the person to give the CSO his name and address.

(4) If in exercise of the power conferred by sub-paragraph (2) the CSO seizes and retains a psychoactive substance, the CSO must—

(*a*) if the person from whom it was seized maintains that he was lawfully in possession of it—

(i) tell the person where inquiries about its recovery may be made, and

(ii) explain the effect of sections 49 to 51 and 53 of the Psychoactive Substances Act 2016 (retention and disposal of items), and

(*b*) comply with a constable's instructions about what to do with it.

(5) Any substance seized in exercise of the power conferred by sub-paragraph (2) is to be treated for the purposes of sections 49 to 53 of the Psychoactive Substances Act 2016 as if it had been seized by a police or customs officer under section 36 of that Act.

(6) A person who fails to comply with a requirement under sub-paragraph (3) is guilty of an offence and is liable, on summary conviction, to a fine not exceeding level 3 on the standard scale.

(7) In this paragraph "police or customs officer" and "psychoactive substance" have the same meaning as in the Psychoactive Substances Act 2016.

**7F.** (1) Sub-paragraph (2) applies where a designation applies this paragraph to any person ("the CSO").

(2) If the CSO imposes a requirement on a person under paragraph 7E(3)—

(*a*) sub-paragraph (3) of paragraph 2 applies in the case of such a requirement as it applies in the case of a requirement under paragraph 1A(3), and

(*b*) sub-paragraphs (4) to (5) of paragraph 2 also apply accordingly.

*Entry to save life or limb or prevent serious damage to property*

**8.** Where a designation applies this paragraph to any person, that person shall have the powers of a constable under section 17 of the 1984 Act to enter and search any premises in the relevant police area for the purpose of saving life or limb or preventing serious damage to property.

*Entry to investigate licensing offences*

**8A.** (1) Where a designation applies this paragraph to any person, that person shall have the powers of a constable under section 180 of the Licensing Act 2003 to enter and search premises other than clubs in the relevant police area, but only in respect of a relevant licensing offence (as defined for the purposes of paragraph 2).

(2) Except as mentioned in sub-paragraph (3), a person to whom this paragraph applies shall not, in exercise of the power conferred by sub-paragraph (1), enter any premises except in the company, and under the supervision, of a constable.

(3) The prohibition in sub-paragraph (2) does not apply in relation to premises in respect of which the person to whom this paragraph applies reasonably believes that a premises licence under Part 3 of the Licensing Act 2003 authorises the sale of alcohol for consumption off the premises.

*Seizure of vehicles used to cause alarm etc*

**9.** (1) Where a designation applies this paragraph to any person—

(*a*) that person shall, within the relevant police area, have all the powers of a constable in uniform under section 59 of this Act which are set out in subsection (3) of that section; and

(*b*) references in that section to a constable, in relation to the exercise of any of those powers by that person, are references to that person.

(2) A person to whom this paragraph applies shall not enter any premises in exercise of the power conferred by section 59(3)(*c*) except in the company, and under the supervision, of a constable.

*Abandoned vehicles*

**10.** Where a designation applies this paragraph to any person, that person shall have any such powers in the relevant police area as are conferred on persons designated under that section by regulations under section 99 of the Road Traffic Regulation Act 1984 (c 27) (removal of abandoned vehicles).

*Power to stop vehicle for testing*

**11.** Where a designation applies this paragraph to any person, that person shall, within the relevant police area, have the power of a constable in uniform to stop a vehicle under subsection (3) of section 67 of the Road Traffic Act 1988 (c 52) for the purposes of a test under subsection (1) of that section.

*Power to stop cycles*

**11A.** (1) Subject to sub-paragraph (2), where a designation applies this paragraph to any person, that person shall, within the relevant police area, have the power of a constable in uniform under section 163(2) of the Road

Traffic Act 1988 to stop a cycle.

(2) The power mentioned in sub-paragraph (1) may only be exercised by that person in relation to a person who he has reason to believe has committed an offence listed in paragraph 1(2B)(*a*) to (*e*), (*f*)(i) or (*g*).

*Power to control traffic for purposes other than escorting a load of exceptional dimensions*

**11B.** (1) Where a designation applies this paragraph to any person, that person shall have, in the relevant police area—

(*a*) the power of a constable engaged in the regulation of traffic in a road to direct a person driving or propelling a vehicle to stop the vehicle or to make it proceed in, or keep to, a particular line of traffic;

(*b*) the power of a constable in uniform engaged in the regulation of vehicular traffic in a road to direct a person on foot to stop proceeding along or across the carriageway.

(2) The purposes for which those powers may be exercised do not include the purpose mentioned in paragraph 12(1).

(3) Where a designation applies this paragraph to any person, that person shall also have, in the relevant police area, the power of a constable, for the purposes of a traffic survey, to direct a person driving or propelling a vehicle to stop the vehicle, to make it proceed in, or keep to, a particular line of traffic, or to proceed to a particular point on or near the road.

(4) Sections 35 and 37 of the Road Traffic Act 1988 (offences of failing to comply with directions of constable engaged in regulation of traffic in a road) shall have effect in relation to the exercise of the powers mentioned in sub-paragraphs (1) and (3), for the purposes for which they may be exercised and by a person whose designation applies this paragraph to him, as if the references to a constable were references to him.

(5) A designation may not apply this paragraph to any person unless a designation also applies paragraph 3A to him.

*Power to control traffic for purposes of escorting a load of exceptional dimensions*

**12.** (1) Where a designation applies this paragraph to any person, that person shall have, for the purpose of escorting a vehicle or trailer carrying a load of exceptional dimensions either to or from the relevant police area, the power of a constable engaged in the regulation of traffic in a road—

(*a*) to direct a vehicle to stop;

(*b*) to make a vehicle proceed in, or keep to, a particular line of traffic; and

(*c*) to direct pedestrians to stop.

(2) Sections 35 and 37 of the Road Traffic Act 1988 (offences of failing to comply with directions of constable engaged in regulation of traffic in a road) shall have effect in relation to the exercise of those powers for the purpose mentioned in sub-paragraph (1) by a person whose designation applies this paragraph to him as if the references to a constable engaged in regulation of traffic in a road were references to that person.

(3) The powers conferred by virtue of this paragraph may be exercised in any police area in England and Wales.

(4) In this paragraph "vehicle or trailer carrying a load of exceptional dimensions" means a vehicle or trailer the use of which is authorised by an order made by the Secretary of State under section 44(1)(*d*) of the Road Traffic Act 1988.

*Carrying out of road checks*

**13.** Where a designation applies this paragraph to any person, that person shall have the following powers in the relevant police area—

(*a*) the power to carry out any road check the carrying out of which by a police officer is authorised under section 4 of the 1984 Act (road checks); and

(*b*) for the purpose of exercising that power, the power conferred by section 163 of the Road Traffic Act 1988 (c 52) (power of police to stop vehicles) on a constable in uniform to stop a vehicle.

*Power to place traffic signs*

**13A.** (1) Where a designation applies this paragraph to any person, that person shall have, in the relevant police area, the powers of a constable under section 67 of the Road Traffic Regulation Act 1984 to place and maintain traffic signs.

(2) Section 36 of the Road Traffic Act 1988 (drivers to comply with traffic directions) shall apply to signs placed in the exercise of the powers conferred by virtue of sub-paragraph (1).

*Cordoned areas*

**14.** Where a designation applies this paragraph to any person, that person shall, in relation to any cordoned area in the relevant police area, have all the powers of a constable in uniform under section 36 of the Terrorism Act 2000 (c 11) (enforcement of cordoned area) to give orders, make arrangements or impose prohibitions or restrictions.

*Power to stop and search vehicles etc in authorised areas*

**15.** (1) Where a designation applies this paragraph to any person—

(*a*) that person shall, in any authorised area within the relevant police area, have all the powers of a constable in uniform by virtue of section 44(1)(*a*) and (*d*) and (2)(*b*) and 45(2) of the Terrorism Act 2000 (powers of stop and search)—

(i) to stop and search vehicles;

(ii) to search anything in or on a vehicle or anything carried by the driver of a vehicle or any passenger in a vehicle;

(iii) to search anything carried by a pedestrian; and

(iv) to seize and retain any article discovered in the course of a search carried out by him or by a constable by virtue of any provision of section 44(1) or (2) of that Act;

and

(*b*) the references to a constable in subsections (1) and (4) of section 45 of that Act (which relate to the exercise of those powers) shall have effect in relation to the exercise of any of those powers by that person as references to that person.

(2) A person shall not exercise any power of stop, search or seizure by virtue of this paragraph except in the company, and under the supervision, of a constable.

*Photographing of persons arrested, detained or given fixed penalty notices*

**15ZA.** Where a designation applies this paragraph to any person, that person shall, within the relevant police area, have the power of a constable under section 64A(1A) of the 1984 Act (photographing of suspects etc) to take a photograph of a person elsewhere than at a police station.

*Power to modify paragraph 1(2A)*

**15A.** (1) The Secretary of State may by order amend paragraph 1(2A) so as to remove a provision from the list or add a provision to the list; but the list must contain only provisions mentioned in the first column of the Table in section 1(1) of the Criminal Justice and Police Act 2001.

(2) The Secretary of State shall not make an order containing (with or without any other provision) any provision authorised by this paragraph unless a draft of that order has been laid before Parliament and approved by a resolution of each House.

## PART 2
## INVESTIGATING OFFICERS

*Search warrants*

**16.** Where a designation applies this paragraph to any person—

(*a*) he may apply as if he were a constable for a warrant under section 8 of the 1984 Act (warrants for entry and search) in respect of any premises whether in the relevant police area or not;

(*b*) the persons to whom a warrant to enter and search any such premises may be issued under that section shall include that person;

(*c*) that person shall have the power of a constable under section 8(2) of that Act in any premises in the relevant police area to seize and retain things for which a search has been authorised under subsection (1) of that section;

(*d*) section 15 of that Act (safeguards) shall have effect in relation to the issue of such a warrant to that person as it has effect in relation to the issue of a warrant under section 8 of that Act to a constable;

(*e*) section 16 of that Act (execution of warrants) shall have effect in relation to any warrant to enter and search premises that is issued (whether to that person or to any other person), but in respect of premises in the relevant police area only, as if references in that section to a constable included references to that person;

(*f*) section 19(6) of that Act (protection for legally privileged material from seizure) shall have effect in relation to the seizure of anything by that person by virtue of sub-paragraph (*c*) as it has effect in relation to the seizure of anything by a constable;

(*g*) section 20 of that Act (extension of powers of seizure to computerised information) shall have effect in relation the power of seizure conferred on that person by virtue of sub-paragraph (*c*) as it applies in relation to the power of seizure conferred on a constable by section 8(2) of that Act;

(*h*) section 21(1) and (2) of that Act (provision of record of seizure) shall have effect in relation to the seizure of anything by that person in exercise of the power conferred on him by virtue of sub-paragraph (*c*) as if the references to a constable and to an officer included references to that person; and

(*i*) sections 21(3) to (8) and 22 of that Act (access, copying and retention) shall have effect in relation to anything seized by that person in exercise of that power, or taken away by him following the imposition of a requirement by virtue of sub-paragraph (*g*)—

(i) as they have effect in relation to anything seized in exercise of the power conferred on a constable by section 8(2) of that Act or taken away by a constable following the imposition of a requirement by virtue of section 20 of that Act; and

(ii) as if the references to a constable in subsections (3), (4) and (5) of section 21 included references to a person to whom this paragraph applies.

**16A.** Where a designation applies this paragraph to any person—

(*a*) the persons to whom a warrant may be addressed under section 26 of the Theft Act 1968 (search for stolen goods) shall, in relation to persons or premises in the relevant police area, include that person; and

(*b*) in relation to such a warrant addressed to him, that person shall have the powers under subsection (3) of that section.

**16B.** Where a designation applies this paragraph to any person, subsection (3), and (to the extent that it applies subsection (3)) subsection (3A), of section 23 of the Misuse of Drugs Act 1971 (powers to search and obtain evidence) shall have effect as if, in relation to premises in the relevant police area, the reference to a constable included a reference to that person.

*Access to excluded and special procedure material*

**17.** Where a designation applies this paragraph to any person—

(*a*) he shall have the powers of a constable under section 9(1) of the 1984 Act (special provisions for access) to obtain access, in accordance with Schedule 1 to that Act and the following provisions of this paragraph, to excluded material and special procedure material;

(*b*) that Schedule shall have effect for the purpose of conferring those powers on that person as if—

(i) the references in paragraphs 1, 4, 5, 12 and 13 of that Schedule to a constable were references to that person; and

(ii) the references in paragraphs 12 and 14 of that Schedule to premises were references to premises in the relevant police area (in the case of a specific premises warrant) or any premises, whether in the relevant police area or not (in the case of an all premises warrant);

(*bb*) section 15 of that Act (safeguards) shall have effect in relation to the issue of any warrant under paragraph 12 of that Schedule to that person as it has effect in relation to the issue of a warrant under that paragraph to a constable;

(*bc*) section 16 of that Act (execution of warrants) shall have effect in relation to any warrant to enter and search premises that is issued under paragraph 12 of that Schedule (whether to that person or to any other person), but in respect of premises in the relevant police area only, as if references in that section to a constable included references to that person;

(*c*) section 19(6) of that Act (protection for legally privileged material from seizure) shall have effect in relation to the seizure of anything by that person in exercise of the power conferred on him by paragraph 13 of Schedule 1 to that Act as it has effect in relation to the seizure of anything under that paragraph by a constable;

(*d*) section 20 of that Act (extension of powers of seizure to computerised information) shall have effect in relation the power of seizure conferred on that person by paragraph 13 of Schedule 1 to that Act as it applies in relation to the power of seizure conferred on a constable by that paragraph;

(*e*) section 21(1) and (2) of that Act (provision of record of seizure) shall have effect in relation to the seizure of anything by that person in exercise of the power conferred on him by paragraph 13 of Schedule 1 to that Act as if the references to a constable and to an officer included references to that person; and

(*f*) sections 21(3) to (8) and 22 of that Act (access, copying and retention) shall have effect in relation to anything seized by that person in exercise of that power or taken away by him following the imposition of a requirement by virtue of sub-paragraph (*d*), and to anything produced to him under paragraph 4(*a*) of Schedule 1 to that Act—

(i) as they have effect in relation to anything seized in exercise of the power conferred on a constable by paragraph 13 of that Schedule or taken away by a constable following the imposition of a requirement by virtue of section 20 of that Act or, as the case may be, to anything produced to a constable under paragraph 4(*a*) of that Schedule; and

(ii) as if the references to a constable in subsections (3), (4) and (5) of section 21 included references to a person to whom this paragraph applies.

*Entry and search after arrest*

**18.** Where a designation applies this paragraph to any person—

(*a*) he shall have the powers of a constable under section 18 of the 1984 Act (entry and search after arrest) to enter and search any premises in the relevant police area and to seize and retain anything for which he may search under that section;

(*b*) subsections (5) and (6) of that section (power to carry out search before arrested person taken to police station and duty to inform senior officer) shall have effect in relation to any exercise by that person of those powers as if the references in those subsections to a constable were references to that person;

(*c*) section 19(6) of that Act (protection for legally privileged material from seizure) shall have effect in relation to the seizure of anything by that person by virtue of sub-paragraph (*a*) as it has effect in relation to the seizure of anything by a constable;

(*d*) section 20 of that Act (extension of powers of seizure to computerised information) shall have effect in relation the power of seizure conferred on that person by virtue of sub-paragraph (*a*) as it applies in relation to the power of seizure conferred on a constable by section 18(2) of that Act;

(*e*) section 21(1) and (2) of that Act (provision of record of seizure) shall have effect in relation to the seizure of anything by that person in exercise of the power conferred on him by virtue of sub-paragraph (*a*) as if the references to a constable and to an officer included references to that person; and

(*f*) sections 21(3) to (8) and 22 of that Act (access, copying and retention) shall have effect in relation to anything seized by that person in exercise of that power or taken away by him following the imposition of a requirement by virtue of sub-paragraph (*d*)—

(i) as they have effect in relation to anything seized in exercise of the power conferred on a constable by section 18(2) of that Act or taken away by a constable following the imposition of a requirement by virtue of section 20 of that Act; and

(ii) as if the references to a constable in subsections (3), (4) and (5) of section 21 included references to a person to whom this paragraph applies.

*Entry and search for evidence of nationality after arrest*

**18A.** Where a designation applies this paragraph to any person—

(*a*) sections 44 to 46 of the UK Borders Act 2007 (entry, search and seizure after arrest) shall apply to that person (with any necessary modifications) as if a reference to a constable included a reference to that person, and

(*b*) a provision of the 1984 Act which applies to constables in connection with any of those sections shall apply (with any necessary modifications) to that person.

*General power of seizure*

**19.** Where a designation applies this paragraph to any person—

(*a*) he shall, when lawfully on any premises in the relevant police area, have the same powers as a constable under section 19 of the 1984 Act (general powers of seizure) to seize things;

(*b*) he shall also have the powers of a constable to impose a requirement by virtue of subsection (4) of that section in relation to information accessible from such premises;

(*c*) subsection (6) of that section (protection for legally privileged material from seizure) shall have effect in relation to the seizure of anything by that person by virtue of sub-paragraph (*a*) as it has effect in relation to the seizure of anything by a constable;

(*d*) section 21(1) and (2) of that Act (provision of record of seizure) shall have effect in relation to the seizure of anything by that person in exercise of the power conferred on him by virtue of sub-paragraph (*a*) as if the references to a constable and to an officer included references to that person; and

(*e*) sections 21(3) to (8) and 22 of that Act (access, copying and retention) shall have effect in relation to anything seized by that person in exercise of that power or taken away by him following the imposition of a requirement by virtue of sub-paragraph (*b*)—

(i) as they have effect in relation to anything seized in exercise of the power conferred on a constable by section 19(2) or (3) of that Act or taken away by a constable following the imposition of a requirement by virtue of section 19(4) of that Act; and

(ii) as if the references to a constable in subsections (3), (4) and (5) of section 21 included references to a person to whom this paragraph applies.

*Access and copying in the case of things seized by constables*

**20.** Where a designation applies this paragraph to any person, section 21 of the 1984 Act (access and copying) shall have effect in relation to anything seized in the relevant police area by a constable or by a person authorised to accompany him under section 16(2) of that Act as if the references to a constable in subsections (3), (4) and (5) of section 21 (supervision of access and photographing of seized items) included references to a person to whom this paragraph applies.

*Arrest at a police station for another offence*

**21.** (1) Where a designation applies this paragraph to any person, he shall have the power to make an arrest at any police station in the relevant police area in any case where an arrest—

(*a*) is required to be made under section 31 of the 1984 Act (arrest for a further offence of a person already at a police station); or

(*b*) would be so required if the reference in that section to a constable included a reference to a person to whom this paragraph applies.

(2) Section 36 of the Criminal Justice and Public Order Act 1994 (c 33) (consequences of failure by arrested person to account for objects etc) shall apply (without prejudice to the effect of any designation applying paragraph 23) in the case of a person arrested in exercise of the power exercisable by virtue of this paragraph as it applies in the case of a person arrested by a constable.

*Power to transfer persons into custody of investigating officers*

**22.** (1) Where a designation applies this paragraph to any person, the custody officer for a designated police station in the relevant police area may transfer or permit the transfer to him of a person in police detention for an offence which is being investigated by the person to whom this paragraph applies.

(2) A person into whose custody another person is transferred under sub-paragraph (1)—

(*a*) shall be treated for all purposes as having that person in his lawful custody;

(*b*) shall be under a duty to keep that person under control and to prevent his escape; and

(*c*) shall be entitled to use reasonable force to keep that person in his custody and under his control.

(3) Where a person is transferred into the custody of a person to whom this paragraph applies, in accordance with sub-paragraph (1), subsections (2) and (3) of section 39 of the 1984 Act shall have effect as if—

(*a*) references to the transfer of a person in police detention into the custody of a police officer investigating an offence for which that person is in police detention were references to that person's transfer into the custody of the person to whom this paragraph applies; and

(*b*) references to the officer to whom the transfer is made and to the officer investigating the offence were references to the person to whom this paragraph applies.

*Powers in respect of detained persons*

**22A.** Where a designation applies this paragraph to any person, he shall be under a duty, when in the course of his employment he is present at a police station—

(*a*) to assist any officer or other designated person to keep any person detained at the police station under control; and

(*b*) to prevent the escape of any such person,

and for those purposes shall be entitled to use reasonable force.

*Power to require arrested person to account for certain matters*

**23.** Where a designation applies this paragraph to any person—

(*a*) he shall have the powers of a constable under sections 36(1)(*c*) and 37(1)(*c*) of the Criminal Justice and Public Order Act 1994 (c 33) to request a person who—

(i) has been arrested by a constable, or by any person to whom paragraph 21 applies, and

(ii) is detained at any place in the relevant police area,

to account for the presence of an object, substance or mark or for the presence of the arrested person at a particular place; and

(*b*) the references to a constable in sections 36(1)(*b*) and (*c*) and (4) and 37(1)(*b*) and (*c*) and (3) of that Act shall have effect accordingly as including references to the person to whom this paragraph is applied.

*Extended powers of seizure*

**24.** Where a designation applies this paragraph to any person—

(*a*) the powers of a constable under Part 2 of the Criminal Justice and Police Act 2001 (c 16) (extension of powers of seizure) that are exercisable in the case of a constable by reference to a power of a constable that is conferred on that person by virtue of the provisions of this Part of this Schedule shall be exercisable by that person by reference to that power to the same extent as in the case of a constable but in relation only to premises in the relevant police area and things found on any such premises; and

(*b*) section 56 of that Act (retention of property seized by a constable) shall have effect as if the property referred to in subsection (1) of that section included property seized by that person at any time when he was lawfully on any premises in the relevant police area.

*Persons accompanying investigating officers*

**24A.** (1) This paragraph applies where a person ("an authorised person") is authorised by virtue of section 16(2) of the 1984 Act to accompany an investigating officer designated for the purposes of paragraph 16 (or 17) in the execution of a warrant.

(2) The reference in paragraph 16(*h*) (or 17(*e*)) to the seizure of anything by a designated person in exercise of a particular power includes a reference to the seizure of anything by the authorised person in exercise of that power by virtue of section 16(2A) of the 1984 Act.

(3) In relation to any such seizure, paragraph 16(*h*) (or 17(*e*)) is to be read as if it provided for the references to a constable and to an officer in section 21(1) and (2) of the 1984 Act to include references to the authorised

person.

(4) The reference in paragraph 16(*i*) (or 17(*f*)) to anything seized by a designated person in exercise of a particular power includes a reference to anything seized by the authorised person in exercise of that power by virtue of section 16(2A) of the 1984 Act.

(5) In relation to anything so seized, paragraph 16(*i*)(ii) (or 17(*f*)(ii)) is to be read as if it provided for—

(*a*) the references to the supervision of a constable in subsections (3) and (4) of section 21 of the 1984 Act to include references to the supervision of a person designated for the purposes of paragraph 16 (or paragraph 17), and

(*b*) the reference to a constable in subsection (5) of that section to include a reference to such a person or an authorised person accompanying him.

(6) Where an authorised person accompanies an investigating officer who is also designated for the purposes of paragraph 24, the references in sub-paragraphs (*a*) and (*b*) of that paragraph to the designated person include references to the authorised person.

## PART 3

## DETENTION OFFICERS

*Attendance at police station for fingerprinting*

**25.** Where a designation applies this paragraph to any person, he shall, in respect of police stations in the relevant police area, have the power of a constable under section 27(1) of the 1984 Act (fingerprinting of suspects) to require a person to attend a police station in order to have his fingerprints taken.

*Non-intimate searches of detained persons*

**26.** (1) Where a designation applies this paragraph to any person, he shall have the powers of a constable under section 54 of the 1984 Act (non-intimate searches of detained persons)—

(*a*) to carry out a search under that section of any person at a police station in the relevant police area or of any other person otherwise in police detention in that area; and

(*b*) to seize or retain, or cause to be seized or retained, anything found on such a search.

(2) Subsections (6C) and (9) of section 54 of that Act (restrictions on power to seize personal effects and searches to be carried out by a member of the same sex) shall apply to the exercise by a person to whom this paragraph is applied of any power exercisable by virtue of this paragraph as they apply to the exercise of the power in question by a constable.

*Searches and examinations to ascertain identity*

**27.** Where a designation applies this paragraph to any person, he shall have the powers of a constable under section 54A of the 1984 Act (searches and examinations to ascertain identity)—

(*a*) to carry out a search or examination at any police station in the relevant police area; and

(*b*) to take a photograph at any such police station of an identifying mark.

*Searches of persons answering to live link bail*

**27A.** (1) Where a designation applies this paragraph to any person, that person has the powers of a constable under section 54B of the 1984 Act (searches of persons answering to live link bail)—

(*a*) to carry out a search of any person attending a police station in the relevant police area; and

(*b*) to seize or retain articles found on such a search.

(2) Anything seized by a person under the power conferred by sub-paragraph (1) must be delivered to a constable as soon as practicable and in any case before the person from whom the thing was seized leaves the police station.

*Intimate searches of detained persons*

**28.** (1) Where a designation applies this paragraph to any person, he shall have the powers of a constable by virtue of section 55(6) of the 1984 Act (intimate searches) to carry out an intimate search of a person at any police station in the relevant police area.

(2) Subsection (7) of section 55 of that Act (no intimate search to be carried out by a constable of the opposite sex) shall apply to the exercise by a person to whom this paragraph applies of any power exercisable by virtue of this paragraph as it applies to the exercise of the power in question by a constable.

*Fingerprinting without consent*

**29.** Where a designation applies this paragraph to any person—

(*a*) he shall have, at any police station in the relevant police area, the power of a constable under section 61 of the 1984 Act (fingerprinting) to take fingerprints without the appropriate consent; and

(*b*) the requirement by virtue of subsection (7A)(*a*) of that section that a person must be informed by an officer that his fingerprints may be the subject of a speculative search shall be capable of being discharged, in the case of a person at such a station, by his being so informed by the person to whom this paragraph applies.

*Warnings about intimate samples*

**30.** Where a designation applies this paragraph to any person, the requirement by virtue of section 62(5)(*c*) of the 1984 Act (intimate samples) that a person must be informed by an officer that a sample taken from him may be the subject of a speculative search shall be capable of being discharged, in the case of a person in a police station in the relevant police area, by his being so informed by the person to whom this paragraph applies.

*Non-intimate samples*

**31.** Where a designation applies this paragraph to any person—

(*a*) he shall have the power of a constable under section 63 of the 1984 Act (non-intimate samples), in the case of a person in a police station in the relevant police area, to take a non-intimate sample without the appropriate consent;

(*b*) the requirement by virtue of subsection (6) of that section (information about authorisation) that a person must be informed by an officer of the matters mentioned in that subsection shall be capable of being discharged, in the case of an authorisation in relation to a person in a police station in the relevant police area, by his being so informed by the person to whom this paragraph applies; and

(*c*) the requirement by virtue of subsection (8B)(*a*) of that section that a person must be informed by an officer that a sample taken from him may be the subject of a speculative search shall be capable of being discharged, in the case of a person in such a police station, by his being so informed by the person to whom this paragraph applies.

*Attendance at police station for the taking of a sample*

**32.** Where a designation applies this paragraph to any person, he shall, as respects any police station in the relevant police area, have the power of a constable Schedule 2A to the 1984 Act (fingerprinting and samples: power to require attendance at a police station) to require a person to attend a police station in order to have a sample taken.

*Photographing persons in police detention*

**33.** Where a designation applies this paragraph to any person, he shall, at police stations in the relevant police area, have the power of a constable under section 64A of the 1984 Act (photographing of suspects etc) to take a photograph of a person detained at a police station.

*Taking of impressions of footwear*

**33A.** Where a designation applies this paragraph to any person—

(*a*) he shall, at any police station in the relevant police area, have the powers of a constable under section 61A of the 1984 Act (impressions of footwear) to take impressions of a person's footwear without the appropriate consent; and

(*b*) the requirement by virtue of section 61A(5)(*a*) of the 1984 Act that a person must be informed by an officer that an impression of his footwear may be the subject of a speculative search shall be capable of being discharged, in the case of a person at such a station, by his being so informed by the person to whom this paragraph applies.

*Powers in respect of detained persons*

**33B.** Where a designation applies this paragraph to any person, he shall be under a duty, when in the course of his employment he is present at a police station—

(*a*) to keep under control any person detained at the police station and for whom he is for the time being responsible;

(*b*) to assist any officer or other designated person to keep any other person detained at the police station under control; and

(*c*) to prevent the escape of any such person as is mentioned in paragraph (*a*) or (*b*),

and for those purposes shall be entitled to use reasonable force.

**33C.** Where a designation applies this paragraph to any person, he shall be entitled to use reasonable force when—

(*a*) securing, or assisting an officer or another designated person to secure, the detention of a person detained at a police station in the relevant police area, or

(*b*) escorting within a police station in the relevant police area, or assisting an officer or another designated person to escort within such a police station, a person detained there.

**33D.** Where a designation applies this paragraph to any person, he is authorised to carry out the duty under—

(*a*) section 55 of the Police and Criminal Evidence Act 1984 of informing a person who is to be subject to an intimate search under that section of the matters of which he is required to be informed in pursuance of subsection (3B) of that section;

(*b*) section 55A of that Act of informing a person who is to be subject to x-ray or ultrasound (as the case may be) under that section of the matters of which he is required to be informed in pursuance of subsection (3) of that section.

## PART 4
## ESCORT OFFICERS

*Power to take an arrested person to a police station*

**34.** (1) Where a designation applies this paragraph to any person—

(*a*) the persons who, in the case of a person arrested by a constable in the relevant police area, are authorised for the purposes of subsection (1A) of section 30 of the 1984 Act (procedure on arrest of person elsewhere than at a police station) to take the person arrested to a police station in that area shall include that person;

(*b*) that section shall have effect in relation to the exercise by that person of the power conferred by virtue of paragraph (*a*) as if the references to a constable in subsections (3), (4)(*a*) and (10) (but not the references in subsections (5) to (9)) included references to that person; and

(*c*) a person who is taking another person to a police station in exercise of the power conferred by virtue of paragraph (*a*)—

(i) shall be treated for all purposes as having that person in his lawful custody;

(ii) shall be under a duty to keep the person under control and to prevent his escape; and

(iii) shall be entitled to use reasonable force to keep that person in his charge and under his control;

(*d*) a person who has taken another person to a police station in exercise of the power conferred by virtue of paragraph (*a*)—

(i) shall be under a duty to remain at the police station until he has transferred control of the other person to the custody officer at the police station;

(ii) until he has so transferred control of the other person, shall be treated for all purposes as having that person in his lawful custody;

(iii) for so long as he is at the police station or in its immediate vicinity in compliance with, or having complied with, his duty under sub-paragraph (i), shall be under a duty to prevent the escape of the other person and to assist in keeping him under control; and

(2) Without prejudice to any application of paragraph 26, where a person has another in his lawful custody by virtue of sub-paragraph (1) of this paragraph—

(*a*) he shall have the same powers under subsections (6A) and (6B) of section 54 of the 1984 Act (non-intimate searches) as a constable has in the case of a person in police detention—

(i) to carry out a search of the other person; and

(ii) to seize or retain, or cause to be seized or retained, anything found on such a search;

(*b*) subsections (6C) and (9) of that section (restrictions on power to seize personal effects and searches to be carried out by a member of the same sex) shall apply to the exercise by a person to whom this paragraph is applied of any power exercisable by virtue of this sub-paragraph as they apply to the exercise of the power in question by a constable.

*Escort of persons in police detention*

**35.** (1) Where a designation applies this paragraph to any person, that person may be authorised by the custody officer for any designated police station in the relevant police area to escort a person in police detention—

(*a*) from that police station to another police station in that or any other police area; or

(*b*) from that police station to any other place specified by the custody officer and then either back to that police station or on to another police station in that area or in another police area.

(2) Where a designation applies this paragraph to any person, that person may be authorised by the custody officer for any designated police station outside the relevant police area to escort a person in police detention—

(*a*) from that police station to a designated police station in that area; or

(*b*) from that police station to any place in that area specified by the custody officer and either back to that police station or on to another police station (whether in that area or elsewhere).

(3) A person who is escorting another in accordance with an authorisation under sub-paragraph (1) or (2)—

(*a*) shall be treated for all purposes as having that person in his lawful custody;

(*b*) shall be under a duty to keep the person under control and to prevent his escape; and

(*c*) shall be entitled to use reasonable force to keep that person in his charge and under his control.

(3A) A person who has escorted another person to a police station or other place in accordance with an authorisation under sub-paragraph (1) or (2)—

(*a*) shall be under a duty to remain at the police station or other place until he has transferred control of the other person to a custody officer or other responsible person there;

(*b*) until he has so transferred control of the other person, shall be treated for all purposes as having that person in his lawful custody;

(*c*) for so long as he is at the police station or other place, or in its immediate vicinity, in compliance with, or having complied with, his duty under paragraph (*a*), shall be under a duty to prevent the escape of the other person and to assist in keeping him under control; and

(*d*) shall be entitled to use reasonable force for the purpose of complying with his duty under paragraph (*c*).

(4) Without prejudice to any application of* paragraph 26, where a person has another in his lawful custody by virtue of sub-paragraph (3) of this paragraph—

(*a*) he shall have the same powers under subsections (6A) and (6B) of section 54 the 1984 Act (non-intimate searches) as a constable has in the case of a person in police detention—

(i) to carry out a search of the other person; and

(ii) to seize or retain, or cause to be seized or retained, anything found on such a search;

(*b*) subsections (6C) and (9) of that section (restrictions on power to seize personal effects and searches to be carried out by a member of the same sex) shall apply to the exercise by a person to whom this paragraph is applied of any power exercisable by virtue of this sub-paragraph as they apply to the exercise of the power in question by a constable.

(5) Section 39(2) of that Act (responsibilities of custody officer transferred to escort) shall have effect where the custody officer for any police station transfers or permits the transfer of any person to the custody of a person who by virtue of this paragraph has lawful custody outside the police station of the person transferred as it would apply if the person to whom this paragraph applies were a police officer.

## Part 4A
## Staff Custody Officers

*Repealed.*

## Part 5
## Interpretation of Schedule

7.9266 **36.** (1) In this Schedule "the relevant police area"—

(*a*) in relation to a person designated under section 38 or 39 by the chief officer of any police force, means the police area for which that force is maintained; and

(*b*) *repealed.*

(2) In Part 1 of this Schedule "a designation" means—

(*a*) a designation under section 38, or

(*b*) an order under section 38A(1) (and, accordingly, the power to make such an order—

(i) is extended by paragraphs 1(3)(*b*), 1A(2) and (7), 2(6) and 4(1)(*b*), but

(ii) is subject to paragraphs 2(2), 4(2) and 11B(5)).

(2A) In Parts 2 and 4A of this Schedule "a designation" means a designation under section 38.

(3) In Parts 3 and 4 of this Schedule "a designation" means a designation under section 38 or 39.

(3A) In this Schedule "specified park" has the same meaning as in section 162 of the Serious Organised Crime and Police Act 2005.

(4) Expressions used in this Schedule and in the 1984 Act have the same meanings in this Schedule as in that Act.

## SCHEDULE 5
### Powers Exercisable by Accredited Persons — Section 41

*(Amended by the Anti-social Behaviour Act 2003, s 89, the Clean Neighbourhoods and Environment Act 2005, s 62, the Police and Justice Act 2006, Sch 5, the Education and Inspections Act 2006, s 107, the Local Government and Public Involvement in Health Act 2007, s 133, the Policing and Crime Act 2009, Sch 7, the Legal Aid, Sentencing and Punishment of Offenders Act 2012, Sch 23 and the Anti-social Behaviour, Crime and Policing Act 2014, Sch 11.)*

*Power to issue fixed penalty notices*

7.9267 **1.** (1) An accredited person whose accreditation specifies that this paragraph applies to him shall have the powers specified in sub-paragraph (2) in relation to any individual who he has reason to believe has committed or is committing a relevant fixed penalty offence at a place within the relevant police area.

(2) Those powers are the following powers so far as exercisable in respect of a relevant fixed penalty offence—

(*a*) the power of a constable in uniform to give a person a fixed penalty notice under section 54 of the Road Traffic Offenders Act 1988 (c 53) (fixed penalty notices) in respect of an offence under section 72 of the Highway Act 1835 (c 50) (riding on a footway) committed by cycling;

(*aa*) the powers of a constable to give a penalty notice under Chapter 1 of Part 1 of the Criminal Justice and Police Act 2001 (fixed penalty notices in respect of offences of disorder);

(*ab*) the power of a constable to give a penalty notice under section 444A of the Education Act 1996 (penalty notice in respect of failure to secure regular attendance at school of registered pupil);

(*ac*) the power of a constable to give a penalty notice under section 105 of the Education and Inspections Act 2006 (penalty notice in respect of presence of excluded pupil in public place);

(*b*) *repealed*;

(*ba*) the power of an authorised officer of a local authority to give a notice under section 43(1) of the Anti-social Behaviour Act 2003 (penalty notices in respect of graffiti or fly-posting); and

(*c*) the power of an authorised officer of a litter authority to give a notice under section 88 of the Environmental Protection Act 1990 (c 43) (fixed penalty notices in respect of litter); and

(*d*) the power of an authorised officer of a primary or secondary authority, within the meaning of section 59 of the Clean Neighbourhoods and Environment Act 2005, to give a notice under that section (fixed penalty notices in respect of offences under dog control orders).

(2A) The reference to the powers mentioned in sub-paragraph (2)(*aa*) does not include those powers so far as they relate to an offence under the provisions in the following list—

section 12 of the Licensing Act 1872,
section 91 of the Criminal Justice Act 1967,
section 1 of the Theft Act 1968,
section 1(1) of the Criminal Damage Act 1971,
section 87 of the Environmental Protection Act 1990.

(3) In this paragraph "relevant fixed penalty offence", in relation to an accredited person, means an offence which—

(*a*) is an offence by reference to which a notice may be given to a person in exercise of any of the powers mentioned in sub-paragraph (2)(*a*) to (*d*); and

(*b*) is specified or described in that person's accreditation as an offence he has been accredited to enforce.

(3A) For the purposes of paragraph (*f*) of section 64A(1B) of the Police and Criminal Evidence Act 1984 (photographing of suspects in relation to fixed penalty offences) "relevant fixed penalty offence", in relation to an accredited person, includes an offence under a relevant byelaw within the meaning of paragraph 1A(4) (and, accordingly, the reference in that paragraph (*f*) to paragraph 1 of this Schedule includes a reference to paragraph 1A of this Schedule).

(4) In its application to an offence which is an offence by reference to which a notice may be given to a person in exercise of the power mentioned in sub-paragraph (2)(*ab*) or (*ac*), sub-paragraph (1) shall have effect as if for the words from "who he has reason to believe" to the end there were substituted "in the relevant police area who he has reason to believe has committed or is committing a relevant fixed penalty offence".

**1A.** (1) This paragraph applies to an accredited person whose accreditation specifies that it applies to him.

(2) The accreditation may specify that, in relation to that person, the application of sub-paragraph (3) is confined to one or more only (and not all) relevant byelaws, being in each case specified in the accreditation.

(3) Where that person has reason to believe that an individual has committed an offence against a relevant byelaw at a place within the relevant police area, he may exercise the power of an authorised officer of an authority to give a notice under section 237A of the Local Government Act 1972 (fixed penalty notices in relation to offences against certain byelaws).

(4) In this paragraph "relevant byelaw", in relation to an accredited person, means a byelaw which—

(*a*) falls within sub-paragraph (5); and

(*b*) is specified or described in that person's accreditation as a byelaw he has been accredited to enforce under this paragraph.

(5) A byelaw falls within this sub-paragraph if—

(*a*) it is a byelaw to which section 237A of the Local Government Act 1972 applies (fixed penalty notices in relation to offences against certain byelaws); and

(*b*) the chief officer of the police force for the relevant police area and the authority who made the byelaw have agreed to include it in a list of byelaws for the purposes of this sub-paragraph.

(6) A list under sub-paragraph (5)(*b*) must be published by the chief officer in such a way as to bring it to the attention of members of the public in localities where the byelaws in the list apply.

(7) The list may be amended from time to time by agreement between the chief officer and the authority, by adding byelaws to it or removing byelaws from it, and the amended list shall also be published by the chief officer as mentioned in sub-paragraph (6).

*Power to require giving of name and address*

**2.** (1) Where an accredited person whose accreditation specifies that this paragraph applies to him has reason to believe that another person has committed a relevant offence in the relevant police area, he may require that other person to give him his name and address.

(2) A person who fails to comply with a requirement under sub-paragraph (1) is guilty of an offence and shall be liable, on summary conviction, to a fine not exceeding level 3 on the standard scale.

(3) In this paragraph "relevant offence", in relation to any accredited person, means any offence which is—

(*a*) a relevant fixed penalty offence for the purposes of any powers exercisable by the accredited person by virtue of paragraph 1; or

(*aa*) an offence under section 3 or 4 of the Vagrancy Act 1824; or

(*aza*) an offence under a relevant byelaw within the meaning of paragraph 1A(4); or

(*b*) an offence the commission of which appears to the accredited person to have caused—

(i) injury, alarm or distress to any other person; or

(ii) the loss of, or any damage to, any other person's property;

but the accreditation of an accredited person may provide that an offence is not to be treated as a relevant offence by virtue of paragraph (*b*) unless it satisfies such other conditions as may be specified in the accreditation.

(4) In its application to an offence which is an offence by reference to which a notice may be given to a person in exercise of the power mentioned in paragraph 1(2)(*ab*) or (*ac*), sub-paragraph (1) of this paragraph shall have effect as if for the words "has committed a relevant offence in the relevant police area" there were substituted "in the relevant police area has committed a relevant offence".

*Power to require name and address of person acting in an anti-social manner*

**3.** An accredited person whose accreditation specifies that this paragraph applies to him shall, in the relevant police area, have the powers of a constable in uniform under section 50 to require a person whom he has reason to believe to have been acting, or to be acting, in an anti-social manner (within the meaning of section 1 of the Crime and Disorder Act 1998 (c 37) (anti-social behaviour orders)) to give his name and address.

*Power to require name and address: road traffic offences*

**3A.** (1) An accredited person whose accreditation specifies that this paragraph applies to him shall, in the relevant police area, have the powers of a constable—

(*a*) under subsection (1) of section 165 of the Road Traffic Act 1988 to require a person mentioned in paragraph (*c*) of that subsection who he has reasonable cause to believe has committed, in the relevant police area, an offence under subsection (1) or (2) of section 35 of that Act (including that section as extended by paragraphs 8B(4) and 9(2) of this Schedule) to give his name and address; and

(*b*) under section 169 of that Act to require a person committing an offence under section 37 of that Act (including that section as extended by paragraphs 8B(4) and 9(2) of this Schedule) to give his name and address.

(2) The reference in section 169 of the Road Traffic Act 1988 to section 37 of that Act is to be taken to include a reference to that section as extended by paragraphs 8B(4) and 9(2) of this Schedule.

*Alcohol consumption in designated public places*

**4.** An accredited person whose accreditation specifies that this paragraph applies to him shall, within the relevant police area, have the powers of a constable under section 12 of the Criminal Justice and Police Act 2001 (c 16) (alcohol consumption in public places)—

(*a*) to impose a requirement under subsection (2) of that section; and

(*b*) to dispose under subsection (3) of that section of anything surrendered to him;

and that section shall have effect in relation to the exercise of those powers by that person as if the references to a constable in subsections (1) and (5) were references to the accredited person.

*Confiscation of alcohol*

**5.** An accredited person whose accreditation specifies that this paragraph applies to him shall, within the relevant police area, have the powers of a constable under section 1 of the Confiscation of Alcohol (Young Persons) Act 1997 (c 33) (confiscation of intoxicating liquor)—

(*a*) to impose a requirement under subsection (1) or (1AA) of that section; and

(*b*) to dispose under subsection (2) of that section of anything surrendered to him;

and that section shall have effect in relation to the exercise of those powers by that person as if the references to a constable in subsections (1), (1AA) and (4) (but not the reference in subsection (1AB) (removal)) were references to the accredited person.

*Confiscation of tobacco etc*

**6.** (1) An accredited person whose accreditation specifies that this paragraph applies to him shall, within the relevant police area, have—

(*a*) the power to seize anything that a constable in uniform has a duty to seize under subsection (3) of section 7 of the Children and Young Persons Act 1933 (c 12) (seizure of tobacco etc from young persons); and

(*b*) the power to dispose of anything that a constable may dispose of under that subsection;

and the power to dispose of anything shall be a power to dispose of it in such manner as the relevant employer of the accredited person may direct.

(2) In this paragraph "relevant employer", in relation to an accredited person, means the person with whom the chief officer of police for the relevant police area has entered into arrangements under section 40.

*Abandoned vehicles*

**7.** An accredited person whose accreditation specifies that this paragraph applies to him shall have all such powers in the relevant police area as are conferred on accredited persons by regulations under section 99 of the Road Traffic Regulation Act 1984 (c 27) (removal of abandoned vehicles).

*Power to stop vehicle for testing*

**8.** A person whose accreditation specifies that this paragraph applies to him shall, within the relevant police area, have the power of a constable in uniform to stop a vehicle under subsection (3) of section 67 of the Road Traffic Act 1988 (c 52) for the purposes of a test under subsection (1) of that section.

*Power to stop cycles*

**8A.** (1) Subject to sub-paragraph (2), a person whose accreditation specifies that this paragraph applies to him shall, within the relevant police area, have the power of a constable in uniform under section 163(2) of the Road Traffic Act 1988 to stop a cycle.

(2) The power mentioned in sub-paragraph (1) may only be exercised by that person in relation to a person who he has reason to believe has committed an offence under section 72 of the Highway Act 1835 (riding on a footway) by cycling.

*Power to control traffic for purposes other than escorting a load of exceptional dimensions*

**8B.** (1) A person whose accreditation specifies that this paragraph applies to him shall have, in the relevant police area—

(*a*) the power of a constable engaged in the regulation of traffic in a road to direct a person driving or propelling a vehicle to stop the vehicle or to make it proceed in, or keep to, a particular line of traffic;

(*b*) the power of a constable in uniform engaged in the regulation of vehicular traffic in a road to direct a person on foot to stop proceeding along or across the carriageway.

(2) The purposes for which those powers may be exercised do not include the purpose mentioned in paragraph 9(1).

(3) A person whose accreditation specifies that this paragraph applies to him shall also have, in the relevant police area, the power of a constable, for the purposes of a traffic survey, to direct a person driving or propelling a vehicle to stop the vehicle, to make it proceed in, or keep to, a particular line of traffic, or to proceed to a particular point on or near the road.

(4) Sections 35 and 37 of the Road Traffic Act 1988 (offences of failing to comply with directions of constable engaged in regulation of traffic in a road) shall have effect in relation to the exercise of the powers mentioned in sub-paragraphs (1) and (3), for the purposes for which they may be exercised and by a person whose accreditation specifies that this paragraph applies to him, as if the references to a constable were references to him.

(5) A person's accreditation may not specify that this paragraph applies to him unless it also specifies that paragraph 3A applies to him.

*Power to control traffic for purposes of escorting a load of exceptional dimensions*

**9.** (1) A person whose accreditation specifies that this paragraph applies to him shall have, for the purpose of escorting a vehicle or trailer carrying a load of exceptional dimensions either to or from the relevant police area, the power of a constable engaged in the regulation of traffic in a road—

(*a*) to direct a vehicle to stop;

(*b*) to make a vehicle proceed in, or keep to, a particular line of traffic; and

(*c*) to direct pedestrians to stop.

(2) Sections 35 and 37 of the Road Traffic Act 1988 (offences of failing to comply with directions of constable engaged in regulation of traffic in a road) shall have effect in relation to the exercise of those powers for the purpose mentioned in sub-paragraph (1) by a person whose accreditation specifies that this paragraph applies to him as if the references to a constable engaged in regulation of traffic in a road were references to that person.

(3) The powers conferred by virtue of this paragraph may be exercised in any police area in England and Wales.

(4) In this paragraph "vehicle or trailer carrying a load of exceptional dimensions" means a vehicle or trailer the use of which is authorised by an order made by the Secretary of State under section 44(1)(*d*) of the Road Traffic Act 1988.

*Photographing of persons given fixed penalty notices*

**9ZA.** An accredited person whose accreditation specifies that this paragraph applies to him shall, within the relevant police area, have the power of a constable under section 64A(1A) of the 1984 Act (photographing of suspects etc) to take a photograph, elsewhere than at a police station, of a person to whom the accredited person has given a penalty notice (or as the case may be a fixed penalty notice) in exercise of any power mentioned in paragraph 1(2) or in exercise of the power mentioned in paragraph 1A(3).

*Power to modify paragraph 1(2A)*

**9A.** (1) The Secretary of State may by order amend paragraph 1(2A) so as to remove a provision from the list or add a provision to the list; but the list must contain only provisions mentioned in the first column of the Table in section 1(1) of the Criminal Justice and Police Act 2001.

(2) The Secretary of State shall not make an order containing (with or without any other provision) any provision authorised by this paragraph unless a draft of that order has been laid before Parliament and approved by a resolution of each House.

*Meaning of "relevant police area"*

**10.** In this Schedule "the relevant police area", in relation to an accredited person, means the police area for which the police force whose chief officer granted his accreditation is maintained.

## SCHEDULE 5A
### Powers Exercisable by Accredited Inspectors

*(Inserted by the Police and Justice Act 2006, Sch 7 and amended by the Legal Aid, Sentencing and Punishment of Offenders Act 2012, Sch 23.)*

*Power to issue fixed penalty notices*

7.9268 **1.** (1) An accredited inspector whose accreditation specifies that this paragraph applies to him shall have the powers specified in sub-paragraph (2) in relation to any individual who he has reason to believe has committed a relevant fixed penalty offence at a place within the relevant police area.

(2) The powers are the powers of a constable to give a penalty notice under Chapter 1 of Part 1 of the Criminal Justice and Police Act 2001 (fixed penalty notices in respect of offences of disorder) so far as exercisable in respect of a relevant fixed penalty offence.

*Power to require giving of name and address*

**2.** (1) Where an accredited inspector whose accreditation specifies that this paragraph applies to him has reason to believe that a person has committed a relevant fixed penalty offence in the relevant police area, he may require the person to give him his name and address.

(2) A person who fails to comply with a requirement under sub-paragraph (1) is guilty of an offence and shall be liable, on summary conviction, to a fine not exceeding level 3 on the standard scale.

*Photographing of persons given fixed penalty notices*

**3.** An accredited inspector whose accreditation specifies that this paragraph applies to him shall, within the relevant police area, have the power of a constable under section 64A(1A) of the 1984 Act (photographing of suspects etc) to take a photograph, elsewhere than at a police station, of a person to whom the accredited inspector has given a penalty notice in exercise of the powers mentioned in paragraph 1(2).

*Interpretation*

**4.** In this Schedule—

"the relevant police area", in relation to an accredited inspector, means the police area for which the police force whose chief officer granted his accreditation is maintained;

"relevant fixed penalty offence", in relation to an accredited inspector, means an offence which—

(*a*) is an offence contained in a provision mentioned in the first column of the Table in section 1(1) of the Criminal Justice and Police Act 2001, and

(*b*) is specified or described in his accreditation as an offence he has been accredited to enforce.

# Railways and Transport Safety Act 2003[1]

(2003 c 20)

## Part 3[2]

## British Transport Police

*Police Authority*

**7.9269 18–19.** *British Transport Police Authority and its functions.*

[1] This Act makes provision about railways, including tramways and transport safety. Reproduced in this title are those provisions relating to the British Transport Police, Part 1 relating to railways is reproduced in Part VI: Transport, title Railways, Part 4 relating to shipping, alcohol and drugs is reproduced in Part VI: Transport, title Merchant Shipping and Part 5 relating to aviation, alcohol and drugs is reproduced in Part VI: Transport, title Aviation.

Sections 104 and 114 came into force on the passing of the Act (10 July 2003) and ss 105 and 112 came into force on 10 September 2003. The remaining provisions come into force in accordance with orders made under s 120. The following commencement orders have been made: (No 1) SI 2003/2681; (No 2) SI 2004/827; (No 3) SI 2004/1572; (No 4) SI 2004/2759; (No 5) 2005/1991. Part 3 was brought into force on 1 July 2004, except ss 34(1) and s 74 (in force 19 June 2004).

[2] Part 3 comprises ss 18–77 and Schs 4 and 5.

*Police Force*

**7.9270 20–23.** *Establishment of police force, Chief Constables, Deputy Chief Constables and Assistant Chief Constables.*

**7.9271 24. Constables** *Appointment and attestation of Constables (modifies the Police Act 1996, s 29).*

**7.9272 25. Special Constables** *Appointment and attestation of Special Constables (modifies the Police Act 1996, s 29).*

**7.9273 26–30.** *Cadets, civilian employees, terms of employment and trade union membership.*

*Jurisdiction*

**7.9274 31. Jurisdiction** (1) A constable of the Police Force shall have all the powers and privileges of a constable—

(*a*) on track,

(*b*) on network,

(*c*) in a station,

(*d*) in a light maintenance depot,

(*e*) on other land used for purposes of or in relation to a railway,

(*f*) on other land in which a person who provides railway services has a freehold or leasehold interest, and

(*g*) throughout Great Britain for a purpose connected to a railway or to anything occurring on or in relation to a railway.

(2) A constable of the Police Force may enter property which is or forms part of anything specified in subsection (3)—

(*a*) without a warrant,

(*b*) using reasonable force if necessary, and

(*c*) whether or not an offence has been committed.

(3) Those things are—

(*a*) track,

(*b*) a network,

(*c*) a station,

(*d*) a light maintenance depot, and

(*e*) a railway vehicle.

(4) In this section "powers" includes powers under an enactment whenever passed or made.

[Railways and Transport Safety Act 2003, s 31.]

7.9275 **32. Prosecution** Where the Police Force investigates an offence in the course of the exercise of its functions, the Chief Constable may institute criminal proceedings in England and Wales in respect of the offence.

[Railways and Transport Safety Act 2003, s 32.]

*Police Services Agreements*

7.9276 **33–35.** *Arrangements with those who provide railway services.*

*Regulation of Police Force*

7.9277 **36–49.** *Regulations and Codes of Practice.*

*Planning*

7.9278 **50–55.** *Policing objectives, policing plans, performance targets, directions and three-year strategy plans.*

*Information, etc*

7.9279 **56–62.** *Reports, inquiries and public consultation.*

*Inspection*

7.9280 **63–67.** *Inspections, directions and action plans.*

*Miscellaneous*

7.9281 **68. Offences** (1) Subsections (1) and (2) of section 89 of the Police Act 1996 (c 16) (assault on constable, etc) shall apply in relation to a constable of the Police Force as they apply in relation to other constables in England and Wales.

(2) Section 90 of that Act (impersonation of constable) shall apply as if—

(*a*) a reference to a member of a police force included a reference to a constable of the Police Force, and

(*b*) a reference to a special constable appointed for a police area included a reference to a special constable of the Police Force.

(3) In their application in relation to the Police Force by virtue of this section, sections 89 and 90 of that Act shall have effect throughout England and Wales and Scotland.

[Railways and Transport Safety Act 2003, s 68.]

*General*

7.9282 **75. Interpretation** (1) For the purposes of this Part (including, except where the context requires otherwise, subsections (2) to (5) below) "railway" means—

(*a*) a railway within the meaning given by section 67(1) of the Transport and Works Act 1992 (c 42) (interpretation), and

(*b*) a tramway within the meaning given by that section.

(2) For the purposes of this Part "railway services" means the management or control, or participation in the management or control, of all or any part or aspect of a railway or railway property.

(3) For the purposes of this Part "railway property" means—

(*a*) a track,

(*b*) a network,

(*c*) a station,

(*d*) a light maintenance depot,

(*e*) a railway vehicle on a network or tramway,

(*f*) rolling stock on a network or tramway,

(*g*) a train used on a network, and

(*h*) a vehicle used on a tramway.

(4) For the purposes of this Part (including subsections (1)(*b*) and (3) above) "tramway" has the meaning given by section 67(1) of the Transport and Works Act 1992 (c 42).

(5) For the purposes of this Part the following expressions have the meaning given by section 82 or 83 of the Railways Act 1993 (c 43) (interpretation) (or, where appropriate, an equivalent meaning in relation to a tramway)—

(*a*) light maintenance depot,

(*b*) network,

(*c*) railway vehicle,

(*d*) rolling stock,

(*e*) station,

(*f*) track, and

(*g*) train.

(6) In this Part unless the context requires otherwise a reference to a constable of the Police Force includes a reference to a constable of any rank.

(7) In this Part a reference to the National Policing Plan is a reference to the plan provided for

in section 36A of the Police Act 1996 (c 16).*

(8) This section is subject to section 77(2).

[Railways and Transport Safety Act 2003, s 75.]

* **Subsection (7) repealed by the Police and Justice Act 2006, Sch 15 from a date to be appointed.**

7.9283 **76. Index of defined expressions** The following expressions are defined for the purposes of this Part by the provisions specified.

| *Expression* | *Provision* |
|---|---|
| The Authority | Section 18 |
| British Transport Police Federation | Section 39 |
| The Chief Constable | Section 21 |
| Constable | Sections 25(6) and 75 |
| Light maintenance depot | Section 75 |
| National Policing Plan | Section 75* |
| Network | Section 75 |
| Police services agreement | Section 33 |
| The Police Force | Section 20 |
| Railway | Section 75 |
| Railway property | Section 75 |
| Railway services | Section 75 |
| Railway vehicle | Section 75 |
| Rolling stock | Section 75 |
| Station | Section 75 |
| Track | Section 75 |
| Train | Section 75 |
| Tramway | Section 75 |

[Railways and Transport Safety Act 2003, s 76.]

* **Entry relating to the "National Policing Plan" repealed by the Police and Justice Act 2006, Sch 15 from a date to be appointed.**

7.9284 77. *Extent.*

SCHEDULE 4
British Transport Police Authority

[Not reproduced]

# Police Reform and Social Responsibility Act 2011

(2011 c 13)

7.9285 *Part 1 relates to police reform and makes provision for there to be an elected police and crime commissioner for each police area outside London who is to secure the maintenance of an efficient and effective police for that area and hold the chief constable to account (**s 1**). Each police force is to have a chief constable (**s 2**). In the metropolitan police district there is the Mayor's office for policing and crime with similar functions. in relation to the Commissioner of Police for the Metropolis (**ss 3–4**).*

*It is a function of a police and crime commissioner (in London the Mayor's office for policing and crime) having consulted the chief constable and relevant police and crime panel to issue and publish an annual police and crime plan which has regard to any strategic policing requirement issued by the Secretary of State (**ss 5–8**). An 'elected local policing body' (ie a policing and crime commissioner or the Mayor's office for policing and crime) must publish such information as may be specified by the Secretary of State by order[1] and such information as it considers necessary to enable persons in its area to assess the performance of the body and the chief officer of police in exercising its functions and an annual report.*

*Outside London there must be a police and crime panel to review the draft police and crime plan, subject the police and crime commissioner to questioning on the plan at an open meeting, review the annual report and review or scrutinise decisions made by the police and crime commissioner. Reports of the panel must be published and sent to local authorities within the panel's area (**s 28**). In London there is to be a London Assembly police and crime panel (**s 32**).*

*Chief officers of police have various duties: to obtain views about crime and disorder from residents and provide them with information and hold regular neighbourhood meetings (**s 34**).*

*Outside London, the police and crime commissioner has responsibility for appointing, suspending or removing a chief constable (**s 38**). Provision is made for the appointment etc. of deputy and assistant chief constables (**ss 39–40**). The Commissioner of Police for the Metropolis is appointed by Her Majesty on recommendation of the Secretary of State (**s 42**). Her Majesty also appoints one Deputy Commissioner (**s 43**). Assistant commissioners, deputy assistant commissioners and commanders are appointed by the Commissioner of Police for the Metropolis in consultation with the Mayor (**ss 45–47**).*

*Detailed provision is made for the election of police and crime commissioners who normally hold office for four years commencing with elections in 2012 and every four years thereafter (**ss 50–76**)[2]. The term of office of a person elected to fill a vacancy ends at the time it would have ended had the person been elected at the most recent ordinary election of police and crime commissioners (**s 51**). Remaining provisions of Part 1 of the Act include a general duty on the Secretary of State to exercise powers under the Act to promote the efficiency and effectiveness of the police (**s 78**); to issue a policing protocol[3] (**s 79**); and obtain advice from representative bodies (**s 80**). Commencement is in accordance with the provisions of s 157 and orders made thereunder[4].*

---

[1] The Elected Local Policing Bodies (Specified Information) Order 2011, SI 2011/3050 amended by SI 2013/1816 has been made.

[2] The Police and Crime Commissioner Elections Order 2012, SI 2012/1917 amended by SI 2014/921 and 1963, SI 2015/643 and 664, SI 2016/300 and 997 and SI 2017/42 (W) has been made which makes detailed provisions for elections of PCCs, creates offences and applies other election legislation.

[3] The Policing Protocol Order 2011, SI 2011/2744 has been made. This sets out to all Police and Crime Commissioners and the Mayor's Office for Policing and Crime, Chief Constables, Police and Crime Panels and the London Assembly Police and Crime Panel how their functions will be exercised in relation to each other.

[4] The following commencement orders have been made: (No 1) SI 2011/2515; (No 2) SI 2011/2834; (No 3 and Transitional Provisions) SI 2011/3019 amended by SI 2012/75; (No 4) SI 2012/896; (No 5) SI 2012/1129; (No 6) SI 2012/209; (No 7 and Transitional Provisions and Commencement No 3 and Transitional Provisions (Amendment)) SI 2012/2892.

7.9286 **101. Crime and disorder reduction** (1) A reference to crime and disorder reduction is a reference to—

(*a*) reduction of crime and disorder (including anti-social and other behaviour adversely affecting the local environment),

(*b*) combating the misuse of drugs, alcohol and other substances, and

(*c*) reduction of re-offending.

(2) In this section "anti-social behaviour" means behaviour by a person which causes or is likely to cause harassment, alarm or distress to one or more other persons not of the same household as the person.

(3) This section applies for the purposes of this Part.

[Police Reform and Social Responsibility Act 2011, s 101.]

7.9287 **102. Interpretation of Part 1** (1) In this Part (unless otherwise specified)—

"chief executive" means—

(*a*) in relation to a police and crime commissioner, the chief executive appointed by the commissioner under Schedule 1;

(*b*) in relation to the Mayor's Office for Policing and Crime, the chief executive appointed by the Office under Schedule 3;

"chief finance officer" means—

(*a*) in relation to a police and crime commissioner, the chief finance officer appointed by the commissioner under Schedule 1;

(*b*) in relation to the chief constable of a police force to which Chapter 1 applies, the chief finance officer appointed by the chief constable under Schedule 2;

(*c*) in relation to the Mayor's Office for Policing and Crime, the chief finance officer appointed by the Office under Schedule 3;

(*d*) in relation to the Commissioner of Police of the Metropolis, the chief finance officer appointed by the Commissioner under Schedule 4;

"chief officer of police" means—

(*a*) in relation to a police force maintained under section 2 of the Police Act 1996, the chief constable of that force;

(*b*) in relation to the metropolitan police force, the Commissioner of Police of the Metropolis;

"crime and disorder reduction" has the meaning given in section 101;

"elected local policing body" means—

(*a*) in relation to a police area listed in Schedule 1 to the Police Act 1996, the police and crime commissioner for the area;

(*b*) in relation to the metropolitan police district, the Mayor's Office for Policing and Crime;

"national or international functions" means functions relating to—

(*a*) the protection of prominent persons or their residences,

(*b*) national security,

(*c*) counter-terrorism, or
(*d*) the provision of services for any other national or international purpose;

"police and crime panel" means—
(*a*) in relation to a police area listed in Schedule 1 to the Police Act 1996, the police and crime panel referred to in subsection (1) of section 28;
(*b*) in relation to the metropolitan police district, the committee established under section 32;

"police and crime plan" has the meaning given in section 7;

"police area" means—
(*a*) a police area listed in Schedule 1 to the Police Act 1996 (police areas outside London), and
(*b*) the metropolitan police district;

"relevant chief officer of police", in relation to—
(*a*) a police area,
(*b*) the police force for a police area,
(*c*) the elected local policing body for a police area, or
(*d*) the police and crime panel for a police area,
means the chief officer of police of the police force for that area;

"relevant elected local policing body", in relation to—
(*a*) a police area,
(*b*) the police force for a police area,
(*c*) the chief officer of police of the police force for a police area, or
(*d*) the police and crime panel for a police area,
means the elected local policing body for that area;

"relevant police and crime panel", in relation to—
(*a*) a police area,
(*b*) the police force for a police area,
(*c*) the chief officer of police of the police force for a police area, or
(*d*) the elected local policing body for a police area, means the police and crime panel for that area;

"relevant police force", in relation to—
(*a*) a police area,
(*b*) a chief officer of police of the police force for a police area,
(*c*) the elected local policing body for a police area, or
(*d*) the police and crime panel for a police area,
means the police force for that area.

(2) References in this Part to a police and crime commissioner's area are references to the police area for which the commissioner is established.

(3)
(*a*) the commissioner's chief executive;
(*b*) the commissioner's chief finance officer; and
(*c*) other staff;
and to the person (if any) appointed as the deputy police and crime commissioner under section 18.

(4) References in this Part to a police force's civilian staff are (except in the case of the metropolitan police force) references to—
(*a*) the chief finance officer appointed by the chief constable of the force under paragraph 4 of Schedule 2, and
(*b*) the other staff appointed by that chief constable under that Schedule.

(5) References in this Part to the staff of the Mayor's Office for Policing and Crime are references to—
(*a*) the Office's chief finance officer appointed under section 127(2) of the Greater London Authority Act 1999;
(*b*) the Office's chief executive appointed under Schedule 3;
(*c*) other staff appointed under Schedule 3; and
(*d*) the person (if any) appointed under section 19 as the Deputy Mayor for Policing and Crime (subject to paragraph 4(4) of Schedule 3 (Deputy Mayor an Assembly member)).

(6) References in this Part to the metropolitan police force's civilian staff are references to—
(*a*) the chief finance officer appointed by the Commissioner of Police of the Metropolis under paragraph 1 of Schedule 4, and
(*b*) the other staff appointed by the Commissioner under that Schedule.

[Police Reform and Social Responsibility Act 2011, s 102.]

SCHEDULE 7

*Regulations*[1] *about complaints and conduct matters*

---

[1] The Elected Local Policing Bodies (Complaints and Misconduct) Regulations 2012, SI 2012/62 have been made.

## Police (Property) Regulations 1997

(SI 1997/1908 amended by SI 2000/1549, SI 2002/2313, SI 2006/594, SI 2011/3058 and SI 2013/2318)

**7.9288** 1. *Citation and commencement.*

[1] Made by the Secretary of State, in exercise of the powers conferred on him by s 2 of the Police (Property) Act 1897, and section 43(5), (6) and (7) of the Powers of Criminal Courts Act 1973.

**7.9289** 2. *Revocation.*

**7.9290** 3. In these Regulations:

"the relevant authority" means

(*a*) in relation to a police area in England and Wales, the or local policing body (within the meaning of section 101(1) of the Police Act 1996);

(*ab*) in relation to the National Crime Agency, that Agency;

(*b*) *revoked*

"the 1897 Act" means the Police (Property) Act 1897.

**7.9291** 4. (1) Subject to regulation 5 below, this regulation applies to property in the possession of the police to which the 1897 Act applies in respect of which the owner has not been ascertained and no order of a competent court has been made.

(2) Subject to section 2(3) of the 1897 Act (which provides for the sale of property which is perishable or the custody of which involves unreasonable expense or inconvenience) property to which this regulation applies shall not be disposed of until it has remained in the possession of the police for a year.

**7.9292** 5. (1) This regulation applies to property which is in the possession of the police by virtue of section 143 of the Powers of Criminal Courts (Sentencing) Act 2000 and in respect of which no application by a claimant has been made within six months of the making of the order under that section or no such application has succeeded.

(2) Subject to section 2(3) of the 1897 Act, property to which this regulation applies shall not be disposed of until the expiration of six months from the date on which the order in respect of the property was made under that section on the conviction of an offender or, if an application by a claimant of the property has been made within that period or the offender has appealed against the conviction or sentence, until that application or appeal has been determined.

**7.9293** 6. (1) After the expiration of the period referred to in regulation 4(2) or 5(2) above, as applicable, property to which these regulations apply (other than money) may be sold.

(2) The proceeds of all sales under these Regulations and any money to which these Regulations apply shall be paid to the relevant authority and shall be kept in a separate account to be called the Police Property Act Fund ("the Fund").

(3) The Fund or any part thereof, may be invested as the relevant authority think fit and the income derived from the investments shall be added to and become part of the Fund.

(4) The moneys, including income from investments standing to the credit of the Fund shall be applicable—

(*a*) to defray expenses incurred in the conveyance, storage and safe custody of the property and in connection with its sale and otherwise in executing these Regulations;

(*b*) to pay reasonable compensation, the amount of which shall be fixed by the relevant authority, to persons by whom property has been delivered to the police;

(*c*) to make payments of such amounts as the relevant authority may determine for such charitable purposes as they may select.

(5) The Chief Officer of Police may, at the request of the relevant authority, exercise the powers and perform the duties of the authority under the foregoing paragraphs of this regulation.

(6) The Fund shall be audited by an auditor nominated for that purpose by the relevant authority.

**7.9294** 7. (1) After the expiration of the period referred to in regulation 4(2) or 5(2) above, as applicable, if in the opinion of the relevant authority to which these Regulations apply (other than money) can be used for police purposes, the relevant authority may determine that the property is to be retained by the authority and the property shall vest in them on the making of the determination.

(2) A determination under paragraph (1) above shall be recorded in writing and published in such manner as the authority think fit and that record shall include the date on which the determination is made.

(3) No determination under paragraph (1) above may be made in relation to any property in relation to which an order has been made under section 145 of the Powers of Criminal Courts (Sentencing) Act 2000.

**7.9295** 8. If the Chief Officer of Police, or in the case of property in the possession of the National Crime Agency the Director General of that Agency, is satisfied that the nature of any property to which these Regulations apply is such that it is not in the public interest that it should be sold or retained, it shall be destroyed or otherwise disposed of in accordance with his directions.

## Police Act 1997 (Criminal Records) Regulations 2002[1]

(SI 2002/233 amended by SI 2003/137, 520 and 1418, SI 2004/367, 1759 and 2592, SI 2005/347, SI 2006/748 and 2181, SI 2007/700, 1892 and 3224 and SI 2008/2143, SI 2009/460, 1882 and 2428, SI 2010/817, 1836 and 2702, SI 2011/719, SI 2012/523, 2114, 2669, 3006 and 3016, SI 2013/1194 and 2669, SI 2014/239, 955, 2103 and 2122, SI 2015/643 and SI 2017/52 (W))

**7.9296** 1. *Citation, commencement and extent* (1) These Regulations may be cited as the

Police Act 1997 (Criminal Records) Regulations 2002 and shall come into force on 1st March 2002.
(2) These Regulations extend to England and Wales.

---

[1] Made by the Secretary of State under:
(a) ss 113(1)(*b*); 114(1)(*b*); 115(1)(*b*) and (10); 116(1)(*b*); 118(3) and 125(5); and
(b) having regard to the meaning of "prescribed" in ss 113(1)(*a*), (3)(*a*), (3A)(*b*) and (5); 114(1)(*a*); 115(1)(*a*), (6)(*a*)(i) and (6A)(*b*); 116(1)(*a*); 118(2)(*a*) and 119(3). See also, the Police Act 1997 (Criminal Records) (Welsh Language) Regulations 2003, SI 2003/117.

**7.9297** 2. *Interpretation* In these Regulations—

"the Act" means the Police Act 1997;

"adult" means a person who has attained the age of 18;

"area committee" has the same meaning as in section 18 of the Local Government Act 2000;

"charity" and "charity trustee" have the same meanings as in the Charities Act 2011;

"childcare" has the meaning given by section 18 of the Childcare Act 2006;

"childcare premises" means any premises on which childcare is provided;

"childminder agency" has the meaning given by section 98(1) of the Childcare Act 2006;

"child minding" for the purposes of regulation 5A(*g*) has the meaning given by section 79A(2) of the Children Act 1989;

"day care" for the purposes of regulation 5A(*g*) has the meaning given by section 79A(6) of the Children Act 1989;

"executive", in relation to a local authority, has the same meaning as in Part 2 of the Local Government Act 2000;

"reprimand" means a reprimand given to a child or young person in accordance with section 65 of the Crime and Disorder Act 1998;

"local authority" has the same meaning as in the Education Act 1996;

"social services functions", in relation to a local authority, has the same meaning as in the Local Authority Social Services Act 1970;

"taxi driver licence" means a licence granted under—
- (i) section 46 of the Town Police Clauses Act 1847;
- (ii) section 8 of the Metropolitan Public Carriage Act 1869;
- (iii) section 9 of the Plymouth City Council Act 1975;
- (iv) section 51 of the Local Government (Miscellaneous Provisions) Act 1976; or
- (v) section 13 of the Private Hire Vehicles (London) Act 1998;

"volunteer" means a person engaged in an activity which involves spending time, unpaid (except for travel and other approved out-of-pocket expenses), doing something which aims to benefit some third party other than or in addition to a close relative;

"warning" means a warning given to a child or young person in accordance with section 65 of the Crime and Disorder Act 1998.

**7.9298** 3. *Application form* The form set out in Schedule 2 to these Regulations, or a form to the like effect, is hereby prescribed for the purposes of sections 113(1)(*a*) (criminal record certificate), 114(1)(*a*) (criminal record certificate: Crown employment), 115(1)(*a*) (enhanced criminal record certificate) and 116(1)(*a*) (enhanced criminal record certificate: judicial appointment and Crown employment) of the Act.

**7.9299** 3A. *Fee for criminal conviction certificates* The fee payable in relation to an application for a criminal conviction certificate is prescribed as £25.

**7.9300** 4. *Fees for criminal record certificates and enhanced criminal record certificates* The fee payable in relation to an application for the issue of a criminal record certificate or an enhanced criminal record certificate is prescribed as—
- (*a*) £26 in the case of a criminal record certificate;
- (*b*) £44 in the case of an enhanced criminal record certificate, and
- (*c*) where an urgent preliminary response is sought under section 113E(3)(*b*) of the Act, an additional £6 in each case;

save that no fee is payable in relation to an application made by a volunteer.

**7.9301** 4B. *Criminal conviction certificates: prescribed details* (1) The following details of a conviction are prescribed for the purposes of section 112(2)(*a*) of the Act—
- (*a*) the date of conviction;
- (*b*) the convicting court;
- (*c*) the offence;
- (*d*) the method of disposal for the offence, including any ancillary order made.

(2) The following details of a conditional caution are prescribed for the purposes of section 112(2)(*a*) of the Act—
- (*a*) the date on which the conditional caution was given;
- (*b*) the offence;
- (*c*) the attached conditions.

**7.9302** 5. *Relevant matters: prescribed details* The following details of a relevant matter for the purposes of sections 113(3)(*a*) and 115(6)(*a*)(i) of the Act (including those provisions as applied by sections 114(3) and 116(3), respectively) are hereby prescribed—
- (*a*) in the case of a conviction within the meaning of the Rehabilitation of Offenders Act 1974, including a spent conviction—
  - (i) the date of conviction;

(ii) the convicting court;
(iii) the offence; and
(iv) the method of disposal for the offence including details of any order made under Part 2 of the Criminal Justice and Court Services Act 2000,

(*b*) in the case of a caution, reprimand or warning—
(i) the date of caution, reprimand or warning;
(ii) the place where the caution, reprimand or warning was issued; and
(iii) the offence which the person issued with a caution, reprimand or warning had admitted.

**7.9303** 5A. *Enhanced criminal record certificates: prescribed purposes* The purposes for which an enhanced criminal record certificate may be required in accordance with a statement made by a registered person under section 113B(2)(*b*) of the Act are prescribed as follows, namely the purposes of—

(*a*) considering the applicant's suitability in the circumstances set out in regulation 5C;
(*aa*) *revoked*
(*b*) considering the applicant's suitability in the circumstances set out in regulation 5B;
(*ba*) *revoked*
(*bb*) *revoked*
(*c*) obtaining or holding an operating licence under Part 5 of the Gambling Act 2005 for the purposes of that Act;
(*d*) obtaining or holding a personal licence under Part 6 of the Gambling Act 2005 for the purposes of that Act;
(*e*) considering an individual's suitability for a position as Commissioner for the Gambling Commission and for any office or employment in the Commissioners' service;
(*f*) obtaining or holding a licence under section 5 or 6 of the National Lottery etc Act 1993 (running or promoting lotteries);
(*g*)–(*u*) *revoked*
(*v*) considering the suitability of any person appointed by the Commissioner for Older People in Wales to assist him in the discharge of his functions or authorised to discharge his functions on his behalf;
(*w*) *revoked*
(*x*) considering the applicant's suitability for work as a person who provides immigration advice or services as defined in section 82(1) of the Immigration and Asylum Act 1999 and is—
(i) a registered person under Part 5 of that Act, or
(ii) a person who acts on behalf of and under the supervision of such a registered person, or
(iii) a person who is exempt by section 84(4)(*a*) to (*c*) of that Act;
(*y*) considering the applicant's suitability to obtain or retain a licence under regulation 5 of the Misuse of Drugs Regulations 2001 or under Article 3(2) of Regulation 2004/273/EC or under Article 6(1) of Regulation 2005/111/EC where the question relates to any person who as a result of his role in the body concerned is required to be named in the application for such a licence (or would have been so required if that person had had that role at the time the application was made);
(*z*) *revoked*
(*za*) *revoked*
(*zb*) *revoked*
(*zc*) *revoked*
(*zd*) considering an individual's suitability to have in their possession, to acquire or to transfer, prohibited weapons or ammunition to which section 5 of the Firearms Act 1968 applies;
(*ze*) assessing the suitability of a person for any office or employment which relates to national security;
(*zf*) considering the applicant's suitability to obtain or hold a taxi driver licence.

**7.9304** 5B. *Work with adults* (1) The circumstances referred to in regulation 5A(*b*) are—

(*a*) any employment or other work which is normally carried out in a hospital used only for the provision of high security psychiatric services within the meaning of section 4(2) of the National Health Service Act 2006;
(*b*) the provision to an adult of regulated activity relating to vulnerable adults within the meaning of Part 2 of Schedule 4 to the Safeguarding Vulnerable Groups Act 2006;
(*c*) the provision of any activity mentioned in paragraph (6) to an adult who receives a health or social care service within the meaning of paragraph (9) or a specified activity within the meaning of paragraph (10), provided that the person carrying out the activity does so—
(i) at any time on more than three days in any period of 30 days;
(ii) at any time between 2 am and 6 am and the activity gives the person the opportunity to have face-to-face contact with the adult; or
(iii) at least once a week on an ongoing basis;
(*d*) the regular day to day management or supervision of a person mentioned in paragraph (*c*) above;
(*e*) the exercise of any of the functions of the Welsh Ministers relating to the inspection of the following so far as the function gives the person exercising the function the opportunity,

in consequence of anything the person is permitted or required to do in exercise of that function, to have contact with an adult who receives a health or social care service within the meaning of paragraph (9) or a specified activity within the meaning of paragraph (10)—

(i) a local authority (within the meaning of section 1 of the Local Authority Social Services Act 1970) in the exercise of its social services functions (within the meaning of that Act);

(ii) an establishment in relation to which a requirement to register arises under section 11 of the Care Standards Act 2000;

(iii) an agency in relation to which such a requirement arises;

(iv) a person to whom Part 2 of that Act applies in pursuance of regulations under section 42 of that Act;

(v) an NHS body within the meaning of section 148 of the Health and Social Care (Community Health and Standards) Act 2003; or

(vi) any person, other than a local authority, providing Welsh local authority social services within the meaning of that section,

in so far as the inspection relates to social services, care, treatment or therapy provided for adults who receive a health or social care service within the meaning of paragraph (9) or a specified activity within the meaning of paragraph (10);

(*f*) the exercise of a function of the Care Quality Commission in so far as the function—

(i) relates to the inspection of anything which is listed in section 60(1) of the Health and Social Care Act 2008 and involves the provision of social services, care, treatment or therapy for adults who receive a health or social care service within the meaning of paragraph (9) or a specified activity within the meaning of paragraph (10); and

(ii) gives the person exercising the function the opportunity, in consequence of anything the person is permitted or required to do in exercise of that function, to have contact with an adult who receives a health or social care service within the meaning of paragraph (9) or a specified activity within the meaning of paragraph (10);

(*g*) the exercise of a function of a person who is—

(i) a member of a local authority and discharges any social services functions of a local authority which relate wholly or mainly to adults who receive a health or social care service within the meaning of paragraph (9) or a specified activity within the meaning of paragraph (10);

(ii) a member of an executive of a local authority which discharges any such functions;

(iii) a member of a committee of an executive of a local authority which discharges any such functions; or

(iv) a member of an area committee, or any other committee, of a local authority which discharges any such functions;

(v) a chief executive of a local authority that has any social services functions;

(vi) a director of adult social services of a local authority in England;

(vii) a director of social services of a local authority in Wales;

(viii) a Commissioner for older people in Wales or deputy Commissioner for older people in Wales;

(ix) a charity trustee of a charity whose workers normally engage in any activity which is work with adults;

(x) a person who is required to register to carry out a regulated activity within the meaning of the Health and Social Care Act 2008 where that activity will be carried out in relation to an adult who receives a health or social care service within the meaning of paragraph (9).

(2) In paragraph (1)(*e*) the reference to an NHS body includes a reference to any person who provides, or is to provide, health care for the body (wherever the health care is or is to be provided).

(3) In paragraph (1)(*g*) any reference to a committee includes a reference to any sub-committee which discharges any functions of that committee.

(4) In paragraph (1)(*g*)(vi) in relation to a local authority which has not appointed a director of children's services under section 18 of the Children Act 2004 the word "adult" must be ignored.

(5) In paragraph (1)(*g*)(ix) an individual is a worker for a charity if he does work under arrangements made by the charity; but the arrangements referred to in this paragraph do not include any arrangements made for purposes which are merely incidental to the purposes for which the charity is established.

(6) For the purposes of this regulation "activity" means—

(*a*) any form of care or supervision;

(*b*) any form of treatment or therapy;

(*c*) any form of training, teaching, instruction, assistance, advice or guidance provided wholly or mainly for adults who receive a health or social care service within the meaning of paragraph (9) or a specified activity within the meaning of paragraph (10);

(*d*) moderating a public electronic interactive communication service which is likely to be used wholly or mainly by adults who receive a health or social care service within the meaning of paragraph (9) or a specified activity within the meaning of paragraph (10);

(*e*) any form of work carried out in a care home (for the purposes of the Care Standards Act 2000) which is exclusively or mainly for adults, whether or not for gain, that gives the person carrying out the work the opportunity to have contact with the adults resident at that care home;

(*f*) representation of, or advocacy services for, adults who receive a health or social care service within the meaning of paragraph (9) or a specified activity within the meaning of paragraph (10), by a service which has been approved by the Secretary of State or created by any enactment, and which is of such a kind as to enable the person to have access to such adults in the course of his normal duties in providing such services;

(*g*) the conveying of an adult who receives a health or social care service within the meaning of paragraph (9) or a specified activity within the meaning of paragraph (10) (whether or not the adult is accompanied by a person caring for them).

(7)

(*a*) For the purposes of paragraph (6)(*d*) a person moderates a public electronic interactive communication service if, for the purposes of protecting the adults mentioned in that sub-paragraph, he has any function relating to—

(i) monitoring the content of matter which forms any part of the service;

(ii) removing matter from, or preventing the addition of matter to, the service; or

(iii) controlling access to, or use of, the service.

(*b*) But a person does not moderate a public electronic interactive communication service as mentioned in sub-paragraph (7)(*a*)(ii) or (iii) unless he has—

(i) access to the content of the matter;

(ii) contact with users of the service.

(8)

(*a*) For the purposes of paragraph (6) "activity" does not include any activity carried out in the course of a family relationship, or carried out in the course of a personal relationship for no commercial consideration.

(*b*) For the purposes of paragraph 8(*a*) "family relationship" includes a relationship between two persons who live in the same household and treat each other as though they were members of the same family.

(*c*) For the purposes of paragraph 8(*a*) a "personal relationship" is a relationship between or among friends, where a "friend" of a person includes a person who is a friend of a member of that person's family.

(9) For the purposes of this regulation "health or social care service" means—

(*a*) residential accommodation provided for an adult in connection with any care or nursing he requires;

(*b*) accommodation provided for an adult who is or has been a pupil attending a residential special school, where that school is—

(i) a special school within the meaning of section 337 of the Education Act 1996;

(ii) an independent school within the meaning of section 463 of that Act which is in England and is specially organised to make special educational provision for pupils with special educational needs (within the meaning of section 579 of that Act) or is in Wales and is approved by the Welsh Ministers under section 347 of that Act;

(iii) an independent school within the meaning of section 463 of that Act not falling within sub-paragraph (*b*)(ii) which, with the consent of the Welsh Ministers, given under section 347(5)(*b*) of that Act, provides places for children with special educational needs (within the meaning of section 579 of that Act);

(iv) an institution within the further education section (within the meaning of section 91 of the Further and Higher Education Act 1992) which provides accommodation for children; or

(v) a 16 to 19 Academy, within the meaning of section 1B of the Academies Act 2010, which provides accommodation for children;

(*c*) sheltered housing;

(*d*) care of any description or assistance provided to an adult by reason of his age, health or any disability he has, which is provided to the adult in the place where he is, for the time being, living, whether provided continuously or not;

(*e*) any form of health care, including treatment, therapy or palliative care of any description;

(*f*) support, assistance or advice for the purpose of developing an adult's capacity to live independently in accommodation, or sustaining their capacity to do so;

(*g*) any service provided specifically for adults because of their age, any disability, physical or mental illness, excluding a service provided specifically for an adult, with one or more of the following disabilities (unless that person has another disability)—

(i) dyslexia;

(ii) dyscalculia;

(iii) dyspraxia;

(iv) Irlen syndrome;

(v) alexia;

(vi) auditory processing disorder;

(vii) dysgraphia;

(*h*) any service provided specifically to an expectant or nursing mother in receipt of residential accommodation pursuant to arrangements made under section 21(1)(aa) of the National Assistance Act 1948 or care pursuant to paragraph 1 of Schedule 20 to the National Health Service Act 2006 or accommodation under Part 1 of the Care Act 2014 (care and support).

(10) For the purposes of this regulation "specified activity" means—

(*a*) the detention of an adult in lawful custody in a prison (within the meaning of the Prison Act 1952), a remand centre, young offender institution or a secure training centre (as mentioned in section 43 of that Act) or an attendance centre (within the meaning of section 53(1) of that Act);

(*b*) the detention of a detained person (within the meaning of Part 8 of the Immigration and Asylum Act 1999) who is detained in a removal centre or short-term holding facility (within the meaning of that Part) or in pursuance of escort arrangements made under section 156 of that Act;

(*c*) the supervision of an adult by virtue of an order of a court by a person exercising functions for the purposes of Part 1 of the Criminal Justice and Court Services Act 2000;

(*d*) the supervision of an adult by a person acting for the purposes mentioned in section 1(1) of the Offender Management Act 2007;

(*e*) the provision to an adult of assistance with the conduct of their affairs in situations where—

(i) a lasting power of attorney is created in respect of the adult in accordance with section 9 of the Mental Capacity Act 2005 or an application is made under paragraph 4 of Schedule 1 to that Act for the registration of an instrument intended to create a lasting power of attorney in respect of the adult;

(ii) an enduring power of attorney (within the meaning of Schedule 4 to that Act) in respect of the adult is registered in accordance with that Schedule or an application is made under that Schedule for the registration of an enduring power of attorney in respect of the adult;

(iii) an order under section 16 of that Act has been made by the Court of Protection in relation to the making of decisions on the adult's behalf, or such an order has been applied for;

(iv) an independent mental capacity advocate is or is to be appointed in respect of the adult in pursuance of arrangements under section 35 of that Act;

(v) independent advocacy services (within the meaning of section 248 of the National Health Service Act 2006 or section 187 of the National Health Service (Wales) Act 2006 are or are to be provided in respect of the adult; or

(vi) a representative is or is to be appointed to receive payments on the adult's behalf in pursuance of regulations made under the Social Security Administration Act 1992;

(*f*) payments are made to the adult or to another person on the adult's behalf under arrangements made under section 57 of the Health and Social Care Act 2001;

(*g*) payments are made to the adult or to another person on the adult's behalf under section 12A(1) or under regulations made under section 12A(*a*) of the National Health Service Act 2006 or under regulations made under section 12A(4) of that Act.

**7.9305** *5C. Work with children* The circumstances referred to in regulation 5A(*a*) are—

(*a*) considering the applicant's suitability to engage in any activity which is a regulated activity relating to children within the meaning of Part 1 of Schedule 4 to the Safeguarding Vulnerable Groups Act 2006 as it had effect immediately before the coming into force of section 64 of the Protection of Freedoms Act 2012;

(*b*) considering the applicant's suitability to engage in any activity which is a regulated activity relating to children within the meaning of Part 1 of Schedule 4 to the Safeguarding Vulnerable Groups Act 2006;

(*c*) a decision made by an adoption agency within the meaning of section 2 of the Adoption and Children Act 2002, or the compiling of a report for the authority making a decision in respect of an application to be a special guardian within the meaning of section 14A of the Children Act 1989, as to a person's suitability to adopt a child or be a special guardian, including obtaining information in respect of any person aged 18 years or over living in the same household as the prospective adopter or special guardian;

(*d*) registration for child minding or providing day care under Part 2 of the Children and Families (Wales) Measure 2010, including assessing the suitability of any person to have regular contact with a child who is—

(i) aged 16 or over and living on the premises at which the child minding or day care is being or is to be provided;

(ii) aged 16 or over and working, or who will be working, on the premises at which the child minding or day care is being or is to be provided at times when such child minding or day care is being or is to be provided;

(*e*) registration under Chapters 2, 3 or 4 of Part 3 of the Childcare Act 2006 (regulation of provision of childcare in England), including assessing the suitability of any person to have regular contact with a child who is—

(i) aged 16 or over and living on the premises at which the childcare is being or is to be provided;

(ii) aged 16 or over and working on the premises at which the childcare is being or is to be provided at times when such childcare is being or is to be provided;

(*f*) placing children with foster parents in accordance with any provision of, or made by virtue of, the Children Act 1989 or the Children (Northern Ireland) Order 1995 or the exercise of any duty under or by virtue of section 67 of that Act or Article 108 of that Order (welfare of privately fostered children), including obtaining information in respect of any person who is—

(i) aged 18 or over and living in the same household as a person who is, or who wishes to be approved as, a foster parent within the meaning of section 53(7)(*a*) or (*b*) of the Safeguarding Vulnerable Groups Act 2006;

(ii) aged 16 or over and living in the same household as a person who fosters, or intends to foster, a child privately within the meaning of section 66(1) of the Children Act 1989 or who is otherwise a private foster parent within the meaning of section 53(7)(*c*) and (8) of the Safeguarding Vulnerable Groups Act 2006;

(*g*) obtaining information in respect of any person who is aged 16 or over and who lives in the same household as an individual who is having or who has had their suitability assessed for the purposes of—

(i) engaging in any activity which is regulated activity relating to children within the meaning of Part 1 of Schedule 4 to the Safeguarding Vulnerable Groups Act 2006 or as it had effect immediately before the coming into force of section 64 of the Protection of Freedoms Act 2012;

(ii) working in a further education institution (within the meaning of section 140 of the Education Act 2002) where the normal duties of that work involve regular contact with children; or

(iii) working in a 16 to 19 Academy (within the meaning of section 1B of the Academies Act 2010) where the normal duties of that work involve regular contact with children

where that individual, and the person who lives in the same household, live on the premises where that activity or work would normally take place;

(*h*) *revoked*

(*i*) work done infrequently which, if done frequently, would be regulated activity relating to children within the meaning of Part 1 of Schedule 4 to the Safeguarding Vulnerable Groups Act 2006 or as it had effect immediately before the coming into force of section 64 of the Protection of Freedoms Act 2012;

(*j*) registration under Part II of the Care Standards Act 2000(*d*) (establishments and agencies);

(*k*) registration under Part 4 of the Regulation and Inspection of Social Care (Wales) Act 2016 (social care workers);

(*l*) considering the applicant's suitability for work in a further education institution (within the meaning of section 140 of the Education Act 2002) or a 16 to 19 Academy (within the meaning of section 1B of the Academies Act 2010) where the normal duties of that work involve regular contact with persons aged under 18.

(*m*) registration as a childminder agency under Chapter 2A or 3A of Part 3 of the Childcare Act 2006;

(*n*) considering the applicant's suitability to manage a childminder agency;

(*o*) considering the applicant's suitability to work for a childminder agency in any capacity which requires the applicant to enter childcare premises and enables that person, in the normal course of duties, to have contact with children for whom childcare is provided or access to sensitive or personal information about children for whom childcare is provided.

**7.9306** 9. *Central records: prescribed details* Information in any form relating to convictions, cautions, reprimands and warnings on a names database held by the Secretary of State for the use of constables is prescribed as "central records" for the purposes of sections 112(3) and 113A(6) of the Police Act 1997 (including section 113A(6) as applied by sections 114(3) and 116(3)).

**7.9307** 11. *Evidence of identity: fingerprinting* (1) Where the Disclosure and Barring Service requires an application under Part V of the Act to be supported by evidence of identity in the form of fingerprints then the place at which they are to be taken is to be determined in accordance with paragraphs (2) and (3) below and he shall notify the applicant—

(*a*) of his requirement; and

(*b*) of the fact that any fingerprints taken from the applicant and provided to the Disclosure and Barring Service in pursuance of the requirement may be the subject of a speculative search.

(2) Any applicant in receipt of such notification shall notify the Secretary of State of whether he wishes to proceed with his application and, if so, notify the Disclosure and Barring Service—

(*a*) that he consents to the taking of his fingerprints; and

(*b*) either—

(i) that he proposes to attend at a police station ("the specified police station") for the purpose of having his fingerprints taken, or

(ii) that he proposes to have his fingerprints taken by the registered person countersigning or acting as the registered person in relation to his application under this Part.

(2A) But a person can only have his fingerprints taken under paragraph (2)(*b*)(ii) with the consent of the Disclosure and Barring Service.

(3) The Disclosure and Barring Service may require the police officer in charge of the specified police station, or any other police station he reasonably determines, to take the applicant's fingerprints at the specified station at such reasonable time as the officer may direct

and notify to the applicant.
(4) Fingerprints taken in connection with an application under Part V of the Act must be destroyed as soon as is practicable after the identity of the applicant is established to the satisfaction of the Disclosure and Barring Service.
(5) If fingerprints are destroyed—
(*a*) any copies of the fingerprints shall also be destroyed; and
(*b*) any chief officer of police controlling access to computer data relating to the fingerprints shall make access to the data impossible, as soon as it is practicable to do so.
(6) Any applicant who asks to be allowed to witness the destruction of his fingerprints or copies of them shall have a right to witness it.
(7) If—
(*a*) paragraph (5)(*b*) above falls to be complied with; and
(*b*) the applicant to whose fingerprints the data relates asks for a certificate that it has been complied with,
such a certificate shall be issued to him, not later than the end of the period of three months beginning with the day on which he asks for it, by the responsible chief officer of police or a person authorised by him or on his behalf for the purposes of this regulation.
(8) In the case of an applicant under the age of 18 years the consent of the applicant's parent or guardian to the taking of the applicant's fingerprints is also required.
(9) In this regulation—
"speculative search" has the same meaning as in Part V of the Police and Criminal Evidence Act 1984; and
"responsible chief officer of police" means the chief officer of police in whose area the computer data were put on to the computer.

**7.9308** *12. Exception to unlawful disclosure provisions* (1) The following purpose is specified for the purposes of subsection (6)(*e*) and (*f*) of section 124 of the Act (exceptions to prohibition of disclosure beyond a registered body), namely disclosure by an employment agency or an employment business, whether or not in response to an exempted question, for the purpose of consideration,
(*a*) by an educational institution, within the meaning given by section 42 of the Criminal Justice and Court Services Act 2000, or
(*b*) by an institution within the further education sector, within the meaning given by section 91(3) of the Further and Higher Education Act 1992,
of a person's suitability for a position at that institution.
(2) In paragraph (1) above the references to an employment agency and an employment business are references to such an agency or business within the meanings given by section 13 of the Employment Agencies Act 1973.

SCHEDULE 1
ENABLING POWERS

**7.9309** These Regulations are made under the following provisions of the Police Act 1997—
(*a*) sections 113(1)(*b*); 114(1)(*b*); 115(1)(*b*) and (10); 116(1)(*b*); 118(3) and 125(5); and
(*b*) having regard to the meaning of "prescribed" in sections 113(1)(*a*), (3)(*a*), (3A)(*b*) and (5); 114(1)(*a*); 115(1)(*a*), (6)(*a*)(i) and (6A)(*b*); 116(1)(*a*); 118(2)(*a*) and 119(3).

# Police Reform Act 2002 (Standard Powers and Duties of Community Support Officers) Order 2007[1]

(SI 2007/3202)

**7.9310** *1. Citation, commencement and extent* (1) This Order may be cited as the Police Reform Act 2002 (Standard Powers and Duties of Community Support Officers) Order 2007 and shall come into force on 1st December 2007.
(2) This Order extends to England and Wales.

[1] Made by the Secretary of State in exercise of the powers conferred by s 38A(1) of and para 1(3)(*b*) of Part 1 and para 36(2) of Part 5 of Sch 4 to the Police Reform Act 2002.

**7.9311** *2. Standard powers and duties of community support officers* The provisions of Part 1 of Schedule 4 to the Police Reform Act 2002 mentioned in the Schedule to this Order shall apply to every person who under section 38 of that Act is designated as a community support officer (a "CSO").

**7.9312** *3.* For the purposes of paragraph 1(3)(*b*) of Part 1 of Schedule 4 to the Police Reform Act 2002, a CSO is designated to enforce the following offences under paragraph 1 of Part 1 of Schedule 4 to that Act—
(*a*) an offence under section 72 of the Highway Act 1835 (riding on a footway) committed by cycling;
(*b*) an offence under section 87 of the Environmental Protection Act 1990 (offence of leaving litter); and
(*c*) an offence under a dog control order within the meaning of section 55 of the Clean Neighbourhoods and Environment Act 2005.

SCHEDULE
STANDARD POWERS AND DUTIES OF COMMUNITY SUPPORT OFFICERS — Article 2

**7.9313** The provisions of Part 1 of Schedule 4 to the Police Reform Act 2002 mentioned in this Schedule are—

(*a*) paragraph 1 (powers to issue fixed penalty notices) in so far as it relates to the powers specified in the following provisions of that paragraph—
  (i) sub-paragraph (2)(*b*) (power to give fixed penalty notices in respect of an offence of riding on a footway committed by cycling);
  (ii) sub-paragraph (2)(*d*) (power to give fixed penalty notices in respect of litter); and
  (iii) sub-paragraph (2)(*e*) (power to give fixed penalty notices in respect of offences under dog control orders);

(*b*) paragraph 1A (power to require name and address);
(*c*) paragraph 3 (power to require name and address of person acting in an anti-social manner);
(*d*) paragraph 3A (power to require name and address: road traffic offences);
(*e*) paragraph 5 (alcohol consumption in designated public places);
(*f*) paragraph 6 (confiscation of alcohol);
(*g*) paragraph 7 (confiscation of tobacco etc);
(*h*) paragraph 7B (power to seize: controlled drugs);
(*i*) paragraph 8 (entry to save life or limb or prevent serious damage to property);
(*j*) paragraph 9 (seizure of vehicles used to cause alarm etc);
(*k*) paragraph 10 (abandoned vehicles);
(*l*) paragraph 11A (power to stop cycles);
(*m*) paragraph 11B (power to control traffic for purposes other than escorting a load of exceptional dimensions);
(*n*) paragraph 13 (carrying out of road checks);
(*o*) paragraph 13A (power to place traffic signs);
(*p*) paragraph 14 (cordoned areas);
(*q*) paragraph 15 (power to stop and search vehicles etc in authorised areas); and
(*r*) paragraph 15ZA (photographing of persons arrested, detained or given fixed penalty notices).

## Police (Conduct) Regulations 2012[1]

(SI 2012/2632)

**7.9314** These Regulations deal with the conduct of members of police forces, including senior officers, the maintenance of discipline, and procedures where conduct fails to meet the appropriate standard which is defined in Sch 2 to the Regulations. Only the Code of Conduct set out in Sch 2 is printed here. The Regulations relate to matters to be dealt with internally by the police, and not by the courts. These regulations have been amended by the Police (Conduct) (Amendment) Regulations 2014, SI 2014/3347 and SI 2015/626 but not in relation to the text reproduced in this Manual.

[1] Made by the Secretary of State, in exercise of the powers conferred by ss 50, 51 and 84 of the Police Act 1996. These regulations have been amended by the Police (Conduct) (Amendment) Regulations 2014, SI 2014/3347 and SI 2015/626 but not in relation to the text reproduced in this *Manual*.

SCHEDULE 2
Standards of Professional Behaviour

Regulation 3

**7.9314A Honesty and Integrity**

Police officers are honest, act with integrity and do not compromise or abuse their position.

**Authority, Respect and Courtesy**

Police officers act with self-control and tolerance, treating members of the public and colleagues with respect and courtesy.

Police officers do not abuse their powers or authority and respect the rights of all individuals.

**Equality and Diversity**

Police officers act with fairness and impartiality. They do not discriminate unlawfully or unfairly.

**Use of Force**

Police officers only use force to the extent that it is necessary, proportionate and reasonable in all the circumstances.

**Orders and Instructions**

Police officers only give and carry out lawful orders and instructions.

Police officers abide by police regulations, force policies and lawful orders.

**Duties and Responsibilities**

Police officers are diligent in the exercise of their duties and responsibilities.

**Confidentiality**

Police officers treat information with respect and access or disclose it only in the proper course of police duties.

**Fitness for Duty**

Police officers when on duty or presenting themselves for duty are fit to carry out their responsibilities.

**Discreditable Conduct**

Police officers behave in a manner which does not discredit the police service or undermine public confidence in it, whether on or off duty.

Police officers report any action taken against them for a criminal offence, any conditions imposed on them by a court or the receipt of any penalty notice.

**Challenging and Reporting Improper Conduct**

Police officers report, challenge or take action against the conduct of colleagues which has fallen below the Standards of Professional Behaviour.

# POSTAL SERVICES

**Contents**



## Postal Services Act 2000[1]

(2000 c 26)

[1] Parts I to VI, ss 101 to 114, ss 116 to 119 (including Sch 7) and s 127(4) and (6) (including Schs 8 and 9) are to come into force on such day as the Secretary of State may by order appoint. At the date of going to press the following orders had been made: Commencement (No 1 and Transitional Provisions) Order 2000, SI 2000/2957; Commencement (No 2) Order 2001, SI 2001/3111; Commencement (No 3 and Transitional and Savings Provisions) Order 2001, SI 2001/878; Commencement (No 4 and Transitional and Savings Provisions) Order 2001, SI 2001/1148; Commencement (No 5) 2007, SI 2007/1181; (No 3 and Savings Provisions) Order 2012, SI 2012/1095.

All the provisions reproduced in this Manual have been in force since 2001.

### Part V[1]

### Offences in relation to Postal Services

*Offences of interfering with the mail*

7.9315 **83. Interfering with the mail: postal operators** (1) A person who is engaged in the business of a postal operator commits an offence if, contrary to his duty and without reasonable excuse, he—

(*a*) intentionally delays or opens a postal packet in the course of its transmission by post, or

(*b*) intentionally opens a mail-bag.

(2) Subsection (1) does not apply to the delaying or opening of a postal packet or the opening of a mail-bag under the authority of—

(*a*) this Act or any other enactment (including, in particular, in pursuance of a warrant issued under any other enactment), or

(*b*) any directly applicable EU provision.

(3) Subsection (1) does not apply to the delaying or opening of a postal packet in accordance with any terms and conditions applicable to its transmission by post.

(4) Subsection (1) does not apply to the delaying of a postal packet as a result of industrial action in contemplation or furtherance of a trade dispute.

(5) In subsection (4) "trade dispute" has the meaning given by section 244 of the Trade Union and Labour Relations (Consolidation) Act 1992 or Article 127 of the Trade Union and Labour Relations (Northern Ireland) Order 1995; and the reference to industrial action shall be construed in accordance with that Act or (as the case may be) that Order.

(6) A person who commits an offence under subsection (1) shall be liable[2]—

(*a*) on summary conviction, to a fine not exceeding the statutory maximum or to imprisonment for a term not exceeding six months or to both,

(*b*) on conviction on indictment, to a fine or to imprisonment for a term not exceeding two years or to both.

[Postal Services Act 2000, s 83 as amended by SI 2011/1043.]

[1] Part V contains ss 83–88.

[2] For mode of trial of this offence which is triable either way, see the Magistrates' Courts Act 1980, ss 17A–21 in Part I: Magistrates' Courts, Procedure, ante.

7.9316 **84. Interfering with the mail: general** (1) A person commits an offence if, without reasonable excuse, he—

(*a*) intentionally delays or opens a postal packet in the course of its transmission by post, or

(*b*) intentionally opens a mail-bag.

(2) Subsections (2) to (5) of section 83 apply to subsection (1) above as they apply to subsection (1) of that section.

(3) A person commits an offence if, intending to act to a person's detriment and without reasonable excuse, he opens a postal packet which he knows or reasonably suspects has been incorrectly delivered to him.

(4) Subsections (2) and (3) of section 83 (so far as they relate to the opening of postal packets) apply to subsection (3) above as they apply to subsection (1) of that section.

(5) A person who commits an offence under subsection (1) or (3) shall be liable on summary conviction to a fine not exceeding level 5 on the standard scale or to imprisonment for a term not exceeding six months or to both.

[Postal Services Act 2000, s 84.]

*Prohibition on sending certain articles by post*

7.9317 **85. Prohibition on sending certain articles by post** (1) A person commits an offence if he sends by post a postal packet which encloses any creature, article or thing of any kind which is likely to injure other postal packets in course of their transmission by post or any person engaged in the business of a postal operator.

(2) Subsection (1) does not apply to postal packets which enclose anything permitted (whether generally or specifically) by the postal operator concerned.

(3) A person commits an offence if he sends by post a postal packet which encloses—

(*a*) any indecent or obscene print, painting, photograph, lithograph, engraving, cinematograph film or other record of a picture or pictures, book, card or written communication, or

(*b*) any other indecent or obscene article (whether or not of a similar kind to those mentioned in paragraph (*a*)).

(4) A person commits an offence if he sends by post a postal packet which has on the packet, or on the cover of the packet, any words, marks or designs which are of an indecent or obscene[1] character.

(5) A person who commits an offence under this section shall be liable[2]—

(*a*) on summary conviction, to a fine not exceeding the statutory maximum,

(*b*) on conviction on indictment, to a fine or to imprisonment for a term not exceeding twelve months or to both.

[Postal Services Act 2000, s 85.]

---

1 These are ordinary words of the English language. It is for a jury or magistrates to set the standard by the recognised standards of propriety of reasonable people. Where the test is properly construed any restriction of the defendant's rights under article 10 of the European Convention on Human Rights would be a permissible restriction under the Convention: *R v Kirk* [2006] EWCA Crim 725, [2006] Crim LR 850.

2 For mode of trial of this offence which is triable either way, see the Magistrates' Courts Act 1980, ss 17A–21 in PART I: MAGISTRATES' COURTS, PROCEDURE, ante.

*Additional protection for universal postal service*

7.9318 **86. Prohibition on affixing advertisements on certain letter boxes etc** (1) A person commits an offence if, without due authority, he affixes any advertisement, document, board or thing in or on any universal postal service post office, universal postal service letter box or other property belonging to, or used by, a universal service provider in connection with the provision of a universal postal service.

(2) A person commits an offence if, without due authority, he paints or in any way disfigures any such office, box or property.

(3) A person who commits an offence under subsection (1) or (2) shall be liable on summary conviction to a fine not exceeding level 3 on the standard scale.

(4) In this Act—

"universal postal service letter box" means any box or receptacle provided by a universal service provider for the purpose of receiving postal packets, or any class of postal packets, for onwards transmission in connection with the provision of a universal postal service, and

"universal postal service post office" includes any house, building, room, vehicle or place used for the provision of any postal services in connection with the provision of a universal postal service or a part of such a service.

[Postal Services Act 2000, s 86.]

7.9319 **87. Prohibition on misleading descriptions** (1) A person commits an offence if, without the authority of the universal service provider concerned, he places or maintains in or on any house, wall, door, window, box, post, pillar or other place belonging to him or under his control, any of the following words, letters or marks—

(*a*) the words "letter box" accompanied with words, letters or marks which signify or imply, or may reasonably lead the public to believe, that it is a universal postal service letter box, or

(*b*) any words, letters or marks which signify or imply or may reasonably lead the public to believe that any house, building, room, vehicle or place is a universal postal service post office, or that any box or receptacle is a universal postal service letter box.

(2) A person commits an offence if, without the authority of the universal service provider concerned, he—

(*a*) places or maintains in or on any ship, vehicle, aircraft or premises belonging to him or under his control, or

(*b*) uses in any document in relation to himself or any other person or in relation to any ship, vehicle, aircraft or premises,

any words, letters or marks which signify or imply, or may reasonably lead the public to believe, any of the things mentioned in subsection (3).

(3) The things are—

(*a*) that he or that other person is authorised by the universal service provider concerned to collect, receive, sort, deliver or convey postal packets in connection with the provision of a universal postal service, (*b*) that the ship, vehicle, aircraft or premises are used by the universal service provider concerned for the purpose of collecting, receiving, sorting, delivering or conveying postal packets in connection with the provision of a universal postal service.

(4) A person commits an offence if, without reasonable excuse, he fails to comply with a notice given to him by the universal service provider concerned requiring him—

(*a*) to remove or efface any words, letters or marks which fall within subsection (1) or (2), or

(*b*) to remove or close up any letter box belonging to him or under his control which has ceased to be a universal postal service letter box.

(5) A person who commits an offence under this section shall be liable on summary conviction to a fine not exceeding level 3 on the standard scale.

[Postal Services Act 2000, s 87.]

**7.9320 88. Obstruction of business of universal service providers** (1) A person commits an offence if, without reasonable excuse, he—

(*a*) obstructs a person engaged in the business of a universal service provider in the execution of his duty in connection with the provision of a universal postal service, or

(*b*) obstructs, while in any universal postal service post office or related premises, the course of business of a universal service provider.

(2) A person who commits an offence under subsection (1) shall be liable on summary conviction to a fine not exceeding level 2 on the standard scale.

(3) A person commits an offence if, without reasonable excuse, he fails to leave a universal postal service post office or related premises when required to do so by a person who—

(*a*) is engaged in the business of a universal service provider, and

(*b*) reasonably suspects him of committing an offence under subsection (1).

(4) A person who commits an offence under subsection (3)—

(*a*) shall be liable on summary conviction to a fine not exceeding level 2 on the standard scale, and

(*b*) may be removed by any person engaged in the business of a universal service provider.

(5) Any constable shall on demand remove, or assist in removing, any such person.

(6) In this section "related premises" means any premises belonging to a universal postal service post office or used together with any such post office.

[Postal Services Act 2000, s 88.]

## PART VI[1]

## POSTAL SERVICES: SUPPLEMENTARY

*Articles in transit*

**7.9321 96. Immunity from prosecution** (1) A universal service provider and a person who is engaged in the business of such a provider shall be entitled to the same immunity from prosecution for conduct in the provision of a universal postal service and falling within subsection (2) as the provider and that person would be entitled to if the provider were a government department.

(2) The following conduct falls within this subsection—

(*a*) possession of anything contained in a postal packet which is in the course of transmission by post where possession of it is prohibited by virtue of any enactment, and

(*b*) failure to comply, in relation to anything contained in a postal packet which is in the course of transmission by post, with any condition or restriction imposed by virtue of any enactment in relation to its possession, conveyance or delivery.

[Postal Services Act 2000, s 96.]

1 Part VI contains ss 89–100 and Schs 5 and 6.

## PART VII[1]

## MISCELLANEOUS AND SUPPLEMENTARY

*Supplementary powers of the Secretary of State*

**7.9322 101. Directions in interests of national security etc** (1) The Secretary of State may give a direction to OFCOM in connection with the exercise of their functions relating to postal services if he considers it necessary or expedient to do so—

(*a*) in the interests of national security or in the interests of encouraging or maintaining the United Kingdom's relations with another country or territory,

(*b*) in order—

(i) to discharge, or facilitate the discharge of, an international obligation,

(ii) to attain, or facilitate the attainment of, any other object which the Secretary of State considers it necessary or expedient to attain in view of Her Majesty's Government in the United Kingdom being a member of an international organisation or a party to an international agreement, or

(iii) to enable Her Majesty's Government in the United Kingdom to become a member of such an organisation or a party to such an agreement.

(2) Directions under subsection (1) may, in particular, require OFCOM—

(*a*) to do or not to do a particular thing, or

(*b*) to secure that a particular thing is done or not done.

(3) The Secretary of State may, if he considers it necessary or expedient to do so for any of the purposes mentioned in subsection (1)(*a*) or (*b*), give a direction (relating to the provision of postal services to—

(*a*) a postal operator,

(*b*) a description of postal operators, or

(*c*) all postal operators.

(4) Directions under subsection (3) may, in particular, require a postal operator—

(*a*) to do or not to do a particular thing, or

(*b*) to secure that a particular thing is done or not done.

(5) Before giving a direction under subsection (1), the Secretary of State shall consult OFCOM.

(6) Before giving a direction under subsection (3) to a particular postal operator (as opposed to all postal operators or a description of them), the Secretary of State must consult the operator.

(7) The Secretary of State—

(*a*) shall send to OFCOM a copy of any direction given under subsection (3), and

(*b*) shall lay before each House of Parliament a copy of any direction given under this section.

(8) Subsection (7)(*b*) does not apply if the Secretary of State considers that the disclosure of the direction would be against the interests of national security or the interests of the United Kingdom's relations with another country or territory or against the commercial interests of any person who has not consented to the disclosure.

(9) A person shall not disclose, and is not required by any enactment or otherwise to disclose, a direction given or other thing done or omitted to be done by virtue of this section if the Secretary of State notifies him that he considers that—

(*a*) disclosure would be against the interests of national security or the interests of the United Kingdom's relations with another country or territory, or

(*b*) disclosure would be against the commercial interests of any person (other than the person notified) who has not consented to the disclosure.

(10) A person commits an offence if—

(*a*) without reasonable excuse he contravenes a direction under this section, or

(*b*) he makes a disclosure in contravention of subsection (9).

(11) A person who commits an offence under this section shall be liable[2]—

(*a*) on summary conviction, to a fine not exceeding the statutory maximum,

(*b*) on conviction on indictment, to a fine or to imprisonment for a term not exceeding two years or to both.

[Postal Services Act 2000, s 101 as amended by the Postal Services Act 2011, Sch 12.]

[1] Part VII contains ss 101–131 and Schs 7–9.

[2] For mode of trial of this offence which is triable either way, see the Magistrates' Courts Act 1980, ss 17A–21 in PART I: MAGISTRATES' COURTS, PROCEDURE, ante.

*Inviolability of mails etc*

7.9323 **104. Inviolability of mails** (1) Subsection (2) applies to—

(*a*) a postal packet,

(*b*) anything contained in a postal packet, and

(*c*) a mail-bag containing a postal packet,

which is not the property of the Crown but which is in the course of transmission by post.

(2) Anything to which this subsection applies shall have the same immunity from—

(*a*) examination, or seizure or detention, under a relevant power conferred by virtue of this Act or any other enactment,

(*b*) seizure under distress or in execution,

(*ba*) in England and Wales, being taken control of under Schedule 12 to the Tribunals, Courts and Enforcement Act 2007,

(*c*) in Scotland, any diligence, and

(*d*) retention by virtue of a lien,

as it would have if it were the property of the Crown.

(3) In subsection (2) "relevant power" means any power other than—

(*a*) *repealed*

(*b*) *repealed*

(*ba*) a power conferred by section 104A,

(*c*) a power conferred by an enactment relating to customs or excise in its application, by virtue of section 105 or any regulations made under that section, to goods contained in postal packets,

(*d*) a power conferred by section 106 or 107, or

(*e*) a power conferred by paragraph 9 of Schedule 7 to the Terrorism Act 2000 (port and border controls).

(4) The Secretary of State may by order modify subsection (3).

[Postal Services Act 2000, s 104 as amended by the Tribunals, Courts and Enforcement Act 2007, Sch 13, the Postal Services Act 2011, Sch 12 and the Counter-Terrorism and Security Act 2015, Sch 8.]

**7.9324 104A. Power to detain packets in respect of unpaid or underpaid postage**

**7.9325 105. Application of customs and excise enactments to certain postal packets**

(1) Subject as follows, the enactments for the time being in force in relation to customs or excise shall apply in relation to goods contained in postal packets to which this section applies which are brought into or sent out of the United Kingdom by post from or to any place outside the United Kingdom as they apply in relation to goods otherwise imported, exported or removed into or out of the United Kingdom from or to any such place.

(2) The Treasury, on the recommendation of the Commissioners of Customs and Excise and the Secretary of State, may make regulations[1] for—

(*a*) specifying the postal packets to which this section applies,

(*b*) making modifications or exceptions in the application of the enactments mentioned in subsection (1) to such packets,

(*c*) enabling persons engaged in the business of a postal operator to perform for the purposes of those enactments and otherwise all or any of the duties of the importer, exporter or person removing the goods,

(*d*) carrying into effect any arrangement with the government or postal administration of any country or territory outside the United Kingdom with respect to foreign postal packets,

(*e*) securing the observance of the enactments mentioned in subsection (1),

(*f*) without prejudice to any liability of any person under those enactments, punishing any contravention of the regulations.

(3) Duties (whether of customs or excise) charged on imported goods or other charges payable in respect of postal packets to which this section applies (whether payable to a postal operator or to a foreign administration) may be recovered by the postal operator concerned and in England and Wales and Northern Ireland may be so recovered as a civil debt due to him.

(4) In any proceedings for the recovery of any charges payable as mentioned in subsection (3), a certificate of the postal operator concerned of the amount of the charges shall be evidence (and, in Scotland, sufficient evidence) of that fact.

(4A) A postal operator may detain a postal packet to which this section applies until any duties and charges in respect of the packet that are recoverable by virtue of subsection (3) have been paid.

(5) In this section "foreign postal packet" means any postal packet either posted in the United Kingdom and sent to a place outside the United Kingdom, or posted in a place outside the United Kingdom and sent to a place within the United Kingdom, or in transit through the United Kingdom to a place outside the United Kingdom.

(6) And in this section "goods" includes cash (within the meaning of section 289(6) and (7) of the Proceeds of Crime Act 2002).

[Postal Services Act 2000, s 105 as amended by the Policing and Crime Act 2009, s 99 and the Postal Services Act 2011, Sch 12.]

---

[1] The Postal Packets (Revenue and Customs) Regulations 2011, SI 2011/3036 have been made.

**7.9326 106. Power to detain postal packets containing contraband** (1) A postal operator may—

(*a*) detain any postal packet if he suspects that it may contain relevant goods,

(*b*) forward any packet so detained to the Commissioners of Customs and Excise.

(2) In this section "relevant goods" means—

(*a*) any goods chargeable with any duty charged on imported goods (whether a customs or an excise duty) which has not been paid or secured, or

(*b*) any goods in the course of importation, exportation or removal into or out of the United Kingdom contrary to any prohibition or restriction for the time being in force by virtue of any enactment.

(3) Subsection (1) is without prejudice to section 105.

(4) The Commissioners may open and examine any postal packet forwarded to them under this section in the presence of a representative of the postal operator.

(5) *Repealed.*

(6) If the Commissioners find any relevant goods on opening and examining a postal packet under this section, they may detain the packet and its contents for the purpose of taking proceedings in relation to them.

(7) If the Commissioners do not find any relevant goods on opening and examining a postal packet under this section, they shall—

(*a*) deliver the packet to the addressee upon his paying any postage and other sums chargeable on it, or

(*b*) forward the packet to him by post.

[Postal Services Act 2000, s 106 as amended by the Finance Act 2010, s 57.]

7.9327 **107. Conditions of transit of postal packets** (1) If a postal operator knows or reasonably suspects that a postal packet is being sent by post in contravention of section 85, he may—

(*a*) refuse the transmission of the packet,

(*b*) detain the packet and open it,

(*c*) subject to any requirements as to additional postage or charges, return the packet to its sender or forward it to its destination,

(*d*) destroy or otherwise dispose of the packet.

(2) Subsection (1) is without prejudice to any other powers which the postal operator may have in relation to the packet (whether under the terms and conditions applicable to its transmission by post or otherwise).

(3) The detention or disposal by a postal operator of any postal packet on the grounds of a contravention of section 85 or of any terms and conditions applicable to its transmission by post shall not exempt the sender from any proceedings which might have been taken if the packet had been delivered in due course of post.

[Postal Services Act 2000, s 107.]

*Evidential provisions*

7.9328 **108. Evidence of amount of postage etc** (1) The mark of—

(*a*) a universal service provider in connection with the provision of a universal postal service, or

(*b*) a foreign postal administration,

of any sum on any postal packet as due in respect of that packet shall, unless the contrary is shown, be sufficient proof in any legal proceedings of the liability of the packet to the sum so marked.

(2) Subsections (3) to (5) apply in relation to any legal proceedings for the recovery of postage or other sums due in respect of postal packets.

(3) In any such proceedings, the production of the packet concerned with a stamp or other endorsement on it of a universal service provider (and made in connection with the provision of a universal postal service) or of a foreign postal administration indicating that the packet—

(*a*) has been refused or rejected,

(*b*) is unclaimed, or

(*c*) cannot for any other reason be delivered,

shall, unless the contrary is shown, be sufficient proof of the fact indicated.

(4) In any such proceedings, a certificate of a universal service provider that any mark, stamp or endorsement is such a mark, stamp or endorsement as is mentioned in subsection (1) or (3) shall, unless the contrary is shown, be sufficient proof of that fact.

(5) In any such proceedings, the person from whom the packet concerned purports to have come shall, unless the contrary is shown, be taken to be the sender of the packet.

[Postal Services Act 2000, s 108.]

7.9329 **109. Evidence of thing being a postal packet** (1) On the prosecution of an offence under this Act (whether summarily or on indictment), evidence that any article is in the course of transmission by post, or has been accepted by a postal operator for transmission by post, shall be sufficient evidence that the article is a postal packet.

(2) In any proceedings in England and Wales for an offence under section 83 or 84 of this Act, section 27(4) of the Theft Act 1968 shall apply as it applies to proceedings for the theft of anything in the course of transmission by post.

(3) In any proceedings in Northern Ireland for an offence under section 83 or 84 of this Act, section 26(5) of the Theft Act (Northern Ireland) 1969 shall apply as it applies to proceedings for the theft of anything in the course of transmission by post.

[Postal Services Act 2000, s 109.]

7.9330 **110. Certificates in relation to universal postal service letter boxes** A certificate given by or on behalf of a universal service provider to the effect that any box or receptacle is or was provided by the provider concerned for the purpose of receiving postal packets, or any class of postal packets, for onwards transmission in connection with the provision of a universal postal service, shall, unless the contrary is shown, be sufficient proof in any legal proceedings of the facts stated.

[Postal Services Act 2000, s 110.]

*General*

7.9331 **120. Offences by bodies corporate** (1) Where an offence under this Act committed by a body corporate is proved to have been committed with the consent or connivance of, or to be attributable to any neglect on the part of—

(*a*) a director, manager, secretary or other similar officer of the body corporate, or

(*b*) a person purporting to act in such a capacity,

he as well as the body corporate commits the offence and shall be liable to be proceeded against and punished accordingly.

(2) Where the affairs of a body corporate are managed by its members, subsection (1) applies in relation to the acts and defaults of a member in connection with his functions of management as if

he were a director of the body corporate.

(3) Where an offence under this Act is committed by a Scottish partnership and is proved to have been committed with the consent or connivance of a partner, he as well as the partnership commits the offence and shall be liable to be proceeded against and punished accordingly.

[Postal Services Act 2000, s 120.]

7.9332 121. **Service of documents** (1) Any document required or authorised by virtue of this Act to be served on any person may be served—

(*a*) by delivering it to him or by leaving it at his proper address or by sending it by post to him at that address,

(*b*) if the person is a body corporate, by serving it in accordance with paragraph (*a*) on the secretary of the body, or

(*c*) if the person is a partnership, by serving it in accordance with paragraph (*a*) on a partner or a person having the control or management of the partnership business.

(2) For the purposes of this section and section 7 of the Interpretation Act 1978 (service of documents by post) in its application to this section, the proper address of any person on whom a document is to be served shall be his last known address, except that—

(*a*) in the case of service on a body corporate or its secretary, it shall be the address of the registered or principal office of the body,

(*b*) in the case of service on a partnership or a partner or a person having the control or management of a partnership business, it shall be the address of the principal office of the partnership.

(3) For the purposes of subsection (2) the principal office of a company constituted under the law of a country or territory outside the United Kingdom or of a partnership carrying on business outside the United Kingdom is its principal office within the United Kingdom.

(4) Subsection (5) applies if a person to be served under this Act with any document by another has specified to that other an address within the United Kingdom other than his proper address (as determined under subsection (2)) as the one at which he or someone on his behalf will accept documents of the same description as that document.

(5) In relation to that document, that address shall be treated as his proper address for the purposes of this section and section 7 of the Interpretation Act 1978 in its application to this section, instead of that determined under subsection (2).

(6) This section does not apply to any document if rules of court make provision about its service.

(7) In this section references to serving include references to similar expressions (such as giving or sending).

[Postal Services Act 2000, s 121.]

7.9333 125. **Interpretation** (1) In this Act, unless the context otherwise requires—

"body" includes an unincorporated association,

"Citizens Advice" means the National Association of Citizens Advice Bureaux,

"Citizens Advice Scotland" means the Scottish Association of Citizens Advice Bureaux,

"contravention", in relation to any requirement, condition, direction, order or regulations, includes any failure to comply with it and cognate expressions shall be construed accordingly,

"correspondent", in relation to a postal packet, means the sender or the person to whom it is addressed,

"employee", in relation to a body corporate, includes any officer or director of the body corporate and any other person taking part in its management, and "employer" and other related expressions shall be construed accordingly,

"enactment" includes an Act of the Scottish Parliament, Northern Ireland legislation (within the meaning of the Northern Ireland Act 1998) and an enactment comprised in subordinate legislation, and includes an enactment whenever passed or made,

"financial year" means a year ending with 31st March,

"foreign postal administration" means a postal administration outside the United Kingdom,

"the GCCNI" means the General Consumer Council for Northern Ireland,

"hovercraft" has the same meaning as in the Hovercraft Act 1968,

"letter" means any communication in written form on any kind of physical medium to be conveyed and delivered otherwise than electronically to the person or address indicated by the sender on the item itself or on its wrapping (excluding any book, catalogue, newspaper or periodical); and includes a postal packet containing any such communication,

"mail-bag" includes any form of container or covering in which postal packets in the course of transmission by post are enclosed by a postal operator in the United Kingdom or a foreign postal administration for the purpose of conveyance by post, whether or not it contains any such packets,

"modify" includes amend or repeal,

"Northern Ireland junior Minister" means a member of the Northern Ireland Assembly appointed as a junior Minister under section 19 of the Northern Ireland Act 1998,

"Northern Ireland Minister" includes the First Minister and the deputy First Minister in Northern Ireland,

"notice" means notice in writing,

"OFCOM" means the Office of Communications,

"post office" includes any house, building, room, vehicle or place used for the provision of any postal services,
"post office letter box" includes any pillar box, wall box, or other box or receptacle provided by a postal operator for the purpose of receiving postal packets, or any class of postal packets, for onwards transmission by post,
"postal operator" has the same meaning as in Part 3 of the Postal Services Act 2011 (see section 27(3) to (5) of that Act),
"postal packet" means a letter, parcel, packet or other article transmissible by post,
"postal services" means the service of conveying postal packets from one place to another by post, the incidental services of receiving, collecting, sorting and delivering such packets and any other service which relates to any of those services and is provided in conjunction with any of them,
"the Postal Services Directive" means the Directive of the European Parliament and the Council of the European Union of 15th December 1997 (No 97/67/EC) on common rules for the development of the internal market of Community postal services and the improvement of quality of service, as amended from time to time,
"public holiday" means Christmas Day, Good Friday or a day which is a bank holiday under the Banking and Financial Dealings Act 1971 in any part of the United Kingdom,
"public post office" means any post office from which any postal services are provided directly to the public (whether or not together with other services),
"registered post service" means a postal service which provides for the registration of postal packets in connection with their transmission by post and for the payment of compensation for any loss or damage,
"sender", in relation to any letter or other communication, means the person whose communication it is,
"ship" includes any boat, vessel or hovercraft,
"subordinate legislation" has the same meaning as in the Interpretation Act 1978 and also includes an instrument made under an Act of the Scottish Parliament and an instrument made under Northern Ireland legislation (within the meaning of section 98(1) of the Northern Ireland Act 1998),
references to the provision of a "universal postal service" are to be read in accordance with sections 30 to 33 and section 65(3) of the Postal Services Act 2011,
"universal postal service letter box" has the meaning given by section 86 of this Act,
"universal postal service post office" has the meaning given by that section,
"universal service provider" has the meaning given by section 65(1) of the Postal Services Act 2011,
"users", in relation to postal services, includes users as addressees and potential users,
"vehicle" includes a railway vehicle, and
"working day" means—

(*a*) in relation to the collection and delivery of letters, any day which is not a Sunday or a public holiday,
(*b*) in relation to the collection and delivery of postal packets other than letters, any day which is not a Saturday, a Sunday or a public holiday.

(2) For the purposes of the definition of "letter" in subsection (1) the reference to a communication to be conveyed and delivered otherwise than electronically shall be construed as a reference to a communication to be conveyed and delivered otherwise than—

(*a*) by means of an electronic communications network, or
(*b*) by other means but while in electronic form.

(3) For the purposes of this Act—

(*a*) a postal packet shall be taken to be in course of transmission by post from the time of its being delivered to any post office or post office letter box to the time of its being delivered to the addressee,
(*b*) the delivery of a postal packet of any description to a letter carrier or other person authorised to receive postal packets of that description for the post or to a person engaged in the business of a postal operator to be dealt with in the course of that business shall be a delivery to a post office, and
(*c*) the delivery of a postal packet—
 (i) at the premises to which it is addressed or redirected, unless they are a post office from which it is to be collected,
 (ii) to any box or receptacle to which the occupier of those premises has agreed that postal packets addressed to persons at those premises may be delivered, or
 (iii) to the addressee's agent or to any other person considered to be authorised to receive the packet,

shall be a delivery to the addressee.

(4) Any reference in this Act to a subsidiary or wholly owned subsidiary shall be construed in accordance with section 1159 of the Companies Act 2006.

[Postal Services Act 2000, s 125 as amended by SI 2002/3050, the Communications Act 2003, Sch 17, the Consumers, Estate Agents and Redress Act 2007, s 30, SI 2009/1941, the Postal Services Act 2011, Sch 12, SI 2014/631.]

*Final*

7.9334 **130. Commencement** (1) Parts I to VI, sections 101 to 114, sections 116 to 119 (including Schedule 7) and section 127(4) and (6) (including Schedules 8 and 9) shall come into force on such day as the Secretary of State may by order appoint; and different days may be appointed for different purposes or different areas.

(2) Section 115 shall come into force at the end of the period of two months beginning with the day on which this Act is passed.

[Postal Services Act 2000, s 130.]

SCHEDULE 6

FURTHER PROVISIONS RELATING TO LAND

*(As amended by SI 2009/1307)* Section 95

*Power to place post-boxes etc in streets*

7.9335 1. (1) A universal service provider may, for any purpose in connection with the provision of a universal postal service, execute in a street works of any of the kinds mentioned in sub-paragraph (2).

(2) The kinds of works are—

(*a*) placing a universal postal service letter box or a universal postal service pouch-box in a street,

(*b*) inspecting, maintaining, adjusting, repairing, altering or renewing such apparatus which has been so placed, changing its position or removing it,

(*c*) works needed for, or incidental to, the purposes of any works falling within paragraph (*a*) or (*b*) (including, in particular, breaking up or opening a street).

(3) Accordingly, Part III of the New Roads and Street Works Act 1991 (street works in England and Wales), and the Street Works (Northern Ireland) Order 1995, apply in relation to undertakers' works in exercise of a power conferred by this paragraph.

(4) For the avoidance of doubt, references in Part III of the Act of 1991 or the Order of 1995 to apparatus shall be construed as including universal postal service letter boxes and universal postal service pouch-boxes.

(5) Subject to sub-paragraphs (6) and (7), sub-paragraph (1) authorises the universal service provider concerned to execute works of any of the kinds mentioned in sub-paragraph (2) without obtaining any consent which would otherwise be required to be given by the street authority in its capacity as such and, in the case of a maintainable highway, in its capacity as owner.

(6) Sub-paragraph (5) is without prejudice to—

(*a*) the provisions of Part III of the Act of 1991, or the provisions of the Order of 1995, as to the making of requirements by the street authority or as to the settlement of a plan and section and the execution of the works in accordance with them,

(*b*) section 61 of the Act of 1991 or Article 21 of the Order of 1995 (consent required for protected streets).

(7) Sub-paragraph (1) does not free the universal service provider concerned from obtaining any other consent, licence or permission which may be required.

(8) This paragraph binds the Crown.

(9) In this paragraph references to doing anything in a street shall be construed as including references to doing anything under, over, across, along or upon the street.

(10) In this paragraph—

"maintainable highway"—

(*a*) in England and Wales, has the same meaning as in Part III of the Act of 1991 and includes a street in respect of which a declaration has been made under section 87 of that Act (prospectively maintainable highways), and

(*b*) in Northern Ireland, means a road (within the meaning of the Order of 1995) and includes a street in respect of which a declaration has been made under Article 46 of that Order (prospective roads),

"street" and "street authority"—

(*a*) in England and Wales, have the same meaning as in Part III of the Act of 1991, and

(*b*) in Northern Ireland, have the same meaning as in the Order of 1995, and

"universal postal service pouch-box" means any box or receptacle provided by a universal service provider for the temporary storage of postal packets in the course of transmission by post pending their collection for immediate delivery by a person who is in the course of delivering postal packets in connection with the provision of a universal postal service.

(11) *Scotland.*

*Entry on land for exploratory purposes*

2. (1) A person authorised in writing by a universal service provider may, at any reasonable time, enter upon and survey any land for the purpose of ascertaining whether the land would be suitable for use for any purpose in connection with the provision of a universal postal service.

(2) The power to survey land conferred by this paragraph includes power to search and bore for the purpose of ascertaining the nature of the subsoil.

(3) The powers conferred by this paragraph shall not be exercisable in relation to land which is covered by a building or will be so covered on the assumption that any planning permission which is in force is acted on.

(4) In this paragraph "building" includes any garden, yard, outhouses and appurtenances belonging to or usually enjoyed with a building.

3. (1) A person authorised to enter upon any land under paragraph 2 shall not demand to do so as of right unless—

(*a*) 28 days notice of the intended entry has been given to the occupier, and

(*b*) if required to do so, he has produced evidence of his authority and has stated the purpose of his entry.

(2) No person may carry out works authorised by paragraph 2(2) unless notice of the proposed works was

included in the notice given under sub-paragraph (1).

(3) If the land in question is held by statutory undertakers and they object to the works on the ground that the carrying out of the works would be seriously detrimental to the carrying on of their undertaking, the authority of the appropriate Minister shall be required for the carrying out of works authorised by paragraph 2(2).

(4) In sub-paragraph (3) as it relates to England and Wales—

"appropriate Minister" means the person indicated by section 265 of the Town and Country Planning Act 1990,

"statutory undertakers" means any persons who, by virtue of section 262 of the Town and Country Planning Act 1990, are or are treated as statutory undertakers for the purposes of that Act or any provision of that Act.

(5) *Scotland.*

(6) *Northern Ireland.*

**4.** (1) Any person who intentionally obstructs a person acting in the exercise of any power conferred by paragraph 2 shall be guilty of an offence.

(2) A person who commits an offence under sub-paragraph (1) shall be liable on summary conviction to a fine not exceeding level 3 on the standard scale.

**5.** (1) If in the exercise of any power conferred by paragraph 2 any damage is caused to land or moveables, any person interested in the land or moveables may recover compensation in respect of that damage from the universal service provider on whose behalf the power is exercised; and if in consequence of the exercise of such a power a person is disturbed in his enjoyment of any land or moveables, he may recover compensation from the universal service provider in respect of that disturbance.

(2) In relation to England and Wales, any question of disputed compensation under sub-paragraph (1) shall be referred to and determined by the Upper Tribunal; and section 4 of the Land Compensation Act 1961 shall apply in relation to the determination subject to any necessary modifications.

(3) *Scotland.*

(4) In relation to Northern Ireland, any question of disputed compensation under sub-paragraph (1) shall be referred to and determined by the Lands Tribunal for Northern Ireland; and the determination shall be deemed to be a determination to which section 31 of the Land Development Values (Compensation) Act (Northern Ireland) 1965 applies.

(5) In this paragraph "moveables" means—

(*a*) in relation to England and Wales and Northern Ireland, chattels, and

(*b*) *Scotland.*

*Acquisition of land by agreement*

**6.** For the purpose of the acquisition by agreement by a universal service provider for any purpose in connection with the provision of a universal postal service of land in England and Wales, the provisions of Part I of the Compulsory Purchase Act 1965 (so far as applicable), other than sections 4 to 8 and section 31, shall apply.

**7.** For the purpose of the acquisition by agreement by a universal service provider for any purpose in connection with the provision of a universal postal service of land in Scotland, section 188(2) of the Town and Country Planning (Scotland) Act 1997 (incorporation of Lands Clauses Acts) shall, with any necessary modifications, apply for the purposes of this Act as it applies for the purposes of that Act.

**8.** For the purpose of the acquisition by agreement by a universal service provider for any purpose in connection with the provision of a universal postal service of land in Northern Ireland, the Lands Clauses Acts shall be incorporated with this Act except for sections 127 to 133 (sale of superfluous land) and sections 150 and 151 (access to the special Act) of the Lands Clauses Consolidation Act 1845.

*Power to sell Duchy of Lancaster land*

**9.** If a universal service provider proposes to acquire by agreement any land belonging to Her Majesty in right of the Duchy of Lancaster for any purpose in connection with the provision of a universal postal service, the Chancellor and Council of the Duchy of Lancaster may sell that land to him.

*Supplementary*

**10.** Any land acquired by agreement by a universal service provider by virtue of any of paragraphs 6 to 9 shall be deemed for all purposes to have been acquired by him for the purposes of his undertaking as a universal service provider.

## Postal Services Act 2011

(2011 c 5)

**7.9336** *This Act makes various provisions for the commercial future of the Royal Mail and the ownership structure of The Post Office Ltd. Part 3 of the Act transfers regulatory responsibility to OFCOM whose primary duty in relation to postal services is to maintain the universal service. The current licensing regime for the provision of postal services is replaced by a general authorisation scheme. Part 4 of the Act contains provisions for a special administration regime to secure the continued provision of the universal postal service in the event that a privately-owned Royal Mail (or other provider of the universal postal service) is at risk of entering insolvency proceedings. Enforcement of regulatory requirements is in Schedule 7 whereby OFCOM may specify things which need to be done or give a direction that the entitlement of the contravening person to provide postal services is suspended (either generally or in relation to particular services), or restricted in the respects set out in the direction. A person in default commits an offence triable either way with a maximum penalty on summary conviction of a fine not exceeding the statutory maximum or on conviction on indictment a fine. Schedule 8 contains provisions for requirements to provide information to OFCOM for the purpose of carrying out any of their functions in relation to postal services. Failure to comply is an offence triable either way with the same penalty as the offence in Schedule 7. It is a defence if it was not reasonably* *practicable to comply with the requirement within the period specified by OFCOM, and the person has taken all reasonable steps to provide the information after the end of that period. Proceedings may be brought in respect of a contravention by a person of a requirement only if OFCOM have given the person a notification under paragraph 5 in respect of the contravention, the period allowed under that paragraph for doing the things mentioned in sub-paragraph (3) of that paragraph has ended without the required information having been provided, and OFCOM have not imposed a financial penalty under paragraph 7 in respect of the contravention. Provision of information that is false in any material particular, which at the time the information is provided, the person knows to be false or is reckless as to whether or not it is false is an offence triable either way with a maximum penalty on summary conviction, of a fine not exceeding the statutory maximum, and on conviction on indictment, of a fine or imprisonment for a term not exceeding two years or both. The provisions referred to in this Manual are to be brought into force in accordance with orders made under s 93*[1].

---

[1] At the date of going to press, the following orders had been made: (No 1 and Transitional Provisions) SI 2011/2329; (No 2) SI 2011/3044; (No 3 and Savings Provisions) Order 2012, SI 2012/1095.

# POUND BREACH

## Offence at common law

**7.9337** Breaking the pound for the purpose of rescuing cattle, etc, distrained for rent or damage feasant, and which have been actually impounded in a public pound, is a misdemeanour, punishable by fine or imprisonment, or both. Ignorance of the distraint is not a defence to a civil action (*Lavell & Co v O'Leary* [1933] 2 KB 200).

It is a misdemeanour to rescue cattle found in the parish lanes, and which the officer appointed by the leet is in the act of driving to the pound (*R v Bradshaw* (1835) 7 C & P 233). The cattle may be retaken without a breach of the peace, wherever found in fresh pursuit and the jury will judge as to the reasonableness of the time; whether the recapture must be on fresh pursuit, where it does not take place by breaking or entering a close, is not quite clear, but it must be within a reasonable time. The offender may be required to find sureties for answering an indictment at the Crown Court (see *Russell v Rider* (1934) 6 C & P 416). If a sum greater than the damage be demanded and paid under protest, the difference may be recovered back (*Green v Duckett* (1883) 11 QBD 275, 47 JP 487).

## Cattle straying on highways

**7.9338** See title Highways, in Part VI: Transport.

# PRINTERS

**Contents**



7.9339 Note: See also the Newspaper Libel and Registration Act 1881 in title Libel, ante; also the Children and Young Persons (Harmful Publications) Act 1955, s 2 in title Obscene Publications, ante, and the Representation of the People Act 1983, s 110.

## Newspapers, Printers and Reading Rooms Repeal Act 1869

(32 & 22 Vict c 24)

SECOND SCHEDULE[1]

7.9340 **Penalty[2] upon printers for not publishing their name and residence on every book, and on persons publishing the same** Every person who shall print any paper or book whatsoever[3] which shall be meant to be published or dispersed, and who shall not print upon the front of every such paper, if the same shall be printed on one side only, or upon the first or last leaf of every paper or book which shall consist of more than one leaf, in legible characters, his or her name and usual place of abode or business, and every person who shall publish or disperse, or assist in publishing or dispersing, any printed paper or book on which the name and place of abode of the person printing the same shall not be printed as aforesaid, shall for every copy of such paper so printed by him[4] or her forfeit a sum not more than **level 1** on the standard scale[5];

Provided always that nothing herein contained shall be construed to impose any penalty upon any person for printing any paper excepted out of the operation of the Unlawful Societies Act 1799[1] either in the said Act or by any Act made for the amendment thereof.

---

1 The Newspapers, Printers and Reading Rooms Repeal Act 1869 consolidated provisions in a number of previous Acts, including the Unlawful Societies Act 1799, the Printers and Publishers Acts 1811 and 1839 and the Seditious Meetings Act 1846. They are here reproduced in, and have force as, the Second Schedule to the 1869 Act (amended by the Criminal Justice Act 1982, s 46).

2 The Second Schedule also requires that the information shall not be prosecuted except *in the name of* the Attorney General (see also *Key v Bastin* [1925] 1 KB 650, 89 JP 74). The provision about publishing name and residence on books originated in 2 & 3 Vict, c 12 of which a repealed provision said that 39 Geo III, c 79 was to be construed as one Act with it. That earlier provision stated that prosecutions should be commenced within three months after the offence, and this limitation still applies to the provision printed here about keeping a copy of every paper etc, but arguably no longer applies to the provision about publishing name and residence on books, as there is now no specific requirement to construe together the different enactments now comprising the Second Schedule to the 1869 Act. Prosecutors may however wish to be prepared to justify using the six month limit under the Magistrates' Courts Act 1980, s 127.

3 Exceptions are made by the next paragraph, *infra*, and the second Schedule also specifically excludes papers printed by authority of Parliament, and makes special provision for books or papers printed at the Oxford University Press and the Pitt Press, Cambridge. It also exempts the printing of the name or the name and address, or business or profession of any person and the articles in which he deals, as well as any papers for the sale of estates or goods by auction or otherwise. See also the Printers Imprint Act 1961, post, which further relaxes the requirements.

4 Despite the wording of the section, it is established that the publisher may be liable to penalties under this section, even though he is not the printer (*A-G v Beauchamp* [1920] 1 KB 650, 84 JP 41; *R v Oakes* [1959] 2 QB 350, [1959] 2 All ER 92.

5 Maximum penalty as amended by the Criminal Law Act 1977, s 31 and the Criminal Justice Act 1982, s 46.

7.9341 **Name and residence of printers not required to be put to bank notes, bills, etc, or to any paper printed by authority of any public office** Nothing in the Unlawful Societies Act 1799[1], or in this Act contained shall extend or be construed to extend to require the name and residence of the printer to be printed upon any bank note of the . . . Bank of England, upon any bill of exchange or promissory note, or upon any bond or other security for payment of money, or upon any bill of lading, policy of insurance, letter of attorney, deed, or agreement, or upon any transfer or assignment of any public stocks, funds, or other securities, or upon any transfer or assignment of the stocks of any public corporation or company authorised or sanctioned by Act of Parliament, or upon any dividend warrant of or for any such public or other stocks, funds, or securities, or upon any receipt for money or goods, or upon any proceeding in any court of law or equity, or in any inferior court, warrant, order, or other papers printed by the authority of any public board or public officer in the execution of the duties of their respective offices, notwithstanding the whole of any part of the said several securities, instruments, proceedings, matters, and things aforesaid shall have been or shall be printed. (Amended by the Statute Law Repeals Acts 1893 and 1973.)

---

1 The Newspapers, Printers and Reading Rooms Repeal Act 1869 consolidated provisions in a number of previous Acts, including the Unlawful Societies Act 1799, the Printers and Publishers Acts 1811 and 1839 and the Seditious Meetings Act 1846. They are here reproduced in, and have force as, the Second Schedule to the 1869 Act (amended by the Criminal Justice Act 1982, s 46).

7.9342 **Printers to keep a copy of every paper they print and write thereon the name and abode of their employer** Penalty[1] **of level 2 on the standard scale for neglect or refusing to produce the copy within six months.**—Every person who shall print any paper for hire, reward, gain, or profit, shall carefully preserve and keep one copy (at least) of every paper so printed by him or her, on which he or she shall write, or cause to be written or printed, in fair and legible characters, the name and place of abode of the person or persons by whom he or she shall be employed to print the same; and every person printing any paper for hire, reward, gain, or profit who shall omit or neglect to write, or cause to be written or printed as aforesaid, the name and place of his or her employer on one of such printed papers, or to keep or preserve the same for the space of six calendar months next after the printing thereof, or to produce and show the same to any justice of the peace who within the said space of six calendar months shall require to see the same, maximum fine for omission, neglect, refusal **level 2** on the standard scale[2].

[1] The Second Schedule also requires that the information shall not be prosecuted except *in the name of* the Attorney General (see also *Key v Bastin* [1925] 1 KB 650, 89 JP 74). The provision about publishing name and residence on books originated in 2 & 3 Vict, c 12 of which a repealed provision said that 39 Geo III, c 79 was to be construed as one Act with it. That earlier provision stated that prosecutions should be commenced within three months after the offence, and this limitation still applies to the provision printed here about keeping a copy of every paper etc, but arguably no longer applies to the provision about publishing name and residence on books, as there is now no specific requirement to construe together the different enactments now comprising the Second Schedule to the 1869 Act. Prosecutors may however wish to be prepared to justify using the six month limit under the Magistrates' Courts Act 1980, s 127.

[2] Maximum penalty as amended by the Criminal Law Act 1977, s 31 and the Criminal Justice Act 1982, s 46.

# Printer's Imprint Act 1961

(9 & 10 Eliz 2 c 31)

7.9343 **1. Relaxation of requirements as to printer's imprint, etc** (1) Nothing in the Newspapers, Printers, and Reading Rooms Repeal Act 1869, shall require a printer to print a statement of his name and usual place of abode or business (in this Act referred to as the "printer's imprint") on any paper or book unless the matter printed by him therein comprises either—

(*a*) words grouped together in a manner calculated to convey a message, other than words calculated to convey only a greeting, invitation or other message in a conventional form; or

(*b*) a drawing, illustration or other picture, other than a picture representing only a geometrical, floral, or other design or a registered trademark[1] or any combination thereof.

(2) Nothing in the said Act of 1869 shall require a printer to preserve or keep, or prohibit any person from publishing or dispersing or assisting in publishing or dispersing a copy of any paper or book which by virtue of that Act or this Act is not required to bear the printer's imprint.

(3) The exemption conferred by section 31 of the Unlawful Societies Act 1799, as set out in the Second Schedule to the said Act of 1869 (which exempts the printing from engravings or by letterpress of the paper's and particulars there mentioned from requirements as to the printer's imprint and the preservation of copies) shall extend to the printing by any process of those papers and particulars and of particulars of the services offered by any person; and accordingly in that section the words "to the impression of any engraving or" and the words "by letter-press" are hereby repealed.

(4) The exemptions conferred by this section shall not prejudice any exemption conferred by the said Act of 1869.

[Printer's Imprint Act 1961, s 1.]

[1] To be construed as a registered trademark within the meaning of the Trademarks Act 1994 (Sch 4).

# PRISONS

**Contents**



## Prison Act 1952

(15 & 16 Geo 6 & 1 Eliz 2 c 52)

**7.9344** This Act[1] consolidates enactments relating to prisons and other institutions for offenders. The Secretary of State has complete responsibility for such establishments[2]. Only the parts of the Act of relevance to magistrates' courts are set out here.

See also the Prison Rules in this title, post.

---

1 For application of any enactment with respect to the treatment of persons detained in prisons or other establishments, to persons sentenced by service courts of visiting forces, see the Visiting Forces and International Headquarters (Application of Law) Order 1965 (SI 1965/1536), Sch 5, para 5. The Act is applied to other institutions for offenders to the extent prescribed by s 43 thereof.

2 Transferred to him by the Prison Commissioners Dissolution Order 1963, SI 1963/597 made under s 24 of the Criminal Justice Act 1961.

*Independent monitoring boards*

**7.9345 6. Independent monitoring boards** (1) *Repealed.*

(2) The Secretary of State shall appoint for every prison a group of independent monitors.

(2A) The groups so appointed are to be known as independent monitoring boards.

(3) Rules made as aforesaid shall prescribe the functions of independent monitoring boards and shall among other things require members to pay frequent visits to the prison and hear any complaints which may be made by the prisoners and report to the Secretary of State any matter which they consider it expedient to report; and any member of an independent monitoring board may at any time enter the prison and shall have free access to every part of it and to every prisoner.

(4) *Repealed.*

[Prison Act 1952, s 6 as amended by the Courts Act 1971, ss 53, 56, Schs 7, 11 and the Offender Management Act 2007, s 26.]

*Prison Officers*

**7.9346 8. Powers of prison officers** Every prison officer while acting as such shall have all the powers, authority, protection and privileges of a constable.

[Prison Act 1952, s 8.]

**7.9347 8A. Powers of search by authorised persons** (1) An authorised person at a prison shall have the power to search any prisoner for the purpose of ascertaining whether he has any unauthorised property on his person.

(2) An authorised person searching a prisoner by virtue of this section—

(*a*) shall not be entitled to require a prisoner to remove any of his clothing other than an outer coat, jacket, headgear, gloves and footwear;

(*b*) may use reasonable force where necessary; and

(*c*) may seize and detain any unauthorised property found on the prisoner in the course of the search.

(3) In this section "authorised person" means a person working at the prison of a description for the time being authorised by the governor to exercise the powers conferred by this section.

(4) The governor of a prison shall take such steps as he considers appropriate to notify to prisoners the descriptions of persons who are for the time being authorised to exercise the powers conferred by this section.

(5) In this section "unauthorised property", in relation to a prisoner, means property which the prisoner is not authorised by prison rules or by the governor to have in his possession or, as the case may be, in his possession in a particular part of the prison.

[Prison Act 1952, s 8A as inserted by the Criminal Justice and Public Order Act 1994, s 152 and amended by the Offender Management Act 2007, s 27.]

7.9348 **11. Ejectment of prison officers and their families refusing to quit** (1) Where any living accommodation is provided for a prison officer or his family by virtue of his office, then, if he ceases to be a prison officer or is suspended from office or dies, he, or as the case may be, his family, shall quit the accommodation when required to do so by notice of the Secretary of State.

(2) Where a prison officer or the family of a prison officer refuses or neglects to quit the accommodation forty-eight hours after the giving of such notice as aforesaid, any two justices of the peace, on proof made to them of the facts authorising the giving of the notice and of the service of the notice and of the neglect or refusal to comply therewith, may, by warrant under their hands and seals, direct any constable, within a period specified in the warrant, to enter by force, if necessary, into the accommodation and deliver possession of it to a person acting on behalf of the Secretary of State.

[Prison Act 1952, s 11 as amended by SI 1963/597.]

*Confinement and treatment of prisoners*

7.9349 **13. Legal custody of prisoner** (1) Every prisoner shall be deemed to be in the legal custody of the governor of the prison.

(2) A prisoner shall be deemed to be in legal custody while he is confined in, or is being taken to or from, any prison and while he is working, or is for any other reason, outside the prison in the custody or under the control of an officer of the prison and while he is being taken to any place to which he is required or authorised by or under this Act or section 95, 98, 99 or 108(5) of the Powers of Criminal Courts (Sentencing) Act 2000* to be taken, or is kept in custody in pursuance of any such requirement or authorisation.

[Prison Act 1952, s 13 as amended by Criminal Justice Act 1961, 4th Sch and the Powers of Criminal Courts (Sentencing) Act 2000, Sch 9.]

* **Amended by the Criminal Justice and Court Services Act 2000, Sch 7 from a date to be appointed.**

7.9350 **16. Photographing and measuring of prisoners** The Secretary of State may make regulations[1].

[Prison Act 1952, s 16.]

1 This section applies to remand centres, young offenders institutions (Prison Act 1952, s 43(1) as amended). Regulations still in force are SR & O 1896 No 762, saved by s 54(3) of the Act. They enable the prisoner to be photographed at any time during imprisonment, in prison dress or any other dress suitable to his position in life, and also to be measured. Finger prints may be taken; so may palm prints (Criminal Justice Act 1967, s 33). The Prison Rules 1999, r 42(2) prohibit the giving of a photograph to a person not authorised to receive it; similar provision is made for young offender institutions.

An untried prisoner may have his photograph, measurements and finger prints taken by order of the Secretary of State, or on written application (stating the purposes of justice for which the records are required) by a police officer of not lower rank than Superintendent, to a magistrate or (in the London metropolitan area) to the commissioner or assistant commissioner of police. An acquitted prisoner without previous convictions shall have all records handed to him, or they will be destroyed.

The above does not apply to prisoners; records can be made before a person is committed to prison provided he does not object.

See also powers contained in the Police and Criminal Evidence Act 1984, s 61 and under the Immigration Act 1971, Sch 2, para 18(2).

7.9351 **16A. Testing prisoners for drugs** (1) If an authorisation is in force for the prison, any prison officer may, at the prison, in accordance with prison rules, require any prisoner who is confined in the prison to provide a sample of urine for the purpose of ascertaining whether he has any drug in his body.

(2) If the authorisation so provides, the power conferred to subsection (1) above shall include power to require a prisoner to provide a sample of any other description specified in the authorisation, not being an intimate sample, whether instead of or in addition to a sample of urine.

(3) In this section—

"authorisation" means an authorisation by the governor;

"drug" means any drug which is a controlled drug for the purposes of the Misuse of Drugs Act 1971 or specified drug;

"intimate sample" has the same meaning as in Part V of the Police and Criminal Evidence Act 1984;

"prison officer" includes a prisoner custody officer within the meaning of Part IV of the Criminal Justice Act 1991;

"prison rules" means rules under section 47 of this Act;

"specified drug" means any substance or product specified in prison rules for the purposes of this section.

[Prison Act 1952, s 16A as inserted by the Criminal Justice and Public Order Act 1994, s 151 and amended by the Criminal Justice and Courts Act 2015, s 16.]

7.9352 **16B. Power to test prisoners for alcohol** (1) If an authorisation is in force for the prison, any prison officer may, at the prison, in accordance with prison rules, require any prisoner who is confined in the prison to provide a sample of breath for the purpose of ascertaining whether he has alcohol in his body.

(2) If the authorisation so provides, the power conferred by subsection (1) above shall include power—

(*a*) to require a prisoner to provide a sample of urine, whether instead of or in addition to a sample of breath, and

(*b*) to require a prisoner to provide a sample of any other description specified in the authorisation, not being an intimate sample, whether instead of or in addition to a sample of breath, a sample of urine or both.

(3) In this section—

"authorisation" means an authorisation by the governor;

"intimate sample" has the same meaning as in Part V of the Police and Criminal Evidence Act 1984;

"prison officer" includes a prisoner custody officer within the meaning of Part IV of the Criminal Justice Act 1991;

"prison rules" means rules under section 47 of this Act.

[Prison Act 1952, s 16B as inserted by the Prisons (Alcohol Testing) Act 1997, s 1.]

7.9353 **19. Right of justice to visit prison** (1) A justice of the peace assigned to any local justice area may at any time visit any prison in that area and any prison in which a prisoner is confined in respect of an offence committed in that area, and may examine the condition of the prison and of the prisoners and enter in the visitors' book, to be kept by the governor of the prison, any observations on the condition of the prison or any abuses.

(2) Nothing in the preceding subsection shall authorise a justice of the peace to communicate with any prisoner except on the subject of his treatment in the prison.

(3) The governor of every prison shall bring any entry in the visitors' book to the attention of the independent monitoring board at their next visit.

[Prison Act 1952, s 19 as amended by the Local Government Act 1972, Sch 30, the Access to Justice Act 1999, Sch 10, the Courts Act 2003, Sch 8 and the Offender Management Act 2007, Sch 3.]

7.9354 **23. Power of constable, etc, to act outside his jurisdiction** For the purpose of taking a person to or from any prison under the order of any authority competent to give the order a constable or other officer may act outside the area of his jurisdiction and shall notwithstanding that he is so acting have all the powers, authority, protection and privileges of his office.

[Prison Act 1952, s 23.]

*Length of sentence, release on licence and temporary discharge*

7.9355 **24. Calculation of term of sentence** (1) In any sentence of imprisonment the word "month" shall, unless the contrary is expressed, be construed as meaning calendar month[1].

(2) *Repealed.*

[Prison Act 1952, s 24 as amended by the Criminal Justice Act 1961, 5th Sch.]

---

[1] A prisoner who would be discharged on Sunday, Christmas Day, Good Friday or any Bank Holiday or (in the case of a person serving a term of more than one month) any Saturday, is discharged on the preceding day (Criminal Justice Act 1961, s 23(3)).

*Offences*

7.9356 **39. Assisting a prisoner to escape** (1) A person who—

(*a*) assists a prisoner in escaping or attempting to escape from a prison, or

(*b*) intending to facilitate the escape of a prisoner—

(i) brings, throws or otherwise conveys anything into a prison,

(ii) causes another person to bring, throw or otherwise convey anything into a prison, or

(iii) gives anything to a prisoner or leaves anything in any place (whether inside or outside a prison),

is guilty of an offence.

(2) A person guilty of an offence under this section is liable on conviction on indictment to imprisonment for a term not exceeding ten years.

[Prison Act 1952, s 39 as substituted by the Offender Management Act 2007, s 21.]

7.9357 **40A. Sections 40B and 40C: classification of articles** (1) This section defines the categories of articles which are referred to in sections 40B and 40C.

(2) A List A article is any article or substance in the following list ("List A")—

(*a*) a controlled drug (as defined for the purposes of the Misuse of Drugs Act 1971);

(*b*) an explosive;

(*c*) any firearm or ammunition (as defined in section 57 of the Firearms Act 1968);

(*d*) any other offensive weapon (as defined in section 1(9) of the Police and Criminal Evidence Act 1984).

(3) A List B article is any article or substance in the following list ("List B")—

(*a*) alcohol (as defined for the purposes of the Licensing Act 2003);

(*b*) a mobile telephone;

(*c*) a camera;

(*d*) a sound-recording device.

(4) In List B—

"camera" includes any device by means of which a photograph (as defined in section 40E) can be produced;

"sound-recording device" includes any device by means of which a sound-recording (as defined in section 40E) can be made.

(5) The reference in paragraph (*b*), (*c*) or (*d*) of List B to a device of any description includes a reference to—

(*a*) a component part of a device of that description; or

(*b*) an article designed or adapted for use with a device of that description (including any disk, film or other separate article on which images, sounds or information may be recorded).

(6) A List C article is any article or substance prescribed for the purposes of this subsection by prison rules.

(7) The Secretary of State may by order amend this section for the purpose of—

(*a*) adding an entry to List A or List B;

(*b*) repealing or modifying any entry for the time being included in List A or List B;

(*c*) adding, repealing or modifying any provision for the interpretation of any such entry.

[Prison Act 1952, s 40A as inserted by the Offender Management Act 2007, s 22.]

7.9358 **40B. Conveyance etc of List A articles into or out of prison** (1) A person who, without authorisation—

(*a*) brings, throws or otherwise conveys a List A article into or out of a prison[1],

(*b*) causes another person to bring, throw or otherwise convey a List A article into or out of a prison,

(*c*) leaves a List A article in any place (whether inside or outside a prison) intending it to come into the possession of a prisoner, or

(*d*) knowing a person to be a prisoner, gives a List A article to him,

is guilty of an offence.

(2) In this section "authorisation" means authorisation given for the purposes of this section—

(*a*) in relation to all prisons or prisons of a specified description, by prison rules or by the Secretary of State; or

(*b*) in relation to a particular prison, by the Secretary of State or by the governor or director of the prison.

In paragraph (*a*) "specified" means specified in the authorisation.

(3) Authorisation may be given to specified persons or persons of a specified description—

(*a*) in relation to specified articles or articles of a specified description;

(*b*) in relation to specified acts or acts of a specified description; or

(*c*) on such other terms as may be specified.

In this subsection "specified" means specified in the authorisation.

(4) Authorisation given by the Secretary of State otherwise than in writing shall be recorded in writing as soon as is reasonably practicable after being given.

(5) Authorisation given by the governor or director of a prison shall—

(*a*) be given in writing; and

(*b*) specify the purpose for which it is given.

(6) A person guilty of an offence under this section is liable on conviction on indictment to imprisonment for a term not exceeding ten years or to a fine (or both).

[Prison Act 1952, s 40B as inserted by the Offender Management Act 2007, s 22.]

---

1 Despite the absence of specific words, offences under (*a*) are not offences of absolute liability and require proof of mens rea, although this does not involve knowledge that the article is a listed prohibited article. The prosecution has to prove the absence of a genuine belief on the part of a defendant that the offence was not being committed. In an offence under s 40(1)(*c*) the defence would be "I honestly believed that I was not bringing it in", and the prosecution would have to proved the absence of an honest belief on the art of a defendant that he was not bringing the article in question with him when he entered the prison: *R v M* [2009] EWCA Crim 2615, [2010] 4 All ER 51, [2011] 1 WLR 822, [2010] 2 Cr App R 33.

7.9359 **40C. Conveyance etc of List B or C articles into or out of prison** (1) A person who, without authorisation—

(*a*) brings, throws or otherwise conveys a List B article into or out of a prison[1],

(*b*) causes another person to bring, throw or otherwise convey a List B article into or out of a prison,

(*c*) leaves a List B article in any place (whether inside or outside a prison) intending it to come into the possession of a prisoner, or

(*d*) knowing a person to be a prisoner, gives a List B article to him,

is guilty of an offence.

(2) A person who, without authorisation—

(*a*) brings, throws or otherwise conveys a List C article into a prison intending it to come into the possession of a prisoner,

(*b*) causes another person to bring, throw or otherwise convey a List C article into a prison intending it to come into the possession of a prisoner, (*c*) brings, throws or otherwise conveys a List C article out of a prison on behalf of a prisoner,

(*d*) causes another person to bring, throw or otherwise convey a List C article out of a prison on behalf of a prisoner,

(*e*) leaves a List C article in any place (whether inside or outside a prison) intending it to come into the possession of a prisoner, or

(*f*) while inside a prison, gives a List C article to a prisoner,

is guilty of an offence.

(3) A person who attempts to commit an offence under subsection (2) is guilty of that offence.

(4) In proceedings for an offence under this section it is a defence for the accused to show that—

(*a*) he reasonably believed that he had authorisation to do the act in respect of which the proceedings are brought, or

(*b*) in all the circumstances there was an overriding public interest which justified the doing of that act.

(5) A person guilty of an offence under subsection (1) is liable—

(*a*) on conviction on indictment, to imprisonment for a term not exceeding two years or to a fine (or both);

(*b*) on summary conviction, to imprisonment for a term not exceeding 12 months or to a fine not exceeding the statutory maximum (or both).

(6) A person guilty of an offence under subsection (2) is liable on summary conviction to a fine not exceeding level 3 on the standard scale.

(7) In this section "authorisation" means authorisation given for the purposes of this section; and subsections (1) to (3) of section 40E apply in relation to authorisations so given as they apply to authorisations given for the purposes of section 40D.

[Prison Act 1952, s 40C as inserted by the Offender Management Act 2007, s 22.]

1 See note to s 40B(1)(*a*), ante.

**7.9359A 40CA. Unauthorised possession in prison of knife or offensive weapon** (1) A person who, without authorisation, is in possession of an article specified in subsection (2) inside a prison is guilty of an offence.

(2) The articles referred to in subsection (1) are—

(*a*) any article that has a blade or is sharply pointed;

(*b*) any other offensive weapon (as defined in section 1(9) of the Police and Criminal Evidence Act 1984).

(3) In proceedings for an offence under this section it is a defence for the accused to show that—

(*a*) he reasonably believed that he had authorisation to be in possession of the article in question, or

(*b*) in all the circumstances there was an overriding public interest which justified his being in possession of the article.

(4) A person guilty of an offence under this section is liable—

(*a*) on conviction on indictment, to imprisonment for a term not exceeding four years or to a fine (or both);

(*b*) on summary conviction, to imprisonment for a term not exceeding 12 months or to a fine (or both).

(5) In this section "authorisation" means authorisation given for the purposes of this section; and subsections (1) to (3) of section 40E apply in relation to authorisations so given as they apply to authorisations given for the purposes of section 40D.

[Prison Act 1952, s 40CA as inserted by the Serious Crime Act 2015, s 78.]

**7.9359B 40CB. Throwing articles into prison** (1) A person who, without authorisation, throws any article or substance into a prison is guilty of an offence.

(2) For the purposes of subsection (1)—

(*a*) the reference to an article or substance does not include a reference to a List A article, a List B article or a List C article (as defined by section 40A);

(*b*) the reference to "throwing" an article or substance into a prison includes a reference to doing anything from outside the prison that results in the article or substance being projected or conveyed over or through a boundary of the prison so as to land inside the prison.

(3) In proceedings for an offence under this section it is a defence for the accused to show that—

(*a*) he reasonably believed that he had authorisation to do the act in respect of which the proceedings are brought, or

(*b*) in all the circumstances there was an overriding public interest which justified the doing of that act.

(4) A person guilty of an offence under subsection (1) is liable—

(*a*) on conviction on indictment, to imprisonment for a term not exceeding two years or to a fine (or both);

(*b*) on summary conviction, to imprisonment for a term not exceeding 12 months or to a fine (or both).

(5) In this section "authorisation" means authorisation given for the purposes of this section; and subsections (1) to (3) of section 40E apply in relation to authorisations so given as they apply to authorisations given for the purposes of section 40D.

[Prison Act 1952, s 40CB as inserted by the Serious Crime Act 2015, s 79.]

7.9360 **40D. Other offences relating to prison security** (1) A person who, without authorisation—

(*a*) takes a photograph, or makes a sound-recording, inside a prison, or

(*b*) transmits, or causes to be transmitted, any image, sound or information from inside a prison by electronic communications for simultaneous reception outside the prison,

is guilty of an offence.

(2) It is immaterial for the purposes of subsection (1)(*a*) where the recording medium is located.

(3) A person who, without authorisation—

(*a*) brings or otherwise conveys a restricted document out of a prison or causes such a document to be brought or conveyed out of a prison,

(*b*) *repealed*,

is guilty of an offence.

(3A) A person who, without authorisation, is in possession of any of the items specified in subsection (3B) inside a prison is guilty of an offence.

(3B) The items referred to in subsection (3A) are—

(*a*) a device capable of transmitting or receiving images, sounds or information by electronic communications (including a mobile telephone);

(*b*) a component part of such a device;

(*c*) an article designed or adapted for use with such a device (including any disk, film or other separate article on which images, sounds or information may be recorded).

(4) In proceedings for an offence under this section it is a defence for the accused to show that—

(*a*) he reasonably believed that he had authorisation to do the act in respect of which the proceedings are brought, or

(*b*) in all the circumstances there was an overriding public interest which justified the doing of that act.

(5) A person guilty of an offence under this section is liable—

(*a*) on conviction on indictment, to imprisonment for a term not exceeding two years or to a fine (or both); or

(*b*) on summary conviction, to imprisonment for a term not exceeding 12 months or to a fine not exceeding the statutory maximum (or both).

[Prison Act 1952, s 40D as inserted by the Offender Management Act 2007, s 23 and amended by the Crime and Security Act 2010, 45.]

7.9361 **40E. Section 40D: meaning of "authorisation" and other interpretation** (1) In section 40D (and the following provisions of this section) "authorisation" means authorisation given for the purposes of that section—

(*a*) in relation to all prisons or prisons of a specified description, by prison rules or by the Secretary of State;

(*b*) in relation to a particular prison—

(i) by the Secretary of State;

(ii) by the governor or director of the prison;

(iii) by a person working at the prison who is authorised by the governor or director to grant authorisation on his behalf.

In paragraph (*a*) "specified" means specified in the authorisation.

(2) Authorisation may be given—

(*a*) to persons generally or to specified persons or persons of a specified description; and

(*b*) on such terms as may be specified.

In this subsection "specified" means specified in the authorisation.

(3) Authorisation given by or on behalf of the governor or director of a prison must be in writing.

(4) In section 40D "restricted document" means the whole (or any part of)—

(*a*) a photograph taken inside the prison;

(*b*) a sound-recording made inside the prison;

(*c*) a personal record (or a document containing information derived from a personal record);

(*d*) any other document which contains—

(i) information relating to an identified or identifiable relevant individual, if the disclosure of that information would or might prejudicially affect the interests of that individual; or

(ii) information relating to any matter connected with the prison or its operation, if the disclosure of that information would or might prejudicially affect the security or operation of the prison.

(5) In subsection (4)—

"personal record" means any record which is required by prison rules to be prepared and maintained in relation to any prisoner (and it is immaterial whether or not the individual concerned is still a prisoner at the time of any alleged offence);

"relevant individual" means an individual who is or has at any time been—

(*a*) a prisoner or a person working at the prison; or

(*b*) a member of such a person's family or household.

(6) In section 40D and this section—

"document" means anything in which information is recorded (by whatever means);

"electronic communications" has the same meaning as in the Electronic Communications Act 2000 (c 7);

"photograph" means a recording on any medium on which an image is produced or from which an image (including a moving image) may by any means be produced; and

"sound-recording" means a recording of sounds on any medium from which the sounds may by any means be reproduced.

[Prison Act 1952, s 40E as inserted by the Offender Management Act 2007, s 23.]

**7.9362 40F. Offences under sections 40B to 40D: extension of Crown immunity** (1) An individual who—

(*a*) works at a prison;

(*b*) does not do that work as a servant or agent of the Crown; and

(*c*) has been designated by the Secretary of State for the purposes of this section,

shall be treated for the purposes of the application of sections 40B to 40D as if he were doing that work as a servant or agent of the Crown.

(2) A designation for the purposes of this section may be given—

(*a*) in relation to persons specified in the designation or persons of a description so specified; and

(*b*) in relation to all work falling within subsection (1)(*a*) or only in relation to such activities as the designation may provide.

[Prison Act 1952, s 40F as inserted by the Offender Management Act 2007, s 24.]

**7.9363 42. Display of notice of penalties** The Prison Commissioners[1] shall cause to be affixed in a conspicuous place outside every prison a notice of the penalties to which persons committing offences under sections 39 to 40D are liable.

[Prison Act 1952, s 42 as amended by the Offender Management Act 2007, s 23.]

---

1 Section 42 has not been specifically amended by the Prison Commissioners Dissolution Order 1963 (see headnote to this Act) but presumably the responsibility for the display of notices has passed to the Secretary of State.

*Disposal of property*

**7.9364 42A. Disposal of unauthorised or unattributable property[1]** (1) The governor or director of a prison may destroy or otherwise dispose of, or arrange for the destruction or other disposal of—

(*a*) an article found in the possession of a prisoner who is not authorised to have it in his or her possession, or

(*b*) an article found inside the prison or in a prisoner escort vehicle, otherwise than in the possession of a prisoner, where—

(i) the owner of the article is a prisoner who is not authorised to have it in his or her possession, or

(ii) the owner of the article cannot be ascertained.

(2) An article which a prisoner is authorised to have in his or her possession is to be treated for the purposes of subsection (1) as not so authorised where the governor or director of the prison reasonably believes that the article is being, has been or may be used for any of the purposes mentioned in subsection (3).

(3) Those purposes are—

(*a*) concealing an article which a prisoner is not authorised to have in his or her possession;

(*b*) causing harm to the prisoner or others;

(*c*) prejudicing the security or operation of the prison.

(4) Where a prisoner is authorised to have an article in his or her possession in a particular part of the prison, subsection (1)(*a*) or (*b*)(i) applies only where the property is found otherwise than in that part.

(5) In this section—

(*a*) "authorised" means authorised in accordance with prison rules or by the governor or director of the prison;

(*b*) "prisoner escort vehicle" means a vehicle used for taking a prisoner to or from a prison or other place while in custody;

(*c*) references to disposing of an article include selling it.

(6) The power under subsection (1)—

(*a*) may be exercised in relation to a relevant article found before the day on which this section comes into force if the article remains unclaimed at the end of six months beginning with that day;

(*b*) may not otherwise be exercised in relation to an article found before that day.

(7) In subsection (6)(*a*) "relevant article" means an article specified in section 40A(3)(*c*) or (*d*) (cameras and sound-recording devices) or section 40D(3B) (devices capable of transmitting or receiving images, sounds or information by electronic communications, etc).

[Prison Act 1952, s 42A as inserted by the Prisons (Property) Act 2013, s 1.]

[1] In force 26 March 2015 (SI 2015/771).

7.9365 **43. Remand centres, detention centres and youth custody centres** (1) The Secretary of State may provide—

(*a*) remand centres, that is to say places for the detention of persons not less than 14 but under 21 years of age who are remanded or committed in custody for trial or sentence*;

(*aa*) young offender institutions, that is to say places for the detention of offenders sentenced to detention in a young offender institution or to custody for life or other persons who may be lawfully detained there;

(*b*), (*c*) *repealed*, and

(*d*) secure training centres, that is to say places in which offenders in respect of whom detention and training orders have been made under section 100 of the Powers of Criminal Courts (Sentencing) Act 2000 may be detained and given training and education and prepared for their release and in which children who have been remanded to youth detention accommodation under section 91(4) of the Legal Aid, Sentencing and Punishment of Offenders Act 2012 may be detained.

(2) The Secretary of State may from time from time direct—

(*a*) that a woman aged 21* years or over who is serving a sentence of imprisonment or who has been committed to prison for default shall be detained in a remand centre or* a youth custody centre instead of a prison;

(*b*) that a woman aged 21 years or over who is remanded in custody or committed in custody for trial or sentence shall be detained in a remand centre instead of a prison;*

(*c*) that a person under 21 but less than 17 years of age who is remanded in custody or committed in custody for trial or sentence shall be detained in a prison instead of a remand centre or a remand centre instead of a prison, notwithstanding anything in section 27 of the Criminal Justice Act 1948 or section 23(3) of the Children and Young Persons Act 1969.**

(3) Notwithstanding subsection (1) above, any person required to be detained in an institution to which this Act applies may be detained in a remand centre for any temporary purpose and a person aged 18 years or over may be detained in such a centre for the purpose of providing maintenance and domestic services for that centre.**

(4) Sections 5A, 6(2) and (3), 16, 22, 25, 36 and 42A of this Act shall apply to remand centres*, detention centres and youth custody centres and to persons detained in them as they apply to prisons and prisoners.

(4A) Sections 16, 22, 36 and 42A of this Act shall apply to secure training centres and to persons detained in them as they apply to prisons and prisoners.

(5) The other provisions of this Act preceding this section, except section 28 above, shall apply to centres of the descriptions specified in subsection (4) above and to persons detained in them as they apply to prisons and prisoners, but subject to such adaptations and modifications as may be specified in rules made by the Secretary of State.

(5A) The other provisions of this Act preceding this section, except sections 5, 5A, 6(2) and (3), 12, 14, 19, 25 and 28 above, shall apply to secure training centres and to persons detained in them as they apply to prisons and prisoners, but subject to such adaptations and modifications as may be specified in rules made by the Secretary of State.

(6) References in the preceding provisions of this Act to imprisonment shall, so far as those provisions apply to institutions provided under this section, be construed as including references to detention in those institutions.

(7) Nothing in this section shall be taken to prejudice the operation of section 108(5) of the Powers of Criminal Courts (Sentencing) Act 2000.**

(8) The application of this Act to a person on whom a custodial sentence (within the meaning of the Armed Forces Act 2006) has been passed in respect of a service offence (within the meaning of that Act) is not affected by the omission from subsection (1) of a reference to that sentence.***

[Prison Act 1952, s 43 as substituted by the Criminal Justice Act 1982, s 11 and amended by the Criminal Justice Act 1988, Schs 15 and 16, the Criminal Justice Act 1991, Sch 8, the Criminal Justice and Public Order Act 1994, s 11, the Crime and Disorder Act 1998, Sch 8, the Powers of Criminal Courts (Sentencing) Act 2000, Sch 9, the Armed Forces Act 2006, Sch 16, the Criminal Justice and Immigration Act 2008, Sch 26, the Legal Aid, Sentencing and Punishment of Offenders Act 2012, Sch 12, the Prisons (Property) Act 2013, s 1 and the Deregulation Act 2015, s 84.]

* **Amended by the Criminal Justice and Court Services Act 2000, Sch 7 from a date to be appointed.**

** **Repealed by the Criminal Justice and Court Services Act 2000, s 59 and Sch 7 from a date to be appointed.**

*** **Substituted by the Criminal Justice and Courts Act 2015, s 38 from a date to be appointed (and as substituted subsequently amended by the Deregulation Act 2015, s 84).**

7.9366 **47.** *Power of Secretary of State to make Rules for the regulation and management of prisons etc*[1].

---

[1] The Prison Rules 1999, and the Young Offenders Institution Rules 2000, post, have been made.

*Miscellaneous*

7.9367 **49. Persons unlawfully at large** (1) Any person who, having been sentenced to imprisonment[1] or custody for life or ordered to be detained in youth detention accommodation or in a young offenders institution, or having been committed to a prison or remand centre, is unlawfully at large[2], may be arrested by a constable without warrant[3] and taken to the place in which he is required in accordance with law to be detained[4].

(2) Where any person sentenced to imprisonment, or ordered to be detained in youth detention accommodation or in a young offenders institution, is unlawfully at large[5] at any time during the period for which he is liable to be detained in pursuance of the sentence or order, then, unless the Secretary of State otherwise directs, no account shall be taken, in calculating the period for which he is liable to be so detained, of any time during which he is absent from the place in which he is required in accordance with law to be detained:

Provided that—

(*a*) this subsection shall not apply to any period during which any such person as aforesaid is detained in pursuance of the sentence or order or in pursuance of any other sentence of any court in the United Kingdom in a prison or remand centre, in youth detention accommodation or in a young offenders institution;

(*b*), (*c*) *repealed*.

(3) The provisions of the last preceding subsection shall apply to a person who is detained in custody in default of payment of any sum of money as if he were sentenced to imprisonment.

(3A) Where—

(*a*) a person is extradited to the United Kingdom from a category 1 territory for the purpose of serving a term of imprisonment or another form of detention mentioned in subsection (2) of this section, and

(*b*) the person was for any time kept in custody in that territory with a view to the extradition (and not also for any other reason),

the Secretary of State shall exercise the power under that subsection to direct that account shall be taken of that time in calculating the period for which the person is liable to be detained.

(3B) In subsection (3A) of this section "category 1 territory" means a territory designated under the Extradition Act 2003 for the purposes of Part 1 of that Act.

(4) For the purposes of this section a person who, after being temporarily released in pursuance of rules made under subsection (5) of section forty-seven of this Act, is at large at any time during the period for which he is liable to be detained in pursuance of his sentence shall be deemed to be unlawfully at large if the period for which he was temporarily released has expired or if an order recalling him has been made by the Secretary of State in pursuance of the rules[6].

(4A) *Repealed.*

(5) In this section "youth detention accommodation" means—

(*a*) a young offender institution;

(*b*) a secure training centre;

(*ba*) a secure college; or

(*c*) any other accommodation that is youth detention accommodation within the meaning given by section 107(1) of the Powers of Criminal Courts (Sentencing) Act 2000 (detention and training orders).*

[Prison Act 1952, s 49 as amended by the Criminal Justice Act 1961, ss 30 and 41, and Sch 4, SI 1963/597, the Criminal Justice Act 1967, s 103 and Sch 7, the Children and Young Persons Act 1969, s 72 and Sch 6, the Criminal Justice Act 1982, ss 77 and 78, and Schs 14 and 16, the Criminal Justice Act 1988, s 123 and Sch 8, the Criminal Justice and Public Order Act 1994, Sch 10, the Crime and Disorder Act 1998, Sch 8, the Powers of Criminal Courts (Sentencing) Act 2000, Sch 9, the Offender Management Act 2007, Sch 3, the Legal Aid, Sentencing and Punishment of Offenders Act 2012, Sch 10, the Anti-social Behaviour, Crime and Policing Act 2014, s 171 and the Criminal Justice and Courts Act 2015, Sch 9.]

---

[1] This expression is extended to a child or young person detained in accordance with the directions of the Secretary of State (Criminal Justice Act 1967, s 67).

[2] A person is unlawfully at large within the meaning of s 49 of the 1952 Act only if he is currently liable to be detained. Thus, where a warrant of commitment as drawn up stated, inaccurately, that two terms were concurrent and not consecutive, the governor had to act in accordance with the order and release the prisoner in accordance with the terms as drafted, and the offender was not "unlawfully at large" between the date of his release and the date on which the order was amended to rectify the error: *R (Lunn) v Governor of Moorland Prison* [2006] EWCA Civ 700, [2006] 1 WLR 2870.

[3] This power of arrest is preserved by the Police and Criminal Evidence Act 1984, s 26 and Sch 2.

[4] See the Criminal Justice Act 1967, s 72, post, for power to issue a warrant.

[5] This includes a prisoner compulsorily detained in hospital under s 3 of the Mental Health Act 1983 on the date when the licence is revoked (*R (on the application of S) v Secretary of State for the Home Department* [2003] EWCA Civ 426, [2003] 25 LS Gaz R 46).

[6] For further provisions relating to the punishment and return to lawful custody of persons unlawfully at large, see the Prisoners (Return to Custody) Act 1995, this PART, post.

# Criminal Justice Act 1961

(9 to 10 Eliz 2 c 39)

## Part II

## Treatment and Supervision of Prisoners and other Detained Persons

7.9368 **22. Harbouring escaped prisoner** (1) *Repealed.*

(2) If any person knowingly harbours[1] a person who has escaped from a prison or other institution[2] to which s 39 of the Prison Act 1952 applies, or who having been sentenced in any part of the United Kingdom or in any of the Channel Islands or the Isle of Man to imprisonment or detention, is otherwise unlawfully at large, or gives to any such person any assistance with intent to prevent, hinder or interfere with his being taken into custody, he shall be liable

(*a*) on summary conviction, to imprisonment for a term not exceeding **six months** or to a fine not exceeding **the statutory maximum**, or to **both**;

(*b*) on conviction on indictment, to imprisonment for a term not exceeding **ten years** or to a **fine** or to **both** [3].

(2A) The reference in subsection (2) to a person who has been sentenced as mentioned there includes—

(*a*) a person on whom a custodial sentence within the meaning of the Armed Forces Act 2006 has been passed (anywhere) in respect of a service offence within the meaning of that Act;

(*b*) a person in respect of whom an order under section 214 of that Act (detention for commission of offence during currency of order) has been made.

(4) *Repealed.*

[Criminal Justice Act 1961, s 22 as amended by the Children and Young Persons Act 1969, s 72 and Sch 6, Criminal Law Act 1977, s 28, the Prison Security Act 1992, s 2 and the Armed Forces Act 2006, Sch 16.]

1. "Harbours" means to shelter or provide refuge, but not merely to assist or support (*Darch v Weight* [1984] 2 All ER 245, [1984] 1 WLR 659, 148 JP 588).
2. This does not extend to an escape from a police yard of a prisoner under escort to a remand centre (*Nicoll v Catron* (1985) 149 JP 424, 81 Cr App Rep 339, [1985] Crim LR 223).
3. For procedure in respect of an offence triable either way, see the Magistrates' Courts Act 1980, ss 17A–21, ante.

7.9369 **23. Prison rules** (1) For the purposes of rules under section forty-seven of the Prison Act 1952 (which authorises the making of rules for the regulation and management of prisons and the discipline and control of persons required to be detained therein) any offence against the rules committed by a prisoner may be treated as committed in the prison in which he is for the time being confined.

(2) Without prejudice to any power to make provision by rules under the said section forty-seven for the confiscation of money or articles conveyed or deposited in contravention of the said Act or of the rules, provision may be made by such rules for the withholding from prisoners (subject to such exceptions as may be prescribed by the rules) of any money or other article sent to them by post, and for the disposal of any such money or article either by returning it to the sender (where the sender's name and address are known) or in such other manner as may be prescribed by or determined under the rules:

Provided that in relation to a prisoner committed to prison in default of payment of any sum of money, the rules shall provide for the application of any money withheld as aforesaid in or towards the satisfaction of the amount due from him unless, upon being informed of the receipt of the money, he objects to its being so applied.

(3) A prisoner who would, apart from this subsection, be discharged on any of the days to which this subsection applies in his case shall be discharged on the next preceding day which is not one of those days.

The days to which this subsection applies are Sunday, Christmas Day, Good Friday and any day which under the Bank Holidays Act 1871 is a bank holiday in England and Wales and, in the case of a person who is serving a term of more than five days, any Saturday.

(3A) *Repealed.*

(4) In this section the references to prisons and prisoners include references respectively to a young offender institution, a secure college, secure training centres and remand centres and to persons detained therein.*

[Criminal Justice Act 1961, s 23 as amended by the Banking and Financial Dealings Act 1971, s 4 and Sch 2, the Criminal Justice Act 1982, s 77 and Sch 14, the Criminal Justice and Public Order Act 1994, Sch 10, SI 2001/1149, the Criminal Justice Act 2003, s 186, the Legal Aid, Sentencing and Punishment of Offenders Act 2012, Sch 10 and the Criminal Justice and Courts Act 2015, Sch 9.]

* **Amended by the Criminal Justice and Court Services Act 2000, Sch 7 from a date to be appointed.**

## Part IV

## Supplemental

7.9370 **35. Legal custody** (1) Any person required or authorised by or under this Act to be taken to any place or to be kept in custody shall, while being so taken or kept, be deemed to be in legal custody.

(2) A constable, or any other person required or authorised by or under this Act to take any

person to or keep him at any place shall, while taking or keeping him there have all the powers, authorities, protection and privileges which a constable has within the area for which he acts as constable.

[Criminal Justice Act 1961, s 35.]

7.9371 **37. Secretary of State's report** In any case where a court is required by this Act to consider a report made by or on behalf of the Secretary of State in respect of an offender, the court shall cause a copy of the report to be given to the offender or his counsel or solicitor.

[Criminal Justice Act 1961, s 37.]

7.9372 **38. Construction of references to sentence of imprisonment, etc** (1) Except as provided by subsection (3) of this section, the expression "sentence" in this Act does not include a committal for default or the fixing of a term to be served in the event of default, or a committal or attachment for contempt of court.

(2) For the purposes of any provisions of this Act referring to a person who is serving or has served a sentence of any description, the expression "sentence" includes—

(*a*) in any case, a sentence of that description passed by a court in Scotland, Northern Ireland, any of the Channel Islands or the Isle of Man; and

(*b*) in the case of imprisonment, a sentence which is treated by virtue of the Colonial Prisoners Removal Act 1884, as a sentence passed by a court in England and Wales.

(3) For the purposes of sections twenty-two and thirty-four of this Act—

(*a*) the expression "imprisonment or detention" means imprisonment, custody for life, detention in a young offender institution or in a secure training centre or secure college or detention under an equivalent sentence passed by a court in the Channel Islands or the Isle of Man;

(*b*) the expression "sentence" includes any order made by any court imposing imprisonment or detention, and "sentenced" shall be construed accordingly;

(*c*) any reference to a person serving a sentence of, or sentenced to, imprisonment or detention shall be construed as including a reference to a person who, under any enactment relating to children and young persons in force in any part of the United Kingdom or any of the Channel Islands or the Isle of Man, has been sentenced by a court to be detained for an offence and is liable to be detained in accordance with a determination of the Secretary of State or of a person authorised by him, in accordance with arrangements made by the Secretary of State or in accordance with directions given by the Secretary of State, or by the Governor of the Isle of Man with the concurrence of the Secretary of State, and any other reference to a sentence of imprisonment or detention shall be construed accordingly.

(4) For the purposes of any reference in this Act to a term of imprisonment or of detention in a young offender institution or to a term of imprisonment or detention, consecutive terms and terms which are wholly or partly concurrent shall be treated as a single term.

(5) *Repealed.*

(6) The Secretary of State may by order[1] designate as equivalent sentences for the purposes of this Act a description of sentence which a court with jurisdiction in one part of the United Kingdom or in the Channel Islands or the Isle of Man may pass and a description of sentence which a court elsewhere in the United Kingdom or in those Islands may pass.

[Criminal Justice Act 1961, s 38 as amended by the Criminal Justice (Scotland) Act 1963, Sch 5, the Criminal Justice Act 1982, Schs 14 and 16, the Criminal Justice Act 1988, Sch 8, the Criminal Justice and Public Order Act 1994, Sch 10, the Crime (Sentences) Act 1997, Sch 6 the Armed Forces Act 2006, Sch 17, the Criminal Justice and Immigration Act 2008, Sch 26 the Criminal Justice and Courts Act 2015, Sch 9.]

---

1 Transfer of Offenders (Designation of Equivalent Sentences) Order 1983, SI 1983/1314, amended by SI 1988/1654, has been made.

7.9373 **39. Interpretation** (1) In this Act, unless the context otherwise requires the following expressions have the meanings hereby assigned to them, that is to say—

"default" means failure to pay, or want of sufficient distress to satisfy, any fine or other sum of money, or failure to do or abstain from doing any thing required to be done or left undone;

"enactment" includes an enactment of the Parliament of Northern Ireland;

"prison" does not include a naval, military or air force prison;*

(1A) *Repealed.*

(1B) Any reference in this Act to a sentence being equivalent to another sentence is to be construed as a reference to its having been so designated under section 38(6) of this Act.

(2) Except as otherwise expressly provided, references in this Act to a court do not include the Court Martial, the Summary Appeal Court, the Service Civilian Court, the Court Martial Appeal Court or the Supreme Court on an appeal brought from the Court Martial Appeal Court.

(3) Where the age of any person at any time is material for the purposes of any provision of this Act regulating the powers of a court or justice of the peace, his age at the material time shall be deemed to be or to have been that which appears to the court or justice, after considering any available evidence, to be or to have been his age at that time.

(4) Any reference in this Act to any other enactment is a reference thereto as amended, and includes a reference thereto as extended or applied, by or under any other enactment, including this Act.

[Criminal Justice Act 1961, s 39 amended by Criminal Justice (Scotland) Act 1963, Sch 5, Powers of Criminal Courts Act 1973, Sch 5, Criminal Law Act 1977, Sch 12, the Criminal Justice Act 1982, Schs 14 and 16, the Crime (Sentences) Act 1997, Sch 6 and the Armed Forces Act 2006, Schs 16 and 17.]

* **New sub-s (1ZA) inserted by the Tribunals, Courts and Enforcement Act 2007, Sch 13 from a date to be appointed.**

## Criminal Justice Act 1967

(1967 c 80)

7.9374 **72. Power of magistrates to issue warrants for arrest of escaped prisoners and mental patients** (1) On an information in writing being laid before a justice of the peace for any area in England and Wales or Northern Ireland and substantiated on oath, or alleging that any person is—

(*a*) an offender unlawfully at large from a prison or other institution to which the Prison Act applies in which he is required to be detained after being convicted of an offence; or

(*b*) a convicted mental patient liable to be retaken under section 18, 38(7) or 138 of the Mental Health Act 1983, s 36 or 106 of the Mental Health (Scotland) Act 1960 or s 30 or 108 of the Mental Health Act (Northern Ireland) 1961 (retaking of mental patients who are absent without leave or have escaped from custody)[1];

the justice may issue a warrant to arrest him and bring him before a magistrates' court for that area.

(2) Where a person is brought before a magistrates' court in pursuance of a warrant for his arrest under this section, the court shall, if satisfied that he is the person named in the warrant and if satisfied as to the facts mentioned in paragraph (*a*) or (*b*) of the foregoing subsection, order him to be returned to the prison or other institution where he is required or liable to be detained or, in the case of a convicted mental patient, order him to be kept in custody or detained in a place of safety pending his admission to hospital.

(3) Section 137 of the Mental Health Act 1983[1], s 105 of the Mental Health (Scotland) Act 1960 and s 107 of the Mental Health Act (Northern Ireland) 1961 (custody, conveyance and detention of certain mental patients) shall apply to a convicted mental patient required by this section to be conveyed to any place or to be kept in custody or detained in a place of safety as they apply to a person required by or by virtue of the said Act of 1983, 1960 or 1961, as the case may be, to be so conveyed or kept.

(4) In this section—

"convicted mental patient" means a person liable after being convicted of an offence to be detained under Part III of the Mental Health Act 1983, Part V of the Mental Health (Scotland) Act 1960 or Part III of the Mental Health Act (Northern Ireland) 1961 in pursuance of a hospital order or transfer direction together with an order or direction restricting his discharge or in pursuance of a hospital direction and a limitation direction or a person liable to be detained under section 38 of the said Act of 1983;

"place of safety" has the same meaning as in Part III of the said Act of 1983 or 1960 or Part III of the said Act of 1961, as the case may be;

"Prison Act" means the Prison Act 1952, the Prisons (Scotland) Act [1989] or the Prison Act (Northern Ireland) 1953, as the case may be.

(5) Section 27 of the Criminal Justice Administration Act 1914 (power to issue warrants for the arrest of persons who may be arrested without a warrant) shall cease to have effect.

(6) References in this section to offences include service offences within the meaning of the Armed Forces Act 2006.

[Criminal Justice Act 1967, s 72 as amended by the Mental Health (Amendment) Act 1982, Sch 3, the Mental Health Act 1983, Sch 4, the Crime (Sentences) Act 1997, Sch 4 and the Armed Forces Act 2006, Sch 16.]

1 See title MENTAL HEALTH, ante.

## Prison Security Act 1992

(1992 c 25)

7.9375 **1. Offence of prison mutiny** (1) Any prisoner who takes part in a prison mutiny shall be guilty of an offence[1] and liable, on conviction on indictment, to imprisonment for a term not exceeding **ten years** or to a **fine** or to **both**.

(2) For the purposes of this section there is a prison mutiny where two or more prisoners, while on the premises of any prison, engage in conduct which is intended to further a common purpose of overthrowing[2] lawful authority in that prison.

(3) For the purposes of this section the intentions and common purpose of prisoners may be inferred from the form and circumstances of their conduct and it shall be immaterial that conduct falling within subsection (2) above takes a different form in the case of different prisoners.

(4) Where there is a prison mutiny, a prisoner who has or is given a reasonable opportunity of submitting to lawful authority[2] and fails, without reasonable excuse, to do so shall be regarded for the purposes of this section as taking part in the mutiny.

(5) Proceedings for an offence under this section shall not be brought except by or with the consent of the Director of Public Prosecutions.

(6) In this section—

"conduct" includes acts and omissions;

"prison" means any prison, young offender institution or remand centre* which is under the general superintendence of, or is provided by, the Secretary of State under the Prison Act 1952, including a contracted out prison within the meaning of Part IV of the Criminal Justice Act 1991;

"prisoner" means any person for the time being in a prison as a result of any requirement imposed by a court or otherwise that he be detained in legal custody.

[Prison Security Act 1992, s 1.]

* **Amended by the Criminal Justice and Court Services Act 2000, Sch 7 from a date to be appointed.**

1 This provision creates only one offence although it may be committed in distinct ways which involve different levels of wrongdoing. Accordingly, any indictment should make clear which type of conduct is alleged (*R v Mason* [2004] EWCA Crim 2173, [2005] 1 Cr App R 11, [2005] Crim LR 140).

2 The concept of "overthrowing" is a stronger one than "subverting" and is not synonymous with a refusal to obey lawful orders and for the offence described in sub-s (4) to be committed, there must already be a mutiny occurring (*R v Mason* supra).

# Prisoners (Return to Custody) Act 1995

(1995 c 16)

7.9376 **1. Remaining at large after temporary release** (1) Subject to subsection (2) below, a person who has been temporarily released in pursuance of rules made under section 47(5) of the Prison Act 1952 (rules for temporary release) is guilty of an offence if—

(*a*) without reasonable excuse, he remains unlawfully at large at any time after becoming so at large by virtue of the expiry of the period for which he was temporarily released; or

(*b*) knowing or believing an order recalling him to have been made and while unlawfully at large by virtue of such an order, he fails, without reasonable excuse, to take all necessary steps for complying as soon as reasonably practicable with that order.

(1A) *Repealed.*

(2) Subsection (1) above shall not apply in the case of a person temporarily released from a secure training centre or secure college.

(3) A person guilty of an offence under this section is liable—

(*a*) on conviction on indictment to imprisonment for a term not exceeding 2 years or a fine (or both), and

(*b*) on summary conviction to imprisonment for a term not exceeding 12 months or a fine (or both).

(4) An offence under this section shall be taken to be committed at the place where the offender was required to be detained immediately before being temporarily released.

(5) A person shall be deemed for the purposes of this section to be unlawfully at large whenever he is deemed to be so at large for the purposes of section 49 of the Prison Act 1952 (which confers powers of arrest).

(6) This section shall not apply where the period of temporary release expired, or the order of recall was made, before the commencement of this section.

(7) In relation to an offence committed before section 154(1) of the Criminal Justice Act 2003 comes into force, the reference in subsection (3)(*b*) to 12 months is to be read as a reference to 6 months.

(8) In relation to an offence committed before section 85 of the Legal Aid, Sentencing and Punishment of Offenders Act 2012 comes into force, the reference in subsection (3)(*b*) to a fine is to be read as a reference to a fine not exceeding the statutory maximum.

[Prisoners (Return to Custody) Act 1995, s 1 as amended by the Criminal Justice Act 2003, s 186, the Legal Aid, Sentencing and Punishment of Offenders Act 2012, Sch 10 and the Criminal Justice and Courts Act 2015, s 13, Sch 9.]

7.9377 **3.** *Short title, commencement and extent.*

# Prisoners' Earnings Act 1996[1]

(1996 c 33)

7.9378 **1. Power to make deductions and impose levies** (1) This section applies where—

(*a*) a prisoner is paid for enhanced wages work done by him; and

(*b*) his net weekly earnings in respect of the work exceed such amount as may be prescribed.

(2) Where the prisoner's net weekly earnings fall to be paid by the governor on behalf of the Secretary of State, the governor may make a deduction from those earnings of an amount not exceeding the prescribed percentage of the excess.

(3) Where those earnings fall to be paid otherwise than as mentioned in subsection (2) above, the governor may impose a levy on those earnings of an amount not exceeding that percentage of the excess.

(4) In this section—

"enhanced wages work", in relation to a prisoner, means any work—

(*a*) which is not directed work, that is to say, work which he is directed to do in pursuance of prison rules; and

(*b*) to which the rates of pay and productivity applicable are higher than those that would be applicable if it were directed work;

"net weekly earnings" means weekly earnings after deduction of such of the following as are applicable, namely—

(*a*) income tax;

(*b*) national insurance contributions;

(*c*) payments required to be made by an order of a court; and

(*d*) payments required to be made by virtue of a maintenance calculation within the meaning of the Child Support Act 1991.*

[Prisoners' Earnings Act 1996, s 1 as amended by the Child Support, Pensions and Social Security Act 2000, Sch 3.]

* **Reproduced as amended by the Child Support, Pensions and Social Security Act 2000, Sch 3 and in force in relation to certain cases: see SI 2003/192.**

[1] For commencement of this Act, see note to s 5, post.

7.9379 **2. Application of amounts deducted or levied** (1) Amounts deducted or levied under section 1 above shall be applied, in such proportions as may be prescribed, for the following purposes, namely—

(*a*) the making of payments (directly or indirectly) to such voluntary organisations concerned with victim support or crime prevention or both as may be prescribed;

(*b*) the making of payments into the Consolidated Fund with a view to contributing towards the cost of the prisoner's upkeep;

(*c*) the making of payments to or in respect of such persons (if any) as may be determined by the governor to be dependants of the prisoner in such proportions as may be so determined; and

(*d*) the making of payments into an investment account of a prescribed description with a view to capital and interest being held for the benefit of the prisoner on such terms as may be prescribed.

(2) Where the governor determines under paragraph (*c*) of subsection (1) above that the prisoner has no dependants, any amount which would otherwise have been applied for the purpose mentioned in that paragraph shall be applied for the purpose mentioned in paragraph (*d*) of that subsection.

(3) Where the prisoner is aggrieved by a determination of the governor under subsection (1)(*c*) above, he may appeal against the determination to the Secretary of State.

(4) On such appeal, the Secretary of State may confirm the governor's determination or direct the governor to vary it, so far as relating to amounts deducted or levied after the after the giving of the direction, in such manner as may be specified in the direction.

[Prisoners' Earnings Act 1996, s 2.]

7.9380 **3. Statements of account** (1) The governor shall, for each week in which an amount is deducted or levied under section 1 above, furnish the prisoner with a statement—

(*a*) showing that amount; and

(*b*) giving details of the manner in which the prescribed proportion of that amount is to be applied for the purpose mentioned in section 2(1)(*c*) above.

(2) Where amounts have been deducted or levied under section 1 above, the governor shall, on a request which is neither frivolous nor vexatious, furnish the prisoner with a statement showing the amount for the time being standing to the credit of the investment account mentioned in section 2(1)(*d*) above.

[Prisoners' Earnings Act 1996, s 3.]

7.9381 **4. Interpretation** (1) In the application of this Act to a contracted out prison—

(*a*) any reference to the governor shall be construed as a reference to the director; and

(*b*) the reference to the Secretary of State in section 1 above shall be construed as a reference to the person running the prison.

(2) In the application of this Act to England and Wales—

"contracted out prison" has the meaning given by section 92(1) of the Criminal Justice Act 1991;

"prescribed" means prescribed by prison rules;

"prisoner" includes a prisoner on temporary release and a person required to be detained in a young offender institution or remand centre;*

"prison rules" means rules made under section 47 of the Prison Act 1952.

(3) Scotland

[Prisoners' Earnings Act 1996, s 4.]

* **Words repealed by the Criminal Justice and Court Services Act 2000, Sch 8 from a date to be appointed.**

7.9382 **5. Short title, commencement and extent** (1) This Act may be cited as the Prisoners' Earnings Act 1996

(2) This Act shall come into force on such day as the Secretary of State may by order made by statutory instrument appoint; and different days may be appointed for different purposes[1].

(3) this Act does not extend to Northern Ireland.

[Prisoners' Earnings Act 1996, s 5.]

[1] 26 September 2011 was the date appointed for the coming into force of this Act (except for s 4(3)) by SI 2011/1658.

# Offender Management Act 2007[1]

(2007 c 21)

## Part 1[2]

## New Arrangements for the Provision of Probation Services

*Probation purposes*

7.9383 **1. Meaning of "the probation purposes"** (1) In this Part "the probation purposes" means the purposes of providing for—

(*a*) courts to be given assistance in determining the appropriate sentences to pass, and making other decisions, in respect of persons charged with or convicted of offences;

(*b*) the giving of assistance to persons determining whether conditional cautions should be given and which conditions to attach to conditional cautions;

(*c*) the supervision and rehabilitation of persons charged with or convicted of offences;

(*d*) the giving of assistance to persons remanded on bail;

(*e*) the supervision and rehabilitation of persons to whom conditional cautions are given;

(*f*) the giving of information to victims of persons charged with or convicted of offences.

(2) The purpose set out in subsection (1)(*c*) includes (in particular)—

(*a*) giving effect to community orders and suspended sentence orders (or, in the case of persons mentioned in subsection (3), any corresponding sentence which is to be carried out in England and Wales);

(*b*) assisting in the rehabilitation of offenders who are being held in prison;

(*c*) supervising persons released from prison on licence;

(*d*) providing accommodation in approved premises.

(3) That purpose also applies in relation to persons who—

(*a*) are convicted of an offence under the law of a country outside England and Wales, and

(*b*) receive a sentence which is to any extent to be served or carried out in England and Wales,

as it applies in relation to persons convicted of offences.

(4) In this section—

"conditional caution" has the same meaning as in Part 3 of the Criminal Justice Act 2003 (c 44);

"community order" means—

(*a*) a community order within the meaning of the Criminal Justice Act 2003 (see section 177 of that Act);

(*aa*) a youth rehabilitation order within the meaning of Part 1 of the Criminal Justice and Immigration Act 2008 (see section 1 of that Act);

(*b*) a community order within the meaning of the Powers of Criminal Courts (Sentencing) Act 2000 (c 6) (as it applies to offences committed before 4th April 2005);

(*c*) a youth community order within the meaning of that Act (as it applies to offences committed before section 1 of the Criminal Justice and Immigration Act 2008 comes into force)

"prison" includes a young offender institution, a secure training centre and a secure college;

"suspended sentence order" has the same meaning as in the Criminal Justice Act 2003 (see section 189 of that Act); and

"victim" includes a person claiming to be a victim of a person charged with or convicted of an offence.

(5) Regulations made by the Secretary of State may extend the purposes mentioned in subsection (1) to include other purposes relating to persons charged with or convicted of offences or persons to whom conditional cautions are given.

[Offender Management Act 2007, s 1 as amended by the Criminal Justice and Immigration Act 2008, Schs 4 and 26 and the Criminal Justice and Courts Act 2015, Sch 9.]

---

[1] This Act is to be brought into force in accordance with orders made under s 41. At the date of going to press the following commencement orders had been made:

(No 1 and Transitional Provisions) SI 2007/3001 (ss 16–20, 25–27, 32–38, 39 (part), 40, Sch 3 Parts 2–4, Sch 4 Part 3, Sch 5 Part 2 entries relating to ss 6(2), 7, 17 and 28(5) of the Prison Act 1952, the Race Relations Act 1976, the Criminal Justice Act 1991, the Criminal Justice and Public Order Act 1994; the Freedom of Information Act 2000; and Sch 5, Part 3 the entries relating to the Criminal Justice and Public Order Act 1994; the Powers of Criminal Courts (Sentencing) Act 2000 on 1 November 2007; ss 31, 39 (part) and Sch 5, Part 3, the entry relating to s 202(3)(*b*) of the Criminal Justice Act 2003 on 1 May 2008);

(No 2 and Transitional Provision) SI 2008/504 (ss 5 and 11(2) and Schs 1 and 2 on 1 March 2008; s 3(6), ss 7(1) and (2), 9, 12(1), (2), 13, 14, 21, 22, 23, 24, 39, Sch 1 Part 3, Sch 4 Parts 1 and 2, Sch 5 Part 1 (part) on 1 April 2008) (other provisions have been brought into force in specified areas only);

(No 3) SI 2009/32 (ss 28, 29 (in the following police areas: Derbyshire; Leicestershire; Lincolnshire; Northamptonshire; Nottinghamshire; Staffordshire; Warwickshire; West Mercia; and West Midlands) and s 30 on 19 January 2009);

(No 4) SI 2009/547 (in certain specified areas, ss 1, 2, 3(1)–(5), (7), 4, 6, 7(3), 8, 10, 11(1), 12(3), 15, 39 (in part), Sch 5, Pt 1 (in part);

(No 5) SI 2010/191 (in so far as not already in force ss 1–4, 6–8, 10–12, 15), s 39 (in part), Sch 5, Pt 1 (in part)); and (No 6) SI 2013/1963 (ss 28 and 29 as from 6 January 2014).

[2] Part 1 comprises ss 1–15.

*Functions of the Secretary of State and miscellaneous*

**2–12.** *Secretary of State to ensure that sufficient provision is made throughout England and Wales probation purposes in accordance with the following aims: protection of the public; reduction of re-offending; proper punishment of offenders; ensuring offenders' awareness of the effects of crime on the victims of crimes and the public; and the rehabilitation of offenders. Contractual or other arrangements with other persons for the making of the probation provision. Probation trusts may be established by order*[1] *for purposes including performance of contracts with the Secretary of State. Grants for probation services. National standards for the management of offenders. Annual plans. National framework for qualification of officers. Abolition of local probation boards and transfers of property etc and staff. Renaming of inspectorate as Her Majesty's Inspectorate of Probation for England and Wales.*

1 The following Offender Management Act (Establishment of Probation Trusts) Orders have been made which established trusts in all areas of England and Wales: SI 2008/598, SI 2009/504 and SI 2010/195 amended by SI 2012/1215. However, all 35 remaining probation trusts across England and Wales were formally dissolved on 31 October 2014 (two trusts: Dyfed Powys and South Wales Probation Trust were previously dissolved in 2010). In accordance with powers in s 11 of and Sch 2 to the 2007 Act probation services have been provided since 1 June 2014 by 21 Community Rehabilitation Companies and the National Probation Service.

7.9384 **13. Approved premises** (1) The Secretary of State may approve[1] premises in which accommodation is provided—

(*a*) for persons granted bail in criminal proceedings (within the meaning of the Bail Act 1976 (c 63)); or

(*b*) for, or in connection with, the supervision or rehabilitation of persons convicted of offences;

and in this section "approved premises" means premises which are for the time being approved under this subsection.

(2)–(7) *Regulations and payments*

[Offender Management Act 2007, s 13.]

1 See the Offender Management Act 2007 (Approved Premises) Regulations 2014, SI 2014/1198.

7.9385 **14. Disclosure for offender management purposes** (1) This section applies to—

(*a*) the Secretary of State;

(*b*) a provider of probation services (other than the Secretary of State);

(*c*) an officer of a provider of probation services; and

(*d*) a person carrying out activities in pursuance of arrangements made by a provider of probation services as mentioned in section 3(3)(*c*).

(2) In this section "listed person" means—

(*a*) a government department;

(*b*) a relevant local authority;

(*c*) the Youth Justice Board for England and Wales;

(*d*) the Parole Board for England and Wales;

(*da*) a recall adjudicator (as defined in section 239A of the Criminal Justice Act 2003);

(*e*) a relevant contractor;

(*f*) a chief officer of police;

(*g*) a person who is responsible for securing the electronic monitoring of an individual; and

(*h*) any other person specified or described in regulations made by the Secretary of State.

(3) Information may be disclosed—

(*a*) by a person to whom this section applies—

(i) to another person to whom this section applies, or

(ii) to a listed person, or

(*b*) by a listed person to a person to whom this section applies,

but only if the disclosure is necessary or expedient for any of the purposes mentioned in subsection (4).

(4) Those purposes are—

(*a*) the probation purposes;

(*b*) the performance of functions relating to prisons or prisoners of—

(i) the Secretary of State;

(ii) any other person to whom this section applies; or

(iii) any listed person; and

(*c*) any other purposes connected with the management of offenders (including the development or assessment of policies relating to matters connected with the management of offenders).

(5) In subsection (4)(*b*)—

(*a*) the reference to prisons or prisoners includes a reference to—

(i) young offender institutions or persons detained in such institutions;

(ii) secure training centres or persons detained in such centres; and

(iii) secure colleges or persons detained in them;

(*b*) the reference to functions, in relation to a listed person who is a relevant contractor, includes activities connected with the making or performance of a contract mentioned in subsection (9).

(6) Nothing in this section—

(*a*) affects any power to disclose information that exists apart from this section; or

(*b*) authorises the disclosure of any information in contravention of any provision contained in an enactment (whenever passed or made) which prevents disclosure of the information.

(7) But the Secretary of State may by order amend or repeal any provision mentioned in subsection (6)(*b*) which is contained in an enactment passed or made before the end of the Session in which this Act is passed so as to enable disclosures that would otherwise be permitted under this section.

(8) In this section "relevant local authority" means a county council in England, a Welsh county council or county borough council, a district council, a London borough council, the Common Council of the City of London or the Council of the Isles of Scilly.

(9) In this section "relevant contractor" means—

(*a*) a person who has entered into a contract for the running of, or of part of—

(i) a prison or young offender institution under section 84 of the Criminal Justice Act 1991 (c 53);

(ii) a secure training centre under section 7 of the Criminal Justice and Public Order Act 1994 (c 33);

(iii) a secure college under paragraph 1 of Schedule 10 to the Criminal Justice and Courts Act 2015;

or a sub-contractor of such a person (within the meaning of the provision in question); or

(*b*) a person who has entered into a contract with the Secretary of State—

(i) under section 80 of the Criminal Justice Act 1991 for the purposes of prisoner escort arrangements (see subsection (2) of that section); or

(ii) under paragraph 1 of Schedule 1 to the Criminal Justice and Public Order Act 1994 for the purposes of escort arrangements.

(10) In this section "enactment" includes any subordinate legislation (within the meaning of the Interpretation Act 1978 (c 30).

[Offender Management Act 2007, s 14 as amended by the Criminal Justice and Courts Act 2015, Schs 3, 9, 10.]

## PART 2[1]
## PRISONS

7.9386 **26. Independent monitoring boards** (1) The boards appointed under section 6 of the Prison Act 1952 (boards of visitors) are renamed as independent monitoring boards.

(2), (3) *Amend the Prison Act 1952, s 6.*

[Offender Management Act 2007, s 26.]

---

[1] Part 2 comprises ss 16–27.

## PART 3[1]
## OTHER PROVISIONS ABOUT THE MANAGEMENT OF OFFENDERS

*Polygraph conditions for certain offenders released on licence*

7.9387 **28. Application of polygraph condition** (1) The Secretary of State may include a polygraph condition in the licence of a person to whom this section applies.

(2) This section applies to a person serving a relevant custodial sentence in respect of a relevant sexual offence who—

(*a*) is released on licence by the Secretary of State under any enactment; and

(*b*) is not aged under 18 on the day on which he is released.

(3) In this section "relevant custodial sentence" means—

(*a*) a sentence of imprisonment for a term of twelve months or more (including such a sentence imposed under section 226A or 227 of the Criminal Justice Act 2003 (c 44));

(*b*) a sentence of detention in a young offender institution for a term of twelve months or more;

(*c*) a sentence of detention under section 90 of the Powers of Criminal Courts (Sentencing) Act 2000 (c 6);

(*d*) a sentence of detention under section 91 of the Powers of Criminal Courts (Sentencing) Act 2000 for a period of twelve months or more;

(*e*) a sentence of custody for life under section 93 or 94 of the Powers of Criminal Courts (Sentencing) Act 2000; or

(*f*) a sentence of detention under section 226, 226B or 228 of the Criminal Justice Act 2003.

(4) In this section "relevant sexual offence" means—

(*a*) an offence specified in Part 2 of Schedule 15 to the Criminal Justice Act 2003 (specified sexual offences);

(b) an offence specified in paragraphs 1 to 21 of Schedule 16 to that Act (offences under the law of Scotland); or

(c) an offence specified in Part 2 of Schedule 17 to that Act (offences under the law of Northern Ireland).

(5) In section 250(4) of the Criminal Justice Act 2003 (licence conditions for prisoners serving sentences of imprisonment of twelve months or more etc), in paragraph (*b*)(i) after "Criminal Justice and Court Services Act 2000" there is inserted "or section 28 of the Offender Management Act 2007".

[Offender Management Act 2007, s 28 as amended by the Legal Aid, Sentencing and Punishment of Offenders Act 2012, Sch 21.]

1 Part 3 comprises ss 28–35.

7.9388 **29. Effect of polygraph condition** (1) For the purposes of section 28, a polygraph condition is a condition which requires the released person—

(*a*) to participate in polygraph sessions conducted with a view to—

(i) monitoring his compliance with the other conditions of his licence; or

(ii) improving the way in which he is managed during his release on licence;

(*b*) to participate in those polygraph sessions at such times as may be specified in instructions given by an appropriate officer; and

(*c*) while participating in a polygraph session, to comply with instructions given to him by the person conducting the session ("the polygraph operator").

(2) A polygraph session is a session during which the polygraph operator—

(*a*) conducts one or more polygraph examinations of the released person; and

(*b*) interviews the released person in preparation for, or otherwise in connection with, any such examination.

(3) For the purposes of subsection (2), a polygraph examination is a procedure in which—

(*a*) the polygraph operator questions the released person;

(*b*) the questions and the released person's answers are recorded; and

(*c*) physiological reactions of the released person while being questioned are measured and recorded by means of equipment of a type approved by the Secretary of State.

(4) In subsection (1)(*b*) "appropriate officer" means an officer of a provider of probation services or an officer of a local probation board.

(5) An appropriate officer giving instructions as mentioned in subsection (1)(*b*) must have regard to any guidance issued by the Secretary of State.

(6) The Secretary of State may make rules[1] relating to the conduct of polygraph sessions.

(7) The rules may, in particular—

(*a*) require polygraph operators to be persons who satisfy such requirements as to qualifications, experience and other matters as are specified in the rules;

(*b*) make provision about the keeping of records of polygraph sessions; and

(*c*) make provision about the preparation of reports on the results of polygraph sessions.

(8) The power to make rules under subsection (6) is exercisable by statutory instrument subject to annulment in pursuance of a resolution of either House of Parliament.

[Offender Management Act 2007, s 29.]

1 The Polygraph Rules 2009, SI 2009/619 have been made.

7.9389 **30. Use in criminal proceedings of evidence from polygraph sessions** (1) Evidence of any matter mentioned in subsection (2) may not be used in any proceedings against a released person for an offence.

(2) The matters so excluded are—

(*a*) any statement made by the released person while participating in a polygraph session; and

(*b*) any physiological reactions of the released person while being questioned in the course of a polygraph examination.

(3) In this section "polygraph examination" and "polygraph session" have the same meaning as in section 29.

[Offender Management Act 2007, s 30.]

## PART 4[1]

## SUPPLEMENTAL

1 Part 4 comprises ss 36–42.

SCHEDULE 4

TRANSITIONAL AND TRANSITORY PROVISIONS AND SAVINGS

Section 39

PART 2

PROVISIONS RELATING TO PART 2

*Penalty for offences under sections 40C & 40D of the Prison Act 1952*

**7.9390** **5.** In the application of section 40C and 40D of the Prison Act 1952 (c 52) (inserted by sections 22 and 23) in relation to offences committed before the commencement of section 154(1) of the Criminal Justice Act 2003 (c 44) (limit on magistrates' court's powers to impose imprisonment), the reference in subsection (5)(*b*) of those sections to 12 months is to be read as a reference to 6 months.

PART 3

PROVISIONS RELATING TO PART 3

*Imprisonment of offenders aged 18 or over but under 21*

**6.** (1) Sub-paragraph (2) applies if section 35(4)(*a*) comes into force before the day on which section 61 of the Criminal Justice and Court Services Act 2000 (c 43) (abolition of sentences of detention in a young offender institution, custody for life, etc) comes into force (or fully into force).

(2) The provision that may be made by order under section 38(1) includes provision modifying the provision inserted by section 35(4)(*a*) of this Act with respect to sentences passed, or other things done, at any time before section 61 of that Act comes into force (or fully into force).

*Remand centres*

**7.** If section 59 of the Criminal Justice and Court Services Act 2000 (abolition of remand centres) has not come into force (or fully into force) before the coming into force of paragraph 18(2) of Schedule 3, that paragraph has effect until section 59 of the Criminal Justice and Court Services Act 2000 comes into force (or comes fully into force) as if after "prison" (in the second place it occurs) there were inserted ", remand centre".

# Prisons (Interference with Wireless Telegraphy) Act 2012[1]

(2012 c 20)

**7.9391** **1. Interference with wireless telegraphy in prisons etc** (1) The appropriate national authority may authorise the person in charge of a relevant institution to interfere with wireless telegraphy.

(2) An interference with wireless telegraphy authorised under subsection (1) may be carried out only for the purpose of—

(*a*) preventing the use within the institution of an item specified in subsection (3), or

(*b*) detecting or investigating the use within the institution of such an item.

(3) The specified items are—

(*a*) a device capable of transmitting or receiving images, sounds or information by electronic communications (including a mobile telephone);

(*b*) a component part of such a device;

(*c*) an article designed or adapted for use with such a device (including any disk, film or other separate article on which images, sounds or information may be recorded).

(4) The interference with wireless telegraphy that may be authorised by virtue of subsection (2)(*b*) is for the collection of traffic data in relation to an electronic communication and (subject to the provisions of this Act) such an authorisation permits the retention, use and disclosure of that data.

(5) Conduct to which this subsection applies is lawful for all purposes.

(6) The conduct to which subsection (5) applies is—

(*a*) interference with wireless telegraphy that—

(i) is authorised under subsection (1), and

(ii) is carried out in accordance with subsection (2) and any direction given under section 2,

(*b*) the retention, use or disclosure of any traffic data, collected as a result of such an interference with wireless telegraphy, which is carried out in accordance with this Act.

(7) Section 8(1) of the Wireless Telegraphy Act 2006 (requirement for a licence to establish or use a wireless telegraphy station or to instal or use wireless telegraphy apparatus) does not apply in relation to anything done for the purposes of carrying out an interference with wireless telegraphy authorised under this section.

(8) An authorisation under this section must be in writing.

[Prisons (Interference with Wireless Telegraphy) Act 2012, s 1.]

---

1 For commencement, see s 5, post.

**7.9392** **2. Safeguards** (1) Before the appropriate national authority authorises an interference with wireless telegraphy under section 1 it must be satisfied any equipment that will be used as a result of the authorisation is fit for the purpose.

(2) Where the appropriate national authority authorises an interference with wireless telegraphy under section 1 it must inform the Office of Communications.

(3) A person in charge of a relevant institution who is authorised to interfere with wireless telegraphy under section 1 must act in accordance with directions given under this section.

(4) Where the appropriate national authority authorises an interference with wireless telegraphy under section 1, it must give directions to the person so authorised—

(*a*) specifying descriptions of information to be provided to the Office of Communications;
(*b*) specifying intervals at, or occurrences on, which such information is to be so provided;
(*c*) as to the circumstances in which the use of equipment for the purposes of an interference with wireless telegraphy authorised under section 1 must be modified or discontinued (and, in particular, directions aimed at ensuring that the authorised interference will not result in disproportionate interference with wireless telegraphy outside the relevant institution).

(5) The appropriate national authority may give such other directions to a person mentioned in subsection (4) as it considers necessary or desirable for the purposes of this Act.

(6) A direction under this section must be in writing.

[Prisons (Interference with Wireless Telegraphy) Act 2012, s 2.]

7.9393 **3. Retention and disclosure of information obtained under section 1** (1) Information obtained by virtue of section 1 must be destroyed no later than 3 months after it was obtained unless the person in charge of the relevant institution has authorised its retention.

(2) The person in charge of a relevant institution may not give an authorisation under subsection (1) unless satisfied—

(*a*) that the retention of the information is necessary on one or more of the grounds specified in subsection (8), and
(*b*) that the retention is proportionate to what is sought to be achieved by it.

(3) Where information is retained under subsection (1) the person in charge of the relevant institution must review, at intervals of not more than 3 months, whether its retention remains in accordance with that subsection.

(4) If, on a review under subsection (3), the person in charge of the relevant institution is not satisfied that the retention of information remains in accordance with subsection (1), that person must arrange for the information to be destroyed.

(5) Information obtained by virtue of section 1(2)(*b*) may be disclosed to—

(*a*) an officer of the relevant institution;
(*b*) an employee authorised for the purposes of this section by the person in charge of the institution;
(*c*) the Secretary of State;
(*d*) if the relevant institution is in Scotland, the Scottish Ministers.

(6) Information obtained by virtue of section 1(2)(*b*) may not be disclosed to any other person unless the person in charge of the relevant institution has authorised its disclosure.

(7) An authorisation under subsection (6) may be given only where the person in charge of the relevant institution is satisfied that—

(*a*) the disclosure is necessary on one or more of the grounds specified in subsection (8), and
(*b*) the disclosure is proportionate to what is sought to be achieved by it.

(8) The specified grounds are—

(*a*) the interests of national security,
(*b*) the prevention, detection, investigation or prosecution of crime,
(*c*) the interests of public safety,
(*d*) securing or maintaining security or good order and discipline in the relevant institution,
(*e*) the protection of health or morals.

(9) An authorisation under this section must be in writing.

[Prisons (Interference with Wireless Telegraphy) Act 2012, s 3.]

7.9394 **4. Interpretation** (1) In this Act—

"the appropriate national authority" means—

(*a*) in relation to a relevant institution in England or Wales, the Secretary of State;
(*b*) in relation to a relevant institution in Scotland, the Scottish Ministers;

"relevant institution" means—

(*a*) a prison in England, Wales or Scotland;
(*b*) a young offender institution in England or Wales;
(*c*) a young offenders institution in Scotland;
(*d*) a secure training centre in England or Wales;
(*e*) a secure college in England or Wales;

"wireless telegraphy" has the same meaning as in the Wireless Telegraphy Act 2006 and, in relation to wireless telegraphy, "interfere" has the same meaning as in that Act.

(2) In this Act reference to the person in charge of a relevant institution is—

(*a*) in relation to a prison, its governor or, in the case of a contracted-out institution in England, Wales or Scotland, its director;
(*b*) in the case of a young offender institution or a secure training centre in England or Wales, its governor or, in the case of a contracted-out institution, its director;
(*ba*) in the case of a secure college in England or Wales, its principal;
(*c*) in the case of a young offenders institution in Scotland, its governor or, in the case of a contracted-out institution, its director.

(3) For the purposes of subsection (2) an institution is "contracted-out" if—

(*a*) in England or Wales, it is a contracted out prison within the meaning of Part 4 of the Criminal Justice Act 1991 (see section 84(4) of that Act);

(*b*) in Scotland, it is a contracted out prison within the meaning of Chapter 2 of Part 8 of the Criminal Justice and Public Order Act 1994 (see section 106(4) of that Act);

(*c*) in the case of a secure training centre in England or Wales, it is provided or run in accordance with a contract made under section 7 of the Criminal Justice and Public Order Act 1994.

(4) In this Act "traffic data" means data—

(*a*) which is comprised in, attached to or logically associated with a communication (whether by the sender or otherwise) for the purposes of a telecommunication system by means of which the communication is being or may be transmitted, and

(*b*) which—

(i) identifies, or purports to identify, any person, apparatus or location to or from which the communication is or may be transmitted,

(ii) identifies or selects, or purports to identify or select, apparatus through which, or by means of which, the communication is or may be transmitted,

(iii) comprises signals for the actuation of apparatus used for the purposes of a telecommunication system for effecting (in whole or in part) the transmission of the communication,

(iv) identifies, or purports to identify, the time at which an event relating to the communication occurs, or

(v) identifies data as comprised in, attached to or logically associated with the communication.

The references in this subsection to a telecommunication system by means of which a communication is being or may be transmitted include, in relation to data comprising signals for the actuation of apparatus, any telecommunication system in which that apparatus is comprised.

(5) Data identifying a computer file or computer program access to which is obtained, or which is run, by means of the communication is not "traffic data" except to the extent that the file or program is identified by reference to the apparatus in which it is stored.

(6) In this section "telecommunication system" has the same meaning as it has for the purposes of the Regulation of Investigatory Powers Act 2000.*

[Prisons (Interference with Wireless Telegraphy) Act 2012, s 4 as amended by the Criminal Justice and Courts Act 2015, Sch 9.]

* **Amended by the Investigatory Powers Act 2016, Sch 10 from a date to be appointed.**

**7.9395** **5. Final provisions** (1) This Act extends to England and Wales and Scotland.

(2) Her Majesty may by Order in Council provide for this Act to extend with modifications to any of the Channel Islands or the Isle of Man.

(3) Sections 1 to 4 of this Act come into force on such day as the appropriate authority may by order[1] appoint.

(4) In subsection (3) "the appropriate authority" means—

(*a*) so far as this Act extends to England and Wales, the Secretary of State;

(*b*) so far as this Act extends to Scotland, the Scottish Ministers.

(5) An order made under subsection (3) by the Secretary of State must be made by statutory instrument.

(6) This Act may be cited as the Prisons (Interference with Wireless Telegraphy) Act 2012.

[Prisons (Interference with Wireless Telegraphy) Act 2012, s 5.]

1 The Prisons (Interference with Wireless Telegraphy) Act 2012 (Commencement) (England and Wales) Order 2013, SI 2013/2460 appointed 21 October 2013 for the coming into force of ss 1 to 4.

## Secure Training Centre Rules 1998[1]

(SI 1998/472 amended by SI 2003/3005 and SI 2007/1709)

**7.9396** 1. *Citation and commencement* These Rules may be cited as the Secure Training Centre Rules 1998 and shall come into force on 16th April 1998.

1 Made by the Secretary of State, in pursuance of s 47 of the Prison Act 1952 and s 7 of the Criminal Justice and Public Order Act 1994. Security Training Orders made under the 1994 Act have been replaced by the Detention and Training Orders made under the Crime and Disorder Act 1998 with effect from 1 April 2000.

**7.9397** 2. *Interpretation* In these Rules unless the contrary intention appears the expression:

"centre" means a secure training centre;

"compulsory school age" has the meaning assigned to it in section 8 of the Education Act 1996;

"convicted trainee" means a trainee who has been ordered to be detained in consequence of his conviction for an offence, and the expression "unconvicted trainee" shall be construed accordingly;

"governor" includes an officer for the time being in charge of a centre;

"independent person" means a person appointed under rule 44 to visit centres and to whom representations may be made by trainees;

"legal adviser" means, in relation to a trainee, his counsel or solicitor, and includes a clerk acting on behalf of his solicitor;
"officer" means an officer of a centre; and
"trainee" means a person detained in a centre.

**7.9398** 3. *Statement of purpose* (1) The aims of a centre shall be—
(*a*) to accommodate trainees in a safe environment within secure conditions; and
(*b*) to help trainees prepare for their return to the outside community.
(2) The aim mentioned in paragraph (1)(*b*) above shall be achieved, in particular, by—
(*a*) providing a positive regime offering high standards of education and training;
(*b*) in the case of convicted trainees, establishing a programme designed to tackle the offending behaviour of each trainee and to assist in his development;
(*c*) fostering links between the trainee and the outside community; and
(*d*) in the case of convicted trainees, co-operating with the services responsible for the trainee's supervision after release.
(3) A statement of the aims mentioned in paragraph (1) above and how they are to be achieved shall be prepared and displayed in each centre and shall be made available on request—
(*a*) to trainees;
(*b*) to any person visiting the centre; and
(*c*) to any person inspecting the centre.

**7.9399** 4. *Classification* Trainees may be classified, in accordance with any direction of the Secretary of State, taking into account their ages, characters and circumstances.

**7.9400** 5. *Temporary release* (1) A trainee may be temporarily released for any period or periods and subject to any conditions.
(2) A trainee released under this rule may be recalled at any time whether any conditions of his release have been broken or not.

**7.9401** 6. *Privileges* (1) There shall be established at every centre systems of privileges, incentives and sanctions approved by the Secretary of State and appropriate to the classes of trainees and their ages, characters and circumstances.
(2) Records shall be kept in writing of any privileges or incentives earned and sanctions awarded.

**7.9402** 7. *Information to trainees*

**7.9403** 8. *Grievance procedure* (1) There shall be established and administered at each centre a comprehensive grievance procedure, approved by the Secretary of State, to which each trainee and his parent shall have access.
(2) Every request by a trainee to see the governor or an independent person shall be recorded by the officer to whom it is made and promptly passed on to the governor.
(3) On every day, the governor shall hear any requests to see him that are made under paragraph (2) above.
(4) Where a trainee has asked to see an independent person, the governor shall ensure that that person is told of the request as soon as possible.
(5) A written request or complaint under the grievance procedure established under this rule may be made in confidence.

**7.9404** 9. *Visits generally* (1) There shall be established at every centre arrangements, approved by the Secretary of State, for trainees to receive visits.
(2) Arrangements established under paragraph (1) above shall take account of—
(*a*) the importance of contact by a trainee with his family, and
(*b*) the need to keep to a minimum any disruption of his education and training.
(3) Subject to the provisions of these Rules, the governor may give such directions as he thinks fit for the supervision of visits to trainees, either generally or in a particular case:
Provided that such directions shall be designed to secure that supervision is not unnecessarily intrusive.

**7.9405** 10. *Letters generally* (1) The Secretary of State may, with a view to securing discipline and good order or the prevention of crime or in the interests of any persons, impose restrictions, either generally or in a particular case, upon the communications to be permitted between a trainee and other persons.
(2) Except as provided by these Rules, a trainee shall not be permitted to communicate with any outside person, or that person with him, without the leave of the Secretary of State.
(3) Except as provided by these Rules, every letter or communication to or from a trainee may be read or examined by the governor or any officer deputed by him and the governor may, at his discretion, stop any communication on the ground that its contents are objectionable or of inordinate length.

**7.9406** 11. *Personal letters, telephone calls and visits* (1) A trainee shall be entitled—
(*a*) to send three letters a week, the cost of which shall be met by the centre; and
(*b*) to receive a visit once a week.
(2) Subject to the provisions of these Rules a trainee shall in addition to his entitlement under paragraph (1) above be entitled to send any number of letters at his own expense, to receive any number of letters, to make and receive any number of telephone calls at his own expense and to receive visits.
(3) The normal duration of a visit to which a trainee is entitled by virtue of paragraph (1)(*b*) above shall be one hour.

**7.9407** *12. Police interviews* A police officer may, on production of an order issued by or on behalf of a chief officer of police, interview any trainee willing to see him.

**7.9408** *13. Legal advisers* (1) The legal adviser of a trainee in any legal proceedings, civil or criminal, to which the trainee is a party shall be afforded reasonable facilities for interviewing him in connection with those proceedings and may do so out of hearing of an officer.
(2) A trainee's legal adviser may, with the leave of the Secretary of State, interview the trainee in connection with any other legal business.

**7.9409** *14. Correspondence with legal advisers and courts* (1) A trainee may correspond with his legal adviser and any court and such correspondence may only be opened, read or stopped by the governor in accordance with the provisions of this rule.
(2) Correspondence to which this rule applies may be opened if the governor has reasonable cause to believe that it contains an illicit enclosure and any such enclosure shall be dealt with in accordance with the other provisions of these Rules.
(3) Correspondence to which this rule applies may be opened, read and stopped if the governor has reasonable cause to believe its contents endanger security in the centre or the safety of others or are otherwise of a criminal nature.
(4) A trainee shall be given the opportunity to be present when any correspondence to which this rule applies is opened and shall be informed if it or any enclosure is to be read or stopped.
(5) A trainee shall on request be provided with any writing materials necessary for the purposes of paragraph (1) of this rule.
(6) In this rule, "court" includes the European Commission of Human Rights, the European Court of Human Rights and the European Court of Justice; and "illicit enclosure" includes any article possession of which has not been authorised in accordance with the other provisions of these Rules and any correspondence to or from a person other than the trainee concerned, his legal adviser or a court.

**7.9410** *15. Clothing*

**7.9411** *16. Food*

**7.9412** *17. Alcohol and tobacco*

**7.9413** *18. Accommodation*

**7.9414** *19. Beds and bedding*

**7.9415** *20. Hygiene*

**7.9416** *21. Library books*

**7.9417** *22. Medical attendance*

**7.9418** *23. Self-harm and suicide assessment* (1) Every trainee shall, as soon as possible after his reception into the centre and in any case within 24 hours, be interviewed by a social worker and by a member of the healthcare staff with a view to assessing whether and, if so, the extent to which he has suicidal intentions or a propensity to harm himself.
(2) A written assessment of the trainee shall be prepared as soon as practicable after such an interview has concluded.
(3) The assessment prepared under paragraph (2) above shall be reviewed at regular intervals throughout the period of the trainee's detention in the centre and each trainee shall be monitored by a social worker or member of healthcare staff for that purpose.

**7.9419** *24. Special illnesses and conditions* (1) The medical officer shall report to the governor on the case of any trainee whose health is likely to be injuriously affected by continued detention or any conditions of detention. The governor shall send the report to the Secretary of State without delay together with his own recommendations.
(2) The medical officer shall pay special attention to any trainee whose mental condition appears to require it, and make any special arrangements which appear necessary for his supervision or care.
(3) The medical officer shall inform the governor immediately if he suspects any trainee of having suicidal intentions or a propensity to harm himself, and the trainee shall be placed under special observation.

**7.9420** *25. Notification of illness or death* (1) If a trainee dies or becomes seriously ill, sustains any serious injury or is removed to hospital on account of mental disorder, the governor shall at once inform the trainee's parent or guardian, and also any person who the trainee may reasonably have asked should be informed.
(2) If a trainee dies, the governor shall give notice immediately to the coroner having jurisdiction, to the Secretary of State and to the person authorised under rule 43(1) to inspect the centre.

**7.9421** *26. Religious observance*

**7.9422** *27. Regime activities* (1) A trainee shall be occupied in education, training, physical education and, in the case of a convicted trainee, programmes designed to tackle offending behaviour provided in accordance with rule 3 of these Rules.
(2) For the purpose of determining the appropriate activities under this rule for individual trainees, each trainee shall be assessed as soon as practicable after the date of his reception into the centre and, within 2 weeks of that date, a training plan shall be prepared.
(3) The training plan for each trainee shall be reviewed—
(*a*) in the case of a trainee who is ordered to be detained for a period of 6 months or less or an unconvicted trainee, every two months; and

(*b*) in the case of a trainee who is ordered to be detained for a period of more than 6 months, every three months.

(4) The preparation and reviewing of a trainee's training plan shall be undertaken in consultation with—

(*a*) in the case of a convicted trainee, the services responsible for the trainee's supervision after release;

(*b*) in the case of an unconvicted trainee, an officer of the local authority which is looking after the trainee (within the meaning of section 22(1) of the Children Act 1989); and

(*c*) in all cases, the trainee's parent or guardian.

(5) An officer of the centre shall be nominated by the governor for the purposes of preparing, supervising and reviewing the training plan of each trainee and carrying out the consultation referred to in paragraph (4) above.

(6) The medical officer or a member of the healthcare staff may excuse a trainee from any activity on medical grounds; and no trainee shall be set to participate in any activity for which he is considered by the medical officer or, as the case may be, member of healthcare staff, to be unfit.

**7.9423** *28. Education and training*

**7.9424** *29. Outside contacts*

**7.9425** *30. After care* (1) From the beginning of his period of detention, consideration shall be given to a trainee's future and the help to be given to him in preparation for and after his return to the community, in consultation with the appropriate supervising service, in the case of a convicted trainee, or an officer of the local authority which is looking after the trainee (within the meaning of section 22(1) of the Children Act 1989), in the case of an unconvicted trainee.

(2) Every convicted trainee shall be given a careful explanation of his liability to supervision after release and the requirements to which he will be subject while under supervision.

(3) The training plan prepared for a trainee under rule 27 of these Rules shall have regard to the need to help the trainee in preparation for and after his return to the community and, in the case of a trainee who will be of compulsory school age at the date of that return, to education in the community.

**7.9426** *31. Maintenance of order and discipline* (1) Order and discipline shall be maintained in a centre, but with no more restriction than is required in the interests of security and well-ordered community life.

(2) In the control of trainees, officers shall seek to influence them through their own example and leadership, and to enlist their willing co-operation.

**7.9427** *32. Custody outside a centre* (1) A trainee being taken to or from a centre in custody shall be exposed as little as possible to public observation and proper care shall be taken to protect him from curiosity and insult.

(2) A trainee required to be taken in custody anywhere outside a centre shall be kept in the custody of a custody officer or of a police officer.

**7.9428** *33. Search* (1) Every trainee shall be searched on his reception into a centre and subsequently as the governor thinks necessary.

(2) A trainee shall be searched in as seemly a manner as is consistent with discovering anything concealed.

(3) No trainee shall be stripped and searched—

(*a*) without the authority of the governor;

(*b*) in the presence of more than two officers; and

(*c*) in the sight of another trainee or in the sight or presence of an officer not of the same sex.

(4) A written record shall be kept of any search to which paragraph (3) above applies which shall specify—

(*a*) the name of the trainee;

(*b*) the reason for the search;

(*c*) when the search was carried out;

(*d*) who authorised the search and who carried it out; and

(*e*) what, if anything, was found as a result of the search.

**7.9429** *34. Record and photograph* (1) A personal record of each trainee shall be prepared, maintained and preserved in such manner and for such period as the Secretary of State may direct, but no part of the record shall be disclosed to any person not authorised to receive it.

(2) Every trainee may be photographed on reception and subsequently, but no copy of the photograph shall be given to any person not authorised to receive it.

**7.9430** *35. Trainees' property* (1) Anything, other than cash, which a trainee has at a centre and which he is not allowed to retain for his own use shall be taken into the governor's custody and shall be listed in an inventory.

(2) Any cash which a trainee has at a centre shall be paid into an account under the control of the governor and the trainee shall be credited with the amount in the books of the centre.

(3) The governor may confiscate any unauthorised article found in the possession of a trainee after his reception into a centre, or concealed or deposited within a centre.

**7.9431** *36. Removal from association* (1) Where it appears to be necessary for the purposes of ensuring good order and discipline or in the interests of preventing him from causing significant harm to himself or to any other person or significant damage to property that a trainee should not associate with other trainees, either generally or for particular purposes, the governor may

arrange for the trainee's removal from association accordingly.
(2) A trainee shall not be removed under this rule unless all other appropriate methods of control have been applied without success.
(3) A trainee who is placed in his own room during normal waking hours in accordance with arrangements made under this rule shall—
(*a*) be observed at least once in every period of 15 minutes;
(*b*) not be left unaccompanied during normal waking hours for a continuous period of more than 3 hours nor for periods which total in aggregate more than 3 hours in any period of 24 hours;
(*c*) be released from the room as soon as it is no longer necessary for the purposes mentioned in paragraph (1) above that he be removed from association; and
(*d*) be informed both orally and in writing of the reasons for such placement.
(4) A record shall be kept of each occasion on which a trainee is removed from association under this rule which shall specify—
(*a*) the name of the trainee;
(*b*) the date and time removal commenced and finished;
(*c*) who authorised it;
(*d*) the reasons for it and that the trainee was informed in accordance with paragraph (3)(*d*) above; and
(*e*) any observations made in accordance with paragraph (3)(*a*) above;
and the record kept in accordance with this paragraph shall be made available, upon request, to the person authorised under rule 43(1) of these Rules to inspect the centre.

**7.9432** 37. *Use of force* (1) An officer in dealing with a trainee shall not use force unnecessarily and, when the application of force to a trainee is necessary, no more force than is necessary shall be used.
(2) No officer shall act deliberately in a manner calculated to provoke a trainee.

**7.9433** 38. *Physical restraint*[1] (1) No trainee shall be physically restrained save where necessary for the purpose of ensuring good order and discipline or for the purpose of preventing him from—
(*a*) escaping from custody;
(*b*) injuring himself or others;
(*c*) damaging property; or
(*d*) inciting another trainee to do anything specified in paragraph (*b*) or (*c*) above,
and then only where no alternative method of ensuring good order and discipline or of preventing the event specified in any of paragraphs (*a*) to (*d*) above is available.
(2) No trainee shall be physically restrained under this rule except in accordance with methods approved by the Secretary of State and by an officer who has undergone a course of training which is so approved.
(3) Particulars of every occasion on which a trainee is physically restrained under this rule shall be recorded within 12 hours of its occurrence.

[1] The Secure Training Centres (Amendment) Rules 2007, SI 2007/1709 which introduced the provision authorising the use of physical restraint for the purposes of ensuring good order and discipline, were declared ultra vires as being in breach of requirements to consult under the Race Relations Act 1976 and the Children Act 2004 and in breach of Convention rights: *R (on the application of C) v Secretary of State for Justice* [2008] EWCA Civ 882, [2009] QB 657, [2009] 2 WLR 1039.

**7.9434** 39. ***Officers of secure training centres***

**7.9435** 40. ***Prohibited articles***

**7.9436** 41. ***Control of persons and vehicles***

**7.9437** 42. *Viewing of secure training centres* (1) No outside person shall be permitted to view a centre unless authorised by the Secretary of State.
(2) No person viewing a centre shall be permitted to take a photograph, make a sketch or communicate with a trainee unless authorised by the Secretary of State.

**7.9438** 43. *Inspection of centres* (1) The Secretary of State may cause any centre to be inspected by persons who are for the time being authorised to conduct inspections under section 80 of the Children Act 1989.
(2) A person conducting an inspection under this rule may be accompanied by Her Majesty's Chief Inspector of Prisons or a person designated by him and by one or more of Her Majesty's Inspectors of Schools in England.
(3) Any person conducting an inspection under this rule or accompanying him in accordance with paragraph (2) above may for that purpose—
(*a*) enter any part of the premises of the centre;
(*b*) conduct an interview with any officer or trainee; and
(*c*) examine any records relating to the centre.
(4) A person who has conducted an inspection under this rule shall report in writing to the Secretary of State and the report shall be published in such manner as the Secretary of State may direct.

**7.9439** 44. *Appointment of independent persons* (1) The Secretary of State may appoint independent persons to visit a centre.
(2) Any trainee may make representations to a person appointed under this rule; and for that purpose the governor shall make arrangements for such a person to interview the trainee and to

receive representations from him.

(3) A person appointed under this rule shall be entitled to have access to any records relating to the centre except that the medical records relating to any trainee or the personal records of any officer shall not be made available to him without the consent of the trainee or, as the case may be, officer concerned.

(4) A person appointed under this rule shall draw to the attention of the Secretary of State any matter which is of concern to him.

**7.9440** *45. Delegation by governor*

**7.9441** *46. Contracted-out secure training centres* (1) In their application to a centre which is a contracted-out secure training centre these Rules shall have effect with the following modifications.

(2) For any reference to the governor there shall be substituted a reference to the director.

(3) For any reference to an officer there shall be substituted a reference to a custody officer.

(4) In rule 6(2), at the end there shall be added the words "and the monitor shall be entitled to have access to such records".

(5) In rule 8, at the end there shall be added the following paragraph:

"(6) Where a person is dissatisfied with the outcome of any request or complaint made by him under the grievance procedure established under this rule he may appeal to the monitor, who shall thereupon consider the request or complaint, and any such appeal may be made in confidence."

(6) In rule 10, at the end there shall be added the following paragraph:

"(4) No letter or communication shall be read or examined, and no communication shall be stopped, under paragraph (3) above without the approval of the monitor."

(7) In rule 15(2), at the end there shall be added the words "and the trainee may appeal from that refusal to the monitor".

(8) In rule 24, at the end there shall be added the following paragraph:

"(4) The monitor shall be informed as soon as practicable and in any event within 12 hours of any trainee having been placed under special observation under paragraph (3) above."

(9) In rule 25—

(*a*) in paragraph (1) after the word "inform" there shall be inserted the words "the monitor,"; and

(*b*) at the end there shall be added the following paragraph:

"(3) If a trainee in respect of whom notification is given under paragraph (1) above has suffered serious harm, or it is alleged that he has been the subject of any form of abuse, notification shall also be given to a constable and, if in the opinion of the director such harm or abuse is caused by the conduct of any custody officer or other member of the staff of the centre, the monitor."

(10) In the rule 29(3), at the end there shall be added the words "and subject to the approval of the monitor".

(11) In rule 33, at the end there shall be added the following paragraph:

"(5) The monitor shall be informed within 24 hours of any search to which paragraph (3) above applies and he shall be provided with a copy of the record kept under paragraph (4) above of that search."

(12) In rule 36, at the end there shall be added the following paragraph:

"(5) The monitor shall be informed within 24 hours of the commencement of any removal from association under this rule and he shall be provided with a copy of the record kept under paragraph (4) above in relation to that removal."

(13) In rule 38(3), after the word "recorded" there shall be inserted the words "and notified to the monitor".

(14) After rule 45 there shall be inserted the following rule:

**"45A** (1) The monitor appointed by the Secretary of State in relation to a contracted-out centre shall have the functions specified in respect of him in the foregoing provisions of these Rules as they have effect in accordance with rule 46 of these Rules.

(2) The director appointed by the contractor in relation to a contracted-out centre shall have—

(*a*) the functions specified in respect of him in the foregoing provisions of these Rules as they have effect in accordance with rule 46 of these Rules; and

(*b*) the following additional functions, namely—

(*i*) to promote and safeguard the welfare of the trainees detained in that centre;

(ii) to co-operate with the monitor appointed in relation to that centre and to facilitate the discharge by him of his duties and functions; and

(iii) to issue a notice to each convicted trainee prior to his release from the centre which specifies the requirements with which he must comply following his release."

## Prison Rules 1999[1]

(SI 1999/728 amended by SI 2000/1794 and 2641, SI 2001/1149, SI 2002/2116, SI 2003/3301, SI 2005/869 and 3437, SI 2006/680, SI 2007/2594 and 3149, SI 2008/597, SI 2009/3082, SI 2011/1663, SI 2013/235 and 2462, SI 2014/2169, SI 2015/1638, SI 2016/583 and 945 and SI 2017/576)

### Part I Interpretation

#### General

**7.9442** *1. Citation and commencement* These Rules may be cited as the Prison Rules 1999 and shall come into force on 1st April 1999.

[1] Made by the Secretary of State under the Prison Act 1962, s 47. Note the amendments introduced by the Prison and Young Offender Institution (Amendment) Rules 2014, SI 2014/2169, SI 2015/1638 and SI 2016/583.

**7.9443** 2. *Interpretation* (1) In these Rules, where the context so admits, the expression—

"adjudicator" means a District Judge (Magistrates' Courts) or Deputy District Judge (Magistrates' Courts) approved[1] by the Lord Chancellor for the purpose of inquiring into a charge which has been referred to him;

"communication" includes any written or drawn communication from a prisoner to any other person, whether intended to be transmitted by means of a postal service or not, and any communication from a prisoner to any other person transmitted by means of a telecommunications system;

"controlled drug" means any drug which is a controlled drug for the purposes of the Misuse of Drugs Act 1971;

"convicted prisoner" means, subject to the provisions of rule 7(3), a prisoner who has been convicted[2] or found guilty of an offence or committed or attached for contempt of court or for failing to do or abstain from doing anything required to be done or left undone, and the expression "unconvicted prisoner" shall be construed accordingly;

"fixed term prisoner has the meaning assigned to it by section 237(1) of the Criminal Justice Act 2003";

"governor" includes an officer for the time being in charge of a prison;

"health care professional" means a person who is a member of a profession regulated by a body mentioned in section 25(3) of the National Health Service Reform and Health Care Professions Act 2002 and who is working within the prison;

"health care provider" includes any provider of health services, whether or not commissioned by an NHS body (within the meaning given by section 275(1) of the National Health Service 2006);

"information technology equipment" includes any laptop or notebook computer, desktop computer, gaming console, handheld computing device, personal organiser or any electronic device containing a computer processor and capable of connecting to the internet, and any reference to information technology equipment includes a reference to–

(*a*) a component part of a device of that description; or

(*b*) any article designed or adapted for use with any information technology equipment (including any disk, film or other separate article on which images, sounds, computer code or other information may be stored or recorded);

"intercepted material" means the contents of any communication intercepted pursuant to these Rules;

"intermittent custody order" has the meaning assigned to it by section 183 of the Criminal Justice Act 2003;

"legal adviser" means, in relation to a prisoner, his counsel or solicitor, and includes a clerk acting on behalf of his solicitor;

"officer" means an officer of a prison and, for the purposes of rule 40(2), includes a prisoner custody officer who is authorised to perform escort functions in accordance with section 89 of the Criminal Justice Act 1991;

"prison minister" means, in relation to a prison, a minister appointed to that prison under section 10 of the Prison Act 1952;

"specified drug" means any product or substance containing one or more of the following—

(a) AB-PINACA (N-[(1S)-1-(aminocarbonyl)-2-methylpropyl]-1-pentyl-1H-indazole- 3-carboxamide);

(b) 5F-AB-PINACA (N-[(1S)-1-(aminocarbonyl)-2-methylpropyl]-1-(5- Fluoropentyl)-1H-indazole-3-carboxamide);

(c) AB-FUBINACA (N-[(1S)-1-(aminocarbonyl)-2-methylpropyl]-1-[(4-fluorophenyl)methyl]-1H-indazole-3-carboxamide);

(d) APICA (1-pentyl-N-tricyclo[3.3.1.13,7]dec-1-yl-1H-indole-3-carboxamide);

(e) 5F-APICA (N-(adamantan-1-yl)-1-(5-fluoropentyl)-1H-indole-3-carboxamide);

(f) APINACA (1-pentyl-N-tricyclo[3.3.1.13,7]dec-1-yl-1H-indazole-3-carboxamide);

(g) 5F-APINACA (1-(5-fluoropentyl)-N-tricyclo[3.3.1.13,7]dec-1-yl-1H-indazole-3-carboxamide);

(h) 5F-PB22 (1-(5-fluoropentyl)-8-quinolinyl ester-1H-indole-3-carboxylic acid),

(i) MDMB-CHMICA (methyl 2-{[1-(cyclohexylmethyl)-1H-indol-3-yl]formamido}- 3,3-dimethylbutanoate);

(j) PB-22 (Quinolin-8-yl-1-pentyl-1H-indole-3-carboxylate);

(k) 5F-MDMB-PINACA (Methyl-[2-(1-(5-fluoropentyl)-1H-indazole-3- carboxamido)-3,3-dimethylbutanoate]);

(l) AB-CHMINACA (N-[-1-(Aminocarbonyl)-2-methylpropyl]-1- (cyclohexylmethyl)-1H-indazole-3-carboxamide);

(m) 5F-AMB (Methyl 2-({[1-(5-fluoropentyl)-1H-indazol-3-yl]carbonyl}amino)-3-methylbutanoate);

(n) AMB-FUBINACA (Methyl-2-(1-(4-fluorobenzyl)-1H-indazole-3-carboxamide)-3-methylbutanoate);

(o) Etizolam (4-(2-Chlorophenyl)-2-ethyl-9-methyl-6H-thieno[3,2- f][1,2,4]triazolo[4,3-a][1,4]diazepine);

(p) ADB-CHMINACA (N-[1-(aminocarbonyl)-2,2-dimethylpropyl]-1-(cyclohexylmethyl)-1H-indazole-3-carboxamide);

"telecommunications system" means any system (including the apparatus comprised in it) which exists for the purpose of facilitating the transmission of communications by any means involving the use of electrical or electro-magnetic energy;

"the 2003 Act" means the Criminal Justice Act 2003.

(2) In these Rules—

(*a*) a reference to an award of additional days means additional days awarded under these Rules by virtue of section 42 of the Criminal Justice Act 1991 or by virtue of section 257 of the 2003 Act;

(*b*) a reference to the Church of England includes a reference to the Church in Wales; and

(*c*) a reference to a numbered rule is, unless otherwise stated, a reference to the rule of that number in these Rules and a reference in a rule to a numbered paragraph is, unless otherwise stated, a reference to the paragraph of that number in that rule.

---

[1] The requirement of the approval of the Lord Chancellor for the appointment of a District Judge (Magistrates' Courts) or Deputy District Judge (Magistrates' Courts) as an adjudicator does not apply to a person who is approved to act as an adjudicator on 18 April 2005, and such a person may continue to act as an adjudicator for so long as he holds office as a District Judge (Magistrates' Courts) or Deputy District Judge (Magistrates' Courts): Prison (Amendment) Rules 2005, SI 2005/789, r 1(2).

[2] A person who has pleaded guilty to an offence but has not yet been sentenced for that offence is a "convicted prisoner" within this rule: *R (Edwards-Sayer) v Secretary of State for Justice* [2008] EWHC 467 (Admin), [2008] 1 WLR 2280.

## Part II Prisoners

### General

**7.9444** 3. *Purpose of prison training and treatment* The purpose of the training and treatment of convicted prisoners shall be to encourage and assist them to lead a good and useful life.

**7.9445** 4. *Outside contacts* (1) Special attention shall be paid to the maintenance of such relationships between a prisoner and his family as are desirable in the best interests of both.

(2) A prisoner shall be encouraged and assisted to establish and maintain such relations with persons and agencies outside prison as may, in the opinion of the governor, best promote the interests of his family and his own social rehabilitation.

**7.9446** 5. *After care* From the beginning of a prisoner's sentence, consideration shall be given, in consultation with the appropriate after-care organisation, to the prisoner's future and the assistance to be given him on and after his release.

**7.9447** 6. *Maintenance of order and discipline* (1) Order and discipline shall be maintained with firmness, but with no more restriction than is required for safe custody and well ordered community life.

(2) In the control of prisoners, officers shall seek to influence them through their own example and leadership, and to enlist their willing co-operation.

(3) At all times the treatment of prisoners shall be such as to encourage their self-respect and a sense of personal responsibility, but a prisoner shall not be employed in any disciplinary capacity.

**7.9448** 7. *Classification of prisoners* (1) Subject to paragraphs (1A) to 1D), prisoners shall be classified, in accordance with any directions of the Secretary of State, having regard to their age, temperament and record and with a view to maintaining good order and facilitating training and, in the case of convicted prisoners, of furthering the purpose of their training and treatment as provided by rule 3.

(1A) Except where paragraph (1D) applies, a prisoner who has the relevant deportation status must not be classified as suitable for open conditions.

(1B) If, immediately before the relevant time—

(*a*) a prisoner has been classified as suitable for open conditions; and

(*b*) the prison has received notice that the prisoner has the relevant deportation status,

the prisoner's classification must be reconsidered in accordance with this rule as soon as practicable after the relevant time.

(1C) If—

(*a*) a prisoner has been classified as suitable for open conditions (whether before or after the relevant time); and

(*b*) t the prison receives notice after the relevant time that the prisoner has the relevant deportation status,

the prisoner's classification must be reconsidered in accordance with this rule as soon as practicable after the prison receives that notice.

(1D) This paragraph applies if a prisoner has been classified as suitable for open conditions and is located in open conditions immediately before the prisoner's classification is reconsidered, whether under paragraph (1B) or (1C) or otherwise.

(1E) For the purposes of this rule, a prisoner has the relevant deportation status if—

(*a*) there is a deportation order against the prisoner under section 5(1) of the Immigration Act 1971; and

(*b*) no appeal under section 82(1) of the Nationality, Immigration and Asylum Act 2002 ("the 2002 Act") that may be brought or continued from within the United Kingdom in relation to the decision to make the deportation order—

(i) could be brought (ignoring any possibility of an appeal out of time with permission), or

(ii) is pending (within the meaning of section 104 of the 2002 Act).

(1F) In paragraph (1E), the reference to the decision to make the deportation order includes a

decision that section 32(5) of the UK Borders Act 2007 applies in respect of the prisoner.
(1G) In this rule, "the relevant time" means 5.00 pm on 13th August 2014.
(2) Unconvicted prisoners:
(*a*) shall be kept out of contact with convicted prisoners as far as the governor considers it can reasonably be done, unless and to the extent that they have consented to share residential accommodation or participate in any activity with convicted prisoners; and
(*b*) shall under no circumstances be required to share a cell with a convicted prisoner.
(3) Prisoners committed or attached for contempt of court, or for failing to do or abstain from doing anything required to be done or left undone:
(*a*) shall be treated as a separate class for the purposes of this rule;
(*b*) notwithstanding anything in this rule, may be permitted to associate with any other class of prisoners if they are willing to do so; and
(*c*) shall have the same privileges as an unconvicted prisoner under rules 20(5), 23(1) and 35(1).
(4) Nothing in this rule shall require a prisoner to be deprived unduly of the society of other persons.

**7.9449** 8. *Privileges* (1) There shall be established at every prison systems of privileges approved by the Secretary of State and appropriate to the classes of prisoners there, which shall include arrangements under which money earned by prisoners in prison may be spent by them within the prison.
(2) Systems of privileges approved under paragraph (1) may include arrangements under which prisoners may be allowed time outside their cells and in association with one another, in excess of the minimum time which, subject to the other provisions of these Rules apart from this rule, is otherwise allowed to prisoners at the prison for this purpose.
(3) Systems of privileges approved under paragraph (1) may include arrangements under which privileges may be granted to prisoners only in so far as they have met, and for so long as they continue to meet, specified standards in their behaviour and their performance in work or other activities.
(4) Systems of privileges which include arrangements of the kind referred to in paragraph (3) shall include procedures to be followed in determining whether or not any of the privileges concerned shall be granted, or shall continue to be granted, to a prisoner; such procedures shall include a requirement that the prisoner be given reasons for any decision adverse to him together with a statement of the means by which he may appeal against it.
(5) Nothing in this rule shall be taken to confer on a prisoner any entitlement to any privilege or to affect any provision in these Rules other than this rule as a result of which any privilege may be forfeited or otherwise lost or a prisoner deprived of association with other prisoners.

**7.9450** 9. *Temporary release* (1) Subject to paragraph (1A), the Secretary of State may, in accordance with the other provisions of this rule, release temporarily a prisoner to whom this rule applies.
(1A) A prisoner who has the relevant deportation status must not be released under this rule unless the prisoner is located in open conditions immediately before the time of release.
(2) A prisoner may be released under this rule for any period or periods and subject to any conditions.
(3) A prisoner may only be released under this rule:
(*a*) on compassionate grounds or for the purpose of receiving medical treatment;
(*b*) to engage in employment or voluntary work;
(*c*) to receive instruction or training which cannot reasonably be provided in the prison;
(*d*) to enable him to participate in any proceedings before any court, tribunal or inquiry;
(*e*) to enable him to consult with his legal adviser in circumstances where it is not reasonably practicable for the consultation to take place in the prison;
(*f*) to assist any police officer in any enquiries;
(*g*) to facilitate the prisoner's transfer between prisons;
(*h*) to assist him in maintaining family ties or in his transition from prison life to freedom; or
(*i*) *revoked.*
(4) A prisoner shall not be released under this rule unless the Secretary of State is satisfied that there would not be an unacceptable risk of his committing offences whilst released or otherwise failing to comply with any condition upon which he is released.
(5) The Secretary of State shall not release under this rule a prisoner serving a sentence of imprisonment if, having regard to:
(*a*) the period or proportion of his sentence which the prisoner has served or, in a case where paragraph (10) does not apply to require all the sentences he is serving to be treated as a single term, the period or proportion of any such sentence he has served; and
(*b*) the frequency with which the prisoner has been granted temporary release under this rule,

the Secretary of State is of the opinion that the release of the prisoner would be likely to undermine public confidence in the administration of justice.
(6) If a prisoner has been temporarily released under this rule during the relevant period and has been sentenced to imprisonment for a criminal offence committed whilst at large following that release, he shall not be released under this rule unless his release, having regard to the circumstances of this conviction, would not, in the opinion of the Secretary of State, be likely to undermine public confidence in the administration of justice.
(7) For the purposes of paragraph (6), "the relevant period":

(*a*) in the case of a prisoner serving a determinate sentence of imprisonment, is the period he has served in respect of that sentence, unless, notwithstanding paragraph (10), the sentences he is serving do not fall to be treated as a single term, in which case it is the period since he was last released in relation to one of those sentences under Part II of the Criminal Justice Act 1991 ("the 1991 Act") or Chapter 6 of Part 12 of the 2003 Act;

(*b*) in the case of a prisoner serving an indeterminate sentence of imprisonment, is, if the prisoner has previously been released on licence under Part II of the Crime (Sentences) Act 1997 or Part II of the 1991 Act or Chapter 6 of Part 12 of the 2003 Act, the period since the date of his last recall to prison in respect of that sentence or, where the prisoner has not been so released, the period he has served in respect of that sentence; or

(*c*) in the case of a prisoner detained in prison for any other reason, is the period for which the prisoner has been detained for that reason;

save that where a prisoner falls within two or more of sub-paragraphs (*a*) to (*c*), the "relevant period", in the case of that prisoner, shall be determined by whichever of the applicable sub-paragraphs produces the longer period.

(8) A prisoner released under this rule may be recalled to prison at any time whether the conditions of his release have been broken or not.

(8A) If, immediately before the relevant time, a prisoner has been released under this rule and the prison has received notice that the prisoner has the relevant deportation status, the prisoner must be recalled unless—

(*a*) the period for which the prisoner has been released is due to expire on 13th August 2014; or

(*b*) the prisoner was released from open conditions.

(8B) If a prisoner has been released under this rule (whether before or after the relevant time) and the prison receives notice after the relevant time that the prisoner has the relevant deportation status, the prisoner must be recalled unless—

(*a*) the period for which the prisoner has been released is due to expire on the day on which the prison receives that notice; or

(*b*) the prisoner was released from open conditions.

(9) This rule applies to prisoners other than persons committed in custody for trial or to be sentenced or otherwise dealt with before or by any Crown Court or remanded in custody by any court.

(10) For the purposes of any reference in this rule to an inmate's sentence, consecutive terms and terms which are wholly or partly concurrent shall be treated as a single term.

(11) In this rule:

(*a*) any reference to a sentence of imprisonment shall be construed as including any sentence to detention or custody; and

(*b*) any reference to release on licence or otherwise under Part II of the 1991 Act includes any release on licence under any legislation providing for early release on licence.

(*c*) any reference to a prisoner who has the relevant deportation status is to be read in accordance with rule 7(1E) and (1F); and

(*d*) any reference to the relevant time is to be read in accordance with rule 7(1G).

**7.9451** 10. *Information to prisoners* (1) Every prisoner shall be provided, as soon as possible after his reception into prison, and in any case within 24 hours, with information in writing about those provisions of these Rules and other matters which it is necessary that he should know, including earnings and privileges, and the proper means of making requests and complaints.

(2) In the case of a prisoner aged less than 18, or a prisoner aged 18 or over who cannot read or appears to have difficulty in understanding the information so provided, the governor, or an officer deputed by him, shall so explain it to him that he can understand his rights and obligations.

(3) A copy of these Rules shall be made available to any prisoner who requests it.

**7.9452** 11. *Requests and complaints* (1) A prisoner may make a request or complaint to the governor or independent monitoring board relating to the prisoner's imprisonment.

(2) The governor shall consider as soon as possible any requests and complaints that are made to him under paragraph (1).

(3) A written request or complaint under paragraph (1) may be made in confidence.

## Women Prisoners

**7.9453** 12. *Women prisoners* (1) Women prisoners shall normally be kept separate from male prisoners.

(2) The Secretary of State may, subject to any conditions he thinks fit, permit a woman prisoner to have her baby with[1] her in prison, and everything necessary for the baby's maintenance and care may be provided there.

[1] For procedural requirements to ensure fairness in any decision whether to transfer a prisoner to a mother and baby unit and the application of article 8 of the European Convention on Human Rights, see *R (on the application of CD) v Secretary of State for the Home Department* [2003] EWHC 155 (Admin), [2003] 1 FLR 979. As the primary decision-maker as to the separation of mother and child is the Secretary of State not the court, any challenge to his decision raises issues of public law and is to be determined whether in the Family Division or the Divisional Court by reference to principles of public law not private law (*CF v Secretary of State for the Home Department* [2004] EWHC 111 (Fam), [2004] 1 FCR 577, [2004] 2 FLR 517).

## Religion

**7.9454** 13. *Religious denomination* A prisoner shall be treated as being of the religious denomination stated in the record made in pursuance of section 10(5) of the Prison Act 1952 but the governor may, in a proper case and after due enquiry, direct that record to be amended.

**7.9455** 14. *Special duties of chaplains and prison ministers* (1) The chaplain or a prison minister of a prison shall—

(*a*) interview every prisoner of his denomination individually soon after the prisoner's reception into that prison and shortly before his release; and

(*b*) if no other arrangements are made, read the burial service at the funeral of any prisoner of his denomination who dies in that prison.

(2) The chaplain shall visit daily all prisoners belonging to the Church of England who are sick, under restraint or undergoing cellular confinement; and a prison minister shall do the same, as far as he reasonably can, for prisoners of his denomination.

(3) The chaplain shall visit any prisoner not of the Church of England who is sick, under restraint or undergoing cellular confinement, and is not regularly visited by a minister of his denomination, if the prisoner is willing.

**7.9456** 15. *Regular visits by ministers of religion* (1) The chaplain shall visit the prisoners belonging to the Church of England.

(2) A prison minister shall visit the prisoners of his denomination as regularly as he reasonably can.

(3) Where a prisoner belongs to a denomination for which no prison minister has been appointed, the governor shall do what he reasonably can, if so requested by the prisoner, to arrange for him to be visited regularly by a minister of that denomination.

**7.9457** 16. *Religious services* (1) The chaplain shall conduct Divine Service for prisoners belonging to the Church of England at least once every Sunday, Christmas Day and Good Friday, and such celebrations of Holy Communion and weekday services as may be arranged.

(2) Prison ministers shall conduct Divine Service for prisoners of their denominations at such times as may be arranged.

**7.9458** 17. *Substitute for chaplain or prison minister* (1) A person approved by the Secretary of State may act for the chaplain in his absence.

(2) A prison minister may, with the leave of the Secretary of State, appoint a substitute to act for him in his absence.

**7.9459** 18. *Sunday work* Arrangements shall be made so as not to require prisoners of the Christian religion to do any unnecessary work on Sunday, Christmas Day or Good Friday, or prisoners of other religions to do any such work on their recognised days of religious observance.

**7.9460** 19. *Religious books* There shall, so far as reasonably practicable, be available for the personal use of every prisoner such religious books recognised by his denomination as are approved by the Secretary of State for use in prisons.

## Medical Attention

**7.9461** 20. *Health services* (1) The governor must work in partnership with local health care providers to secure the provision to prisoners of access to the same quality and range of services as the general public receives from the National Health Service.

(2) Every request by a prisoner to see a health care professional shall be recorded by the officer to whom it was made and promptly communicated to a health care professional.

(3) If an unconvicted prisoner desires the attendance of a named registered medical practitioner or dentist other than one already working in the prison, and will pay any expense incurred, the governor must, if satisfied that there are reasonable grounds for the request and unless the Secretary of State otherwise directs, allow the prisoner to be visited and treated by that practitioner or dentist, in consultation with a registered medical practitioner who works in the prison.

(4) Subject to any directions given in the particular case by the Secretary of State, a registered medical practitioner selected by or on behalf of a prisoner who is a party to any legal proceedings must be afforded reasonable facilities for examining the prisoner in connection with the proceedings, and may do so out of hearing but in the sight of an officer

(5) A prisoner may correspond, in accordance with arrangements made by the Secretary of State for the confidential handling of correspondence, with a registered medical practitioner who has treated the prisoner for a life threatening condition, and such correspondence may not be opened, read or stopped unless the governor has reasonable cause to believe its contents do not relate to the treatment of that condition.

**7.9462** 21. *Special illnesses and conditions* (1) A registered medical practitioner working within the prison shall report to the governor on the case of any prisoner whose health is likely to be injuriously affected by continued imprisonment or any conditions of imprisonment. The governor shall send the report to the Secretary of State without delay, together with his own recommendations.

(2) *Revoked.*

**7.9463** 22. *Notification of illness or death* (1) If a prisoner dies, becomes seriously ill, sustains any severe injury or is removed to hospital on account of mental disorder, the governor shall, if he knows his or her address, at once inform the prisoner's spouse or next of kin, and also any person

who the prisoner may reasonably have asked should be informed.
(2) If a prisoner dies, the governor shall give notice immediately to the coroner having jurisdiction, to the independent monitoring board and to the Secretary of State.

PHYSICAL WELFARE AND WORK

7.9464 23. *Clothing* (1) An unconvicted prisoner may wear clothing of his own if and in so far as it is suitable, tidy and clean, and shall be permitted to arrange for the supply to him from outside prison of sufficient clean clothing:
Provided that, subject to rule 40(3):
(*a*) he may be required, if and for so long as there are reasonable grounds to believe that there is a serious risk of his attempting to escape, to wear items of clothing which are distinctive by virtue of being specially marked or coloured or both; and
(*b*) he may be required, if and for so long as the Secretary of State is of the opinion that he would, if he escaped, be highly dangerous to the public or the police or the security of the State, to wear clothing provided under this rule.
(2) Subject to paragraph (1) above, the provisions of this rule shall apply to an unconvicted prisoner as to a convicted prisoner.
(3) A convicted prisoner shall be provided with clothing adequate for warmth and health in accordance with a scale approved by the Secretary of State.
(4) The clothing provided under this rule shall include suitable protective clothing for use at work, where this is needed.
(5) Subject to rule 40(3), a convicted prisoner shall wear clothing provided under this rule and no other, except on the directions of the Secretary of State or as a privilege under rule 8.
(6) A prisoner may be provided, where necessary, with suitable and adequate clothing on his release.

7.9465 24. *Food* (1) Subject to any directions of the Secretary of State, no prisoner shall be allowed, except as authorised by a health care professional, to have any food other than that ordinarily provided.
(2) The food provided shall be wholesome, nutritious, well prepared and served, reasonably varied and sufficient in quantity.
(3) Any person deemed by the governor to be competent, shall from time to time inspect the food both before and after it is cooked and shall report any deficiency or defect to the governor.
(4) In this rule "food" includes drink.

7.9466 25. *Alcohol and tobacco* (1) No prisoner shall be allowed to have any intoxicating liquor.
(2) No prisoner shall be allowed to smoke or to have any tobacco except as a privilege under rule 8 and in accordance with any orders of the governor.

7.9467 26. *Sleeping accommodation* (1) No room or cell shall be used as sleeping accommodation for a prisoner unless it has been certified in the manner required by section 14 of the Prison Act 1952 in the case of a cell used for the confinement of a prisoner.
(2) A certificate given under that section or this rule shall specify the maximum number of prisoners who may sleep or be confined at one time in the room or cell to which it relates, and the number so specified shall not be exceeded without the leave of the Secretary of State.

7.9468 27. *Beds and bedding* Each prisoner shall be provided with a separate bed and with separate bedding adequate for warmth and health.

7.9469 28. *Hygiene* (1) Every prisoner shall be provided with toilet articles necessary for his health and cleanliness, which shall be replaced as necessary.
(2) Every prisoner shall be required to wash at proper times, have a hot bath or shower on reception and thereafter at least once a week.
(3) A prisoner's hair shall not be cut without his consent.

7.9470 29. *Physical education* (1) If circumstances reasonably permit, a prisoner aged 21 years or over shall be given the opportunity to participate in physical education for at least one hour a week.
(2) The following provisions shall apply to the extent circumstances reasonably permit to a prisoner who is under 21 years of age—
(*a*) provision shall be made for the physical education of such a prisoner within the normal working week, as well as evening and weekend physical recreation; the physical education activities will be such as foster personal responsibility and the prisoner's interests and skills and encourage him to make good use of his leisure on release; and
(*b*) arrangements shall be made for each such prisoner who is a convicted prisoner to participate in physical education for two hours a week on average.
(3) In the case of a prisoner with a need for remedial physical activity, appropriate facilities will be provided.
(4) *Revoked.*

7.9471 30. *Time in the open air* If the weather permits and subject to the need to maintain good order and discipline, a prisoner shall be given the opportunity to spend time in the open air at least once every day, for such period as may be reasonable in the circumstances.

7.9472 31. *Work* (1) A convicted prisoner shall be required to do useful work for not more than 10 hours a day, and arrangements shall be made to allow prisoners to work, where possible, outside the cells and in association with one another.

(2) A registered medical practitioner or registered nurse working within the prison may excuse a prisoner from work on medical grounds.

(3) No prisoner shall be set to do work of a kind not authorised by the Secretary of State.

(4) No prisoner shall work in the service of another prisoner or an officer, or for the private benefit of any person, without the authority of the Secretary of State.

(5) An unconvicted prisoner shall be permitted, if he wishes, to work as if he were a convicted prisoner.

(6) Prisoners may be paid for their work at rates approved by the Secretary of State, either generally or in relation to particular cases.

**7.9473** *31A. Prescription of certain matters in respect of prisoners' earnings* (1) The amount prescribed for the purpose of section 1(1)(*b*) of the Prisoners' Earnings Act 1996 ("the 1996 Act") is £20.[1]

(2) The percentage prescribed for the purpose of section 1(2) of the 1996 Act is 40%.

(3) All amounts deducted or levied under section 1 of the 1996 Act shall be applied for the purpose referred to in section 2(1)(*a*) of the 1996 Act.

(4) Victim Support is prescribed as a voluntary organisation to which payments may be made under section 2(1)(*a*) of the 1996 Act.

---

1 Prison instructions underpinning this rule do not violate art 1 of the First Protocol to the European Convention on Human Rights nor do such deductions engage art 7: *R (on the application of S) v Secretary of State for Justice* [2012] EWHC 1810 (Admin), [2013] 1 All ER 66, (2012) Times, 10 September.

## Education and Library

**7.9474** *32. Education* (1) Every prisoner able to profit from the education facilities provided at a prison shall be encouraged to do so.

(2) Educational classes shall be arranged at every prison and, subject to any directions of the Secretary of State, reasonable facilities shall be afforded to prisoners who wish to do so to improve their education by training by distance learning, private study and recreational classes, in their spare time.

(3) Special attention shall be paid to the education and training of prisoners with special educational needs, and if necessary they shall be taught within the hours normally allotted to work.

(4) In the case of a prisoner of compulsory school age as defined in section 8 of the Education Act 1996, arrangements shall be made for his participation in education or training courses for at least 15 hours a week within the normal working week.

**7.9475** *33. Library* A library shall be provided in every prison and, subject to any directions of the Secretary of State, every prisoner shall be allowed to have library books and to exchange them.

## Communications

**7.9476** *34. Communications generally* (1) Without prejudice to sections 6 and 19 of the Prison Act 1952 and except as provided by these Rules, a prisoner[1] shall not be permitted to communicate with any person outside the prison, or such person with him, except with the leave of the Secretary of State or as a privilege under rule 8.

(2) Notwithstanding paragraph (1) above, and except as otherwise provided in these Rules, the Secretary of State may impose any restriction or condition, either generally or in a particular case, upon the communications to be permitted between a prisoner and other persons if he considers that the restriction or condition to be imposed—

(*a*) Does not interfere with the convention rights of any person; or

(*b*)

(i) is necessary on grounds specified in paragraph (3) below;

(ii) reliance on the grounds is compatible with the convention right to be interfered with; and

(iii) the restriction or condition is proportionate to what is sought to be achieved.

(3) The grounds referred to in paragraph (2) above are—

(*a*) the interests of national security;

(*b*) the prevention, detection, investigation or prosecution of crime;

(*c*) the interests of public safety;

(*d*) securing or maintaining prison security or good order and discipline in prison;

(*e*) the protection of health or morals;

(*f*) the protection of the reputation of others;

(*g*) maintaining the authority and impartiality of the judiciary; or

(*h*) the protection of the rights and freedoms of any person.

(4) Subject to paragraph (2) above, the Secretary of State may require that any visit, or class of visits, shall be held in facilities which include special features restricting or preventing physical contact between a prisoner and a visitor.

(5) Every visit to a prisoner shall take place within the sight of an officer or employee of the prison authorised for the purposes of this rule by the governor (in this rule referred to as an "authorised employee"), unless the Secretary of State otherwise directs, and for the purposes of this paragraph a visit to a prisoner shall be taken to take place within the sight of an officer or authorised employee if it can be seen by an officer or authorised employee by means of an overt closed circuit television system.

(6) Subject to rule 38, every visit to a prisoner shall take place within the hearing of an officer or

authorised employee, unless the Secretary of State otherwise directs.
(7) The Secretary of State may give directions, either generally or in relation to any visit or class of visits, concerning the day and times when prisoners may be visited.
(8) In this rule—
(*a*) references to communications include references to communications during visits;
(*b*) references to restrictions and conditions upon communications include references to restrictions and conditions in relation to the length, duration and frequency of communications; and
(*c*) references to convention rights are to the convention rights within the meaning of the Human Rights Act 1998.

[1] Prisoners must have unimpeded access to a solicitor in order to receive advice and assistance regarding possible civil proceedings, without for example being required by Standing Orders to make an internal complaint first (*R v Secretary of State for the Home Department, ex p Anderson* [1984] QB 778, [1984] 1 All ER 920). "Unimpeded access" does not preclude a closed regime for visitors of exceptional escape risk prisoners whereby physical contact between prisoner and visitor is prevented by an interposed physical barrier (*R v Secretary of State for the Home Department, ex p O'Dhuibhir* (1995)Times, 26 October). A convicted prisoner has no right to communicate orally with the media through a journalist as the loss of that "right" is part and parcel of a sentence of imprisonment. He can no longer speak to those outside prison or receive visits from anyone other than his lawyer and his relatives and friends, If a friend is a journalist the prison is entitled to require an undertaking from the journalist that the material obtained during the visit will not be used for professional purposes (*R v Secretary of State for the Home Department, ex p Simms* [1998] 2 All ER 491, [1998] 3WLR 1169, CA).

**7.9477** *35. Personal letters and visits* (1) Subject to paragraph (8), an unconvicted prisoner may send and receive as many letters and may receive as many visits as he wishes within such limits and subject to such conditions as the Secretary of State may direct, either generally or in a particular case.
(2) Subject to paragraphs (2A) and (8), a convicted prisoner shall be entitled—
(*a*) to send and to receive a letter on his reception into a prison and thereafter once a week; and
(*b*) to receive a visit twice in every period of four weeks, but only once in every such period if the Secretary of State so directs.
(2A) A prisoner serving a sentence of imprisonment to which an intermittent custody order relates shall be entitled to receive a visit only where the governor considers that desirable having regard to the extent to which he has been unable to meet with his friends and family in the periods during which he has been temporarily released on licence.
(3) The governor may allow a prisoner an additional letter or visit as a privilege under rule 8 or where necessary for his welfare or that of his family.
(4) The governor may allow a prisoner entitled to a visit to send and to receive a letter instead.
(5) The governor may defer the right of a prisoner to a visit until the expiration of any period of cellular confinement.
(6) The independent monitoring board may allow a prisoner an additional letter or visit in special circumstances, and may direct that a visit may extend beyond the normal duration.
(7) The Secretary of State may allow additional letters and visits in relation to any prisoner or class of prisoners.
(8) A prisoner shall not be entitled under this rule to receive a visit from:
(*a*) any person, whether or not a relative or friend, during any period of time that person is the subject of a prohibition imposed under rule 73; or
(*b*) any other person, other than a relative or friend, except with the leave of the Secretary of State.
(9) Any letter or visit under the succeeding provisions of these Rules shall not be counted as a letter or visit for the purposes of this rule.

**7.9478** *35A. Interception of communications* (1) The Secretary of State may give directions to any governor concerning the interception in a prison of any communication by any prisoner or class of prisoners if the Secretary of State considers that the directions are—
(*a*) necessary on grounds specified in paragraph (4) below; and
(*b*) proportionate to what is sought to be achieved[1].
(2) Subject to any directions given by the Secretary of State, the governor may make arrangements for any communication by a prisoner or class of prisoners to be intercepted in a prison by an officer or an employee of the prison authorised by the governor for the purposes of this rule (referred to in this rule as an "authorised employee") if he considers that the arrangements are—
(*a*) necessary on grounds specified in paragraph (4) below; and
(*b*) proportionate to what is sought to be achieved.
(2A) The governor may not make arrangements for interception of any communication between a prisoner and
(*a*) the prisoner's legal adviser; or
(*b*) any body or organisation with which the Secretary of State has made arrangements for the confidential handling of correspondence,

unless the governor has reasonable cause to believe that the communication is being made with the intention of furthering a criminal purpose and unless authorised by any one of the following: the chief executive officer of the National Offender Management Service; the director responsible for the national operational services of that service; or the duty director of that service.
(3) Any communication by a prisoner may, during the course of its transmission in a prison, be terminated by an officer or an authorised employee if he considers that to terminate the communication is—

(*a*) necessary on grounds specified in paragraph (4) below; and
(*b*) proportionate to what is sought to be achieved by the termination.
(4) The grounds referred to in paragraphs (1)(*a*),(2)(*a*) and (3)(*a*) above are—
(*a*) the interests of national security;
(*b*) the prevention, detection, investigation or prosecution of crime;
(*c*) the interests of public safety;
(*d*) securing or maintaining prison security or good order and discipline in prison;
(*e*) the protection of health or morals; or
(*f*) the protection of the rights and freedoms of any person.
(5) Any reference to the grounds specified in paragraph (4) above in relation to the interception of a communication by means of a telecommunications system in a prison, or the disclosure or retention of intercepted material from such a communication, shall be taken to be a reference to those grounds with the omission of sub-paragraph (*f*).
(6) For the purposes of this rule "interception"—
(*a*) in relation to a communication by means of a telecommunications system, means any action taken in relation to the system or its operation so as to make some or all of the contents of the communications available, while being transmitted, to a person other than the sender or intended recipient of the communication; and the contents of a communication are to be taken to be made available to a person while being transmitted where the contents of the communication, while being transmitted, are diverted or recorded so as to be available to a person subsequently; and
(*b*) in relation to any written or drawn communication, includes opening, reading, examining and copying the communication.

[1] Rule 34 when read with r 35A creates a regime clearly intended to enable the Secretary of State to impose restrictions and conditions on the telephone calls made by prisoners either across the entire prison estate or by reference to particular prisoners or classes of prisoners. Rule 34 expressly provides that those restrictions and conditions can be applied 'generally' or 'in a particular case'. One of the conditions imposed on the prison population is that any calls they make must be via the PIN system, and by r 35A(1) the Secretary of State is empowered to give directions to any governor concerning the interception of any communication by any prisoner or class of prisoners. The blanket interception and recording of the telephone calls of prisoners at the two prisons the subject of the appeal did not constitute a breach of RIPA as it was not ultra vires r 35A. Although the court stressed it had not considered the extent to which it is necessary for the system to be reconsidered from time to time, in light of the need for measures of this kind to be necessary and proportional: *R v Mahmood* [2013] EWCA Crim 2356, [2014] 1 Cr App R 31 [2014] Crim LR 518.

**7.9479** 35B. *Permanent log of communications* (1) The governor may arrange for a permanent log to be kept of all communications by or to a prisoner.
(2) The log referred to in paragraph (1) above may include, in relation to a communication by means of a telecommunications system in a prison, a record of the destination, duration and cost of the communication and, in relation to any written or drawn communication, a record of the sender and addressee of the communication.

**7.9480** 35C. *Disclosure of material* The governor may not disclose to any person who is not an officer of a prison or of the Secretary of State or an employee of the prison authorised by the governor for the purposes of this rule any intercepted material, information retained pursuant to rule 35B or material obtained by means of an overt closed circuit television system used during a visit unless—
(*a*) he considers that such disclosure is—
(i) necessary on grounds specified in rule 35A(4); and
(ii) proportionate to what is sought to be achieved by the disclosure; or
(*b*)
(i) in the case of intercepted material or material obtained by means of an overt closed circuit television system used during a visit, all parties to the communication or visit consent to the disclosure; or
(ii) in the case of information retained pursuant to rule 35B, the prisoner to whose communication the information relates, consents to the disclosure.

**7.9481** 35D. *Retention of material* (1) The governor shall not retain any intercepted material or material obtained by means of an overt closed circuit television system used during a visit for a period longer than 3 months beginning with the day on which the material was intercepted or obtained unless he is satisfied that continued retention of it is—
(*a*) necessary on grounds specified in rule 35A(4); and
(*b*) proportionate to what is sought to be achieved by the continued retention.
(2) Where such material is retained for longer than 3 months pursuant to paragraph (1) above the governor shall review its continued retention at periodic intervals until such time as it is no longer held by the governor.
(3) The first review referred to in paragraph (2) above shall take place not more than 3 months after the decision to retain the material taken pursuant to paragraph (1) above, and subsequent reviews shall take place not more than 3 months apart thereafter.
(4) If the governor, on a review conducted pursuant to paragraph (2) above or at any other time, is not satisfied that the continued retention of the material satisfies the requirements set out in paragraph (1) above, he shall arrange for the material to be destroyed.

**7.9482** 36. *Police interviews* A police officer may, on production of an order issued by or on behalf of a chief officer of police, interview any prisoner willing to see him.

7.9483 *37. Securing release* A person detained in prison in default of finding a surety, or of payment of a sum of money, may communicate with and be visited at any reasonable time on a weekday by any relative or friend to arrange for a surety or payment in order to secure his release from prison.

7.9484 *38. Visits from legal advisers* (1) Where the legal adviser of a prisoner in any legal proceedings, civil or criminal, to which the prisoner is a party visits the prisoner, the legal adviser shall be afforded reasonable facilities for interviewing him in connection with those proceedings, and may do so out of hearing but in the sight of an officer.
(2) On such a visit prisoner's legal adviser may, subject to any directions given by the Secretary of State, interview the prisoner in connection with any other legal business out of hearing but in the sight of an officer.

7.9485 *39. Delivery and receipt of legally privileged material* (1) A prisoner may deliver to, or receive from, the prisoner's legal adviser and any court, either by post or during a legal visit under rule 38, any legally privileged material and such material may only be opened, read or stopped by the governor in accordance with the provisions of this rule[1].
(2) Material to which this rule applies may be opened if the governor has reasonable cause to believe that it contains an illicit enclosure and any such enclosures shall be dealt with in accordance with the other provision of these Rules.
(3) Material to which this rule applies may be opened, read and stopped if the governor has reasonable cause to believe its contents endanger prison security or the safety of others or are otherwise of a criminal nature.
(4) A prisoner shall be given the opportunity to be present when any material to which this rule applies is opened and shall be informed if it or any enclosure is to be read or stopped.[2]
(5) A prisoner shall on request be provided with any writing materials necessary for the purposes of paragraph (1).
(6) In this rule, "court" includes the European Commission of Human Rights, the European Court of Human Rights and the European Court of Justice; and "illicit enclosure" includes any article possession of which has not been authorised in accordance with the other provisions of these Rules and any material to or from a person other than the prisoner concerned, his legal adviser or a court.

---

1 Although legal professional privilege attaches to correspondence with legal advisers must be protected from unnecessary interference by prison staff, considerations of security may require searches periodically and without notice of cells and everything in them which necessarily will involve examining correspondence so far as it is necessary to ensure that it is bona fide correspondence between a prisoner and a legal adviser and it does not contain anything else (*R v Governor of Whitemoor Prison, ex p Main* [1998] 2 All ER 491, [1998] 3 WLR 1169, CA). Where there is malicious infringement of this rule, a cause of action for misfeasance in public office is complete without proof of special damage (*Watkins v Secretary of State* [2004] EWCA Civ 966, [2004] 4 All ER 1158).

2 For the general right of a prisoner to be present when legal correspondence received or made by a prisoner and kept in his cell is searched and the application of art 8 of the European Convention on Human Rights, see *R v Secretary of State for the Home Department, ex p Daly* [2001] UKHL 26, [2001] 3 All ER 433, [2001] 2 WLR 1622.

## Removal, Search, Record and Property

7.9486 *40. Custody outside prison* (1) A person being taken to or from a prison in custody shall be exposed as little as possible to public observation, and proper care shall be taken to protect him from curiosity and insult.
(2) A prisoner required to be taken in custody anywhere outside a prison shall be kept in the custody of an officer appointed or a police officer.
(3) A prisoner required to be taken in custody to any court shall, when he appears before the court, wear his own clothing or ordinary civilian clothing provided by the governor.

7.9487 *41. Search* (1) Every prisoner shall be searched when taken into custody by an officer, on his reception into a prison and subsequently as the governor thinks necessary or as the Secretary of State may direct.
(2) A prisoner shall be searched in as seemly a manner as is consistent with discovering anything concealed.
(3) No prisoner shall be stripped and searched in the sight of another prisoner, or in the sight of a person of the opposite sex.

7.9488 *42. Record and photograph* (1) A personal record of each prisoner shall be prepared and maintained in such manner as the Secretary of State may direct.
(2) Every prisoner may be photographed on reception and subsequently, but no copy of the photograph or any other personal record shall be given to any person not authorised to receive it.
(2A) In this rule "personal record" may include personal information and biometric records (such as fingerprints or other physical measurements).

7.9489 *43. Prisoners' property* (1) Subject to any directions of the Secretary of State, an unconvicted prisoner may have supplied to him at his expense and retain for his own use books, newspapers, writing materials and other means of occupation, except any that appears objectionable to the independent monitoring board or, pending consideration by them, to the governor.
(2) Anything, other than cash, which a prisoner has at a prison and which he is not allowed to retain for his own use shall be taken into the governor's custody. An inventory of a prisoner's property shall be kept, and he shall be required to sign it, after having a proper opportunity to see that it is correct.
(2A) Where a prisoner is serving a sentence of imprisonment to which an intermittent custody order relates, an inventory as referred to in paragraph (2) shall only be kept where the value of that

property is estimated by the governor to be in excess of £100.
(3) Any cash which a prisoner has at a prison shall be paid into an account under the control of the governor and the prisoner shall be credited with the amount in the books of the prison[1].
(4) Any article belonging to a prisoner which remains unclaimed for a period of more than one year after he leaves prison, or dies, may be sold or otherwise disposed of; and the net proceeds of any sale shall be paid to the National Association for the Care and Resettlement of Offenders, for its general purposes.
(5) The governor may confiscate any unauthorised article found in the possession of a prisoner after his reception into prison, or concealed or deposited anywhere within a prison.

[1] The governor does not hold the cash on trust for the prisoner with an obligation to invest it in an interest bearing account; the relationship created is one of debtor and creditor. There is no specific rule which prevents the prisoner from requesting the cash to be transferred to an interest-bearing account outside the prison (*Duggan v Governor of Full Sutton Prison* [2003] EWHC 361 (Ch), [2003] 2 All ER 678).

**7.9490** *44. Money and articles received by post* (1) Any money or other article (other than a letter or other communication) sent to a convicted prisoner by post shall be dealt with in accordance with the provisions of this rule, and the prisoner shall be informed of the manner in which it is dealt with.
(2) Any cash shall, at the discretion of the governor, be—
(*a*) dealt with in accordance with rule 43(3);
(*b*) returned to the sender; or
(*c*) in a case where the sender's name and address are not known, paid to the National Association for the Care and Resettlement of Offenders, for its general purposes:
Provided that in relation to a prisoner committed to prison in default of payment of any sum of money, the prisoner shall be informed of the receipt of the cash and, unless he objects to its being so applied, it shall be applied in or towards the satisfaction of the amount due from him.
(3) Any security for money shall, at the discretion of the governor, be—
(*a*) delivered to the prisoner or placed with his property at the prison;
(*b*) returned to the sender; or
(*c*) encashed and the cash dealt with in accordance with paragraph (2).
(4) Any other article to which this rule applies shall, at the discretion of the governor, be—
(*a*) delivered to the prisoner or placed with his property at the prison;
(*b*) returned to the sender; or
(*c*) in a case where the sender's name and address are not known or the article is of such a nature that it would be unreasonable to return it, sold or otherwise disposed of, and the net proceeds of any sale applied in accordance with paragraph (2).

## Special Control, Supervision and Restraint and Drug Testing

**7.9491** *45. Removal from association* (1) Where it appears desirable, for the maintenance of good order or discipline or in his own interests, that a prisoner should not associate with other prisoners, either generally or for particular purposes, the governor may arrange for the prisoner's removal from association for up to 72 hours.
(2) Removal for more than 72 hours may be authorised by the governor in writing who may authorise a further period of removal of up to 14 days[1].
(2A) Such authority may be renewed for subsequent periods of up to 14 days.
(2B) But the governor must obtain leave from the Secretary of State in writing to authorise removal under paragraph (2A) where the period in total amounts to more than 42 days starting with the date the inmate was removed under paragraph (1).
(2C) The Secretary of State may only grant leave for a maximum period of 42 days, but such leave may be renewed for subsequent periods of up to 42 days by the Secretary of State.
(3) The governor may arrange at his discretion for a prisoner removed under this rule to resume association with other prisoners at any time.
(3A) In giving authority under paragraphs (2) and (2A) and in exercising the discretion under paragraph (3), the governor must fully consider any recommendation that the prisoner resumes association on medical grounds made by a registered medical practitioner or registered nurse working within the prison.
(4) This rule shall not apply to a prisoner the subject of a direction given under rule 46(1).

[1] This sub rule was amended by SI 2015/1638 to take account of the decision in *R (on the application of Bourgass) v Secretary of State for Justice* [2015] UKSC 54, [2016] AC 384, [2015] 3 WLR 457, [2015] All ER (D) 308 (Jul) which decided that it was implicit in the unamended r 45(2) that the decision of the Secretary of State to extend segregation could not be taken on his behalf by the governor, or by some other officer of the prison in question. It was also held in *Bourgass* that a prisoner should normally have a reasonable opportunity to make representations before a decision is taken by the Secretary of State under the former r 45(2) although the decision would often be sought on the basis of information which could not be disclosed in full without placing at significant risk the safety of others or jeopardising prison security. There might also be cases where other overriding interests might be placed at risk. In such circumstances, fairness did not require the disclosure of information which could compromise the safety of an informant, the integrity of prison security or other overriding interests. It would be sufficient to inform the prisoner in more or less general terms of the gist of the reasons for seeking the authority of the Secretary of State.

**7.9492** *46. Close supervision centres* (1) Where it appears desirable, for the maintenance of good order or discipline or to ensure the safety of officers, prisoners or any other person, that a prisoner should not associate with other prisoners, either generally or for particular purposes, the Secretary of State may direct the prisoner's removal from association accordingly and his placement in a close supervision centre of a prison.
(2) A direction given under paragraph (1) shall be for a period not exceeding one month, but may be renewed from time to time for a like period, and shall continue to apply notwithstanding any

transfer of a prisoner from one prison to another.

(3) The Secretary of State may direct that such a prisoner as aforesaid shall resume association with other prisoners, either within a close supervision centre or elsewhere.

(4) In exercising any discretion under this rule, the Secretary of State shall take account of any relevant medical considerations which are known to him.

(5) A close supervision centre is any cell or other part of a prison designated by the Secretary of State for holding prisoners who are subject to a direction given under paragraph (1).

**7.9492A** *46A. Separation centres* (1) Where it appears desirable, on one or more of the grounds specified in paragraph (2), the Secretary of State may direct that a prisoner be placed in a separation centre within a prison.

(2) The grounds referred to in paragraph (1) are—

(a) the interests of national security;

(b) to prevent the commission, preparation or instigation of an act of terrorism, a terrorism offence, or an offence with a terrorist connection, whether in a prison or otherwise;

(c) to prevent the dissemination of views or beliefs that might encourage or induce others to commit any such act or offence, whether in a prison or otherwise, or to protect or safeguard others from such views or beliefs, or

(d) to prevent any political, religious, racial or other views or beliefs being used to undermine good order and discipline in a prison.

(3) A direction given under paragraph (1) must be reviewed every three months.

(4) The Secretary of State may, at any time, revoke a direction given under paragraph (1) and direct that the prisoner be removed from the separation centre.

(5) In exercising any discretion under this rule, the Secretary of State must take account of any known relevant medical considerations.

(6) In this rule—

"act of terrorism" includes anything constituting an action taken for the purposes of terrorism within the meaning of section 1 of the Terrorism Act 2000;

"offence with a terrorist connection" means an offence listed in Schedule 2 of the Counter-Terrorism Act 2008, which also satisfies the definition in section 93 of that Act;

"separation centre" means any part of a prison for the time being used for holding prisoners who are subject to a direction under paragraph (1);

"terrorism offence" means an offence listed in section 41(1) of the Counter-Terrorism Act 2008.

**7.9493** *47. Use of force* (1) An officer in dealing with a prisoner shall not use force unnecessarily and, when the application of force to a prisoner is necessary, no more force than is necessary shall be used.

(2) No officer shall act deliberately in a manner calculated to provoke a prisoner.

**7.9494** *48. Temporary confinement* (1) The governor may order a refractory or violent prisoner to be confined temporarily in a special cell, but a prisoner shall not be so confined as a punishment, or after he has ceased to be refractory or violent.

(2) A prisoner shall not be confined in a special cell for longer than 24 hours without a direction in writing given by an officer of the Secretary of State. Such a direction shall state the grounds for the confinement and the time during which it may continue.

**7.9495** *49. Restraints* (1) The governor may order a prisoner to be put under restraint where this is necessary to prevent the prisoner from injuring himself or others, damaging property or creating a disturbance.

(2) Notice of such an order shall be given without delay to a member of the independent monitoring board, and to a registered medical practitioner or to a registered nurse working within the prison.

(3) On receipt of the notice, the registered medical practitioner or registered nurse referred to in paragraph (2), shall inform the governor whether there are any medical reasons why the prisoner should not be put under restraint. The governor shall give effect to any recommendation which may be made under this paragraph.

(4) A prisoner shall not be kept under restraint longer than necessary, nor shall he be so kept for longer than 24 hours without a direction in writing given by an officer of the Secretary of State (not being an officer of a prison). Such a direction shall state the grounds for the restraint and the time during which it may continue.

(5) Particulars of every case of restraint under the foregoing provisions of this rule shall be forthwith recorded.

(6) Except as provided by this rule no prisoner shall be put under restraint otherwise than for safe custody during removal, or on medical grounds by direction of a registered medical practitioner or of a registered nurse working within the prison. No prisoner shall be put under restraint as a punishment.

(7) Any means of restraint shall be of a pattern authorised by the Secretary of State, and shall be used in such manner and under such conditions as the Secretary of State may direct.

**7.9496** *50. Compulsory testing for controlled drugs or specified drugs* (1) This rule applies where an officer, acting under the powers conferred by section 16A of the Prison Act 1952 (power to test prisoners for drugs), requires a prisoner to provide a sample for the purpose of ascertaining whether he has any controlled drug or specified drug in his body.

(2) In this rule "sample" means a sample of urine or any other description of sample specified in the authorisation by the governor for the purposes of section 16A of the Prison Act 1952.

(3) When requiring a prisoner to provide a sample, an officer shall, so far as is reasonably practicable, inform the prisoner:

(*a*) that he is being required to provide a sample in accordance with section 16A of the Prison Act 1952; and

(*b*) that a refusal to provide a sample may lead to disciplinary proceedings being brought against him.

(4) An officer shall require a prisoner to provide a fresh sample, free from any adulteration.

(5) An officer requiring a sample shall make such arrangements and give the prisoner such instructions for its provision as may be reasonably necessary in order to prevent or detect its adulteration or falsification.

(6) A prisoner who is required to provide a sample may be kept apart from other prisoners for a period not exceeding one hour to enable arrangements to be made for the provision of the sample.

(7) A prisoner who is unable to provide a sample of urine when required to do so may be kept apart from other prisoners until he has provided the required sample, save that a prisoner may not be kept apart under this paragraph for a period of more than 5 hours.

(8) A prisoner required to provide a sample of urine shall be afforded such degree of privacy for the purposes of providing the sample as may be compatible with the need to prevent or detect any adulteration or falsification of the sample; in particular a prisoner shall not be required to provide such a sample in the sight of a person of the opposite sex.

**7.9497** *50A. Observation of prisoners by means of an overt closed circuit television system* (1) Without prejudice to his other powers to supervise the prison, prisoners and other persons in the prison, whether by use of an overt closed circuit television system or otherwise, the governor may make arrangements for any prisoner to be placed under constant observation by means of an overt closed circuit television system while the prisoner is in a cell or other place in the prison if he considers that—

(*a*) such supervision is necessary for—

(i) the health and safety of the prisoner or any other person;

(ii) the prevention, detection, investigation or prosecution of crime; or

(iii) securing or maintaining prison security or good order and discipline in the prison; and

(*b*) it is proportionate to what is sought to be achieved.

(2) If an overt closed circuit television system is used for the purposes of this rule, the provisions of rules 35C and 35D shall apply to any material obtained.

**7.9498** *50B. Compulsory testing for alcohol* (1) This rule applies where an officer, acting under an authorisation in force under section 16B of the Prison Act 1952 (power to test prisoners for alcohol), requires a prisoner to provide a sample for the purpose of ascertaining whether he has alcohol in his body.

(2) When requiring a prisoner to provide a sample an officer shall, so far as is reasonably practicable, inform the prisoner—

(*a*) that he is being required to provide a sample in accordance with section 16B of the Prison Act 1952; and

(*b*) that a refusal to provide a sample may lead to disciplinary proceedings being brought against him.

(3) An officer requiring a sample shall make such arrangements and give the prisoner such instructions for its provision as may be reasonably necessary in order to prevent or detect its adulteration or falsification.

(4) Subject to paragraph (5) a prisoner who is required to provide a sample may be kept apart from other prisoners for a period not exceeding one hour to enable arrangements to be made for the provision of the sample.

(5) A prisoner who is unable to provide a sample of urine when required to do so may be kept apart from other prisoners until he has provided the required sample, except that a prisoner may not be kept apart under this paragraph for a period of more than 5 hours.

(6) A prisoner required to provide a sample of urine shall be afforded such degree of privacy for the purposes of providing the sample as may be compatible with the need to prevent or detect any adulteration or falsification of the sample; in particular a prisoner shall not be required to provide such a sample in the sight of a person of the opposite sex.

## Offences against Discipline

**7.9499** *51. Offences against discipline* A prisoner is guilty of an offence against discipline if he—

(1) commits any assault;

(1A) commits any racially aggravated assault;

(2) detains any person against his will;

(3) denies access to any part of the prison to any officer or any person (other than a prisoner) who is at the prison for the purpose of working there;

(4) fights with any person;

(5) intentionally endangers the health or personal safety of others or, by his conduct, is reckless whether such health or personal safety is endangered;

(6) intentionally obstructs an officer in the execution of his duty, or any person (other than a prisoner) who is at the prison for the purpose of working there, in the performance of his work;

(7) escapes or absconds from prison or from legal custody;

(8) fails to comply with any condition upon which he is temporarily released under rule 9;

(9) is found with any substance in his urine which demonstrates that a controlled drug or specified drug has, whether in prison or while on temporary release under rule 9, been administered to him by himself or by another person (but subject to rule 52);;

(10) is intoxicated as a consequence of consuming any alcoholic beverage (but subject to

rule 52A);

(11) consumes any alcoholic beverage whether or not provided to him by another person (but subject to rule 52A);

(12) has in his possession—

(*a*) any unauthorised article, or

(*b*) a greater quantity of any article than he is authorised to have;

(13) sells or delivers to any person any unauthorised article;

(14) sells or, without permission, delivers to any person any article which he is allowed to have only for his own use;

(15) takes improperly any article belonging to another person or to a prison;

(16) intentionally or recklessly sets fire to any part of a prison or any other property, whether or not his own;

(17) destroys or damages any part of a prison or any other property, other than his own;

(17A) causes racially aggravated damage to, or destruction of, any part of a prison or any other property, other than his own;

(18) absents himself from any place he is required to be or is present at any place where he is not authorised to be;

(19) is disrespectful to any officer, or any person (other than a prisoner) who is at the prison for the purpose of working there, or any person visiting a prison;

(20) uses threatening, abusive or insulting words or behaviour;

(20A) uses threatening, abusive or insulting racist words or behaviour;

(21) intentionally fails to work properly or, being required to work, refuses to do so;

(22) disobeys any lawful order;

(23) disobeys or fails to comply with any rule or regulation applying to him;

(24) receives any controlled drug or specified drug, or, without the consent of an officer, any other article, during the course of a visit (not being an interview such as is mentioned in rule 38);

(24A) displays, attaches or draws on any part of a prison, or on any other property, threatening, abusive or insulting racist words, drawings, symbols or other material;

(25)

(*a*) attempts to commit,

(*b*) incites another prisoner to commit, or

(*c*) assists another prisoner to commit or to attempt to commit, any of the foregoing offences.

**7.9500** *51A. Interpretation of rule 51* (2) For the purposes of rule 51 words, behaviour or material are racist if they demonstrate, or are motivated (wholly or partly) by, hostility to members of a racial group (whether identifiable or not) based on their membership (or presumed membership) of a racial group, and "membership", "presumed", "racial group" and "racially aggravated", shall have the meanings assigned to them by section 28 of the Crime and Disorder Act 1998.

**7.9501** *52. Defences to rule 51(9)* It shall be a defence for a prisoner charged with an offence under rule 51(9) to show that:

(*a*) the controlled drug or specified drug had been, prior to its administration, lawfully in his possession for his use or was administered to him in the course of a lawful supply of the drug to him by another person;

(*b*) the controlled drug or specified drug was administered by or to him in circumstances in which he did not know and had no reason to suspect that such a drug was being administered; or

(*c*) the controlled drug or specified drug was administered by or to him under duress or to him without his consent in circumstances where it was not reasonable for him to have resisted.

**7.9502** *52A. Defences to rule 51(10) and rule 51(11)* It shall be a defence for a prisoner charged with an offence under rule 51(10) or (11) to show that—

(*a*) the alcohol was consumed by him in circumstances in which he did not know and had no reason to suspect that he was consuming alcohol;

(*b*) the alcohol was consumed by him without his consent in circumstances where it was not reasonable for him to have resisted; or

(*c*) *revoked.*

**7.9503** *53. Disciplinary charges*[1] (1) Where a prisoner is to be charged with an offence against discipline, the charge shall be laid as soon as possible and, save in exceptional circumstances, within 48 hours of the discovery of the offence[2].

(2) Every charge shall be inquired into by the governor[3] or, as the case may be, the adjudicator.

(3) Every charge shall be first inquired into not later, save in exceptional circumstances or in accordance with rule 55A(5), than:

(*a*) where it is inquired into by the governor, the next day, not being a Sunday or public holiday, after it is laid

(*b*) where it is referred to the adjudicator under rule 53A(2) or 60(3)(*b*), 28 days after it is so referred.

(4) A prisoner who is to be charged with an offence against discipline may be kept apart from other prisoners pending the governor's first inquiry or determination under rule 53A.

---

[1] Where disciplinary proceedings may result in the award of additional days, they are criminal proceedings for the purpose of the European Convention on Human Rights and art 6 applies. Therefore the refusal to allow a prisoner to be legally represented is a breach of art 6(3)(*b*) (*Ezeh v United Kingdom* (Application 39665/98); and *Connors v United Kingdom* (Application 40086/98) [2004] Crim LR 472).

Prisoners do not have a 'civil right' to associate with other prisoners; this is a normal privilege rather than a right and is subject to withdrawal in accordance with the Rules, particularly those permitting cellular confinement or segregation, which invest governors with discretionary powers. This administrative decision and the process of review by the SRBs are amenable to judicial review which, among other things, will secure Convention rights such as those under arts 3 and 8: *R (on the application of King) v Secretary of State* [2012] EWCA Civ 376, [2012] 4 All ER 44, [2012] 1 WLR 3602.

[2] The authorities have 48 hours in any event, and longer if there are exceptional circumstances making it impossible to lay the charge within that time. As the rule means 'not later than 48 hours after', a charge which is laid on the stroke of the forty-eighth hour is laid within 48 hours: *R (on the application of Garland) v Secretary of State for Justice* [2011] EWCA Civ 1335, [2012] 1 WLR 1879.

[3] An informed and fair-minded observer would regard prison governors, or their deputies, as being quite capable of interpreting and applying the prison rules fairly and independently. However, in the unusual case where a deputy governor had been present when the governor approved a general order for a squat search which the prisoner refused to obey and had not dissented from that approval, an informed and fair-minded observer could infer that he had thereby tacitly accepted that the order was lawful and there was a real possibility that he would be biased if he later had to adjudicate on the defendant's challenge to the validity of the order (*R (Al-Hasan) v Secretary of State for the Home Department* [2005] UKHL 13, [2005] 1 All ER 927, [2005] 1 WLR 688). See also *R (Greenfield) v Secretary of State for the Home Department* [2005] UKHL 14, [2005] 1 WLR 673 (no damages awarded for breach of art 6 where on the facts the adjudication should not have been by a deputy controller).

**7.9504** 53A. *Determination of mode of inquiry* (1) Before inquiring into a charge the governor shall determine—

(i) whether the charge is so serious that additional days should be awarded for the offence, if the prisoner is found guilty, or

(ii) whether it is necessary or expedient for some other reason for the charge to be inquired into by the adjudicator.

(2) Where the governor determines:

(*a*) that it is so serious, or that it is necessary or expedient for some other reason for the charge to be inquired into by the adjudicator he shall:

(i) refer the charge to the adjudicator forthwith for him to inquir into it;

(ii) refer any other charge arising out of the same incident to the adjudicator forthwith for him to inquire into it; and

(iii) inform the prisoner who has been charged that he has done so;

(*b*) that it is not so serious, or that it is not so necessary or expedient for some other reason for the charge to be inquired into by the adjudicator he shall proceed to inquire into the charge.

(3) If:

(*a*) at any time during an inquiry into a charge by the governor; or

(*b*) following such an inquiry, after the governor has found the prisoner guilty of an offence but before he has imposed a punishment for that offence,

it appears to the governor either that the charge is so serious that additional days should be awarded for the offence if (where sub-paragraph (*a*) applies) the prisoner is found guilty or that it is necessary or expedient for some other reason for the charge to be inquired into by the adjudicator, the governor shall act in accordance with paragraph (2)(*a*)(i) to (iii) and the adjudicator shall first inquire into any charge referred to him under this paragraph not later than, save in exceptional circumstances, 28 days after the charge was referred.

**7.9505** 54. *Rights of prisoners charged* (1) Where a prisoner is charged with an offence against discipline, he shall be informed of the charge as soon as possible and, in any case, before the time when it is inquired into by the governor or, as the case may be, the adjudicator.

(2) At an inquiry into a charge against a prisoner he shall be given a full opportunity of hearing what is alleged against him and of presenting his own case.

(3) At an inquiry into a charge which has been referred to the adjudicator, the prisoner who has been charged shall be given the opportunity to be legally represented.

**7.9506** 55. *Governor's punishments* (1) If he finds a prisoner guilty of an offence against discipline the governor may, subject to paragraph (2) and to rule 57, impose one or more of the following punishments:

(*a*) caution;

(*b*) forfeiture for a period not exceeding 42 days of any of the privileges under rule 8;

(*c*) exclusion from associated work for a period not exceeding 21 days;

(*d*) stoppage of or deduction from earnings for a period not exceeding 84 days and of an amount not exceeding 42 days earnings;

(*e*) cellular confinement for a period not exceeding 21 days;

(*f*) *revoked*;

(*g*) in the case of a prisoner otherwise entitled to them, forfeiture for any period of the right, under rule 43(1), to have the articles there mentioned;

(*h*) removal from his wing or living unit for a period of 28 days.

(2) A caution shall not be combined with any other punishment for the same charge.

(3) If a prisoner is found guilty of more than one charge arising out of an incident, punishments under this rule may be ordered to run consecutively but in the case of a punishment of cellular confinement, the total period shall not exceed 21 days.

(4) In imposing a punishment under this rule, the governor shall take into account any guidelines that the Secretary of State may from time to time issue as to the level of punishment that should normally be imposed for a particular offence against discipline.

**7.9507** 55A. *Adjudicator's punishment* (1) If he finds a prisoner guilty of an offence against discipline the adjudicator may, subject to paragraph (2) and to rule 57, impose one or more of the following punishments:

(*a*) any of the punishments mentioned in rule 55(1);

(*b*) in the case of a fixed-term prisoner, an award of additional days not exceeding 42 days.
(2) A caution shall not be combined with any other punishment for the same charge.
(3) If a prisoner is found guilty of more than one charge arising out of an incident, punishments under this rule may be ordered to run consecutively but, in the case of an award of additional days, the total period added shal not exceed 42 days and, in the case of a punishment of cellular confinement, the total period shall not exceed 21 days.
(4) This rule applies to a prisoner who has been charged with having committed an offence against discipline before the date on which the rule came into force, in the same way as it applies to a prisoner who has been charged with having committed an offence against discipline on or after that date, provided the charge is referred to the adjudicator no later than 60 days after that date.
(5) Rule 53(3) shall not apply to a charge where, by virtue of paragraph (4), this rule applies to the prisoner who has been charged.

**7.9508** *55AB. Requirement to pay for damage to prison property* (1) This rule applies where a prisoner is found guilty of an offence under rule 51(17) or 51(17A) in respect of destroying or damaging any part of a prison or any other property belonging to a prison ("the relevant disciplinary offence").
(2) The governor or, as the case may be, the adjudicator must require the prisoner to pay for the cost of making good the damage from, or replacing any property destroyed as a result of, the commission of the relevant disciplinary offence.
(3) A requirement imposed under paragraph (2) is referred to in this rule and in rules 55B, 61 and 61A as a "compensation requirement".
(4) The amount required to be paid under a compensation requirement must not exceed the cost of making good the damage from, or replacing any property destroyed as a result of, the commission of the relevant disciplinary offence and, in any event, must not exceed £2,000.
(5) A compensation requirement may be imposed instead of or in addition to any punishment imposed under rule 55 or 55A.
(6) A compensation requirement ceases to have effect after two years from the date on which it was imposed regardless of whether or not the full amount has been paid.

**7.9509** *55B. Review of adjudicator's punishment* (1) A reviewer means the Senior District Judge (Chief Magistrate) or any deputy of such a judge as nominated by that judge.
(2) Where an adjudicator imposes a punishment under rule 55A(1), a compensation requirement under rule 55AB(2) or both, a prisoner may, within 14 days of receipt of the punishment or the imposition of the compensation requirement, whichever is later, request in writing that a reviewer conducts a review.
(3) The review must be commenced within 14 days of receipt of the request and must be conducted on the papers alone.
(4) The review may be of the punishment, the compensation requirement or both (whether or not the prisoner requested a review of both) but must not be a review of the finding of guilt under rule 55A.
(5) On completion of the review, if it appears to the reviewer that the [imposition of the punishment, the compensation requirement or both was manifestly unreasonable he may do such of the following as he considers appropriate—
(*a*) reduce the number of any additional days awarded;
(*b*) for whatever punishment has been imposed by the adjudicator, substitute another punishment which is, in his opinion, less severe;
(*c*) quash the punishment entirely.
(*d*) reduce the amount of the compensation requirement
(6) A prisoner requesting a review shall serve any additional days awarded under rule 55A(1)(*b*) unless and until they are reduced.

**7.9510** *56. Forfeiture of remission to be treated as an award of additional days* (1) In this rule, "existing prisoner" and "existing licensee" have the meanings assigned to them by paragraph 8(1) of Schedule 12 to the Criminal Justice Act 1991.
(2) In relation to any existing prisoner or existing licensee who has forfeited any remission of his sentence, the provisions of Part II of the Criminal Justice Act 1991 shall apply as if he had been awarded such number of additional days as equals the numbers of days of remission which he has forfeited.

**7.9511** *57. Offences committed by young persons* (1) In the case of an offence against discipline committed by an inmate who was under the age of 21 when the offence was committed (other than an offender in relation to whom the Secretary of State has given a direction under section 13(1) of the Criminal Justice Act 1982 that he shall be treated as if he had been sentenced to imprisonment) rule 55 or, as the case may be, rule 55A shall have effect, but—
(*a*) the maximum period of forfeiture of privileges under rule 8 shall be 21 days;
(*b*) the maximum period of stoppage of or deduction from earnings shall be 42 days;
(*c*) the maximum period of cellular confinement shall be ten days
(*d*) the maximum period of removal from his cell or living unit shall be 21 days.
(2) In the case of an inmate who has been sentenced to a term of youth custody or detention in a young offender institution, and by virtue of a direction of the Secretary of State under section 99 of the Powers of Criminal Courts (Sentencing) Act 2000, is treated as if he had been sentenced to imprisonment for that term, any punishment imposed on him for an offence against discipline before the said direction was given shall, if it has not been exhausted or remitted, continue to have effect:
(*a*) if imposed by a governor, as if made pursuant to rule 55

(*b*) if imposed by an adjudicator, as if made pursuant to rule 55A.

**7.9512** 58. *Cellular confinement* Before deciding whether to impose a punishment of cellular confinement the governor, adjudicator or reviewer shall first enquire of a registered medical practitioner or registered nurse, working within the prison, as to whether there are any medical reasons why the punishment is unsuitable and shall take this advice into account when making his decision.

**7.9513** 59. *Prospective award of additional days* (1) Subject to paragraph (2), where an offence against discipline is committed by a prisoner who is detained only on remand, additional days may be awarded by the adjudicator notwithstanding that the prisoner has not (or had not at the time of the offence) been sentenced.

(2) An award of additional days under paragraph (1) shall have effect only if the prisoner in question subsequently becomes a fixed-term prisoner whose sentence is reduced, under section 67 of the Criminal Justice Act 1967 or section 240 of the 2003 Act, by a period which includes the time when the offence against discipline was committed.

**7.9514** 59A. *Removal from a cell or living unit* Following the imposition of a punishment of removal from his cell or living unit, a prisoner shall be accommodated in a separate part of the prison under such restrictions of earnings and activities as the Secretary of State may direct.

**7.9515** 60. *Suspended punishments* (1) Subject to any directions given by the Secretary of State, the power to impose a disciplinary punishment (other than a caution) shall include power to direct that the punishment is not to take effect unless, during a period specified in the direction (not being more than six months from the date of the direction), the prisoner commits another offence against discipline and a direction is given under paragraph (2).

(2) Where a prisoner commits an offence against discipline during the period specified in a direction given under paragraph (1) the person dealing with that offence may—

(*a*) direct that the suspended punishment shall take effect;

(*b*) reduce the period or amount of the suspended punishment and direct that it shall take effect as so reduced;

(*c*) vary the original direction by substituting for the period specified a period expiring not later than six months from the date of variation; or

(*d*) give no direction with respect to the suspended punishment.

(3) Where an award of additional days has been suspended under paragraph (1) and a prisoner is charged with committing an offence against discipline during the period specified in a direction given under that paragraph, the governor shall either:

(*a*) inquire into the charge and give no direction with respect to the suspended award; or

(*b*) refer the charge to the adjudicator for him to inquire into it.

**7.9516** 61. *Remission and mitigation of punishments, variation of compensation requirements and quashing of findings of guilt* (1) Except in the case of a finding of guilt made, or a punishment imposed, by an adjudicator under rule 55A(1), the Secretary of State may quash any finding of guilt and may remit any punishment or mitigate it either by reducing it or by substituting another award which is, in his opinion, less severe.

(1A) Where a compensation requirement has been imposed by a governor under rule 55AB(2), the Secretary of State may reduce the amount of the requirement.]

(2) Subject to any directions given by the Secretary of State, the governor may, on the grounds of good behaviour, remit or mitigate any punishment already imposed by an adjudicator or governor.

**7.9517** 61A. *Enforcement of compensation requirements* (1) Where a compensation requirement has been imposed under rule 55AB(2), the governor may debit any amount of money with which the prisoner has been credited in the books of the prison under rule 43(3) in order to recover the whole or part of the amount required to be paid under the compensation requirement.

(2) The amount debited under paragraph (1) on any occasion must not be such as to reduce below £5 the amount with which the prisoner is credited in the books of the prison under rule 43(3).

(3) Where—

(*a*) a compensation requirement has been imposed under rule 60AB(2) of the Young Offender Rules 2000, and

(*b*) the person against whom the compensation requirement was imposed is detained in a prison,

the compensation order may be enforced under paragraph (1) as if it was a compensation requirement imposed under rule 55AB(2).

## Part III Officers of Prisons

**7.9518** 62. *General duty of officers* (1) It shall be the duty of every officer to conform to these Rules and the rules and regulations of the prison, to assist and support the governor in their maintenance and to obey his lawful instructions.

(2) An officer shall inform the governor promptly of any abuse or impropriety which comes to his knowledge.

**7.9519** 63. *Gratuities forbidden* No officer shall receive any unauthorised fee, gratuity or other consideration in connection with his office.

**7.9520** 64. *Search of officers* An officer shall submit himself to be searched in the prison if the governor so directs. Any such search shall be conducted in as seemly a manner as is consistent with discovering anything concealed.

**7.9521** 65. *Transactions with prisoners* (1) No officer shall take part in any business or pecuniary transaction with or on behalf of a prisoner without the leave of the Secretary of State.

(2) No officer shall without authority bring in or take out, or attempt to bring in or take out, or knowingly allow to be brought in or taken out, to or for a prisoner, or deposit in any place with intent that it shall come into the possession of a prisoner, any article whatsoever.

**7.9522** *66. Contact with former prisoners* No officer shall, without the knowledge of the governor, communicate with any person whom he knows to be a former prisoner or a relative or friend of a prisoner or former prisoner.

**7.9523** *67. Communications to the press* (1) No officer shall make, directly or indirectly, any unauthorised communication to a representative of the press or any other person concerning matters which have become known to him in the course of his duty.

(2) No officer shall, without authority, publish any matter or make any public pronouncement relating to the administration of any institution to which the Prison Act 1952 applies or to any of its inmates.

**7.9524** *68. Code of discipline* The Secretary of State may approve a code of discipline to have effect in relation to officers, or such classes of officers as it may specify, setting out the offences against discipline, the awards which may be made in respect of them and the procedure for dealing with charges.

**7.9525** *69. Emergencies* Where any constable or member of the armed forces of the Crown is employed by reason of any emergency to assist the governor of a prison by performing duties ordinarily performed by an officer of a prison, any reference in Part II of these Rules to such an officer (other than a governor) shall be construed as including a reference to a constable or a member of the armed forces of the Crown so employed.

## Part IV Persons having Access to a Prison

**7.9526** *70. Prohibited articles* No person shall, without authority, convey into or throw into or deposit in a prison, or convey or throw out of a prison, or convey to a prisoner, or deposit in any place with intent that it shall come into the possession of a prisoner, any article whatever. Anything so conveyed, thrown or deposited may be confiscated by the governor.

**7.9527** *70A. List C Articles* A List C article is any article or substance in the following list—

(*a*) tobacco;
(*b*) money;
(*c*) clothing;
(*d*) food;
(*e*) drink;
(*f*) letters;
(*g*) paper;
(*h*) books;
(*i*) tools;
(*j*) information technology equipment.

**7.9528** *71. Control of persons and vehicles* (1) Any person or vehicle entering or leaving a prison may be stopped, examined and searched and in addition any such person may be photographed, fingerprinted or required to submit to other physical measurement.

(1A) Any such search of a person shall be carried out in as seemly a manner as is consistent with discovering anything concealed about the person or their belongings.

(2) The governor may direct the removal from a prison of any person who does not leave on being required to do so.

**7.9529** *72. Viewing of prisons* (1) No outside person shall be permitted to view a prison unless authorised by statute or the Secretary of State.

(2) No person viewing the prison shall be permitted to take a photograph, make a sketch or communicate with a prisoner unless authorised by statute or the Secretary of State.

**7.9530** *73. Visitors* (1) Without prejudice to any other powers to prohibit or restrict entry to prisons, or his powers under rules 34 and 35, the Secretary of State may prohibit visits by a person to a prison or to a prisoner in a prison for such periods of time as he considers necessary if the Secretary of State considers that such a prohibition is—

(*a*) necessary on grounds specified in rule 35A(4); and
(*b*) is proportionate to what is sought to be achieved by the prohibition.

(2) Paragraph (1) shall not apply in relation to any visit to a prison or prisoner by a member of the independent monitoring board of the prison, or justice of the peace, or to prevent any visit by a legal adviser for the purposes of an interview under rule 38 or visit allowed by the independent monitoring board under rule 35(6).

## Part V Independent Monitoring Board

**7.9531** *74. Disqualification for membership* Any person, directly or indirectly interested in any contract for the supply of goods or services to a prison, shall not be a member of the independent monitoring board for that prison and any member who becomes so interested in such a contract shall vacate office as a member.

**7.9532** *75. Independent Monitoring Board* (1) A member of the independent monitoring board for a prison appointed by the Secretary of State under section 6(2) of the Prison Act 1952 shall subject to paragraphs (3) and (4) hold office for three years, or such lesser period as the Secretary of State may appoint.

(2) A member—

(*a*) appointed for the first time to the independent monitoring board for a particular prison; or

(*b*) reappointed to the board following a gap of a year or more in his membership of it,

shall, during the period of 12 months following the date on which he is so appointed or (as the case may be) reappointed, undertake such training as may reasonably be required by the Secretary of State.

(3) The Secretary of State may terminate the appointment of a member if he is satisfied that—

(*a*) he has failed satisfactorily to perform his duties;

(*b*) he has failed to undertake training he has been required to undertake under paragraph (2), by the end of the period specified in that paragraph;

(*c*) he is by reason of physical or mental illness, or for any other reason, incapable of carrying out his duties;

(*d*) he has been convicted of such a criminal offence, or his conduct has been such, that it is not in the Secretary of State's opinion fitting that he should remain a member; or

(*e*) there is, or appears to be or could appear to be, any conflict of interest between the member performing his duties as a member and any interest of that member, whether personal, financial or otherwise.

(4) Where the Secretary of State:

(*a*) has reason to suspect that a member of the independent monitoring board for a prison may have so conducted himself that his appointment may be liable to be terminated under paragraph (3)(*a*) or (*d*); and

(*b*) is of the opinion that the suspected conduct is of such a serious nature that the member cannot be permitted to continue to perform his functions as a member of the board pending the completion of the Secretary of State's investigations into the matter and any decision as to whether the member's appointment should be terminated,

he may suspend the member from office for such period or periods as he may reasonably require in order to complete his investigations and determine whether or not the appointment of the member should be so terminated; and a member so suspended shall not, during the period of his suspension, be regarded as being a member of the board, other than for the purposes of this paragraph and paragraphs (1) and (3).

(5) A board shall have a chairman and a vice chairman who shall be members of the board.

(6) The Secretary of State shall—

(*a*) upon the constitution of a board for the first time, appoint a chairman and a vice chairman to hold office for a period not exceeding twelve months;

(*b*) thereafter appoint, before the date of the first meeting of the board in any year of office of the board, a chairman and vice chairman for that year, having first consulted the board; and

(*c*) promptly fill, after first having consulted the board, any casual vacancy in the office of chairman or vice chairman.

(7) The Secretary of State may terminate the appointment of a member as chairman or vice chairman of the board if he is satisfied that the member has—

(*a*) failed satisfactorily to perform his functions as chairman (or as the case may be) vice chairman;

(*b*) has grossly misconducted himself while performing those functions.

**7.9533** 76. *Proceedings of boards* (1) The independent monitoring board for a prison shall meet at the prison once a month or, if they resolve for reasons specified in the resolution that less frequent meetings are sufficient, not fewer than eight times in twelve months.

(2) The board may fix a quorum of not fewer than three members for proceedings.

(3) The board shall keep minutes of their proceedings.

(4) The proceedings of the board shall not be invalidated by any vacancy in the membership or any defect in the appointment of a member.

**7.9534** 77. *General duties of boards* (1) The independent monitoring board for a prison shall satisfy themselves as to the state of the prison premises, the administration of the prison and the treatment of the prisoners.

(2) The board shall inquire into and report upon any matter into which the Secretary of State asks them to inquire.

(3) The board shall direct the attention of the governor to any matter which calls for his attention, and shall report to the Secretary of State any matter which they consider it expedient to report.

(4) The board shall inform the Secretary of State immediately of any abuse which comes to their knowledge.

(5) Before exercising any power under these Rules the board and any member of the board shall consult the governor in relation to any matter which may affect discipline.

**7.9535** 78. *Particular duties* (1) The independent monitoring board for a prison and any member of the board shall hear any complaint or request which a prisoner wishes to make to them or him.

(2) The board shall arrange for the food of the prisoners to be inspected by a member of the board at frequent intervals.

(3) The board shall inquire into any report made to them, whether or not by a member of the board, that a prisoner's health, mental or physical, is likely to be injuriously affected by any conditions of his imprisonment.

7.9536 *79. Members visiting prisons* (1) The members of the independent monitoring board for a prison shall visit the prison frequently, and the board shall arrange a rota whereby at least one of its members visits the prison between meetings of the board.

(2) A member of the board shall have access at any time to every part of the prison and to every prisoner, and he may interview any prisoner out of the sight and hearing of officers.

(3) A member of the board shall have access to the records of the prison, except that members of the board shall not have access to any records held for the purposes of or relating to conduct authorised in accordance with Part 2 of the Regulation of Investigatory Powers Act 2000.

7.9537 *80. Annual report* (1) The independent monitoring board for a prison shall, in accordance with paragraphs (2) and (3) below, from time to time make a report to the Secretary of State concerning the state of the prison and its administration, including in it any advice and suggestions they consider appropriate.

(2) The board shall comply with any directions given to them from time to time by the Secretary of State as to the following matters:

(*a*) the period to be covered by a report under paragraph (1);

(*b*) the frequency with which such a report is to be made; and

(*c*) the length of time from the end of the period covered by such a report within which it is to be made;

either in respect of a particular report or generally; providing that no directions may be issued under this paragraph if they would have the effect of requiring a board to make or deliver a report less frequently than once in every 12 months.

(3) Subject to any directions given to them under paragraph (2), the board shall, under paragraph (1), make an annual report to the Secretary of State as soon as reasonably possible after 31st December each year, which shall cover the period of 12 months ending on that date or, in the case of a board constituted for the first time during that period, such part of that period during which the board has been in existence.

## PART VI SUPPLEMENTAL

7.9538 *81. Delegation by governor* The governor of a prison may, with the leave of the Secretary of State, delegate any of his powers and duties under these Rules to another officer of that prison.

7.9539 *82. Contracted out prisons* (1) Where the Secretary of State has entered into a contract for the running of a prison under section 84 of the Criminal Justice Act 1991 ("the 1991 Act") these Rules shall have effect in relation to that prison with the following modifications—

(*a*) references to an officer in the Rules shall include references to a prisoner custody officer certified as such under section 89(1) of the 1991 Act and performing custodial duties;

(*b*) references to a governor in the Rules shall include references to a director approved by the Secretary of State for the purposes of section 85(1)(*a*) of the 1991 Act except—

(i) in rule 81 the reference to a governor shall include a reference to a controller appointed by the Secretary of State under section 85(1)(*b*) of the 1991 Act; and

(ii) in rules 62(1), 66 and 77 where references to a governor shall include references to the director and the controller;

(iii) in rules 45, 48, 49, 53, 53A, 54, 55, 55AB, 57, 60, 61 and 61A where references to a governor shall include a reference to the director or the controller;

(*c*) rule 68 shall not apply in relation to a prisoner custody officer certified as such under section 89(1) of the 1991 Act and performing custodial duties.

(1A) The director of a prison may, with the leave of the Secretary of State, delegate any of his powers and duties under rules 45, 48, 49, 53, 53A, 55, 55AB, 57, 60, 61 and 61A to another officer of that prison.

(2) *Repealed.*

7.9540 *83. Contracted out parts of prisons* Where the Secretary of State has entered into a contract for the running of part of a prison under section 84(1) of the Criminal Justice Act 1991, that part and the remaining part shall each be treated for the purposes of Parts II to IV and Part VI of these Rules as if they were separate prisons.

7.9541 *84. Contracted out functions at directly managed prisons* (1) Where the Secretary of State has entered into a contract under section 88A(1) of the Criminal Justice Act 1991 ("the 1991 Act") for any functions at a directly managed prison to be performed by prisoner custody officers who are authorised to perform custodial duties under section 89(1) of the 1991 Act, references to an officer in these Rules shall, subject to paragraph (2), include references to a prisoner custody officer who is so authorised and who is performing contracted out functions for the purposes of, or for purposes connected with, the prison.

(2) Paragraph (1) shall not apply to references to an officer in rule 68.

(3) In this rule, "directly managed prison" has the meaning assigned to it by section 88A(5) of the 1991 Act.

7.9542 *85. Revocations and savings* (1) Subject to paragraphs (2) and (3) below, the Rules specified in the Schedule to these Rules are hereby revoked.

(2) Without prejudice to the Interpretation Act 1978, where a prisoner committed an offence against discipline contrary to rule 47 of the Prison Rules 1964 prior to the coming into force of these Rules, those rules shall continue to have effect to permit the prisoner to be charged with such an offence, disciplinary proceedings in relation to such an offence to be continued, and the governor to impose punishment for such an offence.

(3) Without prejudice to the Interpretation Act 1978, any award of additional days or other punishment or suspended punishment for an offence against discipline awarded or imposed

under any provision of the rules revoked by this rule, or those rules as saved by paragraph (2), or treated by any such provision as having been awarded or imposed under the rules revoked by this rule, shall have effect as if awarded or imposed under the corresponding provision of these Rules.

SCHEDULE Rule 85

**7.9543** *Revocations.*

## Young Offender Institution Rules 2000[1]

(SI 2000/3371 amended by SI 2002/2117, SI 2005/897 and 3438, SI 2006/680, SI 2007/2953 and 3220, SI 2008/599 and 3155, SI 2009/3082, SI 2011/1663, SI 2013/235 and 2462, SI 2014/2169, SI 2015/1638 and SI 2016/583 and 945)

### Part I Preliminary

**7.9544** 1. *Citation and commencement* (*a*) These Rules may be cited as the Young Offender Institution Rules 2000 and shall come into force on 1st April 2001.

(*b*) The Rules set out in the Schedule to this Order are hereby revoked.

[1] These rules were made by the Secretary of State under s 47 of the Prison Act 1952.

**7.9545** 2. *Interpretation* (1) In these Rules, where the context so admits, the expression-

"adjudicator" means a District Judge (Magistrates' Courts) or Deputy District Judge (Magistrates' Courts) approved[1] by the Lord Chancellor for the purpose of inquiring into a charge which has been referred to him;

"communication" includes any written or drawn communication from an inmate to any other person, whether intended to be transmitted by means of a postal service or not, and any communication from an inmate to any other person transmitted by means of a telecommunications system;

"compulsory school age" has the same meaning as in the Education Act 1996;

"controlled drug" means any drug which is a controlled drug for the purposes of the Misuse of Drugs Act 1971;

"fixed-term prisoner" has the meaning assigned to it by section 237(1) of the Criminal Justice Act 2003;

"governor" includes an officer for the time being in charge of a young offender institution;

"health care professional" means a person who is a member of a profession regulated by a body mentioned in section 25(3) of the National Health Service Reform and Health Care Professions Act 2002 and who is working within the young offender institution;

"health care provider" includes any provider of health services, whether or not commissioned by an NHS body (within the meaning given by section 275(1) of the National Health Service 2006);

"information technology equipment" includes any laptop or notebook computer, desktop computer, gaming console, handheld computing device, personal organiser or any electronic device containing a computer processor and capable of connecting to the internet, and any reference to information technology equipment includes a reference to–

(*a*) a component part of a device of that description; or

(*b*) any article designed or adapted for use with any information technology equipment (including any disk, film or other separate article on which images, sounds, computer code or other information may be stored or recorded);

"inmate" means a person who is required to be detained in a young offender institution;

"intercepted material" means the contents of any communication intercepted pursuant to these Rules;

"legal adviser" means, in relation to an inmate, his counsel or solicitor, and includes a clerk acting on behalf of his solicitor;

"minister appointed to a young offender institution" means a minister so appointed under section 10 of the Prison Act 1952;

"officer" means an officer of a young offender institution;

"specified drug" means any product or substance containing one or more of the following—

(a) AB-PINACA (N-[(1S)-1-(aminocarbonyl)-2-methylpropyl]-1-pentyl-1H-indazole- 3-carboxamide);

(b) 5F-AB-PINACA (N-[(1S)-1-(aminocarbonyl)-2-methylpropyl]-1-(5- Fluoropentyl)-1H-indazole-3-carboxamide);

(c) AB-FUBINACA (N-[(1S)-1-(aminocarbonyl)-2-methylpropyl]-1-[(4-fluorophenyl)methyl]-1H-indazole-3-carboxamide);

(d) APICA (1-pentyl-N-tricyclo[3.3.1.13,7]dec-1-yl-1H-indole-3-carboxamide);

(e) 5F-APICA (N-(adamantan-1-yl)-1-(5-fluoropentyl)-1H-indole-3-carboxamide);

(f) APINACA (1-pentyl-N-tricyclo[3.3.1.13,7]dec-1-yl-1H-indazole-3-carboxamide);

(g) 5F-APINACA (1-(5-fluoropentyl)-N-tricyclo[3.3.1.13,7]dec-1-yl-1H-indazole-3-carboxamide);

(h) 5F-PB22 (1-(5-fluoropentyl)-8-quinolinyl ester-1H-indole-3-carboxylic acid),

(i) MDMB-CHMICA (methyl 2-{[1-(cyclohexylmethyl)-1H-indol-3-yl]formamido}- 3,3-dimethylbutanoate);

(j) PB-22 (Quinolin-8-yl-1-pentyl-1H-indole-3-carboxylate);

(k) 5F-MDMB-PINACA (Methyl-[2-(1-(5-fluoropentyl)-1H-indazole-3- carboxamido)-3,3-dimethylbutanoate]);

(l) AB-CHMINACA (N-[-1-(Aminocarbonyl)-2-methylpropyl]-1- (cyclohexylmethyl)-1H-indazole-3-carboxamide);
(m) 5F-AMB (Methyl 2-({[1-(5-fluoropentyl)-1H-indazol-3-yl]carbonyl}amino)-3-methylbutanoate);
(n) AMB-FUBINACA (Methyl-2-(1-(4-fluorobenzyl)-1H-indazole-3-carboxamide)-3-methylbutanoate);
(o) Etizolam (4-(2-Chlorophenyl)-2-ethyl-9-methyl-6H-thieno[3,2- f][1,2,4]triazolo[4,3-a][1,4]diazepine);
(p) ADB-CHMINACA (N-[1-(aminocarbonyl)-2,2-dimethylpropyl]-1- (cyclohexylmethyl)-1H-indazole-3-carboxamide);

"telecommunications system" means any system (including the apparatus comprised in it) which exists for the purpose of facilitating the transmission of communications by any means involving the use of electrical or electro-magnetic energy;
"the 2003 Act" means the Criminal Justice Act 2003.

(2) In these Rules a reference to—
(*a*) an award of additional days means additional days awarded under these Rules by virtue of section 42 of the Criminal Justice Act 1991 or by virtue of section 257 of the 2003 Act";
(*b*) the Church of England includes a reference to the Church of Wales; and
(*c*) a reference to a numbered rule is, unless otherwise stated, a reference to the rule of that number in these Rules and a reference to a numbered paragraph is in a rule, unless otherwise stated, a reference to the paragraph of that number in that rule.

[1] The requirement of the approval of the Lord Chancellor for the appointment of a District Judge (Magistrates' Courts) or Deputy District Judge (Magistrates' Courts) as an adjudicator does not apply to a person who is approved to act as an adjudicator on 18 April 2005, and such a person may continue to act as an adjudicator for so long as he holds office as a District Judge (Magistrates' Courts) or Deputy District Judge (Magistrates' Courts): Young Offender Institution (Amendment) Rules 2005, SI 2005/897, r 1(2).

## PART II INMATES

### *General*

**7.9546** 3. *Aims and general principles of young offender institutions* (1) The aim of a young offender institution shall be to help offenders to prepare for their return to the outside community.
(2) The aim mentioned in paragraph (1) shall be achieved, in particular, by—
(*a*) providing a programme of activities, including education, training and work designed to assist offenders to acquire or develop personal responsibility, self-discipline, physical fitness, interests and skills and to obtain suitable employment after release;
(*b*) fostering links between the offender and the outside community; and
(*c*) co-operating with the services responsible for the offender's supervision after release.

**7.9547** 4. *Classification of inmates* (1) Subject to paragraphs (2) to (5), inmates may be classified, in accordance with any directions of the Secretary of State, taking into account their ages, characters and circumstances.
(2) Except where paragraph (5) applies, an inmate who has the relevant deportation status must not be classified as suitable for open conditions.
(3) If, immediately before the relevant time—
(*a*) an inmate has been classified as suitable for open conditions; and
(*b*) the young offender institution has received notice that the inmate has the relevant deportation status,

the inmate's classification must be reconsidered in accordance with this rule as soon as practicable after the relevant time.
(4) If—
(*a*) an inmate has been classified as suitable for open conditions (whether before or after the relevant time); and
(*b*) the young offender institution receives notice after the relevant time that the inmate has the relevant deportation status,

the inmate's classification must be reconsidered in accordance with this rule as soon as practicable after the young offender institution receives that notice.
(5) This paragraph applies if an inmate has been classified as suitable for open conditions and is located in open conditions immediately before the inmate's classification is reconsidered, whether under paragraph (3) or (4) or otherwise.
(6) For the purposes of this rule, an inmate has the relevant deportation status if—
(*a*) there is a deportation order against the inmate under section 5(1) of the Immigration Act 1971; and
(*b*) no appeal under section 82(1) of the Nationality, Immigration and Asylum Act 2002 ("the 2002 Act") that may be brought or continued from within the United Kingdom in relation to the decision to make the deportation order—
  (i) could be brought (ignoring any possibility of an appeal out of time with permission), or
  (ii) is pending (within the meaning of section 104 of the 2002 Act).
(7) In paragraph (6), the reference to the decision to make a deportation order includes a decision that section 32(5) of the UK Borders Act 2007 applies in respect of the inmate.
(8) In this rule, "the relevant time" means 5.00 pm on 13th August 2014.

### *Release*

**7.9548** 5. *Temporary release* (1) Subject to paragraph (1A), the Secretary of State may, in accordance with the other provisions of this rule, release temporarily an inmate to whom this rule applies.

(1A) An inmate who has the relevant deportation status must not be released under this rule unless the inmate is located in open conditions immediately before the time of release.

(2) An inmate may be released under this rule for any period or periods and subject to any conditions.

(3) An inmate may only be released under this rule:

(*a*) on compassionate grounds or for the purpose of receiving medical treatment;

(*b*) to engage in employment or voluntary work;

(*c*) to receive instruction or training which cannot reasonably be provided in the young offender institution;

(*d*) to enable him to participate in any proceedings before any court, tribunal or inquiry;

(*e*) to enable him to consult with his legal adviser in circumstances where it is not reasonably practicable for the consultation to take place in the young offender institution;

(*f*) to assist any police officer in any enquiries;

(*g*) to facilitate the inmate's transfer between the young offender institution and another penal establishment;

(*h*) to assist him in maintaining family ties or in his transition from life in the young offender institution to freedom; or

(*i*) *revoked.*

(4) An inmate shall not be released under this rule unless the Secretary of State is satisfied that there would not be an unacceptable risk of his committing offences whilst released or otherwise of his failing to comply with any condition upon which he is released.

(5) Where at any time an offender is subject concurrently:

(*a*) to a detention and training order; and

(*b*) to a sentence of detention in a young offender institution,

he shall be treated for the purposes of paragraphs (6) and (7) as if he were subject only to the one of them that was imposed on the later occasion.

(6) The Secretary of State shall not release under this rule an inmate if, having regard to:

(*a*) the period or proportion of his sentence which the inmate has served or, in a case where paragraph (10) does not apply to require all the sentences he is serving to be treated as a single term, the period or proportion of any such sentence he has served; and

(*b*) the frequency with which the inmate has been granted temporary release under this rule,

the Secretary of State is of the opinion that the release of the inmate would be likely to undermine public confidence in the administration of justice.

(7) If an inmate has been temporarily released under this rule during the relevant period and has been sentenced to any period of detention, custody or imprisonment for a criminal offence committed whilst at large following that release, he shall not be released under this rule unless his release, having regard to the circumstances of his conviction, would not, in the opinion of the Secretary of State, be likely to undermine public confidence in the administration of justice; and for this purpose "the relevant period":

(*a*) in the case of an inmate serving a determinate sentence of imprisonment, detention or custody, is the period he has served in respect of that sentence, unless, notwithstanding paragraph (10), the sentences he is serving do not fall to be treated as a single term, in which case it is the period since he was last released in relation to one of those sentences under Part II of the Criminal Justice Act 1991 ("the 1991 Act") or section 100 of the Powers of the Criminal Courts (Sentencing) Act 2000 ("the 2000 Act") or Chapter 6 of Part 12 of the 2003 Act; or

(*b*) in the case of an inmate serving an indeterminate sentence of imprisonment, detention or custody, is, if the inmate has previously been released on licence under Part II of the 1991 Act or Part II of the Crime (Sentences) Act 1997 or Chapter 6 of Part 12 of the 2003 Act, the period since the date of his last recall to a penal establishment in respect of that sentence or, where the inmate has not been so released, the period he has served in respect of that sentence,

save that where an inmate falls within both of sub-paragraphs (*a*) and (*b*) above, the "relevant period", in the case of that inmate, shall be determined by whichever of the applicable sub-paragraphs that produces the longer period.

(8) An inmate released under this rule may be recalled at any time whether the conditions of his release have been broken or not.

(8A) If, immediately before the relevant time, an inmate has been released under this rule and the young offender institution has received notice that the inmate has the relevant deportation status, the inmate must be recalled unless—

(*a*) the period for which the inmate has been released is due to expire on 13th August 2014; or

(*b*) the inmate was released from open conditions.

(8B) If an inmate has been released under this rule (whether before or after the relevant time) and the young offender institution receives notice after the relevant time that the inmate has the relevant deportation status, the inmate must be recalled unless—

(*a*) the period for which the inmate has been released is due to expire on the day on which the young offender institution receives that notice; or (*b*) the inmate was released from open conditions.

(9) This rule applies to inmates other than persons committed in custody for trial or to be sentenced or otherwise dealt with before or by the Crown Court or remanded in custody by any court.

(10) For the purposes of any reference in this rule to an inmate's sentence, consecutive terms and terms which are wholly or partly concurrent shall be treated as a single term.

(11) In this rule, any reference to release on licence under Part II of the 1991 Act includes any release on licence under any earlier legislation providing for early release on licence.

(12) In this rule—

(*a*) any reference to an inmate who has the relevant deportation status is to be read in accordance with rule 4(6) and (7); and

(*b*) any reference to the relevant time is to be read in accordance with rule 4(8).

*Conditions*

**7.9549** *6. Privileges* (1) There shall be established at every young offender institution systems of privileges approved by the Secretary of State and appropriate to the classes of inmates thereof and their ages, characters and circumstances, which shall include arrangements under which money earned by inmates may be spent by them within the young offender institution.

(2) Systems of privileges approved under paragraph (1) may include arrangements under which inmates may be allowed time outside the cells and in association with one another, in excess of the minimum time which, subject to the other provisions of these Rules apart from this rule, is otherwise allowed to inmates at the young offender institution for this purpose.

(3) Systems of privileges approved under paragraph (1) may include arrangements under which privileges may be granted to inmates only in so far as they have met, and for so long as they continue to meet, specified standards in their behaviour and their performance in work or other activities.

(4) Systems of privileges which include arrangements of the kind referred to in paragraph (3) shall include procedures to be followed in determining whether or not any of the privileges concerned shall be granted, or shall continue to be granted, to an inmate; such procedures shall include a requirement that the inmate be given reasons for any decision adverse to him together with a statement of the means by which he may appeal against it.

(5) Nothing in this rule shall be taken to confer on an inmate any entitlement to any privilege or to affect any provision in these Rules other than this rule as a result of which any privilege may be forfeited or otherwise lost or an inmate deprived of association with other inmates.

**7.9550** *7. Information to inmates* (1) Every inmate shall be provided, as soon as possible after his reception into the young offender institution, and in any case within 24 hours, with information in writing about those provisions of these Rules and other matters which it is necessary that he should know, including earnings and privileges, and the proper method of making requests and complaints.

(2) In the case of an inmate aged under 18, or an inmate aged 18 or over who cannot read or appears to have difficulty in understanding the information so provided, the governor, or an officer deputed by him, shall so explain it to him that he can understand his rights and obligations.

(3) A copy of these Rules shall be made available to any inmate who requests it.

**7.9551** *8. Requests and complaints* (1) An inmate may make a request or complaint to the governor or independent monitoring board relating to an inmate's detention.

(2) The governor shall consider as soon as possible any requests and complaints that are made to him under paragraph (1).

(3) A written request or complaint under paragraph (1) may be made in confidence.

**7.9552** *9. Communications generally* (1) Without prejudice to sections 6 and 19 of the Prison Act 1952 and except as provided by these Rules, an inmate shall not be permitted to communicate with any person outside the young offender institution, or such person with him, except with the leave of the Secretary of State or as a privilege under rule 7.

(2) Notwithstanding paragraph (1), and except as otherwise provided in these Rules, the Secretary of State may impose any restriction or condition, either generally or in a particular case, upon the communications to be permitted between an inmate and other persons if he considers that the restriction or condition to be imposed—

(*a*) does not interfere with the Convention rights of any person; or

(*b*) is necessary on grounds specified in paragraph (3) below, provided that:

(i) reliance on the grounds is compatible with the Convention right to be interfered with; and

(ii) the restriction or condition is proportionate to what is sought to be achieved.

(3) The grounds referred to in paragraph (2) are—

(*a*) the interests of national security;

(*b*) the prevention, detection, investigation or prosecution of crime;

(*c*) the interests of public safety;

(*d*) securing or maintaining security or good order and discipline in the young offender institution;

(*e*) the protection of health or morals;

(*f*) the protection of the reputation of others;

(*g*) maintaining the authority and impartiality of the judiciary; or

(*h*) the protection of the rights and freedoms of any person.

(4) Subject to paragraph (2), the Secretary of State may require that any visit, or class of visits, shall be held in facilities which include special features restricting or preventing physical contact

between an inmate and a visitor.
(5) Every visit to an inmate shall take place within the sight of an officer or employee of the young offender institution authorised for the purposes of this rule by the governor (in this rule referred to as an "authorised employee"), unless the Secretary of State otherwise directs, and for the purposes of this paragraph a visit to an inmate shall be taken to take place within the sight of an officer or authorised employee if it can be seen by an officer or authorised employee by means of an overt closed circuit television system.
(6) Subject to rule 13, every visit to an inmate shall take place within the hearing of an officer or authorised employee, unless the Secretary of State otherwise directs.
(7) The Secretary of State may give directions, either generally or in relation to any visit or class of visits, concerning the day and times when inmates may be visited.
(8) In this rule—
(*a*) references to communications include references to communications during visits;
(*b*) references to restrictions and conditions upon communications include references to restrictions and conditions in relation to the length, duration and frequency of communications; and
(*c*) references to Convention rights are to the Convention rights within the meaning of the Human Rights Act 1998.

**7.9553** 10. *Personal letters and visits* (1) Subject to paragraph (7) an inmate shall be entitled—
(*a*) to send and to receive a letter on his reception into a young offender institution and thereafter once a week; and
(*b*) to receive a visit twice in every period of four weeks, but only once in every such period if the Secretary of State so directs.
(2) The governor may allow an inmate an additional letter or visit as a privilege under rule 6 or when necessary for his welfare or that of his family.
(3) The governor may allow an inmate entitled to a visit to send and to receive a letter instead.
(4) The governor may defer the right of an inmate to a visit until the expiration of any period of confinement to a cell or room.
(5) The independent monitoring board may allow an inmate an additional letter or visit in special circumstances, and may direct that a visit may extend beyond the normal duration.
(6) The Secretary of State may allow additional letters and visits in relation to any inmate or class of inmates.
(7) An inmate shall not be entitled under this rule to receive a visit from—
(*a*) any person, whether or not a relative or friend, during any period of time that person is the subject of a prohibition imposed under rule 77; or
(*b*) any other person, other than a relative or friend, except with the leave of the Secretary of State.
(8) Any letter or visit under the succeeding provisions of these Rules shall not be counted as a letter or visit for the purposes of this rule.

**7.9554** 11. *Interception of communications* (1) The Secretary of State may give directions to any governor concerning the interception in a young offender institution of any communication by any inmate or class of inmates if the Secretary of State considers that the directions are—
(*a*) necessary on grounds specified in paragraph (4); and
(*b*) proportionate to what is sought to be achieved.
(2) Subject to any directions given by the Secretary of State, the governor may make arrangements for any communication by an inmate or class of inmates to be intercepted in a young offender institution by an officer or an employee of the young offender institution authorised by the governor for the purposes of this rule (referred to in this rule as an "authorised employee") if he considers that the arrangements are—
(*a*) necessary on grounds specified in paragraph (4); and
(*b*) proportionate to what is sought to be achieved.
(2A) The governor may not make arrangements for interception of any communication between an inmate and
(*a*) the inmate's legal adviser; or
(*b*) any body or organisation with which the Secretary of State has made arrangements for the confidential handling of correspondence,
unless the governor has reasonable cause to believe that the communication is being made with the intention of furthering a criminal purpose and unless authorised by any one of the following: the chief executive officer of the National Offender Management Service; the director responsible for the national operational services of that service; or the duty director of that service.
(3) Any communication by an inmate may, during the course of its transmission in a young offender institution, be terminated by an officer or an authorised employee if he considers that to terminate the communication is—
(*a*) necessary on grounds specified in paragraph (4); and
(*b*) proportionate to what is sought to be achieved by the termination.
(4) The grounds referred to in paragraphs (1)(*a*), (2)(*a*) and (3)(*a*) are—
(*a*) the interests of national security;
(*b*) the prevention, detection, investigation or prosecution of crime;
(*c*) the interests of public safety;
(*d*) securing or maintaining security or good order and discipline in the young offender institution;
(*e*) the protection of health or morals; or

(*f*) the protection of the rights and freedoms of any person.

(5) Any reference to the grounds specified in paragraph (4) in relation to the interception of a communication by means of a telecommunications system in a young offender institution, or the disclosure or retention of intercepted material from such a communication, shall be taken to be a reference to those grounds with the omission of sub-paragraph (f).

(6) For the purposes of this rule "interception"—

(*a*) in relation to a communication by means of a telecommunications system, means any action taken in relation to the system or its operation so as to make some or all of the contents of the communications available, while being transmitted, to a person other than the sender or intended recipient of the communication; and the contents of a communication are to be taken to be made available to a person while being transmitted where the contents of the communication, while being transmitted, are diverted or recorded so as to be available to a person subsequently; and

(*b*) in relation to any written or drawn communication, includes opening, reading, examining and copying the communication.

**7.9555** 12. *Permanent log of communications* (1) The governor may arrange for a permanent log to be kept of all communications by or to an inmate.

(2) The log referred to in paragraph (1) may include, in relation to a communication by means of a telecommunications system in a young offender institution, a record of the destination, duration and cost of the communication and, in relation to any written or drawn communication, a record of the sender and addressee of the communication.

**7.9556** 13. *Disclosure of material* (1) Except in accordance with paragraph (2), the governor may not disclose to any person who is not

(*a*) an officer of a young offender institution;

(*b*) an officer of the Secretary of State;

(*c*) an officer of the Youth Justice Board for England and Wales, where the Board has entered into a contract for the provision or running, or both, of the young offender institution; or

(*d*) an employee of the young offender institution authorised by the governor for the purpose of this rule,

any intercepted material, information retained pursuant to rule 12 or material obtained by means of an overt closed circuit television system used during a visit.

(2) The governor may disclose the material and information identified in paragraph (1) to persons, other than those mentioned in that paragraph, if:

(*a*) he considers that such disclosure is—

(i) necessary on the grounds specified in rule 11(4); and

(ii) proportionate to what is sought to be achieved by the disclosure;

(*b*) in the case of intercepted material or material obtained by means of an overt closed circuit television system used during a visit, all parties to the communication or visit consent to the disclosure; or

(*c*) in the case of information retained pursuant to rule 12, the inmate to whose communication the information relates, consents to the disclosure.

**7.9557** 14. *Retention of material* (1) The governor shall not retain any intercepted material or material obtained by means of an overt closed circuit television system used during a visit for a period longer than 3 months beginning with the day on which the material was intercepted or obtained unless he is satisfied that continued retention of it is—

(*a*) necessary on grounds specified in rule 11(4); and

(*b*) proportionate to what is sought to be achieved by the continued retention.

(2) Where such material is retained for longer than three months pursuant to paragraph (1) the governor shall review its continued retention at periodic intervals until such time as it is no longer held by the governor.

(3) The first review referred to in paragraph (2) shall take place not more than three months after the decision to retain the material taken pursuant to paragraph (1) and subsequent reviews shall take place not more than three months apart thereafter.

(4) If the governor, on a review conducted pursuant to paragraph (2) or at any other time, is not satisfied that the continued retention of the material satisfies the requirements set out in paragraph (1), he shall arrange for the material to be destroyed.

**7.9558** 15. *Police interviews* A police officer may, on production of an order issued by or on behalf of a chief officer of police, interview any inmate willing to see him.

**7.9559** 16. *Visits from legal advisers* (1) Where the legal adviser of an inmate in any legal proceedings, civil or criminal, to which the inmate is a party visits the inmate, the legal adviser shall be afforded reasonable facilities for interviewing him in connection with those proceedings, and may do so out of hearing of an officer.

(2) On such a visit, an inmate's legal adviser may, with the leave of the Secretary of State, interview the inmate in connection with any other legal business.

**7.9560** 17. *Delivery and receipt of legally privileged material* (1) An inmate may deliver to, or receive from, the inmate's legal adviser and any court, either by post or during a legal visit under rule 16, any legally privileged material and such material may only be opened, read or stopped by the governor in accordance with the provisions of this rule.

(2) Material to which this rule applies may be opened if the governor has reasonable cause to believe that it contains an illicit enclosure and any such enclosure shall be dealt with in accordance

with the other provisions of these Rules. (3) Material to which this rule applies may be opened, read and stopped if the governor has reasonable cause to believe its contents endanger prison or young offender institution security or the safety of others or are otherwise of a criminal nature.
(4) An inmate shall be given the opportunity to be present when any material to which this rule applies is opened and shall be informed if it or any enclosure is to be read or stopped.
(5) An inmate shall on request be provided with any writing materials necessary for the purposes of paragraph (1).
(6) In this rule, "court" includes the European Court of Human Rights and the European Court of Justice; and "illicit enclosure" includes any article possession of which has not been authorised in accordance with the other provisions of these Rules and any material to or from a person other than the inmate concerned, his legal adviser or a court.

**7.9561** *18. Securing release of defaulters* An inmate detained in a young offender institution in default of payment of a fine or any other sum of money may communicate with, and be visited at any reasonable time on a weekday by, any relative or friend for payment in order to secure his release.

**7.9562** *19. Clothing*

**7.9563** *20. Food*

**7.9564** *21. Alcohol and tobacco*

**7.9565** *22. Sleeping accommodation*

**7.9566** *23. Beds and bedding*

**7.9567** *24. Hygiene*

**7.9568** *25. Female inmates*

**7.9569** *26. Library books*

**7.9570** *27–29. Medical attention*

**7.9571** *30–36. Religion*

**7.9572** *37–42. Occupation and Links with the Community*

**7.9573** *43. After-care* (1) From the beginning of his sentence, consideration shall be given, in consultation with the appropriate supervising service, to an inmate's future and the help to be given to him in preparation for and after his return to the community.
(2) Every inmate who is liable to supervision after release shall be given a careful explanation of his liability and the requirements to which he will be subject while under supervision.

*Discipline and Control*

**7.9574** *44. Maintenance of order and discipline* (1) Order and discipline shall be maintained, but with no more restriction than is required in the interests of security and well-ordered community life.
(2) Notwithstanding paragraph (1), regimes may be established at young offender institutions under which stricter order and discipline are maintained and which emphasise strict standards of dress, appearance and conduct; provided that no inmate shall be required to participate in such a regime unless he has been first assessed as being suitable for it and no inmate shall be required to continue with such a regime if at any time it appears that he is no longer suitable for it.
(3) For the purposes of paragraph (2), whether an inmate is suitable for a stricter regime is to be assessed by reference to whether he is sufficiently fit in mind and body to undertake it and whether, in the opinion of the Secretary of State, experience of the regime will further his rehabilitation.
(4) In the control of inmates, officers shall seek to influence them through their own example and leadership, and to enlist their willing co-operation.

**7.9575** *45. Custody outside a young offender institution* (1) A person being taken to or from a young offender institution in custody shall be exposed as little as possible to public observation and proper care shall be taken to protect him from curiosity and insult.
(2) An inmate required to be taken in custody anywhere outside a young offender institution shall be kept in the custody of an officer appointed under section 3 of the Prison Act 1952 or of a police officer.
(3) An inmate required to be taken in custody to any court shall, when he appears before the court, wear his own clothing or ordinary civilian clothing provided by the governor.

**7.9576** *46. Search* (1) Every inmate shall be searched when taken into custody by an officer, on his reception into a young offender institution and subsequently as the governor thinks necessary or as the Secretary of State may direct.
(2) An inmate shall be searched in as seemly a manner as is consistent with discovering anything concealed.
(3) No inmate shall be stripped and searched in the sight of another inmate or in the sight of a person of the opposite sex.

**7.9577** *47. Record and photograph* (1) A personal record of each inmate shall be prepared and maintained in such manner as the Secretary of State may direct, but no part of the record shall be disclosed to any person not authorised to receive it.
(2) Every inmate may be photographed on reception and subsequently, but no copy of the

photograph or any other personal record shall be given to any person not authorised to receive it.
(2A) In this rule "personal record" may include personal information and biometric records (such as fingerprints or other physical measurements).

**7.9578** *48. Inmates' property* (1) Anything, other than cash, which an inmate has at a young offender institution and which he is not allowed to retain for his own use shall be taken into the governor's custody.
(2) Any case which an inmate has at a young offender institution shall be paid into an account under the control of the governor and the inmate shall be credited with the amount in the books of the institution.
(3) Any article belonging to an inmate which remains unclaimed for a period of more than one year after he is released, or dies, may be sold or otherwise disposed of; and the net proceeds of any sale shall be paid to the National Association for the Care and Resettlement of Offenders, for its general purposes.
(4) The governor may confiscate any unauthorised article found in the possession of an inmate after his reception into a young offender institution, or concealed or deposited within a young offender institution.

**7.9579** *49. Removal from association* (1) Where it appears desirable, for the maintenance of good order or discipline or in his own interests, that an inmate should not associate with other inmates, either generally or for particular purposes, the governor may arrange for the inmate's removal from association for up to 72 hours.
(2) Removal for more than 72 hours may be authorised by the governor in writing who may authorise a further period of removal of up to 14 days.[1]
(2A) Such authority may be renewed for subsequent periods of up to 14 days.
(2B) But the governor must obtain leave from the Secretary of State in writing to authorise removal under paragraph (2A) where the period in total amounts to more than 42 days starting with the date the inmate was removed under paragraph (1).
(2C) The Secretary of State may only grant leave for a maximum period of 42 days, but such leave may be renewed for subsequent periods of up to 42 days by the Secretary of State.
(3) The governor may arrange at his discretion for an inmate removed under this rule to resume association with other inmates at any time.
(4) In giving authority under paragraphs (2) and (2A) and in exercising the discretion under paragraph (3), the governor must fully consider any recommendation that the inmate resumes association on medical grounds made by a registered medical practitioner or registered nurse working within the young offender institution.

---

[1] See note to the Prison Rules, r 45, ante.

**7.9580** *50. Use of force* (1) An officer in dealing with an inmate shall not use force unnecessarily and, when the application of force to an inmate is necessary, no more force than is necessary shall be used.
(2) No officer shall act deliberately in a manner calculated to provoke an inmate.

**7.9581** *51. Temporary confinement* (1) The governor may order an inmate who is refractory or violent to be confined temporarily in a special cell or room, but an inmate shall not be so confined as a punishment, or after he has ceased to be refractory or violent.
(2) A cell or room shall not be used for the purpose of this rule unless it has been certified by an officer of the Secretary of State (not being an officer of a young offender institution) that it is suitable for the purpose, that its size, lighting, heating, ventilation and fittings are adequate for health, and that it allows the inmate to communicate at any time with an officer.
(3) In relation to any young offender institution, section 14(6) of the Prison Act 1952 shall have effect so as to enable the provision of special rooms instead of special cells for the temporary confinement of refractory or violent inmates.
(4) An inmate shall not be confined under this rule for longer than 24 hours without a direction in writing given by an officer of the Secretary of State.

**7.9582** *52. Restraints* (1) The governor may order an inmate to be put under restraint where this is necessary to prevent the inmate from injuring himself or others, damaging property or creating a disturbance.
(2) The governor may not order an inmate aged under 17 to be put under restraint, except that he may order such an inmate be placed in handcuffs where this is necessary to prevent the inmate from injuring himself or others, damaging property or creating a disturbance.
(3) Notice of such an order shall be given without delay to a member of the independent monitoring board and to a registered medical practitioner or registered nurse working within the institution.
(4) On receipt of the notice, the registered medical practitioner or registered nurse referred to in paragraph (3), shall inform the governor whether there are any reasons why the inmate should not be put under restraint. The governor shall give effect to any recommendation which may be made under this paragraph.
(5) An inmate shall not be kept under restraint longer than necessary, nor shall he be so kept for longer than 24 hours without a direction in writing given by an officer of the Secretary of State (not being an officer of a young offender institution). Such a direction shall state the grounds for the restraint and the time during which it may continue.
(6) Particulars of every case of restraint under the foregoing provisions of this rule shall be

forthwith recorded.

(7) Except as provided by this rule no inmate shall be put under restraint otherwise than for safe custody during removal, or on medical grounds by direction of a registered medical practitioner or registered nurse working within the institution.. No inmate shall be put under restraint as a punishment.

(8) Any means of restraint shall be of a pattern authorised by the Secretary of State, and shall be used in such manner and under such conditions as the Secretary of State may direct.

**7.9583** 53. *Compulsory Testing for controlled drugs or specified drugs* (1) This rule applies where an officer, acting under the powers conferred by section 16A of the Prison Act 1952 (power to test inmates for drugs), requires an inmate to provide a sample for the purposes of ascertaining whether he has any controlled drug or specified drug in his body.

(2) In this rule "sample" means a sample of urine or any other description of sample specified in the authorisation by the governor for the purposes of section 16A.

(3) When requiring an inmate to provide a sample, an officer shall, so far as is reasonably practicable, inform the inmate:

(*a*) that he is being required to provide a sample in accordance with section 16A of the Prison Act 1952; and

(*b*) that a refusal to provide a sample may lead to disciplinary proceedings being brought against him.

(4) An officer shall require an inmate to provide a fresh sample, free from any adulteration.

(5) An officer requiring a sample shall make such arrangements and give the inmate such instructions for its provision as may be reasonably necessary in order to prevent or detect its adulteration or falsification.

(6) An inmate who is required to provide a sample may be kept apart from other inmates for a period not exceeding one hour to enable arrangements to be made for the provision of the sample.

(7) An inmate who is unable to provide a sample of urine when required to do so may be kept apart from other inmates until he has provided the required sample, save that an inmate may not be kept apart under this paragraph for a period of more than five hours.

(8) An inmate required to provide a sample of urine shall be afforded such degree of privacy for the purposes of providing the sample as may be compatible with the need to prevent or detect any adulteration or falsification of the sample; in particular an inmate shall not be required to provide such a sample in the sight of a person of the opposite sex.

**7.9584** 54. *Supervision of inmates by means of an overt closed circuit television system* (1) Without prejudice to his powers to make arrangements for the supervision of inmates in his custody, the governor may make arrangements for any inmate to be placed under constant supervision by means of an overt closed circuit television system placed in a cell, dormitory or other place in the young offender institution if he considers that—

(*a*) such supervision is necessary for—

(i) the health and safety of the inmate or any other person;

(ii) the prevention, detection or prosecution of crime; or

(iii) securing or maintaining security or good order and discipline in the young offender institution; and

(*b*) it is proportionate to what is sought to be achieved.

(2) If an overt closed circuit television system is used for the purposes of this rule, the provisions of rules 13 and 14 shall apply to any material obtained.

**7.9585** 54A. *Compulsory testing for alcohol* (1) This rule applies where an officer, acting under an authorisation in force under section 16B of the Prison Act 1952 (power to test prisoners for alcohol), requires an inmate to provide a sample for the purpose of ascertaining whether he has alcohol in his body.

(2) When requiring an inmate to provide a sample an officer shall, so far as is reasonably practicable, inform the inmate—

(*a*) that he is being required to provide a sample in accordance with section 16B of the Prison Act 1952; and

(*b*) that a refusal to provide a sample may lead to disciplinary proceedings being brought against him.

(3) An officer requiring a sample shall make such arrangements and give the inmate such instructions for its provision as may be reasonably necessary in order to prevent or detect its adulteration or falsification.

(4) Subject to paragraph (5) an inmate who is required to provide a sample may be kept apart from other inmates for a period not exceeding one hour to enable arrangements to be made for the provision of the sample.

(5) An inmate who is unable to provide a sample of urine when required to do so may be kept apart from other inmates until he has provided the required sample, except that an inmate may not be kept apart under this paragraph for a period of more than 5 hours.

(6) An inmate required to provide a sample of urine shall be afforded such degree of privacy for the purposes of providing the sample as may be compatible with the need to prevent or detect any adulteration or falsification of the sample; in particular an inmate shall not be required to provide such a sample in the sight of a person of the opposite sex.

**7.9586** 55. *Offences against discipline* An inmate is guilty of an offence against discipline if he—

(1) commits any assault;

(2) commits any racially aggravated assault;

(3) detains any person against his will;

(4) denies access to any part of the young offender institution to any officer or any person (other than an inmate) who is at the young offender institution for the purpose of working there;

(5) fights with any person;

(6) intentionally endangers the health or personal safety of others or, by his conduct, is reckless whether such health or personal safety is endangered;

(7) intentionally obstructs an officer in the execution of his duty, or any person (other than an inmate) who is at the young offender institution for the purpose of working there, in the performance of his work;

(8) escapes or absconds from a young offender institution or from legal custody;

(9) fails to comply with any condition upon which he was temporarily released under rule 5 of these rules;

(10) is found with any substance in his urine which demonstrates that a controlled drug or specified drug has, whether in prison or while on temporary release under rule 5, been administered to him by himself or by another person (but subject to rule 56);

(11) is intoxicated as a consequence of consuming any alcoholic beverage (but subject to rule 56A);

(12) consumes any alcoholic beverage whether or not provided to him by another person (but subject to rule 56A);

(13) has in his possession—

(*a*) any unauthorised article, or

(*b*) a greater quantity of any article than he is authorised to have;

(14) sells or delivers to any person any unauthorised article;

(15) sells or, without permission, delivers to any person any article which he is allowed to have only for his own use;

(16) takes improperly any article belonging to another person or to a young offender institution;

(17) intentionally or recklessly sets fire to any part of a young offender institution or any other property, whether or not his own;

(18) destroys or damages any part of a young offender institution or any other property other than his own;

(19) causes racially aggravated damage to, or destruction of, any part of a young offender institution or any other property, other than his own;

(20) absents himself from any place where he is required to be or is present at any place where he is not authorised to be;

(21) is disrespectful to any officer, or any person (other than an inmate) who is at the young offender institution for the purpose of working there, or any person visiting a young offender institution;

(22) uses threatening, abusive or insulting words or behaviour;

(23) uses threatening, abusive or insulting racist words or behaviour;

(24) intentionally fails to work properly or, being required to work, refuses to do so;

(25) disobeys any lawful order;

(26) disobeys or fails to comply with any rule or regulation applying to him;

(27) receives any controlled drug or specified drug or, without the consent of an officer, any other article, during the course of a visit (not being an interview such as is mentioned in rule 16);

(28) displays, attaches or draws on any part of a young offender institution, or on any other property, threatening, abusive, or insulting racist words, drawings, symbols or other material;

(29)

(*a*) attempts to commit,

(*b*) incites another inmate to commit, or

(*c*) assists another inmate to commit or to attempt to commit,

any of the foregoing offences.

**7.9587** *56. Defences to rule 55(10)* It shall be a defence for an inmate charged with an offence under rule 55(10) to show that—

(*a*) the controlled drug or specified drug had been, prior to its administration, lawfully in his possession for his use or was administered to him in the course of a lawful supply of the drug to him by another person;

(*b*) the controlled drug or specified drug was administered by or to him in circumstances in which he did not know and had no reason to suspect that such a drug was being administered; or

(*c*) the controlled drug or specified drug was administered by or to him under duress or to him without his consent in circumstances where it was not reasonable for him to have resisted.

**7.9588** *56A. Defences to rule 55(11) and rule 55(12)* It shall be a defence for an inmate charged with an offence under rule 55(11) or (12) to show that—

(*a*) the alcohol was consumed by him in circumstances in which he did not know and had no reason to suspect that he was consuming alcohol; or (*b*) the alcohol was consumed by him without his consent in circumstances where it was not reasonable for him to have resisted; or

(*c*) *revoked.*

**7.9589** *57. Interpretation of rule 55* For the purposes of rule 55 words, behaviour or material shall be racist if they demonstrate or are motivated (wholly or partly) by hostility to members of a racial group (whether identifiable or not) based on their membership (or presumed membership) of a racial group, and "membership", "presumed", "racial group" and "racially aggravated", shall have the meanings assigned to them by section 28 of the Crime and Disorder Act 1998

**7.9590** *58. Disciplinary charges* (1) Where an inmate is to be charged with an offence against discipline, the charge shall be laid as soon as possible and, save in exceptional circumstances, within 48 hours of the discovery of the offence.

(2) Every charge shall be inquired into by the governor or, as the case may be, the adjudicator.

(3) Every charge shall be first inquired into not later, save in exceptional circumstances or in accordance with rule 60A(5) or rule 65(4), than:

(*a*) where it is inquired into by the governor, the next day, not being a Sunday or public holiday, after it is laid;

(*b*) where it is referred to the adjudicator under rule 58A(2) or 63(3)(*b*), 28 days after it is so referred.

(4) An inmate who is to be charged with an offence against discipline may be kept apart from other inmates pending the governor's first inquiry or determination under rule 58A.

**7.9591** *58A. Determination of mode of inquiry* (1) Before inquiring into a charge the governor shall determine —

(i) whether the charge is so serious that additional days should be awarded for the offence, if the prisoner is found guilty, or

(ii) whether it is necessary or expedient for some other reason for the charge to be inquired into by the adjudicator.

(2) Where the governor determines:

(*a*) that it is so serious or that it is necessary or expedient for some other reason for the charge to be inquired into by the adjudicator, he shall:

(i) refer the charge to the adjudicator forthwith for him to inquire into it;

(ii) refer any other charge arising out of the same incident to the adjudicator forthwith for him to inquire into it; and

(iii) inform the inmate who has been charged that he has done so;

(*b*) that it is not so serious or that it is not necessary or expedient for some other reason for the charge to be inquired into by the adjudicator, he shall proceed to inquire into the charge.

(3) If:

(*a*) at any time during an inquiry into a charge by the governor; or

(*b*) following such an inquiry, after the governor has found the inmate guilty of an offence but before he has imposed a punishment for that offence,

it appears to the governor either that the charge is so serious that additional days should be awarded for the offence if (where sub-paragraph (*a*) applies) the inmate is found guilty or that it is necessary or expedient for some other reason for the charge to be inquired into by the adjudicator, the governor shall act in accordance with paragraph (2)(*a*)(i) to (iii) and the adjudicator shall first inquire into any charge referred to him under this paragraph not later than, save in exceptional circumstances, 28 days after the charge was referred.

**7.9592** *59. Rights of inmates charged* (1) Where an inmate is charged with an offence against discipline, he shall be informed of the charge as soon as possible and, in any case, before the time when it is inquired into by the governor or, as the case may be, the adjudicator.

(2) At an inquiry into charge against an inmate he shall be given a opportunity of hearing what is alleged against him and of presenting his own case.

(3) At an inquiry into a charge which has been referred to the adjudicator, the inmate who has been charged shall be given the opportunity to be legally represented.

**7.9593** *60. Governor's punishments* (1) If he finds an inmate guilty of an offence against discipline the governor may, subject to paragraph (3) and rule 65, impose one or more of the following punishments:

(*a*) caution;

(*b*) forfeiture for a period not exceeding 21 days of any of the privileges under rule 6;

(*c*) removal for a period not exceeding 21 days from any particular activity or activities of the young offender institution, other than education, training courses, work and physical education in accordance with rules 37, 38, 39, 40 and 41;

(*d*) extra work outside the normal working week for a period not exceeding 21 days and for not more than two hours on any day;

(*e*) stoppage of or deduction from earnings for a period not exceeding 42 days;

(*f*) in the case of an offence against discipline committed by an inmate who was aged 18 or over at the time of commission of the offence, other than an inmate who is serving the period of detention and training under a detention and training order pursuant to section 100 of the Powers of Criminal Courts (Sentencing) Act 2000, confinement to a cell or room for a period not exceeding ten days;

(*g*) removal from his wing or living unit for a period not exceeding 21 days;

(*h*) *revoked.*
(2) If an inmate is found guilty of more than one charge arising out of an incident punishments under this rule may be ordered to run consecutively, but, in the case of a punishment of cellular confinement the total period shall not exceed ten days.
(3) A caution shall not be combined with any other punishment for the same charge.
(4) In imposing a punishment under this rule, the governor shall take into account any guidelines that the Secretary of State may from time to time issue as to the level of punishment that should normally be imposed for a particular offence against discipline.

**7.9594** *60A. Adjudicator's punishments* (1) If he finds a inmate guilty of an offence against discipline the adjudicator may, subject to paragraph (2) and to rule 65, impose one or more of the following punishments:
(*a*) any of the punishments mentioned in rule 60(1);
(*b*) in the case of an inmate who is a fixed-term prisoner, an award of additional days not exceeding 42 days.
(2) A caution shall not be combined with any other punishment for the same charge.
(3) If an inmate is found guilty of more than one charge arising out of an incident, punishments under this rule may be ordered to run consecutively but, in the case of an award of additional days, the total period added shall not exceed 42 days and, in the case of a punishment of cellular confinement, the total period shall not exceed ten days.
(4) This rule applies to an inmate who has been charged with having committed an offence against discipline before the date on which the rule came into force, in the same way as it applies to an inmate who has been charged with having committed an offence against discipline on or after that date, provided the charge is referred to the adjudicator no later than 60 days after that date.
(5) Rule 58(3) shall not apply to a charge where, by virtue of paragraph (4), this rule applies to the inmate who has been charged.

**7.9595** *60AB. Requirement to pay for damage to young offender institution property* (1) This rule applies where an inmate is found guilty of an offence under rule 55(18) or 55(19) in respect of destroying or damaging any part of a young offender institution or any other property belonging to a young offender institution ("the relevant disciplinary offence").
(2) The governor or, as the case may be, the adjudicator must require the inmate to pay for the cost of making good the damage from, or replacing any property destroyed as a result of, the commission of the relevant disciplinary offence.
(3) A requirement imposed under paragraph (2) is referred to in this rule and in rules 60B, 64 and 64A as a "compensation requirement".
(4) The amount required to be paid under a compensation requirement must not exceed the cost of making good the damage from, or replacing any property destroyed as a result of, the relevant disciplinary offence and, in any event, must not exceed £2,000.
(5) A compensation requirement may be imposed instead of or in addition to any punishment imposed under rule 60, 60A or 65.
(6) A compensation requirement ceases to have effect after two years from the date on which it was imposed regardless of whether or not the full amount has been paid.

**7.9596** *60B. Review of adjudicator's punishment* (1) A reviewer means the Senior District Judge (Chief Magistrate) or any deputy of such a judge as nominated by that judge.
(2) Where an adjudicator imposes a punishment under rule 60A(1) or rule 65(1A), a compensation requirement under rule 60AB(2), or both an inmate may, within 14 days of receipt of the punishment [or the imposition of the compensation requirement, whichever is later, request in writing that a reviewer conducts a review.
(3) The review must be commenced within 14 days of receipt of the request and must be conducted on the papers alone.
(4) The review may be of the punishment, the compensation requirement or both (whether or not the inmate requested a review of both) but must not be a review of the finding of guilt.]
(5) On completion of the review, if it appears to the reviewer that the imposition of the punishment, the compensation requirement or both was manifestly unreasonable, he may do such of the following as he considers appropriate—
(*a*) reduce the number of any additional days awarded;
(*b*) for whatever punishment has been imposed by the adjudicator, substitute another punishment which is, in his opinion, less severe;
(*c*) quash the punishment entirely;
(*d*) reduce the amount of the compensation requirement.
(6) An inmate requesting a review shall serve any additional days awarded under rule 60A(1)(*b*) or 65(1A)(*b*) unless and until they are reduced.

**7.9597** *61. Confinement to a cell or room* (1) Before deciding whether to impose a punishment of confinement to a cell or room, the governor, adjudicator or reviewer shall first enquire of a registered medical practitioner or registered nurse, working within the young offender institution, as to whether there are any medical reasons why the punishment is unsuitable and shall take this into account when making his decision.
(2) No cell or room shall be used as a detention cell or room for the purpose of a punishment of confinement to a cell or room unless it has been certified by an officer of the Secretary of State (not being an officer of a young offender institution) that it is suitable for the purpose; that its size, lighting, heating, ventilation and fittings are adequate for health; and that it allows the inmate to communicate at any time with an officer.

**7.9598** *62. Removal from wing or living unit* Following the imposition of a punishment of removal from his wing or living unit, an inmate shall be accommodated in a separate part of the young offender institution under such restrictions of earnings and activities as the Secretary of State may direct.

**7.9599** *63. Suspended punishments* (1) Subject to any directions of the Secretary of State, the power to impose a disciplinary punishment (other than a caution) shall include a power to direct that the punishment is not to take effect unless, during a period specified in the direction (not being more than six months from the date of the direction), the inmate commits another offence against discipline and a direction is given under paragraph (2).

(2) Where an inmate commits an offence against discipline during the period specified in a direction given under paragraph (1), the person dealing with that offence may—

(*a*) direct that the suspended punishment shall take effect; or

(*b*) reduce the period or amount of the suspended punishment and direct that it shall take effect as so reduced; or

(*c*) vary the original direction by substituting for the period specified therein a period expiring not later than six months from the date of variation; or

(*d*) give no direction with respect to the suspended punishment.

(3) Where an award of additional days has been suspended under paragraph (1) and an inmate is charged with committing an offence against discipline during the period specified in a direction given under that paragraph, the governor shall either:

(*a*) inquire into the charge and give no direction with respect to the suspended award; or

(*b*) refer the charge to the adjudicator for him to inquire into it.

**7.9600** *64. Remission and mitigation of punishments, variation of compensation requirements and quashing of findings of guilt* (1) Except in the case of a finding of guilt made, or a punishment imposed, by an adjudicator under rule 60A(1)(*b*) or rule 65(1A)(*b*) the Secretary of State may quash any findings of guilt and may remit a disciplinary punishment or mitigate it either by reducing it or by substituting a punishment which is, in his opinion, less severe.

(1A) Where a compensation requirement has been imposed by a governor under rule 60AB(2), the Secretary of State may reduce the amount of the requirement.

(2) Subject to any directions given by the Secretary of State, the governor may, on the grounds of good behaviour, remit or mitigate any punishment already imposed by an adjudicator or governor.

**7.9601** *64A. Enforcement of compensation requirements* (1) Where a compensation requirement has been imposed under rule 60AB(2), the governor may debit any amount of money with which the inmate has been credited in the books of the young offender institution under rule 48(2) in order to recover the whole or part of the amount required to be paid under the compensation requirement.

(2) The amount debited under paragraph (1) on any occasion must not be such as to reduce below £5 the amount with which the inmate is credited in the books of the young offender institution under rule 48(2).

**7.9602** *65. Adult female inmates: disciplinary punishments* (1) In the case of a female inmate aged 21 years or over, rule 60 shall not apply, but the governor may, if he finds the inmate guilty of an offence against discipline, impose one or more of the following punishments:

(*a*) caution;

(*b*) forfeiture for a period not exceeding 42 days of any of the privileges under rule 6;

(*c*) removal for a period not exceeding 21 days from any particular activity or activities of the young offender institution, other than education, training courses, work and physical education in accordance with rules 37, 38, 39, 40 and 41;

(*d*) stoppage of or deduction from earnings for a period not exceeding 84 days;

(*e*) confinement to a cell or room for a period not exceeding 21 days;

(*f*) *revoked.*

(1A) In the case of a female inmate aged 21 years or over, where a charge has been referred to the adjudicator, rule 60A shall not apply, but the adjudicator may if he finds the inmate guilty of an offence against discipline, impose one or more of the following punishments:

(*a*) any of the punishments mentioned in paragraph (1);

(*b*) in the case of an inmate who is a fixed-term prisoner, an award of additional days not exceeding 42 days.

(2) Subject to any directions given by the Secretary of State, the governor may, on the grounds of good behaviour, remit or mitigate any punishment already imposed by an adjudicator, governor or the independent monitoring board.

(3) Paragraph (1A) applies to an inmate who has been charged with having committed an offence against discipline before the date on which that paragraph came into force, in the same was as it applies to an inmate who has been charged with having committed an offence against discipline on or after that date, provided the charge is referred to the adjudicator no later than 60 days after that date.

(4) Rule 58(3) shall not apply to a charge where, by virtue of paragraph (3), paragraph (1A) applies to the inmate who has been charged.

**7.9603** *66. Forfeiture of remission to be treated as an award of additional days* (1) In this rule, "existing prisoner" and "existing licensee" have the meanings assigned to them by paragraph 8(1) of Schedule 12 to the Criminal Justice Act 1991.

(2) In relation to any existing prisoner or existing licensee who has forfeited any remission of his

sentence, the provisions of Part II of the Criminal Justice Act 1991 shall apply as if he had been awarded such number of additional days as equals the number of days of remission which he has forfeited.

PART III OFFICERS OF YOUNG OFFENDER INSTITUTIONS

PART IV PERSONS HAVING ACCESS TO A YOUNG OFFENDER INSTITUTION

PART V INDEPENDENT MONITORING BOARD

7.9604 *78. Disqualification for membership* Any person directly or indirectly interested in any contract for the supply of goods or services to a young offender institution shall not be a member of the independent monitoring board for that institution and any member who becomes so interested in such a contract shall vacate office as a member.

7.9605 *79. Appointment* (1) A member of the independent monitoring board for a young offender institution appointed by the Secretary of State under section 6(2) of the Prison Act 1952 shall subject to paragraphs (3) and (4) hold office for three years or such shorter period as the Secretary of State may appoint.

(2) A member—

(*a*) appointed for the first time to the independent monitoring board for a particular young offender institution; or

(*b*) re-appointed to the board following a gap of a year or more in his membership of it,

shall, during the period of 12 months following the date on which he is so appointed or (as the case may be) re-appointed, undertake such training as may reasonably be required by the Secretary of State.

(3) The Secretary of State may terminate the appointment of a member if satisfied that—

(*a*) he has failed satisfactorily to perform his duties;

(*b*) he has failed to undertake training he has been required to undertake under paragraph (2), by the end of the period specified in that paragraph;

(*c*) he is by reason of physical or mental illness, or for any other reason, incapable of carrying out his duties;

(*d*) he has been convicted of such a criminal offence, or his conduct has been such, that it is not in the Secretary of State's opinion fitting that he should remain a member; or

(*e*) there is, or appears to be, or could appear to be, any conflict of interest between the member performing his duties as a member and any interest of that member, whether personal, financial or otherwise.

(4) Where the Secretary of State:

(*a*) has reason to suspect that a member of the independent monitoring board for a young offender institution may have so conducted himself that his appointment may be liable to be terminated under paragraph (3)(*a*) or (*d*); and

(*b*) is of the opinion that the suspected conduct is of such a serious nature that the member cannot be permitted to continue to perform his functions as a member of the board pending the completion of the Secretary of State's investigations into the matter and any decision as to whether the member's appointment should be terminated,

he may suspend the member from office for such period or periods as he may reasonably require in order to complete his investigations and determine whether or not the appointment of the member should be so terminated; and a member so suspended shall not, during the period of the suspension, be regarded as being a member of the board, other than for the purposes of this paragraph and paragraphs (1) and (2).

(5) A board shall have a chairman and a vice chairman, who shall be members of the board.

(6) The Secretary of State shall—

(*a*) upon the constitution of a board for the first time, appoint a chairman and a vice chairman to hold office for a period not exceeding 12 months;

(*b*) thereafter appoint, before the date of the first meeting of the board in any year of office of the board, a chairman and a vice chairman for that year, having first consulted the board; and

(*c*) promptly fill, after having first consulted the board, any casual vacancy in the office of chairman or vice chairman.

(7) The Secretary of State may terminate the appointment of a member as chairman or vice chairman of the board if he is satisfied that the member has—

(*a*) failed satisfactorily to perform his functions as chairman or (as the case may be) vice-chairman; or

(*b*) has grossly misconducted himself whilst performing those functions.

7.9606 *80. Proceedings of boards* (1) The independent monitoring board for a young offender institution shall meet at the institution at least once a month.

(2) The board may fix a quorum of not fewer than three members for proceedings.

(3) The board shall keep minutes of their proceedings.

(4) The proceedings of the board shall not be invalidated by any vacancy in the membership or any defect in the appointment of a member.

7.9607 *81. General duties of boards* (1) The independent monitoring board for a young offender institution shall satisfy themselves as to the state of the premises, the administration of the institution and the treatment of the inmates.

(2) The board shall inquire into and report upon any matter into which the Secretary of State asks

them to inquire.

(3) The board shall direct the attention of the governor to any matter which calls for his attention, and shall report to the Secretary of State any matters which they consider it expedient to report.

(4) The board shall inform the Secretary of State immediately of any abuse which comes to their knowledge.

(5) Before exercising any power under these Rules, the board and any member of the board shall consult the governor in relation to any matter which may affect discipline.

**7.9608** *82. Particular duties* (1) The independent monitoring board for a young offender institution and any member of the board shall hear any complaint or request which an inmate wishes to make to them or him.

(2) The board shall arrange for the food of the inmates to be inspected by a member of the board at frequent intervals.

(3) The board shall inquire into any report made to them, whether or not by a member of the board, that an inmate's health, mental or physical, is likely to be injuriously affected by any conditions of his detention.

**7.9609** *83. Members visiting young offender institutions* (1) The members of the independent monitoring board for a young offender institution shall visit the institution frequently, and the board shall arrange a rota for the purpose.

(2) A member of the board shall have access at any time to every part of the institution and to every inmate, and he may interview any inmate out of the sight and hearing of officers.

(3) A member of the board shall have access to the records of the prison, except that members of the board shall not have access to any records held for the purposes of or relating to conduct authorised in accordance with Part 2 of the Regulation of Investigatory Powers Act 2000.

**7.9610** *84. Annual report*

## Part VI Supplemental

**7.9611** *85. Delegation by governor*

**7.9612** *86. Contracted out young offender institutions* (1) Where the Secretary of State has entered into a contract for the running of a young offender institution under section 84 of the Criminal Justice Act 1991 (in this rule "the 1991 Act") these Rules shall have effect in relation to that young offender institution with the following modifications—

(*a*) references to an officer shall include references to a prisoner custody officer certified as such under section 89(1) of the 1991 Act;

(*b*) references to a governor shall include references to a director approved by the Secretary of State for the purposes of section 85(1)(*a*) of the 1991 Act except—

- (i) in rule 85 the reference to a governor shall include a reference to a controller appointed by the Secretary of State under section 85(1)(*b*) of the 1991 Act; and
- (ii) in rules 67(1), 71 and 81 where references to a governor shall include references to a director and a controller;
- (iii) in rules 49, 51, 52, 58, 58A, 60, 60AB, 63, 64, 64A and 65 where references to a governor shall include a reference to the director or the controller;

(*c*) rule 73 shall not apply in relation to a prisoner custody officer certified as such under section 89(1) of the 1991 Act and performing custodial duties.

(1A) The director of a prison may, with the leave of the Secretary of State, delegate any of his powers and duties under rules 49, 51, 52, 58, 58A, 60, 60AB, 63, 64, 64A and 65 to another officer of that prison.

(2) *Revoked.*

**7.9613** *87. Contracted out parts of young offender institutions* Where the Secretary of State has entered into a contract for the running of part of a young offender institution under section 84(1) of the Criminal Justice Act 1991, that part and the remaining part shall each be treated for the purposes of Parts I to IV and Part VI of these Rules as if they were separate young offender institutions.

**7.9614** *88. Contracted out functions at directly managed young offender institutions* (1) Where the Secretary of State has entered into a contract under section 88A(1) of the Criminal Justice Act 1991 for any functions at a directly managed young offender institution too be performed by prisoner custody officers who are authorised to perform custodial duties under section 89(1) of that Act, references to an officer in these Rules shall, subject to paragraph (2), include references to a prisoner custody officer who is so authorised and who is performing contracted out functions for the purposes of, or for purposes connected with, the young offender institution.

(2) Paragraph (1) shall not apply to references to an officer in rule 73.

(3) In this rule "directly managed young offender institution" means a young offender institution which is not a contracted out young offender institution.

**7.9615** *89. Revocations and savings*

# PROPERTY, OFFENCES AGAINST

**Contents**



## Inclosure Act 1857

(1857 c 31)

7.9616 **12. Proceedings for prevention of nuisances in town and village greens and allotments for exercise and recreation** And whereas it is expedient to provide summary means of preventing nuisances in town greens and village greens, and on land allotted and awarded upon any inclosure under the said Acts as a place for exercise and recreation[1]. If any person wilfully cause any injury or damage to any fence of any such town or village green or land, or wilfully and without lawful authority lead or drive any cattle or animal thereon, or wilfully lay any manure, soil, ashes, or rubbish, or other matter or thing thereon, or do any other act whatsoever to the injury of such town or village green or land, or to the interruption of the use or enjoyment thereof as a place for exercise and recreation, such person shall for every such offence, upon a summary conviction thereof before two justices, upon the information of any churchwarden or overseer[2] of the parish in which such town or village green or land is situate, or of the person in whom the soil of such town or village green or land may be vested, forfeit and pay, in any of the cases aforesaid, and for each and every such offence, over and above the damages occasioned thereby, any sum not exceeding **level 1** on the standard scale; and it shall be lawful for any such churchwarden or overseer[2] or other person as aforesaid to sell and dispose of any such manure, soil, ashes, and rubbish, or other matter or thing as aforesaid; and the proceeds arising from the sale thereof, and every such penalty[3] as aforesaid, shall, as regards any such town, or village green not awarded under the said Acts or any of them to be used as a place for exercise and recreation, be applied in aid of the rates for the repair of the public highways in the parish, and shall, as regards the land so awarded, be applied by the persons or person in whom the soil thereof may be vested in the due maintenance of such land as a place for exercise and recreation; and if any manure, soil, ashes, or rubbish be not of sufficient value to defray the expense of removing the same, the person who laid or deposited such manure, soil, ashes, or rubbish shall repay to such churchwarden or overseer[2] or other person as aforesaid the money necessarily expended in the removal thereof; and every such penalty as aforesaid shall be recovered in manner provided by the [Magistrates' Courts Act 1980]; and the amount of damage occasioned by any such offence as aforesaid shall, in case of dispute, be determined by the justices by whom the offender is convicted; and the payment of the amount of such damage, and the repayments of the money necessarily expended in the removal of any manure, soil, ashes, or rubbish, shall be enforced in like manner as any such penalty.

[Inclosure Act 1857, s 12 as amended by the Criminal Justice Act 1967, Sch 3 and the Criminal Justice Act 1982, ss 38 and 46.]

---

1 Section 30 of the Inclosure Act 1845 makes provision for such allotment.

2 By s 189(3) of the Local Government Act 1972, references in this section to a churchwarden or overseer shall be construed with respect to a green or land (*a*) in a parish as reference to the parish council or if there is none, to the parish meeting; (*b*) in a community where there is a community council, to that council; (*c*) otherwise to the council of the district in which the green or land is situated. Any inhabitant of the parish may lay an information (Commons Act 1876, s 29).

3 For application of penalties, see now the Courts Act 2003, s 38 (and see also, s 39), in Part I Magistrates' Courts Procedure, ante.

## Malicious Damage Act 1861

(24 & 25 Vict c 97)

7.9617 **58. Malice against owner unnecessary** Every punishment and forfeiture by this Act imposed on any person maliciously[1] committing any offence, whether the same be punishable upon indictment or upon summary conviction, shall equally apply and be enforced whether the offence shall be committed from malice conceived against the owner of the property in respect of which it shall be committed or otherwise[2].

[Malicious Damage Act 1861, s 58.]

[1] For meaning of "maliciously", see *R v Cunningham* [1957] 2 QB 396, [1957] 2 All ER 412, 121 JP 451.
[2] See *R v Pembliton* (1874) LR 2 CCR 119, 38 JP 454, and cf *R v Latimer* (1886) 17 QBD 359, 51 JP 184.

7.9618 72. **Offences committed within the jurisdiction of the Admiralty** All indictable offences mentioned in this Act which shall be committed within the jurisdiction of the Admiralty of England or Ireland shall be liable to the same punishments as if they had been committed upon the land in England or Ireland.

[Malicious Damage Act 1861, s 72 as amended by the Criminal Law Act 1967, Sch 3.]

# Town Gardens Protection Act 1863[1]

(26 Vict c 13)

7.9619 5. **Penalty for injuring garden** Any person who throws any rubbish into any such garden, or trespasses therein, or gets over the railings or fence, or steals or damages the flowers or plants, or commits any nuisance therein, shall be guilty of an offence and shall be liable on summary conviction for each and every offence aforesaid to a penalty not exceeding **level 1** on the standard scale or to imprisonment for not exceeding **fourteen days***; and in case it shall be necessary to state in any proceedings the ownership of the property of such garden, flowers, or plants, it shall be sufficient to describe the same as the property of the committee by the name A B and others.

[Town Gardens Protection Act 1863, s 5 as amended by the Criminal Law Act 1977, s 31, the Criminal Justice Act 1982, s 46, the Police and Criminal Evidence Act 1984, Sch 6 and the Statute Law (Repeals) Act 1993, Sch 2.]

* **Words repealed by the Criminal Justice Act 2003, Sch 37 from a date to be appointed.**

[1] Section 7 provides that nothing in this Act shall extend to or include any garden, ornamental ground or other land belonging to the Crown or under the management of (now) the Secretary of State for the Environment or for which special provision is made for the due care and protection thereof by any public or private Act of Parliament. Apart from this, it has been held that this act applies in any city or borough to any enclosed garden or ornamental garden set apart in any public square, crescent, circus, street or other public place for the use or enjoyment of the inhabitants, not being Crown property or under the protection of any public or private Act. See *Tulk v Metropolitan Board of Works* (1868) LR 3 QB 682, 32 JP 548.

# Public Stores Act 1875

(38 & 39 Vict c 25)

7.9620 4. **Marks in schedule appropriated for public stores** The marks described in the First Schedule to this Act may be applied in or on stores in order to denote Her Majesty's property in stores so marked; and it shall be lawful for any public department, and the contractors, officers and workmen of such department, to apply those marks, or any of them, in or on any such stores[1]; and if any person without lawful authority (proof of which authority shall lie on the party accused) applies any of those marks in or on any such stores he shall be guilty of a misdemeanour, and shall on conviction thereof be liable to be imprisoned for any term not exceeding **two years**.

[Public Stores Act 1875, s 4 as amended by the Statute Law (Repeals) Act 1993, Sch 1.]

[1] "Stores" includes all goods and chattels, and any single store or article (s 2).

7.9621 5. **Obliteration with intent to concealment** If any person with intent to conceal Her Majesty's property in any stores takes out, destroys, or obliterates, wholly or in part, any such mark as aforesaid, or any mark whatsoever denoting the property of Her Majesty in any stores, he shall be guilty of an offence[1], and on conviction thereof be liable, in the discretion of the court before which he is convicted, to imprisonment for any term not exceeding **seven years**.

[Public Stores Act 1875, s 5.]

[1] "Offence" is substituted for "felony" to accord with the Criminal Law Act 1967, s 12(5). Triable either way; see the Magistrates' Courts Act 1980, s 17A and Sch 1, also ss 17A–21 (procedure) and s 32 (penalty).

7.9622 6. **Power to stop suspected boats, persons, etc** A constable of the metropolitan police force may, within the limits for which he is constable, and any constable, if deputed[1] by a public department, may, within the limits for which he is constable, stop, search, and detain any vessel, boat or vehicle in or on which there is reason to suspect that any of Her Majesty's stores stolen or unlawfully obtained may be found, or any person reasonably suspected of having or conveying in any manner any of Her Majesty's stores stolen or unlawfully obtained.

A constable shall be deemed to be deputed by a public department within the meaning of this section if he is deputed by any writing signed by the person who is the head of such department, or who is authorised to sign documents on behalf of such a department.

[Public Stores Act 1875, s 6.]

[1] A special constable, within premises in the possession or control of the United Kingdom Atomic Energy Authority, is deemed to be so deputed (Atomic Energy Authority Act 1954, Sch 3).

7.9623 8. *Prohibition of sweeping, etc, near dockyards, artillery ranges, etc.*

7.9624 12. **Power of arrest and issue of search warrant** (1) *Repealed.*

(2) If it is made to appear by information on oath before a justice of the peace that there is reasonable cause to believe that any person has in his custody or possession or on his premises any stores in respect of which an offence against section 5 of this Act has been committed, the justice

may issue a warrant to a constable to search for and seize the stores as in the case of stolen goods, and the Police (Property) Act 1897, shall apply as if this subsection were among the enactments mentioned in section 1(1) of that Act.

[Public Stores Act 1875, s 12 as substituted by the Theft Act 1968, Sch 2 and amended by the Serious Organised Crime and Police Act 2005, Sch 7.]

7.9625 13. **Provisions for regimental necessaries, etc** The provisions of this Act relative to the taking out, destroying, or obliterating of marks, shall not apply to stores issued as regimental necessaries or otherwise for any soldier, or volunteer[1]; but nothing herein shall relieve any person from any obligation or liability to which he may be subject under any other Act in respect of such stores.

[Public Stores Act 1875, s 13 as amended by the Statute Law (Repeals) Act 1993, Sch 1.]

1 By Orders in Council made under the Territorial and Reserve Forces Acts, all volunteers have been transferred to the Territorial Army.

# Criminal Damage Act 1971

(1971 c 48)

7.9626 1. **Destroying or damaging property** (1) A person who without lawful excuse[1] destroys or damages[2] any property[3] belonging to another[4] intending to destroy or damage any such property or being reckless[5] as to whether any such property would be destroyed or damaged shall be guilty of an offence.

(2) A person who without lawful excuse destroys or damages any property, whether belonging to himself or another—

(*a*) intending to destroy or damage any property or being reckless[5] as to whether any property would be destroyed or damaged; and

(*b*) intending by the destruction or damage[6] to endanger the life[7] of another or being reckless[5] as to whether the life of another would be thereby endangered[8];

shall be guilty of an offence.

(3) An offence committed under this section by destroying or damaging property by fire shall be charged as arson[9].

[Criminal Damage Act 1971, s 1.]

1 See s 5, post, for defence of "lawful excuse". A person does not commit an offence under s 1(1) and (3) if he destroys or damages his own property, even though he does so with the intent later to commit a fraud by dishonestly claiming against his insurers, see *R v Denton* [1982] 1 All ER 65, [1981] 1 WLR 1446, 146 JP 138, CA; distinguished in *R v Appleyard* (1985) 81 Cr App Rep 319 (managing director setting fire to company premises). A defendant who damaged padlocks in order to remove a clamp on his car which he had unlawfully parked in a private car park, was held not to have a lawful excuse and, therefore, no defence to a charge of criminal damage (*Lloyd v DPP* [1992] 1 All ER 982, [1991] Crim LR 904). Although the scope of the ancient self-help remedy of recaption was unclear it appeared to apply when a person entered private land to reclaim a chattel that had been wrongly taken on to that land but did not appear to apply where the chattel had come on to the land by consensual means such as the lawful parking of a car (*R v Mitchell* [2003] EWCA Crim 2188, [2004] RTR 14, [2004] Crim LR 139, where on the facts the car was not parked in accordance with the instructions for people who wished to park lawfully). As to whether self-help could apply for the immediate protection from clamping of a car lawfully parked, see the commentary to [2004] Crim LR 139. A person did not have a "lawful excuse" for damaging the outer perimeter fence at an atomic weapons establishment on the grounds that the possession of nuclear weapons was contrary to customary international law; nor did her belief that she was acting out of necessity, self-defence, in the public interest or in order to prevent a nuisance provide a lawful justification or excuse for her action: *Hutchinson v Newbury Magistrates' Court* CO/663/2000. DC.

2 What constitutes criminal damage is a matter of fact and degree; the damage need not be permanent (*Roe v Kingerlee* [1986] Crim LR 735). It can include permanent or temporary impairment of value or usefulness (*Morphitis v Salmon* (1989) 154 JP 365—removal of scaffold clip and bar from upright).

3 A computer "hacker" who obtains unauthorised entry to a computer system and makes alterations impairing its proper use can be convicted of criminal damage, although the damage to the magnetic particles in the disk are not perceptible without using the computer. Tangible property has been damaged even though the damage itself is not tangible. Impairment of usefulness does not require breaking, cutting or removal of a part (*R v Whiteley* [1991] Crim LR 436).

4 Informant need not be a person who actually saw the offence committed, and if ownership be incorrectly described the information should be amended or the hearing adjourned, but not dismissed (*Ralph v Hurrell* (1875) 40 JP 119). No offence is committed if done in the honest though mistaken belief that the property is one's own (*R v David Smith* [1974] 1 All ER 632, [1974] QB 354, 138 JP 236). Where the charge alleges damage to property belonging to the defendant's wife or husband, the prior consent of the Director of Public Prosecutions is necessary: see the Theft Act 1968, s 30(4), post, and *R v Withers* [1975] Crim LR 647. Section 30(3) of the Theft Act 1968 also regulates the presentation of evidence as between husband and wife in such proceedings.

5 It was held in *Metropolitan Police Comr v Caldwell* [1982] AC 341, [1981] 1 All ER 961, [1981] 2 WLR 509 that "reckless" here meant (1) doing an act which in fact creates an obvious risk that property will be destroyed or damaged and (2) when so acting the doer either has not given any thought to the possibility of there being any such risk or has recognised that there was some risk involved and has none the less gone on to do it. In *R v G* [2003] UKHL 50, [2003] 4 All ER 765, [2003] 3 WLR 1060, 167 JP 621, however, the House of Lords departed from its earlier decision in *Caldwell* and held that that foresight of consequences remained an essential ingredient of recklessness in the context of the offence of criminal damage. Therefore, it had to be shown that the defendant's state of mind was culpable in that he acted recklessly in respect of a circumstance if he was aware of a risk which did or would exist, or in respect of a result if he was aware of a risk that it would occur, and it was, in the circumstances known to him, unreasonable to take the risk. Accordingly, a defendant could not be convicted of the offence if, due to his age or personal characteristics, he genuinely did not appreciate or foresee the risks involved in his actions.

If a defendant closes his mind to a risk he must realise that there is a risk and, on the evidence, that will usually be decisive as to whether he was "reckless". (This was the view of Lord Edmund Davies, who dissented in *Caldwell*, and it was cited approvingly in *R v G*.) See also *Booth v CPS* [2006] EWHC 192 (Admin), (2006) 170 JP 305 where the defendant, who ran into the path of a car aware of the risk of a collision causing damage, though that risk was not uppermost in his mind, was held to have been "reckless" within the *R v G* test. Where, however, a defendant realises there is a risk but dismisses it as negligible it cannot be said that he is taking an obvious and significant risk; the court must consider his subjective perception of the risk: *R v Cooper* [2004] EWCA Crim 1382, [2004] All ER (D) 180 (Jun), 168 JPN 507.

It is submitted that self-induced intoxication, in cases that are brought on the basis of recklessness rather than specific intent, continues to be irrelevant.

If the relevant awareness was not present when the defendant did the act by which the risk of damage was created, he is nonetheless guilty if he subsequently gained that awareness before the risk materialised but failed to do anything to prevent it (*R v Miller* [1983] 2 AC 161, [1983] 1 All ER 978 (which in this respect, it is submitted, remains good law post *R v G*, supra)).

[6] The words "destruction or damage" in s 1(2)(*b*) refer back to the destruction or damage intended, or as to which there was recklessness, in s 1(2)(*a*); the words do not refer to the destruction or damage actually caused (*R v Dudley* [1989] Crim LR 57, CA followed in *R v Webster* [1995] 2 All ER 168, CA).

[7] It is not necessary to establish that a life was in fact endangered (*R v Parker* [1993] Crim LR 856).

[8] Although there are two elements of the offence in paragraphs (*a*) and (*b*), the court is concerned with the defendant's state of mind at one stage only, namely when he does the relevant act. The word "thereby" refers to the damage to the property and not to the act which caused the damage; the intention of recklessness must be with regard to the dangers caused by the destroyed or damaged property and not those inherent in the method of causing the destruction or damage (*R v Steer* [1988] AC 111, [1987] 2 All ER 833, 85 Cr App Rep 352, HL followed in *R v Webster* [1995] 2 All ER 168, CA and see *R v Wenton* [2010] EWCA Crim 2361, 174 JP 577 (act of breaking window separate from the insertion of petrol canister through the broken window).

On a charge of *attempted* arson in the aggravated form contemplated by s 1(2), in addition to establishing a specific intent to cause damage by fire, it is sufficient to prove that the defendant was reckless as to whether life would thereby be endangered (*A-G's Reference (No 3 of 1992)* [1994] 2 All ER 121, [1994] 1 WLR 409, [1994] RTR 122, 98 Cr App Rep 383).

[9] Where the charge states "damage by fire" rather than "arson" it is nonetheless a valid charge: *R v Drayton* [2005] EWCA Crim 2013, 169 JP 593, [2006] Crim LR 243.

7.9627 2. **Threats to destroy or damage property**[1] A person who without lawful excuse makes to another a threat, intending that that other would fear it would be carried out—

(*a*) to destroy or damage any property belonging to that other or a third person; or

(*b*) to destroy or damage his own property in a way which he knows is likely to endanger the life of that other or a third person;

shall be guilty of an offence.

[Criminal Damage Act 1971, s 2.]

[1] The gist of the offence under both parts of s 2 is the threat; the nature of the threat has to be considered objectively so that it does not matter what the person threatened thought was embraced within the threat or whether he feared the threat would be carried out, though the prosecution must prove that the defendant intended that the person threatened would fear that the threat would be carried out (*R v Cakmak* [2002] EWCA Crim 500, [2002] 2 Cr App Rep 158, [2002] Crim LR 581). It is sufficient if the defendant's intention was to create in the mind of an objective listener the genuine fear that the threat might be carried; the words of the statute are plain and require no further exegesis: *R v Ankerson* [2015] EWCA Crim 432, 179 JP 219, [2015] All ER (D) 234 (Mar).

7.9628 3. **Possessing anything with intent to destroy or damage property** A person who has anything in his custody or under his control intending[1] without lawful excuse to use it or cause or permit another to use it—

(*a*) to destroy or damage any property belonging to some other person; or

(*b*) to destroy or damage his own or the user's property in a way which he knows is likely to endanger the life of some other person;

shall be guilty of an offence.

[Criminal Damage Act 1971, s 3.]

[1] It is not enough that the defendant realises that the thing may be so used; he must intend or permit such use. But it is unnecessary that the defendant should intend an immediate use of the thing (*R v Buckingham* (1975) 63 Cr App Rep 159).

7.9629 4. **Punishment of offences** (1) A person guilty of arson under section 1 above or of an offence[1] under section 1(2) above (whether arson or not) shall on conviction on indictment be liable to imprisonment for **life**.

(2) A person guilty of any other offence[1] under this Act shall on conviction on indictment be liable to imprisonment for a term not exceeding **ten years**.

[Criminal Damage Act 1971, s 4.]

[1] Offences under ss 1(1) and (3), 2 and 3 are triable either way; see the Magistrates' Courts Act 1980, s 17 and Sch 1, also ss 17A–21 (procedure) and s 32 (penalty) in PART I: MAGISTRATES' COURTS, PROCEDURE, ante. Offences under s 1(2) are not triable summarily. As to having in possession any firearm at the time of committing or at the time of apprehension for an offence under s 1 of this Act, or aiding and abetting or attempting to commit any such offence, see the Firearms Act 1968, s 17 and Sch 1, ante.

7.9630 5. **"Without lawful excuse"** (1) This section applies to any offence under section 1(1) above and any offence under section 2 or 3 above other than one involving a threat by the person charged to destroy or damage property in a way which he knows is likely to endanger the life of another or involving an intent by the person charged to use or cause or permit the use of something in his custody or under his control so to destroy or damage property.

(2) A person charged with an offence to which this section applies shall, whether or not he would be treated for the purposes of this Act as having a lawful excuse apart from this subsection[1], be treated for those purposes as having a lawful excuse—

(*a*) if at the time of the act or acts alleged to constitute the offence he believed that the person or persons whom he believed to be entitled to consent to the destruction of or damage to the property in question had so consented, or would have so consented to it if he or they had known of the destruction or damage and its circumstances[2]; or

(*b*) if he destroyed or damaged or threatened to destroy or damage the property in question or, in the case of a charge of an offence under section 3 above, intended to use or cause or permit the use of something to destroy or damage it, in order to protect[3] property belonging to himself or another or a right or interest[4] in property which was or which he believed to be vested in himself or another, and at the time of the act or acts alleged to constitute the offence he believed—

(i) that the property, right or interest was in immediate need of protection; and

(ii) that the means of protection adopted or proposed to be adopted were or would be reasonable having regard to all the circumstances.

(3) For the purposes of this section it is immaterial whether a belief is justified or not if it is honestly held[2].

(4) For the purposes of subsection (2) above a right or interest in property includes any right or privilege in or over land, whether created by grant, licence or otherwise.

(5) This section shall not be construed as casting doubt on any defence recognised by law as a defence to criminal charges.

[Criminal Damage Act 1971, s 5.]

---

1 In *Stear v Scott* [1992] RTR 226 the Divisional Court was unable to find any authority suggesting a right to use force and cause damage in order to recover property from land upon which property was trespassing (damage to a wheel clamp used to immobilise a vehicle parked on private land without permission).

2 A woman suffering from self-induced intoxication was held to be entitled to the defence under s 5(2) when charged with damaging a house which she mistook for another (*Jaggard v Dickinson* [1981] QB 527, [1980] 3 All ER 716. It has been stated, however, that the continuing validity of Jaggard was questionable, and in a case of failing to stop after an accident where D was intoxicated and was found to have genuinely believed that there had been no accident the conviction was upheld – there was no reason why D should be allowed to pray in aid her own state of drunkenness as the reason for the mistake: *Magee v Crown Prosecution Service* [2014] EWHC 4089 (Admin), 179 JP 261.

A vicar who had a genuine belief in the consent of God and thence the law of England to damage property was held not to have had a lawful excuse (*Blake v DPP* [1993] Crim LR 586).

3 The question whether or not a particular act was done in order to protect property must be an objective test (*R v Hunt* (1977) 66 Cr App Rep 105). The court has to decide first what was in the defendant's mind—a subjective test, and secondly whether it can be said as a matter of law that, on the facts as believed by him, the act was done in order to protect property—an objective test (*R v Hill* [1989] Crim LR 136, CA; applied in *Johnson v DPP* [1994] Crim LR 673). See also *Chamberlain v Lindon* [1998] 2 All ER 538, [1998] 1 WLR 1252, DC (defendant had a lawful excuse to demolish a wall which restricted his right of way as he had an honest belief that it was necessary to do so to protect his right or interest in property. The fact that he chose abatement because he hoped to avoid litigation did not convert the avoidance of litigation into his purpose). See further *R v Jones* [2004] EWCA Crim 1981, [2005] QB 259, [2004] 4 All ER 955, [2005] 1 Cr App R 12 (damage to military airbase to prevent allegedly unlawful warfare being waged against Iraq: held that the only objective element in the defence in s 5(2)(*b*) was whether it could be said that on the facts as believed by the defendant the criminal damage alleged could amount to something done to protect property).

4 Every man has a right at common law by any means he pleases to protect his own land or property, provided he does not invade or interfere with the legal rights of his neighbour (*Deane v Clayton* (1817) 7 Taunt 489; *Jordin v Crump* (1841) 8 M & W 782. See also article at 41 JP 737. The test is whether he acted reasonably (*Goodway v Becher* [1951] 2 All ER 349, 115 JP 435). The defence does not arise in circumstances where damage is caused in order to recover a child (*R v Baker and Wilkins* [1997] Crim LR 497).

For an (unsuccessful) attempt to plead this defence in relation to the destruction of badger traps to protect badgers, see *Cresswell v DPP; Currie v DPP* [2006] EWHC 3379 (Admin), 171 JP 233. The court also considered the common law defence of protecting the property of another and held that it had survived the Act, but with a concept of "property" no wider than that under s 5(2).

See s 7(2), post, for jurisdiction of magistrates' courts to try offences where a dispute of title to property is involved.

7.9631 **6. Search for things intended for use in committing offences of criminal damage**

(1) If it is made to appear by information on oath before a justice of the peace that there is reasonable cause to believe that any person has in his custody or under his control or on his premises anything which there is reasonable cause to believe has been used or is intended for use without lawful excuse—

(*a*) to destroy or damage property belonging to another; or

(*b*) to destroy or damage any property in a way likely to endanger the life of another,

the justice may grant a warrant authorising any constable to search for and seize that thing.

(2) A constable who is authorised under this section to search premises for anything, may enter (if need be by force) and search the premises accordingly and may seize anything which he believes to have been used or to be intended to be used as aforesaid.

(3) The Police (Property) Act 1897 (disposal of property in the possession of the police) shall apply to property which has come into the possession of the police under this section as it applies to property which has come into the possession of the police in the circumstances mentioned in that Act.

[Criminal Damage Act 1971, s 6.]

7.9632 **7. Jurisdiction of magistrates' courts** (1) *Repealed.*

(2) No rule of law ousting the jurisdiction of magistrates' courts to try offences where a dispute of title to property is involved shall preclude magistrates' courts from trying offences under this Act, or any other offences of destroying or damaging property.

[Criminal Damage Act 1971, s 7 as amended by the Criminal Justice Act 1972, Sch 6.]

7.9633 **9. Evidence in connection with offences under this Act** A person shall not be excused, by reason that to do so may incriminate that person or the spouse or civil partner of that person of an offence under this Act—

(*a*) from answering any question put to that person in proceedings for the recovery of administration or any property, for the execution of any trust or for an account of any property or dealings with property; or

(*b*) from complying with any order made in any such proceedings;

but no statement or admission made by a person in answering a question put or complying with an order made as aforesaid shall, in proceedings for an offence under this Act, be admissible in evidence against that person or (unless they married or became civil partners after the making of the statement or admission) against the spouse or civil partner of that person.

[Criminal Damage Act 1971, s 9 as amended by the Civil Partnership Act 2004, Sch 27.]

7.9634 **10. Interpretation** (1) In this Act "property" means property of a tangible nature[1], whether real or personal, including money and—

(*a*) including wild creatures which have been tamed or are ordinarily[2] kept in captivity, and any other wild creatures or their carcasses if, but only if, they have been reduced into possession which has not been lost or abandoned or are in the course of being reduced into possession[3]; but

(*b*) not including mushrooms growing wild on any land or flowers, fruit or foliage of a plant growing wild on any land.

For the purposes of this subsection "mushroom" includes any fungus and "plant" includes any shrub or tree.

(2) Property shall be treated for the purposes of this Act as belonging to any person—

(*a*) having the custody of control of it;

(*b*) having in it any proprietary right or interest (not being an equitable interest arising only from an agreement to transfer or grant an interest); or

(*c*) having a charge on it.

(3) Where property is subject to a trust, the persons to whom it belongs shall be so treated as including any person having a right to enforce the trust.

(4) Property of a corporation sole shall be so treated as belonging to the corporation notwithstanding a vacancy in the corporation.

(5) For the purposes of this Act a modification of the contents of a computer shall not be regarded as damaging any computer or computer storage medium unless its effect on that computer or computer storage medium impairs its physical condition.

[Criminal Damage Act 1971, s 10 as amended by the Police and Justice Act 2006, Sch 14.]

1 This can include a plastic circuit card from which the accused has erased a computer program (*Cox v Riley* [1986] Crim LR 460).

2 It is not necessary for the prosecution to prove that the particular animal was so kept; it is sufficient if the particular animal belonged to a class of animals ordinarily so kept, eg cats (*Nye v Niblett* [1918] 1 KB 23, 82 JP 57).

3 Something more immediate to the taking of possession of wild animals (badgers) than placing traps to catch them is required for those animals to be seen as being "in the course of being reduced into possession"; during the period before that moment the animals cannot be said to belong to somebody, which the defence under s 5(2)(*b*) requires: *Cresswell v DPP; Currie v DPP* [2006] EWHC 3379 (Admin), 171 JP 233.

## Protection of Wrecks Act 1973

(1973 c 33)

7.9635 **1. Protection of sites of historic wrecks** (1) If the Secretary of State is satisfied with respect to any site in United Kingdom waters[1] that—

(*a*) it is, or may prove to be, the site of a vessel lying wrecked on or in the sea bed[1]; and

(*b*) on account of the historical, archaeological or artistic importance of the vessel, or of any objects contained or formerly contained in it which may be lying on the sea bed[1] in or near the wreck, the site ought to be protected from unauthorised interference,

he may by order[2] designate an area round the site as a restricted area.

(2) An order[2] under this section shall identify the site where the vessel lies or formerly lay, or is supposed to lie or have lain, and—

(*a*) the restricted area shall be all within such distance of the site (so identified) as is specified in the order, but excluding any area above high water mark of ordinary spring tides; and

(*b*) the distance specified for the purposes of paragraph (*a*) above shall be whatever the Secretary of State thinks appropriate to ensure protection for the wreck.

(3) Subject to section 3(3) below, a person commits an offence[3], if, in a restricted area[4], he does any of the following things otherwise than under the authority of a licence granted by the Secretary of State—

(*a*) he tampers with, damages or removes any part of a vessel lying wrecked on or in the sea bed[1], or any object formerly contained in such a vessel; or

(*b*) he carries out diving or salvage operations directed to the exploration of any wreck or to removing objects from it or from the sea bed[1], or uses equipment constructed or adapted for any purpose of diving or salvage operations; or (*c*) he deposits, so as to fall and lie abandoned on the sea bed[1], anything which, if it were to fall on the site of a wreck (whether it so falls or not), would wholly or partly obliterate the site or obstruct access to it, or damage any part of the wreck;

and also commits an offence[3] if he causes or permits any of those things to be done by others in a restricted area, otherwise than under the authority of such a licence.

(4) Before making an order under this section, the Secretary of State shall consult with such persons as he considers appropriate having regard to the purposes of the order; but this consultation may be dispensed with if he is satisfied that the case is one in which an order should be made as a matter of immediate urgency.

(5) A licence granted by the Secretary of State for the purposes of subsection (3) above shall be in writing and—

(*a*) the Secretary of State shall in respect of a restricted area grant licences only to persons who appear to him either—

(i) to be competent, and properly equipped, to carry out salvage operations in a manner appropriate to the historical, archaeological or artistic importance of any wreck which may be lying in the area and of any objects contained or formerly contained in a wreck, or

(ii) to have any other legitimate reason for doing in the area that which can only be done under the authority of a licence;

(*b*) a licence may be granted subject to conditions or restrictions, and may be varied or revoked by the Secretary of State at any time after giving not less than one week's notice to the licensee; and

(*c*) anything done contrary to any condition or restriction of a licence shall be treated for purposes of subsection (3) above as done otherwise than under the authority of the licence.

(6) Where a person is authorised, by a licence of the Secretary of State granted under this section, to carry out diving or salvage operations, it is an offence for any other person to obstruct him, or cause or permit him to be obstructed, in doing anything which is authorised by the licence, subject however to section 3(3) below.

[Protection of Wrecks Act 1973, s 1.]

1 Defined in s 3, post.
2 A number of Orders have been made.
3 For penalty, see s 3(4), and note also defences under s 3(3).
4 See s 1, ante.

**7.9636 2. Prohibition on approaching dangerous wrecks** (1) If the Secretary of State is satisfied with respect to a vessel lying wrecked in United Kingdom waters[1] that—

(*a*) because of anything contained in it, the vessel is in a condition which makes it a potential danger to life or property; and

(*b*) on that account it ought to be protected from unauthorised interference,

he may by order designate an area round the vessel as a prohibited area.

(2) An order under this section shall identify the vessel and the place where it is lying and—

(*a*) the prohibited area shall be all within such distance of the vessel as is specified by the order, excluding any area above high water mark of ordinary spring tides; and

(*b*) the distance specified for the purpose of paragraph (*a*) above shall be whatever the Secretary of State thinks appropriate to ensure that unauthorised persons are kept away from the vessel.

(3) Subject to section 3(3) below, a person commits an offence[2] if, without authority in writing granted by the Secretary of State, he enters a prohibited area, whether on the surface or under water.

[Protection of Wrecks Act 1973, s 2.]

1 Defined in s 3 post.
2 For penalties and defences see s 3 post.

**7.9637 3. Supplementary provisions** (1) In this Act—

"United Kingdom waters" means any part of the sea within the seaward limits of United Kingdom territorial waters and includes any part of a river within the ebb and flow of ordinary spring tides;

"the sea" includes any estuary or arm of the sea; and references to the sea bed include any area submerged at high water of ordinary spring tides.

(2) An order under section 1 or section 2 above shall be made by statutory instrument subject to annulment in pursuance of a resolution of either House of Parliament and may be varied or revoked by a subsequent order under the section; and the Secretary of State shall revoke any such order if—

(*a*) in the case of an order under section 1 designating a restricted area, he is of opinion that there is not, or is no longer, any wreck in the area which requires protection under this Act;

(*b*) in the case of an order under section 2 designating a prohibited area, he is satisfied that the vessel is no longer in a condition which makes it a potential danger to life or property.

(3) Nothing is to be regarded as constituting an offence under this Act where it is done by a person—

(*a*) in the course of any action taken by him for the sole purpose of dealing with an emergency of any description; or

(*b*) in exercising, or seeing to the exercise of, functions conferred by or under an enactment (local or other) on him or a body for which he acts; or

(*c*) out of necessity due to stress of weather or navigational hazards.

(4) A person guilty of an offence[1] under section 1 or section 2 above shall be liable on summary conviction to a fine of not more than **the statutory maximum** or on conviction on indictment to a **fine**; and proceedings for such an offence may be taken, and the offence may for all incidental purposes be treated as having been committed, at any place in the United Kingdom where he is for the time being.

[Protection of Wrecks Act 1973, s 3 as amended by the Criminal Law Act 1977, s 28.]

1. For procedure in respect of an offence triable either way, see the Magistrates' Courts Act 1980, ss 17A–21, in PART I: MAGISTRATES' COURTS, PROCEDURE, ante.

## Supply Powers Act 1975

(1975 c 9)

7.9638 Note.—This Act consolidates provisions of the Ministry of Supply Act 1939 and amendments thereto, giving the Secretary of State power to deal with public service articles. He is enabled to make grants or loans to induce the augmentation of stocks or to improve storage facilities (s 3). He can require returns of stocks, and production and storage facilities (s 4). Information gained as to an individual business can only be disclosed with the consent of the person carrying on that business (s 5).

7.9639 **6. Offences and penalties** (1) If any person knowingly or recklessly makes any untrue statement or untrue representation for the purpose of obtaining a payment under section 3 above, either for himself or for any other person, or discloses any information in contravention of section 5 above, he shall be guilty of an offence and liable[1]—

(*a*) on summary conviction, to imprisonment for a term not exceeding **three months** or to a fine not exceeding the prescribed sum, or to **both**; or

(*b*) on conviction on indictment, to imprisonment for a term not exceeding **two years** or to a **fine** of any amount or to both.

(2) If any person—

(*a*) fails to make any return which he is required to make under section 4 above; or

(*b*) knowingly or recklessly makes any untrue statement in any such return,

he shall be guilty of an offence and liable on summary conviction to a fine not exceeding **level 3** on the standard scale, and, if he is convicted in respect of a failure to make a return and the failure continues after the conviction, he shall be guilty of a further offence and liable on summary conviction to a fine not exceeding **£50** for each day on which the failure continues.

(3) Where any offence under this section committed by a body corporate is proved to have been committed with the consent or connivance of any director, manager, secretary or other officer of the body corporate, he, as well as the body corporate, shall be guilty of the offence and shall be liable to be proceeded against and punished accordingly.

[Supply Powers Act 1975, s 6 as amended by the Criminal Law Act 1977, s 28 and the Criminal Justice Act 1982, ss 38 and 46.]

1. For procedure in respect of an offence triable either way, see the Magistrates' Courts Act 1980, ss 17A–21, in PART I: MAGISTRATES' COURTS, PROCEDURE, ante.

## Criminal Law Act 1977

(1977 c 45)

### PART II

### OFFENCES RELATING TO ENTERING AND REMAINING ON PROPERTY

7.9640 **6. Violence for securing entry** (1) Subject to the following provisions of this section, any person who, without lawful authority, uses or threatens violence for the purpose of securing entry into any premises for himself or for any other person is guilty of an offence, provided that—

(*a*) there is someone present on those premises at the time who is opposed to the entry which the violence is intended to secure; and

(*b*) the person using or threatening the violence knows that that is the case.

(1A) Subsection (1) above does not apply to a person who is a displaced residential occupier or a protected intending occupier of the premises in question or who is acting on behalf of such an occupier; and if the accused adduces sufficient evidence that he was, or was acting on behalf of, such an occupier he shall be presumed to be, or to be acting on behalf of, such an occupier unless the contrary is proved by the prosecution.

(2) Subject to subsection (1A) above, the fact that a person has any interest in or right to

possession or occupation of any premises shall not for the purposes of subsection (1) above constitute lawful authority for the use or threat of violence by him or anyone else for the purpose of securing his entry into those premises.

(3) *Repealed.*

(4) It is immaterial for the purposes of this section—

(*a*) whether the violence in question is directed against the person or against property; and

(*b*) whether the entry which the violence is intended to secure is for the purpose of acquiring possession of the premises in question or for any other purpose.

(5) A person guilty of an offence under this section shall be liable on summary conviction to imprisonment for a term not exceeding **six months** or to a fine not exceeding **level 5** on the standard scale or to **both**.

(6) *Repealed.*

(7) Section 12 below contains provisions which apply for determining when any person is to be regarded for the purposes of this Part of this Act as a displaced residential occupier of any premises or of any access to any premises and section 12A below contains provisions which apply for determining when any person is to be regarded for the purposes of this Part of this Act as a protected intending occupier of any premises or of any access to any premises.

[Criminal Law Act 1977, s 6 as amended by the Criminal Justice Act 1982, s 46, the Criminal Justice and Public Order Act 1994, s 72 and Sch 11 and the Serious Organised Crime and Police Act 2005, Sch 7.]

7.9641 7. **Adverse occupation of residential premises** (1) Subject to the following provisions of this section and to section 12A(9) below, any person who is on any premises as a trespasser after having entered as such is guilty of an offence if he fails to leave those premises on being required to do so by or on behalf of—

(*a*) a displaced residential occupier of the premises; or

(*b*) an individual who is a protected intending occupier of the premises.

(2) In any proceedings for an offence under this section it shall be a defence for the accused to prove that he believed that the person requiring him to leave the premises was not a displaced residential occupier or protected intending occupier of the premises or a person acting on behalf of a displaced residential occupier or protected intending occupier.

(3) In any proceedings for an offence under this section it shall be a defence for the accused to prove—

(*a*) that the premises in question are or form part of premises used mainly for non-residential purposes; and

(*b*) that he was not on any part of the premises used wholly or mainly for residential purposes.

(4) Any reference in the preceding provisions of this section to any premises includes a reference to any access to them, whether or not any such access itself constitutes premises, within the meaning of this Part of this Act.

(5) A person guilty of an offence under this section shall be liable on summary conviction to imprisonment for a term not exceeding **six months** or to a fine not exceeding **level 5** on the standard scale or to **both**.

(6) *Repealed.*

(7) Section 12 below contains provisions which apply for determining when any person is to be regarded for the purposes of this Part of this Act as a displaced residential occupier of any premises or of any access to any premises and section 12A below contains provisions which apply for determining when any person is to be regarded for the purposes of this Part of this Act as a protected intending occupier of any premises or of any access to any premises.

[Criminal Law Act 1977, s 7 as substituted by the Criminal Justice and Public Order Act 1994, s 73 and amended by the Serious Organised Crime and Police Act 2005, Sch 7.]

7.9642 8. **Trespassing with a weapon of offence** (1) A person who is on any premises as a trespasser, after having entered as such, is guilty of an offence if, without lawful authority or reasonable excuse, he has with him on the premises any weapon of offence.

(2) In subsection (1) above "weapon of offence" means any article made or adapted for use for causing injury to or incapacitating a person, or intended by the person having it with him for such use.

(3) A person guilty of an offence under this section shall be liable on summary conviction to imprisonment for a term not exceeding **three months** * or to a fine not exceeding **level 5** on the standard scale or to **both**.

(4) *Repealed.*

[Criminal Law Act 1977, s 8 as amended by the Criminal Justice Act 1982, s 46 and the Serious Organised Crime and Police Act 2005, Sch 7.]

---

* **Words substituted by the Criminal Justice Act 2003, Sch 26, from a date to be appointed.**

7.9643 9. **Trespassing on premises of foreign missions, etc** (1) Subject to subsection (3) below, a person who enters or is on any premises to which this section applies as a trespasser is guilty of an offence.

(2) This section applies to any premises which are or form part of—

(*a*) the premises of a diplomatic mission within the meaning of the definition in Article 1(*i*) of the Vienna Convention on Diplomatic Relations signed in 1961 as that Article has effect in the United Kingdom by virtue of section 2 of and Schedule 1 to the Diplomatic Privileges Act 1964;

(*aa*) the premises of a closed diplomatic mission; and

(*b*) consular premises within the meaning of the definition in paragraph 1(*j*) of Article 1 of the Vienna Convention on Consular Relations signed in 1963 as that Article has effect in the United Kingdom by virtue of section 1 of and Schedule 1 to the Consular Relations Act 1968;

(*bb*) the premises of a closed consular post;

(*c*) any other premises in respect of which any organisation or body is entitled to inviolability by or under any enactment; and

(*d*) any premises which are the private residence of a diplomatic agent (within the meaning of Article 1(*e*) of the Convention mentioned in paragraph (*a*) above) or of any other person who is entitled to inviolability of residence by or under any enactment.

(2A) In subsection (2) above—

"the premises of a closed diplomatic mission" means premises which fall within Article 45 of the Convention mentioned in subsection 2(*a*) above (as that Article has effect in the United Kingdom by virtue of the section and Schedule mentioned in that paragraph); and

"the premises of a closed consular post" means premises which fall within Article 27 of the Convention mentioned in subsection (2)(*b*) above (as that Article has effect in the United Kingdom by virtue of the section and Schedule mentioned in that paragraph);

(3) In any proceedings for an offence under this section it shall be a defence for the accused to prove that he believed that the premises in question were not premises to which this section applies.

(4) In any proceedings for an offence under this section a certificate issued by or under the authority of the Secretary of State stating that any premises were or formed part of premises of any description mentioned in paragraphs (*a*) to (*d*) of subsection (2) above at the time of the alleged offence shall be conclusive evidence that the premises were or formed part of premises of that description at that time.

(5) A person guilty of an offence under this section shall be liable on summary conviction to imprisonment for a term not exceeding **six months** or to a fine not exceeding **level 5** on the standard scale or to **both**.

(6) Proceedings for an offence under this section shall not be instituted against any person except by or with the consent of the Attorney General.

(7) *Repealed.*

[Criminal Law Act 1977, s 9 as amended by the Criminal Justice Act 1982, s 46, the Diplomatic and Consular Premises Act 1987, s 7 and the Serious Organised Crime and Police Act 2005, Sch 7.]

7.9644 **10. Obstruction of enforcement officers and court officers executing High Court or county court process** (A1) A person is guilty of an offence if he resists or intentionally obstructs any person who—

(*a*) is an enforcement officer, or is acting under the authority of an enforcement officer; and

(*b*) is engaged in executing a writ issued from the High Court.

(1) Without prejudice to section 8(2) of the Sheriffs Act 1887 but subject to the following provisions of this section, a person is guilty of an offence if he resists or intentionally obstructs any person who is in fact an officer of a court engaged in executing any process issued by the High Court or by any county court for the purpose of enforcing any judgment or order for the recovery of any premises or for the delivery of possession of any premises.

(2) Subsection (1) above does not apply unless the judgment or order in question was given or made in proceedings brought under any provisions of rules of court applicable only in circumstances where the person claiming possession of any premises alleges that the premises in question are occupied solely by a person or persons (not being a tenant or tenants holding over after the termination of the tenancy) who entered into or remained in occupation of the premises without the licence or consent of the person claiming possession or any predecessor in title of his.

(3) In any proceedings for an offence under this section it shall be a defence for the accused to prove that he believed that the person he was resisting or obstructing was not an officer of a court.

(4) A person guilty of an offence under this section shall be liable on summary conviction to imprisonment for a term not exceeding **six months** or to a fine not exceeding **level 5** on the standard scale or to **both**.

(5) An enforcement officer or any officer of a court may arrest[1] without warrant anyone who is, or whom he, with reasonable cause, suspects to be, guilty of an offence under this section.

(6) In this section—

"enforcement officer" means an individual who is authorised to act as an enforcement officer under the Courts Act 2003;

"officer of a court" means—

(*a*) any sheriff, under sheriff, deputy sheriff, bailiff or officer of a sheriff; and

(*b*) any bailiff or other person who is an officer of a county court within the meaning of the County Courts Act 1984.

[Criminal Law Act 1977, s 10 as amended by the Criminal Justice Act 1982, s 46, the Courts Act 2003, Sch 8 and the Serious Organised Crime and Police Act 2005, Sch 7.]

1 This power of arrest is preserved by the Police and Criminal Evidence Act 1984, s 26 and Sch 2.

7.9645 12. **Supplementary provisions** (1) In this Part of this Act—

(*a*) "premises" means any building, any part of a building under separate occupation, any land ancillary to a building, the site comprising any building or buildings together with any land ancillary thereto, and (for the purposes only of sections 10 and 11 above) any other place; and

(*b*) "access" means, in relation to any premises, any part of any site or building within which those premises are situated which constitutes an ordinary means of access to those premises (whether or not that is its sole or primary use).

(2) References in this section to a building shall apply also to any structure other than a movable one, and to any movable structure, vehicle or vessel designed or adapted for use for residential purposes; and for the purposes of subsection (1) above—

(*a*) part of a building is under separate occupation if anyone is in occupation or entitled to occupation of that part as distinct from the whole; and

(*b*) land is ancillary to a building if it is adjacent to it and used (or intended for use) in connection with the occupation of that building or any part of it.

(3) Subject to subsection (4) below, any person who was occupying any premises as a residence immediately before being excluded from occupation by anyone who entered those premises, or any access to those premises, as a trespasser is a displaced residential occupier of the premises for the purposes of this Part of this Act so long as he continues to be excluded from occupation of the premises by the original trespasser or by any subsequent trespasser.

(4) A person who was himself occupying the premises in question as a trespasser immediately before being excluded from occupation shall not by virtue of subsection (3) above be a displaced residential occupier of the premises for the purposes of this Part of this Act.

(5) A person who by virtue of subsection (3) above is a displaced residential occupier of any premises shall be regarded for the purposes of this Part of this Act as a displaced residential occupier also of any access to those premises.

(6) Anyone who enters or is on or in occupation of any premises by virtue of—

(*a*) any title derived from a trespasser; or

(*b*) any licence or consent given by a trespasser or by a person deriving title from a trespasser,

shall himself be treated as a trespasser for the purposes of this Part of this Act (without prejudice to whether or not he would be a trespasser apart from this provision); and references in this Part of this Act to a person's entering or being on or occupying any premises as a trespasser shall be construed accordingly.

(7) Anyone who is on any premises as a trespasser shall not cease to be a trespasser for the purposes of this Part of this Act by virtue of being allowed time to leave the premises, nor shall anyone cease to be a displaced residential occupier of any premises by virtue of any such allowance of time to a trespasser.

(8) No rule of law ousting the jurisdiction of magistrates' courts to try offences where a dispute of title to property is involved shall preclude magistrates' courts from trying offences under this Part of this Act.

[Criminal Law Act 1977, s 12.]

7.9646 12A. **Protected intending occupiers: supplementary provisions** (1) For the purposes of this Part of this Act an individual is a protected intending occupier of any premises at any time if at that time he falls within subsection (2), (4) or (6) below.

(2) An individual is a protected intending occupier of any premises if[1]—

(*a*) he has in those premises a freehold interest or a leasehold interest with not less than two years still to run;

(*b*) he requires the premises for his own occupation as a residence;

(*c*) he is excluded from occupation of the premises by a person who entered them, or any access to them, as a trespasser; and

(*d*) he or a person acting on his behalf holds a written statement—

(i) which specifies his interest in the premises;

(ii) which states that he requires the premises for occupation as a residence for himself; and

(iii) with respect to which the requirements in subsection (3) below are fulfilled.

(3) The requirements referred to in subsection (2)(*d*)(iii) above are—

(*a*) that the statement is signed by the person whose interest is specified in it in the presence of a justice of the peace or commissioner for oaths; and

(*b*) that the justice of the peace or commissioner for oaths has subscribed his name as a witness to the signature.

(4) An individual is also a protected intending occupier of any premises if—

(*a*) he has a tenancy of those premises (other than a tenancy falling within subsection (2)(*a*) above or (6)(*a*) below) or a licence to occupy those premises granted by a person with a freehold interest or a leasehold interest with not less than two years still to run in the premises;

(*b*) he requires the premises for his own occupation as a residence;
(*c*) he is excluded from occupation of the premises by a person who entered them, or any access to them, as a trespasser; and
(*d*) he or a person acting on his behalf holds a written statement—
(i) which states that he has been granted a tenancy of those premises or a licence to occupy those premises;
(ii) which specifies the interest in the premises of the person who granted that tenancy or licence to occupy ("the landlord");
(iii) which states that he requires the premises for occupation as a residence for himself; and
(iv) with respect to which the requirements in subsection (5) below are fulfilled.

(5) The requirements referred to in subsection (4)(*d*)(iv) above are—
(*a*) that the statement is signed by the landlord and by the tenant or licensee in the presence of a justice of the peace or commissioner for oaths;
(*b*) that the justice of the peace or commissioner for oaths has subscribed his name as a witness to the signatures.

(6) An individual is also a protected intending occupier of any premises if—
(*a*) he has a tenancy of those premises (other than a tenancy falling within subsection (2)(*a*) or (4)(*a*) above) or a licence to occupy those premises granted by an authority to which this subsection applies;
(*b*) he requires the premises for his own occupation as a residence;
(*c*) he is excluded from occupation of the premises by a person who entered the premises, or any access to them, as a trespasser; and
(*d*) there has been issued to him by or on behalf of the authority referred to in paragraph (*a*) above a certificate stating that—
(i) he has been granted a tenancy of those premises or a licence to occupy those premises as a residence by the authority; and
(ii) the authority which granted that tenancy or licence to occupy is one to which this subsection applies, being of a description specified in the certificate.

(7) Subsection (6) above applies to the following authorities—
(*a*) any body mentioned in section 14 of the Rent Act 1977 (landlord's interest belonging to local authority etc);
(*b*) the Housing Corporation;
(*c*) *repealed*; and
(*d*) a registered social landlord within the meaning of the Housing Act 1985 (see section 5(4) and (5) of that Act).

(7A) Subsection (6) also applies to the Secretary of State if the tenancy or licence is granted by him under Part III of the Housing Associations Act 1985.

(8) A person is guilty of an offence if he makes a statement for the purposes of subsection (2)(*d*) or (4)(*d*) above which he knows to be false in a material particular or if he recklessly makes such a statement which is false in a material particular.

(9) In any proceedings for an offence under section 7 of this Act where the accused was requested to leave the premises by a person claiming to be or to act on behalf of a protected intending occupier of the premises—
(*a*) it shall be a defence for the accused to prove that, although asked to do so by the accused at the time the accused was requested to leave, that person failed at that time to produce to the accused such a statement as is referred to in subsection (2)(*d*) or (4)(*d*) above or such a certificate as is referred to in subsection (6)(*d*) above; and
(*b*) any document purporting to be a certificate under subsection (6)(*d*) above shall be received in evidence and, unless the contrary is proved, shall be deemed to have been issued by or on behalf of the authority stated in the certificate.

(10) A person guilty of an offence under subsection (8) above shall be liable on summary conviction to imprisonment for a term not exceeding **six months** or to a fine not exceeding **level 5** on the standard scale or to **both**.

(11) A person who is a protected intending occupier of any premises shall be regarded for the purposes of this Part of this Act as a protected intending occupier also of any access to those premises.

[Criminal Law Act 1977, s 12A as inserted by the Criminal Justice and Public Order Act 1994, s 74 and amended by SI 1996/2325, and the Government of Wales Act 1998, Schs 16 and 18.]

[1] The provisions of s 12A(2) are cumulative: *Wakolo v DPP* [2012] All ER (D) 04 (Feb)

7.9647 **13. Abolitions and repeals** *Common law offences of forcible entry and forcible detainer, and forcible entry enactments abolished and repealed.*

## Protection of Military Remains Act 1986

(1986 c 35)

7.9648 **1. Application of Act** (1) This Act applies to any aircraft which has crashed (whether before or after the passing of this Act) while in military service.

(2)–(5) Secretary of State may by Order designate vessels, controlled sites[1].

(6) For the purposes of this Act a place (whether in the United Kingdom, in United Kingdom waters or in international waters) is a protected place if—

(*a*) it comprises the remains of, or of a substantial part of, an aircraft, or vessel to which this Act applies; and

(*b*) it is on or in the sea bed or is the place, or in the immediate vicinity of the place, where the remains were left by the crash, sinking or stranding of that aircraft or vessel;

but no place in international waters shall be a protected place by virtue of its comprising remains of an aircraft or vessel which has crashed, sunk or been stranded while in service with, or while being used for the purposes of, any of the armed forces of a country or territory outside the United Kingdom.

(7) Powers apply to Crown land.

(8) Secretary of State may by Order substitute references to a date later than 4 August 1914 in sub-s (3).

[Protection of Military Remains Act 1986, s 1 with sub-ss (2)–(5), (7), (8)—summarised.]

---

[1] These subsections impose limits on the extent of effect of such Orders. The Protection of Military Remains Act 1986 (Designation of Vessels and Controlled Sites) Order 2012, SI 2012/1110 has been made.

**7.9649 2. Offences in relation to remains and prohibited operations** (1) Subject to the following provisions of this section and to section 3 below, a person shall be guilty of an offence—

(*a*) if he contravenes subsection (2) below in relation to any remains of an aircraft or vessel which are comprised in a place which is part of a controlled site;

(*b*) if, believing or have reasonable grounds for suspecting that any place comprises any remains of an aircraft or vessel which has crashed, sunk or been stranded while in military service, he contravenes that subsection in relation to any remains by virtue of which that place is a protected place.

(*c*) if he knowingly takes part in, or causes or permits any other person to take part in, the carrying out of any excavation or diving or salvage operation which is prohibited by subsection (3) below; or

(*d*) if he knowingly uses, or causes or permits any other person to use, any equipment in connection with the carrying out of any such excavation or operation.

(2) A person contravenes this subsection in relation to any remains—

(*a*) if he tampers with, damages, moves, removes or unearths the remains;

(*b*) if he enters any hatch or other opening in any of the remains which enclose any part of the interior of an aircraft or vessel; or

(*c*) if he causes or permits any other person to do anything falling within paragraph (*a*) or (*b*) above.

(3) An excavation or diving or salvage operation is prohibited by this subsection—

(*a*) if it is carried out at a controlled site for the purpose of investigating or recording details of any remains of an aircraft or vessel which are comprised in a place which is part of that site; or

(*b*) if it is carried out for the purpose of doing something that constitutes, or is likely to involve, a contravention of subsection (2) above in relation to any remains of an aircraft or vessel which are comprised in a protected place or in a place which is part of such a site; or

(*c*) in the case of an excavation, if it is carried out for the purpose of discovering whether any place in the United Kingdom or United Kingdom waters comprises any remains of an aircraft or vessel which has crashed, sunk or been stranded while in military service.

(4) In proceedings against any person for an offence under this section, it shall be a defence for that person to show that what he did or, as the case may be, what he caused or permitted to be done was done under and in accordance with a licence under section 4 below.

(5) In proceedings against any person for an offence under this section in respect of anything done at or in relation to a place which is not part of a controlled site it shall be a defence for that person to show that he believed on reasonable grounds that the circumstances were such that (if those had been the circumstances) the place would not have been a protected place.

(6) In proceedings against any person for an offence under this section it shall be a defence for that person to show that what he did or, as the case may be, what he caused or permitted to be done was urgently necessary in the interests of safety or health or to prevent or avoid serious damage to property.

(7) A person who is guilty of an offence under this section shall be liable[1]—

(*a*) on summary conviction, to a fine not exceeding the **statutory maximum**;

(*b*) on conviction on indictment, to a **fine**.

(8) Nothing in this section shall be construed as restricting any power to carry out works which is conferred by or under any enactment.

(9) References in this section to any remains which are comprised in a protected place or to any remains which are comprised in a place which is part of a controlled site include references to remains other than those by virtue of which that place is a protected place or, as the case may be, to remains other than those in respect of which that site was or could have been designated.

[Protection of Military Remains Act 1986, s 2.]

[1] For procedure in respect of an offence triable either way, see the Magistrates' Courts Act 1980, ss 17A–21, in PART I: MAGISTRATES' COURTS, PROCEDURE, ante.

7.9650 **3. Extraterritorial jurisdiction** (1) Where a contravention of subsection (2) of section 2 above occurs in international waters or an excavation or operation prohibited by subsection (3) of that section is carried out in international waters, a person shall be guilty of an offence under that section in respect of that contravention, excavation or operation only—

(*a*) if the acts or omissions which constitute the offence are committed in the United Kingdom, in United Kingdom waters or on board a British-controlled ship; or

(*b*) in a case where those acts or omissions are committed in international waters but not on board a British-controlled ship, if that person is—

(i) a British citizen, a British overseas territories citizen or a British Overseas citizen; or

(ii) a person who under the British Nationality Act 1981 is a British subject; or

(iii) a British protected person (within the meaning of that Act); or

(iv) a company registered under the Companies Act 2006.

(2) Subject to subsection (1) above, an offence under section 2 above shall, for the purpose only of conferring jurisdiction on any court, be deemed to have been committed in any place where the offender may for the time being be.

(3) Where subsection (1) above applies in relation to any contravention, excavation or operation, no proceedings for an offence under section 2 above in respect of that contravention, excavation or operation shall be instituted—

(*a*) in England and Wales, except by or with the consent of the Director of Public Prosecutions;

(*b*) *Northern Ireland.*

[Protection of Military Remains Act 1986, s 3 as amended by the British Overseas Territories Act 2002, s 2(3) and SI 2009/1941.]

7.9651 **4, 5.** *Secretary of State has power to grant licences to carry out otherwise prohibited operations; it is an offence triable either way to make false or reckless statements to obtain a licence.*

7.9652 **6.** *Powers of boarding by authorised persons.*

7.9653 **7.** *Section 43 of the Powers of Criminal Courts Act 1973 (power to deprive offenders of property used, or intended for use for purposes of crime, to apply; director manager, secretary etc of body corporate liable as well as body corporate.*

7.9654 **9. Interpretation** (1) In this Act, except in so far as the context otherwise requires—

"aircraft" includes a hovercraft, glider or balloon;

"British-controlled ship" means a ship registered in the United Kingdom or a ship exempted from such registration under the Merchant Shipping Act 1995;

"controlled site" means any area which is designated as such a site under section 1 above;

"Crown land" has the same meaning as in section 50 of the Ancient Monuments and Archaeological Areas Act 1979;

"international waters" means any part of the sea outside the seaward limits of the territorial waters adjacent to any country or territory;

"military service" shall be construed in accordance with subsection (2) below;

"nautical miles" means international nautical miles of 1,852 metres;

"protected place" shall be construed in accordance with section 1(6) above;

"remains", in relation to, or to part of, an aircraft or vessel which has crashed, sunk or been stranded, includes any cargo, munitions, apparel or personal effects which were on board the aircraft or vessel during its final flight or voyage (including, in the case of a vessel, any aircraft which were on board) and any human remains associated with the aircraft or vessel;

"sea" includes the sea bed and, so far as the tide flows at mean high water springs, any estuary or arm of the sea and the waters of any channel, creek, bay or river;

"sea bed" includes any area submerged at mean high water springs;

"United Kingdom waters" means any part of the sea within the seaward limits of the territorial waters adjacent to the United Kingdom.

(2) For the purposes of this Act an aircraft or vessel shall be regarded as having been in military service at a particular time if at that time it was—

(*a*) in service with, or being used for the purposes of, any of the armed forces of the United Kingdom or any other country or territory; or

(*b*) in the case of an aircraft, being taken from one place to another for delivery into service with any of the armed forces of the United Kingdom.

(3) Where a place comprising the remains of, or of a substantial part of, an aircraft or vessel which has crashed, sunk or been stranded while in military service is situated only partly in United Kingdom waters, that place shall be treated for the purposes of this Act as if the part which is situated in United Kingdom waters and the part which is situated in the United Kingdom or in international waters were separate places each of which comprised the remains of a substantial part of the aircraft or vessel.

[Protection of Military Remains Act 1986, s 9 as amended by the Merchant Shipping Act 1995, Sch 13.]

# Criminal Justice and Public Order Act 1994[1]

(1994 c 33)

## PART V[2]

## PUBLIC ORDER: COLLECTIVE TRESPASS OR NUISANCE ON LAND

*Powers to remove trespassers on land*

7.9655 **61. Power to remove trespassers on land[3]** (1) If the senior police officer present at the scene reasonably believes that two or more persons are trespassing on land and are present there with the common purpose of residing there for any period, that reasonable steps have been taken by or on behalf of the occupier to ask them to leave[4] and—

(*a*) that any of those persons has caused damage to the land[5] or to property on the land or used threatening, abusive or insulting words or behaviour towards the occupier, a member of his family or an employee or agent of his, or

(*b*) that those persons have between them six or more vehicles on the land,

he may direct those persons, or any of them, to leave the land and to remove any vehicles or other property they have with them on the land.

(2) Where the persons in question are reasonably believed by the senior police officer to be persons who were not originally trespassers but have become trespassers on the land, the officer must reasonably believe that the other conditions specified in subsection (1) are satisfied after those persons became trespassers before he can exercise the power conferred by that subsection.

(3) A direction under subsection (1) above, if not communicated to the persons referred to in subsection (1) by the police officer giving the direction, may be communicated to them by any constable at the scene.

(4) If a person knowing that a direction under subsection (1) above has been given which applies to him—

(*a*) fails to leave the land as soon as reasonably practicable, or

(*b*) having left again enters the land as a trespasser within the period of three months beginning with the day on which the direction was given,

he commits an offence and is liable on summary conviction to imprisonment for a term not exceeding **three months** * or a fine not exceeding **level 4** on the standard scale, or **both**.

(4A) *Scotland.*

(4B) *Scotland.*

(5) *Repealed.*

(6) In proceedings for an offence under this section it is a defence for the accused to show—

(*a*) that he was not trespassing on the land, or

(*b*) that he had a reasonable excuse for failing to leave the land as soon as reasonably practicable or, as the case may be, for again entering the land as a trespasser.

(7) In its application in England and Wales to common land this section has effect as if in the preceding subsections of it—

(*a*) references to trespassing or trespassers were references to acts and persons doing acts which constitute either a trespass as against the occupier or an infringement of the commoners' rights; and

(*b*) references to "the occupier" included the commoners or any of them or, in the case of common land to which the public has access, the local authority as well as any commoner.

(8) Subsection (7) above does not—

(*a*) require action by more than one occupier; or

(*b*) constitute persons trespassers as against any commoner or the local authority if they are permitted to be there by the other occupier.

(9) In this section—

"common land" means common land, as defined in section 22 of the Commons Registration Act 1965;**

"commoner" means a person with rights of common as defined in section 22 of the Commons Registration Act 1965;**

"land" does not include—

(*a*) buildings other than—

(i) agricultural buildings within the meaning of, in England and Wales, paragraphs 3 to 8 of Schedule 5 to the Local Government Finance Act 1988 or, in Scotland, section 7(2) of the Valuation and Rating (Scotland) Act 1956, or

(ii) scheduled monuments within the meaning of the Ancient Monuments and Archaeological Areas Act 1979;

(*b*) land forming part of—

(i) a highway unless it is a footpath, bridleway or byway open to all traffic within the meaning of Part III of the Wildlife and Countryside Act 1981, is a restricted byway within the meaning of Part II of the Countryside and Rights of Way Act 2000 or is a cycle track under the Highways Act 1980 or the Cycle Tracks Act 1984; or

(ii) *Scotland;*

"the local authority", in relation to common land, means any local authority which has powers in relation to the land under section 9 of the Commons Registration Act 1965 **;

"occupier" (and in subsection (8) "the other occupier") means—

(*a*) in England and Wales, the person entitled to possession of the land by virtue of an estate or interest held by him; and

(*b*) *Scotland*;

"property", in relation to damage to property on land, means—

(*a*) in England and Wales, property within the meaning of section 10(1) of the Criminal Damage Act 1971; and

(*b*) *Scotland*

and "damage" includes the deposit of any substance capable of polluting the land;

"trespass" means, in the application of this section—

(*a*) in England and Wales, subject to the extensions effected by subsection (7) above, trespass as against the occupier of the land;

(*b*) *Scotland*; and

"trespassing" and "trespasser" shall be construed accordingly;

"vehicle" includes—

(*a*) any vehicle, whether or not it is in a fit state for use on roads, and includes any chassis or body, with or without wheels, appearing to have formed part of such a vehicle, and any load carried by, and anything attached to, such a vehicle; and

(*b*) a caravan as defined in section 29(1) of the Caravan Sites and Control of Development Act 1960;

and a person may be regarded for the purposes of this section as having a purpose of residing in a place notwithstanding that he has a home elsewhere.

[Criminal Justice and Public Order Act 1994, s 61 as amended by the Land Reform (Scotland) Act 2003, Sch 2, the Serious Organised Crime and Police Act 2005, Sch 17 and the Countryside and Rights of Way Act 2000, Sch 5.]

---

* **Words substituted by the Criminal Justice Act 2003, Sch 26 from a date to be appointed.**

** **Amended by the Commons Act 2006, Sch 5 from a date to be appointed.**

1 The Criminal Justice and Public Order Act 1994 is reproduced partly in PART VIII under this title, and partly in PARTS I, II AND V of this Manual.

2 PART V contains ss 61–80.

3 The police are entitled to assume, in the absence of material to the contrary, that a local authority seeking the assistance of the police under s 61 is not acting in breach of human rights; the right to a fair trial under art 6 is not engaged by making it an offence to fail to comply with a s 61 direction, nor is there any infringement of the right to peaceful enjoyment of possessions under art 1 of the First Protocol to the Convention (*R (on the application of Fuller) v Chief Constable of Dorset* [2001] EWHC 1057, [2003] QB 480, [2002] 3 All ER 57, [2002] 3 WLR 1133.

4 The power to issue a direction under s 61 cannot lawfully be exercised until trespassers have failed to comply with steps taken by the occupier to ask them to leave, and the direction must require the trespassers to leave the land and to remove their vehicles immediately (*R (on the application of Fuller) v Chief Constable of Dorset*, supra).

5 The opening words of s 61(9) make clear that the exclusion of buildings from the meaning of "land" (other than those buildings which are specified) applies only to s 61 and not to other sections: *DPP v Chivers* [2010] EWHC 1814 (Admin), [2011] 1 All ER 367, (2010) 174 JP 587.

7.9656 **62. Supplementary powers of seizure** (1) If a direction has been given under section 61 and a constable reasonably suspects that any person to whom the direction applies has, without reasonable excuse—

(*a*) failed to remove any vehicle on the land which appears to the constable to belong to him or to be in his possession or under his control; or

(*b*) entered the land as a trespasser with a vehicle within the period of three months beginning with the day on which the direction was given,

the constable may seize and remove that vehicle.

(2) In this section, "trespasser" and "vehicle" have the same meaning as in section 61.*

[Criminal Justice and Public Order Act 1994, s 62.]

---

* **Words substituted by the Criminal Justice Act 2003, Sch 26 from a date to be appointed.**

7.9657 **62A. Power to remove trespassers: alternative site available** (1) If the senior police officer present at a scene reasonably believes that the conditions in subsection (2) are satisfied in relation to a person and land, he may direct the person—

(*a*) to leave the land;

(*b*) to remove any vehicle and other property he has with him on the land.

(2) The conditions are—

(*a*) that the person and one or more others ("the trespassers") are trespassing on the land;

(*b*) that the trespassers have between them at least one vehicle on the land;

(*c*) that the trespassers are present on the land with the common purpose of residing there for any period;

(*d*) if it appears to the officer that the person has one or more caravans in his possession or under his control on the land, that there is a suitable pitch on a relevant caravan site for that caravan or each of those caravans;

(*e*) that the occupier of the land or a person acting on his behalf has asked the police to remove the trespassers from the land.

(3) A direction under subsection (1) may be communicated to the person to whom it applies by

any constable at the scene.

(4) Subsection (5) applies if—

(*a*) a police officer proposes to give a direction under subsection (1) in relation to a person and land, and

(*b*) it appears to him that the person has one or more caravans in his possession or under his control on the land.

(5) The officer must consult every local authority within whose area the land is situated as to whether there is a suitable pitch for the caravan or each of the caravans on a relevant caravan site which is situated in the local authority's area.

(6) In this section—

"caravan" and "caravan site" have the same meanings as in Part 1 of the Caravan Sites and Control of Development Act 1960;

"relevant caravan site" means a caravan site which is—

(*a*) situated in the area of a local authority within whose area the land is situated, and

(*b*) managed by a relevant site manager;

"relevant site manager" means—

(*a*) a local authority within whose area the land is situated;

(*b*) a registered social landlord;

"registered social landlord" means a body registered as a social landlord under Chapter 1 of Part 1 of the Housing Act 1996.

(7) The Secretary of State may by order amend the definition of "relevant site manager" in subsection (6) by adding a person or description of person.

(8) An order under subsection (7) must be made by statutory instrument and is subject to annulment in pursuance of a resolution of either House of Parliament.

[Criminal Justice and Public Order Act 1994, s 62A as inserted by the Anti-social Behaviour Act 2003, s 60.]

7.9658 **62B. Failure to comply with direction under section 62A: offences** (1) A person commits an offence if he knows that a direction under section 62A(1) has been given which applies to him and—

(*a*) he fails to leave the relevant land as soon as reasonably practicable, or

(*b*) he enters any land in the area of the relevant local authority as a trespasser before the end of the relevant period with the intention of residing there.

(2) The relevant period is the period of 3 months starting with the day on which the direction is given.

(3) A person guilty of an offence under this section is liable on summary conviction to imprisonment for a term not exceeding 3 months * or a fine not exceeding level 4 on the standard scale or both.

(4) *Repealed.*

(5) In proceedings for an offence under this section it is a defence for the accused to show—

(*a*) that he was not trespassing on the land in respect of which he is alleged to have committed the offence, or

(*b*) that he had a reasonable excuse—

(i) for failing to leave the relevant land as soon as reasonably practicable, or

(ii) for entering land in the area of the relevant local authority as a trespasser with the intention of residing there, or

(*c*) that, at the time the direction was given, he was under the age of 18 years and was residing with his parent or guardian.

[Criminal Justice and Public Order Act 1994, s 62B as inserted by the Anti-social Behaviour Act 2003, s 61 and amended by the Serious Organised Crime and Police Act 2005, Sch 7.]

* **Words substituted by the Criminal Justice Act 2003, Sch 26 from a date to be appointed.**

7.9659 **62C. Failure to comply with direction under section 62A: seizure** (1) This section applies if a direction has been given under section 62A(1) and a constable reasonably suspects that a person to whom the direction applies has, without reasonable excuse—

(*a*) failed to remove any vehicle on the relevant land which appears to the constable to belong to him or to be in his possession or under his control; or

(*b*) entered any land in the area of the relevant local authority as a trespasser with a vehicle before the end of the relevant period with the intention of residing there.

(2) The relevant period is the period of 3 months starting with the day on which the direction is given.

(3) The constable may seize and remove the vehicle.

[Criminal Justice and Public Order Act 1994, s 62C as inserted by the Anti-social Behaviour Act 2003, s 62.]

7.9660 **62D. Common land: modifications** (1) In their application to common land sections 62A to 62C have effect with these modifications.

(2) References to trespassing and trespassers have effect as if they were references to acts, and persons doing acts, which constitute—

(*a*) a trespass as against the occupier, or

(*b*) an infringement of the commoners' rights.

(3) References to the occupier—

(*a*) in the case of land to which the public has access, include the local authority and any commoner;

(*b*) in any other case, include the commoners or any of them.

(4) Subsection (1) does not—

(*a*) require action by more than one occupier, or

(*b*) constitute persons trespassers as against any commoner or the local authority if they are permitted to be there by the other occupier.

(5) In this section "common land", "commoner" and "the local authority" have the meanings given by section 61.

[Criminal Justice and Public Order Act 1994, s 62D as inserted by the Anti-social Behaviour Act 2003, s 63.]

7.9661 **62E. Sections 62A to 62D: interpretation** (1) Subsections (2) to (8) apply for the interpretation of sections 62A to 62D and this section.

(2) "Land" does not include buildings other than—

(*a*) agricultural buildings within the meaning of paragraphs 3 to 8 of Schedule 5 to the Local Government Finance Act 1988, or

(*b*) scheduled monuments within the meaning of the Ancient Monuments and Archaeological Areas Act 1979.

(3) "Local authority" means—

(*a*) in Greater London, a London borough or the Common Council of the City of London;

(*b*) in England outside Greater London, a county council, a district council or the Council of the Isles of Scilly;

(*c*) in Wales, a county council or a county borough council.

(4) "Occupier", "trespass", "trespassing" and "trespasser" have the meanings given by section 61 in relation to England and Wales.

(5) "The relevant land" means the land in respect of which a direction under section 62A(1) is given.

(6) "The relevant local authority" means—

(*a*) if the relevant land is situated in the area of more than one local authority (but is not in the Isles of Scilly), the district council or county borough council within whose area the relevant land is situated;

(*b*) if the relevant land is situated in the Isles of Scilly, the Council of the Isles of Scilly;

(*c*) in any other case, the local authority within whose area the relevant land is situated.

(7) "Vehicle" has the meaning given by section 61.

(8) A person may be regarded as having a purpose of residing in a place even if he has a home elsewhere.

[Criminal Justice and Public Order Act 1994, s 62E as inserted by the Anti-social Behaviour Act 2003, s 64.]

*Powers in relation to raves*

7.9662 **63. Powers to remove persons attending or preparing for a rave** (1) This section applies to a gathering on land in the open air of 20 or more persons (whether or not trespassers) at which amplified music is played during the night (with or without intermissions) and is such as, by reason of its loudness and duration and the time at which it is played, is likely to cause serious distress to the inhabitants of the locality; and for this purpose—

(*a*) such a gathering continues during intermissions in the music and, where the gathering extends over several days, throughout the period during which amplified music is played at night (with or without intermissions); and

(*b*) "music" includes sounds wholly or predominantly characterised by the emission of a succession of repetitive beats.

(1A) This section also applies to a gathering if—

(*a*) it is a gathering on land of 20 or more persons who are trespassing on the land; and

(*b*) it would be a gathering of a kind mentioned in subsection (1) above if it took place on land in the open air.

(2) If, as respects any land, a police officer of at least the rank of superintendent reasonably believes that—

(*a*) two or more persons are making preparations for the holding there of a gathering to which this section applies,

(*b*) ten or more persons are waiting for such a gathering to begin there, or

(*c*) ten or more persons are attending such a gathering which is in progress,

he may give a direction that those persons and any other persons who come to prepare or wait for or to attend the gathering are to leave the land and remove any vehicles or other property which they have with them on the land.*

(3) A direction under subsection (2) above, if not communicated to the persons referred to in subsection (2) by the police officer giving the direction, may be communicated to them by any constable at the scene.

(4) Persons shall be treated as having had a direction under subsection (2) above communicated to them if reasonable steps have been taken to bring it to their attention.

(5) A direction under subsection (2) above does not apply to an exempt person.

(6) If a person knowing that a direction has been given which applies to him—

(*a*) fails to leave the land as soon as reasonably practicable, or

(*b*) having left again enters the land within the period of 7 days beginning with the day on which the direction was given,

he commits an offence and is liable on summary conviction to imprisonment for a term not exceeding **three months** ** or a fine not exceeding **level** 4 on the standard scale, or **both**.

(7) In proceedings for an offence under this section ** it is a defence for the accused to show that he had a reasonable excuse for failing to leave the land as soon as reasonably practicable or, as the case may be, for again entering the land.

(7A) A person commits an offence if—

(*a*) he knows that a direction under subsection (2), and

(*b*) he makes preparations for or attends a gathering to which this section applies within the period of 24 hours starting when the direction was given.

(8) *Repealed.*

(9) This section does not apply—

(*a*) in England and Wales, to a gathering in relation to a licensable activity within section 1(1)(*c*) of the Licensing Act 2003 (provision of certain forms of entertainment) carried on under and in accordance with an authorisation within the meaning of section 136 of that Act; or

(*b*) *Scotland.*

(10) In this section—

"exempt person", in relation to land (or any gathering on land), means the occupier, any member of his family and any employee or agent of his and any person whose home is situated on the land;

"land in the open air" includes a place partly open to the air;

and

"occupier", "trespasser" and "vehicle" have the same meaning as in section 61.

(11) *Repealed.*

[Criminal Justice and Public Order Act 1994, s 63 as amended the Anti-social Behaviour Act 2003, s 58, the Licensing Act 2003, Sch 7 and the Serious Organised Crime and Police Act 2005, Sch 7.]

---

* **Reproduced as in force in England and Wales.**

** **Words in sub-ss (6) and (7) substituted by the Criminal Justice Act 2003, s 336 from a date to be appointed.**

7.9663 **64. Supplementary powers of entry and seizure** (1) If a police officer of at least the rank of superintendent reasonably believes that circumstances exist in relation to any land which would justify the giving of a direction under section 63 in relation to a gathering to which that section applies he may authorise any constable to enter the land for any of the purposes specified in subsection (2) below.

(2) Those purposes are—

(*a*) to ascertain whether such circumstances exist; and

(*b*) to exercise any power conferred on a constable by section 63 or subsection (4) below.

(3) A constable who is so authorised to enter land for any purpose may enter the land without a warrant.

(4) If a direction has been given under section 63 and a constable reasonably suspects that any person to whom the direction applies has, without reasonable excuse—

(*a*) failed to remove any vehicle or sound equipment on the land which appears to the constable to belong to him or to be in his possession or under his control; or

(*b*) entered the land as a trespasser with a vehicle or sound equipment within the period of 7 days beginning with the day on which the direction was given,

the constable may seize and remove that vehicle or sound equipment.

(5) Subsection (4) above does not authorise the seizure of any vehicle or sound equipment of an exempt person.

(5A) *Scotland.*

(6) In this section—

"exempt person" has the same meaning as in section 63;

"sound equipment" means equipment designed or adapted for amplifying music and any equipment suitable for use in connection with such equipment, and "music" has the same meaning as in section 63; and

"vehicle" has the same meaning as in section 61.

[Criminal Justice and Public Order Act 1994, s 64 as amended by the Land Reform (Scotland) Act 2003, Sch 2.]

7.9664 **65. Raves: power to stop persons from proceeding** (1) If a constable in uniform reasonably believes that a person is on his way to a gathering to which section 63 applies in relation to which a direction under section 63(2) is in force, he may, subject to subsections (2) and (3) below—

(*a*) stop that person, and

(*b*) direct him not to proceed in the direction of the gathering.

(2) The power conferred by subsection (1) above may only be exercised at a place within 5 miles of the boundary of the site of the gathering.

(3) No direction may be given under subsection (1) above to an exempt person.

(4) If a person knowing that a direction under subsection (1) above has been given to him fails to comply with that direction, he commits an offence and is liable on summary conviction to a fine not exceeding **level 3** on the standard scale.

(5) *Repealed.*

(6) In this section, "exempt person" has the same meaning as in section 63.

[Criminal Justice and Public Order Act 1994, s 65 as amended by the Serious Organised Crime and Police Act 2005, Sch 7.]

7.9665 **66. Power of court to forfeit sound equipment** (1) Where a person is convicted of an offence under section 63 in relation to a gathering to which that section applies and the court is satisfied that any sound equipment which has been seized from him under section 64(4), or which was in his possession or under his control at the relevant time, has been used at the gathering the court may make an order for forfeiture under this subsection in respect of that property.

(2) The court may make an order under subsection (1) above whether or not it also deals with the offender in respect of the offence in any other way and without regard to any restrictions on forfeiture in any enactment.

(3) In considering whether to make an order under subsection (1) above in respect of any property a court shall have regard—

- (*a*) to the value of the property; and
- (*b*) to the likely financial and other effects on the offender of the making of the order (taken together with any other order that the court contemplates making).

(4) An order under subsection (1) above shall operate to deprive the offender of his rights, if any, in the property to which it relates, and the property shall (if not already in their possession) be taken into the possession of the police.

(5) Except in a case to which subsection (6) below applies, where any property has been forfeited under subsection (1) above, a magistrates' court may, on application by a claimant of the property, other than the offender from whom it was forfeited under subsection (1) above, make an order for delivery of the property to the applicant if it appears to the court that he is the owner of the property.

(6) In a case where forfeiture under subsection (1) above has been by order of a Scottish court, a claimant such as is mentioned in subsection (5) above may, in such manner as may be prescribed by act of adjournal, apply to that court for an order for the return of the property in question.

(7) No application shall be made under subsection (5), or by virtue of subsection (6), above by any claimant of the property after the expiration of 6 months from the date on which an order under subsection (1) above was made in respect of the property.

(8) No such application shall succeed unless the claimant satisfies the court either that he had not consented to the offender having possession of the property or that he did not know, and had no reason to suspect, that the property was likely to be used at a gathering to which section 63 applies.

(9) An order under subsection (5), or by virtue of subsection (6), above shall not affect the right of any person to take, within the period of 6 months from the date of an order under subsection (5), or as the case may be by virtue of subsection (6), above, proceedings for the recovery of the property from the person in possession of it in pursuance of the order, but on the expiration of that period the right shall cease.

(10) The Secretary of State may make regulations[1] for the disposal of property, and for the application of the proceeds of sale of property, forfeited under subsection (1) above where no application by a claimant of the property under subsection (5), or by virtue of subsection (6), above has been made within the period specified in subsection (7) above or no such application has succeeded.

(11) The regulations[1] may also provide for the investment of money and for the audit of accounts.

(12) The power to make regulations under subsection (10) above shall be exercisable by statutory instrument which shall be subject to annulment in pursuance of a resolution of either House of Parliament.

(13) In this section—

"relevant time", in relation to a person—

- (*a*) convicted in England and Wales of an offence under section 63, means the time of his arrest for the offence or of the issue of a summons in respect of it;
- (*b*) *Scotland*;

"sound equipment" has the same meaning as in section 64.

[Criminal Justice and Public Order Act 1994, s 66.]

---

1. See the Police (Disposal of Sound Equipment) Regulations 1995, this title, post.

*Retention and charges for seized property*

7.9666 **67. Retention and charges for seized property** (1) Any vehicles which have been seized and removed by a constable under section 62(1)* or 64(4) may be retained in accordance with regulations made by the Secretary of State under subsection (3) below.

(2) Any sound equipment which has been seized and removed by a constable under section 64(4) may be retained until the conclusion of proceedings against the person from whom it

was seized for an offence under section 63.

(3) The Secretary of State may make regulations[1]—

(*a*) regulating the retention and safe keeping and the disposal and the destruction in prescribed circumstances of vehicles; and

(*b*) prescribing charges in respect of the removal, retention, disposal and destruction of vehicles.

(4) Any authority shall be entitled to recover from a person from whom a vehicle has been seized such charges as may be prescribed in respect of the removal, retention, disposal and destruction of the vehicle by the authority.

(5) Regulations under subsection (3) above may make different provisions for different classes of vehicles or for different circumstances.

(6) Any charges under subsection (4) above shall be recoverable as a simple contract debt.

(7) Any authority having custody of vehicles under regulations under subsection (3) above shall be entitled to retain custody until any charges under subsection (4) are paid.

(8) The power to make regulations under subsection (3) above shall be exercisable by statutory instrument which shall be subject to annulment in pursuance of a resolution of either House of Parliament.

(9) In this section—

"conclusion of proceedings" against a person means—

(*a*) his being sentenced or otherwise dealt with for the offence or his acquittal;

(*b*) the discontinuance of the proceedings; or

(*c*) the decision not to prosecute him,

whichever is the earlier;

"sound equipment" has the same meaning as in section 64; and

"vehicle" has the same meaning as in section 61.

[Criminal Justice and Public Order Act 1994, s 67.]

---

* **Words inserted by the Anti-social Behaviour Act 2003, s 62 from a date to be appointed.**

1 See the Police (Retention and Disposal of Vehicles) Regulations 1995, this title, post.

*Disruptive trespassers*

**7.9667** **68. Offence of aggravated trespass** (1) A person commits the offence of aggravated trespass[1] if he trespasses on land and, in relation to any lawful activity[2] which persons are engaging in or are about to engage in on that or adjoining land, does there anything which is intended by him to have the effect[3]—

(*a*) of intimidating those persons or any of them so as to deter them or any of them from engaging in that activity,

(*b*) of obstructing that activity, or

(*c*) of disrupting that activity[4].

(1A) *Scotland.*

(2) Activity on any occasion on the part of a person or persons on land is "lawful" for the purposes of this section if he or they may engage in the activity on the land on that occasion without committing an offence[5] or trespassing on the land.

(3) A person guilty of an offence under this section is liable on summary conviction to imprisonment for a term not exceeding **three months** * or a fine not exceeding **level 4** on the standard scale, or **both**.

(4) *Repealed.*

(5) In this section "land[6]" does not include—

(*a*) the highways and roads excluded from the application of section 61 by paragraph (*b*) of the definition of "land" in subsection (9) of that section; or

(*b*) a road within the meaning of the Roads (Northern Ireland) Order 1993.

[Criminal Justice and Public Order Act 1994, s 68 as amended by the Anti-social Behaviour Act 2003, s 59, the Land Reform (Scotland) Act 2003, Sch 2 and the Serious Organised Crime and Police Act 2005, Sch 7.]

---

* **Words substituted by the Criminal Justice Act 2003, Sch 26 from a date to be appointed.**

1 Where the common law private defence of property is raised the court must first ask itself whether the defendants are contending that they used reasonable force in order to defend property from actual or imminent damage, which constituted or would constitute an unlawful or criminal act. If the answer to that is "no" then the defence is not available. If the answer is "yes" then the court has to go on to consider the facts as the defendants honestly believed them to be and then has to determine objectively whether the force that was used was reasonable in all the circumstances. Thus, in a case where it was clear that the defendants knew quite well that there was nothing unlawful about the drilling of GM maize on the land, even if the seed might be transferred by one means or another to the neighbouring land; they acted as they had because they believed strongly that the seed represented a danger to neighbouring property and they knew that the law would not help them because what was going on was not unlawful or criminal, then, as a matter of law that the private defence of property simply was not available to the defendants on the facts (*DPP v Bayer* [2003] EWHC 2567 (Admin), (2003) 167 JP 666).

2 "Activity" means that something is being done or about to be done by a person and is a more particular definition than "carry on" eg of an enterprise such as farming. Accordingly, the persons engaged in the "lawful activity" must be physically present on the land so that persons who had trespassed on a field and damaged genetically modified crops were not guilty of an offence contrary to s 68(1) where neither the farmer nor anyone responsible for cultivation was present (*Tilly v DPP* [2001] EWCA Admin 821, 166 JP 22, [2002] Crim LR 128).

"Lawful activity" includes activities carried on by a body corporate: *Richardson v DPP; Nero v DPP* [2012] EWHC 1238 (Admin), 176 JP 451.

[3] Since s 68(1) has criminalised an *actus reus* with three effects, the three effects do not need to be the subject of three separate charges (*Nelder v DPP* (1998) Times, 11 June). Where there is no allegation of any second distinct act beyond the trespass itself an information alleging aggravated trespass will be defective (*DPP v Barnard* [2000] Crim LR 371, DC).

In *Peppersharp v DPP* [2012] EWHC 474 (Admin), 176 JP 257 a large number of demonstrators entered a building and caused significant damage. Their behaviour prevented persons in the building from working, and significant fear was caused. Eventually police evacuated the occupants. Later that day an officer saw a group of people detained by other officers. One of the group was the appellant, who was dressed in a black hat and hooded jacket and was carrying a banner. He was arrested, gave a "no comment" interview and did not give evidence at his trial. He was convicted on the basis that having entered or remained in the premises as a trespasser at a time when significant damage was caused or being caused it could be inferred that his presence encouraged the criminal behaviour of others. The conviction was upheld on appeal by way of case stated. What had happened was much more than mere trespass and was capable of constituting a "distinct and overt act". The court had been entitled to infer that, absent any innocent explanation for being in the building, the appellant's presence had encouraged the criminal behaviour of others to disrupt and obstruct the lawful activity of the occupiers.

*Peppersharp* was considered in *Bauer v DPP* [2013] EWHC 634 (Admin), [2013] 1 WLR 3616, 177 JP 177, where a group of 130 persons belonging to a group called "UK Uncut" forced their way into a shop premises in a protest against tax avoidance. Some of the customers remained in the store and were "terrified, frightened, confused, angry, intimidated and tearful" in consequence of some of the behaviour of members of the group, but there was no evidence that the appellants, who remained in the store for two-and-half hours had engaged in any of that behaviour. Nevertheless, the convictions were upheld. By virtue of their lengthy presence, the court had been entitled to infer that the demonstration had been a second act, distinct from the trespass; "intimidate" bore its ordinary meaning and the chaotic scene inside the store provided ample evidence from which the court had been entitled to infer that demonstrators who had chosen to remain in the store after it had closed had had an intention to intimidate. There had been nothing "mere" about the presence of those participating as demonstrators. They had been committing the conduct element of the offence, and in those circumstances there had been no need to consider whether the appellants had encouraged others since they had been guilty as the rest of the demonstrators as joint principals:

> "35. Looking at this case and *Peppersharp*, it appears to me that those prosecuting protesters for aggravated trespass have not properly focused on the question whether those taking part in the protest were guilty of the conduct element of that offence. If they can prove that, then, in my view, it is wrong and misleading to suggest that they are guilty of encouraging others. The question of whether they were encouraging others only arises on the hypothesis that they themselves have not committed the conduct element of aggravated trespass. In the context of the invasion of a building in force, it makes no sense to distinguish any of those participating in that invasion by categorizing some of them as principal offenders and others as accessories . . .
>
> 38. It seems to me that it will maintain and protect the rights enshrined in arts 10 and 11, in the context of peaceful protests, to focus on the question whether those participating in a demonstration are themselves guilty of the conduct element of the crime of aggravated trespass. If the prosecution cannot prove that their presence as part of the demonstration itself constituted that criminal conduct, then it should not fall back on the far more difficult proposition that, whilst their presence was itself peaceful, it encouraged others to commit the criminal offence of aggravated trespass. I, of course, exclude from that consideration those who are properly identified as accessories, namely those not themselves present who have procured or encouraged the demonstration which amounts to aggravated trespass." (per Moses LJ)

[4] Defendants who, having taken part in a mass protest against fox hunting, as trespassers, were running towards a hunt with the intention of disrupting it, were held to have been properly convicted of an offence under s 68(1) because the running after the hunt was sufficiently closely connected to the intended disruption as to be more than merely preparatory within the meaning of the Criminal Attempts Act 1981 (*Winder v DPP* (1996) 160 JP 713).

[5] "Offence" here means an offence under domestic law, and the crime "against peace" or "of aggression" is not a domestic crime and does not fall within this provision: *R v Jones (Margaret), Ayliffe v DPP, Swain v DPP* [2006] UKHL 16, [2007] 1 AC 136, [2006] 2 All ER 741, [2006] 2 WLR 772, [2006] 2 Cr App R 9. The true meaning of this provision lies in examining the activity which was (or was to be) carried out on the land. The intention of the section was to criminalise trespass where, in addition to the invasion of someone else's property, the defendant there disrupted an activity which the occupant was entitled to pursue. The additional criminal sanction is removed when the activity which was disrupted was, in itself, unlawful, which might be either because the occupant was himself trespassing, or because his activity was criminal. But not every incidental or collateral criminal offence could properly be said to affect the lawfulness of the activity, nor render it criminal. It would do so only when the criminal offence was integral to, and not remote from, the core activity carried on: *Richardson v DPP* [2014] UKSC 8, [2014] 2 All ER 20, [2014] 2 WLR 288.

[6] "Land" includes buildings. In its unamended form s 68 did not include buildings within the definition of "land" because of the inclusion of the phrase "in the open air", and the purpose and effect of the amendment was to negative the exclusion of buildings; the exclusion of most kinds of buildings in s 61(9)(*a*) applies only for the purposes of s 61: *DPP v Chivers* [2010] EWHC 1814 (Admin), [2011] 1 All ER 367, [2011] 1 WLR 2324, 174 JP 587.

7.9668 **69. Powers to remove persons committing or participating in aggravated trespass**

(1) If the senior police officer present at the scene reasonably believes—

(*a*) that a person is committing, has committed or intends to commit the offence of aggravated trespass on land; or

(*b*) that two or more persons are trespassing on land and are present there with the common purpose of intimidating persons so as to deter them from engaging in a lawful activity or of obstructing or disrupting a lawful activity,

he may direct that person or (as the case may be) those persons (or any of them) to leave the land.

(2) A direction under subsection (1) above, if not communicated to the persons referred to in subsection (1) by the police officer giving the direction may be communicated to them by any constable at the scene.

(3) If a person knowing that a direction under subsection (1) above has been given which applies to him—

(*a*) fails to leave the land as soon as practicable[1], or

(*b*) having left again enters the land as a trespasser within the period of three months beginning with the day on which the direction was given,

he commits an offence and is liable on summary conviction to imprisonment for a term not exceeding **three months** * or a fine not exceeding **level 4** on the standard scale, or both.

(4) In proceedings for an offence under subsection (3) it is a defence for the accused to show—

(*a*) that he was not trespassing on the land, or

(*b*) that he had a reasonable excuse for failing to leave the land as soon as practicable or, as the case may be, for again entering the land as a trespasser.

(5) *Repealed.*

(6) In this section "lawful activity" and "land" have the same meaning as in section 68[2].

[Criminal Justice and Public Order Act 1994, s 69 as amended by the Anti-social Behaviour Act 2003, s 59 and the Serious Organised Crime and Police Act 2005, Sch 7.]

* **Words substituted by the Criminal Justice Act 2003, Sch 26 from a date to be appointed.**

1 Where defendants tied themselves together in a concrete tube before the direction was given it was punishable, if at all, only as an offence contrary to s 68: *Nero v DPP, Richardson v DPP* [2012] EWHC 1238 (Admin), (2012) 176 JP 450.

2 "Land" includes buildings. In its unamended form s 68 did not include buildings within the definition of "land" because of the inclusion of the phrase "in the open air", and the purpose and effect of the amendment was to negative the exclusion of buildings; the exclusion of most kinds of buildings in s 61(9)(*a*) applies only for the purposes of s 61: *DPP v Chivers* [2010] EWHC 1814 (Admin), [2011] 1 All ER 367, (2010) 174 JP 587.

*Squatters*

7.9669 75. **Interim possession orders: false or misleading statements** (1) A person commits an offence if, for the purpose of obtaining an interim possession order, he—

(*a*) makes a statement which he knows to be false or misleading in a material particular; or

(*b*) recklessly makes a statement which is false or misleading in a material particular.

(2) A person commits an offence if, for the purpose of resisting the making of an interim possession order, he—

(*a*) makes a statement which he knows to be false or misleading in a material particular; or

(*b*) recklessly makes a statement which is false or misleading in a material particular.

(3) A person guilty of an offence under this section shall be liable[1]—

(*a*) on conviction on indictment, to imprisonment for a term not exceeding **two years** or a **fine** or **both**;

(*b*) on summary conviction, to imprisonment for a term not exceeding **six months** or a fine not exceeding **the statutory maximum** or **both**.

(4) In this section—

"interim possession order" means an interim possession order (so entitled) made under rules of court for the bringing of summary proceedings for possession of premises which are occupied by trespassers;

"premises" has the same meaning as in Part II of the Criminal Law Act 1977 (offences relating to entering and remaining on property); and

"statement", in relation to an interim possession order, means any statement, in writing or oral and whether as to fact or belief, made in or for the purposes of the proceedings.

[Criminal Justice and Public Order Act 1994, s 75.]

1 For procedure in respect of this offence which is triable either way, see the Magistrates' Courts Act 1980, ss 17A–21, in PART I: MAGISTRATES' COURTS, PROCEDURE, ante.

7.9670 76. **Interim possession orders: trespassing during currency of order** (1) This section applies where an interim possession order has been made in respect of any premises and served in accordance with rules of court; and references to "the order" and "the premises" shall be construed accordingly.

(2) Subject to subsection (3), a person who is present on the premises as a trespasser at any time during the currency of the order commits an offence.

(3) No offence under subsection (2) is committed by a person if—

(*a*) he leaves the premises within 24 hours of the time of service of the order and does not return; or

(*b*) a copy of the order was not fixed to the premises in accordance with rules of court.

(4) A person who was in occupation of the premises at the time of service of the order but leaves them commits an offence if he re-enters the premises as a trespasser or attempts to do so after the expiry of the order but within the period of one year beginning with the day on which it was served.

(5) A person guilty of an offence under this section shall be liable on summary conviction to imprisonment for a term not exceeding **six months** or a fine not exceeding **level 5** on the standard scale or both.

(6) A person who is in occupation of the premises at the time of service of the order shall be treated for the purposes of this section as being present as a trespasser.

(7) *Repealed.*

(8) In this section—

"interim possession order" has the same meaning as in section 75 above and "rules of court" is to be construed accordingly; and

"premises" has the same meaning as in that section, that is to say, the same meaning as in Part II of the Criminal Law Act 1977 (offences relating to entering and remaining on property).

[Criminal Justice and Public Order Act 1994, s 76 as amended by the Serious Organised Crime and Police Act 2005, Sch 7.]

*Powers to remove unauthorised campers*

7.9671 **77. Power of local authority to direct unauthorised campers to leave land**[1]

(1) If it appears to a local authority that persons are for the time being residing in a vehicle or vehicles within that authority's area—

(*a*) on any land forming part of a highway;

(*b*) on any other unoccupied land; or

(*c*) on any occupied land without the consent of the occupier,

the authority may give a direction that those persons and any others with them[2] are to leave the land and remove the vehicle or vehicles and any other property they have with them on the land.

(2) Notice of a direction under subsection (1) must be served on the persons to whom the direction applies, but it shall be sufficient for this purpose for the direction to specify the land and (except where the direction applies to only one person) to be addressed to all occupants of the vehicles on the land, without naming them.

(3) If a person knowing that a direction under subsection (1) above has been given which applies to him—

(*a*) fails, as soon as practicable, to leave the land or remove from the land any vehicle or other property which is the subject of the direction, or

(*b*) having removed any such vehicle or property again enters the land with a vehicle within the period of three months beginning with the day on which the direction was given,

he commits an offence and is liable on summary conviction to a fine not exceeding **level 3** on the standard scale.

(4) A direction under subsection (1) operates to require persons who re-enter the land within the said period with vehicles or other property to leave and remove the vehicles or other property as it operates in relation to the persons and vehicles or other property on the land when the direction was given.

(5) In proceedings for an offence under this section it is a defence for the accused to show that his failure to leave or to remove the vehicle or other property as soon as practicable or his re-entry with a vehicle was due to illness, mechanical breakdown or other immediate emergency.

(6) In this section—

"land" means land in the open air;

"local authority" means—

(*a*) in Greater London, a London borough or the Common Council of the City of London;

(*b*) in England outside Greater London, a county council, a district council or the Council of the Isles of Scilly;

(*c*) in Wales, a county council or a county borough council;

"occupier" means the person entitled to possession of the land by virtue of an estate or interest held by him;

"vehicle" includes—

(*a*) any vehicle, whether or not it is in a fit state for use on roads, and includes any body, with or without wheels, appearing to have formed part of such a vehicle, and any load carried by, and anything attached to, such a vehicle; and

(*b*) a caravan as defined in section 29(1) of the Caravan Sites and Control of Development Act 1960;

and a person may be regarded for the purposes of this section as residing on any land notwithstanding that he has a home elsewhere.

(7) Until 1st April 1996, in this section "local authority" means, in Wales, a county council or a district council.

[Criminal Justice and Public Order Act 1994, s 77.]

---

1 When deciding whether to make a removal order under this section, the local authority must consider the relationship of its proposed action to the various statutory provisions and humanitarian considerations that would arise, such as those outlined in the Departmental Circular *Gypsy Sites and Unauthorised Camping* DOE 18/94, Welsh Office 76/94). These considerations should be kept under review so far as there are any changes in circumstances after a removal order has been made, when deciding whether to make a complaint to the justices under s 78 of the Act (*R v Wealden District Council, ex p Wales* (1995) Times, 22 September).

The local authority should make inquiries into personal circumstances before and not after making the order. Magistrates are restricted to considering whether the formalities under the Act have been carried out and it is not part of their function to review the merits of the local authority's decision (*R v Wolverhampton Metropolitan Borough Council, ex p Dunne* (1996) 29 HLR 745, DC).

2 A removal notice applies only to persons who were on the land at the time when the direction was made and can be contravened only by such persons (*R v Wealden District Council, ex p Wales* (1995) Times, 22 September).

7.9672 **78. Orders for removal of persons and their vehicles unlawfully on land** (1) A magistrates' court may[1], on a complaint made by a local authority, if satisfied that persons and vehicles in which they are residing are present on land within that authority's area in contravention of a direction[2] given under section 77, make an order requiring the removal of any vehicle or other property which is so present on the land and any person residing in it.

(2) An order under this section may authorise the local authority to take such steps as are reasonably necessary to ensure that the order is complied with and, in particular, may authorise the authority, by its officers and servants—

(*a*) to enter upon the land specified in the order; and

(*b*) to take, in relation to any vehicle or property to be removed in pursuance of the order, such steps for securing entry and rendering it suitable for removal as may be so specified.

(3) The local authority shall not enter upon any occupied land unless they have given to the owner and occupier at least 24 hours notice of their intention to do so or unless after reasonable inquiries they are unable to ascertain their names and addresses.

(4) A person who wilfully obstructs any person in the exercise of any power conferred on him by an order under this section commits an offence and is liable on summary conviction to a fine not exceeding **level 3** on the standard scale.

(5) Where a complaint is made under this section, a summons issued by the court requiring the person or persons to whom it is directed to appear before the court to answer to the complaint may be directed—

(*a*) to the occupant of a particular vehicle on the land in question; or

(*b*) to all occupants of vehicles on the land in question, without naming him or them.

(6) Section 55(2) of the Magistrates' Courts Act 1980 (warrant for arrest of defendant failing to appear) does not apply to proceedings on a complaint made under this section.

(7) Section 77(6) of this Act applies also for the interpretation of this section.

[Criminal Justice and Public Order Act 1994, s 78.]

1 Where a local authority has made a direction under s 77, the question of reasonableness is a matter for the local authority to decide and there is no discretion for magistrates to review the reasonableness of the council's action. Only a limited discretion exists to refuse to make an order in special circumstances, for example when it is unnecessary to do so because the occupier has made an acceptable undertaking to leave by a certain time (*Shropshire County Council v Wynne* (1997) 96 LGR 689, DC). See also the reference to *R v Wolverhampton Metropolitan Borough Council, ex p Dunne* in note 1 to s 77, ante).

2 We would suggest that the legality of any direction is not to be challenged before the justices but by way of judicial review of the local authority's decision (see, for example, *R v Wealden District Council, ex p Wales* (1995) Times, 22 September).

**7.9673 79. Provisions as to directions under s 77 and orders under s 78** (1) The following provisions apply in relation to the service of notice of a direction under section 77 and of a summons under section 78, referred to in those provisions as a "relevant document".

(2) Where it is impracticable to serve a relevant document on a person named in it, the document shall be treated as duly served on him if a copy of it is fixed in a prominent place to the vehicle concerned; and where a relevant document is directed to the unnamed occupants of vehicles, it shall be treated as duly served on those occupants if a copy of it is fixed in a prominent place to every vehicle on the land in question at the time when service is thus effected.

(3) A local authority shall take such steps as may be reasonably practicable to secure that a copy of any relevant document is displayed on the land in question (otherwise than by being fixed to a vehicle) in a manner designed to ensure that it is likely to be seen by any person camping on the land.

(4) Notice of any relevant document shall be given by the local authority to the owner of the land in question and to any occupier of that land unless, after reasonable inquiries, the authority is unable to ascertain the name and address of the owner or occupier; and the owner of any such land and any occupier of such land shall be entitled to appear and to be heard in the proceedings.

(5) Section 77(6) applies also for the interpretation of this section.

[Criminal Justice and Public Order Act 1994, s 79.]

**7.9674 80.** *Repeal of certain provisions relating to gipsy sites.*

## Police (Disposal of Sound Equipment) Regulations 1995[1]

(SI 1995/722 amended by SI 2000/1549 and SI 2011/3058)

### *Extent, citation and commencement*

**7.9675** *1.* These Regulations, which extend to England and Wales and Scotland, may be cited as the Police (Disposal of Sound Equipment) Regulations 1995 and shall come into force on 10th April 1995.

1 Made by the Secretary of State in exercise of the powers conferred on him by s 66(10) and (11) of the Criminal Justice and Public Order Act 1994.

### *Property to which Regulations apply*

**7.9676** *2.* (1) Subject to paragraph (2) below, these Regulations apply to property in the possession of the police which has been forfeited by order under section 66(1) of the Criminal Justice and Public Order Act 1994 ("the 1994 Act") provided that—

(*a*) not less than six months have expired from the date on which the order was made, and

(*b*) either—

(i) no application by a claimant of the property has been made under section 66(5) of the 1994 Act, or by virtue of section 66(6); or

(ii) no such application has succeeded.

(2) Where, within the period specified in paragraph (1)(*a*) above—

(*a*) an application by a claimant of the property has been made under section 66(5) of the 1994 Act or by virtue of section 66(6), or

(*b*) the person upon whose conviction the court ordered the forfeiture of the property under section 66(1) of that Act has appealed against his conviction or sentence, these Regulations shall not apply to the property until the application or appeal has been determined.

*Disposal of property*

**7.9677** *3.* Property to which these Regulations apply shall be disposed of by sale or, if a police officer not below the rank of superintendent is satisfied that the nature of the property is such that it is not in the public interest that it should be sold, by other means in accordance with his directions.

*Application of proceeds of sale*

**7.9678** *4.* (1) The proceeds of any sale under regulation 3 above shall be paid to the police authority or local policing body and shall be kept in a separate account (referred to in this regulation as "the Fund").

(2) The Fund, or any part thereof, may be invested as the police authority or local policing body think fit and the income derived from the investments shall be added to and become part of the Fund.

(3) The money, including income from investments, standing to the credit of the Fund shall be applicable—

(*a*) to defray expenses incurred in the conveyance, storage and safe custody of the property to which these Regulations apply and in connection with its sale and otherwise in executing these Regulations;

(*b*) to make such payments of such amounts as the police authority or local policing body may determine for such charitable purposes as they may select.

(4) The Fund shall be audited by an auditor nominated for that purpose by the police authority or local policing body.

(5) *Revoked.*

## Police (Retention and Disposal of Vehicles) Regulations 1995[1]

(SI 1995/723 as amended by SI 1997/2971)

*Extent, citation and commencement*

**7.9679** *1.* These Regulations, which extend to England and Wales and Scotland, may be cited as the Police (Retention and Disposal of Vehicles) Regulations 1995 and shall come into force on 10th April 1995.

1 Made by the Secretary of State in exercise of the powers conferred on him by s 67(3) of the Criminal Justice and Public Order Act 1994.

*Application and interpretation*

**7.9680** *2.* (1) These Regulations apply to vehicles which have been seized and removed by a constable under section 62(1) or 64(4) of the 1994 Act.

(2) In these Regulations—

"the 1994 Act" means the Criminal Justice and Public Order Act 1994;

"the authority" means a police officer or other person authorised by the chief officer under regulation 3(1);

"G.B. registration mark" means a registration mark issued in relation to a vehicle under the Vehicle Excise and Registration Act 1994;

"local authority" means—

(*a*) in relation to England—

(i) a county council or, in a county where there is no county council, a district council;

(ii) a London borough council, or the Common Council of the City of London; or

(iii) the Council of the Isles of Scilly;

(*b*) *Scotland.*

(*c*) in relation to Wales—

(i) until 1st April 1996, a county council;

(ii) on or after that date, a county council or county borough council;

"owner" includes—

(*a*) the person by whom, according to the records maintained by the Secretary of State for the Environment, Transport and the Regions in connection with any functions exercisable by him by virtue of the Vehicle Excise and Registration Act 1994, the vehicle is kept and used;

(*b*) in relation to a vehicle which is the subject of a hiring agreement or a hire-purchase agreement, the person entitled to possession of the vehicle under the agreement;

"removal notice" means a notice complying with regulation 4;

"specified information", in relation to a vehicle, means such of the following information as can be or could have been ascertained from an inspection of the vehicle, or has been ascertained from any other source, that is to say:

(*a*) in the case of a vehicle which carries a G.B. registration mark, or a mark indicating registration in a place outside Great Britain, particulars of that mark; and

(*b*) the make of the vehicle.

*Retention and safe keeping of vehicles*

**7.9681** *3.* (1) After a vehicle has been seized and removed under section 62(1) or 64(4) of the 1994 Act, it shall be passed into and remain in the custody of a police officer or other person authorised under this regulation by the chief officer of the police force for the area in which the vehicle was seized ("the authority") until—

(*a*) the authority permit it to be removed from their custody by a person appearing to them to be the person from whom the vehicle was seized or the owner of the vehicle; or

(*b*) it has been disposed of or destroyed under these Regulations.

(2) While the vehicle is in the custody of the authority, they shall be under a duty to take such steps as are reasonably necessary for its safe keeping.

*Service of removal notice*

**7.9682** *4.* (1) The authority shall, as soon as they are able after the vehicle has been taken into their custody, take such steps as are practicable to serve a removal notice on the person from whom the vehicle was seized, except where the vehicle has been removed from their custody under regulation 5 below.

(2) A removal notice required to be served under this regulation or under regulation 6(3) below shall comply with, and shall be served in accordance with, the following provisions of this regulation.

(3) The removal notice shall, in respect of the vehicle to which it relates, contain the specified information and shall state:

(*a*) the place where the vehicle was seized;

(*b*) the place where it is now being kept;

(*c*) that the person to whom the notice is directed is required to claim the vehicle from the authority on or before the date specified in the notice, being a date not less than 21 days from the day when the notice is served on him;

(*d*) that unless the vehicle is claimed on or before that date the authority intend to destroy or dispose of it;

(*e*) that charges are payable under these Regulations by the person from whom the vehicle was seized in respect of the removal and retention of the vehicle, and that the vehicle may be retained until such charges are paid.

(4) The removal notice shall be served—

(*a*) by delivering it to the person to whom it is directed;

(*b*) by leaving it at his usual or last known place of abode;

(*c*) by sending it in a prepaid registered letter, or by the recorded delivery service, addressed to him at his usual or last known place of abode; or

(*d*) if the person is—

(i) a body corporate, by delivering it to the secretary or clerk of the body at its registered or principal office, or sending it in a prepaid registered letter, or by the recorded delivery service, addressed to the secretary or clerk of the body at that office;

(ii) a Scottish partnership, by delivering it to any member of, or manager employed by, the partnership at the usual place of business of the partnership, or sending it in a prepaid registered letter, or by the recorded delivery service, addressed to such a person at that place.

*Removal of vehicles from custody*

**7.9683** *5.* (1) Subject to section 67(4) and (7) of the 1994 Act and the following provisions of these Regulations, if at any time a person satisfies the authority that he is the person from whom the vehicle was seized the authority shall permit him to remove the vehicle from their custody.

(2) Paragraph (1) above does not—

(*a*) impose a duty on the authority where they reasonably believe that the person referred to is not the owner of the vehicle or authorised by the owner to remove the vehicle; or

(*b*) prevent the authority, in those circumstances, from returning the vehicle to its owner.

*Disposal and destruction of vehicles*

**7.9684** *6.* (1) Where the authority have been unable to serve a removal notice on the person from whom the vehicle was seized or, following the service of a removal notice, the vehicle has not been removed from their custody under these Regulations, the authority may dispose of or destroy the vehicle in accordance with the following provisions of this regulation.

(2) If the authority are satisfied that the person on whom they have served or attempted to serve a removal notice is the owner of the vehicle, they may dispose of or destroy the vehicle at any time, subject to paragraph (5) below.

(3) Where the authority are not so satisfied, they may, after taking steps under paragraph (4) below to find a person who may be the owner of the vehicle and any other steps for that purpose which appear to them to be practicable, in such manner as they think fit dispose of or destroy the vehicle at any time, subject to paragraph (5) below, if—

(*a*) they fail to find such a person, allowing a reasonable time for any person or body from whom they have requested information to respond to the request; or

(*b*) they find such a person but he fails to comply with a removal notice served on him under this paragraph but complying with, and served in accordance with, regulation 4 above; or

(*c*) they find such a person but he is a person on whom the authority have already served or attempted to serve a removal notice under regulation 4 above.

(4) The steps to be taken under this paragraph to find a person who may be the owner of the vehicle shall be such of the following as are applicable to the vehicle—

(*a*) if the vehicle carries a G.B. registration mark—

(i) the authority shall ascertain from the records maintained by the Secretary of State for the Environment, Transport and the Regions in connection with any functions exercisable by him by virtue of the Vehicle Excise and Registration Act 1994 the name and address of the person by whom the vehicle is kept and used; and

(ii) they shall give, where practicable, the specified information to a relevant agency and shall enquire of them whether they can make any enquiries to find the owner of the vehicle;

(*b*) if the vehicle carries a mark indicating registration in Northern Ireland, the authority shall give the specified information and a description of the place where the vehicle was seized to the Secretary of State for the Environment, Transport and the Regions and, where practicable, the specified information to a relevant agency shall enquire of them whether they can make any enquiries to find the owner of the vehicle;

(*c*) if the vehicle carries a mark indicating registration in the Republic of Ireland, the authority shall give the specified information and a description of the place where the vehicle was seized to the Secretary of State for the Environment, Transport and the Regions, and shall enquire of him whether he can make any enquiries to find the owner of the vehicle;

(*d*) if the vehicle carries a registration mark other than one mentioned in sub-paragraphs (*a*) to (*c*) above, the authority shall, where practicable, give the specified information to a relevant agency and shall enquire of them whether they can make any enquiries to find the owner of the vehicle.

(5) The authority may not destroy or dispose of the vehicle under this regulation—

(*a*) during the period of 3 months starting with the date on which the vehicle was seized;

(*b*) if the period in sub-paragraph (*a*) above has expired, until after the date specified by virtue of regulation 4(3)(*c*) above; or

(*c*) if not otherwise covered by sub-paragraph (*a*) or (*b*) above, during the period of 7 days starting with the date on which the vehicle is claimed under regulation 5 above

(6) In this regulation "relevant agency" means such agency maintaining records of hire purchase agreements about vehicles as the authority considers appropriate.

*Information to be given relating to the disposal of a vehicle*

**7.9685** 7. (1) Where the authority dispose of or destroy a vehicle pursuant to these Regulations they shall, where it is possible to do so, give information relating to the disposal or destruction of the vehicle to the person from whom the vehicle was seized, to any person who appears to the authority to have been the owner of the vehicle immediately before it was disposed of, and—

(*a*) if the vehicle carried a GB registration mark, to the Secretary of State for the Environment, Transport and the Regions;

(*b*) if the vehicle carried a mark indicating registration in Northern Ireland, to the Secretary of State for the Environment, Transport and the Regions and to the Secretary of State for Northern Ireland;

(*c*) if the vehicle carried a mark indicating registration in the Republic of Ireland, to the Secretary of State for the Environment, Transport and the Regions and to the Commissioners of Customs and Excise;

(*d*) if the vehicle carried a registration mark other than one mentioned in sub-paragraphs (*a*) to (*c*) above, to the Commissioners of Customs and Excise.

(2) In this regulation "information relating to the disposal or destruction of a vehicle" means—

(*a*) any information which is sufficient to relate the information now being given to any information previously given to the same person in respect of the removal, retention, disposal or destruction of the vehicle; and

(*b*) such of the specified information as has not been previously given to the same person in respect of the removal, retention, disposal or destruction of the vehicle.

*Payment of proceeds of sale to owner of vehicle*

**7.9686** 8. (1) Where the authority dispose of a vehicle in pursuance of these Regulations by means of sale, they shall pay the net proceeds of sale to any person who, before the end of the period of one year beginning with the date on which the vehicle is sold, satisfies the authority that at the time of the sale he was the owner of the vehicle.

(2) If it appears to the authority that more than one person is the owner of a particular vehicle, such one of them as the authority think fit shall be treated as its owner for the purposes of paragraph (1) above.

(3) In this regulation, "the net proceeds of sale" means any sum by which the proceeds of sale exceed the aggregate of such sums as may be payable under these Regulations in respect of the removal and retention of the vehicle.

*Charges for removal, retention and disposal of vehicles*

**7.9687** 9. (1) The prescribed sums for the purpose of section 67(3) of the 1994 Act shall, for any vehicle, be—

(*a*) in respect of removal, £105;

(*b*) in respect of retention, £12 for each period of 24 hours or a part thereof during which the vehicle is in the custody of the authority.

(2) For the purposes of paragraph (1)(*b*) above, each period of 24 hours shall be reckoned from noon on the first day after removal during which the place at which the vehicle is stored is open for the claiming of vehicles before noon.

# PUBLIC HEALTH

**Contents**



## European Communities Act 1972: regulations

**7.9688** Within the scope of the title Public Health would logically fall the subject matter of a number of regulations made under the very wide enabling power provided in s 2(2) of the European Communities Act 1972. Where such regulations create offences they are noted below in chronological order:

- Sludge (Use in Agriculture) Regulations 1989, SI 1989/1263 amended by SI 1990/880, SI 1996/593, SI 2000/656 and SI 2010/1159 (E) and 1820 (W);
- Household Appliances (Noise Emission) Regulations 1990, SI 1990/161 amended by SI 1994/1386 and SI 2004/693;
- Offshore Petroleum Production and Pipe-lines (Assessment of Environmental Effects) Regulations 1999, SI 1999/360 amended by SI 2007/933, SI 2010/1513, SI 2015/1431 and SI 2016/529 and 912;
- Non-Road Mobile Machinery (Emission of Gaseous and Particulate Pollutants) Regulations 1999, SI 1999/1053 amended by SI 2002/1649, SI 2004/693 and 2034, SI 2006/29, SI 2008/2011, SI 2011/2134, SI 2013/1687 and SI 2014/1309;
- Environmental Protection (Disposal of Polychlorinated Biphenyls and other Dangerous Substances) (England and Wales) Regulations 2000, SI 2000/1043 amended by SI 2000/3359, SI 2005/894 and 1806 (W), SI 2010/1159 (E) and 1820 (W) and SI 2011/988;
- Noise Emission in the Environment by Equipment for Use Outdoors Regulations 2001, SI 2001/1701 amended by SI 2001/3958, SI 2005/3525, SI 2007/3224, SI 2008/1597, SI 2009/2748 and SI 2015/98;
- Agricultural or Forestry Tractors and Tractor (Emission of Gaseous and Particulate Pollutants) Regulations 2002, SI 2002/1891 amended by SI 2006/2393, SI 2013/3171 and SI 2015/1350;
- End-of-Life Vehicles Regulations 2003, SI 2003/2635 amended by SI 2005/263, SI 2007/3538, SI 2010/675 and SI 2011/988 and SI 2016/738 and 1154;
- Genetically Modified Organisms (Traceability and Labelling) (England) Regulations 2004, SI 2004/2412 amended by SI 2008/2598;
- Genetically Modified Organisms (Transboundary Movements) (England) Regulations 2004, SI 2004/2692 amended by SI 2008/2598;
- End-of Life Vehicles (Producer Responsibility) Regulations 2005, SI 2005/263 amended by SI 2010/1095, SI 2011/988 and SI 2016/738;

- Greenhouse Gas Emissions Trading Scheme Regulations 2005, SI 2005/925 amended by SI 2005/2903, SI 2006/737, SI 2007/1096, SI 2007/3433 and SI 2007/3538, 3433 and 3538, SI 2010/675 and 1513, SI 2011/1506 and 2911 and SI 2012/2788;
- Hazardous Waste (England and Wales) Regulations 2005, SI 2005/894 amended by SI 2006/937, SI 2007/3476 and 3538, SI 2009/507, SI 2010/675 and 1159 (E), SI 2011/988, SI 2015/1360 and 1640 and SI 2016/58, 336, 691, 721, 738 and 1154;
- Hazardous Waste (Wales) Regulations 2005, SI 2005/1806 amended by SI 2006/937, SI 2007/3538, SI 2009/2861, SI 2010/675 and 1820, SI 2011/971, SI 2015/1417 and 1640 and SI 2016/58, 696, 721 and 1154;
- List of Wastes (Wales) Regulations 2005, SI 2005/1820 amended by SI 2011/971;
- Genetically Modified Organisms (Transboundary Movement) (Wales) Regulations 2005, SI 2005/1912;
- Genetically Modified Organisms (Traceability and Labelling) (Wales) Regulations 2005, SI 2005/1914;
- Waste (Household Waste Duty of Care) (England and Wales) Regulations 2005, SI 2005/2900 amended by SI 2012/811;
- Greenhouse Gas Emissions Trading Scheme (Amendment) and National Emissions Inventory Regulations 2005, SI 2005/2903 amended by SI 2007/3538, SI 2011/727, SI 2013/3135 and SI 2014/3075;
- Waste Management (England and Wales) Regulations 2006, SI 2006/937 amended by SI 2009/3381, SI 2010/675, SI 2011/600 (E) and 988 and SI 2012/811;
- Sulphur Content of Liquid Fuels (England and Wales) Regulations 2007, SI 2007/79 amended by SI 2014/1975;
- Producer Responsibility Obligations (Packaging Waste) Regulations 2007, SI 2007/871 amended by SI 2007/3538, SI 2008/413 and 1941, SI 2010/675, 1159 (E) and 1820 (W) and 2849, SI 2011/988, SI 2012/3082, SI 2013/1857, SI 2014/2890 and SI 2016/241, 645, 738, 1146 and 1154;
- Environmental Impact Assessment and Natural Habitats (Extraction of Minerals by Marine Dredging) (England and Northern Ireland) Regulations 2007, SI 2007/1067;
- Marine Works (Environmental Impact Assessment) Regulations 2007, SI 2007/1518 amended by SI 2009/2258 and SI 2015/446;
- Transfrontier Shipment of Waste Regulations 2007, SI 2007/1711 amended by SI 2007/3538, SI 2008/9, SI 2010/675 and 1159 (E) and SI 2011/988;
- Environmental Impact Assessment and Natural Habitats (Extraction of Minerals by Marine Dredging) (Wales) Regulations 2007, SI 2007/2610;
- Persistent Organic Pollutants Regulations 2007, SI 2007/3106 amended by SI 2010/675 and SI 2016/1154;
- Nitrate Pollution Prevention Regulations 2008, SI 2008/2349 amended by SI 2009/3160, SI 2010/1159 (E), SI 2012/1849 and SI 2013/1001 and 2619;
- REACH[1] Enforcement Regulations 2008, SI 2008/2852 amended by SI 2009/716, SI 2010/1513, SI 2011/3058, SI 2012/632, SI 2013/1948, 2919 and SI 2014/469, 1638 and 2882 and SI 2015/21, 51 and 1682;
- Waste Batteries and Accumulators Regulations 2009, SI 2009/890 amended by SI 2010/675, SI 2011/988, SI 2013/3134, SI 2015/1360 and SI 2016/1154;
- Environmental Damage (Prevention and Remediation) (Wales) Regulations 2009, SI 2009/995 amended by SI 2011/971 and 2131, SI 2012/2897, SI 2015/1394 and SI 2016/1154;
- Mercury Export and Data (Enforcement) Regulations 2010, SI 2010/265 amended by SI 2012/630 and SI 2016/1154;
- Detergents Regulations 2010, SI 2010/740 amended by SI 2013/1244 and SI 2016/1154 and 1165;
- Waste (England and Wales) Regulations 2011[2], SI 2011/988 amended by SI 2011/600 (W), SI 2012/767 (E) and 1889, SI 2013/141, SI 2014/517, SI 2015/483, 1360, 1417 (W), 1640 and SI 2016/58, 691 (W), 738 and 1154;
- Greenhouse Gas Emissions Trading Scheme (Nitrous Oxide) Regulations 2011, SI 2011/1506;
- Storage of Carbon Dioxide (Access to Infrastructure) Regulations 2011, SI 2011/2305;
- Controlled Waste Regulations 2012, SI 2012/811 amended by SI 2012/2320 and SI 2015/1360 and 1417 (W);
- Volatile Organic Compounds in Paints, Varnishes and Vehicle Refinishing Products Regulations 2012, SI 2012/1715 amended by SI 2013/390 and SI 2016/1154;
- Greenhouse Gas Emissions Trading Scheme (Amendment) (Charging Schemes) Regulations 2012, SI 2012/2788;
- Restriction of the Use of Certain Hazardous Substances in Electrical and Electronic Equipment Regulations 2012, SI 2012/3032 amended by SI 2014/1771;
- Motor Fuel (Road Vehicle and Mobile Machinery) Greenhouse Gas Emissions Reporting Regulations 2012, SI 2012/3030;
- Greenhouse Gas Emissions Trading Scheme Regulations 2012, SI 2012/3038 amended by SI 2013/1037 and 3135, SI 2014/3125, SI 2015/1388 (W) and 1849 and SI 2016/1154;
- Energy Performance of Buildings (England and Wales) Regulations 2012, SI 2012/3118 amended by SI 2013/10, 181 and 603, SI 2014/880 and 1681, SI 2015/609 and SI 2016/284 and 888;
- Waste and Emissions Trading Act 2003 (Amendment etc.) Regulations 2013, SI 2013/141 amended by SI 2016/738;
- Timber and Timber Products (Placing on the Market) Regulations 2013, SI 2013/233;

- Construction Products Regulations 2013, SI 2013/1387 amended by SI 2016/618;
- Nitrate Pollution Prevention (Wales) Regulations 2013, SI 2013/2506 amended by SI 2015/2020;
- Waste Electrical and Electronic Equipment Regulations 2013, SI 2013/3113 amended by SI 2014/1771, SI 2015/1968 and SI 2016/738 and 1154;
- Ozone-Depleting Substances Regulations 2015, SI 2015/168;
- Fluorinated Greenhouse Gases Regulations 2015, SI 2015/310 amended by SI 2016/1105;
- Environmental Damage (Prevention and Remediation) Regulations 2015, SI 2015/810 amended by SI 2015/1391 and SI 2016/1154;
- Nagoya Protocol (Compliance) Regulations 2015, SI 2015/821 amended by SI 2015/1691;
- Packaging (Essential Requirements) Regulations 2015, SI 2015/1640;
- Environmental Permitting (England and Wales) Regulations 2016.

1 "REACH" means Regulation (EC) No 1907/2006 of the European Parliament and of the Council concerning the Registration, Evaluation, Authorisation and Restriction of Chemicals (reg 2(1)).

2 A challenge to the provisions of regs 10 and 11 which transpose the requirements of Council Directive (EC) 2008/98 (the Waste Framework Directive) imposing an obligation to set up separate collection of paper, metal, plastic and glass waste from 2015 where economically practicable and not be mixed with other waste or other material with different properties has been dismissed: *R (UK Recyclate Ltd and others) v Secretary of State for Environment, Food and Rural Affairs* [2013] EWHC 425 (Admin), [2013] 3 All ER 561.

7.9689 **Wales** The Natural Resources Body for Wales (Establishment) Order 2012, SI 2012/1903 established the Natural Resources Body for Wales which assumed responsibility for the Welsh devolved functions of the Environment Agency and the Forestry Commissioners and the functions of the (abolished) Countryside Council for Wales. See also, the Natural Resources Body for Wales (Consequential Provision) Order 2013, SI 2013/1821.

# Public Health Act 1875

(38 & 39 Vict c 55)

## Water Supply

7.9690 **68. Causing water to be corrupted[1] by gas washings[1]** *Penalty*, **level 4** on the standard scale and **£20** a day for every day it continues.

[Public Health Act 1875, s 68 as amended by the Criminal Justice Act 1982, ss 38 and 46.]

1 A person shall not be guilty of an offence under this section in respect of any entry of matter into any controlled waters (within the meaning of Pt III of the Water Resources Act 1991) which occurs—(*a*) under and in accordance with a consent under Ch II of Pt III of the Water Resources Act 1991 or under Pt II of the Control of Pollution Act 1974 (which makes corresponding provision for Scotland); or (*b*) as a result of any act or omission under and in accordance with such a consent. (Water Consolidation (Consequential Provisions) Act 1991, Sch 1, para 1).

## Public Pleasure Grounds, etc

7.9691 **164. Bye-laws** The urban authority may make[1] bye-laws for the regulation of any public walk or pleasure ground[2] (provided supported, or contributed to by them), and may by such bye-laws provide for the removal from such public walk or pleasure ground of any person infringing any such bye-law by any officer of the urban authority or constable[3].

[Public Health Act 1875, s 164.]

1 See Treat 43 JP 457, as to model "Bye-laws," and *De Morgan v Metropolitan Board of Works* (1880) 5 QBD 155, 44 JP 296, as to validity of bye-laws against the delivery of a public speech, etc, in the ground. A bye-law "that a person shall not suffer any fowl, etc, belonging to him to enter or remain in the pleasure grounds," was held to be repugnant to the common law and not warranted by the statute, therefore invalid (*Torquay Local Board v Bridle* (1882) 47 JP 183). By the Criminal Justice Act 1967, Sch 3, Pt II, the maximum penalty permissible under such bye-laws was increased from £5 to £20, then to £50 under the Criminal Law Act 1977 s 31(2) and (3), now **level 2** on the standard scale (Criminal Justice Act 1982, ss 38 and 46).

2 As to gardens and ornamental grounds in public squares, etc, in cities and boroughs, see the Town Gardens Protection Act 1863, s 5, title Property, Offences Against, ante, and as to making available for the use of the inhabitants certain open spaces, etc, and their acquisition and maintenance by local authorities, see Open Spaces Act 1906, 6 Edw 7, c 25. As to construction of the words "public walks and pleasure grounds," and the use to which such places may be applied, see *A-G v Sunderland Corpn* (1876) 2 Ch D 634, 40 JP 564. See also the Commons Act 1876, as to appropriation of allotments and regulation of commons. A local authority may close the grounds for charitable or public purposes not exceeding 12 days in any one year, nor six consecutive days on any one occasion, but not on Sunday and only subject to prescribed restrictions on certain holidays, and may authorise a charge to be made for admission (Public Health Acts Amendment Act 1890, s 44(1), (amended by the Public Health Act 1961, s 53)). This provision applies throughout the district of every local authority (Public Health Act 1961, s 53(2)). Similar provisions relating to public parks and pleasure grounds are contained in the Public Health Acts Amendment Act 1907, s 76, post.

3 These powers are now exercisable by a local authority within the meaning of s 180 of the Local Government Act 1972 (see Sch 14, para 27 of that Act). The powers of a council abolished by the Local Government Act 1985 (namely the Greater London Council or a metropolitan county council) to make byelaws under this section are conferred on any body to which is transferred by or under that Act any land in respect of which such power was exercisable by such a council (Local Government Reorganisation (Property etc) (No 2) Order 1986, SI 1986/413).

## Police Regulations

7.9692 **171. Town Police Clauses Act 1847** The provisions of the Town Police Clauses Act 1847, with respect (1) To obstructions and nuisances in the street; and (2) To fires; and (3) To places of public resort; and (4) To hackney carriages[1]; shall, for the purpose of regulating such matters in districts[2] be incorporated with this Act[3]. The expression "the superintendent constable" and the expression "any constable or other officer appointed by virtue of this or the special Act" shall include any superintendent of police, and any constable or officer of police acting for or in the district of any authority, and the expression "within the prescribed distance" shall mean within any district.

[Public Health Act 1875, s 171 as amended by Public Health Act 1936, 3rd Sch and the Local Government Act 1972, s 179 and Sch 14.]

1 Licences to drive are to be in force for one year only from the date of the licence, or until the general licensing meeting, when one is appointed.

2 The reference was formerly to "urban districts" but now refers to all metropolitan and non-metropolitan districts except in relation to para (4)—hackney carriages; for power of a local authority to apply or disapply para (4), see the Local Government Act 1972, Sch 14, para 25.

3 Section 251 of the Public Health Act 1875 is not repealed for the purposes of the Town Police Clauses Act 1847 (Public Health Act 1936, Sch 3). This section relates to the prosecution of offences and is similar to s 296 of the Public Health Act 1936, post.

## Public Health Acts Amendment Act 1890

(53 & 54 Vict c 59)

7.9693 **37. Safety of platforms, etc, erected or used on public occasions**[1] (1) Whenever large numbers of persons are likely to assemble on the occasion of any show, entertainment, public procession, open-air meeting, or other like occasion, every roof of a building, and every platform, balcony, or other structure or part thereof let or used or intended to be let or used for the purpose of affording sitting or standing accommodation for a number of persons, shall be safely constructed or secured to the satisfaction of the surveyor of the urban authority.

(2) Any person who uses or allows to be used in contravention of this section any roof of a building, platform, balcony, or structure not so safely constructed or secured, or who neglects to comply with the provisions of this section in respect thereof, shall be liable to a *penalty* not exceeding **level 3** on the standard scale.

[Public Health Acts Amendment Act 1890, s 37 as amended by the Criminal Justice Act 1982, ss 38 and 46.]

1 This provision is excluded by s 9(1) of the Safety of Sports Grounds Act 1975 from applying where a general safety certificate under the 1975 Act is in force in relation to a stadium.

## Public Health Acts Amendment Act 1907[1]

(7 Edw 7 c 53)

### Part I

### General

7.9694 **2. Existing bye-laws** (4) Any bye-laws made under any enactment for which any provisions of this Act are substituted shall remain in force as if the bye-laws had been made under the corresponding provisions of this Act.

[Public Health Acts Amendment Act 1907, s 2(4).]

1 To be construed as one with the Public Health Acts 1875–1925.

7.9695 **7. Appeals to Crown Court, etc** (1) Except where this Act otherwise expressly provides any person aggrieved[1]—

(*a*) By any order, judgment, determination, or requirement of a local authority under this Act;

(*b*) By the withholding[2] of any order, certificate, licence, consent, or approval, which may be made, granted, or given by a local authority under this Act;

(*c*) By any conviction or order of a court of summary jurisdiction under any provision of this Act;

may appeal[3] to the Crown Court.

[Public Health Acts Amendment Act 1907, s 7 as amended by the Courts Act 1971, Sch 9, and the Crown Court Rules, 1971.]

1 See note 2 to s 301 of the Public Health Act 1936, post.

2 An appeal is available where a local authority fails to determine an application for a hackney carriage vehicle licence (*Kelly v Wirral Metropolitan Borough Council* (1996) Times, 13 May, CA).

3 See now the Magistrates' Courts Act 1980, s 108, ante. Although there may be a right of appeal under this section, yet the defendant is not precluded from raising before the justices some questions which can form the subject of appeal (*Eccles v Wirral Rural Sanitary Authority* (1886) 17 QBD 107, 50 JP 596; *Shoeburyness UDC v Burgess* (1924) 22 LGR 684). Seemingly, on a successful appeal the order of the Crown Court operates to give the licence, consent or approval withheld by the local authority (*Marshall v Blackpool Corpn* [1935] AC 16, 98 JP 376). Cf the Public Health Act 1936, s 302, post.

7.9696 **9. Bye-laws** All the provisions with respect to bye-laws contained in sections[1] one hundred and eighty-two to one hundred and eighty-six of the Public Health Act 1875 and any enactment amended or extended by those sections shall apply to all bye-laws from time to time made by a local authority under the provisions of this Act, provided that the Secretary of State shall be the confirming authority for bye-laws made under Part VII (Police) of this Act.

[Public Health Acts Amendment Act 1907, s 9.]

[1] Sections 182, 185 and 186 were repealed by the Local Government Act 1933. See now ss 235–237 of the Local Government Act 1972. By the Criminal Law Act 1977, s 31, the maximum penalty permissible under such bye-laws was increased to £50 (**level 2** on the standard scale under s 46 of the Criminal Justice Act 1982). See note 1 to s 237 of the Local Government Act 1972, ante.

7.9697 **10. Compensation, how determined** Where any compensation, costs, damages or expenses is or are by this Act directed to be paid, and the method for determining the amount thereof is not otherwise provided for, such amount shall in case of dispute be ascertained in the manner provided[1] by the Public Health Acts.

[Public Health Acts Amendment Act 1907, s 10.]

[1] This section is repealed, except for the purposes of any unrepealed enactment (Public Health Act 1936, Sch 3). See now s 276 thereof, post.

7.9698 **12. Crown rights** Nothing in this Act affects prejudicially any estate, right, power, privilege, or exemption of the Crown[1], and in particular nothing herein contained authorises any local authority to take, use, or in any manner interfere with any portion of the shore or bed of the sea or of any river, channel, creek, bay, or estuary, or any land, hereditaments, subjects, or right of whatsoever description belonging to Her Majesty in right of Her Crown, and under the management of the Commissioners of Woods[2] or of the Board of Trade respectively, without the consent in writing of the Commissioners of Woods[2] or the Board of Trade, as the case may be, on behalf of Her Majesty first had and obtained for that purpose (which consent the said Commissioners and Board are hereby respectively authorised to give).

[Public Health Acts Amendment Act 1907, s 12.]

[1] Extended to any works or apparatus belonging to the Post Office authority or any power conferred on the Minister of Transport by the London Traffic Act 1924 (*repealed and replaced by the Road Traffic Act* 1960) (Public Health Act 1925, ss 10 and 1(3), as amended by the Public Health Act 1936, Sch 3).

[2] Now the Commissioners of Crown Lands (SR & O 1924, No 1370).

## Part II
## Streets and Buildings

7.9699 **21. Power to alter names of streets[1]** The local authority[2] may, with the consent of two-thirds in number of the ratepayers and persons who are liable to pay an amount in respect of council tax in any street, alter the name of such street or any part of such street. The local authority may cause the name of any street or of any part of any street to be painted or otherwise marked on a conspicuous part of any building or other erection.

Any person who shall wilfully and without the consent of the local authority, obliterate, deface, obscure, remove, or alter any such name, shall be liable to a penalty not exceeding **level 1** on the standard scale.

[Public Health Acts Amendment Act 1907, s 21 as amended by the Criminal Law Act 1977, s 31, the Criminal Justice Act 1982, s 46, SI 1990/776 and the Local Government Finance Act 1982, Sch 13.]

[1] Upon the coming into operation in an area of s 18 of the Public Health Act 1925, post, this section will cease to have effect therein. Section 21 does not apply to Greater London.

[2] "Local authority" means the council or a district of London borough, the Common Council of the City of London, the Sub-Treasurer of the Inner Temple and the Under Treasurer of the Middle Temple (Local Government Act 1972, s 180). For application to local government areas, see the Local Government Act 1972, Sch 14, paras 24–26.

7.9700 **31. Fencing lands adjoining streets** If any land (other than land forming part of any common) adjoining any street is allowed to remain unfenced or if the fences of any such land are allowed to be or remain out of repair, and such land is used for any immoral or indecent purposes, or for any purpose, causing inconvenience or annoyance to the public, in that case, at any time after the expiration of fourteen days from the service upon the owner or occupier of notice in writing by the local authority requiring the land to be fenced or any fence of the land to be repaired, the local authority may cause the land to be fenced or may cause the fences to be repaired in such manner as they think fit, and the reasonable expenses thereby incurred shall be recoverable from such owner or occupier summarily as a civil debt.

[Public Health Acts Amendment Act 1907, s 31 as amended by the Highways Act 1959, 25th Sch and the Local Government Act 1972, Sch 30.]

## Part VI
## Recreation Grounds[1]

7.9701 **76. Parks and pleasure gardens** (1) The local authority[2] shall, in addition to any powers under any general Act, have the powers detailed in this section with respect to any public park or pleasure ground provided by them or under their management and control.

(4) No power given by this section shall be exercised in such a manner as to contravene any covenant or condition subject to which a gift or lease of a public park or pleasure ground has been accepted or made, without the consent of the donor, grantor, lessor, or other person or persons entitled in law to the benefit of such covenant or condition.

[Public Health Acts Amendment Act 1907, s 76 as amended by the Local Government Act 1972, Sch 30 (summarised).]

[1] Sections 76, 77 shall be in force throughout the district of every local authority (Public Health Act 1961, s 52(1)). These sections are extended by Pt VI of the Public Health Act 1925 and s 52(2), (3) of the Public Health Act 1961. Section 54 of the 1961 Act contains provisions relating to boating pools and lakes in parks and pleasure gardens. See also s 164 of the Public Health Act 1875 (public pleasure grounds, etc), ante.

[2] For definition of "local authority", see footnote 2 to s 21, ante.

7.9702 77. **Power to appoint officers** The local authority may appoint officers for securing the observance of this Part of this Act, and of the regulations and bye-laws made thereunder, and may procure such officers to be sworn in as constables for that purpose, but any such officer shall not act as a constable unless in uniform or provided with a warrant.

[Public Health Acts Amendment Act 1907, s 77.]

## PART VII
## POLICE

7.9703 80. **Leading or driving animals** The local authority may, by order, prescribe the streets in which, and the manner according to which, the leading or driving of animals shall be permitted within their district, provided that the route or routes which it shall be lawful for the local authority so to prescribe shall not be such as would prevent the passage of cattle between any market on the one hand, and any railway station or landing wharf in the district, or any place beyond the district, on the other hand, when such animals are merely passing between such market and railway station, landing wharf, or other place aforesaid, and the local authority shall be bound to allow at all times a reasonably short and efficient route or routes for the passage of such animals. Provided also that any such order shall only operate between the hours of nine in the morning and nine in the evening, and shall not prevent the owner of any animals driving the same to or from his own premises, and nothing in this enactment contained shall authorise the local authority to interfere with the leading or driving of any animals to any duly licensed slaughter-house.

[Public Health Acts Amendment Act 1907, s 80.]

7.9704 81. **Definition of public place and street** Any place of public resort or recreation ground belonging to, or under the control of the local authority[1], and any unfenced ground adjoining or abutting upon any street in an urban district[2] shall for the purpose of the Vagrancy Act 1824, and of any Act for the time being in force altering or amending the same, be deemed to be an open and public place, and shall be deemed to be a street for the purposes of section twenty-nine of the Town Police Clauses Act 1847, and also for the purposes of so much of section twenty-eight of that Act as relates to the following offences:

Every person who suffers to be at large any unmuzzled ferocious dog, or urges any dog or other animal to attack, worry, or put in fear any person or animal:

Every person who rides or drives furiously any horse or carriage, or drives furiously any cattle:

Every person who wilfully and indecently exposes his person:

Every person who publicly offers for sale or distribution, or exhibits to public view, any profane book, paper, print, drawing, painting, or representation, or sings any profane or obscene song or ballad, or uses any profane or obscene language:

Every person who wantonly discharges any firearm or discharges any missile or makes any bonfire:

Every person who throws or lays any dirt, litter, ashes, or night soil, or any carrion, fish, offal, or rubbish on any street.

[Public Health Acts Amendment Act 1907, s 81 as amended by the Street Offences Act 1959, Sch and the Indecent Displays (Control) Act 1981, Sch.]

[1] For definition of "local authority", see footnote 2 to s 21, ante.

[2] The Local Government Act 1972, Sch 14, para 23 provides that, with the qualifications set out in that Schedule, all the provisions of the Public Health Acts 1875–1925 extend throughout England and Wales. By para 26 so much of s 81 as relates to the Town Police Clauses Act 1847 does not extend to Greater London.

7.9705 82. **Byelaws as to sea-shore**[1] *The local authority for the prevention of danger, obstruction or annoyance to persons using the sea-shore may make and enforce byelaws*[2].

[1] This section was repealed by the Public Health Act 1936, s 346 and Sch 3, so far as regards matters with respect to which byelaws can be made under Part VIII of that Act.

[2] For considerations to be applied in the interpretation of byelaws under this section, such as their extent, the meaning of "low water line", and the public right to take fish or dig for worms from the sea-shore, see *Anderson v Alnwick District Council* [1993] 3 All ER 613.

7.9706 83. **Bye-laws as to promenades** The local authority[1] may, for the prevention of danger, obstruction, or annoyance to persons using the esplanades or promenades within the district, make bye-laws prescribing the nature of the traffic for which they may be used, regulating the selling and hawking of any article, commodity, or thing thereon, and for the preservation of order and good conduct among the persons using the same.

[Public Health Acts Amendment Act 1907, s 83.]

[1] For definition of "local authority", see footnote 2 to s 21, ante.

## PART X
## MISCELLANEOUS

7.9707 **94. Power to license pleasure boats**[1] (1) The local authority[2] may grant upon such terms and conditions as they may think fit licences for pleasure boats and pleasure vessels to be let for hire or to be used for carrying passengers for hire, and to the persons in charge of or navigating such boats and vessels, and may charge for each type of licence such annual fee as appears to them to be appropriate.

(2) Any such licence may be granted for such period as the local authority may think fit, and may be suspended or revoked by the local authority whenever they shall deem such suspension or revocation to be necessary or desirable in the interests of the public:

Provided that the existence of the power to suspend or revoke the licence shall be plainly set forth in the licence itself.

(3) No person shall let for hire any pleasure boat or pleasure vessel not so licensed or at any time during the suspension of the licence for the boat or vessel, nor shall any person carry or permit to be carried passengers for hire in any pleasure boat or vessel unless—

(*a*) the boat or vessel is so licensed and the licence is not suspended; and

(*b*) the person in charge of the boat or vessel and any other person navigating it is so licensed and his licence is not suspended and the conditions of his licence are complied with.

(4) A licence under this section shall not be required for any boat or vessel duly licensed by or under any regulations of the Board of Trade or for a person in charge of or navigating such a boat or vessel.

(5) No person shall carry or permit to be carried in any pleasure boat or pleasure vessel a greater number of passengers for hire than shall be specified in the licence applying to such boat or vessel, and every owner of any such boat or vessel shall, before permitting the same to be used for carrying passengers for hire, paint or cause to be painted, in letters and figures not less than one inch in height and three quarters of an inch in breadth, on a conspicuous part of the said boat or vessel, his own name and also the number of persons which it is licensed to carry in the form "Licensed to carry . . . . . . . . . . persons."

(6) Every person who shall act in contravention of the provisions of this section shall for each offence be liable to a penalty not exceeding **level 3** on the standard scale; but a person shall not be guilty of an offence under this subsection by reason of a failure to comply with such conditions as are mentioned in subsection (3)(*b*) of this section if it is shown that there is a reasonable excuse for the failure.

(7) Any person deeming himself aggrieved by the withholding, suspension, or revocation of any licence under the provisions of this section may appeal to a petty sessional court held after the expiration of two clear days after such withholding, suspension, or revocation:

Provided that the person so aggrieved shall give twenty-four hours' written notice of such appeal, and the ground thereof, to the designated officer for the court, and the court shall have power to make such order as they see fit and to award costs, such costs to be recoverable summarily as a civil debt[3].

(8) No licence under this section shall be required in respect of pleasure boats and pleasure vessels on any inland waterway owned or managed by the British Waterways Board.

(9) In subsections (1) and (3) of this section "let for hire" means let for hire to the public.

[Public Health Acts Amendment Act 1907, s 94 amended by the Criminal Justice Act 1967, 3rd Sch, the Local Government Act 1974, Sch 6, the Local Government (Miscellaneous Provisions) Act 1976, s 18, the Local Government, Planning and Land Act 1980, s 186, the Criminal Justice Act 1982, ss 38 and 46, the Access to Justice Act 1999, s 90 and Sch 13, SI 1997/1187 and the Courts Act 2003, Sch 8.]

---

1 This section extends the power under s 172 of the Public Health Act 1875 as amended: proceedings if taken under the 1875 Act carry a maximum penalty not exceeding **level 2** on the standard scale (Criminal Law Act 1977, s 31(2) and the Criminal Justice Act 1982, s 46.)

2 For definition of "local authority", see footnote 2 to s 21, ante.

3 The procedure is regulated by the Magistrates' Courts Rules 1981, r 34, in PART I: MAGISTRATES' COURTS, PROCEDURE, ante.

# Public Health Act 1925[1]

(15 & 16 Geo 5 c 71)

## PART I[2]

7.9708 **8. Appeals to petty sessional court** Where any enactment, in this Act provides for an appeal[3] to a petty sessional court against a notice, determination, requirement, order or intended order of a local authority[4] under this Act.

(1) Notice in writing of the appeal and of the grounds thereof shall be given by the appellant[3] to the clerk to the local authority;

(2) The court may make such order in the matter as they consider reasonable, and may award costs to be recoverable as a civil debt[5];

(3) No proceeding shall be taken by the local authority, or work executed, until after the determination or abandonment of the appeal;

(4) Notice of the right of appeal should be endorsed on the order of the local authority and on any notice communicating their determination, requirement or intended order.

[Public Health Act 1925, s 8.]

---

[1] Parts I to VIII of this Act and the Public Health Acts 1875–1907 may be cited together as the Public Health Acts 1875 to 1925 (s 1(2)). Parts I to VIII of this Act shall be construed as one with the Public Health Acts 1875 to 1907 (s 1(3)). Accordingly, the right of appeal to the Crown Court under s 7 of the Public Health Acts Amendment Act 1907, ante, will also apply to any conviction or order of a magistrates' court under this Act. The National Rivers Authority, every water undertaker and every sewerage undertaker is deemed to be a statutory undertaker for the purposes of this Act (Water Act 1989, Sch 25, para 1). As to the persons who can prosecute, see the Local Government Act 1972, s 223, ante.

[2] Part I is not adoptive.

[3] "Local authority" or "urban authority" shall be the council of a district or London borough, the Common Council of the City of London, the Sub-Treasurer of the Inner Temple and the Under Treasurer of the Middle Temple (Local Government Act 1972, s 180). For application to local government areas, see the Local Government Act 1972, Sch 14, paras 24–26.

[4] The procedure shall be by way of complaint for an order (Magistrates' Courts Rules 1981, r 34, in PART I: MAGISTRATES' COURTS, PROCEDURE, ante).

[5] See the Magistrates' Courts Act 1980, s 58 in PART I: MAGISTRATES' COURTS, PROCEDURE, ante.

## PART II[1]

7.9709 **17. Notice to urban authority before street is named** Before any street is given a name, notice of the proposed name shall be sent to the urban authority[2] by the person proposing to name the street.

(2) The urban authority,[2] within one month after the receipt of such notice, may, by notice in writing served on the person by whom notice of the proposed name of the street was sent, object to the proposed name.

(3) It shall not be lawful to set up in any street an inscription of the name thereof

(*a*) until the expiration of one month after notice of the proposed name has been sent to the urban authority[2] under this section; and

(*b*) where the urban authority have objected to the proposed name, unless and until such objection has been withdrawn by the urban authority or overruled on appeal; and any person acting in contravention of this provision shall be liable to a penalty not exceeding **level 1** on the standard scale, and to a daily penalty not exceeding **£1**.

(4) Where the urban authority[2] serve a notice of objection under this section, the person proposing to name the street may, within twenty-one days after the serving of the notice, appeal against the objection to a petty sessional court[3].

[Public Health Act 1925, s 17 as amended by the Decimal Currency Act 1969, s 10, the Criminal Law Act 1977, s 31 and the Criminal Justice Act 1982, s 46.]

---

[1] Part II extends throughout England and Wales, with the exception of ss 17 to 19 which are adoptive (but do not apply to Greater London) under the Local Government Act 1972, Sch 14, Pt II.

[2] "Local authority" or "urban authority" shall be the council of a district or London borough, the Common Council of the City of London, the Sub-Treasurer of the Inner Temple and the Under Treasurer of the Middle Temple (Local Government Act 1972, s 180). For application to local government areas, see the Local Government Act 1972, Sch 14, paras 24–26.

[3] For procedure on such appeal, see the Public Health Act 1925, s 8, supra, and notes thereto.

7.9710 **18. Alteration of name of street** (1) The urban authority[1] by order may alter the name of any street, or part of a street, or may assign a name to any street, or part of a street, to which a name has not been given.

(2) Not less than one month before making an order under this section, the urban authority[1] shall cause notice of the intended order to be posted at each end of the street, or part of the street, or in some conspicuous position in the street or part affected.

(3) Every such notice shall contain a statement that the intended order may be made by the urban authority[1] on or at any time after the day named in the notice, and that an appeal will lie under this Act to a petty sessional court against the intended order at the instance of any person aggrieved.

(4) Any person aggrieved by the intended order of the local authority may, within twenty-one days after the posting of the notice, appeal[2] to a petty sessional court.

[Public Health Act 1925, s 18 as amended by the Local Government Act 1972, Sch 30.]

---

[1] See note to "local authority" in s 8, ante.

[2] For procedure on such appeal, see the Public Health Act 1925, s 8, supra, and notes thereto.

7.9711 **19. Indication of name of street** The urban authority[1] shall cause the name of every street to be painted, or otherwise marked, in a conspicuous position on any house, building or erection in or near the street and shall from time to time alter or renew such inscription of the name of any street; if and when the name of the street is altered or the inscription becomes illegible.

(2) If any person pulls down any inscription of the name of a street, which has lawfully been set up, or sets up in any street any name different from the name lawfully given to the street, or places or affixes any notice or advertisement within twelve inches of any name of a street marked on a house, building, or erection in pursuance of this section, he shall be liable to a penalty not exceeding **level 1** on the standard scale, and to a daily penalty not exceeding **£1**.

[Public Health Act 1925, s 19 as amended by the Decimal Currency Act 1969, s 10, the Criminal Damage Act 1971, Schedule, the Local Government Act 1972, Sch 30, the Criminal Law Act 1977, s 31 and the Criminal Justice Act 1982, s 46.]

---

[1] See note to "local authority" in s 8, ante.

7.9712 **26. Bye-laws as to wires, etc, connected with wireless installations** (1) The local authority may make bye-laws[1] for the prevention of danger or obstruction to persons using any street or public place from posts, wires, tubes, aerials or, any other apparatus, in connection with or for the purposes of wireless telegraphy or telephony installations, stretched or placed, whether before or after the commencement of this section, on or over any premises and liable to fall on to any street or public place. In this section the expression "public place" includes any public park or garden, and any ground to which the public have or are permitted to have access, whether on payment or otherwise.

(2) Nothing in any bye-laws made under this section shall extend to any apparatus belonging to any statutory undertakings[2].

[Public Health Act 1925, s 26.]

---

1 Penalties may be imposed under the Local Government Act 1972, s 237, in this PART: title LOCAL GOVERNMENT, ante.

2 For the purposes of this section the holder of a licence under s 6 of the Electricity Act 1989 who is entitled to exercise any power conferred by para 1 of Sch 4 to that Act (street works, etc) shall be deemed to be a statutory undertaker and his undertaking a statutory undertaking (Electricity Act 1989, Sch 16, para 2(4)).

PART VIII[1]

7.9713 **75. Bye-laws as to persons waiting to enter public vehicles** (1) The local authority may make bye-laws[1] for regulating the conduct of persons waiting in the streets[2] to enter public vehicles, and the priority of entry into such vehicles, and may by such bye-laws require queues[3] or lines to be formed and kept by such persons.

[Public Health Act 1925, s 75.]

---

1 The bye-laws may impose fines. If they do not, the maximum fine is at **level 3** on the standard scale (Local Government Act 1972, s 237, the Criminal Law Act 1977, s 31(2) and the Criminal Justice Act 1982, s 46).

2 For definition, see the Public Health Act 1875, s 4.

3 As to the power to erect in a street barriers and posts for such queues, see the Public Health Act 1875, s 75(2), (3).

## Public Health Act 1936[1]

(26 Geo 5 & Edw 8 c 49)

PART I.—LOCAL ADMINISTRATION

7.9714 **1. Local authorities[2] under a duty to carry the Act into execution** (1) *Duty of local authority to carry this Act, excluding Part VI except* s 198, *into execution.*

(2) In this Act—

"community", in relation to a common community council acting for two or more grouped communities, means those communities;

"district", in relation to a local authority in Greater London, means a London Borough, the City of London, the Inner Temple or the Middle Temple, as the case may be and, in relation to a local authority in Wales, means a county or (as the case may be) county borough;

"local authority" means the council of a district or London borough, the Common Council of the City of London, the Sub-Treasurer of the Inner Temple and the Under Treasurer of the Middle Temple but, in relation to Wales, means the council of a county or county borough;

"parish", in relation to a common parish council acting for two or more grouped parishes, means those parishes.

[Public Health Act 1936, s 1 as substituted by the Local Government Act 1972, Sch 14 and amended by the National Health Service Reorganisation Act 1973, Sch 4 and the Local Government (Wales) Act 1994, Sch 9.]

---

1 For application of this and other public health Acts to London, see the London Government Act 1963, s 40 and Sch 11. The Environment Agency, every water undertaker and every sewerage undertaker is deemed to be a statutory undertaker for the purposes of this Act (Water Act 1989, Sch 25, para 1).

2 Any reference to an urban authority or rural authority in the 1936 Act shall be construed as a reference to a local authority (Local Government Act 1972, Sch 14, para 2). Sections 2–10 of the 1936 Act constitute Port Health Authorities and joint boards (incorporated). See the Port Health Authorities (England) Order 1974, SI 1974/215 and note also s 263 of the Local Government Act 1972.

PART II.—SANITATION AND BUILDINGS [1]

---

1 The Public Health Act 1961, s 1(1) provides that Pt II of that Act (post) shall be construed as one with Pt II of this Act.

SANITARY CONVENIENCES FOR BUILDINGS

7.9715 **45. Buildings having defective closets capable of repair[1]** (1) If it appears to a local authority that any closets provided for or in connection with a building are in such a state as to be prejudicial to health or a nuisance, but that they can without reconstruction be put into a satisfactory condition, the authority shall by notice require the owner or the occupier of the building to execute such works, or to take such steps by cleansing the closets or otherwise, as may be necessary for that purpose.

(2) In so far as a notice under this section requires a person to execute works, the provisions of Part XII of this Act with respect to appeals against, and the enforcement of, notices requiring the execution of works shall apply in relation to the notice.

(3) In so far as such a notice requires a person to take any steps other than the execution of

works, he shall, if he fails to comply with the notice, be liable to a fine not exceeding **level 1** on the standard scale and to a further fine not exceeding **£2** for each day on which the offence continues after conviction therefor:

Provided that in any proceedings under this subsection it shall be open to the defendant to question the reasonableness of the authority's requirements or of their decision to address their notice to him and not to the occupier or, as the case may be, the owner of the building.

(4) This section shall not apply to a factory, or to a building to which the next succeeding section applies.

[Public Health Act 1936, s 45 as amended by the Factories Act 1937, Sch 4, the Offices, Shops and Railway Premises Act 1963, Sch 2, the Decimal Currency Act 1969, s 10, the Criminal Law Act 1977, s 31, the Criminal Justice Act 1982, s 46 and the Statute Law (Repeals) Act 1993, Sch 1.]

1 This section does not apply to premises to which the Offices, Shops and Railway Premises Act 1963, applies (Offices, Shops and Railway Premises Act 1963, s 9(6)).

## SUPPLEMENTAL PROVISIONS AS TO DRAINS, SANITARY CONVENIENCES, CESSPOOLS, ETC

7.9716 **48. Power of relevant authority to examine and test drains, etc, believed to be defective** (1) Where it appears to a local authority that there are reasonable grounds for believing that a sanitary convenience[1], drain, private sewer or cesspool is in such a condition as to be prejudicial to health[2] or a nuisance, or that a drain or private sewer communicating indirectly with a public sewer is so defective as to admit subsoil water, they may examine its condition, and for that purpose may apply any test, other than a test by water under pressure, and, if they deem it necessary, open the ground.

(1A) *Repealed.*

(2) If on examination the convenience, drain, sewer, or cesspool is found to be in proper condition[3], the authority shall, as soon as possible, reinstate any ground which has been opened by them and make good any damage done by them.

[Public Health Act 1936, s 48 as amended by the Water Act 1973, Sch 8, the Water Act 1989, Sch 8 and the Water Consolidation (Consequential Provisions) Act 1991, Schs 1 and 3.]

1 "Sanitary conveniences" mean closets and urinals (s 90(1)).
2 "Prejudicial to health" means injurious, or likely to cause injury to health (s 343(1)).
3 For remedying defects found on examination, the authority will act under s 39, ante, or s 17 of the Public Health Act 1961, post.

7.9717 **49. Rooms over closets of certain types, or over ashpits, etc, not to be used as living, sleeping or workrooms** (1) A room which, or any part of which, is immediately over a closet, other than a watercloset or earthcloset, or immediately over a cesspool, midden or ashpit, shall not be occupied as a living room, sleeping room or workroom.

(2) Any person who, after seven days' notice from the local authority, occupies any room in contravention of the provisions of this section, or who permits any room to be so occupied, shall be liable to a fine not exceeding **level 1** on the standard scale, and to a further fine not exceeding **£2** for each day on which the offence continues after conviction therefor.

[Public Health Act 1936, s 49 as amended by the Decimal Currency Act 1969, s 10, the Criminal Law Act 1977, s 31 and the Criminal Justice Act 1982, s 46.]

7.9718 **50. Overflowing and leaking cesspools** (1) If the contents of any cesspool soak therefrom or overflow, the local authority may by notice require the person by whose act, default or sufferance the soakage or overflow occurred or continued to execute such works, or to take such steps by periodically emptying the cesspool or otherwise, as may be necessary for preventing the soakage or overflow:

Provided that this subsection shall not apply in relation to the effluent from a properly constructed tank for the reception and treatment of sewage, if that effluent is of such a character, and is so conveyed away and disposed of, as not to be prejudicial to health[1] or a nuisance.

(2) In so far as notice under this section requires a person to execute works, the provisions of Part XII[2] of this Act with respect to appeals against, and the enforcement of, notices requiring the execution of works shall apply in relation to the notice.

(3) In so far as such a notice requires a person to take any steps other than the execution of works, he shall, if he fails to comply with the notice, be liable to a fine not exceeding **level 1** on the standard scale, and to a further fine not exceeding **£2** for each day on which the offence continues after conviction therefor:

Provided that in any proceeding under this subsection it shall be open to the defendant to question the reasonableness of the authority's requirements.

[Public Health Act 1936, s 50 as amended by the Decimal Currency Act 1969, s 10, the Water Act 1973, Sch 8, the Criminal Law Act 1977, s 31, the Criminal Justice Act 1982, s 46 and the Water Act 1989, Sch 8.]

1 See note 2 to s 48, ante.
2 See ss 290 and 300, post.

7.9719 **51. Care of closets** (1) The occupier of every building in, or in connection with, which a watercloset[1] or an earth-closet[2] is provided shall, in the case of a watercloset, cause the flushing apparatus thereof to be kept supplied with water sufficient for flushing and where necessary to be properly protected against frost, and shall, in the case of an earth-closet, cause it to be kept supplied with dry earth or other suitable deodorising material.

(2) A person who fails to comply with any of the provisions of this section shall be liable to a fine not exceeding **level 1** on the standard scale.

[Public Health Act 1936, s 51 as amended by the Criminal Law Act 1977, s 31 and the Criminal Justice Act 1982, s 46.]

---

1 "Watercloset" means a closet which has a separate fixed receptacle connected to a drainage system and separate provision for flushing from a supply of clean water either by the operation of mechanism or by automatic action (s 90(1)).

2 "Earth closet" means a closet having a movable receptacle for the reception of faecal matter and its deodorisation by the use of earth, ashes or chemicals, or by other methods (s 90(1)).

7.9720 **52. Care of sanitary conveniences used in common** Where a sanitary convenience[1] is used in common by the members of two or more families, the following provisions shall have effect—

(*a*) if any person injures or improperly fouls the convenience, or anything used in connection therewith, or wilfully or by negligence causes an obstruction in the drain therefrom, he shall be liable to a fine not exceeding **level 1** on the standard scale;

(*b*) if the convenience, or the approach thereto, is, for want of proper cleansing or attention, in such a condition as to be insanitary, such of the persons having the use thereof in common as are in default, or, in the absence of satisfactory proof as to which of them is in default, each of them, shall be liable to a fine not exceeding **level 1** on the standard scale, and to a further fine not exceeding **25p** for each day on which the offence continues after conviction therefor.

[Public Health Act 1936, s 52 as amended by the Decimal Currency Act 1969, s 10, the Criminal Law Act 1977, s 31 and the Criminal Justice Act 1982, s 46.]

---

1 See note 1 to s 48, ante.

## REMOVAL OF REFUSE, SCAVENGING, KEEPING OF ANIMALS, ETC

7.9721 **78. Scavenging of common courts and passages** (1) If any court, yard or passage which is used in common by the occupants of two or more buildings, but is not a highway repairable by the inhabitants at large, is not regularly swept and kept clean and free from rubbish or other accumulation to the satisfaction of the local authority, the authority may cause it to be swept and cleansed.

(2) The local authority may recover any expenses reasonably incurred by them under this section from the occupiers of the buildings which front or abut on the court or yard, or to which the passage affords access, in such proportions as may be determined[1] by the authority, or, in case of dispute, by a court of summary jurisdiction.

[Public Health Act 1936, s 78.]

---

1 See ss 300–302, post.

7.9722 **79. Power to require removal of noxious matter by occupier of premises in urban district** (1) If in a borough or urban district, or in a rural district or contributory place[1] in which section 49 of the Public Health Act 1875, was in force immediately before the commencement[2] of this Act[3] it appears to the public health inspector that any accumulation of noxious matter ought to be removed, he shall serve notice on the owner[4] thereof, or on the occupier of the premises on which it is found, requiring him to remove it, and, if the notice is not complied with within twenty-four hours after service thereof, the inspector may remove the matter referred to.

(2) A local authority may recover[5] the expenses of any action reasonably taken by their inspector under the preceding subsection from the owner or occupier in default.*

[Public Health Act 1936, s 79.]

---

* **Repealed by the Control of Pollution Act 1974, Schs 3 and 4 from a date to be appointed.**

1 For definition of contributory place, see note 2 to s 46.

2 1 October 1937 (s 347(1)).

3 This section applies throughout the district of every local authority (Local Government Act 1972, Sch 14, para 4).

4 That is, the owner of the accumulation.

5 Under s 293, post.

7.9723 **80. Power to require periodical removal of manure, etc, from stables, etc, in urban district** (1) In a borough or urban district, and in a rural district or contributory place in which section 50 of the Public Health Act 1875, was in force immediately before the commencement[1] of this Act,[2] the local authority may by public or other notice require the periodical removal, at such intervals as may be specified in the notice, of manure or refuse from mews, stables or other premises.

(2) If a person on whom a notice has been served under this section fails to comply therewith, he shall be liable to a fine not exceeding level 1 on the standard scale.*

[Public Health Act 1936, s 80 as amended by the Criminal Law Act 1977, s 31 and the Criminal Justice Act 1982, s 46.]

---

* **Repealed by the Control of Pollution Act 1974, Schs 3 and 4 from a date to be appointed.**

1 1 October 1937 (s 347(1)).

2 This section applies throughout the district of every local authority (Local Government Act 1972, Sch 14, para 4).

7.9724 **81. Bye-laws for the prevention of certain nuisances** A local authority may make bye-laws for preventing—

(*a*) the occurrence of nuisance from snow[1], filth, dust, ashes and rubbish;

(*b*) the keeping[2] of animals so as to be prejudicial to health.

[Public Health Act 1936, s 81.]

[1] The accumulation of snow on a roof of premises overhanging a street is a nuisance. The occupier is liable for any danger due to falling snow if, with knowledge, nothing is done within a reasonable time to abate the nuisance (*Slater v Worthington's Cash Stores (1930) Ltd* [1941] 1 KB 488, [1941] 3 All ER 28).

[2] This is a statutory nuisance under s 79(1)(*f*) of the Environmental Protection Act 1990, post.

7.9725 **82. Bye-laws as to removal through streets of offensive matter or liquid** (1) A local authority may make bye-laws—

(*a*) prescribing the times for the removal or carriage through the streets, of any fæcal or offensive or noxious matter or liquid, whether that matter or liquid is in course of removal or carriage from within, or from without, or through, their district;

(*b*) requiring that the receptacle or vehicle used for the removal or carriage of any such matter or liquid shall be properly constructed and covered so as to prevent the escape of any such matter or liquid;

(*c*) requiring the cleansing of any place whereon any such matter or liquid has been dropped or spilt in the course of removal or carriage.

(2) If and so far as a bye-law made under the preceding subsection is inconsistent with an order under section 6 of the Road Traffic Regulation Act 1984, the order shall prevail.

[Public Health Act 1936, s 82 as amended by the London Government Act 1963, 11th Sch.]

FILTHY OR VERMINOUS PREMISES OR ARTICLES, AND VERMINOUS PERSONS

7.9726 **83. Cleansing of filthy or verminous premises[1]** (1) Where a local authority upon consideration of a report from any of their officers or other information in their possession are satisfied that any premises[2]—

(*a*) are in such a filthy or unwholesome condition as to be prejudicial to health[3]; or

(*b*) are verminous[4],

the local authority shall give notice to the owner or occupier of the premises requiring him to take such steps as may be specified in the notice to remedy the condition of the premises by cleansing and disinfecting them and the notice may require among other things the removal of wallpaper or other covering of the walls, or, in the case of verminous premises, the taking of such steps as may be necessary for the purpose of destroying or removing vermin.

(1 A) A notice under the foregoing subsection may require—

(*a*) the interior surface of premises used for human habitation or as shops or offices to be papered, painted or distempered, and

(*b*) the interior surface of any other premises to be painted, distempered or whitewashed,

and shall allow the person on whom the notice is served, or the local authority acting in his default, to choose, in a case under paragraph (*a*) of this subsection, between papering, painting and distempering and, in a case under paragraph (*b*) of this subsection, between painting, distempering and whitewashing.

(2) If a person on whom a notice under this section is served fails to comply with the requirements thereof, the authority may themselves carry out the requirements and recover[5] from him the expenses reasonably incurred by them in so doing, and, without prejudice to the right of the authority to exercise that power, he shall be liable to a fine not exceeding **level 1** on the standard scale and to a further fine not exceeding **£2** for each day on which the offence continues after conviction therefor:

Provided that in any proceedings under this subsection it shall be open to the defendant to question the reasonableness of the authority's requirements or of their decision to address their notice to him and not to the occupier or, as the case may be, the owner of the premises.

(3) Where a local authority take action under paragraph (*b*) of subsection (1) of this section, their notice may require that they shall be allowed to employ gas for the purpose of destroying vermin on the premises[6] but in that case the notice shall be served both on the owner and on the occupier of the premises, and the authority shall bear the cost of their operations and may provide temporary shelter or house accommodation for any person compelled to leave the premises by reason of their operations.

(4) This section shall not apply to any premises forming part of a factory or a mine or quarry within the meaning of the Mines and Quarries Act 1954.

[Public Health Act 1936, s 83 as amended by the Public Health Act 1961, s 35, the Decimal Currency Act 1969, s 10, the Criminal Justice Act 1967, 3rd Sch and the Criminal Justice Act 1982, ss 38 and 46.]

[1] This section is applied to ships and boats and to tents, vans, sheds, etc, by ss 267, 268, post. See also the Hydrogen Cyanide (Fumigation) Act 1937, in this PART: title HEALTH AND SAFETY, ante.

[2] "Premises" includes messuages, buildings, lands, easements and hereditaments of any tenure (s 343(1)).

[3] "Prejudicial to health" means injurious, or likely to cause injury to health (s 343(1)). See also s 92, post.

[4] "Vermin" in its application to insects and parasites, include their eggs, larvæ and pupæ, and "verminous" shall be construed accordingly (s 90(1)).

[5] Under s 293, post.

[6] For extended powers when this requirement is contained in the notice, see the Public Health Act 1961, s 36, post.

7.9727 **85. Cleansing of verminous persons and their clothing** (1) Upon the application of any person, a county council or a local authority may take such measures as are, in their opinion, necessary to free him and his clothing[1] from vermin[2].

(2) Where it appears to a county council or a local authority, upon a report from their medical officer of health or, in the case of a local authority, from their public health inspector, that any person, or the clothing of any person, is verminous, then, if that person consents to be removed to a cleansing station, they may cause him to be removed to such a station, and, if he does not so consent, they may apply to a court of summary jurisdiction, and the court, if satisfied that it is necessary that he or his clothing should be cleansed, may make an order[3] for his removal to such a station and for his detention therein for such period and subject to such conditions as may be specified in the order.

(3) Where a person has been removed to a cleansing station in pursuance of the last preceding subsection, the county council or local authority shall take such measures as may, in their opinion, be necessary to free him and his clothing from vermin.

(4) The cleansing of females under this section shall be carried out only by a registered medical practitioner, or by a woman duly authorised by the medical officer of health.

(5) Any consent required to be given for the purposes of this section may, in the case of a person under the age of sixteen years, be given on his behalf by his parent or guardian.

(6) No charge shall be made in respect of the cleansing of a person or his clothing, or in respect of his removal to, or maintenance in, a cleansing station under this section.

(7) The powers conferred on a county council or local authority by this section shall be in addition to, and not in derogation of, any power[4] in relation to the cleansing of children which may be exercisable by them as a local education authority.

[Public Health Act 1936, s 85.]

---

1 As to cleansing or destruction of filthy or verminous articles, see s 84. A county council or local authority may provide cleansing stations (s 86). The sale of verminous household articles (including clothing) is prohibited (Public Health Act 1961, s 37, post).

2 For definition of "vermin", see note 4 to s 83, supra.

3 As to enforcement of this order, see the Magistrates' Courts Act 1980, s 63 in PART I: MAGISTRATES' COURTS, PROCEDURE, ante. This section is applied to ships and boats, and to tents, vans, sheds, etc, by ss 267, 268, post.

4 See the Education Act 1996, ss 521–526, in this PART: title EDUCATION.

## PART IV—WATER SUPPLY

### PROVISIONS FOR THE PROTECTION OF PUBLIC FROM POLLUTED WATER

7.9728 **140. Power to close, or restrict water from, polluted source of supply** (1) If a local authority are of opinion that the water in or obtained from any well, tank, or other source of supply not vested in them, being water which is, or is likely to be, used for domestic purposes, or in the preparation of food or drink for human consumption, is, or is likely to become, so polluted as to be prejudicial to health[1], the authority may apply to a court of summary jurisdiction and thereupon a summons may be issued to the owner or occupier of the premises to which the source of supply belongs or[2] to any other person alleged in the application to have control thereof.

(2) Upon the hearing of the summons, the court may make an order directing the source of supply to be permanently or temporarily closed or cut off, or the water therefrom to be used for certain purposes only, or such other order as appears to the court to be necessary to prevent injury or danger to the health of persons using the water, or consuming food or drink prepared therewith or therefrom.

The court shall hear any user of the water who claims to be heard, and may cause the water to be analysed at the cost of the local authority.

(3) If a person on whom an order is made under this section fails to comply therewith, the court may, on the application of the local authority, authorise them to do whatever may be necessary for giving effect to the order, and any expenses reasonably incurred by the authority in so doing may be recovered[3] by them from the person in default.

[Public Health Act 1936, s 140.]

---

1 See note 3 to s 83, ante.

2 The court may select, after considering the local authority's views.

3 See s 293, post.

7.9729 **141. Power to deal with insanitary cisterns, etc[1]** Any well, tank, cistern, or water-butt used for the supply of water for domestic purposes which is so placed, constructed or kept as to render the water therein liable to contamination prejudicial to health, shall be a statutory nuisance for the purpose of Part III of the Environmental Protection Act 1990.

[Public Health Act 1936 s 141 as amended by the Environmental Protection Act 1990, Sch 151.]

---

1 For the purposes of the operation of this provision and the exercise or performance of any power or duty conferred or imposed by this provision, no account shall be taken of any radioactivity possessed by any substance or article or by any part of any premises (Radioactive Substances Act 1960, s 9(1), Sch 1).

## PART V—PREVENTION, NOTIFICATION AND TREATMENT OF DISEASE [1]

7.9730 **143.** *Power of Minister[2] to make regulations with a view to the treatment of certain diseases[3] and for preventing the spread of such diseases.*

[Public Health Act 1936, s 143 amended by the London Government Act 1963, Sch 18, the National Health Service Reorganisation Act 1973, ss 57, 58, Schs 4 and 5, the Health Services Act 1980, ss 1, 2, and Sch 1, the Civil Aviation Act

1982, s 36, the Criminal Justice Act 1982, ss 39 and 46, and Sch 3, the Health and Social Services and Social Security Adjudications Act 1983, Schs 9 and 10 and the Public Health (Control of Disease) Act 1984 Sch 3.]

1 The Public Health Act 1961, s 1(2) provides that Pt III of that Act, post, shall be construed as one with Pt V of this Act.

2 For Ministerial responsibility, see now the Secretary of State for Social Services Order 1968, SI 1968/1699, and the Transfer of Functions (Wales) Order 1969, SI 1969/388. Additional provisions are contained in Part III of the Public Health Act 1961, post. Section 143(1)–(7) and (10) is repealed by the Public Health (Control of Disease) Act 1984 Sch 3 and replaced by s 13 thereof.

3 The maximum penalty which may be provided by regulations is a fine at level 5 on the standard scale. The Public Health (Infectious Diseases) Regulations 1968 (SI 1968/1366, SI 1969/844, SI 1974/274, SI 1976/1226 and 1955), the Public Health (Aircraft) Regulations 1979, SI 1979/1434 amended by SI 2007/1447 (E), 1603 (E) and 1900 (W), SI 2010/1593 (W) and 2982 and the Public Health (Ships) Regulations 1979, SI 1979/1435 amended by SI 2007/1446 (E), 1603 (E), 1901 (W) and SI 2010/1593 (W) and 2982 and the Public Health (Aircraft and Ships) (Isle of Man) Order 2010, SI 2010/2982 amended by SI 2011/1212, have been made. For notifiable diseases see post the Health Services and Public Health Act 1968, s 48, listing diseases covered by these regulations.

## PART VI—HOSPITALS, NURSING HOMES, ETC

7.9731 **198. Bye-laws as to mortuaries and post-mortem rooms** A local authority, or a parish council, may make bye-laws[1] with respect to the management, and charges for the use of a mortuary or post-mortem room, provided by them.

[Public Health Act 1936, s 198.]

1 The bye-laws may prescribe the fines; if they do not, the penalty is not exceeding **level 2** on the standard scale (Local Government Act 1972, s 237, the Criminal Law Act 1977, s 31(2) and the Criminal Justice Act 1982, s 46, ante). Ministerial functions under s 198 were transferred to the Minister of Local Government and Planning by the Transfer of Functions (Minister of Health and Minister of Local Government and Planning) (No 2) Order 1951, SI 1951/753. The name of the Minister of Local Government and Planning has now been changed to the Secretary of State for the Environment.

## PART VII—NOTIFICATION OF BIRTHS

7.9732 **205. Women not to be employed in factories or workshops within four weeks after birth of a child** If the occupier of a factory[1] knowingly allows a woman to be employed therein within four weeks after she has given birth to a child, he shall be liable to a fine not exceeding **level 1** on the standard scale.

[Public Health Act 1936, s 205 as amended by the Criminal Law Act 1977, s 31, the Criminal Justice Act 1982, ss 35, 38 and 46, the Statute Law (Repeals) Act 1993, Sch 1 and the Statute Law (Repeals) Act 2004.]

1 "Factory" means a factory within the meaning of the Factory and Workshop Acts 1901–1929. This Act was repealed by, and re-enacted in, the Factories Act 1937, and the division has ceased. See now s 175 of the Factories Act 1961, in this PART: TITLE HEALTH AND SAFETY, ante.

## PART VIII—BATHS, WASHHOUSES, BATHING PLACES, ETC

### PROVISION OF BATHS, ETC

*Bye-laws for regulation of baths, etc, with respect to public bathing*[1] *and with respect to swimming baths and bathing pools not under the management of a local authority, and for use of baths and bathing places during winter months.*—The local authority may make these bye-laws.

[Public Health Act 1936, ss 223, 226(2), 231, and 233.]

7.9733 **234. Baths, etc, to be public places for certain purposes** Any baths, washhouses, swimming bath or bathing place under the management of a local authority shall be deemed to be a public and open place for the purposes of any enactment relating to offences against decency.

[Public Health Act 1936, s 234.]

1 For extension of power to make bye-laws about bathing, see s 17 of the Local Government (Miscellaneous Provisions) Act 1976, post.

## PART XI—MISCELLANEOUS

### WATERCOURSES, DITCHES, PONDS, ETC

7.9734 **259. Nuisances in connection with watercourses, ditches, ponds, etc** (1) The following matters shall be statutory nuisances for the purposes of Part III[1] of the Environmental Protection Act 1990, that is to say—

(*a*) any pond, pool, ditch, gutter or watercourse[2] which is so foul or in such a state as to be prejudicial to health[3] or a nuisance;

(*b*) any part of a watercourse, not being a part ordinarily navigated by vessels employed in the carriage of goods by water, which is so choked[4] or silted up as to obstruct or impede the proper flow of water and thereby to cause a nuisance, or give rise to conditions prejudicial to health:

Provided that in the case of an alleged nuisance under paragraph (*b*) nothing in this subsection shall be deemed to impose any liability on any person other than the person by whose act or default[5] the nuisance arises or continues.

(2) *Repealed.*

[Public Health Act 1936, s 259 as amended by the Criminal Law Act 1977, s 31, the Control of Pollution Act 1974, Sch 4, the Criminal Justice Act 1982, s 46 and the Environmental Protection Act 1990, Sch 15.]

[1] As to statutory nuisances, see s 79 of the Environmental Protection Act 1990, post.

[2] "Watercourse" does not include estuaries or tidal waters (*R v Falmouth and Truro Port Health Authority, ex p South West Water Ltd* [2001] QB 445, [2000] 3 All ER 306, [2000] 3 WLR 1464, CA).

[3] "Prejudicial to health" means injurious, or likely to cause injury to health (s 343(1)). As to power of local authority to obtain an order from a court of summary jurisdiction for cleansing offensive ditches lying near to, or forming, boundary of district, see s 261.

[4] A watercourse can be said to be "choked" within the meaning of the section where there is an obstruction or an artificial obstruction causing a statutory nuisance. Nor does the statutory nuisance caused by the choking have to be ever present and continuous. The subsection is capable of addressing an intermittent state or a series of events or occurrences. By its nature, the "proper flow of water" in a watercourse is not itself a constant. The piers of a bridge and perhaps other works associated with those piers or other parts of the bridge are capable of being "artificial" obstructions in a watercourse or river (*R (on the application of Robinson) v Torridge District Council* [2006] EWHC 877 (Admin), [2006] 3 All ER 1148, [2007] 1 WLR 871).

[5] The owner of land is under no duty at common law to remove obstructions arising by natural causes in a natural watercourse; therefore, such an obstruction, not arising or contained by his act or default, is not a statutory nuisance under s 93, ante (*Neath RDC v Williams* [1951] 1 KB 115, [1950] 2 All ER 625, 114 JP 464).

7.9737 **264. Urban authority may require repair and cleansing of culverts** The owner or occupier of any land shall repair, maintain and cleanse any culvert in, on or under that land, and, if it appears to the local authority that any person has failed to fulfil his obligations under this section they may by notice require him to execute such works of repair, maintenance or cleansing as may be necessary.

The provisions of Part XII of this Act with respect to appeal against, and the enforcement of, notices requiring the execution of works[5] shall apply in relation to any notice given under this section.

[Public Health Act 1936, s 264 as amended by the Statute Law (Repeals) Act 2004.]

7.9738 **266. Saving for land drainage authorities, railway companies and dock undertakers** (1) The powers conferred by the foregoing provisions of this Part of this Act shall not be exercised—(i) with respect to any stream, watercourse, ditch or culvert within the jurisdiction of a land drainage authority[1], except after consultation with that authority; Provided that nothing in this subsection shall apply in relation to the taking of proceedings in respect of a statutory nuisance.

(2) Nothing in the foregoing provisions of this Part of this Act shall prejudice or affect the powers of any railway company[2] or dock undertakers to culvert or cover in any stream or watercourse, or, without the consent of the railway company or dock undertakers concerned, extend to any culvert or covering of a stream or watercourse constructed by a railway company and used by them for the purposes of their railway, or constructed by dock undertakers and used by them for the purposes of their undertaking.

[Public Health Act 1936, s 266 as amended by London Government Act 1963, 18th Sch.]

[1] Under s 343 as amended by the Water Consolidation (Consequential Provisions) Act 1991, Sch 1, "land drainage authority" means the National Rivers Authority or an internal drainage board.

[2] "Railway company" means persons who are statutory undertakers in respect of a railway undertaking (s 343(1)).

## Ships and Boats

7.9739 **267. Application to ships and boats of certain provisions of this Act[1]** (1) For the purposes of such of the provisions of this Act specified in subsection (4) of this section as are provisions for the execution of which local authorities are responsible, a vessel[2] lying in any inland or coastal water[3] shall—

*(a)* if those waters are within a port health district, be subject to the jurisdiction of the port health authority for that district;

*(b)* if those waters are within the district of a local authority but not within a port health district, be subject to the jurisdiction of that local authority;

*(c)* if those waters are not within the district of any local authority or any port health district, be subject to the jurisdiction of such local authority as the Minister[4] may from time to time by order direct or, if no such direction is given, within the jurisdiction of the local authority whose district includes that point on land which is nearest to the spot where the vessel is lying.

(2) For the purposes of such of the said provisions as are provisions for the execution of which county councils are responsible, a vessel when lying in any inland or coastal waters not within a county shall be subject to the jurisdiction of the council of the county which includes that point on land which is nearest to the spot where the vessel is lying.

(2A) Subsection (2) of this section does not apply if the point on land which is nearest to the spot where the vessel is lying is Wales.

(3) In relation to any vessel the said provisions shall have effect as if—

*(a)* the vessel were a house, building or premises within the district, or, as the case may be, the county, of the port health authority or local authority or county council to whose jurisdiction it is subject; and

*(b)* the master, or other officer or person in charge, of the vessel were the occupier.

(4) The provisions of this Act referred to in the preceding subsections are Parts VI and XII[5] and, so far as regards boats used for human habitation, the provisions of Part II relating to filthy or

verminous premises or articles and verminous persons[6].

(5) This section does not apply to any vessel belonging to His Majesty or under the command or charge of an officer holding His Majesty's commission, or to any vessel belonging to a foreign government.

(6) In determining for the purposes of subsection (1) above what provisions of this Act specified in subsection (4) above are provisions for the execution of which local authorities are responsible, no account shall be taken of any enactment (whether contained in this Act or not) relating to port health authorities or joint boards or to any particular port health authority or joint board or of any instrument made under any such enactment.

[Public Health Act 1936, s 267 as amended by the Clean Air Act 1956, 4th Sch, the Local Government (Miscellaneous Provisions) Act 1982, Sch 6, the Public Health (Control of Disease) Act 1984, Sch 3 the Environmental Protection Act 1990, Sch 16, and the Local Government (Wales) Act 1994, Sch 9.]

1 In its application to a council which is a local health authority, this section shall be construed as applying to that council in their capacity of local health authority as well as in other capacities (National Health Service Act 1946, Sch 10).

2 "Vessel" has the same meaning as "ship" in the Merchant Shipping Act 1995 (s 343(1)), see s 313 thereof in PART VI: TRANSPORT, ante.

3 "Inland waters" include rivers, harbours and creeks; "Coastal waters" mean waters within a distance of three nautical miles from any point on the coast measured from low-water mark of ordinary spring tides (s 343(1)).

4 Now the Secretary of State for the Environment.

5 Part VI, ss 181–199, deals with hospitals, nursing homes, etc, and Pt XII, ss 271–347, is headed "General". Many of the sections mentioned were repealed by the National Health Service Act 1946, Sch 10.

6 See ss 83–86, ante.

## TENTS, VANS, SHEDS, ETC

7.9740 **268. Nuisances arising from, and bye-laws and other matters relating to, tents, vans, etc** (1) The provisions of Part III of the Environmental Protection Act 1990 and Parts VII[1] and XII of this Act, and the provisions of Part II relating to filthy or verminous premises or articles and verminous persons, shall apply in relation to tents, vans, sheds and similar structures used for human habitation as they apply in relation to other premises and as if a tent, van, shed or similar structure used for human habitation were a house or a building so used.

(2) For the purposes of Part III of the Environmental Protection Act 1990, a tent, van, shed or similar structure used for human habitation—

- (*a*) which is in such a state, or so overcrowded, as to be prejudicial to the health of the inmates; or
- (*b*) the use of which, by reason of the absence of proper sanitary accommodation or otherwise, gives rise, whether on the site or on other land, to a nuisance or to conditions prejudicial to health,

shall be a statutory nuisance[2], and the expression "occupier" in relation to a tent, van, shed or similar structure shall include any person for the time being in charge thereof.

(3) Where such a nuisance as is mentioned in paragraph (*b*) of the preceding subsection is alleged to arise, wholly or in part, from the use for human habitation of any tent, van, shed or similar structure, then, without prejudice to the liability of the occupants or other users thereof, an abatement notice[3] may be served on, and proceedings under Part III of the Environmental Protection Act 1990 may be taken against the occupier of the land on which the tent, van, shed or other structure is erected or stationed:

Provided that it shall be a defence for him to prove that he did not authorise the tent, van, shed, or other structure to be stationed or erected on the land.

(4) A local authority may make bye-laws for promoting cleanliness in, and the habitable condition of, tents, vans, sheds and similar structures used for human habitation, and generally for the prevention of nuisances in connection therewith.

(5) The powers of a court before which proceedings are brought—

- (*a*) in respect of a statutory nuisance caused by, or arising in connection with, a tent, van, shed or similar structure used for human habitation; or
- (*b*) in respect of any contravention of bye-laws made under this section,

shall include power to make an order prohibiting the use for human habitation of the tent, van, shed or other structure in question at such places, or within such area, as may be specified in the order.

[Public Health Act 1936, s 268 as amended by the Public Health (Control of Disease) Act 1984, Sch 3 and the Environmental Protection Act 1990, Sch 15.]

1 As to Pt XII, see note 5 to s 267, supra. Part VII, ss 200–205, deals with notification of births.

2 As to statutory nuisances, see s 79 of the Environmental Protection Act 1990, post.

3 See s 80 of the Environmental Protection Act 1990, post.

7.9741 **269. Power of local authority to control use of moveable dwellings[1]** (1) For the purpose of regulating in accordance with the provisions of this section[2] the use of moveable dwellings within their district, a local authority may grant—

- (i) licences authorising persons to allow land occupied by them within the district to be used as sites for moveable dwellings; and
- (ii) licences authorising persons to erect or station, and use, such dwellings within the district;

and may attach to any such licence such conditions as they think fit—

(*a*) in the case of a licence authorising the use of land, with respect to the number and classes of moveable dwellings which may be kept thereon at the same time, and the space to be kept free between any two such dwellings, with respect to water supply, and for securing sanitary conditions;

(*b*) in the case of a licence authorising the use of a moveable dwelling, with respect to the use of that dwelling (including the space to be kept free between it and any other such dwelling) and its removal at the end of a specified period, and for securing sanitary conditions.

(2) Subject to the provisions of this section, a person shall not allow any land occupied by him to be used for camping purposes on more than 42 consecutive days or more than 60 days in any 12 consecutive months, unless either he holds in respect of the land so used such a licence from the local authority of the district as is mentioned in paragraph (i) of the preceding subsection, or each person using the land as a site for a moveable dwelling holds in respect of that dwelling such a licence from that authority as is mentioned in paragraph (ii) of the said subsection.

For the purposes of this subsection, land which is in the occupation of the same person as, and within 100 yards of, a site on which there is during any part of any day a moveable dwelling shall be regarded as being used for camping purposes on that day.

(3) Subject to the provisions of this section, a person shall not keep a moveable dwelling on any one site, or on two or more sites in succession, if any one of those sites is within 100 yards of another of them, on more than 42 consecutive days, or 60 days in any 12 consecutive months, unless either he holds in respect of that dwelling such a licence from the local authority of the district as is mentioned in paragraph (ii) of subsection (1) of this section, or the occupier of each piece of land on which the dwelling is kept holds in respect of that land such a licence from that authority as is mentioned in paragraph (i) of the said subsection.

(4) Where under this section an application for a licence is made to a local authority, the authority shall be deemed to have granted it unconditionally, unless within 4 weeks from the receipt thereof they give notice to the applicant stating that his application is refused, or stating the conditions subject to which a licence is granted, and, if an applicant is aggrieved by the refusal of the authority to grant him a licence, or by any condition attached to a licence granted, he may appeal[3] to a court of summary jurisdiction.

(5) Nothing in this section applies—(i) to a moveable dwelling which—(*a*) is kept by its owner on land occupied by him in connection with his dwelling-house and is used for habitation only by him or by members of his household; or (*b*) is kept by its owner on agricultural land occupied by him and is used for habitation only at certain seasons and only by persons employed in farming operations on that land; (iii) to a moveable dwelling while it is not in use for human habitation and is being kept on premises the occupier of which permits no moveable dwellings to be kept thereon except such as are for the time being not in use for human habitation.

(6) If an organisation satisfies the Minister that it takes reasonable steps for securing—(*a*) that camping sites belonging to or provided by it, or used by its members, are properly managed and kept in good sanitary condition; and (*b*) that moveable dwellings used by its members are so used as not to give rise to any nuisance, the Minister may grant to that organisation a certificate of exemption.

A certificate so granted may be withdrawn at any time, but while in force shall for the purpose of this section have the effect of a licence—(i) authorising the use as a site for moveable dwellings of any camping ground belonging to, provided by or used by members of, the organisation; (ii) authorising any member of the organisation to erect or station on any site, and use, a moveable dwelling.

In this subsection the expression "member" in relation to an organisation includes a member of any branch or unit of, or formed by, the organisation.

(7) A person who contravenes any of the provisions of this section or fails to comply with any condition attached to a licence granted to him under this section, shall be liable to a fine not exceeding **level 1** on the standard scale, and to a further fine not exceeding **£2** for each day on which the offence continues after conviction therefor.

(8) For the purposes of this section—

(i) the expression "moveable dwelling" includes any tent, any van or other conveyance whether on wheels or not, and, subject as hereinafter provided, any shed or similar structure, being a tent, conveyance or structure which is used either regularly, or at certain seasons only, or intermittently, for human habitation:

Provided that it does not include a structure to which building regulations apply;

(ii) the owner of land which is not let shall be deemed to be the occupier thereof;

(iii) if a moveable dwelling is removed from the site on which it stands, but within 48 hours is brought back to the same site or to another site within 100 yards thereof, then, for the purpose of reckoning any such period of 42 consecutive days as is mentioned in subsection (2) or subsection (3) of this section, it shall be deemed not to have been removed or, as the case may be, to have been moved direct from the one site to the other.

(9) Subject as hereinafter provided, this section shall not apply to any district in which at the commencement of this Act there was in force a local Act containing provisions enabling the local authority to regulate, by means of bye-laws or licences or otherwise, the use of moveable dwellings

or camping grounds:

Provided that, on the application of the local authority, the Minister may declare this section to be in force in their district, and upon the declaration taking effect, such of the provisions of the local Act as may be specified in the declaration shall be repealed or, as the case may be, shall be repealed as respects the district of that authority.

[Public Health Act 1936, s 26 as amended by the Caravan Sites and Control of Development Act 1960, Fourth Sch, the Public Health Act 1961, Sch 1, Part III, the Criminal Justice Act 1967, 3rd Sch, the Decimal Currency Act 1969, s 10, the Criminal Justice Act 1982, ss 38 and 46 and the Building Act 1984, Sch 67.]

---

1 Subject to certain transitional provisions, this section has ceased to apply to caravans (Caravan Sites and Control of Development Act 1960, s 30). See title TOWN AND COUNTRY PLANNING, post for relevant provisions of that Act.

2 The section deals with public health and sanitary conditions at the site; the local authority may not take into account any question of local amenities in refusing to grant a licence under this section (*Pilling v Abergele UDC* [1950] 1 KB 636, [1950] 1 All ER 76, 114 JP 69).

3 See s 300, post.

## HOP-PICKERS, ETC

7.9742 270. **Bye-laws as to hop-pickers and persons engaged in similar work** A local authority may make bye-laws for securing the decent lodging and accommodation of hop-pickers and other persons engaged temporarily in picking, gathering or lifting fruit, flowers, bulbs, roots or vegetables within their district.

[Public Health Act 1936, s 270.]

## PART XII—GENERAL[1]

## SUPPLEMENTAL AS TO POWERS OF COUNCILS

7.9743 278. **Compensation to individuals for damage resulting from exercise of powers under this Act** A local authority shall make compensation[2], and in case of dispute the amount shall be determined by arbitration. If not exceeding **£50** be claimed, all questions may on the application of either party be determined by and the amount recovered before a court of summary jurisdiction.

[Public Health Act 1936, s 278 as amended by the Water Consolidation (Consequential Provisions) Act 1991, Sch 3 (summarised).]

---

1 For application of certain sections in this Part to Pts IV and VI of the Public Health Act 1961, post, see s 1(4) thereof. In its application to a council which is a local health authority, this Part of the Act shall be construed as applying to that council in their capacity of local health authority as well as in other capacities (National Health Service Act 1946, Sch 10). Part XII of this Act shall have effect as if so much of Pt II of the Public Health Act 1961 (sanitation and buildings) as does not relate to building regulations were contained in Pt II of the Public Health Act 1936 (Housing and Building Control Act 1984, s 60(1)). This section may apply to a sewerage undertaker; see the Water Industry Act 1991, s 115.

2 This section may be applied for the purposes of the Town and Country Planning Act 1990, ss 178(3), (4), 209(3), (4) and 219(3), (4) and the Planning (Listed Buildings and Conservation Areas) Act 1990, s 42(3).

## NOTICES, ETC

7.9744 283. **Notices to be in writing; forms of notices, etc** (1) All notices, orders, consents, demands and other documents authorised or required by or under this Act to be given, made or issued by a council[1], and all notices and applications authorised or required by or under this Act to be given or made to, or to any officer of, a council shall be in writing[2].

(2) The Minister[3] may by regulations prescribe the form of any notice, advertisement, certificate or other document to be used for any of the purposes of this Act and, if forms are so prescribed, those forms or forms to the like effect may be used in all cases to which those forms are applicable.[4]

[Public Health Act 1936, s 283.]

---

1 This section may apply to a sewerage undertaker; see the Water Industry Act 1991, s 115.

2 See the Interpretation Act 1978, Sch 1, in PART II: EVIDENCE, ante.

3 By the Transfer of Functions (Minister of Health and Minister of Local Government and Planning) (No 1) Order 1951, SI 1951/142, the majority of the functions under the Public Health Act 1936, formerly exercised by the Minister of Health were transferred to the Minister of Local Government and Planning (now the Secretary of State for the Environment). Certain functions have been retained by the Minister of Health. In this section and others that follow the expression "Minister" means whichever of these two Ministers is appropriate having regard to the functions that are being discharged. Ministerial functions relating to the control of building are exercised by the Minister of Public Building and Works.

4 Section 266 and Sch 4 of the Public Health Act 1875 (which contain similar provisions), are not repealed for the purposes of any unrepealed enactment (Public Health Act 1936, Sch 3).

7.9745 284. **Authentication of documents[1]** (1) Any notice, order, consent, demand or other document which a council are authorised or required by or under this Act to give, make or issue may be signed on behalf of the council—(*a*) by the clerk of the council; (*b*) by the surveyor, the medical officer of health, the public health inspector or the chief financial officer, of the council as respects documents relating to matters within their respective provinces; (*c*) by any officer of the council authorised by them in writing to sign documents of the particular kind or, as the case may be, the particular document.

(2) Any document purporting to bear the signature of an officer expressed to hold an office by virtue of which he is under this section empowered to sign such a document, or expressed to be duly

authorised by the council to sign such a document or the particular document, shall for the purposes of this Act, and of any byelaws, building regulations and orders made thereunder, be deemed, until the contrary is proved, to have been duly given, made or issued by authority of the council.

In this subsection the expression "signature" includes a facsimile of a signature by whatever process reproduced.

[Public Health Act 1936, s 284 as amended by the Public Health Act 1961, Sch 1, Part III.]

1 The authentication provided by this section is permissive and not imperative: it does not invalidate any other method of signing a document; cf *Tennant v LCC* (1957) 121 JP 428. Section 266 of the Public Health Act 1875 is not repealed for the purposes of any unrepealed enactment (Public Health Act 1936, Sch 3).

7.9746 285. **Service of notices, etc** Any notice, order, consent, demand or other document[1] which is required or authorised by or under this Act to be given to or served on any person may, in any case for which no other provision is made by this Act, be given or served[2] either—

(*a*) by delivering it to that person; or

(*b*) in the case of a coroner, or a medical officer of health, by leaving it or sending it in a prepaid[3] letter addressed to him at either his residence or his office and, in the case of any other officer of a council, by leaving it or sending it in a prepaid letter addressed to him, at his office; or

(*c*) in the case of any other person, by leaving it or sending it in a prepaid letter addressed to him, at his usual or last known residence[4]; or

(*d*) in the case of an incorporated company or body, by delivering it to their secretary or clerk at their registered or principal office, or by sending it in a prepaid letter addressed to him at that office; or

(*e*) in the case of a document to be given to or served on a person as being the owner of any premises by virtue of the fact that he receives the rackrent thereof as agent for another, or would so receive it if the premises were let at a rackrent, by leaving it, or sending it in a prepaid letter addressed to him, at his place of business; or

(*f*) in the case of a document to be given to or served on the owner or the occupier of any premises, if it is not practicable after reasonable inquiry to ascertain the name and address of the person to or on whom it should be given or served, or if the premises are unoccupied, by addressing it to the person concerned by the description of "owner" or "occupier" of the premises (naming them) to which it relates, and delivering it to some person on the premises, or, if there is no person on the premises to whom it can be delivered, by affixing it, or a copy of it, to some conspicuous[5] part of the premises.[6]

[Public Health Act 1936, s 285.]

1 This has been held to include a summons (*R v Braithwaite, ex p Dowling* [1918] 2 KB 319, 82 JP 242—for non-payment of rates; *R v Hastings Justices, ex p Mitchell* (1925) 89 JP JO 86—for employing an unlicensed hackney carriage driver). Inasmuch as s 296, post, requires that prosecutions shall be in accordance with (what is now) the Magistrates' Courts Act 1980, we think it safer that summonses for *offences* should be served and service proved in accordance with the Criminal Procedure Rules 2005, Part 4, in the *Key Materials*. This section does not apply to county court summonses (*Wealdstone UDC v Evershed* (1905) 69 JP 258), nor to High Court writs (*Friern Barnet UDC v Adams* [1927] 2 Ch 25, 91 JP 60).

2 Notices duly served under this section are deemed to have been duly served, although in point of fact they never reach the person to whom they are addressed (*Woodford UDC v Henwood* (1900) 64 JP 148). Cf *Re Levy* [1924] 68 Sol Jo 419.

3 It is a condition precedent that the postage should be prepaid. Where there was no evidence of prepayment an action in the Chancery Division failed (*Walthamstow UDC v Henwood* [1897] 1 Ch 41, 61 JP 23).

4 In *R v Braithwaite, ex p Dowling* note 1, supra, residence was held to include his place of business.

5 See *R v Mead* [1894] 2 QB 124, 58 JP 448; *Butler v Gravesend Urban Authority* (1894) 58 JP 446, and *West Ham Corpn v Thomas* (1908) 73 JP 65.

6 Section 267 of the Public Health Act 1875 (which contains similar provisions), is not repealed for the purposes of any unrepealed enactment (Public Health Act 1936, Sch 3).

## Entry and Obstruction

7.9747 287. **Power to enter premises** (1) Subject to the provisions of this section, any authorised officer[1] of a council shall, on producing, if so required, some duly authenticated document showing his authority, have a right to enter any premises[2] at all reasonable hours—

(*a*) for the purpose of ascertaining whether there is, or has been, on or in connection with the premises any contravention of the provisions of this Act or of any bye-laws or building regulations made thereunder, being provisions which it is the duty of the council to enforce;

(*b*) for the purpose of ascertaining whether or not circumstances exist which would authorise or require the council to take any action, or execute any work, under this Act or any such bye-laws or building regulations;

(*c*) for the purpose of taking any action, or executing any work, authorised or required by this Act or any such bye-laws or building regulations, or any order made under this Act, to be taken, or executed, by the council;

(*d*) generally, for the purpose of the performance by the council of their functions under this Act or any such bye-laws or building regulations:

Provided that admission to any premises not being a factory or workplace, shall not be demanded as of right unless twenty-four hours' notice[3] of the intended entry has been given to the occupier.

(2) If it is shown to the satisfaction of a justice of the peace on sworn information in writing—

(*a*) that admission to any premises has been refused, or that refusal is apprehended, or that the premises are unoccupied or the occupier is temporarily absent, or that the case is one of urgency, or that an application for admission would defeat the object of the entry; and

(*b*) that there is reasonable ground for entry into the premises for any such purpose as aforesaid,

the justice may by warrant[4] under his hand authorise the council by any authorised officer to enter the premises, if need be by force:

Provided that such a warrant shall not be issued unless the justice is satisfied either that notice of the intention to apply for a warrant has been given to the occupier, or that the premises are unoccupied, or that the occupier is temporarily absent, or that the case is one of urgency, or that the giving of such notice would defeat the object of the entry.

(3) An authorised officer entering any premises by virtue of this section, or of a warrant issued thereunder, may take with him such other persons as may be necessary and on leaving any unoccupied premises which he has entered by virtue of such a warrant shall leave them as effectually secured against trespassers as he found them.

(4) Every warrant granted under this section shall continue in force until the purpose for which the entry is necessary has been satisfied.

(5) If any person who in compliance with the provisions of this section or of a warrant issued thereunder is admitted into a factory or workplace discloses to any person any information obtained by him in the factory or workplace with regard to any manufacturing process or trade secret, he shall, unless such disclosure was made in the performance of his duty, be liable to a fine not exceeding **level 3** on the standard scale or to imprisonment for a term not exceeding **three months***.

(6) *Repealed.*

[Public Health Act 1936, s 287 as amended by the Public Health Act 1961, Sch 1, Part III, the Criminal Justice Act 1982, ss 38 and 46, the Statute Law (Repeals) Act 1989, Sch 1 and the Statute Law (Repeals) Act 1993, Sch 1.]

* **Words repealed by the Criminal Justice Act 2003, Sch 37 from a date to be appointed.**

1 A like power is given to any member of a fire brigade duly authorised in writing by the authority maintaining the brigade to enter premises for the purpose of obtaining information required for fire-fighting purposes, with respect to the character of the buildings and other property and available water supplies and the means of access thereto (Fire Service Act 1947, s 1(2)). Section 287 applies in relation to a sewerage undertaker for the purposes of provisions of this Act 1989 and of s 27 of this Act as it applies in relation to a local authority; the words "if so required" in s 287(1) are, however, omitted.

2 In *Senior v Twelves* (1958) 122 JP Jo 379, the Divisional Court held that the right of entry conferred by paras (*b*) and (*c*) of this subsection are not limited to those premises where there may have been a contravention of the Act or bye-laws (see para (*a*)), but may extend, in appropriate cases, to adjoining property. Presumably, this decision would apply to the right conferred by para (*d*).

3 The notice of intended entry must be certain in its terms (cf *Stroud v Bradbury* [1952] 2 All ER 76, 116 JP 386).

4 Note also the power to issue a warrant under s 61 of the Public Health (Control of Disease) Act 1984, post.

7.9748 **288. Penalty for obstructing execution of Act** A person who wilfully obstructs any person acting in the execution of this Act or of any bye-law, building regulation, order or warrant made or issued thereunder shall, in any case for which no other provision is made by this Act, be liable[1] to a fine not exceeding **level 1** on the standard scale.[2]

[Public Health Act 1936, s 288 as amended by the Public Health Act 1961, Sch 1, Part III, and the Criminal Justice Act 1967, 3rd Sch and the Criminal Justice Act 1982, ss 35, 38 and 462.]

1 See ss 296 and 297, post.

2 Section 306 of the Public Health Act 1875 (which contains similar provisions to this section) is not repealed for the purposes of any unrepealed enactment (Public Health Act 1936, Sch 3).

7.9749 **289. Power to require occupier to permit works to be executed by owner** If on a complaint made by the owner of any premises[1], it appears to a court of summary jurisdiction that the occupier of those premises prevents the owners from executing any work which he is by or under this Act required to execute, the court may order the occupier to permit the execution of the work.[2]

[Public Health Act 1936, s 289.]

1 See note 1 to s 73, ante.

2 Section 306 of the Public Health Act 1875 (which contains similar provisions to this section) is not repealed for the purposes of any unrepealed enactment (Public Health Act 1936, Sch 3).

## Notices Requiring the Execution of Works

7.9750 **290. Provisions as to appeals against, and enforcement of, notices requiring execution of works[1]** (1) The following provisions of this section shall, subject to any express modifications specified in the section under which the notice is given, apply in relation to any notice given under this Act which is expressly declared to be a notice in relation to which the provisions of this Part of this Act with respect to appeals against, and the enforcement of, notices requiring the execution of works are to apply[2].

(2) Any such notice shall indicate[3] the nature of the works to be executed, and state the time

within which they are to be executed.

(3) A person served with such a notice as aforesaid may appeal[4] to a court of summary jurisdiction on any of the following grounds which are appropriate in the circumstances of the particular case:

(*a*) that the notice or requirement is not justified by the terms of the section under which it purports to have been given or made;

(*b*) that there has been some informality, defect or error in, or in connection with, the notice;

(*c*) that the authority have refused unreasonably to approve the execution of alternative works, or that the works required by the notice to be executed are otherwise unreasonable in character or extent, or are unnecessary;

(*d*) that the time within which the works are to be executed is not reasonably sufficient[5] for the purpose;

(*e*) that the notice might lawfully have been served on the occupier of the premises in question instead of on the owner, or on the owner instead of on the occupier, and that it would have been equitable for it to have been so served;

(*f*) where the work is work for the common benefit of the premises in question and other premises, that some other person, being the owner or occupier of premises to be benefited, ought to contribute towards the expenses of executing any works required.

(4) If and in so far as an appeal under this section is based on the ground of some informality, defect or error in or in connection with the notice, the court shall dismiss the appeal, if it is satisfied that the informality, defect or error was not a material one.

(5) Where the grounds upon which an appeal under this section is brought include a ground specified in paragraph (*e*) or paragraph (*f*) of subsection (3) of this section, the appellant shall serve a copy of his notice of appeal on each other person referred to, and in the case of any appeal under this section may serve a copy of his notice of appeal on any other person having an estate or interest in the premises in question, and on the hearing of the appeal the court may make such order as it thinks fit with respect to the person by whom any work is to be executed and the contribution to be made by any other person towards the cost of the work, or as to the proportions in which any expenses which may become recoverable by the local authority are to be borne by the appellant and such other person.

In exercising its powers under this subsection, the court shall have regard—

(*a*) as between an owner and an occupier, to the terms and conditions, whether contractual or statutory, of the tenancy and to the nature of the works required; and

(*b*) in any case, to the degree of benefit to be derived by the different persons concerned.

(6) Subject to such right of appeal as aforesaid, if the person required by the notice to execute the works fails to execute the works indicated within the time thereby limited, the local authority may themselves execute the works and recover from that person the expenses reasonably incurred by them in so doing and, without prejudice to their right to exercise that power, he shall be liable[6] to a fine not exceeding **level 4** on the standard scale, and to a further fine not exceeding £2 for each day on which the default continues after conviction thereof.

(7) In proceedings by the local authority against the person served with the notice for the recovery of any expenses which the authority are entitled to recover from him, it shall not be open to him to raise any question which he could have raised on an appeal under this section.

[Public Health Act 1936, s 290 as amended by the Decimal Currency Act 1969, s 10, the Criminal Law Act 1977, Sch 6 and the Criminal Justice Act 1982, s 46.]

---

1 Subsections (2) to (7) of this section are applied, subject to certain modifications, to the service of a notice under s 167(5) of the Highways Act 1980 (powers relating to retaining walls near streets); see the Highways Act 1980, s 167, in PART VI: TRANSPORT title HIGHWAYS, ante.

2 The sections are ss 25, 39(1), 40, 44(2), 45(2), 46(3), 47(5), 50(2), 56(1), 59(2), 60(2), 88(4) and 264.

3 This is less precise than the word "specify".

4 See s 300, post.

5 See *Bristol Corpn v Sinnott* [1917] 2 Ch 340, 81 JP 258; *Macclesfield Corpn v Macclesfield Grammar School* [1921] 2 Ch 189, and *Ryall v Cubitt Heath* [1922] 1 KB 275, 86 JP 15.

6 See ss 296 and 297, post.

## PROVISIONS AS TO RECOVERY OF EXPENSES, ETC

7.9751 **291. Certain expenses recoverable from owners to be a charge on the premises; power to order payment by instalments** (1) Where a local authority[1] have incurred expenses for the repayment of which the owner of the premises[2] in respect of which the expenses were incurred is liable, either under this Act or under any enactment repealed thereby, or by agreement with the authority, those expenses, together with interest from the date of service of a demand for the expenses, may be recovered by the authority from the person who is the owner of the premises at the date when the works are completed, or, if he has ceased to be the owner of the premises before the date when a demand for the expenses is served, either from him or from the person who is the owner at the date when the demand is served, and, as from the date of the completion of the works, the expenses and interest accrued due thereon shall, until recovered, be a charge[3] on the premises and on all estates and interests therein.

(2) A local authority may by order declare any expenses recoverable by them under this section to be payable with interest by instalments within a period not exceeding thirty years, until

the whole amount is paid; and any such instalments and interest, or any part thereof, may be recovered from the owner or occupier for the time being of the premises in respect of which the expenses were incurred, and, if recovered from the occupier, may be deducted by him from the rent of the premises:

Provided that an occupier shall not be required to pay at any one time any sum in excess of the amount which was due from him on account of rent at, or has become due from him on account of rent since, the date on which he received a demand from the local authority together with a notice requiring him not to pay rent to his landlord without deducting the sum so demanded.

An order may be made under this subsection at any time with respect to any unpaid balance of expenses and accrued interest so, however, that the period for repayment shall not in any case extend beyond thirty years from the service of the first demand for the expenses.

(3) The rate of interest chargeable under subsection (1) or subsection (2) of this section shall be such reasonable rate as the authority may determine:

(4) A local authority shall, for the purpose of enforcing a charge under this section, have all the same powers and remedies under the Law of Property Act 1925, and otherwise as if they were mortgagees by deed having powers of sale and lease, of accepting surrenders of leases and of appointing a receiver.

[Public Health Act 1936, s 291 as amended by the Local Government, Planning and Land Act 1980, Schs 6 and 34.]

---

1 For definition of "local authority", see s 1(2), ante. This section may apply to a sewerage undertaker; see the Water Industry Act 1991, ss 107 and 109.

2 For definition of "premises", see note 1 to s 73, ante.

3 The charge is on the property (see *Altrincham UDC v O'Brien* (1927) 91 JP 149), and not on the interest of any particular owner, but on the total ownership, and it overrides all other proprietary interests (*Birmingham Corpn v Baker* (1881) 17 Ch D 782; *Paddington Borough Council v Finucane* [1928] Ch 567, 92 JP 68; *Bristol Corpn v Virgin* [1928] 2 KB 622, 92 JP 145). The local authority cannot sell free from restrictive covenants (*Tendring Union v Dowton* [1891] 3 Ch 265). The charge is enforced by writ for foreclosure or sale, or by originating summons. For summary proceedings, see s 293, post.

7.9752 **293. Recovery of expenses, etc** (1) Any sum which a council[1] are entitled to recover under this Act, and with respect to the recovery of which provision is not made by any other section of this Act, may be recovered as a simple contract debt in any court of competent jurisdiction.

(2) *Repealed.*

[Public Health Act 1936, s 293 as amended by the Local Government (Miscellaneous Provisions) Act 1976, s 27.]

---

1 This section may apply to a sewerage undertaker; see the Water Industry Act 1991, ss 107 and 109.

7.9753 **294. Limitation of liability of agents or trustees for other persons** Where a council[1] claim to recover any expenses under this Act from a person as being the owner of the premises in respect of which the expenses were incurred and that person proves that he—

(*a*) is receiving the rent of those premises merely as agent or trustee for some other person; and

(*b*) has not, and since the date of the service on him of a demand for payment has not had, in his hands on behalf of that other person sufficient money to discharge the whole demand of the authority,

his liability shall be limited to the total amount of the money which he has or has had in his hands as aforesaid, but a council who are, or would be, debarred by the foregoing provisions from recovering the whole of any such expenses from an agent or trustee may recover the whole or any unpaid balance thereof from the person on whose behalf the agent or trustee receives the rent.[2]

[Public Health Act 1936, s 2942.]

---

1 This section may apply to a sewerage undertaker; see the Water Industry Act 1991, ss 107 and 109.

2 This meets the case of *St Helen's Corpn v Kirkham* (1885) 16 QBD 403, 50 JP 647. As to power of the local authority to grant charging orders, see s 295.

## Prosecution of Offences, etc

7.9754 **296. Summary proceedings for offences** All offences under this Act may be prosecuted under the Summary Jurisdiction Acts.[1]

[Public Health Act 1936, s 296.]

---

1 The Summary Jurisdiction Acts are consolidated in the Magistrates' Courts Act 1980 in Part I: Magistrates' Courts, Procedure, ante. The corresponding s 251 of the Public Health Act 1875 is not repealed for the purposes of any unrepealed enactment (Public Health Act 1936, Sch 3).

7.9755 **297. Continuing offences and penalties** Where provision is made by or under this Act for the imposition of a daily penalty in respect of a continuing offence, the court by which a person is convicted of the original offence may fix a reasonable period from the date of conviction for compliance by the defendant with any directions given by the court and, where a court has fixed such a period, the daily penalty shall not be recoverable in respect of any day before the expiration thereof.

[Public Health Act 1936, s 297.]

7.9756 **298. Restriction on right to prosecute[1]** Proceedings in respect of an offence created by or under this Act shall not, without the written consent of the Attorney-General[2], be taken by any person other than a party aggrieved[3], or a council or a body whose function it is to enforce the provisions or bye-laws in question, or by whom or by whose predecessors the bye-law in question was made.

[Public Health Act 1936, s 298.]

---

[1] For a relaxation of the provisions of this section in relation to proceedings brought by a constable in respect of an offence against a bye-law, see the Local Government (Miscellaneous Provisions) Act 1982, s 12, in this PART, title LOCAL GOVERNMENT, ante.

[2] See PART I: MAGISTRATES' COURTS, PROCEDURE, para 1.112 **Criminal prosecutions**, ante.

[3] A person is not a party aggrieved by merely being a ratepayer (*Boyce v Higgins* (1853) 14 CB 1, 17 JP 808), nor by having been a defeated candidate at a local election (*Hollis v Marshall* (1858) 2 H & N 755, 22 JP 210). See also *R v Blanshard* (1866) 30 JP 280, and *Fletcher v Hudson* (1881) 7 QBD 611, 46 JP 372. A candidate against whom votes are fabricated is such a party (*Verdin v Wray* (1877) 2 QBD 608, 41 JP 484). A person who has the same interest in land as the person convicted is a party aggrieved (*Drapers' Co v Hadder* (1892) 57 JP 200). A rival omnibus company is not aggrieved by a local authority running unlicensed omnibus on another route (*Sheffield Corpn v Kitson* [1929] 2 KB 322, 93 JP 135). This section may apply to a sewerage undertaker; see the Water Industry Act 1991, s 115.

7.9757 **300. Appeals and applications to courts of summary jurisdiction** (1) Where any enactment in this Act provides—

(*a*) for an appeal to a court of summary jurisdiction against a requirement, refusal or other decision of a council[1]; or

(*b*) for any matter to be determined by, or an application in respect of any matter to be made to, a court of summary jurisdiction,

the procedure shall be by way of complaint for an order[2], and the Summary Jurisdiction Acts[3] shall apply to the proceedings.

(2) The time within which any such appeal may be brought shall be twenty-one days[4] from the date on which notice of the council's requirement, refusal or other decision was served upon the person desiring to appeal, and for the purpose of this subsection the making of the complaint[5] shall be deemed to be the bringing of the appeal.

(3) In any case where such an appeal lies, the document notifying to the person concerned the decision of the council in the matter shall state[6] the right of appeal to a court of summary jurisdiction and the time within which such an appeal may be brought.

[Public Health Act 1936, s 300.]

---

[1] This section may apply to a sewerage undertaker; see the Water Industry Act 1991, ss 106 and 113.

[2] See also the Magistrates' Courts Rules 1981, r 34, in PART I: MAGISTRATES' COURTS, PROCEDURE, ante.

[3] Now the Magistrates' Courts Act 1980.

[4] But note however different limitations in s 138(2A) ante and in s 36(3) of the Public Health Act 1961, post.

[5] This section does not also require the service of a notice containing the grounds of appeal, as is required by the Public Health Act 1925, s 8.

[6] See *Rayner v Stepney Corpn* [1911] 2 Ch 312, 75 JP 468; *Nalder v Ilford Corpn* [1951] 1 KB 822, [1950] 2 All ER 908, 114 JP 594.

7.9758 **301. Appeals to Crown Court against decisions of justices**[1] Subject as hereinafter provided, where a person aggrieved[2] by any order, determination or other decision of a court of summary jurisdiction under this Act is not by any other enactment authorised to appeal to the Crown Court, he may appeal to such a court:

Provided that nothing in this section shall be construed as conferring a right of appeal from the decision of a court of summary jurisdiction in any case if each of the parties concerned might under this Act have required that the dispute should be determined by arbitration instead of by such a court.

[Public Health Act 1936, s 301 as amended by the Courts Act 1971, Sch 9.]

---

[1] This section applies to an appeal against the refusal to grant a music etc licence under the Public Health Acts (Amendment) Act 1890, s 51 (*R v East Riding of Yorkshire Quarter Sessions, ex p Newton* [1968] 1 QB 32, [1967] 3 All ER 118).

[2] This expression includes a successful party wrongly deprived of his costs (*R v Lancashire Quarter Sessions Appeal Committee, ex p Huyton-with-Roby UDC* [1955] 1 QB 52, [1954] 3 All ER 225, 118 JP 526). Normally a public authority is entitled to be treated as a "person aggrieved"; see *Cook v Southend Borough Council* [1990] 2 QB 1, [1990] 1 All ER 243, 154 JP 145, CA. This section may apply to a sewerage undertaker; see the Water Industry Act 1991, ss 106 and 113.

7.9759 **302. Effect of decision of court upon appeal** Where upon an appeal under this Act a court varies or reverses any decision of a council[1], it shall be the duty of the council to give effect to the order of the court and, in particular, to grant or issue any necessary consent, certificate or other document, and to make any necessary entry in any register.

[Public Health Act 1936, s 302.]

---

[1] This section may apply to a sewerage undertaker; see the Water Industry Act 1991, ss 106 and 113.

7.9760 **304. Judges and justices not to be disqualified by liability to rates** A judge of any court or a justice of the peace shall not be disqualified from acting in cases arising under this Act by reason only of his being as one of several ratepayers, or as one of any other class of persons, liable in common with the others to contribute to, or be benefited by, any rate or fund out of which any expenses of a council are to be defrayed.[1]

[Public Health Act 1936, s 304.]

[1] Section 258 of the Public Health Act 1875 (which contains similar provisions), is not repealed for the purposes of any unrepealed enactment (Public Health Act 1936, 3rd Sch).

### Savings

7.9761 **328. Powers of Act to be cumulative** All powers and duties conferred or imposed by this Act shall be deemed to be in addition to, and not in derogation of, any other powers and duties conferred or imposed by Act of Parliament, law or custom, and, subject to any repeal effected by, or other express provision of, this Act, all such other powers and duties may be exercised and shall be performed in the same manner as if this Act had not been passed.

[Public Health Act 1936, s 328.]

# Prevention of Damage by Pests Act 1949

(12, 13 & 14 Geo 6 c 55)

## Part I

## Rats and Mice

7.9762 **1. Local authorities for the purposes of Part I** (1) The local authorities for the purposes of this Part of this Act in England and Wales shall be the Common Council of the City of London and the councils of London boroughs and county districts:

Provided that

(*a*) the local authority for any port health district, whether constituted before or after the commencement of this Act, shall be the port health authority; and

(*b*) in relation to sewers vested in the council of any county or in the Greater London Council, the functions of the local authority under this Part of this Act shall be exercisable by that council and not by any other authority.

(2) *Scotland.*

(3) Section 6 of the Public Health Act 1936 (which provides for the constitution of united districts for any of the purposes of that Act) shall have effect as if the purposes of this Part of this Act were purposes of that Act.

[Prevention of Damage by Pests Act 1949, s 1 amended by the London Government Act 1963, Sch 17 and the Local Government Act 1972, Sch 30.]

7.9763 **2. Duties of local authorities** (1) It shall be the duty of every local authority to take such steps as may be necessary to secure so far as practicable that their district is kept free from rats and mice, and in particular—

(*a*) from time to time carry out such inspections as may be necessary for the purpose aforesaid;

(*b*) to destroy rats and mice on land of which they are the occupier and otherwise to keep such land so far as practicable free from rats and mice;

(*c*) to enforce the duties of owners and occupiers of land under the following provisions of this Part of this Act, and to carry out such operations as are authorised by those provisions.

(2) *Repealed.*

[Prevention of Damage by Pests Act 1949, s 2 as amended by the Local Government, Planning and Land Act 1980, Sch 34.]

7.9764 **3. Obligation of occupiers of land to notify local authority of rats and mice**

(1) Subject to the provisions of this section, the occupier of any land shall give to the local authority forthwith notice in writing if it comes to his knowledge that rats or mice are living on or resorting to the land in substantial numbers.

(2) The foregoing subsection shall not apply to agricultural land.

(3) A person shall not be required to give notice under this section to the local authority of any matter of which notice is given to the Minister in pursuance of Part II of this Act.

(4) Any person who fails to give a notice which he is required to give under this section shall be liable on summary conviction to a fine not exceeding **level 1** on the standard scale.

[Prevention of Damage by Pests Act 1949, s 3 as amended by the Criminal Justice Act 1982, ss 38 and 46 and the Statute Law (Repeals) Act 2004.]

7.9765 **4. Power of local authority to require action** (1) If in the case of any land it appears to the local authority, whether in consequence of a notice given in respect of the land under the last foregoing section or otherwise, that steps should be taken for the destruction of rats or mice on the land or otherwise for keeping the land free from rats and mice, they may serve on the owner[1] or occupier of the land a notice[2] requiring him to take, within such reasonable period as may be specified in the notice, such reasonable steps[3] for the purpose aforesaid as may be so specified; and where the owner of any land is not also the occupier thereof separate notices may be served under this section on the owner and on the occupier.

(2) Any such notice may in particular require—

(*a*) the application to the land of any form of treatment specified in the notice;

(*b*) the carrying out on the land of any structural repairs or other works so specified,

and may prescribe the times at which any treatment required by the notice is to be carried out.

(3) *Repealed.*

(4) If on a complaint made by the owner of any land it appears to a court of summary jurisdiction that the occupier of the land prevents the owner from carrying out any work which he is required to carry out by a notice under this section, the court may order the occupier to permit the carrying out of the work.

(5) Subsections (3) to (5) of section 290 of the Public Health Act 1936 (which provides for an appeal to a court of summary jurisdiction against certain notices requiring the execution of works under that Act) shall apply to any notice served under this section requiring the carrying out of any structural works as they apply to any such notice as is mentioned in subsection (1) of that section; and sections 300 to 302 of that Act (which contain supplementary provisions relating to such appeals) shall have effect accordingly.

(6) *Scotland.*

[Prevention of Damage by Pests Act 1949, s 4 as amended by the Agriculture (Miscellaneous Provisions) Act 1972, Sch 6.]

1 "Owner" has the same meaning as in the Public Health Act 1936, s 28. See s 343 of that Act, post. As to notices, see s 10, post.

2 There are no statutory provisions prescribing the form of the notice so that even though the signature on the notice is not that of a local authority's environmental officer but that of another member of staff on his behalf the notice is valid. So long as the source and authenticity of the notice are apparent to the recipient, the notice need not be signed at all, see *Basildon District Council v Railtrack plc* (1998) Times, 27 February, DC.

3 The notice must specify the thing required to be done: a notice to apply poison treatment to the land or to carry out "other work of a not less effectual character" was held not to comply with the section (*Perry v Garner* [1953] 1 QB 335, [1953] 1 All ER 285, 117 JP 104).

7.9766 **5. Remedies for failure to comply with notice under section 4** (1) Subject to the provisions of the last foregoing section with respect to appeals, if any person on whom a notice is served by the local authority under that section fails to take any steps required by the notice at the time or within the period prescribed by the notice, the local authority may themselves take those steps and recover from him any expenses reasonably incurred by them in doing so.

(2) Without prejudice to the provisions of subsection (1) of this section, but subject to the provisions of the last foregoing section with respect to appeals, a person who fails to take any such steps as aforesaid shall be guilty of an offence and liable on summary conviction to a fine not exceeding **level 3** on the standard scale.

[Prevention of Damage by Pests Act 1949, s 5 as amended by the Criminal Justice Act 1982, s 35, 38 and 46.]

7.9767 **6. Additional powers of local authorities in relation to groups of premises** (1) If it appears to the local authority that rats or mice are found in substantial numbers on any land comprising premises in the occupation of different persons and that it is expedient to deal with the land as one unit for the purpose of destroying rats or mice or keeping the land so far as practicable free from rats and mice, they may, without serving notices under s 4 of this Act on the occupiers or owners of those premises, themselves take in relation to the land such steps as they consider necessary or expedient for the purpose aforesaid:

Provided that the steps taken by the local authority under this section shall not include the carrying out of any structural work.

(2) Without prejudice to the provisions of section 22 of this Act requiring notice to be given before entry upon land under that section, a local authority shall, before taking any steps under this section in relation to any premises, give to the occupier at least seven days' notice of their intention to do so, specifying the steps proposed to be taken.

(3) Any expenses reasonably incurred by a local authority in taking steps under this section in relation to any land may be recovered by that authority from the several occupiers of the premises comprised in that land in such proportion as may be just having regard to the cost of the work done on the several premises.

(4) For the purposes of this section, any premises which are unoccupied shall be deemed to be in the occupation of the owner, and references in this section to the occupier shall be construed accordingly.

[Prevention of Damage by Pests Act 1949, s 6.]

7.9768 **7. Recovery of expenses under section 5 or section 6** (1) Any expenses recoverable by a local authority under section 5 or section 6 of this Act may be recovered as a simple contract debt in any court of competent[1] jurisdiction.

(2) Sections 291 and 294 of the Public Health Act 1936 (which provide respectively for charging on the premises expenses recoverable under that Act from the owner, and for limiting the liability for expenses recoverable under that Act of owner receiving rent as agent or trustee) shall so far as applicable apply to expenses recoverable by a local authority under section 5 or section 6 of this Act as they apply to expenses recoverable under that Act by a local authority within the meaning of that Act.

(3) In proceedings under this section by a local authority for the recovery of any expenses incurred by them under section 5 of this Act, it shall not be open to the defendant to raise by way of defence any question which he could have raised on an appeal under section 4 of this Act.

(4) *Scotland.*

[Prevention of Damage by Pests Act 1949, s 7 as amended by the Local Government Act 1974, Sch 8.]

1 Note that this debt is not recoverable summarily as a civil debt.

7.9769 **10. Authentication of documents, service of notices, etc** (1) Sections 284 to 286 of the Public Health Act 1936 (which relate to the authentication of documents, the service of notices and the proof of proceedings of local authorities) shall apply to documents, notices and proceedings of local authorities in England and Wales under this Part of this Act (whether or not they are local authorities within the meaning of that Act) as they apply to documents, notices and proceedings of local authorities under that Act.

[Prevention of Damage by Pests Act 1949, s 10.]

## PART II

### INFESTATION [1] OF FOOD [2]

7.9770 **13. Obligation of certain undertakers to give notice of occurrence of infestation**[3] (1) Subject to the provisions of this section, every person whose business consists of or includes the manufacture[4], storage, transport or sale of food, shall give to the Minister[5] forthwith notice in writing if it comes to his knowledge that any infestation is present—

(*a*) in any premises or vehicles, or any equipment belonging to any premises or vehicle, used or likely to be used in the course of that business for the manufacture, storage, transport or sale of food;

(*b*) in any food manufactured, stored, transported or sold in the course of that business, or in any other goods for the time being in his possession which are in contact or likely to come into contact with food so manufactured, stored, transported or sold.

(2) Subject to the provisions of this section, every person whose business consists of or includes the manufacture, sale, repair or cleaning of containers[6] shall forthwith give notice in writing to the Minister if it comes to his knowledge that any infestation is present in any container for the time being in his possession which is to be used for the reception of food in the course of any such business as is mentioned in subsection (1) of this section.

(3) The Minister may after consultation with such associations or bodies (if any) as appear to him to be representative of persons affected, make regulations—

(*a*) for relaxing or excluding the requirements of this section in such cases and subject to such conditions (if any) as may be prescribed by or under the regulations;

(*b*) for prohibiting or restricting the delivery in the course of business of any food or other goods in respect of which notice is or is required to be given to the Minister under this section.

[Prevention of Damage by Pests Act 1949, s 13.]

---

1 "Infestation" means the presence of rats, mice, insects or mites in numbers or under conditions which involve an immediate or potential risk of substantial loss of or damage to food, and "infested" shall be construed accordingly (s 28).

2 "Food" includes any substance ordinarily used in the composition or preparation of food, the seeds of any cereal or vegetable, and any feeding stuffs for animals, but does not include growing crops (s 28).

3 For penalty for contravention, etc, see s 17, post.

4 "Manufacture" includes processing (s 28).

5 "Minister" means the Minister of Agriculture and Fisheries (s 28), now the Minister of Agriculture, Fisheries and Food (SI 1955/554) or the Secretary of State for Wales (SI 1978/272).

6 "Container" includes sacks, boxes, tins and other similar articles (s 28).

7.9771 **14. Power of Minister to give directions to certain undertakers for preventing or mitigating infestation** (1) Without prejudice to the provisions of any regulations made under the last foregoing section, the Minister may, if he is satisfied, whether in consequence of a notice under the last foregoing section or otherwise, that it is necessary to do so for the purpose of preventing or mitigating damage to food, give such directions[1] under the following provisions of this section as he thinks expedient.

(2) Directions may be given under this section to any person whose business consists of or includes the manufacture, storage, transport or sale of food—

(*a*) prohibiting or restricting the use for the manufacture, storage, transport or sale of food in the course of that business of any premises or vehicle, or any equipment belonging to any premises or vehicles, which is or is likely to become infested;

(*b*) prohibiting or restricting the acceptance, delivery, retention or removal in the course of that business of any infested food or of any other infested goods which are likely to come into contact with food manufactured, stored, transported or sold as aforesaid;

(*c*) requiring the carrying out, within such time as may be specified in the directions, of any structural works, or the application of any form of treatment, being works or treatment appearing to the Minister to be necessary for preventing or remedying infestation in any such premises, vehicles, equipment, food or other goods as aforesaid.

(3) Directions may be given under this section to any person whose business consists of or includes the manufacture, sale, repair or cleaning of containers, requiring the treatment of any infested container, or of any infested premises in which the business is carried on, in such manner as may be specified in the directions, and prohibiting the removal of any such container until it has been so treated.

(4) Where the Minister is satisfied that any food or container in the possession of a person carrying on any such business as is mentioned in subsection (2) or subsection (3) of this section is so infested that the infestation cannot reasonably be remedied by any form of treatment, he may give directions under this section to that person requiring him to destroy it within such time and by such means as may be specified in the directions.

[Prevention of Damage by Pests Act 1949, s 14.]

1 For penalty for non-compliance with directions, see s 17, post.

7.9772 15. **Appeal against directions under section 14** (1) Where directions are given under the last foregoing section requiring the carrying out of any structural works, or the destruction of any food or container, any person who is aggrieved thereby may—

(*a*) in the case of directions requiring the carrying out of any structural works, within twenty-one days from the service of the directions;

(*b*) in the case of directions requiring the destruction of any food or container, within seven days from the service of the directions,

appeal[1] to a court of summary jurisdiction.

(2) Upon any such appeal the court, if satisfied that the directions are for any reason invalid, or that any requirement thereof is excessive or unreasonable, may quash or amend the directions, as the case may be, but in any other case shall dismiss the appeal:
Provided that if and so far as the appeal is based on the ground of some informality, defect or error in or in connection with the directions, the court shall dismiss the appeal if satisfied that the informality, defect or error was not a material one.

(3) Any directions given under the last foregoing section requiring the carrying out of any structural works, or the destruction of any food or container, shall include a statement of the right of appeal under this section, and of the time within which such an appeal may be brought.

(4) An appeal shall lie to the Crown Court from the decision of a court of summary jurisdiction under this section in respect of directions requiring the carrying out of any structural works.

[Prevention of Damage by Pests Act 1949, s 15 as amended by the Courts Act 1971, Sch 9 and the Courts Act 2003, Sch 8.]

1 See the Magistrates' Courts Rules 1981, r 34, in PART I: MAGISTRATES' COURTS, PROCEDURE, ante.

7.9773 16. **Powers of Minister in case of failure to comply with directions** (1) Subject to the provisions of the last foregoing section with respect to appeals, if any person to whom directions are given by the Minister under section 14 of this Act fails to comply with any requirement of the directions within the period prescribed thereby, then, without prejudice to any proceedings which may be taken against him in respect of an offence under this Part of this Act, the Minister may by order authorise any person named in the order to take, on behalf of the person in default, such steps as the Minister considers necessary for securing compliance with that requirement.

(2) The amount of any expenses reasonably incurred by a person authorised as aforesaid in carrying out works under this section may be recovered by the Minister from the person in default.

(3) In proceedings for the recovery of any expenses under this section, it shall not be open to the defendant to raise by way of defence any question which he could have raised on an appeal under the last foregoing section.

[Prevention of Damage by Pests Act 1949, s 16.]

7.9774 17. **Offences against Part II** Subject to the provisions of this Part of this Act with respect to appeals, any person who contravenes or fails to comply with this Part of this Act or any directions given thereunder shall be guilty of an offence and liable on summary conviction to a fine not exceeding **level 4** on the standard scale.

[Prevention of Damage by Pests Act 1949, s 17 as amended by the Criminal Justice Act 1982, ss 35, 38 and 46.]

## PART III
## SUPPLEMENTAL

7.9775 22. **Powers of entry** (1) Any person duly authorised in writing by a local authority[1] for the purposes of Part I of this Act, or by a person empowered by the Minister[2] to exercise functions of a local authority under that Part, may, at any reasonable time, enter upon any land—

(*a*) for the purpose of carrying out any inspection required by the said Part I to be carried out by the local authority;

(*b*) for the purpose of ascertaining whether there is or has been, on or in connection with the land, any failure to comply with any requirement of the said Part I or of any notice served thereunder;

(*c*) for the purpose of taking any steps authorised by section 5 or section 6 of this Act to be taken by the local authority on or in relation to the land.

(2) Any person duly authorised in writing by the Minister, or by a local authority to whom functions of the Minister under Part II of this Act are delegated, may, at any reasonable time, enter upon any land—

(*a*) for the purpose of ascertaining whether there is or has been, on or in connection with the land or any vehicle thereon, any failure to comply with any requirement of the said Part II or of any directions given thereunder;

(*b*) for the purpose of taking any steps authorised to be taken on or in relation to the land under the said Part II by a person named in an order made by the Minister or by that authority thereunder,

and where any such person has entered on any premises for the purposes specified in paragraph (*a*) of this subsection, he may take samples of any food found on those premises.

(3) Any person authorised under this section to enter upon any land shall, if so required,

produce evidence of his authority before so entering, and shall not demand admission as of right to any land which is occupied unless twenty-four hours' notice of the intended entry has been given to the occupier.

(4) Any person who wilfully obstructs the exercise of powers conferred by this section or by section 5, section 6(1) or section 16(1) of this Act shall be liable on summary conviction, to a fine not exceeding **level 1** on the standard scale.

(5) If any person who, in compliance with the provisions of this section, is admitted into a factory, workshop or work place, discloses to any person any information obtained by him therein as to any manufacturing process or trade secret, he shall, unless the disclosure is made in the course of performing his duty in connection with the purpose for which he was authorised to enter the premises, be liable on summary conviction to a fine not exceeding **level 3** on the standard scale or to imprisonment for a term not exceeding **three months** *.

(6) If any land is damaged in the exercise of a power of entry conferred under this section, compensation in respect of that damage may be recovered by any person interested in the land from the local authority on whose behalf the entry was effected, or from the Minister, as the case may be.

[Prevention of Damage by Pests Act 1949, s 22 as amended by the Pests Act 1954, s 5(3) and the Criminal Justice Act 1982, ss 35, 38 and 46.]

* **Words repealed by the Criminal Justice Act 2003, Sch 37 from a date to be appointed.**

1 See s 1, ante.

2 "The Minister" means the Minister of Agriculture and Fisheries (s 28), now the Minister of Agriculture, Fisheries and Food (SI 1955/554) or the Secretary of State for Wales (SI 1978/272).

7.9776 **26. Legal proceedings** (1) Proceedings for an offence under this Act shall not, in England and Wales, be instituted except by or with the consent of the Minister[1] or the local authority.

(2) Where an offence under this Act is committed by a body corporate, every person who, at the time of the commission of the offence, was a director, general manager, secretary or other similar officer of the body corporate, or was purporting to act in any such capacity, shall be deemed to be guilty of that offence unless he proves that it was committed without his consent or connivance and that he exercised any such diligence to prevent its commission as he ought to have exercised having regard to the nature of his functions in that capacity and to all the circumstances.

(3) For the purposes of the last foregoing subsection, the expression "director", in relation to any body corporate established by or under any enactment for the purpose of carrying on under national ownership any industry or part of an industry or undertaking, being a body corporate whose affairs are managed by the members thereof, means a member of that body.

[Prevention of Damage by Pests Act 1949, s 26.]

1 "The Minister" means the Minister of Agriculture and Fisheries (s 28), now the Minister of Agriculture, Fisheries and Food (SI 1955/554) or the Secretary of State for Wales (SI 1978/272).

## Public Health Act 1961[1]

(9 & 10 Eliz 2 c 64)

### PART II[2]

### SANITATION AND BUILDINGS

*Sewers, drains and sanitary conveniences*

7.9777 **17. Powers to repair drains etc and to remedy stopped-up drains etc** (1) If it appears to a local authority that a drain, private sewer, water-closet, waste pipe or soil pipe—

(*a*) is not sufficiently maintained and kept in good repair, and

(*b*) can be sufficiently repaired at a cost not exceeding £250,

the local authority may, after giving not less than seven days notice to the person or persons concerned, cause the drain, private sewer, water-closet or pipe to be repaired and, subject to subsections (7) and (8) below, recover[1] the expenses reasonably incurred in so doing, so far as they do not exceed £250, from the person or persons concerned, in such proportions, if there is more than one such person, as the local authority may determine.

(2) In subsection (1) above "person concerned" means—

(*a*) in relation to a water-closet, waste pipe or soil pipe, the owner or occupier of the premises on which it is situated, and

(*b*) in relation to a drain or private sewer, any person owning any premises drained by means of it and also, in the case of a sewer, the owner of the sewer.

(3) If it appears to a local authority that on any premises a drain, private sewer, water-closet, waste pipe or soil pipe is stopped up, they may by notice in writing require the owner or occupier of the premises to remedy the defect within forty-eight hours from the service of the notice.

(4) If a notice under subsection (3) of this section is not complied with, the local authority may themselves carry out the work necessary to remedy the defect and, subject to subsections (7) and (8) below, may recover the expenses reasonably incurred in so doing from the person on whom the notice was served.

(5) Where the expenses recoverable by a local authority under subsection (1) or (4) of this section do not exceed £10, the local authority may, if they think fit, remit the payment of the

expenses.

(6) In proceedings to recover expenses under this section—

(*a*) where the expenses were incurred under subsection (1) of this section, the court—

(i) shall inquire whether the local authority were justified in concluding that the drain, private sewer, water-closet, waste pipe or soil pipe was not sufficiently maintained and kept in good repair; and

(ii) may inquire whether any apportionment of expenses by the local authority under that subsection was fair;

(*b*) where the expenses were incurred under subsection (4) of this section, the court may inquire—

(i) whether any requirement contained in a notice served under subsection (3) of this section was reasonable; and

(ii) whether the expenses ought to be borne wholly or in part by some person other than the defendant in the proceedings.

(7) Subject to subsection (8) below, the court may make such order concerning the expenses or their apportionment as appears to the court to be just.

(8) Where the court determines that the local authority were not justified in concluding that a drain, private sewer, water-closet, waste pipe or soil pipe was not sufficiently maintained and kept in good repair, the local authority shall not recover expenses incurred by them under subsection (1) of this section.

(9) The court shall not revise an apportionment unless it is satisfied that all persons affected by the apportionment or by an order made by virtue of subsection (6)(*b*)(ii) above have had notice of the proceedings and an opportunity of being heard.

(10) Subject to subsection (11) of this section, the provisions of subsection (1) of this section shall not authorise a local authority to carry out works on land which belongs to any statutory undertakers[2] and is held or used by them for the purposes of their undertaking.

(11) Subsection (10) of this section does not apply to houses, or to buildings used as offices or showrooms, other than buildings so used which form part of a railway station.

(12) The Secretary of State may by order made by statutory instrument increase any amount specified in this section.

(13) Nothing in an order made under subsection (12) of this section shall apply to a notice given under this section before the commencement of the order.

(14) A statutory instrument containing an order under subsection (12) of this section shall be subject to annulment in pursuance of a resolution of either House of Parliament.

(15) The provisions of this section shall be without prejudice to section 59 of the Building Act 1984 (which empowers a local authority to serve notices as regards defective drains).

[Public Health Act 1961, s 17 as substituted by the Local Government (Miscellaneous Provisions) Act 1982, s 27 and amended by the Building Act 1984, Sch 6.]

---

1 In accordance with the Public Health Act 1936, s 293, ante.

2 The National Rivers Authority, every water undertaker and every sewerage undertaker is deemed to be a statutory undertaker for the purposes of this Act (Water Act 1989, Sch 25, para 1).

**7.9778 22. Power to cleanse or repair drains** A local authority may, on the application of the owner or occupier of any premises, undertake the cleansing or repair of any drains, water closets, sinks or gullies in or connected with the premises, and may recover[1] from the applicant such reasonable charge, if any, for so doing as they think fit.

[Public Health Act 1961, s 22.]

---

1 In accordance with the Public Health Act 1936, s 293, ante.

*Accumulations of rubbish*

**7.9779 34. Accumulations of rubbish** (1) If it appears to a local authority that there is on any land in the open air in their area any rubbish which is seriously detrimental to the amenities of the neighbourhood, the local authority may, subject to the provisions of this section, take such steps for removing the rubbish as they may consider necessary in the interests of amenity.

(2) Not less than twenty-eight days before taking any action under this section, the local authority shall serve on the owner and occupier of the land a notice stating the steps which they propose to take and giving particulars of the following provisions of this subsection; and a person on whom the notice is served and any other person having an interest in the land may within twenty-eight days from the service of the notice—

(*a*) serve a counter-notice on the local authority stating that he intends to take those steps himself; or

(*b*) appeal to a magistrates' court[1] on the ground that the local authority were not justified in concluding that action should be taken under this section, or that the steps proposed to be taken are unreasonable.

(3) If a counter-notice is served under the last foregoing subsection, the local authority shall take no further action in the matter under this section unless the person who served the counter-notice either—

(*a*) fails within what seems to the local authority a reasonable time to begin to take the steps stated in the notice, or (*b*) having begun to take those steps fails to make such progress towards their completion as seems to the local authority reasonable.

(4) If an appeal is brought under subsection (2) of this section, the local authority shall take no further action in the matter under this section until the appeal is finally determined or withdrawn; and on the hearing of the appeal the court may direct the local authority to take no further action or may permit the local authority to take such steps as the court may direct or may dismiss the appeal.

(5) In this section "rubbish" means rubble, waste paper, crockery and metal, and any other kind of refuse (including organic matter), but does not include any material accumulated for, or in the course of, any business.

[Public Health Act 1961, s 34 as amended by the Civic Amenities Act 1967, s 26 and SI 2007/3538.]

1 In accordance with the Public Health Act 1936, s 300, ante.

*Filthy or verminous premises or articles*

7.9780 **36. Power to require vacation of premises during fumigation**[1] (1) If a local authority serve a notice under section 83(3) of the Public Health Act 1936, as amended by the last foregoing section[2], on the owner and occupier of any premises requiring that they shall be allowed to employ gas for the purpose of destroying vermin on the premises—

(*a*) the notice to the occupier may also require that the premises shall, as from such date as may be specified in the notice, be vacated until the local authority give the occupier further notice that the premises can safely be reoccupied; and

(*b*) the local authority may also serve notice on the occupiers of any other premises having any floor, wall or ceiling contiguous with the first-mentioned premises, or into which there is reason to apprehend that the gas may penetrate, requiring that those other premises shall be vacated as aforesaid.

(2) No person shall be required under this section to vacate any premises used for human habitation for any period unless alternative shelter or other accommodation has been provided for him by the local authority free of charge for that period; and any notice given under this section shall specify the alternative shelter or other accommodation so provided.

(3) A person on whom a notice is served under this section may within the period of seven days from the date on which the notice was served on him appeal to a magistrates' court[3], and the requirements included in the notice in pursuance of this section shall not take effect until the expiration of that period or, where an appeal is brought within that period, before the appeal is disposed of or withdrawn.

The provisions of this subsection as to the period within which an appeal shall be brought shall have effect notwithstanding anything in section 300(2) of the Public Health Act 1936, as applied to this Part of this Act.

(4) So much of subsection (2) of the said section 83 as imposes a penalty for failure to comply with the requirements of a notice under that section shall also apply to the requirements included in the notice by virtue of this section[4].

(5) The local authority shall defray any reasonable expenses incurred in removing from and returning to any premises in compliance with a notice served under paragraph (*b*) of subsection (1) of this section, and may, if they think fit, defray any such expenses incurred in compliance with a notice under paragraph (*a*) of that subsection.

[Public Health Act 1961, s 36.]

1 This section should be considered in conjunction with s 83 of the Public Health Act 1936, ante.
2 These amendments have been carried into the text of s 83, ante.
3 In accordance with the Public Health Act 1936, s 300, ante.
4 Section 83(2) provides for a fine not exceeding **level 1** on the standard scale and a further fine not exceeding **£2** for each day on which the offence continues after conviction.

7.9781 **37. Prohibition of sale of verminous articles** (1) No dealer shall—

(*a*) prepare for sale, or

(*b*) sell or offer or expose for sale, or

(*c*) deposit with any person for sale or preparation for sale,

any household article[1] if it is to his knowledge verminous, or if by taking reasonable precautions he could have known it to be verminous.

(2) If a household article which is verminous is on any premises—

(*a*) being prepared by a dealer for sale, or

(*b*) offered or exposed by a dealer for sale, or

(*c*) deposited by a dealer with any person for sale or preparation for sale,

the medical officer of health or public health inspector may cause the article to be disinfested or destroyed as the case may require, and if necessary for that purpose to be removed from the premises; and the local authority may recover from the dealer the expenses[2] reasonably incurred by the local authority in taking any action under this subsection.

(3) If any person contravenes the provisions of subsection (1) of this section he shall be liable to a fine not exceeding **level 1** on the standard scale[3].

(4) In this section—

(*a*) "dealer" means a person who trades or deals in any household articles;

(*b*) "household article" means an article of furniture, bedding or clothing or any similar article;

(*c*) references to preparation for sale do not include references to disinfestation.

[Public Health Act 1961, s 37 as amended by the Criminal Justice Act 1982, ss 38 and 46.]

---

1 Defined in sub-s (4), infra.

2 In accordance with the Public Health Act 1936, s 293, ante.

3 Prosecution will be under the Magistrates' Courts Act 1980, consolidating the Summary Jurisdiction Acts (Public Health Act 1936, s 296).

## PART IV
## STREETS AND PUBLIC PLACES[1]

### *Streets*

**7.9782 45. Attachment of street lamps to buildings** (1) Subject to the provisions of this section, a county council, local authority or parish council or parish meeting (hereafter in this section referred to as a "street lighting authority") may affix to any building such lamps, brackets, pipes, electric lines and apparatus (hereafter in this section referred to as "attachments") as may be required for the purposes of street lighting.

(2) A street lighting authority shall not under this section affix attachments to a building without the consent of the owner[2] of the building:
Providing that, where in the opinion of the street lighting authority any consent required under this subsection is unreasonably withheld, they may apply to the appropriate authority[3] who may either allow the attachments subject to such conditions, if any, as to rent or otherwise as the appropriate authority thinks fit, or disallow the attachments.

(3) Where any attachments have been affixed to a building under this section and the person who gave his consent under subsection (2) of this section, or who was the owner of the building when the attachments were allowed by the appropriate authority, ceases to be the owner of the building, the subsequent owner may give to the street lighting authority notice requiring them to remove the attachments; and subject to the provisions of this subsection, the street lighting authority shall comply with the requirements within three months after the service of the notice:
Provided that, where in the opinion of the street lighting authority any such requirement is unreasonable, they may apply to the appropriate authority[3] who may either annul the notice subject to such conditions, if any, as to rent or otherwise as the appropriate authority thinks fit or confirm the notice subject to such extension, if any, of the said period of three months as the appropriate authority thinks fit.

(4) Where any attachments have been affixed to a building under this section, the owner of the building may give the street lighting authority by whom they were affixed not less than fourteen days notice requiring them at their own expense temporarily to remove the attachments where necessary during any reconstruction or repair of the building.

(5) Where attachments are affixed to a building under this section, the street lighting authority shall have the right as against any person having an interest in the building to alter or remove them, or to repair or maintain them.

(6) (*Consequential damage to building is recoverable by owner. Disputes relating thereto are determined by Upper Tribunal.*)

(7) A street lighting authority shall not do anything under this section which would, to their knowledge, be in contravention of a building preservation order under s 29 of the Town and Country Planning Act 1947[4].

(8) In this section "appropriate authority" means a magistrates' court, except that in relation to buildings of the descriptions in the Fourth Schedule to this Act it has the meaning there given.

(9) In this section—

"building" includes a structure and a bridge or aqueduct over a street;

"owner"—

(*a*) in relation to a building occupied under a tenancy for a term of years whereof five years or more remain unexpired, means the occupier of the building, and

(*b*) in relation to any other building, has the same meaning as in the Public Health Act 1936, and

"owned" shall be construed accordingly;

"street lighting" includes the lighting of markets and public buildings under s 161 of the Public Health Act 1875 (which relates to the powers conferred on urban authorities within the meaning of that Act), and the lighting of public places under s 3 of the Parish Councils Act 1957,

and the definitions in this section shall apply for the purposes of the Fourth Schedule of this Act.

(10) Section 5 of the Parish Councils Act 1957 (which contains provisions as to the consents required for the exercise of the powers of street lighting conferred by that Act), shall not apply in relation to the affixing after the commencement of this Act of any attachments to a building within the meaning of this section but those powers shall not be taken to authorise anything to be done without consent for which consent is required by this section.

[Public Health Act 1961, s 45 as amended by SI 2009/1307.]

[1] By s 1(4) of the Act, certain provisions of Pt XII of the Public Health Act 1936, apply to this Part. These include ss 283–285, 288, 304, 305, ante, and s 343, Interpretation. Other provisions of the 1936 Act are specifically applied in the several sections contained in this Part of the Act.

[2] In this section "owner" is defined by sub-s (9) thereof, infra.

[3] Except in relation to buildings specified in the Sch 4, this expression means a magistrates' court (sub-s (8)).

[4] See now the Planning (Listed Buildings and Conservation Areas) Act 1990, post.

## PART VI
## MISCELLANEOUS[1]

7.9783 **73. Derelict petrol tanks** (1) Where a fixed tank or other fixed container which has been used for the storage of petroleum spirit[2], and is no longer used for that purpose, is kept on any premises, the occupier of the premises shall take all such steps as may be reasonably necessary to prevent danger from the container.

(2) An officer of the local authority[3] duly authorised by them may, on producing, if so required, some duly authenticated document showing his authority, require the occupier of premises on which there is any tank or other container to which subsection (1) of this section applies to show it to him and permit him to ascertain whether steps have been taken to comply with the provision, of this section.

(3) The local authority[3] may by notice require the occupier of the premises to take any steps reasonably necessary to prevent danger from any tank or other container to which subsection (1) of this section applies.

(4) The provisions of Part XII of the Public Health Act 1936, with respect to appeals against, and the enforcement of, notices requiring the execution of works shall apply in relation to any notice under subsection (3) of this section, and shall so apply as if this section were contained in that Act.

(5) This section shall apply in relation to premises which are unoccupied with the substitution for the references to the occupier of the premises of references to their owner (as defined in section 343(1) of the Public Health Act 1936); and this section shall not apply to premises situated within the jurisdiction of a harbour authority (as defined in section 23 of the Petroleum (Consolidation) Act 1928[4]).

(6) In this section the expression "petroleum spirit" has the same meaning as in the said Act of 1928[4].

[Public Health Act 1961, s 73.]

[1] By s 1(4) of the Act, certain provisions of Pt XII of the Public Health Act 1936, apply to this Part. These include ss 283–285, 288, 304, 305, ante, and s 343, Interpretation. Other provisions of the 1936 Act are specifically applied in the several sections contained in this Part of the Act.

[2] See sub-s (6), infra.

[3] The functions of a local authority under s 73 of this Act shall be functions:
(a) in Greater London or a metropolitan county, of the fire authority;
(b) elsewhere, of the county council,
and references in the section, and in the provisions of the Act applied by it, to a local authority shall be construed accordingly.
(Local Government Act 1985, Sch 11, para 5).

[4] See this PART: title HEALTH AND SAFETY, ante.

7.9784 **75–77. Additional byelaws[1]** A local authority may make byelaws as to pleasure fairs and roller skating rinks; as to seaside pleasure boats[2]; and as to hairdressers and barbers.

[Public Health Act 1961, ss 75–77 as amended by the Local Government (Miscellaneous Provisions) Act 1976, s 22, the Fire and Rescue Services Act 2004, s 53(1), Sch 1 and SI 2005/1541—summarised.]

[1] The power to make byelaws under s 75 as to pleasure fairs replaces that under s 38 of the Public Health Acts Amendment Act 1890, without prejudice to byelaws in force thereunder. So far as penalties are concerned, the Criminal Law Act 1977, s 31(4) and the Criminal Justice Act 1982, s 46, provides that any byelaws under s 75 of the Public Health Act 1961 relating to pleasure fairs and roller skating rinks, and any byelaws under s 76 of the Public Health Act 1961 relating to seaside pleasure boats, may provide for a fine on summary conviction not exceeding **level 3** on the standard scale and in the case of a continuing offence a further fine of £5 a day. If a byelaw in force at 17 July 1978 specifies a maximum fine of £20 or less, it shall have effect as if it specified **level 3** on the standard scale (maximum daily fines, if any, remaining unchanged). For penalties for other byelaws, see s 237 of the Local Government Act 1972, ante, and notes thereto.

[2] For extension of power to make byelaws about boating, see s 17 of the Local Government (Miscellaneous Provisions) Act 1976, post.

7.9785 **81. Summary recovery of damages for negligence** Damages recoverable by a county council, local authority or parish council or parish meeting for damage caused by negligence to any lamp, lamp-post, notice board, fence, rail, post, shelter or other apparatus or equipment provided by them in a street or public place shall, if the amount thereof does not exceed **£20**, be recoverable summarily as a civil debt[1].

[Public Health Act 1961, s 81 as amended by the London Government Act 1963, Sch 11 and the Local Government Act 1985, Sch 17.]

[1] Section 58 of the Magistrates' Courts Act 1980 in PART I: MAGISTRATES' COURTS, PROCEDURE, ante, will apply.

SCHEDULE 4

ATTACHMENT OF STREET LIGHTING EQUIPMENT TO CERTAIN BUILDINGS Section 45

**7.9786** As regards buildings of the descriptions in the first column of the following Table the appropriate authority for the purposes of s 45 of this Act shall be the person specified in the second column of that Table (and not a magistrates' court).

*TABLE*

| | |
|---|---|
| A building which is for the time being included in a list published under section 12 of the Ancient Monuments Consolidation and Amendment Act 1913. | The Secretary of State. |
| A building which is included in a list compiled or approved under section 1 of the Planning (Listed Buildings and Conservation Areas) Act 1990. | The Secretary of State. |
| A building owned by railway, canal, dock, harbour or inland navigation undertakers. | The Secretary of State. |
| A building owned by electricity or gas undertakers[1] | The Secretary of State. |
| A building owned by statutory water undertakers. | The Secretary of State. |
| A building forming part of an aerodrome licensed under the Civil Aviation Act 1949, or any enactment repealed by that Act. | The Secretary of State. |
| A building owned by a county council, local authority or parish council or parish meeting who are not the street lighting authority concerned. | The Secretary of State. |
| A building owned by a development corporation established under the New Towns Act 1946, or the Homes and Communities Agency so far as exercising functions in relation to anything transferred (or to be transferred) to it as mentioned in section 52(1)(*a*) to (*d*) of the Housing and Regeneration Act 2008 or the Greater London Authority so far as exercising its new towns and urban development functions. | The Secretary of State. |
| A building owned by British Telecommunications. | The Secretary of State. |

[Public Health Act 1961, Sch 4 as amended by the Post Office Act 1969, Sch 4, the Town and Country Planning Act 1971, Sch 23, the British Telecommunications Act 1981, Sch 3, the Planning (Consequential Provisions) Act 1990, Sch 2, the Coal Industry Act 1994, Sch 9, SI 2001/1149, SI 2003/2908, the Housing and Regeneration Act 2008, Sch 8 and the Localism Act 2011, Sch 19.]

[1] The reference to "gas undertakers" shall have effect as a reference to a public gas transporter (Gas Act 1995, Sch 4).

# Prevention of Oil Pollution Act 1971[1]

(1971 c 60)

*General provisions for preventing oil pollution*

**7.9787 1. Discharge of certain oils into sea outside territorial waters** (1) *Repealed.*

(2) This section applies—

(*a*) to crude oil, fuel oil and lubricating oil; and

(*b*) to heavy diesel oil, as defined by regulations made under this section by the Secretary of State[2];

and shall also apply to any other description of oil which may be specified by regulations made by the Secretary of State, having regard to the provisions of any Convention accepted by Her Majesty's Government in the United Kingdom in so far as it relates to the prevention of pollution of the sea by oil or having regard to the persistent character of oil of that description and the likelihood that it would cause pollution if discharged from a ship into any part of the sea outside the territorial waters of the United Kingdom.

(3)–(4) *Repealed.*

[Prevention of Oil Pollution Act 1971, s 1 as amended by SI 1983/1106.]

[1] This Act consolidated the Oil in Navigable Waters Acts 1955 to 1971 and s 5 of the Continental Shelf Act 1964 with effect from 1 March 1973. For other statutory control see the Merchant Shipping Act 1995, in PART VI: TRANSPORT, ante.

[2] See SI 1967/710 which has effect as if made hereunder by reason of s 33 (repeals and savings).

**7.9788 2. Discharge of oil into United Kingdom waters** (1) If any oil or mixture containing oil is discharged as mentioned in the following paragraphs into waters to which this section applies, then, subject to the provisions of this Act, the following shall be guilty of an offence[1], that is to say—

(*a*)–(*b*) *repealed*;

(*c*) if the discharge is from a place on land, the occupier of that place, unless he proves[2] that the discharge was caused as mentioned in paragraph (*d*) of this subsection;

(*d*) if the discharge is from a place on land and is caused by the act of a person who is in that place without the permission (express or implied) of the occupier, that person;

(*e*) if the discharge takes place otherwise than as mentioned in the preceding paragraphs and is the result of any operations for the exploration of the sea-bed and subsoil or the exploitation of their natural resources, the person carrying on the operations.

(2) This section applies to the following waters, that is to say—

(*a*) the whole of the sea within the seaward limits of the territorial waters of the United Kingdom; and

(*b*) all other waters (including inland waters) which are within those limits and are navigable by sea-going ships.

(3) In this Act "place on land" includes anything resting on the bed or shore of the sea, or of any other waters to which this section applies, and also includes anything afloat (other than a vessel) if it is anchored or attached to the bed or shore of the sea or of any such waters; and "occupier", in relation to any such thing as is mentioned in the preceding provisions of this subsection, if it has no occupier, means the owner thereof, and, in relation to a railway wagon or road vehicle, means the person in charge of the wagon or vehicle and not the occupier of the land on which the wagon or vehicle stands.

(4) A person guilty of an offence under this section shall be liable on summary conviction, or on conviction on indictment, to a fine [3].

[Prevention of Oil Pollution Act 1971, s 2 as amended by SI 1983/1106, the Prevention of Oil Pollution Act 1986, s 1, the Merchant Shipping Act 1995, Sch 12 and SI 2015/664.]

---

1 See special defences in ss 5–8, post, provisions relating to the prosecution of offences in s 19, post, and enforcement and application of fines (which can be used to pay expenses and make good damage) in s 20, post.

2 On a preponderance of probabilities: *R v Carr-Briant* [1943] KB 607, [1943] 2 All ER 156, 107 JP 167.

3 For procedure in respect of an offence triable either way, see the Magistrates' Courts Act 1980, ss 17A–21 in PART I: MAGISTRATES' COURTS, PROCEDURE, ante.

7.9789 **3. Discharge of certain oils from pipe-lines or as the result of exploration etc in designated areas** (1) If any oil to which section 1 of this Act applies, or any mixture containing such oil, is discharged into any part of the sea—

(*a*) from a pipe-line; or

(*b*) (otherwise than from a ship) as the result of any operation for the exploration of the sea-bed and subsoil or the exploitation of their natural resources in a designated area,

then, subject to the following provisions of this Act, the owner of the pipe-line or, as the case may be, the person carrying on the operations shall be guilty of an offence[1] unless the discharge was from a place in his occupation and he proves[2] that it was due to the act of a person who was there without his permission (express or implied).

(2) In this section "designated area" means an area for the time being designated by an Order made under section 1 of the Continental Shelf Act 1964.

(3) A person guilty of an offence under this section shall be liable on summary conviction, or on conviction on indictment, to a fine[3].

[Prevention of Oil Pollution Act 1971, s 3 as amended by SI 2015/664.]

---

1 See note 1 to s 2, ante.

2 On a preponderance of probabilities: *R v Carr-Briant* [1943] KB 607, [1943] 2 All ER 156, 107 JP 167.

3 For procedure in respect of an offence triable either way, see the Magistrates' Courts Act 1980, ss 17A–21 in PART I: MAGISTRATES' COURTS, PROCEDURE, ante.

7.9790 **5. Defences of owner or master, charged with offence under section 1 or section 2**

(1) Where a person is charged with an offence under section 1 of this Act, or is charged with an offence under section 2 of this Act as the owner or master of a vessel, it shall be a defence to prove that the oil or mixture was discharged for the purpose of securing the safety of any vessel, or of preventing damage to any vessel or cargo, or of saving life, unless the court is satisfied that the discharge of the oil or mixture was not necessary for that purpose or was not a reasonable step to take in the circumstances.

(2) Where a person is charged as mentioned in subsection (1) of this section, it shall also be a defence to prove—

(*a*) that the oil or mixture escaped in consequence of damage to the vessel, and that as soon as practicable after the damage occurred all reasonable steps were taken for preventing, or (if it could not be prevented) for stopping or reducing, the escape of the oil or mixture, or

(*b*) that the oil or mixture escaped by reason of leakage, that neither the leakage nor any delay in discovering it was due to any want of reasonable care, and that as soon as practicable after the escape was discovered all reasonable steps were taken for stopping or reducing it.*

[Prevention of Oil Pollution Act 1971, s 5.]

---

* **The repeal of s 5 by the Merchant Shipping Act 1995, Sch 12 does not apply so far as this section relates to s 2(1) and (3) of this Act.**

7.9791 **6. Defences of other persons charged with offences under section 2 or section 3**

(1) Where a person is charged, in respect of the escape of any oil or mixture containing oil, with an offence under section 2 or 3 of this Act—

(*a*) as the occupier of a place on land; or*

(*b*) as a person carrying on operations for the exploration of the seabed and subsoil or the exploitation of their natural resources; or

(*c*) as the owner of a pipe-line,

it shall be a defence to prove that neither the escape nor any delay in discovering it was due to any want of reasonable care and that as soon as practicable after it was discovered all reasonable steps were taken for stopping or reducing it.

(2) Where a person is charged with an offence under section 2 of this Act in respect of the discharge of a mixture containing oil from a place on land, it shall also, subject to subsection (3) of this section, be a defence to prove—

(*a*) that the oil was contained in an effluent produced by operations for the refining of oil;

(*b*) that it was not reasonably practicable to dispose of the effluent otherwise than by discharging it into waters to which that section applies; and

(*c*) that all reasonably practicable steps had been taken for eliminating oil from the effluent.

(3) If it is proved that, at a time to which the charge relates, the surface of the waters into which the mixture was discharged from the place on land, or land adjacent to those waters, was fouled by oil, subsection (2) of this section shall not apply unless the court is satisfied that the fouling was not caused, or contributed to, by oil contained in any effluent discharged at or before that time from that place.

[Prevention of Oil Pollution Act 1971, s 6 as amended by the Merchant Shipping Act 1955, Sch 12.]

---

*** The repeal of sub-s (1)( *a*) by the Merchant Shipping Act 1995, Sch 12 does not apply so far as this subsection relates to s 2(1) and (3) of this Act.**

**7.9792 7. Protection of acts done in exercise of certain powers of harbour authorities etc**

(1) Where any oil, or mixture containing oil, is discharged in consequence of—

(*a*) the exercise of any power conferred by sections 530 to 532 of the Merchant Shipping Act 1894 (which relate to the removal of wrecks by harbour, conservancy and lighthouse authorities); or

(*b*) the exercise, for the purpose of preventing an obstruction or danger to navigation, of any power to dispose of sunk, stranded or abandoned vessels which is exercisable by a harbour authority under any local enactment;

and apart from this subsection the authority exercising the power, or a person employed by or acting on behalf of the authority, would be guilty of an offence under section 1 or section 2 of this Act in respect of that discharge, the authority or person shall not be convicted of that offence unless it is shown that they or he failed to take such steps (if any) as were reasonable in the circumstances for preventing, stopping or reducing the discharge.

(2) Subsection (1) of this section shall apply to the exercise of any power conferred by section 13 of the Dockyard Ports Regulation Act 1865 (which relates to the removal of obstructions to dockyard ports) as it applies to the exercise of any such power as is mentioned in paragraph (*a*) of that subsection, and shall, as so applying, have effect as if references to the authority exercising the power were references to the Queen's harbour master for the port in question.*

[Prevention of Oil Pollution Act 1971, s 7.]

---

*** The repeal of s 7 by the Merchant Shipping Act 1995, Sch 12 does not apply so far as this section relates to s 2(1) and (3) of this Act.**

**7.9793 11. Duty to report discharge of oil into waters of harbours** (1) If any oil or mixture containing oil—

(*a*) *repealed*

(*b*) *repealed.*

(*c*) is found to be escaping or to have escaped into any such waters from a place on land;

the occupier of the place on land shall forthwith report the occurrence to the harbour master, or, if the harbour has no harbour master, to the harbour authority.

(2) *Repealed.*

(3) If a person fails to make a report as required by this section he shall be liable on summary conviction to a fine not exceeding **level 5** on the standard scale.

[Prevention of Oil Pollution Act 1971, s 11 as amended by the Merchant Shipping Act 1979, Sch 6, Criminal Justice Act 1982, s 46 and the Merchant Shipping Act 1995, Sch 12.]

**7.9794 11A. Certain provisions not to apply where a discharge or escape is authorised under Part I of the Environmental Protection Act 1990** (1) The provisions of sections 2(1) and 3(1) of this Act shall not apply to any discharge which is made under, and the provisions of section 11(1) of this Act shall not apply to any escape which is authorised by, an authorisation granted under Part I of the Environmental Protection Act 1990 or * a permit granted under section 2 of the Pollution Prevention and Control Act 1999.

(2) This section does not extend to Northern Ireland.

[Prevention of Oil Pollution Act 1971, s 11A as inserted by the Environment Act 1995, Sch 22 and amended by the Pollution Prevention and Control Act 1999, Sch 2.]

---

*** Words repealed by the Pollution Prevention and Control Act 1999, Sch 3 from a date to be appointed.**

**7.9795 18. Powers of inspection[1]** (1) The Secretary of State may appoint any person as an inspector to report to him—

(a) whether the prohibitions, restrictions and obligations imposed by virtue of this Act (including prohibitions so imposed by the creation of offences under any provision of this Act other than section 3) have been complied with;

(b) what measures (other than measures made obligatory by regulations made under section 4 of this Act) have been taken to prevent the escape of oil and mixtures containing oil;

(c) whether the oil reception facilities provided in harbours are adequate;

and any such inspector may be so appointed to report either in a particular case or in a class of cases specified in his appointment.

(2) Every surveyor of ships shall be taken to be a person appointed generally under the preceding subsection to report to the Secretary of State in every kind of case falling within that subsection.

(3) Sections 27 and 28(1), (3) and (4) of the Merchant Shipping Act 1979 (powers of inspectors) shall apply to persons appointed or taken to be appointed under subsection (1) of this section as it applies to the inspectors referred to in that section and shall, as so applying, have effect as if—

(a) any reference to a ship included any vessel, any reference to the Merchant Shipping Acts (except the second reference in sub-paragraph (iii) of section 27(1)(*h*)) were a reference to this Act and the reference in that sub-paragraph to regulations were omitted;

(b) any power under that section to inspect premises included power to inspect any apparatus used for transferring oil.

(4) *Repealed.*

(5) Any power of an inspector, under section 27 as so applied, to require the production of any oil record book required to be carried or records required to be kept in pursuance of regulations made under section 17 of this Act shall include power to copy any entry therein and require the master to certify the copy as a true copy of the entry.

(6) Without prejudice to any powers exercisable by virtue of the preceding provisions of this section, in the case of a vessel which is for the time being in a harbour in the United Kingdom the harbour master, and any other person appointed by the Secretary of State under this subsection (either generally or in relation to a particular vessel), shall have power—

(a) to go on board and inspect the vessel or any part thereof, or any of the machinery, boats, equipment or articles on board the vessel, for the purpose of ascertaining the circumstances relating to an alleged discharge of oil or a mixture containing oil from the vessel into the waters of the harbour;

(b) to require the production of any oil record book required to be carried or records required to be kept in pursuance of regulations made under section 17 of this Act; and

(c) to copy any entry in any such book or record and require the master to certify the copy as a true copy of the entry.

(7) A person exercising any powers conferred by subsection (6) of this section shall not unnecessarily detain or delay the vessel from proceeding on any voyage.

(8) If any person fails to comply with any requirement duly made in pursuance of paragraph (*b*) or paragraph (*c*) of subsection (6) of this section, he shall be liable on summary conviction to a fine not exceeding **level 3** on the standard scale; and if any person wilfully obstructs a person acting in the exercise of any power conferred by virtue of this section and the obstruction is not punishable by virtue of the said section 28(1), he shall be liable on summary conviction to a fine not exceeding **level 4** on the standard scale.

[Prevention of Oil Pollution Act 1971, s 18 as amended by the Merchant Shipping Act 1979, s 28 and Schs 6 and 7, the Criminal Justice Act 1982, s 46 and the Merchant Shipping Act 1995, Sch 12.]

[1] Section 18 is repealed by the Merchant Shipping (Registration, etc) Act 1993, Sch 5 except in its application to ss 2(1) and 3. For the purposes of the Prevention of Oil Pollution Act 1971 other than ss 2(1) and 3 see the Merchant Shipping Act 1894, s 728 as modified by the Merchant Shipping (Registration, etc) Act 1993, Sch 4. For the purposes of the Act other than ss 2(1) and 3 the powers of inspectors and harbour masters are modified by the Merchant Shipping (Registration, etc) Act 1993, Sch 4.

**7.9796 19. Prosecutions** (1) Proceedings for an offence under this Act may, in England or Wales, be brought only—

(a) by or with the consent of the Attorney General[1], or

(b) if the offence is one to which subsection (2) of this section applies, by the harbour authority, or

(c) unless the offence is one mentioned in paragraph (*b*), (*c*) or (*d*) of subsection (2) of this section, by the Secretary of State or a person authorised by any general or special direction of the Secretary of State.

(2) This subsection applies to the following offences—

(a) any offence under section 2 of this Act which is alleged to have been committed by the discharge of oil, or a mixture containing oil, into the waters of a harbour in the United Kingdom;

(b), (c) *repealed.*

(d) any offence under section 18 of this Act in respect of a failure to comply with a requirement of a harbour master, or in respect of obstruction of a harbour master acting in the exercise of any power conferred by virtue of that section.

(3) The preceding provisions of this section shall apply in relation to any part of a dockyard port within the meaning of the Dockyard Ports Regulation Act 1865 as follows, that is to say—

(*a*) if that part is comprised in a harbour in the United Kingdom, the reference to the harbour authority shall be construed as including a reference to the Queen's harbour master for the port;

(*b*) if that part is not comprised in a harbour in the United Kingdom, the references to such a harbour shall be construed as references to such a dockyard port and the reference to the harbour authority as a reference to the Queen's harbour master for the port.

(4) [2].

(4A) Any document required or authorised, by virtue of any statutory provision, to be served on a foreign company for the purposes of the institution of, or otherwise in connection with, proceedings for an offence under section 2(2A) of this Act alleged to have been committed by the company as the owner of a vessel shall be treated as duly served on that company if the document is served on the master of the vessel; and any person authorised to serve any document for the purposes of the institution of, or otherwise in connection with, proceedings for an offence under this Act (whether or not in pursuance of the foregoing provisions of this subsection) shall, for that purpose, have the right to go on board the vessel in question.

(4B) In subsection (4A) of this section a "foreign company" means a company or body which is not one to which section 1139 of the Companies Act 2006 applies so as to authorise service of the document in question.

(5) Proceedings for any offence under this Act may (without prejudice to any jurisdiction exercisable apart from this subsection) be taken against a person at any place at which he is for the time being.[3]

(5A) If an inshore fisheries and conservation authority for a district established under section 149 of the Marine and Coastal Access Act 2009, or any inshore fisheries and conservation officer appointed by the authority under section 165 of that Act, is authorised in that behalf under subsection (1) of this section, the authority may institute proceedings for any offence under this Act committed within the district.

(6) *Repealed.*

(7) The preceding provisions of this section do not apply in relation to an offence under section 3 of this Act, but proceedings for such an offence may—

(*a*) in England and Wales, be brought only by or with the consent of the Director of Public Prosecutions; and

(*b*) *Northern Ireland*;

and any such proceedings may be taken, and the offence may for all incidental purposes be treated as having been committed, in any place in the United Kingdom.

(8) Where a body corporate is guilty of an offence under section 3 of this Act and the offence is proved to have been committed with the consent or connivance of, or to be attributable to any neglect on the part of, any director, manager, secretary or other similar officer of the body corporate or any person who was purporting to act in any such capacity he, as well as the body corporate, shall be guilty of the offence and shall be liable to be proceeded against and punished accordingly.
In this subsection, "director" in relation to a body corporate established for the purpose of carrying on under national ownership any industry or part of an industry or undertaking, being a body corporate whose affairs are managed by its members, means a member of that body corporate.

[Prevention of Oil Pollution Act 1971, s 19 as amended by the Environmental Protection Act 1990, s 148 and Sch 14, the Merchant Shipping Act 1995, Sch 12, the Marine and Coastal Access Act 2009, Schs 14 and 22 and SI 2009/1941.]

---

1 See PART I: MAGISTRATES' COURTS, PROCEDURE at para 1.112 **Criminal prosecutions**, ante.

2 The time limit provisions of ss 274 and 275 of the Merchant Shipping Act 1995 apply in place of those previous contained in sub-s (4) (Merchant Shipping (Registration, etc) Act 1993, Sch 4).

3 The jurisdiction provisions of s 279 of the Merchant Shipping Act 1995 shall apply in place of those previously contained in s 19(5) (Merchant Shipping (Registration, etc) Act 1993, Sch 4).

7.9797 **29. Interpretation** (1) In this Act—

"harbour authority" and "harbour in the United Kingdom", have the meanings assigned to them by section 8(2) of this Act;

"harbour master" includes a dock master or pier master, and any person specially appointed by a harbour authority for the purpose of enforcing the provisions of this Act in relation to the harbour;

"local enactment" means a local or private Act, or an order confirmed by Parliament or brought into operation in accordance with special parliamentary procedure;

"oil" means oil of any description and includes spirit produced from oil of any description, and also includes coal tar;

"oil reception facilities" has the meaning assigned to it by section 9(1) of this Act;

"oil residues" means any waste consisting of, or arising from, oil or a mixture containing oil;

"petroleum-spirit" has the same meaning as in the Petroleum (Consolidation) Act 1928;

"place on land" has the meaning assigned to it by section 2(3) of this Act;

"sea" includes any estuary or arm of the sea;

"transfer", in relation to oil, means transfer in bulk.

(2) Any reference in any provision of this Act to a mixture containing oil shall be construed as a reference to any mixture of oil (or, as the case may be, of oil of a description referred to in that provision) with water or with any other substance.*

(3) Any reference in the provisions of this Act other than section 11 to the discharge of oil or a mixture containing oil, or to its being discharged, from a vessel, place or thing, except where the reference is to its being discharged for a specified purpose, includes a reference to the escape of the oil or mixture, or (as the case may be) to its escaping, from that vessel, place or thing.

(4) *Repealed.*

(5) *Repealed.*

(6) *Repealed.*

(7) Except in so far as the context otherwise requires, any reference in this Act to an enactment shall be construed as a reference to that enactment as amended by or under any other enactment.

[Prevention of Oil Pollution Act 1971, s 29 as amended by the Merchant Shipping Act 1995, Sch 12.]

* **The repeal of s 29(2) by the Merchant Shipping Act 1995, Sch 12 does not apply so far as this subsection relates to s 2(1) and (3) of this Act.**

7.9798 **31. Application to hovercraft** The enactments and instruments with respect to which provision may be made by an Order[1] in Council under section 1(1)(*h*) of the Hovercraft Act 1968 shall include this Act and any instrument made under it.

[Prevention of Oil Pollution Act 1971, s 31.]

1 The Hovercraft (Application of Enactments) Order 1989, SI 1989/1350, applies ss 2(2A), (2B) and (4), 5, 7, 11, 20, 23, 24 and 30 in relation to hovercraft subject to modifications contained in art 3 of the Order.

7.9799 **32. Saving for other restrictions, rights of action etc** Subject to section 33 of the Interpretation Act 1889[1] (offence under two or more laws) nothing in this Act shall affect any restriction imposed by or under any other enactment, whether contained in a public general Act or in a local or private Act, or shall derogate from any right of action or other remedy (whether civil or criminal) in proceedings instituted otherwise than under this Act.

[Prevention of Oil Pollution Act 1971, s 32.]

1 Now s 18 of the Interpretation Act 1978.

# Control of Pollution Act 1974

(1974 c 40)

## PART I[1]

## WASTE ON LAND

*Licensing of disposal of controlled waste*

7.9800 **3. Prohibition of unlicensed disposal of waste[2]** (1) Except in prescribed[3] cases, a person shall not—

(*a*) deposit[4] controlled waste[5] on any land[6] or cause or knowingly permit controlled waste to be deposited on any land; or

(*b*) use any plant or equipment, or cause or knowingly permit any plant or equipment to be used, for the purpose of disposing of controlled waste[3] or of dealing in a prescribed manner with controlled waste,

unless the land[6] on which the waste[7] is deposited or, as the case may be, which forms the site of the plant or equipment is occupied by the holder of a licence issued in pursuance of section 5 of this Act (in this Part of this Act referred to as a "disposal licence") which authorises the deposit or use in question and the deposit or use is in accordance with the conditions, if any, specified in the licence[8].

(2) Except in a case falling within the following subsection, a person who contravenes any of the provisions of the preceding subsection shall, subject to subsection (4) of this section, be guilty of an offence[9] and liable on summary conviction to a fine of an amount not exceeding the statutory maximum or on conviction on indictment to imprisonment for a term not exceeding two years or a fine or both.

(3) A person who contravenes paragraph (*a*) of subsection (1) of this section in a case where—

(*a*) the waste in question is of a kind which is poisonous, noxious or polluting[10]; and

(*b*) its presence on the land is likely to give rise to an environmental hazard[10]; and

(*c*) it is deposited on the land in such circumstances or for such a period that whoever deposited it there may reasonably be assumed to have abandoned it there or to have brought it there for the purpose of its being disposed of (whether by himself or others) as waste[10],

shall, subject to the following subsection, be guilty of an offence[11] and liable on summary conviction to imprisonment for a term not exceeding six months or a fine not exceeding the statutory maximum or both or on conviction on indictment to imprisonment for a term not exceeding five years or a fine or both.

(4) It shall be a defence for a person charged with an offence under this section to prove—

(*a*) that he—

(i) took care to inform himself, from persons who were in a position to provide the information, as to whether the deposit or use to which the charge relates would be in contravention of subsection (1) of this section, and

(ii) did not know and had no reason to suppose that the information given to him was false or misleading and that the deposit or use might be in contravention of that subsection; or

(*b*) that he acted under instructions from his employer and neither knew nor had reason to suppose that the deposit or use was in contravention of the said subsection (1); or

(*c*) in the case of an offence of making, causing or permitting a deposit or use otherwise than in accordance with conditions specified in a disposal licence, that he took all such steps as were reasonably open to him to ensure that the conditions were complied with; or

(*d*) that the acts specified in the charge were done in an emergency in order to avoid danger to the public and that, as soon as reasonably practicable after they were done, particulars of them were furnished to the disposal authority in whose area the acts were done.

(5) In this section and in subsections (5) and (6) of the following section "land" includes land covered with waters where the land is above the law-water mark of ordinary spring tides and the waters are not inland waters (within the meaning of Chapter I of Part III of the Water Act 1989).*

[Control of Pollution Act 1974, s 3 as amended by the Criminal Law Act 1977, s 28 and the Water Act 1989 Sch 25.]

---

* **Repealed by the Environmental Protection Act 1990, but with transitional provisions and savings as set out in SI 1994/1096, arts 2(2), (3), 3, as read with the Environmental Protection (Prescribed Processes and Substances) Regulations 1991, SI 1991/472.**

1 Part I contains ss 1–30. In Greater London or a metropolitan county, functions conferred on the local authorities by Pt I of this Act may be discharged by a single authority established by order of the Secretary of State to act on behalf of the councils where joint arrangements for waste disposal can with advantage be made (Local Government Act 1985, s 10).

2 Separate controls exist in relation to sewage sludge used in agriculture which is controlled by the Sludge (Use in Agriculture) Regulations 1989, SI 1989/1263 amended by SI 1990/880, SI 1996/593, SI 2000/656 and SI 2010/1159 (E) and 1820 (W) implementing EEC Council Directives.

3 The Collection and Disposal of Waste Regulations 1988, SI 1988/819 amended by SI 1989/1968 and SI 1994/1056 and modified by the Waste Disposal (Authorities) Order 1985, SI 1985/1884 have been made; reg 7 and Sch 5 prescribe the manner of dealing with waste for the purposes of s 3(1)(*b*).

4 "Deposit" does not mean final deposit, the fact that waste was not to remain on a site was no bar to conviction (*R v Metropolitan Stipendiary Magistrate, ex p London Waste Regulation Authority* [1993] 3 All ER 113). A reasonable bench of magistrates was entitled on the facts to conclude that barrels containing less than 1 per cent of original volume of solid phenol waste were empty (*Durham County Council v Thomas Swan and Co Ltd* [1995] Crim LR 319).

5 Defined by s 30(1), post.

6 Special provision is made for land occupied by disposal authorities ibid, s 11.

7 Defined by s 30(3), post.

8 It is not necessary for the prosecution to prove that the defendant knowingly permitted a breach of a condition of a waste disposal licence in addition to proving that he knowingly permitted the deposit of controlled waste (*Ashcroft v Cambro Waste Products Ltd* [1981] 3 All ER 699, [1981] 1 WLR 1349).

9 For procedure in respect of offences triable either way, see the Magistrates' Courts Act 1980, ss 17A–21, PART I: MAGISTRATES' COURTS, PROCEDURE, ante.

10 See s 4(5), post (waste in containers, and "environmental hazard") and s 4(6) as to the degree of risk relevant thereunder.

11 For procedure in respect of offences triable either way, see the Magistrates' Courts Act 1980, ss 17A–21, PART I: MAGISTRATES' COURTS, PROCEDURE, ante. Civil liability following a contravention of s 3(3) is dealt with by s 88 of this Act.

7.9801 4. **Provisions supplementary to section 3** (1) Where activities for which a disposal licence is required apart from this subsection have been carried on on any land during the period of six months ending with the date when subsection (1) of the preceding section comes into force[1], nothing in that subsection shall apply to the carrying on of those activities on the land during the period of one year beginning with that date and, where at the end of that period an appeal is pending in pursuance of section 10 of this Act against a rejection of an application for a disposal licence in respect of those activities on the land or against a decision to issue such a licence which specifies conditions, until the appeal is determined.

(2) Nothing in subsection (1) of the preceding section applies to household waste from a private dwelling[2] which is deposited, disposed of or dealt with within the curtilage of the dwelling by or with the permission of the occupier of the dwelling.

(3) Duty of Secretary of State in prescribing exceptions.

(4) *Repealed.*

(5) For the purposes of subsection (3) of the preceding section—

(*a*) the presence of waste on land gives rise to an environmental hazard if the waste has been deposited in such a manner or in such a quantity (whether that quantity by itself or cumulatively with other deposits of the same or different substances) as to subject persons or animals to a material risk of death, injury or impairment of health or as to threaten the pollution (whether on the surface or underground) of any water supply; and

(*b*) the fact that waste is deposited in containers shall not of itself be taken to exclude any risk which might be expected to arise if the waste were not in containers.

(6) In the case of any deposit of waste, the degree of risk relevant for the purposes of the preceding subsection shall be assessed with particular regard—

(*a*) to the measures, if any taken by the person depositing the waste, or by the owner or occupier of the land, or by others, for minimising the risk; and

(*b*) to the likelihood of the waste, or any container in which it is deposited, being tampered with by children or others.*

[Control of Pollution Act 1974, s 4 as amended by the Water Act 1989, Sch 27.]

* **See note to s 3, ante.**

[1] Section 3(1) came into force on 14 June 1976.

[2] Defined by s 30(1), post.

7.9802 **5. Licences to dispose of waste** (1)–(5) Applications for disposal licences.

(6) A person who, in an application for a disposal licence, makes any statement which he knows to be false in a material particular or recklessly makes any statement which is false in a material particular shall be guilty of an offence[1] and liable on summary conviction to a fine not exceeding the statutory maximum or on conviction on indictment to imprisonment for a term not exceeding two years or a fine or both.*

[Control of Pollution Act 1974, s 5 as amended by the Criminal Law Act 1977, s 28, the Local Government, Planning and Land Act 1980, Schs 2 and 34, the Local Government Act 1985, Sch 6, the Water Act 1989, Sch 25, the Planning (Consequential Provisions) Act 1990, Sch 2 and the Environment Act 1995, Schs 22 and 24.]

* **See note to s 3, ante.**

[1] For procedure in respect of an offence triable either way, see the Magistrates' Courts Act 1980, ss 17A–21, PART I: MAGISTRATES' COURTS, PROCEDURE, ante.

7.9803 **6. Provisions supplementary to section 5** (1)–(2) Regulations may prescribe conditions[1] in a disposal licence.

(3) The holder of a disposal licence who without reasonable excuse contravenes a condition of the licence which in pursuance of regulations made by virtue of subsection (1) of this section is to be disregarded for the purposes mentioned in that subsection[2] shall be guilty of an offence and liable on summary conviction to a fine not exceeding **level 5** on the standard scale; but no proceedings for such an offence shall be brought in England and Wales except by or with the consent of the Director of Public Prosecutions or by the Environment Agency.

(4)–(5) Register of licences, disposal of applications.

(6) References to land in the preceding section and this section include such water as is mentioned in section 4(4) of this Act.*

[Control of Pollution Act 1974, s 6 as amended by the Local Government, Planning and Land Act 1980, Schs 2 and 34, the Criminal Justice Act 1982, ss 38 and 46, the Environment Act 1995, Sch 22 and SI 1996/593.]

* **See note to s 3, ante.**

[1] Including conditions to carry out works or do something which the licence holder is not entitled as of right to do (sub-s (2)). The disposal authority does not have power to impose a condition prohibiting public nuisances of any and all kinds, whether or not they pollute water, endanger public health or constitute a serious detriment to the amenities of the locality in which the licensed activities are carried on (*A-G's Reference (No 2 of 1988)* [1990] 1 QB 77, [1989] 3 WLR 397, 89 Cr App Rep 314, CA).

[2] That is, for the purposes of s 3(1) of this Act.

7.9804 **13. Dustbins etc**[1] (1) Where a collection authority[2] has a duty by virtue of subsection (1)(*a*) of the preceding section[3] to arrange for the collection of household waste4 from any premises, the authority may, by a notice served on the occupier of the premises, require him to place the waste for collection in receptacles which are of a kind and number reasonably specified in the notice.

(1A) A person who fails to comply with any of the requirements of such a notice shall be guilty of an offence and liable on summary conviction to a fine of an amount not exceeding **level 3** on the standard scale.

(2) A notice served by an authority in pursuance of the preceding subsection may provide for the receptacles in question to be provided by the authority free of charge or—

(*a*) if the recipient of the notice agrees, by the authority on payment by the recipient of the notice of such a single payment or such periodical payments as he agrees with the authority; or

(*b*) by the recipient of the notice if he does not enter into an agreement in pursuance of the preceding paragraph within a period specified in the notice or the notice does not propose such an agreement.

(3) Where by virtue of such a notice the recipient of it is required to provide any receptacles he may within the period of twenty-one days beginning with the last day of the period specified in the notice in pursuance of paragraph (*b*) of the preceding subsection or, where no period is so specified, beginning with the day on which the notice is served on him, appeal to a magistrates' court against the notice on the ground that any requirement specified in the notice is unreasonable or on the ground that the receptacles in which household waste in the premises in question is placed for collection are adequate; and where an appeal against a notice is brought in pursuance of this subsection—

(*a*) the notice shall be of no effect pending the determination of the appeal; and

(*b*) the court shall either quash or modify the notice or dismiss the appeal; and

(*c*) no question as to whether any requirement specified in the notice is unreasonable shall be entertained in any proceedings for an offence under this section in respect of the notice.

(4) An English county disposal authority and any collection authority may at the request of any person supply him with receptacles for commercial waste or industrial waste[4] which he 1has requested the authority to arrange to collect and shall make a reasonable charge for any receptacle supplied in pursuance of this subsection unless in the case of a receptacle for commercial waste the authority considers it appropriate not to make a charge.

(5) If it appears to a collection authority that there is likely to be situated, on any premises in its area, commercial waste or industrial waste of a kind which, if the waste is not stored in receptacles of a particular kind, is likely to cause a nuisance or to be detrimental to the amenities of the locality in which the premises are situated, the authority may, by a notice served on the occupier of the premises, require him to provide at the premises receptacles for the storage of such waste which are of a kind and number reasonably specified in the notice.

(5A) A person who fails to comply with any requirement specified in a notice shall be guilty of an offence and liable on summary conviction to a fine of an amount not exceeding **level 3** on the standard scale.

(6) A person on whom a notice is served in pursuance of the preceding subsection may, within the period of twenty-one days beginning with the day on which the notice is served on him, appeal to a magistrates' court against the notice on the grounds that any requirement specified in the notice is unreasonable or that the waste is not likely to cause a nuisance or be detrimental to the amenities of the locality in which the premises are situated; and where an appeal against a notice is brought in pursuance of this subsection, paragraphs *(a)* to *(c)* of subsection (3) of this section shall apply in relation to the notice as they apply in relation to such a notice as is mentioned in that subsection.

(7) A notice under subsection (1) or (5) of this section may make provision with respect to—

*(a)* the size, construction and maintenance of receptacles for controlled waste[5]

*(b)* the placing of the receptacles on premises for the purpose of facilitating the emptying of them, and access to the receptacles for that purpose;

*(c)* the placing of the receptacles for that purpose on highways;

*(d)* the substances which may and may not be put into the receptacles and the precautions to be taken where particular substances are put into them; and

*(e)* the steps to be taken by occupiers of premises for the purposes of facilitating the collection of waste from receptacles for controlled waste which are provided in connection with the premises.

(7A) A notice under subsection (1) or (5) of this section shall not require receptacles to be placed on a highway unless—

*(a)* the relevant highway authority have given their consent to their being so placed; and

*(b)* arrangements have been made as to the liability for any damage arising out of their being so placed.

(8) References to receptacles in the preceding provisions of this section include references to holders for receptacles.*

[Control of Pollution Act 1974, s 13 as amended by the Local Government, Planning and Land Act 1980, Sch 2, the Criminal Justice Act 1982, ss 38 and 46 and the Local Government Act 1985, Sch 6.]

* **Repealed for certain purposes and prospectively repealed for remaining purposes, as from a day to be appointed, by the Environmental Protection Act 1990, s 162, Sch 16, Part II; for those purposes see SI 1992/266.**

1 Of this section, subsections (5), (6), (7) and (8), and subsection (3) so far as it applies to an appeal under subsection (6), were brought into force on 1 August 1978 (SI 1978/954) and the remainder on 6 June 1988 (SI 1988/818).

2 Defined by s 30(1), post.

3 That is, except for waste at a place so isolated or inaccessible that the cost of collection would be unreasonably high, and as to which adequate arrangements can reasonably be expected to be made by a person who controls the waste.

4 Defined by s 30(3), post.

5 Defined by s 30(1), post.

7.9805 **16. Removal of waste deposited in breach of licensing provisions** (1) If any controlled waste[1] is deposited on any land in contravention of section 3(1) of this Act, any authority to which this section applies may serve a notice on the occupier of the land requiring him—

*(a)* to remove the waste from the land within a period specified in the notice, which shall not be less than twenty-one days beginning with the date of service of the notice; or

*(b)* to take within such a period such steps as are so specified with a view to eliminating or reducing the consequences of the deposit of the waste;

or requiring him both to remove the waste as mentioned in paragraph *(a)* of this subsection and to take such steps as are mentioned in paragraph *(b)* of this subsection within such a period as aforesaid.

(2) A person served with a notice in pursuance of the preceding subsection may within the twenty-one days aforesaid appeal to a magistrates' court against the notice; and on any such appeal the court shall quash the notice if it is satisfied that—

*(a)* the appellant neither deposited nor caused nor knowingly permitted the deposit of the waste on the land; or

*(b)* service of the notice on the appellant was not authorised by the preceding subsection; or

*(c)* there is a material defect in the notice;

and in any other case shall either modify the notice or dismiss the appeal.

(3) Where a person appeals against a notice in pursuance of this section, the notice shall be of no effect pending the determination of the appeal; and where the court modifies the notice or dismisses the appeal it may extend the period specified in the notice.

(4) If a person on whom a notice if served in pursuance of subsection (1) of this section fails to comply with the notice, then—

*(a)* he shall be guilty of an offence and liable on summary conviction to a fine not exceeding **level 5** on the standard scale and a further fine not exceeding £50 for each day on which the failure continues after conviction for the offence and before the authority which served the notice has begun to exercise its powers in pursuance of the following paragraph; and

*(b)* the said authority may do what that person was required by the notice to do and may recover from him any expenses reasonably incurred by the authority in doing it.

(5)–(7) Power to remove waste and recover cost.

(8) The authorities to which this section applies are—

*(a)* the appropriate Agency;

*(b)* any collection authority in whose area the land mentioned in subsection (1) above is situated.*

[Control of Pollution Act 1974, s 16 as amended by the Criminal Justice Act 1982, ss 38 and 46 and the Environment Act 1995, Sch 22.]

* **Repealed by the Environmental Protection Act 1990, s 162, Sch 16 from a date to be appointed.**

1 Defined by s 30(1), post.

7.9806 **17. Special provisions with respect to certain dangerous or intractable waste** (1) If the Secretary of State considers that controlled waste of any kind is or may be so dangerous or difficult to dispose of that special provision in pursuance of this subsection is required for the disposal of waste of that kind by disposal authorities or other persons, it shall be his duty to make provision by regulations for the disposal of waste of that kind (hereafter in this section referred to as "special waste"); and, without prejudice to the generality of the Secretary of State's power to make regulations in pursuance of the preceding provisions of this subsection, any such regulations[1] may include provision—

*(a)–(d)* specific requirements;

*(e)* providing that a contravention of the regulations shall be an offence and prescribing the maximum penalty for the offence[1] (which shall not exceed, on summary conviction, a fine of the statutory maximum and, on conviction on indictment, imprisonment for a term of two years and a fine).

(2) Further specific requirements for inclusion in regulations.

(3) Provisions may also be made by regulations—

*(a)* for the giving of a direction, in respect of any place in respect of which a disposal licence or a resolution in pursuance of section 11[2] of this Act is in force, requiring the holder of the licence or the authority which passed the resolution to accept and dispose of at the place, on such terms as are specified in the direction (including terms as to the making of payments to the recipient of the direction), such special waste as is so specified;

*(b)* as to the consents to be obtained and the other steps to be taken before a direction may be given in pursuance of the regulations and as to appeals to the Secretary of State against a direction so given;

*(c)* providing that a failure to comply with such a direction shall be an offence punishable on summary conviction by a fine not exceeding **level 5** on the standard scale or such less amount as is prescribed and that a person shall not be guilty of an offence under any prescribed enactment by reason only of anything necessarily done or omitted in order to comply with such a direction.*

[Control of Pollution Act 1974, s 17 as amended by the Criminal Law Act 1977, s 28 and the Criminal Justice Act 1982, ss 38 and 46.]

* **Repealed by the Environmental Protection Act 1990, s 162, Sch 16 from a date to be appointed.**

1 For procedure in respect of an offence triable either way, see the Magistrates' Courts Act 1980, ss 17A–21, PART I: MAGISTRATES' COURTS, PROCEDURE, ante.

2 That is, a resolution specifying the conditions in accordance with which land occupied by the disposal authority itself is to be used for the deposit or disposal of controlled waste.

*Waste other than controlled waste*

7.9807 **18. Application of preceding provisions to other waste** (1) The Secretary of State may, after consultation with such bodies as he considers appropriate, make regulations providing that prescribed provisions of sections 1 to 11 and 14 to 17 of this Act shall have effect in a prescribed area—

*(a)* as if references in those provisions to controlled waste or controlled waste of a kind specified in the regulations included references to such waste as is mentioned in section 30(3)*(c)*(ii) of this Act which is of a kind so specified; and

*(b)* with such other modifications as are prescribed;

and regulations made in pursuance of this subsection may make such modifications of any enactment other than the sections aforesaid as the Secretary of State considers appropriate in connection with the regulations.

(2) A person who—

(*a*) deposits on any land any waste other than controlled waste; or

(*b*) causes or knowingly permits the deposit on any land of any waste other than controlled waste,

in a case where, if the waste were controlled waste and any disposal licence relating to the land were not in force, he would be guilty of an offence under section 3(3) of this Act shall be guilty of such an offence[1] and punishable accordingly unless the act charged was done in pursuance of and in accordance with the terms of any consent, licence, approval or authority granted under any enactment (excluding any planning permission under the enactments relating to town and country planning); and in this subsection "land" includes such water as is mentioned in section 4(4) of this Act.

(3) Subsection (2) of section 12[2] and subsection (4) of section 13 of this Act shall apply to waste other than controlled waste as the subsections apply to controlled waste.*

[Control of Pollution Act 1974, s 18.]

* **See note to s 3, ante.**

1 The limitation period will also be the same as for an offence under s 3(3), ie one year (s 87(3), post). Civil liability is dealt with by s 88 of this Act.

2 This enables a disposal authority or collection authority to arrange for the collection of industrial waste if so requested by the occupier of premises in its area.

**7.9808 27. Interference with refuse tins and dustbins etc** (1) No person shall sort over or disturb—

(*a*) anything deposited at a place provided by a disposal authority or a collection authority for the deposit of waste or in a receptacle for waste which is provided by such an authority or a parish or community council for public use; or

(*b*) the contents of any receptacle for waste which, in accordance with a notice under section 13(1) or (5) of this Act, is placed on any highway or in any other place with a view to its being emptied;

unless he is authorised to do so by the authority or council in the case of anything deposited as mentioned in paragraph (*a*) above or, in the case of such a receptacle as is mentioned in paragraph (*b*) above, unless he is a person entitled to the custody of the receptacle or is authorised to do so by such a person or is a person having the function of emptying the receptacle.

(2) A person who contravenes any of the provisions of the preceding subsection shall be guilty of an offence and liable on summary conviction to a fine of an amount not exceeding **level 3** on the standard scale.*

[Control of Pollution Act 1974, s 27 as amended by the Local Government, Planning and Land Act 1980, Sch 2 as amended by the Criminal Justice Act 1982, ss 38 and 46.]

* **See note to s 3, ante.**

**7.9809 30. Interpretation etc of Part I** (1) Subject to the following subsection and to subsection (6) below, in this Part of this Act—

"the appropriate Agency" means—

(*a*) in relation to England, the Environment Agency;

(*aa*) in relation to Wales, the Natural Resources Body for Wales; and

(*b*) *Scotland*;

"collection authority" means the council of a district or a London borough, the Common Council of the City of London, the Sub-Treasurer of the Inner Temple and the Under Treasurer of the Middle Temple and "English collection authority" means a collection authority of which the area is in the area of an English county disposal authority;

"controlled waste" means household, industrial and commercial waste or any such waste;

"disposal authority" means the council of a county or metropolitan district in England, the council of a district in Wales, the council of a London borough and the Common Council of the City of London, "English county disposal authority" means the council of a county in England and "relevant disposal authority" in relation to an English collection authority, means the English county disposal authority whose area includes that of the collection authority;

"disposal licence" has the meaning assigned to it by section 3(1) of this Act, and "holder" in relation to such a licence shall be construed in accordance with section 8(3) of this Act;

"private dwelling" means—

(*a*) a hereditament or premises used wholly for the purposes of a private dwelling or private dwellings as determined in accordance with Schedule 13 to the General Rate Act 1967[1]; and

(*b*) a caravan as defined in section 29(1) of the Caravan Sites and Control of Development Act 1960 (disregarding the amendment made by section 13(2) of the Caravan Sites Act 1968) which usually and for the time being is situated on a caravan site within the meaning of that Act;

"relevant land" means—

*(a)* in relation to a proposal to issue a disposal licence, the land on which activities may be carried on in pursuance of the licence if it is issued in accordance with the proposal; and

*(b)* in relation to a disposal licence, the land on which activities may be carried on in pursuance of the licence,

and references to land in the preceding paragraphs include such water as is mentioned in section 4(4) of this Act;

"waste" has the same meaning as it has in Part II of the Environmental Protection Act 1990 by virtue of section 75(2) of that Act;

"waste disposal provisions" means—

*(a)* sections 1 and 2 (waste disposal arrangements and plans);

*(b)* section 12 (collection of waste;

*(c)* section 13(4) (provision of receptacles for industrial or commercial waste);

*(d)* section 14 (disposal of waste);

*(e)* section 17(2)*(a)* and *(c)* (disposal of dangerous or intractable waste);

*(f)* sections 19 to 21 (powers in relation to disposal of waste which is not controlled waste, reclamation of waste and production of heat and electricity from waste); and

*(g)* section 27(1) (interference with refuse tips and dustbins etc);

"waste regulation provisions" means—

*(a)* sections 3 to 11 (disposal licences);

*(b)* section 16 (removal of waste deposited in breach of licensing provisions); and

*(c)* section 17(1)*(a)* and (2)*(b)* to *(d)* (directions as to disposal of dangerous or intractable waste, supervision of certain activities, recovery of expenses and charges and appeals to the Secretary of State);

(2) *Scotland.*

(3) Subject to the following subsection, or the purposes of this Part of this Act—

*(a)* household waste consists of waste from a private dwelling or residential home or from premises forming part of a university or school or other educational establishment or forming part of a hospital or nursing home;

*(b)* industrial waste[2] consists of waste from any factory within the meaning of the Factories Act 1961 and any premises occupied by a body corporate established by or under any enactment for the purpose of carrying on under national ownership any industry or part of an industry or any undertaking, excluding waste from any mine or quarry; and

*(c)* commercial waste[2] consists of waste from premises used wholly or mainly for the purposes of a trade or business or the purposes of sport, recreation or entertainment excluding—

(i) household and industrial waste, and

(ii) waste from any mine or quarry and waste from premises used for agriculture within the meaning of the Agriculture Act 1947 or, (Scotland), and

(iii) waste of any other description prescribed for the purposes of this sub-paragraph.

(4) Regulations[3] may provide that waste of a prescribed description shall be treated for the purposes of prescribed provisions of this Part of this Act as being or not being household waste or industrial waste or commercial waste; but no regulations shall be made by virtue of the preceding provisions of this subsection in respect of such waste as is mentioned in paragraph *(c)*(ii) of the preceding subsection and references in those provisions and in the preceding subsection to waste do not include sewage except so far as regulations provide otherwise. In this subsection "sewage" includes matter in or from a privy within the meaning[4] of section 12(5) of this Act.

(5) Except as provided by regulations[3] made by virtue of this subsection, nothing in this Part of this Act applies to radioactive waste within the meaning of the Radioactive Substances Act 1960; but regulations may—

*(a)* provide for prescribed provisions of this Part of this Act to have effect with such modifications as the Secretary of State considers appropriate for the purposes of dealing with such radioactive waste;

*(b)* make such modifications of the said Act of 1960 and any other Act as the Secretary of State considers appropriate in consequence of the passing of this Part of this Act or in connection with regulations made by virtue of the preceding paragraph.

(6) In the application of this Part of this Act to Wales—

"collection authority" means a county council; or county borough council; and

"disposal authority" means a county council or county borough council.*

[Control of Pollution Act 1974, s 30 as amended by the Local Government Act 1985, Sch 6, the Local Government (Wales) Act 1994, Sch 9 and the Environment Act 1995, Schs 22 and 24 and SI 2013/755.]

---

* **Repealed by the Environmental Protection Act 1990, s 162, Sch 16 from a date to be appointed.**

1 The General Rate Act 1967 has been repealed by the Local Government Finance Act 1988.

2 Material which was waste when removed from its original site is not changed by sorting or its usefulness for infill purposes (*Kent County Council v Queenborough Rolling Mill Co Ltd* (1990) 154 JP 530).

3 Part I of the Act divides controlled waste into three categories: household, industrial and commercial. The Collection and Disposal of Waste Regulations 1988, SI 1988/819 amended by SI 1989/1968 and SI 1994/1056 and modified by

the Waste Disposal (Authorities) Order 1985, SI 1985/1884, provides that certain types of waste are to be treated as belonging to a particular category.

[4] That is, a latrine which has a moveable receptacle for faecal matter.

## PART III[1]
## NOISE

*Construction sites*

7.9810 **60. Control of noise on construction sites** (1) This section applies to works of the following description, that is to say—

(*a*) the erection, construction, alteration, repair or maintenance of buildings, structures or roads;

(*b*) breaking up, opening or boring under any road or adjacent land in connection with the construction, inspection, maintenance or removal of works;

(*c*) demolition or dredging work; and

(*d*) (whether or not also comprised in paragraph (*a*), (*b*) or (*c*) above) any work of engineering construction[2].

(2) Where it appears to a local authority that works to which this section applies are being, or are going to be, carried out on any premises, the local authority may serve a notice imposing requirements as to the way in which the works are to be carried out and may if it thinks fit publish notice of the requirements in such way as appears to the local authority to be appropriate.

(3) The notice may in particular—

(*a*) specify the plant or machinery which is or is not to be used;

(*b*) specify the hours during which the works may be carried out;

(*c*) specify the level of noise which may be emitted from the premises in question or at any specified point on those premises or which may be so emitted during specified hours; and

(*d*) provide for any change of circumstances.

(4) In acting under this section the local authority shall have regard—

(*a*) to the relevant provisions of any code of practice[3] issued under this Part of this Act;

(*b*) to the need for ensuring that the best practicable means[4] are employed to minimise noise;

(*c*) before specifying any particular methods or plant or machinery, to the desirability in the interests of any recipients of the notice in question of specifying other methods or plant or machinery which would be substantially as effective in minimising noise and more acceptable to them;

(*d*) to the need to protect any persons in the locality in which the premises in question are situated from the effects of noise.

(5) A notice under this section shall be served on the person who appears to the local authority to be carrying out, or going to carry out, the works, and on such other persons appearing to the local authority to be responsible for, or to have control over, the carrying out of the works as the local authority thinks fit.

(6) A notice under this section may specify the time within which the notice is to be complied with, and may require the execution of such works, and the taking of such other steps, as may be necessary for the purpose of the notice, or as may be specified in the notice.

(7) A person served with a notice under this section may appeal[5] against the notice to a magistrates' court within twenty-one days from the service of the notice.

(8) If a person on whom a notice is served under this section without reasonable excuse contravenes any requirement[6] of the notice he shall be guilty of an offence[7] against this Part of this Act.

[Control of Pollution Act 1974, s 60.]

---

[1] Part III contains ss 57–74.

[2] Defined in s 73, post.

[3] Section 71 enables the Secretary of State to issue or approve codes of practice for minimising noise.

[4] "Best practicable means" is defined in s 72, post.

[5] For procedure on appeal, see s 70, post.

[6] requirements in a notice may only apply to works under way at the date of the notice and do not apply, for example, to works undertaken under a subsequent contract in respect of the same premises (*Walter Lilly & Co Ltd v Westminster City Council* (1994) 158 JP 805).

[7] For penalty, see s 74, post. Note also the defence available under s 61(8), post.

7.9811 **61. Prior consent for work on construction sites** (1)–(3) *Application may be made before work begins, and consent granted.*

(5) In acting under this section a local authority shall have regard to the considerations set out in subsection (4) of the preceding section and shall have power to—

(*a*) attach any conditions to a consent; and

(*b*) limit or qualify a consent to allow for any change in circumstances; and

(*c*) limit the duration of a consent;

and any person who knowingly carries out the works, or permits the works to be carried out, in contravention of any conditions attached to a consent under this section shall be guilty of an offence[1] against this Part of this Act.

(6) The local authority shall inform the applicant of its decision on the application within twenty-eight days from receipt of the application; and if the local authority gives its consent to the application it may if it thinks fit publish notice of the consent, and of the works to which it relates, in such way as appears to the local authority to be appropriate.

(7) If—

(*a*) the local authority does not give a consent within the said period of twenty-eight days; or

(*b*) the local authority gives its consent within the said period of twenty-eight days but attaches any condition to the consent or limits or qualifies the consent in any way;

the applicant may appeal[2] to a magistrates' court within twenty-one days from the end of that period.

(8) In any proceedings for an offence under section 60(8) of this Act it shall be a defence to prove that the alleged contravention amounted to the carrying out of the works in accordance with a consent given under this section.

(9) A consent given under this section shall contain a statement to the effect that the consent does not of itself constitute any ground of defence against any proceedings instituted under section 82 of the Environmental Protection Act 1990.

(10) Where a consent has been given under this section and the works are carried out by a person other than the applicant for the consent, it shall be the duty of the applicant to take all reasonable steps to bring the consent to the notice of that other person; and if he fails to comply with this subsection he shall be guilty of an offence[1] against this Part of this Act.

[Control of Pollution Act 1974, s 61 as amended by the Building Act 1984, Sch 7, the Environmental Protection Act 1990, Sch 15 and the Environment Act 1995, Sch 24.]

---

1 For penalty see s 74, post.

2 For procedure on appeal, see s 70, post.

*Noise in streets*

7.9812 **62. Noise in streets** (1) Subject to the provisions of this section, a loudspeaker in a street[1] shall not be operated—

(*a*) between the hours of nine in the evening and eight in the following morning, for any purpose;

(*b*) at any other time, for the purpose of advertising any entertainment, trade or business;

and any person who operates or permits the operation of a loudspeaker in contravention of this subsection shall be guilty of an offence[2] against this Part of this Act.

In this section "street"[1] means a highway and any other road, footway, square or court which is for the time being open to the public.

(1A) Subject to subsection (1B) of this section, the Secretary of State may by order amend the times specified in subsection (1)(*a*) of this section.

(1B) An order under subsection (1A) of this section shall not amend the times so as to permit the operation of a loudspeaker in a street at any time between the hours of nine in the evening and eight in the following morning.

(2) Subsection (1) of this section shall not apply to the operation of a loudspeaker—

(*a*) for police, fire and rescue authority or ambulance purposes or for purposes relating to the functions of Ministry of Defence firefighters (as defined in section 16 of the Armed Forces Act 2016), by the Environment Agency, a water undertaker or a sewerage undertaker in the exercise of any of its functions, or by a local authority within its area;

(*b*) for communicating with person on a vessel for the purpose of directing the movement of that or any other vessel;

(*c*) if the loudspeaker forms part of a public telephone system;

(*d*) if the loudspeaker—

(i) is in or fixed to a vehicle, and

(ii) is operated solely for the entertainment of or for communicating with the driver or a passenger of the vehicle or, where the loudspeaker is or forms part of the horn or similar warning instrument of the vehicle, solely for giving warning to other traffic, and

(iii) is so operated as not to give reasonable cause for annoyance to persons in the vicinity;

(*e*) otherwise than on a highway, by persons employed in connection with a transport undertaking used by the public in a case where the loudspeaker is operated solely for making announcements to passengers or prospective passengers or to other persons so employed;

(*f*) by a travelling showman on land which is being used for the purposes of a pleasure fair;

(*g*) in case of emergency.

(3) Subsection (1)(*b*) of this section shall not apply to the operation of a loudspeaker between the hours of noon and seven in the evening on the same day if the loudspeaker—

(*a*) is fixed to a vehicle which is being used for the conveyance of a perishable commodity for human consumption; and (*b*) is operated solely for informing members of the public (otherwise than by means of words) that the commodity is on sale from the vehicle; and

(*c*) is so operated as not to give reasonable cause for annoyance to persons in the vicinity.

(3A) Subsection (1) of this section shall not apply to the operation of a loudspeaker in accordance with a consent granted by a local authority under Schedule 2 to the Noise and Statutory Nuisance Act 1993.

[Control of Pollution Act 1974, s 62 as amended by the Water Act 1989, Sch 25, the Noise and Statutory Nuisance Act 1993, s 7, the Environment Act 1995, Sch 22, the Fire and Rescue Services Act 2004, Sch 1 and the Armed Forces Act 2016, s 17.]

---

1 For a judicial consideration of the meaning of "street" within s 62(1), see *Tower Hamlets London Borough Council v Creitzman* (1984) 148 JP 630. Where equipment was attached by suckers to a street-facing window and had the effect of turning the windows into loudspeakers, this amounted to operating a loudspeaker in a street: *Westminster City Council v French Connection Ltd* [2005] EWHC Admin 933, (2005) 169 JP 312.

2 For penalty see s 74, post.

*Noise from plant or machinery*

7.9816 **68. Noise from plant or machinery** (1)–(2) *Power of Secretary of State to make regulations.*

(3) Any person who contravenes or causes or permits another person to contravene regulations under this section shall be guilty of an offence[1] against this Part of this Act; but in any proceedings for a contravention of regulations made in pursuance of paragraph (*a*) of subsection (1) of this section it shall be a defence to prove that means were used for the purpose of reducing the noise in question which were not less effective for that purpose than the means required by the regulations.

(4)–(5) *Local authority to enforce; no derogation to other provisions of Act.*

[Control of Pollution Act 1974, s 68.]

---

1 For penalty, see s 74, post.

*Supplemental*

7.9818 **70. Appeals to Secretary of State and magistrates' court** (1) Where any provision in this Part of this Act provides for an appeal to a magistrates' court, the procedure shall be by way of complaint for an order and the Magistrates' Courts Act 1980 shall apply to the proceedings.

(2)–(3) *Regulations to be made as to appeals to the Secretary of State and to magistrates' courts.*[1]

(4) In entertaining any appeal under this Part of this Act the Secretary of State, or as the case may be the magistrates' court, shall have regard to any duty imposed by law on the appellant which concerns the activities in the course of which the noise is emitted.

[Control of Pollution Act 1974, s 70.]

---

1 See the Control of Noise (Appeals) Rules 1975 and the Statutory Nuisance (Appeals) Regulations 1990, post.

7.9819 **71.** *Power to prepare and approve codes of practice for minimising noise*[1].

---

1 The Control of Noise (Code of Practice on Noise from Ice-Cream Van Chimes Etc) Order 1981, SI 1981/1828 (revoked in relation to England by SI 2013/2036), the Control of Noise (Code of Practice on Noise from Model Aircraft) Order 1981, SI 1981/1830, the Control of Noise (Code of Practice on Noise from Ice-Cream Van Chimes Etc) (England) Order 2013, SI 2013/2036, the Control of Noise (Codes of Practice for Construction and Open Sites) (England) Order 2015, SI 2015/227 and the Noise from Audible Intruder Alarms (Wales) (Revocation) and Control of Noise (Codes of Practice for Construction and Open Sites) (Wales) Order 2017, SI 2017/81 have been made.

7.9820 **72. "Best practicable means"** (1) This section shall apply for the construction of references in this Part of this Act to best practicable means.

(2) In that expression "practicable" means reasonably practicable having regard among other things to local conditions and circumstances, to the current state of technical knowledge and to the financial implications.

(3) The means to be employed include the design, installation, maintenance and manner and periods of operation of plant and machinery, and the design, construction and maintenance of buildings and acoustic structures.

(4) The test of best practicable means is to apply only so far as compatible with any duty imposed by law, and in particular is to apply to statutory undertakers only so far as compatible with the duties imposed on them in their capacity of statutory undertakers.

(5) The said test is to apply only so far as compatible with safety and safe working conditions, and with the exigencies of any emergency or unforeseen circumstances.

(6) Subject to the preceding provisions of this section, regard shall be had, in construing references to "best practicable means", to any relevant provision of a code of practice approved under the preceding section.

[Control of Pollution Act 1974, s 72.]

7.9821 **73. Interpretation and other supplementary provisions** (1) Except where the context otherwise requires, in this Part of this Act—

"contravention" includes a failure to comply with the provision in question, and "contravene" shall be construed accordingly;

"local authority" means—

(*a*) in England, the council of a district or a London borough, the Common Council of the City of London, the Sub-Treasurer of the Inner Temple and the Under Treasurer of the Middle Temple;
(*aa*) in Wales, the council of a county or a county borough; and
(*b*) *Scotland*;

"noise" includes vibration;

"statutory undertakers" means persons authorised by any enactment to carry on any railway, light railway, tramway, road transport, water transport, canal, inland navigation, dock, harbour, pier or lighthouse undertaking, or any undertaking for the supply of hydraulic power, and includes a universal service provider (within the meaning of the Postal Services Act 2000) in his capacity as a person who provides a universal service provider (within the meaning of that Act);

"work of engineering construction" means the construction, structural alteration, maintenance or repair of any railway line or siding or any dock, harbour, inland navigation, tunnel, bridge, viaduct, waterworks, reservoir, pipeline, aqueduct, sewer, sewage works or gas-holder.

(2) The area of a local authority which includes part of the seashore shall also include for the purposes of this Part of this Act, except section 62, the territorial sea lying seawards from that part of the shore; and—

(*a*) *repealed*;
(*b*) this Part of this Act (except section 62 and this subsection) shall have effect, in relation to any area included in the area of a local authority by virtue of this subsection—
(i) as if references to premises and the occupier of premises included respectively a vessel and the master of a vessel, and
(ii) with such other modifications, if any, as are prescribed.

(3) Where more than one person is responsible for noise, this Part of this Act shall apply to each of those persons whether or not what any one of them is responsible for would by itself amount to a nuisance, or would result in a level of noise justifying action under this Part of this Act.

(4) This Part of this Act does not apply to noise caused by aircraft other than model aircraft and does not confer functions on port health authorities.

[Control of Pollution Act 1974, s 73 as amended by the Local Government, Planning and Land Act 1980, Schs 2 and 34, the Gas Act 1986, Sch 9 the Water Act 1989, Sch 25, the Electricity Act 1989, Sch 18, the Local Government (Wales) Act 1994, Sch 9, the Environment Act 1995, Sch 24, SI 2001/1149 and the Deregulation Act 2015, Sch 13.]

7.9822 74. **Penalties** (1) A person guilty of an offence against this Part of this Act shall be liable on summary conviction to a fine not exceeding **level 5** on the standard scale, together, in any case, with a further fine not exceeding **£50** for each day on which the offence continues after the conviction.

(2) In determining whether an offence is a second or subsequent offence against this Part of this Act, account shall be taken of any offence—

(*a*) under section 24 of the Public Health (Scotland) Act 1897 by way of contravening a decree or interdict relating to noise; or
(*b*) under section 95 of the Public Health Act 1936 by way of contravening a nuisance order relating to noise; or
(*c*) under section 80(4) of the Environmental Protection Act 1990,

as if it were an offence against this Part of this Act.

[Control of Pollution Act 1974, s 74 as amended by the Criminal Justice Act 1982, ss 35, 38 and 46 and the Environmental Protection Act 1990, Sch 15.]

## PART V[1]

## SUPPLEMENTARY PROVISIONS

### *Legal proceedings*

7.9823 85. **Appeals to Crown Court or Court of Session against decisions of magistrates' court or sheriff** (1) An appeal against any decision of a magistrates' court in pursuance of this Act (other than a decision made in criminal proceedings) shall lie to the Crown Court at the instance of any party to the proceedings in which the decision was given if such an appeal does not lie to the Crown Court by virtue of any other enactment.

(2) *Scotland.*

(3) Where a person appeals to the Crown Court or the Court of Session against a decision of a magistrates' court or the sheriff dismissing an appeal against a notice served in pursuance of this Act which was suspended pending determination of that appeal, the notice shall again be suspended pending the determination of the appeal to the Crown Court or Court of Session.

1 Part V contains ss 85–98.

7.9824 87. **Miscellaneous provisions relating to legal proceedings** (1) When an offence under this Act which has been committed by a body corporate is proved to have been committed with the consent or connivance of, or to be attributable to any neglect on the part of, any director, manager, secretary or other similar officer of the body corporate or any person who was purporting to act in any such capacity, he as well as the body corporate shall be guilty of that offence and be

liable to be proceeded against and punished accordingly.
Where the affairs of a body corporate are managed by its members the preceding provisions of this subsection shall apply in relation to the acts and defaults of a member in connection with his functions of management as if he were a director of the body corporate.

(2) Where the commission by any person of an offence under this Act is due to the act or default of some other person, that other person shall be guilty of the offence; and a person may be charged with and convicted of an offence by virtue of this subsection whether or not proceedings for the offence are taken against any other person.

(3) *Scotland.*

(4) Where an appeal against a decision of a relevant authority lies to a magistrates' court by virtue of any provision of this Act, it shall be the duty of the authority to include in any document by which it notifies the decision to the person concerned a statement indicating that such an appeal lies as aforesaid and specifying the time within which it must be brought.

(5) Where on an appeal to any court against or arising out of a decision of a relevant authority in pursuance of this Act the court varies or reverses the decision it shall be the duty of the authority to act in accordance with the court's decision.

(6) A judge of any court and a justice of the peace shall not be disqualified from acting, in cases arising under this Act by reason of his being, as one of several ratepayers or as one of any other class of persons, liable in common with the others to contribute to or be benefited by any rate or fund out of which any expenses of a relevant authority are to be defrayed.

[Control of Pollution Act 1974, s 87 as amended by the Criminal Law Act 1977, Sch 13, the Magistrates' Courts Act 1980, Sch 7 and the Environment Act 1995, Sch 24.]

*Miscellaneous*

7.9825 **91. Rights of entry and inspection etc** (1) Any person authorised in writing in that behalf by a relevant authority may at any reasonable time—

(*a*) enter upon any land or vessel for the purpose of—

(i) performing any function conferred on the authority or that person by virtue of this Act, or

(ii) determining whether, and if so what manner, such a function should be performed, or

(iii) determining whether any provision of this Act or of an instrument made by virtue of this Act is being complied with;

(*b*) carry out such inspections, measurements and tests on the land or vessel or of any articles on it and take away such samples of the land or articles as he considers appropriate for such a purpose.

(2) If it is shown to the satisfaction of a justice of the peace on sworn information in writing—

(*a*) that admission to any land or vessel which a person is entitled to enter in pursuance of the preceding subsection has been refused to that person or that refusal is apprehended or that the land or vessel is unoccupied or that the occupier is temporarily absent or that the case is one of emergency or that an application for admission would defeat the object of the entry; and

(*b*) that there is reasonable ground for entry upon the land or vessel for the purpose for which entry is required,

then, subject to the following subsection, the justice may by warrant under his hand authorise that person to enter the land or vessel, if need be by force.

(3) A justice of the peace shall not issue a warrant in pursuance of the preceding subsection in respect of any land or vessel unless he is satisfied—

(*a*) that admission to the land or vessel in pursuance of subsection (1) of this section was sought after not less than seven days notice of the intended entry had been served on the occupier; or

(*b*) that admission to the land or vessel in pursuance of that subsection was sought in an emergency and was refused by or on behalf of the occupier; or

(*c*) that the land or vessel is unoccupied; or

(*d*) that an application for admission to the land or vessel would defeat the object of the entry.

(4) A warrant issued in pursuance of this section shall continue in force until the purpose for which the entry is required has been satisfied.

[Control of Pollution Act 1974, s 91.]

7.9826 **92. Provisions supplementary to s 91** (1) A person authorised to enter upon any land or vessel in pursuance of the preceding section shall, if so required, produce evidence of his authority before he enters upon the land or vessel.

(2) A person so authorised may take with him on to the land or vessel in question such other persons and such equipment as may be necessary.

(3) Admission to any land or vessel used for residential purposes and admission with heavy equipment to any other land or vessel shall not, except in an emergency or in a case where the land or vessel is unoccupied, be demanded as of right in pursuance of subsection (1) of the preceding section unless a notice of the intended entry has been served on the occupier not less than seven

days before the demand.

(4) A person who, in the exercise of powers conferred on him by virtue of the preceding section or this section, enters upon any land or vessel which is unoccupied or of which the occupier is temporarily absent shall leave the land or vessel as effectually secured against trespassers as he found it.

(5) *Compensation.*

(6) A person who wilfully obstructs another person acting in the exercise of any powers conferred on the other person by virtue of the preceding section or this section shall be guilty of an offence and liable on summary conviction to a fine not exceeding **level 3** on the standard scale.

(7) In the preceding section and this section any reference to an emergency is a reference to a case where a person requiring entry to any land or vessel has reasonable cause to believe that circumstances exist which are likely to endanger life or health and that immediate entry to the land or vessel is necessary to verify the existence of those circumstances or to ascertain their cause or to effect a remedy.

[Control of Pollution Act 1974, s 92 as amended by the Criminal Justice Act 1982, ss 38 and 46.]

7.9827 **93. Power of authorities to obtain information** (1) Subject to the following subsection, a relevant authority may serve on any person a notice requiring him to furnish to the authority, within a period or at times specified in the notice and in a form so specified, any information so specified which the authority reasonably considers that it needs for the purposes of any function conferred on the authority by this Act.

(2) Provision may be made by regulations for restricting the information which may be required in pursuance of the preceding subsection and for determining the form in which the information is to be so required.

(3) A person who—

(*a*) fails without reasonable excuse to comply with the requirements of a notice served on him in pursuance of this section; or

(*b*) in furnishing any information in compliance with such a notice, makes any statement which he knows to be false or misleading in a material particular or recklessly makes any statement which is false or misleading in a material particular,

shall be guilty of an offence.

(3A) A person guilty of an offence under this section shall be liable[1]—

(*a*) on summary conviction, to a fine not exceeding **the statutory maximum**; or

(*b*) on conviction on indictment, to a **fine** or to imprisonment for a term not exceeding **two years**, or to **both**.

[Control of Pollution Act 1974, s 93 as amended by the Criminal Justice Act 1982, ss 38 and 46 and the Environment Act 1995, Sch 19.]

---

1 For procedure in respect of an offence which is triable either way, see the Magistrates' Courts Act 1980 ss 17A–21, in PART I: MAGISTRATES' COURTS, PROCEDURE, ante.

7.9828 **94. Prohibition of disclosure of information** (1) If a person discloses information relating to any trade secret used in carrying on a particular undertaking and the information has been given to him or obtained by him by virtue of this Act he shall, subject to the following subsection, be guilty of an offence and liable on summary conviction to a fine not exceeding **level 5** on the standard scale.

(2) A person shall not be guilty of an offence under the preceding subsection by virtue of the disclosure of any information if—

(*a*) the disclosure is made—

(i) in the performance of his duty, or

(ii) in pursuance of section 79(1)(*b*)[1] of this Act, or

(iii) with the consent in writing of a person having a right to disclose the information; or

(*b*) the information is of a kind prescribed for the purposes of this paragraph and, if regulations made for those purposes provide that information of that kind may only be disclosed in pursuance of the regulations to prescribed persons, the disclosure is to a prescribed person.

[Control of Pollution Act 1974, s 94 as amended by the Criminal Justice Act 1982, ss 38 and 46.]

---

1 Section 79(1)(*b*) relates to arrangements by a local authority for the publication of information on the problem of air pollution.

7.9829 **98. Interpretation of Part V** In this Part of this Act—

"functions" includes powers and duties; and

"relevant authority" means—

(*a*) in England, the Secretary of State, a county council, a district council, a London borough council, the Common Council of the City of London, the Sub-Treasurer of the Inner Temple and Under Treasurer of the Middle Temple and, for the purposes of sections 91 to 93 of this Act, a sewerage undertaker, any authority established by the Waste Regulation and Disposal (Authorities) Order 1985;

(*aa*) in Wales, the Secretary of State, a county council or a county borough council and, for the purposes of sections 91 to 93 of this Act, a sewerage undertaker; and

(*b*) *Scotland.*

[Control of Pollution Act 1974, s 98 as amended by the Local Government Act 1985, Sch 17, the Water Act 1989, Schs 25 and 27 and the Local Government (Wales) Act 1994, Sch 9.]

## PART VI[1]

## MISCELLANEOUS AND GENERAL

*Miscellaneous*

7.9830 **105. Interpretation etc—general** (1) In this Act—

"the Alkali Act" means the Alkali, etc Works Regulation Act 1906;*

"county", "county borough" and "district", except in relation to Scotland, have the same meanings as in the Local Government Act 1972;

"mine" and "quarry" have the same meanings as in the Mines and Quarries Act 1954;

"modifications" includes additions, omissions and amendments and "modify" and cognate expressions shall be construed accordingly;

"notice" means notice in writing;

"owner", except in relation to Scotland, means the person for the time being receiving the rackrent of the premises in connection with which the word is used, whether on his own account or as agent or trustee for another person, or who would so receive the rackrent if the premises were let at a rackrent;

"premises" includes land;

"prescribed" means prescribed by regulations;

"regulations" means regulations made by the Secretary of State;

"trade effluent" includes any liquid (either with or without particles of matter in suspension in it) which is discharged from premises used for carrying on any trade or industry, other than surface water and domestic sewage, and for the purposes of this definition any premises wholly or mainly used (whether for profit or not) for agricultural or horticultural purposes or for scientific research or experiment shall be deemed to be premises used for carrying on a trade; and

"vessel" includes a hovercraft within the meaning of the Hovercraft Act 1968.

(2) Except so far as this Act expressly provides otherwise and subject to the provisions of section 33 of the Interpretation Act 1889[2] (which relates to offences under two or more laws), nothing in this Act—

(*a*) confers a right of action in any civil proceedings (other than proceedings for the recovery of a fine) in respect of any contravention of this Act or an instrument made in pursuance of this Act;

(*b*) affects any restriction imposed by or under any other enactment, whether public, local or private; or

(*c*) derogates from any right of action or other remedy (whether civil or criminal) in proceedings instituted otherwise than under this Act.

(3) In so far as any interest in Crown land is not an interest belonging to Her Majesty or a Crown interest or a Duchy interest, this Act shall apply to the land as if it were not Crown land; and expressions used in this subsection and subsection (1) of section 293 of the Town and Country Planning Act 1990 or, in relation to Scotland, subsection (7) of section 253 of the Town and Country Planning (Scotland) Act 1972 have the same meanings in this subsection as in that subsection.

(4) References in this Act to any enactment are references to it as amended by or under any other enactment.

[Control of Pollution Act 1974, s 105 as amended by the Planning (Consequential Provisions) Act 1990, Sch 2 and the Local Government (Wales) Act 1994, Sch 9.]

* **Definition repealed by the Environmental Protection Act 1990, Sch 16 from a day to be appointed.**

1 Part VI contains ss 99–109.

2 Now s 18 of the Interpretation Act 1978.

# Refuse Disposal (Amenity) Act 1978

(1978 c 3)

*Control of dumping*

7.9831 ***1. Provision by local authorities for disposal of refuse*** *Duty on local authority[1] to provide places for deposit of non-business refuse.**

[Refuse Disposal (Amenity) Act 1978, s 1 amended by the Local Government Act 1985, Sch 6, SI 1985/1984 and SI 1986/564—summarised.]

* **Section 1 was repealed by The Environmental Protection Act 1990 (Commencement No 19) Order 2012, SI 2012/898.**

1 In Greater London or a metropolitan county, functions conferred on local authorities by this Act may be discharged by a single authority established by order of the Secretary of State to act on behalf of the councils where joint arrangements for waste disposal can with advantage be made (Local Government Act 1985, s 10).

7.9832 **2. Penalty for unauthorised dumping** (1) Any person who, without lawful authority—

(*a*) abandons on any land in the open air, or on any other land forming part of a highway, a motor vehicle or anything which formed part of a motor vehicle and was removed from it in the course of dismantling the vehicle on the land; or

(*b*) abandons on any such land any thing other than a motor vehicle, being a thing which he has brought to the land for the purpose of abandoning it there,

shall be guilty of an offence and liable on summary conviction to a fine of an amount not exceeding **level 4** on the standard scale or imprisonment for a term not exceeding **three months** * or **both**.

(2) For the purposes of subsection (1) above, a person who leaves any thing on any land in such circumstances or for such a period that he may reasonably be assumed to have abandoned it or to have brought it to the land for the purpose of abandoning it there shall be deemed to have abandoned it there or, as the case may be, to have brought it to the land for the purpose unless the contrary is shown.

(3) *Scotland.*

[Refuse Disposal (Amenity) Act 1978, s 2 as amended by the Criminal Justice Act 1982, ss 35, 38 and 46.]

* **Words substituted by the Criminal Justice Act 2003, Sch 37 from a date to be appointed.**

7.9833 **2A. Fixed penalty notices for offence of abandoning vehicles** (1) Where on any occasion it appears to an authorised officer of a local authority that a person has committed an offence under section 2(1)(*a*) above in the area of that authority, the officer may give that person a notice offering him the opportunity of discharging any liability to conviction for the offence by payment of a fixed penalty to the authority.

(2) Where a person is given a notice under this section in respect of an offence—

(*a*) no proceedings may be instituted for that offence before the expiration of the period of fourteen days following the date of the notice; and

(*b*) he may not be convicted of that offence if he pays the fixed penalty before the expiration of the period.

(3) A notice under this section must give such particulars of the circumstances alleged to constitute the offence as are necessary for giving reasonable information of the offence.

(4) A notice under this section must also state—

(*a*) the period during which, by virtue of subsection (2) above, proceedings will not be taken for the offence;

(*b*) the amount of the fixed penalty; and

(*c*) the person to whom and the address at which the fixed penalty may be paid.

(5) Without prejudice to payment by any other method, payment of the fixed penalty may be made by pre-paying and posting a letter containing the amount of the penalty (in cash or otherwise) to the person mentioned in subsection (4)(*c*) above at the address so mentioned.

(6) Where a letter is sent in accordance with subsection (5) above payment is to be regarded as having been made at the time at which that letter would be delivered in the ordinary course of post.

(7) The form of a notice under this section is to be such as the appropriate person may by order prescribe.

(8) The fixed penalty payable to a local authority under this section is, subject to subsection (9) below, £200.

(9) The appropriate person may by order substitute a different amount for the amount for the time being specified in subsection (8) above.

(10) The local authority to which a fixed penalty is payable under this section may make provision for treating it as having been paid if a lesser amount is paid before the end of a period specified by the authority.

(11) The appropriate person may by regulations[1] restrict the extent to which, and the circumstances in which, a local authority may make provision under subsection (10) above.

(12) An order or regulations under this section may make different provision for different purposes and in relation to different areas.

(13) In any proceedings a certificate which—

(*a*) purports to be signed on behalf of the chief finance officer of the local authority, and

(*b*) states that payment of a fixed penalty was or was not received by a date specified in the certificate,

is evidence of the facts stated.

(14) In this section—

"authorised officer", in relation to a local authority, means an employee of the authority who is authorised in writing by the authority for the purposes of giving notices under this section;

"chief finance officer", in relation to a local authority, means the person having responsibility for the financial affairs of the authority.

[Refuse Disposal (Amenity) Act 1978, s 2A as inserted by the Clean Neighbourhoods and Environment Act 2005, s 10.]

1 The Environmental Offences (Fixed Penalties) (Miscellaneous Provisions) Regulations 2007, SI 2007/175 amended by SI 2012/1151; the Environmental Offences (Use of Fixed Penalty Receipts) (Wales) Regulations 2007, SI 2007/739 amended by SI 2008/663; the Environmental Offences (Use of Fixed Penalty Receipts) Regulations 2007, SI

2007/901 and the Environmental Offences (Fixed Penalties) (Miscellaneous Provisions) (Wales) Regulations 2008, SI 2008/663 have been made.

7.9834 **2B. Fixed penalty notices: power to require name and address** (1) If an authorised officer of a local authority proposes to give a person a notice under section 2A above, the officer may require the person to give him his name and address.

(2) A person commits an offence if—

(*a*) he fails to give his name and address when required to do so under subsection (1) above, or

(*b*) he gives a false or inaccurate name or address in response to a requirement under that subsection.

(3) A person guilty of an offence under subsection (2) above is liable on summary conviction to a fine not exceeding level 3 on the standard scale.

(4) In this section "authorised officer" has the same meaning as in section 2A above.

[Refuse Disposal (Amenity) Act 1978, s 2B as inserted by the Clean Neighbourhoods and Environment Act 2005, s 10.]

7.9835 **2C. Use of fixed penalties under section 2A** (1) This section applies in relation to amounts paid to a local authority in pursuance of notices under section 2A above (its "fixed penalty receipts").

(2) A local authority may use its fixed penalty receipts only for the purposes of—

(*a*) its functions under this Act;

(*b*) its functions under sections 99 to 102 of the Road Traffic Regulation Act 1984;

(*c*) its functions relating to the enforcement of sections 3 and 4 of the Clean Neighbourhoods and Environment Act 2005; and

(*d*) such other of its functions as may be specified in regulations made by the appropriate person.

(3) Regulations under subsection (2)(*d*) above may in particular have the effect that a local authority may use its fixed penalty receipts for the purposes of any of its functions.

(4) A local authority must supply the appropriate person with such information relating to its use of its fixed penalty receipts as the appropriate person may require.

(5) The appropriate person may by regulations—

(*a*) make provision for what a local authority is to do with its fixed penalty receipts—

(i) pending their being used for the purposes of functions of the authority referred to in subsection (2) above;

(ii) if they are not so used before such time after their receipt as may be specified by the regulations;

(*b*) make provision for accounting arrangements in respect of a local authority's fixed penalty receipts.

(6) The provision that may be made under subsection (5)(*a*)(ii) above includes (in particular) provision for the payment of sums to a person (including the appropriate person) other than the authority.

(7) Before making regulations under this section, the appropriate person must consult—

(*a*) the authorities to which the regulations are to apply;

(*b*) such other persons as the appropriate person thinks fit.

(8) The powers to make regulations conferred by this section are, for the purposes of subsection (1) of section 100 of the Local Government Act 2003, to be regarded as included among the powers mentioned in subsection (2) of that section.

[Refuse Disposal (Amenity) Act 1978, s 2C as inserted by the Clean Neighbourhoods and Environment Act 2005, s 10.]

*Abandoned vehicles and other refuse*

7.9836 **3, 4, 4A.** *Removal and disposal of abandoned vehicles*[1]*, guidance.*

---

1 The removal of other refuse, which does not affect the courts, is dealt with by s 7. There is no provision similar to s 5(3) applying to refuse other than a motor vehicle. The Removal and Disposal of Vehicles Regulations 1986, SI 1986/183 amended by SI 1993/278 and 1708, SI 1994/1503, SI 1996/1003, SI 2004/746 and 2777 (E), SI 2005/3252 (W) and SI 2008/612 (W) have been made.

7.9837 **5. Recovery of expenses connected with removed vehicles** (1) Where a vehicle is removed in pursuance of section 3(1) above the appropriate authority shall be entitled to recover from any person responsible—

(*a*) such charges as may be prescribed[1] in respect of the removal of the vehicle; and

(*b*) charges ascertained by reference to a prescribed scale in respect of any period during which the vehicle is in the custody of the authority; and

(*c*) where the vehicle is disposed of in pursuance of section 4 above, charges determined in the prescribed manner in respect of its disposal.

(2) Any sum recoverable by virtue of this section shall be recoverable as a simple contract debt in any court of competent jurisdiction.

(3) Without prejudice to subsection (2) above, the court by which a person is convicted of an offence under section 2(1) above in respect of a motor vehicle may, on the application of the

appropriate authority and in addition to any other order made by the court in relation to that person, order him to pay to the authority any sum which, in the opinion of the court, the authority are entitled to recover from him under this section in respect of the vehicles.

(4) In this section—

"the appropriate authority" means—

(*a*) in the case of a vehicle removed in pursuance of section 3(1) above by a local authority in England other than the council of a non-metropolitan district, or by a local authority in Wales, the local authority; and

(*b*) in the case of a vehicle so removed by the council of a non-metropolitan district in England, the county council; and

"person responsible", in relation to a vehicle, means—

(*a*) the owner of the vehicle at the time when it was put in the place from which it was so removed, unless he shows that he was not concerned in and did not know of its being put there;

(*b*) any person by whom it was put in the place aforesaid;

(*c*) any person convicted of an offence under section 2(1) above in consequence of the putting of the vehicle in the place aforesaid.

(5) For the purposes of subsection (1)(*b*) above—

(*a*) *Repealed*;

(*b*) a vehicle so removed by the council of a non-metropolitan district in England shall be treated as in the custody of the county council while it was in the custody of the district council by whom it was so removed.

[Refuse Disposal (Amenity) Act 1978, s 5 as amended by the Local Government Act 1985, Schs 6 and 17.]

---

1 These are contained in the Removal, Storage and Disposal of Vehicles (Prescribed Sums and Charges) Regulations 2008, SI 2008/2095.

7.9838 11. **Interpretation** (1) In this Act, unless the contrary intention appears, the following expressions have the following meanings, that is to say—

"appropriate person" means—

(*a*) in relation to a local authority in England, the Secretary of State;

(*b*) in relation to a local authority in Wales, the National Assembly for Wales;

"the Common Council" means the Common Council of the City of London;

"licence" means in relation to a vehicle, a licence issued for the vehicle under the Vehicle Excise and Registration Act 1994 (including a nil licence within the meaning of that Act);

"local authority" means—

(*a*) in relation to England, a district council, London borough council or the Common Council;

(*b*) *Scotland*;

(*c*) in relation to Wales, a county council or county borough council;

"motor vehicle" means a mechanically propelled vehicle intended or adapted for use on roads, whether or not it is in a fit state for such use, and includes any trailer intended or adapted for use as an attachment to such a vehicle, any chassis or body, with or without wheels, appearing to have formed part of such a vehicle or trailer and anything attached to such a vehicle or trailer;

"London waste disposal authority" means an authority established by Part II, III, IV or V of Schedule 1 to the Waste Regulation and Disposal (Authorities) Order 1985;

"motor vehicle" means a mechanically propelled vehicle intended or adapted for use on roads, whether or not it is in a fit state for such use, and includes any trailer intended or adapted for use as an attachment to such a vehicle, any chassis or body, with or without wheels, appearing to have formed part of such a vehicle or trailer and anything attached to such a vehicle or trailer;

"owner", in relation to a motor vehicle which is the subject of a hiring agreement or hire-purchase agreement, includes the person entitled to possession of the vehicle under the agreement;

"prescribed" means prescribed by regulations made by the Secretary of State;

"the relevant date" has the meaning given to it by section 13(3) below.

(2) Any reference in this Act to an enactment is a reference to it as amended or applied by or under any other enactment, including this Act.

[Refuse Disposal (Amenity) Act 1978, s 11 as amended by the Local Government (Wales) Act 1994, Sch 9, the Vehicle Excise and Registration Act 1994, Sch 3 and the Clean Neighbourhoods and Environment Act 2005, ss 12 and 14.]

## Litter Act 1983

(1983 c 35)

7.9839 5. **Litter bins in England and Wales**[1] (1) A litter authority[2] in England and Wales may provide and maintain in any street or public place receptacles for refuse or litter (in this section referred to as "litter bins").

(2) It shall be the duty of a litter authority in England and Wales to make arrangements for the regular emptying and cleansing of any litter bins provided or maintained by them under this section or under section 185 of the Highways Act 1980; and such an authority shall have power to

cleanse and empty litter bins provided in any street or public place by them or any other person.

(3) The regular emptying mentioned in subsection (2) above shall be sufficiently frequent to ensure that no such litter bin or its contents shall become a nuisance or give reasonable ground for complaint.

(4) In any place where a litter bin may be provided or maintained under this section or under section 185 of the Highways Act 1980, a litter authority may put up notices about the leaving of refuse and litter, and for that purpose may, subject to the provisions of this section, erect and maintain notice boards.

(5) Subject to section 13 of the City of London (Various Powers) Act 1971 (which empowers the Common Council of the City of London to affix litter bins), a litter authority shall not have power under this section to place any litter bin or any notice board—

(*a*) on any land forming part of an open space as defined in the Open Spaces Act 1906 which is provided by or under the management and control of some other litter authority or a parish meeting, without the consent of that authority or meeting, or

(*b*) on any other land not forming part of a street, without the consent of the owner and of the occupier of that land.

(6) The powers conferred by this section shall only be exercisable with the consent of the persons mentioned in the Table in paragraph 1 of Schedule 1 to this Act, and paragraphs 2 and 3 of that Schedule shall have effect in relation to those consents.

(7) A litter authority may sell refuse or litter removed by them from any litter bins.

(8) A litter authority may not, under this section, do anything that is unlawful under the law relating to ancient monuments or to town and country planning.

(9) Any person who wilfully removes or otherwise interferes with any litter bin or notice board provided or erected under this section or section 185 of the Highways Act 1980 shall be liable on summary conviction to a fine not exceeding **level 1** on the standard scale.

(10) The court by which a person is convicted under subsection (9) above may order him to pay a sum not exceeding **£20** as compensation to the litter authority concerned, and any such order shall be enforceable in the same way as an order for costs to be paid by the offender.

(11) This section applies to a receptacle provided under section 76 of the Public Health Act 1936 or section 51 of the Public Health Act 1961 as if it had been provided under this section.

[Litter Act 1983, s 5.]

---

[1] Sections 283–285, 288, 304, 305, 341 and 343 of the Public Health Act 1936, title PUBLIC HEALTH, post, apply in relation to this section, s 6 and Sch 1 to this Act as if ss 5 and 6 and that Schedule were contained in the Act of 1936 (s 6(7)). In Greater London or a metropolitan county, functions conferred by ss 5 and 6 of this Act may be discharged by a single authority established by order of the Secretary of State to act on behalf of the councils where joint arrangements for waste disposal can with advantage be made (Local Government Act 1985, s 10).

[2] In this section "litter authority" includes the Council of the Isles of Scilly (s 6(8)).

**7.9840 6.** *Provisions supplementary to section 5.*

**7.9841 9.** *Orders.*

**7.9842 10. Interpretation** (1) In this Act—

"joint body" means a joint body constituted solely of two or more such councils as are mentioned in paragraphs (*a*) to (*f*) of the definition of "litter authority" below;

"litter authority", in relation to England and Wales, means, except so far as is otherwise provided—

(*a*) a county council,

(*b*) a district council,

(*c*) a London borough council,

(*d*) the Common Council of the City of London,

(*e*) a parish council,

(*f*) a community council,

(*g*) a joint body,

(*h*) *repealed,*

(*i*) the Sub-Treasurer of the Inner Temple, or

(*j*) the Under Treasurer of the Middle Temple;

(2) In the application of this Act in relation to Wales, any reference to a county shall be read as including a reference to a county borough and any reference to a county council shall be read as including a reference to a county borough council.

[Litter Act 1983, s 10 as amended by the Statute Law (Repeals) Act 1993, Sch 1, the Local Government (Wales) Act 1994, s 6 and Sch 9 and the Environment Act 1995, Sch 24.]

**7.9843 11. Isles of Scilly** Sections 3 and 4 above shall have effect in their application to the Isles of Scilly with such modifications, additions, omissions and amendments as the Secretary of State may by order specify.

[Litter Act 1983, s 11.]

**7.9844 12–13.** *Consequential amendments and repeals; Short title commencement and extent.*

SCHEDULE 1

*Consents required under Section 5*

# Public Health (Control of Disease) Act 1984

(1984 c 22)

## Part I

## Administrative Provisions

7.9845 Part I of the Act (ss 1–9) provides for local authorities to carry the Act into execution, with certain powers being assigned to port health authorities as constituted by Order of the Secretary of State. Vessels in inland and coastal waters are subject to the jurisdiction of the appropriate authority, as if they were houses, buildings or premises and the master were the occupier; this does not apply to naval and foreign government vessels, nor to certain provisions of the Act such as those applying to common lodging houses, burial and cremation, Part V (other than s 56) and Part VI.

## Part II[1]

## Control of Disease

*General*

[1] Part II comprises ss 10–45.

7.9846 **13. Regulations for control of certain diseases** Powers of the Secretary of State to make regulations[1].*

[Public Health (Control of Disease) Act 1984, s 13 amended by the National Health Service and Community Care Act 1990, Sch 9, the Local Government (Wales) Act 1994, Sch 9, and the Health Authorities Act 1995, Sch 1 and SI 2000/90—summarised.]

* **Repealed by the Health and Social Care Act 2008, Sch 15 from a date to be appointed.**

[1] The Public Health (Infectious Diseases) Regulations 1988, SI 1988/1546 amended by SI 2002/2469 apply certain sections of this Act to certain diseases. In particular s 38 is applied, with modification, to the acquired immune deficiency syndrome.

7.9847 **15. Contravention of regulations under s 13** Any person who wilfully neglects or refuses to obey or carry out, or obstructs the execution of, any regulations made under section 13 above shall, in a case where no provision is made in the regulations for his punishment, be liable on summary conviction—

(*a*) to a fine not exceeding **level 5** on the standard scale, and

(*b*) in the case of a continuing offence, to a further fine not exceeding £50 for every day on which the offence continues after conviction.*

[Public Health (Control of Disease) Act 1984, s 15.]

* **Repealed by the Health and Social Care Act 2008, Sch 15 from a date to be appointed.**

## Part 2A

## Public Health Protection

*Introductory*

7.9848 **45A. Infection or contamination** (1) The following provisions have effect for the interpretation of this Part.

(2) "Contamination" includes radiation.

(3) Any reference to infection or contamination is a reference to infection or contamination which presents or could present significant harm to human health.

(4) Any reference to the spread of contamination includes a reference to the spread of any source of contamination.

(5) Any reference to disinfection or decontamination includes a reference to the removal of any vector, agent or source of the infection or contamination.

(6) Related expressions are to be read accordingly.

[Public Health (Control of Disease) Act 1984, s 45A as inserted by the Health and Social Care Act 2008, s 129.]

*Power to make regulations*

7.9849 **45B-45F.** *Power of the Minster to make regulations in relation to international travel and for the purpose of preventing, protection against, controlling or providing a public health response to the incidence of or spread of infection or contamination in England and Wales. Regulations may create summary offences punishable by a fine.*

*Orders that may be made by justice of the peace*

7.9850 **45G. Power to order health measures in relation to persons** (1) A justice of the peace may make an order under subsection (2) in relation to a person ("P") if the justice is satisfied that—

(*a*) P is or may be infected or contaminated,

(*b*) the infection or contamination is one which presents or could present significant harm to human health,

(*c*) there is a risk that P might infect or contaminate others, and
(*d*) it is necessary to make the order in order to remove or reduce that risk.

(2) The order may impose on or in relation to P one or more of the following restrictions or requirements—
(*a*) that P submit to medical examination;
(*b*) that P be removed to a hospital or other suitable establishment;
(*c*) that P be detained in a hospital or other suitable establishment;
(*d*) that P be kept in isolation or quarantine;
(*e*) that P be disinfected or decontaminated;
(*f*) that P wear protective clothing;
(*g*) that P provide information or answer questions about P's health or other circumstances;
(*h*) that P's health be monitored and the results reported;
(*i*) that P attend training or advice sessions on how to reduce the risk of infecting or contaminating others;
(*j*) that P be subject to restrictions on where P goes or with whom P has contact;
(*k*) that P abstain from working or trading.

(3) A justice of the peace may make an order under subsection (4) in relation to a person ("P") if the justice is satisfied that—
(*a*) P is or may be infected or contaminated,
(*b*) the infection or contamination is one which presents or could present significant harm to human health,
(*c*) there is a risk that a related party might infect or contaminate others, and
(*d*) it is necessary to make the order in order to remove or reduce that risk.

(4) The order may impose on or in relation to P a requirement that P provide information or answer questions about P's health or other circumstances (including, in particular, information or questions about the identity of a related party).

(5) "Related party" means—
(*a*) a person who has or may have infected or contaminated P, or
(*b*) a person whom P has or may have infected or contaminated.

(6) An order under this section may also order a person with parental responsibility (within the meaning of the Children Act 1989) for P to secure that P submits to or complies with the restrictions or requirements imposed by the order.

(7) The appropriate Minister must by regulations make provision about the evidence that must be available to a justice of the peace before the justice can be satisfied as mentioned in subsection (1) or (3).

(8) Any reference in this section to a person who is infected or contaminated includes a reference to a person who carries the source of an infection or contamination, and any reference to infecting or contaminating others includes a reference to passing that source to others.

[Public Health (Control of Disease) Act 1984, s 45G as inserted by the Health and Social Care Act 2008, s 129.]

7.9851 **45H. Power to order health measures in relation to things** (1) A justice of the peace may make an order under subsection (2) in relation to a thing if the justice is satisfied that—
(*a*) the thing is or may be infected or contaminated,
(*b*) the infection or contamination is one which presents or could present significant harm to human health,
(*c*) there is a risk that the thing might infect or contaminate humans, and
(*d*) it is necessary to make the order in order to remove or reduce that risk.

(2) The order may impose in relation to the thing one or more of the following restrictions or requirements—
(*a*) that the thing be seized or retained;
(*b*) that the thing be kept in isolation or quarantine;
(*c*) that the thing be disinfected or decontaminated;
(*d*) in the case of a dead body, that the body be buried or cremated;
(*e*) in any other case, that the thing be destroyed or disposed of.

(3) A justice of the peace may make an order under subsection (4) in relation to a thing if the justice is satisfied that—
(*a*) the thing is or may be infected or contaminated,
(*b*) the infection or contamination is one which presents or could present significant harm to human health,
(*c*) there is a risk that a related person or related thing might infect or contaminate humans, and
(*d*) it is necessary to make the order in order to remove or reduce that risk.

(4) The order may require—
(*a*) the owner of the thing, or
(*b*) any person who has or has had custody or control of the thing,

to provide information or answer questions about the thing (including, in particular, information or questions about where the thing has been or about the identity of any related person or the whereabouts of any related thing).

(5) "Related person" means—

(*a*) a person who has or may have infected or contaminated the thing mentioned in subsection (3)(*a*), or

(*b*) a person whom the thing has or may have infected or contaminated.

(6) "Related thing" means—

(*a*) a thing which has or may have infected or contaminated the thing mentioned in subsection (3)(*a*), or

(*b*) a thing which the thing mentioned in subsection (3)(*a*) has or may have infected or contaminated.

(7) The appropriate Minister may by regulations make provision about the evidence that must be available to a justice of the peace before the justice can be satisfied as mentioned in subsection (1) or (3).

(8) In this section—

(*a*) any reference to being infected or contaminated includes a reference to carrying the source of an infection or contamination, and

(*b*) any reference to infecting or contaminating humans, or a person or thing, includes a reference to passing the source of an infection or contamination to humans, or to the person or thing.

[Public Health (Control of Disease) Act 1984, s 45H as inserted by the Health and Social Care Act 2008, s 129.]

7.9852 **45I. Power to order health measures in relation to premises** (1) A justice of the peace may make an order under subsection (2) in relation to premises if the justice is satisfied that—

(*a*) the premises are or may be infected or contaminated,

(*b*) the infection or contamination is one which presents or could present significant harm to human health,

(*c*) there is a risk that the premises might infect or contaminate humans, and

(*d*) it is necessary to make the order in order to remove or reduce that risk.

(2) The order may impose in relation to the premises one or more of the following restrictions or requirements—

(*a*) that the premises be closed;

(*b*) that, in the case of a conveyance or movable structure, the conveyance or structure be detained;

(*c*) that the premises be disinfected or decontaminated;

(*d*) that, in the case of a building, conveyance or structure, the premises be destroyed.

(3) A justice of the peace may make an order under subsection (4) in relation to premises if the justice is satisfied that—

(*a*) the premises are or may be infected or contaminated or are or may be a place where infection or contamination was spread between persons or things,

(*b*) the infection or contamination is one which presents or could present significant harm to human health,

(*c*) there is a risk that a related person or related thing might infect or contaminate humans, and

(*d*) it is necessary to make the order in order to remove or reduce that risk.

(4) The order may require the owner or any occupier of the premises to provide information or answer questions about the premises (including, in particular, information about the identity of any related person or the whereabouts of any related thing).

(5) "Related person" means—

(*a*) a person who has or may have infected or contaminated the premises,

(*b*) a person who has or may have infected or contaminated a person who or thing which is or has been on the premises,

(*c*) a person whom the premises have or may have infected or contaminated, or

(*d*) a person who has or may have been infected or contaminated by a person who or thing which is or has been on the premises.

(6) "Related thing" means—

(*a*) a thing which has or may have infected or contaminated the premises,

(*b*) a thing which has or may have infected or contaminated a person who or thing which is or has been on the premises,

(*c*) a thing which the premises have or may have infected or contaminated, or

(*d*) a thing which has or may have been infected or contaminated by a person who or thing which is or has been on the premises.

(7) The appropriate Minister may by regulations make provision about the evidence that must be available to a justice of the peace before the justice can be satisfied as mentioned in subsection (1) or (3).

(8) In this section—

(*a*) any reference to being infected or contaminated includes a reference to carrying the source of an infection or contamination, and

(*b*) any reference to infecting or contaminating humans, or a person, thing or premises, includes a reference to passing the source of an infection or contamination to humans, or to the person, thing or premises.

[Public Health (Control of Disease) Act 1984, s 45I as inserted by the Health and Social Care Act 2008, s 129.]

**7.9853 45J. Orders in respect of groups** (1) The powers in sections 45G, 45H and 45I include power to make an order in relation to a group of persons, things or premises.

(2) For those purposes, the sections have effect as follows.

(3) In section 45G—

(*a*) in subsections (1)(*a*) and (*c*) and (3)(*a*), the reference to P is a reference to each person in the group, and

(*b*) in subsections (2) and (4), any reference to P is a reference to any one or more of the persons in the group.

(4) In section 45H—

(*a*) in subsections (1)(*a*) and (*c*) and (3)(*a*), the reference to the thing is a reference to each thing in the group, and

(*b*) in subsections (2) and (4) any reference to the thing is a reference to any one or more of the things in the group.

(5) In section 45I—

(*a*) in subsections (1)(*a*) and (*c*) and (3)(*a*), the reference to the premises is a reference to each set of premises in the group, and

(*b*) in subsections (2) and (4), any reference to the premises is a reference to any one or more of the sets of premises in the group.

[Public Health (Control of Disease) Act 1984, s 45J as inserted by the Health and Social Care Act 2008, s 129.]

**7.9854 45K. Part 2A orders: supplementary** (1) This section makes further provision about orders under sections 45G, 45H and 45I (referred to in this Part as "Part 2A orders").

(2) A Part 2A order may include, in addition to the restrictions or requirements mentioned in the provision under which it is made, such other restrictions or requirements as the justice considers necessary for the purpose of reducing or removing the risk in question.

(3) A restriction or requirement contained in a Part 2A order may be expressed to take effect subject to conditions specified in the order.

(4) Two or more Part 2A orders may be combined in a single order.

(5) A Part 2A order may contain such directions as the justice considers appropriate to give effect to it.

(6) Without prejudice to subsection (5)—

(*a*) a Part 2A order may, if the justice is satisfied as mentioned in subsection (4) of section 61, authorise anything which may be authorised by warrant under subsection (3) of that section, and

(*b*) if the order does so, section 62(1) and (1A) have effect as if—

(i) the order were a warrant issued under section 61, and

(ii) the person so authorised were a proper officer.

(7) A Part 2A order may order the payment of compensation or expenses in connection with the taking of measures pursuant to the order.

(8) A Part 2A order is authority for those persons to whom it is addressed to do such things as may be necessary to give effect to it.

[Public Health (Control of Disease) Act 1984, s 45K as inserted by the Health and Social Care Act 2008, s 129.]

**7.9855 45L. Period for which Part 2A order may be in force** (1) A Part 2A order must specify the period for which any restriction or requirement imposed by or under the order is to remain in force.

(2) That period may be extended by further order of a justice of the peace.

(3) In relation to restrictions or requirements mentioned in section 45G(2)(*c*) or (*d*), neither the period specified under subsection (1) nor the period of any extension under subsection (2) may exceed 28 days or such shorter period as the appropriate Minister may by regulations prescribe.

(4) The appropriate Minister may by regulations prescribe, in relation to any other restrictions or requirements, the maximum period which may be specified under subsection (1) and the maximum period of any extension under subsection (2).

[Public Health (Control of Disease) Act 1984, s 45L as inserted by the Health and Social Care Act 2008, s 129.]

**7.9856 45M. Procedure for making, varying and revoking Part 2A orders** (1) The power of a justice of the peace to make a Part 2A order is exercisable on the application of a local authority.

(2) Local authorities must co-operate with each other in deciding which of them should apply for a Part 2A order in any particular case.

(3) The appropriate Minister must by regulations require a local authority to give notice to such persons as may be prescribed by the regulations of the making of an application for a Part 2A order, but this is subject to subsection (4).

(4) If a justice of the peace considers it necessary to do so, the justice may make a Part 2A order without a person having been given such notice as is otherwise required to be given to that

person under rules of court or regulations under subsection (3).

(5) A Part 2A order may be varied or revoked by a justice of the peace on the application of—

(*a*) an affected person,

(*b*) a local authority, or

(*c*) any other authority with the function of executing or enforcing the order in question.

(6) In the case of an order under section 45G, the following persons are affected persons—

(*a*) P,

(*b*) a person with parental responsibility (within the meaning of the Children Act 1989) for P,

(*c*) P's husband, wife or civil partner,

(*d*) a person living with P as P's husband, wife or civil partner, and

(*e*) such other persons as may be prescribed by regulations.

(7) In the case of an order under section 45H(2), the following persons are affected persons—

(*a*) the owner of the thing,

(*b*) any person with custody or control of the thing, and

(*c*) such other persons as may be prescribed by regulations.

(8) In the case of an order under section 45I(2), the following persons are affected persons—

(*a*) the owner of the premises,

(*b*) any occupier of the premises, and

(*c*) such other persons as may be prescribed by regulations.

(9) In the case of an order under section 45H(4) or 45I(4), the person required to provide information or answer questions and such other persons as may be prescribed by regulations are affected persons.

(10) Variation or revocation of a Part 2A order does not invalidate anything done under the order prior to the variation or revocation.

(11) In this section "regulations" means regulations made by the appropriate Minister.

[Public Health (Control of Disease) Act 1984, s 45M as inserted by the Health and Social Care Act 2008, s 129.]

7.9857 **45N. Power to make further provision by regulations** (1) The appropriate Minister may by regulations make provision about the taking of measures pursuant to Part 2A orders.

(2) The regulations may in particular make provision about—

(*a*) the type of investigation which may be carried out as part of a medical examination;

(*b*) the manner in which measures are to be taken;

(*c*) who is to be responsible for executing and enforcing measures;

(*d*) who is to be liable for the costs of measures;

(*e*) the payment of compensation or expenses in connection with the taking of measures.

(3) But the regulations may not confer functions on officers of Revenue and Customs to execute or enforce Part 2A orders unless the regulations are made with the consent of the Commissioners for Her Majesty's Revenue and Customs.

[Public Health (Control of Disease) Act 1984, s 45N as inserted by the Health and Social Care Act 2008, s 129.]

7.9858 **45O. Enforcement of Part 2A orders** (1) A person commits an offence if the person—

(*a*) fails without reasonable excuse to comply with a restriction or requirement imposed by or under a Part 2A order, or

(*b*) wilfully obstructs anyone acting in the execution of a Part 2A order.

(2) A person guilty of an offence under subsection (1) is liable on summary conviction to a fine.

(3) If—

(*a*) a person is convicted of an offence under subsection (1), and

(*b*) the court by which the person is convicted is satisfied that the failure or wilful obstruction constituting the offence has caused premises or things to become infected or contaminated or otherwise damaged them in a material way,

the court may, if it considers it appropriate to do so, order the person to take or pay for such remedial action as may be specified in the order.

(4) Subsection (5) applies if—

(*a*) a Part 2A order imposes a requirement that a person be detained or kept in isolation or quarantine in a place, and

(*b*) the person leaves that place contrary to the requirement.

(5) A constable may take the person into custody and return the person to that place.

(6) But a person may not be taken into custody under subsection (5) after expiry of the period for which the requirement is in force.

[Public Health (Control of Disease) Act 1984, s 45O as inserted by the Health and Social Care Act 2008, s 129 and amended by SI 2015/664.]

**45P–45R.** *General provisions about procedure for making regulations.*

*General*

**7.9859 45S. Application to territorial sea** The provisions of this Part have effect in relation to the territorial sea adjacent to England or Wales.

[Public Health (Control of Disease) Act 1984, s 45S as inserted by the Health and Social Care Act 2008, s 129.]

**7.9860 45T. Part 2A: further definitions** (1) This Part is to be read in accordance with this section.

(2) "Enactment" means an enactment whenever passed or made, and includes an enactment comprised in subordinate legislation (within the meaning of the Interpretation Act 1978).

(3) "Medical examination" includes microbiological, radiological and toxicological tests.

(4) "Special restriction or requirement" has the meaning given by section 45C(6).

(5) "Thing" includes—

(*a*) human tissue,

(*b*) a dead body or human remains,

(*c*) animals, and

(*d*) plant material.

(6) "The appropriate Minister" means—

(*a*) the Secretary of State, as respects England (including the sea adjacent to England out as far as the seaward boundary of the territorial sea);

(*b*) the Welsh Ministers, as respects Wales (including the sea adjacent to Wales out as far as that boundary).

(7) An order made under section 158(3) of the Government of Wales Act 2006 (orders to determine boundary of the sea adjacent to Wales) applies for the purposes of subsection (6) as it applies for the purposes of that Act.

(8) Any reference to amending an enactment includes a reference to repealing, revoking or modifying the application of an enactment, and "amendment" is to be read accordingly.

(9) Any reference to giving effect to an international agreement or arrangement includes a reference to giving effect to a recommendation issued under such an agreement or arrangement.

[Public Health (Control of Disease) Act 1984, s 45T as inserted by the Health and Social Care Act 2008, s 129.]

## PART III[1]
## DISPOSAL OF DEAD BODIES

**7.9861 46.** *Burial and cremation.*

[1] Part III comprises ss 46–48.

**7.9862 47.** *Regulations about dead bodies.*

**7.9863 48. Removal of body to mortuary or for immediate burial** (1) If a justice of the peace (acting, if he deems it necessary, ex parte) is satisfied, on a certificate of the proper officer of the local authority for the district in which a dead body lies, that the retention of the body in any place would endanger the health of any person, he may order—

(*a*) that the body be removed by, and at the cost of, the local authority to a mortuary, and

(*b*) that the necessary steps be taken to secure that it is buried within a time limited by the order or, if he considers immediate burial necessary, immediately.

(2) Where an order is made under subsection (1) above, relatives or friends of the deceased person shall be deemed to comply with the order if they cause the body to be cremated within the time limited by the order or, as the case may be, immediately.

(3) An order under this section shall be an authority to any officer named in it to do all acts necessary for giving effect to the order.

[Public Health (Control of Disease) Act 1984, s 48 as amended by the Health and Social Care Act 2008, Sch 11.]

## PART IV[1]
## CANAL BOATS

**7.9864 49. Regulations as to canal boats** (1), (2) *Duty of the Secretary of State to make regulations*[2].

(3) If any regulation in force under this section is not complied with as respects a canal boat, the master of the boat, and also the owner, if he is himself in default, shall be liable on summary conviction to a fine not exceeding **level 1** on the standard scale, and to a further fine not exceeding £2 for each day after conviction on which the non-compliance continues.

[Public Health (Control of Disease) Act 1984, s 49 as amended by the Health and Social Care Act 2008, Sch 11.]

[1] Part IV comprises ss 49–53.

[2] The Canal Boats Regulations 1878 (made 20 March 1878) have effect under this provision.

**7.9865 51.** *Duties of local authorities and port health authorities under Part IV.*

**7.9866 53. Interpretation of Part IV** In this Part of this Act—

"canal" includes any river, inland navigation or lake, and any other waters situated wholly or partly within a county or county borough, whether those waters are or are not within the ebb and flow of the tide;

"canal boat" means any vessel, however propelled, which is used for the conveyance of goods along a canal, not being—

(*a*) a sailing barge which belongs to the class generally known as "Thames sailing barge" and is registered under the Merchant Shipping Act 1995, either in the Port of London or elsewhere, or

(*b*) a sea-going ship so registered, or

(*c*) a vessel used for pleasure purposes only;

"master", in relation to a canal boat, means the person having command or charge of the boat; and

"owner", in relation to a canal boat, includes a person who, though only the hirer of the boat, appoints the master and other persons working the boat.

[Public Health (Control of Disease) Act 1984, s 53, as amended by the Local Government (Wales) Act 1994, Sch 9 and the Merchant Shipping Act 1995, Sch 13.]

## PART VI[1]
## GENERAL

7.9867 **58. Form of notices and other documents** (1) All notices, orders and other documents authorised or required by or under this Act to be given, made or issued by a relevant health protection authority, and all notices and applications authorised or required by or under this Act to be given or made to or to any officer of a relevant health protection authority, shall be in writing.

(2) The Secretary of State may by regulations made by statutory instrument prescribe the form of any notice, certificate or other document to be used for the purposes of this Act, and, if forms are so prescribed, those forms or forms to the like effect may be used in all cases to which those forms are applicable.

[Public Health (Control of Disease) Act 1984, s 58 as amended by the Health and Social Care Act 2008, Sch 11.]

---

1 Part VI comprises ss 57–79.

7.9868 **59. Authentication of documents** (1) Any notice, order or other document which a relevant health protection authority are authorised or required by or under this Act to give, make or issue may be signed on behalf of the authority—

(*a*) by the proper officer of the authority as respects documents relating to matters within his province, or

(*b*) by any officer of the authority authorised by them in writing to sign documents of the particular kind or, as the case may be, the particular document.

(2) Any document purporting to bear the signature of an officer—

(*a*) expressed to hold an office by virtue of which he is under this section empowered to sign such a document, or

(*b*) expressed to be duly authorised by the relevant health protection authority to sign such a document or the particular document,

shall, for the purposes of this Act, and of any regulations and orders made under it, be deemed, until the contrary is proved, to have been duly given, made or issued by authority of the relevant health protection authority.

(3) In subsection (2) above, "signature" includes a facsimile of a signature by whatever process reproduced.

[Public Health (Control of Disease) Act 1984, s 59 as amended by the Health and Social Care Act 2008, Sch 11.]

7.9869 **60. Service of notices and other documents** Any notice, order or other document which is required or authorised by or under this Act to be given to or served on any person may, in any case for which no other provision is made by or under this Act, be given or served either—

(*a*) by delivering it to that person, or

(*b*) in the case of a coroner or the proper officer of a local authority, by leaving it or sending it in a prepaid letter addressed to him, at either his residence or his office, and, in the case of any other officer of a local authority, by leaving it, or sending it in a prepaid letter addressed to him, at his office, or

(*c*) in the case of any other person, by leaving it, or sending it in a prepaid letter addressed to him, at his usual or last known residence, or

(*d*) in the case of an incorporated company or body, by delivering it to their secretary or clerk at their registered or principal office, or by sending it in a prepaid letter addressed to him at that office, or

(*e*) in the case of a document to be given to or served on a person as being the owner of any premises by virtue of the fact that he receives the rackrent of the premises as agent for another, or would so receive it if the premises were let at a rackrent, by leaving it, or sending it in a prepaid letter addressed to him, at his place of business, or

(*f*) in the case of a document to be given to or served on the owner or the occupier of any premises, if it is not practicable after reasonable inquiry to ascertain the name and address of the person to or on whom it should be given or served, or if the premises are unoccupied, by addressing it to the person concerned by the description of "owner" or "occupier" of the premises (naming them) to which it relates, and delivering it to some person on the premises, or, if there is no person on the premises to whom it can be delivered, by affixing it, or a copy of it, to some conspicuous part of the premises.

[Public Health (Control of Disease) Act 1984, s 60 as amended by the Health and Social Care Act 2008, Sch 11.]

**7.9870 60A.** *Minister may make regulations enabling notices, orders and other documents to be given or served by an electronic communication.*

**7.9871 61. Power to enter premises** (1) Subject to the provisions of this section, any proper officer of a relevant health protection authority shall, on producing, if so required, some duly authenticated document showing his authority, have a right to enter any premises at all reasonable hours—

(*a*) for the purposes of ascertaining whether there is, or has been, any contravention of a relevant provision of this Act, or of an order made by a justice of the peace under Part 2A of this Act, which it is the function of the relevant health protection authority to enforce,

(*b*) for the purpose of ascertaining whether or not circumstances exist which would authorise or require the relevant health protection authority to take any action, or execute any work, under such a provision or in relation to such an order,

(*c*) for the purpose of taking any action, or executing any work, authorised or required by such a provision or in relation to such an order, or by any order made under such a provision, to be taken, or executed, by the relevant health protection authority, or

(*d*) generally, for the purpose of the performance by the relevant health protection authority of their functions under such a provision or in relation to such an order.

(2) Admission to any premises, shall not be demanded as of right unless twenty-four hours' notice of the intended entry has been given to the occupier.

(2A) Subsection (1) does not authorise entry to any part of premises which is used as a private dwelling (but this does not affect the power of a justice of the peace under subsection (3) to issue a warrant authorising entry to a private dwelling or to any part of premises used as a private dwelling).

(3) If it is shown to the satisfaction of a justice of the peace on sworn information in writing—

(*a*) that admission to any premises has been refused, or that refusal is apprehended, or that the premises are unoccupied or the occupier is temporarily absent, or that the case is one of urgency, or that an application for admission would defeat the object of the entry, and

(*b*) that there is reasonable ground for entry into the premises for any such purpose as is mentioned in subsection (1) above,

the justice may by warrant under his hand authorise the relevant health protection authority by any proper officer to enter the premises, if need be by force.

(4) Such a warrant shall not be issued unless the justice is satisfied either that notice of the intention to apply for a warrant has been given to the occupier, or that the premises are unoccupied, or that the occupier is temporarily absent, or that the case is one of urgency, or that the giving of such notice would defeat the object of the entry.

[Public Health (Control of Disease) Act 1984, s 61 as amended by the Health and Social Care Act 2008, Sch 11.]

**7.9872 62. Supplementary provisions as to entry** (1) A proper officer ("the officer") entering any premises by virtue of section 61 above, or of a warrant issued under that section, may take with him such other persons and such equipment and materials as may be necessary, and on leaving any unoccupied premises which he has entered by virtue of such a warrant he shall leave them as effectively secured against trespassers as he found them.

(1A) The officer may for the purpose for which entry is authorised—

(*a*) search the premises,

(*b*) carry out measurements and tests of the premises or of anything found on them,

(*c*) take and retain samples of the premises or of anything found on them,

(*d*) inspect and take copies or extracts of any documents or records found on the premises,

(*e*) require information stored in an electronic form and accessible from the premises to be produced in a form in which it can be taken away and in which it is visible and legible or from which it can readily be produced in a visible and legible form, and

(*f*) seize and detain or remove anything which the officer reasonably believes to be evidence of any contravention relevant to the purpose for which entry is authorised.

(2) Every warrant issued under that section shall continue in force until the purpose for which the entry is necessary has been satisfied.

(3) *Repealed.*

(4) Nothing in section 61 or this section limits the provisions of Parts 2A and 4, and of regulations made under Part 2A, with respect to entry into or upon, and inspection of, any premises.

[Public Health (Control of Disease) Act 1984, s 62 as amended by the Health and Social Care Act 2008, Sch 11.]

**7.9873 63. Offence of wilful obstruction** (1) A person commits an offence if the person wilfully obstructs any person acting in the execution of a provision of Part 3 or 4 or this Part, or of any regulations, order or warrant made or issued under such a provision.

(2) A person guilty of an offence under subsection (1) is liable on summary conviction—

(*a*) in the case of an offence of wilfully obstructing a person in the execution of a provision of Part 4 or of any regulations made under a provision of that Part, to a fine not exceeding level 1 on the standard scale, and

(*b*) in any other case, to a fine.

[Public Health (Control of Disease) Act 1984, s 63 as substituted by the Health and Social Care Act 2008, Sch 11 and amended by SI 2015/664.]

7.9874 **63A. Offences by bodies corporate** (1) If an offence created by or under this Act is committed by a body corporate and is proved—

(*a*) to have been committed with the consent or connivance of an officer, or

(*b*) to be attributable to any neglect on the part of an officer,

the officer (as well as the body corporate) is guilty of the offence and liable to be proceeded against and punished accordingly.

(2) "Officer", in relation to a body corporate, means a director, manager, secretary or other similar officer of the body, or a person purporting to act in any such capacity.

(3) If the affairs of a body corporate are managed by its members, subsection (1) applies to the acts and defaults of a member in connection with the member's functions of management as if the member were a director of the body corporate.

[Public Health (Control of Disease) Act 1984, s 63A as inserted by the Health and Social Care Act 2008, Sch 11.]

7.9875 **63B. Unincorporated associations** (1) Proceedings for an offence alleged to have been committed by an unincorporated association are to be brought in the name of the association (and not in that of any of the members).

(2) Rules of court relating to the service of documents have effect as if the unincorporated association were a body corporate.

(3) In proceedings for an offence brought against an unincorporated association, Schedule 3 to the Magistrates' Courts Act 1980 applies as it applies to a body corporate.

(4) A fine imposed on an unincorporated association on its conviction for an offence is to be paid out of the funds of the association.

(5) If an offence committed by an unincorporated association is proved—

(*a*) to have been committed with the consent or connivance of an officer of the association or a member of its governing body, or

(*b*) to be attributable to any neglect on the part of such an officer or member,

the officer or member (as well as the association) is guilty of the offence and liable to be proceeded against and punished accordingly.

(6) In this section, "offence" means an offence created by or under this Act.

[Public Health (Control of Disease) Act 1984, s 63B as inserted by the Health and Social Care Act 2008, Sch 11.]

7.9876 **64. Restriction on right to prosecute** (1) Proceedings in respect of an offence created by a provision of, or regulations under, this Act may not be taken by any person other than—

(*a*) a relevant health protection authority,

(*b*) a body whose function it is to enforce the provision or regulation in question, or

(*c*) a person who made (or whose predecessors made) the regulation in question.

(2) *Repealed.*

[Public Health (Control of Disease) Act 1984, s 64, as amended by the Local Government (Wales) Act 1994, Sch 9 and the Health and Social Care Act 2008, Sch 11.]

7.9877 **64A. Time limits for prosecutions** (1) Notwithstanding anything in section 127(1) of the Magistrates' Courts Act 1980, a magistrates' court may try an information (or written charge) relating to an offence created by or under this Act if the information is laid (or the charge is issued)—

(*a*) before the end of the period of 3 years beginning with the date of the commission of the offence, and

(*b*) before the end of the period of 6 months beginning with the date on which evidence which the prosecutor thinks is sufficient to justify the proceedings comes to the prosecutor's knowledge.

(2) For the purposes of subsection (1)(*b*)—

(*a*) a certificate signed by or on behalf of the prosecutor and stating the date on which such evidence came to the prosecutor's knowledge is conclusive evidence of that fact, and

(*b*) a certificate stating that matter and purporting to be so signed is to be treated as so signed unless the contrary is proved.

[Public Health (Control of Disease) Act 1984, s 64A as inserted by the Health and Social Care Act 2008, Sch 11.]

7.9878 **65. Daily penalties for continuing offences** Where by or under this Act provision is made for the imposition of a daily penalty in respect of a continuing offence, the court by which a person is convicted of the original offence may fix a reasonable period from the date of conviction for compliance by the defendant with any directions given by the court; and, where the court has fixed such a period, the daily penalty shall not be recoverable in respect of any day before that period expires.

[Public Health (Control of Disease) Act 1984, s 65.]

7.9879 **67. Applications to, and appeals from, magistrates' courts** (1) Where this Act or a provision contained in regulations made under this Act provides for any matter to be determined by, or for an application in respect of a matter to be made to, a magistrates' court, the procedure shall be by way of complaint for an order.

(2) Where a person aggrieved by any order, determination or other decision of a magistrates' court under a relevant provision of this Act is not by any other enactment authorised to appeal to the Crown Court, he may appeal to the Crown Court.

(3) *Repealed.*

[Public Health (Control of Disease) Act 1984, s 67 as amended by the Health and Social Care Act 2008, Sch 11.]

7.9880 **68. Judges and justices not to be disqualified by liability to rates** A judge of any court or a justice of the peace shall not be disqualified from acting in cases arising under this Act by reason only of his being, as one of several ratepayers, or as one of any other class of persons, liable in common with the others to contribute to, or be benefited by, any rate or fund out of which any expenses of a local authority are to be defrayed.

[Public Health (Control of Disease) Act 1984, s 68.]

7.9881 **72. Cumulative effect of Act** Powers and duties under Act are in addition to other powers and duties elsewhere.

[Public Health (Control of Disease) Act 1984, s 72—summarised.]

7.9882 **73. Crown property** Act may be applied by agreement to Crown property.

[Public Health (Control of Disease) Act 1984, s 73—summarised.]

7.9883 **74. Interpretation** In this Act, unless the context otherwise requires—

"authorised officer", in relation to a local authority, means—

- (*a*) an officer of the authority authorised by them in writing, either generally or specially, to act in matters of a specified kind or in a specified matter, or
- (*b*) by virtue of his appointment and for the purpose of matters within his province, a proper officer of the authority, appointed for purposes corresponding to any of those of the former medical officers of health, surveyors and sanitary inspectors;

"district", in relation to a local authority in Greater London, means a London borough, the City of London, the Inner Temple or the Middle Temple and, in relation to a local authority in Wales, means a county or county borough;

"district" means—

- (*a*) in relation to a local authority in Greater London, a London borough, the City of London, the Inner Temple or the Middle Temple,
- (*b*) in relation to a local authority in England for an area for which there is no district council, that area,
- (*c*) in relation to a local authority in Wales, a county or county borough,
- (*d*) in relation to the Council of the Isles of Scilly, those Isles;

"functions" includes powers and duties;

"local authority" has the meaning given by section 1(1) above;

"London port health authority" and "London port health district" have the meanings given by section 7 above;

"officer" includes servant;

"owner" means the person for the time being receiving the rackrent of the premises in connection with which the word is used, whether on his own account or as agent or trustee for any other person, or who would so receive the rackrent if those premises were let at a rackrent;

"port" has the meaning given by section 2(1) above;

"Port of London" has the meaning given by section 6 above;

"premises" includes any place and, in particular, includes—

- (*a*) any vehicle, train, vessel or aircraft,
- (*b*) any tent or movable structure, and
- (*c*) any offshore installation (as defined in section 12(1) of the Mineral Workings (Offshore Installations) Act 1971);

"proper officer" means, in relation to a purpose and to an authority, an officer appointed for that purpose by that authority;

"public authority" has the meaning given in section 6(3) of the Human Rights Act 1998;

"rackrent" in relation to any property means a rent which is not less than two-thirds of the rent at which the property might reasonably be expected to let from year to year, free from all usual tenant's rates and taxes, and deducting from it the probable average annual cost of the repairs, insurance and other expenses (if any) necessary to maintain the property in a state to command such a rent;

"relevant health protection authority" means—

- (*a*) a local authority, port health authority or joint board with functions under a relevant provision of this Act, and
- (*b*) if regulations under Part 2A confer functions on a public authority of any other description and state that the authority is to be regarded as a relevant health protection authority with respect to those functions, that authority;

"relevant provision of this Act" means a provision of this Act (including a provision in regulations made under this Act) other than section 46;

"riparian authority" has the meaning given by section 2(2) above;

"vessel" has the same meaning as "ship" in the Merchant Shipping Act 1995 except that it includes a hovercraft within the meaning of the Hovercraft Act 1968, and "master" shall be construed accordingly.

[Public Health (Control of Disease) Act 1984, s 74 as amended by the Statute Law (Repeals) Act 1993, Sch 1, the Local Government (Wales) Act 1994, Sch 9, the Merchant Shipping Act 1995, Sch 13, the National Health Service and Community Care Act 1990, Sch 9, the National Health Service (Consequential Provisions) Act 2006, Sch 1 and the Health and Social Care Act 2008, Schs 11 and 15.]

# Building Act 1984[1]

(1984 c 55)

## Part I[2]

## Building Regulations

*Power to make building regulations*

7.9884 **1. Power to make building regulations** (1) The Secretary of State may, for any of the purposes of—

(*a*) securing the health, safety, welfare and convenience of persons in or about buildings and of others who may be affected by buildings or matters connected with buildings,

(*b*) furthering the conservation of fuel and power,

(*c*) preventing waste, undue consumption, misuse or contamination of water,

(*d*) furthering the protection or enhancement of the environment,

(*e*) facilitating sustainable development, or

(*f*) furthering the prevention or detection of crime,

make regulations[3] with respect to the matters mentioned in subsection (1A) below.

(1A) Those matters are—

(*a*) the design and construction of buildings;

(*b*) the demolition of buildings;

(*c*) services, fittings and equipment provided in or in connection with buildings.

(2) Regulations made under subsection (1) above are known as building regulations.

(3) Schedule 1 to this Act has effect with respect to the matters as to which building regulations may provide.

(4) The power to make building regulations is exercisable by statutory instrument, which is subject to annulment in pursuance of a resolution of either House of Parliament.*

[Building Act 1984, s 1, as amended by the Sustainable and Secure Buildings Act 2004, s 1.]

---

* **Amended by the Infrastructure Act 2015, s 37 from a date to be appointed.**

1 This Act is to be brought into force in accordance with the provisions of s 134, post. For the purposes of this Act, the holder of a licence under s 6(1) of the Electricity Act 1989 shall be deemed to be a statutory undertaker and his undertaking a statutory undertaking (Electricity Act 1989, Sch 16, para 1).

The Building (Local Authority Charges) Regulations 2010, SI 2010/404 amended by SI 2012/3119 (amended by SI 2013/181) have also been made in exercise of powers under s 1 and other sections of this Act which authorise a local authority to levy charges in relation to their building control functions. However, s 35 of the Act (penalty for breach) does not apply to any breach of these regulations (reg 13).

2 Part I contains ss 1–46. In addition to the powers in s 1, Parts I–II of this Act contain a number of regulation-making powers under which the following regulations have been made. We also list regulations under the particular section under which they have been made:

Building (Inner London) Regulations 1985, SI 1985/1936 amended by SI 1987/798 and SI 1991/2768;

Building (Repeal of Provisions of Local Acts) Regulations 2003, SI 2003/3030;

Building Regulations 2010, SI 2010/2214 amended by SI 2011/1515 and 3058, SI 2012/718, 3118 and 3119 and SI 2013/10, 181, 747 (W), 1105, 1959 and 2730 (W), SI 2014/110(W); 579, 1638 and 2362, SI 2015/767 and 1486 (W) and SI 2016/285, 361 (W), 490, 611(W) and 1101;

Building (Approved Inspectors etc.) Regulations 2010, SI 2010/2215 amended by SI 2012/3119 (amended by SI 2013/181) and SI 2013/747 (W), 1959 and 2730 (W), SI 2014/58 (W) and 579 and SI 2015/767 and SI 2016/285 and 611 (W).

3 See the Building (Inner London) Regulations 1985, SI 1985/1936; Building Regulations 2000, SI 2000/2531; Building (Approved Inspectors etc) Regulations 2000, SI 2000/2532; Building (Repeal of Provisions of Local Acts) Regulations 2003, SI 2003/3030. (For amending instruments, see note 2 to this section, ante).

*Exemption from building regulations*

7.9885 **3. Exemption of particular classes of buildings etc** (1) Building regulations may exempt a prescribed class of buildings, services, fittings or equipment from all or any of the provisions of building regulations[1].

(2) The Secretary of State may by direction exempt from all or any of the provisions of building regulations—

(*a*) a particular building, or

(*b*) buildings of a particular class at a particular location,

either unconditionally or subject to compliance with any conditions specified in the direction.

(3) A person who contravenes a condition specified in a direction given under subsection (2) above, or permits such a condition to be contravened, is liable on summary conviction to a fine not

exceeding **level 5** on the standard scale, and to a further fine not exceeding **£50** for each day on which the offence continues after he is convicted.

[Building Act 1984, s 3.]

[1] See the Building (Inner London) Regulations 1985, SI 1985/1936; Building Regulations 2010, SI 2010/2214. (For amending instruments, see note 2 to s 1, ante.)

*Approved documents*

**7.9886 6.** *Secretary of State or body acting on his behalf may approve and issue documents for the purpose of providing practical guidance with respect to the requirements of any provision of building regulations.*

**7.9887 7. Compliance or non-compliance with approved documents** (1) A failure on the part of a person to comply with an approved document does not of itself render him liable to any civil or criminal proceedings; but if, in any proceedings whether civil or criminal, it is alleged that a person has at any time contravened a provision of building regulations—

(*a*) a failure to comply with a document that at that time was approved for the purposes of that provision may be relied upon as tending to establish liability, and

(*b*) proof of compliance with such a document may be relied on as tending to negative liability.

(2) In any proceedings, whether civil or criminal—

(*a*) a document purporting to be a notice issued as mentioned in section 6(3) above shall be taken to be such a notice unless the contrary is proved, and

(*b*) a document that appears to the court to be the approved document to which such a notice refers shall be taken to be that approved document unless the contrary is proved.

[Building Act 1984, s 7.]

*Relaxation of building regulations*

**7.9888 8–10.** *Relaxation of building regulations*[1].

[1] See the Building (Inner London) Regulations 1985, SI 1985/1936; Building Regulations 2010, SI 2010/2214. (For amending instruments, see note 2 to s 1, ante.)

**7.9889 11. Type relaxation of building regulations** (1) If the Secretary of State considers that the operation of a requirement of building regulations would be unreasonable in relation to a particular type of building matter, he may, either on an application made to him or of his own accord, give a direction dispensing with or relaxing that requirement generally in relation to that type of building matter, either—

(*a*) unconditionally, or

(*b*) subject to compliance with any conditions specified in the direction, being conditions with respect to matters directly connected with the dispensation or relaxation.

(2) A direction under subsection (1) above—

(*a*) if it so provides, ceases to have effect at the end of such period as may be specified in the direction,

(*b*) may be varied or revoked by a subsequent direction of the Secretary of State.

(3) Building regulations may require a person making an application under subsection (1) above to pay the Secretary of State the prescribed fee, and—

(*a*) without prejudice to paragraph 10 of Schedule 1 to this Act, regulations made by virtue of this subsection may prescribe different fees for different cases, and

(*b*) the Secretary of State may in a particular case remit the whole or part of a fee payable by virtue of this subsection.

(4) Before giving a direction under subsection (1) above, the Secretary of State shall consult such bodies as appear to him to be representative of the interests concerned.

(5) Where the Secretary of State gives a direction under subsection (1) above, he shall publish notice of that fact in such manner as he thinks fit.

(6) A person who contravenes a condition specified in a direction given under subsection (1) above, or permits such a condition to be contravened, is liable on summary conviction to a fine not exceeding **level 5** on the standard scale and to a further fine not exceeding **£50** for each day on which the offence continues after he is convicted.

(7) If at any time a direction under subsection (1) above dispensing with or relaxing a requirement of building regulations ceases to have effect by virtue of subsection (2)(*a*) above, or is varied or revoked under subsection (2)(*b*) above, that fact does not affect the continued operation of the direction (with any conditions specified in it) in a case in which before that time—

(*a*) plans of the proposed work were, in accordance with building regulations, deposited with a local authority,

(*b*) *repealed*.

(8) In this section, "building matter" means any building or other matter whatsoever to which building regulations are in any circumstances applicable.

[Building Act 1984, s 11 as amended by the Local Government Act 1985, Sch 17 and the Statute Law (Repeals) Act 2004.]

*Passing of plans*

7.9890 **16. Passing or rejection of plans** (1) Where plans of any proposed work are, in accordance with building regulations, deposited with a local authority, it is the duty of the local authority, subject to any other section of this Act that expressly requires or authorises them in certain cases to reject plans, to pass the plans unless—

(*a*) they are defective, or

(*b*) they show that the proposed work would contravene any of the building regulations.

(2) If the plans—

(*a*) are defective, or

(*b*) show that the proposed work would contravene any of the building regulations,

the local authority may—

(i) reject the plans, or

(ii) subject to subsection (4) below, pass them subject to either or both of the conditions set out in subsection (3) below.

(3) The conditions mentioned in subsection (2) above are—

(*a*) that such modifications as the local authority may specify shall be made in the deposited plans, and

(*b*) that such further plans as they may specify shall be deposited.

(4) A local authority may only pass plans subject to a condition such as is specified in subsection (3) above if the person by whom or on whose behalf they were deposited—

(*a*) has requested them to do so, or

(*b*) has consented to their doing so.

(5) A request or consent under subsection (4) above shall be in writing.

(6) The authority shall within the relevant period from the deposit of the plans give notice to the person by whom or on whose behalf they were deposited whether they have been passed or rejected.

(7) A notice that plans have been rejected shall specify the defects on account of which, or the regulation or section of this Act for non-conformity with which, or under the authority of which, they have been rejected.

(8) A notice that plans have been passed shall—

(*a*) specify any condition subject to which they have been passed, and

(*b*) state that the passing of the plans operates as an approval of them only for the purposes of the requirements of—

(i) the building regulations, and

(ii) any section of this Act (other than this section) that expressly requires or authorises the local authority in certain cases to reject plans.

(9) Where the deposited plans are accompanied by—

(*a*) a certificate given by a person approved for the purposes of this subsection to the effect that the proposed work, if carried out in accordance with the deposited plans, will comply with such provisions of the regulations prescribed for the purposes of this subsection as may be specified in the certificate, and

(*b*) such evidence as may be prescribed that an approved scheme applies, or the prescribed insurance cover has been or will be provided, in relation to the certificate,

the local authority may not, except in prescribed circumstances, reject the plans on the ground that—

(i) they are defective with respect to any provisions of the building regulations that are so specified, or

(ii) they show that the proposed work would contravene any of those provisions.

(10) In any case where a question arises under this section between a local authority and a person who proposes to carry out any work—

(*a*) whether plans of the proposed work are in conformity with building regulations, or

(*b*) whether the local authority are prohibited from rejecting plans of the proposed work by virtue of subsection (9) above,

that person may refer the question to the Secretary of State for his determination; and an application for a reference under this subsection shall be accompanied by such fee as may be prescribed.

(11) Where—

(*a*) deposited plans accompanied by such a certificate and such evidence as are mentioned in subsection (9) above are passed by the local authority, or

(*b*) notice of the rejection of deposited plans so accompanied is not given within the relevant period from the deposit of the plans,

the authority may not institute proceedings under section 35 below for a contravention of building regulations that—

(i) arises out of the carrying out of the proposed work in accordance with the plans, and

(ii) is a contravention of any of the provisions of the regulations specified in the certificate.

(12) For the purposes of this Part of this Act, "the relevant period", in relation to the passing or rejection of plans, means five weeks or such extended period (expiring not later than two months from the deposit of the plans) as may before the expiration of the five weeks be agreed in writing

between the person depositing the plans and the local authority.

(13) *Repealed.*

[Building Act 1984, s 16 as amended by the Statute Law (Repeals) Act 1993, Sch 1.]

**7.9891 17. Approval of persons to give certificates etc** (1)–(5) *Building regulations* [1] *may make provision for the approval of persons for the purposes of section 16 (9).*

(6) Building regulations may—

(*a*) contain provision prescribing the period for which, subject to any provision made by virtue of paragraph (*b*) or (*c*) below, any such approval as is referred to in subsection (1) above continues in force,

(*b*) contain provision precluding the giving of, or requiring the withdrawal of, any such approval as is referred to in subsection (1) above in such circumstances as may be prescribed,

(*c*) contain provision authorising the withdrawal of any such approval or designation as is referred to in subsection (1) above,

(*d*) provide for the maintenance by the Secretary of State of a list of bodies that are for the time being designated by him as mentioned in subsection (1) above and for the maintenance by the Secretary of State and by each designated body of a list of persons for the time being approved by him or them as mentioned in that subsection,

(*e*) make provision for the supply to local authorities of copies of any list of approved persons maintained by virtue of paragraph (*d*) above and for such copy lists to be made available for inspection, and

(*f*) make provision for the supply, on payment of a prescribed fee, of a certified copy of any entry in a list maintained by virtue of paragraph (*d*) above or in a copy list held by a local authority by virtue of paragraph (*e*) above.

(7) Unless the contrary is proved, in any proceedings (whether civil or criminal) a document that appears to the court to be a certified copy of an entry either in a list maintained as mentioned in subsection (6)(*d*) above or in a copy of such a list supplied as mentioned in subsection (6)(*e*) above—

(*a*) is presumed to be a true copy of an entry in the current list so maintained, and

(*b*) is evidence of the matters stated in it.

[Building Act 1984, s 17.]

---

[1] See the Building (Approved Inspectors etc) Regulations 2010, SI 2010/2215.

**7.9892 19. Use of short-lived materials** (1) Where plans of a building are, in accordance with building regulations, deposited with a local authority, and the plans show that it is proposed to construct a building of materials to which this section applies, or to place or assemble on the site a building constructed of such materials, the authority may, notwithstanding that the plans conform with the regulations—

(*a*) reject the plans, or

(*b*) in passing the plans—

(i) fix a period on the expiration of which the building must be removed, and

(ii) impose with respect to the use of the building such reasonable conditions, if any, as having regard to the nature of the materials used in its construction they deem appropriate,

but no condition shall be imposed that conflicts with any condition imposed on the grant of planning permission for that building under Part III of the Town and Country Planning Act 1990.

(2) If a building in respect of which plans ought under the building regulations to have been deposited, but have not been deposited, appears to the authority to be constructed of such materials as aforesaid, the authority, without prejudice to their right to take proceedings in respect of any contravention of the regulations, may—

(*a*) fix a period on the expiration of which the building must be removed, and

(*b*) if they think fit, impose such conditions with respect to the use of the building as might have been imposed under subsection (1) above upon the passing of plans for the building,

and where they fix such a period they shall forthwith give notice thereof, and of any conditions imposed, to the owner of the building.

(3) A local authority may from time to time extend any period fixed, or vary any conditions imposed, under this section; but, unless an application in that behalf is made to them by the owner of the building in question, they shall not exercise their power of varying conditions except when granting an extension, or further extension, of the period fixed with respect to the building.

(4) A person aggrieved by the action of a local authority under this section in rejecting plans, or in fixing or refusing to extend any period, or in imposing or refusing to vary any conditions, may appeal to a magistrates' court.

(5) The owner of a building in respect of which a period has been fixed under this section shall, on the expiration of that period, or, as the case may be, of that period as extended, remove the building, and, if he fails to do so—

(*a*) the local authority shall remove it and may recover from him the expenses reasonably incurred by them in so doing, and (*b*) without prejudice to the right of the authority to exercise that power, he is liable on summary conviction to a fine not exceeding **level 1** on the standard scale and to a further fine not exceeding £5 for each day during which the building is allowed to remain after he is convicted.

(6) A person who uses a building in contravention of a condition imposed under this section, or who permits a building to be so used, is liable on summary conviction to a fine not exceeding **level 1** on the standard scale and to a further fine not exceeding £5 for each day on which the offence continues after he is convicted.

(7) Building regulations may provide that this section applies to any materials specified in the regulations as being materials that are, in the absence of special care, liable to rapid deterioration, or are otherwise unsuitable for use in the construction of permanent buildings.

(8) This section applies in relation to an extension of an existing building as it applies in relation to a new building.

(9) This section ceases to have effect upon the coming into force of section 20 below (which supersedes it).

[Building Act 1984, s 19 as amended by the Planning (Consequential Provisions) Act 1990, Sch 2.]

7.9893 **20. Use of materials unsuitable for permanent building** (1) Where plans of any proposed work are, in accordance with building regulations, deposited with a local authority, and the plans show that the proposed work would include or consist of work to which this section applies, the authority may, notwithstanding that the plans conform with the regulations—

(*a*) reject the plans, or

(*b*) in passing the plans—

(i) fix a period on the expiration of which the work to which this section applies or the relevant building (as the authority may in passing the plans direct) must be removed, and

(ii) if they think fit, impose with respect to the use of the relevant building or with respect to the work to which this section applies such reasonable conditions, if any, as they consider appropriate,

but no condition as to the use of the relevant building shall be imposed that conflicts with any condition imposed or having effect as if imposed under Part III or VIII of the Town and Country Planning Act 1990 or under the Planning (Listed Buildings and Conservation Areas) Act 1990 or the Planning (Hazardous Substances) Act 1990.

(2) If, in the case of any work in respect of which plans ought by virtue of building regulations to have been deposited with a local authority but have not been so deposited, the work appears to the authority to include or consist of work to which this section applies, the authority, without prejudice to their right to take proceedings in respect of any contravention of the regulations, may—

(*a*) fix a period on the expiration of which the work to which this section applies or the relevant building (as the authority may in fixing the period direct) must be removed, and

(*b*) if they think fit, impose any conditions that might have been imposed under subsection (1) above in passing plans for the first-mentioned work,

and where they fix such a period they shall forthwith give notice thereof, and of any conditions imposed, to the owner of the relevant building.

(3) If, in the case of any work appearing to the local authority to fall within subsection (9)(*b*) below, plans of the work were not required by building regulations to be deposited with the authority, and were not so deposited, the authority may at any time within 12 months from the date of completion of the work—

(*a*) fix a period on the expiration of which the work must be removed, and

(*b*) if they think fit, impose any conditions that, if plans of the work had been required to be, and had been, so deposited, might have been imposed under subsection (1) above in passing the plans,

and where they fix such a period they shall forthwith give notice thereof, and of any conditions imposed, to the owner of the relevant building.

(4) A local authority may from time to time extend any period fixed, or vary any conditions imposed, under this section, but, unless an application in that behalf is made to them by the owner of the relevant building, they shall not exercise their power of varying conditions so imposed except when granting an extension or further extension of the period fixed with respect to the work or building, as the case may be.

(5) A person aggrieved by the action of a local authority under this section—

(*a*) in rejecting plans,

(*b*) in fixing or refusing to extend any period, or

(*c*) in imposing or refusing to vary any conditions,

may appeal to the Secretary of State within the prescribed time and in the prescribed manner.

(6) Where a period has been fixed under this section with respect to any work to which this section applies or with respect to the relevant building—

(*a*) the owner of that building shall on the expiration of that period, or, as the case may be, of that period as extended, remove the work or building with respect to which the period was fixed, and (*b*) if he fails to do so, the local authority may remove that work or building, as the case may be, and may recover from him the expenses reasonably incurred by them in doing so.

(7) A person who—

(*a*) contravenes a condition imposed under this section or permits such a condition to be contravened, or

(*b*) contravenes subsection (6) above,

is liable on summary conviction to a fine not exceeding **level 5** on the standard scale and to a further fine not exceeding **£50** for each day on which the offence continues or, as the case may be, on which the work or building is allowed to remain after he is convicted; but this subsection does not prejudice a local authority's rights under subsection (6) above.

(8) In this section, "the relevant building" means, in any particular case, the building mentioned in paragraph (*a*) or, as the case may be, paragraph (*b*) of subsection (9) below.

(9) This section applies to—

(*a*) any work consisting of a part of a building, being a part in the construction of which there is used any material or component of a type that, in relation to a part of that description, is prescribed for the purposes of this paragraph under subsection (10) below, and

(*b*) any work provided in or in connection with a building, being work consisting of a service, fitting or item of equipment of a type so prescribed for the purposes of this paragraph.

(10) *Power of Secretary of State to make building regulations for the purposes of subsection* (9)(*a*)– (*b*).

(11) Upon section 19 above ceasing to have effect—

(*a*) any building regulations made, period fixed, condition imposed or other thing done by virtue of the said section 19 shall be deemed to have been made, fixed, imposed or done by virtue of this section, and

(*b*) anything begun under the said section 19 may be continued under this Act as if begun under this section, but any appeal under section 19(4) that is pending at the time when the said section 19 ceases to have effect, and any proceedings arising out of such an appeal, shall proceed as if that section were still in force.*

[Building Act 1984, s 20 as amended by the Planning (Consequential Provisions) Act 1990, Sch 2.]

---

* **Not yet in force.**

**7.9894 21. Provision of drainage** (1)–(2) *Repealed.*

(3) Any question arising under subsection (4) below between a local authority and the person by whom, or on whose behalf, plans are deposited as to whether a proposed drain shall be required to connect with a sewer may on the application of that person be determined by a magistrates' court.

(4) Where plans of a building or of an extension of a building are, in accordance with building regulations, deposited with a local authority, the local authority, or on appeal a magistrates' court, may require a proposed drain to connect with a sewer where—

(*a*) that sewer is within one hundred feet of the site of the building or, in the case of an extension, the site either of the extension or of the original building, and is at a level that makes it reasonably practicable to construct a drain to communicate with it, and, if it is not a public sewer, is a sewer that the person constructing the drain is entitled to use, and

(*b*) the intervening land is land through which that person is entitled to construct a drain.

(5) Notwithstanding paragraph (*a*) of subsection (4) above, a drain may be required to be made to connect with a sewer that is not within the distance mentioned in that paragraph, but is otherwise such a sewer as is therein mentioned, if the authority undertake to bear so much of the expenses reasonably incurred in constructing, and in maintaining and repairing, the drain as may be attributable to the fact that the distance of the sewer exceeds the distance so mentioned.

(6) If any question arises as to the amount of a payment to be made to a person under subsection (5) above, that question may on his application be determined by a magistrates' court, or he may require it to be referred to arbitration.

[Building Act 1984, s 21 as amended by SI 2001/3335.]

**7.9895 22. Drainage of buildings in combination** (1) Where—

(*a*) a local authority might under section 21 above require each of two or more buildings to be drained separately into an existing sewer, but

(*b*) it appears to the authority that those buildings may be drained more economically or advantageously in combination,

the authority may, when the drains of the buildings are first laid, require that the buildings be drained in combination into the existing sewer by means of a private sewer to be constructed either by the owners of the buildings in such manner as the authority may direct or, if the authority so elect, by the authority on behalf of the owners.

(2) A local authority shall not, except by agreement with the owners concerned, exercise the power conferred by subsection (1) above in respect of any building for whose drainage plans have been previously passed by them.

(3) A local authority who make such a requirement as aforesaid shall fix—

(*a*) the proportions in which the expenses of constructing, and of maintaining and repairing, the private sewer are to be borne by the owners concerned, or

(*b*) in a case in which the distance of the existing sewer from the site of any of the buildings in question is or exceeds one hundred feet, the proportions in which those expenses are to borne by the owners concerned and the local authority,

and shall forthwith give notice of their decision to each owner affected.

(4) An owner aggrieved by the decision of a local authority under subsection (3) above may appeal to a magistrates' court.

(5) Subject to any such appeal—

(*a*) any expenses reasonably incurred in constructing, or maintaining or repairing, the private sewer shall be borne in the proportions so fixed, and

(*b*) those expenses, or, as the case may be, contributions to them, may be recovered accordingly by the persons, whether the local authority or the owners, by whom they were incurred in the first instance.

(6) A sewer constructed by a local authority under this section is not deemed a public sewer by reason of the fact that the expenses of its construction are in the first instance defrayed by the authority, or that some part of those expenses is borne by them.

[Building Act 1984, s 22.]

**7.9896 23. Provision of facilities for refuse** (1)–(2) *Repealed.*

(3) It is unlawful for any person except with the consent of the local authority to close or obstruct the means of access by which refuse or faecal matter is removed from a building, and the local authority in giving their consent may impose such conditions as they think fit with respect to the improvement of an alternative means of access or the substitution of other means of access.

(4) A person who contravenes subsection (3) above is liable on summary conviction to a fine not exceeding **level** 4 on the standard scale.

[Building Act 1984, s 23 as amended by SI 1985/1065.]

**7.9897 24. Provision of exits etc** (1) Where—

(*a*) plans of a building or of an extension of a building are, in accordance with building regulations, deposited with a local authority, and

(*b*) the building or, as the case may be, the building as extended will be a building to which this section applies,

the authority shall reject the plans unless they show that the building, or, as the case may be, the building as extended, will be provided with such means of ingress and egress and passages or gangways as the authority, after consultation with the fire and rescue authority, deem satisfactory, regard being had to the purposes for which the building is intended to be, or is, used and the number of persons likely to resort to it at any one time.

(2) Any question arising under subsection (1) above between a local authority and the person by whom, or on whose behalf, plans are deposited as to whether the means of ingress or egress or passages or gangways already existing, or proposed to be provided, ought to be accepted by the authority as satisfactory may on the application of that person be determined by a magistrates' court.

(3) Where building regulations imposing requirements as to the provision of means of escape in case of fire are applicable to a proposed building or proposed extension of a building, or would be so applicable but for a direction under section 8 above dispensing with such requirements—

(*a*) this section, and

(*b*) any provision of a local Act that has effect in place of this section,

does not apply in relation to the proposed building or extension.

(4) Subject to subsection (3) above, this section applies to—

(*a*) a theatre, and a hall or other building that is used as a place of public resort,

(*b*) a restaurant, shop, store or warehouse to which members of the public are admitted and in which more than twenty persons are employed,

(*c*) premises in respect of which a club premises certificate has effect under the Licensing Act 2003,

(*d*) a school not exempted from the operation of building regulations, and

(*e*) a church, chapel or other place of public worship,

but not—

(i) a private house to which members of the public are admitted occasionally or exceptionally,

(ii) a building that was used as a church, chapel or other place of public worship immediately before the date on which section 36 of the Public Health Acts Amendment Act 1890, or a corresponding provision in a local Act, came into operation in the district or rating district, or

(iii) a building that was so used immediately before the 1st October 1937 (the date of commencement of the Public Health Act 1936) in a district or rating district where neither the said section 36 nor such a corresponding provision ever came into operation.

[Building Act 1984, s 24 as amended by the Fire and Rescue Services Act 2004, Sch 1 and the Licensing Act 2003, Sch 6.]

7.9898 **25. Provision of water supply** (1) Where plans of a house are, in accordance with building regulations, deposited with a local authority, the authority shall reject the plans unless a proposal is put before them that appears to them to be satisfactory for providing the occupants of the house with a supply of wholesome water sufficient for their domestic purposes—

(*a*) by connecting the house to a supply of water in pipes provided by water undertakers,

(*b*) if in all the circumstances it is not reasonable to require the house to be connected as aforesaid, by otherwise taking water into the house by means of a pipe, or

(*c*) if in all the circumstances neither of the preceding alternatives can reasonably be required, by providing a supply of water within a reasonable distance of the house,

and the authority are satisfied that the proposal can and will be carried into effect.

(2) Any question arising under subsection (1) above between a local authority and the person by whom, or on whose behalf, plans are deposited as to whether the local authority ought to pass the plans may on the application of that person be determined by a magistrates' court.

(3) If, after any such plans as aforesaid have been passed, it appears to the local authority that the proposal for providing a supply of water—

(*a*) has not been carried into effect, or

(*b*) has not resulted in a supply of wholesome water sufficient for the domestic purposes of the occupants,

the authority shall give notice to the owner of the house prohibiting him from occupying it, or permitting it to be occupied, until the authority, being satisfied that such a supply has been provided, have granted him a certificate to that effect.

(4) Until a certificate is granted under subsection (3) above, the owner shall not occupy the house or permit it to be occupied.

(5) A person aggrieved by the refusal of the authority to grant such a certificate may apply to a magistrates' court for an order authorising the occupation of the house, and, if the court is of opinion that a certificate ought to have been granted, the court may make an order authorising the occupation of the house, and such an order shall have the like effect as a certificate of the local authority.

(6) A person who contravenes subsection (4) above is liable on summary conviction to a fine not exceeding **level 1** on the standard scale and to a further fine not exceeding **£2** for each day on which the offence continues after he is convicted.

(7) Section 67 of the Water Industry Act 1991 (standards of wholesomeness of water) and any regulations made under that section shall apply for the purposes of subsection (1) above as they apply for the purposes of Chapter III of Part III of that Act.

[Building Act 1984, s 25 as amended by the Water Act 1989, Schs 25 and 27 and the Water Consolidation (Consequential Provisions) Act 1991, Sch 1.]

*Proposed departure from plans*

7.9899 **31. Proposed departure from plans** (1) Where plans of any proposed work have been passed under section 16 above by a local authority, the person by or on whose behalf the plans were in accordance with building regulations deposited with the authority may, and in such cases as may be prescribed shall, for the purpose of obtaining the approval of the authority to any proposed departure or deviation from the plans as passed, deposit plans of the departure or deviation.

(2) Section 16 above applies in relation to plans deposited under subsection (1) above as it applies in relation to the plans originally deposited.*

[Building Act 1984, s 31.]

---

* **Not yet in force**.

*Lapse of deposit of plans*

7.9900 **32. Lapse of deposit of plans** (1) Where plans of any proposed work have, in accordance with building regulations, been deposited with a local authority, and—

(*a*) the plans have been passed by the authority, or

(*b*) notice of rejection of the plans has not been given within the relevant period from their deposit,

and the work to which the plans relate has not been commenced within three years from the deposit of the plans, the local authority may, at any time before the work is commenced, by notice to the person by whom or on whose behalf the plans were deposited, or other the owner for the time being of the land to which the plans relate, declare that the deposit of the plans is of no effect.

(2) Where a notice has been given under subsection (1) above, this Act and the building regulations shall, as respects the proposed work, have effect as if no plans had been deposited.

[Building Act 1984, s 32.]

*Tests for conformity with building regulations*

7.9901 **33. Tests for conformity with building regulations** (1) The following subsection has effect for the purpose of enabling a local authority to ascertain, as regards any work or proposed work to which building regulations for the enforcement of which they are responsible are applicable, whether any provision of building regulations is or would be contravened by, or by anything done or proposed to be done in connection with, that work.

(2) The local authority have power for that purpose—

(a) to require a person by whom or on whose behalf the work was, is being or is proposed to be done to carry out such reasonable tests of or in connection with the work as may be specified in the requirement, or

(b) themselves to carry out any reasonable tests of or in connection with the work, and to take any samples necessary to enable them to carry out such a test.

(3) Without prejudice to the generality of subsection (2) above, the matters with respect to which tests may be required or carried out under that subsection include—

(a) tests of the soil or subsoil of the site of a building,

(b) tests of any material, component or combination of components that has been, is being or is proposed to be used in the construction of a building, and tests of any service, fitting or equipment that has been, is being or is proposed to be provided in or in connection with a building.

(4) A local authority have power, for the purpose of ascertaining whether there is or has been, in the case of a building, a contravention of a continuing requirement that applies in relation to that building—

(a) to require the owner or occupier of the building to carry out such reasonable tests as may be specified in the requirement under this paragraph, or

(b) themselves to carry out any tests that they have power to require under paragraph (a) above, and to take any samples necessary to enable them to carry out such a test;

and in this subsection "continuing requirement" means a continuing requirement imposed by building regulations made by virtue of section 2(1) or (2) or (2A) above.

(5) The expense of carrying out any tests that a person is required to carry out under this section shall be met by that person, except that the local authority, on an application made to them, may, if they think it reasonable to do so, direct that the expense of carrying out any such tests, or such part of that expense as may be specified in the direction, shall be met by the local authority.

(6) Any question arising under this section between a local authority and a person as to the reasonableness of—

(a) a test specified in a requirement imposed on him by the authority under this section,

(b) a refusal by the authority to give a direction under subsection (5) above on an application made by him, or

(c) a direction under that subsection given on such an application,

may on the application of that person be determined by a magistrates' court; and in a case falling within paragraph (b) or (c) above the court may order the expense to which the application relates to be met by the local authority to such extent as the court thinks just.*

[Building Act 1984, s 33 as amended by the Sustainable and Secure Buildings Act 2004, s 4.]

* **Not yet in force.**

*Classification of buildings*

7.9902 34. **Classification of buildings** For the purposes of building regulations and of a direction given or instrument made with reference to building regulations, buildings may be classified by reference to size, description, design, purpose, location or any other characteristic whatsoever.

[Building Act 1984, s 34.]

*Breach of building regulations*

7.9903 35. **Penalty for contravening building regulations** If a person contravenes any provision contained in building regulations[1], other than a provision designated in the regulations as one to which this section does not apply, he is liable on summary conviction to a fine not exceeding **level** 5 on the standard scale and to a further fine not exceeding **£50** for each day on which the default continues[2] after he is convicted.

[Building Act 1984, s 35.]

1 See the Building (Inner London) Regulations 1985, SI 1985/1936; Building Regulations 2010, SI 2010/2214. (For amending instruments, see note 2 to s 1, ante.)

2 Not every offence under the regulation is a continuing offence. Following *Hodgetts v Chiltern District Council* [1983] 2 AC 120 it is necessary to consider whether the regulation requires the doing of something; if it does the offence is not a continuing offence (*Torridge District Council v Turner* (1991) 157 JP 65).

7.9904 35A. **Time limit for prosecution for contravention of building regulations** (1) Despite anything in section 127(1) of the Magistrates' Courts Act 1980 (c 43), an information relating to an offence under section 35 above may be tried by a magistrates' court if it is laid at any time—

(a) within the period of two years beginning with the day on which the offence was committed, and

(b) within the period of six months beginning with the relevant date.

(2) *Repealed.*

(3) *Repealed.*

(4) In subsection (1)(b) above, "the relevant date" means the date on which evidence sufficient to justify the proceedings comes to the knowledge of the person commencing the proceedings.

(5) In the case of proceedings commenced by a local authority—

(*a*) evidence is to be regarded for the purposes of subsection (4) above as sufficient to justify the proceedings if in the opinion of the proper officer or an authorised officer it is sufficient to justify the proceedings, and

(*b*) a certificate of the proper officer or, as the case may be, that authorised officer as to the date on which evidence which, in his opinion, was sufficient to justify the proceedings came to the knowledge of the person commencing the proceedings is to be conclusive evidence of that fact.

(6) *Repealed.*

[Building Act 1984, s 35A as inserted by the Climate Change and Sustainable Energy Act 2006, s 13(1) and amended by the Housing and Regeneration Act 2008, 317 and Sch 16.]

7.9905 36. **Removal or alteration of offending work** (1) If any work to which building regulations are applicable contravenes any of those regulations, the local authority, without prejudice to their right to take proceedings for a fine in respect of the contravention, may by notice require the owner—

(*a*) to pull down or remove the work, or

(*b*) if he so elects, to effect such alterations in it as may be necessary to make it comply with the regulations.

(2) If, in a case where the local authority are, by any section of this Part of this Act other than section 16, expressly required or authorised to reject plans, any work to which building regulations are applicable is executed—

(*a*) without plans having been deposited,

(*b*) notwithstanding the rejection of the plans, or

(*c*) otherwise than in accordance with any requirements subject to which the authority passed the plans,

the authority may by notice to the owner—

(i) require him to pull down or remove the work, or

(ii) require him either to pull down or remove the work or, if he so elects, to comply with any other requirements specified in the notice, being requirements that they might have made under the section in question as a condition of passing plans.

(3) If a person to whom a notice has been given under subsection (1) or (2) above fails to comply with the notice before the expiration of 28 days, or such longer period as a magistrates' court may on his application allow, the local authority may—

(*a*) pull down or remove the work in question, or

(*b*) effect such alterations in it as they deem necessary,

and may recover from him the expenses reasonably incurred by them in doing so.

(4) A notice under subsection (1) or (2) above (called a "section 36 notice") shall not be given after the expiration of 12 months from the date of the completion of the work in question.

(5) A section 36 notice shall not be given, in a case where plans were deposited and the work was shown on them, on the ground that the work contravenes any building regulations or, as the case may be, does not comply with the authority's requirements under any section of this Part of this Act other than section 16, if—

(*a*) the plans were passed by the authority, or

(*b*) notice of their rejection was not given within the relevant period from their deposit,

and if the work has been executed in accordance with the plans and of any requirement made by the local authority as a condition of passing the plans.

(6) This section does not affect the right of a local authority, the Attorney General or any other person to apply for an injunction for the removal or alteration of any work on the ground that it contravenes any regulation or any provision of this Act; but if—

(*a*) the work is one in respect of which plans were deposited,

(*b*) the plans were passed by the local authority, or notice of their rejection was not given within the relevant period from their deposit, and

(*c*) the work has been executed in accordance with the plans,

the court on granting an injunction has power to order the local authority to pay to the owner of the work such compensation as the court thinks just, but before making any such order the court shall in accordance with rules of court cause the local authority, if not a party to the proceedings, to be joined as a party to them.

[Building Act 1984, s 36.]

7.9906 37. **Obtaining of report where section 36 notice given** (1) In a case where—

(*a*) a person to whom a section 36 notice has been given gives to the local authority by whom the notice was given notice of his intention to obtain from a suitably qualified person a written report concerning work to which the section 36 notice relates, and

(*b*) such a report is obtained and submitted to the local authority and, as a result of their consideration of it, the local authority withdraw the section 36 notice,

the local authority may pay to the person to whom the section 36 notice was given such amount as appears to them to represent the expenses reasonably incurred by him in consequence of their having given him that notice including, in particular, his expenses in obtaining the report.

(2) Subject to subsection (3) below, if a person to whom a section 36 notice has been given gives

notice under subsection (1)(*a*) above, then, so far as regards the matters to which the section 36 notice relates, the reference to 28 days in section 36(3) above shall be construed as a reference to 70 days.

(3) Notice under subsection (1)(*a*) above shall be given before the expiry of the period of 28 days referred to in section 36(3) above, or, as the case may be, within such longer period as a court allows under section 36(3); and, where such a longer period has been so allowed before notice is given under subsection (1)(*a*) above, subsection (2) above does not apply.

[Building Act 1984, s 37.]

*Appeals in certain cases*

7.9907 **39. Appeal against refusal etc to relax building regulations** *If a local authority refuse an application to dispense with or relax a requirement in building regulations the applicant may appeal to the Secretary of State.*

7.9908 **40. Appeal against section 36 notice** (1) A person aggrieved by the giving of a section 36 notice may appeal to a magistrates' court.

(2) Subject to subsection (3) below, on an appeal under this section the court shall—

(*a*) if it determines that the local authority were entitled to give the notice, confirm the notice, and

(*b*) in any other case, give the local authority a direction to withdraw the notice.

(3) If, in a case where the appeal is against a notice under section 36(2) above, the court is satisfied that—

(*a*) the local authority were entitled to give the notice, but

(*b*) in all the circumstances of the case the purpose for which was enacted the section of this Act by virtue of which the notice was given has been substantially achieved,

the court may give a direction under subsection (2)(*b*) above.

(4) An appeal under this section shall be brought—

(*a*) within 28 days of the giving of the section 36 notice, or

(*b*) in a case where the person to whom the section 36 notice was given gives notice under section 37(1)(*a*) above, within 70 days of the giving of the section 36 notice.

(5) Where an appeal is brought under this section—

(*a*) the section 36 notice is of no effect pending the final determination or withdrawal of the appeal, and

(*b*) section 36(3) above has effect in relation to that notice as if after the words "28 days" there were inserted the words "(beginning, in a case where an appeal is brought under section 40 below, on the date when the appeal is finally determined or, as the case may be, withdrawn)".

(6) If, on an appeal under this section, there is produced to the court a report that has been submitted to the local authority under section 37(1) above, the court, in making an order as to costs, may treat the expenses incurred in obtaining the report as expenses incurred for the purposes of the appeal.

[Building Act 1984, s 40 as amended by the Courts Act 2003, Sch 8.]

7.9909 **41. Appeal to Crown Court** (1) Where a person—

(*a*) is aggrieved by an order, determination or other decision of a magistrates' court under this Part of this Act, or under Part IV of this Act as it applies in relation to this Part, and

(*b*) is not by any other enactment authorised to appeal to the Crown Court,

he may appeal to the Crown Court.

(2) Subsection (1) above does not confer a right of appeal in a case in which each of the parties concerned might under this Act have required that the dispute should be determined by arbitration instead of by a magistrates' court.

[Building Act 1984, s 41.]

*Inner London*

7.9910 **46. Inner London** In its application to inner London, this Part of this Act has effect subject to Part I of Schedule 3 to this Act.

[Building Act 1984, s 46.]

PART II[1]

SUPERVISION OF BUILDING WORK ETC OTHERWISE THAN BY LOCAL AUTHORITIES

*Supervision of plans and work by approved inspectors*

7.9911 **47. Giving and acceptance of initial notice** (1) If—

(*a*) a notice in the prescribed form (called an "initial notice") is given jointly to a local authority by a person intending to carry out work and a person who is an approved inspector in relation to that work,

(*b*) the initial notice is accompanied by such plans of the work as may be prescribed,

(*c*) the initial notice is accompanied by such evidence as may be prescribed that an approved scheme applies, or the prescribed insurance cover has been or will be provided, in relation to the work, and (*d*) the initial notice is accepted by the local authority,

then, so long as the initial notice continues in force, the approved inspector by whom the notice was given shall undertake such functions as may be prescribed[2] with respect to the inspection of plans of the work to which the notice relates, the supervision of that work and the giving and receiving of certificates and other notices.

(2) A local authority to whom an initial notice is given—

(*a*) may not reject the notice except on prescribed grounds, and

(*b*) shall reject the notice if any of the prescribed grounds exists,

and, in a case where the work to which an initial notice relates is work of such a description that, if plans of it had been deposited with the local authority, the authority could, under any enactment, have imposed requirements as a condition of passing the plans, the local authority may impose the like requirements as a condition of accepting the initial notice.

(3) Unless, within the prescribed period, the local authority to whom an initial notice is given give notice of rejection, specifying the ground or grounds in question, to each of the persons by whom the initial notice was given, the authority is conclusively presumed to have accepted the initial notice and to have done so without imposing any such requirements as are referred to in subsection (2) above.

(4) An initial notice—

(*a*) comes into force when it is accepted by the local authority, either by notice given within the prescribed period to each of the persons by whom it was given or by virtue of subsection (3) above, and

(*b*) subject to section 51(3) below, continues in force until—

(i) it is cancelled by a notice under section 52 below, or

(ii) the occurrence of, or the expiry of a prescribed period of time beginning on the date of, such event as may be prescribed;

and building regulations[3] may empower a local authority to extend (whether before or after its expiry) any such period of time as is referred to in paragraph (ii) above.

(5) The form prescribed for an initial notice may be such as to require—

(*a*) either or both of the persons by whom the notice is to be given to furnish information relevant for the purposes of this Act, Part II or IV of the Public Health Act 1936 or any provision of building regulations, and

(*b*) the approved inspector by whom the notice is to be given to enter into undertakings with respect to his performance of any of the functions referred to in subsection (1) above.

(6) The Secretary of State may approve for the purposes of this section any scheme that appears to him to secure the provision of adequate insurance cover in relation to any work to which an initial notice relates and is work to which the scheme applies.

(7) Building regulations may prescribe for the purposes of this section the insurance cover that is to be provided in relation to any work to which an initial notice relates and is not work to which an approved scheme applies and may, in particular, prescribe the form and content of policies of insurance.

[Building Act 1984, s 47 as amended by SI 1996/1905 and the Sustainable and Secure Buildings Act 2004, s 8.]

1 Part II contains ss 47–58.

2 See the Building (Approved Inspectors etc) Regulations 2010, SI 2010/2215. (For amending instruments, see note 2 to s 1, ante).

3 See the Building (Inner London) Regulations 1985, SI 1985/1936; Building Regulations 2010, SI 2010/2214. (For amending instruments, see note 2 to s 1, ante).

7.9912 48. **Effect of initial notice** (1) So long as an initial notice continues in force, the function of enforcing building regulations that is conferred on a local authority by section 91(2) below is not exercisable in relation to the work to which the notice relates, and accordingly—

(*a*) a local authority may not give a notice under section 36(1) above in relation to that work, and

(*b*) a local authority may not institute proceedings under section 35 above for a contravention of building regulations that arises out of the carrying out of that work.

(2) For the purposes of the enactments specified in subsection (3) below—

(*a*) the giving of an initial notice accompanied by such plans as are referred to in section 47(1)(*b*) above shall be treated as the deposit of plans,

(*b*) the plans accompanying an initial notice shall be treated as the deposited plans,

(*c*) the acceptance or rejection of an initial notice shall be treated as the passing or, as the case may be, the rejection of plans, and

(*d*) the cancellation of an initial notice under section 52(5) below shall be treated as a declaration under section 32 above that the deposit of plans is of no effect.

(3) The enactments referred to in subsection (2) above are—

(*a*) section 36(2) above,

(*b*) section 36(5) above, in so far as it relates to a notice under section 36(2) above and to non-compliance with any such requirement as is referred to in that subsection,

(*c*) section 36(6) above, in so far as it relates to a contravention of this Act,

(*d*) section 18(2) above, and

(e) sections 219 to 225 of the Highways Act 1980 (the advance payments code).

(4) *Repealed.*

[Building Act 1984, s 48 as amended by SI 1996/1905 and SI 2005/1541.]

7.9913 **49. Approved inspectors** (1) In this Act, "approved inspector" means a person who, in accordance with building regulations[1], is approved for the purposes of this Part of this Act—

(a) by the Secretary of State, or

(b) by a body (corporate or unincorporated) that, in accordance with the regulations, is designated by the Secretary of State for the purpose.

(2) Any such approval as is referred to in subsection (1) above may limit the description of work in relation to which the person concerned is an approved inspector.

(3) Any such designation as is referred to in subsection (1)(*b*) above may limit the cases in which and the terms on which the body designated may approve a person and, in particular, may provide that any approval given by the body shall be limited as mentioned in subsection (2) above.

(4) There shall be paid on an application for any such approval as is referred to in subsection (1) above—

(a) where the application is made to the Secretary of State, such fee as may be prescribed,

(b) where the application is made to a body designated by him as mentioned in that subsection, such fee as that body may determine.

(5) Building regulations may—

(a) contain provision prescribing the period for which, subject to any provision made by virtue of paragraph (*b*) or (*c*) below, any such approval as is referred to in subsection (1) above continues in force,

(b) contain provision precluding the giving of, or requiring the withdrawal of, any such approval as is referred to in subsection (1) above in such circumstances as may be prescribed,

(c) contain provision authorising the withdrawal of any such approval or designation as is referred to in subsection (1) above,

(d) provide for the maintenance—

(i) by the Secretary of State of a list of bodies that are for the time being designated by him as mentioned in subsection (1) above, and

(ii) by the Secretary of State and by each designated body of a list of persons for the time being approved by him or them as mentioned in that subsection,

(e) make provision for the supply to local authorities of copies of any list of approved inspectors maintained by virtue of paragraph (*d*) above and for such copy lists to be made available for inspection, and

(f) make provision for the supply, on payment of a prescribed fee, of a certified copy of any entry in a list maintained by virtue of paragraph (*d*) above or in a copy list held by a local authority by virtue of paragraph (*e*) above.

(6) Unless the contrary is proved, in any proceedings (whether civil or criminal) a document that appears to the court to be a certified copy of an entry either in a list maintained as mentioned in subsection (5)(*d*) above or in a copy of such a list supplied as mentioned in subsection (5)(*e*) above—

(a) is presumed to be a true copy of an entry in the current list so maintained, and

(b) is evidence of the matters stated in it.

(7) An approved inspector may make such charges in respect of the carrying out of the functions referred to in section 47(1) above as may in any particular case be agreed between him and the person who intends to carry out the work in question or, as the case may be, by whom that work is being or has been carried out.

(8) Nothing in this Part of this Act prevents an approved inspector from arranging for plans or work to be inspected on his behalf by another person; but such a delegation—

(a) shall not extend to the giving of a certificate under section 50 or 51 below, and

(b) shall not affect any liability, whether civil or criminal, of the approved inspector which arises out of functions conferred on him by this Part of this Act or by building regulations,

and, without prejudice to the generality of paragraph (*b*) above, an approved inspector is liable for negligence on the part of a person carrying out an inspection on his behalf in like manner as if it were negligence by a servant of his acting in the course of his employment.

[Building Act 1984, s 49.]

---

[1] See the Building (Inner London) Regulations 1985, SI 1985/1936; Building Regulations 2010, SI 2010/2214; Building (Approved Inspectors etc) Regulations 2010, SI 2010/2215. (For amending instruments, see note 2 to this section, ante).

7.9914 **50. Plans certificates** (1) Where an approved inspector—

(a) has inspected plans of the work to which an initial notice given by him relates,

(b) is satisfied that the plans neither are defective nor show that work carried out in accordance with them would contravene any provision of building regulations[1], and

(c) has complied with any prescribed requirements as to consultation or otherwise,

he shall, if requested to do so by the person intending to carry out the work, give a certificate in the prescribed[2] form (called a "plans certificate") to the local authority and to that person.

(2) If any question arises under subsection (1) above between an approved inspector and a person who proposes to carry out any work whether plans of the work are in conformity with building regulations, that person may refer the question to the Secretary of State for his determination.

(3) An application for a reference under subsection (2) above shall be accompanied by such fee as may be prescribed.

(4) Building regulations may authorise the giving of an initial notice combined with a certificate under subsection (1) above, and may prescribe a single form for such a combined notice and certificate; and where such a prescribed form is used—

(*a*) a reference in this Part of this Act to an initial notice or to a plans certificate includes a reference to that form, but

(*b*) should the form cease to be in force as an initial notice by virtue of section 47(4) above, nothing in that subsection affects the continuing validity of the form as a plans certificate.

(5) A plans certificate—

(*a*) may relate either to the whole or to part only of the work to which the initial notice concerned relates, and

(*b*) does not have effect unless it is accepted by the local authority to whom it is given.

(6) A local authority to whom a plans certificate is given—

(*a*) may not reject the certificate except on prescribed grounds, and

(*b*) shall reject the certificate if any of the prescribed grounds exists.

(7) Unless, within the prescribed period, the local authority to whom a plans certificate is given give notice of rejection, specifying the ground or grounds in question, to—

(*a*) the approved inspector by whom the certificate was given, and

(*b*) the other person to whom the approved inspector gave the certificate,

the authority shall be conclusively presumed to have accepted the certificate.

(8) If it appears to a local authority by whom a plans certificate has been accepted that the work to which the certificate relates has not been commenced within the period of three years beginning on the date on which the certificate was accepted, the authority may rescind their acceptance of the certificate by notice, specifying the ground or grounds in question, given—

(*a*) to the approved inspector by whom the certificate was given, and

(*b*) to the person shown in the initial notice concerned as the person intending to carry out the work.

[Building Act 1984, s 50 as amended by SI 1996/1905.]

1 See the Building (Inner London) Regulations 1985, SI 1985/1936; Building Regulations 2010, SI 2010/2214. (For amending instruments, see note 2 to s 1, ante).

2 See the Building (Approved Inspectors etc) Regulations 2010, SI 2010/2215. (For amending instruments, see note 2 to s 1, ante).

**7.9915 51. Final certificates** (1) Where an approved inspector is satisfied that any work to which an initial notice given by him relates has been completed, he shall give to the local authority by whom the initial notice was accepted such certificate with respect to the completion of the work and the discharge of his functions as may be prescribed (called a "final certificate").

(2) Section 50(5) to (7) above has effect in relation to a final certificate as if any reference in those subsections to a plans certificate were a reference to a final certificate.

(3) Where a final certificate—

(*a*) has been given with respect to any of the work to which an initial notice relates, and

(*b*) has been accepted by the local authority concerned,

the initial notice ceases to apply to that work, but section 48(1) above continues to apply, by virtue of this subsection, in relation to that work as if the initial notice continued in force in relation to it.

[Building Act 1984, s 51 as amended by SI 1996/1905.]

**7.9916 51A. Variation of work to which initial notice relates** (1) This section applies where it is proposed that the work to which an initial notice relates should be varied.

(2) If—

(*a*) a notice in the prescribed form (called an "amendment notice")—

(i) is given to the local authority by whom the initial notice was accepted, and

(ii) is jointly given by the approved inspector who gave the initial notice and by the person shown in the amendment notice as the person intending to carry out the relevant work,

(*b*) the amendment notice is accompanied by such plans of the proposed variation as may be prescribed,

(*c*) the amendment notice is accompanied by such evidence as may be prescribed that—

(i) a scheme approved for the purposes of section 47 above applies, or

(ii) the insurance cover prescribed for those purposes has been, or will be provided, in relation to the relevant work, and

(*d*) the amendment notice—

(i) is accepted by the local authority giving notice of acceptance within the prescribed period to each of the persons by whom the amendment notice was given, or

(ii) is deemed to have been accepted by the local authority by virtue of subsection (5) below,

the work to which the initial notice relates shall be treated as varied as proposed in the amendment notice.

(3) A local authority to whom an amendment notice is given—

(*a*) may not reject the notice except on prescribed grounds, and—

(*b*) shall reject the notice if any of the prescribed grounds exists.

(4) Where the relevant work is of such a description that, if plans of it had been deposited with the local authority, the authority could, under any enactment, have imposed requirements as a condition of passing the plans, the local authority may impose the like requirements as a condition of accepting the amendment notice.

(5) Unless, within the prescribed period, the local authority to whom an amendment notice is given give notice of rejection, specifying the ground or grounds in question, to each of the persons by whom the notice was given, the authority is conclusively presumed to have accepted it and to have done so without imposing any such requirements as are referred to in subsection (4) above.

(6) Section 47(5) shall apply in relation to the form prescribed for an amendment notice as it applies in relation to the form prescribed for an initial notice.

(7) In this section, references to the relevant work are to the work to which the initial notice, as proposed to be varied, relates.

[Building Act 1984, s 51A as inserted by SI 1996/1905.]

7.9917 **51B. Effect of Amendment Notice** (1) For the purposes of the enactments specified in section 48(3) above—

(*a*) the giving of an amendment notice accompanied by such plans as are referred to in section 51A(2)(*b*) above shall be treated as the deposit of plans,

(*b*) the acceptance or rejection of an amendment notice shall be treated as the passing, or, as the case may be, the rejection of plans,

(*c*) where an initial notice is varied by an amendment notice, the deposited plans shall be treated—

(i) as including the plans accompanying the amendment notice, and

(ii) as excluding such of the plans previously treated as the deposited plans as are superseded by the plans accompanying the amendment notice, and

(*d*) where an initial notice has been varied by an amendment notice, the cancellation of the initial notice under section 52(5) below shall be treated as a declaration under section 32 above that the deposit of plans constituted by the giving of the amendment notice is of no effect.

(2) *Repealed.*

[Building Act 1984, s 51B as inserted by SI 1996/1905 and amended by SI 2005/1541.]

7.9918 **51C. Change of person intending to carry out work** (1) This section applies where it is proposed that the work to which an initial notice relates should be carried out by a different person.

(2) If—

(*a*) the approved inspector who gave the initial notice, and

(*b*) the person who now proposes to carry out the work to which the initial notice relates,

jointly give written notice of the proposal to the local authority by whom the initial notice was accepted, the initial notice shall be treated as showing as the person intending to carry out the work to which it relates the person mentioned in the notice under this section.

[Building Act 1984, s 51C as inserted by SI 1996/1905.]

7.9919 **52. Cancellation of initial notice** (1) If, at a time when an initial notice is in force—

(*a*) the approved inspector becomes or expects to become unable to carry out (or to continue to carry out) his functions with respect to any of the work to which the initial notice relates,

(*b*) the approved inspector is of the opinion that any of the work is being so carried out that he is unable adequately to carry out his functions with respect to it, or

(*c*) the approved inspector is of the opinion that there is a contravention of any provision of building regulations[1] with respect to any of that work and the circumstances are as mentioned in subsection (2) below,

the approved inspector shall cancel the initial notice by notice in the prescribed[2] form given to the local authority concerned and to the person carrying out or intending to carry out the work.

(2) The circumstances referred to in subsection (1)(*c*) above are—

(*a*) that the approved inspector has, in accordance with building regulations, given notice of the contravention to the person carrying out the work or intending to carry out the work, and

(*b*) that, within the prescribed period, the prescribed steps are not taken by the person who, in accordance with building regulations, is required to take them.

(3) If, at a time when an initial notice is in force, it appears to the person carrying out or intending to carry out the work to which the initial notice relates that the approved inspector is no longer willing or able to carry out his functions with respect to any of that work, he shall cancel the initial notice by notice in the prescribed[2] form given to the local authority concerned and, if it is practicable to do so, to the approved inspector.

(4) If a person fails without reasonable excuse to give to a local authority a notice that he is required to give by subsection (3) above, he is liable on summary conviction to a fine not exceeding **level 5** on the standard scale.

(5) If, at a time when an initial notice is in force, it appears to the local authority by whom the initial notice was accepted that the work to which the initial notice relates has not been commenced within the period of three years beginning on the date on which the initial notice was accepted, the authority may cancel the initial notice by notice in the prescribed form given—

(*a*) to the approved inspector by whom the initial notice was given, and

(*b*) to the person shown in the initial notice as the person intending to carry out the work.

(6) A notice under subsection (1), (3) or (5) above has the effect of cancelling the initial notice to which it relates with effect from the day on which the notice is given.

[Building Act 1984, s 52 as amended by SI 1996/1905 and the Sustainable and Secure Buildings Act 2004, s 8.]

---

1 See the Building (Inner London) Regulations 1985, SI 1985/1936; Building Regulations 2010, SI 2010/2214. (For amending instruments, see note 2 to s 1, ante).

2 See the Building (Approved Inspectors etc) Regulations 2010, SI 2010/2215. (For amending instruments, see note 2 to s 1, ante).

7.9920 **53. Effect of initial notice ceasing to be in force** (1) This section applies where an initial notice ceases to be in force by virtue of section 47(4)(*b*)(i) or (ii) above.

(2) Building regulations[1] may provide that, if—

(*a*) a plans certificate was given before the day on which the initial notice ceased to be in force,

(*b*) that certificate was accepted by the local authority (before, on or after that day), and

(*c*) before that day, that acceptance was not rescinded by a notice under section 50(8) above,

then, with respect to the work specified in the certificate, such of the functions of a local authority referred to in section 48(1) above as may be prescribed for the purposes of this subsection either are not exercisable or are exercisable only in prescribed circumstances.

(3) If, before the day on which the initial notice ceased to be in force, a final certificate—

(*a*) was given in respect of part of the work to which the initial notice relates, and

(*b*) was accepted by the local authority (before, on or after that day),

the fact that the initial notice has ceased to be in force does not affect the continuing operation of section 51(3) above in relation to that part of the work.

(4) Notwithstanding anything in subsections (2) and (3) above, for the purpose of enabling the local authority to perform the functions referred to in section 48(1) above in relation to any part of the work not specified in a plans certificate or final certificate, as the case may be, building regulations may require the local authority to be provided with plans that relate not only to that part but also to the part to which the certificate in question relates.

(5) In any case where this section applies, the reference in subsection (4) of section 36 above to the date of the completion of the work in question has effect, in relation to a notice under subsection (1) of that section, as if it were a reference to the date on which the initial notice ceased to be in force.

(6) Subject to any provision of building regulations made by virtue of subsection (2) above, if, before the initial notice ceased to be in force, an offence under section 35 above was committed with respect to any of the work to which that notice relates, proceedings for that offence may be commenced by the local authority at any time within six months beginning with the day on which the function of the local authority referred to in section 48(1) above became exercisable with respect to the provision of building regulations to which the offence relates.

(6A) Subsection (6) above is without prejudice to any ability which, after that function has become exercisable, the local authority may have under section 35A above to commence proceedings for the offence after the end of that period of six months.

(7) The fact that an initial notice has ceased to be in force does not affect the right to give a new initial notice relating to any of the work to which the original notice related and in respect of which no final certificate has been given and accepted; but where—

(*a*) a plans certificate has been given in respect of any of that work,

(*b*) the conditions in paragraphs (*a*) to (*c*) of subsection (2) above are fulfilled with respect to that certificate, and

(*c*) such a new initial notice is given and accepted,

section 50(1) above does not apply in relation to so much of the work to which the new initial notice relates as is work specified in the plans certificate.

[Building Act 1984, s 53 as amended by SI 1996/1905 and the Climate Change and Sustainable Energy Act 2006, s 13.]

[1] See the Building (Inner London) Regulations 1985, SI 1985/1936; Building Regulations 2010, SI 2010/2214. (For amending instruments, see note 2 to s 1, ante).

*Supervision of their own work by public bodies*

7.9921 **54. Giving, acceptance and effect of public body's notice** (1) This section applies where a body (corporate or unincorporated) that acts under an enactment for public purposes and not for its own profit and is, or is of a description that is, approved by the Secretary of State in accordance with building regulations[1] (in this Part of this Act referred to as a "public body")—

(*a*) intends to carry out in relation to a building belonging to it work to which the substantive requirements of building regulations apply,

(*b*) considers that the work can be adequately supervised by its own servants or agents, and

(*c*) gives to the local authority in whose district the work is to be carried out notice in the prescribed[2] form (called a "public body's notice") together with such plans of the work as may be prescribed.

(2) A public body's notice is of no effect unless it is accepted by the local authority to whom it is given; and that local authority—

(*a*) may not reject the notice except on prescribed grounds, and

(*b*) shall reject the notice if any of the prescribed grounds exists,

and, in a case where the work to which the public body's notice relates is work of such a description that, if plans of it had been deposited with the local authority, the authority could, under an enactment, have imposed requirements as a condition of passing the plans, the local authority may impose the like requirements as a condition of accepting the public body's notice.

(3) Unless, within the prescribed period, the local authority to whom a public body's notice is given give notice of rejection, specifying the ground or grounds in question, the authority is conclusively presumed to have accepted the public body's notice and to have done so without imposing any such requirements as are referred to in subsection (2) above.

(4) Section 48 above has effect for the purposes of this section—

(*a*) with the substitution of a reference to a public body's notice for any reference to an initial notice, and

(*b*) with the substitution, in subsection (2)(*a*), of a reference to subsection (1)(*c*) of this section for the reference to section 47(1)(*b*).

(5) The form prescribed for a public body's notice may be such as to require the public body by whom it is to be given—

(*a*) to furnish information relevant for the purposes of this Act, Part II or IV of the Public Health Act 1936 or any provision of building regulations, and

(*b*) to enter into undertakings with respect to consultation and other matters.

(6) Where a public body's notice is given and accepted by the local authority to whom it is given, the provisions of Schedule 4 to this Act have effect, being provisions that correspond, as nearly as may be, to those made by the preceding provisions of this Part of this Act for the case where an initial notice is given and accepted.

[Building Act 1984, s 54.]

[1] See the Building (Inner London) Regulations 1985, SI 1985/1936; Building Regulations 2010, SI 2010/2214. (For amending instruments, see note 2 to s 1, ante).

[2] See the Building (Approved Inspectors etc) Regulations 2010, SI 2010/2215. (For amending instruments, see note 2 to s 1, ante).

*Supplementary*

7.9922 **55. Appeals** (1) A person aggrieved by the local authority's rejection of—

(*a*) an initial notice, amendment notice or a public body's notice, or

(*b*) a plans certificate, a final certificate, a public body's plans certificate or a public body's final certificate,

may appeal to a magistrates' court.

(2) On an appeal under subsection (1) above, the court shall—

(*a*) if it determines that the notice or certificate was properly rejected, confirm the rejection, and

(*b*) in any other case, give a direction to the local authority to accept the notice or certificate.

(3) Where a person is aggrieved by a determination, confirmation, direction or other decision of a magistrates' court under this section, he may appeal to the Crown Court.

[Building Act 1984, s 55 as amended by SI 1996/1905 and the Courts Act 2003, Sch 8.]

7.9923 **56. Recording and furnishing of information** (1) Every local authority shall keep, in such manner as may be prescribed[1], a register containing such information as may be prescribed with respect to initial notices, amendment notices, notices under section 51C above, public body's notices and certificates given to them, including information (where applicable) as to whether such notices or certificates have been accepted or rejected.*

(2) The information that may be prescribed under subsection (1) above with respect to an initial notice or amendment notice includes information about the insurance cover provided with

respect to the work to which the notice relates.*

(3) The reference in subsection (1) above to certificates is a reference to plans certificates, final certificates, public body's plans certificates, public body's final certificates and certificates given under section 16(9) above.*

(4) Every register kept under this section shall be available for inspection by the public at all reasonable hours.*

(5) Where an initial notice or a public body's notice has continued in force for any period, the local authority by whom it was accepted may require the approved inspector or public body by whom it was given to furnish them with any information that—

(*a*) they would have obtained themselves if during that period their function of enforcing building regulations had continued to be exercisable in relation to the work to which the notice relates, and

(*b*) they require for the purpose of performing their duty under section 230 of the Local Government Act 1972 (reports and returns),

and that section shall have effect as if during that period that function had continued to be so exercisable.

[Building Act 1984, s 56 as amended by SI 1996/1905.]

* **Repealed by the Sustainable and Secure Buildings Act 2004, s 11 from a date to be appointed.**

1 See the Building (Inner London) Regulations 1985, SI 1985/1936; Building Regulations 2010, SI 2010/2214; Building (Approved Inspectors etc) Regulations 2010, SI 2010/2215. (For amending instruments, see note 2 to s 1, ante).

7.9924 **57. Offences** (1) If a person—

(*a*) gives a notice or certificate that—

(i) purports to comply with the requirements of this Part of this Act, section 16(9) above or building regulations falling within paragraph 4A(1)(*a*) or (*b*) of Schedule 1 to this Act, and

(ii) contains a statement that he knows to be false or misleading in a material particular, or

(*b*) recklessly gives a notice or certificate that—

(i) purports to comply with those requirements, and

(ii) contains a statement that is false or misleading in a material particular,

he is guilty of an offence.

(2) A person guilty of an offence under subsection (1) above is liable[1]—

(*a*) on summary conviction, to a fine not exceeding **the statutory maximum** or imprisonment for a term not exceeding **six months** or **both**, and

(*b*) on conviction on indictment, to a **fine** or imprisonment for a term not exceeding **two years** or **both**.

(3) Where an approved inspector or person approved for the purposes of section 16(9) above is convicted of an offence under this section, the court by or before which he is convicted shall, within one month of the date of conviction, forward a certificate of the conviction to the person by whom the approval was given.

[Building Act 1984, s 57 as amended by the Sustainable and Secure Buildings Act 2004, s 8.]

1 For procedure in respect of an offence triable either way, see the Magistrates' Courts Act 1980, ss 17A–21, in PART I: MAGISTRATES' COURTS, PROCEDURE, ante.

7.9925 **58. Construction of Part II** (1) In this Part of this Act—

"amendment notice" has the meaning given by section 51A(2) above;

"final certificate" has the meaning given by section 51(1) above;

"initial notice" has the meaning given by section 47(1) above;

"plans certificate" has the meaning given by section 50(1) above;

"public body" and "public body's notice" have the meanings given by section 54(1) above;

"public body's final certificate" has the meaning given by paragraph 3 of Schedule 4 to this Act;

"public body's plans certificate" has the meaning given by paragraph 2 of Schedule 4 to this Act.

(2) A reference in this Part of this Act to the carrying out of work includes a reference to the making of a material change of use, as defined by and for the purposes of building regulations.

(3) A reference in this Part of this Act to an initial notice given by an approved inspector is a reference to a notice given by him jointly with another person as mentioned in section 47(1)(*a*) above.

[Building Act 1984, s 58 as amended by SI 1996/1905.]

## PART III[1]

## OTHER PROVISIONS ABOUT BUILDINGS

### *Drainage*

7.9926 **59. Drainage of building** (1) If it appears to a local authority that in the case of a building—

(*a*) satisfactory provision has not been, and ought to be, made for drainage, (*b*) a cesspool, private sewer, drain, soil pipe, rain-water pipe, spout, sink or other necessary appliance provided for the building is insufficient or, in the case of a private sewer or drain communicating directly or indirectly with a public sewer, is so defective as to admit subsoil water,

(*c*) a cesspool or other such work or appliance as aforesaid provided for the building is in such a condition as to be prejudicial to health or a nuisance,[2] or

(*d*) a cesspool, private sewer or drain formerly used for the drainage of the building, but no longer used for it, is prejudicial to health or a nuisance,

they shall by notice require the owner of the building to make satisfactory provision for the drainage of the building, or, as the case may be, require either the owner or the occupier of the building to do such work as may be necessary for renewing, repairing or cleansing the existing cesspool, sewer, drain, pipe, spout, sink or other appliance, or for filling up, removing or otherwise rendering innocuous the disused cesspool, sewer or drain.

(2) Sections 99 and 102 below apply in relation to a notice given under subsection (1) above.

(3) Subsections (4), (5) and (6) of section 21 above apply in relation to a drain that a local authority require to be constructed under this section as they apply in relation to such a proposed drain as is mentioned in that section.

(4) Subsection (1) above, so far as it empowers a local authority to take action in the cases mentioned in paragraphs (*a*) and (*b*) of the subsection, does not apply in relation to a building belonging to statutory undertakers, the Civil Aviation Authority or a person who holds a licence under Chapter I of Part I of the Transport Act 2000 (air traffic services) and held or used by such a body or person for the purpose of that body's or that person's undertaking, unless it is—

(*a*) a house, or

(*b*) a building used as offices or showrooms, and not forming part of a railway station or in the case of the Civil Aviation Authority not being on an aerodrome owned by the Authority.*

(5) For the purposes of subsection (4) above, the undertaking of a person who holds a licence under Chapter I of Part I of the Transport Act 2000 shall be taken to be the person's undertaking as licence holder.*

(6) In subsection (1) above, "drainage" includes the conveyance, by means of a sink and any other necessary appliance, of refuse water and the conveyance of rainwater from roofs.

[Building Act 1984, s 59 as amended by the Airports Act 1986, Sch 6, SI 2001/3335 and 4050 and SI 2002/440.]

* **Repealed by the Sustainable and Secure Buildings Act 2004, s 11 from a date to be appointed.**

1 Part III contains ss 59–90.

2 A notice under s 59(1)(*c*) alleging that a sewer is defective, and requiring works to be executed, must be served not only on the owner or occupier on whose premises the break has occurred, but also on all other persons whose premises are upstream of those premises (*Swansea City Council v Jenkins* (1994) 158 JP 952).

7.9927 **60. Use and ventilation of soil pipes** (1) A pipe for conveying rain-water from a roof shall not be used for the purpose of conveying the soil or drainage from a sanitary convenience.

(2) The soil pipe from a water-closet shall be properly ventilated.

(3) A pipe for conveying surface water from premises shall not be permitted to act as a ventilating shaft to a drain or sewer conveying foul water.

(4) If it appears to the local authority that there is on any premises a contravention of any provision of this section, they may by notice require the owner or the occupier of those premises to execute such work as may be necessary to remedy the matter.

(5) Sections 99 and 102 below apply in relation to a notice given under subsection (4) above.

[Building Act 1984, s 60 as amended by the Water Act 1989, Sch 8.]

7.9928 **61. Repair etc of drain** (1) No person shall—

(*a*) except in case of emergency, repair, reconstruct or alter the course of an underground drain that communicates with a sewer, or with a cesspool or other receptacle for drainage, or

(*b*) where in a case of emergency any such works have been executed without notice, cover over the drain or sewer,

without giving to the local authority at least 24 hours' notice of his intention to do so.

(2) While any such work as aforesaid is being executed, all persons concerned shall permit the proper officer, or any other authorised officer, of the local authority to have free access to the work.

(3) A person who fails to comply with this section is liable on summary conviction to a fine not exceeding **level 3** on the standard scale.

(4) This section does not apply to—

(*a*) so much of a drain or sewer constructed by, or belonging to, a railway company as runs under, across or along their railway, or

(*b*) so much of a drain or sewer constructed by, or belonging to, dock undertakers as is situated in or on land of the undertakers that is held or used by them for the purposes of their undertaking.

[Building Act 1984, s 61.]

7.9929 **62. Disconnection of drain** (1) Where a person—

(*a*) reconstructs in the same or a new position a drain that communicates with a sewer or another drain, (*b*) executes any works to such a drain so as permanently to discontinue its use, or

(*c*) executes any works on premises served by such a drain so as permanently to discontinue its use,

he shall cause any drains or parts of drains thereby becoming disused or unnecessary to be disconnected and sealed at such points as the local authority may reasonably require.

(2) Any question as to the reasonableness of a requirement of a local authority under this section shall be determined by a magistrates' court, and the court may vary the requirement as it thinks fit.

(3) No one shall be required under this section to carry out any work in land outside the premises served by the drain if he has no right to carry out that work, but, subject to section 101 below, the person undertaking the reconstruction of the drain or the execution of the works may break open any street for the purpose of complying with a requirement under this section.

(4) Before a person complies with a requirement under this section, he shall give at least 48 hours' notice to the local authority, and a person who fails to comply with this subsection is liable on summary conviction to a fine not exceeding **level 1** on the standard scale.

(5) A person who knowingly fails to comply with subsection (1) above is liable on summary conviction to a fine not exceeding **level 1** on the standard scale and to a further fine not exceeding **£1** for each day on which the default continues after he is convicted.

(6) This section does not apply in relation to anything done in the course of the demolition of a building, or of part of a building, being a demolition as respects which the local authority have power under section 81 below to serve a notice on the person undertaking the demolition.

[Building Act 1984, s 62.]

**7.9930 63. Improper construction or repair of water-closet or drain** (1) If a water-closet, drain or soil pipe is so constructed or repaired as to be prejudicial to health or a nuisance, the person who undertook or executed the construction or repair is liable on summary conviction to a fine not exceeding **level 1** on the standard scale, unless he shows that the prejudice to health or nuisance could not have been avoided by the exercise of reasonable care.

(2) A person charged with an offence under this section (hereafter in this section referred to as "the original defendant") is entitled, upon information duly laid by him and on giving to the prosecutor not less than three clear days' notice of his intention, to have any other person, being his agent or servant, to whose act or default he alleges that the offence was due brought before the court at the time appointed for the hearing of the charge; and—

(*a*) if after the commission of the offence has been proved the original defendant proves that the offence was due to the act or default of that other person, that other person may be convicted of the offence, and

(*b*) if the original defendant further proves that he used all due diligence to secure that the water-closet, drain or soil pipe in question was so constructed or repaired as not to be prejudicial to health or a nuisance, he shall be acquitted of the offence.

(3) Where the original defendant seeks to avail himself of subsection (2) above—

(*a*) the prosecutor as well as the person whom the original defendant charges with the offence has the right to cross-examine the original defendant, if he gives evidence, and any witness called by him in support of his pleas, and to call rebutting evidence, and

(*b*) the court may make such order as it thinks fit for the payment of costs by any party to the proceedings to any other party to them.

(4) In this section in its application to Greater London, a reference to a water-closet includes a reference to a urinal.

[Building Act 1984, s 63.]

*Provision of sanitary conveniences*

**7.9931 64. Provision of closets in building** (1) If it appears to a local authority—

(*a*) that a building is without sufficient closet accommodation,

(*b*) that a part of a building, being a part that is occupied as a separate dwelling, is without sufficient closet accommodation, or

(*c*) that any closets provided for or in connection with a building are in such a state as to be prejudicial to health or a nuisance and cannot without reconstruction be put into a satisfactory condition,

the authority shall, by notice to the owner of the building, require him to provide the building with such closets or additional closets, or such substituted closets, being in each case either water-closets or earth-closets, as may be necessary.

(2) Unless a sufficient water supply and sewer are available, the authority shall not require the provision of a water-closet except in substitution for an existing water-closet.

(3) Sections 99 and 102 below apply in relation to a notice given under subsection (1) above.

(4) Among the grounds on which an appeal may be brought under section 102 below against such a notice is that—

(*a*) the need for the works to be executed under the notice would not, in whole or in part, arise but for the occupation of part of the building as a separate dwelling, and the occupation of that part as a separate dwelling is a matter in respect of which the appellant has a cause of action, and

(*b*) the person against whom the appellant has a cause of action ought to contribute towards the expenses of executing the works.

(5) Where the grounds on which an appeal under section 102 below is brought include the ground specified in subsection (4) above—

(*a*) the appellant shall serve a copy of his notice of appeal on the person or persons referred to in that ground of appeal, and

(*b*) on the hearing of the appeal the court may make such order as it thinks fit with respect to—

(i) the contribution to be made by any such person towards the cost of the works, or

(ii) the proportion in which any expenses that may be recoverable by the local authority are to be borne by the appellant and any such other person.

(6) This section does not apply to—

(*a*) a factory,

(*b*) a building that is used as a workplace, or

(*c*) premises to which the Offices, Shops and Railway Premises Act 1963 applies.

[Building Act 1984, s 64.]

7.9932 **65. Provision of sanitary conveniences in workplace** (1) A building that is used as a workplace shall be provided with—

(*a*) sufficient and satisfactory accommodation in the way of sanitary conveniences, regard being had to the number of persons employed in, or in attendance at, the building, and

(*b*) where persons of both sexes are employed or in attendance, sufficient and satisfactory separate accommodation for persons of each sex, unless the local authority are satisfied that in the circumstances of the particular case the provision of such separate accommodation is unnecessary.

(2) If it appears to the local authority that subsection (1) above is not complied with in the case of any building, they shall by notice require the owner or the occupier of the building to make such alterations in the existing conveniences, and to provide such additional conveniences, as may be necessary.

(3) Sections 99 to 102 below apply in relation to a notice given under subsection (2) above.

(4) This section does not apply to premises to which the Offices, Shops and Railway Premises Act 1963 applies.

[Building Act 1984, s 65.]

7.9933 **66. Replacement of earth-closets etc** (1) If a building has a sufficient water supply and sewer available, the local authority may, subject to this section, by notice to the owner of the building require that any closets, other than water-closets, provided for, or in connection with, the building shall be replaced by water-closets, notwithstanding that the closets are not insufficient in number and are not prejudicial to health or a nuisance.

(2) A notice under subsection (1) above shall—

(*a*) require the owner to execute the necessary works, or

(*b*) require that the authority themselves shall be allowed to execute them,

and shall state the effect of subsection (3) below.

(3) Where the local authority give a notice under subsection (1) above—

(*a*) if it requires the owner to execute the works, the owner is entitled to recover from them one-half of the expenses reasonably incurred by him in the execution of the works, and

(*b*) if it requires that they shall be allowed to execute the works, they are entitled to recover from the owner one-half of the expenses reasonably incurred by them in the execution of the works.

(4) Where the owner of a building proposes to provide it with a water-closet in substitution for a closet of any other type, the local authority may, if they think fit, agree to pay him a part, not exceeding one-half, of the expenses reasonably incurred in effecting the replacement, notwithstanding that a notice has not been given by them under subsection (1) above.

(5) Sections 99 and 102 below apply in relation to a notice given under subsection (1) above, subject to the following modifications—

(*a*) no appeal lies on the ground that the works are unnecessary, and

(*b*) any reference in the said section 99 to the expenses reasonably incurred in executing works is a reference to one-half of those expenses.

[Building Act 1984, s 66.]

7.9934 **67. Loan of temporary sanitary conveniences** (1) A local authority may, at the request of the occupier of any premises connected with a cesspool, sewer or drain on which any work of maintenance, improvement or repair that necessitates the disconnection of the sanitary conveniences provided for or in connection with the premises is to be carried out—

(*a*) by a local authority, or

(*b*) by the owner or occupier of the premises in pursuance of section 59 above,

supply on loan temporary sanitary conveniences in substitution for any sanitary conveniences so disconnected.

(2) Subject to the following provisions of this section, the local authority may make reasonable charges for supplying, removing and cleansing any temporary sanitary conveniences lent under this

section for more than seven days.

(3) No charge may be made under subsection (2) above—

(*a*) for the use of the temporary sanitary conveniences for the first seven days, or

(*b*) in a case where the work is made necessary by a defect in a public sewer.

(4) No charge may be made under subsection (2) above where the work is made necessary—

(*a*) *repealed*;

(*b*) by a defect in a cesspool, private sewer or drain in respect of which the local authority have served a notice under section 59 above,

but, if the temporary sanitary conveniences are provided for a period of more than seven days, the reasonable expenses of supplying, removing and cleansing them are recoverable from the owner of the premises (but not any charge for the use of them for the first seven days).

(5) In proceedings to recover expenses under subsection (4) above, the court may—

(*a*) inquire whether the expenses ought to be borne wholly or in part by some person other than the defendant in the proceedings, and

(*b*) make such order concerning the expenses or their apportionment as appears to the court to be just,

but the court shall not order the expenses or any part of them to be borne by any person other than the defendant in the proceedings unless the court is satisfied that that other person has had notice of the proceedings and an opportunity of being heard.

[Building Act 1984, s 67 as amended by the Water Act 1989, Sch 27.]

7.9935 **68. Erection of public conveniences** (1) No person shall erect a public sanitary convenience in, or so as to be accessible from, a street without the consent of the local authority, who may give their consent upon such terms as to the use of the convenience or its removal at any time, if required by them, as they think fit.

(2) A person who contravenes subsection (1) above is liable on summary conviction to a fine not exceeding **level 1** on the standard scale, without prejudice to the right of the authority under subsection (4) below to require the convenience to be removed.

(3) A person aggrieved by the refusal of a local authority to give a consent under subsection (1) above, or by any terms imposed by them, may appeal to a magistrates' court.

(4) The local authority may by notice require—

(*a*) the owner of a sanitary convenience—

(i) that has been erected in contravention of subsection (1) above, or

(ii) that the authority are, by virtue of the terms of a consent given under that subsection, entitled to require to be removed,

to remove it, or

(*b*) the owner of a sanitary convenience that opens on a street, and is so placed or constructed as to be a nuisance or offensive to public decency, to remove it or permanently close it.

(5) Sections 99 and 102 below apply in relation to a notice given under subsection (4) above.

(6) In this section, a reference to a local authority, in relation to a street that is a highway for which the local authority are not the highway authority, is a reference to the highway authority.

(7) Subsection (1) above does not apply to a sanitary convenience erected—

(*a*) by a railway company within their railway station or its yard or approaches, or

(*b*) by dock undertakers in or on land that belongs to them and is held or used by them for the purposes of their undertaking.

(8) This section does not affect the powers of—

(*a*) a county council under section 87 of the Public Health Act 1936,

(*b*) the Secretary of State under section 112 of the Highways Act 1980, or

(*c*) a county council under section 114(1) of the Highways Act 1980.

[Building Act 1984, s 68 as amended by the Local Government Act 1985, Sch 17.]

7.9936 **70. Provision of food storage accommodation in house** (1) If it appears to a local authority that a house, or part of a building that is occupied as a separate dwelling, is without sufficient and suitable accommodation for the storage of food, the local authority may by notice require the owner of the house or building to provide the house or building with sufficient and suitable accommodation for that purpose.

(2) Sections 99 and 102 below apply in relation to a notice given under subsection (1) above.

(3) Among the grounds on which an appeal may be brought under section 102 below against such a notice are—

(*a*) that it is not reasonably practicable to comply with the notice;

(*b*) that—

(i) the need for the works to be executed under the notice would not, in whole or in part, arise but for the occupation of part of the building as a separate dwelling, and that the occupation of that part as a separate dwelling is a matter in respect of which the appellant has a cause of action, and

(ii) the person against whom the appellant has a cause of action ought to contribute towards the expenses of executing the works.

(4) Where the grounds on which an appeal under section 102 below is brought include the ground specified in subsection (3)(*b*) above—

(*a*) the appellant shall serve a copy of his notice of appeal on the person or persons referred to in that ground of appeal, and

(*b*) on the hearing of the appeal the court may make such order as it thinks fit with respect to—

(i) the contribution to be made by any such person towards the cost of the works, or

(ii) the proportion in which any expenses that may be recoverable by the local authority are to be borne by the appellant and any such other person.

[Building Act 1984, s 70.]

7.9937 72. **Means of escape from fire** (1) If it appears to a local authority, after consultation with the fire and rescue authority, that—

(*a*) a building to which this section applies is not provided, or

(*b*) a proposed building that will be a building to which this section applies will not be provided,

with such means of escape in case of fire as the local authority, after such consultation, deem necessary from each storey whose floor is more than twenty feet above the surface of the street or ground on any side of the building, the authority shall by notice require the owner of the building, or, as the case may be, the person proposing to erect the building, to execute such work or make such other provision in regard to the matters aforesaid as may be necessary.

(2) Sections 99 and 102 below apply in relation to a notice given under subsection (1) above in so far as it requires a person to execute works.

(3) In so far as such a notice requires a person to make provision otherwise than by the execution of works, he is, if he fails to comply with the notice, liable on summary conviction to a fine not exceeding **level 4** on the standard scale and to a further fine not exceeding **£2** for each day on which the offence continues after he is convicted.

(4) In proceedings under subsection (3) above, it is open to the defendant to question the reasonableness of the authority's requirements.

(5) Where building regulations imposing requirements as to the provision of means of escape in case of fire are applicable to a proposed building or proposed extension of a building, or would be so applicable but for a direction under section 8 above dispensing with such requirements—

(*a*) this section, and

(*b*) any provision of a local Act that has effect in place of this section,

does not apply in relation to the proposed building or extension.

(6) This section applies to a building that exceeds two storeys in height and in which the floor of any upper storey is more than twenty feet above the surface of the street or ground on any side of the building and that—

(*a*) *repealed.*

(*b*) *repealed.*

(*c*) *repealed.*

(7) *Repealed.*

[Building Act 1984, s 72 as amended by the Fire and Rescue Services Act 2004, Sch 1, the Housing Act 2004, Sch 16 and SI 2005/1541.]

7.9938 73. **Raising of chimney** (1) Where, after the 3rd October 1961 (which was the date of commencement of the relevant provisions of the Public Health Act 1961)—

(*a*) a person erects or raises a building (in this section referred to as "the taller building") to a greater height than an adjoining building, and

(*b*) any chimneys or flues of an adjoining building are in a party wall between the two buildings or are six feet or less from the nearest part of the taller building,

the local authority may by notice—

(i) require that person, within such time as may be specified in the notice, to build up those chimneys and flues, if it is reasonably practicable so to do, so that their top will be of the same height as the top of the chimneys of the taller building or the top of the taller building, whichever is the higher, and

(ii) require the owner or occupier of the adjoining building to allow the first-mentioned person to enter on that building and carry out such work as may be necessary to comply with the notice served on him,

except that, if the said owner or occupier, within fourteen days from the date of service of the notice on him, serves on the first-mentioned person and on the local authority a notice (in this section referred to as a "counter-notice") that he elects to carry out the work himself, the owner or occupier shall comply with the notice served under paragraph (i) above instead of the first-mentioned person and may recover the expenses reasonably incurred in so doing from that person.

(2) A person on whom a notice is served under paragraph (i) or paragraph (ii) of subsection (1) above may appeal to a magistrates' court.

(3) If—

(*a*) a person on whom a notice is served under paragraph (i) of subsection (1) above fails to comply with the notice, except in a case where the owner or occupier of an adjoining building has refused to allow entry on that building, or has refused to allow the carrying out of any such work as may be necessary to comply with the notice, or has served a counter-notice, or

(*b*) a person on whom a notice is served under paragraph (ii) of subsection (1) above fails to comply with the notice or, having served a counter-notice, fails to comply with the notice served under paragraph (i) of that subsection,

he is liable on summary conviction to a fine not exceeding **level 1** on the standard scale, and the local authority may themselves carry out such work as may be necessary to comply with the notice served under the said paragraph (1), and recover the expenses reasonably incurred in doing so from the person on whom that notice was served.

[Building Act 1984, s 73.]

7.9939 **74. Cellars and rooms below subsoil water level** (1) No person shall without the consent of the local authority construct a cellar or room in, or as part of, a house, shop, inn, hotel or office if the floor level of the cellar or room is lower than the ordinary level of the subsoil water on, under or adjacent to the site of the house, shop, inn, hotel or office.

(2) Subsection (1) above does not apply to—

(*a*) *repealed*

(*b*) the construction of a cellar or room in connection with a shop, inn, hotel or office that forms part of a railway station.

(3) If a person constructs a cellar or room in contravention of subsection (1) above, or of any condition attached to a consent under this section—

(*a*) he is liable on summary conviction to a fine not exceeding **level 1** on the standard scale, and

(*b*) the local authority may by notice require him either to alter the cellar or room so that its construction will no longer contravene the said subsection or condition or, if he so elects, to fill it in or otherwise make it unusable.

(4) Sections 99 and 102 below apply in relation to a notice given under subsection (3) above, subject to the following modifications—

(*a*) section 99(1) requires the notice to indicate the nature of the works of alteration and that of the works for making the cellar or room unusable, and

(*b*) section 99(2) authorises the local authority to execute, subject to that subsection, at their election either the works of alteration or the works for making the cellar or room unusable.

(5) If the owner for the time being of the house, shop, inn, hotel or office causes or permits a cellar or room forming part of it to be used in a manner that he knows to be in contravention of a condition attached to a consent under this section, he is liable on summary conviction to a fine not exceeding **level 1** on the standard scale.

[Building Act 1984, s 74 as amended by the Licensing Act 2003, Sch 6.]

7.9940 **75. Consents under section** 74 (1) A consent under section 74 above may be given subject to such conditions as to the construction or use of the premises as may be specified in it, and conditions specified in such a consent are binding on successive owners of the house, shop, inn, hotel or office.

(2) If a local authority—

(*a*) refuse an application for such a consent, or

(*b*) attach any conditions to such a consent,

the person applying for the consent may appeal to a magistrates' court against the refusal or, as the case may be, against any of the conditions, and if a magistrates' court allows an appeal against a refusal to grant a consent it may direct the local authority to give their consent subject to such conditions, if any, as appear to the court to be appropriate.

(3) An application may be made at any time to the local authority for the variation or withdrawal of a condition attached to such a consent, and, if the local authority refuse the application, the applicant may appeal to a magistrates' court.

[Building Act 1984, s 75.]

*Defective premises, demolition etc*

7.9941 **76. Defective premises** (1) If it appears to a local authority that—

(*a*) any premises are in such a state (in this section referred to as a "defective state") as to be prejudicial to health or a nuisance, and

(*b*) unreasonable delay in remedying the defective state would be occasioned by following the procedure prescribed by section 80 of the Environmental Protection Act 1990,

the local authority may serve on the person on whom it would have been appropriate to serve an abatement notice under the said section 93 (if the local authority had proceeded under that section) a notice stating that the local authority intend to remedy the defective state and specifying the defects that they intend to remedy.

(2) Subject to subsection (3) below, the local authority may, after the expiration of nine days after service of a notice under subsection (1) above, execute such works as may be necessary to remedy the defective state, and recover the expenses reasonably incurred in so doing from the

person on whom the notice was served.

(3) If, within seven days after service of a notice under subsection (1) above, the person on whom the notice was served serves a counter-notice that he intends to remedy the defects specified in the first-mentioned notice, the local authority shall take no action in pursuance of the first-mentioned notice unless the person who served the counter-notice—

(*a*) fails within what seems to the local authority a reasonable time to begin to execute works to remedy the said defects, or

(*b*) having begun to execute such works fails to make such progress towards their completion as seems to the local authority reasonable.

(4) In proceedings to recover expenses under subsection (2) above, the court—

(*a*) shall inquire whether the local authority were justified in concluding that the premises were in a defective state, or that unreasonable delay in remedying the defective state would have been occasioned by following the procedure prescribed by section 80 of the Environmental Protection Act 1990, and

(*b*) if the defendant proves that he served a counter-notice under subsection (3) above, shall inquire whether the defendant failed to begin the works to remedy the defects within a reasonable time, or failed to make reasonable progress towards their completion,

and if the court determines that—

(i) the local authority were not justified in either of the conclusions mentioned in paragraph (*a*) of this subsection, or

(ii) there was no failure under paragraph (*b*) of this subsection,

the local authority shall not recover the expenses or any part of them.

(5) Subject to subsection (4) above, in proceedings to recover expenses under subsection (2) above, the court may—

(*a*) inquire whether the said expenses ought to be borne wholly or in part by some person other than the defendant in the proceedings, and

(*b*) make such order concerning the expenses or their apportionment as appears to the court to be just,

but the court shall not order the expenses or any part of them to be borne by a person other than the defendant in the proceedings unless the court is satisfied that that other person has had due notice of the proceedings and an opportunity of being heard.

(6) A local authority shall not serve a notice under subsection (1) above, or proceed with the execution of works in accordance with a notice so served, if the execution of the works would, to their knowledge, be in contravention of a building preservation order under section 29 of the Town and Country Planning Act 1947[1].

(7) The power conferred on a local authority by subsection (1) above may be exercised notwithstanding that the local authority might instead have proceeded under Part VI of the Housing Act 1985 (repair notices).

[Building Act 1984, s 76 as amended by the Housing (Consequential Provisions) Act 1985, Sch 2 and the Environmental Protection Act 1990, Sch 15.]

---

[1] The issue of building preservation notices by local planning authorities and the listing of special buildings is now governed by the Planning (Listed Buildings and Conservation Areas) Act 1990, post.

7.9942 77. **Dangerous building** (1) If it appears to a local authority that a building or structure, or part of a building or structure, is in such a condition, or is used to carry such loads, as to be dangerous, the authority may apply to a magistrates' court, and the court may—

(*a*) where danger arises from the condition of the building or structure, make an order requiring the owner thereof—

(i) to execute such work as may be necessary to obviate the danger or,

(ii) if he so elects, to demolish the building or structure, or any dangerous part of it, and remove any rubbish resulting from the demolition, or

(*b*) where danger arises from overloading of the building or structure, make an order restricting its use until a magistrates' court, being satisfied that any necessary works have been executed, withdraws or modifies the restriction.

(2) If the person on whom an order is made under subsection (1)(*a*) above fails to comply with the order within the time specified, the local authority may—

(*a*) execute the order in such manner as they think fit, and

(*b*) recover the expenses reasonably incurred by them in doing so from the person in default,

and, without prejudice to the right of the authority to exercise those powers, the person is liable on summary conviction to a fine not exceeding **level 1** on the standard scale.

(3) This section has effect subject to the provisions of the Planning (Listed Buildings and Conservation Areas) Act 1990 relating to listed buildings, buildings subject to building preservation notices and buildings in conservation areas.

[Building Act 1984, s 77 as amended by the Housing and Planning Act 1986, Sch 9 and the Planning (Consequential Provisions) Act 1990, Sch 2.]

7.9943 **78. Dangerous building—emergency measures** (1) If it appears to a local authority that—

(*a*) a building or structure, or part of a building or structure, is in such a state, or is used to carry such loads, as to be dangerous, and

(*b*) immediate action should be taken to remove the danger,

they may take such steps as may be necessary for that purpose.

(2) Before exercising their powers under this section, the local authority shall, if it is reasonably practicable to do so, give notice of their intention to the owner and occupier of the building, or of the premises on which the structure is situated.

(3) Subject to this section, the local authority may recover from the owner the expenses reasonably incurred by them under this section.

(4) So far as expenses incurred by the local authority under this section consist of expenses of fencing off the building or structure, or arranging for it to be watched, the expenses shall not be recoverable in respect of any period—

(*a*) after the danger has been removed by other steps under this section, or

(*b*) after an order made under section 77(1) above for the purpose of its removal has been complied with or has been executed as mentioned in subsection (2) of that section.

(5) In proceedings to recover expenses under this section, the court shall inquire whether the local authority might reasonably have proceeded instead under section 77(1) above, and, if the court determines that the local authority might reasonably have proceeded instead under that subsection, the local authority shall not recover the expenses or any part of them.

(6) Subject to subsection (5) above, in proceedings to recover expenses under this section, the court may—

(*a*) inquire whether the expenses ought to be borne wholly or in part by some person other than the defendant in the proceedings, and

(*b*) make such order concerning the expenses or their apportionment as appears to the court to be just,

but the court shall not order the expenses or any part of them to be borne by any person other than the defendant in the proceedings unless it is satisfied that that other person has had due notice of the proceedings and an opportunity of being heard.

(7) Where in consequence of the exercise of the powers conferred by this section the owner or occupier of any premises sustains damage, but section 106(1) below does not apply because the owner or occupier has been in default—

(*a*) the owner or occupier may apply to a magistrates' court to determine whether the local authority were justified in exercising their powers under this section so as to occasion the damage sustained, and

(*b*) if the court determines that the local authority were not so justified, the owner or occupier is entitled to compensation, and section 106(2) and (3) below applies in relation to any dispute as regards compensation arising under this subsection.

(8) The proper officer of a local authority may, as an officer of the local authority, exercise the powers conferred on the local authority by subsection (1) above.

(9) This section does not apply to premises forming part of a mine or quarry within the meaning of the Mines and Quarries Act 1954.

[Building Act 1984, s 78.]

7.9944 **79. Ruinous and dilapidated buildings and neglected sites** (1) If it appears to a local authority that a building or structure is by reason of its ruinous or dilapidated condition seriously detrimental to the amenities of the neighbourhood, the local authority may by notice require the owner thereof—

(*a*) to execute such works of repair or restoration, or

(*b*) if he so elects, to take such steps for demolishing the building or structure, or any part thereof, and removing any rubbish or other material resulting from or exposed by the demolition,

as may be necessary in the interests of amenity.

(2) If it appears to a local authority that—

(*a*) rubbish or other material resulting from, or exposed by, the demolition or collapse of a building or structure is lying on the site or on any adjoining land, and

(*b*) by reason thereof the site or land is in such a condition as to be seriously detrimental to the amenities of the neighbourhood,

the local authority may by notice require the owner of the site or land to take such steps for removing the rubbish or material as may be necessary in the interests of amenity.

(3) Sections 99 and 102 below apply in relation to a notice given under subsection (1) or (2) above, subject to the following modifications—

(*a*) section 99(1) requires the notice to indicate the nature of the works of repair or restoration and that of the works of demolition and removal of rubbish or material, and

(*b*) section 99(2) authorises the local authority to execute, subject to that subsection, at their election either the works of repair or restoration or the works of demolition and removal of rubbish or material.

(4) This section does not apply to an advertisement as defined in section 336(1) of the Town

and Country Planning Act 1990.

(5) This section has effect subject to the provisions of the Planning (Listed Buildings and Conservation Areas) Act 1990 relating to listed buildings, buildings subject to building preservation notices and buildings in conservation areas.

[Building Act 1984, s 79 as amended by the Housing and Planning Act 1986, Sch 9 and the Planning (Consequential Provisions) Act 1990, Sch 2.]

7.9945 **80. Notice to local authority of intended demolition** (1) This section applies to any demolition of the whole or part of a building except—

(*a*) a demolition in pursuance of a demolition order or obstructive building order made under Part IX of the Housing Act 1985, and

(*b*) a demolition—

(i) of an internal part of a building, where the building is occupied and it is intended that it should continue to be occupied,

(ii) of a building that has a cubic content (as ascertained by external measurement) of not more than 1,750 cubic feet, or, where a greenhouse, conservatory, shed or prefabricated garage forms part of a larger building, of that greenhouse, conservatory, shed or prefabricated garage, or

(iii) without prejudice to sub-paragraph (ii) above, of an agricultural building (within the meaning of any paragraphs 3 to 7 of Schedule 5 to the Local Government Finance Act 1988), unless it is contiguous to another building that is not itself an agricultural building or a building of a kind mentioned in that sub-paragraph.

(2) No person shall begin a demolition to which this section applies unless—

(*a*) he has given the local authority notice of his intention to do so, and

(*b*) either—

(i) the local authority have given a notice to him under section 81 below, or

(ii) the relevant period (as defined in that section) has expired.

(3) A notice under subsection (2) above shall specify the building to which it relates and the works of demolition intended to be carried out, and it is the duty of a person giving such a notice to a local authority to send or give a copy of it to—

(*a*) the occupier of any building adjacent to the building,

(*b*) any public gas supplier[1] (as defined in Part I of the Gas Act 1986) in whose authorised area (as so defined) the building is situated,

(*c*) the public electricity supplier (as defined in Part I of the Electricity Act 1989) in whose authorised area (as so defined) the building is situated and any other person authorised by a licence under that Part to supply electricity to the building.

(4) A person who contravenes subsection (2) above is liable on summary conviction to a fine not exceeding **level 4** on the standard scale.

[Building Act 1984, s 80, as amended by the Housing (Consequential Provisions) Act 1985, Sch 2, the Gas Act 1986, Sch 7, the Housing and Planning Act 1986, Sch 5, the Electricity Act 1989, Sch 16 and SI 1990/1285.]

---

1 The reference to a "public gas supplier" shall have effect as a reference to a "public gas transporter" as defined in Pt I of the Gas Act 1986 (Gas Act 1995, Sch 4).

7.9946 **81. Local authority's power to serve notice about demolition** (1) A local authority may give a notice under this section to—

(*a*) a person on whom a demolition order or obstructive building order has been served under Part IX of the Housing Act 1985,

(*b*) a person who appears to them not to be intending to comply with an order made under section 77 above or a notice given under section 79 above, and

(*c*) a person who appears to them to have begun or to be intending to begin a demolition to which section 80 above otherwise applies.

(2) Nothing contained in a notice under this section prejudices or affects the operation of any of the relevant statutory provisions, as defined in section 53(1) of the Health and Safety at Work etc Act 1974; and accordingly, if a requirement of such a notice is inconsistent with a requirement imposed by or under the said Act of 1974, the latter requirement prevails.

(3) Where—

(*a*) a person has given a notice under section 80 above, or

(*b*) the local authority have served a demolition order or obstructive building order on a person under Part IX of the Housing Act 1985,

a notice under this section may only be given to the person in question within the relevant period.

(4) In this section and section 80 above, "the relevant period" means—

(*a*) in a case such as is mentioned in subsection (3)(*a*) above, six weeks from the giving of the notice under section 80 above, or such longer period as the person who gave that notice may in writing allow, and

(*b*) in a case such as is mentioned in subsection (3)(*b*) above, seven days after the local authority served a copy of the demolition order or obstructive building order in accordance with Part IX of the Housing Act 1985, or such longer period as the person on whom the copy was served may in writing allow.

(5) It is the duty of the local authority to send or give a copy of a notice under this section to the

owner and occupier of any building adjacent to the building to which the notice relates.

(6) It is also the duty of the local authority to send or give a copy of a notice under this section—

(*a*) if it contains such a requirement as is specified in section 82(1)(*h*) below, to the statutory undertakers concerned, and

(*b*) if it contains such a requirement as is specified in section 82(1)(*i*) below, to the fire and rescue authority, if they are not themselves the fire and rescue authority.

(7) *Repealed.*

[Building Act 1984, s 81 as amended by the Housing (Consequential Provisions) Act 1985, Sch 2, the Housing and Planning Act 1986, Sch 5, the Fire and Rescue Services Act 2004, Sch 1 and SI 2005/1541.]

**7.9947 82. Notices under section 81** (1) A notice under section 81(1) above may require the person to whom it is given—

(*a*) to shore up any building adjacent to the building to which the notice relates,

(*b*) to weatherproof any surfaces of an adjacent building that are exposed by the demolition,

(*c*) to repair and make good any damage to an adjacent building caused by the demolition or by the negligent act or omission of any person engaged in it,

(*d*) to remove material or rubbish resulting from the demolition and clearance of the site,

(*e*) to disconnect and seal, at such points as the local authority may reasonably require, any sewer or drain in or under the building,

(*f*) to remove any such sewer or drain, and seal any sewer or drain with which the sewer or drain to be removed is connected,

(*g*) to make good to the satisfaction of the local authority the surface of the ground disturbed by anything done under paragraph (*e*) or (*f*) above,

(*h*) to make arrangements with the relevant statutory undertakers for the disconnection of the supply of gas, electricity and water to the building,

(*i*) to make such arrangements with regard to the burning of structures or materials on the site as may be reasonably required by the fire and rescue authority.

(*j*) to take such steps relating to the conditions subject to which the demolition is to be undertaken, and the condition in which the site is to be left on completion of the demolition, as the local authority may consider reasonably necessary for the protection of the public and the preservation of public amenity.

(2) No one shall be required under paragraph (*c*), (*e*) or (*f*) of subsection (1) above to carry out any work in land outside the premises on which the works of demolition are being carried out if he has no right to carry out that work, but, subject to section 101 below, the person undertaking the demolition, or the local authority acting in his default, may break open any street for the purpose of complying with any such requirement.

(3) Before a person complies with a requirement under paragraph (*e*), (*f*) or (*g*) of subsection (1) above, he shall give to the local authority—

(*a*) at least 48 hours' notice, in the case of a requirement under paragraph (*e*) or (*f*), or

(*b*) at least 24 hours' notice, in the case of a requirement under paragraph (*g*),

and a person who fails to comply with this subsection is liable on summary conviction to a fine not exceeding **level 2** on the standard scale.

(4) This section does not authorise interference with apparatus or works of statutory undertakers authorised by an enactment to carry on an undertaking for the supply of electricity[1], or gas[2] with apparatus or works of a water undertaker or sewage undertaker.

(5) Without prejudice to the generality of subsection (4) above, this section does not exempt a person from—

(*a*) the obligation to obtain any consent required under section 174 of the Water Industry Act 1991 or section 176 of the Water Resources Act 1991 (interference with water supplies or with waterworks),

(*b*) criminal liability under any enactment relating to the supply of gas or electricity, or

(*c*) the requirements of regulations under section 31 of the Gas Act 1972 (public safety).

(6) Section 99 below applies in relation to a notice given under section 81(1) above.

[Building Act 1984, s 82 as amended by the Water Act 1989, the Water Consolidation (Consequential Provisions) Act 1991, Sch 1 and SI 2005/1541.]

---

[1] The reference to a person authorised by an enactment to carry on an undertaking for the supply of electricity shall be construed as a reference to the holder of a licence under s 6 of the Electricity Act 1989 (Electricity Act 1989, Sch 16, para 1(7)).

[2] The reference to a person authorised to carry on an undertaking for the supply of gas shall be construed as a reference to a public gas transporter (Gas Act 1995, Sch 4).

**7.9948 83. Appeal against notice under section 81** (1) Section 102 below applies in relation to a notice given under section 81 above.

(2) Among the grounds on which an appeal may be brought under section 102 below against such a notice are—

(*a*) in the case of a notice requiring an adjacent building to be shored up, that the owner of the building is not entitled to the support of that building by the building that is being demolished, and ought to pay, or contribute towards, the expenses of shoring it up, (*b*) in the case of a notice requiring any surfaces of an adjacent building to be weatherproofed, that the owner of the adjacent building ought to pay, or contribute towards, the expenses of weatherproofing those surfaces.

(3) Where the grounds on which an appeal under section 102 below is brought include a ground specified in subsection (2) above—

(*a*) the appellant shall serve a copy of his notice of appeal on the person or persons referred to in that ground of appeal, and

(*b*) on the hearing of the appeal the court may make such order as it thinks fit—

(i) in respect of the payment of, or contribution towards, the cost of the works by any such person, or

(ii) as to how any expenses that may be recoverable by the local authority are to be borne between the appellant and any such person.

[Building Act 1984, s 83.]

*Yards and passages*

7.9949 **84. Paving and drainage of yards and passages** (1) If a court or yard appurtenant to, or a passage giving access to, buildings to which this section applies—

(*a*) is not so formed, flagged, asphalted or paved, or

(*b*) is not provided with such works on, above or below its surface,

as to allow of the satisfactory drainage of its surface or subsoil to a proper outfall, the local authority may by notice require any person who is the owner of any of the buildings to execute all such works as may be necessary to remedy the defect.

(2) Sections 99 and 102 below apply in relation to a notice given under subsection (1) above.

(3) The buildings to which this section applies are houses and industrial and commercial buildings.

(4) This section applies in relation to any court, yard or passage that is used in common by the occupiers of two or more houses, or a house and a commercial or industrial building, but is not a highway maintainable at the public expense.

[Building Act 1984, s 84.]

7.9950 **85. Maintenance of entrances to courtyards** (1) Except with the consent of the local authority—

(*a*) an entrance to a court or yard on which two or more houses front or abut shall not be closed, narrowed, reduced in height or otherwise altered so as to impede the free circulation of air through the entrance, and

(*b*) no permanent structure shall be erected so as to impede the free circulation of air through such an entrance.

(2) A local authority in giving a consent under this section may impose such conditions as they think fit with respect to the provision of other openings or means of access, or other means for securing free circulation of air throughout the court or yard.

(3) A person aggrieved by the refusal of a local authority to give a consent under this section, or by a condition imposed by them, may appeal to a magistrates' court.

(4) A person who contravenes this section is liable on summary conviction to a fine not exceeding **level 1** on the standard scale and to a further fine not exceeding **£2** for each day on which the offence continues after he is convicted.

[Building Act 1984, s 85.]

*Appeal to Crown Court*

7.9951 **86. Appeal to Crown Court** (1) Where a person—

(*a*) is aggrieved by an order, determination or other decision of a magistrates' court under this Part of this Act, or under Part IV of this Act as it applies in relation to this Part, and

(*b*) is not by any other enactment authorised to appeal to the Crown Court,

he may appeal to the Crown Court.

(2) Subsection (1) above does not confer a right of appeal in a case in which each of the parties concerned might under this Act have required that the dispute should be determined by arbitration instead of by a magistrates' court.

[Building Act 1984, s 86.]

*Application of provisions to Crown property*

7.9952 **87. Application of provisions to Crown property** (1) This section applies to any house, building or other premises being property belonging to Her Majesty in right of the Crown or of the Duchy of Lancaster, or belonging to the Duchy of Cornwall, or belonging to a government department, or held in trust for Her Majesty for purposes of a government department.

(2) In relation to any such property, the appropriate authority may agree with—

(*a*) the council of the county, or

(*b*) the local authority of the district,

in which the property is situated that any particular provisions of this Part of this Act, and of Part IV of this Act so far as it relates to this Part, shall apply to the property; and, while the agreement is in force, those provisions shall apply to that property accordingly, subject to the terms of the agreement.

(2A) Subsection (2) above shall apply in relation to property in Wales as if—

(*a*) in paragraph (*a*) the reference to a county included a reference to a county borough; and

(*b*) paragraph (*b*) were omitted.

(3) Any such agreement may contain such consequential and incidental provisions (including, with the approval of the Treasury, provisions of a financial character) as appear to the appropriate authority to be necessary or equitable.

(4) In this section, "the appropriate authority" means—

(*a*) in the case of property belonging to Her Majesty in right of the Crown, the Crown Estate Commissioners or other government department having the management of the property,

(*b*) in the case of property belonging to Her Majesty in right of the Duchy of Lancaster, the Chancellor of the Duchy,

(*c*) in the case of property belonging to the Duchy of Cornwall, such person as the Duke of Cornwall, or the possessor for the time being of the Duchy of Cornwall, appoints, and

(*d*) in the case of property belonging to a government department or held in trust for Her Majesty for purposes of a government department, that department,

and, if a question arises as to what authority is the appropriate authority in relation to any property, that question shall be referred to the Treasury, whose decision is final.

[Building Act 1984, s 87 as amended by the Local Government (Wales) Act 1994, Sch 9.]

*Inner London*

**7.9953 88. Inner London** (1) In its application to inner London, this Part of this Act has effect subject to Part II of Schedule 3 to this Act.

(2) Part III of Schedule 3 to this Act has effect with respect to building and the drainage of buildings in the inner London boroughs.

(3) Part IV of Schedule 3 to this Act has effect with respect to the making of byelaws—

(*a*) for the inner London boroughs, with respect to certain matters, and

(*b*) for the inner London boroughs, the Inner Temple and the Middle Temple, with respect to certain other matters.

[Building Act 1984, s 88 as amended by the Local Government Act 1985, Sch 17.]

*Miscellaneous*

**7.9954 89. References in Acts to building byelaws** (1) Subject to subsection (2) below, for any reference to—

(*a*) building byelaws as defined in section 343 of the Public Health Act 1936, or

(*b*) byelaws made under Part II of that Act with respect to buildings, works and fittings,

that occurs in an Act, or in an instrument having effect under an Act, there is substituted a reference to building regulations.

(2) *Repealed.*

[Building Act 1984, s 89 as amended by the Housing (Consequential Provisions) Act 1985, Sch 1.]

**7.9955 90. Facilities for inspecting local Acts** (1) In an area in which there is in force a local Act containing provisions that impose an obligation or restriction as to the construction, nature or situation of buildings, the local authority shall keep a copy of those provisions at their offices for inspection by the public at all reasonable times free of charge.

(2) Any question as to what provisions of a local Act are provisions of which a copy is to be so kept shall, on the application of the local authority, be determined by the Secretary of State.

[Building Act 1984, s 90.]

## PART IV[1]
## GENERAL

*Duties of local authorities*

**7.9956 91. Duties of local authorities** (1) It is the duty of local authorities to carry this Act into execution in their areas, subject to—

(*a*) the provisions of this Act relating to certain other authorities or persons,

(*b*) the provisions of Part I of the Public Health Act 1936 relating to united districts and joint boards,

(*c*) section 151 of the Local Government, Planning and Land Act 1980 (urban development areas), and

(*d*) section 1(3) of the Public Health (Control of Disease) Act 1984 (port health authorities).

(2) It is the function of local authorities to enforce building regulations in their areas, subject to sections 5(3), 48(1) and 53(2) above.

[Building Act 1984, s 91 as amended by the Local Government Act 1985, Sch 17.]

1 Part IV contains ss 91–131.

*Documents*

7.9957 **92. Form of documents** (1) All—

(*a*) notices, orders, consents, demands and other documents authorised or required by or under this Act to be given, made or issued by a local authority, and

(*b*) notices and applications authorised or required by or under this Act to be given or made to, or to any officer of, a local authority,

shall be in writing.

(2) The Secretary of State may, by regulations made by statutory instrument, prescribe the form of any notice, advertisement, certificate or other document to be used for any of the purposes of this Act, and if forms are so prescribed those forms or forms to the like effect may be used in all cases to which those forms are applicable.

[Building Act 1984, s 92.]

7.9958 **93. Authentication of documents** (1) A notice, order, consent, demand or other document that a local authority are authorised or required by or under this Act to give, make or issue may be signed on behalf of the authority—

(*a*) by the proper officer of the authority or the district surveyor, as respects documents relating to matters within his province, or

(*b*) by an officer of the authority authorised by them in writing to sign documents of the particular kind or, as the case may be, the particular document.

(2) A document purporting to bear the signature of an officer—

(*a*) expressed to hold an office by virtue of which he is under this section empowered to sign such a document, or

(*b*) expressed to be authorised by the local authority to sign such a document or the particular document,

is deemed, for the purposes of this Act and of any building regulations and orders made under it, to have been duly given, made or issued by authority of the local authority, until the contrary is proved.

(3) In subsection (2) above, "signature" includes a facsimile of a signature by whatever process reproduced.

[Building Act 1984, s 93.]

7.9959 **94. Service of documents** A notice, order, consent, demand or other document that is authorised or required by or under this Act to be given to or served on a person may, in any case for which no other provision is made by this Act, be given or served either—

(*a*) by delivering it to that person,

(*b*) in the case of an officer of a local authority, by leaving it, or sending it in a prepaid letter addressed to him, at his office,

(*c*) in the case of any other person, by leaving it, or sending it in a prepaid letter addressed to him, at his usual or last known residence,

(*d*) in the case of an incorporated company or body, by delivering it to their secretary or clerk at their registered or principal office, or by sending it in a prepaid letter addressed to him at that office,

(*e*) in the case of a document to be given to or served on a person as being the owner of any premises by virtue of the fact that he receives the rackrent thereof as agent for another, or would so receive it if the premises were let at a rackrent, by leaving it, or sending it in a prepaid letter addressed to him, at his place of business,

(*f*) in the case of a document to be given to or served on the owner or the occupier of any premises, if it is not practicable after reasonable inquiry to ascertain the name and address of the person to or on whom it should be given or served, or if the premises are unoccupied, by addressing it to the person concerned by the description of "owner" or "occupier" of the premises (naming them) to which it relates, and delivering it to some person on the premises, or, if there is no person on the premises to whom it can be delivered, by affixing it, or a copy of it, to some conspicuous part of the premises.

[Building Act 1984, s 94.]

*Entry on premises*

7.9960 **95. Power to enter premises** (1) Subject to this section, an authorised officer of a local authority, on producing, if so required, some duly authenticated document showing his authority, has a right to enter any premises at all reasonable hours—

(*a*) for the purpose of ascertaining whether there is, or has been, on or in connection with the premises, a contravention of this Act, or of any building regulations, that it is the duty of the local authority to enforce,

(*b*) for the purpose of ascertaining whether or not circumstances exist that would authorise or require the local authority to take any action, or execute any work, under this Act or under building regulations,

(*c*) for the purpose of taking any action, or executing any work, authorised or required by this Act, or by building regulations, or by an order made under this Act, to be taken, or executed, by the local authority, or

(*d*) generally for the purpose of the performance by the local authority of their functions under this Act or under building regulations.

(2) Admission to premises, other than a factory or workplace, shall not be demanded as of right unless 24 hours' notice of the intended entry has been given to the occupier.

(3) If it is shown to the satisfaction of a justice of the peace on sworn information in writing that—

(*a*) admission to any premises has been refused, or refusal is apprehended, or the premises are unoccupied, or the occupier is temporarily absent, or the case is one of urgency, or an application for admission would defeat the object of the entry, and

(*b*) there is reasonable ground for entry into the premises for any of the purposes mentioned in subsection (1) above,

the justice may by warrant under his hand authorise the local authority by any authorised officer to enter the premises, if need be by force.

(4) A warrant shall not be issued under subsection (3) above unless the justice is satisfied that—

(*a*) notice of the intention to apply for a warrant has been given to the occupier, or

(*b*) the premises are unoccupied, or the occupier is temporarily absent, or the case is one of urgency, or the giving of the notice would defeat the object of the entry.

[Building Act 1984, s 95.]

7.9961 **96. Supplementary provisions as to entry** (1) An authorised officer entering premises by virtue of section 95 above, or of a warrant issued under it, may take with him such other persons as may be necessary, and on leaving unoccupied premises that he has entered by virtue of such a warrant he shall leave them as effectually secured against trespassers as he found them.

(2) A warrant issued under that section shall continue in force until the purpose for which the entry is necessary has been satisfied.

(3) A person who—

(*a*) is admitted into a factory or workplace in compliance with that section or a warrant issued under it, and

(*b*) discloses to another person information obtained by him in the factory or workplace with regard to a manufacturing process or trade secret,

is liable on summary conviction to a fine not exceeding **level 3** on the standard scale or to imprisonment for a term not exceeding **three months** *, unless the disclosure was made in the performance of his duty.

[Building Act 1984, s 96.]

---

* **Words repealed by the Criminal Justice Act 2003, Sch 37 from a date to be appointed.**

*Execution of works*

7.9962 **97. Power to execute work** A local authority may, by agreement with the owner or occupier of any premises, themselves execute at his expense—

(*a*) any work that they have under this Act required him to execute, or

(*b*) any work in connection with the construction, laying, alteration or repair of a sewer or drain that he is entitled to execute,

and for that purpose they have all the rights that he would have.

[Building Act 1984, s 97.]

7.9963 **98. Power to require occupier to permit work** If, on a complaint made by the owner of premises, it appears to a magistrates' court that the occupier of those premises prevents the owner from executing any work that he is by or under this Act required to execute, the court may order the occupier to permit the execution of the work.

[Building Act 1984, s 98.]

7.9964 **99. Content and enforcement of notice requiring works** (1) A notice in relation to which it is declared by any provision of this Act that this section applies shall indicate the nature of the works to be executed and state the time within which they are to be executed.

(2) Subject to any right of appeal conferred by section 102 below, if the person required by such a notice to execute works fails to execute them within the time limited by the notice—

(*a*) the local authority may themselves execute the works and recover from that person the expenses reasonably incurred by them in doing so, and

(*b*) without prejudice to that power, he is liable on summary conviction to a fine not exceeding **level 4** on the standard scale and to a further fine not exceeding **£2** for each day on which the default continues after he is convicted.

(3) This section has effect subject to any modification specified in the provision under which the notice is given.

[Building Act 1984, s 99.]

7.9965 **100. Sale of materials** (1) A local authority may sell any materials that—

(*a*) have been removed by them from any premises, including a street, when executing works under this Act or otherwise carrying this Act into effect, and

(*b*) are not before the expiration of three days from the date of their removal claimed by the owner and taken away by him.

(2) Where a local authority sell materials under this section, they shall pay the proceeds to the person to whom the materials belonged, after deducting the amount of any expenses recoverable by them from him.

(3) This section does not apply to refuse removed by a local authority.

[Building Act 1984, s 100.]

7.9966 **101. Breaking open of streets** (1) For the purposes of any section of this Act that confers powers on local authorities to construct, lay or maintain sewers, drains or pipes, section 158 of the Water Industry Act 1991 (street works) shall apply, with the necessary modifications, as it applies for the purpose of conferring power on a water undertaker or sewerage undertaker to lay a relevant pipe, within the meaning of that section.

(2) That section shall also so apply so far as necessary for the purposes of any power to lay or maintain a sewer or drain which is conferred by this Act on a person other than a local authority.

[Building Act 1984, s 101 as amended by the Water Act 1989, Sch 25 and the Water Consolidation (Consequential Provisions) Act 1991, Sch 1.]

*Appeal against notice requiring works*

7.9967 **102. Appeal against notice requiring works** (1) Where a person is given a notice in relation to which it is declared by any provision of this Act that this section applies, he may appeal to a magistrates' court on any of the following grounds that are appropriate in the circumstances of the particular case—

(*a*) that the notice or requirement is not justified by the terms of the provision under which it purports to have been given,

(*b*) that there has been some informality, defect or error in, or in connection with, the notice,

(*c*) that the authority have refused unreasonably to approve the execution of alternative works, or that the works required by the notice to be executed are otherwise unreasonable in character or extent, or are unnecessary,

(*d*) that the time within which the works are to be executed is not reasonably sufficient for the purpose,

(*e*) that the notice might lawfully have been served on the occupier of the premises in question instead of on the owner, or on the owner instead of on the occupier, and that it would have been equitable for it to have been so served,

(*f*) where the works are works for the common benefit of the premises in question and other premises, that some other person, being the owner or occupier of premises to be benefited, ought to contribute towards the expenses of executing any works required.

(2) If and in so far as an appeal under this section is based on the ground of some informality, defect or error in or in connection with the notice, the court shall dismiss the appeal, if it is satisfied that the informality, defect or error was not a material one.

(3) The appellant—

(*a*) shall, where the grounds upon which the appeal is brought include a ground specified in subsection (1)(*e*) or (*f*) above, serve a copy of his notice of appeal on each other person referred to, and

(*b*) may, in the case of any appeal under this section, serve a copy of his notice of appeal on any other person having an estate or interest in the premises in question,

and on the hearing of the appeal the court may make such order as it thinks fit with respect to—

(i) the person by whom any works are to be executed and the contribution to be made by any other person towards the cost of the works, or

(ii) the proportions in which any expenses that may become recoverable by the local authority are to be borne by the appellant and such other person.

(4) In exercising its powers under subsection (3) above, the court shall have regard—

(*a*) as between an owner and an occupier, to the terms and conditions, whether contractual or statutory, of the tenancy and to the nature of the works required, and

(*b*) in any case, to the degree of benefit to be derived by the different persons concerned.

(5) This section has effect subject to any modification specified in the provision under which the notice is given.

[Building Act 1984, s 102.]

*General provisions about appeals and applications*

7.9968 **103. Procedure on appeal or application to magistrates' court** (1) Where this Act provides—

(*a*) for an appeal to a magistrates' court against a requirement, refusal or other decision of a local authority, or

(*b*) for a matter to be determined by, or for an application in respect of a matter to be made to, a magistrates' court,

the procedure shall be by way of complaint for an order.

(2) The time within which such an appeal may be brought is 21 days from the date on which

notice of the local authority's requirement, refusal or other decision was served upon the person desiring to appeal, and for the purposes of this subsection the making of the complaint is deemed to be the bringing of the appeal.

(3) In a case where such an appeal lies, the document notifying to the person concerned the local authority's decision in the matter shall state the right of appeal to a magistrates' court and the time within which such an appeal may be brought.

[Building Act 1984, s 103.]

7.9969 **104. Local authority to give effect to appeal** Where upon an appeal under this Act a court varies or reverses a decision of a local authority, it is the duty of the local authority to give effect to the order of the court and, in particular, to grant or issue any necessary consent, certificate or other document, and to make any necessary entry in any register.

[Building Act 1984, s 104.]

7.9970 **105. Judge not disqualified by liability to rates** A judge of a court or a justice of the peace is not disqualified from acting in cases arising under this Act by reason only of his being, as one of several ratepayers, or as one of any other class of persons, liable in common with the others to contribute to, or be benefited by, a rate or fund out of which expenses of a local authority are to be defrayed.

[Building Act 1984, s 105.]

*Compensation, and recovery of sums*

7.9971 **106. Compensation for damage** (1) A local authority shall make full compensation to a person who has sustained damage by reason of the exercise by the authority, in relation to a matter as to which he has not himself been in default, of any of their powers under this Act.

(2) Subject to subsection (3) below, any dispute arising under this section as to the fact of damage, or as to the amount of compensation, shall be determined by arbitration.

(3) If the compensation claimed does not exceed £50, all questions as to the fact of damage, liability to pay compensation and the amount of compensation may on the application of either party be determined by, and any compensation awarded may be recovered before, a magistrates' court.

[Building Act 1984, s 106.]

7.9972 **107. Recovery of expenses etc** (1) Where a local authority have incurred expenses for whose repayment the owner of the premises in respect of which the expenses were incurred is liable, either under this Act or by agreement with the authority, those expenses, together with interest from the date of service of a demand for the expenses, may be recovered by the authority—

(*a*) from the person who is the owner of the premises at the date on which the works are completed, or

(*b*) if he has ceased to be the owner of the premises before the date on which a demand for the expenses is served, either from him or from the person who is the owner at the date on which the demand is served,

and, as from the date of the completion of the works, the expenses and interest accrued due thereon are, until recovered, a charge on the premises and on all estates and interests in them.

(2) A local authority, for the purpose of enforcing a charge under subsection (1) above, have all the same powers and remedies under the Law of Property Act 1925 and otherwise as if they were mortgagees by deed having powers of sale and lease, of accepting surrenders of leases and of appointing a receiver.

(3) The rate of interest chargeable under subsection (1) above is such reasonable rate as the authority may determine.

(4) A sum that a local authority are entitled to recover under this Act, and with respect to whose recovery provision is not made by any other section of this Act, may be recovered as a simple contract debt in any court of competent jurisdiction.

(5) Where—

(*a*) a person has been given a notice in relation to which section 102 above applies, and

(*b*) the local authority take proceedings against him for the recovery of expenses that they are entitled to recover from him,

it is not open to him to raise any question that he could have raised on an appeal under that section.

[Building Act 1984, s 107.]

*Obstruction*

7.9973 **112. Obstruction** A person who wilfully obstructs a person acting in the execution of this Act, or of building regulations, or of an order or warrant made or issued under this Act, is, in a case for which no other provision is made by this Act, liable on summary conviction to a fine not exceeding **level 1** on the standard scale.

[Building Act 1984, s 112.]

*Prosecutions*

7.9974 **113. Prosecution of offences** Proceedings in respect of an offence created by or under this Act shall not, without the written consent of the Attorney General, be taken by any person other than—

(*a*) a party aggrieved, or

(*b*) a local authority or a body whose function it is to enforce the provision in question.

[Building Act 1984, s 113.]

7.9975 **114. Continuing offences** Where provision is made by or under this Act for the imposition of a daily penalty in respect of a continuing offence—

(*a*) the court by which a person is convicted of the original offence may fix a reasonable period from the date of conviction for the defendant to comply with any directions given by the court, and

(*b*) where the court has fixed such a period, the daily penalty is not recoverable in respect of any day before the period expires.

[Building Act 1984, s 114.]

*Default powers*

7.9976 **116. Default powers of Secretary of State** (1) If the Secretary of State is satisfied that a local authority or joint board have failed to discharge their functions under this Act in a case in which they ought to have discharged them, he may make an order declaring them to be in default and directing them for the purpose of removing the default to discharge such of their functions, in such manner and within such time or times, as may be specified in the order.

(2) If a local authority or joint board with respect to whom an order has been made under subsection (1) above fail to comply with a requirement of the order within the time limited by the order for compliance with that requirement, the Secretary of State, in lieu of enforcing the order by mandamus or otherwise, may make an order transferring to himself such of the functions of the body in default as may be specified in his order.

[Building Act 1984, s 116.]

*Orders*

7.9977 **120. Orders** (1) The power to make an order under section 16(13), 30(3) or (4), 42(7), 69(6) or 134(1) above, or under paragraph 5(2) of Schedule 1 to this Act, is exercisable by statutory instrument, and different days may be appointed by such an order for different provisions or for different purposes.

(2) An order under section 30(3) above or 134(1)(*a*), (*b*) or (*c*) below may contain such transitional provisions and savings as appear to the Secretary of State to be necessary or expedient in connection with the provisions thereby brought into force, including such adaptations of those provisions as appear to him necessary or expedient in consequence of the partial operation of this Act (whether before or after the day appointed by the order).

[Building Act 1984, s 120.]

*Interpretation*

7.9978 **121. Meaning of "building"** (1) The word "building", for the purposes of—

(*a*) Part I of this Act, and

(*b*) any other enactment (whether or not contained in this Act) that relates to building regulations, or that mentions "buildings" or "a building" in a context from which it appears that those expressions are there intended to have the same meaning as in Part I of this Act,

means any permanent or temporary building, and, unless the context otherwise requires, it includes any other structure or erection of whatever kind or nature (whether permanent or temporary).

(2) In subsection (1) above, "structure or erection" includes a vehicle, vessel, hovercraft, aircraft or other movable object of any kind in such circumstances as may be prescribed (being circumstances that in the opinion of the Secretary of State justify treating it for those purposes as a building).

(3) For the purposes mentioned in subsection (1) above, unless the context otherwise requires—

(*a*) a reference to a building includes a reference to part of a building, and

(*b*) a reference to the provision of services, fittings and equipment in or in connection with buildings, or to services, fittings and equipment so provided, includes a reference to the affixing of things to buildings or, as the case may be, to things so affixed.

[Building Act 1984, s 121.]

7.9979 **122. Meaning of "building regulations"** In this Act—

(*a*) "building regulations" means, subject to paragraph (*b*) below, regulations made under section 1 above;

(*b*) a reference to building regulations, in a particular case in relation to which a requirement of building regulations is for the time being dispensed with, waived, relaxed or modified by virtue of section 8 or 11 above or any other enactment, is a reference to building regulations as they apply in that case, unless the context otherwise requires.

[Building Act 1984, s 122.]

7.9980 **123. Meaning of "construct" and "erect"** (1) For the purposes of—

(*a*) Part I of this Act, and

(*b*) any other enactment (whether or not contained in this Act) that relates to building regulations, or that mentions “buildings” or “a building” in a context from which it appears that those expressions are there intended to have the same meaning as in the said Part I,

references to the construction or erection of a building include references to—

(i) the carrying out of such operations (whether for the reconstruction of a building, the roofing over of an open space between walls or buildings, or otherwise) as may be designated in building regulations as operations falling to be treated for those purposes as the construction or erection of a building, and

(ii) the conversion of a movable object into what is by virtue of section 121(1) and (2) above a building,

and “construct” and “erect” shall be construed accordingly.

(2) For the purposes of Part III of this Act, each of the following operations is deemed to be the erection of a building—

(*a*) the re-erection of a building or part of a building when an outer wall of that building or, as the case may be, that part of a building has been pulled down, or burnt down, to within 10 feet of the surface of the ground adjoining the lowest storey of the building or of that part of the building,

(*b*) the re-erection of a frame building or part of a frame building when that building or part of a building has been so far pulled down, or burnt down, as to leave only the framework of the lowest storey of the building or of that part of the building,

(*c*) the roofing over of an open space between walls or buildings,

and “erect” shall be construed accordingly.

[Building Act 1984, s 123.]

7.9981 124. **Meaning of deposit of plans** In this Act, a reference to the deposit of plans in accordance with building regulations is a reference to the deposit of plans in accordance with building regulations for the purposes of section 16 above, unless the context otherwise requires.

[Building Act 1984, s 124.]

7.9982 125. **Construction and availability of sewers** (1) A reference in Part I of this Act to the construction of a sewer includes a reference to the extension of an existing sewer.

(2) For the purposes of sections 64(2) and 66(1) above, a building or proposed building—

(*a*) is not deemed to have a sufficient water supply available unless—

(i) it has a sufficient supply of water laid on, or

(ii) such a supply can be laid on to it from a point within 100 feet of the site of the building or proposed building, and the intervening land is land through which the owner of the building or proposed building is, or will be, entitled to lay a communication pipe, and

(*b*) is not deemed to have a sewer available unless—

(i) there is within 100 feet of the site of the building or proposed building, and at a level that makes it reasonably practicable to construct a drain to communicate with it, a public sewer or other sewer that the owner of the building or proposed building is, or will be, entitled to use, and

(ii) the intervening land is land through which he is entitled to construct a drain.

(3) The limit of 100 feet does not apply, for the purposes of subsection (2) above, if the local authority undertake to bear so much of the expenses reasonably incurred in—

(*a*) constructing, and maintaining and repairing, a drain to communicate with a sewer, or

(*b*) laying, and maintaining and repairing, a pipe for the purpose of obtaining a supply of water,

as the case may be, as is attributable to the fact that the distance of the sewer, or of the point from which a supply of water can be laid on, exceeds 100 feet.

[Building Act 1984, s 125.]

7.9983 126. **General interpretation** In this Act, unless the context otherwise requires—

“Act” includes an enactment contained in a local Act;

“approved inspector” has the meaning given by section 49(1) above;

“authorised officer”, in relation to a local authority, means—

(*a*) an officer of the local authority authorised by them in writing, either generally or specially, to act in matters of a specified kind or in a specified matter, or

(*b*) by virtue of his appointment and for the purpose of matters within his province, a proper officer of the local authority;

“cesspool” includes a settlement tank or other tank for the reception or disposal of foul matter from buildings;

“closet” includes privy;

“contravention” includes failure to comply, and “contravene” has a corresponding meaning;

“drain” means a drain used for the drainage of one building or of buildings or yards appurtenant to buildings within the same curtilage, and includes any manholes, ventilating shafts, pumps or other accessories belonging to the drain;

"earth-closet" means a closet having a movable receptacle for the reception of faecal matter and its deodorisation by the use of earth, ashes or chemicals, or by other methods;
"enactment" includes an enactment contained in a local Act;
"factory" has the meaning given by section 175 of the Factories Act 1961;
"fire and rescue authority" in relation to any premises or proposed premises, means—
(*a*) where the Regulatory Reform (Fire Safety) Order 2005 applies to the premises or proposed premises, the enforcing authority within the meaning given by article 25 of that Order;
(*b*) in any other case, the fire and rescue authority under the Fire and Rescue Services Act 2004 for the area in which the premises are or are to be situated;
"functions" includes powers and duties;
"highway authority" means, in the case of a highway repairable by the inhabitants at large, the council in whom the highway is vested;
"house" means a dwelling-house, whether a private dwelling-house or not;
"inner London" means the area comprising the inner London boroughs, the City of London, the Inner Temple and the Middle Temple;
"joint board" has the meaning given by section 343(1) of the Public Health Act 1936;
"local Act" includes a provisional order confirmed by Parliament, and the confirming Act so far as it relates to that order;
"local authority" means the council of a district or London borough, the Common Council of the City of London, the Sub-Treasurer of the Inner Temple, the Under Treasurer of the Middle Temple or, for the purposes of Parts I and II above and of this Part so far as it relates to them, the Council of the Isles of Scilly but in relation to Wales, means the council of a county or a county or county borough
"modifications" includes additions, omissions and amendments, and related expressions shall be construed accordingly;
"officer" includes servant;
"owner" means the person for the time being receiving the rackrent of the premises in connection with which the word is used, whether on his own account or as agent or trustee for another person, or who would so receive it if those premises were let at a rackrent;
"plans" includes drawings of any other description, and also specifications or other information in any form;
"prejudicial to health" means injurious, or likely to cause injury, to health;
"premises" includes buildings, land, easements and hereditaments of any tenure;
"prescribed" means prescribed by building regulations;
"private sewer" means a sewer that is not a public sewer;
"proper officer", in relation to a purpose and to a local authority, means an officer appointed for that purpose by that authority;
"public sewer" has the same meaning as in the Water Industry Act 1991;
"rackrent", in relation to property, means a rent that is not less than two-thirds of the rent at which the property might reasonably be expected to let from year to year, free from all usual tenant's rates and taxes, and deducting from it the probable average annual cost of the repairs, insurance and other expenses (if any) necessary to maintain the property in a state to command such rent;
"rating district" has the meaning given by section 115(1) of the General Rate Act 1967[1];
"relevant period" has the meaning given by section 16(12) or 81(4) above, as the case may require;
"sanitary convenience" means closet or urinal;
"school" includes a Sunday school or a Sabbath school;
"sewer" does not include a drain as defined in this section, but otherwise it includes all sewers and drains used for the drainage of buildings and yards appurtenant to buildings, and any manholes, ventilating shafts, pumps or other accessories belonging to the sewer;
"statutory undertakers" means persons authorised by an enactment or statutory order to construct, work or carry on a railway, canal, inland navigation, dock harbour, tramway, or other public undertaking; but does not include a universal service provider (within the meaning of the Postal Services Act 2000), the Post Office Company (within the meaning of Part IV of that Act) or any subsidiary or wholly-owned subsidiary (within the meaning given by section 1159 of the Companies Act 2006) of the Post Office company;
"street" includes a highway, including a highway over a bridge, and a road, lane, footway, square, court, alley or passage, whether a thoroughfare or not;
"substantive requirements", in relation to building regulations, means the requirements of building regulations with respect to the matters mentioned in section 1(1A) above (including requirements imposed by virtue of section 2(1) or (2)(*a*) or (*b*) above and requirements that are of a kind mentioned in subsection (2)(*a*), (*b*) or (*c*) of section 2A above and are imposed by virtue of subsection (1) of that section), as distinct from procedural requirements;
"surface water" includes water from roofs;

"water-closet" means a closet that has a separate fixed receptacle connected to a drainage system and separate provision for flushing from a supply of clean water either by the operation of mechanism or by automatic action;

"workplace" does not include a factory, but otherwise it includes any place in which persons are employed otherwise than in domestic service.

[Building Act 1984, s 126 as amended by the Local Government Act 1985, Schs 8 and 17, the Gas Act 1986, Sch 9 the Water Act 1989, Schs 25 and 27, the Electricity Act 1989, Sch 18, the Water Consolidation (Consequential Provisions) Act 1991, Sch 1, the Statute Law (Repeals) Act 1993, Sch 1, the Local Government (Wales) Act 1994, Sch 9, SI 2001/1149, the Fire and Rescue Services Act 2004, Sch 1, SI 2005/1541 and SI 2009/1941.]

[1] The General Rate Act 1967 has been repealed by the Local Government Finance Act 1988 in this PART: title LOCAL GOVERNMENT, ante.

7.9984 **127. Construction of certain references concerning Temples** In relation to the Inner Temple and the Middle Temple, a reference in a provision of this Part of this Act to the proper officer or an officer or authorised officer of a local authority is a reference to an officer authorised by the Sub-Treasurer or the Under Treasurer, as the case may be, to act for the purposes of that provision.

[Building Act 1984, s 127.]

*Savings*

7.9985 **128. Protection for dock and railway undertakings** Section 333 of the Public Health Act 1936 applies in relation to local authorities acting under this Act as it applies in relation to local authorities acting under that Act.

[Building Act 1984, s 128.]

7.9986 **129. Saving for Local Land Charges Act 1975** Nothing in this Act about the recovery of expenses from owners of premises affects the Local Land Charges Act 1975.

[Building Act 1984, s 129.]

7.9987 **130. Saving for other laws** All powers and duties conferred or imposed by this Act are in addition to, and not in derogation of, any other powers and duties conferred or imposed by Act, law or custom, and, subject to any express provision of this Act, all such other powers and duties may be exercised and shall be performed in the same manner as if this Act had not been passed.

[Building Act 1984, s 130.]

7.9988 **131. Restriction of application of Part IV to Schedule 3** This Part has effect subject to paragraph 13 of Schedule 3 to this Act.

[Building Act 1984, s 131.]

## PART V[1]

## SUPPLEMENTARY

7.9989 **135. Short title and extent** (1) This Act may be cited as the Building Act 1984.

(2) This Act does not extend to Scotland or to Northern Ireland.

[Building Act 1984, s 135.]

[1] Part V contains ss 132–135.

# SCHEDULES

## SCHEDULE 3

### INNER LONDON

Sections 46, 88 and 91(2)

7.9990

*(Amended by the Local Government Act 1985, Schs 8 and 17, SI 1985/1936 and SI 1987/798.)*

## PART I

## APPLICATION OF PART I OF THIS ACT

1. **Application to inner London** Sections 24(1), (2) and (4), 25 of this Act do not apply to inner London.

2. **Application of provisions by building regulations** (1) Where, by section 91(2) above or by building regulations made under paragraph 6 of Schedule 1 to this Act or paragraph 14(1) of this Schedule, local authorities, or a prescribed person or class of persons other than local authorities, are made responsible for—

(*a*) enforcing, or

(*b*) performing prescribed functions under or in connection with,

building regulations in force in inner London, then, without prejudice to the said paragraphs 6 and 14(1), building regulations[1] may in that connection provide for any relevant provision to apply (with any prescribed modifications, and notwithstanding paragraph 1 above) in relation to any such authority, person or class of persons as that provision applies in relation to a local authority outside inner London.

(2) In sub-paragraph (1) above, "relevant provision" means any of the following provisions of this Act that may be prescribed for the purposes of sub-paragraph (1) above: sections 4, 8 to 10, 16, 18(1), (4) and (5), 21 to 23, 24(1), (2) and (4), 26 to 29, 32, 36, 37, 39 and 40.

3. **Repeal and modification of Acts** Without prejudice to the generality of paragraph 11(1) of Schedule 1 to this Act, building regulations may repeal or modify—

(*a*) any provision of the London Building Acts 1930 to 1939,

(*b*) any provision of an Act passed before the 20th September 1974, in so far as that provision—

(i) applies to or to any part of inner London, and

(ii) relates to, or to the making of, byelaws for or for any part of inner London with respect to any matter for or in connection with which provision can be made by building regulations, or

(*c*) any provision of byelaws made or having effect under the said Acts or of any such byelaws as are mentioned in sub-paragraph (*b*)(ii) above,

if it appears to the Secretary of State that the repeal or, as the case may be, the modification of that provision is expedient—

(i) in consequence of the application of any of sections 61, 62 and 67 of the Public Health Act 1936, sections 4(2), (5), (6) and (7), 5 and 9 of the Public Health Act 1961 and sections 61 to 74 and 76 of the Health and Safety at Work etc Act 1974 to inner London by virtue of section 70(1) of the said Act of 1974 (which section is repealed by and incorporated in this Act),

(ii) in consequence of paragraph 2 or 14 of this Schedule, or

(iii) in connection with any provision contained in building regulations that apply to or to any part of inner London.

4. **Consultation** Before making any building regulations that provide for the repeal or modification of any such provision the Secretary of State shall (without prejudice to the requirements as to consultation in section 14(3) of this Act) consult any local authority who appear to him to be concerned.

## Part II
## Application of Part III of this Act

5. **Application to inner London** Sections 71, 72(1) to (4), (6) and (7), 73 to 75, 77 to 83, 85 and 90 of this Act do not apply to inner London.

6. **Application to Temples** Sections 59 to 61 of this Act do not apply to the Inner Temple or the Middle Temple.

## Part IV
## Byelaws

10. **Byelaws about demolition** (1) The council of an inner London borough may make byelaws in relation to the demolition of buildings in the borough—

(*a*) requiring the fixing of fans at the level of each floor of a building undergoing demolition,

(*b*) requiring the hoarding up of windows in a building from which sashes and glass have been removed,

(*c*) regulating the demolition of internal parts of buildings before any external walls are taken down,

(*d*) requiring the placing of screens or mats, the use of water or the taking of other precautions to prevent nuisances arising from dust,

(*e*) regulating the hours during which ceilings may be broken down and mortar may be shot, or be allowed to fall, into any lower floor,

(*f*) requiring any person proposing to demolish a building to give to the borough council such notice of his intention to do so as may be specified in the byelaws.

(2) Byelaws under this paragraph may make different provision for different cases, and in particular may provide that, in their application to an area specified in the byelaws, the byelaws shall have effect subject to such modifications or exceptions as may be so specified.

(3) No byelaws under this paragraph shall apply to a building (not being a dwelling-house) belonging to a board carrying on a railway undertaking and used by that board as a part of, or in connection with, that undertaking.

11, 12. *Repealed.*

13. **Restriction of application of Part IV of Act** Part IV of this Act does not apply in relation to this Part of this Schedule.

## Part V
## Enforcement of Building Regulations

14. *Repealed.*

---

[1] The following provisions of the Building Act 1984 are prescribed for the purposes of para 2(1) of Sch 3 to the Act and apply in relation to a local authority in inner London as they apply to a local authority outside inner London—
s 8 (relaxation of building regulations);
s 9 (application for relaxation);
s 10 (advertisement of proposal for relaxation of building regulations);
s 16 (passing or rejection of plans);
section 32 (lapse of deposit of plans);
s 36 (removal or alteration of offending work);
s 37 (obtaining of report where s 36 notice given);
s 39 (appeal against refusal etc to relax building regulations);
s 40 (appeal against s 36 notice).
(Building (Inner London) Regulations 1985 SI 1985/1936, reg 2(3), as amended by SI 1986/452).

## SCHEDULE 4
## Provisions Consequential Upon Public Body's Notice [1]

Section 54

*Duration of notice*

7.9991 1. (1) A public body's notice comes into force when it is accepted by the local authority, either by notice given within the prescribed period to the public body by which it was given or by virtue of section 54(3) of this Act, and, subject to paragraph 3(3) below, continues in force until the occurrence of, or the expiry of a prescribed period of time beginning on the date of such event as may be prescribed.

(2) Building regulations may empower a local authority to extend (whether before or after its expiry) any such period of time as is referred to in sub-paragraph (1) above.

*Public body's plans certificates*

2. (1) Where a public body—

(*a*) is satisfied that plans of the work specified in a public body's notice given by it have been inspected by a servant or agent of the body who is competent to assess the plans, (*b*) in the light of that inspection is satisfied that the plans neither are defective nor show that work carried out in accordance with them would contravene any provision of building regulations, and

(*c*) has complied with any prescribed requirements as to consultation or otherwise,

the body may give to the local authority a certificate in the prescribed form (called a "public body's plans certificate").

(2) Building regulations may authorise the giving of a public body's notice combined with a public body's plans certificate, and may prescribe a single form for such a combined notice and certificate; and where such a prescribed form is used—

(*a*) a reference in this Schedule or in any other provision of Part II of this Act to a public body's notice or to a public body's plans certificate includes a reference to that form, but

(*b*) should the form cease to be in force as a public body's notice by virtue of paragraph 1(1) above, nothing in that paragraph affects the continuing validity of the form as a public body's plans certificate.

(3) A public body's plans certificate—

(*a*) may relate either to the whole or to part only of the work specified in the public body's notice concerned, and

(*b*) does not have effect unless it is accepted by the local authority to whom it is given.

(4) A local authority to whom a public body's plans certificate is given—

(*a*) may not reject the certificate except on prescribed grounds, and

(*b*) shall reject the certificate if any of the prescribed grounds exists.

(5) Unless, within the prescribed period, the local authority to whom a public body's plans certificate is given give notice of rejection, specifying the ground or grounds in question, to the public body by which the certificate was given, the authority are conclusively presumed to have accepted the certificate.

(6) If it appears to a local authority by whom a public body's plans certificate has been accepted that the work to which the certificate relates has not been commenced within the period of three years beginning on the date on which the certificate was accepted, the authority may rescind their acceptance of the certificate by notice, specifying the ground or grounds in question, given to the public body.

*Public body's final certificates*

3. (1) Where a public body is satisfied that any work specified in a public body's notice given by it has been completed, the body may give to the local authority such certificate with respect to the completion of the work and compliance with building regulations as may be prescribed (called a "public body's final certificate").

(2) Sub-paragraphs (3) to (5) of paragraph 2 above have effect in relation to a public body's final certificate as if any reference in those sub-paragraphs to a public body's plans certificate were a reference to a public body's final certificate.

(3) Where a public body's final certificate has been given with respect to any of the work specified in a public body's notice and that certificate has been accepted by the local authority concerned, the public body's notice ceases to apply to that work, but the provisions of section 48(1) of this Act, as applied by section 54(4), continue, by virtue of this sub-paragraph, to apply in relation to that work as if the public body's notice continued in force in relation to it.

*Effects of public body's notice ceasing to be in force*

4. (1) This paragraph applies where a public body's notice ceases to be in force by virtue of paragraph 1 above.

(2) Building regulations may provide that if—

(*a*) a public body's plans certificate was given before the day on which the public body's notice ceased to be in force, and

(*b*) that certificate was accepted by the local authority (before, on or after that day), and

(*c*) before that day, that acceptance was not rescinded by a notice under paragraph 2(6) above,

then, with respect to the work specified in the certificate, such of the functions of a local authority referred to in section 48(1) of this Act as may be prescribed for the purposes of this sub-paragraph either are not exercisable or are exercisable only in prescribed circumstances.

(3) If, before the day on which the public body's notice ceased to be in force, a public body's final certificate was given in respect of part of the work specified in the notice and that certificate was accepted by the local authority (before, on or after that day), the fact that the public body's notice has ceased to be in force does not affect the continuing operation of paragraph 3(3) above in relation to that part of the work.

(4) Notwithstanding anything in sub-paragraphs (2) and (3) above, for the purpose of enabling the local authority to perform the functions referred to in section 48(1) of this Act in relation to any part of the work not specified in a public body's plans certificate or final certificate, as the case may be, building regulations may require the local authority to be provided with plans that relate not only to that part but also to the part to which the certificate in question relates.

(5) In any case where this paragraph applies, the reference in subsection (4) of section 36 of this Act to the date of the completion of the work in question has effect, in relation to a notice under subsection (1) of that section, as if it were a reference to the date on which the public body's notice ceased to be in force.

(6) Subject to any provision of building regulations made by virtue of sub-paragraph (2) above, if, before the public body's notice ceased to be in force, an offence under section 35 of this Act was committed with respect to any of the work specified in that notice, summary proceedings for that offence may be commenced by the local authority at any time within six months beginning with the day on which the functions of the local authority referred to in section 48(1) of this Act became exercisable with respect to the provision of building regulations to which the offence relates.

(7) Any reference in the preceding provisions of this paragraph to section 48(1) of this Act is a reference to that section as applied by section 54(2) of this Act.

*Consultation*

5. Building regulations may make provision for requiring, in such circumstances as may be prescribed, a public body that has given a public body's notice to consult any prescribed person before taking any prescribed step in connection with any work specified in the notice.

[1] For provisions "prescribed" by virtue of this Schedule, see the Building (Approved Inspectors etc) Regulations 2002, SI 2000/2532 amended by SI 2001/3336, SI 2002/2872, SI 2003/3133, SI 2004/1466 and 3168, SI 2005/1541 and 2929 (W) and SI 2006/652 and 3318.

# Control of Pollution (Amendment) Act 1989[1]

(1989 c 14)

7.9992 1. **Offence of transporting controlled waste without registering** (1) Subject to the following provisions of this section, it shall be an offence for any person who is not a registered carrier[2] of controlled waste, in the course of any business of his or otherwise with a view to profit, to transport any controlled waste to or from any place in Great Britain.

(2) A person shall not be guilty of an offence under this section in respect of—

(*a*) the transport of controlled waste within the same premises between different places in those premises;

(*b*) the transport to a place in Great Britain of controlled waste which has been brought from a country or territory outside Great Britain and is not landed in Great Britain until it arrives at that place;

(*c*) the transport by air or sea of controlled waste from a place in Great Britain to a place outside Great Britain.

(3) The Secretary of State may by regulations provide that a person shall not be required for the purposes of this section to be a registered carrier of controlled waste if—

(*a*) he is a prescribed person or a person of such a description as may be prescribed[3]; or

(*b*) without prejudice to paragraph (*a*) above, he is a person in relation to whom the prescribed requirements under the law of any other member State are satisfied.

(4) In proceedings against any person for an offence under this section in respect of the transport of any controlled waste it shall be a defence for that person to show—

(*a*) that the waste was transported in an emergency of which notice was given, as soon as practicable after it occurred, to the regulation authority in whose area the emergency occurred; or

(*b*) that he neither knew nor had reasonable grounds for suspecting that what was being transported was controlled waste and took all such steps as it was reasonable to take for ascertaining whether it was such waste; or

(*c*) *repealed.*

(5) A person guilty of an offence under this section shall be liable on summary conviction to a fine not exceeding **level 5** on the standard scale.

(6) In this section "emergency", in relation to the transport of any controlled waste, means any circumstances in which, in order to avoid, remove or reduce any serious danger to the public or serious risk of damage to the environment, it is necessary for the waste to be transported from one place to another without the use of a registered carrier of such waste.

[Control of Pollution (Amendment) Act 1989, s 1 as amended by the Environmental Protection Act 1990, Sch 15 and the Clean Neighbourhoods and Environment Act 2005, s 35.]

[1] This Act shall come into force on such day or days as the Secretary of State may by order appoint (s 11(2), post). The Control of Pollution (Amendment) Act 1989 (Commencement) Order 1991, SI 1991/1618 brought the following provisions into force: ss 1(3), 2, 3, 4, 5(3) and (6) (in part), 6 (in part), 7–11. By virtue of that Order, the remaining provisions of the Act came into force on 1 April 1992.

[2] Registration under the Act is of carriers, not of vehicles; accordingly, an owner of a vehicle used by someone who has hired it to transport controlled waste does not commit an offence by virtue of not himself being registered (*Cosmick Transport v Bedfordshire County Council* [1997] RTR 132).

[3] See the Controlled Waste (Registration of Carriers and Seizure of Vehicles) Regulations 1991, SI 1991/1624 amended by SI 1992/588, SI 1994/1056 and 1137, SI 1996/593 and 972, SI 1998/605, SI 2005/894 and 1806 (W), SI 2006/937, SI 2007/3538, SI 2010/675, SI 2011/660 (W), 881 (E) and 988 and SI 2013/2952; and the Waste Management (England and Wales) Regulations 2006, SI 2006/937 amended by SI 2009/3381 and SI 2010/675.

7.9993 2. **Registration of carriers** (1) Subject to section 3 below, the Secretary of State may by regulations make provision for the registration of persons with regulation authorities[1] as carriers of controlled waste and, for that purpose, for the establishment and maintenance by such authorities, in accordance with the regulations, of such registers as may be prescribed[2].

(2)–(5) *Supplementary provisions relating to regulations.*

[Control of Pollution (Amendment) Act 1989, s 2 as amended by the Environmental Protection Act 1990, Sch 15, the Environment Act 1995, Schs 22 and 24 and the Clean Neighbourhoods and Environment Act 2005, s 36.]

[1] For the meaning of "regulation authority", see s 9, post.

[2] See the Controlled Waste (Registration of Carriers and Seizure of Vehicles) Regulations 1991, SI 1991/1624 (for amending instruments, see note to s 1, ante).

7.9994 4. **Appeals against refusal of registration etc** (1) Where a person has applied to a regulation authority to be registered in accordance with any regulations under section 2 above, he may appeal to the Secretary of State if—

(*a*) his application is refused; or

(*b*) the relevant period from the making of the application has expired without his having been registered;

and for the purposes of this subsection the relevant period is two months or, except in the case of an application for the renewal of his registration by a person who is already registered, such longer period as may be agreed between the applicant and the regulation authority in question.

(2) A person whose registration as a carrier of controlled waste has been revoked may appeal against the revocation to the Secretary of State.

(3) On an appeal under this section the Secretary of State may, as he thinks fit, either dismiss the appeal or give the regulation authority in question a direction to register the appellant or, as the case may be, to cancel the revocation.

(4) Where on an appeal made by virtue of subsection (1)(*b*) above the Secretary of State dismisses an appeal, he shall direct the regulation authority in question not to register the appellant.

(5) It shall be the duty of a regulation authority to comply with any direction under this section.

(6) The Secretary of State may by regulations[1] make provision as to the manner in which and time within which an appeal under this section is to be made and as to the procedure to be followed on any such appeal.

(7) Where an appeal under this section is made in accordance with regulations under this section—

(*a*) by a person whose appeal is in respect of such an application for the renewal of his registration as was made, in accordance with regulations under section 2 above, at a time when he was already registered; or

(*b*) by a person whose registration has been revoked,

that registration shall continue in force, notwithstanding the expiry of the prescribed period or the revocation, until the appeal is disposed of.

(8) For the purposes of subsection (7) above an appeal is disposed of when any of the following occurs, that is to say—

(*a*) the appeal is withdrawn;

(*b*) the appellant is notified by the Secretary of State or the regulation authority in question that his appeal has been dismissed; or

(*c*) the regulation authority comply with any direction of the Secretary of State to renew the appellant's registration or to cancel the revocation.

(9) This section is subject to section 114 of the Environment Act 1995 (delegation or reference of appeals etc).

[Control of Pollution (Amendment) Act 1989, s 4 as amended by the Environmental Protection Act 1990, Sch 15 and the Environment Act 1995, Sch 22.]

---

[1] See the Controlled Waste (Registration of Carriers and Seizure of Vehicles) Regulations 1991, SI 1991/1624 (for amending instruments, see note to s 1, ante).

7.9995 **5. Power to require production of authority, stop and search etc** (1) This section applies where an authorised officer of a regulation authority or a constable reasonably believes that controlled waste has been, is being or is about to be transported in contravention of section 1(1) above.

(2) The authorised officer or constable may—

(*a*) require any person appearing to him to be or to have been engaged in transporting that waste to produce his (or, as the case may be, his employer's) authority to do so;

(*b*) search any vehicle that appears to him to be a vehicle that has been, is being or is about to be used for transporting that waste;

(*c*) carry out tests on anything found in any such vehicle (including by taking away samples for testing of anything so found);

(*d*) seize any such vehicle and any of its contents.

(3) For the purposes of subsection (2)(*a*) above, a person's authority for transporting controlled waste is—

(*a*) his certificate of registration as a carrier of controlled waste;

(*b*) such copy of that certificate as satisfies requirements specified in regulations made by the appropriate person; or

(*c*) such evidence as may be so specified that he is not required to be registered as a carrier of controlled waste.

(4) Where an authorised officer or constable has required a person to produce an authority under subsection (2)(*a*) above, the person must do so—

(*a*) by producing it forthwith to the authorised officer or constable;

(*b*) by producing it at a place and within a period specified in regulations made by the appropriate person; or

(*c*) by sending it to that place and within that period.

(5) In acting under subsection (2) above an authorised officer or constable may—

(*a*) stop any vehicle as referred to in paragraph (*b*) of that subsection (but only a constable in uniform may stop a vehicle on any road);

(*b*) enter any premises for the purpose specified in paragraph (*b*) or (*d*) of that subsection.

(6) A vehicle or its contents seized under subsection (2)(*d*) above—

(*a*) by an authorised officer of a regulation authority, are seized on behalf of that authority;

(*b*) by a constable in the presence of an authorised officer of a regulation authority, are seized on behalf of that authority;

(*c*) by a constable without such an officer present, are seized on behalf of the waste collection authority in whose area the seizure takes place.

(7) A person commits an offence if—

(*a*) he fails without reasonable excuse to comply with a requirement imposed under paragraph (*a*) of subsection (2) above;

(*b*) he fails without reasonable excuse to give any assistance that an authorised officer or constable may reasonably request in the exercise of a power under that subsection;

(*c*) he otherwise intentionally obstructs an authorised officer or constable in the exercise of a power under that subsection.

(8) A person is not guilty of an offence by virtue of subsection (7)(*a*) above unless it is shown—

(*a*) that the waste in question was controlled waste; and

(*b*) that the waste was or was being transported to or from a place in Great Britain.

(9) Where an authorised officer or constable has stopped a vehicle under subsection (5) above, he may (in addition to any requirement that may be imposed under paragraph (*a*) of subsection (2) above) require any occupant of the vehicle to give him—

(*a*) the occupant's name and address;

(*b*) the name and address of the registered owner of the vehicle;

(*c*) any other information he may reasonably request.

(10) A person commits an offence if—

(*a*) he fails without reasonable excuse to comply with a requirement under subsection (9) above;

(*b*) he gives information required under that subsection that is—

(i) to his knowledge false or misleading in a material way, or

(ii) given recklessly and is false or misleading in a material way.

(11) A person guilty of an offence under this section is liable on summary conviction to a fine not exceeding level 5 on the standard scale.*

[Control of Pollution (Amendment) Act 1989, s 5 as substituted by the Clean Neighbourhoods and Environment Act 2005, s 37.]

* **Substituted, and new s 5A inserted, in relation to England and Wales, by the Clean Neighbourhoods and Environment Act 2005, s 37 from a date to be appointed. In force for certain purposes from 16 March 2006 (W), 6 April 2006 (E), and 27 October 2006 (W).**

**7.9996 5A. Seizure of vehicles etc: supplementary** (1) Where under section 5 above an authorised officer of a regulation authority or a constable seizes a vehicle or its contents ("seized property") on behalf of a regulation authority, the authority may remove the seized property to such a place as the authority consider appropriate.

(2) A regulation authority must deal with any seized property in accordance with regulations[1] made by the appropriate person.

(3)–(5) *Supplementary provision as to regulations.*

[Control of Pollution (Amendment) Act 1989, s 5A as inserted by the Clean Neighbourhoods and Environment Act 2005, s 37.]

[1] The Control of Waste (Dealing with Seized Property) (England and Wales) Regulations 2015, SI 2015/426 have been made.

* **New s 5A in force for certain purposes as noted to s 5 above.**

**7.9997 5B. Fixed penalty notices for offences under section 5** (1) This section applies where it appears to a regulation authority that a person has failed without reasonable excuse to comply with a requirement under section 5(2)(*a*) above (requirement to produce authority to transport waste).

(2) The regulation authority may give that person a notice offering him the opportunity of discharging any liability to conviction for an offence under section 5(7)(*a*) above by payment of a fixed penalty.

(3) Where a person is given a notice under this section in respect of an offence—

(*a*) no proceedings may be instituted for that offence before expiration of the period of fourteen days following the date of the notice; and

(*b*) he may not be convicted of that offence if he pays the fixed penalty before the expiration of the period.

(4) A notice under this section must give such particulars of the circumstances alleged to constitute the offence as are necessary for giving reasonable information of the offence.

(5) A notice under this section must also state—

(*a*) the period during which, by virtue of subsection (3) above, proceedings will not be taken for the offence;

(*b*) the amount of the fixed penalty; and

(*c*) the person to whom and the address at which the fixed penalty may be paid.

(6) Without prejudice to payment by any other method, payment of the fixed penalty may be made by pre-paying and posting a letter containing the amount of the penalty (in cash or otherwise) to the person mentioned in subsection (5)(*c*) above at the address so mentioned.

(7) Where a letter is sent in accordance with subsection (6) above payment is to be regarded as having been made at the time at which that letter would be delivered in the ordinary course of post.

(8) The form of a notice under this section must be such as the appropriate person may by

order prescribe.

(9) The fixed penalty payable to a regulation authority under this section is, subject to subsection (10) below, £300.

(10) The appropriate person may by order substitute a different amount for the amount for the time being specified in subsection (9) above.

(11) The regulation authority to which a fixed penalty is payable under this section may make provision for treating it as having been paid if a lesser amount is paid before the end of a period specified by the authority.

(12) The appropriate person may by regulations[1] restrict the extent to which, and the circumstances in which, a regulation authority may make provision under subsection (11) above.

(13) In any proceedings a certificate which—

(*a*) purports to be signed on behalf of the chief finance officer of the regulation authority, and

(*b*) states that payment of a fixed penalty was or was not received by a date specified in the certificate,

is evidence of the facts stated.

(14) In this section "chief finance officer", in relation to a regulation authority, means the person having responsibility for the financial affairs of the authority.

[Control of Pollution (Amendment) Act 1989, s 5B as inserted by the Clean Neighbourhoods and Environment Act 2005, s 38.]

---

1 The Environmental Offences (Fixed Penalties) (Miscellaneous Provisions) Regulations 2007, SI 2007/175, the Environmental Offences (Use of Fixed Penalty Receipts) (Wales) Regulations 2007, SI 2007/739 amended by SI 2008/663; the Environmental Offences (Use of Fixed Penalty Receipts) Regulations 2007, SI 2007/901 and the Environmental Offences (Fixed Penalties) (Miscellaneous Provisions) (Wales) Regulations 2008, SI 2008/663 have been made. For amending instruments, see the note to the Refuse Disposal (Amenity) Act 1978, s 2A, ante.

**7.9998 5C. Use of fixed penalties under section 5B** *Where received by Environment Agency, payable to Secretary of State; waste collection authority for functions under s 5 or in accordance with regulations[1].*

[Control of Pollution (Amendment) Act 1989, s 5C as inserted by the Clean Neighbourhoods and Environment Act 2005, s 38.]

---

1 The Environmental Offences (Fixed Penalties) (Miscellaneous Provisions) Regulations 2007, SI 2007/175 have been made. For amending instruments, see the note to the Refuse Disposal (Amenity) Act 1978, s 2A, ante.

**7.9999 6. Seizure and disposal of vehicles used for illegal waste disposal** (1) A justice of the peace or, in Scotland, a sheriff or a justice of the peace may issue a warrant to a regulation authority for the seizure of any vehicle if he is satisfied, on sworn information in writing—

(*a*) that there are reasonable grounds for believing—

(i) that an offence under section 3 of the Control of Pollution Act 1974 or section 33 of the Environmental Protection Act 1990 (prohibition on unlicensed deposit, treatment or disposal of waste) has been committed; and

(ii) that that vehicle was used in the commission of the offence;

(*b*) that proceedings for that offence have not yet been brought against any person; and

(*c*) that the authority have failed, after taking the prescribed[1] steps, to ascertain the name and address of any person who is able to provide them with the prescribed information about who was using the vehicle at the time when the offence was committed.

(2) Subject to subsections (3) and (4) below, where a warrant under this section has been issued to a regulation authority in respect of any vehicle, any duly authorised officer of the regulation authority or any constable may stop the vehicle and, on behalf of the authority, seize the vehicle and its contents.

(3) Nothing in this section shall authorise any person other than a constable in uniform to stop a vehicle on any road; and a duly authorised officer of a regulation authority shall not be entitled to seize any property under this section unless he is accompanied by a constable.

(4) A warrant under this section shall continue in force until its purpose is fulfilled; and any person seizing any property under this section shall, if required to do so, produce both the warrant and any authority in pursuance of which he is acting under the warrant.

(5) Where any property has been seized under this section on behalf of a regulation authority, the authority may, in accordance with regulations[1] made by the Secretary of state, remove it to such place as the authority consider appropriate and may retain custody of it until either—

(*a*) it is returned, in accordance with the regulations, to a person who establishes that he is entitled to it; or

(*b*) it is disposed of by the authority in exercise of a power conferred by the regulations to sell or destroy the property or to deposit it at any place.

(6)–(7) *Regulations under this section.*

(8) Subject to their powers by virtue of any regulations under this section to sell or destroy any property or to dispose of it by depositing it at any place, it shall be the duty of a regulation authority, while any property is in their custody by virtue of a warrant under this section, to take such steps as are reasonably necessary for the safe custody of that property.

(9) Any person who intentionally obstructs any authorised officer of a regulation authority or

constable in the exercise of any power conferred by virtue of a warrant under this section shall be guilty of an offence and liable, on summary conviction, to a fine not exceeding **level 5** on the standard scale.*

[Control of Pollution (Amendment) Act 1989, s 6 as amended by the Environmental Protection Act 1990, Sch 15 and the Environment Act 1995, Sch 22.]

* **Repealed, in relation to England and Wales, by the Clean Neighbourhoods and Environment Act 2005, s 37 from a date to be appointed.**

[1] The Control of Waste (Dealing with Seized Property) (England and Wales) Regulations 2015, SI 2015/426 have been made.

7.10000 **7. Further enforcement provisions** (1) Subject to subsection (2) below, the provisions of section 71 of the Environmental Protection Act 1990 (powers of entry, of dealing with imminent pollution and to obtain information and duty not to disclose information) shall have effect as if the provisions of this Act were provisions of that Act and as if, in those sections, references to a relevant authority were references to a regulation authority.

(2) *Repealed.*

(3) A person shall be guilty of an offence under this subsection if he—

(*a*) fails, without reasonable excuse, to comply with any requirement in pursuance of regulations under this Act to provide information to the Secretary of State or a regulation authority; or

(*b*) in complying with any such requirement, provides information which he knows to be false or misleading in a material particular or recklessly provides information which is false or misleading in a material particular;

and in paragraph (*a*) above the words "without reasonable excuse" shall be construed in their application to Scotland, as in their application to England and Wales, as making it a defence for a person against whom proceedings for the failure are brought to show that there was a reasonable excuse for the failure, rather than as requiring the person bringing the proceedings to show that there was no such excuse.

(4) A person guilty of an offence under subsection (3) above shall be liable on summary conviction to a fine not exceeding **level 5** on the standard scale.

(5) Where the commission by any person of an offence under this Act is due to the act or default of some other person, that other person shall also be guilty of the offence; and a person may be charged with and convicted of an offence by virtue of this subsection whether or not proceedings for the offence are taken against any other person.

(6) Where a body corporate is guilty of an offence under this Act (including where it is so guilty by virtue of subsection (5) above) in respect of any act or omission which is shown to have been committed with the consent or connivance of, or to be attributable to any neglect on the part of, any director, manager, secretary or other similar officer of the body corporate or any person who was purporting to act in any such capacity, he, as well as the body corporate, shall be guilty of that offence and shall be liable to be proceeded against and punished accordingly.

(7) Where the affairs of a body corporate are managed by its members, subsection (6) above shall apply in relation to the acts and defaults of a member in connection with his functions of management as if he were a director of the body corporate.

(8) *Repealed.*

[Control of Pollution (Amendment) Act 1989, s 7 as amended by the Environmental Protection Act 1990, Schs 15 and 16 and the Environment Act 1995, Schs 19, 22 and 24.]

7.10001 **9. Interpretation** (1) In this Act—

"appropriate person" means—

(*a*) the Secretary of State, in relation to England;

(*b*) the National Assembly for Wales, in relation to Wales.

"controlled waste" has, at any time, the same meaning as for the purposes of Part II of the Environmental Protection Act 1990[1];

"prescribed" means prescribed by regulations made by the Secretary of State;

"regulation authority" means—

(*a*) in relation to England and Wales, the Environment Agency; and

(*b*) *Scotland*;

and any reference to the area of a regulation authority shall accordingly be construed as a reference to any area in England and Wales or, as the case may be, in Scotland;

"road" has the same meaning as in the Road Traffic Act 1988;

"transport", in relation to any controlled waste, includes the transport of that waste by road or rail or by air, sea or inland waterway but does not include moving that waste from one place to another by means of any pipe or other apparatus that joins those two places.

"vehicle" means any motor vehicle or trailer within the meaning of the Road Traffic Regulation Act 1984.

(1A) In sections 5 to 7 above "regulation authority" also means a waste collection authority falling within section 30(3)(*a*), (*b*) or (*bb*) of the Environmental Protection Act 1990.

(1AA) But, in the case of a waste collection authority that is a regulation authority by virtue of subsection (1A), the powers conferred on that authority under sections 5 to 7 above are not exercisable by that authority in relation to specified persons (within the meaning of Part 8 of the

Waste (England and Wales) Regulations 2011).

(1B) For the purposes of any provision of this Act, "authorised officer" in relation to any authority means an officer of the authority who is authorised in writing for the purposes of that provision.

(2) *Repealed.*

[Control of Pollution (Amendment) Act 1989, s 9 as amended by the Environmental Protection Act 1990, Schs 15 and 16, the Environment Act 1995, Sch 22, the Anti-Social Behaviour Act 2003, s 55, the Clean Neighbourhoods and Environment Act 2005, s 39 and SI 2011/988.]

[1] See this title, post.

7.10002 **11. Short title, commencement and extent** (1) This Act may be cited as the Control of Pollution (Amendment) Act 1989.

(2) *Repealed.*

(3) *Repealed.*

(4) This Act shall not extend to Northern Ireland.

[Control of Pollution (Amendment) Act 1989, s 11 as amended by the Environment Act 1995, s 118 and Sch 24 and the Statute Law (Repeals) Act 2004.]

# Environmental Protection Act 1990[1]

(1990 c 43)

## PART I[2]

## INTEGRATED POLLUTION CONTROL AND AIR POLLUTION CONTROL BY LOCAL AUTHORITIES*

*Preliminary*

7.10003 **1. Preliminary** (1) The following provisions have effect for the interpretation of this Part.

(2) The "environment" consists of all, or any, of the following media, namely, the air, water and land; and the medium of air includes the air within buildings and the air within other natural or man-made structures above or below ground.

(3) "Pollution of the environment" means pollution of the environment due to the release (into any environmental medium) from any process of substances which are capable of causing harm to man or any other living organisms supported by the environment.

(4) "Harm" means harm to the health of living organisms or other interference with the ecological systems of which they form part and, in the case of man, includes offence caused to any of his senses or harm to his property; and "harmless" has a corresponding meaning.

(5) "Process" means any activities carried on in Great Britain, whether on premises or by means of mobile plant, which are capable of causing pollution of the environment and "prescribed process" means a process prescribed under section 2(1) below.

(6) For the purposes of subsection (5) above—

"activities" means industrial or commercial activities or activities of any other nature whatsoever (including, with or without other activities, the keeping of a substance);

"Great Britain" includes so much of the adjacent territorial sea as is, or is treated as, relevant territorial waters for the purposes of Part III of the Water Resources Act 1991 or, as respects Scotland, Part II of the Control of Pollution Act 1974; and

"mobile plant" means plant which is designed to move or to be moved whether on roads or otherwise.

(7) The "enforcing authority", in relation to England and Wales, is the Environment Agency or the local authority by which, under section 4 below, the functions conferred or imposed by this Part otherwise than on the Secretary of State are for the time being exercisable in relation respectively to releases of substances into the environment or into the air; and "local enforcing authority" means any such local authority.

(8) *Scotland.*

(9) "Authorisation" means an authorisation for a process (whether on premises or by means of mobile plant) granted under section 6 below; and a reference to the conditions of an authorisation is a reference to the conditions subject to which at any time the authorisation has effect.

(10) A substance is "released" into any environmental medium whenever it is released directly into that medium whether it is released into it within or outside Great Britain and "release" includes—

(*a*) in relation to air, any emission of the substance into the air;

(*b*) in relation to water, any entry (including any discharge) of the substance into water;

(*c*) in relation to land, any deposit, keeping or disposal of the substance in or on land;

and for this purpose "water" and "land" shall be construed in accordance with subsections (11) and (12) below.

(11) For the purpose of determining into what medium a substance is released—

(*a*) any release into—

(i) the sea or the surface of the seabed,

(ii) any river, watercourse, lake, loch or pond (whether natural or artificial or above or below ground) or reservoir or the surface of the riverbed or of other land supporting such waters, or

(iii) ground waters,

is a release into water;

(*b*) any release into—

(i) land covered by water falling outside paragraph (*a*) above or the water covering such land; or

(ii) the land beneath the surface of the seabed or of other land supporting waters falling within paragraph (*a*)(ii) above,

is a release into land; and

(*c*) any release into a sewer (within the meaning of the Water Industry Act 1991 or, in relation to Scotland, of the Sewerage (Scotland) Act 1968) shall be treated as a release into water;

but a sewer and its contents shall be disregarded in determining whether there is pollution of the environment at any time.

(12) In subsection (11) above "ground waters" means any waters contained in underground strata, or in—

(*a*) a well, borehole or similar work sunk into underground strata, including any adit or passage constructed in connection with the well, borehole or work for facilitating the collection of water in the well, borehole or work; or

(*b*) any excavation into underground strata where the level of water in the excavation depends wholly or mainly on water entering it from the strata.

(13) "Substance" shall be treated as including electricity or heat and "prescribed substance" has the meaning given by section 2(7) below.

(14) In this Part "the appropriate Agency" means—

(*a*) in relation to England and Wales, the Environment Agency; and

(*b*) *Scotland* *.

[Environmental Protection Act 1990, s 1 as amended by the Water Consolidation (Consequential Provisions) Act 1991, Sch 1 and the Environment Act 1995, Sch 22.]

* **Repealed by the Pollution Prevention and Control Act 1999, Sch 3 from a date to be appointed.**

1 The Act is to come into force in accordance with s 164. For commencement orders made thereunder, see note 1 to s 164, post.

2 Part I consists of ss 1–28.

**2–4.** *The Secretary of State may, by regulations, prescribe any description of process as a process for the carrying on of which after a prescribed date an authorisation is required under section 6 below; establish standards, objectives or requirements in relation to particular prescribed processes or particular substances; in relation to releases of any substance from prescribed processes into any environmental medium, prescribe standard limits for the concentration, the amount or the amount in any period of that substance which may be so released; and any other characteristic of that substance in any circumstances in which it may be so released; prescribe standard requirements for the measurement or analysis of, or of releases of, substances for which limits have been set; and in relation to any prescribed process, prescribe standards or requirements as to any aspect of the process. Functions under this Part to be those of the appropriate agency*

*Authorisations*

7.10004 **6. Authorisations: general provisions** (1) No person shall carry on a prescribed process after the date prescribed or determined for that description of process by or under regulations under section 2(1) above (but subject to any transitional provision made by the regulations) except under an authorisation granted by the enforcing authority and in accordance with the conditions to which it is subject.

(2) An application for an authorisation shall be made to the enforcing authority in accordance with Part I of Schedule 1 to this Act and shall be accompanied by

(*a*) in a case where, by virtue of section 41 of the Environment Act 1995, a charge prescribed by a charging scheme under that section is required to be paid to the appropriate Agency in respect of the application, the charge so prescribed; or

(*b*) in any other case,

the fee prescribed under section 8(2)(*a*) below.

(3) Where an application is duly made to the enforcing authority, the authority shall either grant the authorisation subject to the conditions required or authorised to be imposed by section 7 below or refuse the application.

(4)–(8) Duties etc of Enforcing authority.*

[Environmental Protection Act 1990, s 6 as amended by the Environment Act 1995, Sch 22.]

* **See note to s 1, ante.**

7.10005 **7. Conditions of authorisations** (1) There shall be included in an authorisation—

(*a*) subject to paragraph (*b*) below, such specific conditions as the enforcing authority considers appropriate, when taken with the general condition implied by subsection (4) below, for achieving the objectives[1] specified in subsection (2) below;

(*b*) such conditions as are specified in directions given by the Secretary of State under subsection (3) below; and

(*c*) such other conditions (if any) as appear to the enforcing authority to be appropriate;

but no conditions shall be imposed for the purpose only of securing the health of persons at work (within the meaning of Part I of the Health and Safety at Work etc Act 1974).

(2) Those objectives are—

(*a*) ensuring that, in carrying on a prescribed process, the best available techniques not entailing excessive cost will be used—

(i) for preventing the release of substances prescribed for any environmental medium into that medium or, where that is not practicable by such means, for reducing the release of such substances to a minimum and for rendering harmless any such substances which are so released; and

(ii) for rendering harmless any other substances which might cause harm if released into any environmental medium;

(*b*) compliance with any directions by the Secretary of State given for the implementation of any obligations of the United Kingdom under the Community Treaties or international law relating to environmental protection;

(*c*) compliance with any limits or requirements and achievement of any quality standards or quality objectives prescribed by the Secretary of State under any of the relevant enactments;

(*d*) compliance with any requirements applicable to the grant of authorisations specified by or under a plan made by the Secretary of State under section 3(5) above.

(3) Except as respects the general condition implied by subsection (4) below, the Secretary of State may give directions to the enforcing authorities as to the conditions which are, or are not, to be included in all authorisations, in authorisations of any specified description or in any particular authorisation.

(4) Subject to subsections (5) and (6) below, there is implied in every authorisation a general condition that, in carrying on the process to which the authorisation applies, the person carrying it on must use the best available techniques not entailing excessive cost—

(*a*) for preventing the release of substances prescribed for any environmental medium into that medium or, where that is not practicable by such means, for reducing the release of such substances to a minimum and for rendering harmless any such substances which are so released; and

(*b*) for rendering harmless any other substances which might cause harm if released into any environmental medium.

(5) In the application of subsections (1) to (4) above to authorisations granted by a local enforcing authority references to the release of substances into any environmental medium are to be read as references to the release of substances into the air.

(6) The obligation implied by virtue of subsection (4) above shall not apply in relation to any aspect of the process in question which is regulated by a condition imposed under subsection (1) above.

(7) The objectives referred to in subsection (2) above shall, where the process—

(*a*) is one designated for central control; and

(*b*) is likely to involve the release of substances into more than one environmental medium;

include the objective of ensuring that the best available techniques not entailing excessive cost will be used for minimising the pollution which may be caused to the environment taken as a whole by the releases having regard to the best practicable environmental option available as respects the substances which may be released.

(8) An authorisation for carrying on a prescribed process may, without prejudice to the generality of subsection (1) above, include conditions—

(*a*) imposing limits on the amount or composition of any substance produced by or utilised in the process in any period; and

(*b*) requiring advance notification of any proposed change in the manner of carrying on the process.

(9) This section has effect subject to section 28 below.

(10) References to the best available techniques not entailing excessive cost, in relation to a process, include (in addition to references to any technical means and technology) references to the number, qualifications, training and supervision of persons employed in the process and the design, construction, lay-out and maintenance of the buildings in which it is carried on.

(11) It shall be the duty of enforcing authorities to have regard to any guidance issued to them by the Secretary of State for the purposes of the application of subsections (2) and (7) above as to the techniques and environmental options that are appropriate for any description of prescribed process.

(12) In subsection (2) above "the relevant enactments" are any enactments or instruments contained in or made for the time being under—

(*a*) section 2 of the Clean Air Act 1968;

(*b*) section 2 of the European Communities Act 1972;

(*c*) Part I of the Health and Safety at Work etc Act 1974;

(*d*) Parts II, III or IV of the Control of Pollution Act 1974;

(*e*) the Water Resources Act 1991;

(*f*) section 3 of this Act; and

(g) section 87 of the Environment Act 1995.*

[Environmental Protection Act 1990, s 7 as amended by the Water Consolidation (Consequential Provisions) Act 1991, Sch 1 and the Environment Act 1995, Schs 22 and 24.]

* **See note to s 1, ante.**

[1] The obligation under art 4 of Council Directive 75/442/EEC (states must take measures to ensure that waste is recovered/disposed of without endangering human health or using process/methods that could harm the environment) is a material consideration for competent authorities when deciding applications involving environmental issues under s 7(2) below (*R (Thornby Farms Ltd) v Daventry District Council and R (Murray) v Derbyshire County Council* [2002] EWCA Civ 31, [2003] QB 503, [2002] 3 WLR 875).

7.10006 **9. Transfer of authorisations** (1) An authorisation for the carrying on of any prescribed process may be transferred by the holder to a person who proposes to carry on the process in the holder's place.

(2) Where an authorisation is transferred under this section, the person to whom it is transferred shall notify the enforcing authority in writing of that fact not later than the end of the period of twenty-one days beginning with the date of the transfer.

(3) An authorisation which is transferred under this section shall have effect on and after the date of the transfer as if it had been granted to that person under section 6 above, subject to the same conditions as were attached to it immediately before that date.*

[Environmental Protection Act 1990, s 9.]

* **See note to s 1, ante.**

7.10007 **10. Variation of authorisations by enforcing authority** (1) The enforcing authority may at any time, subject to the requirements of section 7 above, and, in cases to which they apply, the requirements of Part II of Schedule 1 to this Act, vary an authorisation and shall do so if it appears to the authority at that time that that section requires conditions to be included which are different from the subsisting conditions.

(2) Where the enforcing authority has decided to vary an authorisation under subsection (1) above the authority shall notify the holder of the authorisation and serve a variation notice on him.

(3) In this Part a "variation notice" is a notice served by the enforcing authority on the holder of an authorisation—

(a) specifying variations of the authorisation which the enforcing authority has decided to make; and

(b) specifying the date or dates on which the variations are to take effect;

and, unless the notice is withdrawn or is varied under subsection (3A) below, the variations specified in a variation notice shall take effect on the date or dates so specified.

(3A) An enforcing authority which has served a variation notice may vary that notice by serving on the holder of the authorisation in question a further notice—

(a) specifying the variations which the enforcing authority has decided to make to the variation notice; and

(b) specifying the date or dates on which the variations specified in the variation notice, as varied by the further notice, are to take effect;

and any reference in this Part to a variation notice, or to a variation notice served under subsection (2) above, includes a reference to such a notice as varied by a further notice served under this subsection.

(4) A variation notice served under subsection (2) above shall also—

(a) require the holder of the authorisation, within such period as may be specified in the notice, to notify the authority what action (if any) he proposes to take to ensure that the process is carried on in accordance with the authorisation as varied by the notice; and

(b) require the holder to pay, within such period as may be specified in the notice,—

(i) in a case where the enforcing authority is the Environment Agency or SEPA, the charge (if any) prescribed for the purpose by a charging scheme under section 41 of the Environment Act 1995; or

(ii) in any other case, the fee (if any) prescribed by a scheme under section 8 above.

(5) Where in the opinion of the enforcing authority any action to be taken by the holder of an authorisation in consequence of a variation notice served under subsection (2) above will involve a substantial change in the manner in which the process is being carried on, the enforcing authority shall notify the holder of its opinion.

(6) The Secretary of State may, if he thinks fit in relation to authorisations of any description or particular authorisations, direct the enforcing authorities—

(a) to exercise their powers under this section, or to do so in such circumstances as may be specified in the directions, in such manner as may be so specified; or

(b) not to exercise those powers, or not to do so in such circumstances or such manner as may be so specified;

and the Secretary of State shall have the corresponding power of direction in respect of the powers of the enforcing authorities to vary authorisations under section 11 below.

(7) In this section and section 11 below a "substantial change", in relation to a prescribed process being carried on under an authorisation, means a substantial change in the substances released from the process or in the amount or any other characteristic of any substance so released;

and the Secretary of State may give directions to the enforcing authorities as to what does or does not constitute a substantial change in relation to processes generally, any description of process or any particular process.

(8) In this section and section 11 below—

"prescribed" means prescribed in regulations made by the Secretary of State;

"vary",

(*a*) in relation to the subsisting conditions or other provisions of an authorisation, means adding to them or varying or rescinding any of them; and

(*b*) in relation to a variation notice, means adding to, or varying or rescinding the notice or any of its contents;

and "variation" shall be construed accordingly.*

[Environmental Protection Act 1990, s 10 as amended by the Environment Act 1995, Sch 22.]

* **See note to s 1, ante.**

7.10008 **11. Variation of conditions etc: applications by holders of authorisations** (1) A person carrying on a prescribed process under an authorisation who wishes to make a relevant change in the process may at any time—

(*a*) notify the enforcing authority in the prescribed form of that fact, and

(*b*) request the enforcing authority to make a determination, in relation to the proposed change, of the matters mentioned in subsection (2) below;

and a person making a request under paragraph (*b*) above shall furnish the enforcing authority with such information as may be prescribed or as the authority may by notice require.

(2) On receiving a request under subsection (1) above the enforcing authority shall determine—

(*a*) whether the proposed change would involve a breach of any condition of the authorisation;

(*b*) if it would not involve such a breach, whether the authority would be likely to vary the conditions of the authorisation as a result of the change;

(*c*) if it would involve such a breach, whether the authority would consider varying the conditions of the authorisation so that the change may be made; and

(*d*) whether the change would involve a substantial change in the manner in which the process is being carried on;

and the enforcing authority shall notify the holder of the authorisation of its determination of those matters.

(3) Where the enforcing authority has determined that the proposed change would not involve a substantial change, but has also determined under paragraph (*b*) or (*c*) of subsection (2) above that the change would lead to or require the variation of the conditions of the authorisation, then—

(*a*) the enforcing authority shall (either on notifying its determination under that subsection or on a subsequent occasion) notify the holder of the authorisation of the variations which the authority is likely to consider making; and

(*b*) the holder may apply in the prescribed1 form to the enforcing authority for the variation of the conditions of the authorisation so that he may make the proposed change.

(4) Where the enforcing authority has determined that a proposed change would involve a substantial change that would lead to or require the variation of the conditions of the authorisation, then—

(*a*) the authority shall (either on notifying its determination under subsection (2) above or on a subsequent occasion) notify the holder of the authorisation of the variations which the authority is likely to consider making; and

(*b*) the holder of the authorisation shall, if he wishes to proceed with the change, apply in the prescribed form to the enforcing authority for the variation of the conditions of the authorisation.

(5) The holder of an authorisation may at any time, unless he is carrying on a prescribed process under the authorisation and wishes to make a relevant change in the process, apply to enforcing authority in the prescribed form for the variation of the conditions of the authorisation.

(6) A person carrying on a process under an authorisation who wishes to make a relevant change in the process may, where it appears to him that the change will require the variation of the conditions of the authorisation, apply to the enforcing authority in the prescribed form for the variation of the conditions of the authorisation specified in the application.

(7) A person who makes an application for the variation of the conditions of an authorisation shall furnish the authority with such information as may be prescribed1 or as the authority may by notice require.

(8) On an application for variation of the conditions of an authorisation under any provision of this section—

(*a*) the enforcing authority may, having fulfilled the requirements of Part II of Schedule 1 to this Act in cases to which they apply, as it thinks fit either refuse the application or, subject to the requirements of section 7 above, vary the conditions or, in the case of an application under subsection (6) above, treat the application as a request for a determination under subsection (2) above; and

(*b*) if the enforcing authority decides to vary the conditions, it shall serve a variation notice on the holder of the authorisation.

(9) *Fees.*

(10) This section applies to any provision other than a condition which is contained in an authorisation as it applies to a condition with the modification that any reference to the breach of a condition shall be read as a reference to acting outside the scope of the authorisation.

(11) For the purposes of this section a relevant change in a prescribed process is a change in the manner of carrying on the process which is capable of altering the substances released from the process or of affecting the amount or any other characteristic of any substance so released.*

[Environmental Protection Act 1990, s 11 as amended by the Environment Act 1995, Sch 22.]

* **See note to s 1, ante.**

7.10009 **12. Revocation of authorisation** (1) The enforcing authority may at any time revoke an authorisation by notice in writing to the person holding the authorisation.

(2) Without prejudice to the generality of subsection (1) above, the enforcing authority may revoke an authorisation where it has reason to believe that a prescribed process for which the authorisation is in force has not been carried on or not for a period of twelve months.

(3) The revocation of an authorisation under this section shall have effect from the date specified in the notice; and the period between the date on which the notice is served and the date so specified shall not be less than twenty-eight days.

(4) The enforcing authority may, before the date on which the revocation of an authorisation takes effect, withdraw the notice or vary the date specified in it.

(5) The Secretary of State may, if he thinks fit in relation to an authorisation, give to the enforcing authority directions as to whether the authority should revoke the authorisation under this section.*

[Environmental Protection Act 1990, s 12.]

* **See note to s 1, ante.**

*Enforcement*

7.10010 **13. Enforcement notices** (1) If the enforcing authority is of the opinion that the person carrying on a prescribed process under an authorisation is contravening any condition of the authorisation, or is likely to contravene any such condition, the authority may serve on him a notice ("an enforcement notice").

(2) An enforcement notice shall—

(*a*) state that the authority is of the said opinion;

(*b*) specify the matters constituting the contravention or the matters making it likely that the contravention will arise, as the case may be;

(*c*) specify the steps that must be taken to remedy the contravention or to remedy the matters making it likely that the contravention will arise, as the case may be; and

(*d*) specify the period within which those steps must be taken.

(3) The Secretary of State may, if he thinks fit in relation to the carrying on by any person of a prescribed process, give to the enforcing authority directions as to whether the authority should exercise its powers under this section and as to the steps which are to be required to be taken under this section.

(4) The enforcing authority may, as respects any enforcement notice it has issued to any person, by notice in writing served on that person, withdraw the notice.*

[Environmental Protection Act 1990, s 13 as amended by the Environment Act 1995, Sch 22.]

* **See note to s 1, ante.**

7.10011 **14. Prohibition notices** (1) If the enforcing authority is of the opinion, as respects the carrying on of a prescribed process under an authorisation, that the continuing to carry it on, or the continuing to carry it on in a particular manner, involves an imminent risk of serious pollution of the environment the authority shall serve a notice (a "prohibition notice") on the person carrying on the process.

(2) A prohibition notice may be served whether or not the manner of carrying on the process in question contravenes a condition of the authorisation and may relate to any aspects of the process, whether regulated by the conditions of the authorisation or not.

(3) A prohibition notice shall—

(*a*) state the authority's opinion;

(*b*) specify the risk involved in the process;

(*c*) specify the steps that must be taken to remove it and the period within which they must be taken; and

(*d*) direct that the authorisation shall, until the notice is withdrawn, wholly or to the extent specified in the notice cease to have effect to authorise the carrying on of the process;

and where the direction applies to part only of the process it may impose conditions to be observed in carrying on the part which is authorised to be carried on.

(4) The Secretary of State may, if he thinks fit in relation to the carrying on by any person of a prescribed process, give to the enforcing authority directions as to—

*(a)* whether the authority should perform its duties under this section; and

*(b)* the matters to be specified in any prohibition notice in pursuance of subsection (3) above which the authority is directed to issue.

(5) The enforcing authority shall, as respects any prohibition notice it has issued to any person, by notice in writing served on that person, withdraw the notice when it is satisfied that the steps required by the notice have been taken.*

[Environmental Protection Act 1990, s 14.]

* **See note to s 1, ante.**

7.10012 **15. Appeals as respects authorisations and against variation, enforcement and prohibition notices** (1)–(7) (Appeals to the Secretary of State).

(8) Where an appeal is brought under subsection (1) above against the revocation of an authorisation, the revocation shall not take effect pending the final determination or the withdrawal of the appeal.

(9) Where an appeal is brought under subsection (2) above against a notice, the bringing of the appeal shall not have the effect of suspending the operation of the notice.

(10) *Regulations.**

[Environmental Protection Act 1990, s 15 as amended by the Environment Act 1995, Sch 22.]

* **See note to s 1, ante.**

7.10013 **19. Obtaining of information from persons and authorities** (1) For the purposes of the discharge of his functions under this Part, the Secretary of State may, by notice in writing served on an enforcing authority, require the authority to furnish such information about the discharge of its functions as an enforcing authority under this Part as he may require.

(2) For the purposes of the discharge of their respective functions under this Part, the following authorities, that is to say—

*(a)* the Secretary of State,

*(b)* a local enforcing authority,

*(c)* the Environment Agency, and

*(d)* SEPA,

may, by notice in writing served on any person, require that person to furnish to the authority such information which the authority reasonably considers that it needs as is specified in the notice, in such form and within such period following service of the notice, or at such time, as is so specified.

(3) For the purposes of this section the discharge by the Secretary of State of an obligation of the United Kingdom under the Community Treaties or any international agreement relating to environmental protection shall be treated as a function of his under this Part.*

[Environmental Protection Act 1990, s 19 as amended by the Environment Act 1995, Sch 22.]

* **See note to s 1, ante.**

*Provisions as to offences*

7.10014 **23. Offences** (1) It is an offence for a person—

*(a)* to contravene section 6(1) above;

*(b)* to fail to give the notice required by section 9(2) above;

*(c)* to fail to comply with or contravene any requirement or prohibition imposed by an enforcement notice or a prohibition notice;

*(d)–(f)* *Repealed*;

*(g)* to fail, without reasonable excuse, to comply with any requirement imposed by a notice under section 19(2) above;

*(h)* to make a statement which he knows to be false or misleading in a material particular, or recklessly to make a statement which is false or misleading in a material particular, where the statement is made—

(i) in purported compliance with a requirement to furnish any information imposed by or under any provision of this Part; or

(ii) for the purpose of obtaining the grant of an authorisation to himself or any other person or the variation of an authorisation;

(i) intentionally to make a false entry in any record required to be kept under section 7 above;

*(j)* with intent to deceive, to forge or use a document issued or authorised to be issued under section 7 above or required for any purpose thereunder or to make or have in his possession a document so closely resembling any such document as to be likely to deceive;

*(k)* *Repealed*;

(*l*) to fail to comply with an order made by a court under section 26 below.

(2) A person guilty of an offence under paragraph (*a*), (*c*) or (*l*) of subsection (1) above shall be liable[1]:

(*a*) on summary conviction, to a fine or to imprisonment for a term not exceeding three months, or to both;

(*b*) on conviction on indictment, to a fine or to imprisonment for a term not exceeding two years, or to both.

(3) A person guilty of an offence under paragraph (*b*), (*g*), (*h*), (i) or (*j*) of subsection (1) above shall be liable[1]—

(*a*) on summary conviction, to a fine not exceeding the statutory maximum;

(*b*) on conviction on indictment, to a fine or to imprisonment for a term not exceeding two years, or to both.

(4)–(5) *Repealed.**

[Environmental Protection Act 1990, s 23 as amended by the Environment Act 1995, Schs 22 and 24 and SI 2015/664.]

* **See note to s 1, ante.**

1 For procedure in respect of an offence triable either way; see the Magistrates' Courts Act 1980, ss 17A–21 in PART I: MAGISTRATES' COURTS, PROCEDURE, ante.

7.10015 **25. Onus of proof as regards techniques and evidence** (1) In any proceedings for an offence under section 23(1)(*a*) above consisting in a failure to comply with the general condition implied in every authorisation by section 7(4) above, it shall be for the accused to prove that there was no better available technique not entailing excessive cost than was in fact used to satisfy the condition.

(2) Where—

(*a*) an entry is required under section 7 above to be made in any record as to the observance of any condition of an authorisation; and

(*b*) the entry has not been made;

that fact shall be admissible as evidence that that condition has not been observed.*

[Environmental Protection Act 1990, s 25.]

* **See note to s 1, ante.**

7.10016 **26. Power of court to order cause of offence to be remedied** (1) Where a person is convicted of an offence under section 23(1)(*a*) or (*c*) above in respect of any matters which appear to the court to be matters which it is in his power to remedy, the court may, in addition to or instead of imposing any punishment, order him, within such time as may be fixed by the order, to take such steps as may be specified in the order for remedying those matters.

(2) The time fixed by an order under subsection (1) above may be extended or further extended by order of the court on an application made before the end of the time as originally fixed or as extended under this subsection, as the case may be.

(3) Where a person is ordered under subsection (1) above to remedy any matters, that person shall not be liable under section 23 above in respect of those matters in so far as they continue during the time fixed by the order or any further time allowed under subsection (2) above.*

[Environmental Protection Act 1990, s 26.]

* **See note to s 1, ante.**

7.10017 **27. Power of appropriate Agency to remedy harm** (1) Where the commission of an offence under section 23(1)(*a*) or (*c*) above causes any harm which it is possible to remedy, the appropriate Agency may subject to subsection (2) below—

(*a*) arrange for any reasonable steps to be taken towards remedying the harm; and

(*b*) recover the cost of taking those steps from any person convicted of that offence.

(2) The Environment Agency or SEPA, as the case may be, shall not exercise its powers under this section except with the approval in writing of the Secretary of State and, where any of the steps are to be taken on or will affect land in the occupation of any person other than the person on whose land the prescribed process is being carried on, with the permission of that person.*

[Environmental Protection Act 1990, s 27 as amended by the Environment Act 1995, Sch 22.]

* **See note to s 1, ante.**

*Authorisations and other statutory controls*

7.10018 **28. Authorisations and other statutory controls** (1) No condition shall at any time be attached to an authorisation so as to regulate the final disposal by deposit in or on land of controlled waste (within the meaning of Part II), nor shall any condition apply to such a disposal.

(2) Where any of the activities comprising a prescribed process are regulated both by an authorisation granted by the enforcing authority under this Part and by a an environmental permit granted under the Environmental Permitting (England and Wales) Regulations 2010 in relation to a radioactive substances activity within the meaning of those Regulations, then, if different obligations are imposed as respects the same matter by a condition attached to the authorisation under this Part and a condition attached to the registration or authorisation under that Act, the condition imposed by the authorisation under this Part shall be treated as not binding the person carrying on the

process.

(3)–(4) *Repealed.**

[Environmental Protection Act 1990, s 28 as amended by the Water Consolidation (Consequential Provisions) Act 1991, Sch 1, the Radioactive Substances Act 1993, Sch 4, the Environment Act 1995, Schs 22 and 24 and SI 2010/675.]

* **See note to s 1, ante.**

## PART II[1]

## WASTE ON LAND

### *Preliminary*

7.10019 **29. Preliminary** (1) The following provisions have effect for the interpretation of this Part.

(1A) "Appropriate person" means—

(*a*) in relation to England, the Secretary of State;

(*b*) in relation to Wales, the National Assembly for Wales.

(2) The "environment" consists of all, or any, of the following media, namely land, water and the air.

(3) "Pollution of the environment" means pollution of the environment due to the release or escape (into any environment medium) from—

(*a*) the land on which controlled waste or extractive waste is treated,

(*b*) the land on which controlled waste or extractive waste is kept,

(*c*) the land in or on which controlled waste or extractive waste is deposited,

(*d*) fixed plant by means of which controlled waste or extractive waste is treated, kept or disposed of,

of substances or articles constituting or resulting from the waste and capable (by reason of the quantity or concentrations involved) of causing harm to man or any other living organisms supported by the environment.

(4) Subsection (3) above applies in relation to mobile plant by means of which controlled waste or extractive waste is treated or disposed of as it applies to plant on land by means of which controlled waste or extractive waste is treated or disposed of.

(5) For the purposes of subsections (3) and (4) above "harm" means harm to the health of living organisms or other interference with the ecological systems of which they form part and in the case of man includes offence to any of his senses or harm to his property; and "harmless" has a corresponding meaning.

(6) The "disposal" of waste includes its disposal by way of deposit in or on land and, subject to subsection (7) below, waste is "treated" when it is subjected to any process, including making it re-usable or reclaiming substances from it and "recycle" (and cognate expressions) shall be construed accordingly.

(7) Regulations made by the Secretary of State may prescribe activities as activities which constitute the treatment of waste for the purposes of this Part or any provision of this Part prescribed in the regulations.

(8) "Land" includes land covered by waters where the land is above the low water mark of ordinary spring tides and references to land on which controlled waste or extractive waste is treated, kept or deposited are references to the surface of the land (including any structure set into the surface).

(9) "Mobile plant" means plant which is designed to move or be moved whether on roads or other land.

(10) *Repealed.*

(11) "Substance" means any natural or artificial substance, whether in solid or liquid form or in the form of a gas or vapour.

(12) "The Environmental Permitting Regulations" means the Environmental Permitting (England and Wales) Regulations 2010.

(13) The following expressions have the same meaning as in the Environmental Permitting Regulations —

"environmental permit";

"exempt waste operation";

"extractive waste";

"mining waste operation";

"the Mining Waste Directive";

"waste operation".

[Environmental Protection Act 1990, s 29 as amended by the Clean Neighbourhoods and Environment Act 2005, s 51, SI 2007/3538, SI 2009/1799 and SI 2010/675.]

1. Part II consists of ss 29–78.

Part II of this Act contains a number of regulation-making powers under which a number of regulations have been made. In the table below we list all the regulations made under ss 29–78 together with amending instruments. We also list regulations under the particular section under which they have been made:

Environmental Protection (Waste Recycling Payments) Regulations 1992, SI 1992/462 amended by SI 1994/522, SI 1996/634 and SI 1997/351;

Waste (Foot-and-Mouth Disease) (England) Regulations 2001, SI 2001/1478 amended by SI 2001/3189 (England);

Environmental Offences (Use of Fixed Penalty Receipts) (Wales) Regulations 2007, SI 2007/739 amended by SI 2008/663.

7.10020 **30. Authorities for purposes of this Part** (1) Any reference in this Part to a waste regulation authority—

(*a*) in relation to England, is a reference to the Environment Agency;

(*aa*) in relation to Wales, is a reference to the Natural Resources Body for Wales; and

(*b*) *Scotland*;

and any reference in this Part to the area of a waste regulation authority shall accordingly be taken as a reference to the area over which the Environment Agency, the Natural Resources Body for Wales or the Scottish Environment Protection Agency, as the case may be, exercises its functions or, in the case of any particular function, the function in question.

(2) For the purposes of this Part the following authorities are waste disposal authorities, namely—

(*a*) for any non-metropolitan county in England, the county council;

(*b*) in Greater London, the following—

(i) for the area of a London waste disposal authority, the authority constituted as the waste disposal authority for that area;

(ii) for the City of London, the Common Council;

(iii) for any other London borough, the council of the borough;

(*c*) in the metropolitan county of Greater Manchester, the following—

(i) for the metropolitan district of Wigan, the district council;

(ii) for all other areas in the county, the authority constituted as the Greater Manchester Waste Disposal Authority;

(*d*) for the metropolitan county of Merseyside, the authority constituted as the Merseyside Waste Disposal Authority;

(*e*) for any district in any other metropolitan county in England, the council of the district;

(*f*) for any county or county borough in Wales, the council of the county or county borough;

(*g*) *Scotland.*

(3) For the purposes of this Part the following authorities are waste collection authorities—

(*a*) for any district in England not within Greater London, the council of the district;

(*b*) in Greater London, the following—

(i) for any London borough, the council of the borough;

(ii) for the City of London, the Common Council;

(iii) for the Temples, the Sub-Treasurer of the Inner Temple and the Under Treasurer of the Middle Temple respectively;

(*bb*) for any county or county borough in Wales, the council of the county or county borough;

(*c*) *Scotland.*

(4) In this section references to particular authorities having been constituted as waste disposal authorities are references to their having been so constituted by the Waste Regulation and Disposal (Authorities) Order 1985 made by the Secretary of State under section 10 of the Local Government Act 1985 and the reference to London waste disposal authorities is a reference to the authorities named in Parts I, II, III, IV and V of Schedule 1 to that Order and this section has effect subject to any order made under the said section 10.

(5)–(8) *Repealed.*

[Environmental Protection Act 1990, s 30 as amended by the Local Government (Wales) Act 1994, Sch 9, the Environment Act 1995, Schs 22 and 24, the Clean Neighbourhoods and Environment Act 2005, Sch 5 and SI 2013/755.]

*Prohibition on unauthorised or harmful depositing, treatment or disposal of waste*

7.10021 **33. Prohibition on unauthorised or harmful deposit, treatment or disposal etc of waste** (1) Subject to subsections (1A), (1B), (2) and (3) below and, in relation to Scotland, to section 54 below*, a person shall not—

(*a*) deposit controlled waste[1] or extractive waste, or knowingly[2] cause or knowingly[2] permit controlled waste or extractive waste to be deposited in or on any land unless[3] an environmental permit authorising the deposit is in force and the deposit is in accordance with the permit;

(*b*) submit controlled waste or extractive waste, or knowingly cause or knowingly permit controlled waste to be submitted, to any listed operation (other than an operation within subsection (1)(*a*)) that—

(i) is carried out in or on any land, or by means of any mobile plant, and

(ii) is not carried out under and in accordance with an environmental permit;

(*c*) treat, keep or dispose of controlled waste in a manner likely to cause pollution of the environment or harm to human health.

(1A) Paragraphs (*a*) and (*b*) of subsection (1) above do not apply in relation to a waste operation that is an exempt waste operation.

(1B) Subsection (1) does not apply in relation to the carrying on of any waste operation which is or forms part of an operation which—

(*a*) is the subject of a licence under Part 2 of the Food and Environment Protection Act 1985; or

(*b*) by virtue of an order under section 7 of that Act, does not require such a licence;

(2) Subject to subsection (2A) below, paragraphs (*a*) and (*b*) of subsection (1) above do not apply in relation to household waste from a domestic property which is treated, kept or disposed of within the curtilage of the dwelling.

(2A) Subsection (2) above does not extend to the treatment, keeping or disposal of household waste by an establishment or undertaking.

(3) Subsection (1)(*a*), (*b*) or (*c*) above do not apply in cases prescribed in regulations made by the Secretary of State and the regulations may make different exceptions for different areas.

(4) The Secretary of State, in exercising his power under subsection (3) above, shall have regard in particular to the expediency of excluding from the prohibitions in subsection (1)—

(*a*) any deposits which are small enough or of such a temporary nature that they may be so excluded;

(*b*) any means of treatment or disposal which are innocuous enough to be so excluded;

(*c*) cases for which adequate controls are provided by another enactment than this section.

(5) Where controlled waste is carried in and deposited from a motor vehicle, the person who controls or is in a position to control the use of the vehicle shall, for the purposes of subsection (1)(*a*) above, be treated as knowingly causing the waste to be deposited whether or not he gave any instructions for this to be done[4].

(6) A person[5] who contravenes subsection (1) above commits an offence.

(7) It shall be a defence for a person charged with an offence under this section to prove—

(*a*) that he took all reasonable precautions and exercised all due diligence to avoid the commission of the offence; or

(*b*) *repealed*

(*c*) that the acts alleged to constitute the contravention were done in an emergency in order to avoid danger to human health in a case where—

(i) he took all such steps as were reasonably practicable in the circumstances for minimising pollution of the environment and harm to human health; and

(ii) particulars of the acts were furnished to the waste regulation authority as soon as reasonably practicable after they were done.

(8) Subject to subsection (9) below, a person who commits an offence under this section is liable—

(*a*) on summary conviction, to imprisonment for a term not exceeding 12 months or a fine or both;

(*b*) on conviction on indictment, to imprisonment for a term not exceeding **five years** or a **fine** or **both**.

(9) A person (other than an establishment or undertaking) who commits a relevant offence shall be liable[6] on summary conviction, or on conviction on indictment, to a fine.

(10) In this section, "relevant offence" means an offence under this section in respect of a contravention of subsection (1)(*c*) above consisting of the treatment, keeping or disposal within the curtillage of a domestic property of household waste from that property.

(11) For the purposes of subsection (1)(*a*) above, the deposit of waste in or on land includes any listed operation involving such a deposit.

(12) For the purposes of subsection (1)(*c*) above, treating, keeping or disposing of controlled waste includes submitting it to any listed operation.

(13) For the purposes of this section, a "listed operation" is an operation listed in Annex I or II of Directive 2008/98/EC of the European Parliament and of the Council on waste.

[Environmental Protection Act 1990, s 33 as amended by the Environment Act 1995, Sch 22, the Antisocial Behaviour etc (Scotland) Act 2004, Sch 2, SI 2005/894, the Clean Neighbourhoods and Environment Act 2005, s 41 and Sch 5, SI 2006/937, SI 2007/3538, SI 2009/1799, SI 2010/675, SI 2011/988 and SI 2015/664.]

---

* **Amended by the Environment Act 1995, Sch 24 from a date to be appointed.**

1 "Controlled waste" is defined in the 1990 Act and subsidiary legislation as meaning or including waste within the meaning of Council Directive 75/442/EEC on waste, as amended, but "waste waters" "covered by other legislation" are excluded from the scope of the Directive by article 2(1)(*b*); for waste to be covered by other legislation, however, and thus be excluded from the scope of Directive 75/442/EEC by article 2 the domestic legislation has to contain precise provisions organising the management of the waste in question and ensure a level of protection of the environment equivalent to that guaranteed by the Directive; domestic legislation does not meet that standard in relation to the management of waste which escaped unintentionally from the sewerage system; therefore, escaping waste water is not covered by other domestic legislation and so is controlled waste within the meaning of s 33: *R (Thames Water Utilities Ltd) v Bromley Magistrates' Court (Water Services Regulation Authority intervening)* [2008] EWHC 1763 (Admin), [2009] 1 WLR 1247.

2 The defendant is only required to have knowledge of the fact of the deposit and not of the breach of conditions. Therefore a company was liable where a site supervisor had wrongly discharged waste in breach of the licence conditions where it had knowledge that controlled waste was being caused or permitted to be deposited on its land. It was not necessary to prove that it had knowingly breached the conditions of the waste management licence or that it had any knowledge of the particular deposit of waste (*Shanks & McEwan (Teeside) Ltd v Environment Agency* [1997] 2 All ER 332, [1998] 2 WLR 452, [1997] Crim LR 684, DC). See also *Walker & Son (Hauliers) Ltd v Environment Agency* sub nom *R v Walker & Son (Hauliers) Ltd* [2014] EWCA Crim 100, [2014] 4 All ER 825, [2014] 1 Cr App Rep 427.

3 In *Environment Agency v ME Foley Contractors Ltd* [2002] EWHC 258 (Admin), [2002] 1 WLR 1754 the first defendant transported controlled waste to two sites, a waste disposal landfill site and the second defendant's sea wall reinforcement works site. The former was the subject of a waste disposal licence which authorised the deposit of controlled waste at that site, but the licence specifically excluded "special waste", as defined by the Control of Pollution (Special

Waste) Regulations 1980, the disposal of which required written approval. The second defendant's site was exempt from waste management licensing, save in respect of special waste. The defendants were charged, respectively, with knowingly causing and knowingly permitting special waste to be deposited. Both contended that the waste deposited was not of the type alleged. The justices held that since their case did not involve reliance on an exception or proviso if was for the prosecution to prove that the waste was of the type alleged, and the informations were dismissed.

In the resulting appeal by way of case stated it was submitted on behalf of the appellant that once the prosecutor had proved that the defendants had knowingly caused or permitted the deposit of controlled waste on any land, the burden shifted to them to prove on a balance of probabilities that there was a waste management licence authorising the deposit, and that the deposit was in accordance with the licence, or that it was exempt from any licensing requirements at all. It was held:

> "28 In the case of the first defendant, when delivering to the Cardiff landfill site, it was for the prosecution to prove that it had delivered special waste, namely contaminated soil, but not that it had done so without prior written approval. The latter negative averment was of a matter peculiarly within the first defendant's knowledge and it was for it to establish the requisite approval on a balance of probabilities if it sought to challenge the prosecution case in that respect.
>
> 29 In the case of the first defendant, when delivering to the sea wall reinforcement works site, and for the second defendant when accepting deliveries to that site, it was for the prosecution to prove that the waste respectively delivered and accepted contained special waste, namely contaminated soil, thus taking it outside the exemption.
>
> 30 It will be noted that I have reached this conclusion without further reference to section 101 of the Magistrates' Courts Act 1980. That is because, as the justices rightly concluded, this was not a case which, on the structure of section 33(1)(a), or the issue in play, was truly concerned with an exception or proviso. I agree with (counsel for the respondent's) contentions that a court, before resorting to section 101 in a section 33(1) case, should consider the particular exemption in play. There are a number of them in Schedule 3 to the Waste Management Licensing Regulations 1994, the regulations." (per Auld LJ).

In *R v Jagger (Michael Edward)* [2015] Crim 348, [2015] Env LR 25 the defendant contractor admitted depositing material, but raised at trial the issue of categorisation where potential re-use of the material might take it out of the category of waste provided such re-use was consistent with the aims and objectives of the Act and Directive 2008/98, art 3(1). The failure of the trial judge to give the jury sufficient direction as to whether an event had occurred which had changed the status of the waste – he did not assist the jury by referring to the facts to indicate factors which might have borne on whether such an alteration had occurred – resulted in the appeal being allowed. What is waste at any given time may not be clear cut and in such fact sensitive cases the jury must be given sufficient directions.

See further s 75 (Meaning of "waste", etc) and the notes thereto, post.

[4] Evidence that the defendant is the owner or keeper of a vehicle, such as in a response to a request for information by a notice under s 71, post, is capable, depending on the particular facts and absent evidence that the vehicle was stolen, or had been lent to another or was hired, of amounting to a prima facie case that the defendant controlled or was in a position to control the vehicle at the material time (*Environment Agency v Melland* [2002] EWHC 904 (Admin), [2002] RTR 425).

[5] Any person and not only the licence holder is liable for prosecution so that where the operator is the person by whom the offence is committed, the licence holder who was not the operator, cannot be guilty of the offence (*Shanks McEwan (Midlands) Ltd v Wrexham Maelor Borough Council* (1996) Times, 10 April).

[6] For procedure in respect of an offence triable either way, see the Magistrates' Courts Act 1980, ss 17A–21 in PART I: MAGISTRATES' COURTS, PROCEDURE, ante.

**7.10021A 33ZA. Fixed penalty notices for contravention of section 33(1)(a): England**

(1) Where an authorised officer of an English waste collection authority has reason to believe that a person has committed a waste deposit offence in the area of the authority, the officer may give the person a notice under this section in respect of the offence.

(2) In subsection (1), "waste deposit offence" means an offence under section 33 in respect of a contravention of subsection (1)(*a*) of that section.

(3) A notice under this section is a notice offering the opportunity of discharging any liability to conviction for the offence to which it relates by payment of a fixed penalty.

(4) Where a person is given a notice under this section in respect of an offence—

(*a*) no proceedings may be instituted for the offence before the end of the period of 14 days following the date of the notice; and

(b) the person may not be convicted of the offence if the person pays the fixed penalty before the end of that period.

(5) A notice under this section must give such particulars of the circumstances alleged to constitute the offence as are necessary for giving reasonable information about the offence and must state—

(*a*) the period during which, by virtue of subsection (4)(*a*), proceedings will not be taken for the offence;

(*b*) the amount of the fixed penalty; and

(*c*) the person to whom and the address at which the fixed penalty may be paid.

(6) If an authorised officer proposes to give a person a notice under this section, the officer may require the person to give the person's name and address.

(7) It is an offence to—

(*a*) fail to give a name or address when required to do so under subsection (6), or

(*b*) give a false or inaccurate name or address in response to a requirement under that subsection.

(8) A person guilty of an offence under subsection (7) is liable on summary conviction to a fine not exceeding level 3 on the standard scale.

(9) The fixed penalty payable in pursuance of a notice under this section—

(*a*) is an amount not less than £150 and not more than £400, as specified by the English waste collection authority whose authorised officer gave the notice, or (*b*) if no amount is specified by that authority, is £200.

(10) An English waste collection authority to whom a fixed penalty is payable pursuant to a notice under this section may make provision for treating the fixed penalty as having been paid if a lesser amount of not less than £120 is paid before the end of the period of 10 days following the date of the notice.

(11) In any proceedings a certificate which—

(*a*) purports to be signed by or on behalf of the chief finance officer of an English waste collection authority to whom a fixed penalty is payable pursuant to a notice under this section, and

(*b*) states that the payment of a fixed penalty was or was not received by a date specified in the certificate,

is evidence of the facts stated

(12) In this section—

"authorised officer", in relation to an English waste collection authority, means—

(*a*) an employee of the authority who is authorised in writing by the authority for the purposes of giving notices under this section;

(b) a person who, in pursuance of arrangements made with the authority, has the function of giving such notices and is authorised in writing by the authority to perform that function;

(*c*) an employee of such a person who is authorised in writing by the authority for the purpose of giving such notices;

"chief finance officer", in relation to an English waste collection authority, means the person having responsibility for the financial affairs of the authority;

"English waste collection authority" means a waste collection authority whose area is in England.]

[Environmental Protection Act 1990, s 33ZA as inserted by SI 2016/334.]

7.10022 **33A. Section 33 offences: investigation and enforcement costs** (1) This section applies where a person is convicted of an offence—

(*a*) under section 33 above, in respect of a contravention of subsection (1) of that section;

(*b*) under regulation 38(1) of the Environmental Permitting Regulations, in respect of a waste operation or a mining waste operation.

(2) The court by or before which the offender is convicted may make an order requiring him to pay to an enforcement authority a sum which appears to the court not to exceed the costs arising from—

(*a*) investigations of the enforcement authority which resulted in the conviction; and

(*b*) the seizure by the enforcement authority under section 34B below of a vehicle involved in the offence.

(3) The costs arising from the seizure of a vehicle as specified in subsection (2)(*b*) above may include the cost of disposing of the contents of the vehicle.

(4) The power of a court to make an order under this section is in addition to its power to make an order under section 18 of the Prosecution of Offences Act 1985 (award of costs against accused).

(5) In this section "enforcement authority" means the Environment Agency, the Natural Resources Body for Wales or a waste collection authority.

[Environmental Protection Act 1990, s 33A as inserted by the Clean Neighbourhoods and Environment Act 2005, s 42 and amended by SI 2007/3538, SI 2009/1799, SI 2010/675 and SI 2013/755.]

7.10023 **33B. Section 33 offences: clean-up costs** (1) This section applies where a person is convicted of an offence—

(*a*) under section 33 above, in respect of a contravention of subsection (1) of that section consisting of the deposit or disposal of controlled waste or extractive waste;

(*b*) under regulation 38(1) of the Environmental Permitting Regulations, in respect of a contravention of regulation 12 of those Regulations consisting of the disposal of waste.

(2) The reference in section 130(1)(*a*) of the Powers of Criminal Courts (Sentencing) Act 2000 (compensation orders) to loss or damage resulting from the offence includes costs incurred or to be incurred by a relevant person in—

(*a*) removing the waste deposited or disposed of in or on the land;

(*b*) taking other steps to eliminate or reduce the consequences of the deposit or disposal; or

(*c*) both.

(3) In subsection (2) above "relevant person" means—

(*a*) the Environment Agency;

(*aa*) the Natural Resources Body for Wales;

(*b*) a waste collection authority;

(*c*) the occupier of the land;

(*d*) the owner of the land (within the meaning of section 78A(9) below).

(4) The reference in subsection (2) above to costs incurred does not, in the case of the Environment Agency, the Natural Resources Body for Wales or a waste collection authority, include any costs which the Agency, Body or authority has already recovered under section 59(8) below.

(5) Subject to subsection (6) below, in relation to the costs referred to in subsection (2) above,

the reference in section 131(1) of the Powers of Criminal Courts (Sentencing) Act 2000 (limit on amount payable in case of young offender) to £5000 is instead to be construed as a reference to the amount of those costs (or, if the costs have not yet been incurred, the likely amount).

(6) Subsection (5) above does not apply where a person (other than an establishment or undertaking) is convicted of a relevant offence within the meaning of section 33 above.

[Environmental Protection Act 1990, s 33B as inserted by the Clean Neighbourhoods and Environment Act 2005, s 43 and amended by SI 2006/937, SI 2007/3538, SI 2009/1799, SI 2010/675, the Crime and Courts Act 2013, Sch 16 and SI 2013/755.]

7.10024 **33C. Section 33 offences: forfeiture of vehicles** (1) This section applies where—

(*a*) subject to subsection (1A) below, a person is convicted of an offence under section 33 above in respect of a contravention of subsection (1) of that section consisting of the deposit or disposal of controlled waste;

(*b*) a person is convicted of an offence under regulation 38(1) of the Environmental Permitting Regulations in respect of a contravention of regulation 12 of those Regulations consisting of the disposal of waste.

(1A) This section does not apply where a person (other than an establishment or undertaking) is convicted of a relevant offence within the meaning of section 33 above.

(2) The court by or before which the offender is convicted may make an order under this section if—

(*a*) the court is satisfied that a vehicle was used in or for the purposes of the commission of the offence; and

(*b*) at the time of his conviction the offender has rights in the vehicle.

(3) An order under this section operates to deprive the offender of his rights in the vehicle (including its fuel) at the time of his conviction and to vest those rights in the relevant enforcement authority.

(4) In a case where a vehicle has been seized under section 34B below and the offender retains rights in any of the vehicle's contents, an order under this section may, if and to the extent that it so specifies, deprive the offender of those rights and vest them in the relevant enforcement authority.

(5) Where an order under this section is made, the relevant enforcement authority may take possession of the vehicle (if it has not already done so under section 34C below).

(6) The court may make an order under this section whether or not it also deals with the offender in any other way in respect of the offence of which he is convicted.

(7) In considering whether to make an order under this section a court must in particular have regard to—

(*a*) the value of the vehicle;

(*b*) the likely financial and other effects on the offender of the making of the order (taken together with any other order that the court contemplates making);

(*c*) the offender's need to use the vehicle for lawful purposes;

(*d*) whether, in a case where it appears to the court that the offender is engaged in a business which consists wholly or partly in activities which are unlawful by virtue of section 33 above or regulation 38(1) or (2) of the Environmental Permitting Regulations, the making of the order is likely to inhibit the offender from engaging in further such activities.

(8) Section 143 of the Powers of Criminal Courts (Sentencing) Act 2000 (power to deprive offender of property) does not apply in any case where this section applies.

(9) For the purposes of this section, where a vehicle or its contents have been seized under section 34B below in connection with the offence referred to in subsection (1) above, any transfer by the offender after the seizure and before his conviction of any of his rights in the vehicle or its contents is of no effect.

(10) In this section—

"relevant enforcement authority" means—

(*a*) the Environment Agency, where the proceedings in respect of the offence have been brought by or on behalf of the Agency,

(*aa*) the Natural Resources Body for Wales, where the proceedings in respect of the offence have been brought by or on behalf of that Body, or

(*b*) in any other case, the waste collection authority in whose area the offence was committed;

"vehicle" means any motor vehicle or trailer within the meaning of the Road Traffic Regulation Act 1984 or any mobile plant.

[Environmental Protection Act 1990, s 33C as inserted by the Clean Neighbourhoods and Environment Act 2005, s 44 and amended by SI 2006/937, SI 2007/3538, SI 2010/675 and SI 2013/755.]

*Duty of care etc as respects waste*

7.10025 **34. Duty of care etc as respects waste**[1] (1) Subject to subsection (2) below, it shall be the duty of any person who imports, produces, carries, keeps, treats or disposes of controlled waste or, as a dealer or broker, has control of such waste, to take all such measures applicable to him in that capacity as are reasonable in the circumstances—

(*a*) to prevent any contravention by any other person of section 33 above;

(*aa*) to prevent any contravention by any other person of regulation 12 of the Environmental Permitting Regulations or of a condition of an environmental permit;

(*b*) to prevent the escape[2] of the waste from his control or that of any other person; and

(*c*) on the transfer of the waste, to secure—

(i) that the transfer is only to an authorised person or to a person for authorised transport purposes; and

(ii) that there is transferred such a written description of the waste as will enable other persons to avoid a contravention of that section or regulation 12 of the Environmental Permitting Regulations, or a contravention of a condition of an environmental permit, and to comply with the duty under this subsection as respects the escape of waste.

(1A) It shall be the duty of any person who is responsible for the management of extractive waste to take all such measures applicable to him in that capacity as are reasonable in the circumstances—

(*a*) to prevent any contravention by any other person of section 33 above;

(*b*) to prevent any contravention by another person of regulation 12 of the Environmental Permitting Regulations or of a condition of an environmental permit; and

(*c*) to prevent the escape of the waste from his control or that of any other person.

(2) The duty imposed by subsection (1) above does not apply to an occupier of domestic property as respects the household waste produced on the property.

(2A) It shall be the duty of the occupier of any domestic property in England or Wales to take all such measures available to him as are reasonable in the circumstances to secure that any transfer by him of household waste produced on the property is only to an authorised person or to a person for authorised transport purposes.

(3) The following are authorised persons for the purposes of subsection (1)(*c*) and (2A) above—

(*a*) any authority which is a waste collection authority for the purposes of this Part;

(*b*) any person who is the holder of an environmental permit in relation to a waste operation;

(*ba*) any person who is carrying on an exempt waste operation;

(*c*) any person to whom section 33(1) above does not apply by virtue of regulations under subsection (3) of that section or by virtue of regulations under section 2 of the Pollution Prevention and Control Act 1999;

(*d*) any person registered as a carrier of controlled waste under section 2 of the Control of Pollution (Amendment) Act 1989;

(*e*) any person who is not required to be so registered by virtue of regulations under section 1(3) of that Act; and

(*f*) *Scotland.*

(3A) The Secretary of State may by regulations amend subsection (3) above so as to add, whether generally or in such circumstances as may be prescribed in the regulations, any person specified in the regulations, or any description of person so specified, to the persons who are authorised persons for the purposes of subsection (1)(*c*) and (2A) above.

(4) The following are authorised transport purposes for the purposes of subsection (1)(*c*) and (2A) above—

(*a*) the transport of controlled waste within the same premises between different places in those premises;

(*b*) the transport to a place in Great Britain of controlled waste which has been brought from a country or territory outside Great Britain not having been landed in Great Britain until it arrives at that place; and

(*c*) the transport by air or sea of controlled waste from a place in Great Britain to a place outside Great Britain;

and "transport" has the same meaning in this subsection as in the Control of Pollution (Amendment) Act 1989.

(4A) For the purposes of subsection (1)(*c*)(ii) above—

(*a*) a transfer of waste in stages shall be treated as taking place when the first stage of the transfer takes place, and

(*b*) a series of transfers between the same parties of waste of the same description shall be treated as a single transfer taking place when the first of the transfers in the series takes place[3].

(5) The Secretary of State may, by regulations, make provision imposing requirements on any person who is subject to the duty imposed by subsection (1) above as respects the making and retention of documents and the furnishing of documents or copies of documents.

(6) Any person who fails to comply with the duty imposed by subsection (1), (1A) or (2A) above or with any requirement imposed under subsection (5) above shall be liable—

(*a*) on summary conviction, to a fine not exceeding the **statutory maximum**; and

(*b*) on conviction on indictment, to a **fine**.

(7) The Secretary of State shall, after consultation with such persons or bodies as appear to him

representative of the interests concerned, prepare and issue a code of practice for the purpose of providing to persons practical guidance on how to discharge the duty imposed on them by subsection (1) above.

(8) The Secretary of State may from time to time revise a code of practice issued under subsection (7) above by revoking, amending or adding to the provisions of the code.

(9) A code of practice prepared in pursuance of subsection (7) above shall be laid before:

(*a*) both Houses of Parliament; or

(*b*) if it relates only to Scotland before the Scottish Parliament.

(10) A code of practice issued under subsection (7) above shall be admissible in evidence and if any provision of such a code appears to the court to be relevant to any question arising in the proceedings it shall be taken into account in determining that question.

(11) Different codes of practice may be prepared and issued under subsection (7) above for different areas.

[Environmental Protection Act 1990, s 34 as amended by the Deregulation and Contracting Out Act 1994, s 33, the Environment Act 1995, Sch 22, SI 1999/1820, SI 2000/1973, SI 2005/2900, SI 2006/123 (W), SI 2007/3538, SI 2009/1799, SI 2010/675 and SI 2011/988.]

---

1 For form of information and issues as to local authority prosecution policies and abuse of process, see, *Wandsworth London Borough Council v Rashid* [2009] EWHC 1844 (Admin), 173 JP 547 and para 1.152 Abuse of the process of the court, ante.

2 The offence under s 34(6) is the failure to take reasonable measures as required by the duty imposed under this subsection. Accordingly, the prosecution does not have to establish that an escape has taken place, rather that there had been a failure to exercise the statutory duty of care (*Camden London Borough Council v Mortgage Times Group Ltd* [2006] EWHC 1615 (Admin), (2006) Times, 15 August).

3 This provision does not apply in relation to any proceedings for failure to comply with the duty imposed by s 34(1) which were commenced before 3 November 1994 and, where any proceedings have not been disposed of before that date, it shall be a defence to show that the conduct in question would not have constituted a breach of the duty prior to that date.

7.10026 **34A. Fixed penalty notices for certain offences under section 34** (1) This section applies where it appears to an enforcement authority that a person has failed to comply with a duty to furnish documents to that authority imposed under regulations made at any time under section 34(5) above.

(2) The authority may serve on that person a notice offering him the opportunity of discharging any liability to conviction for an offence under section 34(6) above by payment of a fixed penalty.

(3) Where a person is given a notice under this section in respect of an offence—

(*a*) no proceedings may be instituted for that offence before expiration of the period of fourteen days following the date of the notice; and

(*b*) he may not be convicted of that offence if he pays the fixed penalty before the expiration of the period.

(4) A notice under this section must give such particulars of the circumstances alleged to constitute the offence as are necessary for giving reasonable information of the offence.

(5) A notice under this section must also state—

(*a*) the period during which, by virtue of subsection (3) above, proceedings will not be taken for the offence;

(*b*) the amount of the fixed penalty; and

(*c*) the person to whom and the address at which the fixed penalty may be paid.

(6) Without prejudice to payment by any other method, payment of the fixed penalty may be made by pre-paying and posting a letter containing the amount of the penalty (in cash or otherwise) to the person mentioned in subsection (5)(*c*) above at the address so mentioned.

(7) Where a letter is sent in accordance with subsection (6) above payment is to be regarded as having been made at the time at which that letter would be delivered in the ordinary course of post.

(8) The form of a notice under this section is to be such as the appropriate person may by order prescribe.

(9) The fixed penalty payable to an enforcement authority under this section is, subject to subsection (10) below, £300.

(10) The appropriate person may by order substitute a different amount for the amount for the time being specified in subsection (9) above.

(11) The enforcement authority to which a fixed penalty is payable under this section may make provision for treating it as having been paid if a lesser amount is paid before the end of a period specified by the authority.

(12) The appropriate person may by regulations[1] restrict the extent to which, and the circumstances in which, an enforcement authority may make provision under subsection (11) above.

(13) In any proceedings a certificate which—

(*a*) purports to be signed on behalf of the chief finance officer of the enforcement authority, and

(*b*) states that payment of a fixed penalty was or was not received by a date specified in the certificate,

is evidence of the facts stated.

(14) In this section—

"chief finance officer", in relation to an enforcement authority, means the person having responsibility for the financial affairs of the authority;

"enforcement authority" means the Environment Agency, the Natural Resources Body for Wales or a waste collection authority.

[Environmental Protection Act 1990, s 34A as inserted by the Clean Neighbourhoods and Environment Act 2005, s 45 and amended by SI 2013/755.]

---

[1] The Environmental Offences (Fixed Penalties) (Miscellaneous Provisions) Regulations 2007, SI 2007/175, the Environmental Offences (Use of Fixed Penalty Receipts) (Wales) Regulations 2007, SI 2007/739 amended by SI 2008/663; the Environmental Offences (Use of Fixed Penalty Receipts) Regulations 2007, SI 2007/901 and the Environmental Offences (Fixed Penalties) (Miscellaneous Provisions) (Wales) Regulations 2008, SI 2008/663 have been made. For amending instruments, see the note to the Refuse Disposal (Amenity) Act 1978, s 2A, ante.

*Offences under sections 33 and 34: powers of seizure etc*

7.10027 **34B. Power to search and seize vehicles etc** (1) This section applies where an authorised officer of an enforcement authority or a constable reasonably believes that the grounds in subsection (2) or (3) below exist.

(2) The grounds in this subsection are that—

(*a*) a relevant offence under section 33 or 34 above has been committed, or an offence under regulation 38(1) or (2) of the Environmental Permitting Regulations has been committed in relation to a waste operation,

(*b*) a vehicle was used in the commission of the offence, and

(*c*) proceedings for the offence have not yet been brought against any person.

(3) The grounds in this subsection are that—

(*a*) a relevant offence under section 33 or 34 above is being or is about to be committed, or an offence under regulation 38(1) or (2) of the Environmental Permitting Regulations is being or is about to be committed in relation to a waste operation, and

(*b*) a vehicle is being or is about to be used in the commission of the offence.

(4) The authorised officer or constable may—

(*a*) search the vehicle;

(*b*) seize the vehicle and any of its contents.

(5) In acting under subsection (4) above the authorised officer or constable may—

(*a*) stop the vehicle (but only a constable in uniform may stop a vehicle on any road);

(*b*) enter any premises for the purpose of searching or seizing the vehicle.

(6) A vehicle or its contents seized under subsection (4) above—

(*a*) by an authorised officer of an enforcement authority, are seized on behalf of that authority;

(*b*) by a constable in the presence of an authorised officer of an enforcement authority, are seized on behalf of that authority;

(*c*) by a constable without such an officer present, are seized on behalf of the waste collection authority in whose area the seizure takes place.

(7) A person commits an offence if—

(*a*) he fails without reasonable excuse to give any assistance that an authorised officer or constable may reasonably request in the exercise of a power under subsection (4) or (5) above;

(*b*) he otherwise intentionally obstructs an authorised officer or constable in exercising that power.

(8) Where an authorised officer or constable has stopped a vehicle under subsection (5)(*a*) above, he may require any occupant of the vehicle to give him—

(*a*) the occupant's name and address;

(*b*) the name and address of the registered owner of the vehicle;

(*c*) any other information he may reasonably request.

(9) A person commits an offence if—

(*a*) he fails without reasonable excuse to comply with a requirement under subsection (8) above;

(*b*) he gives information required under that subsection that is—

(i) to his knowledge false or misleading in a material way, or

(ii) given recklessly and is false or misleading in a material way.

(10) A person guilty of an offence under this section is liable on summary conviction to a fine not exceeding level 5 on the standard scale.

(11) In this section and section 34C below—

"authorised officer" means an officer of an enforcement authority who is authorised in writing by the authority for the purposes of this section;

"enforcement authority" means—

(*a*) the Environment Agency,

(*aa*) the Natural Resources Body for Wales, or

(*b*) a waste collection authority;

"relevant offence" means—

(*a*) an offence under section 33 above, or

(*b*) an offence under section 34 above consisting of a failure to comply with the duty imposed by subsection (1) of that section;

"road" has the same meaning as in the Road Traffic Regulation Act 1984;

"vehicle" means any motor vehicle or trailer within the meaning of that Act or any mobile plant.*

[Environmental Protection Act 1990, s 34B as inserted by the Clean Neighbourhoods and Environment Act 2005, s 46 and amended by SI 2005/2900, SI 2007/3538, SI 2010/675 and SI 2013/755.]

* **In force for certain purposes in Wales from 16 March 2006; from a date to be appointed in England and for remaining purposes in Wales.**

7.10028 **34C. Seizure vehicles etc: supplementary** (1) Where under section 34B above an authorised officer or constable seizes a vehicle or its contents ("seized property") on behalf of an enforcement authority, the authority may remove the seized property to such a place as it considers appropriate.

(2) An enforcement authority must deal with any seized property in accordance with regulations[1] made by the appropriate person.

(3) Regulations under subsection (2) above may in particular include provision as to—

(*a*) the duties of enforcement authorities in relation to the safe custody of seized property;

(*b*) the circumstances in which they must return any such property to a person claiming entitlement to it;

(*c*) the manner in which such persons, and the seized property to which they are entitled, may be determined;

(*d*) the circumstances in which an enforcement authority may sell, destroy or otherwise dispose of seized property;

(*e*) the uses to which the proceeds of any such sale may be put.

(4) Regulations making provision under subsection (3)(*d*) above—

(*a*) must (subject to paragraph (*c*) below) require the enforcement authority to publish a notice in such form, and to take any other steps, as may be specified in the regulations for informing persons who may be entitled to the seized property that it has been seized and is available to be claimed;

(*b*) must (subject to paragraph (*c*) below) prohibit the authority from selling, destroying or otherwise disposing of any seized property unless a period specified in the regulations has expired without any obligation arising under the regulations for the authority to return the property to any person;

(*c*) may allow for the requirements in paragraphs (*a*) and (*b*) above to be dispensed with if the condition of the seized property requires its disposal without delay.

(5) The appropriate person may issue guidance to enforcement authorities in relation to the performance of their functions under regulations under subsection (2) above.*

1 The Control of Waste (Dealing with Seized Property) (England and Wales) Regulations 2015, SI 2015/426 have been made.

[Environmental Protection Act 1990, s 34C as inserted by the Clean Neighbourhoods and Environment Act 2005, s 46.]

* **In force for certain purposes in Wales from 16 March 2006; from a date to be appointed in England and for remaining purposes in Wales.**

*Waste Management Licences*

7.10028A **44. Offences of making false or misleading statements or false entries** (1) A person who—

(*a*) in purported compliance with a requirement to furnish any information imposed by or under any provision of this Part,

(*b*) *repealed*,

makes a statement which he knows to be false or misleading in a material particular, or recklessly makes any statement which is false or misleading in a material particular, commits an offence.

(2) *Repealed.*

(3) A person who commits an offence under this section shall be liable[1]—

(*a*) on summary conviction, to a fine not exceeding **the statutory maximum**;

(*b*) on conviction on indictment, to a fine or to imprisonment for a term not exceeding **two years**, or to **both**.

[Environmental Protection Act 1990, s 44 as substituted by the Environment Act 1995, Sch 19 and amended by SI 2007/3538.]

1 For procedure in respect of an offence which is triable either way, see the Magistrates' Courts Act 1980, ss 17A–21, in PART I: MAGISTRATES' COURTS, PROCEDURE, ante.

*Collection, disposal or treatment of controlled waste*

7.10029 **45. Collection of controlled waste** (1) It shall be the duty of each waste collection authority—

(*a*) to arrange for the collection of household waste in its area except waste—

(i) which is situated at a place which in the opinion of the authority is so isolated or inaccessible that the cost of collecting it would be unreasonably high, and

(ii) as to which the authority is satisfied that adequate arrangements for its disposal have been or can reasonably be expected to be made by a person who controls the waste; and

(*b*) if requested by the occupier of premises in its area to collect any commercial waste from the premises, to arrange for the collection of the waste.

(2) Each waste collection authority may, if requested by the occupier of premises in its area to collect any industrial waste from the premises, arrange for the collection of the waste; but a collection authority in England and Wales shall not exercise the power except with the consent of the waste disposal authority whose area includes the area of the waste collection authority.

(3) *No charge shall be made for the collection of household waste except in cases prescribed in regulations*[1] *made by the Secretary of State.*

(4) *Charges for the collection and disposal of waste other than household waste.*

(5)–(7) *Duty of each waste collection authority to make arrangements for the emptying of privies, and on request, cesspools.*

(8) A waste collection authority may contribute towards the cost incurred by another person in providing or maintaining plant or equipment intended to deal with commercial or industrial waste before it is collected under arrangements made by the authority under subsection (1)(*b*) or (2) above.

(9) Subject to section 48(1) below, anything collected under arrangements made by a waste collection authority under this section shall belong to the authority and may be dealt with accordingly.

(10)–(11) *Scotland.*

(12) *Meaning of "privy" and "cesspool".*

[Environmental Protection Act 1990, s 45.]

---

1 The Controlled Waste Regulations 2012, SI 2012/811 have been made, amending regulations are noted in the list of regulations made under s 2 of the European Communities Act 1972, ante.

7.10030 **45A. Arrangements for separate collection of recyclable waste** (1) This section applies to any waste collection authority whose area is in England (an "English waste collection authority").

(2) Where an English waste collection authority has a duty by virtue of section 45(1)(*a*) above to arrange for the collection of household waste from any premises, the authority shall ensure that the arrangements it makes in relation to those premises include the arrangements mentioned in subsection (3) below, unless it is satisfied that (in that case)—

(*a*) the cost of doing so would be unreasonably high; or

(*b*) comparable alternative arrangements are available.

(3) The arrangements are arrangements for the collection of at least two types of recyclable waste together or individually separated from the rest of the household waste.

(4) The requirement in subsection (2) above shall apply from 31st December 2010.

(5) The Secretary of State may, if requested to do so by an English waste collection authority, direct the authority that subsection (4) above shall have effect in relation to that authority as if the date mentioned there were such later date as may be specified in the direction (being a date no later than 31st December 2015).

(6) In this section, "recyclable waste" means household waste which is capable of being recycled or composted.

[Environmental Protection Act 1990, s 45A as inserted by the Household Waste Recycling Act 2003, s 3.]

7.10031 **45B. Power to apply section 45A to Welsh waste collection authorities** (1) The National Assembly for Wales may by order made by statutory instrument provide that section 45A above shall apply, subject to subsection (2) below, to all waste collection authorities whose areas are in Wales, as it applies to English waste collection authorities.

(2) Where the Assembly provides as mentioned in subsection (1) above, the reference to the Secretary of State in section 45A(5) above shall be read for these purposes as a reference to the National Assembly for Wales.

Section 161(3) below (which relates to order-making powers) shall not apply to the making of an order under this section.

[Environmental Protection Act 1990, s 45B as inserted by the Household Waste Recycling Act 2003, s 3.]

7.10032 **46. Receptacles for household waste** (1) Where a waste collection authority has a duty by virtue of section 45(1)(*a*) above to arrange for the collection of household waste from any premises, the authority may, by notice served on him, require the occupier to place the waste for collection in receptacles of a kind and number specified.

(2) The kind and number of the receptacles required under subsection (1) above to be used shall be such only as are reasonable but, subject to that, separate receptacles or compartments of receptacles may be required to be used for waste which is to be recycled and waste which is not.

(3) In making requirements under subsection (1) above the authority may, as respects the provision of the receptacles—

(*a*) determine that they be provided by the authority free of charge;

(*b*) propose that they be provided, if the occupier agrees, by the authority on payment by him of such a single payment or such periodical payments as he agrees with the authority;

(*c*) require the occupier to provide them if he does not enter into an agreement under paragraph (*b*) above within a specified period; or

(*d*) require the occupier to provide them.

(4) In making requirements as respects receptacles under subsection (1) above, the authority may, by the notice under that subsection, make provision with respect to—

(*a*) the size, construction and maintenance of the receptacles;

(*b*) the placing of the receptacles for the purpose of facilitating the emptying of them, and access to the receptacles for that purpose;

(*ba*) the placing of the receptacles for the purpose of avoiding nuisance or detriment to the amenities of the area;

(*c*) the placing of the receptacles for that purpose on highways or, in Scotland, roads;

(*d*) the substances or articles which may or may not be put into the receptacles or compartments of receptacles of any description and the precautions to be taken where particular substances or articles are put into them; and

(*e*) the steps to be taken by occupiers of premises to facilitate the collection of waste from the receptacles.

(5) No requirement shall be made under subsection (1) above for receptacles to be placed on a highway or, as the case may be, road, unless—

(*a*) the relevant highway authority or roads authority have given their consent to their being so placed; and

(*b*) arrangements have been made as to the liability for any damage arising out of their being so placed.

(6) A person who fails, without reasonable excuse, to comply with any requirements imposed by a waste collection authority in Scotland or Wales under subsection (1), (3)(*c*) or (*d*) or (4) above shall be liable on summary conviction to a fine not exceeding **level 3** on the standard scale.

(7) Where an occupier is required under subsection (1) above to provide any receptacles he may, within the period allowed by subsection (8) below, appeal to a magistrates' court or, in Scotland, to the sheriff by way of summary application against any requirement imposed under subsection (1), subsection (3)(*c*) or (*d*) or (4) above on the ground that—

(*a*) the requirement is unreasonable; or

(*b*) the receptacles in which household waste is placed for collection from the premises are adequate.

(8) The period allowed to the occupier of premises for appealing against such a requirement is the period of twenty-one days beginning—

(*a*) in a case where a period was specified under subsection (3)(*c*) above, with the end of that period; and

(*b*) where no period was specified, with the day on which the notice making the requirement was served on him.

(9) Where an appeal against a requirement is brought under subsection (7) above—

(*a*) the requirement shall be of no effect pending the determination of the appeal;

(*b*) the court shall either quash or modify the requirement or dismiss the appeal; and

(*c*) no question as to whether the requirement is, in any respect, unreasonable shall be entertained in any proceedings for an offence under subsection (6) above.

(10) In this section—

"receptacle" includes a holder for receptacles; and

"specified" means specified in a notice under subsection (1) above.

(11) A waste collection authority is not obliged to collect household waste that is placed for collection in contravention of a requirement under this section.*

[Environmental Protection Act 1990, s 46 as amended by the London Local Authorities Act 2007, s 19, the Climate Change Act 2008, s 76 and the Deregulation Act 2015, s 58.]

---

* **Amended by the Climate Change Act 2008, Sch 5 from a date to be appointed.**

**7.10032A 46A. Written warnings and penalties for failure to comply with requirements relating to household waste receptacles: England** (1) This section applies where an authorised officer of a waste collection authority in England is satisfied that—

(a) a person has failed without reasonable excuse to comply with a requirement imposed by the authority under section 46(1), (3)(*c*) or (*d*) or (4) (a "section 46 requirement"), and

(b) the person's failure to comply—

(i) has caused, or is or was likely to cause, a nuisance, or

(ii) has been, or is or was likely to be, detrimental to any amenities of the locality.

(2) Where this section applies, the authorised officer may give a written warning to the person.

(3) A written warning must—

(*a*) identify the section 46 requirement with which the person has failed to comply,

(*b*) explain the nature of the failure to comply,

(*c*) explain how the failure to comply has had, or is or was likely to have, the effect described in subsection (1)(*b*), (*d*) if the failure to comply is continuing, specify the period within which the requirement must be complied with and explain the consequences of the requirement not being complied with within that period, and

(*e*) whether or not the failure to comply is continuing, explain the consequences of the person subsequently failing to comply with the same or a similar section 46 requirement.

(4) Where a written warning has been given in respect of a failure to comply that is continuing, an authorised officer of the waste collection authority may require the person to whom the written warning was given to pay a fixed penalty to the authority if satisfied that the person has failed to comply with the section 46 requirement identified in the warning within the period specified by virtue of subsection (3)(*d*).

(5) Where a person has been required to pay a fixed penalty under subsection (4) and that requirement has not been withdrawn on appeal, an authorised officer of the authority may require the person to pay a further fixed penalty to the authority if satisfied that the failure to comply is still continuing at the end of a relevant period which falls within the period of one year beginning with the day the written warning was given.

(6) For the purposes of subsection (5)—

(*a*) a "relevant period" is a period beginning with the day a final notice is served on the person under section 46C(5) in respect of the failure to comply that is continuing and ending with—

(i) where the person appeals against the requirement to pay a fixed penalty imposed by the final notice, the day on which the appeal that is the final appeal made by the person against the requirement is dismissed or withdrawn;

(ii) where the person does not appeal, the day on which the period for appealing expires;

(*b*) there is no relevant period where the person appeals as mentioned in paragraph (*a*)(i) and the requirement to pay the fixed penalty is withdrawn on appeal.

(7) Where a written warning has been given, whether or not in respect of a failure to comply that is continuing, an authorised officer of the waste collection authority may require the person to whom the written warning was given to pay a fixed penalty to the authority if satisfied that, within the period of one year beginning with the day the written warning was given —

(*a*) the person has again failed without reasonable excuse to comply with the section 46 requirement identified in the warning and the person's failure to comply has had, or is or was likely to have, the effect described in subsection (1)(*b*), or

(*b*) the person has failed without reasonable excuse to comply with a section 46 requirement that is similar to the one identified in the warning and the person's failure to comply has had, or is or was likely to have, the effect described in subsection (1)(*b*).

(8) An authorised officer may require a person to pay a fixed penalty under subsection (5) or (7) each time that the authorised officer is satisfied of the matters mentioned in the subsection.

(9) An authorised officer imposing a requirement to pay a fixed penalty under subsection (4), (5) or (7) must act in accordance with section 46C.

(10) A "fixed penalty" means a monetary penalty of an amount determined in accordance with section 46B.

(11) An "authorised officer", in relation to a waste collection authority, means—

(*a*) an employee of the authority who is authorised in writing by the authority for the purpose of giving written warnings and requiring payment of fixed penalties under this section;

(*b*) any person who, under arrangements made with the authority, has the function of giving such warnings and requiring such payments and is authorised in writing by the authority to perform that function;

(*c*) any employee of such a person who is authorised in writing by the authority for the purpose of giving such warnings and requiring such payments.

[Environmental Protection Act 1990, s 46A as inserted by the Deregulation Act 2015, s 58.]

**7.10032B 46B. Amount of penalty under section 46A and recovery of penalty** (1) The amount of the monetary penalty that a person may be required to pay to a waste collection authority under section 46A is—

(*a*) the amount specified by the waste collection authority in relation to the authority's area, or

(*b*) if no amount is so specified, £60.

(2) A waste collection authority may make provision for treating a fixed penalty under section 46A as having been paid if a lesser amount is paid before the end of a period specified by the authority.

(3) The Secretary of State may by regulations make provision in connection with the powers conferred on waste collection authorities in England under subsections (1)(*a*) and (2).

(4) Regulations under subsection (3) may (in particular)—

(*a*) require an amount specified under subsection (1)(*a*) to fall within a range prescribed in the regulations;

(*b*) restrict the extent to which, and the circumstances in which, a waste collection authority may make provision under subsection (2).

(5) The Secretary of State may by order substitute a different amount for the amount for the time being specified in subsection (1)(b).

(6) A fixed penalty under section 46A—

(*a*) is recoverable summarily as a civil debt;

(*b*) is recoverable as if it were payable under an order of the High Court or the county court, if the court in question so orders.

[Environmental Protection Act 1990, s 46B as inserted by the Deregulation Act 2015, s 58.]

7.10032C **46C. Penalties under section 46A: procedure regarding notices of intent and final notices** (1) Before requiring a person to pay a fixed penalty under section 46A, an authorised officer must serve on the person notice of intention to do so (a "notice of intent") in accordance with subsections (2) to (4).

(2) A notice of intent must contain information about—

(*a*) the grounds for proposing to require payment of a fixed penalty,

(*b*) the amount of the penalty that the person would be required to pay, and

(*c*) the right to make representations under subsection (3).

(3) A person on whom a notice of intent is served may make representations to the authorised officer as to why payment of a fixed penalty should not be required.

(4) Representations under subsection (3) must be made within the period of 28 days beginning with the day service of the notice of intent is effected.

(5) In order to require a person to pay a fixed penalty under section 46A, an authorised officer must serve on the person a further notice (the "final notice") in accordance with subsections (6) to (8).

(6) A final notice may not be served on a person by an authorised officer before the expiry of the period of 28 days beginning with the day service of the notice of intent on the person was effected.

(7) Before serving a final notice on a person, an authorised officer must consider any representations made by the person under subsection (3).

(8) The final notice must contain information about—

(*a*) the grounds for requiring payment of a fixed penalty,

(*b*) the amount of the penalty,

(*c*) how payment may be made,

(*d*) the period within which payment is required to be made (which must not be less than the period of 28 days beginning with the day service of the final notice is effected),

(*e*) any provision giving a discount for early payment made by virtue of section 46B(2),

(*f*) the right to appeal under section 46D, and

(*g*) the consequences of not paying the penalty.

[Environmental Protection Act 1990, s 46C as inserted by the Deregulation Act 2015, s 58.]

7.10032D **46D. Appeals against penalties under section 46A** (1) A person on whom a final notice is served under section 46C may appeal to the First-tier Tribunal against the decision to require payment of a fixed penalty.

(2) On an appeal under this section the First-tier Tribunal may withdraw or confirm the requirement to pay the fixed penalty.

(3) The requirement to pay the fixed penalty is suspended pending the determination or withdrawal of the appeal that is the final appeal made by the person against the decision to require payment of the penalty.

(This is subject to subsection (4).)

(4) Where the requirement to pay the fixed penalty is confirmed at any stage in the proceedings on appeal, payment must be made before the end of the period of 28 days beginning with the day on which the requirement is so confirmed unless the person makes a further appeal before the end of that period.

(5) The reference in subsection (4) to the requirement to pay the fixed penalty being confirmed on appeal includes a reference to an appeal decision confirming the requirement to pay the fixed penalty being upheld on a further appeal.

[Environmental Protection Act 1990, s 46D as inserted by the Deregulation Act 2015, s 58.]

7.10033 **47. Receptacles for commercial or industrial waste** (1) A waste collection authority may, at the request of any person, supply him with receptacles for commercial or industrial waste which he has requested the authority to arrange to collect and shall make a reasonable charge for any receptacle supplied unless in the case of a receptacle for commercial waste the authority considers it appropriate not to make a charge.

(2) If it appears to a waste collection authority that there is likely to be situated, on any premises in its area, commercial waste or industrial waste of a kind which, if the waste is not stored in receptacles of a particular kind, is likely to cause a nuisance or to be detrimental to the amenities of the locality, the authority may, by notice served on him, require the occupier of the premises to provide at the premises receptacles for the storage of such waste of a kind and number specified.

(3) The kind and number of the receptacles required under subsection (2) above to be used shall be such only as are reasonable.

(4) In making requirements as respects receptacles under subsection (2) above, the authority may, by the notice under that subsection, make provision with respect to—

(*a*) the size, construction and maintenance of the receptacles;
(*b*) the placing of the receptacles for the purpose of facilitating the emptying of them, and access to the receptacles for that purpose;
(*ba*) the placing of the receptacles for the purpose of avoiding nuisance or detriment to the amenities of the area;
(*c*) the placing of the receptacles for that purpose on highways or, in Scotland, roads;
(*d*) the substances or articles which may or may not be put into the receptacles and the precautions to be taken where particular substances or articles are put into them; and
(*e*) the steps to be taken by occupiers of premises to facilitate the collection of waste from the receptacles.

(5) No requirement shall be made under subsection (2) above for receptacles to be placed on a highway or, as the case may be, road unless—
(*a*) the relevant highway authority or roads authority have given their consent to their being so placed; and
(*b*) arrangements have been made as to the liability for any damage arising out of their being so placed.

(6) A person who fails, without reasonable excuse, to comply with any requirements imposed under subsection (2) or (4) above shall be liable on summary conviction to a fine not exceeding **level 3** on the standard scale.

(7) Where an occupier is required under subsection (2) above to provide any receptacles he may, within the period allowed by subsection (8) below, appeal to a magistrates' court or, in Scotland, to the sheriff by way of summary application against any requirement imposed under subsection (2) or (4) above on the ground that—
(*a*) the requirement is unreasonable; or
(*b*) the waste is not likely to cause a nuisance or be detrimental to the amenities of the locality.

(8) The period allowed to the occupier of premises for appealing against such a requirement is the period of twenty-one days beginning with the day on which the notice making the requirement was served on him.

(9) Where an appeal against a requirement is brought under subsection (7) above—
(*a*) the requirement shall be of no effect pending the determination of the appeal;
(*b*) the court shall either quash or modify the requirement or dismiss the appeal; and
(*c*) no question as to whether the requirement is, in any respect, unreasonable shall be entertained in any proceedings for an offence under subsection (6) above.

(10) In this section—
"receptacle" includes a holder for receptacles; and
"specific" means specified in a notice under subsection (2) above.

[Environmental Protection Act 1990, s 47 as amended by the London Local Authorities Act 2007, s 21.]

7.10034 **47ZA. Fixed penalty notices for offences under sections 46 and 47** (1) This section applies where on any occasion an authorised officer of a waste collection authority has reason to believe that a person has committed an offence under section 46 or 47 above in the area of that authority.

(2) The authorised officer may give that person a notice offering him the opportunity of discharging any liability to conviction for the offence by payment of a fixed penalty to the waste collection authority.

(3) Where a person is given a notice under this section in respect of an offence—
(*a*) no proceedings may be instituted for that offence before the expiration of the period of fourteen days following the date of the notice; and
(*b*) he may not be convicted of that offence if he pays the fixed penalty before the expiration of that period.

(4) A notice under this section must give such particulars of the circumstances alleged to constitute the offence as are necessary for giving reasonable information of the offence.

(5) A notice under this section must also state—
(*a*) the period during which, by virtue of subsection (3) above, proceedings will not be taken for the offence;
(*b*) the amount of the fixed penalty; and
(*c*) the person to whom and the address at which the fixed penalty may be paid.

(6) Without prejudice to payment by any other method, payment of the fixed penalty may be made by pre-paying and posting a letter containing the amount of the penalty (in cash or otherwise) to the person mentioned in subsection (5)(*c*) above at the address so mentioned.

(7) Where a letter is sent in accordance with subsection (6) above payment is to be regarded as having been made at the time at which that letter would be delivered in the ordinary course of post.

(8) The form of a notice under this section is to be such as the appropriate person may by order prescribe.

(9) In any proceedings a certificate which—
(*a*) purports to be signed on behalf of the chief finance officer of the waste collection authority, and
(*b*) states that payment of a fixed penalty was or was not received by a date specified in the

certificate,

is evidence of the facts stated.

(10) In this section—

"authorised officer", in relation to a waste collection authority, means—

(*a*) an employee of the authority who is authorised in writing by the authority for the purposes of giving notices under this section;

(*b*) any person who, in pursuance of arrangements made with the authority, has the function of giving such notices and is authorised in writing by the authority to perform that function;

(*c*) any employee of such a person who is authorised in writing by the authority for the purpose of giving such notices;

"chief finance officer", in relation to a waste collection authority, means the person having responsibility for the financial affairs of the authority.

[Environmental Protection Act 1990, s 47ZA as inserted by the Clean Neighbourhoods and Environment Act 2005, s 48.]

**7.10035 47ZB. Amount of fixed penalty under section 47ZA** (1) This section applies in relation to a fixed penalty payable to a waste collection authority in pursuance of a notice under section 47ZA above.

(2) The amount of the fixed penalty—

(*a*) is the amount specified by the waste collection authority in relation to the authority's area, or

(*b*) if no amount is so specified[1]—

(i) *repealed*

(ii) is £100[2].

(3) The waste collection authority may make provision for treating the fixed penalty as having been paid if a lesser amount is paid before the end of a period specified by the authority.

(4) The appropriate person may by regulations[3] make provision in connection with the powers conferred on waste collection authorities under subsections (2)(*a*) and (3) above.

(5) Regulations[2] under subsection (4) may (in particular)—

(*a*) require an amount specified under subsection (2)(*a*) above to fall within a range prescribed in the regulations;

(*b*) restrict the extent to which, and the circumstances in which, a waste collection authority can make provision under subsection (3) above.

(6) The appropriate person may by order substitute a different amount for the amount for the time being specified in subsection (2)(*b*) above.

[Environmental Protection Act 1990, s 47ZB as inserted by the Clean Neighbourhoods and Environment Act 2005, s 48 and amended by SI 2012/1150 and the Deregulation Act 2015, s 58.]

---

1 For permissible range of penalties, see the Environmental Offences (Fixed Penalties) (Miscellaneous Provisions) Regulations 2007, SI 2008/175 and the Environmental Offences (Fixed Penalties) (Miscellaneous Provisions) (Wales) Regulations 2008, SI 2008/663. For amending instruments, see the note to the Refuse Disposal (Amenity) Act 1978, s 2A, ante.

2 Sub-s (2)(*b*) is printed as amended by the Environmental Protection Act 1990 (Amendment of Fixed Penalty Amount) (England) Order 2012, SI 2012/1150.

3 The Environmental Offences (Fixed Penalties) (Miscellaneous Provisions) Regulations 2007, SI 2007/175; the Environmental Offences (Use of Fixed Penalty Receipts) (Wales) Regulations 2007, SI 2007/739 as amended by SI 2008/663; and the Environmental Offences (Fixed Penalties) (Miscellaneous Provisions) (Wales) Regulations 2008, SI 2008/663 have been made. For amending instruments, see the note to the Refuse Disposal (Amenity) Act 1978, s 2A, ante.

**7.10036 47A. Recycling and composting: duty to report to Parliament** (1) Not later than 31st October 2004, the Secretary of State shall lay before each House of Parliament a report of the performance—

(*a*) of each English waste authority in meeting its recycling and composting standards (if any); and

(*b*) of each English waste collection authority towards meeting the requirement imposed by section 45A(2) above.

(2) In this section—

"English waste authority" means a waste collection authority or a waste disposal authority whose area is in England;

"English waste collection authority" means a waste collection authority whose area is in England; and

"recycling and composting standards" means, in relation to an English waste authority, such performance standards and performance indicators (if any) as may be specified for that authority in an order made under section 4 of the Local Government Act 1999 in connection with the recycling and composting of household waste.

[Environmental Protection Act 1990, s 47A as inserted by the Household Waste Recycling Act 2003, s 3.]

**7.10037 57. Power of Secretary of State to require waste to be accepted, treated, disposed of or delivered** (1) The Secretary of State may, by notice in writing, direct the holder of any environmental permit authorising a waste operation to accept and keep, or accept and treat or dispose of, waste at specified places on specified terms.

(2) The Secretary of State may, by notice in writing, direct any person who is keeping waste on any land to deliver the waste to a specified person on specified terms with a view to its being treated or disposed of by that other person.

(3) A direction under this section may impose a requirement as respects waste of any specified kind or as respects any specified consignment of waste.

(4) A direction under subsection (2) above may require the person who is directed to deliver the waste to pay to the specified person his reasonable costs of treating or disposing of the waste.

(5) A person who fails, without reasonable excuse, to comply with a direction under this section shall be liable on summary conviction to a fine not exceeding **level 5** on the standard scale.

(6) A person shall not be guilty of an offence under any other enactment prescribed by the Secretary of State by regulations[1] made for the purposes of this subsection by reason only of anything necessarily done or omitted in order to comply with a direction under this section.

(7) The Secretary of State may, where the costs of the treatment or disposal of waste are not paid or not fully paid in pursuance of subsection (4) above to the person treating or disposing of the waste, pay the costs or the unpaid costs, as the case may be, to that person.

(7A) *Repealed.*

(8) In this section—

"specified" means specified in a direction under this section; and

"waste" means anything that is waste within the meaning of Article 3(1) of Directive 2008/98/EC of the European Parliament and of the Council on waste including anything excluded from the scope of that Directive by Article 2(1)(*f*) or 2(2)(*b*) or (*c*), but not including anything excluded by the remainder of that Article.

[Environmental Protection Act 1990, s 57 as amended by SI 2005/3026, SI 2007/3538 and SI 2011/988.]

1 The Waste (Foot-and-Mouth Disease) (England) Regulations 2001, SI 2001/1478 have been made (for amending instruments, see note to s 29, ante).

7.10038 **59. Powers to require removal of waste unlawfully deposited** (1) If any controlled waste or extractive waste is deposited in or on any land in the area of a waste regulation authority or waste collection authority in contravention of section 33(1) above or regulation 12 of the Environmental Permitting Regulations, the authority may, by notice served on him, require the occupier to do either or both of the following, that is—

(*a*) to remove the waste from the land within a specified period not less than a period of twenty-one days beginning with the service of the notice;

(*b*) to take within such a period specified steps with a view to eliminating or reducing the consequences of the deposit of the waste.

(2) A person on whom any requirements are imposed under subsection (1) above may, within the period of twenty-one days mentioned in that subsection, appeal against the requirement to a magistrates' court or, in Scotland, to the sheriff by way of summary application.

(3) On any appeal under subsection (2) above the court shall quash the requirement if it is satisfied that—

(*a*) the appellant neither deposited nor knowingly caused nor knowingly permitted the deposit of the waste; or

(*b*) there is a material defect in the notice;

and in any other case shall either modify the requirement or dismiss the appeal.

(4) Where a person appeals against any requirement imposed under subsection (1) above, the requirement shall be of no effect pending the determination of the appeal; and where the court modifies the requirement or dismisses the appeal it may extend the period specified in the notice.

(5) If a person on whom a requirement imposed under subsection (1) above fails, without reasonable excuse, to comply with the requirement he shall be liable, on summary conviction, to a fine not exceeding **level 5** on the standard scale and to a further fine of an amount equal to one-tenth of the greater of £5,000 or level 4 on the standard scale for each day on which the failure continues after conviction of the offence and before the authority has begun to exercise its powers under subsection (6) below.

(6) Where a person on whom a requirement has been imposed under subsection (1) above by an authority fails to comply with the requirement the authority may do what that person was required to do and may recover from him any expenses reasonably incurred by the authority in doing it.

(7) If it appears to a waste regulation authority or waste collection authority that waste has been deposited in or on any land in contravention of section 33(1) above or regulation 12 of the Environmental Permitting Regulations, and that—

(*a*) in order to remove or prevent pollution of land, water or air or harm to human health it is necessary that the waste be forthwith removed or other steps taken to eliminate or reduce the consequences of the deposit or both; or

(*b*) there is no occupier of the land or the occupier cannot be found without the authority incurring unreasonable expense; or

(*c*) the occupier neither made nor knowingly permitted the deposit of the waste;

the authority may remove the waste from the land or take other steps to eliminate or reduce the consequences of the deposit or, as the case may require, to remove the waste and take those steps.

(8) Where an authority exercises any of the powers conferred on it by subsection (7) above it shall be entitled to recover the cost incurred by it in removing the waste or taking the steps or both and in disposing of the waste—

(*a*) in a case falling within subsection (7)(*a*) above, from the occupier of the land unless he proves that he neither made nor knowingly caused nor knowingly permitted the deposit of the waste;

(*b*) in any case, from any person who deposited or knowingly caused or knowingly permitted the deposit of any of the waste;

except such of the cost as the occupier or that person shows was incurred unnecessarily.

(8A)An authority may not recover costs under subsection (8) above if a compensation order has been made under section 130 of the Powers of Criminal Courts (Sentencing) Act 2000 in favour of the authority in respect of any part of those costs.*

(8B)Subsection (8A) does not apply if the order is set aside on appeal.*

(9) Any waste removed by an authority under subsection (7) above shall belong to that authority and may be dealt with accordingly.

[Environmental Protection Act 1990, s 59 as amended by the Clean Neighbourhoods and Environment Act 2005, s 43, 50, SI 2007/3538, SI 2009/1799, SI 2010/675 and SI 2015/664.]

* **Inserted in relation to England and Wales only.**

7.10039 **60. Interference with waste sites and receptacles for waste** (1) No person shall sort over or disturb—

(*a*) anything deposited at a place for the deposit of waste provided by a waste collection authority, by or under arrangements made with a waste disposal authority or by any other local authority or person;

(*b*) anything deposited in a receptacle for waste, whether for public or private use, provided by a waste collection authority, by or under arrangements made with a waste disposal authority, by a parish or community council or by a holder of a waste management licence; or

(*c*) the contents of any receptacle for waste which, in accordance with a requirement under section 46 or 47 above, is placed on any highway or, in Scotland, road or in any other place with a view to its being emptied;

unless he has the relevant consent or right to do so specified in subsection (2) below.

(2) The consent or right that is relevant for the purposes of subsection (1)(*a*), (*b*) or (*c*) above is—

(*a*) in the case of paragraph (*a*), the consent of the authority or other person who provides the place for the deposit of the waste;

(*b*) in the case of paragraph (*b*), the consent of the authority or other person who provides the receptacle for the deposit of the waste;

(*c*) in the case of paragraph (*c*), the right to the custody of the receptacle, the consent of the person having the right to the custody of the receptacle or the right conferred by the function by or under this Part of emptying such receptacles.

(3) A person who contravenes subsection (1) above shall be liable on summary conviction to a fine of an amount not exceeding **level 3** on the standard scale.* **

[Environmental Protection Act 1990, s 60 as amended by the Clean Neighbourhoods and Environment Act 2005, Sch 4.]

* **Section reproduced as in force in England and Wales.**

** **New s 60A inserted by the Climate Change Act 2008, Sch 5 from a date to be appointed.**

*Supervision and enforcement*

7.10040 **71. Obtaining of information from persons and authorities** (1) *Repealed.*

(2) For the purpose of the discharge of their respective functions under this Part—

(*a*) the Secretary of State, and

(*b*) a waste regulation authority,

may, by notice in writing served on him, require any person to furnish such information specified in the notice as the Secretary of State or the authority, as the case may be, reasonably considers he or it needs, in such form and within such period following service of the notice, or at such time as is so specified[1].

(2A) A waste collection authority has the power referred to in subsection (2) for the purpose of the discharge of its functions under sections 34B and 34C above.

(3) A person who—

(*a*) fails, without reasonable excuse, to comply with a requirement imposed under subsection (2) or (2A) above;

(*b*) *repealed.*

shall be liable[2]—

(i) on summary conviction, to a fine not exceeding the **statutory maximum**;

(ii) on conviction on indictment, to a **fine** or to imprisonment for a term not exceeding **two**

**years**, or to **both**.

(4) The Secretary of State may, by notice in writing, require a waste regulation authority or waste collection authority in England and Wales to supply to him, or to such other person as may be specified in the notice, such information as may be so specified in respect of—

(*a*) cases where the authority has exercised any powers under section 59 above, and

(*b*) cases where the authority has taken action under any other enactment in respect of any deposit or other disposal of controlled waste in contravention of section 33(1) above.*

[Environmental Protection Act 1990, s 71, as amended by the Environment Act 1995, Schs 19, 22 and 24, the Anti-social Behaviour Act 2003, s 55 and the Clean Neighbourhoods and Environment Act 2005, s 46.]

---

* **Amended by the Investigatory Powers Act 2016, Sch 2 from a date to be appointed.**

1 The power given by s 71(2) has been conferred not merely for the purpose of obtaining evidence against offenders but also for the broad public purpose of protecting public health and the environment. Accordingly, persons who are required under s 71(2) to provide information cannot rely on the privilege against self-incrimination under English law or the principles under the European Convention on Human Rights for refusing to do so, although the question of exclusion on the ground of prejudice of any potentially incriminating answers may arise in any subsequent criminal proceedings (*R v Hertfordshire County Council, ex p Green Environmental Industries Ltd* [2000] 2 AC 412, [2000] 1 All ER 773, [2000] 2 WLR 373, HL).

2 For procedure in respect of an offence triable either way, see the Magistrates' Courts Act 1980, ss 17A–21 in PART I: MAGISTRATES' COURTS, PROCEDURE, ante.

*Supplemental*

**7.10041 73. Appeals and other provisions relating to legal proceedings and civil liability**

(1) An appeal against any decision of a magistrates' court under this Part (other than a decision made in criminal proceedings) shall lie to the Crown Court at the instance of any party to the proceedings in which the decision was given if such an appeal does not lie to the Crown Court by virtue of any other enactment.

(2) *Scotland.*

(3) Where a person appeals to the Crown Court or the Court of Session against a decision of a magistrates' court or the sheriff dismissing an appeal against any requirement imposed under this Part which was suspended pending determination of that appeal, the requirement shall again be suspended pending the determination of the appeal to the Crown Court or Court of Session.

(4) Where an appeal against a decision of any authority lies to a magistrates' court or to the sheriff by virtue of any provision of this Part, it shall be the duty of the authority to include in any document by which it notifies the decision to the person concerned a statement indicating that such an appeal lies and specifying the time within which it must be brought.

(5) Where on an appeal to any court against or arising out of a decision of any authority under this Part the court varies or reverses the decision it shall be the duty of the authority to act in accordance with the court's decision.

(6)–(9) *Civil liability.*

[Environmental Protection Act 1990, s 73.]

**7.10042 75. Meaning of "waste" and household, commercial and industrial waste and hazardous waste** (1) The following provisions apply for the interpretation of this Part.

(2) "Waste"[1] means anything that is waste within the meaning of Article 3(1) of Directive 2008/98/EC of the European Parliament and of the Council on waste[2].

(3) *Repealed.*

(4) "Controlled waste"[3] means household, industrial and commercial waste or any such waste.

(5) Subject to subsection (8) below, "household waste" means waste from—

(*a*) domestic property, that is to say, a building or self-contained part of a building which is used wholly for the purposes of living accommodation;

(*b*) a caravan (as defined in section 29(1) of the Caravan Sites and Control of Development Act 1960) which usually and for the time being is situated on a caravan site (within the meaning of that Act);

(*c*) a residential home;

(*d*) premises forming part of a university or school or other educational establishment;

(*e*) premises forming part of a hospital or nursing home.*

(6) Subject to subsection (8) below, "industrial waste" means waste from any of the following premises—

(*a*) any factory (within the meaning of the Factories Act 1961);

(*b*) any premises used for the purposes of, or in connection with, the provision to the public of transport services by land, water or air;

(*c*) any premises used for the purposes of, or in connection with, the supply to the public of gas, water or electricity or the provision of sewerage services;

(*d*) any premises used for the purposes of, or in connection with, the provision to the public of postal or telecommunications services; or

(*e*) any mine or quarry or any premises used for agriculture within the meaning of the Agriculture Act 1947.

(7) Subject to subsection (8) below, "commercial waste" means waste from premises used wholly or mainly for the purposes of a trade or business or the purposes of sport, recreation or entertainment excluding—

(*a*) household waste;
(*b*) industrial waste; and
(*c*) *repealed*
(*d*) waste of any other description prescribed[4] by regulations made by the Secretary of State for the purposes of this paragraph.

(8) Regulations[5] made by the Secretary of State may provide that waste of a description prescribed in the regulations shall be treated for the purposes of provisions of this Part prescribed in the regulations as being or not being household waste or industrial waste or commercial waste; and references to waste in subsection (7) above and this subsection do not include sewage (including matter in or from a privy) except so far as the regulations provide otherwise.

(8A) "Hazardous waste"—
(*a*) in the application of this Part to England, means any waste which is a hazardous waste for the purposes of the Hazardous Waste (England and Wales) Regulations 2005;
(*b*) in the application of this Part to Wales, means any waste which is a hazardous waste for the purposes of the Hazardous Waste (Wales) Regulations 2005.

(8B) *Repealed.*
(9) *Repealed.*
(10) *Repealed.*
(11) *Repealed.*
(12) *Repealed.*

[Environmental Protection Act 1990, s 75 as amended by the Environment Act 1985, Sch 22 and SI 2005/894 and 1806, SI 2006/937 and SI 2011/988.]

* **Section heading and para (5)(*e*) text differ in relation to Scotland by virtue of the Regulations of Care (Scotland) Act 2002, s 79 and SI 2005/894.**

1 The European Court on a preliminary reference has held that "waste" within the meaning of Council Directive 75/442/ EEC, art 1(*a*) includes stone left over after quarrying even though the residue stone could be put to use directly, without further processing (*Application by Palin Granit Oy* (Case C-9/00) [2002] 1 WLR 2644). There is a distinction, however, between depositing material for storage pending proposed re-use and depositing it for use more or less straight away; in the case of the latter, at the time of the deposit the material is not "controlled waste": *Environment Agency v Inglenorth Ltd* [2009] EWHC 670 (Admin), [2009] Env LR 33.

2 Article 3 provides '1. "waste" means any substance or object which the holder discards or intends or is required to discard. The term 'discard' is to be interpreted in the light of the aims of the Directive and material which was originally waste will continue to be so treated until acceptable recovery or disposal has been achieved in accordance with the aims of the Directive. Whether that occurs is a question of fact. The possibility that the material might be reused at some time does not alter its status. Actual re-use might do so, but only if consistent with the aims and objectives of the 1990 Act and of the Directive to avoid harm to persons or the environment: *R v W* [2010] EWCA Crim 927, [2011] 3 All ER 691. See also *R v Jagger* [2015] EWCA Crim 348, [2015] All ER (D) 229 (Feb), considered at para 7.10021, ante.

3 It was decided under the Control of Pollution Act 1974 that seaweed was not controlled waste for the purpose of the predecessor legislation (*Thanet District Council v Kent County Council* [1993] Crim LR 703.

4 See note 3, supra.

5 The Controlled Waste Regulations 2012, SI 2012/811 have been made, amending regulations are noted in the list of regulations made under s 2 of the European Communities Act 1972, ante.

7.10043 **78. This Part and radioactive substances** Except as provided by regulations made by the Secretary of State under this section, nothing in this Part applies to radioactive waste within the meaning of Schedule 23 to the Environmental Permitting Regulations (radioactive substances activities); but regulations[1] may—
(*a*) provide for prescribed provisions of this Part to have effect with such modifications as the Secretary of State considers appropriate for the purposes of dealing with such radioactive waste;
(*b*) make such modifications of the Environmental Permitting Regulations in relation to such radioactive waste, and any Act or other enactment as the Secretary of State considers appropriate.

[Environmental Protection Act 1990, s 78 as amended by the Radioactive Substances Act 1993, Sch 4 and SI 2010/675.]

## PART IIA[1]
## CONTAMINATED LAND

7.10044 **78A. Preliminary[1]** (1) The following provisions have effect for the interpretation of this Part.

(2) "Contaminated land" is any land which appears to the local authority in whose area it is situated to be in such a condition, by reason of substances in, on or under the land, that—
(*a*) significant harm is being caused or there is a significant possibility of such harm being caused; or
(*b*) significant pollution of controlled waters is being caused or there is a significant possibility of such pollution being caused;

and, in determining whether any land appears to be such land, a local authority shall, subject to subsection (5) below, act in accordance with guidance issued by the Secretary of State in accordance with section 78YA below with respect to the manner in which that determination is to be made.

(3) A "special site" is any contaminated land—

(*a*) which has been designated as such a site by virtue of section 78C(7) or 78D(6) below; and

(*b*) whose designation as such has not been terminated by the appropriate Agency under section 78Q(4) below.

(4) "Harm" means harm to the health of living organisms or other interference with the ecological systems of which they form part and, in the case of man, includes harm to his property.

(5) The questions—

(*a*) what harm or pollution of controlled waters is to be regarded as "significant",

(*b*) whether the possibility of significant harm or of significant pollution of controlled waters being caused is "significant",

(*c*) *revoked*

shall be determined in accordance with guidance issued for the purpose by the Secretary of State in accordance with section 78YA below.

(6) Without prejudice to the guidance that may be issued under subsection (5) above, guidance under paragraph (*a*) of that subsection may make provision for different degrees of importance to be assigned to, or for the disregard of,—

(*a*) different descriptions of living organisms or ecological systems, or of poisonous, noxious or polluting matter or solid waste matter;

(*b*) different descriptions of places or controlled waters, or different degrees of pollution; or

(*c*) different descriptions of harm to health or property, or other interference;

and guidance under paragraph (*b*) of that subsection may make provision for different degrees of possibility to be regarded as "significant" (or as not being "significant") in relation to different descriptions of significant harm or of significant pollution.

(7) "Remediation" means—

(*a*) the doing of anything for the purpose of assessing the condition of—

(i) the contaminated land in question;

(ii) any controlled waters affected by that land; or

(iii) any land adjoining or adjacent to that land;

(*b*) the doing of any works, the carrying out of any operations or the taking of any steps in relation to any such land or waters for the purpose—

(i) of preventing or minimising, or remedying or mitigating the effects of, any significant harm, or any significant pollution of controlled waters, by reason of which the contaminated land is such land; or

(ii) of restoring the land or waters to their former state; or

(*c*) the making of subsequent inspections from time to time for the purpose of keeping under review the condition of the land or waters;

and cognate expressions shall be construed accordingly.

(8) Controlled waters are "affected by" contaminated land if (and only if) it appears to the enforcing authority that the contaminated land in question is, for the purposes of subsection (2) above, in such a condition, by reason of substances in, on or under the land, that significant pollution of those waters is being caused or there is a significant possibility of such pollution being caused.

(9) The following expressions have the meaning respectively assigned to them—

"the appropriate Agency" means—

(*a*) in relation to England, the Environment Agency;

(*b*) *Scotland*;

(*c*) in relation to Wales, the Natural Resources Body for Wales;

"appropriate person" means any person who is an appropriate person, determined in accordance with section 78F below, to bear responsibility for anything which is to be done by way of remediation in any particular case;

"charging notice" has the meaning given by section 78P(3)(*b*) below;

"controlled waters"—

(*a*) in relation to England and Wales, has the same meaning as in Part III of the Water Resources Act 1991 except that "ground waters" does not include waters contained in underground strata but above the saturation zone; and

(*b*) *Scotland*;

"creditor" has the same meaning as in the Conveyancing and Feudal Reform (Scotland) Act 1970;

"enforcing authority" means—

(*a*) in relation to a special site, the appropriate Agency;

(*b*) in relation to contaminated land other than a special site, the local authority in whose area the land is situated;

"heritable security" has the same meaning as in the Conveyancing and Feudal Reform (Scotland) Act 1970;

"local authority" in relation to England and Wales means—

(*a*) any unitary authority;

(*b*) any district council, so far as it is not a unitary authority;

(*c*) the Common Council of the City of London and, as respects the Temples, the Sub-Treasurer of the Inner Temple and the Under-Treasurer of the Middle Temple respectively;

and in relation to Scotland means a council for an area constituted under section 2 of the Local Government etc. (Scotland) Act 1994;

"notice" means notice in writing;

"notification" means notification in writing;

"owner", in relation to any land in England and Wales, means a person (other than a mortgagee not in possession) who, whether in his own right or as trustee for any other person, is entitled to receive the rack rent of the land, or, where the land is not let at a rack rent, would be so entitled if it were so let;

"owner", in relation to any land in Scotland, means a person (other than a creditor in a heritable security not in possession of the security subjects) for the time being entitled to receive or who would, if the land were let, be entitled to receive, the rents of the land in connection with which the word is used and includes a trustee, factor, guardian or curator and in the case of public or municipal land includes the persons to whom the management of the land is entrusted;

"pollution of controlled waters" means the entry into controlled waters of any poisonous, noxious or polluting matter or any solid waste matter;

"prescribed" means prescribed by regulations;

"regulations" means regulations[2] made by the Secretary of State;

"remediation declaration" has the meaning given by section 78H(6) below;

"remediation notice" has the meaning given by section 78E(1) below;

"remediation statement" has the meaning given by section 78H(7) below;

"required to be designated as a special site" shall be construed in accordance with section 78C(8) below;

"substance" means any natural or artificial substance, whether in solid or liquid form or in the form of a gas or vapour;

"unitary authority" means—

(*a*) the council of a county, so far as it is the council of an area for which there are no district councils;

(*b*) the council of any district comprised in an area for which there is no county council;

(*c*) the council of a London borough;

(*d*) the council of a county borough in Wales

[Environmental Protection Act, 1990, s 78A as inserted by the Environment Act 1995, s 57 and amended by the Water Act 2003, s 86 and SI 2013/755.]

---

1 Part IIA contains ss 78A–78YC.

2 The Radio-active Contaminated Land (Enabling Powers) (England) Regulations 2005, SI 2005/3467 amended by SI 2010/2214, the Radioactive Contaminated Land (Modifications of Enactments) (England) Regulations 2006, SI 2006/1379 amended by SI 2007/3245, SI 2008/520, SI 2010/2147 and SI 2016/1154, the Contaminated Land (England) Regulations 2006, SI 2006/1380 amended by SI 2007/353, SI 2009/1307, SI 2010/675, SI 2012/263 and SI 2016/1154, the Radioactive Contaminated Land (Modification of Enactments) (Wales) Regulations 2006, SI 2006/2988 amended by SI 2007/3250, SI 2008/521, SI 2010/2146 and SI 2016/1154 and the Contaminated Land (Wales) Regulations 2006/2989 amended by SI 2007/3538, SI 2010/675, SI 2012/283 and SI 2016/1154 have been made.

**78B–78D** *Duty of local authority to inspect and identify contaminated land and decide whether such land is required to be designated a special site. Notice to be given to the appropriate Agency, the landowner, occupier and any person the authority deems to be appropriate. Referral of special site decisions to Secretary of State.*

7.10045 **78E. Duty of enforcing authority to require remediation of contaminated land etc** (1) In any case where—

(*a*) any land has been designated as a special site by virtue of section 78C(7) or 78D(6) above, or

(*b*) a local authority has identified any contaminated land (other than a special site) in its area,

the enforcing authority shall, in accordance with such procedure as may be prescribed and subject to the following provisions of this Part, serve on each person who is an appropriate person a notice (in this Part referred to as a "remediation notice") specifying what that person is to do by way of remediation and the periods within which he is required to do each of the things so specified.

(2) Different remediation notices requiring the doing of different things by way of remediation may be served on different persons in consequence of the presence of different substances in, on or under any land or waters.

(3) Where two or more persons are appropriate persons in relation to any particular thing which is to be done by way of remediation, the remediation notice served on each of them shall state the proportion, determined under section 78F(7) below, of the cost of doing that thing which each of them respectively is liable to bear.

(4) The only things by way of remediation which the enforcing authority may do, or require to be done, under or by virtue of this Part are things which it considers reasonable, having regard to—

(*a*) the cost which is likely to be involved; and

(*b*) the seriousness of the harm, or of the pollution of controlled waters, in question.

(5) In determining for any purpose of this Part—

(*a*) what is to be done (whether by an appropriate person, the enforcing authority or any other person) by way of remediation in any particular case,

(*b*) the standard to which any land is, or waters are, to be remediated pursuant to the notice, or

(*c*) what is, or is not, to be regarded as reasonable for the purposes of subsection (4) above,

the enforcing authority shall have regard to any guidance issued for the purpose by the Secretary of State.

(6) Regulations[1] may make provision for or in connection with—

(*a*) the form or content of remediation notices; or

(*b*) any steps of a procedural nature which are to be taken in connection with, or in consequence of, the service of a remediation notice.

[Environmental Protection Act 1990, s 78E as inserted by the Environment Act 1995, s 57 and amended by the Water Act 2003, s 86.]

---

1 See the Contaminated Land Regulations 2000, SI 2000/227 as amended and the Contaminated Land (Wales) Regulations 2006, SI 2006/2989 as amended. For amending instruments, see the note to s 78A, ante.

**7.10046 78F. Determination of the appropriate person[1] to bear responsibility for remediation** (1) This section has effect for the purpose of determining who is the appropriate person to bear responsibility for any particular thing which the enforcing authority determines is to be done by way of remediation in any particular case.

(2) subject to the following provisions of this section, any person, or any of the persons, who caused or knowingly permitted the substances, or any of the substances, by reason of which the contaminated land in question is such land to be in, on or under that land is an appropriate person.

(3) A person shall only be an appropriate person by virtue of subsection (2) above in relation to things which are to be done by way of remediation which are to any extent referable to substances which he caused or knowingly permitted to be present in, on or under the contaminated land in question.

(4) If no person has, after reasonable inquiry, been found who is by virtue of subsection (2) above an appropriate person to bear responsibility for the things which are to be done by way of remediation, the owner or occupier for the time being of the contaminated land in question is an appropriate person.

(5) If, in consequence of subsection (3) above, there are things which are to be done by way of remediation in relation to which no person has, after reasonable inquiry, been found who is an appropriate person by virtue of subsection (2) above, the owner or occupier for the time being of the contaminated land in question is an appropriate person in relation to those things.

(6) Where two or more persons would, apart from this subsection, be appropriate persons in relation to any particular thing which is to be done by way of remediation, the enforcing authority shall determine in accordance with guidance issued for the purpose by the Secretary of State whether any, and if so which, of them is to be treated as not being an appropriate person in relation to that thing,

(7) Where two or more persons are appropriate persons in relation to any particular thing which is to be done by way of remediation, they shall be liable to bear the cost of doing that thing in proportions determined by the enforcing authority in accordance with guidance issued for the purpose by the Secretary of State.

(8) Any guidance issued for the purposes of subsection (6) or (7) above shall be issued in accordance with section 78YA below.

(9) A person who has caused or knowingly permitted any substance ("substance A") to be in, on or under any land shall also be taken for the purposes of this section to have caused or knowingly permitted there to be in, on or under that land any substance which is there as a result of a chemical reaction or biological process affecting substance A.

(10) A thing which is to be done by way of remediation may be regarded for the purposes of this Part as referable to the presence of any substance notwithstanding that the thing in question would not have to be done—

(*a*) in consequence only of the presence of that substance in any quantity; or

(*b*) in consequence only of the quantity of that substance which any particular person caused or knowingly permitted to be present.

[Environmental Protection Act 1990, s 78F as inserted by the Environment Act 1995, s 57.]

---

1 The term "appropriate person" in this section refers to the person who caused or knowingly permitted the relevant contamination and not to a successor to the business of that person; although the transfers of gas undertakings effected by s 17(1) of the Gas Act 1948 Act and s 49(1) of the Gas Act 1986 Act had in each case included a transfer of the liabilities of the predecessor, such transfer had been limited to liabilities existing immediately before the relevant vesting date and did not encompass a liability created in 1995 by the amendment of the 1990 Act to remedy pollution caused by those predecessors: *R (National Grid Gas plc) v Environment Agency* [2007] UKHL 30, [2007] 1 WLR 1780.

**7.10047 78G. Grant of, and compensation for, rights of entry etc** (1) A remediation notice may require an appropriate person to do things by way of remediation, notwithstanding that he is not entitled to do those things.

(2) Any person whose consent is required before any thing required by a remediation notice may be done shall grant, or join in granting, such rights in relation to any of the relevant land or waters as will enable the appropriate person to comply with any requirements imposed by the

remediation notice.

(3) Before serving a remediation notice, the enforcing authority shall reasonably endeavour to consult every person who appears to the authority—

(*a*) to be the owner or occupier of any of the relevant land or waters, and

(*b*) to be a person who might be required by subsection (2) above to grant, or join in granting, any rights,

concerning the rights which that person may be so required to grant.

(4) Subsection (3) above shall not preclude the service of a remediation notice in any case where it appears to the enforcing authority that the contaminated land in question is in such a condition, by reason of substances in, on or under the land, that there is imminent danger of serious harm, or serious pollution of controlled waters, being caused.

(5) A person who grants, or joins in granting, any rights pursuant to subsection (2) above shall be entitled, on making an application within such period as may be prescribed[1] and in such manner as may be prescribed[1] to such person as may be prescribed, to be paid by the appropriate person compensation of such amount as may be determined in such manner as may be prescribed.

(6) Without prejudice to the generality of the regulations[1] that may be made by virtue of subsection (5) above, regulations by virtue of that subsection may make such provision in relation to compensation under this section as may be made by regulations by virtue of subsection (4) of section 35A above in relation to compensation under that section.

(7) In this section, "relevant land or waters" means—

(*a*) the contaminated land in question;

(*b*) any controlled waters affected by that land; or

(*c*) any land adjoining or adjacent to that land or those waters.

[Environmental Protection Act 1990, s 78G as inserted by the Environment Act 1995, s 57.]

---

[1] See the Contaminated Land Regulations 2000, SI 2000/227 as amended and the Contaminated Land (Wales) Regulations 2006, SI 2006/2989 as amended. For amending instruments, see the note to s 78A, ante.

7.10048 **78H. Restrictions and prohibitions on serving remediation notices** (1) Before serving a remediation notice, the enforcing authority shall reasonably endeavour to consult—

(*a*) the person on whom the notice is to be served,

(*b*) the owner of any land to which the notice relates,

(*c*) any person who appears to that authority to be in occupation of the whole or any part of the land, and

(*d*) any person of such other description as may be prescribed,

concerning what is to be done by way of remediation.

(2) Regulations may make provision for, or in connection with, steps to be taken for the purposes of subsection (1) above.

(3) No remediation notice shall be served on any person by reference to any contaminated land during any of the following periods, that is to say—

(*a*) the period—

(i) beginning with the identification of the contaminated land in question pursuant to section 78B(1) above, and

(ii) ending with the expiration of the period of three months beginning with the day on which the notice required by subsection (3)(*d*) or, as the case may be, (4) of section 78B above is given to that person in respect of that land;

(*b*) if a decision falling within paragraph (*b*) of section 78C(1) above is made in relation to the contaminated land in question, the period beginning with the making of the decision and ending with the expiration of the period of three months beginning with—

(i) in a case where the decision is not referred to the Secretary of State under section 78D above, the day on which the notice required by section 78C(6) above is given, or

(ii) in a case where the decision is referred to the Secretary of State under section 78D above, the day on which he gives the notice required by subsection (4)(*b*) of that section;

(*c*) if the appropriate Agency gives a notice under subsection (4) of section 78C above to a local authority in relation to the contaminated land in question, the period beginning with the day on which that notice is given and ending with the expiration of the period of three months beginning with—

(i) in a case where notice is given under subsection (6) of that section, the day on which that notice is given;

(ii) in a case where the authority makes a decision falling within subsection (5)(*b*) of that section and the appropriate Agency fails to give notice under paragraph (*b*) of section 78D(1) above, the day following the expiration of the period of twenty-one days mentioned in that paragraph; or

(iii) in a case where the authority makes a decision falling within section 78C(5)(*b*) above which is referred to the Secretary of State under section 78D above, the day on which the Secretary of State gives the notice required by subsection

(4)(*b*) of that section.

(4) Neither subsection (1) nor subsection (3) above shall preclude the service of a remediation notice in any case where it appears to the enforcing authority that the land in question is in such a condition, by reason of substances in, on or under the land, that there is imminent danger of serious harm, or serious pollution of controlled waters, being caused.

(5) The enforcing authority shall not serve a remediation notice on a person if and so long as any one or more of the following conditions is for the time being satisfied in the particular case, that is to say—

(*a*) the authority is satisfied, in consequence of section 78E(4) and (5) above, that there is nothing by way of remediation which could be specified in a remediation notice served on that person;

(*b*) the authority is satisfied that appropriate things are being, or will be, done by way of remediation without the service of a remediation notice on that person;

(*c*) it appears to the authority that the person on whom the notice would be served is the authority itself; or

(*d*) the authority is satisfied that the powers conferred on it by section 78N below to do what is appropriate by way of remediation are exercisable.

(6) Where the enforcing authority is precluded by virtue of section 78E(4) or (5) above from specifying in a remediation notice any particular thing by way of remediation which it would otherwise have specified in such a notice, the authority shall prepare and publish a document (in this Part referred to as a "remediation declaration") which shall record—

(*a*) the reasons why the authority would have specified that thing; and

(*b*) the grounds on which the authority is satisfied that it is precluded from specifying that thing in such a notice.

(7) In any case where the enforcing authority is precluded, by virtue of paragraph (*b*), (*c*) or (*d*) of subsection (5) above, from serving a remediation notice, the responsible person shall prepare and publish a document (in this Part referred to as a "remediation statement") which shall record—

(*a*) the things which are being, have been, or are expected to be, done by way of remediation in the particular case;

(*b*) the name and address of the person who is doing, has done, or is expected to do, each of those things; and

(*c*) the periods within which each of those things is being, or is expected to be, done.

(8) For the purposes of subsection (7) above, the "responsible person" is—

(*a*) in a case where the condition in paragraph (*b*) of subsection (5) above is satisfied, the person who is doing or has done, or who the enforcing authority is satisfied will do, the things there mentioned; or

(*b*) in a case where the condition in paragraph (*c*) or (*d*) of that subsection is satisfied, the enforcing authority.

(9) If a person who is required by virtue of subsection (8)(*a*) above to prepare and publish a remediation statement fails to do so within a reasonable time after the date on which a remediation notice specifying the things there mentioned could, apart from subsection (5) above, have been served, the enforcing authority may itself prepare and publish the statement and may recover its reasonable costs of doing so from that person.

(10) Where the enforcing authority has been precluded by virtue only of subsection (5) above from serving a remediation notice on an appropriate person but—

(*a*) none of the conditions in that subsection is for the time being satisfied in the particular case, and

(*b*) the authority is not precluded by any other provision of this Part from serving a remediation notice on that appropriate person,

the authority shall serve a remediation notice on that person; and any such notice may be so served without any further endeavours by the authority to consult persons pursuant to subsection (1) above, if and to the extent that that person has been consulted pursuant to that subsection concerning the things which will be specified in the notice.

[Environmental Protection Act 1990, s 78H as inserted by the Environment Act 1995, s 57.]

**7.10049 78J. Restrictions on liability relating to the pollution of controlled waters**

(1) This section applies where any land is contaminated land by virtue of paragraph (*b*) of subsection (2) of section 78A above (whether or not the land is also contaminated land by virtue of paragraph (*a*) of that subsection).

(2) Where this section applies, no remediation notice given in consequence of the land in question being contaminated land shall require a person who is an appropriate person by virtue of section 78F(4) or (5) above to do anything by way of remediation to that or any other land, or any waters, which he could not have been required to do by such a notice had paragraph (*b*) of section 78A(2) above (and all other references to pollution of controlled waters) been omitted from this Part.

(3) If, in a case where this section applies a person permits, has permitted, or might permit, water from an abandoned mine or part of a mine—

(*a*) to enter any controlled waters, or

(*b*) to reach a place from which it is or, as the case may be, was likely, in the opinion of the enforcing authority, to enter such waters,

no remediation notice shall require him in consequence to do anything by way of remediation (whether to the contaminated land in question or to any other land or waters) which he could not have been required to do by such a notice had paragraph (*b*) of section 78A(2) above (and all other references to pollution of controlled waters) been omitted from this Part.

(4) Subsection (3) above shall not apply to the owner or former operator of any mine or part of a mine if the mine or part in question became abandoned after 31st December 1999.

(5) In determining for the purposes of subsection (4) above whether a mine or part of a mine became abandoned before, on or after 31st December 1999 in a case where the mine or part has become abandoned on two or more occasions, of which—

(*a*) at least one falls on or before that date, and

(*b*) at least one falls after that date,

the mine or part shall be regarded as becoming abandoned after that date (but without prejudice to the operation of subsection (3) above in relation to that mine or part at, or in relation to, any time before the first of those occasions which falls after that date).

(6) Where, immediately before a part of a mine becomes abandoned, that part is the only part of the mine not falling to be regarded as abandoned for the time being, the abandonment of that part shall not be regarded for the purposes of subsection (4) or (5) above as constituting the abandonment of the mine, but only of that part of it.

(7) Nothing in subsection (2) or (3) above prevents the enforcing authority from doing anything by way of remediation under section 78N below which it could have done apart from that subsection, but the authority shall not be entitled under section 78P below to recover from any person any part of the cost incurred by the authority in doing by way of remediation anything which it is precluded by subsection (2) or (3) above from requiring that person to do.

(8) In this section "mine" has the same meaning as in the Mines and Quarries Act 1954.

[Environmental Protection Act 1990, s 78J as inserted by the Environment Act 1995, s 57.]

7.10050 **78K. Liability in respect of contaminating substances which escape to other land**

(1) A person who has caused or knowingly permitted any substances to be in, on or under any land shall also be taken for the purposes of this Part to have caused or, as the case may be, knowingly permitted those substances to be in, on or under any other land to which they appear to have escaped.

(2) Subsections (3) and (4) below apply in any case where it appears that any substances are or have been in, on or under any land (in this section referred to as "land A") as a result of their escape, whether directly or indirectly, from other land in, on or under which a person caused or knowingly permitted them to be.

(3) Where this subsection applies, no remediation notice shall require a person—

(*a*) who is the owner or occupier of land A, and

(*b*) who has not caused or knowingly permitted the substances in question to be in, on or under that land,

to do anything by way of remediation to any land or waters (other than land or waters of which he is the owner or occupier) in consequence of land A appearing to be in such a condition, by reason of the presence of those substances in, on or under it, that significant harm, or significant pollution of controlled waters, is being caused, or there is a significant possibility of such harm or pollution being caused.

(4) Where this subsection applies, no remediation notice shall require a person—

(*a*) who is the owner or occupier of land A, and

(*b*) who has not caused or knowingly permitted the substances in question to be in, on or under that land,

to do anything by way of remediation in consequence of any further land in, on or under which those substances or any of them appear to be or to have been present as a result of their escape from land A ("land B") appearing to be in such a condition, by reason of the presence of those substances in, on or under it, that significant harm, or significant pollution of controlled waters, is being caused, or there is a significant possibility of such harm or pollution being caused, unless he is also the owner or occupier of land B.

(5) In any case where—

(*a*) a person ("person A") has caused or knowingly permitted any substances to be in, on, or under any land,

(*b*) another person ("person B") who has not caused or knowingly permitted those substances to be in, on or under that land becomes the owner or occupier of that land, and

(*c*) the substances, or any of the substances, mentioned in paragraph (*a*) above appear to have escaped to other land,

no remediation notice shall require person B to do anything by way of remediation to that other land in consequence of the apparent acts or omissions of person A, except to the extent that person B caused or knowingly permitted the escape.

(6) Nothing in subsection (3), (4) or (5) above prevents the enforcing authority from doing anything by way of remediation under section 78N below which it could have done apart from that

subsection, but the authority shall not be entitled under section 78P below to recover from any person any part of the cost incurred by the authority in doing by way of remediation anything which it is precluded by subsection (3), (4) or (5) above from requiring that person to do.

(7) In this section, "appear" means appear to the enforcing authority, and cognate expressions shall be construed accordingly.

[Environmental Protection Act 1990, s 78K as inserted by the Environment Act 1995, s 57 and amended by the Water Act 2003, s 86.]

7.10051 78L. **Appeals against remediation notices** (1) A person on whom a remediation notice is served may, within the period of twenty-one days beginning with the day on which the notice is served, appeal against the notice—

(*a*) if it was served by a local authority in England or by the Environment Agency, to the Secretary of State;

(*b*) if it was served by a local authority in Wales or by the Natural Resources Body for Wales, to the National Assembly for Wales;

and in the following provisions of this section "the appellate authority" means the Secretary of State or the National Assembly for Wales, as the case may be.

(2) On any appeal under subsection (1) above the appellate authority—

(*a*) shall quash the notice, if it is satisfied that there is a material defect in the notice; but

(*b*) subject to that, may confirm the remediation notice, with or without modification, or quash it.

(3) Where an appellate authority confirms a remediation notice, with or without modification it may extend the period specified in the notice for doing what the notice requires to be done.

(4) Regulations[1] may make provision with respect to—

(*a*) the grounds on which, appeals under subsection (1) above may be made;

(*b*) *repealed*

(*c*) the procedure on an appeal under subsection (1) above.

(5) Regulations[1] under subsection (4) above may (among other things)—

(*a*) include provisions comparable to those in section 290 of the Public Health Act 1936 (appeals against notices requiring the execution of works);

(*b*) prescribe the cases in which a remediation notice is, or is not, to be suspended until the appeal is decided, or until some other stage in the proceedings;

(*c*) prescribe the cases in which the decision on an appeal may in some respects be less favourable to the appellant than the remediation notice against which he is appealing;

(*d*) prescribe the cases in which the appellant may claim that a remediation notice should have been served on some other person and prescribe the procedure to be followed in those cases;

(*e*) make provision as respects—

(i) the particulars to be included in the notice of appeal;

(ii) the persons on whom notice of appeal is to be served and the particulars, if any, which are to accompany the notice; and

(iii) the abandonment of an appeal;

(*f*) make different provision for different cases or classes of case.

(6) This section, is subject to section 114 of the Environment Act 1995 (delegation or reference of appeals etc).

[Environmental Protection Act 1990, s 78L as inserted by the Environment Act 1995, s 57 and amended by the Clean Neighbourhoods and Environment Act 2005, Sch 5 and SI 2013/755.]

---

1 See the Contaminated Land Regulations 2000, SI 2000/227 as amended and the Contaminated Land (Wales) Regulations 2006, SI 2006/2989 as amended. For amending instruments, see the note to s 78A, ante.

7.10052 78M. **Offences of not complying with a remediation notice** (1) If a person on whom an enforcing authority serves a remediation notice fails, without reasonable excuse, to comply with any of the requirements of the notice, he shall be guilty of an offence.

(2) Where the remediation notice in question is one which was required by section 78E(3) above to state, in relation to the requirement which has not been complied with, the proportion of the cost involved which the person charged with the offence is liable to bear, it shall be a defence for that person to prove that the only reason why he has not complied with the requirement is that one or more of the other persons who are liable to bear a proportion of that cost refused, or was not able, to comply with the requirement.

(3) Except in a case falling within subsection (4) below, a person who commits an offence under subsection (1) above shall be liable, on summary conviction, to a fine not exceeding **level 5** on the standard scale and to a further fine of an amount equal to one-tenth of the greater of £5,000 or level 4 on the standard scale for each day on which the failure continues after conviction of the offence and before the enforcing authority has begun to exercise its powers by virtue of section 78N(3)(*c*) below.

(4) A person who commits an offence under subsection (1) above in a case where the contaminated land to which the remediation notice relates is industrial, trade or business premises shall be liable on summary conviction to a fine and to a further fine of an amount equal to **one-tenth of that sum** for each day on which the failure continues after conviction of the offence and

before the enforcing authority has begun to exercise its powers by virtue of section 78N(3)(*c*) below.

(5) If the enforcing authority is of the opinion that proceedings for an offence under this section would afford an ineffectual remedy against a person who has failed to comply with any of the requirements of a remediation notice which that authority has served on him, that authority may take proceedings in the High Court or, in Scotland, in any court of competent jurisdiction, for the purpose of securing compliance with the remediation notice.

(6) In this section, "industrial, trade or business premises" means premises used for any industrial, trade or business purposes or premises not so used on which matter is burnt in connection with any industrial, trade or business process, and premises are used for industrial purposes where they are used for the purposes of any treatment or process as well as where they are used for the purpose of manufacturing.

(7) No order shall be made under subsection (4) above unless a draft of the order has been laid before, and approved by a resolution of, each House of Parliament.

[Environmental Protection Act 1990, s 78M as inserted by the Environment Act 1995, s 57 and amended by SI 2015/664.]

7.10053 **78N. Powers of the enforcing authority to carry out remediation** (1) Where this section applies, the enforcing authority shall itself have power, in a case falling within paragraph (*a*) or (*b*) of section 78E(1) above, to do what is appropriate by way of remediation to the relevant land or waters.

(2) Subsection (1) above shall not confer power on the enforcing authority to do anything by way of remediation if the authority would, in the particular case, be precluded by section 78YB below from serving a remediation notice requiring that thing to be done.

(3) This section applies in each of the following cases, that is to say—

(*a*) where the enforcing authority considers it necessary to do anything itself by way of remediation for the purpose of preventing the occurrence of any serious harm, or serious pollution of controlled waters, of which there is imminent danger;

(*b*) where an appropriate person has entered into a written agreement with the enforcing authority for that authority to do, at the cost of that person, that which he would otherwise be required to do under this Part by way of remediation;

(*c*) where a person on whom the enforcing authority serves a remediation notice fails to comply with any of the requirements of the notice;

(*d*) where the enforcing authority is precluded by section 78J or 78K above from including something by way of remediation in a remediation notice;

(*e*) where the enforcing authority considers that, were it to do some particular thing by way of remediation, it would decide, by virtue of subsection (2) of section 78P below or any guidance issued under that subsection,—

(i) not to seek to recover under subsection (1) of that section any of the reasonable cost incurred by it in doing that thing; or

(ii) to seek so to recover only a portion of that cost;

(*f*) where no person has, after reasonable inquiry, been found who is an appropriate person in relation to any particular thing.

(4) Subject to section 78E(4) and (5) above, for the purposes of this section, the things which it is appropriate for the enforcing authority to do by way of remediation are—

(*a*) in a case falling within paragraph (*a*) of subsection (3) above, anything by way of remediation which the enforcing authority considers necessary for the purpose mentioned in that paragraph;

(*b*) in a case falling within paragraph (*b*) of that subsection, anything specified in, or determined under, the agreement mentioned in that paragraph;

(*c*) in a case falling within paragraph (*c*) of that subsection, anything which the person mentioned in that paragraph was required to do by virtue of the remediation notice;

(*d*) in a case falling within paragraph (*d*) of that subsection, anything by way of remediation which the enforcing authority is precluded by section 78J or 78K above from including in a remediation notice;

(*e*) in a case falling within paragraph (*e*) or (*f*) of that subsection, the particular thing mentioned in the paragraph in question.

(5) In this section "the relevant land or waters" means—

(*a*) the contaminated land in question;

(*b*) any controlled waters affected by that land; or

(*c*) any land adjoining or adjacent to that land or those waters.

[Environmental Protection Act 1990, s 78N as inserted by the Environment Act 1995, s 57.]

7.10054 **78P.** *Recovery of, and security for, the cost of remediation by the enforcing authority.*

7.10055 **78Q. Special sites** (1) If, in a case where a local authority has served a remediation notice, the contaminated land in question becomes a special site, the appropriate Agency may adopt the remediation notice and, if it does so,—

(*a*) it shall give notice of its decision to adopt the remediation notice to the appropriate person and to the local authority;

(*b*) the remediation notice shall have effect, as from the time at which the appropriate Agency decides to adopt it, as a remediation notice given by that Agency; and

(*c*) the validity of the remediation notice shall not be affected by—

(i) the contaminated land having become a special site;

(ii) the adoption of the remediation notice by the appropriate Agency; or

(iii) anything in paragraph (*b*) above.

(2) Where a local authority has, by virtue of section 78N above, begun to do anything, or any series of things, by way of remediation—

(*a*) the authority may continue doing that thing, or that series of things, by virtue of that section, notwithstanding that the contaminated land in question becomes a special site; and

(*b*) section 78P above shall apply in relation to the reasonable cost incurred by the authority in doing that thing or those things as if that authority were the enforcing authority.

(3) If and so long as any land is a special site, the appropriate Agency may from time to time inspect that land for the purpose of keeping its condition under review.

(4) If it appears to the appropriate Agency that a special site is no longer land which is required to be designated as such a site, the appropriate Agency may give notice—

(*a*) to the Secretary of State, and

(*b*) to the local authority in whose area the site is situated,

terminating the designation of the land in question as a special site as from such date as may be specified in the notice.

(5) A notice under subsection (4) above shall not prevent the land, or any of the land, to which the notice relates being designated as a special site on a subsequent occasion.

(6) In exercising its functions under subsection (3) or (4) above; the appropriate Agency shall act in accordance with any guidance given for the purpose by the Secretary of State.

[Environmental Protection Act 1990, s 78Q as inserted by the Environment Act 1995, s 57.]

**7.10056 78R. Registers** (1) Every enforcing authority shall maintain a register containing prescribed particulars of or relating to—

(*a*) remediation notices served by that authority;

(*b*) appeals against any such remediation notices;

(*c*) remediation statements or remediation declarations prepared and published under section 78H above;

(*d*) in relation to an enforcing authority in England and Wales, appeals against charging notices served by that authority;

(*e*) notices under subsection (1)(*b*) or (5)(*a*) of section 78C above which have effect by virtue of subsection (7) of that section as the designation of any land as a special site;

(*f*) notices under subsection (4)(*b*) of section 78D above which have effect by virtue of subsection (6) of that section as the designation of any land as a special site;

(*g*) notices given by or to the enforcing authority under section 78Q(4) above terminating the designation of any land as a special site;

(*h*) notifications given to that authority by persons—

(i) on whom a remediation notice has been served, or

(ii) who are or were required by virtue of section 78H(8)(*a*) above to prepare and publish a remediation statement,

of what they claim has been done by them by way of remediation;

(*j*) notifications given to that authority by owners or occupiers of land—

(i) in respect of which a remediation notice has been served, or

(ii) in respect of which a remediation statement has been prepared and published.

of what they claim has been done on the land in question by way of remediation;

(*k*) convictions for such offences under section 78M above as may be prescribed;

(*l*) such other matters relating to contaminated land as may be prescribed;

but that duty is subject to section 78S and 78T below.

(2) The form of, and the descriptions of information to be contained in, notifications for the purposes of subsection (1)(*h*) or (*j*) above may be prescribed by the Secretary of State.

(3) No entry made in a register by virtue of subsection (1)(*h*) or (*j*) above constitutes a representation by the body maintaining the register or, in a case where the entry is made by virtue of subsection (6) below, the authority which sent the copy of the particulars in question pursuant to subsection (4) or (5) below—

(*a*) that what is stated in the entry to have been done has in fact been done; or

(*b*) as to the manner in which it has been done.

(4) Where any particulars are entered on a register maintained under this section by the appropriate Agency, the appropriate Agency shall send a copy of those particulars to the local authority in whose area is situated the land to which the particulars relate.

(5) In any case where—

(*a*) any land is treated by virtue of section 78X(2) below as situated in the area of a local authority other than the local authority in whose area it is in fact situated, and (*b*) any particulars relating to that land are entered on the register maintained under this section by the local authority in whose area the land is so treated as situated,

that authority shall send a copy of those particulars to the local authority in whose area the land is in fact situated.

(6) Where a local authority receives a copy of any particulars sent to it pursuant to subsection (4) or (5) above, it shall enter those particulars on the register maintained by it under this section.

(7) Where information of any description is excluded by virtue of section 78T below from any register maintained under this section, a statement shall be entered in the register indicating the existence of information of that description.

(8) It shall be the duty of each enforcing authority—

(*a*) to secure that the registers maintained by it under this section are available, at all reasonable times, for inspection by the public free of charge; and

(*b*) to afford to members of the public facilities for obtaining copies of entries, on payment of reasonable charges;

and, for the purposes of this subsection, places may be prescribed by the Secretary of State at which any such registers or facilities as are mentioned in paragraph (*a*) or (*b*) above are to be available or afforded to the public in pursuance of the paragraph in question.

(9) Registers under this section may be kept in any form.

[Environmental Protection Act 1990, s 78R as inserted by the Environment Act 1995, s 57.]

**7.10057 78X. Supplementary provisions** (1) Where it appears to a local authority that two or more different sites, when considered together, are in such a condition, by reason of substances in, on or under the land, that—

(*a*) significant harm is being caused or there is a significant possibility of such harm being caused, or

(*b*) significant pollution of controlled waters, is being caused, or there is a significant possibility of such pollution being caused,

this Part shall apply in relation to each of those sites, whether or not the condition of the land at any of them, when considered alone, appears to the authority to be such that significant harm or significant pollution of controlled waters, is being caused, or there is a significant possibility of such harm or pollution being caused.

(2) Where it appears to a local authority that any land outside, but adjoining or adjacent to, its area is in such a condition, by reason of substances in, on or under the land, that significant harm, or significant pollution of controlled waters, is being caused, or there is a significant possibility of such harm or pollution being caused within its area—

(*a*) the authority may, in exercising its functions under this Part, treat that land as if it were land situated within its area; and

(*b*) except in this subsection, any reference—

(i) to land within the area of a local authority, or

(ii) to the local authority in whose area any land is situated,

shall be construed accordingly;

but this subsection is without prejudice to the functions of the local authority in whose area the land is in fact situated.

(3) A person acting in a relevant capacity—

(*a*) shall not thereby be personally liable, under this Part, to bear the whole or any part of the cost of doing any thing by way of remediation, unless that thing is to any extent referable to substances whose presence in, on or under the contaminated land in question is a result of any act done or omission made by him which it was unreasonable for a person acting in that capacity to do or make; and

(*b*) shall not thereby be guilty of an offence under or by virtue of section 78M above unless the requirement which has not been complied with is a requirement to do some particular thing for which he is personally liable to bear the whole or any part of the cost.

(4) In subsection (3) above, "person acting in a relevant capacity" means—

(*a*) a person acting as an insolvency practitioner, within the meaning of section 388 of the Insolvency Act 1986 (including that section as it applies in relation to an insolvent partnership by virtue of any order made under section 421 of that Act);

(*b*) the official receiver acting in a capacity in which he would be regarded as acting as an insolvency practitioner within the meaning of section 388 of the Insolvency Act 1986 if subsection (5) of that section were disregarded;

(*c*) the official receiver acting as receiver or manager;

(*d*) a person acting as a special manager under section 177 or 370 of the Insolvency Act 1986;

(*e*) the Accountant in Bankruptcy acting as permanent or interim trustee in a sequestration (within the meaning of the Bankruptcy (Scotland) Act 1985);

(*f*) a person acting as a receiver or receiver and manager—

(i) under or by virtue of any enactment; or

(ii) by virtue of his appointment as such by an order of a court or by any other instrument.

(5) Regulations may make different provision for different cases or circumstances.

[Environmental Protection Act 1990, s 78X as inserted by the Environment Act 1995, s 57 and amended by the Water Act 2003, s 86.]

7.10058 **78Y. Application to the Isles of Scilly** (1) Subject to the provisions of any order under this section, this Part shall not apply in relation to the Isles of Scilly.

(2) The Secretary of State may, after consultation with the Council of the Isles of Scilly, by order provide for the application of any provisions of this Part to the Isles of Scilly; and any such order may provide for the application of those provisions to those Isles with such modifications as may be specified in the order[1].

(3) An order under this section may—

(*a*) make different provision for different cases, including different provision in relation to different persons, circumstances or localities; and

(*b*) contain such supplemental, consequential and transitional provision as the Secretary of State considers appropriate, including provision saving provision repealed by or under any enactment.

[Environmental Protection Act 1990, s 78Y as inserted by the Environment Act 1995, s 57.]

---

1 The Environmental Protection Act 1990 (Isles of Scilly) Order 2006, SI 2006/1381 has been made.

7.10059 **78YB. Interaction of this Part with other enactments** (1) A remediation notice shall not be served if and to the extent that it appears to the enforcing authority that the powers of the appropriate Agency under section 27 above may be exercised in relation to—

(*a*) the significant harm (if any), and

(*b*) the significant pollution of controlled waters (if any),

by reason of which the contaminated land in question is such land.

(2) Nothing in this Part shall apply in relation to any land in respect of which there is for the time being in force a site licence under Part II above, except to the extent that any significant harm, or significant pollution of controlled waters, by reason of which that land would otherwise fall to be regarded as contaminated land is attributable to causes other than—

(*a*) breach of the conditions of the licence; or

(*b*) the carrying on in accordance with the conditions of the licence, of any activity authorised by the licence.

(2A) This Part shall not apply if and to the extent that—

(*a*) any significant harm, or pollution of controlled waters, by reason of which the land would otherwise fall to be regarded as contaminated, is attributable to the final disposal by deposit in or on land of controlled waste, and

(*b*) enforcement action may be taken in relation to that disposal.

(2B) A remediation notice shall not be served in respect of contaminated land if and to the extent that—

(*a*) the significant harm, or pollution of controlled waters, by reason of which the contaminated land is such land is attributable to an activity other than the final disposal by deposit in or on land of controlled waste, and

(*b*) enforcement action may be taken in relation to that activity.

(2C) In subsections (2A) and (2B) above—

"controlled waste" has the meaning given in section 75(4) of this Act; and

"enforcement action" means action under regulation 24 (enforcement notices) or regulation 26(2)(power of regulator to remedy pollution) of the Pollution Prevention and Control (England and Wales) Regulations 2000.

(3) If, in a case falling within subsection (1) or (7) of section 59 above, the land in question is contaminated land, or becomes such land by reason of the deposit of the controlled waste in question, a remediation notice shall not be served in respect of that land by reason of that waste or any consequences of its deposit, if and to the extent that it appears to the enforcing authority that the powers of a waste regulation authority or waste collection authority under that section may be exercised in relation to that waste or the consequences of its deposit.

(4) No remediation notice shall require a person to do anything the effect of which would be to impede or prevent the making of a discharge in pursuance of an environmental permit or, in relation to Scotland, in pursuance of a consent given under Part II of the Control of Pollution Act 1974.

(5) In this section—

"enforcement action" means action under regulation 36, 37 or 42 of the Environmental Permitting (England and Wales) Regulations 2010;

"regulated facility" has the meaning given in regulation 8 of those Regulations.

[Environmental Protection Act 1990, s 78YB as inserted by the Environment Act 1995, s 57 and amended by SI 2000/1973, the Water Act 2003, s 86, SI 2007/3538 and SI 2010/675.]

7.10060 **78YC. This Part and radioactivity** Except as provided by regulations, nothing in this Part applies in relation to harm, or pollution of controlled waters, so far as attributable to any radioactivity possessed by any substance; but regulations[1] may—

(a) provide for prescribed provisions of this Part to have effect with such modifications as the Secretary of State considers appropriate for the purpose of dealing with harm, or pollution of controlled waters, so far as attributable to any radioactivity possessed by any substances; or

(b) make such modifications of the Environmental Permitting (England and Wales) Regulations 2010 or any Act or other enactment as the Secretary of State considers appropriate.

[Environmental Protection Act 1990, s 78YC as inserted by the Environment Act 1995, s 57 and amended by SI 2010/675.]

1 The Radio-active Contaminated Land (Enabling Powers) (England) Regulations 2005, SI 2005/3467 amended by SI 2010/2147, the Radioactive Contaminated Land (Modifications of Enactments) (England) Regulations 2006, SI 2006/1379 amended by SI 2007/3245, SI 2008/520, SI 2010/2147 and SI 2016/1154 and the Radioactive Contaminated Land (Modification of Enactments) (Wales) Regulations 2006, SI 2006/2988 amended by SI 2007/3250, SI 2008/521, SI 2010/2146 and SI 2016/1154 have been made.

## Part III[1]

## Statutory Nuisances and Clean Air

### *Statutory nuisances*

7.10061 79. **Statutory nuisances and inspection therefor**[2] (1) Subject to subsections (1A) to (6A) below, the following matters constitute "statutory nuisances" for the purposes of this Part, that is to say—

(a) any premises in such a state as to be prejudicial to health[3] or a nuisance;

(b) smoke emitted from premises so as to be prejudicial to health or a nuisance;

(c) fumes or gases emitted from premises so as to be prejudicial to health or a nuisance;

(d) any dust, steam, smell or other effluvia arising on industrial, trade or business premises and being prejudicial to health or a nuisance;

(e) any accumulation or deposit which is prejudicial to health or a nuisance;

(f) any animal kept in such a place or manner as to be prejudicial to health or a nuisance;

(fa) any insects emanating from relevant industrial, trade or business premises and being prejudicial to health or a nuisance;

(fb) artificial light emitted from premises so as to be prejudicial to health or a nuisance;

(g) noise[4] emitted from premises so as to be prejudicial to health or a nuisance;

(ga) noise that is prejudicial to health or a nuisance and is emitted from or caused by a vehicle, machinery or equipment in a street or in Scotland, road;

(h) any other matter declared by any enactment to be a statutory nuisance;

and it shall be the duty of every local authority to cause its area to be inspected from time to time to detect any statutory nuisances which ought to be dealt with under section 80 below or sections 80 and 80A below and, where a complaint of a statutory nuisance is made to it by a person living within its area, to take such steps as are reasonably practicable to investigate the complaint.

(1A) No matter shall constitute a statutory nuisance to the extent that it consists of, or is caused by, any land being in a contaminated state.

(1B) Land is in a "contaminated state" for the purposes of subsection (1A) above if, and only if, it is in such a condition, by reason of substances in, on or under the land, that—

(a) harm is being caused or there is a possibility of harm being caused; or

(b) pollution of controlled waters is being, or is likely to be, caused;

and in this subsection "harm", "pollution of controlled waters" and "substance" have the same meaning as in Part IIA of this Act.

(2) Subsection (1)(b), (fb) and (g) above do not apply in relation to premises—

(a) occupied on behalf of the Crown for naval, military or air force purposes or for the purposes of the department of the Secretary of State having responsibility for defence, or

(b) occupied by or for the purposes of a visiting force;

and "visiting force" means any such body, contingent or detachment of the forces of any country as is a visiting force for the purposes of any of the provisions of the Visiting Forces Act 1952.

(3) Subsection (1)(b) above does not apply to—

(i) smoke emitted from a chimney of a private dwelling within a smoke control area,

(ii) dark smoke emitted from a chimney of a building or a chimney serving the furnace of a boiler or industrial plant attached to a building or for the time being fixed to or installed on any land,

(iii) smoke emitted from a railway locomotive steam engine, or

(iv) dark smoke emitted otherwise than as mentioned above from industrial or trade premises.

(4) Subsection (1)(c) above does not apply in relation to premises other than private dwellings.

(5) Subsection (1)(d) above does not apply to steam emitted from a railway locomotive engine.

(5A) Subsection (1)(fa) does not apply to insects that are wild animals included in Schedule 5 to the Wildlife and Countryside Act 1981 (animals which are protected), unless they are included in respect of section 9(5) of that Act only.

(5B) Subsection (1)(*fb*) does not apply to artificial light emitted from—

(*a*) an airport;

(*b*) harbour premises;

(*c*) railway premises, not being relevant separate railway premises;

(*d*) tramway premises;

(*e*) a bus station and any associated facilities;

(*f*) a public service vehicle operating centre;

(*g*) a goods vehicle operating centre;

(*h*) a lighthouse;

(*i*) a prison.

(6) Subsection (1)(*g*) above does not apply to noise caused by aircraft other than model aircraft.

(6A) Subsection (1)(*ga*) above does not apply to noise made—

(*a*) by traffic,

(*b*) by any naval, military or air force of the Crown or by a visiting force (as defined in subsection (2) above), or

(*c*) by a political demonstration or a demonstration supporting or opposing a cause or campaign.

(7) In this Part—

"airport" has the meaning given by section 95 of the Transport Act 2000;

"appropriate person" means—

(*a*) in relation to England, the Secretary of State;

(*b*) in relation to Wales, the National Assembly for Wales;

"associated facilities", in relation to a bus station, has the meaning given by section 83 of the Transport Act 1985;

"bus station" has the meaning given by section 83 of the Transport Act 1985;

"chimney" includes structures and openings of any kind from or through which smoke may be emitted;

"dust" does not include dust emitted from a chimney as an ingredient of smoke;

"equipment" includes a musical instrument;

"fumes" means any airborne solid matter smaller than dust;

"gas" includes vapour and moisture precipitated from vapour;

"goods vehicle operating centre", in relation to vehicles used under an operator's licence, means a place which is specified in the licence as an operating centre for those vehicles, and for the purposes of this definition "operating centre" and "operator's licence" have the same meaning as in the Goods Vehicles (Licensing of Operators) Act 1995;

"harbour premises" means premises which form part of a harbour area and which are occupied wholly or mainly for the purposes of harbour operations, and for the purposes of this definition "harbour area" and "harbour operations" have the same meaning as in Part 3 of the Aviation and Maritime Security Act 1990;

"industrial, trade or business premises" means premises used for any industrial, trade or business purposes or premises not so used on which matter is burnt in connection with any industrial, trade or business process, and premises are used for industrial purposes where they are used for the purposes of any treatment or process as well as where they are used for the purposes of manufacturing[5];

"lighthouse" has the same meaning as in Part 8 of the Merchant Shipping Act 1995;

"local authority" means, subject to subsection (8) below,—

(*a*) in Greater London, a London borough council, the Common Council of the City of London and, as respects the Temples, the Sub-Treasurer of the Inner Temple and the Under-Treasurer of the Middle Temple respectively;

(*b*) in England and Wales outside Greater London, a district council in England;

(*bb*) in Wales, a county council or county borough council;

(*c*) the Council of the Isles of Scilly; and

(*d*) *Scotland*;

"noise" includes vibration;

"person responsible—

(*a*) in relation to a statutory nuisance, means the person to whose act, default or sufferance the nuisance is attributable;

(*b*) in relation to a vehicle, includes the person in whose name the vehicle is for the time being registered under the Vehicles Excise and Registration Act 1994 and any other person who is for the time being the driver of the vehicle;

(*c*) in relation to machinery or equipment, includes any person who is for the time being the operator of the machinery or equipment;

"prejudicial to health" means injurious, or likely to cause injury, to health[6];

"premises" includes land and, in relation to England and Wales, subject to subsection (12) and section 81A(9) below, any vessel;

"prison" includes a young offender institution;

"private dwelling" means any building, or part of a building, used or intended to be used, as a dwelling;

"public service vehicle operating centre", in relation to public service vehicles used under a PSV operator's licence, means a place which is an operating centre of those vehicles, and for the purposes of this definition "operating centre", "PSV operator's licence" and "public service vehicle" have the same meaning as in the Public Passenger Vehicles Act 1981;
"railway premises" means any premises which fall within the definition of "light maintenance depot", "network", "station" or "track" in section 83 of the Railways Act 1993;
"relevant separate railway premises" has the meaning given by subsection (7A);
"road" has the same meaning as in Part IV of the New Roads and Street Works Act 1991;
"smoke" includes soot, ash, grit and gritty particles emitted in smoke[7];
"street" means a highway and any other road, footway, square or court that is for the time being open to the public;
"tramway premises" means any premises which, in relation to a tramway, are the equivalent of the premises which, in relation to a railway, fall within the definition of "light maintenance depot", "network", "station" or "track" in section 83 of the Railways Act 1993;
and any expression used in this section and in the Clean Air Act 1993 have the same meaning in this section as in that Act and section 3 of the Clean Air Act 1993 shall apply for the interpretation of the expression "dark smoke" and the operation of this Part in relation to it.

(7A) Railway premises are relevant separate railway premises if—
- (*a*) they are situated within—
  - (i) premises used as a museum or other place of cultural, scientific or historical interest, or
  - (ii) premises used for the purposes of a funfair or other entertainment, recreation or amusement, and
- (*b*) they are not associated with any other railway premises.

(7B) For the purposes of subsection (7A)—
- (*a*) a network situated as described in subsection (7A)(*a*) is associated with other railway premises if it is connected to another network (not being a network situated as described in subsection (7A)(*a*));
- (*b*) track that is situated as described in subsection (7A)(*a*) but is not part of a network is associated with other railway premises if it is connected to track that forms part of a network (not being a network situated as described in subsection (7A)(*a*));
- (*c*) a station or light maintenance depot situated as described in subsection (7A)(*a*) is associated with other railway premises if it is used in connection with the provision of railway services other than services provided wholly within the premises where it is situated.

In this subsection "light maintenance depot", "network", "railway services", "station" and "track" have the same meaning as in Part 1 of the Railways Act 1993.

(7C) In this Part "relevant industrial, trade or business premises" means premises that are industrial, trade or business premises as defined in subsection (7), but excluding—
- (*a*) land used as arable, grazing, meadow or pasture land,
- (*b*) land used as osier land, reed beds or woodland,
- (*c*) land used for market gardens, nursery grounds or orchards,
- (*d*) land forming part of an agricultural unit, not being land falling within any of paragraphs (*a*) to (*c*), where the land is of a description prescribed by regulations[8] made by the appropriate person, and
- (*e*) land included in a site of special scientific interest (as defined in section 52(1) of the Wildlife and Countryside Act 1981),

and excluding land covered by, and the waters of, any river or watercourse, that is neither a sewer nor a drain, or any lake or pond.

(7D) For the purposes of subsection (7C)—
"agricultural" has the same meaning as in section 109 of the Agriculture Act 1947;
"agricultural unit" means land which is occupied as a unit for agricultural purposes;
"drain" has the same meaning as in the Water Resources Act 1991;
"lake or pond" has the same meaning as in section 104 of that Act;
"sewer" has the same meaning as in that Act.

(8) Where, by an order under section 2 of the Public Health (Control of Disease) Act 1984, a port health authority has been constituted for any port health district or in Scotland where by an order under section 172 of the Public Health (Scotland) Act 1897 a port local authority or a joint port local authority has been constituted for the whole or part of a port, the port health authority, port local authority or joint port local authority, as the case may be shall have by virtue of this subsection, as respects its district, the functions conferred or imposed by this Part in relation to statutory nuisance other than a nuisance falling within paragraph *(fb)*, (*g*) or (*ga*) of subsection (1) above and no such order shall be made assigning those functions; and "local authority" and "area" shall be construed accordingly.

(9) In this Part "best practicable means" is to be interpreted by reference to the following provisions—
- (*a*) "practicable" means reasonably practicable having regard among other things to local conditions and circumstances, to the current state of technical knowledge and to the financial implications;

(*b*) the means to be employed include the design, installation, maintenance and manner and periods of operation of plant and machinery, and the design, construction and maintenance of buildings and structures;

(*c*) the test is to apply only so far as compatible with any duty imposed by law;

(*d*) the test is to apply only so far as compatible with safety and safe working conditions, and with the exigencies of any emergency or unforseeable circumstances;

and, in circumstances where a code of practice under section 71 of the Control of Pollution Act 1974 (noise minimisation) is applicable, regard shall also be had to guidance given in it.

(10) A local authority shall not without the consent of the Secretary of State institute summary proceedings under this Part in respect of a nuisance falling within paragraph (*b*), (*d*), (*e*), (*fb*) or (*g*) and, in relation to Scotland, paragraph (*ga*), of subsection (1) above if proceedings in respect thereof might be instituted under Part I or under regulations under section 2 of the Pollution Prevention and Control Act 1999.

(11) The area of a local authority which includes part of the seashore shall also include for the purposes of this Part the territorial sea lying seawards from that part of the shore; and subject to subsection (12) and, in relation to England and Wales section 81A(9) below, this Part shall have effect, in relation to any area included in the area of a local authority by virtue of this subsection—

(*a*) as if references to premises and the occupier of premises included respectively a vessel and the master of a vessel; and

(*b*) with such other modifications, if any, as are prescribed in regulations made by the Secretary of State.

(12) A vessel powered by steam reciprocating machinery is not a vessel to which this Part of this Act applies.

[Environmental Protection Act 1990, s 79 as amended by Sch 16 to that Act, the Clean Air Act 1993, Sch 4, the Noise and Statutory Nuisance Act 1993, ss 2 and 10, the Local Government (Wales) Act 1994, Sch 9, the Vehicle Excise and Registration Act 1994, Sch 3, the Environment Act 1995, Sch 17, the Pollution Prevention and Control Act 1999, Schs 2 and 3, SI 2000/1973 and the Clean Neighbourhoods and Environment Act 2005, ss 101 and 102.]

---

1 Part III consists of ss 79–85.

2 The application of this section to London Boroughs is modified by the London Local Authorities Act 1996, s 24 in this PART: title LONDON, ante.

3 The expressions "prejudicial to health" and "injurious or likely to cause injury to health" are aimed at the effect on people's health of filthy or unwholesome premises and the like: in particular, the risk of disease or illness. There is nothing in s 79 to suggest that the powers were intended to protect against the danger of accidental physical injury; accordingly, premises that are in such a state as to create the likelihood of accident causing personal injury are not as a matter of law capable of giving rise to a statutory nuisance within s 79 (1)(*a*) (*R v Bristol City Council, ex p Everett* [1999] 2 All ER 193, [1999] 1 WLR 1170, CA). The powers in this provision do not extend to a lack of adequate sound insulation for which there is a separate statutory code under which local authorities have express powers and, in serious cases, duties to deal with sound insulation (*R (Vella) v Lambeth Borough Council* [2005] TLR 533, QBD).

The powers in this section are directed to the presence of some feature which in itself is prejudicial to health in that it is the source of possible infection or disease or illness such as dampness, mould, dirt or evil-smelling accumulations or the presence of rats. They do not extend to the arrangement of rooms otherwise not in themselves insanitary so as to be prejudicial to health, such as where the nearest facility for washing hands after use of a lavatory required access through kitchen or use of the kitchen sink (*Birmingham City Council v Oakley* [2001] 1 All ER 385, [2000] 3 WLR 1936, HL).

Evidence given by experts about the condition of premises is sufficient by itself, in the absence of evidence relating to the health and medical condition of the tenant, to establish a prima facie case that premises were prejudicial to health and a statutory nuisance (*O'Toole v Knowsley Metropolitan Borough Council* [1999] LS Gaz R 36).

Traffic noise from vehicles, machinery or equipment in the street which renders premises to be in such a state as to be prejudicial to health or a nuisance does not constitute a statutory nuisance within the meaning of s 79(1)(*a*) because s 79(1)(*ga*) subject to the limitations in s 79(6A), deals directly with vehicle noise (*Haringey London Borough Council v Jowett* (1999) 78 P & CR D24, [1999] EGCS 64).

4 It is wrong for justices to refuse to convict of an offence under s 80(4) and (5) merely on the basis that no reliable acoustic measurement evidence has been adduced; however, where the evidence of the environmental enforcement officer is that the nuisance was "marginal" justices are perfectly entitled to say that they are not sure and to acquit (*Lewisham Borough Council v Hall* [2002] EWHC 960 (Admin), [2002] All ER (D) 83 (May), [2002] JPN 378.

5 This definition includes a sewage treatment works (*Hounslow London Borough Council v Thames Water Utilities Ltd* [2003] EWHC 1197 (Admin), [2004] QB 212, [2003] 3 WLR 1243.

6 See note 3 ante.

7 Whilst "smoke" has a primary meaning of "the visible volatile product given off by burning or smouldering substance" the term can also be applied to the smell of smoke (*Griffiths v Pembrokeshire County Council* [2000] 18 LS Gaz R 36, DC).

8 The Statutory Nuisance (Insects) Regulations 2006, SI 2006/770 and the Statutory Nuisances (Miscellaneous Provisions) (Wales) Regulations 2007, SI 2007/117 have been made.

**7.10062 80. Summary proceedings for statutory nuisances** (1) Subject to subsection (2A) where a local authority is satisfied that a statutory nuisance exists, or is likely to occur or recur, in the area of the authority, the local authority shall serve a notice[1] ("an abatement notice") imposing all or any of the following requirements—

(*a*) requiring the abatement of the nuisance of prohibiting or restricting its occurrence or recurrence;

(*b*) requiring the execution of such works, and the taking of such other steps, as may be necessary for any of those purposes,

and the notice shall specify the time or times within[2] which the requirements of the notice are to be complied with.

(2) Subject to section 80A(1) below, the abatement notice shall be served[3]—

(*a*) except in a case falling within paragraph (*b*) or (*c*) below, on the person responsible for the nuisance;

(*b*) where the nuisance arises from any defect of a structural character, on the owner[4] of the premises;

(*c*) where the person responsible for the nuisance cannot be found or the nuisance has not yet occurred, on the owner or occupier of the premises.

(2A) Where a local authority is satisfied that a statutory nuisance falling within paragraph (*g*) of section 79(1) above exists, or is likely to occur or recur, in the area of the authority, the authority shall—

(*a*) serve an abatement notice in respect of the nuisance in accordance with subsections (1) and (2) above; or

(*b*) take such other steps as it thinks appropriate for the purpose of persuading the appropriate person to abate the nuisance or prohibit or restrict its occurrence or recurrence.

(2B) If a local authority has taken steps under subsection (2A)(*b*) above and either of the conditions in subsection (2C) below is satisfied, the authority shall serve an abatement notice in respect of the nuisance.

(2C) The conditions are—

(*a*) that the authority is satisfied at any time before the end of the relevant period that the steps taken will not be successful in persuading the appropriate person to abate the nuisance or prohibit or restrict its occurrence or recurrence;

(*b*) that the authority is satisfied at the end of the relevant period that the nuisance continues to exist, or continues to be likely to occur or recur, in the area of the authority.

(2D) The relevant period is the period of seven days starting with the day on which the authority was first satisfied that the nuisance existed, or was likely to occur or recur.

(2E) The appropriate person is the person on whom the authority would otherwise be required under subsection (2A)(*a*) above to serve an abatement notice in respect of the nuisance.

(3) A person served with an abatement notice may appeal[5] against the notice to a magistrates' court or in Scotland, the sheriff within the period of twenty-one days beginning with the date on which he was served with the notice.

(4) If a person on whom an abatement notice[6] is served, without reasonable excuse[7], contravenes[8] or fails to comply with any requirement or prohibition imposed by the notice, he shall be guilty of an offence[9].

(5) Except in a case falling within subsection (6) below, a person who commits an offence under subsection (4) above shall be liable on summary conviction to a fine not exceeding **level 5** on the standard scale together with a further fine of an amount equal to one-tenth of the greater of £5,000 or level 4 on the standard scale for each day on which the offence continues after the conviction.

(6) A person who commits an offence under subsection (4) above on industrial, trade or business premises shall be liable on summary conviction to a fine.

(7) Subject to subsection (8) below, in any proceedings for an offence under subsection (4) above in respect of a statutory nuisance it shall be a defence to prove that the best practicable means[10] were used to prevent, or to counteract the effects of, the nuisance.

(8) The defence under subsection (7) above is not available—

(*a*) in the case of a nuisance falling within paragraph (*a*), (*d*), (*e*), (*f*), (*fa*) or (*g*) of section 79(1) above except where the nuisance arises on industrial, trade or business premises;

(*aza*) in the case of a nuisance falling within paragraph (*fb*) of section 79(1) above except where—

(i) the artificial light is emitted from industrial, trade or business premises, or

(ii) the artificial light (not being light to which sub-paragraph (i) applies) is emitted by lights used for the purpose only of illuminating an outdoor relevant sports facility;

(*aa*) in the case of a nuisance falling within paragraph (*ga*) of section 79(1) above except where the noise is emitted from or caused by a vehicle, machinery or equipment being used for industrial, trade or business purposes;

(*b*) in the case of a nuisance falling within paragraph (*b*) of section 79(1) above except where the smoke is emitted from a chimney; and

(*c*) in the case of a nuisance falling within paragraph (*c*) or (*h*) of section 79(1) above.

(8A) For the purposes of subsection (8)(*aza*) a relevant sports facility is an area, with or without structures, that is used when participating in a relevant sport, but does not include such an area comprised in domestic premises.

(8B) For the purposes of subsection (8A) "relevant sport" means a sport that is designated for those purposes by order[11] made by the Secretary of State, in relation to England, or the National Assembly for Wales, in relation to Wales.

A sport may be so designated by reference to its appearing in a list maintained by a body specified in the order.

(8C) In subsection (8A) "domestic premises" means—

(*a*) premises used wholly or mainly as a private dwelling, or

(*b*) land or other premises belonging to, or enjoyed with, premises so used.

(9) In proceedings for an offence under subsection (4) above in respect of a statutory nuisance

falling within paragraph (*g*) or (*ga*) of section 79(1) above where the offence consists in contravening requirements imposed by virtue of subsection (1)(*a*) above it shall be a defence to prove—

(*a*) that the alleged offence was covered by a notice served under section 60 or a consent given under section 61 or 65 of the Control of Pollution Act 1974 (construction sites, etc); or

(*b*) where the alleged offence was committed at a time when the premises were subject to a notice under section 66 of that Act (noise reduction notice), that the level of noise emitted from the premises at that time was not such as to constitute a contravention of the notice under that section; or

(*c*) where the alleged offence was committed at a time when the premises were not subject to a notice under section 66 of that Act, and when a level fixed under section 67 of that Act (new buildings liable to abatement order) applied to the premises, that the level of noise emitted from the premises at that time did not exceed that level.

(10) Paragraphs (*b*) and (*c*) of subsection (9) above apply whether or not the relevant notice was subject to appeal at the time when the offence was alleged to have been committed.

[Environmental Protection Act 1990, s 80 as amended by the Noise and Statutory Nuisance Act 1993, s 3, the Environment Act 1995, Sch 17, the Clean Neighbourhoods and Environment Act 2005, ss 86, 103 and SI 2015/664.]

---

1 An abatement notice must inform the person on whom it is served the nature of the nuisance complained of, but it need not specify the works or other steps to be taken to abate the nuisance. In all cases the local authority has a discretion to leave the choice of means of abatement to the perpetrator of the nuisance. If, however, the means of abatement are required by the local authority, then they must be specified in the notice (*R v Falmouth and Truro Port Health Authority, ex p South West Water Ltd* [2001] QB 445, [2000] 3 All ER 306, [2000] 3 WLR 1464, CA).

The local authority has an implied power to withdraw an abatement notice after it has been served (*R v Bristol City Council, ex p Everett* [1999] 2 All ER 193, [1999] 1 WLR 1170, CA). However, a local authority is entitled to serve a notice simply requiring the recipient to abate a nuisance created by barking dogs without specifying the manner of abatement or the level of barking, either which constituted the nuisance or the level of barking which would be acceptable (*Budd v Colchester Borough Council* (1999) 97 LGR 601).

2 In relation to a similarly worded provision in the predecessor to this section, namely s 58(1) of the Control of Pollution Act 1974, it was held that the notice must specify a period within which a nuisance is to be abated or within which works are to be executed or other steps taken, but the notice does not have to state a period within which a prohibition on recurrence has to be complied with (*R v Birmingham City Justices, ex p Guppy* (1987) 86 LGR 264, 152 JP 159) and see *R v Tunbridge Wells Justices, ex p Tunbridge Wells Borough Council* (1995) 160 JP 574, DC.

3 For service of notices, see s 160, post.

4 The word "owner" includes a managing agent who receives rack rent for the premises (*Camden London Borough Council v Gunby* [1999] 4 All ER 602, [2000] 1 WLR 465, DC).

5 For further provisions with respect to such an appeal, see s 81 and Sch 3, post, and the Statutory Nuisance (Appeals) Regulations 1995, this title, post. In deciding whether a statutory nuisance exists, the decision is that of the court which is not obliged to accept the evidence of a witness, expert or otherwise, even if unchallenged (*Hackney London Borough Council v Rottenberg* (2007) Times, 9 February, DC).

In considering the validity of a noise abatement notice served by a local authority under s 80, a magistrates' court or the Crown Court on appeal are required to consider the facts at the time the notice was served and not at the time of the appeal (*SFI Group plc (formerly Surrey Free Inns plc) v Gosport Borough Council* [1999] EGCS 51, CA).

6 The effectiveness of a notice served under the repealed Control of Pollution Act 1974, s 58(1) is preserved by the Interpretation Act 1978, s 16(1) and may be enforced under s 58(4) of the 1974 Act (*Aitken v South Hams District Council* [1995] 1 AC 262, [1994] 3 All ER 400, 159 JP 25).

7 "Reasonable excuse" does not include matters that should have been raised on an appeal under sub-s (3) challenging the validity of the notice, unless there has been some special reason for not entering an appeal (*A Lambert Flat Management Ltd v Lomas* [1981] 2 All ER 280, [1981] 1 WLR 898). Mitigating factors, such as loud reggae music playing to celebrate a birthday, do not amount to a reasonable excuse if other ingredients of a nuisance are established (*Wellingborough Borough Council v Gordon* (1990) 155 JP 494). The burden is on the prosecution to disprove reasonable excuse once raised by the defendant (as distinct from the defences in subsections (7) and (9)) (*Polychronakis v Richards and Jerrom* [1998] JPL B35, [1998] Env LR 346, DC).

8 When proving that noise amounting to a nuisance has occurred or recurred in contravention of a notice served under s 80, the prosecution need not necessarily prove that a particular occupier of property has actually suffered interference with his reasonable enjoyment of his property, but, depending on the circumstances of a particular case, may seek to rely on other evidence including expert evidence (*Cooke v Adatia* (1988) 153 JP 129).

9 Whether or not the defendant is dealt with in any other way, in the case of a noise offence, the court may make a forfeiture order in respect of any seized equipment used or alleged to have been used in the commission of the offence (Noise Act 1996, Schedule, this title, post).

A person guilty of an offence under s 80(4) is not also liable in a civil action for damages at the suit of any person who thereby suffers loss or damage (*Issa v Hackney London Borough Council* [1997] 1 WLR 956).

10 "Best practicable means" is defined in s 79(9), ante.

11 The Statutory Nuisances (Artificial Lighting) (Designation of Relevant Sports) (England) Order 2006, SI 2006/781 and the Statutory Nuisances (Miscellaneous Provisions) (Wales) Order 2007, SI 2007/120 has have been made.

**7.10063 80A. Abatement notice in respect of noise in street[1]** (1) In the case of a statutory nuisance within section 79(1)(*ga*) above that—

(*a*) has not yet occurred, or

(*b*) arises from noise emitted from or caused by an unattended vehicle or unattended machinery or equipment,

the abatement notice shall be served in accordance with subsection (2) below,

(2) The notice shall be served—

(*a*) where the person responsible for the vehicle, machinery or equipment can be found, on that person;

(*b*) where that person cannot be found or where the local authority determines that this paragraph should apply, by fixing the notice to the vehicle, machinery or equipment.

(3) Where—

(*a*) an abatement notice is served in accordance with subsection (2)(*b*) above by virtue of a determination of the local authority, and

(*b*) the person responsible for the vehicle, machinery or equipment can be found and served with a copy of the notice within an hour of the notice being fixed to the vehicle, machinery or equipment,

a copy of the notice shall be served on that person accordingly.

(4) Where an abatement notice is served in accordance with subsection (2)(*b*) above by virtue of a determination of the local authority, the notice shall state that, if a copy of the notice is subsequently served under subsection (3) above, the time specified in the notice as the time within which its requirements are to be complied with is extended by such further period as is specified in the notice.

(5) Where an abatement notice is served in accordance with subsection (2)(*b*) above, the person responsible for the vehicle, machinery or equipment may appeal against the notice under section 80(3) above as if he had been served with the notice on the date on which it was fixed to the vehicle, machinery or equipment.

(6) Section 80(4) above shall apply in relation to a person on whom a copy of an abatement notice is served under subsection (3) above as if the copy were the notice itself.

(7) A person who removes or interferes with a notice fixed to a vehicle, machinery or equipment in accordance with subsection (2)(*b*) above shall be guilty of an offence, unless he is the person responsible for the vehicle, machinery or equipment or he does so with the authority of that person.

(8) A person who commits an offence under subsection (7) above shall be liable on summary conviction to a fine not exceeding **level 3** on the standard scale.

[Environmental Protection Act 1990, s 80A as inserted by the Noise and Statutory Nuisance Act 1993, s 3.]

---

1 The application of this section to London Boroughs is modified by the London Local Authorities Act 1996, s 24 in this PART: title LONDON, ante.

7.10064 **81. Supplementary provisions** (1) Subject to subsection (1A) below, where more than one person is responsible for a statutory nuisance section 80 above shall apply to each of those persons whether or not what any one of them is responsible for would by itself amount to a nuisance.

(1A) In relation to a statutory nuisance within section 79(1)(*ga*) above for which more than one person is responsible (whether or not what any one of those persons is responsible for would by itself amount to such a nuisance), section 80(2)(*a*) above shall apply with the substitution of "any one of the persons" for "the person".

(1B) In relation to a statutory nuisance within section 79(1)(*ga*) above caused by noise emitted from or caused by an unattended vehicle or unattended machinery or equipment for which more than one person is responsible, section 80A above shall apply with the substitution—

(*a*) in subsection (2)(*a*), of "any of the persons" for "the person" and of "one such person" for "that person",

(*b*) in subsection (2)(*b*), of "such a person" for "that person",

(*c*) in subsection (3), of "any of the persons" for "the person" and of "one such person" for "that person",

(*d*) in subsection (5), of "any person" for "the person", and

(*e*) in subsection (7), of "a person;" for "the person", and of "such a person" for "that person".

(2) Where a statutory nuisance which exists or has occurred within the area of a local authority, or which has affected any part of that area, appears to the local authority to be wholly or partly caused by some act or default committed or taking place outside the area, the local authority may act under section 80 above as if the act or default were wholly within that area, except that any appeal shall be heard by a magistrates' court or in Scotland, the sheriff having jurisdiction where the act or default is alleged to have taken place.

(3) Where an abatement notice has not been complied with the local authority may, whether or not they take proceedings for an offence or, in Scotland, whether or not proceedings have been taken for an offence, under section 80(4) above, abate the nuisance and do whatever may be necessary[1] in execution of the notice.

(4) Any expenses reasonably incurred by a local authority in abating, or preventing the recurrence of, a statutory nuisance under subsection (3) above may be recovered by them from the person by whose act or default the nuisance was caused and, if that person is the owner of the premises, from any person who is for the time being the owner thereof; and the court or sheriff may apportion the expenses between persons by whose acts or defaults the nuisance is caused in such manner as the court consider or sheriff considers fair and reasonable.

(5) If a local authority is of opinion that proceedings for an offence under section 80(4) above would afford an inadequate remedy in the case of any statutory nuisance, they may, subject to subsection (6) below, take proceedings[2] in the High Court or, in Scotland, in any court of competent jurisdiction, for the purpose of securing the abatement, prohibition or restriction of the nuisance, and the proceedings shall be maintainable notwithstanding the local authority have suffered no damage from the nuisance.

(6) In any proceedings under subsection (5) above in respect of a nuisance falling within

paragraph (*g*) or (*ga*) of section 79(1) above, it shall be a defence to prove that the noise was authorised by a notice under section 60 or a consent under section 61 (construction sites) of the Control of Pollution Act 1974.

(7) The further supplementary provisions in Schedule 3 to this Act shall have effect.

[Environmental Protection Act 1990, s 81 as amended by the Noise and Statutory Nuisance Act 1993, s 4 and the Environment Act 1995, Sch 17.]

---

1 In the case of nuisance by noise, the local authority has the power to seize and remove any equipment which appears to the authority as being or has been used in the emission of the noise in question (Noise Act 1996, s 10(7), this title, post).

2 This remedy is additional to those available summarily, and a local authority may seek an injunction notwithstanding that the statutory procedure for appealing to a magistrates' court has not been exhausted (*Hammersmith London Borough Council v Magnum Automated Forecourts Ltd* [1978] 1 All ER 401, 142 JP 130).

7.10065 **82. Summary proceedings by persons aggrieved by statutory nuisances** (1) A magistrates' court may act under this section on a complaint[1] or, in Scotland, the sheriff may act under this section on a summary application made by any person on the ground that he is aggrieved by the existence of a statutory nuisance[2].

(2) If the magistrates' court or, in Scotland, the sheriff is satisfied that the alleged nuisance exists, or that although abated it is likely to recur on the same premises or, in the case of a nuisance within section 79(1)(*ga*) above, in the same street or, in Scotland, road, the court or the sheriff shall make an order for either or both of the following purposes—

(*a*) requiring the defendant[3] or, in Scotland, defender to abate the nuisance, within a time specified in the order, and to execute any works necessary for that purpose;

(*b*) prohibiting a recurrence of the nuisance, and requiring the defendant or defender, within a time specified in the order, to execute any works necessary to prevent the recurrence;

and, in England and Wales may also impose on the defendant a fine not exceeding **level 5** on the standard scale.

(3) If the magistrates' court, or the sheriff is satisfied that the alleged nuisance exists and is such as, in the opinion of the court, or of the sheriff to render premises unfit for human habitation, an order under subsection (2) above may prohibit the use of the premises for human habitation until the premises are, to the satisfaction of the court or of the sheriff, rendered fit for that purpose.

(4) Proceedings for an order under subsection (2) above shall be brought—

(*a*) except in a case falling within paragraph (*b*), (*c*) or (*d*) below, against the person responsible for the nuisance;

(*b*) where the nuisance arises from any defect of a structural character, against the owner of the premises;

(*c*) where the person responsible for the nuisance cannot be found, against the owner or occupier of the premises;

(*d*) in the case of a statutory nuisance within section 79(1)(*ga*) above caused by noise emitted from or caused by an unattended vehicle or unattended machinery or equipment, against the person responsible for the vehicle, machinery or equipment.

(5) Subject to subsection (5A) below, where more than one person is responsible for a statutory nuisance, subsections (1) to (4) above shall apply to each of those persons whether or not what any one of them is responsible for would by itself amount to a nuisance.

(5A) In relation to a statutory nuisance within section 79(1)(*ga*) above for which more than one person is responsible (whether or not what any one of those persons is responsible for would by itself amount to such a nuisance), subsection (4)(*a*) above shall apply with the substitution of "each person responsible for the nuisance who can be found" for "the person responsible for the nuisance".

(5B) In relation to a statutory nuisance within section 79(1)(*ga*) above caused by noise emitted from or caused by an unattended vehicle or unattended machinery or equipment for which more than one person is responsible, subsection (4)(*d*) above shall apply with the substitution of "any person" for "the person".

(6) Before instituting proceedings for an order under subsection (2) above against any person, the person aggrieved by the nuisance shall give to that person such notice[4] in writing of his intention to bring the proceedings as is applicable to proceedings in respect of a nuisance of that description and the notice shall specify the matter complained of.

(7) The notice of the bringing of proceedings in respect of a statutory nuisance required by subsection (6) above which is applicable is—

(*a*) in the case of a nuisance falling within paragraph (*g*) or (*ga*) of section 79(1) above, not less than three days' notice; and

(*b*) in the case of a nuisance of any other description, not less than twenty-one days' notice;

but the Secretary of State may, by order, provide that this subsection shall have effect as if such period as is specified in the order were the minimum period of notice applicable to any description of statutory nuisance specified in the order.

(8) A person who, without reasonable excuse, contravenes any requirement or prohibition imposed by an order under subsection (2) above shall be guilty of an offence and liable on summary conviction to a fine not exceeding **level 5** on the standard scale together with a further fine of an amount equal to one-tenth of the greater of £5,000 or level 4 on the standard scale for each day on

which the offence continues after the conviction.

(9) Subject to subsection (10) below, in any proceedings for an offence under subsection (8) above in respect of a statutory nuisance it shall be a defence to prove that the best practicable means were used to prevent, or to counteract the effects of, the nuisance.

(10) The defence under subsection (9) above is not available—

(*a*) in the case of a nuisance falling within paragraph (*a*), (*d*), (*e*), (*f*), (*fa*) or (*g*) of section 79(1) above except where the nuisance arises on industrial, trade or business premises;

(*aza*) in the case of a nuisance falling within paragraph (fb) of section 79(1) above except where—

(i) the artificial light is emitted from industrial, trade or business premises, or

(ii) the artificial light (not being light to which sub-paragraph (i) applies) is emitted by lights used for the purpose only of illuminating an outdoor relevant sports facility

(*aa*) in the case of a nuisance falling within paragraph (*ga*) of section 79(1) above except where the noise is emitted from or caused by a vehicle, machinery or equipment being used for industrial, trade or business purposes;

(*b*) in the case of a nuisance falling within paragraph (*b*) of section 79(1) above except where the smoke is emitted from a chimney;

(*c*) in the case of a nuisance falling within paragraph (*c*) or (*h*) of section 79(1) above; and

(*d*) in the case of a nuisance which is such as to render the premises unfit for human habitation.

(10A) For the purposes of subsection (10)(*aza*) "relevant sports facility" has the same meaning as it has for the purposes of section 80(8)(*aza*).

(11) If a person is convicted of an offence under subsection (8) above, a magistrates' court or the sheriff may, after giving the local authority in whose area the nuisance has occurred an opportunity of being heard, direct the authority to do anything which the person convicted was required to do by the order to which the conviction relates.

(12) Where on the hearing of proceedings for an order under subsection (2) above it is proved that the alleged nuisance existed at the date of the making of the complaint or summary application, then, whether or not at the date of the hearing it still exists or is likely to recur, the court or the sheriff shall[5] order the defendant or defender (or defendants or defenders in such proportions as appears fair and reasonable) to pay to the person bringing the proceedings such amount as the court or the sheriff considers reasonably sufficient to compensate him for any expenses properly incurred[6] by him in the proceedings.

(13) If it appears to the magistrates' court or to the sheriff that neither the person responsible for the nuisance nor the owner or occupier of the premises or (as the case may be) the person responsible for the vehicle, machinery or equipment can be found the court or the sheriff may, after giving the local authority in whose area the nuisance has occurred an opportunity of being heard, direct the authority to do anything which the court or the sheriff would have ordered that person to do.

[Environmental Protection Act 1990, s 82 as amended by the Noise and Statutory Nuisance Act 1993, s 5, the Environment Act 1995, Sch 17, the Clean Neighbourhoods and Environment Act 2005, s 103 and SI 2015/664.]

---

1 Where an order may require work to be done which cannot be required of a landlord under a contractual or other statutory duty, there is no ground for refusal to issue a summons. It would be otherwise if the two sets of proceedings were co-extensive and it is clear that no bench of magistrates could or would impose a fine (*R v Highbury Corner Magistrates' Court, ex p Edwards* [1995] Crim LR 65).

Notwithstanding that proceedings are commenced by way of complaint, they are criminal in nature and the court has power to make a compensation order under s 35 of the Powers of Criminal Courts Act 1973 (*Botross v Hammersmith and Fulham London Borough Council* (1994) 27 HLR 179). The combined effect of this and s 50 of the Magistrates' Courts Act 1980 is that s 82 must be read as if the word "information" was substituted for "complaint"; consequently, the only power to award costs in favour of a successful defendant (other than wasted costs) is under s 16(1) of the Prosecution of Offences Act 1985: *R (on the application of Desouza) v Croydon Magistrates' Court* [2012] EWHC 1362 (Admin), (2012) 176 JP 624.

The justices have no power to adjourn the hearing without taking a plea when to do so would avoid the consequence of a conviction under s 82(2) and the right to compensation under s 35 of the Powers of Criminal Courts Act 1973 (*R v Dudley Magistrates' Court, ex p Hollis* [1998] 1 All ER 759).

2 Note also the defence available in relation to an "authorised project" within the scope of the Planning Act 2008 under the Infrastructure Planning (Model Provisions) (England and Wales) Order 2009, SI 2009/2265.

3 It is open to the defendant to avoid liability by showing that he was not a person by whose act, default or sufferance the nuisance arose or continued (*Carr v Hackney London Borough Council* (1995) 160 JP 402).

4 It is important that ordinary members of the public who might not have any legal expertise, such as tenants, are not deterred from pursuing complaints which are well founded on the merits over technical requirements. Accordingly, it is not necessary for a s 82(6) notice to specify the works required to remedy the complaint, nor does it need to identify the capacity in which the proposed defendant is to be proceeded against (*East Staffordshire Borough Council v Fairless* [1998] 41 LS Gaz R 46).

When assessing compensation pursuant to s 35 of the Powers of Criminal Courts Act 1973, in PART III: SENTENCING, ante, in respect of an offence of statutory nuisance by a landlord under s 82 of this Act, the court should take into account only the injury, loss or damage caused by the continuation of the nuisance from the date when the period stated in the complainant's s 82(6) notice expired to the date of the hearing. However, if the complainant should delay for more than six months after the expiry of the s 82(6) notice before making complaint to the magistrates, then the offence which could form the basis for compensation would not commence earlier than a date six months before the complaint was made (*R v Crown Court at Liverpool, ex p Cooke* [1996] 4 All ER 589). For service of notices see s 160, post.

5 The court is bound to order costs provided that it is satisfied that the statutory nuisance existed at the time of the complaint. The court is not entitled to refuse costs on the grounds that it considers it was unnecessary for the complainant

to institute proceedings or because the nuisance has since been abated. The courts consideration is limited to questions as to whether a particular items of expenditure were unnecessary and as to whether the amounts claimed are more than those warranted by the particular proceedings before the court, such as the engagement of unduly expensive solicitors or counsel or a excessive number of experts (*R v Dudley Magistrates' Court, ex p Hollis* [1998] 1 All ER 759, [1999] 1 WLR 642, DC).

6 See note 4 ante.

*Termination of existing controls over offensive trades and businesses*

**7.10066 84. Termination of Public Health Act controls over offensive trades etc**

(1) Where a person carries on, in the area or part of the area of any local authority—

(*a*) in England or Wales, a trade which—

(i) is an offensive trade within the meaning of section 107 of the Public Health Act 1936 in that area or part of that area, and

(ii) constitutes a prescribed process designated for local control for the carrying on of which an authorisation is required under section 6 of this Act; or

(*b*) *Scotland.*

subsection (2) below shall have effect in relation to that trade or business as from the date on which an authorisation is granted under section 6 of this Act or, if that person has not applied for such an authorisation within the period allowed under section 2(1) above for making applications under that section, as from the end of that period.

(2) Where this subsection applies in relation to the trade or business carried on by any person—

(*a*) nothing in section 107 of the Public Health Act 1936 or in section 32 of the Public Health (Scotland) Act 1897 shall apply in relation to it, and

(*b*) no byelaws or further byelaws made under section 108(2) of the said Act of 1936, or under subsection (2) of the said section 32, with respect to a trade or business of that description shall apply in relation to it;

but without prejudice to the continuance of, and imposition of any penalty in, any proceedings under the said section 107 or the said section 32 which were instituted before the date as from which this subsection has effect in relation to the trade or business.

(3) Subsection (2)(*b*) above shall apply in relation to the trade of fish frying as it applies in relation to an offensive trade.

(4) When the Secretary of State considers it expedient to do so, having regard to the operation of Part I and the preceding provisions of this Part of this Act in relation to offensive trades or businesses, he may by order[1] repeal—

(*a*) sections 107 and 108 of the Public Health Act 1936; and

(*b*) *Scotland*;

and different days may be so appointed in relation to trades or businesses which constitute prescribed processes and those which do not.

(5) In this section—

"prescribed process" has the same meaning as in Part I of this Act; and

"offensive trade" or "trade" has the same meaning as in section 107 of the Public Health Act 1936.*

[Environmental Protection Act 1990, s 84.]

---

* **Reproduced as in force in England and Wales.**

1 The Repeal of Offensive Trades or Business Provisions Order 1995, SI 1995/205, which repeals ss 107 and 108 of the Public Health Act 1936 has been made.

## PART IV[1]
## LITTER ETC

*Provisions relating to litter*

**7.10067 86. Preliminary** (1) The following provisions have effect for the purposes of this Part.

(2) In England and Wales the following are "principal litter authorities"—

(*a*) a county council,

(*aa*) a county borough council,

(*b*) a district council,

(*c*) a London borough council,

(*d*) the Common Council of the City of London, and

(*e*) the Council of the Isles of Scilly;

but the Secretary of State may, by order, designate other descriptions of local authorities as litter authorities for the purposes of this Part; and any such authority shall also be a principal litter authority.

(3) *Scotland.*

(4) Subject to subsection (8) below, land is "relevant land" of a principal litter authority if, not being relevant land falling within subsection (7) below, it is open to the air and is land (but not a highway or in Scotland a public road) which is under the direct control of such an authority to which the public are entitled or permitted to have access with or without payment.

(5) Land is "Crown land" if it is land—

(a) occupied by the Crown Estate Commissioners as part of the Crown Estate,
(b) occupied by or for the purposes of a government department or for naval, military or air force purposes, or
(c) occupied or managed by any body acting on behalf of the Crown;

is "relevant Crown land" if it is Crown land which is open to the air and is land (but not a highway or in Scotland a public road) to which the public are entitled or permitted to have access with or without payment; and "the appropriate Crown authority" for any Crown land is the Crown Estate Commissioners, the Minister in charge of the government department or the body which occupies or manages the land on the Crown's behalf, as the case may be.

(6) Subject to subsection (8) below, land is "relevant land" of a designated statutory undertaker if it is land which is under the direct control of any statutory undertaker or statutory undertaker of any description which may be designated by the Secretary of State, by order[2], for the purposes of this Part, being land to which the public are entitled or permitted to have access with or without payment or, in such cases as may be prescribed in the designation order, land in relation to which the public have no such right or permission.

(7) Subject to subsection (8) below, land is "relevant land" of a designated[3] educational institution if it is open to the air and is land which is under the direct control of the governing body of or, in Scotland, of such body or of the education authority responsible for the management of, any educational institution or educational institution of any description which may be designated by the Secretary of State, by order, for the purposes of this Part.

(8) The Secretary of State may, by order[4], designate descriptions of land which are not to be treated as relevant Crown land or as relevant land of principal litter authorities, of designated statutory undertakers or of designated educational institutions or of any description of any of them.

(9) Every highway maintainable at the public expense other than a trunk road which is a special road is a "relevant highway" and the local authority which is, for the purposes of this Part, "responsible" for so much of it as lies within its area is, subject to any order under subsection (11) below—

(a) in Greater London, the council of the London borough or the Common Council of the City of London;
(b) in England outside Greater London, the council of the district;
(bb) in Wales, the council of the county or county borough;
(c) the Council of the Isles of Scilly.

(10) *Scotland.*

(11) The Secretary of State may, by order[5], as respects relevant highways or relevant roads, relevant highways or relevant roads of any class or any part of a relevant highway or relevant road specified in the order, transfer the responsibility for the discharge of the duties imposed by section 89 below from the local authority to the highway or roads authority; but he shall not make an order under this subsection unless—

(a) (except where he is the highway or roads authority) he is requested to do so by the highway or roads authority;
(b) he consults the local authority; and
(c) it appears to him to be necessary or expedient to do so in order to prevent or minimise interference with the passage or with the safety of traffic along the highway or, in Scotland, road in question;

and where, by an order under this subsection, responsibility for the discharge of those duties is transferred, the authority to which the transfer is made is, for the purposes of this Part, "responsible" for the highway, road or part specified in the order.

(12) *Repealed.*

(13) A place on land shall be treated as "open to the air" notwithstanding that it is covered if it is open to the air on at least one side.

(14) The Secretary of State may, by order[6], apply the provisions of this Part which apply to refuse to any description of animal droppings in all or any prescribed circumstances subject to such modifications as appear to him to be necessary.

(15) Any power under this section may be exercised differently as respects different areas, different descriptions of land or for different circumstances.

[Environmental Protection Act 1990, s 86 as amended by the Local Government (Wales) Act 1994, Sch 9 and the Clean Neighbourhoods and Environment Act 2005, Sch 5.]

---

1 Part IV consists of ss 86–99.

2 See the Litter (Statutory Undertakers) (Designation and Relevant Land) Order 1991 in this PART, post.

3 See the Litter (Designated Educational Institutions) Order 1991, SI 1991/561.

4 The Litter (Relevant Land of Principal Litter Authorities and Relevant Crown Land) Order 1991, SI 1991/476 has been made.

5 Certain highways and lengths of highway are the subject of the Highway Litter Clearance and Cleaning (Transfer of Duties) Order transferring duties under s 89(1)(*a*) and (2)(*a*) to the Secretary of State. See SI 1991/337, SI 1997/2960, SI 1998/467, SI 1999/1007, SI 2009/2677 amended by SI 2010/2401.

6 The Litter (Animal Droppings) Order 1991, SI 1991/961, provides that Pt IV of the Act will apply to dog faeces on the kinds of land prescribed in the Order.

7.10068 **87. Offence of leaving litter** (1) A person is guilty of an offence if he throws down, drops or otherwise deposits any litter in[1] any place to which this section applies and leaves it.

(2) This section applies to any place in the area of a principal litter authority which is open to

the air, subject to subsection (3) below.

(3) This section does not apply to a place which is "open to the air"[2] for the purposes of this Part by virtue of section 86(13) above if the public does not have access to it, with or without payment.

(4) It is immaterial for the purposes of this section whether the litter is deposited on land or in water.

(4A) No offence is committed under subsection (1) above where the depositing of the litter is—

(*a*) authorised by law; or

(*b*) done by or with the consent of the owner, occupier or other person having control of the place where it is deposited.

(4B) A person may only give consent under subsection (4A)(*b*) above in relation to the depositing of litter in a lake or pond or watercourse if he is the owner, occupier or other person having control of—

(*a*) all the land adjoining that lake or pond or watercourse; and

(*b*) all the land through or into which water in that lake or pond or watercourse directly or indirectly discharges, otherwise than by means of a public sewer.

(4C) In subsection (4B) above, "lake or pond", "watercourse" and "public sewer" have the same meanings as in section 104 of the Water Resources Act 1991.[3]

(5) A person who is guilty of an offence under this section shall be liable on summary conviction to a fine not exceeding **level 4** on the standard scale.

(6) A local authority, with a view to promoting the abatement of litter, may take such steps as the authority think appropriate for making the effect of subsection (5) above known to the public in their area.

(7) *Scotland.*

[Environmental Protection Act 1990, s 87 as amended by the Clean Neighbourhoods and Environment Act 2005, s 18.]

---

[1] The words "otherwise deposits in" are extremely wide and "deposits" means no more than places or puts; see *Felix v DPP* [1998] Crim LR 657.

[2] A telephone kiosk which was enclosed on three sides, had a roof and a door which was normally closed was held not to be a "place in the open air"; see *Felix v DPP* [1998] Crim LR 657.

[3] Subsections (1)–(4), (4A)–(4C) reproduced as substituted in relation to England and Wales by the Clean Neighbourhoods and Environment Act 2005, s 18.

**7.10069 88. Fixed penalty notices for leaving litter** (1) Where on any occasion—

(*a*) an authorised officer of a litter authority finds a person who he has reason to believe has on that occasion committed an offence under section 87 above in the area of that authority; or

(*b*) a constable has reason to believe that a person has committed an offence under that section,

he may give that person a notice offering him the opportunity of discharging any liability to conviction for that offence by payment of a fixed penalty.

(1A) Where a constable gives a notice under this section to a person, he shall, no later than 24 hours after the giving of the notice, send a copy of it to the litter authority in whose area the offence was committed.

(2) Where a person is given a notice under this section in respect of an offence—

(*a*) no proceedings shall be instituted for that offence before the expiration of fourteen days following the date of the notice; and

(*b*) he shall not be convicted of that offence if he pays the fixed penalty before the expiration of that period.

(3) A notice under this section shall give such particulars of the circumstances alleged to constitute the offence as are necessary for giving reasonable information of the offence and shall state—

(*a*) the period during which, by virtue of subsection (2) above, proceedings will not be taken for the offence;

(*b*) the amount of the fixed penalty; and

(*c*) the person to whom and the address at which the fixed penalty may be paid;

and, without prejudice to payment by any other method, payment of the fixed penalty may be made by pre-paying and posting to that person at that address a letter containing the amount of the penalty (in cash or otherwise).

(4) Where a letter is sent in accordance with subsection (3) above payment shall be regarded as having been made at the time at which that letter would be delivered in the ordinary course of post.

(5) The form of notices under this section shall be such as the Secretary of State may by order[1] prescribe.

(6) The fixed penalty payable in pursuance of a notice under this section is payable to the litter authority whose authorised officer gave the notice.

(6A) The amount of a fixed penalty payable in pursuance of a notice under this section—

(*a*) is the amount specified[2] by a principal litter authority in relation to its area (whether the penalty is payable to that or another authority), or

(*b*) if no amount is so specified, is £75.

(6B) The reference in subsection (6A) above to a principal litter authority does not include an

English county council for an area for which there is also a district council.

(7) The litter authority to which a fixed penalty is payable under this section may make provision for treating it as having been paid if a lesser amount is paid before the end of a period specified by the authority.

(8) In any proceedings a certificate which—

(*a*) purports to be signed by or on behalf of—

(i) in England and Wales, the chief finance officer of the litter authority; or

(ii) *Scotland*; and

(*b*) states that payment of a fixed penalty was or was not received by a date specified in the certificate,

shall be evidence of the facts stated.

(8A) If an authorised officer of a litter authority proposes to give a person a notice under this section, the officer may require the person to give him his name and address.

(8B) A person commits an offence if—

(*a*) he fails to give his name and address when required to do so under subsection (8A) above, or

(*b*) he gives a false or inaccurate name or address in response to a requirement under that subsection.

(8C) A person guilty of an offence under subsection (8B) above is liable on summary conviction to a fine not exceeding level 3 on the standard scale.

(9) For the purposes of this section the following are "litter authorities"—

(*a*) any principal litter authority, other than an English county council or a joint board;

(*b*) any English county council or joint board designated by the Secretary of State, by order, in relation to such area as is specified in the order (not being an area in a National Park);

(*c*), (*d*) *repealed*;

(*e*) the Broads Authority;

(*f*) a parish or community council.

(10) In this section—

"authorised officer", in relation to a litter authority, means—

(*a*) an employee of the authority who is authorised in writing by the authority for the purpose of giving notices under this section;

(*b*) any person who, in pursuance of arrangements made with the authority, has the function of giving such notices and is authorised in writing by the authority to perform that function; and

(*c*) any employee of such a person who is authorised in writing by the authority for the purpose of giving such notices;

"chief finance officer", in relation to a litter authority, means the person having responsibility for the financial affairs of the authority;

"proper officer" means the officer who has, as respects the authority, the responsibility mentioned in section 95 of the Local Government (Scotland) Act 1973 (financial administration).

(11) The appropriate person may by regulations prescribe conditions to be satisfied by a person before a parish or community council may authorise him in writing for the purpose of giving notices under this section.

[Environmental Protection Act 1990, s 88 as amended by the Local Government (Wales) Act 1994, Schs 6 and 16; the Environment Act 1995, Sch 24, SI 1996/3055, SI 2002/424, SI 2004/909, the Local Government Act 2003, Sch 8 and the Clean Neighbourhoods and Environment Act 2005, s 19.]

---

1 The Litter (Fixed Penalty Notices) Order 1991, SI 1991/111 revoked in relation to England by the Litter (Fixed Penalty Notices) Order 1991 and the Dog Fouling (Fixed Penalties) Order 1996 (Revocation) (England) Order 2005, SI 2005/3223, prescribes the form of notice which may be given by an authorised officer of a litter authority. The Dogs Fouling (Fixed Penalties) Order 1996, SI 1996/2763 amended by SI 2002/425 and SI 2004/909 (W) revoked in relation to England by the Litter (Fixed Penalty Notices) Order 1991 and the Dog Fouling (Fixed Penalties) Order 1996 (Revocation) (England) Order 2005, SI 2005/3223 has also been made.

2 For permissible range of penalties, see the Environmental Offences (Fixed Penalties) (Miscellaneous Provisions) Regulations 2007, SI 2008/175 and the Environmental Offences (Fixed Penalties) (Miscellaneous Provisions) (Wales) Regulations 2008, SI 2008/663.

7.10070 **89. Duty to keep land and highways clear of litter etc** (1) It shall be the duty of—

(*a*) each local authority, as respects any relevant highway or, in Scotland, relevant road for which it is responsible,

(*b*) the Secretary of State, as respects any trunk road which is a special road (other than one to which paragraph (*ba*)(i) applies) and any relevant highway or relevant road for which he is responsible,

(*ba*) a strategic highways company as respects—

(i) any trunk road which is a special road for which it is the highway authority, and

(ii) any relevant highway for which it is responsible,

(*c*) each principal litter authority, as respects its relevant land,

(*d*) the appropriate Crown authority, as respects its relevant Crown land,

(*e*) each designated statutory undertaker, as respects its relevant land, and (*f*) the governing body of each designated educational institution or in Scotland such body or, as the case may be, the education authority responsible for the management of the institution, as respects its relevant land,

(*g*) *repealed,*

to ensure that the land is, so far as is practicable, kept clear of litter and refuse.

(2) Subject to subsection (6) below, it shall also be the duty of—

(*a*) each local authority, as respects any relevant highway or relevant road for which it is responsible,

(*b*) the Secretary of State, as respects any trunk road which is a special road (other than one to which paragraph (*c*)(i) applies) and any relevant highway or relevant road for which he is responsible,

to ensure that the highway or road is, so far as is practicable, kept clean.

(c) a strategic highways company as respects—

(i) any trunk road which is a special road for which it is the highway authority, and

(ii) any relevant highway for which it is responsible.

(3) In determining what standard is required, as respects any description of land, highway or road, for compliance with subsections (1) and (2) above, regard shall be had to the character and use of the land, highway or road as well as the measures which are practicable in the circumstances.

(4) Matter of any description prescribed by regulations made by the Secretary of State for the purposes of subsections (1)(*a*) and (2) above shall be litter or refuse to which the duties imposed by those subsections apply as respects relevant highways or relevant roads whether or not it would be litter or refuse apart from this subsection.

(5) It shall be the duty of a local authority, when discharging its duty under subsection (1)(*a*) or (2) above as respects any relevant highway or relevant road, to place and maintain on the highway or road such traffic signs and barriers as may be necessary for giving warning and preventing danger to traffic or for regulating it and afterwards to remove them as soon as they cease to be necessary for those purposes; but this subsection has effect subject to any directions given under subsection (6) below.

(6) In discharging its duty under subsection (1)(*a*) or (2) above to keep clear of litter and refuse or to clean any relevant highway or relevant road for which it is responsible, the local authority shall comply with any directions given to it by the highway or roads authority with respect to—

(*a*) the placing and maintenance of any traffic signs or barriers;

(*b*) the days or periods during which clearing or cleaning shall not be undertaken or undertaken to any extent specified in the direction;

and for the purpose of enabling it to discharge its duty under subsection (1)(*a*) or (2) above as respects any relevant highway or relevant road the local authority may apply to the highway authority or roads authority for that authority to exercise its powers under section 14(1) or (3) of the Road Traffic Regulation Act 1984 (temporary prohibition or restriction of traffic).

(7) The Secretary of State shall prepare and issue a code of practice for the purpose of providing practical guidance on the discharge of the duties imposed by subsections (1) and (2) above.

(8) Different codes of practice may be prepared and issued under subsection (7) above for different areas.

(9) The Secretary of State may issue modifications of, or withdraw, a code issued under subsection (7) above; but where a code is withdrawn, he shall prepare and issue a new code under that subsection in substitution for it.

(10) Any person subject to any duty imposed by subsection (1) or (2) above shall have regard to the code of practice in force under subsection (7) above in discharging that duty.

(11) A draft code prepared under subsection (7) above shall be laid before both Houses of Parliament and shall not be issued until after the end of the period of 40 days beginning with the day on which the code was so laid, or if the draft is laid on different days, the later of the two days.

(12) If, within the period mentioned in subsection (11) above, either House resolves that the code the draft of which was laid before it should not be issued, the Secretary of State shall not issue that code.

(13) No account shall be taken in reckoning any period of 40 days for the purposes of subsection (11) above of any time during which Parliament is dissolved or prorogued or during which both Houses are adjourned for more than four days.

(13A) Subsections (11) to (13) shall not apply in respect of a draft code prepared under subsection (7) above which relates only to Scotland and such a code shall be laid before the Scottish Parliament and shall not be issued until after the end of the period of 40 days beginning with the day on which the code was so laid.

(13B) If within the period mentioned in subsection (13A) above the Scottish Parliament resolves that the code, the draft of which was laid before it, should not be issued the Scottish Ministers shall not issue that code.

(13C) No account shall be taken in reckoning any period of 40 days for the purposes of subsection (13A) above of any time during which the Scottish Parliament is dissolved or is in recess for more than 4 days.

(14) In this section "traffic sign" has the meaning given in section 64(1) of the Road Traffic Regulation Act 1984.

[Environmental Protection Act 1990, s 89 as amended by SI 1999/1820, the Clean Neighbourhoods and Environment Act 2005, s 106 and the Infrastructure Act 2015, Sch 1.]

7.10071 **91. Summary proceedings by persons aggrieved by litter** (1) A magistrates' court may act under this section on a complaint made by any person on the ground that he is aggrieved by the defacement, by litter or refuse, of—

(*a*) any relevant highway;
(*b*) any trunk road which is a special road;
(*c*) any relevant land of a principal litter authority;
(*d*) any relevant Crown land;
(*e*) any relevant land of a designated statutory undertaker; or
(*f*) any relevant land of a designated educational institution;
(*g*) *repealed.*

(2) A magistrates' court may also act under this section on a complaint made by any person on the ground that he is aggrieved by the want of cleanliness of any relevant highway or any trunk road which is a special road.

(3) A principal litter authority shall not be treated as a person aggrieved for the purposes of proceedings under this section.

(4) Proceedings under this section shall be brought against the person who has the duty to keep the land clear under section 89(1) above or to keep the highway clean under section 89(2) above, as the case may be.

(5) Before instituting proceedings under this section against any person, the complainant shall give to the person not less than five days written notice of his intention to make the complaint and the notice shall specify the matter complained of.

(6) If the magistrates' court is satisfied that the highway or land in question is defaced by litter or refuse or, in the case of a highway, is wanting in cleanliness, the court may, subject to subsections (7) and (8) below, make an order ("a litter abatement order") requiring the defendant to clear the litter or refuse away or, as the case may be, clean the highway within a time specified in the order.

(7) The magistrates' court shall not make a litter abatement order if the defendant proves that he has complied, as respects the highway or land in question, with his duty under section 89(1) and (2) above.

(8) The magistrates' court shall not make a litter abatement order where it appears that the matter complained of is the result of directions given to the local authority under section 89(6) above by the highway authority.

(9) A person who, without reasonable excuse, fails to comply with a litter abatement order shall be guilty of an offence and liable on summary conviction to a fine not exceeding **level 4** on the standard scale together with a further fine of an amount equal to **one-twentieth of that level** for each day on which the offence continues after the conviction.

(10) In any proceedings for an offence under subsection (9) above it shall be a defence for the defendant to prove that he has complied, as respects the highway or land in question, with his duty under section 89(1) and (2) above.

(11) A code of practice under section 89(7) shall be admissible in evidence in any proceedings under this section and if any provision of such a code appears to the court to be relevant to any question in the proceedings it shall be taken into account in determining that question.

(12) Where a magistrates' court is satisfied on the hearing of a complaint under this section—

(*a*) that, when the complaint was made to it, the highway or land in question was defaced by litter or refuse or, as the case may be, was wanting in cleanliness, and
(*b*) that there were reasonable grounds for bringing the complaint,

the court shall order the defendant to pay such reasonable sum to the complainant as the court may determine in respect of the expenses incurred by the complainant in bringing the complaint and the proceedings before the court.

(13) *Scotland.*

[Environmental Protection Act 1990, s 91 as amended by the Clean Neighbourhoods and Environment Act 2005, s 106.]

7.10079 **94B. Free distribution of printed matter** Schedule 3A (distribution of printed matter on designated land) has effect.

[Environmental Protection Act 1990, s 94B as inserted by the Clean Neighbourhoods and Environment Act 2005, s 22.]

7.10080 **96. Application of Part II** (1) This section applies to litter and refuse collected—

(*a*) by any authority or person in pursuance of section 89(1) above;
(*b*) by a principal litter authority in pursuance of section 92(9) or 92C(3) above; or
(*c*) by any person in pursuance of section 93 above.

(2) The Secretary of State may make regulations[1] providing that prescribed provisions of Part II shall have effect, with such modifications (if any) as may be prescribed—

(*a*) as if references to controlled waste or controlled waste of a prescribed description included references to litter and refuse to which this section applies or any description of such litter and refuse;
(*b*) as if references to controlled waste or controlled waste of a prescribed description collected under section 45 above included references to litter and refuse collected as mentioned in subsection (1) above or any description of such litter and refuse.

(3) The powers conferred by this section are exercisable in relation to litter and refuse to which

it applies whether or not the circumstances are such that the litter or refuse would be treated as controlled waste apart from this section and this section is not to affect the interpretation of the expressions defined in section 75 above.

[Environmental Protection Act 1990, s 96 as amended by the Clean Neighbourhoods and Environment Act 2005, Sch 4.]

[1] The Controlled Waste Regulations 2012, SI 2012/811 have been made, amending regulations are noted in the list of regulations made under s 2 of the European Communities Act 1972, ante.

7.10081 **97. Transitional provision relating to section 89** (1) The Secretary of State may, for the purposes of the transition to the duties imposed by section 89 above on local authorities and educational bodies, by regulations[1], make provision—

(*a*) modifying that section, or

(*b*) modifying Part I of the Local Government Act 1988 (competition rules for functional work or works contracts).

(2) Regulations under this section may make different provision for different descriptions of authorities, different areas or other different circumstances or cases.

(3) In this section—

"educational bodies" means the governing bodies and education authorities mentioned in section 89(1)(*f*) above; and

"local authorities" means the local authorities mentioned in section 89(1)(*a*) and (*c*) and (2)(*a*) above.

[Environmental Protection Act 1990, s 97.]

[1] The Litter Etc (Transitional Provisions) Regulations 1991, SI 1991/719, have been made.

7.10082 **97A. Fixed penalty notices: supplementary** (1) The appropriate person may by regulations[1] make provision in connection with the powers conferred under—

(*a*) section 88(6A)(*a*) and (7) above;

(*b*) section 94A(4)(*a*) and (5) above;

(*c*) paragraph 7(4)(*a*) and (5) of Schedule 3A.

(2) Regulations under subsection (1) may (in particular)—

(*a*) require an amount specified under section 88(6A)(*a*), 94A(4)(*a*) or paragraph 7(4)(*a*) of Schedule 3A to fall within a range prescribed in the regulations;

(*b*) restrict the extent to which, and the circumstances in which, an authority can make provision under section 88(7), 94A(5) or paragraph 7(5) of Schedule 3A.

(3) The appropriate person may by order substitute a different amount for the amount for the time being specified in section 88(6A)(*b*), 94A(4)(*b*) or paragraph 7(4)(*b*) of Schedule 3A.

(4) Regulations or an order under this section may make different provision for different purposes.

[Environmental Protection Act 1990, s 97A as inserted by the Clean Neighbourhoods and Environment Act 2005, s 24.]

[1] The Environmental Offences (Fixed Penalties) (Miscellaneous Provisions) Regulations 2007, SI 2007/175, the Environmental Offences (Use of Fixed Penalty Receipts) (Wales) Regulations 2007, SI 2007/739 amended by SI 2008/663; the Environmental Offences (Use of Fixed Penalty Receipts) Regulations 2007, SI 2007/901 and the Environmental Offences (Fixed Penalties) (Miscellaneous Provisions) (Wales) Regulations 2008, SI 2008/663 have been made. For amending instruments, see the note to the Refuse Disposal (Amenity) Act 1978, s 2A, ante.

7.10083 **97B. Exclusion of liability** (1) None of the persons mentioned in subsection (2) below is to have any liability to an occupier or owner of land for damages or otherwise (whether at common law or otherwise) arising out of anything done or omitted to be done in the exercise or purported exercise of the power in section 92(9), 92A(9) or 92C(3) above.

(2) Those persons are—

(*a*) the principal litter authority and any employee of the authority; and

(*b*) in the case of the power in section 92C(3) above, any person authorised by the authority under that provision and the employer or any employee of that person.

(3) Subsection (1) above does not apply—

(*a*) if the act or omission is shown to be in bad faith;

(*b*) to liability arising out of a failure to exercise due care and attention;

(*c*) so as to prevent an award of damages in respect of an act or omission on the ground that the act or omission was unlawful by virtue of section 6(1) of the Human Rights Act 1998.

(4) This section does not affect any other exemption from liability (whether at common law or otherwise).

[Environmental Protection Act 1990, s 97B as inserted by the Clean Neighbourhoods and Environment Act 2005, s 25.]

7.10084 **98. Definitions** (1) The following definitions apply for the interpretation of this Part.

(1A) "Appropriate person" means—

(*a*) in relation to England, the Secretary of State;

(*b*) in relation to Wales, the National Assembly for Wales.

(2) "Educational institution", in relation to England and Wales, means—

(*a*) *repealed*;
(*b*) the Open University;
(*c*) any institution which provides higher education or further education (or both) which is full-time education being an institution which—
(i) is maintained by grants made by the Secretary of State under section 485 of the Education Act 1996;
(ii) *repealed*
(iii) is maintained by a local education authority;
(*d*) any institution within the higher education sector within the meaning of section 91(5) of the Further and Higher Education Act 1992;
(*da*) any institution within the further education sector within the meaning of section 91(3) of the Further and Higher Education Act 1992;
(*e*) any city technology college, city college for the technology of the arts or Academy;
(*f*) any community, foundation or voluntary school;
(*g*) any community or foundation special school.

(3)–(4) *Scotland.*

(5) "Highway" (and "highway maintainable at the public expense") highway authority, "special road" and "trunk road", in relation to England and Wales, have the same meaning as in the Highways Act 1980 and "public road", "special road" and "trunk road", in relation to Scotland, have the same meaning as in the Roads (Scotland) Act 1984.

(5A) "Litter" includes—
(*a*) the discarded ends of cigarettes, cigars and like products, and
(*b*) discarded chewing-gum and the discarded remains of other products designed for chewing.

(5B) "Strategic highways company" means a company for the time being appointed under Part 1 of the Infrastructure Act 2015.

(6) "Statutory undertaker" means—
(*a*) any person authorised by any enactment to carry on any railway, light railway, tramway or road transport undertaking;
(*aa*) any operator of a relevant railway asset;
(*b*) any person authorised by any enactment to carry on any canal, inland navigation, dock, harbour or pier undertaking; or
(*c*) any relevant airport operator (within the meaning of Part V of the Airports Act 1986).

(7) Subject to subsection (8) below, "relevant railway asset" means—
(*a*) a transferred network, that is to say a network which was transferred by virtue of a transfer scheme made under section 85 of the Railways Act 1993 from the British Railways Board and vested in the company formed and registered under the Companies Act 1985 and known, at the date of the vesting, as Railtrack PLC,
(*b*) a station which is used in connection with the provision of services for the carriage of passengers on a transferred network and is operated by a provider of such services or by the operator of such a network, or
(*c*) a light maintenance depot which is used to provide light maintenance services for rolling stock which is used on a transferred network.

(8) A transferred network shall not cease to be such a network where it is modified by virtue of having any network or part of a network added to or removed from it.

(9) Expressions used in subsections (6)(*aa*), (7) and (8) above and in Part I of the Railways Act 1993 have the same meaning in those subsections as they have in that Part.

[Environmental Protection Act 1990, s 98 as amended by the Further and Higher Education Act 1992, Sch 8, the Education Act 1996, Sch 37, the School Standards and Framework Act 1998, Sch 30, SI 1999/1443, the Learning and Skills Act 2000, Sch 9, the Education Act 2002, Schs 21 and 22, SI 2002/2002, the Clean Neighbourhoods and Environment Act 2005, ss 26, 27 and the Infrastructure Act 2015, Sch 1.]

## PART VI[1]
## GENETICALLY MODIFIED ORGANISMS

### *Preliminary*

7.10085 **106. Purpose of Part VI and meaning of "genetically modified organisms" and related expressions** (1) This Part has effect for the purpose of ensuring that all appropriate measures are taken to avoid damage to the environment which may arise from the escape or release from human control of genetically modified organisms.

(2) In this Part the term "organism" means any acellular, unicellular or multicellular entity (in any form), other than humans, human embryos or human admixed embryos; and, unless the context otherwise requires, the term also includes any article or substance consisting of or including biological matter.

(3) For the purpose of subsection (2) above "biological matter" means anything (other than an entity mentioned in that subsection) which consists of or includes—
(*a*) tissue or cells (including gametes or propagules) or subcellular entities, of any kind, capable of replication or of transferring genetic material, or
(*b*) genes or other genetic material, in any form, which are so capable,

and it is immaterial, in determining if something is or is not an organism or biological matter, whether it is the product of natural or artificial processes of reproduction and, in the case of biological matter, whether it has ever been part of a whole organism.

(3A) For the purposes of subsection (2) above—

(*a*) "human embryo" means an embryo within the meaning given in the provisions of the Human Fertilisation and Embryology Act 1990 (apart from section 4A) by virtue of section 1(1) and (6) of that Act, and

(*b*) "human admixed embryo" has the same meaning as it has in that Act by virtue of section 4A(6) and (11) of that Act.

(4) For the purposes of this Part an organism is "genetically modified" if any of the genes or other genetic material in the organism—

(*a*) have been artificially modified; or

(*b*) are inherited or otherwise derived, through any number of replications, from genes or other genetic material (from any source) which were so modified.

(4A) Genes or other genetic material in an organism are "artificially modified" for the purposes of subsection (4) above if they are altered otherwise than by a process which occurs naturally in mating or natural recombination.

This subsection is subject to subsections (4B) and (4C) below.

(4B) For the purposes of subsection (4) above—

(*a*) genes or other genetic material shall be taken to be artificially modified if they are altered using such techniques as may be prescribed for the purposes of this paragraph;

(*b*) genes or other genetic material shall not be regarded as artificially modified by reason only of being altered by the use of such techniques as may be prescribed for the purposes of this paragraph.

(4C) An organism shall be taken not to be a genetically modified organism for the purposes of this Part if it is an organism of a prescribed description.

(4D) In subsections (4B) and (4C) above "prescribed" means prescribed by regulations made by the Secretary of State.

(5) *Repealed.*

(6) *Repealed.*

(7) In this Part, where the context permits, a reference to "reproduction", in relation to an organism, includes a reference to its replication or its transferring genetic material.

[Environmental Protection Act 1990, s 106 as amended by SI 2002/2443 and the Human Fertilisation and Embryology Act 2008, s 60.]

---

[1] Part VI contains ss 106–127.

**7.10086 107. Meaning of "damage to the environment", "control" and related expressions in Part VI** (1) The following provisions have effect for the interpretation of this Part.

(2) The "environment" includes land, air and water and living organisms supported by any of those media.

(3) "Damage to the environment" is caused by the presence in the environment of genetically modified organisms which have (or of a single such organism which has) escaped or been released from a person's control and are (or is) capable of causing harm.

(4) An organism shall be regarded as present in the environment notwithstanding that it is present in or on any human or other organism, or any other thing, which is itself present in the environment.

(5) Genetically modified organisms present in the environment are capable of causing harm if—

(*a*) they are individually capable, or are present in numbers such that together they are capable, of causing harm; or

(*b*) they are able to produce descendants which will be capable, or which will be present in numbers such that together they will be capable, of causing harm;

and a single organism is capable of causing harm either if it is itself capable of causing harm or if it is able to produce descendants which will be so capable.

(6) "Harm" means adverse effects as regards the health of humans or the environment.

(7) "Harmful" and "harmless" mean respectively, in relation to genetically modified organisms, their being capable or their being incapable of causing harm.

(8) The Secretary of State[1] may by regulations provide, in relation to genetically modified organisms of any description specified in the regulations, that—

(*a*) the capacity of those organisms for causing harm of any description so specified, or

(*b*) harm of any description so specified,

shall be disregarded for such purposes of this Part as may be so specified.

(9) Organisms of any description are under the "control" of a person where he keeps them contained measures designed to limit their contact with humans and the environment and to prevent or minimise the risk of harm.

(10) An organism under a person's control is "released" if he deliberately causes or permits it to cease to be under his control or the control of any other person and to enter the environment; and such an organism "escapes" if, otherwise than by being released, it ceases to be under his control or

that of any other person and enters the environment.

(11) Genetically modified organisms of any description are "marketed" by a person when products consisting of or including such organisms are placed on the market by being made available to other persons, whether or not for consideration.

[Environmental Protection Act 1990, s 107 as amended by SI 2002/2443 (E) and SI 2002/3188 (W).]

1 The functions of the Secretary of State under Part VI of this Act, so far as exercisable in relation to Wales, have been transferred to the National Assembly for Wales (Transfer of Functions) Order 2000, SI 2000/253, art 2, Sch 1.

*General controls*

7.10087 **108. Risk assessment and notification requirements** (1) Subject to subsections (2) and (7) below, no person shall import or acquire, release or market any genetically modified organisms unless, before doing that act—

(*a*) he has carried out an assessment of any risks there are (by reference to the nature of the organisms and the manner in which he intends to keep them after their importation or acquisition or, as the case may be, to release or market them) of damage to the environment being caused as a result of doing that act; and

(*b*) in such cases and circumstances as may be prescribed, he has given the Secretary of State such notice of his intention of doing that act and such information as may be prescribed.

(2) Subsection (1) above does not apply to a person proposing to do an act mentioned in that subsection who is required under section 111(1)(*a*) below to have a consent before doing that act.

(3) Subject to subsections (4) and (7) below, a person who is keeping genetically modified organisms shall, in such cases or circumstances and at such times or intervals as may be prescribed—

(*a*) carry out an assessment of any risks there are of damage to the environment being caused as a result of his continuing to keep them;

(*b*) give the Secretary of State notice of the fact that he is keeping the organisms and such information as may be prescribed.

(4) Subsection (3) above does not apply to a person who is keeping genetically modified organisms and is required under section 111(2) below to have a consent authorising him to continue to keep the organisms.

(5) It shall be the duty of a person who carries out an assessment under subsection (1)(*a*) or (3)(*a*) above to keep, for the prescribed period, such a record of the assessment as may be prescribed.

(6) A person required by subsection (1)(*b*) or (3)(*b*) above to give notice to the Secretary of State shall give the Secretary of State[1] such further information as the Secretary of State may by notice in writing require.

(7) Regulations under this section may provide for exemptions, or for the granting by the Secretary of State, or by the Secretary of State and the Food Standards Agency acting jointly, of exemptions to particular persons or classes of person, from the requirements of subsection (1) or (3) above in such cases or circumstances, and to such extent, as may be prescribed.

(8) The Secretary of State may at any time—

(*a*) give directions to a person falling within subsection (1) above requiring that person to apply for a consent before doing the act in question; or

(*b*) give directions to a person falling within subsection (3) above requiring that person, before such date as may be specified in the direction, to apply for a consent authorising him to continue keeping the organisms in question;

and a person given directions under paragraph (*a*) above shall then, and a person given directions under paragraph (*b*) above shall from the specified date, be subject to section 111 below in place of the requirements of this section.

(9) Regulations[2] under this section may—

(*a*) prescribe the manner in which assessments under subsection (1) or (3) above are to be carried out and the matters which must be investigated and assessed;

(*b*) prescribe minimum periods of notice between the giving of a notice under subsection (1)(*b*) above and the doing of the act in question;

(*c*) make provision allowing the Secretary of State to shorten or to extend any such period;

(*d*) prescribe maximum intervals at which assessments under subsection (3)(*a*) above must be carried out;

and the regulations may make different provision for different cases and different circumstances.

(10) In this section "prescribed" means prescribed by the Secretary of State in regulations under this section.

[Environmental Protection Act 1990, s 108 as amended by the Food Standards Act 1999, Sch 3.]

1 The functions of the Secretary of State under Part VI of this Act, so far as exercisable in relation to Wales, have been transferred to the National Assembly for Wales (Transfer of Functions) Order 2000, SI 2000/253 art 2, Sch 1.

2 The Genetically Modified Organisms (Risk Assessment) (Records and Exemptions) Regulations 1996, SI 1996/1106, amended by SI 1997/1900, SI 2000/2831 and SI 2005/2759, have been made.

7.10088 **109. General duties relating to importation, acquisition, keeping, release or marketing of organisms** (1) A person who—

(*a*) is proposing to import or acquire any genetically modified organisms, or
(*b*) is keeping any such organisms, or
(*c*) is proposing to release or market any such organisms,

shall, subject to subsection (5) below, be subject to the duties specified in subsection (2), (3) or (4) below, as the case may be.

(2) A person who proposes to import or acquire genetically modified organisms—

(*a*) shall take all reasonable steps to identify, by reference to the nature of the organisms and the manner in which he intends to keep them (including any precautions to be taken against their escaping or causing damage to the environment), what risks there are of damage to the environment being caused as a result of their importation or acquisition; and

(*b*) shall not import or acquire the organisms if it appears that, despite any precautions which can be taken, there is a risk of damage to the environment being caused as a result of their importation or acquisition.

(3) A person who is keeping genetically modified organisms—

(*a*) shall take all reasonable steps to keep himself informed of any damage to the environment which may have been caused as a result of his keeping the organisms and to identify what risks there are of damage to the environment being caused as a result of his continuing to keep them;

(*b*) shall cease keeping the organisms if, despite any additional precautions which can be taken, it appears, at any time, that there is a risk of damage to the environment being caused as a result of his continuing to keep them; and

(*c*) shall use the best available techniques not entailing excessive cost for keeping the organisms under this control and for preventing any damage to the environment being caused as a result of his continuing to keep the organisms;

and where a person is required by paragraph (*b*) above to cease keeping the organisms he shall dispose of them as safely and as quickly as practicable and paragraph (*c*) above shall continue to apply until he has done so.

(4) A person who proposes to release genetically modified organisms—

(*a*) shall take all reasonable steps to keep himself informed, by reference to the nature of the organisms and the extent and manner of the release (including any precautions to be taken against their causing damage to the environment), what risks there are of damage to the environment being caused as a result of their being released;

(*b*) shall not release the organisms if it appears that, despite the precautions which can be taken, there is a risk of damage to the environment being caused as a result of their being released; and

(*c*) subject to paragraph (*b*) above, shall use the best available techniques not entailing excessive cost for preventing any damage to the environment being caused as a result of their being released;

and this subsection applies, with the necessary modifications, to a person proposing to market organisms as it applies to a person proposing to release organisms.

(5) This section does not apply—

(*a*) to persons proposing to import or acquire, to release or to market any genetically modified organisms, in cases or circumstances where, under section 108 above, they are not required to carry out a risk assessment before doing that act;

(*b*) to persons who are keeping any genetically modified organisms and who—

(i) were not required under section 108 above to carry out a risk assessment before importing or acquiring them;

(ii) have not been required under that section to carry out a risk assessment in respect of the keeping of those organisms since importing or acquiring them; or

(*c*) to holders of consents, in the case of acts authorised by those consents.

[Environmental Protection Act 1990, s 109.]

**7.10089 110. Prohibition notices** (1) The Secretary of State[1] may serve a notice under this section (a "prohibition notice") on any person he has reason to believe—

(*a*) is proposing to import or acquire, release or market any genetically modified organisms; or

(*b*) is keeping any such organisms;

if he is of the opinion that doing any such act in relation to those organisms or continuing to keep them, as the case may be, would involve a risk of causing damage[2] to the environment.

(2) A prohibition notice may prohibit a person from doing an act mentioned in subsection (1)(*a*) above in relation to any genetically modified organisms or from continuing to keep them; and the prohibition may apply in all cases or circumstances or in such cases or circumstances as may be specified in the notice.

(3) A prohibition notice shall—

(*a*) state that the Secretary of State is, in relation to the person on whom it is served, of the opinion mentioned in subsection (1) above;

(*b*) specify what is, or is to be, prohibited by the notice; and

(c) if the prohibition is not to be effective on being served, specify the date on which the prohibition is to take effect;

and a notice may be served on a person notwithstanding that he may have a consent authorising any act which is, or is to be, prohibited by the notice.

(4) Where a person is prohibited by a prohibited notice from continuing to keep any genetically modified organisms, he shall dispose of them as quickly and safely as practicable or, if the notice so provides, as may be specified in the notice.

(5) The Secretary of State may at any time withdraw a prohibition notice served on any person by notice given to that person.

[Environmental Protection Act 1990, s 110.]

---

1 The functions of the Secretary of State under Part VI of this Act, so far as exercisable in relation to Wales, have been transferred to the National Assembly for Wales (Transfer of Functions) Order 2000, SI 2000/253 art 2, Sch 1.

2 For the circumstances in which the capacity of organisms for causing harm is to be disregarded see the Genetically Modified Organisms (Deliberate Release) Regulations 2002, SI 2002/2443 amended by SI 2004/2411, SI 2005/2759 and SI 2009/1892 and the Genetically Modified Organisms (Deliberate Release) (Wales) Regulations 2002, SI 2002/3188 amended by SI 2005/1913 and 2759.

*Consents*

7.10090 **111. Consents required by certain persons** (1) Subject to subsection (7) below, no person shall import or acquire, release or market any genetically modified organisms—

(a) in such cases or circumstances as may be prescribed[1] in relation to that act, or

(b) in any case where he has been given directions under section 108(8)(a) above,

except in pursuance of a consent[2] granted by the Secretary of State and in accordance with any limitations and conditions to which the consent is subject.

(2) Subject to subsection (7) below, no person who has imported or acquired any genetically modified organisms (whether under a consent or not) shall continue to keep the organisms—

(a) in such cases or circumstances as may be prescribed, after the end of the prescribed period, or

(b) if he has been given directions under section 108(8)(b) above, after the date specified in the directions,

except in pursuance of a consent granted by the Secretary of State[3] and in accordance with any limitations or conditions to which the consent is subject.

(3) A person who is required under subsection (2) above to cease keeping any genetically modified organisms shall dispose of them as quickly and safely as practicable.

(4) An application for a consent must contain such information and be made and advertised in such manner as may be prescribed and shall be accompanied by the fee required under section 113 below.

(5) The applicant shall, in prescribed circumstances, give such notice of his application to such persons as may be prescribed.

(6) The Secretary of State may by notice to the applicant require him to furnish such further information specified in the notice, within such period as may be so specified, as he may require for the purpose of determining the application; and if the applicant fails to furnish the information within the specified period the Secretary of State may refuse to proceed with the application. A notice under this subsection must state the reasons for requiring the further information specified in the notice.

(6A) Where an applicant for consent for releasing or marketing genetically modified organisms becomes aware, before his application is either granted or rejected, of any new information with regard to any risks there are of damage to the environment being caused as a result of the organisms being released or marketed, he shall notify the Secretary of State of that new information forthwith.

(7) Regulations under this section may provide for exemptions, or for the granting by the Secretary of State, or by the Secretary of State and the Food Standards Agency acting jointly, of exemptions to particular persons or classes of person, from—

(a) any requirement under subsection (1) or (2) above to have a consent, or

(b) any of the requirements to be fulfilled under the regulations by an applicant for a consent,

in such cases or circumstances as may be prescribed.

(8) Where an application for a consent is duly made to him, the Secretary of State may grant the consent subject to such limitations and conditions as may be imposed under section 112 below or he may refuse the application.

(9) The conditions attached to a consent may include conditions which are to continue to have effect notwithstanding that the holder has completed or ceased the act or acts authorised by the consent.

(10) The Secretary of State may at any time, by notice given to the holder of a consent, revoke the consent or vary the consent (whether by attaching new limitations and conditions or by revoking or varying any limitations and conditions to which it is at that time subject).

(11) Regulations under this section may make different provision for different cases and different circumstances; and in this section "prescribed" means prescribed in regulations under this section.

[Environmental Protection Act 1990, s 111 as amended by SI 1992/3280, the Food Standards Act 1999, Sch 3, SI 2002/2443 (E) and SI 2002/3188 (W).]

[1] The Genetically Modified Organisms (Deliberate Release) Regulations 2002, SI 2002/2443 amended by SI 2004/2411, SI 2005/2759 and SI 2009/1892 and the Genetically Modified Organisms (Deliberate Release) (Wales) Regulations 2002, SI 2002/3188 amended by SI 2005/1913 and 2759 prescribe any cases or circumstances other than the release of an approved product in accordance with the conditions and limitations to which the use of the product is subject.

[2] For applications for consent and the conditions on which consents are held see s 112 below and the Genetically Modified Organisms (Deliberate Release) Regulations 2002, SI 2002/2443 amended by SI 2004/2411, SI 2005/2759 and SI 2009/1892 and the Genetically Modified Organisms (Deliberate Release) (Wales) Regulations 2002, SI 2002/3188 amended by SI 2005/1913 and 2759.

[3] The functions of the Secretary of State under Part VI of this Act, so far as exercisable in relation to Wales, have been transferred to the National Assembly for Wales (Transfer of Functions) Order 2000, SI 2000/253 art 2, Sch 1.

7.10091 **112. Consents: limitations and conditions** (1) The Secretary of State[1] may include in a consent such limitations and conditions as he may think fit for the purpose of ensuring that all appropriate measures are taken to avoid damage to the environment which may arise from the activity permitted by the consent.

(2) Without prejudice to the generality of subsection (1) above, the conditions included in a consent may—

(*a*) require the giving of notice of any fact to the Secretary of State; or

(*b*) prohibit or restrict the keeping, releasing or marketing of genetically modified organisms under the consent in specified cases or circumstances;

and where, under any condition, the holder of a consent is required to cease keeping any genetically modified organisms, he shall dispose of them, if no manner is specified in the conditions, as quickly and safely as practicable.

(3) Subject to subsection (6) below, there is implied in every consent for the importation or acquisition of genetically modified organisms a general condition that the holder of the consent shall—

(*a*) take all reasonable steps to keep himself informed (by reference to the nature of the organisms and the manner in which he intends to keep them after their importation or acquisition) of any risks there are of damage to the environment being caused as a result of their importation or acquisition; and

(*b*) if at any time it appears that any such risks are more serious than were apparent when the consent was granted, notify the Secretary of State forthwith.

(4) Subject to subsection (6) below, there is implied in every consent for keeping genetically modified organisms a general condition that the holder of the consent shall—

(*a*) take all reasonable steps to keep himself informed of any damage to the environment which may have been caused as a result of his keeping the organisms and of any risks there are of such damage being caused as a result of his continuing to keep them;

(*b*) if at any time it appears that any such risks are more serious than were apparent when the consent was granted, notify the Secretary of State forthwith; and

(*c*) use the best available techniques not entailing excessive cost for keeping the organisms under his control and for preventing any damage to the environment being caused as a result of his continuing to keep them.

(5) Subject to subsection (6) below, there is implied in every consent for releasing or marketing genetically modified organisms a general condition that the holder of the consent shall—

(*a*) take all reasonable steps to keep himself informed (by reference to the nature of the organisms and the extent and manner of the release or marketing) of any risks there are of damage[2] to the environment being caused as a result of their being released or, as the case may be, marketed;

(*b*) notify the Secretary of State forthwith of—

(i) any new information which becomes available with regard to any risks there are of damage[1] to the environment being so caused, and

(ii) *repealed*,

(iii) any unforeseen event, occurring in connection with a release by him, which might affect the risks there are of damage to the environment being caused as a result of their being released.

(*c*) take such measures as are necessary to prevent damage[2] to the environment being caused as a result of the release or, as the case may be, the marketing of the organisms;

(*d*) notify the Secretary of State of the measures (if any) taken as a result of new information becoming available or an unforeseen event occurring as described in paragraph (*b*)(ii) above; and

(*e*) in a case where new information becomes available or an unforeseen event so occurs, revise the information contained in his application for a consent accordingly and supply the revised information to the Secretary of State.

(6) The general condition implied into a consent under subsection (3), (4) or (5) above has effect subject to any conditions imposed under subsection (1) above; and the obligations imposed by virtue of subsection (4)(*c*) or (5)(*c*) above shall not apply to any aspect of an act authorised by a

consent which is regulated by such a condition.

(7) There shall be implied in every consent for keeping, releasing or marketing genetically modified organisms of any description a general condition that the holder of the consent—

(*a*) shall take all reasonable steps to keep himself informed of developments in the techniques which may be available in his case for preventing damage[2] to the environment being caused as a result of the doing of the act authorised by the consent in relation to organisms of that description; and

(*b*) if it appears at any time that any better techniques are available to him than is required by any condition included in the consent under subsection (1) above, shall notify the Secretary of State of that fact forthwith.

But this general condition shall have effect subject to any conditions imposed under subsection (1) above.

[Environmental Protection Act 1990, s 112 as amended by SI 1992/2617 and 3280, SI 1993/152, SI 2002/2443 (E) and 3188(W).]

[1] The functions of the Secretary of State under Part VI of this Act, so far as exercisable in relation to Wales, have been transferred to the National Assembly for Wales (Transfer of Functions) Order 2000, SI 2000/253, art 2, Sch 1.

[2] For the circumstances in which the capacity of organisms for causing harm is to be disregarded see the Genetically Modified Organisms (Deliberate Release) Regulations 2002, SI 2002/2443 amended by SI 2004/2411, SI 2005/2759 and SI 2009/1892 and the Genetically Modified Organisms (Deliberate Release) (Wales) Regulations 2002, SI 2002/3188 amended by SI 2005/1913 and 2759.

*Inspectors*

7.10092 **114. Appointment etc of inspectors** (1) The Secretary of State[1] may appoint as inspectors, for carrying this Part into effect, such number of persons appearing to him to be qualified for the purpose as he may consider necessary.

(2) The Secretary of State may make to or in respect of any person so appointed such payments by way of remuneration, allowances or otherwise as he may with the approval of the Treasury determine.

(3) An inspector shall not be personally liable in any civil or criminal proceedings for anything done in the purported exercise of any power under section 115 or 117 below if the court is satisfied that the act was done in good faith and that there were reasonable grounds for doing it.

(4) In England and Wales an inspector, if authorised to do so by the Secretary of State, may prosecute before a magistrates' court proceedings for an offence under section 118(1) below.

(5) In this Part "inspector" means, subject to section 125 below, a person appointed as an inspector under subsection (1) above.

[Environmental Protection Act 1990, s 114 as amended by the Legal Services Act 2007, Sch 21.]

[1] The functions of the Secretary of State under Part VI of this Act, so far as exercisable in relation to Wales, have been transferred to the National Assembly for Wales (Transfer of Functions) Order 2000, SI 2000/253, art 2, Sch 1.

7.10093 **115. Rights of entry and inspection** (1) An inspector may, on production (if so required) of his authority, exercise any of the powers specified in subsection (3) below for the purposes of the discharge of the functions of the Secretary of State[1] under this Part.

(2) Those powers are exercisable—

(*a*) in relation to premises—

(i) on which the inspector has reason to believe a person is keeping or has kept any genetically modified organisms, or

(ii) from which he has reason to believe any such organisms have been released or have escaped; and

(*b*) in relation to premises on which the inspector has reason to believe there may be harmful genetically modified organisms or evidence of damage to the environment caused by genetically modified organisms;

but they are not exercisable in relation to premises used wholly or mainly for domestic purposes.

(3) The powers of an inspector are—

(*a*) at any reasonable time (or, in a situation in which in his opinion there is an immediate risk of damage to the environment, at any time)—

(i) to enter premises which he has reason to believe it is necessary for him to enter and to take with him any person duly authorised by the Secretary of State and, if the inspector has reasonable cause to apprehend any serious obstruction in the execution of his duty, a constable; and

(ii) to take with him any equipment or materials required for any purpose for which the power of entry is being exercised;

(*b*) to carry out such tests and inspections (and to make such recordings), as may in any circumstances be necessary;

(*c*) to direct that any, or any part of, premises which he has power to enter, or anything in or on such premises, shall be left undisturbed (whether generally or in particular respects) for so long as is reasonably necessary for the purpose of any test or inspection;

(*d*) to take samples of any organisms, articles or substances found in or on any premises which he has power to enter, and of the air, water or land in, on, or in the vicinity of, the premises;

(*e*) in the case of anything found in or on any premises which he has power to enter, which appears to him to contain or to have contained genetically modified organisms which have caused or are likely to cause damage to the environment, to cause it to be dismantled or subjected to any process or test (but not so as to damage or destroy it unless this is necessary);

(*f*) in the case of anything mentioned in paragraph (*e*) above or anything found on premises which he has power to enter which appears to be a genetically modified organism or to consist of or include genetically modified organisms, to take possession of it and detain it for so long as is necessary for all or any of the following purposes, namely—

(i) to examine it and do to it anything which he has power to do under that paragraph;

(ii) to ensure that it is not tampered with before his examination of it is completed; and

(iii) to ensure that it is available for use as evidence in any proceedings for an offence under section 118 below;

(*g*) to require any person whom he has reasonable cause to believe to be able to give any information relevant to any test or inspection under this subsection to answer (in the absence of persons other than a person nominated to be present and any persons whom the inspector may allow to be present) such questions as the inspector thinks fit to ask and to sign a declaration of the truth of his answers;

(*h*) to require the production of, or where the information is recorded in computerised form, the furnishing of extracts from, any records which are required to be kept under this Part or it is necessary for him to see for the purposes of any test or inspection under this subsection and to inspect, and take copies of, or of any entry in, the records;

(*i*) to require any person to afford him such facilities and assistance with respect to any matters or things within that person's control or in relation to which that person has responsibilities as are necessary to enable the inspector to exercise any of the powers conferred on him by this section;

(*j*) any other power for the purpose mentioned in subsection (1) above which is conferred by regulations made by the Secretary of State.

(4) The Secretary of State may by regulations make provision as to the procedure to be followed in connection with the taking of, and the dealing with, samples under subsection (3)(*d*) above.

(5) Where an inspector proposes to exercise the power conferred by subsection (3)(*e*) above, he shall, if so requested by a person who at the time is present on and has responsibilities in relation to those premises, cause anything which is to be done by virtue of that power to be done in the presence of that person.

(6) Before exercising the power conferred by subsection (3)(*e*) above, an inspector shall consult such persons as appear to him appropriate for the purpose of ascertaining what dangers, if any, there may be in doing anything which he proposes to do under the power.

(7) Where under the power conferred by subsection (3)(*f*) above an inspector takes possession of anything found on any premises, he shall leave there, either with a responsible person or, if that is impracticable, fixed in a conspicuous position, a notice giving particulars sufficient to identify what he has seized and stating that he has taken possession of it under that power; and before taking possession under that power of—

(*a*) any thing that forms part of a batch of similar things, or

(*b*) any substance,

an inspector shall, if it is practical and safe for him to do so, take a sample of it and give to a responsible person at the premises a portion of the sample marked in a manner sufficient to identify it.

(8) No answer given by a person in pursuance of a requirement imposed under subsection (3)(*g*) above shall be admissible in evidence—

(*a*) in any proceedings in England and Wales against that person; or

(*b*) *Scotland.*

(9) The powers conferred by subsection (3)(*a*), (*b*), (*c*), (*d*), (*e*) and (*h*) above shall also be exercisable (subject to subsections (4), (5) and (6) above) by any person authorised for the purpose in writing by the Secretary of State.

(10) Nothing in this section shall be taken to compel the production by any person of a document of which he would on grounds of legal professional privilege be entitled to withhold production on an order for discovery in an action in the High Court or, in relation to Scotland, on an order for the production of documents in an action in the Court of Session.

[Environmental Protection Act 1990, s 115.]

---

1 The functions of the Secretary of State under Part VI of this Act, so far as exercisable in relation to Wales, have been transferred to the National Assembly for Wales (Transfer of Functions) Order 2000, SI 2000/253, art 2, Sch 1.

*Enforcement powers and offences*

7.10094 **116. Obtaining of information from persons** (1) For the purposes of the discharge of his functions under this Part, the Secretary of State[1] may, by notice in writing served on any person who appears to him—

(*a*) to be involved in the importation, acquisition, keeping, release or marketing of genetically modified organisms; or

(*b*) to be about to become, or to have been, involved in any of those activities;

require that person to furnish such relevant information available to him as is specified in the notice, in such form and within such period following service of the notice as is so specified.

(2) For the purposes of this section "relevant information" means information concerning any aspects of the activities in question, including any damage to the environment which may be or have been caused thereby; and the discharge by the Secretary of State of an obligation of the United Kingdom under the Community Treaties or any international agreement concerning the protection of the environment from harm caused by genetically modified organisms shall be treated as a function of his under this Part.

[Environmental Protection Act 1990, s 116.]

1 The functions of the Secretary of State under Part VI of this Act, so far as exercisable in relation to Wales, have been transferred to the National Assembly for Wales (Transfer of Functions) Order 2000, SI 2000/253, art 2, Sch 1.

7.10095 **117. Power to deal with cause of imminent danger of damage to the environment**

(1) Where, in the case of anything found by him on any premises which he has power to enter, an inspector has reason to believe that it is a genetically modified organism or that it consists of or includes genetically modified organisms and that, in the circumstances in which he finds it, it is a cause of imminent danger of damage[1] to the environment, he may seize it and cause it to be rendered harmless (whether by destruction, by bringing it under proper control or otherwise).

(2) Before there is rendered harmless under this section—

(*a*) any thing that forms part of a batch of similar things, or

(*b*) any substance,

the inspector shall, if it is practicable and safe for him to do so, take a sample of it and give to a responsible person at the premises a portion of the sample marked in a manner sufficient to identify it.

(3) As soon as may be after anything has been seized and rendered harmless under this section, the inspector shall prepare and sign a written report giving particulars of the circumstances in which it was seized and so dealt with by him, and shall—

(*a*) give a signed copy of the report to a responsible person at the premises where it was found by him; and

(*b*) unless that person is the owner of it, also serve a signed copy of the report on the owner;

and if, where paragraph (*b*) above applies, the inspector cannot after reasonable inquiry ascertain the name or address of the owner, the copy may be served on him by giving it to the person to whom a copy was given under paragraph (*a*) above.

[Environmental Protection Act 1990, s 117.]

1 For the circumstances in which the capacity of organisms for causing harm is to be disregarded see the Genetically Modified Organisms (Deliberate Release) Regulations 2002, SI 2002/2443 amended by SI 2004/2411, SI 2005/2759 and SI 2009/1892 and the Genetically Modified Organisms (Deliberate Release) (Wales) Regulations 2002, SI 2002/3188 amended by SI 2005/1913 and 2759.

7.10096 **118. Offences** (1) It is an offence for a person—

(*a*) to do anything in contravention of section 108(1) above in relation to something which is, and which he knows or has reason to believe is, a genetically modified organism;

(*b*) to fail to comply with section 108(3) above when keeping something which is, and which he knows or has reason to believe is, genetically modified organism;

(*c*) to do anything in contravention of section 111(1) or (2) above in relation to something which is, and which he knows or has reason to believe is, a genetically modified organism;

(*d*) to fail to comply with any requirement of subsection (2), (3)(*a*), (*b*) or (*c*) or (4) of section 109 above in relation to something which is, and which he knows or has reason to believe is, a genetically modified organism;

(*e*) to fail, without reasonable excuse, to comply with section 108(5) or (6) or section 111(6A) above;

(*f*) to contravene any prohibition imposed on him by a prohibition notice;

(*g*) without reasonable excuse, to fail to comply with any requirement imposed under section 115 above;

(*h*) to prevent any other person from appearing before or from answering any question to which an inspector may, by virtue of section 115(3) above, require an answer;

(*i*) intentionally to obstruct an inspector in the exercise or performance of his powers or duties, other than his powers or duties under section 117 above;

(*j*) intentionally to obstruct an inspector in the exercise of his powers or duties under section 117 above;

(*k*) to fail, without reasonable excuse, to comply with any requirement imposed by a notice under section 116 above;

(*l*) to make a statement which he knows to be false or misleading in a material particular, or recklessly to make a statement which is false or misleading in a material particular, where the statement is made—

(i) in purported compliance with a requirement to furnish any information imposed by or under any provision of this Part; or

(ii) for the purpose of obtaining the grant of a consent to himself or any other person or the variation of a consent;

(*m*) intentionally to make a false entry in any record required to be kept under section 108 or 111 above;

(*n*) with intent to deceive, to forge or use a document purporting to be issued under section 111 above or required for any purpose thereunder or to make or have in his possession a document so closely resembling any such document as to be likely to deceive;

(*o*) falsely to pretend to be an inspector.

(2) It shall be a defence for a person charged with an offence under paragraph (*a*), (*b*), (*c*), (*d*) or (*f*) of subsection (1) above to prove that he took all reasonable precautions and exercised all due diligence to avoid the commission of the offence.

(3) A person guilty of an offence under paragraph (*c*) or (*d*) of subsection (1) above shall be liable[1]—

(*a*) on summary conviction, to a fine or to imprisonment for a term not exceeding **six months**, or to **both**;

(*b*) on conviction on indictment, to a **fine** or to imprisonment for a term not exceeding **five years**, or to **both**.

(4) A person guilty of an offence under paragraph (*f*) of subsection (1) above shall be liable[1]—

(*a*) on summary conviction, to a fine or to imprisonment for a term not exceeding **six months**, or to **both**;

(*b*) on conviction on indictment, to a **fine** or to imprisonment for a term not exceeding **two years**, or to **both**.

(5) A person guilty of an offence under paragraph (*a*) or (*b*) of subsection (1) above shall be liable[1]—

(*a*) on summary conviction, to a fine not exceeding the **statutory maximum** or to imprisonment for a term not exceeding **six months**, or to **both**;

(*b*) on conviction on indictment, to a **fine** or to imprisonment for a term not exceeding **five years**, or to **both**.

(6) A person guilty of an offence under paragraph (*e*), (*j*), (*k*), (*l*), (*m*) or (*n*) of subsection (1) above shall be liable[1]—

(*a*) on summary conviction, to a fine not exceeding the **statutory maximum** or to imprisonment for a term not exceeding **six months**, or to **both**;

(*b*) on conviction on indictment, to a **fine** or to imprisonment for a term not exceeding **two years**, or to **both**.

(7) A person guilty of an offence under paragraph (*g*), (*h*) or (*i*) of subsection (1) above shall be liable on summary conviction to a fine not exceeding the **statutory maximum** or to imprisonment for a term not exceeding **three months**, or to **both***.

(8) A person guilty of an offence under paragraph (*o*) of subsection (1) above shall be liable on summary conviction to a fine not exceeding **level 5** on the standard scale.

(9) Where a person is convicted of an offence under paragraph (*b*) of subsection (1) above in respect of his keeping any genetically modified organism, then, if the contravention in respect of which he was convicted is continued after he was convicted he shall be guilty of a further offence and liable on summary conviction to a fine of one-tenth of the greater of £5,000 or level 4 on the standard scale for each day on which the contravention is so continued.

(10) Proceedings in respect of an offence under this section shall not be instituted in England and Wales except by the Secretary of State or with the consent of the Director of Public Prosecutions or in Northern Ireland except with the consent of the Director of Public Prosecutions for Northern Ireland.

[Environmental Protection Act 1990, s 118 as amended by SI 1992/3280 and SI 2015/664.]

* **Words repealed by the Criminal Justice Act 2003, Sch 37 from a date to be appointed.**

1 For procedure in respect of an offence triable either way, see the Magistrates' Courts Act 1980, ss 17A–21 in PART I: MAGISTRATES' COURTS, PROCEDURE, ante.

7.10097 **119. Onus of proof as regards techniques and evidence** (1) In any proceedings for either of the following offences, that is to say—

(*a*) an offence under section 118(1)(*c*) above consisting in a failure to comply with the general condition implied by section 112(4)(*c*) or (5)(*c*) above; or

(*b*) an offence under section 118(1)(*d*) above consisting in a failure to comply with section 109(3)(*c*) or (4)(*c*) above;

it shall be for the accused to prove the matters described in subsection (1A) below.

(1A) The matters referred to in subsection (1) above are—

(*a*) in the case of an offence under section 118(1)(*c*) above consisting in a failure to comply with the general condition implied by section 112(5)(*c*) above—

(i) that no measures, other than the measures taken by him, were necessary to prevent damage being caused to the environment from the release or, as the case may be, marketing of the organisms, or

(ii) in a case where he took no measures, that no measures were necessary; and

(*b*) in any other case.

(2) Where an entry is required by a condition in a consent to be made in any record as to the observance of any other condition and the entry has not been made, that fact shall be admissible as evidence that that other condition has not been observed.

[Environmental Protection Act 1990, s 119 as amended by SI 2002/2443 (E) and 3188 (W).]

**7.10098 120. Power of court to order cause of offence to be remedied** (1) Where a person is convicted of an offence under section 118(1)(*a*), (*b*), (*c*), (*d*), (*e*) or (*f*) above in respect of any matters which appear to the court to be matters which it is in his power to remedy, the court may, in addition to or instead of imposing any punishment, order him, within such time as may be fixed by the order, to take such steps as may be specified in the order for remedying those matters.

(2) The time fixed by an order under subsection (1) above may be extended or further extended by order of the court on an application made before the end of the time as originally fixed or as extended under this subsection, as the case may be.

(3) Where a person is ordered under subsection (1) above to remedy any matters, that person shall not be liable under section 118 above in respect of those matters, in so far as they continue during the time fixed by the order or any further time allowed under subsection (2) above.

[Environmental Protection Act 1990, s 120.]

**7.10099 125. Delegation of enforcement functions** (1) The Secretary of State[1] may, by an agreement made with any public authority, delegate to that authority or to any officer appointed by an authority exercising functions on behalf of that authority any of his enforcement functions under this Part, subject to such restrictions and conditions as may be specified in the agreement.

(2) For the purposes of this section the following are "enforcement functions" of the Secretary of State, that is to say, his functions under—

section 110;

section 114(1) and (4);

section 116;

section 118(10); and

section 121;

and "inspector" in sections 115 and 117 includes, to the extent of the delegation, any inspector appointed by an authority other than the Secretary of State by virtue of an agreement under this section.

(3) The Secretary of State shall, if and so far as an agreement under this section so provides, make payments to the authority to reimburse the authority the expenses incurred in the performance of functions delegated under this section; but no such agreement shall be made without the approval of the Treasury.

[Environmental Protection Act 1990, s 125.]

---

1 The functions of the Secretary of State under Part VI of this Act, so far as exercisable in relation to Wales, have been transferred to the National Assembly for Wales (Transfer of Functions) Order 2000, SI 2000/253, art 2, Sch 1.

**7.10100 127. Definitions** (1) In this Part—

"acquire", in relation to genetically modified organisms, includes any method by which such organisms may come to be in a person's possession, other than by their being imported;

"consent" means a consent granted under section 111 above, and a reference to the limitations or conditions to which a consent is subject is a reference to the limitations or conditions subject to which the consent for the time being has effect;

"descendant", in relation to a genetically modified organism, means any other organism whose genes or other genetic material is derived, through any number of generations, from that organism by any process of reproduction;

"import" means import into the United Kingdom;

"premises" includes any land;

"prohibition notice" means a notice under section 110 above.

(2) This Part, except in so far as it relates to importations of genetically modified organisms, applies to the territorial sea adjacent to England as it applies in England, and applies to the territorial sea adjacent to Wales as it applies in Wales, and applies to any area for the time being designated under section 1(7) of the Continental Shelf Act 1964, as it applies in England.

[Environmental Protection Act 1990, s 127 as amended by SI 2002/2443 (E) and 3188 (W).]

## PART VIII[1]
## MISCELLANEOUS

*Other controls on substances, articles or waste*

7.10101 **140. Power to prohibit or restrict the importation, use, supply or storage of injurious substances or articles**[2] (1) The Secretary of State may by regulations[3] prohibit or restrict—

(*a*) the importation into and the landing and unloading in the United Kingdom,
(*b*) the use for any purpose,
(*c*) the supply for any purpose, and
(*d*) the storage,

of any specified substance or article if he considers it appropriate to do so for the purpose of preventing the substance or article from causing pollution of the environment or harm to human health or to the health of animals or plants.

(2)–(8) *Supplementary provision as to regulations.*

(9) Regulations under this section may provide that a person who contravenes or fails to comply with a specified provision of the regulations or causes or permits another person to contravene or fail to comply with a specified provision of the regulations commits an offence and may prescribe the maximum penalty for the offence.

(10) No offence under the regulations shall be made punishable with imprisonment for more than two years or punishable on summary conviction with a fine exceeding level 5 on the standard scale (if not calculated on a daily basis) or, in the case of a continuing offence—

(*a*) exceeding one-tenth of the level on the standard scale specified as the maximum penalty for the original offence, or
(*b*) if there is no maximum penalty for the original offence, exceeding one-tenth of the greater of £5,000 or level 4 on the standard scale.

(11) In this section—

"the environment" means the air, water and land, or any of those media, and the medium of air includes the air within buildings and the air within other natural or man-made structures above or below ground;

"specified" means specified in the regulations; and

"substance" means any natural or artificial substance, whether in solid or liquid form or in the form of a gas or vapour and it includes mixtures of substances.

[Environmental Protection Act 1990, s 140 as amended by SI 1999/1108, SI 2011/1043, SI 2012/1923 and SI 2015/664.]

---

1 Part VIII consists of ss 140–155.
2 For the power of the Secretary of State to extend the provisions of this section to give effect to community and other obligations, see s 156, post.
3 The Environmental Protection (Restrictions on Use of Lead Shot) (England) Regulations 1999, SI 1999/2170 amended by SI 2002/2102 and SI 2003/2512, the Environmental Protection (Restriction on Use of Lead Shot) (Wales) Regulations 2002, SI 2002/1730, have been made and the Environmental Protection (Anglers' Lead Weights) (England) Regulations 2015, SI 2015/815.

7.10102 **141. Power to prohibit or restrict the importation or exportation of waste**

(1) The Secretary of State may, for the purpose of preventing any risk of pollution of the environment or of harm to human health arising from waste being imported or exported or of conserving the facilities or resources for dealing with waste, make regulations prohibiting or restricting, or providing for the prohibition or restriction of—

(*a*) the importation into and the landing and unloading in the United Kingdom, or
(*b*) the exportation, or the loading for exportation, from the United Kingdom,

of waste of any description.

(2)–(8) *Supplementary provision as to regulations.*

[Environmental Protection Act 1990, s 141 as amended by the Environment Act 1995, Schs 22 and 24 and SI 2015/664.]

---

* **Words substituted and new sub-s (5A) inserted by the Criminal Justice Act 2003, Sch 27 from a date to be appointed.**

7.10103 **142. Powers to obtain information about potentially hazardous substances**

(1) The Secretary of State may, for the purpose of assessing their potential for causing pollution of the environment or harm to human health, by regulations make provision for and in connection with the obtaining of relevant information relating to substances which may be specified by him by order for the purposes of this section.

(2) The Secretary of State shall not make an order under subsection (1) above specifying any substance—

(*a*) which was first supplied in any member State on or after 18th September 1981; or
(*b*) in so far as it is a regulated substance for the purposes of any relevant enactment.

(3) *Repealed.*

(4) *Supplementary provision as to regulations.*

(5) The Secretary of State shall have regard, in imposing or providing for the imposition of any requirement under subsection (4)(*b*), (*c*), (*d*) or (*e*) above, to the cost likely to be involved in

complying with the requirement.

(6) In this section—

"the environment" means the air, water and land or any of them;

"relevant information", in relation to substances, produces or articles, means information relating to their properties, production, distribution, importation or use or intended use and, in relation to products or articles, to their disposal as waste;

"substance" means any natural or artificial substance, whether in solid or liquid form or in the form of a gas or vapour and it includes mixtures of substances.

(7) The enactments which are relevant for the purposes of subsection (2)(*b*) above are the following—

the Manufacture and Storage of Explosives Regulations 2005;

the Environmental Permitting (England and Wales) Regulations 2010 in relation to radioactive material or radioactive waste;

Parts 3 to 8 and 16 of the Human Medicines Regulations 2012;

Part IV of the Agriculture Act 1970;

the Misuse of Drugs Act 1971;

Part III of the Food and Environment Protection Act 1985;

the Food Safety Act 1990;

the Veterinary Medicines Regulations 2006;

and a substance is a regulated substance for the purposes of any such enactment in so far as any prohibition, restriction or requirement is imposed in relation to it by or under the enactment for the purposes of that enactment.

[Environmental Protection Act 1990, s 142 as amended by the Radioactive Substances Act 1993, Sch 4, SI 2005/1082, SI 2006/2407, SI 2010/675, SI 2012/1916 and SI 2012/1923.]

*Control of Dogs*

7.10104 **149. Seizure of stray dogs** (1) Every local authority shall appoint an officer (under whatever title the authority may determine) for the purpose of discharging the functions imposed or conferred by this section for dealing with stray dogs found in the area of the authority.

(2) The officer may delegate the discharge of his functions to another person but he shall remain responsible for securing that the functions are properly discharged.

(3) Where the officer has reason to believe that any dog found in a public place or on any other land or premises is a stray dog, he shall (if practicable) seize the dog and detain it, but, where he finds it on land or premises which is not a public place, only with the consent of the owner or occupier of the land or premises.

(4) Where any dog seized under this section wears a collar having inscribed thereon or attached thereto the address of any person, or the owner of the dog is known, the officer shall serve on the person whose address is given on the collar, or on the owner, a notice in writing stating that the dog has been seized and where it is being kept and stating that the dog will be liable to be disposed of if it is not claimed within seven clear days after the service of the notice and the amounts for which he would be liable under subsection (5) below are not paid.

(5) A person claiming to be the owner of a dog seized under this section shall not be entitled to have the dog returned to him unless he pays all the expenses incurred by reason of its detention and such further amount as is for the time being prescribed[1].

(6) Where any dog seized under this section has been detained for seven clear days after the seizure or, where a notice has been served under subsection (4) above, the service of the notice and the owner has not claimed the dog and paid the amounts due under subsection (5) above the officer may dispose of the dog—

- (*a*) by selling it or giving it to a person who will, in his opinion, care properly for the dog;
- (*b*) by selling it or giving it to an establishment for the reception of stray dogs; or
- (*c*) by destroying it in a manner to cause as little pain as possible;

but no dog seized under this section shall be sold or given for the purposes of vivisection.

(7) Where a dog is disposed of under subsection (6)(*a*) or (*b*) above to a person acting in good faith, the ownership of the dog shall be vested in the recipient.

(8) The officer shall keep a register containing the prescribed particulars of or relating to dogs seized under this section and the register shall be available, at all reasonable times, for inspection by the public free of charge.

(9) The officer shall cause any dog detained under this section to be properly fed and maintained.

(10) Notwithstanding anything in this section, the officer may cause a dog detained under this section to be destroyed before the expiration of the period mentioned in subsection (6) above where he is of the opinion that this should be done to avoid suffering.

(11) In this section—

"local authority", in relation to England, means a district council, a London borough council, the Common Council of the City of London or the Council of the Isles of Scilly, in relation to Wales, means a county council or a county borough council and, in relation to Scotland, means a council constituted under section 2 of the Local Government etc (Scotland) Act 1994;

"officer" means an officer appointed under subsection (1) above;

"prescribed" means prescribed in regulations[1] made by the Secretary of State; and "public place" means—

(i) as respects England and Wales, any highway and any other place to which the public are entitled or permitted to have access;

(ii) *Scotland*;

and, for the purposes of section 160 below in its application to this section, the proper address of the owner of a dog which wears a collar includes the address given on the collar.

[Environmental Protection Act 1990, s 149 as amended by the Local Government (Wales) Act 1994, Sch 9.]

1 See the Environmental Protection (Stray Dogs) Regulations 1992, SI 1992/288.

7.10105 **150. Delivery of stray dogs to local authority officer*** (1) Any person (in this section referred to as "the finder") who takes possession of a stray dog shall forthwith either—

(*a*) return the dog to its owner; or

(*b*) take the dog—

(i) to the officer of the local authority for the area in which the dog was found;

(ii) *repealed*

and shall inform the officer of the local authority where the dog was found.

(2) Where a dog has been taken under subsection (1) above to the officer of a local authority, then—

(*a*) if the finder desires to keep the dog, he shall inform the officer of this fact and shall furnish his name and address and the officer shall, having complied with the procedure (if any) prescribed under subsection (6) below, allow the finder to remove the dog;

(*b*) if the finder does not desire to keep the dog, the officer shall, unless he has reason to believe it is not a stray, treat it as if it had been seized by him under section 149 above.

(3) Where the finder of a dog keeps the dog by virtue of this section he must keep it for not less than one month.

(4) *Scotland.*

(5) If the finder of a dog fails to comply with the requirements of subsection (1) or (3) above he shall be liable on summary conviction to a fine not exceeding **level 2** on the standards scale.

(6) The Secretary of State may, by regulations, prescribe the procedure to be followed under subsection (2)(*a*) above.

(7) In this section "local authority" and "officer" have the same meaning as in section 149 above.

[Environmental Protection Act 1990, s 150 as amended by the Clean Neighbourhoods and Environment Act 2005, Sch 5.]

* **Reproduced as in force in relation to England and Wales.**

*Straw and stubble burning*

7.10106 **152. Burning of straw and stubble etc** (1) The appropriate Minister may by regulations[1] prohibit or restrict the burning of crop residues on agricultural land by persons engaged in agriculture and he may (by the same or other regulations) provide exemptions from any prohibition or restriction so imposed.

(2) Regulations providing an exemption from any prohibition or restriction may make the exemption applicable—

(*a*) in all, or only in specified, areas;

(*b*) to all, or only to specified, crop residues; or

(*c*) in all, or only in specified, circumstances.

(3) Any power to make regulations under this section includes power—

(*a*) to make different provision for different areas or circumstances;

(*b*) where burning of a crop residue is restricted, to impose requirements to be complied with before or after the burning;

(*c*) to create offences subject to the limitation that no offence shall be made punishable otherwise than on summary conviction and the fine prescribed for the offence shall not exceed level 5 on the standard scale; and

(*d*) to make such incidental, supplemental and transitional provision as the appropriate Minister considers appropriate.

(4) Where it appears to the appropriate Minister appropriate to do so in consequence of any regulations made under the foregoing provisions of this section, the appropriate Minister may, by order, repeal any byelaws of local authorities dealing with the burning of crop residues on agricultural land.

(5) In this section—

"agriculture" and "agricultural land" have, as respects England or as respects Wales, the same meaning as in the Agriculture Act 1947 and, as respects Scotland, the same meaning as in the Agriculture (Scotland) Act 1948;

"crop residue" means straw or stubble or any other crop residue;

"the appropriate Minister" means the Minister of Agriculture, Fisheries and Food or the Secretary of State or both of them.

[Environmental Protection Act 1990, s 152.]

1. The Crop Residues (Restrictions on Burning) Regulations 1993, SI 1993/1366 have been made.

## PART IX[1]
## GENERAL

7.10107 **156. Power to give effect to EU and other international obligations etc** (1) The Secretary of State may by regulations[2] provide that the provisions to which this section applies shall have effect with such modifications as may be prescribed for the purpose of enabling Her Majesty's Government in the United Kingdom—

(*a*) to give effect to any EU obligation or exercise any related right; or

(*b*) to give effect to any obligation or exercise any related right under any international agreement to which the United Kingdom is for the time being a party.

(2) This section applies to the following provisions of this Act—

(*a*) Part I;

(*b*) Part II;

(*c*) Part VI; and

(*d*) in Part VIII, sections 140, 141 or 142.

(3) In this section—

"modifications" includes additions, alterations and omissions;

"prescribed" means prescribed in regulations under this section; and

"related right", in relation to an obligation, includes any derogation or other right to make more onerous provisions available in respect of that obligation.

(4) *Northern Ireland.*

[Environmental Protection Act 1990, s 156, as amended by the Radioactive Substances Act 1993, Sch 4, SI 2010/675 and SI 2011/1043.]

1. Part IX consists of ss 156–164.

2. The Environmental Protection Act 1990 (Extension of s 140) Regulations 1999, SI 1999/396 have been made for the purpose of implementing Council Directive 96/56/EC, on the disposal of polychlorinated biphenyls and polychlorinated terphenyls (PCB/PCT) and under PARCOM Decision 92/3 on the phasing out of PCBs and Hazardous PCB substitutes.

7.10108 **157. Offences by bodies corporate** (1) Where an offence under any provision of this Act committed by a body corporate is proved to have been committed with the consent or connivance of, or to have been attributable to any neglect on the part of, any director, manager, secretary or other similar officer of the body corporate or a person who was purporting to act in any such capacity, he as well as the body corporate shall be guilty of that offence and shall be liable to be proceeded against and punished accordingly.

(2) Where the affairs of a body corporate are managed by its members, subsection (1) above shall apply in relation to the acts or defaults of a member in connection with his functions of management as if he were a director of the body corporate.

[Environmental Protection Act 1990, s 157.]

7.10109 **158. Offences under Parts I, II, IV, VI, etc due to fault of others** Where the commission by any person of an offence under Part I, II, IV, or VI, or section 140, 141 or 142 above is due to the act or default of some other person, that other person may be charged with and convicted of the offence by virtue of this section whether or not proceedings for the offence are taken against the first-mentioned person.

[Environmental Protection Act 1990, s 158.]

7.10110 **159. Application to Crown** (1) Subject to the provisions of this section, the provisions of this Act and of regulations and orders made under it shall bind the Crown.

(2) No contravention by the Crown of any provision of this Act or of any regulations or order made under it shall make the Crown criminally liable; but the High Court or, in Scotland, the Court of Session may, on the application of any public or local authority charged with enforcing that provision, declare unlawful any act or omission of the Crown which constitutes such a contravention.

(3) Notwithstanding anything in subsection (2) above, the provisions of this Act and of regulations and orders made under it shall apply to persons in the public service of the Crown as they apply to other persons.

(4) If the Secretary of State certifies that it appears to him, as respects any Crown premises and any powers of entry exercisable in relation to them specified in the certificate that it is requisite or expedient that, in the interests of national security, the powers should not be exercisable in relation to the premises, those powers shall not be exercisable in relation to those premises; and in this subsection "Crown premises" means premises held or used by or on behalf of the Crown.

(5) Nothing in this section shall be taken as in any way affecting Her Majesty in her private capacity; and this subsection shall be construed as if section 38(3) of the Crown Proceedings Act 1947 (interpretation of references in that Act to Her Majesty in her private capacity) were contained in this Act.

(6) References in this section to regulations or orders are references to regulations or

orders made by statutory instrument.

(7) For the purposes of this section in its application to Part II and Part IV the authority charged with enforcing the provisions of those parts in its area is—

(*a*) in the case of Part II, any waste regulation authority, and

(*b*) in the case of Part IV, any principal litter authority.

[Environmental Protection Act 1990, s 159.]

7.10111 **160. Service of notices** (1) Any notice required or authorised by or under this Act to be served on or given to an inspector may be served or given by delivering it to him or by leaving it at, or sending it by post to, his office.

(2) Any such notice required or authorised to be served on or given to a person other than an inspector may be served or given by delivering it to him, or by leaving it at his proper address, or by sending it by post to him at that address.

(3) Any such notice may—

(*a*) in the case of a body corporate, be served on or given to the secretary or clerk of that body;

(*b*) in the case of a partnership, be served on or given to a partner or a person having the control of management of the partnership business.

(4) For the purposes of this section and of section 7 of the Interpretation Act 1978 (service of documents by post) in its application to this section, the proper address of any person on or to whom any such notice is to be served or given shall be his last known address, except that—

(*a*) in the case of a body corporate or their secretary or clerk, it shall be the address of the registered or principal office of that body;

(*b*) in the case of a partnership or person having the control or the management of the partnership business, it shall be the principal office of the partnership;

and for the purposes of this subsection the principal office of a company registered outside the United Kingdom or of a partnership carrying on business outside the United Kingdom shall be their principal office within the United Kingdom.

(5) If the person[1] to be served with or given any such notice has specified an address in the United Kingdom other than his proper address within the meaning of subsection (4) above as the one at which he or someone on his behalf will accept notices of the same description as that notice, that address shall also be treated for the purposes of this section and section 7 of the Interpretation Act 1978 as his proper address.

(6) The preceding provisions of this section shall apply to the sending or giving of a document as they apply to the giving of a notice.

[Environmental Protection Act 1990, s 160.]

1 Where the landlord is a body corporate, such as a local authority, although notice may be served on the secretary or clerk of the local authority, the persons through whom a local authority could specify an alternative address are not confined to the secretary or clerk, so that a letter emanating from some other appropriate source will be effective, *Hall v Kingston upon Hull City Council* [1999] 2 All ER 609, 164 JP 9, QBD. The provisions as to notice in this section are permissive rather than mandatory and are not to put technical obstacles in the way of ordinary citizens using a summary procedure to gain relief from statutory nuisances. Accordingly where a company knew full well what was being alleged against it, there was effective service of a notice where the complainant wrote to a company's director and general manager at the principal office identified on the company notepaper although that office was not at the company's registered office as specified in sub-s (4) (*Hewlings v McLean Homes East Anglia Ltd* ([2001] 2 All ER 281, DC).

7.10112 **161. Regulations, orders and directions** (1) Any power of the Secretary of State, National Assembly for Wales or the Minister of Agriculture, Fisheries and Food under this Act to make regulations or orders shall be exercisable by statutory instrument; but this subsection does not apply to a statutory instrument—

(*a*) which contains an order under section 78M(4) above, or

(*b*) by reason only that it contains to orders under section 72 above or paragraph 4 of Schedule 3.

(2) A statutory instrument containing regulations under this Act shall be subject to annulment in pursuance of a resolution of either House of Parliament.

(2A) Subsection (2) does not apply to a statutory instrument made solely by the National Assembly for Wales.

(3) Except in the cases specified in subsection (4) below, a statutory instrument containing an order under this Act shall be subject to annulment in pursuance of a resolution of either House of Parliament.

(4) Subsection (3) above does not apply to a statutory instrument—

(*a*) which contains an order under s 78M(4) above, or

(*b*) by reason only that it contains an order under section 128(3), 130(4), 131(3) or 138(2) above or section 164 (3) below, or

(*c*) which is made solely by the National Assembly for Wales.

(5) Any power conferred by this Act to give a direction shall include power to vary or revoke the direction.

(6) Any direction given under this Act shall be in writing.*

[Environmental Protection Act 1990, s 161 as amended by the Environment Act 1995, Sch 22, the Clean Neighbourhoods and Environment Act 2005, Sch 4 and the Natural Environment and Rural Communities Act 2006, Sch 11.]

* Amended by the Climate Change Act 2008, Sch 5 from a date to be appointed.

7.10113 **162. Consequential and minor amendments and repeals** (1) The enactments specified in Schedule 15 to this Act shall have effect subject to the amendments specified in that Schedule.

(2) The enactments specified in Schedule 16 to this Act are hereby repealed subject to section 77 above, Schedule 11 to this Act and any provision made by way of a note in Schedule 16.

(3) *Scotland.*

(4) The Secretary of State may by order repeal or amend any provision of any local Act passed before this Act (including an Act confirming a provisional order) or of any order or other instrument made under an Act so passed if it appears to him that the provision is inconsistent with, or has become unnecessary or requires alteration in consequence of, any provision of this Act or corresponds to any provision repealed by this Act.

(5) Any regulations made under section 100 of the Control of Pollution Act 1974 shall have effect after the repeal of that section by subsection (2) above as if made under section 140 of this Act.

[Environmental Protection Act 1990, s 162.]

7.10114 **164. Short title, commencement[1] and extent** (1) This Act may be cited as the Environmental Protection Act 1990.

[Environmental Protection Act 1990, s 164(1).]

[1] The Act is fully in force.

## SCHEDULE 3
STATUTORY NUISANCES: SUPPLEMENTARY PROVISIONS Section 81

*(Amended by the Noise and Statutory Nuisance Act 1993, s 4, the Environment Act 1995, Sch 17 and the Audit Commission Act 1998, Sch 3.)*

*Appeals to magistrates' court*

7.10115 1. (1) This paragraph applies in relation to appeals under section 80(3) against an abatement notice to a magistrates' court.

(2) An appeal to which this paragraph applies shall be by way of complaint for an order and the Magistrates' Courts Act 1980 shall apply to the proceedings.

(3) An appeal against any decision of a magistrates' court in pursuance of an appeal to which this paragraph applies shall lie to the Crown Court at the instance of any party to the proceedings in which the decision was given.

(4) The Secretary of State may make regulations[1] as to appeals to which this paragraph applies and the regulations may in particular—

(*a*) include provisions comparable to those in section 290 of the Public Health Act 1936 (appeals against notices requiring the execution of works);

(*b*) prescribe the cases in which an abatement notice is, or is not, to be suspended until the appeal is decided, or until some other stage in the proceedings;

(*c*) prescribe the cases in which the decision on appeal may in some respects be less favourable to the appellant than the decision from which he is appealing;

(*d*) prescribe the cases in which the appellant may claim that an abatement notice should have been served on some other person and prescribe the procedure to be followed in those cases.

[1] The Statutory Nuisance (Appeals) Regulations 1995 are contained in this title, post.

*Powers of entry etc*

2. (1) Subject to sub-paragraph (2) below, any person authorised by a local authority may, on production (if so required) of his authority, enter any premises at any reasonable time—

(*a*) for the purpose of ascertaining whether or not a statutory nuisance exists; or

(*b*) for the purpose of taking any action, or executing any work, authorised or required by Part III.

(2) Admission by virtue of sub-paragraph (1) above to any premises used wholly or mainly for residential purposes shall not except in an emergency be demanded as of right unless twenty-four hours notice of the intended entry has been given to the occupier.

(3) If it is shown to the satisfaction of a justice of the peace on sworn information in writing—

(*a*) that admission to any premises has been refused, or that refusal is apprehended, or that the premises are unoccupied or the occupier is temporarily absent, or that the case is one of emergency, or that an application for admission would defeat the object of the entry; and

(*b*) that there is reasonable ground for entry into the premises for the purpose for which entry is required,

the justice may by warrant under his hand authorise the local authority by any authorised person to enter the premises, if need be by force.

(4) An authorised person entering any premises by virtue of sub-paragraph (1) or a warrant under sub-paragraph (3) above may—

(*a*) take with him such other persons and such equipment as may be necessary;

(*b*) carry out such inspections, measurements and tests as he considers necessary for the discharge of any of the local authority's functions under Part III; and

(*c*) take away such samples or articles as he considers necessary for that purpose.

(5) On leaving any unoccupied premises which he has entered by virtue of sub-paragraph (1) above or a warrant under sub-paragraph (3) above the authorised person shall leave them as effectually secured against trespassers as he found them.

(6) A warrant issued in pursuance of sub-paragraph (3) above shall continue in force until the purpose for

which the entry is required has been satisfied.

(7) Any reference in this paragraph to an emergency is a reference to a case where the person requiring entry has reasonable cause to believe that circumstances exist which are likely to endanger life or health and that immediate entry is necessary to verify the existence of those circumstances or to ascertain their cause and to effect a remedy.

(8) *Scotland.*

**2A.** (1) Any person authorised by a local authority may on production (if so required) of his authority—

(*a*) enter or open a vehicle, machinery or equipment, if necessary by force, or

(*b*) remove a vehicle, machinery or equipment from a street or, in Scotland, road to a secure place,

for the purpose of taking any action, or executing any work, authorised by or required under Part III in relation to a statutory nuisance within section 79(1)(*ga*) above caused by noise emitted from or caused by the vehicle, machinery or equipment.

(2) On leaving any unattended vehicle, machinery or equipment that he has entered or opened under sub-paragraph (1) above, the authorised person shall (subject to sub-paragraph (3) below) leave it secured against interference or theft in such manner and as effectually as he found it.

(3) If the authorised person is unable to comply with sub-paragraph (2) above, he shall for the purpose of securing the unattended vehicle, machinery or equipment either—

(*a*) immobilise it by such means as he considers expedient, or

(*b*) remove it from the street to a secure place.

(4) In carrying out any function under sub-paragraph (1), (2) or (3) above, the authorised person shall not cause more damage than is necessary.

(5) Before a vehicle, machinery or equipment is entered, opened or removed under sub-paragraph (1) above, the local authority shall notify the police of the intention to take action under that sub-paragraph.

(6) After a vehicle, machinery or equipment has been removed under sub-paragraph (1) or (3) above, the local authority shall notify the police of its removal and current location.

(7) Notification under sub-paragraph (5) or (6) above may be given to the police at any police station in the local authority's area or, in the case of the Temples, at any police station of the City of London Police.

(8) For the purposes of section 81(4) above, any expenses reasonably incurred by a local authority under sub-paragraph (2) or (3) above shall be treated as incurred by the authority under section 81(3) above in abating or preventing the recurrence of the statutory nuisance in question.

*Offences relating to entry*

**3.** (1) A person who wilfully obstructs any person acting in the exercise of any powers conferred by paragraph 2 or 2A above shall be liable, on summary conviction, to a fine not exceeding **level 3** on the standard scale.

(2) If a person discloses any information relating to any trade secret obtained in the exercise of any powers conferred by paragraph 2 above he shall, unless the disclosure was made in the performance of his duty or with the consent of the person having the right to disclose the information, be liable, on summary conviction, to a fine not exceeding **level 5** on the standard scale.

*Default powers*

**4.** (1) This paragraph applies to the following functions of a local authority, that is to say its duty under section 79 to cause its area to be inspected to detect any statutory nuisance which ought to be dealt with under section 80 or sections 80 and 80A and its powers under paragraph 2 or 2A above.

(2) If the Secretary of State is satisfied that any local authority has failed, in any respect, to discharge the function to which this paragraph applies which it ought to have discharged, he may make an order declaring the authority to be in default.

(3) An order made under sub-paragraph (2) above which declares an authority to be in default may, for the purpose of remedying the default, direct the authority ("the defaulting authority") to perform the function specified in the order and may specify the manner in which and the time or times within which the function is to be performed by the authority.

(4) If the defaulting authority fails to comply with any direction contained in such an order the Secretary of State may, instead of enforcing the order by mandamus, make an order transferring to himself the function of the authority specified in the order.

(5) Where the function of a defaulting authority is transferred under sub-paragraph (4) above, the amount of any expenses which the Secretary of State certifies were incurred by him in performing the function shall on demand be paid to him by the defaulting authority.

(6) Any expenses required to be paid by a defaulting authority under sub-paragraph (5) above shall be defrayed by the authority in like manner, and shall be debited to the like account, as if the function had not been transferred and the expenses had been incurred by the authority in performing them.

(7) The Secretary of State may by order vary or revoke any order previously made by him under this paragraph.

(8) Any order under this paragraph may include such incidental, supplemental and transitional provisions as the Secretary of State considers appropriate.

(9) This paragraph does not apply to Scotland.

*Protection from personal liability*

**5.** Nothing done by, or by a member of, a local authority or by any officer of or other person authorised by a local authority shall, if done in good faith for the purpose of executing Part III, subject them or any of them personally to any action, liability, claim or demand whatsoever (other than any liability under section 17 or 18 of the Audit Commission Act 1998 (powers of district auditor and court)).

*Statement of right of appeal in notices*

**6.** Where an appeal against a notice served by a local authority lies to a magistrates' court or, in Scotland, the sheriff by virtue of section 80, it shall be the duty of the authority to include in such a notice a statement indicating that such an appeal lies as aforesaid and specifying the time within which it must be brought.

## SCHEDULE 3A

### Free distribution of printed matter on designated land

*(Inserted by the Clean Neighbourhoods and Environment Act 2005, s 23 and amended by SI 2011/1396.)*

*Offence of unauthorised distribution*

7.10122 **1.** (1) A person commits an offence if he distributes any free printed matter without the consent of a principal litter authority on any land which is designated by the authority under this Schedule, where the person knows that the land is so designated.

(2) A person commits an offence if he causes another person to distribute any free printed matter without the consent of a principal litter authority on any land designated by the authority under this Schedule.

(3) A person is not guilty of an offence under sub-paragraph (2) if he took reasonable steps to ensure that the distribution did not occur on any land designated under this Schedule.

(4) Nothing in this paragraph applies to the distribution of printed matter—

(*a*) by or on behalf of a charity, where the printed matter relates to or is intended for the benefit of the charity;

(*b*) where the distribution is for political purposes or for the purposes of a religion or belief.

(5) A person guilty of an offence under this paragraph is liable on summary conviction to a fine not exceeding level 4 on the standard scale.

(6) For the purposes of this Schedule—

(*a*) to "distribute" printed matter means to give it out to, or offer or make it available to, members of the public and includes placing it on or affixing it to vehicles, but does not include putting it inside a building or letter-box;

(*b*) printed matter is "free" if it is distributed without charge to the persons to whom it is distributed.

(7) For the purposes of this Schedule a person does not distribute printed matter if the distribution takes place inside a public service vehicle (within the meaning of the Public Passenger Vehicles Act 1981).

*Designation*

**2.** (1) A principal litter authority may by order in accordance with this paragraph designate land in its area for the purposes of this Schedule.

(2) The land designated must consist of—

(*a*) relevant land of the authority;

(*b*) all or part of any relevant highway for which the authority is responsible; or

(*c*) both.

(3) A principal litter authority may only designate land where it is satisfied that the land is being defaced by the discarding of free printed matter which has been distributed there.

(4) Where a principal litter authority proposes to make an order under sub-paragraph (1) above in respect of any land, it must—

(*a*) publish a notice of its proposal in at least one newspaper circulating in an area which includes the land; and

(*b*) post such a notice on the land.

(5) A notice under sub-paragraph (4) above must specify—

(*a*) the land proposed to be designated;

(*b*) the date on which it is proposed that the order is to come into force (which may not be earlier than the end of a period of 28 days beginning with the day on which the notice is given);

(*c*) the fact that objections may be made to the proposal, how they may be made and the period within which they may be made (being a period of at least 14 days beginning with the day on which the notice is given).

(6) Where after giving notice under sub-paragraph (4) above and taking into account any objections duly made pursuant to sub-paragraph (5)(*c*) above an authority decides to make an order under sub-paragraph (1) above in respect of any or all of the land in respect of which the notice was given, the authority must—

(*a*) publish a notice of its decision in at least one newspaper circulating in an area which includes the land; and

(*b*) post such a notice on the land.

(7) A notice under sub-paragraph (6) above must specify the date on which the order is to come into force, being a date not earlier than—

(*a*) the end of the period of 14 days beginning with the day on which the notice is given; and

(*b*) the date referred to in sub-paragraph (5)(*b*) above.

(8) A principal litter authority may at any time revoke an order under sub-paragraph (1) above in respect of any land to which the order relates.

(9) A principal litter authority must—

(*a*) publish a notice of any revocation under sub-paragraph (8) above in at least one newspaper circulating in an area which includes the land in question; and

(*b*) post such a notice on the land.

(10) Sub-paragraph (1) above does not apply to an English county council for an area for which there is a district council.

*Consent and conditions*

**3.** (1) A principal litter authority may on the application of any person consent to that person or any other person (identified specifically or by description) distributing free printed matter on any land designated by the authority under this Schedule.

(2) Consent under this paragraph may be given without limitation or may be limited—

(*a*) by reference to the material to be distributed;

(*b*) by reference to a particular period, or particular times or dates;

(*c*) by reference to any part of the designated land;

(*d*) to a particular distribution.

(3) A principal litter authority need not give consent under this paragraph to any applicant where it considers that the proposed distribution would in all the circumstances be likely to lead to defacement of the

designated land.

(4) Consent need not be given to any applicant if within the period of five years ending on the date of his application—

(*a*) he has been convicted of an offence under paragraph 1 above; or

(*b*) he has paid a fixed penalty under paragraph 7 below.

(5) Consent may be given under this paragraph subject to such conditions as the authority consider necessary or desirable for—

(*a*) protecting the designated land from defacement; or

(*b*) the effective operation and enforcement of this Schedule.

(6) The conditions which may be imposed by a principal litter authority under this paragraph include conditions requiring any person distributing printed matter pursuant to consent given under this paragraph to produce on demand written evidence of the consent to an authorised officer of the authority.

(7) Consent given by a principal litter authority under this paragraph may at any time be revoked (entirely or to any extent) by notice to the person to whom it was given, where—

(*a*) he has failed to comply with any condition subject to which it was given; or

(*b*) he is convicted of an offence under paragraph 1 above or pays a fixed penalty under paragraph 7 below.

(8) Any condition imposed under this paragraph in relation to any consent may be varied or revoked by notice given to the person to whom the consent was given.

*Fees*

**4.** (1) A principal litter authority may require the payment of a fee before giving consent under paragraph 3 above.

(2) The amount of a fee under this paragraph is to be such as the authority may determine, but may not be more than, when taken together with all other fees charged by the authority under this paragraph, is reasonable to cover the costs of operating and enforcing this Schedule.

*Appeals*

**5.** (1) Any person aggrieved by a decision of a principal litter authority under paragraph 3 above—

(*a*) to refuse consent,

(*b*) to impose any limitation or condition subject to which consent is given,

(*c*) to revoke consent (or to revoke it to any extent),

may appeal against the decision to a magistrates' court.

(2) A magistrates' court may on an appeal under this paragraph—

(*a*) uphold any refusal of consent or require the authority to grant consent (without limitation or condition or subject to any limitation or condition);

(*b*) require the authority to revoke or vary any condition;

(*c*) uphold or quash revocation of consent (or uphold or quash revocation to any extent).

*Seizure of material*

**6.** (1) Where it appears to an authorised officer of a principal litter authority that a person distributing any printed matter is committing an offence under paragraph 1 above, he may seize all or any of it.

(2) Any person claiming to own any printed matter seized under this paragraph may apply to a magistrates' court for an order that the printed matter be released to him.

(3) On an application under sub-paragraph (2) above, if the magistrates' court considers that the applicant does own the printed matter, the court shall order the principal litter authority to release it to him, except to the extent that the court considers that the authority needs to retain it for the purposes of proceedings relating to an offence under paragraph 1 above.

(4) Any printed matter seized under this paragraph (and not released under sub-paragraph (3) above) must be returned to the person from whom it is seized—

(*a*) at the conclusion of proceedings for the offence (unless the court orders otherwise);

(*b*) at the end of the period in which proceedings for the offence may be instituted, if no such proceedings have been instituted in that period (or have been instituted but discontinued).

(5) Where it is not possible to return any printed matter under sub-paragraph (4) above because the name and address of the person from whom it was seized are not known, a principal litter authority may dispose of or destroy it.

*Fixed penalty notices*

**7.** (1) This paragraph applies where on any occasion it appears to an authorised officer of a principal litter authority that a person has committed an offence under paragraph 1 above on any land designated by the authority under this Schedule.

(2) The authorised officer may give that person a notice offering him the opportunity of discharging any liability to conviction for the offence by payment of a fixed penalty to the principal litter authority.

(3) Subsections (2) to (5) of section 88 above apply in relation to notices given under this paragraph as they apply to notices under that section.

(4) The amount of the fixed penalty payable to a principal litter authority under this paragraph—

(*a*) is the amount specified[1] by the authority in relation to its area; or

(*b*) if no amount is so specified, is £75.

(5) The principal litter authority to which a fixed penalty is payable under this paragraph may make provision for treating it as having been paid if a lesser amount is paid before the end of a period specified by the authority.

(6) In any proceedings a certificate which—

(*a*) purports to be signed on behalf of the chief finance officer of a principal litter authority, and

(*b*) states that payment of a fixed penalty was or was not received by a date specified in the certificate,

is evidence of the facts stated.

(7) If an authorised officer of a principal litter authority proposes to give a person a notice under this paragraph, the officer may require the person to give him his name and address.

(8) A person commits an offence if—

(*a*) he fails to give his name and address when required to do so under sub-paragraph (7) above; or

(b) he gives a false or inaccurate name or address in response to a requirement under that sub-paragraph.

(9) A person guilty of an offence under sub-paragraph (8) above is liable on summary conviction to a fine not exceeding level 3 on the standard scale.

(10) In this paragraph, "chief finance officer", in relation to a principal litter authority, means the person having responsibility for the financial affairs of that authority.

*Supplementary*

8. In this Schedule "authorised officer", in relation to a principal litter authority, means—

(a) an employee of the authority who is authorised in writing by the authority for the purpose of giving notices under paragraph 7 above;

(b) any person who, in pursuance of arrangements made with the authority, has the function of giving such notices and is authorised in writing by the authority to perform that function; and

(c) any employee of such a person who is authorised in writing by the authority for the purpose of giving such notices.

---

[1] For permissible range of penalties, see the Environmental Offences (Fixed Penalties) (Miscellaneous Provisions) Regulations 2007, SI 2008/175 and the Environmental Offences (Fixed Penalties) (Miscellaneous Provisions) (Wales) Regulations 2008, SI 2008/663.

# Clean Air Act 1993[1]

(1993 c 11)

## PART I[2]

## DARK SMOKE

7.10123 1. **Prohibition of dark smoke from chimneys** (1) Dark smoke shall not be emitted from a chimney of any building, and if, on any day, dark smoke is so emitted, the occupier of the building shall be guilty of an offence.

(2) Dark smoke shall not be emitted from a chimney (not being a chimney of a building) which serves the furnace of any fixed boiler or industrial plant, and if, on any day, dark smoke is so emitted, the person having possession of the boiler or plant shall be guilty of an offence.

(3) This section does not apply to emissions of smoke from any chimney, in such classes of case and subject to such limitations as may be prescribed in regulations[3] made by the Secretary of State, lasting for not longer than such periods as may be so prescribed.

(4) In any proceedings for an offence under this section, it shall be a defence to prove—

(a) that the alleged emission was solely due to the lighting up of a furnace which was cold and that all practicable steps had been taken to prevent or minimise the emission of dark smoke;

(b) that the alleged emission was solely due to some failure of a furnace, or of apparatus used in connection with a furnace, and that—

(i) the failure could not reasonably have been foreseen, or, if foreseen, could not reasonably have been provided against; and

(ii) the alleged emission could not reasonably have been prevented by action taken after the failure occurred; or

(c) that the alleged emission was solely due to the use of unsuitable fuel and that—

(i) suitable fuel was unobtainable and the least unsuitable fuel which was available was used; and

(ii) all practicable steps had been taken to prevent or minimise the emission of dark smoke as the result of the use of that fuel;

or that the alleged emission was due to the combination of two or more of the causes specified in paragraphs (a) to (c) and that the other conditions specified in those paragraphs are satisfied in relation to those causes respectively.

(5) A person guilty of an offence under this section shall be liable on summary conviction—

(a) in the case of a contravention of subsection (1) as respects a chimney of a private dwelling, to a fine not exceeding **level 3** on the standard scale; and

(b) in any other case, to a fine not exceeding **level 5** on the standard scale.

(6) This section has effect subject to section 51 (duty to notify offences to occupier or other person liable).[4]

[Clean Air Act 1993, s 1.]

---

[1] This Act consolidates the Clean Air Acts 1956 and 1968 and certain related enactments, with amendments to give effect to recommendations of the Law Commission. Until the coming into force of the repeal by the Environmental Protection Act 1990 of the Alkali, etc Works Regulation Act 1906, the application of this Act to any work subject or potentially subject to the Alkali Act is modified by s 66 and Sch 3, post.

[2] Part I contains ss 1–3.

[3] See the Dark Smoke (Permitted Periods) Regulations and Dark Smoke (Vessels) Regulations 1958, SI 1958/498 and 878 revoked and replaced in respect of England by the Clean Air (Miscellaneous Provisions) (England) Regulations 2014, SI 2014/3318.

[4] For the application of this section to railway locomotive engines, see s 43, post, and to vessels, see s 44, post.

7.10124 2. **Prohibition of dark smoke from industrial or trade premises** (1) Dark smoke shall not be emitted[1] from any industrial or trade premises and if, on any day, dark smoke is so emitted the occupier of the premises and any person who causes or permits the emission shall be guilty of an offence.

(2) This section does not apply—

(*a*) to the emission of dark smoke from any chimney to which section 1 above applies; or

(*b*) to the emission of dark smoke caused by the burning of any matter prescribed in regulations[2] made by the Secretary of State, subject to compliance with such conditions (if any) as may be so prescribed.

(3) In proceedings for an offence under this section, there shall be taken to have been an emission of dark smoke from industrial or trade premises in any case where—

(*a*) material is burned on those premises; and

(*b*) the circumstances are such that the burning would be likely to give rise to the emission of dark smoke,

unless the occupier or any person who caused or permitted the burning shows that no dark smoke was emitted.

(4) In proceedings for an offence under this section, it shall be a defence to prove—

(*a*) that the alleged emission was inadvertent; and

(*b*) that all practicable steps had been taken to prevent or minimise the emission of dark smoke.

(5) A person guilty of an offence under this section shall be liable on summary conviction to a fine.

(6) In this section "industrial or trade premises" means—

(*a*) premises used for any industrial or trade purposes; or

(*b*) premises not so used on which matter is burnt in connection with any industrial or trade process[3].

(7) This section has effect subject to section 51 (duty to notify offences to occupier or other person liable).

[Clean Air Act 1993, s 2 as amended by the Environment Act 1995, Sch 22 and SI 2015/664.]

---

1 Where the premises consist of land (read with s 64, post), it is unnecessary for the prosecutor to prove that dark smoke was emitted over and beyond the territorial boundary of the land. Therefore, if the fire was on open ground not served by a chimney, to establish the offence it is sufficient for the prosecutor to prove that dark smoke was emitted from the fire on land into the air occupying the space above the land (*O'Fee v Copeland Borough Council* (1995) 160 JP 20).

2 See the Waste Management (Miscellaneous Provisions) (England and Wales) Regulations 2007, SI 2007/1156.

3 A vacant site is capable of being "premises" within the meaning of this subsection, and the burning of rubble as part of a demolition scheme has been held to be a trade process within the subsection (*Sheffield City Council v ADH Demolition Ltd* [1983] LS Gaz R 1919).

7.10125 **3. Meaning of "dark smoke"** (1) In this Act "dark smoke" means smoke which, if compared in the appropriate manner with a chart of the type known on 5th July 1956 (the date of the passing of the Clean Air Act 1956) as the Ringelmann Chart, would appear to be as dark as or darker than shade 2 on the chart.

(2) For the avoidance of doubt it is hereby declared that in proceedings—

(*a*) for an offence under section 1 or 2 (prohibition of emissions of dark smoke);

(*b*) *repealed*,

the court may be satisfied that smoke is or is not dark smoke as defined in subsection (1) notwithstanding that there has been no actual comparison of the smoke with a chart of the type mentioned in that subsection.

(3) Without prejudice to the generality of subsections (1) and (2), if the Secretary of State by regulations prescribes any method of ascertaining whether smoke is dark smoke as defined in subsection (1), proof in any such proceedings as are mentioned in subsection (2)—

(*a*) that that method was properly applied, and

(*b*) that the smoke was thereby ascertained to be or not to be dark smoke as so defined,

shall be accepted as sufficient.

[Clean Air Act 1993, s 3 as amended by the Environment Act 1995, Sch 24.]

## PART II[1]

## SMOKE, GRIT, DUST AND FUMES

### *Installation of furnaces*

7.10126 **4. Requirement that new furnaces shall be so far as practicable smokeless** (1) No furnace shall be installed in a building or in any fixed boiler or industrial plant unless notice of the proposal to install it has been given to the local authority.

(2) No furnace shall be installed in a building or in any fixed boiler or industrial plant unless the furnace is so far as practicable capable of being operated continuously without emitting smoke when burning fuel of a type for which the furnace was designed.

(3) Any furnace installed in accordance with plans and specifications submitted to, and approved for the purposes of this section by, the local authority shall be treated as complying with the provisions of subsection (2).

(4) Any person who installs a furnace in contravention of subsection (1) or (2) or on whose instructions a furnace is so installed shall be guilty of an offence and liable on summary conviction—

(*a*) in the case of a contravention of subsection (1), to a fine not exceeding **level 3** on the standard scale; and

(*b*) in the case of a contravention of subsection (2), to a fine not exceeding **level 5** on that scale.

(5) This section does not apply to the installation of domestic furnaces.

(6) This section applies in relation to—

(*a*) the attachment to a building of a boiler or industrial plant which already contains a furnace; or

(*b*) the fixing to or installation on any land of any such boiler or plant;

as it applies in relation to the installation of a furnace in any fixed boiler or industrial plant.

[Clean Air Act 1993, s 4.]

1 Part II contains ss 4–17.

*Limits on rate of emission of grit and dust*

7.10127 5. **Emission of grit and dust from furnaces** (1) This section applies to any furnace other than a domestic furnace.

(2) The Secretary of State may by regulations[1] prescribe limits on the rates of emission of grit and dust from the chimneys of furnaces to which this section applies.

(3) If on any day grit or dust is emitted from a chimney serving a furnace to which this section applies at a rate exceeding the relevant limit prescribed under subsection (2), the occupier of any building in which the furnace is situated shall be guilty of an offence.

(4) In proceedings for an offence under subsection (3) it shall be a defence to prove that the best practicable means had been used for minimising the alleged emission.

(5) If, in the case of a building containing a furnace to which this section applies and which is served by a chimney to which there is no limit applicable under subsection (2), the occupier fails to use any practicable means there may be for minimising the emission of grit or dust from the chimney, he shall be guilty of an offence.

(6) A person guilty of an offence under this section shall be liable on summary conviction to a fine not exceeding **level 5** on the standard scale.

[Clean Air Act 1993, s 5.]

1 See the Clean Air (Emission of Grit and Dust from Furnaces) Regulations 1971, SI 1971/162.

*Arrestment plant for furnaces*

7.10128 6. **Arrestment plant for new non-domestic furnaces** (1) A furnace other than a domestic furnace shall not be used in a building—

(*a*) to burn pulverised fuel; or

(*b*) to burn, at a rate of 45.4 kilograms or more an hour, any other solid matter; or

(*c*) to burn, at a rate equivalent to 366.4 kilowatts or more, any liquid or gaseous matter,

unless the furnace is provided with plant for arresting grit and dust which has been approved by the local authority or which has been installed in accordance with plans and specifications submitted to and approved by the local authority, and that plant is properly maintained and used.

(2) Subsection (1) has effect subject to any exemptions prescribed or granted under section 7.

(3) The Secretary of State may by regulations substitute for any rate mentioned in subsection (1)(*b*) or (*c*) such other rate as he thinks fit: but no regulations shall be made so as to reduce any rate unless a draft of the regulations has been laid before and approved by each House of Parliament.

(4) Regulations under subsection (3) reducing any rate shall not apply to a furnace which has been installed, the installation of which has been begun, or an agreement for the purchase or installation of which has been entered into, before the date on which the regulations come into force.

(5) If on any day a furnace is used in contravention of subsection (1), the occupier of the building shall be guilty of an offence and liable on summary conviction to a fine not exceeding **level 5** on the standard scale.

[Clean Air Act 1993, s 6.]

7.10129 7. **Exemptions from section 6** (1) The Secretary of State may by regulations provide that furnaces of any class prescribed in the regulations[1] shall, while used for a purpose so prescribed, be exempted from the operation of section 6(1).

(2) If on the application of the occupier of a building a local authority are satisfied that the emission of grit and dust from any chimney serving a furnace in the building will not be prejudicial to health or a nuisance if the furnace is used for a particular purpose without compliance with section 6(1), they may exempt the furnace from the operation of that subsection while used for that purpose.

(3) If a local authority to whom an application is duly made for an exemption under subsection (2) fail to determine the application and to give a written notice of their decision to the applicant within—

(*a*) eight weeks of receiving the application; or

(*b*) such longer period as may be agreed in writing between the applicant and the authority,

the furnace shall be treated as having been granted an exemption from the operation of section 6(1) while used for the purpose specified in the application.

(4) If a local authority decide not to grant an exemption under subsection (2), they shall give the applicant a written notification of their decision stating their reasons, and the applicant may within twenty-eight days of receiving the notification appeal against the decision to the Secretary of State.

(5) On an appeal under this section the Secretary of State—

(*a*) may confirm the decision appealed against; or

(*b*) may grant the exemption applied for or vary the purpose for which the furnace to which the application relates may be used without compliance with section 6(1);

and shall give the appellant a written notification of his decision, stating his reasons for it.

(6) If on any day a furnace which is exempt from the operation of section 6(1) is used for a purpose other than a prescribed purpose or, as the case may be, a purpose for which the furnace may be used by virtue of subsection (2), (3) or (5), the occupier of the building shall be guilty of an offence and liable on summary conviction to a fine not exceeding **level 5** on the standard scale.

[Clean Air Act 1993, s 7.]

[1] The Clean Air (Miscellaneous Provisions) (England) Regulations 2014, SI 2014/3318 have been made.

7.10130 **8. Requirement to fit arrestment plant for burning solid fuel in other cases**

(1) A domestic furnace shall not be used in a building—

(*a*) to burn pulverised fuel; or

(*b*) to burn, at a rate of 1.02 tonnes an hour or more, solid fuel in any other form or solid waste;

unless the furnace is provided with plant for arresting grit and dust which has been approved by the local authority or which has been installed in accordance with plans and specifications submitted to and approved by the local authority, and that plant is properly maintained and used.

(2) If a furnace is used in a building in contravention of subsection (1), the occupier of the building shall be guilty of an offence and liable on summary conviction to a fine not exceeding **level 5** on the standard scale.

[Clean Air Act 1993, s 8.]

7.10131 **9. Appeal to Secretary of State against refusal of approval** (1) Where a local authority determine an application for approval under section 6 or 8, they shall give the applicant a written notification of their decision and, in the case of a decision not to grant approval, shall state their reasons for not doing so.

(2) A person who—

(*a*) has made such an application to a local authority; or

(*b*) is interested in a building with respect to which such an application has been made,

may, if he is dissatisfied with the decision of the authority on the application, appeal within twenty-eight days after he is notified of the decision to the Secretary of State; and the Secretary of State may give any approval which the local authority might have given.

(3) An approval given by the Secretary of State under this section shall have the like effect as an approval of the local authority.

[Clean Air Act 1993, s 9.]

*Measurement of grit, dust and fumes*

7.10132 **10. Measurement of grit, dust and fumes by occupiers** (1) If a furnace in a building is used—

(*a*) to burn pulverised fuel;

(*b*) to burn, at a rate of 45.4 kilograms or more an hour, any other solid matter; or

(*c*) to burn, at a rate equivalent to 366.4 kilowatts or more, any liquid or gaseous matter,

the local authority may, by notice in writing served on the occupier of the building, direct that the provisions of subsection (2) below shall apply to the furnace, and those provisions shall apply accordingly.

(2) In the case of a furnace to which this subsection for the time being applies, the occupier of the building shall comply with such requirements as may be prescribed as to—

(*a*) making and recording measurements from time to time of the grit, dust and fumes emitted from the furnace;

(*b*) making adaptations for that purpose to the chimney serving the furnace;

(*c*) providing and maintaining apparatus for making and recording the measurements; and

(*d*) informing the local authority of the results obtained from the measurements or otherwise making those results available to them;

and in this subsection "prescribed" means prescribed (whether generally or for any class of furnace) by regulations made by the Secretary of State.

(3) If the occupier of the building fails to comply with those requirements, he shall be guilty of an offence and liable on summary conviction—

(*a*) to a fine not exceeding **level 5** on the standard scale; or

(*b*) to cumulative penalties on continuance in accordance with section 50.

(4) The occupier of a building who by virtue of subsection (2) is under a duty to make and record measurements of grit, dust and fumes emitted from a furnace in the building shall permit the

local authority to be represented during the making and recording of those measurements.

(5) The Secretary of State may by regulations substitute for any rate mentioned in subsection (1)(*b*) or (*c*) such other rate as he thinks fit; but regulations shall not be made under this subsection so as to reduce any rate unless a draft of the regulations has been laid before and approved by each House of Parliament.

(6) Any direction given by a local authority under subsection (1) with respect to a furnace in a building may be revoked by the local authority by a subsequent notice in writing served on the occupier of the building, without prejudice, however, to their power to give another direction under that subsection.

[Clean Air Act 1993, s 10.]

7.10132A **11. Measurement of grit, dust and fumes by local authorities** (1) This section applies to any furnace to which section 10(2) (duty to comply with prescribed requirements) for the time being applies and which is used—

(*a*) to burn, at a rate less than 1.02 tonnes an hour, solid matter other than pulverised fuel; or

(*b*) to burn, at a rate of less than 8.21 Megawatts, any liquid or gaseous matter.

(2) The occupier of the building in which the furnace is situated may, by notice in writing given to the local authority, request that authority to make and record measurements of the grit, dust and fumes emitted from the furnace.

(3) While a notice is in force under subsection (2)—

(*a*) the local authority shall from time to time make and record measurements of the grit, dust and fumes emitted from the furnace; and

(*b*) the occupier shall not be under a duty to comply with any requirements of regulations under subsection (2) of section 10 in relation to the furnace, except those imposed by virtue of paragraph (*b*) of that subsection;

and any such notice given by the occupier of a building may be withdrawn by a subsequent notice in writing given to the local authority by him or any subsequent occupier of that building.

(4) A direction under section 10(1) applying section 10(2) to a furnace which is used as mentioned in subsection (1)(*a*) or (*b*) of this section shall contain a statement of the effect of subsections (1) to (3) of this section.

[Clean Air Act 1993, s 11.]

7.10133 **12. Information about furnaces and fuel consumed** (1) For the purpose of enabling the local authority properly to perform their functions under and in connection with sections 5 to 11, the local authority may, by notice in writing served on the occupier of any building, require the occupier to furnish to them, within fourteen days or such longer time as may be limited by the notice, such information as to the furnaces in the building and the fuel or waste burned in those furnaces as they may reasonably require for that purpose.

(2) Any person who, having been duly served with a notice under subsection (1)—

(*a*) fails to comply with the requirements of the notice within the time limited, or

(*b*) furnishes any information in reply to the notice which he knows to be false in a material particular,

shall be guilty of an offence and liable on summary conviction to a fine not exceeding level 5 on the standard scale.

[Clean Air Act 1993, s 12.]

*Outdoor furnaces*

7.10134 **13. Grit and dust from outdoor furnaces, etc** (1) Sections 5 to 12 shall apply in relation to the furnace of any fixed boiler or industrial plant as they apply in relation to a furnace in a building.

(2) References in those sections to the occupier of the building shall, in relation to a furnace falling within subsection (1), be read as references to the person having possession of the boiler or plant.

(3) The reference in section 6(4) (and the reference in paragraph 6(1) and (3) of Schedule 5) to the installation and to the purchase of a furnace shall, in relation to a furnace which is already contained in any fixed boiler or industrial plant, be read as a reference to attaching the boiler or plant to the building or fixing it to or installing it on any land and to purchasing it respectively.

[Clean Air Act 1993, s 13.]

*Height of chimneys*

7.10135 **14. Height of chimneys for furnaces** (1) This section applies to any furnace served by a chimney.

(2) An occupier of a building shall not knowingly cause or permit a furnace to be used in the building—

(*a*) to burn pulverised fuel;

(*b*) to burn, at a rate of 45.4 kilograms or more an hour, any other solid matter; or

(*c*) to burn, at a rate equivalent to 366.4 kilowatts or more, any liquid or gaseous matter,

unless the height of the chimney serving the furnace has been approved for the purposes of this section and any conditions subject to which the approval was granted are complied with.

(3) If on any day the occupier of a building contravenes subsection (2), he shall be guilty of an offence.

(4) A person having possession of any fixed boiler or industrial plant, other than an exempted boiler or plant, shall not knowingly cause or permit a furnace of that boiler or plant to be used as mentioned in subsection (2), unless the height of the chimney serving the furnace has been approved for the purposes of this section and any conditions subject to which the approval was granted are complied with.

(5) If on any day a person having possession of any boiler or plant contravenes subsection (4), he shall be guilty of an offence.

(6) A person guilty of an offence under this section shall be liable on summary conviction to a fine not exceeding **level 5** on the standard scale.

(7) In this section "exempted boiler or plant" means a boiler or plant which is used or to be used wholly for any purpose prescribed in regulations[1] made by the Secretary of State; and the height of a chimney is approved for the purposes of this section if approval is granted by the local authority or the Secretary of State under section 15.

[Clean Air Act 1993, s 14.]

1 The Clean Air (Miscellaneous Provisions) (England) Regulations 2014, SI 2014/3318 have been made.

## PART III[1]

## SMOKE CONTROL AREAS

*Creation of smoke control areas*

7.10136 18. **Declaration of smoke control area by local authority** (1) A local authority may by order declare the whole or any part of the district of the authority to be a smoke control area; and any order made under this section is referred to in this Act as a "smoke control order".

(2) A smoke control order—

(*a*) may make different provision for different parts of the smoke control area;

(*b*) may limit the operation of section 20 (prohibition of emissions of smoke) to specified classes of building in the area; and

(*c*) may exempt specified buildings or classes of building or specified fireplaces or classes of fireplace in the area from the operation of that section, upon such conditions as may be specified in the order;

and the reference in paragraph (*c*) to specified buildings or classes of building include a reference to any specified, or to any specified classes of, fixed boiler or industrial plant.

(3) A smoke control order may be revoked or varied by a subsequent order.

(4) The provisions of Schedule 1 apply to the coming into operation of smoke control orders.

[Clean Air Act 1993, s 18.]

1 Part III contains ss 18–29.

*Prohibition on emission of smoke in smoke control area*

7.10137 20. **Prohibition on emission of smoke in smoke control area** (1) If, on any day, smoke is emitted from a chimney of any building within a smoke control area, the occupier of the building shall be guilty of an offence.

(2) If, on any day, smoke is emitted from a chimney (not being a chimney of a building) which serves the furnace of any fixed boiler or industrial plant within a smoke control area, the person having possession of the boiler or plant shall be guilty of an offence.

(3) Subsections (1) and (2) have effect—

(*a*) subject to any exemptions for the time being in force under section 18, 21 or 22;

(*b*) subject to section 51 (duty to notify offences to occupier or other person liable).

(4) In proceedings for an offence under this section it shall be a defence to prove that the alleged emission was not caused by the use of any fuel other than an authorised fuel.

(5) A person guilty of an offence under this section shall be liable on summary conviction to a fine not exceeding **level 3** on the standard scale.

(5ZA) In the application of this Part to England, "authorised fuel" means a fuel included in a list of authorised fuels kept by the Secretary of State for the purposes of this Part.

(5ZB) The Secretary of State must—

(*a*) publish the list of authorised fuels, and

(*b*) publish a revised copy of the list as soon as is reasonably practicable after any change is made to it.

(5ZC) The list must be published in such manner as the Secretary of State considers appropriate.

(6) Except as provided by subsection (5ZA), in this Part "authorised fuel" means a fuel declared by regulations[1] of the Secretary of State to be an authorised fuel for the purposes of this Part.

[Clean Air Act 1993, s 20 as amended by the Deregulation Act 2015, s 15.]

1 The Smoke Control Areas (Authorised Fuels) (England) (No 2) Regulations 2014, SI 2014/2336 (inter alia revoking the Smoke Control Areas (Authorised Fuels) (England) Regulations 2014, SI 2014/491) and the Smoke Control Areas (Authorised Fuels) (Wales) Regulations 2016, SI 2016/812 have been made.

7.10138 **21. Power to exempt certain fireplaces** (A1) For the purposes of the application of this Part to England, the Secretary of State may exempt any class of fireplace from the provisions of section 20 (prohibition of smoke emissions in smoke control area) if he is satisfied that such fireplaces can be used for burning fuel other than authorised fuels without producing any smoke or a substantial quantity of smoke.

(A2) An exemption under subsection (A1) may be made subject to such conditions as the Secretary of State considers appropriate.

(A3) The Secretary of State must—

(*a*) publish a list of those classes of fireplace that are exempt under subsection (A1) including details of any conditions to which an exemption is subject;

(*b*) publish a revised copy of the list as soon as is reasonably practicable after any change is made to the classes of fireplace that are so exempt or to the conditions to which an exemption is subject.

(A4) The list must be published in such manner as the Secretary of State considers appropriate.

(1) Except where subsection (A1) applies, the Secretary of State may by order[1] exempt any class of fireplace, upon such conditions as may be specified in the order, from the provisions of section 20 (prohibition of smoke emissions in smoke control area), if he is satisfied that such fireplaces can be used for burning fuel other than authorised fuels without producing any smoke or a substantial quantity of smoke.

[Clean Air Act 1993, s 21 as amended by the Deregulation Act 2015, s 15.]

---

1 The Smoke Control Areas (Exempted Fireplaces) (England) Order 2015, SI 2015/307 and the Smoke Control Areas (Exempted Fireplaces) (Wales) Order 2016, SI 2016/811 have been made which exempt those fireplaces specified in the Schedule thereto which can be used for burning fuel other than authorised fuels without producing smoke or a substantial quantity of smoke.

7.10139 **22. Exemptions relating to particular areas** (1) The Secretary of State may, if it appears to him to be necessary or expedient so to do, by order suspend or relax the operation of section 20 (prohibition of smoke emissions in smoke control area) in relation to the whole or any part of a smoke control area.

(2) Before making an order under subsection (1) the Secretary of State shall consult with the local authority unless he is satisfied that, on account of urgency, such consultation is impracticable.

(3) As soon as practicable after the making of such an order the local authority shall take such steps as appear to them suitable for bringing the effect of the order to the notice of persons affected.

[Clean Air Act 1993, s 22.]

*Dealings with unauthorised fuel*

7.10140 **23. Acquisition and sale of unauthorised fuel in a smoke control area** (1) Any person who—

(*a*) acquires any solid fuel for use in a building in a smoke control area otherwise than in a building or fireplace exempted from the operation of section 20 (prohibition of smoke emissions in smoke control area);

(*b*) acquires any solid fuel for use in any fixed boiler or industrial plant in a smoke control area, not being a boiler or plant so exempted; or

(*c*) sells by retail any solid fuel for delivery by him or on his behalf to—

(i) a building in a smoke control area; or

(ii) premises in such an area in which there is any fixed boiler or industrial plant,

shall be guilty of an offence and liable on summary conviction to a fine not exceeding **level 3** on the standard scale.

(2) In subsection (1), "solid fuel" means any solid fuel other than an authorised fuel.

(3) Subsection (1) shall, in its application to a smoke control area in which the operation of section 20 is limited by a smoke control order to specified classes of buildings, boilers or plant, have effect as if references to a building, boiler or plant were references to a building, boiler or plant of a class specified in the order.

(4) The power of the Secretary of State under section 22 (exemptions relating to particular areas) to suspend or relax the operation of section 20 in relation to the whole or any part of a smoke control area includes power to suspend or relax the operation of subsection (1) in relation to the whole or any part of such an area.

(5) In proceedings for an offence under this section consisting of the sale of fuel for delivery to a building or premises, it shall be a defence for the person accused to prove that he believed and had reasonable grounds for believing—

(*a*) that the building was exempted from the operation of section 20 or, in a case where the operation of that section is limited to specified classes of building, was not of a specified class; or

(*b*) that the fuel was acquired for use in a fireplace, boiler or plant so exempted or, in a case where the operation of that section is limited to specified classes of boilers or plant, in a boiler or plant not of a specified class.

[Clean Air Act 1993, s 23.]

*Adaptation of fireplaces*

7.10141 **24. Power of local authority to require adaptation of fireplaces in private dwellings** (1) The local authority may, by notice in writing served on the occupier or owner of a private dwelling which is, or when a smoke control order comes into operation will be, within a smoke control area, require the carrying out of adaptations in or in connection with the dwelling to avoid contraventions of section 20 (prohibition of smoke emissions in smoke control area).

(2) The provisions of Part XII of the Public Health Act 1936 with respect to appeals against, and the enforcement of, notices requiring the execution of works shall apply in relation to any notice under subsection (1).

(3) Any reference in those provisions to the expenses reasonably incurred in executing the works shall, in relation to a notice under subsection (1), be read as a reference to three-tenths of those expenses or such smaller fraction of those expenses as the local authority may in any particular case determine.

(4) *Scotland.*

[Clean Air Act 1993, s 24.]

7.10142 **25. Expenditure incurred in relation to adaptations in private dwellings** Schedule 2 to this Act shall have effect with respect to certain expenditure incurred in adapting old private dwellings in smoke control areas.

[Clean Air Act 1993, s 25—summarised.]

*Supplementary provisions*

7.10143 **27. References to adaptations for avoiding contraventions of section 20** (1) References in this Part to adaptations in or in connection with a dwelling to avoid contraventions of section 20 (prohibition of smoke emissions from smoke control area) shall be read as references to the execution of any of the following works (whether in or outside the dwelling), that is to say—

- (*a*) adapting or converting any fireplace;
- (*b*) replacing any fireplace by another fireplace or by some other means of heating or cooking;
- (*c*) altering any chimney which serves any fireplace;
- (*d*) providing gas ignition, electric ignition or any other special means of ignition; or
- (*e*) carrying out any operation incidental to any of the operations mentioned in paragraphs (*a*) to (*d*);

being works which are reasonably necessary in order to make what is in all the circumstances suitable provision for heating and cooking without contraventions of section 20.

(2) For the purposes of this section the provision of any igniting apparatus or appliance (whether fixed or not) operating by means of gas, electricity or other special means shall be treated as the execution of works.

(3) Except for the purposes of section 24 (power of local authority to require certain adaptations), works which make such suitable provision as is mentioned in subsection (1) shall not be treated as not being adaptations to avoid contraventions of section 20 of this Act by reason that they go beyond what is reasonably necessary for that purpose, but any expenditure incurred in executing them in excess of the expenditure which would have been reasonably incurred in doing what was reasonably necessary shall be left out of account.

(4) References in this section to a dwelling include references to any premises or part of any premises to which section 26 (grants towards certain adaptations in churches and other buildings) applies.

[Clean Air Act 1993, s 27.]

7.10144 **29. Interpretation of Part III** In this Part, except so far as the context otherwise requires—

"authorised fuel" has the meaning given in section 20;

"conditional sale agreement" means an agreement for the sale of goods under which—

- (*a*) the purchase price or part of it is payable by instalments; and
- (*b*) the property in the goods is to remain in the seller (notwithstanding that the buyer is to be in possession of the goods) until such conditions as to the payment of instalments or otherwise as may be specified in the agreement are fulfilled;

"heating", in relation to a dwelling, includes the heating of water;

"hire-purchase agreement" means an agreement, other than a conditional sale agreement, under which—

- (*a*) goods are bailed or (in Scotland) hired in return for periodical payments by the person to whom they are bailed or hired; and
- (*b*) the property in the goods will pass to that person if the terms of the agreement are complied with and one or more of the following occurs—
  - (i) the exercise of an option to purchase by that person;
  - (ii) the doing of any other specified act by any party to the agreement; and
  - (iii) the happening of any other specified event;

"old private dwelling" has the meaning given in section 25; and "smoke control order" means an order made by a local authority under section 18.

[Clean Air Act 1993, s 29 as amended by the Deregulation Act 2015, s 15.]

PART IV[1]

CONTROL OF CERTAIN FORMS OF AIR POLLUTION

7.10145 30. **Regulations about motor fuel** (1) For the purpose of limiting or reducing air pollution, the Secretary of State may by regulations[2]—

(*a*) impose requirements as to the composition and contents of any fuel of a kind used in motor vehicles; and

(*b*) where such requirements are in force, prevent or restrict the production, treatment, distribution, import, sale or use of any fuel which in any respect fails to comply with the requirements, and which is for use in the United Kingdom.

(2)–(3) *Supplementary provisions as to regulations.*

(4) It shall be duty of every local weights and measures authority to enforce the provisions of regulations under this section within its area; and subsection (2) of section 26 of the Trade Descriptions Act 1968 (reports and inquiries) shall apply as respects those authorities' functions under this subsection as it applies to their functions under that Act.

(5) The following provisions of the Trade Descriptions Act 1968[3] shall apply in relation to the enforcement of regulations under this section as they apply to the enforcement of that Act, that is to say—

section 27 (power to make test purchases);
section 28 (power to enter premises and inspect and seize goods and documents);
section 29 (obstruction of authorised officers);
section 30 (notice of test);

and section 33 of that Act shall apply to the exercise of powers under section 28 as applied by this subsection.

References to an offence under that Act in those provisions as applied by this subsection shall be construed as references to an offence under section 32 of this Act (provisions supplementary to this section) relating to regulations under this section.

(6) *Scotland.*

(7)–(9) *Northern Ireland.*

[Clean Air Act 1993, s 30 as amended by the Statute Law (Repeals) Act 1998 and the Statute Law (Repeals) Act 2004.]

---

1 Part IV contains ss 30–33.

2 See the Motor Fuel (Composition and Content) Regulations 1999, SI 1999/3107 amended by SI 2001/3896, SI 2003/3078, SI 2007/1608, SI 2010/3035, SI 2012/2567, SI 2013/2897, SI 2014/3075 and SI 2015/1796.

3 See this PART: title CONSUMER PROTECTION, ante.

7.10146 31. **Regulations about sulphur content of oil fuel for furnaces or engines**

(1) For the purpose of limiting or reducing air pollution, the Secretary of State may by regulations impose limits on the sulphur content of oil fuel which is used in furnaces or engines.

(2)–(3) *Supplementary provisions with respect to regulations.*

(4) It shall be the duty—

(*a*) of every local authority to enforce the provisions of regulations under this section within its area, except in relation to a furnace which is—

(i) part of a process subject to Part I of the Environmental Protection Act 1990, or

(ii) part of an installation subject to regulation by the appropriate agency under regulations made under section 2 of the Pollution Prevention and Control Act 1999; and

(*b*) of the inspectors appointed under that Part to enforce those provisions in relation to furnaces within sub-paragraph (1) of paragraph (*a*) above and of the appropriate agency to enforce those provision in relation to furnaces within sub-paragraph (ii) of that paragraph;

but nothing in this section shall be taken to authorise a local authority in Scotland to institute proceedings for any offence.

(5) In this section "oil fuel" means any liquid petroleum product produced in a refinery.

(6) In this section, "appropriate agency" means—

(*a*) in relation to England, the Environment Agency;

(*b*) in relation to Wales, the Natural Resources Body for Wales.

[Clean Air Act 1993, s 31 as amended by SI 2000/1973 and SI 2013/755.]

7.10147 32. **Provisions supplementary to sections 30 and 31** (1) Regulations[1] under section 30 or 31 (regulation of content of motor fuel and fuel oil) may authorise the Secretary of State to confer exemptions from any provision of the regulations.

(2) A person who contravenes or fails to comply with any provision of regulations under section 30 or 31 shall be guilty of an offence and liable[2]—

(*a*) on conviction on indictment, to a **fine**; and

(*b*) on summary conviction, to a fine not exceeding **the statutory maximum**;

but the regulations may in any case exclude liability to conviction on indictment or reduce the maximum fine on summary conviction.

(3) Regulations under section 30 or 31 shall, subject to any provision to the contrary in the regulations, apply to fuel used for, and to persons in, the public service of the Crown as they apply to fuel used for other purposes and to other persons.

(4) A local authority shall not be entitled by virtue of subsection (3) to exercise, in relation to fuel used for and persons in that service, any power conferred on the authority by virtue of sections 56 to 58 (rights of entry and inspection and other local authority powers).

[Clean Air Act 1993, s 32.]

---

1 See the Motor Fuel (Lead Content of Petrol) Regulations 1981, SI 1981/1523, amended by SI 1985/1728 and SI 1989/547. See also the Motor Fuel (Sulphur Content of Gas Oil) Regulations 1976, SI 1976/1989, amended by SI 1990/1097 under which a contravention of reg 5(*b*) is punishable only on summary conviction by a fine not exceeding **level 2** on the standard scale (reg 8) and the Oil Fuel (Sulphur Content of Gas Oil) Regulations 1990, SI 1990/1096 under which a contravention of reg 4 is punishable only on summary conviction by a fine not exceeding **level 2** on the standard scale (reg 7).

2 For procedure in respect of an offence which is triable either way, see the Magistrates' Courts Act 1980, ss 17A–21, in PART I: MAGISTRATES' COURTS, PROCEDURE ante.

**7.10148 33. Cable burning** (1) A person who burns insulation from a cable with a view to recovering metal from the cable shall be guilty of an offence unless the burning is part of a process subject to Part I of the Environmental Protection Act 1990 or* an activity subject to regulations under section 2 of the Pollution Prevention and Control Act 1999.

(2) A person guilty of an offence under this section shall be liable on summary conviction to a fine not exceeding **level 5** on the standard scale.

[Clean Air Act 1993, s 33 as amended by the Pollution Prevention and Control Act 1999, Sch 2.]

---

* **Words repealed by the Pollution Prevention and Control Act 1999, Sch 3 from a date to be appointed.**

## PART V[1]

## INFORMATION ABOUT AIR POLLUTION

**7.10149 34. Research and publicity** (1) A local authority may—

(*a*) undertake, or contribute towards the cost of, investigation and research relevant to the problem of air pollution;

(*b*) arrange for the publication of information on that problem;

(*c*) arrange for the delivery of lectures and addresses, and the holding of discussions, on that problem;

(*d*) arrange for the display of pictures, cinematograph films or models, or the holding of exhibitions, relating to that problem; and

(*e*) prepare, or join in or contribute to the cost of the preparation of, pictures, films, models or exhibitions to be displayed or held as mentioned in paragraph (*d*).

(2) In acting under subsection (1)(*b*), a local authority shall ensure that the material published is presented in such a way that no information relating to a trade secret is disclosed, except with the consent in writing of a person authorised to disclose it.

(3) Breach of a duty imposed by subsection (2) shall be actionable.

(4) In any civil or criminal proceedings (whether or not arising under this Act) brought against a local authority, or any member or officer of a local authority, on the grounds that any information has been published, it shall be a defence to show that it was published in compliance with subsections (1) and (2).

[Clean Air Act 1993, s 34.]

---

1 Part V contains ss 34–40.

**7.10150 35. Obtaining information** (1) Without prejudice to the generality of section 34 (research, etc. by local authorities), local authorities may obtain information about the emission of pollutants and other substances into the air—

(*a*) by issuing notices under section 36 (information about emissions from premises);

(*b*) by measuring and recording the emissions, and for that purpose entering on any premises, whether by agreement or in exercise of the power conferred by section 56 (rights of entry and inspection); and

(*c*) by entering into arrangements with occupiers of premises under which they measure and record emissions on behalf of the local authority;

but references to premises in paragraphs (*b*) and (*c*) do not include private dwellings or caravans.

(2) A local authority shall not be entitled to exercise the power of entry mentioned in subsection (1)(*b*) for the purpose of measuring and recording such emissions on any premises unless—

(*a*) the authority has given to the occupier of the premises a notice in writing—

(i) specifying the kind of emissions in question and the steps it proposes to take on the premises for the purpose of measuring and recording emissions of that kind; and

(ii) stating that it proposes to exercise that power for that purpose unless the occupier requests the authority to serve on him a notice under section 36 (information about emissions from premises) with respect to the emissions; and (*b*) the period of twenty-one days beginning with the day on which the notice was given has expired;

and the authority shall not be entitled to exercise that power if, during that period, the occupier gives a notice to the authority requesting it to serve on him a notice under section 36.

(3) Nothing in this section shall authorise a local authority to investigate emissions from any process subject to Part I of the Environmental Protection Act 1990 or* activity subject to regulations under section 2 of the Pollution Prevention and Control Act 1999 otherwise than—

(*a*) by issuing notices under section 36; or

(*b*) by exercising the powers conferred on the authority by section 34(1)(*a*) (investigation and research etc.) without entering the premises concerned.

(4) So long as a local authority exercises any of its powers under subsection (1), it shall from time to time consult the persons mentioned in subsection (5)—

(*a*) about the way in which the local authority exercises those powers (under this section and section 36); and

(*b*) about the extent to which, and the manner in which, any information collected under those powers should be made available to the public.

(5) The consultations required by subsection (4) shall be with—

(*a*) such persons carrying on any trade or business in the authority's area or such organisations appearing to the authority to be representative of those persons; and

(*b*) such persons appearing to the authority to be conversant with problems of air pollution or to have an interest in local amenity;

as appear to the authority to be appropriate.

(6) The consultations shall take place as the authority think necessary, but not less than twice in each financial year.

[Clean Air Act 1993, s 35 as amended by the Pollution Prevention and Control Act 1999, Sch 2.]

---

* **Words repealed by the Pollution Prevention and Control Act 1999, Sch 3 from a date to be appointed.**

7.10151 **36. Notices requiring information about air pollution** (1) A local authority may by notice in writing require the occupier of any premises in its area to furnish, whether by periodical returns or by other means, such estimates or other information as may be specified or described in the notice concerning the emission of pollutants and other substances into the air from the premises.

(2) This section does not apply to premises in so far as they consist of a private dwelling or a caravan.

(2A) If the notice relates to an installation subject to regulation by the appropriate agency under regulations made under section 2 of the Pollution Prevention and Control Act 1999, the person on whom the notice is served shall not be obliged to supply any information which, as certified by the appropriate agency, is not of a kind which is being supplied to the appropriate agency for the purposes of those regulations.

(3) If the notice relates to a process subject to Part I of the Environmental Protection Act 1990, the person on whom the notice is served shall not be obliged to supply any information which, as certified by an inspector appointed under that Part, is not of a kind which is being supplied to the inspector for the purposes of that Part.*

(4) The person on whom a notice is served under this section shall comply with the notice within six weeks of the date of service, or within such longer period as the local authority may by notice allow.

(5) A notice under this section shall not require returns at intervals of less than three months, and no one notice (whether or not requiring periodical returns) shall call for information covering a period of more than twelve months.

(6) Except so far as regulations[1] made by the Secretary of State provide otherwise, this section applies to premises used for, and to persons in, the public service of the Crown as it applies to other premises and persons.

(7) A local authority shall not be entitled by virtue of subsection (6) to exercise, in relation to premises used for and persons in the public service of the Crown, any power conferred on the authority by virtue of sections 56 to 58 (rights of entry and other local authority powers).

(8) A person who—

(*a*) fails without reasonable excuse to comply with the requirements of a notice served on him in pursuance of this section; or

(*b*) in furnishing any estimate or other information in compliance with a notice under this section, makes any statement which he knows to be false in a material particular or recklessly makes any statement which is false in a material particular,

shall be guilty of an offence and liable on summary conviction to a fine not exceeding **level 5** on the standard scale.

(9) Where a person is convicted of an offence under subsection (8) in respect of any premises and information of any kind, nothing in section 35(2) (limits on exercise of power of entry) shall prevent a local authority from exercising the power of entry there mentioned for the purpose of obtaining information of that kind in respect of the premises.

[Clean Air Act 1993, s 36 as amended by SI 2000/1973 and SI 2013/755.]

* **Subsection (3) repealed by the Pollution Prevention and Control Act 1999, Sch 3 from a date to be appointed.**

[1] See the Control of Atmospheric Pollution (Exempted Premises) Regulations 1977, SI 1977/18 revoked and replaced in respect of England by the Clean Air (Miscellaneous Provisions) (England) Regulations 2014, SI 2014/3318.

**7.10152 40. Interpretation of Part V** In this Part—

(*za*) "appropriate agency" means—

(i) in relation to England, the Environment Agency;

(ii) in relation to Wales, the Natural Resources Body for Wales.

(*a*) references to the emission of substances into the atmosphere are to be construed as applying to substances in a gaseous or liquid or solid state, or any combination of those states; and

(*b*) any reference to measurement includes a reference to the taking of samples.

[Clean Air Act 1993, s 40 as amended by SI 2013/755.]

## PART VI[1]

## SPECIAL CASES

**7.10153 41. Relation to Environmental Protection Act 1990** (1) Parts I to III shall not apply to any process which is a prescribed process as from the date which is the determination date for that process.

(2) The "determination date" for a prescribed process is—

(*a*) in the case of a process for which an authorisation is granted, the date on which the enforcing authority grants it, whether in pursuance of the application or, on an appeal, of a direction to grant it, and

(*b*) in the case of a process for which an authorisation is refused, the date of the refusal or, on an appeal, of the affirmation of the refusal.

(3) In this section "authorisation", "enforcing authority" and "prescribed process" have the meaning given in section 1 of the Environmental Protection Act 1990 and the reference to an appeal is a reference to an appeal under section 15 of that Act.*

[Clean Air Act 1993, s 41.]

* **Section repealed by the Pollution Prevention and Control Act 1999, Sch 3 from a date to be appointed.**

[1] Part VI contains ss 41–46.

**7.10154 41A. Relation to the Pollution Prevention and Control Act 1999** (1) Where an activity is subject to regulations under section 2 of the Pollution Prevention and Control Act 1999 (regulation of polluting activities), Parts I to III of this Act shall not apply as from the determination date for the activity in question.

(2) The "determination date", for an activity, is—

(*a*) in the case of an activity for which a permit is granted, the date on which it is granted, whether in pursuance of the application, or on an appeal, of a direction to grant it;

(*b*) in the case of an activity for which a permit is refused, the date of refusal or, on appeal, of the affirmation of the refusal.

(*c*) in the case of an activity that is an exempt waste operation, the date of the entry on the register maintained under paragraph 7 of Schedule 2 (exempt facilities: general) to the Environmental Permitting Regulations of an establishment or undertaking in relation to that operation.

(3) In subsection (2)—

"exempt waste operation" has the meaning given in the Environmental Permitting Regulations;

"permit" means a permit under regulations under section 2 of the Pollution Prevention and Control Act 1999 and the reference to an appeal is a reference to an appeal under those regulations.

(4) In this section—

"activity" includes—

(*a*) a waste operation, or a mining waste operation, within the meaning of the Environmental Permitting Regulations, and

(*b*) a mining waste operation within the meaning of those Regulations; "the Environmental Permitting Regulations" means the Environmental Permitting (England and Wales) Regulations 2010.

[Clean Air Act 1993, s 41A as inserted by SI 2000/1973 and amended by SI 2007/3538, SI 2009/1799 and SI 2010/675.]

**7.10155 42. Colliery spoilbanks** (1) This section applies to any mine or quarry from which coal or shale has been, is being or is to be got.

(2) The owner of a mine or quarry to which this section applies shall employ all practicable means—

(*a*) for preventing combustion of refuse deposited from the mine or quarry; and

(*b*) for preventing or minimising the emission of smoke and fumes from such refuse;

and, if he fails to do so, he shall be guilty of an offence.

(3) A person guilty of an offence under subsection (2) shall be liable on summary conviction—

(*a*) to a fine not exceeding **level 5** on the standard scale; or (*b*) to cumulative penalties on continuance in accordance with section 50.

(4) Neither the provisions of Part III of the Environmental Protection Act 1990 nor any provision of Parts I to III of this Act shall apply in relation to smoke, grit or dust from the combustion of refuse deposited from any mine or quarry to which this section applies.

(5) *Repealed.*

(6) In this section, "mine", "quarry" and "owner" have the same meaning as in the Mines and Quarries Act 1954.

[Clean Air Act 1993, s 42 as amended by the Environment Act 1995, Sch 24.]

7.10156 43. **Railway engines** (1) Section 1 (prohibition of emissions of dark smoke) shall apply in relation to railway locomotive engines as it applies in relation to buildings.

(2) In the application of section 1 to such engines, for the reference in subsection (1) of that section to the occupier of the building there shall be substituted a reference to the owner of the engine.

(3) The owner of any railway locomotive engine shall use any practicable means there may be for minimising the emission of smoke from the chimney on the engine and, if he fails to do so, he shall, if smoke is emitted from that chimney, be guilty of an offence.

(4) A person guilty of an offence under subsection (3) shall be liable on summary conviction—

(*a*) to a fine not exceeding **level 5** on the standard scale; or

(*b*) to cumulative penalties on continuance in accordance with section 50.

(5) Except as provided in this section, nothing in Parts I to III applies to smoke, grit or dust from any railway locomotive engine.

[Clean Air Act 1993, s 43.]

7.10157 44. **Vessels** (1) Section 1 (prohibition of emissions of dark smoke) shall apply in relation to vessels in waters to which this section applies as it applies in relation to buildings.

(2) In the application of section 1 to a vessel—

(*a*) for the reference in subsection (1) of that section to the occupier of the building there shall be substituted a reference to the owner of, and to the master or other officer or person in charge of, the vessel;

(*b*) references to a furnace shall be read as including references to an engine of the vessel; and

(*c*) subsection (5) of that section shall be omitted;

and a person guilty of an offence under that section in relation to a vessel shall be liable on summary conviction to a fine not exceeding **level 5** on the standard scale.

(3) For the purposes of this Act a vessel in any waters to which this section applies which are not within the district of any local authority shall be deemed to be within the district of the local authority whose district includes that point on land which is nearest to the spot where the vessel is.

(4) The waters to which this section applies are—

(*a*) all waters not navigable by sea-going ships; and

(*b*) all waters navigable by sea-going ships which are within the seaward limits of the territorial waters of the United Kingdom and are contained within any port, harbour, river, estuary, haven, dock, canal or other place so long as a person or body of persons is empowered by or under any Act to make charges in respect of vessels entering it or using facilities in it.

(5) In subsection (4) "charges" means any charges with the exception of light dues, local light dues and any other charges payable in respect of lighthouses, buoys or beacons and of charges in respect of pilotage.

(6) Except as provided in this section, nothing in Parts I to III applies to smoke, grit or dust from any vessel.

[Clean Air Act 1993, s 44.]

7.10158 45. **Exemption for purposes of investigations and research** (1) If the local authority are satisfied, on the application of any person interested, that it is expedient to do so for the purpose of enabling investigations or research relevant to the problem of the pollution of the air to be carried out without rendering the applicant liable to proceedings brought under or by virtue of any of the provisions of this Act or the Environmental Protection Act 1990 mentioned below, the local authority may by notice in writing given to the applicant exempt, wholly or to a limited extent,—

(*a*) any chimney from the operation of sections 1 (dark smoke), 5 (grit and dust), 20 (smoke in smoke control area) and 43 (railway engines) of this Act and Part III of the Environmental Protection Act 1990 (statutory nuisances);

(*b*) any furnace, boiler or industrial plant from the operation of section 4(2) (new furnaces to be as far as practicable smokeless);

(*c*) any premises from the operation of section 2 (emissions of dark smoke);

(*d*) any furnace from the operation of sections 6 or 8 (arrestment plant) and 10 (measurement of grit, dust and fumes by occupier), and

(*e*) the acquisition or sale of any fuel specified in the notice from the operation of section 23 (acquisition and sale of unauthorised fuel in smoke control area),

in each case subject to such conditions, if any, and for such period as may be specified in the notice.

(2) Any person who has applied to the local authority for an exemption under this section may,

if he is dissatisfied with the decision of the authority on the application, appeal to the Secretary of State; and the Secretary of State may, if he thinks fit, by notice in writing given to the applicant and the local authority, give any exemption which the authority might have given or vary the terms of any exemption which they have given.

[Clean Air Act 1993, s 45.]

**7.10159 46. Crown premises, etc** (1) It shall be part of the functions of the local authority, in cases where it seems to them proper to do so, to report to the responsible Minister any cases of—

(*a*) emissions of dark smoke, or of grit or dust, from any premises which are under the control of any Government department and are occupied for the public service of the Crown or for any of the purposes of any Government department;

(*b*) emissions of smoke, whether dark smoke or not, from any such premises which are within a smoke control area;

(*c*) emissions of smoke, whether dark smoke or not, from any such premises which appear to them to constitute a nuisance to the inhabitants of the neighbourhood; or

(*d*) emissions of dark smoke from any vessel of Her Majesty's navy, or any Government ship in the service of the Secretary of State while employed for the purposes of Her Majesty's navy, which appear to them to constitute a nuisance to the inhabitants of the neighbourhood,

and on receiving any such report the responsible Minister shall inquire into the circumstances and, if his inquiry reveals that there is cause for complaint, shall employ all practicable means for preventing or minimising the emission of the smoke, grit or dust or for abating the nuisance and preventing a recurrence of it, as the case may be.

(2) Subsection (1) shall apply to premises occupied for the purposes of the Duchy of Lancaster or the Duchy of Cornwall as it applies to premises occupied for the public service of the Crown which are under the control of a Government department, with the substitution, in the case of the Duchy of Cornwall, for references to the responsible Minister of references to such person as the Duke of Cornwall or the possessor for the time being of the Duchy of Cornwall appoints.

(3) The fact that there subsists in any premises an interest belonging to Her Majesty in right of the Crown or of the Duchy of Lancaster, or to the Duchy of Cornwall, or belonging to a Government department or held in trust for Her Majesty for the purposes of a Government department, shall not affect the application of this Act to those premises so long as that interest is not the interest of the occupier of the premises, and this Act shall have effect accordingly in relation to the premises and that and all other interests in the premises.

(4) Section 44 (vessels) shall, with the omission of the reference in subsection (2) of that section to the owner, apply to vessels owned by the Crown, except that it shall not apply to vessels of Her Majesty's navy or to Government ships in the service of the Secretary of State while employed for the purposes of Her Majesty's navy.

(5) This Act (except Parts IV and V) shall have effect in relation to premises occupied for the service of a visiting force as if the premises were occupied for the public service of the Crown and were under the control of the Government department by arrangement with whom the premises are occupied.

(6) In this section—

"Government ship" has the same meaning as in the Merchant Shipping Act 1995; and

"visiting force" means any such body, contingent or detachment of the forces of any country as is a visiting force for the purposes of any of the provisions of the Visiting Forces Act 1952.

[Clean Air Act 1993, s 46, as amended by the Merchant Shipping Act 1995, Sch 13.]

## PART VII[1]

### MISCELLANEOUS AND GENERAL

*Power to apply certain provisions to fumes and gases*

**7.10160 47. Application to fumes and gases of certain provisions as to grit, dust and smoke** (1) The Secretary of State may by regulations—

(*a*) apply all or any of the provisions of sections 5, 6, 7, 42(4) 43(5), 44(6) and 46(1) to fumes or prescribed gases or both as they apply to grit and dust;

(*b*) apply all or any of the provisions of section 4 to fumes or prescribed gases or both as they apply to smoke; and

(*c*) apply all or any of the provisions of section 11 to prescribed gases as they apply to grit and dust,

subject, in each case, to such exceptions and modifications as he thinks expedient.

(2) No regulations shall be made under this section unless a draft of the regulations has been laid before and approved by each House of Parliament.

(3) In the application of any provision of this Act to prescribed gases by virtue of regulations under this section, any reference to the rate of emission of any substance shall be construed as a reference to the percentage by volume or by mass of the gas which may be emitted during a period specified in the regulations.

(4) In this section—

"gas" includes vapour and moisture precipitated from vapour; and

"prescribed" means prescribed in regulations under this section.

[Clean Air Act 1993, s 47.]

[1] Part VII contains ss 47–68.

*Power to give effect to international agreements*

7.10161 **48. Power to give effect to international agreements** The Secretary of State may by regulations provide that any provision of Parts IV and V, or of this Part (apart from this section) so far as relating to those Parts, shall have effect with such modifications as are prescribed in the regulations with a view to enabling the Government of the United Kingdom to give effect to any provision made by or under any international agreement to which the Government is for the time being a party.

[Clean Air Act 1993, s 48.]

*Administration and enforcement*

7.10162 **49. Unjustified disclosures of information** (1) If a person discloses any information relating to any trade secret used in carrying on any particular undertaking which has been given to him or obtained by him by virtue of this Act, he shall, subject to subsection (2), be guilty of an offence and liable on summary conviction to a fine not exceeding **level 5** on the standard scale.

(2) A person shall not be guilty of an offence under subsection (1) by reason of the disclosure of any information if the disclosure is made—

(*a*) in the performance of his duty;

(*b*) in pursuance of section 34(1)(*b*); or

(*c*) with the consent of a person having a right to disclose the information.

[Clean Air Act 1993, s 49.]

7.10163 **50. Cumulative penalties on continuance of certain offences** (1) Where—

(*a*) a person is convicted of an offence which is subject to cumulative penalties on continuance in accordance with this section; and

(*b*) it is shown to the satisfaction of the court that the offence was substantially a repetition or continuation of an earlier offence by him after he had been convicted of the earlier offence,

the penalty provided by subsection (2) shall apply instead of the penalty otherwise specified for the offence.

(2) Where this subsection applies the person convicted shall be liable on summary conviction to a fine not exceeding—

(*a*) **level** 5 on the standard scale; or

(*b*) **£50** for every day on which the earlier offence has been so repeated or continued by him within the three months next following his conviction of that offence,

whichever is the greater.

(3) Where an offence is subject to cumulative penalties in accordance with this section—

(*a*) the court by which a person is convicted of the original offence may fix a reasonable period from the date of conviction for compliance by the defendant with any directions given by the court; and

(*b*) where a court has fixed such a period, the daily penalty referred to in subsection (2) is not recoverable in respect of any day before the end of that period.

[Clean Air Act 1993, s 50.]

7.10164 **51. Duty to notify occupiers of offences** (1) If, in the opinion of an authorised officer of the local authority—

(*a*) an offence is being or has been committed under section 1, 2 or 20 (prohibition of certain emissions of smoke);

(*b*) *repealed*,

he shall, unless he has reason to believe that notice of it has already been given by or on behalf of the local authority, as soon as may be notify the appropriate person, and, if his notification is not in writing, shall before the end of the four days next following the day on which he became aware of the offence, confirm the notification in writing.

(2) For the purposes of subsection (1), the appropriate person to notify is the occupier of the premises, the person having possession of the boiler or plant, the owner of the railway locomotive engine or the owner or master or other officer or person in charge of the vessel concerned, as the case may be.

(3) In any proceedings for an offence under section 1, 2 or 20 it shall be a defence to prove that the provisions of subsection (1) have not been complied with in the case of the offence; and if no such notification as is required by that subsection has been given before the end of the four days next following the day of the offence, that subsection shall be taken not to have been complied with unless the contrary is proved.

[Clean Air Act 1993, s 51 as amended by the Environment Act 1995, Sch 24.]

7.10165 **52. Offences committed by bodies corporate** (1) Where an offence under this Act which has been committed by a body corporate is proved to have been committed with the consent or connivance of, or to be attributable to any neglect on the part of, any director, manager, secretary or other similar officer of the body corporate or any person who was purporting to act in any such capacity, he as well as the body corporate shall be guilty of that offence and be liable to be proceeded against and punished accordingly.

(2) Where the affairs of a body corporate are managed by its members this section shall apply in relation to the acts and defaults of a member in connection with his functions of management as if he were a director of the body corporate.

[Clean Air Act 1993, s 52.]

7.10166 **53. Offence due to act or default of another** (1) Where the commission by any person of an offence under this Act is due to the act or default of some other person, that other person shall be guilty of the offence.

(2) A person may be charged with and convicted of an offence by virtue of this section whether or not proceedings for the offence are taken against any other person.

[Clean Air Act 1993, s 53.]

7.10167 **55. General provisions as to enforcement** (1) It shall be the duty of the local authority to enforce—

(*a*) the provisions of Parts I to III, section 33 and Part VI; and

(*b*) the provisions of this Part so far as relating to those provisions;

but nothing in this section shall be taken as extending to the enforcement of any building regulations.

(2) A local authority in England and Wales may institute proceedings for an offence under section 1 or 2 (prohibition of emissions of dark smoke) in the case of any smoke which affects any part of their district notwithstanding, in the case of an offence under section 1, that the smoke is emitted from a chimney outside their district and, in the case of an offence under section 2, that the smoke is emitted from premises outside their district.

(3) Nothing in this section shall be taken as authorising a local authority in Scotland to institute proceedings for an offence against this Act.

[Clean Air Act 1993, s 55.]

7.10168 **56. Rights of entry and inspection etc** (1) Any person authorised in that behalf by a local authority may at any reasonable time—

(*a*) enter upon any land or vessel for the purpose of—

(i) performing any function conferred on the authority or that person by virtue of this Act,

(ii) determining whether, and if so in what manner, such a function should be performed, or

(iii) determining whether any provision of this Act or of an instrument made under this Act is being complied with; and

(*b*) carry out such inspections, measurements and tests on the land or vessel or of any articles on it and take away such samples of the land or articles as he considers appropriate for such a purpose.

(2) Subsection (1) above does not, except in relation to work under section 24(1) (adaptations to dwellings in smoke control area), apply in relation to a private dwelling.

(3) If it is shown to the satisfaction of a justice of the peace on sworn information in writing—

(*a*) that admission to any land or vessel which a person is entitled to enter in pursuance of subsection (1) has been refused to that person or that refusal is apprehended or that the land or vessel is unoccupied or that the occupier is temporarily absent or that the case is one of emergency or that an application for admission would defeat the object of the entry; and

(*b*) that there is reasonable ground for entry upon the land or vessel for the purpose for which entry is required,

then, subject to subsection (4), the justice may by warrant under his hand authorise that person to enter the land or vessel, if need be by force.

(4) A justice of the peace shall not issue a warrant in pursuance of subsection (3) in respect of any land or vessel unless he is satisfied—

(*a*) that admission to the land or vessel in pursuance of subsection (1) was sought after not less than seven days notice of the intended entry had been served on the occupier; or

(*b*) that admission to the land or vessel in pursuance of that subsection was sought in an emergency and was refused by or on behalf of the occupier; or

(*c*) that the land or vessel is unoccupied; or

(*d*) that an application for admission to the land or vessel would defeat the object of the entry.

(5) A warrant issued in pursuance of this section shall continue in force until the purpose for which the entry is required has been satisfied.

(6) *Scotland.*

[Clean Air Act 1993, s 56.]

7.10169 **57. Provisions supplementary to section 56** (1) A person authorised to enter upon any land or vessel in pursuance of section 56 shall, if so required, produce evidence of his authority before he enters upon the land or vessel.

(2) A person so authorised may take with him on to the land or vessel in question such other persons and such equipment as may be necessary.

(3) Admission to any land or vessel used for residential purposes and admission with heavy equipment to any other land or vessel shall not, except in an emergency or in a case where the land or vessel is unoccupied, be demanded as of right in pursuance of section 56(1) unless notice of the intended entry has been served on the occupier not less than seven days before the demand.

(4) A person who, in the exercise of powers conferred on him by virtue of section 56 or this section, enters upon any land or vessel which is unoccupied or of which the occupier is temporarily absent shall leave the land or vessel as effectually secured against unauthorised entry as he found it.

(5) It shall be the duty of a local authority to make full compensation to any person who has sustained damage by reason of—

(*a*) the exercise by a person authorised by the authority of any of the powers conferred on the person so authorised by virtue of section 56 or this section; or

(*b*) the failure of a person so authorised to perform the duty imposed on him by subsection (4),

except where the damage is attributable to the default of the person who sustained it; and any dispute as to a person's entitlement to compensation in pursuance of this subsection or as to the amount of the compensation shall be determined by arbitration.

(6) A person who wilfully obstructs another person acting in the exercise of any powers conferred on the other person by virtue of section 56 or this section shall be guilty of an offence and liable on summary conviction to a fine not exceeding **level 3** on the standard scale.

(7) In section 56 and this section any reference to an emergency is a reference to a case where a person requiring entry to any land or vessel has reasonable cause to believe that circumstances exist which are likely to endanger life or health and that immediate entry to the land or vessel is necessary to verify the existence of those circumstances or to ascertain their cause or to effect a remedy.

[Clean Air Act 1993, s 57.]

7.10170 **58. Power of local authorities to obtain information** (1) A local authority may serve on any person a notice requiring him to furnish to the authority, within a period or at times specified in the notice and in a form so specified, any information so specified which the authority reasonably considers that it needs for the purposes of any function conferred on the authority by Part IV or V of this Act (or by this Part of this Act so far as relating to those Parts).

(2) The Secretary of State may by regulations provide for restricting the information which may be required in pursuance of subsection (1) and for determining the form in which the information is to be so required.

(3) Any person who—

(*a*) fails without reasonable excuse to comply with the requirements of a notice served on him in pursuance of this section; or

(*b*) in furnishing any information in compliance with such a notice, makes any statement which he knows to be false in a material particular or recklessly makes any statement which is false in a material particular,

shall be guilty of an offence and liable on summary conviction to a fine not exceeding **level 5** on the standard scale.

[Clean Air Act 1993, s 58.]

7.10171 **61. Joint exercise of local authority functions** (1) Sections 6, 7, 9 and 10 of the Public Health Act 1936 (provisions relating to joint boards) shall, so far as applicable, have effect in relation to this Act as if the provisions of this Act were provisions of that Act.

(2) *Repealed.*

(3) Without prejudice to subsections (1) and (2), any two or more local authorities may combine for the purpose of declaring an area to be a smoke control area and in that event—

(*a*) the smoke control area may be the whole of the districts of those authorities or any part of those districts;

(*b*) the references in section 18, Schedule 1 and paragraph 1 of Schedule 2 to the local authority shall be read as references to the local authorities acting jointly;

(*c*) the reference in paragraph 1 of Schedule 1 to a place in the district of the local authority shall be construed as a reference to a place in each of the districts of the local authorities;

but, except as provided in this subsection, references in this Act to the local authority shall, in relation to a building or dwelling, or to a boiler or industrial plant, in the smoke control area, be read as references to that one of the local authorities within whose district the building, dwelling, boiler or plant is situated.

(4) For the avoidance of doubt it is hereby declared that where a port health authority or joint board has functions, rights or liabilities under this Act—

(*a*) any reference in this Act to a local authority or its district includes, in relation to those functions, rights or liabilities, a reference to the port health authority or board or its district;

(*b*) for the purposes of this Act, no part of the district of any such port health authority or board is to be treated, in relation to any matter falling within the competence of the authority or board, as forming part of the district of any other authority.

(5) Any premises which extend into the districts of two or more authorities shall be treated for the purposes of this Act as being wholly within such one of those districts—

(*a*) in England and Wales, as may from time to time be agreed by those authorities; or

(*b*) *Scotland.*

[Clean Air Act 1993, s 61.]

7.10172 **62. Application of certain provisions of Part XII of Public Health Act 1936 and corresponding Scottish legislation** (1) In the application of this Act to England and Wales, the following provisions of Part XII of the Public Health Act 1936 shall have effect in relation to the provisions of this Act (apart from Parts IV and V) as if those provisions were provisions of that Act—

section 275 (power of local authority to execute works);

section 276 (power of local authority to sell materials);

section 278 (compensation to individuals for damage resulting from exercise of powers under Act);

section 283 (form of notices);

section 284 (authentication of documents);

section 285 (service of notices);

section 289 (power to require occupier to permit works to be executed by owner);

section 291 (expenses to be a charge on the premises);

section 293 (recovery of expenses);

section 294 (limitation of liability of certain owners).

(2) *Scotland.*

[Clean Air Act 1993, s 62 as amended by the Statute Law (Repeals) Act 1993.]

*General*

7.10173 **64. General provisions as to interpretation** (1) In this Act, except so far as the context otherwise requires,—

"authorised officer" means any officer of a local authority authorised by them in writing, either generally or specially, to act in matters of any specified kind or in any specified matter;

"building regulations" means as respects Scotland, any statutory enactments, byelaws, rules and regulations or other provisions under whatever authority made, relating to the construction, alteration or extension of buildings;

"caravan" means a caravan within the meaning of Part I of the Caravan Sites and Control of Development Act 1960, disregarding the amendment made by section 13(2) of the Caravan Sites Act 1968, which usually and for the time being is situated on a caravan site within the meaning of that Act;

"chimney" includes structures and openings of any kind from or through which smoke, grit, dust or fumes may be emitted, and, in particular, includes flues, and references to a chimney of a building include references to a chimney which serves the whole or a part of a building but is structurally separate from the building;

"dark smoke" has the meaning given by section 3(1);

"day" means a period of twenty-four hours beginning at midnight;

"domestic furnace" means any furnace which is—

(*a*) designed solely or mainly for domestic purposes, and

(*b*) used for heating a boiler with a maximum heating capacity of less than 16.12 kilowatts;

"fireplace" includes any furnace, grate or stove, whether open or closed;

"fixed boiler or industrial plant" means any boiler or industrial plant which is attached to a building or is for the time being fixed to or installed on any land;

"fumes" means any airborne solid matter smaller than dust;

"industrial plant" includes any still, melting pot or other plant used for any industrial or trade purposes, and also any incinerator used for or in connection with any such purposes;

"local authority" means—

(*a*) in England, the council of a district or a London borough, the Common Council of the City of London, the Sub-Treasurer of the Inner Temple and the Under Treasurer of the Middle Temple;

(*aa*) in Wales, the council of a county or county borough; and

(*b*) *Scotland*;

"owner", in relation to premises—

(*a*) as respects England and Wales, means the person for the time being receiving the rackrent of the premises, whether on his own account or as agent or trustee for another person, or who would so receive the rackrent if the premises were let at a rackrent; and

(*b*) *Scotland*;

"port health authority" means, as respects Scotland, a port local authority constituted under Part X of the Public Health (Scotland) Act 1897 and includes a reference to a joint port health authority constituted under that Part;

"practicable" means reasonably practicable having regard, amongst other things, to local conditions and circumstances, to the financial implications and to the current state of technical knowledge, and "practicable means" includes the provision and maintenance of plant and its proper use;

"premises" includes land;

"smoke", includes soot, ash, grit and gritty particles emitted in smoke; and

"vessel" has the same meaning as "ship" in the Merchant Shipping Act 1995.

(2) Any reference in this Act to the occupier of a building shall, in relation to any building different parts of which are occupied by different persons, be read as a reference to the occupier or other person in control of the part of the building in which the relevant fireplace is situated.

(3) In this Act any reference to the rate of emission of any substance or any reference which is to be understood as such a reference shall, in relation to any regulations or conditions, be construed as a reference to the quantities of that substance which may be emitted during a period specified in the regulations or conditions.

(4) In this Act, except so far as the context otherwise requires, "private dwelling" means any building or part of a building used or intended to be used as such, and a building or part of a building is not to be taken for the purposes of this Act to be used or intended to be used otherwise than as a private dwelling by reason that a person who resides or is to reside in it is or is to be required or permitted to reside in it in consequence of his employment or of holding an office.

(5) In considering for the purposes of this Act whether any and, if so, what works are reasonably necessary in order to make suitable provision for heating and cooking in the case of a dwelling or are reasonably necessary in order to enable a building to be used for a purpose without contravention of any of the provisions of this Act, regard shall be had to any difficulty there may be in obtaining, or in obtaining otherwise than at a high price, any fuels which would have to be used but for the execution of the works.

(6) Any furnaces which are in the occupation of the same person and are served by a single chimney shall, for the purposes of sections 5 to 12, 14 and 15, be taken to be one furnace.

[Clean Air Act 1993, s 64 as amended by the Local Government (Wales) Act 1994, Sch 9, the Merchant Shipping Act 1995, Sch 13 and the Adults with Incapacity (Scotland) Act 2000, Sch 5.]

7.10174 **65. Application to Isles of Scilly** Parts IV and V, and this Part so far as relating to those Parts, shall have effect in their application to the Isles of Scilly with such modifications as the Secretary of State may by order specify.

[Clean Air Act 1993, s 65.]

## Noise and Statutory Nuisance Act 1993

(1993 c 40)

*Loudspeakers*

7.10175 **8. Consent of local authorities to the operation of loudspeakers in streets or roads** (1) A local authority may resolve that Schedule 2 is to apply to its area.

(2) If a local authority does so resolve, Schedule 2 shall come into force in its area on such date as may be specified for that purpose in the resolution, being a date at least one month after the date on which the resolution is passed.

(3) Where a local authority has passed a resolution under this section, the authority shall cause a notice to be published, in two consecutive weeks before the Schedule comes into force in its area, in a local newspaper circulating in the area.

(4) The notice shall—

(*a*) state that the resolution has been passed, and

(*b*) set out the general effect of Schedule 2 and, in particular, the procedure for applying for a consent under that Schedule.

(5) In this section "local authority" means—

(*a*) in relation to England and Wales—

(i) the council of a district,

(ii) the council of a London borough,

(iii) the Common Council of the City of London,

(iv) the Sub-Treasurer of the Inner Temple, or

(v) the Under Treasurer of the Middle Temple, and

(*b*) *Scotland.*

[Noise and Statutory Nuisance Act 1993, s 8.]

### SCHEDULE 2

CONSENT TO THE OPERATION OF LOUDSPEAKERS IN STREETS OR ROADS — Section 8

*(Amended by the Serious Organised Crime and Police Act 2005, s 137.)*

*Local authority consent*

7.10176 **1.** (1) Subject to sub-paragraph (2), on an application made by any person, the local authority may consent to the operation in its area of a loudspeaker in contravention of section 62(1) of the 1974 Act or of section 137(1) of the Serious Organised Crime and Police Act 2005.

(2) A consent shall not be given to the operation of a loudspeaker in connection with any election or for the purpose of advertising any entertainment, trade or business.

**2.** A consent may be granted subject to such conditions as the local authority considers appropriate.

*Procedure*

**3.** An application for a consent shall be made in writing and shall contain such information as the local authority may reasonably require.

**4.** (1) Where an application is duly made to the local authority for a consent, the authority shall determine the application and notify the applicant in writing of its decision within the period of twenty-one days beginning with the day on which the application is received by the authority.

(2) In a case where a consent is granted, the notification under sub-paragraph (1) shall specify the conditions, if any, subject to which the consent is granted.

**5.** An applicant for a consent shall pay such reasonable fee in respect of his application as the local authority may determine.

*Publication of consent*

**6.** Where the local authority grants a consent, the authority may cause a notice giving details of that consent to be published in a local newspaper circulating in its area.

*Interpretation*

7. In this Schedule "a consent" means a consent under paragraph 1.

# Environment Act 1995[1]

(1995 c 25)

## PART I[2]

## THE ENVIRONMENT AGENCY AND THE SCOTTISH ENVIRONMENT PROTECTION AGENCY

### CHAPTER I[3]

### THE ENVIRONMENT AGENCY

*Establishment of the Agency*

7.10177 **1. The Environment Agency** (1) There shall be a body corporate to be known as the Environment Agency or, in Welsh, Asiantaeth yr Amgylchedd (in this Act referred to as "the Agency"), for the purpose of carrying out the functions transferred or assigned to it by or under this Act.

(2)–(4) *Appointment of members of the Agency.*

(5) Subject to the provisions of section 38[4] below, the Agency shall not be regarded—

(*a*) as the servant or agent of the Crown, or as enjoying any status, immunity or privilege of the Crown; or

(*b*) by virtue of any connection with the Crown, as exempt from any tax, duty, rate, levy or other charge whatsoever, whether general or local;

and the Agency's property shall not be regarded as property of, or property held on behalf of, the Crown.

(6) The provisions of Schedule 1[5] to this Act shall have effect with respect to the Agency.

[Environment Act 1995, s 1.]

---

1 The Environment Act 1995 establishes a body corporate to be known as the Environment Agency and abolishes the National Rivers Authority and the London Waste Regulation Authority. With effect from the transfer date the property, right or liabilities of those Authorities are transferred to and vested in the Agency. The Act also makes provision with respect to contaminated land and abandoned mines, and makes further provision for the control of pollution, the conservation of natural resources and the conservation or enhancement of the environment.

The Act is to be brought into force in accordance with s 125, post. Of the provisions set out below, at the date of going to press, certain provisions in the following Schedules had not been brought fully into force: Schs 15, 22 and 24.

Only those provisions of the Environment Act 1995 which are relevant to proceedings in magistrates' courts are contained in this work.

2 Part I contains Ch 1, ss 1–19, Ch II, ss 20–36, and Ch III, ss 37–56.

3 Chapter I contains ss 1–19.

4 Section 38—delegation of functions by Ministers etc. to the new Agencies—is concerned with agreements made between a Minister of the Crown and a new Agency; s 38 is not printed in this work.

5 Schedule 1 is printed in an abridged form, post.

*Transfer of functions, property etc to the Agency*

7.10178 **2. Transfer of functions to the Agency** (1) On the transfer date there shall by virtue of this section be transferred to the Agency—

(*a*) the functions of the National Rivers Authority, that is to say

(i) its functions under or by virtue of Part II (water resources management) of the Water Resources Act 1991 (in this Part referred to as "the 1991 Act");

(ii) its functions under or by virtue of Part III of that Act (control of pollution of water resources);

(iii) its functions under or by virtue of Part IV of that Act (flood defence) and the Land Drainage Act 1991 and the functions transferred to the Authority by virtue of section 136(8) of the Water Act 1989 and paragraph 1(3) of Schedule 15 to that Act (transfer of land drainage functions under local statutory provisions and subordinate legislation);

(iv) its functions under or by virtue of Part VII of the 1991 Act (land and works powers);

(v) its functions under or by virtue of the Sea Fisheries Regulation Act 1966, the Salmon and Freshwater Fisheries Act 1975, Part V of the 1991 Act or any other enactment relating to fisheries;

(vi) the functions as a navigation authority, harbour authority or conservancy authority which were transferred to the Authority by virtue of Chapter V of Part III of the Water Act 1989 or paragraph 23(3) of Schedule 13 to that Act or which have been transferred to the Authority by any order or agreement under Schedule 2 to the 1991 Act;

(vii) its functions under Schedule 2 to the 1991 Act;

(viii) the functions assigned to the Authority by or under any other enactment, apart from this Act;

(*b*) the functions of waste regulation authorities, that is to say, the functions conferred or imposed on them by or under

(i) the Control of Pollution (Amendment) Act 1989, or

(ii) Part II of the Environmental Protection Act 1990 (in this Part referred to as "the 1990 Act"),

or assigned to them by or under any other enactment, apart from this Act;

(*c*) the functions of disposal authorities under or by virtue of the waste regulation provisions of the Control of Pollution Act 1974;

(*d*) the functions of the chief inspector for England and Wales constituted under section 16(3) of the 1990 Act, that is to say, the functions conferred or imposed on him by or under Part I of that Act or assigned to him by or under any other enactment, apart from this Act;

(*e*) the functions of the chief inspector for England and Wales appointed under section 4(2)(*a*) of the Radioactive Substances Act 1993, that is to say, the functions conferred or imposed on him by or under that Act or assigned to him by or under any other enactment, apart from this Act;

(*f*) the functions conferred or imposed by or under the Alkali, etc, Works Regulation Act 1906 (in this section referred to as "the 1906 Act") on the chief, or any other, inspector (within the meaning of that Act), so far as exercisable in relation to England and Wales;

(*g*) so far as exercisable in relation to England and Wales, the functions in relation to improvement notices and prohibition notices under Part I of the Health and Safety at Work etc. Act 1974 (in this section referred to as "the 1974 Act") of inspectors appointed under section 19 of that Act by the Secretary of State in his capacity as the enforcing authority responsible in relation to England and Wales for the Enforcement of the 1906 Act and section 5 of the 1974 Act; and

(*h*) the functions of the Secretary of State specified in subsection (2) below.

(2) The functions of the Secretary of State mentioned in subsection (1)(*h*) above are the following, that is to say—

(*a*) so far as exercisable in relation to England and Wales, his functions under section 30(1) of the Radioactive Substances Act 1993 (power to dispose of radioactive waste);

(*b*) his functions under Chapter III of Part IV of the Water Industry Act 1991 in relation to special category effluent, within the meaning of that Chapter, other than any function of making regulations or of making orders under section 139 of that Act;

(*c*) so far as exercisable in relation to England and Wales, the functions conferred or imposed on him by virtue of his being, for the purposes of Part I of the 1974 Act, the authority which is by any of the relevant statutory provisions made responsible for the enforcement of the 1906 Act and section 5 of the 1974 Act;

(*d*) so far as exercisable in relation to England and Wales, his functions under, or under regulations made by virtue of, section 9 of the 1906 Act (registration of works), other than any functions of his as an appellate authority or any function of making regulations;

(*e*) so far as exercisable in relation to England and Wales, his functions under regulations 7(1) and 8(2) of, and paragraph 2(2)(*c*) of Schedule 2 to, the Sludge (Use in Agriculture) Regulations 1989 (which relate to the provision of information and the testing of soil).

(3) *Repealed.*

[Environment Act 1995, s 2 as amended by the Statute Law (Repeals) Act 2004 and SI 2009/463.]

## Chapter 1A
## General functions of the Agency and the Natural Resources Body for Wales

7.10179 **5. General functions with respect to pollution control** (1) An appropriate agency's pollution control powers shall be exercisable for the purpose of preventing or minimising, or remedying or mitigating the effects of, pollution of the environment.

(2) An appropriate agency shall, for the purpose—

(*a*) of facilitating the carrying out of its pollution control functions, or (*b*) of enabling it to form an opinion of the general state of pollution of the environment, compile information relating to such pollution (whether the information is acquired by the Agency carrying out observations or is obtained in any other way).

(3) If required by the appropriate national authority to do so, an appropriate agency shall—

(*a*) carry out assessments (whether generally or for such particular purpose as may be specified in the requirement) of the effect, or likely effect, on the environment of existing or potential levels of pollution of the environment and report its findings to the appropriate national authority; or

(*b*) prepare and send to the appropriate national authority a report identifying—

(i) the options which the appropriate agency considers to be available for preventing or minimising, or remedying or mitigating the effects of, pollution of the environment, whether generally or in cases or circumstances specified in the requirement; and

(ii) the costs and benefits of such options as are identified by the appropriate agency pursuant to sub-paragraph (i) above.

(4) An appropriate agency shall follow developments in technology and techniques for preventing or minimising, or remedying or mitigating the effects of, pollution of the environment.

(5) In this section, "pollution control powers" and "pollution control functions", in relation to an appropriate agency, mean respectively its powers or its functions under or by virtue of the following enactments, that is to say—

(*a*) the Alkali, etc, Works Regulation Act 1906;

(*b*) Part I of the Health and Safety at Work etc. Act 1974;

(*c*) Part I of the Control of Pollution Act 1974;

(*d*) the Control of Pollution (Amendment) Act 1989;

(*e*) Parts I,* II and IIA of the 1990 Act (integrated pollution control etc, waste on land and contaminated land);

(*f*) Chapter III of Part IV of the Water Industry Act 1991 (special category effluent);

(*g*) Part III and sections 161 to 161D of the 1991 Act (control of pollution of water resources);

(*h*) *repealed*

(*i*) regulations under section 2 of the Pollution Prevention and Control Act 1999;

(*j*) regulations made by virtue of section 2(2) of the European Communities Act 1972, to the extent that the regulations relate to pollution.

(6) But in relation to the Natural Resources Body for Wales, "pollution control powers" and "pollution control functions" do not include powers or functions which—

(*a*) were exercisable by the Countryside Council for Wales or the Forestry Commissioners immediately before 1 April 2013; and

(*b*) are functions of that Body by virtue of the Natural Resources Body for Wales (Functions) Order 2013.

[Environment Act 1995, s 5 as amended by the Pollution Prevention and Control Act 1999, Sch 2, SI 2010/675 and SI 2013/755.]

---

* **Number repealed by the Pollution Prevention and Control Act 1999, Sch 3 from a date to be appointed.**

**7.10180 6. General provisions with respect to water** (1) It shall be the duty of an appropriate agency, to such extent as it considers desirable, generally to promote—

(*a*) the conservation and enhancement of the natural beauty and amenity of inland and coastal waters and of land associated with such waters;

(*b*) the conservation of flora and fauna which are dependent on an aquatic environment; and

(*c*) the use of such waters and land for recreational purposes;

and it shall be the duty of an appropriate agency, in determining what steps to take in performance of the duty imposed by virtue of paragraph (*c*) above, to take into account the needs of persons who are chronically sick or disabled.

This subsection is without prejudice to the duties of the Agency under section 7 below.

(2) It shall be the duty of the Agency to take all such action as it may from time to time consider, in accordance with any directions given under section 40 below, to be necessary or expedient for the purpose—

(*a*) of conserving, redistributing or otherwise augmenting water resources in England; and

(*b*) of securing the proper use of water resources in England including the efficient use of those resources;

but nothing in this subsection shall be construed as relieving any water undertaker of the obligation to develop water resources for the purpose of performing any duty imposed on it by virtue of section 37 of the Water Industry Act 1991 (general duty to maintain water supply system).

(2A) The Natural Resources Body for Wales must take all such action as it may from time to time consider, in accordance with any directions given under article 11 of the Natural Resources Body for Wales (Establishment) Order 2012 (SI 2012/1903), to be necessary or expedient for the purpose—

(*a*) of conserving, redistributing or otherwise augmenting water resources in Wales; and

(b) of securing the proper use of water resources in Wales (including the efficient use of those resources);

but nothing in this subsection shall be construed as relieving any water undertaker of the obligation to develop water resources for the purpose of performing any duty imposed on it by virtue of section 37 of the Water Industry Act 1991 (general duty to maintain water supply system).

(3) The provisions of the 1991 Act relating to the functions of the Agency under Chapter II of Part II of that Act and the related water resources provisions so far as they relate to other functions of the Agency shall not apply to so much of any inland waters as—

(a) are part of the River Tweed;

(b) are part of the River Esk or River Sark at a point where either of the banks of the river is in Scotland; or

(c) are part of any tributary stream of the River Esk or the River Sark at a point where either of the banks of the tributary stream is in Scotland.*

(3A) Subsection (3) above shall apply to—

(a) sections 3 and 4 of the Water Act 2003; and

(b) such of the related water resources provisions as apply in relation to those sections by virtue of section 33(2) of the Water Act 2003,

as it applies to the provisions referred to in that subsection.

(4) Subject to section 106 of the 1991 Act (obligation to carry out flood defence functions through committees), the Agency shall in relation to England and the Natural Resources Body for Wales shall in relation to Wales exercise a general supervision over all matters relating to flood defence.

(5) The Agency's flood defence functions shall extend to the territorial sea adjacent to England and the Natural Resources Body for Wales' flood defence functions shall extend to the territorial sea adjacent to Wales in so far as—

(a) the area of any regional flood defence committee includes any area of that territorial sea; or

(b) section 165(2) or (3) of the 1991 Act (drainage works for the purpose of defence against sea water or tidal water, and works etc to secure an adequate outfall for a main river) provides for the exercise of any power in the territorial sea.

(6) It shall be the duty of the Agency to maintain, improve and develop fisheries—

(a) salmon, trout, eels, lampreys, smelt and freshwater fish, and

(b) fish of such other description as may be specified for the purposes of this subsection by order under section 40A of the Salmon and Freshwater Fisheries Act 1975.

(7) The area in respect of which an appropriate agency shall carry out its functions relating to fisheries shall be the whole of England, together with—

(a) such part of the territorial sea adjacent to England as extends for six miles from the baselines from which the breadth of that sea is measured,

(b) in the case of—

(i) *repealed*

(ii) the Salmon and Freshwater Fisheries Act 1975,

(iii) Part V of the 1991 Act (general control of fisheries), and

(iv) subsection (6) above,

so much of the River Esk, with its banks and tributary streams up to their source, as is situated in Scotland, and

(c) in the case of sections 31 to 34 and 36(2) of the Salmon and Freshwater Fisheries Act 1975 as applied by section 39(1B) of that Act, so much of the catchment area of the River Esk as is situated in Scotland,

but, in the case of the enactments specified in paragraph (b) above, excluding the River Tweed.

(7A) The area in respect of which the Natural Resources Body for Wales shall carry out its functions relating to fisheries shall be the whole of Wales, together with such part of the territorial sea adjacent to Wales as extends for six miles from the baselines from which the breadth of that sea is measured.

(8) In this section—

"miles" means international nautical miles of 1,852 metres;

"the related water resources provisions" has the same meaning as it has in the 1991 Act;

"the River Tweed" means "the river" within the meaning of the Tweed Fisheries Amendment Act 1859 as amended by byelaws.

"salmon", "trout", "eels", "smelt", "fish" and "freshwater fish" have the same meanings as in the Salmon and Freshwater Fisheries Act 1975.

(9) For the purposes of this section, the parts of the territorial sea which are adjacent to Wales, and which are therefore not adjacent to England, are the parts of the sea which are treated as adjacent to Wales for the purposes of section 158 of the Government of Wales Act 2006.

[Environment Act 1995, s 6 as amended by the Water Act 2003, s 72 and Sch 7, SI 2009/463 and the Marine and Coastal Access Act 2009, s 230.]

---

* **Words inserted by the Water Act 2003, s 73 from a date to be appointed.**

## Chapter III[1]

## Miscellaneous, General and Supplemental Provisions relating to the New Agencies

*Supplemental provisions*

7.10181 **54. Appearance in legal proceedings** In England and Wales, a person who is authorised by the Agency to prosecute on its behalf in proceedings before a magistrates' court shall be entitled to prosecute in any such proceedings.

[Environment Act 1995, s 54 as amended by the Legal Services Act 2007, Sch 21.]

[1] Chapter III contains ss 37–56.

7.10182 **55. Continuity of exercise of functions: the new Agencies** (1) The abolition of—

(*a*) the National Rivers Authority

(*b*) the London Waste Regulation Authority, or

(*c*) a river purification board, shall not affect the validity of anything done by that Authority or board before the transfer date.

(2) Anything which, at the transfer date, is in the process of being done by or in relation to a transferor in the exercise of, or in connection with, any of the transferred functions may be continued by or in relation to the transferee.

(3) Anything done by or in relation to a transferor before the transfer date in the exercise of, or otherwise in connection with, any of the transferred functions, shall, so far as is required for continuing its effect on and after that date, have effect as if done by or in relation to the transferee.

(4) Subsection (3) above applies in particular to—

(*a*) any decision, determination, declaration, designation, agreement or instrument made by a transferor;

(*b*) any regulations or byelaws made by a transferor;

(*c*) any licence, permission, consent, approval, authorisation, exemption, dispensation or relaxation granted by or to a transferor;

(*d*) any notice, direction or certificate given by or to a transferor;

(*e*) any application, request, proposal or objection made by or to a transferor;

(*f*) any condition or requirement imposed by or on a transferor;

(*g*) any fee or charge paid by or to a transferor;

(*h*) any appeal allowed by or in favour of or against a transferor;

(*j*) any proceedings instituted by or against a transferor.

(5) Any reference in the foregoing provisions of this section to anything done by or in relation to a transferor includes a reference to anything which, by virtue of any enactment, is treated as having been done by or in relation to that transferor.

(6) Any reference to a transferor in any document constituting or relating to anything to which the foregoing provisions of this section apply shall, so far as is required for giving effect to those provisions, be construed as a reference to the transferee.

(7) The foregoing provisions of this section—

(*a*) are without prejudice to any provision made by this Act in relation to any particular functions; and

(*b*) shall not be construed as continuing in force any contract of employment made by a transferor;

and the Secretary of State may, in relation to any particular functions, by order exclude, modify or supplement any of the foregoing provisions of this section or make such other transitional provisions as he thinks necessary or expedient.

(8) Where, by virtue of any provision of Schedule 15 to this Act, the Minister is the transferor in the case of any functions, he shall have the same powers under subsection (7) above in relation to those functions as the Secretary of State.

(9) The power to make an order under subsection (7) above shall be exercisable by statutory instrument; and any statutory instrument containing such an order shall be subject to annulment pursuant to a resolution of either House of Parliament.

(10) In this section—

"the transferee", in the case of any transferred functions, means the new Agency whose functions they become by virtue of any provision made by or under this Act;

"transferred functions" means any functions which, by virtue of any provision made by or under this Act, become functions of a new Agency; and

"transferor" means any body or person any or all of whose functions become, by virtue of any provision made by or under this Act, functions of a new Agency.

[Environment Act 1995, s 55.]

7.10183 **56. Interpretation of Part I** (1) In this Part of this Act, except where the context otherwise requires—

"the 1990 Act" means the Environmental Protection Act 1990;

"the 1991 Act" means the Water Resources Act 1991;

"appropriate agency" means the Agency or the Natural Resources Body for Wales;

"the appropriate Minister"—

(*a*) in the case of the Agency, means the Secretary of State or the Minister; and (*b*) in the case of SEPA, means the Secretary of State;

"the appropriate Ministers"—

(*a*) in the case of the Agency, means the Secretary of State and the Minister; and

(*b*) in the case of SEPA, means the Secretary of State;

"the appropriate national authority" means—

(*a*) in relation to the Agency, the Secretary of State;

(*b*) in relation to the Natural Resources Body for Wales, the Welsh Ministers

"conservancy authority" has the meaning given by section 221(1) of the 1991 Act;

"costs" includes—

(*a*) costs to any person; and

(*b*) costs to the environment;

"disposal authority"—

(*a*) in the application of this Part in relation to the Agency, has the same meaning as it has in Part I of the Control of Pollution Act 1974 by virtue of section 30(1) of that Act; and

(*b*) in the application of this Part in relation to SEPA, has the meaning assigned to it by section 30(2) of that Act;

"the environment" means all, or any, of the following media, namely, the air, water and land (and the medium of air includes the air within buildings and the air within other natural or man-made structures above or below ground);

"environmental licence", in the application of this Part in relation to an appropriate agency, means any of the following—

(*a*) registration of a person as a carrier of controlled waste under section 2 of the Control of Pollution (Amendment) Act 1989.

(*aa*) a permit granted by the Agency under regulations under section 2 of the Pollution Prevention and Control Act 1999,

(*b*) an authorisation under Part I of the 1990 Act, other than any such authorisation granted by a local enforcing authority,*

(*c*) *repealed*

(*d*) a licence under Chapter II of Part II of the 1991 Act,

(*e*) *repealed*

(*f*) *repealed*

(*g*) *repealed*

(*h*) registration of a person as a broker of or dealer in controlled waste under any provision which gives effect in England and Wales to Article 26(*b*) of Directive 2008/98/EC of the European Parliament and of the Council on waste,

(*j*) registration under Schedule 2 to the Environmental Permitting (England and Wales) Regulations 2007 of an establishment or undertaking in relation to a WEEE operation (as defined by paragraph 1 of Schedule 2 to those Regulations,

(*k*) a greenhouse gas emissions permit granted under the Greenhouse Gas Emissions Trading Scheme Regulations 2005,

(*l*) approval of a scheme under regulation 41 of the Waste Electrical and Electronic Equipment Regulations 2006 ("the WEEE Regulations");

(*m*) compliance with the condition in regulation 43(*e*)(i) of the WEEE Regulations in relation to a scheme mentioned in paragraph (l);

(*n*) approval of an authorised treatment facility or exporter under regulation 47 of the WEEE Regulations; and

(*o*) extension of approval of an exporter under regulation 48 of the WEEE Regulations,

so far as having effect in relation to England and Wales;

"environmental licence", in the application of this Part in relation to SEPA, means any of the following—

(*a*) *repealed*,

(*aa*) a permit granted by the appropriate agency under—

(i) regulations made under section 2 of the Pollution Prevention and Control Act 1999, other than regulations made for the purpose of implementing the EU ETS Directive,

(ii) regulations made under section 61 of the Water Act 2014.

(*b*) registration of a person as a carrier of controlled waste under section 2 of the Control of Pollution (Amendment) Act 1989,

(*c*) an authorisation under Part I of the 1990 Act,*

(*d*) a waste management licence under Part II of that Act,

(*e*) *repealed*

(*f*) registration under the Radioactive Substances Act 1993,

(*g*) an authorisation under that Act,

(*h*) registration of a person as a broker of controlled waste under the Waste Management Licensing Regulations 1994, (*j*) registration in respect of an activity falling within paragraph 7, 8(2), 9, 10, 12, 19, 42, 45(1) or (2), 46 or 47 of Schedule 3 to those Regulations, except where the waste which is the subject of the activity consists of agricultural waste within the meaning of those Regulations,

(*k*) a greenhouse gas emissions permit granted under the Greenhouse Gas Emissions Trading Scheme Regulations 2005

(*l*) approval of a scheme under regulation 41 of the Waste Electrical and Electronic Equipment Regulations 2006 ("the WEEE Regulations");

(*m*) compliance with the condition in regulation 43(*e*)(i) of the WEEE Regulations in relation to a scheme mentioned in paragraph (l);

(*n*) approval of an authorised treatment facility or exporter under regulation 47 of the WEEE Regulations; and

(*o*) extension of approval of an exporter under regulation 48 of the WEEE Regulations,

so far as having effect in relation to Scotland;

"flood defence functions", in relation to an appropriate agency, has the same meaning as in the 1991 Act;

"harbour authority" has the meaning given by section 221(1) of the 1991 Act;

"local authority", in the application of this Part in relation to SEPA, means a district or islands council in Scotland;

"the Minister" means the Minister of Agriculture, Fisheries and Food;

"the Ministers" means the Secretary of State and the Minister;

"navigation authority" has the meaning given by section 221(1) of the 1991 Act;

"new Agency" means the Agency or SEPA;

"river purification authority" means a river purification authority within the meaning of the 1951 Act;

"river purification board" means a river purification board established by virtue of section 135 of the Local Government (Scotland) Act 1973;

"the transfer date" means such date as the Secretary of State may by order[1] made by statutory instrument appoint as the transfer date for the purposes of this Part; and different dates may be appointed for the purposes of this Part—

(i) as it applies for or in connection with transfers under or by virtue of Chapter I above, and

(ii) as it applies for or in connection with transfers under or by virtue of Chapter II above;

"waste regulation authority"—

(*a*) in the application of this Part in relation to the Agency, means any authority in England or Wales which, by virtue of section 30(1) of the 1990 Act, is a waste regulation authority for the purposes of Part II of that Act; and

(*b*) in the application of this Part in relation to SEPA, means any council which, by virtue of section 30(1)(*g*) of the 1990 Act, is a waste regulation authority for the purposes of Part II of that Act.

(2) *Scotland.*

(3) Where by virtue of any provision of this Part any function of a Minister of the Crown is exercisable concurrently by different Ministers, that function shall also be exercisable jointly by any two or more of those Ministers.

[Environment Act 1995, s 56 as amended by the Pollution Prevention and Control Act 1999, Sch 2, SI 2000/1973, SI 2005/925, SI 2005/1728, SSI 2004/275, SSI 2006/181, SSI 2006/541, SI 2006/3289, SI 2007/3538, SI 2009/3381, SI 2010/675, SI 2011/988, SI 2013/755, SI 2016/475.]

---

* **Repealed by the Pollution Prevention and Control Act 1999, Sch 3 from a date to be appointed.**

[1] The Environment Agency (Transfer Date) Order 1996, SI 1996/234, set 1 April 1996 as the transfer date for the purposes of transfers under or by virtue of CHAPTER I of PART I of this Act.

## PART IV[1]

## AIR QUALITY

7.10184 **80. National air quality strategy** *Secretary of State to publish strategy containing policies with respect to the assessment or management of the quality of air.*

---

[1] Part IV contains ss 80–91.

7.10185 **87. Regulations for the purposes of Part IV** *Regulations[1] may make provision for, or in connection with, implementing the strategy or in connection with, implementing obligations under the Community Treaties, or international agreements.*

---

[1] The following regulations have been made: Air Quality (England) Regulations 2000, SI 2000/928 amended by SI 2002/3043, Air Quality (Wales) Regulations 2000, SI 2000/1940; the Road Traffic (Vehicle Emissions) (Fixed Penalty) (England) Regulations 2002, SI 2002/1808; the Road Traffic (Vehicle Emissions) (Fixed Penalty) (Wales) Regulations 2003, SI 2003/300.

7.10186 **90. Supplemental provisions** Schedule 11 to this Act shall have effect.

[Environment Act 1995, s 90.]

7.10187 **91. Interpretation of Part IV** (1) In this Part—

"action plan" shall be construed in accordance with section 84(2) above;

"air quality objectives" means objectives prescribed by virtue of section 87(2)(*b*) above;

"air quality review" means a review under section 82 or 85 above;

"air quality standards" means standards prescribed by virtue of section 87(2)(*a*) above;

"the appropriate new Agency" means—

(*a*) in relation to England and Wales, the Agency;

(*b*) in relation to Scotland, SEPA;

"designated area" has the meaning given by section 83(1) above;

"local authority", in relation to England and Wales, means—

(*a*) any unitary authority,

(*b*) any district council, so far as it is not a unitary authority;

(*c*) the Common Council of the City of London and, as respects the Temples, the Sub-Treasurer of the Inner Temple and the Under-Treasurer of the Middle Temple respectively,

and, in relation to Scotland, means a council for an area constituted under section 2 of the Local Government etc. (Scotland) Act 1994;

"new Agency" means the Agency or SEPA;

"prescribed" means prescribed, or of a description prescribed, by or under regulations;

"regulations" means regulations made by the Secretary of State;

"the relevant period", in the case of any provision of this Part, means such period as may be prescribed for the purposes of that provision;

"the strategy" has the meaning given by section 80(1) above;

"unitary authority" means—

(*a*) the council of a county, so far as it is the council of an area for which there are no district councils;

(*b*) the council of any district comprised in an area for which there is no county council;

(*c*) the council of a London borough;

(*d*) the council of a county borough in Wales.

(2) Any reference in this Part to it appearing that any air quality standards or objectives are not likely within the relevant period to be achieved includes a reference to it appearing that those standards or objectives are likely within that period not to be achieved.

[Environment Act 1995, s 91 as amended by the Deregulation Act 2015, Sch 13.]

## PART V[1]

## MISCELLANEOUS, GENERAL AND SUPPLEMENTAL PROVISIONS

### *Waste*

7.10188 **93. Producer responsibility: general** *Regulations[2] may make provision for, or in connection with, implementing the strategy or in connection with, implementing obligations under the Community Treaties, or international agreements.*

1 Part V contains ss 92–125.

2 The Producer Responsibility Obligations (Packaging Waste) Regulations 2007, SI 2007/871. For amending instruments see the entry in the list of regulations made under the European Communities Act 1972, ante.

7.10189 **95. Producer responsibility: offences** (1) Regulations[1] may make provision for a person who contravenes a prescribed requirement of the regulations to be guilty of an offence and liable—

(*a*) on summary conviction, to a fine not exceeding the statutory maximum;

(*b*) on conviction on indictment, to a fine.

(2) Where an offence under any provision of the regulations committed by a body corporate is proved to have been committed with the consent or connivance of, or to have been attributable to any neglect on the part of, any director, manager, secretary or other similar officer of the body corporate or a person who was purporting to act in any such capacity, he as well as the body corporate shall be guilty of that offence and shall be liable to be proceeded against and punished accordingly.

(3) Where the affairs of a body corporate are managed by its members, subsection (2) above shall apply in relation to the acts or defaults of a member in connection with his functions of management as if he were a director of the body corporate.

(4) Where the commission by any person of an offence under the regulations is due to the act or default of some other person, that other person may be charged with and convicted of the offence by virtue of this section whether or not proceedings for the offence are taken against the first-mentioned person.

(5) Expressions used in this section and in section 93 or 94 above have the same meaning in this section as they have in that section.

[Environment Act 1995, s 95.]

1 The Producer Responsibility Obligations (Packaging Waste) Regulations 2007, SI 2007/871. For amending instruments see the entry in the list of regulations made under the European Communities Act 1972, ante.

*Hedgerows etc*

**7.10190 97. Hedgerows** (1) The appropriate Ministers may by regulations[1] make provision for, or in connection with, the protection of important hedgerows in England or Wales.

(2) The question whether a hedgerow is or is not "important" for the purposes of this section shall be determined in accordance with prescribed criteria.

(3) For the purpose of facilitating the protection of important hedgerows, regulations under subsection (1) above may also make provision in relation to other hedgerows in England or Wales.

(4) Without prejudice to the generality of subsections (1) to (3) above, regulations under subsection (1) above may provide for the application (with or without modifications) of, or include provision comparable to, any provision contained in the planning Acts and may, in particular, make provision—

(*a*) prohibiting, or for prohibiting, the removal of, or the carrying out of prescribed acts in relation to, a hedgerow except in prescribed cases;

(*b*) for or with respect to appeals against determinations or decisions made, or notices given or served, under or by virtue of the regulations, including provision authorising or requiring any body or person to whom an appeal lies to consult prescribed persons with respect to the appeal in prescribed cases;

(*c*) for a person who contravenes, or fails to comply with, any prescribed provision of the regulations to be guilty of an offence;

(*d*) for a person guilty of an offence by virtue of paragraph (*c*) above which consists of the removal, in contravention of the regulations, of a hedgerow of a description prescribed for the purposes of this paragraph to be liable—

(i) on summary conviction, to a fine not exceeding the statutory maximum, or

(ii) on conviction on indictment, to a fine;

(*e*) for a person guilty of any other offence by virtue of paragraph (*c*) above to be liable on summary conviction to a fine not exceeding such level on the standard scale as may be prescribed.

(5) Regulations under this section may make different provision for different cases, including different provision in relation to different descriptions of hedgerow, different descriptions of person, different areas or localities or different circumstances.

(6) *Consultation before making any regulations.*

(7) No statutory instrument containing regulations under this section shall be made unless a draft of the instrument has been laid before, and approved by a resolution of, each House of Parliament.

(8) In this section—

"the appropriate Ministers" means—

(*a*) as respects England, the Secretary of State and the Minister of Agriculture, Fisheries and Food;

(*b*) as respects Wales, the Secretary of State;

"environmental conservation" means conservation—

(*a*) of the natural beauty or amenity, or flora or fauna, of England or Wales; or

(*b*) of features of archaeological or historic interest in England or Wales;

"hedgerow" includes any stretch of hedgerow;

"local authority" means—

(*a*) the council of a county, county borough, district, London borough, parish or community;

(*b*) the Common Council of the City of London;

(*c*) the Council of the Isles of Scilly;

"the planning Acts" has the same meaning as it has in the Town and Country Planning Act 1990 by virtue of section 336(1) of that Act;

"prescribed" means specified, or of a description specified, in regulations;

"regulations" means regulations made by statutory instrument;

"remove", in relation to a hedgerow, means uproot or otherwise destroy, and cognate expressions shall be construed accordingly;

"statutory functions" means functions conferred or imposed by or under any enactment.

(9) Any reference in this section to removing, or carrying out an act in relation to, a hedgerow includes a reference to causing or permitting another to remove, or (as the case may be) carry out an act in relation to, a hedgerow.

[Environment Act 1995, s 97.]

---

1 The Hedgerows Regulations 1997, SI 1997/1160 amended by SI 2003/2155, SI 2006/1177 and SI 2009/1307 have been made. Regulation 6(1)(*j*) of the 1997 regulations permits the removal of any hedgerow to which the regulations apply if it is required for the proper management of the hedgerow and this includes removal of the whole hedgerow if this is required although the regulations are silent as to whether there is a persuasive or evidential burden on the defendant to prove this: *Conway County Borough Council v Lloyd* [2003] EWHC 264 (Admin), 167 JP 223.

**7.10191 98. Grants for purposes conducive to conservation**[1]

---

1 The Countryside Stewardship Regulations 2000, SI 2000/3048 amended by SI 2001/3991 and SI 2004/114.

*Fisheries*

7.10192 105. **Minor and consequential amendments relating to fisheries** Schedule 15 to this Act (which makes minor and consequential amendments relating to fisheries) shall have effect.

[Environment Act 1995, s 105.]

*Powers of entry*

7.10193 108. **Powers of enforcing authorities and persons authorised by them** (1) A person who appears suitable to an enforcing authority may be authorised in writing by that authority to exercise, in accordance with the terms of the authorisation, any of the powers specified in subsection (4) below for the purpose—

(*a*) of determining whether any provision of the pollution control enactments or flood risk activity enactments in the case of that authority is being, or has been, complied with;

(*b*) of exercising or performing one or more of the pollution control functions or flood risk activity functions of that authority; or

(*c*) of determining whether and, if so, how such a function should be exercised or performed.

(2) A person who appears suitable to the Agency, the Natural Resources Body for Wales or SEPA may be authorised in writing by the Agency, the Natural Resources Body for Wales or, as the case may be, SEPA to exercise, in accordance with the terms of the authorisation, any of the powers specified in subsection (4) below for the purpose of enabling the Agency, the Natural Resources Body for Wales or, as the case may be, SEPA to carry out any assessment or prepare any report which the Agency or, as the case may be, SEPA is required to carry out or prepare under section 5(3) or 33(3) above.

(3) Subsection (2) above only applies where the Minister who required the assessment to be carried out, or the report to be prepared, has, whether at the time of making the requirement or at any later time, notified the Agency, the Natural Resources Body for Wales or, as the case may be, SEPA that the assessment or report appears to him to relate to an incident or possible incident involving or having the potential to involve—

(*a*) serious pollution of the environment,

(*b*) serious harm to human health, or

(*c*) danger to life or health.

(4) The powers which a person may be authorised to exercise under subsection (1) or (2) above are—

(*a*) to enter at any reasonable time (or, in an emergency, at any time and, if need be, by force) any premises which he has reason to believe it is necessary for him to enter;

(*b*) on entering any premises by virtue of paragraph (*a*) above, to take with him—

(i) any other person duly authorised by the enforcing authority and, if the authorised person has reasonable cause to apprehend any serious obstruction in the execution of his duty, a constable; and

(ii) any equipment or materials required for any purpose for which the power of entry is being exercised;

(*c*) to make such examination and investigation as may in any circumstances be necessary;

(*d*) as regards any premises which he has power to enter, to direct that those premises or any part of them, or anything in them, shall be left undisturbed (whether generally or in particular respects) for so long as is reasonably necessary for the purpose of any examination or investigation under paragraph (*c*) above;

(*e*) to take such measurements and photographs and make such recordings as he considers necessary for the purpose of any examination or investigation under paragraph (*c*) above;

(*f*) to take samples, or cause samples to be taken, of any articles or substances found in or on any premises which he has power to enter, and of the air, water or land in, on, or in the vicinity of, the premises;

(*g*) in the case of any article or substance found in or on any premises which the person has power to enter, being an article or substance which appears to that person to have caused or to be likely to cause—

(i) pollution of the environment,

(ii) harm to the environment,

(iii) flooding,

(iv) harm to human health, or

(v) a detrimental impact on drainage,

to cause it to be dismantled or subjected to any process or test (but not so as to damage or destroy it, unless that is necessary);

(*h*) in the case of any such article or substance as is mentioned in paragraph (*g*) above, to take possession of it and detain it for so long as is necessary for all or any of the following purposes, namely—

(i) to examine it, or cause it to be examined, and to do, or cause to be done, to it anything which he has power to do under that paragraph;

(ii) to ensure that it is not tampered with before examination of it is completed;

(iii) to ensure that it is available for use as evidence in any proceedings for an offence under the pollution control enactments or flood risk activity enactments in the case of the enforcing authority under whose authorisation he acts or in any other proceedings relating to a variation notice, enforcement notice or prohibition notice under those enactments;

(*j*) to require any person whom he has reasonable cause to believe to be able to give any information relevant to any examination or investigation under paragraph (*c*) above to answer (in the absence of persons other than a person nominated by that person to be present and any persons whom the authorised person may allow to be present) such questions as the authorised person thinks fit to ask and to sign a declaration of the truth of his answers;

(*k*) to require the production of, or where the information is recorded in computerised form, the furnishing of extracts from, any records—

(i) which are required to be kept under the pollution control enactments or flood risk activity enactments for the enforcing authority under whose authorisation he acts, or

(ii) which it is necessary for him to see for the purposes of an examination or investigation under paragraph (*c*) above,

and to inspect and take copies of, or of any entry in, the records;

(*l*) to require any person to afford him such facilities and assistance with respect to any matters or things within that person's control or in relation to which that person has responsibilities as are necessary to enable the authorised person to exercise any of the powers conferred on him by this section;

(*m*) any other power for—

(i) a purpose falling within any paragraph of subsection (1) above, or

(ii) any such purpose as is mentioned in subsection (2) above,

which is conferred by regulations made by the Secretary of State.

(5) The powers which by virtue of subsections (1) and (4) above are conferred in relation to any premises for the purpose of enabling an enforcing authority to determine whether any provision of the pollution control enactments or flood risk activity enactments in the case of that authority is being, or has been, complied with shall include power, in order to obtain the information on which that determination may be made,—

(*a*) to carry out experimental borings or other works on those premises; and

(*b*) to install, keep or maintain monitoring and other apparatus there.

(6) Except in an emergency, in any case where it is proposed to enter any premises used for residential purposes, or to take heavy equipment on to any premises which are to be entered, any entry by virtue of this section shall only be effected—

(*a*) after the expiration of at least seven days' notice of the proposed entry given to a person who appears to the authorised person in question to be in occupation of the premises in question, and[1]

(*b*) either—

(i) with the consent of a person who is in occupation of those premises; or

(ii) under the authority of a warrant by virtue of Schedule 18 to this Act.

(7) Except in an emergency, where an authorised person proposes to enter any premises and—

(*a*) entry has been refused and he apprehends on reasonable grounds that the use of force may be necessary to effect entry, or

(*b*) he apprehends on reasonable grounds that entry is likely to be refused and that the use of force may be necessary to effect entry,

any entry on to those premises by virtue of this section shall only be effected under the authority of a warrant by virtue of Schedule 18 to this Act.

(8) In relation to any premises belonging to or used for the purposes of the United Kingdom Atomic Energy Authority, subsections (1) to (4) above shall have effect subject to section 6(3) of the Atomic Energy Authority Act 1954 (which restricts entry to such premises where they have been declared to be prohibited places for the purposes of the Official Secrets Act 1911).

(9) The Secretary of State may by regulations make provision as to the procedure to be followed in connection with the taking of, and the dealing with, samples under subsection (4)(*f*) above.

(10) Where an authorised person proposes to exercise the power conferred by subsection (4)(*g*) above in the case of an article or substance found on any premises, he shall, if so requested by a person who at the time is present on and has responsibilities in relation to those premises, cause anything which is to be done by virtue of that power to be done in the presence of that person.

(11) Before exercising the power conferred by subsection (4)(*g*) above in the case of any article or substance, an authorised person shall consult—

(*a*) such persons having duties on the premises where the article or substance is to be dismantled or subjected to the process or test, and

(*b*) such other persons,

as appear to him appropriate for the purpose of ascertaining what dangers, if any, there may be in doing anything which he proposes to do or cause to be done under the power.

(12) No answer given by a person in pursuance of a requirement imposed under subsection (4)(*j*) above shall be admissible in evidence in England and Wales against that person in any proceedings, or in Scotland against that person in any criminal proceedings.

(13) Nothing in this section shall be taken to compel the production by any person of a document of which he would on grounds of legal professional privilege be entitled to withhold production on an order for discovery in an action in the High Court or, in relation to Scotland, on an order for the production of documents in an action in the Court of Session.

(14) Schedule 18 to this Act shall have effect with respect to the powers of entry and related powers which are conferred by this section.

(15) In this section—

"authorised person" means a person authorised under subsection (1) or (2) above;

"emergency" means a case in which it appears to the authorised person in question—

(a) that there is an immediate risk of serious harm or that circumstances exist which are likely to endanger life or health, and

(b) that immediate entry to any premises is necessary to verify the existence of that risk or those circumstances or to ascertain the cause of that risk or those circumstances or to effect a remedy,

and for this purpose "serious harm" means—

(i) serious pollution of the environment,

(ii) serious harm to the environment,

(iii) serious flooding,

(iv) serious harm to human health, or

(v) a serious detrimental impact on drainage;

"enforcing authority" means—

(*a*) the Secretary of State;

(*b*) the Agency;

(*bza*) the Natural Resources Body for Wales;

(*ba*) a waste collection authority;

(*c*) SEPA; or

(*d*) a local enforcing authority;

"flood risk activity enactment", in relation to an enforcing authority, means an enactment relating to the flood risk activity functions of that authority;

"flood risk activity functions", in relation to the Agency or the Natural Resources Body for Wales, means the functions relating to flood risk activities conferred or imposed on it by or under regulations made under section 61 of the Water Act 2014;

"local enforcing authority" means—

(*a*) a local enforcing authority, within the meaning of Part I of the Environmental Protection Act 1990;*

(*b*) a local authority, within the meaning of Part IIA of that Act, in its capacity as an enforcing authority for the purposes of that Part;

(*c*) a local authority for the purposes of Part IV of this Act or regulations under that Part;

(*d*) a local authority for the purposes of regulations under section 2 of the Pollution Prevention and Control Act 1999 extending to England and Wales;

"mobile plant" means plant which is designed to move or to be moved whether on roads or otherwise;

"pollution control enactments", in relation to an enforcing authority, means the enactments and instruments relating to the pollution control functions of that authority;*

"pollution control functions", in relation to the Agency, the Natural Resources Body for Wales or SEPA, means the functions conferred or imposed on it by or under—

(*a*) the Alkali, etc, Works Regulations Act 1906;

(*b*) *repealed*;

(*c*) *repealed*;

(*d*) Part I of the Health and Safety at Work etc. Act 1974;

(*e*) Parts I,* IA and II of the Control of Pollution Act 1974;

(*f*) the Control of Pollution (Amendment) Act 1989;

(*g*) Parts I,* II and IIA of the Environmental Protection Act 1990 (integrated pollution control, waste on land and contaminated land);

(*h*) Chapter III of Part IV of the Water Industry Act 1991 (special category effluent);

(*j*) Part III and section 161 to 161D of the Water Resources Act 1991;

(*k*) section 19 of the Clean Air Act 1993

(*l*) *repealed*

(*m*) regulations made by virtue of section 2(2) of the European Communities act 1972, to the extent that the regulations relate to pollution;

and, in relation to the Agency or the Natural Resources Body for Wales, includes the functions conferred or imposed on, or transferred to, it under section 2 of the Pollution Prevention and Control Act 1999 but, in relation to the Natural Resources Body for Wales, does not include any functions which were exercisable by the Countryside Council for Wales or the Forestry Commissioners immediately before 1 April 2013 and are functions of that Body by virtue of the Natural Resources Body for Wales (Functions) Order 2013;

"pollution control functions", in relation to a waste collection authority, means the functions conferred or imposed on it by or under Part 2 of the Environment Protection Act 1990;
"pollution control functions", in relation to a local enforcing authority, means the functions conferred or imposed on, or transferred to, that authority—
- (*a*) by or under Part I or* IIA of the Environmental Protection Act 1990;
- (*b*) by or under regulations made by virtue of Part IV of this Act; or
- (*c*) by or under regulations made by virtue of section 2(2) of the European Communities Act 1972, to the extent that the regulations relate to pollution;

and, in relation to an authority in England or Wales, includes the functions conferred or imposed on, or transferred to, that authority under section 2 of the Pollution Prevention and Control Act 1999;
"pollution control functions", in relation to the Secretary of State, means any functions which are conferred or imposed upon him by or under any enactment or instrument and which relate to the control of pollution;
"premises" includes any land, vehicle, vessel or mobile plant.
"waste collection authority" shall be construed in accordance with section 30(3)(*a*), (*b*) and (*bb*) of the Environmental Protection Act 1990.*

(16) Any power to make regulations under this section shall be exercisable by statutory instrument; and a statutory instrument containing any such regulations shall be subject to annulment pursuant to a resolution of either House of Parliament.

[Environment Act 1995, s 108 as amended by SI 2000/1973, the Anti-social Behaviour Act 2003, s 55, the Clean Neighbourhoods and Environment Act 2005, s 53, SSI 2006/181, SI 2010/675, SI 2013/755, SI 2016/475.]

* **Words repealed by the Pollution Prevention and Control Act 1999, Sch 3 from a date to be appointed.**

[1] In *R (on the application of Allensway Recycling Ltd) v Environment Agency* [2014] EWCA 1638 (Admin), [2014] 1 WLR 3753 it was held that s 108(6) had been drafted inadvertently; read literally it would mean that notice was required even in the case of a warrant issued under condition (c), (d) or (e) in para 2(2) of Sch 18, post. Accordingly, s 108(6) should be construed as requiring notice only when the warrant was issued under condition (a) or condition (b). The decision was reversed on appeal: *R (on the application of Allensway Recycling Ltd) v Environment Agency* [2015] EWCA Civ 1289, [2016] Env LR 16. The link between s 108(6)(a) and (b) was clear, and it was equally clear that Sch 18 was supplemental to the powers conferred by s 108 and did not confer a stand-alone power of entry free from the conditions laid down by s 108. The statutory words were clear and the courts should not read into them an implied qualification which would make them more restrictive of individual rights.

7.10194 **109. Power to deal with cause of imminent danger of serious pollution etc**

(1) Where, in the case of any article or substance found by him on any premises which he has power to enter, an authorised person has reasonable cause to believe that, in the circumstances in which he finds it, the article or substance is a cause of imminent danger of serious pollution of the environment or serious harm to human health, he may seize it and cause it to be rendered harmless (whether by destruction or otherwise).

(2) As soon as may be after any article or substance has been seized and rendered harmless under this section, the authorised person shall prepare and sign a written report giving particulars of the circumstances in which the article or substance was seized and so dealt with by him, and shall—
- (*a*) give a signed copy of the report to a responsible person at the premises where the article or substance was found by him; and
- (*b*) unless that person is the owner of the article or substance, also serve a signed copy of the report on the owner;

and if, where paragraph (*b*) above applies, the authorised person cannot after reasonable inquiry ascertain the name or address of the owner, the copy may be served on him by giving it to the person to whom a copy was given under paragraph (*a*) above.

(3) In this section, "authorised person" has the same meaning as in section 108 above.

[Environment Act 1995, s 109.]

7.10195 **110. Offences** (1) It is an offence for a person intentionally to obstruct an authorised person in the exercise or performance of his powers or duties.

(2) It is an offence for a person, without reasonable excuse,—
- (*a*) to fail to comply with any requirement imposed under section 108 above;
- (*b*) to fail or refuse to provide facilities or assistance or any information or to permit any inspection reasonably required by an authorised person in the execution of his powers or duties under or by virtue of that section; or
- (*c*) to prevent any other person from appearing before an authorised person, or answering any question to which an authorised person may require an answer, pursuant to subsection (4) of that section.

(3) It is an offence for a person falsely to pretend to be an authorised person.

(4) A person guilty of an offence under subsection (1) above shall be liable—
- (*a*) in the case of an offence of obstructing an authorised person in the execution of his powers under section 109 above[1]—
  - (i) on summary conviction, to a fine not exceeding **the statutory maximum**;
  - (ii) on conviction on indictment, to a **fine** or to imprisonment for a term not exceeding **two years**, or to **both**;
- (*b*) in any other case, on summary conviction, to a fine not exceeding **level 5** on the

standard scale.

(5) A person guilty of an offence under subsection (2) or (3) above shall be liable on summary conviction to a fine not exceeding **level 5** on the standard scale.

(6) In this section—

"authorised person" means a person authorised under section 108 above and includes a person designated under paragraph 2 of Schedule 18 to this Act;

"powers and duties" includes powers or duties exercisable by virtue of a warrant under Schedule 18 to this Act.

[Environment Act 1995, s 110.]

---

1 For procedure in respect of this offence which is triable either way, see the Magistrates' Courts Act 1980, ss 17A–21, in PART I: MAGISTRATES' COURTS, PROCEDURE, ante.

*Evidence*

7.10196 **111. Evidence in connection with certain pollution offences** (1) *Repealed.*

(2) Information provided or obtained pursuant to or by virtue of a condition of a relevant licence (including information so provided or obtained, or recorded, by means of any apparatus) shall be admissible in evidence in any proceedings, whether against the person subject to the condition or any other person.

(3) For the purposes of subsection (2) above, apparatus shall be presumed in any proceedings to register or record accurately, unless the contrary is shown or the relevant licence otherwise provides.

(4) Where—

(*a*) by virtue of a condition of a relevant licence, an entry is required to be made in any record as to the observance of any condition of the relevant licence, and

(*b*) the entry has not been made,

that fact shall be admissible in any proceedings as evidence that that condition has not been observed.

(5) In this section—

"apparatus" includes any meter or other device for measuring, assessing, determining, recording or enabling to be recorded, the volume, temperature, radioactivity, rate, nature, origin, composition or effect of any substance, flow, discharge, emission, deposit or abstraction;

"condition of a relevant licence" includes any requirement to which a person is subject under, by virtue of or in consequence of a relevant licence;

"environmental licence" has the same meaning as it has in Part I above as it applies in relation to the Agency, the Natural Resources Body for Wales or SEPA, as the case may be;

"relevant licence" means—

(*a*) any environmental licence;

(*b*) any consent under Part II of the Sewerage (Scotland) Act 1968 to make discharges of trade effluent;

(*c*) any agreement under section 37 of that Act with respect to, or to any matter connected with, the reception, treatment or disposal of such effluent;

(6) In section 25 of the Environmental Protection Act, after subsection (2) (which makes similar provision to subsection (4) above) there shall be inserted—

"(3) Subsection (2) above shall not have effect in relation to any entry required to be made in any record by virtue of a condition of a relevant licence, within the meaning of section 111 of the Environment Act 1995 (which makes corresponding provision in relation to such licences)."*

[Environment Act 1995, s 111 as amended by the Statute Law (Repeals) Act 2004 and SI 2013/755.]

---

* **Subsection (6) repealed by the Pollution Prevention and Control Act 1999, Sch 3 from a date to be appointed.**

*Information*

7.10197 **113. Disclosure of information** (1) Notwithstanding any prohibition or restriction imposed by or under any enactment or rule of law, information of any description may be disclosed—

(*a*) by a relevant agency to a Minister of the Crown, another relevant agency or local enforcing authority,

(*b*) by a Minister of the Crown to a new Agency, another Minister of the Crown or a local enforcing authority,

(*c*) by a local enforcing authority to a Minister of the Crown, a relevant agency or another local enforcing authority, or

(*d*) by the Natural Resources Body for Wales to the Forestry Commissioners,

for the purpose of facilitating the carrying out by any of the relevant agencies of any of its functions, by any such Minister of any of his environmental functions or by any local enforcing authority of any of its relevant functions; and no person shall be subject to any civil or criminal liability in consequence of any disclosure made by virtue of this subsection.

(2) Nothing in this section shall authorise the disclosure to a local enforcing authority by a relevant agency or another local enforcing authority of information—

(*a*) disclosure of which would, in the opinion of a Minister of the Crown, be contrary to the interests of national security; or

(*b*) which was obtained under or by virtue of the Statistics of Trade Act 1947 and which was disclosed to a relevant agency or any of its officers by the Secretary of State.

(3) No information disclosed to any person under or by virtue of this section shall be disclosed by that person to any other person otherwise than in accordance with the provisions of this section, or any provision of any other enactment which authorises or requires the disclosure, if that information is information—

(*a*) which relates to a trade secret of any person or which otherwise is or might be commercially confidential in relation to any person; or

(*b*) whose disclosure otherwise than under or by virtue of this section would, in the opinion of a Minister of the Crown, be contrary to the interests of national security.

(4) Any authorisation by or under this section of the disclosure of information by or to any person shall also be taken to authorise the disclosure of that information by or, as the case may be, to any officer of his who is authorised by him to make the disclosure or, as the case may be, to receive the information.

(5) In this section—

"the environment" means all, or any, of the following media, namely, the air, water and land (and the medium of air includes the air within buildings and the air within other natural or man-made structures above or below ground);

"environmental functions", in relation to a Minister of the Crown, means any function of that Minister, whether conferred or imposed under or by virtue of any enactment or otherwise, relating to the environment; and

"local enforcing authority" means—

(*a*) any local authority within the meaning of Part IIA of the Environmental Protection Act 1990, and the "relevant functions" of such an authority are its functions under or by virtue of that Part;

(*aa*) in relation to England and Wales, any local authority within the meaning of the regulations under section 2 of the Pollution Prevention and Control Act 1999;

(*b*) any local authority within the meaning of Part IV of this Act, and the "relevant functions" of such an authority are its functions under or by virtue of that Part; or

(*c*) in relation to England, any county council for an area for which there are district councils, and the "relevant functions" of such a county council are its functions under or by virtue of Part IV of this Act; or

(*d*) in relation to England and Wales, any local enforcing authority within the meaning of section 1(7) of the Environmental Protection Act 1990, and the "relevant functions" of such an authority are its functions under or by virtue of Part I of that Act.*

"relevant agency" means the Agency, the Natural Resources Body for Wales or SEPA.

[Environment Act 1995, s 113, as amended by the Pollution Prevention and Control Act 1999, Sch 2, SI 2000/1973 and SI 2013/755.]

* **Repealed by the Pollution Prevention and Control Act 1999, Sch 3 from a date to be appointed.**

*Crown application*

**7.10198 115. Application of this Act to the Crown** (1) Subject to the provisions of this section, this Act shall bind the Crown.

(2) Part III of this Act and any amendments, repeals and revocations made by other provisions of this Act (other than those made by Schedule 21, which shall bind the Crown) bind the Crown to the extent that the enactments to which they relate bind the Crown.

(3) No contravention by the Crown of any provision made by or under this Act shall make the Crown criminally liable; but the High Court or, in Scotland, the Court of Session may, on the application of the Agency or, in Scotland, SEPA, declare unlawful any act or omission of the Crown which constitutes such a contravention.

(4) Notwithstanding anything in subsection (3) above, any provision made by or under this Act shall apply to persons in the public service of the Crown as it applies to other persons.

(5) If the Secretary of State certifies that it appears to him, as respects any Crown premises and any powers of entry exercisable in relation to them specified in the certificate, that it is requisite or expedient that, in the interests of national security, the powers should not be exercisable in relation to those premises, those powers shall not be exercisable in relation to those premises; and in this subsection "Crown premises" means premises held or used by or on behalf of the Crown.

(6) Nothing in this section shall be taken as in any way affecting Her Majesty in her private capacity; and this subsection shall be construed as if section 38(3) of the Crown Proceedings Act 1947 (interpretation of references to Her Majesty in her private capacity) were contained in this Act.

[Environment Act 1995, s 115.]

*Isles of Scilly*

**7.10199 117.** *Application of this Act to the Isles of Scilly.*[1]

[1] The Environment Act 1995 (Isles of Scilly) Order 1996, SI 1996/1030, which is made under s 117, gives the Environment Agency certain functions in the Isles of Scilly which it has in other parts of England and Wales. See also the

Environmental Protection Act 1990 (Isles of Scilly) Order 2006, SI 2006/1381.

*Miscellaneous and supplemental*

7.10200 **121. Local statutory provisions; consequential amendments etc** (1) If it appears to the Secretary of State or the Minister to be appropriate to do so—

(*a*) for the purposes of, or in consequence of, the coming into force of any enactment contained in this Act; or

(*b*) in consequence of the effect or operation at any time after the transfer date of any such enactment or of anything done under any such enactment,

he may by order repeal, amend or re-enact (with or without modifications) any local statutory provision, including, in the case of an order by virtue of paragraph (*b*) above, a provision amended by virtue of paragraph (*a*) above.

(2) An order made by the Secretary of State or the Minister under subsection (1) above may—

(*a*) make provision applying generally in relation to local statutory provisions of a description specified in the order;

(*b*) make different provision for different cases, including different provision in relation to different persons, circumstances or localities;

(*c*) contain such supplemental, consequential and transitional provision as the Secretary of State or, as the case may be, the Minister considers appropriate; and

(*d*) in the case of an order made after the transfer date, require provision contained in the order to be treated as if it came into force on that date.

(3) The power under this section to repeal or amend a local statutory provision shall include power to modify the effect in relation to any local statutory provision of any provision of Schedule 23 to this Act.

(4) Nothing in any order under this section may abrogate or curtail the effect of so much of any local statutory provision as confers any right of way or confers on or preserves for the public—

(*a*) any right of enjoyment of air, exercise or recreation on land; or

(*b*) any right of access to land for the purposes of exercise or recreation.

(5) The power to make an order under subsection (1) above shall be exercisable by statutory instrument subject to annulment in pursuance of a resolution of either House of Parliament.

(6) The power to make an order under subsection (1) above shall be without prejudice to any power conferred by any other provision of this Act.

(7) In this section—

"local statutory provision" means—

(*a*) a provision of a local Act (including an Act confirming a provisional order);

(*b*) a provision of so much of any public general Act as has effect with respect to a particular area, with respect to particular persons or works or with respect to particular provisions falling within any paragraph of this definition;

(*c*) a provision of an instrument made under any provision falling within paragraph (*a*) or (*b*) above; or

(*d*) a provision of any other instrument which is in the nature of a local enactment;

"the Minister" means the Minister of Agriculture, Fisheries and Food;

"the transfer date" has the same meaning as in Part I of this Act.

[Environment Act 1995, s 121.]

7.10201 **122. Directions** (1) Any direction given under this Act shall be in writing.

(2) Any power conferred by this Act to give a direction shall include power to vary or revoke the direction.

(3) Subsection (4) and (5) below apply to any direction given—

(*a*) to the Agency or SEPA under any provision of this Act or any other enactment, or

(*b*) to any other body or person under any provision of this Act,

being a direction to any extent so given for the purpose of implementing any obligations of the United Kingdom under the EU Treaties.

(4) A direction to which this subsection applies shall not be varied or revoked unless, notwithstanding the variation or revocation, the obligations mentioned in subsection (3) above, as they have effect for the time being, continue to be implemented, whether by directions or any other instrument or by any enactment.

(5) Any variation or revocation of a direction to which this subsection applies shall be published in such manner as the Minister giving it considers appropriate for the purpose of bring the matters to which it relates to the attention of persons likely to be affected by them; and—

(*a*) copies of the variation or revocation shall be made available to the public; and

(*b*) notice of the variation or revocation, and of where a copy of the variation or revocation may be obtained, shall be given—

(i) if the direction has effect in England and Wales, in the London Gazette;

(ii) *Scotland.*

[Environment Act 1995, s 122 as amended by SI 2011/1043.]

7.10202 **123. Service of documents** (1) Without prejudice to paragraph 17(2)(*d*) of Schedule 7 to this Act, any notice required or authorised by or under this Act to be served (whether the expression "serve" or the expression "give" or "send" or any other expression is used) on any person may be served by delivering it to him, or by leaving it at his proper address, or by sending it by post to him at that address.

(2) Any such notice may—

(*a*) in the case of a body corporate, be served on the secretary or clerk of that body;

(*b*) in the case of a partnership, be served on a partner or a person having the control or management of the partnership business.

(3) For the purposes of this section and of section 7 of the Interpretation Act 1978 (service of documents by post) in its application to this section, the proper address of any person on whom any such notice is to be served shall be his last known address, except that—

(*a*) in the case of a body corporate or their secretary or clerk, it shall be the address of the registered or principal office of that body;

(*b*) in the case of a partnership or person having the control or the management of the partnership business, it shall be the principal office of the partnership;

and for the purposes of this subsection the principal office of a company registered outside the United Kingdom or of a partnership carrying on business outside the United Kingdom shall be their principal office within the United Kingdom.

(4) If the person to be served with any such notice has specified an address in the United Kingdom other than his proper address within the meaning of subsection (3) above as the one at which he or someone on his behalf will accept notices of the same description as that notice, that address shall also be treated for the purposes of this section and section 7 of the Interpretation Act 1978 as his proper address.

(5) Where under any provision of this Act any notice is required to be served on a person who is, or appears to be, in occupation of any premises then—

(*a*) if the name or address of such a person cannot after reasonable inquiry be ascertained, or

(*b*) if the premises appear to be or are unoccupied,

that notice may be served either by leaving it in the hands of a person who is or appears to be resident or employed on the premises or by leaving it conspicuously affixed to some building or object on the premises.

(6) This section shall not apply to any notice in relation to the service of which provision is made by rules of court.

(7) The preceding provisions of this section shall apply to the service of a document as they apply to the service of a notice.

(8) In this section—

"premises" includes any land, vehicle, vessel or mobile plant;

"serve" shall be construed in accordance with subsection (1) above.

[Environment Act 1995, s 123.]

7.10203 **124. General interpretation** (1) In this Act, except in so far as the context otherwise requires—

"the Agency" means the Environment Agency;

"financial year" means a period of twelve months ending with 31st March;

"functions" includes powers and duties;

"modifications" includes additions, alterations and omissions and cognate expressions shall be construed accordingly;

"notice" means notice in writing;

"records", without prejudice to the generality of the expression, includes computer records and any other records kept otherwise than in a document;

"SEPA" means the Scottish Environment Protection Agency.

(2) The amendment by this Act of any provision contained in subordinate legislation shall not be taken to have prejudiced any power to make further subordinate legislation amending or revoking that provision.

(3) In subsection (2) above, "subordinate legislation" has the same meaning as in the Interpretation Act 1978.

[Environment Act 1995, s 124.]

7.10204 **125. Short title, commencement[1], extent, etc** (1) This Act may be cited as the Environment Act 1995.

[Environment Act 1995, s 125(1).]

[1] The Act is fully in force.

## SCHEDULES

### SCHEDULE 1

THE ENVIRONMENT AGENCY Section 1

7.10205 **1–9.** *Membership; staff; delegation of powers; members' interests and minutes.*

*Application of seal and proof of instruments*

**10.** (1) The application of the seal of the Agency shall be authenticated by the signature of any member, officer or employee of the Agency who has been authorised for the purpose, whether generally or specially, by the Agency.

(2) In this paragraph the reference to the signature of a person includes a reference to a facsimile of a signature by whatever process reproduced; and, in paragraph 11 below, the word "signed" shall be construed accordingly.

*Documents served etc by or on the Agency*

**11.** (1) Any document which the Agency is authorised or required by or under any enactment to serve, make or issue may be signed on behalf of the Agency by any member, officer or employee of the Agency who has been authorised for the purpose, whether generally or specially, by the Agency.

(2) Every document purporting to be an instrument made or issued by or on behalf of the Agency and to be duly executed under the seal of the Agency, or to be signed or executed by a person authorised by the Agency for the purpose, shall be received in evidence and be treated, without further proof, as being so made or issued unless the contrary is shown.

(3) Any notice which is required or authorised, by or under any provision of any other Act, to be given, served or issued by, to or on the Agency shall be in writing.

*Interpretation*

**12.** In this Schedule—

"the appropriate Minister", in relation to any person who is or has been a member, means the Minister or the Secretary of State, according to whether that person was appointed as a member by the Minister or by the Secretary of State; and

"member", except where the context otherwise requires, means any member of the Agency (including the chairman and deputy chairman).

## SCHEDULE 11

AIR QUALITY: SUPPLEMENTAL PROVISIONS — Section 90

**7.10209 1–4.** *Consultation requirements; exchange of information with county councils in England; joint exercise of local authority functions; public access to information about air quality.*

*Fixed penalty offences*

**5.** (1) Without prejudice to the generality of paragraph (*o*) of subsection (2) of section 87 of this Act, regulations may, in particular, make provision—

(*a*) for the qualifications, appointment or authorisation of persons who are to issue fixed penalty notices;

(*b*) for the offences in connection with which, the cases or circumstances in which, the time or period at or within which, or the manner in which fixed penalty notices may be issued;

(*c*) prohibiting the institution, before the expiration of the period for paying the fixed penalty, of proceedings against a person for an offence in connection with which a fixed penalty notice has been issued;

(*d*) prohibiting the conviction of a person for an offence in connection with which a fixed penalty notice has been issued if the fixed penalty is paid before the expiration of the period for paying it;

(*e*) entitling, in prescribed cases, a person to whom a fixed penalty notice is issued to give, within a prescribed period, notice requesting a hearing in respect of the offence to which the fixed penalty notice relates;

(*f*) for the amount of the fixed penalty to be increased by a prescribed amount in any case where the person liable to pay the fixed penalty fails to pay it before the expiration of the period for paying it, without having given notice requesting a hearing in respect of the offence to which the fixed penalty notice relates;

(*g*) for or in connection with the recovery of an unpaid fixed penalty as a fine or as a civil debt or as if it were a sum payable under a county court order;

(*h*) for or in connection with execution or other enforcement in respect of an unpaid fixed penalty by prescribed persons;

(*j*) for a fixed penalty notice, and any prescribed proceedings or other prescribed steps taken by reference to the notice, to be rendered void in prescribed cases where a person makes a prescribed statutory declaration, and for the consequences of any notice, proceedings or other steps being so rendered void (including extension of any time limit for instituting criminal proceedings);

(*k*) for or in connection with the extension, in prescribed cases or circumstances, by a prescribed person of the period for paying a fixed penalty;

(*l*) for or in connection with the withdrawal, in prescribed circumstances, of a fixed penalty notice, including—

(i) repayment of any amount paid by way of fixed penalty in pursuance of a fixed penalty notice which is withdrawn; and

(ii) prohibition of the institution or continuation of proceedings for the offence in connection with which the withdrawn notice was issued;

(*m*) for or in connection with the disposition of sums received by way of fixed penalty;

(*n*) for a certificate purporting to be signed by or on behalf of a prescribed person and stating either—

(i) that payment of a fixed penalty was, or (as the case may be) was not, received on or before a date specified in the certificate, or

(ii) that an envelope containing an amount sent by post in payment of a fixed penalty was marked as posted on a date specified in the certificate,

to be received as evidence of the matters so stated and to be treated, without further proof, as being so signed unless the contrary is shown;

(*o*) requiring a fixed penalty notice to give such reasonable particulars of the circumstances alleged to constitute the fixed penalty offence to which the notice relates as are necessary for giving reasonable information of the offence and to state—

(i) the monetary amount of the fixed penalty which may be paid;

(ii) the person to whom, and the address at which, the fixed penalty may be paid and any correspondence relating to the fixed penalty notice may be sent;
(iii) the method of methods by which payment of the fixed penalty may be made;
(iv) the period for paying the fixed penalty;
(v) the consequences of the fixed penalty not being paid before the expiration of that period;

(*p*) similar to any provision made by section 79 of the Road Traffic Offenders Act 1988 (statements by constables in fixed penalty cases);

(*q*) for presuming, in any proceedings, that any document of a prescribed description purporting to have been signed by a person to whom a fixed penalty notice has been issued has been signed by that person;

(*r*) requiring or authorising a fixed penalty notice to contain prescribed information relating to, or for the purpose of facilitating, the administration of the fixed penalty system;

(*s*) with respect to the giving of fixed penalty notices, including, in particular, provision with respect to—
(i) the methods by which,
(ii) the officers, servants or agents by, to or on whom, and
(iii) the places at which,
fixed penalty notices may be given by, or served on behalf of, a prescribed person;

(*t*) prescribing the method or methods by which fixed penalties may be paid;

(*u*) for or with respect to the issue of prescribed documents to persons to whom fixed penalty notices are or have been given;

(*w*) for a fixed penalty notice to be treated for prescribed purposes as if it were an information or summons or any other document of a prescribed description.

(2) The provision that may be made by regulations prescribing fixed penalty offences includes provision for an offence to be a fixed penalty offence—
(*a*) only if it is committed in such circumstances or manner as may be prescribed; or
(*b*) except if it is committed in such circumstances or manner as may be prescribed.

(3) Regulations may provide for any offence which is a fixed penalty offence to cease to be such an offence.

(4) An offence which, in consequence of regulations made by virtue of sub-paragraph (3) above, has ceased to be a fixed penalty offence shall be eligible to be prescribed as such an offence again.

(5) Regulations may make provision for such exceptions, limitations and conditions as the Secretary of State considers necessary or expedient.

(6) In this paragraph—

"fixed penalty" means a penalty of such amount as may be prescribed (whether by being specified in, or made calculable under, regulations);

"fixed penalty notice" means a notice offering a person an opportunity to discharge any liability to conviction for a fixed penalty offence by payment of a penalty of a prescribed amount;

"fixed penalty offence" means, subject to sub-paragraph (2) above, any offence (whether under or by virtue of this Part or any other enactment) which is for the time being prescribed as a fixed penalty offence;

"the fixed penalty system" means the system implementing regulations made under or by virtue of paragraph (*o*) of subsection (2) of section 87 of this Act;

"the period for paying", in relation to any fixed penalty, means such period as may be prescribed for the purpose;

"regulations" means regulations under or by virtue of paragraph (*o*) of subsection (2) of section 87 of this Act.

## SCHEDULE 15

### MINOR AND CONSEQUENTIAL AMENDMENTS RELATING TO FISHERIES

*(As amended by the Marine and Coastal Access Act 2009, Sch 22 and SI 2009/463)* Section 105

*Interpretation*

7.10211 1. In this Schedule—

"local statutory provision" means—
(*a*) a provision of a local Act (including an Act confirming a provisional order);
(*b*) a provision of so much of any public general Act as has effect with respect to particular persons or works or with respect to particular provisions falling within any paragraph of this definition;
(*c*) a provision of an instrument made under any provision falling within paragraph (*a*) or (*b*) above;
(*d*) a provision of any other instrument which is in the nature of a local enactment;

"the Minister" means the Minister of Agriculture, Fisheries and Food;

"subordinate legislation" has the same meaning as in the Interpretation Act 1978;

"the transfer date" has the same meaning as in Part I of this Act.

*General modifications of references to the National Rivers Authority*

2. (1) Subject to—
(*a*) the following provisions of this Schedule,
(*b*) the provisions of sections 102 to 104 of this Act, and
(*c*) any repeal made by this Act,
any provision to which this paragraph applies which contains, or falls to be construed as containing, a reference (however framed and whether or not in relation to an area) to the National Rivers Authority shall have effect on and after the transfer date as if that reference were a reference to the Agency.

(2) Sub-paragraph (1) above is subject to paragraph 1(2)(*a*) of Schedule 17 to the Water Act 1989 (references in certain local statutory provisions or subordinate legislation to the area of a particular water authority to have effect as references to the area which, immediately before the transfer date within the meaning of that Act, was the area of that authority for the purposes of their functions relating to fisheries).

(3) Subject as mentioned in sub-paragraph (1) above, any provision to which this paragraph applies which contains, or falls to be construed as containing, a reference (however framed) to the whole area in relation to

which the National Rivers Authority carries out its functions in relation to fisheries shall have effect on and after the transfer date as if that reference were a reference to the whole area in relation to which the Agency carries out its functions relating to fisheries.

(4) The provisions to which this paragraph applies are the provisions of—

(*a*) *repealed*

(*b*) the Salmon and Freshwater Fisheries Act 1975; and

(*c*) any local statutory provision or subordinate legislation which is in force immediately before the transfer date and—

(i) relates to the carrying out by the National Rivers Authority of any function relating to fisheries; or

(ii) in the case of subordinate legislation, was made by virtue of any provision to which this paragraph applies.

(5) The modifications made by this paragraph shall be subject to any power by subordinate legislation to revoke or amend any provision to which this paragraph applies; and, accordingly, any such power, including the powers conferred by section 121 of this Act and paragraph 3 below, shall be exercisable so as to exclude the operation of this paragraph in relation to the provisions in relation to which the power is conferred.

*Power to amend subordinate legislation etc*

**3.** (1) If it appears to the Minister or the Secretary of State to be appropriate to do so for the purposes of, or in consequence of, the coming into force of any provision of this Schedule, he may by order revoke or amend any subordinate legislation.

(2) An order under this paragraph may—

(*a*) make different provision for different cases, including different provision in relation to different persons, circumstances or localities; and

(*b*) contain such supplemental, consequential and transitional provision as the Minister or the Secretary of State considers appropriate.

(3) The power conferred by virtue of this paragraph in relation to subordinate legislation made under any enactment shall be without prejudice to any other power to revoke or amend subordinate legislation made under that enactment, but—

(*a*) no requirement imposed with respect to the exercise of any such other power shall apply in relation to any revocation or amendment of that legislation by an order under this paragraph; and

(*b*) the power to make an order under this paragraph shall be exercisable (instead of in accordance with any such requirement) by statutory instrument subject to annulment in pursuance of a resolution of either House of Parliament.

## SCHEDULE 18

### Supplemental provisions with respect to powers of entry

Section 108

*Interpretation*

7.10214 **1.** (1) In this Schedule—

"designated person" means an authorised person, within the meaning of section 108 of this Act and includes a person designated by virtue of paragraph 2 below;

"relevant power" means a power conferred by section 108 of this Act, including a power exercisable by virtue of a warrant under this Schedule.

(2) Expressions used in this Schedule and in section 108 of this Act have the same meaning in this Schedule as they have in that section.

*Issue of warrants*

**2.** (1) If it is shown to the satisfaction of a justice of the peace or, in Scotland, the sheriff or a justice of the peace, on sworn information in writing—

(*a*) that there are reasonable grounds for the exercise in relation to any premises of a relevant power; and

(*b*) that one or more of the conditions specified in sub-paragraph (2) below is fulfilled in relation to those premises,

the justice or sheriff may by warrant authorise an enforcing authority to designate a person who shall be authorised to exercise the power in relation to those premises, in accordance with the warrant and, if need be, by force.

(2) The conditions mentioned in sub-paragraph (1)(*b*) above are—

(*a*) that the exercise of the power in relation to the premises has been refused;

(*b*) that such a refusal is reasonably apprehended;

(*c*) that the premises are unoccupied;

(*d*) that the occupier is temporarily absent from the premises and the case is one of urgency; or

(*e*) that an application for admission to the premises would defeat the object of the proposed entry.

(3) In a case where subsection (6) of section 108 of this Act applies[1], a justice of the peace or sheriff shall not issue a warrant under this Schedule by virtue only of being satisfied that the exercise of a power in relation to any premises has been refused, or that a refusal is reasonably apprehended, unless he is also satisfied that the notice required by that subsection has been given and that the period of that notice has expired.

(4) Every warrant under this Schedule shall continue in force until the purposes for which the warrant was issued have been fulfilled.

---

[1] Section 108(6) was drafted inadvertently; read literally it would mean that notice was required even in the case of a warrant issued under condition (c), (d) or (e) in para 2(2) of Sch 18, post. Accordingly, s 108(6) should be construed as requiring notice only when the warrant was issued under condition (a) or condition (b): *R (Allensway Recycling Ltd) v Environment Agency* [2014] 1 WLR 3753.

*Manner of exercise of powers*

**3.** A person designated as the person who may exercise a relevant power shall produce evidence of his designation and other authority before he exercises the power.

*Information obtained to be admissible in evidence*

**4.** (1) Subject to section 108(12) of this Act, information obtained in consequence of the exercise of a relevant power, with or without the consent of any person, shall be admissible in evidence against that or any other person.

(2) Without prejudice to the generality of sub-paragraph (1) above, information obtained by means of monitoring or other apparatus installed on any premises in the exercise of a relevant power, with or without the consent of any person in occupation of the premises, shall be admissible in evidence in any proceedings against that or any other person.

*Duty to secure premises*

**5.** A person who, in the exercise of a relevant power enters on any premises which are unoccupied or whose occupier is temporarily absent shall leave the premises as effectually secured against trespassers as he found them.

*Compensation*

**6.** (1) Where any person exercises any power conferred by section 108(4)(*a*) or (*b*) or (5) of this Act, it shall be the duty of the enforcing authority under whose authorisation he acts to make full compensation to any person who has sustained loss or damage by reason of—

(*a*) the exercise by the designated person of that power; or

(*b*) the performance of, or failure of the designated person to perform, the duty imposed by paragraph 5 above.

(2) Compensation shall not be payable by virtue of sub-paragraph (1) above in respect of any loss or damage if the loss or damage—

(*a*) is attributable to the default of the person who sustained it; or

(*b*) is loss or damage in respect of which compensation is payable by virtue of any other provision of the pollution control enactments.

(3) Any dispute as to a person's entitlement to compensation under this paragraph, or as to the amount of any such compensation, shall be referred to the arbitration of a single arbitrator or, in Scotland, arbiter appointed by agreement between the enforcing authority in question and the person who claims to have sustained the loss or damage or, in default of agreement, by the Secretary of State.

(4) A designated person shall not be liable in any civil or criminal proceedings for anything done in the purported exercise of any relevant power if the court is satisfied that the act was done in good faith and that there were reasonable grounds for doing it.

## Noise Act 1996

(1996 c 37)

*Summary procedure for dealing with noise at night*

7.10220 **1. Application of sections 2 to 9** Sections 2 to 9 apply to the area of every local authority in England and Wales.

[Noise Act 1996, s 1 as substituted by the Anti-social Behaviour Act 2003, s 42.]

7.10221 **2. Investigation of complaints of noise at night** (1) A local authority may, if they receive a complaint of the kind mentioned in subsection (2), arrange for an officer of the authority to take reasonable steps to investigate the complaint.

(2) The kind of complaint referred to is one made by any individual present in a dwelling during night hours (referred to in this Act as "the complainant's dwelling" that excessive noise is being emitted from—

(*a*) another dwelling (referred to in this group of sections as "the offending dwelling"), or

(*b*) any premises in respect of which a premises licence or a temporary event notice has effect (referred to in this group of sections as "the offending premises").

(3) A complaint under subsection (2) may be made by any means.

(4) If an officer of the authority is satisfied, in consequence of an investigation under subsection (1), that—

(*a*) noise is being emitted from the offending dwelling or the offending premises during night hours, and

(*b*) the noise, if it were measured from within the complainant's dwelling, would or might exceed the permitted level,

he may serve a notice about the noise under section 3.

(5) For the purposes of subsection (4), it is for the officer of the authority dealing with the particular case—

(*a*) to decide whether any noise, if it were measured from within the complainant's dwelling, would or might exceed the permitted level, and

(*b*) for the purposes of that decision, to decide whether to assess the noise from within or outside the complainant's dwelling and whether or not to use any device for measuring the noise.

(6) In this group of sections, "night hours" means the period beginning with 11 p.m. and ending with the following 7 a.m.

(7) Where a local authority receive a complaint under subsection (2) and the offending dwelling is, or the offending premises are, within the area of another local authority, the first local authority may act under this group of sections as if the offending dwelling or the offending premises were within their area.

(7A) In this group of sections—

"premises licence" has the same meaning as in the Licensing Act 2003 (c 17);

"temporary event notice" has the same meaning as in the Licensing Act 2003 (and is to be treated as having effect in accordance with section 171(6) of that Act).

(8) In this section and sections 3 to 9, "this group of sections" means this and those sections.

[Noise Act 1996, s 2 as amended by the Anti-social Behaviour Act 2003, s 42 and the Clean Neighbourhoods and Environment Act 2005, Sch 1.]

7.10222 3. **Warning notices** (1) A notice under this section (referred to in this Act as "a warning notice") must—

(*a*) state that an officer of the authority considers—

(i) that noise is being emitted from the offending dwelling or the offending premises during night hours, and

(ii) that the noise exceeds, or may exceed, the permitted level, as measured from within the complainant's dwelling, and

(*b*) give warning—

(i) in a case where the complaint is in respect of a dwelling, that any person who is responsible for noise which is emitted from the offending dwelling in the period specified in the notice and which exceeds the permitted level, as measured from within the complainant's dwelling, may be guilty of an offence;

(ii) in a case where the complaint is in respect of other premises, that the responsible person in relation to the offending premises may be guilty of an offence if noise which exceeds the permitted level, as measured from within the complainant's dwelling, is emitted from the premises in the period specified in the notice.

(2) The period specified in a warning notice must be a period—

(*a*) beginning not earlier than ten minutes after the time when the notice is served, and

(*b*) ending with the following 7 a.m.

(3) In a case where the complaint is in respect of a dwelling, a warning notice must be served—

(*a*) by delivering it to any person present at or near the offending dwelling and appearing to the officer of the authority to be responsible for the noise, or

(*b*) if it is not reasonably practicable to identify any person present at or near the dwelling as being a person responsible for the noise on whom the notice may reasonably be served, by leaving it at the offending dwelling.

(3A) In a case where the complaint is in respect of other premises, a warning notice must be served by delivering it to the person who appears to the officer of the authority to be the responsible person in relation to the offending premises at the time the notice is delivered.

(4) A warning notice must state the time at which it is served.

(5) For the purposes of this group of sections, a person is responsible for noise emitted from a dwelling if he is a person to whose act, default or sufferance the emission of the noise is wholly or partly attributable.

(6) For the purposes of this group of sections, the responsible person in relation to premises at a particular time is—

(*a*) where a premises licence has effect in respect of the premises—

(i) the person who holds the premises licence if he is present at the premises at that time,

(ii) where that person is not present at the premises at that time, the designated premises supervisor under the licence if he is present at the premises at that time, or

(iii) where neither of the persons mentioned in sub-paragraphs (i) and (ii) is present at the premises at that time, any other person present at the premises at that time who is in charge of the premises;

(*b*) where a temporary event notice has effect in respect of the premises—

(i) the premises user in relation to that notice if he is present at the premises at that time, or

(ii) where the premises user is not present at the premises at that time, any other person present at the premises at that time who is in charge of the premises.

[Noise Act 1996, s 3 as amended by the Clean Neighbourhoods and Environment Act 2005, Sch 1.]

7.10223 4. **Offence where noise from a dwelling exceeds permitted level after service of notice** (1) If a warning notice has been served in respect of noise emitted from a dwelling, any person who is responsible for noise which—

(*a*) is emitted from the dwelling in the period specified in the notice, and

(*b*) exceeds the permitted level, as measured from within the complainant's dwelling,

is guilty of an offence.

(2) It is a defence for a person charged with an offence under this section to show that there was a reasonable excuse for the act, default or sufferance in question.

(3) A person guilty of an offence under this section is liable on summary conviction to a fine not exceeding **level 3** on the standard scale[1].

[Noise Act 1996, s 4 as amended by the Clean Neighbourhoods and Environment Act 2005, Sch 1.]

[1] For power of the court to order forfeiture of any seized equipment used in the commission of the offence, see the Schedule to the Act, post.

7.10224 **4A. Offence where noise from other premises exceeds permitted level after service of notice** (1) If—

(*a*) a warning notice has been served under section 3 in respect of noise emitted from premises,

(*b*) noise is emitted from the premises in the period specified in the notice, and

(*c*) the noise exceeds the permitted level, as measured from within the complainant's dwelling,

the responsible person in relation to the offending premises at the time at which the noise referred to in paragraph (*c*) is emitted is guilty of an offence.

(2) A person guilty of an offence under this section is liable on summary conviction to a fine not exceeding level 5 on the standard scale.

[Noise Act 1996, s 4 as inserted by the Clean Neighbourhoods and Environment Act 2005, Sch 1.]

7.10225 **5. Permitted level of noise** (1)–(4) *The appropriate person may give directions as to permitted level of noise.*

[Noise Act 1996, s 5—summarised.]

7.10226 **6.** *Approval of measuring devices.*

7.10227 **7. Evidence** (1) In proceedings for an offence under section 4 or 4A, evidence—

(*a*) of a measurement of noise made by a device, or of the circumstances in which it was made, or

(*b*) that a device was of a type approved for the purposes of section 6, or that any conditions subject to which the approval was given were satisfied,

may be given by the production of a document mentioned in subsection (2).

(2) The document referred to is one which is signed by an officer of the local authority and which (as the case may be)—

(*a*) gives particulars of the measurement or of the circumstances in which it was made, or

(*b*) states that the device was of such a type or that, to the best of the knowledge and belief of the person making the statement, all such conditions were satisfied;

and if the document contains evidence of a measurement of noise it may consist partly of a record of the measurement produced automatically by a device.

(3) In proceedings for an offence under section 4, evidence that noise, or noise of any kind, measured by a device at any time was noise emitted from a dwelling may be given by the production of a document—

(*a*) signed by an officer of the local authority, and

(*b*) stating that he had identified that dwelling as the source at that time of the noise or, as the case may be, the noise of that kind.

(3A) In proceedings for an offence under section 4A, evidence that noise, or noise of any kind, measured by a device at any time was noise emitted from any other premises may be given by the production of a document—

(*a*) signed by an officer of the local authority, and

(*b*) stating that he had identified those premises as the source at that time of the noise or, as the case may be, noise of that kind.

(4) For the purposes of this section, a document purporting to be signed as mentioned in subsection (2), (3)(*a*) or (3A)(*a*) is to be treated as being so signed unless the contrary is proved.

(5) This section does not make a document admissible as evidence in proceedings for an offence unless a copy of it has, not less than seven days before the hearing or trial, been served on the person charged with the offence.

(6) This section does not make a document admissible as evidence of anything other than the matters shown on a record produced automatically by a device if, not less than three days before the hearing or trial or within such further time as the court may in special circumstances allow, the person charged with the offence serves a notice on the prosecutor requiring attendance at the hearing or trial of the person who signed the document.

[Noise Act 1996, s 7 as amended by the Clean Neighbourhoods and Environment Act 2005, Sch 1.]

7.10228 **8. Fixed penalty notices** (1) Where an officer of a local authority who is authorised for the purposes of this section has reason to believe that a person is committing or has just committed an offence under section 4 or 4A, he may give that person a notice (referred to in this Act as a "fixed penalty notice") offering him the opportunity of discharging any liability to conviction for that offence by payment of a fixed penalty.

(2) A fixed penalty notice may be given to a person—

(*a*) by delivering the notice to him, or

(*b*) if it is not reasonably practicable to deliver it to him, by leaving the notice, addressed to him, at the offending dwelling or the offending premises (as the case may be).

(3) Where a person is given a fixed penalty notice in respect of such an offence—

(*a*) proceedings for that offence must not be instituted before the end of the period of fourteen days following the date of the notice, and (*b*) he cannot be convicted of that offence if he pays the fixed penalty before the end of that period.

(4) A fixed penalty notice must give such particulars of the circumstances alleged to constitute the offence as are necessary for giving reasonable information of the offence.

(5) A fixed penalty notice must state—

(*a*) the period during which, because of subsection (3)(*a*), proceedings will not be taken for the offence,

(*b*) the amount of the fixed penalty, and

(*c*) the person to whom and the address at which the fixed penalty may be paid.

(6) Payment of the fixed penalty may (among other methods) be made by pre-paying and posting to that person at that address a letter containing the amount of the penalty (in cash or otherwise).

(7) Where a letter containing the amount of the penalty is sent in accordance with subsection (6), payment is to be regarded as having been made at the time at which that letter would be delivered in the ordinary course of post.

(8) *Repealed.*

[Noise Act 1996, s 8 as amended by the Clean Neighbourhoods and Environment Act 2005, Sch 1.]

7.10229 **8A. Amount of fixed penalty** (1) This section applies in relation to a fixed penalty payable to a local authority in pursuance of a notice under section 8.

(2) In the case of an offence under section 4 the amount of the fixed penalty—

(*a*) is the amount specified[1] by the local authority in relation to the authority's area, or

(*b*) if no amount is so specified, is £100.

(2A) In the case of an offence under section 4A the amount of the fixed penalty is £500.

(3) The local authority may make provision for treating the fixed penalty payable in the case of an offence under section 4 as having been paid if a lesser amount is paid before the end of a period specified by the authority.

(4) The appropriate person may by regulations[2] make provision in connection with the powers conferred on local authorities under subsections (2)(*a*) and (3).

(5) Regulations under subsection (4) may (in particular)—

(*a*) require an amount specified under subsection (2)(*a*) to fall within a range prescribed in the regulations;

(*b*) restrict the extent to which, and the circumstances in which, a local authority can make provision under subsection (3).

(6) The appropriate person may by order substitute a different amount for the amount for the time being specified in subsection (2)(*b*) or (2A).

[Noise Act 1996, s 8A as inserted by the Clean Neighbourhoods and Environment Act 2005, s 82 and amended by the Clean Neighbourhoods and Environment Act 2005, Sch 1.]

---

1. For permissible range of penalties, see the Environmental Offences (Fixed Penalties) (Miscellaneous Provisions) Regulations 2007, SI 2008/175 and the Environmental Offences (Fixed Penalties) (Miscellaneous Provisions) (Wales) Regulations 2008, SI 2008/663. For amending instruments, see the note to the Refuse Disposal (Amenity) Act 1978, s 2A, ante.

2. The Environmental Offences (Fixed Penalties) (Miscellaneous Provisions) Regulations 2007, SI 2007/175, the Environmental Offences (Use of Fixed Penalty Receipts) (Wales) Regulations 2007, SI 2007/739 amended by SI 2008/663; the Environmental Offences (Use of Fixed Penalty Receipts) Regulations 2007, SI 2007/901 and the Environmental Offences (Fixed Penalties) (Miscellaneous Provisions) (Wales) Regulations 2008, SI 2008/663 have been made. For amending instruments, see the note to the Refuse Disposal (Amenity) Act 1978, s 2A, ante.

7.10230 **8B. Fixed penalty notices: power to require name and address** (1) If an officer of a local authority who is authorised for the purposes of section 8 proposes to give a person a fixed penalty notice, the officer may require the person to give him his name and address.

(2) A person commits an offence if—

(*a*) he fails to give his name and address when required to do so under subsection (1), or

(*b*) he gives a false or inaccurate name or address in response to a requirement under that subsection.

(3) A person guilty of an offence under subsection (2) is liable on summary conviction to a fine not exceeding level 3 on the standard scale.

[Noise Act 1996, s 8B as inserted by the Clean Neighbourhoods and Environment Act 2005, s 82.]

7.10231 **9. Section 8: supplementary** (1) If a form for a fixed penalty notice is specified in an order made by the appropriate person, a fixed penalty notice must be in that form.

(2) If a fixed penalty notice is given to a person in respect of noise emitted from a dwelling in any period specified in a warning notice—

(*a*) no further fixed penalty notice may be given to that person in respect of noise emitted from the dwelling during that period, but

(*b*) that person may be convicted of a further offence under section 4 in respect of noise emitted from the dwelling after the fixed penalty notice is given and before the end of that period.

(2A) If a fixed penalty notice is given to a person in respect of noise emitted from other premises in any period in a warning notice—

(*a*) no further fixed penalty notice may be given to that person in respect of noise emitted from the premises during that period, but (*b*) that person may be convicted of a further offence under section 4A in respect of noise emitted from the premises after the fixed penalty notice is given and before the end of that period.

(3) *Repealed.*

(4) A local authority may use any sums it receives under section 8 (its "penalty receipts") only for the purposes of functions of its that are qualifying functions.

(4A) The following are qualifying functions for the purposes of this section—

(*a*) functions under this Act,

(*aa*) functions under Chapter 1 of Part 7 of the Clean Neighbourhoods and Environment Act 2005;

(*ab*) functions under sections 79 to 82 of the Environmental Protection Act 1990 (statutory nuisances) in connection with statutory nuisances falling with section 79(1)(*g*) or (*ga*) (noise) of that Act;

(*b*) functions of a description specified in regulations made by the appropriate person.

(4B) Regulations[1] under subsection (4A)(*b*) may (in particular) have the effect that a local authority may use its penalty receipts for the purposes of any of its functions.

(4C) A local authority must supply the appropriate person with such information relating to the use of its penalty receipts as the appropriate person may require.

(4D) The appropriate person may by regulations—

(*a*) make provision for what a local authority is to do with its penalty receipts—

(i) pending their being used for the purposes of qualifying functions of the authority;

(ii) if they are not so used before such time after their receipt as may be specified by the regulations;

(*b*) make provision for accounting arrangements in respect of a local authority's penalty receipts.

(4E) The provision that may be made under subsection (4D)(*a*)(ii) includes (in particular) provision for the payment of sums to a person (including the appropriate person) other than the local authority.

(4F) Before making regulations under this section, the appropriate person must consult—

(*a*) the local authorities to which the regulations are to apply, and

(*b*) such other persons as the appropriate person considers appropriate.

(4G) The powers to make regulations conferred by this section are, for the purposes of subsection (1) of section 100 of the Local Government Act 2003, to be regarded as included among the powers mentioned in subsection (2) of that section.

(4H) Regulations under this section relating to local authorities in England may—

(*a*) make provision in relation to—

(i) all local authorities,

(ii) particular local authorities, or

(iii) particular descriptions of local authority;

(*b*) make different provision in relation to different local authorities or descriptions of local authority.

(5) In proceedings for an offence under section 4 or 4A, evidence that payment of a fixed penalty was or was not made before the end of any period may be given by the production of a certificate which—

(*a*) purports to be signed by or on behalf of the person having responsibility for the financial affairs of the local authority, and

(*b*) states that payment of a fixed penalty was made on any date or, as the case may be, was not received before the end of that period.

[Noise Act 1996, s 9 as amended by the Anti-social Behaviour Act 2003, s 42 and the Clean Neighbourhoods and Environment Act 2005, s 83 and Sch 1.]

---

1 For permissible range of penalties, see the Environmental Offences (Fixed Penalties) (Miscellaneous Provisions) Regulations 2007, SI 2008/175 and the Environmental Offences (Fixed Penalties) (Miscellaneous Provisions) (Wales) Regulations 2008, SI 2008/663.

*Seizure, etc of equipment used to make noise unlawfully*

7.10232 **10. Powers of entry and seizure etc** (1) The power conferred by subsection (2) may be exercised where an officer of a local authority has reason to believe that—

(*a*) a warning notice has been served in respect of noise emitted from a dwelling or other premises, and

(*b*) at any time in the period specified in the notice, noise emitted from the dwelling or other premises has exceeded the permitted level, as measured from within the complainant's dwelling.

(2) An officer of the local authority, or a person authorised by the authority for the purpose, may enter the dwelling or other premises from which the noise in question is being or has been emitted and may seize and remove any equipment which it appears to him is being or has been used in the emission of the noise.

(3) A person exercising the power conferred by subsection (2) must produce his authority, if he

is required to do so.

(4) If it is shown to a justice of the peace on sworn information in writing that—

(*a*) a warning notice has been served in respect of noise emitted from a dwelling or other premises,

(*b*) at any time in the period specified in the notice, noise emitted from the dwelling or other premises has exceeded the permitted level, as measured from within the complainant's dwelling, and

(*c*) entry of an officer of the local authority, or of a person authorised by the authority for the purpose, to the dwelling or other premises has been refused, or such a refusal is apprehended, or a request by an officer of the authority, or of such a person, for admission would defeat the object of the entry,

the justice may by warrant under his hand authorise the local authority, by any of their officers or any person authorised by them for the purpose, to enter the dwelling or other premises, if need be by force.

(5) A person who enters any dwelling or other premises under subsection (2), or by virtue of a warrant issued under subsection (4), may take with him such other persons and such equipment as may be necessary; and if, when he leaves, the dwelling is, or the other premises are, unoccupied, must leave it or them as effectively secured against trespassers as he found it or them.

(6) A warrant issued under subsection (4) continues in force until the purpose for which the entry is required has been satisfied.

(7) The power of a local authority under section 81(3) of the Environmental Protection Act 1990[1] to abate any matter, where that matter is a statutory nuisance by virtue of section 79(1)(*g*) of that Act (noise emitted from premises so as to be prejudicial to health or a nuisance), includes power to seize and remove any equipment which it appears to the authority is being or has been used in the emission of the noise in question.

(8) A person who wilfully obstructs any person exercising any powers conferred under subsection (2) or by virtue of subsection (7) is liable, on summary conviction, to a fine not exceeding **level 3** on the standard scale.

(9) The Schedule to this Act (which makes further provision in relation to anything seized and removed by virtue of this section) has effect.

[Noise Act 1996, s 10 as amended by the Clean Neighbourhoods and Environment Act 2005, Sch 1.]

---

1 In this title, ante.

*General*

7.10233 **11. Interpretation and subordinate legislation** (1) In this Act, "local authority" means—

(*a*) in Greater London, a London borough council, the Common Council of the City of London and, as respects the Temples, the Sub-Treasurer of the Inner Temple and the Under-Treasurer of the Middle Temple respectively,

(*b*) outside Greater London—

(i) any district council,

(ii) the council of any county so far as they are the council for any area for which there are no district councils,

(iii) in Wales, the council of a county borough, and

(*c*) the Council of the Isles of Scilly.

(2) In this Act—

(*a*) "dwelling" means any building, or part of a building, used or intended to be used as a dwelling,

(*b*) references to noise emitted from a dwelling include noise emitted from any garden, yard, outhouse or other appurtenance belonging to or enjoyed with the dwelling.

(2A) In this Act "appropriate person" means—

(*a*) the Secretary of State, in relation to England;

(*b*) the National Assembly for Wales, in relation to Wales.

(3) The power to make an order or regulations under this Act is exercisable by statutory instrument which (except in the case of an order under section 14 or an order or regulations made solely by the National Assembly for Wales) shall be subject to annulment in pursuance of a resolution of either House of Parliament.

[Noise Act 1996, s 11 as amended by the Anti-social Behaviour Act 2003, s 42 and the Clean Neighbourhoods and Environment Act 2005, s 85.]

7.10234 **12.** *Protection from personal liability.*

7.10235 **13.** *Expenses.*

7.10236 **14. Short title, commencement and extent** (1) This Act may be cited as the Noise Act 1996.

(2) This Act is to come into force on such day as the Secretary of State may by order appoint, and different days may be appointed for different purposes[1].

(3) This Act does not extend to Scotland.

(4) *Northern Ireland.*

[1] This Act was brought into force by the following commencement orders: Commencement (No 1) Order 1996, SI 1996/2219 and Commencement (No 2) Order 1997, SI 1997/1695.

## SCHEDULE

### Powers in Relation to Seized Equipment

*(Amended by the Clean Neighbourhoods and Environment Act 2005, Sch 1.)*

*Introductory*

7.10237 1. In this Schedule—

(*a*) a "noise offence" means—

(i) in relation to equipment seized under section 10(2) of this Act, an offence under section 4 or 4A of this Act, and

(ii) in relation to equipment seized under section 81(3) of the Environmental Protection Act 1990 (as extended by section 10(7) of this Act), an offence under section 80(4) of that Act in respect of a statutory nuisance falling within section 79(1)(*g*) of that Act,

(*b*) "seized equipment" means equipment seized in the exercise of the power of seizure and removal conferred by section 10(2) of this Act or section 81(3) of the Environmental Protection Act 1990 (as so extended),

(*c*) "related equipment", in relation to any conviction of or proceedings for a noise offence, means seized equipment used or alleged to have been used in the commission of the offence,

(*d*) "responsible local authority", in relation to seized equipment, means the local authority by or on whose behalf the equipment was seized.

*Retention*

2. (1) Any seized equipment may be retained—

(*a*) during the period of twenty-eight days beginning with the seizure, or

(*b*) if it is related equipment in proceedings for a noise offence instituted within that period against any person, until—

(i) he is sentenced or otherwise dealt with for the offence or acquitted of the offence, or

(ii) the proceedings are discontinued.

(2) Sub-paragraph (1) does not authorise the retention of seized equipment if—

(*a*) a person has been given a fixed penalty notice under section 8 of this Act in respect of any noise,

(*b*) the equipment was seized because of its use in the emission of the noise in respect of which the fixed penalty notice was given, and

(*c*) that person has paid the fixed penalty before the end of the period allowed for its payment.

*Forfeiture*

3. (1) Where a person is convicted of a noise offence the court may make an order ("a forfeiture order") for forfeiture of any related equipment.

(2) The court may make a forfeiture order whether or not it also deals with the offender in respect of the offence in any other way and without regard to any restrictions on forfeiture in any enactment.

(3) In considering whether to make a forfeiture order in respect of any equipment a court must have regard—

(*a*) to the value of the equipment, and

(*b*) to the likely financial and other effects on the offender of the making of the order (taken together with any other order that the court contemplates making).

(4) A forfeiture order operates to deprive the offender of any rights in the equipment to which it relates.

*Consequences of forfeiture*

4. (1) Where any equipment has been forfeited under paragraph 3, a magistrates' court may, on application by a claimant of the equipment (other than the person in whose case the forfeiture order was made) make an order for delivery of the equipment to the applicant if it appears to the court that he is the owner of the equipment.

(2) No application may be made under sub-paragraph (1) by any claimant of the equipment after the expiry of the period of six months beginning with the date on which a forfeiture order was made in respect of the equipment.

(3) Such an application cannot succeed unless the claimant satisfies the court—

(*a*) that he had not consented to the offender having possession of the equipment, or

(*b*) that he did not know, and had no reason to suspect, that the equipment was likely to be used in the commission of a noise offence.

(4) Where the responsible local authority is of the opinion that the person in whose case the forfeiture order was made is not the owner of the equipment, it must take reasonable steps to bring to the attention of persons who may be entitled to do so their right to make an application under sub-paragraph (1).

(5) An order under sub-paragraph (1) does not affect the right of any person to take, within the period of six months beginning with the date of the order, proceedings for the recovery of the equipment from the person in possession of it in pursuance of the order, but the right ceases on the expiry of that period.

(6) If on the expiry of the period of six months beginning with the date on which a forfeiture order was made in respect of the equipment no order has been made under sub-paragraph (1), the responsible local authority may dispose of the equipment.

*Return etc of seized equipment*

5. If in proceedings for a noise offence no order for forfeiture of related equipment is made, the court (whether or not a person is convicted of the offence) may give such directions as to the return, retention or disposal of the equipment by the responsible local authority as it thinks fit.

6. (1) Where in the case of any seized equipment no proceedings in which it is related equipment are begun within the period mentioned in paragraph 2(1)(*a*)—

(*a*) the responsible local authority must return the equipment to any person who—

(i) appears to them to be the owner of the equipment, and
(ii) makes a claim for the return of the equipment within the period mentioned in sub-paragraph (2), and

(*b*) if no such person makes such a claim within that period, the responsible local authority may dispose of the equipment.

(2) The period referred to in sub-paragraph (1)(*a*)(ii) is the period of six months beginning with the expiry of the period mentioned in paragraph 2(1)(*a*).

(3) The responsible local authority must take reasonable steps to bring to the attention of persons who may be entitled to do so their right to make such a claim.

(4) Subject to sub-paragraph (6), the responsible local authority is not required to return any seized equipment under sub-paragraph (1)(*a*) until the person making the claim has paid any such reasonable charges for the seizure, removal and retention of the equipment as the authority may demand.

(5) If—

(*a*) equipment is sold in pursuance of—
(i) paragraph 4(6),
(ii) directions under paragraph 5, or
(iii) this paragraph, and

(*b*) before the expiration of the period of one year beginning with the date on which the equipment is sold any person satisfies the responsible local authority that at the time of its sale he was the owner of the equipment,

the authority is to pay him any sum by which any proceeds of sale exceed any such reasonable charges for the seizure, removal or retention of the equipment as the authority may demand.

(6) The responsible local authority cannot demand charges from any person under sub-paragraph (4) or (5) who they are satisfied did not know, and had no reason to suspect, that the equipment was likely to be used in the emission of noise exceeding the level determined under section 5.

## Party Wall etc Act 1996[1]

(1996 c 40)

*Rights etc*

7.10242 8. **Rights of entry** (1) A building owner[2], his servants, agents and workmen may during usual working hours enter and remain on any land or premises for the purpose of executing any work in pursuance of this Act and may remove any furniture or fittings or take any other action necessary for that purpose.

(2) If the premises are closed, the building owner, his agents and workmen may, if accompanied by a constable or other police officer, break open any fences or doors in order to enter the premises.

(3) No land or premises may be entered by any person under subsection (1) unless the building owner serves on the owner and the occupier of the land or premises—

(*a*) in case of emergency, such notice[3] of the intention to enter as may be reasonably practicable;

(*b*) in any other case, such notice[3] of the intention to enter as complies with subsection (4).

(4) Notice complies with this subsection if it is served in a period of not less than fourteen days ending with the day of the proposed entry.

(5) A surveyor appointed or selected under section 10[4] may during usual working hours enter and remain on any land or premises for the purpose of carrying out the object for which he is appointed or selected.

(6) No land or premises may be entered by a surveyor under subsection (5) unless the building owner who is a party to the dispute concerned serves on the owner and the occupier of the land or premises—

(*a*) in case of emergency, such notice of the intention to enter as may be reasonably practicable;

(*b*) in any other case, such notice of the intention to enter as complies with subsection (4).

[Party Wall etc Act 1996, s 8.]

1 This Act makes provision for the construction and repair of walls on the line of the junction of lands of different owners (ss 1–2). Before construction or repair, notices must be served and provision is made for adjacent excavation and construction and compensation (ss 3–7).

2 "Building owner" means an owner of land who is desirous of exercising rights under this Act (s 20).
"Owner" includes—
(a) a person in receipt of, or entitled to receive, the whole or part of the rents or profits of land;
(b) a person in possession of land, otherwise than as a mortgagee or as a tenant from year to year or for a lesser term or as a tenant at will;
(c) a purchaser of an interest in land under a contract for purchase or under an agreement for a lease, otherwise than under an agreement for a tenancy from year to year or for a lesser term (s 20).

3 As to service of notice see s 15, post.

4 Section 10 relates to the appointment of surveyors to resolve disputes under the Act.

*Miscellaneous*

7.10243 15. **Service of notices etc** (1) A notice or other document required or authorised to be served under this Act may be served on a person—

(*a*) by delivering it to him in person;

(*b*) by sending it by post[1] to him at his usual or last-known residence or place of business in the United Kingdom; or

(*c*) in the case of a body corporate, by delivering it to the secretary or clerk of the body corporate at its registered or principal office or sending it by post to the secretary or clerk of that body corporate at that office.

(1A) A notice or other document required or authorised to be served under this Act may also be served on a person ("the recipient") by means of an electronic communication, but only if—

(a) the recipient has stated a willingness to receive the notice or document by means of an electronic communication,

(b) the statement has not been withdrawn, and

(c) the notice or document was transmitted to an electronic address specified by the recipient.

(1B) A statement under subsection (1A) may be withdrawn by giving a notice to the person to whom the statement was made.

(1C) For the purposes of subsection (1A)—

"electronic address" includes any number or address used for the purposes of receiving electronic communications;

"electronic communication" means an electronic communication within the meaning of the Electronic Communications Act 2000; and

"specified" means specified in a statement made for the purposes of subsection (1A).

(2) In the case of a notice or other document required or authorised to be served under this Act on a person as owner of premises, it may alternatively be served by—

(*a*) addressing it "the owner" of the premises (naming them), and

(*b*) delivering it to a person on the premises or, if no person to whom it can be delivered is found there, fixing it to a conspicuous part of the premises.

[Party Wall etc Act 1996, s 15 as amended by SI 2016/335.]

---

1 Section 7 of the Interpretation Act 1978 applies, see *Freetown Ltd v Assethold Ltd* [2012] EWCA Civ 1657, [2013] 2 All ER 323.

**7.10244 16. Offences** (1) If—

(*a*) an occupier of land or premises refuses to permit a person to do anything which he is entitled to do with regard to the land or premises under section 8(1) or (5); and

(*b*) the occupier knows or has reasonable cause to believe that the person is so entitled,

the occupier is guilty of an offence.

(2) If—

(*a*) a person hinders or obstructs a person in attempting to do anything which he is entitled to do with regard to land or premises under section 8(1) or (5); and

(*b*) the first-mentioned person knows or has reasonable cause to believe that the other person is so entitled,

the first-mentioned person is guilty of an offence.

(3) A person guilty of an offence under subsection (1) or (2) is liable on summary conviction to a fine of an amount not exceeding **level 3** on the standard scale.

[Party Wall etc Act 1996, s 16.]

**7.10245 17. Recovery of sums** Any sum payable in pursuance of this Act (otherwise than by way of fine) shall be recoverable summarily as a civil debt.

[Party Wall etc Act 1996, s 17.]

**7.10246 18. Exception in case of Temples etc** (1) This Act shall not apply to land which is situated in inner London and in which there is an interest belonging to—

(*a*) the Honourable Society of the Inner Temple,

(*b*) the Honourable Society of the Middle Temple,

(*c*) the Honourable Society of Lincoln's Inn, or

(*d*) the Honourable Society of Gray's Inn.

(2) The reference in subsection (1) to inner London is to Greater London other than the outer London boroughs.

[Party Wall etc Act 1996, s 18.]

**7.10247 19. The Crown** (1) This Act shall apply to land in which there is—

(*a*) an interest belonging to Her Majesty in right of the Crown,

(*b*) an interest belonging to a government department, or

(*c*) an interest held in trust for Her Majesty for the purposes of any such department.

(2) This Act shall apply to—

(*a*) land which is vested in, but not occupied by, Her Majesty in right of the Duchy of Lancaster;

(*b*) land which is vested in, but not occupied by, the possessor for the time being of the Duchy of Cornwall.

[Party Wall etc Act 1996, s 19.]

**7.10248 20.** *Interpretation.*

**7.10249 21.** *Other statutory provisions.*

*General*

**7.10250 22. Short title, commencement and extent** (1) This Act may be cited as the Party

Wall etc Act 1996.

(2) This Act shall come into force in accordance with provision made by the Secretary of State by order[1] made by statutory instrument.

(3) An order under subsection (2) may—

(*a*) contain such savings or transitional provisions as the Secretary of State thinks fit;

(*b*) make different provision for different purposes.

(4) This Act extends to England and Wales only.

[Party Wall etc Act 1996, s 22.]

---

1 The Party Wall etc Act 1996 (Commencement) Order 1997, SI 1997/670 has been made.

## Pollution Prevention and Control Act 1999[1]

(1999 c 24)

7.10251 **1. General purpose of section 2 and definitions** (1) The purpose of section 2 is to enable provision to be made for or in connection with—

(*a*) implementing Council Directive 96/61/EC concerning integrated pollution prevention and control;

(*b*) regulating, otherwise than in pursuance of that Directive, activities which are capable of causing any environmental pollution;

(*c*) otherwise preventing or controlling emissions capable of causing any such pollution.

(2) In this Act—

"activities" means activities of any nature, whether—

(*a*) industrial or commercial or other activities, or

(*b*) carried on on particular premises or otherwise,

and includes (with or without other activities) the depositing, keeping or disposal of any substance;

"environmental pollution" means pollution of the air, water or land which may give rise to any harm; and for the purposes of this definition (but without prejudice to its generality)—

(*a*) "pollution" includes pollution caused by noise, heat or vibrations or any other kind of release of energy, and

(*b*) "air" includes air within buildings and air within other natural or man-made structures above or below ground.

(3) In the definition of "environmental pollution" in subsection (2), "harm" means—

(*a*) harm to the health of human beings or other living organisms;

(*b*) harm to the quality of the environment, including—

(i) harm to the quality of the environment taken as a whole,

(ii) harm to the quality of the air, water or land, and

(iii) other impairment of, or interference with, the ecological systems of which any living organisms form part;

(*c*) offence to the senses of human beings;

(*d*) damage to property; or

(*e*) impairment of, or interference with, amenities or other legitimate uses of the environment (expressions used in this paragraph having the same meaning as in Council Directive 96/61/EC).

[Pollution Prevention and Control Act 1999, s 1.]

---

1 The former system of waste management licensing in Part II of the Environmental Protection Act 1990 and the Waste Management Licensing Regulations 1994 SI 1994/1056, and the system of permitting in the Pollution Prevention and Control (England and Wales) Regulations 2000, SI 2000/1973 was replaced by a new system of environmental permitting in England and Wales in the Environmental Permitting (England and Wales) Regulations 2007, SI 2007/3538 partly revoked by SI 2010/675 superseded by the Environmental Permitting (England and Wales) Regulations 2010, SI 2010/675 in turn now superseded by the 2016 Regulations, SI 2016/1154 in this title, post. At the date of going to press the following commencement order had been made: Commencement No 1, SI 2000/800 bringing into effect s 6(1) and Sch 2.

7.10252 **2. Regulation of polluting activities**[1]

---

1 See the Environmental Permitting (England and Wales) Regulations 2016, SI 2016/1154, in this title, post. The following Pollution Prevention and Control Regulations have been made:

Offshore Chemicals Regulations 2002, SI 2002/1355 amended by SI 2010/1513, SI 2011/982 and SI 2016/912;

Landfill (England and Wales) Regulations 2002, SI 2002/1559 amended by SI 2004/1375, SI 2005/894, 895, 1640, 1806 (W) and 1820 (W), SI 2006/937 and SI 2007/2596;

Foot-and-Mouth Disease (Air Curtain Incinerators) (England and Wales) Regulations 2001, SI 2001/1623;

Offshore Installations (Emergency Pollution Control) Regulations 2002, SI 2002/1861 amended by SI 2010/1513 and SI 2015/664;

Large Combustion Plants (England and Wales) Regulations 2002, SI 2002/2688;

Offshore Petroleum Activities (Oil Pollution Prevention and Control) Regulations 2005, SI 2005/2055 amended by SI 2010/1513, SI 2011/982, SI 2013/971 and SI 2016/912;

Large Combustion Plants (National Emission Reduction Plan) Regulations 2007, SI 2007/2325 amended by SI 2010/675;

Greenhouse Gas Emissions Trading Scheme (Nitrous Oxide) Regulations 2011, SI 2011/1506;

Greenhouse Gas Emissions Trading Scheme Regulations 2012, SI 2012/3038 amended by SI 2013/1037, 3135 and SI 2015/1388 (W) and 1849 and SI 2016/1154;

Offshore Combustion Installations (Pollution Prevention and Control) Regulations 2013, SI 2013/971 amended by SI 2016/912.
Environmental Permitting (England and Wales) Regulations 2016, SI 2016/1154, in this title, post.

**7.10253 3. Prevention etc of pollution after accidents involving offshore installations**

**7.10254 5. Application to Wales and Scotland**

**7.10255 6. Consequential and minor amendments and repeals**

**7.10256 7. Short title, interpretation, commencement and extent**

SCHEDULE 1
PARTICULAR PURPOSES FOR WHICH PROVISION MAY BE MADE UNDER SECTION 2

# Waste and Emissions Trading Act 2003[1]

(2003 c 33)

## PART 1
## WASTE

### CHAPTER 1
### WASTE SENT TO LANDFILLS

7.10257 Part 1 provides for the Secretary of State by regulations to specify the maximum amounts of biodegradable material waste in the United Kingdom allowed to be sent to landfills in specified "target" years (s 1) and "non target" years (ss 2–4). The Secretary of State (or in Wales, the National Assembly) is the "Allocating Authority" which allocates landfill allowances (ss 4–5) and may make provision by regulations for the "banking" or "borrowing" of allowances from year to year (s 6) and for trading of allowances with other authorities (s 7). Supplementary provision for the creating of offences in regulations is made by s 8. Waste disposal authorities which exceed their allowances are subject to a civil penalty to the allocating authority (s 9).

An allocating authority must appoint a person to monitor the operation of the landfill allowances scheme and audit the performance of the waste disposal authorities. Regulations may make further provision for the purposes of landfill allowances (s 11) and record-keeping by waste disposal authorities (s 12).

---

[1] This Act is to be brought into force in accordance with orders made under s 40. At the date of going to press the following orders had been made: (No 1) SI 2004/1163; (No 2) SI 2004/1874; (No 1) (England) SI 2004/3181; (No 3) SI 2004/3192; (No 1) (England and Wales) SI 2004/3319; (No 1) (Great Britain) SI 2004/3320; (No 2) (England) SI 2004/3321).

7.10258 **13. Powers in relation to landfill operators** (1) An allocating authority may, for purposes connected with the sending of biodegradable municipal waste to landfills, by regulations[1] make provision for requiring a person concerned in the operation of a landfill to—

(*a*) maintain prescribed records;

(*b*) gather prescribed information by carrying out prescribed operations on prescribed waste;

(*c*) make prescribed returns, or provide prescribed information or prescribed evidence, to prescribed persons.

(2) A person commits an offence if he fails to comply with a requirement imposed on him under subsection (1).

(3) An allocating authority may by regulations[1] make provision enabling the monitoring authority for its area, or persons authorised by the monitoring authority—

(*a*) to require persons concerned in the operation of a landfill to produce records related to the operation of the landfill for inspection or for removal for inspection elsewhere;

(*b*) to specify the form in which, the place at which and the time at or by which records are to be produced;

(*c*) to copy records that are produced;

(*d*) to enter premises (with or without a constable, with any necessary equipment or material and, if need be, by force) for the purposes of—

(i) finding records relating to the operation of a landfill,

(ii) inspecting them or removing them for inspection elsewhere, and

(iii) copying them;

(*e*) to require persons to afford, to a person exercising any power conferred under paragraphs (*a*) to (*d*), such facilities and assistance within their control or in relation to which they have responsibilities as are necessary to enable the person to exercise the power.

(4) A person commits an offence if—

(*a*) he intentionally obstructs a person exercising a power conferred under subsection (3), or

(*b*) he fails to comply with a requirement imposed on him under that subsection.

(5) A person guilty of an offence under subsection (2) or (4)(*a*) is liable—

(*a*) on summary conviction, to a fine not exceeding the statutory maximum;
(*b*) on conviction on indictment, to imprisonment for a term not exceeding 2 years or to a fine, or to both.

(6) A person guilty of an offence under subsection (4)(*b*) is liable on summary conviction to a fine not exceeding level 5 on the standard scale.

(7) In subsection (1) "prescribed" means prescribed by or under regulations under that subsection.

[Waste and Emissions Trading Act 2003, s 13.]

---

1 The Landfill Allowances Scheme (Wales) Regulations 2004, SI 2004/1490 amended by SI 2005/1820, SI 2011/971 and 3042, SI 2012/65 and SI 2016/691.

7.10259 **14–15.** *Disclosure of information by monitoring and allocating authorities and registers.*

*Scheme operation and monitoring etc*

7.10260 **16. Registers: public access** An allocating authority may, in relation to a register that a person is required to maintain by regulations under this Chapter made by the authority, by regulations[1]—

(*a*) make provision for public inspection of such of the information contained in the register as is of a description specified by the regulations;
(*b*) make provision for members of the public to obtain copies of information in the register that is open to public inspection under paragraph (*a*), including provision for the payment of reasonable charges.

[Waste and Emissions Trading Act 2003, s 16.]

---

1 The Landfill Allowances Scheme (Wales) Regulations 2004, SI 2004/1490 amended by SI 2005/1820, SI 2011/971 and 3042, SI 2012/65 and SI 2016/691 have been made.

7.10261 **17–20.** *Strategies for reducing landfilling of biodegradable waste.*

*Interpretation of Chapter 1*

7.10262 **21. "Biodegradable waste", "municipal waste" and "local authority collected municipal waste"** (1) In this Chapter "biodegradable waste" means any waste that is capable of undergoing anaerobic or aerobic decomposition, such as—

food and garden waste, and
paper and paperboard.

(2) In this Chapter—

(*a*) "biodegradable municipal waste" means waste that is both biodegradable waste and municipal waste; and
(*b*) "biodegradable local authority collected municipal waste" means waste that is both biodegradable waste and local authority collected municipal waste.

(3) In this section "municipal waste" means—

(*a*) waste from households, and
(*b*) other waste that, because of its nature or composition, is similar to waste from households.

(4) In subsection (2) "local authority collected municipal waste" means any municipal waste which is collected under arrangements made by a waste collection authority or a waste disposal authority.

(5) In subsection (4) "waste collection authority"—

(*a*) in relation to England and Wales and Scotland, has the same meaning as in Part 2 of the Environmental Protection Act 1990;
(*b*) in relation to Northern Ireland, means a district council.

[Waste and Emissions Trading Act 2003, s 21 as amended by SI 2011/2499.]

7.10263 **22. "Landfill"** (1) In this Chapter "landfill" means a site for the deposit of waste onto or into land where the site is—

(*a*) a waste disposal site, or
(*b*) used for the storage of waste.

(2) In determining whether a site is a landfill for the purposes of this Chapter, the following activities at the site are to be ignored—

(*a*) the temporary storage of waste if the site is used for such storage for less than one year;
(*b*) the unloading of waste in order to permit the waste to be prepared for further transport for recovery, treatment or disposal elsewhere;
(*c*) the storage of waste, prior to recovery or treatment, for a period of less than three years as a general rule;
(*d*) the storage of waste, prior to disposal, for a period of less than one year.

(3) The fact that a site for the deposit of waste is at the place of production of the waste does not prevent the site from being a landfill for the purposes of this Chapter.

(4) In subsection (2) "treatment" means the physical, thermal, chemical or biological processes, including sorting, that change the characteristics of waste in order to—

(*a*) reduce its volume,

(*b*) reduce its hazardous nature,
(*c*) facilitate its handling, or
(*d*) enhance its recoverability.

[Waste and Emissions Trading Act 2003, s 22.]

**7.10264 23. "Scheme year" and "target year"**[1]

[1] See the Landfill (Scheme Year and Maximum Landfill Amount) Regulations 2004, SI 2004/1936 partly revoked by SI 2011/2299 and the Landfill (Maximum Landfill Amount) Regulations 2011, SI 2011/2299.

**7.10265 24. Other definitions** (1) For the purposes of this Chapter, the "allocating authority"—

(*a*) *repealed*
(*b*) *Scotland,*
(*c*) for Wales is the National Assembly for Wales, and
(*d*) for Northern Ireland is the Department of the Environment.

(2) In this Chapter, any reference to an allocating authority's "area" is to the area for which it is the allocating authority for the purposes of this Chapter.

(3) In this Chapter "landfill allowances" means allowances allocated under section 4(1).

(4) References in this Chapter to the monitoring authority for an area are to the monitoring authority designated for the area by regulations under section 10(1).

(5) In this Chapter "waste disposal authority"—

(*a*) in relation to England, Wales and Scotland has the same meaning as in Part 2 of the Environmental Protection Act 1990 (c 43);
(*b*) in relation to Northern Ireland means a district council.

(6) *Repealed.*

(7) *Repealed.*

[Waste and Emissions Trading Act 2003, s 24 as amended by the Local Government and Public Involvement in Health Act 2007, s 209, SI 2013/141 and the Deregulation Act 2015, Sch 13.]

*Supplementary*

**7.10266 25. Activities to which Chapter 1 does not apply** (1) References in this Chapter to sending biodegradable waste, biodegradable local authority collected municipal waste, or biodegradable municipal waste, to landfills do not include—

(*a*) the spreading of sludges (including sewage sludges and sludges resulting from dredging operations), or similar matter, on the soil for the purposes of fertilisation or improvement,
(*b*) the deposit of non-hazardous dredging sludges alongside small waterways from out of which they have been dredged,
(*c*) the deposit of non-hazardous sludges in surface water or in the bed or subsoil of surface water, or
(*d*) the deposit of unpolluted soil resulting from—
  (i) prospecting for, or the extraction, treatment or storage of, mineral resources, or
  (ii) the operation of quarries.

(2) For the purposes of this section, sludge is "non-hazardous" if it is not hazardous waste within the meaning of regulation 6 of the Hazardous Waste (England and Wales) Regulations 2005[1].

[Waste and Emissions Trading Act 2003, s 25 as amended by SI 2005/894, SI 2005/1806 and SI 2011/2499.]

[1] Reproduced as in force in England and Wales.

**7.10267 26–28.** *Penalties and regulations.*

PART 3
GENERAL

**7.10268 40. Commencement**

**7.10268A 41. Extent**

**7.10268B 42. Short title**

## Clean Neighbourhoods and Environment Act 2005[1]

(2005 c 16)

PART 1[2]
CRIME AND DISORDER

[1] This Act received the Royal Assent on 7 April 2005. It was enacted following a review of the legislative framework for providing and maintaining a clean and safe local environment. The Act tackles various kinds of nuisance and anti-social behaviour, primarily by adding provisions to existing legislation.

The Act contains 10 Parts and 5 Schedules:

Part 1 amends the law relating to crime and disorder reduction partnerships; it also makes provision for the gating of minor highways, and is not reproduced in this Manual.

Part 2 introduces two new offences relating to nuisance parking and amends the law relating to abandoned and illegally parked vehicles.

Part 3 extends the statutory offence of dropping litter and amends the powers and duties of local authorities in relation to litter.

Part 4 amends the law relating to graffiti, fly-posting and the illegal display of advertisements.

Part 5 makes miscellaneous provision about waste.

Part 6 allows local authorities and parish and community councils to create offences relating to the control of dogs; the new system replaces the Dogs (Fouling of Land) Act 1996.

Part 7 addresses various issues relating to nuisance by noise; it also allows local authorities to employ alternative means to resolve complaints prior to issuing an abatement notice.

Part 8 (not reproduced in this work) creates the Commission for Architecture and Built Environment.

Parts 9 and 10 contain miscellaneous and supplementary provisions.

The Act will be brought into force in accordance with commencement orders made under s 108.

At the date of going to press the following commencement orders had been made: Clean Neighbourhoods and Environment Act 2005 (Commencement No 1) Order 2005, SI 2005/1675; Clean Neighbourhoods and Environment Act 2005 (Commencement No 2, Transitional Provisions and Savings) (England and Wales) Order 2005, SI 2005/2896 (amended by SI 2006/1002); Clean Neighbourhoods and Environment Act 2005 (Commencement No 3) Order 2005, SI 2005/3439; Clean Neighbourhoods and Environment Act 2005 (Commencement No 4) Order 2006, SI 2006/656; Clean Neighbourhoods and Environment Act 2005 (Commencement No 1, Transitional and Savings Provisions) (England) Order 2006, SI 2006/795; Clean Neighbourhoods and Environment Act 2005 (Commencement No 1 and Savings) (Wales) Order 2006, SI 2006/768; Clean Neighbourhoods and Environment Act 2005 (Commencement No 2) (England) Order 2006, SI 2006/1361; Clean Neighbourhoods and Environment Act 2005 (Commencement No 3) (England) Order 2006, SI 2006/2006; Clean Neighbourhoods and Environment Act 2005 (Commencement No 2, Transitional Provisions and Savings) (Wales) Order 2006, SI 2006/2797; Statutory Nuisances (Miscellaneous Provisions) (Wales) Order 2007, SI 2007/120; Clean Neighbourhoods and Environment Act 2005 (Commencement No 4) (England) Order, SI 2007/390; Clean Neighbourhoods and Environment Act 2005 (Commencement No 3) (Wales) Order 2007, SI 2007/3371; Clean Neighbourhoods and Environment Act 2005 (Commencement No 5) Order 2008, SI 2008/95; and the Clean Neighbourhoods and Environment Act 2005 (Commencement No 6) Order 2015, SI 2015/425.

The provisions reproduced here are all in force, except s 37 which has not been brought fully into force.

2 Part 1 contains ss 1–2.

## PART 2[1]
## VEHICLES

### *Nuisance parking offences*

7.10269 3. **Exposing vehicles for sale on a road** (1) A person is guilty of an offence if at any time—

(*a*) he leaves two or more motor vehicles parked within 500 metres of each other on a road or roads where they are exposed or advertised for sale, or

(*b*) he causes two or more motor vehicles to be so left.

(2) A person is not to be convicted of an offence under subsection (1) if he proves to the satisfaction of the court that he was not acting for the purposes of a business of selling motor vehicles.

(3) A person guilty of an offence under subsection (1) is liable on summary conviction to a fine not exceeding level 4 on the standard scale.

(4) In this section—

"motor vehicle" has the same meaning as in the Refuse Disposal (Amenity) Act 1978 (c 3);

"road" has the same meaning as in the Road Traffic Regulation Act 1984 (c 27).

[Clean Neighbourhoods and Environment Act 2005, s 3.]

1 Part 2 contains ss 3–17.

7.10270 4. **Repairing vehicles on a road** (1) A person who carries out restricted works on a motor vehicle on a road is guilty of an offence, subject as follows.

(2) For the purposes of this section "restricted works" means—

(*a*) works for the repair, maintenance, servicing, improvement or dismantling of a motor vehicle or of any part of or accessory to a motor vehicle;

(*b*) works for the installation, replacement or renewal of any such part or accessory.

(3) A person is not to be convicted of an offence under this section in relation to any works if he proves to the satisfaction of the court that the works were not carried out—

(*a*) in the course of, or for the purposes of, a business of carrying out restricted works; or

(*b*) for gain or reward.

(4) Subsection (3) does not apply where the carrying out of the works gave reasonable cause for annoyance to persons in the vicinity.

(5) A person is also not to be convicted of an offence under this section in relation to any works if he proves to the satisfaction of the court that the works carried out were works of repair which—

(*a*) arose from an accident or breakdown in circumstances where repairs on the spot or elsewhere on the road were necessary; and

(*b*) were carried out within 72 hours of the accident or breakdown or were within that period authorised to be carried out at a later time by the local authority for the area.

(6) A person guilty of an offence under this section is liable on summary conviction to a fine not exceeding level 4 on the standard scale.

(7) In this section—

"motor vehicle" has the same meaning as in the Refuse Disposal (Amenity) Act 1978;

"road" has the same meaning as in the Road Traffic Regulation Act 1984;

"local authority" has the meaning given in section 9.

[Clean Neighbourhoods and Environment Act 2005, s 4.]

7.10271 **5. Liability of directors etc** (1) Where an offence under section 3 or 4 committed by a body corporate is proved to have been committed with the consent or connivance of, or to have been attributable to any neglect on the part of—

(*a*) any director, manager, secretary or other similar officer of the body corporate, or

(*b*) a person who was purporting to act in any such capacity,

he as well as the body corporate is guilty of the offence and liable to be proceeded against and punished accordingly.

(2) Where the affairs of a body corporate are managed by its members, subsection (1) applies in relation to the acts or defaults of a member in connection with his functions of management as if he were a director of the body.

[Clean Neighbourhoods and Environment Act 2005, s 5.]

*Nuisance parking offences: fixed penalty notices*

7.10272 **6. Power to give fixed penalty notices** (1) Where on any occasion an authorised officer of a local authority has reason to believe that a person has committed an offence under section 3 or 4 in the area of that authority, the officer may give that person a notice offering him the opportunity of discharging any liability to conviction for that offence by payment of a fixed penalty to the local authority.

(2) Where a person is given a notice under this section in respect of an offence—

(*a*) no proceedings may be instituted for that offence before the expiration of the period of fourteen days following the date of the notice; and

(*b*) he may not be convicted of that offence if he pays the fixed penalty before the expiration of that period.

(3) A notice under this section must give such particulars of the circumstances alleged to constitute the offence as are necessary for giving reasonable information of the offence.

(4) A notice under this section must also state—

(*a*) the period during which, by virtue of subsection (2), proceedings will not be taken for the offence;

(*b*) the amount of the fixed penalty; and

(*c*) the person to whom and the address at which the fixed penalty may be paid.

(5) Without prejudice to payment by any other method, payment of the fixed penalty may be made by pre-paying and posting a letter containing the amount of the penalty (in cash or otherwise) to the person mentioned in subsection (4)(*c*) at the address so mentioned.

(6) Where a letter is sent in accordance with subsection (5) payment is to be regarded as having been made at the time at which that letter would be delivered in the ordinary course of post.

(7) The form of a notice under this section is to be such as the appropriate person may by order prescribe.

(8) The fixed penalty payable to a local authority under this section is, subject to subsection (9), £100.

(9) The appropriate person may by order substitute a different amount for the amount for the time being specified in subsection (8).

(10) The local authority to which a fixed penalty is payable under this section may make provision for treating it as having been paid if a lesser amount is paid before the end of a period specified by the authority.

(11) The appropriate person may by regulations[1] restrict the extent to which, and the circumstances in which, a local authority may make provision under subsection (10).

(12) In any proceedings a certificate which—

(*a*) purports to be signed on behalf of the chief finance officer of the local authority, and

(*b*) states that payment of a fixed penalty was or was not received by a date specified in the certificate,

is evidence of the facts stated.

(13) In this section "chief finance officer", in relation to a local authority, means the person having responsibility for the financial affairs of the authority.

[Clean Neighbourhoods and Environment Act 2005, s 6.]

---

1 The Environmental Offences (Fixed Penalties) (Miscellaneous Provisions) Regulations 2007, SI 2007/175, the Environmental Offences (Use of Fixed Penalty Receipts) (Wales) Regulations 2007, SI 2007/739 amended by SI 2008/663; the Environmental Offences (Use of Fixed Penalty Receipts) Regulations 2007, SI 2007/901 and the Environmental Offences (Fixed Penalties) (Miscellaneous Provisions) (Wales) Regulations 2008, SI 2008/663 have been made. For amending instruments, see the note to the Refuse Disposal (Amenity) Act 1978, s 2A, ante.

7.10273 **7. Power to require name and address** (1) If an authorised officer of a local authority proposes to give a person a notice under section 6, the officer may require the person to give him his name and address.

(2) A person commits an offence if—

(*a*) he fails to give his name and address when required to do so under subsection (1), or

(*b*) he gives a false or inaccurate name or address in response to a requirement under that subsection.

(3) A person guilty of an offence under subsection (2) is liable on summary conviction to a fine not exceeding level 3 on the standard scale.

[Clean Neighbourhoods and Environment Act 2005, s 7.]

7.10274 **9. Fixed penalty notices: supplementary** (1) For the purposes of this section, "this group of sections" means sections 6 to 8 and this section.

(2) In this group of sections—

"local authority" means—

(*a*) a district council in England;

(*b*) a county council in England for an area for which there is no district council;

(*c*) a London borough council;

(*d*) the Common Council of the City of London;

(*e*) the Council of the Isles of Scilly;

(*f*) a county or county borough council in Wales;

"appropriate person" means—

(*a*) in relation to England, the Secretary of State;

(*b*) in relation to Wales, the National Assembly for Wales;

"authorised officer", in relation to a local authority, means an employee of the authority who is authorised in writing by the authority for the purposes of giving notices under section 6.

(3) Any order or regulations under this group of sections must be made by statutory instrument.

(4) Any such order or regulations may make different provision for different purposes (including different provision in relation to different authorities or different descriptions of authority).

(5) A statutory instrument containing an order or regulations made by the Secretary of State under this group of sections is subject to annulment in pursuance of a resolution of either House of Parliament.

[Clean Neighbourhoods and Environment Act 2005, s 9.]

## PART 5[3]
## WASTE

### CHAPTER 3[1]
### SITE WASTE

7.10275 **54. Site waste management plans** *Secretary of State may by regulations make provision requiring persons of a specified description to prepare plans for the management and disposal of waste created in the course of specified descriptions of works in England involving construction or demolition; and to comply with such plans.*

[1] Chapter 3 contains s 54.

## PART 6[1]
## DOGS

### CHAPTER 1[2]
### CONTROLS ON DOGS

*Supplementary*

7.10285 **65. Dogs (Fouling of Land) Act 1996** The Dogs (Fouling of Land) Act 1996 (c 20) shall cease to have effect.

[Clean Neighbourhoods and Environment Act 2005, s 65.]

[1] Part 1 contains ss 55–68.
[2] Chapter 1 contains ss 55–67.

### CHAPTER 2[1]
### STRAY DOGS

7.10288 **68. Termination of police responsibility for stray dogs** (1) Section 3 of the Dogs Act 1906 (c 32) (seizure of stray dogs by police) shall, subject to subsection (2), cease to have effect.

(2) The repeal in subsection (1) does not apply for the purposes of section 2(2) and (3) of the Dogs (Protection of Livestock) Act 1953 (c 28).

(3), (4) *Amend the Environmental Protection Act 1990, s 150.*

[Clean Neighbourhoods and Environment Act 2005, s 68.]

[1] Chapter 2 contains s 68.

## PART 7[1]
## NOISE

### CHAPTER 1[2]
### AUDIBLE INTRUDER ALARMS

*Alarm notification areas*

7.10289 **69. Designation of alarm notification areas** (1) A local authority may designate all or any part of its area as an alarm notification area.

(2) If a local authority proposes to designate an area as an alarm notification area it must arrange for notice of the proposal to be published in a newspaper circulating in the area.

(3) The notice must state—

(*a*) that representations may be made to the authority about the proposal;

(*b*) that any such representations must be made before a specified date.

(4) The specified date must be at least 28 days after the date on which the notice is published in accordance with subsection (2).

(5) The local authority must consider any representations about the proposal which it receives before the specified date.

(6) If a local authority decides to designate an area as an alarm notification area it must—

(*a*) arrange for notice of the decision to be published in a newspaper circulating in the area, and

(*b*) send a copy of the notice to the address of all premises in the area.

(7) The notice must specify the date on which the designation is to have effect.

(8) The date specified must be at least 28 days after the date on which the notice is published in accordance with subsection (6)(*a*).

(9) If a local authority decides not to designate an area as an alarm notification area it must arrange for notice of the decision to be published in a newspaper circulating in the area.

[Clean Neighbourhoods and Environment Act 2005, s 69.]

---

1 Part 7 contains ss 69–86.

2 Chapter 1 contains ss 69–81.

7.10290 70. **Withdrawal of designation** (1) A local authority which has designated an area as an alarm notification area may withdraw the designation.

(2) If a local authority decides to withdraw a designation of an area as an alarm notification area, it must—

(*a*) arrange for notice of the decision to be published in a newspaper circulating in the area, and

(*b*) send a copy of the notice to the address of all premises in the area.

(3) The notice must specify the date on which the withdrawal of the designation is to have effect.

[Clean Neighbourhoods and Environment Act 2005, s 70.]

7.10291 71. **Notification of nominated key-holders** (1) This section and section 72 apply in relation to premises if—

(*a*) the premises are in an area designated by a local authority as an alarm notification area, and

(*b*) an audible intruder alarm has been installed in or on the premises.

(2) The responsible person must—

(*a*) nominate a key-holder in respect of the premises in accordance with section 72;

(*b*) notify the local authority in writing before the end of the required period of the name, address and telephone number of the key-holder nominated in respect of the premises in accordance with that section.

(3) The required period for the purposes of subsection (2)(*b*) is the period before the end of which the key-holder is required to be nominated in accordance with section 72.

(4) A person commits an offence if he fails to comply with a requirement of subsection (2).

(5) A person guilty of an offence under subsection (4) is liable on summary conviction to a fine not exceeding level 3 on the standard scale.

[Clean Neighbourhoods and Environment Act 2005, s 71.]

7.10292 72. **Nomination of key-holders** (1) The responsible person must before the end of the required period nominate a person as a key-holder in respect of the premises.

(2) The required period for the purposes of subsection (1) is—

(*a*) if the alarm was installed before the date on which the designation of the area had effect, the period of 28 days starting with that date;

(*b*) if the alarm was installed on or after that date, the period of 28 days starting with the date on which the installation was completed.

(3) A person may be nominated as a key-holder in respect of premises under this section only if—

(*a*) he holds keys sufficient to enable him to gain access to the part of the premises in which the controls for the alarm are situated;

(*b*) he normally resides or is situated in the vicinity of the premises;

(*c*) he has information sufficient to enable him to silence the alarm;

(*d*) he agrees to be a nominated key-holder in respect of the premises;

(*e*) where the premises are residential premises, he falls within subsection (4);

(*f*) where the premises are non-residential premises, he falls within subsection (5).

(4) A person falls within this subsection if he is—

(*a*) an individual who is not the occupier of the premises, or (*b*) a key-holding company.

(5) A person falls within this subsection if he is—

(*a*) an individual who—

(i) is the responsible person, or

(ii) is acting on behalf of the responsible person, if the responsible person is not an individual, or

(*b*) a key-holding company.

(6) If the responsible person becomes aware that a person who has been nominated as a key-holder in respect of premises under this section no longer satisfies one or more of the requirements in subsection (3), the responsible person must before the end of the required period nominate another person as a key-holder in respect of the premises.

(7) The required period for the purposes of subsection (6) is the period of 28 days starting with the date on which the responsible person becomes aware of that fact.

(8) In this section—

"key-holding company" means a body corporate or an unincorporated association—

(*a*) the business of which consists of or includes holding keys, and

(*b*) which is capable of being contacted at any hour of the day;

"non-residential premises" means premises which are not residential premises;

"residential premises" means premises all or part of which comprise a dwelling.

[Clean Neighbourhoods and Environment Act 2005, s 72.]

7.10293 **73. Offences under section 71: fixed penalty notices** (1) This section applies if it appears to an authorised officer of a local authority that a person has committed an offence under section 71(4) in the area of the local authority.

(2) The officer may give the person a notice offering him the opportunity of discharging any liability to conviction for the offence by payment of a fixed penalty.

(3) If a person is given a notice under this section in respect of an offence—

(*a*) no proceedings may be instituted for the offence before the end of the period of 14 days starting with the day after that on which the notice is given, and

(*b*) he may not be convicted of the offence if he pays the fixed penalty before the end of that period.

(4) A notice under this section must give such particulars of the circumstances alleged to constitute the offence as are necessary for giving reasonable information of the offence.

(5) A notice under this section must also state—

(*a*) the period during which, by virtue of subsection (3), proceedings will not be taken for the offence,

(*b*) the amount of the fixed penalty, and

(*c*) the person to whom and the address at which the fixed penalty may be paid.

(6) Payment of the fixed penalty may be made by pre-paying and posting a letter containing the amount of the penalty (in cash or otherwise) to the person mentioned in subsection (5)(*c*) at the address so mentioned.

(7) If a letter is sent in accordance with subsection (6) payment is to be regarded as having been made at the time at which the letter would be delivered in the ordinary course of post.

(8) Subsection (6) does not prevent payment of the fixed penalty being made by another method.

(9) In any proceedings a certificate which—

(*a*) purports to be signed by or on behalf of the chief finance officer of a local authority, and

(*b*) states that payment of a fixed penalty was or was not received by a date specified in the certificate,

is evidence of the facts stated.

(10) The form of a notice under this section is to be such as the appropriate person may by order prescribe.

(11) In this section—

"authorised officer", in relation to a local authority, means—

(*a*) an employee of the authority who is authorised in writing by the authority for the purpose of giving notices under this section;

(*b*) any person who, in pursuance of arrangements made with the authority, has the function of giving such notices and is authorised in writing by the authority to perform that function;

(*c*) any employee of such a person who is authorised in writing by the authority for the purpose of giving such notices;

"chief finance officer", in relation to a local authority, is the person having responsibility for the financial affairs of the authority.

[Clean Neighbourhoods and Environment Act 2005, s 73.]

7.10294 **74. Amount of fixed penalty** (1) This section applies in relation to a penalty payable to a local authority in pursuance of a notice under section 73.

(2) The amount of the penalty is—

(*a*) the amount specified[1] by the local authority in relation to its area, or (*b*) if no amount is so specified, £75.

(3) The local authority may make provision for treating the penalty as having been paid if a lesser amount is paid before the end of a period specified by the authority.

(4) The appropriate person may by regulations[2] make provision in connection with the powers conferred on local authorities under subsections (2)(*a*) and (3).

(5) Regulations under subsection (4) may (in particular)—

(*a*) require an amount specified under subsection (2)(*a*) to fall within a range prescribed in the regulations;

(*b*) restrict the extent to which, and the circumstances in which, an authority can make provision under subsection (3).

(6) The appropriate person may by order substitute a different amount for the amount for the time being specified in subsection (2)(*b*).

[Clean Neighbourhoods and Environment Act 2005, s 74.]

---

1 For permissible range of penalties, see the Environmental Offences (Fixed Penalties) (Miscellaneous Provisions) Regulations 2007, SI 2008/175 and the Environmental Offences (Fixed Penalties) (Miscellaneous Provisions) (Wales) Regulations 2008, SI 2008/663. For amending instruments, see the note to the Refuse Disposal (Amenity) Act 1978, s 2A, ante.

2 The Environmental Offences (Fixed Penalties) (Miscellaneous Provisions) Regulations 2007, SI 2007/175, the Environmental Offences (Use of Fixed Penalty Receipts) (Wales) Regulations 2007, SI 2007/739 amended by SI 2008/663; the Environmental Offences (Use of Fixed Penalty Receipts) Regulations 2007, SI 2007/901 and the Environmental Offences (Fixed Penalties) (Miscellaneous Provisions) (Wales) Regulations 2008, SI 2008/663 have been made. For amending instruments, see the note to the Refuse Disposal (Amenity) Act 1978, s 2A, ante.

**7.10295** **75. Use of fixed penalty receipts** (1) A local authority may use any sums it receives in respect of fixed penalties payable in pursuance of notices given under section 73 (its "penalty receipts") only for the purposes of functions of its that are qualifying functions.

(2) The following are qualifying functions for the purposes of this section—

(*a*) functions under this Chapter;

(*b*) functions under the Noise Act 1996 (c 37);

(*c*) functions under sections 79 to 82 of the Environmental Protection Act 1990 (c 43) (statutory nuisances) in connection with statutory nuisances falling with section 79(1)(*g*) or (ga) (noise) of that Act;

(*d*) functions of a description specified in regulations made by the appropriate person.

(3) Regulations[1] under subsection (2)(*d*) may (in particular) have the effect that a local authority may use its penalty receipts for the purposes of any of its functions.

(4) A local authority must supply the appropriate person with such information relating to the use of its penalty receipts as the appropriate person may require.

(5) The appropriate person may by regulations—

(*a*) make provision for what a local authority is to do with its penalty receipts—

(i) pending their being used for the purposes of qualifying functions of the authority;

(ii) if they are not so used before such time after their receipt as may be specified by the regulations;

(*b*) make provision for accounting arrangements in respect of a local authority's penalty receipts.

(6) The provision that may be made under subsection (5)(*a*)(ii) includes (in particular) provision for the payment of sums to a person (including the appropriate person) other than the local authority.

(7) Before making regulations under this section the appropriate person must consult—

(*a*) the local authorities to which the regulations are to apply, and

(*b*) such other persons as the appropriate person thinks fit.

(8) The powers to make regulations conferred by this section are, for the purposes of subsection (1) of section 100 of the Local Government Act 2003 (c 26), to be regarded as included among the powers mentioned in subsection (2) of that section.

[Clean Neighbourhoods and Environment Act 2005, s 75.]

---

1 The Environmental Offences (Fixed Penalties) (Miscellaneous Provisions) Regulations 2007, SI 2007/175 have been made. For amending instruments, see the note to the Refuse Disposal (Amenity) Act 1978, s 2A, ante.

**7.10296** **76. Fixed penalty notices: power to require name and address** (1) If an authorised officer of a local authority proposes to give a person a notice under section 73, the officer may require the person to give him his name and address.

(2) A person commits an offence if—

(*a*) he fails to give his name and address when required to do so under subsection (1), or

(*b*) he gives a false or inaccurate name or address in response to a requirement under that subsection.

(3) A person guilty of an offence under subsection (2) is liable on summary conviction to a fine not exceeding level 3 on the standard scale.

(4) "Authorised officer" has the meaning given in section 73.

[Clean Neighbourhoods and Environment Act 2005, s 76.]

*Powers in relation to alarms*

7.10297 77. **Power of entry** (1) This section applies if an authorised officer of a local authority is satisfied that the conditions in subsection (2) are met in relation to an audible intruder alarm installed in or on premises in the area of the local authority.

(2) The conditions are—

(*a*) that the alarm has been sounding continuously for more than twenty minutes or intermittently for more than one hour;

(*b*) that the sounding of the alarm is likely to give persons living or working in the vicinity of the premises reasonable cause for annoyance;

(*c*) if the premises are in an alarm notification area, that reasonable steps have been taken to get the nominated key-holder to silence the alarm.

(3) The officer may enter the premises for the purpose of silencing the alarm.

(4) The officer may not enter premises by force under this section.

(5) The officer must, if required, show evidence of his authority to act under this section.

(6) In this section—

"authorised officer" means an officer of a local authority who is authorised by the authority (generally or specifically) for the purposes of this section;

"nominated key-holder", in respect of premises in the area of a local authority, means a person in respect of whom the authority has received notification in accordance with section 71(2)(*b*).

[Clean Neighbourhoods and Environment Act 2005, s 77.]

7.10298 78. **Warrant to enter premises by force** (1) This section applies if, on an application made by an authorised officer of a local authority, a justice of the peace is satisfied—

(*a*) that the conditions in section 77(2)(*a*) and (*b*) are met in relation to an audible intruder alarm installed in or on premises in the area of the local authority,

(*b*) if the premises are in an alarm notification area, that the condition in section 77(2)(*c*) is met, and

(*c*) that the officer is unable to gain entry to the premises without the use of force.

(2) The justice of the peace may issue a warrant authorising the officer to enter the premises, using reasonable force if necessary, for the purpose of silencing the alarm.

(3) Before applying for a warrant under this section, the officer must leave a notice at the premises stating—

(*a*) that the officer is satisfied that the sounding of the alarm is likely to give persons living or working in the vicinity of the premises reasonable cause for annoyance, and

(*b*) that an application is to be made for a warrant authorising the officer to enter the premises, using reasonable force if necessary, for the purpose of silencing the alarm.

(4) The officer must, if required, show evidence of a warrant issued under this section.

(5) "Authorised officer" has the meaning given in section 77.

[Clean Neighbourhoods and Environment Act 2005, s 78.]

7.10299 79. **Powers of entry: supplementary** (1) This section applies where an officer of a local authority enters any premises under section 77 or under a warrant issued under section 78.

(2) The officer may take any steps he thinks necessary for the purpose of silencing the alarm.

(3) The officer may take with him—

(*a*) such other persons, and

(*b*) such equipment,

as he thinks necessary for the purpose of silencing the alarm.

(4) The officer and any person who enters the premises with him by virtue of subsection (3) must not cause more damage to or disturbance at the premises than is necessary for the purpose of silencing the alarm.

(5) If the premises are unoccupied or (where the premises are occupied) the occupier of the premises is temporarily absent the officer must—

(*a*) leave a notice at the premises stating what action has been taken on the premises under this section and section 77 or 78;

(*b*) leave the premises (so far as is reasonably practicable) as effectively secured against entry as he found them.

(6) But the officer is not required by virtue of subsection (5)(*b*) to re-set the alarm.

(7) Any expenses reasonably incurred by the local authority in connection with entering the premises, silencing the alarm and complying with subsection (5) may be recovered by the authority from the responsible person.

(8) A warrant under section 78 continues in force until—

(*a*) the alarm has been silenced, and

(*b*) the officer has complied with subsection (5) (if that subsection applies).

(9) Nothing done by, or by a member of, a local authority or by an officer of or another person authorised by a local authority, if done in good faith for the purposes of section 77, 78 or this section, is to subject the authority or any of those persons personally to any action, liability, claim or demand.

[Clean Neighbourhoods and Environment Act 2005, s 79.]

*Supplementary*

**7.10300 80. Orders and regulations** (1) This section applies to a power conferred on the appropriate person under any provision of this Chapter to make an order or regulations.

(2) The power includes—

(*a*) power to make different provision for different purposes (including different provision for different local authorities and descriptions of local authority);

(*b*) power to make consequential, supplementary, incidental, transitional and saving provision.

(3) The power is exercisable by statutory instrument.

(4) A statutory instrument containing an order or regulations made by the Secretary of State under any provision of this Chapter is subject to annulment in pursuance of a resolution of either House of Parliament.

[Clean Neighbourhoods and Environment Act 2005, s 80.]

**7.10301 81. Interpretation** (1) In this Chapter—

"alarm notification area" means an area in respect of which a designation under section 69 has effect;

"the appropriate person" is—

(*a*) in relation to a local authority in England, the Secretary of State;

(*b*) in relation to a local authority in Wales, the National Assembly for Wales;

"local authority" means—

(*a*) a district council in England;

(*b*) a county council in England for an area for which there is no district council;

(*c*) a London borough council;

(*d*) the Common Council of the City of London;

(*e*) the Council of the Isles of Scilly;

(*f*) a county or county borough council in Wales;

"the occupier" in respect of premises means (subject to subsection (2))—

(*a*) a person occupying the premises, or

(*b*) if the premises are unoccupied, a person entitled to occupy the premises (other than the owner);

"premises" does not include a vehicle;

"the responsible person" in respect of premises means—

(*a*) the occupier, or

(*b*) if there is no occupier, the owner.

(2) The fact that a person is occupying premises is to be disregarded for the purposes of this Chapter if—

(*a*) the premises comprise a building that is being erected, constructed, altered, improved, maintained, cleaned or repaired,

(*b*) the person is occupying the premises in connection with the erection, construction, alteration, improvement, maintenance, cleaning or repair, and

(*c*) the person is doing so by virtue of a licence granted for less than four weeks.

[Clean Neighbourhoods and Environment Act 2005, s 81.]

## PART 9[1]

## MISCELLANEOUS

**96–98.** *Use of fixed penalty receipts.*

**99.** *Abandoned shopping and luggage trolleys.*

[1] Part 9 contains ss 96–105.

**7.10302 100. Section 99: transitional provision** (1) This section applies if, before the commencement date, a local authority in England and Wales has resolved under section 99 of the Environmental Protection Act 1990 that Schedule 4 to that Act is to apply in its area.

(2) If the day specified in the resolution for the coming into force of Schedule 4 in the authority's area falls on or after the commencement date, the resolution is to be of no effect.

(3) If Schedule 4 applies in the authority's area immediately before the commencement date, the Schedule is to continue to apply in the authority's area on and after the commencement date as it applied before that date.

(4) But Schedule 4 shall not so apply in relation to any shopping or luggage trolley seized by the authority on or after the relevant day.

(5) For the purposes of subsection (4) the relevant day is the earlier of—

(*a*) the third anniversary of the commencement date;

(*b*) if the authority resolves under section 99 of the Environmental Protection Act 1990 (c 43) that Schedule 4 (as amended by section 99 of this Act) is to apply in its area, the day specified in the resolution as the day on which the Schedule (as so amended) comes into force in its area.

(6) So long as Schedule 4 continues to apply as described in subsection (3), the reference in section 99(4) of the Environmental Protection Act 1990 to Schedule 4 is to be treated as including

a reference to Schedule 4 as it so applies.

(7) If the authority resolves under section 99 that Schedule 4 (as amended by section 99 of this Act) is to apply in its area, the authority may not in giving effect to paragraph 4(1) of Schedule 4 (as so amended) take into account charges payable in relation to shopping or luggage trolleys seized before the Schedule (as so amended) comes into force in its area.

(8) Nothing in this section prevents the authority from bringing to an end the application of Schedule 4 in its area.

(9) In this section—

"the commencement date" is the day on which section 99 of this Act comes into force;

"local authority" has the same meaning as in section 99 of the Environmental Protection Act 1990;

"luggage trolley" and "shopping trolley" have the same meaning as in Schedule 4 to that Act.

[Clean Neighbourhoods and Environment Act 2005, s 100.]

## PART 10[1]
## GENERAL

7.10303 **108. Commencement** (1) The provisions specified in subsection (2) come into force—

(*a*) in relation to England, in accordance with provision made by order[2] by the Secretary of State; and

(*b*) in relation to Wales, in accordance with provision so made by the National Assembly for Wales.

(2) The provisions referred to in subsection (1) are—

(*a*) section 2;

(*b*) sections 6 to 13 and 15 to 17 and, in Part 1 of Schedule 5, the repeals to the Refuse Disposal (Amenity) Act 1978 (c 3) and the Road Traffic Regulation Act 1984 (c 27);

(*c*) sections 19 to 25, paragraphs 5 to 9 of Schedule 4 and, in Part 2 of Schedule 5, the repeals to the Environmental Protection Act 1990 (c 43);

(*d*) sections 28 to 31, paragraphs 14 to 19 of Schedule 4 and, in Part 3 of Schedule 5, the repeals to the Anti-Social Behaviour Act 2003 (c 38);

(*e*) section 34 and, in Part 3 of Schedule 5, the repeal to the Town and Country Planning Act 1990 (c 8);

(*f*) sections 37 and 38 and, in Part 4 of Schedule 5, the repeal of section 6 of the Control of Pollution (Amendment) Act 1989 (c 14);

(*g*) sections 45 and 46;

(*h*) section 47, paragraph 4 of Schedule 4 and, in Part 4 of Schedule 5, the repeals to the Environmental Protection Act 1990, other than the repeal to section 33 of that Act;

(*i*) section 48;

(*j*) section 50;

(*k*) section 52;

(*l*) section 53;

(*m*) Chapter 1 of Part 6 above and Part 5 of Schedule 5;

(*n*) Part 7 above except sections 83(2) and 85, and in Part 7 of Schedule 5, the repeals to the Noise and Statutory Nuisance Act 1993 (c 40) and the Noise Act 1996 (c 37);

(*o*) sections 96 to 98 and Part 9 of Schedule 5;

(*p*) sections 99 and 100;

(*q*) sections 101 to 103;

(*r*) section 104 and Part 10 of Schedule 5.

(3) These provisions come into force in accordance with provision made by order by the Secretary of State—

(*a*) section 1;

(*b*) section 32;

(*c*) sections 42 to 44;

(*d*) section 49 and paragraph 3 of Schedule 4;

(*e*) section 68 and Part 6 of Schedule 5;

(*f*) Part 8 above and Part 8 of Schedule 5;

(*g*) in Part 1 of Schedule 5, the repeal to section 3 of the London Local Authorities Act 2004 (c i).

(*h*) in Part 2 of Schedule 5, the repeals to the London Local Authorities Act 1994 (c xii) and the City of Newcastle upon Tyne Act 2000 (c viii);

(*i*) in Part 3 of Schedule 5, the repeal to the London Local Authorities Act 1995 (c x);

(*j*) in Part 7 of Schedule 5, the repeal to the London Local Authorities Act 1991 (c xiii).

(4) These provisions come into force at the end of the period of two months beginning with the day on which this Act is passed—

(*a*) sections 3 to 5 and, in Part 1 of Schedule 5, the repeals to the Greater London Council (General Powers) Act 1982 (c i) and section 11 of the London Local Authorities Act 2004 (c i);

(*b*) section 18;
(*c*) section 27;
(*d*) section 33 and, in Part 3 of Schedule 5, the repeal to the London Local Authorities Act 2004 (c i);
(*e*) sections 35 and 36, and in Part 4 of Schedule 5, the repeals to sections 1 and 2 of the Control of Pollution (Amendment) Act 1989 (c 14);
(*f*) section 40 and, in Part 4 of Schedule 5, the repeal to section 33 of the Environmental Protection Act 1990 (c 43);
(*g*) section 41;
(*h*) section 54;
(*i*) section 83(2);
(*j*) section 105.

(5) An order under subsection (1) or (3) may make—
(*a*) transitional, consequential, incidental and supplemental provision, or savings;
(*b*) different provision for different purposes.

(6) Where a provision of this Act comes into force otherwise than under subsection (1) or (3), the Secretary of State may by order make any transitional, consequential, incidental or supplemental provision, or savings, that he considers necessary or expedient in relation to the coming into force of that provision.

(7) An order under subsection (6) may make different provision for different purposes.

(8) An order under this section is to be made by statutory instrument.

[Clean Neighbourhoods and Environment Act 2005, s 108.]

[1] Part 10 contains ss 106–111.
[2] See the note to the title of the Act for details of commencement orders made.

**7.10304** **110. Extent** (1) This Act extends to England and Wales only, subject as follows.

(2) An amendment in Schedule 2 has the same extent as the provision amended.

(3) The repeal in Part 8 of Schedule 5 has the same extent as the provision repealed.

[Clean Neighbourhoods and Environment Act 2005, s 110.]

**7.10305** **111. Short title** This Act may be cited as the Clean Neighbourhoods and Environment Act 2005.

[Clean Neighbourhoods and Environment Act 2005, s 111.]

# Control of Noise (Appeals) Rules 1975[1]

(SI 1975/2116 amended by SI 1990/2276 and SI 2016/279 (E))

*Interpretation*

**7.10306** *2.* (1) The Interpretation Act [1978] shall apply for the interpretation of these regulations, as it applies for the interpretation of an Act of Parliament.

(2) In these regulations, unless the context otherwise requires—
"the Act" means the Control of Pollution Act 1974, and any reference in these regulations to a numbered section shall be construed as a reference to the section bearing that number in the Act;
"best practicable means" shall be construed in accordance with section 72;
"person responsible" has the meaning given to it by section 73(1).

(3) Any reference in these regulations to a numbered regulation shall be construed as a reference to the regulation bearing that number in these regulations.

[1] Made under the Control of Pollution Act 1974, ss 70(2) and (3) and 104(1).

## Part II Appeals to Magistrates' Courts

*Interpretation of Part II*

**7.10307** *3.* This part of these regulations relates only to appeals brought to magistrates' courts under Part III of the Act, and any reference in this part to an appeal or an appellant shall be construed accordingly.

*Appeals under section 60(7)*

**7.10308** *5.* (1) The provisions of this regulation shall apply to an appeal brought by any person under subsection (7) of section 60 (control of noise on construction sites) against a notice served upon him by a local authority under that section.

(2) The grounds on which a person served with such a notice may appeal under the said subsection (7) may include any of the following grounds which are appropriate in the circumstances of the particular case:—
(*a*) that the notice is not justified by the terms of section 60;
(*b*) that there has been some informality, defect or error in, or in connection with, the notice;
(*c*) that the authority have refused unreasonably to accept compliance with alternative requirements, or that the requirements of the notice are otherwise unreasonable in character or extent, or are unnecessary;

(*d*) that the time, or, where more than one time is specified, any of the times, within which the requirements of the notice are to be complied with is not reasonably sufficient for the purpose;

(*e*) that the notice should have been served on some person instead of the appellant, being a person who is carrying out, or going to carry out, the works, or is responsible for, or has control over, the carrying out of the works;

(*f*) that the notice might lawfully have been served on some person in addition to the appellant, being a person who is carrying out, or going to carry out, the works, or is responsible for, or has control over, the carrying out of the works, and that it would have been equitable for it to have been so served;

(*g*) that the authority have not had regard to some or all of the provisions of section 60(4).

(3) If and so far as an appeal is based on the ground of some informality, defect or error in, or in connection with, the notice, the court shall dismiss the appeal, if it is satisfied that the informality, defect or error was not a material one.

(4) Where the grounds upon which an appeal is brought include a ground specified in paragraph (2)(*e*) or (*f*) above, the appellant shall serve a copy of his notice of appeal on any other person referred to, and in the case of any appeal to which this regulation applies he may serve a copy of his notice of appeal on any other person having an estate or interest in the premises in question.

(5) On the hearing of the appeal the court may—

(*a*) quash the notice to which the appeal relates, or

(*b*) vary the notice in favour of the appellant in such manner as it thinks fit, or

(*c*) dismiss the appeal;

and a notice which is varied under sub-paragraph (*b*) above shall be final and shall otherwise have effect, as so varied, as if it had been so made by the local authority.

*Appeals under section 61(7)*

**7.10309** *6.* (1) The provisions of this regulation shall apply to an appeal brought by any person under subsection (7) of section 61 (prior consent for work on construction sites) in relation to a conditional consent given by a local authority under that section or in relation to an authority's refusal or failure to give a consent within the period specified in subsection (6) of that section.

(2) In this regulation, "conditional consent" means a consent given by a local authority under section 61 in respect of which the authority have attached any condition or imposed any limitation or qualification in pursuance of section 61(5)(*a*), (*b*) or (*c*); and "conditions" includes any limitation or qualification so imposed.

(3) The grounds on which a person to whom a local authority give a conditional consent may appeal under the said subsection (7) may include any of the following grounds which are appropriate in the circumstances of the particular case:—

(*a*) that any condition attached or imposed in relation to the consent (in this regulation referred to as "a relevant condition") is not justified by the terms of section 61;

(*b*) that there has been some informality, defect or error in, or in connection with, the consent;

(*c*) that the requirements of any relevant condition are unreasonable in character or extent, or are unnecessary;

(*d*) that the time, or where more than one time is specified, any of the times, within which the requirements of any relevant condition are to be complied with is not reasonably sufficient for the purpose.

(4) If and so far as an appeal is based on the ground of some informality, defect or error in, or in connection with, the consent, the court shall dismiss the appeal, if it is satisfied that the informality, defect or error was not a material one.

(5) Where the appeal relates to a conditional consent given by a local authority, on the hearing of the appeal the court may—

(*a*) vary the consent or any relevant condition in favour of the appellant in such manner as it thinks fit, or

(*b*) quash any relevant condition, or

(*c*) dismiss the appeal;

and a consent or condition which is varied under sub-paragraph (*a*) above shall be final and shall otherwise have effect, as so varied, as if it had been given, attached or imposed in that form by the authority.

(6) Where the appeal relates to a local authority's refusal or failure to give a consent within the period specified in section 61(6), on the hearing of the appeal the court shall afford to the appellant and to the authority an opportunity of making representations to it concerning the application under section 61(1) to which the appeal relates and concerning the terms and conditions of any consent which they consider to be appropriate thereto, and thereafter the court shall either—

(*a*) adjourn the appeal to enable the appellant to submit to the authority a new application under section 61(1) relating to the matters which are the subject of the appeal, or

(*b*) make an order giving consent to the application either unconditionally or subject to such conditions as it thinks fit, having regard to the provisions of section 61(4), (5) and (9), and any other matters which appear to it to be relevant,

and any consent given by an order made under sub-paragraph (*b*) above shall be final and shall otherwise have effect for the purpose of Part III of the Act as if it were a consent given by the local authority under section 61.

PART IV SUSPENSION OF NOTICES

**7.10311** *10.* (1) Subject to paragraph (2) of this regulation, where an appeal is brought against a notice served under section 60 and—

(*a*) the noise to which the notice relates is noise caused in the course of the performance of some duty imposed by law on the appellant, or

(*b*) compliance with the notice would involve any person in expenditure on the carrying out of works before the hearing of the appeal,

the notice shall be suspended until the appeal has been abandoned or decided by the court.

(2) A notice to which this regulation applies shall not be suspended if in the opinion of the local authority—

(*a*) the noise to which the notice relates—

(i) is injurious to health, or

(ii) is likely to be of a limited duration such that suspension of the notice would render the notice of no practical effect, or

(*b*) the expenditure which would be incurred by any person in the carrying out of works in compliance with the notice before any appeal has been decided would not be disproportionate to the public benefit to be expected in that period from such compliance,

and the notice includes a statement that it shall have effect notwithstanding any appeal to a magistrates' court which has not been decided by the court.

(3) Save as provided in this regulation a notice under Part III of the Act shall not be suspended by reason only of the bringing of an appeal to a magistrates' court.

## Litter (Statutory Undertakers) (Designation and Relevant Land) Order 1991[1]

(SI 1991/1043 amended by SI 1992/406, SI 1999/1443 and SI 2003/1615)

*Citation, commencement and interpretation*

**7.10312** *1.* (1) This Order may be cited as the Litter (Statutory Undertakers) (Designation and Relevant Land) Order 1991 and shall come into force on 13th May 1991.

(2) In this Order—

"the Act" means the Environmental Protection Act 1990;

"operational land" means—

(*a*) in relation to any person authorised by any enactment to carry on any railway or light railway undertaking, land required or used for the operation of rail or light rail services,

(*aa*) in relation to any operator of a relevant railway asset, land required or used for the operation of that asset,

(*b*) in relation to any other designated statutory undertaker—

(i) land which is used for the purpose of carrying on their undertaking; and

(ii) land in which an interest is held for that purpose;

but does not include land which, in respect of its nature and situation, is comparable rather with land in general than with land which is used, or in which interests are held, for the purpose of the carrying on of statutory undertakings.

(3) For the purposes of article 3 of this Order, land is in an urban area if it is surrounded by, or adjoins for a continuous distance of not less than one kilometre, built-up sites (other than sites used for horticultural or agricultural purposes) on which there are permanent structures, and—

(*a*) for the purpose of determining whether any distance is continuous, any gap between built-up sites of 50 metres or less shall be disregarded,

(*b*) highways, navigable rivers and operational land which is not relevant land—

(i) shall not be treated as built-up sites for the purposes of determining whether or not land is in an urban area,

(ii) shall be ignored for the purposes of determining whether or not land adjoins built-up sites.

---

[1] Made by the Secretary of State for the Environment, as respects England, the Secretary of State for Wales, as respects Wales, and the Secretary of State for Scotland, as respects Scotland, in exercise of the powers conferred on them by s 86(6), (8) and (15) of the Environmental Protection Act 1990.

*Designation of statutory undertakers*

**7.10313** *2.* The statutory undertakers described below, and statutory undertakers of the descriptions described below, are designated for the purposes of Part IV of the Act—

the British Railways Board and Transport for London, or any of its subsidiaries (within the meaning of the Greater London Authority 1999) or company as respects which Transport for London has, or at any time has had, a beneficial interest (either directly or through nominees or subsidiaries) in not less than 20 per cent of its issued ordinary share capital,

any operator of a relevant railway asset,

any Passenger Transport Executive established pursuant to section 9(1) of the Transport Act 1968, in so far as it is authorised by any enactment to carry on any railway undertaking,

any person authorised by any enactment to carry on any light railway undertaking other than an independent railway undertaking within the meaning of section 83(7) of the Transport Act 1962,

any person authorised by any enactment to carry on any tramway undertaking, any person authorised by any enactment to carry on any road transport undertaking, other than the operator of a licensed taxi or licensed hire car as defined in section 13(3) of the Transport Act 1985.

any person authorised by any enactment to carry on any canal, inland navigation, dock, harbour or pier undertaking,

any relevant airport operator (within the meaning of Part V of the Airports Act 1986).

*Prescribed land of statutory undertakers*

7.10314 *3.* (1) For the purposes of Part IV of the Act, land—

(*a*) which is under the direct control of a designated statutory undertaker,

(*b*) in relation to which the public have no right or permission to have access with or without payment, and

(*c*) which is within the description in paragraph (2) below but not within the description in paragraph (3) below;

is prescribed as relevant land of the designated statutory undertaker under whose control it is.

(2) The land described in this paragraph is operational land which is within 100 metres of a railway station platform to which the public is entitled or permitted to have access with or without payment and any other land which is not so situated but is land in an urban area, being in either case land which—

(*a*) forms an embankment, cutting, siding, level or junction, but is not part of a depot, goods yard, or enclosed area where plant and machinery is kept, or

(*b*) is within the rails or on the tracksides, but is not within a tunnel, or

(*c*) is on a viaduct or bridge.

(3) The land described in this paragraph is land below the place to which the tide flows at mean high water springs.

*Land not to be treated as relevant land*

7.10315 *4.* For the purposes of Part IV of the Act, land to which the public are entitled or permitted to have access with or without payment which is—

land other than operational land,

land used solely for the provision of freight services,

land adjacent to an unpaved towing path or adjacent to a paved towing path where the paving extends for a length of less than 1 kilometre, or

land below the place to which the tide flows at mean high water springs,

is not to be treated as relevant land of any designated statutory undertaker.

## Statutory Nuisance (Appeals) Regulations 1995

(SI 1995/2644 amended by SI 2006/771 and SI 2007/117)

*Citation, commencement and interpretation*

7.10316 *1.* (1) These Regulations may be cited as the Statutory Nuisance (Appeals) Regulations 1995 and shall come into force on 8th November 1995.

(2) In these Regulations—

"the 1974 Act" means the Control of Pollution Act 1974;

"the 1990 Act" means the Environmental Protection Act 1990; and

"the 1993 Act" means the Noise and Statutory Nuisance Act 1993.

*Appeals under section 80(3) of the 1990 Act*

7.10317 *2.* (1) The provisions of this regulation apply in relation to an appeal brought by any person under section 80(3) of the 1990 Act (appeals to magistrates) against an abatement notice served upon him by a local authority.

(2) The grounds on which a person served with such a notice may appeal under section 80(3) are any one or more of the following grounds that are appropriate in the circumstances of the particular case—

(*a*) that the abatement notice is not justified by section 80 of the 1990 Act (summary proceedings for statutory nuisances);

(*b*) that there has been some informality, defect or error in, or in connection with, the abatement notice, or in, or in connection with, any copy of the abatement notice served under section 80A(3) (certain notices in respect of vehicles, machinery or equipment);

(*c*) that the authority have refused unreasonably to accept compliance with alternative requirements, or that the requirements of the abatement notice are otherwise unreasonable in character or extent, or are unnecessary;

(*d*) that the time, or where more than one time is specified, any of the times, within which the requirements of the abatement notice are to be complied with is not reasonably sufficient for the purpose;

(*e*) where the nuisance to which the notice relates—

(i) is a nuisance falling within section 79(1)(*a*), (*d*), (*e*), (*f*), (*fa*) or (*g*) of the 1990 Act and arises on industrial, trade, or business premises, or

(ii) is a nuisance falling within section 79(1)(*b*) of the 1990 Act and the smoke is emitted from a chimney, or

(iii) is a nuisance falling within section 79(1)(*ga*) of the 1990 Act and is noise emitted from or caused by a vehicle, machinery or equipment being used for industrial, trade or business purposes, or

(iv) is a nuisance falling within section 79(1)(*fb*) of the 1990 Act and—
(*aa*) the artificial light is emitted from industrial, trade or business premises, or
(*bb*) the artificial light (not being light to which sub-paragraph (aa) applies) is emitted by lights used for the purpose only of illuminating an outdoor relevant sports facility (within the meaning given by section 80(8A) of the 1990 Act),

that the best practicable means were used to prevent, or to counteract the effects of, the nuisance;

(*f*) that, in the case of a nuisance under section 79(1)(*g*) or (*ga*) of the 1990 Act (noise emitted from premises), the requirements imposed by the abatement notice by virtue of section 80(1)(*a*) of that Act are more onerous than the requirements for the time being in force, in relation to the noise to which the notice relates, of—
(i) any notice served under section 60 or 66 of the 1974 Act (control of noise on construction sites and from certain premises), or
(ii) any consent given under section 61 or 65 of the 1974 Act (consent for work on construction sites and consent for noise to exceed registered level in a noise abatement zone), or
(iii) any determination made under section 67 of the 1974 Act (noise control of new buildings);

(*g*) that, in the case of a nuisance under section 79(1)(*ga*) of the 1990 Act (noise emitted from or caused by vehicles, machinery or equipment), the requirements imposed by the abatement notice by virtue of section 80(1)(*a*) of the Act are more onerous than the requirements for the time being in force, in relation to the noise to which the notice relates, of any condition of a consent given under paragraph 1 of Schedule 2 to the 1993 Act (loudspeakers in streets or roads);

(*h*) that the abatement notice should have been served on some person instead of the appellant, being—
(i) the person responsible for the nuisance, or
(ii) the person responsible for the vehicle, machinery or equipment, or
(iii) in the case of a nuisance arising from any defect of a structural character, the owner of the premises, or
(iv) in the case where the person responsible for the nuisance cannot be found or the nuisance has not yet occurred, the owner or occupier of the premises;

(*i*) that the abatement notice might lawfully have been served on some person instead of the appellant being—
(i) in the case where the appellant is the owner of the premises, the occupier of the premises, or,
(ii) in the case where the appellant is the occupier of the premises, the owner of the premises,

and that it would have been equitable for it to have been so served;

(*j*) that the abatement notice might lawfully have been served on some person in addition to the appellant, being—
(i) a person also responsible for the nuisance, or
(ii) a person who is also owner of the premises, or
(iii) a person who is also an occupier of the premises, or
(iv) a person who is also the person responsible for the vehicle, machinery or equipment,

and that it would have been equitable for it to have been so served.

(3) If and so far as an appeal is based on the ground of some informality, defect or error in, or in connection with, the abatement notice, or in, or in connection with, any copy of the notice served under section 80A(3), the court shall dismiss the appeal if it is satisfied that the informality, defect or error was not a material one.

(4) Where the grounds upon which an appeal is brought include a ground specified in paragraph 2(*i*) or (*j*) above, the appellant shall serve a copy of his notice of appeal on any other person referred to, and in the case of any appeal to which these regulations apply he may serve a copy of his notice of appeal on any other person having an estate or interest in the premises, vehicle, machinery or equipment in question.

(5) On the hearing of the appeal the court may—
(*a*) quash the abatement notice to which the appeal relates, or
(*b*) vary the abatement notice in favour of the appellant in such manner as it thinks fit, or
(*c*) dismiss the appeal;

and an abatement notice that is varied under sub-paragraph (*b*) above shall be final and shall otherwise have effect, as so varied, as if it had been so made by the local authority.

(6) Subject to paragraph (7) below, on the hearing of an appeal the court may make such order as it thinks fit—
(*a*) with respect to the person by whom any work is to be executed and the contribution to be made by any person towards the cost of the work, or
(*b*) as to the proportions in which any expenses which may become recoverable by the authority under Part III of the 1990 Act are to be borne by the appellant and by any other person.

(7) In exercising its powers under paragraph (6) above the court—

(*a*) shall have regard, as between an owner and an occupier, to the terms and conditions, whether contractual or statutory, of any relevant tenancy and to the nature of the works required, and

(*b*) shall be satisfied before it imposes any requirement thereunder on any person other than the appellant, that that person has received a copy of the notice of appeal in pursuance of paragraph (4) above.

*Suspension of notice*

**7.10318** *3.* (1) Where—

(*a*) an appeal is brought against an abatement notice served under section 80 or section 80A of the 1990 Act, and—

(*b*) either—

(i) compliance with the abatement notice would involve any person in expenditure on the carrying out of works before the hearing of the appeal, or

(ii) in the case of a nuisance under section 79(1)(*g*) or (*ga*) of the 1990 Act, the noise to which the abatement notice relates is noise necessarily caused in the course of the performance of some duty imposed by law on the appellant, and

(*c*) either paragraph (2) does not apply, or it does apply but the requirements of paragraph (3) have not been met,

the abatement notice shall be suspended until the appeal has been abandoned or decided by the court.

(2) This paragraph applies where—

(*a*) the nuisance to which the abatement notice relates—

(i) is injurious to health, or

(ii) is likely to be of a limited duration such that suspension of the notice would render it of no practical effect, or

(*b*) the expenditure which would be incurred by any person in the carrying out of works in compliance with the abatement notice before any appeal has been decided would not be disproportionate to the public benefit to be expected in that period from such compliance.

(3) Where paragraph (2) applies the abatement notice—

(*a*) shall include a statement that paragraph (2) applies, and that as a consequence it shall have effect notwithstanding any appeal to a magistrates' court which has not been decided by the court, and

(*b*) shall include a statement as to which of the grounds set out in paragraph (2) apply.

*Revocations*

**7.10319** *4.* The Statutory Nuisance (Appeals) Regulations 1990 and the Statutory Nuisance (Appeals) (Amendment) Regulations 1990 are hereby revoked.

## Health Protection (Part 2A Orders) Regulations 2010

(SI 2010/658 amended by SI 2013/235)

**7.10342** *1. Citation, commencement and application* (1) These Regulations may be cited as the Health Protection (Part 2A Orders) Regulations 2010 and shall come into force on 6th April 2010.

(2) These Regulations apply in relation to England only.

**7.10343** *2. Interpretation* In these Regulations—

"the Act" means the Public Health (Control of Disease) Act 1984;

"child" means a person under the age of 18 years;

"Part 2A application" means an application made to a justice of the peace for an order under Part 2A of the Act;

"Part 2A order" means an order made by a justice of the peace under Part 2A of the Act; and

"a person with parental responsibility" means a person with parental responsibility within the meaning of the Children Act 1989.

**7.10344** *3. Duty on local authorities to give notice of Part 2A applications* (1) This regulation applies where a local authority is making a Part 2A application.

(2) The local authority must make reasonable enquiries as to the existence and location of persons who fall within paragraphs (4) to (7) (as applicable).

(3) Having made reasonable enquiries pursuant to paragraph (2), the local authority must give notice of the application to the persons specified in paragraphs (4) to (7) (as applicable) where such persons are known to the local authority and contactable by it.

(4) In relation to an application for an order under section 45G(2) or (4) of the Act (power to order health measures in relation to persons), the persons specified are—

(*a*) the person subject to the application (P);

(*b*) a person with parental responsibility for P, if P is a child; and

(*c*) P's decision-maker (if any).

(5) Subject to paragraph (6), in relation to an application for an order under section 45H(2) or (4) of the Act (power to order health measures in relation to things), the persons specified are—

(*a*) the owner of the thing; and

(*b*) the person with custody or control of the thing.

(6) In relation to an application for an order under section 45H(2) of the Act in respect of a dead body or human remains, the person specified is the deceased's next of kin (or where the deceased

has more than one next of kin, any one of those persons).

(7) In relation to an application for an order under section 45I(2) or (4) (power to order health measures in relation to premises), the persons specified are—

(*a*) the owner of the premises; and

(*b*) the occupier of the premises, if any.

(8) The local authority is not required to give notice under paragraph (3) where P, in the reasonable view of the local authority, is likely to abscond or otherwise take steps to undermine the order applied for.

(9) The local authority is not required to give notice under paragraph (3) to a person specified in paragraph (4)(*b*) where exceptional circumstances exist which mean that notifying such a person would not be in P's best interests.

(10) In this regulation—

"next of kin" means the person accorded highest rank in the following list (but if two or more persons are accorded equal ranking then each of those persons is to be treated as next of kin)—

(*a*) a person with parental responsibility for the deceased person (P);

(*b*) P's husband, wife or civil partner;

(*c*) a person who had been living with P up to the time of P's death as P's husband, wife or civil partner;

(*d*) P's child where aged 18 years or over;

(*e*) P's parent;

(*f*) P's brother or sister where aged 18 years or over; and

"P's decision-maker" means P's donee of enduring power of attorney or lasting power of attorney under the Mental Capacity Act 2005 or a deputy appointed by the Court of Protection in relation to P, where decisions in connection with Part 2A applications or orders are within the scope of that person's authority.

**7.10345** 4. *Evidence required for a Part 2A application in relation to persons* (1) A justice of the peace cannot be satisfied that the criteria in section 45G(1) or (3) of the Act (power to order health measures in relation to persons) are met unless the evidence listed in paragraph (2) is available to the justice.

(2) That evidence is—

(*a*) a report which gives details (insofar as known and relevant), or gives reasons for the omission of details, of—

(i) the signs and symptoms of the infection or contamination in the person (P) who is the subject of the application,

(ii) P's diagnosis,

(iii) the outcome of clinical or laboratory tests, and

(iv) P's recent contacts with, or proximity to, a source or sources of infection or contamination;

(*b*) a summary of the characteristics and effects of the infection or contamination which P has or may have which includes an explanation of—

(i) the mechanism by which the infection or contamination spreads,

(ii) how easily the infection or contamination spreads amongst humans, and

(iii) the impact of the infection or contamination on human health (by reference to pain, disability and the likelihood of death);

(*c*) in relation to applications seeking an order under section 45G(2), an assessment of the risk to human health that P presents, including a description of any acts or omissions, or anticipated acts or omissions, of P which affect that risk;

(*d*) in relation to applications seeking an order under section 45G(4), an assessment of the risk to human health that the related party presents, including any acts or omissions, or anticipated acts or omissions, of the related party which affect that risk;

(*e*) in relation to applications seeking an order under section 45G(2), an assessment of the options available to deal with the risk that P presents; and

(*f*) in relation to applications seeking an order under section 45G(4), an assessment of the options available to deal with the risk that the related party presents.

(3) A report under paragraph (2)(*a*) must include the details mentioned in at least one of paragraphs (2)(*a*)(i) to (iv).

(4) The evidence must be given by persons who are suitably qualified to give the evidence.

(5) The evidence may be given orally or in writing.

**7.10346** 5. *Period for which Part 2A order in relation to persons may be in force* (1) This regulation applies in relation to Part 2A orders imposing a restriction or requirement under section 45G(2)(*a*) and (*b*) and (*e*) to (*k*) (power to order health measures in relation to persons) of the Act.

(2) The period for which the restriction or requirement imposed by or under the order may be in force must not exceed 28 days beginning with the day on which the order was made.

(3) The period of any extension of a restriction or requirement must not exceed 28 days.

(4) Where a Part 2A order is varied to impose a new restriction or requirement, the period for which that new restriction or requirement may be in force must not exceed 28 days beginning with the day on which the order was varied.

**7.10347** 6. *Affected persons in relation to Part 2A orders in relation to persons and dead bodies or human remains* (1) The following persons are affected persons (in addition to those prescribed in

section 45M of the Act) for the purposes of Part 2A orders.
(2) In the case of a Part 2A order under section 45G of the Act in relation to a person (P), P's decision-maker (if any).
(3) In the case of a Part 2A Order under section 45H(2) of the Act in relation to a dead body or human remains, the deceased's next of kin.
(4) In this regulation, "next of kin" and "P's decision-maker" have the meaning given to them in regulation 3.

**7.10348** 7. *Discretionary power for local authorities to charge in connection with Part 2A orders in relation to things and premises* (1) This regulation applies where a local authority has incurred costs taking measures pursuant to a Part 2A order under section 45H (health measures in relation to things) or 45I (health measures in relation to premises) of the Act.
(2) Subject to paragraph (4), the local authority may impose a charge on—
(*a*) the owner or person with custody or control of the thing which is the subject of an order under section 45H of the Act; or
(*b*) the owner or occupier of the premises which are the subject of an order under section 45I of the Act.
(3) The amount of the charge imposed—
(*a*) must not exceed the actual costs (including staff costs) incurred by the local authority in taking measures in relation to the thing or premises pursuant to the order; and
(*b*) must be reasonable in the circumstances.
(4) A local authority may not impose a charge in connection with orders under section 45H of the Act which relate to a dead body or human remains.

**7.10349** 8. *Duty on local authorities to provide information in relation to Part 2A orders in relation to persons* (1) This regulation applies where a local authority has made a Part 2A application and a justice of the peace has made a Part 2A order under section 45G (health measures in relation to persons) in respect of that application.
(2) The local authority must take all reasonable steps to ensure that the person who is the subject of the order (P) understands—
(*a*) the effect of the order, the reason it has been made, the power under which it has been made and P's right to apply for a variation or revocation of the order; and
(*b*) the relevant support services available to P (and how to access them).
(3) The local authority must take the steps as soon as reasonably practicable after the order is made.
(4) Where P is under the age of 18 years, the duty under paragraph (2) is to ensure that a person with parental responsibility for P understands the matters set out in sub-paragraphs (*a*) and (*b*) of that paragraph.

**7.10350** 9. *Duty on local authorities to have regard to welfare following a Part 2A order in relation to persons* (1) This regulation applies where a person (P)—
(*a*) is detained in a hospital or other suitable establishment pursuant to a Part 2A order under section 45G(2)(*c*) (health measures in relation to persons); or
(*b*) is kept in isolation or quarantine pursuant to a Part 2A order under section 45G(2)(*d*) (health measures in relation to persons).
(2) The local authority which made the application for the Part 2A order must have regard to the impact of the order on the welfare of P and P's dependants, if any, for the duration of the order.

**7.10351** 10. *Duty on local authorities to report Part 2A applications to Public Health England* (1) A local authority must provide a written report to the chief executive of Public Health England, an executive agency of the Department of Health, each time it makes a Part 2A application.
(2) The report must include—
(*a*) the name of the local authority;
(*b*) contact details for the officer of the local authority responsible for the report;
(*c*) a copy of the Part 2A application (with information that would enable the identification of the person who is the subject of the application removed);
(*d*) if an order is made, a copy of that order (with information that would enable the identification of the person who is the subject of the order removed); and
(*e*) if a Part 2A order is not made, the reason for it not being made.
(3) The report must be provided as soon as practicable after the application is determined and no later than 10 days beginning with the day on which the application is determined.
(4) In this regulation, "the application is determined" when either an order is made pursuant to the application or the application is dismissed or withdrawn.

**7.10352** 11. *Duty on local authorities to report variations or revocations of Part 2A Orders to Public Health England* (1) A local authority must provide a written report to the chief executive of Public Health England, an executive agency of the Department of Health, each time a Part 2A Order made pursuant to a Part 2A application it has made is varied or revoked.
(2) The report must include—
(*a*) the name of the local authority;
(*b*) contact details for the officer of the local authority responsible for the report;
(*c*) a copy of the order varying or revoking the Part 2A order (with information that would enable the identification of the person who is the subject of the order removed); and
(*d*) a copy of the original order (with information that would enable the identification of the

person who is the subject of the order removed).

(3) The report must be provided as soon as practicable after the Part 2A order is varied or revoked and no later than 10 days beginning with the day on which the local authority becomes aware that the Part 2A order has been varied or revoked.

# Environmental Permitting (England and Wales) Regulations 2016

(SI 2016/1154)

## PART 1 GENERAL

**7.10352A** ***1. Citation, commencement, extent and application*** (1) These Regulations may be cited as the Environmental Permitting (England and Wales) Regulations 2016 and come into force 21 days after the day on which these Regulations are made.

(2) These Regulations extend to England and Wales only.

(3) They apply in relation to—

(*a*) England and the sea adjacent to England out as far as the seaward boundary of the territorial sea, and

(*b*) Wales, within the meaning given by section 158 of the Government of Wales Act 2006.

(4) In paragraph (3)(*a*), the sea adjacent to England is so much of the sea adjacent to Great Britain as—

(*a*) is not the sea adjacent to Scotland, and

(*b*) does not form part of Wales.

(5) In paragraph (4)(*a*), the sea adjacent to Scotland has the same meaning as the internal waters and territorial sea of the United Kingdom adjacent to Scotland has by virtue of section 126(2) of the Scotland Act 1998[1].

---

[1] Made by the Secretary of State and the Welsh Ministers in exercise of the powers conferred by ss 2 and 7(9) of, and Sch 1 to, the Pollution Prevention and Control Act 1999; ss 61 and 90 of, and Sch 8 to, the Water Act 2014; and para 1A of Sch 2 to the European Communities Act 1972. Also made by the Secretary of State in exercise of the powers conferred by s 62 of the Regulatory Enforcement and Sanctions Act 2008.

**7.10352B** ***2. Interpretation: general*** (1) In these Regulations—

"the 1980 Act" means the Highways Act 1980;

"the 1990 Act" means the Environmental Protection Act 1990;

"the 1991 Act" means the Water Resources Act 1991;

"the 1993 Act" means the Radioactive Substances Act 1993;

"the 1995 Act" means the Environment Act 1995;

"the 2007 Regulations" means the Environmental Permitting (England and Wales) Regulations 2007;

"the 2010 Regulations" means the Environmental Permitting (England and Wales) Regulations 2010;

"the Agency" means the Environment Agency;

"agricultural waste" means waste from premises used for agriculture within the meaning of the Agriculture Act 1947;

"appropriate agency" means—

(*a*) in relation to England, the Agency, and

(*b*) in relation to Wales, the NRBW,

and references to the "area" of an appropriate agency are to be construed accordingly;

"appropriate authority" means—

(*a*) in relation to England, the Secretary of State, and

(*b*) in relation to Wales, the Welsh Ministers;

"Category A mining waste facility" means a mining waste facility that is classified as Category A under Article 9 of the Mining Waste Directive;

"class", in relation to a regulated facility, is to be construed in accordance with regulation 8;

"coastal waters" has the meaning given in section 104 of the 1991 Act;

"confidential information" means information that is commercially or industrially confidential in relation to any person;

"culvert" has the meaning given in paragraph 3(3) of Part 1 of Schedule 25;

"disposal"—

(*a*) except in relation to a radioactive substances activity, has the meaning given in paragraph 2 of Part 1 of Schedule 9;

(*b*) in relation to a radioactive substances activity, has the meaning given in paragraph 1 of Part 2 of Schedule 23;

"drainage" has the meaning given in paragraph 2(1) of Part 1 of Schedule 25;

"effluent" has the same meaning as in the 1991 Act;

"emission" means—

(*a*) in relation to a Part A installation, the direct or indirect release of substances, vibrations, heat or noise from individual or diffuse sources in the installation into the air, water or land;

(*b*) in relation to a Part B installation, the direct release of substances or heat from individual or diffuse sources in the installation into the air;

(*c*) in relation to a solvent emission activity, the direct or indirect release of substances from individual or diffuse sources in the regulated facility into the air;

(*d*) in relation to Part B mobile plant, the direct release of substances or heat from the mobile plant into the air;

(*e*) in relation to a waste operation, the direct or indirect release of substances, vibrations, heat or noise from individual or diffuse sources related to the operation into the air, water or land;

(*f*) in relation to a mining waste operation, the direct or indirect release of substances, vibrations, heat or noise from individual or diffuse sources related to the operation into the air, water or land;

(*g*) in relation to a radioactive substances activity, the direct or indirect release of radioactive material or radioactive waste;

(*h*) in relation to a small waste incineration plant, the direct or indirect release of substances from individual or diffuse sources in the regulated facility into the air or water;

"enforcement notice" means a notice served under regulation 36;
"enforcement undertaking" has the meaning given in paragraph 1(3) of Schedule 26;
"environmental permit" has the meaning given in regulation 13(1);
"environmental permit condition" means a condition of an environmental permit;
"establishment" has the same meaning as in the Waste Framework Directive;
"excluded flood risk activity" has the meaning given in paragraph 4 of Part 1 of Schedule 25;
"excluded waste operation" means any part of a waste operation not carried on at an installation or by means of Part B mobile plant—

(*a*) that—

(i) requires a marine licence under the Marine and Coastal Access Act 2009, or
(ii) does not require such a licence by virtue of any provision made by or under section 74, 75 or 77 of that Act and does not involve the dismantling of a ship that is waste, or

(*b*) that relates to waste described in regulation 3(2) of the Controlled Waste (England and Wales) Regulations 2012;

"exempt facility" has the meaning given in regulation 5;
"exempt flood risk activity" has the meaning given in regulation 5;
"exempt groundwater activity" has the meaning given in regulation 5;
"exempt waste operation" has the meaning given in regulation 5;
"exempt water discharge activity" has the meaning given in regulation 5;
"exemption authority" has the meaning given in paragraph 2 of Schedule 2;
"exemption registration authority" has the meaning given in paragraph 2 of Schedule 2;
"existing mining waste facility" means a mining waste facility in operation on 1st May 2008;
"extractive waste" means waste within the meaning of Article 2(1) of the Mining Waste Directive, except where it is excluded from the scope of that Directive by Article 2(2)(*a*) and (*b*);
"flood defence structure" has the meaning given in paragraph 2(1) of Part 1 of Schedule 25;
"flood risk activity" has the meaning given in paragraph 3 of Part 1 of Schedule 25;
"flood risk activity emergency works notice" means a notice served under paragraph 7 of Part 1 of Schedule 25;
"flood risk activity notice of intent" means a notice served under paragraph 9(2) of Part 1 of Schedule 25;
"flood risk activity remediation notice" means a notice served under paragraph 8 of Part 1 of Schedule 25;
"groundwater" means all water which is below the surface of the ground in the saturation zone and in direct contact with the ground or subsoil;
"groundwater activity" has the meaning given in paragraph 3 of Schedule 22;
"hazardous substance" has the meaning given in paragraph 4 of Schedule 22;
"hazardous waste", subject to paragraph (7)—

(*a*) in relation to England, has the meaning given in regulation 6 of the Hazardous Waste (England and Wales) Regulations 2005;

(*b*) in relation to Wales, has the meaning given in regulation 6 of the Hazardous Waste (Wales) Regulations 2005;

"highway drain" means a drain which a highway authority or other person is entitled to keep open by virtue of section 100 of the 1980 Act;
"household waste" has the meaning given in section 75(5) of the 1990 Act;
"inland freshwaters" has the meaning given in section 104 of the 1991 Act;
"installation" has the meaning given in paragraph 1(1) of Part 1 of Schedule 1;
"lake or pond" and "waters of any lake or pond" have the same meaning as in section 104 of the 1991 Act;
"landfill" has the meaning given in paragraph 2(1)(*d*) of Schedule 10;
"landfill closure notice" means a closure notice served under paragraph 10 of Schedule 10;
"local authority" has the meaning given in regulation 6;
"main river" has the meaning given in paragraph 2(1) of Part 1 of Schedule 25;
"mining waste facility" has the meaning given in paragraph 2(1) of Schedule 20;

"mining waste facility closure notice" means a closure notice served under paragraph 10 of Schedule 20;
"mining waste operation" has the meaning given in paragraph 2(1) of Schedule 20;
"mobile plant" means either of the following—
(*a*) Part B mobile plant;
(*b*) waste mobile plant;
"mobile radioactive apparatus" has the meaning given in paragraph 1 of Part 2 of Schedule 23;
"the NRBW" means the Natural Resources Body for Wales;
"net rated thermal input" has the meaning given in paragraph 1(1) of Part 1 of Schedule 1;
"non-hazardous waste", subject to paragraph (7), means waste which is not hazardous waste;
"non-tidal main river" has the meaning given in paragraph 2(1) of Part 1 of Schedule 25;
"nuclear site", in relation to a radioactive substances activity, has the meaning given in paragraph 1 of Part 2 of Schedule 23;
"operate a regulated facility" and "operator" have the meaning given in regulation 7;
"Part A(1) activity" means an activity falling within Part A(1) of any Section in Part 2 of Schedule 1;
"Part A(2) activity" means an activity falling within Part A(2) of any Section in Part 2 of Schedule 1;
"Part A installation" means a Part A(1) installation or a Part A(2) installation;
"Part A(1) installation" means an installation where a Part A(1) activity is carried on either alone or in combination with any or all of the following—
(*a*) a Part A(2) activity;
(*b*) a Part B activity;
(*c*) the operation of a small waste incineration plant;
(*d*) a solvent emission activity;
"Part A(2) installation" means an installation where a Part A(2) activity is carried on either alone or in combination with any or all of the following—
(*a*) a Part B activity;
(*b*) the operation of a small waste incineration plant;
(*c*) a solvent emission activity;
"Part B activity" means an activity falling within Part B of any Section in Part 2 of Schedule 1;
"Part B installation" means, subject to Sections 2.2, 5.1 and 6.4 in Part 2 of Schedule 1, an installation, not being a Part A installation, where a Part B activity is carried on either alone or in combination with either or both of the following—
(*a*) the operation of a small waste incineration plant;
(*b*) a solvent emission activity;
"Part B mobile plant" means plant that is designed to move or be moved whether on roads or other land and that is used to carry on a Part B activity;
"pollutant" means any substance liable to cause pollution;
"pollution", in relation to a water discharge activity or groundwater activity, means the direct or indirect introduction, as a result of human activity, of substances or heat into the air, water or land which may—
(*a*) be harmful to human health or the quality of aquatic ecosystems or terrestrial ecosystems directly depending on aquatic ecosystems,
(*b*) result in damage to material property, or
(*c*) impair or interfere with amenities or other legitimate uses of the environment;
"pollution", other than in relation to a water discharge activity or groundwater activity, means any emission as a result of human activity which may—
(*a*) be harmful to human health or the quality of the environment,
(*b*) cause offence to a human sense,
(*c*) result in damage to material property, or
(*d*) impair or interfere with amenities or other legitimate uses of the environment;
"prescribed statutory provision" means—
(*a*) Part 4 of the Marine and Coastal Access Act 2009,
(*b*) section 163 of the 1991 Act,
(*c*) section 165 of the Water Industry Act 1991, or
(*d*) any local statutory provision (within the meaning given in section 221 of the 1991 Act) or statutory order which expressly confers power to discharge effluent into water;
"prohibition notice" means a notice served under paragraph 9 of Schedule 22;
"proposed transferee" means the person to whom an operator or a regulator proposes to transfer an environmental permit in whole or in part;
"public participation provisions" means regulations 26, 29 and 60, and paragraphs 6 and 8 of Part 1 of Schedule 5;
"public register" has the meaning given in regulation 46(1);
"radioactive material" has the meaning given in paragraph 3 of Part 2 of Schedule 23;
"radioactive substances activity" has the meaning given in paragraph 11 of Part 2 of Schedule 23;
"radioactive substances exemption" means an exemption under Part 6 of Schedule 23 from the requirement for an environmental permit in respect of a radioactive substances activity;

"radioactive waste" has the meaning given in paragraph 3 of Part 2 of Schedule 23;
"recovery" has the meaning given in paragraph 2 of Part 1 of Schedule 9;
"register" and "registered", in relation to an exempt facility, have the meanings given in paragraph 1(1) of Schedule 2;
"regulated facility" has the meaning given in regulation 8;
"regulator" means the authority on whom functions are conferred by regulation 32, or by a direction under regulation 33;
"regulator-initiated variation" means the variation of an environmental permit on the initiative of the regulator under regulation 20(1);
"relevant function" has the meaning given in regulation 9;
"relevant territorial waters" has the meaning given in section 104(1) of the 1991 Act;
"remote defence" has the meaning given in paragraph 3(3) of Part 1 of Schedule 25;
"revocation notice" means a notice served under regulation 22(3);
"river control works" has the meaning given in paragraph 3(3) of Part 1 of Schedule 25;
"rule-making authority" means—

(*a*) in relation to a regulated facility for which a local authority is the regulator, the appropriate authority, and

(*b*) in relation to any other regulated facility, the appropriate agency;

"sea defence" has the meaning given in paragraph 3(3) of Part 1 of Schedule 25;
"sewage effluent" has the meaning given in section 221 of the 1991 Act;
"sewer" has the same meaning as in the 1991 Act;
"small waste incineration plant" means a waste incineration plant or waste co-incineration plant with a capacity less than or equal to 10 tonnes per day for hazardous waste or 3 tonnes per hour for non-hazardous waste;
"solvent emission activity" means an activity to which Chapter V of the Industrial Emissions Directive applies;
"standard facility" means a regulated facility described in standard rules published under regulation 26(5);
"stand-alone flood risk activity" means a flood risk activity that is not carried on as part of the operation of a regulated facility of another class;
"stand-alone groundwater activity" means a groundwater activity that is not carried on as part of the operation of a regulated facility of another class;
"stand-alone water discharge activity" means a water discharge activity that is not carried on as part of the operation of a regulated facility of another class;
"suspension notice" means a notice served under regulation 37;
"tidal main river" has the meaning given in paragraph 2(1) of Part 1 of Schedule 25;
"trade effluent" has the meaning given in section 221 of the 1991 Act;
"undertaking", except in relation to a radioactive substances activity, has the same meaning as in the Waste Framework Directive;
"vessel", except in Section 2.2 of Chapter 2 of Part 2 of Schedule 1 and in paragraph 14 of Part 2 of Schedule 23, has the same meaning as in the 1991 Act;
"waste", subject to paragraph (6), and except where otherwise defined—

(*a*) in relation to Chapter 5 of Part 2 of Schedule 1 and Schedules 13 to 15, 17 and 19, means anything that—

(i) is waste within the meaning of Article 3(1) of the Waste Framework Directive, and

(ii) is not excluded from the scope of that Directive by Article 2(1)(*d*) of that Directive;

(*b*) in any other case means anything that—

(i) is waste within the meaning of Article 3(1) of the Waste Framework Directive, and

(ii) is not excluded from the scope of that Directive by Article 2(1), (2) or (3) of that Directive;

"waste battery" and "accumulator" have the meaning given in Article 3(7) of the Batteries Directive, but do not include any waste which is excluded from the scope of that Directive by Article 2(2);
"waste co-incineration plant" means a stationary or mobile technical unit whose main purpose is the generation of energy or production of material products and which uses waste as a regular or additional fuel or in which waste is thermally treated for the purpose of disposal through the incineration by oxidation of waste as well as other thermal treatment processes, such as pyrolysis, gasification or plasma process, if the substances resulting from the treatment are subsequently incinerated;
"waste incineration plant" means a stationary or mobile technical unit and equipment dedicated to the thermal treatment of waste, with or without recovery of the combustion heat generated, through the incineration by oxidation of waste as well as other thermal treatment processes, such as pyrolysis, gasification or plasma process, if the substances resulting from the treatment are subsequently incinerated;
"waste mobile plant" means plant that is—

(*a*) designed to move or be moved whether on roads or other land,

(*b*) used to carry on a waste operation, and

(*c*) not an installation or Part B mobile plant;

"waste oil" means mineral-based lubricating or industrial oil which has become unfit for the use for which it was originally intended and, in particular, used combustion engine oil, gearbox oil, mineral lubricating oil, oil for turbines and hydraulic oil;

"waste operation" means recovery or disposal of waste;

"watercourse" has the meaning given in paragraph 2(1) of Part 1 of Schedule 25;

"water discharge activity" has the meaning given in paragraph 3 of Schedule 21;

"WEEE" has the meaning given in Article 3(1)(e) of the WEEE Directive;

"working day" means a day other than—

(*a*) a Saturday or a Sunday,

(*b*) Good Friday or Christmas Day, or

(*c*) a day which is a bank holiday under the Banking and Financial Dealings Act 1971.

(2) In paragraph (1), "statutory order" means any order, byelaw, scheme or award made under any enactment, including an order or scheme confirmed by Parliament or the National Assembly for Wales, or brought into operation in accordance with special parliamentary procedure or special procedure in the Assembly.

(3) For the purpose of calculating a period of time from one event to another event, that period—

(*a*) starts at the beginning of the day on which the first event occurs, and

(*b*) ends at the end of the day on which the second event occurs.

(4) In these Regulations, a power to give a direction includes a power to vary or revoke it.

(5) Paragraph (6) applies where a person ("A")—

(*a*) carries on a radioactive substances activity described in paragraph 11(2)(*b*) or (*c*) or (4) of Part 2 of Schedule 23 in respect of radioactive waste,

(*b*) is exempt under regulation 12(3) from the requirement for an environmental permit in respect of that activity and that waste ("the relevant exemption"), and

(*c*) the waste ("the applicable radioactive waste") is—

(i) NORM waste (as that term is defined in paragraph 2 of Part 6 of Schedule 23), or

(ii) the waste described in the first, second or sixth row of column 1 of Table 6 in Part 6 of Schedule 23.

(6) Where this paragraph applies, for so long as the relevant exemption applies to A, the applicable radioactive waste must be treated for the purposes of these Regulations as if it were waste other than radioactive waste.

(7) In relation to an activity that falls within Chapter 5 of Part 2 of Schedule 1 or Schedule 13, hazardous waste means waste which displays any of the characteristics listed in Annex III to the Waste Framework Directive.'

**7.10352C** *3.* ***Interpretation: Directives*** In these Regulations—

"the Asbestos Directive" means Council Directive 87/217/EEC on the prevention and reduction of environmental pollution by asbestos;

"the Basic Safety Standards Directive" means Council Directive 96/29/Euratom laying down basic safety standards for the protection of the health of workers and the general public against the dangers arising from ionising radiation;

"the Batteries Directive" means Directive 2006/66/EC of the European Parliament and of the Council on batteries and accumulators and waste batteries and accumulators;

"the End-of-Life Vehicles Directive" means Directive 2000/53/EC of the European Parliament and of the Council on end-of-life vehicles;

"the Energy Efficiency Directive" means Directive 2012/27/EU of the European Parliament and of the Council on energy efficiency;

"the Groundwater Directive" means Directive 2006/118/EC of the European Parliament and of the Council on the protection of groundwater against pollution and deterioration;

"the HASS Directive" means Council Directive 2003/122/Euratom on the control of high-activity sealed radioactive sources and orphan sources;

"the Industrial Emissions Directive" means Directive 2010/75/EU of the European Parliament and of the Council on industrial emissions (integrated pollution prevention and control);

"the Landfill Directive" means Council Directive 1999/31/EC on the landfill of waste, as read with Council Decision 2003/33/EC establishing criteria and procedures for the acceptance of waste at landfills pursuant to Article 16 of, and Annex II to, Directive 1999/31/EC;

"the Mining Waste Directive" means Directive 2006/21/EC of the European Parliament and of the Council on the management of waste from extractive industries;

"PVR I" means European Parliament and Council Directive 94/63/EC on the control of volatile organic compound (VOC) emissions resulting from the storage of petrol and its distribution from terminals to service stations;

"PVR II" means Directive 2009/126/EC of the European Parliament and of the Council on Stage II petrol vapour recovery during refuelling of motor vehicles at service stations;

"the Waste Framework Directive" means Directive 2008/98/EC of the European Parliament and of the Council on waste;

"the Water Framework Directive" means Directive 2000/60/EC of the European Parliament and of the Council establishing a framework for Community action in the field of water policy;

"the WEEE Directive" means Directive 2012/19/EU of the European Parliament and of the Council on waste electrical and electronic equipment (WEEE).

**7.10352D** *4.* ***Exempt facilities and the application of section 33(1)(a) of the 1990 Act***

(1) Schedule 2 (exempt facilities: general) has effect.

(2) Schedule 3 (exempt facilities and waste operations to which section 33(1)(*a*) of the 1990 Act

does not apply: descriptions and conditions) has effect.

(3) Section 33(1)(*a*) of the 1990 Act—

(*a*) does not apply to an operation which—

(i) falls within a description in Part 5 of Schedule 3, and

(ii) meets the conditions specified in that Part for that description, and

(*b*) does not apply to extractive waste at any time before the requirement for an environmental permit under regulation 12 applies in respect of the deposit of that waste.

7.10352E **5. *Interpretation: exempt facilities*** In these Regulations—

"exempt facility" means—

(*a*) an exempt waste operation,

(*b*) an exempt water discharge activity,

(*c*) an exempt groundwater activity, or

(*d*) an exempt flood risk activity;

"exempt flood risk activity" means a flood risk activity that meets the requirements of paragraph 9 of Schedule 2;

"exempt groundwater activity" means—

(*a*) a stand-alone groundwater activity that meets the requirements of—

(i) in relation to Wales only, paragraph 7 of Schedule 2;

(ii) in relation to England only, paragraph 8 of Schedule 2, or

(*b*) a groundwater activity that—

(i) is a groundwater tracer test as defined in paragraph 1 of Part 3 of Schedule 3,

(ii) is also a radioactive substances activity by virtue of the using of radioactive material as a part of that test, and

(iii) meets the requirements of—

(*aa*) in relation to Wales only, paragraph 7 of Schedule 2;

(*bb*) in relation to England only, paragraph 8 of Schedule 2;

"exempt waste operation" means a waste operation—

(*a*) that is not carried on at an installation, and

(*b*) that meets the requirements of paragraph 4(1) of Schedule 2;

"exempt water discharge activity" means a stand-alone water discharge activity that meets the requirements of—

(*a*) in relation to Wales only, paragraph 5 of Schedule 2;

(*b*) in relation to England only, paragraph 6 of Schedule 2.

7.10352F **6. *Interpretation: local authority*** (1) In these Regulations, "local authority" means—

(*a*) in England outside Greater London—

(i) a district council,

(ii) where there is a county council but no district council, the county council, or

(iii) the Council of the Isles of Scilly;

(*b*) in Greater London—

(i) the council of a London borough,

(ii) the Common Council of the City of London,

(iii) the Sub-Treasurer of the Inner Temple, or

(iv) the Under-Treasurer of the Middle Temple;

(*c*) in Wales—

(i) a county council, or

(ii) a county borough council.

(2) Where a port health authority has been constituted for a port health district by an order under section 2 of the Public Health (Control of Disease) Act 1984 that authority is the local authority for the area covered by that district in relation to a Part B installation, a small waste incineration plant or a solvent emission activity.

7.10352G **7. *Interpretation: operate a regulated facility and operator*** In these Regulations—

"operate a regulated facility" means—

(*a*) operate an installation or mobile plant, or

(*b*) carry on a waste operation, mining waste operation, radioactive substances activity, water discharge activity, groundwater activity, small waste incineration plant operation, solvent emission activity or flood risk activity;

"operator", in relation to a regulated facility, means—

(*a*) the person who has control over the operation of the regulated facility,

(*b*) if the regulated facility has not yet been put into operation, the person who will have control over the regulated facility when it is put into operation, or

(*c*) if a regulated facility authorised by an environmental permit ceases to be in operation, the person who holds the environmental permit.

7.10352H **8. *Interpretation: regulated facility and class of regulated facility*** (1) In these Regulations, "regulated facility" means any of the following—

(*a*) an installation;

(*b*) mobile plant;

(*c*) a waste operation;

(*d*) a mining waste operation;

(*e*) a radioactive substances activity;
(*f*) a water discharge activity;
(*g*) a groundwater activity;
(*h*) a small waste incineration plant;
(*i*) a solvent emission activity;
(*j*) a flood risk activity.
(2) But the following are not regulated facilities—
(*a*) an exempt facility;
(*b*) an excluded waste operation;
(*c*) the disposal or recovery of household waste from a domestic property within the curtilage of that property by a person other than an establishment or undertaking;
(*d*) an excluded flood risk activity.
(3) In these Regulations, a reference to a class of regulated facility is a reference to a class in paragraph (1).
(4) A regulated facility of any of the following classes may be carried on as part of the operation of a regulated facility of another class—
(*a*) a waste operation;
(*b*) a mining waste operation;
(*c*) a water discharge activity;
(*d*) a groundwater activity;
(*e*) a small waste incineration plant;
(*f*) a solvent emission activity;
(*g*) a flood risk activity.

**7.10352I** *9.* ***Interpretation: relevant function*** In these Regulations, "relevant function" means any of the following functions—
(*a*) determining an application—
(i) for the grant of an environmental permit under regulation 13(1);
(ii) for the variation of an environmental permit under regulation 20(1);
(iii) for the transfer of an environmental permit in whole or in part under regulation 21(1);
(iv) for the surrender of an environmental permit in whole or in part under regulation 25(2);
(*b*) varying an environmental permit—
(i) on the initiative of the regulator under regulation 20(1);
(ii) in relation to a transfer in whole or in part under regulation 21(1) or (3);
(iii) in relation to a partial revocation under regulation 22(1);
(iv) in relation to a partial surrender under regulation 24(2) or 25(2);
(*c*) revoking an environmental permit in whole or in part under regulation 22(1);
(*d*) exercising the power to serve a notice under Schedule 21 or 25 requiring a person to hold an environmental permit;
(e) exercising the following powers or duty—
(i) any power in relation to standard rules in Chapter 4 of Part 2;
(ii) the duty to vary an environmental permit after revocation of standard rules in regulation 30(3);
(*f*) exercising any of the following powers relating to enforcement—
(i) the power to serve an enforcement notice;
(ii) the power to serve a suspension notice;
(iii) the power to serve a prohibition notice;
(iv) the power to serve a landfill closure notice;
(v) the power to serve a mining waste facility closure notice;
(*g*) exercising the power to serve a flood risk activity emergency works notice, a flood risk activity notice of intent or a flood risk activity remediation notice;
(*h*) exercising the power to take steps under paragraph 9(1) of Part 1 of Schedule 25.

**7.10352J** *10.* ***Giving notices, notifications and directions, and the submission of forms*** (1) In this regulation, "instrument" means a notice, notification, certificate, direction or form under these Regulations.
(2) An instrument must be in writing.
(3) An instrument may be served on or given to a person by—
(*a*) personal delivery,
(*b*) leaving it at the person's proper address, or
(*c*) sending it by post or electronic means to the person's proper address.
(4) In the case of a body corporate, an instrument may be served on or given to a director of that body or the secretary or clerk.
(5) In the case of a partnership, an instrument may be served on or given to a partner or a person having control or management of the partnership business.
(6) In paragraph (3), "proper address" means—
(*a*) in the case of a body corporate, a director of the body or the secretary or clerk—
(i) the registered or principal office of that body, or
(ii) the email address of the director, secretary or clerk;

(*b*) in the case of a partnership or a partner or person having control or management of the partnership business—
(i) the principal office of the partnership, or
(ii) the email address of a partner or a person having that control or management;
(*c*) in any other case, a person's last known address, which includes an email address.
(7) For the purposes of paragraph (6), the principal office of a company registered outside the United Kingdom or of a partnership established outside the United Kingdom is their principal office in the United Kingdom.
(8) A form provided by the regulator which specifies an electronic address for submission may be submitted electronically to that address.
(9) A form provided by the regulator for completion and submission through a website may be submitted through that site.

## PART 2 ENVIRONMENTAL PERMITS

### CHAPTER 1 APPLICATION TO THE CROWN AND REQUIREMENT FOR AN ENVIRONMENTAL PERMIT

**7.10352K** *12.* ***Requirement for an environmental permit*** (1) A person must not, except under and to the extent authorised by an environmental permit—
(*a*) operate a regulated facility, or
(*b*) cause or knowingly permit a water discharge activity or groundwater activity.
(2) Paragraph (1)(*b*) does not apply if the water discharge activity or groundwater activity is an exempt facility.
(3) In respect of a radioactive substances activity, paragraph (1) does not apply to a person to whom a radioactive substances exemption applies for that activity.
(4) Paragraph (5) applies to a person ("A") who—
(*a*) receives radioactive waste from another person ("B") for the purposes of A disposing of that waste, and
(*b*) subsequently disposes of that waste.
(5) Where this paragraph applies, A does not require an environmental permit—
(*a*) for the receipt of waste from B, where B holds an environmental permit which allows B to dispose of the waste to A, or
(*b*) for the subsequent disposal of that waste by A, where the waste is disposed of in accordance with the permit held by B.

## PART 4 ENFORCEMENT AND OFFENCES

**7.10352L** *36.* ***Enforcement notices*** (1) If the regulator considers that an operator has contravened, is contravening, or is likely to contravene an environmental permit condition, the regulator may serve a notice on the operator.
(2) The notice must—
(*a*) state the regulator's view under paragraph (1),
(*b*) specify the matters constituting the contravention or making a contravention likely,
(*c*) specify the steps that must be taken to remedy the contravention or to ensure that the likely contravention does not occur, and
(*d*) specify the period within which those steps must be taken.
(3) Steps that may be specified in the notice include steps—
(*a*) to make the operation of a regulated facility comply with the environmental permit conditions, and
(*b*) to remedy the environmental effects caused by the contravention.
(4) In paragraph (3)(*b*) "environmental effects" means—
(*a*) in relation to a flood risk activity—
(i) flooding or risk of flooding;
(ii) detrimental impact on drainage or risk of detrimental impact on drainage;
(iii) harm to the environment or risk of harm to the environment;
(*b*) in relation to any other class of regulated facility, the effects of pollution.
(5) In the case of a regulated facility to which Schedule 7, 13 or 14 applies, if the regulator considers that an incident or accident significantly affecting the environment has occurred as the result of the operation of that regulated facility, the regulator may serve a notice on the operator of that facility.
(6) A notice served under paragraph (5) must—
(*a*) specify the measures necessary to limit the environmental consequences of the incident or accident, and
(*b*) specify the measures necessary to prevent further incidents or accidents.
(7) The regulator may withdraw a notice under this regulation at any time by further notice served on the operator.

**7.10352K** *37.* ***Suspension notices*** (1) The regulator may suspend an environmental permit by serving a notice (a "suspension notice") on the operator under this regulation.
(2) If the regulator considers that the operation of a regulated facility under an environmental permit involves a risk of serious pollution or, in the case of a flood risk activity, a risk specified in paragraph (3), it may serve a suspension notice on the operator.
(3) The following are risks specified for the purposes of paragraph (2)—
(*a*) risk of serious flooding;

(*b*) risk of serious detrimental impact on drainage;
(*c*) risk of serious harm to the environment.
(4) Paragraph (2) applies whether or not the manner of operating the regulated facility which involves the risk is subject to or contravenes an environmental permit condition.
(5) If the regulator considers that the manner of operating a regulated facility contravenes an environmental permit condition, and that such contravention involves a risk of pollution or, in the case of a flood risk activity, a risk specified in paragraph (6), it may serve a suspension notice on the operator.
(6) The following are risks specified for the purposes of paragraph (5)—
(*a*) risk of flooding;
(*b*) risk of detrimental impact on drainage;
(*c*) risk of harm to the environment.
(7) A suspension notice served for the purpose of paragraph (2) or (5) must—
(*a*) specify—
(i) the risk mentioned in paragraph (2) or (5),
(ii) the steps that must be taken to remove that risk,
(iii) in a case where paragraph (5) applies, the matters constituting the contravention mentioned in that paragraph,
(iv) in a case where paragraph (5) applies, the steps that must be taken to remedy that contravention, and
(v) the period within which the steps mentioned in paragraph (ii) or (iv) must be taken,
(*b*) state that the environmental permit ceases to have effect to the extent specified in the notice until the notice is withdrawn, and
(*c*) if the environmental permit continues to authorise the operation of a regulated facility, state any steps (in addition to those already required to be taken by the environmental permit conditions) that are to be taken when operating that regulated facility.
(8) The regulator may suspend an environmental permit under regulation 66(5) by serving a suspension notice on the operator.
(9) A suspension notice served for the purpose of paragraph (8) must—
(*a*) specify the reason for the suspension,
(*b*) state the sum payable by the operator and the period within which it is to be paid, and
(*c*) state that the environmental permit ceases to have effect to the extent specified in the notice until the notice is withdrawn.
(10) If a suspension notice is served, the environmental permit ceases to have effect to the extent stated in the notice.
(11) Where a suspension notice has the effect of preventing waste of a specified description being accepted at a regulated facility, the notice may require the operator of that facility to display appropriate signs at such places as may be specified in the notice, informing the public that no further waste of a specified description may be accepted at that facility.
(12) The regulator—
(*a*) may withdraw a suspension notice at any time by further notice served on the operator, and
(*b*) must withdraw a notice when satisfied that the steps specified in it have been taken.

**7.10352L** ***38. Offences*** (1) It is an offence for a person to—
(*a*) contravene regulation 12(1), or
(*b*) knowingly cause or knowingly permit the contravention of regulation 12(1)(a).
(2) It is an offence for a person to fail to comply with or to contravene an environmental permit condition.
(3) It is an offence for a person to fail to comply with the requirements of an enforcement notice or of a prohibition notice, suspension notice, landfill closure notice, mining waste facility closure notice, flood risk activity emergency works notice or flood risk activity remediation notice.
(4) It is an offence for a person—
(*a*) to fail to comply with a notice under regulation 61(1) requiring the provision of information, without reasonable excuse;
(*b*) to make a statement which the person knows to be false or misleading in a material particular, or recklessly to make a statement which is false or misleading in a material particular, where the statement is made—
(i) in purported compliance with a requirement to provide information imposed by or under a provision of these Regulations,
(ii) for the purpose of obtaining the grant of an environmental permit to any person, or the variation, transfer in whole or in part, or surrender in whole or in part of an environmental permit, or
(iii) for the purpose of obtaining, renewing or amending the registration of an exempt facility;
(c) intentionally to make a false entry in a record required to be kept under an environmental permit condition;
(d) with intent to deceive—
(i) to forge or use a document issued or authorised to be issued or required for any purpose under an environmental permit condition, or
(ii) to make or have in the person's possession a document so closely resembling such a document as to be likely to deceive.
(5) It is an offence for an establishment or undertaking to—

(*a*) fail to comply with paragraph 17(3) or (4) of Schedule 2, or
(*b*) intentionally make a false entry in a record required to be kept under that paragraph.

(6) If an offence committed by a person under this regulation is due to the act or default of some other person, that other person is also guilty of the offence and liable to be proceeded against and punished accordingly, whether or not proceedings for the offence are taken against the first-mentioned person.

**7.10352M** *39.* ***Penalties and enforcement undertakings*** (1) Subject to paragraph (2), a person guilty of an offence under regulation 38(1), (2) or (3) is liable—
(*a*) on summary conviction to a fine or imprisonment for a term not exceeding 12 months, or to both;
(*b*) on conviction on indictment to a fine or imprisonment for a term not exceeding 5 years, or to both.

(2) A person guilty of offence under regulation 38(1), (2) or (3) in respect of a flood risk activity is liable—
(*a*) on summary conviction to a fine or imprisonment for a term not exceeding 12 months, or to both;
(*b*) on conviction on indictment to a fine or imprisonment for a term not exceeding 2 years, or both.

(3) In relation to an offence committed before the commencement of section 154(1) of the Criminal Justice Act 2003, paragraphs (1)(*a*) and (2)(*a*) have effect as if for "12 months" there were substituted "6 months".

(4) A person guilty of an offence under regulation 38(4) is liable—
(*a*) on summary conviction to a fine;
(*b*) on conviction on indictment to a fine or imprisonment for a term not exceeding 2 years, or to both.

(5) An establishment or undertaking guilty of an offence under regulation 38(5) is liable on summary conviction to a fine not exceeding level 2 on the standard scale.

(6) Schedule 26 (enforcement undertakings) has effect.

**7.10352N** *40.* ***Defences*** (1) It is a defence for a person charged with an offence under regulation 38(1), (2) or (3) to prove that the acts alleged to constitute the contravention were done in an emergency in order to avoid danger to human health in a case where—
(*a*) the person took all such steps as were reasonably practicable in the circumstances for minimising pollution, and
(*b*) particulars of the acts were furnished to the regulator as soon as reasonably practicable after they were done.

(2) A person who knowingly permits a water discharge activity or groundwater activity where the discharge is water from an abandoned mine or an abandoned part of a mine is not guilty of an offence under regulation 38(1) unless—
(*a*) the person is the owner or former operator of the mine or that part of it, and
(*b*) the mine or the part of the mine was abandoned after 31st December 1999.

(3) In paragraph (2), "abandoned", in relation to a mine, and "mine" have the meaning given in section 91A of the 1991 Act.

**7.10352O** *41.* ***Offences by bodies corporate*** (1) If an offence committed under these Regulations by a body corporate is proved—
(*a*) to have been committed with the consent or connivance of an officer, or
(*b*) to be attributable to any neglect on the part of an officer,

the officer as well as the body corporate is guilty of the offence and liable to be proceeded against and punished accordingly.

(2) If the affairs of a body corporate are managed by its members, paragraph (1) applies in relation to the acts and defaults of a member in connection with the member's functions of management as if the member were a director of the body.

(3) In paragraph (1), "officer", in relation to a body corporate, means a director, member of the committee of management, chief executive, manager, secretary or other similar officer of the body, or a person purporting to act in any such capacity.

**7.10352P** *42.* ***Enforcement by the High Court*** The regulator may take proceedings in the High Court for the purpose of securing compliance with an enforcement notice, suspension notice, prohibition notice, landfill closure notice, mining waste facility closure notice, flood risk activity emergency works notice or flood risk activity remediation notice (whether or not it has taken other steps for that purpose).

**7.10352Q** *43.* ***Admissibility of evidence*** Where, pursuant to an environmental permit granted by a local authority, an entry is required to be made in any record as to the observance of a condition of the environmental permit and the entry has not been made, that fact is admissible as evidence that the condition has not been observed.

**7.10352R** *44.* ***Power of court to order cause of offence to be remedied*** (1) This regulation applies where a person is convicted of an offence under regulation 38(1), (2) or (3) in respect of a matter which appears to the court to be a matter which it is in the person's power to remedy.

(2) In addition to or instead of a punishment imposed under regulation 39, the court may order the person to take such steps for remedying the matter within such period as may be specified in the order.

(3) The period may be extended, or further extended, by order of the court on an application

made before the end of the period or the extended period, as the case may be.

(4) If a person is ordered to remedy a matter, that person is not liable under regulation 38 in respect of that matter during the period or the extended period.

## PART 6 POWERS AND FUNCTIONS OF THE REGULATOR AND THE APPROPRIATE AUTHORITY

**7.10352S** ***61. Power to require the provision of information*** (1) For the purposes of discharging its functions under these Regulations, an appropriate authority, regulator, exemption registration authority or exemption authority, by notice served on any person, may require that person to provide such information in such form and within such period as is specified in the notice.

(2) A notice under paragraph (1) may require a person to provide any information on emissions where that requirement is reasonable, including the provision of information—

(*a*) not in the person's possession, and

(*b*) which would not usually come into the person's possession.

(3) For the purposes of this regulation the discharge by the appropriate authority of—

(*a*) an obligation of the United Kingdom under the EU Treaties, or

(*b*) an international obligation of the United Kingdom,

must be treated as a function of the authority under these Regulations.

(4) For the purposes of this regulation the compilation of an inventory of emissions (whether or not from a regulated facility) must be treated as a function of the regulator under these Regulations.

## PART 7 MISCELLANEOUS PROVISIONS

### CHAPTER 3 REPEAL, REVOCATIONS, SAVING AND AMENDMENTS

Text is not reproduced

### CHAPTER 4 TRANSITIONAL PROVISIONS

Text is not reproduced

### SCHEDULE 2
Exempt Facilities: General — Regulation 4

Text is not reproduced

### SCHEDULE 3
Exempt Facilities and Waste Operations to which section 33(1)(a) of the 1990 Act Does not Apply: Descriptions and Conditions — Regulation 4

Text is not reproduced

### SCHEDULE 7
Part a Installations: Industrial Emissions Directive — Regulation 35(1)

Text is not reproduced

### SCHEDULE 9
Waste Operations and Materials Facilities — Regulation 35(1)

Text is not reproduced

### SCHEDULE 11
Waste Motor Vehicles — Regulation 35(1)

Text is not reproduced

### SCHEDULE 12
Waste Electrical and Electronic Equipment — Regulation 35(1)

Text is not reproduced

### SCHEDULE 13
Waste Incineration: Industrial Emissions Directive — Regulation 35(1)

Text is not reproduced

### SCHEDULE 14
Solvent Emission Activities — Regulation 35(1)

Text is not reproduced

### SCHEDULE 15
Large Combustion Plants: Industrial Emissions Directive — Regulation 35(1)

Text is not reproduced

### SCHEDULE 16
Asbestos — Regulation 35(1)

Text is not reproduced

### SCHEDULE 17
Titanium Dioxide: Industrial Emissions Directive — Regulation 35(1)

Text is not reproduced

### SCHEDULE 18
Petrol Vapour Recovery — Regulation 35(1)

Text is not reproduced

SCHEDULE 19
Waste Batteries and Accumulators
Regulation 35(1)

Text is not reproduced

SCHEDULE 20
Mining Waste Operations
Regulation 35(1)

Text is not reproduced

SCHEDULE 21
Water Discharge Activities
Regulation 35(1)

Text is not reproduced

SCHEDULE 22
Groundwater Activities
Regulation 35(1)

Text is not reproduced

SCHEDULE 23
Radioactive Substances Activities
Regulation 35(1)

Text is not reproduced

SCHEDULE 26
Enforcement Undertakings
Regulation 39(6)

Text is not reproduced

# PUBLIC MEETING AND PUBLIC ORDER

**Contents**



## European Communities Act 1972: regulations

7.10353 Within the scope of the title Public Meeting and Public Order would logically fall the subject matter of the following regulations made under the very wide enabling power provided in section 2(2) of the European Communities Act 1972.

Electronic Commerce Directive (Racial and Religious Hatred Act 2006) Regulations 2010, SI 2010/894

## Licensing Act 1872

(35 & 36 Vict c 94)

*Offences against Public Order*

7.10354 12. **Penalty on persons found drunk**[1] Every person[2] found drunk in any highway[3] or other public place[4], whether a building or not, or on any licensed premises[5], shall be liable to a penalty not exceeding **level 1** on the standard scale[6].

Every person who is drunk[7] while in charge on any highway or other public place[4] of any carriage[8], horse, cattle[9], or steam engine, or who is drunk when in possession of any loaded firearms[10], may be apprehended[11], and shall be liable to a penalty not exceeding **level 1** on the standard scale or in the discretion of the court to imprisonment . . . for any term not exceeding **one month***.

[Licensing Act 1872, s 12, as amended by the Statute Law Revision Act 1953, the Penalties for Drunkenness Act 1962, s 1, the Criminal Justice Act 1967, Sch 7, the Criminal Law Act 1977, Sch 6, the Criminal Justice Act 1982, ss 38 and 46 and the Serious Organised Crime and Police Act 2005, Schs 7 and 17.]

---

* **Words substituted by the Criminal Justice Act 2003, Sch 26 from a date to be appointed.**

1 The Criminal Justice Act 1967, s 91, this title, post, has effect in place of this section where a person is guilty whilst drunk of disorderly behaviour ( Criminal Justice Act 1967, s 91(2)). Note also the power of a constable on arresting a drunken offender to take him to a treatment centre (Criminal Justice Act 1972, s 34 in Part III: Sentencing, ante).

2 One justice may deal with the offence (Criminal Justice Administration Act 1914, s 38), but may not in any case impose a greater penalty than £1 (Magistrates' Courts Act 1980, s 121, in Part I: Magistrates' Courts Procedure, ante). As it is not strictly necessary for the exact language of the statute to be used in the charge sheet if the words used are sufficient to embody the elements of the offence, a person may be rightly convicted under this section though the word "found" be omitted from the charge sheet. "Found" means ascertained to be (*Thomas v Powell* (1893) 57 JP 329; *Moran v Jones* (1911) 75 JP 411; *Martin v McIntyre* 1910 47 SLR 645, 74 JP Jo 482; *Davis v Sly* (1910) 26 TLR 460; *R v Judge Radcliffe, ex p Oxfordshire County Council* [1915] 3 KB 418, 79 JP 540; *R v Goodwin* [1944] KB 518, [1944] 1 All ER 506, 108 JP 159). A person is to be regarded as drunk if he had consumed intoxicating liquor to the extent that he had lost the power of self-control; if he had taken drugs as well, the justices must be satisfied that he would in any event have been deprived of his self-control as a result of having consumed the intoxicating liquor, before convicting under this provision (*Lanham v Rickwood* (1984) 148 JP 737).

3 An offence is committed if a person is in a highway and, while there, is ascertained or perceived to be drunk; the fact that his presence there was momentary or involuntary is immaterial (*Winzar v Chief Constable of Kent* [1983] LS Gaz R 1205).

4 "Public place" includes any place to which the public have access whether on payment or otherwise (Licensing Act 1902, s 8, post). A man in a tramcar was held to be in the street (*Martin v McIntyre* 1910 47 SLR 645, 74 JP Jo 482). A hackney carriage in the street was held a "public place" under a repealed statute (*R v Weller* (1894) 58 JP 286).

5 The expression "licensed premises" means premises in respect of which a premises licence has effect (Licensing Act 2003, s 193).

It was held that a publican could not be convicted of being found drunk on his own licensed premises after the house was closed, it being then his private place (*Lester v Torrens* (1877) 2 QBD 403, 41 JP 821). And the same applies to a lodger (*Young v Gentle* [1915] 2 KB 661, 79 JP 347). But a person who enters the house to use it as licensed premises, and not as a lodger or inmate, found drunk in the house after that time may be convicted (*R v Pelly* [1897] 2 QB 33, 61 JP 373). A resident on licensed premises who was found drunk on the premises at an hour when they were lawfully open for the sale of non-intoxicants and might have been open for the sale of intoxicants but for the restrictions imposed by the Regulations of the Central Control Board (Liquor Traffic), was held liable to conviction (*Lewis v Dodd* [1919] 1 KB 1, 83 JP 25). And where the front door was wide open, and a non-resident found therein, a conviction was ordered (*Evans v Fletcher* (1926) 90 JP 157). We think that residents in licensed premises cannot be convicted of being drunk thereon during the period when intoxicants cannot legally be sold if the licensed premises are actually closed to the public. Whether actually closed or not, the licensee's liability to be convicted for permitting drunkenness is the same (*Thompson v McKenzie* [1908] 1 KB 905, 72 JP 150). A part of the premises which has been let for a private party does not thereby cease to be "licensed premises" (*Stevens v Dickson* [1952] 2 All ER 246, 116 JP 439).

[6] A person found drunk in a highway or public place is liable to arrest if he appears to be incapable of taking care of himself (Licensing Act 1902, s 1, post).

[7] There is no varying standard of drunkenness depending on the occupation carried on by the accused (*R v Presdee* (1927) 20 Cr App Rep 95).

[8] A motor vehicle or trailer is a carriage (Road Traffic Act 1988, s 191, in PART IV: ROAD TRAFFIC, ante). A person liable to be charged with an offence of driving or being in charge of a motor vehicle when under the influence of drink or drugs, shall not be liable to be charged under this section (Road Traffic Act 1988, s 5, in PART IV: ROAD TRAFFIC, post). A bicycle, whether ridden or pushed, is a carriage within the meaning of this section (*Corkery v Carpenter* [1951] 1 KB 102, [1950] 2 All ER 745, 114 JP 481).

[9] Including pigs and sheep (*Child v Hearn* (1874) LR 9 Exch 176).

[10] The Act does not define "firearms"; adopting the ordinary modern meaning, the term would include an airgun (*Seamark v Prouse* [1980] 3 All ER 26, 70 Cr App Rep 236).

[11] For powers of arrest see the Police and Criminal Evidence Act 1984, s 25 in PART I: MAGISTRATES' COURTS, PROCEDURE, ante.

# Inebriates Act 1898[1]

(61 & 62 Vict c 60)

FIRST SCHEDULE Sections 2, 24

*(As amended by the Licensing Act 1902, s 2, the Criminal Justice Act 1967, Sch 7, the Statute Law (Repeals) Act 1976, Sch 1 and the Licensing Act 2003, Schs 6 and 7.)*

7.10355

| Description of Offence | Statute enacting Offence |
|---|---|
| Being found drunk in a highway or other public place, whether a building or not, or on licensed premises. | Licensing Act 1872 (35 & 36 Vict c 94), s 12 |
| Being guilty while drunk of riotous or disorderly behaviour in a highway or other public place, whether a building or not. | |
| Being drunk while in charge, on any highway or other public place, of any carriage, horse, cattle, or steam-engine. | |
| Being drunk when in possession of any loaded firearms. | |
| Being intoxicated while driving a hackney carriage. | Town Police Clauses Act 1847 (10 & 11 Vict c 89), s 61. |
| Being drunk during employment as a driver of a hackney carriage, or as a driver or conductor of a stage carriage in the Metropolitan Police District. | London Hackney Carriages Act 1843 (6 & 7 Vict c 86), s 28. |
| Being drunk and persisting, after being refused admission on that account, in attempting to enter a passenger steamer. | Merchant Shipping Act 1894 (57 & 58 Vict c 60), s 287. |
| Being drunk on board a passenger steamer, and refusing to leave such steamer when requested. | |
| Failing to leave licensed premises, etc when asked to do so. | Licensing Act 2003, s 143. |
| Entering, or attempting to enter, licensed premises, etc when asked not to do so. | |

[1] With the exception of s 30 (Short title) and the First Schedule, the whole of this Act has been repealed. Section 30 as amended by the Statute Law (Repeals) Act 1976, Sch 2, provides that the First Schedule shall have effect for the purposes of the Licensing Act 1902, s 6, post.

# Licensing Act 1902

(2 Edw 7 c 28)

## PART I

*Amendment of Law as to Drunkenness*

7.10356 **1. Apprehension of person found drunk and incapable in public place**[1] If a person is found drunk in any highway or other public place[2], whether a building or not, or on any licensed premises, and appears to be incapable of taking care of himself, he may be dealt with according to law.

[Licensing Act 1902, s 1 as amended by the Serious Organised Crime and Police Act 2005, Schs 7 and 17.]

[1] This section is complementary to s 12 of the Licensing Act 1872, ante. Where a constable has power to arrest a person under this section, the constable may take him to a treatment centre for alcoholics; see the Criminal Justice Act 1972, s 34, in PART III: SENTENCING, ante.

[2] For meaning of "public place", see s 8, post.

7.10357 **2. Penalty for being drunk while in charge of child** (1) If any person is found drunk in any highway or other public place[1], whether a building or not, or on any licensed premises, while having the charge of a child apparently under the age of seven years, he shall, if the child is under that age, be liable, on summary conviction, to a fine not exceeding **level 2** on the standard scale, or to imprisonment, for any period not exceeding **one month***.

(2) If the child appears to the court to be under the age of seven, the child shall, for the purposes of this section, be deemed to be under that age unless the contrary is proved.

(3) The offence under this section shall be included in the list of offences mentioned in the First Schedule to the Inebriates Act, 1898[2].

[Licensing Act 1902, s 2 as amended by the Penalties for Drunkenness Act 1962, s 1, the Statute Law (Repeals) Act 1976, Sch 1, the Criminal Law Act 1977, Sch 6, the Criminal Justice Act 1982, s 46 and the Serious Organised Crime and Police Act 2005, Schs 7 and 17.]

---

* **Words substituted by the Criminal Justice Act 2003, Sch 26 from a date to be appointed.**

[1] For meaning of "public place", see s 8, post.

[2] See this title, ante.

7.10358 **6. Prohibition of sale of liquor to persons declared to be habitual drunkards** (1) Where a person is convicted of an offence mentioned in the First Schedule to the Inebriates Act 1898[1] and such person has during the period of twelve months immediately preceding the date of the offence, been convicted on three occasions of an offence mentioned in the said Schedule, the court may order that notice of the conviction, with such particulars as may be prescribed[2] by the Secretary of State, be sent to the local policing body for the police area in which the court is situate.

(2) Subsections (2A) to (2C) apply where a court, in pursuance of this Act, orders notice of a conviction to be sent to a local policing body.

(2A) The court shall inform[3] the convicted person that the notice is to be sent to a local policing body.

(2B) The convicted person commits an offence if, within the three year period, he buys[4] or obtains, or attempts to buy or obtain, alcohol on relevant premises.

(2C) A person to whom subsection (2D) applies commits an offence if, within the three year period, he knowingly—

- (*a*) sells, supplies or distributes alcohol on relevant premises, or
- (*b*) allows the sale, supply or distribution of alcohol on relevant premises,

to, or for consumption by, the convicted person.

(2D) This subsection applies—

- (*a*) to any person who works at the premises in a capacity, whether paid or unpaid, which gives him authority to sell, supply or distribute the alcohol concerned,
- (*b*) in the case of licensed premises, to—
  - (i) the holder of a premises licence which authorises the sale or supply of alcohol, and
  - (ii) the designated premises supervisor (if any) under such a licence,
- (*c*) in the case of premises in respect of which a club premises certificate authorising the sale or supply of alcohol has effect, to any member or officer of the club which holds the certificate who at the time the sale, supply or distribution takes place is present on the premises in a capacity which enables him to prevent it, and
- (*d*) in the case of premises which may be used for a permitted temporary activity by virtue of Part 5 of the Licensing Act 2003, the premises user in respect of a temporary event notice authorising the sale or supply of alcohol.

(2E) A person guilty of an offence under this section is liable on summary conviction—

- (*a*) in the case of an offence under subsection (2B), to a fine not exceeding level 1 on the standard scale, and
- (*b*) in the case of an offence under subsection (2C), to a fine not exceeding level 2 on the standard scale.

(3) Regulations shall be made by the local policing body for the purpose of securing the giving of information to persons to whom subsection (4) applies, of orders made under this section, and for assisting in the identification of the convicted persons.

(4) This subsection applies to—

- (*a*) the holder of a premises licence which authorises the sale or supply of alcohol,
- (*b*) the designated premises supervisor (if any) under such a licence,
- (*c*) the holder of a club premises certificate authorising the sale or supply of alcohol, and
- (*d*) the premises user in relation to a temporary event notice authorising the sale or supply or alcohol.

(5) In this section—

"alcohol", "club premises certificate", "designated premises supervisor", "licensed premises", "permitted temporary activity", "premises licence", "premises user" and "temporary event notice" have the same meaning as in the Licensing Act 2003,

"relevant premises" means premises which are relevant premises within the meaning of section 159 of that Act and on which alcohol may be lawfully sold or supplied, and "the three year period", in relation to the convicted person, means the period of three years beginning with the day of the conviction."

[Licensing Act 1902, s 6 as amended by the Statute Law (Repeals) Act 1976, Sch 2, the Criminal Law Act 1977, s 31, the Criminal Justice Act 1982, ss 35 and 46, the Police and Magistrates' Courts Act 1994, Sch 9, the Licensing Act 2003, Sch 6 and the Police Reform and Social Responsibility Act 2011, Sch 16.]

1 See this title, ante.

2 These have been prescribed by SR & O 1902/831 amended by SI 2001/1098 and are as follows: date of conviction, date of order directing notice to police authority, name of person convicted, age, address of person convicted, place of business or where employed, offence of which convicted, sentence, licensed premises or clubs usually frequented (if known).

3 If the defendant is not present then presumably he should be sent a notice by registered post. The order of the court should be recorded in the court register.

4 Under this section prior to its amendment by the Licensing Act 2003, it was held that a habitual drunkard placed on the "black list" who sends another person to purchase intoxicating liquor for him is liable to be convicted under this section (*Darbyshire v Downes* (1905) 40 L Jo 299).

7.10359 **8. Interpretation of "public place"** For the purposes of section twelve of the Licensing Act, 1872, and of sections one and two of this Act, the expression "public place" shall include any place to which the public have access, whether on payment or otherwise[1].

[Licensing Act 1902, s 8.]

1 A man in a tramcar was held to be in the street (*Martin v McIntyre* 1910 47 SLR 645, 74 JP Jo 482). A hackney carriage in the street was held a "public place" under a repealed statute (*R v Weller* (1894) 58 JP 286).

7.10360 **8A. Interpretation of "licensed premises"** For those purposes, "licensed premises" includes—

(*a*) any licensed premises within the meaning of section 193 of the Licensing Act 2003, and

(*b*) any premises which may be used for a permitted temporary activity by virtue of Part 5 of that Act.

[Licensing Act 1902, s 8A as inserted by the Licensing Act 2003, Sch 6.]

7.10361 **34. Short title, construction and extent** (1) This Act may be cited as the Licensing Act, 1902, and may be cited, and shall be construed, as one with the Licensing Acts, 1828 to 1886.

(2) This Act shall not extend to Scotland or Ireland.

(3) *Repealed.*

[Licensing Act 1902, s 34 as amended by the Statute Law Revision Act 1927.]

## Public Meeting Act 1908

(8 Edw 7 c 66)

7.10362 **1. Breaking up public meeting** (1) Any person who at a lawful[1] public meeting acts in a disorderly manner for the purpose of preventing the transaction of the business for which the meeting was called together shall be guilty of an offence and shall on summary conviction be liable to imprisonment for a term not exceeding six months or to a fine not exceeding £1,000 or to both.

(2) Any person who incites others to commit an offence under this section shall be guilty of a like offence[2].

(3) If any constable reasonably suspects any person of committing an offence under the foregoing provisions of this section, he may, if requested so to do by the chairman of the meeting, require that person to declare to him immediately his name and address, and if that person refuses or fails so to declare his name and address or gives a false name and address he shall be guilty of an offence[3] under this subsection and liable on summary conviction thereof to a fine not exceeding **level 1** on the standard scale.

(4) This section does not apply as respects meetings to which section 97 of the Representation of the People Act 1983 applies.

[Public Meeting Act 1908, s 1 as amended by the Public Order Act 1936, s 6, the Representation of the People Act 1949, the Public Order Act 1963, s 1(2), the Criminal Law Act 1977, s 31, the Criminal Justice Act 1982, s 46, the Representation of the People Act 1983, Sch 8 and the Police and Criminal Evidence Act 1984, Sch 7.]

1 If they reasonably apprehend a breach of the peace, the police have a right to enter private premises at which the public have been invited to attend (*Thomas v Sawkins* [1935] 2 KB 249, [1935] All ER Rep 655, 99 JP 295). As to removal of a disorderly person (cf *Marshall v Tinnelly* (1937) 81 Sol Jo 902). A public meeting on the highway is not necessarily unlawful (*Burden v Rigler* [1911] 1 KB 337, 75 JP 36). The test is whether there will be a nuisance or danger of breach of the peace (*R v Prebble* (1858) 1 F & F 325). In *Beatty v Gillbanks* (1882) 9 QBD 308, 46 JP 789), where the defendant was charged with an unlawful assembly, Field, J, said there was no authority for the proposition that a man may be punished for acting lawfully if he knows that his so doing may induce another man to act unlawfully. In *Duncan v Jones* [1936] 1 KB 218, 99 JP 399, it was held that it is the duty of the police to prevent any action likely to result in a breach of the peace by any one, and that refusing to desist was obstructing the police in the execution of their duty. Cf *Great Central Rly Co v Bates* [1921] 3 KB 578, and *Davis v Lisle* [1936] 2 KB 434, [1936] 2 All ER 213, 100 JP 280.

For admission of the public to meetings of public bodies, see the Public Bodies (Admission to Meetings) Act 1960 and to meetings of local authorities, see the Local Government Act 1972, s 100A. Both provisions are without prejudice to any power of exclusion to suppress or prevent disorderly conduct or other misbehaviour at a meeting: 1960 Act, s 1(8) and 1972 Act, s 100A(8). The power to exclude is at common law, see *R v Brent Health Authority, ex p Francis* [1985] QB 869, [1985] 1 All ER 74, [1984] 3 WLR 1317 and *Laporte v Comr of Police of the Metropolis* [2014] EWHC 3574 (QB), [2015] 3 All ER 438 (QB). The following propositions are derived from the authorities and basic principles:

(1) Those running a public meeting, including local authorities, have a common law power (or perhaps duty in certain circumstances) to exclude attendees whose disorderly conduct or other misbehaviour disrupts or threatens to disrupt the business of the meeting.

(2) This power extends to the exclusion of all members of the general public in those cases where the attendance of the public as a whole is liable to give rise to disorderly conduct or other misbehaviour which would disrupt or threatens to disrupt the business of the meeting.
(3) The power to exclude, particularly where it is directed at all or most members of the public, will and must be exercised particularly sparingly and only in the absence of a reasonably viable alternative but, in appropriate cases, can be used either in advance of the meeting (as in Brent) or on the occasion of the meeting itself.
(4) The power may be exercised by the deployment of such force (if any) as may be necessary and proportionate to achieve and maintain the exclusion of those against whom it is directed.
(5) It is not necessary that a breach of the peace should have occurred or be imminent to justify laying hands on a trespasser; although in any given case passive resistance may often become active and result in a subsequent breach of the peace.
(6) If the police are called upon to assist in the exercise of the common law power they are acting lawfully in the use of force so long as such force is necessary and not excessive. per Turner J in *Laporte v MPC*, supra.

[2] Triable summarily and punishable by **six months** imprisonment or a fine not exceeding **level 5** on the standard scale (Criminal Law Act 1977, Sch 1).

[3] See the Police and Criminal Evidence Act 1984, s 25, ante in PART I: MAGISTRATES' COURTS, PROCEDURE, for power of arrest.

# Public Order Act 1936

(1 Edw 8 & 1 Geo 6 c 6)

7.10363 **1. Prohibition of uniforms in connection with political objects** (1) Subject as hereinafter provided, any person who in any public place, or at any public meeting[1] wears uniform[2] signifying his association with any political organisation or with the promotion of any political object shall be guilty of an offence[3]:

Provided that if the chief officer of police[4] is satisfied that the wearing of any such uniform as aforesaid on any ceremonial, anniversary or other special occasion will not be likely to involve risk of public disorder, he may, with the consent of a Secretary of State by order[5], permit the wearing of such uniform on that occasion either absolutely or subject to such conditions as may be specified in the order.

(2) Where any person is charged before any court with an offence under this section, no further proceedings in respect thereof shall be taken against him without the consent of the Attorney-General except such as are authorised by section 6 of the Prosecution of Offences Act 1979[6], so, however, that if that person is remanded in custody he shall, after the expiration of a period of eight days from the date on which he was so remanded, be entitled to be released on bail without sureties unless within that period the Attorney-General has consented to such further proceedings as aforesaid.

[Public Order Act 1936, s 1 as amended by the Bail Act 1976, Sch 2 and the Prosecution of Offences Act 1979, Sch 1.]

[1] "Meeting" means a meeting held for the purpose of the discussion of matters of public interest or for the purpose of the expression of views on such matters; "Public meeting" includes any meeting in a public place and any meeting which the public or any section thereof are permitted to attend, whether on payment or otherwise; "Public place" includes any highway and any other premises or place to which at the material time the public have or are permitted to have access, whether on payment or otherwise (s 9(1), as amended by the Criminal Justice Act 1972, s 33). Where an establishment such as a football ground is involved, it should be treated as a public place in its entirety. Accordingly a speedway track surrounding a football pitch was held to be part of premises constituting a public place (*Cawley v Frost* [1978] 3 All ER 743, 141 JP 30). The front garden of a house in which an altercation occurred was held not to be a public place (*R v Roberts* (1978) 67 Cr App Rep 228). A public house with open doors inviting the public to enter is a public place (*Lawrenson v Oxford* [1982] Crim LR 185).

[2] See *O'Moran v DPP* [1975] QB 864, [1975] 1 All ER 473, 139 JP 245, for circumstances where a black beret, dark glasses, black pullover and other dark clothing was held to be a uniform.

[3] For penalty and power of arrest on reasonable suspicion, see s 7(2), (3), post.

[4] "Chief officer of police" is now defined by the Police Act 1964, Sch 8 in this PART: title POLICE, ante. In the event of a vacancy in the office or in the event of the chief officer being unable to act owing to illness or absence, these powers may be exercised by the person duly appointed to act as his deputy authorised in accordance with directions given by a Secretary of State to exercise those powers on behalf of the chief officer of police (s 9(4)).

[5] This order should be in writing. It may be revoked or varied by a subsequent order, made in like manner (s 9(3)).

[6] Now replaced by the Prosecution of Offences Act 1985, s 25(2) in PART I: MAGISTRATES' COURTS, PROCEDURE, ante.

7.10364 **2. Prohibition of quasi-military organisations, evidence and search warrant** (1) If the members or adherents of any association of persons, whether incorporated or not, are—

(*a*) organised or trained or equipped for the purpose of enabling them to be employed in usurping the functions of the police or of the armed forces of the Crown; or

(*b*) organised and trained or organised and equipped either for the purpose of enabling them to be employed for the use or display of physical force in promoting any political object, or in such manner as to arouse reasonable apprehension that they are organised and either trained or equipped for that purpose;

then any person who takes part in the control or management of the association, or in so organising or training as aforesaid any members or adherents thereof, shall be guilty of an offence[1] under this section:

Provided that in any proceedings against a person charged with the offence of taking part in the control or management of such an association as aforesaid it shall be a defence to that charge to prove that he neither consented to nor connived at the organisation, training, or equipment of members or adherents of his association in contravention of the provisions of this section.

(2) No prosecution shall be instituted under this section without the consent of the Attorney-General.

(3) *Disposal of property belonging to any association within subsection (2) by order of the High Court*

*upon the application of the Attorney-General.*

(4) In any criminal or civil proceedings under this section proof of things done or of words written, spoken or published (whether or not in the presence of any party to the proceedings) by any person taking part in the control or management of an association or in organising, training or equipping members or adherents of an association shall be admissible as evidence of the purposes for which, or the manner in which members or adherents of the association (whether those persons or others) were organised, or trained or equipped.

(5) If a judge of the High Court is satisfied by information on oath that there is reasonable ground for suspecting that an offence under this section has been committed, and that evidence of the commission thereof is to be found at any premises or place specified in the information, he may, on an application made by an officer of police of a rank not lower than that of inspector, grant a search warrant authorising any such officer as aforesaid named in the warrant together with any other persons named in the warrant and any other officers of police to enter the premises or place at any time within three months from the date of the warrant, if necessary by force, and to search the premises or place and every person found therein, and to seize[2] anything found on the premises or place or on any such person which the officer has reasonable ground for suspecting to be evidence of the commission of such an offence as aforesaid:

Provided that no woman shall, in pursuance of a warrant issued under this subsection, be searched except by a woman.

(6) Nothing in this section shall be construed as prohibiting the employment of a reasonable number of persons as stewards to assist in the preservation of order at any public meeting held upon private premises[3], or the making of arrangements for that purpose or the instruction of the persons to be so employed in their lawful duties as such stewards, or their being furnished with badges or other distinguishing signs.

[Public Order Act 1936, s 2 as amended by the Serious Organised Crime and Police Act 2005, Sch 16.]

---

1 For penalty, see s 7(1), post.

2 As to the common law powers of seizure under a search warrant, see *Elias v Pasmore* [1934] 2 KB 164, 98 JP 92.

3 "Private premises" means premises to which the public have access (whether on payment or otherwise) only by permission of the owner, occupier or lessee of the premises (s 9(1)).

7.10365 **7. Enforcement and power of arrest** (1) Any person who commits an offence under section 2 of this Act shall be liable on summary conviction to imprisonment for a term not exceeding **six months**[1], or to a fine not exceeding **the statutory maximum**, or to **both** such imprisonment and fine, or, on conviction on indictment, to imprisonment for a term not exceeding **two years** or to a **fine**, or to **both** such imprisonment and fine.

(2) Any person guilty of any offence under this Act other than an offence under s 2 shall be liable on summary conviction to imprisonment for a term not exceeding **three months*** or to a fine not exceeding **level 4** on the standard scale or to **both** such imprisonment and fine.

(3) *Repealed.*

[Public Order Act 1936, s 7 as amended by the Public Order Act 1963, s 1(2), the Race Relations Act 1976, s 70, the Criminal Law Act 1977, s 28, Sch 6, the Criminal Justice Act 1982, s 46, the Public Order Act 1986 Sch 3 and the Serious Organised Crime and Police Act 2005, Sch 7.]

---

* **Words substituted by the Criminal Justice Act 2003, Sch 26 from a date to be appointed.**

1 For procedure in respect of an offence triable either way, see the Magistrates' Courts Act 1980, ss 17A–21, in PART I: MAGISTRATES' COURTS, PROCEDURE, ante.

# Criminal Justice Act 1967[1]

(1967 c 80)

## PART VI

## MISCELLANEOUS AND GENERAL

### *Offences*

7.10366 **91. Drunkenness in a public place** (1) Any person who in any public place[2] is guilty, while drunk[3], of disorderly behaviour shall be liable on summary conviction to a fine not exceeding **level 3** on the standard scale[4].

(2) The foregoing subsection shall have effect instead of any corresponding provision contained in s 12 of the Licensing Act 1872, s 58 of the Metropolitan Police Act 1839, s 37 of the City of London Police Act 1839, and 29 of the Town Police Clauses Act 1847 (being enactments which authorise the imposition of a short term of imprisonment or of a fine not exceeding [£10 or £25] or both for the corresponding offence) and instead of any corresponding provisions contained in any local Act.

(3) The Secretary of State may by order repeal any provision of a local Act which appears to him to be a provision corresponding to subsection (1) of this section or to impose a liability to imprisonment for an offence of drunkenness or of being incapable while drunk.

(4) In this section "public place" includes any highway and any other premises or place to which at the material time the public have or are permitted to have access, whether on payment or otherwise.

(5) *Repealed.*[5]

[Criminal Justice Act 1967, s 91 as amended by the Criminal Law Act 1977, Sch 13, the Criminal Justice Act 1982, ss 38 and 46 and the Serious Organised Crime and Police Act 2005, Sch 7.]

[1] For other provisions of this Act, see PART I: MAGISTRATES' COURTS, PROCEDURE, ante.

[2] A landing in a block of flats, to which access was gained by way of key, security code, tenants' intercom or caretaker, was held not to be a public place because only those admitted by or with the implied consent of the occupiers had access (*Williams (Richard) v DPP* (1992) 156 JP 804, [1992] Crim LR 503).

[3] "Drunk" refers to a person who has taken intoxicating liquor to excess so that he has lost the power of self-control; it does not apply to a person who is disorderly as a result of sniffing glue *(Neale v E (a minor)* (1983) 80 Cr App Rep 20, [1984] Crim LR 485).

[4] The elements of the offence are: (1) the defendant was drunk; (2) he was in a public place; and (3) he was guilty of disorderly behaviour. There is no mental element to be proved in relation to "disorderly behaviour"; the requisite mens rea of the offence is limited to the voluntary consumption of alcohol: *Carroll v DPP* [2009] EWHC 554 (Admin), (2009) 173 JP 285.

[5] Where a constable has power to arrest a person under this section, the constable may take him to a treatment centre for alcoholics; see the Criminal Justice Act 1972, s. 34, in PART III: SENTENCING, ante. This statutory power of arrest was not repealed by the Police and Criminal Evidence Act 1984 (*DPP v Kitching* (1989) 154 JP 293).

# Sporting Events (Control of Alcohol etc) Act 1985

(1985 c 57)

7.10367 **1. Offences in connection with alcohol on coaches and trains** (1) This section applies to a vehicle which—

(*a*) is a public service vehicle or railway passenger vehicle, and

(*b*) is being used for the principal purpose of carrying passengers for the whole or part of a journey to or from a designated sporting event.

(2) A person who knowingly causes or permits alcohol to be carried on a vehicle to which this section applies is guilty of an offence—

(*a*) if the vehicle is a public service vehicle and he is the operator of the vehicle or the servant or agent of the operator, or

(*b*) if the vehicle is a hired vehicle and he is the person to whom it is hired or the servant or agent of that person.

(3) A person who has alcohol in his possession while on a vehicle to which this section applies is guilty of an offence.

(4) A person who is drunk on a vehicle to which this section applies is guilty of an offence.

(5) In this section "public service vehicle" and "operator" have the same meaning as in the Public Passenger Vehicles Act 1981.

[Sporting Events (Control of Alcohol etc) Act 1985, s 1 as amended by the Licensing Act 2003, Sch 6.]

7.10368 **1A. Alcohol on certain other vehicles** (1) This section applies to a motor vehicle which—

(*a*) is not a public service vehicle but is adapted to carry more than 8 passengers, and

(*b*) is being used for the principal purpose of carrying two or more passengers for the whole or part of a journey to or from a designated sporting event.

(2) A person who knowingly causes or permits alcohol to be carried on a motor vehicle to which this section applies is guilty of an offence—

(*a*) if he is its driver, or

(*b*) if he is not its driver but is its keeper, the servant or agent of its keeper, a person to whom it is made available (by hire, loan or otherwise) by its keeper or the keeper's servant or agent, or the servant or agent of a person to whom it is so made available.

(3) A person who has alcohol in his possession while on a motor vehicle to which this section applies is guilty of an offence.

(4) A person who is drunk on a motor vehicle to which this section applies is guilty of an offence.

(5) In this section—

"keeper", in relation to a vehicle, means the person having the duty to take out a licence for it under the Vehicle Excise and Registration Act 1994,

"motor vehicle" means a mechanically propelled vehicle intended or adapted for use on roads, and

"public service vehicle" has the same meaning as in the Public Passenger Vehicles Act 1981.

[Sporting Events (Control of Alcohol etc) Act 1985, s 1A as inserted by the Public Order Act 1986, Sch 1 and amended by the Vehicle Excise and Registration Act 1994, Sch 3 and the Licensing Act 2003, Sch 6.]

7.10369 **2. Offences in connection with alcohol, containers etc at sports grounds** (1) A person who has alcohol or an article to which this section applies in his possession—

(*a*) at any time during the period of a designated sporting event when he is in any area of a designated sports ground from which the event may be directly viewed, or

(*b*) while entering or trying to enter a designated sports ground at any time during the period of a designated sporting event at that ground,

is guilty of an offence.

(1A) *Repealed.*

(2) A person who is drunk in a designated sports ground at any time during the period of a designated sporting event at that ground or is drunk while entering or trying to enter such a ground

at any time during the period of a designated sporting event at that ground is guilty of an offence.

(3) This section applies to any article capable of causing injury to a person struck by it, being—

(*a*) a bottle, can or other portable container (including such an article when crushed or broken) which—

(i) is for holding any drink, and

(ii) is of a kind which, when empty, is normally discarded or returned to, or left to be recovered by, the supplier, or

(*b*) part of an article falling within paragraph (*a*) above;

but does not apply to anything that is for holding any medicinal product (within the meaning of the Medicines Act 1968) or any veterinary medicinal product (within the meaning of the Veterinary Medicines Regulations 2006).

[Sporting Events (Control of Alcohol etc) Act 1985, s 2 as amended by the Public Order Act 1986, Sch 1, the Licensing Act 2003, Sch 6 and SI 2006/2407.]

7.10370 2A. **Fireworks etc** (1) A person is guilty of an offence if he has an article or substance to which this section applies in his possession—

(*a*) at any time during the period of a designated sporting event when he is in any area of a designated sports ground from which the event may be directly viewed, or

(*b*) while entering or trying to enter a designated sports ground at any time during the period of a designated sporting event at the ground.

(2) It is a defence for the accused to prove that he had possession with lawful authority.

(3) This section applies to any article or substance whose main purpose is the emission of a flare for purposes of illuminating or signalling (as opposed to igniting or heating) or the emission of smoke or a visible gas; and in particular its applies to distress flares, fog signals, and pellets and capsules intended to be used as fumigators or for testing pipes, but not to matches, cigarette lighters or heaters.

(4) This section also applies to any article which is a firework.

[Sporting Events (Control of Alcohol etc) Act 1985, s 2A as inserted by the Public Order Act 1986, Sch 1.]

7.10371 7. **Powers of enforcement** (1) A constable may, at any time during the period of a designated sporting event at any designated sports ground, enter any part of the ground for the purpose of enforcing the provisions of this Act.

(2) A constable may search a person he has reasonable grounds to suspect is committing or has committed an offence under this Act.

(3) A constable may stop a public service vehicle (within the meaning of section 1 of this Act) or a motor vehicle to which section 1A of this Act applies and may search such a vehicle or a railway passenger vehicle if he has reasonable grounds to suspect that an offence under that section is being or has been committed in respect of the vehicle.

[Sporting Events (Control of Alcohol etc) Act 1985, s 7 as amended by the Public Order Act 1986, Sch 1 and the Serious Organised Crime and Police Act 2005, Schs 7 and 17.]

7.10372 8. **Penalties for offences** A person guilty of an offence under this Act shall be liable on summary conviction—

(*a*) in the case of an offence under section 1(2) or 1A(2), to a fine not exceeding **level 4** on the standard scale,

(*b*) in the case of an offence under section 1(3), 1A(3), 2(1) or 2A(1), to a fine not exceeding **level 3** on the standard scale or to imprisonment for a term not exceeding **three months* or both**,

(*c*) in the case of an offence under section 1(4), 1A(4) or 2(2), to a fine not exceeding **level 2** on the standard scale.

(*d*) *repealed,*

(*e*) *repealed.*

[Sporting Events (Control of Alcohol etc) Act 1985, s 8 as amended by the Public Order Act 1986, Schs 1 and 3 and the Licensing Act 2003, Sch 6.]

---

* **Words substituted by the Criminal Justice Act 2003, Sch 26 from a date to be appointed.**

7.10373 9. **Interpretation** (1) The following provisions shall have effect for the interpretation of this Act.

(2) "Designated sports ground" means any place—

(*a*) used (wholly or partly) for sporting events where accommodation is provided for spectators, and

(*b*) for the time being designated, or of a class designated, by order[1] made by the Secretary of State;

and an order under this subsection may include provision for determining for the purposes of this Act the outer limit of any designated sports ground.

(3) "Designated sporting event"—

(*a*) means a sporting event or proposed sporting event for the time being designated, or of a class designated, by order[1] made by the Secretary of State, and

(*b*) includes a designated sporting event within the meaning of Part V of the Criminal Justice (Scotland) Act 1980;

and an order under this subsection may apply to events or proposed events outside Great Britain as well as those in England and Wales.

(4) The period of a designated sporting event is the period beginning two hours before the start of the event or (if earlier) two hours before the time at which it is advertised to start and ending one hour after the end of the event, but—

- (*a*) where an event advertised to start at a particular time on a particular day is postponed to a later day, the period includes the period in the day on which it is advertised to take place beginning two hours before and ending one hour after that time, and
- (*b*) where an event advertised to start at a particular time on a particular day does not take place, the period is the period referred to in paragraph (*a*) above.

(5) *Repealed.*

(6) This Act does not apply to any sporting event or proposed sporting event—

- (*a*) where all competitors are to take part otherwise than for reward, and
- (*b*) to which all spectators are to be admitted free of charge.

(7) An expression used in this Act and in the Licensing Act 2003 has the same meaning in this Act as in that Act.

(8) Any power to make an order under this section shall be exercisable by statutory instrument subject to annulment in pursuance of a resolution of either House of Parliament.

[Sporting Events (Control of Alcohol etc) Act 1985, s 9 as amended by the Licensing Act 2003, Sch 6.]

1 The Sports Grounds and Sporting Events (Designation) Order 2005, SI 2005/3204 in this title, post, has been made.

# Public Order Act 1986

(1986 c 64)

## PART I[1]

## NEW OFFENCES

7.10374 **1. Riot** (1) Where 12 or more persons who are present together use or threaten unlawful violence[2] for a common purpose and the conduct of them (taken together) is such as would cause a person of reasonable firmness present at the scene to fear for his personal safety, each of the persons using unlawful violence for the common purpose is guilty of riot[3].

(2) It is immaterial whether or not the 12 or more use or threaten unlawful violence simultaneously.

(3) The common purpose may be inferred from conduct.

(4) No person of reasonable firmness need actually be, or be likely to be, present at the scene.

(5) Riot may be committed in private as well as in public places.

(6) A person guilty of riot is liable on conviction on indictment to imprisonment for a term not exceeding ten years or a fine or both.

[Public Order Act 1986, s 1.]

1 Part I contains ss 1–10.

2 As to the mental element, see s 6, post.

3 See s 7 post as to the consent necessary for instituting prosecutions.

An indictment charging an offence of riot should reflect the two parts of s 1(1) of the Act, first stating the statutory context and second the commission, within that context, of the offence as defined (*R v Jefferson* [1994] 1 All ER 270, 158 JP 76, 99 Cr App Rep 13).

By the Riot (Damages) Act 1886 (as amended by the Police Act 1964) claims for compensation for damage due to riot may be made against a police authority. The Riot (Damages) Regulations 1921, SR & O 1921/1536 as amended by SI 1986/76 and SI 2011/2002 and 2009 have been made, prescribing the procedure to be followed for a claim. See *J W Dwyer Ltd v Metropolitan Police District Receiver* [1967] 2 QB 970, [1967] 2 All ER 1051, 131 JP 416, for an analysis of the basis for such a claim. By the Merchant Shipping Act 1995, s 235, similar claims may be made in respect of the riotous plundering of wrecked vessels.

The Queen's Regulations for the Army provide that should the assistance of the Armed Forces be called for to maintain peace and public order, the officer to whom the application is made is at once to inform the Ministry of Defence and his immediate superior authority. Assistance will normally be requested by the Chief Officer of Police and is to be confirmed in writing. Where a request is received from a source other than the Chief Officer of Police, the Service Commander on the spot is to refer the request to the Chief Officer of Police and report it to his superiors. It is possible, however, in very exceptional circumstances for grave and sudden emergencies to arise which in the opinion of the commander demand his immediate intervention to protect life and property. In such emergencies he is to act on his own responsibility and is to report as early as possible the matter and the action he has taken to the Service authorities mentioned above and to the Chief Officer of Police.

The "Chief Officer of Police" means in England and Wales, the Commissioner of Police for the City of London, the Commissioner of Police of the Metropolis or the Chief Constable of a county or a combined area (Police Act 1964, s 62).

See also the Reserve Forces Act 1980, s 23, Army and air force reserves in aid of civil power.

7.10375 **2. Violent disorder** (1) Where 3 or more persons[1] who are present together[2] use or threaten unlawful[3] violence[4] and the conduct of them (taken together) is such as would cause a person of reasonable firmness present at the scene to fear for his personal safety, each of the persons using or threatening unlawful violence is guilty of violent disorder.

(2) It is immaterial whether or not the 3 or more use or threaten unlawful violence simultaneously.

(3) No person of reasonable firmness need actually be, or be likely to be, present at the scene.

(4) Violent disorder may be committed in private as well as in public places.

(5) A person guilty of violent disorder is liable on conviction on indictment to imprisonment for

a term not exceeding 5 years or a fine or both, or on summary conviction to imprisonment for a term not exceeding **6 months** or a fine not exceeding the **statutory maximum** or **both**[5].

[Public Order Act 1986, s 2.]

[1] Where the allegation involves only three named defendants, acquittal of one or two would seem to necessitate acquittal of the remainder; see *R v Mahroof* (1988) 88 Cr App Rep 317, and commentary thereon in [1989] Crim LR 72, CA. See also *R v Fleming and Robinson* (1989) 153 JP 517, [1989] Crim LR 658, CA and *R v McGuigan and Cameron* [1991] Crim LR 719.

[2] The expression "present together" means no more than being in the same place at the same time. There is no requirement for any degree of co-operation between those who are using or threatening violence, nor any common aim or common motive; all that is required is that they be present in the same place at the same time using or threatening violence (*R v NW* [2010] EWCA Crim 404, [2010] 1 WLR 1426, [2010] 2 Cr App Rep 54).

[3] Self defence, reasonable defence of another and actions which were no more than necessary to restore the peace are three examples of lawful action which could amount to defences (*R v Rothwell and Barton* [1993] Crim LR 626).

[4] As to the mental element see s 6, post.

[5] For procedure in respect of an offence triable either way, see the Magistrates' Courts Act 1980, ss 17A–21, ante in PART I: MAGISTRATES' COURTS PROCEDURE, ante.

7.10376 **3. Affray** (1) A person is guilty of affray[1] if he uses or threatens[2] unlawful violence[3] towards another[4] and his conduct is such as would cause a person[5] of reasonable firmness present at the scene[6] to fear for his personal safety[7].

(2) Where 2 or more persons use or threaten the unlawful violence, it is the conduct of them taken together that must be considered for the purposes of subsection (1).

(3) For the purposes of this section a threat cannot be made by the use of words[8] alone.

(4) No person of reasonable firmness need actually be, or be likely to be, present at the scene.

(5) Affray may be committed in private as well as in public places.

(6) *Repealed.*

(7) A person guilty of affray is liable on conviction on indictment to imprisonment for a term not exceeding 3 years or a fine or both, or on summary conviction to imprisonment for a term not exceeding **6 months** or a fine not exceeding the **statutory maximum** or **both**[9].

[Public Order Act 1986, s 3 as amended by the Serious Organised Crime and Police Act 2005, Schs 7 and 17.]

[1] Affray typically involves a continuous course of conduct, the criminal character of which depends on the general nature and effect of the conduct as a whole. In such cases the prosecution does not have to identify and prove particular incidents. However where the conduct is not continuous but falls into separate sequences, before there can be a conviction based on any one sequence the court must be satisfied on that sequence and it does not suffice that some members of the court are satisfied on one sequence and others on another sequence, *R v Smith* [1997] 1 Cr App Rep 14, CA. For the purposes of s 3(1), the carrying of dangerous weapons by a group of persons can in some circumstances constitute a threat of violence without those weapons being waved or brandished, but the mere possession of a weapon, without threatening circumstances, is insufficient to constitute such a threat. Nor can carrying a concealed weapon itself be such a threat. However, the visible carrying in public of primed petrol bombs by a large number of what is obviously a gang out for no good is clearly capable of constituting a threat of unlawful violence: *I v DPP, M v DPP, H v DPP* [2001] UKHL 10, [2002] AC 285, [2001] 2 All ER 583, [2001] 2 WLR 765.

[2] What amounts to a threat is essentially a question of fact in each case. Where a threat of violence takes the form of a gathering of armed persons in a public place, it is not necessary to prove that a person or persons present actually felt threatened, but it must be shown that there was someone at or in the vicinity towards whom the threat of violence could be said to have been directed (*I v DPP* [2001] UKHL 10, [2002] AC 285, [2001] 2 All ER 583, [2001] 2 WLR 765 – the visible carrying in public of primed petrol bombs by a large number of youths held to be capable of constituting a threat of unlawful violence).

[3] As to the mental element, see s 6, post.

[4] The threat of unlawful violence must be directed towards a person or persons present at the scene, and it does not necessarily follow that because a person is present at a location where a gang are carrying petrol bombs there is a threat of violence towards that person; whether the latter is the case will depend on the facts of the actual case: *I v DPP, M v DPP, H v DPP* (supra).

[5] The court must consider the reaction of the hypothetical reasonable bystander, not that of the victim of any violent conduct (*R v Sanchez* (1996) 160 JP 321, [1996] Crim LR 572, CA). Affray is a Public Order Act offence and not a supplementary offence against the person; the circumstances must be such that the notional bystander would fear for his own safety rather than for the safety of one or both or two parties engaged in a fight: *Leeson v DPP* [2010] EWHC 994 (Admin), (2010) 174 JP 367, [2010] 17 LS Gaz R 16.

[6] The concept of presence at the scene suggests that the notional bystander would be in the presence of both the offender and the victim: *I v DPP, M v DPP, H v DPP* (supra).

[7] Where an information charging affray includes specific allegations such as causing damage or assault, it is not necessary for the prosecution to prove these allegations since they are not essential elements of the offence (*Cobb v DPP* (1992) 156 JP 746).

[8] As to the application of sub-s (3) see *R v Robinson* [1993] Crim LR 581.

[9] For procedure in respect of an offence triable either way, see the Magistrates' Courts Act 1980, ss 17A–21 in PART I: MAGISTRATES' COURTS PROCEDURE, ante.

7.10377 **4. Fear or provocation of violence** (1) A person is guilty of an offence[1] if he—

(*a*) uses towards another person[2] threatening, abusive or insulting words or behaviour[3], or

(*b*) distributes or displays to another person any writing, sign or other visible representation[3] which is threatening, abusive or insulting,

with intent to cause that person to believe[4] that immediate[5] unlawful violence will be used against him or another by any person, or to provoke the immediate use of unlawful violence by that person or another, or whereby that person is likely to believe that such violence[6] will be used or it is likely that such violence will be provoked[7].

(2) An offence under this section may be committed in a public or a private place, except that no offence is committed where the words or behaviour are used, or the writing, sign or other visible representation is distributed or displayed, by a person inside a dwelling[8] and the other person is also

inside that or another dwelling.

(3) *Repealed.*

(4) A person guilty of an offence under this section is liable on summary conviction to imprisonment for a term not exceeding **6 months** or a fine not exceeding **level 5** on the standard scale or **both**.

[Public Order Act 1986, s 4 as amended by the Serious Organised Crime and Police Act 2005, Schs 7 and 17.]

---

1 Although s 4(1) creates only one offence, that offence may be committed in four different ways. Common to all four is the requirement that the accused must intend or be aware that his words or behaviour are or may be threatening, abusive or insulting, and must be directed to another person; see *Winn v DPP* (1992) 156 JP 881. Where D delivers a blow to P in such a way as to give P no advance warning of the attack it cannot be said that he had the intent required by the section: *Hughes v DPP* [2012] EWHC 606 (Admin) , 176 JP 237 (defence appeal by way of case stated succeeded where D had delivered a blow in such a way that P could have had no prior perception of it).

2 The words "uses towards another person" mean that threatening words must be addressed directly to another person who is present and either in earshot or aimed at as being putatively in earshot (*Atkin v DPP* (1989) 153 JP 383, [1989] Crim LR 581, DC). It is inappropriate to use the words "another person" in an information charging an offence under s 4 because the person in whom the belief that unlawful violence would be used has to be the same person as the person threatened, abused or insulted; see *Loade v DPP* (1990) 90 Cr App Rep 162.

3 As to the mental element, see s 6, post.

4 To establish the offence it does not have to be shown what the other person believed; it has to be shown that the defendant had the intention to cause that person to believe. This can be proved by any admissible evidence and it is not necessary for the person to whom the threats or insulting behaviour were directed to give evidence (*Swanston v DPP* (1996) 161 JP 203).

Where there had been a serious violent incident in a nightclub of which the appellant's friend was the victim and two security staff wrongly believed the appellant had been responsible and retrained him, and the appellant struggled violently to break free, the justices were entitled to infer that his state of mind was "Unless you let me through, unless you let me get to my friend, I will assault you" and there was evidence to support a conviction of a s 4 offence: *Knight v DPP* [2012] EWHC 605 (Admin), 176 JP 177.

5 Provided the victim believes and is likely to believe that something will happen at any time, there is a case to answer (*DPP v Ramos* [2000] Crim LR 768, DC (letters sent threatening a bombing hate campaign and that the recipient, if seen, would be killed).

6 "Such violence" must be "immediate", and the phrase refers back to the words "immediate unlawful violence" (*R v Horseferry Road Metropolitan Stipendiary Magistrate, ex p Siadatan* [1991] 1 QB 260, [1991] 1 All ER 324).

7 For the position under the European Convention on Human Rights see para 7.10379, footnote (1), post.

8 A communal landing in a block of flats has been held not to be a dwelling for this purpose, since the common parts were not part of the structure occupied as a person's home (*Rukwira v DPP* (1993) 158 JP 65, [1993] Crim LR 882.

7.10378 **4A. Intentional harassment, alarm or distress** (1) A person is guilty of an offence if, with intent to cause a person harassment, alarm or distress, he—

(*a*) uses threatening, abusive or insulting words or behaviour, or disorderly behaviour, or

(*b*) displays any writing, sign or other visible representation which is threatening, abusive or insulting,

thereby causing that or another person harassment, alarm or distress[1].

(2) An offence under this section may be committed in a public or a private place, except that no offence is committed where the words or behaviour are used, or the writing, sign or other visible representation is displayed, by a person inside a dwelling[2] and the person who is harassed, alarmed or distressed is also inside that or another dwelling.

(3) It is a defence for the accused to prove—

(*a*) that he was inside a dwelling and had no reason to believe that the words or behaviour used, or the writing, sign or other visible representation displayed, would be heard or seen by a person outside that or any other dwelling, or

(*b*) that his conduct was reasonable.

(4) *Repealed.*

(5) A person guilty of an offence under this section is liable on summary conviction to imprisonment for a term not exceeding **6 months** or a fine not exceeding **level 5** on the standard scale or **both**.

[Public Order Act 1986, s 4A as inserted by the Criminal Justice and Public Order Act 1994, s 154 and amended by the Serious Organised Crime and Police Act 2005, Schs 7 and 17.]

---

1 In *Dehal v CPS* [2005] EWHC 2154, 169 JP 581, the defendant faced a charge under s 4A ante, on facts that he had entered a Sikh temple and affixed a notice to a notice board that stated, inter alia, that the president of the temple was a hypocrite. It was held that to justify such an interference with art 10 the prosecution had to demonstrate that the criminal proceedings were being brought in pursuance of a legitimate aim and were the minimum necessary to achieve that aim. However, there were indications in *Bauer v DPP (Liberty intervening)* [2013] EWHC 634 (Admin), [2013] 1 WLR 3617, 177 JP 297 by the same judge (Moses LJ) at para 40 that the imposition of such a burden on the prosecution might be open to question, and it is submitted that it is difficult to reconcile with the well established line of authority that it is not for courts to question how prosecutorial discretion is exercised. Since no such reasoning had been given in the case stated it had not been open to the court to find that the prosecution had been a proportionate response to the defendant's conduct. *Dehal* and *Bauer* were considered in *James v Director of Public Prosecutions* [2015] EWHC 3296 (Admin), [2016] 1 WLR 2118, 180 JP 1, [2016] Crim LR 212 in which it was held that the decision in *Bauer* more than qualified *Dehal* and was "a considered disavowal" in the way it focused consideration of proportionality on the decision to prosecution. " . . . all that can be extracted now from *Dehal* is a much more general point about the interaction between free speech, which may be insulting, and proof of the ingredients of the 'reasonable excuse' defence" (per Ouseley J at para 20). His Lordship then added: "24 I am satisfied that *Dehal* was wrongly decided, perhaps misunderstanding some comments in *Hammond*, and should no longer be applied or cited". It is for the prosecutor to decide whether or not to prosecute and it is not for the trial court to review the proportionality of a decision to prosecute unless it amounts to an abuse of process.

Where the charge arises from material posted on the Internet, neither the fact that the complainant did not see it until some months (five) later nor the fact that it was a police officer showed him the material breaks the chain of causation; once the defendant with the requisite intent had posted the image to the website, he took the chance that the intended harassment, alarm or distress would be caused to the complainant: *S v DPP* [2008] Admin 438, [2008] 1 WLR 2847.

[2] A police cell is not a "dwelling" for the purpose of this exception: *R v Francis* [2006] EWCA Crim 3323, [2007] 1 Cr App R 36, [2007] Crim LR 574.

7.10379 **5. Harassment, alarm or distress** (1) A person is guilty of an offence if he—

(*a*) uses threatening or abusive [1] words or behaviour[2], or disorderly[3] behaviour, or

(*b*) displays any writing, sign or other visible representation which is threatening or abusive[4],

within the hearing or sight[5] of a person likely to be caused harassment[6], alarm[7] or distress[8] thereby[9].

(2) An offence under this section may be committed in a public or a private place, except that no offence is committed where the words or behaviour are used, or the writing, sign or other visible representation is displayed, by a person inside a dwelling and the other person is also inside that or another dwelling.

(3) It is a defence for the accused to prove[10]—

(*a*) that he had no reason to believe that there was any person within hearing or sight who was likely to be caused harassment, alarm or distress, or

(*b*) that he was inside a dwelling and had no reason to believe that the words or behaviour used, or the writing, sign or other visible representation displayed, would be heard or seen by a person outside that or any other dwelling, or

(*c*) that his conduct was reasonable[11].

(4) *Repealed.*

(5) *Repealed.*

(6) A person guilty of an offence under this section is liable on summary conviction to a fine not exceeding **level 3** on the standard scale.

[Public Order Act 1986, s 5 as amended by the Public Order (Amendment) Act 1996, s 1, the Serious Organised Crime and Police Act 2005, Schs 7 and 17 and the Crime and Courts Act 2013, s 57.]

---

[1] The words "or insulting" were removed from this offence by s 57 of the Crime and Courts Act 2013, which came into effect on 1 February 2014. For relevant case law on the meaning of "insulting" and related ECHR issues, readers should refer to the 2013 edn of this work.

[2] As to the mental element, see s 6, post. Section 5 is not limited to rowdy or obscene behaviour in a public context, but will cover the behaviour of a person who peeps between the curtain of a changing room and watches his customers undressing, or who installs a video camera to film customers in a state of undress (*Vigon v DPP* (1997) 162 JP 115, [1998] Crim LR 289 approved *Kay v Metropolitan Police Comr* [2007] EWCA Civ 477, [2007] 4 All ER 31, [2007] 1 WLR 2915).

[3] A court is entitled to conclude that walking naked through a town centre violates public order and is thus "disorderly": *Gough v Director Of Public Prosecutions* [2013] EWHC 3267 (Admin), 177 JP 669, [2014] Crim LR 371.

[4] Only those elements of the offence in either paragraph (*a*) or (*b*) of s 5(1) are reflected in s 6(4), post; see *DPP v Clarke* (1991) 156 JP 267. The structure of the s 5(1)(*b*) limb of the offence was considered by the Divisional Court in *Norwood v DPP* [2002] EWHC 1564 (Admin), [2002] Crim LR 888, 167 JPN 522. It requires proof by the prosecution of the following four elements: (1) a fact – display by a defendant of a visible representation; (2) a value judgment that the representation is threatening, abusive or insulting; (3) a fact – that the defendant either intended, or was aware that it might be, threatening, abusive or insulting; and (4) a mixed fact and value judgment – that the display was within sight of a person likely to be caused, harassment, alarm or distress by it.

[5] The prosecution must show that some person actually saw the abusive or insulting words or behaviour (*Holloway v DPP* [2004] EWHC Admin 2621, (2005) 169 JP 14), though it is not necessary for the prosecution to call that person, provided the court can draw the inference to the criminal standard that what the defendant was doing was visible or audible to a person who was in the vicinity at the relevant time (per Collins LJ at para 32). See also *R (on the application of Reda) v DPP* [2011] EWHC 1550, 175 JP 329.

It was held that an offence under s 5(1)(*a*) was not committed merely by causing some "writing, sign or other visible representation" to be delivered through the letter box of an intended recipient, because the sender was not a person who "uses . . . words or behaviour . . . within the hearing or sight of a person" who received it (*Chappell v DPP* (1988) 89 Cr App Rep 82). The latter was confirmed in *Taylor v DPP* [2006] EWHC 1202 (Admin), 170 JP 485.

[6] No element of apprehension about one's personal safety is necessary for there to be harassment (*Chambers and Edwards v DPP* [1995] Crim LR 896).

[7] It is not necessary that the person alarmed should be concerned at physical danger to himself; it may be alarm about the safety of an unconnected third party (*Lodge v DPP* (1988) Times, 26 October).

[8] A police officer might be the person caused harassment, alarm or distress, although on the facts the magistrates might equally well decide that the words and behaviour did not have this effect (*DPP v Orum* [1988] 3 All ER 449, [1989] 1 WLR 88, 153, JP 85). See also *Harvey v DPP* [2011] EWHC 3992 (Admin), 176 JP 265, [2012] Crim LR 553. The defendant used the word "fuck" twice and "fucking" once to police officers searching him and his two friends in a public area in the middle of a block of flats. The language was capable of falling within s 5, but it had not been open to the justices to infer that the officers, or a group of young bystanders who witnessed the incident, or persons who may have been in the open area or residents in their homes, were persons likely to have been caused harassment, etc, in the absence of specific evidence that the officers had felt threatened, harassed, alarmed or distressed, or that it was likely that the young bystanders would have so felt, and in the absence of any evidence that anybody other than the young bystanders had in fact been within earshot.

[9] Under the Human Rights Act 1998, this provision, so far as it is possible to do so, must be read and given effect in a way which is compatible with the Convention rights. Article 10(1) of the European Convention on Human Rights applies "not only to ideas that are favourably received, or regarded as inoffensive or as a matter of indifference, but also to those that offend, shock or disturb the State or any sector of the population": *Handyside v United Kingdom* (1976) 1 EHRR 737.

[10] The burden of proof rests on the defence on the balance of probabilities (*DPP v Clarke* (1991) 156 JP 267). This would seem to remain the case after commencement of the Human Rights Act 1998 (*Norwood v DPP*, supra, where the court indicated a predilection for a legal burden, but did not come to a firm conclusion on the point).

In *Norwood* Auld LJ stated, in relation to the defence under s 5(3):

> "[20] However, in this statutory context, whatever the nature of the burden cast on the defence, it is, in any event, hard to find much of a role for any of the s 5(3) defences, directed, as they are, to an objective assessment by the court of the reasonableness of the accused's conduct. That is because the essentials of

the basic s 5 offence require the court to be satisfied as to the accused's subjective state of mind, namely that he intended that the representation should be, or was aware that it might be, threatening, abusive or insulting. See eg *DPP v Clarke* (1991) 94 Cr App Rep 359, per Nolan LJ. If the s 5(3) burden on the defence is to be "read down" to an evidential burden so as to make it Convention compliant, with the result of casting upon the prosecution the burden of disproving it, it would be harder to find any sensible role for s 5(3) . . .

[*Norwood* concerned a racially aggravated s 5 offence]

[21] Add now the fifth element that the prosecution must prove on this religiously aggravated charge, that the appellant, in displaying the poster within the hearing or sight of a person to whom it was likely to cause harassment, harm or distress, was motivated by hostility towards a religious group, and it is even harder to see much of a role for s 5(3) once the prosecution has proved its case under s 5(1) and 6 (4)."

As for the impact of art 10 (freedom of expression) his lordship stated:

"[35] . . . often, and certainly in the circumstances of this case, the question whether a defendant's conduct is objectively reasonable necessarily includes consideration of his right to freedom of expression under art 10 . . . [37] As this Court said in *Percy*, a prosecution under s 5 does not per se engage art 10. It depends on the facts and the drawing of an appropriate balance of competing interests under art 10.1 and 10.2, bearing always in mind that the restrictions in art 10.2 should be narrowly construed and convincingly established. As I have indicated earlier in this judgment, in the absence of a challenge to the compatibility of s 5 with the Convention, the mechanics of the Article's operation on a prosecution under it seem to me to be confined to the objective defence of reasonableness in s 5(3). It cannot bear in any reasoned way on whether the prosecution have proved the two limbs under s 5(1), first, intentional or foreseen insulting conduct and, second, an objective likelihood of harassment, alarm or distress. Putting aside for the moment, questions as to the nature of the reverse burden of proof provided by s 5(3), the way in which art 10 intrudes on the operation of a s 5 prosecution is whether the defendant's conduct was objectively reasonable, having regard to all the circumstances, including importantly those for which the art 10.2 itself provides. These will include consideration whether to mark as criminal the accused's conduct in displaying the poster as a necessary restriction of his freedom of expression for the prevention of disorder or crime and/or for the protection of the rights of others. Hallett J, who gave the leading judgment in *Percy*, identified, at para 11 of her judgment, two of a number of relevant factors in that case, which seem to me to be of general application in this context: namely: whether the accused's conduct went beyond legitimate protest and whether the behaviour had not formed part of an open expression of opinion on a matter of public interest, but had become disproportionate and unreasonable."

In *Abdul v DPP* [2011] EWHC 247 (Admin), 175 JP 190, [2011] Crim L R 553 the relevant principles between s 5 and art 10 were held to be these:

"i) The starting point is the importance of the right to freedom of expression.

ii) . . . legitimate protest can be offensive at least to some – and on occasions must be, if it is to have impact. Moreover, the right to freedom of expression would be unacceptably devalued if it did no more than protect those holding popular, mainstream views; it must plainly extend beyond that so that minority views can be freely expressed, even if distasteful.

iii) . . . interference with the right to freedom of expression must be convincingly established. Art 10 does not confer an unqualified right to freedom of expression, but the restrictions contained in Art 10.2 are to be narrowly construed.

iv) There is not and cannot be any universal test for resolving when speech goes beyond legitimate protest, so attracting the sanction of the criminal law. The justification for invoking the criminal law is the threat to public order. Inevitably, the context of the particular occasion will be of the first importance.

v) The relevance of the threat to public order should not be taken as meaning that the risk of violence by those reacting to the protest is, without more, determinative; sometimes it may be that protesters are to be protected. That said in striking the right balance when determining whether speech is 'threatening, abusive or insulting', the focus on minority rights should not result in overlooking the rights of the majority.

vi) Plainly, if there is no prima facie case that speech was 'threatening, abusive or insulting' or that the other elements of the s 5 offence can be made good, then no question of prosecution will arise. However, even if there is otherwise a prima facie case for contending that an offence has been committed under s 5, it is still for the Crown to establish that prosecution is a proportionate response, necessary for the preservation of public order.

vii) If the line between legitimate freedom of expression and a threat to public order has indeed been crossed, freedom of speech will not have been impaired by 'ruling . . . out' threatening, abusive or insulting speech: per Lord Reid, in Brutus v Cozens [1973] AC 854, at p862.

viii) [The High Court] should not interfere [with decisions of the magistrates] unless, on well-known grounds, the appellants can establish that the decision to which the district judge has come is one she could not properly have reached."

[49] per Gross LJ.

One of the judges in *Abdul* was Davis LJ. His Lordship took the opportunity in *James v Director of Public Prosecutions* [2015] EWHC 3296 (Admin), [2016] 1 WLR 2118, 180 JP 1, [2016] Crim LR 212 to reconsider whether or not it was proper for the court to consider the proportionality of a decision to prosecute (see para vi, above) as a separate issue. The decision in *Abdul* had, in this respect, followed that of *Dehal v CPS* [2005] EWHC 2154 (Admin), 169 JP 581. His Lordship referred to a number of cases on various POA 1986 offences, which held that Convention rights were capable of being considered within the express words of the statute and did not superimpose a separate legal test of proportionality by which a decision to prosecute might be challenged:

"52. It is a pity that this approach — which provides a workable approach for magistrates — became somewhat muddied by the further approach indicated in *Dehal*, and followed in *Abdul*. Those cases in effect gave a green light to courts, in such cases, being additionally required to assess the proportionality of the decision to prosecute itself.

53. It is a pity for a number of reasons.

i) First, the necessary element of proportionality and the need for its consideration are to be found, in cases such as this one, in the provisions of the statute relating to the offence itself and/or to the available defences, as applied to the facts.

ii) Second, it potentially makes the task of the magistrates immeasurably more complex. That is not desirable in a situation where magistrates may already sometimes have quite difficult decisions to make, in balancing the importance of the rights of freedom of expression and assembly against the rights of others, and in making their assessment of reasonableness accordingly by reference to the facts of the particular case.

iii) Third, it has the potential for converting a magistrates' court in effect into a court exercising powers of judicial review: something the magistrates court is neither equipped to do nor, indeed, empowered to do: see the *Barons Pub Company* case.

54. In my view, the court in *Bauer* was correct not to follow or apply the decision in *Dehal* on this point. Whilst Moses LJ did say that, in effect, his own previous decision in *Dehal* was a decision to be explained on its own facts — and certainly, on its facts, the decision can readily be supported — it seems to me that in reality Moses LJ in *Bauer* was recanting from the legal approach previously indicated by him as appropriate in *Dehal*. In my view, he was right to do so for the reasons given by him in paragraph 40 of his judgment in *Bauer* (with which Kenneth Parker J agreed); as well as for the further reasons given by Ouseley J in his judgment in the present case.

55. It follows that I myself recant from what in effect was an unduly deferential and insufficiently critical endorsement in *Abdul* of this aspect of the *Dehal* approach: albeit that approach was in response to one of the specific forms of question posed in the case stated in *Abdul*. (It may perhaps also be added that it had not been troublesome to do so in that particular case of *Abdul*, given the careful and cogent appraisal of the position, on that basis, by the District Judge at first instance.) But be that as it may, the appropriate approach is henceforth to be taken as that set out in *Bauer*. Accordingly, in cases such as this the prosecution do not have to prove, in addition to the facts establishing the guilt of the defendant, the proportionality of the decision to prosecute itself.

56. In the 2015 edition of Archbold at paras 29–44 it is suggested that the *Dehal* approach accords with the approach of the European Court of Human Rights in *Gul v Turkey (Application No 4870/02)* (2010) 52 EHRR 1085, [2010] ECHR 4870/02, ECtHR. As I read it, however, the latter decision was one on its own facts, by no means requiring an endorsement of a general proposition that the proportionality of a decision to prosecute, as well as proof of guilt, must always be established.

57. That does not mean that proportionality has no part to play in prosecution decisions in cases of this kind. It does. This is because of the sensible provisions contained in the Crown Prosecution Service Code of Practice relating to potential prosecutions in public protest cases. The guidance given requires prosecutors in such cases to focus, among other things, on (a) whether prosecution is necessary and (b) whether prosecution is proportionate. The point remains that that is a matter for the decision of the Crown Prosecution Service, whose function it is to make such decisions. The magistrates' court is not itself thereafter required to review such a decision.

58. It further follows that it would be improper for defendants, under the guise of an abuse of process application made to the magistrates' court, to advance arguments which are in truth simply directed at considerations of the proportionality of the decision to prosecute. Applications for a stay on the grounds of abuse of process are to be circumscribed and orders of stay are, when made, granted only exceptionally. Applications for a stay on the ground of abuse of process must not themselves be permitted to become an abuse."

The prosecution of an offence under s 5 of the Public Order Act 1986 of a man who walked naked through a town centre, knowing that this would cause many members of the public to be alarmed and distressed, was a proportionate response to his behaviour; the defendant's minority view on public nudity had to be respected, but did not entitle him to trample over the rights of the majority to enjoy a public space without being alarmed or distressed: *Gough v DPP* [2013] EWHC 3267 (Admin), 177 JP 669.

See further footnote 11, infra.

[11] The defence of reasonable conduct is to be viewed objectively (*DPP v Clarke* (1991) 156 JP 267). In a case involving the defacement of the American flag (the defendant's own property) near the gate of an RAF base, in the course of a protest against the use of weapons of mass destruction and American military policy including the national missile defence system, it was held that the court had to presume that the defendant's conduct was protected by art 10 unless and until is was established that a restriction on her freedom was strictly necessary. While the district judge had been entitled to find that there was a pressing social need in a multicultural society to prevent the denigration of objects veneration and symbolic importance for one social group, the next stage was to assess whether or not interference, by means of prosecution, with the defendant's right to free expression by using her own property to convey a lawful message, was a proportionate response to that aim, and the fact that the defendant could have demonstrated in other ways was only one factor to be taken into account when determining the overall reasonableness of the defendant's behaviour and the state's response to it: *Percy v DPP* [2001] EWHC Admin 1125, 166 JP 93, [2002] Crim LR 835.

7.10380 6. **Mental element: miscellaneous**[1] (1) A person is guilty of riot only if he intends to use violence or is aware that his conduct may be violent.

(2) A person is guilty of violent disorder or affray only if he intends to use or threaten violence or is aware that his conduct may be violent or threaten violence.

(3) A person is guilty of an offence under section 4 only if he intends his words or behaviour, or the writing, sign or other visible representation, to be threatening, abusive or insulting, or is aware that it may be threatening, abusive or insulting.

(4) A person is guilty of an offence under section 5 only if he intends his words or behaviour, or the writing, sign or other visible representation, to be threatening or abusive or is aware that it may be threatening or abusive or (as the case may be) he intends his behaviour to be or is aware that it may be disorderly[2].

(5) For the purposes of this section a person whose awareness is impaired by intoxication shall be taken to be aware of that of which he would be aware if not intoxicated, unless he shows either that his intoxication was not self-induced or that it was caused solely by the taking or administration of a substance in the course of medical treatment.

(6) In subsection (5) "intoxication" means any intoxication, whether caused by drink, drugs or other means, or by a combination of means.

(7) Subsections (1) and (2) do not affect the determination for the purposes of riot or violent disorder of the number of persons who use or threaten violence.

[Public Order Act 1986, s 6 as amended by the Crime and Courts Act 2013, s 57.]

---

[1] The offences created by the Public Order Act 1986 may be committed by aiders and abettors as well as by principals. Section 6 of the Act is concerned only with identifying the requisite *mens rea* for each of the offences under ss 1–5, and it does not exclude in relation to any of those offences the liability of an aider and abettor who is aware of and party to the requisite intent of the principal offender (*R v Jefferson* [1994] 1 All ER 270, 158 JP 76, 99 Cr App Rep 13).

[2] The burden of proof in relation to the mental element in s 6(4) rests on the prosecution the standard of proof being beyond reasonable doubt (*DPP v Clarke* (1991) 156 JP 267).

7.10381 7. **Procedure: miscellaneous** (1) No prosecution for an offence of riot or incitement to riot may be instituted except by or with the consent of the Director of Public

Prosecutions.

(2) For the purposes of the rules against charging more than one offence in the same count or information, each of sections 1 to 5 creates one offence.

(3) If on the trial on indictment of a person charged with violent disorder or affray the jury find him not guilty of the offence charged, they may (without prejudice to section 6(3) of the Criminal Law Act 1967) find him guilty of an offence under section 4.

(4) The Crown Court has the same powers and duties in relation to a person who is by virtue of subsection (3) convicted before it of an offence under section 4 as a magistrates' court would have on convicting him of the offence.

[Public Order Act 1986, s 7.]

7.10382 8. **Interpretation** In this Part—

"dwelling" means any structure or part of a structure occupied as a person's home or as other living accommodation[1] (whether the occupation is separate or shared with others) but does not include any part not so occupied, and for this purpose "structure" includes a tent, caravan, vehicle, vessel or other temporary or movable structure;

"violence" means any violent conduct, so that—

(*a*) except in the context of affray, it includes violent conduct towards property as well as violent conduct towards persons, and

(*b*) it is not restricted to conduct causing or intended to cause injury or damage but includes any other violent conduct (for example, throwing at or towards a person a missile of a kind capable of causing injury which does not hit or falls short).

[Public Order Act 1986, s 8.]

---

1 A communal laundry room in the basement of a sheltered housing block containing a number of self-contained flats is not a dwelling or other living accommodation for the purposes of s 8: *Levine v DPP* [2010] EWHC 1128 (Admin), 174 JP 337.

7.10383 9. **Offences abolished** (1) The common law offences of riot, rout, unlawful assembly and affray are abolished.

(2) The offences under the following enactments are abolished—

(*a*) section 1 of the Tumultuous Petitioning Act 1661 (presentation of petition to monarch or Parliament accompanied by excessive number of persons),

(*b*) section 1 of the Shipping Offences Act 1793 (interference with operation of vessel by persons riotously assembled),

(*c*) section 23 of the Seditious Meetings Act 1817 (prohibition of certain meetings within one mile of Westminster Hall when Parliament sitting), and

(*d*) section 5 of the Public Order Act 1936 (conduct conducive to breach of the peace).

[Public Order Act 1986, s 9.]

7.10384 10. **Construction of other instruments** (1) In the Riot (Damages) Act 1886 (compensation for riot damage) "riotous" and "riotously" shall be construed in accordance with section 1 above.

(2) In Schedule 1 to the Marine Insurance Act 1906 (form and rules for the construction of certain insurance policies) "rioters" in rule 8 and "riot" in rule 10 shall, in the application of the rules to any policy taking effect on or after the coming into force of this section, be construed in accordance with section 1 above unless a different intention appears.

(3) "Riot" and cognate expressions in any enactment in force before the coming into force of this section (other than the enactments mentioned in subsections (1) and (2) above) shall be construed in accordance with section 1 above if they would have been construed in accordance with the common law offence of riot apart from this Part.

(4) Subject to subsections (1) to (3) above and unless a different intention appears, nothing in this Part affects the meaning of "riot" or any cognate expression in any enactment in force, or other instrument taking effect, before the coming into force of this section.

[Public Order Act 1986, s 10 as amended by the Merchant Shipping Act 1995, Sch 12.]

## Part II[1]

## Processions and Assemblies

7.10385 11. **Advance notice of public processions**[2] (1) Written notice shall be given in accordance with this section of any proposal to hold a public procession intended—

(*a*) to demonstrate support for or opposition to the views or actions of any person or body of persons,

(*b*) to publicise a cause or campaign, or

(*c*) to mark or commemorate an event,

unless it is not reasonably practicable[3] to give any advance notice of the procession.

(2) Subsection (1) does not apply where the procession is one commonly or customarily held[4] in the police area (or areas) in which it is proposed to be held or is a funeral procession organised by a funeral director acting in the normal course of his business.

(3) The notice must specify the date when it is intended to hold the procession, the time when it is intended to start it, its proposed route, and the name and address of the person (or of one of the

persons) proposing to organise it.

(4) Notice must be delivered to a police station—

(*a*) in the police area in which it is proposed the procession will start, or

(*b*) where it is proposed the procession will start in Scotland and cross into England, in the first police area in England on the proposed route.

(5) If delivered not less than 6 clear days before the date when the procession is intended to be held, the notice may be delivered by post by the recorded delivery service; but section 7 of the Interpretation Act 1978 (under which a document sent by post is deemed to have been served when posted and to have been delivered in the ordinary course of post) does not apply.

(6) If not delivered in accordance with subsection (5), the notice must be delivered by hand not less than 6 clear days before the date when the procession is intended to be held or, if that is not reasonably practicable, as soon as delivery is reasonably practicable.

(7) Where a public procession is held, each of the persons organising it is guilty of an offence if—

(*a*) the requirements of this section as to notice have not been satisfied, or

(*b*) the date when it is held, the time when it starts, or its route, differs from the date, time or route specified in the notice.

(8) It is a defence for the accused to prove that he did not know of, and neither suspected nor had reason to suspect, the failure to satisfy the requirements or (as the case may be) the difference of date, time or route.

(9) To the extent that an alleged offence turns on a difference of date, time or route, it is a defence for the accused to prove that the difference arose from circumstances beyond his control or from something done with the agreement of a police officer or by his direction.

(10) A person guilty of an offence under subsection (7) is liable on summary conviction to a fine not exceeding **level 3** on the standard scale.

[Public Order Act 1986, s 11.]

---

[1] Part II contains ss 11–16.

[2] An obligation to notify the police or to seek authorisation in relation to marches and assemblies will not necessarily infringe art 10 (freedom of expression) or art 11 (the right to peaceful assembly) of the European Convention on Human Rights: *Rassemblement Jurassien and Unite Jurassienne v Switzerland* (1979) 17 DR 93.

In the first instance decision in *Kay v Metropolitan Police Comr* [2006] EWHC 1536 (Admin), [2006] RTR 469 it was held that a procession with no planned route and no organiser might still be the subject of the notice requirements of s 11; this view was doubted, however, when the case came before the House of Lords in *Kay v Metropolitan Police Comr* [2008] UKHL 69, [2009] 2 All ER 935, [2008] 1 WLR 2793.

[3] This exemption is designed to accommodate demonstrations occurring in relation to sudden events; it does not apply simply because some of the necessary details cannot be given, eg there is no planned route or organiser: see both the first instance and House of Lords decisions in *Kay v Metropolitan Police Comr*, supra.

[4] A procession can become "commonly or customarily held" even though lacking a fixed and known route: *Kay v Metropolitan Police Comr* [2008] UKHL 69, [2009] 2 All ER 935, [2008] 1 WLR 2793.

7.10386 **12. Imposing conditions on public processions** (1) If the senior police officer, having regard to the time or place at which and the circumstances in which any public procession is being held or is intended to be held and to its route or proposed route[1], reasonably believes that—

(*a*) it may result in serious public disorder, serious damage to property or serious disruption to the life of the community, or

(*b*) the purpose of the persons organising it is the intimidation of others with a view to compelling them not to do an act they have a right to do, or to do an act they have a right not to do,

he may give directions imposing on the persons organising or taking part in the procession such conditions as appear to him necessary to prevent such disorder, damage, disruption or intimidation, including conditions as to the route of the procession or prohibiting it from entering any public place specified in the directions.

(2) In subsection (1) "the senior police officer" means—

(*a*) in relation to a procession being held, or to a procession intended to be held in a case where persons are assembling with a view to taking part in it, the most senior in rank of the police officers present at the scene, and

(*b*) in relation to a procession intended to be held in a case where paragraph (*a*) does not apply, the chief officer of police.

(3) A direction given by a chief officer of police by virtue of subsection (2)(*b*) shall be given in writing.

(4) A person who organises a public procession and knowingly fails to comply with a condition imposed under this section is guilty of an offence, but it is a defence for him to prove that the failure arose from circumstances beyond his control.

(5) A person who takes part in a public procession[2] and knowingly fails to comply with a condition imposed under this section is guilty of an offence, but it is a defence for him to prove that the failure arose from circumstances beyond his control.

(6) A person who incites another to commit an offence under subsection (5) is guilty of an offence.

(7) *Repealed.*

(8) A person guilty of an offence under subsection (4) is liable on summary conviction to imprisonment for a term not exceeding **3 months*** or a fine not exceeding **level 4** on the standard

scale or both.

(9) A person guilty of an offence under subsection (5) is liable on summary conviction to a fine not exceeding **level 3** on the standard scale.

(10) A person guilty of an offence under subsection (6) is liable on summary conviction to imprisonment for a term not exceeding **3 months*** or a fine not exceeding **level 4** on the standard scale or **both**.

(11) *Scotland.*

[Public Order Act 1986, s 12 as amended by the Serious Crime Act 2007, Schs 6 and 14.]

* **"51 weeks" substituted by the Criminal Justice Act 2003, Sch 26 from a date to be appointed.**

[1] Section 12 is not concerned solely with proposed routes of which advance notice must be given under s 11 above; "proposed route" for the purposes of s 12 includes a route which has not been notified or is not even notifiable. Nor does the route have to be a specifically planned route; for the purposes of s 12, the police can give a direction based on what they understand of the organizers' intentions and based on what they believe to be reasonably possible future routes of the procession, which may result in serious disruption: *Powlesland v DPP* [2013] EWHC 3846 (Admin), [2014] 3 All ER 479, 178 JP 67.

[2] Where persons took part in a procession which was subject to s 12 conditions, but with the intention of breaking away from it and joining a pre-planned arrangement to set up an encampment in Trafalgar Square as part of a different protest, and they were allowed to leave the route of the march once it had reached that point, it remained open for the court to find that the s 12 conditions still applied to them at the time they left the prescribed route and that their arrest an hour later was not for participating in the Trafalgar Square protest (to which the conditions did not apply) but for the earlier breach: *Jukes v DPP; Van El v DPP* [2013] EWHC 195 (Admin), 177 JP 212, [2013] Crim LR 773.

**7.10387** **13. Prohibiting public processions** (1) If at any time the chief officer of police reasonably believes that, because of particular circumstances existing in any district or part of a district, the powers under section 12 will not be sufficient to prevent the holding of public processions in that district or part from resulting in serious public disorder, he shall apply to the council of the district for an order prohibiting for such period not exceeding 3 months as may be specified in the application the holding of all public processions (or of any class of public procession so specified) in the district or part concerned.

(2) On receiving such an application, a council may with the consent of the Secretary of State make an order either in the terms of the application or with such modifications as may be approved by the Secretary of State.

(3) Subsection (1) does not apply in the City of London or the metropolitan police district.

(4) If at any time the Commissioner of Police for the City of London or the Commissioner of Police of the Metropolis reasonably believes that, because of particular circumstances existing in his police area or part of it, the powers under section 12 will not be sufficient to prevent the holding of public processions in that area or part from resulting in serious public disorder, he may with the consent of the Secretary of State make an order prohibiting for such period not exceeding 3 months as may be specified in the order the holding of all public processions (or of any class of public procession so specified) in the area or part concerned.

(5) An order made under this section may be revoked or varied by a subsequent order made in the same way, that is, in accordance with subsections (1) and (2) or subsection (4), as the case may be.

(6) Any order under this section shall, if not made in writing, be recorded in writing as soon as practicable after being made.

(7) A person who organises a public procession the holding of which he knows is prohibited by virtue of an order under this section is guilty of an offence.

(8) A person who takes part in a public procession the holding of which he knows is prohibited by virtue of an order under this section is guilty of an offence.

(9) A person who incites another to commit an offence under subsection (8) is guilty of an offence.

(10) *Repealed.*

(11) A person guilty of an offence under subsection (7) is liable on summary conviction to imprisonment for a term not exceeding **3 months*** or a fine not exceeding **level 4** on the standard scale or **both**.

(12) A person guilty of an offence under subsection (8) is liable on summary conviction to a fine not exceeding **level 3** on the standard scale.

(13) A person guilty of an offence under subsection (9) is liable on summary conviction to imprisonment for a term not exceeding **3 months*** or a fine not exceeding **level 4** on the standard scale or **both**.

[Public Order Act 1986, s 13 as amended by the Serious Organised Crime and Police Act 2005, Schs 7 and 17 and the Serious Crime Act 2007, Schs 6 and 14.]

* **"51 weeks" substituted by the Criminal Justice Act 2003, Sch 26 from a date to be appointed.**

**7.10388** **14. Imposing conditions on public assemblies** (1) If the senior police officer, having regard to the time or place at which and the circumstances in which any public assembly is being held or is intended to be held, reasonably believes that—

(*a*) it may result in serious public disorder, serious damage to property or serious disruption to the life of the community, or

(*b*) the purpose of the persons organising it is the intimidation of others with a view to compelling them not to do an act they have a right to do, or to do an act they have a right not to do, he may give directions imposing on the persons organising or taking part in the assembly such conditions[1] as to the place at which the assembly may be (or continue to be) held, its maximum duration, or the maximum number of persons who may constitute it, as appear to him necessary to prevent such disorder, damage, disruption or intimidation.

(2) In subsection (1) "the senior police officer" means—

(*a*) in relation to an assembly being held, the most senior in rank of the police officers present at the scene, and

(*b*) in relation to an assembly intended to be held, the chief officer of police.

(3) A direction given by a chief officer of police by virtue of subsection (2)(*b*) shall be given in writing.

(4) A person who organises a public assembly and knowingly fails to comply with a condition imposed under this section is guilty of an offence, but it is a defence for him to prove that the failure arose from circumstances beyond his control.

(5) A person who takes part in a public assembly and knowingly fails to comply with a condition imposed under this section is guilty of an offence[2], but it is a defence for him to prove that the failure arose from circumstances beyond his control.

(6) A person who incites another to commit an offence under subsection (5) is guilty of an offence.

(7) *Repealed.*

(8) A person guilty of an offence under subsection (4) is liable on summary conviction to imprisonment for a term not exceeding **3 months*** or a fine not exceeding **level 4** on the standard scale or **both**.

(9) A person guilty of an offence under subsection (5) is liable on summary conviction to a fine not exceeding **level 3** on the standard scale.

(10) A person guilty of an offence under subsection (6) is liable on summary conviction to imprisonment for a term not exceeding **3 months*** or a fine not exceeding **level 4** on the standard scale or **both**.

[Public Order Act 1986, s 14 as amended by the Serious Organised Crime and Police Act 2005, Schs 7 and 17 and the Serious Crime Act 2007, Schs 6 and 14.]

---

* **"51 weeks" substituted by the Criminal Justice Act 2003, Sch 26 from a date to be appointed.**

1 The designation of entrance and exit points that are not within the assembly area falls outside the power contained in s 14; however, such conditions can be severed from other conditions in the notice that envisage a different activity, the test of severance being that which applies to legislation and legislative instruments (*DPP v Jones* [2002] All ER (D) 157 (Jan), [2002] JPN 78).

2 It was held in *James v Director of Public Prosecutions* [2015] EWHC 3296 (Admin), [2016] 1 WLR 2118, 180 JP 1 (which concerned a demonstration outside St Paul's Cathedral which blocked the carriageway) that it was not for the trial court to review the proportionality of a decision to prosecute unless it amounts to an abuse of process (see Note 1 to s 4A of the Public Order Act 1986 at para 7.10378, ante). The court then considered the role of arts 10 and 11 in the trial of an offence under s 14(5):

"33. The fact that the proportionality of a decision to prosecute in relation to arts 10 and 11 cannot be raised before trial Courts, otherwise than as an abuse of process argument, does not mean that arts 10 or 11 cannot play their proper role in the trial.

34. For some POA offences, the position has been clear for some time. *Norwood* and *Hammond* show that these rights and the qualifications to them, and thus the proportionality of the prohibitions or restraints on expression and assembly, form part of the statutory defence that the accused's conduct was reasonable. That is also what should have been decided in *Dehal.* It is the point on which the issue in *Abdul* turned in substance, and where the focus of the legal analysis should have been.

35. There are other CJPOA 1994 offences, of which *Bauer* is an example, where, as the Court held, once the specific ingredients of the offence have been proved, the conduct of the accused has gone beyond what could be regarded as reasonable conduct in the exercise of ECHR rights. The necessary balance for proportionality is struck by the terms of the offence-creating provision, without more ado.

36. The relationship between the offence of obstruction of the highway under s 137 of the Highway Act 1980 and common law rights to freedom of speech and assembly is dealt with by interpreting the words 'without lawful authority or excuse in any way wilfully obstructs . . . free passage' as not prohibiting those acts which involved wilful obstruction of the highway but which were not otherwise of themselves unlawful and which might or might not be reasonable in the circumstances. The focus therefore was on what was reasonable in all the circumstances: *Hirst and Agu v Chief Constable of West Yorkshire* (1986) 151 JP 304, 85 Cr App Rep 143, [1987] Crim LR 330.

37. The same approach was adopted in the related context of an order under s.14A of the POA prohibiting a trespassory assembly on the highway; *DPP v Jones* [1999] 2 AC 240, [1999] 2 All ER 257, 163 JP 285: the public could use the highway for any reasonable purpose so long as the activity did not obstruct the highway by unreasonably impeding the public's primary right to pass and re-pass. It was expressed in a variety of ways but that captures the essence of the thinking. Read in that way, the statutory offence of obstructing the highway allowed for consideration of the common law rights of assembly and expression, and of arts.10 and 11, through a judgment as to reasonable use of the highway, a judgment for the trial court.

38. (Counsel for the appellant) submitted that, in the absence of the specific statutory defence of 'reasonable conduct', or of a provision capable of interpretation in the way s 137 of the Highways Act has been interpreted, words had to be read into s.14 of the POA 1986 to make it compatible with ECHR rights. The wording of s 14(5), the offence-creating provision, simply required the Court to consider whether there had been a knowing failure to comply with a direction. It did not permit the defendant to contend that the direction itself had been a disproportionate interference with arts 10 and 11 rights. The defence relating to circumstances beyond the defendant's control could not cover that issue. Something needed to be done to bring s 14(5) into line with the approach to other public order offences involving freedom of speech and assembly. (Counsel) suggested that the words 'except insofar as a conviction would be disproportionate by reference to arts 10 or 11 of the ECHR' should be read into s.14(5). He likened this to *R v Waya* [2012] UKSC 51, [2013] 1 AC 294, in which a provision of the Proceeds of Crime Act 2002 dealing with confiscation orders was interpreted, by virtue of s.3 Human Rights Act 1998, as containing words disapplying the power to make an order where to do so would be disproportionate with property rights under art.1 of Protocol 1 to the ECHR.

39. To my mind, the starting point is the power to give a direction in s 14(1). It is plain that it requires the senior officer to hold the necessary belief that a public assembly may result in serious public disorder, and to have reasonable grounds for that belief. If, upon challenge by a person accused of an offence under s 14(5), the officer cannot prove that he actually held the necessary belief and did so upon reasonable grounds, his direction would be unlawful. It is necessarily implicit in s 14(5) that the direction containing the conditions must be lawful. Acquittal would follow, if it were not. As with *Bauer*, no other words are necessary to imply proportionality at that stage. Satisfaction of the statutory test is proof of the proportionality of the making of a direction.

40. If the officer holds that belief on reasonable grounds, the conditions imposed by the direction must be such 'as appear to him necessary to prevent such disorder'. Again, that 'necessity' must genuinely appear to him. If no such necessity had appeared to him, the condition would not be lawful; non-compliance with it would not be an offence. If that necessity had appeared, I have some difficulty envisaging the circumstances in which the qualifications to arts.10 and 11 would not also inevitably be satisfied. Rather as in *Bauer*, proof of the ingredients of the offence itself would demonstrate the proportionality of the condition, non-compliance with which underlies the offence. Conviction would require proof of a reasonable belief actually held by the Senior Officer that a public assembly may result in serious disorder, so he had power to make a lawful direction, the purpose of which is to impose conditions on a public assembly; and conviction would then also require proof that it appeared to him that such a condition was necessary to prevent the serious public disorder he reasonably believed may exist.

41. It would only be if the officer reasonably believed that serious disorder might result from an assembly so that the direction was lawful, and genuinely but unreasonably thought that a particular condition was necessary to prevent the serious disorder, that an issue related to the proportionality of the condition could arise. A condition might be wholly out of proportion to the problem to be solved, but it would still be necessary for the officer to have believed that it was necessary before any further issue could arise, and the disproportion of condition to circumstance as known would be relevant to the genuineness of the belief that it was necessary.

42. However, it is clear that a condition imposed under s 14(1) must be a lawful condition, and in this section that must import that it must reasonably appear to be necessary to prevent serious disorder. This reflects the language of the first part of s 14(1). I do not think that Parliament intended to draw the distinction between the two aspects of s 14 — directions and conditions — which the omission of the word 'reasonably' before 'appear to him necessary' in the last part of s 14(1) could suggest. Rather it assumed that the requirement for reasonableness would carry over to the appearance of necessity. So, in my judgment, for a s 14(5) offence, the proportionality of direction and condition for the purposes of arts 10 and 11 ECHR can be raised through testing of the reasonableness of the beliefs which necessarily underpin each.

43. This is not the argument as put to the District Judge. But he accepted the evidence of Chief Inspector Wade as to the seriously disruptive effect on traffic in the Strand which the assembly was having, through blocking the pedestrian crossing. The protestors were only required to go to the pavement, and not to block it. It would have been irrational to conclude that the direction and condition were unreasonable." (per Ouseley J).

**7.10389 14A. Prohibiting trespassory assemblies** (1) If at any time the chief officer of police reasonably believes that an assembly is intended to be held in any district at a place on land to which the public has no right of access or only a limited right of access and that the assembly—

(*a*) is likely to be held without the permission of the occupier of the land or to conduct itself in such a way as to exceed the limits of any permission of his or the limits of the public's right of access, and

(*b*) may result—

(i) in serious disruption to the life of the community, or

(ii) where the land, or a building or monument on it, is of historical, architectural, archaeological or scientific importance, in significant damage to the land, building or monument,

he may apply to the council of the district for an order prohibiting for a specified period the holding of all trespassory assemblies in the district or a part of it, as specified.

(2) On receiving such an application, a council may—

(*a*) in England and Wales, with the consent of the Secretary of State make an order[1] either in the terms of the application or with such modifications as may be approved by the Secretary of State; or

(*b*) *Scotland.*

(3) Subsection (1) does not apply in the City of London or the metropolitan police district.

(4) If at any time the Commissioner of Police for the City of London or the Commissioner of Police of the Metropolis reasonably believes that an assembly is intended to be held at a place on land to which the public has no right of access or only a limited right of access in his police area and that the assembly—

(*a*) is likely to be held without the permission of the occupier of the land or to conduct itself in such a way as to exceed the limits of any permission of his or the limits of the public's right of access, and

(*b*) may result—

(i) in serious disruption to the life of the community, or

(ii) where the land, or a building or monument on it, is of historical, architectural, archaeological or scientific importance, in significant damage to the land, building or monument,

he may with the consent of the Secretary of State make an order prohibiting for a specified period the holding of all trespassory assemblies in the area or a part of it, as specified.

(5) An order[1] prohibiting the holding of trespassory assemblies operates to prohibit any assembly which—

(*a*) is held on land to which the public has no right of access or only a limited right of access, and (*b*) takes place in the prohibited circumstances, that is to say, without the permission of the occupier of the land or so as to exceed the limits of any permission of his or the limits of the public's right of access.

(6) No order under this section shall prohibit the holding of assemblies for a period exceeding 4 days or in an area exceeding an area represented by a circle with a radius of 5 miles from a specified centre.

(7) An order made under this section may be revoked or varied by a subsequent order made in the same way, that is, in accordance with subsection (1) and (2) or subsection (4), as the case may be.

(8) Any order under this section shall, if not made in writing, be recorded in writing as soon as practicable after being made.

(9) In this section and sections 14B and 14C—

"assembly" means an assembly of 20 or more persons;

"land" means land in the open air;

"limited", in relation to a right of access by the public to land, means that their use of it is restricted to use for a particular purpose (as in the case of a highway or road) or is subject to other restrictions;

"occupier" means—

(*a*) in England and Wales, the person entitled to possession of the land by virtue of an estate or interest held by him; or

(*b*) in Scotland, the person lawfully entitled to natural possession of the land,

and in subsections (1) and (4) includes the person reasonably believed by the authority applying for or making the order to be the occupier;

"public" includes a section of the public; and

"specified" means specified in an order under this section.

(9A) *Scotland.*

(10) *Scotland.*

(11) In relation to Wales, the references in subsection (1) above to a district and to the council of the district shall be construed, as respects applications on and after 1st April 1996, as references to a county or county borough and to the council for that county or county borough.

[Public Order Act 1986, s 14A as inserted by the Criminal Justice and Public Order Act 1994, s 70 and amended by the Land Reform (Scotland) Act 2003, s 70.]

---

1 The public highway is a public place which the public may enjoy for any reasonable purpose, provided the activity in question does not amount to a public or private nuisance, and does not obstruct the highway by unreasonably impeding the primary right of the public to pass and re-pass. Within these qualifications, a peaceful and non-obstructive assembly does not necessarily exceed the limits of the public's right of access to the highway; however, it is for the justices in each case to decide whether the user of the highway under consideration is reasonable and, therefore, not a trespass (*DPP v Jones* [1999] 2 All ER 257, [1999] 2 WLR 625, 163 JP 285, HL).

**7.10390 14B. Offences in connection with trespassory assemblies and arrest therefor**

(1) A person who organises an assembly the holding of which he knows is prohibited by an order under section 14A is guilty of an offence.

(2) A person who takes part in an assembly which he knows is prohibited by an order under section 14A is guilty of an offence.

(3) In England and Wales, a person who incites another to commit an offence under subsection (2) is guilty of an offence.

(4) *Repealed.*

(5) A person guilty of an offence under subsection (1) is liable on summary conviction to imprisonment for a term not exceeding **3 months*** or a fine not exceeding **level 4** on the standard scale or both.

(6) A person guilty of an offence under subsection (2) is liable on summary conviction to a fine not exceeding **level 3** on the standard scale.

(7) A person guilty of an offence under subsection (3) is liable on summary conviction to imprisonment for a term not exceeding **3 months*** or a fine not exceeding **level 4** on the standard scale or **both**.

(8) Subsection (3) above is without prejudice to the application of any principle of Scots Law as respects art and part guilt to such incitement as is mentioned in that subsection.

[Public Order Act 1986, s 14B as inserted by the Criminal Justice and Public Order Act 1994, s 70 and amended by the Serious Organised Crime and Police Act 2005, Schs 7 and 17 and the Serious Crime Act 2007, Schs 6 and 14.]

---

* **"51 weeks" substituted by the Criminal Justice Act 2003, Sch 26 from a date to be appointed.**

**7.10391 14C. Stopping persons from proceeding to trespassory assemblies** (1) If a constable in uniform reasonably believes that a person is on his way to an assembly within the area to which an order under section 14A applies which the constable reasonably believes is likely to be an assembly which is prohibited by that order, he may, subject to subsection (2) below—

(*a*) stop that person, and

(*b*) direct him not to proceed in the direction of the assembly.

(2) The power conferred by subsection (1) may only be exercised within the area to which the order applies.

(3) A person who fails to comply with a direction under subsection (1) which he knows has been given to him is guilty of an offence.

(4) *Repealed.*

(5) A person guilty of an offence under subsection (3) is liable on summary conviction to a fine not exceeding **level 3** on the standard scale.

[Public Order Act 1986, s 14C as inserted by the Criminal Justice and Public Order Act 1994, s 71 and amended by the Serious Organised Crime and Police Act 2005, Schs 7 and 17.]

7.10392 **15. Delegation** (1) The chief officer of police may delegate, to such extent and subject to such conditions as he may specify, any of his functions under sections 12 to 14A to an assistant chief constable; and references in those sections to the person delegating shall be construed accordingly.

(2) Subsection (1) shall have effect in the City of London and the metropolitan police district as if "an assistant chief constable" read "an assistant commissioner of police".

[Public Order Act 1986, s 15 as amended by the Police and Magistrates' Courts Act 1994, Sch 5 and the Criminal Justice and Public Order Act 1994, Sch 10.]

7.10393 **16. Interpretation** In this Part—

"the City of London" means the City as defined for the purposes of the Acts relating to the City of London police;

"the metropolitan police district" means that district as defined in section 76 of the London Government Act 1963;

"public assembly" means an assembly of 2[1] or more persons in a public place which is wholly or partly open to the air;

"public place" means—

(*a*) any highway, or in Scotland any road within the meaning of the Roads (Scotland) Act 1984, and

(*b*) any place to which at the material time the public or any section of the public has access, on payment or otherwise, as of right or by virtue of express or implied permission;

"public procession" means a procession in a public place.

[Public Order Act 1986, s 16 as amended by the Anti-Social Behaviour Act 2003, s 57.]

---

1 Reference to "2" substituted for "20", in relation to England and Wales.

## PART III[1]
## RACIAL HATRED

*Meaning of "racial hatred"*

7.10394 **17. Meaning of "racial hatred"** In this Part "racial hatred" means hatred against a group of persons defined by reference to colour, race, nationality (including citizenship) or ethnic or national origins.

[Public Order Act 1986, s 17 as amended by the Anti-terrorism, Crime and Security Act 2001, Sch 8.]

---

1 Part III contains ss 17–29.

*Acts intended or likely to stir up racial hatred*

7.10395 **18. Use of words or behaviour or display of written material[1]** (1) A person who uses threatening, abusive or insulting words or behaviour, or displays any written material which is threatening, abusive or insulting, is guilty of an offence if—

(*a*) he intends thereby to stir up racial hatred, or

(*b*) having regard to all the circumstances racial hatred is likely to be stirred up thereby.

(2) An offence under this section may be committed in a public or a private place, except that no offence is committed where the words or behaviour are used, or the written material is displayed, by a person inside a dwelling and are not heard or seen except by other persons in that or another dwelling.

(3) *Repealed.*

(4) In proceedings for an offence under this section it is a defence for the accused to prove that he was inside a dwelling and had no reason to believe that the words or behaviour used, or the written material displayed, would be heard or seen by a person outside that or any other dwelling.

(5) A person who is not shown to have intended to stir up racial hatred is not guilty of an offence under this section if he did not intend his words or behaviour, or the written material, to be, and was not aware that it might be, threatening, abusive or insulting.

(6) This section does not apply to words or behaviour used, or written material displayed, solely for the purpose of being included in a programme included in a programme service.

[Public Order Act 1986, s 18 as amended by the Broadcasting Act 1990, s 164 and the Serious Organised Crime and Police Act 2005, Sch 7.]

---

1 Restrictions on the expression of racist ideas are legitimate under art 10(2) of the European Convention on Human Rights as being for the protection of the rights of others. They are also specifically provided for in art 17 of the Convention. See further *Glimmerveen and Hagenbeek v Netherlands* (1979) 18 DR 187, *Kuhnen v Germany* (1988) 56 DR 205 and *Jersild v Denmark* (1994) 19 EHRR 1.

7.10396 **19. Publishing or distributing written material[1]** (1) A person who publishes or distributes written material which is threatening, abusive or insulting is guilty of an offence if—

(*a*) he intends thereby to stir up racial hatred, or

(*b*) having regard to all the circumstances racial hatred is likely to be stirred up thereby.

(2) In proceedings for an offence under this section it is a defence for an accused who is not shown to have intended to stir up racial hatred to prove that he was not aware of the content of the material and did not suspect, and had no reason to suspect, that it was threatening, abusive or insulting.

(3) References in this Part to the publication or distribution of written material are to its publication or distribution to the public or a section of the public[2].

[Public Order Act 1986, s 19.]

---

[1] For the position under the European Convention on Human Rights see para 7.10395, footnote (1), ante.

[2] Where material was on a website, the fact that it was readily accessible to all or available to or was placed before, or offered to the public and that that was proved by the evidence of one witness, was sufficient to establish publication to the public etc. There is no need for proof that anybody actually read or heard the material (*R v Sheppard* [2010] EWCA Crim 65, [2010] 2 All ER 850, [2010] 1 WLR 2779, [2010] 1 Cr App R 26).

7.10397 **20. Public performance of play**[1] (1) If a public performance of a play is given which involves the use of threatening, abusive or insulting words or behaviour, any person who presents or directs the performance is guilty of an offence if—

(*a*) he intends thereby to stir up racial hatred, or

(*b*) having regard to all the circumstances (and, in particular, taking the performance as a whole) racial hatred is likely to be stirred up thereby.

(2) If a person presenting or directing the performance is not shown to have intended to stir up racial hatred, it is a defence for him to prove—

(*a*) that he did not know and had no reason to suspect that the performance would involve the use of the offending words or behaviour, or

(*b*) that he did not know and had no reason to suspect that the offending words or behaviour were threatening, abusive or insulting, or

(*c*) that he did not know and had no reason to suspect that the circumstances in which the performance would be given would be such that racial hatred would be likely to be stirred up.

(3) This section does not apply to a performance given solely or primarily for one or more of the following purposes—

(*a*) rehearsal,

(*b*) making a recording of the performance, or

(*c*) enabling the performance to be included in a programme service;

but if it is proved that the performance was attended by persons other than those directly connected with the giving of the performance or the doing in relation to it of the things mentioned in paragraph (*b*) or (*c*), the performance shall, unless the contrary is shown, be taken not to have been given solely or primarily for the purposes mentioned above.

(4) For the purposes of this section—

(*a*) a person shall not be treated as presenting a performance of a play by reason only of his taking part in it as a performer,

(*b*) a person taking part as a performer in a performance directed by another shall be treated as a person who directed the performance if without reasonable excuse he performs otherwise than in accordance with that person's direction, and

(*c*) a person shall be taken to have directed a performance of a play given under his direction notwithstanding that he was not present during the performance;

and a person shall not be treated as aiding or abetting the commission of an offence under this section by reason only of his taking part in a performance as a performer.

(5) In this section "play" and "public performance" have the same meaning as in the Theatres Act 1968.

(6) The following provisions of the Theatres Act 1968 apply in relation to an offence under this section as they apply to an offence under section 2 of that Act—

section 9 (script as evidence of what was performed),

section 10 (power to make copies of script),

section 15 (powers of entry and inspection).

[Public Order Act 1986, s 20 as amended by the Broadcasting Act 1990, s 164.]

---

[1] For the position under the European Convention on Human Rights see para 7.10395, footnote (1), ante.

7.10398 **21. Distributing, showing or playing a recording**[1] (1) A person who distributes, or shows or plays, a recording of visual images or sounds which are threatening, abusive or insulting is guilty of an offence if—

(*a*) he intends thereby to stir up racial hatred, or

(*b*) having regard to all the circumstances racial hatred is likely to be stirred up thereby.

(2) In this Part "recording" means any record from which visual images or sounds may, by any means, be reproduced; and references to the distribution, showing or playing of a recording are to its distribution, showing or playing to the public or a section of the public.

(3) In proceedings for an offence under this section it is a defence for an accused who is not shown to have intended to stir up racial hatred to prove that he was not aware of the content of the recording and did not suspect, and had no reason to suspect, that it was threatening, abusive or

insulting.

(4) This section does not apply to the showing or playing of a recording solely for the purpose of enabling the recording to be included in a programme service.

[Public Order Act 1986, s 21 as amended by the Broadcasting Act 1990, s 164.]

---

1 For the position under the European Convention on Human Rights see para 7.10395, footnote (1), ante.

7.10399 **22. Broadcasting or including programme in programme service**[1] (1) If a programme involving threatening, abusive or insulting visual images or sounds is included in a programme service, each of the persons mentioned in subsection (2) is guilty of an offence if—

(*a*) he intends thereby to stir up racial hatred, or

(*b*) having regard to all the circumstances racial hatred is likely to be stirred up thereby.

(2) The persons are—

(*a*) the person providing the programme service,

(*b*) any person by whom the programme is produced or directed, and

(*c*) any person by whom offending words or behaviour are used.

(3) If the person providing the service, or a person by whom the programme was produced or directed, is not shown to have intended to stir up racial hatred, it is a defence for him to prove that—

(*a*) he did not know and had no reason to suspect that the programme would involve the offending material, and

(*b*) having regard to the circumstances in which the programme was included in a programme service, it was not reasonably practicable for him to secure the removal of the material.

(4) It is a defence for a person by whom the programme was produced or directed who is not shown to have intended to stir up racial hatred to prove that he did not know and had no reason to suspect—

(*a*) that the programme would be included in a programme service, or

(*b*) that the circumstances in which the programme would be so included would be such that racial hatred would be likely to be stirred up.

(5) It is a defence for a person by whom offending words or behaviour were used and who is not shown to have intended to stir up racial hatred to prove that he did not know and had no reason to suspect—

(*a*) that a programme involving the use of the offending material would be included in a programme service, or

(*b*) that the circumstances in which a programme involving the use of the offending material would be so included, or in which a programme so included would involve the use of the offending material, would be such that racial hatred would be likely to be stirred up.

(6) A person who is not shown to have intended to stir up racial hatred is not guilty of an offence under this section if he did not know, and had no reason to suspect, that the offending material was threatening, abusive or insulting.

(7), (8) *Repealed.*

[Public Order Act 1986, s 22 as amended by the Broadcasting Act 1990, s 164 and Sch 21.]

---

1 For the position under the European Convention on Human Rights see para 7.10395, footnote (1), ante.

*Racially inflammatory material*

7.10400 **23. Possession of racially inflammatory material**[1] (1) A person who has in his possession written material which is threatening, abusive or insulting, or a recording of visual images or sounds which are threatening, abusive or insulting, with a view to—

(*a*) in the case of written material, its being displayed, published, distributed, or included in a programme service whether by himself or another, or

(*b*) in the case of a recording, its being distributed, shown, played, or included in a programme service whether by himself or another,

is guilty of an offence if he intends racial hatred to be stirred up thereby or, having regard to all the circumstances, racial hatred is likely to be stirred up thereby.

(2) For this purpose regard shall be had to such display, publication, distribution, showing, playing, or inclusion in a programme service as he has, or it may reasonably be inferred that he has, in view.

(3) In proceedings for an offence under this section it is a defence for an accused who is not shown to have intended to stir up racial hatred to prove that he was not aware of the content of the written material or recording and did not suspect, and had no reason to suspect, that it was threatening, abusive or insulting.

(4) *Repealed.*

[Public Order Act 1986, s 23 as amended by the Broadcasting Act 1990, s 164 and Sch 21.]

---

1 For the position under the European Convention on Human Rights see para 7.10395, footnote (1), ante.

7.10401 **24. Powers of entry and search** (1) If in England and Wales a justice of the peace is satisfied by information on oath laid by a constable that there are reasonable grounds for suspecting that a person has possession of written material or a recording in contravention of section 23, the justice may issue a warrant under his hand authorising any constable to enter and search the premises where it is suspected the material or recording is situated.

(2) *Scotland.*

(3) A constable entering or searching premises in pursuance of a warrant issued under this section may use reasonable force if necessary.

(4) In this section "premises" means any place and, in particular, includes—

(*a*) any vehicle, vessel, aircraft or hovercraft,

(*b*) any offshore installation as defined in section 1(3)(*b*) of the Mineral Workings (Offshore Installations) Act 1971, and

(*c*) any tent or movable structure.

[Public Order Act 1986, s 24.]

7.10402 25. **Power to order forfeiture** (1) A court by or before which a person is convicted of—

(*a*) an offence under section 18 relating to the display of written material, or

(*b*) an offence under section 19, 21 or 23,

shall order to be forfeited any written material or recording produced to the court and shown to its satisfaction to be written material or a recording to which the offence relates.

(2) An order made under this section shall not take effect—

(*a*) in the case of an order made in proceedings in England and Wales, until the expiry of the ordinary time within which an appeal may be instituted or, where an appeal is duly instituted, until it is finally decided or abandoned;

(*b*) in the case of an order made in proceedings in Scotland, until the expiration of the time within which, by virtue of any statute, an appeal may be instituted or, where such an appeal is duly instituted, until the appeal is finally decided or abandoned.

(3) For the purposes of subsection (2)(*a*)—

(*a*) an application for a case stated or for leave to appeal shall be treated as the institution of an appeal, and

(*b*) where a decision on appeal is subject to a further appeal, the appeal is not finally determined until the expiry of the ordinary time within which a further appeal may be instituted or, where a further appeal is duly instituted, until the further appeal is finally decided or abandoned.

(4) For the purposes of subsection (2)(*b*) the lodging of an application for a stated case or note of appeal against sentence shall be treated as the institution of an appeal.

[Public Order Act 1986, s 25.]

*Supplementary provisions*

7.10403 26. **Savings for reports of parliamentary or judicial proceedings** (1) Nothing in this Part applies to a fair and accurate report of proceedings in Parliament or in the Scottish Parliament or in the National Assembly for Wales.

(2) Nothing in this Part applies to a fair and accurate report of proceedings publicly heard before a court or tribunal exercising judicial authority where the report is published contemporaneously with the proceedings or, if it is not reasonably practicable or would be unlawful to publish a report of them contemporaneously, as soon as publication is reasonably practicable and lawful.

[Public Order Act 1986, s 24 as amended by the Scotland Act 1998, Sch 8 and the Government of Wales Act 2006, Sch 10.]

7.10404 27. **Procedure and punishment** (1) No proceedings for an offence under this Part may be instituted in England and Wales except by or with the consent of the Attorney General.

(2) For the purposes of the rules in England and Wales against charging more than one offence in the same count or information, each of sections 18 to 23 creates one offence.

(3) A person guilty of an offence under this Part is liable[1]—

(*a*) on conviction on indictment to imprisonment for a term not exceeding **seven years** or a **fine** or **both**;

(*b*) on summary conviction to imprisonment for a term not exceeding **six months** or a fine not exceeding the **statutory maximum** or **both**.

[Public Order Act 1986, s 27 as amended by the Anti-terrorism, Crime and Security Act 2001, s 40.]

---

1 For procedure in respect of an offence triable either way, see the Magistrates' Courts Act 1980, ss 17A–21 in PART I: MAGISTRATES' COURTS PROCEDURE, ante.

7.10405 28. **Offences by corporations** (1) Where a body corporate is guilty of an offence under this Part and it is shown that the offence was committed with the consent or connivance of a director, manager, secretary or other similar officer of the body, or a person purporting to act in any such capacity, he as well as the body corporate is guilty of the offence and liable to be proceeded against and punished accordingly.

(2) Where the affairs of a body corporate are managed by its members, subsection (1) applies in relation to the acts and defaults of a member in connection with his functions of management as it applies to a director.

[Public Order Act 1986, s 28.]

**7.10406 29. Interpretation** In this Part—

"distribute", and related expressions, shall be construed in accordance with section 19(3) (written material) and section 21(2) (recordings);

"dwelling" means any structure or part of a structure occupied as a person's home or other living accommodation (whether the occupation is separate or shared with others) but does not include any part not so occupied, and for this purpose "structure" includes a tent, caravan, vehicle, vessel or other temporary or movable structure;

"programme" means any item which is included in a programme service;

"programme service" has the same meaning as in the Broadcasting Act 1990;

"publish", and related expressions, in relation to written material, shall be construed in accordance with section 19(3);

"racial hatred" has the meaning given by section 17;

"recording" has the meaning given by section 21(2), and "play" and "show", and related expressions, in relation to a recording, shall be construed in accordance with that provision;

"written material" includes any sign or other visible representation[1].

[Public Order Act 1986, s 29 as amended by the Broadcasting Act 1990, s 164 and Sch 21.]

---

[1] This definition is sufficiently wide to include articles in electronic form (*R v Sheppard* [2010] EWCA Crim 65, [2010] 2 All ER 850, [2010] 1 WLR 2779, [2010] 1 Cr App R 26).

## PART IIIA

## HATRED AGAINST PERSONS ON RELIGIOUS GROUNDS OR GROUNDS OF SEXUAL ORIENTATION[1]

*Meaning of "religious hatred" and "hatred on the grounds of sexual orientation"*

**7.10407 29A. Meaning of "religious hatred"** In this Part "religious hatred" means hatred against a group of persons defined by reference to religious belief or lack of religious belief.*

[Public Order Act 1986, s 29A as inserted by the Racial and Religious Hatred Act 2006, Schedule.]

---

[1] This Part comprises (originally ss 29A–29N) was inserted by the Racial and Religious Hatred Act 2006 with effect from 1 October 2007.

The liability of internet service providers within the EEA under this Part is regulated by Directive 2000/31/EC of 8th June 2000 on certain legal aspects of information society services. The Directive is implemented by the Electronic Commerce Directive (Racial and Religious Hatred Act 2006) Regulations 2010, SI 2010/894. The Directive provides in general terms that "information society services" must be regulated by the law of the EEA state in which the provider of the services is established, rather than the law of the EEA state in which the services are received. Criminal offences are created by the regulations with exceptions for "mere conduits", caching and hosting.

**7.10408 29AB. Meaning of "hatred on the grounds of sexual orientation"** In this Part "hatred on the grounds of sexual orientation" means hatred against a group of persons defined by reference to sexual orientation (whether towards persons of the same sex, the opposite sex or both).

[Public Order Act 1986, s 29AB as inserted by the Criminal Justice and Immigration Act 2008, Sch 16.]

*Acts intended to stir up religious hatred or hatred on the grounds of sexual orientation*

**7.10409 29B. Use of words or behaviour or display of written material** (1) A person who uses threatening words or behaviour, or displays any written material which is threatening, is guilty of an offence if he intends thereby to stir up religious hatred or hatred on the grounds of sexual orientation.

(2) An offence under this section may be committed in a public or a private place, except that no offence is committed where the words or behaviour are used, or the written material is displayed, by a person inside a dwelling and are not heard or seen except by other persons in that or another dwelling.

(3) *Repealed.*

(4) In proceedings for an offence under this section it is a defence for the accused to prove that he was inside a dwelling and had no reason to believe that the words or behaviour used, or the written material displayed, would be heard or seen by a person outside that or any other dwelling.

(5) This section does not apply to words or behaviour used, or written material displayed, solely for the purpose of being included in a programme service.

[Public Order Act 1986, s 29B as inserted by the Racial and Religious Hatred Act 2006, Schedule and amended by the Criminal Justice and Immigration Act 2008, Schs 16 and 28.]

**7.10410 29C. Publishing or distributing written material** (1) A person who publishes or distributes written material which is threatening is guilty of an offence if he intends thereby to stir up religious hatred or hatred on the grounds of sexual orientation.

(2) References in this Part to the publication or distribution of written material are to its publication or distribution to the public or a section of the public.

[Public Order Act 1986, s 29C as inserted by the Racial and Religious Hatred Act 2006, Schedule and amended by the Criminal Justice and Immigration Act 2008, Sch 16.]

**7.10411 29D. Public performance of play** (1) If a public performance of a play is given which involves the use of threatening words or behaviour, any person who presents or directs the performance is guilty of an offence if he intends thereby to stir up religious hatred or hatred on the grounds of sexual orientation.

(2) This section does not apply to a performance given solely or primarily for one or more of the following purposes—

(*a*) rehearsal,

(*b*) making a recording of the performance, or

(*c*) enabling the performance to be included in a programme service;

but if it is proved that the performance was attended by persons other than those directly connected with the giving of the performance or the doing in relation to it of the things mentioned in paragraph (*b*) or (*c*), the performance shall, unless the contrary is shown, be taken not to have been given solely or primarily for the purpose mentioned above.

(3) For the purposes of this section—

(*a*) a person shall not be treated as presenting a performance of a play by reason only of his taking part in it as a performer,

(*b*) a person taking part as a performer in a performance directed by another shall be treated as a person who directed the performance if without reasonable excuse he performs otherwise than in accordance with that person's direction, and

(*c*) a person shall be taken to have directed a performance of a play given under his direction notwithstanding that he was not present during the performance;

and a person shall not be treated as aiding or abetting the commission of an offence under this section by reason only of his taking part in a performance as a performer.

(4) In this section "play" and "public performance" have the same meaning as in the Theatres Act 1968.

(5) The following provisions of the Theatres Act 1968 apply in relation to an offence under this section as they apply to an offence under section 2 of that Act—

section 9 (script as evidence of what was performed),

section 10 (power to make copies of script),

section 15 (powers of entry and inspection).

[Public Order Act 1986, s 29D as inserted by the Racial and Religious Hatred Act 2006, Schedule and amended by the Criminal Justice and Immigration Act 2008, Sch 16.]

7.10412 **29E. Distributing, showing or playing a recording** (1) A person who distributes, or shows or plays, a recording of visual images or sounds which are threatening is guilty of an offence if he intends thereby to stir up religious hatred or hatred on the grounds of sexual orientation.

(2) In this Part "recording" means any record from which visual images or sounds may, by any means, be reproduced; and references to the distribution, showing or playing of a recording are to its distribution, showing or playing to the public or a section of the public.

(3) This section does not apply to the showing or playing of a recording solely for the purpose of enabling the recording to be included in a programme service.

[Public Order Act 1986, s 29E as inserted by the Racial and Religious Hatred Act 2006, Schedule and amended by the Criminal Justice and Immigration Act 2008, Sch 16.]

7.10413 **29F. Broadcasting or including programme in programme service** (1) If a programme involving threatening visual images or sounds is included in a programme service, each of the persons mentioned in subsection (2) is guilty of an offence if he intends thereby to stir up religious hatred or hatred on the grounds of sexual orientation.

(2) The persons are—

(*a*) the person providing the programme service,

(*b*) any person by whom the programme is produced or directed, and

(*c*) any person by whom offending words or behaviour are used.

[Public Order Act 1986, s 29F as inserted by the Racial and Religious Hatred Act 2006, Schedule and amended by the Criminal Justice and Immigration Act 2008, Sch 16.]

*Inflammatory material*

7.10414 **29G. Possession of inflammatory material** (1) A person who has in his possession written material which is threatening, or a recording of visual images or sounds which are threatening, with a view to—

(*a*) in the case of written material, its being displayed, published, distributed, or included in a programme service whether by himself or another, or

(*b*) in the case of a recording, its being distributed, shown, played, or included in a programme service, whether by himself or another,

is guilty of an offence if he intends thereby to stir up religious hatred or hatred on the grounds of sexual orientation.

(2) For this purpose regard shall be had to such display, publication, distribution, showing, playing, or inclusion in a programme service as he has, or it may be reasonably be inferred that he has, in view.

[Public Order Act 1986, s 29G as inserted by the Racial and Religious Hatred Act 2006, Schedule and amended by the Criminal Justice and Immigration Act 2008, Sch 16.]

7.10415 **29H. Powers of entry and search** (1) If a justice of the peace is satisfied by information on oath laid by a constable that there are reasonable grounds for suspecting that a person has possession of written material or a recording in contravention of section 29G, the justice may issue a warrant under his hand authorising any constable to enter and search the premises where it is suspected the material or recording is situated.

(2) *Repealed.*

(3) A constable entering or searching premises in pursuance of a warrant issued under this section may use reasonable force if necessary.

(4) In this section "premises" means any place and, in particular, includes—

(*a*) any vehicle, vessel, aircraft or hovercraft,

(*b*) any offshore installation as defined in section 12 of the Mineral Workings (Offshore Installations) Act 1971, and

(*c*) any tent or movable structure.

[Public Order Act 1986, s 29H as inserted by the Racial and Religious Hatred Act 2006, Schedule and amended by the Criminal Justice and Immigration Act 2008, Schs 16 and 28.]

**7.10416 29I. Power to order forfeiture** (1) A court by or before which a person is convicted of—

(*a*) an offence under section 29B relating to the display of written material, or

(*b*) an offence under section 29C, 29E or 29G,

shall order to be forfeited any written material or recording produced to the court and shown to its satisfaction to be written material or a recording to which the offence relates.

(2) An order made under this section shall not take effect—

(*a*) until the expiry of the ordinary time within which an appeal may be instituted or, where an appeal is duly instituted, until it is finally decided or abandoned;

(*b*) *repealed.*

(3) For the purposes of subsection (2)(*a*)—

(*a*) an application for a case stated or for leave to appeal shall be treated as the institution of an appeal, and

(*b*) where a decision on appeal is subject to a further appeal, the appeal is not finally determined until the expiry of the ordinary time within which a further appeal may be instituted or, where a further appeal is duly instituted, until the further appeal is finally decided or abandoned.

(4) *Repealed.*

[Public Order Act 1986, s 29I as inserted by the Racial and Religious Hatred Act 2006, Schedule and amended by the Criminal Justice and Immigration Act 2008, Schs 16 and 28.]

**7.10417 29J. Protection of freedom of expression** Nothing in this Part shall be read or given effect in a way which prohibits or restricts discussion, criticism or expressions of antipathy, dislike, ridicule, insult or abuse of particular religions or the beliefs or practices of their adherents, or of any other belief system or the beliefs or practices of its adherents, or proselytising or urging adherents of a different religion or belief system to cease practising their religion or belief system.

[Public Order Act 1986, s 29J as inserted by the Racial and Religious Hatred Act 2006, Schedule.]

**7.10418 29JA. Protection of freedom of expression (sexual orientation)** (1) In this Part, for the avoidance of doubt, the discussion or criticism of sexual conduct or practices or the urging of persons to refrain from or modify such conduct or practices shall not be taken of itself to be threatening or intended to stir up hatred.

(2) In this Part, for the avoidance of doubt, any discussion or criticism of marriage which concerns the sex of the parties to marriage shall not be taken of itself to be threatening or intended to stir up hatred.

[Public Order Act 1986, s 29JA as inserted by the Criminal Justice and Immigration Act 2008, Sch 16 and amended by the Marriage (Same Sex Couples) Act 2013, Sch 7.]

*Supplementary provisions*

**7.10419 29K. Savings for reports of parliamentary or judicial proceedings** (1) Nothing in this Part applies to a fair and accurate report of proceedings in Parliament, in the Scottish Parliament or in the National Assembly for Wales.

(2) Nothing in this Part applies to a fair and accurate report of proceedings publicly heard before a court or tribunal exercising judicial authority where the report is published contemporaneously with the proceedings or, if it is not reasonably practicable or would be unlawful to publish a report of them contemporaneously, as soon as publication is reasonably practicable and lawful.

[Public Order Act 1986, s 29K as inserted by the Racial and Religious Hatred Act 2006, Schedule and amended by the Criminal Justice and Immigration Act 2008, Sch 16.]

**7.10420 29L. Procedure and punishment** (1) No proceedings for an offence under this Part may be instituted except by or with the consent of the Attorney General.

(2) For the purposes of the rules against charging more than one offence in the same count or information, each of sections 29B to 29G creates one offence.

(3) A person guilty of an offence under this Part is liable—

(*a*) on conviction on indictment to imprisonment for a term not exceeding seven years or a fine or both;

(*b*) on summary conviction to imprisonment for a term not exceeding 12 months or a fine not exceeding the statutory maximum or both.

(4) In subsection (3)(*b*) the reference to 12 months shall be read as a reference to 6 months in relation to an offence committed before the commencement of section 154(1) of the Criminal Justice Act 2003.

[Public Order Act 1986, s 29L as inserted by the Racial and Religious Hatred Act 2006, Schedule and amended by the Criminal Justice and Immigration Act 2008, Sch 16.]

7.10421 **29M. Offences by corporations** (1) Where a body corporate is guilty of an offence under this Part and it is shown that the offence was committed with the consent or connivance of a director, manager, secretary or other similar officer of the body, or a person purporting to act in any such capacity, he as well as the body corporate is guilty of the offence and liable to be proceeded against and punished accordingly.

(2) Where the affairs of a body corporate are managed by its members, subsection (1) applies in relation to the acts and defaults of a member in connection with his functions of management as it applies to a director.

[Public Order Act 1986, s 29M as inserted by the Racial and Religious Hatred Act 2006, Schedule.]

7.10422 **29N. Interpretation** In this Part—

"distribute", and related expressions, shall be construed in accordance with section 29C(2) (written material) and section 29E(2) (recordings);

"dwelling" means any structure or part of a structure occupied as a person's home or other living accommodation (whether the occupation is separate or shared with others) but does not include any part not so occupied, and for this purpose "structure" includes a tent, caravan, vehicle, vessel or other temporary or movable structure;

"hatred on the grounds of sexual orientation" has the meaning given by section 29AB;

"programme" means any item which is included in a programme service;

"programme service" has the same meaning as in the Broadcasting Act 1990;

"publish", and related expressions, in relation to written material, shall be construed in accordance with section 29C(2);

"religious hatred" has the meaning given by section 29A;

"recording" has the meaning given by section 29E(2), and "play" and "show", and related expressions, in relation to a recording, shall be construed in accordance with that provision;

"written material" includes any sign or other visible representation.

[Public Order Act 1986, s 29N as inserted by the Racial and Religious Hatred Act 2006, Schedule and amended by the Criminal Justice and Immigration Act 2008, Sch 16.]

## PART IV[1]
## EXCLUSION ORDERS

7.10423 **35. Photographs** (1) The court by which a banning order is made may make an order which—

(*a*) requires a constable to take a photograph of the person to whom the banning order relates or to cause such a photograph to be taken, and

(*b*) requires that person to go to a specified police station not later than 7 clear days after the day on which the order under this section is made, and at a specified time of day or between specified times of day, in order to have his photograph taken.

(2) In subsection (1) "specified" means specified in the order made under this section and "banning order" has the same meaning as in Part II of the Football Spectators Act 1989.

(3) No order may be made under this section unless an application to make it is made to the court by or on behalf of the person who is the prosecutor in respect of the offence leading to the banning order or (in the case of a banning order made under section 14B of the Football Spectators Act 1989) the complainant.

(4) If the person to whom the banning order relates fails to comply with an order under this section a constable may arrest him without warrant in order that his photograph may be taken.*

[Public Order Act 1986, s 35 as amended by the Football (Disorder) Act 2000, Sch 2.]

* **Repealed by the Football Spectators Act 1989, s 27 from a date to be appointed.**

1 Part IV comprises ss 30–37 of which ss 30–34 and 36 have been repealed. For Banning Orders, see the Football Spectators Act 1989, Pt II, in this PART, post.

7.10424 **37. Extension to other sporting events** (1) The Secretary of State may by order provide for section 35 of this Act and Part II of the Football Spectators Act 1989 to apply as if—

(*a*) any reference to an association football match included a reference to a sporting event of a kind specified in the order, and

(*b*) any reference to a prescribed football match included a reference to such a sporting event of a description specified in the order.

(2) An order under subsection (1) may make such modifications of that section and that Part, as they apply by virtue of the order, as the Secretary of State thinks fit.

(3) The power to make an order under this section shall be exercisable by statutory instrument, and no such order shall be made unless a draft of the order has been laid before and approved by resolution of each House of Parliament.*

[Public Order Act 1986, s 37 as amended by the Football (Disorder) Act 2000, Sch 2.]

* **Repealed by the Football Spectators Act 1989, s 27 from a date to be appointed.**

PART V[1]
MISCELLANEOUS AND GENERAL

7.10425 **38. Contamination of or interference with goods with intention of causing public alarm or anxiety, etc** (1) It is an offence for a person, with the intention—

(*a*) of causing public alarm or anxiety, or
(*b*) of causing injury to members of the public consuming or using the goods, or
(*c*) of causing economic loss to any person by reason of the goods being shunned by members of the public, or
(*d*) of causing economic loss to any person by reason of steps taken to avoid any such alarm or anxiety, injury or loss,

to contaminate or interfere with goods, or make it appear that goods have been contaminated or interfered with, or to place goods which have been contaminated or interfered with, or which appear to have been contaminated or interfered with, in a place where goods of that description are consumed, used, sold or otherwise supplied.

(2) It is also an offence for a person, with any such intention as is mentioned in paragraph (*a*), (*c*) or (*d*) of subsection (1), to threaten that he or another will do, or to claim that he or another has done, any of the acts mentioned in that subsection.

(3) It is an offence for a person to be in possession of any of the following articles with a view to the commission of an offence under subsection (1)—

(*a*) materials to be used for contaminating or interfering with goods or making it appear that goods have been contaminated or interfered with, or
(*b*) goods which have been contaminated or interfered with, or which appear to have been contaminated or interfered with.

(4) A person guilty of an offence under this section is liable[2]—

(*a*) on conviction on indictment to imprisonment for a term not exceeding **10 years** or a **fine** or **both**, or
(*b*) on summary conviction to imprisonment for a term not exceeding **six months** or a fine not exceeding the **statutory maximum** or **both**.

(5) In this section "goods" includes substances whether natural or manufactured and whether or not incorporated in or mixed with other goods.

(6) The reference in subsection (2) to a person claiming that certain acts have been committed does not include a person who in good faith reports or warns that such acts have been, or appear to have been, committed.

[Public Order Act 1986, s 38.]

1 Part V contains ss 38–43.
2 For procedure in respect of an offence triable either way, see the Magistrates' Courts Act 1980, ss 17A–21 in PART I: MAGISTRATES' COURTS PROCEDURE, ante.

7.10426 **40. Amendments, repeals and savings** (1)–(3) *Amendments and repeals incorporated in text.*

(4) Nothing in this Act affects the common law powers in England and Wales to deal with or prevent a breach of the peace.

(5) *Scotland.*

[Public Order Act 1986, s 40.]

7.10427 **41. Commencement** (1) This Act shall come into force on such day as the Secretary of State may appoint by order made by statutory instrument, and different days may be appointed for different provisions or different purposes.

(2) Nothing in a provision of this Act applies in relation to an offence committed or act done before the provision comes into force.

(3) Where a provision of this Act comes into force for certain purposes only, the references in subsection (2) to the provision are references to it so far as it relates to those purposes.

[Public Order Act 1986, s 41.]

# Football Spectators Act 1989[1]

(1989 c 37)

PART I[2]
FOOTBALL MATCHES IN ENGLAND AND WALES

*Preliminary*

7.10428 **1. Scope and interpretation of this Part** (1) This Part of this Act applies in relation to association football matches played in England and Wales which are regulated football matches and the following provisions have effect for its interpretation.

(2) "Designated football match" means any such match of a description for the time being designated for the purposes of this Part by order[3] made by the Secretary of State or a particular such match so designated.

(3) *Repealed.*

(4) An order under subsection (2) above—

(*a*) may designate descriptions of football matches wherever played or when played at descriptions of ground or in any area specified in the order;

(*b*) *repealed.*

(5) *Repealed.*

(6) A person is not to be regarded as a "spectator" in relation to a designated football match if the principal purpose of his being on the premises is to provide services in connection with the match, or to report on it.

(6A) In this Part "the licensing authority" means the Sports Grounds Safety Authority (see Part 1 of the Sports Grounds Safety Authority Act 2011).

(7) A "licence to admit spectators" is a licence granted in respect of any premises by the licensing authority under this Part of this Act authorising the admission to the premises of spectators for the purpose of watching any regulated football match played at those premises.

(8) Each of the following periods is "relevant to" a regulated football match, that is to say—

(*a*) the period beginning—

(i) two hours before the start of the match, or

(ii) two hours before the time at which it is advertised to start, or

(iii) with the time at which spectators are first admitted to the premises,

whichever is the earliest, and ending one hour after the end of the match;

(*b*) where a match advertised to start at a particular time on a particular day is postponed to a later day, or does not take place, the period in the advertised day beginning two hours before and ending one hour after that time.

(8A) *Repealed.*

(9) *Repealed.*

(10) The power to make an order under subsection (2) above is exercisable by statutory instrument which shall be subject to annulment in pursuance of a resolution of either House of Parliament.

(11) The imposition under this Part of this Act of restrictions on the persons who may attend as spectators at any regulated football match does not affect any other right of any person to exclude persons from admission to the premises at which the match is played.

[Football Spectators Act 1989, s 1 as amended by the Football (Offences and Disorder) Act 1999, s 2, the Football (Disorder) Act 2000, Sch 2, the Criminal Justice Act 2003, Sch 32, the Violent Crime Reduction Act 2006, Schs 3 and 5 and the Sports Grounds Safety Authority Act 2011, Sch 2.]

---

1 This Act, other than s 27, shall come into force on such day or days as may be appointed by order made by the Secretary of State (s 27, post). At the date of going to press all provisions of the Act had been brought into force by SI 1990/690 and 926, and SI 1991/107 and SI 1993/1690 except: ss 1(3), (4)(*b*), (5), (6), 2, 3, 4, 5, 6, 7, 10(6), (7), (8)(*c*), (12)(*a*)–(*b*). Guidance on Football Related Legislation is contained in Home Office Circular 34/2000.

2 Part I contains ss 1–13.

3 The Football Spectators (Designation of Football Matches in England and Wales) Order 2000, SI 2000/3331 designates the following matches:

> "any association football match which is played at Wembley Stadium, at the Millennium Stadium in Cardiff or at a sports ground in England and Wales which is registered with the Football League or the Football Association Premier League as the home ground of a club which is a member of the Football League or the Football Association Premier League at the time the match is played."

*Licences to admit spectators*

7.10429 **9. Offence of admitting spectators to unlicensed premises** (1) Subject to subsection (2) below, if persons are admitted as spectators to, or permitted to remain as spectators on, any premises during a period relevant to a regulated football match without a licence to admit spectators being in force, any responsible person commits an offence.

(2) Where a person is charged with an offence under this section it shall be a defence to prove either that the spectators were admitted in an emergency or—

(*a*) that the spectators were admitted without his consent; and

(*b*) that he took all reasonable precautions and exercised all due diligence to avoid the commission of such an offence.

(3) A person guilty of an offence under this section shall be liable[1]—

(*a*) on summary conviction, to a fine not exceeding **the statutory maximum**; or

(*b*) on conviction on indictment, to a **fine** or to imprisonment for a term not exceeding **two years**, or to both.

[Football Spectators Act 1989, s 9 as amended by the Football (Disorder) Act 2000, Sch 1.]

---

1 For procedure in respect of this offence which is triable either way, see the Magistrates' Courts Act 1980, ss 17A–21, in PART I: MAGISTRATES' COURTS, PROCEDURE, ante.

7.10430 **10. Licences to admit spectators: general** (1) The licensing authority may, on an application duly made by a responsible person, grant a licence to admit spectators to any premises for the purpose of watching any regulated football match played at those premises.

(2) An application for a licence in respect of any premises shall be made in such manner, in such form and accompanied by such fee as may be determined by the Secretary of State.

(3) The licensing authority shall not refuse to grant a licence without—

(*a*) notifying the applicant in writing of the proposed refusal and of the grounds for it;

(*b*) giving him an opportunity to make representations about them within the period of twenty-eight days beginning with the service of the notice; and

(*c*) taking any representations so made into account in making its decision.

(4) A licence to admit spectators to any premises may authorise the admission of spectators to watch all regulated football matches or specified descriptions of regulated football matches or a particular such match.

(5) A licence to admit spectators shall be in writing and shall be granted on such terms and conditions as the licensing authority considers appropriate and, if the Secretary of State gives to the licensing authority a direction under section 11 below, the conditions may include conditions imposing requirements as respects the seating of spectators.

(6) A licence to admit spectators may also include conditions requiring specified descriptions of spectators to be refused admittance to the premises to watch regulated football matches or specified descriptions of regulated football matches or a particular such match.

(7) Where a designation order includes the provision authorised by section 1(4)(*b*) above as respects the admission of spectators to any ground as authorised spectators, the licensing authority may, by notice in writing to the licence holder, direct that, for the purposes of any match or description of match specified in the direction, the licence shall be treated as including such specified terms and conditions as respects the admission of spectators as authorised spectators as the licensing authority considers appropriate; and the licence shall have effect, for that purpose, subject to those terms and conditions.

(8) It shall be a condition of every licence that any authorised person shall be entitled, on production, if so required, of his authority—

(*a*) to enter at any reasonable time any premises on which a regulated football match is being or is to be played;

(*b*) to make such inspection of the premises and such inquiries relating to them as he considers necessary for the purposes of this Part of this Act;

(*c*) *repealed*.

(9) A licence to admit spectators shall, unless revoked or suspended under section 12 below or surrendered, remain in force for a specified period.

(10) Subject to subsection (11) below, the licensing authority may at any time, by notice in writing to the licence holder, vary the terms and conditions of the licence.

(11) The licensing authority shall not vary the terms or conditions of a licence without—

(*a*) notifying the licence holder in writing of the proposed alterations or additions;

(*b*) giving him an opportunity to make representations about them within the period of twenty-one days beginning with the service of the notice; and

(*c*) taking any representations so made into account in making the decision.

(12) In taking any decision under this section the licensing authority shall have regard, among the other relevant circumstances, to the following matters or to such of them as are applicable to the decision, that is to say—

(*a*) whether the premises and the equipment provided and procedures used at the premises are such as to secure that, except (in the case of the procedures) in an emergency, only authorised spectators are admitted to regulated football matches;

(*b*) *repealed*;

(*c*) whether the equipment provided, procedures used and other arrangements in force at the premises are such as are reasonably required to prevent the commission or minimise the effects of offences at regulated football matches; and

(*d*) such other considerations as the Secretary of State determines from time to time and notifies to the licensing authority.

(13) Subject to subsection (14) below, if any term or condition of a licence is contravened any responsible person commits an offence.

(14) Where a person is charged with an offence under subsection (13) above it shall be a defence to prove—

(*a*) that the contravention took place without his consent; and

(*b*) that he took all reasonable precautions and exercised all due diligence to avoid the commission of such an offence.

(15) A person guilty of an offence under subsection (13) above shall be liable, on summary conviction, to a fine not exceeding **level 5** on the standard scale.

(16) The fees charged on the issue of licences—

(*a*) may be fixed so as to reimburse the licensing authority their expenses under this Part of this Act; and

(*b*) shall be paid by the licensing authority to the Secretary of State.

(17) In this section—

"authorised person" means any person authorised by the Secretary of State or the licensing authority;

"specified" means specified in the licence or in the case of subsection (7) in the direction; and

"vary", in relation to a licence, includes the addition of further terms or conditions.

[Football Spectators Act 1989, s 10 as amended by the Football (Disorder) Act 2000, Sch 1 and the Violent Crime Reduction Act 2006, Schs 3 and 5.]

7.10431 **11. Power of Secretary of State to require conditions in licences relating to seating** (1) The Secretary of State may, by order[1], direct the licensing authority to include in any licence to admit spectators to any specified premises a condition imposing requirements as respects the seating of spectators at regulated football matches at the premises; and it shall be the duty of the authority to comply with the direction.

(2) The requirements imposed by a condition in pursuance of this section may relate to the accommodation to be provided at, or the arrangements to be made as respects the spectators admitted to, the premises.

(3) A direction may require the licensing authority to include the condition in the licence when granting it or by way of varying the conditions of a licence.

(4) Before giving a direction under this section in relation to any premises the Secretary of State shall consult the licensing authority which may, if it thinks fit, make recommendations to him.

(5) The licensing authority shall not make any recommendations under subsection (4) above without consulting the local authority in whose area the premises are situated.

(6) The power to make an order containing a direction under this section is exercisable by statutory instrument which shall be subject to annulment in pursuance of a resolution of either House of Parliament.

(7) In this section "local authority" has the same meaning as in the Safety of Sports Grounds Act 1975[2].

[Football Spectators Act 1989, s 11 as amended by the Football (Disorder) Act 2000, Sch 1.]

---

1 The Football Spectators (Seating) Orders, SI 1994/1666, SI 1995/1706, SI 1996/1706, SI 1997/1677, SI 1998/1599, SI 1999/1926, SI 2000/1739, SI 2001/2373, SI 2002/1755, SI 2004/1737, SI 2005/1751, SI 2006/1661, SI 2007/2038, SI 2008/1749, SI 2009/1395, SI 2010/1584, SI 2011/1436, SI 2012/1470, SI 2013/1568 and SI 2016/629 have been made.

2 In this PART, title HEALTH AND SAFETY, ante.

7.10432 **12. Licences to admit spectators: revocation and suspension** (1) The licensing authority may, subject to subsections (2), (3) and (4) below, at any time, by notice in writing to the holder of a licence to admit spectators, revoke the licence or suspend the licence indefinitely or for such period as the authority considers appropriate.

(2) The licensing authority shall not suspend or revoke a licence under this section unless satisfied that it is necessary to do so having regard to the matters which are relevant for the purposes of this section.

(3) The matters which are relevant for the purposes of this section are—

(*a*) the matters specified in paragraphs (*a*), (*b*) and (*c*) of section 10(12) above; and

(*b*) such other considerations as the Secretary of State determines from time to time and notifies to the licensing authority.

(4) The licensing authority shall not revoke or suspend a licence to admit spectators without—

(*a*) notifying the licence holder of the proposed revocation or suspension and of the grounds for it;

(*b*) giving him an opportunity to make representations about the matter within the period of twenty-one days beginning with the date of the service of the notice; and

(*c*) taking any representations so made into account in making the decision.

(5) The licensing authority may, if satisfied that the urgency of the case so requires, suspend a licence under this section without observing the requirements of subsection (4) above but the authority shall, as soon as is practicable, notify the person to whom the licence was granted of the grounds for the suspension.

(6) A licence suspended under this section shall during the time of suspension be of no effect.

(7) Where a licence has been suspended under this section the person to whom the licence was granted may at any time apply to the licensing authority to terminate the suspension and the licensing authority may terminate the suspension if it appears to be appropriate to do so having regard to the relevant matters and after taking into account any representations made by the applicant.

[Football Spectators Act 1989, s 12.]

7.10433 **13. Licensing authority's powers in relation to safety at football grounds** (1) The licensing authority shall have the function of keeping under review the discharge by local authorities of their functions under the Safety of Sports Grounds Act 1975[1] in relation to sports grounds at which regulated football matches are played and shall have the powers conferred in relation to those functions by the following provisions of this section.

(2) The licensing authority may, by notice in writing to the local authority concerned, require the local authority to include in any safety certificate such terms and conditions as are specified in the notice; and it shall be the duty of the local authority to comply with the requirement.

(3) Before exercising its powers under subsection (2) above to require the inclusion of specified terms and conditions in any safety certificate, the licensing authority shall consult—

(*a*) the local authority;

(*b*) the chief officer of police;

(*c*) if the local authority are not the fire and rescue authority, the fire and rescue authority; and

(*d*) if the local authority are not the building authority, the building authority.

(4) As respects those terms and conditions, the local authority need not consult the chief officer

of police, the fire and rescue authority or the building authority under section 3(3) or 4(8) of the Safety of Sports Grounds Act 1975[1] before issuing a safety certificate or about any proposal to amend or replace one.

(5) A notice under subsection (2) above may require the issue under that Act of a safety certificate incorporating the specified terms or conditions or the amendment under that Act of a safety certificate so that it incorporates the specified terms or conditions.

(6) Any inspector appointed by the licensing authority may, for the purposes of the discharge by the licensing authority of its function under subsection (1) above, on production, if so required, of his authority—

(*a*) enter at any reasonable time any sports ground at which regulated football matches are played;

(*b*) make such inspection of the ground and such inquiries relating to the ground as he considers necessary; or

(*c*) examine the safety certificate and any records kept under the Safety of Sports Grounds Act 1975 or this Part of this Act, and take copies of such records.

(7) The licensing authority may, by notice in writing to any local authority, require the local authority to furnish to the licensing authority such information relating to the discharge by the local authority of its functions under the Safety of Sports Grounds Act 1975 as is specified in the notice; and it shall be the duty of the local authority to comply with the requirement.

(8) Section 5(3) of the Safety of Sports Grounds Act 1975[1] (appeals against terms and conditions of safety certificates) shall have effect with the insertion, after paragraph (ii), of the words "but not against the inclusion in a safety certificate of anything required to be included in it by the Football Licensing Authority under section 13(2) of the Football Spectators Act 1989".

(9) Any expression used in this section and in the Safety of Sports Grounds Act 1975[1] has the same meaning in this section as in that Act.

[Football Spectators Act 1989, s 13 as amended by the Fire and Rescue Services Act 2004, Sch 1.]

1 In this PART, title HEALTH AND SAFETY, ante.

## PART II[1]

## REGULATED FOOTBALL MATCHES

### *Preliminary*

7.10434 **14. Main definitions** (1) This section applies for the purposes of this Part.

(2) "Regulated football match" means an association football match (whether in the United Kingdom or elsewhere) which is a prescribed[2] match or a match of a prescribed[2] description.

(3) "External tournament" means a football competition which includes regulated football matches outside the United Kingdom.

(4) "Banning order" means an order made by the court under this Part which—

(*a*) in relation to regulated football matches in the United Kingdom, prohibits the person who is subject to the order from entering any[3] premises for the purpose of attending such matches, and

(*b*) in relation to regulated football matches outside the United Kingdom, requires that person to report at a police station in accordance with this Part.

(5) "Control period", in relation to a regulated football match outside the United Kingdom, means the period—

(*a*) beginning five days before the day of the match, and

(*b*) ending when the match is finished or cancelled.

(6) "Control period", in relation to an external tournament, means any period described in an order[4] made by the Secretary of State—

(*a*) beginning five days before the day of the first football match outside the United Kingdom which is included in the tournament, and

(*b*) ending when the last football match outside the United Kingdom which is included in the tournament is finished or cancelled,

but, for the purposes of paragraph (*a*), any football match included in the qualifying or pre-qualifying stages of the tournament is to be left out of account.

(7) References to football matches are to football matches played or intended to be played.

(8) "Relevant offence" means an offence to which Schedule 1 to this Act applies.

[Football Spectators Act 1989, s 14 as amended by the Football (Disorder) Act 2000, Sch 1 and the Policing and Crime Act 2009, s 103.]

1 Part II contains ss 14–22. For legal advice and assistance in respect of proceedings under this Part, see the Football (Disorder) (Legal Advice and Assistance) Order 2000, in PART I: MAGISTRATES' COURTS, PROCEDURE, ante.

2 The Football Spectators (Prescription) Order 2004, SI 2004/2409 amended by SI 2006/761, SI 2010/584 and SI 2013/1709 has been made which provides—

"**3.**(1) An association football match (in England and Wales) described in paragraphs (2) or (3) shall be a regulated football match for the purposes of Part II of the 1989 Act.

(2) A regulated match is an association football match in which one or both of the participating teams represents—

(a) a club which is for the time being a member (whether a full or associate member) of the Football League, the Football Association Premier League, the Football Conference, the Welsh Premier League, or the or the Scottish Professional Football League;

(b) a club whose home ground is situated outside England and Wales, or
(c) a country or territory.
(3) A regulated football match is an association football match played in the Football Association Cup (other than in a preliminary or qualifying round).

**4.**(1) An association football match (outside England and Wales) described in paragraph (2) shall be a regulated football match for the purposes of Part II of the 1989 Act.
(2) A regulated match is an association football match involving—
(a) a national team appointed by the Football Association to represent England or appointed by the Football Association of Wales to represent Wales;
(b) a team representing a club which is for the time being a member (whether a full or associate member) of the Football League, the Football Association Premier League, the Football Conference, the Welsh Premier League, or the Scottish Professional Football League;
(c) a team representing any country or territory whose football association is for the time being a member of FIFA, where—
(i) the match is part of a competition or tournament organised by, or under the authority of, FIFA or UEFA, and
(ii) the competition or tournament is one in which a team referred to in sub-paragraph (*a*) above is eligible to participate or has participated; or
(d) a team representing a club which is for the time being a member (whether a full or associate member) of, or affiliated to, a national football association which is a member of FIFA, where—
(i) the match is part of a competition or tournament organised by, or under the authority of, FIFA or UEFA, and
(ii) the competition or tournament is one in which a club referred to in sub-paragraph (*b*) above is eligible to participate or has participated.

[3] A person the subject of a football banning order is prohibited by this provision from attending any regulated football matches anywhere in the UK and the court has no power to make an order limited to particular matches or particular teams: *Commissioner of Police of the Metropolis v Thorpe* [2015] EWHC 3339 (Admin), [2016] 4 WLR 7, 180 JP 16.

[4] Various orders extending the duration of a 'control period' in relation to specific tournaments have been made.

### *Banning orders*[1]

7.10435 **14A. Banning orders made on conviction of an offence**[2] (1) This section applies where a person (the "offender") is convicted of a relevant offence[3].

(2) If the court is satisfied that there are reasonable grounds to believe that making a banning order would help to prevent violence or disorder at or in connection with any regulated football matches, it must make such an order in respect of the offender[4].

(3) If the court is not so satisfied, it must in open court state that fact and give its reasons.

(3A) For the purpose of deciding whether to make an order under this section the court may consider evidence led by the prosecution and the defence.

(3B) It is immaterial whether evidence led in pursuance of subsection (3A) would have been admissible in the proceedings in which the offender was convicted.

(4) A banning order may only be made under this section—
(*a*) in addition to a sentence imposed in respect of the relevant offence, or
(*b*) in addition to an order discharging him conditionally.

(4A) The court may adjourn any proceedings in relation to an order under this section even after sentencing the offender.

(4B) If the offender does not appear for any adjourned proceedings, the court may further adjourn the proceedings or may issue a warrant for his arrest.

(4BA) If the court adjourns or further adjourns any proceedings under subsection (4A) or (4B),), the court may remand the offender.

(4BB) A person who, by virtue of subsection (4BA), is remanded on bail may be required by the conditions of his bail—
(*a*) not to leave England and Wales before his appearance before the court, and
(*b*) if the control period relates to a regulated football match outside the United Kingdom or to an external tournament which includes such matches, to surrender his passport to a police constable, if he has not already done so.

(4C) The court may not issue a warrant under subsection (4B) above for the offender's arrest unless it is satisfied that he has had adequate notice of the time and place of the adjourned proceedings.

(5) A banning order may be made as mentioned in subsection (4)(*b*) above in spite of anything in sections 12 and 14 of the Powers of the Criminal Courts (Sentencing) Act 2000 (which relate to orders discharging a person absolutely or conditionally and their effect).

(5A) The prosecution has a right of appeal against a failure by the court to make a banning order under this section—
(*a*) where the failure is by a magistrates' court, to the Crown Court; and
(*b*) where it is by the Crown Court, to the Court of Appeal[5].

(5B) An appeal under subsection (5A)(*b*) may be brought only if the Court of Appeal gives permission or the judge who decided not to make an order grants a certificate that his decision is fit for appeal.

(5C) An order made on appeal under this section (other than one directing that an application be re-heard by the court from which the appeal was brought) is to be treated for the purposes of this Part as if it were an order of the court from which the appeal was brought.

(6) In this section, "the court" in relation to an offender means—
(*a*) the court by or before which he is convicted of the relevant offence, or
(*b*) if he is committed to the Crown Court to be dealt with for that offence, the Crown Court.

[Football Spectators Act 1989, s 14A as inserted by the Football (Disorder) Act 2000, Sch 1 and amended by the Anti-social Behaviour Act 2003, s 86, the Serious Organised Crime and Police Act 2005, s 139 and the Violent Crime Reduction Act 2006, Schs 3 and 5.]

---

[1] For enforcement in England of banning orders made in Scotland, see the Police, Public Order and Criminal Justice (Scotland) Act 2006 (Consequential Provisions and Modifications) Order 2007, SI 2007/1098, in PART I: MAGISTRATES' COURTS, PROCEDURE, ante.

[2] In *Gough v Chief Constable of the Derbyshire Constabulary, R (on the application of Miller) v Leeds Magistrates' Court, Lilley v DPP* [2001] EWHC Admin 554, [2001] 4 All ER 289, [2001] 3 WLR 1392 the Court of Appeal held as follows in relation to the legislative regime on banning orders. The objective of these provisions was sufficiently important to justify their limits on the right of freedom of movement and they did not, therefore, contravene EC law. However, those that have to apply them are under a duty to interpret them in a manner that is compatible with EC law and the ECHR. While banning orders are not "penalties", and proceedings under s 14B post are not "criminal", banning orders fall into the same category as anti-social behaviour orders and sex offender orders. Therefore, magistrates should apply an exacting standard of proof that will, in practice, be hard to distinguish from the criminal standard. This applies to both of the conditions in s 14B. In practice, the second "reasonable grounds" condition will almost inevitably consist of evidence of past conduct, and this may or may not consist of or include the matters that have to be proved under the first condition, but it must be proved to the same strict standard of proof. Furthermore, it must be conduct that gives rise to the likelihood that, if the respondent is not banned from attending prescribed football matches, he will attend them, or the environs of them, and take part in violence or disorder. See further, *R (on the application of White) v Crown Court at Blackfriars* [2008] EWHC 510 (Admin), 172 JP 321.

The requirement of a "special circumstances" as a precondition to granting an applicant permission to go abroad during a prescribed period (see s 20) must not be interpreted as meaning "extraordinary circumstances". When considering whether or not there are "special circumstances" the FBOA or, on appeal, a magistrates' court should do not more than satisfy itself on a balance of probabilities that the reason for going abroad is not to attend a prescribed match. This should not be something that is difficult to prove (eg a bona fide traveller is likely to be in a position to produce some evidence of the proposed trip).

If a banning order, properly made, interferes with the right to respect for private or family life under art 8, the interference is likely to prove justified under art 8(2) on the grounds that it is necessary for the prevention of disorder.

Where the court could make an order on conviction, the procedure and admissibility of hearsay evidence is regulated by the Criminal Procedure Rules 2010, Part 31, in the *Key Materials*.

As to relevant offences and the grounds for making an order, see Sch 1, post.

[3] Defined in Sch 1, post.

[4] Repetition and propensity are not required for the making of an order under s 14A, and the court is entitled to take into account and to give weight to the question of deterrence: *R (on the application of White) v Crown Court at Blackfriars* [2008] EWHC 510 (Admin), (2008) 172 JP 321, [2008] 2 Cr App Rep (S) 97, [2008] Crim LR 575. See also *R v Lewis Cash Curtis* [2009] EWCA Crim 1225, [2010] 1 Cr App R (S) 193: the banning order was upheld even though the behaviour was an isolated first incident in the case of the defendant. It was held in *R v Boggild* [2011] EWCA Crim 1928, [2011] 4 All ER 1285, [2012] 1 WLR 1298, however, that while the court could take deterrence of others into account when deciding whether making an order would help to prevent violence or disorder, it was a matter for the court to reach a conclusion in each case. Where the violence was serious or prolonged, or the offender played a prominent role, there was greater scope for the statutory test to be satisfied on reasonable grounds; but where the defendant was responding to violence from opposing fans and was of good character or only lightly convicted, and the court was satisfied that that there was no future risk of football-related violence, the court was entitled to conclude it was not satisfied that there were reasonable grounds for believing that a banning order would help to prevent violence. In the present case, the sentences included a prohibited activity requirement forbidding the defendants from attending any professional football match other than the home games of the club they supported. This was not, however, the equivalent of a banning order, breach of which was a criminal offence and to which a different regime applied. In respect of banning orders, there was a sophisticated regime for the co-ordination of intelligence concerning those subject to orders. This needed to be considered.

[5] There is no explicit provision, however, which enables the Court Appeal to make a banning order, whereas such a provision conferring ancillary powers accompanies every other kind of criminal appeal. But because the legislation does not direct that an appeal must be heard by the Criminal Division, the jurisdiction of the Civil Division can be exercised and this confers all the authority and jurisdiction of the court from which the appeal has come, including the making of a banning order. The result is that where there are cross appeals – by the defendant against sentence and by the prosecution against a decision not to make a banning order, while these cannot be heard at the same time the Court of Appeal can re-constitute itself in its civil jurisdiction to deal with the latter and, if appropriate, make an order: *R v Boggild*, supra.

7.10436 **14B. Banning orders made on a complaint**[1] (1) An application for a banning order in respect of any person may be made by—

(*a*) the relevant chief officer, or

(*b*) the Director of Public Prosecutions,

if it appears to him that the condition in subsection (2) is met.

(1A) In subsection (1) "the relevant chief officer" means—

(*a*) the chief officer of police of any police force maintained for a police area; or

(*b*) the chief constable of the British Transport Police Force.

(2) That condition is that the respondent has at any time caused or contributed to any violence or disorder in the United Kingdom or elsewhere.

(3) The application is to be made by complaint to a magistrates' court.

(4) If—

(*a*) it is proved on the application that the condition in subsection (2) above is met, and

(*b*) the court is satisfied that there are reasonable grounds to believe that making a banning order would help to prevent violence or disorder at or in connection with any regulated football matches,

the court must make a banning order in respect of the respondent.

(5) If the magistrates' court adjourns proceedings on an application under this section, the court may remand the person in respect of whom the application is made.

(6) A person who, by virtue of subsection (5) above, is remanded on bail under section 128 of the Magistrates' Courts Act 1980 may be required by the conditions of his bail—

(*a*) not to leave England and Wales before his appearance before the court, and
(*b*) if the control period relates to a regulated football match outside the United Kingdom or to an external tournament which includes such matches, to surrender his passport to a police constable, if he has not already done so.[2]

[Football Spectators Act 1989, s 14B as inserted by the Football (Disorder) Act 2000, Sch 1 and amended by the Violent Crime Reduction Act 2006, Sch 3.]

[1] See note 1 to s 14A, above. Proceedings under s 14B of this Act are "criminal proceedings" for the purposes of s 12(2)(*g*) of the Access to Justice Act 1999 by virtue of reg 3 of the Criminal Defence Service (General) (No 2) Regulations 2001 (eligibility for criminal legal aid).

[2] An application under this section might originally be made during the period of one year from 28 August 2001: Football (Disorder) (Duration of Powers) Order 2001, SI 2001/2646 made under s 5(4) of the Football (Disorder) Act 2000. Section 1 of the Football (Disorder) (Amendment) Act 2002 amended s 5 of the Football (Disorder) Act 2000 to enable the making of applications under s 14B (and the exercise of powers under ss 21A and 21B) of the Football Spectators Act 1989 within the period of 5 years beginning with the day on which s 1 of the 2002 Act came into force. Section 1 of the 2002 Act was brought into force on 28 August 2002 by the Football (Disorder) (Amendment) Act 2002 (Commencement) Order 2002, SI 2002/2200.

7.10437 **14C. Banning orders: supplementary** (1) In this Part, "violence" means violence against persons or property and includes threatening violence and doing anything which endangers the life of any person.

(2) In this Part, "disorder" includes—
(*a*) stirring up hatred against a group of persons defined by reference to colour, race, nationality (including citizenship) or ethnic or national origins, or against an individual as a member of such a group,
(*b*) using threatening, abusive or insulting words or behaviour or disorderly behaviour,
(*c*) displaying any writing or other thing which is threatening, abusive or insulting.

(3) In this Part, "violence" and "disorder" are not limited to violence or disorder in connection with football.

(4) The magistrates' court may take into account the following matters (among others), so far as they consider it appropriate to do so, in determining whether to make an order under section 14B above—
(*a*) any decision of a court or tribunal outside the United Kingdom,
(*b*) deportation or exclusion from a country outside the United Kingdom,
(*c*) removal or exclusion from premises used for playing football matches, whether in the United Kingdom or elsewhere,
(*d*) conduct recorded on video or by any other means.

(5) In determining whether to make such an order—
(*a*) the magistrates' court may not take into account anything done by the respondent before the beginning of the period of ten years ending with the application under section 14B(1) above, except circumstances ancillary to a conviction,
(*b*) before taking into account any conviction for a relevant offence, where a court made a statement under section 14A(3) above (or section 15(2A) below or section 30(3) of the Public Order Act 1986), the magistrates' court must consider the reasons given in the statement,

and in this subsection "circumstances ancillary to a conviction" has the same meaning as it has for the purposes of section 4 of the Rehabilitation of Offenders Act 1974 (effect of rehabilitation).

(6) Subsection (5) does not prejudice anything in the Rehabilitation of Offenders Act 1974.

[Football Spectators Act 1989, s 14C as inserted by the Football (Disorder) Act 2000, Sch 1.]

7.10438 **14D. Banning orders made on a complaint: appeals**[1] (1) An appeal lies to the Crown Court against the making by a magistrates' court of a banning order under section 14B above.

(1A) An appeal lies to the Crown Court against the dismissal by a magistrates' court of an application for the making of a banning order under section 14B above.

(2) On an appeal under this section the Crown Court—
(*a*) may make any orders necessary to give effect to its determination of an appeal under this section, and
(*b*) may also make any incidental or consequential orders which appear to it to be just.

(3) An order of the Crown Court made on an appeal under this section (other than one directing that an application be re-heard by a magistrates' court) is to be treated for the purposes of this Part as if it were an order of the magistrates' court from which the appeal was brought.

[Football Spectators Act 1989, s 14D as inserted by the Football (Disorder) Act 2000, Sch 1 and amended by the Violent Crime Reduction Act 2006, Sch 3.]

[1] Proceedings under s 14D of this Act are "criminal proceedings" for the purposes of s 12(2)(*g*) of the Access to Justice Act 1999 by virtue of reg 3 of the Criminal Defence Service (General) (No 2) Regulations 2001 (eligibility for criminal legal aid).

7.10439 **14E. Banning orders: general** (1) On making a banning order, a court must in ordinary language explain its effect to the person subject to the order.

(2) A banning order must require the person subject to the order to report initially at a police station[1] specified in the order within the period of five days beginning with the day on which the

order is made.

(2A) A banning order must require the person subject to the order to give notification of the events mentioned in subsection (2B) to the enforcing authority.

(2B) The events are—

(*a*) a change of any of his names;

(*b*) the first use by him after the making of the order of a name for himself that was not disclosed by him at the time of the making of the order;

(*c*) a change of his home address;

(*d*) his acquisition of a temporary address;

(*e*) a change of his temporary address or his ceasing to have one;

(*f*) his becoming aware of the loss of his passport;

(*g*) receipt by him of a new passport;

(*h*) an appeal made by him in relation to the order;

(*i*) an application made by him under section 14H(2) for termination of the order;

(*j*) an appeal made by him under section 23(3) against the making of a declaration of relevance in respect of an offence of which he has been convicted.

(2C) A notification required by a banning order by virtue of subsection (2A) must be given before the end of the period of seven days beginning with the day on which the event in question occurs and—

(*a*) in the case of a change of a name or address or the acquisition of a temporary address, must specify the new name or address;

(*b*) in the case of a first use of a previously undisclosed name, must specify that name; and

(*c*) in the case of a receipt of a new passport, must give details of that passport.

(3) A banning order must impose a requirement as to the surrender in accordance with this Part, in connection with regulated football matches outside the United Kingdom, of the passport of the person subject to the order.

(4) *Repealed.*

(5) In the case of a person detained in legal custody—

(*a*) the requirement under this section to report at a police station, and

(*b*) any requirement imposed under section 19 below,

is suspended until his release from custody.

(6) If—

(*a*) he is released from custody more than five days before the expiry of the period for which the order has effect, and

(*b*) he was precluded by his being in custody from reporting initially,

the order is to have effect as if it required him to report initially at the police station specified in the order within the period of five days beginning with the date of his release.

(7) *Repealed.*

(8) In this section—

"declaration of relevance" has the same meaning as in section 23;

"home address", in relation to any person, means the address of his sole or main residence;

"loss" includes theft or destruction;

"new" includes replacement;

"temporary address", in relation to any person, means the address (other than his home address) of a place at which he intends to reside, or has resided, for a period of at least four weeks.

[Football Spectators Act 1989, s 14E as inserted by the Football (Disorder) Act 2000, Sch 1 and amended by the Criminal Justice Act 2003, Sch 32, the Violent Crime Reduction Act 2006, Schs 3 and 5, the Policing and Crime Act 2009, Sch 8, the Identity Documents Act 2010, Schedule and the Legal Aid, Sentencing and Punishment of Offenders Act 2012, Sch 10.]

1 The police station may be in England, Wales, Scotland or Northern Ireland (Policing and Crime Act 2009, s 104).

7.10440 **14F. Period of banning orders** (1) Subject to the following provisions of this Part, a banning order has effect for a period beginning with the day on which the order is made.

(2) The period must not be longer than the maximum or shorter than the minimum.

(3) Where the order is made under section 14A above in addition to a sentence of imprisonment taking immediate effect, the maximum is ten years and the minimum is six years; and in this subsection "imprisonment" includes any form of detention.

(4) In any other case where the order is made under section 14A above, the maximum is five years and the minimum is three years.

(5) Where the order is made under section 14B above, the maximum is five years and the minimum is three years.

[Football Spectators Act 1989, s 14F as inserted by the Football (Disorder) Act 2000, Sch 1 and amended by the Violent Crime Reduction Act 2006, Sch 3.]

7.10441 **14G. Additional requirements of orders**[1] (1) A banning order may, if the court making the order thinks fit, impose additional requirements on the person subject to the order in relation to any regulated football matches.

(2) The court by which a banning order was made may, on an application made by—

(*a*) the person subject to the order, or
(*b*) the person who applied for the order or who was the prosecutor in relation to the order,
vary the order so as to impose, replace or omit any such requirements.

(3) In the case of a banning order made by a magistrates' court, the reference in subsection (2) above to the court by which it was made includes a reference to any magistrates' court acting in the same local justice area as that court.

[Football Spectators Act 1989, s 14G as inserted by the Football (Disorder) Act 2000, Sch 1 and amended by the Courts Act 2003, Sch 8.]

---

[1] Proceedings under s 14G of this Act are "criminal proceedings" for the purposes of s 12(2)(*g*) of the Access to Justice Act 1999 by virtue of reg 3 of the Criminal Defence Service (General) (No 2) Regulations 2001 (eligibility for criminal legal aid).

7.10442 **14H. Termination of orders** (1) If a banning order has had effect for at least two-thirds of the period determined under section 14F above, the person subject to the order may apply to the court by which it was made to terminate it.[1]

(2) On the application, the court may by order terminate the banning order as from a specified date or refuse the application.

(3) In exercising its powers under subsection (2) above, the court must have regard to the person's character, his conduct since the banning order was made, the nature of the offence or conduct which led to it and any other circumstances which appear to it to be relevant.

(4) Where an application under subsection (1) above in respect of a banning order is refused, no further application in respect of the order may be made within the period of six months beginning with the day of the refusal.

(5) The court may order the applicant to pay all or any part of the costs of an application under this section.

(6) In the case of a banning order made by a magistrates' court, the reference in subsection (1) above to the court by which it was made includes a reference to any magistrates' court acting in the same local justice area as that court.

[Football Spectators Act 1989, s 14H as inserted by the Football (Disorder) Act 2000, Sch 1 and amended by the Courts Act 2003, Sch 8.]

---

[1] Proceedings under s 14H are "criminal proceedings" for the purposes of s 12(2)(*g*) of the Access to Justice Act 1999 by virtue of reg 3 of the Criminal Defence Service (General) (No 2) Regulations 2001 (eligibility for criminal legal aid).

7.10443 **14J. Offences** (1) A person subject to a banning order who fails to comply with—
(*a*) any requirement imposed by the order, or
(*b*) any requirement imposed under section 19(2B) or (2C) below,
is guilty of an offence.

(2) A person guilty of an offence under this section is liable on summary conviction to imprisonment for a term not exceeding six months, or a fine not exceeding **level 5** on the standard scale, or both.

[Football Spectators Act 1989, s 14J as inserted by the Football (Disorder) Act 2000, Sch 1.]

*Banning orders*

7.10444 **18. Information** (1) Where a court makes a banning order, the designated officer for the court (in the case of a magistrates' court) or the appropriate officer (in the case of the Crown Court)—
(*a*) shall give a copy of it to the person to whom it relates;
(*b*) shall (as soon as reasonably practicable) send a copy of it to the enforcing authority[1] and to any prescribed[1] person;
(*c*) shall (as soon as reasonably practicable) send a copy of it to the police station (addressed to the officer responsible for the police station) at which the person subject to the order is to report initially; and
(*d*) in a case where the person subject to the order detained in legal custody, shall (as soon as reasonably practicable) send a copy of it to the person in whose custody he is detained.

(2) Where a court terminates a banning order under section 14H above, the designated officer for the court (in the case of a magistrates' court) or the appropriate officer (in the case of the Crown Court)—
(*a*) shall give a copy of the terminating order to the person to whom the banning order;
(*b*) shall (as soon as reasonably practicable) send a copy of it to the enforcing authority[1] and to any prescribed person[1]; and
(*c*) in a case where the person subject to the banning order detained in legal custody, shall (as soon as reasonably practicable) send a copy of the terminating order to the person in whose custody he is detained.

(3) Where a person subject to a banning order is released from custody and, in the case of a person who has not reported initially to a police station, is released more than five days before the expiry of the banning order, the person in whose custody he is shall (as soon as reasonably practicable) give notice of his release to the enforcing authority[2].

(4) *Repealed.*

(5) *Repealed*

[Football Spectators Act 1989, s 18 as amended by the Football (Disorder) Act 2000, Sch 2, the Criminal Justice Act 2003, Sch 32, the Courts Act 2003, Sch 8 and the Legal Aid, Sentencing and Punishment of Offenders Act 2012, Sch 10.]

---

[1] See the Football Spectators (Prescription) Order 2004, SI 2004/2409 amended by SI 2006/761, SI 2010/584 and SI 2013/1709 which prescribes for these purposes the Football Banning Orders Authority and the Chief Executive of the Football Association Limited.

[2] The Football Banning Orders Authority is prescribed as the enforcing authority for the purposes of Part II of this Act by the Football Spectators (Prescription) Order 2004, SI 2004/2409 amended by SI 2006/761, SI 2010/584 and SI 2013/1709 which prescribes for these purposes the Football Banning Orders Authority.

*Reporting*

7.10445 **19. Functions of enforcing authority and local police** (1) The enforcing authority[1] and the officer responsible for the police station at which he reports initially shall have the following functions as respects any person subject to a banning order.

(2) On a person reporting initially at the police station, the officer responsible for the station may make such requirements of that person as are determined by the enforcing authority[1] to be necessary or expedient for giving effect to the banning order, so far as relating to regulated football matches outside the United Kingdom.

(2A) If, in connection with any regulated football match outside the United Kingdom, the enforcing authority[1] is of the opinion that requiring any person subject to a banning order to report is necessary or expedient in order to reduce the likelihood of violence or disorder at or in connection with the match, the authority must give him a notice in writing under subsection (2B) below.

(2B) The notice must require that person—

(*a*) to report at a police station[1] specified in the notice at the time, or between the times, specified in the notice,

(*b*) to surrender his passport at a police station[1] specified in the notice at the time, or between the times, specified in the notice,

and may require him to comply with any additional requirements of the order in the manner specified in the notice.

(2C) In the case of any regulated football match, the enforcing authority[2] may by notice in writing require any person subject to a banning order to comply with any additional requirements of the order in the manner specified in the notice.

(2D) The enforcing authority[2] may establish criteria for determining whether any requirement under subsection (2B) or (2C) above ought to be imposed on any person or any class of person.

(2E) A notice under this section—

(*a*) may not require the person subject to the order to report except in the control period in relation to a regulated football match outside the United Kingdom or an external tournament,

(*b*) may not require him to surrender his passport except in the control period in relation to a regulated football match outside the United Kingdom or an external tournament which includes such matches,

(*c*) must require him to notify the enforcing authority within the time period specified in the notice of each address at which he intends to stay, or has stayed, for one night or more in a period which is the control period in relation to a regulated football match.

(2F) Where a notice under this section requires the person subject to the order to surrender his passport, the passport must be returned to him as soon as reasonably practicable after the end of the control period in question.

(3) During the currency of a banning order in force in relation to any person the enforcing authority shall perform the following functions on the occasion of any regulated football match, that is to say—

(*a*) where the match is one for which reporting is obligatory for all persons subject to banning orders, the authority shall, by notice in writing to that person,

(i) require him to report to the police station specified in the notice at the time or between the times specified in the notice; and

(ii) require him to comply with the conditions (if any) imposed by the order;

(*b*) where the match is one for which reporting is obligatory for such persons only as are required to report under this paragraph, the authority shall, if that person is one as respects whom subsection (4) below is satisfied, by notice in writing to that person,

(i) require him to report to the police station specified in the notice at the time or between the times specified in the notice; and

(ii) require him to comply with the conditions (if any) imposed by the order;

(4) No requirements under subsection (3)(*b*) above shall be imposed by the enforcing authority on any person unless imposing them is, in their opinion, necessary or expedient in order to reduce the likelihood of violence or disorder at, or in connection with, the regulated football match; and the authority may establish criteria for determining whether requirements under that paragraph ought to be imposed on any person or class of person.

(5) The enforcing authority[1], in exercising their functions under this section shall have regard to any guidance issued by the Secretary of State under section 21 below.

(6) A person who, without reasonable excuse, fails to comply with any requirement imposed on

him under subsection (2) above shall be guilty of an offence.

(7) A person guilty of an offence under subsection (6) above shall be liable on summary conviction to a fine not exceeding **level 2** on the standard scale.

[Football Spectators Act 1989, s 19 as amended by the Football (Disorder) Act 2000, Schs 1 and 2, the Violent Crime Reduction Act 2006, Schs 3 and 5, the Policing and Crime Act 2009, s 103 and Sch 8 and the Identity Documents Act 2010, Schedule.]

---

1 The police station may be in England, Wales, Scotland or Northern Ireland (Policing and Crime Act 2009, s 104).

2 The Football Banning Orders Authority is prescribed as the enforcing authority for the purposes of Part II of this Act by the Football Spectators (Prescription) Order 2004, SI 2004/2409 amended by SI 2006/761, SI 2010/584 and SI 2013/1709.

7.10446 **20. Exemptions from requirement to report as respects a match**[1] (1) A person who is subject to a banning order may—

(*a*) as respects a particular regulated football match, or

(*b*) as respects regulated football matches played during a period,

apply to the authority empowered to grant exemptions under this section ("the exempting authority") to be exempt from the requirements imposed by or under this Part, or any of them as respects that match or matches played during that period.

(2) The enforcing authority[2] may grant exemptions under this section in all cases; but where the application is made during the control period in relation to any match to which the application applies, the officer responsible for a police station may grant the exemption as respects that match, subject to subsection (3) below.

(3) The officer responsible for a police station shall not grant an exemption without referring the question of exemption to the enforcing authority, unless he considers that it is not reasonably practicable to do so.

(4) The exempting authority shall exempt the applicant from the requirements imposed by or under this Part, or any of them, as respects any match or matches to which the application relates if he shows to the authority's satisfaction—

(*a*) that there are special circumstances which justify his being so exempted; and

(*b*) that, because of those circumstances, he would not attend the match or matches if he were so exempted.

(5) The exempting authority shall, in taking any decision under subsection (4) above, have regard to any guidance issued by the Secretary of State under section 21 below.

(6) Where an exemption is granted by the exempting authority to a person under subsection (4) above the banning order is to have effect subject to the exemption and, accordingly, no requirement is to be imposed under section 19 which is inconsistent with the exemption.

(7) A person who is aggrieved by the refusal of the exempting authority to grant him an exemption under subsection (4) above may, after giving the authority notice in writing of his intention to do so, appeal to a magistrates' court.

(8) On any appeal under subsection (7) above the court may make such order as it thinks fit.

(9) The court may order the appellant to pay all or any part of the costs of an appeal under subsection (7) above.

(10) Any person commits an offence who, in connection with an application under this section to be exempted from the requirements imposed by or under this Part, or any of them—

(*a*) makes a statement which he knows to be false or misleading in a material particular or recklessly makes a statement which is false or misleading in a material particular, or

(*b*) produces, furnishes, signs or otherwise makes use of a document which he knows to be false or misleading in a material particular or recklessly produces, furnishes, signs or otherwise makes use of a document which is false or misleading in a material particular.

(11) A person guilty of an offence under subsection (10) above shall be liable on summary conviction to a fine not exceeding **level 3** on the standard scale.

[Football Spectators Act 1989, s 20 as amended by the Football (Disorder) Act 2000, Sch 2 and the Courts Act 2003, Schs 8 and 10.]

---

1 See note 1 to s 14A above.

2 The Football Banning Orders Authority is prescribed as the enforcing authority for the purposes of Part II of this Act by the Football Spectators (Prescription) Order 2004, SI 2004/2409 amended by SI 2006/761, SI 2010/584 and SI 2013/1709.

7.10447 **21. Functions of enforcing authority: supplementary provisions** (1) The Secretary of State may issue to the enforcing authority[1] such guidance as he considers appropriate for the purposes of the exercise of their functions under sections 19 and 20 above.

(2) The Secretary of State shall make such arrangements as he considers appropriate for publishing the guidance issued from time to time under subsection (1) above.

(3) The Secretary of State may make regulations regulating the giving by the enforcing authority[1] to persons subject to banning orders of notices under section 19 above; and it shall be the duty of the enforcing authority to comply with the regulations.

(4) Regulations under subsection (3) above may exclude the operation of section 25 below.

(5) The power to make regulations under subsection (3) above is exercisable by statutory instrument which shall be subject to annulment in pursuance of a resolution of either House of Parliament.

(6) Where any notice is given under section 19 above by the enforcing authority[1] in accordance

with regulations under subsection (3) above, the notice shall be taken to have been received by the person to whom it was addressed unless he proves that he did not receive the notice and did not know and had no reasonable cause to believe requirements had been imposed on him under section 19 above.

(7) Where any notice is given under section 19 above by the enforcing authority[1] in accordance with section 25 below, subsection (6) above (instead of section 25(1A)) shall apply as it applies to such a notice given in accordance with regulations under subsection (3) above.

(8) The Secretary of State may pay to the enforcing authority[1] any expenses incurred by them in exercising their functions under sections 19 and 20 above.

[Football Spectators Act 1989, s 21 as amended by the Football (Disorder) Act 2000, Sch 1 and the Violent Crime Reduction Act 2006, Sch 3.]

---

[1] The Football Banning Orders Authority is prescribed as the enforcing authority for the purposes of Part II of this Act by the Football Spectators (Prescription) Order 2006, SI 2006/761.

**7.10448 21A. Summary measures: detention**[1] (1) This section and section 21B below apply during any control period in relation to a regulated football match outside the United Kingdom or an external tournament if a constable in uniform—

(*a*) has reasonable grounds for suspecting that the condition in section 14B(2) above is met in the case of a person present before him, and

(*b*) has reasonable grounds to believe that making a banning order in his case would help to prevent violence or disorder at or in connection with any regulated football matches.

(2) The constable may detain the person in his custody (whether there or elsewhere) until he has decided whether or not to issue a notice under section 21B below, and shall give the person his reasons for detaining him in writing.

This is without prejudice to any power of the constable apart from this section to arrest the person.

(3) A person may not be detained under subsection (2) above for more than four hours or, with the authority of an officer of at least the rank of inspector, six hours.

(4) A person who has been detained under subsection (2) above may only be further detained under that subsection in the same control period in reliance on information which was not available to the constable who previously detained him; and a person on whom a notice has been served under section 21B(2) below may not be detained under subsection (2) above in the same control period.

[Football Spectators Act 1989, s 21A as inserted by the Football (Disorder) Act 2000, Sch 1 and amended by the Policing and Crime Act 2009, s 103.]

---

[1] Section 1 of the Football (Disorder) (Amendment) Act 2002 amended s 5 of the Amendment of Football (Disorder) Act 2000 to enable the exercise of powers under ss 21A and 21B (and the making of applications under s 14B) of the Football Spectators Act 1989 within the period of 5 years beginning with the day on which s 1 of the 2002 Act came into force. Section 1 came into force on August 28, 2002 (see Football (Disorder) (Amendment) Act 2002 (Commencement) Order 2002 (SI 2002/2200).

**7.10449 21B. Summary measures: reference to a court**[1] (1) A constable in uniform may exercise the power in subsection (2) below if authorised to do so by an officer of at least the rank of inspector.

(2) The constable may give the person a notice in writing requiring him—

(*a*) to appear before a magistrates' court at a time, or between the times, specified in the notice,

(*b*) not to leave England and Wales before that time (or the later of those times), and

(*c*) if the control period relates to a regulated football match outside the United Kingdom or to an external tournament which includes such matches, to surrender his passport to the constable,

and stating the grounds referred to in section 21A(1) above.

(3) The times for appearance before the magistrates' court must be within the period of 24 hours beginning with—

(*a*) the giving of the notice, or

(*b*) the person's detention under section 21A(2) above,

whichever is the earlier.

(4) For the purposes of section 14B above, the notice is to be treated as an application[2] for a banning order made by complaint by the constable to the court in question and subsection (1) of that section is to have effect as if the references to the relevant chief officer were references to that constable.

(5) A constable may arrest a person to whom he is giving such a notice if he has reasonable grounds to believe that it is necessary to do so in order to secure that the person complies with the notice.

(6) Any passport surrendered by a person under this section must be returned to him in accordance with directions given by the court.

[Football Spectators Act 1989, s 21B as inserted by the Football (Disorder) Act 2000, Sch 1 and amended by the Violent Crime Reduction Act 2006, Sch 3 and the Identity Documents Act 2010, Schedule.]

---

[1] Section 1 of the Football (Disorder) (Amendment) Act 2002 amended s 5 of the Amendment of Football (Disorder) Act 2000 to enable the exercise of powers under ss 21A and 21B (and the making of applications under s 14B) of the Football Spectators Act 1989 within the period of five years beginning with the day on which s 1 of the 2002 Act came into

force. Section 1 came into force on 28 August 2002 (see Football (Disorder) (Amendment) Act 2002 (Commencement) Order 2002 (SI 2002/2200).

2 Proceedings under s 21B of this Act are "criminal proceedings" for the purposes of s 12(2)(*g*) of the Access to Justice Act 1999 by virtue of reg 3 of the Criminal Defence Service (General) (No 2) Regulations 2001 (eligibility for criminal legal aid).

7.10450 **21C. Summary measures: supplementary** (1) The powers conferred by sections 21A and 21B above may only be exercised in relation to a person who is a British citizen.

(2) A person who fails to comply with a notice given to him under section 21B above is guilty of an offence and liable on summary conviction to imprisonment for a term not exceeding six months, or a fine not exceeding level 5 on the standard scale, or both.

(3) Where a person to whom a notice has been given under section 21B above appears before a magistrates' court as required by the notice (whether under arrest or not), the court may remand him.

(4) A person who, by virtue of subsection (3) above, is remanded on bail under section 128 of the Magistrates' Courts Act 1980 may be required by the conditions of his bail—

(*a*) not to leave England and Wales before his appearance before the court, and

(*b*) if the control period relates to a regulated football match outside the United Kingdom or to an external tournament which includes such matches, to surrender his passport to a police constable, if he has not already done so.

[Football Spectators Act 1989, s 21C as inserted by the Football (Disorder) Act 2000, Sch 1 and amended by the Identity Documents Act 2010, Schedule.]

7.10451 **21D. Summary measures: compensation** (1) Where a person to whom a notice has been given under section 21B above appears before a magistrates' court and the court refuses the application for a banning order in respect of him, it may order compensation to be paid to him out of central funds if it is satisfied—

(*a*) that the notice should not have been given,

(*b*) that he has suffered loss as a result of the giving of the notice, and

(*c*) that, having regard to all the circumstances, it is appropriate to order the payment of compensation in respect of that loss.

(2) An appeal lies to the Crown Court against any refusal by a magistrates' court to order the payment of compensation under subsection (1) above.

(3) The compensation to be paid by order of the magistrates' court under subsection (1) above or by order of the Crown Court on an appeal under subsection (2) above shall not exceed £5,000 (but no appeal may be made under subsection (2) in respect of the amount of compensation awarded).

(4) If it appears to the Secretary of State that there has been a change in the value of money since the coming into force of this section or, as the case may be, the last occasion when the power conferred by this subsection was exercised, he may by order substitute for the amount specified in subsection (3) above such other amount as appears to him to be justified by the change.

(5) In this section, "central funds" has the same meaning as in enactments providing for the payment of costs[1].

[Football Spectators Act 1989, s 21D as inserted by the Football (Disorder) Act 2000, Sch 1.]

1 Proceedings under s 21D of this Act are "criminal proceedings" for the purposes of s 12(2)(*g*) of the Access to Justice Act 1999 by virtue of reg 3 of the Criminal Defence Service (General) (No 2) Regulations 2001 (eligibility for criminal legal aid).

*Relevant offences outside England and Wales*

7.10452 **22. Banning orders arising out of offences outside England and Wales** (1) Her Majesty may, by Order[1] in Council, specify offences ("corresponding offences") under the law of any country outside England and Wales which appear to Her to correspond to any offence to which Schedule 1 to this Act applies.

(1A) For the purposes of subsection (1) above, an offence specified in an Order in Council under that subsection shall be regarded as corresponding to an offence to which Schedule 1 to this Act applies notwithstanding that any period specified in the Order is longer than any corresponding period specified in that Schedule.

(2) Upon an information being laid before a justice of the peace that a person has been convicted of a corresponding offence in a country outside England and Wales, the justice may—

(*a*) issue a summons directed to that person requiring him to appear before a magistrates' court to answer to the information; or

(*b*) subject to subsection (3) below, issue a warrant to arrest that person and bring him before a magistrates' court.

(3) No warrant shall be issued under subsection (2) above unless the information is in writing and substantiated on oath.

(4) Where a person appears or is brought before a magistrates' court in pursuance of subsection (2) above, the court, if satisfied that—

(*a*) he is ordinarily resident in England and Wales, and

(*b*) has been convicted in the country outside England and Wales of the corresponding offence,

may, unless it appears that the conviction is the subject of proceedings in a court of law in that country questioning the conviction, make a banning order in relation to him.

(5) A magistrates' court which has power to make a banning order in relation to a person shall be under a duty to make the order in relation to him if it is satisfied that there are reasonable grounds to believe that making the order would help to prevent violence or disorder at or in connection with regulated football matches.

(5A) Where a magistrates' court has power to make a banning order in relation to a person but does not do so, it shall state in open court that it is not satisfied that there are such reasonable grounds as are mentioned in subsection (5) above and give reasons why it is not satisfied.

(6) In proceedings under subsection (4) above, the court shall have the like powers, including power to adjourn the proceedings and meanwhile to remand the defendant on bail (but not in custody), and the proceedings shall be conducted as nearly as may be in the like manner, as if the proceedings were the trial of an information for a summary offence.

(7) Any person aggrieved by the decision of a magistrates' court making a banning order under this section may appeal to the Crown Court against the decision.

(8) Sections 14E to 14J and 18 to 21 shall apply in relation to a person subject to a banning order under this section as they apply in relation to a person subject to a banning order made by a magistrates' court under section 14A.

(9) An Order in Council under subsection (1) above relating to any country may include provision specifying the documentary form in which details are to be given of—

(*a*) the conviction of a person in that country of a corresponding offence,

(*b*) the nature and circumstances of the offence, and

(*c*) whether or not the conviction is the subject of proceedings in that country questioning it.

(10) A document in the form so specified—

(*a*) shall be admissible in any proceedings under this Part of this Act as evidence of the facts stated in it unless the contrary is proved, and

(*b*) shall be taken as such a document unless the contrary is proved.

(11) In proceedings against a person under this section, the facts stated in a document in the form so specified shall, on production of the document and proof that that person is the person whose conviction is set out in the document, be taken to be proved unless the contrary is proved.

(12) Any statutory instrument containing an Order under subsection (1) above shall be subject to annulment in pursuance of a resolution of either House of Parliament.

[Football Spectators Act 1989, s 22 as amended by the Football (Offences and Disorder) Act 1999, ss 1, 3 and 5, the Football (Disorder) Act 2000, Sch 2 and the Courts Act 2003, Schs 8 and 10.]

[1] Orders previous made under this section have been revoked by the Football Spectators (Corresponding Offences) (Revocation) Order 2015, SI 2015/212 as, according to the Explanatory Note to the Order, s 22 has fallen out of use as there are alternative routes to securing a banning order under this Act; in particular via s 14B.

**7.10453 22A. Other interpretation, etc** (1) In this Part—

"British citizen" has the same meaning as in the British Nationality Act 1981,

"country" includes territory,

enforcing authority" means a prescribed organisation established by the Secretary of State under section 57 of the Police Act 1996 (central police organisations),

"passport" means a United Kingdom passport within the meaning of the Immigration Act 1971,

"prescribed" means prescribed by an order made by the Secretary of State;

(2) The Secretary of State may, if he considers it necessary or expedient to do so in order to secure the effective enforcement of this Part, by order[1] provide for section 14(5) and (6) above to have effect in relation to any, or any description of, regulated football match or external tournament as if, for any reference to five days, there were substituted a reference to the number of days (not exceeding ten) specified in the order.

(3) Any power of the Secretary of State to make an order under this Part is exercisable by statutory instrument.

(4) An instrument containing an order made by the Secretary of State under this Part shall be subject to annulment in pursuance of a resolution of either House of Parliament.

[Football Spectators Act 1989, s 22A as inserted by the Football (Disorder) Act 2000, Sch 2 and amended by the Violent Crime Reduction Act 2006, Sch 5 and the Identity Documents Act 2010, Schedule.]

[1] Various orders extending the duration of a 'control period' in relation to specific tournaments have been made.

## PART III[1]

## GENERAL

**7.10454 23. Further provision about, and appeals against, declarations of relevance**

(1) Subject to subsection (2) below, a court may not make a declaration of relevance as respects any offence unless it is satisfied that the prosecutor gave notice to the defendant, at least five days before the first day of the trial, that it was proposed to show that the offence related to football matches, to a particular football match or to particular football matches (as the case may be).

(2) A court may, in any particular case, make a declaration of relevance notwithstanding that notice to the defendant as required by subsection (1) above has not been given if he consents to waive the giving of full notice or the court is satisfied that the interests of justice do not require more

notice to be given.

(3) A person convicted of an offence as respects which the court makes a declaration of relevance may appeal against the making of the declaration of relevance as if the declaration were included in any sentence passed on him for the offence, and accordingly—

*(a)–(c) amendments.*

(4) A banning order made upon a person's conviction of a relevant offence shall be quashed if the making of a declaration of relevance as respects that offence is reversed on appeal.

(5) In this section "declaration of relevance" means a declaration by a court for the purposes of Schedule 1 to this Act that an offence related to football matches, or that it related to one or more particular football matches.

[Football Spectators Act 1989, s 23 as amended by the Football (Offences and Disorder) Act 1999, ss 1 and 2,the Football (Disorder) Act 2000, Sch 2 and the Violent Crime Reduction Act 2006, Sch 3.]

[1] Part III contains ss 23–27.

7.10455 **24. Offences by bodies corporate** (1) Where an offence under this Act which has been committed by a body corporate is proved to have been committed with the consent or connivance of, or to be attributable to any neglect on the part of, a director, manager, secretary or similar officer of the body corporate, or any person purporting to act in that capacity, he, as well as the body corporate, shall be guilty of that offence and be liable to be proceeded against and punished accordingly.

(2) Where the affairs of a body corporate are managed by its members, subsection (1) above shall apply to the acts and defaults of a member in connection with his functions of management as if he were a director of the body corporate.

[Football Spectators Act 1989, s 24.]

7.10456 **25. Service of documents** (1) Any notice or other document required or authorised by or by virtue of this Act to be served on any person may be served on him either by delivering it to him or by leaving it at his proper address or by sending it by post.

(1A) A notice or other document served in accordance with subsection (1) on a person who is the subject of a banning order is to be deemed to be received by him at the time when it is served unless he proves otherwise.

(2) Any notice or other document so required or authorised to be served on a body corporate or a firm shall be duly served if it is served on the secretary or clerk of that body or a partner of that firm.

(3) For the purposes of this section, and of section 7 of the Interpretation Act 1978 in its application to this section, the proper address of a person, in the case of a secretary or clerk of a body corporate, shall be that of the registered office or principal office of that body, in the case of a partner of a firm shall be that of the principal office of the firm, and in any other case shall be the last known address of the person to be served.

(4) This section, and the said section 7 in its application to this section, is subject to section 21(4) and (7) above.

[Football Spectators Act 1989, s 25 as amended by the Violent Crime Reduction Act 2006, Sch 3.]

7.10457 **27. Citation, commencement[1], consequential repeal and extent** (1) This Act may be cited as the Football Spectators Act 1989.

[Football Spectators Act 1989, s 27(1).]

[1] This Act is fully in force.

## SCHEDULES

### SCHEDULE 1

RELEVANT OFFENCES — Sections 7(5), 14(5) and 22(1)

*(As substituted by the Football (Disorder) Act 2000, Sch 1 and amended by the Violent Crime Reduction Act 2006, Schs 3 and 5, the Criminal Justice and Immigration Act 2008, Sch 26, the Policing and Crime Act 2009, s 107 and the Crime and Courts Act 2013, Sch 22.)*

7.10458 1. This Schedule applies to the following offences:

(*a*) any offence under section 2(1), 5(7), 14J(1), 19(6), 20(10) or 21C(2) of this Act or section 68(1) or (5) of the Police, Public Order and Criminal Justice (Scotland) Act 2006 by virtue of section 106 of the Policing and Crime Act 2009,

(*b*) any offence under section 2 or 2A of the Sporting Events (Control of Alcohol etc) Act 1985[1] (alcohol, containers and fireworks) committed by the accused at any football match to which this Schedule applies or while entering or trying to enter the ground,

(*c*) any offence under section 4A or 5 of the Public Order Act 1986[2] (harassment, alarm or distress) or any provision of Part 3 or 3A of that Act (hatred by reference to race etc) committed during a period relevant to a football match to which this Schedule applies at any premises while the accused was at, or was entering or leaving or trying to enter or leave, the premises,

(*d*) any offence involving the use or threat of violence by the accused towards another person committed during a period relevant to a football match to which this Schedule applies at any premises while the accused was at, or was entering or leaving or trying to enter or leave, the premises,

(*e*) any offence involving the use or threat of violence towards property committed during a period relevant to a football match to which this Schedule applies at any premises while the accused was at, or was entering or leaving or trying to enter or leave, the premises, (*f*) any offence involving the use, carrying or possession of an offensive weapon or a firearm committed during a period relevant to a football match to which this Schedule applies at any premises while the accused was at, or was entering or leaving or trying to enter or leave, the premises,

(*g*) any offence under section 12 of the Licensing Act 1872[1] (persons found drunk in public places, etc) of being found drunk in a highway or other public place committed while the accused was on a journey to or from a football match to which this Schedule applies being an offence as respects which the court makes a declaration that the offence related to football matches,

(*h*) any offence under section 91(1) of the Criminal Justice Act 1967[1] (disorderly behaviour while drunk in a public place) committed in a highway or other public place while the accused was on a journey to or from a football match to which this Schedule applies being an offence as respects which the court makes a declaration that the offence related to football matches,

(*j*) any offence under section 1 of the Sporting Events (Control of Alcohol etc) Act 1985[1] (alcohol on coaches or trains to or from sporting events) committed while the accused was on a journey to or from a football match to which this Schedule applies being an offence as respects which the court makes a declaration that the offence related to football matches,

(*k*) any offence under section 4A or 5 of the Public Order Act 1986[2] (harassment, alarm or distress) or any provision of Part 3 or 3A of that Act (hatred by reference to race etc) committed while the accused was on a journey to or from a football match to which this Schedule applies being an offence as respects which the court makes a declaration that the offence related to[3] football matches,

(*l*) any offence under section 4, 5 or 5A of the Road Traffic Act 1988[4] (driving etc when under the influence of drink or drugs or with an alcohol concentration above the prescribed limit or with a concentration of a specified controlled drug above the specified limit) committed while the accused was on a journey to or from a football match to which this Schedule applies being an offence as respects which the court makes a declaration that the offence related to football matches,

(*m*) any offence involving the use or threat of violence by the accused towards another person committed while one or each of them was on a journey to or from a football match to which this Schedule applies being an offence as respects which the court makes a declaration[5] that the offence related to football matches[6],

(*n*) any offence involving the use or threat of violence towards property committed while the accused was on a journey to or from a football match to which this Schedule applies being an offence as respects which the court makes a declaration that the offence related to football matches,

(*o*) any offence involving the use, carrying or possession of an offensive weapon or a firearm committed while the accused was on a journey to or from a football match to which this Schedule applies being an offence as respects which the court makes a declaration that the offence related to football matches,

(*p*) any offence under the Football (Offences) Act 1991,

(*q*) any offence under section 4A or 5 of the Public Order Act 1986 (harassment, alarm or distress) or any provision of Part 3 or 3A of that Act (hatred by reference to race etc)—
  (i) which does not fall within paragraph (*c*) or (*k*) above,
  (ii) which was committed during a period relevant to a football match to which this Schedule applies, and
  (iii) as respects which the court makes a declaration that the offence related to that match or to that match and any other football match which took place during that period,

(*r*) any offence involving the use or threat of violence by the accused towards another person—
  (i) which does not fall within paragraph (*d*) or (*m*) above,
  (ii) which was committed during a period relevant to a football match to which this Schedule applies, and
  (iii) as respects which the court makes a declaration[5] that the offence related to that match or to that match and any other football match which took place during that period[7],

(*s*) any offence involving the use or threat of violence towards property—
  (i) which does not fall within paragraph (*e*) or (*n*) above,
  (ii) which was committed during a period relevant to a football match to which this Schedule applies, and
  (iii) as respects which the court makes a declaration that the offence related to that match or to that match and any other football match which took place during that period,

(*t*) any offence involving the use, carrying or possession of an offensive weapon or a firearm—
  (i) which does not fall within paragraph (*f*) or (*o*) above,
  (ii) which was committed during a period relevant to a football match to which this Schedule applies, and
  (iii) as respects which the court makes a declaration that the offence related to that match or to that match and any other football match which took place during that period.

(*u*) any offence under section 166 of the Criminal Justice and Public Order Act 1994 (sale of tickets by unauthorised persons) which relates to tickets for a football match.

**2.** Any reference to an offence in paragraph 1 above includes—
  (*a*) a reference to any attempt, conspiracy or incitement to commit that offence, and
  (*b*) a reference to aiding and abetting, counselling or procuring the commission of that offence.

**3.** For the purposes of paragraphs 1(*g*) to (*o*) above—
  (*a*) a person may be regarded as having been on a journey to or from a football match to which this Schedule applies whether or not he attended or intended to attend the match, and
  (*b*) a person's journey includes breaks (including overnight breaks).

**4.** In this Schedule, "football match" means a match which is a regulated football match for the purposes of Part II of this Act.

(2) For the purposes of this Schedule each of the following periods is "relevant to" a football match to which this Schedule applies—
  (*a*) in the case of a match which takes place on the day on which it is advertised to take place, the period—
    (i) beginning 24 hours before whichever is the earlier of the start of the match and the time at which it was advertised to start; and
    (ii) ending 24 hours after it ends;

(*b*) in the case of a match which does not take place on the day on which it was advertised to take place, the period—
(i) beginning 24 hours before the time at which it was advertised to start on that day; and
(ii) ending 24 hours after that time.

1 See PART VI: LICENSING, ante.

2 See title PUBLIC MEETING AND PUBLIC ORDER, in this PART, post.

3 "Related to" does not have the same meaning as "relevant to" in s 1(8) and thus the time limits prescribed by the latter are inapplicable; the words should be given their ordinary meaning and be applied in a reasonable way in practice: *DPP v Beaumont, DPP v Dowling* [2008] EWHC 523 (Admin), [2008] 1 WLR 2186, (2008) 172 JP 283, [2008] Crim LR 572, [2008] 2 Cr App Rep (S) 98. In *R v Parkes; R v Cartright* [2010] EWCA Crim 2803, 175 JP 33, [2011] 2 Cr App R (S) 10, the appellants were supporters of Wolverhampton Wanderers FC. On the night in question, West Bromwich Albion FC played Peterborough United. After the game, some WBA supports made their way to a public house in Wednesbury. The police had received intelligence that disorder was being planned between Wolves and WBA fans. The appellants were involved and pleaded guilty to offences contrary to s 4 of the POA 1986. They were made the subject of football banning orders. The orders were upheld on appeal. The appellants had deliberately gone to Wednesbury in that knowledge that some WBA fans would be at the pub after the match. The fact that Wolves had not been involved in the match was of little substance when the whole picture was viewed. The spark was football and the offences were clearly related to the match that had taken place. The opposite conclusion, however, was reached in the case of *R v Doyle* [2012] EWCA Crim 995, [2013] 1 Cr App Rep (S) 197, 176 JP 337 where the appellants, who lived in Reading, were returning by train from a match at West Ham. They were rowdy and foul mouthed and they assaulted another passenger who asked them to stop. They were convicted of affray and made subject to banning orders. The orders were quashed on appeal. The affray arose from drunkenness rather than necessarily having any connection with football, and the judge had not determined that the making of a banning order would help to prevent violence or disorder at or in connection with any regulated football matches. See further note 5, infra.

Where the prosecution and defence advance different accounts which have a material bearing on whether the pre-condition of 'related to' applies, the court should hold a Newton hearing to resolve the matter: *R v Irving and Irving* [2013] EWCA Crim 1932, [2014] 2 Cr App R (S) 6.

4 See PART IV: title ROAD TRAFFIC, ante.

5 Such a declaration is necessary if for this provision to apply: *R v Irving and Irving*, supra.

6 Such a declaration is necessary if for this provision to apply: *R v Irving and Irving*, supra.

7 For a banning order to be made, the violence must relate to a football match; it does not have to be between opposing supporters, but if the violence is sparked by something that has nothing to do with the match the statutory requirements for the making of an order are not satisfied: *R v Gregory Elliot* [2007] EWCA Crim 1002, [2007] 2 Cr App Rep (S) 430 (following, though with the rider that the result of the case was not obvious on the facts, *R v Smith* [2003] EWCA Crim 2480, [2004] 1 Cr App Rep (S) 341). See also *R v Arbery and Mobley* [2008] EWCA Crim 702, (2008) 172 JP 291; and *R v Mabee* [2007] EWCA Crim 3320, [2008] 2 Cr App Rep (S) 25.

# Football (Offences) Act 1991

(1991 c 19)

7.10459 **1. Regulated football matches** (1) In this Act a "regulated football match" means an association football match designated, or of a description designated[1], for the purposes of this Act by order of the Secretary of State.

Any such order shall be made by statutory instrument which shall be subject to annulment in pursuance of a resolution of either House of Parliament.

(2) References in this Act to things done at a regulated football match include anything done at the ground—
(*a*) within the period beginning two hours before the start of the match or (if earlier) two hours before the time at which it is advertised to start and ending one hour after the end of the match; or
(*b*) where the match is advertised to start at a particular time on a particular day but does not take place on that day, within the period beginning two hours before and ending one hour after the advertised starting time.

[Football (Offences) Act 1991, s 1.]

1 The Football (Offences) (Designation of Football Matches) Order 2004, SI 2004/2410 amended by SI 2011/1187 designates football matches for the purpose of this Act. A designated football match is an association football match in which one or both of the participating teams represents a club which is for the time being a member (whether a full or associate member) of the Football League, the Football Association Premier League, the Football Conference, the Scottish Football League or the Welsh Premier League, or whose home ground is for the time being situated outside England and Wales, or represents a country or territory. A designated match is also an association football match in competition for the Football Association Cup (other than in a preliminary or qualifying round).

7.10460 **2. Throwing of missiles** It is an offence for a person at a regulated football match to throw anything at or towards—
(*a*) the playing area, or any area adjacent to the playing area to which spectators are not generally admitted, or
(*b*) any area in which spectators or other persons are or may be present,

without lawful authority or lawful excuse (which shall be for him to prove).

[Football (Offences) Act 1991, s 2.]

7.10461 **3. Indecent or racialist chanting** (1) It is an offence to engage or take part in chanting of an indecent or racialist nature at a regulated football match.

(2) For this purpose—
(*a*) "chanting" means the repeated uttering of any words or sounds (whether alone or in concert with one or more others); and

(*b*) "of a racialist nature" means consisting of or including matter which is threatening, abusive or insulting to a person by reason of his colour, race, nationality (including citizenship) or ethnic or national origins[1].

[Football (Offences) Act 1991, s 3 as amended by the Football (Offences and Disorder Act 1999 s 9.]

[1] Although the use of the word "Paki" must, be considered on a case-by-case basis in the context in which it is used, as a slang expression the modern common understanding of the term is that it is racially offensive. Furthermore, it is immaterial whether persons of the racial group referred to in the offending words are present or, if present, are offended or affected in any way by them. Therefore the chanting by the accused of the words "You're just a town full of Pakis" at supporters of Oldham Athletic was of a racialist nature (*DPP v Stoke on Trent Magistrates' Court* [2003] EWHC 1593 (Admin), [2003] 3 All ER 1086, 167 JP 436, [2003] Crim LR 804).

7.10462 4. **Going onto the playing area** It is an offence for a person at a regulated football match to go onto the playing area, or any area adjacent to the playing area to which spectators are not generally admitted, without lawful authority or lawful excuse (which shall be for him to prove).

[Football (Offences) Act 1991, s 4.]

7.10463 5. **Supplementary provisions** (1) *Repealed.*

(2) A person guilty of an offence under this Act is liable on summary conviction to a fine not exceeding **level 3** on the standard scale.

(3) *Repealed.*

[Football (Offences) Act 1991, s 5 as amended by the Football (Disorder) Act 2000, Sch 3 and the Serious Organised Crime and Police Act 2005, Sch 17.]

7.10464 6. Short title, commencement and extent.

## Confiscation of Alcohol (Young Persons) Act 1997

(1997 c 33)

7.10465 1. **Confiscation of intoxicating liquor** (1) Where a constable reasonably suspects that a person in a relevant place is in possession of alcohol and that either—

(*a*) he is under the age of 18; or

(*b*) he intends that any of the alcohol should be consumed by a person under the age of 18 in that or any other relevant place; or

(*c*) a person under the age of 18 who is, or has recently been, with him has recently consumed alcohol in that or any other relevant place,

the constable may require him to surrender anything in his possession which is, or which the constable reasonably believes to be, alcohol or a container for alcohol.

(1AA) A constable who imposes a requirement on a person under subsection (1) shall also require the person to state the person's name and address.

(1AB) A constable who imposes a requirement on a person under subsection (1) may, if the constable reasonably suspects that the person is under the age of 16, remove the person to the person's place of residence or a place of safety.

(1A) *Repealed.*

(2) A constable may dispose of anything surrendered to him under subsection (1) in such manner as he considers appropriate.

(3) A person who fails without reasonable excuse to comply with a requirement imposed on him under subsection (1) or (1AA) commits an offence and is liable on summary conviction to a fine not exceeding **level 2** on the standard scale.

(4) A constable who imposes a requirement on a person under subsection (1) shall inform him of his suspicion and that failing without reasonable excuse to comply with a requirement imposed under that subsection or (1AA) is an offence.

(5) *Repealed.*

(6) In subsection (1) "relevant place", in relation to a person, means—

(*a*) any public place, other than licensed premises; or

(*b*) any place, other than a public place, to which the person has unlawfully gained access;

and for this purpose a place is a public place if at the material time the public or any section of the public has access to it, on payment or otherwise, as of right or by virtue of express or implied permission.

(7) In this section—

"alcohol"—

(*a*) in relation to England and Wales, has the same meaning as in the Licensing Act 2003;

(*b*) in relation to Northern Ireland, has the same meaning as "intoxicating liquor" in the Licensing (Northern Ireland) Order 1996; and

"licensed premises"—

(*a*) in relation to England and Wales, means premises which may by virtue of Part 3 or Part 5 of the Licensing Act 2003 (premises licence; permitted temporary activity) be used for the supply of alcohol within the meaning of section 14 of that Act;

(*b*) in relation to Northern Ireland, has the same meaning as in the Licensing (Northern Ireland) Order 1996.*

[Confiscation of Alcohol (Young Persons) Act 1997, s 1 as amended by the Criminal Justice and Police Act 2001, s 29 and the Licensing Act 2003, Sch 6, the Serious Organised Crime and Police Act 2005, Sch 17 and the Policing and Crime Act 2009, s 29 and Sch 8.]

7.10466 2. **Short title, commencement and extent** (1) This Act may be cited as the Confiscation of Alcohol (Young Persons) Act 1997.

(2) Section 1 shall not come into force until such day as the Secretary of State may by order[1] made by statutory instrument appoint.

(3) This Act extends to England and Wales and Northern Ireland.

[Confiscation of Alcohol (Young Persons) Act 1997, s 2.]

1 Section 1 came into force on 1 August 1997 (SI 1997/1725).

# Serious Organised Crime and Police Act 2005

(2005 c 15)

## PART 4[1]

## PUBLIC ORDER AND CONDUCT IN PUBLIC PLACES etc

*Trespass on designated site*

7.10467 **128. Offence of trespassing on designated site** (1) A person commits an offence if he enters, or is on, any protected site in England and Wales or Northern Ireland as a trespasser.

(1A) In this section "protected site" means—

(*a*) a nuclear site; or

(*b*) a designated site.

(1B) In this section "nuclear site" means—

(*a*) so much of any premises in respect of which a nuclear site licence (within the meaning of the Nuclear Installations Act 1965) is for the time being in force as lies within the outer perimeter of the protection provided for those premises; and

(*b*) so much of any other premises of which premises falling within paragraph (*a*) form a part as lies within that outer perimeter.

(1C) For this purpose—

(*a*) the outer perimeter of the protection provided for any premises is the line of the outermost fences, walls or other obstacles provided or relied on for protecting those premises from intruders; and

(*b*) that line shall be determined on the assumption that every gate, door or other barrier across a way through a fence, wall or other obstacle is closed.

(2) A "designated site" means a site—

(*a*) specified or described (in any way) in an order[2] made by the Secretary of State, and

(*b*) designated for the purposes of this section by the order[1].

(3) The Secretary of State may only designate a site for the purposes of this section if—

(*a*) it is comprised in Crown land; or

(*b*) it is comprised in land belonging to Her Majesty in Her private capacity or to the immediate heir to the Throne in his private capacity; or

(*c*) it appears to the Secretary of State that it is appropriate to designate the site in the interests of national security.

(4) It is a defence for a person charged with an offence under this section to prove that he did not know, and had no reasonable cause to suspect, that the site in relation to which the offence is alleged to have been committed was a protected site.

(5) A person guilty of an offence under this section is liable on summary conviction—

(*a*) to imprisonment for a term not exceeding 51 weeks[3], or

(*b*) to a fine not exceeding level 5 on the standard scale,

or to both.

(6) No proceedings for an offence under this section may be instituted against any person—

(*a*) in England and Wales, except by or with the consent of the Attorney General, or

(*b*) in Northern Ireland, except by or with the consent of the Attorney General for Northern Ireland.

(7) For the purposes of this section a person who is on any protected site as a trespasser does not cease to be a trespasser by virtue of being allowed time to leave the site.

(8) In this section—

(*a*) "site" means the whole or part of any building or buildings, or any land, or both;

(*b*) "Crown land" means land in which there is a Crown interest or a Duchy interest.

(9) For this purpose—

"Crown interest" means an interest belonging to Her Majesty in right of the Crown, and

"Duchy interest" means an interest belonging to Her Majesty in right of the Duchy of Lancaster or belonging to the Duchy of Cornwall.

(10) In the application of this section to Northern Ireland, the reference to 51 weeks in subsection (5)(*a*) is to be read as a reference to 6 months.

[Serious Organised Crime and Police Act 2005, s 128 as amended by the Terrorism Act 2006, s 12.]

1 Part 4 comprises ss 125–144 and Sch 10. Other provisions of this Act are reproduced in PART I: MAGISTRATES' COURTS, PROCEDURE, ante.

2 The Serious Organised Crime and Police Act 2005 (Designated Sites) Order 2005, SI 2005/3447 and the Serious Organised Crime and Police Act 2005 (Designated Sites under Section 128) Order 2007, SI 2007/930 amended by SI 2007/1387, SI 2012/1769 and 2709, SI 2013/1562 and SI 2014/411 and 2263 have been made.

[3] In relation to an offence committed before the commencement of s 281(5) of the Criminal Justice Act 2003 this is to be read as a reference to "6 months", s 175(3), post.

7.10468 **131. Designated sites: access** (1) The following provisions do not apply to land in respect of which a designation order is in force—

(*a*) section 2(1) of the Countryside and Rights of Way Act 2000 (c 37) (rights of public in relation to access land),

(*b*) Part III of the Countryside (Northern Ireland) Order 1983 (SI 1983/1895 (NI 18)) (access to open country), and

(*c*) section 1 of the Land Reform (Scotland) Act 2003 (asp 2) (access rights).

(2) The Secretary of State may take such steps as he considers appropriate to inform the public of the effect of any designation order, including, in particular, displaying notices on or near the site to which the order relates.

(3) But the Secretary of State may only—

(*a*) display any such notice, or

(*b*) take any other steps under subsection (2),

in or on any building or land, if the appropriate person consents.

(4) The "appropriate person" is—

(*a*) a person appearing to the Secretary of State to have a sufficient interest in the building or land to consent to the notice being displayed or the steps being taken, or

(*b*) a person acting on behalf of such a person.

(5) In this section a "designation order" means—

(*a*) in relation to England and Wales or Northern Ireland, an order under section 128, or

(*b*) *Scotland.*

[Serious Organised Crime and Police Act 2005, s 131.]

*Parental compensation orders*

7.10469 **144. Parental compensation orders** Schedule 10 is to have effect.

[Serious Organised Crime and Police Act 2005, s 144.]

## PART 5[1]

## MISCELLANEOUS

*Protection of activities of certain organisations*

7.10470 **145. Interference with contractual relationships so as to harm animal research organisation** (1) A person (A) commits an offence if, with the intention of harming an animal research organisation, he—

(*a*) does a relevant act, or

(*b*) threatens that he or somebody else will do a relevant act,

in circumstances in which that act or threat is intended or likely to cause a second person (B) to take any of the steps in subsection (2).

(2) The steps are—

(*a*) not to perform any contractual obligation owed by B to a third person (C) (whether or not such non-performance amounts to a breach of contract);

(*b*) to terminate any contract B has with C;

(*c*) not to enter into a contract with C

(3) For the purposes of this section, a "relevant act" is—

(*a*) an act amounting to a criminal offence, or

(*b*) a tortious act causing B to suffer loss or damage of any description;

but paragraph (*b*) does not include an act which is actionable on the ground only that it induces another person to break a contract with B.

(4) For the purposes of this section, "contract" includes any other arrangement (and "contractual" is to be read accordingly).

(5) For the purposes of this section, to "harm" an animal research organisation means—

(*a*) to cause the organisation to suffer loss or damage of any description, or

(*b*) to prevent or hinder the carrying out by the organisation of any of its activities.

(6) This section does not apply to any act done wholly or mainly in contemplation or furtherance of a trade dispute.

(7) In subsection (6) "trade dispute" has the same meaning as in Part 4 of the Trade Union and Labour Relations (Consolidation) Act 1992 (c 52), except that section 218 of that Act shall be read as if—

(*a*) it made provision corresponding to section 244(4) of that Act, and

(*b*) in subsection (5), the definition of "worker" included any person falling within paragraph (*b*) of the definition of "worker" in section 244(5).

[Serious Organised Crime and Police Act 2005, s 145.]

---

[1] Part 5 comprises ss 145–171 and Schs 11–15.

7.10471 **146. Intimidation of persons connected with animal research organisation** (1) A person (A) commits an offence if, with the intention of causing a second person (B) to abstain from doing something which B is entitled to do (or to do something which B is entitled to abstain from doing)—

(*a*) A threatens B that A or somebody else will do a relevant act, and

(*b*) A does so wholly or mainly because B is a person falling within subsection (2).

(2) A person falls within this subsection if he is—

(*a*) an employee or officer of an animal research organisation;

(*b*) a student at an educational establishment that is an animal research organisation;

(*c*) a lessor or licensor of any premises occupied by an animal research organisation;

(*d*) a person with a financial interest in, or who provides financial assistance to, an animal research organisation;

(*e*) a customer or supplier of an animal research organisation;

(*f*) a person who is contemplating becoming someone within paragraph (*c*), (*d*) or (*e*);

(*g*) a person who is, or is contemplating becoming, a customer or supplier of someone within paragraph (*c*), (*d*), (*e*) or (*f*);

(*h*) an employee or officer of someone within paragraph (*c*), (*d*), (*e*), (*f*) or (*g*);

(*i*) a person with a financial interest in, or who provides financial assistance to, someone within paragraph (*c*), (*d*), (*e*), (*f*) or (*g*);

(*j*) a spouse, civil partner, friend or relative of, or a person who is known personally to, someone within any of paragraphs (*a*) to (*i*);

(*k*) a person who is, or is contemplating becoming, a customer or supplier of someone within paragraph (*a*), (*b*), (*h*), (*i*) or (*j*); or

(*l*) an employer of someone within paragraph (*j*).

(3) For the purposes of this section, an "officer" of an animal research organisation or a person includes—

(*a*) where the organisation or person is a body corporate, a director, manager or secretary;

(*b*) where the organisation or person is a charity, a charity trustee (within the meaning of the Charities Act 2011);

(*c*) where the organisation or person is a partnership, a partner.

(4) For the purposes of this section—

(*a*) a person is a customer or supplier of another person if he purchases goods, services or facilities from, or (as the case may be) supplies goods, services or facilities to, that other; and

(*b*) "supplier" includes a person who supplies services in pursuance of any enactment that requires or authorises such services to be provided.

(5) For the purposes of this section, a "relevant act" is—

(*a*) an act amounting to a criminal offence, or

(*b*) a tortious act causing B or another person to suffer loss or damage of any description.

(6) The Secretary of State may by order amend this section so as to include within subsection (2) any description of persons framed by reference to their connection with—

(*a*) an animal research organisation, or

(*b*) any description of persons for the time being mentioned in that subsection.

(7) This section does not apply to any act done wholly or mainly in contemplation or furtherance of a trade dispute.

(8) In subsection (7) "trade dispute" has the meaning given by section 145(7).

[Serious Organised Crime and Police Act 2005, s 146 as amended by the Charities Act 2011, Sch 7.]

7.10472 **147. Penalty for offences under sections 145 and 146** (1) A person guilty of an offence under section 145 or 146 is liable[1]—

(*a*) on summary conviction, to imprisonment for a term not exceeding 12 months[2] or to a fine not exceeding the statutory maximum, or to both;

(*b*) on conviction on indictment, to imprisonment for a term not exceeding five years or to a fine, or to both.

(2) No proceedings for an offence under either of those sections may be instituted except by or with the consent of the Director of Public Prosecutions.

[Serious Organised Crime and Police Act 2005, s 147.]

1 For procedure in respect of an offence triable either way, see the Magistrates' Courts Act 1980, ss 17A–21, in PART I: MAGISTRATES' COURTS, PROCEDURE, ante.

2 In relation to an offence committed before the commencement of s 154(1) of the Criminal Justice Act 2003 this is to be read as a reference to "6 months", s 175(2), post.

7.10473 **148. Animal research organisations** (1) For the purposes of sections 145 and 146 "animal research organisation" means any person or organisation falling within subsection (1A), (2) or (3).

(1A) A person or organisation falls within this subsection if the person or organisation holds a licence granted under section 2C of the 1986 Act (licensing of undertakings involving the use of animals for scientific procedures).

(2) A person or organisation falls within this subsection if he or it is the owner, lessee or licensee of premises constituting or including a place specified in a licence granted under that section or under section 5 of the 1986 Act (licensing of projects involving the use of animals for scientific procedures).

(3) A person or organisation falls within this subsection if he or it employs, or engages under a contract for services, any of the following in his capacity as such—

(*za*) the holder of a licence granted under section 2C of the 1986 Act,

(*zb*) a person specified under section 2C(5) of that Act,

(*a*) the holder of a personal licence granted under section 4 of the 1986 Act, or

(*b*) the holder of a project licence granted under section 5 of that Act,

(*c*) *repealed*

(*d*) *repealed.*

(4) The Secretary of State may by order amend this section so as to include a reference to any description of persons whom he considers to be involved in, or to have a direct connection with persons who are involved in, the application of regulated procedures.

(5) In this section—

"the 1986 Act" means the Animals (Scientific Procedures) Act 1986 (c 14);

"organisation" includes any institution, trust, undertaking or association of persons;

"premises" includes any place within the meaning of the 1986 Act;

"regulated procedures" has the meaning given by section 2 of the 1986 Act.

[Serious Organised Crime and Police Act 2005, s 148 as amended by SI 2012/3039.]

7.10474 **149. Extension of sections 145 to 147** (1) The Secretary of State may by order provide for sections 145, 146 and 147 to apply in relation to persons or organisations of a description specified in the order as they apply in relation to animal research organisations.

(2) The Secretary of State may, however, only make an order under this section if satisfied that a series of acts has taken place and—

(*a*) that those acts were directed at persons or organisations of the description specified in the order or at persons having a connection with them, and

(*b*) that, if those persons or organisations had been animal research organisations, those acts would have constituted offences under section 145 or 146.

(3) In this section "organisation" and "animal research organisation" have the meanings given by section 148.

[Serious Organised Crime and Police Act 2005, s 149.]

# Policing and Crime Act 2009[1]

(2009 c 26)

7.10475 **30. Offence of persistently possessing alcohol in a public place** (1) A person under the age of 18 is guilty of an offence if, without reasonable excuse, the person is in possession of alcohol in any relevant place on 3 or more occasions within a period of 12 consecutive months.

(2) "Relevant place", in relation to a person, means—

(*a*) any public place, other than excluded premises, or

(*b*) any place, other than a public place, to which the person has unlawfully gained access.

(3) A person guilty of an offence under this section is liable on summary conviction to a fine not exceeding level 2 on the standard scale.

(4) For the purposes of subsection (2) a place is a public place if at the material time the public or any section of the public has access to it, on payment or otherwise, as of right or by virtue of express or implied permission.

(5) In subsection (2) "excluded premises"—

(*a*) in relation to England and Wales, means—

(i) premises which may by virtue of Part 3 or 5 of the Licensing Act 2003 (c 17) (premises licence or permitted temporary activity) be used for the supply of alcohol,

(ii) premises which may by virtue of Part 4 of that Act (club premises certificate) be used for the supply of alcohol to members or guests,

(*b*) in relation to Northern Ireland, means—

(i) licensed premises within the meaning of the 1996 Licensing Order,

(ii) premises of a club registered under the Registration of Clubs (Northern Ireland) Order 1996 (SI 1996/3159 (NI 23)),

(iii) premises for which an occasional licence (within the meaning of the 1996 Licensing Order) has been granted.

(6) In this section "alcohol"—

(*a*) in relation to England and Wales, has the same meaning as in the Licensing Act 2003,

(*b*) in relation to Northern Ireland, has the same meaning as "intoxicating liquor" in the 1996 Licensing Order.

(7) References in this section to the 1996 Licensing Order are to the Licensing (Northern Ireland) Order 1996 (SI 1996/3158 (NI 22)).

[Policing and Crime Act 2009, s 30.]

[1] This Act is reproduced partly in this title (ss 30 and 106) and partly in the titles IMMIGRATION AND ASYLUM, (s 101), ante and SEXUAL OFFENCES (Sch 3), post. The Act also amends and inserts new provisions into a number of statutes which are reproduced in this Manual as amended. The Act is brought into force in accordance with the provisions of s 116 and orders made thereunder. At the date of going to press, the following orders had been made: (No 1 and Transitional and Saving Provisions) SI 2009/3096; (No 2) SI 2010/52; (No 3) SI 2010/125; (No 4) SI 2010/507; (No 1 and Transitional and Saving Provisions) (England) SI 2010/722; (No 5) SI 2010/999 amended by SI 2010/1986; (No 1) (Wales) SI 2010/1375; (No 6 and Commencement No 5 (Amendment)) SI 2010/1986; (No 7) SI 2010/2988; (No 8) SI 2012/2235; and (No 9) SI 2014/3101; (No 10 Transitional and Savings) SI 2015/983, (No 11) SI 2016/147. Section 30 was brought into force on 29 January 2010 and Part 4 was brought into force on 31 January 2011. Section 106 was brought into effect on 1 April 2010 (SI 2010/507).

## PART 4[1]

## INJUNCTIONS: GANG-RELATED VIOLENCE AND DRUG DEALING ACTIVITY

*Power to grant injunctions*

7.10476 *On application by the police or transport police or a local authority (s 37), the High Court or a county court may grant an injunction which may last for up to two years where the court is satisfied on the balance of probabilities that the respondent has engaged in, or has encouraged or assisted, gang-related violence or gang-related drug-dealing activity and the court thinks it is necessary to grant the injunction to prevent the respondent from engaging in, or encouraging or assisting, gang-related violence or gang-related drug-dealing activity; and/or to protect the respondent from gang-related violence or gang-related drug-dealing activity (s 34). Something is "gang-related" if it occurs in the course of, or is otherwise related to, the activities of a group that consists of at least three people, and has one or more characteristics that enable its members to be identified by others as a group. "Violence" includes a threat of violence. "Drug-dealing activity" means the unlawful production, supply, importation or exportation of a controlled drug, or the unlawful production, supply, importation or exportation of a psychoactive substance. The prohibitions included in the injunction may, in particular, have the effect of prohibiting the respondent from being in a particular place; being with particular persons in a particular place; being in charge of a particular species of animal in a particular place; wearing particular descriptions of articles of clothing in a particular place; using the internet to facilitate or encourage violence or drug-dealing activity. The requirements included in the injunction may, in particular, have the effect of requiring the respondent to notify the person who applied for the injunction of the respondent's address and of any change to that address; be at a particular place between particular times (for up to 8 hours) on particular days; present himself or herself to a particular person at a place where he or she is required to be between particular times on particular days; participate in particular activities between particular times on particular days (s 35). The court may attach a power of arrest in relation to any prohibition in the injunction, or any requirement in the injunction, other than one which has the effect of requiring the respondent to participate in particular activities (s 36).*

[1] Part 4 comprises ss 34–50 and Sch 5. Jurisdiction in relation to persons under 18 years resides in the youth court. See para 5.74A **Injunctions: gang-related violence and drug-dealing activity**, and the provisions of Part 4 reproduced in PART V: YOUTH COURTS, ante.

## PART 8[1]

## MISCELLANEOUS

## CHAPTER 2[2]

## OTHER

*Football spectators*

7.10477 **106. Enforcement of 2006 Act in England and Wales and Northern Ireland**

(1) The following provisions of the Police, Public Order and Criminal Justice (Scotland) Act 2006[3] extend to England and Wales and Northern Ireland—

(*a*) section 68(1) and (2) (offences of failing to comply with a requirement imposed by a football banning order, under section 61(1) or by a notice under section 61(4), and defence of reasonable excuse),

(*b*) section 68(5) (offence of making a false statement, etc in connection with an application for exemption from a notice under section 61(4)).

(2) A person guilty of an offence under section 68(1)(*a*) or (*c*) of that Act by virtue of subsection (1)(*a*) is liable on summary conviction—

(*a*) in England and Wales, to imprisonment for a term not exceeding 51 weeks or a fine not exceeding level 5 on the standard scale (or both),

(*b*) in Northern Ireland, to imprisonment for a term not exceeding 6 months or a fine not exceeding level 5 on the standard scale (or both).

But in relation to an offence committed before the commencement of section 281(5) of the Criminal Justice Act 2003 (c 44) the reference in paragraph (*a*) to 51 weeks is to be read as a reference to 6 months.

(3) A person guilty of an offence under section 68(1)(*b*) of the Police, Public Order and Criminal Justice (Scotland) Act 2006 (asp 10) by virtue of subsection (1)(*a*) is liable on summary conviction to a fine not exceeding level 2 on the standard scale.

(4) A person guilty of an offence by virtue of subsection (1)(*b*) is liable on summary conviction

to a fine not exceeding level 3 on the standard scale.

(5) Omit articles 1(5) and 5 of the Police, Public Order and Criminal Justice (Scotland) Act 2006 (Consequential Provisions and Modifications) Order 2007 (SI 2007/1098).

[Policing and Crime Act 2009, s 106.]

---

1 Part 8 comprises ss 81–111.

2 Chapter 2 comprises ss 98–111.

3 The Police, Public Order and Criminal Justice (Scotland) Act 2006, ss 61, 62 and 68 provide:

**61. Foreign matches: reporting and other requirements** (1) The constable responsible for the police station at which a person subject to a football banning order reports initially may make such requirements of the person as are determined by the football banning orders authority to be necessary or expedient for giving effect to the football banning order, so far as relating to regulated football matches outside the United Kingdom.

(2) Subject to section 64, if, in connection with any regulated football match outside the United Kingdom, the football banning orders authority is of the opinion mentioned in subsection (3) in relation to a person subject to a football banning order, the authority must cause the person to be served with a notice in writing under subsection (4).

(3) That opinion is that requiring the person to report in accordance with a notice under subsection (4) is necessary or expedient in order to reduce the likelihood of violence or disorder at or in connection with the match.

(4) A notice under this subsection is a notice requiring the person—

(*a*) to report at a specified police station at the time, or between the times, specified; and

(*b*) if the order imposes a requirement as to the surrender of the person's passport, to attend at a specified police station at the time, or between the times, specified and—

(i) if the person has a passport, to surrender it; or

(ii) if the person does not have a passport, to make a declaration to that effect.

(5) In subsection (4), "specified" means specified in the notice.

(6) The football banning orders authority may establish criteria for determining whether a notice under subsection (4) ought to be imposed on any person or on persons of a particular description.

**62. Notices under section 61(4): further provision** (1) A notice under section 61(4) may not require the person subject to the order to report or surrender the person's passport except in the control period in relation to—

(*a*) a regulated football match outside the United Kingdom; or

(*b*) a designated external tournament which includes such matches.

(2) In subsection (1)—

"control period" in relation to a regulated football match outside the United Kingdom means the period—

(*a*) beginning 5 days before the day of the match; and

(*b*) ending when the match is finished or cancelled;

"control period" in relation to a designated external tournament means the period—

(*a*) beginning 5 days before the day of the first football match outside the United Kingdom which is included in the tournament;

(*b*) ending when the last football match outside the United Kingdom which is included in the tournament is finished or cancelled;

(but, for the purposes of paragraph (*a*), any football match included in the qualifying or pre-qualifying stages of the tournament is to be left out of account);

"designated" means designated by the Scottish Ministers by order; and

"external tournament" means a football competition which includes regulated football matches outside the United Kingdom.

(3) Where a notice under section 61(4) requires the person subject to the order to surrender the person's passport, the passport must be returned to the person as soon as reasonably practicable after the control period in question.

**68. Offences under this Chapter** (1) A person who fails to comply with any requirement imposed on the person—

(*a*) by a football banning order;

(*b*) under section 61(1); or

(*c*) by a notice under section 61(4),

commits an offence.

(2) It is a defence for a person charged with an offence under subsection (1) to prove that the person had a reasonable excuse for failing to comply with the requirement.

## Sports Grounds and Sporting Events (Designation) Order 2005

(SI 2005/3204 as amended by SI 2011/1186 and SI 2013/1710)

**7.10478** *1.* This Order may be cited as the Sports Grounds and Sporting Events (Designation) Order 2005 and shall come into force on 14th December 2005.

7.10479 *2.* For the purposes of the Sporting Events (Control of Alcohol etc) Act 1985, there are hereby designated—

(1) the classes of sports ground specified in Schedule 1 to this Order;

(2) the classes of sporting events specified in Part 1 of Schedule 2 to this Order at any sports ground specified in Schedule 1; and

(3) the classes of sporting events specified in Part 2 of Schedule 2.

7.10480 *3.* The Sports Grounds and Sporting Events (Designation) Order 1985, the Sports Grounds and Sporting Events (Designation) (Amendment) Order 1987, and article 2(2)(*a*) of the Sports Grounds and Football (Amendment of Various Orders) Order 1992 are hereby revoked.

SCHEDULE 1
Sports Grounds

Article 2(1)

7.10481 Any sports ground in England or Wales.

SCHEDULE 2
Classes of Sporting Events

PART I

Article 2(1), 2(2)

7.10482 *1.* Association football matches in which one or both of the participating teams represents a club which is for the time being a member (whether a full or associate member) of the Football League, the Football Association Premier League, the Football Conference National Division, the Scottish Professional Football League or Welsh Premier League or whose home ground is situated outside England and Wales, or represents a country or territory.

*2.* Association football matches in competition for the Football Association Cup (other than in a preliminary or qualifying round).

PART 2

Article 2(3)

Association football matches at a sports ground outside England and Wales in which one or both of the participating teams represents a club which is for the time being a member (whether a full or associate member) of the Football League, the Football Association Premier League, the Football Conference National division, the Scottish Professional Football League or Welsh Premier League, or represents the Football Association or the Football Association of Wales.

# PUBLIC OFFICE

## Misconduct in a public office

**7.10483** A public officer who wilfully and without reasonable excuse or justification neglects to perform any duty he is bound to perform by common law or statute is guilty of the common law offence of misconduct in a public office. There are four elements to the offence of misconduct in public office:

(a) a public officer acting as such;
(b) wilfully neglects to perform his duty and/or wilfully misconducts himself;
(c) to such a degree as to amount to an abuse of the public's trust in the office holder; and
(d) without reasonable excuse or justification[1].

"Public officer" embraces everyone who is appointed to discharge a public duty, and receives compensation in whatever shape whether from the Crown or otherwise[2]. This does not mean that the office has to be a remunerated one; the fact that a person is a volunteer may have a bearing, for example in a case of omission, in determining whether or not there has been wilful misconduct, but there are many judicial and public post holders, such as magistrates, who are liable to prosecution if they commit a serious breach of office[3]. In order to decide whether a person is the holder of a public office, the proper approach is to analyse the position of a particular employee or officer by asking three questions. First, what is the position held? Second, what is the nature of the duties undertaken by the employee or officer in that position? Third, does the fulfilment of those duties represent the fulfilment of one of the responsibilities of government such that the public have a significant interest in the discharge of that duty which is additional to or beyond an interest in anyone who might be directly affected by a serious failure in the performance of that duty? If the answer to this last question is "yes", the relevant employee or officer is acting as a public officer; if "no", he or she is not acting as a public officer[4]. The element of culpability required is not restricted to corruption or dishonesty, although it has to be such that the conduct impugned was calculated to injure the public interest and calls for condemnation and punishment. Whether there is such conduct is a matter for the jury on the evidence[5]. The high threshold of criminality is capable of being met in relation to a prison officer who repeatedly divulges information to a journalist about events at the prison for money in breach of his duty. This impacts on morale within the prison of both staff and prisoners; undermines trust and morale amongst and between prisoners and staff; deters prisoners reporting incidents; inhibits constructive internal criticism and debate; and damages the efficient and effective running of the prison and undermines public confidence in its management[6].

The elements of this offence, particularly whether recklessness as to a duty to act is sufficient and whether the concept of "bad faith" has any relevance, were considered in *A-G's Reference (No 3 of 2003)*[7]. The offence may be charged in a great variety of circumstances. However, it consists essentially of a public officer, acting as such, wilfully neglecting to perform his duty and/or wilfully misconducting himself in a way which amounts to an abuse of the public's trust in the office holder, without reasonable excuse or justification. Whether the misconduct is of a sufficiently serious nature depends upon the responsibilities of the office and the office holder, the importance of the public objects which they serve, the nature and extent of the departure from those responsibilities and the seriousness of the consequences which may follow from the misconduct. The relevant mental element is that the office holder is aware of the duty to act or is subjectively reckless as to the existence of the duty. The test of recklessness applies both to the question whether in particular circumstances a duty arises at all and to the conduct of the defendant if it does arise; and that the subjective test applies both to reckless indifference to the legality of the act or omission and in relation to the consequences of the act or omission. The expression "bad faith" should not routinely be introduced into a criminal trial because of the confusion it is liable to cause and the risk it might confuse the jury and deflect them from their task of deciding whether the public office had been abused by the conduct of the office holder, although there may be cases in which the concept of bad faith may be relevant to an assessment of the standard of the defendant's conduct. 'Without justification or reasonable excuse' means no more than acting culpably or in a blameworthy fashion[8].

When the crime of misconduct in public office is committed in circumstances which involve the acquisition of property by theft or fraud, and, in particular, when the holder of a public office is alleged to have made improper claims for public funds in circumstances which are said to be criminal, an essential ingredient of the offence is proof that the defendant has been dishonest[9].

---

1 *A-Gl's Reference (No 3 of 2003)* [2004] EWCA Crim 868; [2005] QB 73; *R v Chapman* [2015] EWCA Crim 539; [2015] QB 88.

2 *R v Bowden* [1995] 4 All ER 505, [1996] 1 WLR 98, [1996] 1 Cr App Rep 104 (maintenance manager in a local authority's direct labour organisation held to be a public officer).

3 *R v Belton* [2010] EWCA Crim 2857, [2011] 1 All ER 700, [2011] 2 WLR 1434, [2011] 1 Cr App R 20. See also *R v Cosford* [2013] EWCA Crim 466, [2013] 3 All ER 649, [2013] 2 Cr App Rep 8. The responsibilities of nurses in a prison were not only for their patients, but also for the public, and it made no difference whether or not the prison was run directly by the state or indirectly through a private company paid by the state. The responsibilities to the public were the same.

4 *R v Mitchell* [2014] EWCA Crim 318, [2014] 2 Cr App Rep 7 (paramedic employed by an NHS Trust did not owe duty to the public which was different from, or additional to, the general duty owed to the individual).

5 *R v Dytham* [1979] QB 722, [1979] 3 All ER 641 where the deliberate and wilful neglect of a police officer to perform his duty amounted to an offence of misconduct in a public office. See also *R v Wyat* (1705) 1 Salk 380; *R v Bembridge* (1783) 3 Doug KB 327 and *R v Llewellyn-Jones and Lougher* (1966) 51 Cr App Rep 4.

[6] *R v Norman* [2016] EWCA Crim 1564, [2017] 4 WLR 16, [2017] 1 Cr App R 8.

[7] [2005] 1 QB 73, [2004] EWCA Crim 868, [2004] 3 WLR 451, [2004] 2 Cr App R 23.

[8] *R v L (D)* [2011] EWCA Crim 1259, [2011] 2 Cr App R 14.

[9] *R v W* [2010] EWCA Crim 372, [2010] QB 787, [2010] 1 Cr App Rep 421 (use of police credit card by defendant police officer for personal purchases defence being it was "the culture in the office at the time").

# RELIGION

## Ecclesiastical Courts Jurisdiction Act 1860

(1860 c 32)

7.10484 **2. Penalty for making a disturbance in churches, chapels, churchyards etc** Any[1] person who shall be guilty[2] of riotous, violent, or indecent[3] behaviour in England in any cathedral church, parish or district church, or chapel of the Church of England, or in any chapel of any religious denomination, or in England in any place[4] of religious worship duly certified[5] under the Places of Worship Registration Act 1855, 18 & 19 Vict c 81, whether during the celebration of[6] Divine service, or at any other time, or in any churchyard, or burial-ground, or who shall molest, let[7], disturb, vex, or trouble, or by any other unlawful means disquiet or misuse any preacher duly authorised to preach therein, or any clergyman in Holy Orders[8] ministering or celebrating any sacrament or any Divine service, rite, or office in any cathedral church or chapel, churchyard, or burial ground shall on conviction thereof by a magistrates' court, be liable to a fine not exceeding **level 1** on the standard scale or to imprisonment for a term not exceeding **two months***.**

[Ecclesiastical Courts Jurisdiction Act 1860 s 2 as amended by Criminal Justice Act 1967, Sch 3, the Criminal Justice Act 1982, ss 38 and 46 and the Courts Act 2003, Sch 8.]

---

* **Words repealed by the Criminal Justice Act 2003, Sch 37 from a date to be appointed.**

** **Reproduced as in force in England and Wales.**

1 In an appeal from a conviction by justices of a clergyman for violent and indecent behaviour in the churchyard of his own church, the Queen's Bench Division held without hesitation that the Act applies to persons in holy orders just as much as to laymen, and confirmed the view of the justices that violent and indecent conduct could not be justified by a claim of right (*Vallancey v Fletcher* [1897] 1 QB 265, 61 JP 183).

2 The offender may be apprehended by a churchwarden (Ecclesiastical Courts Jurisdiction Act 1860, s 3), note also the powers of a constable under s 25 of the Police and Criminal Evidence Act 1984, ante, and the common law powers generally to arrest for a breach of the peace, see para 1.73 in Part I: Magistrates Courts, Procedure ante.

3 Interrupting and shouting and creating disturbance is "indecent behaviour" in the context of this section (*Abrahams v Cavey* [1968] 1 QB 479, [1967] 3 All ER 179). A churchwarden has no right forcibly to exclude an inhabitant from entering a church to attend Divine service, although in his opinion the person cannot be conveniently accommodated (*Taylor v Timson* (1888) 20 QBD 671, 52 JP 135). Churchwardens have authority, for preserving order and decorum, to direct where any member of the congregation shall sit who wishes to occupy a free seat (*Asher v Calcraft* (1887) 18 QBD 607, 51 JP 598).

4 Any place actually used as the "chapel of any religious deonomination", whether certified or not, will be within the protection of the statute (34 JP 12). The law officers of the Crown (Sir R E Webster and Sir Edward Clarke, 28 January 1892) gave an opinion that if the place of meeting is a defined and enclosed area, which can be defined by metes and bounds, and does not form part of an open space to which the public have access, it is a place of meeting to which a certificate may be granted, although there may be no building thereon (56 JP 154).

5 The certificate contains the words "at the date hereof the certificate of registration remained uncancelled," and is not evidence that the place was certified after the date of the certificate.

6 The celebration of a sacrament is a "divine service". The question whether the clergyman or celebrant complied with the ceremonial law of the Church of England is immaterial (*Matthews v King* [1934] 1 KB 505, 97 JP 345). The London Quarter Sessions held that questions as to the nature of the services used were immaterial, and should not be allowed (*Kensit v Rose* (1898) 62 JP 489).

7 See *Kensit v St Paul's (Dean and Chapter)* [1905] 2 KB 249, 69 JP 250.

8 Molesting a clergyman while engaged in collecting alms after a sermon is not an offence under these words, the Rubric not contemplating the collecting of alms is to be done by him (*Cope v Barber* (1872) LR 7 CP 393, 36 JP 439).

# RESCUE

## Rescue of persons

**7.10485** Rescue is the forcible liberation of another from legal custody. To constitute this offence, the party must be in actual custody, though whether in that of a constable or private individual is not material, but in the latter case the party should know that the prisoner is in lawful custody, while in the former he is bound to take notice at his peril (1 *Hale* 606). Punishable on indictment by a fine and imprisonment. See s 39 of the Prison Act 1952—assisting prisoner to escape in this Part: title Prisons, ante.

## Rescue of goods

**7.10486** The forcible rescue of goods distrained, and the rescuing of cattle by the breach of the pound in which they have been placed, are offences at common law, and have been made the subject of indictment. An indictment will lie for taking goods forcibly if such taking be proved to be a breach of the peace, but if a mere trespass, without circumstances of violence, it is not indictable. See this Part: title Pound Breach, ante.

# ROYAL PARKS AND GARDENS

## Contents



7.10487 The **Parks Regulation Acts 1872 to 1974** have for their object the protection from injury of the parks under the management of the Secretary of State for Culture, Media and Sport, and securing the public from molestation and annoyance while enjoying the same. The 1872 Act provides for the powers under the Act to be exercised by a duly attested park constable or a police constable and creates an offence of assaulting such a park constable. The 1872 Act does not apply to those parks specified by order made under s 162 of the Serious Organised Crime and Police Act 2005 for which there are no park constables and which are policed by the Metropolitan Police (and community support officers).

Regulations are made under s 2 of the Parks Regulation (Amendment) Act 1926 which apply to parks to which the 1872 Act applies and to specified parks and which create offences punishable by a fine not exceeding **level 1** on the standard scale (**level 3** in the case of park trading offences).

## Parks Regulation Act 1872[1]

(35 & 36 Vict c 15)

7.10488 **1. Short title** This Act may be cited for all purposes as "The Parks Regulation Act 1872".

[Parks Regulation Act 1872, s 1.]

[1] This Act came into force on Royal Assent (27 June 1872).

7.10489 **3. Definition of park constable** "Park constable" shall mean any person who, previously to the passing of this Act, has been or may hereafter be appointed park constable of a park as defined by this Act.

[Parks Regulation Act 1872, s 3 as amended by the Parks Regulation (Amendment) Act 1974, Schedule.]

7.10490 **3A. Attestation of park constables** Every park constable shall on appointment be attested as a constable by making a declaration before a justice of the peace that he will duly execute the office of constable.

[Parks Regulation Act 1872, s 3A as inserted by the Parks Regulation (Amendment) Act 1974, Schedule.]

7.10491 **5. Park constable may apprehend any offender whose name or residence is not known** Any person who—

(*a*) within the view of a park constable acts in contravention of any of the said regulations in the park where the park constable has jurisdiction; and

(*b*) when required by any park constable or by any police constable to give his name and address gives a false name or false address,

shall be liable on summary conviction to a penalty of an amount not exceeding level 1 on the standard scale.

[Parks Regulation Act 1872, s 5 as substituted by the Police and Criminal Evidence Act 1984, Sch 6 and amended by the Statute Law (Repeals) Act 1993.]

7.10492 **6. Penalty on assaults on park constable** Where any person is convicted of an assault on any park constable when in the execution of his duty, such person shall, on conviction by a court of summary jurisdiction, in the discretion of the court, be liable either to pay a penalty not exceeding level 2 on the standard scale, or to be imprisoned for any term not exceeding six months with or without hard labour.

[Parks Regulation Act 1872, s 6 as amended by the Parks Regulation (Amendment) Act 1974, Schedule, the Criminal Law Act 1977, s 31(6), the Criminal Justice Act 1982, ss 37, 46 and the Statute Law (Repeals) Act 1993.]

7.10493 **7. Powers, duties, and privileges of park constable** Every park constable in addition to any powers and immunities specially conferred on him by this Act, shall, within the limits of the park of which he is park constable, have all such powers, privileges, and immunities, and be liable to all such duties and responsibilities, as any police constable has within the police area in which such park is situated; and any person so appointed a park constable as aforesaid shall obey such lawful commands as he may from time to time receive from the Commissioners in respect of his conduct in the execution of his office.

[Parks Regulation Act 1872, s 7 as amended by the Parks Regulation (Amendment) Act 1974, Schedule and the Police Act 1996, s 103, Sch 7, para 7.]

7.10494 **8. Police constables to have the same powers, etc, as park constables** Every police constable belonging to the police force for the police area in which any park to which this Act applies is situate shall have the powers, privileges, and immunities of a park constable within such park.

[Parks Regulation Act 1872, s 8 as amended by the Police Act 1996, Sch 7, the Parks Regulation (Amendment) Act 1926, Schedule and the Parks Regulation (Amendment) Act 1974, Schedule.]

7.10495 **10. Publication of regulations** Copies of regulations to be observed in pursuance of this Act by persons using a park to which this Act applies shall be put up in such park in such conspicuous manner as the Commissioners may deem best calculated to give information to the persons using the park.

[Parks Regulation Act 1872, s 10 as amended by the Parks Regulation (Amendment) Act 1926, Schedule.]

7.10496 **11. Saving of certain rights** Nothing in this Act shall authorise any interference with any rights of way or any right whatever to which any person or persons may be by law entitled.

[Parks Regulation Act 1872, s 11.]

7.10497 **12. Act to be cumulative** All powers conferred by this Act shall be deemed to be in addition to and not in derogation of any powers conferred by any other Act of Parliament, and any such powers may be exercised as if this Act had not been passed.

[Parks Regulation Act 1872, s 12.]

7.10498 **13. Saving of the rights of the Crown** Nothing in this Act contained shall be deemed to prejudice or affect any prerogative or right of Her Majesty, or any power, right, or duty of the Commissioners, or any powers or duties of any officers, clerks, or servants, appointed by Her Majesty or by the Commissioners.

[Parks Regulation Act 1872, s 13.]

7.10499 **14. Saving of 30 & 31 Vict c 134** Nothing in this Act contained shall affect the Metropolitan Streets Act 1867, or the application thereof to any park to which it is by law applicable.

[Parks Regulation Act 1872, s 14.]

## Parks Regulation (Amendment) Act 1926[1]

(16 & 17 Geo 5 c 36)

7.10500 **1. Application** The Parks Regulation Act 1872 (hereinafter referred to as the principal Act), shall apply to all parks, gardens, recreation grounds, open spaces and other land for the time being vested in, or under the control or management of, the Commissioners of Works, and accordingly in that Act the expression "park" shall include all such parks, gardens, recreation grounds, open spaces and land as aforesaid.

[Parks (Amendment) Act 1926, s 1 as amended by the Statute Law (Repeals) Act 1989.]

---

[1] This Act came into force on Royal Assent (15 December 1926).

7.10501 **2. Power to make regulations** (1) Subject to the provisions of this Act, the Commissioners of Works may make such regulations[1] to be observed by persons using any park to which the principal Act applies, as they consider necessary for securing the proper management of the park, and the preservation of order and prevention of abuses therein, and if any person fails to comply with, or acts in contravention of, any regulations so made, he shall be guilty of an offence against the principal Act and shall be liable on conviction thereof by a court of summary jurisdiction to a penalty not exceeding level 1 on the standard scale.

(1A) Regulations under subsection (1) may include provision applying (with any necessary modifications) sections 4 to 6 of the Royal Parks (Trading) Act 2000 (seizure, retention, disposal and forfeiture of property) in relation to offences under that subsection that are not park trading offences for the purposes of that Act.

(2) Before any regulation made under this Act comes into operation, a draft thereof shall be laid before each House of Parliament for a period of not less than twenty-one days on which that House has sat, and if either House before the expiration of that period presents an Address to His Majesty against the draft or any part thereof, no further proceedings shall be taken thereon, but without prejudice to the making of any new draft regulation.

(3) As from and after the date upon which regulations made under this Act come into operation as respects any park, all references in the principal Act to regulations shall, as respects that park, be construed as references to regulations made under this Act.

(4) The Documentary Evidence Act 1868, as amended by the Documentary Evidence Act 1882, shall apply to the Commissioners of Works as though the Commissioners were included in the first column of the Schedule to the first-mentioned Act, and any Commissioner or the Secretary, or any person authorised to act on behalf of the Secretary, were mentioned in the second column of that Schedule, and as if the regulations referred to in those Acts included any regulations made under this Act.

[Parks (Amendment) Act 1926, s 2 as amended by the Criminal Justice Act 1982, ss 37, 38, 46 and the Police Reform and Social Responsibility Act 2011, s 150.]

---

[1] The following regulations have been made:
Osborne Regulations 1952, SI 1952/1468;
Hampton Court and Bushy Park (Outer Areas) Regulations 1973, SI 1973/214;
Royal Botanic Gardens, Kew Regulations 1977, SI 1977/2088;
Royal Parks and Other Open Spaces Regulations 1997, SI 1997/1639 amended by SI 2000/2949, SI 2004/1308 and 3168, SI 2010/1194 and 2695 and SI 2012/98 and 957;
Hyde Park and The Regents Park (Vehicle Parking) (Amendment) Regulations 1999, SI 1999/392;
Royal Parks and Other Open Spaces (Park Trading) Regulations 2000, SI 2000/2949;
Royal Parks and Other Open Spaces (Amendment) Regulations 2004, SI 2004/1308.

# Royal Parks (Trading) Act 2000[1]

(2000 c 13)

7.10502 **1. Park trading offence** (1) Regulations under section 2 of the Parks Regulation (Amendment) Act 1926 may designate specified provisions of the regulations as park trading regulations.

(2) An offence under that section which is committed by failing to comply with or acting in contravention of a park trading regulation is a park trading offence[2] for the purposes of this Act.

[Royal Parks (Trading) Act 2000, s 1.]

---

1 This Act came into force on Royal Assent (20 July 2000).

2 The maximum penalty for an offence under park trading regulations is a fine not exceeding **level 3** on the standard scale (s 2).

7.10503 **3. Offence by body corporate** (1) Where a park trading offence committed by a body corporate is proved—

(*a*) to have been committed with the consent or connivance of an officer, or

(*b*) to be attributable to any neglect on the part of an officer,

he as well as the body corporate is guilty of the offence and liable to be proceeded against and punished accordingly.

(2) For the purposes of this section the following are officers of a body corporate—

(*a*) a director,

(*b*) a manager,

(*c*) a secretary,

(*d*) another similar officer,

(*e*) a person purporting to act in any of the capacities listed in paragraphs (*a*) to (*d*).

[Royal Parks (Trading) Act 2000, s 3.]

7.10504 **4. Seizure of property** (1) A park constable who reasonably suspects that a person has committed a park trading offence may, subject to subsection (2), seize anything of a non-perishable nature which—

(*a*) the person has in his possession or under his control, and

(*b*) the constable reasonably believes to have been used in the commission of the offence.

(2) A park constable may exercise the power conferred by subsection (1) only in the park where he has jurisdiction.

(3) In this section "park constable" has the meaning given by section 3 of the Parks Regulation Act 1872.

(4) In the application of this section to a specified park—

(*a*) the reference in subsection (1) to a park constable has effect as a reference to a constable, and

(*b*) subsections (2) and (3) do not apply.

(5) In subsection (4) "specified park" has the same meaning as in section 162 of the Serious Organised Crime and Police Act 2005.

[Royal Parks (Trading) Act 2000, s 4 as amended by the Serious Organised Crime and Police Act 2005, Sch 13.]

7.10505 **5. Retention and disposal** (1) The Secretary of State may retain anything which has been seized under section 4 until the end of the period of 28 days beginning with the date of the seizure.

(2) Subsection (3) applies where before the end of that period an information for a park trading offence is laid—

(*a*) against the person from whom the thing was seized, and

(*b*) in respect of his activities at the time of the seizure.

(3) Where this subsection applies—

(*a*) the Secretary of State may retain the thing seized until the conclusion of proceedings relating to the offence (including any appeal), and

(*b*) if an award is made of costs to be paid by the accused to the Secretary of State, the Secretary of State may retain the thing seized until the costs have been paid.

(4) Subsection (3) has effect subject to any order for forfeiture under section 6.

(5) If the Secretary of State has retained a thing in reliance on subsection (3)(*b*) for the period of 28 days beginning with the date of the conclusion of proceedings relating to the offence (including any appeal)—

(*a*) he may sell it for the best price which he can reasonably obtain and apply the proceeds in discharge of the award of costs, and

(*b*) if he does so, he shall pay any balance to the person whom he believes to have owned the thing immediately before the sale.

(6) Where the Secretary of State ceases to be entitled to retain a thing under this section he shall, subject to any order for forfeiture under section 6, return it to the person whom he believes to be its owner.

(7) If the Secretary of State cannot after reasonable inquiry identify a person for the purposes of subsection (5)(*b*) or (6)—

(*a*) he shall apply to a magistrates' court for directions, and (*b*) the court shall make an order about the treatment of the thing or the balance of its price.

[Royal Parks (Trading) Act 2000, s 5.]

7.10506 **6. Forfeiture** (1) A court which convicts a person of a park trading offence may order anything to which subsection (2) applies to be forfeited and dealt with in a manner specified in the order.

(2) This subsection applies to anything which—

(*a*) was seized under section 4,

(*b*) is retained by the Secretary of State under section 5, and

(*c*) the court believes to have been used in the commission of the offence.

(3) Before making an order for the forfeiture of a thing a court shall—

(*a*) permit anyone who claims to be its owner or to have an interest in it to make representations, and

(*b*) consider its value and the likely consequences of forfeiture.

[Royal Parks (Trading) Act 2000, s 6.]

## Serious Organised Crime and Police Act 2005[1]

(2005 c 15)

7.10507 **162. Regulation of specified parks** (1) From the appointed day[1] the Parks Regulation Act 1872 (c 15) does not apply to the specified parks.

(2) But from the appointed day[1] section 2 of the Parks Regulation (Amendment) Act 1926 (c 36) applies in relation to the specified parks in the same way as it applies in relation to parks to which the Parks Regulation Act 1872 applies.

(3) The Secretary of State must ensure that copies of any regulations made under section 2 of the Parks Regulation (Amendment) Act 1926 (c 36) which are in force in relation to a specified park are displayed in a suitable position in that park.

(4) In this section "specified park" means a park, garden, recreation ground, open space or other land in the metropolitan police district—

(*a*) which is specified in an order[2] made by the Secretary of State before the appointed day[1], and

(*b*) to which the Parks Regulation Act 1872 (c 15) then applied by virtue of section 1 of the Parks Regulation (Amendment) Act 1926.

[Serious Organised Crime and Police Act 2005, s 162.]

---

1 1st July 2005 was appointed by SI 2005/1521.

2 The Royal Parks (Regulation of Specified Parks) Order 2005, SI 2005/1522 has been made.

# SEXUAL OFFENCES

**Contents**



## Keeping a disorderly house

**7.10508** This is an ancient offence at common law. Its elements were reviewed in *R v Court*[1]:

[8] (In) the Sexual Offences Act 2003 . . . there are now 35 different statutory provisions which relate to what can loosely be described as the sex trade. Comprehensive as it appears to be, the statute did not abolish the common law offence of keeping a disorderly house.

[9] In the context of such detailed statutory provisions relating to sexual crime in its many different manifestations, an ancient common law offence should not normally be expanded beyond well established parameters by judicial decision . . . .

[10] Our attention was focused on *R v Tan* [1983] QB 1053, [1983] 2 All ER 12, 147 JP 257. Tan and others were accused of keeping a disorderly house. The difference between the facts of that case and the present are encapsulated in the advertisements, of which one example in Tan read "Humiliation enthusiast, my favourite past time is humiliating and disciplining mature male submissives, in strict bondage, lovely tan coloured mistress invites humble Applicants, TV, CP, BD and rubber wear...."

[11] Services of this kind were indeed provided. According to the judgment, they were: "of a particularly revolting and perverted kind... with the aid of a mass of equipment, some manual (such as whips and chains), some mechanical and some electrical, clients were subjected at their own wish and with their full consent, to a variety of forms of humiliation, flagellation, bondage and torture...."

[12] In one of the earlier cases referred to in the judgment, *R v Berg* (1927) 20 Cr App Rep 38, the activities in the disorderly house involved exhibitions of a perverted nature, and in *R v Quinn* [1962] 2 QB 245, [1961] 3 All ER 88, 125 JP 565 the premises were used for the performance of acts which were "seriously indecent and, in some respects, revolting", and the public was invited to resort to the premises for indulging in "perverted and revolting practices".

[13] In *R v Tan* itself the court indicated that before a Defendant could be convicted the jury had to be satisfied that the services provided were open to members of the public who wished to partake of them, and were:

"of such a character and conducted in such a manner (whether by advertisement or otherwise) that their provision amounts to an outrage of public decency, or is otherwise calculated to injure the public interest to such an extent as to call for condemnation and punishment."

The entire judgment proceeds on the basis that the provision of what was described as "straightforward sexual intercourse" would not be sufficient to constitute this offence.

[15] . . . The criminality which should have been alleged was that the Appellants allowed the premises of which they were tenants to be used for prostitution. That however cannot be an appropriate basis for upholding the use of the common law charge[2].

[1] [2012] EWCA Crim 133, [2012] 1 WLR 2260, [2012] 1 Cr App Rep 499.
[2] Per Lord Judge CJ.

# Sexual Offences Act 1956

(4 & 5 Eliz 2 c 69)

## Part I

## Offences, and the Prosecution and Punishments of Offences

*Suppression of brothels*

7.10509 33. **Keeping a brothel** It is an offence[1] for a person to keep a brothel[2], or to manage or act or assist in the management[3] of, a brothel.[4]

[Sexual Offences Act 1956, s 33.]

---

1 For mode of prosecution and penalty, see Sch 2, post. The evidence of a police officer that he knew women who visited a house to be prostitutes is admissible (*R v Korie* [1966] 1 All ER 50). If the information charges a single transaction, taking place over a period of time within the preceding 6 months, it will not be bad for duplicity (*Anderton v Cooper* (1981) 145 JP 128, [1981] Crim LR 177).

2 A brothel is a place where people of opposite sexes are allowed to resort for illicit intercourse, whether the women are common prostitutes or not (*Winter v Woolfe* [1931] 1 KB 549, 95 JP 20). A house occupied by one woman and used by her for prostitution but not allowed by her to be used by other women for a like purpose, is not a brothel (*Singleton v Ellison* [1895] 1 QB 607, 59 JP 119). This was followed in *Caldwell v Leech* (1913) 77 JP 254, where the defendant, the wife of the occupier of the premises, was charged with managing a brothel: she allowed her sister, a prostitute, to use the premises for prostitution with different men, no other woman so using the premises; but the facts justified a finding that premises were used as a brothel where two women, one being the tenant and occupier both used the premises for prostitution (*Gorman v Standen, Palace-Clark v Standen* [1964] 1 QB 294, [1963] 3 All ER 627, 128 JP 28). On other facts it has been held that two flats in one building, separately let to prostitutes, did not justify a finding that the building was used as a brothel (*Strath v Foxon* [1956] 1 QB 67, [1955] 3 All ER 398, 119 JP 581); but a block of flats, inhabited by different women and used by them for prostitution was held, on the facts, to be a brothel (*Durose v Wilson* (1907) 71 JP 263); and where there was use by three prostitutes in separate rooms, separately let to them, in such proximity as to constitute a "nest" of prostitutes, it was held that the premises were a brothel (*Donovan v Gavin* [1965] 2 QB 648, [1965] 2 All ER 611, 129 JP 404, approving *Abbott v Smith* [1965] 2 QB 662n, [1964] 3 All ER 762, 129 JP 3). Similarly where premises were used by a team of different prostitutes, but no more than one used the premises each day, the premises were held to constitute a brothel (*Stevens v Christy* (1987) 151 JP 366, [1987] Crim LR 503).

Premises which are resorted to for the purposes of lewd homosexual practices shall be treated as a brothel for the purposes of ss 33–35 of this Act. See the Sexual Offences Act 1967, s 6, post.

3 Evidence of normal sexual intercourse provided on the premises is not essential to prove a charge of assisting in the management of a brothel: it is sufficient to prove that more than one woman offered herself as a participant in physical acts of indecency for the sexual gratification of men (*Kelly v Purvis* [1983] QB 663, [1983] 1 All ER 525, 76 Cr App Rep 165). Women in a massage parlour, who not only performed lewd acts, but also discussed the nature of the acts to be performed and negotiated the terms of payment for their services, were held to be assisting in the management of a brothel (*Elliott v DPP* (1989) Times, 19 January, DC). To establish the offence of assisting in the management it is not necessary to show that the defendant exercised some sort of control over the management, nor is it necessary to show there was a specific act of management for that would be acting in the management (*Jones and Wood v DPP* (1992) 156 JP 866).

4 The wife or husband of the accused may be called as a witness by the defence or the prosecution, see Police and Criminal Evidence Act 1984, s 80 in Part II: Evidence, ante.

7.10510 33A. **Keeping a brothel used for prostitution** (1) It is an offence for a person to keep, or to manage, or act or assist in the management of, a brothel to which people resort for practices involving prostitution (whether or not also for other practices).

(2) In this section "prostitution" has the meaning given by section 51(2) of the Sexual Offences Act 2003.

[Sexual Offences Act 1956, s 33A as inserted by the Sexual Offences Act 2003, s 55.]

7.10511 34. **Landlord letting premises for use as brothel** It is an offence[1] for the lessor or landlord of any premises or his agent to let the whole or part of the premises with the knowledge[2] that it is to be used, in whole or in part, as a brothel, or, where the whole or part of the premises is used as a brothel, to be wilfully a party[3] to that use continuing.[4]

[Sexual Offences Act 1956, s 34.]

---

1 For mode of prosecution and penalty, see Sch 2, post.

2 The use of the premises as a brothel is a finding of fact: the whole or part of a house may be so used where there is use by more than one prostitute; see *Donovan v Gavin* [1965] 2 QB 648, [1965] 2 All ER 611, 129 JP 404, supra, approving *Abbott v Smith* [1965] 2 QB 662n, [1964] 3 All ER 762, 129 JP 3, supra.

3 It is our view that to be wilfully a party requires something in the nature of a positive act, and more than mere negative acquiescence; cf *Bell v Alfred Franks & Barlett Co Ltd* [1980] 1 All ER 356, [1980] 1 WLR 340.

4 The wife or husband of the accused may be called as a witness by the defence or the prosecution, see the Police and Criminal Evidence Act 1984, s 80 in Part II: Evidence, ante.

7.10512 35. **Tenant permitting premises to be used as brothel** (1) It is an offence[1] for the tenant or occupier, or person in charge, of any premises knowingly to permit the whole or part of the premises to be used as a brothel.

(2) Where the tenant or occupier of any premises is convicted of knowingly permitting the whole or part of the premises to be used as a brothel, the First Schedule to this Act shall apply to enlarge the rights of the lessor or landlord with respect to the assignment or determination of the lease or other contract under which the premises are held by the person convicted.

(3) Where the tenant or occupier of any premises is so convicted, and either—

(*a*) the lessor or landlord, after having the conviction brought to his notice, fails or failed to exercise his statutory rights in relation to the lease or contract under which the premises are or were held by the person convicted; or

(*b*) the lessor or landlord, after exercising his statutory rights so as to determine that lease or contract, grants or granted a new lease or enters or entered into a new contract of tenancy of the premises to, with or for the benefit of the same person, without having all reasonable provisions to prevent the recurrence of the offence inserted in the new lease or contract;

then, if subsequently an offence under this section is committed in respect of the premises during the subsistence of the lease or contract referred to in paragraph (*a*) of this subsection or (where paragraph (*b*) applies) during the subsistence of the new lease or contract, the lessor or landlord shall be deemed to be a party to that offence unless he shows that he took all reasonable steps to prevent the recurrence of the offence.

References in this subsection to the statutory rights of a lessor or landlord refer to his rights under the First Schedule to this Act.[2]

[Sexual Offences Act 1956, s 35 as amended by the Statute Law (Repeals) Act 2008, Sch 1.]

---

1 For mode of prosecution and penalty, see Sch 2, post.

2 The wife or husband of the accused may be called as a witness by the defence or the prosecution, see the Police and Criminal Evidence Act 1984, s 80 in PART II: EVIDENCE, ante.

7.10513 **36. Tenant permitting premises to be used for prostitution** It is an offence[1] for the tenant or occupier of any premises knowingly to permit[2] the whole or part of the premises to be used for the purposes of habitual prostitution (whether any prostitute involved is male or female).

[Sexual Offences Act 1956, s 36(1) as amended by the Sexual Offences Act 2003, s 56.]

---

1 For mode of prosecution and penalty, see Sch 2, post. The wife or husband of the accused may be called as a witness for the prosecution or the defence, see the Police and Criminal Evidence Act 1984, s 80 in PART II: EVIDENCE, ante.

2 This implies a permission by the tenant or occupier given to some other woman or women: a woman who is the sole occupier, using the premises for her own habitual prostitution, cannot be convicted of "permitting" the premises to be so used (*Mattison v Johnson* (1916) 80 JP 243).

*Powers and procedure for dealing with offenders*

7.10514 **37.** Prosecution and punishment of offences. —*Sub-ss* (1) *to* (6) *refer to the Second Schedule in which is tabulated all offences under the Act.*

(7) Nothing in this section or in the Second Schedule to this Act shall exclude the application to any of the offences referred to in the first column of the Schedule—

(*a*) of s 24 of the Magistrates' Courts Act 1980 (which relates to the summary trial of young offenders for indictable offences); or

(*b*) of subsection (5) of s 121 of the Magistrates' Courts Act 1980 (which limits the punishment which may be imposed by a magistrates' court sitting in an occasional courthouse); or

(*c*) of any enactments[1] or rule of law restricting a court's power to imprison; or

(*d*) of any enactment[2] or rule of law authorising an offender to be dealt with in a way not authorised by the enactments specially relating to his offence; or

(*e*) of any enactment or rule of law[3] authorising a jury to find a person guilty of an offence other than that with which he is charged.

[Sexual Offences Act 1956, s 37 as amended by the Magistrates' Courts Act 1980, Sch 7.]

---

1 See, for example, s 1 of the Criminal Justice Act 1991 in PART III: SENTENCING, ante.

2 Examples of this occur in a court's power to impose a fine, or to make a probation order or an order of absolute or conditional discharge.

3 See, eg, *R v Simmonite* [1916] 2 KB 821, 31 JP 80.

## FIRST SCHEDULE

RIGHTS OF LANDLORD WHERE TENANT CONVICTED OF PERMITTING USE OF PREMISES AS BROTHEL

*(As amended by the Local Government and Housing Act 1989, Sch 11.)*

7.10515 **1.** Upon the conviction[1] of the tenant or occupier (in this Schedule referred to as "the tenant"), the lessor or landlord may require the tenant to assign the lease or other contract under which the premises are held by him to some person approved by the lessor or landlord.

**2.** If the tenant fails to do so within three months, the lessor or landlord may determine the lease or contract (but without prejudice to the rights or remedies of any party thereto accrued before the date of the determination).

**3.** Where the lease or contract is determined under this Schedule, the court by which the tenant was convicted may make a summary order for delivery of possession of the premises to the lessor or landlord.

**4.** The approval of the lessor or landlord for the purposes of paragraph 1 of this Schedule shall not be unreasonably withheld.

**5.** This Schedule shall have effect subject to the Rent and Mortgage Interest Restrictions Acts 1920 to 1939, the Furnished Houses (Rent Control) Act 1946, Part II of the Reserve and Auxiliary Forces (Protection of Civil Interests) Act 1951, Part I of the Landlord and Tenant Act 1954, Part I of the Housing Act 1988 and Sch 10 to the Local Government and Housing Act 1989.

---

1 Convicted under s 35 of the Act, ante.

## SECOND SCHEDULE

TABLE OF OFFENCES, MODE OF PROSECUTION, PUNISHMENTS, ETC Section 37

*(As amended by the Criminal Law Act 1977, Sch 13, the Criminal Justice Act 1982, s 38 and the Sexual Offences Act 2003, s 55 and Schs 6 and 7.)*

### PART I

*Paras 1–6: Repealed.*

### PART II

| *Offence* | *Mode of Prosecution* | *Punishment* |
|---|---|---|
| 7.–32. *Repealed.* | | |
| 33. Keeping a brothel (section 33). | Summarily. | For an offence committed after a previous conviction[1], **6 months or level 4** on the standard scale **or both**; otherwise **three months or level 3** on the standard scale **or both.** |
| 33A. Keeping a brothel used for prostitution (section 33A). | (i) on indictment | Seven years |
| | (ii) summarily[2] | Six months, or the statutory maximum, or both. |
| 34. Letting premises for use as brothel (section 34). | Summarily. | For an offence committed after a previous conviction[1], **6 months or level 4** on the standard scale **or both**; otherwise **three months or level 3** on the standard scale **or both.** |
| 35. Tenant permitting premises to be used as brothel (section 35). | Summarily. | For an offence committed after a previous conviction[1], **6 months or level 4** on the standard scale **or both**; otherwise **three months or level 3** on the standard scale **or both.** |
| 36. Tenant permitting premises to be used for prostitution (section 36). | Summarily. | For an offence committed after a previous conviction[1], **6 months or level 4** on the standard scale **or both**; otherwise **three months or level 3** on the standard scale **or both.** |

[1] For prosecutions under ss 33–36 of this Act, previous convictions under any of the said four sections count for the purposes of rendering the accused liable to the heavier penalty.

[2] For procedure in respect of an offence triable either way, see the Magistrates' Courts Act 1980, ss 17A–21, In PART I: MAGISTRATES' COURTS, PROCEDURE, ante.

# Street Offences Act 1959

(7 & 8 Eliz 2 c 57)

7.10518 1. **Loitering or soliciting for purposes of prostitution** (1) It shall be an offence for a person aged 18 or over (whether male or female) persistently[1] to loiter or t[2] in a street[3] or public place[4] for the purpose of prostitution.

(2) A person guilty of an offence under this section shall be liable on summary conviction to a fine of an amount not exceeding **level 2** on the standard scale or, for an offence committed after a previous conviction, to a fine of an amount not exceeding **level 3** on that scale.

(2A) The court may deal with a person convicted of an offence under this section by making an order requiring the offender to attend three meetings with the person for the time being specified in the order ("the supervisor") or with such other person as the supervisor may direct[5].

(2B) The purpose of an order under subsection (2A) is to assist the offender, through attendance at those meetings, to—

(*a*) address the causes of the conduct constituting the offence, and

(*b*) find ways to cease engaging in such conduct in the future.

(2C) Where the court is dealing with an offender who is already subject to an order under subsection (2A), the court may not make a further order under that subsection unless it first revokes the existing order.

(2D) If the court makes an order under subsection (2A) it may not impose any other penalty in respect of the offence.

(3) *Repealed.*

(4) For the purposes of this section—

(*a*) conduct is persistent if it takes place on two or more occasions in any period of three months;

(*b*) any reference to a person loitering or soliciting for the purposes of prostitution is a reference to a person loitering or soliciting for the purposes of offering services as a prostitute;

(*c*) "street" includes any bridge, road, lane, footway, subway, square, court, alley or passage, whether a thoroughfare or not, which is for the time being open to the public; and the doorways and entrances of premises abutting on a street (as hereinbefore defined), and any ground adjoining and open to a street, shall be treated as forming part of the street.

(5) *Repealed*.

[Street Offences Act 1959, s 1 as amended by the Criminal Law Act 1977, Sch 6, the Criminal Justice Act 1982, ss 46 and 71, the Statute Law (Repeals) Act 1989, Sch 1 and the Statute Law (Repeals) Act 1993, Sch 1, the Sexual Offences Act 2003, Sch 1, the Serious Organised Crime and Police Act 2005, Sch 7, the Policing and Crime Act 2009, ss 16 and 17 and the Serious Crime Act 2015, s 68.]

---

[1] The Policing and Crime Act 2009, s 16(5) provides that in determining whether a person's conduct is persistent, any conduct that takes place before the commencement of that section is to be disregarded.

[2] A prostitute who does not make any active approach by gesture, word or signal may solicit in the sense of tempting or alluring prospective customers to come in for the purposes of prostitution and project her solicitation to passers by (*Behrendt v Burridge* [1976] 3 All ER 285, 140 JP 613).

[3] An offence is committed if the person solicited is in a street or public place, although the prostitute may be on a balcony or at a window of a house adjoining the street or public place (*Smith v Hughes* [1960] 2 All ER 859, 124 JP 430); but not where a prostitute offers her services by displaying a notice board, she not being present and importuning prospective customers (*Weiss v Monahan* [1962] 1 All ER 664, 126 JP 184; *Burge v DPP* [1962] 1 All ER 666n).

[4] "Public place" is not defined, but it must be construed *ejusdem generis* with the extended definition of "street" set out in sub-s (4); cf *R v Collinson* (1931) 23 Cr App Rep 49, in which a field to which the public were admitted (for one day) was held to be a public place; *Elkins v Cartlidge* [1947] 1 All ER 829, where an enclosure at the rear of an inn, entered through an open gateway, and in which cars were parked, was held to be a public place; *Glynn v Simmonds* [1952] 2 All ER 47, 116 JP 389, in which it was held that Tattersall's enclosure at a racecourse was a "place of public resort" notwithstanding a charge for admission and a right to exclude any person.

[5] For notice of requirements of suspended sentence and community, etc. orders, see the Criminal Procedure Rules, r 28.2 in the *Key Materials*.

**7.10519 1A. Orders under section 1(2A): supplementary** (1) This section applies to an order under section 1(2A).

(2) The order may not be made unless a suitable person has agreed to act as supervisor in relation to the offender.

(3) In subsection (2) "suitable person" means a person appearing to the court to have appropriate qualifications or experience for helping the offender to make the best use of the meetings for the purpose mentioned in section 1(2B).

(4) The order must specify—

(*a*) a date (not more than six months after the date of the order) by which the meetings required by the order must take place;

(*b*) the local justice area in which the offender resides or will reside while the order is in force.

(5) The supervisor must determine—

(*a*) the times of the meetings required by the order and their duration, and

(*b*) the places at which they are held.

(6) The supervisor must—

(*a*) make any arrangements that are necessary to enable the meetings required by the order to take place; and

(*b*) once the order has been complied with, notify the court which made the order of that fact.

(7) The court making the order must provide copies of it to the offender and the supervisor.

(8) Subsection (9) applies where—

(*a*) the order is made by the Crown Court, or

(*b*) the order is made by a magistrates' court but specifies a local justice area for which the court making the order does not act.

(9) The court must provide to a magistrates' court acting for the local justice area specified in the order—

(*a*) a copy of the order, and

(*b*) any documents and information relating to the case that it considers likely to be of assistance to that court in the exercise of any functions in relation to the order.

(10) The order ceases to be in force (unless revoked earlier under section 1(2C) or under the Schedule to this Act)—

(*a*) at the end of the day on which the supervisor notifies the court that the order has been complied with, or

(*b*) at the end of the day specified in the order under subsection (4)(*a*),

whichever first occurs.

(11) The Schedule to this Act (which relates to failure to comply with orders under section 1(2A) and to the revocation or amendment of such orders) has effect.

[Street Offences Act 1959, s 1A as inserted by the Policing and Crime Act 2009, s 17.]

# Protection of Children Act 1978[1]

(1978 c 37)

7.10520 **1. Indecent photographs of children** (1) Subject to sections 1A and 1B, it is an offence for a person—

(*a*) to take, or permit to be taken or to make[2], any indecent[3] photograph or pseudo-photograph of a child; or

(*b*) to distribute[4] or show such indecent photographs or pseudo-photographs; or

(*c*) to have in his possession[5] such indecent photographs or pseudo-photographs, with a view to their being distributed or shown[6] by himself or others; or

(*d*) to publish or cause to be published any advertisement likely to be understood as conveying that the advertiser distributes or shows such indecent photographs or pseudo-photographs, or intends to do so.

(2) For the purposes of this Act, a person is to be regarded as distributing an indecent photograph or pseudo-photographs if he parts with possession of it to, or exposes or offers it for acquisition by, another person.

(3) Proceedings for an offence under this Act shall not be instituted except by or with the consent of the Director of Public Prosecutions.

(4) Where a person is charged with an offence under subsection (1) (*b*) or (*c*), it shall be a defence[7] for him to prove—

(*a*) that he had a legitimate reason for distributing or showing the photographs or pseudo-photographs or (as the case may be) having them in his possession; or

(*b*) that he had not himself seen the photographs or pseudo-photographs and did not know, nor had any cause to suspect, them to be indecent.

(5)–(7) *References to Children and Young Persons Act* 1933; *Visiting Forces Act* 1952.

[Protection of Children Act 1978, s 1 as amended by the Criminal Justice Act 1988, Sch 16, the Extradition Act 1989, Sch 2, the Criminal Justice and Public Order Act 1994, s 84 and Sch 11 and the Sexual Offences Act 2003, s 141.]

---

[1] For a summary offence of possession of an indecent photograph of a child, see the Criminal Justice Act 1988, s 160, this title post, to which specified provisions of this Act are applied.

[2] Section 1(1)(*a*) renders unlawful the making of not only a photograph or pseudo-photograph but also, by virtue of s 7 post, negatives, copies of photographs and data stored on computer disk. Accordingly, a person who downloads indecent images from the Internet on to a disk or prints them off is "making an indecent photograph" within the meaning of s 1(1)(*a*), even where he was doing so only for his own use (*R v Bowden* [2000] 2 All ER 418, [2000] 2 WLR 1083, [2000] 1 Cr App Rep 438, CA). See also *Atkins v DPP* [2000] 2 All ER 425, [2000] 1 WLR 1427, [2000] 2 Cr App Rep 248, DC. However, s 1(1)(*a*) does not create an absolute offence. Therefore a person who opens an attachment to an unsolicited e-mail not knowing that the e-mail or attachment contained or was likely to contain indecent photographs of a child is not guilty of the offence of making those photographs. But the act of voluntarily down loading an indecent image from a Web page on to a computer screen is an act of making a photograph or pseudo-photograph; there is no need for an intention to store the images with a view to future retrieval (*R v Smith, R v Jayson* [2002] EWCA Crim 683, [2002] Crim LR 659, [2003] 1 Cr App Rep 212).

There are different approaches to the mens rea of the s 1(1)(*a*) offence between what is meant by "makes" in the context of images made by being downloaded to a computer or phone from the internet or via email and the making of an image by the act of photographing or filming. Given particular considerations relating to a phone or computer user's awareness as to what he is downloading, a different approach has been adopted for that situation; the mens rea includes a requirement of knowledge that the image made was likely to be an indecent one of a child. But where the making of an indecent image takes place through the more direct action of photographing or filming, the offence is made out by the deliberate act of photographing or filming without more: *R v W* [2016] EWCA Crim 745, [2016] 2 Cr App R 27.

[3] The age of the child is a material consideration for the court in determining whether the photograph of the child was in fact indecent (*R v Owen* [1988] 1 WLR 134, 86 Cr App Rep 291, CA). In order to convict a person of taking an indecent photograph, it must be proved that the defendant took the photograph deliberately and intentionally. If so satisfied, the court must then decide whether the photograph was indecent by applying the recognised standards of propriety, but for this purpose the circumstances in which the photograph was taken and the motivation of the taker are irrelevant (*R v Graham-Kerr* [1988] 1 WLR 1098, 153 JP 171, CA). Except in a clear case, where the images do not surmount the obstacle of being capable of sustaining a conviction if left to a jury properly directed, it is for the jury to decide whether an image is indecent. That question is to be decided by them and not by any pre-conceived categorisation of images into various levels, which is only useful for sentencing purposes once the jury have convicted the accused: *R v M* [2015] EWCA Crim 353, [2015] 2 Cr App Rep 307, [2015] All ER (D) 130 (Mar). Articles 8 and 10 of the European Convention on Human Rights do not require a reconsideration of the interpretation of s 1 of the 1978 Act as the exceptions in art 8(2) and 10(2) apply as the Act is there for the prevention of crime, for the protection of morals, and in particular for the protection of children from being exploited, which is a matter necessary in a democratic society (*R v Smethurst* [2001] EWCA 772, 165 JP 377, [2001] Crim LR 657, [2002] 1 Cr App Rep 50). Whilst the 1978 Act does not impede an accused from engaging in sexual intercourse with a person who is aged 17, he is not permitted to make such a person the subject of pornography. The defence does not apply to a "one night stand" as a defence which includes a "brief sexual relationship" would diminish the protection provided and would risk the re-introduction of issues as to the circumstances in which the photograph was taken and the motivation for taking or making it. The legislation strikes the balance between keeping interference by the State in the private lives of individuals to the minimum and maintaining under the law maximum protection for children from sexual abuse and exploitation: *R v M* [2011] EWCA Crim 2752, [2012] Crim LR 789.

[4] Where a defendant responded to an advertisement for the sale of pornographic videos by writing to request a compilation tape showing very young girls (aged 7–13) he could be guilty in law of inciting or attempting to incite the distribution of indecent photographs of children, contrary to s 1(1) of the Criminal Attempts Act 1981; the fact that the advertiser was willing to supply its wares was nothing to the point: *R v Goldman* [2001] Crim LR 822, CA.

[5] The concept of "possession" varies according to its statutory context and in this legislation an employee in a shop who knowingly has custody or control of a video, has possession of it. If he maintains that he is unaware of its obscene nature, it is open to him to rely on the defence in s 1(4)(*b*) (*R v Matrix* [1997] Crim LR 901, CA).

[6] To be guilty of the offence the defendant must have had possession of the indecent photograph with a view either to its being distributed to third parties or to its being shown to persons other than himself (*R v ET* (1999) 163 JP 349, [1999] Crim LR 749). There is a distinction between "with a view to" and "with the intention of"; the former is made out if the defendant was in possession of the images in a shared folder and one of his reasons, though not necessarily the primary

reason, for allowing them to remain there was to enable others to have access to the shared folder: *R v Dooley* [2005] EWCA Crim 3093, [2006] 1 WLR 775, [2006] 1 Cr App Rep 349, [2006] Crim LR 544.

7 The statutory defences under s 1(4) are limited to persons who distribute or are in possession of such material for a legitimate reason (eg the police) or an individual who was ignorant of and had no reason to believe that he was in possession of or distributing indecent material or in the case of simple possession, who received it unsolicited and gets rid of it with reasonable promptness. No statutory defence is available for the person who creates the material or advertises its availability. If Parliament had intended to provide a defence for an individual who, because of the apparent maturity of the person depicted in the photographs, failed to appreciate that a child was involved it would have been very simple to make appropriate provision in s 1(4)(*b*) of the 1978 Act and extend the statutory defences to the person who did not know nor had any reason to suspect that the pictures were of a child or, alternatively, reasonably believed that they depicted persons who were 16 years or older. Accordingly, in the absence of such provision, once it was or should have been appreciated that the material was indecent then its continued retention or distribution was subject to the risk of prosecution if the source of it proved to be a child or children: *R v Land* [1998] 1 All ER 403, [1998] 3 WLR 322, [1998] 1 Cr App Rep 30.

**7.10521 1A. Marriage and other relationships** (1) This section applies where, in proceedings for an offence under section 1(1)(*a*) of taking or making an indecent photograph or pseudo-photograph of a child, or for an offence under section 1(1)(*b*) or (*c*) relating to an indecent photograph or pseudo-photograph of a child, the defendant proves that the photograph or pseudo-photograph was of the child aged 16 or over, and that at the time of the offence charged the child and he—

(*a*) were married or civil partners of each other, or

(*b*) lived together as partners in an enduring family relationship.

(2) Subsections (5) and (6) also apply where, in proceedings for an offence under section 1(1)(*b*) or (*c*) relating to an indecent photograph or pseudo-photograph of a child, the defendant proves that the photograph or pseudo-photograph was of the child aged 16 or over, and that at the time when he obtained it the child and he—

(*a*) were married or civil partners of each other, or

(*b*) lived together as partners in an enduring family relationship.

(3) This section applies whether the photograph or pseudo-photograph showed the child alone or with the defendant, but not if it showed any other person.

(4) In the case of an offence under section 1(1)(*a*), if sufficient evidence is adduced to raise an issue as to whether the child consented to the photograph or pseudo-photograph being taken or made, or as to whether the defendant reasonably believed that the child so consented, the defendant is not guilty of the offence unless it is proved that the child did not so consent and that the defendant did not reasonably believe that the child so consented.

(5) In the case of an offence under section 1(1)(*b*), the defendant is not guilty of the offence unless it is proved that the showing or distributing was to a person other than the child.

(6) In the case of an offence under section 1(1)(*c*), if sufficient evidence is adduced to raise an issue both—

(*a*) as to whether the child consented to the photograph or pseudo-photograph being in the defendant's possession, or as to whether the defendant reasonably believed that the child so consented, and

(*b*) as to whether the defendant had the photograph or pseudo-photograph in his possession with a view to its being distributed or shown to anyone other than the child,

the defendant is not guilty of the offence unless it is proved either that the child did not so consent and that the defendant did not reasonably believe that the child so consented, or that the defendant had the photograph or pseudo-photograph in his possession with a view to its being distributed or shown to a person other than the child.

[Protection of Children Act 1978, s 1A as inserted by the Sexual Offences Act 2003, s 45 and amended by the Civil Partnership Act 2004, Sch 27 and the Coroners and Justice Act 2009, s 69.]

**7.10522 1B. Exception for criminal proceedings, investigations etc** (1) In proceedings for an offence under section 1(1)(*a*) of making an indecent photograph or pseudo-photograph of a child, the defendant is not guilty of the offence if he proves that—

(*a*) it was necessary for him to make the photograph or pseudo-photograph for the purposes of the prevention, detection or investigation of crime, or for the purposes of criminal proceedings, in any part of the world,

(*b*) at the time of the offence charged he was a member of the Security Service or the Secret Intelligence Service, and it was necessary for him to make the photograph or pseudo-photograph for the exercise of any of the functions of that Service, or

(*c*) at the time of the offence charged he was a member of GCHQ, and it was necessary for him to make the photograph or pseudo-photograph for the exercise of any of the functions of GCHQ.

(2) In this section "GCHQ" has the same meaning as in the Intelligence Services Act 1994.

[Protection of Children Act 1978, s 1B as inserted by the Sexual Offences Act 2003, s 46 and amended by the Criminal Justice and Immigration Act 2008, s 69.]

**7.10523 2. Evidence** (1), (2) *Repealed.*

(3) In proceedings under this Act relating to indecent photographs of children a person is to be taken as having been a child at any material time if it appears from the evidence as a whole that he was then under the age of 18[1].

[Protection of Children Act 1978, s 2 as amended by the Magistrates' Courts Act 1980, Sch 9, the Police and Criminal Evidence Act 1984, Sch 7, the Criminal Justice and Public Order Act 1994, Sch 10 and the Sexual Offences Act 2003, s 45.]

1 It is a matter for the court to decide whether an unknown person depicted in a photograph is under the age of (18) years. There is no requirement for paediatric or other expert evidence which in any event will be inadmissible (*R v Land* [1998]) 1 All ER 403, [1998] 3 WLR 322, [1998] 1 Cr App Rep 301).

7.10524 3. **Offences by corporations** (1) Where a body corporate is guilty of an offence under this Act and it is proved that the offence occurred with the consent or connivance of, or was attributable to any neglect on the part of, any director, manager, secretary or other officer of the body, or any person who was purporting to act in any such capacity he, as well as the body corporate, shall be deemed to be guilty of that offence and shall be liable to be proceeded against and punished accordingly.

(2) Where the affairs of a body corporate are managed by its members, subsection (1) shall apply in relation to the acts and defaults of a member in connection with his functions of management as if he were a director of the body corporate.

[Protection of Children Act 1978, s 3.]

7.10525 4. **Entry, search and seizure** (1) The following applies where a justice of the peace is satisfied by information on oath, laid by or on behalf of the Director of Public Prosecutions or by a constable, that there is reasonable ground for suspecting that, in any premises, there is an indecent photograph or pseudo-photograph of a child.

(2) The justice may issue a warrant under his hand authorising any constable to enter (if need be by force) and search the premises, and to seize and remove any articles which he believes (with reasonable cause) to be or include indecent photographs or pseudo-photographs of children.

(3) *Repealed.*

(4) In this section "premises" has the same meaning as in the Police and Criminal Evidence Act 1984 (see section 23 of that Act).

[Protection of Children Act 1978, s 4 as amended by the Criminal Justice Act 1988, Schs 15 and 16, the Criminal Justice and Public Order Act 1994, Schs 9, 10 and 11, the Courts Act 2003, Sch 8 and the Police and Justice Act 2006, s 39 and Sch 15.]

7.10526 5. **Forfeiture** The Schedule to this Act makes provision about the forfeiture of indecent photographs and pseudo-photographs

[Protection of Children Act 1978, s 5 as substituted by the Police and Justice Act 2006, s 39.]

7.10527 6. **Punishments** (1) Offences under this Act shall be punishable either on conviction on indictment or on summary conviction.

(2) A person convicted on indictment of any offence under this Act shall be liable to imprisonment for a term of not more than **ten years**, or to a **fine** or to **both**.

(3) A person convicted summarily of any offence under this Act shall be liable[1]—

(*a*) to imprisonment for a term not exceeding **six months**; or

(*b*) to a fine not exceeding **the prescribed sum** for the purposes of section 32 of the Magistrates' Courts Act 1980 (punishment on summary conviction of offences triable either way: **£1,000** or other sum substituted by order under that Act), or to **both**.

[Protection of Children Act 1978, s 6 as amended by the Magistrates' Courts Act 1980, Sch 7 and the Criminal Justice and Court Services Act 2000, s 41.]

1 For procedure with respect to an offence triable either way, see the Magistrates' Courts Act 1980, ss 17A–21, in PART I, MAGISTRATES' COURTS, PROCEDURE, ante.

7.10528 7. **Interpretation** (1) The following subsections apply for the interpretation of the Act.

(2) References to an indecent photograph include an indecent film, a copy of an indecent photograph or film, and an indecent photograph comprised in a film.

(3) Photographs (including those comprised in a film) shall, if they show children and are indecent, be treated for all purposes of this Act as indecent photographs of children and so as respects pseudo-photographs.

(4) References to a photograph include—

(*a*) the negative as well as the positive version; and

(*b*) data stored on a computer disc or by other electronic means which is capable of conversion into a photograph.

(4A) References to a photograph also include—

(*a*) a tracing or other image, whether made by electronic or other means (of whatever nature)—

(i) which is not itself a photograph or pseudo-photograph, but

(ii) which is derived from the whole or part of a photograph or pseudo-photograph (or a combination of either or both); and

(*b*) data stored on a computer disc or by other electronic means which is capable of conversion into an image within paragraph (*a*);

and subsection (8) applies in relation to such an image as it applies in relation to a pseudo-photograph.

(5) "Film" includes any form of video-recording.

(6) "Child", subject to subsection (8), means a person under the age of 18.

(7) "Pseudo-photograph" means an image, whether made by computer-graphics or otherwise howsoever, which appears to be a photograph.

(8) If the impression conveyed by a pseudo-photograph is that the person shown is a child, the pseudo-photograph shall be treated for all purposes of this Act as showing a child and so shall a pseudo-photograph where the predominant impression conveyed is that the person shown is a child notwithstanding that some of the physical characteristics shown are those of an adult.

(9) References to an indecent pseudo-photograph include—

(*a*) a copy of an indecent pseudo-photograph; and

(*b*) data stored on a computer disc or by other electronic means which is capable of conversion into an indecent pseudo-photograph.

[Protection of Children Act 1978, s 7 as amended by the Criminal Justice and Public Order Act 1994, s 84, the Sexual Offences Act 2003, s 45 and the Criminal Justice and Immigration Act 2008, s 69.]

## SCHEDULE

## FORFEITURE OF INDECENT PHOTOGRAPHS OF CHILDREN

*(As inserted by the Police and Justice Act 2006, Sch 11)* Section 5

7.10529 1. **Application of Schedule** (1) This Schedule applies where—

(*a*) property which has been lawfully seized in England and Wales is in the custody of a constable,

(*b*) ignoring this Schedule, there is no legitimate reason for the constable to retain custody of the property,

(*c*) the constable is satisfied that there are reasonable grounds for believing that the property is or is likely to be forfeitable property, and

(*d*) ignoring this Schedule, the constable is not aware of any person who has a legitimate reason for possessing the property or any readily separable part of it.

(2) The following property is "forfeitable property"—

(*a*) any indecent photograph or pseudo-photograph of a child;

(*b*) any property which it is not reasonably practicable to separate from any property within paragraph (*a*).

(3) For the purposes of this paragraph—

(*a*) a part of any property is a "readily separable part" of the property if, in all the circumstances, it is reasonably practicable for it to be separated from the remainder of that property, and

(*b*) it is reasonably practicable for a part of any property to be separated from the remainder if it is reasonably practicable to separate it without prejudicing the remainder of the property or another part of it.

(4) The circumstances mentioned in sub-paragraph (3)(*a*) include the time and costs involved in separating the property.

2. **Possession pending forfeiture** (1) The property must be retained in the custody of a constable until it is returned or otherwise disposed of in accordance with this Schedule.

(2) Nothing in the Police (Property) Act 1897 (property seized in the investigation of an offence) applies to property held under this Schedule.

3. **The relevant officer** "The relevant officer", in relation to any property, is the constable who for the time being has custody of the property.

4. **Notice of intended forfeiture** (1) The relevant officer must give notice of the intended forfeiture of the property ("notice of intended forfeiture") to—

(*a*) every person whom he believes to have been the owner of the property, or one of its owners, at the time of the seizure of the property,

(*b*) where the property was seized from premises, every person whom the relevant officer believes to have been an occupier of the premises at that time, and

(*c*) where the property was seized as a result of a search of any person, that person.

(2) The notice of intended forfeiture must set out—

(*a*) a description of the property, and

(*b*) how a person may give a notice of claim under this Schedule and the period within which such a notice must be given.

(3) The notice of intended forfeiture may be given to a person only by—

(*a*) delivering it to him personally,

(*b*) addressing it to him and leaving it for him at the appropriate address, or

(*c*) addressing it to him and sending it to him at that address by post.

(4) But a notice given in accordance with sub-paragraph (1)(*b*) may, where it is not practicable to give the notice in accordance with sub-paragraph (3), be given by—

(*a*) addressing it to "the occupier" of those premises, without naming him, and

(*b*) leaving it for him at those premises or sending it to him at those premises by post.

(5) Property may be treated or condemned as forfeited under this Schedule only if—

(*a*) the requirements of this paragraph have been complied with in the case of the property, or

(*b*) it was not reasonably practicable for them to be complied with.

(6) In this paragraph "the appropriate address", in relation to a person, means—

(*a*) in the case of a body corporate, its registered or principal office in the United Kingdom;

(*b*) in the case of a firm, the principal office of the partnership;

(*c*) in the case of an unincorporated body or association, the principal office of the body or association;

(*d*) in any other case, his usual or last known place of residence in the United Kingdom or his last known place of business in the United Kingdom.

(7) In the case of—

(*a*) a company registered outside the United Kingdom,

(*b*) a firm carrying on business outside the United Kingdom, or

(*c*) an unincorporated body or association with offices outside the United Kingdom,

the references in this paragraph to its principal office include references to its principal office within the United Kingdom (if any).

**5. Notice of claim** (1) A person claiming that he has a legitimate reason for possessing the property or a part of it may give notice of his claim to a constable at any police station in the police area in which the property was seized.

(2) Oral notice is not sufficient for these purposes.

**6.** (1) A notice of claim may not be given more than one month after—

(*a*) the date of the giving of the notice of intended forfeiture, or

(*b*) if no such notice has been given, the date on which the property began to be retained under this Schedule (see paragraph 2).

(2) A notice of claim must specify—

(*a*) the name and address of the claimant;

(*b*) a description of the property, or part of it, in respect of which the claim is made;

(*c*) in the case of a claimant who is outside the United Kingdom, the name and address of a solicitor in the United Kingdom who is authorised to accept service, and to act, on behalf of the claimant.

(3) Service upon a solicitor so specified is to be taken to be service on the claimant for the purposes of any proceedings by virtue of this Schedule.

(4) In a case in which notice of intended forfeiture was given to different persons on different days, the reference in this paragraph to the day on which that notice was given is a reference—

(*a*) in relation to a person to whom notice of intended forfeiture was given, to the day on which that notice was given to that person, and

(*b*) in relation to any other person, to the day on which notice of intended forfeiture was given to the last person to be given such a notice.

**7. Automatic forfeiture in a case where no claim is made** (1) If the property is unclaimed it is treated as forfeited.

(2) The property is "unclaimed" if, by the end of the period for the giving of a notice of claim—

(*a*) no such notice has been given in relation to it or any part of it, or

(*b*) the requirements of paragraphs 5 and 6 have not been complied with in relation to the only notice or notices of claim that have been given.

(3) Sub-paragraph (1) applies in relation to a readily separable part of the property as it applies in relation to the property, and for this purpose sub-paragraph (2) applies as if references to the property were to the part.

(4) In this paragraph "readily separable part" has the meaning given by paragraph 1.

**8. Decision whether to take court proceedings to condemn property as forfeited** (1) Where a notice of claim in respect of the property, or a part of it, is duly given in accordance with paragraphs 5 and 6, the relevant officer must decide whether to take proceedings to ask the court to condemn the property or a part of it as forfeited.

(2) The decision whether to take such proceedings must be made as soon as reasonably practicable after the giving of the notice of claim.

**9. Return of property if no forfeiture proceedings** (1) This paragraph applies if, in a case in which a notice of claim has been given, the relevant officer decides—

(*a*) not to take proceedings for condemnation of the property, or

(*b*) not to take proceedings for condemnation of a part of the property.

(2) The relevant officer must return the property or part to the person who appears to him to have a legitimate reason for possessing the property or, if there is more than one such person, to one of those persons.

(3) Any property required to be returned in accordance with sub-paragraph (2) must be returned as soon as reasonably practicable after the decision not to take proceedings for condemnation.

**10. Forfeiture proceedings** (1) This paragraph applies if, in a case in which a notice of claim has been given, the relevant officer decides to take proceedings for condemnation of the property or a part of it ("the relevant property").

(2) The court must condemn the relevant property if it is satisfied—

(*a*) that the relevant property is forfeitable property, and

(*b*) that no-one who has given a notice of claim has a legitimate reason for possessing the relevant property.

This is subject to sub-paragraphs (5) and (7).

(3) If the court is not satisfied that the relevant property is forfeitable property, the court must order its return to the person who appears to the court to have a legitimate reason for possessing it or, if there is more than one such person, to one of those persons.

(4) If the court is satisfied—

(*a*) that the relevant property is forfeitable property, and

(*b*) that a person who has given a notice of claim has a legitimate reason for possessing the relevant property, or that more than one such person has such a reason,

the court must order the return of the relevant property to that person or, as the case may be, to one of those persons.

(5) Where the court is satisfied that any part of the relevant property is a separable part, sub-paragraphs (2) to (4) apply separately in relation to each separable part of the relevant property as if references to the relevant property were references to the separable part.

(6) For this purpose a part of any property is a "separable part" of the property if—

(*a*) it can be separated from the remainder of that property, and

(*b*) where a person has a legitimate reason for possessing the remainder of that property or any part of it, the separation will not prejudice the remainder or part.

(7) Where the court is satisfied—

(*a*) that a person who has given a notice of claim has a legitimate reason for possessing part of the relevant property, and

(*b*) that, although the part is not a separable part within the meaning given by sub-paragraph (6), it can be separated from the remainder of the relevant property,

the court may order the return of that part to that person.

(8) Sub-paragraph (7) does not apply to any property required to be returned to a person under sub-paragraph (4).

**11. Supplementary orders** (1) Where the court condemns property under paragraph 10(2)—

(*a*) it may order the relevant officer to take such steps in relation to the property or any part of it as it thinks appropriate, and (*b*) where it orders a step to be taken, it may make that order conditional on specified costs relating to the taking of that step being paid by a specified person within a specified period.

(2) A court order under paragraph 10(3), (4), (5) or (7) requiring the return of a part of the relevant property to a person may be made conditional on specified costs relating to the separation of the part from the remainder of the relevant property being paid by that person within a specified period.

(3) Where the court makes an order under paragraph 10(7) for the return of a part of the relevant property—

(*a*) it may order the relevant officer to take such steps as it thinks appropriate in relation to any property which will be prejudiced by the separation of that part, and

(*b*) where it orders a step to be taken, it may make that order conditional on specified costs relating to the taking of that step being paid by a specified person within a specified period.

(4) For the purposes of this paragraph "specified" means specified in, or determined in accordance with, the court order.

**12. Supplementary provision about forfeiture proceedings** Proceedings by virtue of this Schedule are civil proceedings and may be instituted in a magistrates' court which has jurisdiction in relation to the place where the property to which the proceedings relate was seized.

**13.** (1) Either party may appeal against the decision of the magistrates' court to the Crown Court.

(2) This paragraph does not affect any right to require the statement of a case for the opinion of the High Court.

**14.** Where an appeal has been made (whether by case stated or otherwise) against the decision of the magistrates' court in proceedings by virtue of this Schedule in relation to property, the property is to be left in the custody of a constable pending the final determination of the matter.

**15. Effect of forfeiture** Where property is treated or condemned as forfeited under this Schedule the forfeiture is to be treated as having taken effect as from the time of the seizure.

**16. Disposal of property which is not returned** (1) This paragraph applies where any property is required to be returned to a person under this Schedule.

(2) If—

(*a*) the property is (without having been returned) still in the custody of the relevant officer after the end of the period of 12 months beginning with the day on which the requirement to return it arose, and

(*b*) it is not practicable to dispose of it by returning it immediately to the person to whom it is required to be returned,

the relevant officer may dispose of it in any manner he thinks fit.

**17.** (1) This paragraph applies where any property would be required to be returned to a person under this Schedule but for a failure to satisfy a condition imposed by virtue of paragraph 11(2) (return of property conditional on payment of costs within specified period).

(2) The relevant officer may dispose of the property in any manner he thinks fit.

**18. Provisions as to proof** In proceedings under this Schedule, the fact, form and manner of the seizure are to be taken, without further evidence and unless the contrary is shown, to have been as set forth in the process.

**19.** In proceedings, the condemnation by a court of property as forfeited under this Schedule may be proved by the production of either—

(*a*) the order of condemnation, or

(*b*) a certified copy of the order purporting to be signed by an officer of the court by which the order was made or granted.

**20. Saving for owner's rights** Neither the imposition of a requirement by virtue of this Schedule to return property to a person nor the return of it to a person in accordance with such a requirement affects—

(*a*) the rights in relation to that property, or any part of it, of any other person, or

(*b*) the right of any other person to enforce his rights against the person to whom it is returned.

**21. Interpretation** (1) In this Schedule—

"the court" is to be construed in accordance with paragraph 12;

"forfeitable property" is to be construed in accordance with paragraph 1(2);

"premises" has the same meaning as in the Police and Criminal Evidence Act 1984 (see section 23 of that Act); and

"the relevant officer" is to be construed in accordance with paragraph 3.

(2) For the purposes of this Schedule the circumstances in which a person ("P") has a legitimate reason for possessing an indecent photograph of a child ("C") include where—

(*a*) the photograph was of C aged 16 or over,

(*b*) one or both of the following sub-paragraphs apply—

(i) P and C are married, are civil partners of each other or are living together as partners in an enduring family relationship,

(ii) P and C were married, were civil partners of each other or were so living together at the time P obtained the photograph,

(*c*) the photograph shows C alone or with P, but does not show any other person,

(*d*) C has consented to the photograph being in P's possession (and that consent has not been withdrawn), and

(*e*) P owns, or is authorised (directly or indirectly) by the owner, to possess the photograph.

# Criminal Justice Act 1988[1]

(1988 c 33)

## PART XI[2]

## MISCELLANEOUS

*Possession of indecent photograph of child*

7.10530 **160. Possession of indecent photograph of child** (1) Subject to section 160A, it is an offence[3] for a person to have any indecent photograph or pseudo-photograph of a child in his possession[4].

(2) Where a person is charged with an offence under subsection (1) above, it shall be a defence for him to prove—

(*a*) that he had a legitimate reason for having the photograph or pseudo-photograph in his possession; or

(*b*) that he had not himself seen the photograph or pseudo-photograph and did not know, nor had any cause to suspect, it[5] to be indecent; or

(*c*) that the photograph or pseudo-photograph was sent to him without any prior request made by him or on his behalf and that he did not keep it for an unreasonable time.

(2A) A person shall be liable on conviction on indictment of an offence under this section to imprisonment for a term not exceeding **five years** or a fine, or **both**.

(3) A person shall be liable[6] on summary conviction of an offence under this section to imprisonment for a term not exceeding **six months** or a fine not exceeding **level 5** on the standard scale, or **both**.

(4) Sections 1(3), 2(3), 3 and 7 of the Protection of Children Act 1978[7] shall have effect as if any reference in them to that Act included a reference to this section.

(5) *Repealed.*

[Criminal Justice Act 1988, s 160 as amended by the Criminal Justice and Public Order Act 1994, ss 84 and 86 and Sch 11, the Criminal Justice and Court Services Act 2000, s 41(3) and the Criminal Justice and Immigration Act 2008, Sch 26.]

---

1 For other provisions of the Criminal Justice Act 1988, see in particular PART I: MAGISTRATES' COURTS, PROCEDURE, ante.

2 Part XI contains ss 133–167.

3 In *R v Richard Thompson* [2004] EWCA Crim 669, [2005] 1 Cr App R (S) 1, the Court of Appeal gave the following guidance on the drafting of indictments and informations: (1) in cases where there are significant numbers of photographs, in addition to the specific counts there should be a comprehensive count dealing with the remainder; (2) the specific counts should reflect the range of images in the comprehensive count; (3) where it is impractical to present the court with specific counts that are agreed to be representative of the comprehensive count, there needs to be an approximate breakdown, best achieved by means of a prosecution schedule, of the number of images at each level; (4) each of the counts should make clear whether the image is a real image or a pseudo image; (5) each image charged in a specific count should be identified by a reference; and (6) the estimated age range of the child shown in each of the images should where possible be provided.

4 The offence of possession under s 160(1) is not committed unless the defendant knows that he has the photographs in his possession (*Atkins v DPP* [2000] 2 All ER 425, [2000] 1 WLR 1427, [2000] 2 Cr App Rep 248, DC).

"Possession" means physically in one's custody or under one's physical control. A defendant is not in "possession" of indecent images which he has deleted from his computer, if he could not retrieve or gain access to them as he no longer has custody or control of them. Whether he is able to retrieve items deleted from the recycle bin will depend on a finding of fact about his computer skills and ownership of the requisite software. There may also be practical reasons why an accused is not charged with possession at the time when he viewed the images until he deleted them: *R v Porter* [2006] EWCA Crim 560, [2007] 2 All ER 625, [2006] 1 WLR 2633, [2006] 2 Cr App R 25. See also *R v Rowe* [2008] EWCA Crim 2712, 172 JP 585. Problems can be resolved if the indictment addresses the deletion issue by alleging possession of the indecent image over a period covering either the date of the deletion (if it can be established) or between the dates when the defendant assumed control of the computer and the date when the images were found. If that were done, it would not be the end of the case as it would be open to the defendant to advance any of the statutory defences provided in s 160(2), and, if convicted, if the defendant had truly tried to rid himself of the material, that would be likely to provide substantial mitigation: *R v Leonard* [2012] EWCA Crim 277, [2012] 2 Cr App Rep 138, 176 CL&J 466.

"Pop-ups" that occur when a computer user visits particular websites are made by the user and not the website designer; and in "pop-up" cases the offence of possession is committed where: (*a*) the images stored there are of persons under age and are of an indecent nature; and (*b*) the defendant was the person responsible for accessing the images, and he knew that such material would then be automatically stored to the hard drive and that his browsing would or could access illegal images, or be likely to do so: *R v Harrison* [2007] EWCA Crim 2976, [2008] 1 Cr App R 29.

5 The "it" in s 160(2)(*b*) refers to an indecent image of a child and not an indecent image alone; thus, the defence is available where the defendant had reason to suspect that the image was indecent but not that it was an indecent image of a child: *R v Collier* [2004] EWCA Crim 1411, [2005] 1 WLR 843, [2004] Crim LR 1039, [2005] 1 Cr App R 9.

6 For procedure in respect of an offence triable either way, see the Magistrates' Courts Act 1980, ss 17A–21 in PART I: MAGISTRATES' COURTS, PROCEDURE, ante.

7 See this title, ante.

7.10531 **160A. Marriage and other relationships** (1) This section applies where, in proceedings for an offence under section 160 relating to an indecent photograph or pseudo-photograph of a child, the defendant proves that the photograph or pseudo-photograph was of the child aged 16 or over, and that at the time of the offence charged the child and he—

(*a*) were married or civil partners of each other, or

(*b*) lived together as partners in an enduring family relationship.

(2) This section also applies where, in proceedings for an offence under section 160 relating to an indecent photograph or pseudo-photograph of a child, the defendant proves that the photograph or pseudo-photograph was of the child aged 16 or over, and that at the time when he obtained it the child and he—

(*a*) were married or civil partners of each other, or

(*b*) lived together as partners in an enduring family relationship.

(3) This section applies whether the photograph or pseudo-photograph showed the child alone or with the defendant, but not if it showed any other person.

(4) If sufficient evidence is adduced to raise an issue as to whether the child consented to the photograph or pseudo-photograph being in the defendant's possession, or as to whether the

defendant reasonably believed that the child so consented, the defendant is not guilty of the offence unless it is proved that the child did not so consent and that the defendant did not reasonably believe that the child so consented.

[Criminal Justice Act 1988, s 160A as inserted by the Sexual Offences Act 2003, s 45 and amended by the Civil Partnership Act 2004, Sch 27 and the Coroners and Justice Act 2009, s 69.]

## Sexual Offences (Amendment) Act 1992

(1992 c 34)

**7.10532 1. Anonymity of victims of certain offences**[1] (1) Where an allegation has been made that an offence to which this Act applies has been committed against a person, No matter relating to that person shall during that person's lifetime be included in any publication, if it is likely to lead members of the public to identify that person as the person against whom the offence is alleged to have been committed.

(2) Where a person is accused of an offence to which this Act applies, no matter likely to lead members of the public to identify a person as the person against whom the offence is alleged to have been committed ("the complainant") shall during the complainant's lifetime be included in any publication.

(3) This section—

(*a*) does not apply in relation to a person by virtue of subsection (1) at any time after a person has been accused of the offence, and

(*b*) in its application in relation to a person by virtue of subsection (2), has effect subject to any direction given under section 3.

(3A) The matters relating to a person in relation to which the restrictions imposed by subsection (1) or (2) apply (if their inclusion in any publication is likely to have the result mentioned in that subsection) include in particular—

(*a*) the person's name,

(*b*) the person's address,

(*c*) the identity of any school or other educational establishment attended by the person,

(*d*) the identity of any place of work, and

(*e*) any still or moving picture of the person.

(4) Nothing in this section prohibits the publication or inclusion in a relevant programme of matter consisting only of a report of criminal proceedings other than proceedings at, or intended to lead to, or on an appeal arising out of, a trial at which the accused is charged with the offence.*

[Sexual Offences (Amendment) Act 1992, s 1 as amended by the Youth Justice and Criminal Evidence Act 1999, Sch 2.]

* **Section reproduced as amended by the Youth Justice and Criminal Evidence Act 1999 in force 7 October 2004 in England and Wales.**

1 The 1992 Act confers no express power on the court to make an order restricting publication of a defendant's name to protect or enforce a complainant's right to anonymity and no such power is to be inferred: *R (on the application of the Press Association) v Cambridge Crown Court* [2012] EWCA Crim 2434, [2013] 1 All ER 1361, [2013] Crim LR 323.

**7.10533 2. Offences to which this Act applies** (1) This Act applies to the following offences against the law of England and Wales—

(*aa*) rape;

(*ab*) burglary with intent to rape;

(*a*) any offence under any of the provisions of the Sexual Offences Act 1956 mentioned in subsection (2);

(*b*) any offence under section 128 of the Mental Health Act 1959 (intercourse with mentally handicapped person by hospital staff etc);

(*c*) any offence under section 1 of the Indecency with Children Act 1960 (indecent conduct towards young child);

(*d*) any offence under section 54 of the Criminal Law Act 1977 (incitement by man of his grand-daughter, daughter or sister under the age of 16 to commit incest with him);

(*da*) any offence under any of the provisions of Part 1 of the Sexual Offences Act 2003 except section 64, 65, 69 or 71;

(*db*) any offence under section 2 of the Modern Slavery Act 2015 (human trafficking);

(*e*) any attempt to commit any of the offences mentioned in paragraphs (*aa*) to (*db*).

(*f*) any conspiracy to commit any of those offences;

(*g*) any incitement of another to commit any of those offences;

(*h*) aiding, abetting, counselling or procuring the commission of any of the offences mentioned in paragraphs (*aa*) to (*e*) and (*g*);

(2) The provisions of the Act of 1956 are—

(*a*) section 2 (procurement of a woman by threats);

(*b*) section 3 (procurement of a woman by false pretences);

(*c*) section 4 (administering drugs to obtain intercourse with a woman);

(*d*) section 5 (intercourse with a girl under the age of 13);

(*e*) section 6 (intercourse with a girl between the ages of 13 and 16);

(*f*) section 7 (intercourse with a mentally handicapped person);

(*g*) section 9 (procurement of a mentally handicapped person);
(*h*) section 10 (incest by a man);
(*i*) section 11 (incest by a woman);
(*j*) section 12 (buggery);
(*k*) section 14 (indecent assault on a woman);
(*l*) section 15 (indecent assault on a man);
(*m*) section 16 (assault with intent to commit buggery).
(*n*) section 17 (abduction of woman by force).

(3) This Act applies to the following offences against the law of Northern Ireland—

(*a*) rape;
(*b*) burglary with intent to rape;
(*c*) any offence under any of the following provisions of the Offences against the Person Act 1861—
  (i) section 52 (indecent assault on a female);
  (ii) section 53 so far as it relates to abduction of a woman against her will;
  (iii) section 61 (buggery);
  (iv) section 62 (attempt to commit buggery, assault with intent to commit buggery or indecent assault on a male);
(*d*) any offence under any of the following provisions of the Criminal Law Amendment Act 1885—
  (i) section 3 (procuring unlawful carnal knowledge of woman by threats, false pretences or administering drugs);
  (ii) section 4 (unlawful carnal knowledge, or attempted unlawful carnal knowledge, of a girl under 14);
  (iii) section 5 (unlawful carnal knowledge of a girl under 17);
(*e*) any offence under any of the following provisions of the Punishment of Incest Act 1908—
  (i) section 1 (incest, attempted incest by males);
  (ii) section 2 (incest by females over 16);
(*f*) any offence under section 22 of the Children and Young Persons Act (Northern Ireland) 1968 (indecent conduct towards child);
(*g*) any offence under Article 9 of the Criminal Justice (Northern Ireland) Order 1980 (inciting girl under 16 to have incestuous sexual intercourse);
(*h*) any offence under any of the following provisions of the Mental Health (Northern Ireland) Order 1986—
  (i) Article 122(1)(*a*) (unlawful sexual intercourse with a woman suffering from severe mental handicap);
  (ii) Article 122(1)(*b*) (procuring a woman suffering from severe mental handicap to have unlawful sexual intercourse);
  (iii) Article 123 (unlawful sexual intercourse by hospital staff, etc with a person receiving treatment for mental disorder);
(*hh*) any offence under any of the following provisions of the Criminal Justice (Northern Ireland) Order 2003—
  (i) Article 19 (buggery);
  (ii) Article 20 (assault with intent to commit buggery);
  (iii) Article 21 (indecent assault on a male);]
(*ha*) any offence under any of sections 15 to 21, 47 to 53, 57 to 59, 66, 67, 70 and 72 of the Sexual Offences Act 2003;
(*i*) any attempt to commit any of the offences mentioned in paragraphs (*a*) to (*ha*);
(*j*) any conspiracy to commit any of those offences;
(*k*) any incitement of another to commit any of those offences;
(*l*) aiding, abetting, counselling or procuring the commission of any of the offences mentioned in paragraphs (*a*) to (*i*) and (*k*).

(4) *Application to a service offence.*

[Sexual Offences (Amendment) Act 1992, s 2 as amended by the Criminal Justice and Public Order Act 1994, Sch 9, the Armed Forces Act 2001, Sch 6, the Youth Justice and Criminal Evidence Act 1999, s 48 and Sch 2, the Sexual Offences Act 2003, Sch 6, SI 2003/1247, the Armed Forces Act 2006, Sch 16 and the Modern Slavery Act 2015, Sch 5.]

7.10534 3. **Power to displace section 1** (1) If, before the commencement of a trial at which a person is charged with an offence to which this Act applies, he or another person against whom the complainant may be expected to give evidence at the trial, applies to the judge for a direction under this subsection and satisfies the judge—

(*a*) that the direction is required for the purpose of inducing persons who are likely to be needed as witnesses at the trial to come forward; and
(*b*) that the conduct of the applicant's defence at the trial is likely to be substantially prejudiced if the direction is not given,

the judge shall direct that section 1 shall not, by virtue of the accusation alleging the offence in question, apply in relation to the complainant.

(2) If at a trial the judge is satisfied—

(*a*) that the effect of section 1 is to impose a substantial and unreasonable restriction upon the reporting of proceedings at the trial, and

(*b*) that it is in the public interest to remove or relax the restriction,

he shall direct that that section shall not apply to such matter as is specified in the direction.

(3) A direction shall not be given under subsection (2) by reason only of the outcome of the trial.

(4) If a person who has been convicted of an offence and has given notice of appeal against the conviction, or notice of an application for leave so to appeal, applies to the appellate court for a direction under this subsection and satisfies the court—

(*a*) that the direction is required for the purpose of obtaining evidence in support of the appeal; and

(*b*) that the applicant is likely to suffer substantial injustice if the direction is not given,

the court shall direct that section 1 shall not, by virtue of an accusation which alleges an offence to which this Act applies and is specified in the direction, apply in relation to a complainant so specified.

(5) A direction given under any provision of this section does not affect the operation of section 1 at any time before the direction is given.

(6) In subsections (1) and (2), "judge" means—

(*a*) in the case of an offence which is to be tried summarily or for which the mode of trial has not been determined, any justice of the peace; and

(*b*) in any other case, any judge of the Crown Court in England and Wales.

(6A) In its application to Northern Ireland, this section has effect as if—

(*a*) in subsections (1) and (2) for any reference to the judge there were substituted a reference to the court; and

(*b*) subsection (6) were omitted.

(6B) Where a person is charged with an offence to which this Act applies by virtue of section 2(4), this section applies as if—

(*a*) in subsections (1) and (2) for any reference to the judge there were substituted a reference to the court; and

(*b*) subsections (6) and (6A) were omitted.

(7) If, after the commencement of a trial at which a person is charged with an offence to which this Act applies, a new trial of the person for that offence is ordered, the commencement of any previous trial shall be disregarded for the purposes of subsection (1).

[Sexual Offences (Amendment) Act 1992, s 3 as amended by the Youth Justice and Criminal Evidence Act 1999, s 48, Sch 2, SI 2005/886 and the Armed Forces Act 2006, Sch 16.]

**7.10535 4. Special rules for cases of incest or buggery** (1) In this section—

"section 10 offence" means an offence under section 10 of the Sexual Offences Act 1956 (incest by a man) or an attempt to commit that offence;

"section 11 offence" means an offence under section 11 of that Act (incest by a woman) or an attempt to commit that offence;

"section 12 offence" means an offence under section 12 of that Act (buggery) or an attempt to commit that offence.

(2) Section 1 does not apply to a woman against whom a section 10 offence is alleged to have been committed if she is accused of having committed a section 11 offence against the man who is alleged to have committed the section 10 offence against her.

(3) Section 1 does not apply to a man against whom a section 11 offence is alleged to have been committed if he is accused of having committed a section 10 offence against the woman who is alleged to have committed the section 11 offence against him.

(4) Section 1 does not apply to a person against whom a section 12 offence is alleged to have been committed if that person is accused of having committed a section 12 offence against the person who is alleged to have committed the section 12 offence against him.

(5) Subsection (2) does not affect the operation of this Act in relation to anything done at any time before the woman is accused.

(6) Subsection (3) does not affect the operation of this Act in relation to anything done at any time before the man is accused.

(7) Subsection (4) does not affect the operation of this Act in relation to anything done at any time before the person mentioned first in that subsection is accused.

(8) In its application to Northern Ireland, this section has effect as if—

(*a*) subsection (1) were omitted;

(*b*) for references to a section 10 offence there were substituted references to an offence under section 1 of the Punishment of Incest Act 1908 (incest by a man) or an attempt to commit that offence;

(*c*) for references to a section 11 offence there were substituted references to an offence under section 2 of that Act (incest by a woman) or an attempt to commit that offence; and

(*d*) for references to a section 12 offence there were substituted references to an offence under Article 19 of the Criminal Justice (Northern Ireland) Order 2003 (buggery) or an attempt to commit that offence.

(9) *Repealed.*

[Sexual Offences (Amendment) Act 1992, s 4 as amended by the Armed Forces Act 2001, Sch 6, the Youth Justice and Criminal Evidence Act 1999, Sch 2 and the Armed Forces Act 2006, Sch 17.]

7.10536 5. **Offences** (1) If any matter is included in a publication in contravention of section 1, the following persons shall be guilty of an offence and liable on summary conviction to a fine not exceeding **level 5** on the standard scale—

(*a*) where the publication is a newspaper or periodical, any proprietor, any editor and any publisher of the newspaper or periodical;

(*b*) where the publication is a relevant programme—

(i) any body corporate or Scottish partnership engaged in providing the programme service in which the programme is included; and

(ii) any person having functions in relation to the programme corresponding to those of an editor of a newspaper;

(*c*) in the case of any other publication, any person publishing it.

(2) Where a person is charged with an offence under this section in respect of the inclusion of any matter in a publication, it shall be a defence, subject to subsection (3), to prove that the publication in which the matter appeared was one in respect of which the person against whom the offence mentioned in section 1 is alleged to have been committed had given written consent to the appearance of matter of that description.

(3) Written consent is not a defence if it is proved that any person interfered unreasonably with the peace or comfort of the person giving the consent, with intent to obtain it, or that person was under the age of 16 at the time when it was given.

(4) Proceedings for an offence under this section shall not be instituted except by or with the consent of the Attorney General if the offence is alleged to have been committed in England and Wales or of the Attorney General for Northern Ireland if the offence is alleged to have been committed in Northern Ireland.

(5) Where a person is charged with an offence under this section it shall be a defence to prove that at the time of the alleged offence he was not aware, and neither suspected nor had reason to suspect, that the publication included the matter in question.

(5A) Where—

(*a*) a person is charged with an offence under this section, and

(*b*) the offence relates to the inclusion of any matter in a publication in contravention of section 1(1),

it shall be a defence to prove that at the time of the alleged offence he was not aware, and neither suspected nor had reason to suspect, that the allegation in question had been made.

(6) Where an offence under this section committed by a body corporate is proved to have been committed with the consent or connivance of, or to be attributable to any neglect on the part of—

(*a*) a director, manager, secretary or other similar officer of the body corporate, or

(*b*) a person purporting to act in any such capacity,

he as well as the body corporate shall be guilty of the offence and liable to be proceeded against and punished accordingly.

(7) In relation to a body corporate whose affairs are managed by its members "director", in subsection (6), means a member of the body corporate.

(8) Where an offence under this section is committed by a Scottish partnership and is proved to have been committed with the consent or connivance of a partner, he as well as the partnership shall be guilty of the offence and shall be liable to be proceeded against and punished accordingly.*

[Sexual Offences (Amendment) Act 1992, s 5 as amended by the Youth Justice and Criminal Evidence Act 1999, Sch 2.]

---

* **Section reproduced as amended by the Youth Justice and Criminal Evidence Act 1999 in force 7 October 2004 in England and Wales.**

7.10537 6. **Interpretation etc** (1) In this Act—

"complainant" has the meaning given in section 1(2);

"picture" includes a likeness however produced;

"publication" includes any speech, writing, relevant programme or other communication in whatever form, which is addressed to the public at large or any section of the public (and for this purpose every relevant programme shall be taken to be so addressed), but does not include an indictment or other document prepared for use in particular legal proceedings;

"relevant programme" means a programme included in a programme service, within the meaning of the Broadcasting Act 1990; and

(1A) Section 48 of the Armed Forces Act 2006 (attempts, conspiracy, encouragement and assistance and aiding and abetting outside England and Wales) applies for the purposes of this Act as if the reference in subsection (3)(*b*) of that section to any of the following provisions of that Act were a reference to any provision of this Act.

(2) For the purposes of this Act—

(*a*) where it is alleged that an offence to which this Act applies has been committed, the fact that any person has consented to an act which, on any prosecution for that offence, would fall to be proved by the prosecution, does not prevent that person from being regarded as a person against whom the alleged offence was committed; and

(*b*) where a person is accused of an offence of incest or buggery, the other party to the act in question shall be taken to be a person against whom the offence was committed even though he consented to that act.

(2A) For the purposes of this Act, where it is alleged or there is an accusation—

(*a*) that an offence of conspiracy or incitement of another to commit an offence mentioned in section 2(1)(*aa*) to (*d*) or (3)(*a*) to (*hh*) has been committed, or

(*b*) that an offence of aiding, abetting, counselling or procuring the commission of an offence of incitement of another to commit an offence mentioned in section 2(1)(*aa*) to (*d*) or (3)(*a*) to (*hh*) has been committed,

the person against whom the substantive offence is alleged to have been intended to be committed shall be regarded as the person against whom the conspiracy or incitement is alleged to have been committed.

In this subsection, "the substantive offence" means the offence to which the alleged conspiracy or incitement related.

(3) For the purposes of this Act, a person is accused of an offence, other than an offence under section 42 of the Armed Forces Act 2006, if—

(*a*) an information is laid, or, (in Northern Ireland) a complaint is made, alleging that he has committed the offence,

(*b*) he appears before a court charged with the offence,

(*c*) a court before which he is appearing sends him to the Crown Court for trial on a new charge alleging the offence, or

(*d*) a bill of indictment charging him with the offence is preferred before a court in which he may lawfully be indicted for the offence,

and references in subsection (2A) and in section 3 to an accusation alleging an offence shall be construed accordingly.

(3A) *Application to a service offence.*

(4) Nothing in this Act affects any prohibition or restriction imposed by virtue of any other enactment upon a publication or upon matter included in a relevant programme.

[Sexual Offences (Amendment) Act 1992, s 6 as amended by the Criminal Justice and Public Order Act 1994, Sch 9, the Youth Justice and Criminal Evidence Act 1999, s 48 and Sch 2, the Armed Forces Act 2001, Sch 6, the Criminal Justice Act 2003, Sch 3, SI 2003/1247, the Armed Forces Act 2006, Schs 16 and 17 and the Serious Crime Act 2007, Sch 5.]

# Sexual Offences Act 1993

(1993 c 30)

7.10538 **1. Abolition of presumption of sexual incapacity** The presumption of criminal law that a boy under the age of fourteen is incapable of sexual intercourse (whether natural or unnatural) is hereby abolished.

[Sexual Offences Act 1993, s 1.]

7.10539 **2. Short title, commencement and extent** (1) This Act may be cited as the Sexual Offences Act 1993.

(2) This Act shall come into force at the end of the period of two months beginning with the day on which it is passed.

(3) This Act does not apply to acts done before its commencement.

(4) This Act extends to England and Wales only.

[Sexual Offences Act 1993, s 2.]

# Sexual Offences (Conspiracy and Incitement) Act 1996[1]

(1996 c 29)

*England and Wales and Northern Ireland*

7.10540 **2. Incitement to commit certain sexual acts outside the United Kingdom**

(1) This section applies where—

(*a*) any act done by a person in England and Wales would amount to the offence of incitement to commit a listed sexual offence but for the fact that what he had in view would not be an offence triable in England and Wales,

(*b*) the whole or part of what he had in view was intended to take place in a country or territory outside the United Kingdom, and

(*c*) what he had in view would involve the commission of an offence under the law in force in that country or territory.

(2) Where this section applies—

(*a*) what he had in view is to be treated as that listed sexual offence for the purposes of any charge of incitement brought in respect of that act, and

(*b*) any such charge is accordingly triable in England and Wales.

(3) Any act done by means of a message (however communicated) is to be treated as done in England and Wales if the message is sent or received in England and Wales.

[Sexual Offences (Conspiracy and Incitement) Act 1996, s 2 as amended by the Serious Crime Act 2007, Sch 6.]

[1] The Sexual Offences (Conspiracy and Incitement) Act 1996 was brought into force on 1 October 1996 by the Sexual Offences (Conspiracy and Incitement) Act 1996 (Commencement) Order 1996, SI 1996/2262.

7.10541 **3. Sections 1 and 2: supplementary** (1) Conduct punishable under the law in force in any country or territory is an offence under the law for the purposes of section 2, however it is described in that law.

(2) Subject to subsection (3), a condition in section 2(1)(*c*) is to be taken to be satisfied unless, not later than rules of court may provide, the defence serve on the prosecution a notice—

(*a*) stating that, on the facts as alleged with respect to what the accused had in view, the condition is not in their opinion satisfied,

(*b*) showing their grounds for that opinion, and

(*c*) requiring the prosecution to show that it is satisfied.

(3) *Repealed.*

(4) The court, if it thinks fit, may permit the defence to require the prosecution to show that the condition is satisfied without the prior service of a notice under subsection (2).

(5) In the Crown Court the question whether the condition is satisfied is to be decided by the judge alone.

(6) In any proceedings in respect of any offence triable by virtue of section 2, it is immaterial to guilt whether or not the accused was a British citizen at the time of any act or other event proof of which is required for conviction of the offence.

(7) *Repealed.*

(8) References to an offence of incitement to commit a listed sexual offence include an offence triable in England and Wales as such an incitement by virtue of section 2 (without prejudice to subsection (2) of that section).

(9) Subsection (8) applies to references in any enactment, instrument or document (except those in section 2 of this Act and in Part I of the Criminal Law Act 1977).

[Sexual Offences (Conspiracy and Incitement) Act 1996, s 3 as amended by the Criminal Justice (Terrorism and Conspiracy) Act 1998, Schs 1 and 2.]

7.10542 **5. Interpretation** In this Act "listed sexual offence" has the meaning given by the Schedule.

[Sexual Offences (Conspiracy and Incitement) Act 1996, s 5.]

*General*

7.10543 **7. Short title, commencement and extent** (1) This Act may be cited as the Sexual Offences (Conspiracy and Incitement) Act 1996.

(2) This Act is to come into force on such day as the Secretary of State may by order made by statutory instrument appoint[1], and different days may be appointed for different purposes and for different areas.

(3) Nothing in section 2 or 6 applies to any act or other event occurring before the coming into force of that section.

(4) This Act, except sections 4 and 6, extends to England and Wales.

(5) Section 6 and this section extend to Scotland.

(6) This Act, except section 6, extends to Northern Ireland.

[Sexual Offences (Conspiracy and Incitement) Act 1996, s 7 as amended by the Criminal Justice (Terrorism and Conspiracy) Act 1998, Schs 1 and 2.]

[1] As to commencement, see note 1 to the short title of this Act, ante.

SCHEDULE

LISTED SEXUAL OFFENCES

Section 5

*(Amended by the Sexual Offences Act 2003, Sch 6.)*

*England and Wales*

7.10544 **1.** (1) In relation to England and Wales, the following are listed sexual offences:

(*a*) *repealed*

(*b*) an offence under any of sections 1 to 12, 14 and 15 to 26 of the Sexual Offences Act 2003.

(2) Sub-paragraph (1)(*b*) does not apply where the victim of the offence has attained the age of sixteen years.

**2.** *Northern Ireland.*

# Sexual Offences (Protected Material) Act 1997[1]

(1997 c 39)

*Introductory*

7.10546 **1. Meaning of "protected material"** (1) In this Act "protected material", in relation to proceedings for a sexual offence, means a copy (in whatever form) of any of the following material, namely—

(*a*) a statement relating to that or any other sexual offence made by any victim of the offence (whether the statement is recorded in writing or in any other form),

(*b*) a photograph or pseudo-photograph of any such victim, or

(*c*) a report of a medical examination of the physical condition of any such victim, which is a copy given by the prosecutor to any person under this Act.

(2) For the purposes of subsection (1) a person is, in relation to any proceedings for a sexual offence, a victim of that offence if—

(*a*) the charge, summons or indictment by which the proceedings are instituted names that person as a person in relation to whom that offence was committed; or

(*b*) that offence can, in the prosecutor's opinion, be reasonably regarded as having been committed in relation to that person;

and a person is, in relation to any such proceedings, a victim of any other sexual offence if that offence can, in the prosecutor's opinion, be reasonably regarded as having been committed in relation to that person.

(3) In this Act, where the context so permits (and subject to subsection (4))—

(*a*) references to any protected material include references to any part of any such material; and

(*b*) references to a copy of any such material include references to any part of any such copy.

(4) Nothing in this Act—

(*a*) so far as it refers to a defendant making any copy of—

(i) any protected material, or

(ii) a copy of any such material,

applies to a manuscript copy which is not a verbatim copy of the whole of that material or copy; or

(*b*) so far as it refers to a defendant having in his possession any copy of any protected material, applies to a manuscript copy made by him which is not a verbatim copy of the whole of that material.

[Sexual Offences (Protected Material) Act 1997, s 1.]

[1] This Act is to be brought into force in accordance with orders made under s 11. At the date of going to press no commencement order has been made.

7.10547 2. **Meaning of other expressions** (1) In this Act

"contracted out prison" means a contracted out prison within the meaning of Part IV of the Criminal Justice Act 1991;

"defendant", in relation to any proceedings for a sexual offence, means any person charged with that offence (whether or not he has been convicted);

"governor", in relation to a contracted out prison, means the director of the prison;

"inform" means inform in writing;

"legal representative", in relation to a defendant, means a person who, for the purposes of the Legal Services Act 2007, is an authorised person in relation to an activity which constitutes the exercise of a right of audience or the conduct of litigation (within the meaning of that Act) and who is acting for the defendant in connection with any proceedings for the sexual offence in question;

"photograph" and "pseudo-photograph" shall be construed in accordance with section 7(4) and (7) of the Protection of Children Act 1978;

"prison" means any prison, young offender institution or remand centre which is under the general superintendence of, or is provided by, the Secretary of State under the Prison Act 1952, including a contracted out prison;*

"proceedings" means (subject to subsection (2)) criminal proceedings;

"the prosecutor", in relation to any proceedings for a sexual offence, means any person acting as prosecutor (whether an individual or a body);

"relevant proceedings", in relation to any material which has been disclosed by the prosecutor under this Act, means any proceedings for the purposes of which it has been so disclosed or any further proceedings for the sexual offence in question;

"sexual offence" means one of the offences listed in the Schedule to this Act.

(2) For the purposes of this Act references to proceedings for a sexual offence include references to—

(*a*) any appeal or application for leave to appeal brought or made by or in relation to a defendant in such proceedings;

(*b*) any application made to the Criminal Cases Review Commission for the reference under section 9 or 11 of the Criminal Appeal Act 1995 of any conviction, verdict, finding or sentence recorded or imposed in relation to any such defendant; and

(*c*) any petition to the Secretary of State requesting him to recommend the exercise of Her Majesty's prerogative of mercy in relation to any such defendant.

(3) In this Act, in the context of the prosecutor giving a copy of any material to any person—

(*a*) references to the prosecutor include references to a person acting on behalf of the prosecutor; and

(*b*) where any such copy falls to be given to the defendant's legal representative, references to the defendant's legal representative include references to a person acting on behalf of the defendant's legal representative.

[Sexual Offences (Protected Material) Act 1997, s 2 as amended by the Legal Services Act 2007, Sch 21.]

* **Amended by the Criminal Justice and Court Services Act 2000, Sch 7 from a date to be appointed.**

*Regulation of disclosures to defendant*

7.10548 **3. Regulation of disclosures by prosecutor** (1) Where, in connection with any proceedings for a sexual offence, any statement or other material falling within any of paragraphs (*a*) to (*c*) of section 1(1) would (apart from this section) fall to be disclosed by the prosecutor to the defendant—

(*a*) the prosecutor shall not disclose that material to the defendant; and

(*b*) it shall instead be disclosed under this Act in accordance with whichever of subsection (2) and (3) below is applicable.

(2) If—

(*a*) the defendant has a legal representative, and

(*b*) the defendant's legal representative gives the prosecutor the undertaking required by section 4 (disclosure to defendant's legal representative),

the prosecutor shall disclose the material in question by giving a copy of it to the defendant's legal representative.

(3) If subsection (2) is not applicable, the prosecutor shall disclose the material in question by giving a copy of it to the appropriate person for the purposes of section 5 (disclosure to unrepresented defendant) in order for that person to show that copy to the defendant under that section.

(4) Where under this Act a copy of any material falls to be given to any person by the prosecutor, any such copy—

(*a*) may be in such form as the prosecutor thinks fit, and

(*b*) where the material consists of information which has been recorded in any form, need not be in the same form as that in which the information has already been recorded.

(5) Once a copy of any material is given to any person under this Act by the prosecutor, the copy shall (in accordance with section 1(1)) be protected material for the purposes of this Act.

[Sexual Offences (Protected Material) Act 1997, s 3.]

7.10549 **4. Disclosure to defendant's legal representative** (1) For the purposes of this Act the undertaking which a defendant's legal representative is required to give in relation to any protected material given to him under this Act is an undertaking by him to discharge the obligations set out in subsections (2) to (7).

(2) He must take reasonable steps to ensure—

(*a*) that the protected material, or any copy of it, is only shown to the defendant in circumstances where it is possible to exercise adequate supervision to prevent the defendant retaining possession of the material or copy or making a copy of it, and

(*b*) that the protected material is not shown and no copy of it is given, and its contents are not otherwise revealed, to any person other than the defendant, except so far as it appears to him necessary to show the material or give a copy of it to any such person—

(i) in connection with any relevant proceedings, or

(ii) for the purposes of any assessment or treatment of the defendant (whether before or after conviction).

(3) He must inform the defendant—

(*a*) that the protected material is such material for the purposes of this Act,

(*b*) that the defendant can only inspect that material, or any copy of it, in circumstances such as are described in subsection (2)(*a*), and

(*c*) that it would be an offence for the defendant—

(i) to have material, or any copy of it, in his possession otherwise than while inspecting it or the copy in such circumstances, or

(ii) to give that material or any copy of it, or otherwise reveal its contents, to any other person.

(4) He must, where the protected material or a copy of it has been shown or given in accordance with subsection (2)(*b*)(i) or (ii) to a person other than the defendant, inform that person—

(*a*) that that person must not give any copy of that material, or otherwise reveal its contents—

(i) to any other person other than the defendant, or

(ii) to the defendant otherwise than in circumstances such as are described in subsection (2)(*a*); and

(*b*) that it would be an offence for that person to do so.

(5) He must, where he ceases to act as the defendant's legal representative at a time when any relevant proceedings are current or in contemplation—

(*a*) inform the prosecutor of that fact, and

(*b*) if he is informed by the prosecutor that the defendant has a new legal representative who has given the prosecutor the undertaking required by this section, give the protected material, and any copies of it in his possession, to the defendant's new legal representative.

(6) He must, at the time of giving the protected material to the new legal representative under subsection (5), inform that person—

(*a*) that that material is protected material for the purposes of this Act, and

(*b*) of the extent to which—

(i) that material has been shown by him, and

(ii) any copies of it have been given by him,

to any other person (including the defendant).

(7) He must keep a record of every occasion on which the protected material was shown, or a copy of it was given, as mentioned in subsection (6)(*b*).

[Sexual Offences (Protected Material) Act 1997, s 4.]

**7.10550** **5. Disclosure to unrepresented defendant** (1) This section applies where, in accordance with section 3(3), a copy of any material falls to be given by the prosecutor to the appropriate person for the purposes of this section in order for that person to show that copy to the defendant under this section.

(2) Subject to subsection (3), the appropriate person in such a case is—

(*a*) if the defendant is detained in a prison, the governor of the prison or any person nominated by the governor for the purposes of this section; and

(*b*) otherwise the officer in charge of such police station as appears to the prosecutor to be suitable for enabling the defendant to have access to the material in accordance with this section or any person nominated by that officer for the purposes of this section.

(3) The Secretary of State may by regulations provide that, in such circumstances as are specified in the regulations, the appropriate person for the purposes of this section shall be a person of any description so specified.

(4) The appropriate person shall take reasonable steps to ensure—

(*a*) that the protected material, or any copy of it, is only shown to the defendant in circumstances where it is possible to exercise adequate supervision to prevent the defendant retaining possession of the material or copy or making a copy of it,

(*b*) that, subject to paragraph (*a*), the defendant is given such access to that material, or a copy of it, as he reasonably requires in connection with any relevant proceedings, and

(*c*) that that material is not shown and no copy of it is given, and its contents are not otherwise revealed, to any person other than the defendant.

(5) The prosecutor shall, at the time of giving the protected material to the appropriate person, inform him—

(*a*) that that material is protected material for the purposes of this Act, and

(*b*) that he is required to discharge the obligations set out in subsection (4) in relation to that material.

(6) The prosecutor shall at that time also inform the defendant—

(*a*) that that material is protected material for the purposes of this Act,

(*b*) that the defendant can only inspect that material, or any copy of it, in circumstances such as are described in subsection (4)(*a*), and

(*c*) that it would be an offence for the defendant—

(i) to have that material, or any copy of it, in his possession otherwise than while inspecting it or the copy in such circumstances, or

(ii) to give that material or any copy of it, or otherwise reveal its contents, to any other person,

as well as inform him of the effect of subsection (7).

(7) If—

(*a*) the defendant requests the prosecutor in writing to give a further copy of the material mentioned in subsection (1) to some other person, and

(*b*) it appears to the prosecutor to be necessary to do so—

(i) in connection with any relevant proceedings, or

(ii) for the purposes of any assessment or treatment of the defendant (whether before or after conviction),

the prosecutor shall give such a copy to that other person.

(8) The prosecutor may give such a copy to some other person where no request has been made under subsection (7) but it appears to him that in the interests of the defendant it is necessary to do so as mentioned in paragraph (*b*) of that subsection.

(9) The prosecutor shall, at the time of giving such a copy to a person under subsection (7) or (8), inform that person—

(*a*) that the copy is protected material for the purposes of this Act,

(*b*) that he must not give any copy of the protected material or otherwise reveal its contents—

(i) to any person other than the defendant, or

(ii) to the defendant otherwise than in circumstances such as are described in subsection (4)(*a*); and (*c*) that it would be an offence for him to do so.

(10) If the prosecutor—

(*a*) receives a request from the defendant under subsection (7) to give a further copy of the material in question to another person, but

(*b*) does not consider it to be necessary to do so as mentioned in paragraph (*b*) of that subsection and accordingly refuses the request,

he shall inform the defendant of his refusal.

(11) Any regulations under subsection (3) shall be made by statutory instrument subject to annulment in pursuance of a resolution of either House of Parliament.

[Sexual Offences (Protected Material) Act 1997, s 5.]

7.10551 6. **Further disclosures by prosecutor** (1) Where—

(*a*) any material has been disclosed in accordance with section 3(2) to the defendant's legal representative, and

(*b*) at a time when any relevant proceedings are current or in contemplation the legal representative either—

(i) ceases to act as the defendant's legal representative in circumstances where section 4(5)(*b*) does not apply, or

(ii) dies or becomes incapacitated,

that material shall be further disclosed under this Act in accordance with whichever of section 3(2) or (3) is for the time being applicable.

(2) Where—

(*a*) any material has been disclosed in accordance with section 3(3), and

(*b*) at a time when any relevant proceedings are current or in contemplation the defendant acquires a legal representative who gives the prosecutor the undertaking required by section 4,

that material shall be further disclosed under this Act, in accordance with section 3(2), to the defendant's legal representative.

[Sexual Offences (Protected Material) Act 1997, s 6.]

7.10552 7. *Regulation of disclosures by Criminal Cases Review Commission.*

*Supplementary*

7.10553 8. **Offences** (1) Where any material has been disclosed under this Act in connection with any proceedings for a sexual offence, it is an offence for the defendant—

(*a*) to have the protected material, or any copy of it, in his possession otherwise than while inspecting it or the copy in circumstances such as are described in section 4(2)(*a*) or 5(4)(*a*), or

(*b*) to give that material or any copy of it, or otherwise reveal its contents, to any other person.

(2) Where any protected material, or any copy of any such material, has been shown or given to any person in accordance with section 4(2)(*b*)(i) or (ii) or section 5(7) or (8), it is an offence for that person to give any copy of that material or otherwise reveal its contents—

(*a*) to any person other than the defendant, or

(*b*) to the defendant otherwise than in circumstances such as are described in section 4(2)(*a*) or 5(4)(*a*).

(3) Subsections (1) and (2) apply whether or not any relevant proceedings are current or in contemplation (and references to the defendant shall be construed accordingly).

(4) A person guilty of an offence under this section is liable[1]—

(*a*) on summary conviction, to imprisonment for a term not exceeding **six months** or a fine not exceeding the **statutory maximum** or **both**;

(*b*) on conviction on indictment, to imprisonment for a term not exceeding **two years** or a **fine** or **both**.

(5) Where a person is charged with an offence under this section relating to any protected material or copy of any such material, it is a defence to prove that, at the time of the alleged offence, he was not aware, and neither suspected nor had reason to suspect, that the material or copy in question was protected material or (as the case may be) a copy of any such material.

(6) The court before which a person is tried for an offence under this section may (whether or not he is convicted of that offence) make an order requiring him to return any protected material, or any copy of any such material, in his possession to the prosecutor.

(7) Nothing in subsection (1) or (2) shall be taken to apply to—

(*a*) any disclosure made in the course of any proceedings before a court or in any report of any such proceedings, or

(*b*) any disclosure made or copy given by a person when returning any protected material, or a copy of any such material, to the prosecutor or the defendant's legal representative;

and accordingly nothing in section 4 or 5 shall be read as precluding the making of any disclosure or the giving of any copy in circumstances falling within paragraph (*a*) or (as the case may be) paragraph (*b*) above.

[Sexual Offences (Protected Material) Act 1997, s 8.]

[1] For procedure in respect of this offence which is triable either way, see the Magistrates' Courts Act 1980, ss 17A–21, in PART I: MAGISTRATES' COURTS, PROCEDURE, ante.

7.10554 9. *Modification and amendment of other enactments.*

7.10555 10. *Financial provision.*

7.10556 11. **Short title, commencement and extent** (1) *Short title.*

(2) This Act shall come into force on such day as the Secretary of State may appoint by order[1] made by statutory instrument.

(3) Nothing in this Act applies to any proceedings for a sexual offence where the defendant was charged with the offence before the commencement of this Act.

(4) This Act extends to England and Wales only.

[Sexual Offences (Protected Material) Act 1997, s 11.]

[1] As to commencement, see note 1 to the short title of this Act, ante.

SCHEDULE

SEXUAL OFFENCES FOR PURPOSES OF THIS ACT — Section 2(1)

*(As amended by the Sexual Offences Act 2003, Sch 7.)*

7.10557 1–4. *Repealed.*

5. Any offence under section 1 of the Protection of Children Act 1978 or section 160 of the Criminal Justice Act 1988 (indecent photographs of children).

5A. Any offence under any provision of Part 1 of the Sexual Offences Act 2003 except section 64, 65, 69 or 71.

6. Any offence under section 1 of the Criminal Law Act 1977 of conspiracy to commit any of the offences mentioned in paragraphs 5 and 5A.

7. Any offence under section 1 of the Criminal Attempts Act 1981 of attempting to commit any of those offences.

8. Any offence of inciting another to commit any of those offences.

# Sexual Offences Act 2003[1]

(2003 c 42)

## PART 1[2]

## SEXUAL OFFENCES

*Rape*

7.10563 1. **Rape** (1) A person (A) commits an offence[3] if—

(*a*) he intentionally penetrates[4] the vagina[4], anus or mouth of another person (B) with his penis,

(*b*) B does not consent[5] to the penetration, and

(*c*) A does not reasonably[6] believe that B consents.

(2) Whether a belief is reasonable is to be determined having regard to all the circumstances, including any steps A has taken to ascertain whether B consents.

(3) Sections 75[7] and 76[8] apply to an offence under this section.

(4) A person guilty of an offence under this section is liable, on conviction on indictment, to imprisonment for life.

[Sexual Offences Act 2003, s 1.]

[1] This Act, with the exception of ss 138, 141, 142 and 143 which came into force on Royal Assent (20 November 2003), is to be brought into force in accordance with commencement orders made under s 141, post. The Sexual Offences Act 2003 (Commencement) Order 2004, SI 2004/874 brought the remaining provisions into force on 1 May 2004. For continuity of sexual offences law, see the Violent Crime Reduction Act 2006, s 55, in this title, post.

[2] Part 1 comprises ss 1–79 and Schs 1 and 2.

[3] This section creates one offence of rape which is described in s 1(1)(*a*), it is therefore not duplicitous to charge alleged rape by "penetrating the complainant vaginally or anally": *R v K (Robert)* [2008] EWCA Crim 1923, [2009] 1 Cr App R 24.

[4] For "penetration" and "vagina", see s 79, post.

[5] For "consent", see s 74, post.

[6] As to the relevance of mental illness, see *R v Braham* [2013] EWCA Crim 3, [2013] 1 Cr App Rep 481, [2014] Crim LR 312. A genuine belief in consent is not enough. Unless the state of mind amounts to insanity in law, beliefs in consent arising from conditions such as delusional psychotic illness or personality disorders had to be judged by objective standards of reasonableness and not by taking into account a mental disorder which induced a belief which could not reasonably arise without it.

[7] Evidential presumptions about consent, post.

[8] Conclusive presumptions about consent, post.

*Assault*

7.10564 2. **Assault by penetration** (1) A person (A) commits an offence if—

(*a*) he intentionally penetrates[1] the vagina[1] or anus of another person (B) with a part of his body[1] or anything else,

(*b*) the penetration is sexual[2],

(*c*) B does not consent[3] to the penetration, and

(*d*) A does not reasonably believe that B consents.

(2) Whether a belief is reasonable is to be determined having regard to all the circumstances, including any steps A has taken to ascertain whether B consents.

(3) Sections 75[4] and 76[5] apply to an offence under this section.

(4) A person guilty of an offence under this section is liable, on conviction on indictment, to imprisonment for life.

[Sexual Offences Act 2003, s 2.]

1 For "penetration", "vagina" and "part of his body" see s 79, post.
2 For "sexual", see s 78, post.
3 For "consent", see s 74, post.
4 Evidential presumptions about consent, post.
5 Conclusive presumptions about consent, post.

7.10565 3. **Sexual assault** (1) A person (A) commits an offence if—

(*a*) he intentionally[1] touches[2] another person (B),

(*b*) the touching is sexual[3],

(*c*) B does not consent[4] to the touching, and

(*d*) A does not reasonably believe that B consents.

(2) Whether a belief is reasonable is to be determined having regard to all the circumstances, including any steps A has taken to ascertain whether B consents.

(3) Sections 75[5] and 76[6] apply to an offence under this section.

(4) A person guilty of an offence under this section is liable[7]—

(*a*) on summary conviction, to imprisonment for a term not exceeding 6 months or a fine not exceeding the statutory maximum or both;

(*b*) on conviction on indictment, to imprisonment for a term not exceeding 10 years.

[Sexual Offences Act 2003, s 3.]

1 If, whether intoxicated or otherwise, the touching is unintentional the offence is not committed. Thus, to flail about resulting in unintended touching, objectively sexual, does not make out the offence. However, the offence under s 3 is not an offence of "specific intent", since purpose is not an element that falls under consideration. Therefore, voluntary intoxication preventing the defendant from intending to touch is not available as a defence: *R v Heard* [2007] EWCA Crim 125, [2008] QB 43, [2007] 3 All ER 306, [2007] 3 WLR 475, [2007] 1 Cr App R 37.
2 For "touching", see s 79, post.
3 For "sexual", see s 78, post.
4 For "consent", see s 74, post.
5 Evidential presumptions about consent, post.
6 Conclusive presumptions about consent, post.
7 For procedure in respect of this offence which is triable either way, see the Magistrates' Courts Act 1980, ss 17A–21 in PART I: MAGISTRATES' COURTS, PROCEDURE, ante.

*Causing sexual activity without consent*

7.10566 4. **Causing a person to engage in sexual activity without consent** (1) A person (A) commits an offence if—

(*a*) he intentionally causes another person (B) to engage in an activity,

(*b*) the activity is sexual[1],

(*c*) B does not consent[2] to engaging in the activity, and

(*d*) A does not reasonably believe that B consents.

(2) Whether a belief is reasonable is to be determined having regard to all the circumstances, including any steps A has taken to ascertain whether B consents.

(3) Sections 75[3] and 76[4] apply to an offence under this section.

(4) A person guilty of an offence under this section, if the activity caused involved—

(*a*) penetration[6] of B's anus or vagina[5],

(*b*) penetration of B's mouth with a person's penis,

(*c*) penetration of a person's anus or vagina with a part of B's body or by B with anything else, or

(*d*) penetration of a person's mouth with B's penis,

is liable, on conviction on indictment, to imprisonment for life.

(5) Unless subsection (4) applies, a person guilty of an offence under this section is liable[6]—

(*a*) on summary conviction, to imprisonment for a term not exceeding 6 months or to a fine not exceeding the statutory maximum or both;

(*b*) on conviction on indictment, to imprisonment for a term not exceeding 10 years.

[Sexual Offences Act 2003, s 4.]

1 For "sexual", see s 78, post.
2 For "consent", see s 74, post.
3 Evidential presumptions about consent, post.
4 Conclusive presumptions about consent, post.
5 For "penetration" and "vagina", see s 79, post.
6 For procedure in respect of this offence which is triable either way, see the Magistrates' Courts Act 1980, ss 17A–21 in PART I: MAGISTRATES' COURTS, PROCEDURE, ante.

*Rape and other offences against children under 13*

7.10567 **5. Rape of a child under 13**[1] (1) A person commits an offence if—

(*a*) he intentionally penetrates[2] the vagina[2], anus or mouth of another person with his penis, and

(*b*) the other person is under 13.

(2) A person guilty of an offence under this section is liable, on conviction on indictment, to imprisonment for life.

[Sexual Offences Act 2003, s 5.]

[1] Section 5 creates an offence of absolute liability in these in that all that need be proved is the intentional penetration of a child under the age of 13; this is not incompatible with art 6(2) of the ECHR since art 6(2) is not concerned with the mental or other elements of offences: *R v G* [2008] UKHL 37, [2009] 1 AC 32, [2008] 3 All ER 1071, [2008] 1 WLR 1379, [2008] Crim LR 818, [2009] 1 Cr App R 8. Where the agreed facts bring a s 5 case within the scope of s 13, it is not incompatible with the child defendant's rights under art 8 to convict him under the former provision: *R v G* (supra).

[2] For "penetration" and "vagina", see s 79, post.

7.10568 **6. Assault of a child under 13 by penetration** (1) A person commits an offence if—

(*a*) he intentionally penetrates[1] the vagina[1] or anus of another person with a part of his body[1] or anything else,

(*b*) the penetration is sexual[2], and

(*c*) the other person is under 13.

(2) A person guilty of an offence under this section is liable, on conviction on indictment, to imprisonment for life.

[Sexual Offences Act 2003, s 6.]

[1] For "penetration", "vagina" and "part of his body", see s 79, post.

[2] For "sexual", see s 78, post.

7.10569 **7. Sexual assault of a child under 13** (1) A person commits an offence if—

(*a*) he intentionally touches another person,

(*b*) the touching[1] is sexual[2], and

(*c*) the other person is under 13.

(2) A person guilty of an offence under this section is liable[3]—

(*a*) on summary conviction, to imprisonment for a term not exceeding 6 months or a fine not exceeding the statutory maximum or both;

(*b*) on conviction on indictment, to imprisonment for a term not exceeding 14 years.

[Sexual Offences Act 2003, s 7.]

[1] For "touching", see s 79, post.

[2] For "sexual", see s 78, post.

[3] For procedure in respect of this offence which is triable either way, see the Magistrates' Courts Act 1980, ss 17A–21 in PART I: MAGISTRATES' COURTS, PROCEDURE, ante.

7.10570 **8. Causing or inciting a child under 13 to engage in sexual activity** (1) A person commits an offence if—

(*a*) he intentionally causes or incites[1] another person[2] (B) to engage in an activity,

(*b*) the activity is sexual[3], and

(*c*) B is under 13.

(2) A person guilty of an offence under this section, if the activity caused or incited involved—

(*a*) penetration[4] of B's anus or vagina,

(*b*) penetration of B's mouth with a person's penis,

(*c*) penetration of a person's anus or vagina[4] with a part of B's body[4] or by B with anything else, or

(*d*) penetration of a person's mouth with B's penis,

is liable, on conviction on indictment, to imprisonment for life.

(3) Unless subsection (2) applies, a person guilty of an offence under this section is liable[5]—

(*a*) on summary conviction, to imprisonment for a term not exceeding 6 months or to a fine not exceeding the statutory maximum or both;

(*b*) on conviction on indictment, to imprisonment for a term not exceeding 14 years.

[Sexual Offences Act 2003, s 8.]

[1] The following propositions are derived from the case of *R v Grout* [2011] EWCA Crim 299, 175 JP 209, [2011] 1 Cr App R 38, [2011] Crim L R 584:

(1) Section 8(1) creates two basic offences. The first is intentionally causing a child to engage in sexual activity. The second is intentionally inciting a child to engage in sexual activity. Intentional incitement means the intentional seeking by encouragement or persuasion to bring something about, namely the child engaging in sexual activity, though it is unnecessary to prove that the defendant intended that sexual activity should take place.

(2) The offences are not concerned with whether the defendant engages in sexual activity.

(3) There is no definition of "activity". (For the purposes of the appeal it was accepted that it could embrace conversation or text or other messages.)

(4) The questions to be considered when deciding whether or not a particular "activity" is "sexual" were set out in *R v H* [2005] EWCA Crim 732, [2005] 2 All ER 859, [2005] 1 WLR 2005, [2005] 2 Cr App R 9 (see para 7.10640, post).

(5) Because s 8 creates two, if not four (by reason of the higher penalties prescribed for cases within s 8(2)), offences a charge must be drawn with particular care to avoid duplicity.

2 The offence under s 8 can be committed by a person who, with the requisite intention, makes a statement which in specific terms directly incites a child or children under the age of 13 to engage in sexual activity; it does not matter that it is not possible to identify any specific or identifiable person to whom the statement was addressed: *R v Jones* [2007] EWCA Crim 1118, [2008] QB 460, [2007] 4 All ER 112, [2007] 3 WLR 907, [2007] 2 Cr App Rep 267 (where the defendant left explicit messages on trains, etc, seeking girls aged between 8 and 13 for sex, offering payment and including a contact text number).

3 For "sexual", see s 78, post.

4 For "penetration", "vagina" and "part of his body", see s 79, post.

5 For procedure in respect of this offence which is triable either way, see the Magistrates' Courts Act 1980, ss 17A–21 in PART I: MAGISTRATES' COURTS, PROCEDURE, ante.

*Child sex offences*

7.10571 **9. Sexual activity with a child** (1) A person aged 18 or over (A) commits an offence if—

(*a*) he intentionally touches[1] another person (B),

(*b*) the touching is sexual[2], and

(*c*) either—

(i) B is under 16 and A does not reasonably believe that B is 16 or over, or

(ii) B is under 13.

(2) A person guilty of an offence under this section, if the touching involved—

(*a*) penetration[3] of B's anus or vagina[3] with a part of A's body[3] or anything else,

(*b*) penetration of B's mouth with A's penis,

(*c*) penetration of A's anus or vagina with a part of B's body, or

(*d*) penetration of A's mouth with B's penis,

is liable, on conviction on indictment, to imprisonment for a term not exceeding 14 years.

(3) Unless subsection (2) applies, a person guilty of an offence under this section is liable[4]—

(*a*) on summary conviction, to imprisonment for a term not exceeding 6 months or to a fine not exceeding the statutory maximum or both;

(*b*) on conviction on indictment, to imprisonment for a term not exceeding 14 years.

[Sexual Offences Act 2003, s 9.]

1 For "touching", see s 79, post.

2 For "sexual", see s 78, post.

3 For "penetration", "vagina" and "part of his body", see s 79, post.

4 For procedure in respect of this offence which is triable either way, see the Magistrates' Courts Act 1980, ss 17A–21 in PART I: MAGISTRATES' COURTS, PROCEDURE, ante.

7.10572 **10. Causing or inciting a child to engage in sexual activity** (1) A person aged 18 or over (A) commits an offence if—

(*a*) he intentionally causes or incites another person (B) to engage in an activity,

(*b*) the activity is sexual[1], and

(*c*) either—

(i) B is under 16 and A does not reasonably believe that B is 16 or over, or

(ii) B is under 13.

(2) A person guilty of an offence under this section, if the activity caused or incited involved—

(*a*) penetration[3] of B's anus or vagina[2],

(*b*) penetration of B's mouth with a person's penis,

(*c*) penetration of a person's anus or vagina with a part of B's body[2] or by B with anything else, or

(*d*) penetration of a person's mouth with B's penis,

is liable, on conviction on indictment, to imprisonment for a term not exceeding 14 years.

(3) Unless subsection (2) applies, a person guilty of an offence under this section is liable[3]—

(*a*) on summary conviction, to imprisonment for a term not exceeding 6 months or to a fine not exceeding the statutory maximum or both;

(*b*) on conviction on indictment, to imprisonment for a term not exceeding 14 years.

[Sexual Offences Act 2003, s 10.]

1 For "sexual", see s 78, post.

2 For "penetration", "vagina" and "part of his body", see s 79, post.

3 For procedure in respect of this offence which is triable either way, see the Magistrates' Courts Act 1980, ss 17A–21 in PART I: MAGISTRATES' COURTS, PROCEDURE, ante.

7.10573 **11. Engaging in sexual activity in the presence of a child** (1) A person aged 18 or over (A) commits an offence if—

(*a*) he intentionally engages in an activity,

(*b*) the activity is sexual[1],

(*c*) for the purpose of obtaining sexual gratification, he engages in it—

(i) when another person (B) is present or is in a place from which A can be observed, and

(ii) knowing or believing that B is aware, or intending that B should be aware, that he is engaging in it, and

(*d*) either—

(i) B is under 16 and A does not reasonably believe that B is 16 or over, or

(ii) B is under 13.

(2) A person guilty of an offence under this section is liable[2]—

(*a*) on summary conviction, to imprisonment for a term not exceeding 6 months or a fine not exceeding the statutory maximum or both;

(*b*) on conviction on indictment, to imprisonment for a term not exceeding 10 years.

[Sexual Offences Act 2003, s 11.]

---

1 For "sexual", see s 78, post.

2 For procedure in respect of this offence which is triable either way, see the Magistrates' Courts Act 1980, ss 17A–21 in PART I: MAGISTRATES' COURTS, PROCEDURE, ante.

7.10574 **12. Causing a child to watch a sexual act** (1) A person aged 18 or over (A) commits an offence if—

(*a*) for the purpose of obtaining sexual gratification[1], he intentionally causes another person (B) to watch a third person engaging in an activity, or to look at an image[2] of any person engaging in an activity,

(*b*) the activity is sexual[3], and

(*c*) either—

(i) B is under 16 and A does not reasonably believe that B is 16 or over, or

(ii) B is under 13.

(2) A person guilty of an offence under this section is liable[4]—

(*a*) on summary conviction, to imprisonment for a term not exceeding 6 months or a fine not exceeding the statutory maximum or both;

(*b*) on conviction on indictment, to imprisonment for a term not exceeding 10 years.

[Sexual Offences Act 2003, s 12.]

---

1 "There is . . . nothing in the language of section 12 to suggest that the offence can only be committed if the sexual gratification and the display of the images are simultaneous, or contemporaneous, or synchronised. Unsurprisingly the form which the perpetrator's sexual activity may take is not defined. Provided the purpose is indeed his sexual gratification, it may take any of the myriad forms which sexual pleasure or indulgence, or to use a colloquialism, a sexual thrill may take. Indeed, even if the hope is that at a later stage things may go further, the sexual gratification may simply involve, for example, the perpetrator enjoying the sight of the child looking at the images and his or her reactions or responses, whatever they may be. Whatever form it may take, we can find nothing in the section which suggests that sexual gratification must be taken immediately, or putting the same point the other way round, that it cannot extend to a longer term plan to obtain further or greater sexual gratification in the form of the eventual working out of a particular sexual fantasy or activity involving the child. The purpose may involve both short-term and long-term sexual gratification; immediate or deferred, or immediate and deferred gratification", per Sir Igor Judge P in *R v Abdullahi* [2006] EWCA Crim 2060, [2007] 1 WLR 225, [2007] 1 Cr App R 14, [2007] Crim LR 184 at para 117.

2 For "image", see s 79, post.

3 For "sexual", see s 78, post.

4 For procedure in respect of this offence which is triable either way, see the Magistrates' Courts Act 1980, ss 17A–21 in PART I: MAGISTRATES' COURTS, PROCEDURE, ante.

7.10575 **13. Child sex offences committed by children or young persons** (1) A person under 18 commits an offence if he does anything which would be an offence under any of sections 9 to 12 if he were aged 18.

(2) A person guilty of an offence under this section is liable[1]—

(*a*) on summary conviction, to imprisonment for a term not exceeding 6 months or a fine not exceeding the statutory maximum or both;

(*b*) on conviction on indictment, to imprisonment for a term not exceeding 5 years[2].

[Sexual Offences Act 2003, s 13.]

---

1 For procedure in respect of this offence which is triable either way, see the Magistrates' Courts Act 1980, ss 17A–21 in PART I: MAGISTRATES' COURTS, PROCEDURE, ante. For mode of trial where the defendant is under 18 years, see the Magistrates' Courts Act 1980, s 24, ante and para 5.10 ff **Jurisdiction of the magistrates' and Crown Courts** in PART V: YOUTH COURTS, ante.

2 Accordingly, the offence is not a "serious specified offence" for the purposes of the Criminal Justice Act 2003: *R v B* [2008] EWCA Crim 830, [2009] 1 Cr App Rep (S) 6, [2008] Crim LR 730.

7.10576 **14. Arranging or facilitating commission of a child sex offence[1]** (1) A person commits an offence if—

(*a*) he intentionally arranges or facilitates something that he intends to do, intends another person to do, or believes that another person will do, in any part of the world, and

(*b*) doing it will involve the commission of an offence under any of sections 9 to 13.

(2) A person does not commit an offence under this section if—

(*a*) he arranges or facilitates something that he believes another person will do, but that he does not intend to do or intend another person to do, and

(*b*) any offence within subsection (1)(*b*) would be an offence against a child for whose protection he acts.

(3) For the purposes of subsection (2), a person acts for the protection of a child if he acts for the purpose of—

(*a*) protecting the child from sexually transmitted infection,
(*b*) protecting the physical safety of the child,
(*c*) preventing the child from becoming pregnant, or
(*d*) promoting the child's emotional well-being by the giving of advice,

and not for the purpose of obtaining sexual gratification or for the purpose of causing or encouraging the activity constituting the offence within subsection (1)(*b*) or the child's participation in it.

(4) A person guilty of an offence under this section is liable[2]—

(*a*) on summary conviction, to imprisonment for a term not exceeding 6 months or a fine not exceeding the statutory maximum or both;
(*b*) on conviction on indictment, to imprisonment for a term not exceeding 14 years.

[Sexual Offences Act 2003, s 14.]

---

1 This section introduces an offence more than and wider than a criminal attempt and imposes criminal liability on preparatory steps. An "arrangement" may be made without the consent or acquiescence of anyone else. A request to another, which was refused, to find the defendant a 12 year old girl working as a prostitute might constitute the substantive offence. Alternatively, if more than preparatory, it was capable of amounting to an attempt to commit an offence contrary to this section as being more than a preparatory act; it was the last thing the defendant needed to do before committing the substantive offence (*R v Robson* [2008] EWCA Crim 619, [2009] 1 WLR 713, [2008] 2 Cr App R 38, 172 JP 441).

2 For procedure in respect of this offence which is triable either way, see the Magistrates' Courts Act 1980, ss 17A–21 in PART I: MAGISTRATES' COURTS, PROCEDURE, ante.

7.10577 **15. Meeting a child following sexual grooming etc**[1] (1) A person aged 18 or over (A) commits an offence if—

(*a*) A has met or communicated with another person (*b*) on one or more occasions and subsequently—
(i) A intentionally meets B,
(ii) A travels with the intention of meeting B in any part of the world or arranges to meet B in any part of the world, or
(iii) B travels with the intention of meeting A in any part of the world,
(*b*) A intends to do anything to or in respect of B, during or after the meeting mentioned in paragraph (*a*)(i) to (iii) and in any part of the world, which if done will involve the commission by A of a relevant offence,
(*c*) B is under 16, and
(*d*) A does not reasonably believe that B is 16 or over.

(2) In subsection (1)—

(*a*) the reference to A having met or communicated with B is a reference to A having met B in any part of the world or having communicated with B by any means from, to or in any part of the world;
(*b*) "relevant offence" means—
(i) an offence under this Part[2],
(ii) *repealed*, or
(iii) anything done outside England and Wales which is not an offence within sub-paragraph (i) but would be an offence within sub-paragraph (i) if done in England and Wales.

(3) *Repealed.*

(4) A person guilty of an offence under this section is liable[3]—

(*a*) on summary conviction, to imprisonment for a term not exceeding 6 months or a fine not exceeding the statutory maximum or both;
(*b*) on conviction on indictment, to imprisonment for a term not exceeding 10 years.

[Sexual Offences Act 2003, s 15 as amended by the Criminal Justice and Immigration Act 2008, Sch 15, SI 2008/1779 and the Criminal Justice and Courts Act 2015, s 36.]

---

1 The heading might be taken to suggest that the behaviour antecedent to any arranged meeting had to be sexual in nature, but the language of s 15 is far wider. The only requirement prior to the intentional meeting referred to in s 15(1)(*a*) is meeting or communication "on at least two occasions". The aim was to penalise those who used a relationship they had developed, whether innocently or otherwise, as a platform from which to launch sexual offending. An offence is committed whether or not a meeting takes place if it was the defendant's intention to engage in a child sex offence on the victim during or after the meeting. Section 15 is not engaged, however, if the meeting started without any such intention and the defendant then decides to take advantage of the situation and commit an offence (the crime would then be the commission of the offence or the attempt to commit it): *R v G* [2010] EWCA Crim 1693, [2011] Crim L R 339.

2 "This Part" means ss 1–79 and Schs 1 and 2.

3 For procedure in respect of this offence which is triable either way, see the Magistrates' Courts Act 1980, ss 17A–21 in PART I: MAGISTRATES' COURTS, PROCEDURE, ante.

7.10577A **15A. Sexual communication with a child** (1) A person aged 18 or over (A) commits an offence if—

(*a*) for the purpose of obtaining sexual gratification, A intentionally communicates with another person (B),
(*b*) the communication is sexual or is intended to encourage B to make (whether to A or to another) a communication that is sexual, and
(*c*) B is under 16 and A does not reasonably believe that B is 16 or over.

(2) For the purposes of this section, a communication is sexual if—

(*a*) any part of it relates to sexual activity, or

(*b*) a reasonable person would, in all the circumstances but regardless of any person's purpose, consider any part of the communication to be sexual;

and in paragraph (*a*) "sexual activity" means an activity that a reasonable person would, in all the circumstances but regardless of any person's purpose, consider to be sexual.

(3) A person guilty of an offence under this section is liable—

(*a*) on summary conviction, to imprisonment for a term not exceeding 12 months or a fine or both;

(*b*) on conviction on indictment, to imprisonment for a term not exceeding 2 years.

[Sexual Offences Act 2003, s 15A as inserted by the Serious Crime Act 2015, s 67.]

*Abuse of position of trust*

7.10578 **16. Abuse of position of trust: sexual activity with a child** (1) A person aged 18 or over (A) commits an offence[1] if—

(*a*) he intentionally touches[2] another person (B),

(*b*) the touching is sexual[3],

(*c*) A is in a position of trust[4] in relation to B,

(*d*) where subsection (2) applies, A knows or could reasonably be expected to know of the circumstances by virtue of which he is in a position of trust in relation to B, and

(*e*) either—

(i) B is under 18 and A does not reasonably believe that B is 18 or over, or

(ii) B is under 13.

(2) This subsection applies where A—

(*a*) is in a position of trust in relation to B by virtue of circumstances within section 21(2), (3), (4) or (5), and

(*b*) is not in such a position of trust by virtue of other circumstances.

(3) Where in proceedings for an offence under this section it is proved that the other person was under 18, the defendant is to be taken not to have reasonably believed that that person was 18 or over unless sufficient evidence is adduced to raise an issue as to whether he reasonably believed it.

(4) Where in proceedings for an offence under this section—

(*a*) it is proved that the defendant was in a position of trust in relation to the other person by virtue of circumstances within section 21(2), (3), (4) or (5), and

(*b*) it is not proved that he was in such a position of trust by virtue of other circumstances,

it is to be taken that the defendant knew or could reasonably have been expected to know of the circumstances by virtue of which he was in such a position of trust unless sufficient evidence is adduced to raise an issue as to whether he knew or could reasonably have been expected to know of those circumstances.

(5) A person guilty of an offence under this section is liable[5]—

(*a*) on summary conviction, to imprisonment for a term not exceeding 6 months or a fine not exceeding the statutory maximum or both;

(*b*) on conviction on indictment, to imprisonment for a term not exceeding 5 years.

[Sexual Offences Act 2003, s 16.]

---

1 For marriage exception, see s 23, post.

2 For "touching", see s 79, post.

3 For "sexual", see s 78, post.

4 For "position of trust", see ss 21 and 22 and for sexual relationships which pre-date position of trust, see s 24, post.

5 For procedure in respect of this offence which is triable either way, see the Magistrates' Courts Act 1980, ss 17A–21 in PART I: MAGISTRATES' COURTS, PROCEDURE, ante.

7.10579 **17. Abuse of position of trust: causing or inciting a child to engage in sexual activity** (1) A person aged 18 or over (A) commits an offence if—

(*a*) he intentionally causes or incites another person (B) to engage in an activity,

(*b*) the activity is sexual[1],

(*c*) A is in a position of trust[2] in relation to B,

(*d*) where subsection (2) applies, A knows or could reasonably be expected to know of the circumstances by virtue of which he is in a position of trust in relation to B, and

(*e*) either—

(i) B is under 18 and A does not reasonably believe that B is 18 or over, or

(ii) B is under 13.

(2) This subsection applies where A—

(*a*) is in a position of trust in relation to B by virtue of circumstances within section 21(2), (3), (4) or (5), and

(*b*) is not in such a position of trust by virtue of other circumstances.

(3) Where in proceedings for an offence under this section it is proved that the other person was under 18, the defendant is to be taken not to have reasonably believed that that person was 18 or over unless sufficient evidence is adduced to raise an issue as to whether he reasonably believed it.

(4) Where in proceedings for an offence under this section—

(*a*) it is proved that the defendant was in a position of trust in relation to the other person by virtue of circumstances within section 21(2), (3), (4) or (5), and

(*b*) it is not proved that he was in such a position of trust by virtue of other circumstances,

it is to be taken that the defendant knew or could reasonably have been expected to know of the circumstances by virtue of which he was in such a position of trust unless sufficient evidence is adduced to raise an issue as to whether he knew or could reasonably have been expected to know of those circumstances.

(5) A person guilty of an offence under this section is liable[3]—

(*a*) on summary conviction, to imprisonment for a term not exceeding 6 months or a fine not exceeding the statutory maximum or both;

(*b*) on conviction on indictment, to imprisonment for a term not exceeding 5 years.

[Sexual Offences Act 2003, s 17.]

[1] For "sexual", see s 78, post.
[2] For "position of trust", see ss 21 and 22 and for sexual relationships which pre-date position of trust, see s 24, post.
[3] For procedure in respect of this offence which is triable either way, see the Magistrates' Courts Act 1980, ss 17A–21 in PART I: MAGISTRATES' COURTS, PROCEDURE, ante.

7.10580 **18. Abuse of position of trust: sexual activity in the presence of a child** (1) A person aged 18 or over (A) commits an offence if—

(*a*) he intentionally engages in an activity,

(*b*) the activity is sexual[1],

(*c*) for the purpose of obtaining sexual gratification, he engages in it—

(i) when another person (B) is present or is in a place from which A can be observed, and

(ii) knowing or believing that B is aware, or intending that B should be aware, that he is engaging in it,

(*d*) A is in a position of trust[2] in relation to B,

(*e*) where subsection (2) applies, A knows or could reasonably be expected to know of the circumstances by virtue of which he is in a position of trust in relation to B, and

(*f*) either—

(i) B is under 18 and A does not reasonably believe that B is 18 or over, or

(ii) B is under 13.

(2) This subsection applies where A—

(*a*) is in a position of trust in relation to B by virtue of circumstances within section 21(2), (3), (4) or (5), and

(*b*) is not in such a position of trust by virtue of other circumstances.

(3) Where in proceedings for an offence under this section it is proved that the other person was under 18, the defendant is to be taken not to have reasonably believed that that person was 18 or over unless sufficient evidence is adduced to raise an issue as to whether he reasonably believed it.

(4) Where in proceedings for an offence under this section—

(*a*) it is proved that the defendant was in a position of trust in relation to the other person by virtue of circumstances within section 21(2), (3), (4) or (5), and

(*b*) it is not proved that he was in such a position of trust by virtue of other circumstances,

it is to be taken that the defendant knew or could reasonably have been expected to know of the circumstances by virtue of which he was in such a position of trust unless sufficient evidence is adduced to raise an issue as to whether he knew or could reasonably have been expected to know of those circumstances.

(5) A person guilty of an offence under this section is liable[3]—

(*a*) on summary conviction, to imprisonment for a term not exceeding 6 months or a fine not exceeding the statutory maximum or both;

(*b*) on conviction on indictment, to imprisonment for a term not exceeding 5 years.

[Sexual Offences Act 2003, s 18.]

[1] For "sexual", see s 78, post.
[2] For "position of trust", see ss 21 and 22 and for sexual relationships which pre-date position of trust, see s 24, post.
[3] For procedure in respect of this offence which is triable either way, see the Magistrates' Courts Act 1980, ss 17A–21 in PART I: MAGISTRATES' COURTS, PROCEDURE, ante.

7.10581 **19. Abuse of position of trust: causing a child to watch a sexual act** (1) A person aged 18 or over (A) commits an offence if—

(*a*) for the purpose of obtaining sexual gratification, he intentionally causes another person (B) to watch a third person engaging in an activity, or to look at an image of any person engaging in an activity,

(*b*) the activity is sexual[1],

(*c*) A is in a position of trust[2] in relation to B,

(*d*) where subsection (2) applies, A knows or could reasonably be expected to know of the circumstances by virtue of which he is in a position of trust in relation to B, and

(*e*) either—

(i) B is under 18 and A does not reasonably believe that B is 18 or over, or

(ii) B is under 13.

(2) This subsection applies where A—

(*a*) is in a position of trust in relation to B by virtue of circumstances within section 21(2), (3), (4) or (5), and

(*b*) is not in such a position of trust by virtue of other circumstances.

(3) Where in proceedings for an offence under this section it is proved that the other person was under 18, the defendant is to be taken not to have reasonably believed that that person was 18 or over unless sufficient evidence is adduced to raise an issue as to whether he reasonably believed it.

(4) Where in proceedings for an offence under this section—

(*a*) it is proved that the defendant was in a position of trust in relation to the other person by virtue of circumstances within section 21(2), (3), (4) or (5), and

(*b*) it is not proved that he was in such a position of trust by virtue of other circumstances,

it is to be taken that the defendant knew or could reasonably have been expected to know of the circumstances by virtue of which he was in such a position of trust unless sufficient evidence is adduced to raise an issue as to whether he knew or could reasonably have been expected to know of those circumstances.

(5) A person guilty of an offence under this section is liable[3]—

(*a*) on summary conviction, to imprisonment for a term not exceeding 6 months or a fine not exceeding the statutory maximum or both;

(*b*) on conviction on indictment, to imprisonment for a term not exceeding 5 years.

[Sexual Offences Act 2003, s 19.]

---

1 For "sexual", see s 78, post.

2 For "position of trust", see ss 21 and 22 and for sexual relationships which pre-date position of trust, see s 24, post.

3 For procedure in respect of this offence which is triable either way, see the Magistrates' Courts Act 1980, ss 17A–21 in PART I: MAGISTRATES' COURTS, PROCEDURE, ante.

**7.10582 20. Abuse of position of trust: acts done in Scotland** Anything which, if done in England and Wales, would constitute an offence under any of sections 16 to 19 also constitutes that offence if done in Scotland or Northern Ireland.

[Sexual Offences Act 2003, s 20 as amended by SI 2008/1779.]

**7.10583 21. Positions of trust** (1) For the purposes of sections 16 to 19, a person (A) is in a position of trust in relation to another person (B) if—

(*a*) any of the following subsections applies, or

(*b*) any condition specified in an order made by the Secretary of State is met.

(2) This subsection applies if A looks after persons under 18 who are detained in an institution by virtue of a court order or under an enactment, and B is so detained in that institution.

(3) This subsection applies if A looks after persons under 18 who are resident in a home or other place in which—

(*a*) accommodation and maintenance are provided by an authority in accordance with section 22C(6) of the Children Act 1989 (c 41) or section 81(6) of the Social Services and Well-being (Wales) Act 2014, or

(*b*) accommodation is provided by a voluntary organisation under section 59(1) of that Act,

and B is resident, and is so provided with accommodation and maintenance or accommodation, in that place.

(4) This subsection applies if A looks after persons under 18 who are accommodated and cared for in one of the following institutions—

(*a*) a hospital,

(*b*) in Wales, an independent clinic,

(*c*) a care home,

(*d*) a community home, voluntary home or children's home, or

(*e*) a home provided under section 82(5) of the Children Act 1989,

(*f*) *repealed*

and B is accommodated and cared for in that institution.

(5) This subsection applies if A looks after persons under 18 who are receiving education at an educational institution and B is receiving, and A is not receiving, education at that institution.

(6) *Repealed.*

(7) This subsection applies if A is engaged in the provision of services under, or pursuant to anything done under—

(*a*) sections 8 to 10 of the Employment and Training Act 1973 (c 50), or

(*b*) section 68, 70(1)(*b*) or 74 of the Education and Skills Act 2008,,

and, in that capacity, looks after B on an individual basis.

(8) This subsection applies if A regularly has unsupervised contact with B (whether face to face or by any other means)—

(*a*) in the exercise of functions of a local authority under section 20 or 21 of the Children Act 1989 (c 41) or section 76 or 77 of the Social Services and Well-being (Wales) Act 2014,

(b) *repealed.*

(9) This subsection applies if A, as a person who is to report to the court under section 7 of the Children Act 1989 on matters relating to the welfare of B, regularly has unsupervised contact with B (whether face to face or by any other means).

(10) This subsection applies if A is a personal adviser appointed for B under—

(a) section 23B(2) of, or paragraph 19C of Schedule 2 to, the Children Act 1989, or

(aa) section 106(1) of the Social Services and Well-being (Wales) Act 2014 in respect of category 1 or 2 young persons within the meaning of that Act,

(b) *repealed,*

and, in that capacity, looks after B on an individual basis.

(11) This subsection applies if—

(a) B is subject to a care order, a supervision order or an education supervision order, and

(b) in the exercise of functions conferred by virtue of the order on an authorised person or the authority designated by the order, A looks after B on an individual basis.

(12) This subsection applies if A—

(a) is an officer of the Service or Welsh family proceedings officer (within the meaning given by section 35 of the Children Act 2004) appointed for B under section 41(1) of the Children Act 1989,

(b) is appointed a children's guardian of B under rule 6 or rule 18 of the Adoption Rules 1984 (SI 1984/265),

(c) is appointed to be the guardian ad litem of B under rule 9.5 of the Family Proceedings Rules 1991 (SI 1991/1247), or

(d) is appointed to be the children's guardian of B under rule 59 of the Family Procedure (Adoption) Rules 2005 (SI 2005/2795) or rule 16.3(1)(ii) or rule 16.4 of the Family Procedure Rules 2010 (SI 2010/2955),

and, in that capacity, regularly has unsupervised contact with B (whether face to face or by any other means).

(13) This subsection applies if—

(a) B is subject to requirements imposed by or under an enactment on his release from detention for a criminal offence, or is subject to requirements imposed by a court order made in criminal proceedings, and

(b) A looks after B on an individual basis in pursuance of the requirements.

[Sexual Offences Act 2003, s 21 as amended by the Children Act 2004, Sch 3, the Education and Skills Act 2008, Sch 1, the Children and Young Persons Act 2008, Sch 1, SI 2008/1779, SI 2010/813, SI 2011/1045 and SI 2016/413.]

7.10584 **22. Positions of trust: interpretation** (1) The following provisions apply for the purposes of section 21.

(2) Subject to subsection (3), a person looks after persons under 18 if he is regularly involved in caring for, training, supervising or being in sole charge of such persons.

(3) A person (A) looks after another person (B) on an individual basis if—

(a) A is regularly involved in caring for, training or supervising B, and

(b) in the course of his involvement, A regularly has unsupervised contact with B (whether face to face or by any other means).

(4) A person receives education at an educational institution if—

(a) he is registered or otherwise enrolled as a pupil or student at the institution, or

(b) he receives education at the institution under arrangements with another educational institution at which he is so registered or otherwise enrolled.

(5) In section 21—

"authority"—

(a) in relation to England and Wales, means a local authority;

(b) *repealed*

"care home" means an establishment which is a care home for the purposes of the Care Standards Act 2000 (c 14);

"care order" has—

(a) in relation to England and Wales, the same meaning as in the Children Act 1989 (c 41),

(b) *repealed*

"children's home" has—

(a) in relation to England and Wales, the meaning given by section 1 of the Care Standards Act 2000,

(b) *repealed*

"community home" has the meaning given by section 53 of the Children Act 1989;

"education supervision order" has—

(a) in relation to England and Wales, the meaning given by section 36 of the Children Act 1989,

(b) *repealed*

"hospital"—

(a) in relation to England and Wales, means a hospital within the meaning given by section 275(1) of the National Health Service Act 2006 or section 206(1) of the

National Health Service Act 2006, or any other establishment which is a hospital within the meaning given by section 2(3) of the Care Standards Act 2000 (c 14);

(*b*) *repealed*

"independent clinic" has—

(*a*) in relation to England and Wales, the meaning given by section 2 of the Care Standards Act 2000;

(*b*) *repealed*;

"supervision order" has—

(*a*) in relation to England and Wales, the meaning given by section 31(11) of the Children Act 1989 (c 41),

(*b*) *repealed*

"voluntary home" has—

(*a*) in relation to England and Wales, the meaning given by section 60(3) of the Children Act 1989,

(*b*) *repealed*

[Sexual Offences Act 2003, s 22 as amended by the Health Service (Consequential Provisions) Act 2006, Sch 1 and SI 2008/1779.]

7.10585 **23. Sections 16 to 19: exception for spouses and civil partners** (1) Conduct by a person (A) which would otherwise be an offence under any of sections 16 to 19 against another person (B) is not an offence under that section if at the time—

(*a*) B is 16 or over, and

(*b*) A and B are lawfully married or civil partners of each other.

(2) In proceedings for such an offence it is for the defendant to prove that A and B were at the time lawfully married or civil partners of each other.

[Sexual Offences Act 2003, s 23 as amended by the Civil Partnership Act 2004, Sch 27.]

7.10586 **24. Sections 16 to 19: sexual relationships which pre-date position of trust** (1) Conduct by a person (A) which would otherwise be an offence under any of sections 16 to 19 against another person (B) is not an offence under that section if, immediately before the position of trust arose, a sexual relationship existed between A and B.

(2) Subsection (1) does not apply if at that time sexual intercourse between A and B would have been unlawful.

(3) In proceedings for an offence under any of sections 16 to 19 it is for the defendant to prove that such a relationship existed at that time.

[Sexual Offences Act 2003, s 24.]

*Familial child sex offences*

7.10587 **25. Sexual activity with a child family member** (1) A person (A) commits an offence[1] if—

(*a*) he intentionally touches another person (B),

(*b*) the touching[2] is sexual[3],

(*c*) the relation of A to B is within section 27,

(*d*) A knows or could reasonably be expected to know that his relation to B is of a description falling within that section, and

(*e*) either—

(i) B is under 18 and A does not reasonably believe that B is 18 or over, or

(ii) B is under 13.

(2) Where in proceedings for an offence under this section it is proved that the other person was under 18, the defendant is to be taken not to have reasonably believed that that person was 18 or over unless sufficient evidence is adduced to raise an issue as to whether he reasonably believed it.

(3) Where in proceedings for an offence under this section it is proved that the relation of the defendant to the other person was of a description falling within section 27, it is to be taken that the defendant knew or could reasonably have been expected to know that his relation to the other person was of that description unless sufficient evidence is adduced to raise an issue as to whether he knew or could reasonably have been expected to know that it was.

(4) A person guilty of an offence under this section, if aged 18 or over at the time of the offence, is liable—

(*a*) where subsection (6) applies, on conviction on indictment to imprisonment for a term not exceeding 14 years;

(*b*) in any other case[4]—

(i) on summary conviction, to imprisonment for a term not exceeding 6 months or a fine not exceeding the statutory maximum or both;

(ii) on conviction on indictment, to imprisonment for a term not exceeding 14 years.

(5) Unless subsection (4) applies, a person guilty of an offence under this section is liable[4]—

(*a*) on summary conviction, to imprisonment for a term not exceeding 6 months or a fine not exceeding the statutory maximum or both;

(*b*) on conviction on indictment, to imprisonment for a term not exceeding 5 years.

(6) This subsection applies where the touching involved—

(*a*) penetration[2] of B's anus or vagina[2] with a part of A's body[2] or anything else,

(*b*) penetration of B's mouth with A's penis,
(*c*) penetration of A's anus or vagina with a part of B's body, or
(*d*) penetration of A's mouth with B's penis.

[Sexual Offences Act 2003, s 25.]

1 For marriage exception and sexual relationships which pre-date family relationships, see ss 28 and 29, post.
2 For "touching", "penetration", "vagina" and "part of his body", see s 79, post.
3 For "sexual", see s 78, post.
4 For procedure in respect of this offence which is triable either way, see the Magistrates' Courts Act 1980, ss 17A–21 in PART I: MAGISTRATES' COURTS, PROCEDURE, ante.

7.10588 26. **Inciting a child family member to engage in sexual activity** (1) A person (A) commits an offence[1] if—

(*a*) he intentionally incites another person (B) to touch[2], or allow himself to be touched by, A,
(*b*) the touching is sexual[3],
(*c*) the relation of A to B is within section 27,
(*d*) A knows or could reasonably be expected to know that his relation to B is of a description falling within that section, and
(*e*) either—
(i) B is under 18 and A does not reasonably believe that B is 18 or over, or
(ii) B is under 13.

(2) Where in proceedings for an offence under this section it is proved that the other person was under 18, the defendant is to be taken not to have reasonably believed that that person was 18 or over unless sufficient evidence is adduced to raise an issue as to whether he reasonably believed it.

(3) Where in proceedings for an offence under this section it is proved that the relation of the defendant to the other person was of a description falling within section 27, it is to be taken that the defendant knew or could reasonably have been expected to know that his relation to the other person was of that description unless sufficient evidence is adduced to raise an issue as to whether he knew or could reasonably have been expected to know that it was.

(4) A person guilty of an offence under this section, if he was aged 18 or over at the time of the offence, is liable—

(*a*) where subsection (6) applies, on conviction on indictment to imprisonment for a term not exceeding 14 years;
(*b*) in any other case[4]—
(i) on summary conviction, to imprisonment for a term not exceeding 6 months or a fine not exceeding the statutory maximum or both;
(ii) on conviction on indictment, to imprisonment for a term not exceeding 14 years.

(5) Unless subsection (4) applies, a person guilty of an offence under this section is liable[4]—

(*a*) on summary conviction, to imprisonment for a term not exceeding 6 months or a fine not exceeding the statutory maximum or both;
(*b*) on conviction on indictment, to imprisonment for a term not exceeding 5 years.

(6) This subsection applies where the touching to which the incitement related involved—

(*a*) penetration[2] of B's anus or vagina[2] with a part of A's body[2] or anything else,
(*b*) penetration of B's mouth with A's penis,
(*c*) penetration of A's anus or vagina with a part of B's body, or
(*d*) penetration of A's mouth with B's penis.

[Sexual Offences Act 2003, s 26.]

1 For marriage exception and sexual relationships which pre-date family relationships, see ss 28 and 29, post.
2 For "touching", "penetration", "vagina" and "part of his body", see s 79, post.
3 For "sexual", see s 78, post.
4 For procedure in respect of this offence which is triable either way, see the Magistrates' Courts Act 1980, ss 17A–21 in PART I: MAGISTRATES' COURTS, PROCEDURE, ante.

7.10589 27. **Family relationships** (1) The relation of one person (A) to another (B) is within this section if—

(*a*) it is within any of subsections (2) to (4), or
(*b*) it would be within one of those subsections but for section 39 of the Adoption Act 1976 or section 67 of the Adoption and Children Act 2002 (c 38) (status conferred by adoption).

(2) The relation of A to B is within this subsection if—

(*a*) one of them is the other's parent, grandparent, brother, sister, half-brother, half-sister, aunt or uncle, or
(*b*) A is or has been B's foster parent.

(3) The relation of A to B is within this subsection if A and B live or have lived in the same household, or A is or has been regularly involved in caring for, training, supervising or being in sole charge of B, and—

(*a*) one of them is or has been the other's step-parent,
(*b*) A and B are cousins,
(*c*) one of them is or has been the other's stepbrother or stepsister, or

(*d*) the parent or present or former foster parent of one of them is or has been the other's foster parent.

(4) The relation of A to B is within this subsection if—

(*a*) A and B live in the same household, and

(*b*) A is regularly involved in caring for, training, supervising or being in sole charge of B.

(5) For the purposes of this section—

(*a*) "aunt" means the sister or half-sister of a person's parent, and "uncle" has a corresponding meaning;

(*b*) "cousin" means the child of an aunt or uncle;

(*c*) a person is a child's foster parent if—

(i) he is a person with whom the child has been placed under section 22C of the Children Act 1989 in a placement falling within subsection (6)(a) or (b) of that section (placement with local authority foster parent),

(ia) he is a person with whom the child has been placed under section 59(1)(a) of that Act (placement by voluntary organisation),

(ib) he is a person with whom the child has been placed under section 81 of the Social Services and Well-being (Wales) Act 2014 in a placement falling within subsection (6)(a) or (b) of that section (placement with a local authority foster parent), or

(ii) he fosters the child privately, within the meaning given by section 66(1)(b) of that Act;

(*d*) a person is another's partner (whether they are of different sexes or the same sex) if they live together as partners in an enduring family relationship;

(*e*) "step-parent" includes a parent's partner and "stepbrother" and "stepsister" include the child of a parent's partner.

[Sexual Offences Act 2003, s 27 as amended by the Criminal Justice and Immigration Act 2008, Sch 15, the Children and Young Persons Act 2008, Sch 1 and SI 2016/413.]

**7.10590 28. Sections 25 and 26: exception for spouses and civil partners** (1) Conduct by a person (A) which would otherwise be an offence under section 25 or 26 against another person (B) is not an offence under that section if at the time—

(*a*) B is 16 or over, and

(*b*) A and B are lawfully married or civil partners of each other.

(2) In proceedings for such an offence it is for the defendant to prove that A and B were at the time lawfully married or civil partners of each other.

[Sexual Offences Act 2003, s 28 as amended by the Civil Partnership Act 2004, Sch 27.]

**7.10591 29. Sections 25 and 26: sexual relationships which pre-date family relationships** (1) Conduct by a person (A) which would otherwise be an offence under section 25 or 26 against another person (B) is not an offence under that section if—

(*a*) the relation of A to B is not within subsection (2) of section 27,

(*b*) it would not be within that subsection if section 39 of the Adoption Act 1976 or section 67 of the Adoption and Children Act 2002 (c 38) did not apply, and

(*c*) immediately before the relation of A to B first became such as to fall within section 27, a sexual relationship existed between A and B.

(2) Subsection (1) does not apply if at the time referred to in subsection (1)(*c*) sexual intercourse between A and B would have been unlawful.

(3) In proceedings for an offence under section 25 or 26 it is for the defendant to prove the matters mentioned in subsection (1)(*a*) to (*c*).

[Sexual Offences Act 2003, s 29 as amended by the Criminal Justice and Immigration Act 2008, Sch 15.]

*Offences against persons with a mental disorder impeding choice*

**7.10592 30. Sexual activity with a person with a mental disorder impeding choice**

(1) A person (A) commits an offence if—

(*a*) he intentionally touches[1] another person (B),

(*b*) the touching is sexual[2],

(*c*) B is unable to refuse because of or for a reason related to a mental disorder[1], and

(*d*) A knows or could reasonably be expected to know that B has a mental disorder and that because of it or for a reason related to it B is likely to be unable to refuse.

(2) B is unable to refuse if—

(*a*) he lacks the capacity to choose whether to agree to the touching (whether because he lacks sufficient understanding of the nature or reasonably foreseeable consequences of what is being done, or for any other reason)[3], or

(*b*) he is unable to communicate such a choice to A[4].

(3) A person guilty of an offence under this section, if the touching involved—

(*a*) penetration[1] of B's anus or vagina[1] with a part of A's body or anything else,

(*b*) penetration of B's mouth with A's penis,

(*c*) penetration of A's anus or vagina with a part of B's body[1], or

(*d*) penetration of A's mouth with B's penis,

is liable, on conviction on indictment, to imprisonment for life.

(4) Unless subsection (3) applies, a person guilty of an offence under this section is liable[5]—

(*a*) on summary conviction, to imprisonment for a term not exceeding 6 months or to a fine not exceeding the statutory maximum or both;

(*b*) on conviction on indictment, to imprisonment for a term not exceeding 14 years.

[Sexual Offences Act 2003, s 30.]

---

[1] For "touching", "mental disorder", "penetration", "vagina" and "part of his body", see s 79, post. As to evidence capable of fulfilling this element of the offence, see *Hulme v DPP* [2006] EWHC 1347 (Admin), 170 JP 598 (in which the following evidence sufficed: when sexually touched the complainant, a vulnerable person of limited mental capacity, did not know what to do or say, and when the defendant placed her hand on his penis, her mental condition prevented her from communicating that she did not want to).

[2] For "sexual", see s 78, post.

[3] 'The bracketed words reflect the provisions of ss 2(1) and 3(1) of the Mental Capacity Act 2005, and lead us to determine that the difference in definition of capacity in the civil and criminal jurisprudence is a difference without distinction' (per Macur LJ in *R v A (G)* [2014] EWCA Crim 299 at para 25, [2014] 1 WLR 2469 at para 25[2014] 2 Cr App Rep 73 at para 25). His Lordship then added:

> '26 However, the similarity of definition does not, in our view, dictate the same standard of proof. We observe that the adjudications of the Court of Protection will look to the future in generality; the criminal law looks retrospectively to specific acts of the past.
>
> 27 The fact that capacity is lacking in relation to one area of decision making at the material time does not necessarily translate into another area or another time. The criminal court concerned with offences created by the Sexual Offences Act 2003 must adjudge, if in dispute, capacity to understand and consent to sexual relations. The weight to be given to the complainant's understanding of the circumstances will therefore vary enormously as between a sexual encounter and consent to invasive medical treatment. This must be fully borne in mind not only by those "experts" who venture away from the Court of Protection into the criminal courts but also the judges who must be careful to appraise the expertise and therefore competence of those called to give "expert" evidence of competence before the jury. At this time there is no better source of reference than *IM v LM* ([2014] EWCA Civ 37).
>
> 28 The requirement that a complainant should understand the nature of the act of the sexual engagement involved will be a relatively simple issue to address. The question relating to the understanding of reasonably foreseeable consequences obviously should not become divorced from the actual decision-making process carried out in that regard on a daily basis by persons of full capacity. In the opinion of this court, adopting the opinion of the Court of Appeal, Civil Division, in IM, this process is "largely visceral rather than cerebral, and owes more to instinct and emotion rather than to analysis".
>
> 29 Section 1(2) of the Mental Capacity Act 2005 provides that "A person must be assumed to have capacity unless it is established that he lacks capacity." When capacity to consent is in issue in criminal proceedings, the burden of proving incapacity falls upon the party asserting it and will inevitably be the prosecution. We consider that, other than in criminal proceedings pursuant to s 44 of the Mental Capacity Act 2005 , the prosecution must discharge that burden to the criminal standard of proof; that is, they must make the jury sure that the complainant did not have capacity to consent. If the jury cannot be sure that the relevant complainant lacks capacity, then they must be directed to assume that he or she does. The issue for them then will be an examination of all the facts and circumstances to determine whether or not the complainant consented to the act or acts in question and whether the alleged assailant knew they did not consent or did not believe that they did so or were unreasonable in their belief that there was consent."

[4] In *R v Cooper (Gary Anthony)* [2009] UKHL 42, [2009] 4 All ER 1033, [2009] 1 WLR 1736, [2010] 1 Cr App R 7 the Court of Appeal had held "Irrational fear that prevents the exercise of choice cannot be equated with lack of capacity to choose . . . a lack of capacity to choose to agree to sexual activity cannot be "person specific" or, we would add, "situation specific".

The questions certified in the appeal to the House of Lords were:

> "Whether the decision of the Court of Appeal . . . has unduly limited the scope of section 30(1) of the Sexual Offences Act 2003 beyond that which Parliament intended. Specifically: (*a*) in holding that a lack of capacity to choose cannot be person- or situation-specific; (*b*) in holding that an irrational fear that prevents the exercise of choice cannot be equated with a lack of capacity to choose; (*c*) in holding that to fall within section 30(2)(*b*) a complainant must be physically unable to communicate by reason of his mental disorder."

Their Lordships answered all three questions in the affirmative:

> "26 The 2003 Act also makes it clear that the question is whether the complainant has the capacity to choose whether to agree to 'the touching', that is, the specific act of sexual touching of which the defendant is accused . . . capacity can fluctuate, so that a person may have the required degree of understanding one day but not another. But that is because of a fluctuation in the mental disorder rather than a fluctuation in the circumstances. Once it is accepted that choice is an exercise of free will, and that mental disorder may rob a person of free will in a number of different ways and in a number of different situations, then a mentally disordered person may be quite capable of exercising choice in one situation but not in another. The complainant here, even in her agitated and aroused state, might have been quite capable of deciding whether or not to have sexual intercourse with a person who had not put her in the vulnerable and terrifying situation in which she found herself on 27 June 2007. The question is whether, in the state that she was in that day, she was capable of choosing whether to agree to the touching demanded of her by the defendant (per Baroness Hale)".

As to inability to communicate, " . . . it is quite clear that in the 2003 Act Parliament had in mind an inability to communicate which was the result of or associated with a disorder of the mind. There is no warrant at all for limiting it to a physical inability to communicate. It must include a person with such a degree of learning difficulty that they have never acquired the gift of speech, so that it is impossible to discover whether or not they can understand or make a choice (per Baroness Hale at para 30)".

[5] For procedure in respect of this offence which is triable either way, see the Magistrates' Courts Act 1980, ss 17A–21 in PART I: MAGISTRATES' COURTS, PROCEDURE, ante.

7.10593 **31. Causing or inciting a person, with a mental disorder impeding choice, to engage in sexual activity** (1) A person (A) commits an offence if—

(*a*) he intentionally causes or incites another person (B) to engage in an activity,

(*b*) the activity is sexual[1],

(*c*) B is unable to refuse because of or for a reason related to a mental disorder[2], and

(*d*) A knows or could reasonably be expected to know that B has a mental disorder and that because of it or for a reason related to it B is likely to be unable to refuse.

(2) B is unable to refuse if—

(*a*) he lacks the capacity to choose whether to agree to engaging in the activity caused or incited (whether because he lacks sufficient understanding of the nature or reasonably foreseeable consequences of the activity, or for any other reason)[3], or

(*b*) he is unable to communicate such a choice to A.

(3) A person guilty of an offence under this section, if the activity caused or incited involved—

(*a*) penetration[2] of B's anus or vagina[2],

(*b*) penetration of B's mouth with a person's penis,

(*c*) penetration of a person's anus or vagina with a part of B's body[2] or by B with anything else, or

(*d*) penetration of a person's mouth with B's penis,

is liable, on conviction on indictment, to imprisonment for life.

(4) Unless subsection (3) applies, a person guilty of an offence under this section is liable[4]—

(*a*) on summary conviction, to imprisonment for a term not exceeding 6 months or to a fine not exceeding the statutory maximum or both;

(*b*) on conviction on indictment, to imprisonment for a term not exceeding 14 years.

[Sexual Offences Act 2003, s 31.]

1 For "sexual", see s 78, post.
2 For "mental disorder", "penetration", "vagina" and "part of his body", see s 79, post.
3 See the note to s 30(2)(*a*), ante.
4 For procedure in respect of this offence which is triable either way, see the Magistrates' Courts Act 1980, ss 17A–21 in PART I: MAGISTRATES' COURTS, PROCEDURE, ante.

7.10594 **32. Engaging in sexual activity in the presence of a person with a mental disorder impeding choice** (1) A person (A) commits an offence if—

(*a*) he intentionally engages in an activity,

(*b*) the activity is sexual[1],

(*c*) for the purpose of obtaining sexual gratification, he engages in it—

(i) when another person (B) is present or is in a place from which A can be observed, and

(ii) knowing or believing that B is aware, or intending that B should be aware, that he is engaging in it,

(*d*) B is unable to refuse because of or for a reason related to a mental disorder[2], and

(*e*) A knows or could reasonably be expected to know that B has a mental disorder and that because of it or for a reason related to it B is likely to be unable to refuse.

(2) B is unable to refuse if—

(*a*) he lacks the capacity to choose whether to agree to being present (whether because he lacks sufficient understanding of the nature of the activity, or for any other reason)[3], or

(*b*) he is unable to communicate such a choice to A.

(3) A person guilty of an offence under this section is liable[4]—

(*a*) on summary conviction, to imprisonment for a term not exceeding 6 months or a fine not exceeding the statutory maximum or both;

(*b*) on conviction on indictment, to imprisonment for a term not exceeding 10 years.

[Sexual Offences Act 2003, s 32.]

1 For "sexual", see s 78, post.
2 For "mental disorder", see s 79, post.
3 See the note to s 30(2)(*a*), ante.
4 For procedure in respect of this offence which is triable either way, see the Magistrates' Courts Act 1980, ss 17A–21 in PART I: MAGISTRATES' COURTS, PROCEDURE, ante.

7.10595 **33. Causing a person, with a mental disorder impeding choice, to watch a sexual act** (1) A person (A) commits an offence if—

(*a*) for the purpose of obtaining sexual gratification, he intentionally causes another person (B) to watch a third person engaging in an activity, or to look at an image of any person engaging in an activity,

(*b*) the activity is sexual[1],

(*c*) B is unable to refuse because of or for a reason related to a mental disorder[2], and

(*d*) A knows or could reasonably be expected to know that B has a mental disorder and that because of it or for a reason related to it B is likely to be unable to refuse.

(2) B is unable to refuse if—

(*a*) he lacks the capacity to choose whether to agree to watching or looking (whether because he lacks sufficient understanding of the nature of the activity, or for any other reason)[3], or

(*b*) he is unable to communicate such a choice to A.

(3) A person guilty of an offence under this section is liable[4]—

(*a*) on summary conviction, to imprisonment for a term not exceeding 6 months or a fine not exceeding the statutory maximum or both;

(*b*) on conviction on indictment, to imprisonment for a term not exceeding 10 years.

[Sexual Offences Act 2003, s 33.]

1 For "sexual", see s 78, post.

2 For "mental disorder", see s 79, post.

3 See the note to s 30(2)(*a*), ante.

4 For procedure in respect of this offence which is triable either way, see the Magistrates' Courts Act 1980, ss 17A–21 in PART I: MAGISTRATES' COURTS, PROCEDURE, ante.

*Inducements etc to persons with a mental disorder*

7.10596 **34. Inducement, threat or deception to procure sexual activity with a person with a mental disorder** (1) A person (A) commits an offence if—

(*a*) with the agreement of another person (B) he intentionally touches[1] that person,

(*b*) the touching is sexual[2],

(*c*) A obtains B's agreement by means of an inducement offered or given, a threat made or a deception practised by A for that purpose,

(*d*) B has a mental disorder[1], and

(*e*) A knows or could reasonably be expected to know that B has a mental disorder.

(2) A person guilty of an offence under this section, if the touching involved—

(*a*) penetration[1] of B's anus or vagina[1] with a part of A's body[1] or anything else,

(*b*) penetration of B's mouth with A's penis,

(*c*) penetration of A's anus or vagina with a part of B's body, or

(*d*) penetration of A's mouth with B's penis,

is liable, on conviction on indictment, to imprisonment for life.

(3) Unless subsection (2) applies, a person guilty of an offence under this section is liable[3]—

(*a*) on summary conviction, to imprisonment for a term not exceeding 6 months or a fine not exceeding the statutory maximum or both;

(*b*) on conviction on indictment, to imprisonment for a term not exceeding 14 years.

[Sexual Offences Act 2003, s 34.]

1 For "touching", "mental disorder", "penetration", "vagina" and "part of his body", see s 79, post.

2 For "sexual", see s 78, post.

3 For procedure in respect of this offence which is triable either way, see the Magistrates' Courts Act 1980, ss 17A–21 in PART I: MAGISTRATES' COURTS, PROCEDURE, ante.

7.10597 **35. Causing a person with a mental disorder to engage in or agree to engage in sexual activity by inducement, threat or deception** (1) A person (A) commits an offence if—

(*a*) by means of an inducement offered or given, a threat made or a deception practised by him for this purpose, he intentionally causes another person (B) to engage in, or to agree to engage in, an activity,

(*b*) the activity is sexual[1],

(*c*) B has a mental disorder, and

(*d*) A knows or could reasonably be expected to know that B has a mental disorder.

(2) A person guilty of an offence under this section, if the activity caused or agreed to involved—

(*a*) penetration[2] of B's anus or vagina[2],

(*b*) penetration of B's mouth with a person's penis,

(*c*) penetration of a person's anus or vagina with a part of B's body[2] or by B with anything else, or

(*d*) penetration of a person's mouth with B's penis,

is liable, on conviction on indictment, to imprisonment for life.

(3) Unless subsection (2) applies, a person guilty of an offence under this section is liable[3]—

(*a*) on summary conviction, to imprisonment for a term not exceeding 6 months or a fine not exceeding the statutory maximum or both;

(*b*) on conviction on indictment, to imprisonment for a term not exceeding 14 years.

[Sexual Offences Act 2003, s 35.]

1 For "sexual", see s 78, post.

2 For "mental disorder", "penetration", "vagina" and "part of his body", see s 79, post.

3 For procedure in respect of this offence which is triable either way, see the Magistrates' Courts Act 1980, ss 17A–21 in PART I: MAGISTRATES' COURTS, PROCEDURE, ante.

7.10598 **36. Engaging in sexual activity in the presence, procured by inducement, threat or deception, of a person with a mental disorder** (1) A person (A) commits an offence if—

(*a*) he intentionally engages in an activity,

(*b*) the activity is sexual[1],

(*c*) for the purpose of obtaining sexual gratification, he engages in it—

(i) when another person (B) is present or is in a place from which A can be observed, and

(ii) knowing or believing that B is aware, or intending that B should be aware, that he is engaging in it, (*d*) B agrees to be present or in the place referred to in paragraph (*c*)(i) because of an inducement offered or given, a threat made or a deception practised by A for the purpose of obtaining that agreement,

(*e*) B has a mental disorder[2], and

(*f*) A knows or could reasonably be expected to know that B has a mental disorder.

(2) A person guilty of an offence under this section is liable[3]—

(*a*) on summary conviction, to imprisonment for a term not exceeding 6 months or a fine not exceeding the statutory maximum or both;

(*b*) on conviction on indictment, to imprisonment for a term not exceeding 10 years.

[Sexual Offences Act 2003, s 36.]

[1] For "sexual", see s 78, post.

[2] For "mental disorder", see s 79, post.

[3] For procedure in respect of this offence which is triable either way, see the Magistrates' Courts Act 1980, ss 17A–21 in PART I: MAGISTRATES' COURTS, PROCEDURE, ante.

**7.10599 37. Causing a person with a mental disorder to watch a sexual act by inducement, threat or deception** (1) A person (A) commits an offence if—

(*a*) for the purpose of obtaining sexual gratification, he intentionally causes another person (B) to watch a third person engaging in an activity, or to look at an image of any person engaging in an activity,

(*b*) the activity is sexual[1],

(*c*) B agrees to watch or look because of an inducement offered or given, a threat made or a deception practised by A for the purpose of obtaining that agreement,

(*d*) B has a mental disorder[2], and

(*e*) A knows or could reasonably be expected to know that B has a mental disorder.

(2) A person guilty of an offence under this section is liable[3]—

(*a*) on summary conviction, to imprisonment for a term not exceeding 6 months or a fine not exceeding the statutory maximum or both;

(*b*) on conviction on indictment, to imprisonment for a term not exceeding 10 years.

[Sexual Offences Act 2003, s 37.]

[1] For "sexual", see s 78, post.

[2] For "mental disorder", see s 79, post.

[3] For procedure in respect of this offence which is triable either way, see the Magistrates' Courts Act 1980, ss 17A–21 in PART I: MAGISTRATES' COURTS, PROCEDURE, ante.

*Care workers for persons with a mental disorder*

**7.10600 38. Care workers: sexual activity with a person with a mental disorder** (1) A person (A) commits an offence[1] if—

(*a*) he intentionally touches another person (B),

(*b*) the touching[2] is sexual[3],

(*c*) B has a mental disorder[2],

(*d*) A knows or could reasonably be expected to know that B has a mental disorder, and

(*e*) A is involved in B's care in a way that falls within section 42.

(2) Where in proceedings for an offence under this section it is proved that the other person had a mental disorder, it is to be taken that the defendant knew or could reasonably have been expected to know that that person had a mental disorder unless sufficient evidence is adduced to raise an issue as to whether he knew or could reasonably have been expected to know it.

(3) A person guilty of an offence under this section, if the touching involved—

(*a*) penetration[2] of B's anus or vagina[2] with a part of A's body[2] or anything else,

(*b*) penetration of B's mouth with A's penis,

(*c*) penetration of A's anus or vagina with a part of B's body, or

(*d*) penetration of A's mouth with B's penis,

is liable, on conviction on indictment, to imprisonment for a term not exceeding 14 years.

(4) Unless subsection (3) applies, a person guilty of an offence under this section is liable[4]—

(*a*) on summary conviction, to imprisonment for a term not exceeding 6 months or a fine not exceeding the statutory maximum or both;

(*b*) on conviction on indictment, to imprisonment for a term not exceeding 10 years.

[Sexual Offences Act 2003, s 38.]

[1] For marriage exception and sexual relationships which pre-date care relationships, see ss 43 and 44, post.

[2] For "touching", "mental disorder", "penetration", "vagina" and "part of his body", see s 79, post.

[3] For "sexual", see s 78, post.

[4] For procedure in respect of this offence which is triable either way, see the Magistrates' Courts Act 1980, ss 17A–21 in PART I: MAGISTRATES' COURTS, PROCEDURE, ante.

**7.10601 39. Care workers: causing or inciting sexual activity** (1) A person (A) commits an offence[1] if—

(*a*) he intentionally causes or incites another person (B) to engage in an activity,

(*b*) the activity is sexual[2],

(*c*) B has a mental disorder[3],

(*d*) A knows or could reasonably be expected to know that B has a mental disorder, and

(*e*) A is involved in B's care in a way that falls within section 42.

(2) Where in proceedings for an offence under this section it is proved that the other person had a mental disorder, it is to be taken that the defendant knew or could reasonably have been expected to know that that person had a mental disorder unless sufficient evidence is adduced to raise an issue as to whether he knew or could reasonably have been expected to know it.

(3) A person guilty of an offence under this section, if the activity caused or incited involved—

(*a*) penetration[3] of B's anus or vagina[3],

(*b*) penetration of B's mouth with a person's penis,

(*c*) penetration of a person's anus or vagina with a part of B's body[3] or by B with anything else, or

(*d*) penetration of a person's mouth with B's penis,

is liable, on conviction on indictment, to imprisonment for a term not exceeding 14 years.

(4) Unless subsection (3) applies, a person guilty of an offence under this section is liable[4]—

(*a*) on summary conviction, to imprisonment for a term not exceeding 6 months or a fine not exceeding the statutory maximum or both;

(*b*) on conviction on indictment, to imprisonment for a term not exceeding 10 years.

[Sexual Offences Act 2003, s 39.]

---

1 For marriage exception and sexual relationships which pre-date care relationships, see ss 43 and 44, post.
2 For "sexual", see s 78, post.
3 For "mental disorder", "penetration", "vagina" and "part of his body", see s 79, post.
4 For procedure in respect of this offence which is triable either way, see the Magistrates' Courts Act 1980, ss 17A–21 in PART I: MAGISTRATES' COURTS, PROCEDURE, ante.

7.10602 **40. Care workers: sexual activity in the presence of a person with a mental disorder** (1) A person (A) commits an offence[1] if—

(*a*) he intentionally engages in an activity,

(*b*) the activity is sexual[2],

(*c*) for the purpose of obtaining sexual gratification, he engages in it—

(i) when another person (B) is present or is in a place from which A can be observed, and

(ii) knowing or believing that B is aware, or intending that B should be aware, that he is engaging in it,

(*d*) B has a mental disorder[3],

(*e*) A knows or could reasonably be expected to know that B has a mental disorder, and

(*f*) A is involved in B's care in a way that falls within section 42.

(2) Where in proceedings for an offence under this section it is proved that the other person had a mental disorder, it is to be taken that the defendant knew or could reasonably have been expected to know that that person had a mental disorder unless sufficient evidence is adduced to raise an issue as to whether he knew or could reasonably have been expected to know it.

(3) A person guilty of an offence under this section is liable[4]—

(*a*) on summary conviction, to imprisonment for a term not exceeding 6 months or a fine not exceeding the statutory maximum or both;

(*b*) on conviction on indictment, to imprisonment for a term not exceeding 7 years.

[Sexual Offences Act 2003, s 40.]

---

1 For marriage exception and sexual relationships which pre-date care relationships, see ss 43 and 44, post.
2 For "sexual", see s 78, post.
3 For "mental disorder", see s 79, post.
4 For procedure in respect of this offence which is triable either way, see the Magistrates' Courts Act 1980, ss 17A–21 in PART I: MAGISTRATES' COURTS, PROCEDURE, ante.

7.10603 **41. Care workers: causing a person with a mental disorder to watch a sexual act** (1) A person (A) commits an offence[1] if—

(*a*) for the purpose of obtaining sexual gratification, he intentionally causes another person (B) to watch a third person engaging in an activity, or to look at an image of any person engaging in an activity,

(*b*) the activity is sexual[2],

(*c*) B has a mental disorder,

(*d*) A knows or could reasonably be expected to know that B has a mental disorder[3], and

(*e*) A is involved in B's care in a way that falls within section 42.

(2) Where in proceedings for an offence under this section it is proved that the other person had a mental disorder, it is to be taken that the defendant knew or could reasonably have been expected to know that that person had a mental disorder unless sufficient evidence is adduced to raise an issue as to whether he knew or could reasonably have been expected to know it.

(3) A person guilty of an offence under this section is liable[4]—

(*a*) on summary conviction, to imprisonment for a term not exceeding 6 months or a fine not exceeding the statutory maximum or both;

(*b*) on conviction on indictment, to imprisonment for a term not exceeding 7 years.

[Sexual Offences Act 2003, s 41.]

1 For marriage exception and sexual relationships which pre-date care relationships, see ss 43 and 44, post.
2 For "sexual", see s 78, post.
3 For "mental disorder", see s 79, post.
4 For procedure in respect of this offence which is triable either way, see the Magistrates' Courts Act 1980, ss 17A–21 in PART I: MAGISTRATES' COURTS, PROCEDURE, ante.

**7.10604 42. Care workers: interpretation** (1) For the purposes of sections 38 to 41, a person (A) is involved in the care of another person (B) in a way that falls within this section if any of subsections (2) to (4) applies.

(2) This subsection applies if—

(*a*) B is accommodated and cared for in a care home, community home, voluntary home or children's home, and

(*b*) A has functions to perform in the home in the course of employment which have brought him or are likely to bring him into regular face to face contact with B.

(3) This subsection applies if B is a patient for whom services are provided—

(*a*) by a National Health Service body or an independent medical agency;

(*b*) in an independent hospital; or

(*c*) in Wales, in an independent clinic,

and A has functions to perform for the body or agency or in the hospital or clinic in the course of employment which have brought A or are likely to bring A into regular face to face contact with B.

(4) This subsection applies if A—

(*a*) is, whether or not in the course of employment, a provider of care, assistance or services to B in connection with B's mental disorder, and

(*b*) as such, has had or is likely to have regular face to face contact with B.

(5) In this section—

"care home" means an establishment which is a care home for the purposes of the Care Standards Act 2000 (c 14);

"children's home" has the meaning given by section 1 of that Act;

"community home" has the meaning given by section 53 of the Children Act 1989 (c 41);

"employment" means any employment, whether paid or unpaid and whether under a contract of service or apprenticeship, under a contract for services, or otherwise than under a contract;

"independent clinic" has the meaning given by section 2 of the Care Standards Act 2000;

"independent hospital"—

(*a*) in England, means—

(i) a hospital as defined by section 275 of the National Health Service Act 2006 that is not a health service hospital as defined by that section; or

(ii) any other establishment in which any of the services listed in section 22(6) are provided and which is not a health service hospital as so defined; and

(*b*) in Wales, has the meaning given by section 2 of the Care Standards Act 2000;

"independent medical agency" means an undertaking (not being an independent hospital, or in Wales an independent clinic) which consists of or includes the provision of services by medical practitioners;

"National Health Service body" means—

(*a*) a Local Health Board,

(*b*) a National Health Service trust,

(*c*) a Primary Care Trust, or

(*d*) a Special Health Authority;

"voluntary home" has the meaning given by section 60(3) of the Children Act 1989.

(6) In subsection (5), in the definition of "independent medical agency", "undertaking" includes any business or profession and—

(*a*) in relation to a public or local authority, includes the exercise of any functions of that authority; and

(*b*) in relation to any other body of persons, whether corporate or unincorporate, includes any of the activities of that body.

[Sexual Offences Act 2003, s 42 as amended by SI 2007/961 and SI 2010/813.]

**7.10605 43. Sections 38 to 41: exception for spouses and civil partners** (1) Conduct by a person (A) which would otherwise be an offence under any of sections 38 to 41 against another person (B) is not an offence under that section if at the time—

(*a*) B is 16 or over, and

(*b*) A and B are lawfully married or civil partners of each other.

(2) In proceedings for such an offence it is for the defendant to prove that A and B were at the time lawfully married or civil partners of each other.

[Sexual Offences Act 2003, s 43 as amended by the Civil Partnership Act 2004, Sch 27.]

**7.10606 44. Sections 38 to 41: sexual relationships which pre-date care relationships** (1) Conduct by a person (A) which would otherwise be an offence under any of sections 38 to 41 against another person (B) is not an offence under that section if, immediately before A became involved in B's care in a way that falls within section 42, a sexual relationship existed between A and

B.

(2) Subsection (1) does not apply if at that time sexual intercourse between A and B would have been unlawful.

(3) In proceedings for an offence under any of sections 38 to 41 it is for the defendant to prove that such a relationship existed at that time.

[Sexual Offences Act 2003, s 44.]

*Sexual exploitation of children*

7.10607 **47. Paying for sexual services of a child** (1) A person (A) commits an offence if—

(*a*) he intentionally obtains for himself the sexual[1] services of another person (B),

(*b*) before obtaining those services, he has made or promised payment for those services to B or a third person, or knows that another person has made or promised such a payment, and

(*c*) either—

(i) B is under 18, and A does not reasonably believe that B is 18 or over, or

(ii) B is under 13.

(2) In this section, "payment" means any financial advantage, including the discharge of an obligation to pay or the provision of goods or services (including sexual services) gratuitously or at a discount.

(3) A person guilty of an offence under this section against a person under 13, where subsection (6) applies, is liable on conviction on indictment to imprisonment for life.

(4) Unless subsection (3) applies, a person guilty of an offence under this section against a person under 16 is liable—

(*a*) where subsection (6) applies, on conviction on indictment, to imprisonment for a term not exceeding 14 years;

(*b*) in any other case[2]—

(i) on summary conviction, to imprisonment for a term not exceeding 6 months or a fine not exceeding the statutory maximum or both;

(ii) on conviction on indictment, to imprisonment for a term not exceeding 14 years.

(5) Unless subsection (3) or (4) applies, a person guilty of an offence under this section is liable[2]—

(*a*) on summary conviction, to imprisonment for a term not exceeding 6 months or a fine not exceeding the statutory maximum or both;

(*b*) on conviction on indictment, to imprisonment for a term not exceeding 7 years.

(6) This subsection applies where the offence involved—

(*a*) penetration[3] of B's anus or vagina[3] with a part of A's body or anything else,

(*b*) penetration of B's mouth with A's penis,

(*c*) penetration of A's anus or vagina with a part of B's body or by B with anything else, or

(*d*) penetration of A's mouth with B's penis.

(7) *Repealed.*

[Sexual Offences Act 2003, s 47 as amended by SI 2008/1779 and the Serious Crime Act 2015, s 68.]

---

1 For "sexual", see s 78, post.

2 For procedure in respect of this offence which is triable either way, see the Magistrates' Courts Act 1980, ss 17A–21 in PART I: MAGISTRATES' COURTS, PROCEDURE, ante.

3 For "penetration" and "vagina", see s 79, post.

7.10608 **48. Causing or inciting sexual exploitation of a child** (1) A person (A) commits an offence if—

(*a*) he intentionally causes or incites another person (B) to be sexually exploited, in any part of the world, and

(*b*) either—

(i) B is under 18, and A does not reasonably believe that B is 18 or over, or

(ii) B is under 13.

(2) A person guilty of an offence under this section is liable[1]—

(*a*) on summary conviction, to imprisonment for a term not exceeding 6 months or a fine not exceeding the statutory maximum or both;

(*b*) on conviction on indictment, to imprisonment for a term not exceeding 14 years.

[Sexual Offences Act 2003, s 48 as amended by the Serious Crime Act 2015, s 68.]

---

1 For procedure in respect of this offence which is triable either way, see the Magistrates' Courts Act 1980, ss 17A–21 in PART I: MAGISTRATES' COURTS, PROCEDURE, ante.

7.10609 **49. Controlling a child in relation to sexual exploitation** (1) A person (A) commits an offence if—

(*a*) he intentionally controls any of the activities of another person (B) relating to B's sexual exploitation in any part of the world, and

(*b*) either—

(i) B is under 18, and A does not reasonably believe that B is 18 or over, or

(ii) B is under 13.

(2) A person guilty of an offence under this section is liable[1]—

(*a*) on summary conviction, to imprisonment for a term not exceeding 6 months or a fine not exceeding the statutory maximum or both;

(*b*) on conviction on indictment, to imprisonment for a term not exceeding 14 years.

[Sexual Offences Act 2003, s 49 as amended by the Serious Crime Act 2015, s 68.]

---

1 For procedure in respect of this offence which is triable either way, see the Magistrates' Courts Act 1980, ss 17A–21 in PART I: MAGISTRATES' COURTS, PROCEDURE, ante.

7.10610 **50. Arranging or facilitating sexual exploitation of a child** (1) A person (A) commits an offence if—

(*a*) he intentionally arranges or facilitates the sexual exploitation in any part of the world of another person (B), and

(*b*) either—

(i) B is under 18, and A does not reasonably believe that B is 18 or over, or

(ii) B is under 13.

(2) A person guilty of an offence under this section is liable[1]—

(*a*) on summary conviction, to imprisonment for a term not exceeding 6 months or a fine not exceeding the statutory maximum or both;

(*b*) on conviction on indictment, to imprisonment for a term not exceeding 14 years.

[Sexual Offences Act 2003, s 50 as amended by the Serious Crime Act 2015, s 68.]

---

1 For procedure in respect of this offence which is triable either way, see the Magistrates' Courts Act 1980, ss 17A–21 in PART I: MAGISTRATES' COURTS, PROCEDURE, ante.

7.10611 **51. Sections 48 to 50: interpretation** (1) *Repealed.*

(2) For the purposes of sections 48 to 50, a person (B) is sexually exploited if—

(*a*) on at least one occasion and whether or not compelled to do so, B offers or provides sexual services to another person in return for payment or a promise of payment to B or a third person, or

(*b*) an indecent image of B is recorded;

and "sexual exploitation" is to be interpreted accordingly.

(3) In subsection (2), "payment" means any financial advantage, including the discharge of an obligation to pay or the provision of goods or services (including sexual services) gratuitously or at a discount.

[Sexual Offences Act 2003, s 51 as amended by the Serious Crime Act 2015, s 68.]

*Prostitution*

7.10612 **51A. Soliciting** (1) It is an offence for a person in a street or public place to solicit another (B) for the purpose of obtaining B's sexual services as a prostitute.

(2) The reference to a person in a street or public place includes a person in a vehicle in a street or public place.

(3) A person guilty of an offence under this section is liable on summary conviction to a fine not exceeding level 3 on the standard scale.

(4) In this section "street" has the meaning given by section 1(4) of the Street Offences Act 1959.

[Sexual Offences Act 2003, s 51A as inserted by the Policing and Crime Act 2009, s 19.]

7.10613 **52. Causing or inciting prostitution for gain** (1) A person commits an offence if—

(*a*) he intentionally causes or incites another person to become a prostitute[1] in any part of the world, and

(*b*) he does so for or in the expectation of gain[2] for himself or a third person.

(2) A person guilty of an offence under this section is liable[3]—

(*a*) on summary conviction, to imprisonment for a term not exceeding 6 months or a fine not exceeding the statutory maximum or both;

(*b*) on conviction on indictment, to imprisonment for a term not exceeding 7 years.

[Sexual Offences Act 2003, s 52.]

---

1 For "prostitute", see s 54(2), post.

2 For "gain", see s 54(1), post.

3 For procedure in respect of this offence which is triable either way, see the Magistrates' Courts Act 1980, ss 17A–21 in PART I: MAGISTRATES' COURTS, PROCEDURE, ante.

7.10614 **53. Controlling prostitution for gain** (1) A person commits an offence if—

(*a*) he intentionally controls[1] any of the activities of another person relating to that person's prostitution[2] in any part of the world, and

(*b*) he does so for or in the expectation of gain[3] for himself or a third person.

(2) A person guilty of an offence under this section is liable[4]—

(*a*) on summary conviction, to imprisonment for a term not exceeding 6 months or a fine not exceeding the statutory maximum or both;

(*b*) on conviction on indictment, to imprisonment for a term not exceeding 7 years.

[Sexual Offences Act 2003, s 53.]

1 "Control" includes but is not limited to one who forces another to carry out the relevant activity. "Control" may be exercised in a variety of ways. It is enough where a defendant instructs or directs the other person to carry out the relevant activity or do it in a particular way. There may be a variety of reasons why the other person does as instructed: physical violence or threats of violence emotional blackmail, because the defendant has a dominating personality and the woman who acts under his direction is psychologically damaged and fragile. It may be because the defendant is an older person, and the other person is emotionally immature. It may be because the defendant holds out the lure of gain, or the hope of a better life. Or there may be other reasons: *R v Massey* [2007] EWCA Crim 2664, [2008] 2 All ER 969, [2008] 1 WLR 937, [2008] 1 Cr App Rep 28.

2 For "prostitute", see s 54(2), post.

3 For "gain", see s 54(1), post.

4 For procedure in respect of this offence which is triable either way, see the Magistrates' Courts Act 1980, ss 17A–21 in PART I: MAGISTRATES' COURTS, PROCEDURE, ante.

7.10615 **53A. Paying for sexual services of a prostitute subjected to force etc** (1) A person (A) commits an offence if—

(*a*) A makes or promises payment for the sexual services of a prostitute (B),

(*b*) a third person (C) has engaged in exploitative conduct of a kind likely to induce or encourage B to provide the sexual services for which A has made or promised payment, and

(*c*) C engaged in that conduct for or in the expectation of gain for C or another person (apart from A or B).

(2) The following are irrelevant—

(*a*) where in the world the sexual services are to be provided and whether those services are provided,

(*b*) whether A is, or ought to be, aware that C has engaged in exploitative conduct.

(3) C engages in exploitative conduct if—

(*a*) C uses force, threats (whether or not relating to violence) or any other form of coercion, or

(*b*) C practises any form of deception.

(4) A person guilty of an offence under this section is liable on summary conviction to a fine not exceeding level 3 on the standard scale.

[Sexual Offences Act 2003, s 53A as inserted by the Policing and Crime Act 2009, s 14.]

7.10616 **54. Sections 51A to 53A: interpretation** (1) In sections 52, 53 and 53A, "gain" means—

(*a*) any financial advantage, including the discharge of an obligation to pay or the provision of goods or services (including sexual services) gratuitously or at a discount; or

(*b*) the goodwill of any person which is or appears likely, in time, to bring financial advantage.

(2) In sections 51A, 52, 53 and 53A "prostitute" means a person (A) who, on at least one occasion and whether or not compelled to do so, offers or provides sexual services to another person in return for payment or a promise of payment to A or a third person; and "prostitution" is to be interpreted accordingly.

(3) In subsection (2) and section 53A, "payment" means any financial advantage, including the discharge of an obligation to pay or the provision of goods or services (including sexual services) gratuitously or at a discount.

[Sexual Offences Act 2003, s 54 as amended by the Policing and Crime Act 2009, Sch 7 and the Serious Crime Act 2015, Sch 4.]

*Preparatory offences*

7.10622 **61. Administering a substance with intent** (1) A person commits an offence if he intentionally administers a substance to, or causes a substance to be taken by, another person (B)—

(*a*) knowing that B does not consent[1], and

(*b*) with the intention of stupefying or overpowering B, so as to enable any person to engage in a sexual activity that involves B.

(2) A person guilty of an offence under this section is liable[2]—

(*a*) on summary conviction, to imprisonment for a term not exceeding 6 months or a fine not exceeding the statutory maximum or both;

(*b*) on conviction on indictment, to imprisonment for a term not exceeding 10 years.

[Sexual Offences Act 2003, s 61.]

1 For "consent", see s 74, post.

2 For procedure in respect of this offence which is triable either way, see the Magistrates' Courts Act 1980, ss 17A–21 in PART I: MAGISTRATES' COURTS, PROCEDURE, ante

7.10623 **62. Committing an offence with intent to commit a sexual offence** (1) A person commits an offence under this section if he commits any offence with the intention of committing a relevant sexual offence.

(2) In this section, "relevant sexual offence" means any offence under this Part (including an offence of aiding, abetting, counselling or procuring such an offence).

(3) A person guilty of an offence under this section is liable on conviction on indictment, where

the offence is committed by kidnapping or false imprisonment, to imprisonment for life.

(4) Unless subsection (3) applies, a person guilty of an offence under this section is liable[1]—

(*a*) on summary conviction, to imprisonment for a term not exceeding 6 months or a fine not exceeding the statutory maximum or both;

(*b*) on conviction on indictment, to imprisonment for a term not exceeding 10 years.

[Sexual Offences Act 2003, s 62.]

1 For procedure in respect of this offence which is triable either way, see the Magistrates' Courts Act 1980, ss 17A–21 in PART I: MAGISTRATES' COURTS, PROCEDURE, ante.

7.10624 **63. Trespass with intent to commit a sexual offence** (1) A person commits an offence if—

(*a*) he is a trespasser on any premises,

(*b*) he intends to commit a relevant sexual offence[1] on the premises, and

(*c*) he knows that, or is reckless as to whether, he is a trespasser.

(2) In this section—

"premises" includes a structure or part of a structure;

"relevant sexual offence" has the same meaning as in section 62;

"structure" includes a tent, vehicle or vessel or other temporary or movable structure.

(3) A person guilty of an offence under this section is liable[2]—

(*a*) on summary conviction, to imprisonment for a term not exceeding 6 months or a fine not exceeding the statutory maximum or both;

(*b*) on conviction on indictment, to imprisonment for a term not exceeding 10 years.

[Sexual Offences Act 2003, s 63.]

1 "Relevant sexual offence" is defined in s 62 (s 63(2)). In relation to a statement of offence in an information, a charge or an indictment, the Criminal Procedure Rules provide that it must contain a statement of the offence that describes the offence in ordinary language and identifies any legislation that creates it and 'such particulars of the conduct constituting the commission of the offence as to make clear what the prosecutor alleges against the defendant'. Where the evidence points to a specific sexual offence intended, the prosecution will be in a position to make clear what is alleged, by identifying the offence alleged in the particulars of the offence. Where the prosecution alleges it is obvious from all the circumstances that the defendant intended to commit a sexual offence but it is impossible to specify precisely which one and upon whom, s 63 covers both situations, provided, any prosecution and trial can be fair. Prosecutors may obviate an objection by narrowing the offences and putting more details into the body of the particulars. It is not necessary for a bench or jury to agree on the sexual offence intended, provided they are all agreed that the ingredients of the offence are made out, namely that he trespassed with the intent to commit a relevant sexual offence: *R v Pacurar* [2016] EWCA (Crim) 569, [2016] 1 WLR 3913, [2016] 2 Cr App R 26.

2 For procedure in respect of this offence which is triable either way, see the Magistrates' Courts Act 1980, ss 17A–21 in PART I: MAGISTRATES' COURTS, PROCEDURE, ante.

*Sex with an adult relative*

7.10625 **64. Sex with an adult relative: penetration** (1) A person aged 16 or over (A) (subject to subsection (3A)) commits an offence if—

(*a*) he intentionally penetrates[1] another person's vagina[1] or anus with a part of his body[1] or anything else, or penetrates another person's mouth with his penis,

(*b*) the penetration is sexual[2],

(*c*) the other person (B) is aged 18 or over,

(*d*) A is related to B in a way mentioned in subsection (2), and

(*e*) A knows or could reasonably be expected to know that he is related to B in that way.

(2) The ways that A may be related to B are as parent, grandparent, child, grandchild, brother, sister, half-brother, half-sister, uncle, aunt, nephew or niece.

(3) In subsection (2)—

(*za*) "parent" includes an adoptive parent;

(*zb*) "child" includes an adopted person within the meaning of Chapter 4 of Part 1 of the Adoption and Children Act 2002;

(*a*) "uncle" means the brother of a person's parent, and "aunt" has a corresponding meaning;

(*b*) "nephew" means the child of a person's brother or sister, and "niece" has a corresponding meaning.

(3A) Where subsection (1) applies in a case where A is related to B as B's child by virtue of subsection (3)(*zb*), A does not commit an offence under this section unless A is 18 or over.

(4) Where in proceedings for an offence under this section it is proved that the defendant was related to the other person in any of those ways, it is to be taken that the defendant knew or could reasonably have been expected to know that he was related in that way unless sufficient evidence is adduced to raise an issue as to whether he knew or could reasonably have been expected to know that he was.

(5) A person guilty of an offence under this section is liable[3]—

(*a*) on summary conviction, to imprisonment for a term not exceeding 6 months or a fine not exceeding the statutory maximum or both;

(*b*) on conviction on indictment, to imprisonment for a term not exceeding 2 years.

(6) Nothing in—

(*a*) section 47 of the Adoption Act 1976 (which disapplies the status provisions in section 39 of that Act for the purposes of this section in relation to adoptions before 30 December 2005), or

(*b*) section 74 of the Adoption and Children Act 2002 (which disapplies the status provisions in section 67 of that Act for those purposes in relation to adoptions on or after that date),

is to be read as preventing the application of section 39 of the Adoption Act 1976 or section 67 of the Adoption and Children Act 2002 for the purposes of subsection (3)(*za*) and (*zb*) above.

[Sexual Offences Act 2003, s 64 as amended by the Criminal Justice and Immigration Act 2008, Sch 15.]

1 For "penetration", "vagina" and "part of his body", see s 79, post.
2 For "sexual", see s 78, post.
3 For procedure in respect of this offence which is triable either way, see the Magistrates' Courts Act 1980, ss 17A–21 in Part I: Magistrates' Courts, Procedure, ante.

7.10626 **65. Sex with an adult relative: consenting to penetration** (1) A person aged 16 or over (A) (subject to subsection (3A)) commits an offence if—

(*a*) another person (B) penetrates[1] A's vagina[1] or anus with a part of B's body[1] or anything else, or penetrates A's mouth with B's penis,
(*b*) A consents[2] to the penetration,
(*c*) the penetration is sexual[3],
(*d*) B is aged 18 or over,
(*e*) A is related to B in a way mentioned in subsection (2), and
(*f*) A knows or could reasonably be expected to know that he is related to B in that way.

(2) The ways that A may be related to B are as parent, grandparent, child, grandchild, brother, sister, half-brother, half-sister, uncle, aunt, nephew or niece.

(3) In subsection (2)—

(*za*) "parent" includes an adoptive parent;
(*zb*) "child" includes an adopted person within the meaning of Chapter 4 of Part 1 of the Adoption and Children Act 2002;
(*a*) "uncle" means the brother of a person's parent, and "aunt" has a corresponding meaning;
(*b*) "nephew" means the child of a person's brother or sister, and "niece" has a corresponding meaning.

(3A) Where subsection (1) applies in a case where A is related to B as B's child by virtue of subsection (3)(*zb*), A does not commit an offence under this section unless A is 18 or over.

(4) Where in proceedings for an offence under this section it is proved that the defendant was related to the other person in any of those ways, it is to be taken that the defendant knew or could reasonably have been expected to know that he was related in that way unless sufficient evidence is adduced to raise an issue as to whether he knew or could reasonably have been expected to know that he was.

(5) A person guilty of an offence under this section is liable[4]—

(*a*) on summary conviction, to imprisonment for a term not exceeding 6 months or a fine not exceeding the statutory maximum or both;
(*b*) on conviction on indictment, to imprisonment for a term not exceeding 2 years.

(6) Nothing in—

(*a*) section 47 of the Adoption Act 1976 (which disapplies the status provisions in section 39 of that Act for the purposes of this section in relation to adoptions before 30 December 2005), or
(*b*) section 74 of the Adoption and Children Act 2002 (which disapplies the status provisions in section 67 of that Act for those purposes in relation to adoptions on or after that date),

is to be read as preventing the application of section 39 of the Adoption Act 1976 or section 67 of the Adoption and Children Act 2002 for the purposes of subsection (3)(*za*) and (*zb*) above.

[Sexual Offences Act 2003, s 65 as amended by the Criminal Justice and Immigration Act 2008, Sch 15.]

1 For "penetration", "vagina" and "part of his body", see s 79, post.
2 For "consent", see s 74, post.
3 For "sexual", see s 78, post.
4 For procedure in respect of this offence which is triable either way, see the Magistrates' Courts Act 1980, ss 17A–21 in Part I: Magistrates' Courts, Procedure, ante.

*Other offences*

7.10627 **66. Exposure** (1) A person commits an offence if—

(*a*) he intentionally exposes his genitals, and
(*b*) he intends that someone will see them and be caused alarm or distress.

(2) A person guilty of an offence under this section is liable[1]—

(*a*) on summary conviction, to imprisonment for a term not exceeding 6 months or a fine not exceeding the statutory maximum or both;
(*b*) on conviction on indictment, to imprisonment for a term not exceeding 2 years.

[Sexual Offences Act 2003, s 66.]

[1] For procedure in respect of this offence which is triable either way, see the Magistrates' Courts Act 1980, ss 17A–21 in PART I: MAGISTRATES' COURTS, PROCEDURE, ante.

**7.10628** **67. Voyeurism** (1) A person commits an offence if—

(*a*) for the purpose of obtaining sexual gratification[1], he observes another person doing a private act[2], and

(*b*) he knows that the other person does not consent[3] to being observed for his sexual gratification.

(2) A person commits an offence if—

(*a*) he operates equipment with the intention of enabling another person to observe[4], for the purpose of obtaining sexual gratification, a third person (B) doing a private act, and

(*b*) he knows that B does not consent[3] to his operating equipment with that intention.

(3) A person commits an offence if—

(*a*) he records another person (B) doing a private act,

(*b*) he does so with the intention that he or a third person will, for the purpose of obtaining sexual gratification, look at an image[4] of B doing the act, and

(*c*) he knows that B does not consent[3] to his recording the act with that intention.

(4) A person commits an offence if he installs equipment, or constructs or adapts a structure[5] or part of a structure, with the intention of enabling himself or another person to commit an offence under subsection (1).

(5) A person guilty of an offence under this section is liable[6]—

(*a*) on summary conviction, to imprisonment for a term not exceeding 6 months or a fine not exceeding the statutory maximum or both;

(*b*) on conviction on indictment, to imprisonment for a term not exceeding 2 years.

[Sexual Offences Act 2003, s 67.]

[1] The purpose of obtaining sexual gratification forms part of the relevant act; thus, where a defendant was unfit to plead and the jury had to determine whether or not he had committed the relevant act, it was necessary for the jury to find both deliberate observation and the purpose of sexual gratification (but not the mental element specified in (1)(*b*)): *R v B* [2012] EWCA Crim 770, [2012] 3 All ER 1093, [2013] 1 WLR 499.

[2] For "private act", see s 68(1), post.

[3] For "consent", see s 74, post.

[4] For "observes" and "image", see s 79, post.

[5] For "structure", see s 68(2), post.

[6] For procedure in respect of this offence which is triable either way, see the Magistrates' Courts Act 1980, ss 17A–21 in PART I: MAGISTRATES' COURTS, PROCEDURE, ante.

**7.10629** **68. Voyeurism: interpretation** (1) For the purposes of section 67, a person is doing a private act if the person is in a place which, in the circumstances, would reasonably be expected to provide privacy, and—

(*a*) the person's genitals, buttocks or breasts[1] are exposed or covered only with underwear,

(*b*) the person is using a lavatory, or

(*c*) the person is doing a sexual act that is not of a kind ordinarily done in public.

(2) In section 67, "structure" includes a tent, vehicle or vessel or other temporary or movable structure.

[Sexual Offences Act 2003, s 68.]

[1] This refers to female breasts and does not include an exposed male chest: *R v Bassett* [2008] EWCA (Crim) 1174, [2009] 1 WLR 1032, [2009] 1 Cr App Rep 90.

**7.10630** **69. Intercourse with an animal** (1) A person commits an offence if—

(*a*) he intentionally performs an act of penetration with his penis,

(*b*) what is penetrated is the vagina or anus[1] of a living animal, and

(*c*) he knows that, or is reckless as to whether, that is what is penetrated.

(2) A person (A) commits an offence if—

(*a*) A intentionally causes, or allows, A's vagina or anus to be penetrated,

(*b*) the penetration is by the penis of a living animal, and

(*c*) A knows that, or is reckless as to whether, that is what A is being penetrated by.

(3) A person guilty of an offence under this section is liable[2]—

(*a*) on summary conviction, to imprisonment for a term not exceeding 6 months or a fine not exceeding the statutory maximum or both;

(*b*) on conviction on indictment, to imprisonment for a term not exceeding 2 years.

[Sexual Offences Act 2003, s 69.]

[1] In relation to an animal, references to the vagina or anus include references to any similar part (s 79(10), post).

[2] For procedure in respect of this offence which is triable either way, see the Magistrates' Courts Act 1980, ss 17A–21 in PART I: MAGISTRATES' COURTS, PROCEDURE, ante.

**7.10631** **70. Sexual penetration of a corpse** (1) A person commits an offence if—

(*a*) he intentionally performs an act of penetration[1] with a part of his body or anything else,

(*b*) what is penetrated is a part of the body of a dead person,

(*c*) he knows that, or is reckless as to whether, that is what is penetrated, and (*d*) the penetration is sexual[2].

(2) A person guilty of an offence under this section is liable[3]—

(*a*) on summary conviction, to imprisonment for a term not exceeding 6 months or a fine not exceeding the statutory maximum or both;

(*b*) on conviction on indictment, to imprisonment for a term not exceeding 2 years.

[Sexual Offences Act 2003, s 70.]

---

1 For "penetration", see s 79, post.

2 For "sexual", see s 78, post.

3 For procedure in respect of this offence which is triable either way, see the Magistrates' Courts Act 1980, ss 17A–21 in PART I: MAGISTRATES' COURTS, PROCEDURE, ante.

7.10632 **71. Sexual activity in a public lavatory** (1) A person commits an offence if—

(*a*) he is in a lavatory to which the public or a section of the public has or is permitted to have access, whether on payment or otherwise,

(*b*) he intentionally engages in an activity, and,

(*c*) the activity is sexual.

(2) For the purposes of this section, an activity is sexual if a reasonable person would, in all the circumstances but regardless of any person's purpose, consider it to be sexual.

(3) A person guilty of an offence under this section is liable on summary conviction, to imprisonment for a term not exceeding 6 months or a fine not exceeding level 5 on the standard scale or both.

[Sexual Offences Act 2003, s 71.]

*Offences outside the United Kingdom*

7.10633 **72. Offences outside the United Kingdom** (1) If—

(*a*) a United Kingdom national does an act in a country outside the United Kingdom, and

(*b*) the act, if done in England and Wales, would constitute a sexual offence to which this section applies,

the United Kingdom national is guilty in England and Wales of that sexual offence.

(2) If—

(*a*) a United Kingdom resident does an act in a country outside the United Kingdom,

(*b*) the act constitutes an offence under the law in force in that country, and

(*c*) the act, if done in England and Wales, would constitute a sexual offence to which this section applies,

the United Kingdom resident is guilty in England and Wales of that sexual offence.

(3) If—

(*a*) a person does an act in a country outside the United Kingdom at a time when the person was not a United Kingdom national or a United Kingdom resident,

(*b*) the act constituted an offence under the law in force in that country,

(*c*) the act, if done in England and Wales, would have constituted a sexual offence to which this section applies, and

(*d*) the person meets the residence or nationality condition at the relevant time,

proceedings may be brought against the person in England and Wales for that sexual offence as if the person had done the act there.

(4) The person meets the residence or nationality condition at the relevant time if the person is a United Kingdom national or a United Kingdom resident at the time when the proceedings are brought.

(5) An act punishable under the law in force in any country constitutes an offence under that law for the purposes of subsections (2) and (3) however it is described in that law.

(6) The condition in subsection (2)(*b*) or (3)(*b*) is to be taken to be met unless, not later than rules of court may provide, the defendant serves on the prosecution a notice—

(*a*) stating that, on the facts as alleged with respect to the act in question, the condition is not in the defendant's opinion met,

(*b*) showing the grounds for that opinion, and

(*c*) requiring the prosecution to prove that it is met.

(7) But the court, if it thinks fit, may permit the defendant to require the prosecution to prove that the condition is met without service of a notice under subsection (6).

(8) In the Crown Court the question whether the condition is met is to be decided by the judge alone.

(9) In this section—

"country" includes territory;

"United Kingdom national" means an individual who is—

(*a*) a British citizen, a British overseas territories citizen, a British National (Overseas) or a British Overseas citizen;

(*b*) a person who under the British Nationality Act 1981 is a British subject; or

(*c*) a British protected person within the meaning of that Act;

"United Kingdom resident" means an individual who is resident in the United Kingdom.

(10) Schedule 2 lists the sexual offences to which this section applies.

[Sexual Offences Act 2003, s 72 as substituted by the Criminal Justice and Immigration Act 2008, s 72 and amended by SI 2008/1779.]

*Supplementary and general*

7.10634 **73. Exceptions to aiding, abetting and counselling** (1) A person is not guilty of aiding, abetting or counselling the commission against a child of an offence to which this section applies if he acts for the purpose of—

(*a*) protecting the child from sexually transmitted infection,

(*b*) protecting the physical safety of the child,

(*c*) preventing the child from becoming pregnant, or

(*d*) promoting the child's emotional well-being by the giving of advice,

and not for the purpose of obtaining sexual gratification or for the purpose of causing or encouraging the activity constituting the offence or the child's participation in it.

(2) This section applies to—

(*a*) an offence under any of sections 5 to 7 (offences against children under 13);

(*b*) an offence under section 9 (sexual activity with a child);

(*c*) an offence under section 13 which would be an offence under section 9 if the offender were aged 18;

(*d*) an offence under any of sections 16, 25, 30, 34 and 38 (sexual activity) against a person under 16.

(3) This section does not affect any other enactment or any rule of law restricting the circumstances in which a person is guilty of aiding, abetting or counselling an offence under this Part.

[Sexual Offences Act 2003, s 73.]

7.10635 **74. "Consent"** For the purposes of this Part, a person consents if he agrees by choice, and has the freedom and capacity[1] to make that choice[2].

[Sexual Offences Act 2003, s 74.]

[1] Then burden of proving incapacity falls on the prosecution and the standard of proof is proof beyond reasonable doubt: *R v Avanzi* [2014] WLR (D) 55. Some deceptions (such as, for example, in relation to wealth) would obviously not be sufficient to vitiate consent. The evidence relating to "choice' and the "freedom' to make any particular choice must be approached in a broad commonsense way. Depending on the circumstances, deception as to gender can vitiate consent such as where the defendant, a girl, impersonated a male and had obtained consent by fraudulent deception and the complainant, had she known the truth, would not have consented to acts of vaginal penetration: *R v McNally* [2013] EWCA Crim 1051, [2014] QB 593, [2014] 2 WLR 200, [2013] 2 Cr App R 28. See also the note to s 30(2)(*a*), ante.

In *R v Ali* [2015] EWCA Crim 1279, [2015] 2 Cr App Rep 457, [2015] All ER (D) 202 (Jul) the defendants were charged with various sexual offences, including rape and trafficking within the UK for sexual exploitation. The prosecution case was that defendants targeted young girls, often from troubled backgrounds, whom they groomed for sexual purposes. It was alleged that they drove the victims to a variety of out-of-the-way locations where they sexually assaulted and raped them, usually having first plied them with alcohol. The prosecution contended that, as the result of such grooming, the victims became sexually compliant and that any apparent consent on their part was not genuine or real. The defendants were convicted and the first defendant appealed, contending, in relation to the rape convictions, that the prosecution had impermissibly invited the jury to ignore the evidence of the alleged victims, which was too the effect that they had consented, and to substitute their own moral judgment as to the sexual relations which had occurred:

> "56 It is necessary to consider certain aspects of the principles that apply in these circumstances. There are many instances when the complainant's evidence as to whether she consented will determine if there is a case to go to the jury. In our judgment, however, in particular situations such as the present the prosecution is not obliged to call overt evidence from the alleged victim to the effect that he or she did not consent, given it is possible that the circumstances may have limited or distorted the individual's appreciation or understanding of his or her role in the sexual relations and the true nature of what occurred. This issue was explored in *R v Malone* [1998] 2 Cr App R. 447, when Roch LJ in giving the judgment of the court observed (at 457):
>
> > 'No doubt in order to obtain a conviction there will have to be some evidence of lack of consent to go before the jury. But what that evidence will be will depend on the particular circumstances of the case that the jury is trying. The evidence may be of widely differing kinds as a few illustrations will show. It may be the complainant's simple assertion "I did not consent to sexual intercourse with the defendant". It may be evidence of threats uttered by the defendant. It may be evidence of the use of physical force by the defendant. It may be evidence that the complainant was by reason of drink or drugs incapable of giving consent or incapable of being aware of what was occurring. It may be evidence that by reason of age or lack of understanding due to mental handicap the complainant did not give consent. The jury may accept that the complainant was asleep when sexual intercourse occurred or that she was tricked into giving her consent in the belief that the defendant was her husband or partner. We do not for a moment suggest that these examples exhaust the possible factual situations which may arise. They suffice to demonstrate that it is not the law that the prosecution in order to obtain a conviction for rape have to show that the complainant was either incapable of saying no or putting up some physical resistance or did say no or put up some physical resistance.'
>
> 57 One of the consequences when vulnerable people are groomed for sexual exploitation is that compliance can mask the lack of true consent on the part of the victim. As the judge directed the jury in the summing-up in this case, where there is evidence of exploitation of a young and immature person who may not understand the full significance of what he or she is doing, that is a factor the jury can take into

account in deciding whether or not there was genuine consent. This was directly recognised by this court in *R v Robinson* [2011] EWCA Crim 916, [2011] All ER (D) 264 (Mar) (per Elias LJ):

'21. Grooming is not a term of art, but it suggests cynical and manipulative behaviour designed to achieve a particular sexual objective. Not all relationships with underage children can fairly be characterised as involving grooming, although many will. But even where they can, the fact of grooming plainly does not necessarily vitiate consent. Many a seducer achieves his objectives with the liberal and cynical employment of gifts, insincere compliments and false promises. But such manipulative and deceitful methods could not be relied upon to establish a lack of consent whenever the seduction was successful. The situation will often be no different where the complainant is under age. But where the exploitation is of a girl who is of an age where she does not, or may not, have the capacity to understand the full significance of what she is doing, and in particular, where, as here, there was evidence of acquiescence or acceptance rather than positive consent, we think that, as the judge found, it would be open to the jury to conclude that the complainant, perhaps out of embarrassment or some other reason, had in reality unwillingly gone along with the acts which she did not in fact wish to engage in.'

58 Although, as Elias LJ observed, grooming does not necessarily vitiate consent, it starkly raises the possibility that a vulnerable or immature individual may have been placed in a position in which he or she is led merely to acquiesce rather than to give proper or real consent. One of the consequences of grooming is that it has a tendency to limit or subvert the alleged victim's capacity to make free decisions, and it creates the risk that he or she simply submitted because of the environment of dependency created by those responsible for treating the alleged victim in this way. Indeed, the individual may have been manipulated to the extent that he or she is unaware of, or confused about, the distinction between acquiescence and genuine agreement at the time the incident occurred.

59 The critical distinction between consent and submission was explored in *R v Olugboja* (1981) 73 Cr. App. R. 344. Dunn LJ in giving the judgment of the court observed (at 350):

'Although "consent" is an equally common word it covers a wide range of states of mind in the context of intercourse between a man and a woman, ranging from actual desire on the one hand to reluctant acquiescence on the other. We do not think that the issue of consent should be left to a jury without some further direction. What this should be will depend on the circumstances of each case. The jury will have been reminded of the burden and standard of proof required to establish each ingredient, including lack of consent, of the offence. They should be directed that consent, or the absence of it, is to be given its ordinary meaning and if need be, by way of example, that there is a difference between consent and submission; every consent involves a submission, but it by no means follows that a mere submission involves consent (per Coleridge J. in *Day* (1841) 9 C. & P. 722, 724). In the majority of cases, where the allegation is that the intercourse was had by force or the fear of force, such a direction coupled with specific references to and comments on the evidence relevant to the absence of real consent will clearly suffice. In the less common type of case where intercourse takes place after threats not involving violence or the fear of it, . . . we think that an appropriate direction to a jury will have to be fuller. They should be directed to concentrate on the state of mind of the victim immediately before the act of sexual intercourse, having regard to all the relevant circumstances, and in particular the events leading up to the act, and her reaction to them showing their impact on her mind. Apparent acquiescence after penetration does not necessarily involve consent, which must have occurred before the act takes place. In addition to the general direction about consent . . . the jury will probably be helped in such cases by being reminded that in this context consent does comprehend . . . (a) wide spectrum of states of mind . . . , and that the dividing line in such circumstances between real consent on the one hand and mere submission on the other may not be easy to draw. Where it is to be drawn in a given case is for the jury to decide, applying their combined good sense, experience and knowledge of human nature and modern behaviour to all the relevant facts of that case.'

60 Hallett LJ indicated in *R v H* [2007] EWCA Crim 2056 that questions of capacity and consent should normally be left to the jury. It is, therefore, only in clear cases that a judge should conclude that there is no evidence on which the jury could properly convict in a case of this kind and accede to a submission of no case.

61 In summary, in a case in these circumstances in which a vulnerable or immature individual has allegedly been groomed by the defendant, the question of whether real or proper consent was given will usually be for the jury unless the evidence clearly indicates that proper consent was given." (per Fulford LJ)

[2] Prior to the enactment of the Sexual Offences Act 2003, where a person suffering from HIV had sexual intercourse without disclosing his condition to the other party that did not vitiate the other party's consent to that intercourse: *R v Dica* [2004] EWCA Crim 1103, [2004] QB 1257, [2004] 2 Cr App Rep 467. It was held in *R v B* [2006] EWCA Crim 2945, [2007] 1 WLR 1567, [2007] 1 Cr App Rep 388 that the 2003 Act had not changed the position.

As to the relevance of voluntary intoxication by the complainant, it was held in *R v Bree* [2007] EWCA Crim 804, [2008] QB 131, [2007] 3 WLR 600, [2007] 2 All ER 676, [2007] 1 WLR 1567 (per Sir Igor Judge P):

"[25] . . . There is nothing abnormal, surprising, or even unusual about men and women having consensual intercourse when one, or other, or both have voluntarily consumed a great deal of alcohol. Provided intercourse is indeed consensual, it is not rape. [26] In cases which are said to arise after voluntary consumption of alcohol the question is not whether the alcohol made either or both less inhibited than they would have been if sober, nor whether either or both might afterwards have regretted what had happened, and indeed wished that it had not. If the complainant consents, her consent cannot be revoked . . . [34] In our judgment, the proper construction of s 74 of the 2003 Act, as applied to the problem now under discussion, leads to clear conclusions. If, through drink (or for any other reason) the complainant has temporarily lost her capacity to choose whether to have intercourse on the relevant occasion, she is not consenting, and subject to questions about the defendant's state of mind, if intercourse takes place, this would be rape. However, where the complainant has voluntarily consumed even substantial quantities of alcohol, but nevertheless remains capable of choosing whether or not to have intercourse, and in drink agrees to do so, this would not be rape. We should perhaps underline that, as a matter of practical reality, capacity to consent may evaporate well before a complainant becomes unconscious. Whether this is so or not, however, is fact specific, or more accurately, depends on the actual state of mind of the individuals involved on the particular occasion. [35] Considerations like these underline the fact that it would be unrealistic to endeavour to create some kind of grid system which would enable the answer to these questions to be related to some prescribed level of alcohol consumption.

Experience shows that different individuals have a greater or lesser capacity to cope with alcohol than others, and indeed the ability of a single individual to do so may vary from day to day. The practical reality is that there are some areas of human behaviour which are inapt for detailed legislative structures. In this context, provisions intended to protect women from sexual assaults might very well be conflated into a system which would provide patronising interference with the right of autonomous adults to make personal decisions for themselves. [36] For these reasons, notwithstanding criticisms of the statutory provisions, in our view the 2003 Act provides a clear definition of 'consent' for the purposes of the law of rape, and by defining it with reference to 'capacity to make that choice', sufficiently addresses the issue of consent in the context of voluntary consumption of alcohol by the complainant. The problems do not arise from the legal principles. They lie with infinite circumstances of human behaviour, usually taking place in private without independent evidence, and the consequent difficulties of proving this very serious offence". (per Sir Igor Judge P).

In *R v Jheeta* [2007] EWCA Crim 1699, [2008] 1 WLR 2582, [2007] 2 Cr App Rep 32, [2008] Crim LR 144, the defendant created a bizarre and fictitious fantasy which, because it was real enough to the complainant, pressurised her to have intercourse with him more frequently than she otherwise would have done. She was not, however, deceived as to the nature or purpose of intercourse, but deceived as to the situation in which she found herself; accordingly, the conclusive presumption within s 76(2)(*a*) of the 2003 Act had no application. However, the appellant had accepted that there had been occasions when sexual intercourse had taken place when the complainant had not been truly consenting, acknowledging that he had persuaded the complainant to have intercourse with him more frequently than she would otherwise have done and the persuasion had taken the form of the pressures imposed on her by the complicated and unpleasant scheme which he had fabricated. That was not a free choice or consent for the purposes of the 2003 Act, and in those circumstances, there was no doubt that on some occasions at least the complainant had not consented to intercourse for the purposes of s 74 and that the appellant had been perfectly well aware of that fact. In *R (on the application of F) v DPP* [2013] EWHC 945 (Admin), [2014] QB 581, [2014] 2 WLR 190 the claimant challenged a decision of the DPP not to prosecute an offence of rape where the claimant had claimed that she had consented to intercourse only on the basis that her partner would not ejaculate inside her vagina and the DPP had taken this to be a true account. It was held:

"Ejaculation is irrelevant to this definition: so is pregnancy. If ejaculation occurs it may be an aggravating feature relevant to sentence: it is irrelevant to proof of the offence itself.

22 At the time when the review was written (the senior CPS lawyer) did not have the advantage of the judgment of the Divisional Court in *Assange v Swedish Prosecution Authority* [2011] EWHC 2849 (Admin). It was submitted to the Divisional Court that as the complainant had consented to sexual intercourse only on the basis that Assange would use a condom, even if he did not, that fact was or would be irrelevant. She had consented to intercourse. Sir John Thomas (President of the Queen's Bench Division) explained, at [86]:

'The question of consent in the present case is to be determined by reference to s 74. The allegation is clear and covers the alternative; it is not an allegation that the condom came off accidentally or was damaged accidentally. It would plainly be open to a jury to hold that, if (the complainant) had made clear that she would only consent to sexual intercourse if Mr Assange used a condom, then there would be no consent if, without her consent, he did not use a condom, or removed or tore the condom without her consent. His conduct in having sexual intercourse without a condom in circumstances where she had made clear she would only have sexual intercourse if he used a condom would therefore amount to an offence under the Sexual Offences Act 2003, whatever the position may have been prior to that Act.'

23 Having reached that conclusion, the Divisional Court addressed the question whether Mr Assange's conduct in having sexual intercourse without a condom, or in continuing with it after removing, damaging or tearing the condom was 'deceptive'. The point did not require a firm conclusion, but it was accepted that 'it could be argued that sexual intercourse without a condom was different from sexual intercourse with a condom, given the presence of a physical barrier, a perceived difference in the threat in the degree of intimacy, the risks of disease and the prevention of a pregnancy; moreover the editors of Smith and Hogan (12th ed. at p. 866) commented that it had been argued that unprotected sexual intercourse should be treated as being different in nature to protected sexual intercourse'. However, the court was not inclined to accept this approach, noting that the editors of Smith and Hogan approached the possible deception in relation to the use of a condom as 'likely to be held to remove any purported free agreement by the complainant under s 74'. The court further noted a view to similar effect expressed in the well-known text book Rook and Ward on Sexual Offences (4th ed. at para. 1.216.)

24 We must emphasise that we are not addressing the situation in which sexual intercourse occurs consensually when the man, intending to withdraw in accordance with his partner's wishes, or their understanding, nevertheless ejaculates prematurely, or accidentally, within rather than outside his partner's vagina. These things happen. They always have and they always will, and no offence is committed when they do. They underline why withdrawal is not a safe method of contraception. Equally we are not addressing the many fluctuating ways in which sexual relationships may develop, as couples discover and renew their own levels of understanding and tolerance, their codes of communication, express or understood, and mutual give and take, experimentation and excitement. These are intensely private matters, personal to the couple in question.

25 The facts suggested by the evidence in this case are quite different. It is inappropriate to examine the incident of sexual intercourse in February 2010 in isolation from the well evidenced history (including his own admissions) of the intervener's sexual dominance of the claimant and her unenthusiastic acquiescence to his demands. Given that essential background, the evidence about the incident in February 2010 is reasonably open to this analysis. Consensual penetration occurred. The claimant consented on the clear understanding that the intervener would not ejaculate within her vagina. She believed that he intended and agreed to withdraw before ejaculation. The intervener knew and understood that this was the only basis on which she was prepared to have sexual intercourse with him. There is evidence from the history of the relationship, as well as what he said when sexual intercourse was taking place, and his observations to the claimant afterwards, that although he never disclosed his intention to her (because if she had known he knew that she would have never have consented), either from the outset of penetration, or after penetration had begun, he intended that this occasion of sexual intercourse would culminate in ejaculation within her vagina, whatever her wishes and their understanding. In short, there is evidence that he deliberately ignored the basis of her consent to penetration as a manifestation of his control over her.

26 In law, the question which arises is whether this factual structure can give rise to a conviction of rape. Did the claimant consent to this penetration? She did so, provided, in the language of s 74 of the 2003 Act, she agreed by choice, when she had the freedom and capacity to make the choice. What *Assange* underlines is that 'choice' is crucial to the issue of 'consent', and indeed we underline that the statutory definition of consent provided in s 74 applies equally to s 1(1)(*c*) as it does to s 1(1)(*b*). The evidence relating to 'choice' and the 'freedom' to make any particular choice must be approached in a broad commonsense way. If before penetration began the intervener had made up his mind that he would penetrate and ejaculate within the claimant's vagina, or even, because 'penetration is a continuing act from entry to withdrawal' (see s 79(2) of the 2003 Act) he decided that he would not withdraw at all, just because he deemed the

claimant subservient to his control, she was deprived of choice relating to the crucial feature on which her original consent to sexual intercourse was based. Accordingly her consent was negated. Contrary to her wishes, and knowing that she would not have consented, and did not consent to penetration or the continuation of penetration if she had any inkling of his intention, he deliberately ejaculated within her vagina. In law, this combination of circumstances falls within the statutory definition of rape.

27 The entire body of evidence, both in relation to the nature and history of the relationship between these two people, and as it applies to each of the individual, specific occasions of complaint, requires re-examination in the light of these observations. This decision should be reviewed in the light of the legal principles explained in this judgment. This is an appropriate case in which to order a judicial review. (Per Lord Judge LCJ)"

See also *R v McNally* [2013] EWCA Crim 1051, [2014] QB 593, [2014] 2 WLR 200 where the defendant pretended to be male and the issue was whether this deception vitiated the complainant's consent to a number of acts of assault by penetration. The Court affirmed that the evidence relating to choice and freedom to choose had to be approached in a broad and commonsense way. While digital penetration was the same in a physical sense whether performed by a male or a female, the act was different when the complainant was deceived as in the present case and consent was vitiated because her freedom to choose whether or not to have a sexual account with a girl was removed by the deception.

7.10636 **75. Evidential presumptions about consent** (1) If in proceedings for an offence to which this section applies it is proved—

(*a*) that the defendant did the relevant act,

(*b*) that any of the circumstances specified in subsection (2) existed, and

(*c*) that the defendant knew that those circumstances existed,

the complainant is to be taken not to have consented to the relevant act unless sufficient evidence[1] is adduced to raise an issue as to whether he consented, and the defendant is to be taken not to have reasonably believed that the complainant consented unless sufficient evidence[1] is adduced to raise an issue as to whether he reasonably believed it.

(2) The circumstances are that—

(*a*) any person was, at the time of the relevant act or immediately before it began, using violence against the complainant or causing the complainant to fear that immediate violence would be used against him;

(*b*) any person was, at the time of the relevant act or immediately before it began, causing the complainant to fear that violence was being used, or that immediate violence would be used, against another person;

(*c*) the complainant was, and the defendant was not, unlawfully detained at the time of the relevant act;

(*d*) the complainant was asleep or otherwise unconscious at the time of the relevant act;

(*e*) because of the complainant's physical disability, the complainant would not have been able at the time of the relevant act to communicate to the defendant whether the complainant consented;

(*f*) any person had administered to or caused to be taken by the complainant, without the complainant's consent, a substance which, having regard to when it was administered or taken, was capable of causing or enabling the complainant to be stupefied or overpowered at the time of the relevant act.

(3) In subsection (2)(*a*) and (*b*), the reference to the time immediately before the relevant act began is, in the case of an act which is one of a continuous series of sexual activities, a reference to the time immediately before the first sexual activity began.

[Sexual Offences Act 2003, s 75.]

1 This does not reverse the burden of proof, but merely provides for evidential presumptions in circumstances where, as a matter of reality and common sense, the strong likelihood is that the complainant was not consenting. Evidence which is merely speculative or fanciful is not, however, 'sufficient' to raise either of the two issues; nor is a mere assertion by the defendant of his belief in consent. Thus, where the complainant and the defendant, who were effectively strangers, had been at the house of a mutual friend, the defendant claimed that the complainant 'made an advance', the defendant and his girlfriend took the drunk complainant back to their flat, the complainant fell asleep in the spare bedroom and the defendant saw she was asleep and touched her sexually before waking her up, the judge had been right to rule that no sufficient evidence to raise reasonable belief in consent had been adduced: *R v Ciccarelli* [2011] EWCA Crim 2665, [2012] 1 Cr App Rep 190, 175 CL&J 678.

7.10637 **76. Conclusive presumptions about consent** (1) If in proceedings for an offence to which this section applies it is proved that the defendant did the relevant act and that any of the circumstances specified in subsection (2) existed, it is to be conclusively presumed—

(*a*) that the complainant did not consent to the relevant act, and

(*b*) that the defendant did not believe that the complainant consented to the relevant act.

(2) The circumstances are that—

(*a*) the defendant intentionally deceived the complainant as to the nature or purpose of the relevant act[1];

(*b*) the defendant intentionally induced the complainant to consent to the relevant act by impersonating a person known personally to the complainant.

[Sexual Offences Act 2003, s 76.]

1 For the limited ambit of this provision, see *R v Jheeta*, para 7.10635, ante. The deceit must go to the purpose of the act; thus, where the complainant knew the purpose of the act was sexual gratification s 76(2)(*a*) did not apply even though the defendant (the complainant's boyfriend) deceived her as to his identity when blackmailing her (by threatening to publish certain photographs of her topless which she had sent to him as her boyfriend) into performing sexual acts over the internet: *R v B* [2013] EWCA Crim 823, [2013] 2 Cr App Rep 29.

7.10638 **77. Sections 75 and 76: relevant acts** In relation to an offence to which sections 75 and 76 apply, references in those sections to the relevant act and to the complainant are to be read as follows—

| ***Offence*** | ***Relevant Act*** |
|---|---|
| An offence under section 1 (rape). | The defendant intentionally penetrating, with his penis, the vagina, anus or mouth of another person ("the complainant"). |
| An offence under section 2 (assault by penetration). | The defendant intentionally penetrating, with a part of his body or anything else, the vagina or anus of another person ("the complainant"), where the penetration is sexual. |
| An offence under section 3 (sexual assault). | The defendant intentionally touching another person ("the complainant"), where the touching is sexual. |
| An offence under section 4 (causing a person to engage in sexual activity without consent). | The defendant intentionally causing another person ("the complainant") to engage in an activity, where the activity is sexual. |

[Sexual Offences Act 2003, s 77.]

7.10639 **78. "Sexual"** For the purposes of this Part (except sections 15A and 71), penetration, touching or any other activity is sexual if a reasonable person would consider that—

(*a*) whatever its circumstances or any person's purpose in relation to it, it is because of its nature sexual, or

(*b*) because of its nature it may be sexual and because of its circumstances or the purpose of any person in relation to it (or both) it is sexual.

[Sexual Offences Act 2003, s 78 as amended by the Serious Crime Act 2015, Sch 4.]

7.10640 **79. Part 1: general interpretation** (1) The following apply for the purposes of this Part.

(2) Penetration is a continuing act from entry to withdrawal.[1]

(3) References to a part of the body include references to a part surgically constructed (in particular, through gender reassignment surgery).

(4) "Image" means a moving or still image and includes an image produced by any means and, where the context permits, a three-dimensional image.

(5) References to an image of a person include references to an image of an imaginary person.

(6) "Mental disorder" has the meaning given by section 1 of the Mental Health Act 1983 (c 20).

(7) References to observation (however expressed) are to observation whether direct or by looking at an image.

(8) Touching[2] includes touching—

(*a*) with any part of the body,

(*b*) with anything else,

(*c*) through anything,

and in particular includes touching amounting to penetration.

(9) "Vagina" includes vulva.

(10) In relation to an animal, references to the vagina or anus include references to any similar part.

[Sexual Offences Act 2003, s 79.]

[1] See the observations of Lord Judge LCJ at para 26 of his judgment in *R (F) v Director of Public Prosecutions* [2013] EWHC 945 (Admin), [2013] 2 Cr App Rep 21, quoted in the Note 1 to s 74 of the SOA 2003 at para 7.10635, ante, where the claimant had consented to intercourse only the basis that the other party would not ejaculate inside her and he had done so.

[2] The matters referred to in s 79(8) are not exhaustive and s 78 is not a definition section; where a person is wearing clothing, touching of that clothing constitutes "touching" for the purposes of the offence contrary to s 3 of the Act: *R v H* [2005] EWCA Crim 732, [2005] 2 All ER 859, [2005] 2 Cr App R 9, [2005] Crim LR 735. Where touching is not inevitably sexual because of its nature, s 78(*b*) of the Act applies and in such a case, two distinct questions should be identified for the court/jury (both of which must be answered in the affirmative to find the defendant guilty), namely: (i) whether they, as reasonable people, consider that the touching, in the particular circumstances before them, because of its nature, may be sexual; and (ii) whether they, as 12 reasonable people, consider that the touching, in view of its circumstances, or the purpose of any person in relation to it, or both, was in fact sexual. In relation to the first question, evidence as to the circumstances before and after the touching, and evidence of the purpose of any person in relation to that touching is irrelevant. However, in most cases, the answer will be same whether the two-stage approach is adopted or whether the matter is looked at as a whole: *R v H*, supra.

## PART 2[1]

## NOTIFICATION AND ORDERS

### *Notification requirements*

7.10641 **80. Persons becoming subject to notification requirements** (1) A person is subject to the notification requirements of this Part for the period set out in section 82 ("the notification period") if—

(a) he is convicted[2] of an offence listed in Schedule 3;

(b) he is found not guilty of such an offence by reason of insanity;

(c) he is found to be under a disability and to have done the act charged against him in respect of such an offence; or

(d) in England and Wales or Northern Ireland, he is cautioned in respect of such an offence.

(2) A person for the time being subject to the notification requirements of this Part is referred to in this Part as a "relevant offender".

[Sexual Offences Act 2003, s 80.]

---

1 Part 2 comprises ss 80–136 and Schs 3–5.

2 The notification requirement arises on the date of conviction, and not the date of sentence if this occurs later; but in the case of an offender sentenced to an absolute discharge the notification requirement does not arise if sentencing occurs on the date of conviction, or survive if sentence is passed on a later date: *R v Longworth* [2006] UKHL 1, [2006] 1 All ER 887, [2006] 1 WLR 313, [2006] 2 Crim App Rep (S) 401.

7.10642 **81. Persons formerly subject to Part 1 of the Sex Offenders Act 1997** (1) A person is, from the commencement of this Part until the end of the notification period, subject to the notification requirements of this Part if, before the commencement of this Part—

(a) he was convicted[1] of an offence listed in Schedule 3;

(b) he was found not guilty of such an offence by reason of insanity;

(c) he was found to be under a disability and to have done the act charged against him in respect of such an offence; or

(d) in England and Wales or Northern Ireland, he was cautioned in respect of such an offence.

(2) Subsection (1) does not apply if the notification period ended before the commencement of this Part.

(3) Subsection (1)(*a*) does not apply to a conviction before 1st September 1997 unless, at the beginning of that day, the person—

(a) had not been dealt with in respect of the offence;

(b) was serving a sentence of imprisonment or was subject to a community order, in respect of the offence;

(c) was subject to supervision, having been released from prison after serving the whole or part of a sentence of imprisonment in respect of the offence; or

(d) was detained in a hospital or was subject to a guardianship order, following the conviction.

(4) Paragraphs (*b*) and (*c*) of subsection (1) do not apply to a finding made before 1st September 1997 unless, at the beginning of that day, the person—

(a) had not been dealt with in respect of the finding; or

(b) was detained in a hospital, following the finding.

(5) Subsection (1)(*d*) does not apply to a caution given before 1st September 1997.

(6) A person who would have been within subsection (3)(*b*) or (*d*) or (4)(*b*) but for the fact that at the beginning of 1st September 1997 he was unlawfully at large or absent without leave, on temporary release or leave of absence, or on bail pending an appeal, is to be treated as being within that provision.

(7) Where, immediately before the commencement of this Part, an order under a provision within subsection (8) was in force in respect of a person, the person is subject to the notification requirements of this Part from that commencement until the order is discharged or otherwise ceases to have effect.

(8) The provisions are—

(a) section 5A of the Sex Offenders Act 1997 (c 51) (restraining orders);

(b) section 2 of the Crime and Disorder Act 1998 (c 37) (sex offender orders made in England and Wales);

(c) section 2A of the Crime and Disorder Act 1998 (interim orders made in England and Wales);

(d) section 20 of the Crime and Disorder Act 1998 (sex offender orders and interim orders made in Scotland);

(e) *Northern Ireland*;

(f) *Northern Ireland*.

[Sexual Offences Act 2003, s 81 as amended by the Armed Forces Act 2006, Sch 17.]

---

1 A person sentenced to an absolute or conditional discharge for a pre-commencement offence is not subject to the notification requirements of the 1997 Act and, consequently, is not subject to the notification requirements of the 2003 Act: *R v Longworth* [2006] UKHL 1, [2006] 1 All ER 887, [2006] 1 WLR 313.

7.10643 **82. The notification period** (1) The notification period for a person within section 80(1) or 81(1) is the period in the second column of the following Table opposite the description that applies to him.

*Table*

| ***Description of relevant offender***[1] | ***Notification period*** |
|---|---|
| A person who, in respect of the offence, is or has been sentenced to imprisonment for life, to imprisonment for public protection under section 225 of the Criminal Justice Act 2003 or to imprisonment for a term of 30 months or more[2] | An indefinite period[3] beginning with the relevant date |
| A person who, in respect of the offence, has been made the subject of an order under section 210F(1) of the Criminal Procedure (Scotland) Act 1995 (order for lifelong restriction) | An indefinite period[3] beginning with that date |
| A person who, in respect of the offence or finding, is or has been admitted to a hospital subject to a restriction order | An indefinite period[3] beginning with that date |
| A person who, in respect of the offence, is or has been sentenced to imprisonment for a term of more than 6 months but less than 30 months | 10 years beginning with that date |
| A person who, in respect of the offence, is or has been sentenced to imprisonment for a term of 6 months or less | 7 years beginning with that date |
| A person who, in respect of the offence or finding, is or has been admitted to a hospital without being subject to a restriction order | 7 years beginning with that date |
| A person within section 80(1)(*d*) | 2 years beginning with that date |
| A person in whose case an order for conditional discharge or, in Scotland, a probation order, is made in respect of the offence | The period of conditional discharge or, in Scotland, the probation period |
| A person of any other description | 5 years beginning with the relevant date |

(2) Where a person is under 18 on the relevant date, subsection (1) has effect as if for any reference to a period of 10 years, 7 years, 5 years or 2 years there were substituted a reference to one-half of that period.

(3) Subsection (4) applies where a relevant offender within section 80(1)(*a*) or 81(1)(*a*) is or has been sentenced, in respect of two or more offences listed in Schedule 3—

(*a*) to consecutive terms of imprisonment; or

(*b*) to terms of imprisonment which are partly concurrent.

(4) Where this subsection applies, subsection (1) has effect as if the relevant offender were or had been sentenced, in respect of each of the offences, to a term of imprisonment which—

(*a*) in the case of consecutive terms, is equal to the aggregate of those terms;

(*b*) in the case of partly concurrent terms (X and Y, which overlap for a period Z), is equal to X plus Y minus Z.

(5) Where a relevant offender the subject of a finding within section 80(1)(*c*) or 81(1)(*c*) is subsequently tried for the offence, the notification period relating to the finding ends at the conclusion of the trial.

(6) In this Part, "relevant date" means—

(*a*) in the case of a person within section 80(1)(*a*) or 81(1)(*a*), the date of the conviction;

(*b*) in the case of a person within section 80(1)(*b*) or (*c*) or 81(1)(*b*) or (*c*), the date of the finding;

(*c*) in the case of a person within section 80(1)(*d*) or 81(1)(*d*), the date of the caution;

(*d*) in the case of a person within section 81(7), the date which, for the purposes of Part 1 of the Sex Offenders Act 1997 (c 51), was the relevant date in relation to that person.

[Sexual Offences Act 2003, s 82 as amended by the Violent Crime Reduction Act 2006, s 57.]

---

1 For the application of the term "imprisonment" to custodial sentences imposed on young offenders, see s 131, post.

2 In the case of an extended sentence, the term is the aggregate of the period to be served and the extension period; and it was not a violation of art 14 of the ECHR that, owing to the "raising of the bar" for extended sentences to a minimum custodial term of four years, only offenders sentenced to an extended sentence before 14 July 2008 could be caught by this: *R (Minter) v Chief Constable of Hampshire Constabulary* [2013] EWCA 697, [2014] 1 WLR 179.

3 The failure of the notification regime of the Sexual Offences Act 2003 to provide any mechanism for the review of an indefinite notification requirement meant that the scheme was incompatible with art 8: *R v F* [2010] UKSC 17, [2011] 1 AC 331. See below for provisions subsequently inserted which now provide for review of indefinite notification requirements.

7.10644 **83. Notification requirements: initial notification** (1) A relevant offender must, within the period of 3 days beginning with the relevant date (or, if later, the commencement of this Part), notify to the police the information set out in subsection (5).

(2) Subsection (1) does not apply to a relevant offender in respect of a conviction, finding or caution within section 80(1) if—

(*a*) immediately before the conviction, finding or caution, he was subject to the notification requirements of this Part as a result of another conviction, finding or caution or an order of a court ("the earlier event"),

(*b*) at that time, he had made a notification under subsection (1) in respect of the earlier event, and

(*c*) throughout the period referred to in subsection (1), he remains subject to the notification requirements as a result of the earlier event.

(3) Subsection (1) does not apply to a relevant offender in respect of a conviction, finding or caution within section 81(1) or an order within section 81(7) if the offender complied with section 2(1) of the Sex Offenders Act 1997 in respect of the conviction, finding, caution or order.

(4) Where a notification order is made in respect of a conviction, finding or caution, subsection (1) does not apply to the relevant offender in respect of the conviction, finding or caution if—

(*a*) immediately before the order was made, he was subject to the notification requirements of this Part as a result of another conviction, finding or caution or an order of a court ("the earlier event"),

(*b*) at that time, he had made a notification under subsection (1) in respect of the earlier event, and

(*c*) throughout the period referred to in subsection (1), he remains subject to the notification requirements as a result of the earlier event.

(5) The information is—

(*a*) the relevant offender's date of birth;

(*b*) his national insurance number;

(*c*) his name on the relevant date and, where he used one or more other names on that date, each of those names;

(*d*) his home address on the relevant date;

(*e*) his name on the date on which notification is given and, where he uses one or more other names on that date, each of those names;

(*f*) his home address on the date on which notification is given;

(*g*) the address of any other premises in the United Kingdom at which, at the time the notification is given, he regularly resides or stays;

(*h*) whether he has any passports and, in relation to each passport he has, the details set out in subsection (5A);

(*i*) such other information, about him or his personal affairs, as the Scottish Ministers may prescribe in regulations.

(5A) The details are—

(*a*) the issuing authority;

(*b*) the number;

(*c*) the dates of issue and expiry;

(*d*) the name and date of birth given as being those of the passport holder.

(6) When determining the period for the purpose of subsection (1), there is to be disregarded any time when the relevant offender is—

(*a*) remanded in or committed to custody by an order of a court or kept in service custody;

(*b*) serving a sentence of imprisonment or a term of service detention;

(*c*) detained in a hospital; or

(*d*) outside the United Kingdom.

(7) In this Part, "home address" means, in relation to any person—

(*a*) the address of his sole or main residence in the United Kingdom, or

(*b*) where he has no such residence, the address or location of a place in the United Kingdom where he can regularly be found and, if there is more than one such place, such one of those places as the person may select.

(8) *Scotland.*

[Sexual Offences Act 2003, s 83 as amended by the Criminal Justice and Immigration Act 2008, s 142 and Sch 26.]

7.10645 **84. Notification requirements: changes** (1) A relevant offender must, within the period of 3 days beginning with—

(*a*) his using a name which has not been notified to the police under section 83(1), this subsection, or section 2 of the Sex Offenders Act 1997 (c 51),

(*b*) any change of his home address,

(*c*) his having resided or stayed, for a qualifying period, at any premises in the United Kingdom the address of which has not been notified to the police under section 83(1), this subsection, or section 2 of the Sex Offenders Act 1997, or

(*ca*) any prescribed change of circumstances,

(*d*) his release from custody pursuant to an order of a court or from imprisonment, service detention or detention in a hospital

(*e*)– (*g*) *Scotland*,

notify to the police that name, the new home address, the address of those premises, the prescribed details or (as the case may be) the fact that he has been released, and (in addition) the information set out in section 83(5).

(1A) *Scotland.*

(2) A notification under subsection (1) may be given before the name is used, the change of home address or the prescribed change of circumstances occurs or the qualifying period ends, but in that case the relevant offender must also specify the date when the event is expected to occur.

(3) If a notification is given in accordance with subsection (2) and the event to which it relates occurs more than 2 days before the date specified, the notification does not affect the duty imposed by subsection (1).

(4) If a notification is given in accordance with subsection (2) and the event to which it relates has not occurred by the end of the period of 3 days beginning with the date specified—

(*a*) the notification does not affect the duty imposed by subsection (1), and

(*b*) the relevant offender must, within the period of 6 days beginning with the date specified, notify to the police the fact that the event did not occur within the period of 3 days beginning with the date specified.

(5) Section 83(6) applies to the determination of the period of 3 days mentioned in subsection (1) and the period of 6 days mentioned in subsection (4)(*b*), as it applies to the determination of the period mentioned in section 83(1).

(5A) In this section—

(*a*) "prescribed change of circumstances" means any change—

(i) occurring in relation to any matter in respect of which information is required to be notified by virtue of section 83(5)(*h*), and

(ii) of a description prescribed by regulations[1] made by the Secretary of State;

(*b*) "the prescribed details", in relation to a prescribed change of circumstances, means such details of the change as may be so prescribed.

(6) In this section, "qualifying period" means—

(*a*) a period of 7 days, or

(*b*) two or more periods, in any period of 12 months, which taken together amount to 7 days.

[Sexual Offences Act 2003, s 84 as amended by the Criminal Justice and Immigration Act 2008, s 142.]

---

1 See the Sexual Offences Act 2003 (Notification Requirements) (England and Wales) Regulations 2012, SI 2012/1876, in this title, post.

7.10646 **85. Notification requirements: periodic notification** (1) A relevant offender must, within the applicable period after each event within subsection (2), notify to the police the information set out in section 83(5), unless within that period he has given a notification under section 84(1).

(2) The events are—

(*a*) the commencement of this Part (but only in the case of a person who is a relevant offender from that commencement);

(*b*) any notification given by the relevant offender under section 83(1) or 84(1); and

(*c*) any notification given by him under subsection (1).

(3) Where the applicable period would (apart from this subsection) end whilst subsection (4) applies to the relevant offender, that period is to be treated as continuing until the end of the period of 3 days beginning when subsection (4) first ceases to apply to him.

(4) This subsection applies to the relevant offender if he is—

(*a*) remanded in or committed to custody by an order of a court or kept in service custody,

(*b*) serving a sentence of imprisonment or a term of service detention,

(*c*) detained in a hospital, or

(*d*) outside the United Kingdom.

(5) In this section, "the applicable period" means—

(*a*) in any case where subsection (6) applies to the relevant offender, such period as may be prescribed by regulations[1] made by the Secretary of State, and

(*b*) in any other case, the period of one year.

(6) This subsection applies to the relevant offender if the last home address notified by him under section 83(1) or 84(1) or subsection (1) was the address or location of such a place as is mentioned in section 83(7)(*b*).

[Sexual Offences Act 2003, s 85 as amended by the Criminal Justice and Immigration Act 2008, s 142 and Sch 26.]

---

1 See the Sexual Offences Act 2003 (Notification Requirements) (England and Wales) Regulations 2012, SI 2012/1876, in this title, post.

7.10647 **86. Notification requirements: travel outside the United Kingdom** (1) The Secretary of State may by regulations[1] make provision requiring relevant offenders who leave the United Kingdom, or any description of such offenders—

(*a*) to give in accordance with the regulations, before they leave, a notification under subsection (2);

(*b*) if they subsequently return to the United Kingdom, to give in accordance with the regulations a notification under subsection (3).

(2) A notification under this subsection must disclose—

(*a*) the date on which the offender will leave the United Kingdom;

(*b*) the country (or, if there is more than one, the first country) to which he will travel and his point of arrival (determined in accordance with the regulations) in that country;

(*c*) any other information prescribed by the regulations which the offender holds about his departure from or return to the United Kingdom or his movements while outside the United Kingdom.

(3) A notification under this subsection must disclose any information prescribed by the regulations about the offender's return to the United Kingdom.

(4) *Repealed.*

[Sexual Offences Act 2003, s 86 as amended by the Criminal Justice and Immigration Act 2008, Sch 28.]

---

[1] See the Sexual Offences Act 2003 (Travel Notification Requirements) Regulations 2004 and the Sexual Offences Act 2003 (Notification Requirements) (England and Wales) Regulations 2012, in this title, post.

7.10648 **87. Method of notification and related matters** (1) A person gives a notification under section 83(1), 84(1) or 85(1) by—

(*a*) attending at such police station in his local police area as the Secretary of State may by regulations[1] prescribe or, if there is more than one, at any of them, and

(*b*) giving an oral notification to any police officer, or to any person authorised for the purpose by the officer in charge of the station.

(2) A person giving a notification under section 84(1)—

(*a*) in relation to a prospective change of home address, or

(*b*) in relation to premises referred to in subsection (1)(*c*) of that section,

may give the notification at a police station that would fall within subsection (1) above if the change in home address had already occurred or (as the case may be) if the address of those premises were his home address.

(3) Any notification under this section must be acknowledged; and an acknowledgement under this subsection must be in writing, and in such form as the Secretary of State may direct.

(4) Where a notification is given under section 83(1), 84(1) or 85(1), the relevant offender must, if requested to do so by the police officer or person referred to in subsection (1)(*b*), allow the officer or person to—

(*a*) take his fingerprints,

(*b*) photograph any part of him, or

(*c*) do both these things.

(5) The power in subsection (4) is exercisable for the purpose of verifying the identity of the relevant offender.

(5A)–(5C) *Scotland.*

(6) *Repealed.*

[Sexual Offences Act 2003, s 87 as amended by the Criminal Justice and Immigration Act 2008, Sch 28.]

---

[1] Sexual Offences Act 2003 (Prescribed Police Stations) (No 2) Regulations 2015, SI 2015/1523.

7.10649 **88. Section 87: interpretation** (1) Subsections (2) to (4) apply for the purposes of section 87.

(2) "Photograph" includes any process by means of which an image may be produced.

(2A) *Scotland.*

(3) "Local police area" means, in relation to a person—

(*a*) the police area in which his home address is situated;

(*b*) in the absence of a home address, the police area in which the home address last notified is situated;

(*c*) in the absence of a home address and of any such notification, the police area in which the court which last dealt with the person in a way mentioned in subsection (4) is situated.

(4) The ways are—

(*a*) dealing with a person in respect of an offence listed in Schedule 3 or a finding in relation to such an offence;

(*b*) dealing with a person in respect of an offence under section 128 or a finding in relation to such an offence;

(*c*) making, in respect of a person, a notification order, interim notification order, sexual harm prevention order, interim sexual harm prevention order, sexual offences prevention order or interim sexual offences prevention order;

(*d*) making, in respect of a person, an order under section 2, 2A or 20 of the Crime and Disorder Act 1998 (c 37) (sex offender orders and interim orders made in England and Wales or Scotland) or Article 6 or 6A of the Criminal Justice (Northern Ireland) Order 1998 (SI 1998/2839 (NI 20)) (sex offender orders and interim orders made in Northern Ireland);

and in paragraphs (*a*) and (*b*), "finding" in relation to an offence means a finding of not guilty of the offence by reason of insanity or a finding that the person was under a disability and did the act or omission charged against him in respect of the offence.

(5) Subsection (3) applies as if Northern Ireland were a police area.

[Sexual Offences Act 2003, s 88 as amended by the Anti-social Behaviour, Crime and Policing Act 2014, Sch 11.]

7.10650 **89. Young offenders: parental directions** (1) Where a person within the first column of the following Table ("the young offender") is under 18 (or, in Scotland, 16) when he is before the court referred to in the second column of the Table opposite the description that applies to him, that court may direct that subsection (2) applies in respect of an individual ("the parent") having parental responsibility for (or, in Scotland, parental responsibilities in relation to) the young offender.

*Table*

| *Description of person* | ***Court which may make the direction*** |
|---|---|
| A relevant offender within section 80(1)(*a*) to (*c*) or 81(1)(*a*) to (*c*) | The court which deals with the offender in respect of the offence or finding |
| A relevant offender within section 129(1)(*a*) to (*c*) | The court which deals with the offender in respect of the offence or finding |
| A person who is the subject of a notification order, interim notification order, sexual harm prevention order, interim sexual harm prevention order, sexual offences prevention order or interim sexual offences prevention order | The court which makes the order |
| A relevant offender who is the defendant to an application under subsection (4) (or, in Scotland, the subject of an application under subsection (5)) | The court which hears the application |

(2) Where this subsection applies—

(*a*) the obligations that would (apart from this subsection) be imposed by or under sections 83 to 86 on the young offender are to be treated instead as obligations on the parent, and

(*b*) the parent must ensure that the young offender attends at the police station with him, when a notification is being given.

(3) A direction under subsection (1) takes immediate effect and applies—

(*a*) until the young offender attains the age of 18 (or, where a court in Scotland gives the direction, 16); or

(*b*) for such shorter period as the court may, at the time the direction is given, direct.

(4) A chief officer of police may, by complaint to any magistrates' court whose commission area includes any part of his police area, apply for a direction under subsection (1) in respect of a relevant offender ("the defendant")—

(*a*) who resides in his police area, or who the chief officer believes is in or is intending to come to his police area, and

(*b*) who the chief officer believes is under 18.

(5) *Scotland.*

[Sexual Offences Act 2003, s 89 as amended by the Anti-social Behaviour, Crime and Policing Act 2014, Sch 11.]

7.10651 **90. Parental directions: variations, renewals and discharges** (1) A person within subsection (2) may apply to the appropriate court for an order varying, renewing or discharging a direction under section 89(1).

(2) The persons are—

(*a*) the young offender;

(*b*) the parent;

(*c*) the chief officer of police for the area in which the young offender resides;

(*d*) a chief officer of police who believes that the young offender is in, or is intending to come to, his police area;

(*e*) *Scotland.*

and in any other case, the prosecutor;

(*f*) where the direction was made on an application under section 89(4), the chief officer of police who made the application;

(*g*) where the direction was made on an application under section 89(5), the chief constable who made the application.

(3) An application under subsection (1) may be made—

(*a*) where the appropriate court is the Crown Court (or in Scotland a criminal court), in accordance with rules of court;

(*b*) in any other case, by complaint (or, in Scotland, by summary application).

(4) On the application the court, after hearing the person making the application and (if they wish to be heard) the other persons mentioned in subsection (2), may make any order, varying, renewing or discharging the direction, that the court considers appropriate.

(5) In this section, the "appropriate court" means—

(*a*) where the Court of Appeal made the order, the Crown Court;

(*b*) in any other case, the court that made the direction under section 89(1).

[Sexual Offences Act 2003, s 90.]

7.10652 **91. Offences relating to notification** (1) A person commits an offence if he—

(*a*) fails, without reasonable excuse, to comply with section 83(1), 84(1), 84(4)(*b*), 85(1), 87(4) or 89(2)(*b*) or any requirement imposed by regulations made under section 86(1); or

(*b*) notifies to the police, in purported compliance with section 83(1), 84(1) or 85(1) or any requirement imposed by regulations made under section 86(1), any information which he knows to be false.

(2) A person guilty of an offence under this section is liable[1]—

(*a*) on summary conviction, to imprisonment for a term not exceeding 6 months or a fine not exceeding the statutory maximum or both;

(*b*) on conviction on indictment, to imprisonment for a term not exceeding 5 years.

(3) A person commits an offence under paragraph (*a*) of subsection (1) on the day on which he first fails, without reasonable excuse, to comply with section 83(1), 84(1) or 85(1) or a requirement imposed by regulations made under section 86(1), and continues to commit it throughout any period during which the failure continues; but a person must not be prosecuted under subsection (1) more than once in respect of the same failure.

(4) Proceedings for an offence under this section may be commenced in any court having jurisdiction in any place where the person charged with the offence resides or is found.

[Sexual Offences Act 2003, s 91.]

---

1 For procedure in respect of this offence which is triable either way, see the Magistrates' Courts Act 1980, ss 17A–21 in PART I: MAGISTRATES' COURTS, PROCEDURE, ante.

7.10653 **91A. Review of indefinite notification requirements: qualifying relevant offender**

(1) A qualifying relevant offender may apply to the relevant chief officer of police for a determination that the qualifying relevant offender is no longer subject to the indefinite notification requirements ("an application for review").

(2) A qualifying relevant offender means a relevant offender who, on the date on which he makes an application for review, is—

(*a*) subject to the indefinite notification requirements; and

(*b*) not subject to a sexual harm prevention order under section 103A, an interim sexual harm prevention order under section 103F, a sexual offences prevention order under section 104(1) or an interim sexual offences prevention order under section 109(3).

(3) The "indefinite notification requirements" mean the notification requirements of this Part for an indefinite period by virtue of—

(*a*) section 80(1);

(*b*) section 81(1); or

(*c*) a notification order made under section 97(5).

(4) In this Part, the "relevant chief officer of police" means, subject to subsection (5), the chief officer of police for the police area in which a qualifying relevant offender is recorded as residing or staying in the most recent notification given by him under section 84(1) or 85(1).

(5) Subsection (6) applies if a qualifying relevant offender is recorded as residing or staying at more than one address in the most recent notification given by him under section 84(1) or 85(1).

(6) If this subsection applies, the "relevant chief officer of police" means the chief officer of police for the police area in which, during the relevant period, the qualifying relevant offender has resided or stayed on a number of days which equals or exceeds the number of days on which he has resided or stayed in any other police area.

(7) In subsection (6), "the relevant period" means the period of 12 months ending on the day on which the qualifying relevant offender makes an application for review.

[Sexual Offences Act 2003, s 91A as inserted by SI 2012/1883 and amended by the Anti-social Behaviour, Crime and Policing Act 2014, Sch 11.]

7.10654 **91B. Review of indefinite notification requirements: application for review and qualifying dates** (1) An application for review must be in writing and may be made on or after the qualifying date or, as the case may be, the further qualifying date.

(2) Subject to subsection (7), the qualifying date is—

(*a*) where the qualifying relevant offender was 18 or over on the relevant date, the day after the end of the 15 year period beginning with the day on which the qualifying relevant offender gives the relevant notification; or

(*b*) where the qualifying relevant offender was under 18 on the relevant date, the day after the end of the 8 year period beginning with the day on which the qualifying relevant offender gives the relevant notification.

(3) Subject to subsections (4) to (6), the further qualifying date is the day after the end of the 8 year period beginning with the day on which the relevant chief officer of police makes a determination under section 91C to require a qualifying relevant offender to remain subject to the indefinite notification requirements.

(4) Subsection (5) applies if the relevant chief officer of police, when making a determination under section 91C to require a qualifying relevant offender to remain subject to the indefinite notification requirements, considers that the risk of sexual harm posed by a qualifying relevant offender is sufficient to justify a continuation of those requirements after the end of the 8 year period

beginning with the day on which the determination is made.

(5) If this subsection applies, the relevant chief officer of police may make a determination to require a qualifying relevant offender to remain subject to the indefinite notification requirements for a period which may be no longer than the 15 year period beginning with the day on which the determination is made.

(6) If subsection (5) applies, the further qualifying date is the day after the end of the period determined under that subsection.

(7) The qualifying date must not be earlier than the expiry of the fixed period specified in a notification continuation order made in relation to a qualifying relevant offender in accordance with sections 88A to 88I.

(8) The relevant chief officer of police within 14 days of receipt of an application for review—

(*a*) must give an acknowledgment of receipt of the application to the qualifying relevant offender, and

(*b*) may notify a responsible body that the application has been made.

(9) Where a responsible body is notified of the application for review under subsection (8)(*b*) and holds information which it considers to be relevant to the application, the responsible body must give such information to the relevant chief officer of police within 28 days of receipt of the notification.

(10) In this section "the relevant notification" means the first notification which the relevant offender gives under section 83, 84 or 85 when he is first released after—

(*a*) being remanded in or committed to custody by an order of a court in relation to the conviction for the offence giving rise to the indefinite notification requirements;

(*b*) serving a sentence of imprisonment or a term of service detention in relation to that conviction;

(*c*) being detained in hospital in relation to that conviction.

(11) For the purposes of this Part—

(*a*) "responsible body" means—

(i) the probation trust for any area that includes any part of the police area concerned,

(ii) in relation to any part of the police area concerned for which there is no probation trust, each provider of probation services which has been identified as a relevant provider of probation services for the purposes of section 325 of the Criminal Justice Act 2003 by arrangements under section 3 of the Offender Management Act 2007,

(iii) the Minister of the Crown exercising functions in relation to prisons (and for this purpose "prison" has the same meaning as in the Prison Act 1952), and

(iv) each body mentioned in section 325(6) of the Criminal Justice Act 2003, but as if the references in that subsection to the relevant area were references to the police area concerned;

(*b*) "risk of sexual harm" means a risk of physical or psychological harm to the public in the United Kingdom or any particular members of the public caused by the qualifying relevant offender committing one or more of the offences listed in Schedule 3.

[Sexual Offences Act 2003, s 91B as inserted by SI 2012/1883.]

**7.10655 91C. Review of indefinite notification requirements: determination of application for review** (1) The relevant chief officer of police[1] must, within 6 weeks of the latest date on which any body to which a notification has been given under section 91B(8)(*b*) may give information under section 91B(9)—

(*a*) determine the application for review, and

(*b*) give notice of the determination to the qualifying relevant offender.

(2) For the purposes of the determination of an application for review under this section, a qualifying relevant offender must satisfy[2] the relevant chief officer of police that it is not necessary for the purpose of protecting the public or any particular members of the public from sexual harm for the qualifying relevant offender to remain subject to the indefinite notification requirements.

(3) If the relevant chief officer of police determines under this section that the qualifying relevant offender should remain subject to the indefinite notification requirements, the notice of the determination must—

(*a*) contain a statement of reasons for the determination, and

(*b*) inform the qualifying relevant offender that he may appeal the determination in accordance with section 91E.

(4) If the relevant chief officer of police determines under this section that a qualifying relevant offender should not remain subject to the indefinite notification requirements, the qualifying relevant offender ceases to be subject to the indefinite notification requirements on the date of receipt of the notice of determination.

(5) The Secretary of State may by order amend the period in subsection (1).

[Sexual Offences Act 2003, s 91C as inserted by SI 2012/1883.]

---

1 The determination may be delegated to an officer of appropriate seniority having regard to the nature of the duty: *R (Hamill) v Chelmsford Magistrates' Court. Chief Constable of Essex (Interested Party)* [2014] EWCA 2799 (Admin), 178 JP 401.

[2] The burden of proof is thus on the relevant offender and, while the standard of proof is the balance of probabilities, 'the hurdle is high': *R (on the application of NE) v Birmingham Magistrates Court; R (on the application of NM) v Birmingham Magistrates Court* [2015] EWHC 688 (Admin), [2015] 2 Cr App Rep (S) 230, 179 JP 187. See further the note to the title of s 91E, post.

7.10656 **91D. Review of indefinite notification requirements: factors applying to determination under section 91C** (1) In determining an application for review under section 91C, the relevant chief officer of police must—

(*a*) have regard to information (if any) received from a responsible body;

(*b*) consider the risk of sexual harm posed by the qualifying relevant offender and the effect of a continuation of the indefinite notification requirements on the offender; and

(*c*) take into account the matters listed in subsection (2).

(2) The matters are—

(*a*) the seriousness of the offence in relation to which the qualifying relevant offender became subject to the indefinite notification requirements;

(*b*) the period of time which has elapsed since the qualifying relevant offender committed the offence (or other offences);

(*c*) where the qualifying relevant offender falls within section 81(1), whether the qualifying relevant offender committed any offence under section 3 of the Sex Offenders Act 1997;

(*d*) whether the qualifying relevant offender has committed any offence under section 91;

(*e*) the age of the qualifying relevant offender at the qualifying date or further qualifying date;

(*f*) the age of the qualifying relevant offender at the time the offence referred to in paragraph (*a*) was committed;

(*g*) the age of any person who was a victim of any such offence (where applicable) and the difference in age between the victim and the qualifying relevant offender at the time the offence was committed;

(*h*) any assessment of the risk posed by the qualifying relevant offender which has been made by a responsible body under the arrangements for managing and assessing risk established under section 325 of the Criminal Justice Act 2003;

(*i*) any submission or evidence from a victim of the offence giving rise to the indefinite notification requirements;

(*j*) any convictions or findings made by a court (including by a court in Scotland, Northern Ireland or countries outside the United Kingdom) in respect of the qualifying relevant offender for any offence listed in Schedule 3 other than the one referred to in paragraph (*a*);

(*k*) any caution which the qualifying relevant offender has received for an offence (including for an offence in Northern Ireland or countries outside the United Kingdom) which is listed in Schedule 3;

(*l*) any convictions or findings made by a court in Scotland, Northern Ireland or countries outside the United Kingdom in respect of the qualifying relevant offender for any offence listed in Schedule 5 where the behaviour of the qualifying relevant offender since the date of such conviction or finding indicates a risk of sexual harm;

(*m*) any other submission or evidence of the risk of sexual harm posed by the qualifying relevant offender;

(*n*) any evidence presented by or on behalf of the qualifying relevant offender which demonstrates that the qualifying relevant offender does not pose a risk of sexual harm; and

(*o*) any other matter which the relevant chief officer of police considers to be appropriate.

(3) In this section, a reference to a conviction, finding or caution for an offence committed in a country outside the United Kingdom means a conviction, finding or caution for an act which—

(*a*) constituted an offence under the law in force in the country concerned, and

(*b*) would have constituted an offence listed in Schedule 3 or Schedule 5 if it had been done in any part of the United Kingdom.

[Sexual Offences Act 2003, s 91D as inserted by SI 2012/1883.]

7.10657 **91E. Review of indefinite notification requirements: appeals[1]** (1) A qualifying relevant offender may appeal against a determination of the relevant chief officer of police under section 91C.

(2) An appeal under this section may be made by complaint to a magistrates' court within the period of 21 days beginning with the day of receipt of the notice of determination.

(3) A qualifying relevant offender may appeal under this section to any magistrates' court in a local justice area which includes any part of the police area for which the chief officer is the relevant chief officer of police.

(4) If the court makes an order that a qualifying relevant offender should not remain subject to the indefinite notification requirements, the qualifying relevant offender ceases to be subject to the indefinite notification requirements on the date of the order.

[Sexual Offences Act 2003, s 91E as inserted by SI 2012/1883.]

[1] The magistrates' court must focus on the statutory test as set out in s 91C(2) and take full account, as it affects the appellant, of the matters set out in s 91D(1)–(2); the appellant must 'satisfy' the court that he should cease to be subject to notification requirements, but the court must also examine the effect that the continuation of the requirements for a further eight years if the appeal fails will have on the appellant's art 8 rights and consider whether or not that interference is proportionate: *R (Hamill) v Chelmsford Magistrates' Court, Chief Constable of Essex (Interested Party)* [2014] EWCA 2799 (Admin), 178 JP 401.

However, the opposite conclusion on proportionality was reached in *R (NE and NM) v Birmingham Magistrates' Court and The Chief Constable of West Midlands Police* [2015] EWHC 688 (Admin), [2015] 1 WLR 4771, [2015] 2 Cr App R (S) 25, 179 JP 187:

> "21. . . . With respect to Aikens LJ (in *Hamill,* above) (before whom no contrary argument was advanced), I do not accept that s.91(D)(1)(b) imports a proportionality test which was neither suggested by the Supreme Court (in *R (on the application by JF (by his litigation friend OF)) v Secretary of State for the Home Department* [2010] UKSC 17, [2011] 1 AC 331, [2010] 2 All ER 707, [2010] All ER (D) 123 (Apr)) nor identified within the Order which utilized the Human Rights Act 1998 to modify the law for the purposes of achieving compatibility as required by the Supreme Court. Furthermore, the wording is not to require the chief officer to consider the risk of sexual harm posed by the offender together with the effect on the offender of a continuation of the indefinite notification requirements but, rather, the effect of continuation of the requirements for the purposes of s 91C.
>
> 22. This construction is supported by a consideration of the possible circumstances in which this issue might arise. Take the case of an offender for whom it is legitimately considered that there remains a risk of his causing sexual harm unless appropriately monitored (ie, by compliance with the notification provisions). It is, in my view, unarguable that a different conclusion would be reached in relation to such an offender for whom the continuation of the requirements of notification posed little additional burden, (perhaps because the offender was unemployed or had no children) to that in relation to an offender for whom the burden was very greatly increased (because of the risk, raised in one of these cases, of information seeping out and affecting employment, family or both). In both cases, if there is a risk of causing sexual harm, the high threshold test is not met and the notification provisions must remain in place. It might be appropriate to take account of the impact on private life when deciding where to fix the point at which a further application can be made (on the spectrum between eight and 15 years) but the line to be drawn between those who must continue to be subject to the notification provisions and those who are relieved of that responsibility cannot depend on the impact of notification on private and family life; the test remains necessity for the purpose of protecting the public or any particular members of the public from sexual harm."(per Sir Brian Leveson P)

As to the relevance of subsequent, unrelated offences, see *R (NE and NM) v Birmingham Magistrates' Court and The Chief Constable of West Midlands Police* paras 48 and 49. Offences subsequent to the index offence, where they indicate a blatant disregard for the law, may, if the offender fails adequately to address that concern, lead the court to conclude that the disregard could extend to sexual matters.

Save for exceptional cases, judicial review is not the appropriate way to challenge a decision of the magistrates' court. The better course is to appeal by way of case stated, where the aggrieved party can identify the decisions of law with which issue is taken and both parties can ensure that all the facts are set out, along with the relevant findings on those facts made by the magistrates' court: *R (NE and NM) v Birmingham Magistrates' Court and The Chief Constable of West Midlands Police* paras 52-54.

**7.10658 91F. Review of indefinite notification requirements: guidance** (1) The Secretary of State must issue guidance to relevant chief officers of police in relation to the determination by them of applications made under section 91B.

(2) The Secretary of State may, from time to time, revise the guidance issued under subsection (1).

(3) The Secretary of State must arrange for any guidance issued or revised under this section to be published in such manner as the Secretary of State considers appropriate.

[Sexual Offences Act 2003, s 91F as inserted by SI 2012/1883.]

**7.10659 92. Certificates for purposes of Part 2** (1) Subsection (2) applies where on any date a person is—

(*a*) convicted of an offence listed in Schedule 3;

(*b*) found not guilty of such an offence by reason of insanity; or

(*c*) found to be under a disability and to have done the act charged against him in respect of such an offence.

(2) If the court by or before which the person is so convicted or found—

(*a*) states in open court—

(i) that on that date he has been convicted, found not guilty by reason of insanity or found to be under a disability and to have done the act charged against him, and

(ii) that the offence in question is an offence listed in Schedule 3, and

(*b*) certifies those facts, whether at the time or subsequently,

the certificate is, for the purposes of this Part, evidence (or, in Scotland, sufficient evidence) of those facts.

(3) Subsection (4) applies where on any date a person is, in England and Wales or Northern Ireland, cautioned in respect of an offence listed in Schedule 3.

(4) If the constable—

(*a*) informs the person that he has been cautioned on that date and that the offence in question is an offence listed in Schedule 3, and

(*b*) certifies those facts, whether at the time or subsequently, in such form as the Secretary of State may by order prescribe,

the certificate is, for the purposes of this Part, evidence (or, in Scotland, sufficient evidence) of those facts.

[Sexual Offences Act 2003, s 92.]

7.10660 **93. Abolished homosexual offences** Schedule 4 (procedure for ending notification requirements for abolished homosexual offences) has effect.

[Sexual Offences Act 2003, s 93.]

*Information for verification*

7.10661 **94. Part 2: supply of information to Secretary of State etc for verification**

(1) This section applies to information notified to the police under—

(*a*) section 83, 84 or 85, or

(*b*) section 2(1) to (3) of the Sex Offenders Act 1997 (c 51).

(2) A person within subsection (3) may, for the purposes of the prevention, detection, investigation or prosecution of offences under this Part, supply information to which this section applies to—

(*a*) the Secretary of State,

(*aa*) *repealed*

(*b*) a Northern Ireland Department, or

(*c*) a person providing services to the Secretary of State or a Northern Ireland Department in connection with a relevant function,

for use for the purpose of verifying the information.

(3) The persons are—

(*a*) a chief officer of police (in Scotland, a chief constable),

(*b*) the Director General of the National Crime Agency

(4) In relation to information supplied under subsection (2) to any person, the reference to verifying the information is a reference to—

(*a*) checking its accuracy by comparing it with information held—

(i) where the person is the Secretary of State or a Northern Ireland Department, by him or it in connection with the exercise of a relevant function, or

(ii) where the person is within subsection (2)(*c*), by that person in connection with the provision of services referred to there, and

(*b*) compiling a report of that comparison.

(5) Subject to subsection (6), the supply of information under this section is to be taken not to breach any restriction on the disclosure of information (however arising or imposed).

(6) This section does not authorise the doing of anything that contravenes the Data Protection Act 1998 (c 29).

(7) This section does not affect any power existing apart from this section to supply information.

(8) In this section—

"Northern Ireland Department" means the Department for Employment and Learning, the Department of the Environment or the Department for Social Development;

"relevant function" means—

(*a*) a function relating to social security, child support, employment or training,

(*aa*) *repealed*

(*b*) a function relating to passports,

(*c*) a function under Part 3 of the Road Traffic Act 1988 (c 52) or Part 2 of the Road Traffic (Northern Ireland) Order 1981 (SI 1981/154 (NI 1)).

[Sexual Offences Act 2003, s 94 as amended by the Serious Organised Crime and Police Act 2005, Sch 4, the Police and Justice Act 2006, Sch 1, SI 2008/2656, SI 2012/2007 and the Crime and Courts Act 2013, Sch 8.]

7.10662 **95. Part 2: supply of information by Secretary of State etc** (1) A report compiled under section 94 may be supplied by—

(*a*) the Secretary of State,

(*aa*) *repealed*

(*b*) a Northern Ireland Department, or

(*c*) a person within section 94(2)(*c*),

to a person within subsection (2).

(2) The persons are—

(*a*) a chief officer of police (in Scotland, a chief constable),

(*b*) Serious Organised Crime Agency.

(3) Such a report may contain any information held—

(*a*) by the Secretary of State or a Northern Ireland Department in connection with the exercise of a relevant function, or

(*b*) by a person within section 94(2)(*c*) in connection with the provision of services referred to there.

(4) Where such a report contains information within subsection (3), the person within subsection (2) to whom it is supplied—

(*a*) may retain the information, whether or not used for the purposes of the prevention, detection, investigation or prosecution of an offence under this Part, and

(*b*) may use the information for any purpose related to the prevention, detection, investigation or prosecution of offences (whether or not under this Part), but for no other purpose.

(5) Subsections (5) to (8) of section 94 apply in relation to this section as they apply in relation to section 94.

[Sexual Offences Act 2003, s 95 as amended by the Serious Organised Crime and Police Act 2005, Sch 4 and SI 2008/2656.]

*Information about release or transfer*

**7.10663** **96. Information about release or transfer** (1) This section applies to a relevant offender who is serving a sentence of imprisonment or a term of service detention, or is detained in a hospital.

(2) The Secretary of State may by regulations make provision requiring notice to be given by the person who is responsible for that offender to persons prescribed by the regulations, of any occasion when the offender is released or a different person becomes responsible for him.

(2A), (2B) *Scotland.*

(3) The regulations may make provision for determining who is to be treated for the purposes of this section as responsible for an offender.

(4) *Scotland.*

[Sexual Offences Act 2003, s 96.]

*Entry and search of home address*

**7.10664** **96B. Power of entry and search of relevant offender's home address** (1) If on an application made by a senior police officer of the relevant force a justice of the peace is satisfied that the requirements in subsection (2) are met in relation to any premises, he may issue a warrant authorising a constable of that force—

(*a*) to enter the premises for the purpose of assessing the risks posed by the relevant offender to which the warrant relates; and

(*b*) to search the premises for that purpose.

(2) The requirements are—

(*a*) that the address of each set of premises specified in the application is an address falling within subsection (3);

(*b*) that the relevant offender is not one to whom subsection (4) applies;

(*c*) that it is necessary for a constable to enter and search the premises for the purpose mentioned in subsection (1)(*a*); and

(*d*) that on at least two occasions a constable has sought entry to the premises in order to search them for that purpose and has been unable to obtain entry for that purpose.

(3) An address falls within this subsection if—

(*a*) it is the address which was last notified in accordance with this Part by a relevant offender to the police as his home address; or

(*b*) there are reasonable grounds to believe that a relevant offender resides there or may regularly be found there.

(4) This subsection applies to a relevant offender if he is—

(*a*) remanded in or committed to custody by order of a court;

(*b*) serving a sentence of imprisonment or a term of service detention;

(*c*) detained in a hospital; or

(*d*) outside the United Kingdom.

(5) A warrant issued under this section must specify the one or more sets of premises to which it relates.

(6) The warrant may authorise the constable executing it to use reasonable force if necessary to enter and search the premises.

(7) The warrant may authorise entry to and search of premises on more than one occasion if, on the application, the justice of the peace is satisfied that it is necessary to authorise multiple entries in order to achieve the purpose mentioned in subsection (1)(*a*).

(8) Where a warrant issued under this section authorises multiple entries, the number of entries authorised may be unlimited or limited to a maximum.

(9) In this section a reference to the relevant offender to whom the warrant relates is a reference to the relevant offender—

(*a*) who has in accordance with this Part notified the police that the premises specified in the warrant are his home address; or

(*b*) in respect of whom there are reasonable grounds to believe that he resides there or may regularly be found there.

(10) In this section—

"the relevant force" means the police force maintained for the police area in which the premises in respect of which the application is made or the warrant is issued are situated;

"senior police officer" means a constable of the rank of superintendent or above.

[Sexual Offences Act 2003, s 96B as inserted by the Violent Crime Reduction Act 2006, s 58.]

*Notification orders*

**7.10665** **97. Notification orders: applications and grounds** (1) A chief officer of police may, by complaint to any magistrates' court whose commission area includes any part of his police area, apply[1] for an order under this section (a "notification order") in respect of a person ("the defendant") if—

(*a*) it appears to him that the following three conditions are met with respect to the defendant, and

(*b*) the defendant resides in his police area or the chief officer believes that the defendant is in, or is intending to come to, his police area.

(2) The first condition is that under the law in force in a country outside the United Kingdom—

(*a*) he has been convicted of a relevant offence (whether or not he has been punished for it),

(*b*) a court exercising jurisdiction under that law has made in respect of a relevant offence a finding equivalent to a finding that he is not guilty by reason of insanity,

(*c*) such a court has made in respect of a relevant offence a finding equivalent to a finding that he is under a disability and did the act charged against him in respect of the offence, or

(*d*) he has been cautioned in respect of a relevant offence.

(3) The second condition is that—

(*a*) the first condition is met because of a conviction, finding or caution which occurred on or after 1st September 1997,

(*b*) the first condition is met because of a conviction or finding which occurred before that date, but the person was dealt with in respect of the offence or finding on or after that date, or has yet to be dealt with in respect of it, or

(*c*) the first condition is met because of a conviction or finding which occurred before that date, but on that date the person was, in respect of the offence or finding, subject under the law in force in the country concerned to detention, supervision or any other disposal equivalent to any of those mentioned in section 81(3) (read with sections 81(6) and 131).

(4) The third condition is that the period set out in section 82 (as modified by subsections (2) and (3) of section 98) in respect of the relevant offence has not expired.

(5) If on the application it is proved that the conditions in subsections (2) to (4) are met, the court must make a notification order.

(6) In this section and section 98, "relevant offence" has the meaning given by section 99.

[Sexual Offences Act 2003, s 97.]

---

1 For form of application and procedure, see the Magistrates' Courts (Notification Orders) Rules 2004, in PART I: MAGISTRATES' COURTS, PROCEDURE, ante.

7.10666 **98. Notification orders: effect** (1) Where a notification order is made—

(*a*) the application of this Part to the defendant in respect of the conviction, finding or caution to which the order relates is subject to the modifications set out below, and

(*b*) subject to those modifications, the defendant becomes or (as the case may be) remains subject to the notification requirements of this Part for the notification period set out in section 82.

(2) The "relevant date" means—

(*a*) in the case of a person within section 97(2)(*a*), the date of the conviction;

(*b*) in the case of a person within section 97(2)(*b*) or (*c*), the date of the finding;

(*c*) in the case of a person within section 97(2)(*d*), the date of the caution.

(3) In section 82—

(*a*) references, except in the Table, to a person (or relevant offender) within any provision of section 80 are to be read as references to the defendant;

(*b*) the reference in the Table to section 80(1)(*d*) is to be read as a reference to section 97(2)(*d*);

(*c*) references to an order of any description are to be read as references to any corresponding disposal made in relation to the defendant in respect of an offence or finding by reference to which the notification order was made;

(*d*) the reference to offences listed in Schedule 3 is to be read as a reference to relevant offences.

(4) In sections 83 and 85, references to the commencement of this Part are to be read as references to the date of service of the notification order.

[Sexual Offences Act 2003, s 98.]

7.10667 **99. Sections 97 and 98: relevant offences** (1) "Relevant offence" in sections 97 and 98 means an act which—

(*a*) constituted an offence under the law in force in the country concerned, and

(*b*) would have constituted an offence listed in Schedule 3 (other than at paragraph 60) if it had been done in any part of the United Kingdom.

(2) An act punishable under the law in force in a country outside the United Kingdom constitutes an offence under that law for the purposes of subsection (1) however it is described in that law.

(3) Subject to subsection (4), on an application for a notification order the condition in subsection (1)(*b*) is to be taken as met unless, not later than rules of court[1] may provide, the defendant serves on the applicant a notice—

(*a*) stating that, on the facts as alleged with respect to the act concerned, the condition is not in his opinion met,

(*b*) showing his grounds for that opinion, and

(*c*) requiring the applicant to prove that the condition is met.

(4) The court, if it thinks fit, may permit the defendant to require the applicant to prove that the condition is met without service of a notice under subsection (3).

[Sexual Offences Act 2003, s 99.]

---

1 See the Magistrates' Courts (Notification Orders) Rules 2004, in PART I: MAGISTRATES' COURTS, PROCEDURE, ante.

**7.10668** **100. Interim notification orders** (1) This section applies where an application for a notification order ("the main application") has not been determined.

(2) An application[1] for an order under this section ("an interim notification order")—

(*a*) may be made in the complaint containing the main application, or

(*b*) if the main application has been made, may be made by the person who has made that application, by complaint to the court to which that application has been made.

(3) The court may, if it considers it just to do so, make an interim notification order.

(4) Such an order—

(*a*) has effect only for a fixed period, specified in the order;

(*b*) ceases to have effect, if it has not already done so, on the determination of the main application.

(5) While such an order has effect—

(*a*) the defendant is subject to the notification requirements of this Part;

(*b*) this Part applies to the defendant, subject to the modification set out in subsection (6).

(6) The "relevant date" means the date of service of the order.

(7) The applicant or the defendant may by complaint apply to the court that made the interim notification order for the order to be varied, renewed or discharged.

[Sexual Offences Act 2003, s 100.]

---

1 For form of application and procedure, see the Magistrates' Courts (Notification Orders) Rules 2004, in PART I: MAGISTRATES' COURTS, PROCEDURE, ante.

**7.10669** **101. Notification orders and interim notification orders: appeals** A defendant may appeal to the Crown Court against the making of a notification order or interim notification order.

[Sexual Offences Act 2003, s 101.]

*Sexual harm prevention orders (England and Wales)*

**7.10669A** **103A. Sexual harm prevention orders: applications and grounds** (1) A court may make an order under this section (a "sexual harm prevention order") in respect of a person ("the defendant") where subsection (2) or (3) applies to the defendant.

(2) This subsection applies to the defendant where—

(*a*) the court deals with the defendant in respect of—

(i) an offence listed in Schedule 3 or 5, or

(ii) a finding that the defendant is not guilty of an offence listed in Schedule 3 or 5 by reason of insanity, or

(iii) a finding that the defendant is under a disability and has done the act charged against the defendant in respect of an offence listed in Schedule 3 or 5,

and

(*b*) the court is satisfied that it is necessary to make a sexual harm prevention order, for the purpose of—

(i) protecting the public or any particular members of the public from sexual harm from the defendant, or

(ii) protecting children or vulnerable adults generally, or any particular children or vulnerable adults, from sexual harm from the defendant outside the United Kingdom.

(3) This subsection applies to the defendant where—

(*a*) an application under subsection (4) has been made in respect of the defendant and it is proved on the application that the defendant is a qualifying offender, and

(*b*) the court is satisfied that the defendant's behaviour since the appropriate date makes it necessary to make a sexual harm prevention order, for the purpose of—

(i) protecting the public or any particular members of the public from sexual harm from the defendant, or

(ii) protecting children or vulnerable adults generally, or any particular children or vulnerable adults, from sexual harm from the defendant outside the United Kingdom.

(4) A chief officer of police or the Director General of the National Crime Agency ("the Director General") may by complaint to a magistrates' court apply for a sexual harm prevention order in respect of a person if it appears to the chief officer or the Director General that—

(*a*) the person is a qualifying offender, and

(*b*) the person has since the appropriate date acted in such a way as to give reasonable cause to believe that it is necessary for such an order to be made.

(5) A chief officer of police may make an application under subsection (4) only in respect of a person—

(*a*) who resides in the chief officer's police area, or

(*b*) who the chief officer believes is in that area or is intending to come to it.

(6) An application under subsection (4) may be made to any magistrates' court acting for a local justice area that includes—

(*a*) any part of a relevant police area, or

(*b*) any place where it is alleged that the person acted in a way mentioned in subsection (4)(*b*).

(7) The Director General must as soon as practicable notify the chief officer of police for a relevant police area of any application that the Director has made under subsection (4).

(8) Where the defendant is a child, a reference in this section to a magistrates' court is to be taken as referring to a youth court (subject to any rules of court made under section 103K(1)).

(9) In this section "relevant police area" means—

(*a*) where the applicant is a chief officer of police, the officer's police area;

(b) where the applicant is the Director General—

(i) the police area where the person in question resides, or

(ii) a police area which the Director General believes the person is in or is intending to come to.

[Sexual Offences Act 2003, s 103A as inserted by the Anti-social Behaviour, Crime and Policing Act 2014, Sch 5.]

**7.10669B 103B. Section 103A: supplemental** (1) In section 103A—

"appropriate date", in relation to a qualifying offender, means the date or (as the case may be) the first date on which the offender was convicted, found or cautioned as mentioned in subsection (2) or (3) below;

"child" means a person under 18;

"the public" means the public in the United Kingdom;

"sexual harm" from a person means physical or psychological harm caused—

(*a*) by the person committing one or more offences listed in Schedule 3, or

(*b*) (in the context of harm outside the United Kingdom) by the person doing, outside the United Kingdom, anything which would constitute an offence listed in Schedule 3 if done in any part of the United Kingdom;

"qualifying offender" means a person within subsection (2) or (3) below;

"vulnerable adult" means a person aged 18 or over whose ability to protect himself or herself from physical or psychological harm is significantly impaired through physical or mental disability or illness, through old age or otherwise.

(2) A person is within this subsection if, whether before or after the commencement of this Part, the person—

(*a*) has been convicted of an offence listed in Schedule 3 (other than at paragraph 60) or in Schedule 5,

(*b*) has been found not guilty of such an offence by reason of insanity,

(*c*) has been found to be under a disability and to have done the act charged against him in respect of such an offence, or

(*d*) has been cautioned in respect of such an offence.

(3) A person is within this subsection if, under the law in force in a country outside the United Kingdom and whether before or after the commencement of this Part—

(*a*) the person has been convicted of a relevant offence (whether or not the person has been punished for it),

(*b*) a court exercising jurisdiction under that law has made in respect of a relevant offence a finding equivalent to a finding that the person is not guilty by reason of insanity,

(*c*) such a court has made in respect of a relevant offence a finding equivalent to a finding that the person is under a disability and did the act charged against the person in respect of the offence, or

(*d*) the person has been cautioned in respect of a relevant offence.

(4) In subsection (3), "relevant offence" means an act which—

(*a*) constituted an offence under the law in force in the country concerned, and

(*b*) would have constituted an offence listed in Schedule 3 (other than at paragraph 60) or in Schedule 5 if it had been done in any part of the United Kingdom.

For this purpose an act punishable under the law in force in a country outside the United Kingdom constitutes an offence under that law, however it is described in that law.

(5) For the purposes of section 103A, acts, behaviour, convictions and findings include those occurring before the commencement of this Part.

(6) Subject to subsection (7), on an application under section 103A(4) the condition in subsection (4)(*b*) above (where relevant) is to be taken as met unless, not later than rules of court may provide, the defendant serves on the applicant a notice—

(*a*) stating that, on the facts as alleged with respect to the act concerned, the condition is not in the defendant's opinion met,

(*b*) showing the grounds for that opinion, and

(*c*) requiring the applicant to prove that the condition is met.

(7) The court, if it thinks fit, may permit the defendant to require the applicant to prove that the condition is met without service of a notice under subsection (6).

(8) Subsection (9) applies for the purposes of section 103A and this section.

(9) In construing any reference to an offence listed in Schedule 3, any condition subject to which an offence is so listed that relates—

(*a*) to the way in which the defendant is dealt with in respect of an offence so listed or a relevant finding (as defined by section 132(9)), or

(*b*) to the age of any person,

is to be disregarded.

[Sexual Offences Act 2003, s 103B as inserted by the Anti-social Behaviour, Crime and Policing Act 2014, Sch 5.]

**7.10669C 103C. SHPOs: effect** (1) A sexual harm prevention order prohibits the defendant from doing anything described in the order.

(2) Subject to section 103D(1), a prohibition contained in a sexual harm prevention order has effect—

(*a*) for a fixed period, specified in the order, of at least 5 years, or

(*b*) until further order.

(3) A sexual harm prevention order—

(*a*) may specify that some of its prohibitions have effect until further order and some for a fixed period;

(*b*) may specify different periods for different prohibitions.

(4) The only prohibitions that may be included in a sexual harm prevention order are those necessary for the purpose of—

(*a*) protecting the public or any particular members of the public from sexual harm from the defendant, or

(*b*) protecting children or vulnerable adults generally, or any particular children or vulnerable adults, from sexual harm from the defendant outside the United Kingdom.

(5) In subsection (4) "the public", "sexual harm", "child" and "vulnerable adult" each has the meaning given in section 103B(1).

(6) Where a court makes a sexual harm prevention order in relation to a person who is already subject to such an order (whether made by that court or another), the earlier order ceases to have effect.

[Sexual Offences Act 2003, s 103C as inserted by the Anti-social Behaviour, Crime and Policing Act 2014, Sch 5.]

**7.10669D 103D. SHPOs: prohibitions on foreign travel** (1) A prohibition on foreign travel contained in a sexual harm prevention order must be for a fixed period of not more than 5 years.

(2) A "prohibition on foreign travel" means—

(*a*) a prohibition on travelling to any country outside the United Kingdom named or described in the order,

(*b*) a prohibition on travelling to any country outside the United Kingdom other than a country named or described in the order, or

(*c*) a prohibition on travelling to any country outside the United Kingdom.

(3) Subsection (1) does not prevent a prohibition on foreign travel from being extended for a further period (of no more than 5 years each time) under section 103E.

(4) A sexual harm prevention order that contains a prohibition within subsection (2)(*c*) must require the defendant to surrender all of the defendant's passports at a police station specified in the order—

(*a*) on or before the date when the prohibition takes effect, or

(*b*) within a period specified in the order.

(5) Any passports surrendered must be returned as soon as reasonably practicable after the person ceases to be subject to a sexual harm prevention order containing a prohibition within subsection (2)(*c*) (unless the person is subject to an equivalent prohibition under another order).

(6) Subsection (5) does not apply in relation to—

(*a*) a passport issued by or on behalf of the authorities of a country outside the United Kingdom if the passport has been returned to those authorities;

(*b*) a passport issued by or on behalf of an international organisation if the passport has been returned to that organisation.

(7) In this section "passport" means—

(*a*) a United Kingdom passport within the meaning of the Immigration Act 1971;

(*b*) a passport issued by or on behalf of the authorities of a country outside the United Kingdom, or by or on behalf of an international organisation;

(*c*) a document that can be used (in some or all circumstances) instead of a passport.

[Sexual Offences Act 2003, s 103D as inserted by the Anti-social Behaviour, Crime and Policing Act 2014, Sch 5.]

**7.10669E 103E. SHPOs: variations, renewals and discharges** (1) A person within subsection (2) may apply to the appropriate court for an order varying, renewing or discharging a sexual harm prevention order.

(2) The persons are—

(*a*) the defendant;

(*b*) the chief officer of police for the area in which the defendant resides;

(*c*) a chief officer of police who believes that the defendant is in, or is intending to come to, that officer's police area;

(*d*) where the order was made on an application by a chief officer of police under section 103A(4), that officer.

(3) An application under subsection (1) may be made—

(*a*) where the appropriate court is the Crown Court, in accordance with rules of court;

(*b*) in any other case, by complaint.

(4) Subject to subsections (5) and (7), on the application the court, after hearing the person making the application and (if they wish to be heard) the other persons mentioned in subsection (2), may make any order, varying, renewing or discharging the sexual harm prevention order, that the court considers appropriate.

(5) An order may be renewed, or varied so as to impose additional prohibitions on the defendant, only if it is necessary to do so for the purpose of—

(*a*) protecting the public or any particular members of the public from sexual harm from the defendant, or

(*b*) protecting children or vulnerable adults generally, or any particular children or vulnerable adults, from sexual harm from the defendant outside the United Kingdom.

Any renewed or varied order may contain only such prohibitions as are necessary for this purpose.

(6) In subsection (5) "the public", "sexual harm", "child" and "vulnerable adult" each has the meaning given in section 103B(1).

(7) The court must not discharge an order before the end of 5 years beginning with the day on which the order was made, without the consent of the defendant and—

(*a*) where the application is made by a chief officer of police, that chief officer, or

(*b*) in any other case, the chief officer of police for the area in which the defendant resides.

(8) Subsection (7) does not apply to an order containing a prohibition on foreign travel and no other prohibitions.

(9) In this section "the appropriate court" means—

(*a*) where the Crown Court or the Court of Appeal made the sexual harm prevention order, the Crown Court;

(*b*) where an adult magistrates' court made the order, that court, an adult magistrates' court for the area in which the defendant resides or, where the application is made by a chief officer of police, any adult magistrates' court acting for a local justice area that includes any part of the chief officer's police area;

(*c*) where a youth court made the order and the defendant is under the age of 18, that court, a youth court for the area in which the defendant resides or, where the application is made by a chief officer of police, any youth court acting for a local justice area that includes any part of the chief officer's police area;

(*d*) where a youth court made the order and the defendant is aged 18 or over, an adult magistrates' court for the area in which the defendant resides or, where the application is made by a chief officer of police, any adult magistrates' court acting for a local justice area that includes any part of the chief officer's police area.

In this subsection "adult magistrates' court" means a magistrates' court that is not a youth court.

[Sexual Offences Act 2003, s 103E as inserted by the Anti-social Behaviour, Crime and Policing Act 2014, Sch 5.]

**7.10669F 103F. Interim SHPOs** (1) This section applies where an application under section 103A(4) ("the main application") has not been determined.

(2) An application for an order under this section ("an interim sexual harm prevention order")—

(*a*) may be made by the complaint by which the main application is made, or

(*b*) if the main application has been made, may be made by the person who has made that application, by complaint to the court to which that application has been made.

(3) The court may, if it considers it just to do so, make an interim sexual harm prevention order, prohibiting the defendant from doing anything described in the order.

(4) Such an order—

(*a*) has effect only for a fixed period, specified in the order;

(*b*) ceases to have effect, if it has not already done so, on the determination of the main application.

(5) The applicant or the defendant may by complaint apply to the court that made the interim sexual harm prevention order for the order to be varied, renewed or discharged.

[Sexual Offences Act 2003, s 103F as inserted by the Anti-social Behaviour, Crime and Policing Act 2014, Sch 5.]

**7.10669G 103G. SHPOs and interim SHPOs: notification requirements** (1) Where—

(*a*) a sexual harm prevention order is made in respect of a defendant who was a relevant offender immediately before the making of the order, and (*b*) the defendant would (apart from this subsection) cease to be subject to the notification requirements of this Part while the order (as renewed from time to time) has effect,

the defendant remains subject to the notification requirements.

(2) Where a sexual harm prevention order is made in respect of a defendant who was not a relevant offender immediately before the making of the order—

(*a*) the order causes the defendant to become subject to the notification requirements of this Part from the making of the order until the order (as renewed from time to time) ceases to have effect, and

(*b*) this Part applies to the defendant, subject to the modification set out in subsection (3).

(3) The "relevant date" is the date of service of the order.

(4) Subsections (1) to (3) apply to an interim sexual harm prevention order as if references to a sexual harm prevention order were references to an interim sexual harm prevention order, and with the omission of "(as renewed from time to time)" in both places.

(5) Where—

(*a*) a sexual harm prevention order is in effect in relation to a relevant sex offender (within the meaning of section 88A), and

(*b*) by virtue of section 88F or 88G the relevant sex offender ceases to be subject to the notification requirements of this Part,

the sexual harm prevention order ceases to have effect.

(6) On an application for a sexual harm prevention order made by a chief officer of police, the court must make a notification order in respect of the defendant (either in addition to or instead of a sexual harm prevention order) if—

(*a*) the applicant invites the court to do so, and

(*b*) it is proved that the conditions in section 97(2) to (4) are met.

(7) On an application for an interim sexual harm prevention order made by a chief officer of police, the court may, if it considers it just to do so, make an interim notification order (either in addition to or instead of an interim sexual harm prevention order).

[Sexual Offences Act 2003, s 103G as inserted by the Anti-social Behaviour, Crime and Policing Act 2014, Sch 5.]

**7.10669H 103H. SHPOs and interim SHPOs: appeals** (1) A defendant may appeal against the making of a sexual harm prevention order—

(*a*) where the order was made by virtue of section 103A(2)(*a*)(i), as if the order were a sentence passed on the defendant for the offence;

(*b*) where the order was made by virtue of section 103A(2)(*a*)(ii) or (iii), as if the defendant had been convicted of the offence and the order were a sentence passed on the defendant for that offence;

(*c*) where the order was made on an application under section 103A(4), to the Crown Court.

(2) A defendant may appeal to the Crown Court against the making of an interim sexual harm prevention order.

(3) A defendant may appeal against the making of an order under section 103E, or the refusal to make such an order—

(*a*) where the application for such an order was made to the Crown Court, to the Court of Appeal;

(*b*) in any other case, to the Crown Court.

(4) On an appeal under subsection (1)(*c*), (2) or (3)(*b*), the Crown Court may make such orders as may be necessary to give effect to its determination of the appeal, and may also make such incidental or consequential orders as appear to it to be just.

(5) Any order made by the Crown Court on an appeal under subsection (1)(*c*) or (2) (other than an order directing that an application be re-heard by a magistrates' court) is for the purposes of section 103E(9) or 103F(5) (respectively) to be treated as if it were an order of the court from which the appeal was brought (and not an order of the Crown Court).

[Sexual Offences Act 2003, s 103H as inserted by the Anti-social Behaviour, Crime and Policing Act 2014, Sch 5.]

**7.10669I 103I. Offence: breach of SHPO or interim SHPO etc** (1) A person who, without reasonable excuse, does anything that the person is prohibited from doing by—

(*a*) a sexual harm prevention order,

(*b*) an interim sexual harm prevention order,

(*c*) a sexual offences prevention order,

(*d*) an interim sexual offences prevention order, or

(*e*) a foreign travel order,

commits an offence.

(2) A person commits an offence if, without reasonable excuse, the person fails to comply with a requirement imposed under section 103D(4).

(3) A person guilty of an offence under this section is liable—

(*a*) on summary conviction, to imprisonment for a term not exceeding 6 months or a fine or both;

(*b*) on conviction on indictment, to imprisonment for a term not exceeding 5 years.

(4) Where a person is convicted of an offence under this section, it is not open to the court by or before which the person is convicted to make, in respect of the offence, an order for conditional discharge.

[Sexual Offences Act 2003, s 103I as inserted by the Anti-social Behaviour, Crime and Policing Act 2014, Sch 5.]

**7.10669J 103J. SHPOs and interim SHPOs: guidance** (1) The Secretary of State must issue guidance to chief officers of police and to the Director General of the National Crime Agency in relation to the exercise by them of their powers with regard to sexual harm prevention orders and interim sexual harm prevention orders.

(2) The Secretary of State may, from time to time, revise the guidance issued under subsection (1).

(3) The Secretary of State must arrange for any guidance issued or revised under this section to be published in such manner as the Secretary of State considers appropriate.

[Sexual Offences Act 2003, s 103J as inserted by the Anti-social Behaviour, Crime and Policing Act 2014, Sch 5.]

**7.10669K 103K. SHPOs and interim SHPOs: supplementary** (1) Rules of court—

(*a*) may provide for a youth court to give permission for an application under section 103A(4) against a person aged 18 or over to be made to the youth court if—

(i) an application to the youth court has been made, or is to be made, under that section against a person aged under 18, and

(ii) the youth court thinks that it would be in the interests of justice for the applications to be heard together;

(*b*) may, in relation to a person attaining the age of 18 after proceedings against that person by virtue of section 103A, 103E, 103F or 103G(6) or (7) have begun—

(i) prescribe circumstances in which the proceedings may or must remain in the youth court;

(ii) make provision for the transfer of the proceedings from the youth court to a magistrates' court that is not a youth court (including provision applying section 103F with modifications).

(2) A person's age is treated for the purposes of sections 103A to 103J and this section as being that which it appears to the court to be after considering any available evidence.

[Sexual Offences Act 2003, s 103K as inserted by the Anti-social Behaviour, Crime and Policing Act 2014, Sch 5.]

*Sexual risk orders (England and Wales)*

**7.10684A 122A. Sexual risk orders: applications, grounds and effect** (1) A chief officer of police or the Director General of the National Crime Agency ("the Director General") may by complaint to a magistrates' court apply for an order under this section (a "sexual risk order") in respect of a person ("the defendant") if it appears to the chief officer or the Director General that the following condition is met.

(2) The condition is that the defendant has, whether before or after the commencement of this Part, done an act of a sexual nature as a result of which there is reasonable cause to believe that it is necessary for a sexual risk order to be made.

(3) A chief officer of police may make an application under subsection (1) only in respect of a person—

(*a*) who resides in the chief officer's police area, or

(*b*) who the chief officer believes is in that area or is intending to come to it.

(4) An application under subsection (1) may be made to any magistrates' court acting for a local justice area that includes—

(*a*) any part of a relevant police area, or

(*b*) any place where it is alleged that the person acted in a way mentioned in subsection (2).

(5) The Director General must as soon as practicable notify the chief officer of police for a relevant police area of any application that the Director has made under subsection (1).

(6) On an application under subsection (1), the court may make a sexual risk order if it is satisfied that the defendant has, whether before or after the commencement of this Part, done an act of a sexual nature as a result of which it is necessary to make such an order for the purpose of—

(*a*) protecting the public or any particular members of the public from harm from the defendant, or

(*b*) protecting children or vulnerable adults generally, or any particular children or vulnerable adults, from harm from the defendant outside the United Kingdom.

(7) Such an order—

(*a*) prohibits the defendant from doing anything described in the order;

(*b*) has effect for a fixed period (not less than 2 years) specified in the order or until further order.

(8) A sexual risk order may specify different periods for different prohibitions.

(9) The only prohibitions that may be imposed are those necessary for the purpose of—

(*a*) protecting the public or any particular members of the public from harm from the defendant, or

(*b*) protecting children or vulnerable adults generally, or any particular children or vulnerable adults, from harm from the defendant outside the United Kingdom.

(10) Where a court makes a sexual risk order in relation to a person who is already subject to such an order (whether made by that court or another), the earlier order ceases to have effect.

[Sexual Offences Act 2003, s 122A as inserted by the Anti-social Behaviour, Crime and Policing Act 2014, Sch 5.]

**7.10684B 122B. Section 122A: interpretation** (1) In section 122A—

"child" means a person under 18;

"harm" from the defendant means physical or psychological harm caused by the defendant doing an act of a sexual nature;

"the public" means the public in the United Kingdom;

"vulnerable adult" means a person aged 18 or over whose ability to protect himself or herself from physical or psychological harm is significantly impaired through physical or mental disability or illness, through old age or otherwise.

(2) Where the defendant is a child, a reference in that section to a magistrates' court is to be taken as referring to a youth court (subject to any rules of court made under section 122K(1)).

(3) In that section "relevant police area" means—

(*a*) where the applicant is a chief officer of police, the officer's police area;

(*b*) where the applicant is the Director General of the National Crime Agency—

(i) the police area where the person in question resides, or

(ii) a police area which the Director General believes the person is in or is intending to come to.

[Sexual Offences Act 2003, s 122B as inserted by the Anti-social Behaviour, Crime and Policing Act 2014, Sch 5.]

**7.10684C 122C. Sexual risk orders: prohibitions on foreign travel** (1) A prohibition on foreign travel contained in a sexual risk order must not be for a period of more than 5 years.

(2) A "prohibition on foreign travel" means—

(*a*) a prohibition on travelling to any country outside the United Kingdom named or described in the order,

(*b*) a prohibition on travelling to any country outside the United Kingdom other than a country named or described in the order, or

(*c*) a prohibition on travelling to any country outside the United Kingdom.

(3) Subsection (1) does not prevent a prohibition on foreign travel from being extended for a further period (of no more than 5 years each time) under section 122D.

(4) A sexual risk order that contains a prohibition within subsection (2)(*c*) must require the defendant to surrender all of the defendant's passports at a police station specified in the order—

(*a*) on or before the date when the prohibition takes effect, or

(*b*) within a period specified in the order.

(5) Any passports surrendered must be returned as soon as reasonably practicable after the person ceases to be subject to a sexual risk order containing such a prohibition (unless the person is subject to an equivalent prohibition under another order).

(6) Subsection (5) does not apply in relation to—

(*a*) a passport issued by or on behalf of the authorities of a country outside the United Kingdom if the passport has been returned to those authorities;

(*b*) a passport issued by or on behalf of an international organisation if the passport has been returned to that organisation.

(7) In this section "passport" means—

(*a*) a United Kingdom passport within the meaning of the Immigration Act 1971;

(*b*) a passport issued by or on behalf of the authorities of a country outside the United Kingdom, or by or on behalf of an international organisation;

(*c*) a document that can be used (in some or all circumstances) instead of a passport.

[Sexual Offences Act 2003, s 122C as inserted by the Anti-social Behaviour, Crime and Policing Act 2014, Sch 5.]

**7.10684D 122D. Sexual risk order: variations, renewals and discharges** (1) A person within subsection (2) may by complaint to the appropriate court apply for an order varying, renewing or discharging a sexual risk order.

(2) The persons are—

(*a*) the defendant;

(*b*) the chief officer of police for the area in which the defendant resides;

(*c*) a chief officer of police who believes that the defendant is in, or is intending to come to, that officer's police area;

(*d*) where the order was made on an application by a chief officer of police, that officer.

(3) Subject to subsections (4) and (5), on the application the court, after hearing the person making the application and (if they wish to be heard) the other persons mentioned in subsection (2), may make any order, varying, renewing or discharging the sexual risk order, that the court considers appropriate.

(4) An order may be renewed, or varied so as to impose additional prohibitions on the defendant, only if it is necessary to do so for the purpose of—

(*a*) protecting the public or any particular members of the public from harm from the defendant, or (*b*) protecting children or vulnerable adults generally, or any particular children or vulnerable adults, from harm from the defendant outside the United Kingdom.

Any renewed or varied order may contain only such prohibitions as are necessary for this purpose.

(5) The court must not discharge an order before the end of 2 years beginning with the day on which the order was made, without the consent of the defendant and—

(*a*) where the application is made by a chief officer of police, that chief officer, or

(*b*) in any other case, the chief officer of police for the area in which the defendant resides.

(6) Section 122B(1) applies for the purposes of this section.

(7) In this section "the appropriate court" means—

(*a*) where an adult magistrates' court made the sexual risk order, that court, any adult magistrates' court for the area in which the defendant resides or, where the application is made by a chief officer of police, any adult magistrates' court acting for a local justice area that includes any part of the chief officer's police area;

(*b*) where a youth court made the order and the defendant is under the age of 18, that court, a youth court for the area in which the defendant resides or, where the application is made by a chief officer of police, any youth court acting for a local justice area that includes any part of the chief officer's police area;

(*c*) where a youth court made the order and the defendant is aged 18 or over, an adult magistrates' court for the area in which the defendant resides or, where the application is made by a chief officer of police, any adult magistrates' court acting for a local justice area that includes any part of the chief officer's police area.

In this subsection "adult magistrates' court" means a magistrates' court that is not a youth court.

[Sexual Offences Act 2003, s 122D as inserted by the Anti-social Behaviour, Crime and Policing Act 2014, Sch 5.]

7.10684E **122E. Interim sexual risk orders** (1) This section applies where an application for a sexual risk order ("the main application") has not been determined.

(2) An application for an order under this section ("an interim sexual risk order")—

(*a*) may be made by the complaint by which the main application is made, or

(*b*) if the main application has been made, may be made by the person who has made that application, by complaint to the court to which that application has been made.

(3) The court may, if it considers it just to do so, make an interim sexual risk order, prohibiting the defendant from doing anything described in the order.

(4) Such an order—

(*a*) has effect only for a fixed period, specified in the order;

(*b*) ceases to have effect, if it has not already done so, on the determination of the main application.

(5) The applicant or the defendant may by complaint apply to the court that made the interim sexual risk order for the order to be varied, renewed or discharged.

[Sexual Offences Act 2003, s 122E as inserted by the Anti-social Behaviour, Crime and Policing Act 2014, Sch 5.]

7.10684F **122F. Sexual risk orders and interim sexual risk orders: notification requirements** (1) A person in respect of whom a court makes—

(*a*) a sexual risk order (other than one that replaces an interim sexual risk order), or

(*b*) an interim sexual risk order,

must, within the period of 3 days beginning with the date of service of the order, notify to the police the information set out in subsection (2) (unless the person is subject to the notification requirements of this Part on that date).

(2) The information is—

(*a*) the person's name and, where the person uses one or more other names, each of those names;

(*b*) the person's home address.

(3) A person who—

(*a*) is subject to a sexual risk order or an interim sexual risk order (but is not subject to the notification requirements of this Part), and

(*b*) uses a name which has not been notified under this section (or under any other provision of this Part), or changes home address,

must, within the period of 3 days beginning with the date on which that happens, notify to the police that name or (as the case may be) the new home address.

(4) Sections 87 (method of notification and related matters) and 91 (offences relating to notification) apply for the purposes of this section—

(*a*) with references to section 83(1) being read as references to subsection (1) above,

(*b*) with references to section 84(1) being read as references to subsection (3) above, and

(*c*) with the omission of section 87(2)(*b*).

[Sexual Offences Act 2003, s 122F as inserted by the Anti-social Behaviour, Crime and Policing Act 2014, Sch 5]

7.10684G **122G. Sexual risk orders and interim sexual risk orders: appeals** (1) A defendant may appeal to the Crown Court—

(*a*) against the making of a sexual risk order;

(*b*) against the making of an interim sexual risk order; or

(*c*) against the making of an order under section 122D, or the refusal to make such an order.

(2) On any such appeal, the Crown Court may make such orders as may be necessary to give effect to its determination of the appeal, and may also make such incidental or consequential orders as appear to it to be just.

(3) Any order made by the Crown Court on an appeal under subsection (1)(*a*) or (*b*) (other than an order directing that an application be re-heard by a magistrates' court) is for the purposes of section 122D(7) or 122E(5) (respectively) to be treated as if it were an order of the court from which the appeal was brought (and not an order of the Crown Court).

[Sexual Offences Act 2003, s 122G as inserted by the Anti-social Behaviour, Crime and Policing Act 2014, Sch 5.]

**7.10684H 122H. Offence: breach of sexual risk order or interim sexual risk order etc**

(1) A person who, without reasonable excuse, does anything that the person is prohibited from doing by—

(*a*) a sexual risk order,

(*b*) an interim sexual risk order,

(*c*) a risk of sexual harm order,

(*d*) an interim risk of sexual harm order,

(*e*) an order under section 2 of the Protection of Children and Prevention of Sexual Offences (Scotland) Act 2005 (risk of sexual harm orders in Scotland), or

(*f*) an order under section 5 of that Act (interim risk of sexual harm orders in Scotland),

commits an offence.

(2) A person commits an offence if, without reasonable excuse, the person fails to comply with a requirement imposed under section 122C(4).

(3) A person guilty of an offence under this section is liable—

(*a*) on summary conviction, to imprisonment for a term not exceeding 6 months or a fine or both;

(*b*) on conviction on indictment, to imprisonment for a term not exceeding 5 years.

(4) Where a person is convicted of an offence under this section, it is not open to the court by or before which the person is convicted to make, in respect of the offence, an order for conditional discharge.

[Sexual Offences Act 2003, s 122H as inserted by the Anti-social Behaviour, Crime and Policing Act 2014, Sch 5.]

**7.10684I 122I. Effect of conviction etc of an offence under section 122H etc** (1) This section applies to a person ("the defendant") who—

(*a*) is convicted of an offence mentioned in subsection (2);

(*b*) is found not guilty of such an offence by reason of insanity;

(*c*) is found to be under a disability and to have done the act charged against him in respect of such an offence; or

(*d*) is cautioned in respect of such an offence.

(2) Those offences are—

(*a*) an offence under section 122H or 128 of this Act;

(*b*) an offence under section 7 of the Protection of Children and Prevention of Sexual Offences (Scotland) Act 2005 (contravention of risk of sexual harm order or interim risk of sexual harm order in Scotland).

(3) Where—

(*a*) a defendant was a relevant offender immediately before this section applied to the defendant, and

(*b*) the defendant would (apart from this subsection) cease to be subject to the notification requirements of this Part while the relevant order (as renewed from time to time) has effect,

the defendant remains subject to the notification requirements.

(4) Where the defendant was not a relevant offender immediately before this section applied to the defendant—

(*a*) this section causes the defendant to become subject to the notification requirements of this Part from the time the section first applies to the defendant until the relevant order (as renewed from time to time) ceases to have effect, and

(*b*) this Part applies to the defendant, subject to the modification set out in subsection (5).

(5) The "relevant date" is the date on which this section first applies to the defendant.

(6) In this section "relevant order" means—

(*a*) where the conviction, finding or caution within subsection (1) is in respect of a breach of a sexual risk order or a risk of sexual harm order, that order;

(*b*) where the conviction, finding or caution within subsection (1) is in respect of a breach of an interim sexual risk order or an interim risk of sexual harm order, any sexual risk order or risk of sexual harm order made on the hearing of the application to which the interim order relates or, if no such order is made, the interim order.

(7) In subsection (6) "risk of sexual harm order" and "interim risk of sexual harm order" include orders under sections 2 and 5 (respectively) of the Protection of Children and Prevention of Sexual Offences (Scotland) Act 2005.

[Sexual Offences Act 2003, s 122I as inserted by the Anti-social Behaviour, Crime and Policing Act 2014, Sch 5.]

7.10684J **122J. Sexual risk orders and interim sexual risk orders: guidance** (1) The Secretary of State must issue guidance to chief officers of police and to the Director General of the National Crime Agency in relation to the exercise by them of their powers with regard to sexual risk orders and interim sexual risk orders.

(2) The Secretary of State may, from time to time, revise the guidance issued under subsection (1).

(3) The Secretary of State must arrange for any guidance issued or revised under this section to be published in such manner as the Secretary of State considers appropriate.

[Sexual Offences Act 2003, s 122J as inserted by the Anti-social Behaviour, Crime and Policing Act 2014, Sch 5.]

7.10684K **122K. Sexual risk orders and interim sexual risk orders: supplementary** (1) Rules of court—

(*a*) may provide for a youth court to give permission for an application under section 122A against a person aged 18 or over to be made to the youth court if—
   (i) an application to the youth court has been made, or is to be made, under that section against a person aged under 18, and
   (ii) the youth court thinks that it would be in the interests of justice for the applications to be heard together;

(*b*) may, in relation to a person attaining the age of 18 after proceedings against that person by virtue of section 122A, 122D or 122E have begun—
   (i) prescribe circumstances in which the proceedings may or must remain in the youth court;
   (ii) make provision for the transfer of the proceedings from the youth court to a magistrates' court that is not a youth court (including provision applying section 122E with modifications).

(2) A person's age is treated for the purposes of sections 122A to 122J and this section as being that which it appears to the court to be after considering any available evidence.

[Sexual Offences Act 2003, s 122K as inserted by the Anti-social Behaviour, Crime and Policing Act 2014, Sch 5.]

*Power to amend Schedules 3 and 5*

7.10691 **130. Power to amend Schedules 3 and 5** *Secretary of State may by order amend Schedules 3 and 5.*

*General*

7.10692 **131. Young offenders: application** This Part applies to—

(*a*) a period of detention which a person is liable to serve[1] under a detention and training order (including an order under section 211 of the Armed Forces Act 2006), or a secure training order,

(*b*) a period for which a person is ordered to be detained in residential accommodation under section 44(1) of the Criminal Procedure (Scotland) Act 1995 (c 46),

(*c*) a period of training in a training school, or of custody in a remand centre, which a person is liable to undergo or serve by virtue of an order under section 74(1)(*a*) or (*e*) of the Children and Young Persons Act (Northern Ireland) 1968 (c 34 (NI)),

(*d*) a period for which a person is ordered to be detained in a juvenile justice centre under Article 39 of the Criminal Justice (Children) (Northern Ireland) Order 1998 (SI 1998/1504 (NI 9)),

(*e*) a period for which a person is ordered to be kept in secure accommodation under Article 44A of the Order referred to in paragraph (*d*),

(*f*) a sentence of detention in a young offender institution, a young offenders institution or a young offenders centre,

(*g*) a sentence under a custodial order within the meaning of section 71AA of, or paragraph 10(1) of Schedule 5A to, the Army Act 1955 (3 & 4 Eliz 2 c 18) or the Air Force Act 1955 (3 & 4 Eliz 2 c 19) or section 43AA of, or paragraph 10(1) of Schedule 4A to, the Naval Discipline Act 1957 (c 53),

(*h*) a sentence of detention under section 90 or 91 of the Powers of Criminal Courts (Sentencing) Act 2000 (c 6), section 209 or 218 of the Armed Forces Act 2006, section 208 of the Criminal Procedure (Scotland) Act 1995 or Article 45 of the Criminal Justice (Children) (Northern Ireland) Order 1998,

(*i*) a sentence of custody for life under section 93 or 94 of the Powers of Criminal Courts (Sentencing) Act 2000 (c 6),

(*j*) a sentence of detention, or custody for life, under section 71A of the Army Act 1955 (3 & 4 Eliz 2 c 18) or the Air Force Act 1955 (3 & 4 Eliz 2 c 19) or section 43A of the Naval Discipline Act 1957 (c 53),

(*k*) a sentence of detention for public protection under section 226 of the Criminal Justice Act 2003 (including one passed as a result of section 221 of the Armed Forces Act 2006),

(*l*) an extended sentence under section 226B or 228 of the Criminal Justice Act 2003 (including one passed as a result of section 221A or 222 of the Armed Forces Act 2006),

(*m*) *Northern Ireland*

as it applies to an equivalent sentence of imprisonment; and references in this Part to prison or imprisonment are to be interpreted accordingly.

[Sexual Offences Act 2003, s 131 as amended by the Criminal Justice Act 2003, Sch 32, the Armed Forces Act 2006, Sch 16 and the Legal Aid, Sentencing and Punishment of Offenders Act 2012, Sch 21.]

---

[1] This refers to the period of detention and training and not to the entire term of the detention and training: *R v Slocombe* [2005] EWCA Crim 2297, [2006] 1 All ER 670, [2006] 1 WLR 313.

7.10693 **132. Offences with thresholds** (1) This section applies to an offence which in Schedule 3 is listed subject to a condition relating to the way in which the defendant is dealt with in respect of the offence or (where a relevant finding has been made in respect of him) in respect of the finding (a "sentencing condition").

(2) Where an offence is listed if either a sentencing condition or a condition of another description is met, this section applies only to the offence as listed subject to the sentencing condition.

(3) For the purposes of this Part (including in particular section 82(6))—

(*a*) a person is to be regarded as convicted of an offence to which this section applies, or

(*b*) (as the case may be) a relevant finding in relation to such an offence is to be regarded as made,

at the time when the sentencing condition is met.

(4) In the following subsections, references to a foreign offence are references to an act which—

(*a*) constituted an offence under the law in force in a country outside the United Kingdom ("the relevant foreign law"), and

(*b*) would have constituted an offence to which this section applies (but not an offence, listed in Schedule 3, to which this section does not apply) if it had been done in any part of the United Kingdom.

(5) In relation to a foreign offence, references to the corresponding UK offence are references to the offence (or any offence) to which subsection (3)(*b*) applies in the case of that foreign offence.

(6) For the purposes of this Part, a person is to be regarded as convicted under the relevant foreign law of a foreign offence at the time when he is, in respect of the offence, dealt with under that law in a way equivalent to that mentioned in Schedule 3 as it applies to the corresponding UK offence.

(7) Where in the case of any person a court exercising jurisdiction under the relevant foreign law makes in respect of a foreign offence a finding equivalent to a relevant finding, the court's finding is, for the purposes of this Part, to be regarded as made at the time when the person is, in respect of the finding, dealt with under that law in a way equivalent to that mentioned in Schedule 3 as it applies to the corresponding UK offence.

(8) Where (by virtue of an order under section 130 or otherwise) an offence is listed in Schedule 5 subject to a sentencing condition, this section applies to that offence as if references to Schedule 3 were references to Schedule 5.

(9) In this section, "relevant finding", in relation to an offence, means—

(*a*) a finding that a person is not guilty of the offence by reason of insanity, or

(*b*) a finding that a person is under a disability and did the act charged against him in respect of the offence.

[Sexual Offences Act 2003, s 132.]

7.10694 **132A. Disapplication of time limit for complaints** Section 127 of the Magistrates' Courts Act 1980 (time limits) does not apply to a complaint under any provision of this Part.

[Sexual Offences Act 2003, s 132A as inserted by the Policing and Crime Act 2009, s 22.]

7.10695 **133. Part 2: general interpretation** (1) In this Part—

"admitted to a hospital" means admitted to a hospital under—

(*a*) section 37 of the Mental Health Act 1983 (c 20), *Scotland and Northern Ireland*;

(*b*) Schedule 1 to the Criminal Procedure (Insanity and Unfitness to Plead) Act 1991 (c 25); or

(*c*) section 46 of the Mental Health Act 1983, *Scotland and Northern Ireland*;

"cautioned" means—

(*a*) cautioned (or, in Northern Ireland, cautioned by a police officer) after the person concerned has admitted the offence,

(*b*) *repealed*

and "caution" is to be interpreted accordingly;

"community order" means—

(*a*) a community order within the meaning of the Powers of Criminal Courts (Sentencing) Act 2000 (c 6) as that Act had effect before the passing of the Criminal Justice Act 2003);

(*b*) a probation order or community service order under the Criminal Procedure (Scotland) Act 1995 or a supervised attendance order made in pursuance of section 235 of that Act;

(*c*) *Northern Ireland*; or

(*d*) a community supervision order;

"community supervision order" means an order under paragraph 4 of Schedule 5A to the Army Act 1955 or the Air Force Act 1955 or Schedule 4A to the Naval Discipline Act 1957;
"country" includes territory;
"detained in a hospital" means detained in a hospital under—
- (*a*) Part 3 of the Mental Health Act 1983, *Scotland and Northern Ireland*;
- (*b*) Schedule 1 to the Criminal Procedure (Insanity and Unfitness to Plead) Act 1991; or
- (*c*) section 46 of the Mental Health Act 1983, *Scotland and Northern Ireland*;

"guardianship order" means a guardianship order under section 37 of the Mental Health Act 1983 (c 20), section 58 of the Criminal Procedure (Scotland) Act 1995 (c 46) or Article 44 of the Mental Health (Northern Ireland) Order 1986 (SI 1986/595 (NI 4));
"home address" has the meaning given by section 83(7);
"interim notification order" has the meaning given by section 100(2);
"interim risk of sexual harm order" has the meaning given by section 126(2);
"interim sexual harm prevention order" has the meaning given by section 103F(2);
"interim sexual risk order" has the meaning given by section 122E(2);
"interim sexual offences prevention order" has the meaning given by section 109(2);
"kept in service custody" means kept in service custody by virtue of an order under section 105(2) of the Armed Forces Act 2006 (but see also subsection (3));
"local police area" has the meaning given by section 88(3);
"local probation board" has the same meaning as in the Criminal Justice and Court Services Act 2000 (c 43);
"notification order" has the meaning given by section 97(1);
"notification period" has the meaning given by section 80(1);
"order for conditional discharge" means an order under any of the following provisions discharging the offender conditionally—
- (*a*) section 12 of the Powers of Criminal Courts (Sentencing) Act 2000;
- (*b*) Article 4 of the Criminal Justice (Northern Ireland) Order 1996;
- (*c*) section 185 of the Armed Forces Act 2006;
- (*d*) paragraph 3 of Schedule 5A to the Army Act 1955 or Air Force Act 1955 or Schedule 4A to the Naval Discipline Act 1957;

"parental responsibility" has the same meaning as in the Children Act 1989 (c 41) or the Children (Northern Ireland) Order 1995 (SI 1995/ 755 (NI 2)), and "parental responsibilities" has the same meaning as in Part 1 of the Children (Scotland) Act 1995 (c 36);
"the period of conditional discharge" has the meaning given by each of the following—
- (*a*) section 12(3) of the Powers of Criminal Courts (Sentencing) Act 2000;
- (*b*) Article 2(2) of the Criminal Justice (Northern Ireland) Order 1996;
- (*c*) section 185(2) of the Armed Forces Act 2006;

"probation order" has the meaning given by section 228(1) of the Criminal Procedure (Scotland) Act 1995;
"probation period" has the meaning given by section 307(1) of the Criminal Procedure (Scotland) Act 1995;
"prohibition on foreign travel" has the meaning given by section 103D(2) or 122C(2);
"relevant date" has the meaning given by section 82(6) (save in the circumstances mentioned in sections 98, 100, 107, 109 and 129);
"relevant offender" has the meaning given by section 80(2);
"restriction order" means—
- (*a*) an order under section 41 of the Mental Health Act 1983, section 57(2)(*b*) or 59 of the Criminal Procedure (Scotland) Act 1995 or Article 47(1) of the Mental Health (Northern Ireland) Order 1986;
- (*b*) a direction under paragraph 2(1)(*b*) of Schedule 1 to the Criminal Procedure (Insanity and Unfitness to Plead) Act 1991 (c 25) or Article 50A(3)(*b*) of the Mental Health (Northern Ireland) Order 1986 (SI 1986/595 (NI 4)); or
- (*c*) a direction under section 46 of the Mental Health Act 1983, section 69 of the Mental Health (Scotland) Act 1984 or Article 52 of the Mental Health (Northern Ireland) Order 1986;

"risk of sexual harm order" has the meaning given by section 123(1);
"service detention" has the meaning given by section 374 of the Armed Forces Act 2006;
"sexual harm prevention order" has the meaning given by section 103A(1);
"sexual offences prevention order" has the meaning given by section 106(1);
"sexual risk order" has the meaning given by section 122A(1);
"supervision" means supervision in pursuance of an order made for the purpose or, in the case of a person released from prison on licence, in pursuance of a condition contained in his licence;

(1A) A reference to a provision specified in paragraph (*a*) of the definition of "admitted to a hospital", "detained in a hospital" or "restriction order" includes a reference to the provision as it applies by virtue of—
- (*a*) section 5 of the Criminal Procedure (Insanity) Act 1964,
- (*b*) section 6 or 14 of the Criminal Appeal Act 1968,
- (*ba*) Schedule 4 to the Armed Forces Act 2006 (including as applied by section 16(2) of the Court Martial Appeals Act 1968),

(*c*) section 116A of the Army Act 1955 or the Air Force Act 1955 or section 63A of the Naval Discipline Act 1957, or

(*d*) section 16 or 23 of the Courts-Martial (Appeals) Act 1968.

(2) Where under section 141 different days are appointed for the commencement of different provisions of this Part, a reference in any such provision to the commencement of this Part is to be read (subject to section 98(4)) as a reference to the commencement of that provision.

(3) In relation to any time before the commencement of section 105(2) of the Armed Forces Act 2006, "kept in service custody" means being kept in military, air-force or naval custody by virtue of an order made under section 75A(2) of the Army Act 1955 or of the Air Force Act 1955 or section 47G(2) of the Naval Discipline Act 1957 (as the case may be).

[Sexual Offences Act 2003, s 133 as amended by the Domestic Violence, Crime and Victims Act 2004, Sch 10, the Armed Forces Act 2006, Schs 16 and 17, the Criminal Justice and Immigration Act 2008, Sch 26, the Legal Aid, Sentencing and Punishment of Offenders Act 2012, Sch 24 and the Anti-social Behaviour, Crime and Policing Act 2014, Sch 11.]

7.10696 **134. Conditional discharges and probation orders**[1] (1) The following provisions do not apply for the purposes of this Part to a conviction for an offence in respect of which an order for conditional discharge or, in Scotland, a probation order is made—

(*a*) section 14(1) of the Powers of Criminal Courts (Sentencing) Act 2000 (c 6) (conviction with absolute or conditional discharge deemed not to be a conviction);

(*b*) *Northern Ireland*;

(*c*) *Scotland*;

(*ca*) section 187(1) of the Armed Forces Act 2006 (conviction with absolute or conditional discharge deemed not to be a conviction);

(*d*) paragraph 5(1) of Schedule 5A to the Army Act 1955 (3 & 4 Eliz 2 c 18) or the Air Force Act 1955 (3 & 4 Eliz 2 c 19) or Schedule 4A to the Naval Discipline Act 1957 (c 53) (conviction with absolute or conditional discharge or community supervision order deemed not to be a conviction).

(2) Subsection (1) applies only to convictions after the commencement of this Part.

(3) The provisions listed in subsection (1)(*d*) do not apply for the purposes of this Part to a conviction for an offence in respect of which a community supervision order is or has (before or after the commencement of this Part) been made.

[Sexual Offences Act 2003, s 134 as amended by the Armed Forces Act 2006, Sch 16.]

---

1 Section 134 does not refer to absolute discharges; consequently, the notification does not arise, or survive is sentence is passed on a later date than the date of conviction, if the offender is so sentenced: *R v Longworth* [2006] UKHL 1, [2006] 1 All ER 887, [2006] 1 WLR 313.

7.10697 **135. Interpretation: mentally disordered offenders** (1) In this Part, a reference to a conviction includes a reference to a finding of a court in summary proceedings, where the court makes an order under an enactment within subsection (2), that the accused did the act charged; and similar references are to be interpreted accordingly.

(2) The enactments are—

(*a*) section 37(3) of the Mental Health Act 1983 (c 20);

(*b*) section 58(3) of the Criminal Procedure (Scotland) Act 1995 (c 46);

(*c*) *Northern Ireland*.

(3) In this Part, a reference to a person being or having been found to be under a disability and to have done the act charged against him in respect of an offence includes a reference to his being or having been found—

(*a*) unfit to be tried for the offence;

(*b*) to be insane so that his trial for the offence cannot or could not proceed; or

(*c*) unfit to be tried and to have done the act charged against him in respect of the offence.

(4) In section 133—

(*a*) a reference to admission or detention under Schedule 1 to the Criminal Procedure (Insanity and Unfitness to Plead) Act 1991 (c 25), and the reference to a direction under paragraph 2(1)(*b*) of that Schedule, include respectively—

(i) a reference to admission or detention under Schedule 1 to the Criminal Procedure (Insanity) Act 1964 (c 84); and

(ii) a reference to a restriction order treated as made by paragraph 2(1) of that Schedule;

(*b*) a reference to admission or detention under any provision of Part 6 of the Criminal Procedure (Scotland) Act 1995, and the reference to an order under section 57(2)(*b*) or 59 of that Act, include respectively—

(i) a reference to admission or detention under section 174(3) or 376(2) of the Criminal Procedure (Scotland) Act 1975 (c 21); and

(ii) a reference to a restriction order made under section 178(1) or 379(1) of that Act;

(*c*) *repealed*.

[Sexual Offences Act 2003, s 135 as amended by the Domestic Violence, Crime and Victims Act 2004, Sch 10.]

**7.10698 136. *Northern Ireland***

**7.10698A 136ZA. Application of orders throughout the United Kingdom** (1) In this section "relevant order" means—

(*a*) a sexual harm prevention order;
(*b*) an interim sexual harm prevention order;
(*c*) a sexual offences prevention order;
(*d*) an interim sexual offences prevention order;
(*e*) a foreign travel order;
(*f*) a sexual risk order;
(*g*) an interim sexual risk order;
(*h*) a risk of sexual harm order;
(*i*) an interim risk of sexual harm order;
(*j*) an order under section 2 of the Protection of Children and Prevention of Sexual Offences (Scotland) Act 2005 (risk of sexual harm orders in Scotland);
(*k*) an order under section 5 of that Act (interim risk of sexual harm orders in Scotland).

(2) For the purposes of sections 103I, 113, 122, 122H and 128, prohibitions imposed by a relevant order made in one part of the United Kingdom apply (unless expressly confined to particular localities) throughout that and every other part of the United Kingdom.

[Sexual Offences Act 2003, s 136ZA as inserted by the Anti-social Behaviour, Crime and Policing Act 2014, Sch 5.]

**7.10698B 136ZB. Order ceases to have effect when new order made** (1) Where a court in England and Wales makes an order listed in the first column of the following Table in relation to a person who is already subject to an order listed opposite it in the second column, the earlier order ceases to have effect (whichever part of the United Kingdom it was made in) unless the court orders otherwise.

| New order | Earlier order |
|---|---|
| Sexual harm prevention order | —sexual offences prevention order;<br>—foreign travel order. |
| Sexual risk order | —risk of sexual harm order;<br>—foreign travel order. |

(2) Where a court in Northern Ireland or Scotland makes an order listed in the first column of the following Table in relation to a person who is already subject to an order or prohibition listed opposite it in the second column, the earlier order or prohibition ceases to have effect (even though it was made or imposed by a court in England and Wales) unless the court orders otherwise.

| New order | Earlier order or prohibition |
|---|---|
| Sexual offences prevention order | —sexual harm prevention order not containing a prohibition on foreign travel;<br>—in the case of a sexual harm prevention order containing a prohibition on foreign travel, each of its other prohibitions. |
| Foreign travel order | —prohibition on foreign travel contained in a sexual harm prevention order. |
| Risk of sexual harm order | —sexual risk order not containing a prohibition on foreign travel;<br>—in the case of a sexual risk order containing a prohibition on foreign travel, each of its other prohibitions. |

(3) In this section—

(*a*) "court", in Scotland, includes sheriff;
(*b*) "risk of sexual harm order" includes an order under section 2 of the Protection of Children and Prevention of Sexual Offences (Scotland) Act 2005.

[Sexual Offences Act 2003, s 136ZB as inserted by the Anti-social Behaviour, Crime and Policing Act 2014, Sch 5.]

**136ZC, 136ZD. *Northern Ireland***

PART 2A[1]

CLOSURE ORDERS[2]

*Basic definitions*

**7.10699 136A. Meaning of specified prostitution offence etc** (1) This section applies for the purposes of this Part.

(2) The specified prostitution offences are—

(*a*) an offence under Article 37 of the Sexual Offences (Northern Ireland) Order 2008 ("the Northern Ireland Order");

(*aa*) an offence under section 48 of this Act committed by causing or inciting a child to be sexually exploited within the meaning given by section 51(2)(a);

(*b*) an offence under Article 38 of the Northern Ireland Order, committed by causing or inciting a child to become a prostitute;

(*ba*) an offence under section 49 of this Act committed by controlling the activities of a child in relation to sexual exploitation within the meaning given by section 51(2)(*a*);

(*c*) an offence under Article 39 of the Northern Ireland Order, committed by controlling the activities of a child relating to the child's prostitution;

(*ca*) an offence under section 50 of this Act committed by arranging or facilitating the sexual exploitation, within the meaning given by section 51(2)(*a*), of a child;

(*d*) an offence under Article 40 of the Northern Ireland Order, committed by arranging or facilitating a child's prostitution;

(*e*) an offence under section 52 of this Act or Article 62 of the Northern Ireland Order;

(*f*) an offence under section 53 of this Act or Article 63 of the Northern Ireland Order.

(3) The specified pornography offences are—

(*za*) an offence under section 48 of this Act committed by causing or inciting a child to be sexually exploited within the meaning given by section 51(2)(b);

(*a*) an offence under Article 38 of the Northern Ireland Order, committed by causing or inciting a child to be involved in pornography;

(*aa*) an offence under section 49 of this Act committed by controlling the activities of a child in relation to sexual exploitation within the meaning given by section 51(2)(b);

(*b*) an offence under Article 39 of the Northern Ireland Order, committed by controlling the activities of a child relating to the child's involvement in pornography;

(*ba*) an offence under section 50 of this Act committed by arranging or facilitating the sexual exploitation, within the meaning given by section 51(2)(*b*), of a child;

(*c*) an offence under Article 40 of the Northern Ireland Order, committed by arranging or facilitating a child's involvement in pornography.

(3A) The specified child sex offences are—

(*a*) an offence under any of the following sections of this Act—

sections 5 to 13;
sections 16 to 19;
sections 25 and 26;
sections 47 to 50;

(*b*) an offence under section 1 of the Protection of Children Act 1978 (indecent photographs of children);

(*c*) an offence under any of the following sections of this Act committed against a person under 18—

sections 1 to 4;
sections 30 to 41;
section 59A;
section 61;
sections 66 and 67;

(*d*) an offence under section 2 of the Modern Slavery Act 2015 (human trafficking) committed against a person under 18 with a view to exploitation that consists of or includes behaviour within section 3(3) of that Act (sexual exploitation).

(4) Premises are being used for activities related to a specified prostitution offence—

(*a*) in the case of an offence under Article 37 of the Northern Ireland Order, at any time when the sexual services mentioned in paragraph (1)(*a*) of that Article are being provided on the premises, and

(*b*) in the case of any other specified prostitution offence, at any time when the person in respect of whom the offence is committed is providing sexual services as a prostitute on the premises.

(5) Premises are being used for activities related to a specified pornography offence at any time when the person in respect of whom the offence is committed is doing anything on the premises which enables an indecent image of himself or herself to be recorded.

(5A) Premises are being used for activities related to a specified child sex offence at any time when the premises are used—

(*a*) to commit the offence, or

(*b*) for activities intended to arrange or facilitate the commission of the offence.

(6) Any reference to an offence under this Act includes a reference to—

(*a*) an offence under section 70 of the Army Act 1955, section 70 of the Air Force Act 1955 or section 42 of the Naval Discipline Act 1957 of which the corresponding civil offence (within the meaning of the Act in question) is such an offence;

(*b*) an offence under section 42 of the Armed Forces Act 2006 as respects which the corresponding offence under the law of England and Wales (within the meaning given by that section) is such an offence.

[Sexual Offences Act 2003, s 136A as inserted by the Policing and Crime Act 2009, Sch 2 and amended by the Anti-social Behaviour, Crime and Policing Act 2014, Sch 6, the Serious Crime Act 2015, Sch 4 and SI 2016/244.]

1 Part 2A comprises ss 136A–136R.

2 See the analogous provisions in relation to closure orders under the Anti-social Behaviour Act 2003 and cases decided thereunder, in PART I: MAGISTRATES' COURTS, PROCEDURE, ante.

*Closure notices*

7.10700 **136B. Power to authorise issue of closure notice: prostitution or pornography offences** (1) A member of a police force not below the rank of superintendent ("the authorising officer") may authorise the issue of a closure notice in respect of any premises if three conditions are met.

(2) The first condition is that the officer has reasonable grounds for believing that either subsection (3) or (4) (or both) applies.

(3) This subsection applies[1] if, during the relevant period, the premises were used for activities related to one or more specified prostitution offences.

But this subsection does not apply if only one person obtained all of the sexual services in question (whether or not on a single occasion).

(4) This subsection applies[1] if, during the relevant period, the premises were used for activities related to one or more specified pornography offences.

(5) In subsections (3) and (4), "the relevant period" means the period of 3 months ending with the day on which the officer is considering whether to authorise the issue of the notice.

(6) The second condition is that the officer has reasonable grounds for believing that the making of a closure order under section 136D is necessary to prevent the premises being used for activities related to one or more specified prostitution or pornography offences.

(7) The third condition is that the officer is satisfied—

(*a*) that the local authority for the area in which the premises are situated has been consulted, and

(*b*) that reasonable steps have been taken to establish the identity of any person who resides on the premises or who has control of or responsibility for or an interest in the premises.

(8) For the purposes of the second condition, it does not matter whether the officer believes that the offence or offences in question have been committed or that they will be committed (or will be committed unless a closure order is made).

(9) An authorisation under subsection (1) may be given orally or in writing, but if it is given orally the authorising officer must confirm it in writing as soon as it is practicable.

(10) The issue of a closure notice may be authorised whether or not a person has been convicted of any specified prostitution or pornography offence that the authorising officer believes has been committed.

(11) The Secretary of State may by regulations specify premises or descriptions of premises to which this section does not apply.

[Sexual Offences Act 2003, s 136B as inserted by the Policing and Crime Act 2009, Sch 2 and amended by the Anti-social Behaviour, Crime and Policing Act 2014, Sch 6.]

1 For the purposes of s 136B(3) and (4), it does not matter whether the offence or offences were committed before, or on or after, the date on which s 21(2) of the Policing and Crime Act 2009 was commenced.

7.10700A **136BA. Power to authorise issue of closure notice: child sex offences in England and Wales** (1) A member of a police force not below the rank of superintendent ("the authorising officer") may authorise the issue of a closure notice in respect of any premises in England and Wales if three conditions are met.

(2) The first condition is that the officer has reasonable grounds for believing that—

(*a*) during the relevant period, the premises were used for activities related to one or more specified child sex offences, or

(*b*) the premises are likely to be used (unless a closure order is made) for activities related to one or more specified child sex offences.

(3) In subsection (2)(*a*), "the relevant period" means the period of 3 months ending with the day on which the officer is considering whether to authorise the issue of the notice.

(4) The second condition is that the officer has reasonable grounds for believing that the making of a closure order under section 136D is necessary to prevent the premises being used for activities related to one or more specified child sex offences.

(5) For the purposes of the second condition, it does not matter whether the officer believes that the offence or offences in question have been committed or that they will be committed (or will be committed unless a closure order is made).

(6) The third condition is that the officer is satisfied that reasonable efforts have been made—

(*a*) to consult the local authority for the area in which the premises are situated, and

(*b*) to establish the identity of any person who resides on the premises or who has control of or responsibility for or an interest in the premises.

(7) If the local authority has not been consulted when the notice is issued, it must be consulted

as soon as possible afterwards.

(8) An authorisation under subsection (1) may be given orally or in writing, but if it is given orally the authorising officer must confirm it in writing as soon as it is practicable.

(9) The issue of a closure notice may be authorised whether or not a person has been convicted of any specified child sex offence that the authorising officer believes has been committed.

(10) The Secretary of State may by regulations specify premises or descriptions of premises to which this section does not apply.

[Sexual Offences Act 2003, s 136BA as inserted by the Anti-social Behaviour, Crime and Policing Act 2014, Sch 6.]

7.10701 **136C. Contents and service of closure notice** (1) A closure notice must—

(*a*) state that no-one other than a person who regularly resides on, or owns, the premises may enter or remain on them,

(*b*) state that failure to comply with the notice amounts to an offence,

(*c*) specify the offence or offences in respect of which the authorising officer considers that the first and second conditions in section 136B or 136BA are met,

(*d*) state that an application will be made under section 136D for the closure of the premises,

(*e*) specify the date and time when, and the place at which, that application will be heard, and

(*f*) explain the effects of an order under section 136D.

(2) A closure notice must be served by a constable.

(3) Service is effected by—

(*a*) fixing a copy of the notice to at least one prominent place on the premises,

(*b*) fixing a copy of the notice to each normal means of access to the premises,

(*c*) fixing a copy of the notice to any outbuildings which appear to the constable to be used with or as part of the premises, and

(*d*) giving a copy of the notice to the persons identified in pursuance of section 136B(7)(*b*) or 136BA(6)(b) and to any other person appearing to the constable to be a person of a description mentioned in that provision.

(4) A constable must also serve a copy of the notice on any person who occupies any other part of a building or other structure in which the premises are situated if, at the time of acting under subsection (3), the constable reasonably believes that the person's access to the other part of the building or structure will be impeded if a closure order is made.

(5) Subsection (3)(*d*) or (4) does not require a constable to serve a copy of the notice on a person if it is not reasonably practicable to do so.

(6) A constable acting under subsection (3) may enter any premises, using reasonable force if necessary, for the purpose of complying with subsection (3)(*a*) to (*c*).

(7) A closure notice has effect until an application for a closure order is determined under section 136D.

(8) But, if the hearing of an application for a closure order is adjourned, the closure notice ceases to have effect unless the court makes an order under section 136E(2).

[Sexual Offences Act 2003, s 136C as inserted by the Policing and Crime Act 2009, Sch 2 and amended by the Anti-social Behaviour, Crime and Policing Act 2014, Sch 6.]

*Closure orders*

7.10702 **136D. Power to make a closure order** (1) If a closure notice has been issued, a constable must apply under this section to a magistrates' court for a closure order.

(2) A closure order is an order that the premises in respect of which the order is made are closed to all persons for such period not exceeding 3 months as is specified in the order.

(3) The application must be heard by the magistrates' court not later than 48 hours after the notice was served in pursuance of section 136C(3)(*a*).

(4) The magistrates' court may make a closure order if three conditions are met.

(5) The first condition is that the court is satisfied that at least one of subsections (6), (7) and (7A) applies.

(6) This subsection applies[1] if, during the relevant period, the premises were used for activities related to one or more specified prostitution offences.

But this subsection does not apply if only one person obtained all of the sexual services in question (whether or not on a single occasion).

(7) This subsection applies[1] if, during the relevant period, the premises were used for activities related to one or more specified pornography offences.

(7A) This subsection applies if—

(*a*) during the relevant period, the premises were used for activities related to one or more specified child sex offences, or

(*b*) the premises are likely to be used (unless a closure order is made) for activities related to one or more specified child sex offences.

(8) In subsections (6), (7) and (7A)(*a*), "the relevant period" means the period of 3 months ending with the day on which the issue of the closure notice was authorised.

(9) The second condition is that the court is satisfied that the making of the closure order is necessary to prevent the premises being used for activities related to one or more specified

prostitution, pornography or child sex offences during the period to be specified in the order.

(10) The third condition is that the court is satisfied that—

(*a*) before the issue of the closure notice was authorised, reasonable steps were taken to establish the identity of any person of a description mentioned in section 136B(7)(*b*) or 136BA(6)(*b*), and

(*b*) a constable complied with section 136C(3)(*d*) in relation to the persons so identified.

(11) For the purposes of the second condition, it does not matter whether the court is satisfied that the offence or offences in question have been committed or that they will be committed (or will be committed unless a closure order is made).

(12) A closure order may be made whether or not a person has been convicted of any specified prostitution, pornography or child sex offences that the court is satisfied has been committed.

[Sexual Offences Act 2003, s 136D as inserted by the Policing and Crime Act 2009, Sch 2 and amended by the Anti-social Behaviour, Crime and Policing Act 2014, Sch 6.]

[1] For the purposes of ss 136D(6) and (7), it does not matter whether the offence or offences were committed before, or on or after, the date on which s 21(2) of the Policing and Crime Act 2009 was commenced.

7.10703 **136E. Making of closure orders: supplementary provision** (1) The magistrates' court may adjourn the hearing of an application for a closure order for a period of not more than 14 days to enable any of the following to show why a closure order should not be made—

(*a*) an occupier of the premises;

(*b*) a person who has control of or responsibility for the premises;

(*c*) any other person with an interest in the premises.

(2) If the court adjourns the hearing, it may order that the closure notice continues in effect until the end of the period of the adjournment.

(3) A closure order may include such provision as the court thinks appropriate relating to access to any other part of a building or other structure in which the premises are situated.

(4) A closure order may be made in respect of the whole or any part of the premises in respect of which the closure notice was issued.

[Sexual Offences Act 2003, s 136E as inserted by the Policing and Crime Act 2009, Sch 2.]

*Enforcement*

7.10704 **136F. Closure order: enforcement** (1) This section applies if a closure order is made.

(2) A constable or an authorised person may—

(*a*) enter the premises in respect of which the order is made;

(*b*) do anything reasonably necessary to secure the premises against entry by any person.

(3) A constable or an authorised person seeking to enter premises for the purposes of subsection (2) must, if required to do so by or on behalf of the owner, occupier or other person in charge of the premises, produce evidence of the constable's or (as the case may be) the authorised person's identity and authority before entering the premises.

(4) A constable or an authorised person may also enter the premises at any time while the order has effect for the purpose of carrying out essential maintenance of, or repairs to, the premises.

(5) A constable or an authorised person acting under subsection (2) or (4) may use reasonable force.

(6) In this section "authorised person"—

(*a*) in the application of this section to England and Wales, means a person authorised by the chief officer of police for the area in which the premises are situated;

(*b*) in the application of this section to Northern Ireland, means a person authorised by the Chief Constable of the Police Service of Northern Ireland.

[Sexual Offences Act 2003, s 136F as inserted by the Policing and Crime Act 2009, Sch 2.]

7.10705 **136G. Closure of premises: offences** (1) A person who remains on or enters premises in contravention of a closure notice commits an offence.

(2) A person who remains on or enters premises in contravention of a closure order commits an offence.

(3) A person does not commit an offence under subsection (1) or (2) if the person has a reasonable excuse for remaining on or entering the premises.

(4) A person who obstructs a constable or an authorised person acting under section 136C(3) or (4) or 136F(2) or (4) commits an offence.

(5) A person guilty of an offence under this section is liable on summary conviction—

(*a*) to imprisonment for a period not exceeding 51 weeks, or

(*b*) to a fine not exceeding level 5 on the standard scale,

or to both.

(6) In relation to an offence committed before the commencement of section 281(5) of the Criminal Justice Act 2003, the reference in subsection (5)(*a*) to 51 weeks is to be read as a reference to 6 months.

(7) In the application of this section to Northern Ireland—

(*a*) the reference in subsection (5)(*a*) to 51 weeks is to be read as a reference to 6 months, and (*b*) subsection (6) is omitted.

(8) In this section "authorised person" has the same meaning as in section 136F.

[Sexual Offences Act 2003, s 136G as inserted by the Policing and Crime Act 2009, Sch 2.]

*Extension and discharge of closure orders*

7.10706 **136H. Applications for extension of closure order** (1) At any time before the end of the period for which a closure order is made or extended a constable may make a complaint to the appropriate judicial officer for an extension or further extension of the period for which it has effect.

(2) A complaint may not be made under subsection (1) unless it is authorised by a member of a police force not below the rank of superintendent.

(3) Authorisation may be given under subsection (2) if two conditions are met.

(4) The first condition is that the officer has reasonable grounds for believing that it is necessary to extend the period for which the order has effect to prevent the premises being used for activities related to any of the specified prostitution, pornography or child sex offences in respect of which section 136D(9) applied.

(5) The second condition is that the officer is satisfied that the local authority has been consulted about the intention to make a complaint.

(6) If a complaint is made under subsection (1) the appropriate judicial officer may issue a summons directed to—

(*a*) any person on whom the closure notice relating to the closed premises was served under section 136C(3)(*d*) or (4), or

(*b*) any other person who appears to the judicial officer to have an interest in the closed premises but on whom the closure notice was not served,

requiring such person to appear before the magistrates' court to answer to the complaint.

(7) If a summons is issued in accordance with subsection (6), a notice stating the date and time when, and the place at which, the complaint will be heard must be served on—

(*a*) the persons to whom the summons is directed,

(*b*) such constable as the judicial officer thinks appropriate (unless the complainant is a constable), and

(*c*) the local authority.

(8) In this section "the appropriate judicial officer" means—

(*a*) in the application of this section to England and Wales, a justice of the peace;

(*b*) in the application of this section to Northern Ireland, a lay magistrate.

[Sexual Offences Act 2003, s 136H as inserted by the Policing and Crime Act 2009, Sch 2 and amended by the Anti-social Behaviour, Crime and Policing Act 2014, Sch 6.]

7.10707 **136I. Orders extending closure orders** (1) This section applies where a complaint is made under section 136H.

(2) The court may make an order extending the period for which the closure order has effect by a period specified in the order if the court is satisfied that the extension is necessary to prevent the premises being used for activities related to any of the specified prostitution, pornography or child sex offences in respect of which section 136D(9) applied.

(3) The period specified in the order may not exceed 3 months.

(4) The total period for which a closure order has effect may not exceed 6 months.

(5) An order under this section may include such provision as the court thinks appropriate relating to access to any other part of a building or other structure in which the premises are situated.

[Sexual Offences Act 2003, s 136I as inserted by the Policing and Crime Act 2009, Sch 2 and amended by the Anti-social Behaviour, Crime and Policing Act 2014, Sch 6.]

7.10708 **136J. Discharge of closure order** (1) Any of the following persons may make a complaint to an appropriate judicial officer for an order that a closure order be discharged—

(*a*) a constable;

(*b*) the local authority;

(*c*) a person on whom the closure notice relating to the closed premises was served under section 136C(3)(*d*) or (4);

(*d*) any other person who has an interest in the closed premises but on whom the closure notice was not served.

(2) If a complaint is made under subsection (1) by a person other than a constable the judicial officer may issue a summons directed to such constable as the judicial officer thinks appropriate requiring the constable to appear before the magistrates' court to answer to the complaint.

(3) The court may not make an order discharging a closure order unless it is satisfied that the order is no longer necessary to prevent the premises being used for activities related to any of the specified prostitution, pornography or child sex offences in respect of which section 136D(9) applied.

(4) If a complaint is made under subsection (1), a notice stating the date and time when, and the place at which, the complaint will be heard must be served on—

(*a*) the persons mentioned in subsection (1)(*c*) and (*d*) (other than the complainant),

(*b*) a constable (unless a constable is the complainant), and (*c*) the local authority (unless it is the complainant).

(5) In this section "appropriate judicial authority" has the same meaning as in section 136H.

[Sexual Offences Act 2003, s 136J as inserted by the Policing and Crime Act 2009, Sch 2 and amended by the Anti-social Behaviour, Crime and Policing Act 2014, Sch 6.]

*Appeals against closure orders etc*

7.10709 **136K. Appeals** (1) An appeal against an order under section 136D or 136I, or an appeal against a decision not to be make an order under section 136J, may be made to the appropriate appeal court by—

(*a*) a person on whom the closure notice relating to the closed premises was served under section 136C(3)(*d*), or

(*b*) any other person who has an interest in the closed premises but on whom the closure notice was not served.

(2) An appeal against a decision of a court not to make an order under section 136D or 136I, or an appeal against an order under section 136J, may be made to the appropriate appeal court by—

(*a*) a constable, or

(*b*) the local authority.

(3) An appeal under subsection (1) or (2) must be made before the end of the period of 21 days beginning with the day on which the order or decision is made.

(4) On an appeal under this section the court may make such order as it thinks appropriate.

(5) In this section "the appropriate appeal court" means—

(*a*) in the application of this section to England and Wales, the Crown Court;

(*b*) in the application of this section to Northern Ireland, a county court.

[Sexual Offences Act 2003, s 136K as inserted by the Policing and Crime Act 2009, Sch 2.]

*Access to other premises*

7.10710 **136L. Access to other premises** (1) This section applies to any person who occupies or has an interest in any part of a building or other structure—

(*a*) in which closed premises are situated, and

(*b*) in respect of which the closure order does not have effect.

(2) A person to whom this section applies may at any time while a closure order has effect apply to—

(*a*) the magistrates' court in respect of an order made under section 136D or 136I, or

(*b*) the appropriate appeal court in respect of an order made by that court under section 136K.

(3) If an application is made under this section notice of the date and time when, and the place at which, the hearing to consider the application will take place must be given to—

(*a*) a constable,

(*b*) the local authority.

(*c*) each person on whom the closure notice relating to the closed premises was served under section 136C(3)(*d*) or (4), and

(*d*) any other person who appears to the court to have an interest in the closed premises but on whom the closure notice was not served.

(4) On an application under this section the court may make such order as it thinks appropriate in relation to access to any other part of a building or other structure in which the closed premises are situated.

(5) It is immaterial whether any provision has been made as mentioned in section 136E(3) or 136I(5).

(6) In this section "appropriate appeal court" has the same meaning as in section 136K.

[Sexual Offences Act 2003, s 136L as inserted by the Policing and Crime Act 2009, Sch 2.]

*Reimbursement of costs, compensation etc*

7.10711 **136M. Reimbursement of costs** (1) A local policing body or a local authority which incurs expenditure for the purpose of clearing, securing, repairing or maintaining closed premises may apply to the court which made the closure order for an order under this section.

(2) On an application under this section, the court may make such order as it thinks appropriate in the circumstances for the reimbursement (in full or in part) by the owner of the premises of the expenditure mentioned in subsection (1).

(3) An application under this section must not be entertained unless it is made before the end of the period of three months beginning with the day the closure order ceases to have effect.

(4) An application under this section must be served on—

(*a*) the local policing body for the area in which the premises are situated, if the application is made by the local authority,

(*b*) the local authority, if the application is made by a local policing body, and

(*c*) the owner of the premises.

(5) In the application of this section to Northern Ireland references to the local policing body are to be read as references to the Northern Ireland Policing Board.

[Sexual Offences Act 2003, s 136M as inserted by the Policing and Crime Act 2009, Sch 2 and amended by the Police Reform and Social Responsibility Act 2011, Sch 16.]

7.10712 **136N. Exemption from liability for certain damages** (1) A constable is not liable for relevant damages in respect of anything done or omitted to be done by the constable in the performance or purported performance of the constable's functions under this Part.

(2) A chief officer of police who has direction or control of a constable is not liable for relevant damages in respect of anything done or omitted to be done by the constable in the performance or purported performance of the constable's functions under this Part.

(3) An authorised person is not liable for relevant damages in respect of anything done or omitted to be done by the authorised person in the performance or purported performance of the authorised person's functions under this Part.

(4) No person is vicariously liable for anything done or omitted to be done by an authorised person as mentioned in subsection (3).

(5) Subsections (1) to (4) do not apply—

(*a*) if the act or omission is shown to have been in bad faith;

(*b*) so as to prevent an award of damages made in respect of an act or omission on the ground that the act or omission was unlawful by virtue of section 6(1) of the Human Rights Act 1998.

(6) This section does not affect any other exemption from liability for damages (whether at common law or otherwise).

(7) In this section—

(*a*) "authorised person" has the same meaning as in section 136F;

(*b*) "relevant damages" means damages in proceedings for judicial review or for the tort of negligence or misfeasance in public office.

(8) In the application of this section to Northern Ireland, the reference in subsection (2) to the chief officer of police is to be read as a reference to the Chief Constable of the Police Service of Northern Ireland.

[Sexual Offences Act 2003, s 136N as inserted by the Policing and Crime Act 2009, Sch 2.]

7.10713 **136O. Compensation** (1) A person who claims to have incurred financial loss in consequence of a closure notice or closure order may apply for compensation.

(2) The application must be made—

(*a*) to the appropriate appeal court, if the closure order was made or extended by an order of that court on an appeal under section 136K;

(*b*) in any other case, to the magistrates' court which considered the application for a closure order.

(3) In a case where a closure notice is issued but a closure order is not made, the application must not be entertained unless it is made before the end of the period of three months beginning with—

(*a*) the day the magistrates' court decides not to make a closure order, or

(*b*) if there is an appeal against that decision, the day the appropriate appeal court dismisses that appeal.

(4) In a case where a closure order is made, the application must not be entertained unless it is made before the end of the period of three months beginning with the day the closure order ceases to have effect.

(5) The court which hears the application may order the payment of compensation out of central funds if it is satisfied—

(*a*) that the person was not associated with the use of the premises for the activities in relation to which the first condition in section 136B or 136BA was met,

(*b*) if the person is the owner or occupier of the premises, that the person took reasonable steps to prevent that use,

(*c*) that the person has incurred financial loss as mentioned in subsection (1), and

(*d*) having regard to all the circumstances it is appropriate to order payment of compensation in respect of that loss.

(6) In this section—

(*a*) "appropriate appeal court" has the same meaning as in section 136K;

(*b*) "central funds" has the same meaning as in enactments providing for the payment of costs.

(7) In the application of this section to Northern Ireland—

(*a*) the reference in subsection (5) to "central funds" is to be read as a reference to monies provided by Parliament, and

(*b*) subsection (6)(*b*) is omitted.

[Sexual Offences Act 2003, s 136O as inserted by the Policing and Crime Act 2009, Sch 2 and amended by the Anti-social Behaviour, Crime and Policing Act 2014, Sch 6.]

*General*

7.10714 **136P. Guidance** (1) The Secretary of State may issue guidance relating to the discharge of any functions under or for the purposes of this Part by a constable or by an authorised person (within the meaning of section 136F).

(2) A person discharging a function to which guidance under this section relates must have regard to the guidance in discharging the function.

[Sexual Offences Act 2003, s 136P as inserted by the Policing and Crime Act 2009, Sch 2.]

**7.10715 136Q. Issue of closure notices by persons other than police officers** (1) The Secretary of State may by order amend this Part so as to extend the power to authorise the issue of a closure notice to persons other than members of police forces.

(2) An order under subsection (1) may make such further amendments of this Part as the Secretary of State thinks appropriate in consequence of the extension of that power to persons other than members of police forces.

[Sexual Offences Act 2003, s 136Q as inserted by the Policing and Crime Act 2009, Sch 2.]

**7.10716 136R. Interpretation** (1) This section applies for the purposes of this Part.

(2) "A closure notice" means a notice issued under section 136B or 136BA.

(3) "A closure order" means—

(*a*) an order made under section 136D;

(*b*) an order extended under section 136I;

(*c*) an order made or extended under section 136K which has the like effect as an order made or extended under section 136D or 136I (as the case may be).

(4) "Closed premises" means premises in respect of which a closure order has effect.

(5) "Local authority", in relation to England, means—

(*a*) a district council;

(*b*) a London borough council;

(*c*) a county council for an area for which there is no district council;

(*d*) the Common Council of the City of London in its capacity as a local authority;

(*e*) the Council of the Isles of Scilly.

(6) "Local authority", in relation to Wales, means—

(*a*) a county council;

(*b*) a county borough council.

(7) "Local authority", in relation to Northern Ireland, means a district council.

(8) In the application of this Part to England and Wales, references to the local authority in relation to—

(*a*) any premises,

(*b*) a closure notice relating to any premises, or

(*c*) a closure order relating to any premises,

are references to the local authority for the area in which the premises are situated.

(8A) In the application of this Part to Northern Ireland, references to the Secretary of State are to be read as references to the Department of Justice in Northern Ireland.

(9) In the application of this Part to Northern Ireland, references to the local authority in relation to—

(*a*) any premises,

(*b*) a closure notice relating to any premises, or

(*c*) a closure order relating to any premises,

are references to the council for the district in which the premises are situated.

(10) In the application of this Part to Northern Ireland, the reference in section 136B(7)(*a*) to the area is to be read as a reference to the district.

(11) "The owner", in relation to premises, means—

(*a*) a person who, whether alone or jointly with another person, is for the time being entitled to dispose of the fee simple in the premises, whether in possession or in reversion (apart from a mortgagee not in possession);

(*b*) a person who, whether alone or jointly with another person, holds or is entitled to the rents and profits of the premises under a lease which (when granted) was for a term of not less than 3 years.

(12) "Premises" includes—

(*a*) any land or other place (whether enclosed or not);

(*b*) any outbuildings which are, or are used as, part of the premises.

(13) "Specified prostitution offence" means an offence listed in section 136A(2).

(14) "Specified pornograph offence" means an offence listed in section 136A(3).

(15) In the application of this Part to England and Wales, references to specified pornography offences are to be ignored.

(16) "Specified child sex offence" means an offence listed in section 136A(3A).

(17) In the application of this Part to Northern Ireland, references to specified child sex offences and to section 136BA are to be ignored.

[Sexual Offences Act 2003, s 136R as inserted by the Policing and Crime Act 2009, Sch 2 and amended by SI 2010/976 and the Anti-social Behaviour, Crime and Policing Act 2014, Sch 6.]

## PART 3
## GENERAL

**7.10717 137. Service courts** (1) In this Act—

(*a*) a reference to a court order or a conviction or finding includes a reference to an order of or a conviction or finding by a service court,

(*b*) a reference to an offence includes a reference to an offence triable by a service court,
(*c*) "proceedings" includes proceedings before a service court, and
(*d*) a reference to proceedings for an offence under this Act includes a reference to proceedings for the offence an offence under section 42 of the Armed Forces Act 2006 as respects which the corresponding offence under the law of England and Wales (within the meaning given by that section) is that offence. (2) In sections 92 and 104(1), "court" includes a service court.

(3) Where the court making a sexual offences prevention order is a service court—
(*a*) sections 104(1)(*a*) and (4) to (6), 105, 109, 111 and 112 do not apply,
(*b*) in section 108, "the appropriate court" means the Crown Court in England and Wales, and
(*c*) in section 110(3)(*a*), the references to the Crown Court and Court of Appeal are references to the Crown Court and Court of Appeal in England and Wales.

(4) In this section "service court" means the Court Martial or the Service Civilian Court.

(5) In subsection (1)(*a*) the reference to a service court includes a reference to the following—
(*a*) the Court Martial Appeal Court;
(*b*) the Supreme Court on an appeal brought from the Court Martial Appeal Court;
(*c*) a court-martial;
(*d*) a Standing Civilian Court.

[Sexual Offences Act 2003, s 137 as amended by the Armed Forces Act 2006, Sch 16.]

**7.10717.1 138. Orders and regulations**

**7.10717.2 139. Minor and consequential amendments**

**7.10717.3 140. Repeals and revocations**

**7.10718 141. Commencement** (1) This Act, except this section and sections 138, 142 and 143, comes into force in accordance with provision made by the Secretary of State by order[1].

(2) An order under subsection (1) may—
(*a*) make different provision for different purposes;
(*b*) include supplementary, incidental, saving or transitional provisions.*

[Sexual Offences Act 2003, s 141.]

---

[1] For orders made under this provision, see the note to the title of this Act, ante.

**7.10718A 142. Extent, saving etc**

**7.10718B 143. Short title**

SCHEDULE 1

Extension of Gender-Specific Prostitution Offences

7.10719 *Amends the Sexual Offences Act 1956, the Street Offences Act 1959 and the Sexual Offences Act 1985 to extend prostitution offences including soliciting for the purposes of prostitution to male prostitution.*

SCHEDULE 2

Sexual Offences to which Section 72 Applies

7.10720

*(Amended by the Criminal Justice and Immigration Act 2008, s 72 and Sch 28 and SI 2008/1779.)* Section 72(7)

*England and Wales*

1. In relation to England and Wales, the following are sexual offences to which section 72 applies—
(*a*) an offence under any of sections 5 to 19, 25 and 26 and 47 to 50;
(*b*) an offence under any of sections 1 to 4, 30 to 41 and 61 where the victim of the offence was under 18 at the time of the offence;
(*c*) an offence under section 62 or 63 where the intended offence was an offence against a person under 18;
(*d*) an offence under—
(i) section 1 of the Protection of Children Act 1978 (c 37) (indecent photographs of children), or
(ii) section 160 of the Criminal Justice Act 1988 (c 33) (possession of indecent photograph of child).

2. *Repealed.*

*General*

3. A reference in paragraph 1 to an offence includes—
(*a*) a reference to an attempt, conspiracy or incitement to commit that offence; and
(*b*) a reference to aiding and abetting, counselling or procuring the commission of that offence.

SCHEDULE 3

Sexual Offences for Purposes of Part 2 Section 80

7.10721

*(Amended by the Protection of Children and Prevention of Sexual Offences (Scotland) Act 2004, Schedule, the Armed Forces Act 2006, Schs 16 and 17, SI 2007/296, the Serious Crime Act 2007, Sch 6, the Criminal Justice and Immigration Act 2008, Sch 26, the Coroners and Justice Act 2009, Sch 21 and the Serious Crime Act 2015, Sch 4.)*

*England and Wales*

**1.** An offence under section 1 of the Sexual Offences Act 1956 (c 69) (rape).
**2.** An offence under section 5 of that Act (intercourse with girl under 13).
**3.** An offence under section 6 of that Act (intercourse with girl under 16), if the offender was 20 or over.
**4.** An offence under section 10 of that Act (incest by a man), if the victim or (as the case may be) other party was under 18.
**5.** An offence under section 12 of that Act (buggery) if—
(*a*) the offender was 20 or over, and
(*b*) the victim or (as the case may be) other party was under 18.
**6.** An offence under section 13 of that Act (indecency between men) if—
(*a*) the offender was 20 or over, and
(*b*) the victim or (as the case may be) other party was under 18.
**7.** An offence under section 14 of that Act (indecent assault on a woman) if—
(*a*) the victim or (as the case may be) other party was under 18, or
(*b*) the offender, in respect of the offence or finding, is or has been—
(i) sentenced to imprisonment for a term of at least 30 months; or
(ii) admitted to a hospital subject to a restriction order.
**8.** An offence under section 15 of that Act (indecent assault on a man) if—
(*a*) the victim or (as the case may be) other party was under 18, or
(*b*) the offender, in respect of the offence or finding, is or has been—
(i) sentenced to imprisonment for a term of at least 30 months; or
(ii) admitted to a hospital subject to a restriction order.
**9.** An offence under section 16 of that Act (assault with intent to commit buggery), if the victim or (as the case may be) other party was under 18.
**10.** An offence under section 28 of that Act (causing or encouraging the prostitution of, intercourse with or indecent assault on girl under 16).
**11.** An offence under section 1 of the Indecency with Children Act 1960 (c 33) (indecent conduct towards young child).
**12.** An offence under section 54 of the Criminal Law Act 1977 (c 45) (inciting girl under 16 to have incestuous sexual intercourse).
**13.** An offence under section 1 of the Protection of Children Act 1978 (c 37) (indecent photographs of children), if the indecent photographs or pseudo-photographs showed persons under 16 and—
(*a*) the conviction, finding or caution was before the commencement of this Part, or
(*b*) the offender—
(i) was 18 or over, or
(ii) is sentenced in respect of the offence to imprisonment for a term of at least 12 months.
**14.** An offence under section 170 of the Customs and Excise Management Act 1979 (c 2) (penalty for fraudulent evasion of duty etc) in relation to goods prohibited to be imported under section 42 of the Customs Consolidation Act 1876 (c 36) (indecent or obscene articles), if the prohibited goods included indecent photographs of persons under 16 and—
(*a*) the conviction, finding or caution was before the commencement of this Part[1], or
(*b*) the offender—
(i) was 18 or over, or
(ii) is sentenced in respect of the offence to imprisonment for a term of at least 12 months.
**15.** An offence under section 160 of the Criminal Justice Act 1988 (c 33) (possession of indecent photograph of a child), if the indecent photographs or pseudo-photographs showed persons under 16 and—
(*a*) the conviction, finding or caution was before the commencement of this Part, or
(*b*) the offender—
(i) was 18 or over, or
(ii) is sentenced in respect of the offence to imprisonment for a term of at least 12 months.
**16.** An offence under section 3 of the Sexual Offences (Amendment) Act 2000 (c 44) (abuse of position of trust), if the offender was 20 or over.
**17.** An offence under section 1 or 2 of this Act (rape, assault by penetration).
**18.** An offence under section 3 of this Act (sexual assault) if—
(*a*) where the offender was under 18, he is or has been sentenced, in respect of the offence, to imprisonment for a term of at least 12 months;
(*b*) in any other case—
(i) the victim was under 18, or
(ii) the offender, in respect of the offence or finding, is or has been—
(*a*) sentenced to a term of imprisonment,
(*b*) detained in a hospital, or
(*c*) made the subject of a community sentence of at least 12 months[2].
**19.** An offence under any of sections 4 to 6 of this Act (causing sexual activity without consent, rape of a child under 13, assault of a child under 13 by penetration).
**20.** An offence under section 7 of this Act (sexual assault of a child under 13) if the offender—
(*a*) was 18 or over, or
(*b*) is or has been sentenced in respect of the offence to imprisonment for a term of at least 12 months.
**21.** An offence under any of sections 8 to 12 of this Act (causing or inciting a child under 13 to engage in sexual activity, child sex offences committed by adults).
**22.** An offence under section 13 of this Act (child sex offences committed by children or young persons), if the offender is or has been sentenced, in respect of the offence, to imprisonment for a term of at least 12 months.
**23.** An offence under section 14 of this Act (arranging or facilitating the commission of a child sex offence) if the offender—
(*a*) was 18 or over, or
(*b*) is or has been sentenced, in respect of the offence, to imprisonment for a term of at least 12 months.
**24.** An offence under section 15 of this Act (meeting a child following sexual grooming etc).
**24A.** An offence under section 15A of this Act (sexual communication with a child).

**25.** An offence under any of sections 16 to 19 of this Act (abuse of a position of trust) if the offender, in respect of the offence, is or has been—

(*a*) sentenced to a term of imprisonment,

(*b*) detained in a hospital, or

(*c*) made the subject of a community sentence of at least 12 months[2].

**26.** An offence under section 25 or 26 of this Act (familial child sex offences) if the offender—

(*a*) was 18 or over, or

(*b*) is or has been sentenced in respect of the offence to imprisonment for a term of at least 12 months.

**27.** An offence under any of sections 30 to 37 of this Act (offences against persons with a mental disorder impeding choice, inducements etc to persons with mental disorder).

**28.** An offence under any of sections 38 to 41 of this Act (care workers for persons with mental disorder) if—

(*a*) where the offender was under 18, he is or has been sentenced in respect of the offence to imprisonment for a term of at least 12 months;

(*b*) in any other case, the offender, in respect of the offence or finding, is or has been—

(i) sentenced to a term of imprisonment,

(ii) detained in a hospital, or

(iii) made the subject of a community sentence of at least 12 months[2].

**29.** An offence under section 47 of this Act (paying for sexual services of a child) if the victim or (as the case may be) other party was under 16, and the offender—

(*a*) was 18 or over, or

(*b*) is or has been sentenced in respect of the offence to imprisonment for a term of at least 12 months.

**29A.** An offence under section 48 of this Act (causing or inciting child prostitution or pornography) if the offender—

(*a*) was 18 or over, or

(*b*) is or has been sentenced in respect of the offence to imprisonment for a term of at least 12 months.

**29B.** An offence under section 49 of this Act (controlling a child prostitute or a child involved in pornography) if the offender—

(*a*) was 18 or over, or

(*b*) is or has been sentenced in respect of the offence to imprisonment for a term of at least 12 months.

**29C.** An offence under section 50 of this Act (arranging or facilitating child prostitution or pornography) if the offender—

(*a*) was 18 or over, or

(*b*) is or has been sentenced in respect of the offence to imprisonment for a term of at least 12 months.

**30.** An offence under section 61 of this Act (administering a substance with intent).

**31.** An offence under section 62 or 63 of this Act (committing an offence or trespassing, with intent to commit a sexual offence) if—

(*a*) where the offender was under 18, he is or has been sentenced in respect of the offence to imprisonment for a term of at least 12 months;

(*b*) in any other case—

(i) the intended offence was an offence against a person under 18, or

(ii) the offender, in respect of the offence or finding, is or has been—

(*a*) sentenced to a term of imprisonment,

(*b*) detained in a hospital, or

(*c*) made the subject of a community sentence of at least 12 months[2].

**32.** An offence under section 64 or 65 of this Act (sex with an adult relative) if—

(*a*) where the offender was under 18, he is or has been sentenced in respect of the offence to imprisonment for a term of at least 12 months;

(*b*) in any other case, the offender, in respect of the offence or finding, is or has been—

(i) sentenced to a term of imprisonment, or

(ii) detained in a hospital.

**33.** An offence under section 66 of this Act (exposure) if—

(*a*) where the offender was under 18, he is or has been sentenced in respect of the offence to imprisonment for a term of at least 12 months;

(*b*) in any other case—

(i) the victim was under 18, or

(ii) the offender, in respect of the offence or finding, is or has been—

(*a*) sentenced to a term of imprisonment,

(*b*) detained in a hospital, or

(*c*) made the subject of a community sentence of at least 12 months[2].

**34.** An offence under section 67 of this Act (voyeurism) if—

(*a*) where the offender was under 18, he is or has been sentenced in respect of the offence to imprisonment for a term of at least 12 months;

(*b*) in any other case—

(i) the victim was under 18, or

(ii) the offender, in respect of the offence or finding, is or has been—

(*a*) sentenced to a term of imprisonment,

(*b*) detained in a hospital, or

(*c*) made the subject of a community sentence of at least 12 months[2].

**35.** An offence under section 69 or 70 of this Act (intercourse with an animal, sexual penetration of a corpse) if—

(*a*) where the offender was under 18, he is or has been sentenced in respect of the offence to imprisonment for a term of at least 12 months;

(*b*) in any other case, the offender, in respect of the offence or finding, is or has been—

(i) sentenced to a term of imprisonment, or

(ii) detained in a hospital.

**35A.** An offence under section 63 of the Criminal Justice and Immigration Act 2008 (possession of extreme pornographic images) if the offender—

(*a*) was 18 or over, and

(*b*) is sentenced in respect of the offence to imprisonment for a term of at least 2 years.

**35B.** An offence under section 62(1) of the Coroners and Justice Act 2009 (possession of prohibited images of children) if the offender—

(*a*) was 18 or over, and

(*b*) is sentenced in respect of the offence to imprisonment for a term of at least 2 years.

**35C.** An offence under section 69 of the Serious Crime Act 2015 (possession of paedophile manual) if the offender—

(*a*) was 18 or over, or

(*b*) is sentenced in respect of the offence to imprisonment for a term of at least 12 months.

**36–60.** *Scotland.*

*Northern Ireland*

**61.** Rape.

**62.** An offence under section 52 of the Offences against the Person Act 1861 (c 100) (indecent assault upon a female) if—

(*a*) where the offender was under 18, he is or has been sentenced, in respect of the offence, to imprisonment for a term of at least 12 months;

(*b*) in any other case—

(i) the victim was under 18, or

(ii) the offender, in respect of the offence or finding, is or has been—

(*a*) sentenced to a term of imprisonment,

(*b*) detained in a hospital, or

(*c*) made the subject of a community sentence of at least 12 months[2].

**63.** An offence under section 53 or 54 of that Act (abduction of woman by force for unlawful sexual intercourse) if the offender—

(*a*) was 18 or over, or

(*b*) is or has been sentenced in respect of the offence to imprisonment for a term of at least 12 months.

**64.** An offence under section 61 of that Act (buggery) if—

(*a*) the offender was 20 or over, and

(*b*) the victim or (as the case may be) other party was under 18.

**65.** An offence under section 62 of that Act of assault with intent to commit buggery if the victim or (as the case may be) other party was under 18, and the offender—

(*a*) was 18 or over, or

(*b*) is or has been sentenced in respect of the offence to imprisonment for a term of at least 12 months.

**66.** An offence under section 62 of that Act of indecent assault upon a male person if—

(*a*) where the offender was under 18, he is or has been sentenced, in respect of the offence, to imprisonment for a term of at least 12 months;

(*b*) in any other case—

(i) the victim was under 18, or

(ii) the offender, in respect of the offence or finding, is or has been—

(*a*) sentenced to a term of imprisonment,

(*b*) detained in a hospital, or

(*c*) made the subject of a community sentence of at least 12 months[2].

**67.** An offence under section 2 of the Criminal Law Amendment Act 1885 (c 69) (procuration) if the offender—

(*a*) was 18 or over, or

(*b*) is or has been sentenced in respect of the offence to imprisonment for a term of at least 12 months.

**68.** An offence under section 3 of that Act (procuring defilement of woman by threats or fraud, etc) if the offender—

(*a*) was 18 or over, or

(*b*) is or has been sentenced in respect of the offence to imprisonment for a term of at least 12 months.

**69.** An offence under section 4 of that Act of unlawful carnal knowledge of a girl under 14 if the offender—

(*a*) was 18 or over, or

(*b*) is or has been sentenced in respect of the offence to imprisonment for a term of at least 12 months.

**70.** An offence under section 5 of that Act of unlawful carnal knowledge of a girl under 17, if the offender was 20 or over.

**71.** An offence under section 7 of that Act (abduction of girl under 18) if the offender—

(*a*) was 18 or over, or

(*b*) is or has been sentenced in respect of the offence to imprisonment for a term of at least 12 months.

**72.** An offence under section 11 of that Act (homosexual offences) if—

(*a*) the offender was 20 or over, and

(*b*) the victim or (as the case may be) other party was under 18.

**73.** An offence under section 1 of the Punishment of Incest Act 1908 (c 45) (incest by males), if—

(*a*) where the offender was under 18, he is or has been sentenced in respect of the offence to imprisonment for a term of at least 12 months;

(*b*) in any other case—

(i) the victim or (as the case may be) other party was under 18, or

(ii) the offender, in respect of the offence or finding, is or has been—

(*a*) sentenced to a term of imprisonment, or

(*b*) detained in a hospital.

**74.** An offence under section 2 of that Act (incest by females), if—

(*a*) where the offender was under 18, he is or has been sentenced in respect of the offence to imprisonment for a term of at least 12 months;

(*b*) in any other case—

(i) the victim or (as the case may be) other party was under 18, or

(ii) the offender, in respect of the offence or finding, is or has been—

(*a*) sentenced to a term of imprisonment, or

(*b*) detained in a hospital.

**75.** An offence under section 21 of the Children and Young Persons Act (Northern Ireland) 1968 (c 34) (causing or encouraging seduction or prostitution of a girl under 17) if the offender—

(*a*) was 18 or over, or

(*b*) is or has been sentenced in respect of the offence to imprisonment for a term of at least 12 months.

**76.** An offence under section 22 of that Act (indecent conduct towards a child) if the offender—

(*a*) was 18 or over, or

(*b*) is or has been sentenced in respect of the offence to imprisonment for a term of at least 12 months.

**77.** An offence under Article 3 of the Protection of Children (Northern Ireland) Order 1978 (SI 1978/1047 (NI 17)) (indecent photographs of children) if the offender—

(*a*) was 18 or over, or

(*b*) is or has been sentenced in respect of the offence to imprisonment for a term of at least 12 months.

**78.** An offence under section 170 of the Customs and Excise Management Act 1979 (c 2) (penalty for fraudulent evasion of duty etc) in relation to goods prohibited to be imported under section 42 of the Customs Consolidation Act 1876 (c 36) (indecent or obscene articles), if the prohibited goods included indecent photographs of persons under 16, and the offender—

(*a*) was 18 or over, or

(*b*) is or has been sentenced in respect of the offence to imprisonment for a term of at least 12 months.

**79.** An offence under Article 9 of the Criminal Justice (Northern Ireland) Order 1980 (SI 1980/704 (NI 6)) (inciting girl under 16 to have incestuous sexual intercourse) if the offender—

(*a*) was 18 or over, or

(*b*) is or has been sentenced in respect of the offence to imprisonment for a term of at least 12 months.

**80.** An offence under Article 122 of the Mental Health (Northern Ireland) Order 1986 (SI 1986/595 (NI 4)) (offences against women suffering from severe mental handicap).

**81.** An offence under Article 123 of that Order (offences against patients) if—

(*a*) where the offender was under 18, he is or has been sentenced in respect of the offence to imprisonment for a term of at least 12 months;

(*b*) in any other case, the offender, in respect of the offence or finding, is or has been—

(i) sentenced to a term of imprisonment,

(ii) detained in a hospital, or

(iii) made the subject of a community sentence of at least 12 months[2].

**82.** An offence under Article 15 of the Criminal Justice (Evidence, etc) (Northern Ireland) Order 1988 (SI 1988/1847 (NI 17) (possession of indecent photographs of children) if the offender—

(*a*) was 18 or over, or

(*b*) is or has been sentenced in respect of the offence to imprisonment for a term of at least 12 months.

**83.** An offence under section 3 of the Sexual Offences (Amendment) Act 2000 (c 44) (abuse of position of trust), if the offender, in respect of the offence or finding, is or has been—

(*a*) sentenced to a term of imprisonment,

(*b*) detained in a hospital, or

(*c*) made the subject of a community sentence of at least 12 months[2].

**84.** An offence under Article 19 of the Criminal Justice (Northern Ireland) Order 2003 (SI 2003/1247 (NI 13)) (buggery) if—

(*a*) the offender was 20 or over, and

(*b*) the victim or (as the case may be) other party was under 17.

**85.** An offence under Article 20 of that Order (assault with intent to commit buggery) if the victim was under 18 and the offender—

(*a*) was 18 or over, or

(*b*) is or has been sentenced in respect of the offence to imprisonment for a term of at least 12 months.

**86.** An offence under Article 21 of that Order (indecent assault upon a male) if—

(*a*) where the offender was under 18, he is or has been sentenced, in respect of the offence, to imprisonment for a term of at least 12 months;

(*b*) in any other case—

(i) the victim was under 18, or

(ii) the offender, in respect of the offence or finding, is or has been—

(*a*) sentenced to a term of imprisonment,

(*b*) detained in a hospital, or

(*c*) made the subject of a community sentence of at least 12 months[2].

**87.** An offence under section 15 of this Act (meeting a child following sexual grooming etc).

**88.** An offence under any of sections 16 to 19 of this Act (abuse of trust) if the offender, in respect of the offence or finding, is or has been—

(*a*) sentenced to a term of imprisonment,

(*b*) detained in a hospital, or

(*c*) made the subject of a community sentence of at least 12 months[2].

**89.** An offence under section 47 of this Act (paying for sexual services of a child) if the victim or (as the case may be) other party was under 17 and the offender—

(*a*) was 18 or over, or

(*b*) is or has been sentenced in respect of the offence to a term of imprisonment of at least 12 months.

**89A.** An offence under section 48 of this Act (causing or inciting child prostitution or pornography) if the offender—

(*a*) was 18 or over, or

(*b*) is or has been sentenced in respect of the offence to imprisonment for a term of at least 12 months.

**89B.** An offence under section 49 of this Act (controlling a child prostitute or a child involved in pornography) if the offender—

(*a*) was 18 or over, or

(*b*) is or has been sentenced in respect of the offence to imprisonment for a term of at least 12 months.

**89C.** An offence under section 50 of this Act (arranging or facilitating child prostitution or pornography) if the offender—

(*a*) was 18 or over, or

(*b*) is or has been sentenced in respect of the offence to imprisonment for a term of at least 12 months.

**90.** An offence under section 66 of this Act (exposure) if—

(*a*) where the offender was under 18, he is or has been sentenced in respect of the offence to imprisonment for a term of at least 12 months;

(*b*) in any other case—

(i) the victim was under 18, or

(ii) the offender, in respect of the offence or finding, is or has been—

(*a*) sentenced to a term of imprisonment,

(*b*) detained in a hospital, or

(*c*) made the subject of a community sentence of at least 12 months[2].

**91.** An offence under section 67 of this Act (voyeurism) if—

(*a*) where the offender was under 18, he is or has been sentenced in respect of the offence to imprisonment for a term of at least 12 months;

(*b*) in any other case—

(i) the victim was under 18, or

(ii) the offender, in respect of the offence or finding, is or has been—

(*a*) sentenced to a term of imprisonment,

(*b*) detained in a hospital, or

(*c*) made the subject of a community sentence of at least 12 months[2].

**92.** An offence under section 69 or 70 of this Act (intercourse with an animal, sexual penetration of a corpse) if—

(*a*) where the offender was under 18, he is or has been sentenced in respect of the offence to imprisonment for a term of at least 12 months;

(*b*) in any other case, the offender, in respect of the offence or finding, is or has been—

(i) sentenced to a term of imprisonment, or

(ii) detained in a hospital.

**92A.** An offence under section 63 of the Criminal Justice and Immigration Act 2008 (possession of extreme pornographic images) if the offender—

(*a*) was 18 or over, and

(*b*) is sentenced in respect of the offence to imprisonment for a term of at least 2 years.

**92B–92X.** *Northern Ireland.*

**92Y.** An offence under section 69 of the Serious Crime Act 2015 (possession of paedophile manual) if the offender—

(*a*) was 18 or over, or

(*b*) is sentenced in respect of the offence to imprisonment for a term of at least 12 months.

*Service offences*

**93.** (1) An offence under—

(*a*) section 70 of the Army Act 1955 (3 & 4 Eliz 2 c 18),

(*b*) section 70 of the Air Force Act 1955 (3 & 4 Eliz 2 c 19), or

(*c*) section 42 of the Naval Discipline Act 1957 (c 53),

of which the corresponding civil offence (within the meaning of that Act) is an offence listed in any of paragraphs 1 to 35B.

(2) A reference in any of those paragraphs to being made the subject of a community sentence of at least 12 months[2] is to be read, in relation to an offence under an enactment referred to in sub-paragraph (1), as a reference to being sentenced to a term of detention of at least 112 days.

(3) In sub-paragraph (2), the reference to detention is to detention awarded under section 71(1)(*e*) of the Army Act 1955 or Air Force Act 1955 or section 43(1)(*e*) of the Naval Discipline Act 1957.

**93A.** (1) An offence under section 42 of the Armed Forces Act 2006 as respects which the corresponding offence under the law of England and Wales (within the meaning given by that section) is an offence listed in any of paragraphs 1 to 35B.

(2) A reference in any of those paragraphs to being made the subject of a community sentence of at least 12 months is to be read, in relation to an offence under that section, as a reference to—

(*a*) being made the subject of a service community order or overseas community order under the Armed Forces Act 2006 of at least 12 months; or

(*b*) being sentenced to a term of service detention of at least 112 days.

(3) Section 48 of that Act (attempts, conspiracy, encouragement and assistance and aiding and abetting outside England and Wales) applies for the purposes of this paragraph as if the reference in subsection (3)(*b*) to any of the following provisions of that Act were a reference to this paragraph.

*General*

**94.** A reference in a preceding paragraph to an offence includes—

(*a*) a reference to an attempt, conspiracy or incitement to commit that offence, and

(*b*) except in paragraphs 36 to 43, a reference to aiding, abetting, counselling or procuring the commission of that offence.

**94A.** A reference in a preceding paragraph to an offence ("offence A") includes a reference to an offence under Part 2 of the Serious Crime Act 2007 in relation to which offence A is the offence (or one of the offences) which the person intended or believed would be committed.

**95.** A reference in a preceding paragraph to a person's age is—

(*a*) in the case of an indecent photograph, a reference to the person's age when the photograph was taken;

(*b*) in any other case, a reference to his age at the time of the offence.

**96.** In this Schedule "community sentence" has—

(*a*) in relation to England and Wales, the same meaning as in the Powers of Criminal Courts (Sentencing) Act 2000 (c 6), and

(*b*) in relation to Northern Ireland, the same meaning as in the Criminal Justice (Northern Ireland) Order 1996 (SI 1996/3160 (NI 24)).

**97.** For the purposes of paragraphs 14, 44 and 78—

(*a*) a person is to be taken to have been under 16 at any time if it appears from the evidence as a whole that he was under that age at that time;

(*b*) section 7 of the Protection of Children Act 1978 (c 37) (interpretation), subsections (2) to (2C) and (8) of section 52 of the Civic Government (Scotland) Act 1982 (c 45), and Article 2(2) and (3) of the Protection of Children (Northern Ireland) Order 1978 (SI 1978/1047 (NI 17)) (interpretation) (respectively) apply as each provision applies for the purposes of the Act or Order of which it forms part.

**98.** A determination under paragraph 60 constitutes part of a person's sentence, within the meaning of the Criminal Procedure (Scotland) Act 1995 (c 46), for the purposes of any appeal or review.

---

[1] This provision is not incompatible with the rights provided by art 8 of the European Convention on Human Rights: *Forbes v Secretary of State for the Home Department* [2006] EWCA Civ 962, [2006] 4 All ER 799, [2006] 1 WLR 3075, [2006] Crim LR 1085, [2007] 1 Cr App Rep (S) 418.

[2] The length of a community sentence must be set; where the sentence contains a sole requirement of unpaid work to be completed within 12 months, the duration of the order is 12 months whether or not the work is completed sooner: *R v Davison* [2008] EWCA Crim 2795, [2009] 2 Cr Ap Rep (S) 76, [2009] Crim LR 208 (cf *R v Odam* [2008] EWCA Crim 1087, [2009] 1 Cr App Rep (S) 120).

## SCHEDULE 4

### Procedure for Ending Notification Requirements for Abolished Homosexual Offences — Section 93

*Scope of Schedule*

7.10722 **1.** This Schedule applies where a relevant offender is subject to the notification requirements of this Part as a result of a conviction, finding or caution in respect of an offence under—

(*a*) section 12 or 13 of the Sexual Offences Act 1956 (c 69) (buggery or indecency between men), or

(*b*) section 61 of the Offences against the Person Act 1861 (c 100) or section 11 of the Criminal Law Amendment Act 1885 (c 69) (corresponding Northern Ireland offences).

*Application for decision*

**2.** (1) The relevant offender may apply to the Secretary of State for a decision as to whether it appears that, at the time of the offence, the other party to the act of buggery or gross indecency—

(*a*) where paragraph 1(*a*) applies, was aged 16 or over,

(*b*) where paragraph 1(*b*) applies, was aged 17 or over,

and consented to the act.

(2) An application must be in writing and state—

(*a*) the name, address and date of birth of the relevant offender,

(*b*) his name and address at the time of the conviction, finding or caution,

(*c*) so far as known to him, the time when and the place where the conviction or finding was made or the caution given and, for a conviction or finding, the case number,

(*d*) such other information as the Secretary of State may require.

(3) An application may include representations by the relevant offender about the matters mentioned in sub-paragraph (1).

*Decision by Secretary of State*

**3.** (1) In making the decision applied for, the Secretary of State must consider—

(*a*) any representations included in the application, and

(*b*) any available record of the investigation of the offence and of any proceedings relating to it that appears to him to be relevant,

but is not to seek evidence from any witness.

(2) On making the decision the Secretary of State must—

(*a*) record it in writing, and

(*b*) give notice in writing to the relevant offender.

*Effect of decision*

**4.** (1) If the Secretary of State decides that it appears as mentioned in paragraph 2(1), the relevant offender ceases, from the beginning of the day on which the decision is recorded under paragraph 3(2)(*a*), to be subject to the notification requirements of this Part as a result of the conviction, finding or caution in respect of the offence.

(2) Sub-paragraph (1) does not affect the operation of this Part as a result of any other conviction, finding or caution or any court order.

*Right of appeal*

**5.** (1) If the Secretary of State decides that it does not appear as mentioned in paragraph 2(1), and if the High Court gives permission, the relevant offender may appeal to that court.

(2) On an appeal the court may not receive oral evidence.

(3) The court—

(*a*) if it decides that it appears as mentioned in paragraph 2(1), must make an order to that effect,

(*b*) otherwise, must dismiss the appeal.

(4) An order under sub-paragraph (3)(*a*) has the same effect as a decision of the Secretary of State recorded under paragraph 3(2)(*a*) has under paragraph 4.

(5) There is no appeal from the decision of the High Court.

*Interpretation*

**6.** (1) In this Schedule a reference to an offence includes—

(*a*) a reference to an attempt, conspiracy or incitement to commit that offence, and

(*b*) a reference to aiding, abetting, counselling or procuring the commission of that offence.

(2) In the case of an attempt, conspiracy or incitement, references in paragraph 2 to the act of buggery or gross indecency are references to the act of buggery or gross indecency to which the attempt, conspiracy or incitement related (whether or not that act occurred).

*Transitional provision*

7. Until the coming into force of the repeal by this Act of Part 1 of the Sex Offenders Act 1997 (c 51), this Schedule has effect as if references to this Part of this Act were references to Part 1 of that Act.

## SCHEDULE 5
### Other Offences for Purposes of Part 2

Section 104

7.10723

*(Amended by the Domestic Violence, Crime and Victims Act 2004, Sch 10, SI 2004/702, the Armed Forces Act 2006, Sch 16, SI 2007/296, the Serious Crime Act 2007, Schs 5 and 6, the Policing and Crime Act 2009, Sch 7, the Domestic Violence, Crime and Victims (Amendment) Act 2012, Schedule, the Protection of Freedoms Act 2012, Sch 9 and the Modern Slavery Act 2015, Sch 5.)*

*England and Wales*

**1.** Murder.
**2.** Manslaughter.
**3.** Kidnapping.
**4.** False imprisonment.
**4A.** Outraging public decency.
**5.** An offence under section 4 of the Offences against the Person Act 1861 (c 100) (soliciting murder).
**6.** An offence under section 16 of that Act (threats to kill).
**7.** An offence under section 18 of that Act (wounding with intent to cause grievous bodily harm).
**8.** An offence under section 20 of that Act (malicious wounding).
**9.** An offence under section 21 of that Act (attempting to choke, suffocate or strangle in order to commit or assist in committing an indictable offence).
**10.** An offence under section 22 of that Act (using chloroform etc to commit or assist in the committing of any indictable offence).
**11.** An offence under section 23 of that Act (maliciously administering poison etc so as to endanger life or inflict grievous bodily harm).
**12.** An offence under section 27 of that Act (abandoning children).
**13.** An offence under section 28 of that Act (causing bodily injury by explosives).
**14.** An offence under section 29 of that Act (using explosives etc with intent to do grievous bodily harm).
**15.** An offence under section 30 of that Act (placing explosives with intent to do bodily injury).
**16.** An offence under section 31 of that Act (setting spring guns etc with intent to do grievous bodily harm).
**17.** An offence under section 32 of that Act (endangering the safety of railway passengers).
**18.** An offence under section 35 of that Act (injuring persons by furious driving).
**19.** An offence under section 37 of that Act (assaulting officer preserving wreck).
**20.** An offence under section 38 of that Act (assault with intent to resist arrest).
**21.** An offence under section 47 of that Act (assault occasioning actual bodily harm).
**22.** An offence under section 2 of the Explosive Substances Act 1883 (c 3) (causing explosion likely to endanger life or property).
**23.** An offence under section 3 of that Act (attempt to cause explosion, or making or keeping explosive with intent to endanger life or property).
**24.** An offence under section 1 of the Infant Life (Preservation) Act 1929 (c 34) (child destruction).
**25.** An offence under section 1 of the Children and Young Persons Act 1933 (c 12) (cruelty to children).
**26.** An offence under section 1 of the Infanticide Act 1938 (c 36) (infanticide).
**27.** An offence under section 16 of the Firearms Act 1968 (c 27) (possession of firearm with intent to endanger life).
**28.** An offence under section 16A of that Act (possession of firearm with intent to cause fear of violence).
**29.** An offence under section 17(1) of that Act (use of firearm to resist arrest).
**30.** An offence under section 17(2) of that Act (possession of firearm at time of committing or being arrested for offence specified in Schedule 1 to that Act).
**31.** An offence under section 18 of that Act (carrying a firearm with criminal intent).
**31A.** An offence under section 1 of the Theft Act 1968 (c 60) (theft).
**32.** An offence under section 8 of that Act (robbery or assault with intent to rob).
**33.** An offence under section 9(1)(*a*) of that Act (burglary with intent to steal, inflict grievous bodily harm or do unlawful damage).
**34.** An offence under section 10 of that Act (aggravated burglary).
**35.** An offence under section 12A of that Act (aggravated vehicle-taking) involving an accident which caused the death of any person.
**36.** An offence of arson under section 1 of the Criminal Damage Act 1971 (c 48).
**37.** An offence under section 1(2) of that Act (destroying or damaging property) other than an offence of arson.
**38.** An offence under section 1 of the Taking of Hostages Act 1982 (c 28) (hostage-taking).
**39.** An offence under section 1 of the Aviation Security Act 1982 (c 36) (hijacking).
**40.** An offence under section 2 of that Act (destroying, damaging or endangering safety of aircraft).
**41.** An offence under section 3 of that Act (other acts endangering or likely to endanger safety of aircraft).
**42.** An offence under section 4 of that Act (offences in relation to certain dangerous articles).
**43.** An offence under section 127 of the Mental Health Act 1983 (c 20) (ill-treatment of patients).
**43A.** An offence under section 1 of the Child Abduction Act 1984 (c 37) (offence of abduction of child by parent, etc).
**43B.** An offence under section 2 of that Act (offence of abduction of child by other persons).
**44.** An offence under section 1 of the Prohibition of Female Circumcision Act 1985 (c 38) (prohibition of female circumcision).
**45.** An offence under section 1 of the Public Order Act 1986 (c 64) (riot).
**46.** An offence under section 2 of that Act (violent disorder).
**47.** An offence under section 3 of that Act (affray).
**48.** An offence under section 134 of the Criminal Justice Act 1988 (c 33) (torture).
**49.** An offence under section 1 of the Road Traffic Act 1988 (c 52) (causing death by dangerous driving).
**50.** An offence under section 3A of that Act (causing death by careless driving when under influence of drink or drugs).

**51.** An offence under section 1 of the Aviation and Maritime Security Act 1990 (c 31) (endangering safety at aerodromes).
**52.** An offence under section 9 of that Act (hijacking of ships).
**53.** An offence under section 10 of that Act (seizing or exercising control of fixed platforms).
**54.** An offence under section 11 of that Act (destroying fixed platforms or endangering their safety).
**55.** An offence under section 12 of that Act (other acts endangering or likely to endanger safe navigation).
**56.** An offence under section 13 of that Act (offences involving threats).
**56A.** An offence under section 2 or 2A of the Protection from Harassment Act 1997 (c 40) (offences of harassment and stalking).
**57.** An offence under section 4 or 4A of that Act (putting people in fear of violence and stalking involving fear of violence or serious alarm or distress).
**58.** An offence under section 29 of the Crime and Disorder Act 1998 (c 37) (racially or religiously aggravated assaults).
**59.** An offence falling within section 31(1)(*a*) or (*b*) of that Act (racially or religiously aggravated offences under section 4 or 4A of the Public Order Act 1986 (c 64)).
**60.** An offence under Part II of the Channel Tunnel (Security) Order 1994 (SI 1994/570) (offences relating to Channel Tunnel trains and the tunnel system).
**60ZA.** An offence under section 53 or 54 of the Regulation of Investigatory Powers Act 2000 (contravention of notice relating to encrypted information or tipping off in connection with such a notice).
**60A.** An offence under section 85(3) or (4) of the Postal Services Act 2000 (c 26) (prohibition on sending certain articles by post).
**61.** An offence under section 51 or 52 of the International Criminal Court Act 2001 (c 17) (genocide, crimes against humanity, war crimes and related offences), other than one involving murder.
**61A.** An offence under section 127(1) of the Communications Act 2003 (c 21) (improper use of public electronic communications network).
**62.** An offence under section 47 of this Act, where the victim or (as the case may be) other party was 16 or over.
**63.** An offence under any of sections 51 to 53 or 57 to 59A of this Act.
**63A.** An offence under section 5 of the Domestic Violence, Crime and Victims Act 2004 (causing or allowing a child or vulnerable adult to die or suffer serious physical harm).
**63B.** An offence under section 2 of the Modern Slavery Act 2015 (human trafficking).
**64–111.** *Scotland.*
**112–171B.** *Northern Ireland.*

*Service offences*

**172.** An offence under—
(*a*) section 70 of the Army Act 1955 (3 & 4 Eliz 2 c 18),
(*b*) section 70 of the Air Force Act 1955 (3 & 4 Eliz 2 c 19), or
(*c*) section 42 of the Naval Discipline Act 1957 (c 53),
of which the corresponding civil offence (within the meaning of that Act) is an offence under a provision listed in any of paragraphs 1 to 63A.
**172A.** (1) An offence under section 42 of the Armed Forces Act 2006 as respects which the corresponding offence under the law of England and Wales (within the meaning given by that section) is an offence listed in any of paragraphs 1 to 63A.
(2) Section 48 of that Act (attempts, conspiracy, encouragement and assistance and aiding and abetting outside England and Wales) applies for the purposes of this paragraph as if the reference in subsection (3)(*b*) to any of the following provisions of that Act were a reference to this paragraph.

*General*

**173.** A reference in a preceding paragraph to an offence includes—
(*a*) a reference to an attempt, conspiracy or incitement to commit that offence, and
(*b*) a reference to aiding, abetting, counselling or procuring the commission of that offence.
**173A.** A reference in a preceding paragraph to an offence ("offence A") includes a reference to an offence under Part 2 of the Serious Crime Act 2007 in relation to which offence A is the offence (or one of the offences) which the person intended or believed would be committed.
**174.** A reference in a preceding paragraph to a person's age is a reference to his age at the time of the offence.

# Violent Crime Reduction Act 2006[1]

(2006 c 38)

## PART 3[2]

## MISCELLANEOUS

*Sexual offences*

**7.10724 55. Continuity of sexual offences law** (1) This section applies where, in any proceedings—
(*a*) a person ("the defendant") is charged in respect of the same conduct both with an offence under the Sexual Offences Act 2003 ("the 2003 Act offence") and with an offence specified in subsection (2) ("the pre-commencement offence");
(*b*) the only thing preventing the defendant from being found guilty of the 2003 Act offence is the fact that it has not been proved beyond a reasonable doubt that the time when the conduct took place was after the coming into force of the enactment providing for the offence; and
(*c*) the only thing preventing the defendant from being found guilty of the pre-commencement offence is the fact that it has not been proved beyond a reasonable doubt that that time was before the coming into force of the repeal of the enactment

providing for the offence.

(2) The offences referred to in subsection (1)(*a*) are—

(*a*) any offence under the Sexual Offences Act 1956 (c 69);

(*b*) an offence under section 4 of the Vagrancy Act 1824 (c 83) (obscene exposure);

(*c*) an offence under section 28 of the Town Police Clauses Act 1847 (c 89) (indecent exposure);

(*d*) an offence under section 61 or 62 of the Offences against the Person Act 1861 (c 100) (buggery etc);

(*e*) an offence under section 128 of the Mental Health Act 1959 (c 72) (sexual intercourse with patients);

(*f*) an offence under section 1 of the Indecency with Children Act 1960 (c 33) (indecency with children);

(*g*) an offence under section 4 or 5 of the Sexual Offences Act 1967 (procuring an man to commit buggery and living on the earnings of male prostitution);

(*h*) an offence under section 9 of the Theft Act 1968 (c 60) (burglary, including entering premises with intent to commit rape);

(*i*) an offence under section 54 of the Criminal Law Act 1977 (c 45) (incitement of girl under 16 to commit incest);

(*j*) an offence under section 1 of the Protection of Children Act 1978 (c 37) (indecent photographs of children);

(*k*) an offence under section 3 of the Sexual Offences (Amendment) Act 2000 (c 44) (abuse of position of trust);

(*l*) an offence under section 145 of the Nationality, Immigration and Asylum Act 2002 (c 41) (traffic in prostitution).

(3) For the purpose of determining the guilt of the defendant it shall be conclusively presumed that the time when the conduct took place was—

(*a*) if the maximum penalty for the pre-commencement offence is less than the maximum penalty for the 2003 Act offence, a time before the coming into force of the repeal of the enactment providing for the pre-commencement offence; and

(*b*) in any other case, a time after the coming into force of the enactment providing for the 2003 Act offence.

(4) In subsection (3) the reference, in relation an offence, to the maximum penalty is a reference to the maximum penalty by way imprisonment or other detention that could be imposed on the defendant on conviction of the offence in the proceedings in question.

(5) A reference in this section to an offence under the Sexual Offences Act 2003 (c 42) or to an offence specified in subsection (2) includes a reference to—

(*a*) inciting the commission of that offence;

(*b*) conspiracy to commit that offence; and

(*c*) attempting to commit that offence;

and, in relation to an offence falling within paragraphs (*a*) to (*c*), a reference in this section to the enactment providing for the offence so falling has effect as a reference to the enactment providing for the offence under that Act or, as the case may be, for the offence so specified.

(6) This section applies to any proceedings, whenever commenced, other than proceedings in which the defendant has been convicted or acquitted of the 2003 Act offence or the pre-commencement offence before the commencement of this section.

[Violent Crime Reduction Act 2006, s 55.]

---

[1] The Violent Crime Reduction Act 2006 is reproduced partly in Part I and partly in Part VIII of this Manual. For the provisions of the Act which are not reproduced in this Part, reference should be made to the following: ss 1–27, 59–63. Sch 5 in PART I: MAGISTRATES' COURTS, PROCEDURE, ante; ss 28, 29, 32, 35–39, 50, in the title Firearms, post; and ss 43, 47 in the title OFFENSIVE WEAPONS, post.

This Act is brought into effect in accordance with s 66, and orders made thereunder. Section 55 was brought into force on 12 February 2007, s 56 came into force on Royal Assent 8 November 2006.

[2] Part 3 comprises ss 52–63 and Schs 3 and 4.

7.10725 **56. Cross-border provisions relating to sexual offences** (1) The following provisions of the Protection of Children and Prevention of Sexual Offences (Scotland) Act 2005 (asp 9) extend to England and Wales and to Northern Ireland, as well as to Scotland—

(*a*) section 17 (which relates to the making of sexual offences prevention orders in Scotland); and

(*b*) section 18 and the Schedule, so far as they provide for the amendment of the Sexual Offences Act 2003 (c 42) (see paragraph 3 of the Schedule, which relates to the offences in respect of which powers are exercisable under Part 2 of the 2003 Act).

(2) *Repealed.*

(3) *Amends s 129 of the Sexual Offences Act 2003.*

(4) Subsection (3) of section 282 of the Criminal Justice Act 2003 (c 44) (increase of maximum sentence on summary conviction of an either way offence), so far as it applies to offences under the Sexual Offences Act 2003, applies to them as amended, extended or applied by virtue of this section.

[Violent Crime Reduction Act 2006, s 56 as amended by the Anti-social Behaviour, Crime and Policing Act 2014, Sch 11.]

## Policing and Crime Act 2009[1]

(2009 c 26)

SCHEDULE 3

Lap Dancing and Other Sexual Entertainment Venues etc: Transitional Provision

Section 27

*Effect of section 27: cases where no existing resolutions passed*

7.10726 **1.** A resolution made on or after the coming into force of section 27 by a local authority under section 2 of the 1982 Act that Schedule 3 to that Act is to apply to the area of the local authority applies to that Schedule as amended by section 27.

[1] This Act is reproduced partly in this title (Sch 3) and partly in the titles IMMIGRATION AND ASYLUM (s 101), and PUBLIC MEETING AND PUBLIC ORDER (ss 30 and 106), ante. The Act also amends and inserts new provisions into a number of statutes which are reproduced in this Manual as amended. The Act is brought into force in accordance with the provisions of s 116 and orders made thereunder. At the date of going to press, the following orders had been made: (No 1 and Transitional and Saving Provisions) SI 2009/3096; (No 2) SI 2010/52; (No 3) SI 2010/125; (No 4) SI 2010/507; (No 1 and Transitional and Saving Provisions) (England) SI 2010/722; (No 5) SI 2010/999 amended by SI 2010/1986; (No 1 Wales) SI 2010/1375; (No 6) SI 2010/1986; (No 7) SI 2010/2988; (No 8) SI 2012/2235; (No 9) SI 2014/3101; (No 10) SI 2015/983; (No 11) SI 2016/147. At the date of going to press, this schedule had been brought into force in England.

*Effect of section 27: cases where existing resolutions in force*

**2.** (1) Sub-paragraph (2) applies if a local authority has, before the coming into force of section 27, resolved under section 2 of the 1982 Act that Schedule 3 to that Act is to apply to the area of the local authority.

(2) The amendments made by section 27 do not apply to the area of the local authority concerned and the resolution concerned does not apply to the Schedule as amended by section 27 but the local authority may resolve that the Schedule as amended by section 27 is to apply to their area.

(3) Section 2 of the 1982 Act has effect in relation to a resolution under sub-paragraph (2) that Schedule 3 to that Act as amended by section 27 is to apply to the area of a local authority as section 2 of that Act has effect in relation to any resolution under that section that the Schedule is to apply to the area of a local authority.

(4) The definition of "the appropriate authority" in paragraph 5 of Schedule 3 to the 1982 Act has effect as if the reference to a resolution under section 2 of that Act included a reference to a resolution under sub-paragraph (2).

*Power to make transitional provision on adoption of Schedule 3 to the 1982 Act as amended*

**3.** (1) The relevant national authority may by order make such transitional, transitory or saving provision as the relevant national authority considers appropriate in connection with the coming into force, in consequence of a resolution of a local authority under section 2 of the 1982 Act or paragraph 2(2) above, of Schedule 3 to that Act as amended by section 27.

(2) An order under this paragraph may, in particular, make different provision from that made by paragraphs 28 and 29 of Schedule 3 to that Act (and may accordingly provide for those paragraphs not to apply).

(3) The power of the relevant national authority under this paragraph—

(*a*) is exercisable by statutory instrument,

(*b*) may be exercised so as to make different provision for different purposes or different areas,

(*c*) includes power to make supplementary, incidental or consequential provision.

*Duty to consult about adopting Schedule 3 to the 1982 Act as amended*

**4.** (1) Sub-paragraph (2) applies if a local authority has not made a resolution under section 2 of the 1982 Act or (as the case may be) paragraph 2(2) above within the period of one year beginning with the coming into force of section 27.

(2) The local authority must, as soon as reasonably practicable, consult local people about whether the local authority should make such a resolution.

(3) In sub-paragraph (2) "local people" means persons who live or work in the area of the local authority.

*Interpretation*

**5.** In this Schedule—

"the 1982 Act" means the Local Government (Miscellaneous Provisions) Act 1982 (c 30),

"relevant national authority" means—

(*a*) in relation to England, the Secretary of State, and

(*b*) in relation to Wales, the Welsh Ministers,

"local authority" has the same meaning as in Part 2 of the 1982 Act (see section 2(5) of that Act);

and references in this Schedule to the coming into force of section 27 are references to the coming into force of that section for purposes other than the purposes of the Secretary of State or the Welsh Ministers making orders.

## Sexual Offences Act 2003 (Travel Notification Requirements) Regulations 2004[1]

(SI 2004/1220 amended by SI 2012/1876)

7.10727 *1. Citation and extent* (1) These Regulations may be cited as the Sexual Offences Act 2003 (Travel Notification Requirements) Regulations 2004.

(2) These Regulations do not extend to Scotland.

[1] Made by the Secretary of State, in exercise of the powers conferred upon him by s 86 of the Sexual Offences Act 2003.

7.10728 *2. Interpretation* In these Regulations:

(*a*) a reference to a numbered section is to the section of that number in the Sexual Offences Act 2003, and

(*b*) a reference to the "2001 Regulations" is to the Sex Offenders (Notice Requirements) (Foreign Travel) Regulations 2001.

7.10729 3. *Commencement, revocation and transitional provision* (1) Subject to paragraph (2), these Regulations shall come into force on 1st May 2004.

(2) A relevant offender who intends to leave the United Kingdom for a period of less than eight days is not required to give a notification pursuant to regulation 5(1) if his intended date of departure is on or before 9th May 2004.

(3) Subject to paragraphs (4) and (5), the 2001 Regulations are hereby revoked.

(4) Where a relevant offender has given notice in accordance with section 2(6E) of the Sex Offenders Act 1997 before the coming into force of these Regulations, the requirements of the 2001 Regulations shall apply to the departure and return so notified as if these Regulations had not been made.

(5) Where a relevant offender subject to the notice requirements of the 2001 Regulations whose intended date of departure is on or before 9th May 2004 has not given notice in accordance with section 2(6E) of the Sex Offenders Act 1997 before the coming into force of these Regulations, the requirements of the 2001 Regulations shall apply to the departure and return as if these Regulations had not been made.

7.10730 4. *Determination of point of arrival* (1) For the purposes of section 86(2)(*b*) and of these Regulations, a relevant offender's point of arrival in a country is to be determined in accordance with this regulation.

(2) In a case in which a relevant offender will arrive in a country by rail, sea or air, his point of arrival is the station, port or airport at which he will first disembark.

(3) In a case in which a relevant offender will arrive in a country by any means other than those mentioned in paragraph (2) above, his point of arrival is the place at which he will first enter the country.

7.10731 5. *Notification to be given before leaving the United Kingdom* (1) A relevant offender who intends to leave the United Kingdom must give a notification under section 86(2) in accordance with these Regulations.

(2) Where a relevant offender to whom these Regulations apply knows the information required to be disclosed by section 86(2)(*a*) and (*b*) more than seven days before the date of his intended departure, he shall give a notification which sets out that information and as much of the information required by regulation 6 as he holds—

(*a*) not less than seven days before that date (the seven day notification requirement); or

(*b*) as soon as reasonably practicable but not less than 24 hours before that date, if and only if the relevant offender has a reasonable excuse for not complying with the seven day notification requirement.

(3) Where the relevant offender does not know the information required to be disclosed by section 86(2)(*a*) and (*b*) more than seven days before the date of his intended departure, he shall give not less than 12 hours before that date, a notification which sets out that information and as much of the information required by regulation 6 as he holds.

7.10732 6. *Information to be disclosed in a notification under section 86(2)* In addition to the information required by section 86(2)(*a*) and (*b*), a relevant offender to whom these Regulations apply must disclose, where he holds such information—

(*a*) where he intends to travel to more than one country outside the United Kingdom, his intended point of arrival in each such additional country,

(*b*) the dates on which he intends to stay in any country to which he intends to travel,

(*c*) details of his accommodation arrangements in any country to which he intends to travel,

(*d*) the identity of any carrier or carriers he intends to use for the purposes of his departure from and return to the United Kingdom, and of travelling to any other point of arrival,

(*e*) in a case in which he intends to return to the United Kingdom on a particular date, that date, and

(*f*) in a case in which he intends to return to the United Kingdom at a particular point of arrival, that point of arrival.

7.10733 7. *Change to information disclosed in a notification under section 86(2)* (1) Where—

(*a*) a relevant offender has given a notification under section 86(2), and

(*b*) at any time prior to his intended departure from the United Kingdom, the information disclosed in that notification becomes inaccurate or incomplete as a statement of all the information mentioned in section 86(2)(*a*) and (*b*) and regulation 6 which he currently holds,

he must give a further notification under section 86(2).

(2) A further notification under paragraph (1) above must be given not less than 12 hours before the relevant offender's intended departure from the United Kingdom.

(3) The relevant offender may not give notification under paragraph (2) less than 24 hours before the date of his intended departure unless he has a reasonable excuse for being unable to give such notification before that time.

7.10734 8. *Notification to be given on return to the United Kingdom* (1) This regulation applies to a relevant offender who—

(*a*) is required to give a notification under section 86(2),

(*b*) has left the United Kingdom, and

(*c*) subsequently returns to the United Kingdom.

(2) Except as provided by paragraph (3) below, every relevant offender to whom this regulation applies must give a notification under section 86(3) within three days of his return to the United Kingdom.

(3) A relevant offender to whom this regulation applies need not give a notification under section 86(3) in any case in which he gave a relevant notification under 86(2) which—

(*a*) disclosed a date under the provisions of regulation 6(*e*) above, and

(*b*) disclosed a point of arrival under the provisions of regulation 6(*f*) above,

provided his return to the United Kingdom was on that date and at that point of arrival.

**7.10735** 9. *Information to be disclosed in a notification under section 86(3)* A notification under section 86(3) must disclose the date of the relevant offender's return to the United Kingdom and his point of arrival in the United Kingdom.

**7.10736** 10. *Giving a notification* (1) Subject to paragraph (2) below, for the purpose of giving a notification under section 86(2) or 86(3), a relevant offender must attend at a police station—

(*a*) which is in his local police area within the meaning of section 88(3), and

(*b*) at which, pursuant to the provisions of section 87, notifications under section 83, 84 or 85 may be made.

(2) For the purpose of giving a notification under section 86(2) as required by regulation 5(3) or 7 above, a relevant offender must attend at a police station prescribed under section 87, but such a police station need not be in his local police area.

(3) A notification under section 86(2) or 86(3) must be given to a police officer, or to a person authorised by the officer in charge of the station under section 87(1)(*b*) for the purpose of receiving a notification under that section.

(4) A relevant offender giving a notification under section 86(2) or 86(3) must inform the person to whom he gives the notice of—

(*a*) his name and other names he is using,

(*b*) his home address, and

(*c*) his date of birth,

as currently notified under Part 2 of the Act.

(5) A relevant offender giving a further notification under section 86(2) as required by regulation 7 above must inform the person to whom he gives the notification of the police station at which he first gave a notification in respect of the journey in question under section 86(2).

# Sexual Offences Act 2003 (Notification Requirements) (England and Wales) Regulations 2012[1]

(SI 2012/1876)

**7.10737** 1. *Citation, commencement and extent* (1) These Regulations may be cited as the Sexual Offences Act 2003 (Notification Requirements) (England and Wales) Regulations 2012.

(2) These Regulations come into force 28 days after the day on which they are made.

(3) These Regulations extend to England and Wales only.

---

[1] Made by the Secretary of State, in exercise of the powers conferred by ss 83(5) and (5A), 84(1) and (5A), 85(5), 86 and 138(4) of the Sexual Offences Act 2003.

The obligation of a person on the sex offenders' register to provide bank account details does not contravene art 8. The Sexual Offences Act 2003 (Notification Requirements) (England and Wales) Regulations 2012 have a legitimate policy objective, namely the ability to trace an offender quickly, to guard against the risk of an offender using another identity or to have a means of obtaining quick access to a credit card account, and the means employed are practical and proportionate to provide further protection to prevent other persons from becoming potential victims of those on the register: *R (on the application of Prothero) v Secretary of State for the Home Department* [2013] EWHC 2830 (Admin), [2014] 1 WLR 1195, [2014] 1 WLR 1195, 155 Sol Jo (no 37) 37.

**7.10738** 2. *Interpretation* In these Regulations—

"the 2003 Act" means the Sexual Offences Act 2003;

"the 2004 Regulations" means the Sexual Offences Act 2003 (Travel Notification Requirements) Regulations 2004;

"banking institution" means a bank, building society or other institution which provides banking services;

"business" includes any trade, profession or vocation;

"child" means a person aged under 18 years;

"credit card" means a card which is a credit-token within the meaning of section 14(1)(*b*) of the Consumer Credit Act 1974;

"credit card provider" means a bank, building society or other institution which provides a credit card;

"debit card" means a card the use of which by its holder to make a payment results in a current account of the holder at a banking institution being debited with the payment;

"identity document" has the same meaning as in the Identity Documents Act 2010 but does not include a stamp or label; and

"relevant household" means a household or other place—

(*a*) where a child resides or stays, and

(*b*) to which the public do not have access (whether for payment or not).

**7.10739** 3. *Transitional provision: travel notification requirements* A relevant offender who intends to leave the United Kingdom for a period of less than three days is not required to give notification in accordance with regulation 5(1) of the 2004 Regulations if his intended date of departure is on or before the date 14 days after these Regulations come into force.

7.10740 *9. Periodic notification of address where there is no sole or main residence* For the purposes of section 85(5)(*a*) of the 2003 Act, the applicable period means the period of seven days.

7.10741 *10. Notification to be given by relevant offender residing or staying at a relevant household* (1) The information set out in paragraph (2) is prescribed for the purposes of section 83(5)(h) of the 2003 Act in a case where a relevant offender (R) resides, or stays for a period of at least 12 hours, at a relevant household.

(2) The information which R must notify is—

(*a*) the date on which R begins to reside or stay at a relevant household,

(*b*) the address of the relevant household, and

(*c*) where R holds such information, the period or periods for which R intends to reside or stay at the relevant household.

7.10742 *11.* (1) The changes in circumstances set out in paragraph (2) are prescribed for the purposes of section 84(1)(ca) of the 2003 Act.

(2) The changes of circumstance are where the relevant offender (R)—

(*a*) resides, or stays for a period of at least 12 hours, at a relevant household in relation to which there has been no notification under section 83(1);

(*b*) ceases to reside or stay at a relevant household in relation to which there has been a notification under section 83(1).

(3) A notification given under section 84(1) of the 2003 Act must disclose the date from which R resides or stays, or the date on which R ceases to reside or stay, at a relevant household.

7.10743 *12. Notification of information about bank accounts and credit cards*[1] (1) The information set out in paragraphs (2) to (7) is prescribed for the purposes of section 83(5)(h) of the 2003 Act in a case where a relevant offender (R) holds—

(*a*) an account with a banking institution in R's name, or in R's name and the name of another person, and in relation to each such account, the information specified in paragraph (2);

(*b*) an account with a banking institution in the name of an unincorporated business which is run by R, or run by R and another person, and in relation to each such account, the information specified in paragraph (3);

(*c*) a debit card in relation to any account of which notification is given in accordance with sub-paragraph (*a*) or (*b*), and in relation to each such debit card, the information specified in paragraph (4);

(*d*) an account with a credit card provider in R's name, or in R's name and the name of another person, and in relation to each such account, the information specified in paragraph (5);

(*e*) an account with a credit card provider in the name of an unincorporated business which is run by R, or run by R and another person, and in relation to each such account, the information specified in paragraph (6); or

(*f*) a credit card in relation to any account of which notification is given in accordance with sub-paragraph (*d*) or (*e*), and in relation to each such credit card, the information specified in paragraph (7).

(2) The information specified for the purposes of paragraph (1)(*a*) is—

(*a*) the name of each banking institution with which R holds an account;

(*b*) the address of the office at which each account is held and, if that office is outside the United Kingdom, the address of the principal office in the United Kingdom (if any) of the banking institution;

(*c*) the number of each account; and

(*d*) the sort code in relation to each account.

(3) The information specified for the purposes of paragraph (1)(*b*) is—

(*a*) the information specified in paragraph (2); and

(*b*) the name of the business in whose name the account is held.

(4) The information specified for the purposes of paragraph (1)(*c*) is—

(*a*) the card number in relation to each debit card;

(*b*) the validation date of each debit card;

(*c*) the expiry date of each debit card; and

(*d*) the name of the business (if any) in whose name the card is held.

(5) The information specified for the purposes of paragraph (1)(*d*) is—

(*a*) the name of each credit card provider with which R holds an account;

(*b*) the address of the office at which each account is held and, if that office is outside the United Kingdom, the address of the principal office in the United Kingdom (if any) of the credit card provider; and

(*c*) the number of each account.

(6) The information specified for the purposes of paragraph (1)(*e*) is—

(*a*) the information specified in paragraph (5); and

(*b*) the name of the business in whose name the card is held.

(7) The information specified for the purposes of paragraph (1)(*f*) is—

(*a*) the card number in relation to each credit card;

(*b*) the validation date of each credit card;

(*c*) the expiry date of each credit card; and

(*d*) the name of the business (if any) in whose name the card is held.

[1] The 2012 Regulations are not incompatible with article 8 of the European Convention on Human Rights. These requirements are very valuable in achieving the legitimate aims and are both necessary and proportionate for the achievement of those aims *R (on the application of Prothero) v Secretary of State for the Home Department* [2013] EWHC 2830 (Admin), [2014] 1 WLR 1195, 155 Sol Jo (no 37) 37.

**7.10744** *13.* (1) The changes in circumstances set out in paragraph (2) are prescribed for the purposes of section 84(1)(ca) of the 2003 Act.

(2) The changes of circumstance are where—

(*a*) an account which a relevant offender (R) holds with a banking institution, as specified in regulation 12(1)(*a*) or (*b*), has been—

(i) opened, or

(ii) closed;

(*b*) a debit card R holds in relation to any account specified in regulation 12(1)(*a*) or (*b*)—

(i) has been obtained by R, or

(ii) is no longer held by R;

(*c*) an account R holds with a credit card provider, as specified in regulation 12(1)(*d*) or (*e*), has been—

(i) opened, or

(ii) closed;

(*d*) a credit card R holds in relation to any account specified in regulation 12(1)(*d*) or (*e*)—

(i) has been obtained by R, or

(ii) is no longer held by R;

(*e*) any information previously notified by R under regulation 12(1) has—

(i) altered, or

(ii) become inaccurate or incomplete.

(3) A notification given under section 84(1) of the 2003 Act must include the information specified in regulation 12(2) to (7) in relation to that account, or debit or credit card.

**7.10745** *14. Notification of information about passport or other form of identification* (1) The information set out in paragraph (2) is prescribed for the purposes of section 83(5)(h) of the 2003 Act in a case where a relevant offender (R) holds any passport, other identity document or (in a case where R does not hold any passport or other identity document) any other document in which R's full name appears.

(2) The information which R must notify is—

(*a*) where R holds any passport, and in relation to each passport R holds—

(i) the passport number, and

(ii) R's full name as it appears in the passport;

(*b*) where R does not hold a passport, in relation to any other identity document R holds—

(i) the description of the identity document,

(ii) the issue number (if any) of the identity document, and

(iii) R's full name as it appears in the identity document;

(*c*) where R does not hold a passport or other identity document, in relation to another document R holds—

(i) the description of the document (including the name of any issuing authority),

(ii) the issue number (if any) of the document; and

(iii) R's full name as it appears in the document.

**7.10746** *15.* (1) The changes in circumstances set out in paragraph (2) are prescribed for the purposes of section 84(1)(ca) of the 2003 Act.

(2) The changes of circumstance are where the relevant offender—

(*a*) obtains a passport, other identity document or other document in relation to which there has been no notification under section 83(1); and

(*b*) ceases to hold a passport, other identity document or other document in relation to which there has been a notification under section 83(1).

# SHOPS

## Contents



# Sunday Trading Act 1994

(1994 c 20)

**7.10747** **2. Loading and unloading at large shops on Sunday morning** (1) A local authority may by resolution designate their area as a loading control area for the purposes of this section with effect from a date specified in the resolution, which must be a date at least one month after the date on which the resolution is passed.

(2) A local authority may by resolution revoke any designation made by them under subsection (1) above.

(3) It shall be the duty of a local authority, before making or revoking any designation under subsection (1) above, to consult persons appearing to the local authority to be likely to be affected by the proposed designation or revocation (whether as the occupiers of shops or as local residents) or persons appearing to the local authority to represent such persons.

(4) Where a local authority make or revoke a designation under this section, they shall publish notice of the designation or revocation in such manner as they consider appropriate.

(5) Schedule 3 to this Act (which imposes restrictions on loading and unloading on Sunday before 9 am at large shops in loading control areas) shall have effect.

[Sunday Trading Act 1994, s 2.]

**7.10748** **8. Meaning of "local authority"** (1) In this Act "local authority" means any unitary authority or any district council so far as they are not a unitary authority.

(2) In subsection (1) above "unitary authority" means—

(*a*) the council of any county so far as they are the council for an area for which there are no district councils,

(*b*) the council of any district comprised in an area for which there is no county council.

(*c*) a county borough council,

(*d*) a London borough council,

(*e*) the Common Council of the City of London, or

(*f*) the Council of the Isles of Scilly.

(3) Until 1st April 1996, the definition of "unitary authority" in subsection (2) above shall have effect with the omission of paragraph (*c*).

[Sunday Trading Act 1994, s 8.]

## SCHEDULES

### SCHEDULE 1

RESTRICTIONS ON SUNDAY OPENING OF LARGE SHOPS[1] Section 1(1)

**7.10749**

*(Amended by the Licensing Act 2003, Sch 6, the Christmas Day (Trading) Act 2004, s 4, SI 2004/470, SI 2006/2407 and SI 2015/664)*

*Interpretation*

1. In this Schedule—

"alcohol" has the same meaning as in the Licensing Act 2003,

"large shop" means a shop which has a relevant floor area exceeding 280 square metres,

"medicinal product" and "registered pharmacy" have the same meaning as in the Medicines Act 1968,

"relevant floor area", in relation to a shop, means the internal floor area of so much of the shop as consists of or is comprised in a building, but excluding any part of the shop which, throughout the week ending with the Sunday in question, is used neither for the serving of customers in connection with the sale of goods nor for the display of goods,

"retail customer" means a person who purchases goods retail,

"retail sale" means any sale other than a sale for use or resale in the course of a trade or business, and references to retail purchase shall be construed accordingly,

"sale of goods" does not include—

(*a*) the sale of meals, refreshments or alcohol for consumption on the premises on which they are sold, or

(*b*) the sale of meals or refreshments prepared to order for immediate consumption off those premises,

"shop" means any premises where there is carried on a trade or business consisting wholly or mainly of the sale of goods, and

"stand", in relation to an exhibition, means any platform, structure, space or other area provided for exhibition purposes "veterinary medicinal product" has the same meaning as in regulation 2 of the Veterinary Medicines Regulations 2006.

*Restrictions on Sunday opening hours of large shops*

**2.** (1) Subject to sub-paragraphs (2) and (3) below, a large shop[2] shall not be open on Sunday for the serving of retail customers[3].

(2) Sub-paragraph (1) above does not apply in relation to–

(*a*) any of the shops mentioned in paragraph 3(1) below, or

(*b*) any shop in respect of which a notice under paragraph 8(1) of Schedule 2 to this Act (shops occupied by persons observing the Jewish Sabbath) has effect

(3) Sub-paragraph (1) above does not apply in relation to the opening of a large shop during any continuous period of six hours on a Sunday beginning no earlier than 10 am and ending no later than 6 pm, but this sub-paragraph has effect subject to sub-paragraph (4) below.

(4) The exemption conferred by sub-paragraph (3) above does not apply where the Sunday is Easter Day.

(5) Nothing in this paragraph applies where the Sunday is Christmas Day (the opening of large shops on Christmas Day being prohibited by section 1 of the Christmas Day (Trading) Act 2004).

*Exemptions*

**3.** (1) The shops referred to in paragraph 2(2)(*a*) above are—

(*a*) any shop which is at a farm and where the trade or business carried on consists wholly or mainly of the sale of produce from that farm,

(*b*) any shop where the trade or business carried on consists wholly or mainly of the sale of alcohol,

(*c*) any shop where the trade or business carried on consists wholly or mainly of the sale of any one or more of the following—

(i) motor supplies and accessories[4], and

(ii) cycle supplies and accessories,

(*d*) any shop which—

(i) is a registered pharmacy, and

(ii) is not open for the retail sale of any goods other than medicinal products, veterinary medicinal products and medical and surgical appliances,

(*e*) any shop at a designated airport which is situated in a part of the airport to which sub-paragraph (3) below applies,

(*f*) any shop in a railway station,

(*g*) any shop at a service area within the meaning of the Highways Act 1980,

(*h*) any petrol filling station,

(*j*) any shop which is not open for the retail sale of any goods other than food, stores or other necessaries required by any person for a vessel or aircraft on its arrival at, or immediately before its departure from, a port, harbour or airport, and

(*k*) any stand used for the retail sale of goods during the course of an exhibition.

(2) In determining whether a shop falls within sub-paragraph (1)(*a*), (*b*) or (*c*) above, regard shall be had to the nature of the trade or business carried on there on weekdays as well as to the nature of the trade or business carried on there on Sunday.

(3) This sub-paragraph applies to every part of a designated airport, except any part which is not ordinarily used by persons travelling by air to or from the airport.

(4) In this paragraph "designated airport" means an airport designated for the purposes of this paragraph by an order made by the Secretary of State, as being an airport at which there appears to him to be a substantial amount of international passenger traffic.

(5) The power to make an order under sub-paragraph (4) above shall be exercisable by statutory instrument.

(6) Any order made under section 1(2) of the Shops (Airports) Act 1962[5] and in force at the commencement of this Schedule shall, so far as it relates to England and Wales, have effect as if made also under sub-paragraph (4) above, and may be amended or revoked as it has effect for the purposes of this paragraph by an order under sub-paragraph (4) above.

**4–5.** *Repealed.*

*Duty to display notice*

**6.** At any time when—

(*a*) a large shop is open on Sunday for the serving of retail customers, and

(*b*) the prohibition in sub-paragraph (1) of paragraph 2 above is excluded only by sub-paragraph (3) of that paragraph,

a notice specifying the Sunday opening hours shall be displayed in a conspicuous position inside and outside the shop[3].

*Offences*

**7.** (1) If paragraph 2(1)[6] above is contravened in relation to a shop, the occupier of the shop shall be liable on summary conviction to a fine.

(2) If paragraph 6 above is contravened in relation to a shop, the occupier of the shop shall be liable on summary conviction to a fine not exceeding **level 2** on the standard scale.

**8.** Where a person is charged with having contravened paragraph 2(1) above, in relation to a large shop which was permitted to be open for the serving of retail customers on the Sunday in questionby reason of his having served a retail customer after the end of the period during which the shop is permitted to be open by virtue of paragraph 2(3) above, it shall be a defence to prove that the customer was in the shop before the end of that period and left not later than half an hour after the end of that period.

**9.** *Repealed.*

---

[1] It has been held that the prohibition in Art 30 of the EEC Treaty on quantitative restrictions on imports does not apply to national legislation, prohibiting retailers from opening their premises on Sundays (*Stoke on Trent City Council v B & Q plc* [1993] 2 All ER 297n).

[2] Whether a shop is a "large shop", must be determined in the light of the situation which continues for a period of time. Accordingly, a shop in which only part of the premises were open on a particular day did not thereby cease to be a

"large shop" when on most other days the whole of the premises were open; see *Haskins Garden Centres Ltd v East Dorset District Council* (1998) Times, 7 May.

For penalty for contravention, see para 7, post. The Channel Tunnel (Sunday Trading Act 1994) (Disapplication) Order 1994, SI 1994/3286, excludes the application of para 2(1) of Sch 1 in relation to any shops situated in a specified part of the terminal area of the Channel Tunnel system at Cheriton, Folkestone.

[3] The justices must ask themselves whether in the ordinary and natural use of language an item is capable of being a motor supply or accessory; evidence of capacity is not necessary; there is a difference between an object capable of being used as a motor accessory and an object which is properly speaking a motor accessory (*Hadley v Texas Homecare Ltd* (1987) 152 JP 268).

[4] The Airports Shops Order 1977, SI 1977/1397, designates the following airports in England and Wales: Birmingham, Liverpool, London—Gatwick, Heathrow and Stansted—Manchester International and Southend, the Airports Shops Order 1985, SI 1985/654, similarly designates Leeds, Bradford, Luton and Southampton Airports and the Airports Shops (No 2) Order 1985, SI 1985/1739, designates Bournemouth (Hurn), Humberside, Liverpool, Norwich and Teesside, and orders have also been made for Exeter (SI 1986/981), London City (SI 1987/1983) and Manston (SI 1990/1044).

[5] For statutory defence that goods were supplied to a customer who was in the shop before the end of permitted Sunday opening hours, see para 8, post.

[6] For defence of due diligence, see Sch 2, para 7, post. For offences due to default of other person and for liability of director, manager etc for acts of a body corporate, see Sch 2, paras 5 and 6, post.

## SCHEDULE 2

### SUPPLEMENTARY PROVISIONS

Section 1(1)

(*As amended by the Consumer Rights Act 2015, Sch 6.*)

## PART I

### GENERAL ENFORCEMENT PROVISIONS

*Duty to enforce Act*

7.10750 **1.** It shall be the duty[1] of every local authority to enforce within their area the provisions of Schedules 1 and 3 to this Act and Part II of this Schedule.

*Inspectors*

**2.** For the purposes of their duties under paragraph 1 above it shall be the duty of every local authority to appoint inspectors.

**3, 4.** *Repealed.*

*Investigatory powers*

**4A.** For the investigatory powers available to a local authority and the inspectors appointed by it under paragraph 2 for the purposes of the duty in paragraph 1, see Schedule 5 to the Consumer Rights Act 2015.

*Offences due to fault of other person*

**5.** Where the commission by any person of an offence under this Act is due to the act or default of some other person, that other person shall be guilty of the offence, and a person may be charged with and convicted of the offence by virtue of this paragraph whether or not proceedings are taken against the first-mentioned person.

*Offences by bodies corporate*

**6.** (1) Where an offence under this Act committed by a body corporate is proved to have been committed with the consent or connivance of, or to be attributable to any neglect on the part of, any director, manager, secretary or other similar officer of the body corporate, or any person who was purporting to act in any such capacity, he as well as the body corporate shall be guilty of the offence and shall be liable to be proceeded against and punished accordingly.

(2) Where the affairs of a body corporate are managed by its members, sub-paragraph (1) above shall apply in relation to the acts and defaults of a member in connection with his functions of management as if he were a director of the body corporate.

*Defence of due diligence*

**7.** (1) In any proceedings for an offence under this Act it shall, subject to sub-paragraph (2) below, be a defence for the person charged to prove that he took all reasonable precautions and exercised all due diligence to avoid the commission of the offence by himself or by a person under his control.

(2) If in any case the defence provided by sub-paragraph (1) above involves the allegation that the commission of the offence was due to the act or default of another person, the person charged shall not, without leave of the court, be entitled to rely on that defence unless, at least seven clear days before the hearing, he has served on the prosecutor a notice in writing giving such information identifying or assisting in the identification of that other person as was then in his possession.

[1] For the duty of a local authority and its powers to seek an injunction in the civil courts to restrain a person acting in contravention of the legislation. See *Stoke-on-Trent City Council v B & Q (Retail) Ltd* [1984] AC 754, [1984] 2 All ER 332, HL (decided under the Shops Act 1950).

## PART II

### SHOPS OCCUPIED BY PERSONS OBSERVING THE JEWISH SABBATH

*Shops occupied by persons of the Jewish religion*

7.10751 **8.** (1) A person of the Jewish religion who is the occupier of a large shop may give to the local authority for the area in which the shop is situated a notice signed by him stating—

(*a*) that he is a person of the Jewish religion, and

(*b*) that he intends to keep the shop closed for the serving of customers on the Jewish Sabbath.

(2) For the purposes of this paragraph, a shop occupied by a partnership or company shall be taken to be occupied by a person of the Jewish religion if, and only if, the majority of the partners or of the directors, as the case may be, are persons of that religion.

(3) A notice under sub-paragraph (1) above shall be accompanied by a certificate signed by an authorised

person that the person giving the notice is a person of the Jewish religion.

(4) Where the occupier of the shop is a partnership or company—

(*a*) any notice under sub-paragraph (1) above shall be given by the majority of the partners or directors and, if not given by all of them, shall specify the names of the other partners or directors;

(*b*) a certificate under sub-paragraph (3) above is required in relation to each of the persons by whom such a notice is given.

(5)–(6) *Register.*

(7) If there is any change—

(*a*) in the occupation of a shop in respect of which a notice under sub-paragraph (1) above has effect, or

(*b*) in any partnership or among the directors of any company by which such a shop is occupied,

the notice shall be taken to be cancelled at the end of the period of 14 days beginning with the day on which the change occurred, unless during that period, or within such further time as may be allowed by the local authority, a fresh notice is given under sub-paragraph (1) above in respect of the shop.

(8) Where a fresh notice is given under sub-paragraph (1) above by reason of a change of the kind mentioned in sub-paragraph (7) above, the local authority may dispense with the certificate required by sub-paragraph (3) above in the case of any person in respect of whom such a certificate has been provided in connection with a former notice in respect of that shop or any other shop in the area of the local authority.

(9) A notice given under sub-paragraph (1) above in respect of any shop shall be cancelled on application in that behalf being made to the local authority by the occupier of the shop.

(10) A person who, in a notice or certificate given for the purposes of this paragraph, makes a statement which is false in a material respect and which he knows to be false or does not believe to be true shall be liable on summary conviction to a fine not exceeding **level** 5 on the standard scale.

(11) Where a person is convicted of an offence under sub-paragraph (10) above, the local authority may cancel any notice under sub-paragraph (1) above to which the offence relates.

(12) In this paragraph—

"authorised person", in relation to a notice under sub-paragraph (1) above, means—

(*a*) the Minister of the synagogue of which the person giving the notice is a member,

(*b*) the secretary of that synagogue, or

(*c*) any other person nominated for the purposes of this paragraph by the President of the London Committee of Deputies of the British Jews (otherwise known as the Board of Deputies of British Jews),

"large shop" and "shop" have the same meaning as in Schedule 1 to this Act, and

"secretary of a synagogue" has the same meaning as in Part IV of the Marriage Act 1949.

*Members of other religious bodies observing the Jewish Sabbath*

**9.** Paragraph 8 above shall apply to persons who are members of any religious body regularly observing the Jewish Sabbath as it applies to persons of the Jewish religion, and accordingly—

(*a*) references to persons of the Jewish religion shall be construed as including any person who is a member of such a body, and

(*b*) in the application of that paragraph to such persons "authorised person" means a Minister of the religious body concerned.

**10.** *Transitional provisions.*

## SCHEDULE 3

### Loading and Unloading at Large Shops on Sunday Morning

Section 2

7.10752

*(Amended by the Christmas Day (Trading) Act 2004, s 4 and SI 2004/470.)*

*Shops to which Schedule applies*

**1.** This Schedule applies to any shop—

(*a*) which is a large shop, within the meaning of Schedule 1 to this Act, that is permitted to be open on a Sunday by virtue of paragraph 2(3) of that Schedule and which the occupier opens on Sunday for the serving of retail customers, and

(*b*) which is situated in an area designated as a loading control area under section 2 of this Act.

*Consent required for early Sunday loading and unloading*

**2.** The occupier of a shop to which this Schedule applies shall not load or unload, or permit any other person to load or unload, goods from a vehicle at the shop before 9 am on Sunday in connection with the trade or business carried on in the shop, unless the loading or unloading is carried on—

(*a*) with the consent of the local authority for the area in which the shop is situated granted under this Schedule, and

(*b*) in accordance with any conditions subject to which that consent is granted.

**3.** (1) A consent under this Schedule may be granted subject to such conditions as the local authority consider appropriate.

(2) The local authority may at any time vary the conditions subject to which a consent is granted, and shall give notice of the variation to the person to whom the consent was granted.

*Offence*

**9.** A person who contravenes paragraph 2 above shall be liable on summary conviction to a fine not exceeding **level 3** on the standard scale[1].

*Christmas Day*

**10.** Paragraph 2 does not apply where the Sunday is Christmas Day (loading and unloading at large shops on Christmas Day being regulated by section 2 of the Christmas Day (Trading) Act 2004).

---

[1] For defence of due diligence, see Sch 2, para 7, ante. For offences due to default of other person and for liability of director, manager etc for acts of a body corporate, see Sch 2, paras 5 and 6, ante.

# Christmas Day (Trading) Act 2004

(2004 c 26)

7.10753 **1. Prohibition of opening of large shops on Christmas Day** (1) A large shop must not be open on Christmas Day for the serving of retail customers.

(2) Subsection (1) does not apply to any of the shops mentioned in paragraph 3(1) of Schedule 1 to the 1994 Act (shops exempt from restrictions on Sunday trading).

(3) If subsection (1) is contravened in relation to a shop, the occupier of the shop is liable on summary conviction to a fine.

(4) In its application for the purposes of subsection (2), paragraph 3(2) of Schedule 1 to the 1994 Act (which relates to the interpretation of paragraph 3(1) of that Schedule) has effect as if—

(*a*) the reference to weekdays were a reference to days of the year other than Christmas Day, and

(*b*) the reference to Sunday were a reference to Christmas Day.

(5) In this section—

"large shop" has the same meaning as in Schedule 1 to the 1994 Act, except that for the purposes of this section the definition of "relevant floor area" in paragraph 1 of that Schedule is to be read as if the reference to the week ending with the Sunday in question were a reference to the period of seven days ending with the Christmas Day in question;

"retail customer" and "shop" have the same meaning as in that Schedule.

[Christmas Day (Trading) Act 2004, s 1 as amended by SI 2015/664.]

7.10754 **2. Loading and unloading early on Christmas Day** (1) Where a shop which is prohibited by section 1 from opening on Christmas Day is located in a loading control area, the occupier of the shop must not load or unload, or permit any other person to load or unload, goods from a vehicle at the shop before 9am on Christmas Day in connection with the trade or business carried on in the shop, unless the loading or unloading is carried on—

(*a*) with the consent of the local authority for the area in which the shop is situated, granted in accordance with this section, and

(*b*) in accordance with any conditions subject to which that consent is granted.

(2) The provisions of paragraphs 3 to 8 of Schedule 3 to the 1994 Act shall apply in relation to consent under subsection (1) as they apply in relation to consent under that Schedule, but as if—

(*a*) the reference in paragraph 6(1) to Sunday were a reference to Christmas Day, and

(*b*) the reference in paragraph 7(*a*) to an offence under paragraph 9 of that Schedule were a reference to an offence under subsection (3).

(3) A person who contravenes subsection (1) is liable on summary conviction to a fine not exceeding level 3 on the standard scale.

(4) In this section, "loading control area" means any area designated by a local authority as a loading control area in accordance with section 2 of the 1994 Act.

[Christmas Day (Trading) Act 2004, s 2.]

7.10755 **3. Enforcement** (1) It is the duty of every local authority to enforce within their area the provisions of sections 1 and 2.

(2) For the purposes of their duties under subsection (1), it is the duty of every local authority to appoint inspectors, who may be the same persons as those appointed as inspectors by the local authority under paragraph 2 of Schedule 2 to the 1994 Act.

(3) Paragraphs 3 and 4 of Schedule 2 to the 1994 Act (powers of entry and obstruction of inspectors) apply in respect of inspectors appointed under subsection (2) as they apply to inspectors appointed under paragraph 2 of that Schedule and, for the purposes of paragraph 3 of that Schedule as so applied, the reference in that paragraph to the provisions of Schedules 1 and 3 to the 1994 Act is to be taken to be a reference to the provisions of sections 1 and 2 of this Act.

(4) Paragraphs 5, 6 and 7 of Schedule 2 to the 1994 Act (offences due to fault of other person, offences by body corporate and defence of due diligence) apply in respect of the offences under sections 1 and 2 as they apply in respect of offences under the 1994 Act.

(5) In this section "local authority" has the meaning given by section 8 of the 1994 Act.

[Christmas Day (Trading) Act 2004, s 3.]

# SOCIAL SECURITY

**Contents**



## National Assistance Act 1948

(11 & 12 Geo 6 c 29)

### Part III
### Local Authority Services

*Provision of Accommodation*

7.10756 **21. Duty of local authorities to provide accommodation** (1) Subject to and in accordance with the provisions of this Part of this Act[1], a local authority may with the approval of the Secretary of State, and to such extent as he may direct shall, make arrangements[2] for providing—

(*a*) residential accommodation[3] for persons aged eighteen or over who by reason of age, illness, disability or any other circumstances are in need of care and attention[4] which is not otherwise available to them; and

(*aa*) residential accommodation for expectant and nursing mothers who are in need of care and attention which is not otherwise available to them.

(*b*) *repealed.*

(1A) A person to whom section 115 of the Immigration and Asylum Act 1999 (exclusion from benefits) applies may not be provided with residential accommodation under subsection (1)(*a*) if his need for care and attention has arisen solely—

(*a*) because he is destitute; or

(*b*) because of the physical effects, or anticipated physical effects, of his being destitute.

(1B) Subsections (3) and (5) to (8) of section 95 of the Immigration and Asylum Act 1999, and paragraph 2 of Schedule 8 to that Act, apply for the purposes of subsection (1A) as they apply for the purposes of that section, but for the references in subsections (5) and (7) of that section and in that paragraph to the Secretary of State substitute references to a local authority.*

(2) In making any such arrangements a local authority shall have regard to the welfare of all persons for whom accommodation is provided, and in particular to the need for providing accommodation of different descriptions suited to different descriptions of such persons as are mentioned in the last foregoing subsection.

(2A) In determining for the purposes of paragraph (*a*) or (aa) of subsection (1) of this section whether care and attention are otherwise available to a person, a local authority shall disregard so much of the person's resources as may be specified in, or determined in accordance with, regulations[5] made by the Secretary of State for the purposes of this subsection.

(2B) In subsection (2A) of this section the reference to a person's resources is a reference to his resources within the meaning of regulations made for the purposes of that subsection.

(3) *Repealed.*

(4) Subject to the provisions of section 26 of this Act, accommodation provided by a local authority in the exercise of their functions under this section shall be provided in premises managed by the authority or, to such extent as may be determined in accordance with the arrangements under this section, in such premises managed by another local authority, including a local authority in England, as may be agreed between the two authorities and on such terms, including terms as to

the reimbursement of expenditure incurred by the said other authority, as may be so agreed.

(5) References in this Act to accommodation provided under this Part thereof shall be construed as references to accommodation provided in accordance with this and the five next following sections, and as including references to board and other services, amenities and requisites provided in connection with the accommodation except where in the opinion of the authority managing the premises their provision is unnecessary.

(6) References in this Act to a local authority providing accommodation shall be construed, in any case where a local authority agree with another local authority for the provision of accommodation in premises managed by the said other authority, as references to the first-mentioned local authority.

(7) Without prejudice to the generality of the foregoing provisions of this section, a local authority may—

(*a*) provide, in such cases as they may consider appropriate, for the conveyance of persons to and from premises in which accommodation is provided for them under this Part of the Act;

(*b*) make arrangements for the provision on the premises in which accommodation is being provided of such other services as appear to the authority to be required.

(8) Nothing in this section shall authorise or require a local authority to make any provision authorised or required to be made (whether by that or by any other authority) by or under any enactment not contained in this Part of this Act or authorised or required to be provided under the National Health Service Act 2006 or the National Health Service (Wales) Act 2006.

[National Assistance Act 1948, s 21 as amended by the Local Government Act 1972, Schs 23 and 30, the National Health Service Reorganisation Act 1973, Schs 4 and 5, the Housing (Homeless Persons) Act 1977, Sch, the Health Services Act 1980, Sch 1, the Children Act 1989, Sch 13, the National Health Service and Community Care Act 1990, s 42(1), Schs 9 and 10 and the Community Care (Residential Accommodation) Act 1998, s 1, the Immigration and Asylum Act 1999, s 116, the Health and Social Care Act 2001, s 53 and the National Health Service (Consequential Provisions) Act 2006, Sch 1 and SI 2015/914.]

---

* **Subsection (1B) substituted by the Nationality, Immigration and Asylum Act 2002, s 45 from a date to be appointed.**

1 Section 26A, added by the National Health Service and Community Care Act 1990, s 43 excludes the power to provide accommodation in certain cases.

2 This duty may be discharged by arrangements made with third parties either wholly or in part under s 26, post (see *R v Wandsworth London Borough Council, ex p Beckwith* [1996] 1 All ER 129, [1996] 1 WLR 60, HL).

3 Power to make rules for the preservation of order is contained in s 23(1).

4 "Care and attention" in this context means "looking after" ie doing something for the person being cared for which he cannot or should not be expected to do for himself eg household tasks which an old person can no longer perform or can only perform with great difficulty or protection from risks which a mentally disabled person cannot perceive or personal care, such as feeding, washing or toileting: *R (on the application of M) v Slough Borough Council* [2008] UKHL 52, [2008] 4 All ER 831. But something well beyond mere monitoring of an individual's condition is required. The care and attention has to be of a sort which is normally provided in the home (whether ordinary or specialised) or will be effectively useless if the claimant has no home: *R (on the application of S) v Westminster City Council* [2013] UKSC 27, [2013] 3 All ER 191, [2013] 1 WLR 1445.

5 The National Assistance (Residential Accommodation) (Disregarding of Resources) (England) Regulations 2001, SI 2001/3067 and the National Assistance (Residential Accommodation) (Disregarding of Resources) (Wales) Regulations 2003, SI 2003/969 have been made.

**7.10757** 22. **Charges to be made for accommodation** Such persons shall pay[1] for the accommodation in accordance with the rates provided by the Act and regulations[2] prescribed from time to time by the Secretary of State, giving effect to relevant provisions. In the case of a child under 16 years, accompanied by a person over that age, payment shall be made by the person by whom the child is accompanied.

[National Assistance Act 1948, s 22 amended by the Ministry of Social Security Act 1966, 6th Sch, the Social Security Act 1980, Sch 5, the Health and Social Services and Social Security Adjudications Act 1983, s 20, the Social Security Act 1986, Sch 10, the National Health Service and Community Care Act 1990, s 44 and Sch 10 and the Community Care (Delayed Discharges etc) Act 2003, s 17—summarised.]

---

1 For recovery of cost, see s 56, post. The Health and Social Services and Social Security Adjudications Act 1983, ss 21–24 makes further provision for the recovery of charges where persons in residential accommodation have disposed of assets or have a beneficial interest in land.

2 National Assistance (Assessment of Resources) Regulations 1992, SI 1992/2977 as amended have been made. See also the National Assistance (Residential Accommodation) (Disregarding of Resources) (England) Regulations 2001, SI 2001/3067 also the following regulations made under the Health and Social Care Act 2001: National Assistance (Residential Accommodation) (Relevant Contributions) (England) Regulations 2001, SI 2001/3069; the National Assistance (Residential Accommodation) (Additional Payments and Assessment of Resources) (Amendment) (England) Regulations 2001, SI 2001/3441; the National Assistance (Sums for Personal Requirements) (England) Regulations 2003, SI 2003/628 as amended; the National Assistance (Residential Accommodation) (Additional Payments, Relevant Contributions and Assessment of Resources) (Wales) Regulations 2003, SI 2003/931 as amended.

**7.10758** 26. **Provision of accommodation in premises maintained by voluntary organisations** (1) Subject to subsections (1A) and (1C) below, arrangements under section 21 of this Act may include arrangements with a voluntary organisation or with any other person who is not a local authority where—

(*a*) that organisation or person manages premises which provide for reward accommodation falling within subsection (1)(*a*) or (*aa*) of that section, and

(*b*) the arrangements are for the provision of such accommodation in those premises.

(1A) Arrangements must not be made by virtue of this section for the provision of accommodation together with nursing or personal care for persons such as are mentioned in section 3(2) of the Care Standards Act 2000 (care homes) unless—

(*a*) the accommodation is to be provided, under the arrangements, in a care home (within the meaning of that Act) which is managed by the organisation or person in question; and

(*b*) that organisation or person is registered under Part II of that Act in respect of the home.

(1C) Subject to subsection (1D) below, no arrangements may be made by virtue of this section for the provision of accommodation together with nursing without the consent of such clinical commissioning group or Local Health Board as may be determined in accordance with regulations.

(1D) Subsection (1C) above does not apply to the making by an authority of temporary arrangements for the accommodation of any person as a matter of urgency; but, as soon as practicable after any such temporary arrangements have been made, the authority shall seek the consent required by subsection (1C) above to the making of appropriate arrangements for the accommodation of the person concerned.

(1E) *Repealed.*

(2) Any arrangements made by virtue of this section shall provide for the making by the local authority to the other party thereto of payments in respect of the accommodation provided at such rates as may be determined by or under the arrangements[1] and subject to subsection (3A) below the local authority shall recover from each person for whom accommodation is provided under the arrangements the amount of the refund which he is liable to make in accordance with the following provisions of this section.

(3) Subject to subsection (3A) below, a person for whom accommodation is provided under any such arrangements shall, in lieu of being liable to make payment therefor in accordance with section twenty-two of this Act, refund to the local authority any payments made in respect of him under the last foregoing subsection[2]:

Provided that where a person for whom accommodation is provided, or proposed to be provided, under any such arrangements satisfies the local authority that he is unable to make a refund at the full rate determined under that subsection, subsections (3) to (5) of section twenty-two of this Act shall, with the necessary modifications, apply as they apply where a person satisfies the local authority of his inability to pay at the standard rate as mentioned in the said subsection (3).

(3A) Where accommodation in any premises is provided for any person under arrangements made by virtue of this section and the local authority, the person concerned and the voluntary organisation or other person managing the premises (in this subsection referred to as "the provider") agree that this subsection shall apply—

(*a*) so long as the person concerned makes the payments for which he is liable under paragraph (*b*) below, he shall not be liable to make any refund under subsection (3) above and the local authority shall not be liable to make any payment under subsection (2) above in respect of the accommodation provided for him;

(*b*) the person concerned shall be liable to pay to the provider such sums as he would otherwise (under subsection (3) above) be liable to pay by way of refund to the local authority; and

(*c*) the local authority shall be liable to pay to the provider the difference between the sums paid by virtue of paragraph (*b*) above and the payments which, but for paragraph (*a*) above, the authority would be liable to pay under subsection (2) above.

(4) Subsections (5A), (7) and (9) of the said section twenty-two shall, with the necessary modifications, apply for the purposes of the last foregoing subsection as they apply for the purposes of the said section twenty-two.

(4AA) Subsections (2) to (4) shall have effect subject to any regulations under section 15 of the Community Care (Delayed Discharges etc) Act 2003 (power to require certain community care services and services for carers to be free of charge).

(4A) Section 21(5) of this Act shall have effect as respects accommodation provided under arrangements made by virtue of this section with the substitution for the reference to the authority managing the premises of a reference to the authority making the arrangements.

(4AA) Subsections (2) to (4) shall have effect subject to any regulations under section 15 of the Community Care (Delayed Discharges etc) Act 2003 (power to require certain community care services and services for carers to be free of charge).

(5) Where in any premises accommodation is being provided under this section in accordance with arrangements made by any local authority, any person authorised in that behalf by the authority may at all reasonable times enter and inspect the premises.

(6) *Repealed.*

(7) In this section the expression "voluntary organisation" includes any association which is a housing association for the purposes of the Housing Act, 1936 and "exempt body" means an authority or body constituted by an Act of Parliament or incorporated by Royal Charter.

[National Assistance Act 1948, s 26 as amended by the Health Services and Public Health Act 1968, s 44, the Social Work (Scotland) Act 1968, s 95 and Sch 9, the Local Government Act 1972, Sch 23, the Housing (Homeless Persons) Act 1977, s 20 and Sch, the Health and Social Services and Social Security Adjudications Act 1983, s 20, the Registered Homes (Amendment) Act 1991, s 2(5), the National Health Service and Community Care Act 1990, s 42 and Schs 9 and 10, the Community Care (Residential Accommodation) Act 1992, s 1 and the Health Authorities Act 1995, Sch 1, the Care Standards Act 2000, s 116, the Community Care (Delayed Discharges etc) Act 2003, s 17, SI 2007/961 and the Health and Social Care Act 2012, s 55(2), Sch 5, paras 2, 4(*a*).]

[1] If the arrangements for transfer to a voluntary organization of the local authority's obligations to provide "residential accommodation" do not include arrangements for the local authority to make payments to the voluntary organization at rates determined by or under the arrangements, "residential accommodation" is not provided under Pt III of the Act. Accordingly the rate of benefit payable under the Social Security legislation will be at the rate applicable to claimants in a "residential care home" rather than to those in residential accommodation (*Chief Adjudication Officer v Quinn* [1996] 4 All ER 72, [1996] 1 WLR 1184, HL).

[2] Section 26(3) is not to be construed as meaning that, whatever the figure and however wrongly a local authority may make payments for the provision of accommodation, the resident has to reimburse them under the section. The ordinary principles of construction involve putting in the words "any payments properly made in respect of him" (*Dorset County Council v Greenham* (1981) 145 JP 125).

7.10759 **45. Recovery in cases of misrepresentation or non-disclosure** (1) If, whether fraudulently or otherwise, any person misrepresents or fails to disclose any material fact, and in consequence of the misrepresentation or failure—

(*a*) a local authority incur any expenditure under Part III of this Act, or

(*b*) any sum recoverable under this Act by a local authority is not recovered, the authority shall be entitled to recover the amount thereof from the said person[1].

[National Assistance Act 1948, s 45 as amended by Ministry of Social Security Act 1966, 8th Sch.]

[1] Recoverable summarily as a civil debt, see s 56(1), post.

7.10760 **47. Removal to suitable premises of persons in need of care and attention** (1) The following provisions of this section shall have effect for the purposes of securing the necessary care and attention for persons in Wales who—

(*a*) are suffering from grave chronic disease or, being aged, infirm or physically incapacitated, are living in insanitary conditions, and

(*b*) are unable to devote to themselves, and are not receiving from other persons, proper care and attention.

(1A) But this section does not apply to a person ("P") in either of the following cases.

(1B) The first case is where an order of the Court of Protection authorises the managing authority of a hospital or care home (within the meaning of Schedule A1 to the Mental Capacity Act 2005) to provide P with proper care and attention.

(1C) The second case is where—

(*a*) an authorisation under Schedule A1 to the Mental Capacity Act 2005 is in force, or

(*b*) the managing authority of a hospital or care home are under a duty under paragraph 24 of that Schedule to request a standard authorisation, and

P is, or would be, the relevant person in relation to the authorisation.

(2) If the medical officer of health[1] certifies in writing to the appropriate authority[2] that he is satisfied after thorough inquiry and consideration that in the interests of any such person as aforesaid residing in the area of the authority or for preventing injury to the health of, or serious nuisance to, other persons, it is necessary to remove any such person as aforesaid from the premises in which he is residing, the appropriate authority may apply to the court for an order under the next following subsection.

(3) [3] On any such application the court may, if satisfied on oral evidence of the allegations in the certificate, and that it is expedient so to do, order the removal of the persons to whom the application relates by such officer of the appropriate authority as may be specified in the order, to a suitable hospital[4] or other place in, or within convenient distance of, the area of the appropriate authority, and his detention and maintenance therein:

Provided[3] that the court shall not order the removal of a person to any premises, unless either the person managing the premises has been heard in the proceedings or seven[5] clear days' notice has been given to him of the intended application and of the time and place at which it is proposed to be made.

(4) An order under the last foregoing subsection may be made so as to authorise a person's detention for any period not exceeding three months, and the court may from time to time by order extend that period for such further period, not exceeding three months, as the court may determine[3].

(5) An order under subsection (3) of this section may be varied by an order of the Court so as to substitute for the place referred to in that subsection such other suitable place in, or within convenient distance of, the area of the appropriate authority as the court may determine, so however that the proviso in the said subsection (3) shall with the necessary modification apply to any proceedings under this subsection[3].

(6) [3] At any time after the expiration of six clear weeks from the making of an order under subsection (3) or (4) of this section an application may be made to the court by or on behalf of the person in respect of whom the order was made, and on any such application the court may, if in the circumstances it appears expedient so to do, revoke the order.

(7) [3] No application under this section shall be entertained by the court unless, seven clear days before the making of the application, notice has been given of the intended application and of the time and place at which it is proposed to be made—

(*a*) where the application is for an order under subsection (3) or (4) of this section, to the person in respect of whom the application is made or to some person in charge of him;

(*b*) where the application is for the revocation of such an order, to the medical officer of health.

(8) Where in pursuance of an order under this section a person is maintained neither in hospital accommodation provided by the Minister of Health under the National Health Service Act 2006 or the National Health Service (Wales) Act 2006, nor by the Secretary of State under the National Health Service (Scotland) Act 1947, nor in premises where accommodation is provided by, or by arrangement with, a local authority under Part III of this Act, the cost of his maintenance shall be borne by the appropriate authority.

(9) Any expenditure incurred under the last foregoing subsection shall be recoverable from the person maintained; and any expenditure incurred by virtue of this section in connection with the maintenance of a person in premises where accommodation is provided under Part III of this Act shall be recoverable[6] in like manner as expenditure incurred in providing accommodation under the said Part III.

(11) Any person who wilfully disobeys, or obstructs the execution of, an order under this section shall be guilty of an offence and liable on summary conviction to a fine not exceeding **level 1** on the standard scale.

(12) For the purposes of this section, the appropriate authorities shall be in Wales the councils of counties and county boroughs and in Scotland the councils constituted under section 2 of the Local Government etc (Scotland) Act 1994.

(12A) In this section, "the court"—

(*a*) in Wales, means a magistrates' court acting in the local justice area where the premises are situated;

(*b*) *Scotland.*

(13) The foregoing provisions of this section shall have effect in substitution for any provisions for the like purposes contained in, or having effect under, any public general or local Act passed before the passing of this Act: Provided that nothing in this subsection shall be construed as affecting any enactment providing for the removal to, or detention in, hospital of persons suffering from notifiable or infectious diseases[7].

(14) Any notice under this section may be served by post.

[National Assistance Act 1948, s 47 as amended by the Local Government Act 1972, Sch 29, the National Health Service Reorganisation Act 1973, Sch 5, the National Health Service Act 1977, Sch 15, the Criminal Law Act 1977, s 31, the Criminal Justice Act 1982, s 46, the Local Government (Scotland) Act 1973, s 214, Sch 7, Pt II, the Local Government (Wales) Act 1994, Sch 10, the Courts Act 2003, Sch 8, the National Health Service (Consequential Provisions) Act 2006, Sch 1, the Mental Health Act 2007, Sch 9 and the Health and Social Care Act 2008, Sch 15 and SI 2015/914.]

---

1 The reference to the medical officer of health must now be read as a reference to "the proper officer" by reason of the effect of the Local Government Act 1972, Sch 29, Pt I, paras 1 and 4.

2 "Appropriate authority" is defined in sub-s (12), infra.

3 Note amendments to this section appropriate to a case where it is certified by the medical officer of health and another registered medical practitioner that in their opinion it is necessary in the interests of the person concerned to remove him without delay, contained in the National Assistance (Amendment) Act 1951, post.

4 "Hospital" has the meaning assigned to it by s 79 of the National Health Service Act 1946 (s 64) (now s 128 of the National Health Service Act 1977)—that is, any institution for the reception and treatment of persons suffering from illness, any maternity home, and any institution for the reception and treatment of persons during convalescence or persons requiring medical rehabilitation, and includes clinics, dispensaries and out-patient departments, maintained in connection with any such institution or home as aforesaid.

5 That is, seven perfect intervening days (*Mitchell v Foster* (1840) 12 Ad & El 472).

6 For procedure for recovery, see s 43, ante.

7 See the Public Health (Control of Disease) Act 1984, ss 37, 38 in this PART: title PUBLIC HEALTH, ante.

**7.10761 48. Duty of councils to provide temporary protection for property of persons admitted to hospitals, etc** (1) Where a person—

(*a*) is admitted as a patient to any hospital[1], or

(*b*) is admitted to accommodation provided under Part III of this Act, or

(*c*) is removed to any other place under an order made under subsection (3) of the last foregoing section;

and it appears to the council in the case of any moveable property of that person that is for the time being situated in Wales, that there is danger of loss of, or damage to, the property by reason of his temporary or permanent inability to protect or deal with the property, and that no other suitable arrangements have been or are being made for the purposes of this subsection, it shall be the duty of the council to take reasonable steps to prevent or mitigate the loss or damage.

(2) For the purposes of discharging the said duty the council shall have power at all reasonable times to enter[2] any premises which immediately before the person was admitted or removed as aforesaid were his place of residence or usual place of residence, and to dealt with any movable property of his in any way which is reasonably necessary to prevent or mitigate loss thereof or damage thereto.

(3) A council may recover[3] from a person admitted or removed as aforesaid, any reasonable expenses incurred by the council in relation to him under the foregoing provisions of this section.

(4) In this section the expression "council" means in relation to any property the council which is the local authority for the purposes of the Local Authority Social Services Act 1970 and in the area of which the property is for the time being situated.

[National Assistance Act 1948, s 48 as amended by the Local Government Act 1972, Sch 23 and the Health and Social Care Act 2008, Sch 15 and SI 2015/914.]

[1] For definition of "hospital" see note 4 to s 47, ante.
[2] The person proposing to exercise the power to enter should have with him a written authority to do so (s 55(1)): for penalty for obstructing such a person, see s 55(2) post.
[3] The sum is recoverable summarily as a civil debt, see s 56, post.

7.10762 **51. Failure to maintain** (1) Where a person persistently refuses or neglects to maintain himself, and in consequences of his refusal or neglect, accommodation under Part III thereof is provided for him, he shall be guilty of an offence.

(2) For the purposes of this section, a person shall not be deemed to refuse or neglect to maintain himself by reason only of anything done or omitted in furtherance of a trade dispute[1].

(3) A person guilty of an offence under this section shall be liable on summary conviction[2]—

(*a*) to imprisonment for a term not exceeding **three months***;[3]

(*b*) *repealed.*

[National Assistance Act 1948, s 51 as amended by Ministry of Social Security Act 1966, 8th Sch, the Criminal Justice Act 1982, ss 38 and 46 and the Health and Social Care Act 2008, Sch 15.]

* **"51 weeks" substituted by the Criminal Justice Act 2003, Sch 26 from a date to be appointed.**
[1] "Trade dispute" has the same meaning as in (what is now) s 27(3)(*b*) of the Social Security Contributions and Benefits Act 1992; that is, any dispute between employers and employees or between employees and employees which is connected with the employment or non-employment or the terms of employment or the conditions of employment of any persons, whether employees in the employment of the employer with whom the dispute arises or not (s 64(1) amended by Sch 2 of the Social Security (Consequential Provisions) Act 1992).
[2] While proceedings must be commenced within six months of the last refusal or neglect to maintain, evidence of earlier refusals or neglect may be given to prove persistence, cf *Donkin v Donkin* [1933] P 17, [1932] All ER Rep 582, 96 JP 472.
[3] A fine not exceeding **level 3** on the standard scale may be imposed (Magistrates' Courts Act 1980, s 34(3) in PART I: MAGISTRATES' COURTS, PROCEDURE, ante.

7.10763 **52. False statements** (1) If any person—

(*a*) for the purpose of obtaining, either for himself or for another person, any benefit under Part III of this Act; or

(*b*) for the purpose of avoiding or reducing any liability under this Act,

makes any statement or representation which he knows to be false, he shall be guilty of an offence and liable on summary conviction to a fine not exceeding **level 3** on the standard scale or to imprisonment for a term not exceeding **three months*** or to both such imprisonment and such fine.

(2) Notwithstanding anything in any enactment, proceedings for an offence under this section may be begun at any time within three months from the date on which evidence sufficient in the opinion of the local authority concerned to justify a prosecution for an offence comes to the knowledge of the local authority, or within twelve months from the commission of the offence, whichever period is the longer.

(3) For the purposes of the last foregoing subsection, a certificate of the local authority as to the date on which such evidence as aforesaid came to the knowledge of the local authority, as the case may be, shall be conclusive[1] proof thereof.

[National Assistance Act 1948, s 52 as amended by Ministry of Social Security Act 1966, 8th Sch and the Criminal Justice Act 1982, ss 38 and 46.]

* **"51 weeks" substituted by the Criminal Justice Act 2003, Sch 26 from a date to be appointed.**
[1] Therefore, where a proper certificate is produced, it will not be for the court to investigate, or to admit evidence casting doubt upon, its accuracy.

7.10764 **55. Provisions as to entry and inspection** (1) A person who proposes to exercise any power of entry or inspection[1] conferred by this Act shall if so required produce some duly authenticated document showing his authority to exercise the power.

(2) Any person who obstructs the exercise of any such power as aforesaid shall be guilty of an offence and liable on summary conviction to a fine not exceeding **level 4** on the standard scale.

[National Assistance Act 1948, s 55 as amended by the Criminal Law Act 1977, Sch 6 and the Criminal Justice Act 1982, ss 38 and 46.]

[1] See s 26(5), premises maintained by voluntary organisations; s 39, ante, disabled persons' and old persons' homes; s 48(2), ante, to provide protection for property of persons admitted to hospitals, etc.

7.10765 **56. Legal proceedings** (1) Without prejudice to any other method of recovery, any sum due under this Act[1] to a local authority shall be recoverable summarily as a civil debt.

(2) Notwithstanding anything in any Act, proceedings for the recovery of any sum in the manner provided by the last foregoing subsection may be brought at any time within three years after the sum became due.

(3) Offences under this Act, other than offences under s 47(11) of this Act, may be prosecuted by any council which is a local authority for the purposes of the Local Authority Social Services Act 1970 in Wales and offences under s 47(11) of this Act may be prosecuted by the councils referred to in s 47(12) of this Act.

(4) *Repealed.*

(5) *Scotland.*

[National Assistance Act 1948, s 56 as amended by the Ministry of Social Security Act 1966, 8th Sch, the Local Government Act 1972, Sch 23, the Family Law Reform Act 1987, Sch 2 and the Health and Social Care Act 2008, Sch 15 and SI 2015/914.]

1 See eg s 22, ante, recovery of cost of accommodation provided by local authority; s 45, ante, recovery in cases of misrepresentation or non-disclosure; s 48, ante, recovery of reasonable expenses of providing protection for property of persons admitted to hospitals, etc.

## National Assistance (Amendment) Act 1951

(14 & 15 Geo 6 c 57)

7.10766 1. **Amendments to section 47 of the National Assistance Act 1948** (1) An order under subsection (3) of section forty-seven of the National Assistance Act 1948, for the removal of any such person as is mentioned in subsection (1) of that section may be made without the notice required by subsection (7) of that section if it is certified by the medical officer of health[1] and another registered medical practitioner that in their opinion it is necessary in the interests of that person to remove him without delay.

(2) If in any such case it is shown by the applicant that the manager of any such hospital or place as is mentioned in the said subsection (3) agrees to accommodate therein the person in respect of whom the application is made, the proviso to that subsection (which requires that the manager of the premises to which a person is to be removed must be heard in the proceedings or receive notice of the application) shall not apply in relation to an order for the removal of that person to that hospital or place.

(3) Any such order as is authorised by this section may be made on the application either of the appropriate authority within the meaning of the said section forty-seven or, if the medical officer of health[1] is authorised by that authority to make such applications, by that officer, and may be made either by a court of summary jurisdiction having jurisdiction in the place where the premises are situated in which the person in respect of whom the application is made resides, or by a single justice having such jurisdiction; and the order may, if the court or justice thinks it necessary, be made *ex parte*.

(4) In relation to any such order as is authorised by this section the provision of the said section forty-seven shall have effect subject to the following modifications:

(*a*) in subsection (4) (which specifies the period for which a person may be detained pursuant to an order) for the words "three months" in the first place where those words occur, there shall be substituted the words "three weeks" and subsection (6) (which enables an application to be made for the revocation of an order) shall not apply:

(*b*) where the order is made by a single justice, any reference in subsections (4) and (5) to the court shall be construed as a reference to a court of summary jurisdiction having jurisdiction in the same place as that justice.

[National Assistance (Amendment) Act 1951, s 1.]

1 Now the "proper officer"; see footnote to the National Assistance Act 1948, s 47(2), ante.

## Pneumoconiosis etc (Workers' Compensation) Act 1979

(1979 c 41)

7.10767 This Act makes provision for lump sum payments in respect of persons disabled by pneumoconiosis, byssinosis and diffuse mesothelioma. Knowingly making a false representation, or producing or furnishing or causing or knowingly allowing to be produced or furnished any document or information known to be false in a material particular; penalty on summary conviction a fine not exceeding **level** 5 on the standard scale.

## Health and Social Services and Social Security Adjudications Act 1983[1]

(1983 c 41)

### PART VII[1]

### CHARGES FOR LOCAL AUTHORITY SERVICES

7.10768 17. **Charges for local authority services in England and Wales.** (1) Subject to subsection (3) below, an authority providing a service to which this section applies may recover such charge (if any) for it as they consider reasonable.

(2) This section applies to services provided under the following enactments—

(*a*) *repealed*;

(*b*) *repealed*;

(*c*) *repealed*;

(*d*) *repealed*

(*e*) paragraph 1 of Part II of Schedule 9 to this Act.

(*f*) *repealed*.

(3) If a person—

(a) avails himself of a service to which this section applies or a service within subsection (2A), and

(b) satisfies the authority providing the service that his means are insufficient for it to be reasonably practicable for him to pay for the service the amount which he would otherwise be obliged to pay for it,

the authority shall not require him to pay more for it than it appears to them that it is reasonably practicable for him to pay.

(4) Any charge under this section may, without prejudice to any other method of recovery, be recovered summarily[2] as a civil debt.

(5) Subsection (2A), and subsections (3) and (4) so far as they relate to it, have effect subject to any regulations under the Community Care (Delayed Discharges etc) Act 2003 (power to require certain community care services and services for carers to be free of charge).

[Health and Social Services and Social Security Adjudications Act 1983, s 17 as amended by the National Health Service and Community Care Act 1990, Sch 9, the Community Care (Delayed Discharges etc) Act 2003, s 17, the National Health Service (Consequential Provisions) Act 2006, Sch 1 and SI 2015/914.]

---

1. Part VII contains 17–24.
2. See the Magistrates' Courts Act 1980, s 58, in PART I: MAGISTRATES' COURTS, PROCEDURE, ante, for procedure to obtain order for payment of civil debt, and the Magistrates' Courts Act 1980, s 96 for the enforcement of such order.

## Social Security Act 1986

(1986 c 50)

7.10769 **54. Breach of regulations** (1) Regulations under any of the benefit Acts may provide for contravention of, or failure to comply with, any provision contained in regulations made under that Act to be an offence under that Act and for the recovery, on summary conviction of any such offence, of penalties not exceeding—

(a) for any one offence, **level 3** on the standard scale; or

(b) for an offence of continuing any such contravention or failure after conviction, **£40 for each day** on which it is so continued.

(2) *Repealed.*

[Social Security Act 1986, s 54 as amended by the Social Security (Consequential Provisions) Act 1992, Sch 1.]

7.10770 **56. Legal proceedings** (1) Any person authorised by the Secretary of State[1] in that behalf may conduct any proceedings under the benefit Acts before a magistrates' court.

(2) Notwithstanding anything in any Act—

(a) proceedings for an offence under the benefit Acts may be begun[2] at any time within the period of three months from the date on which evidence, sufficient in the opinion of the Secretary of State to justify a prosecution for the offence, comes to his knowledge or within a period of twelve months from the commission of the offence, whichever period last expires;

(b) *repealed.*

(3) For the purposes of subsection (2) above—

(a) a certificate purporting to be signed by or on behalf of the Secretary of State as to the date on which such evidence as is mentioned in paragraph (a) of that subsection came to his knowledge shall be conclusive evidence of that date;

(b) *repealed.*

(4)–(5) *Repealed.*

[Social Security Act 1986, s 56 as amended by the Local Government Finance Act 1988, Sch 10, the Social Security (Consequential Provisions) Act 1992, Sch 1 and the Legal Services Act 2007, Sch 21.]

---

1. The authority to conduct proceedings is proved by the production of a copy of the original, certified under the Documentary Evidence Act 1868 (in PART II: EVIDENCE, ante) which Act is applied to any documents issued by the Secretary of State: see Secretary of State for Social Services Order 1968, art 5(3). An officer who did not lay the information may conduct the prosecution (*R v Northumberland Justices, ex p Thompson* (1923) 87 JP 95).
2. Proceedings begin when an information is laid or a complaint made (*Brooks v Bagshaw* [1904] 2 KB 798, 68 JP 514).

7.10771 **57. Offences by bodies corporate** (1) Where an offence under any of the benefit Acts which has been committed by a body corporate is proved to have been committed with the consent or connivance of, or to be attributable to any neglect on the part of, a director[1], manager, secretary or other similar officer of the body corporate, or any person who was purporting to act in any such capacity, he, as well as the body corporate, shall be guilty of that offence and be liable to be proceeded against accordingly.

(2) Where the affairs of a body corporate are managed by its members, subsection (1) above applies in relation to the acts and defaults of a member in connection with his functions of management as if he were a director of the body corporate.

[Social Security Act 1986, s 57.]

---

1. This means a director properly appointed; in the case of a limited company, in accordance with the Companies Acts. It is not sufficient merely that he acted as a director (*Dean v Hiesler* [1942] 2 All ER 340, 106 JP 282). The director or other officer is liable to the same maximum penalty as the body corporate.

# National Health Service and Community Care Act 1990

(1990 c 19)

7.10772 47. **Assessment of needs for community care service** (1) Subject to subsections (5) and (6) below, where it appears to a local authority that any person for whom they may provide or arrange for the provision of community care services may be in need of any such services, the authority—

(*a*) shall carry out an assessment of his needs for those services; and

(*b*) having regard to the results of that assessment, shall then decide whether his needs call for the provision by them of any such services.

(2)–(7) *Procedure on assessment.*

[National Health Service and Community Care Act 1990, s 47 as amended by the Health Authorities Act 1995, Sch 1.]

7.10773 48. **Inspection of premises used for provision of community care services**

(1) Any person authorised by the Secretary of State may at any reasonable time enter and inspect any premises (other than regulated premises) in which community care services are or are proposed to be provided by a local authority, whether directly or under arrangements made with another person.

(1A) In subsection (1) "regulated premises" means—

(*a*) in relation to England, premises used for the carrying on of a regulated activity within the meaning of Part 1 of the Health and Social Care Act 2008 by a person who is registered under Chapter 2 of that Part in respect of the activity; and

(*b*) in relation to Wales, premises in respect of which a person is registered under Part 2 of the Care Standards Act 2000.

(2) Any person inspecting any premises under this section may—

(*a*) make such examination into the state and management of the premises and the facilities and services provided therein as he thinks fit;

(*b*) inspect any records (in whatever form they are held) relating to the premises, or any person for whom community care services have been or are to be provided there; and

(*c*) require the owner of, or any person employed in, the premises to furnish him with such information as he may request.

(3) Any person exercising the power to inspect records conferred by subsection (2)(*b*) above—

(*a*) shall be entitled at any reasonable time to have access to, and inspect and check the operation of, any computer and any associated apparatus or material which is or has been in use in connection with the records in question; and

(*b*) may require—

(i) the person by whom or on whose behalf the computer is or has been so used; or

(ii) any person having charge of or otherwise concerned with the operation of the computer, apparatus or material,

to give him such reasonable assistance as he may require.

(4) Any person inspecting any premises under this section—

(*a*) may interview any person residing there in private—

(i) for the purpose of investigating any complaint as to those premises or the community care services provided there, or

(ii) if he has reason to believe that the community care services being provided there for that person are not satisfactory; and

(*b*) may examine any such person in private.

(5) No person may—

(*a*) exercise the power conferred by subsection (2)(*b*) above so as to inspect medical records; or

(*b*) exercise the power conferred by subsection (4)(*b*) above,

unless he is a registered medical practitioner and, in the case of the power conferred by subsection (2)(b) above, the records relate to medical treatment given at the premises in question.

(6) Any person exercising the power of entry under subsection (1) above shall, if so required, produce some duly authenticated documented showing his authority to do so.

(7) Any person who intentionally obstructs another in the exercise of that power shall be guilty of an offence and liable on summary conviction to a fine not exceeding **level 3** on the standard scale.

(8) In this section "local authority" and "community care services" have the same meanings as in section 46 above.

[National Health Service and Community Care Act 1990, s 48 as amended by the Care Standards Act 2000, s 116 and SI 2010/813]

# Social Security Contributions and Benefits Act 1992[1]

(1992 c 4)

7.10774 Part I (ss 1–19A) provides for contributions by earners, employers and others to funds for paying social security benefits and payments towards the National Health Service. There are six classes of contributions—

(*a*) Class 1, earnings-related, being—

(i) primary Class 1 contributions from employed earners; and
(ii) secondary Class 1 contributions from employers and other persons paying earnings;

(*b*) Class 1A, payable in respect of cars made available for private use and car fuel by persons liable to pay secondary Class 1 contributions and certain other persons;

(*bb*) Class 1B, payable under section 10A by persons who are accountable to the Inland Revenue in respect of income tax on emoluments in accordance with PAYE settlement agreement;

(*c*) Class 2, flat-rate, payable weekly by self-employed earners;

(*d*) Class 3, payable by earners and others voluntarily with a view to providing entitlement to benefit, or making up entitlement; and

(*e*) Class 4, payable in respect of the profits or gains of a trade, profession or vocation, in respect of equivalent earnings.

**7.10775** The Act defines limits and liability. Part II (ss 20–62) describes contributory benefits, being unemployment benefit, incapacity benefit maternity allowance, benefits for widows and widowers, retirement pensions, and child's special allowance.

**7.10776** Part III (ss 63–79) describes non-contributory benefits, being attendance allowance, severe disablement allowance, invalid care allowance, disability living allowance, guardians allowance, and benefits for the aged.

**7.10777** Part IV (ss 80–93) provides for benefit increases for child and adult dependants.

**7.10778** Part V (ss 94–111) provides for benefit for industrial injuries.

**7.10779** Part VII (ss 123–137) sets out income-related benefits, being income support, working families' tax credit, disabled person's tax credit, housing benefit, and community charge benefits.

**7.10780** Part VIII (ss 138–140) governs the operation of the social fund.

**7.10781** Part IX (ss 141–147) is concerned with child benefit, Part X (ss 148–150) with the Christmas bonus for pensioners, Part XI (ss 151–163) with statutory sick pay, and Part XII (ss 164–171) with statutory maternity pay.

S 175 enables the making of subordinate legislation under the Act.

[1] This Act is part of a consolidation measure: the other two Acts are the Social Security Administration Act 1992 (post) and the Social Security (Consequential Provisions) Act 1992 (s 6) which provides for continuity of the law, repeals, and transitional, provision and savings.

## Social Security Administration Act 1992

(1992 c 5)

### Part III[1]

### Overpayments and Adjustments of Benefit[2]

**7.10782** 78. **Recovery of social fund awards** (1)–(5) *Recovery.*

(6) For the purposes of this section[3]—

(*a*) a man shall be liable to maintain his wife or civil partner and any children of whom he is the father;

(*b*) a woman shall be liable to maintain her husband or civil partner and any children of whom she is the mother;

(*c*) a person shall be liable to maintain another person throughout any period in respect of which the first-mentioned person has, on or after 23rd May 1980 (the date of the passing of the Social Security Act 1980) and either alone or jointly with a further person, given an undertaking in writing in pursuance of immigration rules within the meaning of the Immigration Act 1971 to be responsible for the maintenance and accommodation of the other person; and

(*d*) "child" includes a person who has attained the age of 16 but not the age of 19 and in respect of whom either parent, or some person acting in the place of either parent, is receiving universal credit, income support or an income-based jobseeker's allowance.

(7) Any reference in subsection (6) above to children of whom the man or the woman is the father or the mother shall be construed in accordance with section 1 of the Family Law Reform Act 1987.

(8) Subsection (7) above does not apply in Scotland, and in the application of subsection (6) above to Scotland any reference to children of whom the man or the woman is the father or the mother shall be construed as a reference to any such children whether or not their parents have ever been married to one another.

(9) A document bearing a certificate which—

(*a*) is signed by a person authorised in that behalf by the Secretary of State; and (*b*) states that the document apart from the certificate is, or is a copy of, such an undertaking as is mentioned in subsection (6)(*c*) above,

shall be conclusive of the undertaking in question for the purposes of this section; and a certificate purporting to be so signed shall be deemed to be so signed until the contrary is proved.*

[Social Security Administration Act 1992, s 78 as amended by the Jobseekers Act 1995, s 32 and Sch 2, the Civil Partnership Act 2004, Sch 24 and the Welfare Reform Act 2012, Sch 2.]

* **Amended by the Welfare Reform Act 2009, Sch 7 from a date to be appointed. Sub-ss (6)–(9) repealed by the Welfare Reform Act 2012, Sch 14 from a date to be appointed.**

1 Part III contains ss 71–80.

2 Overpayment will usually be recovered by deduction from benefit, but other methods may sometimes be used. As to the Secretary of State's deduction power not surviving the making either of a Debt Relief Order under Pt VIIA of the Insolvency Act 1986 or of a bankruptcy order, see *Payne v Secretary of State for Work and Pensions* [2011] UKSC 60, [2012] 2 AC 1, [2012] 2 All ER 46.

3 Section 78(6)–(9) has effect for the purposes of Pt V, post, as well; see s 105, post.

## PART V[1]

## INCOME SUPPORT AND THE DUTY TO MAINTAIN

7.10783 **105. Failure to maintain—general** (1) If—

(*a*) any person persistently refuses or neglects to maintain himself or any person whom he is liable to maintain; and

(*b*) in consequence of his refusal or neglect universal credit, income support, an income-based jobseeker's allowance or an income-related employment and support allowance is paid to or in respect of him or such a person,

he shall be guilty of an offence and liable on summary conviction[2] to imprisonment for a term not exceeding **3 months** or** to a fine of an amount not exceeding **level 4** on the standard scale or to both.**

(2) For the purposes of subsection (1) above a person shall not be taken to refuse or neglect to maintain himself or any other person by reason only of anything done or omitted in furtherance of a trade dispute.

(3) Subject to subsection (4), for the purposes of this Part, a person shall be liable to maintain another person if that other person is—

(*a*) his or her spouse or civil partner, or

(*b*) a person whom he or she would be liable to maintain if sections 78(6)(*c*) and (9) had effect for the purposes of this Part.

(4) For the purposes of this section, in its application to an income-based jobseekers' allowance or an income-related employment and support allowance, subsection (3)(*b*) shall not apply.*

[Social Security Administration Act 1992, s 105 as amended by the Jobseekers Act 1995, Sch 2 and the Civil Partnership Act 2004, Sch 24, the Welfare Reform Act 2007, Sch 3, the Child Maintenance and Other Payments Act 2008, s 45 and the Welfare Reform Act 2012, Sch 2.]

* **Section amended by the Welfare Reform Act 2009, Sch 7 and the Welfare Reform Act 2012, Schs 7, 14 from a date to be appointed.**

** **Words repealed by the Criminal Justice Act 2003, Sch 37 from a date to be appointed.**

1 Part V contains ss 105–109.

2 For legal proceedings see s 116, post.

7.10784 **106. Recovery of expenditure on benefit from person liable for maintenance** (1) Subject to the following provisions of this section, if income support or is claimed by or in respect of a person whom another person is liable to maintain or paid to or in respect of such a person, the Secretary of State may make against the liable person to for an order under this section.

(1) Subject to the following provisions of this section, if income support or universal credit is claimed by or in respect of a person whom another person is liable to maintain[1] or paid to or in respect of such a person, the Secretary of State may make an application against the liable person to the family court for an order under this section.

(2) On the hearing of an application under this section the court shall have regard to all the circumstances[2] and, in particular, to the income of the liable person, and may order him to pay such sum, weekly or otherwise, as it may consider appropriate[3], except that in a case falling within section 78(6)(*c*) above that sum shall not include any amount which is not attributable to income support or universal credit (whether paid before or after the making of the order).

(3) In determining whether to order any payments to be made in respect of income support or universal credit for any period before the application was made, or the amount of any such payments, the court shall disregard any amount by which the liable person's income exceeds the income which was his during that period.

(4) Any payments ordered to be made under this section shall be made—

(*a*) to the Secretary of State in so far as they are attributable to any income support or universal credit (whether paid before or after the making of the order);

(*b*) to the person claiming income support or universal credit or (if different) the dependant; or

(*c*) to such other person as appears to the court expedient in the interests of the dependant.

(5) *Repealed.*

(6) *Scotland.*

(7) *Repealed.**

[Social Security Administration Act 1992, s 106 as amended by the Child Maintenance and Other Payments Act 2008, Sch 8, the Welfare Reform Act 2012, Sch 2 and the Crime and Courts Act 2013, Sch 11.]

* **Section repealed by the Welfare Reform Act 2009, Sch 7 from a date to be appointed and amended by the Welfare Reform Act 2012, Sch 14 from a date to be appointed.**

1 See ss 78 and 105(3), ante.

2 See also notes to s 43 of the National Assistance Act 1948, ante, and *Windas v Bell* (1981) 2 FLR 109 (conduct of parents and delay in bringing proceedings are relevant).

3 For costs, see the Magistrates' Courts Act 1980, s 64 in PART I: MAGISTRATES' COURTS, PROCEDURE, ante. A divorce consent order for no maintenance will not prevent an order under this section (*Hulley v Thompson* [1981] 1 All ER 1128, [1981] 1 WLR 159).

7.10785 **108. Reduction of expenditure on income support: certain maintenance orders to be enforceable by the Secretary of State** (1) This section applies where—

(*a*) a person ("the claimant") who is the parent of one or more children is in receipt of universal credit or income support either in respect of those children or in respect of both himself and those children; and

(*b*) there is in force a maintenance order made against the other parent ("the liable person")—

(i) in favour of the claimant or one or more of the children, or

(ii) in favour of some other person for the benefit of the claimant or one or more of the children;

and in this section "the primary recipient" means the person in whose favour that maintenance order was made.

(2) If, in a case where this section applies, the liable person fails to comply with any of the terms of the maintenance order—

(*a*) the Secretary of State may bring any proceedings or take any other steps to enforce the order that could have been brought or taken by or on behalf of the primary recipient; and

(*b*) any court before which proceedings are brought by the Secretary of State by virtue of paragraph (*a*) above shall have the same powers in connection with those proceedings as it would have had if they had been brought by the primary recipient.

(3) The Secretary of State's powers under this section are exercisable at his discretion and whether or not the primary recipient or any other person consents to their exercise; but any sums recovered by virtue of this section shall be payable to or for the primary recipient, as if the proceedings or steps in question had been brought or taken by him or on his behalf.

(4) The powers conferred on the Secretary of State by subsection (2)(*a*) above include power—

(*a*) to apply for the registration of the maintenance order under—

(i) section 17 of the Maintenance Orders Act 1950;

(ii) section 2 of the Maintenance Orders Act 1958; or

(iii) the Civil Jurisdiction and Judgments Act 1982;

(iv) *repealed*

(*aa*) to apply for recognition and enforcement of the maintenance order under the Maintenance Regulation, to the extent permitted by Article 4 of that Regulation;

(*ab*) to apply for recognition and enforcement of the maintenance order under the Convention on the International Recovery of Child Support and other forms of Family Maintenance done at The Hague on 23rd November 2007, to the extent permitted by Article 36 of that Convention; and

(*b*) to make an application under section 2 of the Maintenance Orders (Reciprocal Enforcement) Act 1972 (application for enforcement in reciprocating country).

(5) Where this section applies, the prescribed person shall in prescribed circumstances give the Secretary of State notice of any application—

(*a*) to alter, vary, suspend, discharge, revoke, revive or enforce the maintenance order in question; or

(*b*) to remit arrears under that maintenance order;

and the Secretary of State shall be entitled to appear and be heard on the application.

(6) Where, by virtue of this section, the Secretary of State commences any proceedings to enforce a maintenance order, he shall, in relation to those proceedings, be treated for the purposes of any enactment or instrument relating to maintenance orders as if he were a person entitled to payment under the maintenance order in question (but shall not thereby become entitled to any such payment).

(7) *Duty to notify Lord Chancellor.*

(8) In this section "maintenance order"—

(*a*) in England and Wales, means—

(i) any order for the making of periodical payments which is, or has at any time been, a maintenance order within the meaning of the Attachment of Earnings Act 1971;

(ii) any order under Part 3 of the Matrimonial and Family Proceedings Act 1984 (overseas divorce) for the making of periodical payments;

(iii) any order under Schedule 7 to the Civil Partnership Act 2004 for the making of periodical payments;

(*b*) *Scotland.**

(9) In this section "the Maintenance Regulation" means Council Regulation (EC) No 4/2009 including as applied in relation to Denmark by virtue of the Agreement made on 19th December 2005 between the European Community and the Kingdom of Denmark.

[Social Security Administration Act 1992, s 108 as amended by the Access to Justice Act 1999, Sch 4, SI 2001/3929, SI 2007/1655, the Child Maintenance and Other Payments Act 2008, Sch 7, SI 2011/1484, SI 2012/2814 and the Welfare Reform Act 2012, Sch 2.]

* **Section repealed by the Welfare Reform Act 2009, Sch 7 from a date to be appointed and amended by the Welfare Reform Act 2012, Sch 14 from a date to be appointed.**

## PART VI

## ENFORCEMENT[1]

7.10786 **109A. Authorisations for investigators** (1) An individual who for the time being has the Secretary of State's authorisation for the purposes of this Part shall be entitled, for any one or more of the purposes mentioned in subsection (2) below, to exercise any of the powers which are conferred on an authorised officer by sections 109B and 109C below.

(2) Those purposes are—

(*a*) ascertaining in relation to any case whether a benefit is or was payable in that case in accordance with any provision of the relevant social security legislation;

(*b*) investigating the circumstances in which any accident, injury or disease which has given rise, or may give rise, to a claim for—

(i) industrial injuries benefit, or

(ii) any benefit under any provision of the relevant social security legislation,

occurred or may have occurred, or was or may have been received or contracted;

(*c*) ascertaining whether provisions of the relevant social security legislation are being, have been or are likely to be contravened (whether by particular persons or more generally);

(*d*) preventing, detecting and securing evidence of the commission (whether by particular persons or more generally) of benefit offences.

(3) An individual has the Secretary of State's authorisation for the purposes of this Part if, and only if, the Secretary of State has granted him an authorisation for those purposes and he is—

(*a*) an official of a Government department;

(*b*) an individual employed by an authority administering housing benefit or council tax benefit;

(*c*) an individual employed by an authority or joint committee that carries out functions relating to housing benefit or council tax benefit on behalf of the authority administering that benefit; or

(*d*) an individual employed by a person authorised by or on behalf of any such authority or joint committee as is mentioned in paragraph (*b*) or (*c*) above to carry out functions relating to housing benefit or council tax benefit for that authority or committee.

(4) An authorisation granted for the purposes of this Part to an individual of any of the descriptions mentioned in subsection (3) above—

(*a*) must be contained in a certificate provided to that individual as evidence of his entitlement to exercise powers conferred by this Part;

(*b*) may contain provision as to the period for which the authorisation is to have effect; and

(*c*) may restrict the powers exercisable by virtue of the authorisation so as to prohibit their exercise except for particular purposes, in particular circumstances or in relation to particular benefits or particular provisions of the relevant social security legislation.

(5) An authorisation granted under this section may be withdrawn at any time by the Secretary of State.

(6) Where the Secretary of State grants an authorisation for the purposes of this Part to an individual employed by a local authority, or to an individual employed by a person who carries out functions relating to housing benefit or council tax benefit on behalf of a local authority—

(*a*) the Secretary of State and the local authority shall enter into such arrangements (if any) as they consider appropriate with respect to the carrying out of functions conferred on that individual by or in connection with the authorisation granted to him; and

(*b*) the Secretary of State may make to the local authority such payments (if any) as he thinks fit in respect of the carrying out by that individual of any such functions.

(7) The matters on which a person may be authorised to consider and report to the Secretary of State under section 139A below shall be taken to include the carrying out by any such individual as is mentioned in subsection (3)(*b*) to (*d*) above of any functions conferred on that individual by virtue of any grant by the Secretary of State of an authorisation for the purposes of this Part.

(8) The powers conferred by sections 109B and 109C below shall be exercisable in relation to persons holding office under the Crown and persons in the service of the Crown, and in relation to premises owned or occupied by the Crown, as they are exercisable in relation to other persons and premises.

(9) This section and sections 109B to 109C below apply as if—

(*a*) the Tax Credits Act 2002 were relevant social security legislation, and (*b*) accordingly, child tax credit and working tax credit were relevant social security benefits for the purposes of the definition of "benefit offence".

[Social Security Administration Act 1992, s 109A as substituted by the Child Support, Pensions and Social Security Act 2000, Sch 6 and amended by the Welfare Reform Act 2012, s 122.]

[1] Part VI comprises ss 109A–121.

7.10787 **109B. Power to require information**[1] (1) An authorised officer who has reasonable grounds for suspecting that a person—

(*a*) is a person falling within subsection (2) or (2A) below, and

(*b*) has or may have possession of or access to any information about any matter that is relevant for any one or more of the purposes mentioned in section 109A(2) above,

may, by written notice, require that person to provide all such information described in the notice as is information of which he has possession, or to which he has access, and which it is reasonable for the authorised officer to require for a purpose so mentioned.

(2) The persons who fall within this subsection are—

(*a*) any person who is or has been an employer or employee within the meaning of any provision made by or under the Contributions and Benefits Act;

(*b*) any person who is or has been a self-employed earner within the meaning of any such provision;

(*c*) any person who by virtue of any provision made by or under that Act falls, or has fallen, to be treated for the purposes of any such provision as a person within paragraph (*a*) or (*b*) above;

(*d*) any person who is carrying on, or has carried on, any business involving the supply of goods for sale to the ultimate consumers by individuals not carrying on retail businesses from retail premises;

(*e*) any person who is carrying on, or has carried on, any business involving the supply of goods or services by the use of work done or services performed by persons other than employees of his;

(*f*) any person who is carrying on, or has carried on, an agency or other business for the introduction or supply, to persons requiring them, of persons available to do work or to perform services;

(*g*) any local authority acting in their capacity as an authority responsible for the granting of any licence;

(*h*) any person who is or has been a trustee or manager of a personal or occupational pension scheme;

(*i*) any person who is or has been liable to make a compensation payment or a payment to the Secretary of State under section 6 of the Social Security (Recovery of Benefits) Act 1997 (payments in respect of recoverable benefits);

(*ia*) a person of a prescribed[2] description;] and

(*j*) the servants and agents of any such person as is specified in any of paragraphs (*a*) to (*ia*) above.

(2A) The persons who fall within this subsection are—

(*a*) any bank;

(*aa*) the Director of National Savings;

(*b*) any person carrying on a business the whole or a significant part of which consists in the provision of credit (whether secured or unsecured) to members of the public;

(*c*) any insurer;

(*d*) any credit reference agency (within the meaning given by section 145(8) of the Consumer Credit Act 1974 (c 39));

(*e*) any body the principal activity of which is to facilitate the exchange of information for the purpose of preventing or detecting fraud;

(*f*) any person carrying on a business the whole or a significant part of which consists in the provision to members of the public of a service for transferring money from place to place;

(*g*) any water undertaker or sewerage undertaker, Scottish Water or any local authority which is to collect charges by virtue of an order under section 37 of the Water Industry (Scotland) Act 2002 (asp 3);

(*h*) any person who—

(i) is the holder of a licence under section 7 of the Gas Act 1986 (c 44) to convey gas through pipes, or

(ii) is the holder of a licence under section 7A(1) of that Act to supply gas through pipes;

(*i*) any person who (within the meaning of the Electricity Act 1989 (c 29)) distributes or supplies electricity;

(*j*) any person who provides a telecommunications service;

(*k*) any person conducting any educational establishment or institution;

(*l*) any body the principal activity of which is to provide services in connection with admissions to educational establishments or institutions;

(*m*) the Student Loans Company;

(*n*) any servant or agent of any person mentioned in any of the preceding paragraphs.

(2B) Subject to the following provisions of this section, the powers conferred by this section on an authorised officer to require information from any person by virtue of his falling within subsection (2A) above shall be exercisable for the purpose only of obtaining information relating to a particular person identified (by name or description) by the officer.

(2C) An authorised officer shall not, in exercise of those powers, require any information from any person by virtue of his falling within subsection (2A) above unless it appears to that officer that there are reasonable grounds for believing that the identified person to whom it relates is—

(*a*) a person who has committed, is committing or intends to commit a benefit offence; or

(*b*) a person who (within the meaning of Part 7 of the Contributions and Benefits Act) is a member of the family of a person falling within paragraph (*a*) above.

(2D) Nothing in subsection (2B) or (2C) above shall prevent an authorised officer who is an official of a Government department and whose authorisation states that his authorisation applies for the purposes of this subsection from exercising the powers conferred by this section for obtaining from—

(*a*) a water undertaker or Scottish Water,

(*b*) any person who (within the meaning of the Gas Act 1986) supplies gas conveyed through pipes,

(*c*) any person who (within the meaning of the Electricity Act 1989) supplies electricity conveyed by distribution systems, or

(*d*) any servant or agent of a person mentioned in any of the preceding paragraphs,

any information which relates exclusively to whether and in what quantities water, gas or electricity are being or have been supplied to residential premises specified or described in the notice by which the information is required.

(2E) The powers conferred by this section shall not be exercisable for obtaining from any person providing a telecommunications service any information other than information which (within the meaning of section 21 of the Regulation of Investigatory Powers Act 2000 (c 23)) is communications data but not traffic data.

(2F) Nothing in subsection (2B) or (2C) above shall prevent an authorised officer from exercising the powers conferred by this section for requiring information, from a person who provides a telecommunications service, about the identity and postal address of a person identified by the authorised officer solely by reference to a telephone number or electronic address used in connection with the provision of such a service.

(3) The obligation of a person to provide information in accordance with a notice under this section shall be discharged only by the provision of that information, at such reasonable time and in such form as may be specified in the notice, to the authorised officer who—

(*a*) is identified by or in accordance with the terms of the notice; or

(*b*) has been identified, since the giving of the notice, by a further written notice given by the authorised officer who imposed the original requirement or another authorised officer.

(4) The power of an authorised officer under this section to require the provision of information shall include a power to require the production and delivery up and (if necessary) creation of, or of copies of or extracts from, any such documents containing the information as may be specified or described in the notice imposing the requirement.

(5) No one shall be required under this section to provide—

(*a*) any information that tends to incriminate either himself or, in the case of a person who is married or is a civil partner, his spouse or civil partner; or

(*b*) any information in respect of which a claim to legal professional privilege or, in Scotland, confidentiality as between client and professional legal adviser, would be successful in any proceedings;

and for the purposes of this subsection it is immaterial whether the information is in documentary form or not.

(6) Provision may be made by order—

(*a*) adding any person to the list of persons falling within subsection (2A) above;

(*b*) removing any person from the list of persons falling within that subsection;

(*c*) modifying that subsection for the purpose of taking account of any change to the name of any person for the time being falling within that subsection.

(7) In this section—

"bank" means—

(*a*) a person who has permission under Part IV of the Financial Services and Markets Act 2000 (c 8) to accept deposits;

(*b*) an EEA firm of the kind mentioned in paragraph 5(*b*) of Schedule 3 to that Act which has permission under paragraph 15 of that Schedule (as a result of qualifying for authorisation under paragraph 12 of that Schedule) to accept deposits or other repayable funds from the public; or

(c) a person who does not require permission under that Act to accept deposits, in the course of his business in the United Kingdom;

"credit" includes a cash loan or any form of financial accommodation, including the cashing of a cheque;

"insurer" means—

(a) a person who has permission under Part IV of the Financial Services and Markets Act 2000 to effect or carry out contracts of insurance; or

(b) an EEA firm of the kind mentioned in paragraph 5(*d*) of Schedule 3 to that Act, which has permission under paragraph 15 of that Schedule (as a result of qualifying for authorisation under paragraph 12 of that Schedule) to effect or carry out contracts of insurance;

"residential premises", in relation to a supply of water, gas or electricity, means any premises which—

(a) at the time of the supply were premises occupied wholly or partly for residential purposes, or

(b) are premises to which that supply was provided as if they were so occupied; and

"telecommunications service" has the same meaning as in the Regulation of Investigatory Powers Act 2000 (c 23).

(7A) The definitions of "bank" and "insurer" in subsection (7) must be read with—

(a) section 22 of the Financial Services and Markets Act 2000;

(b) any relevant order under that section; and

(c) Schedule 2 to that Act.*

[Social Security Administration Act 1992, s 109B as inserted by the Child Support, Pensions and Social Security Act 2000, Sch 6 and amended by the Social Security Fraud Act 2001, s 1, SI 2004/1822, the Civil Partnership Act 2004, Sch 2 and the Welfare Reform Act 2012, s 110.]

* **Amended by the Investigatory Powers Act 2016, Sch 2 from a date to be appointed.**

1 The Secretary of State is required by s 3 of the Social Security Fraud Act 2001 to issue a Code of Practice relating to the exercise of the powers that are exercisable by an authorized officer under this section in relation to the persons mentioned in sub-s (2A) and the powers conferred on an authorized officer by ss 109BA and 110AA.

2 See the Social Security (Persons Required to Provide Information) Regulations 2013, SI 2013/1510.

**7.10788 109BA. Power of Secretary of State to require electronic access to information**[1]

(1) Subject to subsection (2) below, where it appears to the Secretary of State—

(a) that a person falling within section 109B(2A) keeps any electronic records,

(b) that the records contain or are likely, from time to time, to contain information about any matter that is relevant for any one or more of the purposes mentioned in section 109A(2) above, and

(c) that facilities exist under which electronic access to those records is being provided, or is capable of being provided, by that person to other persons,

the Secretary of State may require that person to enter into arrangements under which authorised officers are allowed such access to those records.

(2) An authorised officer—

(a) shall be entitled to obtain information in accordance with arrangements entered into under subsection (1) above only if his authorisation states that his authorisation applies for the purposes of that subsection; and

(b) shall not seek to obtain any information in accordance with any such arrangements other than information which relates to a particular person and could be the subject of a requirement under section 109B above.

(3) The matters that may be included in the arrangements that a person is required to enter into under subsection (1) above may include—

(a) requirements as to the electronic access to records that is to be made available to authorised officers;

(b) requirements as to the keeping of records of the use that is made of the arrangements;

(c) requirements restricting the disclosure of information about the use that is made of the arrangements; and

(d) such other incidental requirements as the Secretary of State considers appropriate in connection with allowing access to records to authorised officers.

(4) An authorised officer who is allowed access in accordance with any arrangements entered into under subsection (1) above shall be entitled to make copies of, and to take extracts from, any records containing information which he is entitled to require under section 109B.

[Social Security Administration Act 1992, s 109BA as inserted by the Social Security Fraud Act 2001, Sch.]

1 See note to s 109B ante.

**7.10789 109C. Powers of entry** (1) An authorised officer shall be entitled, at any reasonable time and either alone or accompanied by such other persons as he thinks fit, to enter any premises which—

(a) are liable to inspection under this section; and

(b) are premises to which it is reasonable for him to require entry in order to exercise the powers conferred by this section.

(2) An authorised officer who has entered any premises liable to inspection under this section may—

(*a*) make such an examination of those premises, and

(*b*) conduct any such inquiry there,

as appears to him appropriate for any one or more of the purposes mentioned in section 109A(2) above.

(3) An authorised officer who has entered any premises liable to inspection under this section may—

(*a*) question any person whom he finds there;

(*b*) require any person whom he finds there to do any one or more of the following—

(i) to provide him with such information,

(ii) to produce and deliver up and (if necessary) create such documents or such copies of, or extracts from, documents,

as he may reasonably require for any one or more of the purposes mentioned in section 109A(2) above; and

(*c*) take possession of and either remove or make his own copies of any such documents as appear to him to contain information that is relevant for any of those purposes.

(4) The premises liable to inspection under this section are any premises (including premises consisting in the whole or a part of a dwelling house) which an authorised officer has reasonable grounds for suspecting are—

(*a*) premises which are a person's place of employment;

(*b*) premises from which a trade or business is being carried on or where documents relating to a trade or business are kept by the person carrying it on or by another person on his behalf;

(*c*) premises from which a personal or occupational pension scheme is being administered or where documents relating to the administration of such a scheme are kept by the person administering the scheme or by another person on his behalf;

(*d*) premises where a person who is the compensator in relation to any such accident, injury or disease as is referred to in section 109A(2)(*b*) above is to be found;

(*e*) premises where a person on whose behalf any such compensator has made, may have made or may make a compensation payment is to be found.

(5) An authorised officer applying for admission to any premises in accordance with this section shall, if required to do so, produce the certificate containing his authorisation for the purposes of this Part.

(6) Subsection (5) of section 109B applies for the purposes of this section as it applies for the purposes of that section.*

[Social Security Administration Act 1992, s 109C as inserted by the Child Support, Pensions and Social Security Act 2000, Sch 6.]

* **Amended by the Investigatory Powers Act 2016, Sch 2 from a date to be appointed.**

**7.10790 110ZA. Class 1, 1A, 1B or 2 contributions: powers to call for documents etc**

(1) Schedule 36 to the Finance Act 2008 (information and inspection powers) applies for the purpose of checking a person's position as regards relevant contributions as it applies for the purpose of checking a person's tax position, subject to the modifications in subsection (2).

(2) That Schedule applies as if—

(*a*) references to any provision of the Taxes Acts were to any provision of this Act or the Contributions and Benefits Act relating to relevant contributions,

(*b*) references to prejudice to the assessment or collection of tax were to prejudice to the assessment of liability for, and payment of, relevant contributions,

(*c*) the reference to information relating to the conduct of a pending appeal relating to tax were a reference to information relating to the conduct of a pending appeal relating to relevant contributions, and

(*d*) paragraphs 21, 21A, 35(4A)(*c*), 36, 37(2) and (2A), 37A and 37B of that Schedule (restrictions on giving taxpayer notice where taxpayer has made tax return) were omitted.

(3) In this section "relevant contributions" means Class 1, Class 1A, Class 1B or Class 2 contributions.

[Social Security Administration Act 1992, s 110ZA as inserted by the Social Security Contributions (Transfer of Functions, etc) Act 1999, Sch 5, substituted by the National Insurance Contributions and Statutory Payments Act 2004, s 7 and amended by the Finance Act 2008, Sch 36, SI 2009/2035 and SI 2009/3054.]

**7.10791 110A. Authorisations by local authorities** (1) An individual who for the time being has the authorisation for the purposes of this Part of an authority administering housing benefit or council tax benefit ("a local authority authorisation") shall be entitled, for a relevant purpose, to exercise any of the powers which, subject to subsection (8) below, are conferred on an authorised officer by sections 109B and 109C above.

(1A) Each of the following is a relevant purpose—

(*a*) a purpose mentioned in subsection (2) below;

(*b*) a purpose mentioned in section 109A(2)(*a*), (*c*) or (*d*).

(1B) If the Secretary of State prescribes conditions for the purposes of this section, an authority must not proceed under this section for a purpose mentioned in section 109A(2)(*a*), (*c*) or (*d*) unless any such condition is satisfied.

(1C) An authorisation made for a purpose mentioned in section 109A(2)(*a*), (*c*) or (*d*)—

(*a*) is subject to such restrictions as may be prescribed;

(b) is not valid in such circumstances as may be prescribed.

(2) The purposes in this subsection are—

(*a*) ascertaining in relation to any case whether housing benefit or council tax benefit is or was payable in that case;

(*b*) ascertaining whether provisions of the relevant social security legislation that relate to housing benefit or council tax benefit are being, have been or are likely to be contravened (whether by particular persons or more generally);

(*c*) preventing, detecting and securing evidence of the commission (whether by particular persons or more generally) of benefit offences relating to housing benefit or council tax benefit.

(3) An individual has the authorisation for the purposes of this Part of an authority administering housing benefit or council tax benefit if, and only if, that authority have granted him an authorisation for those purposes and he is—

(*a*) an individual employed by that authority;

(*b*) an individual employed by another authority or joint committee that carries out functions relating to housing benefit or council tax benefit on behalf of that authority;

(*c*) an individual employed by a person authorised by or on behalf of—

(i) the authority in question,

(ii) any such authority or joint committee as is mentioned in paragraph (*b*) above,

to carry out functions relating to housing benefit or council tax benefit for that authority or committee;

(*d*) an official of a Government department.

(4) Subsection (4) of section 109A above shall apply in relation to a local authority authorisation as it applies in relation to an authorisation under that section.

(5) A local authority authorisation may be withdrawn at any time by the authority that granted it or by the Secretary of State.

(6) The certificate or other instrument containing the grant or withdrawal by any local authority of any local authority authorisation must be issued under the hand of either—

(*a*) the officer designated under section 4 of the Local Government and Housing Act 1989 as the head of the authority's paid service; or

(*b*) the officer who is the authority's chief finance officer (within the meaning of section 5 of that Act).

(7) It shall be the duty of any authority with power to grant local authority authorisations to comply with any directions of the Secretary of State as to—

(*a*) whether or not such authorisations are to be granted by that authority;

(*b*) the period for which authorisations granted by that authority are to have effect;

(*c*) the number of persons who may be granted authorisations by that authority at any one time; and

(*d*) the restrictions to be contained by virtue of subsection (4) above in the authorisations granted by that authority for those purposes.

(8) The powers conferred by sections 109B and 109C above shall have effect in the case of an individual who is an authorised officer by virtue of this section as if those sections had effect—

(*a*) with the substitution for every reference to the purposes mentioned in section 109A(2) above of a reference to the purposes mentioned in subsection (2) above;

(*b*) with the substitution for every reference to the relevant social security legislation of a reference to so much of it as relates to housing benefit or council tax benefit; and

(*c*) with the omission of section 109B(2D)

but paragraphs (*a*) and (*b*) above do not apply in any case where the relevant purpose is as mentioned in subsection (1A)(*b*) above.

(9) Nothing in this section conferring any power on an authorised officer in relation to housing benefit or council tax benefit shall require that power to be exercised only in relation to cases in which the authority administering the benefit is the authority by whom that officer's authorisation was granted.

[Social Security Administration Act 1992, s 110A as inserted by the Child Support, Pensions and Social Security Act 2000, Sch 6 and amended by the Social Security Fraud Act 2001, s 1 and the Welfare Reform Act 2007, s 46.]

**7.10792 110AA. Power of local authority to require electronic access to information[1]**

(1) Subject to subsection (2) below, where it appears to an authority administering housing benefit or council tax benefit—

(*a*) that a person falling within section 109B(2A) keeps any electronic records,

(*b*) that the records contain or are likely, from time to time, to contain information about any matter that is relevant for any one or more of the purposes mentioned in section 110A(2) above, and (*c*) that facilities exist under which electronic access to those records is being provided, or is capable of being provided, by that person to other persons,

that authority may require that person to enter into arrangements under which authorised officers are allowed such access to those records.

(2) An authorised officer—

(*a*) shall be entitled to obtain information in accordance with arrangements entered into under subsection (1) above only if his authorisation states that his authorisation applies for the purposes of that subsection; and

(*b*) shall not seek to obtain any information in accordance with any such arrangements other than information which—

(i) relates to a particular person; and

(ii) could be the subject of any such requirement under section 109B above as may be imposed in exercise of the powers conferred by section 110A(8) above.

(3) The matters that may be included in the arrangements that a person is required to enter into under subsection (1) above may include—

(*a*) requirements as to the electronic access to records that is to be made available to authorised officers;

(*b*) requirements as to the keeping of records of the use that is made of the arrangements;

(*c*) requirements restricting the disclosure of information about the use that is made of the arrangements; and

(*d*) such other incidental requirements as the authority in question considers appropriate in connection with allowing access to records to authorised officers.

(4) An authorised officer who is allowed access in accordance with any arrangements entered into under subsection (1) above shall be entitled to make copies of, and to take extracts from, any records containing information which he is entitled to make the subject of a requirement such as is mentioned in subsection (2)(*b*) above.

(5) An authority administering housing benefit or council tax benefit shall not—

(*a*) require any person to enter into arrangements for allowing authorised officers to have electronic access to any records; or

(*b*) otherwise than in pursuance of a requirement under this section, enter into any arrangements with a person specified in section 109B(2A) above for allowing anyone acting on behalf of the authority for purposes connected with any benefit to have electronic access to any private information contained in any records,

except with the consent of the Secretary of State and subject to any conditions imposed by the Secretary of State by the provisions of the consent.

(6) A consent for the purposes of subsection (5) may be given in relation to a particular case, or in relation to any case that falls within a particular description of cases.

(7) In this section "private information", in relation to an authority administering housing benefit or council tax benefit, means any information held by a person who is not entitled to disclose it to that authority except in compliance with a requirement imposed by the authority in exercise of their statutory powers.

[Social Security Administration Act 1992, s 110AA as inserted by the Social Security Fraud Act 2001, s 2.]

7.10793 **111. Delay, obstruction etc of inspector** (1) If a person—

(*a*) intentionally delays or obstructs an authorised officer in the exercise of any power under this Act other than an Inland Revenue power; or

(*ab*) refuses or neglects to comply with any requirement under section 109BA or 110AA or with the requirements of any arrangements entered into in accordance with subsection (1) of that section, or

(*b*) refuses or neglects to answer any question or to furnish any information or to produce any document when required to do so under this Act otherwise than in the exercise of an Inland Revenue power,

he shall be guilty of an offence and liable on summary conviction to a fine not exceeding **level 3** on the standard scale.

(2) Where a person is convicted of an offence under subsection (1)(*ab*) or (*b*) above and the refusal or neglect is continued by him after his conviction, he shall be guilty of a further offence and liable on summary conviction to a fine not exceeding £40 for each day on which it is continued.

(3) In subsection (1) "Inland Revenue power" means any power conferred on an officer of the Inland Revenue by virtue of section 110ZA above or by virtue of an authorisation granted under section 109A or 110A above.

(4) *Repealed.*

[Social Security Administration Act 1992, s 111 as amended by Social Security Contributions (Transfer of Functions, etc) Act 1999, Sch 5 and the Child Support, Pensions and Social Security Act 2000, Sch 6 and the Social Security Fraud Act 2001, s 1 and the National Insurance Contributions and Statutory Payments Act 2004, Sch 1.]

7.10794 **111A. Dishonest representations for obtaining benefit etc**[1] (1) If a person dishonestly—

(*a*) makes a false statement or representation or;

(*b*) produces or furnishes, or causes or allows to be produced or furnished, any document or information which is false in a material particular;

(*c*) *repealed*;
(*d*) *repealed*,

with a view to obtaining any benefit or other payment or advantage under the relevant social security legislation (whether for himself or for some other person), he shall be guilty of an offence.

(1A) A person shall be guilty of an offence if—

(*a*) there has been a change of circumstances affecting[1] any entitlement of his to any benefit or other payment or advantage under any provision of the relevant social security legislation;
(*b*) the change is not a change that is excluded by regulations from the changes that are required to be notified;
(*c*) he knows that the change affects an entitlement of his to such a benefit or other payment or advantage; and
(*d*) he dishonestly fails to give a prompt notification of that change in the prescribed[2] manner to the prescribed[2] person.

(1B) A person shall be guilty of an offence if—

(*a*) there has been a change of circumstances affecting any entitlement of another person to any benefit or other payment or advantage under any provision of the relevant social security legislation;
(*b*) the change is not a change that is excluded by regulations from the changes that are required to be notified;
(*c*) he knows that the change affects an entitlement of that other person to such a benefit or other payment or advantage; and
(*d*) he dishonestly causes or allows[2] that other person to fail to give a prompt notification of that change in the prescribed[3] manner to the prescribed[2] person.

(1C) This subsection applies where—

(*a*) there has been a change of circumstances affecting any entitlement of a person ("the claimant") to any benefit or other payment or advantage under any provision of the relevant social security legislation;
(*b*) the benefit, payment or advantage is one in respect of which there is another person ("the recipient") who for the time being has a right to receive payments to which the claimant has, or (but for the arrangements under which they are payable to the recipient) would have, an entitlement; and
(*c*) the change is not a change that is excluded by regulations from the changes that are required to be notified.

(1D) In a case where subsection (1C) above applies, the recipient is guilty of an offence if—

(*a*) he knows that the change affects an entitlement of the claimant to a benefit or other payment or advantage under a provision of the relevant social security legislation;
(*b*) the entitlement is one in respect of which he has a right to receive payments to which the claimant has, or (but for the arrangements under which they are payable to the recipient) would have, an entitlement; and
(*c*) he dishonestly fails to give a prompt notification of that change in the prescribed[3] manner to the prescribed[2] person.

(1E) In a case where that subsection applies, a person other than the recipient is guilty of an offence if—

(*a*) he knows that the change affects an entitlement of the claimant to a benefit or other payment or advantage under a provision of the relevant social security legislation;
(*b*) the entitlement is one in respect of which the recipient has a right to receive payments to which the claimant has, or (but for the arrangements under which they are payable to the recipient) would have, an entitlement; and
(*c*) he dishonestly causes or allows the recipient to fail to give a prompt notification of that change in the prescribed[2] manner to the prescribed[3] person.

(1F) In any case where subsection (1C) above applies but the right of the recipient is confined to a right, by reason of his being a person to whom the claimant is required to make payments in respect of a dwelling, to receive payments of housing benefit—

(*a*) a person shall not be guilty of an offence under subsection (1D) or (1E) above unless the change is one relating to one or both of the following—
  (i) the claimant's occupation of that dwelling;
  (ii) the claimant's liability to make payments in respect of that dwelling;
  but
(*b*) subsections (1D)(*a*) and (1E)(*a*) above shall each have effect as if after "knows" there were inserted "or could reasonably be expected to know".

(1G) For the purposes of subsections (1A) to (1E) above a notification of a change is prompt if, and only if, it is given as soon as reasonably practicable after the change occurs.

(2) *Repealed.*

(3) A person guilty of an offence under this section shall be liable[4]—

(*a*) on summary conviction, to imprisonment for a term not exceeding **six months**, or to a fine not exceeding the **statutory maximum**, or to **both**; or
(*b*) on conviction on indictment, to imprisonment for a term not exceeding **seven years**,

or to a **fine**, or to **both**.

(4) *Scotland.*

[Social Security Administration Act 1992, s 111A as inserted by the Social Security Administration (Fraud) Act 1997, s 13, as amended by the Child Support, Pensions and Social Security Act 2000, Sch 6, the Child Support, Pensions and Social Security Act 2000, Sch 6 and the Social Security Fraud Act 2001, Schedule.]

---

[1] The change of circumstances must have made a difference to the amount of benefit which the recipient was entitled to claim: *R v Passmore* [2007] EWCA Crim 2053, [2008] 1 Cr App Rep 165, 171 JP 519. Where a defendant has more than one new source of income arising from her gaining employment eg. tax credits and child tax credits, all those sources are disclosable if at the time each would have made a difference to the computation of the defendant's entitlement to benefit. But if there had been disclosure of one source which extinguished liability, there would be no requirement to notify further sources: *London Borough of Croydon v Shanahan* [2010] EWCA Crim 98, 174 JP 172.

[2] "Allowing" means something less than "causing". An example of the situation this provision is designed to catch is where a claimant is in receipt of unemployed job seekers' allowance and has a partner in part time work and the latter's earnings increase but he does not tell the claimant. Where the claimant is as aware of the change of circumstances that needed to be reported as the defendant third party, for the defendant to be liable under this subsection there has to be some action that he could have taken that would have resulted in the claimant discharging her primary obligation to report. The subsection does not require the reporting of the claimant to the authorities, or instructing the claimant to stop as this implies some control and power of compulsion: *R v Tilley* [2009] EWCA Crim 1426, [2010] 1 WLR 605, [2009] 2 Cr App R 31, 173 JP 393.

[3] The following regulations have been made under this provision: the Social Security (Notification of Change of Circumstances) Regulations 2001, SI 2001/3252 amended by SI 2003/3209, SI 2006/832 and SI 2010/444, the Child Benefit and Guardians Allowance (Administration) Regulations 2003, SI 2003/492, the Social Security (Notification of Change of Circumstances) Regulations 2003, SI 2003/3209 and the Social Security (Notification of Changes of Circumstances) Regulations 2010, SI 2010/444, the effect of which is notice must be given to the Secretary of State at the appropriate office (a) in writing or by telephone (unless the Secretary of State determines in any particular case that notice must be in writing or may be given otherwise than in writing or by telephone); or (b) in writing if in any class of case he requires written notice (unless he determines in any particular case to accept notice given otherwise than in writing)and the Social Security (Notification of Changes of Circumstances) Regulations 2010, SI 2010/444; also (*a*) where the change of circumstances is a birth or death, through a relevant authority, or a county council in England, by personal attendance at an office specified by that authority or county council, provided the Secretary of State has agreed with that authority or county council for it to facilitate such notification; or (*b*) where the change of circumstances is a death, by telephone to a telephone number specified for that purpose by the Secretary of State.

[4] For procedure in respect of this offence which is triable either way, see the Magistrates' Courts Act 1980, ss 17A–21, in PART I: MAGISTRATES' COURTS, PROCEDURE, ante.

**7.10795** **112. False representations for obtaining benefit etc** (1) If a person for the purpose of obtaining any benefit or other payment under the relevant social security legislation whether for himself or some other person, or for any other purpose connected with that legislation—

(*a*) makes a statement or representation which he knows to be false[1]; or

(*b*) produces or furnishes, or knowingly causes or knowingly allows to be produced or furnished, any document or information which he knows to be false in a material particular,

he shall be guilty of an offence[2].

(1A) A person shall be guilty of an offence[3] if—

(*a*) there has been a change of circumstances affecting[4] any entitlement of his to any benefit or other payment or advantage under any provision of the relevant social security legislation;

(*b*) the change is not a change that is excluded by regulations from the changes that are required to be notified;

(*c*) he knows that the change affects an entitlement of his to such a benefit or other payment or advantage; and

(*d*) he fails to give a prompt notification of that change in the prescribed[5] manner to the prescribed[5] person.

(1B) A person is guilty of an offence under this section if—

(*a*) there has been a change of circumstances affecting any entitlement of another person to any benefit or other payment or advantage under any provision of the relevant social security legislation;

(*b*) the change is not a change that is excluded by regulations from the changes that are required to be notified;

(*c*) he knows that the change affects an entitlement of that other person to such a benefit or other payment or advantage; and

(*d*) he causes or allows that other person to fail to give a prompt notification of that change in the prescribed[5] manner to the prescribed[5] person.

(1C) In a case where subsection (1C) of section 111A above applies, the recipient is guilty of an offence if—

(*a*) he knows that the change affects an entitlement of the claimant to a benefit or other payment or advantage under a provision of the relevant social security legislation;

(*b*) the entitlement is one in respect of which he has a right to receive payments to which the claimant has, or (but for the arrangements under which they are payable to the recipient) would have, an entitlement; and

(*c*) he fails to give a prompt notification of that change in the prescribed[5] manner to the prescribed[5] person.

(1D) In a case where that subsection applies, a person other than the recipient is guilty of an offence if—

(*a*) he knows that the change affects an entitlement of the claimant to a benefit or other payment or advantage under a provision of the relevant social security legislation;

(*b*) the entitlement is one in respect of which the recipient has a right to receive payments to which the claimant has, or (but for the arrangements under which they are payable to the recipient) would have, an entitlement; and

(*c*) he causes or allows the recipient to fail to give a prompt notification of that change in the prescribed[5] manner to the prescribed[5] person.

(1E) Subsection (1F) of section 111A above applies in relation to subsections (1C) and (1D) above as it applies in relation to subsections (1D) and (1E) of that section.

(1F) For the purposes of subsections (1A) to (1D) above a notification of a change is prompt if, and only if, it is given as soon as reasonably practicable after the change occurs.

(2) A person guilty of an offence under this section shall be liable on summary conviction to a fine not exceeding **level 5** on the standard scale, or to imprisonment for a term not exceeding **3 months***, or to **both**.

(3) *Repealed.*

[Social Security Administration Act 1992, s 112 as amended by the Social Security Administration (Fraud) Act 1997, s 14 and Sch 1, the Child Support, Pensions and Social Security Act 2000, Sch 6 and the Social Security Fraud Act 2001, s 16(3).]

---

* **"51 weeks" substituted by the Criminal Justice Act 2003, Sch 26 from a date to be appointed.**

1 It is an offence under this section to obtain benefit by signing a postal draft on which the claimant represents he is entitled to the sum stated when he is not entitled to the whole sum even though the original award was not induced by any false statement or representation (*Tolfree v Florence* [1971] 1 All ER 125, [1971] 1 WLR 141). In cases decided under earlier legislation in similar terms it was established that the offence is committed when there is a false representation made which the person claiming benefit knows to be false; the proof of an intent to defraud is not necessary (*Barrass v Reeve* [1980] 3 All ER 705, [1981] 1 WLR 408; *Clear v Smith* [1981] 1 WLR 399). "Constructive knowledge" ie that the defendant neglected to make such inquiries as a reasonable and prudent person would make (as distinct from deliberately closing his eyes to an obvious means of knowledge) is insufficient to establish criminal liability for this offence (*Flintshire County Council v Reynolds* [2006] EWHC 195 (Admin), 170 JP 73).

2 The offence under s 112 does not require the prosecution to proved dishonesty (*Flintshire County Council v Reynolds* [2006] EWHC 195 (Admin), 170 JP 73). More serious offences may well be charged under the Theft Act 1968, s 15, post. As to sentencing, see comments in *R v Stewart* [1987] 2 All ER 383, [1987] 1 WLR 559, CA (noted in para 3.136, ante).

3 An offence under this subsection may be framed as a continuing offence. The issue of promptness is not relevant where there has been no notification at any time: *Smith v North Somerset Council* [2007] EWHC 1767 (Admin), 171 JP 509.

4 The change of circumstances must have made a difference to the amount of benefit which the recipient was entitled to claim: *R v Passmore* [2007] EWCA Crim 2053, 171 JP 519.

5 For methods of giving notice, see note to s 111A, ante.

**7.10796 113.** *Breach of Regulations.*

**7.10797 113A.** *Statutory sick pay and statutory maternity pay: breach of regulations*

**7.10798 113B.** *Statutory sick pay and statutory maternity pay: fraud and negligence*

**7.10799 114. Offences relating to contributions** (1) Any person who is knowingly concerned in the fraudulent evasion of any contributions which he or any other person is liable to pay shall be guilty of an offence.

(2) A person guilty of an offence under this section shall be liable—

(*a*) on conviction on indictment, to imprisonment for a term not exceeding seven years or to a fine or to both;

(*b*) on summary conviction, to a fine not exceeding the statutory maximum.

[Social Security Administration Act 1992, s 114 as substituted by the Social Security Act 1998, s 61.]

**7.10800 115. Offences by bodies corporate** (1) Where an offence under this Act, or under the Jobseekers Act 1995, which has been committed by a body corporate is proved to have been committed with the consent or connivance of, or to be attributable to any neglect on the part of, a director[1], manager, secretary or other similar officer of the body corporate, or any person who was purporting to act in any such capacity, he, as well as the body corporate, shall be guilty of that offence and be liable to be proceeded against accordingly.

(2) Where the affairs of a body corporate are managed by its members, subsection (1) above applies in relation to the acts and defaults of a member in connection with his functions of management as if he were a director of the body corporate.

[Social Security Administration Act 1992, s 115 as amended by the Jobseekers Act 1995, Sch 2.]

---

1 This means a director properly appointed; in the case of a limited company, in accordance with the Companies Acts. It is not sufficient merely that he acted as a director (*Dean v Hiesler* [1942] 2 All ER 340, 106 JP 282). The director or other officer is liable to the same maximum penalty as the body corporate.

**7.10801 115A.** *Penalty as alternative to prosecution.*

**7.10802 115B.** *Penalty as alternative to prosecution: colluding employers etc*

*Legal proceedings*

7.10803 **116. Legal proceedings** (1) Any person authorised by the Secretary of State[1] in that behalf may conduct any proceedings under this Act or under any provision of this Act other than section 114 or under any provision of the Jobseekers Act 1995 before a magistrates' court although not a barrister or solicitor.

(2) Notwithstanding anything in any Act—

(*a*) proceedings for an offence under this Act (other than proceedings to which paragraph (b) applies), or for an offence under the Jobseekers Act 1995, may be begun[2] at any time within the period of 3 months from the date on which evidence, sufficient in the opinion of the Secretary of State to justify a prosecution for the offence, comes to his knowledge or within a period of 12 months from the commission of the offence, whichever period last expires; and

(*b*) proceedings brought by the appropriate authority for an offence under this Act relating to housing benefit or council tax benefit may be begun at any time within the period of 3 months from the date on which evidence, sufficient in the opinion of the appropriate authority to justify a prosecution for the offence, comes to the authority's knowledge or within a period of 12 months from the commission of the offence, whichever period last expires.

(2A) Subsection (2) above shall not be taken to impose any restriction on the time when proceedings may be begun for an offence under section 111A above.

(3) For the purposes of subsection (2) above—

(*a*) a certificate purporting to be signed by or on behalf of the Secretary of State as to the date on which such evidence as is mentioned in paragraph (*a*) of that subsection came to his knowledge shall be conclusive evidence of that date; and

(*b*) a certificate of the appropriate authority as to the date on which such evidence as is mentioned in paragraph (*b*) of that subsection came to the authority's knowledge shall be conclusive evidence of that date.

(4) In subsections (2) and (3) above "the appropriate authority" means, in relation to an offence which relates to housing benefit and concerns any dwelling—

(*a*) if the offence relates to rate rebate, the authority who are the appropriate rating authority by virtue of section 134 below; and*

(*b*) if it relates to a rent rebate, the authority who are the appropriate housing authority by virtue of that subsection; and

(*c*) if it relates to rent allowance, the authority who are the appropriate local authority by virtue of that subsection.

(5) In subsections (2) and (3) above "the appropriate authority" means, in relation to an offence relating to council tax benefit, such authority as is prescribed in relation to the offence.

(5A) In relation to proceedings for an offence under section 114 above, the references in subsections (2)(*a*) and (3)(*a*) to the Secretary of State shall have effect as references to the Inland Revenue.

(6) Any proceedings in respect of any act or omission of an adjudication officer which, apart from this subsection, would fall to be brought against a person appointed by virtue of section 38(1)(*b*) above who is resident in Northern Ireland, other than proceedings for an offence, may instead be brought against the Chief Adjudication Officer; and, for the purposes of any proceedings so brought, the acts or omissions of the adjudication officer shall be treated as the acts or omissions of the Chief Adjudication Officer.*

(7) *Scotland.*

[Social Security Administration Act 1992, s 116 as amended by the Local Government Finance Act 1992, Sch 9, the Jobseekers Act 1995, Sch 2, the Housing Act 1996, Sch 16, the Social Security Administration (Fraud) Act 1997, Sch 1, the Social Security Contributions (Transfer of Functions, etc) Act 1999, Sch 1, the Welfare Reform and Pensions Act 1999, Sch 11 and the Welfare Reform Act 2012, s 111.]

---

* **Subsection (6) repealed by the Social Security Act 1998, Sch 7 as from 29 November 1999 for certain purposes (see SI 1999/3178) and from a date to be appointed for remaining purposes.**

1 The authority to conduct proceedings is proved by the production of a copy of the original, certified under the Documentary Evidence Act 1868 (in PART II: EVIDENCE, ante) which Act is applied to any documents issued by the Secretary of State: see Secretary of State for Social Services Order 1968, Art 5(3). An officer who did not lay the information may conduct the prosecution (*R v Northumberland Justices, ex p Thompson* (1923) 87 JP 95).

2 Proceedings begin when an information is laid or a complaint made (*Brooks v Bagshaw* [1904] 2 KB 798, 98 JP 514). Section 116(2) does not require the prosecution to comply with the three-month time limit for a prosecution set out in s 116(2), if they can do. A prosecution can be begun at any time within the period of three months from when the Secretary of State knows of evidence to justify a prosecution, or within 12 months from the offence itself, 'whichever period last expires'. Thus, if shortly after an offence is committed, the Secretary of State could prosecute, he has six months longer than with the more run-of-the-mill summary offence to proceed: *Bennett v Secretary of State for Work and Pensions* [2012] EWHC 371 (Admin), 176 JP 181.

7.10804 **116ZA. Local authority powers to prosecute housing benefit and council tax benefit fraud** (1) This section applies to an authority administering housing benefit or council tax benefit.

(2) The authority may not bring proceedings against a person for a benefit offence relating to either of those benefits unless—

(*a*) the authority has already started an investigation in relation to that person in respect of the offence,

(*b*) in a case where the proceedings relate to housing benefit, the authority has already started an investigation in relation to the person in respect of a benefit offence relating to council tax benefit, or has already brought proceedings against the person in respect of such an offence,

(*c*) in a case where the proceedings relate to council tax benefit, the authority has already started an investigation in relation to the person in respect of a benefit offence relating to housing benefit, or has already brought proceedings against the person in respect of such an offence,

(*d*) the proceedings arise in prescribed circumstances or are of a prescribed description, or

(*e*) the Secretary of State has directed that the authority may bring the proceedings.

(3) The Secretary of State may direct that in prescribed circumstances, an authority may not bring proceedings by virtue of subsection (2)(*a*), (*b*) or (*c*) despite the requirements in those provisions being met.

(4) A direction under subsection (2)(*e*) or (3) may relate to a particular authority or description of authority or to particular proceedings or any description of proceedings.

(5) If the Secretary of State prescribes conditions for the purposes of this section, an authority may bring proceedings in accordance with this section only if any such condition is satisfied.

(6) The Secretary of State may continue proceedings which have been brought by an authority in accordance with this section as if the proceedings had been brought in his name or he may discontinue the proceedings if—

(*a*) the proceedings were brought by virtue of subsection (2)(*a*), (*b*) or (*c*),

(*b*) he makes provision under subsection (2)(*d*) which has the effect that the authority would no longer be entitled to bring the proceedings in accordance with this section,

(*c*) he withdraws a direction under subsection (2)(*e*) in relation to the proceedings, or

(*d*) a condition prescribed under subsection (5) ceases to be satisfied in relation to the proceedings.

(7) In exercising a power to bring proceedings in accordance with this section, a local authority must have regard to the Code for Crown Prosecutors issued by the Director of Public Prosecutions under section 10 of the Prosecution of Offences Act 1985—

(*a*) in determining whether the proceedings should be instituted;

(*b*) in determining what charges should be preferred;

(*c*) in considering what representations to make to a magistrates' court about mode of trial;

(*d*) in determining whether to discontinue proceedings.

(8) Regulations shall define "an investigation in respect of a benefit offence" for the purposes of this section.

(9) This section does not apply to Scotland.

7.10805 **116A. Local authority powers to prosecute benefit fraud** (1) This section applies if an authority administering housing benefit or council tax benefit has power to bring proceedings for a benefit offence relating to that benefit.

(2) The authority may bring proceedings for a benefit offence relating to any other relevant social security benefit unless—

(*a*) the proceedings relate to any benefit or circumstances or any description of benefit or circumstances which the Secretary of State prescribes for the purposes of this paragraph, or

(*b*) the Secretary of State has directed that the authority must not bring the proceedings,

and a direction under paragraph (b) may relate to a particular authority or description of authority or to particular proceedings or any description of proceedings.

(3) If the Secretary of State prescribes conditions for the purposes of this section, an authority must not bring proceedings under this section unless any such condition is satisfied.

(4) The Secretary of State may continue proceedings which have been brought by an authority under this section as if the proceedings had been brought in his name or he may discontinue the proceedings if—

(*a*) he makes provision under subsection (2)(*a*), such that the authority would no longer be entitled to bring the proceedings under this section,

(*b*) he gives a direction under subsection (2)(*b*) in relation to the proceedings, or

(*c*) a condition prescribed under subsection (3) ceases to be satisfied in relation to the proceedings.

(5) In the exercise of its power under subsection (2), a local authority must have regard to the Code for Crown Prosecutors issued by the Director of Public Prosecutions under section 10 of the Prosecution of Offences Act 1985—

(*a*) in determining whether the proceedings should be instituted;

(*b*) in determining what charges should be preferred;

(*c*) in considering what representations to make to a magistrates' court about mode of trial;

(*d*) in determining whether to discontinue proceedings.

(6) An authority must not bring proceedings for a benefit offence which does not relate to

housing benefit or council tax benefit otherwise than in accordance with this section.

(7) In subsection (2), "relevant social security benefit" has the same meaning as in section 121DA below.

(8) This section does not apply to Scotland.

[Social Security Administration Act 1992, s 116A as inserted by the Welfare Reform Act 2007, s 47.]

7.10806 **117. Issues arising in proceedings** (1) This section applies to proceedings before a court—

(*a*) for an offence under this Act or the Jobseekers Act 1995; or

(*b*) involving any question as to the payment of contributions (other than a Class 4 contribution recoverable by the Inland Revenue); or

(*c*) for the recovery of any sums due to the Secretary of State, the Inland Revenue or the National Insurance Fund[1].

(2) A decision of the Secretary of State which—

(*a*) falls within Part II of Schedule 3 to the Social Security Act 1988 ("the 1998 Act"); and;

(*b*) relates to or affects an issue arising in the proceedings, shall be conclusive for the purposes of the proceedings.

(3) If—

(*a*) any such decision is necessary for the determination of the proceedings; and

(*b*) the decision of the Secretary of State has not been obtained or an application with respect to the decision has been made under section 9 or 10 of the 1998 Act;

the decision shall be referred to the Secretary of State to be made in accordance (subject to any necessary modification) with Chapter II of Part I of that Act.

(4) Subsection (2) above does not apply where, in relation to the decision—

(*a*) an appeal has been brought but not determined;

(*b*) an application for leave to appeal has been made but not determined;

(*c*) an appeal has not been brought (or, as the case may be, an application for leave to appeal has not been made) but the time for doing so has not yet expired; or

(*d*) an application has been made under section 9 or 10 of the 1998 Act.

(5) In a case falling within subsection (4) above the court shall adjourn the proceedings until such time as the final decision is known; and that decision shall be conclusive for the purposes of the proceedings*.

[Social Security Administration Act 1992, s 117 as amended by the Jobseekers Act 1995, Sch 2.]

---

*** A new s 117 is substituted by the Social Security Act 1998, Sch 7 from a date to be appointed. Until Chapter II of the Social Security Act 1998 is in force, s 117 has effect as if, in subsection (1) para (b) were omitted (SI 1999/978).**

1 The court has no jurisdiction to determine questions as to insurability: they must be referred to the Inland Revenue (*Wood v Burke* (1927) 91 JP 144). This decision, under repealed enactments, is still good law: see *Ministry of Social Security v John Bryant & Co Ltd* [1968] 3 All ER 175, [1968] 1 WLR 1260, and also *Department of Health and Social Security v Walker Dean Walker Ltd* [1970] 2 QB 74, [1970] 1 All ER 757, where the question of whether National Insurance contributions had in fact been made by correctly affixing National Insurance stamps to employees' cards which were then delivered, duly stamped to the Department, was to be referred for the decision of the Inland Revenue. A form that may be used for the purpose of referring the question to the Inland Revenue is contained in Oke's Magisterial Formulist.

7.10807 **117A. Issues arising in proceedings: contributions, etc** (1) This section applies to proceedings before a court—

(*a*) for an offence under this Act or the Jobseekers Act 1995; or

(*b*) involving any question as to the payment of contributions (other than a Class 4 contribution recoverable in accordance with section 15 of the Contributions and Benefits Act); or

(*c*) for the recovery of any sums due to the Inland Revenue or the National Insurance Fund.

(2) A decision of an officer of the Inland Revenue which—

(*a*) falls within section 8(1) of the Social Security Contributions (Transfer of Functions, etc) Act 1999; and

(*b*) relates to or affects an issue arising in the proceedings,

shall be conclusive for the purposes of the proceedings.

(3) If—

(*a*) any such decision is necessary for the determination of the proceedings, and

(*b*) the decision of an officer of the Inland Revenue has not been obtained under section 8 of the Social Security Contributions (Transfer of Functions, etc) Act 1999,

the decision shall be referred to such an officer to be made in accordance (subject to any necessary modifications) with Part II of the Social Security Contributions (Transfer of Functions, etc) Act 1999.

(4) Subsection (2) above does not apply where, in relation to the decision—

(*a*) an appeal has been brought but not determined;

(*b*) an appeal has not been brought (or, as the case may be, an application for leave to appeal has not been made) but the time for doing so has not yet expired; or

(*c*) an application for variation of the decision has been made under regulations made under section 10 of the Social Security Contributions (Transfer of Functions, etc) Act

1999.

(5) In a case falling within subsection (4) above the court shall adjourn the proceedings until such time as the final decision is known; and that decision shall be conclusive for the purposes of the proceedings.

[Social Security Administration Act 1992, s 117A as inserted by the Social Security Contributions (Transfer of Functions, etc) Act 1999, Sch 7.]

*Unpaid contributions etc*[1]

7.10808 **118. Evidence of non-payment** (1) *Repealed.*

(2) *Repealed.*

(3) *Repealed.*

(4) A statutory declaration by an officer of the Inland Revenue that the searches specified in the declaration for a record of the payment of a particular contribution have been made, and that a record of the payment of the contribution in question has not been found, is admissible in any proceedings for an offence as evidence of the facts stated in the declaration.

(5) Nothing in subsection (4) above makes a statutory declaration admissible as evidence in proceedings for an offence except in a case where, and to the extent to which, oral evidence to the like effect would have been admissible in those proceedings.

(6) Nothing in subsections (4) and (5) above makes a statutory declaration admissible as evidence in proceedings for an offence—

(*a*) unless a copy of it has, not less than 7 days before the hearing or trial, been served[2] on the person charged with the offence in any manner in which a summons or, in Scotland, a citation in a summary prosecution may be served; or

(*b*) if that person, not later than 3 days before the hearing or trial or within such further time as the court may in special circumstances allow, gives notice to the prosecutor requiring the attendance at the trial of the person by whom the declaration was made.

(7) *Repealed.*

[Social Security Administration Act 1992, s 118 as amended by the Social Security Act 1998, s 63, the Social Security Contributions (Transfer of Functions, etc) Act 1999, Sch 5 and the Finance Act 2008, Sch 44.]

1 Sections 118–120 and 121(1) to (4) apply to any secondary Class 1 contribution with which a surcharge under the National Insurance Surcharge Act 1976 is payable as if the surcharge were part of the contribution (National Insurance Surcharge Act 1976, s 1(3)).

2 See the Criminal Procedure Rules, Part 4, in the *Key Materials*.

7.10809 **119. Recovery of unpaid contributions on prosecution** (1) Where—

(*a*) a person has been convicted of an offence under section 114(1) above of failing to pay a contribution at or within the time prescribed for the purpose; and

(*b*) the contribution remains unpaid at the date of the conviction,

he shall be liable to pay to the Inland Revenue a sum equal to the amount which he failed to pay.

(2) *Repealed.*

[Social Security Administration Act 1992, s 119 as amended by the Social Security Act 1998, Sch 7 and the Social Security Contributions (Transfer of Functions, etc) Act 1999, Sch 1.]

7.10810 **120. Proof of previous offences** (1) Subject to and in accordance with subsections (2) to (5) below, where a person is convicted of an offence mentioned in section 119(1) above, evidence may be given of any previous failure by him to pay contributions within the time prescribed for the purpose; and in those subsections "the conviction" and "the offence" mean respectively the conviction referred to in this subsection and the offence of which the person is convicted.

(2) Such evidence may be given only if notice of intention to give it is served with the summons or warrant or, in Scotland, the complaint on which the person appeared before the court which convicted him.

(3) If the offence is one of failure to pay a Class 1 contribution, evidence may be given of failure on his part to pay (whether or not in respect of the same person) such contributions or any Class 1A or Class 1B contributions or contributions equivalent premiums on the date of the offence, or during the 6 years preceding that date.

(4) If the offence is one of failure to pay Class 1A or Class 1B contribution, evidence may be given of failure on his part to pay (whether or not in respect of the same person or the same amount) such contributions, or any Class 1 contributions or contributions equivalent premiums, on the date of the offence, or during the 6 years preceding that date.

(4A) If the offence is one of failure to pay a Class 1B contribution, evidence may be given of failure on his part to pay such contributions, or any Class 1 or Class 1A contributions or contributions equivalent premiums, on the date of the offence, or during the 6 years preceding that date.

(5) If the offence—

(*a*) is one of failure to pay Class 2 contributions;

(*b*) *repealed*

evidence may be given of his failure to pay such contributions during those 6 years.

(6) On proof of any matter of which evidence may be given under subsection (3), (4), (4A), or

(5) above, the person convicted shall be liable to pay to the Inland Revenue a sum equal to the total of all amounts which he is so proved to have failed to pay and which remain unpaid at the date of the conviction[1].

[Social Security Administration Act 1992, s 120 as amended by the Pensions Act 1995, Sch 5, the Social Security Act 1998, Sch 7, the Social Security Contributions (Transfer of Functions, etc) Act 1999, Sch 1 and the Child Support, Pensions and Social Security Act 2000, s 74.]

---

[1] The sum ordered to be paid is recoverable as a penalty (see s 121(4), post). Where, following a conviction under s 14, evidence is given in accordance with s 120 of further arrears of contributions which the defendant has failed to pay, it is the duty of the magistrates to make an order for payment of those arrears. The words "shall be liable to pay" do not confer a discretion upon the magistrates. Once such an order has been made by the magistrates against a limited company, it is not appropriate for the prosecutor to be requested by the Court to commence civil proceedings against the company for the recovery of the arrears of contributions which have formed the subject of the order. This is because the Act gives a special remedy against the directors of a limited company which is a remedy which does not exist under the ordinary civil law. This additional remedy is available once the order has been made by the magistrates (*Morgan v Quality Tools Engineering (Stowbridge) Ltd* [1972] 1 All ER 744, [1972] 1 WLR 196, DC, followed in *R v Melksham Justices, ex p Williams* (1983) 147 JP 283). The justices have no power to mitigate any part of the contributions due (*Leach v Litchfield* [1960] 3 All ER 739, [1960] 1 WLR 1392, 125 JP 115); nor may they be remitted in accordance with s 85 of the Magistrates' Courts Act 1980 in PART I: MAGISTRATES' COURTS, PROCEDURE, ante.

7.10811 **121. Unpaid contributions—supplementary** (1) Where in England and Wales a person charged with an offence mentioned in section 119(1) above is convicted of that offence in his absence under section 12(5) of the Magistrates' Courts Act 1980, then if—

(*a*) it is proved to the satisfaction of the court, on oath or in the manner prescribed by Criminal Procedure Rules, that notice under section 120(2) above has been duly served specifying the other contributions in respect of which the prosecutor intends to give evidence; and

(*b*) the designated officer for the court has received a statement in writing purporting to be made by the accused or by a solicitor acting on his behalf to the effect that if the accused is convicted in his absence of the offence charged he desires to admit failing to pay the other contributions so specified or any of them,

section 120 above shall have effect as if the evidence had been given and the failure so admitted had been proved, and the court shall proceed accordingly.

(2) In England and Wales, where a person is convicted of an offence mentioned in section 119(1) above and an order is made under section 12 of the Powers of Criminal Courts (Sentencing) Act 2000 placing the offender on probation or discharging him absolutely or conditionally, sections 119 and 120 above, and subsection (1) above, shall apply as if it were a conviction for all purposes.

(3) *Scotland.*

(4) In England and Wales, any sum which a person is liable to pay under section 119 or 120 above or under subsection (1) above shall be recoverable from him as a penalty[1].

(5) Sums recovered by the Inland Revenue under the provisions mentioned in subsection (4) above, so far as representing contributions of any class, are to be treated for all purposes of the Contributions and Benefits Act and this Act (including in particular the application of section 162 below) as contributions of that class received by the Inland Revenue.

(6) Without prejudice to subsection (5) above, in so far as such sums represent primary Class 1 or Class 2 contributions, they are to be treated as contributions paid in respect of the person in respect of whom they were originally payable; and enactments relating to earnings factors shall apply accordingly.

[Social Security Administration Act 1992, s 121 as amended by the Magistrates' Courts (Procedure) Act 1998, s 4, the Social Security Act 1998, Sch 7, the Social Security Contributions (Transfer of Functions, etc) Act 1999, Sch 1, the Access to Justice Act 1999, s 90, the Powers of Criminal Courts (Sentencing) Act 2000, Sch 9, and the Courts Act 2003, Sch 8.]

---

[1] This does not mean that the sum ordered to be paid is a penalty, but that it is recoverable in the same way as if it were a penalty; hence s 34(1) of the Magistrates' Courts Act 1980 (mitigation of penalties) does not apply and justices have no power to order an amount less than the full sum (*Leach v Litchfield*, ante). As to satisfaction and enforcement, see the Magistrates' Courts Act 1980, Part III (s 75 et seq). Note that contributions due may not be remitted in accordance with s 85(1) of the Magistrates' Courts Act 1980 (Magistrates' Courts Act 1980, s 85(2), ante).

A sum so ordered to be paid is no longer enforceable as a civil debt (*R v Marlow (Bucks) Justices, ex p Schiller* [1957] 2 QB 508, [1957] 2 All ER 783, 121 JP 519) therefore a defendant who fails to comply with an order is liable to be committed to prison under the Magistrates' Courts Act 1980, Sch 4, ante in PART I: MAGISTRATES' COURTS, PROCEDURE.

7.10813 **121C. Liability of directors etc for company's contributions** (1) This section applies to contributions which a body corporate is liable to pay, where—

(*a*) the body corporate has failed to pay the contributions at or within the time prescribed for the purpose; and

(*b*) the failure appears to the Inland Revenue to be attributable to fraud or neglect on the part of one or more individuals who, at the time of the fraud or neglect, were officers of the body corporate ("culpable officers").

(2) The Inland Revenue may issue and serve on any culpable officer a notice (a "personal liability notice")—

(*a*) specifying the amount of the contributions to which this section applies ("the specified amount");

(*b*) requiring the officer to pay to the Inland Revenue—

(i) a specified sum in respect of that amount; and
(ii) specified interest on that sum; and

(*c*) where that sum is given by paragraph (*b*) of subsection (3) below, specifying the proportion applied by the Inland Revenue for the purposes of that paragraph.

(3) The sum specified in the personal liability notice under subsection (2)(*b*)(I) above shall be—

(*a*) in a case where there is, in the opinion of the Inland Revenue, no other culpable officer, the whole of the specified amount; and

(*b*) in any other case, such proportion of the specified amount as, in the opinion of the Inland Revenue, the officer's culpability for the failure to pay that amount bears to that of all the culpable officers taken together.

(4) In assessing an officer's culpability for the purposes of subsection (3)(*b*) above, the Inland Revenue may have regard both to the gravity of the officer's fraud or neglect and to the consequences of it.

(5) The interest specified in the personal liability notice under subsection (2)(*b*) (ii) above shall be at the prescribed rate and shall run from the date on which the notice is issued.

(6) An officer who is served with a personal liability notice shall be liable to pay to the Inland Revenue the sum and the interest specified in the notice under subsection (2)(*b*) above.

(7) Where, after the issue of one or more personal liability notices, the amount of contributions to which this section applies is reduced by a payment made by the body corporate—

(*a*) the amount that each officer who has been served with such a notice is liable to pay under this section shall be reduced accordingly;

(*b*) the Inland Revenue shall serve on each such officer a notice to that effect; and

(*c*) where the reduced liability of any such officer is less than the amount that he has already paid under this section, the difference shall be repaid to him together with interest on it at the prescribed rate.

(8) Any amount paid under a personal liability notice shall be deducted from the liability of the body corporate in respect of the specified amount.

(8A) The amount which an officer is liable to pay under this section is to be recovered in the same manner as a Class 1 contribution to which regulations under paragraph 6 of Schedule 1 to the Contributions and Benefits Act apply and for this purpose references in those regulations to Class 1 contributions are to be construed accordingly.

(9) In this section—

"contributions" includes any interest or penalty in respect of contributions;

"officer", in relation to a body corporate, means—

(*a*) any director, manager, secretary or other similar officer of the body corporate, or any person purporting to act as such; and

(*b*) in a case where the affairs of the body corporate are managed by its members, any member of the body corporate exercising functions of management with respect to it or purporting to do so;

"the prescribed rate" means the rate from time to time prescribed by regulations under section 178 of the Finance Act 1989 for the purposes of the corresponding provision of Schedule 1 to the Contributions and Benefits Act, that is to say—

(*a*) in relation to subsection (5) above, paragraph 6(2)(*a*);

(*b*) in relation to subsection (7) above, paragraph 6(2)(*b*).

[Social Security Administration Act 1992, s 121C as inserted by the Social Security Act 1998, s 64 and amended by the Social Security Contributions (Transfer of Functions, etc) Act 1999, Sch 5 and the National Insurance Contributions and Statutory Payments Act 2004, s 5.]

7.10814 **121D. Appeals in relation to personal liability notices** (1) No appeal shall lie in relation to a personal liability notice except as provided by this section.

(2) An individual who is served with a personal liability notice may appeal against the Inland Revenue's decision as to the issue and content of the notice on the ground that—

(*a*) the whole or part of the amount specified under subsection (2)(*a*) of section 121C above (or the amount so specified as reduced under subsection (7) of that section) does not represent contributions to which that section applies;

(*b*) the failure to pay that amount was not attributable to any fraud or neglect on the part of the individual in question;

(*c*) the individual was not an officer of the body corporate at the time of the alleged fraud or neglect; or

(*d*) the opinion formed by the Inland Revenue under subsection (3)(*a*) or (*b*) of that section was unreasonable.

(3) The Inland Revenue shall give a copy of any notice of an appeal under this section, within 28 days of the giving of the notice, to each other individual who has been served with a personal liability notice.

(4) On an appeal under this section, the burden of proof as to any matter raised by a ground of appeal shall be on the Inland Revenue.

(5) Where an appeal under this section—

(*a*) is brought on the basis of evidence not considered by the Inland Revenue, or on the ground mentioned in subsection (2)(*d*) above; and (*b*) is not allowed on some other basis or ground,

and is notified to the tribunal, the tribunal shall either dismiss the appeal or remit the case to the Inland Revenue, with any recommendations the tribunal sees fit to make, for the Inland Revenue to consider whether to vary their decision as to the issue and content of the personal liability notice.

(6) In this section—

"officer", in relation to a body corporate, has the same meaning as in section 121C above;

"personal liability notice" has the meaning given by subsection (2) of that section;

"tribunal" means the First-tier Tribunal or, where determined under Tribunal Procedure Rules, the Upper Tribunal;

"vary" means vary under regulations made under section 10 of the Social Security Contributions (Transfer of Functions, etc) Act 1999.

[Social Security Administration Act 1992, s 121D as inserted by the Social Security Act 1998, s 64 and amended by the Social Security Contributions (Transfer of Functions, etc) Act 1999, Sch 5 and SI 2009/56.]

**7.10815 121DA. Interpretation of Part VI** (1) In this Part "the relevant social security legislation" means the provisions of any of the following, except so far as relating to contributions, statutory sick pay or statutory maternity pay, that is to say—

(*a*) the Contributions and Benefits Act;

(*b*) this Act;

(*c*) the Pensions Act, except Part III;

(*d*) section 4 of the Social Security (Incapacity for Work) Act 1994;

(*e*) the Jobseekers Act 1995;

(*f*) the Social Security (Recovery of Benefits) Act 1997;

(*g*) Parts I and IV of the Social Security Act 1998;

(*h*) Part V of the Welfare Reform and Pensions Act 1999;

(*hh*) the State Pension Credit Act 2002;

(*hi*) Part 1 of the Welfare Reform Act 2007;

(*i*) the Social Security Pensions Act 1975;

(*j*) the Social Security Act 1973;

(*k*) any subordinate legislation made, or having effect as if made, under any enactment specified in paragraphs (*a*) to (*j*) above.

(2) In this Part "authorised officer" means a person acting in accordance with any authorisation for the purposes of this Part which is for the time being in force in relation to him.

(3) For the purposes of this Part—

(*a*) references to a document include references to anything in which information is recorded in electronic or any other form;

(*b*) the requirement that a notice given by an authorised officer be in writing shall be taken to be satisfied in any case where the contents of the notice—

(i) are transmitted to the recipient of the notice by electronic means; and

(ii) are received by him in a form that is legible and capable of being recorded for future reference.

(4) In this Part "premises" includes—

(*a*) moveable structures and vehicles, vessels, aircraft and hovercraft;

(*b*) installations that are offshore installations for the purposes of the Mineral Workings (Offshore Installations) Act 1971; and

(*c*) places of all other descriptions whether or not occupied as land or otherwise;

and references in this Part to the occupier of any premises shall be construed, in relation to premises that are not occupied as land, as references to any person for the time being present at the place in question.

(5) In this Part—

"benefit" includes any allowance, payment, credit or loan;

"benefit offence" means a criminal offence committed in connection with a claim for benefit under a provision of the relevant social security legislation, or in connection with the receipt or payment of such a benefit; and

"compensation payment" has the same meaning as in the Social Security (Recovery of Benefits) Act 1997.

(6) In this Part—

(*a*) any reference to a person authorised to carry out any function relating to housing benefit or council tax benefit shall include a reference to a person providing services relating to the benefit directly or indirectly to an authority administering it; and

(*b*) any reference to the carrying out of a function relating to such a benefit shall include a reference to the provision of any services relating to it.

(7) In this section—

"relevant social security benefit" means a benefit under any provision of the relevant social security legislation; and

"subordinate legislation" has the same meaning as in the Interpretation Act 1978.

[Social Security Administration Act 1992, s 121D as inserted by the Child Support, Pensions and Social Security Act 2000, Sch 6, the Social Security Fraud Act 2001, Schedule, the Tax Credits Act 2002, 60, the State Pension Credits Act 2002, Sch 2 and the Welfare Reform Act 2007, Sch 3.]

## PART VII[1]

## INFORMATION

7.10816 Inland Revenue and Customs and Excise may disclose information to the Secretary of State or an authorised officer for use in the prevention, detection, investigation or prosecution of offences relating to social security, checking social security records or in connection with the operation of the Contributions and Benefits Act or this Act (**ss 122–122AA**). Other government information relating to passports, immigration and emigration, nationality or prisoners and other prescribed matter may be disclosed for the purpose of social security fraud prevention or verification (**s 122B**). Social Security information may be disclosed to authorities administering housing benefit and council tax benefit (**s 122C**) and such authorities may make reciprocal disclosure for the purpose of preventing social security fraud (**s 122D**) and may make disclosure between themselves (**s 122E**). Rent officers may be required to supply housing benefit information held by the rent officer to, or to a person providing services to, the Secretary of State for use for purposes relating to any of the following social security; child support; war pensions; employment or training; private pensions policy or retirement planning (**s 122F**). Unauthorised disclosure is an offence triable either way (with certain defences stated) (**s 123**). Further particular provisions are made for information to be provided to and by the Secretary of State (**ss 124–132**) including the furnishing of addresses for maintenance proceedings (**s 133**).

1 Part VII contains ss 122–133.

## PART XV[1]

## MISCELLANEOUS

*Offences*

7.10817 **181. Impersonation of officers** If any person, with intent to deceive, falsely represents himself to be a person authorised by the Secretary of State for Work and Pensions to act in any capacity (whether under this Act or otherwise) he shall be guilty of an offence[2] and liable on summary conviction to a fine not exceeding **level 4** on the standard scale.

[Social Security Administration Act 1992, s 181 as amended by SI 2002/1397.]

1 Part XV contains ss 180–188.
2 As to legal proceedings see s 116, ante.

7.10818 **182. Illegal possession of documents** (1) If any person—

(*a*) as a pledge or a security for a debt; or

(*b*) with a view to obtaining payment from the person entitled to it of a debt due either to himself or to any other person,

receives, detains or has in his possession any document issued by or on behalf of the Secretary of State for Work and Pensions in connection with any benefit, pension or allowance (whether payable under the Contributions and Benefits Act or otherwise) he shall be guilty of an offence.

(2) If any such person has such a document in his possession without lawful authority or excuse (the proof whereof shall lie on him) he shall be guilty of an offence.

(3) A person guilty of an offence[1] under this section shall be liable on summary conviction to imprisonment for a term not exceeding **3 months** or* to a fine not exceeding **level 4** on the standard scale or to **both***.

[Social Security Administration Act 1992, s 182 as amended by SI 2002/1397.]

* **Words repealed by the Criminal Justice Act 2003, Sch 37 from a date to be appointed.**
1 As to legal proceedings see s 116, ante.

# Pension Schemes Act 1993

(1993 c 48)

## PART III[1]

## CERTIFICATION OF PENSION SCHEMES AND EFFECTS ON MEMBERS' STATE SCHEME RIGHTS AND DUTIES

### CHAPTER III[2]

### TERMINATION OF CONTRACTED-OUT OR APPROPRIATE SCHEME STATUS: STATE SCHEME PREMIUMS

*State scheme premiums*

7.10819 **67. Non-payment of contributions equivalent premiums** (1) If a person fails to pay[3] any contributions equivalent premium[4] which is payable by him at or within the time prescribed for the purpose, he shall be liable on summary conviction to a fine of not more than **level 3** on the standard scale.

(2) Where—

(*a*) a person is convicted of the offence under subsection (1) of failing to pay a premium, and

(*b*) the premium remains unpaid at the date of the conviction, he shall be liable to pay to the Inland Revenue a sum equal to the amount which he failed to pay.

(3) Subject to subsection (4), where a person is convicted of an offence mentioned in subsection (2), evidence may be given of any previous failure by him to pay contributions equivalent premiums within the time prescribed for the purpose; and in that subsection "the conviction" and "the offence" mean respectively the conviction referred to in this subsection and the offence of which the person is convicted.

(4) Such evidence may be given only if notice of intention to give it is served with the summons or warrant or, in Scotland, the complaint on which the person appeared before the court which convicted him.

[Pension Schemes Act 1993, s 67 as amended by the Pensions Act 1995, Sch 5 and the Social Security Contributions (Transfer of Functions, etc) Act 1999, Sch 1.]

1 Part III contains ss 7–68.

2 Chapter III contains ss 50–68.

3 Where in any proceedings for an offence under this Act there arises any question as to whether a state scheme premium is payable or has been paid in any case or as to the amount of any such premium, the decision of the Secretary of State shall be conclusive for the purpose of the proceedings (ss 170(1) and 171(1), post).

4 "Contributions equivalent premium" means a contributions equivalent premium payable under Chapter III of Pt III (s 181(1)).

A contributions equivalent premium is payable where an earner in contracted-out employment with reference to an occupational pension scheme (other than a contracted-out money purchase scheme) leaves the scheme within 2 years or the scheme ceases to be a contracted out scheme (whether by being wound up or otherwise (s 55(2)). The amount of the contributions equivalent premium is the difference between the amount of the Class 1 contributions payable in respect of the earner's employment which was contracted-out by reference to the scheme and the amount of those contributions which would have been payable if the employment had not been contracted-out (s 58(4)). The person paying the premium may deduct a specified amount (within defined limits) from the refund of contributions to the earner (s 61).

## PART XI[1]

## GENERAL AND MISCELLANEOUS PROVISIONS

*Information about schemes*

7.10821 **157. Power of Secretary of State to obtain information in connection with applications under section 124** (1) Where an application is made to the Secretary of State under section 124[2] in respect of contributions to an occupational pension scheme or personal pension scheme falling to be made, by an employer, the Secretary of State may require—

(*a*) the employer to provide him with such information as the Secretary of State may reasonably require for the purpose of determining whether the application is well founded; and

(*b*) any person having the custody or control of any relevant records or other documents to produce for examination on behalf of the Secretary of State any such document in that person's custody or under his control which is of such a description as the Secretary of State may require.

(2) Any such requirement shall be made in writing given to the person on whom the requirement is imposed and may be varied or revoked by a subsequent notice so given.

(3) If a person refuses or wilfully neglects to furnish any information or produce any document which he has been required to furnish or produce by a notice under this section he shall be liable on summary conviction to a fine not exceeding **level 3** on the standard scale.

(4) If a person, in purporting to comply with a requirement of a notice under this section, knowingly or recklessly makes any false statement, he shall be liable on summary conviction to a fine not exceeding **level 5** on the standard scale.

(5) This section shall be construed as if it were in Chapter II of Part VII.

[Pension Schemes Act 1993, s 157.]

1 Part XI contains ss 153–177.

2 Section 124 imposes, subject to the provisions of the section and s 125, a duty on the Secretary of State to pay into the resources of an occupational pension scheme or a personal pension scheme a sum which in his opinion is payable in respect of unpaid relevant contributions. This obligation arises if, on an application made to him in writing by the persons competent to act in respect of the scheme, the Secretary of State is satisfied (a) that an employer has become insolvent; and (b) that at the time he did so there remained unpaid relevant contributions falling to be paid by him to the scheme.

*General provisions as to offences*

7.10822 **168. Breach of regulations** (1) Regulations under any provision of this Act (other than Chapter II of Part VII) may make such provision as is referred to in subsection (2) or (4) for the contravention of any provision contained in regulations made or having effect as if made under any provision of this Act.

(2) The regulations may provide for the contravention to be an offence under this Act and for the recovery on summary conviction of a fine not exceeding **level 5** on the standard scale.

(3) An offence under any provision of the regulations may be charged by reference to any day or longer period of time; and a person may be convicted of a second or subsequent offence under such a provision by reference to any period of time following the preceding conviction of the offence.

(4)–(9) *Regulations may provide for a person in contravention of the provisions to pay a penalty to the Regulatory Authority.*

(10) Where by reason of the contravention of any provision contained in regulations made, or having effect as if made, under this Act—

(*a*) a person is convicted of an offence under this Act, or

(*b*) a person pays a penalty under subsection (4),

then, in respect of that contravention he shall not, in a case within paragraph (*a*), be liable to pay such a penalty or, in a case within paragraph (*b*), be convicted of such an offence.

(11) In this section "contravention" means a partnership constituted under the law of Scotland.

[Pension Schemes Act 1993, s 168 as substituted by the Pensions Act 1995, s 155 and amended by the Pensions Act 2004, Sch 12.]

7.10823 **169. Offences by bodies corporate** (1) Where an offence under this Act which has been committed by a body corporate is proved to have been committed with the consent or connivance of, or to be attributable to any neglect on the part of, a director, manager, secretary or other similar officer of the body corporate, or any person who was purporting to act in any such capacity, he as well as the body corporate shall be guilty of that offence and be liable to be proceeded against accordingly.

(2) Where the affairs of a body corporate are managed by its members, subsection (1) applies in relation to the acts and defaults of a member in connection with his functions of management as if he were a director of the body corporate.

[Pension Schemes Act 1993, s 169.]

*General provisions as to determinations and appeals*

7.10824 **170. Decisions and appeals** (1) Section 2 (use of computers) of the Social Security Act 1998 ("the 1998 Act") applies as if, for the purposes of subsection (1) of that section, this Act were a relevant enactment.

(2) It shall be for an officer of the Inland Revenue—

(*a*) to make any decision that falls to be made under or by virtue of Part III of this Act, other than a decision which under or by virtue of that Part falls to be made by the Secretary of State;

(*b*) to decide any issue arising in connection with payments under section 7 of the Social Security Act 1986 (occupational pension schemes becoming contracted-out between 1986 and 1993); and

(*c*) to decide any issue arising by virtue of regulations made under paragraph 15 of Schedule 3 to the Social Security (Consequential Provisions) Act 1992 (continuing in force of certain enactments repealed by the Social Security Act 1973).

(3) In the following provisions of this section a "relevant decision" means any decision which under subsection (2) falls to be made by an officer of the Inland Revenue, other than a decision under section 53 or 54.

(4) Sections 9 and 10 of the 1998 Act (revision of decisions and decisions superseding earlier decisions) apply as if—

(*a*) any reference in those sections to a decision of the Secretary of State under section 8 of that Act included a reference to a relevant decision; and

(*b*) any other reference in those sections to the Secretary of State were, in relation to a relevant decision, a reference to an officer of the Inland Revenue.

(5) Regulations may make provision—

(*a*) generally with respect to the making of relevant decisions;

(*b*) with respect to the procedure to be adopted on any application made under section 9 or 10 of the 1998 Act by virtue of subsection (4); and

(*c*) generally with respect to such applications, revisions under section 9 and decisions under section 10;

but may not prevent a revision under section 9 or decision under section 10 being made without such an application.

(6) Section 12 of the 1998 Act (appeal to First-tier Tribunal) applies as if, for the purposes of subsection (1)(*b*) of that section, a relevant decision were a decision of the Secretary of State falling within Schedule 3 to the 1998 Act.

(7) The following provisions of the 1998 Act (which relate to decisions and appeals)—

sections 13 to 18,

sections 25 and 26,

section 28, and

Schedules 4 and 5,

shall apply in relation to any appeal under section 12 of the 1998 Act by virtue of subsection (6) above as if any reference to the Secretary of State were a reference to an officer of the Inland Revenue.

[Pension Schemes Act 1993, s 170 as amended by the Social Security Act 1998, Sch 7, the Social Security Contributions (Transfer of Functions, etc) Act 1999, s 16(2), the Welfare Reform and Pensions Act 1999, Sch 11, SI 2001/3649 and SI 2008/2833.]

7.10825 **171. Questions arising in proceedings** (1) Where in any proceedings—

(*a*) for an offence under this Act; or

(*b*) involving any question as to the payment of a contributions equivalent premium;

any relevant decision as defined by section 170(3) is made by the Inland Revenue, the decision shall be conclusive for the purpose of the proceedings.

(2) If—

(*a*) any such decision is necessary for the determination of the proceedings, and

(*b*) the decision of the Inland Revenue has not been obtained or an application with respect to the decision has been made under section 9 or 10 of the Social Security Act 1998,

the decision shall be referred to the Inland Revenue to be made in accordance (subject to any necessary modifications) with Chapter II of Part I of that Act.

(3) Subsection (1) does not apply where, in relation to the decision—

(*a*) an appeal has been brought but not determined,

(*b*) an application for leave to appeal has been made but not determined,

(*c*) an appeal has not been brought (or, as the case may be, an application for leave to appeal has not been made) but the time for doing so has not yet expired, or

(*d*) an application has been made under section 9 or 10 of that Act.

(4) In a case falling within subsection (3) the court shall adjourn the proceedings until such time as the final decision is known and that decision shall be conclusive for the purposes of the proceedings.

[Pension Schemes Act 1993, s 17 as amended by the Pensions Act 1995, Sch 5 and the Social Security Contributions (Transfer of Functions, etc) Act 1999, Sch 7.]

## PART XII[1]
## SUPPLEMENTARY PROVISIONS

**7.10826 181.** *General interpretation.*

[1] Part XII contains ss 178–193.

**7.10827 182.** *Orders and regulations (general provisions).*

**7.10828 193.** *Short title and commencement.*

# Jobseekers Act 1995[1]
(1995 c 18)

## PART I[2]
## THE JOBSEEKER'S ALLOWANCE

### *Entitlement*

**7.10829 1. The jobseeker's allowance** (1) An allowance, to be known as a jobseeker's allowance, shall be payable in accordance with the provisions of this Act.

(2) Subject to the provisions of this Act, a claimant is entitled to a jobseeker's allowance if he—

(*a*) is available for employment;

(*b*) has entered into a jobseeker's agreement which remains in force;

(*c*) is actively seeking employment;

(*d*) satisfies the conditions set out in section 2;

(*e*) is not engaged in remunerative work;

(*f*) does not have limited capability for work;

(*g*) is not receiving relevant education;

(*h*) is under pensionable age; and

(*i*) is in Great Britain.

(2A) Subject to the provisions of this Act, a claimant who is not a member of a joint-claim couple is entitled to a jobseeker's allowance if he satisfies—

(*a*) the conditions set out in paragraphs (*a*) to (*c*) and (*e*) to (*i*) of subsection (2); and

(*b*) the conditions set out in section 3.

(2B) Subject to the provisions of this Act, a joint-claim couple are entitled to a jobseeker's allowance if—

(*a*) a claim for the allowance is made jointly by the couple;

(*b*) each member of the couple satisfies the conditions set out in paragraphs (*a*) to (*c*) and (*e*) to (*i*) of subsection (2); and

(*c*) the conditions set out in section 3A are satisfied in relation to the couple.

(2C) Regulations may prescribe circumstances in which subsection (2A) is to apply to a claimant who is a member of a joint-claim couple.

(2D) Regulations may, in respect of cases where a person would (but for the regulations) be a member of two or more joint-claim couples, make provision for only one of those couples to be a joint-claim couple; and the provision which may be so made includes provision for the couple which is to be the joint-claim couple to be nominated—

(*a*) by the persons who are the members of the couples, or

(*b*) in default of one of the couples being so nominated, by the Secretary of State.

(3) A jobseeker's allowance is payable in respect of a week.

(4) In this Act—

"a contribution-based jobseeker's allowance" means a jobseeker's allowance entitlement to which is based on the claimant's satisfying conditions which include those set out in section 2;
"an income-based jobseeker's allowance" means a jobseeker's allowance entitlement to which is based on the claimant's satisfying conditions which include those set out in section 3 or a joint-claim jobseeker's allowance;
"a joint-claim couple" means a couple who—
(*a*) are not members of any family whose members include a person in respect of whom a member of the couple is entitled to child benefit, and
(*b*) are of a prescribed description;
"a joint-claim jobseeker's allowance" means a jobseeker's allowance entitlement to which arises by virtue of subsection (2B).

[Jobseekers Act 1995, s 1 as amended by the Welfare Reform and Pensions Act 1999, Sch 7, the Civil Partnership Act 2004, Sch 24 and the Welfare Reform Act 2007, Sch 3.]

[1] The Jobseekers Act 1995 provides for a jobseeker's allowance and makes other provision to promote the employment of the unemployed and the assistance of persons without a settled way of life.
This Act shall come into force in accordance with the provisions of s 41, post.
Only those provisions of the Act which are relevant to the work of magistrates' courts are contained in this Manual.
[2] Part I contains ss 1–25.

*Miscellaneous*

7.10830 **23. Recovery of sums in respect of maintenance** (1) Regulations[1] may make provision for the court to have power to make a recovery order against any person where an award of income-based jobseeker's allowance has been made to that person's spouse or civil partner.

(2) In this section "recovery order" means an order requiring the person against whom it is made to make payments to the Secretary of State or to such other person or persons as the court may determine.

(3) Regulations[1] under this section may make provision for the transfer by the Secretary of State of the right to receive payments under, and to exercise rights in relation to, a recovery order.

(4) Regulations[1] made under this section may, in particular, include provision—
(*a*) as to the matters to which the court is, or is not, to have regard in determining any application under the regulations; and
(*b*) as to the enforcement of recovery orders.

(5) In this section, "the court" means—
(*a*) in relation to England and Wales, a magistrates' court; and
(*b*) *Scotland.*

[Jobseekers Act 1995, s 23 as amended by the Civil Partnership Act 2004, Sch 24.]

[1] The Jobseeker's Allowance Regulations 1996, SI 1996/207 as amended have been made. Regulation 169 thereof—recovery orders—makes the following provision with respect to the recovery of maintenance under s 23 of the Act:

"**169. Recovery orders.—** (1) Where an award of income-based jobseeker's allowance has been made to a person ('the claimant'), the Secretary of State may apply to the court for a recovery order against the claimant's spouse or civil partner ('the liable person').

(2) On making a recovery order the court may order the liable person to pay such amount at such intervals as it considers appropriate, having regard to all the circumstances of the liable person and in particular his income.

(3) Except in Scotland, a recovery order shall be treated for all purposes as if it were a maintenance order within the meaning of section 150(1) of the Magistrates Court Act 1980.

(4) Where a recovery order requires the liable person to make payments to the Secretary of State, the Secretary of State may, by giving notice in writing to the court which made the order, the liable person, and the claimant, transfer to the claimant the right to receive payments under the order and to exercise the relevant rights in relation to the order.

(5) In this regulation—
the expression 'the court' and 'recovery order' have the same meanings as in section 23 of the Act; and
'the relevant rights' means, in relation to a recovery order, the right to bring any proceedings, take any steps or do any other thing under or in relation to the order".

## PART II[1]
## BACK TO WORK SCHEMES

7.10831 **26. The back to work bonus** (1) Regulations may make provision for the payment, in prescribed circumstances, of sums to or in respect of persons who are or have been entitled to a jobseeker's allowance or to income support.

(2) A sum payable under the regulations shall be known as "a back to work bonus".

(3) Subject to section 677 of the Income Tax (Earnings and Pensions) Act 2003 (which provides for a back to work bonus not to be taxable), a back to work bonus shall be treated for all purposes as payable by way of a jobseeker's allowance or (as the case may be) income support.

(4) *Supplementary provisions as to regulations.*

[Jobseekers Act 1995, s 26 as amended by the Income Tax (Earnings and Pensions) Act 2003, Sch 6.]

[1] Part II contains ss 26–29.

7.10832 27. **Employment of long-term unemployed: deductions by employers** (1) An employee is a "qualifying employee" in relation to his employer for the purposes of this section if, immediately before beginning his employment with that employer, he had been entitled to a jobseeker's allowance for a continuous period of not less than two years.

(2) An employee is also a "qualifying employee" in relation to his employer for the purposes of this section if—

(*a*) immediately before beginning his employment with that employer, he had been unemployed for a continuous period of not less than two years;

(*b*) he is under pensionable age; and

(*c*) he falls within a prescribed description of person.

(3) Regulations[1] may make provision for any employer who employs a person who is a qualifying employee in relation to him, to make deductions from the employer's contributions payments in accordance with the regulations and in prescribed circumstances.

(4) Those regulations may, in particular, make provision as to the period for which deductions may be made by an employer.

(5) Regulations[1] may provide, in relation to cases where an employee is a qualifying employee in relation to more than one employer at the same time, for the right to make deductions to be confined to one employer—

(*a*) determined in accordance with the regulations; and

(*b*) certified by the Commissioners of Inland Revenue, in accordance with the regulations, to be the employer entitled to make those deductions.

(6) *Supplementary provisions as to regulations.*

(7) Where, in accordance with any provision of regulations made under this section, an amount has been deducted from an employer's contributions payments, the amount so deducted shall (except in such cases as may be prescribed) be treated for the purposes of any provision made by or under any enactment in relation to primary or secondary Class 1 contributions as having been—

(*a*) paid (on such date as may be determined in accordance with the regulations); and

(*b*) received by the Commissioners of Inland Revenue,

towards discharging the employer's liability in respect of such contributions.

(8) In this section—

"contributions payments", in relation to an employer, means the aggregate of the payments which he is required to make by way of primary and secondary Class 1 contributions;

"deductions" means deductions made in accordance with regulations under subsection (3);

"employee" and "employer" have such meaning as may be prescribed;

"prescribed" means specified in or determined in accordance with regulations; and

"regulations" means regulations made by the Treasury.

[Jobseekers Act 1995, s 27 as amended by the Social Security Contributions (Transfer of Functions, etc) Act 1999, Sch 1, Sch 3.]

---

[1] The Employers Contributions Re-imbursement Regulations 1996, SI 1996/195 amended by SI 1999/286 have been made.

## PART III[1]

## MISCELLANEOUS AND SUPPLEMENTAL

7.10833 35. **Interpretation** (1) In this Act—

"the Administration Act" means the Social Security Administration Act 1992;

"applicable amount" means the applicable amount determined in accordance with regulations under section 4;

"benefit year" has the meaning given by section 2(4);

"the Benefits Act" means the Social Security Contributions and Benefits Act 1992;

"child" means a person under the age of 16;

"claimant" means a person who claims a jobseeker's allowance except that in relation to a joint-claim couple claiming a joint-claim jobseeker's allowance it means the couple, or each member of the couple, as the context requires;

"continental shelf operations" has the same meaning as in section 120 of the Benefits Act;

"contribution-based conditions" means the conditions set out in section 2;

"contribution-based jobseeker's allowance" has the meaning given in section 1(4);

"couple" means-

(*a*) a man and woman who are married to each other and are members of the same household;

(*b*) a man and woman who are not married to each other but are living together as husband and wife otherwise than in prescribed circumstances;

(*c*) two people of the same sex who are civil partners of each other and are members of the same household;

(*d*) two people of the same sex who are not civil partners but are living together as if they were civil partners otherwise than in prescribed circumstances;

"employed earner" has the meaning prescribed for the purposes of this Act;

"employment", except in section 7, has the meaning prescribed for the purposes of this Act;

"entitled", in relation to a jobseeker's allowance, is to be construed in accordance with—

(*a*) the provisions of this Act relating to entitlement; and (*b*) section 1 of the Administration Act and section 27 of the Social Security Act 1998;

"family" means—

(*a*) a couple;

(*b*) a couple and a member of the same household for whom one of them is, or both are, responsible and who is a child or a person of a prescribed description;

(*c*) except in prescribed circumstances, a person who is not a member of a couple and a member of the same household for whom that person is responsible and who is a child or a person of a prescribed description;

"FAS payments" means payments made under the Financial Assistance Scheme Regulations 2005;

"Great Britain" includes the territorial waters of the United Kingdom adjacent to Great Britain;

"income-based conditions" means the conditions set out in section 3;

"income-based jobseeker's allowance" has the meaning given in section 1(4);

"income-related employment and support allowance" means an income-related allowance under Part 1 of the Welfare Reform Act 2007 (employment and support allowance);

"jobseeker's agreement" has the meaning given by section 9(1);

"jobseeking period" has the meaning prescribed for the purposes of this Act;

"joint-claim couple" and "joint-claim jobseeker's allowance" have the meanings given by section 1(4);

"the nominated member", in relation to a joint-claim couple, shall be construed in accordance with section 3B(4);

"occupational pension scheme" has the same meaning as it has in the Pension Schemes Act 1993 by virtue of section 1 of that Act;

"pensionable age" has the meaning prescribed for the purposes of this Act;

"pension payments" means—

(*a*) periodical payments made in relation to a person, under a personal pension scheme or, in connection with the coming to an end of an employment of his, under an occupational pension scheme or a public service pension scheme; and

(*b*) such other payments as may be prescribed;

"personal pension scheme" means—

(*a*) a personal pension scheme as defined by section 1 of the Pension Schemes Act 1993;

(*b*) an annuity contract or trust scheme approved under section 620 or 621 of the Income and Corporation Taxes Act 1988 or a substituted contract within the meaning of section 622(3) of that Act which is treated as having become a registered pension scheme by virtue of paragraph 1(1)(*f*) of Schedule 36 to the Finance Act 2004; and

(*c*) a personal pension scheme approved under Chapter 4 of Part 14 of the Income and Corporation Taxes Act 1988 which is treated as having become a registered pension scheme by virtue of paragraph 1(1)(*g*) of Schedule 36 to the Finance Act 2004;

"PPF payments" means any payments made in relation to a person—

(*a*) payable under the pension compensation provisions as specified in section 162(2) of the Pensions Act 2004 or Article 146(2) of the Pensions (Northern Ireland) Order 2005 (the pension compensation provisions); or

(*b*) payable under section 166 of the Pensions Act 2004 or Article 150 of the Pensions (Northern Ireland) Order 2005 (duty to pay scheme benefits unpaid at assessment date etc);

"prescribed", except in section 27 (and in section 36 so far as relating to regulations under section 27), means specified in or determined in accordance with regulations;

"public service pension scheme" has the same meaning as it has in the Pension Schemes Act 1993 by virtue of section 1 of that Act;

"regulations", except in section 27 (and in section 36 so far as relating to regulations under section 27), means regulations made by the Secretary of State;

"tax year" means the 12 months beginning with 6th April in any year;

"trade dispute" means any dispute between employers and employees[2], or between employees and employees, which is connected with the employment or non-employment or the terms of employment or the conditions of employment of any persons, whether employees in the employment of the employer with whom the dispute arises, or not;

"training" has the meaning prescribed for the purposes of this Act and, in relation to prescribed provisions of this Act, if regulations so provide, includes assistance to find training or employment, or to improve a person's prospects of being employed, of such a kind as may be prescribed;

"week" means a period of 7 days beginning with a Sunday or such other period of 7 days as may be prescribed;

"work" has the meaning prescribed for the purposes of this Act;

"year", except in the expression "benefit year", means a tax year.

(1A) *Repealed.*

(2) The expressions "limited capacity for work", "linked period", "relevant education" and

"remunerative work" are to be read with paragraphs 2, 3, 14 and 1 of Schedule 1.*

(3) Subject to any regulations made for the purposes of this subsection, "earnings" is to be construed for the purposes of this Act in accordance with section 3 of the Benefits Act and paragraph 6 of Schedule 1 to this Act.

[Jobseekers Act 1995, s 35 as amended by the Social Security Contributions (Transfer of Functions, etc) Act 1999, Sch 3, the Welfare Reform and Pensions Act 1999, Sch 7, the Social Security Act 1998, Schs 7 and 8, the Civil Partnership Act 2004, Sch 24, SI 2006/343, and 745 and the Welfare Reform Act 2007, Sch 3 and SI 2014/560.]

1 Part III contains ss 30–41.

2 Modified in respect of share fishermen by the Jobseeker's Allowance Regulations 1996, SI 1996/207, reg 160 to provide that the owner or managing owner shall be treated as the employer of the other share fishermen who for these purposes are to be treated as his employees. See also the Jobseekers Allowance Regulations 2013, SI 2013/378, Pt 9.

7.10834 **36.** *Regulations and orders.*

7.10835 **41. Short title, commencement, extent etc** (1) This Act may be cited as the Jobseekers Act 1995.

(2) Section 39 and this section (apart from subsections (4) and (5)) come into force on the passing of this Act, but otherwise the provisions of this Act come into force on such day as the Secretary of State may by order[1] appoint.

(3) Different days may be appointed for different purposes.

(4) Schedule 2 makes consequential amendments.

(5) The repeals set out in Schedule 3 shall have effect.

(6) Apart from this section, section 39 and paragraphs 11 to 16, 28, 67 and 68 of Schedule 2, this Act does not extend to Northern Ireland.

[Jobseekers Act 1995, s 41.]

1 At the date of going to press the Jobseekers Act 1995 (Commencement No 1) Order 1995, SI 1995/3228, Commencement No 2) Order 1996, SI 1996/1126, (Commencement No 3) Order 1996, SI 1996/1509, and (Commencement No 4) Order 1996, SI 1996/2208, had been made.

# Pensions Act 1995[1]

(1995 c 26)

## Part I

## Occupational Pensions[2]

### *Supervision by the Authority*

7.10836 **3. Prohibition orders** (1) The Authority[3] may by order prohibit a person from being a trustee of—

(*a*) a particular trust scheme[4],

(*b*) a particular description of trust schemes, or

(*c*) trust schemes in general,

if they are satisfied that he is not a fit and proper person to be a trustee of the scheme or schemes to which the order relates.

(2) Where a prohibition order is made under subsection (1) against a person in respect of one or more schemes of which he is a trustee, the order has the effect of removing him.

(3) The Authority may, on the application of any person prohibited under this section, by order revoke the order either generally or in relation to a particular scheme or description of schemes.

(4) An application under subsection (3) may not be made—

(*a*) during the period within which the determination to exercise the power to make the prohibition order may be referred to a tribunal under section 96(3) or 99(7) of the Pensions Act 2004, and

(*b*) if the determination is so referred, until the reference, and any appeal against the determination of the tribunal concerned, has been finally disposed of.

(5) A revocation made at any time under this section cannot affect anything done before that time.

(6) The Authority must prepare and publish a statement of the policies they intend to adopt in relation to the exercise of their powers under this section.

(7) The Authority may revise any statement published under subsection (6) and must publish any revised statement.

(8) *Repealed.*

[Pensions Act 1995, s 3 as substituted by the Pensions Act 2004, s 33 and amended by SI 2010/22.]

1 The Act makes provision for amendment of the law relating to pensions. In particular, Pt I prescribes measures regulating the management of funds held by occupational pension schemes to protect the interests of the beneficiaries of such schemes. An Occupational Pensions Regulatory Authority is established (ss 1–2) which has wide powers over the appointment of trustees including powers to prohibit, suspend, and remove persons from appointment and to wind up schemes (ss 3–15). The description and functions of trustees are prescribed together with investment principles and the role of advisers and auditors (ss 16–61). There is a requirement for equal treatment of scheme members (ss 62–66) and restrictions on the power to modify schemes and for winding-up (ss 67–77). The Pensions Compensation Board is established (ss 78–80) which may make awards of compensation to members of an occupational scheme whose pension provision has suffered as a result of malpractice in the administration of the scheme (ss 81–86). The Authority and

the Compensation Board are enabled to require and obtain information in order to fulfil their functions (ss 98–114). Pt II (ss 126–134) relates to state pensions and Pt III (ss 135–151) makes provision for the relationship between certified pension schemes and members' state scheme rights and duties. Part IV (ss 152–181) contains miscellaneous and general matters.

With some exceptions, the provisions of the Act are to be brought into force by orders made under s 180. At the time of going to press the following commencement orders had been made: Pensions Act 1995 (Commencement No 1) Order 1995, SI 1995/2548; (Commencement No 2) Order 1995, SI 1995/3104; (Commencement No 3) Order 1996, SI 1996/778; (Commencement No 4) Order 1996, SI 1996/1412; (Commencement No 5) Order 1996, SI 1996/1675; (Commencement No 6) Order 1996, SI 1996/1843 (*provisions applicable only to Scotland*); (Commencement No 7) Order 1996, SI 1996/1853 as amended by SI 1996/2150; Commencement (No 8) Order 1996, SI 1996/2637; Commencement (No 9) Order 1997, SI 1997/216; Commencement (No 10) Order 1997, SI 1997/664. All the provisions reproduced here are in force.

2 Part I contains ss 1–125.

3 The Occupational Pensions Regulatory Authority (s 1).

4 An occupational pension scheme established under a trust (s 124).

*Trustees: general*

7.10837 **27. Trustee not to be auditor or actuary of the scheme** (1) A trustee of a trust scheme[1], and any person who is connected with, or an associate of, such a trustee, is ineligible to act as an auditor or actuary of the scheme.

(2) Subsection (1) does not make a person who is a director, partner or employee of a firm of actuaries ineligible to act as an actuary of a trust scheme merely because another director, partner or employee of the firm is a trustee of the scheme.

(3) Subsection (1) does not make a person who falls within a prescribed class or description ineligible to act as an auditor or actuary of a trust scheme.

(4) A person must not act as an auditor or actuary of a trust scheme if he is ineligible under this section to do so[2].

(5) In this section and section 28 references to a trustee of a trust scheme do not include—

(*a*) a trustee, or

(*b*) a trustee of a scheme,

falling within a prescribed class or description.

[Pensions Act 1995, s 27.]

1 An occupational pension scheme established under a trust (s 124).

2 For provisions as to offences, see 28, post.

7.10838 **28. Section 27: consequences** (1) Any person[1] who acts as an auditor or actuary of a trust scheme in contravention of section 27(4) is guilty of an offence and liable—

(*a*) on summary conviction, to a fine not exceeding the **statutory maximum**, and

(*b*) on conviction on indictment, to **imprisonment** or a **fine**, or **both**[2].

(2) An offence under subsection (1) may be charged by reference to any day or longer period of time; and a person may be convicted of a second or subsequent offence under that subsection by reference to any period of time following the preceding conviction of the offence.

(3) Acts done as an auditor or actuary of a trust scheme by a person who is ineligible under section 27 to do so are not invalid merely because of that fact.

(4) *Repealed.*

[Pensions Act 1995, s 28 as amended by the Pensions Act 2004, Sch 12.]

1 For offences by bodies corporate and partnerships, see s 115, post.

2 For procedure in respect of an offence triable either way, see the Magistrates' Courts Act 1980, ss 17A–21, in PART I: MAGISTRATES' COURTS, PROCEDURE, ante.

7.10839 **29. Persons disqualified for being trustees** (1) Subject to subsection (5), a person is disqualified for being a trustee of any trust scheme[1] if—

(*a*) he has been convicted of any offence involving dishonesty or deception,

(*b*) he has been adjudged bankrupt or sequestration of his estate has been awarded and (in either case) he has not been discharged or he is the subject of a bankruptcy restrictions order or an interim order.

(*ba*) a moratorium period under a debt relief order (under Part 7A of the Insolvency Act 1986) applies in relation to him or he is the subject of a debt relief restrictions order or an interim debt relief restrictions order (under Schedule 4ZB of the Insolvency Act 1986),

(*c*) where the person is a company, if any director of the company is disqualified under this section,

(*d*) where the person is a Scottish partnership, if any partner is disqualified under this section.

(*e*) he has made a composition contract or an arrangement with, or granted a trust deed for the behoof of, his creditors and has not been discharged in respect of it, or

(*f*) he is subject to a disqualification order or disqualification undertaking under the Company Directors Disqualification Act 1986 or the Company Directors Disqualification (Northern Ireland) Order 2002 or to an order made under section 429(2)(*b*) of the Insolvency Act 1986 (failure to pay under county court administration order)*.

(2) In subsection (1)—

(*a*) paragraph (*a*) applies whether the conviction occurred before or after the coming into force of that subsection, but does not apply in relation to any conviction which is a spent conviction for the purposes of the Rehabilitation of Offenders Act 1974,

(*b*) paragraph (*b*) applies whether the adjudication of bankruptcy or the sequestration or the making of the bankruptcy restrictions order or an interim order occurred before or after the coming into force of that subsection,

(*c*) paragraph (*e*) applies whether the composition contract or arrangement was made, or the trust deed was granted, before or after the coming into force of that subsection, and

(*d*) paragraph (*f*) applies in relation to orders made before or after the coming into force of that subsection.

(3)–(6) *Disqualification by the Authority.*

[Pensions Act 1995, s 29 as amended by the Insolvency Act 2000, s 8, SI 2004/1941, the Pensions Act 2004, Schs 12 and 13, SI 2006/1722, SI 2009/1941 and SI 2012/2404.]

---

1 An occupational pension scheme established under a trust (s 124).

* **Words substituted by the Tribunals, Courts and Enforcement Act 2007, Sch 16 from a date to be appointed.**

**7.10840 30. Persons disqualified: consequences** (1) Where a person who is a trustee of a trust scheme[1] becomes disqualified under section 29 in relation to the scheme, his becoming so disqualified has the effect of removing him as a trustee.

(2) Where—

(*a*) a trustee of a trust scheme becomes disqualified under section 29,

(*b*) *repealed.*

the Authority[2] may exercise the same jurisdiction and powers as are exercisable by order by the High Court or, in relation to a trust scheme subject to the law of Scotland, the Court of Session for vesting any property in, or transferring any property to, the trustees.*

(3) A person[3] who purports to act as a trustee of a trust scheme while he is disqualified under section 29 is guilty of an offence and liable—

(*a*) on summary conviction to a fine not exceeding the **statutory maximum**, and

(*b*) on conviction on indictment, to a **fine** or **imprisonment** or **both**[4].

(4) An offence under subsection (3) may be charged by reference to any day or longer period of time; and a person may be convicted of a second or subsequent offence under that subsection by reference to any period of time following the preceding conviction of the offence.

(5) Things done by a person disqualified under section 29 while purporting to act as trustee of a trust scheme are not invalid merely because of that disqualification.

(6) Nothing in section 29 or this section affects the liability of any person for things done, or omitted to be done, by him while purporting to act as trustee of a trust scheme.

(7)–(8) *Repealed.*

[Pensions Act 1995, s 30, as amended by the Child Support, Pensions and Social Security Act 2000, Sch 5 and the Pensions Act 2004, s 37 and Sch 12, 13.]

---

1 An occupational pension scheme established under a trust (s 124).

2 The Occupational Pensions Regulatory Authority (s 1).

3 For offences by bodies corporate and partnerships, see s 115, post.

4 For procedure in respect of an offence triable either way, see the Magistrates' Courts Act 1980, ss 17A–21 in PART I: MAGISTRATES' COURTS, PROCEDURE, ante.

*General*

**7.10841 115. Offences by bodies corporate and partnerships** (1) Where an offence under this Part committed by a body corporate is proved to have been committed with the consent or connivance of, or to be attributable to any neglect on the part of, a director, manager, secretary or other similar officer of the body, or a person purporting to act in any such capacity, he as well as the body corporate is guilty of the offence and liable to be proceeded against and punished accordingly.

(2) Where the affairs of a body corporate are managed by its members, subsection (1) applies in relation to the acts and defaults of a member in connection with his functions of management as to a director of a body corporate.

(3) Where an offence under this Part committed by a Scottish partnership is proved to have been committed with the consent or connivance of, or to be attributable to any neglect on the part of, a partner, he as well as the partnership is guilty of the offence and liable to be proceeded against and punished accordingly.

[Pensions Act 1995, s 115.]

**7.10842 116. Breach of regulations** (1) *Regulations.*

(2) An offence under any provision of the regulations may be charged by reference to any day or longer period of time; and a person may be convicted of a second or subsequent offence under such a provision by reference to any period of time following the preceding conviction of the offence.

(3) Where by reason of the contravention of any provision contained in regulations made by virtue of this Part—

(*a*) a person is convicted of an offence under this Part, or

(*b*) a person pays a penalty under section 10,

then, in respect of that contravention, he shall not, in a case within paragraph (*a*), be liable to pay such a penalty or, in a case within paragraph (*b*), be convicted of such an offence.

[Pensions Act 1995, s 116.]

## PART IV
## MISCELLANEOUS AND GENERAL
### *General*

7.10843 **176. Interpretation** In this Act—

"enactment" includes an enactment comprised in subordinate legislation (within the meaning of the Interpretation Act 1978),

"occupational pension scheme" and "personal pension scheme" have the meaning given by section 1 of the Pension Schemes Act 1993,

and the definition of "enactment" shall apply for the purposes of section 114 as if "Act" in section 21(1) of the Interpretation Act 1978 included any enactment.

[Pensions Act 1995, s 176.]

7.10844 **177.** *Repeals.*

7.10845 **178.** *Extent.*

7.10846 **180. Commencement** (1) Subject to the following provisions, this Act shall come into force on such day as the Secretary of State may by order[1] made by statutory instrument appoint and different days may be appointed for different purposes.

(2) The following provisions shall come into force on the day this Act is passed—

(*a*) subject to the provisions of Schedule 4, Part II,

(*b*) section 168,

(*c*) sections 170 and 171,

(*d*) section 179,

and any repeal in Schedule 7 for which there is a note shall come into force in accordance with that note.

(3) Section 166 shall come into force on such day as the Lord Chancellor may by order made by statutory instrument appoint and different days may be appointed for different purposes.

(4) Without prejudice to section 174(3), the power to make an order under this section includes power—

(*a*) to make transitional adaptations or modifications—

(i) of the provisions brought into force by the order, or

(ii) in connection with those provisions, of any provisions of this Act, or the Pension Schemes Act 1993, then in force, or

(*b*) to save the effect of any of the repealed provisions of that Act, or those provisions as adapted or modified by the order,

as it appears to the Secretary of State expedient, including different adaptations or modifications for different periods.

[Pensions Act 1995, s 180.]

[1] As to commencement orders which had been made at the date of going to press, see note 1 to the short title of this Act, ante.

7.10847 **181.** *Title.*

## Social Security Contributions (Transfer of Functions, etc) Act 1999

(1999 c 2)

7.10848 **4. Recovery of contributions where income tax recovery provisions not applicable**[1] The provisions of Schedule 4 shall have effect with respect to the recovery of—

(*a*) those Class 1, Class 1A, Class 1B and Class 2 contributions to which regulations under paragraph 6 or 7BZA of Schedule 1 to the Social Security Contributions and Benefits Act 1992 or paragraph 6 or 7BZA of Schedule 1 to the Social Security Contributions and Benefits (Northern Ireland) Act 1992 (power to combine collection of contributions with income tax) do not apply,

(*b*) *repealed*

(*c*) interest or penalties payable under regulations made under paragraph 7A of Schedule 1 to the Social Security Contributions and Benefits Act 1992 or paragraph 7A of Schedule 1 to the Social Security Contributions and Benefits (Northern Ireland) Act 1992 and

(*d*) interest or penalties—

(i) payable under regulations made under paragraph 7B of Schedule 1 to the Social Security Contributions and Benefits Act 1992 and to which regulations under paragraph 7BZA of that Schedule do not apply, or

(ii) payable under regulations made under paragraph 7B of Schedule 1 to the Social Security Contributions and Benefits (Northern Ireland) Act 1992 and to which regulations under paragraph 7BZA of that Schedule do not apply.

[Social Security Contributions (Transfer of Functions, etc) Act 1999, s 4 as amended by the Welfare Reform and Pensions Act 1999, Sch 11 the National Insurance Contributions and Statutory Payments Act 2004, Sch 1.]

[1] The Social Security Contributions (Transfer of Functions, etc) Act 1999 provides for the transfer of certain functions from the Secretary of State to the Commissioners of Inland Revenue or the Treasury relating to national insurance contributions, the National Insurance Fund, statutory sick pay, statutory maternity pay or pension schemes and certain associated functions relating to benefits and to make further provision, in connection with the functions transferred, as to the powers of the Commissioners of Inland Revenue, and the making of decisions and appeals. The Act is brought in to force in accordance with s 28.

## PART III
## MISCELLANEOUS AND SUPPLEMENTAL

7.10849 28. **Short title, commencement and extent** (1) This Act may be cited as the Social Security Contributions (Transfer of Functions, etc) Act 1999.

(2) The following provisions of this Act—

(*a*) section 1(1) (with Schedule 1), so far as enabling the Secretary of State to make subordinate legislation conferring functions on the Board,

(*b*) sections 8 to 15, so far as conferring any power to make subordinate legislation,

(*c*) section 17,

(*d*) section 20,

(*e*) section 22(4), so far as conferring the power to make an order,

(*f*) sections 24 and 25,

(*g*) section 26(1) (with Schedule 8), and

(*h*) section 27 and this section,

shall come into force on the passing of this Act.

(3) Except as provided by subsection (2) above, the provisions of this Act shall come into force on such day as the Secretary of State may by order appoint; and different days may be appointed for different purposes[1].

(4)–(7) *Further provisions as to orders and extent*

[Social Security Contributions (Transfer of Functions, etc) Act 1999, s 4 as amended by the Welfare Reform and Pensions Act 1999, Sch 11.]

[1] At the date of going the following orders had been made:

Social Security Contributions (Transfer of Functions, etc) Act 1999 (Commencement No 1 and Transitional Provisions) Order 1999, SI 1999/527;

Social Security Contributions (Transfer of Functions, etc) Act 1999 (Commencement No 2 and Consequential and Transitional Provisions) Order 1999, SI 1999/1662.

## SCHEDULE 4
### RECOVERY OF CONTRIBUTIONS WHERE INCOME TAX RECOVERY PROVISIONS NOT APPLICABLE

*Interpretation*

7.10850 1. In any provision of this Schedule "authorised officer" means an officer of the Board authorised by them for the purposes of that provision.

*Magistrates' courts*

2. (1) Any amount which—

(*a*) is due by way of contributions or by way of interest or penalty in respect of contributions, and

(*b*) does not exceed the prescribed sum,

shall, without prejudice to any other remedy, be recoverable summarily as a civil debt in proceedings commenced in the name of an authorised officer.

(2) All or any of the sums due from any one person in respect of contributions, or interest or penalties in respect of contributions, (being sums which are by law recoverable summarily) may be included in the same complaint, summons, order, warrant or other document required by law to be laid before justices or to be issued by justices, and every such document shall, as respects each such sum, be construed as a separate document and its invalidity as respects any one such sum shall not affect its validity as respects any other such sum.

(3) Proceedings under this paragraph in England and Wales may be brought—

(*a*) in the case of Class 2 contributions or interest or penalties in respect of such contributions, at any time before the end of the year following the tax year in which the contributor becomes liable to pay the contributions, and

(*b*) in any other case, not later than the first anniversary of the day on which the contributions became due.

(4) In sub-paragraph (1) above, the expression "recoverable summarily as a civil debt" in respect of proceedings in Northern Ireland means recoverable in proceedings under Article 62 of the Magistrates' Courts (Northern Ireland) Order 1981.

(5) In this paragraph—

"the prescribed sum" means the sum for the time being specified in section 65(1) of the Taxes Management Act 1970 (recovery of income tax, etc in magistrates' courts);

"tax year" means the twelve months beginning with 6th April in any year.

*General*

5. (1) Proceedings may be brought for the recovery of the total amount of Class 1 or Class 1A contributions which an employer has become liable to pay on a particular date and any sum due by way of interest or penalty in respect of those contributions without distinguishing the amounts which the employer is liable to pay in respect of each employee and without specifying the employees in question; and for the purposes of proceedings under

any of paragraphs 2 to 4 above that total amount shall be one cause of action or one matter of complaint.

(2) Nothing in sub-paragraph (1) above shall prevent the bringing of separate proceedings for the recovery of each of the several amounts of Class 1 or Class 1A contributions which the employer is liable to pay.

# Social Security Fraud Act 2001[1]

(2001 c 11)

*Loss of benefit provisions*

7.10853 **6A. Meaning of "disqualifying benefit" and "sanctionable benefit" for purposes of sections 6B and 7** (1) In this section and sections 6B and 7—

"disqualifying benefit" means (subject to any regulations under section 10(1))—

(*za*) any benefit under Part 1 of the Welfare Reform Act 2012 (universal credit) or under any provision having effect in Northern Ireland corresponding to that Part;

(*a*) any benefit under the Jobseekers Act 1995 or the Jobseekers (Northern Ireland) Order 1995;

(*b*) any benefit under the State Pension Credit Act 2002 or the State Pension Credit Act (Northern Ireland) 2002;

(*c*) any benefit under Part 1 of the Welfare Reform Act 2007 or Part 1 of the Welfare Reform Act (Northern Ireland) 2007 (employment and support allowance);

(*ca*) any benefit under Part 4 of the Welfare Reform Act 2012 (personal independence payment) or under any provision in Northern Ireland which corresponds to that Part;]

(*d*) any benefit under the Social Security Contributions and Benefit Act 1992 or the Social Security Contributions and Benefits (Northern Ireland) Act 1992 other than—

(i) maternity allowance;

(ii) statutory sick pay and statutory maternity pay;

(*e*) any war pension;

(*f*) "child tax credit;

(*g*) working tax credit;

"sanctionable benefit" means (subject to subsection (2) and to any regulations under section 10(1)) any disqualifying benefit other than—

(*a*) joint-claim jobseeker's allowance;

(*b*) any retirement pension;

(*c*) graduated retirement benefit;

(*d*) disability living allowance;

(*e*) attendance allowance;

(*f*) child benefit;

(*fa*) child tax credit;

(*fb*) working tax credit;

(*g*) guardian's allowance;

(*h*) a payment out of the social fund in accordance with Part 8 of the Social Security Contributions and Benefits Act 1992;

(*i*) a payment under Part 10 of that Act (Christmas bonuses).

(2) In their application to Northern Ireland sections 6B and 7 shall have effect as if references to a sanctionable benefit were references only to a war pension.

[Social Security Fraud Act 2001, s 6A as inserted by the Welfare Reform Act 2009, s 24 and amended by the Welfare Reform Act 2012, s 117, Schs 2, 9.]

7.10854 **6B. Loss of benefit in case of conviction, penalty or caution for benefit offence**

(1) Subsection (4) applies where a person ("the offender")—

(*a*) is convicted of one or more benefit offences in any proceedings,

(*b*) after being given a notice under subsection (2) of the appropriate penalty provision by an appropriate authority, agrees in the manner specified by the appropriate authority to pay a penalty under the appropriate penalty provision to the appropriate authority, in a case where the offence to which the notice relates is a benefit offence, or

(*c*) is cautioned in respect of one or more benefit offences.

(2) In subsection (1)(*b*)—

(*a*) "the appropriate penalty provision" means section 115A of the Administration Act (penalty as alternative to prosecution) or section 109A of the Social Security Administration (Northern Ireland) 1992 (the corresponding provision for Northern Ireland);

(*b*) "appropriate authority" means—

(i) in relation to section 115A of the Administration Act, the Secretary of State or an authority which administers housing benefit or council tax benefit, and

(ii) in relation to section 109A of the Social Security Administration (Northern Ireland) Act 1992, the Department (within the meaning of that Act) or the Northern Ireland Housing Executive.

(3) Subsection (4) does not apply by virtue of subsection (1)(*a*) if, because the proceedings in which the offender was convicted constitute the current set of proceedings for the purposes of

section 7, the restriction in subsection (2) of that section applies in the offender's case.

(4) If this subsection applies and the offender is a person with respect to whom the conditions for an entitlement to a sanctionable benefit are or become satisfied at any time within the disqualification period, then, even though those conditions are satisfied, the following restrictions shall apply in relation to the payment of that benefit in the offender's case.

(5) Subject to subsections (5A) (6) to (10), the sanctionable benefit shall not be payable in the offender's case for any period comprised in the disqualification period.*

(5A) The Secretary of State may by regulations provide that, where the sanctionable benefit is universal credit, the benefit shall be payable, during the whole or a part of any period comprised in the disqualification period, as if one or more of the following applied—

(*a*) the amount payable were reduced in such manner as may be prescribed;

(*b*) he benefit were payable only if there is compliance by the offender with such obligations with respect to the provision of information as may be imposed by the regulations;

(*c*) the benefit were payable only if the circumstances are otherwise such as may be prescribed;

(*d*) any amount of the benefit payable in prescribed circumstances were recoverable by the Secretary of State.

(6) Where the sanctionable benefit is income support, the benefit shall be payable in the offender's case for any period comprised in the disqualification period as if the applicable amount used for the determination under section 124(4) of the Social Security Contributions and Benefits Act 1992 of the amount of the offender's entitlement for that period were reduced in such manner as may be prescribed.*

(7) The Secretary of State may by regulations provide that, where the sanctionable benefit is jobseeker's allowance, any income-based jobseeker's allowance shall be payable, during the whole or a part of any period comprised in the disqualification period, as if one or more of the following applied—

(*a*) the rate of the allowance were such reduced rate as may be prescribed;

(*b*) the allowance were payable only if there is compliance by the offender with such obligations with respect to the provision of information as may be imposed by the regulations;

(*c*) the allowance were payable only if the circumstances are otherwise such as may be prescribed.

(8) The Secretary of State may by regulations provide that, where the sanctionable benefit is state pension credit, the benefit shall be payable in the offender's case for any period comprised in the disqualification period as if the rate of the benefit were reduced in such manner as may be prescribed.

(9) The Secretary of State may by regulations provide that, where the sanctionable benefit is employment and support allowance, any income-related allowance shall be payable, during the whole or a part of any period comprised in the disqualification period, as if one or more of the following applied—

(*a*) the rate of the allowance were such reduced rate as may be prescribed;

(*b*) the allowance were payable only if there is compliance by the offender with such obligations with respect to the provision of information as may be imposed by the regulations;

(*c*) the allowance were payable only if the circumstances are otherwise such as may be prescribed.

(10) The Secretary of State may by regulations provide that, where the sanctionable benefit is housing benefit or council tax benefit, the benefit shall be payable, during the whole or a part of any period comprised in the disqualification period, as if one or more of the following applied—

(*a*) the rate of the benefit were reduced in such manner as may be prescribed;

(*b*) the benefit were payable only if the circumstances are such as may be prescribed.

(11) For the purposes of this section the disqualification period, in relation to any disqualifying event, means the relevant period beginning with such date, falling after the date of the disqualifying event, as may be determined by or in accordance with regulations made by the Secretary of State.

(11A) For the purposes of subsection (11) the relevant period is—

(*a*) in a case falling within subsection (1)(*a*) where the benefit offence, or one of them, is a relevant offence, the period of three years,

(*b*) in a case falling within subsection (1)(*a*) (but not within paragraph (*a*) above)), the period of 13 weeks, or

(*c*) in a case falling within subsection (1)(*b*) or (*c*), the period of four weeks.

(12) This section has effect subject to section 6C.

(13) In this section and section 6C—

"benefit offence" means—

(*a*) any post-commencement offence in connection with a claim for a disqualifying benefit;

(*b*) any post-commencement offence in connection with the receipt or payment of any amount by way of such a benefit;

(*c*) any post-commencement offence committed for the purpose of facilitating the commission (whether or not by the same person) of a benefit offence;

(*d*) any post-commencement offence consisting in an attempt or conspiracy to commit a benefit offence;

"disqualifying event" means the conviction falling within subsection (1)(*a*), the agreement falling within subsection (1)(*b*) or the caution falling within subsection (1)(*c*);

"post-commencement offence" means any criminal offence committed after the commencement of this section.

(14) In this section and section 7 "relevant offence" means—

(*a*) in England and Wales, the common law offence of conspiracy to defraud, or

(*b*) a prescribed offence which, in the offender's case, is committed in such circumstances as may be prescribed, and which, on conviction—

(i) is found by the court to relate to an overpayment (as defined in section 115A(8) of the Administration Act) of at least £50,000,

(ii) is punished by a custodial sentence of at least one year (including a suspended sentence as defined in section 189(7)(*b*) of the Criminal Justice Act 2003), or

(iii) is found by the court to have been committed over a period of at least two years.

(15) The Secretary of State may by order amend subsection (11A)(*a*), (*b*) or (*c*), or (14)(*b*)(i), (ii) or (iii) to substitute a different period or amount for that for the time being specified there.

[Social Security Fraud Act 2001, s 6B as inserted by the Welfare Reform Act 2009, s 24 and amended by the Welfare Reform Act 2012, ss 113, 118, 119, Sch 2.]

---

*** Section amended by the Welfare Reform Act 2009, s 9 and the Welfare Reform Act 2012, s 121, Schs 3, 14 from a date to be appointed.**

7.10855 **6C. Section 6B: supplementary provisions** (1) Where—

(*a*) the conviction of any person of any offence is taken into account for the purposes of the application of section 6B in relation to that person, and

(*b*) that conviction is subsequently quashed,

all such payments and other adjustments shall be made as would be necessary if no restriction had been imposed by or under section 6B that could not have been imposed if the conviction had not taken place.

(2) Where, after the agreement of any person ("P") to pay a penalty under the appropriate penalty provision is taken into account for the purposes of the application of section 6B in relation to that person—

(*a*) P's agreement to pay the penalty is withdrawn under subsection (5) of the appropriate penalty provision, or

(*b*) it is decided on an appeal or in accordance with regulations under the Social Security Act 1998 or the Social Security (Northern Ireland) Order 1998 that the overpayment to which the agreement relates is not recoverable or due,

all such payments and other adjustments shall be made as would be necessary if no restriction had been imposed by or under section 6B that could not have been imposed if P had not agreed to pay the penalty.

(3) Where, after the agreement ("the old agreement") of any person ("P") to pay a penalty under the appropriate penalty provision is taken into account for the purposes of the application of section 6B in relation to P, the amount of the overpayment to which the penalty relates is revised on an appeal or in accordance with regulations under the Social Security Act 1998 or the Social Security (Northern Ireland) Order 1998—

(*a*) section 6B shall cease to apply by virtue of the old agreement, and

(*b*) subsection (4) shall apply.

(4) Where this subsection applies—

(*a*) if there is a new disqualifying event consisting of—

(i) P's agreement to pay a penalty under the appropriate penalty provision in relation to the revised overpayment, or

(ii) P being cautioned in relation to the offence to which the old agreement relates,

the disqualification period relating to the new disqualifying event shall be reduced by the number of days in so much of the disqualification period relating to the old agreement as had expired when section 6B ceased to apply by virtue of the old agreement, and

(*b*) in any other case, all such payments and other adjustments shall be made as would be necessary if no restriction had been imposed by or under section 6B that could not have been imposed if P had not agreed to pay the penalty.

(5) For the purposes of section 6B—

(*a*) the date of a person's conviction in any proceedings of a benefit offence shall be taken to be the date on which the person was found guilty of that offence in those proceedings (whenever the person was sentenced) or in the case mentioned in paragraph (*b*)(ii) the date of the order for absolute discharge; and

(*b*) references to a conviction include references to—

(i) a conviction in relation to which the court makes an order for absolute or conditional discharge or a court in Scotland makes a probation order,

(ii) an order for absolute discharge made by a court of summary jurisdiction in Scotland under section 246(3) of the Criminal Procedure (Scotland) Act 1995 without proceeding to a conviction, and

(iii) a conviction in Northern Ireland.

(6) In this section "the appropriate penalty provision" has the meaning given by section 6B(2)(*a*).

[Social Security Fraud Act 2001, s 6C as inserted by the Welfare Reform Act 2009, s 24.]

7.10856 7. **Loss of benefit for repeated benefit fraud**[1] (1) If—

(a) a person ("the offender") is convicted of one or more benefit offences in a set of proceedings ("the current set of proceedings"),

(*b*) within the period of five years ending on the date on which the benefit offence was, or any of them were, committed, one or more disqualifying events occurred in relation to the offender (the event, or the most recent of them, being referred to in this section as "the earlier disqualifying event"),

(*c*) the current set of proceedings has not been taken into account for the purposes of any previous application of this section or section 8 or 9 in relation to the offender or any person who was then a member of his family,

(*d*) the earlier disqualifying event has not been taken into account as an earlier disqualifying event for the purposes of any previous application of this section or either of those sections in relation to the offender or any person who was then a member of his family, and

(*e*) the offender is a person with respect to whom the conditions for an entitlement to a sanctionable benefit are or become satisfied at any time within the disqualification period,

then, even though those conditions are satisfied, the following restrictions shall apply in relation to the payment of that benefit in the offender's case.

(1A) The following restrictions do not apply if the benefit offence referred to in subsection (1)(*a*), or any of them, is a relevant offence.

(2) Subject to subsections (3) to (5), the sanctionable benefit shall not be payable in the offender's case for any period comprised in the disqualification period.

(3) Where the sanctionable benefit is income support, the benefit shall be payable in the offender's case for any period comprised in the disqualification period as if the applicable amount used for the determination under section 124(4) of the Social Security Contributions and Benefits Act 1992 (c 4) of the amount of the offender's entitlement for that period were reduced in such manner as may be prescribed.

(4) The Secretary of State may by regulations provide that, where the sanctionable benefit is jobseeker's allowance, any income-based jobseeker's allowance shall be payable, during the whole or a part of any period comprised in the disqualification period, as if one or more of the following applied—

(*a*) the rate of the allowance were such reduced rate as may be prescribed;

(*b*) the allowance were payable only if there is compliance by the offender with such obligations with respect to the provision of information as may be imposed by the regulations;

(*c*) the allowance were payable only if the circumstances are otherwise such as may be prescribed.

(4A) The Secretary of State may by regulations provide that, where the sanctionable benefit is state pension credit, the benefit shall be payable in the offender's case for any period comprised in the disqualification period as if the rate of the benefit were reduced in such manner as may be prescribed.

(4B) The Secretary of State may by regulations provide that, where the sanctionable benefit is employment and support allowance, any income-related allowance shall be payable, during the whole or a part of any period comprised in the disqualification period, as if one or more of the following applied—

(*a*) the rate of the allowance were such reduced rate as may be prescribed;

(*b*) the allowance were payable only if there is compliance by the offender with such obligations with respect to the provision of information as may be imposed by the regulations;

(*c*) the allowance were payable only if the circumstances are otherwise such as may be prescribed.

(5) The Secretary of State may by regulations provide that, where the sanctionable benefit is housing benefit or council tax benefit, the benefit shall be payable, during the whole or a part of any period comprised in the disqualification period, as if one or both of the following applied—

(*a*) the rate of the benefit were reduced in such manner as may be prescribed;

(*b*) the benefit were payable only if the circumstances are such as may be prescribed.

(6) For the purposes of this section the disqualification period, in an offender's case, means the relevant period beginning with a prescribed date falling after the date of the conviction in the current set of proceedings.

(6A) For the purposes of subsection (6) the relevant period is—

(a) in a case where, within the period of five years ending on the date on which the earlier disqualifying event occurred, a previous disqualifying event occurred in relation to the offender, the period of three years;

(b) in any other case, 26 weeks.

(7) Where—

(a) the conviction of any person of any offence is taken into account for the purposes of the application of this section in relation to that person, and

(b) that conviction is subsequently quashed,

all such payments and other adjustments shall be made as would be necessary if no restriction had been imposed by or under this section that could not have been imposed if the conviction had not taken place.

(7A) Subsection (7B) applies where, after the agreement of any person ("P") to pay a penalty under the appropriate penalty provision is taken into account for the purposes of the application of this section in relation to that person—

(a) P's agreement to pay the penalty is withdrawn under subsection (5) of the appropriate penalty provision,

(b) it is decided on an appeal or in accordance with regulations under the Social Security Act 1998 or the Social Security (Northern Ireland) Order 1998 (SI 1998/1506 (N.I. 10)) that any overpayment to which the agreement relates is not recoverable or due, or

(c) the amount of any overpayment to which the penalty relates is revised on an appeal or in accordance with regulations under the Social Security Act 1998 or the Social Security (Northern Ireland) Order 1998 and there is no new agreement by P to pay a penalty under the appropriate penalty provision in relation to the revised overpayment.

(7B) In those circumstances, all such payments and other adjustments shall be made as would be necessary if no restriction had been imposed by or under this section that could not have been imposed if P had not agreed to pay the penalty.

(8) In this section—

"appropriate penalty provision" has the meaning given in section 6B(2)(*a*);

"benefit offence" means—

(a) any post-commencement offence in connection with a claim for a disqualifying benefit;

(b) any post-commencement offence in connection with the receipt or payment of any amount by way of such a benefit;

(c) any post-commencement offence committed for the purpose of facilitating the commission (whether or not by the same person) of a benefit offence;

(d) any post-commencement offence consisting in an attempt or conspiracy to commit a benefit offence;

"disqualifying benefit" means (subject to any regulations under section 10(1))—

(a) any benefit under the Jobseekers Act 1995 (c 18) or the Jobseekers (Northern Ireland) Order 1995 (SI 1995/2705 (NI 15));

(aa) any benefit under the State Pension Credit Act 2002 or under any provision having effect in Northern Ireland corresponding to that Act;

(ab) any benefit under Part 1 of the Welfare Reform Act 2007 (employment and support allowance) or under any provision having effect in Northern Ireland corresponding to that Part;

(b) any benefit under the Social Security Contributions and Benefits Act 1992 (c 4) or the Social Security Contributions and Benefits (Northern Ireland) Act 1992 (c 7) other than—

(i) maternity allowance;

(ii) *repealed*

(iii) *repealed*

(iv) statutory sick pay and statutory maternity pay;

(c) any war pension;

"disqualifying event" has the meaning given in section 6B(13);

"sanctionable benefit" means (subject to subsection (11) and to any regulations under section 10(1)) any disqualifying benefit other than—

(a) joint-claim jobseeker's allowance;

(b) any retirement pension;

(c) graduated retirement benefit;

(d) disability living allowance;

(e) attendance allowance;

(f) child benefit;

(g) guardian's allowance;

(h) a payment out of the social fund in accordance with Part 8 of the Social Security Contributions and Benefits Act 1992;

(i) a payment under Part X of that Act (Christmas bonuses).

(8A) Where a person is convicted of more than one benefit offence in the same set of proceedings, there is to be only one disqualifying event in respect of that set of proceedings for the purposes of this section and—

(*a*) subsection (1)(*b*) is satisfied if any of the convictions take place in the five year periods mentioned there;

(*b*) the event is taken into account for the purposes of subsection (1)(d) if any of the convictions have been taken into account as mentioned there;

(*c*) in the case of the earlier disqualifying event mentioned in subsection (6A)(*a*), the reference there to the date on which the earlier disqualifying event occurred is a reference to the date on which any of the convictions take place;

(*d*) in the case of the previous disqualifying event mentioned in subsection (6A)(*a*), that provision is satisfied if any of the convictions take place in the five year period mentioned there.

(9) For the purposes of this section—

(*a*) the date of a person's conviction in any proceedings of a benefit offence shall be taken to be the date on which he was found guilty of that offence in those proceedings (whenever he was sentenced); and

(*b*) references to a conviction include references to a conviction in relation to which the court makes an order for a conditional discharge or a court in Scotland makes a probation order and to a conviction in Northern Ireland.

(10) In this section references to any previous application of this section or section 8 or 9—

(*a*) include references to any previous application of a provision having an effect in Northern Ireland corresponding to provision made by this section, or either of those sections; but

(*b*) do not include references to any previous application of this section, or of either of those sections, the effect of which was to impose a restriction for a period comprised in the same disqualification period.

(10A) The Secretary of State may by order amend subsection (6A) to substitute different periods for those for the time being specified there.

(10B) An order under subsection (10A) may provide for different periods to apply according to the type of earlier disqualifying event or events occurring in any case.

(11) In its application to Northern Ireland this section shall have effect as if references to a sanctionable benefit were references only to a war pension.

[Social Security Fraud Act 2001, s 7 as amended by the Tax Credits Act 2002, s 14, the State Pension Credit Act 2002, Sch 2, the Welfare Reform Act 2007, s 49 and Sch 3 and the Welfare Reform Act 2012, ss 118, 119.]

---

[1] As to commencement of this Act, see s 20 and commencement orders made thereunder, post.

**7.10857 8. *Effect of offence on joint-claim jobseeker's allowance***

**7.10858 9. *Effect of offence on benefits for members of offender's family***

**7.10859 10. *Power to supplement and mitigate loss of benefit provisions***

**7.10860 11. *Loss of benefit regulations***

**7.10861 12. *Consequential amendments***

**7.10862 13. Interpretation of sections 7 to 12** In this section and sections 7 to 12—

"benefit" includes any allowance, payment, credit or loan;

"disqualification period" has the meaning given by section 7(6);

"family" has the same meaning as in Part 7 of the Social Security Contributions and Benefits Act 1992 (c 4);

"income-based jobseeker's allowance", "joint-claim jobseeker's allowance" and "joint-claim couple" have the same meanings as in the Jobseekers Act 1995 (c 18);

"income-related allowance" has the same meaning as in Part 1 of the Welfare Reform Act 2007 (employment and support allowance);

"post-commencement offence" means any criminal offence committed after the commencement of section 7;

"sanctionable benefit" has the meaning given by section 7(8);

"state pension credit" means state pension credit under the State Pension Credit Act 2002;

"war pension" has the same meaning as in section 25 of the Social Security Act 1989 (c 24) (establishment and functions of war pensions committees).

[Social Security Fraud Act 2001, s 13 as amended by the State Pension Credit Act 2002, Sch 2 and the Welfare Reform Act 2007, Sch 3.]

*Supplemental*

**7.10863 18. Meaning of "the Administration Act"** In this Act "the Administration Act" means the Social Security Administration Act 1992 (c 5).

[Social Security Fraud Act 2001, s 18.]

**7.10864 19. Repeals**

**7.10865 20. Commencement** (1) The preceding provisions of this Act shall come into force on such day as the Secretary of State may by order[1] made by statutory instrument appoint.

(2) Subject to subsection (3), different days may be appointed under this section for different purposes.

(3) The power under this section to appoint a day for the coming into force of the provisions of

sections 1 and 2 shall not authorise the appointment for those purposes of any day before the issue of the code of practice that must be issued under section 3.

[Social Security Fraud Act 2001, s 20.]

[1] At the date of going to press the following commencement orders had been made: (No 1) SI 2001/3251; (No 2) SI 2001/3689; (No 3), SI 2002/117; (No 4) SI 2002/403; (No 5) SI 2002/1222; (No 6) SI 2003/273. All the provisions reproduced here are in force.

7.10866 **21. Short title and extent**

# Tax Credits Act 2002[1]

(2002 c 21)

## PART 1
## TAX CREDITS

*Fraud*

7.10867 **35. Offence of fraud** (1) A person commits an offence if he is knowingly concerned in any fraudulent activity undertaken with a view to obtaining payments of a tax credit by him or any other person.

(2) A person who commits an offence under subsection (1) is liable[2]—

(*a*) on summary conviction, to imprisonment for a term not exceeding six months, or a fine not exceeding the statutory maximum, or both, or

(*b*) on conviction on indictment, to imprisonment for a term not exceeding seven years, or a fine, or both.

[Tax Credits Act 2002, s 35.]

[1] Administrative penalties may be levied under ss 31–34 in respect of incorrect statements, failure to comply with requirements and failure by employers to make correct payments. Provision is made for commencement of this Act by orders made under ss 61 and 62. At the date of going to press the following commencement orders had been made: (No 1) SI 2002/1727; (No 2) SI 2003/392; (No 3 and Transitional Provisions and Savings) SI 2003/938; (No 4, Transitional Provisions and Savings) SI 2003/962 (amended by SI 2011/2910); (Commencement and Transitional Provisions) SI 2006/3369. All the provisions reproduced here are in force. See also the Tax Credits Act (Transitional Provisions) Orders: 2005, SI 2005/2910; 2008, SI 2008/3151.

[2] For procedure in respect of this offence, which is triable either way, see the Magistrates' Courts Act 1980, ss 17A–21, in PART I: MAGISTRATES' COURTS, PROCEDURE, ante.

7.10868 **36. Powers in relation to documents** (1) Section 20BA of the Taxes Management Act 1970 (c 9) (orders for delivery of documents) applies (with Schedule 1AA and section 20BB) in relation to offences involving fraud in connection with, or in relation to, tax credits as in relation to offences involving serious fraud in connection with, or in relation to, tax.

(2), (3) *Repealed.*

(4) Any regulations under Schedule 1AA to the Taxes Management Act 1970 which are in force immediately before the commencement of subsection (1) apply, subject to any necessary modifications, for the purposes of that Schedule as they apply by virtue of that subsection (until amended or revoked).

[Tax Credits Act 2002, s 36 as amended by the Finance Act 2007, Sch 22.]

*Loss of tax credit provisions*

7.10869 **36A. Loss of working tax credit in case of conviction etc for benefit offence**

(1) Subsection (4) applies where a person ("the offender")—

(*a*) is convicted of one or more benefit offences in any proceedings, or

(*b*) after being given a notice under subsection (2) of the appropriate penalty provision by an appropriate authority, agrees in the manner specified by the appropriate authority to pay a penalty under the appropriate penalty provision to the appropriate authority, in a case where the offence to which the notice relates is a benefit offence, or

(*c*) is cautioned in respect of one or more benefit offences.

(2) In subsection (1)(*b*)—

(*a*) "the appropriate penalty provision" means section 115A of the Social Security Administration Act 1992 (penalty as alternative to prosecution) or section 109A of the Social Security Administration (Northern Ireland) Act 1992 (the corresponding provision for Northern Ireland);

(*b*) "appropriate authority" means—

(i) in relation to section 115A of the Social Security Administration Act 1992, the Secretary of State or an authority which administers housing benefit or council tax benefit, and

(ii) in relation to section 109A of the Social Security Administration (Northern Ireland) Act 1992, the Department (within the meaning of that Act) or the Northern Ireland Housing Executive.

(3) Subsection (4) does not apply by virtue of subsection (1)(*a*) if, because the proceedings in which the offender was convicted constitute the current set of proceedings for the purposes of section 36C, the restriction in subsection (3) of that section applies in the offender's case.

(4) If this subsection applies and the offender is a person who would, apart from this section, be

entitled (whether pursuant to a single or joint claim) to working tax credit at any time within the disqualification period, then, despite that entitlement, working tax credit shall not be payable for any period comprised in the disqualification period—

(*a*) in the case of a single claim, to the offender, or

(*b*) in the case of a joint claim, to the offender or the other member of the couple.

(5) Regulations may provide in relation to cases to which subsection (4)(*b*) would otherwise apply that working tax credit shall be payable, for any period comprised in the disqualification period, as if the amount payable were reduced in such manner as may be prescribed.

(6) For the purposes of this section, the disqualification period, in relation to any disqualifying event, means the relevant period beginning with such date, falling after the date of the disqualifying event, as may be determined by or in accordance with regulations.

(7) For the purposes of subsection (6) the relevant period is—

(*a*) in a case falling within subsection (1)(*a*) where the benefit offence, or one of them, is a relevant offence, the period of three years,

(*b*) in a case falling within subsection (1)(*a*) (but not within paragraph (*a*) above)), the period of 13 weeks, or

(*c*) in a case falling within subsection (1)(*b*) or (*c*), the period of 4 weeks.

(8) The Treasury may by order amend subsection (7)(*a*), (*b*) or (*c*) to substitute a different period for that for the time being specified there.

(9) This section has effect subject to section 36B.

(10) In this section and section 36B—

"benefit offence" means any of the following offences committed on or after the day specified by order made by the Treasury—

(*a*) an offence in connection with a claim for a disqualifying benefit;

(*b*) an offence in connection with the receipt or payment of any amount by way of such a benefit;

(*c*) an offence committed for the purpose of facilitating the commission (whether or not by the same person) of a benefit offence;

(*d*) an offence consisting in an attempt or conspiracy to commit a benefit offence;

"disqualifying benefit" has the meaning given in section 6A(1) of the Social Security Fraud Act 2001;

"disqualifying event" means—

(*a*) the conviction falling within subsection (1)(*a*);

(*b*) the agreement falling within subsection (1)(*b*);

(*c*) the caution falling within subsection (1)(*c*);

"relevant offence" has the meaning given in section 6B of the Social Security Fraud Act 2001.

[Tax Credits Act 2002, s 36A as inserted by the Welfare Reform Act 2012, s 120.]

**7.10870 36B. Section 36A: supplementary** (1) Where—

(*a*) the conviction of any person of any offence is taken in account for the purposes of the application of section 36A in relation to that person, and

(*b*) that conviction is subsequently quashed,

all such payments and other adjustments shall be made as would be necessary if no restriction had been imposed by or under section 36A that could not have been imposed if the conviction had not taken place.

(2) Where, after the agreement of any person ("P") to pay a penalty under the appropriate penalty provision is taken into account for the purposes of the application of section 36A in relation to that person—

(*a*) P's agreement to pay the penalty is withdrawn under subsection (5) of the appropriate penalty provision, or

(*b*) it is decided on an appeal or in accordance with regulations under the Social Security Act 1992 or the Social Security (Northern Ireland) Order 1998 (SI 1998/1506 (N.I. 10)) that the overpayment to which the agreement relates is not recoverable or due,

all such payments and other adjustments shall be made as would be necessary if no restriction had been imposed by or under section 36A that could not have been imposed if P had not agreed to pay the penalty.

(3) Where, after the agreement ("the old agreement") of any person ("P") to pay a penalty under the appropriate penalty provision is taken into account for the purposes of the application of section 36A in relation to P, the amount of any overpayment made to which the penalty relates is revised on an appeal or in accordance with regulations under the Social Security Act 1998 or the Social Security (Northern Ireland) Order 1998—

(*a*) section 36A shall cease to apply by virtue of the old agreement, and

(*b*) subsection (4) shall apply.

(4) Where this subsection applies—

(*a*) if there is a new disqualifying event consisting of—

(i) P's agreement to pay a penalty under the appropriate penalty regime in relation to the revised overpayment, or

(ii) P being cautioned in relation to the offence to which the old agreement relates, the disqualification period relating to the new disqualifying event shall be reduced by the number of days in so much of the disqualification period relating to the old agreement as had expired when subsection 36A ceased to apply by virtue of the old agreement, and

(*b*) in any other case, all such payments and other adjustments shall be made as would be necessary if no restriction had been imposed by or under section 36A that could not have been imposed if P had not agreed to pay the penalty.

(5) For the purposes of section 36A—

(*a*) the date of a person's conviction in any proceedings of a benefit offence shall be taken to be the date on which the person was found guilty of that offence in those proceedings (whenever the person was sentenced) or in the case mentioned in paragraph (*b*)(ii) the date of the order for absolute discharge, and

(*b*) references to a conviction include references to—

(i) a conviction in relation to which the court makes an order for absolute or conditional discharge,

(ii) an order for absolute discharge made by a court of summary jurisdiction in Scotland under section 246(3) of the Criminal Procedure (Scotland) Act 1995 without proceeding to a conviction, and

(iii) a conviction in Northern Ireland.

(6) In this section "the appropriate penalty provision" has the meaning given by section 36A(2)(*a*).

[Tax Credits Act 2002, s 36B as inserted by the Welfare Reform Act 2012, s 120.]

7.10871 **36C. Loss of working tax credit for repeated benefit fraud** (1) If—

(*a*) a person ("the offender") is convicted of one or more benefit offences in a set of proceedings ("the current set of proceedings"),

(*b*) within the period of five years ending on the date on which the benefit offence was, or any of them were, committed, one or more disqualifying events occurred in relation to the offender (the event, or the most recent of them, being referred to in this section as "the earlier disqualifying event"),

(*c*) the current set of proceedings has not been taken into account for the purposes of any previous application of this section in relation to the offender,

(*d*) the earlier disqualifying event has not been taken into account as an earlier disqualifying event for the purposes of any previous application of this section in relation to the offender, and

(*e*) the offender is a person who would, apart from this section, be entitled (whether pursuant to a single or joint claim) to working tax credit at any time within the disqualification period,

then, despite that entitlement, the restriction in subsection (3) shall apply in relation to the payment of that benefit in the offender's case.

(2) The restriction in subsection (3) does not apply if the benefit offence referred to in subsection (1)(*a*), or any of them, is a relevant offence.

(3) Working tax credit shall not be payable for any period comprised in the disqualification period—

(*a*) in the case of a single claim, to the offender, or

(*b*) in the case of a joint claim, to the offender or the other member of the couple.

(4) Regulations may provide in relation to cases to which subsection (3)(*b*) would otherwise apply that working tax credit shall be payable, for any period comprised in the disqualification period, as if the amount payable were reduced in such manner as may be prescribed.

(5) For the purposes of this section the disqualification period, in an offender's case, means the relevant period beginning with a prescribed date falling after the date of the conviction in the current set of proceedings.

(6) For the purposes of subsection (5) the relevant period is—

(*a*) in a case where, within the period of five years ending on the date on which the earlier disqualifying event occurred, a previous disqualifying event occurred in relation to the offender, the period of three years;

(*b*) in any other case, 26 weeks.

(7) In this section and section 36D—

"appropriate penalty provision" has the meaning given in section 36A(2)(*a*);

"benefit offence" means any of the following offences committed on or after the day specified by order made by the Treasury—

(*a*) an offence in connection with a claim for a disqualifying benefit;

(*b*) an offence in connection with the receipt or payment of any amount by way of such a benefit;

(*c*) an offence committed for the purpose of facilitating the commission (whether or not by the same person) of a benefit offence;

(*d*) an offence consisting in an attempt or conspiracy to commit a benefit offence;

"disqualifying benefit" has the meaning given in section 6A(1) of the Social Security Fraud Act 2001;

"disqualifying event" has the meaning given in section 36A(10);

"relevant offence" has the meaning given in section 6B of the Social Security Fraud Act 2001.

(8) Where a person is convicted of more than one benefit offence in the same set of proceedings, there is to be only one disqualifying event in respect of that set of proceedings for the purposes of this section and—

(*a*) subsection (1)(*b*) is satisfied if any of the convictions take place in the five year period there;

(*b*) the event is taken into account for the purposes of subsection (1)(*d*) if any of the convictions have been taken into account as mentioned there;

(*c*) in the case of the earlier disqualifying event mentioned in subsection (6)(*a*), the reference there to the date on which the earlier disqualifying event occurred is a reference to the date on which any of the convictions take place;

(*d*) in the case of the previous disqualifying event mentioned in subsection (6)(*a*), that provision is satisfied if any of the convictions take place in the five year period mentioned there.

(9) The Treasury may by order amend subsection (6) to substitute different periods for those for the time being specified there.

(10) An order under subsection (9) may provide for different periods to apply according to the type of earlier disqualifying event or events occurring in any case.

(11) This section has effect subject to section 36D.

[Tax Credits Act 2002, s 36C as inserted by the Welfare Reform Act 2012, s 120.]

**7.10872 36D. Section 36C: supplementary** (1) Where—

(*a*) the conviction of any person of any offence is taken into account for the purposes of the application of section 36C in relation to that person, and

(*b*) that conviction is subsequently quashed,

all such payments and other adjustments shall be made as would be necessary if no restriction had been imposed by or under section 36C that could not have been imposed if the conviction had not taken place.

(2) Subsection (3) applies where, after the agreement of any person ("P") to pay a penalty under the appropriate penalty provision is taken into account for the purposes of the application of section 36C in relation to that person—

(*a*) P's agreement to pay the penalty is withdrawn under subsection (5) of the appropriate penalty provision,

(*b*) it is decided on an appeal or in accordance with regulations under the Social Security Act 1998 or the Social Security (Northern Ireland) Order 1998 (SI 1998/1506 (N.I. 10)) that any overpayment made to which the agreement relates is not recoverable or due, or

(c) the amount of any over payment to which the penalty relates is revised on an appeal or in accordance with regulations under the Social Security Act 1998 or the Social Security (Northern Ireland) Order 1998 and there is no new agreement by P to pay a penalty under the appropriate penalty provision in relation to the revised overpayment.

(3) In those circumstances, all such payments and other adjustments shall be made as would be necessary if no restriction had been imposed by or under section 36C that could not have been imposed if P had not agreed to pay the penalty.

(4) For the purposes of section 36C—

(*a*) the date of a person's conviction in any proceedings of a benefit offence shall be taken to be the date on which the person was found guilty of that offence in those proceedings (whenever the person was sentenced) or in the case mentioned in paragraph (*b*)(ii) the date of the order for absolute discharge, and

(*b*) references to a conviction include references to—

(i) a conviction in relation to which the court makes an order for absolute or conditional discharge,

(ii) an order for absolute discharge made by a court of summary jurisdiction in Scotland under section 246(3) of the Criminal Procedure (Scotland) Act 1995 without proceeding to a conviction, and

(iii) a conviction in Northern Ireland.

(5) In section 36C references to any previous application of that section—

(*a*) include references to any previous application of a provision having an effect in Northern Ireland corresponding to provision made by that section, but

(*b*) do not include references to any previous application of that section the effect of which was to impose a restriction for a period comprised in the same disqualification period.

[Tax Credits Act 2002, s 36D as inserted by the Welfare Reform Act 2012, s 120.]

# Pensions Act 2004[1]

(2004 c 35)

*Gathering information*

7.10873 **72. Provision of information** (1) The Regulator may, by notice in writing, require any person to whom subsection (2) applies to produce any document, or provide any other information, which is—

(*a*) of a description specified in the notice, and

(*b*) relevant to the exercise of the Regulator's functions.

(1A) If the Regulator requires information which is relevant to the exercise of its functions under Chapter 2 of Part 1 of the Pensions Act 2008 or section 51 of that Act, the Regulator may, by notice in writing, require a person to whom subsection (2) applies—

(*a*) to furnish the Regulator with an explanation of any document or information required under subsection (1);

(*b*) to attend before the Regulator at such time and place as may be specified in the notice under that subsection to furnish any such explanation.

(1B) The Regulator may not require a person to answer any question or furnish any information which might incriminate the person or, if that person is married or a civil partner, the person's spouse or civil partner.

(2) This subsection applies to—

(*a*) a trustee or manager of an occupational or personal pension scheme,

(*b*) a professional adviser in relation to an occupational pension scheme,

(*c*) the employer in relation to—

(i) an occupational pension scheme, or

(ii) a personal pension scheme where direct payment arrangements exist in respect of one or more members of the scheme who are employees, and

(*d*) any other person appearing to the Regulator to be a person who holds, or is likely to hold, information relevant to the exercise of the Regulator's functions.

(3) Where the production of a document, or the provision of information, is required by a notice given under subsection (1), the document must be produced, or information must be provided, in such a manner, at such a place and within such a period as may be specified in the notice.

[Pensions Act 2004, s 72 as amended by the Pensions Act 2008, s 61.]

---

[1] The provisions reproduced here have been brought into force in accordance with commencement orders made under s 322: s 190 (partially) (No 2, Transitional Provisions and Consequential Amendments) Order 2005, SI 2005/275 (10 February 2005); s 193 (partially) (Commencement No. 1 and Consequential and Transitional Provisions) Order 2004, SI 2004/3350); ss 72-79, 190 (partially), 192, 193 (partially), 194, 195, 204(1)(2) (No 2, Transitional Provisions and Consequential Amendments) Order 2005, SI 2005/275 (6 April 2005); s 204(3) (No 9) Order 2005, SI 2005/560 (6 April 2006).

7.10874 **73. Inspection of premises** (1) An inspector may, for the purposes of investigating whether, in the case of any occupational pension scheme, the occupational scheme provisions are being, or have been, complied with, at any reasonable time enter premises liable to inspection.

(2) In subsection (1), the "occupational scheme provisions" means provisions contained in or made by virtue of—

(*a*) any of the following provisions of this Act—
this Part;
Part 3 (scheme funding);
sections 241 to 243 (member-nominated trustees and directors);
sections 247 to 249 (requirement for knowledge and understanding);
section 252 (UK-based scheme to be trust with effective rules);
section 253 (non-European scheme to be trust with UK-resident trustee);
section 255 (activities of occupational pension schemes);
section 256 (no indemnification for fines or civil penalties);
sections 259 and 261 (consultation by employers);
Part 7 (cross-border activities within European Union);
Part 9 (miscellaneous and supplementary);

(*b*) either of the following provisions of the Welfare Reform and Pensions Act 1999 (c 30)—
section 33 (time for discharge of pension credit liability);
section 45 (information);

(*c*) any of the provisions of Part 1 of the Pensions Act 1995 (c 26) (occupational pension schemes), other than—

(i) sections 51 to 54 (indexation), and

(ii) sections 62 to 65 (equal treatment);

(*d*) any of the following provisions of the Pension Schemes Act 1993 (c 48)—
Chapter 4 of Part 4 (transfer values);
Chapter 5 of Part 4 (early leavers: cash transfer sums and contribution refunds);
Chapter 2 of Part 4A (pension credit transfer values);
section 113 (information);

section 175 (levy);

(*e*) any provisions in force in Northern Ireland corresponding to any provisions within paragraphs (*a*) to (*d*).

(3) An inspector may, for the purposes of investigating whether, in the case of a stakeholder scheme—

(*a*) sections 1 and 2(4) of the Welfare Reform and Pensions Act 1999 (stakeholder pension schemes: registration etc), or

(*b*) any corresponding provisions in force in Northern Ireland,

are being, or have been, complied with, at any reasonable time enter premises liable to inspection.

(4) An inspector may, for the purposes of investigating whether, in the case of any trust-based personal stakeholder scheme, the trust-based scheme provisions are being, or have been, complied with, at any reasonable time enter premises liable to inspection.

(5) In subsection (4)—

"trust-based personal stakeholder scheme" means a personal pension scheme which—

(*a*) is a stakeholder scheme, and

(*b*) is established under a trust;

the "trust-based scheme provisions" means any provisions contained in or made by virtue of—

(*a*) any provision which applies in relation to trust-based personal stakeholder schemes by virtue of paragraph 1 of Schedule 1 to the Welfare Reform and Pensions Act 1999 (c 30), as the provision applies by virtue of that paragraph, or

(*b*) any corresponding provision in force in Northern Ireland.

(6) Premises are liable to inspection for the purposes of this section if the inspector has reasonable grounds to believe that—

(*a*) members of the scheme are employed there,

(*b*) documents relevant to the administration of the scheme are being kept there, or

(*c*) the administration of the scheme, or work connected with that administration, is being carried out there.

(7) In this section, "stakeholder scheme" means an occupational pension scheme or a personal pension scheme which is or has been registered under—

(*a*) section 2 of the Welfare Reform and Pensions Act 1999 (register of stakeholder schemes), or

(*b*) any corresponding provision in force in Northern Ireland.

[Pensions Act 2004, s 73.]

7.10875 74. **Inspection of premises in respect of employers' obligations** (A1) An inspector may, for the purposes of investigating whether an employer is contravening, or has contravened—

(*a*) any provision of, or of regulations under, Chapter 1 of Part 1, or section 50 or 54, of the Pensions Act 2008, or

(*b*) any corresponding provision in force in Northern Ireland,

at any reasonable time enter premises liable to inspection.

(B1) Premises are liable to inspection for the purposes of subsection (A1) if the inspector has reasonable grounds to believe that—

(*a*) the employer employs workers there,

(*b*) documents relevant to any of the following are being kept there—

(i) the administration of the employer's business,

(ii) the duties of the employer under Chapter 1 of Part 1 of the Pensions Act 2008 or under any corresponding provision in force in Northern Ireland,

(iii) the administration of a pension scheme that is relevant to the discharge of those duties, or

(*c*) the administration of the employer's business, or work connected with that administration, is being carried out there.

(C1) In subsections (A1) and (B1) "employer" and "worker" have the meaning given by section 88 of the Pensions Act 2008.

(D1) In the application of subsections (A1) and (B1) in relation to any provision mentioned in subsection (A1)(*b*) (a "corresponding Northern Ireland provision"), references in those subsections to "employer" or "worker" are to be read as having the meaning that they have for the purposes of the corresponding Northern Ireland provision.]

(1) An inspector may, for the purposes of investigating whether an employer is complying, or has complied, with the requirements under—

(*a*) section 3 of the Welfare Reform and Pensions Act 1999 (duty of employers to facilitate access to stakeholder pension schemes), or

(*b*) any corresponding provision in force in Northern Ireland,

at any reasonable time enter premises liable to inspection.

(2) Premises are liable to inspection for the purposes of subsection (1) if the inspector has reasonable grounds to believe that—

(*a*) employees of the employer are employed there,

(*b*) documents relevant to the administration of the employer's business are being kept there, or (*c*) the administration of the employer's business, or work connected with that administration, is being carried out there.

(3) In subsections (1) and (2), "employer" has the meaning given by section 3(9) of the Welfare Reform and Pensions Act 1999 (or, where subsection (1)(*b*) applies, by any corresponding provision in force in Northern Ireland).

(4) An inspector may, for the purposes of investigating whether, in the case of any direct payment arrangements relating to a personal pension scheme, any of the following provisions—

(*a*) regulations made by virtue of sections 260 and 261 (consultation by employers),

(*b*) section 111A of the Pension Schemes Act 1993 (c 48) (monitoring of employers' payments to personal pension schemes), or

(*c*) any corresponding provisions in force in Northern Ireland,

is being, or has been, complied with, at any reasonable time enter premises liable to inspection.

(5) Premises are liable to inspection for the purposes of subsection (4) if the inspector has reasonable grounds to believe that—

(*a*) employees of the employer are employed there,

(*b*) documents relevant to the administration of—

(i) the employer's business,

(ii) the direct payment arrangements, or

(iii) the scheme to which those arrangements relate,

are being kept there, or

(*c*) either of the following is being carried out there—

(i) the administration of the employer's business, the arrangements or the scheme;

(ii) work connected with that administration.

(6) In the application of subsections (4) and (5) in relation to any provision mentioned in subsection (4)(c) (a "corresponding Northern Ireland provision"), references in those subsections to—

direct payment arrangements,
a personal pension scheme,
the employer, or
employees of the employer,

are to be read as having the meanings that they have for the purposes of the corresponding Northern Ireland provision.

[Pensions Act 2004, s 74 as amended by the Pensions Act 2008, s 61.]

7.10876 **75. Inspection of premises: powers of inspectors** (1) Subsection (2) applies where, for a purpose mentioned in subsection (1), (3) or (4) of section 73 or subsection (A1), (1) or (4) of section 74, an inspector enters premises which are liable to inspection for the purposes of that provision.

(2) While there, the inspector—

(*a*) may make such examination and inquiry as may be necessary for the purpose for which he entered the premises,

(*b*) may require any person on the premises to produce, or secure the production of, any document relevant to compliance with the regulatory provisions for his inspection,

(*c*) may take copies of any such document,

(*d*) may take possession of any document appearing to be a document relevant to compliance with the regulatory provisions or take in relation to any such document any other steps which appear necessary for preserving it or preventing interference with it,

(*e*) may, in the case of any such document which consists of information which is stored in electronic form and is on, or accessible from, the premises, require the information to be produced in a form—

(i) in which it can be taken away, and

(ii) in which it is legible or from which it can readily be produced in a legible form,

and

(*f*) may, as to any matter relevant to compliance with the regulatory provisions, examine, or require to be examined, either alone or in the presence of another person, any person on the premises whom he has reasonable cause to believe to be able to give information relevant to that matter.

[Pensions Act 2004, s 75 as amended by the Pensions Act 2008, s 61.]

7.10877 **76. Inspection of premises: supplementary** (1) This section applies for the purposes of sections 73 to 75.

(2) Premises which are a private dwelling-house not used by, or by permission of, the occupier for the purposes of a trade or business are not liable to inspection.

(3) Any question whether—

(*a*) anything is being or has been done or omitted which might by virtue of any of the regulatory provisions give rise to a liability for a civil penalty under or by virtue of section 10 of the Pensions Act 1995 (c 26) or section 168(4) of the Pension Schemes Act 1993 (c 48) (or under or by virtue of any provision in force in Northern Ireland corresponding to either of them), or (*b*) an offence is being or has been committed under any of the regulatory provisions,

is to be treated as a question whether the regulatory provision is being, or has been, complied with.

(4) An inspector applying for admission to any premises for the purposes of section 73 or 74 must, if so required, produce his certificate of appointment.

(5) When exercising a power under section 73, 74 or 75 an inspector may be accompanied by such persons as he considers appropriate.

(6) Any document of which possession is taken under section 75 may be retained—

(*a*) if the document is relevant to proceedings against any person for any offence which are commenced before the end of the retention period, until the conclusion of those proceedings, and

(*b*) otherwise, until the end of the retention period.

(7) In subsection (6), "the retention period" means the period comprising—

(*a*) the period of 12 months beginning with the date on which possession was taken of the document, and

(*b*) any extension of that period under subsection (8).

(8) The Regulator may, by a direction made before the end of the retention period (including any extension of it under this subsection), extend it by such period not exceeding 12 months as the Regulator considers appropriate.

(9) "The regulatory provisions", in relation to an inspection under subsection (1), (3) or (4) of section 73 or subsection (A1), (1) or (4) of section 74, means the provision or provisions referred to in that subsection.

[Pensions Act 2004, s 76 as amended by the Pensions Act 2008, s 61.]

**7.10878 77. Penalties relating to sections 72 to 75** (1) A person who, without reasonable excuse, neglects or refuses to provide information or produce a document when required to do so under section 72 is guilty of an offence.

(2) A person who without reasonable excuse—

(*a*) intentionally delays or obstructs an inspector exercising any power under section 73, 74 or 75,

(*b*) neglects or refuses to produce, or secure the production of, any document when required to do so under section 75, or

(*c*) neglects or refuses to answer a question or to provide information when so required,

is guilty of an offence.

(3) A person guilty of an offence under subsection (1) or (2) is liable on summary conviction to a fine not exceeding level 5 on the standard scale.

(4) An offence under subsection (1) or (2)(*b*) or (*c*) may be charged by reference to any day or longer period of time; and a person may be convicted of a second or subsequent offence by reference to any period of time following the preceding conviction of the offence.

(5) Any person who intentionally and without reasonable excuse alters, suppresses, conceals or destroys any document which he is or is liable to be required to produce under section 72 or 75 is guilty of an offence.

(6) Any person guilty of an offence under subsection (5) is liable—

(*a*) on summary conviction, to a fine not exceeding the statutory maximum;

(*b*) on conviction on indictment, to a fine or imprisonment for a term not exceeding two years, or both.

[Pensions Act 2004, s 77.]

**7.10879 78. Warrants** (1) A justice of the peace may issue a warrant under this section if satisfied on information on oath given by or on behalf of the Regulator that there are reasonable grounds for believing—

(*a*) that there is on, or accessible from, any premises any document—

(i) whose production has been required under section 72 or 75, or any corresponding provision in force in Northern Ireland, and

(ii) which has not been produced in compliance with that requirement,

(*b*) that there is on, or accessible from, any premises any document whose production could be so required and, if its production were so required, the document—

(i) would not be produced, but

(ii) would be removed, or made inaccessible, from the premises, hidden, tampered with or destroyed, or

(*c*) that—

(i) an offence has been committed,

(ii) a person will do any act which constitutes a misuse or misappropriation of the assets of an occupational pension scheme or a personal pension scheme,

(iii) a person is liable to pay a penalty under or by virtue of section 10 of the Pensions Act 1995 (c 26) (civil penalties) or section 168(4) of the Pension Schemes Act 1993 (c 48) (civil penalties for breach of regulations), or under or by virtue of any provision in force in Northern Ireland corresponding to either of them, or

(iv) a person is liable to be prohibited from being a trustee of an occupational or personal pension scheme under section 3 of the Pensions Act 1995 (prohibition orders), including that section as it applies by virtue of paragraph 1 of Schedule 1 to the Welfare Reform and Pensions Act 1999 (c 30) (stakeholder schemes), or under or by virtue of any corresponding provisions in force in Northern Ireland,

and that there is on, or accessible from, any premises any document which relates to whether the offence has been committed, whether the act will be done or whether the person is so liable, and whose production could be required under section 72 or 75 or any corresponding provision in force in Northern Ireland.

(2) A warrant under this section shall authorise an inspector—

(*a*) to enter the premises specified in the information, using such force as is reasonably necessary for the purpose,

(*b*) to search the premises and—

(i) take possession of any document appearing to be such a document as is mentioned in subsection (1), or

(ii) take in relation to such a document any other steps which appear necessary for preserving it or preventing interference with it,

(*c*) to take copies of any such document,

(*d*) to require any person named in the warrant to provide an explanation of any such document or to state where it may be found or how access to it may be obtained, and

(*e*) in the case of any such document which consists of information which is stored in electronic form and is on, or accessible from, the premises, to require the information to be produced in a form—

(i) in which it can be taken away, and

(ii) in which it is legible or from which it can readily be produced in a legible form.

(3) In subsection (1), any reference in paragraph (*a*) or (*b*) to a document does not include any document which is relevant to whether a person has complied with—

(*a*) subsection (3) of section 238 (information and advice to employees) or regulations under subsection (4) of that section, or

(*b*) any provision in force in Northern Ireland which corresponds to that subsection (3) or is made under provision corresponding to that subsection (4),

and is not relevant to the exercise of the Regulator's functions for any other reason.

(4) For the purposes of subsection (1)(*c*)(iii), any liability to pay a penalty under—

(*a*) section 10 of the Pensions Act 1995 (c 26), or

(*b*) any corresponding provision in force in Northern Ireland,

which might arise out of a failure to comply with any provision within subsection (3)(*a*) or (*b*) is to be disregarded.

(5) References in subsection (2) to such a document as is mentioned in subsection (1) are to be read in accordance with subsections (3) and (4).

(6) When executing a warrant under this section, an inspector may be accompanied by such persons as he considers appropriate.

(7) A warrant under this section continues in force until the end of the period of one month beginning with the day on which it is issued.

(8) Any document of which possession is taken under this section may be retained—

(*a*) if the document is relevant to proceedings against any person for any offence which are commenced before the end of the retention period, until the conclusion of those proceedings, and

(*b*) otherwise, until the end of the retention period.

(9) In subsection (8), "the retention period" means the period comprising—

(*a*) the period of 12 months beginning with the date on which possession was taken of the document, and

(*b*) any extension of that period under subsection (10).

(10) The Regulator may, by a direction made before the end of the retention period (including any extension of it under this subsection), extend it by such period not exceeding 12 months as the Regulator considers appropriate.

(11) *Scotland.*

[Pensions Act 2004, s 78.]

7.10880 **79. Sections 72 to 78: interpretation** (1) This section applies for the purposes of sections 72 to 78.

(2) "Document" includes information recorded in any form, and any reference to production of a document, in relation to information recorded otherwise than in a legible form, is to producing a copy of the information—

(*a*) in a legible form, or

(*b*) in a form from which it can readily be produced in a legible form.

(3) "Inspector" means a person appointed by the Regulator as an inspector.

[Pensions Act 2004, s 79.]

7.10881 **190. Information to be provided to the Board etc** (1) Regulations[1] may require such persons as may be prescribed to provide—

(*a*) to the Board, or

(*b*) to a person—
(i) with whom the Board has made arrangements under paragraph 18 of Schedule 5, and
(ii) who is authorised by the Board for the purposes of the regulations,
information of a prescribed description at such times, or in such circumstances, as may be prescribed.

(2) Regulations under subsection (1) may in particular make provision for requiring such persons as may be prescribed to provide any information or evidence needed for a determination of entitlement to compensation under Chapter 3 of this Part.

(3) Regulations made by virtue of paragraph (b) of that subsection must make provision regarding the manner in which the persons required to provide information are to be notified of the identity of the person authorised as mentioned in sub-paragraph (ii) of that paragraph.

[Pensions Act 2004, s 190.]

---

[1] See the Pension Protection Fund (Provision of Information) Regulations 2005, SI 2005/674 amended by SI 2010/196. The Financial Assistance Scheme (Miscellaneous Provisions) Regulations 2009, SI 2009/1851 have been made under this provision.

7.10882 191. **Notices requiring provision of information** (1) Any person to whom subsection (3) applies may be required by a notice in writing to produce any document, or provide any other information, which is—
(*a*) of a description specified in the notice, and
(*b*) relevant to the exercise of the Board's functions in relation to an occupational pension scheme.

(2) A notice under subsection (1) may be given by—
(*a*) the Board, or
(*b*) a person authorised by the Board for the purposes of this section in relation to the scheme.

(3) This subsection applies to—
(*a*) a trustee or manager of the scheme,
(*b*) a professional adviser in relation to the scheme,
(*c*) the employer in relation to the scheme,
(*d*) an insolvency practitioner in relation to the employer, and
(*e*) any other person appearing to the Board, or person giving the notice, to be a person who holds, or is likely to hold, information relevant to the discharge of the Board's functions in relation to the scheme.

(4) Where the production of a document, or the provision of information, is required by a notice given under subsection (1), the document must be produced, or information must be provided, in such a manner, at such a place and within such a period as may be specified in the notice.

[Pensions Act 2004, s 191.]

7.10883 192. **Entry of premises** (1) An appointed person may, for the purpose of enabling or facilitating the performance of any function of the Board in relation to an occupational pension scheme, at any reasonable time enter scheme premises and, while there—
(*a*) may make such examination and inquiry as may be necessary for such purpose,
(*b*) may require any person on the premises to produce, or secure the production of, any document relevant to that purpose for inspection by the appointed person,
(*c*) may take copies of any such document,
(*d*) may take possession of any document appearing to be such a document or take in relation to any such document any other steps which appear necessary for preserving it or preventing interference with it,
(*e*) may, in the case of any such document which consists of information which is stored in electronic form and is on, or accessible from, the premises, require the information to be produced in a form—
(i) in which it can be taken away, and
(ii) in which it is legible or from which it can readily be produced in a legible form, and
(*f*) may, as to any matter relevant to the exercise of the Board's functions in relation to the scheme, examine, or require to be examined, either alone or in the *presence* of another person, any person on the premises whom he has reasonable cause to believe to be able to give information relevant to that matter.

(2) Premises are scheme premises for the purposes of subsection (1) if the appointed person has reasonable grounds to believe that—
(*a*) they are being used for the business of the employer,
(*b*) an insolvency practitioner in relation to the employer is acting there in that capacity,
(*c*) documents relevant to—
(i) the administration of the scheme, or
(ii) the employer,
are being kept there, or

(*d*) the administration of the scheme, or work connected with the administration of the scheme, is being carried out there,

unless the premises are a private dwelling-house not used by, or by permission of, the occupier for the purposes of a trade or business.

(3) An appointed person applying for admission to any premises for the purposes of this section must, if so required, produce his certificate of appointment.

(4) When exercising a power under this section an appointed person may be accompanied by such persons as he considers appropriate.

(5) Any document of which possession is taken under this section may be retained until the end of the period comprising—

(*a*) the period of 12 months beginning with the date on which possession was taken of the document, and

(*b*) any extension of that period under subsection (6).

(6) The Board may before the end of the period mentioned in subsection (5) (including any extension of it under this subsection) extend it by such period not exceeding 12 months as the Board considers appropriate.

(7) In this section "appointed person" means a person appointed by the Board for the purposes of this section in relation to the scheme.

[Pensions Act 2004, s 192.]

7.10884 **193. Penalties relating to sections 191 and 192** (1) A person who, without reasonable excuse, neglects or refuses to provide information or produce a document when required to do so under section 191 is guilty of an offence.

(2) A person who without reasonable excuse—

(*a*) intentionally delays or obstructs an appointed person exercising any power under section 192,

(*b*) neglects or refuses to produce, or secure the production of, any document when required to do so under that section, or

(*c*) neglects or refuses to answer a question or to provide information when so required,

is guilty of an offence.

(3) In subsection (2)(a) "appointed person" has the same meaning as it has in section 192.

(4) A person guilty of an offence under subsection (1) or (2) is liable on summary conviction to a fine not exceeding level 5 on the standard scale.

(5) An offence under subsection (1) or (2)(*b*) or (*c*) may be charged by reference to any day or longer period of time; and a person may be convicted of a second or subsequent offence by reference to any period of time following the preceding conviction of the offence.

(6) Any person who intentionally and without reasonable excuse alters, suppresses, conceals or destroys any document which he is or is liable to be required to produce under section 191 or 192 is guilty of an offence.

(7) Any person guilty of an offence under subsection (6) is liable—

(*a*) on summary conviction, to a fine not exceeding the statutory maximum;

(*b*) on conviction on indictment, to a fine or imprisonment for a term not exceeding two years, or both.

[Pensions Act 2004, s 193.]

7.10885 **194. Warrants** (1) A justice of the peace may issue a warrant under this section if satisfied on information on oath given by or on behalf of the Board that there are reasonable grounds for believing—

(*a*) that there is on, or accessible from, any premises any document—

(i) whose production has been required under section 191 or 192, or any corresponding provision in force in Northern Ireland, and

(ii) which has not been produced in compliance with that requirement,

(*b*) that there is on, or accessible from, any premises any document relevant to the exercise of the Board's functions in relation to an occupational pension scheme whose production could be so required and, if its production were so required, the document—

(i) would not be produced, but

(ii) would be removed, or made inaccessible, from the premises, hidden, tampered with or destroyed, or

(*c*) that a person will do any act which constitutes a misuse or misappropriation of the assets of an occupational pension scheme and that there is on, or accessible from, any premises any document—

(i) which relates to whether the act will be done, and

(ii) whose production could be required under section 191 or 192, or any corresponding provision in force in Northern Ireland.

(2) A warrant under this section shall authorise an inspector—

(*a*) to enter the premises specified in the information, using such force as is reasonably necessary for the purpose,

(*b*) to search the premises and—

(i) take possession of any document appearing to be such a document as is mentioned in subsection (1), or
(ii) take in relation to such a document any other steps which appear necessary for preserving it or preventing interference with it,

(*c*) to take copies of any such document,

(*d*) to require any person named in the warrant to provide an explanation of any such document or to state where it may be found or how access to it may be obtained, and

(*e*) in the case of any such document which consists of information which is stored in electronic form and is on, or accessible from, the premises, to require the information to be produced in a form—
(i) in which it can be taken away, and
(ii) in which it is legible or from which it can readily be produced in a legible form.

(3) When executing a warrant under this section, an inspector may be accompanied by such persons as he considers appropriate.

(4) A warrant under this section continues in force until the end of the period of one month beginning with the day on which it is issued.

(5) Any document of which possession is taken under this section may be retained until the end of the period comprising—

(*a*) the period of 12 months beginning with the date on which possession was taken of the document, and

(*b*) any extension of that period under subsection (6).

(6) The Board may before the end of the period mentioned in subsection (5) (including any extension of it under this subsection) extend it by such period not exceeding 12 months as the Board considers appropriate.

(7) In this section "inspector" means a person appointed by the Board as an inspector.

(8) *Scotland.*

[Pensions Act 2004, s 194.]

*Provision of false or misleading information*

7.10886 **195. Offence of providing false or misleading information to the Board**

(1) Any person who knowingly or recklessly provides information which is false or misleading in a material particular is guilty of an offence if the information—

(*a*) is provided in purported compliance with a requirement under—
(i) section 190 (information to be provided to the Board etc),
(ii) section 191 (notices requiring provision of information), or
(iii) section 192 (entry of premises), or

(*b*) is provided otherwise than as mentioned in paragraph (a) but in circumstances in which the person providing the information intends, or could reasonably be expected to know, that it would be used by the Board for the purposes of exercising its functions under this Act.

(2) Any person guilty of an offence under subsection (1) is liable—

(*a*) on summary conviction, to a fine not exceeding the statutory maximum;

(*b*) on conviction on indictment, to a fine or imprisonment for a term not exceeding two years, or both.

[Pensions Act 2004, s 195.]

*Interpretation*

7.10887 **204. Sections 190 to 203: interpretation** (1) This section applies for the purposes of sections 190 to 203.

(2) "Document" includes information recorded in any form, and any reference to production of a document, in relation to information recorded otherwise than in a legible form, is to producing a copy of the information—

(*a*) in a legible form, or

(*b*) in a form from which it can readily be produced in a legible form.

(3) Where the Board has assumed responsibility for a scheme—

(*a*) any reference to the Board's functions in relation to the scheme includes a reference to the functions which it has by virtue of having assumed responsibility for the scheme, and

(*b*) any reference to a trustee, manager, professional adviser or employer in relation to the scheme is to be read as a reference to a person who held that position in relation to the scheme before the Board assumed responsibility for it.

[Pensions Act 2004, s 204.]

7.10888 **322. Commencement** (1) Subject to subsections (2) to (4), the provisions of this Act come into force in accordance with provision made by the Secretary of State by order.

(2) The following provisions come into force on the day this Act is passed—

(*a*) in Part 4, sections 234, 235 and 236 and Schedule 10 (provisions relating to retirement planning);

(*b*) in Part 5, section 281 (exemption from statutory revaluation requirement);

(*c*) in Part 8—
  (i) section 296 (entitlement to more than one state pension),
  (ii) section 297(3) (commencement of amendments of state pension deferment provisions made by Pensions Act 1995),
  (iii) section 298 (disclosure of state pension information), except subsections (4) and (5)(*b*), and
  (iv) section 299 (claims for certain benefits following termination of reciprocal agreement with Australia);

(*d*) in this Part (miscellaneous and general)—
  (i) sections 303 to 305 (service of notifications etc and electronic working), and
  (ii) this section and sections 313, 315 (other than subsection (6)), 316, 317, 318 (other than subsections (4) and (5)) and 323 to 325;

(*e*) the repeal by this Act of section 50(2) of the Welfare Reform and Pensions Act 1999.

(3) Section 297 (and Schedule 11) (deferral of retirement pensions and shared additional pensions), other than the provisions coming into force in accordance with subsection (2)—

(*a*) come into force on the day this Act is passed so far as is necessary for enabling the making of any regulations for which they provide, and

(*b*) otherwise, come into force on 6th April 2005.

(4) The repeals by this Act of section 134(3) of, and paragraph 21(14) of Schedule 4 to, the Pensions Act 1995 (c 26) come into force on 6th April 2005.

(5) Without prejudice to section 315(5), the power to make an order under this section includes power—

(*a*) to make transitional adaptations or modifications—
  (i) of the provisions brought into force by the order, or
  (ii) in connection with those provisions, of any provisions of Parts 1 to 7 of this Act or of the Pension Schemes Act 1993 (c 48), the Pensions Act 1995, Parts 1, 2 or 4 of the Welfare Reform and Pensions Act 1999 (c 30) or Chapter 2 of Part 2 of the Child Support, Pensions and Social Security Act 2000 (c 19), or

(*b*) to save the effect of any of the repealed provisions of those Acts, or those provisions as adapted or modified by the order,

as it appears to the Secretary of State expedient, including different adaptations or modifications for different periods.

[Pensions Act 2004, s 322.]

# Welfare Reform Act 2007[1]

(2007 c 5)

## PART 1[2]

## EMPLOYMENT AND SUPPORT ALLOWANCE

### *Entitlement*

7.10889 1. **Employment and support allowance** (1) An allowance, to be known as an employment and support allowance, shall be payable in accordance with the provisions of this Part.

(2) Subject to the provisions of this Part, a claimant is entitled to an employment and support allowance if he satisfies the basic conditions and either—

(*a*) the first and the second conditions set out in Part 1 of Schedule 1 (conditions relating to national insurance) or the third condition set out in that Part of that Schedule (condition relating to youth), or

(*b*) the conditions set out in Part 2 of that Schedule (conditions relating to financial position).

(3) The basic conditions are that the claimant—

(*a*) has limited capability for work,

(*b*) is at least 16 years old,

(*c*) has not reached pensionable age,

(*d*) is in Great Britain,

(*e*) is not entitled to income support, and

(*f*) is not entitled to a jobseeker's allowance (and is not a member of a couple who are entitled to a joint-claim jobseeker's allowance).

(4) For the purposes of this Part, a person has limited capability for work if—

(*a*) his capability for work is limited by his physical or mental condition, and

(*b*) the limitation is such that it is not reasonable to require him to work.

(5) An employment and support allowance is payable in respect of a week.

(6) In subsection (3)—

"joint-claim jobseeker's allowance" means a jobseeker's allowance entitlement to which arises by virtue of section 1(2B) of the Jobseekers Act 1995 (c 18);

"pensionable age" has the meaning given by the rules in paragraph 1 of Schedule 4 to the Pensions Act 1995 (c 26).

(7) In this Part—

"contributory allowance" means an employment and support allowance entitlement to which is based on subsection (2)(*a*);

"income-related allowance" means an employment and support allowance entitlement to which is based on subsection (2)(*b*).

[Welfare Reform Act 2007, s 1.]

---

[1] This Act implements proposals in the Green Paper *'A new deal for welfare – Empowering people to work'* (Cm 6730) (January 2006) and the Consultation Report (Cm 6859) (June 2006). Provision is made for an employment and support allowance which replaces incapacity benefit and income support on grounds of incapacity for work or disability. The new benefit incorporates both a contributory allowance and an income-related allowance. For some claimants receipt of benefit will be conditional on satisfying either a National Insurance contribution test or an income-related test and being assessed to be limited in their capability for work because of their physical or mental condition and satisfying certain other conditions. The Act is to be brought into force in accordance s 70, post and with orders made thereunder with the exception of ss 1 and 23 which came fully into force on 1 April 2008 and s 46 which came fully into force on 7 April 2008; s 42 came into force for the purpose of making regulations on 5 August 2008 and fully in force together with ss 42 and 43 on 1 September 2008. At the date of going to press the following commencement orders had been made: (No 1) SI 2007/1721; (No 2) SI 2007/1991; (No 3) SI 2007/2819; (No 4 and Savings and Transitional Provisions) SI 2007/2872; (No 5) SI 2008/411; (No 6 and Consequential Provisions) SI 2008/787; (No 7, Transitional and Savings Provisions) Order 2008, SI 2008/2101; (No 8) SI 2008/2772; (No 9) SI 2008/3167; (No 10, Transitional and Savings Provisions) SI 2009/775; (No 11) SI 2009/1608; (No 12) SI 2010/1905; (No 13) SI 2011/330. The provisions reproduced in this Manual came into force as follows: ss 1, 2–16 (27 October 2008); s 23 (fully) (27 October 2008); s 42 (fully) (1 September 2008); s 43 (1 September 2008); s 46 (fully) (7 April 2008); s 49 (1 April 2008).

[2] Part 1 comprises ss 1–29 and Schs 1–4.

**2–16.** *Amounts of and deductions from contributory and income-related benefits. Assessments relating to entitlement. Work-focused health-related assessments, work focused interviews.*

*Miscellaneous*

7.10890 **23. Recovery of sums in respect of maintenance** (1) Regulations may make provision for the court to have power to make a recovery order against any person where an award of income-related allowance[1] has been made to that person's spouse or civil partner.

(2) The reference in subsection (1) to a recovery order is to an order requiring the person against whom it is made to make payments to the Secretary of State or to such other person or persons as the court may determine.

(3) *Further provisions about regulations.*

(4) In this section, "the court" means—

(*a*) in relation to England and Wales, a magistrates' court;

(*b*) *Scotland.*

[Welfare Reform Act 2007, s 23.]

---

[1] "Income-related allowance" has the meaning given by section 1(7) (s 24).

## Part 3[1]

## Social Security Administration: General

*Sharing of social security information*

7.10891 **42. Information relating to certain benefits** (1) Information falling within subsection (3) may be supplied by the person who holds it to a person falling within subsection (4) for purposes connected with the application of grant paid under a relevant enactment towards expenditure incurred by the recipient of the grant—

(*a*) in providing, or contributing to the provision of, welfare services, or

(*b*) in connection with such welfare services.

(2) Information falling within subsection (3) which is held for a prescribed purpose by a person falling within any of paragraphs (*c*) to (*h*) of subsection (4) may be—

(*a*) used by that person for another prescribed purpose;

(*b*) provided to another such person for use in relation to the same or another prescribed purpose.

(3) The information is any information which is held by a person falling within subsection (4) relating to—

(*a*) income support;

(*b*) income-based jobseeker's allowance;

(*c*) income-related employment and support allowance;

(*d*) state pension credit;

(*e*) housing benefit;

(*f*) welfare services.

(4) The persons are—

(*a*) the Secretary of State;

(*b*) a person providing services to the Secretary of State;

(*c*) an authority administering housing benefit;

(*d*) a person authorised to exercise any function of such an authority relating to housing benefit;

(*e*) a person providing to such an authority services relating to housing benefit;

(*f*) a local authority to which any grant is or will be paid as mentioned in subsection (1);
(*g*) a person authorised to exercise any function of such an authority relating to the grant;
(*h*) a person providing to such an authority services relating to any such function.

(5) Information which is supplied under subsection (1) to an authority or other person falling within subsection (4)(*f*), (*g*) or (*h*) may be supplied by the authority or person to a person who provides qualifying welfare services for purposes connected with the provision of those services.

(6) A person provides qualifying welfare services if—
(*a*) he provides welfare services,
(*b*) a local authority contribute or will contribute to the expenditure incurred by him in providing those services, and
(*c*) that contribution is or will be derived (in whole or in part) from any grant which is or will be paid to the authority as mentioned in subsection (1).

(7) A relevant enactment is an enactment specified by order[2] made by the Secretary of State; and the power to make an order under this subsection is exercisable by statutory instrument subject to annulment in pursuance of a resolution of either House of Parliament.

(8) In subsection (2) a prescribed purpose is a purpose relating to housing benefit or welfare services which is prescribed by regulations[3] made by the Secretary of State by statutory instrument subject to annulment in pursuance of a resolution of either House of Parliament.

(9) The power to make an order or regulations under this section includes power—
(*a*) to make different provision for different purposes;
(*b*) to make such incidental, supplementary, consequential, transitional or saving provision as the Secretary of State thinks necessary or expedient.

(10) In this section—
"income-based jobseeker's allowance" has the same meaning as in the Jobseekers Act 1995 (c 18);
"income-related employment and support allowance" means an income-related allowance under Part 1;
"local authority" means—
(*a*) in relation to England, a county council, a district council, a London borough council, the Common Council of the City of London or the Council of the Isles of Scilly;
(*b*) in relation to Wales, a county council or a county borough council;
"welfare services" includes services which provide support, assistance, advice or counselling to individuals with particular needs.

(11) In the Local Government Act 2000 (c 22), sections 94 (disclosure of information) and 95 (unauthorised disclosure of information) are omitted.

[Welfare Reform Act 2007, s 42.]

---

1 Part 3 comprises ss 41–49.
2 The Welfare Reform Act (Relevant Enactment) Order 2009, SI 2009/2162 has been made which specifies s 31 of the Local Government Act 2003 (power to pay grant). Provision for Wales is made by the Welfare Reform Act (Relevant Enactment) (Wales) Order 2009, SI 2009/22687.
3 The Social Security (Use of Information for Housing Benefit and Welfare Services Purposes) Regulations 2008, SI 2008/2112 have been made.

7.10892 **43. Unlawful disclosure of certain information** (1) A person to whom subsection (2) applies is guilty of an offence if he discloses without lawful authority any information—
(*a*) which comes to him by virtue of section 42(1), (2) or (5), and
(*b*) which relates to a particular person.

(2) This subsection applies to—
(*a*) a person mentioned in section 42(4)(*f*) to (*h*);
(*b*) a person who provides qualifying welfare services (within the meaning of section 42(6));
(*c*) a person who is or has been a director, member of the committee of management, manager, secretary or other similar officer of a person mentioned in paragraph (*a*) or (*b*);
(*d*) a person who is or has been an employee of a person mentioned in paragraph (*a*) or (*b*).

(3) A person guilty of an offence under this section shall be liable—
(*a*) on conviction on indictment, to imprisonment for a term not exceeding 2 years or a fine or both, or
(*b*) on summary conviction, to imprisonment for a term not exceeding 12 months or a fine not exceeding the statutory maximum or both.

(4) It is not an offence under this section—
(*a*) to disclose information in the form of a summary or collection of information so framed as not to enable information relating to any particular person to be ascertained from it;
(*b*) to disclose information which has previously been disclosed to the public with lawful authority.

(5) It is a defence for a person charged with an offence under this section to prove that at the time of the alleged offence—

(*a*) he believed that he was making the disclosure in question with lawful authority and had no reasonable cause to believe otherwise, or

(*b*) he believed that the information in question had previously been disclosed to the public with lawful authority and had no reasonable cause to believe otherwise.

(6) A disclosure is made with lawful authority if it is so made for the purposes of section 123 of the Administration Act.

(7) This section does not affect that section.

(8) Until the commencement of section 282 of the Criminal Justice Act 2003 (c 44) (increase in maximum term that may be imposed on summary conviction of offence triable either way) the reference in subsection (3)(*b*) to 12 months must be taken to be a reference to 6 months.

[Welfare Reform Act 2007, s 43.]

## PART 5[1]
## GENERAL

7.10893 **70. Commencement** (1) The following provisions shall come into force at the end of the period of 2 months beginning with the day on which this Act is passed—

(*a*) sections 41(2) and (3), 44, 45, 54, 55, 59, 61(1)(*b*) and (2) to (6) and 62,

(*b*) paragraphs 1 to 4, 10, 11 and 14 of Schedule 5, and section 40 so far as relating thereto,

(*c*) paragraphs 2(1) and (3), 3 and 4 of Schedule 7, and section 63 so far as relating thereto, and

(*d*) Schedule 8, so far as relating to—

(i) section 3(5) of the Pneumoconiosis etc (Workers' Compensation) Act 1979 (c 41),

(ii) section 140(1A) of the Contributions and Benefits Act,

(iii) sections 71(5), 71ZA(2), 134(8)(*a*) and 168(3)(*d*) of the Administration Act,

(iv) section 69(5) of the Social Security Administration (Northern Ireland) Act 1992,

(v) Schedule 13 to the Local Government etc (Scotland) Act 1994 (c 39),

(vi) section 38(7)(*a*) of, and paragraph 81(2) of Schedule 7 to, the Social Security Act 1998 (c 14), and

(vii) paragraph 65 of Schedule 24 to the Civil Partnership Act 2004 (c 33),

and section 67 so far as relating thereto.

(2) The remaining provisions of this Act, except—

(*a*) this section,

(*b*) sections 64, 65, 66, 68, 69 and 71, and

(*c*) paragraph 8 of Schedule 5, and section 40 so far as relating thereto,

shall come into force on such day as the Secretary of State may by order[2] made by statutory instrument appoint, and different days may be so appointed for different purposes.

[Welfare Reform Act 2007, s 70.]

---

1 Part 5 comprises ss 64–71 and Sch 8.

2 For orders made under this provision, see the note to s 1, ante.

# Pensions Act 2008[1]

(2008 c 30)

*Offences and monitoring*

7.10894 **45. Offences of failing to comply** (1) An offence is committed by an employer who wilfully fails to comply with—

(*a*) the duty under section 3(2) (automatic enrolment),

(*b*) the duty under section 5(2) (automatic re-enrolment), or

(*c*) the duty under section 7(3) (jobholder's right to opt in).

(2) A person guilty of an offence under this section is liable[2]—

(*a*) on conviction on indictment, to imprisonment for a term not exceeding two years, or to a fine, or both;

(*b*) on summary conviction to a fine not exceeding the statutory maximum.

[Pensions Act 2008, s 45.]

---

1 The provisions of this Act referred to in this Manual are to be brought into force in accordance with orders made by the Secretary of State under s 149. The following commencement orders had been made: (No 1 and Consequential Provisions) SI 2008/3241; (No 2) SI 2009/82; (No 3 and Consequential Provisions) SI 2009/809; (No 4) SI 2009/1566; (No 5) SI 2010/10; (No 6) SI 2010/467; (No 7 and Saving, Consequential and Incidental Provisions) SI 2010/1145; (No 8) SI 2010/1221; (No 9) SI 2011/664; (No 10) SI 2011/1266; (No 11) SI 2011/3033; (No 12) SI 2012/683; (No 13) SI 2012/1682 (ss 45–47 on 30 June 2012); (No 14 and Supplementary Provisions) SI 2012/2480; (No 15) SI 2014/463.

2 For procedure in respect of this offence which is triable either way, see the Magistrates' Courts Act 1980, ss 17A–21 in PART I: MAGISTRATES' COURTS, PROCEDURE, ante.

7.10895 **46. Offences by bodies corporate** (1) Subsection (2) applies where an offence under section 45 committed by a body corporate is proved—

(a) to have been committed with the consent or connivance of an officer of the body corporate, or

(b) to be attributable to any neglect on the part of an officer of the body corporate.

(2) The officer, as well as the body corporate, is guilty of the offence and is liable to be proceeded against and punished accordingly.

(3) "Officer" in this section means—

(a) a director, manager, secretary or other similar officer, or

(b) a person purporting to act in such a capacity.

(4) Where the affairs of a body corporate are managed by its members, this section applies in relation to the acts and defaults of a member in connection with the member's functions of management as if the member were an officer of the body corporate.

[Pensions Act 2008, s 46.]

7.10896 47. **Offences by partnerships and unincorporated associations** (1) Proceedings for an offence under section 45 alleged to have been committed by a partnership or an unincorporated association may be brought in the name of the partnership or association.

(2) For the purposes of such proceedings—

(a) rules of court relating to the service of documents are to have effect as if the partnership or association were a body corporate;

(b) the following provisions apply in relation to the partnership or association as they apply in relation to a body corporate—

(i) section 33 of the Criminal Justice Act 1925 (c 86) and Schedule 3 to the Magistrates' Courts Act 1980 (c 43);

(ii) section 70 of the Criminal Procedure (Scotland) Act 1995 (c 46).

(3) A fine imposed on a partnership or association on its conviction of an offence under section 45 is to be paid out of the funds of the partnership or association.

(4) Subsection (5) applies where an offence under section 45 committed by a partnership is proved—

(a) to have been committed with the consent or connivance of a partner, or

(b) to be attributable to any neglect on the part of a partner.

(5) The partner, as well as the partnership, is guilty of the offence and is liable to be proceeded against and punished accordingly.

(6) Subsection (7) applies where an offence under section 45 committed by an unincorporated association is proved—

(a) to have been committed with the consent or connivance of an officer of the association, or

(b) to be attributable to any neglect on the part of an officer of the association.

(7) The officer, as well as the association, is guilty of the offence and is liable to be proceeded against and punished accordingly.

(8) "Officer" in this section means—

(a) an officer of the association or a member of its governing body, or

(b) a person purporting to act in such capacity.

(9) "Partner" in this section includes a person purporting to act as a partner.

[Pensions Act 2008, s 47.]

# Welfare Reform Act 2012[1]

(2012 c 5)

## Part 5

## Social Security: General

*Information-sharing: Secretary of State and HMRC*

7.10897 127. **Information-sharing between Secretary of State and HMRC** (1) This subsection applies to information which is held for the purposes of any HMRC functions—

(a) by the Commissioners for Her Majesty's Revenue and Customs, or

(b) by a person providing services to them.

(2) Information to which subsection (1) applies may be supplied—

(a) to the Secretary of State, or to a person providing services to the Secretary of State, or

(b) to a Northern Ireland Department, or to a person providing services to a Northern Ireland Department,

for use for the purposes of departmental functions.

(3) This subsection applies to information which is held for the purposes of any departmental functions—

(a) by the Secretary of State, or by a person providing services to the Secretary of State, or

(b) by a Northern Ireland Department, or by a person providing services to a Northern Ireland Department.

(4) Information to which subsection (3) applies may be supplied—

(a) to the Commissioners for Her Majesty's Revenue and Customs, or

(b) to a person providing services to them,

for use for the purposes of HMRC functions.

(5) Information supplied under this section must not be supplied by the recipient of the information to any other person or body without—

(*a*) the authority of the Commissioners for Her Majesty's Revenue and Customs, in the case of information supplied under subsection (2);

(*b*) the authority of the Secretary of State, in the case of information held as mentioned in subsection (3)(*a*) and supplied under subsection (4);

(*c*) the authority of the relevant Northern Ireland Department, in the case of information held as mentioned in subsection (3)(*b*) and supplied under subsection (4).

(6) Where information supplied under this section has been used for the purposes for which it was supplied, it is lawful for it to be used for any purposes for which information held for those purposes could be used.

(7) In this section—

"departmental functions" means functions relating to—

(*a*) social security,

(*b*) employment or training, or

(*c*) the investigation or prosecution of offences relating to tax credits, or

(*d*) child support;

"HMRC function" means any function—

(*a*) for which the Commissioners for Her Majesty's Revenue and Customs are responsible by virtue of section 5 of the Commissioners for Revenue and Customs Act 2005, or

(*b*) which relates to a matter listed in Schedule 1 to that Act;

"Northern Ireland Department" means any of the following—

(*a*) the Department for Social Development;

(*b*) the Department of Finance and Personnel;

(*c*) the Department for Employment and Learning.

(8) For the purposes of this section any reference to functions relating to social security includes a reference to functions relating to—

(*a*) statutory payments as defined in section 4C(11) of the Social Security Contributions and Benefits Act 1992;

(*b*) maternity allowance under section 35 of that Act;

(*c*) statutory payments as defined in section 4C(11) of the Social Security Contributions and Benefits (Northern Ireland) Act 1992;

(*d*) maternity allowance under section 35 of that Act.

(9) This section does not limit the circumstances in which information may be supplied apart from this section.

(10) *Amends section 3 of the Social Security Act 1998.*

[Welfare Reform Act 2012, s 127 as amended by SI 2012/2007.]

[1] Sections 128, 129, 133(1)-(4) were brought into force on 20 March 2012; ss 130, 131 and 132 fully in force by 8 May 2012 Welfare Reform Act 2012 (Commencement No 1) Order 2012, SI 2012/863; s 127 on 8 May 2012 (Welfare Reform Act 2012, s 150(2)(f)); s 133(6) on 2 July 2012 (Welfare Reform Act 2012 (Commencement No 3, Savings Provision) Order 2012, SI 2012/1651).

*Information-sharing: Secretary of State and DPP*

7.10898 **128. Information-sharing between Secretary of State and DPP** (1) The Secretary of State may supply social security information or child support information to a person specified in subsection (2) for use for a purpose specified in subsection (3).

(2) The persons referred to in subsection (1) are—

(*a*) the Director of Public Prosecutions;

(*b*) a person appointed under section 5 of the Prosecution of Offences Act 1985 (conduct of prosecutions on behalf of Crown Prosecution Service).

(3) The purposes referred to in subsection (1) are—

(*a*) the institution or conduct of criminal proceedings which relate wholly or partly to social security matters or child support;

(*b*) the giving of advice to any person on any matter relating to criminal proceedings, or criminal offences, which relate wholly or partly to social security matters or child support;

(*c*) the exercise in relation to social security matters or child support of functions assigned to the Director of Public Prosecutions under section 3(2)(g) of the Prosecution of Offences Act 1985;

(*d*) the exercise of functions of the Director of Public Prosecutions under Part 2, 5 or 8 of the Proceeds of Crime Act 2002.

(4) The reference in subsection (1) to the Secretary of State includes a person providing services to the Secretary of State.

(5) This section does not limit the circumstances in which information may be supplied apart from this section.

(6) In this section—

"child support information" means information held for the purposes of any of the Secretary of State's functions relating to child support;

"social security information" means information held for the purposes of any of the Secretary of State's functions relating to social security matters;

"social security matters" means—

(*a*) social security (including the payments and allowances referred to in section 127(8)),

(*b*) tax credits, and

(*c*) schemes and arrangements under section 2 of the Employment and Training Act 1973.

[Welfare Reform Act 2012, s 128 as amended by SI 2012/2007.]

7.10899 **129. Unlawful disclosure of information supplied under section 128** (1) A person to whom information is supplied under section 128, or an employee or former employee of such a person, may not disclose the information if it relates to a particular person.

(2) Subsection (1) does not apply to—

(*a*) a disclosure of a summary or collection of information so framed as not to enable information relating to any particular person to be ascertained from it;

(*b*) a disclosure made for the purposes of a function of the Director of Public Prosecutions, where the disclosure does not contravene any restriction imposed by the Director;

(*c*) a disclosure made to the Secretary of State, or a person providing services to the Secretary of State, for the purposes of the exercise of functions relating to social security matters or child support (within the meaning of section 128);

(*d*) a disclosure made for the purposes of a criminal investigation or criminal proceedings (whether or not in the United Kingdom);

(*e*) a disclosure made for the purposes of—

(i) the exercise of any functions of the prosecutor under Parts 2, 3 and 4 of the Proceeds of Crime Act 2002;

(ii) the exercise of any functions of the Serious Organised Crime Agency under that Act;

(iii) the exercise of any functions of the Director of the Serious Fraud Office, the Director of Public Prosecutions for Northern Ireland or the Scottish Ministers under, or in relation to, Part 5 or 8 of that Act;

(iv) investigations or proceedings outside the United Kingdom which have led or may lead to the making of an external order within the meaning of section 447 of that Act;

(*f*) a disclosure made to a person exercising public functions of law enforcement for the purposes of the exercise of those functions in civil proceedings;

(*g*) a disclosure which in the opinion of the Director of Public Prosecutions is desirable for the purpose of safeguarding national security;

(*h*) a disclosure made in pursuance of an order of a court;

(*i*) a disclosure made with the consent of each person to whom the information relates.

(3) Subsection (1) does not apply in relation to information relating to schemes and arrangements under section 2 of the Employment and Training Act 1973.

(4) Subsection (1) is subject to any other Act or to an instrument made under an Act.

(5) A person who contravenes subsection (1) commits an offence.

(6) It is a defence for a person charged with an offence under this section of disclosing information to prove that he or she reasonably believed—

(*a*) that the disclosure was lawful, or

(*b*) that the information had already and lawfully been made available to the public.

(7) A person guilty of an offence under this section is liable—

(*a*) on conviction on indictment, to imprisonment for a term not exceeding two years or a fine or both, or

(*b*) on summary conviction, to imprisonment for a term not exceeding twelve months or a fine not exceeding the statutory maximum or both.

(8) A prosecution for an offence under this section may be instituted only with the consent of the Director of Public Prosecutions.

(9) In relation to an offence under this section committed before the commencement of section 154(1) of the Criminal Justice Act 2003 (increase in maximum term that may be imposed on summary conviction of offence triable either way), the reference in subsection (7)(*b*) to twelve months shall have effect as if it were a reference to six months.

[Welfare Reform Act 2012, s 129 as amended by SI 2012/2007.]

*Information-sharing involving local authorities etc*

7.10900 **130. Information-sharing in relation to provision of overnight care etc**

(1) This section applies where a local authority holds information falling within subsection (2) in relation to a person who is receiving or is likely to receive a relevant service.

(2) The information referred to in subsection (1) is—

(*a*) information as to the fact of the provision or likely provision of the service;
(*b*) information about when the provision of the service begins or ends or is likely to do so;
(*c*) other prescribed information relating to the service provided and how it is funded (including the extent to which it is funded by the recipient).

(3) In this section "relevant service means—
(*a*) a service consisting of overnight care in the individual's own home provided by or on behalf of a local authority;
(*b*) a residential care service provided by or on behalf of a local authority;
(*c*) a service consisting of overnight hospital accommodation.

(4) In subsection (3)(*c*) "hospital accommodation" means—
(*a*) in relation to England, hospital accommodation within the meaning of the National Health Service Act 2006 which is provided by a Primary Care Trust, an NHS trust or an NHS foundation trust;
(*b*) in relation to Wales, hospital accommodation within the meaning of the National Health Service (Wales) Act 2006 which is provided by a Local Health Board or an NHS trust;
(*c*) in relation to Scotland, hospital accommodation within the meaning of the National Health Service (Scotland) Act 1978 which is provided by a Health Board or Special Health Board but excluding accommodation in an institution for providing dental treatment maintained in connection with a dental school.

(5) The local authority may—
(*a*) itself use the information for purposes relating to the payment of a relevant benefit to the individual, or
(*b*) supply the information to a person specified in subsection (6) for those purposes.

(6) The persons referred to in subsection (5) are—
(*a*) the Secretary of State;
(*b*) a person providing services to the Secretary of State;
(*c*) a local authority;
(*d*) a person authorised to exercise any function of a local authority relating to a relevant benefit;
(*e*) a person providing services relating to a relevant benefit to a local authority.

(7) In this section "relevant benefit" means—
(*a*) universal credit;
(*b*) housing benefit;
(*c*) council tax benefit;
(*d*) any prescribed benefit.

(8) Regulations under subsection (7)(*d*) may not prescribe a benefit provision for which is within the legislative competence of the Scottish Parliament.

[Welfare Reform Act 2012, s 130.]

7.10901 **131. Information-sharing in relation to welfare services etc** (1) The Secretary of State, or a person providing services to the Secretary of State, may supply relevant information to a qualifying person for prescribed purposes relating to welfare services or council tax.

(2) A qualifying person who holds relevant information for a prescribed purpose relating to welfare services may supply that information to—
(*a*) the Secretary of State, or
(*b*) a person providing services to the Secretary of State,

for a prescribed purpose relating to a relevant social security benefit.

(3) A qualifying person who holds relevant information for a prescribed purpose relating to welfare services, council tax or housing benefit may—
(*a*) use the information for another prescribed purpose relating to welfare services, council tax or housing benefit;
(*b*) supply it to another qualifying person for use in relation to the same or another prescribed purpose relating to welfare services, council tax or housing benefit.

(4) Relevant information supplied under subsection (1) or (3) to a qualifying person may be supplied by that person to a person who provides qualifying welfare services for purposes connected with the provision of those services.

(5) In subsection (4) services are qualifying welfare services if—
(*a*) a local authority, or
(b) a person who is a qualifying person by virtue of subsection (11)(*g*),

contributes or will contribute to the expenditure incurred in their provision.

(6) The Secretary of State may not exercise the power in subsection (3) to prescribe purposes for which information may be supplied by a qualifying person so as to prescribe an excepted purpose in relation to excepted information held by a Welsh body.

(7) In subsection (6)—
(*a*) excepted information is information held by the Welsh body that—

(i) is not supplied by, or derived from information supplied to another person by, the Secretary of State or a person providing services to the Secretary of State or a person engaged in the administration of housing benefit, and

(ii) is held only for an excepted purpose;

(*b*) an excepted purpose is a purpose relating to a matter provision for which—

(i) is within the legislative competence of the National Assembly for Wales, or

(ii) is made by the Welsh Ministers, the First Minister for Wales or the Counsel General to the Welsh Assembly Government.

(8) The Secretary of State may not exercise the power in subsection (3) to prescribe purposes for which information may be supplied by a qualifying person so as to prescribe an excepted purpose in relation to excepted information held by a Scottish body.

(9) In subsection (8)—

(*a*) excepted information is information held by the Scottish body that—

(i) is not supplied by, or derived from information supplied to another person by, the Secretary of State or a person providing services to the Secretary of State or a person engaged in the administration of housing benefit, and

(ii) is held only for an excepted purpose;

(*b*) an excepted purpose is a purpose relating to a matter provision for which is within the legislative competence of the Scottish Parliament.

(10) Subsections (1) to (4) do not apply in a case where the supply or use of information is authorised by section 130.

(11) In this section "qualifying person" means—

(*a*) a local authority;

(*b*) a person authorised to exercise any function of such an authority relating to welfare services or council tax;

(*c*) a person providing services to a local authority relating to welfare services or council tax;

(*d*) an authority which administers housing benefit;

(*e*) a person authorised to exercise any function of such an authority relating to housing benefit;

(*f*) a person providing to such an authority services relating to housing benefit; or

(*g*) a person prescribed or of a description prescribed by the Secretary of State.

(12) In this section—

"council tax" includes any local tax to fund local authority expenditure;

"person engaged in the administration of housing benefit" means—

(*a*) an authority which administers housing benefit,

(*b*) a person authorised to exercise any function of such an authority relating to housing benefit, or

(*c*) a person providing to such an authority services relating to housing benefit;

"relevant information" means information relating to—

(*a*) any relevant social security benefit, or

(*b*) welfare services;

"relevant social security benefit" has the meaning given in section 121DA(7) of the Social Security Administration Act 1992;

"Scottish body" means—

(*a*) a local authority in Scotland,

(*b*) a person authorised to exercise any function of such an authority relating to welfare services,

(*c*) a person providing to a local authority in Scotland services relating to welfare services, or

(*d*) a person prescribed or of a description prescribed by the Secretary of State;

"welfare services" includes services which provide accommodation, support, assistance, advice or counselling to individuals with particular needs, and for these purposes "assistance" includes assistance by means of a grant or loan or the provision of goods or services;

"Welsh body" means—

(*a*) a local authority in Wales,

(*b*) a person authorised to exercise any function of such an authority relating to welfare services,

(*c*) a person providing to a local authority in Wales services relating to welfare services, or

(*d*) a person prescribed or of a description prescribed by the Secretary of State.

[Welfare Reform Act 2012, s 131.]

7.10902 **132. Unlawful disclosure of information supplied under section 131** (1) A person to whom subsection (2) applies is guilty of an offence if the person discloses without lawful authority any information—

(*a*) which comes to the person by virtue of section 131(1), (3) or (4), and (*b*) which relates to a particular person.

(2) This subsection applies to—

(*a*) a person mentioned in section 131(11)(*a*) to (*c*);

(*b*) a person who provides qualifying welfare services (within the meaning of section 131);

(*c*) a person who is or has been a director, member of the committee of management, manager, secretary or other similar officer of a person mentioned in paragraph (*a*) or (*b*);

(*d*) a person who is or has been an employee of a person mentioned in paragraph (*a*) or (*b*).

(3) A person guilty of an offence under this section is liable—

(*a*) on conviction on indictment, to imprisonment for a term not exceeding two years or a fine or both, or

(*b*) on summary conviction, to imprisonment for a term not exceeding twelve months or a fine not exceeding the statutory maximum or both.

(4) It is not an offence under this section—

(*a*) to disclose information in the form of a summary or collection of information so framed as not to enable information relating to any particular person to be ascertained from it;

(*b*) to disclose information which has previously been disclosed to the public with lawful authority.

(5) It is a defence for a person ("D") charged with an offence under this section to prove that at the time of the alleged offence—

(*a*) D believed that D was making the disclosure in question with lawful authority and had no reasonable cause to believe otherwise, or

(*b*) D believed that the information in question had previously been disclosed to the public with lawful authority and had no reasonable cause to believe otherwise.

(6) A disclosure is made with lawful authority if it is so made for the purposes of section 123 of the Social Security Administration Act 1992.

(7) This section does not affect that section.

(8) Regulations under section 131(11)(*g*) may include provision for applying the provisions of this section to—

(*a*) a person who is a qualifying person within the meaning of section 131 by virtue of the regulations, or

(*b*) a person associated with such a qualifying person by reason of the person's office or employment or otherwise.

(9) In relation to an offence under this section committed in England and Wales before the commencement of section 154(1) of the Criminal Justice Act 2003 (increase in maximum term that may be imposed on summary conviction of offence triable either way) the reference in subsection (3)(*b*) to twelve months must be taken to be a reference to six months.

[Welfare Reform Act 2012, s 132.]

**7.10903 133. Sections 130 to 132: supplementary** (1) In sections 130 and 131—

"benefit" includes any allowance, payment, credit or loan;

"local authority" means—

(*a*) a county or district council in England;

(*b*) an eligible parish council (within the meaning of Chapter 1 of Part 1 of the Localism Act 2011);

(*c*) a London borough council;

(*d*) the Common Council of the City of London in its capacity as a local authority;

(*e*) the Council of the Isles of Scilly;

(*f*) a county or county borough council in Wales;

(*g*) a council constituted under section 2 of the Local Government etc (Scotland) Act 1994;

"prescribed" means prescribed in regulations[1] made by the Secretary of State.

(2) Any power to make regulations under sections 130 and 131 includes power—

(*a*) to make different provision for different purposes, cases and areas;

(*b*) to make such incidental, supplemental, consequential, transitional or saving provision as the Secretary of State thinks necessary or expedient.

(3) Regulations under sections 130 and 131 must be made by statutory instrument.

(4) A statutory instrument containing regulations under section 130 or 131 is subject to annulment in pursuance of a resolution of either House of Parliament.

(5) Until the coming into force of provision for identifying eligible parish councils within the meaning of Chapter 1 of Part 1 of the Localism Act 2011, the reference in subsection (1) to an eligible parish council within the meaning of that Chapter is to be read as a reference to an eligible parish council within the meaning of Part 1 of the Local Government Act 2000.

(6) The following are repealed—

(*a*) sections 42 and 43 of the Welfare Reform Act 2007;

(*b*) section 69(2)(*a*) of that Act.

[Welfare Reform Act 2012, s 133.]

[1] The Social Security (Information-sharing in relation to Welfare Services etc.) Regulations 2012, SI 2012/1483 amended by SI 2013/41 and 454 and the Social Security (Information-sharing in relation to Welfare Services etc.) Amendment and Prescribed Bodies Regulations 2013, SI 2013/454 have been made.

## Social Security (Claims and Payments) Regulations 1979[1]

(SI 1979/628 as amended by SI 1979/781 and 1199, SI 1980/1101, 1136, 1621, and 1943, SI 1982/699, 1241, 1344, and 1362, SI 1983/186, and 1015, SI 1984/458, 550, 1303, and 1699, SI 1985/600, SI 1986/903, SI 1993/495 and 405, SI 1993/2113 and SI 2002/1397)

*Information to be given when making a claim for benefit*

**7.10904** *7.* (1) Every person who makes a claim for benefit[2] shall furnish such certificates, documents, information and evidence for the purpose of determining the claim as may be required by the Secretary of State and, if reasonably so required, shall for that purpose attend at such office or place as the Secretary of State may direct.

(2) Every person who makes a claim for a widowed mother's allowance, child's special allowance, benefit in respect of a child or for an increase of benefit in respect of a child, shall, in particular, furnish such certificate relating to the birth of the child and such other information to show that that person is entitled or may be treated by regulations as if he were entitled to child benefit in respect of that child as the Secretary of State may require.

(3) Every person who makes a claim for an increase of benefit in respect of an adult dependant shall, in particular, furnish, if required, the following information concerning such dependant—

(*a*) his identity, date of birth, usual place of residence, occupation and relationship to the claimant;

(*b*) his position in regard to benefit under the Act, available sources of income and the amounts contributed by any person towards his maintenance; and

(*c*) in the case of an increase in respect of a wife or a husband, a certificate of the marriage;

together with a declaration signed by the dependant confirming the information given.

(4) Every person who makes a claim for a death grant shall, in particular, furnish the following information—

(*a*) if required by the Secretary of State, a death certificate relating to the deceased; and, where the claim is in respect of the death of a child, such certificate relating to the birth of the child, and such other information as the Secretary of State may reasonably require in support of a contention that immediately before the death of the child or the person by whom the contribution condition is to be satisfied, as the case may be, that person was entitled to child benefit in respect of that child; in this sub-paragraph a child includes a person referred to in section 32(4) (*a*) or (*b*);

(*b*) if required by the Secretary of State, the estimate or account of the undertaker.

(5) In this regulation the expression "child benefit" means benefit under Part 1 of the Child Benefit Act 1975.

[1] Made by the Secretary of State for Social Services under ss 45(4), 79–81, 88–90 and 146(5) of the Social Security Act 1975 and paras 9(1) (*a*) and (*c*) of Sch 3 to the Social Security (Consequential Provisions) Act 1975. Only those parts of the Regulations of direct concern to magistrates' courts are included here.

[2] "Claim for benefit" includes an application for a declaration that an accident was an industrial accident and an application for the review of an award or a decision for the purpose of obtaining any increase of benefit mentioned in Sch 1 to these regulations but does not include any other application for the review of an award or a decision; and the expression "claims benefit" and every reference to a claim shall be construed accordingly (reg 2(1)).

*Information to be given when obtaining payment of benefit*

**7.10905** *23.* (1) Every beneficiary and every person by whom or on whose behalf sums payable by way of benefit are receivable shall furnish in such manner and at such times as the Secretary of State may determine such certificates and other documents and such information of facts affecting the right to benefit or to its receipt as the Secretary of State may require (either as a condition on which any sum or sums shall be receivable or otherwise), and in particular shall notify the Secretary of State in writing of any change of circumstances which he might reasonably be expected to know might affect the right to benefit, or to its receipt, as soon as reasonably practicable after the occurrence thereof.

(2) Where any sum is receivable on account of an increase of benefit in respect of an adult dependant the beneficiary shall, in such cases or classes of case as the Secretary of State may direct, furnish a declaration signed by such dependant confirming the particulars respecting him furnished by the claimant.

*Breach of regulations*

**7.10906** *31.* If any person contravenes or fails to comply with any requirement of these regulations (not being a requirement to give notice of an accident or a requirement to submit himself to medical treatment or examination) in respect of which no special penalty is provided, he shall for such offence be liable on summary conviction to a penalty not exceeding **level 3** or, where the offence consists of continuing any such contravention or failure after conviction thereof, **£20** for each day on which it is so continued.

# Income Support (Liable Relatives) Regulations 1990[1]

(SI 1990/1777 as amended by SI 2002/2497)

*Citation, commencement and interpretation*

**7.10907** *1.* (1) *Citation and commencement.*

(2) In these Regulations—

"the Act" means the Social Security Act 1986; and

"the Income Support Regulations" means the Income Support (General) Regulations 1987.

---

[1] Made by the Secretary of State for Social Security, in exercise of the powers conferred by section 166(1) to (3A) of the Social Security Act 1975 and ss 24A(1), 24B(5) and 84(1) of the Social Security Act 1986.

*Prescribed amounts for the purposes of section 24A of the Act*

**7.10908** *2.* (1) For the purposes of section 24A of the Act (recovery of expenditure on income support: additional amounts and transfer of orders) the amount which may be included in the sum which the court may order the other parent to pay under section 24(4) of the Act shall be the whole of the following amounts which are payable to or for the claimant—

(*a*) any personal allowance under paragraph 2 of Part 1 of Schedule 2 to the Income Support Regulations for each of the children whom the other parent is liable to maintain;

(*b*) any family premium under paragraph 3 of Part II of that Schedule;

(*c*) any lone parent premium under paragraph 8 of Part III of that Schedule;

(*d*) any disabled child premium under paragraph 14 of Part III of that Schedule in respect of a child whom the other parent is liable to maintain; and

(*e*) any carer premium under paragraph 14ZA of Part III of that Schedule if, but only if, that premium is payable because the claimant is in receipt, or is treated as being in receipt, of carer's allowance by reason of the fact that he is caring for a severely disabled child or young person whom the other parent is liable to maintain.

(2) If the court is satisfied that in addition to the amounts specified in paragraph (1) above the liable parent has the means to pay, the sum which the court may order him to pay under section 24 of the Act may also include all or some of the amount of any personal allowance payable to or for the claimant under paragraph 1 of Part I of Schedule 2 to the Income Support Regulations.

*Notice to the Secretary of State of applications to alter etc maintenance orders*

**7.10909** *3.* (1) For the purposes of section 24B(5) of the Act (prescribed person in prescribed circumstances to notify the Secretary of State of application to alter etc a maintenance order) the prescribed person is, and in paragraph (2) below that expression means—

(*a*) in England and Wales—

(i) in relation to the High Court, where the case is proceeding in the deputy principal registry the senior registrar of that registry, and where the case is proceeding in a district registry the district registrar;

(ii) in relation to a county court, the proper officer of that court within the meaning of Order 1, Rule 3 of the County Court Rules 1981; and

(iii) in relation to a magistrates' court, the clerk to the justices of that court; and

(*b*) Scotland.

(2) For the purposes of that subsection the prescribed circumstances are that before the final determination of the application the Secretary of State has made a written request to the prescribed person that he be notified of any such application, and has not made a written withdrawal of that request.

# SOLICITORS

**Contents**



## European lawyers

**7.10910** The European Communities (Lawyer's Practice) Regulations 2000, SI 2000/1119 amended by SI 2001/644, SI 2004/1628, SI 2008/81, SI 2009/1587, SI 2009/3348, SI 2010/21, SI 2013/534, 1605 and 3176 and SI 2015/401 made under s 2(2) of the European Communities Act 1972, give effect to European Communities Council Directive 98/5/EC. The purpose of the Directive is to facilitate the practice of the profession of lawyer on a permanent basis in a member State of the European Community other than the State in which the qualification was obtained. A European lawyer may apply to register with the solicitors' or the barristers' professional bodies. It is an offence punishable on summary conviction with a fine not exceeding **level 4** on the standard scale to pretend to be a registered European lawyer (reg 21). A certificate purporting to be signed by an officer of a professional body is evidence that a person is or is not registered with that professional body unless the contrary is proved (reg 23). A registered European lawyer is subject to the rules of professional conduct and disciplinary proceedings applicable to the professional body with which he is registered (regs 25 and 26). A registered European lawyer may apply for entry into the profession of solicitor or barrister (reg 29). Enactments relating to the provision of legal advice and assistance and legal aid, certain enactments reserving certain activities to solicitors, barristers and other qualified persons are modified accordingly (Sch 3); and certain enactments extended in relation to the registration of European lawyers with the Law Society (Sch 4).

## Apparent bias by legal representatives

**7.10911** Where a firm of solicitors has acted for one party in proceedings where they have previously acted for another party to them, an injunction may be issued to restrain the solicitors from acting based on the protection of confidential information, relevant to the proceedings, which the firm received when acting for the other party unless the solicitors establish that there is no real risk that the information is or will become known to those within the firm now proposing to act[1]. In care proceedings where the solicitor for the children had previously represented the father in the juvenile court and in other criminal proceedings but the solicitor had no recollection of the juvenile court proceedings nor any knowledge of the latter criminal proceedings, the court rightly refused not to continue to hear the solicitor[2]. It is generally undesirable for husband and wife, or other partners living together, to appear as advocates against each other in a contested criminal matter[3]. The particular sensitivity of care proceedings places a premium on impartiality and cohabitation by advocates for the local authority and one of the parties would give rise to a reasonable lay apprehension of bias in the other parties[4].

1 *Bolkiah (Prince Jefri) v KPMG (a firm)* [1999] 2 AC 222, [1999] 1 All ER 517, [1999] 2 WLR 215, HL.
2 *Re T and A (children) (risk of disclosure)* [2000] 1 FCR 659, [2000] 1 FLR 859, CA.
3 *R v Batt* [1996] Crim LR 910, CA.
4 *In re L (Minors) (care proceedings: solicitors)* [2001] 1 WLR 100, [2000] 3 FCR 71, [2000] 2 FLR 887, FD.

# Solicitors Act 1974[1]

(1974 c 47)

**7.10912 20. Unqualified person[2] not to act as solicitor** (1) No unqualified person is to act as a solicitor.

(2) Any person who contravenes subsection (1) is guilty of an offence and liable on conviction on indictment to imprisonment for not more than 2 years or to a fine, or to both.

[Solicitors Act 1974, s 20 as substituted by the Legal Services Act 2007, Sch 16.]

1 See also Part I: Magistrates' Courts, Procedure, para 1.48 *Appearance by legal representative*, ante.
2 No person shall be qualified to act as a solicitor unless his name is on the roll—ie the list of solicitors kept in accordance with this Act, s 6(1)—and he has in force a practising certificate (s 1) and a person who is not so qualified is referred to in this Part as an "unqualified person" (s 87). A practising certificate has effect from the date which it bears until 31 October 31 (s 14). The certificate is suspended if an order is made by the Solicitors Disciplinary Tribunal (s 14) or the court suspending the solicitor from practice or if he is adjudicated bankrupt (s 15). Any list published by authority of the Law Society containing the names of solicitors holding practising certificates is prima facie evidence whether or not

he holds a certificate (s 18). For European Lawyers see para 7.10910, ante.

7.10913 **21. Unqualified person not to pretend to be a solicitor**[1] Any unqualified person[1], who wilfully pretends[2] to be, or takes or uses any name, title, addition or description implying that he is, qualified or recognised by law as qualified[3] to act as a solicitor, shall be guilty of an offence and liable on summary conviction to a fine not exceeding the **fourth level** on the standard scale.

[Solicitors Act 1974, s 21 as amended by the Criminal Justice Act 1982, ss 38 and 46 and the Administration of Justice Act 1985, Sch 1.]

---

1 See note 2 to s 20, supra.

2 B, a person in the employ of a tailor, was in the habit of issuing county court summonses for his employer, and applying for debts on a printed form sent from and bearing his own address, under the orders of his master, headed "Notice of intention to take proceedings in the county court for recovery of small debts," and ending with the words, "Unless you pay forthwith I shall proceed against you under the above Act." In a case where he demanded 9s. 6d. larger than the debt, and the receiver believed the letter came from a solicitor, the Queen's Bench Division held it was a question of fact whether B, intended falsely to represent himself as a solicitor, and the magistrate was not bound to convict upon the evidence (*Incorporated Law Society v Bedford* (1885) 49 JP 215). A notice in a printed form, "Final notice before proceeding in the county court," or "I hereby give you notice that unless the sum of £1 2s. 6d., due by you to Messrs. H and L, be paid on or before 21st inst., I shall proceed against you under the above Act," was sent by a partner of the firm, but did not on the face of it show he applied for payment of the debt as a member of the firm. The Queen's Bench Division held justices were wrong in convicting (*Symonds v Incorporated Law Society* (1884) 49 JP 212). Convictions were upheld when an unqualified person advertised that a society of which he was general secretary would do conveyancing business at cheap rates for any who would become members (*Carter v Butcher* [1966] 1 QB 326, [1965] 1 All ER 994).

3 Where a solicitor, while suspended from practice, on being approached on a matter of legal business, merely described himself as a solicitor, it was held that he held himself out as a person qualified to act as such. On the other hand, there may be occasions when the use of that word would not have that implication (*Taylor v Richardson* [1938] 2 All ER 681, 102 JP 341).

A person who not being duly qualified or authorised sues out any writ or process, or carries on any such proceeding as a solicitor is alone authorised to carry on, in effect acts as a solicitor, whether he acts in his own name or that of another (*Re Simmons* (1885) 15 QB 348, 49 JP 741). An unqualified person who gives notice of appearance on behalf of a defendant is carrying on a proceeding within what is now s 20(1) of the Solicitors Act 1974 (*Re Ainsworth, ex p Law Society* [1905] 2 KB 103).

7.10914 **24. Application of penal provisions to body corporate**[1] (1) If any act is done by a body corporate or by any director, officer, or servant of a body corporate, and is of such a nature or is done in such a manner as to be calculated[2] to imply that the body corporate is qualified or recognised by law as qualified to act as a solicitor, (*a*) the body corporate shall be guilty of an offence and liable on summary conviction to a fine not exceeding the **fourth level** on the standard scale, and (*b*), in the case of an act done by a director, officer, or servant of the body corporate, he shall be guilty of an offence and liable on summary conviction to a fine not exceeding the **fourth level** on the standard scale.

(2) For the avoidance of doubt it is hereby declared that in section 20 the reference to an unqualified person and the reference to a person both include a reference to a body corporate.

[Solicitors Act 1974, s 24 as amended by the Criminal Law Act 1977, s 31, the Criminal Justice Act 1982, ss 38 and 46, the Administration of Justice Act 1985, Sch 1 and the Legal Services Act 2007, Sch 16.]

---

1 See *Dean v Hiesler* [1942] 2 All ER 340, 106 JP 282. See also *Beeston and Stapleford UDC v Smith* [1949] 1 KB 656, [1949] 1 All ER 394, 113 JP 160.

2 This means likely to deceive—not intended to deceive (cf *Re London and Globe Finance Corpn Ltd* [1903] 1 Ch 728, 82 JP 447; *R v Wines* [1953] 2 All ER 1497, [1954] 1 WLR 64, 118 JP 49).

7.10915 **35–36A. Intervention in solicitor's practice and Compensation Fund** The Law Society has established and administers a compensation fund from which grants are paid to mitigate losses sustained in consequence of the act or omission of a solicitor (or former solicitor) or his employees (or former employees). The Law Society may intervene in a solicitor's practice in circumstances and to the extent set out in Schedule 1.

[Solicitors Act 1974, ss 35, 36 and 36A (as amended by the Legal Services Act 2007, Sch 16—summarised).]

*Inadequate professional services*

7.10916 **38. Solicitor who is justice of the peace not to act in certain proceedings** (1) Subject to the provisions of this section, it shall not be lawful for any solicitor who is one of the justices of the peace assigned to any local justice area, or for any partner of his, to act in connection with proceedings before any justice of the peace acting in that area as solicitor or agent for the solicitor of any person concerned in those proceedings.

(2) *Repealed.*

(3) *Repealed.*

(3A) Subsection (1) does not apply where a solicitor is a Deputy District Judge (Magistrates' Courts); but where a solicitor is acting as a Deputy District Judge (Magistrates' Courts) in any local justice area it shall not be lawful for him, or for any partner of his, to act in connection with proceedings before any justice of the peace acting in that area as solicitor or agent for the solicitor of any person concerned in those proceedings.

(4) *Repealed.*

[Solicitors Act 1974, s 38 as amended by the Justices of the Peace Act 1997, Sch 5, the Access to Justice Act 1999, Schs 10, 11 and 15 and the Courts Act 2003, Sch 8.]

7.10917 **42. Failure to disclose fact of having been struck off or suspended** (1) Any person who, while he is disqualified from practising as a solicitor by reason of the fact that (*a*) his name has been struck off the roll, or (*b*) he is suspended from practising as a solicitor, or (*c*) his practising certificate is suspended while he is an undischarged bankrupt, seeks or accepts employment by a solicitor in connection with that solicitor's practice without previously informing him that he is so disqualified, shall be guilty of an offence and liable on summary conviction to a fine not exceeding **level 3** on the standard scale.

(1A) Any person—

(*a*) with respect to whom a direction is in force under section 47(2)(*g*); and

(*b*) who seeks or accepts employment by a solicitor in connection with that solicitor's practice without previously informing him of the direction,

shall be guilty of an offence and liable on summary conviction to a fine not exceeding level three on the standard scale.

(2) Notwithstanding anything in the Magistrates' Courts Act 1980, proceedings under this section may be commenced at any time before the expiration of six months after the first discovery of the offence by the prosecutor, but no such proceedings shall be commenced except by, or with the consent[1] of, the Attorney-General.

[Solicitors Act 1974, s 42 as amended by the Criminal Law Act 1977, s 31, the Magistrates' Courts Act 1980, Sch 7, the Criminal Justice Act 1982, s 46 and the Courts and Legal Services Act 1990, Sch 18.]

---

1 As to the consent of the Solicitor-General, see para 1.112 Criminal Prosecutions, ante, and as to proof of such consent, see the Prosecution of Offences Act 1985, s 26 in PART I: MAGISTRATES' COURTS, PROCEDURE, ante.

7.10918 43. **Control of solicitors' employees and consultants** (1) Where a person who is or was involved in a legal practice but is not a solicitor—

(*a*) has been convicted of a criminal offence which is such that in the opinion of the Society it would be undesirable for the person to be involved in a legal practice in one or more of the ways mentioned in subsection (1A), or

(*b*) has, in the opinion of the Society, occasioned or been a party to, with or without the connivance of a solicitor, an act or default in relation to a legal practice which involved conduct on his part of such a nature that in the opinion of the Society it would be undesirable for him to be involved in a legal practice in one or more of the ways mentioned in subsection (1A),

the Society[1] may either make, or make an application to the Tribunal[2] for it to make, an order under subsection (2) with respect to that person.

(1A) A person is involved in a legal practice for the purposes of this section if the person—

(*a*) is employed or remunerated by a solicitor in connection with the solicitor's practice;

(*b*) is undertaking work in the name of, or under the direction or supervision of, a solicitor;

(*c*) is employed or remunerated by a recognised body;

(*d*) is employed or remunerated by a manager or employee of a recognised body in connection with that body's business;

(*e*) is a manager of a recognised body;

(*f*) has or intends to acquire an interest in such a body.

(2) An order made by the Society or the Tribunal under this subsection is an order which states one or more of the following—

(*a*) that as from the specified date—

(i) no solicitor shall employ or remunerate, in connection with his practice as a solicitor, the person with respect to whom the order is made,

(ii) no employee of a solicitor shall employ or remunerate, in connection with the solicitor's practice, the person with respect to whom the order is made,

(iii) no recognised body shall employ or remunerate that person, and

(iv) no manager or employee of a recognised body shall employ or remunerate that person in connection with the business of that body,

except in accordance with a Society permission;

(*b*) that as from the specified date no recognised body or manager or employee of such a body shall, except in accordance with a Society permission, permit the person with respect to whom the order is made to be a manager of the body;

(*c*) that as from the specified date no recognised body or manager or employee of such a body shall, except in accordance with a Society permission, permit the person with respect to whom the order is made to have an interest in the body.

(2A) The Society may make regulations prescribing charges to be paid to the Society by persons who are the subject of an investigation by the Society as to whether there are grounds for the Society—

(*a*) to make an order under subsection (2), or

(*b*) to make an application to the Tribunal for it to make such an order.

(2B) Regulations under subsection (2A) may—

(*a*) make different provision for different cases or purposes;

(*b*) provide for the whole or part of a charge payable under the regulations to be repaid in such circumstances as may be prescribed by the regulations.

(2C) Any charge which a person is required to pay under regulations under subsection (2A) is recoverable by the Society as a debt due to the Society from the person.

(3) Where an order has been made under subsection (2) with respect to a person by the Society or the Tribunal—

(*a*) that person or the Society may make an application to the Tribunal for it to be reviewed, and

(*b*) whichever of the Society and the Tribunal made it may at any time revoke it.

(3A) On the review of an order under subsection (3) the Tribunal may order—

(*a*) the quashing of the order;

(*b*) the variation of the order; or

(*c*) the confirmation of the order;

and where in the opinion of the Tribunal no prima facie case for quashing or varying the order is shown, the Tribunal may order its confirmation without hearing the applicant.

(4) The Tribunal, on the hearing of any application under this section, may make an order as to the payment of costs by any party to the application.

(7) For the purposes of this section an order discharging a person absolutely or conditionally shall, notwithstanding anything in section 14 of the Powers of Criminal Courts (Sentencing) Act 2000, be deemed to be a conviction of the offence for which the order was made.

[Solicitors Act 1974, s 43 as amended by the Administration of Justice Act 1985, Sch 1, the Criminal Justice Act 1991, Sch 11, the Access to Justice Act 1999, Sch 7, the Powers of Criminal Courts (Sentencing) Act 2000, Sch 9 and the Legal Services Act 2007, Sch 16.]

---

[1] Ie, the Law Society (s 87).

[2] The "Tribunal" is the Solicitors Disciplinary Tribunal appointed under s 46 of the Solicitors Act 1974.

**7.10919 44. Offences in connection with orders controlling employment of certain clerks**

(1) It is an offence for a person in respect of whom there is in force an order under section 43(2) which contains provision within section 43(2)(*a*)—

(*a*) to seek or accept any employment or remuneration from a solicitor, or an employee of a solicitor, in connection with the practice carried on by that solicitor without previously informing the solicitor or employee of the order;

(*b*) to seek or accept any employment or remuneration from a recognised body, or a manager or employee of a recognised body, in connection with that body's business, without previously informing the body, or manager or employee, of the order.

(1A) It is an offence for a person in respect of whom there is in force an order under section 43(2) which contains provision within section 43(2)(*b*) to seek or accept a position as a manager of a recognised body, without previously informing that body of the order.

(1B) It is an offence for a person in respect of whom there is in force an order under section 43(2) which contains provision within section 43(2)(*c*) to seek or accept an interest in a recognised body from any person, without previously informing that person and (if different) the recognised body of the order.

(1C) A person guilty of an offence under subsection (1), (1A) or (1B) is liable on summary conviction to a fine not exceeding level 3 on the standard scale.

(2) Where an order under section 43(2) is in force in respect of a person, then, if any solicitor knowingly acts in contravention of that order or of any conditions subject to which permission for the taking of any action has been granted under it, a complaint in respect of that contravention may be made to the Tribunal by or on behalf of the Society.

(3) Any document purporting to be an order under section 43(2) and to be duly signed in accordance with s 48(1)[1] of this Act shall be received in evidence in any proceedings under this section and be deemed to be such an order without further proof unless the contrary is shown.

(4) Notwithstanding anything in the Magistrates' Courts Act 1980, proceedings under subsection (1) may be commenced at any time before the expiration of six months from the first discovery of the offence by the prosecutor, but no such proceedings shall be commenced, except with the consent[2] of the director of Public Prosecutions, by any person other than the Society or a person acting on behalf of the Society.

(5) In this section—

"manager" has the same meaning as in section 43;

"recognised body" means a body recognised under section 9 of the Administration of Justice Act 1985;

and for the purposes of subsection (1B) a person seeks or accepts an interest in a recognised body if the person seeks or accepts an interest which if it were obtained by the person would result in the person having an interest in that body within the meaning of Part 5 of the Legal Services Act 2007 (see sections 72 and 109 of that Act).

[Solicitors Act 1974, s 44 as amended by the Magistrates' Courts Act 1980, Sch 7, the Criminal Justice Act 1982, ss 38 and 46, the Access to Justice Act 1999, Sch 7 and the Legal Services Act 2007, Sch 16.]

---

[1] Section 48(1) requires that an order of the Tribunal shall be filed with the Society, and a statement of its findings signed by the Chairman or by some other member of the Tribunal authorised by him, shall be attached.

[2] For proof of this consent, see the Prosecution of Offences Act 1985, s 26 in PART I: MAGISTRATES' COURTS, PROCEDURE, ante.

**7.10920 44B, 44BA–44BC.** *Provision of information and documents*

**7.10921 44C.** *Power to charge for costs of investigations*

*Disciplinary Powers of the Society*

**44D, 44E.** *Disciplinary Powers of the Society and appeals*

*Disciplinary Proceedings before Solicitors Disciplinary Tribunal*

7.10922 **46, 46A.** *Applications and complaints under the Act made to Solicitors Disciplinary Tribunal*[1].

[1] The Solicitors (Disciplinary Proceedings) Rules 2007, SI 2007/3588 amended by SI 2011/2346 and the Solicitors Disciplinary Tribunal (Appeals and Amendment) Rules 2011, SI 2011/2346 amended by SI 2011/3070 have been made which regulate the way in which applications are to be made and heard.

7.10923 **47. Jurisdiction and powers of Tribunal** (1) Any application—

(*a*) to strike the name of a solicitor off the roll;

(*b*) to require a solicitor to answer allegations contained in an affidavit;

(*c*) to require a former solicitor whose name has been removed from or struck off the roll to answer allegations contained in an affidavit relating to a time when he was a solicitor;

(*d*) by a solicitor who has been suspended from practice for an unspecified period, by order of the Tribunal, for the termination of that suspension;

(*e*) by a former solicitor whose name has been struck off the roll to have his name restored to the roll;

(*ea*) by a solicitor who has been suspended from practice as a sole solicitor for an unspecified period, by order of the Tribunal, for the termination of that suspension;

(*f*) by a former solicitor in respect of whom a direction has been given under subsection (2)(*g*) to have his name restored to the roll.

shall be made to the Tribunal; but nothing in this subsection shall affect any jurisdiction over solicitors exercisable by the Master of the Rolls, or by any judge of the High Court, by virtue of section 50.

(2) Subject to subsections (2E) and (3) and to section 54, on the hearing of any application or complaint made to the Tribunal under this Act, other than an application under section 43, the Tribunal shall have power to make such order as it may think fit, and any such order may in particular include provision for any of the following matters—

(*a*) the striking off the roll of the name of the solicitor to whom the application or complaint relates;

(*b*) the suspension of that solicitor from practice indefinitely or for a specified period;

(*ba*) the revocation of that solicitor's sole solicitor endorsement (if any);

(*bb*) the suspension of that solicitor from practice as a sole solicitor indefinitely or for a specified period;

(*c*) the payment by that solicitor or former solicitor of a penalty which shall be forfeit to Her Majesty;

(*d*) in the circumstances referred to in subsection (2A), the exclusion of that solicitor from providing representation funded by the Legal Services Commission as part of the Criminal Defence Service (either permanently or for a specified period);

(*e*) the termination of that solicitor's unspecified period of suspension from practice;

(*ea*) the termination of that solicitor's unspecified period of suspension from practice as a sole solicitor;

(*f*) the restoration to the roll of the name of a former solicitor whose name has been struck off the roll and to whom the application relates;

(*g*) in the case of a former solicitor whose name has been removed from the roll, a direction prohibiting the restoration of his name to the roll except by order of the Tribunal;

(*h*) in the case of an application under subsection (1)(*f*), the restoration of the applicant's name to the roll;

(*i*) the payment by any party of costs or a contribution towards, costs of such amount as the Tribunal may consider reasonable.

(2A) An order of the Tribunal may make provision for the exclusion of a solicitor from providing representation as mentioned in subsection (2)(*d*) where the Tribunal determines that there is good reason for doing so arising out of—

(*a*) his conduct, including conduct in the capacity of agent for another solicitor, in connection with the provision for any person of services funded by the Legal Services Commission as part of the Community Legal Service or Criminal Defence Service; or

(*b*) his professional conduct generally.

(2B) Where the Tribunal makes any such order as is referred to in subsection (2A) in the case of a solicitor who is a member of a firm of solicitors, the Tribunal may, if it thinks fit, order that any other person who is for the time being a member of the firm shall be excluded (either permanently or for a specified period) from providing representation funded by the Legal Services Commission as part of the Criminal Defence Service.

(2C) The Tribunal shall not make an order under subsection (2B) unless an opportunity is given to him to show cause why the order should not be made.

(2D) Any person excluded from providing representation funded by the Legal Services Commission as part of the Criminal Defence Service by an order under this section may make an application to the Tribunal for an order terminating his exclusion.

(2E) On the hearing of any complaint made to the Tribunal by virtue of section 34A(2) or (3), the Tribunal shall have power to make one or more of the following—

- (*a*) an order directing the payment by the employee to whom the complaint relates of a penalty to be forfeited to Her Majesty;
- (*b*) an order requiring the Society to consider taking such steps as the Tribunal may specify in relation to that employee;
- (*c*) if that employee is not a solicitor, an order which states one or more of the matters mentioned in paragraphs (*a*) to (*c*) of section 43(2);
- (*d*) an order requiring the Society to refer to an appropriate regulator any matter relating to the conduct of that employee.

(2F) Subsections (1) to (1C), (3) and (4) of section 44 apply in relation to an order under subsection (2E)(*c*) as they apply in relation to an order under section 43(2).

(2G) Section 44(2), paragraph 16(1)(*d*) and (1A)(*d*) of Schedule 2 to the Administration of Justice Act 1985 and paragraph 15(3A) of Schedule 14 to the Courts and Legal Services Act 1990 apply in relation to an order under subsection (2E)(*c*) as they apply in relation to an order under section 43(2).

(2H) For the purposes of subsection (2E)(*d*) an "appropriate regulator" in relation to an employee means—

- (*a*) if the employee is an authorised person in relation to a reserved legal activity (within the meaning of the Legal Services Act 2007), any relevant approved regulator (within the meaning of that Act) in relation to that employee, and
- (*b*) if the employee carries on activities which are not reserved legal activities (within the meaning of that Act), any body which regulates the carrying on of such activities by the employee.

(3) On proof of the commission of an offence with respect to which express provision is made by any section of this Act, the Tribunal shall, without prejudice to its power of making an order as to costs, impose the punishment, or one of the punishments, specified in that section.

(3A) Where, on the hearing of any application or complaint under this Act, the Tribunal is satisfied that more than one allegation is proved against the person to whom the application or complaint relates it may impose a separate penalty (by virtue of subsection (2)(*c*)) with respect to each such allegation.*

(4) *Repealed.*

(5) *Repealed.*

(6) *Repealed.**

[Solicitors Act 1974, s 47 as amended by the Administration of Justice Act 1982, s 56, the Administration of Justice Act 1985, s 44 and Sch 7, the Legal Aid Act 1988, Sch 5, the Courts and Legal Services Act 1990, s 92, the Access to Justice Act 1999, Schs 4 and 5, SI 2003/1887 and the Legal Services Act 2007, Sch 16.]

---

* **Subsection (3B) inserted by the Legal Services Act 2007, Sch 16 from a date to be appointed.**

7.10924 **48–55.** *Orders of Tribunal; appeals from Tribunal; disciplinary proceedings and jurisdiction of the Supreme Court.*

7.10925 **88. Savings for solicitors to public departments and City of London**

(1) Nothing in this Act shall prejudice or affect any rights or privileges of the solicitor to the Treasury[1], any other public department, the Church Commissioners or the Duchy of Cornwall, or require any such officer or any clerk or officer appointed to act for him to be admitted or enrolled or to hold a practising certificate in any case where it would not have been necessary for him to be admitted or enrolled or to hold such a certificate if this Act had not been passed.

(1A) The exemption from the requirement to hold a practising certificate conferred by subsection (1) above shall not apply to solicitors who are Crown Prosecutors.]

(2) Sections 31 and 32(1) shall not apply to, and nothing in this Act shall prejudice or affect any rights or privileges which immediately before the commencement of this Act attached to the office of, the Solicitor of the City of London.

[Solicitors Act 1974, s 88 as amended by the Prosecution of Offences Act 1985, s 4.]

---

1 Where the Treasury solicitor acts under the directions of the Crown as solicitor for an individual, he is to be considered duly qualified for all purposes, including the right of his client to recover costs (*R v Archbishop of Canterbury* [1903] 1 KB 289).

## SCHEDULE 1

(*As amended by the Criminal Justice Act 1982, ss 38 and 46 and the Legal Services Act 2007, Sch 16.*)

7.10926 **9.** (1) The Society may give notice to the solicitor or his firm requiring the production or delivery to any person appointed by the Society at a time and place to be fixed by the Society—

- (*a*) where the powers conferred by this Part of this Schedule are exercisable by virtue of paragraph 1, of all documents in the possession or under the control of the solicitor or his firm in connection with his practice or former practice or with any trust of which the solicitor is or was a trustee; and (*b*) where they are exercisable by virtue of paragraph 3, of all documents in the possession or under the control of the solicitor or his firm in connection with the trust or other matters of which the Society is satisfied (whether or not they relate also to other matters).

(2) The person appointed by the Society may take possession of any such documents on behalf of the Society.

(3) Except in a case where an application has been made to the High Court under sub-paragraph (4), if the person having possession or control of any such documents refuses, neglects or otherwise fails to comply with a requirement under sub-paragraph (1), he shall be guilty of an offence and liable on summary conviction to a fine not exceeding **level 3** on the standard scale.

(4) The High Court, on the application of the Society, may order a person required to produce or deliver documents under sub-paragraph (1) to produce or deliver them to any person appointed by the Society at such time and place as may be specified in the order, and authorise him to take possession of them on behalf of the Society.

[Solicitors Act 1974, Sch 1, para 9(1)–(4).]

# Courts and Legal Services Act 1990[1]

(1990 c 41)

## PART II[2]

## LEGAL SERVICES

[1] This Act is to be brought into force in accordance with s 124, post. For commencement orders, see s 124, post. Of the provisions of the Act printed below, ss 36, 37, 47, 48, 49, 50, 54, 55, 70, 104, 105, 106 and 107 had not been brought into force at the date of going to press.

[2] Part II comprises ss 17–70.

7.10927 **31B. Advocates and litigators employed by Lord Chancellor** (1) This section applies where a person—

(*a*) is authorised by a relevant approved regulator ("the regulator") to carry on an activity which constitutes the exercise of a right of audience or the conduct of litigation, and

(*b*) is employed by the Lord Chancellor, or by any body established and maintained by the Lord Chancellor, under arrangements made for the purposes of Part 1 of the Legal Aid, Sentencing and Punishment of Offenders Act 2012.

(1A) Any rules of the regulator which fall within subsection (2) shall not have effect in relation to that person.

(2) Rules of a regulator fall within this subsection if they are—

(*a*) conduct rules prohibiting or limiting the exercise of the right on behalf of members of the public by members of the regulator who are employees; or

(*b*) rules of any other description prohibiting or limiting the provision of legal services to members of the public by such members of the regulator,

and either of the conditions specified in subsection (3) is satisfied.

(3) Those conditions are—

(*a*) that the prohibition or limitation is on the exercise of the right, or the provision of the services, otherwise than on the instructions of solicitors (or other persons acting for the members of the public); and

(*b*) that the rules do not impose the same prohibition or limitation on members of the regulator who have the right but are not employees.

(4) For the purposes of this section "relevant approved regulator" is to be construed in accordance with section 20(3) of the Legal Services Act 2007.

[Courts and Legal Services Act 1990, s 31B as inserted by the Access to Justice Act 1999, s 38 and amended by the Legal Services Act 2007, Sch 21 and the Legal Aid, Sentencing and Punishment of Offenders Act 2012, Sch 5.]

7.10928 **31C. Change of authorised body** (1) Where a person—

(*a*) has at any time been authorised by a relevant approved regulator to exercise a right of audience before a court in relation to proceedings of a particular description, and

(*b*) becomes authorised by another relevant approved regulator to exercise a right of audience before that court in relation to that description of proceedings,

any qualification regulations of the relevant approved regulator mentioned in paragraph (*b*) which relate to that right are not to have effect in relation to the person.

(2) Subsection (1) does not apply in relation to any qualification regulations to the extent that they impose requirements relating to continuing education or training which have effect in relation to the exercise of the right by all members of the relevant approved regulator who have the right.

(3) Subsection (1) does not apply to a person if he has been banned from exercising the right of audience by the relevant approved regulator mentioned in paragraph (*a*) of that subsection as a result of disciplinary proceedings and that relevant approved regulator has not lifted the ban.

(4) For the purposes of this section "relevant approved regulator" is to be construed in accordance with section 20(3) of the Legal Services Act 2007.

[Courts and Legal Services Act 1990, s 31C as inserted by the Access to Justice Act 1999, s 39 and amended by the Legal Services Act 2007, Sch 21.]

*Probate Services*

**7.10929 56. Administration of oaths etc by justices in certain probate business**

(1) Every justice shall have power to administer any oath or take any affidavit which is required for the purposes of an application for a grant of probate or letters of administration made in any non-contentious or common form probate business.

(2) A justice before whom any oath or affidavit is taken or made under this section shall state in the jurat or attestation at what place and on what date the oath or affidavit is taken or made.

(3) No justice shall exercise the powers conferred by this section in any proceedings in which he is interested.

(4) A document purporting to be signed by a justice administering an oath or taking an affidavit shall be admitted in evidence without proof of the signature and without proof that he is a justice.

(5) In this section—

"affidavit" has the same meaning as in the Commissioners for Oaths Act 1889;

"justice" means a justice of the peace;

"letters of administration" includes all letters of administration of the effects of deceased persons, whether with or without a will annexed, and whether granted for general, special or limited purposes; and

"non-contentious or common form probate business" has the same meaning as in section 128 of the Senior Courts Act 1981.

[Courts and Legal Services Act 1990, s 56 as amended by the Constitutional Reform Act 2005, Sch 11.]

*Miscellaneous*

**7.10930 58. Conditional fee agreements** (1) A conditional fee agreement which satisfies all of the conditions applicable to it by virtue of this section shall not be unenforceable by reason only of its being a conditional fee agreement; but (subject to subsection (5)) any other conditional fee agreement shall be unenforceable.

(2) For the purposes of this section and section 58A—

(*a*) a conditional fee agreement is an agreement with a person providing advocacy or litigation services which provides for his fees and expenses, or any part of them, to be payable only in specified circumstances; and

(*b*) a conditional fee agreement provides for a success fee if it provides for the amount of any fees to which it applies to be increased, in specified circumstances, above the amount which would be payable if it were not payable only in specified circumstances.

(3) The following conditions are applicable to every conditional fee agreement—

(*a*) it must be in writing;

(*b*) it must not relate to proceedings which cannot be the subject of an enforceable conditional fee agreement; and

(*c*) it must comply with such requirements (if any) as may be prescribed by the Lord Chancellor.

(4) The following further conditions are applicable to a conditional fee agreement which provides for a success fee—

(*a*) it must relate to proceedings of a description specified by order made by the Lord Chancellor;

(*b*) it must state the percentage by which the amount of the fees which would be payable if it were not a conditional fee agreement is to be increased; and

(*c*) that percentage must not exceed the percentage specified in relation to the description of proceedings to which the agreement relates by order made by the Lord Chancellor.

(5) If a conditional fee agreement is an agreement to which section 57 of the Solicitors Act 1974 (non-contentious business agreements between solicitor and client) applies, subsection (1) shall not make it unenforceable.

[Courts and Legal Services Act 1990, s 58 as substituted by the Access to Justice Act 1999, s 27 and amended by SI 2003/1887 and SI 2005/3429.]

**7.10931 58A. Conditional fee agreements: supplementary** (1) The proceedings which cannot be the subject of an enforceable conditional fee agreement are—

(*a*) criminal proceedings, apart from proceedings under section 82 of the Environmental Protection Act 1990; and

(*b*) family proceedings.

(2) In subsection (1) "family proceedings" means proceedings under any one or more of the following—

(*a*) the Matrimonial Causes Act 1973;

(*b*) the Adoption and Children Act 2002;

(*c*) the Domestic Proceedings and Magistrates' Courts Act 1978;

(*d*) Part III of the Matrimonial and Family Proceedings Act 1984;

(*e*) Parts I, II and IV of the Children Act 1989;

(*f*) Parts 4 and 4A of the Family Law Act 1996;

(*fza*) Part 1 of Schedule 2 to the Female Genital Mutilation Act 2003;

(*fa*) Chapter 2 of Part 2 of the Civil Partnership Act 2004 (proceedings for dissolution etc of civil partnership);

(*fb*) Schedule 5 to the 2004 Act (financial relief in the High Court or a county court etc);
(*fc*) Schedule 6 to the 2004 Act (financial relief in magistrates' courts etc); and
(*fd*) Schedule 7 to the 2004 Act (financial relief in England and Wales after overseas dissolution etc of a partnership); and
(*g*) the inherent jurisdiction of the High Court in relation to children.

(3) The requirements which the Lord Chancellor may prescribe[1] under section 58(3)(*c*)—
(*a*) include requirements for the person providing advocacy or litigation services to have provided prescribed information before the agreement is made; and
(*b*) may be different for different descriptions of conditional fee agreements (and, in particular, may be different for those which provide for a success fee and those which do not).

(4) In section 58 and this section (and in the definitions of "advocacy services" and "litigation services" as they apply for their purposes) "proceedings" includes any sort of proceedings for resolving disputes (and not just proceedings in a court), whether commenced or contemplated.

(5) Before making an order under section 58(4), (4A) or (4B), the Lord Chancellor shall consult
(*a*) the designated judges;
(*b*) the General Council of the Bar;
(*c*) the Law Society; and
(*d*) such other bodies as he considers appropriate.

(6) A costs order made in proceedings may not include provision requiring the payment by one party of all or part of a success fee payable by another party under a conditional fee agreement.

(7) Rules of court may make provision with respect to the assessment of any costs which include fees payable under a conditional fee agreement (including one which provides for a success fee).

[Courts and Legal Services Act 1990, s 58A as substituted, together with s 58 for s 58 as originally enacted, by the Access to Justice Act 1999, s 27 and amended by SI 2003/1887, the Adoption and Children Act 2002, Sch 3, the Civil Partnership Act 2004, Sch 27, SI 2005/3429, the Forced Marriage (Civil Protection) Act 2007, Sch 2, the Legal Aid, Sentencing and Punishment of Offenders Act 2012, s 44 and the Serious Crime Act 2015, Sch 4.]

**7.10932 58AA. Damages-based agreements relating to employment matters** (1) A damages-based agreement which relates to an employment matter and satisfies the conditions in subsection (4) is not unenforceable by reason only of its being a damages-based agreement.

(2) But a damages-based agreement which relates to an employment matter and does not satisfy those conditions is unenforceable.

(3) For the purposes of this section—
(*a*) a damages-based agreement is an agreement between a person providing advocacy services, litigation services or claims management services and the recipient of those services which provides that—
(i) the recipient is to make a payment to the person providing the services if the recipient obtains a specified financial benefit in connection with the matter in relation to which the services are provided, and
(ii) the amount of that payment is to be determined by reference to the amount of the financial benefit obtained;
(*b*) a damages-based agreement relates to an employment matter if the matter in relation to which the services are provided is a matter that is, or could become, the subject of proceedings before an employment tribunal.

(4) The agreement—
(*a*) must be in writing;
(*b*) must not provide for a payment above a prescribed amount or for a payment above an amount calculated in a prescribed manner;
(*c*) must comply with such other requirements as to its terms and conditions as are prescribed; and
(*d*) must be made only after the person providing services under the agreement has provided prescribed information.

(5) Regulations under subsection (4) are to be made by the Lord Chancellor and may make different provision in relation to different descriptions of agreements.

(6) Before making regulations under subsection (4) the Lord Chancellor must consult—
(*a*) the designated judges,
(*b*) the General Council of the Bar,
(*c*) the Law Society, and
(*d*) such other bodies as the Lord Chancellor considers appropriate.

(7) In this section—
"payment" includes a transfer of assets and any other transfer of money's worth (and the reference in subsection (4)(*b*) to a payment above a prescribed amount, or above an amount calculated in a prescribed manner, is to be construed accordingly);
"claims management services" has the same meaning as in Part 2 of the Compensation Act 2006 (see section 4(2) of that Act).

(8) Nothing in this section applies to an agreement entered into before the coming into force of the first regulations made under subsection (4).]

[Courts and Legal Services Act 1990, s 58AA as inserted by the Coroners and Justice Act 2009, s 154.]

7.10933 **58B. 58B Litigation funding agreements** (1) A litigation funding agreement which satisfies all of the conditions applicable to it by virtue of this section shall not be unenforceable by reason only of its being a litigation funding agreement.

(2) For the purposes of this section a litigation funding agreement is an agreement under which—

(*a*) a person ("the funder") agrees to fund (in whole or in part) the provision of advocacy or litigation services (by someone other than the funder) to another person ("the litigant"); and

(*b*) the litigant agrees to pay a sum to the funder in specified circumstances.

(3) The following conditions are applicable to a litigation funding agreement—

(*a*) the funder must be a person, or person of a description, prescribed by the Lord Chancellor;

(*b*) the agreement must be in writing;

(*c*) the agreement must not relate to proceedings which by virtue of section 58A(1) and (2) cannot be the subject of an enforceable conditional fee agreement or to proceedings of any such description as may be prescribed by the Lord Chancellor;

(*d*) the agreement must comply with such requirements (if any) as may be so prescribed;

(*e*) the sum to be paid by the litigant must consist of any costs payable to him in respect of the proceedings to which the agreement relates together with an amount calculated by reference to the funder's anticipated expenditure in funding the provision of the services; and

(*f*) that amount must not exceed such percentage of that anticipated expenditure as may be prescribed by the Lord Chancellor in relation to proceedings of the description to which the agreement relates.

(4) Regulations under subsection (3)(*a*) may require a person to be approved by the Lord Chancellor or by a prescribed person.

(5) The requirements which the Secretary of State may prescribe under subsection (3)(*d*)—

(*a*) include requirements for the funder to have provided prescribed information to the litigant before the agreement is made; and

(*b*) may be different for different descriptions of litigation funding agreements.

(6) In this section (and in the definitions of "advocacy services" and "litigation services" as they apply for its purposes) "proceedings" includes any sort of proceedings for resolving disputes (and not just proceedings in a court), whether commenced or contemplated.

(7) Before making regulations under this section, the Lord Chancellor shall consult—

(*a*) the designated judges;

(*b*) the General Council of the Bar;

(*c*) the Law Society; and

(*d*) such other bodies as he considers appropriate.

(8) A costs order made in any proceedings may, subject in the case of court proceedings to rules of court, include provision requiring the payment of any amount payable under a litigation funding agreement.

(9) Rules of court may make provision with respect to the assessment of any costs which include fees payable under a litigation funding agreement.*

[Courts and Legal Services Act 1990, s 58B as inserted by the Access to Justice Act 1999, s 28 and amended by SI 2005/3429.]

---

* **Reproduced as prospectively inserted by the Access to Justice Act 1999, s 28 from a date to be appointed.**

## PART VI[1]

## MISCELLANEOUS AND SUPPLEMENTAL

### *Miscellaneous*

### *Tying-in[1]*

7.10934 **104. Tying-in arrangements in connection with residential property loans** (1) In this section and sections 105 and 106 "residential property loan" means any loan which—

(*a*) is secured on land in the United Kingdom; and

(*b*) is made to an individual in respect of the acquisition of land which is for his residential use or the residential use of a dependant of his.

(2) No person ("the lender") shall provide a residential property loan together with one or more controlled services to another person ("the borrower") unless the conditions mentioned in subsection (3) are complied with before a relevant step is taken with respect to any of those services or the loan.

(3) The conditions are that the lender—

(*a*) informs the borrower by notice that the residential property loan, and each of the controlled services in question, are separate services;

(*b*) informs the borrower by notice whether the terms and conditions of the residential property loan will be capable of being varied by the lender after it is made;

(*c*) provides the borrower with a statement of—

(i) the price which will be payable by the borrower for each of the controlled services if they are all provided in accordance with the terms proposed by the lender; and

(ii) the extent to which (if at all) the terms and conditions of the residential property loan would differ if it were to be provided by the lender without the controlled services in question being provided by the lender; and

(*d*) informs the borrower by notice that, if the borrower declines to take from the lender any of the controlled services in question, the lender will not on that account refuse to provide the residential property loan.

(4) A person who—

(*a*) in the course of his business provides, or makes arrangements for the provision of, controlled services together with residential property loans; and

(*b*) advertises or in any other manner promotes—

(i) the provision of any controlled service or any residential property loan; or

(ii) the making by him of any such arrangements,

shall comply with such requirements as to the information to be given, or which may not be given, in any such advertisement or promotion as the Secretary of State may by regulations impose.

[Courts and Legal Services Act 1990, s 104.]

[1] At the date of going to press, ss 104–107 had not been brought into force.

**7.10935 105. Tying-in arrangements: supplemental provisions** (1) In section 104, this section and section 106 "controlled services" means any services of a description prescribed by order made by the Secretary of State.

(2) The order may, in particular, prescribe any description of—

(*a*) banking, insurance, investment, trusteeship, executorship or other financial services;

(*b*) services relating to the acquisition, valuation, surveying or disposal of property;

(*c*) conveyancing services; or

(*d*) removal services.

(3) For the purposes of section 104(1), the Secretary of State may by order specify—

(*a*) the circumstances in which land is to be treated as being for a person's residential use; and

(*b*) who are to be treated as a person's dependants.

(4) Section 104(2) shall not apply in relation to the provision of a controlled service if the lender proves—

(*a*) that the provision of that service was not connected with the transaction in respect of which the borrower required the residential property loan in question; or

(*b*) where it was so connected, that the lender did not know, and had no reasonable cause to know, that it was.

(5) For the purposes of section 104, this section and section 106—

(*a*) where the lender is a member of a group of companies, the lender and all the other members of the group shall be treated as one; and

(*b*) where the lender derives any financial benefit from the provision of a controlled service by any other person, the lender shall be treated as providing that service.

(6) In subsection (5), "a group of companies" means a holding company and its subsidiaries within the meaning of section 1159 of the Companies Act 2006.

(7) The Secretary of State may by order provide that, in such cases or for such purposes as may be prescribed by the order, paragraph (*a*) or (*b*) of subsection (5) shall not have effect.

(8) For the purposes of section 104—

"notice" means a notice in writing given in the form prescribed by regulations made by the Secretary of State;

"price" shall have the meaning given by order made by the Secretary of State;

"relevant step", in relation to any controlled service or residential property loan, means such step as may be prescribed by order made by the Secretary of State in relation to that service or loan (taken by such person as may be so prescribed); and

"statement" means a statement in writing given in the form prescribed by regulations made by the Secretary of State.

(9) Scotland

(10) Before making any order or regulations under section 104 or this section the Secretary of State shall consult the OFT and such other persons as he considers appropriate.

[Courts and Legal Services Act 1990, s 105 as amended by the Enterprise Act 2002, Sch 25 and SI 2009/1941.]

**7.10936 106. Tying-in: offences** (1) If any person contravenes section 104(2) or (4) he shall be guilty of an offence.

(2) Subsection (3) applies where—

(*a*) a person ("the lender") has, in relation to the proposed provision to any person ("the borrower") of a residential property loan together with one or more controlled services, complied with the conditions mentioned in section 104(3); and

(*b*) the borrower has declined to take from the lender one or more of the controlled services.

(3) The lender shall be guilty of an offence if he refuses to provide the borrower with the residential property loan or refuses to provide it to him—

(*a*) on the terms applicable if it were provided together with the controlled services; or

(*b*) where they differ, on terms which are compatible with the statement required by section 104(3)(*c*)(ii),

unless he proves that his reason for so refusing was unconnected with the borrower's having declined as mentioned in subsection (2)(*b*).

(4) Any person guilty of an offence under this section shall be liable[1]—

(*a*) on summary conviction, to a fine not exceeding the **statutory maximum**; and

(*b*) on conviction on indictment, to a **fine**.

(5) Subsection (6) applies where an offence under this section is committed by a body corporate.

(6) If the offence is proved to have been committed with the consent or connivance of or to be attributable to any neglect on the part of—

(*a*) any director, secretary or other similar officer of the body corporate; or

(*b*) any person who was purporting to act in any such capacity,

he (as well as the body corporate) shall be guilty of the offence and shall be liable to be proceeded against and punished accordingly.

(7) The fact that a person has committed an offence under this section in connection with any agreement shall not make the agreement void, or unenforceable (whether as a whole or in part) or otherwise affect its validity or give rise to any cause of action for breach of statutory duty.

[Courts and Legal Services Act 1990, s 106.]

[1] For procedure in respect of an offence which is triable either way, see the Magistrates' Courts Act 1980, ss 17A–21, in PART I: MAGISTRATES' COURTS, PROCEDURE, ante.

7.10937 **107. Tying-in: enforcement** (1) Every local weights and measures authority ("an authority") and the OFT shall have the duty of enforcing sections 104 to 106 and any regulations made under them.

(2) Nothing in subsection (1) is to be taken as authorising a local weights and measures authority in Scotland to institute proceedings for an offence.

(3) Where an authority propose to institute proceedings for an offence under section 106 they shall give the OFT notice of the intended proceedings together with a summary of the facts on which the charges are to be founded.

(4) Where an authority are under a duty to give such a notice and summary they shall not institute the proceedings until—

(*a*) the end of the period of 28 days beginning with the date on which they gave the required notice and summary; or

(*b*) if earlier, the date on which the OFT notifies them of receipt of the notice and summary.

(5) Every authority shall, whenever the OFT requires, report to it in such form and with such particulars as it requires on the exercise of their functions under this section.

(6) A duly authorised officer of the OFT or of an authority ("an authorised officer") who has reasonable cause to suspect that an offence may have been committed under section 106 may, at any reasonable time—

(*a*) enter any premises which are not used solely as a dwelling;

(*b*) require any officer, agent or other competent person on the premises who is, or may be, in possession of information relevant to an investigation in connection with the provision made by section 104 or 105 to provide such information;

(*c*) require the production of any document which may be relevant to such an investigation;

(*d*) take copies, or extracts, of any such documents;

(*e*) seize and retain any document which he has reason to believe may be required as evidence in proceedings for an offence under section 106.

(7) Any authorised officer exercising any power given by subsection (6) shall, if asked to do so, produce evidence that he is such an officer.

(8) A justice of the peace may issue a warrant under this section if satisfied, on information on oath given by an authorised officer, that there is reasonable cause to believe that an offence may have been committed under section 106 and that—

(*a*) entry to the premises concerned, or production of any documents which may be relevant to an investigation in connection with the provision made by section 104 or 105, has been or is likely to be refused to the authorised officer; or (*b*) there is reasonable cause to believe that, if production of any such document were to be required by the authorised officer without a warrant having been issued under this section, the document would not be produced but would be removed from the premises or hidden, tampered with or destroyed.

(9) Scotland.

(10) A warrant issued under this section shall authorise the authorised officer (accompanied, where he considers it appropriate, by a constable or any other person)—

(*a*) to enter the premises specified in the information, using such force as is reasonably necessary; and

(*b*) to exercise any of the powers given to the authorised officer by subsection (6).

(11) If a person—

(*a*) intentionally obstructs an authorised officer in the exercise of any power under this section;

(*b*) intentionally fails to comply with any requirement properly imposed on him by an authorised officer in the exercise of any such power;

(*c*) fails, without reasonable excuse, to give to an authorised officer any assistance or information which he may reasonably require of him for the purpose of exercising any such power; or

(*d*) in giving to an authorised officer any information which he has been required to give to an authorised officer exercising any such power, makes any statement which he knows to be false or misleading in a material particular,

he shall be guilty of an offence.

(12) A person guilty of an offence under subsection (11)(*a*), (*b*) or (*c*) shall be liable on summary conviction to a fine not exceeding **level 3** on the standard scale.

(13) A person guilty of an offence under subsection (11)(*d*) shall be liable on summary conviction to a fine not exceeding **level 4** on the standard scale.

(14) Nothing in this section shall be taken to require any person to answer any question put to him by an authorised officer, or to give any information to an authorised officer, if to do so might incriminate him.

(15) In this section "document" includes information recorded in any form.

(16) In relation to information recorded otherwise than in legible form, references in this section to its production include references to producing a copy of the information in legible form.

[Courts and Legal Services Act 1990, s 107 as amended by the Enterprise Act 2002, Sch 25.]

## Access to Justice Act 1999[1]

(1999 c 22)

### Part II[2]

### Other Funding of Legal Services

*Costs*

**7.10938 29–30.** *Repealed by the Legal Aid, Sentencing and Punishment of Offenders Act 2012, s 47(1) as from 1 April 2013.*

### Part III[1]

### Provision of Legal Services

*Barristers and solicitors*

**7.10940 44. 44 Barristers employed by solicitors etc** (1) Where a barrister —

(*a*) is employed by an authorised person, or

(*b*) is a manager of such a person,

any rules of the General Council of the Bar which impose a prohibition or limitation on the provision of legal services shall not operate to prevent him from providing legal services to clients of the authorised person of which the barrister is an employee or a manager if either of the conditions specified in subsection (2) is satisfied.

(2) Those conditions are—

(*a*) that the prohibition or limitation is on the provision of the services otherwise than on the instructions of a solicitor (or other person acting for the client), and

(*b*) that the prohibition or limitation does not apply to barristers who provide legal services but are not employees or managers of an authorised person.

(3) In this section—

"authorised person" means a person who, for the purposes of the Legal Services Act 2007, is an authorised person in relation to an activity which is a reserved legal activity (within the meaning of that Act), and

"manager" has the same meaning as in that Act (see section 207 of that Act).

[Access to Justice Act 1999, s 44 as amended by the Legal Services Act 2007, Sch 21.]

**7.10941 46. Bar practising certificates** (1) If the General Council of the Bar makes rules prohibiting barristers from practising as specified in the rules unless authorised by a certificate issued by the Council (a "practising certificate"), the rules may include provision requiring the payment of fees to the Council by applicants for practising certificates.

(2) *Rules*

[Access to Justice Act 1999, s 46.]

7.10942 **48. Law Society's powers in relation to conduct of solicitors etc** Schedule 7 (which extends the powers of the Law Society in relation to the conduct of solicitors and their employees and consultants) has effect.

[Access to Justice Act 1999, s 48.]

*Public notaries*

7.10943 **53. Abolition of scriveners' monopoly** A public notary may practise as a notary in, or within three miles of, the City of London whether or not he is a member of the Incorporated Company of Scriveners of London (even if he is admitted to practise only outside that area).

[Access to Justice Act 1999, s 53.]

# Legal Services Act 2007[1]

(2007 c 29)

## PART 1[2]

## THE REGULATORY OBJECTIVES

## PART 2[3]

## THE LEGAL SERVICES BOARD

## PART 3[4]

## RESERVED LEGAL ACTIVITIES

[1] This Act follows the publication of the White Paper, The Future of Legal Services: Putting Consumers First (2006) which in turn had its origins in the Office of Fair Trading report Competition in the Professions – A Report by the Director General of Fair Trading (2001) recommending that rules governing the legal professions should be subject to competition law and that unjustified restrictions on competition be removed. This was followed by Government consultation and a report Competition and Regulation in the Legal Services Market – A Report Following the Consultation "In the Public Interest?" (Department for Constitutional Affairs, 2003). The 2004 Review of the Regulatory Framework for Legal Services in England and Wales – Final Report (Sir David Clementi (2004)) highlighted concerns about the current regulatory framework; complaints systems, and restrictive nature of business structures.

The 2007 Act establishes the Legal Services Board, a single oversight body, independent from both Government and approved regulators eg the Law Society and Bar Council. It has a duty to promote the regulatory objectives set out in Part 1. There is an Office for Legal Complaints which has statutory powers to handle complaints about services provided by persons and to award redress in appropriate circumstances. The explanatory notes to the legislation state that it is expected to address concerns about the quality, independence, and consistency of complaints handling by the legal professions.

The Act identifies and covers six existing forms of legal service or activity: the right of audience in the courts; the right to conduct litigation; reserved instrument activities; probate activities; notarial services; and the administration of oaths. Current regulators of these services include the Law Society and the Bar Council and these will continue as "approved regulators". The Act will not directly affect the Legal Services Commission. The Act also aims to facilitate a regulatory framework in which different types of lawyer and non-lawyer are able to form businesses together, and in which regulators can be given effective powers to regulate such businesses.

The Act is brought into force in accordance with the provisions of s 211, post. Sections 208(2)–(5), 211, 212 and 214 came into force on Royal Assent, 30 October 2007. The remaining provisions are to be brought into force by commencement orders. At the date of going to press, the following commencement orders had been made: (No 1 and Transitional Provisions) SI 2008/222; (No 2 and Transitory Provisions) Order 2008, SI 2008/1436 amended by SI 2008/1591; (No 3 and Transitory Provisions) SI 2008/3149; (No 4, Transitory and Transitional Provisions and Appointed Day) SI 2009/503; (No 5, Transitory and Transitional Provisions) Order 2009, SI 2009/1365; (No 6, Transitory and Transitional and Saving Provisions) SI 2009/3250; (No 7) Order 2010, SI 2010/1118; (No 8, Transitory and Transitional Provisions) Order 2010, SI 2010/2089; and (No 9) Order 2010, SI 2010/2842. Of the material reproduced here the following are in force: ss 48(6) to (9) 79(6) to (10) (1 January 2009), ss 12–17, 18, 19, 48 (fully), 181, 183, 188–190, 192, 193, 197, 197, 198, Schs 2 and 3 (1 January 2010), s 207 (various dates); (No 10) SI 2011/720 (ss 175(2)(*e*) and 186; Sch 4, para 19(2)(*f*); Parts 1 and 2 of Sch 18); (No 11, Transitory and Transitional Provisions and Related Amendments) SI 2011/2196; (No 12, Supplementary and Transitory Provision) Order 2012, SI 2012/3307.

[2] Part 1 comprises s 1.

[3] Part 2 comprises ss 2–11 and Sch 1.

[4] Part 3 comprises ss 12–26 and Schs 2–6.

*Reserved legal activities*

7.10944 **12. Meaning of "reserved legal activity" and "legal activity"** (1) In this Act "reserved legal activity" means—

(*a*) the exercise of a right of audience;

(*b*) the conduct of litigation[1];

(*c*) reserved instrument activities;

(*d*) probate activities;

(*e*) notarial activities;

(*f*) the administration of oaths.

(2) Schedule 2 makes provision about what constitutes each of those activities.

(3) In this Act "legal activity" means—

(*a*) an activity which is a reserved legal activity within the meaning of this Act as originally enacted, and

(*b*) any other activity which consists of one or both of the following—
(i) the provision of legal advice or assistance in connection with the application of the law or with any form of resolution of legal disputes;
(ii) the provision of representation in connection with any matter concerning the application of the law or any form of resolution of legal disputes.

(4) But "legal activity" does not include any activity of a judicial or quasi-judicial nature (including acting as a mediator).

(5) For the purposes of subsection (3) "legal dispute" includes a dispute as to any matter of fact the resolution of which is relevant to determining the nature of any person's legal rights or liabilities.

(6) Section 24 makes provision for adding legal activities to the reserved legal activities.

[Legal Services Act 2007, s 12.]

[1] The laying of an information amounts to the commencement of proceedings and is, therefore, within the term "conduct of litigation" and, consequently, a "reserved legal activity". Where an information was laid by a person, not as a litigant acting on his own behalf but as a director of a company acting for reward for a client, he acted as a solicitor within the meaning of and in breach of the Solicitors Act 1974, s 20. He was not an authorised litigator. The company could not, therefore, bring itself within Sch 2, para 4(2) (see post): *Media Protection Services Ltd v Crawford* [2012] EWHC 2373 (Admin), [2013] 1 WLR 1068, 177 JP 54, [2013] Crim LR 155.

*Carrying on the activities*

7.10945 **13. Entitlement to carry on a reserved legal activity** (1) The question whether a person is entitled to carry on an activity which is a reserved legal activity is to be determined solely in accordance with the provisions of this Act.

(2) A person is entitled to carry on an activity ("the relevant activity") which is a reserved legal activity where—
(*a*) the person is an authorised person in relation to the relevant activity, or
(*b*) the person is an exempt person in relation to that activity.

(3) Subsection (2) is subject to section 23 (transitional protection for non-commercial bodies).

(4) Nothing in this section or section 23 affects section 84 of the Immigration and Asylum Act 1999 (c 33) (which prohibits the provision of immigration advice and immigration services except by certain persons).

[Legal Services Act 2007, s 13.]

*Offences*

7.10946 **14. Offence to carry on a reserved legal activity if not entitled** (1) It is an offence for a person to carry on an activity ("the relevant activity") which is a reserved legal activity unless that person is entitled to carry on the relevant activity.

(2) In proceedings for an offence under subsection (1), it is a defence for the accused to show that the accused did not know, and could not reasonably have been expected to know, that the offence was being committed.

(3) A person who is guilty of an offence under subsection (1) is liable—
(*a*) on summary conviction, to imprisonment for a term not exceeding 12 months or a fine not exceeding the statutory maximum (or both), and
(*b*) on conviction on indictment, to imprisonment for a term not exceeding 2 years or a fine (or both).

(4) A person who is guilty of an offence under subsection (1) by reason of an act done in the purported exercise of a right of audience, or a right to conduct litigation, in relation to any proceedings or contemplated proceedings is also guilty of contempt of the court concerned and may be punished accordingly.

(5) In relation to an offence under subsection (1) committed before the commencement of section 154(1) of the Criminal Justice Act 2003 (c 44), the reference in subsection (3)(*a*) to 12 months is to be read as a reference to 6 months.

[Legal Services Act 2007, s 14.]

7.10947 **15. Carrying on of a reserved legal activity: employers and employees etc**

(1) This section applies for the interpretation of references in this Act to a person carrying on an activity which is a reserved legal activity.

(2) References to a person carrying on an activity which is a reserved legal activity include a person ("E") who—
(*a*) is an employee of a person ("P"), and
(*b*) carries on the activity in E's capacity as such an employee.

(3) For the purposes of subsection (2), it is irrelevant whether P is entitled to carry on the activity.

(4) P does not carry on an activity ("the relevant activity") which is a reserved legal activity by virtue of E carrying it on in E's capacity as an employee of P, unless the provision of relevant services to the public or a section of the public (with or without a view to profit) is part of P's business.

(5) Relevant services are services which consist of or include the carrying on of the relevant activity by employees of P in their capacity as employees of P.

(6) Where P is an independent trade union, persons provided with relevant services do not constitute the public or a section of the public where—

(*a*) the persons are provided with the relevant services by virtue of their membership or former membership of P or of another person's membership or former membership of P, and

(*b*) the services are excepted membership services.

(7) Subject to subsection (8), "excepted membership services" means relevant services which relate to or have a connection with—

(*a*) relevant activities of a member, or former member, of the independent trade union;

(*b*) any other activities carried on for the purposes of or in connection with, or arising from, such relevant activities;

(*c*) any event which has occurred (or is alleged to have occurred) in the course of or in connection with such relevant activities or activities within paragraph (*b*);

(*d*) activities carried on by a person for the purposes of or in connection with, or arising from, the person's membership of the independent trade union;

and such other relevant services as the Lord Chancellor may by order specify.

(8) The Lord Chancellor may by order make provision about the circumstances in which relevant services do or do not relate to, or have a connection with, the matters mentioned in paragraphs (*a*) to (*d*) of subsection (7).

(9) Subject to that, the Lord Chancellor may by order make provision about—

(*a*) what does or does not constitute a section of the public;

(*b*) the circumstances in which the provision of relevant services to the public or a section of the public does or does not form part of P's business.

(10) The Lord Chancellor may make an order under subsection (7), (8) or (9) only on the recommendation of the Board.

(11) If P is a body, references to an employee of P include references to a manager of P.

(12) In subsection (7), "relevant activities", in relation to a person who is or was a member of an independent trade union, means any employment (including self-employment), trade, occupation or other activity to which the person's membership of the trade union relates or related.

[Legal Services Act 2007, s 15.]

7.10948 **16. Offence to carry on reserved legal activity through person not entitled**

(1) Where subsection (2) applies it is an offence for a person ("P") to carry on an activity ("the relevant activity") which is a reserved legal activity, despite P being entitled to carry on the relevant activity.

(2) This subsection applies if—

(*a*) P carries on the relevant activity by virtue of an employee of P ("E") carrying it on in E's capacity as such an employee, and

(*b*) in carrying on the relevant activity, E commits an offence under section 14.

(3) If P is a body, references in subsection (2) to an employee of P include references to a manager of P.

(4) In proceedings for an offence under subsection (1), it is a defence for the accused to show that the accused took all reasonable precautions and exercised all due diligence to avoid committing the offence.

(5) A person who is guilty of an offence under subsection (1) is liable—

(*a*) on summary conviction, to imprisonment for a term not exceeding 12 months or a fine not exceeding the statutory maximum (or both), and

(*b*) on conviction on indictment, to imprisonment for a term not exceeding 2 years or a fine (or both).

(6) A person who is guilty of an offence under subsection (1) by reason of an act done in the purported exercise of a right of audience, or a right to conduct litigation, in relation to any proceedings or contemplated proceedings is also guilty of contempt of the court concerned and may be punished accordingly.

(7) In relation to an offence under subsection (1) committed before the commencement of section 154(1) of the Criminal Justice Act 2003 (c 44), the reference in subsection (5)(*a*) to 12 months is to be read as a reference to 6 months.

[Legal Services Act 2007, s 16.]

7.10949 **17. Offence to pretend to be entitled** (1) It is an offence for a person—

(*a*) wilfully to pretend to be entitled to carry on any activity which is a reserved legal activity when that person is not so entitled, or

(*b*) with the intention of implying falsely that that person is so entitled, to take or use any name, title or description.

(2) A person who is guilty of an offence under subsection (1) is liable—

(*a*) on summary conviction, to imprisonment for a term not exceeding 12 months or a fine not exceeding the statutory maximum (or both), and

(*b*) on conviction on indictment, to imprisonment for a term not exceeding 2 years or a fine (or both).

(3) In relation to an offence under subsection (1) committed before the commencement of section 154(1) of the Criminal Justice Act 2003 (c 44), the reference in subsection (2)(*a*) to 12 months is to be read as a reference to 6 months.

[Legal Services Act 2007, s 17.]

*Interpretation*

**7.10950 18. Authorised persons** (1) For the purposes of this Act "authorised person", in relation to an activity ("the relevant activity") which is a reserved legal activity, means—

(*a*) a person who is authorised to carry on the relevant activity by a relevant approved regulator in relation to the relevant activity (other than by virtue of a licence under Part 5), or

(*b*) a licensable body which, by virtue of such a licence, is authorised to carry on the relevant activity by a licensing authority in relation to the reserved legal activity.

(2) A licensable body may not be authorised to carry on the relevant activity as mentioned in subsection (1)(*a*).

(3) But where a body ("A") which is authorised as mentioned in subsection (1)(*a*) becomes a licensable body, the body is deemed by virtue of this subsection to continue to be so authorised from that time until the earliest of the following events—

(*a*) the end of the period of 90 days beginning with the day on which that time falls;

(*b*) the time from which the relevant approved regulator determines this subsection is to cease to apply to A;

(*c*) the time when A ceases to be a licensable body.

(4) Subsection (2) is subject to Part 2 of Schedule 5 (by virtue of which licensable bodies may be deemed to be authorised as mentioned in subsection (1)(*a*) in relation to certain activities during a transitional period).

(5) A person other than a licensable body may not be authorised to carry on the relevant activity as mentioned in subsection (1)(*b*).

(6) But where a body ("L") which is authorised as mentioned in subsection (1)(*b*) ceases to be a licensable body, the body is deemed by virtue of this subsection to continue to be so authorised from that time until the earliest of the following events—

(*a*) the end of the period of 90 days beginning with the day on which that time falls;

(*b*) the time from which the relevant licensing authority determines this subsection is to cease to apply to L;

(*c*) the time when L becomes a licensable body.

[Legal Services Act 2007, s 18.]

**7.10951 19. Exempt persons** In this Act, "exempt person", in relation to an activity ("the relevant activity") which is a reserved legal activity, means a person who, for the purposes of carrying on the relevant activity, is an exempt person by virtue of—

(*a*) Schedule 3 (exempt persons), or

(*b*) paragraph 13 or 18 of Schedule 5 (additional categories of exempt persons during transitional period).

[Legal Services Act 2007, s 19.]

**10951A 42. Intervention directions: further provision** (1) This section applies where an intervention direction has effect in respect of a function of an approved regulator ("the relevant function").

(2) The approved regulator must give the specified person all such assistance, in connection with the proposed exercise of the relevant function by the specified person in pursuance of the direction, as the approved regulator is reasonably able to give.

(3) On an application by the specified person (or a person appointed by the specified person to act on its behalf) a judge of the High Court, Circuit judge or justice of the peace may issue a warrant authorising that person to—

(*a*) enter and search the premises of the approved regulator, and

(*b*) take possession of any written or electronic records found on the premises.

(4) The person so authorised may, for the purpose of the exercise by the specified person of the relevant function, take copies of written or electronic records found on a search carried out by virtue of the warrant.

(5) The judge or justice of the peace may not issue the warrant unless satisfied that its issue is necessary or desirable for the exercise by the specified person of the relevant function.

(6) The Lord Chancellor must make regulations[1]—

(*a*) specifying further matters which a judge or justice of the peace must be satisfied of, or matters which a judge or justice of the peace must have regard to, before issuing a warrant, and

(*b*) regulating the exercise of a power conferred by a warrant issued under subsection (3) or by subsection (4) (whether by restricting the circumstances in which a power may be exercised, by specifying conditions to be complied with in the exercise of a power, or otherwise).

(7) Regulations under subsection (6)(*b*) must in particular make provision as to the circumstances in which written or electronic records of which a person has taken possession by virtue of a warrant issued under subsection (3) may be copied or must be returned.

(8) But the Lord Chancellor may not make regulations under subsection (6) unless—

(*a*) they are made in accordance with a recommendation made by the Board, or (*b*) the Lord Chancellor has consulted the Board about the making of the regulations.

(9) In this section "the specified person" means the Board or, where a person is nominated by it as mentioned in section 41(2), that person.

(10) The Board must make rules as to the persons a specified person may appoint for the purposes of subsection (3).

[Legal Services Act 2007, s 42.]

---

1 The Legal Services Act 2007 (Warrant) (Approved Regulator) Regulations 2015, SI 2015/935 have been made, in this title, post.

10951B **43. Intervention directions: enforcement** (1) If at any time it appears to the Board that an approved regulator has failed to comply with an obligation imposed on it by, or by virtue of, an intervention direction or section 42(2), the Board may make an application to the High Court under this section.

(2) If, on an application under subsection (1), the High Court decides that the approved regulator has failed to comply with the obligation in question, it may order the approved regulator to take such steps as the High Court directs for securing that the obligation is complied with.

(3) This section is without prejudice to any other powers conferred on the Board by this Part.

[Legal Services Act 2007, s 43.]

## PART 4[1]

## REGULATION OF APPROVED REGULATORS

7.10952 **48. Cancellation of designation: powers of entry etc** (1) This section applies where a body ("the former regulator") has its designation in relation to one or more reserved legal activities cancelled by an order under section 45.

(2) The Board may request the former regulator to provide assistance to the new regulator and the Board, for the purpose of continuing regulation.

(3) On an application by a person appointed by the Board to act on its behalf, a judge of the High Court, Circuit judge or justice of the peace may issue a warrant authorising that person to—

(*a*) enter and search the premises of the former regulator, and

(*b*) take possession of any written or electronic records found on the premises.

(4) A person so authorised may, for the purpose of continuing regulation, take copies of written or electronic records found on a search carried out by virtue of the warrant.

(5) The judge or justice of the peace may not issue the warrant unless satisfied that its issue is necessary or desirable for the purpose of continuing regulation.

(6) The Lord Chancellor must make regulations[2]—

(*a*) specifying further matters which a judge or justice of the peace must be satisfied of, or matters which a judge or justice of the peace must have regard to, before issuing a warrant, and

(*b*) regulating the exercise of a power conferred by a warrant issued under subsection (3) or by subsection (4) (whether by restricting the circumstances in which a power may be exercised, by specifying conditions to be complied with in the exercise of a power, or otherwise).

(7) Regulations under subsection (6)(*b*) must in particular make provision as to circumstances in which written or electronic records of which a person has taken possession by virtue of a warrant issued under subsection (3) may be copied or must be returned.

(8) But the Lord Chancellor may not make regulations under subsection (6) unless—

(*a*) they are made in accordance with a recommendation made by the Board, or

(*b*) the Lord Chancellor has consulted the Board about the making of the regulations.

(9) The Board must make rules as to the persons it may appoint for the purposes of subsection (3).

(10) For the purposes of this section—

"authorised by the former regulator", "protected activity" and "new regulator" have the same meaning as for the purposes of section 46;

"the purpose of continuing regulation" means the purpose of enabling persons authorised by the former regulator to continue to be authorised and regulated in relation to the protected activity.

[Legal Services Act 2007, s 48.]

---

1 Part 4 comprises ss 27–70 and Schs 7–9.

2 The Legal Services Act 2007 (Warrant) (Approved Regulator) Regulations 2015, SI 2015/935 have been made, in this title, post.

## PART 5[1]

## ALTERNATIVE BUSINESS STRUCTURES

7.10953 **79. Cancellation of designation: powers of entry etc** (1) This section applies where an approved regulator ("the former authority") has its designation in relation to one or more reserved legal activities cancelled by virtue of section 75 or an order under section 76.

(2) The Board may request the former authority to provide assistance to the new authority and

the Board, for the purpose of continuing regulation.

(3) On an application by a person appointed by the Board to act on its behalf, a judge of the High Court, Circuit judge or justice of the peace may issue a warrant authorising that person to—

(*a*) enter and search the premises of the former authority, and

(*b*) take possession of any written or electronic records found on the premises.

(4) A person so authorised may, for the purpose of continuing regulation, take copies of written or electronic records found on a search carried out by virtue of the warrant.

(5) The judge or justice of the peace may not issue the warrant unless satisfied that its issue is necessary or desirable for the purpose of continuing regulation.

(6) The Lord Chancellor must make regulations[2]—

(*a*) specifying further matters which a judge or justice of the peace must be satisfied of, or matters which a judge or justice of the peace must have regard to, before issuing a warrant, and

(*b*) regulating the exercise of a power conferred by a warrant issued under subsection (3) or by subsection (4) (whether by restricting the circumstances in which a power may be exercised, by specifying conditions to be complied with in the exercise of a power, or otherwise).

(7) Regulations under subsection (6)(*b*) must in particular make provision as to circumstances in which written or electronic records of which a person has taken possession by virtue of a warrant issued under subsection (3) may be copied or must be returned.

(8) But the Lord Chancellor may not make regulations under subsection (6) unless—

(*a*) they are made in accordance with a recommendation made by the Board, or

(*b*) the Lord Chancellor has consulted the Board about the making of the regulations.

(9) The Board must make rules as to the persons it may appoint for the purposes of subsection (3).

(10) For the purposes of this section—

"authorised by the former authority", "protected activity" and "new authority" have the same meaning as for the purposes of section 77;

"the purpose of continuing regulation" means the purpose of enabling bodies authorised by the former authority to continue to be authorised and regulated in relation to the protected activity.

[Legal Services Act 2007, s 79.]

1 Part 5 comprises ss 71–111 and Schs 10–14.

2 The Legal Services Act 2007 (Warrant) (Licensing Authority) Regulations 2015, SI 2015/938 have been made, in this title, post.

## PART 6[1]

## LEGAL COMPLAINTS

## PART 7[2]

## FURTHER PROVISIONS RELATING TO THE BOARD AND THE OLC

1 Part 6 comprises ss 112–161 and Sch 15.

2 Part 7 comprises ss 162–175.

## PART 8[1]

## MISCELLANEOUS PROVISIONS ABOUT LAWYERS ETC

7.10954 181. **Unqualified person not to pretend to be a barrister** (1) It is an offence for a person who is not a barrister—

(*a*) wilfully to pretend to be a barrister, or

(*b*) with the intention of implying falsely that that person is a barrister to take or use any name, title or description.

(2) A person who is guilty of an offence under subsection (1) is liable—

(*a*) on summary conviction, to imprisonment for a term not exceeding 12 months or a fine not exceeding the statutory maximum (or both), and

(*b*) on conviction on indictment, to imprisonment for a term not exceeding 2 years or a fine (or both).

(3) In relation to an offence under subsection (1) committed before the commencement of section 154(1) of the Criminal Justice Act 2003 (c 44), the reference in subsection (2)(*a*) to 12 months is to be read as a reference to 6 months.

[Legal Services Act 2007, s 181.]

1 Part 8 comprises ss 176–196 and Schs 16–20.

7.10955 183. **Commissioners for oaths** (1) For the purposes of any enactment or instrument (including an enactment passed or instrument made after the passing of this Act) "commissioner for oaths" includes an authorised person in relation to the administration of oaths ("a relevant authorised person").

(2) A relevant authorised person has the right to use the title "Commissioner for Oaths".

(3) A relevant authorised person may not carry on the administration of oaths in any proceedings in which that person represents any of the parties or is interested.

(4) A relevant authorised person before whom an oath or affidavit is taken or made must state in

the jurat or attestation at which place and on what date the oath or affidavit is taken or made.

(5) A document containing such a statement and purporting to be sealed or signed by a relevant authorised person must be admitted in evidence without proof of the seal or signature, and without proof that that person is a relevant authorised person.

(6) The Lord Chancellor may by order prescribe the fees to be charged by relevant authorised persons in respect of the administration of an oath or the taking of an affidavit.

(7) The Lord Chancellor may make an order under subsection (6) only—

(*a*) after consultation with the Board, and

(*b*) with the consent of the Lord Chief Justice and the Master of the Rolls.

(8) In this section "affidavit" has the same meaning as in the Commissioners for Oaths Act 1889 (c 10).

[Legal Services Act 2007, s 183.]

7.10956 188. **Duties of advocates and litigators** (1) This section applies to a person who—

(*a*) exercises before any court a right of audience, or

(*b*) conducts litigation in relation to proceedings in any court,

by virtue of being an authorised person in relation to the activity in question.

(2) A person to whom this section applies has a duty to the court in question to act with independence in the interests of justice.

(3) That duty, and the duty to comply with relevant conduct rules imposed on the person by section 176(1), override any obligations which the person may have (otherwise than under the criminal law) if they are inconsistent with them.

(4) "Relevant conduct rules" are the conduct rules of the relevant authorising body which relate to the exercise of a right of audience or the conduct of litigation.

(5) The relevant authorising body is—

(*a*) the approved regulator by which the person is authorised to exercise the right of audience or conduct the litigation, or

(*b*) where the person is authorised to exercise the right of audience or conduct the litigation by the Board in its capacity as a licensing authority, the Board.

[Legal Services Act 2007, s 188.]

7.10957 189. **Employed advocates** (1) This section applies where an authorised person in relation to the exercise of a right of audience is employed as a Crown Prosecutor or in any other description of employment.

(2) Qualification regulations or conduct rules of the approved regulator by whom the person is authorised to carry on that activity which relate to the right of audience do not have effect in relation to the person if—

(*a*) they—

(i) limit the courts before which, or proceedings in which, that activity may be carried on by persons who are employed, or

(ii) limit the circumstances in which that activity may be carried on by persons who are employed by requiring such persons to be accompanied by some other person when carrying on that activity, and

(*b*) they do not impose the same limitation on persons who are authorised persons in relation to the activity in question but are not employed.

[Legal Services Act 2007, s 189.]

7.10958 190. **Legal professional privilege** (1) Subsection (2) applies where an individual ("P") who is not a barrister or solicitor—

(*a*) provides advocacy services as an authorised person in relation to the exercise of rights of audience,

(*b*) provides litigation services as an authorised person in relation to the conduct of litigation,

(*c*) provides conveyancing services as an authorised person in relation to reserved instrument activities, or

(*d*) provides probate services as an authorised person in relation to probate activities.

(2) Any communication, document, material or information relating to the provision of the services in question is privileged from disclosure in like manner as if P had at all material times been acting as P's client's solicitor.

(3) Subsection (4) applies where—

(*a*) a licensed body provides services to a client, and

(*b*) the individual ("E") through whom the body provides those services—

(i) is a relevant lawyer, or

(ii) acts at the direction and under the supervision of a relevant lawyer ("the supervisor").

(4) Any communication, document, material or information relating to the provision of the services in question is privileged from disclosure only if, and to the extent that, it would have been privileged from disclosure if—

(*a*) the services had been provided by E or, if E is not a relevant lawyer, by the supervisor, and (*b*) at all material times the client had been the client of E or, if E is not a relevant lawyer, of the supervisor.

(5) "Relevant lawyer" means an individual who is—

(*a*) a solicitor;

(*b*) a barrister;

(*c*) a solicitor in Scotland;

(*d*) an advocate in Scotland;

(*e*) a solicitor of the Court of Judicature of Northern Ireland;

(*f*) a member of the Bar of Northern Ireland;

(*g*) a registered foreign lawyer (within the meaning of section 89 of the Courts and Legal Services Act 1990 (c 41));

(*h*) an individual not within paragraphs (*a*) to (*g*) who is an authorised person in relation to an activity which is a reserved legal activity; or

(*i*) a European lawyer (within the meaning of the European Communities (Services of Lawyers) Order 1978 (SI 1978/1910)).

(6) In this section—

"advocacy services" means any services which it would be reasonable to expect a person who is exercising, or contemplating exercising, a right of audience in relation to any proceedings, or contemplated proceedings, to provide;

"litigation services" means any services which it would be reasonable to expect a person who is exercising, or contemplating exercising, a right to conduct litigation in relation to any proceedings, or contemplated proceedings, to provide;

"conveyancing services" means the preparation of transfers, conveyances, contracts and other documents in connection with, and other services ancillary to, the disposition or acquisition of estates or interests in land;

"probate services" means the preparation of any papers on which to found or oppose a grant of probate or a grant of letters of administration and the administration of the estate of a deceased person.

(7) This section is without prejudice to any other enactment or rule of law by virtue of which a communication, a document, material or information is privileged from disclosure.

[Legal Services Act 2007, s 190.]

**7.10959 192. Powers of court in respect of rights of audience and conduct of litigation**

(1) Nothing in this Act affects the power of any court in any proceedings to refuse to hear a person (for reasons which apply to that person as an individual) who would otherwise have a right of audience before the court in relation to those proceedings.

(2) Where a court refuses to hear a person as mentioned in subsection (1), it must give its reasons for refusing.

(3) Where—

(*a*) immediately before the commencement of section 13 (entitlement to carry on reserved legal activities), or

(*b*) by virtue of any provision made by or under an enactment passed subsequently,

a court does not permit the appearance of advocates, or permits the appearance of advocates only with leave, no person may exercise a right of audience before the court, in relation to any proceedings, solely by virtue of being entitled to do so under this Act.

(4) But a court may not limit the right to appear before the court in any proceedings to only some of those who are entitled to exercise that right by virtue of this Act.

(5) A court may not limit the right to conduct litigation in relation to proceedings before the court to only some of those who are entitled to exercise that right by virtue of this Act.

(6) In this section "advocate", in relation to any proceedings, means a person exercising a right of audience as a representative of, or on behalf of, any party to the proceedings.

[Legal Services Act 2007, s 192.]

**7.10960 193. Solicitors to public departments and the City of London** (1) Nothing in this Act is to prejudice or affect any rights or privileges of—

(*a*) the Treasury Solicitor,

(*b*) the solicitor to any other public department,

(*c*) the solicitor to the Church Commissioners, or

(*d*) the solicitor to the Duchy of Cornwall.

(2) Nothing in this Act requires a person to whom subsection (1) applies, or any clerk or officer appointed to act for such a person, to be entitled to carry on an activity which is a reserved legal activity in any case where, by virtue of section 88(1) of the Solicitors Act 1974 (c 47), it would not have been necessary for that person to be admitted and enrolled and to hold a practising certificate under that Act if this Act had not been passed.

(3) Nothing in this Act is to prejudice or affect any rights or privileges which immediately before the commencement of this Act attached to the office of Solicitor of the City of London.

(4) Nothing in section 17 (offence to pretend to be entitled) applies to a person to whom subsection (1) applies, or any clerk or officer appointed to act for such a person, or to the Solicitor of the City of London.

(5) A person who—

(*a*) exercises before any court a right of audience, or
(*b*) conducts litigation in relation to proceedings in any court,

by virtue of this section has a duty to the court in question to act with independence in the interests of justice.

(6) That duty overrides any obligations which the person may have (otherwise than under the criminal law) if it is inconsistent with them.

[Legal Services Act 2007, s 193.]

## PART 9[1]
## GENERAL

### *Offences*

7.10961 **197. Offences committed by bodies corporate and unincorporated bodies** (1) Where an offence committed by a body corporate is proved to have been committed with the consent or connivance of or to be attributable to any neglect on the part of an officer of the body corporate, that officer (as well as the body corporate) is guilty of the offence and is liable to be proceeded against and punished accordingly.

(2) Where the affairs of a body corporate are managed by its members, subsection (1) applies in relation to the acts and defaults of a member in connection with the member's functions of management as it applies to an officer of the body corporate.

(3) Proceedings for an offence alleged to have been committed by an unincorporated body are to be brought in the name of that body (and not in that of any of its members) and, for the purposes of any such proceedings, any rules of court relating to the service of documents have effect as if that body were a corporation.

(4) A fine imposed on an unincorporated body on its conviction of an offence is to be paid out of the funds of that body.

(5) If an unincorporated body is charged with an offence, section 33 of the Criminal Justice Act 1925 (c 86) and Schedule 3 to the Magistrates' Courts Act 1980 (c 43) (procedure on charge of an offence against a corporation) have effect in like manner as in the case of a corporation so charged.

(6) Where an offence committed by an unincorporated body (other than a partnership) is proved to have been committed with the consent or connivance of, or to be attributable to any neglect on the part of, any officer of the body or any member of its governing body, that officer or member as well as the unincorporated body is guilty of the offence and liable to be proceeded against and punished accordingly.

(7) Where an offence committed by a partnership is proved to have been committed with the consent or connivance of, or to be attributable to any neglect on the part of, a partner, that partner as well as the partnership is guilty of the offence and liable to be proceeded against and punished accordingly.

(8) In this section—

"offence" means an offence under this Act;

"officer", in relation to a body corporate, means—

(*a*) any director, secretary or other similar officer of the body corporate, or
(*b*) any person who was purporting to act in any such capacity.

[Legal Services Act 2007, s 197.]

1 Part 9 comprises ss 197–214 and Schs 21–24.

7.10962 **198. Local weights and measures authorities** (1) A local weights and measures authority may institute proceedings for an offence under section 14 if the activity which it is alleged that the accused was not entitled to carry on constitutes reserved instrument activities.

(2) A local weights and measures authority may institute proceedings for an offence under section 16 if the activity which it is alleged that E was not entitled to carry on constitutes reserved instrument activities.

"E" has the same meaning as in that section.

(3) In this section—

"relevant offence" means an offence in relation to which proceedings may be instituted by virtue of subsection (1) or (2);

"weights and measures officer" means an officer of a local weights and measures authority who is authorised by the authority to exercise the powers conferred by subsection (4).

(4) A weights and measures officer who has reasonable cause to suspect that a relevant offence may have been committed may, at any reasonable time—

(*a*) enter any premises which are not used solely as a dwelling;
(*b*) require any officer, agent or other competent person on the premises who is, or may be, in possession of information relevant to an investigation of the suspected offence to provide such information;
(*c*) require the production of any document which may be relevant to such an investigation;
(*d*) take copies, or extracts, of any such documents;
(*e*) seize and retain any document which the weights and measures officer has reason to believe may be required as evidence in proceedings for a relevant offence.

(5) Any person exercising a power given by subsection (4) must, if asked to do so, produce

evidence that that person is a weights and measures officer.

(6) A justice of the peace may issue a warrant under this section if satisfied, on information on oath given by a weights and measures officer, that there is reasonable cause to believe that a relevant offence may have been committed and that—

(*a*) entry to the premises concerned, or production of any documents which may be relevant to an investigation of the relevant offence, has been or is likely to be refused to a weights and measures officer, or

(*b*) there is reasonable cause to believe that, if production of any such document were to be required by the weights and measures officer without a warrant having been issued under this section, the document would not be produced but would be removed from the premises or hidden, tampered with or destroyed.

(7) A warrant issued under this section must authorise the weights and measures officer accompanied, where that officer considers it appropriate, by a constable or other person—

(*a*) to enter the premises specified in the information, using such force as is reasonably necessary, and

(*b*) to exercise any of the powers given to the weights and measures officer by subsection (4).

(8) It is an offence for a person ("P")—

(*a*) intentionally to obstruct a weights and measures officer in the exercise of any power under this section;

(*b*) intentionally to fail to comply with any requirement properly imposed on P by a weights and measures officer in the exercise of any such power;

(*c*) to fail, without reasonable excuse, to give a weights and measures officer any assistance or information which the weights and measures officer may reasonably require of P for the purpose of exercising any such power; or

(*d*) in giving to a weights and measures officer any information which P has been required to give a weights and measures officer exercising any such power, to make any statement which P knows to be false or misleading in a material particular.

(9) A person who is guilty of an offence under subsection (8) is liable on summary conviction to a fine not exceeding level 3 on the standard scale.

(10) Nothing in this section is to be taken to require any person to answer any question put to that person by a weights and measures officer, or to give any information to such an officer, if to do so might incriminate that person.

[Legal Services Act 2007, s 198.]

7.10963 207. **Interpretation** (1) In this Act, except where the context otherwise requires—

"barrister" means an individual who—

(*a*) has been called to the Bar by an Inn of Court, and

(*b*) is not disbarred by order of an Inn of Court;

"consumers" means (subject to subsection (3)) persons—

(*a*) who use, have used or are or may be contemplating using, services within subsection (2),

(*b*) who have rights or interests which are derived from, or are otherwise attributable to, the use of such services by other persons, or

(*c*) who have rights or interests which may be adversely affected by the use of such services by persons acting on their behalf or in a fiduciary capacity in relation to them;

"conveyancing services" has the same meaning as in Part 2 of the Administration of Justice Act 1985 (c 61) (licensed conveyancing) (see section 11(3) of that Act);

"court" includes—

(*a*) a tribunal that is (to any extent) a listed tribunal for, or for any of, the purposes of Schedule 7 to the Tribunals, Courts and Enforcement Act 2007 (functions etc of Administrative Justice and Tribunals Council);

(*b*) a court-martial;

(*c*) a statutory inquiry within the meaning of section 16(1) of the Tribunals and Inquiries Act 1992 (c 53);

(*d*) an ecclesiastical court (including the Court of Faculties);

"functions" includes powers and duties;

"immigration advice" and "immigration services" have the meaning given by section 82 of the Immigration and Asylum Act 1999 (c 33) (interpretation of Part 5) (see also subsection (4) below);

"independent trade union" has the same meaning as in the Trade Union and Labour Relations (Consolidation) Act 1992 (c 52) (see section 5 of that Act);

"manager", in relation to a body, means (subject to subsection (5)) a person who—

(*a*) if the body is a body corporate whose affairs are managed by its members, is a member of the body,

(*b*) if the body is a body corporate and paragraph (*a*) does not apply, is a director of the body,

(*c*) if the body is a partnership, is a partner, and

(*d*) if the body is an unincorporated body (other than a partnership), is a member of its governing body;

"modify" includes amend, add to or revoke, and references to "modifications" are to be construed accordingly;

"non-commercial legal services" means—

(*a*) legal services carried on otherwise than with a view to profit;

(*b*) legal services carried on by a not for profit body, a community interest company or an independent trade union;

"not for profit body" means a body which, by or by virtue of its constitution or any enactment—

(*a*) is required (after payment of outgoings) to apply the whole of its income, and any capital which it expends, for charitable or public purposes, and

(*b*) is prohibited from directly or indirectly distributing amongst its members any part of its assets (otherwise than for charitable or public purposes);

"the OFT" means the Office of Fair Trading;

"person" includes a body of persons (corporate or unincorporate);

"reserved legal services" means services provided by a person which consist of or include reserved legal activities carried on by, or on behalf of, that person;

"solicitor" means solicitor of the Senior Courts.

(2) The services within this subsection are—

(*a*) any services provided by a person who is an authorised person in relation to an activity which is a reserved legal activity, and

(*b*) any other services provided by a person which consist of or include a legal activity carried on by, or on behalf of, that person.

(3) For the purposes of the definition of "consumers" in subsection (1)—

(*a*) if a person ("A") is carrying on an activity in A's capacity as a trustee, the persons who are, have been or may be beneficiaries of the trust are to be treated as persons who use, have used or are or may be contemplating using services provided by A in A's carrying on of that activity, and

(*b*) a person who deals with another person ("B") in the course of B's carrying on of an activity is to be treated as using services provided by B in carrying on that activity.

(4) The references in this Act (other than section 195) to the provision of immigration advice or immigration services are to the provision of such advice or services by a person—

(*a*) in England and Wales (regardless of whether the persons to whom they are provided are in England and Wales or elsewhere), and

(*b*) in the course of a business carried on (whether or not for profit) by the person or another person.

(5) The Lord Chancellor may by order make provision modifying the definition of "manager" in its application to a body of persons formed under, or in so far as the body is recognised by, law having effect outside England and Wales.

(6) In this section "enactment" means a provision of—

(*a*) an Act of Parliament;

(*b*) an Act of the Scottish Parliament;

(*c*) a Measure or Act of the National Assembly for Wales;

(*d*) Northern Ireland legislation.

[Legal Services Act 2007, s 207.]

**7.10964 211. Commencement** (1) This section and sections 208(2) to (5), 212 and 214 come into force on the day this Act is passed.

(2) Subject to that, the provisions of this Act come into force on such day as may be appointed by order of the Lord Chancellor.

[Legal Services Act 2007, s 211.]

## SCHEDULE 2
The Reserved Legal Activities

Section 12

*Introduction*

**7.10965 1.** This Schedule makes provision about the reserved legal activities.

**2.** In this Schedule "the appointed day" means the day appointed for the coming into force of section 13 (entitlement to carry on reserved legal activities).

*Rights of audience*

**3.** (1) A "right of audience" means the right to appear before and address a court, including the right to call and examine witnesses.

(2) But a "right of audience" does not include a right to appear before or address a court, or to call or examine witnesses, in relation to any particular court or in relation to particular proceedings, if immediately before the appointed day no restriction was placed on the persons entitled to exercise that right.

*Conduct of litigation*

**4.** (1) The "conduct of litigation" means—

(*a*) the issuing of proceedings before any court in England and Wales,

(*b*) the commencement, prosecution and defence of such proceedings, and

(*c*) the performance of any ancillary functions in relation to such proceedings (such as entering appearances to actions).

(2) But the "conduct of litigation" does not include any activity within paragraphs (*a*) to (*c*) of sub-paragraph (1), in relation to any particular court or in relation to any particular proceedings, if immediately before the appointed day no restriction was placed on the persons entitled to carry on that activity.

*Administration of oaths*

**8.** The "administration of oaths" means the exercise of the powers conferred on a commissioner for oaths by—

(*a*) the Commissioners for Oaths Act 1889 (c 10);

(*b*) the Commissioners for Oaths Act 1891 (c 50);

(*c*) section 24 of the Stamp Duties Management Act 1891 (c 38).

## SCHEDULE 3

Exempt Persons

Section 19

*Rights of audience*

**7.10966** **1.** (1) This paragraph applies to determine whether a person is an exempt person for the purpose of exercising a right of audience before a court in relation to any proceedings (subject to paragraph 7).

(2) The person is exempt if the person—

(*a*) is not an authorised person in relation to that activity, but

(*b*) has a right of audience granted by that court in relation to those proceedings.

(3) The person is exempt if the person—

(*a*) is not an authorised person in relation to that activity, but

(*b*) has a right of audience before that court in relation to those proceedings granted by or under any enactment.

(4) The person is exempt if the person is the Attorney General or the Solicitor General and—

(*a*) the name of the person is on the roll kept by the Law Society under section 6 of the Solicitors Act 1974 (c 47), or

(*b*) the person has been called to the Bar by an Inn of Court.

(5) The person is exempt if the person is the Advocate General for Scotland and is admitted—

(*a*) as a solicitor in Scotland under section 6 of the Solicitors (Scotland) Act 1980 (c 46), or

(*b*) to practise as an advocate before the courts of Scotland.

(6) The person is exempt if the person—

(*a*) is a party to those proceedings, and

(*b*) would have a right of audience, in the person's capacity as such a party, if this Act had not been passed.

(7) The person is exempt if—

(*a*) the person is an individual whose work includes assisting in the conduct of litigation,

(*b*) the person is assisting in the conduct of litigation—

(i) under instructions given (either generally or in relation to the proceedings) by an individual to whom sub-paragraph (8) applies, and

(ii) under the supervision of that individual, and

(*c*) the proceedings are being heard in chambers in the High Court or a county court and are not reserved family proceedings.

(8) This sub-paragraph applies to—

(*a*) any authorised person in relation to an activity which constitutes the conduct of litigation;

(*b*) any person who by virtue of section 193 is not required to be entitled to carry on such an activity.

(9) The person is an exempt person in relation to the exercise of a right of audience in proceedings on an appeal from the Comptroller-General of Patents, Designs and Trade Marks to the Patents Court under the Patents Act 1977 (c 37), if the person is a solicitor of the Court of Judicature of Northern Ireland.

(10) For the purposes of this paragraph—

"family proceedings" has the same meaning as in the Matrimonial and Family Proceedings Act 1984 (c 42) and also includes any other proceedings which are family proceedings for the purposes of the Children Act 1989 (c 41);

"reserved family proceedings" means such category of family proceedings as the Lord Chancellor may, after consulting the President of the Law Society and with the concurrence of the President of the Family Division, by order prescribe;

and any order made under section 27(9) of the Courts and Legal Services Act 1990 (c 41) before the day appointed for the coming into force of this paragraph is to have effect on and after that day as if it were an order made under this sub-paragraph.

*Conduct of litigation*

**2.** (1) This paragraph applies to determine whether a person is an exempt person for the purpose of carrying on any activity which constitutes the conduct of litigation in relation to any proceedings (subject to paragraph 7).

(2) The person is exempt if the person—

(*a*) is not an authorised person in relation to that activity, but

(*b*) has a right to conduct litigation granted by a court in relation to those proceedings.

(3) The person is exempt if the person—

(*a*) is not an authorised person in relation to that activity, but

(*b*) has a right to conduct litigation in relation to those proceedings granted by or under any enactment.

(4) The person is exempt if the person—

(*a*) is a party to those proceedings, and

(*b*) would have a right to conduct the litigation, in the person's capacity as such a party, if this Act had not been passed.

(5) The person is an exempt person in relation to any activity which is carried on in or in connection with proceedings on an appeal from the Comptroller-General of Patents, Designs and Trade Marks to the Patents Court under the Patents Act 1977 (c 37), if the person is a solicitor of the Court of Judicature of Northern Ireland.

*Administration of oaths*

**6.** (1) This paragraph applies to determine whether a person is an exempt person for the purpose of carrying on any activity which constitutes the administration of oaths (subject to paragraph 7).

(2) The person is exempt if the person is not an authorised person in relation to that activity under this Act, but is authorised to carry on that activity by or by virtue of any other enactment.

(3) The person is exempt if the person has a commission under section 1(1) of the Commissioners for Oaths Act 1889 (c 10).

*European lawyers*

**7.** A European lawyer (within the meaning of the European Communities (Services of Lawyers) Order 1978 (SI 1978/1910)) is an exempt person for the purposes of carrying on an activity which is a reserved legal activity and which the European lawyer is entitled to carry on by virtue of that order.

*Employers etc acting through exempt person*

**8.** (1) This paragraph applies where—

(*a*) a person ("P") carries on an activity ("the relevant activity") which is a reserved legal activity,

(*b*) P carries on the relevant activity by virtue of an employee of P ("E") carrying it on in E's capacity as such an employee, and

(*c*) E is an exempt person in relation to the relevant activity.

(2) P is an exempt person in relation to the relevant activity to the extent that P carries on that activity by virtue of E so carrying it on.

(3) This paragraph does not apply where E—

(*a*) carries on the relevant activity at the direction and under the supervision of an authorised person in relation to that activity, and

(*b*) is exempt in relation to that activity by virtue of paragraph 1(7), 3(3) or 4(2).

(4) If P is a body, in this paragraph references to an employee of P include references to a manager of P.

*Further exempt persons*

**9.** (1) The Lord Chancellor may, by order, amend this Schedule so as to provide—

(*a*) for persons to be exempt persons in relation to any activity which is a reserved legal activity (including any activity which is a reserved legal activity by virtue of an order under section 24 (extension of reserved legal activities)),

(*b*) for persons to cease to be such persons, or

(*c*) for the amendment of any provision made in respect of an exempt person.

(2) The Lord Chancellor may make an order under sub-paragraph (1) only on the recommendation of the Board.

## SCHEDULE 4
## Approved Regulators

7.10967

*(Amended by SI 2009/3233)* Section 20

### PART 1
### EXISTING REGULATORS

**1.** (1) Each body listed in the first column of the Table in this paragraph is an approved regulator.

(2) Each body so listed is an approved regulator in relation to the reserved legal activities listed in relation to it in the second column of the Table.

*Table*

| *Approved regulator* | *Reserved legal activities* |
|---|---|
| The Law Society | The exercise of a right of audience.<br>The conduct of litigation.<br>Reserved instrument activities.<br>Probate activities.<br>The administration of oaths. |
| The General Council of the Bar | The exercise of a right of audience.<br>The conduct of litigation.<br>Reserved instrument activities.<br>Probate activities.<br>The administration of oaths. |
| The Master of the Faculties | Reserved instrument activities.<br>Probate activities.<br>Notarial activities.<br>The administration of oaths. |
| The Institute of Legal Executives | The exercise of a right of audience.<br>The administration of oaths. |
| The Council for Licensed Conveyancers | Reserved instrument activities.<br>The administration of oaths.<br>Probate activities. |
| The Chartered Institute of Patent Attorneys | The exercise of a right of audience.<br>The conduct of litigation. |

| *Approved regulator* | *Reserved legal activities* |
|---|---|
| | Reserved instrument activities.<br>The administration of oaths. |
| The Institute of Trade Mark Attorneys | The exercise of a right of audience.<br>The conduct of litigation.<br>Reserved instrument activities.<br>The administration of oaths. |
| The Association of Law Costs Draftsmen | The exercise of a right of audience.<br>The conduct of litigation.<br>The administration of oaths. |
| The Institute of Chartered Accountants of Scotland | Probate activities. |
| The Association of Chartered Certified Accountants | Probate activities. |

[1] The Legal Services Act (Approved Regulators) Order 2011, SI 2011/1118 designates the Institute of Legal Executives as an approved regulator in relation to the conduct of litigation.

PART 2
DESIGNATION OF BODIES BY ORDER[1]

## Legal Services Act 2007 (Warrant) (Approved Regulator) Regulations 2015
(SI 2015/935)

**7.10967A** 1. *Citation, commencement and interpretation* (1) These Regulations may be cited as the Legal Services Act 2007 (Warrant) (Approved Regulator) Regulations 2015 and come into force 21 days after the day on which they are made.

(2) In these Regulations—

"the 2007 Act" means the Legal Services Act 2007;

"appointed person" means—

(*a*) in relation to an application made under section 42(3) of the 2007 Act, the specified person (within the meaning of section 42 of the 2007 Act) or a person appointed by the specified person to act on its behalf; and

(*b*) in relation to an application made under section 48(3) of the 2007 Act, the person appointed by the Board to act on its behalf;

"judicial officer" means—

(*a*) a judge of the High Court;

(*b*) a Circuit judge; or

(*c*) a justice of the peace;

"relevant regulator" means—

(*a*) in relation to a warrant issued under section 42(3) of the 2007 Act (intervention directions), the approved regulator in respect of whose premises that warrant was issued;

(*b*) in relation to a warrant issued under section 48(3) of the 2007 Act (cancellation of designation), the former approved regulator which has had its designation cancelled under section 45 of the 2007 Act in respect of whose premises that warrant was issued.

(3) A reference in these regulations to a warrant is a reference to a warrant which has been or may be issued under sections 42(3) or 48(3) of the 2007 Act.

**7.10967B** 2. *Conditions for issuing a warrant* A judicial officer may issue a warrant only if satisfied that—

(*a*) the Board has made reasonable attempts to obtain the written or electronic records sought by other means, or that such attempts would be likely to result in the records being removed, hidden, tampered with or destroyed; and

(*b*) no judicial officer has refused to issue a warrant based on another application that is in substance the same.

**7.10967C** 3. *Execution of a warrant* (1) Entry and search under a warrant must be—

(*a*) within a period of one month beginning on the date of its issue; and

(*b*) at a reasonable hour unless it appears to the appointed person exercising the power conferred by the warrant that the purpose of entry may be frustrated by entry at a reasonable hour.

(2) If there is a person ("P") present at the premises of the relevant regulator when the appointed person seeks to exercise the power conferred by the warrant, and P is the occupier or appears to be in charge of the premises, the appointed person must—

(*a*) show P documentary evidence of identity;

(*b*) show the warrant to P; and

(*c*) give P a certified copy of the warrant.

(3) If there is no occupier or person present at the premises who appears to be in charge of them, the appointed person must leave a certified copy of the warrant in a prominent place on the premises.

(4) The appointed person who exercises the power conferred by the warrant must make an endorsement on it stating—

(*a*) the date on which the power conferred by the warrant was exercised;
(*b*) whether any of the records sought were found;
(*c*) whether any written or electronic records have been copied; and
(*d*) whether possession has been taken of any written or electronic records.

(5) In the case of a warrant that authorises entry to and search of two or more premises of a relevant regulator, the appointed person exercising the power conferred by the warrant—
(*a*) must make a separate endorsement in accordance with paragraph (4) for each premises entered and searched; and
(*b*) must specify in each endorsement the premises to which the endorsement relates.

**7.10967D** *4. Legal privilege* (1) The powers conferred by a warrant must not be exercised to take possession of or copy any written or electronic record subject to legal privilege (within the meaning of section 10 of the Police and Criminal Evidence Act 1984).

(2) If possession is taken in error of any record of the kind referred to in paragraph (1), the record must be returned, and any copies taken must be destroyed, as soon as it is identified that the record is subject to legal privilege.

**7.10967E** *5. Notice and return of records taken* An appointed person who takes possession of any written or electronic record in the exercise of the power conferred by a warrant must—
(*a*) provide a list of what was taken to the relevant regulator within a reasonable time, which must be no longer than a period of 21 days beginning on the date the record was taken; and
(*b*) return that record to the relevant regulator—
  (i) within a period of 3 months beginning on the date on which the appointed person took possession of it;
  (ii) in the case of a warrant issued under section 42(3) of the 2007 Act, where the relevant regulator requests a record on the grounds that the record is required by that regulator to discharge a regulatory function, within a period of 7 days beginning with receipt of that request; or
  (iii) when an intervention direction given under section 41 of the 2007 Act is revoked under section 44 of that Act,

whichever is earliest, unless the relevant regulator agrees otherwise in writing.

**7.10967F** *6. Copying of records* (1) This regulation applies to any record of which an appointed person has taken possession in the exercise of a power conferred by a warrant.

(2) Where the record taken is electronic, the appointed person may produce records from it in a form that —
(*a*) is visible and legible; and
(*b*) can be copied,

for the purpose of determining whether the record may be copied in accordance with section 42(4) or 48(4) of the 2007 Act.

(3) As soon as it is identified that a record has been copied in error or otherwise than for the purpose in—
(*a*) section 42(4) of the 2007 Act, in the case of a warrant issued under section 42(3); or
(*b*) section 48(4) of the 2007 Act, in the case of a warrant issued under section 48(3),

any copies taken of that record must be destroyed.

**7.10967G** *7. Notice to be given of records copied* An appointed person who copies any written or electronic record under section 42(4) or 48(4) of the 2007 Act must, at the request of the relevant regulator, provide a list of what was copied and the date on which it was copied.

**7.10967H** *8. Retention of copies* A copy of a written or electronic record taken in the exercise of a power conferred by a warrant may not be retained for longer than is necessary in all the circumstances.

## Legal Services Act 2007 (Warrant) (Licensing Authority) Regulations 2015[1]

(SI 2015/938)

**7.10967I** *1. Citation, commencement and interpretation* (1) These Regulations may be cited as the Legal Services Act 2007 (Warrant) (Licensing Authority) Regulations 2015 and come into force 21 days after the day on which they are made.

(2) In these Regulations—

"the 2007 Act" means the Legal Services Act 2007;

"appointed person" means a person appointed by the Board to act on its behalf;

"former authority" means an approved regulator which has had its designation as a licensing authority in relation to one or more reserved legal activities cancelled by virtue of section 75 of the 2007 Act or an order under section 76;

"judicial officer" means—
  (*a*) a judge of the High Court;
  (*b*) a Circuit judge; or
  (*c*) a justice of the peace.

(3) A reference in these regulations to a warrant is a reference to a warrant which has been or may be issued under section 79(3) of the 2007 Act.

---

1 Made by the Lord Chancellor in exercise of the powers conferred by ss 79(6) and (7) and 204(3) of the Legal Services Act 2007.

**7.10967J** 2. *Conditions for issuing a warrant* A judicial officer may issue a warrant only if satisfied that—

(*a*) the Board has made reasonable attempts to obtain the written or electronic records sought by other means, or that such attempts would be likely to result in the records being removed, hidden, tampered with or destroyed; and

(*b*) no judicial officer has refused to issue a warrant based on another application that is in substance the same.

**7.10967K** 3. *Execution of a warrant* (1) Entry and search under a warrant must be—

(*a*) within a period of one month beginning on the date of its issue; and

(*b*) at a reasonable hour unless it appears to the appointed person exercising the power conferred by the warrant that the purpose of entry may be frustrated by entry at a reasonable hour.

(2) If there is a person ("P") present at the premises of the former authority when the appointed person seeks to exercise the power conferred by the warrant, and P is the occupier or appears to be in charge of the premises, the appointed person must—

(*a*) show P documentary evidence of identity;

(*b*) show the warrant to P; and

(*c*) give P a certified copy of the warrant.

(3) If there is no occupier or person present at the premises who appears to be in charge of them, the appointed person must leave a certified copy of the warrant in a prominent place on the premises.

(4) The appointed person who exercises the power conferred by the warrant must make an endorsement on it stating—

(*a*) the date on which the power conferred by the warrant was exercised;

(*b*) whether any of the records sought were found;

(*c*) whether any written or electronic records have been copied; and

(*d*) whether possession has been taken of any written or electronic records.

(5) In the case of a warrant that authorises entry to and search of two or more premises of a former authority, the appointed person exercising the power conferred by the warrant—

(*a*) must make a separate endorsement in accordance with paragraph (4) for each premises entered and searched; and

(*b*) must specify in each endorsement the premises to which the endorsement relates.

**7.10967L** 4. *Legal privilege* (1) The powers conferred by a warrant must not be exercised to take possession of or copy any written or electronic record subject to legal privilege (within the meaning of section 10 of the Police and Criminal Evidence Act 1984).

(2) If possession is taken in error of any record of the kind referred to in paragraph (1), the record must be returned, and any copies taken must be destroyed, as soon as it is identified that the record is subject to legal privilege.

**7.10967M** 5. *Notice and return of records taken* An appointed person who takes possession of any written or electronic record in the exercise of the power conferred by the warrant must—

(*a*) provide a list of what was taken to the former authority within a reasonable time, which must be no longer than a period of 21 days beginning on the date the record was taken; and

(*b*) return that record to the former authority within a period of 3 months beginning on the date on which the appointed person took possession of it, unless the former authority agrees otherwise in writing.

**7.10967N** 6. *Copying of records* (1) This regulation applies to any record of which an appointed person has taken possession in the exercise of a power conferred by the warrant.

(2) Where the record taken is electronic, the appointed person may produce records from it in a form that —

(*a*) is visible and legible; and

(*b*) can be copied,

for the purpose of determining whether the record may be copied in accordance with section 79(4) of the 2007 Act.

(3) As soon as it is identified that a record has been copied in error or otherwise than for the purpose in section 79(4) of the 2007 Act, any copies taken of that record must be destroyed.

**7.10967O** 7. *Notice to be given of records copied* An appointed person who copies any written or electronic record under section 79(4) of the 2007 Act must, at the request of the former authority, provide a list of what was copied and the date on which it was copied.

**7.10967P** 8. *Retention of copies* A copy of a written or electronic record taken in the exercise of a power conferred by a warrant may not be retained for longer than is necessary in all the circumstances.

# STREET AND HOUSE TO HOUSE COLLECTIONS

**Contents**



## Police, Factories, etc (Miscellaneous Provisions) Act 1916

(6 & 7 Geo 5 c 31)

7.10968 **5. Regulations as to street collections** (1) Each of the authorities specified in subsection (1A) below may make regulations[1] with respect to the places where and the conditions under which persons may be permitted in any[2] street or public place[3], within their area, to collect money or sell articles for the benefit of charitable or other purposes, and any person who acts in contravention of any such regulation shall be liable on summary conviction to a fine not exceeding **level 1** on the standard scale.

Provided that—

(*a*) Regulations made under this section shall not come into operation until they have been confirmed by the Secretary of State or the Minister for the Cabinet Office, and published for such time and in such manner as the Secretary of State or the Minister for the Cabinet Office may direct; and

(*b*) Regulations made under this section shall not apply to the selling of articles in any street or public place where the articles are sold in the ordinary course of trade, and for the purpose of earning a livelihood, and no representation is made by or on behalf of the sellers that any part of the proceeds of sale will be devoted to any charitable purpose.

(1A) The authorities referred to in subsection (1) above are—

(*a*) the Common Council of the City of London

(*b*) the Mayor's Office for Policing and Crime, and

(*c*) the council of each district

but any regulations made by a district council under that subsection shall not have effect with respect to any street or public place which is within the Metropolitan Police District as well as within the district.*

[Police, Factories, etc (Miscellaneous Provisions) Act 1916, s 5 as amended by the Local Government Act 1972, Sch 29, the Criminal Law Act 1977, s 31, the Criminal Justice Act 1982, s 46, SI 2006/2951 and the Police Reform and Social Responsibility Act 2011, Sch 16.]

* **Amended by the Charities Act 2006, Schs 8 and 9 from a date to be appointed.**

1 With the exception of those relating to the Metropolitan Police District, the regulations made under this section are not contained in the Statutory Instruments. For regulations covering the Metropolitan Police District, see the Street Collections (Metropolitan Police District) Regulations 1979, SI 1979/1230 amended by SI 1986/1696.

2 "Street" includes any highway and any public bridge, road, lane, footway, square, court, alley, or passage, whether a thoroughfare or not (s 5(4)).

3 The Act contains no definition of "public place". Cf the Licensing Act 1902, s 8, in PART VII, title PUBLIC MEETING AND PUBLIC ORDER, ante.

## House to House Collections Act 1939[1]

(2 & 3 Geo 6 c 44)

7.10969 **1. Charitable collections from house to house to be licensed** (1) Subject to the provisions of this Act, no collection[2] for charitable purpose[3] shall be made unless the requirements of this Act[4] as to a licence[5] for the promotion thereof are satisfied.

(2) If a person promotes[6] a collection for a charitable purpose, and a collection for that purpose is made in any locality pursuant to his promotion[6], then, unless there is in force, throughout the period during which the collection is made in that locality, a licence[5] authorising him, or authorising another under whose authority he acts, to promote[6] a collection therein for that purpose, he shall be guilty of an offence[7].

(3) If a person acts as a collector[8] in any locality[9] for the purposes of a collection for a charitable purpose, then, unless there is in force, at all times when he so acts, a licence[5] authorising a promoter[6] under whose authority he acts, or authorising the collector himself, to promote[6] a collection therein for that purpose, he shall be guilty of an offence[10].

(4) If the chief officer of police[11] for the police area[11] comprising a locality in which a collection for a charitable purpose is being, or is proposed to be, made is satisfied that that purpose is local in character and that the collection is likely to be completed within a short period of time, he may grant to the person who appears to him to be principally concerned in the promotion of the collection a certificate[12] in the prescribed[13] form, and, where a certificate is so granted, the provisions of this Act, except the provisions of sections five and six thereof and the provisions of section eight thereof in so far as they relate to those sections, shall not apply, in relation to a collection made for that purpose within such locality and within such period as may be specified in the certificate, to the person to whom the certificate is granted or to any person authorised by him to promote[14] the collection or to act as a collector[8] for the purposes thereof.*

[House to House Collections Act 1939, s 1.]

* **Repealed by the Charities Act 1992, Sch 7 from a date to be appointed.**

[1] This Act should be construed within its own ambit and not in conjunction with the provisions of the Trading Representations (Disabled Persons) Act 1958, title CONSUMER PROTECTION, ante; see *Cooper v Coles* [1987] QB 230, [1987] 1 All ER 91.

[2] "Collection" means an appeal to the public, made by means of visits from house to house, to give, whether for consideration or not, money or other property; and "collector" means, in relation to a collection, a person who makes the appeal in the course of such visits as aforesaid (s 11(1)). For the purposes of this Act, a collection shall be deemed to be made for a particular purpose where the appeal is made in association with a representation that the money or other property appealed for, or part thereof, will be applied for that purpose (s 11(2)). See also *Emmanuel v Smith, Hird v Smith*, and *Carasu Ltd v Smith* [1968] 2 QB 383, [1968] 2 All ER 529. A promotion for a charitable purpose which involves the exchange of goods for money is a "collection" within the meaning of the Act (*Cooper v Coles* [1987] QB 230, [1987] 1 All ER 91).

[3] "Charitable purpose" means any charitable, benevolent or philanthropic purpose, whether or not the purpose is charitable within the meaning of any rule of law (s 11(1)).

[4] A licence is granted by the district council or, in the Metropolitan Police District, the Commissioner of Police for the Metropolis or, in the City of London, by the Common Council (s 2). An appeal lies to the Secretary of State against the refusal to grant a licence or its revocation (sub-s (4)).

[5] "Licence" means a licence under this Act (s 11(1)). An order of exemption granted under s 3, post, has the same effect as a licence. An application for a licence is made to the licensing authority under s 2, which sets out the grounds on which the authority may refuse it, broadly speaking so as to ensure that a proper amount of the proceeds are applied to the charity and to exclude persons of bad character. Notification of the grounds of refusal must be given in writing by the authority.

[6] "Promoter" means, in relation to a collection, a person who causes others to act, whether for remuneration or otherwise, as collectors for the purposes of the collection; and "promote" and "promotion" have corresponding meanings (s 11(1)). A promoter may be exempt from the provisions of s 1(2) (s 3, post).

[7] As to penalty, see s 8(1), post; and as to an offence committed by a corporation, see s 8(7), post.

[8] As to the meaning of "collector", see note 2, supra, and as to the effect where a promoter is exempted see s 3, post.

[9] Collecting in one establishment on one occasion is not "collecting in a locality" unless there is evidence that the defendant was about to go on to other houses (*Hankinson v Dowland* [1974] 3 All ER 655, [1974] 1 WLR 1327). "Locality" can include two public houses a mile apart (*Davison v Richards* [1976] Crim LR 46).

[10] As to penalty, see s 8(2), post.

[11] These expressions are now defined by the Police Act 1996, s 1, in title POLICE, ante. A chief officer of police may delegate his functions to any police officer not below the rank of inspector (s 7). The Commissioner of Police is the police authority for the metropolitan police district. He cannot delegate his functions (s 9).

[12] See the House to House Collections Regulations 1947, SR & O 1947/2662, as amended by SI 1963/684.

[13] "Prescribed" means prescribed by regulations made under this Act (s 11(1)).

[14] See note 6, supra.

7.10970 **3. Exemptions in the case of collections over wide areas** (1) Where the Minister for the Cabinet Office is satisfied that a person pursues a charitable purpose[1] throughout the whole of England or a substantial part thereof and is desirous of promoting[2] collections[3] for that purpose, the Minister for the Cabinet Office may by order direct that he shall be exempt from the provisions of subsection (2) of section one of this Act as respects all collections for that purpose in such localities as may be described in the order, and whilst an order so made in the case of any person is in force as respects collections in any locality, the provisions of this Act shall have effect in relation to the person exempted, to a promoter[2] of a collection[3] in that locality for that purpose who acts under the authority of the person exempted, and to a person who so acts as a collector[3] for the purposes of any such collection, as if a licence[4] authorising the person exempted to promote[2] a collection in that locality for that purpose had been in force.

(2) Any order made under this section may be revoked or varied by a subsequent order made by the Minister for the Cabinet Office.*

[House to House Collections Act 1939, s 3 as amended by SI 2006/2951.]

* **Repealed by the Charities Act 1992, Sch 7 from a date to be appointed.**

[1] "Charitable purpose" means any charitable, benevolent or philanthropic purpose, whether or not the purpose is charitable within the meaning of any rule of law (s 11(1)).

[2] See note 6 to s 1, supra.

[3] See note 2 to s 1, supra.

[4] See note 5 to s 1, supra.

7.10971 **4. Regulations** (1) The Minister for the Cabinet Office may make regulations[1] for prescribing anything which by this Act is required to be prescribed, and for regulating the manner in which collections, in respect of which licences have been granted or orders have been made under the last foregoing section, may be carried out and the conduct of promoters and collectors in relation to such collections.

(2) Without prejudice to the generality of powers conferred by the foregoing subsection, regulations made thereunder may make provision for all or any of the following matters, that is to say—*(a)* to *(e)* (prescribing badges, minimum age for collectors and other matters).

(3) Any person who contravenes or fails to comply with the provisions of a regulation made under this Act shall be guilty of an offence[2].*

[House to House Collections Act 1939, s 4 as amended by SI 2006/2951.]

* **Repealed by the Charities Act 1992, Sch 7 from a date to be appointed.**

[1] See the House to House Collections Regulations 1947, SR & O 1947/2662 as amended by SI 1963/684.

[2] See s 8(3), post.

7.10972 **5. Unauthorised use of badges, &c** If any person, in connection with any appeal[1] made by him, to the public in association with a representation that the appeal is for a charitable purpose[2], displays or uses—

(*a*) a prescribed badge[3] or a prescribed certificate of authority[3], not being a badge or certificate for the time being held by him for the purposes of the appeal pursuant to regulations made under this Act, or

(*b*) any badge or device, or any certificate or other document, so nearly resembling a prescribed badge[3] or, as the case may be, a prescribed certificate of authority as to be calculated to deceive[4],

he shall be guilty of an offence[5].*

[House to House Collections Act 1939, s 5.]

* **Repealed by the Charities Act 1992, Sch 7 from a date to be appointed.**

1 This section applies to any appeal made to the public in association with a representation which is for a charitable purpose and is not limited to house to house collections (*R v Davison* [1972] 3 All ER 1121, [1972] 1 WLR 1540).

2 See note 1 to s 3, supra.

3 See House to House Collections Regulations 1947, SR & O 1947 No 2662, as amended by SI 1963/684.

4 This means "likely to deceive" (*R v Davison* [1972] 3 All ER 1121, [1972] 1 WLR 1540).

5 See s 8(4), post.

7.10973 **6. Collector to give name, etc, to police on demand** A police constable may require any person whom he believes to be acting as a collector[1] for the purposes of a collection[1] for a charitable purpose[2] to declare to him immediately his name and address and to sign his name, and if any person fails to comply with a requirement duly made to him under this section, he shall be guilty of an offence[3].*

[House to House Collections Act 1939, s 6.]

* **Repealed by the Charities Act 1992, Sch 7 from a date to be appointed.**

1 See note 2 to s 1, ante.

2 See note 1 to s 3, supra.

3 See s 8(5), post.

7.10974 **8. Penalties** (1) Any promoter[1] guilty of an offence under subsection (2) of section one of this Act shall be liable, on summary conviction, to imprisonment for a term not exceeding six months or to a fine not exceeding **level 3** on the standard scale or to both[2] such imprisonment and such fine.

(2) Any collector guilty of an offence under subsection (3) of section one of this Act shall be liable, on summary conviction, to imprisonment for a term not exceeding three months** or to a fine not exceeding **level 2** on the standard scale or to both[2] such imprisonment and such fine.

(3) Any person guilty of an offence under subsection (3) of section four of this Act shall be liable, on summary conviction, to a fine not exceeding **level 1** on the standard scale.

(4) Any person guilty of an offence under section five of this Act shall be liable, on summary conviction, to imprisonment for a term not exceeding six months or to a fine not exceeding **level 3** on the standard scale, or to both[2] such imprisonment and such fine.

(5) Any person guilty of an offence under section six of this Act shall be liable, on summary conviction, to a fine not exceeding **level 1** on the standard scale.

(6) If any person in furnishing any information for the purposes of this Act knowingly or recklessly makes a statement false in a material particular, he shall be guilty of an offence, and shall be liable, on summary conviction, to imprisonment for a term not exceeding six months or to a fine not exceeding **level 3** on the standard scale, or to both[2] such imprisonment and such fine.

(7) Where an offence under this Act committed by a corporation is proved to have been committed with the consent or connivance of, or to be attributable to any culpable neglect of duty on the part of, any director[3], manager, secretary, or other officer of the corporation, he, as well as the corporation, shall be deemed to be guilty of that offence and shall be liable to be proceeded against and punished accordingly.*

[House to House Collections Act 1939, s 8 as amended by the Criminal Law Act 1977, s 31 and the Criminal Justice Act 1982, ss 35, 38 and 46.]

* **Repealed by the Charities Act 1992, Sch 7 from a date to be appointed.**

** **"Three months" substituted by "51 weeks" by the Criminal Justice Act 2003, Sch 26 from a date to be appointed.**

1 See note 6 to s 1, ante.

2 As to consecutive sentences, see the Magistrates' Courts Act 1980, s 133, ante.

3 See *Dean v Hiesler* [1942] 2 All ER 340, 106 JP 282.

# TAX AND DUTIES

**Contents**



## CHEATING THE PUBLIC REVENUE

**7.10975** Cheating is a common law offence punishable by imprisonment. Although s 32(1) of the Theft Act 1968[1] abolished cheating, it did so only "except as regards offences relating to the public revenue".

*Hawkins*[2] defined cheating as " . . . deceitful practices, in defrauding or endeavouring to defraud another of his own right by means of some artful device, contrary to the plain rules of common honesty." The offence may be committed not only by a public officer, but also by a private individual who acts in such a way as to defraud the Crown[3]. The Court of Criminal Appeal upheld a conviction on a charge of making false statements to the prejudice of the Crown and the public revenue with intent to defraud where the defendant had falsely stated to the Inland Revenue the profits of his business[3]. The offence does not necessarily require a false representation, either by words or conduct. Cheating can include any form of fraudulent conduct which results in diverting money from the Revenue and in depriving the Revenue of money to which it is entitled[4]. This will include omissions to act having the purpose and effect of depriving the revenue of money due to it (*R v Dimsey* [2000] QB 744, [2000] 3 WLR 273, CA (convictions confirmed by the House of Lords [2001] UKHL 46, [2002] 1 AC 509)).

1 See this PART: title THEFT, post.
2 1 PC 318.
3 *R v Hudson* [1956] 2 QB 252, [1956] 1 All ER 814.
4 *R v Mavji* (1987) 84 Cr App Rep 34, [1987] Crim LR 39.

## INCOME TAX AND MAINTENANCE ORDERS

**7.10976** Section 65 of the Income and Corporation Taxes Act 1970 which made provision for the making of "small maintenance payments" without deduction of tax but enabled larger payments to be made less tax, was repealed by the Income and Corporation Taxes Act 1988; s 351 of which, re-enacting the s 65 provisions, was in turn repealed by the Finance Act 1988.

For new maintenance orders, the Income and Corporation Taxes Act 1988 s 347A, this title, post, (added by s 36 of the Finance Act 1988) provides that as a general rule annual payments (held to include a permanent order although expressed in weekly or monthly terms: see *Re Janes' Settlement, Wasmuth v Janes* [1918] 2 Ch 54; *Smith v Smith (No 2)* [1923] P 191) should not be deducted when computing the payer's income for tax purposes (ie there is no "tax relief"). The payment shall not form part of the income of the person to whom it is made or of any other person (ie the recipient is not liable to pay tax on such payments).

However, s 347B, this title, post, of the Income and Corporation Taxes Act 1988 (also added by the Finance Act 1988 s 36 and amended by the Finance (No 2) Act 1992, ss 61 and 62) allows the payer to deduct "qualifying maintenance payments" when assessing income for tax purposes (but *not* to deduct it from the payments made under an order). As a consequence of further amendments made to s 347B made by the Finance Act 1999, s 36, with respect to any payment falling due on or after 6 April 2000 a periodical payment is not a qualifying maintenance payment unless either of the parties to the marriage which has been dissolved or annulled was born before 6 April 1935.

## Stamp Duties Management Act 1891

(54 & 55 Vict c 38)

**7.10977 13. Offences in relation to dies and stamps[1]** (1) A person commits an offence who does, or causes or procures to be done, or knowingly aids, abets, or assists in doing, any of the acts following; that is to say:

(1), (2) *Repealed*
(3) fraudulently prints or makes an impression upon any material[2] from a genuine die[3];
(4) fraudulently cuts, tears, or in any way removes from any material any stamp[4] with intent that any use should be made of such stamp or of any part thereof;

(5) fraudulently mutilates any stamp, with intent that any use should be made of any part of such stamp;

(6) fraudulently fixes or places upon any material or upon any stamp, any stamp or part of a stamp which, whether fraudulently or not, has been cut, torn, or in any way removed from any other material, or out of or from any other stamp[5];

(7) fraudulently erases or otherwise either really or apparently removes from any stamped[6] material any name, sum, date, or other matter or thing whatsoever thereon written, with the intent that any use should be made of the stamp upon such material;

(8) knowingly sells or exposes for sale or utters or uses any stamp which has been fraudulently printed or impressed from a genuine die;

(9) knowingly[7] and without lawful excuse (the proof whereof shall lie on the person accused) has in his possession any stamp which has been fraudulently printed or impressed from a genuine die, or any stamp or part of a stamp which has been fraudulently cut, torn, or otherwise removed from any material, or any stamp which has been fraudulently mutilated, or any stamped material out of which any name, sum, date, or other matter or thing has been fraudulently erased or otherwise either really or apparently removed.

(10) A person guilty of an offence under this section is liable[8]—

(*a*) on summary conviction, to imprisonment for a term not exceeding six months or a fine not exceeding the statutory maximum, or both;

(*b*) on conviction on indictment, to imprisonment for a term not exceeding ten years or a fine, or both.

[Stamp Duties Management Act 1891, s 13 as amended by Forgery Act 1913, s 20, and Sch 1, the Criminal Justice Act 1948, s 1 and the Finance Act 1999, Schs 18 and 20.]

1 Section 13 is applied to offences in respect of contribution stamps by the Social Security (Contributions) Regulations 1979, this PART: title Social Security, ante. These Regulations also apply s 26 of the 1891 Act, relating to recovery of fines, to social security proceedings. For recovery of contributions in proceedings under the Social Security Administration Act 1992, see s 119 thereof.

2 "Material" includes every sort of material upon which words or figures can be expressed (Stamp Duties Management Act 1891, s 27).

3 "Die" includes any plate, type, tool, or implement whatever used under the direction of the Comrs (of Inland Revenue) for expressing or denoting any duty, or rate of duty, or the fact that any duty or rate of duty or penalty has been paid, or that an instrument is duly stamped, or is not chargeable with any duty or for denoting any fee, and also any part of any such plate, type, tool, or implement (Stamp Duties Management Act 1891, s 27). The reference to the Comrs of Inland Revenue is to be construed as including the Post Office and "duty" includes "postage" (Post Office Act 1969, s 118). The reference includes the Secretary of State in the case of proceedings under the Social Security Administration Act 1992, see s 119 thereof.

4 "Stamp" means as well a stamp impressed by means of a die as an adhesive stamp for denoting any duty or fee (Stamp Duties Management Act 1891, s 27).

5 For the offence of fixing a used social security contribution stamp to any contribution card, see Social Security Administration Act 1992, s 114.

6 The expression "stamped" is applicable as well to instruments and material impressed with stamps by means of a die as to instruments and material having adhesive stamps affixed thereto (Stamp Duties Management Act 1891, s 27).

7 Knowledge is necessary both of the fact of possession and of the fraudulent removal etc (*R v Hallam* [1957] 1 QB 569, [1957] 1 All ER 665, 121 JP 254).

8 For procedure in respect of this offence which is triable either way, see the Magistrates, Courts Act 1980, ss 17A–21, in PART I: MAGISTRATES' COURTS, PROCEDURE, ante.

## Finance Act 1931

(1931 c 28)

7.10978 **28. Production to commissioners of instruments transferring land**[1] (1) On the occasion of (*a*) any transfer on sale of the fee simple of land; (*b*) the grant of any lease of land for a term of seven or more years; (*c*) any transfer on sale of any such lease; it shall be the duty of the transferee, lessee, or proposed lessee to produce to the Commissioners the instrument by means of which the transfer is effected, or the lease granted or agreed to be granted, as the case may be, and to comply with the requirements of the Second Schedule to this Act, and if he fails so to produce any such instrument within thirty days after the execution thereof, or in the case of an instrument first executed at any place out of Great Britain, after the instrument is first received in Great Britain, or fails to comply with the requirements of the said Schedule, he shall be liable on summary conviction to a fine not exceeding **level 3** on the standard scale.

(3) This section shall not apply with respect to any instrument which relates—

(*a*) solely to incorporeal hereditaments or to a grave or right of burial; or

(*b*) to an SDLT transaction within the meaning of paragraph 1(2) of Schedule 19 to the Finance Act 2003.

[Finance Act 1931, s 28 as amended by the Land Commission Act 1967, Sch 14, the Criminal Justice Act 1982, ss 38 and 46 and SI 2003/2867.]

1 This section shall not apply in relation to any instrument (an "exempt instrument") which falls within any class prescribed for the purposes of s 89 of the Finance Act 1985 by regulations made by the Commissioners. Regulations under s 89 may provide that the particulars mentioned in Sch 2 to the Finance Act 1931 shall be furnished to the Commissioners, in accordance with the requirements of the regulations, in respect of exempt instruments or such descriptions of exempt instruments as may be prescribed by the regulations. Any person who fails to comply with any requirement imposed by regulations made under s 89 shall be liable on summary conviction to a fine not exceeding **level 3** on the standard scale (Finance Act 1985, s 89).

# Taxes Management Act 1970

(1970 c 9)

## PART III[1]

## OTHER RETURNS AND INFORMATION

*Production of accounts, books and other information*

[1] Part III contains ss 13–28.

[2] Section 20(1) and the Hansard Procedure (which provides a mechanism for settling tax liabilities without recourse to criminal or civil proceedings) provide legitimate means of furthering the core function of the revenue to collect taxes in a prompt, fair and complete manner and they underpin the revenue's selective prosecution policy; both the s 20(1) notice and the Hansard Procedure are civil in nature, they do not constituted "criminal" proceedings for the purpose of the Convention and they belong to an investigative process to which art 6 does not apply; moreover, the notice under s 20(1) cannot constitute a violation of the right against self-incrimination (*R v Dimsey* [2001] UKHL 46, [2002] 1 AC 509, [2002] 1 Cr App Rep 167). Section 20(1) does not entitle an inspector of taxes to require a taxpayer to deliver to him material that is subject to legal professional privilege (*R (on the application of Morgan Grenfell & Co Ltd) v Special Comr of Income Tax* [2002] UKHL 21, [2002] 3 All ER 1).

7.10981 **20BA. Orders for the delivery of documents** (1) The appropriate judicial authority may make an order under this section if satisfied on information on oath given by an authorised officer of the Board—

(*a*) that there is reasonable ground for suspecting that an offence involving serious fraud in connection with, or in relation to, tax is being, has been or is about to be committed, and

(*b*) that documents which may be required as evidence for the purposes of any proceedings in respect of such an offence are or may be in the power or possession of any person.

(2) An order under this section is an order requiring the person who appears to the authority to have in his possession or power the documents specified or described in the order to deliver them to an officer of the Board within—

(*a*) ten working days after the day on which notice of the order is served on him, or

(*b*) such shorter or longer period as may be specified in the order.

For this purpose a "working day" means any day other than a Saturday, Sunday or public holiday.

(3) *Scotland.*

(4) Schedule 1AA[1] to this Act contains provisions supplementing this section.

[Taxes Management Act 1970, s 20BA as inserted by the Finance Act 2000, s 149.]

[1] See, post.

7.10982 **20BB. Falsification etc of documents** (1) Subject to subsections (2) to (3) below, a person shall be guilty of an offence if he intentionally falsifies, conceals, destroys or otherwise disposes of, or causes or permits the falsification, concealment, destruction or disposal of, a document which—

(*a*) he has been required by an order under section 20BA above,

(*b*) *repealed,*

to deliver, or to deliver or make available for inspection.

(2) A person does not commit an offence under subsection (1) above if he acts—

(*a*) with the written permission of the tribunal or an officer of the Board, or

(*b*) after the document has been delivered or,

(*c*) *repealed.*

(3) A person does not commit an offence under subsection (1)(*a*) above if he acts after the end of the period of two years beginning with the date on which the order is made, unless before the end of that period an officer of Revenue and Customs has notified the person in writing that the order has not been complied with to the officer's satisfaction.

(4) *Repealed.*

(5) A person guilty of an offence under subsection (1) above shall be liable[1]—

(*a*) on summary conviction, to a fine not exceeding the **statutory maximum;**

(*b*) on conviction on indictment, to imprisonment for a term not exceeding **two years** or to a **fine** or to **both**.

[Taxes Management Act 1970, s 20BB as inserted by the Finance Act 1989, s 145 and amended by the Finance Act 2000, s 149, the Finance Act 2008, Sch 36, SI 2009/56 and the Finance Act 2012, Sch 38.]

[1] For procedure in respect of an offence triable either way, see the Magistrates' Courts Act 1980, ss 17A–21, in PART I: MAGISTRATES' COURTS, PROCEDURE, ante.

7.10983 **20D. Interpretation of ss 20 to 20C** (1) For the purposes of section 20BA above, "the appropriate judicial authority" is—

(*a*) in England and Wales, a Circuit judge*;

(*b*) *Scotland;*

(*c*) *Northern Ireland.*

(2) *Repealed*

(3) *Repealed.*

[Taxes Management Act 1970, s 20D as inserted by the Finance Act 1976, Sch 6, and amended by the Finance Act 1989, s 148, the Civil Evidence Act 1995, Sch 1, the Finance Act 2000, s 149, the Finance Act 2007, Sch 22, the Finance Act 2008, Sch 36 and the Finance Act 2012, Sch 38.]

* **Words inserted by the Courts Act 2003, Sch 4 from a date to be appointed.**

## PART VI[1]

## COLLECTION AND RECOVERY

7.10984 **60. Issue of demand notes and receipts** (1) Every collector shall, when the tax becomes due and payable, make demand of the respective sums given to him in charge to collect, from the persons charged therewith, or at the places of their last abode, or on the premises in respect of which the tax is charged, as the case may require.

(2) On payment of the tax, the collector shall if so requested give a receipt.

[Taxes Management Act 1970, s 60.]

[1] Part VI contains ss 60–70.

*Distraint and poinding*

7.10985 **61. Distraint by collectors** (1) If a person neglects or refuses to pay the sum charged, upon demand made by the collector, the collector may—

(*a*) *repealed*

*b*) *repealed*

distrain upon the goods and chattels of the person charged (in this section referred to as "the person in default").

(1A) *Repealed.*

(2) For the purpose of levying any such distress, a justice of the peace, on being satisfied by information on oath that there is reasonable ground for believing that a person is neglecting or refusing to pay a sum charged, may issue a warrant in writing authorising a collector to break open, in the daytime, any house or premises, calling to his assistance any constable. Every such constable shall when so required, aid and assist the collector in the execution of the warrant and in levying the distress in the house or premises.

(3) A levy or warrant to break open shall be executed by, or under the direction of, and in the presence of, the collector.

(4) A distress levied by the collector shall be kept for five days, at the costs and charges of the person in default.

(5) If the person in default does not pay the sum due, together with the costs and charges, the distress shall be appraised by one or more independent persons appointed by the collector, and shall be sold by public auction by the collector for payment of the sum due and all costs and charges. Any overplus coming by the distress, after the deduction of the costs and charges and of the sum due, shall be restored to the owner of the goods distrained.

(6) The Treasury may by regulations[1] make provision with respect to—

(*a*) the fees chargeable on or in connection with the levying of distress, and

(*b*) the costs and charges recoverable where distress has been levied;

and any such regulations shall be made by statutory instrument which shall be subject to annulment in pursuance of a resolution of the House of Commons.

(7) This section extends only to Northern Ireland.

[Taxes Management Act 1970, s 61 as amended by the Finance Act 1989, s 152, Sch 17 and the Finance Act 2008, Sch 43.]

[1] The Distraint by Collectors (Fees, Costs and Charges) Regulations 1994, SI 1994/236 amended by SI 1995/2151, have been made.

7.10986 **62. Priority of claim for tax** (1) If at any time at which any goods or chattels belonging to any person (in this section referred to as "the person in default") are liable to be taken by virtue of any execution or other process, warrant, or authority whatever, or by virtue of any assignment, on any account or pretence whatever, except at the suit of the landlord for rent, the person in default is in arrears in respect of any such sums as are referred to in subsection (1A) below, the goods or chattels may not be taken unless on demand made by the collector the person at whose suit the execution or seizure is made, or to whom the assignment was made, pays or causes to be paid to the collector, before the sale or removal of the goods or chattels, all such sums as have fallen due at or before the date of seizure.

(1A) The sums referred to in subsection (1) above are—

(*a*) sums due from the person in default on account of deductions of income tax from taxable earnings (as defined by section 10 of ITEPA 2003) paid during the period of twelve months next before the date of seizure, being deductions which the person in default was liable to make under PAYE regulations less the amount of the repayments of income tax which he was liable to make during that period; and

(*b*) sums due from the person in default in respect of deductions required to be made by him for that period under section 61 of the Finance Act 2004 (sub-contractors in the construction industry).

(2) If the sums referred to in subsection (1) above are not paid within ten days of the date of the

demand referred to in that subsection, the collector may distrain the goods and chattels notwithstanding the seizure or assignment, and may proceed to the sale thereof, as prescribed by this Act, for the purpose of obtaining payment of the whole of those sums, and the reasonable costs and charges attending such distress and sale, and every collector so doing shall be indemnified by virtue of this Act.

(3) *Repealed.*

(4) This section does not extend to England and Wales.

[Taxes Management Act 1970, s 62 as amended by the Finance Act 1989, s 153 and Sch 17, the Income Tax (Earnings and Pensions) Act 2003, s 722, the Finance Act 2004, Sch 12 and the Tribunals, Courts and Enforcement Act 2007, Sch 13.]

*Court proceedings*

7.10987 **65. Magistrates' courts** (1) Any amount due and payable[1] by way of income tax, capital gains tax or corporation tax which does not exceed £2,000 shall, without prejudice to any other remedy, be recoverable summarily as a civil debt[2] by proceedings commenced in the name of a collector[3].

(2) All or any of the sums due in respect of tax from any one person and payable to any one collector (being sums which are by law recoverable summarily) may, whether or not they are due under one assessment, be included in the same complaint, summons, order, warrant, or other document required by law to be laid before justices or to be issued by justices, and every such document as aforesaid shall, as respects each such sum, be construed as a separate document and its invalidity as respects any one such sum shall not affect its validity as respects any other such sum.

(3) Proceedings under this section may be brought in England and Wales at any time within one year from the time when the matter complained of arose.

(4) *Northern Ireland.*

(5) The Treasury may by order made by statutory instrument increase the sum specified in subsection (1) above; and any such statutory instrument shall be subject to annulment in pursuance of a resolution of the Commons House of Parliament.

[Taxes Management Act 1970, s 65 as amended by the Finance Act 1984, s 57, SI 1989/1300, SI 1991/1625, the Finance Act 1994, Sch 19 and the Finance Act 1998, Schs 19 and 27.]

---

[1] Section 203 of the Income and Corporation Taxes Act 1988 and the Income Tax (Employments) Regulations 1973 (SI 1973/334) provide for collecting tax due under Schedule E by means of deductions from current earnings (PAYE). Regulation 28 as amended by SI 1984/1858 and SI 1985/350 relates to the recovery of tax deducted by an employer; its purport is similar to that of s 65 of the Taxes Management Act 1970 and the maximum amount recoverable summarily is £500. A similar limit also applies to deductions from payment to sub-contractors in the construction industry made by contractors under the Income Tax (Sub-contractors in the Construction Industry) Regulations 1975, SI 1975/1960.

The Social Security Contributions and Benefits Act 1992, provides for the payment of earnings related contributions in respect of employed persons. The employer is liable to account therefor in the same manner as for deductions of tax. The Social Security (Contributions) Regulations 1979, SI 1979/591, apply reg 28 of the Income Tax (Employments) Regulations 1973, supra, so that any graduated contributions not accounted for may be recovered summarily. A certificate of non-payment given by a collector of taxes is admissible in evidence (Social Security Administration Act 1992, s 119); see this PART: title Social Security, ante.

[2] See the Magistrates' Courts Act 1980, ss 58, 96, in PART I, ante. See also in connection with the recovery in magistrates' courts of income tax or any other tax or liability recoverable under this section, the Administration of Justice Act 1970, s 12 and Sch 4, and the Magistrates' Courts Act 1980, s 92, in PART I: MAGISTRATES' COURTS, PROCEDURE, ante. An attachment of earnings order may be made only by a county court and not a magistrates' court; see Attachment of Earnings Act 1971, ss 1 and 2, in PART I: MAGISTRATES' COURTS, PROCEDURE, ante.

[3] Proceedings begun by one collector may be continued by another and any collector may act for any division or area (s 1(3) of the Taxes Management Act 1970).

*Supplemental*

7.10988 **69. Recovery of penalty or interest** (1) This section applies to—

(*a*) penalties imposed under Part II, VA or X of this Act or Schedule 18 to the Finance Act 1998;

(*b*) penalties imposed under any paragraph of Schedule 56 to the Finance Act 2009 in respect of an amount falling within any of the following items of the Table in paragraph 1 of that Schedule—

(i) item 1, 12, 18 or 19, or

(ii) insofar as the tax falls within item 1, item 17, 23 or 24; and

(*c*) interest charged under any provision of this Act (or recoverable as if it were interest so charged); and

(*d*) interest charged under section 101 of the Finance Act 2009.

(2) An amount by way of penalty or interest to which this section applies shall be treated for the purposes of the following provisions as if it were an amount of tax.

(3) Those provisions are—

(*a*) sections 61, 63 and 65 to 68 of this Act;

(*b*) section 35(2)(*g*)(i) of the Crown Proceedings Act 1947 (rules of court: restriction of set-off or counterclaim where proceedings, or set-off or counterclaim, relate to tax) and any rules of court imposing any such restriction;

(*c*) section 35(2)(*b*) of that Act as set out in section 50 of that Act (which imposes corresponding restrictions in Scotland).

[Taxes Management Act 1970, s 69 as substituted by the Finance Act 2001, s 89 and SI 2011/702.]

7.10989 **70. Evidence** (1)–(3) *Repealed.*

(4) A written statement as to the wages, salaries, fees, and other earnings or amounts treated as earnings paid for any period to the person against whom proceedings are brought under section 65, 66 or 67 of this Act, purporting to be signed by his employer for that period, or by any responsible person in the employment of the employer, shall in such proceedings be *prima facie* evidence that the wages, salaries, fees and other earnings or amounts treated as earnings therein stated to have been paid to the person charged have in fact been so paid.

(5) *Repealed.*

[Taxes Management Act 1970, s 70 as amended by the Finance Act 1985, s 93 and Sch 25, Part II, the Finance (No 2) Act 1987, s 84, the Finance Act 1989, s 160 and Sch 17, the Finance Act 1994, Sch 19, the Finance Act 1998, Sch 19, the Finance Act 2001, s 89 and the Finance Act 2008, Sch 44.]

## Part X[1]

## Penalties, Etc

7.10990 **105. Admissibility of evidence not affected by offer of settlement etc**

(1) Statements made of documents produced by or on behalf of a person shall not be inadmissible[2] in any such proceedings as are mentioned in subsection (2) below by reason only that it has been drawn to his attention that—

(*a*) that where serious tax fraud had been committed the Board may accept a money settlement and that the Board will accept such a settlement, and will not pursue a criminal prosecution, if he makes a full confession of all tax irregularities, or

(*b*) that the extent to which he is helpful and volunteers information is a factor that will be taken into account in determining the amount of the penalty,

and that he was or may have been induced thereby to make the statements or produce the documents.

(2) The proceedings mentioned in subsection (1) above are—

(*a*) any criminal proceedings against the person in question for any form of fraudulent conduct in connection with or in relation to tax, and

(*b*) any proceedings against him for the recovery of any tax due from him, and

(*c*) any proceedings for a penalty or on appeal against the determination of a penalty.

[Taxes Management Act 1970, s 105 as amended by the Finance Act 1989, ss 149 and 168 and the Finance Act 2003, s 206.]

---

[1] Part X contains ss 93–106.

[2] If, in response to the Hansard statement (ie a statement made pursuant to the Hansard Procedure, which provides a mechanism for settling tax liabilities without recourse to criminal or civil proceedings) true and accurate information is disclosed that reveals earlier cheating, and the taxpayer is then prosecuted in respect of that earlier dishonesty, he will have a strong argument that the criminal proceedings are unfair and an even stronger argument that the Crown should not be able to rely on evidence of his admission; but that does not apply where the reverse occurs, ie the information that is provided is not true and accurate (*R v Dimsey* [2001] UKHL 46, [2002] 1 AC 509).

## SCHEDULE 1AA

### Orders for Production of Documents

Section 20BA(4)

*(As inserted by the Finance Act 2000, s 149 and Sch 39.)*

*Introduction*

7.10991 **1.** The provisions of this Schedule supplement section 20BA.

*Authorised officer of the Board*

**2.** (1) In section 20BA(1) an "authorised officer of the Board" means an officer of the Board authorised by the Board for the purposes of that section.

(2) The Board may make provision by regulations as to—

(*a*) the procedures for approving in any particular case the decision to apply for an order under that section, and

(*b*) the descriptions of officer by whom such approval may be given.

*Notice of application for order*

**3.** (1) A person is entitled—

(*a*) to notice of the intention to apply for an order against him under section 20BA, and

(*b*) to appear and be heard at the hearing of the application,

unless the appropriate judicial authority is satisfied that this would seriously prejudice the investigation of the offence.

(2) The Board may make provision by regulations as to the notice to be given, the contents of the notice and the manner of giving it.

*Obligations of person given notice of application*

**4.** (1) A person who has been given notice of intention to apply for an order under section 20BA(4) shall not—

(*a*) conceal, destroy, alter or dispose of any document to which the application relates, or

(*b*) disclose to any other person information or any other matter likely to prejudice the investigation of the offence to which the application relates.

This is subject to the following qualifications.

(2) Sub-paragraph (1)(*a*) does not prevent anything being done—

(*a*) with the leave of the appropriate judicial authority,

(*b*) with the written permission of an officer of the Board,
(*c*) after the application has been dismissed or abandoned, or
(*d*) after any order made on the application has been complied with.

(3) Sub-paragraph (1)(*b*) does not prevent a professional legal adviser from disclosing any information or other matter—

(*a*) to, or to a representative of, a client of his in connection with the giving by the adviser of legal advice to the client; or
(*b*) to any person—
(i) in contemplation of, or in connection with, legal proceedings; and
(ii) for the purpose of those proceedings.

This sub-paragraph does not apply in relation to any information or other matter which is disclosed with a view to furthering a criminal purpose.

(4) A person who fails to comply with the obligation in sub-paragraph (1)*a*) or *b*) above may be dealt with as if he had failed to comply with an order under section 20BA.

*Exception of items subject to legal privilege*

**5.** (1) Section 20BA does not apply to items subject to legal privilege.

(2) For this purpose "items subject to legal privilege" means—

(*a*) communications between a professional legal adviser and his client or any person representing his client made in connection with the giving of legal advice to the client;
(*b*) communications between a professional legal adviser and his client or any person representing his client or between such an adviser or his client or any such representative and any other person made in connection with or in contemplation of legal proceedings and for the purposes of such proceedings; and
(*c*) items enclosed with or referred to in such communications and made—
(i) in connection with the giving of legal advice; or
(ii) in connection with or in contemplation of legal proceedings and for the purposes of such proceedings,

when they are in the possession of a person who is entitled to possession of them.

(3) Items held with the intention of furthering a criminal purpose are not subject to legal privilege.

*Resolution of disputes as to legal privilege*

**6.** (1) The Board may make provision by regulations for the resolution of disputes as to whether a document, or part of a document, is an item subject to legal privilege.

(2) The regulations may, in particular, make provision as to—

(*a*) the custody of the document whilst its status is being decided;
(*b*) the appointment of an independent, legally qualified person to decide the matter;
(*c*) the procedures to be followed; and
(*d*) who is to meet the costs of the proceedings.

*Complying with an order*

**7.** (1) The Board may make provision by regulations as to how a person is to comply with an order under section 20BA.

(2) The regulations may, in particular, make provision as to—

(*a*) the officer of the Board to whom the documents are to be produced,
(*b*) the address to which the documents are to be taken or sent, and
(*c*) the circumstances in which sending the documents by post complies with the order.

(3) Where an order under section 20BA applies to a document in electronic or magnetic form, the order shall be taken to require the person to deliver the information recorded in the document in a form in which it is visible and legible.

*Procedure where documents are delivered*

**8.** (1) The provisions of section 20CC(3) to (9) apply in relation to a document delivered to an officer of the Board in accordance with an order under section 20BA as they apply to a thing removed by an officer of the Board as mentioned in subsection (1) of section 20CC.

(2) In section 20CC(9) as applied by sub-paragraph (1) above the reference to the warrant concerned shall be read as a reference to the order concerned.

*Sanction for failure to comply with order*

**9.** (1) If a person fails to comply with an order made under section 20BA, he may be dealt with as if he had committed a contempt of the court.

(2) For this purpose "the court" means—

(*a*) in relation to an order made by a Circuit judge*, the Crown Court;
(*b*) in relation to an order made by a sheriff, a sheriff court;
(*c*) in relation to an order made by a county court judge, a county court in Northern Ireland.

*Notice of order etc*

**10.** The Board may make provision by regulations as to the circumstances in which notice of an order under section 20BA, or of an application for such an order, is to be treated as having been given.

*General provisions about regulations*

**11.** Regulations under this Schedule—

(*a*) may contain such incidental, supplementary and transitional provision as appears to the Board to be appropriate, and
(*b*) shall be made by statutory instrument which shall be subject to annulment in pursuance of a resolution of either House of Parliament.

---

* **Words inserted by the Courts Act 2003, Sch 4 from a date to be appointed.**

# Finance Act 1989
(1989 c 26)

## Part III[1]
## Miscellaneous and General

*Miscellaneous*

7.11002 **182. Disclosure of information[2]** (1) A person who discloses any information which he holds or has held in the exercise of tax functions, tax credit functions, child trust fund functions or social security functions is guilty of an offence if it is information about any matter relevant, for the purposes of any of those functions—

(*a*) to tax or duty in the case of any identifiable person,
(*aa*) to a tax credit in respect of any identifiable person,
(*ab*) to a child trust fund of any identifiable person,
(*b*) to contributions payable by or in respect of any identifiable person, or
(*c*) to statutory sick pay, statutory maternity pay, statutory paternity pay, statutory adoption pay or statutory shared parental pay in respect of any identifiable person.

(2) In this section "tax functions" means functions relating to tax or duty—
(*a*) of the Commissioners, the Board and their officers,
(*b*) of any person carrying out the administrative work of the First-tier Tribunal or Upper Tribunal, and
(*c*) of any other person providing, or employed in the provision of, services to any person mentioned in paragraph (*a*) or (*b*) above.

(2ZA) In this section "tax credit functions" means the functions relating tax credits—
(*a*) of the Board,
(*b*) of any person carrying out the administrative work of the First-tier Tribunal or Upper Tribunal, and
(*c*) of any other person providing, or employed in the provision of, services to any person mentioned in paragraph (*b*) above.

(2ZB) In this section "child trust fund functions" means the functions relating to child trust funds—
(*a*) of the Board and their officers,
(*b*) of any person carrying out the administrative work of the First-tier Tribunal or an appeal tribunal constituted under Chapter 1 of Part 2 of the Social Security (Northern Ireland) Order 1998, or
(*c*) of any person providing, or employed in the provision of, services to the Board or any person mentioned in paragraph (*b*) above.

(2A) In this section "social security functions" means—
(*a*) the functions relating to contributions, child benefit, guardian's allowance, statutory sick pay, statutory maternity pay, statutory paternity pay, statutory adoption pay or statutory shared parental pay—
(i) of the Board and their officers,
(ii) of any person carrying out the administrative work of the First-tier Tribunal or Upper Tribunal, and
(iii) of any other person providing, or employed in the provision of, services to any person mentioned in sub-paragraph (i) or (ii) above, and
(*b*) the functions under Part III of the Pension Schemes Act 1993 or Part III of the Pension Schemes (Northern Ireland) Act 1993 of the Board and their officers and any other person providing, or employed in the provision of, services to the Board or their officers.

(3) *Repealed.*

(4) A person who discloses any information which—
(*a*) he holds or has held in the exercise of functions—
(i) of the Comptroller and Auditor General and any member of the staff of the National Audit Office,
(ii) of the Parliamentary Commissioner for Administration and his officers,
(iii) of the Auditor General for Wales and any member of his staff, or
(iv) of the Public Services Ombudsman for Wales and any member of his staff, or
(v) of the Scottish Public Services Ombudsman and any member of his staff,
(*b*) is, or is derived from, information which was held by any person in the exercise of tax functions, tax credit functions, child trust fund functions or social security functions and
(*c*) is information about any matter relevant, for the purposes of tax functions, tax credit functions, child trust fund functions or social security functions—
(i) to tax or duty in the case of any identifiable person,
(ia) to a tax credit in respect of any identifiable person,
(ib) to a child trust fund of any identifiable person,

(ii) to contributions payable by or in respect of any identifiable person, or
(iii) to child benefit, guardian's allowance, statutory sick pay, statutory maternity pay, statutory paternity pay, statutory adoption pay or statutory shared parental pay in respect of any identifiable person in respect of any identifiable person

is guilty of an offence.

(5) Subsections (1) and (4) above do not apply to any disclosure of information—

(*a*) with lawful authority,

(*b*) with the consent of any person in whose case the information is about a matter relevant to tax or duty, to a tax credit or to a child trust fund or to contributions, statutory sick pay, statutory maternity pay, statutory paternity pay, statutory adoption pay or statutory shared parental pay, or

(*c*) which has been lawfully made available to the public before the disclosure is made.

(6) For the purposes of this section a disclosure of any information is made with lawful authority if, and only if, it is made—

(*a*) by a Crown servant in accordance with his official duty,

(*b*) by any other person for the purposes of the function in the exercise of which he holds the information and without contravening any restriction duly imposed by the person responsible,

(*c*) to, or in accordance with an authorisation duly given by, the person responsible,

(*d*) in pursuance of any enactment or of any order of a court, or

(*e*) in connection with the institution of or otherwise for the purposes of any proceedings relating to any matter within the general responsibility of the Commissioners or, as the case requires, the Board,

and in this subsection "the person responsible" means the Commissioners, the Board, the Comptroller, the Parliamentary Commissioner, the Auditor General for Wales, the Public Services Ombudsman for Wales or the Scottish Public Services Ombudsman, as the case requires.

(7) It is a defence for a person charged with an offence under this section to prove that at the time of the alleged offence—

(*a*) he believed that he had lawful authority to make the disclosure in question and had no reasonable cause to believe otherwise, or

(*b*) he believed that the information in question had been lawfully made available to the public before the disclosure was made and had no reasonable cause to believe otherwise.

(8) A person of an offence under this section is liable[2]

(*a*) on conviction on indictment, to imprisonment for a term not exceeding **two years** or a **fine** or **both**, and

(*b*) on summary conviction, to imprisonment for a term not exceeding **six months** or a fine not exceeding the **statutory maximum** or **both**.

(9) No prosecution for an offence under this section shall be instituted in England and Wales or in Northern Ireland except—

(*a*) by the Commissioners or the Board, as the case requires, or

(*b*) by or with the consent of the Director of Public Prosecutions or, in Northern Ireland, the Director of Public Prosecutions for Northern Ireland.

(10) In this section—

"the Board" means the Commissioners of Inland Revenue,

"child trust fund" has the same meaning as in the Child Trust Funds Act 2004,

"the Commissioners" means the Commissioners of Customs and Excise,

"contributions" means contributions under Part I of the Social Security Contributions and Benefits Act 1992 or Part I of the Social Security Contributions and Benefits (Northern Ireland) Act 1992;

"Crown servant" has the same meaning as in the Official Secrets Act 1989,

"tax credit" means a tax credit under the Tax Credits Act 2002,

"tax or duty" means ant tax or duty within the general responsibility of the Commissioners or the Board.

(10A) In this section, in relation to the disclosure of information "identifiable person" means a person whose identity is specified in the disclosure or can be deduced from it.

(11) In this section—

(*a*) references to the Comptroller and Auditor General include the Comptroller and Auditor General for Northern Ireland,

(*b*) references to the National Audit Office include the Northern Ireland Audit Office, and

(*c*) reference to the Parliamentary Commissioner for Administration include the Health Service Commissioner for England, the Northern Ireland Parliamentary Commissioner for Administration and the Northern Ireland Commissioner for complaints.

(11A) In this section, references to statutory paternity pay, statutory adoption pay or statutory shared parental pay include statutory pay under Northern Ireland legislation corresponding to Part 12ZA, Part 12ZB or Part 12ZC of the Social Security Contributions and Benefits Act 1992 (c 4).

(12) *Commencement*.

[Finance Act 1989, s 182 as amended by the Finance Act 1995, Sch 29, the Government of Wales Act 1998, Sch 12 and Sch 18, the Tax Credits Act 1999, s 12, the Social Security Contributions (Transfer of Functions, etc) Act 1999, Sch 6, the Tax Credits Act 2002, s 59, the Employment Act 2002, Sch 7, the Statute Law (Repeals) Act 2004, SI 2004/1823, the Child Trust Funds Act 2004, s 18, the Public Services Ombudsman (Wales) Act 2005, Sch 6, the Work and Families Act 2006, Sch 1, the Income Tax Act 2007, Sch 1, SI 2009/56 and the Children and Families Act 2014, Sch 7.]

1 Part III contains ss 171–188.

2 For procedure in respect of an offence which is triable either way, see the Magistrates' Courts Act 1980, ss 17A–21, in PART I: MAGISTRATES' COURTS, PROCEDURE, ante.

7.11003 **182A. Double taxation: disclosure of information** (1) A person who discloses any information acquired by him in the exercise of his functions as a member of an advisory commission set up under the Arbitration Convention is guilty of an offence.

(2) Subsection (1) above does not apply to any disclosure of information—

(*a*) with the consent of the person who supplied the information to the commission, or

(*b*) which has been lawfully made available to the public before the disclosure is made.

(3) It is a defence for a person charged with an offence under this section to prove that at the time of the alleged offence he believed that the information in question had been lawfully made available to the public before the disclosure was made and had no reasonable cause to believe otherwise.

(4) A person guilty of an offence under this section is liable[1]—

(*a*) on conviction on indictment to imprisonment for a term not exceeding **two years** or a **fine** or **both**;

(*b*) on summary conviction, to imprisonment for a term not exceeding **six months** or a fine not exceeding **the statutory maximum** or **both**.

(5) No prosecution for an offence under this section shall be instituted in England and Wales or in Northern Ireland except—

(*a*) by the Board, or

(*b*) by or with the consent of the Director of Public Prosecutions or, in Northern Ireland, the Director of Public Prosecutions for Northern Ireland.

(6) In this section—

"the Arbitration Convention" has the meaning given by section 815B(4) of the Taxes Act 1988;

"the Board" means the Commissioners of Inland Revenue."

[Finance Act 1989, s 182A as inserted by the Finance (No 2) Act 1992, s 51.]

1 For procedure in respect of an offence which is triable either way, see the Magistrates' Courts Act 1980, ss 17A–21, in PART I: MAGISTRATES' COURTS, PROCEDURE, ante.

## Value Added Tax Act 1994

(1994 c 23)

7.11004 Value added tax is charged on the supply of goods or services in the United Kingdom, the acquisition in the United Kingdom from other member states of any goods or on the importation of goods from places outside the member states (s 1). The scope of VAT on taxable supplies is defined by s 4 and the meaning of "supply" is defined by s 5 and Sch 4. The time of supply (and when VAT is due) is defined by s 6 and the place of supply by s 7. Further provision in respect of acquisition from member states is made by ss 10–14 and for goods imported from outside member states by ss 15–17. Specific provision is made for the determination of value by ss 19–23. The rate of tax is established by s 2.

A taxable person may offset VAT paid on goods supplied etc to him (input) against tax which he must pay (output tax) and must pay VAT in accordance with accounting periods prescribed by regulations.

Relief is available for zero rated supplies (s 30 and Sch 8), exempt supplies (s 31 and Sch 9) and certain second hand goods (s 32), capital goods (s 34) and other reliefs specified in Pt II. Application of the Act to particular cases such as the Crown and local authorities is provided for in Pt III (ss 41–57).

Administration, enforcement and collection is provided for by Pt IV (ss 58–81 and Sch 11). The Act contains extensive powers to make regulations under which, inter alia, the Value Added Tax Regulations 1995[1] have been made. The Commissioners of Customs and Excise may assess tax due where there has been failure to make proper returns; they may require the keeping of records, the furnishing of information and the production of documents by s 58 and Sch 11.

The Commissioners are empowered to impose surcharges in respect of default in payment (s 59) and penalties where there is evasion of VAT involving dishonesty (s 60). Other forms of misconduct liable to a penalty are prescribed by ss 62–69. Penalties may be mitigated by the Commissioners (s 70). Criminal liability may also arise under s 72.

Appeals in disputes including registration, assessment, tax chargeable and the deduction known as "input tax" lie to local value added tax tribunals (Pt V, ss 82–87, Sch 12); these and not magistrates' courts are the proper forum for the settlement of such disputes.

Only the parts of the Act concerned with entry and search facilities, and with offences and penalties, are included in this work.

*Note that the comprehensive code governing proceedings, which is contained in ss* 145–155 *of the Customs and Excise Management Act* 1979, *in this* PART: title CUSTOMS AND EXCISE, *ante, applies here.*

---

[1] SI 1995/2518 amended by SI 1996/210, 1198, 1250, 2098 and 2960, SI 1997/1086, 1525, 1614, 2437 and 2887, SI 1998/59 and 765, SI 1999/438, 599, 1374, 3029 and 3114, SI 2000/258, 634 and 794, SI 2001/630, 677, and SI 2002/1074, 1142, 2918 and 3027, SI 2003/532, 1069, 1114, 1485, 2318 and 3220, SI 2004/767, 1082, 1675 and 3140 and SI 2005/762, 2231, SI 2006/587, 2902 and 3292, SI 2007/313, 768, 599, 1418, 2085, 2922 and 3099, SI 2008/556, 954 and 3021, SI 2009/586, 820 and 1967, 2978 and 3241, SI 2010/559, 2240, 2940, 3022 and SI 2011/254 and 2085, SI 2012/33, 1899 and 2951, SI 2013/701, 2241 and 3211, SI 2014/548,1497 and 2430, SI 2015/1978 and SI 2016/989.

## PART I
## THE CHARGE TO TAX

*Imposition and rate of VAT*

7.11005 1. **Value added tax** (1) Value added tax shall be charged, in accordance with the provisions of this Act—

(*a*) on the supply of goods or services in the United Kingdom (including anything treated as such a supply),

(*b*) on the acquisition in the United Kingdom from other member States of any goods, and

(*c*) on the importation of goods from places outside the member States,

and references in this Act to VAT are references to value added tax.

(2) VAT on any supply of goods or services is a liability of the person making the supply and (subject to provisions about accounting and payment) becomes due at the time of supply.

(3) VAT on any acquisition of goods from another member State is a liability of the person who acquires the goods and (subject to provisions about accounting and payment) becomes due at the time of acquisition.

(4) VAT on the importation of goods from places outside the member States shall be charged and payable as if it were a duty of customs.

[Value Added Tax Act 1994, s 1.]

7.11006 3. **Taxable persons and registration** (1) A person is a taxable person for the purposes of this Act while he is, or is required to be, registered[1] under this Act.

(2) Schedules 1 to 3A[2] shall have effect with respect to registration.

(3) Persons registered under any of those Schedules shall be registered in a single register kept by the Commissioners for the purposes of this Act; and, accordingly, references in this Act to being registered under this Act are references to being registered under any of those Schedules.

(4) The Commissioners may by regulations make provision as to the inclusion and correction of information in that register with respect to the Schedule under which any person is registered.

[Value Added Tax Act 1994, s 3 as amended by the Finance Act 2000, s 136.]

---

[1] Registration of one firm name is registration of those who are carrying on business in partnership as such, and covers the taxable activities of the same individuals trading alternatively under another firm name (*Customs and Excise Comrs v Glassborow* [1975] QB 465, [1974] 1 All ER 1041).

[2] Schedules 1–3A to this Act are not printed in this work.

7.11007 3A. **Supply of electronic services in member States: special accounting scheme**

(1) Schedule 3B (scheme enabling persons who supply electronically supplied services in any member State but who are not established in a member State, to account for and pay VAT in the United Kingdom on those supplies) has effect.

(2) The Treasury may by order amend Schedule 3B.

(3) The power of the Treasury by order to amend Schedule 3B includes power to make such incidental, supplemental, consequential and transitional provision in connection with any amendment of that Schedule as they think fit.

[Value Added Tax Act 1994, s 3A as inserted by the Finance Act 2003, Sch 2]

*Supply of goods or services in the United Kingdom*

7.11008 4. **Scope of VAT on taxable supplies** (1) VAT shall be charged on any supply of goods or services made in the United Kingdom, where it is a taxable supply made by a taxable person in the course or furtherance of any business carried on by him.

(2) A taxable supply is a supply of goods or services made in the United Kingdom other than an exempt supply.

[Value Added Tax Act 1994, s 4.]

*Acquisition of goods from member States*

7.11009 10. **Scope of VAT on acquisitions from member States** (1) VAT shall be charged on any acquisition from another member State of any goods where—

(a) the acquisition is a taxable acquisition and takes place in the United Kingdom;
(b) the acquisition is otherwise than in pursuance of a taxable supply; and
(c) the person who makes the acquisition is a taxable person or the goods are subject to a duty of excise or consist in a new means of transport.

(2) An acquisition of goods from another member State is a taxable acquisition if—
(a) it falls within subsection (3) below or the goods consist in a new means of transport; and
(b) it is not an exempt acquisition.

(3) An acquisition of goods from another member State falls within this subsection if—
(a) the goods are acquired in the course or furtherance of—
(i) any business carried on by any person; or
(ii) any activities carried on otherwise than by way of business by any body corporate or by any club, association, organisation or other unincorporated body;
(b) it is the person who carries on that business or, as the case may be, those activities who acquires the goods; and
(c) the supplier—
(i) is taxable in another member State at the time of the transaction in pursuance of which the goods are acquired; and
(ii) in participating in that transaction, acts in the course or furtherance of a business carried on by him.

[Value Added Tax Act 1994, s 10.]

*Importation of goods from outside the member States*

7.11010 **15. General provisions relating to imported goods** (1) For the purposes of this Act goods are imported from a place outside the member States where—
(a) having been removed from a place outside the member States, they enter the territory of the Community;
(b) they enter that territory by being removed to the United Kingdom or are removed to the United Kingdom after entering that territory; and
(c) the circumstances are such that it is on their removal to the United Kingdom or subsequently while they are in the United Kingdom that any Community customs debt in respect of duty on their entry into the territory of the Community would be incurred.

(2) Accordingly—
(a) goods shall not be treated for the purposes of this Act as imported at any time before a Community customs debt in respect of duty on their entry into the territory of the Community would be incurred, and
(b) the person who is to be treated for the purposes of this Act as importing any goods from a place outside the member States is the person who would be liable to discharge any such Community customs debt.

(3) Subsections (1) and (2) above shall not apply, except in so far as the context otherwise requires or provision to the contrary is contained in regulations under section 16(1), for construing any references to importation or to an importer in any enactment or subordinate legislation applied for the purposes of this Act by section 16(1).

[Value Added Tax Act 1994, s 15.]

7.11011 **72. Offences**[1] (1) If any person is knowingly[2] concerned in, or in the taking of steps with a view to, the fraudulent evasion[3] of VAT by him or any other person, he shall be liable[4]—
(a) on summary conviction, to a penalty of the **statutory maximum or of three times the amount of the VAT, whichever is the greater,** or to imprisonment for a term not exceeding **6 months** or to **both**[5]; or
(b) on conviction on indictment, to a **penalty of any amount** or to imprisonment for a term not exceeding **7 years** or to **both**.

(2) Any reference in subsection (1) above or subsection (8) below to the evasion of VAT includes a reference to the obtaining of—
(a) the payment of a VAT credit; or
(b) a refund under section 35, 36 or 40 of this Act or section 22 of the 1983 Act; or
(c) a refund under any regulations made by virtue of section 13(5); or
(d) a repayment under section 39;

and any reference in those subsections to the amount of the VAT shall be construed—
(i) in relation to VAT itself or a VAT credit, as a reference to the aggregate of the amount (if any) falsely claimed by way of credit for input tax and the amount (if any) by which output tax was falsely understated, and
(ii) in relation to a refund or repayment falling within paragraph (b), (c) or (d) above, as a reference to the amount falsely claimed by way of refund or repayment.

(3) If any person—
(a) with intent to deceive produces, furnishes or sends for the purposes of this Act or otherwise makes use for those purposes of any document which is false in a material particular; or

(*b*) in furnishing any information for the purposes of this Act makes any statement which he knows to be false in a material particular or recklessly makes a statement which is false in a material particular,

he shall be liable[4]—

(i) on summary conviction, to a penalty of the **statutory maximum** or, where subsection (4) or (5) below applies, to the alternative penalty specified in that subsection if it is greater, or to imprisonment for a term not exceeding **6 months** or to **both**; or

(ii) on conviction on indictment, to a **penalty of any amount** or to imprisonment for a term not exceeding 7 **years** or to **both**.

(4) In any case where—

(*a*) the document referred to in subsection (3)(*a*) above is a return required under this Act, or

(*b*) the information referred to in subsection (3)(*b*) above is contained in or otherwise relevant to such a return,

the alternative penalty referred to in subsection (3)(i) above is a penalty equal to three times the aggregate of the amount (if any) falsely claimed by way of credit for input tax and the amount (if any) by which output tax was falsely understated.

(5) In any case where—

(*a*) the document referred to in subsection (3)(*a*) above is a claim for a refund under section 35, 36 or 40 of this Act or section 22 of the 1983 Act, for a refund under any regulations made by virtue of section 13(5) or for a repayment under section 39, or

(*b*) the information referred to in subsection (3)(*b*) above is contained in or otherwise relevant to such a claim,

the alternative penalty referred to in subsection (3)(i) above is a penalty equal to 3 times the amount falsely claimed.

(6) The reference in subsection (3)(*a*) above to furnishing, sending or otherwise making use of a document which is false in a material particular, with intent to deceive, includes a reference to furnishing, sending or otherwise making use of such a document, with intent to secure that a machine will respond to the document as if it were a true document.

(7) Any reference in subsection (3)(*a*) or (6) above to producing, furnishing or sending a document includes a reference to causing a document to be produced, furnished or sent.

(8) Where a person's conduct during any specified period must have involved the commission by him of one or more offences under the preceding provisions of this section, then, whether or not the particulars of that offence or those offences are known, he shall, by virtue of this subsection, be guilty of an offence[5] and liable[4]—

(*a*) on summary conviction, to a penalty of the **statutory maximum or, if greater, 3 times the amount of any VAT** that was or was intended to be evaded by his conduct, or to imprisonment for a term not exceeding **6 months** or to **both**,[6] or

(*b*) on conviction on indictment to a penalty of any amount or to imprisonment for a term not exceeding 7 **years** or to **both**.

(9) *Repealed.*

(10) If any person acquires possession of or deals with any goods, or accepts the supply of any services, having reason to believe that VAT on the supply of the goods or services, on the accession of the goods from another member State or on the importation of the goods from a place outside the member States has been or will be evaded, he shall be liable on summary conviction to a penalty of **level 5** on the standard scale or **three times the amount of the VAT, whichever is the greater**.

(11) If any person supplies or is supplied with goods or services in contravention of paragraph 4(2) of Schedule 11, he shall be liable on summary conviction to a penalty of **level 5** on the standard scale.

(12) Subject to subsection (13) below, sections 145 to 155 of the Management Act (proceedings for offences, mitigation of penalties and certain other matters) shall apply in relation to offences under this Act (which include any act or omission in respect of which a penalty is imposed) and penalties imposed under this Act as they apply in relation to offences and penalties under the customs and excise Acts as defined in that Act; and accordingly in section 154(2) as it applies by virtue of this subsection the reference to duty shall be construed as a reference to VAT.

(13) In subsection (12) above the references to penalties do not include references to penalties under sections 60 to 70.

[Value Added Tax Act 1994, s 72 as amended by the Finance Act 2003, s 17 and the Finance Act 2007, Sch 22.]

---

1 As to time limits for the prosecution of offences under the custom and excise acts, see the Customs and Excise Management Act 1979, s 146A, in this PART, ante.

2 A person may act "knowingly" if, intending what is happening, he deliberately looks the other way (*Ross v Moss* [1965] 2 QB 396, [1965] 3 All ER 145, 129 JP 537). See also *R v Cohen* [1951] 1 KB 505, [1951] 1 All ER 203 (an offence of knowingly harbouring uncustomed goods).

3 Evasion in this section means a deliberate non-payment when payment is due. There is no need for the Crown to prove in addition an intention permanently to deprive (*R v Dealy* [1995] 1 WLR 658, [1995] 2 Cr App Rep 398, CA).

4 For procedure in respect of an offence triable either way, see the Magistrates' Courts Act 1980, ss 17A–21 in PART I: MAGISTRATES' COURTS, PROCEDURE, ante.

5 The offence under sub-s (8) relates to a person's conduct during a specified period, and creates one offence embracing the commission of numerous offences which themselves, if the details were known, could be individually

charged under s 38(1) and (2) (*R v Asif* (1985) 82 Cr App Rep 123).

6 Where an offender is sentenced to imprisonment and a fine, with an alternative period of imprisonment in default of payment of the fine, the aggregate of the terms of imprisonment must not exceed 15 months (Customs and Excise Management Act 1979, s 149).

7.11012 **94. Meaning of "business" etc** (1) In this Act "business" includes any trade, profession or vocation.

(2) Without prejudice to the generality of anything else in this Act, the following are deemed to be the carrying on of a business—

(*a*) the provision by a club, association or organisation (for a subscription or other consideration) of the facilities or advantages available to its members; and

(*b*) the admission, for a consideration, of persons to any premises.

(3) *Repealed.*

(4) Where a person, in the course or furtherance of a trade, profession or vocation, accepts any office, services supplied by him as the holder of that office are treated as supplied in the course or furtherance of the trade, profession or vocation.

(5) Anything done in connection with the termination or intended termination of a business is treated as being done in the course or furtherance of that business.

(6) The disposition of a business, or part of a business, as a going concern, or of the assets or liabilities of the business or part of the business (whether or not in connection with its reorganisation or winding up), is a supply made in the course or furtherance of the business.

[Value Added Tax Act 1994, s 94 as amended by the Finance Act 1999, s 20 and Sch 20 and the Finance Act 2007, s 100.]

7.11013 **96. Other interpretative provisions** (1) In this Act—

"the 1983 Act" means the Value Added Tax Act 1983;

"another member State" means, subject to section 93(1), any member State other than the United Kingdom, and "other member States" shall be construed accordingly;

"assignment", in relation to Scotland, means assignation;

"authorised person" means any person acting under the authority of the Commissioners;

"the Commissioners" means the Commissioners of Customs and Excise;

"copy", in relation to a document, means anything onto which information recorded in the document has been copied, by whatever means and whether directly or indirectly;

"document" means anything in which information of any description is recorded;

"fee simple"—

(*a*) in relation to Scotland, means the interest of the owner;

(*b*) in relation to Northern Ireland, includes the estate of a person who holds land under a fee farm grant;

"HMRC" means Her Majesty's Revenue and Customs;

"invoice" includes any document similar to an invoice;

"input tax" has the meaning given by section 24;

"interim trustee" has the same meaning as in the Bankruptcy (Scotland) Act 1985;

"local authority" has the meaning given by subsection (4) below;

"major interest", in relation to land, means the fee simple or a tenancy for a term certain of not less than 21 years, and in relation to Scotland means the interest of the owner, or the lessee's interest under a lease for a period of not less than 20 years;

"the Management Act" means the Customs and Excise Management Act 1979;

"money" includes currencies other than sterling;

"output tax" has the meaning given by section 24;

"permanent trustee" has the same meaning as in the Bankruptcy (Scotland) Act 1985;

"the Post Office company" has the same meaning as in Part IV of the Postal Services Act 2000;

"prescribed" means prescribed by regulations;

"prescribed accounting period" has the meaning given by section 25(1);

"quarter" means a period of 3 months ending at the end of March, June, September or December;

"regulations" means regulations made by the Commissioners under this Act;

"relevant business person" has the meaning given by section 7A(4);

"ship" includes hovercraft;

"subordinate legislation" has the same meaning as in the Interpretation Act 1978;

"tax" means VAT;

"taxable acquisition" has the meaning given by section 10(2);

"taxable person" means a person who is a taxable person under section 3;

"taxable supply" has the meaning given by section 4(2)

"the Taxes Act" means the Income and Corporation Taxes Act 1988;

"tribunal" has the meaning given by section 82;

"VAT" means value added tax charged in accordance with this Act or, where the context requires, with the law of another member State;

"VAT credit" has the meaning given by section 25(3);

"VAT invoice" has the meaning given by section 6(15);

"VAT representative" has the meaning given by section 48;

and any reference to a particular section, Part or Schedule is a reference to that section or Part of, or

Schedule to, this Act.

(2) Any reference in this Act to being registered shall be construed in accordance with section 3(3).

(3) Subject to section 93—

(*a*) the question whether or not goods have entered the territory of the Community;

(*b*) the time when any Community customs debt in respect of duty on the entry of any goods into the territory of the Community would be incurred; and

(*c*) the person by whom any such debt would fall to be discharged,

shall for the purposes of this Act be determined (whether or not the goods in question are themselves subject to any such duties) according to the Community legislation applicable to goods which are in fact subject to such duties.

(4) In this Act "local authority" means the council of a county, county borough, district, London borough, parish or group of parishes (or, in Wales, community or group of communities), the Common Council of the City of London, the Council of the Isles of Scilly, and any joint committee or joint board established by two or more of the foregoing and, in relation to Scotland, a council constituted under section 2 of the Local Government etc (Scotland) Act 1994, any two or more such councils and any joint committee or joint board within the meaning of section 235(1) of the Local Government (Scotland) Act 1973.

established by of the foregoing and any joint board to which section 226 of that Act applies.

(5) Any reference in this Act to the amount of any duty of excise on any goods shall be taken to be a reference to the amount of duty charged on those goods with any addition or deduction falling to be made under section 1 of the Excise Duties (Surcharges or Rebates) Act 1979.

(6)–(7) *Repealed.*

(8) The question whether, in relation to any supply of services, the supplier or the recipient of the supply belongs in one country or another shall be determined in accordance with section 9.

(9) Schedules 7A, 8 and 9 shall be interpreted in accordance with the notes contained in those Schedules; and accordingly the powers conferred by this Act to vary those Schedules include a power to add to, delete or vary those notes.

(10) The descriptions of Groups in those Schedules are for ease of reference only and shall not affect the interpretation of the descriptions of items in those Groups.

(10A) Where—

(*a*) the grant of any interest, right, licence or facilities gives rise for the purposes of this Act to supplies made at different times after the making of the grant, and

(*b*) a question whether any of those supplies is zero-rated or exempt falls to be determined according to whether or not the grant is a grant of a description specified in Schedule 8 or 9 or any of paragraphs 5 to 11 of Schedule 10.

that question shall be determined according to whether the description is applicable as at the time of supply, rather than by reference to the time of the grant.

(10B) Notwithstanding subsection (10A) above—

(*a*) item 1 of Group 1 of Schedule 9 does not make exempt any supply that arises for the purposes of this Act from the prior grant of a fee simple falling within paragraph (*a*) of that item; and

(*b*) that paragraph does not prevent the exemption of a supply that arises for the purposes of this Act from the prior grant of a fee simple not falling within that paragraph.

(11) References in this Act to the United Kingdom include the territorial sea of the United Kingdom.

[Value Added Tax Act 1994, s 96 as amended by the Civil Evidence Act 1995, Schs 1 and 2, SI 1995/1510, SI 1996/739, the Finance Act 1997, s 35, the Finance Act 1998, s 19, SI 2001/1149, the Finance Act 2003, s 20, the Abolition of Feudal Tenure etc (Scotland) Act 2000, Schs 12 and 13, SI 2008/1146, SI 2009/56 and the Finance Act 2009, Sch 36.]

*Supplementary provisions*

7.11014 **97. Orders, rules and regulations** (1) Any order made by the Treasury under this Act and any regulations or rules under this Act shall be made by statutory instrument.

[Value Added Tax Act 1994, s 97 as amended by the Finance Act 1995, s 21, the Finance Act 1996, s 33 and Sch 41, the Finance Act 2004, Sch 31, the Finance Act 2004, ss 19, 20 and 22, the Finance Act 2006, s 19, the Finance Act 2007, s 98 and SI 2009/56—summarised.]

7.11015 **101. Commencement and extent** (1) This Act shall come into force on 1st September 1994 and Part I shall have effect in relation to the charge to VAT on supplies, acquisitions and importations in prescribed accounting periods ending on or after that date.

(2) Without prejudice to section 16 of the Interpretation Act 1978 (continuation of proceedings under repealed enactments) except in so far as it enables proceedings to be continued under repealed enactments, section 72 shall have effect on the commencement of this Act to the exclusion of section 39 of the 1983 Act.

(3) This Act extends to Northern Ireland.

(4) Paragraph 23 of Schedule 13 and paragraph 7 of Schedule 14 shall extend to the Isle of Man but no other provision of this Act shall extend there.

7.11016 **102. Short title** This Act may be cited as the Value Added Tax Act 1994.

## SCHEDULE 11

### Administration, Collection and Enforcement

Section 58

*(As amended by the Criminal Procedure (Consequential Provisions) (Scotland) Act 1995, Sch 4, the Finance Act 1996, s 38 and Sch 3, the Civil Evidence Act 1995, Sch 2, SI 1997/2983, the Finance Act 1999, the Youth Justice and Criminal Evidence Act 1999, Sch 6, the Finance Act 2002, s 24, the Criminal Justice and Police Act 2001, Sch 2, the Criminal Justice Act 2003, Sch 37, the Commissioners for Revenue and Customs 2005, Sch 4, the Finance Act 2006, ss 20 and 21, the Finance Act 2007, Sch 27, the Finance Act 2008, Schs 36, 37 and 44 and the Finance Act 2009, s 78.)*

*Power to require security and production of evidence*

7.11017 4. (1) The Commissioners may, as a condition of allowing or repaying input tax[1] to any person, require the production of such evidence relating to VAT as they may specify.

(1A) If they think it necessary for the protection of the revenue, the Commissioners may require, as a condition of making any VAT credit, the giving of such security for the amount of the payment as appears to them appropriate.

(2) If they think it necessary for the protection of the revenue, the Commissioners may require a taxable person, as a condition of his supplying or being supplied with goods or services under a taxable supply, to give security, or further security, for the payment of any VAT that is or may become due from—

(*a*) the taxable person, or

(*b*) any person by or to whom relevant goods or services are supplied.

(3) In sub-paragraph (2) above "relevant goods or services" means goods or services supplied by or to the taxable person.

(4) Security under sub-paragraph (2) above shall be of such amount, and shall be given in such manner, as the Commissioners may determine.

(5) The powers conferred on the Commissioners by sub-paragraph (2) above are without prejudice to their powers under section 48(7).

[1] Input tax is defined by s 24. It is tax already charged on goods or services acquired as part of his business (including goods imported); when he furnishes his return, and accounts for the tax due on supplies by him of goods or services, he is entitled to take credit for the input tax on supplies of goods or services made to him during the period to which the return relates. If input tax exceeds output tax, the Commissioners will repay the excess.

Section 24 also enables the Treasury by order to make provisions for exceptions to the entitlement to claim input tax, and this power has been extensively exercised.

*Duty to keep records*

6. (1) Every taxable person shall keep such records as the Commissioners may by regulations require, and every person who, at a time when he is not a taxable person, acquires in the United Kingdom from another member State any goods which are subject to a duty of excise or consist in a new means of transport shall keep such records with respect to the acquisition (if it is a taxable acquisition and is not in pursuance of a taxable supply) as the Commissioners may so require.

(2) Regulations under sub-paragraph (1) above may make different provision for different cases and may be framed by reference to such records as may be specified in any notice published by the Commissioners in pursuance of the regulations and not withdrawn by a further notice.

(3) The Commissioners may require any records kept in pursuance of this paragraph to be preserved for such period not exceeding 6 years as they may specify in writing (and different periods may be specified for different cases).

(4) The duty under this paragraph to preserve records may be discharged—

(*a*) by preserving them in any form and by any means, or

(*b*) by preserving the information contained in them in any form and by any means,

subject to any conditions or exceptions specified in writing by the Commissioners for Her Majesty's Revenue and Customs.]

**6A.** (1) The Commissioners may direct any taxable person named in the direction to keep such records as they specify in the direction in relation to such goods as they so specify.

(2) A direction under this paragraph may require the records to be compiled by reference to VAT invoices or any other matter.

(3) The Commissioners may not make a direction under this paragraph unless they have reasonable grounds for believing that the records specified in the direction might assist in identifying taxable supplies in respect of which the VAT chargeable might not be paid.

(4) The taxable supplies in question may be supplies made by—

(*a*) the person named in the direction, or

(*b*) any other person.

(5) A direction under this paragraph—

(*a*) must be given by notice in writing to the person named in it,

(*b*) must warn that person of the consequences under section 69B of failing to comply with it, and

(*c*) remains in force until it is revoked or replaced by a further direction.

(6) The Commissioners may require any records kept in pursuance of this paragraph to be preserved for such period not exceeding 6 years as they may require.

(7) Sub-paragraph (4) of paragraph 6 (preservation of information) applies for the purposes of this paragraph as it applies for the purposes of that paragraph.

(8) This paragraph is without prejudice to the power conferred by paragraph 6(1) to make regulations requiring records to be kept.

(9) Any records required to be kept by virtue of this paragraph are in addition to any records required to be kept by virtue of paragraph 6.

*Furnishing of information and production of documents*

7. (1) The Commissioners may be regulations make provision for requiring taxable persons to notify to the Commissioners such particulars of changes in circumstances relating to those persons or any business[1] carried on by them as appear to the Commissioners required for the purpose of keeping the register kept under this Act up to date.

(2)–(9) *Repealed.*

[1] See s 94, ante.

*Power to take samples*

**8.** (1) An authorised person, if it appears to him necessary for the protection of the revenue against mistake or fraud, may at any time take, from the goods in the possession of any person who supplies goods or acquires goods from another member State, or in the possession of a fiscal warehousekeeper, such samples as the authorised person may require with a view to determining how the goods or the materials of which they are made ought to be or to have been treated for the purposes of VAT.

(2) Any sample taken under this paragraph shall be disposed of and accounted for in such manner as the Commissioners may direct.

(3) Where a sample is taken under this paragraph from the goods in any person's possession and is not returned to him within a reasonable time and in good condition the Commissioners shall pay him by way of compensation a sum equal to the cost of the sample to him or such larger sum as they may determine.

*Power to require opening of gaming machines*

**9.** An authorised person may at any reasonable time require a person making such a supply as is referred to in section 23(1) or any person acting on his behalf—

(*a*) to open any gaming machine, within the meaning of that section; and

(*b*) to carry out any other operation which may be necessary to enable the authorised person to ascertain the amount which, in accordance with subsection (2) of that section, is to be taken as the value of supplies made in the circumstances mentioned in subsection (1) of that section in any period.

*Entry and search of premises and persons*

**10.** *Repealed.*

*Order for access to recorded information etc*

**11.** (1) Where, on an application[1] by an authorised person, a justice of the peace or, in Scotland, a justice (within the meaning of section 308 of the Criminal Procedure (Scotland) Act 1995) is satisfied[2] that there are reasonable grounds for believing—

(*a*) that an offence in connection with VAT is being, has been or is about to be committed, and

(*b*) that any recorded information (including any document of any nature whatsoever) which may be required as evidence for the purpose of any proceedings in respect of such an offence is in the possession of any person,

he may make an order[3] under this paragraph.

(2) An order under this paragraph is an order that the person who appears to the justice to be in possession of the recorded information to which the application relates shall—

(*a*) give an authorised person access to it, and

(*b*) permit an authorised person to remove and take away any of it which he reasonably considers necessary,

not later than the end of the period of 7 days beginning on the date of the order or the end of such longer period as the order may specify.

(3) The reference in sub-paragraph (2)(*a*) above to giving an authorised person access to the recorded information to which the application relates includes a reference to permitting the authorised person to take copies of it or to make extracts from it.

(4) Where the recorded information consists of information stored in any electronic form, an order under this paragraph shall have effect as an order to produce the information in a form in which it is visible and legible or from which it can readily be produced in a visible and legible form and, if the authorised person wishes to remove it, in a form in which it can be removed.

(5) This paragraph is without prejudice to paragraphs 7 and 10 above.

[1] In certain circumstances an *ex parte* application will be justified, even when a charge has been made. However, it is normally desirable that the application should be made on notice, even where a charge has not been made. In appropriate circumstances, instead of proceeding under para 11, resort should be had to the procedure under the Bankers' Books Evidence Act 1879 (in PART II: EVIDENCE, ante); see *R v Epsom Justices, ex p Bell* [1989] STC 169, [1988] Crim LR 684.

When an application is made for an order *ex parte*, the justice must consider whether it is appropriate to proceed in that way, bearing in mind that the balance is in favour of proceeding *inter partes* unless there is a real reason to believe something of value to the investigation may be lost. If it is decided to proceed *inter partes* it will normally be appropriate to give notice not only to those from whom access is sought but to others likely to be directly affected by the order, such as suspects (*R v City of London Magistrates' Court, ex p Asif* [1996] Crim LR 725).

[2] The justice himself must be satisfied that there are reasonable grounds and not merely rely on a statement of belief by a customs officer. Any order made ought not to be without limit of subject-matter or time. Where an offence has been charged, the application should specify the grounds upon which it is believed that such an offence has been committed (*R v Epsom Justices, ex p Bell* [1989] STC 169, [1988] Crim LR 684, DC).

[3] Where following an *inter partes* application an access order under paragraph 11 is made, the justice has no jurisdiction to make an order for costs in favour of the person against whom the order is made under s 19 of the Prosecution of Offences Act 1985 or regulation 3 of the Costs in Criminal Cases (General) Regulations 1986 because such application does not constitute criminal proceedings (*Customs and Excise Comrs v City of London Magistrates' Court* [2000] 1 WLR 2020, [2000] 2 Cr App Rep 348, [2000] Crim LR 841, DC).

*Procedure where documents etc are removed*

**12.** (1) An authorised person who removes anything in the exercise of a power conferred by or under paragraph 10 or 11 above shall, if so requested by a person showing himself—

(*a*) to be the occupier of premises from which it was removed, or

(*b*) to have had custody or control of it immediately before the removal,

provide that person with a record of what he removed.

(2) The authorised person shall provide the record within a reasonable time from the making of the request for it.

(3) Subject to sub-paragraph (7) below, if a request for permission to be granted access to anything which—

(*a*) has been removed by an authorised person, and
(*b*) is retained by the Commissioners for the purposes of investigating an offence,

is made to the officer in overall charge of the investigation by a person who had custody or control of the thing immediately before it was so removed or by someone acting on behalf of such a person, the officer shall allow the person who made the request access to it under the supervision of an authorised person.

(4) Subject to sub-paragraph (7) below, if a request for a photograph or copy of any such thing is made to the officer in overall charge of the investigation by a person who had custody or control of the thing immediately before it was so removed, or by someone acting on behalf of such a person, the officer shall—

(*a*) allow the person who made the request access to it under the supervision of an authorised person for the purpose of photographing it or copying it, or
(*b*) photograph or copy it, or cause it to be photographed or copied.

(5) Where anything is photographed or copied under sub-paragraph (4)(*b*) above the photograph or copy shall be supplied to the person who made the request.

(6) The photograph or copy shall be supplied within a reasonable time from the making of the request.

(7) There is no duty under this paragraph to grant access to, or to supply a photograph or copy of, anything if the officer in overall charge of the investigation for the purposes of which it was removed has reasonable grounds for believing that to do so would prejudice—

(*a*) that investigation;
(*b*) the investigation of an offence other than the offence for the purposes of the investigation of which the thing was removed; or
(*c*) any criminal proceedings which may be brought as a result of—
 (i) the investigation of which he is in charge, or
 (ii) any such investigation as is mentioned in paragraph (*b*) above.

(8) Any reference in this paragraph to the officer in overall charge of the investigation is a reference to the person whose name and address are endorsed on the warrant or order concerned as being the officer so in charge.

**13.** (1) Where, on an application made as mentioned in sub-paragraph (2) below, the appropriate judicial authority is satisfied that a person has failed to comply with a requirement imposed by paragraph 12 above, the authority may order that person to comply with the requirement within such time and in such manner as may be specified in the order.

(2) An application under sub-paragraph (1) above shall be made—

(*a*) in the case of a failure to comply with any of the requirements imposed by paragraph 12(1) and (2) above, by the occupier of the premises from which the thing in question was removed or by the person who had custody or control of it immediately before it was so removed, and
(*b*) in any other case, by the person who had such custody or control.

(3) In this paragraph "the appropriate judicial authority" means—

(*a*) in England and Wales, a magistrates' court;
(*b*) in Scotland, the sheriff; and
(*c*) in Northern Ireland, a court of summary jurisdiction.

(4) In England and Wales and Northern Ireland, an application for an order under this paragraph shall be made by way of complaint; and sections 21 and 42(2) of the Interpretation Act (Northern Ireland) 1954 shall apply as if any reference in those provisions to any enactment included a reference to this paragraph.

*Evidence by certificate, etc*

**14.** (1) A certificate of the Commissioners—

(*a*) that a person was or was not, at any date, registered under this Act; or
(*b*) that any return required by or under this Act has not been made or had not been made at any date; or
(*c*) that any statement or notification required to be submitted or given to the Commissioners in accordance with any regulations under paragraph 2(3) or (4) above has not been submitted or given or had not been submitted or given at any date;
(*d*) *repealed*;

shall be sufficient evidence of that fact until the contrary is proved.

(2) A photograph of any document furnished to the Commissioners for the purposes of this Act and certified by them to be such a photograph shall be admissible in any proceedings, whether civil or criminal, to the same extent as the document itself.

(3) Any document purporting to be a certificate under sub-paragraph (1) or (2) above shall be deemed to be such a certificate until the contrary is proved.

## Commissioners for Revenue and Customs Act 2005[1]

(2005 c 11)

*Information*

7.11027 **17. Use of information** (1) Information acquired by the Revenue and Customs in connection with a function may be used by them in connection with any other function.

(2) Subsection (1) is subject to any provision which restricts or prohibits the use of information and which is contained in—

(*a*) this Act,
(*b*) any other enactment, or
(*c*) an international or other agreement to which the United Kingdom or Her Majesty's Government is party.

(3) In subsection (1) "the Revenue and Customs" means—

(*a*) the Commissioners,
(*b*) an officer of Revenue and Customs,
(*c*) a person acting on behalf of the Commissioners or an officer of Revenue and Customs,
(*d*) a committee established by the Commissioners,
(*e*) a member of a committee established by the Commissioners,

(*f*) the Commissioners of Inland Revenue (or any committee or staff of theirs or anyone acting on their behalf),

(*g*) the Commissioners of Customs and Excise (or any committee or staff of theirs or anyone acting on their behalf), and

(*h*) a person specified in section 6(2) or 7(3).

(4) In subsection (1) "function" means a function of any of the persons listed in subsection (3).

(5) In subsection (2) the reference to an enactment does not include—

(*a*) an Act of the Scottish Parliament or an instrument made under such an Act, or

(*b*) an Act of the Northern Ireland Assembly or an instrument made under such an Act.

(6) Part 2 of Schedule 2 (which makes provision about the supply and other use of information in specified circumstances) shall have effect.

[Commissioners for Revenue and Customs Act 2005, s 17.]

---

1 This Act creates a new department integrating the Inland Revenue and HM Customs and Excise. The title of the new department is "Her Majesty's Revenue and Customs" (HMRC). Like its predecessors, the new department is a non-ministerial government department.

The Customs and Excise Prosecutions Office was created in 2003. The Act puts this office on a statutory footing and it now undertakes all the prosecutions of the new department. The new prosecutions office is called the "Revenue and Customs Prosecutions Office" (RCPO). It was merged with the Crown Prosecution Service on 1 January 2010. The provisions reproduced below are in force.

Sections 1–16 deal with the appointment and functions of Commissioners for HMRC and are not reproduced in this work.

**7.11028 18. Confidentiality** (1) Revenue and Customs officials may not disclose information which is held by the Revenue and Customs in connection with a function of the Revenue and Customs.

(2) But subsection (1) does not apply to a disclosure—

(*a*) which—

(i) is made for the purposes of a function of the Revenue and Customs, and

(ii) does not contravene any restriction imposed by the Commissioners,

(*b*) which is made in accordance with section 20 or 21,

(*c*) which is made for the purposes of civil proceedings (whether or not within the United Kingdom) relating to a matter in respect of which the Revenue and Customs have functions,

(*d*) which is made for the purposes of a criminal investigation or criminal proceedings (whether or not within the United Kingdom) relating to a matter in respect of which the Revenue and Customs have functions,

(*e*) which is made in pursuance of an order of a court,

(*f*) which is made to Her Majesty's Inspectors of Constabulary, the Scottish inspectors or the Northern Ireland inspectors for the purpose of an inspection by virtue of section 27,

(*g*) which is made to the Independent Police Complaints Commission, or a person acting on its behalf, for the purpose of the exercise of a function by virtue of section 28, or

(*h*) which is made with the consent of each person to whom the information relates; or

(*I*)which is made to the Scottish Ministers in connection with the collection and management of a devolved tax within the meaning of the Scotland Act 1998.

(2A) Information disclosed in reliance on subsection (2)(*i*) may not be further disclosed without the consent of the Commissioners (which may be general or specific).

(3) Subsection (1) is subject to any other enactment permitting disclosure.

(4) In this section—

(*a*) a reference to Revenue and Customs officials is a reference to any person who is or was—

(i) a Commissioner,

(ii) an officer of Revenue and Customs,

(iii) a person acting on behalf of the Commissioners or an officer of Revenue and Customs, or

(iv) a member of a committee established by the Commissioners,

(*b*) a reference to the Revenue and Customs has the same meaning as in section 17,

(*c*) a reference to a function of the Revenue and Customs is a reference to a function of—

(i) the Commissioners, or

(ii) an officer of Revenue and Customs,

(*d*) a reference to the Scottish inspectors or the Northern Ireland inspectors has the same meaning as in section 27, and

(*e*) a reference to an enactment does not include—

(i) an Act of the Scottish Parliament or an instrument made under such an Act, or

(ii) an Act of the Northern Ireland Assembly or an instrument made under such an Act.

[Commissioners for Revenue and Customs Act 2005, s 18 amended by the Scotland Act 2012, s 44(2)(b).]

7.11029 **19. Wrongful disclosure** (1) A person commits an offence if he contravenes section 18(1) or 20(9) by disclosing revenue and customs information relating to a person whose identity—

(*a*) is specified in the disclosure, or

(*b*) can be deduced from it.

(2) In subsection (1) "revenue and customs information relating to a person" means information about, acquired as a result of, or held in connection with the exercise of a function of the Revenue and Customs (within the meaning given by section 18(4)(*c*)) in respect of the person; but it does not include information about internal administrative arrangements of Her Majesty's Revenue and Customs (whether relating to Commissioners, officers or others).

(3) It is a defence for a person charged with an offence under this section of disclosing information to prove that he reasonably believed—

(*a*) that the disclosure was lawful, or

(*b*) that the information had already and lawfully been made available to the public.

(4) A person guilty of an offence under this section shall be liable—

(*a*) on conviction on indictment, to imprisonment for a term not exceeding two years, to a fine or to both, or

(*b*) on summary conviction, to imprisonment for a term not exceeding 12 months, to a fine not exceeding the statutory maximum or to both.

(5) A prosecution for an offence under this section may be instituted in England and Wales only by or with the consent of the Director of Public Prosecutions.

(6) A prosecution for an offence under this section may be instituted in Northern Ireland only—

(*a*) by the Commissioners, or

(*b*) with the consent of the Director of Public Prosecutions for Northern Ireland.

(7) *Scotland, Northern Ireland.*

(8) This section is without prejudice to the pursuit of any remedy or the taking of any action in relation to a contravention of section 18(1) or 20(9) (whether or not this section applies to the contravention).

[Commissioners for Revenue and Customs Act 2005, s 19 as amended by SI 2014/834.]

7.11030 **20. Public interest disclosure** (1) Disclosure is in accordance with this section (as mentioned in section 18(2)(*b*)) if—

(*a*) it is made on the instructions of the Commissioners (which may be general or specific),

(*b*) it is of a kind—

(i) to which any of subsections (2) to (7) applies, or

(ii) specified in regulations made by the Treasury, and

(*c*) the Commissioners are satisfied that it is in the public interest.

(2) This subsection applies to a disclosure made—

(*a*) to a person exercising public functions (whether or not within the United Kingdom),

(*b*) for the purposes of the prevention or detection of crime, and

(*c*) in order to comply with an obligation of the United Kingdom, or Her Majesty's Government, under an international or other agreement relating to the movement of persons, goods or services.

(3) This subsection applies to a disclosure if—

(*a*) it is made to a body which has responsibility for the regulation of a profession,

(*b*) it relates to misconduct on the part of a member of the profession, and

(*c*) the misconduct relates to a function of the Revenue and Customs.

(4) This subsection applies to a disclosure if—

(*a*) it is made to a constable, and

(*b*) either—

(i) the constable is exercising functions which relate to the movement of persons or goods into or out of the United Kingdom, or

(ii) the disclosure is made for the purposes of the prevention or detection of crime.

(5) This subsection applies to a disclosure if it is made—

(*a*) to the National Criminal Intelligence Service, and

(*b*) for a purpose connected with its functions under section 2(2) of the Police Act 1997 (c 50) (criminal intelligence).

(6) This subsection applies to a disclosure if it is made—

(*a*) to a person exercising public functions in relation to public safety or public health, and

(*b*) for the purposes of those functions.

(7) This subsection applies to a disclosure if it—

(*a*) is made to the National Policing Improvement Agency for the purpose of enabling information to be entered in a computerised database, and

(*b*) relates to—

(i) a person suspected of an offence,

(ii) a person arrested for an offence,

(iii) the results of an investigation, or

(iv) anything seized.

(8) Regulations under subsection (1)(*b*)(ii)—

(*a*) may specify a kind of disclosure only if the Treasury are satisfied that it relates to—

(i) national security,

(ii) public safety,

(iii) public health, or

(iv) the prevention or detection of crime;

(*b*) may make provision limiting or restricting the disclosures that may be made in reliance on the regulations; and that provision may, in particular, operate by reference to—

(i) the nature of information,

(ii) the person or class of person to whom the disclosure is made,

(iii) the person or class of person by whom the disclosure is made,

(iv) any other factor, or

(v) a combination of factors;

(*c*) shall be made by statutory instrument;

(*d*) may not be made unless a draft has been laid before and approved by resolution of each House of Parliament.

(9) Information disclosed in reliance on this section may not be further disclosed without the consent of the Commissioners (which may be general or specific); (but the Commissioners shall be taken to have consented to further disclosure by use of the computerised database of information disclosed by virtue of subsection (7)).

[Commissioners for Revenue and Customs Act 2005, s 20 as amended by the Police and Justice Act 2006, Sch 1.]

7.11031 **21. Disclosure to prosecuting authority** (1) Disclosure is in accordance with this section (as mentioned in section 18(2)(*b*)) if made—

(*a*) to a prosecuting authority, and

(*b*) for the purpose of enabling the authority—

(i) to consider whether to institute criminal proceedings in respect of a matter considered in the course of an investigation conducted by or on behalf of Her Majesty's Revenue and Customs,

(ii) to give advice in connection with a criminal investigation or criminal proceedings, or

(iii) in the case of the Director of Public Prosecutions, to exercise his functions under, or in relation to, Part 5 or 8 of the Proceeds of Crime Act 2002 (c 29).

(2) In subsection (1) "prosecuting authority" means—

(*a*) the Director of Public Prosecutions,

(*b*) in Scotland, the Lord Advocate or a procurator fiscal, and

(*c*) in Northern Ireland, the Director of Public Prosecutions for Northern Ireland.

(2A) In subsection (1) "criminal investigation" means any process—

(i) for considering whether an offence has been committed,

(ii) for discovering by whom an offence has been committed, or

(iii) as a result of which an offence is alleged to have been committed.

(3) Information disclosed to a prosecuting authority in accordance with this section may not be further disclosed except—

(*a*) for a purpose connected with the exercise of the prosecuting authority's functions, or

(*b*) with the consent of the Commissioners (which may be general or specific).

(4) A person commits an offence if he contravenes subsection (3).

(5) It is a defence for a person charged with an offence under this section to prove that he reasonably believed—

(*a*) that the disclosure was lawful, or

(*b*) that the information had already and lawfully been made available to the public.

(6) A person guilty of an offence under this section shall be liable—

(*a*) on conviction on indictment, to imprisonment for a term not exceeding two years, to a fine or to both, or

(*b*) on summary conviction, to imprisonment for a term not exceeding 12 months, to a fine not exceeding the statutory maximum or to both[1].

(7) A prosecution for an offence under this section may be instituted in England and Wales only by or with the consent of the Director of Public Prosecutions.

(8) A prosecution for an offence under this section may be instituted in Northern Ireland only—

(*a*) by the Commissioners, or

(*b*) with the consent of the Director of Public Prosecutions for Northern Ireland.

(9) In the application of this section to Scotland or Northern Ireland the reference in subsection (6)(*b*) to 12 months shall be taken as a reference to six months.

[Commissioners for Revenue and Customs Act 2005, s 21 as amended by the Serious Crime Act 2007, Sch 8 and SI 2014/834.]

---

1 For procedure in respect of an offence triable either way, see the Magistrates' Courts Act 1908, ss 17A–21, in PART I: MAGISTRATES' COURTS, PROCEDURE, ante.

7.11032 **22. Data protection, &c** Nothing in sections 17 to 21 authorises the making of a disclosure which—

(*a*) contravenes the Data Protection Act 1998 (c 29), or

(*b*) is prohibited by Part 1 of the Regulation of Investigatory Powers Act 2000 (c 23).*

[Commissioners for Revenue and Customs Act 2005, s 22.]

* **Amended by the Investigatory Powers Act 2016, Sch 10 from a date to be appointed.**

7.11033 **23. Freedom of information** (1) Revenue and customs information relating to a person, the disclosure of which is prohibited by section 18(1), is exempt information by virtue of section 44(1)(*a*) of the Freedom of Information Act 2000 (c 36) (prohibitions on disclosure) if its disclosure—

(*a*) would specify the identity of the person to whom the information relates, or

(*b*) would enable the identity of such a person to be deduced.

(1A) Subsections (2) and (3) of section 18 are to be disregarded in determining for the purposes of subsection (1) of this section whether the disclosure of revenue and customs information relating to a person is prohibited by subsection (1) of that section.

(2) Except as specified in subsection (1), information the disclosure of which is prohibited by section 18(1) is not exempt information for the purposes of section 44(1)(*a*) of the Freedom of Information Act 2000.

(3) In subsection (1) "revenue and customs information relating to a person" has the same meaning as in section 19.

[Commissioners for Revenue and Customs Act 2005, s 23 as amended by the Borders, Citizenship and Immigration Act 2009, s 19.]

*Proceedings*

7.11034 **24. Evidence** (1) A document that purports to have been issued or signed by or with the authority of the Commissioners—

(*a*) shall be treated as having been so issued or signed unless the contrary is proved, and

(*b*) shall be admissible in any legal proceedings.

(2) A document that purports to have been issued by the Commissioners and which certifies any of the matters specified in subsection (3) shall (in addition to the matters provided for by subsection (1)(*a*) and (*b*)) be treated as accurate unless the contrary is proved.

(3) The matters mentioned in subsection (2) are—

(*a*) that a specified person was appointed as a commissioner on a specified date,

(*b*) that a specified person was appointed as an officer of Revenue and Customs on a specified date,

(*c*) that at a specified time or for a specified purpose (or both) a function was delegated to a specified Commissioner,

(*d*) that at a specified time or for a specified purpose (or both) a function was delegated to a specified committee, and

(*e*) that at a specified time or for a specified purpose (or both) a function was delegated to another specified person.

(4) A photographic or other copy of a document acquired by the Commissioners shall, if certified by them to be an accurate copy, be admissible in any legal proceedings to the same extent as the document itself.

(5) Section 2 of the Documentary Evidence Act 1868 (c 37) (proof of documents) shall apply to a Revenue and Customs document as it applies in relation to the documents mentioned in that section.

(6) In the application of that section to a Revenue and Customs document the Schedule to that Act shall be treated as if—

(*a*) the first column contained a reference to the Commissioners, and

(*b*) the second column contained a reference to a Commissioner or a person acting on his authority.

(7) In this section—

(*a*) "Revenue and Customs document" means a document issued by or on behalf of the Commissioners, and

(*b*) a reference to the Commissioners includes a reference to the Commissioners of Inland Revenue and to the Commissioners of Customs and Excise.

[Commissioners for Revenue and Customs Act 2005, s 24.]

7.11035 **25. Conduct of civil proceedings** (1) An officer of Revenue and Customs or a person authorised by the Commissioners may conduct civil proceedings, in a magistrates' court or in the sheriff court, relating to a function of the Revenue and Customs.

(1A) An officer of Revenue and Customs or a person authorised by the Commissioners may conduct county court proceedings for the recovery of an amount payable to the Commissioners under or by virtue of an enactment or under a contract settlement.

(2) A solicitor member of the Commissioners' staff may act as a solicitor in connection with civil proceedings relating to a function of the Revenue and Customs.

(3) A legally qualified member of the Commissioners' staff may conduct county court

proceedings relating to a matter specified in section 7.

(4) A court shall grant any rights of audience necessary to enable a person to exercise a function under this section.

(5) In this section—

(*a*) a reference to a function of the Revenue and Customs is a reference to a function of—
(i) the Commissioners, or
(ii) an officer of Revenue and Customs,

(*b*) a reference to civil proceedings is a reference to proceedings other than proceedings in respect of an offence,

(*c*) a reference to county court proceedings is a reference to civil proceedings in a county court,

(*d*) the reference to a legally qualified member of the Commissioners' staff is a reference to a member of staff who has been admitted as a solicitor, or called to the Bar, whether or not he holds a practising certificate, and

(*e*) the reference to a solicitor member of the Commissioners' staff—
(i) except in relation to Scotland, is a reference to a member of staff who has been admitted as a solicitor, whether or not he holds a practising certificate,
(ii) *Scotland.*

(6) In this section "contract settlement" means an agreement made in connection with any person's liability to make a payment to the Commissioners under or by virtue of an enactment.

[Commissioners for Revenue and Customs Act 2005, s 25 as amended by the Finance Act 2008, s 137.]

**7.11036 25A. Certificates of debt** (1) A certificate of an officer of Revenue and Customs that, to the best of that officer's knowledge and belief, a relevant sum has not been paid is sufficient evidence that the sum mentioned in the certificate is unpaid.

(2) In subsection (1) "relevant sum" means a sum payable to the Commissioners under or by virtue of an enactment or under a contract settlement (within the meaning of section 25).

(3) Any document purporting to be such a certificate shall be treated as if it were such a certificate until the contrary is proved.

(4) Subsection (1) has effect subject to any provision treating the certificate as conclusive evidence.

[Commissioners for Revenue and Customs Act 2005, s 25A as inserted by the Finance Act 2008, s 138.]

**7.11037 26. Rewards** The Commissioners may pay a reward to a person in return for a service which relates to a function of—

(*a*) the Commissioners, or

(*b*) an officer of Revenue and Customs.

[Commissioners for Revenue and Customs Act 2005, s 26.]

*Inspection and complaints*

**7.11038 27. Inspection** (1) The Treasury may make regulations conferring functions on Her Majesty's Inspectors of Constabulary, the Scottish inspectors or the Northern Ireland inspectors in relation to—

(*a*) the Commissioners for Her Majesty's Revenue and Customs, and

(*b*) officers of Revenue and Customs.

(2) Regulations under subsection (1)—

(*a*) may—
(i) in relation to Her Majesty's Inspectors of Constabulary, apply (with or without modification) or make provision similar to any provision of sections 54 to 56 of the Police Act 1996 (c 16) (inspection);
(ii) in relation to the Scottish inspectors, apply (with or without modification) or make provision similar to any provision of section 33 or 34 of the Police (Scotland) Act 1967 (c 77) (inspection);
(iii) in relation to the Northern Ireland inspectors, apply (with or without modification) or make provision similar to any provision of section 41 or 42 of the Police (Northern Ireland) Act 1998 (c 32) (inspection);

(*b*) may enable a Minister of the Crown or the Commissioners to require an inspection to be carried out;

(*c*) shall provide for a report of an inspection to be made and, subject to any exceptions required or permitted by the regulations, published;

(*d*) shall provide for an annual report by Her Majesty's Inspectors of Constabulary;

(*e*) may make provision for payment by the Commissioners to or in respect of Her Majesty's Inspectors of Constabulary, the Scottish inspectors or the Northern Ireland inspectors.

(3) An inspection carried out by virtue of this section may not address a matter of a kind which the Comptroller and Auditor General may examine under section 6 of the National Audit Act 1983 (c 44).

(4) An inspection carried out by virtue of this section shall be carried out jointly by Her Majesty's Inspectors of Constabulary and the Scottish inspectors—

(*a*) if it is carried out wholly in Scotland, or

(*b*) in a case where it is carried out partly in Scotland, to the extent that it is carried out there.

(5) Regulations under subsection (1)—

(*a*) shall be made by statutory instrument, and

(*b*) shall be subject to annulment in pursuance of a resolution of either House of Parliament.

(6) In this section—

(*a*) "the Scottish inspectors" means the inspectors of constabulary appointed under section 33(1) of the Police (Scotland) Act 1967, and

(*b*) "the Northern Ireland inspectors" means the inspectors of constabulary appointed under section 41(1) of the Police (Northern Ireland) Act 1998.

[Commissioners for Revenue and Customs Act 2005, s 27.]

**7.11039 28. Complaints and misconduct: England and Wales** (1) The Treasury may make regulations conferring functions on the Independent Police Complaints Commission in relation to—

(*a*) the Commissioners for Her Majesty's Revenue and Customs, and

(*b*) officers of Revenue and Customs.

(2) Regulations under subsection (1)—

(*a*) may apply (with or without modification) or make provision similar to any provision of or made under Part 2 of the Police Reform Act 2002 (c 30) (complaints);

(*b*) may confer on the Independent Police Complaints Commission, or on a person acting on its behalf, a power of a kind conferred by this Act or another enactment on an officer of Revenue and Customs;

(*c*) may make provision for payment by the Commissioners to or in respect of the Independent Police Complaints Commission.

(3) The Independent Police Complaints Commission and the Parliamentary Commissioner for Administration may disclose information to each other for the purposes of the exercise of a function—

(*a*) by virtue of this section, or

(*b*) under the Parliamentary Commissioner Act 1967 (c 13).

(4) The Independent Police Complaints Commission and the Parliamentary Commissioner for Administration may jointly investigate a matter in relation to which—

(*a*) the Independent Police Complaints Commission has functions by virtue of this section, and

(*b*) the Parliamentary Commissioner for Administration has functions by virtue of the Parliamentary Commissioner Act 1967.

(5) Regulations under subsection (1)—

(*a*) shall be made by statutory instrument, and

(*b*) shall be subject to annulment in pursuance of a resolution of either House of Parliament.

(6) Regulations under subsection (1) shall relate to the Commissioners or officers of Revenue and Customs only in so far as their functions are exercised in or in relation to England and Wales.

[Commissioners for Revenue and Customs Act 2005, s 28.]

**7.11040 29. Confidentiality, &c** (1) Where Her Majesty's Inspectors of Constabulary, the Scottish inspectors or the Northern Ireland inspectors obtain information in the course of exercising a function by virtue of section 27—

(*a*) they may not disclose it without the consent of the Commissioners, and

(*b*) they may not use it for any purpose other than the exercise of the function by virtue of section 27.

(2) A report of an inspection by virtue of section 27 may not include information relating to a specified person without his consent.

(3) Where the Independent Police Complaints Commission or a person acting on its behalf obtains information from the Commissioners or an officer of Revenue and Customs, or from the Parliamentary Commissioner for Administration, in the course of exercising a function by virtue of section 28—

(*a*) the Commission or person shall comply with any restriction on disclosure imposed by regulations under that section (and those regulations may, in particular, prohibit disclosure generally or only in specified circumstances or only without the consent of the Commissioners), and

(*b*) the Commission or person may not use the information for any purpose other than the exercise of the function by virtue of that section.

(4) A person commits an offence if he contravenes a provision of this section.

(5) It is a defence for a person charged with an offence under this section of disclosing or using information to prove that he reasonably believed—

(*a*) that the disclosure or use was lawful, or

(*b*) that the information had already and lawfully been made available to the public.

(6) A person guilty of an offence under this section shall be liable—

(*a*) on conviction on indictment, to imprisonment for a term not exceeding two years, to a fine or to both, or

(*b*) on summary conviction, to imprisonment for a term not exceeding 12 months, to a fine not exceeding the statutory maximum or to both[1].

(7) A prosecution for an offence under this section may be instituted in England and Wales only by or with the consent of the Director of Public Prosecutions.

(8) A prosecution for an offence under this section may be instituted in Northern Ireland only—

(*a*) by the Commissioners, or

(*b*) with the consent of the Director of Public Prosecutions for Northern Ireland.

(9) *Scotland, Northern Ireland.*

(10) In this section a reference to the Scottish inspectors or the Northern Ireland inspectors has the same meaning as in section 27.

[Commissioners for Revenue and Customs Act 2005, s 29 as amended by SI 2014/834.]

---

1 For procedure in respect of an offence triable either way, see the Magistrates' Courts Act 1908, ss 17A–21, in PART I: MAGISTRATES' COURTS, PROCEDURE, ante.

*Offences*

7.11041 **30. Impersonation** (1) A person commits an offence if he pretends to be a Commissioner or an officer of Revenue and Customs with a view to obtaining—

(*a*) admission to premises,

(*b*) information, or

(*c*) any other benefit.

(2) A person guilty of an offence under this section shall be liable on summary conviction to—

(*a*) imprisonment for a period not exceeding 51 weeks,

(*b*) a fine not exceeding level 5 on the standard scale, or

(*c*) both.

(3) *Scotland, Northern Ireland.*

[Commissioners for Revenue and Customs Act 2005, s 30.]

7.11042 **31. Obstruction** (1) A person commits an offence if without reasonable excuse he obstructs—

(*a*) an officer of Revenue and Customs,

(*b*) a person acting on behalf of the Commissioners or an officer of Revenue and Customs, or

(*c*) a person assisting an officer of Revenue and Customs.

(2) A person guilty of an offence under this section shall be liable on summary conviction to—

(*a*) imprisonment for a period not exceeding 51 weeks,

(*b*) a fine not exceeding level 3 on the standard scale, or

(*c*) both.

(3) *Scotland, Northern Ireland.*

[Commissioners for Revenue and Customs Act 2005, s 31.]

7.11043 **32. Assault** (1) A person commits an offence if he assaults an officer of Revenue and Customs.

(2) A person guilty of an offence under this section shall be liable on summary conviction to—

(*a*) imprisonment for a period not exceeding 51 weeks,

(*b*) a fine not exceeding level 5 on the standard scale, or

(*c*) both.

(3) *Scotland, Northern Ireland.*

[Commissioners for Revenue and Customs Act 2005, s 32.]

7.11044 **33. Power of arrest** (1) An authorised officer of Revenue and Customs may arrest a person without warrant if the officer reasonably suspects that the person—

(*a*) has committed an offence under section 30, 31 or 32,

(*b*) is committing an offence under any of those sections, or

(*c*) is about to commit an offence under any of those sections.

(2) In subsection (1) "authorised" means authorised by the Commissioners.

(3) Authorisation for the purposes of this section may be specific or general.

(4) *Scotland, Northern Ireland.*

[Commissioners for Revenue and Customs Act 2005, s 33.]

*Prosecutions*

7.11051 **40. Confidentiality** (1) The Crown Prosecution Service may not disclose information which—

(*a*) is held by the Service in connection with any of the Director of Public Prosecution's functions, (*b*) relates to a person whose identity is specified in the disclosure or can be deduced from it, and

(*c*) was disclosed to the Director of Public Prosecutions by Her Majesty's Revenue and Customs for use in connection with a Revenue and Customs function of the Director of Public Prosecutions.

(2) But subsection (1)—

(*a*) does not apply to a disclosure which—

(i) is made for the purposes of a function of the Director of Public Prosecutions, and

(ii) does not contravene any restriction imposed by the Director of Public Prosecutions,

(*b*) does not apply to a disclosure made to Her Majesty's Revenue and Customs in connection with a function of the Revenue and Customs (within the meaning of section 25),

(*c*) does not apply to a disclosure made for the purposes of a criminal investigation or criminal proceedings (whether or not within the United Kingdom),

(*ca*) does not apply to a disclosure made for the purposes of—

(i) the exercise of any functions of the prosecutor under Parts 2, 3 and 4 of the Proceeds of Crime Act 2002 (c 29),

(ii) the exercise of any functions of the Serious Organised Crime Agency under that Act,

(iii) the exercise of any functions of the Director of the Serious Fraud Office, the Director of Public Prosecutions for Northern Ireland or the Scottish Ministers under, or in relation to, Part 5 or 8 of that Act,

(iv) the exercise of any functions of an officer of Revenue and Customs, an accredited financial investigator or a constable under Chapter 3 of Part 5 of that Act, or

(v) investigations or proceedings outside the United Kingdom which have led or may lead to the making of an external order within the meaning of section 447 of that Act,

(*cb*) *repealed*

(*d*) does not apply to a disclosure which in the opinion of the Director of Public Prosecutions is desirable for the purpose of safeguarding national security,

(*e*) does not apply to a disclosure made in pursuance of an order of a court,

(*ea*) does not apply to a disclosure made with the consent of the Commissioners (which may be general or specific),

(*f*) does not apply to a disclosure made with the consent of each person to whom the information relates, and

(*g*) is subject to any other enactment.

(3) A person commits an offence if he contravenes subsection (1).

(4) Subsection (3) does not apply to the disclosure of information about internal administrative arrangements of the Crown Prosecution Service (whether relating to a member of the Service or to another person).

(5) It is a defence for a person charged with an offence under this section of disclosing information to prove that he reasonably believed—

(*a*) that the disclosure was lawful, or

(*b*) that the information had already and lawfully been made available to the public.

(6) In this section a reference to the Crown Prosecution Service includes a reference to—

(*za*) former members of the Crown Prosecution Service,

(*zb*) persons who hold or have held appointment under section 5 of the Prosecution of Offences Act 1985,

(*a*) former members of the Revenue and Customs Prosecutions Office, and

(*b*) persons who have held appointment under section 38.

(6A) In this section "Revenue and Customs function of the Director of Public Prosecutions" means—

(*a*) a function of the Director of Public Prosecutions under section 3(2)(*ab*), (*bb*) or (*ee*) of the Prosecution of Offences Act 1985, or

(b) a function of the Director of Public Prosecutions under the Proceeds of Crime Act 2002 that relates to a function of the Commissioners for Her Majesty's Revenue and Customs or an officer of Revenue and Customs.

(7) A person guilty of an offence under this section shall be liable—

(*a*) on conviction on indictment, to imprisonment for a term not exceeding two years, to a fine or to both, or

(*b*) on summary conviction, to imprisonment for a term not exceeding 12 months, to a fine not exceeding the statutory maximum or to both[1].

(8) A prosecution for an offence under this section may be instituted in England and Wales only

by or with the consent of the Director of Public Prosecutions.

(9) A prosecution for an offence under this section may be instituted in Northern Ireland only—

(*a*) by the Commissioners, or

(*b*) with the consent of the Director of Public Prosecutions for Northern Ireland.

(10) *Scotland, Northern Ireland.*

(10A) *Repealed.*

(11) In subsection (2) the reference to an enactment does not include—

(*a*) an Act of the Scottish Parliament or an instrument made under such an Act, or

(*b*) an Act of the Northern Ireland Assembly or an instrument made under such an Act.

[Commissioners for Revenue and Customs Act 2005, s 40 as amended by the Serious Crime Act 2007, Schs 8 and 11 and SI 2014/834.]

---

1 For procedure in respect of an offence triable either way, see the Magistrates' Courts Act 1908, ss 17A–21, in PART I: MAGISTRATES' COURTS, PROCEDURE, ante.

*General*

7.11054 **51. Interpretation** (1) In this Act—

except where otherwise expressly provided, "enactment" includes—

(*a*) an Act of the Scottish Parliament,

(*b*) an instrument made under an Act of the Scottish Parliament,

(*c*) Northern Ireland legislation, and

*d*) an instrument made under Northern Ireland legislation,

"officer of Revenue and Customs" means a person appointed under section 2, and

"revenue" has the meaning given by section 5(4).

(2) In this Act—

(*a*) "function" means any power or duty (including a power or duty that is ancillary to another power or duty), and

(*b*) a reference to the functions of the Commissioners or of officers of Revenue and Customs is a reference to the functions conferred—

(i) by or by virtue of this Act, or

(ii) by or by virtue of any enactment passed or made after the commencement of this Act.

(3) A reference in this Act, in an enactment amended by this Act or, subject to express provision to the contrary, in any future enactment, to responsibility for collection and management of revenue has the same meaning as references to responsibility for care and management of revenue in enactments passed before this Act.

(4) In this Act a reference to information acquired in connection with a matter includes a reference to information held in connection with that matter.

[Commissioners for Revenue and Customs Act 2005, s 51.]

7.11055 **53. Commencement** (1) This Act shall come into force in accordance with provision made by order[1] of the Treasury.

(2) An order under subsection (1)—

(*a*) may make provision generally or only in relation to specified provisions or purposes,

(*b*) may include transitional, consequential or incidental provision or savings, and

(*c*) shall be made by statutory instrument.

[Commissioners for Revenue and Customs Act 2005, s 53.]

---

1 The Commissioners for Revenue and Customs Act 2005 (Commencement) Order 2005, SI 2005/1126, brought the Act fully into force.

7.11056 **55. Transitional: penalties** (1) In relation to an offence under section 19 committed before the commencement of section 282 of the Criminal Justice Act 2003 (c 44) (short sentences) the reference in section 19(4)(*b*) to 12 months shall have effect as if it were a reference to six months.

(2) In relation to an offence under section 21 committed before the commencement of section 282 of the Criminal Justice Act (short sentences), the reference in section 21(6)(*b*) to 12 months shall have effect as if it were a reference to six months.

(3) In relation to an offence under section 29 committed before the commencement of section 282 of the Criminal Justice Act 2003 (c 44) (short sentences) the reference in section 29(6)(*b*) to 12 months shall have effect as if it were a reference to six months.

(4) In relation to an offence under section 30 committed before the commencement of section 281(4) and (5) of the Criminal Justice Act 2003 (51 week maximum term of sentences) the reference in section 30(2)(*a*) to 51 weeks shall have effect as if it were a reference to six months.

(5) In relation to an offence under section 31 committed before the commencement of section 281(4) and (5) of the Criminal Justice Act 2003 (51 week maximum term of sentences) the reference in section 31(2)(*a*) to 51 weeks shall have effect as if it were a reference to one month.

(6) In relation to an offence under section 32 committed before the commencement of section 281(4) and (5) of the Criminal Justice Act 2003 (51 week maximum term of sentences) the

reference in section 32(2)(*a*) to 51 weeks shall have effect as if it were a reference to six months.

(7) In relation to an offence under section 40 committed before the commencement of section 282 of the Criminal Justice Act 2003 (short sentences) the reference in section 40(7)(*b*) to 12 months shall have effect as if it were a reference to six months.

[Commissioners for Revenue and Customs Act 2005, s 55.]

7.11057 56. **Extent** (1) This Act extends to the United Kingdom.

(2) But an amendment, modification or repeal effected by this Act has the same extent as the enactment (or the relevant part of the enactment) to which it relates.

[Commissioners for Revenue and Customs Act 2005, s 56.]

7.11058 57. **Short title** This Act may be cited as the Commissioners for Revenue and Customs Act 2005.

[Commissioners for Revenue and Customs Act 2005, s 57.]

# Finance Act 2014[1]

(2014 c 26)

## Part 5
## Promoters of Tax Avoidance Schemes

[1] Part 5 contains ss 234–283. It is concerned with tax avoidance schemes. Within this PART offences are created. The relevant provisions are reproduced below. As to the application of Part 5 to partnerships, see s 281 and Sch 36 (not reproduced in this work).

*Obtaining information and documents*

7.11058A 255. **Power to obtain information and documents** (1) An authorised officer, or an officer of Revenue and Customs with the approval of an authorised officer, may by notice in writing require any person ("P") to whom this section applies—

(*a*) to provide information, or

(*b*) to produce a document,

if the information or document is reasonably required by the officer for any of the purposes in subsection (3).

(2) This section applies to—

(*a*) any person who is a monitored promoter, and

(*b*) any person who is a relevant intermediary in relation to a monitored proposal of a monitored promoter,

and in either case that monitored promoter is referred to below as "the relevant monitored promoter".

(3) The purposes mentioned in subsection (1) are—

(*a*) considering the possible consequences of implementing a monitored proposal of the relevant monitored promoter for the tax position of persons implementing the proposal,

(*b*) checking the tax position of any person who the officer reasonably believes has implemented a monitored proposal of the relevant monitored promoter, or

(*c*) checking the tax position of any person who the officer reasonably believes has entered into transactions forming monitored arrangements of the relevant monitored promoter.

(4) A person is a "relevant intermediary" in relation to a monitored proposal if the person meets the conditions in section 236(*a*) to (*c*) (meaning of "intermediary") in relation to the proposal at any time after the person has been notified of a promoter reference number of a person who is a promoter in relation to the proposal.

(5) In this section "checking" includes carrying out an investigation or enquiry of any kind.

(6) In this section "tax position", in relation to a person, means the person's position as regards any tax, including the person's position as regards—

(*a*) past, present and future liability to pay any tax,

(*b*) penalties and other amounts that have been paid, or are or may be payable, by or to the person in connection with any tax,

(*c*) claims, elections, applications and notices that have been or may be made or given in connection with the person's liability to pay any tax,

(*d*) deductions or repayments of tax, or of sums representing tax, that the person is required to make—

(i) under PAYE regulations, or

(ii) by or under any other provision of the Taxes Acts, and

(*e*) the withholding by the person of another person's PAYE income (as defined in section 683 of ITEPA 2003).

(7) In this section the reference to the tax position of a person—

(*a*) includes the tax position of a company that has ceased to exist and an individual who has died, and (*b*) is to the person's tax position at any time or in relation to any period.

(8) A notice under subsection (1) which is given for the purpose of checking the tax position of a person mentioned in subsection (3)(*b*) or (*c*) may not be given more than 4 years after the person's death.

(9) A notice under subsection (1) may specify or describe the information or documents to be provided or produced.

(10) Information or a document required as a result of a notice under subsection (1) must be provided or produced within—

(*a*) the period of 10 days beginning with the day on which the notice was given, or

(*b*) such longer period as the officer who gives the notice may direct.

[Finance Act 2014, s 255.]

**7.11058B 256. Tribunal approval for certain uses of power under section 255** (1) An officer of Revenue and Customs may not, without the approval of the tribunal, give a notice under section 255 requiring a person ("A") to provide information or produce a document which relates (in whole or in part) to a person who is neither A nor an undertaking in relation to which A is a parent undertaking.

(2) An officer of Revenue and Customs may apply to the tribunal for the approval required by subsection (1); and an application for approval may be made without notice.

(3) The tribunal may approve the giving of the notice only if—

(*a*) the application for approval is made by, or with the agreement of, an authorised officer,

(*b*) the tribunal is satisfied that, in the circumstances, the officer giving the notice is justified in doing so,

(*c*) the person to whom the notice is to be given has been informed that the information or documents referred to in the notice are required and given a reasonable opportunity to make representations to an officer of Revenue and Customs, and

(*d*) the tribunal has been given a summary of any representations made by that person.

(4) Where a notice is given under section 255 with the approval of the tribunal, it must state that it is given with that approval.

(5) Paragraphs (*c*) and (*d*) of subsection (3) do not apply to the extent that the tribunal is satisfied that taking the action specified in those paragraphs might prejudice the assessment or collection of tax.

(6) In subsection (1) "parent undertaking" and "undertaking" have the same meaning as in the Companies Acts (see section 1161 and 1162 of, and Schedule 7 to, the Companies Act 2006).

(7) A decision of the tribunal under this section is final (despite the provisions of sections 11 and 13 of the Tribunals, Courts and Enforcement Act 2007).

[Finance Act 2014, s 256.]

**7.11058C 257. Ongoing duty to provide information following HMRC notice** (1) An authorised officer, or an officer of Revenue and Customs with the approval of an authorised officer, may give a notice to a person ("P") in relation to whom a monitoring notice has effect.

(2) A person to whom a notice is given under subsection (1) must provide prescribed information and produce prescribed documents relating to—

(*a*) all the monitored proposals and all the monitored arrangements in relation to which the person is a promoter at the time of the notice, and

(*b*) all the monitored proposals and all the monitored arrangements in relation to which the person becomes a promoter after that time.

(3) The duty under subsection (2)(*b*) does not apply in relation to any proposals or arrangements in relation to which the person first becomes a promoter after the monitoring notice ceases to have effect.

(4) A notice under subsection (1) must specify the time within which information must be provided or a document produced and different times may be specified for different cases.

[Finance Act 2014, s 257.]

**7.11058D 258. Duty of person dealing with non-resident monitored promoter** (1) This section applies where a monitored promoter who is resident outside the United Kingdom has failed to comply with a duty under section 255 or 257 to provide information about a monitored proposal or monitored arrangements.

(2) An authorised officer, or an officer of Revenue and Customs with the approval of an authorised officer, may give a notice to a relevant person which—

(*a*) specifies or describes the information which the monitored promoter has failed to provide, and

(*b*) requires the person to provide the information.

(3) A "relevant person" means—

(*a*) any person who is an intermediary in relation to the monitored proposal concerned, and

(*b*) any person ("A") to whom the monitored promoter has made a firm approach in relation to the monitored proposal concerned with a view to making the proposal available for implementation by a person other than A.

(4) If an authorised officer is not aware of any person to whom a notice could be given under

subsection (2) the authorised officer, or an officer of Revenue and Customs with the approval of the authorised officer, may give a notice to any person who has implemented the proposal which—

(*a*) specifies or describes the information which the monitored promoter has failed to provide, and

(*b*) requires the person to provide the information.

(5) If the duty mentioned in subsection (1) relates to monitored arrangements an authorised officer, or an officer of Revenue and Customs with the approval of an authorised officer, may give a notice to any person who has entered into any transaction forming part of the monitored arrangements concerned which—

(*a*) specifies or describes the information which the monitored promoter has failed to provide, and

(*b*) requires the person to provide the information.

(6) A notice under this section may be given only if the officer giving the notice reasonably believes that the person to whom the notice is given is able to provide the information requested.

(7) Information required as a result of a notice under this section must be provided within—

(*a*) the period of 10 days beginning with the day on which the notice was given, or

(*b*) such longer period as the officer who gives the notice may direct.

[Finance Act 2014, s 258.]

**7.11058E 259. Monitored promoters: duty to provide information about clients** (1) An authorised officer, or an officer of Revenue and Customs with the approval of an authorised officer, may give notice to a person in relation to whom a monitoring notice has effect ("the monitored promoter").

(2) A person to whom a notice is given under subsection (1) must, for each relevant period, give the officer who gave the notice the information set out in subsection (9) in respect of each person who was its client with reference to that relevant period (see subsections (5) to (8)).

(3) Each of the following is a "relevant period"—

(*a*) the calendar quarter in which the notice under subsection (1) was given but not including any time before the monitoring notice takes effect,

(*b*) the period (if any) beginning with the date the monitoring notice takes effect and ending immediately before the beginning of the period described in paragraph (*a*), and

(*c*) each calendar quarter after the period described in paragraph (*a*) but not including any time after the monitoring notice ceases to have effect.

(4) Information required as a result of a notice under subsection (1) must be given—

(*a*) within the period of 30 days beginning with the end of the relevant period concerned, or

(*b*) in the case of a relevant period within subsection (3)(*b*), within the period of 30 days beginning with the day on which the notice under subsection (1) was given if that period would expire at a later time than the period given by paragraph (a).

(5) A person ("C") is a client of the monitored promoter with reference to a relevant period if—

(*a*) the promoter did any of the things mentioned in subsection (6) in relation to C at any time during that period, or

(*b*) the person falls within subsection (7).

(6) Those things are that the monitored promoter—

(*a*) made a firm approach to C in relation to a relevant proposal with a view to the promoter making the proposal available for implementation by C or another person;

(*b*) made a relevant proposal available for implementation by C;

(*c*) took part in the organisation or management of relevant arrangements entered into by C.

(7) A person falls within this subsection if the person has entered into transactions forming part of relevant arrangements and those arrangements—

(*a*) enable the person to obtain a tax advantage either in that relevant period or a later relevant period, and

(*b*) are either relevant arrangements in relation to which the monitored promoter is or was a promoter, or implement a relevant proposal in relation to which the monitored promoter was a promoter.

(8) But a person is not a client of the monitored promoter with reference to a relevant period if—

(*a*) the person has previously been a client of the monitored promoter with reference to a different relevant period,

(*b*) the promoter complied with the duty in subsection (2) in respect of the person for that relevant period, and

(*c*) the information provided as a result of complying with that duty remains accurate.

(9) The information mentioned in subsection (2) is—

(*a*) the person's name and address, and

(*b*) such other information about the person as may be prescribed.

(10) Where the monitoring notice mentioned in subsection (1) is a replacement monitoring notice, subsection (5)(*b*) does not impose a duty on the monitored promoter concerned to provide information about a person who has entered into transactions forming part of relevant

arrangements (as described in subsection (7)) if the monitored promoter reasonably believes that information about that person has, in relation to those arrangements, already been provided under the original monitoring notice.

[Finance Act 2014, s 259.]

**7.11058F 260. Intermediaries: duty to provide information about clients** (1) An authorised officer, or an officer of Revenue and Customs with the approval of an authorised officer, may give notice to a person ("the intermediary") who is an intermediary in relation to a relevant proposal which is a monitored proposal of a person in relation to whom a monitoring notice has effect ("the monitored promoter").

(2) A person to whom a notice is given under subsection (1) must, for each relevant period, give the officer who gave the notice the information set out in subsection (7) in respect of each person who was its client with reference to that relevant period (see subsections (5) to (6)).

(3) Each of the following is a "relevant period"—

(*a*) the calendar quarter in which the notice under subsection (1) was given but not including any time before the intermediary was first notified under section 250, 251 or 252 of the promoter reference number of the monitored promoter,

(*b*) the period (if any) beginning with the date of the notification under section 250, 251 or 252 and ending immediately before the beginning of the period described in paragraph (*a*), and

(*c*) each calendar quarter after the period described in paragraph (*a*) but not including any time after the monitoring notice mentioned in subsection (1) ceases to have effect.

(4) Information required as a result of a notice under subsection (1) must be given—

(*a*) within the period of 30 days beginning with the end of the relevant period concerned, or

(*b*) in the case of a relevant period within subsection (3)(*b*), within the period of 30 days beginning with the day on which the notice under subsection (1) was given if that period would expire at a later time than the period given by paragraph (a).

(5) A person ("C") is a client of the intermediary with reference to a relevant period if during that period—

(*a*) the intermediary communicated information to C about a monitored proposal in the course of a business, and

(*b*) the communication was made with a view to C, or any other person, entering into transactions forming part of the proposed arrangements.

(6) But a person is not a client of the intermediary with reference to a relevant period if—

(*a*) the person has previously been a client of the intermediary with reference to a different relevant period,

(*b*) the intermediary complied with the duty in subsection (2) in respect of the person for that relevant period, and

(*c*) the information provided as a result of complying with that duty remains accurate.

(7) The information mentioned in subsection (2) is—

(*a*) the person's name and address, and

(*b*) such other information about the person as may be prescribed.

[Finance Act 2014, s 260.]

**7.11058G 261. Enquiry following provision of client information** (1) This section applies where—

(*a*) a person ("the notifying person") has provided information under section 259 or 260 about a person who was a client of the notifying person with reference to a relevant period (within the meaning of the section concerned) in connection with a particular relevant proposal or particular relevant arrangements, and

(*b*) an authorised officer suspects that a person in respect of whom information has not been provided under section 259 or 260—

(i) has at any time been, or is likely to be, a party to transactions implementing the proposal, or

(ii) is a party to a transaction forming (in whole or in part) particular relevant arrangements.

(2) The authorised officer may by notice in writing require the notifying person to provide prescribed information in relation to any person whom the notifying person might reasonably be expected to know—

(*a*) has been, or is likely to be, a party to transactions implementing the proposal, or

(*b*) is a party to a transaction forming (in whole or in part) the relevant arrangements.

(3) But a notice under subsection (2) does not impose a requirement on the notifying person to provide information which the notifying person has already provided to an authorised officer under section 259 or 260.

(4) The notifying person must comply with a requirement under subsection (2) within—

(*a*) 10 days of the notice, or

(*b*) such longer period as the authorised officer may direct.

[Finance Act 2014, s 261.]

**7.11058H 262. Information required for monitoring compliance with conduct notice**
(1) This section applies where a conduct notice has effect in relation to a person.

(2) An authorised officer, or an officer of Revenue and Customs with the approval of an authorised officer, may (as often as is necessary for the purpose mentioned below) by notice in writing require the person—

(*a*) to provide information, or

(*b*) to produce a document,

if the information or document is reasonably required for the purpose of monitoring whether and to what extent the person is complying with the conditions in the conduct notice.

[Finance Act 2014, s 262.]

**7.11058I 263. Duty to notify HMRC of address** If, on the last day of a calendar quarter, a monitoring notice has effect in relation to a person ("the monitored promoter") the monitored promoter must within 30 days of the end of the calendar quarter inform an authorised officer of its current address.

[Finance Act 2014, s 263.]

**7.11058J 264. Failure to provide information: application to tribunal** (1) This section applies where—

(*a*) a person ("P") has provided information or produced a document in purported compliance with section 255, 257, 258, 259, 260, 261 or 262, but

(*b*) an authorised officer suspects that P has not provided all the information or produced all the documents required under the section concerned.

(2) The authorised officer, or an officer of Revenue and Customs with the approval of the authorised officer, may apply to the tribunal for an order requiring P to—

(*a*) provide specified information about persons who are its clients for the purposes of the section to which the application relates,

(*b*) provide specified information, or information of a specified description, about a monitored proposal or monitored arrangements,

(*c*) produce specified documents relating to a monitored proposal or monitored arrangements.

(3) The tribunal may make an order under subsection (2) in respect of information or documents only if satisfied that the officer has reasonable grounds for suspecting that the information or documents—

(*a*) are required under section 255, 257, 258, 259, 260, 261 or 262 (as the case may be), or

(*b*) will support or explain information required under the section concerned.

(4) A requirement by virtue of an order under subsection (2) is to be treated as part of P's duty under section 255, 257, 258, 259, 260, 261 or 262 (as the case may be).

(5) Information or a document required as a result of subsection (2) must be provided, or the document produced, within the period of 10 days beginning with the day on which the order under subsection (2) was made.

(6) An authorised officer may, by direction, extend the 10 day period mentioned in subsection (5).

[Finance Act 2014, s 264.]

**7.11058K 265. Duty to provide information to monitored promoter** (1) This section applies where a person has been notified of a promoter reference number—

(*a*) under section 250 by reason of being a person falling within subsection (2)(*b*) of that section, or

(*b*) under section 251 or 252.

(2) The person notified ("C") must within 10 days notify the person whose promoter reference number it is of—

(*a*) C's national insurance number (if C has one), and

(*b*) C's unique tax reference number (if C has one).

(3) If C has neither a national insurance number nor a unique tax reference number, C must within 10 days inform the person whose promoter reference number it is of that fact.

(4) A unique tax reference number is an identification number allocated to a person by HMRC.

(5) Subsection (2) or (3) does not impose a duty on C to provide information which C has already provided to the person whose promoter reference number it is.

[Finance Act 2014, s 265.]

*Obtaining information and documents: appeals*

**7.11058L 266. Appeals against notices imposing information etc requirements**
(1) This section applies where a person is given a notice under section 255, 257, 258, 259, 260, 261 or 262.

(2) The person to whom the notice is given may appeal against the notice or any requirement under the notice.

(3) Subsection (2) does not apply—

(*a*) to a requirement to provide any information or produce any document that forms part of the person's statutory records, or (*b*) if the tribunal has approved the giving of the notice under section 256.

(4) For the purposes of this section, information or a document forms part of a person's statutory records if it is information or a document which the person is required to keep and preserve under or by virtue of—

(*a*) the Taxes Acts, or

(*b*) any other enactment relating to a tax.

(5) Information and documents cease to form part of a person's statutory records when the period for which they are required to be preserved by the enactments mentioned in subsection (4) has expired.

(6) Notice of appeal must be given—

(*a*) in writing to the officer who gave the notice, and

(*b*) within the period of 30 days beginning with the day on which the notice was given.

(7) The notice of appeal must state the grounds of the appeal.

(8) On an appeal that is notified to the tribunal, the tribunal may—

(*a*) confirm the notice or a requirement under the notice,

(*b*) vary the notice or such a requirement, or

(*c*) set aside the notice or such a requirement.

(9) Where the tribunal confirms or varies the notice or a requirement, the person to whom the notice was given must comply with the notice or requirement—

(*a*) within such period as is specified by the tribunal, or

(*b*) if the tribunal does not specify a period, within such period as is reasonably specified in writing by an officer of Revenue and Customs following the tribunal's decision.

(10) A decision of the tribunal on an appeal under this section is final (despite the provisions of sections 11 and 13 of the Tribunals, Courts and Enforcement Act 2007).

(11) Subject to this section, the provisions of Part 5 of TMA 1970 relating to appeals have effect in relation to an appeal under this section.

[Finance Act 2014, s 266.]

*Obtaining information and documents: supplementary*

**7.11058M 267. Form and manner of providing information** (1) The Commissioners may specify the form and manner in which information required to be provided or documents required to be produced by sections 255 to 264 must be provided or produced if the provision is to be complied with.

(2) The Commissioners may specify that a document must be produced for inspection—

(*a*) at a place agreed between the person and an officer of Revenue and Customs, or

(*b*) at such place (which must not be a place used solely as a dwelling) as an officer of Revenue and Customs may reasonably specify.

(3) The production of a document in compliance with a notice under this Part is not to be regarded as breaking any lien claimed on the document.

[Finance Act 2014, s 267.]

**7.11058N 268. Production of documents: compliance** (1) Where the effect of a notice under section 255, 257 or 262 is to require a person to produce a document, the person may comply with the requirement by producing a copy of the document, subject to any conditions or exceptions that may be prescribed.

(2) Subsection (1) does not apply where—

(*a*) the effect of the notice is to require the person to produce the original document, or

(*b*) an authorised officer, or an officer of Revenue and Customs with the approval of an authorised officer, subsequently makes a request in writing to the person for the original document.

(3) Where an officer requests a document under subsection (2)(*b*), the person to whom the request is made must produce the document—

(*a*) within such period, and

(*b*) at such time and by such means,

as is reasonably requested by the officer.

[Finance Act 2014, s 268.]

**7.11058O 269. Exception for certain documents or information** (1) Nothing in this Part requires a person to provide or produce—

(*a*) information that relates to the conduct of a pending appeal relating to tax or any part of a document containing such information,

(*b*) journalistic material (as defined in section 13 of the Police and Criminal Evidence Act 1984) or information contained in such material, or

(*c*) personal records (as defined in section 12 of the Police and Criminal Evidence Act 1984) or information contained in such records (but see subsection (2)).

(2) A notice under this Part may require a person—

(*a*) to produce documents, or copies of documents, that are personal records, omitting any information whose inclusion (whether alone or with other information) makes the original documents personal records ("personal information"), and (*b*) to provide any information contained in such records that is not personal information.

[Finance Act 2014, s 269.]

**7.11058P 270. Limitation on duty to produce documents** Nothing in this Part requires a person to produce a document—

(*a*) which is not in the possession or power of that person, or

(*b*) if the whole of the document originates more than 6 years before the requirement to produce it would, if it were not for this section, arise.

[Finance Act 2014, s 270.]

**7.11058Q 271. Legal professional privilege** (1) Nothing in this Part requires any person to disclose to HMRC any privileged information.

(2) "Privileged information" means information with respect to which a claim to legal professional privilege by the person who would (ignoring the effect of this section) be required to disclose it, could be maintained in legal proceedings.

(3) In the case of legal proceedings in Scotland, the reference in subsection (2) to legal professional privilege is to be read as a reference to confidentiality of communications.

[Finance Act 2014, s 271.]

**7.11058R 272. Tax advisers** (1) This section applies where a notice is given under section 258(4) or (5) and the person to whom the notice is given is a tax adviser.

(2) The notice does not require a tax adviser—

(*a*) to provide information about relevant communications, or

(*b*) to produce documents which are the tax adviser's property and consist of relevant communications.

(3) Subsection (2) does not have effect in relation to—

(*a*) information explaining any information or document which the person to whom the notice is given has, as tax accountant, assisted any person in preparing for, or delivering to, HMRC, or

(*b*) a document which contains such information.

(4) But subsection (2) is not disapplied by subsection (3) if the information in question has already been provided, or a document containing the information has already been produced, to an officer of Revenue and Customs.

(5) In this section—

"relevant communications" means communications between the tax adviser and—

(*a*) a person in relation to whose tax affairs the tax adviser has been appointed, or

(*b*) any other tax adviser of such a person,

the purpose of which is the giving or obtaining of advice about any of those tax affairs, and

"tax adviser" means a person appointed to give advice about the tax affairs of another person (whether appointed directly by that person or by another tax adviser of that person).

[Finance Act 2014, s 272.]

**7.11058S 273. Confidentiality** (1) No duty of confidentiality or other restriction on disclosure (however imposed) prevents the voluntary disclosure by a relevant client or a relevant intermediary to HMRC of information or documents about—

(*a*) a monitored promoter, or

(*b*) relevant proposals or relevant arrangements in relation to which a monitored promoter is a promoter.

(2) "Relevant client" means a person in relation to whom the monitored promoter mentioned in subsection (1)(*a*) or (*b*)—

(*a*) has made a firm approach in relation to a relevant proposal with a view to making the proposal available for implementation by that person or another person;

(*b*) has made a relevant proposal available for implementation by that person;

(*c*) took part in the organisation or management of relevant arrangements entered into by that person.

(3) "Relevant intermediary" means a person who is an intermediary in relation to a relevant proposal in relation to which the monitored promoter mentioned in subsection (1)(*a*) or (*b*) is a promoter.

(4) The relevant proposal or relevant arrangements mentioned in subsection (2) or (3) need not be the relevant proposals or relevant arrangements to which the disclosure relates.

[Finance Act 2014, s 273.]

*Offences*

**7.11058T 278. Offence of concealing etc documents** (1) A person is guilty of an offence if—

(*a*) the person is required to produce a document by a notice given under section 255,

(*b*) the tribunal approved the giving of the notice under section 256, and

(*c*) the person conceals, destroys or otherwise disposes of, or arranges for the concealment, destruction or disposal of, that document.

(2) Subsection (1) does not apply if the person acts after the document has been produced to an

officer of Revenue and Customs in accordance with section 255, unless the officer has notified the person in writing that the document must continue to be available for inspection (and has not withdrawn the notification).

(3) Subsection (1) does not apply, in a case to which section 268(1) applies, if the person acts after the end of the expiry of 6 months beginning with the day on which a copy of the document was produced in accordance with that section unless, before the expiry of that period, an officer of Revenue and Customs makes a request for the original document under section 268(2)(*b*).

[Finance Act 2014, s 278.]

**7.11058U 279. Offence of concealing etc documents following informal notification**
(1) A person is guilty of an offence if the person conceals, destroys or otherwise disposes of, or arranges for the concealment, destruction or disposal of, a document after an officer of Revenue and Customs has informed the person in writing that—

(*a*) the document is, or is likely, to be the subject of a notice under section 255, and

(*b*) the officer of Revenue and Customs intends to seek the approval of the tribunal to the giving of the notice.

(2) A person is not guilty of an offence under this section if the person acts after—

(*a*) at least 6 months has expired since the person was, or was last, informed as described in subsection (1), or

(*b*) a notice has been given to the person under section 255, requiring the document to be produced.

[Finance Act 2014, s 279.]

**7.11058V 280. Penalties for offences** (1) A person who is guilty of an offence under section 278 or 279 is liable—[1]

(*a*) on summary conviction, to—

(i) in England and Wales, a fine, or

(ii) in Scotland or Northern Ireland, a fine not exceeding the statutory maximum, or

(*b*) on conviction on indictment, to imprisonment for a term not exceeding 2 years or to a fine or both.

(2) In relation to an offence committed before section 85(1) of the Legal Aid, Sentencing and Punishment of Offenders Act 2012 comes into force, subsection (1)(*a*)(i) has effect as if the reference to "a fine" were a reference to "a fine not exceeding the statutory maximum".

---

1 For procedure in respect of offences triable either way, see Magistrates' Courts Act 1980, ss 17–20A (procedure) and s 32 (penalty) in Part I Magistrates; Courts, Procedure, above.

[Finance Act 2014, s 280.]

# TELECOMMUNICATIONS AND BROADCASTING

**Contents**



## Privacy and Electronic Communications (EC Directive) Regulations 2003, SI 2003/2426

(amended by SI 2004/1039, SI 2010/22, SI 2011/1208, SI 2015/355 and SI 2016/524 and 1177)

**7.11059** These Regulations implement arts 2, 4, 5(3), 6 to 13, 15 and 16 of Directive 2002/58/EC of the European Parliament and of the Council of 12 July 2002 concerning the processing of personal data and the protection of privacy in the electronic communications sector (Directive on privacy and electronic communications). No criminal offences are created but remedies for non-compliance are provided in damages (reg 30). Further, the Regulations do not relieve a person of any of his obligations under the Data Protection Act 1998.

A provider of a public electronic communications service has a duty to take measures to safeguard the security of the service, and to comply with the service provider's reasonable requests made for the purposes of taking the measures (reg 5).

An electronic communications network may not be used to store or gain access to information in the terminal equipment of a subscriber or user ("user" is defined as "any individual using a public electronic communications service") unless the subscriber or user is provided with certain information and is given the opportunity to refuse the storage of or access to the information in his terminal equipment (reg 6). Certain restrictions on the processing of traffic data relating to a subscriber or user are imposed on a public communications provider (regs 7 and 8).

Providers of public electronic communications services are to provide subscribers with non-itemised bills on request; with a means of preventing the presentation of calling line identification on a call-by-call basis; and with a means of preventing the presentation of such identification on a per-line basis (regs 9–11).

Restrictions are imposed on the processing of location data, ie data which indicates the geographical position of the terminal equipment of a user of a public electronic communications service (reg 14).

Provision is made for the tracing of malicious or nuisance calls and there is provision in relation to emergency calls, ie 999 or the European emergency call number 112 (regs 15 and 16) and for emergency alerts (reg 16A).

The provider of an electronic communications service is required to stop, on request, the automatic forwarding of calls to a subscriber's line and conditions are set out in relation to directories of subscribers including rights for subscribers to verify, correct or withdraw their data in directories (regs 17 and 18).

Provision is made which prevents calls for direct marketing purposes by an automated calling system without the consent of the subscriber, similarly there are restrictions on the unsolicited use for direct marketing of facsimile machines, unsolicited calls or unsolicited e-mails for these purposes and a prohibition on making calls (whether solicited or unsolicited) for direct marketing purposes where the caller prevents presentation of the identity of the calling line on the called line (regs 19–22). Also, direct marketing by e-mail is prohibited where the identity of the person on whose behalf the communication is made has been disguised or concealed or an address to which requests for such communications to cease may be sent has not been provided (reg 23).

## European Communities Act 1972: regulations

**7.11060** Within the scope of the title Telecommunications and Broadcasting would logically fall the subject matter of a number of regulations made under the very wide enabling power provided in s 2(2) of the European Communities Act 1972. Where such regulations create offences they are noted below:

- Radio Equipment and Telecommunications Terminal Equipment Regulations 2000, SI 2000/730 amended by SI 2003/1903 and 3144, SI 2004/693, SI 2005/281 and SI 2016/1101;
- Authorisation of Frequency Use for the Provision of Mobile Satellite Services (European Union) Regulations 2010, SI 2010/672 amended by SI 2013/174;
- Open Internet Access (EU Regulation) Regulations 2016, SI 2016/607;
- Electromagnetic Compatibility Regulations 2016, SI 2016/1091.

# Telecommunications Act 1984

(1984 c 12)

## Part VII[1]

## Miscellaneous and Supplemental

*Supplemental*

**7.11061 101. General restrictions on disclosure of information** (1) Subject to the following provisions of this section, no information with respect to any particular business which—

(*a*) has been obtained under or by virtue of the provisions of this Act; and

(*b*) relates to the private affairs of any individual or to any particular business,

shall during the lifetime of that individual or so long as that business continues to be carried on, be disclosed without the consent of that individual or the person for the time being carrying on that business.

(2) Subsection (1) above does not apply to any disclosure of information which is made—

(*a*) for the purpose of facilitating the performance of any functions assigned to the Secretary of State or OFCOM by or under this Act;

(*b*) for the purpose of facilitating the performance of any functions of any Minister, any Northern Ireland department, the head of any such department, the Office of Fair Trading, the Commission, the Water Services Regulation Authority, the Gas and Electricity Markets Authority, (*Northern Ireland*), the Office of Rail Regulation, OFCOM, the Civil Aviation Authority or a local weights and measures authority in Great Britain under any of the enactments or subordinate legislation specified in subsection (3) below;

(*bb*) for the purpose of facilitating the carrying out by the Comptroller and Auditor General of any of his functions under any enactment;

(*c*) in connection with the investigation of any criminal offence or for the purposes of any criminal proceedings;

(*d*) for the purpose of any civil proceedings brought under or by virtue of this Act or any of the enactments or subordinate legislation specified in subsection (3) below; or

(*e*) in pursuance of an EU obligation.

(3) The enactments and subordinate legislation referred to in subsection (2) above are—

(*a*) the Trade Descriptions Act 1968;

(*b*) the 1973 Act;

(*c*) the Consumer Credit Act 1974;

(*d*)–(*e*) *repealed*;

(*f*) the Estate Agents Act 1979;

(*g*) the 1980 Act;

(*h*) the Consumer Protection Act 1987;

(*i*) *repealed*;

(*j*) the Water Act 1989, the Water Industry Act 1991 or any of the other consolidation Acts (within the meaning of section 206 of that Act of 1991), or the Water Act 2003;

(*k*) the Electricity Act 1989;

(*l*), (*ll*) *Northern Ireland*;

(*m*) the Railways Act 1993;

(*n*) the Competition Act 1998;

(*o*) Part I of the Transport Act 2000;

(*p*) the Enterprise Act 2002;

(*q*) the Communications Act 2003;

(*r*) the Railways Act 2005;

(*s*), (*t*) *Northern Ireland*;

(*u*) the Business Protection from Misleading Marketing Regulations 2008;

(*v*) the Consumer Protection from Unfair Trading Regulations 2008.

(4) *Repealed.*

(5) Any person who discloses any information in contravention of this section shall be guilty of an offence[2] and liable—

(*a*) on summary conviction, to a fine not exceeding **the statutory maximum**;

(*b*) on conviction on indictment, to imprisonment for a term not exceeding **two years** or to a **fine** or to **both**.

(6) Information obtained by OFCOM in the exercise of functions which are exercisable concurrently with the Office of Fair Trading under Part I of the Competition Act 1998 is subject to Part 9 of the Enterprise Act 2002 (information) and not to subsections (1) to (5) of this section.

[Telecommunications Act 1984, s 101 as amended by the Consumer Protection Act 1987, Schs 4 and 5, SI 1988/915, the Water Act 1989, Sch 25, the Electricity Act 1989, Sch 16, the Water Consolidation (Consequential Provisions) Act 1991, Sch 1, the Competition and Service (Utilities) Act 1992, Sch 1, the Railways Act 1993, Sch 12, the Competition Act 1998, Schs 10 and 14, SI 1999/506, the Utilities Act 2000, s 3(2), SI 2001/4050, the Communications Act 2003, s 406, the Enterprise Act 2002, Sch 25, the Railways Act 2005, Sch 12, the Water Act 2003, Sch 7, the Wireless Telegraphy Act 2006, Sch 9, SI 2008/1277 and SI 2011/1043.]

---

1 Part VII comprises ss 93–110.

2 For procedure in respect of an offence triable either way, see the Magistrates' Courts Act 1980, ss 17A–21 of the Magistrates' Courts Act 1980 in PART I: MAGISTRATES' COURTS, PROCEDURE, ante.

7.11062 **103. Summary proceedings** (1) Proceedings for any offence under this Act which is punishable on summary conviction may be commenced at any time within twelve months next after the commission of the offence.

(2) Subsection (1) above shall not apply for the purposes of an offence under any provision of the Enterprise Act 2002 as applied by virtue of section 13B above.

[Telecommunications Act 1984, s 103 as amended by the Enterprise Act 2002, Sch 25.]

7.11063 **106. General interpretation** (1) In this Act, unless the context otherwise requires—

"the 1973 Act" means the Fair Trading Act 1973;

"the 1980 Act" means the Competition Act 1980;

"the 1981 Act" means the British Telecommunications Act 1981;

"the appointed day" has the meaning given by section 2 above;

"the Commission" means the Competition Commission;

"the excepted liabilities" has the meaning given by section 60(2) above;

"modifications" includes additions, alterations and omissions and cognate expressions shall be construed accordingly;

"OFCOM" means the Office of Communications;

"the successor company" and "the transfer date" have the meanings given by section 60(1) above;

(2), (3) *Repealed.*

(4) Any power conferred on the Secretary of State by this Act to give a direction if it appears to him to be requisite or expedient to do so in the interests of national security or relations with the government of a country or territory outside the United Kingdom includes power to give the direction if it appears to him to be requisite or expedient to do so in order—

(*a*) to discharge, or facilitate the discharge of, an obligation binding on Her Majesty's Government in the United Kingdom by virtue of it being a member of an international organisation or a party to an international agreement;

(*b*) to attain, or facilitate the attainment of, any other objects the attainment of which is, in the Secretary of State's opinion, requisite or expedient in view of Her Majesty's Government in the United Kingdom being a member of such an organisation or a party to such an agreement; or

(*c*) to enable Her Majesty's Government in the United Kingdom to become a member of such an organisation or a party to such an agreement.

(5) For the purposes of any licence granted, approval given or order made under this Act any description or class may be framed by reference to any circumstances whatsoever.

[Telecommunications Act 1984, s 106 as amended by the Statute Law (Repeals) Act 1993, Sch 1, the Communications Act 2003, Sch 19 and SI 1999/506.]

# Broadcasting Act 1990

(1990 c 42)

## PART I[1]

## INDEPENDENT TELEVISION SERVICES

### CHAPTER I

### REGULATION BY COMMISSION OF TELEVISION SERVICES GENERALLY

*Prohibition on providing unlicensed television services*

7.11064 **13. Prohibition on providing television services without a licence** (1) Subject to subsection (2), any person who provides any relevant regulated television service without being authorised to do so by or under a licence under this Part or Part I of the Broadcasting Act 1996 shall be guilty of an offence.

(1A) In subsection (1) "relevant regulated television service" means a service falling, in pursuance of section 211(1) of the Communications Act 2003, to be regulated by OFCOM, other than a television multiplex service.

(2) The Secretary of State may, after consultation with OFCOM by order[1] provide that subsection (1) shall not apply to such services or descriptions of services as are specified in the order.

(3) A person guilty of an offence under this section shall be liable[2]—

(*a*) on summary conviction, to a fine not exceeding the **statutory maximum**;

(*b*) on conviction on indictment, to a **fine**.

(4) No proceedings in respect of an offence under this section shall be instituted—

(*a*) in England and Wales, except by or with the consent of the Director of Public Prosecutions;

(*b*) *Northern Ireland.*

(5) Without prejudice to subsection (3), compliance with this section shall be enforceable by civil proceedings by the Crown for an injunction or interdict or for any other appropriate relief.

(6) Any order under this section shall be subject to annulment in pursuance of a resolution of either House of Parliament.

[Broadcasting Act 1990, s 13 as amended by the Broadcasting Act 1996, Sch 10, SI 1997/1682, SI 2000/54 and the Communications Act 2003, Sch 15.]

---

1 See the Broadcasting Act 1990 (Independent Television Services: Exceptions) Order 1990, SI 1990/2537 and the Broadcasting and (Unlicensed Television Services) Exemption (Revocation) Order 1999, SI 1999/2628.

2 For procedure in respect of an offence which is triable either way, see the Magistrates' Courts Act 1980, ss 17A–21, in PART I: MAGISTRATES' COURTS, PROCEDURE, ante.

## CHAPTER VII
## SUPPLEMENTAL

7.11065 **71. Interpretation of Part I** (1) In this Part (unless the context otherwise requires)—

"the 1981 Act" means the Broadcasting Act 1981;

"additional service" and "additional services licence" have the meaning given by section 48(1) and section 49(10) respectively;

"the appropriate percentage", in relation to any year, has the meaning given by section 19(10);

"cash bid", in relation to a licence, has the meaning given by section 15(7);

"Channel 3" means the system of television broadcasting services established under section 14, and "a Channel 3 licence" means a licence to provide one of the services comprised within that system;

"Channel 4" means the television broadcasting service referred to in section 24(1), and "on Channel 4" means in that service;

"Channel 5" means the television broadcasting service referred to in section 28(1), and "a Channel 5 licence" means a licence to provide that service;

"the Corporation" means the Channel Four Television Corporation established by section 23;

"licence" means a licence under this Part, and "licensed" shall be construed accordingly;

"national Channel 3 service" has the meaning given by section 14(6), and "a national Channel 3 licence" means a licence to provide a national Channel 3 service;

"regional Channel 3 service" has the meaning given by section 14(6), and "a regional Channel 3 licence" means a licence to provide a regional Channel 3 service;

"restricted service" has the meaning given by section 42A;

"S4C" and "S4C Digital" each has the same meaning as in Part 3 of the Communications Act 2003;

"spare capacity" shall be construed in accordance with section 48(2);

"television broadcasting service", "television licensable content service" and "television programme service" each has the same meaning as in Part 3 of the Communications Act 2003.

(2) Where the person who is for the time being the holder of any licence ("the present licence holder") is not the person to whom the licence was originally granted, any reference in this Part (however expressed) to the holder of the licence shall be construed, in relation to any time falling before the date when the present licence holder became the holder of it, as including a reference to a person who was previously the holder of the licence.

[Broadcasting Act 1990, s 71 as amended by the Broadcasting Act 1996, Sch 10 and SI 1997/1682, the Communications Act 2003, Schs 15 and 19 and SI 2009/1968.]

## Part III[1]
## Independent Radio Services

### Chapter I
### Regulations by Authority of Independent Radio Services Generally

*Prohibition on providing unlicensed independent radio services*

7.11066 **97. Prohibition on providing independent radio services without a licence**
(1) Subject to subsection (2), any person who provides any relevant regulated radio service without being authorised to do so by or under a licence under this Part or Part II of the Broadcasting Act 1996 shall be guilty of an offence.

(1A) In subsection (1) "relevant regulated radio service" means a service falling to be regulated by OFCOM under section 245 of the Communications Act 2003, other than a radio multiplex service.

(2) The Secretary of State may, after consultation with OFCOM, by order[2] provide that subsection (1) shall not apply to such services or descriptions of services as are specified in the order.

(3) A person guilty of an offence under this section shall be liable[3]—

(*a*) on summary conviction, to a fine not exceeding the **statutory maximum**;
(*b*) on conviction on indictment, to a **fine**.

(4) No proceedings in respect of an offence under this section shall be instituted—

(*a*) in England and Wales, except by or with the consent of the Director of Public Prosecutions;
(*b*) *Northern Ireland.*

(5) Without prejudice to subsection (3) above, compliance with this section shall be enforceable by civil proceedings by the Crown for an injunction or interdict or for any other appropriate relief.

(6) Any order under this section shall be subject to annulment in pursuance of a resolution of either House of Parliament.

[Broadcasting Act 1990, s 97 as amended by the Broadcasting Act 1996, Sch 10 and the Communications Act 2003, Sch 15.]

---

1 Part III contains Chs I–V, ss 83–126.

2 See the Broadcasting Act 1990 (Independent Radio Services: Exceptions) Orders 1990, SI 1990/2536 and 2007, SI 2007/272.

3 For procedure in respect of an offence which is triable either way, see the Magistrates' Courts Act 1980, ss 17A–21, in Part I: Magistrates' Courts, Procedure, ante.

## Part VII[1]
## Prohibition on Inclusion of Obscene and Other Material in Programme Services

*Supplementary*

7.11067 **167. Power to make copies of recordings** (1) If a justice of the peace is satisfied by information on oath laid by a constable that there is reasonable ground for suspecting that a relevant offence has been committed by any person in respect of a programme included in a programme service, he may make an order authorising any constable to require that person—

(*a*) to produce to the constable a visual or sound recording of any matter included in that programme, if and so far as that person is able to do so; and
(*b*) on the production of such a recording, to afford the constable an opportunity of causing of copy of it to be made.

(2) An order made under this section shall describe the programme to which it relates in a manner sufficient to enable that programme to be identified.

(3) A person who without reasonable excuse fails to comply with any requirement of a constable made by virtue of subsection (1) shall be guilty of an offence and liable on summary conviction to a fine not exceeding the **third level** on the standard scale.

(4) No order shall be made under this section in respect of any recording in respect of which a warrant could be granted under any of the following provisions, namely—

(*a*) section 3 of the Obscene Publications Act 1959;
(*b*) section 24 or 29H of the Public Order Act 1986; and
(*c*) Article 14 of the Public Order (Northern Ireland) Order 1987.

(5) In the application of subsection (1) to England and Wales "relevant offence" means an offence under—

(*a*) section 2 of the Obscene Publications Act 1959; or
(*b*) section 22 or 29F of the Public Order Act 1986.

(6)–(7) *Scotland and Northern Ireland.*

[Broadcasting Act 1990, s 167 as amended by the Criminal Justice and Immigration Act 2008, Sch 26.]

---

1 Part VII contains ss 162–167.

## Part X[1]
## Miscellaneous and General

*Foreign satellite services*

7.11068 **177. Orders proscribing unacceptable foreign satellite services** (1) Subject to the following provisions of this section, the Secretary of State may make an order[2] proscribing a foreign satellite service for the purposes of section 178.

(2) If OFCOM consider that the quality of any relevant foreign satellite service which is brought to their attention is unacceptable and that the service should be the subject of an order under this section, they shall notify to the Secretary of State details of the service and their reasons why they consider such an order should be made.

(3) OFCOM shall not consider a foreign satellite service to be unacceptable for the purposes of subsection (2) unless they are satisfied that there is repeatedly contained in programmes included in the service matter which offends against good taste or decency or is likely to encourage or incite to crime or to lead to disorder or to be offensive to public feeling.

(4) Where the Secretary of State has been notified under subsection (2), he shall not make an order under this section unless he is satisfied that the making of the order—

(*a*) is in the public interest; and

(*b*) is compatible with any international obligations of the United Kingdom.

(5) An order under this section—

(*a*) may make such provision for the purpose of identifying a particular foreign satellite service as the Secretary of State thinks fit; and

(*b*) shall be subject to annulment in pursuance of a resolution of either House of Parliament.

(6) In this section and section 178—

"foreign satellite service" means—

(*a*) a service which is provided by a person who is not for the purposes of the Audiovisual Media Services Directive under the jurisdiction of the United Kingdom and which consists wholly or mainly in the transmission by satellite of television programmes which are capable of being received in the United Kingdom, or

(*b*) a service which consists wholly or mainly in the transmission by satellite from a place outside the United Kingdom of sound programmes which are capable of being received in the United Kingdom.

[Broadcasting Act 1990, s 177 as amended by SI 1997/1682, SI 1998/3196, the Communications Act 2003, Sch 15 and SI 2010/1883.]

---

[1] Part X contains ss 177–204.

[2] The following Foreign Satellite Service Proscription Orders have been made: 1993, SI 1993/1024; 1995, SI 1995/2917; 1996, SI 1996/2557 and 1997, SI 1997/1150, SI 1998/1865 and 3083, SI 2005/220.

7.11069 **178. Offence of supporting proscribed foreign satellite services** (1) This section applies to any foreign satellite service which is proscribed for the purposes of this section by virtue of an order under section 177; and references in this section to a proscribed service are references to any such service.

(2) Any person who in the United Kingdom does any of the acts specified in subsection (3) shall be guilty of an offence.

(3) Those acts are—

(*a*) supplying any equipment or other goods for use in connection with the operation or day-to-day running of a proscribed service;

(*b*) supplying, or offering to supply, programme material to be included in any programme transmitted in the provision of a proscribed service;

(*c*) arranging for, or inviting, any other person to supply programme material to be so included;

(*d*) advertising, by means of programmes transmitted in the provision of a proscribed service, goods supplied by him or services provided by him;

(*e*) publishing the times or other details of any programmes which are to be transmitted in the provision of a proscribed service or (otherwise than by publishing such details) publishing an advertisement of matter calculated to promote a proscribed service (whether directly or indirectly);

(*f*) supplying or offering to supply any decoding equipment which is designed or adapted to be used primarily for the purpose of enabling the reception of programmes transmitted in the provision of a proscribed service.

(4) In any proceedings against a person for an offence under this section, it is a defence for him to prove that he did not know, and had no reasonable cause to suspect, that the service in connection with which the act was done was a proscribed service.

(5) A person who is guilty of an offence under this section shall be liable[1]—

(*a*) on summary conviction, to imprisonment for a term not exceeding **six months** or to a fine not exceeding the **statutory maximum**, or **both**;

(*b*) on conviction on indictment, to imprisonment for a term not exceeding **two years** or to a **fine**, or **both**.

(6) For the purposes of this section a person exposing decoding equipment for supply or having such equipment in his possession for supply shall be deemed to offer to supply it.

(7) Section 46 of the Consumer Protection Act 1987 shall have effect for the purpose of construing references in this section to the supply of any thing as it has effect for the purpose of construing references in that Act to the supply of any goods.

(8) In this section "programme material" includes—

(*a*) a film (within the meaning of Part I of the Copyright, Designs and Patents Act 1988);

(*b*) any other recording; and

(*c*) any advertisement or other advertising material.

[Broadcasting Act 1990, s 178.]

---

1 For procedure in respect of an offence which is triable either way, see the Magistrates' Courts Act 1980, ss 17A–21, in PART I: MAGISTRATES' COURTS, PROCEDURE, ante.

*General*

7.11070 **195. Offences by bodies corporate** (1) Where a body corporate is guilty of an offence under this Act and that offence is proved to have been committed with the consent or connivance of, or to be attributable to any neglect on the part of, any director, manager, secretary or other similar officer of the body corporate or any person who was purporting to act in any such capacity, then he, as well as the body corporate, shall be guilty of that offence and shall be liable to be proceeded against and punished accordingly.

(2) Where the affairs of a body corporate are managed by its members, subsection (1) above shall apply in relation to the acts and defaults of a member in connection with his functions of management as if he were a director of the body corporate.

[Broadcasting Act 1990, s 195.]

7.11071 **196. Entry and search of premises** (1) If a justice of the peace is satisfied by information on oath—

(*a*) that there is reasonable ground for suspecting that an offence under section 13 or 97 has been or is being committed on any premises specified in the information, and

(*b*) that evidence of the commission of the offence is to be found on those premises,

he may grant a search warrant conferring power on any person or persons authorised in that behalf by OFCOM to enter and search the premises specified in the information at any time within one month from the date of the warrant.

(2) *Repealed.*

(3) A person who intentionally obstructs a person in the exercise of powers conferred on him under this section shall be guilty of an offence and liable on summary conviction to a fine not exceeding the fifth level on the standard scale.

(4) A person who discloses, otherwise than for the purposes of any legal proceedings or of a report of any such proceedings, any information obtained by means of an exercise of powers conferred by this section shall be guilty of an offence and liable[1]—

(*a*) on summary conviction, to a fine not exceeding the **statutory maximum**;

(*b*) on conviction on indictment, to imprisonment for a term not exceeding **two years** or to a **fine**, or **both**.

(5) *Scotland.*

(6) *Northern Ireland.*

[Broadcasting Act 1990, s 196 as amended by the Communications Act 2003, Schs 15 and 19.]

---

1 For procedure in respect of an offence which is triable either way, see ss 18–21 of the Magistrates' Courts Act 1980, ss 17A–21 in PART I: MAGISTRATES' COURTS, PROCEDURE, ante.

7.11072 **201. Programme services** (1) In this Act "programme service" means any of the following services (whether or not it is, or it requires to be, licensed), namely—

(*aa*) any service which is a programme service within the meaning of the Communications Act 2003;

(*c*) any other service which consists in the sending, by means of an electronic communications network (within the meaning of the Communications Act 2003), of sounds or visual images or both either—

(i) for reception at two or more places in the United Kingdom (whether they are so sent for simultaneous reception or at different times in response to requests made by different users of the service); or

(ii) for reception at a place in the United Kingdom for the purpose of being presented there to members of the public or to any group of persons.

(2A) Subsection (1)(*c*) does not apply to so much of a service consisting only of sound programmes as—

(*a*) is a two-way service (within the meaning of section 248(4) of the Communications Act 2003);

(*b*) satisfies the conditions in section 248(5) of that Act; or

(*c*) is provided for the purpose only of being received by persons who have qualified as users of the service by reason of being persons who fall within paragraph (*a*) or (*b*) of section 248(7) of that Act.

(2B) Subsection (1)(*c*) does not apply to so much of a service not consisting only of sound programmes as—

(*a*) is a two-way service (within the meaning of section 232 of the Communications Act 2003);

(*b*) satisfies the conditions in section 233(5) of that Act; or

(*c*) is provided for the purpose only of being received by persons who have qualified as users of the service by reason of being persons who fall within paragraph (*a*) or (*b*) of section 233(7) of that Act.

[Broadcasting Act 1990, s 201 as amended by the Broadcasting Act 1996, Sch 10 and the Communications Act 2003, s 360 and Sch 19.]

7.11073 **202. General interpretation** (1) In this Act (unless the context otherwise requires)—

"advertising agent" shall be construed in accordance with subsection (7);

"the Audiovisual Media Services Directive" means Directive 2010/13/EU of the European Parliament and of the Council on the coordination of certain provisions laid down by law, regulation or administrative action in Member States concerning the provision of audiovisual media services;

"the BBC" means the British Broadcasting Corporation;

"a BBC company" means—

(*a*) any body corporate which is controlled by the BBC, or

(*b*) any body corporate in which the BBC or any body corporate falling within paragraph (*a*) above is (to any extent) a participant (as defined in paragraph 1(1) of Part I of Schedule 2);

"body", without more, means a body of persons whether incorporated or not, and includes a partnership;

"broadcast" means broadcast by wireless telegraphy;

"a Channel 4 company" means—

(*a*) any body corporate which is controlled by the Channel Four Television Corporation, or

(*b*) any body corporate in which the Corporation or any body corporate falling within paragraph (*a*) above is (to any extent) a participant (as defined in paragraph 1(1) of Part I of Schedule 2);

"connected", in relation to any person, shall be construed in accordance with paragraph 3 in Part I of Schedule 2;

"control", in relation to a body, has the meaning given by paragraph 1(1) in that Part of that Schedule;

"dwelling-house" includes a hotel, inn, boarding-house or other similar establishment;

"EEA Agreement" and "EEA State" have the meaning given by Schedule 1 to the Interpretation Act 1978;

"financial year" shall be construed in accordance with subsection (2);

"frequency" includes frequency band;

"modifications" includes additions, alterations and omissions;

"OFCOM" means the Office of Communications;

"pension scheme" means a scheme for the payment of pensions, allowances or gratuities;

"product placement" has the meaning given by paragraph 1 of Schedule 11A to the Communications Act 2003;

"programme" includes an advertisement and, in relation to any service, includes any item included in that service;

"an S4C company" means—

(*a*) any body corporate which is controlled by the Welsh Authority, or

(*b*) any body corporate in which the Welsh Authority or any body corporate falling within paragraph (*a*) above is (to any extent) a participant (as defined in paragraph 1(1) of Part I of Schedule 2);

"the Welsh Authority" means the authority renamed Sianel Pedwar Cymru by section 56(1);

"wireless telegraphy" and "wireless telegraphy station" each has the same meaning as in the Wireless Telegraphy Act 2006.

(2) In any provision of—

(*a*) *repealed*; or

(*b*) Schedule 2, 3, 6, or 19,

"financial year" means a financial year of the body with which that provision is concerned; and in any other provision of this Act "financial year" means the twelve months ending with 31st March.

(3) In this Act—

(*a*) references to pensions, allowances or gratuities include references to like benefits to be given on death or retirement; and

(*b*) any reference to the payment of pensions, allowances or gratuities to or in respect of any persons includes a reference to the making of payments towards provision for the payment of pensions, allowances or gratuities to or in respect of those persons.

(4) Any reference in this Act (however expressed) to a licence under this Act being in force is a reference to its being in force so as to authorise the provision under the licence of the licensed service; and any such reference shall accordingly not be construed as prejudicing the operation of any provisions of such a licence which are intended to have effect otherwise than at a time when the licensed service is authorised to be so provided.

(4A) *Repealed.*

(5) It is hereby declared that, for the purpose of determining for the purposes of any provision of this Act whether a service is—

(*a*) capable of being received, within the United Kingdom or elsewhere, or

(*b*) for reception at any place or places, or in any area, in the United Kingdom,

the fact that the service has been encrypted to any extent shall be disregarded.

(6) Any reference in this Act, in relation to a service consisting of programmes transmitted by satellite—

(*a*) to a person by whom the programmes are transmitted, or

(*b*) to a place from which the programmes are transmitted,

is a reference to a person by whom, or a place from which, the programmes are transmitted to the satellite by means of which the service is provided.

(6A) Subsections (2) and (3) of section 362 of the Communications Act 2003 (persons by whom services provided) are to apply for the purposes of this Act as they apply for the purposes of Part 3 of that Act.

(7) For the purposes of this Act—

(*a*) a person shall not be regarded as carrying on business as an advertising agent, or as acting as such an agent, unless he carries on a business involving the selection and purchase of advertising time or space for persons wishing to advertise;

(*b*) a person who carries on such a business shall be regarded as carrying on business as an advertising agent irrespective of whether in law he is the agent of those for whom he acts;

(*c*) a person who is the proprietor of a newspaper shall not be regarded as carrying on business as an advertising agent by reason only that he makes arrangements on behalf of advertisers whereby advertisements appearing in the newspaper are also to appear in one or more other newspapers;

(*d*) a company or other body corporate shall not be regarded as carrying on business as an advertising agent by reason only that its objects or powers include or authorise that activity.

[Broadcasting Act 1990, s 202 as amended by the Broadcasting Act 1996, Schs 10 and 11, SI 1997/1682, SI 1998/3196, the Communications Act 2003, Sch 5, the Wireless Telegraphy Act 2006, Sch 7, SI 2010/831, SI 2010/1883 and SI 2013/2217.]

7.11074 **203. Consequential and transitional provisions** (1) *Consequential amendments.*

(2) Unless the context otherwise requires, in any enactment amended by this Act—

"programme", in relation to a programme service, includes any item included in that service; and

"television programme" includes a teletext transmission.

(3)–(4) *Repeals and transitional provisions.*

[Broadcasting Act 1990, s 203.]

## SCHEDULE 15

APPLICATION OF 1959 ACT TO TELEVISION AND SOUND PROGRAMMES — Section 162

*Interpretation*

7.11075 1. In this Schedule—

"the 1959 Act" means the Obscene Publications Act 1959;

"relevant programme" means a programme included in a programme service;

and other expressions used in this Schedule which are also used in the 1959 Act have the same meaning as in that Act.

*Liability of person providing live programme material*

2. Where—

(*a*) any matter is included by any person in a relevant programme in circumstances falling within section 1(5) of the 1959 Act, and

(*b*) that matter has been provided, for inclusion in that programme, by some other person,

the 1959 Act shall have effect as if that matter had been included in that programme by that other person (as well as by the person referred to in sub-paragraph (*a*)).

*Obscene articles kept for inclusion in programmes*

3. It is hereby declared that where a person has an obscene article in his ownership, possession or control with a view to the matter recorded on it being included in a relevant programme, the article shall be taken for the purposes of the 1959 Act to be an obscene article had or kept by that person for publication for gain.

*Requirement for consent of Director of Public Prosecutions*

4. (1) Proceedings for an offence under section 2 of the 1959 Act for publishing an obscene article shall not be instituted except by or with the consent of the Director of Public Prosecutions in any case where—

(*a*) the relevant publication, or
(*b*) the only other publication which followed from the relevant publication,

took place in the course of the inclusion of a programme in a programme service; and in this sub-paragraph "the relevant publication" means the publication in respect of which the defendant would be charged if the proceedings were brought.

(2) Proceedings for an offence under section 2 of the 1959 Act for having an obscene article for publication for gain shall not be instituted except by or with the consent of the Director of Public Prosecutions in any case where—

(*a*) the relevant publication, or
(*b*) the only other publication which could reasonably have been expected to follow from the relevant publication,

was to take place in the course of the inclusion of a programme in a programme service; and in this sub-paragraph "the relevant publication" means the publication which, if the proceedings were brought, the defendant would be alleged to have had in contemplation.

(3) Without prejudice to the duty of a court to make an order for the forfeiture of an article under section 1(4) of the Obscene Publications Act 1964 (orders on conviction), in a case where by virtue of sub-paragraph (2) above proceedings under section 2 of the 1959 Act for having an article for publication for gain could not be instituted except by or with the consent of the Director of Public Prosecutions, no order for the forfeiture of the article shall be made under section 3 of the 1959 Act (power of search and seizure) unless the warrant under which the article was seized was issued on an information laid by or on behalf of the Director of Public Prosecutions.

*Defences*

5. (1) A person shall not be convicted of an offence under section 2 of the 1959 Act in respect of the inclusion of any matter in a relevant programme if he proves that he did not know and had no reason to suspect that the programme would include matter rendering him liable to be convicted of such an offence.

(2) Where the publication in issue in any proceedings under that Act consists of the inclusion of any matter in a relevant programme, section 4(1) of that Act (general defence of public good) shall not apply; but—

(*a*) a person shall not be convicted of an offence under section 2 of that Act, and
(*b*) an order for forfeiture shall not be made under section 3 of that Act,

if it is proved that the inclusion of the matter in question in a relevant programme is justified as being for the public good on the ground that it is in the interests of—

(i) drama, opera, ballet or any other art,
(ii) science, literature or learning, or
(iii) any other objects of general concern.

(3) Section 4(2) of that Act (admissibility of opinions of experts) shall apply for the purposes of sub-paragraph (2) above as it applies for the purposes of section 4(1) and (1A) of that Act.

*Exclusion of proceedings under common law*

6. Without prejudice to section 2(4) of the 1959 Act, a person shall not be proceeded against for an offence at common law—

(*a*) in respect of a relevant programme or anything said or done in the course of a such a programme, where it is of the essence of the common law offence that the programme or (as the case may be) what was said or done was obscene, indecent, offensive, disgusting or injurious to morality; or
(*b*) in respect of an agreement to cause a programme to be included in a programme service or to cause anything to be said or done in the course of a programme which is to be so included, where the common law offence consists of conspiring to corrupt public morals or to do any act contrary to public morals or decency.

# Broadcasting Act 1996

(1996 c 55)

## PART VIII[1]

## MISCELLANEOUS AND GENERAL

*Provision of false information, etc.*

7.11076 **144. Offence of providing false information in certain circumstances** (1) A person who, in connection with an application by him for, or his continued holding of, a licence under the 1990 Act or this Act—

(*a*) makes a statement to OFCOM which he knows to be false in a material particular, or
(*b*) recklessly makes a statement to OFCOM which is false in a material particular,

is guilty of an offence if the statement relates to a matter which would be relevant in determining whether he is by virtue of any of the provisions specified in subsection (3) a disqualified person, and he is by virtue of any of those provisions a disqualified person in relation to that licence.

(2) A person who, in connection with an application by him for, or his continued holding of, a licence under the 1990 Act or this Act, withholds any information with the intention of causing OFCOM to be misled is guilty of an offence if—

(*a*) the information would be relevant in determining whether he is by virtue of any of the provisions specified in subsection (3) a disqualified person, and
(*b*) he is by virtue of any of those provisions a disqualified person in relation to that licence.

(3) The provisions referred to in subsection (1) and (2) are the following provisions of paragraph 1(1) of Part II of Schedule 2 to the 1990 Act—

(*a*) paragraphs (*d*) to (*g*),
(*b*) paragraph (*h*) so far as relating to participating by bodies falling within paragraph (*d*), (*e*) or (*g*),

(*c*) paragraph (*hh*) so far as relating to a body corporate controlled by a body corporate in which a body falling within paragraph (*d*), (*e*) or (*g*) is a participant with more than a 5 per cent. interest,

(*d*) paragraph (i) so far as relating to control by a person falling within any of paragraphs (*d*) to (*g*) or by two or more such persons, and

(*e*) paragraph (*j*) so far as relating to participation by a body corporate which is controlled by a person falling within any of paragraphs (*d*) to (*g*) or by two or more such persons.

(4) A person guilty of an offence under this section is liable on summary conviction to imprisonment for a term not exceeding **three months** or * to a fine not exceeding **level 5** on the standard scale or to **both** *.

(5) *Repealed.*

[Broadcasting Act 1996, s 144 as amended by the Communications Act 2003, Schs 15 and 19.]

[1] Part VIII contains ss 142–150.

* **Words repealed by the Criminal Justice Act 2003, Sch 37 from a date to be appointed.**

7.11077 **145. Disqualification for offence of supplying false information, etc** (1) Where a person is convicted of an offence under section 144 the court by which he is convicted may make an order (in this section referred to as a "disqualification order") disqualifying him from holding a licence during a period specified in the order.

(2) The period specified in a disqualification order shall not exceed five years beginning with the date on which the order takes effect.

(3) Where an individual is disqualified from holding a licence by virtue of a disqualification order, any body corporate—

(*a*) of which he is a director, or

(*b*) in the management of which he is directly or indirectly concerned,

is also disqualified from holding a licence.

(4) Where the holder of a licence is disqualified by virtue of a disqualification order, the licence shall be treated as being revoked with effect from the time when the order takes effect.

(5) For the purposes of any of the provisions specified in subsection (6) (which relate to the imposition of a financial penalty on the revocation of a licence), a licence which is revoked by virtue of subsection (4) shall be taken to have been revoked by OFCOM as mentioned in that provision.

(6) The provisions referred to in subsection (5) are as follows—

(*a*) section 18(3) of the 1990 Act,

(*b*) section 101(3) of the 1990 Act,

(*c*) section 11(5), and

(*d*) section 53(5).

(7) In sections 5(1)(*a*) and (2)(db), and 88(1)(*a*) and (2)(db) of the 1990 Act and sections 5(1)(*a*) and (2)(db) and 44(1)(*a*) and (2)(db) of this Act, the reference to a person who is a disqualified person by virtue of Part II of Schedule 2 to the 1990 Act includes a reference to a person who is disqualified by virtue of a disqualification order.

(8) In this section—

"licence" means a licence under Part 1 or 3 of the 1990 Act or under Part 1 or 2 of this Act.

[Broadcasting Act 1996, s 145 as amended by the Communications Act 2003, Schs 15 and 19 and SI 2003/3299.]

7.11078 **146. Supplementary provisions as to disqualification orders** (1) A person disqualified by a disqualification order may appeal against the order in the same manner as against a conviction.

(2) A disqualification order made by a court in England and Wales or Northern Ireland—

(*a*) shall not take effect until the end of the period within which the person on whose conviction the order was made can appeal against the order, and

(*b*) if he so appeals, shall not take effect until the appeal has been determined or abandoned.

(3) A disqualification order made by a court in Scotland—

(*a*) shall not take effect until the end of the period within which the person on whose conviction the order was made can appeal against the order, and

(*b*) if an appeal against the order or the conviction is taken within that period, shall not take effect until the date when that appeal is determined or abandoned or deemed to have been abandoned.

(4) In this section "disqualification order" means an order under section 145.

[Broadcasting Act 1996, s 146.]

*General*

7.11079 **147. General interpretation** (1) In this Act—

"the 1990 Act" means the Broadcasting Act 1990;

"the BBC" means the British Broadcasting Corporation;

"OFCOM" means the Office of Communications.

(2) The 1990 Act and the following provisions of this Act—

(*a*) Parts I and II and Schedule 1,

(*b*) Part IV,

(*c*) Part V and Schedules 3 and 4, and
(*d*) sections 142 to 146,

shall be construed as if those provisions were contained in that Act.

[Broadcasting Act 1996, s 147 as amended by the Communications Act 2003, Sch 15.]

# Electronic Communications Act 2000[1]

(2000 c 7)

## PART II[2]

## FACILITATION OF ELECTRONIC COMMERCE, DATA STORAGE, ETC

7.11080 7. **Electronic signatures and related certificates** (1) In any legal proceedings—

(*a*) an electronic signature[3] incorporated into or logically associated with a particular electronic communication or particular electronic data, and

(*b*) the certification by any person of such a signature,

shall each be admissible in evidence in relation to any question as to the authenticity of the communication or data or as to the integrity of the communication or data.

(2) For the purposes of this section an electronic signature is so much of anything in electronic form as—

(*a*) is incorporated into or otherwise logically associated with any electronic communication or electronic data; and

(*b*) purports to be so incorporated or associated for the purpose of being used in establishing the authenticity of the communication or data, the integrity of the communication or data, or both.

(3) For the purposes of this section an electronic signature incorporated into or associated with a particular electronic communication or particular electronic data is certified by any person if that person (whether before or after the making of the communication) has made a statement confirming that—

(*a*) the signature,

(*b*) a means of producing, communicating or verifying the signature, or

(*c*) a procedure applied to the signature,

is (either alone or in combination with other factors) a valid means of establishing the authenticity of the communication or data, the integrity of the communication or data, or both.

[Electronic Communications Act 2000, s 7.]

---

1. This Act makes provision to facilitate the use of electronic communications and electronic data storage, and makes provision about the modification of licences granted under s 7 of the Telecommunications Act 1984. Only those provisions of the Act that are relevant to the work of magistrates' courts are included in this Manual. The Act is to be brought into force in accordance with the provisions of s 16, post.
2. Part II comprises ss 7–10.
3. For regulation of electronic signature certificate providers, see the Electronic Signatures Regulations 2002, SI 2002/318 made under s 2 of the European Communities Act 1972.

## PART III[1]

## MISCELLANEOUS AND SUPPLEMENTAL

### *Supplemental*

7.11081 15. **General interpretation** (1) In this Act, except in so far as the context otherwise requires—

"document" includes a map, plan, design, drawing, picture or other image;

"communication" includes a communication comprising sounds or images or both and a communication effecting a payment;

"electronic communication" means a communication transmitted (whether from one person to another, from one device to another or from a person to a device or vice versa)—

(*a*) by means of an electronic communications network; or
(*b*) by other means but while in an electronic form;

"enactment" includes—

(*a*) an enactment passed after the passing of this Act,
(*b*) an enactment comprised in an Act of the Scottish Parliament, and
(*c*) an enactment contained in Northern Ireland legislation,

but does not include an enactment contained in Part I or II of this Act;

"modification" includes any alteration, addition or omission, and cognate expressions shall be construed accordingly;

"record" includes an electronic record; and

"subordinate legislation" means—

(*a*) any subordinate legislation (within the meaning of the Interpretation Act 1978);
(*b*) any instrument made under an Act of the Scottish Parliament; or
(*c*) any statutory rules (within the meaning of the Statutory Rules (Northern Ireland) Order 1979).

(2) In this Act—

(*a*) references to the authenticity of any communication or data are references to any one or more of the following—
(i) whether the communication or data comes from a particular person or other source;
(ii) whether it is accurately timed and dated;
(iii) whether it is intended to have legal effect;
and
(*b*) references to the integrity of any communication or data are references to whether there has been any tampering with or other modification of the communication or data.

(3) References in this Act to something's being put into an intelligible form include references to its being restored to the condition in which it was before any encryption or similar process was applied to it.

[Electronic Communications Act 2000, s 15 as amended by the Communications Act 2003, Sch 17.]

[1] Part III comprises ss 11–16.

7.11082 **16. Short title, commencement, extent** (1) This Act may be cited as the Electronic Communications Act 2000.

(2) Part I of this Act and sections 7, 11 and 12 shall come into force on such day as the Secretary of State may by order[1] made by statutory instrument appoint; and different days may be appointed under this subsection for different purposes.

(3) An order shall not be made for bringing any of Part I of this Act into force for any purpose unless a draft of the order has been laid before Parliament and approved by a resolution of each House.

(4) If no order for bringing Part I of this Act into force has been made under subsection (2) by the end of the period of five years beginning with the day on which this Act is passed, that Part shall, by virtue of this subsection, be repealed at the end of that period.

(5) This Act extends to Northern Ireland.

[Electronic Communications Act 2000, s 16.]

[1] At the date of going to press, the Electronic Communications Act 2000 (Commencement No 1) Order, SI 2000/1798, had been made, bringing ss 7, 11 and 12 of the Act into force on 25 July 2000.

# Regulation of Investigatory Powers Act 2000[1]

(2000 c 23)

## PART I[2]
## COMMUNICATIONS

### CHAPTER I[3]
### INTERCEPTION

*Unlawful and authorised interception*

7.11083 1. **Unlawful interception** (1) It shall be an offence for a person intentionally and without lawful authority to intercept, at any place in the United Kingdom, any communication in the course of its transmission by means of—
(*a*) a public postal service; or
(*b*) a public telecommunication system.

(1A) The Interception of Communications Commissioner may serve a monetary penalty notice on a person if the Commissioner—
(*a*) considers that the person—
(i) has without lawful authority intercepted, at any place in the United Kingdom, any communication in the course of its transmission by means of a public telecommunication system, and
(ii) was not, at the time of the interception, making an attempt in accordance with an interception warrant which might, in the opinion of the Commissioner, explain the interception concerned, and
(*b*) does not consider that the person has committed an offence under subsection (1).

(1B) Schedule A1 (which makes further provision about monetary penalty notices) has effect.

(2) It shall be an offence for a person—
(*a*) intentionally and without lawful authority, and
(*b*) otherwise than in circumstances in which his conduct is excluded by subsection (6) from criminal liability under this subsection,

to intercept, at any place in the United Kingdom, any communication in the course of its transmission by means of a private telecommunication system.

(3) Any interception of a communication which is carried out at any place in the United Kingdom by, or with the express or implied consent of, a person having the right to control the operation or the use of a private telecommunication system shall be actionable at the suit or instance of the sender or recipient, or intended recipient, of the communication if it is without lawful authority and is either—

(a) an interception of that communication in the course of its transmission by means of that private system; or

(b) an interception of that communication in the course of its transmission, by means of a public telecommunication system, to or from apparatus comprised in that private telecommunication system.

(4) Where the United Kingdom is a party to an international agreement which—

(a) relates to the provision of mutual assistance in connection with, or in the form of, the interception of communications,

(b) requires the issue of a warrant, order or equivalent instrument in cases in which assistance is given, and

(c) is designated for the purposes of this subsection by an order[4] made by the Secretary of State,

it shall be the duty of the Secretary of State to secure that no request for assistance in accordance with the agreement is made on behalf of a person in the United Kingdom to the competent authorities of a country or territory outside the United Kingdom except with lawful authority.

(5) Conduct has lawful authority[5] for the purposes of this section if, and only if—

(a) it is authorised by or under section 3 or 4;

(b) it takes place in accordance with a warrant under section 5 ("an interception warrant"); or

(c) it is in exercise, in relation to any stored communication, of any statutory power that is exercised (apart from this section) for the purpose of obtaining information or of taking possession of any document or other property;

and conduct (whether or not prohibited by this section) which has lawful authority for the purposes of this section by virtue of paragraph (*a*) or (*b*) shall also be taken to be lawful for all other purposes.

(6) The circumstances in which a person makes an interception of a communication in the course of its transmission by means of a private telecommunication system are such that his conduct is excluded from criminal liability under subsection (2) if—

(a) he is a person with a right to control[6] the operation or the use of the system; or

(b) he has the express or implied consent of such a person to make the interception.

(7) A person who is guilty of an offence under subsection (1) or (2) shall be liable[7]—

(a) on conviction on indictment, to imprisonment for a term not exceeding two years or to a fine, or to both;

(b) on summary conviction, to a fine not exceeding the statutory maximum.

(8) No proceedings for any offence which is an offence by virtue of this section shall be instituted—

(a) in England and Wales, except by or with the consent of the Director of Public Prosecutions;

(b) in Northern Ireland, except by or with the consent of the Director of Public Prosecutions for Northern Ireland.*

[Regulation of Investigatory Powers Act 2000, s 1 as amended by SI 2011/1340.]

---

* **Section repealed by the Investigatory Powers Act 2016, Sch 10 from a date to be appointed.**

[1] The main purpose of this Act is to ensure that relevant investigatory powers are used in accordance with the European Convention on Human Rights namely: interception of communications; acquisition of communications data (eg billing data); intrusive surveillance on residential premises or in private vehicles; covert surveillance in the course of specific operations; use of agents, informants, undercover officers; access to encrypted data. The background to this Act was fully considered in *A-G's Reference (No 5 of 2002)* [2004] UKHL 40, [2005] 1 AC 167, [2004] 4 All ER 901, [2004] 3WLR 957 (see Note 1 to s 17, post). The Act works in conjunction with other legislation such as the Intelligence Services Act 1994, the Police Act 1997 and the Human Rights Act 1998. The rules in this Act together with the Codes of Practice provide sufficient safeguards against arbitrariness to comply with the Convention (*Kennedy v United Kingdom* Application 26839/05, [2010] Crim LR 868, ECtHR). The provisions of the Act implement art 5 of the Telecommunications Data Protection Directive 97/66, and are to be brought into force in accordance with commencement orders made under section 83. At the date of going to press the following orders had been made: Commencement (No 1 and Transitional Provisions) Order 2000, SI 2000/2543 which brought into effect s 1 (except (3)), 2–20, 21(4) (partially), 26–48, 57–59 (all partially), 60, s 61, 62 (except (1)(*b*) and (*c*)), 63, 64, 65 (partially), 67 (partially), 68 (partially), 69, 70, 71 and 72 (partially), 73, 74–78, 79, 80, 81, 82, Schs 1, 3, 4, 5; Commencement (No 2) Order 2001, SI 2001/2684 which brought into force ss 71 and 72 to the extent they relate to Chapter II of Part I of the Act; Commencement (No 3) Order 2003, SI 2003/3140 which brought into force 5 January 2004: Chapter II of Part I (Acquisition and disclosure of communications data) (ss 21–25); s 57(2)(*b*); s 58(1)(*g*), (*h*) and (*j*); ss 65(5)(*c*) and (8)(*b*); and s 68(7)(*g*) and (*h*); Commencement (No 4) Order 2007, SI 2007/2196 which brought into force on 1 October 2007 Part 3 (ss 49–56, Sch 2); 57(2)(*c*), (*d*)(ii), 58(1)(i), 59(2)(*b*) to the extent that it is not already in force, 62(1)(*b*) and (*c*), 65(3)(*c*), (5)(*e*), (8)(*d*) and (*e*), and (10), 68(7)(*m*) and, in respect of paragraph (*m*), (*n*); 71 and 72, to the extent that they relate to Part 3.

[2] Part I contains ss 1–25.

[3] Chapter I contains ss 1–20.

[4] The Regulation of Investigatory Powers (Designation of an International Agreement) Order 2004, SI 2004/158 has been made which designates the Convention on Mutual Assistance in Criminal Matters between the Member States of the European Union established by Council Act of 29 May 2000 (2000/C197/01).

[5] Where a company is served with notice of an application pursuant to s 9 of and Sch 1 to the Police and Criminal Evidence Act 1984 for an order to produce special procedure material in the form of e-mails addressed to a particular customer and the notice warns that the company cannot destroy or dispose of that material except with the leave of the court and, due to its auto deletion system (for reasons of storage) the company can only comply by transferring copies of the e-mails to another e-mail address, which amounts to an offence under s 1 above, the company has implicit power to preserve the e-mails and this provides it with lawful authority for the purposes of s 1(5)(*c*) below (*R (NTL Group Ltd) v Crown Court at Ipswich* [2002] EWHC 1585 (Admin), [2003] QB 131).

[6] "Control" extends to controlling how the system is used and operated by others and not to those who merely have

the right to access or to operate the system (*R v Stanford* [2006] EWCA Crim 258, [2006] 1WLR 1554, [2006] 2 Cr App R 5, [2006] Crim LR 1068).

[7] For procedure in respect of an offence triable either way, see the Magistrates' Courts Act 1980, ss 17A–21, in PART I: MAGISTRATES' COURTS, PROCEDURE, ante.

**7.11084 2. Meaning and location of "interception"[1] etc** (1) In this Act—

"postal service" means any service which—

(*a*) consists in the following, or in any one or more of them, namely, the collection, sorting, conveyance, distribution and delivery (whether in the United Kingdom or elsewhere) of postal items; and

(*b*) is offered or provided as a service the main purpose of which, or one of the main purposes of which, is to make available, or to facilitate, a means of transmission from place to place of postal items containing communications;

"private telecommunication system" means any telecommunication system which, without itself being a public telecommunication system, is a system in relation to which the following conditions are satisfied—

(*a*) it is attached, directly or indirectly and whether or not for the purposes of the communication in question, to a public telecommunication system; and

(*b*) there is apparatus comprised in the system which is both located in the United Kingdom and used (with or without other apparatus) for making the attachment to the public telecommunication system;

"public postal service" means any postal service which is offered or provided to, or to a substantial section of, the public in any one or more parts of the United Kingdom;

"public telecommunications service" means any telecommunications service which is offered or provided to, or to a substantial section of, the public in any one or more parts of the United Kingdom;

"public telecommunication system" means any such parts of a telecommunication system by means of which any public telecommunications service is provided as are located in the United Kingdom;

"telecommunications service" means any service that consists in the provision of access to, and of facilities for making use of, any telecommunication system (whether or not one provided by the person providing the service); and

"telecommunication system" means any system (including the apparatus comprised in it) which exists (whether wholly or partly in the United Kingdom or elsewhere) for the purpose of facilitating the transmission of communications by any means involving the use of electrical or electro-magnetic energy.

(2) For the purposes of this Act, but subject to the following provisions of this section, a person intercepts a communication in the course of its transmission by means of a telecommunication system if, and only if, he—

(*a*) so modifies or interferes with the system, or its operation,

(*b*) so monitors transmissions made by means of the system, or

(*c*) so monitors transmissions made by wireless telegraphy to or from apparatus comprised in the system,

as to make some or all of the contents of the communication available, while being transmitted, to a person other than the sender or intended recipient[2] of the communication.

(3) References in this Act to the interception of a communication do not include references to the interception of any communication broadcast for general reception.

(4) For the purposes of this Act the interception of a communication takes place in the United Kingdom if, and only if, the modification, interference or monitoring or, in the case of a postal item, the interception is effected by conduct within the United Kingdom and the communication is either—

(*a*) intercepted in the course of its transmission by means of a public postal service or public telecommunication system; or

(*b*) intercepted in the course of its transmission by means of a private telecommunication system in a case in which the sender or intended recipient of the communication is in the United Kingdom.

(5) References in this Act to the interception of a communication in the course of its transmission by means of a postal service or telecommunication system do not include references to—

(*a*) any conduct that takes place in relation only to so much of the communication as consists in any traffic data comprised in or attached to a communication (whether by the sender or otherwise) for the purposes of any postal service or telecommunication system by means of which it is being or may be transmitted; or

(*b*) any such conduct, in connection with conduct falling within paragraph (*a*), as gives a person who is neither the sender nor the intended recipient only so much access to a communication as is necessary for the purpose of identifying traffic data so comprised or attached.

(6) For the purposes of this section references to the modification of a telecommunication system include references to the attachment of any apparatus to, or other modification of or interference with—

(*a*) any part of the system; or

(b) any wireless telegraphy apparatus used for making transmissions to or from apparatus comprised in the system.

(7) For the purposes of this section the times while a communication is being transmitted by means of a telecommunication system shall be taken to include any time when the system by means of which the communication is being, or has been, transmitted is used for storing it in a manner that enables the intended recipient to collect it or otherwise to have access to it[3].

(8) For the purposes of this section the cases in which any contents of a communication are to be taken to be made available to a person while being transmitted shall include any case in which any of the contents of the communication, while being transmitted, are diverted or recorded so as to be available to a person subsequently.

(9) In this section "traffic data", in relation to any communication, means—

(a) any data identifying, or purporting to identify, any person, apparatus or location to or from which the communication is or may be transmitted,

(b) any data identifying or selecting, or purporting to identify or select, apparatus through which, or by means of which, the communication is or may be transmitted,

(c) any data comprising signals for the actuation of apparatus used for the purposes of a telecommunication system for effecting (in whole or in part) the transmission of any communication, and

(d) any data identifying the data or other data as data comprised in or attached to a particular communication,

but that expression includes data identifying a computer file or computer program access to which is obtained, or which is run, by means of the communication to the extent only that the file or program is identified by reference to the apparatus in which it is stored.

(10) In this section—

(a) references, in relation to traffic data comprising signals for the actuation of apparatus, to a telecommunication system by means of which a communication is being or may be transmitted include references to any telecommunication system in which that apparatus is comprised; and

(b) references to traffic data being attached to a communication include references to the data and the communication being logically associated with each other;

and in this section "data", in relation to a postal item, means anything written on the outside of the item.

(11) In this section "postal item" means any letter, postcard or other such thing in writing as may be used by the sender for imparting information to the recipient, or any packet or parcel.*

[Regulation of Investigatory Powers Act 2000, s 2.]

* **Section repealed by the Investigatory Powers Act 2016, Sch 10 from a date to be appointed.**

1 The natural meaning of "interception" denotes some interference or abstraction of the signal, whether it is passing along wires or by wireless telegraphy, during the process of transmission; accordingly, a listening device (fitted in a car) that picked up what a person said, including words spoken on his mobile telephone, but not what was said by persons at the other end of the telephone, was not an 'interception': *R v E* [2004] EWCA Crim 1243, [2004] 2 Cr App Rep 484.

2 The tape recording by undercover police officers of their telephone conversations with a suspect does not constitute the interception of a communication within the meaning of s 2(2); it is not telephone tapping by a third party, but the same as a secret recording of a face-to-face meeting of a suspect (*R v Hardy* [2002] EWCA Crim 3012, [2003] 1 Cr App Rep 494).

3 Section 2(7) was clearly intended to extend the scope of the course of transmission. There was no justification for limiting the extension to periods of transient storage, nor was there any basis for reading into the statutory language a limitation restricting it by reference to the first occasion when the intended recipient had access to it. Furthermore, the language used made clear that the course of transmission might continue notwithstanding that the voicemail message had already been received and read by the intended recipient: *R v Coulson* [2013] EWCA Crim 1026, [2013] 4 All ER 999, [2014] 1 WLR 1119, sub nom *R v Edmonson* [2013] 3 CMLR 1371).

7.11085 **3. Lawful interception without an interception warrant** (1) Conduct by any person consisting in the interception of a communication is authorised by this section if the communication is one which is both—

(a) a communication sent by a person who has consented to the interception; and

(b) a communication the intended recipient of which has so consented.

(2) Conduct by any person consisting in the interception of a communication is authorised by this section if—

(a) the communication is one sent by, or intended for, a person who has consented to the interception; and

(b) surveillance by means of that interception has been authorised under Part II.

(3) Conduct consisting in the interception of a communication is authorised by this section if—

(a) it is conduct by or on behalf of a person who provides a postal service or a telecommunications service; and

(b) it takes place for purposes connected with the provision or operation of that service or with the enforcement, in relation to that service, of any enactment relating to the use of postal services or telecommunications services.

(3A) Conduct consisting in the interception of a communication in the course of its transmission by means of a public postal service is authorised by this section if it is conduct—

(a) under section 159 of the Customs and Excise Management Act 1979 as applied by virtue of—

(i) section 105 of the Postal Services Act 2000 (power to open postal items etc); or
(ii) that section 105 and another enactment; and

(*b*) by an officer of Revenue and Customs.

(4) Conduct by any person consisting in the interception of a communication in the course of its transmission by means of wireless telegraphy is authorised by this section if it takes place—

(*a*) with the authority of a designated person under section 48 of the Wireless Telegraphy Act 2006 (interception and disclosure of wireless telegraphy messages); and
(*b*) for purposes connected with anything falling within subsection (5).

(5) Each of the following falls within this subsection—

(*a*) the grant of wireless telegraphy licences under the Wireless Telegraphy Act 2006;
(*b*) the prevention or detection of anything which constitutes interference with wireless telegraphy; and
(*c*) the enforcement of—
(i) any provision of Part 2 (other than Chapter 2 and sections 27 to 31) or Part 3 of that Act, or
(ii) any enactment not falling within sub-paragraph (i),
that relates to such interference.*

[Regulation of Investigatory Powers Act 2000, s 3 as amended by the Wireless Telegraphy Act 2006, Sch 7, the Policing and Crime Act 2009, s 100 and SI 2011/1340.]

---

* **Section repealed by the Investigatory Powers Act 2016, Sch 10 from a date to be appointed.**

7.11086 **4. Power to provide for lawful interception** (1) Conduct by any person ("the interceptor") consisting in the interception of a communication in the course of its transmission by means of a telecommunication system is authorised by this section if—

(*a*) the interception is carried out for the purpose of obtaining information about the communications of a person who, or who the interceptor has reasonable grounds for believing, is in a country or territory outside the United Kingdom;
(*b*) the interception relates to the use of a telecommunications service provided to persons in that country or territory which is either—
(i) a public telecommunications service; or
(ii) a telecommunications service that would be a public telecommunications service if the persons to whom it is offered or provided were members of the public in a part of the United Kingdom;
(*c*) the person who provides that service (whether the interceptor or another person) is required by the law of that country or territory to carry out, secure or facilitate the interception in question;
(*d*) the situation is one in relation to which such further conditions as may be prescribed by regulations made by the Secretary of State are required to be satisfied before conduct may be treated as authorised by virtue of this subsection; and
(*e*) the conditions so prescribed are satisfied in relation to that situation.

(2) Subject to subsection (3), the Secretary of State may by regulations[1] authorise any such conduct described in the regulations as appears to him to constitute a legitimate practice reasonably required for the purpose, in connection with the carrying on of any business, of monitoring or keeping a record of—

(*a*) communications by means of which transactions are entered into in the course of that business; or
(*b*) other communications relating to that business or taking place in the course of its being carried on.

(3) Nothing in any regulations under subsection (2) shall authorise the interception of any communication except in the course of its transmission using apparatus or services provided by or to the person carrying on the business for use wholly or partly in connection with that business.

(4) Conduct taking place in a prison is authorised by this section if it is conduct in exercise of any power conferred by or under any rules made under section 47 of the Prison Act 1952[2], section 39 of the Prisons (Scotland) Act 1989 or section 13 of the Prison Act (Northern Ireland) 1953 (prison rules).

(5) Conduct taking place in any hospital premises where high security psychiatric services are provided is authorised by this section if it is conduct in pursuance of, and in accordance with, any direction given under section 4(3A)(*a*) of the National Health Service Act 2006, or section 19 or 23 of the National Health Service (Wales) Act 2006 (directions as to the carrying out of their functions by health bodies) to the body providing those services at those premises.

(6) Conduct taking place in a state hospital is authorised by this section if it is conduct in pursuance of, and in accordance with, any direction given to the State Hospitals Board for Scotland under section 2(5) of the National Health Service (Scotland) Act 1978 (regulations and directions as to the exercise of their functions by health boards) as applied by Article 5(1) of and the Schedule to The State Hospitals Board for Scotland Order 1995 (which applies certain provisions of that Act of 1978 to the State Hospitals Board).

(7) In this section references to a business include references to any activities of a government department, of any public authority or of any person or office holder on whom functions are

conferred by or under any enactment.

(8) In this section—

"government department" includes any part of the Scottish Administration, a Northern Ireland department and the Welsh Assembly Government;

"high security psychiatric services" has the same meaning as in section 4 of the National Health Service Act 2006;

"hospital premises" has the same meaning as in section 4(3) of that Act; and

"state hospital" has the same meaning as in the National Health Service (Scotland) Act 1978.

(9) In this section "prison" means—

(*a*) any prison, young offender institution, young offenders centre or remand centre which is under the general superintendence of, or is provided by, the Secretary of State under the Prison Act 1952 or the Prison Act (Northern Ireland) 1953, or

(*b*) any prison, young offenders institution or remand centre which is under the general superintendence of the Scottish Ministers under the Prisons (Scotland) Act 1989,

and includes any contracted out prison, within the meaning of Part IV of the Criminal Justice Act 1991 or section 106(4) of the Criminal Justice and Public Order Act 1994, and any legalised police cells within the meaning of section 14 of the Prisons (Scotland) Act 1989.*

[Regulation of Investigatory Powers Act 2000, s 4 as amended by the National Health Service (Consequential Provisions) Act 2006, Sch 1, SI 2007/1388 and the Health and Social Care Act 2012, Sch 5.]

---

* **Section repealed by the Investigatory Powers Act 2016, Sch 10 from a date to be appointed.**

[1] The Telecommunications (Lawful Business Practice) (Interception of Communications) Regulations 2000 have been made, in this title, post.

[2] For the rules made under s 47 of the Prison Act 1952, see this PART: title PRISONS, ante.

7.11087 **5. Interception with a warrant** (1) Subject to the following provisions of this Chapter, the Secretary of State may issue a warrant authorising or requiring the person to whom it is addressed, by any such conduct as may be described in the warrant, to secure any one or more of the following—

(*a*) the interception in the course of their transmission by means of a postal service or telecommunication system of the communications described in the warrant;

(*b*) the making, in accordance with an international mutual assistance agreement, of a request for the provision of such assistance in connection with, or in the form of, an interception of communications as may be so described;

(*c*) the provision, in accordance with an international mutual assistance agreement, to the competent authorities of a country or territory outside the United Kingdom of any such assistance in connection with, or in the form of, an interception of communications as may be so described;

(*d*) the disclosure, in such manner as may be so described, of intercepted material obtained by any interception authorised or required by the warrant, and of related communications data.

(2) The Secretary of State shall not issue an interception warrant unless he believes—

(*a*) that the warrant is necessary on grounds falling within subsection (3); and

(*b*) that the conduct authorised by the warrant is proportionate to what is sought to be achieved by that conduct.

(3) Subject to the following provisions of this section, a warrant is necessary on grounds falling within this subsection if it is necessary—

(*a*) in the interests of national security;

(*b*) for the purpose of preventing or detecting serious crime;

(*c*) for the purpose of safeguarding the economic well-being of the United Kingdom; or

(*d*) for the purpose, in circumstances appearing to the Secretary of State to be equivalent to those in which he would issue a warrant by virtue of paragraph (*b*), of giving effect to the provisions of any international mutual assistance agreement.

(4) The matters to be taken into account in considering whether the requirements of subsection (2) are satisfied in the case of any warrant shall include whether the information which it is thought necessary to obtain under the warrant could reasonably be obtained by other means.

(5) A warrant shall not be considered necessary on the ground falling within subsection (3)(*c*) unless the information which it is thought necessary to obtain is information relating to the acts or intentions of persons outside the British Islands.

(6) The conduct authorised by an interception warrant shall be taken to include—

(*a*) all such conduct (including the interception of communications not identified by the warrant) as it is necessary to undertake in order to do what is expressly authorised or required by the warrant;

(*b*) conduct for obtaining related communications data; and

(*c*) conduct by any person which is conduct in pursuance of a requirement imposed by or on behalf of the person to whom the warrant is addressed to be provided with assistance with giving effect to the warrant.*

[Regulation of Investigatory Powers Act 2000, s 5.]

---

* **Section repealed by the Investigatory Powers Act 2016, Sch 10 from a date to be appointed.**

*Interception warrants*

An interception warrant may only be made on application by specified persons (**s 6**) and may only be issued by the Secretary of State or, in prescribed circumstances, under the hand of a senior official (**s 7**). An interception warrant must contain prescribed particulars including the name or description of one person as the interception subject or a single set of premises in relation to which the interception is to take place (**s 8**). A warrant ceases to have effect at the end of the 'relevant period' as defined but may be renewed on certain grounds (**s 9**), and may be modified (**s 10**). The person to whom the warrant is addressed may give effect to the warrant himself or with persons he may require to assist him (**s 11**).

*Interception capability*

The Secretary of State may by order provide for the imposition by him on persons who are providing public postal services or public telecommunications services of reasonable obligations to provide assistance in relation to interception warrants (**s 12**). A Technical Advisory Board is established (**s 13**) and grants may be made for fair contributions towards the costs imposed (**s 14**).*

* **Ss 6–14 are repealed by the Investigatory Powers Act 2016, Sch 10 from a date to be appointed.**

*Restrictions on use of intercepted material etc*

**7.11088 15. General safeguards** (1) Subject to subsection (6), it shall be the duty of the Secretary of State to ensure, in relation to all interception warrants, that such arrangements are in force as he considers necessary for securing—

(*a*) that the requirements of subsections (2) and (3) are satisfied in relation to the intercepted material and any related communications data; and

(*b*) in the case of warrants in relation to which there are section 8(4) certificates, that the requirements of section 16 are also satisfied.

(2) The requirements of this subsection are satisfied in relation to the intercepted material and any related communications data if each of the following—

(*a*) the number of persons to whom any of the material or data is disclosed or otherwise made available,

(*b*) the extent to which any of the material or data is disclosed or otherwise made available,

(*c*) the extent to which any of the material or data is copied, and

(*d*) the number of copies that are made,

is limited to the minimum that is necessary for the authorised purposes.

(3) The requirements of this subsection are satisfied in relation to the intercepted material and any related communications data if each copy made of any of the material or data (if not destroyed earlier) is destroyed as soon as there are no longer any grounds for retaining it as necessary for any of the authorised purposes.

(4) For the purposes of this section something is necessary for the authorised purposes if, and only if—

(*a*) it continues to be, or is likely to become, necessary as mentioned in section 5(3);

(*b*) it is necessary for facilitating the carrying out of any of the functions under this Chapter of the Secretary of State;

(*c*) it is necessary for facilitating the carrying out of any functions in relation to this Part of the Interception of Communications Commissioner or of the Tribunal;

(*d*) it is necessary to ensure that a person conducting a criminal prosecution has the information he needs to determine what is required of him by his duty to secure the fairness of the prosecution; or

(*e*) it is necessary for the performance of any duty imposed on any person by the Public Records Act 1958 or the Public Records Act (Northern Ireland) 1923.

(5) The arrangements for the time being in force under this section for securing that the requirements of subsection (2) are satisfied in relation to the intercepted material or any related communications data must include such arrangements as the Secretary of State considers necessary for securing that every copy of the material or data that is made is stored, for so long as it is retained, in a secure manner.

(6) Arrangements in relation to interception warrants which are made for the purposes of subsection (1)—

(*a*) shall not be required to secure that the requirements of subsections (2) and (3) are satisfied in so far as they relate to any of the intercepted material or related communications data, or any copy of any such material or data, possession of which has been surrendered to any authorities of a country or territory outside the United Kingdom; but

(*b*) shall be required to secure, in the case of every such warrant, that possession of the intercepted material and data and of copies of the material or data is surrendered to authorities of a country or territory outside the United Kingdom only if the requirements of subsection (7) are satisfied.

(7) The requirements of this subsection are satisfied in the case of a warrant if it appears to the Secretary of State—

(a) that requirements corresponding to those of subsections (2) and (3) will apply, to such extent (if any) as the Secretary of State thinks fit, in relation to any of the intercepted material or related communications data possession of which, or of any copy of which, is surrendered to the authorities in question; and

(b) that restrictions are in force which would prevent, to such extent (if any) as the Secretary of State thinks fit, the doing of anything in, for the purposes of or in connection with any proceedings outside the United Kingdom which would result in such a disclosure as, by virtue of section 17, could not be made in the United Kingdom.

(8) In this section "copy", in relation to intercepted material or related communications data, means any of the following (whether or not in documentary form)—

(a) any copy, extract or summary of the material or data which identifies itself as the product of an interception, and

(b) any record referring to an interception which is a record of the identities of the persons to or by whom the intercepted material was sent, or to whom the communications data relates,

and "copied" shall be construed accordingly.*

[Regulation of Investigatory Powers Act 2000, s 15.]

* **Section repealed by the Investigatory Powers Act 2016, Sch 10 from a date to be appointed.**

7.11089 **16. Extra safeguards in the case of certificated warrants** (1) For the purposes of section 15 the requirements of this section, in the case of a warrant in relation to which there is a section 8(4) certificate, are that the intercepted material is read, looked at or listened to by the persons to whom it becomes available by virtue of the warrant to the extent only that it—

(a) has been certified as material the examination of which is necessary as mentioned in section 5(3)(a), (b) or (c); and

(b) falls within subsection (2).

(2) Subject to subsections (3) and (4), intercepted material falls within this subsection so far only as it is selected to be read, looked at or listened to otherwise than according to a factor which—

(a) is referable to an individual who is known to be for the time being in the British Islands; and

(b) has as its purpose, or one of its purposes, the identification of material contained in communications sent by him, or intended for him.

(3) Intercepted material falls within subsection (2), notwithstanding that it is selected by reference to any such factor as is mentioned in paragraph (a) and (b) of that subsection, if—

(a) it is certified by the Secretary of State for the purposes of section 8(4) that the examination of material selected according to factors referable to the individual in question is necessary as mentioned in subsection 5(3)(a), (b) or (c); and

(b) the material relates only to communications sent during a period specified in the certificate that is no longer than the permitted maximum.

(3A) In subsection (3)(b) 'the permitted maximum' means—

(a) in the case of material the examination of which is certified for the purposes of section 8(4) as necessary in the interests of national security, six months; and

(b) in any other case, three months.

(4) Intercepted material also falls within subsection (2), notwithstanding that it is selected by reference to any such factor as is mentioned in paragraph (a) and (b) of that subsection, if—

(a) the person to whom the warrant is addressed believes, on reasonable grounds, that the circumstances are such that the material would fall within that subsection; or

(b) the conditions set out in subsection (5) below are satisfied in relation to the selection of the material.

(5) Those conditions are satisfied in relation to the selection of intercepted material if—

(a) it has appeared to the person to whom the warrant is addressed that there has been such a relevant change of circumstances as, but for subsection (4)(b), would prevent the intercepted material from falling within subsection (2);

(b) since it first so appeared, a written authorisation to read, look at or listen to the material has been given by a senior official; and

(c) the selection is made before the end of the permitted period.

(5A) In subsection (5)(c) 'the permitted period' means—

(a) in the case of material the examination of which is certified for the purposes of section 8(4) as necessary in the interests of national security, the period ending with the end of the fifth working day after it first appeared as mentioned in subsection (5)(a) to the person to whom the warrant is addressed; and

(b) in any other case, the period ending with the end of the first working day after it first so appeared to that person.

(6) References in this section to its appearing that there has been a relevant change of circumstances are references to its appearing either—

(a) that the individual in question has entered the British Islands; or

(b) that a belief by the person to whom the warrant is addressed in the individual's presence outside the British Islands was in fact mistaken.*

[Regulation of Investigatory Powers Act 2000, s 16 as amended by the Terrorism Act 2006, s 32.]

* **Section repealed by the Investigatory Powers Act 2016, Sch 10 from a date to be appointed.**

7.11090 **17. Exclusion of matters from legal proceedings**[1] (1) Subject to section 18, no evidence shall be adduced, question asked, assertion or disclosure made or other thing done in, for the purposes of or in connection with any legal proceedings or Inquiries Act proceedings which (in any manner)—

(*a*) discloses, in circumstances from which its origin in anything falling within subsection (2) may be inferred, any of the contents of an intercepted communication or any related communications data; or

(*b*) tends (apart from any such disclosure) to suggest that anything falling within subsection (2) has or may have occurred or be going to occur[2].

(2) The following fall within this subsection—

(*a*) conduct by a person falling within subsection (3) that was or would be an offence under section 1(1) or (2) of this Act or under section 1 of the Interception of Communications Act 1985;

(*b*) a breach by the Secretary of State of his duty under section 1(4) of this Act;

(*c*) the issue of an interception warrant or of a warrant under the Interception of Communications Act 1985;

(*d*) the making of an application by any person for an interception warrant, or for a warrant under that Act;

(*e*) the imposition of any requirement on any person to provide assistance with giving effect to an interception warrant.

(3) The persons referred to in subsection (2)(*a*) are—

(*a*) any person to whom a warrant under this Chapter may be addressed;

(*b*) any person holding office under the Crown;

(*ba*) any person deemed to be the proper officer of Revenue and Customs by virtue of section 8(2) of the Customs and Excise Management Act 1979;

(*c*) *repealed;*

(*ca*) *repealed;*

(*e*) any person employed by or for the purposes of a police force;

(*f*) any person providing a postal service or employed for the purposes of any business of providing such a service; and

(*g*) any person providing a public telecommunications service or employed for the purposes of any business of providing such a service.

(4) In this section—

"Inquiries Act proceedings" means proceedings of an inquiry under the Inquiries Act 2005;

"intercepted communication" means any communication intercepted in the course of its transmission by means of a postal service or telecommunication system.*

[Regulation of Investigatory Powers Act 2000, s 17 as amended by the Inquiries Act 2005, s 48, the Serious Organised Crime and Police Act 2005, Sch 4, SI 2007/1098, the Policing and Crime Act 2009, s 100, the Crime and Courts Act 2013, Sch 8 and SI 2013/602.]

* **Section repealed by the Investigatory Powers Act 2016, Sch 10 from a date to be appointed.**

1 In *A-G's Reference (No 5 of 2002)* [2004] UKHL 40, [2005] 1 AC 167, [2004] 3 WLR 957 the following questions were referred by the Attorney-General: (1) whether s 17(1) operated so as to prevent, in criminal proceedings, any evidence being adduced, question asked, assertion or disclosure made or other thing done so as to ascertain whether a telecommunications system was a public or a private telecommunications system; (2) whether the answer to question (1) was different if the evidence being adduced or question asked related to events which took place before the 2000 Act came into force; (3) whether, where an interception of a communication had taken place on a private telecommunications system, it was permissible in criminal proceedings to ask questions or adduce evidence to establish that the interception had been carried out by or on behalf of the person with the right to control the operation or use of the system (*a*) where the interception took place before the 2000 Act came into force and (*b*) where the interception took place after the 2000 Act came into force. Their lordships upheld the answers to those questions given by the Court of Appeal, namely "No" to questions 1 and 2, "Yes" to question 3(*a*) and "Yes, subject to the facts of the particular case", to question 3(*b*) (adding, however, that the latter qualification might not have been necessary).

2 It was held in *A-G's Reference (No 5 of 2002)* [2004] UKHL 40, [2004] 3 WLR 957 that s 17(1) did not operate so as to prevent, in criminal proceedings, any evidence being adduced, question asked, assertion or disclosure made or other thing done so as to ascertain whether a telecommunications system was a public or private telecommunications system, whether or not the evidence being adduced or question asked related to events which had taken place before the 2000 Act came into force; where an interception of a communication had taken place on a private telecommunications system, it was permissible to in criminal proceedings to ask questions or adduce evidence to establish that the interception had been carried out by or on behalf of the person with the right to control the operation of the system (*a*) where the interception had taken place before the 2000 Act came into force, and (*b*) possibly where it had taken place after that date, subject to the facts of the particular case.

7.11091 **18. Exceptions to section 17** (1) Section 17(1) shall not apply in relation to—

(*a*) any proceedings for a relevant offence;

(*b*) any civil proceedings under section 11(8);

(*c*) any proceedings before the Tribunal;

(*d*) any proceedings on an appeal or review for which provision is made by an order under section 67(8);

(*dza*) any proceedings before an employment tribunal, or (in Northern Ireland) an industrial tribunal, where the applicant or the applicant's representatives are excluded for all or part of the proceedings pursuant to—
(i) a direction to the tribunal by virtue of section 10(5)(*b*) or (*c*) of the Employment Tribunals Act 1996 or (as the case may be) Article 12(5)(*b*) or (*c*) of the Industrial Tribunals (Northern Ireland) Order 1996 (SI 1996/1921 (N.I. 18)) (exclusion from Crown employment proceedings by direction of Minister in interests of national security), or
(ii) a determination of the tribunal by virtue of section 10(6) of that Act or (as the case may be) Article 12(6) of that Order (determination by tribunal in interests of national security),
or any proceedings arising out of such proceedings;
(*dzb*) *Northern Ireland;*
(*da*) *repealed;*
(*db*) any financial restrictions proceedings as defined in section 65 of the Counter-Terrorism Act 2008, or any proceedings arising out of such proceedings;
(*dc*) any proceedings—
(i) on an appeal under section 26, or an application under section 27, of the Terrorist Asset-Freezing etc Act 2010 (appeals and reviews by the court), or
(ii) on a claim arising from any matter to which such an appeal or application relates,
or any proceedings arising out of such proceedings;
(*dd*) any TPIM proceedings (within the meaning of the Terrorism Prevention and Investigation Measures Act 2011) or any proceedings arising out of such proceedings;
(*e*) any proceedings before the Special Immigration Appeals Commission or any proceedings arising out of proceedings before that Commission;
(*f*) any proceedings before the Proscribed Organisations Appeal Commission or any proceedings arising out of proceedings before that Commission; or
(*g*) any section 6 proceedings within the meaning given by section 14(1) of the Justice and Security Act 2013 (certain civil proceedings in which closed material applications may be made)].

(2) Subsection (1) shall not, by virtue of paragraphs (*dza*) to (*g*), authorise the disclosure of anything—
(*zza*) in the case of proceedings falling within paragraph (dza), to—
(i) the person who is or was the applicant in the proceedings before the employment or industrial tribunal, or
(ii) any person who for the purposes of proceedings so falling (but otherwise than by virtue of appointment as a special advocate) represents that person;
(*zzb*) *Northern Ireland;*
(*za*) *repealed*
(*zb*) in the case of proceedings falling within paragraph (*db*) or (*dc*), to—
(i) a person, other than the Treasury, who is or was a party to the proceedings, or
(ii) any person who for the purposes of the proceedings (but otherwise than by virtue of appointment as a special advocate) represents a person falling within sub-paragraph (i);
(*zc*) in the case of proceedings falling within paragraph (*dd*), to—
(i) a person, other than the Secretary of State, who is or was a party to the proceedings, or
(ii) any person who for the purposes of the proceedings (but otherwise than by virtue of appointment as a special advocate under Schedule 4 to the Terrorism Prevention and Investigation Measures Act 2011) represents a person falling within sub-paragraph (i);
(*a*) in the case of any proceedings falling within paragraph (*e*), to—
(i) the appellant or (as the case may be) applicant to the Special Immigration Appeals Commission; or
(ii) any person who for the purposes of any proceedings so falling (but otherwise than by virtue of an appointment under section 6 of the Special Immigration Appeals Commission Act 1997) represents that appellant or applicant;
(*b*) in the case of proceedings falling within paragraph (*f*), to—
(i) the applicant to the Proscribed Organisations Appeal Commission;
(ii) the organisation concerned (if different);
(iii) any person designated under paragraph 6 of Schedule 3 to the Terrorism Act 2000 to conduct proceedings so falling on behalf of that organisation; or
(iv) any person who for the purposes of any proceedings so falling (but otherwise than by virtue of an appointment under paragraph 7 of that Schedule) represents that applicant or that organisation.
(*c*) in the case of proceedings falling within paragraph (*g*) where the only relevant person is the Secretary of State, to—

(i) a person, other than the Secretary of State, who is or was a party to the proceedings; or

(ii) any person who for the purposes of the proceedings (but otherwise than by virtue of appointment as a special advocate) represents a person falling within sub-paragraph (i); or

(*d*) in the case of proceedings falling within paragraph (*g*) where the Secretary of State is not the only relevant person or is not a relevant person but is a party to the proceedings, to—

(i) a person, other than the relevant person concerned or the Secretary of State, who is or was a party to the proceedings; or

(ii) any person who for the purposes of the proceedings (but otherwise than by virtue of appointment as a special advocate) represents a person falling within sub-paragraph (i).

(2A) In subsection (2)(*c*) and (*d*) "relevant person", in relation to proceedings falling within subsection (1)(*g*), has the meaning given by section 14(1) of the Justice and Security Act 2013.

(3) Section 17(1) shall not prohibit anything done in, for the purposes of, or in connection with, so much of any legal proceedings as relates to the fairness or unfairness of a dismissal on the grounds of any conduct constituting an offence under section 1(1) or (2), 11(7) or 19 of this Act, or section 1 of the Interception of Communications Act 1985.

(4) Section 17(1)(*a*) shall not prohibit the disclosure of any of the contents of a communication if the interception of that communication was lawful by virtue of section 1(5)(*c*), 3 or 4.

(5) Where any disclosure is proposed to be or has been made on the grounds that it is authorised by subsection (4), section 17(1) shall not prohibit the doing of anything in, or for the purposes of, so much of any proceedings as relates to the question whether that disclosure is or was so authorised.

(6) Section 17(1)(*b*) shall not prohibit the doing of anything that discloses any conduct of a person for which he has been convicted of an offence under section 1(1) or (2), 11(7) or 19 of this Act, or section 1 of the Interception of Communications Act 1985.

(7) Nothing in section 17(1) shall prohibit any such disclosure of any information that continues to be available for disclosure as is confined to—

(*a*) a disclosure to a person conducting a criminal prosecution for the purpose only of enabling that person to determine what is required of him by his duty to secure the fairness of the prosecution;

(*b*) a disclosure to a relevant judge in a case in which that judge has ordered the disclosure to be made to him alone; or

(*c*) a disclosure to the panel of an inquiry held under the Inquiries Act 2005 or to a person appointed as counsel to such an inquiry where, in the course of the inquiry, the panel has ordered the disclosure to be made to the panel alone or (as the case may be) to the panel and the person appointed as counsel to the inquiry.

(8) A relevant judge shall not order a disclosure under subsection (7)(*b*) except where he is satisfied that the exceptional circumstances of the case make the disclosure essential in the interests of justice.

(8A) The panel of an inquiry shall not order a disclosure under subsection (7)(*c*) except where it is satisfied that the exceptional circumstances of the case make the disclosure essential to enable the inquiry to fulfil its terms of reference.

(9) Subject to subsection (10), where in any criminal proceedings—

(*a*) a relevant judge does order a disclosure under subsection (7)(*b*), and

(*b*) in consequence of that disclosure he is of the opinion that there are exceptional circumstances requiring him to do so,

he may direct the person conducting the prosecution to make for the purposes of the proceedings any such admission of fact as that judge thinks essential in the interests of justice.

(10) Nothing in any direction under subsection (9) shall authorise or require anything to be done in contravention of section 17(1).

(11) In this section "a relevant judge" means—

(*a*) any judge of the High Court or of the Crown Court or any Circuit judge;

(*b*) any judge of the High Court of Justiciary or any sheriff;

(*c*) in relation to proceedings before the Court Martial, the judge advocate for those proceedings; or

(*d*) any person holding any such judicial office as entitles him to exercise the jurisdiction of a judge falling within paragraph (*a*) or (*b*).

(12) In this section "relevant offence" means—

(*a*) an offence under any provision of this Act;

(*b*) an offence under section 1 of the Interception of Communications Act 1985;

(*c*) an offence under section 47 or 48 of the Wireless Telegraphy Act 2006;

(*d*) an offence under section 83 or 84 of the Postal Services Act 2000;

(*e*) *repealed*;

(*f*) an offence under section 4 of the Official Secrets Act 1989 relating to any such information, document or article as is mentioned in subsection (3)(*a*) of that section;

(*g*) an offence under section 1 or 2 of the Official Secrets Act 1911 relating to any sketch, plan, model, article, note, document or information which incorporates or relates to the contents of any intercepted communication or any related communications data or tends to suggest as mentioned in section 17(1)(*b*) of this Act;

(*h*) perjury committed in the course of any proceedings mentioned in subsection (1) or (3) of this section;

(*i*) attempting or conspiring to commit, or aiding, abetting, counselling or procuring the commission of, an offence falling within any of the preceding paragraphs; and

(*j*) contempt of court committed in the course of, or in relation to, any proceedings mentioned in subsection (1) or (3) of this section.

(13) In subsection (12) "intercepted communication" has the same meaning as in section 17.*

[Regulation of Investigatory Powers Act 2000, s 18 as amended by the Inquiries Act 2005, Schs 2 and 3, the Prevention of Terrorism Act 2005, Schedule, the Wireless Telegraphy Act 2006, Sch 7, the Armed Forces Act 2006, Sch 16, the Counter-Terrorism Act 2008, ss 69 and 74, the Terrorist Asset-Freezing etc Act 2010, ss 28, 55, the Terrorism Prevention and Investigation Measures Act 2011, Sch 7 and the Justice and Security Act 2013, s 16, Sch 2.]

* **Section repealed by the Investigatory Powers Act 2016, Sch 10 from a date to be appointed.**

7.11092 **19. Offence for unauthorised disclosures** (1) Where an interception warrant has been issued or renewed, it shall be the duty of every person falling within subsection (2) to keep secret all the matters mentioned in subsection (3).

(2) The persons falling within this subsection are—

(*a*) the persons specified in section 6(2);

(*b*) every person holding office under the Crown;

(*c*) *repealed;*

(*ca*) *repealed;*

(*e*) every person employed by or for the purposes of a police force;

(*f*) persons providing postal services or employed for the purposes of any business of providing such a service;

(*g*) persons providing public telecommunications services or employed for the purposes of any business of providing such a service;

(*h*) persons having control of the whole or any part of a telecommunication system located wholly or partly in the United Kingdom.

(3) Those matters are—

(*a*) the existence and contents of the warrant and of any section 8(4) certificate in relation to the warrant;

(*b*) the details of the issue of the warrant and of any renewal or modification of the warrant or of any such certificate;

(*c*) the existence and contents of any requirement to provide assistance with giving effect to the warrant;

(*d*) the steps taken in pursuance of the warrant or of any such requirement; and

(*e*) everything in the intercepted material, together with any related communications data.

(4) A person who makes a disclosure to another of anything that he is required to keep secret under this section shall be guilty of an offence and liable[1]—

(*a*) on conviction on indictment, to imprisonment for a term not exceeding five years or to a fine, or to both;

(*b*) on summary conviction, to imprisonment for a term not exceeding six months or to a fine not exceeding the statutory maximum, or to both.

(5) In proceedings against any person for an offence under this section in respect of any disclosure, it shall be a defence for that person to show that he could not reasonably have been expected, after first becoming aware of the matter disclosed, to take steps to prevent the disclosure.

(6) In proceedings against any person for an offence under this section in respect of any disclosure, it shall be a defence for that person to show that—

(*a*) the disclosure was made by or to a professional legal adviser in connection with the giving, by the adviser to any client of his, of advice about the effect of provisions of this Chapter; and

(*b*) the person to whom or, as the case may be, by whom it was made was the client or a representative of the client.

(7) In proceedings against any person for an offence under this section in respect of any disclosure, it shall be a defence for that person to show that the disclosure was made by a legal adviser—

(*a*) in contemplation of, or in connection with, any legal proceedings; and

(*b*) for the purposes of those proceedings.

(8) Neither subsection (6) nor subsection (7) applies in the case of a disclosure made with a view to furthering any criminal purpose.

(9) In proceedings against any person for an offence under this section in respect of any disclosure, it shall be a defence for that person to show that the disclosure was confined to a disclosure made to the Interception of Communications Commissioner or authorised—

(*a*) by that Commissioner;

(*b*) by the warrant or the person to whom the warrant is or was addressed;
(*c*) by the terms of the requirement to provide assistance; or
(*d*) by section 11(9).*

[Regulation of Investigatory Powers Act 2000, s 19 as amended by the Serious Organised Crime and Police Act 2005, Sch 4, SI 2007/1098, the Crime and Courts Act 2013, Sch 8 and SI 2013/602.]

* **Section repealed by the Investigatory Powers Act 2016, Sch 10 from a date to be appointed.**

1 For procedure in respect of an offence triable either way, see the Magistrates' Courts Act 1980, ss 17A–21, in PART I: MAGISTRATES' COURTS, PROCEDURE, ante.

*Interpretation of Chapter I*

**7.11093 20. Interpretation of Chapter I** In this Chapter—

"certified", in relation to a section 8(4) certificate, means of a description certified by the certificate as a description of material the examination of which the Secretary of State considers necessary;

"external communication" means a communication sent or received outside the British Islands;

"intercepted material", in relation to an interception warrant, means the contents of any communications intercepted by an interception to which the warrant relates;

"the interception subject", in relation to an interception warrant, means the person about whose communications information is sought by the interception to which the warrant relates;

"international mutual assistance agreement" means an international agreement designated for the purposes of section 1(4);

"related communications data", in relation to a communication intercepted in the course of its transmission by means of a postal service or telecommunication system, means so much of any communications data (within the meaning of Chapter II of this Part) as—

(*a*) is obtained by, or in connection with, the interception; and
(*b*) relates to the communication or to the sender or recipient, or intended recipient, of the communication;

"section 8(4) certificate" means any certificate issued for the purposes of section 8(4).*

[Regulation of Investigatory Powers Act 2000, s 20.]

* **Section repealed by the Investigatory Powers Act 2016, Sch 10 from a date to be appointed.**

## CHAPTER II[1]

## ACQUISITION AND DISCLOSURE OF COMMUNICATIONS DATA

**7.11094 21. Lawful acquisition and disclosure of communications data** (1) This Chapter applies to—

(*a*) any conduct in relation to a postal service or telecommunication system for obtaining communications data, other than conduct consisting in the interception of communications in the course of their transmission by means of such a service or system; and
(*b*) the disclosure to any person of communications data.

(2) Conduct to which this Chapter applies shall be lawful for all purposes if—

(*a*) it is conduct in which any person is authorised or required to engage by an authorisation or notice granted or given under this Chapter; and
(*b*) the conduct is in accordance with, or in pursuance of, the authorisation or requirement.

(3) A person shall not be subject to any civil liability in respect of any conduct of his which—

(*a*) is incidental to any conduct that is lawful by virtue of subsection (2); and
(*b*) is not itself conduct an authorisation or warrant for which is capable of being granted under a relevant enactment and might reasonably have been expected to have been sought in the case in question.

(4) In this Chapter "communications data" means any of the following—

(*a*) any traffic data comprised in or attached to a communication (whether by the sender or otherwise) for the purposes of any postal service or telecommunication system by means of which it is being or may be transmitted;
(*b*) any information which includes none of the contents of a communication (apart from any information falling within paragraph (*a*)) and is about the use made by any person—
  (i) of any postal service or telecommunications service; or
  (ii) in connection with the provision to or use by any person of any telecommunications service, of any part of a telecommunication system;
(*c*) any information not falling within paragraph (*a*) or (*b*) that is held or obtained, in relation to persons to whom he provides the service, by a person providing a postal service or telecommunications service.

(5) In this section "relevant enactment" means—

(*a*) an enactment contained in this Act;
(*b*) section 5 of the Intelligence Services Act 1994 (warrants for the intelligence services); or
(*c*) an enactment contained in Part III of the Police Act 1997 (powers of the police and of

officers of Revenue and Customs).

(6) In this section "traffic data", in relation to any communication, means—

(*a*) any data identifying, or purporting to identify, any person, apparatus or location to or from which the communication is or may be transmitted,

(*b*) any data identifying or selecting, or purporting to identify or select, apparatus through which, or by means of which, the communication is or may be transmitted,

(*c*) any data comprising signals for the actuation of apparatus used for the purposes of a telecommunication system for effecting (in whole or in part) the transmission of any communication, and

(*d*) any data identifying the data or other data as data comprised in or attached to a particular communication,

but that expression includes data identifying a computer file or computer program access to which is obtained, or which is run, by means of the communication to the extent only that the file or program is identified by reference to the apparatus in which it is stored.

(7) In this section—

(*a*) references, in relation to traffic data comprising signals for the actuation of apparatus, to a telecommunication system by means of which a communication is being or may be transmitted include references to any telecommunication system in which that apparatus is comprised; and

(*b*) references to traffic data being attached to a communication include references to the data and the communication being logically associated with each other;

and in this section "data", in relation to a postal item, means anything written on the outside of the item.*

[Regulation of Investigatory Powers Act 2000, s 21 as amended by the Serious Crime Act 2007, Sch 12.]

---

* **Section repealed by the Investigatory Powers Act 2016, Sch 10 from a date to be appointed.**

1 Chapter II contains ss 21–25.

7.11095 22. **Obtaining and disclosing communications data** (1) This section applies where a person designated for the purposes of this Chapter believes that it is necessary on grounds falling within subsection (2) to obtain any communications data[1].

(2) It is necessary on grounds falling within this subsection to obtain communications data if it is necessary—

(*a*) in the interests of national security;

(*b*) for the purpose of preventing or detecting crime or of preventing disorder;

(*c*) in the interests of the economic well-being of the United Kingdom;

(*d*) in the interests of public safety;

(*e*) for the purpose of protecting public health;

(*f*) for the purpose of assessing or collecting any tax, duty, levy or other imposition, contribution or charge payable to a government department;

(*g*) for the purpose, in an emergency, of preventing death or injury or any damage to a person's physical or mental health, or of mitigating any injury or damage to a person's physical or mental health; or

(*h*) for any purpose (not falling within paragraphs (*a*) to (*g*)) which is specified for the purposes of this subsection by an order[2] made by the Secretary of State.

(3) Subject to subsection (5), the designated person may grant an authorisation for persons holding offices, ranks or positions with the same relevant public authority as the designated person to engage in any conduct to which this Chapter applies.

(3A) Subsection (3B) applies if—

(*a*) a person is the designated person by reference to an office, rank or position with a police force; and

(*b*) the chief officer of police of that force has made an agreement under section 23(1) of the Police Act 1996 with the chief officer of police of one or more other police forces.

(3B) The designated person may grant an authorisation for persons holding offices, ranks or positions with a collaborative force to engage in any conduct to which this Chapter applies.

(3C) For the purposes of subsection (3B) a police force is a collaborative force if—

(*a*) its chief officer of police is a party to the agreement mentioned in subsection (3A)(*b*); and

(*b*) the persons holding offices, ranks or positions with it are permitted by the terms of the agreement to be granted authorisations by the designated person.

(3D) A reference in subsections (3A) to (3C) to a police force is to the following—

(*a*) any police force maintained under section 2 of the Police Act 1996 (police forces in England and Wales outside London);

(*b*) the metropolitan police force; and

(*c*) the City of London police force.

(3E) *Repealed.*

(3F) *Repealed.*

(3G) *Repealed.*

(3H) *Repealed.*

(3I) Subsections (3B) is subject to subsection (5).

(4) Subject to subsection (5), where it appears to the designated person that a postal or telecommunications operator is or may be in possession of, or be capable of obtaining, any communications data, the designated person may, by notice to the postal or telecommunications operator, require the operator—

(*a*) if the operator is not already in possession of the data, to obtain the data; and

(*b*) in any case, to disclose all of the data in his possession or subsequently obtained by him.

(5) The designated person shall not grant an authorisation under subsection (3) or (3B), or give a notice under subsection (4), unless he believes that obtaining the data in question by the conduct authorised or required by the authorisation or notice is proportionate to what is sought to be achieved by so obtaining the data.

(6) It shall, subject to section 23A, be the duty of the postal or telecommunications operator to comply with the requirements of any notice given to him under subsection (4).

(7) A person who is under a duty by virtue of subsection (6) shall not be required to do anything in pursuance of that duty which it is not reasonably practicable for him to do.

(8) The duty imposed by subsection (6) shall be enforceable by civil proceedings by the Secretary of State for an injunction, or for specific performance of a statutory duty under section 45 of the Court of Session Act 1988, or for any other appropriate relief.

(9) The Secretary of State shall not make an order under subsection (2)(*h*) unless a draft of the order has been laid before Parliament and approved by a resolution of each House.*

[Regulation of Investigatory Powers Act 2000, s 22 as amended by the Policing and Crime Act 2009, ss 7, 100 and Sch 7 and the Protection of Freedoms Act 2012, Sch 9 and SI 2013/602.]

---

* **Section repealed by the Investigatory Powers Act 2016, Sch 10 from a date to be appointed.**

1 For the applicability of these provisions to cases involving freedom of the press, see *News Group Newspapers v Metropolitan Police Commissioner* [2015] UKIPTrib 14_176_H, [2016] 2 All ER 483.

2 The Regulation of Investigatory Powers (Communications Data) Order 2010, SI 2010/480 amended by SI 2011/2085, SI 2012/2007, SI 2013/472, SI 2014/549, SI 2015/228 and SI 2016/655 has been made.

**7.11095A 23. Form and duration of authorisations and notices***

---

* **Section repealed by the Investigatory Powers Act 2016, Sch 10 from a date to be appointed.**

**7.11096 23A. Authorisations requiring judicial approval[1]** (1) This section applies where a relevant person has—

(*a*) granted or renewed an authorisation under section 22(3) or (3B), or

(*b*) given or renewed a notice under section 22(4).

(2) The authorisation or notice is not to take effect until such time (if any) as the relevant judicial authority has made an order approving the grant or renewal of the authorisation or (as the case may be) the giving or renewal of the notice.

(3) The relevant judicial authority may give approval under this section to the granting or renewal of an authorisation under section 22(3) or (3B) if, and only if, the relevant judicial authority is satisfied that—

(*a*) at the time of the grant or renewal—

(i) there were reasonable grounds for believing that the requirements of section 22(1) and (5) were satisfied in relation to the authorisation, and

(ii) the relevant conditions were satisfied in relation to the authorisation, and

(*b*) at the time when the relevant judicial authority is considering the matter, there remain reasonable grounds for believing that the requirements of section 22(1) and (5) are satisfied in relation to the authorisation.

(4) The relevant judicial authority may give approval under this section to the giving or renewal of a notice under section 22(4) if, and only if, the relevant judicial authority is satisfied that—

(*a*) at the time of the giving or renewal of the notice—

(i) there were reasonable grounds for believing that the requirements of section 22(1) and (5) were satisfied in relation to the notice, and

(ii) the relevant conditions were satisfied in relation to the notice, and

(*b*) at the time when the relevant judicial authority is considering the matter, there remain reasonable grounds for believing that the requirements of section 22(1) and (5) are satisfied in relation to the notice.

(5) For the purposes of subsections (3) and (4) the relevant conditions are—

(*a*) in relation to any grant, giving or renewal by an individual holding an office, rank or position in a local authority in England, Wales or Scotland, that—

(i) the individual was a designated person for the purposes of this Chapter,

(ii) the grant, giving or renewal was not in breach of any restrictions imposed by virtue of section 25(3), and

(iii) any other conditions that may be provided for by an order made by the Secretary of State were satisfied,

(*b*) in relation to a grant, giving or renewal, for any purpose relating to a Northern Ireland excepted or reserved matter, by an individual holding an office, rank or position in a district council in Northern Ireland, that—

(i) the individual was a designated person for the purposes of this Chapter,

(ii) the grant, giving or renewal was not in breach of any restrictions imposed by virtue of section 25(3), and

(iii) any other conditions that may be provided for by an order made by the Secretary of State were satisfied, and

(*c*) in relation to any other grant, giving or renewal by a relevant person, that any conditions that may be provided for by an order made by the Secretary of State were satisfied.

(6) In this section—

"local authority in England" means—

(*a*) a district or county council in England,

(*b*) a London borough council,

(*c*) the Common Council of the City of London in its capacity as a local authority, or

(*d*) the Council of the Isles of Scilly,

"local authority in Scotland" means a council constituted under section 2 of the Local Government etc (Scotland) Act 1994,

"local authority in Wales" means any county council or county borough council in Wales,

"Northern Ireland excepted or reserved matter" means an excepted or reserved matter (within the meaning of section 4(1) of the Northern Ireland Act 1998),

"Northern Ireland transferred matter" means a transferred matter (within the meaning of section 4(1) of the Act of 1998),

"relevant judicial authority" means—

(*a*) in relation to England and Wales, a justice of the peace,

(*b*) in relation to Scotland, a sheriff, and

(*c*) in relation to Northern Ireland, a district judge (magistrates' courts) in Northern Ireland,

"relevant person" means—

(*a*) an individual holding—

(i) an office, rank or position in a local authority in England or Wales, or

(ii) an office, rank or position in a local authority in Scotland (other than an office, rank or position in a fire and rescue authority),

(*b*) also, in relation to a grant, giving or renewal for any purpose relating to a Northern Ireland excepted or reserved matter, an individual holding an office, rank or position in a district council in Northern Ireland, and

(*c*) also, in relation to any grant, giving or renewal of a description that may be prescribed for the purposes of this subsection by an order made by the Secretary of State or every grant, giving or renewal if so prescribed, a person of a description so prescribed.

(7) No order of the Secretary of State—

(*a*) may be made under subsection (6) unless a draft of the order has been laid before Parliament and approved by a resolution of each House;

(*b*) may be made under this section so far as it makes provision which, if it were contained in an Act of the Northern Ireland Assembly, would be within the legislative competence of the Northern Ireland Assembly and would deal with a Northern Ireland transferred matter.*

[Regulation of Investigatory Powers Act 2000, s 23A as inserted by the Protection of Freedoms Act 2012, s 37 and amended by SI 2013/602.]

---

* **Section repealed by the Investigatory Powers Act 2016, Sch 10 from a date to be appointed.**

1 For procedure in respect of applications for judicial approval for obtaining or disclosing communications data in criminal cases, see the Criminal Procedure Rules, Part 47 in *Key Materials*; and in civil cases, see the Magistrates' Courts (Regulation of Investigatory Powers) Rules 2012, SI 2012/2563, in PART I: MAGISTRATES' COURTS, STATUTORY INSTRUMENTS AND PRACTICE DIRECTIONS ON PRACTICE AND PROCEDURE, ante. Detailed guidance for magistrates' courts considering applications under s 23A is given in *Home Office guidance for Magistrates' Courts in England and Wales for a local authority application seeking an order approving the grant or renewal of a RIPA authorisation or notice* (October 2012).

7.11097 **23B. Procedure for judicial approval** (1) The public authority with which the relevant person holds an office, rank or position may apply to the relevant judicial authority for an order under section 23A approving the grant or renewal of an authorisation or (as the case may be) the giving or renewal of a notice.

(2) The applicant is not required to give notice of the application to—

(*a*) any person to whom the authorisation or notice which is the subject of the application relates, or

(*b*) such a person's legal representatives.

(3) Where, on an application under this section, the relevant judicial authority refuses to approve the grant or renewal of the authorisation concerned or (as the case may be) the giving or renewal of the notice concerned, the relevant judicial authority may make an order quashing the

authorisation or notice.

(4) In this section "relevant judicial authority" and "relevant person" have the same meaning as in section 23A.*

[Regulation of Investigatory Powers Act 2000, s 23B as inserted by the Protection of Freedoms Act 2012, s 37.]

* **Section repealed by the Investigatory Powers Act 2016, Sch 10 from a date to be appointed.**

**7.11097A 24. Arrangements for payments***

* **Section repealed by the Investigatory Powers Act 2016, Sch 10 from a date to be appointed.**

**7.11098 25. Interpretation of Chapter II** (1) In this Chapter—

"communications data" has the meaning given by section 21(4);

"designated" shall be construed in accordance with subsection (2);

"postal or telecommunications operator" means a person who provides a postal service or telecommunications service;

"relevant public authority" means (subject to subsection (4)) any of the following—

(*a*) a police force;

(*b*) the National Crime Agency;

(*ba*) *repealed*;

(*d*) Her Majesty's Revenue and Customs;

(*f*) any of the intelligence services;

(*g*) any such public authority not falling within paragraphs (*a*) to (*f*) as may be specified for the purposes of this subsection by an order made by the Secretary of State.

(2) Subject to subsection (3), the persons designated for the purposes of this Chapter are the individuals holding such offices, ranks or positions with relevant public authorities as are prescribed for the purposes of this subsection by an order[1] made by the Secretary of State.

(3) The Secretary of State may by order[1] impose restrictions—

(*a*) on the authorisations and notices under this Chapter that may be granted or given by any individual holding an office, rank or position with a specified public authority; and

(*b*) on the circumstances in which, or the purposes for which, such authorisations may be granted or notices given by any such individual.*

(3A) References in this Chapter to an individual holding an office or position with the Serious Organised Crime Agency include references to any member of the staff of that Agency.

(4) The Secretary of State may by order—

(*a*) remove any person from the list of persons who are for the time being relevant public authorities for the purposes of this Chapter; and

(*b*) make such consequential amendments, repeals or revocations in this or any other enactment as appear to him to be necessary or expedient.

(5) The Secretary of State shall not make an order under this section—

(*a*) that adds any person to the list of persons who are for the time being relevant public authorities for the purposes of this Chapter, or

(*b*) that by virtue of subsection (4)(*b*) amends or repeals any provision of an Act,

unless a draft of the order has been laid before Parliament and approved by a resolution of each House.*

[Regulation of Investigatory Powers Act 2000, s 25 as amended by the Serious Organised Crime and Police Act 2005, Sch 4, SI 2007/1098, the Serious Crime Act 2007, Sch 12, the Crime and Courts Act 2013, Sch 8 and SI 2013/602.]

* **Section repealed by the Investigatory Powers Act 2016, Sch 10 from a date to be appointed.**

1 The Regulation of Investigatory Powers (Communications Data) Order 2010, SI 2010/480 amended by SI 2011/2085, SI 2012/2007, SI 2013/472, SI 2014/549, SI 2015/228 and SI 2016/655 has been made.

## PART II[1]

## SURVEILLANCE AND COVERT HUMAN INTELLIGENCE SOURCES

### *Introductory*

**7.11099 26. Conduct to which Part II applies** (1) This Part applies to the following conduct—

(*a*) directed surveillance;

(*b*) intrusive surveillance; and

(*c*) the conduct and use of covert human intelligence sources.

(2) Subject to subsection (6), surveillance is directed for the purposes of this Part if it is covert but not intrusive and is undertaken—

(*a*) for the purposes of a specific investigation or a specific operation;

(*b*) in such a manner as is likely to result in the obtaining of private information about a person (whether or not one specifically identified for the purposes of the investigation or operation); and

(*c*) otherwise than by way of an immediate response to events or circumstances the nature of which is such that it would not be reasonably practicable for an authorisation under this Part to be sought for the carrying out of the surveillance.

(3) Subject to subsections (4) to (6), surveillance is intrusive for the purposes of this Part if, and only if, it is covert surveillance that—

(a) is carried out in relation to anything taking place on any residential premises or in any private vehicle; and

(b) involves the presence of an individual on the premises or in the vehicle or is carried out by means of a surveillance device.

(4) For the purposes of this Part surveillance is not intrusive to the extent that—

(a) it is carried out by means only of a surveillance device designed or adapted principally for the purpose of providing information about the location of a vehicle; or

(b) it is surveillance consisting in any such interception of a communication as falls within section 48(4).

(5) For the purposes of this Part surveillance which—

(a) is carried out by means of a surveillance device in relation to anything taking place on any residential premises or in any private vehicle, but

(b) is carried out without that device being present on the premises or in the vehicle,

is not intrusive unless the device is such that it consistently provides information of the same quality and detail as might be expected to be obtained from a device actually present on the premises or in the vehicle.

(6) For the purposes of this Part surveillance which—

(a) is carried out by means of apparatus designed or adapted for the purpose of detecting the installation or use in any residential or other premises of a television receiver (within the meaning of Part 4 of the Communications Act 2003), and

(b) is carried out from outside those premises exclusively for that purpose,

is neither directed nor intrusive.

(7) In this Part—

(a) references to the conduct of a covert human intelligence source are references to any conduct of such a source which falls within any of paragraphs (a) to (c) of subsection (8), or is incidental to anything falling within any of those paragraphs; and

(b) references to the use of a covert human intelligence source are references to inducing, asking or assisting a person to engage in the conduct of such a source, or to obtain information by means of the conduct of such a source.

(8) For the purposes of this Part a person is a covert human intelligence source[2] if—

(a) he establishes or maintains a personal or other relationship[3] with a person for the covert purpose of facilitating the doing of anything falling within paragraph (b) or (c);

(b) he covertly uses such a relationship to obtain information or to provide access to any information to another person; or

(c) he covertly discloses information obtained by the use of such a relationship, or as a consequence of the existence of such a relationship.

(9) For the purposes of this section—

(a) surveillance is covert if, and only if, it is carried out in a manner that is calculated to ensure that persons who are subject to the surveillance are unaware that it is or may be taking place;

(b) a purpose is covert, in relation to the establishment or maintenance of a personal or other relationship, if and only if the relationship is conducted in a manner that is calculated to ensure that one of the parties to the relationship is unaware of the purpose; and

(c) a relationship is used covertly, and information obtained as mentioned in subsection (8)(c) is disclosed covertly, if and only if it is used or, as the case may be, disclosed in a manner that is calculated to ensure that one of the parties to the relationship is unaware of the use or disclosure in question.

(10) In this section "private information", in relation to a person, includes any information relating to his private or family life.

(11) References in this section, in relation to a vehicle, to the presence of a surveillance device in the vehicle include references to its being located on or under the vehicle and also include references to its being attached to it.

[Regulation of Investigatory Powers Act 2000, s 26 as amended by the Communications Act 2003, Sch 17.]

---

1 Part II contains ss 26–48 and Sch 1.

2 The tape recording by undercover police officers of their telephone conversations with a suspect constitutes the use of 'a covert human intelligence source' within the meaning of s 26(8), but the complex framework provided for authority for surveillance under the 2000 Act was in no way contrary to the provisions of the European Convention (*R v Hardy* [2002] EWCA Crim 3012, [2003] 1 Cr App R 30).

3 This includes intimate sexual relationships: *AJA v Comr of Police for the Metropolis* [2013] EWCA Civ 1342, [2014] 1 All ER 882, [2014] 1 WLR 28.

*Authorisation of surveillance and human intelligence sources*

7.11100 27. **Lawful surveillance etc** (1) Conduct to which this Part applies shall be lawful for all purposes[1] if—

(a) an authorisation[2] under this Part confers an entitlement to engage in that conduct on the person whose conduct it is; and

(b) his conduct is in accordance with the authorisation.

(2) A person shall not be subject to any civil liability in respect of any conduct of his which—

(*a*) is incidental to any conduct that is lawful by virtue of subsection (1); and
(*b*) is not itself conduct an authorisation or warrant for which is capable of being granted under a relevant enactment and might reasonably have been expected to have been sought in the case in question.

(3) The conduct that may be authorised under this Part includes conduct outside the United Kingdom.

(4) In this section "relevant enactment" means—
(*a*) an enactment contained in this Act;
(*b*) section 5 of the Intelligence Services Act 1994 (warrants for the intelligence services); or
(*c*) an enactment contained in Part III of the Police Act 1997 (powers of the police and of officers of Revenue and Customs).*

[Regulation of Investigatory Powers Act 2000, s 27 as amended by the Serious Crime Act 2007, Sch 12.]

---

* **Amended by the Investigatory Powers Act 2016, Sch 10 from a date to be appointed.**

1 Therefore an authorisation under s 28 of the Act overrode the right of a person to consult in private with a legal or medical adviser but infringed the person's article 8 rights: *Re McE* [2009] UKHL 15, [2009] 4 All ER 335, [2009] Crim LR 524.

2 The authorisation and the terms of it do not attract public interest immunity, see *R v Hardy* [2002] EWCA Crim 3012, [2003] 1 Cr App Rep 494 (an application to exclude the evidence obtained by the surveillance was foreseeable; therefore, this was material that could assist the defence and it should have been disclosed).

**7.11100A 28. Authorisation of directed surveillance** (1) Subject to the following provisions of this Part, the persons designated for the purposes of this section shall each have power to grant authorisations for the carrying out of directed surveillance.

(2) A person shall not grant an authorisation for the carrying out of directed surveillance unless he believes—
(*a*) that the authorisation is necessary on grounds falling within subsection (3); and
(*b*) that the authorised surveillance is proportionate to what is sought to be achieved by carrying it out.

(3) An authorisation is necessary on grounds falling within this subsection if it is necessary—
(*a*) in the interests of national security;
(*b*) for the purpose of preventing or detecting crime or of preventing disorder;
(*c*) in the interests of the economic well-being of the United Kingdom;
(*d*) in the interests of public safety;
(*e*) for the purpose of protecting public health;
(*f*) for the purpose of assessing or collecting any tax, duty, levy or other imposition, contribution or charge payable to a government department; or
(*g*) for any purpose (not falling within paragraphs (a) to (f)) which is specified for the purposes of this subsection by an order made by the Secretary of State.

(4) The conduct that is authorised by an authorisation for the carrying out of directed surveillance is any conduct that—
(*a*) consists in the carrying out of directed surveillance of any such description as is specified in the authorisation; and
(*b*) is carried out in the circumstances described in the authorisation and for the purposes of the investigation or operation specified or described in the authorisation.

(5) The Secretary of State shall not make an order under subsection (3)(g) unless a draft of the order has been laid before Parliament and approved by a resolution of each House.

[Regulation of Investigatory Powers Act 2000, s 28.]

**7.11100B 29. Authorisation of covert human intelligence sources** (1) Subject to the following provisions of this Part, the persons designated for the purposes of this section shall each have power to grant authorisations for the conduct or the use of a covert human intelligence source.

(2) A person shall not grant an authorisation for the conduct or the use of a covert human intelligence source unless he believes—
(*a*) that the authorisation is necessary on grounds falling within subsection (3);
(*b*) that the authorised conduct or use is proportionate to what is sought to be achieved by that conduct or use; and
(*c*) that arrangements exist for the source's case that satisfy—
(i) the requirements of subsection (4A), in the case of a source of a relevant collaborative unit;
(ii) the requirements of subsection (4B), in the case of a source of a relevant Scottish collaborative unit;
(iii) the requirements of subsection (5), in the case of any other source;
and that satisfy such other requirements as may be imposed by order made by the Secretary of State.

(2A) For the purposes of subsection (2)—
(*a*) a relevant collaborative unit is a unit consisting of two or more police forces whose chief officers of police have made an agreement under section 23(1) of the Police Act 1996 which relates to the discharge by persons holding offices, ranks or positions with any of the forces of functions in connection with the conduct or use of the source; and

(b) *repealed*

(3) An authorisation is necessary on grounds falling within this subsection if it is necessary—

(a) in the interests of national security;

(b) for the purpose of preventing or detecting crime or of preventing disorder;

(c) in the interests of the economic well-being of the United Kingdom;

(d) in the interests of public safety;

(e) for the purpose of protecting public health;

(f) for the purpose of assessing or collecting any tax, duty, levy or other imposition, contribution or charge payable to a government department; or

(g) for any purpose (not falling within paragraphs (a) to (f)) which is specified for the purposes of this subsection by an order made by the Secretary of State.

(4) The conduct that is authorised by an authorisation for the conduct or the use of a covert human intelligence source is any conduct that—

(a) is comprised in any such activities involving conduct of a covert human intelligence source, or the use of a covert human intelligence source, as are specified or described in the authorisation;

(b) consists in conduct by or in relation to the person who is so specified or described as the person to whose actions as a covert human intelligence source the authorisation relates; and

(c) is carried out for the purposes of, or in connection with, the investigation or operation so specified or described.

(4A) For the purposes of this Part there are arrangements for the source's case that satisfy the requirements of this subsection if such arrangements are in force as are necessary for ensuring—

(a) that there will at all times be a qualifying person who will have day-to-day responsibility for dealing with the source, and for the source's security and welfare;

(b) that there will at all times be another qualifying person who will have general oversight of the use made of the source;

(c) that there will at all times be a qualifying person who will have responsibility for maintaining a record of the use made of the source;

(d) that the records relating to the source that are maintained by virtue of paragraph (c) will always contain particulars of all such matters (if any) as may be specified for the purposes of this paragraph in regulations made by the Secretary of State; and

(e) that records maintained by virtue of paragraph (c) that disclose the identity of the source will not be available to persons except to the extent that there is a need for access to them to be made available to those persons.

(4B) *Repealed.*

(5) For the purposes of this Part there are arrangements for the source's case that satisfy the requirements of this subsection if such arrangements are in force as are necessary for ensuring—

(a) that there will at all times be a person holding an office, rank or position with the relevant investigating authority who will have day-to-day responsibility for dealing with the source on behalf of that authority, and for the source's security and welfare;

(b) that there will at all times be another person holding an office, rank or position with the relevant investigating authority who will have general oversight of the use made of the source;

(c) that there will at all times be a person holding an office, rank or position with the relevant investigating authority who will have responsibility for maintaining a record of the use made of the source;

(d) that the records relating to the source that are maintained by the relevant investigating authority will always contain particulars of all such matters (if any) as may be specified for the purposes of this paragraph in regulations made by the Secretary of State; and

(e) that records maintained by the relevant investigating authority that disclose the identity of the source will not be available to persons except to the extent that there is a need for access to them to be made available to those persons.

(6) The Secretary of State shall not make an order under subsection (3)(g) unless a draft of the order has been laid before Parliament and approved by a resolution of each House.

(7) The Secretary of State may by order[1]—

(a) prohibit the authorisation under this section of any such conduct or uses of covert human intelligence sources as may be described in the order; and

(b) impose requirements, in addition to those provided for by subsection (2), that must be satisfied before an authorisation is granted under this section for any such conduct or uses of covert human intelligence sources as may be so described.

(7A) For the purposes of subsection (4A) a person is a qualifying person if—

(a) the person holds an office, rank or position with a police force whose chief officer of police is a party to the agreement mentioned in subsection (2A)(a); and

(b) persons holding offices, ranks or positions with that force are permitted by the terms of the agreement to have the responsibility mentioned in paragraph (a) or (c) of subsection (4A) or the general oversight mentioned in paragraph (b) of that subsection (as the case may require).

(7B) *Repealed.*

(8) In this section "relevant investigating authority", in relation to an authorisation for the conduct or the use of an individual as a covert human intelligence source, means (subject to subsection (9)) the public authority for whose benefit the activities of that individual as such a source are to take place.

(9) In the case of any authorisation for the conduct or the use of a covert human intelligence source whose activities are to be for the benefit of more than one public authority, the references in subsection (5) to the relevant investigating authority are references to one of them (whether or not the same one in the case of each reference).

(10) For the purposes of this section—

(*a*) references to a police force are to the following—

(i) any police force maintained under section 2 of the Police Act 1996 (police forces in England and Wales outside London);

(ii) the metropolitan police force; and

(iii) the City of London police force;

(*b*) *repealed.*

[Regulation of Investigatory Powers Act 2000, s 29 as amended by the Policing and Crime Act 2009.]

---

1 The Regulation of Investigatory Powers (Juveniles) Order 2000, SI 2000/2793 has been made which impose restrictions, conditions, requirements and risk assessments in relation to sources under 18 years.

**7.11100C 30. Persons entitled to grant authorisations under ss 28 and 29** (1) Subject to subsection (3), the persons designated for the purposes of sections 28 and 29 are the individuals holding such offices, ranks or positions with relevant public authorities as are prescribed for the purposes of this subsection by an order under this section.

(2) For the purposes of the grant of an authorisation that combines—

(*a*) an authorisation under section 28 or 29; and

(*b*) an authorisation by the Secretary of State for the carrying out of intrusive surveillance,

the Secretary of State himself shall be a person designated for the purposes of that section.

(3) An order under this section may impose restrictions—

(*a*) on the authorisations under sections 28 and 29 that may be granted by any individual holding an office, rank or position with a specified public authority; and

(*b*) on the circumstances in which, or the purposes for which, such authorisations may be granted by any such individual.

(4) A public authority is a relevant public authority for the purposes of this section—

(*a*) in relation to section 28 if it is specified in Part I or II of Schedule 1; and

(*b*) in relation to section 29 if it is specified in Part I of that Schedule.

(5) An order under this section may amend Schedule 1 by—

(*a*) adding a public authority to Part I or II of that Schedule;

(*b*) removing a public authority from that Schedule;

(*c*) moving a public authority from one Part of that Schedule to the other;

(*d*) making any change consequential on any change in the name of a public authority specified in that Schedule.

(6) Without prejudice to section 31, the power to make an order under this section shall be exercisable by the Secretary of State.

(7) The Secretary of State shall not make an order under subsection (5) containing any provision for—

(*a*) adding any public authority to Part I or II of that Schedule, or

(*b*) moving any public authority from Part II to Part I of that Schedule,

unless a draft of the order has been laid before Parliament and approved by a resolution of each House.

[Regulation of Investigatory Powers Act 2000, s 30.]

**7.11100D 31.** *Northern Ireland*

**7.11100E 32. Authorisation of intrusive surveillance** *Power of Secretary of State and "senior authorising officers" to grant authorisations for the carrying out of intrusive surveillance.*

*Authorisations requiring judicial approval*

**7.11101 32A. Authorisations requiring judicial approval[1]** (1) This section applies where a relevant person has granted an authorisation under section 28 or 29.

(2) The authorisation is not to take effect until such time (if any) as the relevant judicial authority has made an order approving the grant of the authorisation.

(3) The relevant judicial authority may give approval under this section to the granting of an authorisation under section 28 if, and only if, the relevant judicial authority is satisfied that—

(*a*) at the time of the grant—

(i) there were reasonable grounds for believing that the requirements of section 28(2) were satisfied in relation to the authorisation, and

(ii) the relevant conditions were satisfied in relation to the authorisation, and

(b) at the time when the relevant judicial authority is considering the matter, there remain reasonable grounds for believing that the requirements of section 28(2) are satisfied in relation to the authorisation.

(4) For the purposes of subsection (3) the relevant conditions are—

(a) in relation to a grant by an individual holding an office, rank or position in a local authority in England or Wales, that—
   (i) the individual was a designated person for the purposes of section 28,
   (ii) the grant of the authorisation was not in breach of any restrictions imposed by virtue of section 30(3), and
   (iii) any other conditions that may be provided for by an order made by the Secretary of State were satisfied,

(b) in relation to a grant, for any purpose relating to a Northern Ireland excepted or reserved matter, by an individual holding an office, rank or position in a district council in Northern Ireland, that—
   (i) the individual was a designated person for the purposes of section 28,
   (ii) the grant of the authorisation was not in breach of any restrictions imposed by virtue of section 30(3), and
   (iii) any other conditions that may be provided for by an order made by the Secretary of State were satisfied, and

(c) in relation to any other grant by a relevant person, that any conditions that may be provided for by an order made by the Secretary of State were satisfied.

(5) The relevant judicial authority may give approval under this section to the granting of an authorisation under section 29 if, and only if, the relevant judicial authority is satisfied that—

(a) at the time of the grant—
   (i) there were reasonable grounds for believing that the requirements of section 29(2), and any requirements imposed by virtue of section 29(7)(b), were satisfied in relation to the authorisation, and
   (ii) the relevant conditions were satisfied in relation to the authorisation, and

(b) at the time when the relevant judicial authority is considering the matter, there remain reasonable grounds for believing that the requirements of section 29(2), and any requirements imposed by virtue of section 29(7)(b), are satisfied in relation to the authorisation.

(6) For the purposes of subsection (5) the relevant conditions are—

(a) in relation to a grant by an individual holding an office, rank or position in a local authority in England or Wales, that—
   (i) the individual was a designated person for the purposes of section 29,
   (ii) the grant of the authorisation was not in breach of any prohibition imposed by virtue of section 29(7)(a) or any restriction imposed by virtue of section 30(3), and
   (iii) any other conditions that may be provided for by an order made by the Secretary of State were satisfied,

(b) in relation to a grant, for any purpose relating to a Northern Ireland excepted or reserved matter, by an individual holding an office, rank or position in a district council in Northern Ireland, that—
   (i) the individual was a designated person for the purposes of section 29,
   (ii) the grant of the authorisation was not in breach of any prohibition imposed by virtue of section 29(7)(a) or any restriction imposed by virtue of section 30(3), and
   (iii) any other conditions that may be provided for by an order made by the Secretary of State were satisfied, and

(c) in relation to any other grant by a relevant person, that any conditions that may be provided for by an order made by the Secretary of State were satisfied.

(7) In this section—

"local authority in England" means—
   (a) a district or county council in England,
   (b) a London borough council,
   (c) the Common Council of the City of London in its capacity as a local authority, or
   (d) the Council of the Isles of Scilly,

"local authority in Wales" means any county council or county borough council in Wales,

"Northern Ireland excepted or reserved matter" means an excepted or reserved matter (within the meaning of section 4(1) of the Northern Ireland Act 1998),

"Northern Ireland transferred matter" means a transferred matter (within the meaning of section 4(1) of the Act of 1998),

"relevant judicial authority" means—
   (a) in relation to England and Wales, a justice of the peace,
   (b) in relation to Scotland, a sheriff, and

(*c*) in relation to Northern Ireland, a district judge (magistrates' courts) in Northern Ireland,

"relevant person" means—

(*a*) an individual holding an office, rank or position in a local authority in England or Wales,

(*b*) also, in relation to a grant for any purpose relating to a Northern Ireland excepted or reserved matter, an individual holding an office, rank or position in a district council in Northern Ireland, and

(*c*) also, in relation to any grant of a description that may be prescribed for the purposes of this subsection by an order made by the Secretary of State or every grant if so prescribed, a person of a description so prescribed.

(8) No order of the Secretary of State—

(*a*) may be made under subsection (7) unless a draft of the order has been laid before Parliament and approved by a resolution of each House;

(*b*) may be made under this section so far as it makes provision which would be within the legislative competence of the Scottish Parliament if it were contained in an Act of the Scottish Parliament;

(*c*) may be made under this section so far as it makes provision which, if it were contained in an Act of the Northern Ireland Assembly, would be within the legislative competence of the Northern Ireland Assembly and would deal with a Northern Ireland transferred matter.

[Regulation of Investigatory Powers Act 2000, s 32A as inserted by the Protection of Freedoms Act 2012, s 38.]

1 For procedure, see the Criminal Procedure Rules, Part 47 in the *Key Materials*. Detailed guidance for magistrates' courts considering applications under s 32A is given in *Home Office guidance for Magistrates' Courts in England and Wales for a local authority application seeking an order approving the grant or renewal of a RIPA authorisation or notice* (October 2012).

**7.11102 32B. Procedure for judicial approval** (1) The public authority with which the relevant person holds an office, rank or position may apply to the relevant judicial authority for an order under section 32A approving the grant of an authorisation.

(2) The applicant is not required to give notice of the application to—

(*a*) any person to whom the authorisation relates, or

(*b*) such a person's legal representatives.

(3) Where, on an application under this section, the relevant judicial authority refuses to approve the grant of the authorisation concerned, the relevant judicial authority may make an order quashing the authorisation.

(4) In this section "relevant judicial authority" and "relevant person" have the same meaning as in section 32A.

[Regulation of Investigatory Powers Act 2000, s 32B as inserted by the Protection of Freedoms Act 2012, s 38.]

**7.11102A 33–46.** *Authorisation on application by Intelligence Services; general rules about grant, renewal and duration.*

*Supplemental provision for Part II*

**7.11103 47. Power to extend or modify authorisation provisions** (1) The Secretary of State may by order[1] do one or both of the following—

(*a*) apply this Part, with such modifications as he thinks fit, to any such surveillance that is neither directed nor intrusive as may be described in the order;

(*b*) provide for any description of directed surveillance to be treated for the purposes of this Part as intrusive surveillance.

(2) No order shall be made under this section unless a draft of it has been laid before Parliament and approved by a resolution of each House.

[Regulation of Investigatory Powers Act 2000, s 47.]

1 The Regulation of Investigatory Powers (British Broadcasting Corporation) Order 2001, SI 2001/1057 has been made which applies Part II of the 2000 Act with modifications, to the carrying out of surveillance to detect whether a television is being used in any residential or other premises. The Regulation of Investigatory Powers (Extension of Authorisation Provisions: Legal Consultations) Order 2010 has also been made, in this title, post.

**7.11104 48. Interpretation of Part II** (1) In this Part—

"CMA" means the Competition and Markets Authority;

"covert human intelligence source" shall be construed in accordance with section 26(8);

"directed" and "intrusive", in relation to surveillance, shall be construed in accordance with section 26(2) to (6);

"private vehicle" means (subject to subsection (7)(*a*)) any vehicle which is used primarily for the private purposes of the person who owns it or of a person otherwise having the right to use it[1];

"residential premises" means (subject to subsection (7)(*b*)) so much of any premises as is for the time being occupied or used by any person, however temporarily, for residential purposes or otherwise as living accommodation (including hotel or prison accommodation that is so occupied or used);

"senior authorising officer" means a person who by virtue of subsection (6) of section 32 is a senior authorising officer for the purposes of that section;

"surveillance" shall be construed in accordance with subsections (2) to (4);

"surveillance device" means any apparatus designed or adapted for use in surveillance.

(2) Subject to subsection (3), in this Part "surveillance" includes—

(*a*) monitoring, observing or listening to persons, their movements, their conversations or their other activities or communications;

(*b*) recording anything monitored, observed or listened to in the course of surveillance; and

(*c*) surveillance by or with the assistance of a surveillance device[2].

(3) References in this Part to surveillance do not include references to—

(*a*) any conduct of a covert human intelligence source for obtaining or recording (whether or not using a surveillance device) any information which is disclosed in the presence of the source;

(*b*) the use of a covert human intelligence source for so obtaining or recording information; or

(*c*) any such entry on or interference with property or with wireless telegraphy as would be unlawful unless authorised under—

(i) section 5 of the Intelligence Services Act 1994 (warrants for the intelligence services); or

(ii) Part III of the Police Act 1997 (powers of the police and of officers of Revenue and Customs).

(4) References in this Part to surveillance include references to the interception of a communication in the course of its transmission by means of a postal service or telecommunication system if, and only if—

(*a*) the communication is one sent by or intended for a person who has consented to the interception of communications sent by or to him; and

(*b*) there is no interception warrant authorising the interception.

(5) References in this Part to an individual holding an office or position with a public authority include references to any member, official or employee of that authority.

(6) For the purposes of this Part the activities of a covert human intelligence source which are to be taken as activities for the benefit of a particular public authority include any conduct of his as such a source which is in response to inducements or requests made by or on behalf of that authority.

(7) In subsection (1)—

(*a*) the reference to a person having the right to use a vehicle does not, in relation to a motor vehicle, include a reference to a person whose right to use the vehicle derives only from his having paid, or undertaken to pay, for the use of the vehicle and its driver for a particular journey; and

(*b*) the reference to premises occupied or used by any person for residential purposes or otherwise as living accommodation does not include a reference to so much of any premises as constitutes any common area to which he has or is allowed access in connection with his use or occupation of any accommodation.

(8) In this section—

"premises" includes any vehicle or moveable structure and any other place whatever, whether or not occupied as land;

"vehicle" includes any vessel, aircraft or hovercraft.

[Regulation of Investigatory Powers Act 2000, s 48 as amended by the Enterprise Act 2002, s 199, the Serious Crime Act 2007, Sch 12 and SI 2014/892.]

---

* **Amended by the Investigatory Powers Act 2016, Sch 10 from a date to be appointed.**

[1] A police vehicle owned by a constabulary and used solely for police purposes in which covert recordings were made was not a private vehicle; it was owned by a state entity and it was not being used for private purposes, but for the purposes of the state: *R v Plunkett* [2013] EWCA Crim 261, [2013] 1 WLR 3121, [2013] 2 Cr App R 2, [2013] Crim LR 765.

[2] Section 48(2) does not provide a comprehensive definition or description of surveillance itself as distinct from the various ways in which it may conducted. Surveillance must be given its ordinary English usage which is adjusted by the subsection to amplify its scope to ensure it includes within the process the various different ways in which the intelligence gathering may be conducted. But every act of observing, or listening to persons, their conversations or communications is not automatically treated as surveillance. Accordingly, the awareness and participation of the interviewee in the process of a voluntary declared interview which was covertly recorded meant that no surveillance of the interviewee by the interviewer was involved: *Re a Complaint of Surveillance* [2014] 2 All ER 576 (Investigatory Powers Tribunal).

## PART III[1]
## INVESTIGATION OF ELECTRONIC DATA PROTECTED BY ENCRYPTION ETC

*Power to require disclosure*

7.11105 **49. Notices requiring disclosure**[2] (1) This section applies where any protected information—

(*a*) has come into the possession of any person by means of the exercise of a statutory power to seize, detain, inspect, search or otherwise to interfere with documents or other property, or is likely to do so;

(*b*) has come into the possession of any person by means of the exercise of any statutory power to intercept communications, or is likely to do so;

(*c*) has come into the possession of any person by means of the exercise of any power conferred by an authorisation under section 22(3) or, (3B) or under Part II, or as a result of the giving of a notice under section 22(4), or is likely to do so;

(*d*) has come into the possession of any person as a result of having been provided or disclosed in pursuance of any statutory duty (whether or not one arising as a result of a request for information), or is likely to do so; or

(*e*) has, by any other lawful means not involving the exercise of statutory powers, come into the possession of any of the intelligence services, the police, the National Crime Agency or Her Majesty's Revenue and Customs, or is likely so to come into the possession of any of those services, the police, the National Crime Agency or Her Majesty's Revenue and Customs.

(2) If any person with the appropriate permission under Schedule 2 believes, on reasonable grounds—

(*a*) that a key to the protected information is in the possession of any person,

(*b*) that the imposition of a disclosure requirement in respect of the protected information is—

(i) necessary on grounds falling within subsection (3), or

(ii) necessary for the purpose of securing the effective exercise or proper performance by any public authority of any statutory power or statutory duty,

(*c*) that the imposition of such a requirement is proportionate to what is sought to be achieved by its imposition, and

(*d*) that it is not reasonably practicable for the person with the appropriate permission to obtain possession of the protected information in an intelligible form without the giving of a notice under this section,

the person with that permission may, by notice to the person whom he believes to have possession of the key, impose a disclosure requirement in respect of the protected information.

(3) A disclosure requirement in respect of any protected information is necessary on grounds falling within this subsection if it is necessary—

(*a*) in the interests of national security;

(*b*) for the purpose of preventing or detecting crime; or

(*c*) in the interests of the economic well-being of the United Kingdom.

(4) A notice under this section imposing a disclosure requirement in respect of any protected information—

(*a*) must be given in writing or (if not in writing) must be given in a manner that produces a record of its having been given;

(*b*) must describe the protected information to which the notice relates;

(*c*) must specify the matters falling within subsection (2)(*b*)(i) or (ii) by reference to which the notice is given;

(*d*) must specify the office, rank or position held by the person giving it;

(*e*) must specify the office, rank or position of the person who for the purposes of Schedule 2 granted permission for the giving of the notice or (if the person giving the notice was entitled to give it without another person's permission) must set out the circumstances in which that entitlement arose;

(*f*) must specify the time by which the notice is to be complied with; and

(*g*) must set out the disclosure that is required by the notice and the form and manner in which it is to be made;

and the time specified for the purposes of paragraph (*f*) must allow a period for compliance which is reasonable in all the circumstances.

(5) Where it appears to a person with the appropriate permission—

(*a*) that more than one person is in possession of the key to any protected information,

(*b*) that any of those persons is in possession of that key in his capacity as an officer or employee of any body corporate, and

(*c*) that another of those persons is the body corporate itself or another officer or employee of the body corporate,

a notice under this section shall not be given, by reference to his possession of the key, to any officer or employee of the body corporate unless he is a senior officer of the body corporate or it appears to the person giving the notice that there is no senior officer of the body corporate and (in the case of an employee) no more senior employee of the body corporate to whom it is reasonably practicable to give the notice.

(6) Where it appears to a person with the appropriate permission—

(*a*) that more than one person is in possession of the key to any protected information,

(*b*) that any of those persons is in possession of that key in his capacity as an employee of a firm, and

(*c*) that another of those persons is the firm itself or a partner of the firm, a notice under this section shall not be given, by reference to his possession of the key, to any employee of the firm unless it appears to the person giving the notice that there is neither a partner of the firm nor a more senior employee of the firm to whom it is reasonably practicable to give the notice.

(7) Subsections (5) and (6) shall not apply to the extent that there are special circumstances of the case that mean that the purposes for which the notice is given would be defeated, in whole or in part, if the notice were given to the person to whom it would otherwise be required to be given by those subsections.

(8) A notice under this section shall not require the making of any disclosure to any person other than—

- (*a*) the person giving the notice; or
- (*b*) such other person as may be specified in or otherwise identified by, or in accordance with, the provisions of the notice.

(9) A notice under this section shall not require the disclosure of any key which—

- (*a*) is intended to be used for the purpose only of generating electronic signatures; and
- (*b*) has not in fact been used for any other purpose.

(10) In this section "senior officer", in relation to a body corporate, means a director, manager, secretary or other similar officer of the body corporate; and for this purpose "director", in relation to a body corporate whose affairs are managed by its members, means a member of the body corporate.

(11) Schedule 2 (definition of the appropriate permission) shall have effect.*

[Regulation of Investigatory Powers Act 2000, s 49 as amended by the Serious Organised Crime and Police Act 2005, Sch 4, the Serious Crime Act 2007, Sch 12, SI 2007/1098, the Policing and Crime Act 2009, Sch 7, the Crime and Courts Act 2013, Sch 8 and SI 2013/602.]

---

* **Amended by the Investigatory Powers Act 2016, Sch 10 from a date to be appointed.**

[1] Part III contains ss 49–56 and Sch 2.

[2] Although a requirement under this Part may engage the privilege against incrimination, the key or password is a fact; it does not constitute an admission of guilt. Only knowledge of it may be incriminating and evidence of this knowledge (as distinct from the key or underlying material) might be excluded under s 78 of the Police and Criminal Evidence Act 1984 if the admission of evidence of the defendant's knowledge of the key were unfair. Procedural safeguards and limitations on the circumstances in which the notice may be served are addressed in a comprehensive structure, and in relation to any subsequent trial, the powers under s 78 of the Police and Criminal Evidence Act 1984 Act to exclude evidence in relation, first, to the underlying material, second, the key or means of access to it, and third, an individual defendant's knowledge of the key or means of access, remain. Neither the process, nor any subsequent trial can realistically be stigmatised as unfair: *R v S and A* [2008] EWCA Crim 2177, [2009] 1 Cr App R 18.

**7.11106 50. Effect of notice imposing disclosure requirement** (1) Subject to the following provisions of this section, the effect of a section 49 notice imposing a disclosure requirement in respect of any protected information on a person who is in possession at a relevant time of both the protected information and a means of obtaining access to the information and of disclosing it in an intelligible form is that he—

- (*a*) shall be entitled to use any key in his possession to obtain access to the information or to put it into an intelligible form; and
- (*b*) shall be required, in accordance with the notice imposing the requirement, to make a disclosure of the information in an intelligible form.

(2) A person subject to a requirement under subsection (1)(*b*) to make a disclosure of any information in an intelligible form shall be taken to have complied with that requirement if—

- (*a*) he makes, instead, a disclosure of any key to the protected information that is in his possession; and
- (*b*) that disclosure is made, in accordance with the notice imposing the requirement, to the person to whom, and by the time by which, he was required to provide the information in that form.

(3) Where, in a case in which a disclosure requirement in respect of any protected information is imposed on any person by a section 49 notice—

- (*a*) that person is not in possession of the information,
- (*b*) that person is incapable, without the use of a key that is not in his possession, of obtaining access to the information and of disclosing it in an intelligible form, or
- (*c*) the notice states, in pursuance of a direction under section 51, that it can be complied with only by the disclosure of a key to the information,

the effect of imposing that disclosure requirement on that person is that he shall be required, in accordance with the notice imposing the requirement, to make a disclosure of any key to the protected information that is in his possession at a relevant time.

(4) Subsections (5) to (7) apply where a person ("the person given notice")—

- (*a*) is entitled or obliged to disclose a key to protected information for the purpose of complying with any disclosure requirement imposed by a section 49 notice; and
- (*b*) is in possession of more than one key to that information.

(5) It shall not be necessary, for the purpose of complying with the requirement, for the person given notice to make a disclosure of any keys in addition to those the disclosure of which is, alone, sufficient to enable the person to whom they are disclosed to obtain access to the information and to put it into an intelligible form.

(6) Where—

(*a*) subsection (5) allows the person given notice to comply with a requirement without disclosing all of the keys in his possession, and

(*b*) there are different keys, or combinations of keys, in the possession of that person the disclosure of which would, under that subsection, constitute compliance,

the person given notice may select which of the keys, or combination of keys, to disclose for the purpose of complying with that requirement in accordance with that subsection.

(7) Subject to subsections (5) and (6), the person given notice shall not be taken to have complied with the disclosure requirement by the disclosure of a key unless he has disclosed every key to the protected information that is in his possession at a relevant time.

(8) Where, in a case in which a disclosure requirement in respect of any protected information is imposed on any person by a section 49 notice—

(*a*) that person has been in possession of the key to that information but is no longer in possession of it,

(*b*) if he had continued to have the key in his possession, he would have been required by virtue of the giving of the notice to disclose it, and

(*c*) he is in possession, at a relevant time, of information to which subsection (9) applies,

the effect of imposing that disclosure requirement on that person is that he shall be required, in accordance with the notice imposing the requirement, to disclose all such information to which subsection (9) applies as is in his possession and as he may be required, in accordance with that notice, to disclose by the person to whom he would have been required to disclose the key.

(9) This subsection applies to any information that would facilitate the obtaining or discovery of the key or the putting of the protected information into an intelligible form.

(10) In this section "relevant time", in relation to a disclosure requirement imposed by a section 49 notice, means the time of the giving of the notice or any subsequent time before the time by which the requirement falls to be complied with.

[Regulation of Investigatory Powers Act 2000, s 50.]

7.11107 **51. Cases in which key required** (1) A section 49 notice imposing a disclosure requirement in respect of any protected information shall not contain a statement for the purposes of section 50(3)(*c*) unless—

(*a*) the person who for the purposes of Schedule 2 granted the permission for the giving of the notice in relation to that information, or

(*b*) any person whose permission for the giving of a such a notice in relation to that information would constitute the appropriate permission under that Schedule,

has given a direction that the requirement can be complied with only by the disclosure of the key itself.

(2) A direction for the purposes of subsection (1) by the police, the National Crime Agency, Her Majesty's Revenue and Customs or a member of Her Majesty's forces shall not be given—

(*a*) in the case of a direction by the police or by a member of Her Majesty's forces who is a member of a police force, except by or with the permission of a chief officer of police;

(*aa*) in the case of a direction by [the National Crime Agency, except by or with the permission of the Director General of the National Crime Agency;

(*ab*) *repealed*

(*b*) in the case of a direction by Her Majesty's Revenue and Customs, except by or with the permission of the Commissioners for Her Majesty's Revenue and Customs; or

(*c*) in the case of a direction by a member of Her Majesty's forces who is not a member of a police force, except by or with the permission of a person of or above the rank of brigadier or its equivalent.

(3) A permission given for the purposes of subsection (2) by a chief officer of police, the Director General of the National Crime Agency, the Commissioners for Her Majesty's Revenue and Customs or a person of or above any such rank as is mentioned in paragraph (*c*) of that subsection must be given expressly in relation to the direction in question.

(4) A person shall not give a direction for the purposes of subsection (1) unless he believes—

(*a*) that there are special circumstances of the case which mean that the purposes for which it was believed necessary to impose the requirement in question would be defeated, in whole or in part, if the direction were not given; and

(*b*) that the giving of the direction is proportionate to what is sought to be achieved by prohibiting any compliance with the requirement in question otherwise than by the disclosure of the key itself.

(5) The matters to be taken into account in considering whether the requirement of subsection (4)(*b*) is satisfied in the case of any direction shall include—

(*a*) the extent and nature of any protected information, in addition to the protected information in respect of which the disclosure requirement is imposed, to which the key is also a key; and

(*b*) any adverse effect that the giving of the direction might have on a business carried on by the person on whom the disclosure requirement is imposed.

(6) Where a direction for the purposes of subsection (1) is given by a chief officer of police, by the Director General of the National Crime Agency, by the Commissioners for Her

Majesty's Revenue and Customs or by a member of Her Majesty's forces, the person giving the direction shall give a notification that he has done so—

(*a*) in a case where the direction is given—

(i) by a member of Her Majesty's forces who is not a member of a police force, and

(ii) otherwise than in connection with activities of members of Her Majesty's forces in Northern Ireland,

to the Intelligences Services Commissioner; and

(*b*) in any other case, to the Chief Surveillance Commissioner.

(7) A notification under subsection (6)—

(*a*) must be given not more than seven days after the day of the giving of the direction to which it relates; and

(*b*) may be given either in writing or by being transmitted to the Commissioner in question by electronic means.*

[Regulation of Investigatory Powers Act 2000, s 51 as amended by the Serious Organised Crime and Police Act 2005, Sch 4, the Serious Crime Act 2007, Sch 12, SI 2007/1098, the Policing and Crime Act 2009, Sch 7, the Crime and Courts Act 2013, Sch 8 and SI 2013/602.]

* **Amended by the Investigatory Powers Act 2016, s 233, Sch 10 from a date to be appointed.**

*Contributions to costs*

7.11108 52. **Arrangements for payments for disclosure** (1) It shall be the duty of the Secretary of State to ensure that such arrangements are in force as he thinks appropriate for requiring or authorising, in such cases as he thinks fit, the making to persons to whom section 49 notices are given of appropriate contributions towards the costs incurred by them in complying with such notices.

(2) For the purpose of complying with his duty under this section, the Secretary of State may make arrangements for payments to be made out of money provided by Parliament.

[Regulation of Investigatory Powers Act 2000, s 52.]

*Offences*

7.11109 53. **Failure to comply with a notice** (1) A person to whom a section 49 notice has been given is guilty of an offence if he knowingly fails, in accordance with the notice, to make the disclosure required by virtue of the giving of the notice.

(2) In proceedings against any person for an offence under this section, if it is shown that that person was in possession of a key to any protected information at any time before the time of the giving of the section 49 notice, that person shall be taken for the purposes of those proceedings to have continued to be in possession of that key at all subsequent times, unless it is shown that the key was not in his possession after the giving of the notice and before the time by which he was required to disclose it.

(3) For the purposes of this section a person shall be taken to have shown that he was not in possession of a key to protected information at a particular time if—

(*a*) sufficient evidence of that fact is adduced to raise an issue with respect to it; and

(*b*) the contrary is not proved beyond a reasonable doubt.

(4) In proceedings against any person for an offence under this section it shall be a defence for that person to show—

(*a*) that it was not reasonably practicable for him to make the disclosure required by virtue of the giving of the section 49 notice before the time by which he was required, in accordance with that notice, to make it; but

(*b*) that he did make that disclosure as soon after that time as it was reasonably practicable for him to do so.

(5) A person guilty of an offence under this section shall be liable—

(*a*) on conviction on indictment, to imprisonment for a term not exceeding the appropriate maximum term or to a fine, or to both;

(*b*) on summary conviction, to imprisonment for a term not exceeding six months or to a fine not exceeding the statutory maximum, or to both.

(5A) In subsection (5) 'the appropriate maximum term' means—

(*a*) in a national security case or a child indecency case, five years; and

(*b*) in any other case, two years.

(5B) In subsection (5A) 'a national security case' means a case in which the grounds specified in the notice to which the offence relates as the grounds for imposing a disclosure requirement were or included a belief that the imposition of the requirement was necessary in the interests of national security.

(6) In subsection (5A) "a child indecency case" means a case in which the grounds specified in the notice to which the offence relates as the grounds for imposing a disclosure requirement were or included a belief that the imposition of the requirement was necessary for the purpose of preventing or detecting an offence under any of the provisions listed in subsection (7).

(7) Those provisions are—

(*a*) section 1 of the Protection of Children Act 1978 (showing or taking etc an indecent photograph of a child: England and Wales);

(*b*) Article 3 of the Protection of Children (Northern Ireland) Order 1978 (SI 1978/1047 (NI 17)) (corresponding offence for Northern Ireland);

(*c*) section 52 or 52A of the Civic Government (Scotland) Act 1982 (showing or taking etc or possessing an indecent photograph of a child: Scotland);

(*d*) section 160 of the Criminal Justice Act 1988 (possessing an indecent photograph of a child: England and Wales);

(*e*) Article 15 of the Criminal Justice (Evidence, Etc) (Northern Ireland) Order 1988 (SI 1988/1847 (NI 17)) (corresponding offence for Northern Ireland).

[Regulation of Investigatory Powers Act 2000, s 53 as amended by Terrorism Act 2006, s 15 and the Policing and Crime Act 2009, s 26.]

**7.11110 54. Tipping-off** (1) This section applies where a section 49 notice contains a provision requiring—

(*a*) the person to whom the notice is given, and

(*b*) every other person who becomes aware of it or of its contents,

to keep secret the giving of the notice, its contents and the things done in pursuance of it.

(2) A requirement to keep anything secret shall not be included in a section 49 notice except where—

(*a*) it is included with the consent of the person who for the purposes of Schedule 2 granted the permission for the giving of the notice; or

(*b*) the person who gives the notice is himself a person whose permission for the giving of such a notice in relation to the information in question would have constituted appropriate permission under that Schedule.

(3) A section 49 notice shall not contain a requirement to keep anything secret except where the protected information to which it relates—

(*a*) has come into the possession of the police, the National Crime Agency, Her Majesty's Revenue and Customs or any of the intelligence services, or

(*b*) is likely to come into the possession of the police, the National Crime Agency, Her Majesty's Revenue and Customs or any of the intelligence services,

by means which it is reasonable, in order to maintain the effectiveness of any investigation or operation or of investigatory techniques generally, or in the interests of the safety or well-being of any person, to keep secret from a particular person.

(4) A person who makes a disclosure to any other person of anything that he is required by a section 49 notice to keep secret shall be guilty of an offence and liable—

(*a*) on conviction on indictment, to imprisonment for a term not exceeding five years or to a fine, or to both;

(*b*) on summary conviction, to imprisonment for a term not exceeding six months or to a fine not exceeding the statutory maximum, or to both.

(5) In proceedings against any person for an offence under this section in respect of any disclosure, it shall be a defence for that person to show that—

(*a*) the disclosure was effected entirely by the operation of software designed to indicate when a key to protected information has ceased to be secure; and

(*b*) that person could not reasonably have been expected to take steps, after being given the notice or (as the case may be) becoming aware of it or of its contents, to prevent the disclosure.

(6) In proceedings against any person for an offence under this section in respect of any disclosure, it shall be a defence for that person to show that—

(*a*) the disclosure was made by or to a professional legal adviser in connection with the giving, by the adviser to any client of his, of advice about the effect of provisions of this Part; and

(*b*) the person to whom or, as the case may be, by whom it was made was the client or a representative of the client.

(7) In proceedings against any person for an offence under this section in respect of any disclosure, it shall be a defence for that person to show that the disclosure was made by a legal adviser—

(*a*) in contemplation of, or in connection with, any legal proceedings; and

(*b*) for the purposes of those proceedings.

(8) Neither subsection (6) nor subsection (7) applies in the case of a disclosure made with a view to furthering any criminal purpose.

(9) In proceedings against any person for an offence under this section in respect of any disclosure, it shall be a defence for that person to show that the disclosure was confined to a disclosure made to a relevant Commissioner or authorised—

(*a*) by such a Commissioner;

(*b*) by the terms of the notice;

(*c*) by or on behalf of the person who gave the notice; or

(*d*) by or on behalf of a person who—

(i) is in lawful possession of the protected information to which the notice relates; and

(ii) came into possession of that information as mentioned in section 49(1).

(10) In proceedings for an offence under this section against a person other than the person to whom the notice was given, it shall be a defence for the person against whom the proceedings are brought to show that he neither knew nor had reasonable grounds for suspecting that the notice contained a requirement to keep secret what was disclosed.

(11) In this section "relevant Commissioner" means the Interception of Communications Commissioner, the Intelligence Services Commissioner or any Surveillance Commissioner or Assistant Surveillance Commissioner.*

[Regulation of Investigatory Powers Act 2000, s 54 as amended by the Serious Organised Crime and Police Act 2005, Sch 4, SI 2007/1098 and the Serious Crime Act 2007, Sch 12, the Crime and Courts Act 2013, Sch 8 and SI 2013/602.]

---

* **Amended by the Investigatory Powers Act 2016, s 233 from a date to be appointed.**

*Safeguards*

7.11111 **55. General duties of specified authorities** (1) This section applies to—

(*a*) the Secretary of State and every other Minister of the Crown in charge of a government department;

(*b*) every chief officer of police;

(*ba*) the Director General of the National Crime Agency;

(*bb*) *repealed;*

(*c*) the Commissioners for Her Majesty's Revenue and Customs; and

(*d*) every person whose officers or employees include persons with duties that involve the giving of section 49 notices.

(2) It shall be the duty of each of the persons to whom this section applies to ensure that such arrangements are in force, in relation to persons under his control who by virtue of this Part obtain possession of keys to protected information, as he considers necessary for securing—

(*a*) that a key disclosed in pursuance of a section 49 notice is used for obtaining access to, or putting into an intelligible form, only protected information in relation to which power to give such a notice was exercised or could have been exercised if the key had not already been disclosed;

(*b*) that the uses to which a key so disclosed is put are reasonable having regard both to the uses to which the person using the key is entitled to put any protected information to which it relates and to the other circumstances of the case;

(*c*) that, having regard to those matters, the use and any retention of the key are proportionate to what is sought to be achieved by its use or retention;

(*d*) that the requirements of subsection (3) are satisfied in relation to any key disclosed in pursuance of a section 49 notice;

(*e*) that, for the purpose of ensuring that those requirements are satisfied, any key so disclosed is stored, for so long as it is retained, in a secure manner;

(*f*) that all records of a key so disclosed (if not destroyed earlier) are destroyed as soon as the key is no longer needed for the purpose of enabling protected information to be put into an intelligible form.

(3) The requirements of this subsection are satisfied in relation to any key disclosed in pursuance of a section 49 notice if—

(*a*) the number of persons to whom the key is disclosed or otherwise made available, and

(*b*) the number of copies made of the key,

are each limited to the minimum that is necessary for the purpose of enabling protected information to be put into an intelligible form.

(3A) The power of the Director General of the National Crime Agency to delegate functions under paragraph 10 of Schedule 1 to the Crime and Courts Act 2013 does not apply in relation to the Director General's duties under this section.

(3B) *Repealed.*

(4) Subject to subsection (5), where any relevant person incurs any loss or damage in consequence of—

(*a*) any breach by a person to whom this section applies of the duty imposed on him by subsection (2), or

(*b*) any contravention by any person whatever of arrangements made in pursuance of that subsection in relation to persons under the control of a person to whom this section applies,

the breach or contravention shall be actionable against the person to whom this section applies at the suit or instance of the relevant person.

(5) A person is a relevant person for the purposes of subsection (4) if he is—

(*a*) a person who has made a disclosure in pursuance of a section 49 notice; or

(*b*) a person whose protected information or key has been disclosed in pursuance of such a notice;

and loss or damage shall be taken into account for the purposes of that subsection to the extent only that it relates to the disclosure of particular protected information or a particular key which, in the case of a person falling with paragraph (*b*), must be his information or key.

(6) For the purposes of subsection (5)—

(*a*) information belongs to a person if he has any right that would be infringed by an unauthorised disclosure of the information; and

(*b*) a key belongs to a person if it is a key to information that belongs to him or he has any right that would be infringed by an unauthorised disclosure of the key.

(7) In any proceedings brought by virtue of subsection (4), it shall be the duty of the court to have regard to any opinion with respect to the matters to which the proceedings relate that is or has been given by a relevant Commissioner.

(8) In this section "relevant Commissioner" means the Interception of Communications Commissioner, the Intelligence Services Commissioner, the Investigatory Powers Commissioner for Northern Ireland or any Surveillance Commissioner or Assistant Surveillance Commissioner.*

[Regulation of Investigatory Powers Act 2000, s 55 as amended by the Serious Organised Crime and Police Act 2005, Sch 4, SI 2007/1098, the Serious Crime Act 2007, Sch 12, the Crime and Courts Act 2013, Sch 8 and SI 2013/602.]

---

* **Amended by the Investigatory Powers Act 2016, s 233 from a date to be appointed.**

*Interpretation of Part III*

**7.11112 56. Interpretation of Part III** (1) In this Part—

"chief officer of police" means any of the following—

(*a*) the chief constable of a police force maintained under or by virtue of section 2 of the Police Act 1996;

(*b*) the Commissioner of Police of the Metropolis;

(*c*) the Commissioner of Police for the City of London;

(*ca*) the chief constable of the Police Service of Scotland;

(*d*) the Chief Constable of the Police Service of Northern Ireland;

(*e*) the Chief Constable of the Ministry of Defence Police;

(*f*) the Provost Marshal of the Royal Navy Police;

(*g*) the Provost Marshal of the Royal Military Police;

(*h*) the Provost Marshal of the Royal Air Force Police;

(*i*) the Chief Constable of the British Transport Police;

(*j*) *repealed*

(*k*) *repealed*

"electronic signature" means anything in electronic form which—

(*a*) is incorporated into, or otherwise logically associated with, any electronic communication or other electronic data;

(*b*) is generated by the signatory or other source of the communication or data; and

(*c*) is used for the purpose of facilitating, by means of a link between the signatory or other source and the communication or data, the establishment of the authenticity of the communication or data, the establishment of its integrity, or both;

"key", in relation to any electronic data, means any key, code, password, algorithm or other data the use of which (with or without other keys)—

(*a*) allows access to the electronic data, or

(*b*) facilitates the putting of the data into an intelligible form;

"the police" means—

(*a*) any constable (except a constable who is a National Crime Agency officer;

(*b*) the Commissioner of Police of the Metropolis or any Assistant Commissioner of Police of the Metropolis; or

(*c*) the Commissioner of Police for the City of London;

"protected information" means any electronic data which, without the key to the data—

(*a*) cannot, or cannot readily, be accessed, or

(*b*) cannot, or cannot readily, be put into an intelligible form;

"section 49 notice" means a notice under section 49;

"warrant" includes any authorisation, notice or other instrument (however described) conferring a power of the same description as may, in other cases, be conferred by a warrant.

(2) References in this Part to a person's having information (including a key to protected information) in his possession include references—

(*a*) to its being in the possession of a person who is under his control so far as that information is concerned;

(*b*) to his having an immediate right of access to it, or an immediate right to have it transmitted or otherwise supplied to him; and

(*c*) to its being, or being contained in, anything which he or a person under his control is entitled, in exercise of any statutory power and without otherwise taking possession of it, to detain, inspect or search.

(3) References in this Part to something's being intelligible or being put into an intelligible form include references to its being in the condition in which it was before an encryption or similar process was applied to it or, as the case may be, to its being restored to that condition.

(4) In this section—

(*a*) references to the authenticity of any communication or data are references to any one or more of the following—
  (i) whether the communication or data comes from a particular person or other source;
  (ii) whether it is accurately timed and dated;
  (iii) whether it is intended to have legal effect;
  and
(*b*) references to the integrity of any communication or data are references to whether there has been any tampering with or other modification of the communication or data.

[Regulation of Investigatory Powers Act 2000, s 56 as amended by the Police (Northern Ireland) Act 2000, s 78 and the Serious Organised Crime and Police Act 2005, Sch 4, the Armed Forces Act 2006, Sch 16, the Serious Crime Act 2007, Sch 12, SI 2007/1098, the Crime and Courts Act 2013, Sch 8 and SI 2013/602.]

## Part IV[1]

## Scrutiny etc of Investigatory Powers and of the Functions of the Intelligence Services*

[1] Part IV contains ss 57–72 and Sch 3.

* **Ss 57, 58, 59, 59A, 60, 62. 63 repealed by the Investigatory Powers Act 2016, s 240 from a date to be appointed.**

*Codes of practice*

### 7.11113 71. *Issue and revision of Codes of Practice*[*1]

* **Amended by the Investigatory Powers Act 2016, Sch 10 from a date to be appointed.**

[1] The Regulation of Investigatory Powers (Covert Surveillance: Code of Practice) Order 2002, SI 2002/1933 has been made which brought into force the code of practice entitled "Covert Surveillance", laid before each House of Parliament on 10 June 2002, relating to covert surveillance under Part II of the 2000 Act, on 1 August 2002.

The Regulation of Investigatory Powers (Investigation of Protected Electronic Information: Code of Practice) Order 2007, SI 2007/2200 has been made which brought into force the code of practice entitled "Investigation of Protected Electronic Information", laid before each House of Parliament in draft on 7 June 2007, relating to the investigation of protected electronic information under Part 3 of the Regulation of Investigatory Powers Act 2000, on 1 October 2007.

The Regulation of Investigatory Powers (Covert Human Intelligence Sources: Code of Practice) Order 2014, SI 2014/3119 has been made which brought into force on 10 December 2014 the code of practice entitled "Covert Human Intelligence Sources", laid before each House of Parliament in draft on 22 July 2014, relating to the conduct and the use of covert human intelligence sources under Part 2 of the Regulation of Investigatory Powers Act 2000.

The Regulation of Investigatory Powers (Covert Surveillance and Property Interference: Code of Practice) Order 2014, SI 2014/3103 has been made which brought into force on 10 December 2014 the code of practice entitled "Covert Surveillance and Property Interference", laid before each House of Parliament in draft on 22 July 2014, relating to the carrying out of covert surveillance under Part 2 of the Regulation of Investigatory Powers Act 2000 and to interference with property or wireless telegraphy under s 5 of the Intelligence Services Act 1994 and Part 3 of the Police Act 1997.

The Retention of Communications Data (Code of Practice) Order 2015, SI 2015/926 has been made which brought into force on 25 March 2015 the Code of Practice entitled "Retention of Communications Data", laid before each House of Parliament on 4 March 2015, relating to the retention of Communications Data under s 1(1) to (6) of the Data Retention and Investigatory Powers Act 2014.

The Regulation of Investigatory Powers (Acquisition and Disclosure of Communications Data: Code of Practice) Order 2015, SI 2015/927 brought into force on 25 March 2015 the Code of Practice entitled "Acquisition and Disclosure of Communications Data", laid before Parliament in draft on 4 March 2015, relating to the acquisition and disclosure of communications data under Chapter 2 of Part 1 of the Regulation of Investigatory Powers Act 2000.

The Regulation of Investigatory Powers (Interception of Communications: Code of Practice) Order 2016, SI 2016/37 has been made which brought into force on 15 January 2016 the code of practice entitled "Interception of Communications", laid before each House of Parliament on 4 November 2015, relating to the interception of communications under Chapter 1 of Part 1 of the 2000 Act.

The Equipment Interference (Code of Practice) Order 2016, SI 2016/38 has been made which brought into force on 15 January 2016 the code of practice entitled "Equipment Interference", laid before each House of Parliament on 4 November 2015, relating to the authorisation of interference with property under s 5 of the Intelligence Services Act 1994.

**7.11114 72. Effect of codes of practice** (1) A person exercising or performing any power or duty in relation to which provision may be made by a code of practice under section 71 shall, in doing so, have regard to the provisions (so far as they are applicable) of every code of practice for the time being in force under that section.

(2) A failure on the part of any person to comply with any provision of a code of practice for the time being in force under section 71 shall not of itself render him liable to any criminal or civil proceedings.

(3) A code of practice in force at any time under section 71 shall be admissible in evidence in any criminal or civil proceedings.

(4) If any provision of a code of practice issued or revised under section 71 appears to—
  (*a*) the court or tribunal conducting any civil or criminal proceedings,
  (*b*) the Tribunal,
  (*c*) a relevant Commissioner carrying out any of his functions under this Act,
  (*d*) a Surveillance Commissioner carrying out his functions under this Act or the Police Act 1997, or
  (*e*) any Assistant Surveillance Commissioner carrying out any functions of his under section 63 of this Act,

to be relevant to any question arising in the proceedings, or in connection with the exercise of that jurisdiction or the carrying out of those functions, in relation to a time when it was in force, that provision of the code shall be taken into account in determining that question.

(5) In this section "relevant Commissioner" means the Interception of Communications Commissioner, the Intelligence Services Commissioner or the Investigatory Powers Commissioner for Northern Ireland.*

[Regulation of Investigatory Powers Act 2000, s 72.]

* **Amended by the Investigatory Powers Act 2016, Sch 10 from a date to be appointed.**

## PART V[1]
## MISCELLANEOUS AND SUPPLEMENTAL

[1] Part V contains ss 73–83 and Schs 4 and 5.

## SCHEDULE 2
### Persons having the Appropriate Permission*

*(Amended by the Courts Act 2003, Sch 4, the Serious Organised Crime and Police Act 2005, Sch 4, SI 2007/1098, the Serious Crime Act 2007, Sch 12, the Protection of Freedoms Act 2012, Sch 9, the Crime and Courts Act 2013, Sch 8 and SI 2013/602.)*

* **Amended by the Investigatory Powers Act 2016, Sch 10 from a date to be appointed.** Section 49

*Requirement that appropriate permission is granted by a judge*

7.11115 1. (1) Subject to the following provisions of this Schedule, a person has the appropriate permission in relation to any protected information if, and only if, written permission for the giving of section 49 notices in relation to that information has been granted—

(*a*) in England and Wales, by a Circuit judge or a District Judge (Magistrates' Courts);
(*b*) in Scotland, by a sheriff; or
(*c*) in Northern Ireland, by a county court judge.

(2) Nothing in paragraphs 2 to 5 of this Schedule providing for the manner in which a person may be granted the appropriate permission in relation to any protected information without a grant under this paragraph shall be construed as requiring any further permission to be obtained in a case in which permission has been granted under this paragraph.

*Data obtained under warrant etc*

**2.** (1) This paragraph applies in the case of protected information falling within section 49(1)(*a*), (*b*) or (*c*) where the statutory power in question is one exercised, or to be exercised, in accordance with—

(*a*) a warrant issued by the Secretary of State or a person holding judicial office; or
(*b*) an authorisation under Part III of the Police Act 1997 (authorisation of otherwise unlawful action in respect of property).

(2) Subject to sub-paragraphs (3) to (5) and paragraph 6(1), a person has the appropriate permission in relation to that protected information (without any grant of permission under paragraph 1) if—

(*a*) the warrant or, as the case may be, the authorisation contained the relevant authority's permission for the giving of section 49 notices in relation to protected information to be obtained under the warrant or authorisation; or
(*b*) since the issue of the warrant or authorisation, written permission has been granted by the relevant authority for the giving of such notices in relation to protected information obtained under the warrant or authorisation.

(3) Only persons holding office under the Crown, the police, the National Crime Agency and Her Majesty's Revenue and Customs shall be capable of having the appropriate permission in relation to protected information obtained, or to be obtained, under a warrant issued by the Secretary of State.

(4) Only a person who—

(*a*) was entitled to exercise the power conferred by the warrant, or
(*b*) is of the description of persons on whom the power conferred by the warrant was, or could have been, conferred,

shall be capable of having the appropriate permission in relation to protected information obtained, or to be obtained, under a warrant issued by a person holding judicial office.

(5) Only the police, the National Crime Agency and Her Majesty's Revenue and Customs shall be capable of having the appropriate permission in relation to protected information obtained, or to be obtained, under an authorisation under Part III of the Police Act 1997.

(6) In this paragraph "the relevant authority"—

(*a*) in relation to a warrant issued by the Secretary of State, means the Secretary of State;
(*b*) in relation to a warrant issued by a person holding judicial office, means any person holding any judicial office that would have entitled him to issue the warrant; and
(*c*) in relation to protected information obtained under an authorisation under Part III of the Police Act 1997, means (subject to sub-paragraph (7)) an authorising officer within the meaning of section 93 of that Act.

(7) Section 94 of the Police Act 1997 (power of other persons to grant authorisations in urgent cases) shall apply in relation to—

(*a*) an application for permission for the giving of section 49 notices in relation to protected information obtained, or to be obtained, under an authorisation under Part III of that Act, and
(*b*) the powers of any authorising officer (within the meaning of section 93 of that Act) to grant such a permission,

as it applies in relation to an application for an authorisation under section 93 of that Act and the powers of such an officer under that section.

(8) References in this paragraph to a person holding judicial office are references to—

(*a*) any judge of the Crown Court or of the High Court of Justiciary;
(*b*) any sheriff;
(*c*) any justice of the peace;

(*d*) any resident magistrate in Northern Ireland; or

(*e*) any person holding any such judicial office as entitles him to exercise the jurisdiction of a judge of the Crown Court or of a justice of the peace.

(9) Protected information that comes into a person's possession by means of the exercise of any statutory power which—

(*a*) is exercisable without a warrant, but

(*b*) is so exercisable in the course of, or in connection with, the exercise of another statutory power for which a warrant is required,

shall not be taken, by reason only of the warrant required for the exercise of the power mentioned in paragraph (*b*), to be information in the case of which this paragraph applies.

*Data obtained by the intelligence services under statute but without a warrant*

**3.** (1) This paragraph applies in the case of protected information falling within section 49(1)(*a*), (*b*) or (*c*) which—

(*a*) has come into the possession of any of the intelligence services or is likely to do so; and

(*b*) is not information in the case of which paragraph 2 applies.

(2) Subject to paragraph 6(1), a person has the appropriate permission in relation to that protected information (without any grant of permission under paragraph 1) if written permission for the giving of section 49 notices in relation to that information has been granted by the Secretary of State.

(3) Sub-paragraph (2) applies where the protected information is in the possession, or (as the case may be) is likely to come into the possession, of both—

(*a*) one or more of the intelligence services, and

(*b*) a public authority which is not one of the intelligence services,

as if a grant of permission under paragraph 1 were unnecessary only where the application to the Secretary of State for permission under that sub-paragraph is made by or on behalf of a member of one of the intelligence services.

*Data obtained under statute by other persons but without a warrant*

**4.** (1) This paragraph applies—

(*a*) in the case of protected information falling within section 49(1)(*a*), (*b*) or (*c*) which is not information in the case of which paragraph 2 or 3 applies; and

(*b*) in the case of protected information falling within section 49(1)(*d*) which is not information also falling within section 49(1)(*a*), (*b*) or (*c*) in the case of which paragraph 3 applies.

(2) Subject to paragraph 6, where—

(*a*) the statutory power was exercised, or is likely to be exercised, by the police, the National Crime Agency, Her Majesty's Revenue and Customs or a member of Her Majesty's forces, or

(*b*) the information was provided or disclosed, or is likely to be provided or disclosed, to the police, the National Crime Agency, Her Majesty's Revenue and Customs or a member of Her Majesty's forces, or

(*c*) the information is in the possession of, or is likely to come into the possession of, the police, the National Crime Agency, Her Majesty's Revenue and Customs or a member of Her Majesty's forces,

the police, the National Crime Agency, Her Majesty's Revenue and Customs or, as the case may be, members of Her Majesty's forces have the appropriate permission in relation to the protected information, without any grant of permission under paragraph 1.

(3) In any other case a person shall not have the appropriate permission by virtue of a grant of permission under paragraph 1 unless he is a person falling within sub-paragraph (4).

(4) A person falls within this sub-paragraph if, as the case may be—

(*a*) he is the person who exercised the statutory power or is of the description of persons who would have been entitled to exercise it;

(*b*) he is the person to whom the protected information was provided or disclosed, or is of a description of person the provision or disclosure of the information to whom would have discharged the statutory duty; or

(*c*) he is a person who is likely to be a person falling within paragraph (*a*) or (*b*) when the power is exercised or the protected information provided or disclosed.

*Data obtained without the exercise of statutory powers*

**5.** (1) This paragraph applies in the case of protected information falling within section 49(1)(*e*).

(2) Subject to paragraph 6, a person has the appropriate permission in relation to that protected information (without any grant of permission under paragraph 1) if—

(*a*) the information is in the possession of any of the intelligence services, or is likely to come into the possession of any of those services; and

(*b*) written permission for the giving of section 49 notices in relation to that information has been granted by the Secretary of State.

(3) Sub-paragraph (2) applies where the protected information is in the possession, or (as the case may be) is likely to come into the possession, of both—

(*a*) one or more of the intelligence services, and

(*b*) the police, the National Crime Agency or Her Majesty's Revenue and Customs,

as if a grant of permission under paragraph 1 were unnecessary only where the application to the Secretary of State for permission under that sub-paragraph is made by or on behalf of a member of one of the intelligence services.

*General requirements relating to the appropriate permission*

**6.** (1) A person does not have the appropriate permission in relation to any protected information unless he is either—

(*a*) a person who has the protected information in his possession or is likely to obtain possession of it; or

(*b*) a person who is authorised (apart from this Act) to act on behalf of such a person.

(2) Subject to sub-paragraph (3), a constable does not by virtue of paragraph 1, 4 or 5 have the appropriate permission in relation to any protected information unless—

(*a*) he is of or above the rank of superintendent; or
(*b*) permission to give a section 49 notice in relation to that information has been granted by a person holding the rank of superintendent, or any higher rank.

(3) In the case of protected information that has come into the police's possession by means of the exercise of powers conferred by—
(*a*) section 47A of the Terrorism Act 2000 (power to stop and search) (including that section as it had effect by virtue of the Terrorism Act 2000 (Remedial) Order 2011 (SI 2011/631), or
(*b*) section 44 of the Terrorism Act 2000 or section 13A or 13B of the Prevention of Terrorism (Temporary Provisions) Act 1989 (which previously had effect for similar purposes),

the permission required by sub-paragraph (2) shall not be granted by any person below the rank mentioned in paragraph 14(1) and (2) of Schedule 6B to that Act of 2000 (see the definition of "senior police officer"), section 44(4) of that Act of 2000 or, as the case may be, section 13A(1) of that Act of 1989.

(3A) A National Crime Agency officer does not by virtue of paragraph 1, 4 or 5 have the appropriate permission in relation to any protected information unless permission to give a section 49 notice in relation to that information has been granted—
(*a*) by the Director General; or
(*b*) by a member of the staff of the Agency of or above such level as the Director General may designate for the purposes of this sub-paragraph.

(3B) *Repealed.*

(4) An officer of Revenue and Customs does not by virtue of paragraph 1, 4 or 5 have the appropriate permission in relation to any protected information unless permission to give a section 49 notice in relation to that information has been granted—
(*a*) by the Commissioners for Her Majesty's Revenue and Customs; or
(*b*) by an officer of Revenue and Customs of or above such level as the Commissioners may designate for the purposes of this sub-paragraph.

(5) A member of Her Majesty's forces does not by virtue of paragraph 1, 4 or 5 have the appropriate permission in relation to any protected information unless—
(*a*) he is of or above the rank of lieutenant colonel or its equivalent; or
(*b*) permission to give a section 49 notice in relation to that information has been granted by a person holding the rank of lieutenant colonel or its equivalent, or by a person holding a rank higher than lieutenant colonel or its equivalent.

(6) In sub-paragraph (2) "constable" does not include a constable who is a National Crime Agency officer.

*Duration of permission*

7. (1) A permission granted by any person under any provision of this Schedule shall not entitle any person to give a section 49 notice at any time after the permission has ceased to have effect.

(2) Such a permission, once granted, shall continue to have effect (notwithstanding the cancellation, expiry or other discharge of any warrant or authorisation in which it is contained or to which it relates) until such time (if any) as it—
(*a*) expires in accordance with any limitation on its duration that was contained in its terms; or
(*b*) is withdrawn by the person who granted it or by a person holding any office or other position that would have entitled him to grant it.

*Formalities for permissions granted by the Secretary of State*

**8.** A permission for the purposes of any provision of this Schedule shall not be granted by the Secretary of State except—
(*a*) under his hand; or
(*b*) in an urgent case in which the Secretary of State has expressly authorised the grant of the permission, under the hand of a senior official.

## Mobile Telephones (Re-programming) Act 2002[1]

(2002 c 31)

7.11116 **1. Re-programming mobile telephone etc** (1) A person commits an offence if—
(*a*) he changes a unique device identifier,
(*b*) he interferes with the operation of a unique device identifier,
(*c*) he offers or agrees to change, or interfere with the operation of, a unique device identifier, or
(*d*) he offers or agrees to arrange for another person to change, or interfere with the operation of, a unique device identifier.

(2) A unique device identifier is an electronic equipment identifier which is unique to a mobile wireless communications device.

(3) But a person does not commit an offence under this section if—
(*a*) he is the manufacturer of the device, or
(*b*) he does the act mentioned in subsection (1) with the written consent of the manufacturer of the device.

(4) A person guilty of an offence under this section is liable[2]—
(*a*) on summary conviction, to imprisonment for a term not exceeding 6 months or to a fine not exceeding the statutory maximum or to both, or
(*b*) on conviction on indictment, to imprisonment for a term not exceeding 5 years or to a fine or to both.

[Mobile Telephones (Re-programming) Act 2002, s 1 as amended by the Violent Crime Reduction Act 2006, s 62 and Sch 5.]

---

[1] Sections 1 and 2 of this Act were brought into effect on 4 October 2002 in accordance with the Mobile Telephones (Re-programming) Act 2002 (Commencement) Order 2002, SI 2002/2294 made under s 3.

[2] For mode of trial of this offence which is triable either way, see the Magistrates' Courts Act 1980, ss 17A–21 in PART I, MAGISTRATES' COURTS, PROCEDURE, ante.

7.11117 **2. Possession or supply of anything for re-programming purposes** (1) A person commits an offence if—

(*a*) he has in his custody or under his control anything which may be used for the purpose of changing or interfering with the operation of a unique device identifier, and

(*b*) he intends to use the thing unlawfully for that purpose or to allow it to be used unlawfully for that purpose.

(2) A person commits an offence if—

(*a*) he supplies anything which may be used for the purpose of changing or interfering with the operation of a unique device identifier, and

(*b*) he knows or believes that the person to whom the thing is supplied intends to use it unlawfully for that purpose or to allow it to be used unlawfully for that purpose.

(3) A person commits an offence if—

(*a*) he offers to supply anything which may be used for the purpose of changing or interfering with the operation of a unique device identifier, and

(*b*) he knows or believes that the person to whom the thing is offered intends if it is supplied to him to use it unlawfully for that purpose or to allow it to be used unlawfully for that purpose.

(4) A unique device identifier is an electronic equipment identifier which is unique to a mobile wireless communications device.

(5) A thing is used by a person unlawfully for a purpose if in using it for that purpose he commits an offence under section 1.

(6) A person guilty of an offence under this section is liable[1]—

(*a*) on summary conviction, to imprisonment for a term not exceeding 6 months or to a fine not exceeding the statutory maximum or to both, or

(*b*) on conviction on indictment, to imprisonment for a term not exceeding 5 years or to a fine or to both.

[Mobile Telephones (Re-programming) Act 2002, s 2.]

---

[1] For mode of trial of this offence which is triable either way, see the Magistrates' Courts Act 1980, For mode of trial of this offence which is triable either way, see the Magistrates' Courts Act 1980, ss 17A–21 in PART I, MAGISTRATES' COURTS, PROCEDURE, ante.

# Communications Act 2003[1]

(2003 c 21)

*Offences relating to networks and services*

7.11119 **125. Dishonestly obtaining electronic communications services** (1) A person who—

(*a*) dishonestly obtains an electronic communications service, and

(*b*) does so with intent to avoid payment of a charge applicable to the provision of that service,

is guilty of an offence.

(2) It is not an offence under this section to obtain a service mentioned in section 297(1) of the Copyright, Designs and Patents Act 1988 (c 48) (dishonestly obtaining a broadcasting service provided from a place in the UK).

(3) A person guilty of an offence under this section shall be liable—

(*a*) on summary conviction, to imprisonment for a term not exceeding six months or to a fine not exceeding the statutory maximum, or to both;

(*b*) on conviction on indictment, to imprisonment for a term not exceeding five years or to a fine, or to both.

[Communications Act 2003, s 125 as amended by SI 2003/2498.]

---

[1] The Act provides a regulatory framework for the communications sector, reflecting the proposals made in the Communications White Paper – A New Future for Communications (Cm 5010) – published on 12 December 2000.

The main provisions of the Act provide for: the transfer of functions to the Office of Communications (OFCOM) from the bodies and office holders that previously regulated the telecommunications and broadcasting and managed the radio spectrum; namely: the Broadcasting Standards Commission; the Director General of Telecommunications; the Independent Television Commission; the Radio Authority; and the Secretary of State, as far as the office included (through the Radio Communications Agency) a regulatory role in respect of the allocation, maintenance and supervision of non-military radio spectrum in the UK.

The Office of Communications Act 2002 established OFCOM and gave it a single initial function – to prepare to assume regulatory functions at a later stage. It also gave the existing regulators additional functions and duties to assist OFCOM to prepare.

Once the transfer to OFCOM of the functions, property, rights and liabilities of the bodies and office holders that previously regulated the communications sector has taken effect OFCOM will develop and maintain new regulatory rules for the communications sector within the context of a single set of regulatory objectives, and in the light of the changing market environment.

In February 2002 the European Parliament and the Council of Ministers adopted four Directives ("the EC Communications Directives"), which set out a package of measures for a common regulatory framework for electronic communications networks and services. Provisions in the Act implement a significant proportion of this new regulatory package in the UK.

**7.11120 126. Possession or supply of apparatus etc for contravening s 125** (1) A person is guilty of an offence if, with an intention falling within subsection (3), he has in his possession or under his control anything that may be used—

(*a*) for obtaining an electronic communications service; or

(*b*) in connection with obtaining such a service.

(2) A person is guilty of an offence if—

(*a*) he supplies or offers to supply anything which may be used as mentioned in subsection (1); and

(*b*) he knows or believes that the intentions in relation to that thing of the person to whom it is supplied or offered fall within subsection (3).

(3) A person's intentions fall within this subsection if he intends—

(*a*) to use the thing to obtain an electronic communications service dishonestly;

(*b*) to use the thing for a purpose connected with the dishonest obtaining of such a service;

(*c*) dishonestly to allow the thing to be used to obtain such a service; or

(*d*) to allow the thing to be used for a purpose connected with the dishonest obtaining of such a service.

(4) An intention does not fall within subsection (3) if it relates exclusively to the obtaining of a service mentioned in section 297(1) of the Copyright, Designs and Patents Act 1988 (c 48).

(5) A person guilty of an offence under this section shall be liable—

(*a*) on summary conviction, to imprisonment for a term not exceeding six months or to a fine not exceeding the statutory maximum, or to both; and

(*b*) on conviction on indictment, to imprisonment for a term not exceeding five years or to a fine, or to both.

(6) In this section, references, in the case of a thing used for recording data, to the use of that thing include references to the use of data recorded by it.

[Communications Act 2003, s 126.]

**7.11121 127. Improper use of public electronic communications network** (1) A person is guilty of an offence if he—

(*a*) sends by means of a public electronic communications network a message or other matter that is grossly offensive[1] or of an indecent, obscene or menacing[2] character; or

(*b*) causes any such message or matter to be so sent.

(2) A person is guilty of an offence if, for the purpose of causing annoyance, inconvenience or needless anxiety to another, he—

(*a*) sends by means of a public electronic communications network, a message that he knows to be false,

(*b*) causes such a message to be sent; or

(*c*) persistently makes use of a public electronic communications network.

(3) A person guilty of an offence under this section shall be liable, on summary conviction, to imprisonment for a term not exceeding six months or to a fine not exceeding level 5 on the standard scale, or to both.

(4) Subsections (1) and (2) do not apply to anything done in the course of providing a programme service (within the meaning of the Broadcasting Act 1990 (c 42)).

(5) An information or complaint relating to an offence under this section may be tried by a magistrates' court in England and Wales or Northern Ireland if it is laid or made—

(*a*) before the end of the period of 3 years beginning with the day on which the offence was committed, and

(*b*) before the end of the period of 6 months beginning with the day on which evidence comes to the knowledge of the prosecutor which the prosecutor considers sufficient to justify proceedings.

(6) Summary proceedings for an offence under this section may be commenced in Scotland—

(*a*) before the end of the period of 3 years beginning with the day on which the offence was committed, and

(*b*) before the end of the period of 6 months beginning with the day on which evidence comes to the knowledge of the prosecutor which the prosecutor considers sufficient to justify proceedings,

and section 136(3) of the Criminal Procedure (Scotland) Act 1995 (date when proceedings deemed to be commenced) applies for the purposes of this subsection as it applies for the purposes of that section.

(7) A certificate of a prosecutor as to the date on which evidence described in subsection (5)(*b*) or (6)(*b*) came to his or her knowledge is conclusive evidence of that fact.

[Communications Act 2003, s 127 as amended by the Criminal Justice and Courts Act 2015, s 51.]

---

1 In *DPP v Collins* [2006] UK 40, [2006] 4 All ER 602, [2006] 1 WLR 2223, (2006) 170 JP 712, [2007] 1 Cr App R 5, [2007] Crim LR 98 the House of Lords held that the purpose and elements of the offence under s 127(1)(*a*) were as follows. The object was to prohibit the use of a service provided and funded by the public for the benefit of the public, for the transmission of communications that contravened the basic standards of society. The proscribed act was the sending of the message of the proscribed character by the defined means, and the offence was complete when the message was sent. It was for the court, applying the standards of an open and just multiracial society and taking account of the context and all relevant circumstances, to determine as a question of fact whether a message was grossly offensive. It was necessary

to show that the defendant intended his words to be grossly offensive to those to whom the message related, or that he was aware that they might be taken to be so. Although s 127(1)(*a*) interfered with the right to freedom of expression under art 10 of the Convention, it went no further than was necessary in a democratic society for achieving the legitimate objective of preventing the use of the public electronic communications network for attacking the reputations and rights of others.

[2] In *Chambers v DPP* [2012] EWHC 2157 (Admin), [2013] 1 All ER 149, [2013] 1 WLR 2157, [2013] 1 Cr App Rep 1 the defendant was a registered user of Twitter and 'tweeted' in his own name. When he learned of the closure of an airport owing to adverse weather conditions he tweeted ' . . . . You've got a week and a bit to get your shit together otherwise I am blowing the airport sky high!!' This was posted onto the public time line, which meant it was available to be read by about 600 Twitter followers of the defendant. The conviction was quashed by the Divisional Court. At the time the tweet was posted it was a 'message' within s 127, but on an objective assessment there was no proper basis for concluding that the tweet constituted or included a message of a menacing character. There was no evidence that any Twitter follower of the defendant, or anyone else who may have seen the tweet, had found it to be menacing or even slightly alarming. 'The message must be credible as an immediate threat to the mind of an ordinary person of normal stability and courage . . . it is difficult to imagine a serious threat in which warning of it is given to a large number of tweet 'followers' in ample time for the threat to be reported and extinguished' (per Lord Judge CJ at paras 30 and 31). His Lordship added this regarding the mental element of the offence. No different test applied to 'menacing' messages than those which were 'grossly offensive'. The mental element is satisfied 'if the offender is proved to have been aware or to have recognised the risk at the time of sending the message that it may create fear or apprehension in any reasonable member of the public who reads or sees it. We would merely emphasise that, even expressed in these terms, the mental element of the offence is directed exclusively to the state of the mind of the offender, and that if he may have intended the message as a joke, even if a joke in bad taste, it is unlikely that the mens rea required before conviction for the offence of sending a message of a menacing character will be established' (at para 37).

See also *Karsten v Wood Green Crown Court* [2014] EWHC 2900 (Admin), [2014] All ER (D) 286 (Oct). Conviction quashed where defendant had used nasty, anti-semitic words, but they could not be regarded as menacing in the sense demanded by authority.

*Powers to deal with emergencies*

**7.11122 132. Powers to require suspension or restriction of a provider's entitlement**

(1) If the Secretary of State has reasonable grounds for believing that it is necessary to do so—

(*a*) to protect the public from any threat to public safety or public health, or

(*b*) in the interests of national security,

he may, by a direction to OFCOM, require them to give a direction under subsection (3) to a person ("the relevant provider") who provides an electronic communications network or electronic communications service or who makes associated facilities available.

(2) OFCOM must comply with a requirement of the Secretary of State under subsection (1) by giving to the relevant provider such direction under subsection (3) as they consider necessary for the purpose of complying with the Secretary of State's direction.

(3) A direction under this section is—

(*a*) a direction that the entitlement of the relevant provider to provide electronic communications networks or electronic communications services, or to make associated facilities available, is suspended (either generally or in relation to particular networks, services or facilities); or

(*b*) a direction that that entitlement is restricted in the respects set out in the direction.

(4) A direction under subsection (3)—

(*a*) must specify the networks, services and facilities to which it relates; and

(*b*) except so far as it otherwise provides, takes effect for an indefinite period beginning with the time at which it is notified to the person to whom it is given.

(5) A direction under subsection (3)—

(*a*) in providing for the effect of a suspension or restriction to be postponed, may provide for it to take effect only at a time determined by or in accordance with the terms of the direction; and

(*b*) in connection with the suspension or restriction contained in the direction or with the postponement of its effect, may impose such conditions on the relevant provider as appear to OFCOM to be appropriate for the purpose of protecting that provider's customers.

(6) Those conditions may include a condition requiring the making of payments—

(*a*) by way of compensation for loss or damage suffered by the relevant provider's customers as a result of the direction; or

(*b*) in respect of annoyance, inconvenience or anxiety to which they have been put in consequence of the direction.

(7) Where OFCOM give a direction under subsection (3), they shall, as soon as practicable after doing so, provide that person with an opportunity of—

(*a*) making representations about the effect of the direction; and

(*b*) proposing steps for remedying the situation.

(8) If OFCOM consider it appropriate to do so (whether in consequence of any representations or proposals made to them under subsection (3) or otherwise), they may, without revoking it, at any time modify the terms of a direction under subsection (3) in such manner as they consider appropriate.

(9) If the Secretary of State considers it appropriate to do so, he may, by a direction to OFCOM, require them to revoke a direction under subsection (3).

(10) Where OFCOM modify or revoke a direction they have given under subsection (3), they may do so—

(a) with effect from such time as they may direct;

(b) subject to compliance with such requirements as they may specify; and

(c) to such extent and in relation to such networks, services or facilities, or parts of a network, service or facility, as they may determine.

(11) It shall be the duty of OFCOM to comply with—

(a) a requirement under subsection (9) to revoke a direction; and

(b) a requirement contained in that direction as to how they should exercise their powers under subsection (10) in the case of the required revocation.

[Communications Act 2003, s 132.]

7.11123 133. **Enforcement of directions under s 132** (1) A person is guilty of an offence if he provides an electronic communications network or electronic communications service, or makes available any associated facility—

(a) while his entitlement to do so is suspended by a direction under section 132; or

(b) in contravention of a restriction contained in such a direction.

(2) A person guilty of an offence under subsection (1) shall be liable—

(a) on summary conviction, to a fine not exceeding the statutory maximum;

(b) on conviction on indictment, to a fine.

(3) The duty of a person to comply with a condition of a direction under section 132 shall be a duty owed to every person who may be affected by a contravention of the condition.

(4) Where a duty is owed by virtue of subsection (3) to a person—

(a) a breach of the duty that causes that person to sustain loss or damage, and

(b) an act which—

(i) by inducing a breach of the duty or interfering with its performance, causes that person to sustain loss or damage, and

(ii) is done wholly or partly for achieving that result,

shall be actionable at the suit or instance of that person.

(5) In proceedings brought against a person by virtue of subsection (4)(*a*) it shall be a defence for that person to show that he took all reasonable steps and exercised all due diligence to avoid contravening the condition in question.

(6) Sections 96A to 99 apply in relation to a contravention of conditions imposed by a direction under section 132 as they apply in relation to a contravention of conditions set under section 45, other than SMP apparatus conditions.

[Communications Act 2003, s 133 as amended by SI 2011/1210.]

7.11124 140. **Suspending service provision for information contraventions** (1) OFCOM may give a direction under this section to a person who is a communications provider or who makes associated facilities available ("the contravening provider") if they are satisfied—

(a) that he is or has been in serious or repeated contravention of requirements imposed under sections 135 and 136, or either of them;

(b) the requirements are not requirements imposed for purposes connected with the carrying out of OFCOM's functions in relation to SMP apparatus conditions;

(c) in the case of a repeated contravention, that an attempt, by the imposition of penalties or the giving of notifications under section 138 and confirmation decisions under section 139A, or both, or the bringing of proceedings for an offence under section 144, to secure compliance with the contravened requirements has failed; and

(d) that the giving of the direction is appropriate and proportionate to the contravention in respect of which it is given.

(2) A direction under this section is—

(a) a direction that the entitlement of the contravening provider to provide electronic communications networks or electronic communications services, or to make associated facilities available, is suspended (either generally or in relation to particular networks, services or facilities); or

(b) a direction that that entitlement is restricted in the respects set out in the direction.

(3) A direction under this section—

(a) must specify the networks, services and facilities to which it relates; and

(b) except so far as it otherwise provides, takes effect for an indefinite period beginning with the time at which it is notified to the person to whom it is given.

(4) A direction under this section—

(a) in providing for the effect of a suspension or restriction to be postponed, may provide for it to take effect only at a time determined by or in accordance with the terms of the direction; and

(b) in connection with the suspension or restriction contained in the direction or with the postponement of its effect, may impose such conditions on the contravening provider as appear to OFCOM to be appropriate for the purpose of protecting that provider's customers.

(5) Those conditions may include a condition requiring the making of payments—

(*a*) by way of compensation for loss or damage suffered by the contravening provider's customers as a result of the direction; or

(*b*) in respect of annoyance, inconvenience or anxiety to which they have been put in consequence of the direction.

(6) If OFCOM consider it appropriate to do so (whether or not in consequence of any representations or proposals made to them), they may revoke a direction under this section or modify its conditions—

(*a*) with effect from such time as they may direct;

(*b*) subject to compliance with such requirements as they may specify; and

(*c*) to such extent and in relation to such networks, services or facilities, or parts of a network, service or facility, as they may determine.

(7) For the purposes of this section there are repeated contraventions by a person of requirements imposed under sections 135 and 136, or either of them, to the extent that—

(*a*) in the case of a previous notification of a contravention given to that person under section 138, OFCOM have given a confirmation decision to that person under section 139A(2) in respect of the contravention; and

(*b*) in the period of 24 months following the giving of that confirmation decision, one or more further confirmation decisions have been given to the person in respect of contraventions of numbering conditions;

and for the purposes of this subsection it shall be immaterial whether the confirmation decisions related to the same contravention or to different contraventions of the same or different requirements or of requirements under different sections.

[Communications Act 2003, s 140 as amended by SI 2011/1210.]

**7.11125 141. Suspending apparatus supply for information contraventions**

(1) OFCOM may give a direction under this section to a person who supplies electronic communications apparatus ("the contravening supplier") if they are satisfied—

(*a*) that he is or has been in serious and repeated contravention of requirements imposed under section 135;

(*b*) that an attempt, by the imposition of penalties under section 139 or the bringing of proceedings for an offence under section 144, to secure compliance with the contravened requirements has failed; and

(*c*) that the giving of the direction is appropriate and proportionate to the seriousness (when repeated as they have been) of the contraventions.

(2) A direction under this section is—

(*a*) a direction to the contravening supplier to cease to act as a supplier of electronic communications apparatus (either generally or in relation to apparatus of a particular description); or

(*b*) a direction imposing such restrictions as may be set out in the direction on the supply by that supplier of electronic communications apparatus (either generally or in relation to apparatus of a particular description).

(3) A direction under this section takes effect, except so far as it otherwise provides, for an indefinite period beginning with the time at which it is notified to the person to whom it is given.

(4) A direction under this section—

(*a*) may provide for a prohibition or restriction to take effect only at a time determined by or in accordance with the terms of the direction; and

(*b*) in connection with a prohibition or restriction contained in the direction or with the postponement of its effect, may impose such conditions on the contravening supplier as appear to OFCOM to be appropriate for the purpose of protecting that supplier's customers.

(5) Those conditions may include a condition requiring the making of payments—

(*a*) by way of compensation for loss or damage suffered by the contravening supplier's customers as a result of the direction; or

(*b*) in respect of annoyance, inconvenience or anxiety to which they have been put in consequence of the direction.

(6) If OFCOM consider it appropriate to do so (whether or not in consequence of representations or proposals made to them), they may revoke a direction under this section or modify its conditions—

(*a*) with effect from such time as they may direct;

(*b*) subject to compliance with such requirements as they may specify; and

(*c*) to such extent and in relation to such apparatus or descriptions of apparatus as they may determine.

(7) For the purposes of this section contraventions by a person of requirements imposed under section 135 are repeated contraventions if—

(*a*) in the case of a previous notification given to that person under section 138, OFCOM have determined for the purposes of section 139(2) that such a contravention did occur; and (*b*) in the period of twelve months following the day of the making of that determination, one or more further notifications have been given to that person in respect of contraventions of such requirements;

and for the purposes of this subsection it shall be immaterial whether the notifications related to the same contravention or to different contraventions of the same or different requirements.

[Communications Act 2003, s 141.]

7.11126 **142. Procedure for directions under ss 140 and 141** (1) Except in an urgent case, or a case where a proposed direction has been notified to a person in accordance with section 138(2)(*f*), OFCOM are not to give a direction under section 140 or 141 unless they have—

(*a*) notified the contravening provider or contravening supplier of the proposed direction and of the conditions (if any) which they are proposing to impose by that direction;

(*b*) provided him with an opportunity of making representations about the proposals and of proposing steps for remedying the situation; and

(*c*) considered every representation and proposal made to them during the period allowed by them for the contravening provider or the contravening supplier to take advantage of that opportunity.

(2A) That period must be—

(*a*) in relation to a direction under section 140, such reasonable period as OFCOM may determine, and

(*b*) in relation to a direction under section 141, a period ending not less than one month after the day of the giving of the notification.

(3) As soon as practicable after giving a direction under section 140 or 141 in an urgent case, OFCOM must provide the contravening provider or contravening supplier with an opportunity of—

(*a*) making representations about the effect of the direction and of any of its conditions; and

(*b*) proposing steps for remedying the situation.

(3A) In relation to a direction under section 140 in an urgent case, as soon as practicable after the period allowed by OFCOM for making those representations has ended (and in any event within 3 months beginning with the day on which the direction was given), they must determine—

(*a*) whether the contravention providing the grounds for the giving of the direction did occur; and

(*b*) whether the circumstances made it an urgent case justifying the giving of the direction.

(3B) The period of 3 months mentioned in subsection (3A) may be extended by up to 3 months if OFCOM—

(*a*) require additional time to consider representations received; or

(*b*) decide that it is necessary to obtain additional information from the person in order to make a determination under subsection (3A).

(4) A case is an urgent case for the purposes of this section if OFCOM—

(*a*) consider that it would be inappropriate, because the contraventions in question fall within subsection (5), to allow time, before giving a direction under section 140 or 141, for the making and consideration of representations; and

(*b*) decide for that reason to act in accordance with subsection (3), instead of subsection (1).

(5) The contraventions fall within this subsection if they have resulted in, or create an immediate risk of—

(*a*) a serious threat to the safety of the public, to public health or to national security;

(*b*) serious economic or operational problems for persons (apart from the contravening provider or contravening supplier) who are communications providers or persons who make associated facilities available; or

(*c*) serious economic or operational problems for persons who make use of electronic communications networks, electronic communications services or associated facilities.

(6) In this section—

"contravening provider" has the same meaning as in section 140; and

"contravening supplier" has the same meaning as in section 141.

[Communications Act 2003, s 142 as amended by SI 2011/1210.]

7.11127 **143. Enforcement of directions under ss 140 and 141** (1) A person is guilty of an offence if he provides an electronic communications network or electronic communications service, or makes available any associated facility—

(*a*) while his entitlement to do so is suspended by a direction under section 140; or

(*b*) in contravention of a restriction contained in such a direction.

(2) A person is guilty of an offence if he supplies electronic communications apparatus—

(*a*) while prohibited from doing so by a direction under section 141; or

(*b*) in contravention of a restriction contained in such a direction.

(3) A person guilty of an offence under this section shall be liable—

(*a*) on summary conviction, to a fine not exceeding the statutory maximum;

(*b*) on conviction on indictment, to a fine.

(4) Sections 96A to 99 apply in relation to a contravention of conditions imposed by a direction under section 139B or 140 as they apply in relation to a contravention of conditions set under section 45, other than SMP apparatus conditions.

(5) Sections 94 to 96 and 97 to 99 apply in relation to a contravention of conditions imposed by a direction under section 141 as they apply in relation to a contravention of SMP apparatus conditions.

[Communications Act 2003, s 143 as amended by SI 2011/1210.]

*Interpretation of Chapter 1*

7.11128 **151. Interpretation of Chapter 1** (1) In this Chapter—

"the Access Directive" means Directive 2002/19/EC of the European Parliament and of the Council on access to, and interconnection of, electronic communications networks and associated facilities, as amended by Directive 2009/140/EC of the European Parliament and of the Council;

"access-related condition" means a condition set as an access-related condition under section 45;

"allocation" and "adoption", in relation to telephone numbers, and cognate expressions, are to be construed in accordance with section 56;

"apparatus market", in relation to a market power determination, is to be construed in accordance with section 46(9)(*b*);

"designated universal service provider" means a person who is for the time being designated in accordance with regulations under section 66 as a person to whom universal service conditions are applicable;

"electronic communications apparatus"—

(*a*) in relation to SMP apparatus conditions and in section 141, means apparatus that is designed or adapted for a use which consists of or includes the sending or receiving of communications or other signals (within the meaning of section 32) that are transmitted by means of an electronic communications network; and

(*b*) in all other contexts, has the same meaning as in the electronic communications code;

"the electronic communications code" has the meaning given by section 106(1);

"end-user", in relation to a public electronic communications service, means—

(*a*) a person who, otherwise than as a communications provider, is a customer of the provider of that service;

(*b*) a person who makes use of the service otherwise than as a communications provider; or

(*c*) a person who may be authorised, by a person falling within paragraph (*a*), so to make use of the service;

"the Framework Directive" means Directive 2002/21/EC of the European Parliament and of the Council on a common regulatory framework for electronic communications networks and services, [, as amended by Directive 2009/140/EC of the European Parliament and of the Council;

"general condition" means a condition set as a general condition under section 45;

"interconnection" is to be construed in accordance with subsection (2);

"market power determination" means—

(*a*) a determination, for the purposes of provisions of this Chapter, that a person has significant market power in an identified services market or an identified apparatus market, or

(*b*) a confirmation for such purposes of a market power determination reviewed on a further analysis under section 84 or 85;

"misuse", in relation to an electronic communications network or electronic communications service, is to be construed in accordance with section 128(5) and (8), and cognate expressions are to be construed accordingly;

"network access" is to be construed in accordance with subsection (3);

"persistent" and "persistently", in relation to misuse of an electronic communications network or electronic communications service, are to be construed in accordance with section 128(6) and (7);

"premium rate service" is to be construed in accordance with section 120(7);

"privileged supplier condition" means a condition set as a privileged supplier condition under section 45;

"provider", in relation to a premium rate service, is to be construed in accordance with section 120(9) to (12), and cognate expressions are to be construed accordingly;

"public communications provider" means—

(*a*) a provider of a public electronic communications network;

(*b*) a provider of a public electronic communications service; or

(*c*) a person who makes available facilities that are associated facilities by reference to a public electronic communications network or a public electronic communications service;

"public electronic communications network" means an electronic communications network provided wholly or mainly for the purpose of making electronic communications services available to members of the public;
"public electronic communications service" means any electronic communications service that is provided so as to be available for use by members of the public;
"regulatory authorities" is to be construed in accordance with subsection (5);
"relevant international standards" means—
(*a*) any standards or specifications from time to time drawn up and published in accordance with Article 17 of the Framework Directive;
(*b*) the standards and specifications from time to time adopted by—
(i) the European Committee for Standardisation,
(ii) the European Committee for Electrotechnical Standardisation; or
(iii) the European Telecommunications Standards Institute; and
(*c*) the international standards and recommendations from time to time adopted by—
(i) the International Telecommunication Union;
(ii) the International Organisation for Standardisation; or
(iii) the International Electrotechnical Committee;
"service interoperability" means interoperability between different electronic communications services;
"services market", in relation to a market power determination or market identification, is to be construed in accordance with section 46(8)(*a*);
"significant market power" is to be construed in accordance with section 78;
"SMP condition" means a condition set as an SMP condition under section 45, and "SMP services condition" and "SMP apparatus condition" are to be construed in accordance with subsections (8) and (9) of that section respectively;
"telephone number" has the meaning given by section 56(5);
"the Universal Service Directive" means Directive 2002/22/EC of the European Parliament and of the Council on universal service and users' rights relating to electronic communications networks and services, as amended by Directive 2009/136/EC of the European Parliament and of the Council;
"universal service condition" means a condition set as a universal service condition under section 45;
"the universal service order" means the order for the time being in force under section 65.

(2) In this Chapter references to interconnection are references to the linking (whether directly or indirectly by physical or logical means, or by a combination of physical and logical means) of one public electronic communications network to another for the purpose of enabling the persons using one of them to be able—
(*a*) to communicate with users of the other one; or
(*b*) to make use of services provided by means of the other one (whether by the provider of that network or by another person).

(3) In this Chapter references to network access are references to—
(*a*) interconnection of public electronic communications networks; or
(*b*) any services, facilities or arrangements which—
(i) are not comprised in interconnection; but
(ii) are services, facilities or arrangements by means of which a person is able, for the purposes of the provision of an electronic communications service (whether by him or by another), to make use of anything mentioned in subsection (4);
and references to providing network access include references to providing any such services, making available any such facilities or entering into any such arrangements.

(4) The things referred to in subsection (3)(*b*) are—
(*a*) any electronic communications network or electronic communications service provided by another communications provider;
(*b*) any apparatus comprised in such a network or used for the purposes of such a network or service;
(*ba*) any electronic communications apparatus;]
(*c*) any facilities made available by another that are associated facilities by reference to any network or service (whether one provided by that provider or by another);
(*d*) any other services or facilities which are provided or made available by another person and are capable of being used for the provision of an electronic communications service.

(4A) In subsections (3)(*b*)(ii) and (4)(*d*), the references to an electronic communications service include the conveyance by means of an electronic communications network of signals, including an information society service or content service so conveyed.

(4B) In subsection (4A)—
"content service" has the meaning given by section 32(7), and
"information society service" has the meaning given by Article 2(*a*) of Directive 2000/31/EC of the European Parliament and of the Council of 8 June 2000 on certain legal aspects of

information society services, in particular electronic commerce, in the Internal Market.

(5) References in this Chapter to the regulatory authorities of member States are references to such of the authorities of the member States as have been notified to the European Commission as the regulatory authorities of those States for the purposes of the Framework Directive.

(6) For the purposes of this Chapter, where there is a contravention of an obligation that requires a person to do anything within a particular period or before a particular time, that contravention shall be taken to continue after the end of that period, or after that time, until that thing is done.

(7) References in this Chapter to remedying the consequences of a contravention include references to paying an amount to a person—

(*a*) by way of compensation for loss or damage suffered by that person; or

(*b*) in respect of annoyance, inconvenience or anxiety to which he has been put.

(8) In determining for the purposes of provisions of this Chapter whether a contravention is a repeated contravention for any purposes, a notification of a contravention under that provision shall be disregarded if it has been withdrawn before the imposition of a penalty in respect of the matters notified.

(9) For the purposes of this section a service is made available to members of the public if members of the public are customers, in respect of that service, of the provider of that service.

[Communications Act 2003, s 151 as amended by SI 2011/1210.]

## PART 4[1]
## LICENSING OF TV RECEPTION

7.11129 **363. Licence required for use of TV receiver** (1) A television receiver[2] must not be installed or used unless the installation and use of the receiver is authorised by a licence under this Part.

(2) A person who installs or uses a television receiver in contravention of subsection (1) is guilty of an offence.

(3) A person with a television receiver in his possession or under his control who—

(*a*) intends to install or use it in contravention of subsection (1), or

(*b*) knows, or has reasonable grounds for believing, that another person intends to install or use it in contravention of that subsection,

is guilty of an offence.

(4) A person guilty of an offence under this section shall be liable, on summary conviction, to a fine not exceeding level 3 on the standard scale.

(5) Subsection (1) is not contravened by anything done in the course of the business of a dealer in television receivers solely for one or more of the following purposes—

(*a*) installing a television receiver on delivery;

(*b*) demonstrating, testing or repairing a television receiver.

(6) The Secretary of State may by regulations exempt from the requirement of a licence under subsection (1) the installation or use of television receivers—

(*a*) of such descriptions,

(*b*) by such persons,

(*c*) in such circumstances, and

(*d*) for such purposes,

as may be provided for in the regulations.

(7) Regulations under subsection (6) may make any exemption for which such regulations provide subject to compliance with such conditions as may be specified in the regulations.

[Communications Act 2003, s 363.]

---

[1] Part 4 comprises ss 363–368.

[2] Defined in the Communications (Television Licensing) Regulations 2004, in this title, post.

7.11130 **364. TV licences** *May be issued by the BBC and must be subject to such restrictions and conditions as the BBC think fit and the Secretary of State may require. A TV licence shall continue in force, unless previously revoked by the BBC, for such period as may be specified in the licence.*

7.11131 **365. TV licence fees** (1) A person to whom a TV licence is issued shall be liable to pay—

(*a*) on the issue of the licence (whether initially or by way of renewal), and

(*b*) in such other circumstances as regulations[1] made by the Secretary of State may provide,

such sum (if any) as may be provided for by any such regulations.

(2) Sums which a person is liable to pay by virtue of regulations under subsection (1) must be paid to the BBC and are to be recoverable by them accordingly.

(3) The BBC are entitled, in such cases as they may determine, to make refunds of sums received by them by virtue of regulations under this section.

(4)–(8) *Concessions and further provisions as to Regulations.*

[Communications Act 2003, s 365.]

---

[1] The Communications (Television Licensing) Regulations 2004 have been made, in this title, post.

7.11132 **366. Powers to enforce TV licensing** (1) If a justice of the peace, a sheriff in Scotland or a lay magistrate in Northern Ireland is satisfied by information on oath that there are reasonable grounds for believing—

(*a*) that an offence under section 363 has been or is being committed,

(*b*) that evidence of the commission of the offence is likely to be on premises specified in the information, or in a vehicle so specified, and

(*c*) that one or more of the conditions set out in subsection (3) is satisfied,

he may grant a warrant under this section.

(2) A warrant under this section is a warrant authorising any one or more persons authorised for the purpose by the BBC or by OFCOM—

(*a*) to enter the premises or vehicle at any time (either alone or in the company of one or more constables); and

(*b*) to search the premises or vehicle and examine and test any television receiver found there.

(3) Those conditions are—

(*a*) that there is no person entitled to grant entry to the premises or vehicle with whom it is practicable to communicate;

(*b*) that there is no person entitled to grant access to the evidence with whom it is practicable to communicate;

(*c*) that entry to the premises or vehicle will not be granted unless a warrant is produced;

(*d*) that the purpose of the search may be frustrated or seriously prejudiced unless the search is carried out by a person who secures entry immediately upon arriving at the premises or vehicle.

(4) A person is not to enter premises or a vehicle in pursuance of a warrant under this section at any time more than one month after the day on which the warrant was granted.

(5) The powers conferred by a warrant under this section on a person authorised by OFCOM are exercisable in relation only to a contravention or suspected contravention of a condition of a TV licence relating to interference with wireless telegraphy.

(6) A person authorised by the BBC, or by OFCOM, to exercise a power conferred by a warrant under this section may (if necessary) use such force as may be reasonable in the exercise of that power.

(7) Where a person has the power by virtue of a warrant under this section to examine or test any television receiver found on any premises, or in any vehicle, it shall be the duty—

(*a*) of a person who is on the premises or in the vehicle, and

(*b*) in the case of a vehicle, of a person who has charge of it or is present when it is searched,

to give the person carrying out the examination or test all such assistance as that person may reasonably require for carrying it out.

(8) A person is guilty of an offence if he—

(*a*) intentionally obstructs a person in the exercise of any power conferred on that person by virtue of a warrant under this section; or

(*b*) without reasonable excuse, fails to give any assistance that he is under a duty to give by virtue of subsection (7).

(9) A person guilty of an offence under subsection (8) shall be liable, on summary conviction, to a fine not exceeding level 5 on the standard scale.

(10) In this section—

"interference", in relation to wireless telegraphy, has the same meaning as in the Wireless Telegraphy Act 2006; and

"vehicle" includes vessel, aircraft or hovercraft.

(11) *Scotland*

(12) *Northern Ireland*

[Communications Act 2003, s 366 as amended by the Wireless Telegraphy Act 2006, Sch 7.]

7.11133 **368. Meanings of "television receiver" and "use"** (1) In this Part "television receiver" means any apparatus of a description specified in regulations[1] made by the Secretary of State setting out the descriptions of apparatus that are to be television receivers for the purposes of this Part.

(2) Regulations under this section defining a television receiver may provide for references to such a receiver to include references to software used in association with apparatus.

(3) References in this Part to using a television receiver are references to using it for—

(a) receiving all or any part of any television programme, or

(b) receiving all or any part of a programme included in an on-demand programme service which is provided by the BBC,

and that reference to the provision of an on-demand programme service by the BBC is to be read in accordance with section 368R(5) and (6).

(4) The power to make regulations under this section defining a television receiver includes power to modify subsection (3).

[Communications Act 2003, s 368 as amended by SI 2016/704.]

---

[1] The Communications (Television Licensing) Regulations 2004 have been made, in this title, post.

## Part 4A[1]

## On-demand Programme Services

*Preliminary*

**7.11134 368A. Meaning of "on-demand programme service"** (1) For the purposes of this Act, a service is an "on-demand programme service" if—

(*a*) its principal purpose is the provision of programmes the form and content of which are comparable to the form and content of programmes normally included in television programme services;

(*b*) access to it is on-demand;

(*c*) there is a person who has editorial responsibility for it;

(*d*) it is made available by that person for use by members of the public; and

(*e*) that person is under the jurisdiction of the United Kingdom for the purposes of the Audiovisual Media Services Directive.

(2) Access to a service is on-demand if—

(*a*) the service enables the user to view, at a time chosen by the user, programmes selected by the user from among the programmes included in the service; and

(*b*) the programmes viewed by the user are received by the user by means of an electronic communications network (whether before or after the user has selected which programmes to view).

(3) For the purposes of subsection (2)(*a*), the fact that a programme may be viewed only within a period specified by the provider of the service does not prevent the time at which it is viewed being one chosen by the user.

(4) A person has editorial responsibility for a service if that person has general control—

(*a*) over what programmes are included in the range of programmes offered to users; and

(*b*) over the manner in which the programmes are organised in that range;

and the person need not have control of the content of individual programmes or of the broadcasting or distribution of the service (and see section 368R(6)).

(5) If an on-demand programme service ("the main service") offers users access to a relevant ancillary service, the relevant ancillary service is to be treated for the purposes of this Part as a part of the main service.

(6) In subsection (5), "relevant ancillary service" means a service or facility that consists of or gives access to assistance for disabled people in relation to some or all of the programmes included in the main service.

(7) In this section "assistance for disabled people" has the same meaning as in Part 3.

[Communications Act 2003, s 368A as inserted by SI 2009/2979.]

[1] Part 4A comprises ss 368A–368R and was inserted by the Audiovisual Media Services Regulations 2009, SI 2009/2979 which came into force on 19 December 2009.

**7.11134A 368B–368C.** *OFCOM or corporate body designated by OFCOM to be regulatory authority. Duties of regulatory authority.*

*Duties of service providers*

**7.11135 368D. Duties of service providers** (1) The provider of an on-demand programme service must ensure that the service complies with the requirements of sections 368E to 368H.

(2) The provider of an on-demand programme service ("P") must supply the following information to users of the service—

(*a*) P's name;

(*b*) P's address;

(*c*) P's electronic address;

(*d*) the name, address and electronic address of any body which is the appropriate regulatory authority for any purpose in relation to P or the service that P provides.

(3) The provider of an on-demand programme service must—

(*za*) pay to the appropriate regulatory authority such fee as that authority may require under section 368NA;

(*zb*) retain a copy of every programme included in the service for at least forty-two days after the day on which the programme ceases to be available for viewing;

(*a*) comply with any requirement under section 368O (provision of information);

(*b*) co-operate fully with the appropriate authority for any purpose within section 368O(2) or (3).

(3A) A copy of a programme retained for the purposes of subsection (3)(zb) must be of a standard and in a format which allows the programme to be viewed as it was made available for viewing.

(4) In this section "electronic address" means an electronic address to which users may send electronic communications, and includes any number or address used for the purposes of receiving such communications.

[Communications Act 2003, s 368D as inserted by SI 2009/2979 and SI 2010/419.]

**7.11136 368E. Harmful material** (1) An on-demand programme service must not contain any material likely to incite hatred based on race, sex, religion or nationality.

(2) An on-demand programme service must not contain any prohibited material.

(3) "Prohibited material" means—

(*a*) a video work which the video works authority has determined for the purposes of the 1984 Act not to be suitable for a classification certificate to be issued in respect of it, or

(*b*) material whose nature is such that it is reasonable to expect that, if the material were contained in a video work submitted to the video works authority for a classification certificate, the video works authority would determine for those purposes that the video work was not suitable for a classification certificate to be issued in respect of it.

(4) An on-demand programme service must not contain any specially restricted material unless the material is made available in a manner which secures that persons under the age of 18 will not normally see or hear it.

(5) "Specially restricted material" means—

(*a*) a video work in respect of which the video works authority has issued a R18 classification certificate,

(*b*) material whose nature is such that it is reasonable to expect that, if the material were contained in a video work submitted to the video works authority for a classification certificate, the video works authority would issue a R18 classification certificate, or

(*c*) other material that might seriously impair the physical, mental or moral development of persons under the age of 18.

(6) In determining whether any material falls within subsection (3)(b) or (5)(*b*), regard must be had to any guidelines issued by the video works authority as to its policy in relation to the issue of classification certificates.

(7) In this section—

"the 1984 Act" means the Video Recordings Act 1984;

"classification certificate" has the same meaning as in the 1984 Act (see section 7 of that Act);

"R18 classification certificate" means a classification certificate containing the statement mentioned in section 7(2)(*c*) of the 1984 Act that no video recording containing the video work is to be supplied other than in a licensed sex shop;

"the video works authority" means the person or persons designated under section 4(1) of the 1984 Act as the authority responsible for making arrangements in respect of video works other than video games;

"video work" has the same meaning as in the 1984 Act (see section 1(2) of that Act).

[Communications Act 2003, s 368E as inserted by SI 2009/2979 and amended by SI 2014/2916.]

**7.11137 368F. Advertising** (1) Advertising of the following products is prohibited in on-demand programme services—

(*a*) cigarettes or other tobacco products;

(*b*) any prescription-only medicine.

(2) Advertising of alcoholic drinks is prohibited in on-demand programme services unless—

(*a*) it is not aimed at persons under the age of eighteen, and

(*b*) it does not encourage excessive consumption of such drinks.

(3) Advertising included in an on-demand programme service—

(*a*) must be readily recognisable as such, and

(*b*) must not use techniques which exploit the possibility of conveying a message subliminally or surreptitiously.

(4) Advertising included in an on-demand programme service must not—

(*a*) prejudice respect for human dignity;

(*b*) include or promote discrimination based on sex, racial or ethnic origin, nationality, religion or belief, disability, age or sexual orientation;

(*c*) encourage behaviour prejudicial to health or safety;

(*d*) encourage behaviour grossly prejudicial to the protection of the environment;

(*e*) cause physical or moral detriment to persons under the age of eighteen;

(*f*) directly exhort such persons to purchase or rent goods or services in a manner which exploits their inexperience or credulity;

(*g*) directly encourage such persons to persuade their parents or others to purchase or rent goods or services;

(*h*) exploit the trust of such persons in parents, teachers or others; or

(*i*) unreasonably show such persons in dangerous situations.

[Communications Act 2003, s 368F as inserted by SI 2009/2979.]

**7.11138 368G. Sponsorship** (1) An on-demand programme service or a programme included in an on-demand programme service must not be sponsored—

(*a*) for the purpose of promoting cigarettes or other tobacco products, or

(*b*) by an undertaking whose principal activity is the manufacture or sale of cigarettes or other tobacco products.

(2) An on-demand programme service or a programme included in an on-demand programme service must not be sponsored for the purpose of promoting a prescription-only medicine.

(3) An on-demand programme service may not include a news programme or current affairs

programme that is sponsored.

(4) Subsections (5) to (11) apply to an on-demand programme service that is sponsored or that includes any programme that is sponsored.

(5) The sponsoring of a service or programme must not influence the content of that service or programme in a way that affects the editorial independence of the provider of the service.

(6) Where a service or programme is sponsored for the purpose of promoting goods or services, the sponsored service or programme and sponsorship announcements relating to it must not directly encourage the purchase or rental of the goods or services, whether by making promotional reference to them or otherwise.

(7) Where a service or programme is sponsored for the purpose of promoting an alcoholic drink, the service or programme and sponsorship announcements relating to it must not—

(*a*) be aimed specifically at persons under the age of eighteen; or

(*b*) encourage the immoderate consumption of such drinks.

(8) A sponsored service must clearly inform users of the existence of a sponsorship agreement.

(9) The name of the sponsor and the logo or other symbol (if any) of the sponsor must be displayed at the beginning or end of a sponsored programme.

(10) Techniques which exploit the possibility of conveying a message subliminally or surreptitiously must not be used in a sponsorship announcement.

(11) A sponsorship announcement must not—

(*a*) prejudice respect for human dignity;

(*b*) include or promote discrimination based on sex, racial or ethnic origin, nationality, religion or belief, disability, age or sexual orientation;

(*c*) encourage behaviour prejudicial to health or safety;

(*d*) encourage behaviour grossly prejudicial to the protection of the environment;

(*e*) cause physical or moral detriment to persons under the age of eighteen;

(*f*) directly encourage such persons to persuade their parents or others to purchase or rent goods or services;

(*g*) exploit the trust of such persons in parents, teachers or others; or

(*h*) unreasonably show such persons in dangerous situations.

(12) For the purposes of this Part a programme included in an on-demand programme service is "sponsored" if a person ("the sponsor") other than—

(*a*) the provider of that service, or

(*b*) the producer of that programme,

has met some or all of the costs of the programme for the purpose of promoting the name, trademark, image, activities, services or products of the sponsor or of another person.

(13) But a programme is not sponsored if it falls within this section only by virtue of the inclusion of product placement (see section 368H(1)) or prop placement (see section 368H(2)).

(14) For the purposes of subsection (12) a person meets some or all of the costs of a programme included in a service only if that person makes a payment or provides other resources for the purpose of meeting or saving some or all of the costs of—

(*a*) producing that programme;

(*b*) transmitting that programme; or

(*c*) making that programme available as part of the service.

(15) For the purposes of this Part an on-demand programme service is "sponsored" if a person ("the sponsor") other than the provider of the service has met some or all of the costs of providing the service for the purpose of promoting the name, trademark, image, activities, services or products of the sponsor or another person.

(16) For the purposes of subsection (15) a person is not to be taken to have met some or all of the costs of providing a service only because a programme included in the service is sponsored by that person.

(17) In this section a "sponsorship announcement" means—

(*a*) anything included for the purpose of complying with subsection (8) or (9), and

(*b*) anything included at the same time as or otherwise in conjunction with anything within paragraph (*a*).

[Communications Act 2003, s 368G as inserted by SI 2009/2979 and amended by SI 2010/419.]

7.11139 **368H. Prohibition of product placement and exceptions** (1) "Product placement", in relation to a programme included in an on-demand programme service, means the inclusion in the programme of, or of a reference to, a product, service or trade mark, where the inclusion—

(*a*) is for a commercial purpose,

(*b*) is in return for the making of any payment, or the giving of other valuable consideration, to any relevant provider or any connected person, and

(*c*) is not prop placement.

(2) "Prop placement", in relation to a programme included in an on-demand programme service, means the inclusion in the programme of, or of a reference to, a product, service or trade mark where—

(*a*) the provision of the product, service or trade mark has no significant value; and (*b*) no relevant provider, or person connected with a relevant provider, has received any payment or other valuable consideration in relation to its inclusion in, or the reference to it in, the programme, disregarding the costs saved by including the product, service or trademark, or a reference to it, in the programme.

(3) Product placement is prohibited in children's programmes included in on-demand programme services.

(4) Product placement is prohibited in on-demand programme services if—

(*a*) it is of cigarettes or other tobacco products,

(*b*) it is by or on behalf of an undertaking whose principal activity is the manufacture or sale of cigarettes or other tobacco products, or

(*c*) it is of prescription-only medicines.

(5) Product placement of alcoholic drinks must not—

(*a*) be aimed specifically at persons under the age of eighteen;

(*b*) encourage immoderate consumption of such drinks.

(6) Product placement is otherwise permitted in programmes included in on-demand programme services provided that—

(*a*) conditions A to F are met, and

(*b*) if subsection (14) applies, condition G is also met.

(7) Condition A is that the programme in which the product, service or trademark, or the reference to it, is included is—

(*a*) a film made for cinema;

(*b*) a film or series made for a television programme service or for an on-demand programme service;

(*c*) a sports programme; or

(*d*) a light entertainment programme.

(8) Condition B is that the product placement has not influenced the content of the programme in a way that affects the editorial independence of the provider of the service.

(9) Condition C is that the product placement does not directly encourage the purchase or rental of goods or services, whether by making promotional reference to those goods or services or otherwise.

(10) Condition D is that the programme does not give undue prominence to the products, services or trade marks concerned.

(11) Condition E is that the product placement does not use techniques which exploit the possibility of conveying a message subliminally or surreptitiously.

(12) Condition F is that the way in which the product, service or trade mark, or the reference to it, is included in the programme by way of product placement does not—

(*a*) prejudice respect for human dignity;

(*b*) promote discrimination based on sex, racial or ethnic origin, nationality, religion or belief, disability, age or sexual orientation;

(*c*) encourage behaviour prejudicial to health or safety;

(*d*) encourage behaviour grossly prejudicial to the protection of the environment;

(*e*) cause physical or moral detriment to persons under the age of eighteen;

(*f*) directly encourage such persons to persuade their parents or others to purchase or rent goods or services;

(*g*) exploit the trust of such persons in parents, teachers or others; or

(*h*) unreasonably show such persons in dangerous situations.

(13) Condition G is that the on-demand programme service in question signals appropriately the fact that product placement is contained in a programme, no less frequently than—

(*a*) at the start and end of such a programme, and

(*b*) in the case of an on-demand programme service which includes advertising breaks within it, at the recommencement of the programme after each such advertising break.

(14) This subsection applies where the programme featuring the product placement has been produced or commissioned by the provider of the service or any connected person.

(15) This section applies only in relation to programmes the production of which begins after 19th December 2009.

(16) In this section—

"connected" has the same meaning as it has in the Broadcasting Act 1990 by virtue of section 202 of that Act;

"film made for cinema" means a film made with a view to its being shown to the general public first in a cinema;

"producer", in relation to a programme, means the person by whom the arrangements necessary for the making of the programme are undertaken;

"relevant provider", in relation to a programme, means—

(*a*) the provider of the on-demand programme service in which the programme is included; and

(*b*) the producer of the programme;

"residual value" means any monetary or other economic value in the hands of the relevant provider other than the cost saving of including the product, service or trademark, or a reference to it, in a programme;

"significant value" means a residual value that is more than trivial; and

"trade mark", in relation to a business, includes any image (such as a logo) or sound commonly associated with that business or its products or services.

[Communications Act 2003, s 368H as inserted by SI 2009/2979.]

7.11139A **368I. Enforcement of section 368D** *Contravention of s 368D enforceable by an enforcement notification under this section or a financial penalty on the provider in accordance with section 368J.*

*Suspension or restriction of service*

7.11139B **368K–N. Suspension or restriction of service for contraventions** *Notice must be served on provider of an on-demand programme service where the provider is in contravention of section 368BA or 368D; an attempt to secure compliance with section 368BA or 368D by the imposition of one or more financial penalties or enforcement notifications under section 368BB or 368I has failed; and that the giving of a direction under this section would be appropriate and proportionate to the seriousness of the contravention. After representations if any, a direction may be made suspending or restricting that the entitlement of the provider to provide an on-demand programme service. Similar provisions apply where the service has failed to comply with any requirement of section 368E to 368H and that accordingly the provider has contravened section 368D(1); the failure is due to the inclusion in the service of material likely to encourage or to incite the commission of crime, or to lead to disorder; and the contravention is such as to justify the giving of a direction under this section.*

7.11139C **368O–Q.** *Provision of information and application of Part 4A to the BBC and the Welsh Authority.*

7.11140 **368R. Interpretation of Part 4A** (1) In this Part—

"appropriate regulatory authority" is to be construed in accordance with 368B;

"children's programme" means a programme made—

(*a*) for a television programme service or for an on-demand programme service, and

(*b*) for viewing primarily by persons under the age of sixteen;

"prescription-only medicine" means a prescription only medicine within the meaning of regulation 5(3) of the Human Medicines Regulations 2012;

"product placement" has the meaning given by section 368H(1);

"sponsorship" is to be construed in accordance with section 368G;

"tobacco product" has the meaning given in section 1 of the Tobacco Advertising and Promotion Act 2002.

(2) For the purposes of this Part, a programme is included in an on-demand programme service if it is included in the range of programmes the service offers to users.

(3) For the purposes of this Part, advertising is included in an on-demand programme service if it can be viewed by a user of the service as a result of the user selecting a programme to view.

(4) The services that are to be taken for the purposes of this Part to be available for use by members of the public include any service which—

(*a*) is made available for use only to persons who subscribe to the service (whether for a period or in relation to a particular occasion) or who otherwise request its provision; but

(*b*) is a service the facility of subscribing to which, or of otherwise requesting its provision, is offered or made available to members of the public.

(5) The person, and the only person, who is to be treated for the purposes of this Part as providing an on-demand programme service is the person who has editorial responsibility for the service (see section 368A(4)).

(6) For the purposes of this Part—

(*a*) the provision of a service by the BBC does not include its provision by a BBC company;

(*b*) the provision of a service by the Welsh Authority does not include its provision by an S4C company;

and, accordingly, control that is or is capable of being exercised by the BBC or the Welsh Authority over decisions by a BBC company or an S4C company about what is to be comprised in a service is to be disregarded for the purposes of determining who has editorial responsibility for the service.

[Communications Act 2003, s 368G as inserted by SI 2009/2979 and amended by SI 2010/831 and SI 2012/1916.]

7.11141 **411. Short title, commencement and extent** (1) This Act may be cited as the Communications Act 2003.

(2) This Act (except the provisions listed in subsection (3), which come into force on the passing of this Act) shall come into force on such day as the Secretary of State may by order[1] appoint; and different days may be appointed under this subsection for different purposes.

(3) Those provisions are sections 31(1) to (4) and (6) and 405 and this section.

(4) An order under subsection (2) may include provision making such transitional or transitory provision, in addition to that made by Schedule 18, as the Secretary of State considers appropriate in connection with the bringing into force of any provisions of this Act; and the power to make transitional or transitory provision includes power to make—

(*a*) different provision for different cases (including different provision in respect of different areas);
(*b*) provision subject to such exemptions and exceptions as the Secretary of State thinks fit; and
(*c*) such incidental, supplemental and consequential provision as he thinks fit.

(5) This Act extends to Northern Ireland.

(6) Subject to subsection (7), Her Majesty may by Order in Council[2] extend the provisions of this Act, with such modifications as appear to Her Majesty in Council to be appropriate, to any of the Channel Islands or to the Isle of Man.

(7) Subsection (6) does not authorise the extension to any place of a provision of this Act so far as it gives effect to an amendment of an enactment that is not itself capable of being extended there in exercise of a power conferred on Her Majesty in Council.

(8) Subsection (3) of section 402 applies to the power to make an Order in Council under this section as it applies to any power of the Secretary of State to make an order under this Act, but as if references in that subsection to the Secretary of State were references to Her Majesty in Council.

[Communications Act 2003, s 411.]

---

1 At the time of going to press the following commencement orders had been made: Communications Act 2003 (Commencement No 1) Order 2003, SI 2003/1900, as amended by SI 2003/3142; Office of Communications Act 2002 (Commencement No 3) and Communications Act 2003 (Commencement No 2) Order 2003, SI 2003/3142, as amended by SI 2004/545, SI 2004/697, SI 2004/1492; Communications Act 2003 (Commencement No 3) Order 2004, SI 2004/3309; and Communications Act 2003 (Commencement No 4) Order 2009, SI 2009/2130.

2 The following orders have been made under this provision: Communications (Bailiwick of Guernsey) Order 2003, SI 2003/3195 amended by SI 2005/856; (No 2) Order 2004, SI 2004/715; (No 3) Order 2004, SI 2004/1116; Broadcasting and Communications (Jersey) Order 2003, SI 2003/3197 amended by SI 2005/855, (No 2) Order 2004, SI 2004/716; (No 3) Order 2004, SI 2004/1114; Broadcasting and Communications (Isle of Man) Order 2003, SI 2003/3198 amended by SI 2007/278, (No 2) Order 2004, SI 2004/718; (No 3) Order 2004, SI 2004/1115; Wireless Telegraphy (Jersey) Order 2006, SI 2006/3324; Wireless Telegraphy (Guernsey) Order 2006, SI 2006/3325; and Wireless Telegraphy (Isle of Man) Order 2007, SI 2007/278.

## SCHEDULE 8
## Decisions not Subject to Appeal

Section 192

*(Amended by the Wireless Telegraphy Act 2006, Schs 7 and 9 and the Digital Economy Act 2010, s 16.)*

*Prosecutions and civil proceedings*

7.11142 **1.** A decision to institute, bring or carry on any criminal or civil proceedings.

**2.** A decision (other than one under section 119) to take preliminary steps for the purpose of enabling any such proceedings to be instituted.

*This Act*

**3.** A decision relating to the making or revision of a statement under section 38.
**4.** A decision required to be published in a notification under section 44(4).
**5.** A decision given effect to by an order under section 55.
**6.** A decision given effect to by regulations under section 66.
**7.** A decision given effect to by regulations under section 71.
**8.** A decision required to be published in a notification under section 108(4).
**9.** A decision given effect to by an order under section 122.
**9A.** A decision relating to any of sections 124A to 124N or to anything done under them.
**10.** A decision relating to the making or revision of a statement under section 131.
**11.** A decision given effect to by an order under section 134(6).
**12.** A decision relating to the making or revision of a statement under section 145.
**13–36.** *Repealed.*

*Wireless Telegraphy Act 2006*

**37.** A decision relating to the publication of the United Kingdom Plan for Frequency Authorisation.
**38.** A decision in exercise of the functions conferred on OFCOM by section 1 as to—
(*a*) the services, records and advice to be provided, maintained or given by them;
(*b*) the research to be carried out or the arrangements made for carrying it out; or
(*c*) the making or terms of any grant.
**39.** A decision under section 4 or 7.
**40.** A decision given effect to—
(*a*) by regulations under section 8(3), 12, 14, 18, 21, 23, 27, 30, 45 or 54 or paragraph 1 of Schedule 1 or paragraph 1 of Schedule 2;
(*b*) by an order under section 29 or 62.
**41.** A decision relating to the recovery of a sum payable to OFCOM under section 15 or 24.
**42.** A decision given effect to by regulations under section 31 and any decision under any such regulations.
**43.** A decision relating to the making or revision of a statement under—
(*a*) section 34, or
(*b*) section 44.
**44.** A decision to impose a penalty under section 42(1).
**45.** A decision for the purposes of section 59.
**46.** A decision relating to an authority under section 62(5).

# Wireless Telegraphy Act 2006[1]

(2006 c 36)

## PART 2[2]

## REGULATION OF RADIO SPECTRUM

### CHAPTER 1[3]

### WIRELESS TELEGRAPHY LICENCES

*Licensing of wireless telegraphy*

7.11143 **8. Licences and exemptions** (1) It is unlawful[4]—

(*a*) to establish or use a wireless telegraphy station[5], or

(*b*) to instal or use wireless telegraphy apparatus[6],

except under and in accordance with a licence[7] (a "wireless telegraphy licence") granted under this section by OFCOM.

(2) Subsection (1) does not apply to—

(*a*) the use of a television receiver (within the meaning of Part 4 of the Communications Act 2003) for receiving a television programme; or

(*b*) the installation of a television receiver for use solely for that purpose.

(3) OFCOM may by regulations[8] exempt from subsection (1) the establishment, installation or use of wireless telegraphy stations or wireless telegraphy apparatus of such classes or descriptions as may be specified in the regulations, either absolutely or subject to such terms, provisions and limitations as may be so specified.

(3A) OFCOM may not make regulations under subsection (3) specifying terms, provisions or limitations in relation to the establishment, installation or use of wireless telegraphy stations or wireless telegraphy apparatus for the provision of an electronic communications network or electronic communications service unless the terms, provisions or limitations are of a kind falling within Part A of the Annex to Directive 2002/20/EC of the European Parliament and of the Council.

(3B) Terms, provisions and limitations specified in regulations under subsection (3) must be—

(*a*) objectively justifiable in relation to the wireless telegraphy stations or wireless telegraphy apparatus to which they relate,

(*b*) not such as to discriminate unduly against particular persons or against a particular description of persons,

(*c*) proportionate to what they are intended to achieve, and

(*d*) in relation to what they are intended to achieve, transparent.

(4) If OFCOM are satisfied that the conditions in subsection (5) are satisfied as respects the use of stations or apparatus of a particular description, they must make regulations under subsection (3) exempting the establishment, installation and use of a station or apparatus of that description from subsection (1).

(5) The conditions are that the use of stations or apparatus of that description is not likely to—

(*a*) involve undue interference with wireless telegraphy;

(*b*) have an adverse effect on technical quality of service;

(*c*) lead to inefficient use of the part of the electromagnetic spectrum available for wireless telegraphy;

(*d*) endanger safety of life;

(*e*) prejudice the promotion of social, regional or territorial cohesion; or

(*f*) prejudice the promotion of cultural and linguistic diversity and media pluralism.]

[Wireless Telegraphy Act 2006, s 8 as amended by SI 2011/1210.]

---

1 This Act, which came into force on 8 February 2007 in accordance with the provisions of s 126, consolidated a number of enactments about wireless telegraphy, notably the Wireless Telegraphy Act 1949 and the Marine etc. Broadcasting (Offences) Act 1967.

Part 1 (ss 1–7) makes general provision about the radio spectrum including the role of OFCOM, one of whose functions is to provide advice and assistance to persons complaining of interference with wireless telegraphy (s 4).

The establishment and installation of stations and apparatus for use by members of visiting forces or international headquarters for service purposes in the course of their duty as such, and the use as aforesaid of such stations or apparatus, are excepted from the provisions of this Part of the Act (Visiting Forces and International Headquarters (Application of Law) Order 1965, SI 1965/1536, art 7.

2 Part 2 comprises ss 8–53 and Schs 1–3.

3 Chapter 1 comprises ss 8–17 and Sch 1.

4 Contravention of this section is an offence contrary to s 35, post. To prove an offence under s 8(1) and s 35 of the Act the prosecution must establish merely that the defendant knew he was making use of apparatus, and do not need to show that he was doing so with a guilty mind because the section creates an absolute offence (*R v Blake* [1997] 1 All ER 963, [1997] 1 WLR 1167, [1997] 1 Cr App Rep 209; [1997] Crim LR 207). For power to order forfeiture of apparatus, see s 103 and Sch 5, post. For power to issue search warrant, see s 97, post.

5 For meaning of "wireless telegraphy," "station for wireless telegraphy", see ss 116 and 117, post.

6 For meaning of "wireless telegraphy apparatus", see s 117, post. The installation and use of cordless telephone apparatus, metal detectors and model control equipment are exempted from the requirements of a licence; see note 8 below.

7 The prosecution does not have to prove the defendant had no licence; see the Magistrates' Courts Act 1980, s 101, ante.

8 Exemptions are provided under the following regulations made under the repealed provisions of s 1 of the Wireless

Telegraphy Act 1949:
Wireless Telegraphy (Reciprocal Exemption of European Radio Amateurs) Regulations 1988, 1988/2090;
Wireless Telegraphy Apparatus (Receivers) (Exemption) Regulations 1989, SI 1989/123;
Wireless Telegraphy Apparatus (Citizens' Band European Users) (Exemption) Regulations 1989, SI 1989/943;
Wireless Telegraphy (Testing and Development Under Suppressed Radiation Conditions) (Exemption) Regulations 1989, SI 1989/1842;
Wireless Telegraphy (Exemption) Regulations 2003, SI 2003/74 amended by SI 2003/2155, SI 2005/3481, SI 2006/2994, SI 2008/236 and 2426, SI 2010/2512 (amending instrument amended by SI 2011/3035 amended by SI 2013/1253 and 1254), SI 2011/2950 and SI 2016/486 and 1075;
Wireless Telegraphy (Radio Frequency Identification Equipment) (Exemption) Regulations 2005, SI 2005/3471 amended by SI 2007/1282.
Exemptions are provided by the following regulations made under this section:
Wireless Telegraphy (Ultra-Wideband Equipment) (Exemption) Regulations 2009, SI 2009/2517 amended by SI 2010/2761;
Wireless Telegraphy (Exemption) Regulations 2010, SI 2010/2512 amended by SI 2013/1253 and SI 2014/1484;
Wireless Telegraphy (Mobile Communication Services on Board Ships) (Exemption) Regulations 2011, SI 2011/316;
Wireless Telegraphy (Intelligent Transport Systems) (Exemption) Regulations 2011, SI 2011/2945;
Wireless Telegraphy (Automotive Short Range Radar) (Exemption) Regulations 2013, SI 2013/1437;
Wireless Telegraphy (Mobile Communication Services on Aircraft) (Exemption) Regulations 2014, SI 2014/953;
Wireless Telegraphy (Ultra-Wideband Equipment) (Exemption) Regulations 2015, SI 2015/591;
Wireless Telegraphy (White Space Devices) (Exemption) Regulations 2015, SI 2015/2066 amended by SI 2016/615;
Wireless Telegraphy (Mobile Satellite System Equipment) (Exemption) Regulations 2016, SI 2016/1074.

**7.11143A 8A.** *Review of long licences*

**7.11143B 8B.** *Restriction on grant of exclusive licence*

**7.11143C 8C.** *Consultation before grant of exclusive licence*

**7.11144 9. Terms, provisions and limitations** (1) A wireless telegraphy licence[1] may be granted subject to such terms, provisions and limitations as OFCOM think fit.

(1A) But a licence in relation to the establishment, installation or use of wireless telegraphy stations or wireless telegraphy apparatus for the provision of an electronic communications network or electronic communications service may not be made subject to a term, provision or limitation unless the term, provision or limitation is of a kind falling within Part B of the Annex to Directive 2002/20/EC of the European Parliament and of the Council.

(2)–(7) *Further provisions as to terms and limitations*

(8) This section has effect subject to regulations under s 14.

[Wireless Telegraphy Act 2006, s 9 as amended by SI 2011/1210.]

[1] The Wireless Telegraphy (Licensing Procedures) Regulations 2010, SI 2010/1823 amended by SI 2016/418 have been made which apply in respect of licences granted under s 8.

**9A.** *Notice to satellite uplinkers*

**10. Procedure** *Procedures for the grant, revocation and variation of wireless telegraphy licences.*

**7.11145 11. Surrender of licence** (1) Where a wireless telegraphy licence has expired or has been revoked, it is the duty of—

(*a*) the person to whom the licence was granted, and

(*b*) any other person in whose possession or under whose control the licence may be,

to cause it to be surrendered to OFCOM if required by them to do so.

(2) Subsection (1) does not apply to a licence that relates solely to receiving apparatus.

(3) A person commits an offence if—

(*a*) he has a duty under subsection (1) to cause a wireless telegraphy licence to be surrendered to OFCOM; and

(*b*) without reasonable excuse he fails or refuses to do so.

(4) A person who commits an offence under this section is liable on summary conviction to a fine not exceeding level 3 on the standard scale.

[Wireless Telegraphy Act 2006, s 11.]

**12–17.** *Charges etc for grant of licence*

## CHAPTER 3[1]
## MANAGEMENT OF RADIO SPECTRUM

*Statistical information*

**7.11146 32. Statistical information** (1) OFCOM may require a person who is using or has established, installed or used a wireless telegraphy station or wireless telegraphy apparatus to provide OFCOM with all such information relating to—

(*a*) the establishment, installation or use of the station or apparatus, and

(*b*) any related matters,

as OFCOM may require for statistical purposes.

(2) Subsection (1) has effect subject to the following provisions of this section.

(3) OFCOM may not require the provision of information under this section except—

(*a*) by a demand for information that sets out OFCOM's reasons for requiring the information and the statistical purposes for which it is required; and

(*b*) where the making of a demand for that information is proportionate to the use to which the information is to be put in the carrying out of OFCOM's functions.

(4) A demand for information required under this section must be contained in a notice given to the person from whom the information is required.

(5) A person required to give information under this section must provide it in such manner and within such reasonable period as may be specified by OFCOM.

[Wireless Telegraphy Act 2006, s 32.]

---

1 Chapter 3 comprises ss 27–34.

7.11147 **33. Failure to provide information etc** (1) A person commits an offence if he fails to provide information in accordance with a requirement of OFCOM under section 32 or 32A.

(2) In proceedings against a person for an offence under subsection (1) it is a defence for the person to show—

(*a*) that it was not reasonably practicable for him to comply with the requirement within the period specified by OFCOM; but

(*b*) that he has taken all reasonable steps to provide the required information after the end of that period.

(3) A person who commits an offence under subsection (1) is liable on summary conviction to—

(*a*) on summary conviction, to a fine not exceeding the statutory maximum; or

(*b*) on conviction on indictment, to a fine.

(4) A person commits an offence if—

(*a*) in pursuance of a requirement under section 32 or 32A, he provides information that is false in any material particular; and

(*b*) at the time he provides it, he knows it to be false or is reckless as to whether or not it is false.

(5) A person who commits an offence under subsection (4) is liable on summary conviction to—

(*a*) on summary conviction, to a fine not exceeding the statutory maximum; or

(*b*) on conviction on indictment, to imprisonment for a term not exceeding 2 years, or to a fine, or to both.

(6) Proceedings for an offence under this section may be brought in respect of a contravention by a person of a requirement imposed under section 32A only if OFCOM have not imposed a financial penalty under sections 32C and 32E in respect of that contravention.

[Wireless Telegraphy Act 2006, s 33 as amended by SI 2011/1210.]

7.11148 **34. Statement of policy** (1) OFCOM must prepare and publish a statement of their general policy with respect to—

(*a*) the exercise of their powers under sections 32 and 32A; and

(*b*) the uses to which they are proposing to put information obtained under that section.

(2) OFCOM may from time to time revise that statement as they think fit.

(3) Where OFCOM make a statement under this section (or revise it), they must publish the statement (or the revised statement) in such manner as they consider appropriate for bringing it to the attention of persons who, in their opinion, are likely to be affected by it.

(4) OFCOM must, in exercising their powers under sections 32 and 32A, have regard to the statement for the time being in force under this section.

[Wireless Telegraphy Act 2006, s 34 as amended by SI 2011/1210.]

## CHAPTER 4[1]

## ENFORCEMENT

*Unauthorised use etc*

7.11149 **35. Unauthorised use etc of wireless telegraphy station or apparatus** (1) A person commits an offence if he contravenes section 8.

(2) A person who commits an offence under this section consisting in the establishment or use of a wireless telegraphy station, or the installation or use of wireless telegraphy apparatus, for the purpose of making a broadcast is liable[2]—

(*a*) on summary conviction, to imprisonment for a term not exceeding 12 months or to a fine not exceeding the statutory maximum or to both;

(*b*) on conviction on indictment, to imprisonment for a term not exceeding two years or to a fine or to both.

(3) In the application of subsection (2) to Scotland or Northern Ireland the reference to 12 months is to be read as a reference to six months.

(4) A person who commits an offence under this section consisting in the installation or use of receiving apparatus is liable on summary conviction to a fine not exceeding level 3 on the standard scale.

(5) A person who commits an offence under this section other than one falling within subsection (2) or (4) is liable on summary conviction to imprisonment for a term not exceeding 51 weeks[3] or to a fine not exceeding level 5 on the standard scale or to both.

(6) In the application of subsection (5) to Scotland or Northern Ireland the reference to 51

weeks is to be read as a reference to six months.

(7) In this section "broadcast" has the same meaning as in Part 5.

[Wireless Telegraphy Act 2006, s 35.]

[1] Chapter 4 comprises ss 35–44.

[2] For procedure in respect of this offence which is triable either way, see the Magistrates' Courts Act 1980, ss 17–21, in PART I: MAGISTRATES' COURTS, PROCEDURE, ante. In relation to an offence committed before the commencement of s 282(3) of the Criminal Justice Act 2003 the reference to 'twelve months' is to be read as "six months" (Sch 8, para 16, post).

[3] In relation to an offence committed on or after 18 September 2003 but before the commencement of s 282(3) of the Criminal Justice Act 2003 the reference to '51 weeks' is to be read as 'six months' (Sch 8 para 18, post).

7.11150 **36. Keeping available for unauthorised use** (1) A person who has a wireless telegraphy station or wireless telegraphy apparatus in his possession or under his control commits an offence if—

(*a*) he intends to use it in contravention of section 8; or

(*b*) he knows, or has reasonable cause to believe, that another person intends to use it in contravention of that section.

(2) A person who commits an offence under this section where the relevant contravention of section 8 would constitute an offence to which section 35(2) applies is liable[1]—

(*a*) on summary conviction, to imprisonment for a term not exceeding 12 months or to a fine not exceeding the statutory maximum or to both;

(*b*) on conviction on indictment, to imprisonment for a term not exceeding two years or to a fine or to both.

(3) In the application of subsection (2) to Scotland or Northern Ireland the reference to 12 months is to be read as a reference to six months.

(4) A person who commits an offence under this section in relation to receiving apparatus is liable on summary conviction to a fine not exceeding level 3 on the standard scale.

(5) A person who commits an offence under this section other than one falling within subsection (2) or (4) is liable on summary conviction to imprisonment for a term not exceeding 51 weeks[2] or to a fine not exceeding level 5 on the standard scale or to both.

(6) In the application of subsection (5) to Scotland or Northern Ireland the reference to 51 weeks is to be read as a reference to six months.

[Wireless Telegraphy Act 2006, s 36.]

[1] For procedure in respect of this offence which is triable either way, see the Magistrates' Courts Act 1980, ss 17–21, in PART I: MAGISTRATES' COURTS, PROCEDURE, ante. In relation to an offence committed before the commencement of s 282(3) of the Criminal Justice Act 2003 the reference to "twelve months" is to be read as "six months" (Sch 8, para 16, post).

[2] In relation to an offence committed on or after 18 September 2003 but before the commencement of s 282(3) of the Criminal Justice Act 2003 the reference to "51 weeks" is to be read as "six months" (Sch 8 para 18, post).

7.11151 **37. Allowing premises to be used for unlawful broadcasting** (1) A person who is in charge of premises that are used for unlawful broadcasting commits an offence if—

(*a*) he knowingly causes or permits the premises to be so used; or

(*b*) he has reasonable cause to believe that the premises are being so used but fails to take such steps as are reasonable in the circumstances of the case to prevent them from being so used.

(2) A person who commits an offence under this section is liable[1]—

(*a*) on summary conviction, to imprisonment for a term not exceeding 12 months or to a fine not exceeding the statutory maximum or to both;

(*b*) on conviction on indictment, to imprisonment for a term not exceeding two years or to a fine or to both.

(3) In the application of subsection (2) to Scotland or Northern Ireland the reference to 12 months is to be read as a reference to six months.

(4) For the purposes of this section a person is in charge of premises if—

(*a*) he is the owner or occupier of the premises; or

(*b*) he has, or acts or assists in, the management or control of the premises.

(5) For the purposes of this section premises are used for unlawful broadcasting if they are used—

(*a*) for making an unlawful broadcast; or

(*b*) for sending signals for the operation or control of apparatus used for the purpose of making an unlawful broadcast from another place.

(6) For the purposes of this section a broadcast is unlawful if—

(*a*) it is made by means of the use of a wireless telegraphy station or wireless telegraphy apparatus in contravention of section 8; or

(*b*) the making of the broadcast contravenes a provision of Part 5.

(7) In this section—

"broadcast" has the same meaning as in Part 5;

"premises" includes any place and, in particular, includes—

(*a*) a vehicle, ship or aircraft; and

(*b*) a structure or other object (whether movable or not, and whether on land or not).

[Wireless Telegraphy Act 2006, s 37.]

[1] For procedure in respect of this offence which is triable either way, see the Magistrates' Courts Act 1980, ss 17–21, in PART I: MAGISTRATES' COURTS, PROCEDURE, ante. In relation to an offence committed before the commencement of s 282(3) of the Criminal Justice Act 2003 the reference to "twelve months" is to be read as "six months" (Sch 8, para 16, post).

7.11152 **38. Facilitating unauthorised broadcasting** (1) This section applies in the case of a broadcasting station from which unauthorised broadcasts are made.

(2) A person commits an offence if—

(*a*) he participates in the management, financing, operation or day-to-day running of the broadcasting station knowing, or having reasonable cause to believe, that unauthorised broadcasts are made by the station;

(*b*) he supplies, instals, repairs or maintains wireless telegraphy apparatus or any other item knowing, or having reasonable cause to believe—

(i) that the apparatus or other item is to be, or is, used for the purpose of facilitating the operation or day-to-day running of the broadcasting station, and

(ii) that unauthorised broadcasts are made by the station;

(*c*) he renders any other service to a person knowing, or having reasonable cause to believe—

(i) that the rendering of the service to the person will facilitate the operation or day-to-day running of the broadcasting station, and

(ii) that unauthorised broadcasts are made by the station;

(*d*) he supplies a film or sound recording knowing, or having reasonable cause to believe, that an unauthorised broadcast of it is to be made by the broadcasting station;

(*e*) he makes a literary, dramatic or musical work knowing, or having reasonable cause to believe, that an unauthorised broadcast of it is to be made by the broadcasting station;

(*f*) he makes an artistic work knowing, or having reasonable cause to believe, that an unauthorised broadcast including that work is to be made by the broadcasting station;

(*g*) he participates in an unauthorised broadcast made by the broadcasting station knowing, or having reasonable cause to believe, that unauthorised broadcasts are made by the station;

(*h*) he advertises, or invites another to advertise, by means of an unauthorised broadcast made by the broadcasting station knowing, or having reasonable cause to believe, that unauthorised broadcasts are made by the station;

(*i*) he publishes the times or other details of unauthorised broadcasts made by the broadcasting station, or (otherwise than by publishing such details) publishes an advertisement of matter calculated to promote the station (whether directly or indirectly), knowing, or having reasonable cause to believe, that unauthorised broadcasts are made by the station.

(3) For the purposes of this section a person participates in a broadcast only if he is actually present—

(*a*) as an announcer;

(*b*) as a performer or one of the performers concerned in an entertainment given; or

(*c*) as the deliverer of a speech.

(4) The cases in which a person is to be taken for the purposes of this section as advertising by means of a broadcast include any case in which he causes or allows it to be stated, suggested or implied that entertainment included in the broadcast—

(*a*) has been supplied by him; or

(*b*) is provided wholly or partly at his expense.

(5) In proceedings for an offence under this section consisting in supplying a thing or rendering a service, it is a defence for the defendant to prove that he was obliged, under or by virtue of any enactment, to supply the thing or render the service.

(6) A person who commits an offence under this section is liable[1]—

(*a*) on summary conviction, to imprisonment for a term not exceeding 12 months or to a fine not exceeding the statutory maximum or to both;

(*b*) on conviction on indictment, to imprisonment for a term not exceeding two years or to a fine or to both.

(7) In the application of subsection (6) to Scotland or Northern Ireland the reference to 12 months is to be read as a reference to six months.

(8) In this section—

"broadcast" has the same meaning as in Part 5;

"broadcasting station" means a business or other operation (whether or not in the nature of a commercial venture) that is engaged in the making of broadcasts;

"unauthorised broadcast" means a broadcast made by means of the use of a wireless telegraphy station or wireless telegraphy apparatus in contravention of section 8.

[Wireless Telegraphy Act 2006, s 38.]

[1] For procedure in respect of this offence which is triable either way, see the Magistrates' Courts Act 1980, ss 17–21, in PART I: MAGISTRATES' COURTS, PROCEDURE, ante. In relation to an offence committed before the commencement of

s 282(3) of the Criminal Justice Act 2003 the reference to "twelve months" is to be read as "six months" (Sch 8, para 16, post).

*Procedures for contraventions*

7.11153 **39. Contravention of terms, etc** (1) Where OFCOM determine that there are reasonable grounds for believing that a person is contravening, or has contravened—

(*a*) a term, provision or limitation of a wireless telegraphy licence, or

(*b*) a term, provision or limitation of an exemption under section 8(3),

they may give that person a notification under this section.

(2) A notification under this section—

(*a*) sets out the determination made by OFCOM;

(*b*) specifies the term, provision or limitation, and the contravention, in respect of which that determination has been made; and

(*c*) specifies the period during which the person notified has an opportunity of making representations.

(3) *Repealed.*

(4) *Repealed.*

(5) *Repealed.*

(6) *Repealed.*

(7) *Repealed.*

(8) *Repealed.*

[Wireless Telegraphy Act 2006, s 39 as amended by SI 2009/2979 and SI 2011/1210]

7.11154 **41. Procedure for prosecutions** (1) This section applies to proceedings against a person ("the defendant") for an offence under section 35 consisting in the contravention of—

(*a*) the terms, provisions or limitations of a wireless telegraphy licence; or

(*b*) the terms, provisions or limitations of an exemption under section 8(3).

(2) Proceedings to which this section applies are not to be brought unless, before they are brought, OFCOM have—

(*a*) given the defendant a notification under section 39 in respect of the contravention to which the proceedings relate; and

(*b*) considered any representations about the matters notified which were made by the defendant within the period allowed under that section.

(3) Proceedings to which this section applies are not to be brought against a person in respect of a contravention if—

(*a*) it is a contravention to which a notification given to that person under section 39 relates; and

(*b*) that person has, during the period allowed under that section, complied with the notified term, provision or limitation.

(4) Subsection (2) does not apply where OFCOM have certified that it would be inappropriate to follow the procedure in section 39 because of an immediate risk of—

(*a*) a serious threat to the safety of the public, to public health or to national security; or

(*b*) serious economic or operational problems for persons (other than the defendant) who—

(i) use wireless telegraphy stations or wireless telegraphy apparatus;

(ii) are communications providers or make associated facilities available; or

(iii) are other users of the radio spectrum.

(5) Where—

(*a*) proceedings to which this section applies are as a result of subsection (4) brought without a notification having been given to the defendant, and

(*b*) the defendant is convicted in those proceedings of the offence under section 35,

the court, in determining how to deal with that person, must have regard, in particular, to the matters specified in subsection (6).

(6) The matters are—

(*a*) whether the defendant has ceased to be in contravention of the terms, provisions or limitations in question and (if so) when; and

(*b*) any steps taken by the defendant (whether before or after the commencement of the proceedings) for securing compliance with the obligations imposed on him by virtue of those terms, provisions or limitations.

(7) Where—

(*a*) OFCOM give a notification under section 39 in respect of a contravention, and

(*b*) that notification is given before the end of six months after the day of the contravention,

the time for the bringing of proceedings for a summary offence in respect of that contravention shall be extended until the end of six months from the end of the period allowed, in the case of that notification, for doing the things mentioned in section 39(3).

(8) Subsection (7) has effect notwithstanding anything in—

(*a*) section 127 of the Magistrates' Courts Act 1980 (c 43) (limitation on time for bringing summary proceedings), or (*b*) Article 19 of the Magistrates' Courts (Northern Ireland) Order 1981 (SI 1981/1675 (NI 26)) (equivalent provision for Northern Ireland).

[Wireless Telegraphy Act 2006, s 41 as amended by SI 2011/1210.]

**42–44.** *OFCOM may impose a penalty for contraventions by multiplex holders. No proceedings under this Chapter may be commenced against a person in respect of a contravention in respect of which a penalty has been imposed by OFCOM under this section.*

## CHAPTER 5[1]
## MISCELLANEOUS

*Regulations about wireless telegraphy*

7.11155 **45. Regulations** (1) OFCOM may make regulations[2] prescribing the things that are to be done, or not done, in connection with the use of a wireless telegraphy station or wireless telegraphy apparatus.

(2) Regulations under subsection (1) may, in particular, require the use of a wireless telegraphy station or wireless telegraphy apparatus to cease on the demand of such persons as may be prescribed by or under the regulations.

(3) OFCOM may make regulations imposing on a person—

(*a*) to whom a wireless telegraphy licence relating to a wireless telegraphy station or wireless telegraphy apparatus is granted, or

(*b*) who is in possession or control of such a station or such apparatus,

the obligations mentioned in subsection (4).

(4) The obligations are—

(*a*) obligations as to permitting and facilitating the inspection of the station or apparatus;

(*b*) obligations as to the condition in which the station or apparatus is to be kept;

(*c*) in the case of a station or apparatus for the establishment, installation or use of which a wireless telegraphy licence is necessary, obligations as to the production of the licence, or of such other evidence of the licensing of the station or apparatus as may be prescribed by the regulations.

(5) OFCOM may make regulations requiring the holder of a wireless telegraphy licence in respect of which sums are or may become due after the grant of the licence, or after its renewal, to keep and produce such accounts and records as may be specified in the regulations.

(6) OFCOM may make regulations requiring the holder of a wireless telegraphy licence authorising the establishment or use of a wireless telegraphy station to exhibit at the station such notices as may be specified in the regulations.

(7) Regulations under this section have effect subject to regulations under section 14.

(8) Nothing in regulations under this section requires a person to concede any form of right of entry into a private dwelling-house for the purpose of permitting or facilitating the inspection of receiving apparatus.

(9) The approval of the Secretary of State is required for the making by OFCOM of regulations under this section.

(10) A statutory instrument containing regulations made by OFCOM under this section is subject to annulment in pursuance of a resolution of either House of Parliament.

[Wireless Telegraphy Act 2006, s 45.]

---

1 Chapter 5 comprises ss 45–53 and Sch 3.

2 The Wireless Telegraphy (Content of Transmission) Regulations 1988, SI 1988/47 amended by SI 2003/2155 prohibits the use of apparatus to send messages etc of a grossly offensive, indecent, obscene or menacing nature. The Wireless Telegraphy (Inspections and Restrictions on Use of Exempt Stations and Apparatus) Regulations 2005, SI 2005/3481 have also been made under the repealed provisions of s 3 of the Wireless Telegraphy Act 1949.

7.11156 **46. Offences** (1) A person commits an offence if—

(*a*) he contravenes regulations made under section 45; or

(*b*) he causes or permits a wireless telegraphy station or wireless telegraphy apparatus to be used in contravention of regulations made under that section.

(2) A person who commits an offence under this section consisting in a contravention, in relation to receiving apparatus, of regulations made under section 45 is liable on summary conviction to a fine not exceeding level 3 on the standard scale.

(3) A person who commits an offence under this section other than one falling within subsection (2) is liable on summary conviction to a fine not exceeding level 5 on the standard scale.

[Wireless Telegraphy Act 2006, s 46.]

*Misuse of wireless telegraphy*

7.11157 **47. Misleading messages** (1) A person commits an offence if, by means of wireless telegraphy, he sends or attempts to send a message to which this section applies.

(2) This section applies to a message which, to the person's knowledge—

(*a*) is false or misleading; and

(*b*) is likely to prejudice the efficiency of a safety of life service or to endanger the safety of a person or of a ship, aircraft or vehicle.

(3) This section applies in particular to a message which, to the person's knowledge, falsely suggests that a ship or aircraft—

(*a*) is in distress or in need of assistance; or

(*b*) is not in distress or not in need of assistance.

(4) A person who commits an offence under this section is liable[1]—

(*a*) on summary conviction, to imprisonment for a term not exceeding 12 months or to a fine not exceeding the statutory maximum or to both;

(*b*) on conviction on indictment, to imprisonment for a term not exceeding two years or to a fine or to both.

(5) In the application of subsection (4) to Scotland or Northern Ireland the reference to 12 months is to be read as a reference to six months.

[Wireless Telegraphy Act 2006, s 47.]

---

1 For procedure in respect of this offence which is triable either way, see the Magistrates' Courts Act 1980, ss 17–21, in PART I: MAGISTRATES' COURTS, PROCEDURE, ante. In relation to an offence committed before the commencement of s 282(3) of the Criminal Justice Act 2003 the reference to "twelve months" is to be read as "six months" (Sch 8, para 16, post).

7.11158 **48. Interception and disclosure of messages** (1) A person commits an offence if, otherwise than under the authority of a designated person—

(*a*) he uses wireless telegraphy apparatus with intent to obtain information[1] as to the contents, sender or addressee of a message[2] (whether sent by means of wireless telegraphy or not) of which neither he nor a person on whose behalf he is acting is an intended recipient, or

(*b*) he discloses information as to the contents, sender or addressee of such a message.

(2) A person commits an offence under this section consisting in the disclosure of information only if the information disclosed by him is information that would not have come to his knowledge but for the use of wireless telegraphy apparatus by him or by another person.

(3) A person does not commit an offence under this section consisting in the disclosure of information if he discloses the information in the course of legal proceedings or for the purpose of a report of legal proceedings.

(4) A person who commits an offence under this section is liable on summary conviction to a fine not exceeding level 5 on the standard scale.

(5) "Designated person" means—

(*a*) the Secretary of State;

(*b*) the Commissioners for Her Majesty's Revenue and Customs; or

(*c*) any other person designated for the purposes of this section by regulations made by the Secretary of State.*

[Wireless Telegraphy Act 2006, s 48.]

---

* **Amended by the Investigatory Powers Act 2016, s 259 from a date to be appointed.**

1 Evidence of mischievous or improper intentions is not necessary; all that is required is evidence of the intent to do the prohibited act (*Paul v Ministry of Posts and Telecommunications* [1973] Crim LR 322). Tuning to a police frequency and listening to police messages is an offence since it is impossible to listen to the channel without obtaining information as the messages transmitted on it. It is otherwise where the listener chances on the channel while tuning a radio and passes over it since he does not intend to obtain information (*DPP v White* (1996) 160 JP 726, sub nom *DPP v Waite* [1997] Crim LR 123, DC).

2 As microwave radio emissions from a police radar speed gun do not constitute a "message" for the purposes of this section, the use by a motorist of an electrical field meter to detect such emissions is not an offence under this provision (*R v Knightsbridge Crown Court, ex p Foot* [1999] RTR 21, DC).

7.11159 **49. Interception authorities** (1) The conduct in relation to which a designated person may give an interception authority is not to include conduct falling within subsection (2), except where he believes that the conduct is necessary on grounds falling within subsection (5).

(2) Conduct falls within this subsection if it is—

(*a*) conduct that, if engaged in without lawful authority, constitutes an offence under section 1(1) or (2) of the Regulation of Investigatory Powers Act 2000 (c 23);

(*b*) conduct that, if engaged in without lawful authority, is actionable under section 1(3) of that Act;

(*c*) conduct that is capable of being authorised by an authorisation or notice granted under Chapter 2 of Part 1 of that Act (communications data); or

(*d*) conduct that is capable of being authorised by an authorisation granted under Part 2 of that Act (surveillance etc).

(3) A designated person may not exercise his power to give an interception authority except where he believes—

(*a*) that the giving of his authority is necessary on grounds falling within subsection (4) or (5); and

(*b*) that the conduct authorised by him is proportionate to what is sought to be achieved by that conduct.

(4) An interception authority is necessary on grounds falling within this subsection if it is necessary—

(*a*) in the interests of national security;

(*b*) for the purpose of preventing or detecting crime or of preventing disorder;

(*c*) in the interests of the economic well-being of the United Kingdom;

(*d*) in the interests of public safety;
(*e*) for the purpose of protecting public health;
(*f*) for the purpose of assessing or collecting a tax, duty, levy or other imposition, contribution or charge payable to a government department; or
(*g*) for any purpose (not falling within paragraphs (*a*) to (*f*)) that is specified for the purposes of this subsection by regulations made by the Secretary of State.

(5) An interception authority is necessary on grounds falling within this subsection if it is not necessary on grounds falling within subsection (4)(*a*) or (*c*) to (*g*) but is necessary for purposes connected with—
(*a*) the grant of wireless telegraphy licences;
(*b*) the prevention or detection of anything that constitutes interference with wireless telegraphy; or
(*c*) the enforcement of—
(i) any provision of this Part (other than Chapter 2 and sections 27 to 31) or Part 3, or
(ii) any enactment not falling within sub-paragraph (i) that relates to interference with wireless telegraphy.

(6) The matters to be taken into account in considering whether the requirements of subsection (3) are satisfied in the case of the giving of an interception authority include whether what it is thought necessary to achieve by the authorised conduct could reasonably be achieved by other means.

(7) An interception authority must be in writing and under the hand of—
(*a*) the Secretary of State;
(*b*) one of the Commissioners for Her Majesty's Revenue and Customs; or
(*c*) a person not falling within paragraph (*a*) or (*b*) who is designated for the purposes of this subsection by regulations[1] made by the Secretary of State.

(8) An interception authority may be general or specific and may be given—
(*a*) to such person or persons, or description of persons,
(*b*) for such period, and
(*c*) subject to such restrictions and limitations,
as the designated person thinks fit.

(9) No regulations may be made under subsection (4)(*g*) unless a draft of them has first been laid before Parliament and approved by a resolution of each House.

(10) For the purposes of this section the question whether a person's conduct is capable of being authorised under Chapter 2 of Part 1 of the Regulation of Investigatory Powers Act 2000 (c 23) or under Part 2 of that Act is to be determined without reference—
(*a*) to whether the person is someone upon whom a power or duty is or may be conferred or imposed by or under that Chapter or that Part; or
(*b*) to whether there are grounds for believing that the requirements for the grant of an authorisation or the giving of a notice under that Chapter or that Part are satisfied.

(11) References in this section to an interception authority are references to an authority for the purposes of section 48 given otherwise than by way of the issue or renewal of a warrant, authorisation or notice under Part 1 or 2 of the Regulation of Investigatory Powers Act 2000.

(12) In this section—
"crime" has the meaning given by section 81(2)(*a*) of the Regulation of Investigatory Powers Act 2000 (c 23);
"designated person" has the same meaning as in section 48.*

[Wireless Telegraphy Act 2006, s 49.]

---

* **Amended by the Investigatory Powers Act 2016, s 259 from a date to be appointed.**

[1] See the Wireless Telegraphy (Interception and Disclosure of Messages) (Designation) Regulations 2003, SI 2003/3104.

*Miscellaneous*

7.11160 **50. Apparatus on foreign-registered ships etc** (1) The Secretary of State may make regulations[1] for regulating the use, on board a foreign-registered ship or aircraft while it is within the limits of the United Kingdom and UK territorial sea, of wireless telegraphy apparatus on board the ship or aircraft.

(2) The regulations may provide—
(*a*) for the punishment of persons contravening the regulations by a fine;
(*b*) for the forfeiture of any wireless telegraphy apparatus in respect of which an offence under the regulations is committed.

(3) The maximum fine for each offence under the regulations is—
(*a*) an amount not exceeding level 5 on the standard scale; or
(*b*) a lesser amount.

(4) The regulations may make different provision for ships or aircraft registered in different countries.

(5) Except as provided by this section or in consequence of an Order in Council under

section 119(3), nothing in sections 8 to 11, 35 to 38, 45 to 49, 105 and 119 operates so as to impose any prohibition or restriction on persons using wireless telegraphy apparatus on board a foreign-registered ship or aircraft.

(6) A foreign-registered ship or aircraft is one that—

(*a*) is not registered in the United Kingdom; and

(*b*) is registered in a country other than the United Kingdom, the Isle of Man or any of the Channel Islands.

[Wireless Telegraphy Act 2006, s 50.]

---

1 The Wireless Telegraphy (Visiting Ships and Aircraft) Regulations 1998, SI 1998/2970 have been made under the repealed provisions of the Wireless Telegraphy Act 1949, s 9.

7.11161 **51. Apparatus in vehicles** (1) This section applies to the power of the Secretary of State under section 7(1) of the Vehicle Excise and Registration Act 1994 (c 22) to specify—

(*a*) the declaration to be made, and

(*b*) the particulars to be furnished,

by a person applying for a vehicle licence (within the meaning of that Act).

(2) The power of the Secretary of State includes power to require that the declaration and particulars extend to any matters relevant for the enforcement of section 8 of this Act in respect of any wireless telegraphy apparatus installed in the vehicle.

(3) Accordingly, the Secretary of State is not required to issue a vehicle licence under the Vehicle Excise and Registration Act 1994 where the applicant fails to comply with a requirement imposed because of subsection (2).

(4) A person commits an offence if in providing information that he is required to provide because of subsection (2)—

(*a*) he makes a statement that he knows to be false in a material particular; or

(*b*) he recklessly makes a statement that is false in a material particular.

(5) A person who commits an offence under subsection (4) is liable on summary conviction to a fine not exceeding level 3 on the standard scale.

(6) Where subsection (4) applies, it applies instead of section 45 of the Vehicle Excise and Registration Act 1994 (c 22) (false or misleading declarations and information).

[Wireless Telegraphy Act 2006, s 51.]

**52. Wireless personnel** *Secretary of State may issue certificates of competence and authorities to persons who are to fill positions in connection with the operation of wireless telegraphy stations or apparatus.*

7.11162 **53. Surrender of authority** (1) Where an authority under section 52(3) has ceased to be in force or has been suspended, it is the duty of—

(*a*) the person to whom the authority was issued, and

(*b*) any other person in whose possession or under whose control the authority may be,

to cause it to be surrendered to the Secretary of State if required by the Secretary of State to do so.

(2) A person commits an offence if—

(*a*) he has a duty under subsection (1) to cause an authority under section 52(3) to be surrendered to the Secretary of State, and

(*b*) without reasonable excuse he fails or refuses to do so.

(3) A person who commits an offence under subsection (2) is liable on summary conviction to a fine not exceeding level 3 on the standard scale.

[Wireless Telegraphy Act 2006, s 53.]

## PART 3[1]
## REGULATION OF APPARATUS

### *Undue interference*

7.11163 **54. Regulations about use and sale etc of apparatus** (1) OFCOM may make regulations[2] prescribing the requirements to be complied with in the case of apparatus specified in the regulations, if the apparatus is to be used.

(2) OFCOM may make regulations[2] prescribing the requirements to be complied with in the case of apparatus specified in the regulations, if the apparatus is to be—

(*a*) sold otherwise than for export,

(*b*) offered or advertised for sale otherwise than for export, or

(*c*) let on hire, or offered or advertised for letting on hire,

by a person who manufactures, assembles or imports such apparatus in the course of business.

(3) The requirements prescribed under subsection (1) or (2) are to be such requirements as OFCOM think fit for the purpose of ensuring that the use of the apparatus does not cause undue interference[3] with wireless telegraphy[4].

(4) In particular, the requirements may include—

(*a*) requirements as to the maximum intensity of electromagnetic energy of specified frequencies that may be radiated in any direction from the apparatus while it is being used;

(*b*) in the case of apparatus the power for which is supplied from electric lines, requirements as to the maximum electromagnetic energy of specified frequencies that may be injected into those lines by the apparatus.

(5) The apparatus which may be specified in the regulations under subsection (1) or (2) is apparatus which generates, or is designed to generate, or is liable to generate fortuitously, electromagnetic energy at frequencies not exceeding 3,000 gigahertz.

(6) In a case where apparatus does not comply with the requirements applicable to it under regulations made under subsection (1) or (2), a person does not act unlawfully only because—

(*a*) he uses the apparatus, or

(*b*) he sells it, or offers or advertises it for sale, or lets it on hire or offers or advertises it for letting on hire.

But the non-compliance is a ground for the giving of a notice under section 55 or 56.

(7) The approval of the Secretary of State is required for the making by OFCOM of regulations under this section.

(8) A statutory instrument containing regulations made by OFCOM under this section is subject to annulment in pursuance of a resolution of either House of Parliament.

[Wireless Telegraphy Act 2006, s 54.]

---

[1] Part 3 comprises ss 54–68.

[2] Regulations have been made as follows:

Wireless Telegraphy (Control of Interference from Ignition Apparatus) Regulations 1952, SI 1952/2023 amended by SI 1957/347;

Wireless Telegraphy (Control of Interference from Electro-Medical Apparatus) Regulations 1963, SI 1963/1895;

Wireless Telegraphy (Control of Interference from Radio-Frequency Heating Apparatus) Regulations 1971, SI 1971/1675;

Wireless Telegraphy (Control of Interference from Ignition Apparatus) Regulations 1973, SI 1973/1217;

Wireless Telegraphy (Control of Interference from Household Appliances, Portable Tools etc) Regulations 1978, SI 1978/1267 amended by SI 1985/808 and SI 1989/562;

Wireless Telegraphy (Control of Interference from Fluorescent Lighting Apparatus) Regulations 1979, SI 1979/1268 amended by SI 1985/807 and SI 1989/561;

Wireless Telegraphy (Control of Interference from Citizens Band Radio Apparatus) Regulations 1982, SI 1982/635 amended by SI 1988/1216;

Wireless Telegraphy (Control of Interference from Apparatus) Regulations 2016, SI 2016/426.

The above regulations ceased to have effect by virtue of the Electromagnetic Compatibility Regulations 2006, SI 2006/3418 except to the extent that they impose requirements for radio frequency spectrum planning or for the prevention of undue interference to wireless telegraphy from relevant apparatus in use.

Under this provision the Wireless Telegraphy (Control of Interference from Apparatus) (The London Olympic Games and Paralympic Games) Regulations 2012, SI 2012/1519 have also been made.

[3] For meaning of "interference," "wireless telegraphy," see ss 116 and 117, post.

[4] The use of any apparatus by members of visiting forces or international headquarters for service purposes, in the course of their duty as such, is excepted from this section and any regulations made thereunder (Visiting Forces and International Headquarters (Application of Law) Order 1965, SI 1965/1586, art 7.

7.11164 **55. Enforcement: use of apparatus** (1) This section applies where, in the opinion of OFCOM—

(*a*) apparatus does not comply with the requirements applicable to it under regulations made under section 54(1); and

(*b*) the first or second condition is satisfied in relation to the apparatus.

(2) The first condition is that the use of the apparatus is likely to cause undue interference with wireless telegraphy used—

(*a*) for the purposes of a safety of life service; or

(*b*) for a purpose on which the safety of a person, or of a ship, aircraft or vehicle, may depend.

(3) The second condition is that—

(*a*) the use of the apparatus is likely to cause undue interference with wireless telegraphy other than wireless telegraphy falling within subsection (2);

(*b*) the use of the apparatus in fact has caused, or is causing, such interference; and

(*c*) the case is one where OFCOM consider that all reasonable steps to minimise interference have been taken in relation to the wireless telegraphy station or wireless telegraphy apparatus receiving the telegraphy interfered with.

(4) OFCOM may give a notice in writing to the person in possession of the apparatus—

(*a*) prohibiting the use of the apparatus after a date fixed by the notice, whether by the person to whom the notice is given or otherwise; or

(*b*) (if OFCOM think fit so to frame the notice) prohibiting the use of the apparatus after a date fixed by the notice except in such way, at such times and in such circumstances as the notice may specify.

(5) The date fixed by a notice under subsection (4) must be not less than 28 days from the date on which the notice is given.

(6) But if OFCOM are satisfied that the use of the apparatus in question is likely to cause such undue interference as is described in subsection (2), the date fixed by a notice under subsection (4) may be the date on which the notice is given.

(7) A notice under subsection (4) may be revoked or varied by a subsequent notice in writing from OFCOM given to the person who is then in possession of the apparatus.

(8) Where a notice under subsection (7) has the effect of imposing additional restrictions on the use of the apparatus, the provisions of this section about the coming into force of notices apply in relation to the notice as if it were a notice under subsection (4).

[Wireless Telegraphy Act 2006, s 55.]

**7.11165 56. Enforcement: sale etc of apparatus** (1) This section applies where, in the opinion of OFCOM, apparatus does not comply with the requirements applicable to it under regulations made under section 54(2).

(2) OFCOM may give a notice in writing to the person who, in the course of business, has manufactured, assembled or imported the apparatus, prohibiting him from—

(*a*) selling the apparatus otherwise than for export;

(*b*) offering or advertising it for sale otherwise than for export; or

(*c*) letting it on hire, or offering or advertising it for letting on hire.

[Wireless Telegraphy Act 2006, s 56.]

**7.11166 57. Appeal against notice under section 55 or 56 etc** (1) Where an appeal with respect to a notice under section 55 (or section 56) is pending—

(*a*) proceedings for an offence under section 58(1) (or section 58(4)) relating to that notice, whether instituted before or after the bringing of the appeal, are to be stayed until the appeal has been finally determined; and

(*b*) the proceedings are to be discharged if the notice is set aside in consequence of the appeal.

(2) But subsection (1) does not affect proceedings in which a person has been convicted at a time when there was no pending appeal.

(3) For the purposes of this section an appeal under section 192 of the Communications Act 2003 (c 21) with respect to a notice under section 55 (or section 56) or a further appeal relating to the decision on such an appeal is pending unless—

(*a*) that appeal has been brought to a conclusion or withdrawn and there is no further appeal pending in relation to the decision on the appeal; or

(*b*) no further appeal against a decision made on the appeal or on any such further appeal may be brought without the permission of the court and—

(i) in a case where there is no fixed period within which that permission can be sought, that permission has been refused or has not been sought, or

(ii) in a case where there is a fixed period within which that permission can be sought, that permission has been refused or that period has expired without permission having been sought.

(4) No proceedings for an offence under section 58(1) (or section 58(4)) relating to a notice under section 55 (or section 56) may be commenced in Scotland—

(*a*) until the time during which an appeal against such a notice may be brought has expired; or

(*b*) where such an appeal has been brought, until that appeal has been determined.

(5) Proceedings in Scotland for such an offence must be commenced—

(*a*) where no appeal has been brought, within six months of the time referred to in subsection (4)(*a*); and

(*b*) where an appeal has been brought and determined, within six months of the date of that determination.

[Wireless Telegraphy Act 2006, s 57.]

**7.11167 58. Contravening notice under section 55 or 56** (1) A person commits an offence if—

(*a*) he uses apparatus, or causes or permits apparatus to be used, knowing that a notice under section 55 is in force with respect to it; and

(*b*) the use of the apparatus contravenes the notice.

(2) A person who commits an offence under subsection (1) is liable on summary conviction—

(*a*) if the offence is one that falls within subsection (6), to a fine not exceeding level 5 on the standard scale;

(*b*) otherwise, to a fine not exceeding level 3 on the standard scale.

(3) In the application of subsection (2) to Scotland or Northern Ireland, paragraph (*a*) has effect as if for the words "to a fine not exceeding level 5 on the standard scale" there were substituted "to imprisonment for a term not exceeding three months or to a fine not exceeding level 5 on the standard scale or to both".

(4) A person commits an offence if he contravenes the provisions of a notice given to him under section 56 (unless the notice has previously been revoked by OFCOM).

(5) A person who commits an offence under subsection (4) is liable on summary conviction—

(*a*) if the offence is one that falls within subsection (6), to a fine not exceeding level 5 on the standard scale;

(*b*) otherwise, to a fine not exceeding level 3 on the standard scale.

(6) An offence falls within this subsection if it involves or consists in a contravention of a notice under section 55 or 56 in relation to apparatus the use of which is likely to cause undue interference with wireless telegraphy used—

(*a*) for the purpose of a safety of life service; or

(*b*) for a purpose on which the safety of a person, or of a ship, aircraft or vehicle, may depend.

[Wireless Telegraphy Act 2006, s 58.]

7.11168 **59. Entry and search of premises etc** (1) A justice of the peace may issue an authorisation under this section if he is satisfied, on an application supported by sworn evidence, that—

(*a*) there is reasonable ground for believing that there is to be found, on specified premises or in a specified ship, aircraft or vehicle, apparatus that does not comply with the requirements applicable to it under regulations made under section 54;

(*b*) it is necessary to enter those premises, or that ship, aircraft or vehicle, for the purpose of obtaining information that will enable OFCOM to decide whether or not to give a notice under section 55 or 56; and

(*c*) within the period of 14 days before the date of the application to the justice, access to the premises, ship, aircraft or vehicle for the purpose of obtaining such information—

(i) has been demanded by a person authorised for the purpose by OFCOM, who has produced sufficient documentary evidence of his identity and authority; but

(ii) has been refused.

(2) But the justice may not issue an authorisation unless the first or second condition is fulfilled as regards the application.

(3) The first condition is that it is shown to the justice that OFCOM are satisfied that there is reasonable ground for believing that the use of the apparatus in question is likely to cause undue interference with wireless telegraphy used—

(*a*) for the purposes of a safety of life service; or

(*b*) for a purpose on which the safety of a person, or of a ship, aircraft or vehicle, may depend.

(4) The second condition is that it is shown to the justice that—

(*a*) at least seven days before the demand was made, notice that access would be demanded was given to the occupier of the premises or (as the case may be) the person in possession or the person in charge of the ship, aircraft or vehicle;

(*b*) the demand for access was made at a reasonable hour; and

(*c*) it was unreasonably refused.

(5) An authorisation under this section is an authorisation empowering a person or persons authorised for the purpose by OFCOM, with or without constables—

(*a*) to enter the premises or (as the case may be) the ship, aircraft or vehicle and any premises on which it may be;

(*b*) to search the premises, ship, aircraft or vehicle with a view to discovering whether apparatus falling within subsection (1)(*a*) is there;

(*c*) if he or they find such apparatus there, to examine and test it with a view to obtaining the information mentioned in subsection (1)(*b*).

(6) An authorisation under this section must be in writing and signed by the justice.

(7) A person authorised by OFCOM to exercise a power conferred by this section may if necessary use reasonable force in the exercise of the power.

(8) Subsection (7) does not affect any power exercisable by the person apart from that subsection.

(9) Where under this section a person has a right to examine and test apparatus on premises or in a ship, aircraft or vehicle, any person who—

(*a*) is on the premises, or

(*b*) is in charge of, or in or in attendance on, the ship, aircraft or vehicle,

must give him whatever assistance he may reasonably require in the examination or testing of the apparatus.

(10) A reference in this section to a justice of the peace is to be read—

(*a*) in Scotland, as a reference to a sheriff;

(*b*) in Northern Ireland, as a reference to a lay magistrate.

[Wireless Telegraphy Act 2006, s 59.]

7.11169 **60. Obstruction and failure to assist** (1) A person commits an offence if—

(*a*) he intentionally obstructs a person in the exercise of the powers conferred on him under section 59; or

(*b*) he fails or refuses, without reasonable excuse, to give to such a person any assistance which, under that section, he is under a duty to give to him.

(2) A person who commits an offence under this section is liable on summary conviction to a fine not exceeding level 5 on the standard scale.

[Wireless Telegraphy Act 2006, s 60.]

7.11170 **61. Sections 54 to 60: interpretation** References in sections 54 to 60 to apparatus include references to any form of electric line.

[Wireless Telegraphy Act 2006, s 61.]

*Restriction orders*

7.11171 **62. Restriction orders** (1) This section applies to wireless telegraphy apparatus and to apparatus designed or adapted for use in connection with wireless telegraphy apparatus.

(2) Where it appears to OFCOM to be expedient to do so for the purpose of preventing or reducing the risk of interference with wireless telegraphy, they may make an order (a "restriction order") imposing restrictions in relation to apparatus to which this section applies of a class or description specified in the order.

(3) The restrictions may relate to the following actions—

(*a*) the manufacture of apparatus (whether or not for sale);

(*b*) selling apparatus or offering it for sale;

(*c*) letting apparatus on hire or offering to let it on hire;

(*d*) indicating (whether by displaying apparatus or by any form of advertisement) willingness to sell apparatus or to let it on hire;

(*e*) having custody or control of apparatus;

(*f*) the importation of apparatus.

(4) A restriction order must specify, in the case of apparatus of any class or description specified in the order, what actions are restricted by it.

(5) An action for the time being restricted by a restriction order is prohibited by this section unless—

(*a*) an authority given by OFCOM relates to it; and

(*b*) it complies with any terms and conditions that OFCOM attach to the authority.

(6) The approval of the Secretary of State is required for the making by OFCOM of an order under this section.

(7) A statutory instrument containing an order made by OFCOM under this section is subject to annulment in pursuance of a resolution of either House of Parliament.

[Wireless Telegraphy Act 2006, s 62.]

7.11172 63. **Authorities** (1) An authority given by OFCOM under section 62(5) in the case of apparatus of a class or description specified in a restriction order may be limited—

(*a*) to such of the actions restricted by the order as may be specified in the authority;

(*b*) to such subsidiary class or description of apparatus, falling within the class or description specified in the order, as may be specified in the authority.

(2) Terms or conditions attached by OFCOM to an authority under section 62(5) for the manufacture or importation of apparatus may relate to a period after, as well as to the time of, or a period before, the manufacture or importation.

(3) An authority under section 62(5) may be given, and terms or conditions may be attached to it—

(*a*) generally by means of a notice published in the London, Edinburgh and Belfast Gazettes; or

(*b*) by an instrument in writing issued to each person authorised to do, in relation to apparatus of a class or description to which a restriction order relates, any action for the time being restricted by the order.

[Wireless Telegraphy Act 2006, s 63.]

7.11173 64. **Compatibility with international obligations** (1) OFCOM may not—

(*a*) make a restriction order,

(*b*) give an authority under section 62(5), or

(*c*) attach a term or condition to such an authority,

unless they are satisfied that the order, authority, term or condition is compatible with the international obligations of the United Kingdom.

(2) Where—

(*a*) a statutory instrument containing a restriction order, or

(*b*) a notice or instrument in writing giving an authority under section 62(5), or attaching a term or condition to such an authority,

contains a statement that OFCOM are satisfied as mentioned in subsection (1), the statement is evidence of that fact (and, in Scotland, sufficient evidence of it).

[Wireless Telegraphy Act 2006, s 64.]

7.11174 65. **Powers of Commissioners for Her Majesty's Revenue and Customs** (1) This section applies where the importation of apparatus of a particular class or description is for the time being restricted by a restriction order.

(2) An officer of Revenue and Customs may require a person with custody or control of apparatus of that class or description which is being or has been imported to provide proof that the importation of the apparatus is or was not unlawful by virtue of section 62.

(3) If the proof required under subsection (2) is not provided to the satisfaction of the Commissioners for Her Majesty's Revenue and Customs, the apparatus is to be treated, unless the contrary is proved, as being prohibited goods, within the meaning of the Customs and Excise Management Act 1979 (c 2), and is liable to forfeiture under that Act.

[Wireless Telegraphy Act 2006, s 65.]

7.11175 66. **Offences** (1) A person commits an offence if—

(*a*) he takes any action falling within section 62(3)(*a*) to (*d*) in relation to apparatus in contravention of section 62(5); or (*b*) without reasonable excuse he has apparatus in his custody or control in contravention of section 62(5).

(2) A person commits an offence if he contravenes or fails to comply with any terms or conditions attached to an authority given by OFCOM under section 62(5) (whatever the action to which the authority relates).

(3) A person who commits an offence under this section is liable on summary conviction to a fine not exceeding level 5 on the standard scale.

(4) This section does not affect any liability to a penalty that may have been incurred under the Customs and Excise Management Act 1979 (c 2).

[Wireless Telegraphy Act 2006, s 66.]

7.11176 67. **Restriction orders: interpretation** In sections 62 to 66—

"manufacture" includes construction by any method and the assembly of component parts;

"restriction order" has the meaning given by section 62.

[Wireless Telegraphy Act 2006, s 67.]

*Deliberate interference*

7.11177 68. **Deliberate interference** (1) A person commits an offence if he uses apparatus for the purpose of interfering with wireless telegraphy.

(2) This section applies—

(*a*) whether or not the apparatus in question is wireless telegraphy apparatus;

(*b*) whether or not it is apparatus specified in regulations under section 54;

(*c*) whether or not a notice under section 55 or 56 has been given with respect to it, or, if given, has been varied or revoked.

(3) A person who commits an offence under this section is liable[1]—

(*a*) on summary conviction, to imprisonment for a term not exceeding 12 months or to a fine not exceeding the statutory maximum or to both;

(*b*) on conviction on indictment, to imprisonment for a term not exceeding two years or to a fine or to both.

(4) In the application of subsection (3) to Scotland or Northern Ireland the reference to 12 months is to be read as a reference to six months.

[Wireless Telegraphy Act 2006, s 68.]

1 For procedure in respect of this offence which is triable either way, see the Magistrates' Courts Act 1980, ss 17–21, in PART I: MAGISTRATES' COURTS, PROCEDURE, ante. In relation to an offence committed before the commencement of s 282(3) of the Criminal Justice Act 2003 the reference to "twelve months" is to be read as "six months" (Sch 8, para 16, post).

PART 4[1]

APPROVAL OF APPARATUS ETC

*Approval of apparatus*

69–71. *Procedures for approvals of apparatus.*

1 Part 4 comprises ss 69–76.

*Marking*

72–73. *OFCOM may require apparatus to be marked with particular information or instruction relating to the apparatus or its installation or use and prohibit the supply of such equipment without such markings and require advertisements to contain prescribed information.*

7.11178 74. **Offences** (1) A person commits an offence if in the course of a trade or business he supplies, or offers to supply, apparatus in contravention of an order under section 72.

(2) A person is to be treated as offering to supply apparatus if—

(*a*) he exposes apparatus for supply, or

(*b*) he has apparatus in his possession for supply.

(3) A person who publishes an advertisement for apparatus to be supplied in the course of a trade or business commits an offence if the advertisement fails to comply with a requirement imposed by an order under section 73.

(4) A person who commits an offence under subsection (1) or (3) is liable on summary conviction to a fine not exceeding level 5 on the standard scale.

(5) Proceedings for an offence under this section may be commenced at any time within the period of 12 months beginning with the day after the commission of the offence.

[Wireless Telegraphy Act 2006, s 74.]

7.11179 75. **Default of third person** (1) Where the commission by one person ("A") of an offence under section 74(1) or (3) is due to the act or default of another ("B"), B also commits the offence; and B may be charged with and convicted of the offence by virtue of this subsection whether or not proceedings are taken against A.

(2) In proceedings for an offence under section 74(1) or (3) it is a defence for the defendant to prove that he took all reasonable steps and exercised all due diligence to avoid committing the

offence.

(3) A person may not rely on a defence under subsection (2) which involves an allegation that the commission of the offence was due to the act or default of another person unless—

(*a*) at least seven clear days before the hearing he has given to the prosecutor a notice in writing giving such information identifying or assisting in the identification of the other person as was then in his possession; or

(*b*) the court grants him leave.

(4) In proceedings for an offence under section 74(3) it is a defence for the defendant to prove that—

(*a*) at the time of the alleged offence he was a person whose business it was to publish or arrange for the publication of advertisements;

(*b*) he received the advertisement for publication in the ordinary course of business; and

(*c*) he did not know and had no reason to suspect that publication of the advertisement would amount to an offence under that subsection.

[Wireless Telegraphy Act 2006, s 75.]

*Interpretation*

7.11180 76. **Part 4: interpretation** In this Part—

"advertisement" includes a catalogue, a circular and a price list;

"relevant apparatus" means wireless telegraphy apparatus or apparatus designed or adapted for use in connection with wireless telegraphy apparatus.

[Wireless Telegraphy Act 2006, s 76.]

## PART 5[1]

## PROHIBITION OF BROADCASTING FROM SEA OR AIR

*Prohibitions*

7.11181 77. **Broadcasting from ships and aircraft** (1) It is unlawful—

(*a*) in the case of any ship or aircraft, to make a broadcast from it while it is in or over the United Kingdom or external waters; or

(*b*) in the case of a British-registered ship or British-registered aircraft, to make a broadcast from it while it is not in or over the United Kingdom or external waters.

(2) If a broadcast is made from a ship in contravention of subsection (1), an offence is committed by—

(*a*) the owner of the ship;

(*b*) the master of the ship; and

(*c*) a person who operates, or participates in the operation of, the apparatus by means of which the broadcast is made.

(3) If a broadcast is made from an aircraft in contravention of subsection (1), an offence is committed by—

(*a*) the operator of the aircraft;

(*b*) the commander of the aircraft; and

(*c*) a person who operates, or participates in the operation of, the apparatus by means of which the broadcast is made.

(4) A person commits an offence if he procures a broadcast to be made in contravention of subsection (1).

(5) In this section—

"master", in relation to a ship, includes any other person (except a pilot) who has command or charge of the ship;

"operator", in relation to an aircraft, means the person who at the relevant time has the management of the aircraft.

[Wireless Telegraphy Act 2006, s 77.]

[1] Part 5 comprises ss 77–95.

7.11182 78. **Broadcasting from marine structures etc** (1) This section applies to—

(*a*) tidal waters in the United Kingdom;

(*b*) external waters;

(*c*) waters in a designated area.

(2) It is unlawful to make a broadcast from—

(*a*) a structure, other than a ship, that is affixed to, or supported by, the bed of waters to which this section applies, or

(*b*) any other object in those waters.

(3) Subsection (2) does not apply by virtue of paragraph (*b*) to a broadcast made from a ship or aircraft.

(4) A person commits an offence if he operates, or participates in the operation of, apparatus by means of which a broadcast is made in contravention of subsection (2).

(5) A person commits an offence if he procures a broadcast to be made in contravention of subsection (2).

[Wireless Telegraphy Act 2006, s 78.]

7.11183 **79. Broadcasting from prescribed areas of high seas** (1) It is unlawful—

(*a*) to make a broadcast that is capable of being received in the United Kingdom, or

(*b*) to make a broadcast that causes interference with any wireless telegraphy in the United Kingdom,

from a ship (other than a British-registered ship) while it is within a prescribed area of the high seas.

(2) If a broadcast is made in contravention of subsection (1), an offence is committed by—

(*a*) the owner of the ship from which the broadcast is made;

(*b*) the master of the ship; and

(*c*) a person who operates, or participates in the operation of, apparatus by means of which the broadcast is made.

(3) A person commits an offence if he procures a broadcast to be made in contravention of subsection (1).

(4) The making of a broadcast does not contravene subsection (1) if it is shown to have been authorised under the law of a country or territory outside the United Kingdom.

(5) "Prescribed" means prescribed for the purposes of this section by an order made by the Secretary of State.

[Wireless Telegraphy Act 2006, s 79.]

7.11184 **80. Acts connected with broadcasting** (1) A British person commits an offence if he operates, or participates in the operation of, apparatus by means of which a broadcast is made—

(*a*) from a ship (other than a British-registered ship) while it is on the high seas;

(*b*) from an aircraft (other than a British-registered aircraft) while it is on or over the high seas;

(*c*) from a structure (other than a ship) that is affixed to, or supported by, the bed of the high seas; or

(*d*) from an object on the high seas (other than a structure falling within paragraph (*c*), a ship or an aircraft).

(2) Subsection (1) does not apply—

(*a*) by virtue of paragraph (*a*), to a broadcast made in contravention of section 79(1);

(*b*) by virtue of paragraph (*c*) or (*d*), to a broadcast made from a structure or other object in waters in a designated area.

(3) A person commits an offence if he procures a broadcast to be made as mentioned in subsection (1).

[Wireless Telegraphy Act 2006, s 80.]

7.11185 **81. Management of station** (1) A person commits an offence if, from anywhere in the United Kingdom or external waters, he participates in the management, financing, operation or day-to-day running of a broadcasting station by which broadcasts are made—

(*a*) in contravention of section 77(1), 78(2) or 79(1); or

(*b*) as mentioned in section 80(1)(*a*).

(2) In this section "broadcasting station" means a business or other operation (whether or not in the nature of a commercial venture) that is engaged in the making of broadcasts.

[Wireless Telegraphy Act 2006, s 81.]

7.11186 **82. Facilitating broadcasting from ships or aircraft** (1) A person commits an offence if he provides a ship or aircraft to another, or agrees to do so, knowing, or having reasonable cause to believe, that broadcasts are to be made from it—

(*a*) in contravention of section 77(1); or

(*b*) while it is on or over the high seas.

(2) A person commits an offence if—

(*a*) he carries wireless telegraphy apparatus in a ship or aircraft, or agrees to do so, or

(*b*) he supplies wireless telegraphy apparatus to a ship or aircraft, or instals such apparatus in a ship or aircraft,

knowing, or having reasonable cause to believe, that by means of the apparatus broadcasts are to be made from the ship or aircraft as mentioned in subsection (1).

(3) A person commits an offence if—

(*a*) he supplies goods or materials—

(i) for the operation or maintenance of a ship or aircraft,

(ii) for the operation or maintenance of wireless telegraphy apparatus installed in a ship or aircraft, or

(iii) for the sustenance or comfort of the persons on board a ship or aircraft,

(*b*) he carries by water or air goods or persons to or from a ship or aircraft, or

(*c*) he engages a person as an officer or one of the crew of a ship or aircraft,

knowing, or having reasonable cause to believe, that broadcasts are made, or are to be made, from the ship or aircraft as mentioned in subsection (1).

(4) In proceedings for an offence under this section consisting in carrying goods or persons to or from a ship or aircraft, it is a defence for the defendant to prove—

(*a*) that the ship or aircraft was, or was believed to be, wrecked, stranded or in distress, and that the goods or persons were carried for the purpose of—

(i) preserving the ship or aircraft, or its cargo or equipment, or

(ii) saving the lives of persons on board the ship or aircraft; or

(*b*) that a person on board the ship or aircraft was, or was believed to be, hurt, injured or ill, and that the goods or persons were carried for the purpose of securing that he received the necessary surgical or medical advice and attendance.

(5) The reference in subsection (4)(*a*) to persons carried for the purpose of saving lives is not to be read as excluding the persons whose lives were to be saved.

(6) The reference in subsection (4)(*b*) to persons carried for the purpose of securing that advice and attendance were received is not to be read as excluding the person who was (or was believed to be) hurt, injured or ill.

(7) In proceedings for an offence under this section consisting in carrying a person ("A") to or from a ship or aircraft, it is a defence for the defendant to prove that A was visiting the ship or aircraft for the purpose of exercising or performing a power or duty conferred or imposed on A by law.

(8) This section is subject to section 86.

[Wireless Telegraphy Act 2006, s 82.]

7.11187 **83. Facilitating broadcasting from structures etc** (1) A person commits an offence if he instals wireless telegraphy apparatus on or in a structure or other object, or supplies such apparatus for installation on or in a structure or other object, knowing, or having reasonable cause to believe, that by means of the apparatus broadcasts are to be made from it—

(*a*) in contravention of section 78(2); or

(*b*) while it is on the high seas.

(2) A person commits an offence if, in the case of a structure or other object—

(*a*) he supplies goods or materials—

(i) for its maintenance,

(ii) for the operation or maintenance of wireless telegraphy apparatus installed in or on it, or

(iii) for the sustenance or comfort of the persons in or on it,

(*b*) he carries goods or persons to or from it by water or air, or

(*c*) he engages a person to render services in or on it,

knowing, or having reasonable cause to believe, that broadcasts are made, or are to be made, from the structure or other object as mentioned in subsection (1).

(3) In proceedings for an offence under this section consisting in carrying goods or persons to or from a structure or other object, it is a defence for the defendant to prove—

(*a*) that it was, or was believed to be, unsafe, and that the goods or persons were carried for the purpose of saving the lives of persons in or on it; or

(*b*) that a person in or on it was, or was believed to be, hurt, injured or ill, and that the goods or persons were carried for the purpose of securing that he received the necessary surgical or medical advice and attendance.

(4) The reference in subsection (3)(*a*) to persons carried for the purpose of saving lives is not to be read as excluding the persons whose lives were to be saved.

(5) The reference in subsection (3)(*b*) to persons carried for the purpose of securing that advice and attendance were received is not to be read as excluding the person who was (or was believed to be) hurt, injured or ill.

(6) In proceedings for an offence under this section consisting in carrying a person ("A") to or from a structure or other object, it is a defence for the defendant to prove that A was visiting it for the purpose of exercising or performing a power or duty conferred or imposed on A by law.

(7) In this section references to a structure or other object do not include references to a ship or aircraft.

(8) This section is subject to section 86.

[Wireless Telegraphy Act 2006, s 83.]

7.11188 **84. Maintaining or repairing apparatus** (1) A person commits an offence if he repairs or maintains wireless telegraphy apparatus knowing, or having reasonable cause to believe, that by means of it broadcasts are made, or are to be made—

(*a*) in contravention of section 77(1), 78(2) or 79(1); or

(*b*) as mentioned in section 80(1).

(2) This section is subject to section 86.

[Wireless Telegraphy Act 2006, s 84.]

7.11189 **85. Acts relating to broadcast material** (1) A person commits an offence if—

(*a*) he supplies a film or sound recording knowing, or having reasonable cause to believe, that an unlawful broadcast is to be made of it;

(*b*) he makes a literary, dramatic or musical work knowing, or having reasonable cause to believe, that an unlawful broadcast is to be made of it;

(*c*) he makes an artistic work knowing, or having reasonable cause to believe, that it is to be included in an unlawful television broadcast;

(*d*) he participates in an unlawful broadcast;

(*e*) he advertises by means of an unlawful broadcast or invites another to advertise by means of an unlawful broadcast that is to be made;

(*f*) he publishes the times or other details of unlawful broadcasts that are to be made, or (otherwise than by publishing such details) publishes an advertisement of matter calculated to promote (whether directly or indirectly) the interests of a business whose activities consist in or include the operation of a station from which unlawful broadcasts are or are to be made.

(2) An unlawful broadcast is a broadcast made—

(*a*) in contravention of section 77(1), 78(2) or 79(1); or

(*b*) as mentioned in section 80(1).

(3) A person participates in a broadcast only if he is actually present—

(*a*) as an announcer;

(*b*) as a performer or one of the performers concerned in an entertainment given; or

(*c*) as the deliverer of a speech.

(4) The cases in which a person is to be taken for the purposes of this section as advertising by means of a broadcast include any case in which he causes or allows it to be stated, suggested or implied that entertainment included in the broadcast—

(*a*) has been supplied by him; or

(*b*) is provided wholly or partly at his expense.

(5) For the purposes of this section advertising by means of a broadcast takes place not only where the broadcast is made but also wherever it is received.

(6) This section is subject to section 86.

[Wireless Telegraphy Act 2006, s 85.]

7.11190 **86. Facilitation offences: territorial scope** (1) A person who does an act mentioned in section 82, 83, 84 or 85 does not commit an offence under that section unless condition A, B, C, D or E is satisfied.

(2) Condition A is satisfied if he does the act in the United Kingdom or external waters.

(3) Condition B is satisfied if he does the act in a British-registered ship or British-registered aircraft while it is not in or over the United Kingdom or external waters.

(4) Condition C is satisfied if, in a case where—

(*a*) neither condition A nor condition B is satisfied, but

(*b*) the broadcasts in question are made, or are to be made, from a structure or other object (which is not a ship or aircraft) in waters in a designated area,

he does the act on that structure or other object within those waters.

(5) Condition D is satisfied if, in a case where—

(*a*) neither condition A nor condition B is satisfied, but

(*b*) the broadcasts in question are made, or are to be made, from a ship in contravention of section 79(1);

he does the act in that ship within an area of the high seas that is prescribed for the purposes of section 79.

(6) Condition E is satisfied if—

(*a*) he is a British person; and

(*b*) he does the act on or over the high seas.

[Wireless Telegraphy Act 2006, s 86.]

7.11191 **87. Procuring person to commit offence abroad** A person commits an offence if he procures, in the United Kingdom, another person to do, outside the United Kingdom, anything that would have constituted an offence under sections 82 to 85 had the other person done it in the United Kingdom.

[Wireless Telegraphy Act 2006, s 87.]

*Enforcement*

7.11192 **88. Enforcement officers** (1) For the purposes of sections 89 to 92 enforcement officers are—

(*a*) persons authorised by the Secretary of State or OFCOM to exercise the powers conferred by sections 89 and 90;

(*b*) police officers;

(*c*) commissioned officers of Her Majesty's armed forces;

(*d*) officers of Revenue and Customs; and

(*e*) other persons who are British sea-fishery officers by virtue of section 7(1) of the Sea Fisheries Act 1968 (c 77).

(2) A reference in sections 89 to 92, in relation to an enforcement officer, to an assistant is a reference to a person assigned to assist the enforcement officer in his duties.

(3) In this section "armed forces" means the Royal Navy, the Royal Marines, the regular army and the regular air force, and a reserve or auxiliary force of any of those services that has been called out on permanent service or embodied.

[Wireless Telegraphy Act 2006, s 88.]

7.11193 **89. Enforcement powers** (1) If conditions A and B are satisfied in the case of a ship, structure or other object, an enforcement officer may, with or without assistants, exercise the powers mentioned in subsection (4) in relation to it.

(2) Condition A is satisfied if the enforcement officer has reasonable grounds for suspecting that—

(*a*) an offence under this Part has been or is being committed by the making of a broadcast—

(i) from a ship, structure or other object in external waters or in tidal waters in the United Kingdom, or

(ii) from a British-registered ship while it is on the high seas;

(*b*) an offence under section 78 has been or is being committed by the making of a broadcast from a structure or other object in waters in a designated area; or

(*c*) an offence under section 79 has been or is being committed by the making of a broadcast from a ship.

(3) Condition B is satisfied if a written authorisation has been issued by the Secretary of State or OFCOM for the exercise of the powers mentioned in subsection (4) in relation to that ship, structure or other object.

(4) The powers are—

(*a*) to board and search the ship, structure or other object;

(*b*) to seize and detain it, and any apparatus or other thing found in the course of the search that appears to him—

(i) to have been used, or to have been intended to be used, in connection with the commission of the suspected offence, or

(ii) to be evidence of the commission of the suspected offence;

(*c*) to arrest and search any person who he has reasonable grounds to suspect has committed or is committing an offence under this Part if—

(i) the person is on board the ship, structure or other object, or

(ii) the officer has reasonable grounds for suspecting that the person was on board at, or shortly before, the time when the officer boarded the object;

(*d*) to arrest any person—

(i) who assaults him, or an assistant of his, while exercising any of the powers mentioned in this subsection, or

(ii) who intentionally obstructs him, or an assistant of his, in the exercise of any of those powers;

(*e*) to require any person on board the ship, structure or other object to produce any documents or other items that are in his custody or possession and are or may be evidence of the commission of an offence under this Part;

(*f*) to require any such person to do anything for the purpose of—

(i) enabling any apparatus or other thing to be rendered safe and, in the case of a ship, enabling the ship to be taken to a port, or

(ii) facilitating in any other way the exercise of any of the powers mentioned in this subsection;

(*g*) to use reasonable force, if necessary, in exercising any of those powers.

(5) In subsection (4)(*a*) to (*c*) and (*e*) a reference to the ship, structure or other object includes a reference to a ship's boat, or other vessel, used from it.

[Wireless Telegraphy Act 2006, s 89.]

7.11194 **90. Enforcement powers: facilitation offences** (1) Subsection (2) applies if—

(*a*) a written authorisation has been issued by the Secretary of State or OFCOM under section 89(3) for the exercise of the powers mentioned in section 89(4) in relation to a ship, structure or other object, and

(*b*) an enforcement officer has reasonable grounds for suspecting that an offence under section 82, 83, 84 or 85 has been or is being committed in connection with the making of a broadcast from that ship, structure or other object.

(2) The enforcement officer may, with or without assistants, exercise the powers mentioned in section 89(4) in relation to any ship, structure or other object which he has reasonable grounds to suspect has been or is being used in connection with the commission of the offence referred to in subsection (1)(*b*).

(3) Subsection (4) applies if—

(*a*) an enforcement officer has reasonable grounds for suspecting that an offence under section 82, 83, 84 or 85 has been or is being committed in connection with the making of a broadcast from a ship, structure or other object, but

(*b*) no written authorisation has been issued under section 89(3) for the exercise of the powers mentioned in section 89(4) in relation to that ship, structure or other object.

(4) The enforcement officer may, with or without assistants, exercise the powers mentioned in section 89(4) in relation to any ship, structure or other object which he has reasonable grounds to suspect has been or is being used in connection with the commission of the offence referred to in

subsection (3)(*a*).

(5) Subsection (4) only applies if a written authorisation under this subsection has been issued by the Secretary of State or OFCOM for the exercise of those powers in relation to that ship, structure or other object.

[Wireless Telegraphy Act 2006, s 90.]

7.11195 **91. Exercise of powers** (1) Except as provided in subsections (2) and (3), the powers mentioned in section 89(4) may be exercised only in tidal waters in the United Kingdom or in external waters.

(2) The powers may in addition—

(*a*) in the case of a suspected offence under this Part committed in a British-registered ship while it is on the high seas, be exercised in relation to the ship on the high seas;

(*b*) in the case of a suspected offence under section 78 committed on a structure or other object within waters in a designated area, be exercised in relation to the structure or other object within those waters;

(*c*) in the case of a suspected offence under section 79 committed in a ship within an area of the high seas prescribed for the purposes of that section, be exercised in relation to the ship within that area of the high seas.

(3) Subsection (2) does not apply so far as the powers are exercisable by virtue of a written authorisation issued by OFCOM.

[Wireless Telegraphy Act 2006, s 91.]

7.11196 **92. Further provisions** (1) A person commits an offence if—

(*a*) he assaults an enforcement officer, or an assistant of his, while he is exercising any of the powers conferred by section 89 or 90;

(*b*) he intentionally obstructs an enforcement officer, or an assistant of his, in the exercise of any of those powers; or

(*c*) he fails or refuses, without reasonable excuse, to comply with such a requirement as is mentioned in section 89(4)(*e*) or (*f*).

(2) Neither an enforcement officer nor an assistant of his is liable in civil or criminal proceedings for anything done in purported exercise of any of the powers conferred by section 89 or 90 if the court is satisfied that the act was done in good faith and that there were reasonable grounds for doing it.

(3) Nothing in sections 89 to 91 or this section affects the exercise of any powers exercisable apart from those sections.

(4) A reference in sections 89 to 91 or this section, in relation to an enforcement officer's assistant, to the exercise of any of the powers mentioned in section 89(4) is a reference to the exercise by the assistant of any of those powers on behalf of the officer.

[Wireless Telegraphy Act 2006, s 92.]

*Penalties and proceedings*

7.11197 **93. Penalties and proceedings** (1) A person who commits an offence under this Part is liable[1]—

(*a*) on summary conviction, to imprisonment for a term not exceeding 12 months or to a fine not exceeding the statutory maximum or to both;

(*b*) on conviction on indictment, to imprisonment for a term not exceeding two years or to a fine or to both.

(2) In the application of subsection (1) to Scotland or Northern Ireland the reference to 12 months is to be read as a reference to six months.

(3) Proceedings in England and Wales for an offence under this Part may be brought only—

(*a*) by OFCOM; or

(*b*) by or with the consent of the Secretary of State or the Director of Public Prosecutions.

(4) Proceedings in Northern Ireland for an offence under this Part may be brought only—

(*a*) by OFCOM; or

(*b*) by or with the consent of the Secretary of State or the Advocate General for Northern Ireland.

(5) Summary proceedings in Scotland for an offence under this Part may be commenced at any time within the period of two years beginning with the day after the commission of the offence.

[Wireless Telegraphy Act 2006, s 93.]

1 For procedure in respect of this offence which is triable either way, see the Magistrates' Courts Act 1980, ss 17–21, in PART I: MAGISTRATES' COURTS, PROCEDURE, ante. In relation to an offence committed before the commencement of s 282(3) of the Criminal Justice Act 2003 the reference to "twelve months" is to be read as "six months" (Sch 8, para 16, post).

*Saving*

7.11198 **94. Saving for certain broadcasts** Nothing in this Part makes it unlawful to do anything under and in accordance with a wireless telegraphy licence, or to procure anything to be so done.

[Wireless Telegraphy Act 2006, s 94.]

*Interpretation*

7.11199 **95. Part 5: interpretation** (1) In this Part—

"British-registered" means registered in the United Kingdom, the Isle of Man or any of the Channel Islands;

"broadcast" means a broadcast by wireless telegraphy of sounds or visual images intended for general reception (whether or not the sounds or images are actually received by anyone), but does not include a broadcast consisting in a message or signal sent in connection with navigation or for the purpose of securing safety;

"designated area" has the meaning given by section 1(7) of the Continental Shelf Act 1964 (c 29);

"external waters" means the whole of the sea adjacent to the United Kingdom that is within the seaward limits of UK territorial sea;

"the high seas" means seas that are not within the seaward limits of UK territorial sea or of the territorial waters adjacent to a country or territory outside the United Kingdom.

(2) For the purposes of this Part references to a "British person" are references to—

(*a*) a British citizen, a British overseas territories citizen, a British National (Overseas) or a British Overseas citizen;

(*b*) a person who under the British Nationality Act 1981 (c 61) is a British subject; or

(*c*) a British protected person within the meaning given by section 50(1) of that Act.

[Wireless Telegraphy Act 2006, s 95.]

## PART 6[1]
## GENERAL

*Fixed penalties*

7.11200 **96. Fixed penalties for summary offences** *OFCOM or a person authorised on its behalf may issue a fixed penalty notice in respect of an offence under this Act other than Part 4[2]). Statements in a notice may be admissible in subsequent criminal proceedings under s 9 of the Criminal Justice Act 1967, see Sch 4, post.*

1 Part 6 comprises ss 96–126 snd Schs 4–9.

2 See also the Wireless Telegraphy (Fixed Penalty) Regulations 2011, SI 2011/2084.

*Entry, search and seizure*

7.11201 **97. Powers of entry and search** (1) A justice of the peace may grant a search warrant under this section if he is satisfied by information on oath that—

(*a*) there is reasonable ground for suspecting that an offence under this Act, other than an offence under Part 4 or section 111, has been or is being committed; and

(*b*) evidence of the commission of the offence is to be found on premises specified in the information, or in a vehicle, ship or aircraft so specified.

(2) A search warrant under this section is a warrant empowering a constable or any person or persons authorised for the purpose by OFCOM or the Secretary of State—

(*a*) to enter, at any time within the relevant period, the premises specified in the information or (as the case may be) the vehicle, ship or aircraft so specified and any premises on which it may be;

(*b*) to search the premises, vehicle, ship or aircraft;

(*c*) to examine and test any apparatus found there.

(3) In subsection (2) "the relevant period" means the period of three months beginning with the day after the date of the warrant.

(4) In the application of subsection (3) to Scotland or Northern Ireland the reference to three months is to be read as a reference to one month.

(5) Where a person authorised by OFCOM or the Secretary of State is empowered by a search warrant under this section to enter any premises, he is to be entitled to exercise that warrant alone or to exercise it accompanied by one or more constables.

(6) A person authorised by OFCOM or the Secretary of State to exercise a power conferred by this section may if necessary use reasonable force in the exercise of the power.

(7) Subsection (6) does not affect any power exercisable apart from that subsection by a person so authorised.

(8) Where under this section a person has a right to examine and test apparatus on premises or in a ship, aircraft or vehicle, any person who—

(*a*) is on the premises, or

(*b*) is in charge of, or in or in attendance on, the ship, aircraft or vehicle,

must give him whatever assistance he may reasonably require in the examination or testing of the apparatus.

(9) In this section—

(*a*) a reference to a justice of the peace is to be read, in Scotland, as a reference to a sheriff and, in Northern Ireland, as a reference to a lay magistrate;

(*b*) a reference to information on oath is to be read, in Northern Ireland, as a reference to complaint on oath.

[Wireless Telegraphy Act 2006, s 97.]

7.11202 **98. Obstruction and failure to assist** (1) A person commits an offence if—

(*a*) he intentionally obstructs a person in the exercise of the powers conferred on him under section 97; or

(*b*) he fails or refuses, without reasonable excuse, to give to such a person any assistance which, under that section, he is under a duty to give to him.

(2) A person who commits an offence under this section is liable on summary conviction to a fine not exceeding level 5 on the standard scale.

[Wireless Telegraphy Act 2006, s 98.]

7.11203 **99. Powers of seizure** (1) This section applies to—

(*a*) an indictable offence under this Act, other than an offence under section 111;

(*b*) an offence under section 35, other than one consisting in the installation or use of receiving apparatus;

(*c*) an offence under section 36, other than one where the relevant contravention of section 8 would constitute an offence consisting in the use of receiving apparatus;

(*d*) an offence under section 48;

(*e*) an offence under section 66.

(2) Where—

(*a*) a search warrant is granted under section 97, and

(*b*) the suspected offence (or any of the suspected offences) is an offence to which this section applies,

the warrant may authorise a person authorised by OFCOM to exercise the power conferred by this subsection to seize and detain, for the purposes of any relevant proceedings, any apparatus or other thing found in the course of the search carried out in pursuance of the warrant that appears to him to be a relevant item.

(3) If a constable or a person authorised by OFCOM to exercise the power conferred by this subsection has reasonable grounds to suspect that an offence to which this section applies has been or is being committed, he may seize and detain, for the purposes of any relevant proceedings, any apparatus or other thing that appears to him to be a relevant item.

(4) A person authorised by OFCOM to exercise a power conferred by this section may if necessary use reasonable force in the exercise of the power.

(5) Subsection (4) does not affect any power exercisable by the person so authorised apart from that subsection.

(6) Nothing in this section affects any power to seize or detain property that is exercisable by a constable apart from this section.

(7) In this section—

"relevant item" means an item that—

(*a*) was used in connection with an offence to which this section applies; or

(*b*) is evidence of the commission of such an offence;

"relevant proceedings" means—

(*a*) proceedings for an offence to which this section applies; or

(*b*) proceedings for condemnation under Schedule 6.

[Wireless Telegraphy Act 2006, s 99.]

7.11204 **100. Obstruction** (1) A person commits an offence if he intentionally obstructs a person in the exercise of the power conferred on him under section 99(3).

(2) A person who commits an offence under this section is liable on summary conviction to a fine not exceeding level 5 on the standard scale.

[Wireless Telegraphy Act 2006, s 100.]

*Disposal and forfeiture*

7.11205 **101. Detention and disposal of property** (1) This section applies to property seized by a person authorised by OFCOM—

(*a*) in pursuance of a warrant under section 97; or

(*b*) in the exercise of the power conferred by section 99(3).

(2) The property may be detained—

(*a*) until the end of the period of six months beginning with the date of seizure; or

(*b*) if proceedings for an offence to which section 99 applies involving that property or proceedings under Schedule 6 for condemnation of that property as forfeited are instituted within that period, until the conclusion of those proceedings.

(3) Subsections (4) to (6) apply in the case of property so detained which, after the end of the period authorised by subsection (2)—

(*a*) remains in the possession of OFCOM; and

(*b*) has not been ordered to be forfeited under Schedule 5 or condemned as forfeited under Schedule 6.

(4) OFCOM must take reasonable steps to deliver the property to the person who appears to them to be its owner.

(5) If the property remains in the possession of OFCOM after the end of one year immediately following the end of the period of detention authorised by subsection (2), OFCOM may dispose of

it in such manner as they think fit.

(6) The delivery of the property in accordance with subsection (4) to the person who appears to OFCOM to be its owner does not affect the right of any other person to take legal proceedings for the recovery of the property—

(*a*) against the person to whom the property is so delivered; or

(*b*) against any person subsequently in possession of the property.

[Wireless Telegraphy Act 2006, s 101.]

7.11206 102. **Section 101: conclusion of proceedings** (1) This section applies to—

(*a*) proceedings for an offence to which section 99 applies;

(*b*) proceedings under Schedule 6 for the condemnation of apparatus as forfeited.

(2) Where proceedings to which this section applies are terminated by an appealable decision, they are not to be regarded as concluded for the purposes of section 101(2)(*b*)—

(*a*) until the end of the ordinary time for appeal against the decision, if no appeal in respect of the decision is brought within that time; or

(*b*) if an appeal in respect of the decision is brought within that time, until the conclusion of the appeal.

(3) Subsection (2) applies for determining, for the purposes of paragraph (*b*) of that subsection, when proceedings on an appeal are concluded as it applies for determining when the original proceedings are concluded.

(4) References in subsection (2) to a decision which terminates proceedings include references to a verdict, sentence, finding or order that puts an end to the proceedings.

(5) An appealable decision is a decision of a description against which an appeal will lie, whether by way of case stated or otherwise and whether with or without permission.

(6) References to an appeal include references to an application for permission to appeal.

[Wireless Telegraphy Act 2006, s 102.]

7.11207 103. **Forfeiture on conviction** Schedule 5 (which makes provision in relation to forfeiture on conviction) has effect.

[Wireless Telegraphy Act 2006, s 103.]

7.11208 104. **Forfeiture etc of restricted apparatus** (1) Apparatus to which this section applies is liable to forfeiture if, immediately before being seized, it was in a person's custody or control in contravention of section 62(5).

(2) This section applies to apparatus if it has been seized—

(*a*) in pursuance of a warrant granted under section 97; or

(*b*) in the exercise of the power conferred by section 99(3).

(3) Apparatus forfeited under this section is to be forfeited to OFCOM and may be disposed of by them in any manner they think fit.

(4) Schedule 6 (which makes provision in relation to the seizure and forfeiture of apparatus) has effect.

[Wireless Telegraphy Act 2006, s 104.]

*Enforcement, proceedings etc*

7.11209 105. **Offences relating to ships or aircraft** (1) This section applies if an offence is committed under any of sections 11, 35 to 38, 46 to 48, 58 and 68.

(2) Where the offence is committed in relation to a station or apparatus on board or released from a ship or aircraft, the captain or person for the time being in charge of the ship or aircraft is guilty of the offence (as well as anyone who is guilty of it apart from this subsection).

(3) This section does not apply where the offence consists in the use by a passenger on board the ship or aircraft of receiving apparatus that is not part of the wireless telegraphy apparatus, if any, of the ship or aircraft.

[Wireless Telegraphy Act 2006, s 105.]

7.11210 106. **Continuing offences** (1) This section applies where—

(*a*) a person is convicted of an offence under Part 2 or 3 consisting in—

(i) the use of a wireless telegraphy station or wireless telegraphy apparatus, or

(ii) a failure or refusal to cause a wireless telegraphy licence or an authority under section 52(3) to be surrendered; and

(*b*) the use, or the failure or refusal, continues after the conviction.

(2) The person is to be treated as committing a separate offence in respect of every day on which the use, or the failure or refusal, so continues.

(3) Subsection (2) does not affect the right to bring separate proceedings for contraventions of this Act taking place on separate occasions.

[Wireless Telegraphy Act 2006, s 106.]

7.11211 107. **Proceedings and enforcement** (1) Proceedings for—

(*a*) an offence under Part 2, 3 or 6 (other than an offence under section 111) that is committed in UK territorial sea, or

(*b*) an offence under Part 5,

may be taken, and the offence may for all incidental purposes be treated as having been committed, in any place in the United Kingdom.

(2) For the purpose of the enforcement of any provision falling within subsection (3), a member of a police force has in any area of the sea within the seaward limits of UK territorial sea all the powers, protection and privileges which he has in the area for which he acts as constable.

(3) The provisions are—

(*a*) sections 8 to 11, 32 to 38 and 45 to 53;

(*b*) Part 3;

(*c*) Part 5;

(*d*) sections 97 to 100, 103, 105 and 106 and Schedule 5.

(4) *Northern Ireland.*

(5) *Scotland.*

[Wireless Telegraphy Act 2006, s 107 as amended by SI 2013/602.]

**7.11211A 108. Civil proceedings**

**7.11211B 109. Fines in Scotland**

**7.11212 110. Criminal liability of company directors etc** (1) Where an offence under this Act is committed by a body corporate and is proved to have been committed with the consent or connivance of, or to be attributable to any neglect on the part of—

(*a*) a director, manager, secretary or other similar officer of the body corporate, or

(*b*) a person who was purporting to act in any such capacity,

he (as well as the body corporate) is guilty of that offence and is liable to be proceeded against and punished accordingly.

(2) Where an offence under this Act—

(*a*) is committed by a Scottish firm, and

(*b*) is proved to have been committed with the consent or connivance of, or to be attributable to any neglect on the part of a partner of the firm,

he (as well as the firm) is guilty of that offence and is liable to be proceeded against and punished accordingly.

(3) "Director", in relation to a body corporate whose affairs are managed by its members, means a member of the body corporate.

[Wireless Telegraphy Act 2006, s 110.]

*Disclosure of information*

**111. General restrictions**

*Notifications etc and electronic working*

**7.11213 112. Service of documents** (1) This section applies where provision made (in whatever terms) by or under this Act authorises or requires—

(*a*) a notification to be given to any person; or

(*b*) a document of any other description (including a copy of a document) to be sent to any person.

(2) The notification or document may be given or sent to the person in question—

(*a*) by delivering it to him;

(*b*) by leaving it at his proper address; or

(*c*) by sending it by post to him at that address.

(3) The notification or document may be given or sent to a body corporate by being given or sent to the secretary or clerk of that body.

(4) The notification or document may be given or sent to a firm by being given or sent to—

(*a*) a partner in the firm; or

(*b*) a person having the control or management of the partnership business.

(5) The notification or document may be given or sent to an unincorporated body or association by being given or sent to a member of the governing body of the body or association.

(6) For the purposes of this section and section 7 of the Interpretation Act 1978 (c 30) (service of documents by post) in its application to this section, the proper address of a person is—

(*a*) in the case of a body corporate, the address of the registered or principal office of the body;

(*b*) in the case of a firm, unincorporated body or association, the address of the principal office of the partnership, body or association;

(*c*) in the case of a person to whom the notification or other document is given or sent in reliance on any of subsections (3) to (5), the proper address of the body corporate, firm or (as the case may be) other body or association in question; and

(*d*) in any other case, the last known address of the person in question.

(7) In the case of—

(*a*) a company registered outside the United Kingdom,

(*b*) a firm carrying on business outside the United Kingdom, or

(*c*) an unincorporated body or association with offices outside the United Kingdom,

the references in subsection (6) to its principal office include references to its principal office within the United Kingdom (if any).

(8) In this section—

"document" includes anything in writing; and

"notification" includes notice;

and references to giving or sending a notification or other document to a person include references to transmitting it to him and to serving it on him.

(9) This section has effect subject to section 113.

[Wireless Telegraphy Act 2006, s 112.]

7.11214 **113. Documents in electronic form** (1) This section applies where—

(*a*) section 112 authorises the giving or sending of a notification or other document by its delivery to a particular person ("the recipient"); and

(*b*) the notification or other document is transmitted to the recipient—

(i) by means of an electronic communications network; or

(ii) by other means but in a form that nevertheless requires the use of apparatus by the recipient to render it intelligible.

(2) For the purposes of subsection (1), something is not to be regarded as in an intelligible form if it cannot be readily understood without being decrypted or having some comparable process applied to it.

(3) The transmission has effect for the purposes of this Act as a delivery of the notification or other document to the recipient, but only if the requirements imposed by or under this section are complied with.

(4) Where the recipient is OFCOM—

(*a*) they must have indicated their willingness to receive the notification or other document in a manner mentioned in subsection (1)(*b*);

(*b*) the transmission must be made in such manner and satisfy such other conditions as they may require; and

(*c*) the notification or other document must take such form as they may require.

(5) Where the person making the transmission is OFCOM, they may (subject to subsection (6)) determine—

(*a*) the manner in which the transmission is made; and

(*b*) the form in which the notification or other document is transmitted.

(6) Where the recipient is a person other than OFCOM—

(*a*) the recipient, or

(*b*) the person on whose behalf the recipient receives the notification or other document,

must have indicated to the person making the transmission the recipient's willingness to receive notifications or documents transmitted in the form and manner used.

(7) An indication to any person for the purposes of subsection (6)—

(*a*) must be given to that person in such manner as he may require;

(*b*) may be a general indication or one that is limited to notifications or documents of a particular description;

(*c*) must state the address to be used and must be accompanied by such other information as that person requires for the making of the transmission; and

(*d*) may be modified or withdrawn at any time by a notice given to that person in such manner as he may require.

(8) An indication, requirement or determination given, imposed or made by OFCOM for the purposes of this section is to be given, imposed or made by being published in such manner as they consider appropriate for bringing it to the attention of the persons who, in their opinion, are likely to be affected by it.

(9) Section 112(8) applies for the purposes of this section as it applies for the purposes of section 112.

[Wireless Telegraphy Act 2006, s 113.]

7.11215 **114. Timing and location of things done electronically** (1) The Secretary of State may by order make provision specifying, for the purposes of this Act, the manner of determining—

(*a*) the times at which things done under this Act by means of electronic communications networks are done; and

(*b*) the places at which such things are so done, and at which things transmitted by means of such networks are received.

(2) The provision made by subsection (1) may include provision as to the country or territory in which an electronic address is to be treated as located.

(3) An order made by the Secretary of State may also make provision about the manner of proving in any legal proceedings—

(*a*) that something done by means of an electronic communications network satisfies the requirements of this Act for the doing of that thing; and

(*b*) the matters mentioned in subsection (1)(*a*) and (*b*).

(4) An order under this section may provide for such presumptions to apply (whether conclusive or not) as the Secretary of State considers appropriate.

[Wireless Telegraphy Act 2006, s 114.]

*Interpretation*

7.11216 **115. General interpretation** (1) In this Act—

"artistic work" has the meaning given by section 4(1) of the Copyright, Designs and Patents Act 1988 (c 48);

"associated facility" has the meaning given by section 32 of the Communications Act 2003 (c 21);

"the Audiovisual Media Services Directive" means Directive 2010/13/EU of the European Parliament and of the Council on the coordination of certain provisions laid down by law, regulation or administrative action in Member States concerning the provision of audiovisual media services;

"broadcast" (except in sections 35 to 38 and Part 5), means broadcast by wireless telegraphy, and cognate expressions are to be construed accordingly;

"business" includes a trade or profession;

"communications provider" has the same meaning as in the Communications Act 2003;

"contravention" includes a failure to comply, and cognate expressions are to be construed accordingly;

"electric line" has the meaning given by section 64(1) of the Electricity Act 1989 (c 29);

"electronic communications network" and "electronic communications service" have the meaning given by section 32 of the Communications Act 2003;

"emission", in relation to electromagnetic energy, is to be construed in accordance with subsection (2);

"the enactments relating to the management of the radio spectrum" has the meaning given by section 405 of the Communications Act 2003;

"film" has the meaning given by section 5B(1) of the Copyright, Designs and Patents Act 1988 (c 48);

"frequency" includes frequency band;

"grant of recognised spectrum access" means a grant made under section 18;

"information" includes accounts, estimates and projections and any document;

"interfere" and "interference", in relation to wireless telegraphy, are to be construed in accordance with subsection (3);

"international obligation of the United Kingdom" includes any EU obligation and any obligation which will or may arise under any international agreement or arrangements to which the United Kingdom is party;

"literary, dramatic or musical work" has the same meaning as in Part 1 of the Copyright, Designs and Patents Act 1988;

"modification" includes omissions, alterations and additions, and cognate expressions are to be construed accordingly;

"OFCOM" means the Office of Communications;

"radio spectrum functions", in relation to OFCOM, means their functions under the enactments relating to the management of the radio spectrum;

"receiving apparatus" means wireless telegraphy apparatus that is not designed or adapted for emission (as opposed to reception);

"satellite uplink apparatus" means wireless telegraphy apparatus, the purpose of which is to emit, to one or more satellites, energy to which section 116(2) applies;

"satellite uplinker" means a person who operates satellite uplink apparatus, but where a person is employed or engaged to operate satellite uplink apparatus under the direction or control of another person, references to a satellite uplinker are references only to that other person;

"ship" includes every description of vessel used in navigation;

"sound recording" has the meaning given by section 5A(1) of the Copyright, Designs and Patents Act 1988;

"speech" includes lecture, address and sermon;

"supply", in relation to any item, is to be construed in accordance with subsection (6);

"UK territorial sea" means the territorial sea adjacent to the United Kingdom;

"wireless telegraphy" is to be construed in accordance with section 116;

"wireless telegraphy apparatus" is to be construed in accordance with section 117;

"wireless telegraphy licence" means a licence granted under section 8;

"wireless telegraphy station" is to be construed in accordance with section 117.

(2) A reference in this Act to the emission of electromagnetic energy, or to emission (as opposed to reception), includes a reference to the deliberate reflection (whether continuous or intermittent) of electromagnetic energy by means of apparatus designed or specially adapted for the purpose.

(3) For the purposes of this Act, wireless telegraphy is interfered with if the fulfilment of the purposes of the telegraphy is prejudiced (either generally or in part and, in particular, as respects all, or as respects any, of the recipients or intended recipients of a message, sound or visual image intended to be conveyed by the telegraphy) by an emission or reflection of electromagnetic energy.

(4) Interference with any wireless telegraphy is not to be regarded as undue for the purposes of this Act unless it is also harmful.

(5) For the purposes of this Act interference is harmful if—

(*a*) it creates dangers, or risks of danger, in relation to the functioning of any service provided by means of wireless telegraphy for the purposes of navigation or otherwise for safety purposes; or

(*b*) it degrades, obstructs or repeatedly interrupts anything which is being broadcast or otherwise transmitted—

(i) by means of wireless telegraphy; and

(ii) in accordance with a wireless telegraphy licence, regulations under section 8(3) or a grant of recognised spectrum access or otherwise lawfully.

(6) Section 46 of the Consumer Protection Act 1987 (c 43) has effect for the purpose of construing references in this Act to the supply of any thing as it has effect for the purpose of construing references in that Act to the supply of goods.

(7) In this Act (except Part 5) a reference to the sending or conveying of a message includes a reference to the making of a signal or the sending or conveying of a warning or information, and a reference to the reception of a message is to be construed accordingly.

(8) A reference in this Act to apparatus on board a ship includes a reference to apparatus on a kite or captive balloon flown from a ship.

[Wireless Telegraphy Act 2006, s 115 as amended by SI 2009/2979, SI 2010/1883 and SI 2011/1043.]

**7.11217 116. "Wireless telegraphy"** (1) In this Act "wireless telegraphy" means the emitting or receiving, over paths that are not provided by any material substance constructed or arranged for the purpose, of energy to which subsection (2) applies.

(2) This subsection applies to electromagnetic energy of a frequency not exceeding 3,000 gigahertz that—

(*a*) serves for conveying messages, sound or visual images (whether or not the messages, sound or images are actually received by anyone), or for operating or controlling machinery or apparatus; or

(*b*) is used in connection with determining position, bearing or distance, or for gaining information as to the presence, absence, position or motion of an object or of a class of objects.

(3) The Secretary of State may by order modify the definition of "wireless telegraphy" by substituting a different frequency for the frequency that is for the time being specified in subsection (2).

(4) No order is to be made containing provision authorised by subsection (3) unless a draft of the order has been laid before Parliament and approved by a resolution of each House.

[Wireless Telegraphy Act 2006, s 116.]

**7.11218 117. "Wireless telegraphy apparatus" and "wireless telegraphy station"** (1) In this Act "wireless telegraphy apparatus" means apparatus for the emitting or receiving, over paths that are not provided by any material substance constructed or arranged for the purpose, of energy to which section 116(2) applies.

(2) In this Act "wireless telegraphy station"—

(*a*) means a station for the emitting or receiving, over paths that are not provided by any material substance constructed or arranged for the purpose, of energy to which section 116(2) applies; and

(*b*) includes the wireless telegraphy apparatus of a ship or aircraft.

[Wireless Telegraphy Act 2006, s 117.]

*Extent and application*

**7.11219 118. Extent** (1) Subject to subsection (2), this Act extends to Northern Ireland.

(2) An amendment, repeal or revocation made by this Act has the same extent as the enactment or other instrument amended, repealed or revoked.

(3) Her Majesty may by Order in Council[1] extend the provisions of this Act, with such modifications as appear to Her Majesty to be appropriate, to the Isle of Man or any of the Channel Islands.

(4) But subsection (3) does not authorise the extension of sections 62 to 67 to any of the Channel Islands.

(5) Section 121(3) applies to the power to make an Order in Council under this section as it applies to a power of the Secretary of State to make an order under this Act, but as if references in section 121(3) to the Secretary of State were references to Her Majesty in Council.

(6) The provisions capable of being extended outside the United Kingdom under—

(*a*) *repealed*

(*b*) section 204(6) of the Broadcasting Act 1990 (c 42),

(*c*) section 12(4) of the Intelligence Services Act 1994 (c 13),

(*d*) section 315(2) of the Merchant Shipping Act 1995 (c 21),

(*e*) section 150(4) of the Broadcasting Act 1996 (c 55), or

(*f*) section 411(6) of the Communications Act 2003 (c 21),

include any amendment of those provisions made by this Act.

[Wireless Telegraphy Act 2006, s 118 as amended by the Enterprise and Regulatory Reform Act 2013, Sch 21.]

---

[1] The provisions of this Act have been applied with modifications to the Isle of Man by the Wireless Telegraphy (Isle of Man) Order 2007, SI 2007/278.

7.11220 **119. Territorial application** (1) The provisions mentioned in subsection (2) apply to—

(*a*) all stations and apparatus in or over, or for the time being in or over, the United Kingdom or UK territorial sea[1];

(*b*) subject to any limitations that the Secretary of State may by regulations determine, all stations and apparatus on board a ship or aircraft that is registered in the United Kingdom but is not for the time being in or over the United Kingdom or UK territorial sea; and

(*c*) subject to any limitations that the Secretary of State may by regulations determine, all apparatus not itself in or over the United Kingdom or UK territorial sea but released—

(i) from within the United Kingdom or UK territorial sea, or

(ii) from a ship or aircraft that is registered in the United Kingdom.

(2) The provisions are—

(*a*) sections 8 to 11, 35 to 38, 45 to 49, 55 to 58 and 68; and

(*b*) regulations under section 54.

(3) Her Majesty may by Order in Council direct that a reference in subsection (1) to a ship or aircraft registered in the United Kingdom is to be construed as including a reference to a ship or aircraft—

(*a*) registered in the Isle of Man, in any of the Channel Islands or in a colony; or

(*b*) registered under the law of any other country or territory outside the United Kingdom that is for the time being administered by Her Majesty's Government in the United Kingdom.

(4) For the purposes of paragraph 4(3) of Schedule 2 to the Interpretation Act 1978 (c 30) (meaning of "colony" in existing enactments), subsection (3) is to be treated as if contained in an Act passed before the commencement of that Act.

[Wireless Telegraphy Act 2006, s 119.]

---

1 See the Territorial Waters Jurisdiction Act 1878 and the Territorial Sea Act 1987 (12 miles). Installations in the English part of the Continental Shelf adjacent to the United Kingdom are treated for the purposes of the civil jurisdiction of the High Court as being in England for the purposes of this Act (Civil Jurisdiction (Offshore Activities) Order 1987, SI 1987/2197 amended by SI 2010/675 (made under the Continental Shelf Act 1964, ss 6 and 7)). For criminal jurisdiction see note to s 2 of the Magistrates' Courts Act 1980, in Part I: Magistrates' Courts, Procedure, ante. For the Isle of Man, see note to s 118(3), ante.

7.11221 **120. Territorial sea and other waters** (1) Her Majesty may by Order in Council provide—

(*a*) for an area of UK territorial sea to be treated, for the purposes of any provision of this Act, as if it were situated in such part of the United Kingdom as may be specified in the Order; and

(*b*) for jurisdiction with respect to questions arising in relation to UK territorial sea under any such provision to be conferred on courts in a part of the United Kingdom so specified.

(2) An Order in Council under section 11 of the Petroleum Act 1998 (c 17) (application of civil law to offshore installations etc) or section 87 of the Energy Act 2004 (c 20) (application of civil law to renewable energy installations etc) may make provision for treating—

(*a*) an installation with respect to which provision is made under that section and which is outside UK territorial sea but in waters to which that section applies, and

(*b*) waters within 500 metres of the installation,

as if, for the purposes of any provision of this Act, they were situated in such part of the United Kingdom as is specified in the Order.

(3) The jurisdiction conferred on a court by an Order in Council under this section is in addition to any jurisdiction exercisable apart from this section by that or any other court.

(4) Section 121(3) applies to the power to make an Order in Council under this section as it applies to any power of the Secretary of State to make an order under this Act, but as if references in section 121(3) to the Secretary of State were references to Her Majesty in Council.

(5) A statutory instrument containing an Order in Council under this section is subject to annulment in pursuance of a resolution of either House of Parliament.

(6) "Installation" includes any floating structure or device maintained on a station by whatever means, and installations in transit.

[Wireless Telegraphy Act 2006, s 120.]

7.11221A **121, 122. Orders and regulations**

7.11222 **126. Short title and commencement** (1) This Act may be cited as the Wireless Telegraphy Act 2006.

(2) This Act comes into force at the end of the period of three months beginning with the day on which it is passed.

[Wireless Telegraphy Act 2006, s 126.]

## SCHEDULE 5
### Forfeiture on Conviction

Section 103

*Power to order forfeiture*

7.11223 **1.** (1) Where a person is convicted of a relevant offence, the court may, as well as imposing any other penalty, order to be forfeited to OFCOM such of the things mentioned in sub-paragraph (2) as the court considers appropriate.

(2) The things are—

(*a*) any vehicle, ship or aircraft, or any structure or other object, that was used in connection with the commission of the offence;

(*b*) any wireless telegraphy apparatus or other apparatus in relation to which the offence was committed;

(*c*) any wireless telegraphy apparatus or other apparatus that was used in connection with the commission of the offence;

(*d*) any wireless telegraphy apparatus or other apparatus (not falling within paragraph (*b*) or (*c*)) that—

(i) was in the possession or under the control of the person convicted of the offence at the time he committed it, and

(ii) was intended to be used (whether or not by that person) in connection with the making of a broadcast or other transmission that would contravene section 8 or any provision of Part 5.

(3) References in sub-paragraph (2)(*b*) to (*d*) to apparatus other than wireless telegraphy apparatus include references to—

(*a*) recordings;

(*b*) equipment designed or adapted for use—

(i) in making recordings, or

(ii) in reproducing sounds or visual images from recordings;

(*c*) any other equipment that is connected, directly or indirectly, to wireless telegraphy apparatus.

(4) A relevant offence is—

(*a*) an offence under Chapter 4 or 5 of Part 2 consisting in a contravention of any provision of that Part in relation to a wireless telegraphy station or wireless telegraphy apparatus (including an offence under section 37 or 38);

(*b*) an offence under section 66;

(*c*) an offence under section 68;

(*d*) an offence under Part 5.

(5) But the following are not relevant offences—

(*a*) an offence under section 35 consisting in the installation or use of receiving apparatus;

(*b*) an offence under section 36 committed in relation to receiving apparatus;

(*c*) an offence under section 51(4).

*Forfeiture in relation to restricted apparatus*

**2.** (1) Where a person is convicted of an offence under Part 2, 3 or 6 involving restricted apparatus, the court must order the apparatus to be forfeited to OFCOM unless the defendant or a person who claims to be the owner of, or otherwise interested in, the apparatus shows cause why it should not be forfeited.

(2) This paragraph does not affect the operation of paragraph 1 in relation to apparatus that is not restricted apparatus.

(3) Apparatus is restricted apparatus if custody or control of apparatus of any class or description to which it belongs is for the time being restricted by a restriction order under section 62.

*Property of third parties*

**3.** Apparatus may be ordered to be forfeited under paragraph 1 or 2 even if it is not the property of the person by whom the offence giving rise to the forfeiture was committed.

*Disposal of apparatus*

**4.** Apparatus ordered to be forfeited under paragraph 1 or 2 may be disposed of by OFCOM in such manner as they think fit.

*Delivery to OFCOM*

**5.** (1) A court that orders apparatus to be forfeited under paragraph 1 or 2 may also order the person by whom the offence giving rise to the forfeiture was committed not to dispose of it except by delivering it up to OFCOM within 48 hours of being so required by them.

(2) A person against whom an order is made under sub-paragraph (1) commits a further offence if—

(*a*) he contravenes the order; or

(*b*) he fails to deliver up the apparatus to OFCOM as required.

(3) An offence under sub-paragraph (2) is punishable as if it were committed under the same provision, and at the same time, as the offence for which the forfeiture was ordered.

*Provisions as to disposal of property disapplied*

**6.** Section 140 of the Magistrates' Courts Act 1980 (c 43) and Article 58 of the Magistrates' Courts (Northern Ireland) Order 1981 (SI 1981/1675 (NI 26)) (under which magistrates sell or dispose of forfeited property) do not apply in relation to apparatus ordered to be forfeited under paragraph 1 or 2.

*Provisions as to deprivation of property disapplied*

**7.** The following provisions (under which a court convicting a person of an offence has power to deprive him of property used etc for purposes of crime) do not apply where a person is convicted of an offence under Part 2, 3 or 5—

(*a*) section 143 of the Powers of Criminal Courts (Sentencing) Act 2000 (c 6);

(*b*) Part 2 of the Proceeds of Crime (Scotland) Act 1995 (c 43);

(*c*) Article 11 of the Criminal Justice (Northern Ireland) Order 1994 (SI 1994/2795 (NI 15)).

## SCHEDULE 6
### Seizure and Forfeiture of Restricted Apparatus

Section 104

*Application of Schedule*

7.11224 **1.** (1) This Schedule applies to restricted apparatus seized—
(*a*) in pursuance of a warrant granted under section 97; or
(*b*) in the exercise of the power conferred by section 99(3).

(2) Apparatus is restricted apparatus for the purposes of this Schedule if custody or control of apparatus of any class or description to which it belongs is for the time being restricted by a restriction order under section 62.

*Notice of seizure*

**2.** (1) OFCOM must give notice of the seizure of the restricted apparatus to every person who, to their knowledge, was at the time of the seizure the owner or one of the owners of the apparatus.

(2) The notice must set out the grounds of the seizure.

(3) Where there is no proper address for the purposes of the service of a notice under sub-paragraph (1) in a manner authorised by section 112, the requirements of that sub-paragraph shall be satisfied by the publication of a notice of the seizure in the London, Edinburgh or Belfast Gazette (according to the part of the United Kingdom where the seizure took place).

(4) Apparatus may be condemned or taken to have been condemned under this Schedule only if the requirements of this paragraph have been complied with in the case of that apparatus.

*Notice of claim*

**3.** A person claiming that the restricted apparatus is not liable to forfeiture must give written notice of his claim to OFCOM.

**4.** (1) A notice of claim must be given within one month after the day of the giving of the notice of seizure.

(2) A notice of claim must specify—
(*a*) the name and address of the claimant; and
(*b*) in the case of a claimant who is outside the United Kingdom, the name and address of a solicitor in the United Kingdom who is authorised to accept service of process and to act on behalf of the claimant.

(3) Service of process upon a solicitor so specified is to be taken to be proper service upon the claimant.

*Condemnation*

**5.** The restricted apparatus is to be taken to have been duly condemned as forfeited if—
(*a*) by the end of the period for the giving of a notice of claim in respect of the apparatus, no notice of claim has been given to OFCOM; or
(*b*) a notice of claim is given which does not comply with the requirements of paragraphs 3 and 4.

**6.** (1) Where a notice of claim in respect of the restricted apparatus is duly given in accordance with paragraphs 3 and 4, OFCOM may take proceedings for the condemnation of the apparatus by the court.

(2) In such proceedings—
(*a*) if the court finds that the apparatus was liable to forfeiture at the time of seizure, it must condemn the apparatus as forfeited unless cause is shown why it should not; and
(*b*) if the court finds that the apparatus was not liable to forfeiture at that time, or cause is shown why it should not be forfeited, the court must order the return of the apparatus to the person appearing to the court to be entitled to it.

(3) If OFCOM decide not to take proceedings for condemnation in a case in which a notice of claim has been so given, they must return the apparatus to the person appearing to them to be the owner of the apparatus, or to one of the persons appearing to them to be the owners of it.

(4) Apparatus required to be returned in accordance with sub-paragraph (3) must be returned as soon as reasonably practicable after the decision not to take proceedings for condemnation.

(5) OFCOM's decision whether to take such proceedings must be taken as soon as reasonably practicable after the receipt of the notice of claim.

**7.** Where the restricted apparatus is condemned or taken to have been condemned as forfeited, the forfeiture is to have effect as from the time of the seizure.

*Proceedings for condemnation by court*

**8.** Proceedings for condemnation are civil proceedings and may be instituted—
(*a*) in England or Wales, in the High Court or in a magistrates' court;
(*b*) in Scotland, in the Court of Session or in the sheriff court;
(*c*) in Northern Ireland, in the High Court or in a court of summary jurisdiction.

**9.** Proceedings for the condemnation of restricted apparatus instituted in a magistrates' court in England or Wales, in the sheriff court in Scotland or in a court of summary jurisdiction in Northern Ireland may be so instituted—
(*a*) in a court having jurisdiction in a place where an offence under section 66 involving that apparatus was committed;
(*b*) in a court having jurisdiction in proceedings for such an offence;
(*c*) in a court having jurisdiction in the place where the claimant resides or, if the claimant has specified a solicitor under paragraph 4, in the place where that solicitor has his office; or
(*d*) in a court having jurisdiction in the place where that apparatus was seized or to which it was first brought after being seized.

**10.** (1) In proceedings for condemnation that are instituted in England and Wales or Northern Ireland, the claimant or his solicitor must make his oath that the seized apparatus was, or was to the best of his knowledge and belief, the property of the claimant at the time of the seizure.

(2) In proceedings for condemnation instituted in the High Court—
(*a*) the court may require the claimant to give such security for the costs of the proceedings as may be determined by the court; and
(*b*) the claimant must comply with such a requirement.

(3) If a requirement of this paragraph is not complied with, the court must give judgment for OFCOM.

**11.** (1) In the case of proceedings for condemnation instituted in a magistrates' court in England or Wales, either party may appeal against the decision of that court to the Crown Court.

(2) In the case of proceedings for condemnation instituted in a court of summary jurisdiction in Northern Ireland, either party may appeal against the decision of that court to the county court.

(3) This paragraph does not affect any right to require the statement of a case for the opinion of the High Court.

**12.** Where an appeal has been made (whether by case stated or otherwise) against the decision of the court in proceedings for the condemnation of restricted apparatus, the apparatus is to be left with OFCOM pending the final determination of the matter.

*Disposal of unclaimed property*

**13.** (1) This paragraph applies where a requirement is imposed by or under this Schedule for apparatus to be returned to a person.

(2) If the apparatus is still in OFCOM's possession after the end of the period of 12 months beginning with the day after the requirement to return it arose, OFCOM may dispose of it in any manner they think fit.

(3) OFCOM may exercise their power under this paragraph to dispose of apparatus only if it is not practicable at the time when the power is exercised to dispose of the apparatus by returning it immediately to the person to whom it is required to be returned.

*Provisions as to proof*

**14.** In proceedings arising out of the seizure of restricted apparatus, the fact, form and manner of the seizure is to be taken, without further evidence and unless the contrary is shown, to have been as set forth in the process.

**15.** In any proceedings, the condemnation by a court of restricted apparatus as forfeited may be proved by the production of—

(*a*) the order or certificate of condemnation; or

(*b*) a certified copy of the order purporting to be signed by an officer of the court by which the order or certificate was made or granted.

*Special provisions as to certain claimants*

**16.** (1) This paragraph applies for the purposes of—

(*a*) a claim to the restricted apparatus; and

(*b*) proceedings for its condemnation.

(2) Where at the time of the seizure the apparatus is—

(*a*) the property of a body corporate,

(*b*) the property of two or more partners, or

(*c*) the property of more than five persons,

the oath required by paragraph 10 to be taken by the claimant, and any other thing required by this Schedule or by rules of court to be done by the owner of the apparatus, may be done by a person falling within sub-paragraph (3) or by a person authorised to act on his behalf.

(3) The persons are—

(*a*) where the owner is a body corporate, the secretary or some duly authorised officer of that body;

(*b*) where the owners are in partnership, any one or more of the owners;

(*c*) where there are more than five owners and they are not in partnership, any two or more of the owners acting on behalf of themselves and any of their co-owners who are not acting on their own behalf.

*Saving for owner's rights*

**17.** Neither the imposition of a requirement by or under this Schedule to return apparatus to a person nor the return of apparatus to a person in accordance with such a requirement affects—

(*a*) the rights in relation to that apparatus of any other person; or

(*b*) the right of any other person to enforce his rights against the person to whom it is returned.

## SCHEDULE 8

Transitional Provisions, Savings and Transitory Modifications — Section 124

**7.11225**

*(Amended by the Legislative and Regulatory Reform Act 2006, Sch.)*

## Part 1
## Transitional Provisions and Savings

*General provisions*

**1.** The substitution of provisions of this Act for provisions repealed or revoked by it does not affect the continuity of the law.

**2.** Anything done, or having effect as if done, under or for the purposes of a provision repealed by this Act (including subordinate legislation so made or having effect as if so made), and in force or effective immediately before the commencement of this Act, has effect after that commencement as if done under or for the purposes of the corresponding provision of this Act.

**3.** A reference (express or implied) in this Act or another enactment, or in an instrument or document, to a provision of this Act is (so far as the context permits) to be read as (according to the context) being or including a reference to the corresponding provision repealed by this Act, in relation to times, circumstances or purposes in relation to which the repealed provision had effect.

**4.** (1) A reference (express or implied) in an enactment, or in an instrument or document, to a provision repealed by this Act is (so far as the context permits) to be read as (according to the context) being or including a reference to the corresponding provision of this Act, in relation to times, circumstances and purposes in relation to which that corresponding provision has effect.

(2) In particular, where a power conferred by an Act is expressed to be exercisable in relation to enactments contained in Acts passed before or in the same Session as the Act conferring the power, the power is also exercisable in relation to provisions of this Act that reproduce such enactments.

**5.** Paragraphs 1 to 4 have effect in place of section 17(2) of the Interpretation Act 1978 (c 30) (but do not affect the application of any other provision of that Act).

6. Paragraphs 2 and 4(1) do not apply to an Order in Council to which paragraph 24(1) applies.

*General rule for old savings*

7. (1) The repeal by this Act of an enactment previously repealed subject to savings does not affect the continued operation of those savings.

(2) The repeal by this Act of a saving on the previous repeal of an enactment does not affect the saving in so far as it remains capable of having effect.

*Use of existing forms etc*

8. A reference to an enactment repealed by this Act which is contained in a document made, served or issued on or after the commencement of that repeal is to be read, except so far as a contrary intention appears, as referring or, as the context may require, including a reference to the corresponding provision of this Act.

9. *Repealed.*

*Contracted-out functions under section 1 of the Wireless Telegraphy Act 1949*

10. An order under Part 2 of the Deregulation and Contracting Out Act 1994 (c 40) which is in force immediately before the commencement of this Act and, by virtue of paragraph 6 of Schedule 18 to the Communications Act 2003 (c 21), has effect as if made by virtue of section 1(7) of that Act shall, so long as the order remains in force, continue to have that effect by virtue of this paragraph.

*Wireless telegraphy licences granted before 18th June 1998*

11. (1) This paragraph has effect in relation to wireless telegraphy licences granted before 18th June 1998 (the date on which section 1 of the Wireless Telegraphy Act 1998 (c 6) came into force).

(2) Where this paragraph has effect, section 12 is the provision of this Act which, for the purposes of paragraph 4(1) of this Schedule, corresponds to section 2(1) of the Wireless Telegraphy Act 1949 (c 54).

*Procedures treated as prescribed by regulations made by OFCOM*

12. (1) Sub-paragraph (2) applies where, immediately before the commencement of this Act, procedures have effect, by virtue of paragraph 20(2) or 21(2) of Schedule 18 to the Communications Act 2003 (c 21), as if prescribed by OFCOM by regulations under—

(*a*) section 1D(3) of the Wireless Telegraphy Act 1949, or
(*b*) section 3 of the Wireless Telegraphy Act 1998.

(2) In relation to times after the commencement of this Act, the procedures are to have effect as if prescribed by OFCOM by regulations under—

(*a*) paragraph 1 of Schedule 1, or
(*b*) section 14.

(3) A notice under—

(*a*) section 1D of the Wireless Telegraphy Act 1949, or
(*b*) regulations under section 3 of the Wireless Telegraphy Act 1998,

which is in force immediately before the commencement of this Act and, by virtue of paragraph 20 or 21 of Schedule 18, has effect as if it authorised or required a thing to be done by or in relation to OFCOM shall, so long as it remains in force, continue to have that effect by virtue of this paragraph.

*Tribunal established under section 9 of the Wireless Telegraphy Act 1949*

13. The repeal by this Act of sections 11 and 12 of the Wireless Telegraphy Act 1949 does not affect the continued operation of section 11 or 12 (without the amendments made in those sections by section 178 of the Communications Act 2003) in relation to a notice under section 11(1) or (2) or section 12(1) that is served before 25th July 2003.

*References to Postmaster General etc*

14. The repeal by this Act of part of section 3(1)(ii) of the Post Office Act 1969 (c 48) is not to affect the continued operation of section 3(1)(ii) in relation to a provision of regulations or a licence where the regulations were made or the licence was granted under the Wireless Telegraphy Act 1949 before 1st October 1969 (the day on which functions of the Postmaster General were transferred to the Minister).

*Procedure for prosecutions*

15. (1) This paragraph has effect in relation to prosecutions to which section 41 of this Act applies.

(2) The restrictions on the bringing of proceedings which are imposed by section 41(2) and (3) do not have effect in relation to proceedings started before 25th July 2003 (the date on which section 174 of the Communications Act 2003 (c 21) came into force).

*Penalties for certain offences triable either way*

16. In relation to an offence committed before the commencement of section 282(3) of the Criminal Justice Act 2003 (c 44), the references in the following provisions to periods of imprisonment of 12 months are to be read as references to periods of imprisonment of six months—

(*a*) section 35(2);
(*b*) section 36(2);
(*c*) section 37(2);
(*d*) section 38(6);
(*e*) section 47(4);
(*f*) section 68(3);
(*g*) section 93(1).

*Penalties for offences: unauthorised use of wireless telegraphy station etc*

17. In relation to an offence committed before 18th September 2003 (the date on which section 179 of the Communications Act 2003 came into force), each of sections 35(5) and 36(5) is to have effect as if for the words from "is liable" to the end there were substituted

"is liable—

(*a*) on summary conviction, to imprisonment for a term not exceeding six months or to a fine not exceeding the statutory maximum or to both;

(*b*) on conviction on indictment, to imprisonment for a term not exceeding two years or to a fine or to both."

**18.** In relation to an offence committed on or after 18th September 2003 but before the commencement of section 281(5) of the Criminal Justice Act 2003, the references in the following provisions to periods of imprisonment of 51 weeks are to be read as references to periods of imprisonment of six months—

(*a*) section 35(5);

(*b*) section 36(5).

*Penalties for offences: contravening notice under section 55 or 56*

**19.** In relation to an offence committed before the commencement of section 280 of the Criminal Justice Act 2003, section 58(2) has effect as if in paragraph (*a*) for the words "to a fine not exceeding level 5 on the standard scale" there were substituted "to imprisonment for a term not exceeding three months or to a fine not exceeding level 5 on the standard scale or to both".

*Fixed penalties for wireless telegraphy offences*

**20.** Schedule 4 to this Act does not apply to offences committed before the day which is the relevant commencement date for the purposes of paragraph 27 of this Schedule.

*Powers of seizure*

**21.** In relation to an offence committed before 18th September 2003 (the date on which section 179 of the Communications Act 2003 (c 21) came into force), section 99(1) of this Act has effect with the omission of paragraph (*c*).

*Forfeiture etc of restricted apparatus*

**22.** Nothing in section 104 of, and Schedule 6 to, this Act applies in relation to apparatus seized before 29th December 2003 (the date on which section 182 of the Communications Act 2003 came into force).

*Appeals of wireless telegraphy decisions*

**23.** The repeals made by this Act do not affect the continued operation of paragraph 23(2) of Schedule 18 to the Communications Act 2003 as regards decisions against which an appeal could have been brought under section 1F of the Wireless Telegraphy Act 1949 (c 54).

*Orders in Council: section 118*

**24.** (1) An Order in Council made under a provision that is repealed by this Act and re-enacted in section 118(3) continues to have effect despite the repeal of that provision.

(2) An Order in Council made under section 118(3) may amend or revoke an Order in Council continued in effect by sub-paragraph (1).

*Orders in Council: continental shelf*

**25.** (1) This paragraph applies in the case of an Order in Council which, as a result of paragraph 63 of Schedule 18 to the Communications Act 2003 (provision relating to Orders in Council under section 6 of the Continental Shelf Act 1964 (c 29)), has effect, immediately before the commencement of this Act, as if made under section 410 of the Communications Act 2003.

(2) An Order in Council to which this paragraph applies is to have effect, after the commencement of this Act, as an Order in Council made in exercise of the powers conferred by section 120.

## PART 2

## TRANSITORY MODIFICATIONS

*Justice (Northern Ireland) Act 2002 (c 26)*

**26.** (1) This paragraph applies if paragraph 25 of Schedule 7 to the Justice (Northern Ireland) Act 2002 has not come into force before the commencement of this Act.

(2) Until the relevant commencement date, section 93(4)(*b*) has effect as if for "the Advocate General for Northern Ireland" there were substituted "the Attorney General for Northern Ireland".

(3) The relevant commencement date is—

(*a*) if an order has been made before the commencement of this Act appointing a day after that commencement as the day for the coming into force of paragraph 25 of Schedule 7 to the Justice (Northern Ireland) Act 2002 (c 26), the day so appointed;

(*b*) otherwise, such day as the Secretary of State may by order appoint.

*Communications Act 2003 (c 21)*

**27.** (1) This paragraph applies if—

(*a*) section 180 of the Communications Act 2003, and

(*b*) Schedule 6 to that Act,

have not come into force before the commencement of this Act.

(2) Until the relevant commencement date, this Act has effect with the omission of—

(*a*) section 96, and

(*b*) Schedule 4.

(3) The relevant commencement date is—

(*a*) if an order has been made before the commencement of this Act appointing a day after that commencement as the day for the coming into force of the provisions mentioned in sub-paragraph (1), the day so appointed;

(*b*) otherwise, such day as the Secretary of State may by order appoint.

*Power to make transitional provision*

**28.** Section 121(3) of this Act does not apply to an order made by the Secretary of State under paragraph 26 or 27, but—

(*a*) an order under paragraph 26 may make such provision as may be made by an order under section 89(1) of the Justice (Northern Ireland) Act 2002 in connection with the coming into force of a provision of that Act, and

(*b*) an order under paragraph 27 may make such provision as, by virtue of section 411(4) of the Communications Act 2003, is authorised to be made by an order under section 411(2) of that Act.

*Saving for old transitional provisions*

**29.** (1) This paragraph applies to any transitional or transitory provision or saving ("the transitional provision") made in connection with the coming into force of any provision of the Justice (Northern Ireland) Act 2002 or the Communications Act 2003 mentioned in sub-paragraph (1) of paragraph 26 or 27 ("the old enactment").

(2) If the old enactment is in force before the commencement of the provision of this Act reproducing its effect ("the corresponding provision of this Act"), the transitional provision is to continue to have effect (so far as capable of doing so) in relation to the corresponding provision of this Act.

(3) Sub-paragraph (4) applies if—

(*a*) sub-paragraph (2) does not apply, but

(*b*) before the commencement of this Act an order has been made appointing a day for the coming into force of the old enactment.

(4) The transitional provision is to have effect from the date so appointed in relation to the corresponding provision of this Act.

## Digital Switchover (Disclosure of Information) Act 2007[1]

(2007 c 8)

7.11226 **1. Disclosure of information** (1) The Secretary of State and the Northern Ireland department may, at the request of a relevant person, supply a relevant person with social security information for use (by the person to whom it is supplied or by another relevant person) in connection with switchover help functions.

(2) The Secretary of State may, at the request of a relevant person, supply a relevant person with war pensions information for use (by the person to whom it is supplied or by another relevant person) in connection with switchover help functions.

(3) A local authority or, in Northern Ireland, a Health and Social Services Board may, at the request of a relevant person, supply a relevant person with visual impairment information for use (by the person to whom it is supplied or by another relevant person) in connection with switchover help functions.

(4) In this Act "relevant person" means—

(*a*) the BBC;

(*b*) any company in respect of which any one or more of the following—

(i) the BBC,

(ii) the Secretary of State, or

(iii) a nominee of the BBC or the Secretary of State,

hold at least 51% of the issued ordinary share capital or possess at least 51% of the voting rights;

(*c*) any person who is engaged by the BBC, the Secretary of State or any company falling within paragraph (*b*) to provide any service connected with switchover help functions, to carry out a switchover help function or to carry out any function connected with switchover help functions.

(5) In this Act "switchover help functions" means—

(*a*) the identification of persons who may be eligible for help under a switchover help scheme;

(*b*) making contact with such persons with a view to the provision of such help; and

(*c*) the establishment of any person's entitlement to such help.

[Digital Switchover (Disclosure of Information) Act 2007, s 1.]

---

1 This Act provides for social security and certain other information to be supplied on request to the BBC or one its agents for use in connection with digital switchover functions. The Act creates in s 3 offences in relation to the disclosure of such information.

7.11227 **2. Kinds of information referred to in section 1** (1) This section applies for the purposes of section 1.

(2) "Social security information" means—

(*a*) in relation to the Secretary of State, information of a prescribed description held by him (or on his behalf) and obtained as a result of, or for the purpose of, the exercise of functions of his in relation to social security;

(*b*) in relation to the Northern Ireland department, information of a prescribed description held by the department (or on its behalf) and obtained as a result of, or for the purpose of, the exercise of the functions of the department in relation to social security.

(3) "War pensions information" means information of a prescribed description held by the Secretary of State (or on his behalf) and obtained as a result of, or for the purpose of, the exercise of functions of his relating to war pensions, as defined by section 25(4) of the Social Security Act 1989

(c 24).

(4) "Visual impairment information" means information of a prescribed description about persons who—

(*a*) are registered as blind or partially sighted in a register maintained by or on behalf of a local authority in England or Wales under section 29 of the National Assistance Act 1948 (c 29) (welfare services),

(*b*) have been certified as blind or partially sighted in Scotland and in consequence are registered as blind or partially sighted in a register maintained by or on behalf of a local authority in Scotland, or

(*c*) have been certified as blind in Northern Ireland and in consequence are registered as blind in a register maintained by or on behalf of a Health and Social Services Board in Northern Ireland.

(5) In this section "prescribed" means prescribed by order[1] made by the Secretary of State by statutory instrument.

(6) A statutory instrument containing an order under this section is subject to annulment in pursuance of a resolution of either House of Parliament.

(7) An order under this section may make different provision in relation to different cases.

[Digital Switchover (Disclosure of Information) Act 2007, s 2.]

---

[1] The Digital Switchover (Disclosure of Information) Act 2007 (Prescription of Information) Order 2007/1768 amended by SI 2008/2557, SI 2010/1881 and SI 2011/677 has been made.

**7.11228 3. Offences** (1) A relevant person must not disclose without lawful authority any information supplied to him or another relevant person under section 1.

(2) A person—

(*a*) who is or who has been employed by a relevant person,

(*b*) who is or who has been engaged—

(i) in the provision of services to a relevant person in connection with the carrying out of a switchover help function, or

(ii) to carry out any switchover help function, or to carry out any function in connection with the carrying out of a switchover help function, or

(*c*) who is or who has been employed by, or who is or who has been engaged in the provision of services to, or to carry out a function for, a person mentioned in paragraph (*b*),

must not disclose without lawful authority information supplied to a relevant person under section 1.

(3) A person who contravenes subsection (1) or (2) commits an offence.

(4) It is not an offence under this section—

(*a*) to disclose information in the form of a summary or collection of information so framed as not to enable information supplied under section 1 relating to any particular person to be ascertained from it; or

(*b*) to disclose information which has previously been disclosed to the public with lawful authority.

(5) It is a defence for a person charged with an offence under this section to prove that at the time of the alleged offence he believed—

(*a*) that he was making the disclosure in question with lawful authority, or

(*b*) that the information in question had previously been disclosed to the public with lawful authority,

and that he had no reasonable cause to believe otherwise.

(6) For the purposes of this section, a disclosure is to be regarded as made with lawful authority if, but only if, it is made—

(*a*) for the purpose of carrying out a switchover help function, or for doing anything connected with the carrying out of a switchover help function;

(*b*) in accordance with any enactment or court order;

(*c*) for the purpose of instituting, or otherwise for the purposes of, proceedings before a court; or

(*d*) with the consent of the person to whom the information relates or of any person authorised to act on that person's behalf.

(7) A person guilty of an offence under this section is liable—

(*a*) on conviction on indictment, to imprisonment for a term not exceeding two years, or to a fine, or both; or

(*b*) on summary conviction to imprisonment for a term not exceeding 12 months or to a fine not exceeding the statutory maximum, or both.

(8) In the application of this section—

(*a*) in England and Wales, in relation to an offence committed before the commencement of section 154(1) of the Criminal Justice Act 2003 (c 44),

(*b*) in Scotland, until the commencement of section 45(1) of the Criminal Proceedings etc (Reform) (Scotland) Act 2007 (asp 6), or

(*c*) in Northern Ireland,

the reference in subsection (7)(*b*) to 12 months is to be read as a reference to 6 months.
[Digital Switchover (Disclosure of Information) Act 2007, s 3.]

7.11229 **4. Liability of directors etc** (1) If an offence under section 3 committed by a body corporate is shown—

(*a*) to have been committed with the consent or connivance of an officer, or

(*b*) to be attributable to any neglect on his part,

the officer as well as the body corporate is guilty of the offence and liable to be proceeded against and punished accordingly.

(2) If the affairs of a body corporate are managed by its members, subsection (1) applies in relation to the acts and defaults of a member in connection with his functions of management as if he were a director of the body.

(3) "Officer", in relation to a body corporate, means a director, member of the committee of management, chief executive, manager, secretary or other similar officer of the body, or a person purporting to act in any such capacity.
[Digital Switchover (Disclosure of Information) Act 2007, s 4.]

7.11230 **5. Interpretation** (1) In this Act—

"the BBC" means the British Broadcasting Corporation;

"local authority" means—

(*a*) in relation to England—

(i) a county council,

(ii) a district council, other than a council for a district in a county for which there is a county council,

(iii) a London borough council,

(iv) the Common Council of the City of London, in its capacity as a local authority, or

(v) the Council of the Isles of Scilly,

(*b*) in relation to Wales, a county council or a county borough council, and

(*c*) in relation to Scotland, a council constituted under section 2 of the Local Government etc (Scotland) Act 1994 (c 39);

"the Northern Ireland department" means the Northern Ireland department having responsibility for social security;

"relevant person" has the meaning given by section 1(4);

"switchover help functions" has the meaning given by section 1(5);

"switchover help scheme" means any scheme for the provision of help to individuals in connection with digital switchover which is agreed between the BBC and the Secretary of State in pursuance of the BBC Charter and Agreement, as the scheme has effect from time to time.

(2) In this section—

"digital switchover" means the replacement of the broadcasting of television services in the United Kingdom in analogue form with their broadcasting in digital form;

"the BBC Charter and Agreement" means the following documents, or any one or more of them, so far as they are for the time being in force—

(*a*) a Royal Charter for the continuance of the BBC;

(*b*) supplemental Charters obtained by the BBC under such a Royal Charter;

(*c*) an agreement between the BBC and the Secretary of State entered into (whether before or after the passing of this Act) for purposes that include the regulation of activities carried on by the BBC;

"broadcasting" means broadcasting by wireless telegraphy (as defined by section 116 of the Wireless Telegraphy Act 2006 (c 36)) otherwise than by satellite.
[Digital Switchover (Disclosure of Information) Act 2007, s 5.]

7.11231 **6. Short title and extent** (1) This Act may be cited as the Digital Switchover (Disclosure of Information) Act 2007.

(2) This Act extends to England and Wales, Scotland and Northern Ireland.

(3) Her Majesty may by Order in Council provide for any of the provisions of this Act to extend, with or without modifications, to the Isle of Man.
[Digital Switchover (Disclosure of Information) Act 2007, s 6.]

## Data Retention and Investigatory Powers Act 2014

(2014 c 27)

*Retention of relevant communications data*

**7.11231A 1–7.**

---

*Ss 1–7 were repealed by virtue of s 8(3) of this Act, as from 31 December 2016. The Investigatory Powers Act 2016, Sch 10, Pt 4, para 63 also provides that ss 1, 2 are repealed as from 31 December 2016.*

---

*Final provisions*

**7.11231D 8. Commencement, duration, extent and short title** (1) Subject to subsection

(2), this Act comes into force on the day on which it is passed.

(2) Section 1(6) comes into force on such day as the Secretary of State may by order made by statutory instrument appoint; and different days may be appointed for different purposes.

(3) Sections 1 to 7 (and the provisions inserted into the Regulation of Investigatory Powers Act 2000 by sections 3 to 6) are repealed on 31 December 2016.

(4) This Act extends to England and Wales, Scotland and Northern Ireland.

(5) This Act may be cited as the Data Retention and Investigatory Powers Act 2014.*

[Data Retention and Investigatory Powers Act 2014, s 8.]

* **Section repealed by the Investigatory Powers Act 2016, Sch 10 from a date to be appointed.**

# Investigatory Powers Act 2016[1]

(2016 c 25)

## PART 1[2]

## GENERAL PRIVACY PROTECTIONS

*Overview and General Privacy Duties*

**7.11231E 1. Overview of Act** (1) This Act sets out the extent to which certain investigatory powers may be used to interfere with privacy.

(2) This Part imposes certain duties in relation to privacy and contains other protections for privacy.

(3) These other protections include offences and penalties in relation to—

(a) the unlawful interception of communications, and

(b) the unlawful obtaining of communications data.

(4) This Part also abolishes and restricts various general powers to obtain communications data and restricts the circumstances in which equipment interference, and certain requests about the interception of communications, can take place.

(5) Further protections for privacy—

(a) can be found, in particular, in the regimes provided for by Parts 2 to 7 and in the oversight arrangements in Part 8, and

(b) also exist—

(i) by virtue of the Human Rights Act 1998,

(ii) in section 55 of the Data Protection Act 1998 (unlawful obtaining etc of personal data),

(iii) in section 48 of the Wireless Telegraphy Act 2006 (offence of interception or disclosure of messages),

(iv) in sections 1 to 3A of the Computer Misuse Act 1990 (computer misuse offences),

(v) in the common law offence of misconduct in public office, and

(vi) elsewhere in the law.

(6) The regimes provided for by Parts 2 to 7 are as follows—

(a) Part 2 and Chapter 1 of Part 6 set out circumstances (including under a warrant) in which the interception of communications is lawful and make further provision about the interception of communications and the treatment of material obtained in connection with it,

(b) Part 3 and Chapter 2 of Part 6 set out circumstances in which the obtaining of communications data is lawful in pursuance of an authorisation or under a warrant and make further provision about the obtaining and treatment of such data,

(c) Part 4 makes provision for the retention of certain communications data in pursuance of a notice,

(d) Part 5 and Chapter 3 of Part 6 deal with equipment interference warrants, and

(e) Part 7 deals with bulk personal dataset warrants.

(7) As to the rest of the Act—

(a) Part 8 deals with oversight arrangements for regimes in this Act and elsewhere, and

(b) Part 9 contains miscellaneous and general provisions including amendments to sections 3 and 5 of the Intelligence Services Act 1994 and provisions about national security and combined warrants and authorisations.

[Investigatory Powers Act 2016, s 1.]

1 This Act provides an updated framework for the use of investigatory powers to obtain communications and communications data. These powers cover: interception, retention and acquisition of communications data; and equipment interference for obtaining communications and other data. The Act also makes provision as to the security and intelligence agencies' retention and examination of bulk personal datasets.

The Act replaces the Data Retention and Investigatory Powers Act 2014 (DRIPA), which was an emergency measure and had a sunset clause of 31 December 2016 (Sch 9 to the IPA prescribes a transitional period). The Act also consolidates and updates powers available to the state to obtain communications and communications data. Previously, these were provided for in a number of statutes, many of which were enacted before the rise of the internet as a means of communication.

Section 1 provides an overview of the Act and describes the regimes provide by PARTS 2-7.

Nearly all of the Act's provisions are prospective and will be brought into force in accordance with regulations made under s 272. At the date at which this work states the law the Investigatory Powers Act 2016 (Commencement No 1 and Transitional Provisions) Regulations 2016, SI 2016/1233 and the Investigatory Powers Act 2016 (Commencement No 2 and Transitional Provisions) Regulations 2017, SI 2017/137 had been made. With the exception of ss 1, 2 (n part), 60 (in part), 61 (in part), 272, Sch 7, Sch 9 (in part), none of the provisions reproduced below is in force save as mentioned in s 272.

2 PART 1 contains ss 1-14.

7.11231F **2. General duties in relation to privacy** (1) Subsection (2) applies where a public authority is deciding whether—

(a) to issue, renew or cancel a warrant under Part 2, 5, 6 or 7,
(b) to modify such a warrant,
(c) to approve a decision to issue, renew or modify such a warrant,
(d) to grant, approve or cancel an authorisation under Part 3,
(e) to give a notice in pursuance of such an authorisation or under Part 4 or section 252, 253 or 257,
(f) to vary or revoke such a notice,
(g) to approve a decision to give or vary a notice under Part 4 or section 252, 253 or 257,
(h) to approve the use of criteria under section 153, 194 or 222,
(i) to give an authorisation under section 219(3)(b),
(j) to approve a decision to give such an authorisation, or
(k) to apply for or otherwise seek any issue, grant, giving, modification, variation or renewal of a kind falling within paragraph (a), (b), (d), (e), (f) or (i).

(2) The public authority must have regard to—

(a) whether what is sought to be achieved by the warrant, authorisation or notice could reasonably be achieved by other less intrusive means,
(b) whether the level of protection to be applied in relation to any obtaining of information by virtue of the warrant, authorisation or notice is higher because of the particular sensitivity of that information,
(c) the public interest in the integrity and security of telecommunication systems and postal services, and
(d) any other aspects of the public interest in the protection of privacy.

(3) The duties under subsection (2)—

(a) apply so far as they are relevant in the particular context, and
(b) are subject to the need to have regard to other considerations that are also relevant in that context.

(4) The other considerations may, in particular, include—

(a) the interests of national security or of the economic well-being of the United Kingdom,
(b) the public interest in preventing or detecting serious crime,
(c) other considerations which are relevant to—
  (i) whether the conduct authorised or required by the warrant, authorisation or notice is proportionate, or
  (ii) whether it is necessary to act for a purpose provided for by this Act,
(d) the requirements of the Human Rights Act 1998, and
(e) other requirements of public law.

(5) For the purposes of subsection (2)(b), examples of sensitive information include—

(a) items subject to legal privilege,
(b) any information identifying or confirming a source of journalistic information, and
(c) relevant confidential information within the meaning given by paragraph 2(4) of Schedule 7 (certain information held in confidence and consisting of personal records, journalistic material or communications between Members of Parliament and their constituents).

(6) In this section "public authority" includes the relevant judicial authority (within the meaning of section 75) where the relevant judicial authority is deciding whether to approve under that section an authorisation under Part 3.

[Investigatory Powers Act 2016, s 2.]

*Prohibitions against Unlawful Interception*

7.11231G **3. Offence of unlawful interception** (1) A person commits an offence if—

(a) the person intentionally intercepts a communication in the course of its transmission by means of—
  (i) a public telecommunication system,
  (ii) a private telecommunication system, or
  (iii) a public postal service,
(b) the interception is carried out in the United Kingdom, and
(c) the person does not have lawful authority to carry out the interception.

(2) But it is not an offence under subsection (1) for a person to intercept a communication in the course of its transmission by means of a private telecommunication system if the person—

(a) is a person with a right to control the operation or use of the system, or

(b) has the express or implied consent of such a person to carry out the interception.

(3) Sections 4 and 5 contain provision about—

(a) the meaning of "interception", and

(b) when interception is to be regarded as carried out in the United Kingdom.

(4) Section 6 contains provision about when a person has lawful authority to carry out an interception.

(5) For the meaning of the terms used in subsection (1)(a)(i) to (iii), see sections 261 and 262.

(6) A person who is guilty of an offence under subsection (1) is liable—

(a) on summary conviction in England and Wales, to a fine;

(b) on summary conviction in Scotland or Northern Ireland, to a fine not exceeding the statutory maximum;

(c) on conviction on indictment, to imprisonment for a term not exceeding 2 years or to a fine, or to both.[1]

(7) No proceedings for any offence which is an offence by virtue of this section may be instituted—

(a) in England and Wales, except by or with the consent of the Director of Public Prosecutions;

(b) in Northern Ireland, except by or with the consent of the Director of Public Prosecutions for Northern Ireland.

[Investigatory Powers Act 2016, s 3.]

---

[1] For procedure in respect of an offence triable either way, see the Magistrates' Courts Act 1980, s 17A-21, in PART 1: MAGISTRATES' COURTS, PROCEDURE, ante.

**7.11231H 4. Definition of "interception" etc** *Interception in relation to telecommunication systems*

(1) For the purposes of this Act, a person intercepts a communication in the course of its transmission by means of a telecommunication system if, and only if—

(a) the person does a relevant act in relation to the system, and

(b) the effect of the relevant act is to make any content of the communication available, at a relevant time, to a person who is not the sender or intended recipient of the communication.

For the meaning of "content" in relation to a communication, see section 261(6).

(2) In this section "relevant act", in relation to a telecommunication system, means—

(a) modifying, or interfering with, the system or its operation;

(b) monitoring transmissions made by means of the system;

(c) monitoring transmissions made by wireless telegraphy to or from apparatus that is part of the system.

(3) For the purposes of this section references to modifying a telecommunication system include references to attaching any apparatus to, or otherwise modifying or interfering with—

(a) any part of the system, or

(b) any wireless telegraphy apparatus used for making transmissions to or from apparatus that is part of the system.

(4) In this section "relevant time", in relation to a communication transmitted by means of a telecommunication system, means—

(a) any time while the communication is being transmitted, and

(b) any time when the communication is stored in or by the system (whether before or after its transmission).

(5) For the purposes of this section, the cases in which any content of a communication is to be taken to be made available to a person at a relevant time include any case in which any of the communication is diverted or recorded at a relevant time so as to make any content of the communication available to a person after that time.

(6) In this section "wireless telegraphy" and "wireless telegraphy apparatus" have the same meaning as in the Wireless Telegraphy Act 2006 (see sections 116 and 117 of that Act).

*Interception in relation to postal services*

(7) Section 125(3) of the Postal Services Act 2000 applies for the purposes of determining for the purposes of this Act whether a postal item is in the course of its transmission by means of a postal service as it applies for the purposes of determining for the purposes of that Act whether a postal packet is in course of transmission by post.

*Interception carried out in the United Kingdom*

(8) For the purposes of this Act the interception of a communication is carried out in the United Kingdom if, and only if—

(a) the relevant act or, in the case of a postal item, the interception is carried out by conduct within the United Kingdom, and

(b) the communication is intercepted—

(i) in the course of its transmission by means of a public telecommunication system or a public postal service, or

(ii) in the course of its transmission by means of a private telecommunication system in a case where the sender or intended recipient of the communication is in the United Kingdom.

[Investigatory Powers Act 2016, s 4.]

**7.11231I 5. Conduct that is not interception** (1) References in this Act to the interception of a communication do not include references to the interception of any communication broadcast for general reception.

(2) References in this Act to the interception of a communication in the course of its transmission by means of a postal service do not include references to—

(a) any conduct that takes place in relation only to so much of the communication as consists of any postal data comprised in, included as part of, attached to, or logically associated with a communication (whether by the sender or otherwise) for the purposes of any postal service by means of which it is being or may be transmitted, or

(b) any conduct, in connection with conduct falling within paragraph (a), that gives a person who is neither the sender nor the intended recipient only so much access to a communication as is necessary for the purpose of identifying such postal data.

For the meaning of "postal data", see section 262.

[Investigatory Powers Act 2016, s 5.]

**7.11231J 6. Definition of "lawful authority"** (1) For the purposes of this Act, a person has lawful authority to carry out an interception if, and only if—

(a) the interception is carried out in accordance with—

(i) a targeted interception warrant or mutual assistance warrant under Chapter 1 of Part 2, or

(ii) a bulk interception warrant under Chapter 1 of Part 6,

(b) the interception is authorised by any of sections 44 to 52, or

(c) in the case of a communication stored in or by a telecommunication system, the interception—

(i) is carried out in accordance with a targeted equipment interference warrant under Part 5 or a bulk equipment interference warrant under Chapter 3 of Part 6,

(ii) is in the exercise of any statutory power that is exercised for the purpose of obtaining information or taking possession of any document or other property, or

(iii) is carried out in accordance with a court order made for that purpose.

(2) Conduct which has lawful authority for the purposes of this Act by virtue of subsection (1)(a) or (b) is to be treated as lawful for all other purposes.

(3) Any other conduct which—

(a) is carried out in accordance with a warrant under Chapter 1 of Part 2 or a bulk interception warrant, or

(b) is authorised by any of sections 44 to 52,

is to be treated as lawful for all purposes.

[Investigatory Powers Act 2016, s 6.]

**7.11231K 9. Restriction on requesting interception by overseas authorities** (1) This section applies to a request for any authorities of a country or territory outside the United Kingdom to carry out the interception of communications sent by, or intended for, an individual who the person making the request believes will be in the British Islands at the time of the interception.

(2) A request to which this section applies may not be made by or on behalf of a person in the United Kingdom unless—

(a) a targeted interception warrant has been issued under Chapter 1 of Part 2 authorising the person to whom it is addressed to secure the interception of communications sent by, or intended for, that individual, or

(b) a targeted examination warrant has been issued under that Chapter authorising the person to whom it is addressed to carry out the selection of the content of such communications for examination.

[Investigatory Powers Act 2016, s 9.]

**7.11231L 10. Restriction on requesting assistance under mutual assistance agreements etc** (1) This section applies to—

(a) a request for assistance under an EU mutual assistance instrument, and

(b) a request for assistance in accordance with an international mutual assistance agreement.

(2) A request to which this section applies may not be made by or on behalf of a person in the United Kingdom to the competent authorities of a country or territory outside the United Kingdom unless a mutual assistance warrant has been issued under Chapter 1 of Part 2 authorising the making of the request.

(3) In this section—

"EU mutual assistance instrument" means an EU instrument which—

(a) relates to the provision of mutual assistance in connection with, or in the form of, the interception of communications,

(b) requires the issue of a warrant, order or equivalent instrument in cases in which assistance is given, and

(c) is designated as an EU mutual assistance instrument by regulations made by the Secretary of State;

"international mutual assistance agreement" means an international agreement which—

(a) relates to the provision of mutual assistance in connection with, or in the form of, the interception of communications,

(b) requires the issue of a warrant, order or equivalent instrument in cases in which assistance is given, and

(c) is designated as an international mutual assistance agreement by regulations made by the Secretary of State.

[Investigatory Powers Act 2016, s 10.]

*Prohibition against unlawful obtaining of communications data*

**7.11231M 11. Offence of unlawfully obtaining communications data** (1) A relevant person who, without lawful authority, knowingly or recklessly obtains communications data from a telecommunications operator or a postal operator is guilty of an offence.

(2) In this section "relevant person" means a person who holds an office, rank or position with a relevant public authority (within the meaning of Part 3).

(3) Subsection (1) does not apply to a relevant person who shows that the person acted in the reasonable belief that the person had lawful authority to obtain the communications data.

(4) A person guilty of an offence under this section is liable—

(a) on summary conviction in England and Wales—

(i) to imprisonment for a term not exceeding 12 months (or 6 months, if the offence was committed before the commencement of section 154(1) of the Criminal Justice Act 2003), or

(ii) to a fine,

or to both;

(b) on summary conviction in Scotland—

(i) to imprisonment for a term not exceeding 12 months, or

(ii) to a fine not exceeding the statutory maximum,

or to both;

(c) on summary conviction in Northern Ireland—

(i) to imprisonment for a term not exceeding 6 months, or

(ii) to a fine not exceeding the statutory maximum,

or to both;

(d) on conviction on indictment, to imprisonment for a term not exceeding 2 years or to a fine, or to both[1].

[Investigatory Powers Act 2016, s 11.]

1 For procedure in respect of an offence triable either way, see the Magistrates' Courts Act 1980, s 17A-21, in PART 1: MAGISTRATES' COURTS, PROCEDURE, ante.

*Abolition or restriction of powers to obtain communications data*

**7.11231N 12. Abolition or restriction of certain powers to obtain communications data**

(1) Schedule 2 (which repeals certain information powers so far as they enable public authorities to secure the disclosure by a telecommunications operator or postal operator of communications data without the consent of the operator) has effect.

(2) Any general information power which—

(a) would (apart from this subsection) enable a public authority to secure the disclosure by a telecommunications operator or postal operator of communications data without the consent of the operator, and

(b) does not involve a court order or other judicial authorisation or warrant and is not a regulatory power or a relevant postal power,

is to be read as not enabling the public authority to secure such a disclosure.

(3) A regulatory power or relevant postal power which enables a public authority to secure the disclosure by a telecommunications operator or postal operator of communications data without the consent of the operator may only be exercised by the public authority for that purpose if it is not possible for the authority to use a power under this Act to secure the disclosure of the data.

(4) The Secretary of State may by regulations modify any enactment in consequence of subsection (2).

(5) In this section "general information power" means—

(a) in relation to disclosure by a telecommunications operator, any power to obtain information or documents (however expressed) which—

(i) is conferred by or under an enactment other than this Act or the Regulation of Investigatory Powers Act 2000, and

(ii) does not deal (whether alone or with other matters) specifically with telecommunications operators or any class of telecommunications operators, and

(b) in relation to disclosure by a postal operator, any power to obtain information or documents (however expressed) which—

(i) is conferred by or under an enactment other than this Act or the Regulation of Investigatory Powers Act 2000, and

(ii) does not deal (whether alone or with other matters) specifically with postal operators or any class of postal operators.

(6) In this section—

"power" includes part of a power,

"regulatory power" means any power to obtain information or documents (however expressed) which—

(a) is conferred by or under an enactment other than this Act or the Regulation of Investigatory Powers Act 2000, and

(b) is exercisable in connection with the regulation of—

(i) telecommunications operators, telecommunications services or telecommunication systems, or

(ii) postal operators or postal services,

"relevant postal power" means any power to obtain information or documents (however expressed) which—

(a) is conferred by or under an enactment other than this Act or the Regulation of Investigatory Powers Act 2000, and

(b) is exercisable in connection with the conveyance or expected conveyance of any postal item into or out of the United Kingdom,

and references to powers include duties (and references to enabling and exercising are to be read as including references to requiring and performing).

[Investigatory Powers Act 2016, s 12.]

*Restrictions on interference with equipment*

**7.11231O 13. Mandatory use of equipment interference warrants** (1) An intelligence service may not, for the purpose of obtaining communications, private information or equipment data, engage in conduct which could be authorised by an equipment interference warrant except under the authority of such a warrant if—

(a) the intelligence service considers that the conduct would (unless done under lawful authority) constitute one or more offences under sections 1 to 3A of the Computer Misuse Act 1990 (computer misuse offences), and

(b) there is a British Islands connection.

(2) For the purpose of this section, there is a British Islands connection if—

(a) any of the conduct would take place in the British Islands (regardless of the location of the equipment which would, or may, be interfered with),

(b) the intelligence service believes that any of the equipment which would, or may, be interfered with would, or may, be in the British Islands at some time while the interference is taking place, or

(c) a purpose of the interference is to obtain—

(i) communications sent by, or to, a person who is, or whom the intelligence service believes to be, for the time being in the British Islands,

(ii) private information relating to an individual who is, or whom the intelligence service believes to be, for the time being in the British Islands, or

(iii) equipment data which forms part of, or is connected with, communications or private information falling within sub-paragraph (i) or (ii).

(3) This section does not restrict the ability of the head of an intelligence service to apply for an equipment interference warrant in cases where—

(a) the intelligence service does not consider that the conduct for which it is seeking authorisation would (unless done under lawful authority) constitute one or more offences under sections 1 to 3A of the Computer Misuse Act 1990, or

(b) there is no British Islands connection.

(4) In this section—

"communications", "private information" and "equipment data" have the same meaning as in Part 5 (see section 135);

"equipment interference warrant" means—

(a) a targeted equipment interference warrant under Part 5;

(b) a bulk equipment interference warrant under Chapter 3 of Part 6.

[Investigatory Powers Act 2016, s 13.]

**7.11231P 14. Restriction on use of section 93 of the Police Act 1997** (1) A person may not, for the purpose of obtaining communications, private information or equipment data, make an application under section 93 of the Police Act 1997 for authorisation to engage in conduct which could be authorised by a targeted equipment interference warrant under Part 5 if the applicant considers that the conduct would (unless done under lawful authority) constitute one or more offences under sections 1 to 3A of the Computer Misuse Act 1990 (computer misuse offences).

(2) In this section, "communications", "private information" and "equipment data" have the same meaning as in Part 5 (see section 135).

[Investigatory Powers Act 2016, s 14.]

## PART 2[1]
## LAWFUL INTERCEPTION OF COMMUNICATIONS

### CHAPTER 1[2]
### INTERCEPTION AND EXAMINATION WITH A WARRANT

*Warrants under this Chapter*

**7.11231Q 15. Warrants that may be issued under this Chapter** (1) There are three kinds of warrant that may be issued under this Chapter—

(a) targeted interception warrants (see subsection (2)),

(b) targeted examination warrants (see subsection (3)), and

(c) mutual assistance warrants (see subsection (4)).

(2) A targeted interception warrant is a warrant which authorises or requires the person to whom it is addressed to secure, by any conduct described in the warrant, any one or more of the following—

(a) the interception, in the course of their transmission by means of a postal service or telecommunication system, of communications described in the warrant;

(b) the obtaining of secondary data from communications transmitted by means of a postal service or telecommunication system and described in the warrant (see section 16);

(c) the disclosure, in any manner described in the warrant, of anything obtained under the warrant to the person to whom the warrant is addressed or to any person acting on that person's behalf.

(3) A targeted examination warrant is a warrant which authorises the person to whom it is addressed to carry out the selection of relevant content for examination, in breach of the prohibition in section 152(4) (prohibition on seeking to identify communications of individuals in the British Islands).

In this Part "relevant content", in relation to a targeted examination warrant, means any content of communications intercepted by an interception authorised or required by a bulk interception warrant under Chapter 1 of Part 6.

(4) A mutual assistance warrant is a warrant which authorises or requires the person to whom it is addressed to secure, by any conduct described in the warrant, any one or more of the following—

(a) the making of a request, in accordance with an EU mutual assistance instrument or an international mutual assistance agreement, for the provision of any assistance of a kind described in the warrant in connection with, or in the form of, an interception of communications;

(b) the provision to the competent authorities of a country or territory outside the United Kingdom, in accordance with such an instrument or agreement, of any assistance of a kind described in the warrant in connection with, or in the form of, an interception of communications;

(c) the disclosure, in any manner described in the warrant, of anything obtained under the warrant to the person to whom the warrant is addressed or to any person acting on that person's behalf.

(5) A targeted interception warrant or mutual assistance warrant also authorises the following conduct (in addition to the conduct described in the warrant)—

(a) any conduct which it is necessary to undertake in order to do what is expressly authorised or required by the warrant, including—

(i) the interception of communications not described in the warrant, and

(ii) conduct for obtaining secondary data from such communications;

(b) any conduct by any person which is conduct in pursuance of a requirement imposed by or on behalf of the person to whom the warrant is addressed to be provided with assistance in giving effect to the warrant;

(c) any conduct for obtaining related systems data from any postal operator or telecommunications operator.

(6) For the purposes of subsection (5)(c)—

"related systems data", in relation to a warrant, means systems data relating to a relevant communication or to the sender or recipient, or intended recipient, of a relevant communication (whether or not a person), and

"relevant communication", in relation to a warrant, means—

(a) any communication intercepted in accordance with the warrant in the course of its transmission by means of a postal service or telecommunication system, or

(b) any communication from which secondary data is obtained under the warrant.

(7) For provision enabling the combination of targeted interception warrants with certain other warrants or authorisations (including targeted examination warrants), see Schedule 8.

[Investigatory Powers Act 2016, s 15.]

---

[1] PART 2 contains ss 15-60.

[2] Chapter 1 contains ss 15-43. The omitted provisions concern: power to issue warrants; approval of warrants by Judicial Commissioners; additional safeguards for MPs, legal privilege and journalistic information; duration, modification and cancellation of warrants; special provision for mutual assistance warrants.

**7.11231R 16. Obtaining secondary data** (1) This section has effect for the purposes of this Part.

(2) In relation to a communication transmitted by means of a postal service, references to obtaining secondary data from the communication are references to obtaining such data in the course of the transmission of the communication (as to which, see section 4(7)).

(3) In relation to a communication transmitted by means of a telecommunication system, references to obtaining secondary data from the communication are references to obtaining such data—

(a) while the communication is being transmitted, or

(b) at any time when the communication is stored in or by the system (whether before or after its transmission).

(4) "Secondary data"—

(a) in relation to a communication transmitted by means of a postal service, means any data falling within subsection (5);

(b) in relation to a communication transmitted by means of a telecommunication system, means any data falling within subsection (5) or (6).

(5) The data falling within this subsection is systems data which is comprised in, included as part of, attached to or logically associated with the communication (whether by the sender or otherwise).

(6) The data falling within this subsection is identifying data which—

(a) is comprised in, included as part of, attached to or logically associated with the communication (whether by the sender or otherwise),

(b) is capable of being logically separated from the remainder of the communication, and

(c) if it were so separated, would not reveal anything of what might reasonably be considered to be the meaning (if any) of the communication, disregarding any meaning arising from the fact of the communication or from any data relating to the transmission of the communication.

(7) For the meaning of "systems data" and "identifying data", see section 263.

[Investigatory Powers Act 2016, s 16.]

**7.11231S 17. Subject-matter of warrants** (1) A warrant under this Chapter may relate to—

(a) a particular person or organisation, or

(b) a single set of premises.

(2) In addition, a targeted interception warrant or targeted examination warrant may relate to—

(a) a group of persons who share a common purpose or who carry on, or may carry on, a particular activity;

(b) more than one person or organisation, or more than one set of premises, where the conduct authorised or required by the warrant is for the purposes of a single investigation or operation;

(c) testing or training activities.

(3) In subsection (2)(c) "testing or training activities" means—

(a) in relation to a targeted interception warrant—

(i) the testing, maintenance or development of apparatus, systems or other capabilities relating to the interception of communications in the course of their transmission by means of a telecommunication system or to the obtaining of secondary data from communications transmitted by means of such a system, or

(ii) the training of persons who carry out, or are likely to carry out, such interception or the obtaining of such data;

(b) in relation to a targeted examination warrant—

(i) the testing, maintenance or development of apparatus, systems or other capabilities relating to the selection of relevant content for examination, or

(ii) the training of persons who carry out, or are likely to carry out, the selection of relevant content for examination.

[Investigatory Powers Act 2016, s 17.]

*Implementation of warrants*

**7.11231T 41. Implementation of warrants** (1) This section applies to targeted interception warrants and mutual assistance warrants.

(2) In giving effect to a warrant to which this section applies, the person to whom it is addressed

("the intercepting authority") may (in addition to acting alone) act through, or together with, such other persons as the intercepting authority may require (whether under subsection (3) or otherwise) to provide the authority with assistance in giving effect to the warrant.

(3) For the purpose of requiring any person to provide assistance in relation to a warrant to which this section applies, the intercepting authority may—

(a) serve a copy of the warrant on any person who the intercepting authority considers may be able to provide such assistance, or

(b) make arrangements for the service of a copy of the warrant on any such person.

(4) A copy of a warrant may be served under subsection (3) on a person outside the United Kingdom for the purpose of requiring the person to provide such assistance in the form of conduct outside the United Kingdom.

(5) For the purposes of this Act, the provision of assistance in giving effect to a warrant to which this section applies includes any disclosure to the intercepting authority, or to persons acting on behalf of the intercepting authority, of anything obtained under the warrant.

(6) References in this section and sections 42 and 43 to the service of a copy of a warrant include—

(a) the service of a copy of one or more schedules contained in the warrant with the omission of the remainder of the warrant, and

(b) the service of a copy of the warrant with the omission of any schedule contained in the warrant.

[Investigatory Powers Act 2016, s 41.]

**7.11231U 42. Service of warrants** (1) This section applies to the service of warrants under section 41(3).

(2) A copy of the warrant must be served in such a way as to bring the contents of the warrant to the attention of the person who the intercepting authority considers may be able to provide assistance in relation to it.

(3) A copy of a warrant may be served on a person outside the United Kingdom in any of the following ways (as well as by electronic or other means of service)—

(a) by serving it at the person's principal office within the United Kingdom or, if the person has no such office in the United Kingdom, at any place in the United Kingdom where the person carries on business or conducts activities;

(b) if the person has specified an address in the United Kingdom as one at which the person, or someone on the person's behalf, will accept service of documents of the same description as a copy of a warrant, by serving it at that address;

(c) by making it available for inspection (whether to the person or to someone acting on the person's behalf) at a place in the United Kingdom (but this is subject to subsection (4)).

(4) A copy of a warrant may be served on a person outside the United Kingdom in the way mentioned in subsection (3)(c) only if—

(a) it is not reasonably practicable for a copy to be served by any other means (whether as mentioned in subsection (3)(a) or (b) or otherwise), and

(b) the intercepting authority takes such steps as the authority considers appropriate for the purpose of bringing the contents of the warrant, and the availability of a copy for inspection, to the attention of the person.

(5) The steps mentioned in subsection (4)(b) must be taken as soon as reasonably practicable after the copy of the warrant is made available for inspection.

(6) In this section "the intercepting authority" has the same meaning as in section 41.

[Investigatory Powers Act 2016, s 42.]

**7.11231V 43. Duty of operators to assist with implementation** (1) A relevant operator that has been served with a copy of a warrant to which section 41 applies by (or on behalf of) the intercepting authority must take all steps for giving effect to the warrant that are notified to the relevant operator by (or on behalf of) the intercepting authority.

This is subject to subsection (4).

(2) In this section—

"relevant operator" means a postal operator or a telecommunications operator;

"the intercepting authority" has the same meaning as in section 41.

(3) Subsection (1) applies whether or not the relevant operator is in the United Kingdom.

(4) The relevant operator is not required to take any steps which it is not reasonably practicable for the relevant operator to take.

(5) In determining for the purposes of subsection (4) whether it is reasonably practicable for a relevant operator outside the United Kingdom to take any steps in a country or territory outside the United Kingdom for giving effect to a warrant, the matters to be taken into account include the following—

(a) any requirements or restrictions under the law of that country or territory that are relevant to the taking of those steps, and

(b) the extent to which it is reasonably practicable to give effect to the warrant in a way that does not breach any of those requirements or restrictions.

(6) Where obligations have been imposed on a relevant operator ("P") under section 253

(technical capability notices), for the purposes of subsection (4) the steps which it is reasonably practicable for P to take include every step which it would have been reasonably practicable for P to take if P had complied with all of those obligations.

(7) A person who knowingly fails to comply with subsection (1) is guilty of an offence and liable—

(a) on summary conviction in England and Wales—
  (i) to imprisonment for a term not exceeding 12 months (or 6 months, if the offence was committed before the commencement of section 154(1) of the Criminal Justice Act 2003), or
  (ii) to a fine,
  or to both;

(b) on summary conviction in Scotland—
  (i) to imprisonment for a term not exceeding 12 months, or
  (ii) to a fine not exceeding the statutory maximum,
  or to both;

(c) on summary conviction in Northern Ireland—
  (i) to imprisonment for a term not exceeding 6 months, or
  (ii) to a fine not exceeding the statutory maximum,
  or to both;

(d) on conviction on indictment, to imprisonment for a term not exceeding 2 years or to a fine, or to both[1].

(8) The duty imposed by subsection (1) is enforceable (whether or not the person is in the United Kingdom) by civil proceedings by the Secretary of State for an injunction, or for specific performance of a statutory duty under section 45 of the Court of Session Act 1988, or for any other appropriate relief.

[Investigatory Powers Act 2016, s 43.]

---

[1] For procedure in respect of an offence triable either way, see the Magistrates' Courts Act 1980, s 17A-21, in PART 1: MAGISTRATES' COURTS, PROCEDURE, ante.

## CHAPTER 2[1]

## OTHER FORMS OF LAWFUL INTERCEPTION

*Interception with consent*

7.11231W 44. **Interception with the consent of the sender or recipient** (1) The interception of a communication is authorised by this section if the sender and the intended recipient of the communication have each consented to its interception.

(2) The interception of a communication is authorised by this section if—

(a) the communication is one sent by, or intended for, a person who has consented to the interception, and

(b) surveillance by means of that interception has been authorised under—
  (i) Part 2 of the Regulation of Investigatory Powers Act 2000, or
  (ii) the Regulation of Investigatory Powers (Scotland) Act 2000 (2000 asp 11).

[Investigatory Powers Act 2016, s 44.]

---

[1] Chapter 2 contains ss 44-52.

*Interception for administrative or enforcement purposes*

7.11231X 45. **Interception by providers of postal or telecommunications services** (1) The interception of a communication is authorised by this section if the interception is carried out—

(a) by, or on behalf of, a person who provides a postal service or a telecommunications service, and

(b) for any of the purposes in subsection (2).

(2) The purposes referred to in subsection (1) are—

(a) purposes relating to the provision or operation of the service;

(b) purposes relating to the enforcement, in relation to the service, of any enactment relating to—
  (i) the use of postal or telecommunications services, or
  (ii) the content of communications transmitted by means of such services;

(c) purposes relating to the provision of services or facilities aimed at preventing or restricting the viewing or publication of the content of communications transmitted by means of postal or telecommunications services.

(3) A reference in this section to anything carried out for purposes relating to the provision or operation of a telecommunications service includes, among other things, a reference to anything done for the purposes of identifying, combating or preventing anything which could affect—

(a) any telecommunication system by means of which the service is provided, or

(b) any apparatus attached to such a system.

[Investigatory Powers Act 2016, s 45.]

**7.11231Y 46. Interception by businesses etc for monitoring and record-keeping purposes**

(1) Conduct is authorised by this section if it is authorised by regulations made under subsection (2).

(2) The Secretary of State may by regulations authorise conduct of a description specified in the regulations if that conduct appears to the Secretary of State to constitute a legitimate practice reasonably required for the purpose, in connection with the carrying on of any relevant activities (see subsection (4)), of monitoring or keeping a record of—

(a) communications by means of which transactions are entered into in the course of the relevant activities, or

(b) other communications relating to the relevant activities or taking place in the course of the carrying on of those activities.

(3) But nothing in any regulations under subsection (2) may authorise the interception of any communication except in the course of its transmission using apparatus or services provided by or to the person carrying on the relevant activities for use (whether wholly or partly) in connection with those activities.

(4) In this section "relevant activities" means—

(a) any business,

(b) any activities of a government department, the Welsh Government, a Northern Ireland department or any part of the Scottish Administration,

(c) any activities of a public authority, and

(d) any activities of any person or office holder on whom functions are conferred by or under any enactment.

[Investigatory Powers Act 2016, s 46.]

**7.11231Z 47. Postal services: interception for enforcement purposes** (1) The interception of a communication in the course of its transmission by means of a public postal service is authorised by this section if it is carried out by an officer of Revenue and Customs under section 159 of the Customs and Excise Management Act 1979, as applied by virtue of—

(a) section 105 of the Postal Services Act 2000 (power to open postal items etc), or

(b) that section and another enactment.

(2) The interception of a communication in the course of its transmission by means of a public postal service is authorised by this section if it is carried out under paragraph 9 of Schedule 7 to the Terrorism Act 2000 (port and border controls).

[Investigatory Powers Act 2016, s 47.]

**7.11231ZA 48. Interception by OFCOM in connection with wireless telegraphy**

(1) Conduct falling within subsection (2) is authorised by this section if it is carried out by OFCOM for purposes connected with a relevant matter (see subsection (3)).

(2) The conduct referred to in subsection (1) is—

(a) the interception of a communication in the course of its transmission by means of a telecommunication system;

(b) the obtaining, by or in connection with the interception, of information about the sender or recipient, or intended recipient, of the communication (whether or not a person);

(c) the disclosure of anything obtained by conduct falling within paragraph (a) or (b).

(3) Each of the following is a relevant matter for the purposes of subsection (1)—

(a) the grant of wireless telegraphy licences under the Wireless Telegraphy Act 2006 ("the 2006 Act");

(b) the prevention or detection of anything which constitutes interference with wireless telegraphy;

(c) the enforcement of—

(i) any provision of Part 2 (other than Chapter 2 and sections 27 to 31) or Part 3 of the 2006 Act, or

(ii) any enactment not falling within sub-paragraph (i) that relates to interference with wireless telegraphy.

(4) In this section—

"interference", in relation to wireless telegraphy, has the same meaning as in the Wireless Telegraphy Act 2006 (see section 115(3) of that Act);

"OFCOM" means the Office of Communications established by section 1 of the Office of Communications Act 2002;

"wireless telegraphy" has the same meaning as in the Wireless Telegraphy Act 2006 (see section 116 of that Act).

[Investigatory Powers Act 2016, s 48.]

*Interception taking place in certain institutions*

**7.11231ZB 49. Interception in prisons** (1) Conduct taking place in a prison is authorised by this section if it is conduct in exercise of any power conferred by or under prison rules.

(2) In this section "prison rules" means any rules made under—

(a) section 47 of the Prison Act 1952,

(b) section 39 of the Prisons (Scotland) Act 1989, or
(c) section 13 of the Prison Act (Northern Ireland) 1953.

(3) In this section "prison" means—

(a) any prison, young offender institution, young offenders centre, secure training centre, secure college or remand centre which—
(i) is under the general superintendence of, or is provided by, the Secretary of State under the Prison Act 1952, or
(ii) is under the general superintendence of, or is provided by, the Department of Justice in Northern Ireland under the Prison Act (Northern Ireland) 1953, or

(b) any prison, young offenders institution or remand centre which is under the general superintendence of the Scottish Ministers under the Prisons (Scotland) Act 1989,

and includes any contracted out prison, within the meaning of Part 4 of the Criminal Justice Act 1991 or section 106(4) of the Criminal Justice and Public Order Act 1994, and any legalised police cells within the meaning of section 14 of the Prisons (Scotland) Act 1989.

[Investigatory Powers Act 2016, s 49.]

**7.11231ZC 50. Interception in psychiatric hospitals etc** (1) Conduct is authorised by this section if—

(a) it takes place in any hospital premises where high security psychiatric services are provided, and
(b) it is conduct in pursuance of, and in accordance with, any relevant direction given to the body providing those services at those premises.

(2) "Relevant direction" means—

(a) a direction under section 4(3A)(a) of the National Health Service Act 2006, or
(b) a direction under section 19 or 23 of the National Health Service (Wales) Act 2006.

(3) Conduct is authorised by this section if—

(a) it takes place in a state hospital, and
(b) it is conduct in pursuance of, and in accordance with, any direction given to the State Hospitals Board for Scotland under section 2(5) of the National Health Service (Scotland) Act 1978 (regulations and directions as to the exercise of their functions by health boards).

The reference to section 2(5) of that Act is to that provision as applied by Article 5(1) of, and the Schedule to, the State Hospitals Board for Scotland Order 1995 (which applies certain provisions of that Act to the State Hospitals Board).

(4) Conduct is authorised by this section if it is conduct in exercise of any power conferred by or under—

(a) section 281 of the Mental Health (Care and Treatment) (Scotland) Act 2003 (2003 asp 13) (power to withhold correspondence of certain persons detained in hospital), or
(b) section 284 of that Act (powers relating to the use of telephones by certain persons detained in hospital).

(5) In this section—

"high security psychiatric services" has the same meaning as in section 4 of the National Health Service Act 2006;

"hospital premises" has the same meaning as in section 4(3) of that Act;

"state hospital" has the same meaning as in the National Health Service (Scotland) Act 1978.

[Investigatory Powers Act 2016, s 50.]

**7.11231ZD 51. Interception in immigration detention facilities** (1) Conduct taking place in immigration detention facilities is authorised by this section if it is conduct in exercise of any power conferred by or under relevant rules.

(2) In this section—

"immigration detention facilities" means any removal centre, short-term holding facility or pre-departure accommodation;

"removal centre", "short-term holding facility" and "pre-departure accommodation" have the meaning given by section 147 of the Immigration and Asylum Act 1999;

"relevant rules" means—
(a) in the case of a removal centre, rules made under section 153 of that Act;
(b) in the case of a short-term holding facility, rules made under, or having effect by virtue of, section 157 of that Act;
(c) in the case of pre-departure accommodation, rules made under, or having effect by virtue of, section 157A of that Act.

[Investigatory Powers Act 2016, s 51.]

*Interception in accordance with overseas requests*

**7.11231ZE 52. Interception in accordance with overseas requests** (1) The interception of a communication in the course of its transmission by means of a telecommunication system is authorised by this section if conditions A to D are met.

(2) Condition A is that the interception—

(a) is carried out by or on behalf of a telecommunications operator, and

(b) relates to the use of a telecommunications service provided by the telecommunications operator.

(3) Condition B is that the interception is carried out in response to a request made in accordance with a relevant international agreement by the competent authorities of a country or territory outside the United Kingdom.

In this subsection "relevant international agreement" means an international agreement to which the United Kingdom is a party and which is designated as a relevant international agreement by regulations made by the Secretary of State.

(4) Condition C is that the interception is carried out for the purpose of obtaining information about the communications of an individual—

(a) who is outside the United Kingdom, or

(b) who each of the following persons believes is outside the United Kingdom—

(i) the person making the request;

(ii) the person carrying out the interception.

(5) Condition D is that any further conditions specified in regulations made by the Secretary of State for the purposes of this section are met.

[Investigatory Powers Act 2016, s 52.]

## CHAPTER 3[1]

## OTHER PROVISIONS ABOUT INTERCEPTION

*Restrictions on use or disclosure of material obtained under warrants etc*

**7.11231ZF 53. Safeguards relating to retention and disclosure of material** (1) The issuing authority must ensure, in relation to every targeted interception warrant or mutual assistance warrant issued by that authority, that arrangements are in force for securing that the requirements of subsections (2) and (5) are met in relation to the material obtained under the warrant.

This is subject to subsection (9).

(2) The requirements of this subsection are met in relation to the material obtained under a warrant if each of the following is limited to the minimum that is necessary for the authorised purposes (see subsection (3))—

(a) the number of persons to whom any of the material is disclosed or otherwise made available;

(b) the extent to which any of the material is disclosed or otherwise made available;

(c) the extent to which any of the material is copied;

(d) the number of copies that are made.

(3) For the purposes of this section something is necessary for the authorised purposes if, and only if—

(a) it is, or is likely to become, necessary on any of the grounds falling within section 20 on which a warrant under Chapter 1 of this Part may be necessary,

(b) it is necessary for facilitating the carrying out of any functions under this Act of the Secretary of State, the Scottish Ministers or the person to whom the warrant is or was addressed,

(c) it is necessary for facilitating the carrying out of any functions of the Judicial Commissioners or the Investigatory Powers Tribunal under or in relation to this Act,

(d) it is necessary to ensure that a person ("P") who is conducting a criminal prosecution has the information P needs to determine what is required of P by P's duty to secure the fairness of the prosecution, or

(e) it is necessary for the performance of any duty imposed on any person by the Public Records Act 1958 or the Public Records Act (Northern Ireland) 1923.

(4) The arrangements for the time being in force under this section for securing that the requirements of subsection (2) are met in relation to the material obtained under the warrant must include arrangements for securing that every copy made of any of that material is stored, for so long as it is retained, in a secure manner.

(5) The requirements of this subsection are met in relation to the material obtained under a warrant if every copy made of any of that material (if not destroyed earlier) is destroyed as soon as there are no longer any relevant grounds for retaining it (see subsection (6)).

(6) For the purposes of subsection (5), there are no longer any relevant grounds for retaining a copy of any material if, and only if—

(a) its retention is not necessary, or not likely to become necessary, on any of the grounds falling within section 20 on which a warrant under Chapter 1 of this Part may be necessary, and

(b) its retention is not necessary for any of the purposes mentioned in paragraphs (b) to (e) of subsection (3) above.

(7) Where—

(a) a communication which has been intercepted in accordance with a targeted interception warrant or mutual assistance warrant is retained, following its examination, for purposes other than the destruction of the communication, and

(b) it is a communication that contains confidential journalistic material or identifies a source of journalistic information,

the person to whom the warrant is addressed must inform the Investigatory Powers Commissioner as soon as is reasonably practicable.

(8) Subsection (9) applies if—

(a) any material obtained under the warrant has been handed over to any overseas authorities, or

(b) a copy of any such material has been given to any overseas authorities.

(9) To the extent that the requirements of subsections (2) and (5) relate to any of the material mentioned in subsection (8)(a), or to the copy mentioned in subsection (8)(b), the arrangements made for the purposes of this section are not required to secure that those requirements are met (see instead section 54).

(10) In this section—

"copy", in relation to material obtained under a warrant, means any of the following (whether or not in documentary form)—

(a) any copy, extract or summary of the material which identifies the material as having been obtained under the warrant, and

(b) any record which—

and "copied" is to be read accordingly;

(i) refers to any interception or to the obtaining of any material, and

(ii) is a record of the identities of the persons to or by whom the material was sent, or to whom the material relates,

"the issuing authority" means—

(a) the Secretary of State, in the case of warrants issued by the Secretary of State;

(b) the Scottish Ministers, in the case of warrants issued by the Scottish Ministers;

"overseas authorities" means authorities of a country or territory outside the United Kingdom.

[Investigatory Powers Act 2016, s 53.]

---

[1] Chapter 3 contains ss 53–60.

7.11231ZG **54. Safeguards relating to disclosure of material overseas** (1) The issuing authority must ensure, in relation to every targeted interception warrant or mutual assistance warrant issued by that authority, that arrangements are in force for securing that—

(a) any material obtained under the warrant is handed over to overseas authorities only if the requirements of subsection (2) are met, and

(b) copies of any such material are given to overseas authorities only if those requirements are met.

(2) The requirements of this subsection are met in the case of a warrant if it appears to the issuing authority—

(a) that requirements corresponding to the requirements of section 53(2) and (5) will apply, to such extent (if any) as the issuing authority considers appropriate, in relation to any of the material which is handed over, or any copy of which is given, to the authorities in question, and

(b) that restrictions are in force which would prevent, to such extent (if any) as the issuing authority considers appropriate, the doing of anything in, for the purposes of or in connection with any proceedings outside the United Kingdom which would result in a prohibited disclosure.

(3) In subsection (2)(b) "prohibited disclosure" means a disclosure which, if made in the United Kingdom, would breach the prohibition in section 56(1).

(4) In this section—

"copy" has the same meaning as in section 53;

"the issuing authority" means—

(a) the Secretary of State, in the case of warrants issued by the Secretary of State;

(b) the Scottish Ministers, in the case of warrants issued by the Scottish Ministers;

"overseas authorities" means authorities of a country or territory outside the United Kingdom.

[Investigatory Powers Act 2016, s 54.]

7.11231ZH **55. Additional safeguards for items subject to legal privilege** (1) This section applies where an item subject to legal privilege which has been intercepted in accordance with a targeted interception warrant or mutual assistance warrant is retained, following its examination, for purposes other than the destruction of the item.

(2) The person to whom the warrant is addressed must inform the Investigatory Powers Commissioner of the retention of the item as soon as is reasonably practicable.

(3) Unless the Investigatory Powers Commissioner considers that subsection (5) applies to the item, the Commissioner must—

(a) direct that the item is destroyed, or

(b) impose one or more conditions as to the use or retention of that item.

(4) If the Investigatory Powers Commissioner considers that subsection (5) applies to the item,

the Commissioner may nevertheless impose such conditions under subsection (3)(b) as the Commissioner considers necessary for the purpose of protecting the public interest in the confidentiality of items subject to legal privilege.

(5) This subsection applies to an item subject to legal privilege if—

(a) the public interest in retaining the item outweighs the public interest in the confidentiality of items subject to legal privilege, and

(b) retaining the item is necessary in the interests of national security or for the purpose of preventing death or significant injury.

(6) The Investigatory Powers Commissioner—

(a) may require an affected party to make representations about how the Commissioner should exercise any function under subsection (3), and

(b) must have regard to any such representations made by an affected party (whether or not as a result of a requirement imposed under paragraph (a)).

(7) Each of the following is an "affected party" for the purposes of subsection (6)—

(a) the person who decided to issue the warrant;

(b) the person to whom the warrant is or was addressed.

[Investigatory Powers Act 2016, s 55.]

7.11231ZI **56. Exclusion of matters from legal proceedings etc** (1) No evidence may be adduced, question asked, assertion or disclosure made or other thing done in, for the purposes of or in connection with any legal proceedings or Inquiries Act proceedings which (in any manner)—

(a) discloses, in circumstances from which its origin in interception-related conduct may be inferred—

(i) any content of an intercepted communication, or

(ii) any secondary data obtained from a communication, or

(b) tends to suggest that any interception-related conduct has or may have occurred or may be going to occur.

This is subject to Schedule 3 (exceptions).

(2) "Interception-related conduct" means—

(a) conduct by a person within subsection (3) that is, or in the absence of any lawful authority would be, an offence under section 3(1) (offence of unlawful interception);

(b) a breach of the prohibition imposed by section 9 (restriction on requesting interception by overseas authorities);

(c) a breach of the prohibition imposed by section 10 (restriction on requesting assistance under mutual assistance agreements etc);

(d) the making of an application by any person for a warrant, or the issue of a warrant, under Chapter 1 of this Part;

(e) the imposition of any requirement on any person to provide assistance in giving effect to a targeted interception warrant or mutual assistance warrant.

(3) The persons referred to in subsection (2)(a) are—

(a) any person who is an intercepting authority (see section 18);

(b) any person holding office under the Crown;

(c) any person deemed to be the proper officer of Revenue and Customs by virtue of section 8(2) of the Customs and Excise Management Act 1979;

(d) any person employed by, or for the purposes of, a police force;

(e) any postal operator or telecommunications operator;

(f) any person employed or engaged for the purposes of the business of a postal operator or telecommunications operator.

(4) Any reference in subsection (1) to interception-related conduct also includes any conduct taking place before the coming into force of this section and consisting of—

(a) conduct by a person within subsection (3) that—

(i) was an offence under section 1(1) or (2) of the Regulation of Investigatory Powers Act 2000 ("RIPA"), or

(ii) would have been such an offence in the absence of any lawful authority (within the meaning of section 1(5) of RIPA);

(b) conduct by a person within subsection (3) that—

(i) was an offence under section 1 of the Interception of Communications Act 1985, or

(ii) would have been such an offence in the absence of subsections (2) and (3) of that section;

(c) a breach by the Secretary of State of the duty under section 1(4) of RIPA (restriction on requesting assistance under mutual assistance agreements);

(d) the making of an application by any person for a warrant, or the issue of a warrant, under—

(i) Chapter 1 of Part 1 of RIPA, or

(ii) the Interception of Communications Act 1985;

(e) the imposition of any requirement on any person to provide assistance in giving effect to a warrant under Chapter 1 of Part 1 of RIPA.

(5) In this section—

"Inquiries Act proceedings" means proceedings of an inquiry under the Inquiries Act 2005;

"intercepted communication" means any communication intercepted in the course of its transmission by means of a postal service or telecommunication system.

[Investigatory Powers Act 2016, s 56.]

**7.11231ZJ 57. Duty not to make unauthorised disclosures** (1) A person to whom this section applies must not make an unauthorised disclosure to another person.

(2) A person makes an unauthorised disclosure for the purposes of this section if—

(a) the person discloses any of the matters within subsection (4) in relation to—

(i) a warrant under Chapter 1 of this Part, or

(ii) a warrant under Chapter 1 of Part 1 of the Regulation of Investigatory Powers Act 2000, and

(b) the disclosure is not an excepted disclosure (see section 58).

(3) This section applies to the following persons—

(a) any person who is an intercepting authority (see section 18);

(b) any person holding office under the Crown;

(c) any person employed by, or for the purposes of, a police force;

(d) any postal operator or telecommunications operator;

(e) any person employed or engaged for the purposes of the business of a postal operator or telecommunications operator;

(f) any person to whom any of the matters within subsection (4) have been disclosed in relation to a warrant mentioned in subsection (2)(a).

(4) The matters referred to in subsection (2)(a) are—

(a) the existence or contents of the warrant;

(b) the details of the issue of the warrant or of any renewal or modification of the warrant;

(c) the existence or contents of any requirement to provide assistance in giving effect to the warrant;

(d) the steps taken in pursuance of the warrant or of any such requirement;

(e) any of the material obtained under the warrant.

[Investigatory Powers Act 2016, s 57.]

**7.11231ZK 58. Section 57: meaning of "excepted disclosure"** (1) For the purposes of section 57 a disclosure made in relation to a warrant is an "excepted disclosure" if it falls within any of the Heads set out in—

(a) subsection (2) (disclosures authorised by warrant etc);

(b) subsection (4) (oversight bodies);

(c) subsection (5) (legal advisers);

(d) subsection (8) (disclosures of a general nature).

(2) Head 1 is—

(a) a disclosure authorised by the warrant;

(b) a disclosure authorised by the person to whom the warrant is or was addressed or under any arrangements made by that person for the purposes of this section;

(c) a disclosure authorised by the terms of any requirement to provide assistance in giving effect to the warrant (including any requirement for disclosure imposed by virtue of section 41(5) or, in the case of a warrant under Chapter 1 of Part 1 of the Regulation of Investigatory Powers Act 2000 ("RIPA"), section 11(9) of RIPA).

(3) But subsection (2)(b) does not apply in the case of a mutual assistance warrant that is or was addressed to a person falling within section 18(1)(h) (competent authorities of overseas countries or territories).

(4) Head 2 is—

(a) in the case of a warrant under Chapter 1 of this Part, a disclosure made to, or authorised by, a Judicial Commissioner;

(b) in the case of a warrant under Chapter 1 of Part 1 of RIPA, a disclosure made to, or authorised by, the Interception of Communications Commissioner or a Judicial Commissioner;

(c) a disclosure made to the Independent Police Complaints Commission for the purposes of facilitating the carrying out of any of its functions;

(d) a disclosure made to the Intelligence and Security Committee of Parliament for the purposes of facilitating the carrying out of any of its functions.

(5) Head 3 is—

(a) a disclosure made by a legal adviser—

(i) in contemplation of, or in connection with, any legal proceedings, and

(ii) for the purposes of those proceedings;

(b) a disclosure made—

(i) by a professional legal adviser ("L") to L's client or a representative of L's client, or

(ii) by L's client, or by a representative of L's client, to L,

in connection with the giving, by L to L's client, of advice about the effect of the relevant provisions (see subsection (7)).

(6) But a disclosure within Head 3 is not an excepted disclosure if it is made with the intention of furthering a criminal purpose.

(7) In subsection (5)(b) "the relevant provisions" means—

(a) in the case of a warrant under Chapter 1 of this Part, the provisions of this Part;

(b) in the case of a warrant under Chapter 1 of Part 1 of RIPA, the provisions of that Chapter.

(8) Head 4 is—

(a) a disclosure that—

(i) is made by a postal operator or a telecommunications operator in accordance with a requirement imposed by regulations made by the Secretary of State, and

(ii) consists of statistical information of a description specified in the regulations;

(b) a disclosure of information that does not relate to any particular warrant under Chapter 1 of this Part or under Chapter 1 of Part 1 of RIPA but relates to any such warrants in general.

(9) Nothing in this section affects the operation of section 56 (which, among other things, prohibits the making of certain disclosures in, for the purposes of or in connection with legal proceedings).

[Investigatory Powers Act 2016, s 58.]

**7.11231ZL 59. Offence of making unauthorised disclosures** (1) A person who fails to comply with section 57(1) commits an offence.

(2) A person who is guilty of an offence under this section is liable—

(a) on summary conviction in England and Wales—

(i) to imprisonment for a term not exceeding 12 months (or 6 months, if the offence was committed before the commencement of section 154(1) of the Criminal Justice Act 2003), or

(ii) to a fine,

or to both;

(b) on summary conviction in Scotland—

(i) to imprisonment for a term not exceeding 12 months, or

(ii) to a fine not exceeding the statutory maximum,

or to both;

(c) on summary conviction in Northern Ireland—

(i) to imprisonment for a term not exceeding 6 months, or

(ii) to a fine not exceeding the statutory maximum,

or to both;

(d) on conviction on indictment, to imprisonment for a term not exceeding 5 years or to a fine, or to both[1].

(3) In proceedings against any person for an offence under this section in respect of any disclosure, it is a defence for the person to show that the person could not reasonably have been expected, after first becoming aware of the matter disclosed, to take steps to prevent the disclosure.

[Investigatory Powers Act 2016, s 59.]

---

1 For procedure in respect of an offence triable either way, see the Magistrates' Courts Act 1980, s 17A-21, in PART 1: MAGISTRATES' COURTS, PROCEDURE, ante.

*Interpretation*

**7.11231ZM 60. Part 2: interpretation** (1) In this Part—

"EU mutual assistance instrument" has the meaning given by section 10(3);

"intercepting authority" is to be read in accordance with section 18;

"international mutual assistance agreement" has the meaning given by section 10(3);

"mutual assistance warrant" has the meaning given by section 15(4);

"police force" means any of the following—

(a) any police force maintained under section 2 of the Police Act 1996;

(b) the metropolitan police force;

(c) the City of London police force;

(d) the Police Service of Scotland;

(e) the Police Service of Northern Ireland;

(f) the Ministry of Defence Police;

(g) the Royal Navy Police;

(h) the Royal Military Police;

(i) the Royal Air Force Police;

(j) the British Transport Police Force;

"relevant content", in relation to a targeted examination warrant, has the meaning given by section 15(3);

"relevant Scottish application" has the meaning given by section 22;

"secondary data" has the meaning given by section 16, and references to obtaining secondary data from a communication are to be read in accordance with that section;

"targeted examination warrant" has the meaning given by section 15(3).

(2) In this Part references to a member of a police force, in relation to the Royal Navy Police, the Royal Military Police or the Royal Air Force Police, do not include any member of that force who is not for the time being attached to, or serving with, that force or another of those police forces.

(3) See also—

section 261 (telecommunications definitions),

section 262 (postal definitions),

section 263 (general definitions),

section 264 (general definitions: "journalistic material" etc),

section 265 (index of defined expressions).

[Investigatory Powers Act 2016, s 60.]

## PART 3[1]
## AUTHORISATIONS FOR OBTAINING COMMUNICATIONS DATA[2]

### *Targeted authorisations for obtaining data*

7.11231ZN **61. Power to grant authorisations** (1) Subsection (2) applies if a designated senior officer of a relevant public authority considers—

(a) that it is necessary to obtain communications data for a purpose falling within subsection (7),

(b) that it is necessary to obtain the data—

(i) for the purposes of a specific investigation or a specific operation, or

(ii) for the purposes of testing, maintaining or developing equipment, systems or other capabilities relating to the availability or obtaining of communications data, and

(c) that the conduct authorised by the authorisation is proportionate to what is sought to be achieved.

(2) The designated senior officer may authorise any officer of the authority to engage in any conduct which—

(a) is for the purpose of obtaining the data from any person, and

(b) relates to—

(i) a telecommunication system, or

(ii) data derived from a telecommunication system.

(3) Subsections (1) and (2) are subject to—

(a) section 62 (restrictions in relation to internet connection records),

(b) section 63 (additional restrictions on grant of authorisations),

(c) sections 70 and 73 to 75 and Schedule 4 (restrictions relating to certain relevant public authorities),

(d) section 76 (requirement to consult a single point of contact), and

(e) section 77 (Commissioner approval for authorisations to identify or confirm journalistic sources).

(4) Authorised conduct may, in particular, consist of an authorised officer—

(a) obtaining the communications data themselves from any person or telecommunication system,

(b) asking any person whom the authorised officer believes is, or may be, in possession of the communications data or capable of obtaining it—

(i) to obtain the data (if not already in possession of it), and

(ii) to disclose the data (whether already in the person's possession or subsequently obtained by that person) to a person identified by, or in accordance with, the authorisation, or

(c) requiring by notice a telecommunications operator whom the authorised officer believes is, or may be, in possession of the communications data or capable of obtaining it—

(i) to obtain the data (if not already in possession of it), and

(ii) to disclose the data (whether already in the operator's possession or subsequently obtained by the operator) to a person identified by, or in accordance with, the authorisation.

(5) An authorisation—

(a) may relate to data whether or not in existence at the time of the authorisation,

(b) may authorise the obtaining or disclosure of data by a person who is not an authorised officer, or any other conduct by such a person, which enables or facilitates the obtaining of the communications data concerned, and

(c) may, in particular, require a telecommunications operator who controls or provides a telecommunication system to obtain or disclose data relating to the use of a telecommunications service provided by another telecommunications operator in relation to that system.

(6) An authorisation—

(a) may not authorise any conduct consisting in the interception of communications in the course of their transmission by means of a telecommunication system, and

(b) may not authorise an authorised officer to ask or require, in the circumstances mentioned in subsection (4)(b) or (c), a person to disclose the data to any person other than—

(i) an authorised officer, or

(ii) an officer of the same relevant public authority as an authorised officer.

(7) It is necessary to obtain communications data for a purpose falling within this subsection if it is necessary to obtain the data—

(a) in the interests of national security,

(b) for the purpose of preventing or detecting crime or of preventing disorder,

(c) in the interests of the economic well-being of the United Kingdom so far as those interests are also relevant to the interests of national security,

(d) in the interests of public safety,

(e) for the purpose of protecting public health,

(f) for the purpose of assessing or collecting any tax, duty, levy or other imposition, contribution or charge payable to a government department,

(g) for the purpose of preventing death or injury or any damage to a person's physical or mental health, or of mitigating any injury or damage to a person's physical or mental health,

(h) to assist investigations into alleged miscarriages of justice,

(i) where a person ("P") has died or is unable to identify themselves because of a physical or mental condition—

(i) to assist in identifying P, or

(ii) to obtain information about P's next of kin or other persons connected with P or about the reason for P's death or condition, or

(j) for the purpose of exercising functions relating to—

(i) the regulation of financial services and markets, or

(ii) financial stability.

(8) The fact that the communications data which would be obtained in pursuance of an authorisation relates to the activities in the British Islands of a trade union is not, of itself, sufficient to establish that it is necessary to obtain the data for a purpose falling within subsection (7).

(9) See—

(a) sections 70 and 73 for the meanings of "designated senior officer" and "relevant public authority";

(b) section 84 for the way in which this Part applies to postal operators and postal services.

[Investigatory Powers Act 2016, s 61.]

---

1 PART 3 contains ss 61-96.

2 Communications data' is defined in s 261(5) and is described in the explanatory notes to the Act as the 'who', 'when', 'where' and 'how' of a communication, but not its content.

**7.11231ZO 62. Restrictions in relation to internet connection records** (1) A designated senior officer of a local authority may not grant an authorisation for the purpose of obtaining data which is, or can only be obtained by processing, an internet connection record.

(2) A designated senior officer of a relevant public authority which is not a local authority may not grant an authorisation for the purpose of obtaining data which is, or can only be obtained by processing, an internet connection record unless condition A, B or C is met.

(3) Condition A is that the designated senior officer considers that it is necessary, for a purpose falling within section 61(7), to obtain the data to identify which person or apparatus is using an internet service where—

(a) the service and time of use are already known, but

(b) the identity of the person or apparatus using the service is not known.

(4) Condition B is that—

(a) the purpose for which the data is to be obtained falls within section 61(7) but is not the purpose falling within section 61(7)(b) of preventing or detecting crime, and

(b) the designated senior officer considers that it is necessary to obtain the data to identify—

(i) which internet communications service is being used, and when and how it is being used, by a person or apparatus whose identity is already known,

(ii) where or when a person or apparatus whose identity is already known is obtaining access to, or running, a computer file or computer program which wholly or mainly involves making available, or acquiring, material whose possession is a crime, or

(iii) which internet service is being used, and when and how it is being used, by a person or apparatus whose identity is already known.

(5) Condition C is that—

(a) the purpose for which the data is to be obtained is the purpose falling within section 61(7)(b) of preventing or detecting crime,
(b) the crime to be prevented or detected is serious crime or other relevant crime, and
(c) the designated senior officer considers that it is necessary to obtain the data to identify—
(i) which internet communications service is being used, and when and how it is being used, by a person or apparatus whose identity is already known,
(ii) where or when a person or apparatus whose identity is already known is obtaining access to, or running, a computer file or computer program which wholly or mainly involves making available, or acquiring, material whose possession is a crime, or
(iii) which internet service is being used, and when and how it is being used, by a person or apparatus whose identity is already known.

(6) In subsection (5) "other relevant crime" means crime which is not serious crime but where the offence, or one of the offences, which is or would be constituted by the conduct concerned is—
(a) an offence for which an individual who has reached the age of 18 (or, in relation to Scotland or Northern Ireland, 21) is capable of being sentenced to imprisonment for a term of 12 months or more (disregarding any enactment prohibiting or restricting the imprisonment of individuals who have no previous convictions), or
(b) an offence—
(i) by a person who is not an individual, or
(ii) which involves, as an integral part of it, the sending of a communication or a breach of a person's privacy.

(7) In this Act "internet connection record" means communications data which—
(a) may be used to identify, or assist in identifying, a telecommunications service to which a communication is transmitted by means of a telecommunication system for the purpose of obtaining access to, or running, a computer file or computer program, and
(b) comprises data generated or processed by a telecommunications operator in the process of supplying the telecommunications service to the sender of the communication (whether or not a person).

[Investigatory Powers Act 2016, s 62.]

**7.11231ZP 63. Additional restrictions on grant of authorisations** (1) A designated senior officer may not grant an authorisation for the purposes of a specific investigation or a specific operation if the officer is working on that investigation or operation.

(2) But, if the designated senior officer considers that there are exceptional circumstances which mean that subsection (1) should not apply in a particular case, that subsection does not apply in that case.

(3) Examples of exceptional circumstances include—
(a) an imminent threat to life or another emergency,
(b) the investigation or operation concerned is one where there is an exceptional need, in the interests of national security, to keep knowledge of it to a minimum,
(c) there is an opportunity to obtain information where—
(i) the opportunity is rare,
(ii) the time to act is short, and
(iii) the need to obtain the information is significant and in the interests of national security, or
(d) the size of the relevant public authority concerned is such that it is not practicable to have a designated senior officer who is not working on the investigation or operation concerned.

[Investigatory Powers Act 2016, s 63.]

**7.11231ZQ 64. Procedure for authorisations and authorised notices** (1) An authorisation must specify—
(a) the office, rank or position held by the designated senior officer granting it,
(b) the matters falling within section 61(7) by reference to which it is granted,
(c) the conduct that is authorised,
(d) the data or description of data to be obtained, and
(e) the persons or descriptions of persons to whom the data is to be, or may be, disclosed or how to identify such persons.

(2) An authorisation which authorises a person to impose requirements by notice on a telecommunications operator must also specify—
(a) the operator concerned, and
(b) the nature of the requirements that are to be imposed,

but need not specify the other contents of the notice.

(3) The notice itself—
(a) must specify—
(i) the office, rank or position held by the person giving it,
(ii) the requirements that are being imposed, and

(iii) the telecommunications operator on whom the requirements are being imposed, and

(b) must be given in writing or (if not in writing) in a manner that produces a record of its having been given.

(4) An authorisation must be applied for, and granted, in writing or (if not in writing) in a manner that produces a record of its having been applied for or granted.

[Investigatory Powers Act 2016, s 64.]

**7.11231ZR 65. Duration and cancellation of authorisations and notices** (1) An authorisation ceases to have effect at the end of the period of one month beginning with the date on which it is granted.

(2) An authorisation may be renewed at any time before the end of that period by the grant of a further authorisation.

(3) Subsection (1) has effect in relation to a renewed authorisation as if the period of one month mentioned in that subsection did not begin until the end of the period of one month applicable to the authorisation that is current at the time of the renewal.

(4) A designated senior officer who has granted an authorisation—

(a) may cancel it at any time, and

(b) must cancel it if the designated senior officer considers that the requirements of this Part would not be satisfied in relation to granting an equivalent new authorisation.

(5) The Secretary of State may by regulations provide for the person by whom any function under subsection (4) is to be exercised where the person who would otherwise have exercised it is no longer available to do so.

(6) Such regulations may, in particular, provide for the person by whom the function is to be exercised to be a person appointed in accordance with the regulations.

(7) A notice given in pursuance of an authorisation (and any requirement imposed by the notice)—

(a) is not affected by the authorisation subsequently ceasing to have effect under subsection (1), but

(b) is cancelled if the authorisation is cancelled under subsection (4).

[Investigatory Powers Act 2016, s 65.]

**7.11231ZS 66. Duties of telecommunications operators in relation to authorisations** (1) It is the duty of a telecommunications operator on whom a requirement is imposed by notice given in pursuance of an authorisation to comply with that requirement.

(2) It is the duty of a telecommunications operator who is obtaining or disclosing communications data, in response to a request or requirement for the data in pursuance of an authorisation, to obtain or disclose the data in a way that minimises the amount of data that needs to be processed for the purpose concerned.

(3) A person who is under a duty by virtue of subsection (1) or (2) is not required to take any steps in pursuance of that duty which it is not reasonably practicable for that person to take.

(4) For the purposes of subsection (3), where obligations have been imposed on a telecommunications operator ("P") under section 253 (maintenance of technical capability), the steps which it is reasonably practicable for P to take include every step which it would have been reasonably practicable for P to take if P had complied with all of those obligations.

(5) The duty imposed by subsection (1) or (2) is enforceable by civil proceedings by the Secretary of State for an injunction, or for specific performance of a statutory duty under section 45 of the Court of Session Act 1988, or for any other appropriate relief.

[Investigatory Powers Act 2016, s 66.]

*Filtering arrangements for obtaining data*

**7.11231ZT 67. Filtering arrangements for obtaining data** (1) The Secretary of State may establish, maintain and operate arrangements for the purposes of—

(a) assisting a designated senior officer, who is considering whether to grant an authorisation, to determine whether the requirements of this Part in relation to granting the authorisation are satisfied, or

(b) facilitating the lawful, efficient and effective obtaining of communications data from any person by relevant public authorities in pursuance of an authorisation.

(2) Arrangements under subsection (1) ("filtering arrangements") may, in particular, involve the obtaining of communications data in pursuance of an authorisation ("the target data") by means of—

(a) a request to the Secretary of State to obtain the target data on behalf of an authorised officer, and

(b) the Secretary of State—

(i) obtaining the target data or data from which the target data may be derived,

(ii) processing the target data or the data from which it may be derived (and retaining data temporarily for that purpose), and

(iii) disclosing the target data to the person identified for this purpose by, or in accordance with, the authorisation.

(3) Filtering arrangements may, in particular, involve the generation or use by the Secretary of State of information—

(a) for the purpose mentioned in subsection (1)(a), or

(b) for the purposes of—

(i) the support, maintenance, oversight, operation or administration of the arrangements, or

(ii) the functions of the Investigatory Powers Commissioner mentioned in subsection (4) or (5).

(4) Filtering arrangements must involve the generation and retention of such information or documents as the Investigatory Powers Commissioner considers appropriate for the purposes of the functions of the Commissioner under section 229(1) of keeping under review the exercise by public authorities of functions under this Part.

(5) The Secretary of State must consult the Investigatory Powers Commissioner about the principles on the basis of which the Secretary of State intends to establish, maintain or operate any arrangements for the purpose mentioned in subsection (1)(a).

[Investigatory Powers Act 2016, s 67.]

7.11231ZU 68. **Use of filtering arrangements in pursuance of an authorisation** (1) This section applies in relation to the use of the filtering arrangements in pursuance of an authorisation.

(2) The filtering arrangements may be used—

(a) to obtain and disclose communications data in pursuance of an authorisation, only if the authorisation specifically authorises the use of the arrangements to obtain and disclose the data,

(b) to process data in pursuance of an authorisation (and to retain the data temporarily for that purpose), only if the authorisation specifically authorises processing data of that description under the arrangements (and their temporary retention for that purpose).

(3) An authorisation must record the designated senior officer's decision as to—

(a) whether the communications data to be obtained and disclosed in pursuance of the authorisation may be obtained and disclosed by use of the filtering arrangements,

(b) whether the processing of data under the filtering arrangements (and its temporary retention for that purpose) is authorised,

(c) if the processing of data under the filtering arrangements is authorised, the description of data that may be processed.

(4) A designated senior officer must not grant an authorisation which authorises—

(a) use of the filtering arrangements, or

(b) processing under the filtering arrangements,

unless the condition in subsection (5) is met.

(5) The condition is that the designated senior officer (as well as considering that the other requirements of this Part in relation to granting the authorisation are satisfied) considers that what is authorised in relation to the filtering arrangements is proportionate to what is sought to be achieved.

[Investigatory Powers Act 2016, s 68.]

7.11231ZV 69. **Duties in connection with operation of filtering arrangements** (1) The Secretary of State must secure—

(a) that no authorisation data is obtained or processed under the filtering arrangements except for the purposes of an authorisation,

(b) that data which—

(i) has been obtained or processed under the filtering arrangements, and

(ii) is to be disclosed in pursuance of an authorisation or for the purpose mentioned in section 67(1)(a),

is disclosed only to the person to whom the data is to be disclosed in pursuance of the authorisation or (as the case may be) to the designated senior officer concerned,

(c) that any authorisation data which is obtained under the filtering arrangements in pursuance of an authorisation is immediately destroyed—

(i) when the purposes of the authorisation have been met, or

(ii) if at any time it ceases to be necessary to retain the data for the purposes or purpose concerned.

(2) The Secretary of State must secure that data (other than authorisation data) which is retained under the filtering arrangements is disclosed only—

(a) for the purpose mentioned in section 67(1)(a),

(b) for the purposes of support, maintenance, oversight, operation or administration of the arrangements,

(c) to the Investigatory Powers Commissioner for the purposes of the functions of the Commissioner mentioned in section 67(4) or (5), or

(d) otherwise as authorised by law.

(3) The Secretary of State must secure that—

(a) only the Secretary of State and designated individuals are permitted to read, obtain or otherwise process data for the purposes of support, maintenance, oversight, operation or administration of the filtering arrangements, and

(b) no other persons are permitted to access or use the filtering arrangements except in pursuance of an authorisation or for the purpose mentioned in section 67(1)(a).

(4) In subsection (3)(a) "designated" means designated by the Secretary of State; and the Secretary of State may designate an individual only if the Secretary of State thinks that it is necessary for the individual to be able to act as mentioned in subsection (3)(a).

(5) The Secretary of State must—

(a) put in place and maintain an adequate security system to govern access to, and use of, the filtering arrangements and to protect against any abuse of the power of access, and

(b) impose measures to protect against unauthorised or unlawful data retention, processing, access or disclosure.

(6) The Secretary of State must—

(a) put in place and maintain procedures (including the regular testing of relevant software and hardware) to ensure that the filtering arrangements are functioning properly, and

(b) report, as soon as possible after the end of each calendar year, to the Investigatory Powers Commissioner about the functioning of the filtering arrangements during that year.

(7) A report under subsection (6)(b) must, in particular, contain information about the destruction of authorisation data during the calendar year concerned.

(8) If the Secretary of State believes that significant processing errors have occurred giving rise to a contravention of any of the requirements of this Part which relate to the filtering arrangements, the Secretary of State must report that fact immediately to the Investigatory Powers Commissioner.

(9) In this section "authorisation data", in relation to an authorisation, means communications data that is, or is to be, obtained in pursuance of the authorisation or any data from which that data is, or may be, derived.

[Investigatory Powers Act 2016, s 69.]

*Relevant Public Authorities other than Local Authorities*

7.11231ZW **70. Relevant public authorities and designated senior officers etc**

(1) Schedule 4 (relevant public authorities and designated senior officers etc) has effect.

(2) A public authority listed in column 1 of the table in the Schedule is a relevant public authority for the purposes of this Part.

(3) In this Part "designated senior officer", in relation to a relevant public authority listed in column 1 of the table, means an individual who holds with the authority—

(a) an office, rank or position specified in relation to the authority in column 2 of the table, or

(b) an office, rank or position higher than that specified in relation to the authority in column 2 of the table (subject to subsections (4) and (5)).

(4) Subsection (5) applies where an office, rank or position specified in relation to a relevant public authority in column 2 of the table is specified by reference to—

(a) a particular branch, agency or other part of the authority, or

(b) responsibility for functions of a particular description.

(5) A person is a designated senior officer by virtue of subsection (3)(b) only if the person—

(a) holds an office, rank or position in that branch, agency or part, or

(b) has responsibility for functions of that description.

(6) A person who is a designated senior officer of a relevant public authority by virtue of subsection (3) and an entry in column 2 of the table may grant an authorisation—

(a) only for obtaining communications data of the kind specified in the corresponding entry in column 3 of the table, and

(b) only if section 61(1)(a) is met in relation to a purpose within one of the paragraphs of section 61(7) specified in the corresponding entry in column 4 of the table.

(7) Where there is more than one entry in relation to a relevant public authority in column 2 of the table, and a person is a designated senior officer of the authority by virtue of subsection (3) as it applies to more than one of those entries, subsection (6) applies in relation to each entry.

[Investigatory Powers Act 2016, s 70.]

7.11231ZX **71. Power to modify section 70 and Schedule 4** (1) The Secretary of State may by regulations modify section 70 or Schedule 4.

(2) Regulations under subsection (1) may in particular—

(a) add a public authority to, or remove a public authority from, the list in column 1 of the table,

(b) modify an entry in column 2 of the table,

(c) impose or remove restrictions on the authorisations that may be granted by a designated senior officer with a specified public authority,

(d) impose or remove restrictions on the circumstances in which or purposes for which such authorisations may be granted by a designated senior officer.

(3) The power to make regulations under subsection (1) includes power to make such

modifications in any enactment (including this Act) as the Secretary of State considers appropriate in consequence of a person becoming, or ceasing to be, a relevant public authority because of regulations under that subsection.

[Investigatory Powers Act 2016, s 71.]

**7.11231ZY 72. Certain regulations under section 71: supplementary** (1) This section applies to regulations under section 71 other than regulations which do only one or both of the following—

(a) remove a public authority from the list in column 1 of the table in Schedule 4 and make consequential modifications,

(b) modify column 2 of the table in a way that does not involve replacing an office, rank or position specified in that column in relation to a particular public authority with a lower office, rank or position in relation to the same authority.

(2) Before making regulations to which this section applies, the Secretary of State must consult—

(a) the Investigatory Powers Commissioner, and

(b) the public authority to which the modifications relate.

(3) A statutory instrument containing regulations to which this section applies may not be made except in accordance with the enhanced affirmative procedure.

[Investigatory Powers Act 2016, s 72.]

*Local authorities*

**7.11231ZZ 73. Local authorities as relevant public authorities** (1) A local authority is a relevant public authority for the purposes of this Part.

(2) In this Part "designated senior officer", in relation to a local authority, means an individual who holds with the authority—

(a) the position of director, head of service or service manager (or equivalent), or

(b) a higher position.

(3) A designated senior officer of a local authority may grant an authorisation for obtaining communications data only if section 61(1)(a) is met in relation to a purpose within section 61(7)(b).

(4) The Secretary of State may by regulations amend subsection (2).

(5) Before making regulations under subsection (4) which amend subsection (2) so as to replace an office, rank or position specified in that subsection with a lower office, rank or position, the Secretary of State must consult—

(a) the Investigatory Powers Commissioner, and

(b) each local authority to which the amendment relates.

(6) A statutory instrument containing regulations under subsection (4) to which subsection (5) applies may not be made except in accordance with the enhanced affirmative procedure.

(7) Sections 74 and 75 impose further restrictions in relation to the grant of authorisations by local authorities.

[Investigatory Powers Act 2016, s 73.]

**7.11231ZZ1 74. Requirement to be party to collaboration agreement** (1) A designated senior officer of a local authority may not grant an authorisation unless—

(a) the local authority is a party to a collaboration agreement (whether as a supplying authority or a subscribing authority or both), and

(b) that collaboration agreement is certified by the Secretary of State (having regard to guidance given by virtue of section 79(6) and (7)) as being appropriate for the local authority.

(2) A designated senior officer of a local authority may only grant an authorisation to a person within subsection (3).

(3) A person is within this subsection if the person is an officer of a relevant public authority which is a supplying authority under a collaboration agreement to which the local authority is a party.

(4) If the local authority is itself a supplying authority under a collaboration agreement with the result that officers of the local authority are permitted to be granted authorisations by a designated senior officer of a subscribing authority, the persons within subsection (3) include officers of the local authority.

(5) In this section "collaboration agreement", "subscribing authority" and "supplying authority" have the same meaning as in section 78.

[Investigatory Powers Act 2016, s 74.]

**7.11231ZZ2 75. Judicial approval for local authority authorisations** (1) This section applies to an authorisation granted by a designated senior officer of a local authority other than an authorisation to which section 77 applies.

(2) The authorisation is not to take effect until such time (if any) as the relevant judicial authority has made an order under this section approving it.

(3) The local authority may apply to the relevant judicial authority for an order under this section approving the authorisation.

(4) The local authority is not required to give notice of the application to—

(a) any person to whom the authorisation relates, or
(b) that person's legal representatives.

(5) The relevant judicial authority may approve the authorisation if, and only if, the relevant judicial authority considers that—

(a) at the time of the grant, there were reasonable grounds for considering that the requirements of this Part were satisfied in relation to the authorisation, and
(b) at the time when the relevant judicial authority is considering the matter, there are reasonable grounds for considering that the requirements of this Part would be satisfied if an equivalent new authorisation were granted at that time.

(6) Where, on an application under this section, the relevant judicial authority refuses to approve the grant of the authorisation, the relevant judicial authority may make an order quashing the authorisation.

(7) In this section "the relevant judicial authority" means—

(a) in relation to England and Wales, a justice of the peace,
(b) in relation to Scotland, a sheriff, and
(c) in relation to Northern Ireland, a district judge (magistrates' courts) in Northern Ireland.

(8) See also sections 77A and 77B of the Regulation of Investigatory Powers Act 2000 (procedure for orders under this section of a sheriff in Scotland or a district judge (magistrates' courts) in Northern Ireland).

[Investigatory Powers Act 2016, s 75.]

*Additional protections*

7.11231ZZ3 **76. Use of a single point of contact** (1) Before granting an authorisation, the designated senior officer must consult a person who is acting as a single point of contact in relation to the granting of authorisations.

(2) But, if the designated senior officer considers that there are exceptional circumstances which mean that subsection (1) should not apply in a particular case, that subsection does not apply in that case.

(3) Examples of exceptional circumstances include—

(a) an imminent threat to life or another emergency, or
(b) the interests of national security.

(4) A person is acting as a single point of contact if that person—

(a) is an officer of a relevant public authority, and
(b) is responsible for advising—
(i) officers of the relevant public authority about applying for authorisations, or
(ii) designated senior officers of the relevant public authority about granting authorisations.

(5) A person acting as a single point of contact may, in particular, advise an officer of a relevant public authority who is considering whether to apply for an authorisation about—

(a) the most appropriate methods for obtaining data where the data concerned is processed by more than one telecommunications operator,
(b) the cost, and resource implications, for—
(i) the relevant public authority concerned of obtaining the data, and
(ii) the telecommunications operator concerned of disclosing the data,
(c) any unintended consequences of the proposed authorisation, and
(d) any issues as to the lawfulness of the proposed authorisation.

(6) A person acting as a single point of contact may, in particular, advise a designated senior officer who is considering whether to grant an authorisation about—

(a) whether it is reasonably practical to obtain the data sought in pursuance of the proposed authorisation,
(b) the cost, and resource implications, for—
(i) the relevant public authority concerned of obtaining the data, and
(ii) the telecommunications operator concerned of disclosing the data,
(c) any unintended consequences of the proposed authorisation, and
(d) any issues as to the lawfulness of the proposed authorisation.

(7) A person acting as a single point of contact may also provide advice about—

(a) whether requirements imposed by virtue of an authorisation have been met,
(b) the use in support of operations or investigations of communications data obtained in pursuance of an authorisation, and
(c) any other effects of an authorisation.

(8) Nothing in this section prevents a person acting as a single point of contact from also applying for, or being granted, an authorisation or, in the case of a designated senior officer, granting an authorisation.

[Investigatory Powers Act 2016, s 76.]

7.11231ZZ4 **77. Commissioner approval for authorisations to identify or confirm journalistic sources** (1) Subsection (2) applies if—

(a) a designated senior officer has granted an authorisation in relation to the obtaining by a relevant public authority of communications data for the purpose of identifying or confirming a source of journalistic information, and

(b) the authorisation is not necessary because of an imminent threat to life.

(2) The authorisation is not to take effect until such time (if any) as a Judicial Commissioner has approved it.

(3) The relevant public authority for which the authorisation has been granted may apply to a Judicial Commissioner for approval of the authorisation.

(4) The applicant is not required to give notice of the application to—

(a) any person to whom the authorisation relates, or

(b) that person's legal representatives.

(5) A Judicial Commissioner may approve the authorisation if, and only if, the Judicial Commissioner considers that—

(a) at the time of the grant, there were reasonable grounds for considering that the requirements of this Part were satisfied in relation to the authorisation, and

(b) at the time when the Judicial Commissioner is considering the matter, there are reasonable grounds for considering that the requirements of this Part would be satisfied if an equivalent new authorisation were granted at that time.

(6) In considering whether the position is as mentioned in subsection (5)(a) and (b), the Judicial Commissioner must, in particular, have regard to—

(a) the public interest in protecting a source of journalistic information, and

(b) the need for there to be another overriding public interest before a relevant public authority seeks to identify or confirm a source of journalistic information.

(7) Where, on an application under this section, the Judicial Commissioner refuses to approve the grant of the authorisation, the Judicial Commissioner may quash the authorisation.

[Investigatory Powers Act 2016, s 77.]

*Collaboration agreements*

7.11231ZZ5 **78. Collaboration agreements** (1) A collaboration agreement is an agreement (other than a police collaboration agreement) under which—

(a) a relevant public authority ("the supplying authority") puts the services of designated senior officers of that authority or other officers of that authority at the disposal of another relevant public authority ("the subscribing authority") for the purposes of the subscribing authority's functions under this Part, and

(b) either—

(i) a designated senior officer of the supplying authority is permitted to grant authorisations to officers of the subscribing authority,

(ii) officers of the supplying authority are permitted to be granted authorisations by a designated senior officer of the subscribing authority, or

(iii) officers of the supplying authority act as single points of contact for officers of the subscribing authority.

(2) The persons by whom, or to whom, authorisations may be granted (or who may act as single points of contact) under a collaboration agreement are additional to those persons by whom, or to whom, authorisations would otherwise be granted under this Part (or who could otherwise act as single points of contact).

(3) In a case falling within subsection (1)(b)(i)—

(a) section 61 has effect as if—

(i) in subsection (2) the reference to an officer of the authority were a reference to an officer of the subscribing authority, and

(ii) in subsection (6)(b)(ii) the reference to an officer of the same relevant public authority as an authorised officer included a reference to an officer of the supplying authority,

(b) section 63(3)(d) has effect as if the reference to the relevant public authority concerned were a reference to both authorities,

(c) this Part has effect as if the designated senior officer of the supplying authority had the power to grant an authorisation to officers of the subscribing authority, and had other functions in relation to the authorisation, which were the same as (and subject to no greater or lesser restrictions than) the power and other functions which the designated senior officer of the subscribing authority who would otherwise have dealt with the authorisation would have had, and

(d) section 75(1) applies to the authorisation as if it were granted by a designated senior officer of the subscribing authority.

(4) In a case falling within subsection (1)(b)(ii)—

(a) section 61 has effect as if—

(i) in subsection (2) the reference to an officer of the authority were a reference to an officer of the supplying authority, and

(ii) in subsection (6)(b)(ii) the reference to an officer of the same relevant public authority as an authorised officer included a reference to an officer of the subscribing authority, and

(b) section 63(3)(d) has effect as if the reference to the relevant public authority concerned were a reference to both authorities.

(5) In a case falling within subsection (1)(b)(iii), section 76(4)(b) has effect as if the references to the relevant public authority were references to the subscribing authority.

(6) In this section—

"force collaboration provision" has the meaning given by paragraph (a) of section 22A(2) of the Police Act 1996 but as if the reference in that paragraph to a police force included the National Crime Agency,

"police collaboration agreement" means a collaboration agreement under section 22A of the Police Act 1996 which contains force collaboration provision.

[Investigatory Powers Act 2016, s 78.]

7.11231ZZ6 **79. Collaboration agreements: supplementary** (1) A collaboration agreement may provide for payments to be made between parties to the agreement.

(2) A collaboration agreement—

(a) must be in writing,

(b) may be varied by a subsequent collaboration agreement, and

(c) may be brought to an end by agreement between the parties to it.

(3) A person who makes a collaboration agreement must—

(a) publish the agreement, or

(b) publish the fact that the agreement has been made and such other details about it as the person considers appropriate.

(4) A relevant public authority may enter into a collaboration agreement as a supplying authority, a subscribing authority or both (whether or not it would have power to do so apart from this section).

(5) The Secretary of State may, after consulting a relevant public authority, direct it to enter into a collaboration agreement if the Secretary of State considers that entering into the agreement would assist the effective exercise by the authority, or another relevant public authority, of its functions under this Part.

(6) A code of practice under Schedule 7 must include guidance to relevant public authorities about collaboration agreements.

(7) The guidance must include guidance about the criteria the Secretary of State will use in considering whether a collaboration agreement is appropriate for a relevant public authority.

[Investigatory Powers Act 2016, s 79.]

7.11231ZZ7 **80. Police collaboration agreements** (1) This section applies if—

(a) the chief officer of police of an England and Wales police force ("force 1") has entered into a police collaboration agreement for the purposes of a collaborating police force's functions under this Part, and

(b) under the terms of the agreement—

(i) a designated senior officer of force 1 is permitted to grant authorisations to officers of the collaborating police force,

(ii) officers of force 1 are permitted to be granted authorisations by a designated senior officer of the collaborating police force, or

(iii) officers of force 1 act as single points of contact for officers of the collaborating police force.

(2) The persons by whom, or to whom, authorisations may be granted (or who may act as single points of contact) under a police collaboration agreement are additional to those persons by whom, or to whom, authorisations would otherwise be granted under this Part (or who could otherwise act as single points of contact).

(3) In a case falling within subsection (1)(b)(i)—

(a) section 61 has effect as if—

(i) in subsection (2) the reference to an officer of the authority were a reference to an officer of the collaborating police force, and

(ii) in subsection (6)(b)(ii) the reference to an officer of the same relevant public authority as an authorised officer included a reference to an officer of force 1,

(b) section 63(3)(d) has effect as if the reference to the relevant public authority concerned were a reference to force 1 and the collaborating police force, and

(c) this Part has effect as if the designated senior officer of force 1 had the power to grant an authorisation to officers of the collaborating police force, and had other functions in relation to the authorisation, which were the same as (and subject to no greater or lesser restrictions than) the power and other functions which the designated senior officer of the collaborating police force who would otherwise have dealt with the authorisation would have had.

(4) In a case falling within subsection (1)(b)(ii)—

(a) section 61 has effect as if—

(i) in subsection (2) the reference to an officer of the authority were a reference to an officer of force 1, and

(ii) in subsection (6)(b)(ii) the reference to an officer of the same relevant public authority as an authorised officer included a reference to an officer of the collaborating police force, and

(b) section 63(3)(d) has effect as if the reference to the relevant public authority concerned were a reference to force 1 and the collaborating police force.

(5) In a case falling within subsection (1)(b)(iii), section 76(4)(b) has effect as if the references to the relevant public authority were references to the collaborating police force.

(6) In this section—

"collaborating police force", in relation to a police collaboration agreement, means a police force (other than force 1) whose chief officer of police is a party to the agreement,

"England and Wales police force" means—

(a) any police force maintained under section 2 of the Police Act 1996 (police forces in England and Wales outside London),

(b) the metropolitan police force, or

(c) the City of London police force,

"police collaboration agreement" has the same meaning as in section 78 (see subsection (6) of that section),

and references in this section to an England and Wales police force or a police force include the National Crime Agency (and references to the chief officer of police include the Director General of the National Crime Agency).

[Investigatory Powers Act 2016, s 80.]

*Further and supplementary provision*

7.11231ZZ8 **81. Lawfulness of conduct authorised by this Part** (1) Conduct is lawful for all purposes if—

(a) it is conduct in which any person is authorised to engage by an authorisation or required to undertake by virtue of a notice given in pursuance of an authorisation, and

(b) the conduct is in accordance with, or in pursuance of, the authorisation or notice.

(2) A person (whether or not the person so authorised or required) is not to be subject to any civil liability in respect of conduct that—

(a) is incidental to, or is reasonably undertaken in connection with, conduct that is lawful by virtue of subsection (1), and

(b) is not itself conduct for which an authorisation or warrant—

(i) is capable of being granted under any of the enactments mentioned in subsection (3), and

(ii) might reasonably have been expected to have been sought in the case in question.

(3) The enactments referred to in subsection (2)(b)(i) are—

(a) an enactment contained in this Act,

(b) an enactment contained in the Regulation of Investigatory Powers Act 2000,

(c) an enactment contained in Part 3 of the Police Act 1997 (powers of the police and of customs officers), or

(d) section 5 of the Intelligence Services Act 1994 (warrants for the intelligence services).

[Investigatory Powers Act 2016, s 81.]

7.11231ZZ9 **82. Offence of making unauthorised disclosure** (1) It is an offence for a telecommunications operator, or any person employed or engaged for the purposes of the business of a telecommunications operator, to disclose, without reasonable excuse, to any person the existence of—

(a) any requirement imposed on the operator by virtue of this Part to disclose communications data relating to that person, or

(b) any request made in pursuance of an authorisation for the operator to disclose such data.

(2) For the purposes of subsection (1), it is, in particular, a reasonable excuse if the disclosure is made with the permission of the relevant public authority which is seeking to obtain the data from the operator (whether the permission is contained in any notice requiring the operator to disclose the data or otherwise).

(3) A person guilty of an offence under this section is liable—

(a) on summary conviction in England and Wales—

(i) to imprisonment for a term not exceeding 12 months (or 6 months, if the offence was committed before the commencement of section 154(1) of the Criminal Justice Act 2003), or

(ii) to a fine,

or to both;

(b) on summary conviction in Scotland—

(i) to imprisonment for a term not exceeding 12 months, or

(ii) to a fine not exceeding the statutory maximum,

or to both;

(c) on summary conviction in Northern Ireland—

(i) to imprisonment for a term not exceeding 6 months, or

(ii) to a fine not exceeding the statutory maximum,

or to both;

(d) on conviction on indictment, to imprisonment for a term not exceeding 2 years or to a fine, or to both[1].

[Investigatory Powers Act 2016, s 82.]

---

[1] For procedure in respect of an offence triable either way, see the Magistrates' Courts Act 1980, s 17A-21, in PART 1: MAGISTRATES' COURTS, PROCEDURE, ante.

**7.11231ZZ10 84. Application of Part 3 to postal operators and postal services** (1) This Part applies to postal operators and postal services as it applies to telecommunications operators and telecommunications services.

(2) In its application by virtue of subsection (1), this Part has effect as if—

(a) any reference to a telecommunications operator were a reference to a postal operator,

(b) any reference to a telecommunications service were a reference to a postal service,

(c) any reference to a telecommunication system were a reference to a postal service,

(d) sections 61(3)(a) and 62 were omitted, and

(e) in Part 2 of Schedule 4, for "which is entity data" there were substituted "within paragraph (c) of the definition of "communications data" in section 262(3)".

[Investigatory Powers Act 2016, s 84.]

**7.11231ZZ11 85. Extra-territorial application of Part 3** (1) An authorisation may relate to conduct outside the United Kingdom and persons outside the United Kingdom.

(2) A notice given in pursuance of an authorisation may relate to conduct outside the United Kingdom and persons outside the United Kingdom.

(3) Where such a notice is to be given to a person outside the United Kingdom, the notice may be given to the person in any of the following ways (as well as by electronic or other means of service)—

(a) by delivering it to the person's principal office within the United Kingdom or, if the person has no such office in the United Kingdom, to any place in the United Kingdom where the person carries on business or conducts activities,

(b) if the person has specified an address in the United Kingdom as one at which the person, or someone on the person's behalf, will accept documents of the same description as a notice, by delivering it to that address,

(c) by notifying the person by such other means as the authorised officer considers appropriate (which may include notifying the person orally).

(4) In determining for the purposes of subsection (3) of section 66 whether it is reasonably practicable for a telecommunications operator outside the United Kingdom to take any steps in a country or territory outside the United Kingdom for the purpose of complying with a duty imposed by virtue of subsection (1) or (2) of that section, the matters to be taken into account include the following—

(a) any requirements or restrictions under the law of that country or territory that are relevant to the taking of those steps, and

(b) the extent to which it is reasonably practicable to comply with the duty in a way that does not breach any of those requirements or restrictions.

(5) Nothing in the definition of "telecommunications operator" limits the type of communications data in relation to which an authorisation, or a request or requirement of a kind which gives rise to a duty under section 66(1) or (2), may apply.

[Investigatory Powers Act 2016, s 85.]

**7.11231ZZ12 86. Part 3: interpretation** (1) In this Part—

"authorisation" means an authorisation under section 61 (including that section as modified by sections 78 and 80),

"designated senior officer"—

(a) in relation to a relevant public authority which is a local authority, has the meaning given by section 73(2), and

(b) in relation to any other relevant public authority, has the meaning given by section 70(3),

"filtering arrangements" means any arrangements under section 67(1),

"officer", in relation to a relevant public authority, means a person holding an office, rank or position with that authority,

"relevant public authority" means a public authority which is a relevant public authority for the purposes of this Part by virtue of section 70(2) or 73(1).

(2) In this Part "local authority" means—

(a) a district or county council in England,

(b) a London borough council,

(c) the Common Council of the City of London in its capacity as a local authority,
(d) the Council of the Isles of Scilly,
(e) a county council or county borough council in Wales,
(f) a council constituted under section 2 of the Local Government etc (Scotland) Act 1994, and
(g) a district council in Northern Ireland.

(3) See also—
section 261 (telecommunications definitions),
section 262 (postal definitions),
section 263 (general definitions),
section 265 (index of defined expressions).

[Investigatory Powers Act 2016, s 86.]

## PART 4
## RETENTION OF COMMUNICATIONS DATA

*Part 4 (not reproduced) contains ss 87-98. It empowers the Secretary of State to require telecommunications operators to retain communications data for a maximum of 12 months. The Secretary of State's decision must be approved by a Judicial Commissioner.*

## PART 5[1]
## EQUIPMENT INTERFERENCE

### *Warrants under this Part*

7.11231ZZ13 **99. Warrants under this Part: general** (1) There are two kinds of warrants which may be issued under this Part—
(a) targeted equipment interference warrants (see subsection (2));
(b) targeted examination warrants (see subsection (9)).

(2) A targeted equipment interference warrant is a warrant which authorises or requires the person to whom it is addressed to secure interference with any equipment for the purpose of obtaining—
(a) communications (see section 135);
(b) equipment data (see section 100);
(c) any other information.

(3) A targeted equipment interference warrant—
(a) must also authorise or require the person to whom it is addressed to secure the obtaining of the communications, equipment data or other information to which the warrant relates;
(b) may also authorise that person to secure the disclosure, in any manner described in the warrant, of anything obtained under the warrant by virtue of paragraph (a).

(4) The reference in subsections (2) and (3) to the obtaining of communications or other information includes doing so by—
(a) monitoring, observing or listening to a person's communications or other activities;
(b) recording anything which is monitored, observed or listened to.

(5) A targeted equipment interference warrant also authorises the following conduct (in addition to the conduct described in the warrant)—
(a) any conduct which it is necessary to undertake in order to do what is expressly authorised or required by the warrant, including conduct for securing the obtaining of communications, equipment data or other information;
(b) any conduct by any person which is conduct in pursuance of a requirement imposed by or on behalf of the person to whom the warrant is addressed to be provided with assistance in giving effect to the warrant.

(6) A targeted equipment interference warrant may not, by virtue of subsection (3), authorise or require a person to engage in conduct, in relation to a communication other than a stored communication, which would (unless done with lawful authority) constitute an offence under section 3(1) (unlawful interception).

(7) Subsection (5)(a) does not authorise a person to engage in conduct which could not be expressly authorised under the warrant because of the restriction imposed by subsection (6).

(8) In subsection (6), "stored communication" means a communication stored in or by a telecommunication system (whether before or after its transmission).

(9) A targeted examination warrant is a warrant which authorises the person to whom it is addressed to carry out the selection of protected material obtained under a bulk equipment interference warrant for examination, in breach of the prohibition in section 193(4) (prohibition on seeking to identify communications of, or private information relating to, individuals in the British Islands).

In this Part, "protected material", in relation to a targeted examination warrant, means any material obtained under a bulk equipment interference warrant under Chapter 3 of Part 6, other than material which is—
(a) equipment data;

(b) information (other than a communication or equipment data) which is not private information.

(10) For provision enabling the combination of targeted equipment interference warrants with certain other warrants or authorisations (including targeted examination warrants), see Schedule 8.

(11) Any conduct which is carried out in accordance with a warrant under this Part is lawful for all purposes.

[Investigatory Powers Act 2016, s 99.]

---

[1] PART 5 contains ss 99–135. The omitted provisions concern: power to issue warrants; restriction on issue of warrants to certain law enforcement officers; approval of warrants; additional safeguards; requirements of warrants and their duration and renewal; modification of warrants; implementation and service of warrants; and duty of telecommunications operators to assist with implementation.

7.11231ZZ14 **100. Meaning of "equipment data"** (1) In this Part, "equipment data" means—

(a) systems data;

(b) data which falls within subsection (2).

(2) The data falling within this subsection is identifying data which—

(a) is, for the purposes of a relevant system, comprised in, included as part of, attached to or logically associated with a communication (whether by the sender or otherwise) or any other item of information,

(b) is capable of being logically separated from the remainder of the communication or the item of information, and

(c) if it were so separated, would not reveal anything of what might reasonably be considered to be the meaning (if any) of the communication or the item of information, disregarding any meaning arising from the fact of the communication or the existence of the item of information or from any data relating to that fact.

(3) In subsection (2), "relevant system" means any system on or by means of which the data is held.

(4) For the meaning of "systems data" and "identifying data", see section 263.

[Investigatory Powers Act 2016, s 100.]

7.11231ZZ15 **101. Subject-matter of warrants** (1) A targeted equipment interference warrant may relate to any one or more of the following matters—

(a) equipment belonging to, used by or in the possession of a particular person or organisation;

(b) equipment belonging to, used by or in the possession of a group of persons who share a common purpose or who carry on, or may carry on, a particular activity;

(c) equipment belonging to, used by or in the possession of more than one person or organisation, where the interference is for the purpose of a single investigation or operation;

(d) equipment in a particular location;

(e) equipment in more than one location, where the interference is for the purpose of a single investigation or operation;

(f) equipment which is being, or may be, used for the purposes of a particular activity or activities of a particular description;

(g) equipment which is being, or may be, used to test, maintain or develop capabilities relating to interference with equipment for the purpose of obtaining communications, equipment data or other information;

(h) equipment which is being, or may be, used for the training of persons who carry out, or are likely to carry out, such interference with equipment.

(2) A targeted examination warrant may relate to any one or more of the following matters—

(a) a particular person or organisation;

(b) a group of persons who share a common purpose or who carry on, or may carry on, a particular activity;

(c) more than one person or organisation, where the conduct authorised by the warrant is for the purpose of a single investigation or operation;

(d) the testing, maintenance or development of capabilities relating to the selection of protected material for examination;

(e) the training of persons who carry out, or are likely to carry out, the selection of such material for examination.

[Investigatory Powers Act 2016, s 101.]

*Supplementary provision*

7.11231ZZ16 **130. Safeguards relating to disclosure of material overseas** (1) The issuing authority must ensure, in relation to every targeted equipment interference warrant, that arrangements are in force for securing that—

(*a*) any material obtained under the warrant is handed over to overseas authorities only if the requirements of subsection (2) are met, and

(*b*) copies of any such material are given to overseas authorities only if those requirements are met.

(2) The requirements of this subsection are met in the case of a warrant if it appears to the issuing authority that requirements corresponding to the requirements of section 129(2) and (5) will apply, to such extent (if any) as the issuing authority considers appropriate, in relation to any of the material which is handed over, or any copy of which is given, to the authorities in question.

(3) In this section—

"copy" has the same meaning as in section 129;

"issuing authority" also has the same meaning as in that section;

"overseas authorities" means authorities of a country or territory outside the United Kingdom.

[Investigatory Powers Act 2016, s 130.]

7.11231ZZ17 **131. Additional safeguards for items subject to legal privilege** (1) This section applies where an item subject to legal privilege which has been obtained under a targeted equipment interference warrant is retained, following its examination, for purposes other than the destruction of the item.

(2) The person to whom the warrant is addressed must inform the Investigatory Powers Commissioner of the retention of the item as soon as is reasonably practicable.

(3) Unless the Investigatory Powers Commissioner considers that subsection (5) applies to the item, the Commissioner must—

(a) direct that the item is destroyed, or

(b) impose one or more conditions as to the use or retention of that item.

(4) If the Investigatory Powers Commissioner considers that subsection (5) applies to the item, the Commissioner may nevertheless impose such conditions under subsection (3)(b) as the Commissioner considers necessary for the purpose of protecting the public interest in the confidentiality of items subject to legal privilege.

(5) This subsection applies to an item subject to legal privilege if—

(a) the public interest in retaining the item outweighs the public interest in the confidentiality of items subject to legal privilege, and

(b) retaining the item is necessary in the interests of national security or for the purpose of preventing death or significant injury.

(6) The Investigatory Powers Commissioner—

(a) may require an affected party to make representations about how the Commissioner should exercise any function under subsection (3), and

(b) must have regard to any such representations made by an affected party (whether or not as a result of a requirement imposed under paragraph (a)).

(7) Each of the following is an "affected party" for the purposes of subsection (6)—

(a) the issuing authority (within the meaning given by section 129(11));

(b) the person to whom the warrant is or was addressed.

[Investigatory Powers Act 2016, s 131.]

7.11231ZZ18 **132. Duty not to make unauthorised disclosures** (1) A person to whom this section applies must not make an unauthorised disclosure to another person.

(2) A person makes an unauthorised disclosure for the purposes of this section if—

(a) the person discloses any of the matters within subsection (4) in relation to a warrant under this Part, and

(b) the disclosure is not an excepted disclosure (see section 133).

(3) This section applies to the following persons—

(a) any person who may apply for a warrant under this Part;

(b) any person holding office under the Crown;

(c) any person employed by, or for the purposes of, a police force;

(d) any telecommunications operator;

(e) any person employed or engaged for the purposes of any business of a telecommunications operator;

(f) any person to whom any of the matters within subsection (4) have been disclosed in relation to a warrant under this Part.

(4) The matters referred to in subsection (2)(a) are—

(a) the existence or contents of the warrant;

(b) the details of the issue of the warrant or of any renewal or modification of the warrant;

(c) the existence or contents of any requirement to provide assistance in giving effect to the warrant;

(d) the steps taken in pursuance of the warrant or of any such requirement;

(e) any of the material obtained under the warrant in a form which identifies it as having been obtained under a warrant under this Part.

[Investigatory Powers Act 2016, s 132.]

7.11231ZZ19 **133. Section 132: meaning of "excepted disclosure"** (1) For the purposes of section 132, a disclosure made in relation to a warrant is an excepted disclosure if it falls within any of the Heads set out in—

(a) subsection (2) (disclosures authorised by warrant etc);

(b) subsection (3) (oversight bodies);
(c) subsection (4) (legal proceedings);
(d) subsection (6) (disclosures of a general nature).

(2) Head 1 is—

(a) a disclosure authorised by the warrant;
(b) a disclosure authorised by the person to whom the warrant is or was addressed or under any arrangements made by that person for the purposes of this section;
(c) a disclosure authorised by the terms of any requirement to provide assistance in giving effect to the warrant (including any requirement for disclosure imposed by virtue of section 126(4)).

(3) Head 2 is—

(a) a disclosure made to, or authorised by, a Judicial Commissioner;
(b) a disclosure made to the Independent Police Complaints Commission for the purposes of facilitating the carrying out of any of its functions;
(c) a disclosure made to the Intelligence and Security Committee of Parliament for the purposes of facilitating the carrying out of any of its functions.

(4) Head 3 is—

(a) a disclosure made—
(i) in contemplation of, or in connection with, any legal proceedings, and
(ii) for the purposes of those proceedings;
(b) a disclosure made—
(i) by a professional legal adviser ("L") to L's client or a representative of L's client, or
(ii) by L's client, or by a representative of L's client, to L,
in connection with the giving, by L to L's client, of advice about the effect of the provisions of this Part.

(5) But a disclosure within Head 3 is not an excepted disclosure if it is made with the intention of furthering a criminal purpose.

(6) Head 4 is—

(a) a disclosure which—
(i) is made by a telecommunications operator in accordance with a requirement imposed by regulations made by the Secretary of State, and
(ii) consists of statistical information of a description specified in the regulations;
(b) a disclosure of information that does not relate to any particular warrant under this Part but relates to such warrants in general.

[Investigatory Powers Act 2016, s 133.]

**7.11231ZZ20 134. Offence of making unauthorised disclosure** (1) A person commits an offence if—

(a) the person discloses any matter in breach of section 132(1), and
(b) the person knew that the disclosure was in breach of that section.

(2) A person who is guilty of an offence under this section is liable—

(a) on summary conviction in England and Wales—
(i) to imprisonment for a term not exceeding 12 months (or 6 months, if the offence was committed before the commencement of section 154(1) of the Criminal Justice Act 2003), or
(ii) to a fine,
or to both;
(b) on summary conviction in Scotland—
(i) to imprisonment for a term not exceeding 12 months, or
(ii) to a fine not exceeding the statutory maximum,
or to both;
(c) on summary conviction in Northern Ireland—
(i) to imprisonment for a term not exceeding 6 months, or
(ii) to a fine not exceeding the statutory maximum,
or to both;
(d) on conviction on indictment, to imprisonment for a term not exceeding 5 years or to a fine, or to both[1].

(3) In proceedings against any person for an offence under this section in respect of any disclosure, it is a defence for the person to show that the person could not reasonably have been expected, after first becoming aware of the matter disclosed, to take steps to prevent the disclosure.

[Investigatory Powers Act 2016, s 134.]

---

1 For procedure in respect of an offence triable either way, see the Magistrates' Courts Act 1980, s 17A-21, in PART 1: MAGISTRATES' COURTS, PROCEDURE, ante.

**7.11231ZZ21 135. Part 5: interpretation** (1) In this Part—

"communication" includes—

(a) anything comprising speech, music, sounds, visual images or data of any description, and

(b) signals serving either for the impartation of anything between persons, between a person and a thing or between things or for the actuation or control of any apparatus;

"equipment" means equipment producing electromagnetic, acoustic or other emissions or any device capable of being used in connection with such equipment;

"equipment data" has the meaning given by section 100;

"private information" includes information relating to a person's private or family life;

"protected material", in relation to a targeted examination warrant, has the meaning given by section 99(9);

"senior official" means—

(a) in the case of a targeted equipment interference warrant which is or may be issued by the Secretary of State or a law enforcement chief, or in the case of a targeted examination warrant which is or may be issued by the Secretary of State, a member of the Senior Civil Service or a member of the Senior Management Structure of Her Majesty's Diplomatic Service;

(b) in the case of a targeted equipment interference warrant or a targeted examination warrant which is or may be issued by the Scottish Ministers, a member of the staff of the Scottish Administration who is a member of the Senior Civil Service;

"targeted examination warrant" has the meaning given by section 99(9).

(2) See also—

section 261 (telecommunications definitions),

section 263 (general definitions),

section 264 (general definitions: "journalistic material" etc),

section 265 (index of defined expressions).

[Investigatory Powers Act 2016, s 135.]

## PART 6[1]
## BULK WARRANTS

## CHAPTER 1[2]
## BULK INTERCEPTION WARRANTS

*Bulk interception warrants*

**7.11231ZZ22 136. Bulk interception warrants** (1) For the purposes of this Act a "bulk interception warrant" is a warrant issued under this Chapter which meets conditions A and B.

(2) Condition A is that the main purpose of the warrant is one or more of the following—

(a) the interception of overseas-related communications (see subsection (3));

(b) the obtaining of secondary data from such communications (see section 137).

(3) In this Chapter "overseas-related communications" means—

(a) communications sent by individuals who are outside the British Islands, or

(b) communications received by individuals who are outside the British Islands.

(4) Condition B is that the warrant authorises or requires the person to whom it is addressed to secure, by any conduct described in the warrant, any one or more of the following activities—

(a) the interception, in the course of their transmission by means of a telecommunication system, of communications described in the warrant;

(b) the obtaining of secondary data from communications transmitted by means of such a system and described in the warrant;

(c) the selection for examination, in any manner described in the warrant, of intercepted content or secondary data obtained under the warrant;

(d) the disclosure, in any manner described in the warrant, of anything obtained under the warrant to the person to whom the warrant is addressed or to any person acting on that person's behalf.

(5) A bulk interception warrant also authorises the following conduct (in addition to the conduct described in the warrant)—

(a) any conduct which it is necessary to undertake in order to do what is expressly authorised or required by the warrant, including—

(i) the interception of communications not described in the warrant, and

(ii) conduct for obtaining secondary data from such communications;

(b) conduct by any person which is conduct in pursuance of a requirement imposed by or on behalf of the person to whom the warrant is addressed to be provided with assistance in giving effect to the warrant;

(c) any conduct for obtaining related systems data from any telecommunications operator.

(6) For the purposes of subsection (5)(c)—

"related systems data", in relation to a warrant, means systems data relating to a relevant communication or to the sender or recipient, or intended recipient, of a relevant communication (whether or not a person), and

"relevant communication", in relation to a warrant, means—

(a) any communication intercepted in accordance with the warrant in the course of its transmission by means of a telecommunication system, or

(b) any communication from which secondary data is obtained under the warrant.

[Investigatory Powers Act 2016, s 136.]

---

[1] PART 6 contains ss 136–198.

[2] Chapter 1 contains ss 136-157. The omitted provisions concern: power to issue warrants and their approval; requirements of warrants; duration, renewal, modification cancellation and implementation of warrants.

7.11231ZZ23 137. **Obtaining secondary data** (1) This section has effect for the purposes of this Chapter.

(2) References to obtaining secondary data from a communication transmitted by means of a telecommunication system are references to obtaining such data—

(a) while the communication is being transmitted, or

(b) at any time when the communication is stored in or by the system (whether before or after its transmission),

and references to secondary data obtained under a bulk interception warrant are to be read accordingly.

(3) "Secondary data", in relation to a communication transmitted by means of a telecommunication system, means any data falling within subsection (4) or (5).

(4) The data falling within this subsection is systems data which is comprised in, included as part of, attached to or logically associated with the communication (whether by the sender or otherwise).

(5) The data falling within this subsection is identifying data which—

(a) is comprised in, included as part of, attached to or logically associated with the communication (whether by the sender or otherwise),

(b) is capable of being logically separated from the remainder of the communication, and

(c) if it were so separated, would not reveal anything of what might reasonably be considered to be the meaning (if any) of the communication, disregarding any meaning arising from the fact of the communication or from any data relating to the transmission of the communication.

(6) For the meaning of "systems data" and "identifying data", see section 263.

[Investigatory Powers Act 2016, s 137.]

*Restrictions on use or disclosure of material obtained under warrants etc*

7.11231ZZ24 150. **Safeguards relating to retention and disclosure of material** (1) The Secretary of State must ensure, in relation to every bulk interception warrant, that arrangements are in force for securing—

(a) that the requirements of subsections (2) and (5) are met in relation to the material obtained under the warrant, and

(b) that the requirements of section 152 are met in relation to the intercepted content or secondary data obtained under the warrant.

This is subject to subsection (8).

(2) The requirements of this subsection are met in relation to the material obtained under a warrant if each of the following is limited to the minimum that is necessary for the authorised purposes (see subsection (3))—

(a) the number of persons to whom any of the material is disclosed or otherwise made available;

(b) the extent to which any of the material is disclosed or otherwise made available;

(c) the extent to which any of the material is copied;

(d) the number of copies that are made.

(3) For the purposes of subsection (2) something is necessary for the authorised purposes if, and only if—

(a) it is, or is likely to become, necessary in the interests of national security or on any other grounds falling within section 138(2),

(b) it is necessary for facilitating the carrying out of any functions under this Act of the Secretary of State, the Scottish Ministers or the head of the intelligence service to whom the warrant is or was addressed,

(c) it is necessary for facilitating the carrying out of any functions of the Judicial Commissioners or the Investigatory Powers Tribunal under or in relation to this Act,

(d) it is necessary to ensure that a person ("P") who is conducting a criminal prosecution has the information P needs to determine what is required of P by P's duty to secure the fairness of the prosecution, or

(e) it is necessary for the performance of any duty imposed on any person by the Public

Records Act 1958 or the Public Records Act (Northern Ireland) 1923.

(4) The arrangements for the time being in force under this section for securing that the requirements of subsection (2) are met in relation to the material obtained under the warrant must include arrangements for securing that every copy made of any of that material is stored, for so long as it is retained, in a secure manner.

(5) The requirements of this subsection are met in relation to the material obtained under a warrant if every copy made of any of that material (if not destroyed earlier) is destroyed as soon as there are no longer any relevant grounds for retaining it (see subsection (6)).

(6) For the purposes of subsection (5), there are no longer any relevant grounds for retaining a copy of any material if, and only if—

(a) its retention is not necessary, or not likely to become necessary, in the interests of national security or on any other grounds falling within section 138(2), and

(b) its retention is not necessary for any of the purposes mentioned in paragraphs (b) to (e) of subsection (3) above.

(7) Subsection (8) applies if—

(a) any material obtained under the warrant has been handed over to any overseas authorities, or

(b) a copy of any such material has been given to any overseas authorities.

(8) To the extent that the requirements of subsections (2) and (5) and section 152 relate to any of the material mentioned in subsection (7)(a), or to the copy mentioned in subsection (7)(b), the arrangements made for the purposes of this section are not required to secure that those requirements are met (see instead section 151).

(9) In this section—

"copy", in relation to material obtained under a warrant, means any of the following (whether or not in documentary form)—

(a) any copy, extract or summary of the material which identifies the material as having been obtained under the warrant, and

(b) any record which—

and "copied" is to be read accordingly;

(i) refers to any interception or to the obtaining of any material, and

(ii) is a record of the identities of the persons to or by whom the material was sent, or to whom the material relates,

"overseas authorities" means authorities of a country or territory outside the United Kingdom.

[Investigatory Powers Act 2016, s 150.]

**7.11231ZZ25 151. Safeguards relating to disclosure of material overseas** (1) The Secretary of State must ensure, in relation to every bulk interception warrant, that arrangements are in force for securing that—

(a) any material obtained under the warrant is handed over to overseas authorities only if the requirements of subsection (2) are met, and

(b) copies of any such material are given to overseas authorities only if those requirements are met.

(2) The requirements of this subsection are met in the case of a warrant if it appears to the Secretary of State—

(a) that requirements corresponding to the requirements of section 150(2) and (5) and section 152 will apply, to such extent (if any) as the Secretary of State considers appropriate, in relation to any of the material which is handed over, or any copy of which is given, to the authorities in question, and

(b) that restrictions are in force which would prevent, to such extent (if any) as the Secretary of State considers appropriate, the doing of anything in, for the purposes of or in connection with any proceedings outside the United Kingdom which would result in a prohibited disclosure.

(3) In subsection (2)(b) "prohibited disclosure" means a disclosure which, if made in the United Kingdom, would breach the prohibition in section 56(1) (see section 156).

(4) In this section—

"copy" has the same meaning as in section 150;

"overseas authorities" means authorities of a country or territory outside the United Kingdom.

[Investigatory Powers Act 2016, s 151.]

**7.11231ZZ26 152. Safeguards relating to examination of material** (1) For the purposes of section 150 the requirements of this section are met in relation to the intercepted content and secondary data obtained under a warrant if—

(a) the selection of any of the intercepted content or secondary data for examination is carried out only for the specified purposes (see subsection (2)),

(b) the selection of any of the intercepted content or secondary data for examination is necessary and proportionate in all the circumstances, and

(c) the selection of any of the intercepted content for examination meets any of the selection conditions (see subsection (3)).

(2) The selection of intercepted content or secondary data for examination is carried out only

for the specified purposes if the intercepted content or secondary data is selected for examination only so far as is necessary for the operational purposes specified in the warrant in accordance with section 142.

In this subsection "specified in the warrant" means specified in the warrant at the time of the selection of the intercepted content or secondary data for examination.

(3) The selection conditions referred to in subsection (1)(c) are—

(a) that the selection of the intercepted content for examination does not breach the prohibition in subsection (4);

(b) that the person to whom the warrant is addressed considers that the selection of the intercepted content for examination would not breach that prohibition;

(c) that the selection of the intercepted content for examination in breach of that prohibition is authorised by subsection (5);

(d) that the selection of the intercepted content for examination in breach of that prohibition is authorised by a targeted examination warrant issued under Chapter 1 of Part 2.

(4) The prohibition referred to in subsection (3)(a) is that intercepted content may not at any time be selected for examination if—

(a) any criteria used for the selection of the intercepted content for examination are referable to an individual known to be in the British Islands at that time, and

(b) the purpose of using those criteria is to identify the content of communications sent by, or intended for, that individual.

It does not matter for the purposes of this subsection whether the identity of the individual is known.

(5) The selection of intercepted content ("the relevant content") for examination is authorised by this subsection if—

(a) criteria referable to an individual have been, or are being, used for the selection of intercepted content for examination in circumstances falling within subsection (3)(a) or (b),

(b) at any time it appears to the person to whom the warrant is addressed that there has been a relevant change of circumstances in relation to the individual (see subsection (6)) which would mean that the selection of the relevant content for examination would breach the prohibition in subsection (4),

(c) since that time, a written authorisation to examine the relevant content using those criteria has been given by a senior officer, and

(d) the selection of the relevant content for examination is made before the end of the permitted period (see subsection (7)).

(6) For the purposes of subsection (5)(b) there is a relevant change of circumstances in relation to an individual if—

(a) the individual has entered the British Islands, or

(b) a belief by the person to whom the warrant is addressed that the individual was outside the British Islands was in fact mistaken.

(7) In subsection (5)—

"senior officer", in relation to a warrant addressed to the head of an intelligence service, means a member of the intelligence service who—

(a) is a member of the Senior Civil Service or a member of the Senior Management Structure of Her Majesty's Diplomatic Service, or

(b) holds a position in the intelligence service of equivalent seniority to such a member;

"the permitted period" means the period ending with the fifth working day after the time mentioned in subsection (5)(b).

(8) In a case where the selection of intercepted content for examination is authorised by subsection (5), the person to whom the warrant is addressed must notify the Secretary of State that the selection is being carried out.

[Investigatory Powers Act 2016, s 152.]

**7.11231ZZ27 153. Additional safeguards for items subject to legal privilege**

(1) Subsection (2) applies if, in a case where intercepted content obtained under a bulk interception warrant is to be selected for examination—

(a) the selection of the intercepted content for examination meets any of the selection conditions in section 152(3)(a) to (c), and

(b) either—

(i) the purpose, or one of the purposes, of using the criteria to be used for the selection of the intercepted content for examination ("the relevant criteria") is to identify any items subject to legal privilege, or

(ii) the use of the relevant criteria is likely to identify such items.

(2) The intercepted content may be selected for examination using the relevant criteria only if a senior official acting on behalf of the Secretary of State has approved the use of those criteria.

(3) In deciding whether to give an approval under subsection (2) in a case where subsection (1)(b)(i) applies, a senior official must have regard to the public interest in the confidentiality of

items subject to legal privilege.

(4) A senior official may give an approval under subsection (2) only if—

(a) the official considers that the arrangements made for the purposes of section 150 (safeguards relating to retention and disclosure of material) include specific arrangements for the handling, retention, use and destruction of items subject to legal privilege, and

(b) where subsection (1)(b)(i) applies, the official considers that there are exceptional and compelling circumstances that make it necessary to authorise the use of the relevant criteria.

(5) For the purposes of subsection (4)(b), there cannot be exceptional and compelling circumstances that make it necessary to authorise the use of the relevant criteria unless—

(a) the public interest in obtaining the information that would be obtained by the selection of the intercepted content for examination outweighs the public interest in the confidentiality of items subject to legal privilege,

(b) there are no other means by which the information may reasonably be obtained, and

(c) obtaining the information is necessary in the interests of national security or for the purpose of preventing death or significant injury.

(6) Subsection (7) applies if, in a case where intercepted content obtained under a bulk interception warrant is to be selected for examination—

(a) the selection of the intercepted content for examination meets any of the selection conditions in section 152(3)(a) to (c),

(b) the purpose, or one of the purposes, of using the criteria to be used for the selection of the intercepted content for examination ("the relevant criteria") is to identify communications that, if they were not made with the intention of furthering a criminal purpose, would be items subject to legal privilege, and

(c) the person to whom the warrant is addressed considers that the communications ("the targeted communications") are likely to be communications made with the intention of furthering a criminal purpose.

(7) The intercepted content may be selected for examination using the relevant criteria only if a senior official acting on behalf of the Secretary of State has approved the use of those criteria.

(8) A senior official may give an approval under subsection (7) only if the official considers that the targeted communications are likely to be communications made with the intention of furthering a criminal purpose.

(9) Where an item subject to legal privilege which has been intercepted in accordance with a bulk interception warrant is retained following its examination, for purposes other than the destruction of the item, the person to whom the warrant is addressed must inform the Investigatory Powers Commissioner as soon as is reasonably practicable.

(For provision about the grounds for retaining material obtained under a warrant, see section 150.)

(10) Unless the Investigatory Powers Commissioner considers that subsection (12) applies to the item, the Commissioner must—

(a) direct that the item is destroyed, or

(b) impose one or more conditions as to the use or retention of that item.

(11) If the Investigatory Powers Commissioner considers that subsection (12) applies to the item, the Commissioner may nevertheless impose such conditions under subsection (10)(b) as the Commissioner considers necessary for the purpose of protecting the public interest in the confidentiality of items subject to legal privilege.

(12) This subsection applies to an item subject to legal privilege if—

(a) the public interest in retaining the item outweighs the public interest in the confidentiality of items subject to legal privilege, and

(b) retaining the item is necessary in the interests of national security or for the purpose of preventing death or significant injury.

(13) The Investigatory Powers Commissioner—

(a) may require an affected party to make representations about how the Commissioner should exercise any function under subsection (10), and

(b) must have regard to any such representations made by an affected party (whether or not as a result of a requirement imposed under paragraph (a)).

(14) Each of the following is an "affected party" for the purposes of subsection (13)—

(a) the Secretary of State;

(b) the person to whom the warrant is or was addressed.

[Investigatory Powers Act 2016, s 153.]

**7.11231ZZ28 154. Additional safeguard for confidential journalistic material** Where—

(a) a communication which has been intercepted in accordance with a bulk interception warrant is retained, following its examination, for purposes other than the destruction of the communication, and

(b) it is a communication containing confidential journalistic material,

the person to whom the warrant is addressed must inform the Investigatory Powers Commissioner as soon as is reasonably practicable.

(For provision about the grounds for retaining material obtained under a warrant, see section 150.)

[Investigatory Powers Act 2016, s 154.]

**7.11231ZZ29 155. Offence of breaching safeguards relating to examination of material**

(1) A person commits an offence if—

(a) the person selects for examination any intercepted content or secondary data obtained under a bulk interception warrant,

(b) the person knows or believes that the selection of that intercepted content or secondary data for examination does not comply with a requirement imposed by section 152 or 153, and

(c) the person deliberately selects that intercepted content or secondary data for examination in breach of that requirement.

(2) A person guilty of an offence under this section is liable—

(a) on summary conviction in England and Wales—

(i) to imprisonment for a term not exceeding 12 months (or 6 months, if the offence was committed before the commencement of section 154(1) of the Criminal Justice Act 2003), or

(ii) to a fine,

or to both;

(b) on summary conviction in Scotland—

(i) to imprisonment for a term not exceeding 12 months, or

(ii) to a fine not exceeding the statutory maximum,

or to both;

(c) on summary conviction in Northern Ireland—

(i) to imprisonment for a term not exceeding 6 months, or

(ii) to a fine not exceeding the statutory maximum,

or to both;

(d) on conviction on indictment, to imprisonment for a term not exceeding 2 years or to a fine, or to both[1].

(3) No proceedings for any offence which is an offence by virtue of this section may be instituted—

(a) in England and Wales, except by or with the consent of the Director of Public Prosecutions;

(b) in Northern Ireland, except by or with the consent of the Director of Public Prosecutions for Northern Ireland.

[Investigatory Powers Act 2016, s 155.]

[1] For procedure in respect of an offence triable either way, see the Magistrates' Courts Act 1980, s 17A-21, in PART 1: MAGISTRATES' COURTS, PROCEDURE, ante.

**7.11231ZZ30 156. Application of other restrictions in relation to warrants** (1) Section 56 and Schedule 3 (exclusion of matters from legal proceedings etc) apply in relation to bulk interception warrants as they apply in relation to targeted interception warrants.

(2) Sections 57 to 59 (duty not to make unauthorised disclosures) apply in relation to bulk interception warrants as they apply in relation to targeted interception warrants, but as if the reference in section 58(2)(c) to a requirement for disclosure imposed by virtue of section 41(5) were a reference to such a requirement imposed by virtue of section 149(4).

[Investigatory Powers Act 2016, s 156.]

*Interpretation*

**7.11231ZZ31 157. Chapter 1: interpretation** (1) In this Chapter—

"intercepted content", in relation to a bulk interception warrant, means any content of communications intercepted by an interception authorised or required by the warrant;

"overseas-related communications" has the meaning given by section 136;

"secondary data" has the meaning given by section 137, and references to obtaining secondary data from a communication are to be read in accordance with that section;

"senior official" means a member of the Senior Civil Service or a member of the Senior Management Structure of Her Majesty's Diplomatic Service;

"the specified operational purposes" has the meaning given by section 142(11).

(2) See also—

section 261 (telecommunications definitions),

section 263 (general definitions),

section 264 (general definitions: "journalistic material" etc),

section 265 (index of defined expressions).

[Investigatory Powers Act 2016, s 157.]

## Chapter 2[1]

## Bulk Acquisition Warrants

### *Bulk acquisition warrants*

7.11231ZZ32 **158. Power to issue bulk acquisition warrants** (1) The Secretary of State may, on an application made by or on behalf of the head of an intelligence service, issue a bulk acquisition warrant if—

(a) the Secretary of State considers that the warrant is necessary—

(i) in the interests of national security, or

(ii) on that ground and on any other grounds falling within subsection (2),

(b) the Secretary of State considers that the conduct authorised by the warrant is proportionate to what is sought to be achieved by that conduct,

(c) the Secretary of State considers that—

(i) each of the specified operational purposes (see section 161) is a purpose for which the examination of communications data obtained under the warrant is or may be necessary, and

(ii) the examination of such data for each such purpose is necessary on any of the grounds on which the Secretary of State considers the warrant to be necessary,

(d) the Secretary of State considers that satisfactory arrangements made for the purposes of section 171 (safeguards relating to the retention and disclosure of data) are in force in relation to the warrant, and

(e) the decision to issue the warrant has been approved by a Judicial Commissioner.

For the meaning of "head of an intelligence service", see section 263.

(2) A warrant is necessary on grounds falling within this subsection if it is necessary—

(a) for the purpose of preventing or detecting serious crime, or

(b) in the interests of the economic well-being of the United Kingdom so far as those interests are also relevant to the interests of national security (but see subsection (3)).

(3) A warrant may be considered necessary on the ground falling within subsection (2)(b) only if the communications data which it is considered necessary to obtain is communications data relating to the acts or intentions of persons outside the British Islands.

(4) The fact that the communications data which would be obtained under a warrant relates to the activities in the British Islands of a trade union is not, of itself, sufficient to establish that the warrant is necessary in the interests of national security or on that ground and a ground falling within subsection (2).

(5) A bulk acquisition warrant is a warrant which authorises or requires the person to whom it is addressed to secure, by any conduct described in the warrant, any one or more of the activities in subsection (6).

(6) The activities are—

(a) requiring a telecommunications operator specified in the warrant—

(i) to disclose to a person specified in the warrant any communications data which is specified in the warrant and is in the possession of the operator,

(ii) to obtain any communications data specified in the warrant which is not in the possession of the operator but which the operator is capable of obtaining, or

(iii) to disclose to a person specified in the warrant any data obtained as mentioned in sub-paragraph (ii),

(b) the selection for examination, in any manner described in the warrant, of communications data obtained under the warrant,

(c) the disclosure, in any manner described in the warrant, of communications data obtained under the warrant to the person to whom the warrant is addressed or to any person acting on that person's behalf.

(7) A bulk acquisition warrant also authorises the following conduct (in addition to the conduct described in the warrant)—

(a) any conduct which it is necessary to undertake in order to do what is expressly authorised or required by the warrant, and

(b) conduct by any person which is conduct in pursuance of a requirement imposed by or on behalf of the person to whom the warrant is addressed to be provided with assistance in giving effect to the warrant.

(8) A bulk acquisition warrant may relate to data whether or not in existence at the time of the issuing of the warrant.

(9) An application for the issue of a bulk acquisition warrant may only be made on behalf of the head of an intelligence service by a person holding office under the Crown.

[Investigatory Powers Act 2016, s 158.]

---

[1] Chapter 2 contains ss 158-175. The omitted provisions concern: approval of warrants; requirements of warrants, their duration, renewal, modification, cancellation and service.

*Implementation of warrants*

7.11231ZZ33 **170. Duty of operators to assist with implementation** (1) A telecommunications operator that has been served with a copy of a bulk acquisition warrant by (or on behalf of) the implementing authority must take all steps for giving effect to the warrant that are notified to the operator by (or on behalf of) the implementing authority.

This is subject to subsection (3).

(2) Subsection (1) applies whether or not the operator is in the United Kingdom.

(3) The operator is not required to take any steps which it is not reasonably practicable for the operator to take.

(4) Where obligations have been imposed on a telecommunications operator ("P") under section 253 (technical capability notices), for the purposes of subsection (3) the steps which it is reasonably practicable for P to take include every step which it would have been reasonably practicable for P to take if P had complied with all of those obligations.

(5) The duty imposed by subsection (1) is enforceable against a person in the United Kingdom by civil proceedings by the Secretary of State for an injunction, or for specific performance of a statutory duty under section 45 of the Court of Session Act 1988, or for any other appropriate relief.

(6) In this section "the implementing authority" has the same meaning as in section 168.

[Investigatory Powers Act 2016, s 170.]

*Restrictions on use or disclosure of data obtained under warrants etc*

7.11231ZZ34 **171. Safeguards relating to the retention and disclosure of data** (1) The Secretary of State must ensure, in relation to every bulk acquisition warrant, that arrangements are in force for securing—

(a) that the requirements of subsections (2) and (5) are met in relation to the communications data obtained under the warrant, and

(b) that the requirements of section 172 are met in relation to that data.

This is subject to subsection (8).

(2) The requirements of this subsection are met in relation to the communications data obtained under a warrant if each of the following is limited to the minimum that is necessary for the authorised purposes (see subsection (3))—

(a) the number of persons to whom any of the data is disclosed or otherwise made available,

(b) the extent to which any of the data is disclosed or otherwise made available,

(c) the extent to which any of the data is copied,

(d) the number of copies that are made.

(3) For the purposes of subsection (2) something is necessary for the authorised purposes if, and only if—

(a) it is, or is likely to become, necessary in the interests of national security or on any other grounds falling within section 158(2),

(b) it is necessary for facilitating the carrying out of any functions under this Act of the Secretary of State, the Scottish Ministers or the head of the intelligence service to whom the warrant is or was addressed,

(c) it is necessary for facilitating the carrying out of any functions of the Judicial Commissioners or the Investigatory Powers Tribunal under or in relation to this Act,

(d) it is necessary to ensure that a person ("P") who is conducting a criminal prosecution has the information P needs to determine what is required of P by P's duty to secure the fairness of the prosecution,

(e) it is necessary for use as evidence in legal proceedings, or

(f) it is necessary for the performance of any duty imposed on any person by the Public Records Act 1958 or the Public Records Act (Northern Ireland) 1923.

(4) The arrangements for the time being in force under subsection (1) for securing that the requirements of subsection (2) are met in relation to the communications data obtained under the warrant must include arrangements for securing that every copy made of any of that data is stored, for so long as it is retained, in a secure manner.

(5) The requirements of this subsection are met in relation to the communications data obtained under a warrant if every copy made of any of that data (if not destroyed earlier) is destroyed as soon as there are no longer any relevant grounds for retaining it (see subsection (6)).

(6) For the purposes of subsection (5), there are no longer any relevant grounds for retaining a copy of any data if, and only if—

(a) its retention is not necessary, or not likely to become necessary, in the interests of national security or on any other grounds falling within section 158(2), and

(b) its retention is not necessary for any of the purposes mentioned in paragraphs (b) to (f) of subsection (3) above.

(7) Subsection (8) applies if—

(a) any communications data obtained under the warrant has been handed over to any overseas authorities, or

(b) a copy of any such data has been given to any overseas authorities.

(8) To the extent that the requirements of subsections (2) and (5) and section 172 relate to any of the data mentioned in subsection (7)(a), or to the copy mentioned in subsection (7)(b), the arrangements made for the purposes of subsection (1) are not required to secure that those requirements are met.

(9) But the Secretary of State must instead ensure that arrangements are in force for securing that communications data obtained under a bulk acquisition warrant, or any copy of such data, is handed over or given to an overseas authority only if the Secretary of State considers that requirements corresponding to the requirements of subsections (2) and (5) and section 172 will apply, to such extent (if any) as the Secretary of State considers appropriate, in relation to such data or copy.

(10) In this section—

"copy", in relation to communications data obtained under a warrant, means any of the following (whether or not in documentary form)—

(a) any copy, extract or summary of the data which identifies the data as having been obtained under the warrant, and

(b) any record referring to the obtaining of the data which is a record of the identities of the persons to whom the data relates,

and "copied" is to be read accordingly,

"overseas authorities" means authorities of a country or territory outside the United Kingdom.

[Investigatory Powers Act 2016, s 171.]

**7.11231ZZ35 172. Safeguards relating to examination of data** (1) For the purposes of section 171 the requirements of this section are met in relation to the communications data obtained under a warrant if—

(a) any selection of the data for examination is carried out only for the specified purposes (see subsection (2)), and

(b) the selection of any of the data for examination is necessary and proportionate in all the circumstances.

(2) The selection of communications data for examination is carried out only for the specified purposes if the data is selected for examination only so far as is necessary for the operational purposes specified in the warrant in accordance with section 161.

(3) In subsection (2) "specified in the warrant" means specified in the warrant at the time of the selection of the data for examination.

[Investigatory Powers Act 2016, s 172.]

**7.11231ZZ36 173. Offence of breaching safeguards relating to examination of data**

(1) A person commits an offence if—

(a) the person selects for examination any communications data obtained under a bulk acquisition warrant,

(b) the person knows or believes that the selection of that data for examination does not comply with a requirement imposed by section 172, and

(c) the person deliberately selects that data for examination in breach of that requirement.

(2) A person guilty of an offence under this section is liable—

(a) on summary conviction in England and Wales—

(i) to imprisonment for a term not exceeding 12 months (or 6 months, if the offence was committed before the commencement of section 154(1) of the Criminal Justice Act 2003), or

(ii) to a fine,

or to both;

(b) on summary conviction in Scotland—

(i) to imprisonment for a term not exceeding 12 months, or

(ii) to a fine not exceeding the statutory maximum,

or to both;

(c) on summary conviction in Northern Ireland—

(i) to imprisonment for a term not exceeding 6 months, or

(ii) to a fine not exceeding the statutory maximum,

or to both;

(d) on conviction on indictment, to imprisonment for a term not exceeding 2 years or to a fine, or to both[1].

(3) No proceedings for any offence which is an offence by virtue of this section may be instituted—

(a) in England and Wales, except by or with the consent of the Director of Public Prosecutions;

(b) in Northern Ireland, except by or with the consent of the Director of Public Prosecutions for Northern Ireland.

[Investigatory Powers Act 2016, s 173.]

---

1 For procedure in respect of an offence triable either way, see the Magistrates' Courts Act 1980, s 17A-21, in PART 1: MAGISTRATES' COURTS, PROCEDURE, ante.

*Supplementary provision*

7.11231ZZ37 **174. Offence of making unauthorised disclosure** (1) It is an offence for—

(a) a telecommunications operator who is under a duty by virtue of section 170 to assist in giving effect to a bulk acquisition warrant, or

(b) any person employed or engaged for the purposes of the business of such an operator,

to disclose to any person, without reasonable excuse, the existence or contents of the warrant.

(2) For the purposes of subsection (1), it is, in particular, a reasonable excuse if the disclosure is made with the permission of the Secretary of State.

(3) A person guilty of an offence under this section is liable—

(a) on summary conviction in England and Wales—

(i) to imprisonment for a term not exceeding 12 months (or 6 months, if the offence was committed before the commencement of section 154(1) of the Criminal Justice Act 2003), or

(ii) to a fine,

or to both;

(b) on summary conviction in Scotland—

(i) to imprisonment for a term not exceeding 12 months, or

(ii) to a fine not exceeding the statutory maximum,

or to both;

(c) on summary conviction in Northern Ireland—

(i) to imprisonment for a term not exceeding 6 months, or

(ii) to a fine not exceeding the statutory maximum,

or to both;

(d) on conviction on indictment, to imprisonment for a term not exceeding 2 years or to a fine, or to both[1].

[Investigatory Powers Act 2016, s 174.]

---

[1] For procedure in respect of an offence triable either way, see the Magistrates' Courts Act 1980, s 17A-21, in PART 1: MAGISTRATES' COURTS, PROCEDURE, ante.

7.11231ZZ38 **175. Chapter 2: interpretation** (1) In this Chapter—

"communications data" does not include communications data within the meaning given by section 262(3),

"senior official" means—

(a) a member of the Senior Civil Service, or

(b) a member of the Senior Management Structure of Her Majesty's Diplomatic Service,

"the specified operational purposes" has the meaning given by section 161(11).

(2) See also—

section 261 (telecommunications definitions),

section 263 (general definitions),

section 265 (index of defined expressions).

[Investigatory Powers Act 2016, s 175.]

## CHAPTER 3[1]

## BULK EQUIPMENT INTERFERENCE WARRANTS

*Bulk equipment interference warrants*

7.11231ZZ39 **176. Bulk equipment interference warrants: general** (1) For the purposes of this Act, a warrant is a "bulk equipment interference warrant" if—

(a) it is issued under this Chapter;

(b) it authorises or requires the person to whom it is addressed to secure interference with any equipment for the purpose of obtaining—

(i) communications (see section 198);

(ii) equipment data (see section 177);

(iii) any other information; and

(c) the main purpose of the warrant is to obtain one or more of the following—

(i) overseas-related communications;

(ii) overseas-related information;

(iii) overseas-related equipment data.

(2) In this Chapter—

"overseas-related communications" means—

(a) communications sent by individuals who are outside the British Islands, or

(b) communications received by individuals who are outside the British Islands;

"overseas-related information" means information of individuals who are outside the British Islands.

(3) For the purpose of this Chapter, equipment data is "overseas-related equipment data" if—

(a) it forms part of, or is connected with, overseas-related communications or overseas-related information;

(b) it would or may assist in establishing the existence of overseas-related communications or overseas-related information or in obtaining such communications or information;

(c) it would or may assist in developing capabilities in relation to obtaining overseas-related communications or overseas-related information.

(4) A bulk equipment interference warrant—

(a) must authorise or require the person to whom it is addressed to secure the obtaining of the communications, equipment data or other information to which the warrant relates;

(b) may also authorise or require the person to whom it is addressed to secure—

(i) the selection for examination, in any manner described in the warrant, of any material obtained under the warrant by virtue of paragraph (a);

(ii) the disclosure, in any manner described in the warrant, of any such material to the person to whom the warrant is addressed or to any person acting on that person's behalf.

(5) A bulk equipment interference warrant also authorises the following conduct (in addition to the conduct described in the warrant)—

(a) any conduct which it is necessary to undertake in order to do what is expressly authorised or required by the warrant, including conduct for securing the obtaining of communications, equipment data or other information;

(b) any conduct by any person which is conduct in pursuance of a requirement imposed by or on behalf of the person to whom the warrant is addressed to be provided with assistance in giving effect to the warrant.

(6) A bulk equipment interference warrant may not, by virtue of subsection (4)(a), authorise a person to engage in conduct, in relation to a communication other than a stored communication, which would (unless done with lawful authority) constitute an offence under section 3(1) (unlawful interception).

(7) Subsection (5)(a) does not authorise a person to engage in conduct which could not be expressly authorised under the warrant because of the restriction imposed by subsection (6).

(8) In subsection (6), "stored communication" means a communication stored in or by a telecommunication system (whether before or after its transmission).

(9) Any conduct which is carried out in accordance with a bulk equipment interference warrant is lawful for all purposes.

[Investigatory Powers Act 2016, s 176.]

---

[1] Chapter 3 contains ss 176-198. The omitted provisions concern: power to issue and approval of warrants; requirements of warrants; duration, renewal, modification, cancellation and implementation of warrants.

7.11231ZZ40 **177. Meaning of "equipment data"** (1) In this Chapter, "equipment data" means—

(a) systems data;

(b) data which falls within subsection (2).

(2) The data falling within this subsection is identifying data which—

(a) is, for the purposes of a relevant system, comprised in, included as part of, attached to or logically associated with a communication (whether by the sender or otherwise) or any other item of information,

(b) is capable of being logically separated from the remainder of the communication or the item of information, and

(c) if it were so separated, would not reveal anything of what might reasonably be considered to be the meaning (if any) of the communication or the item of information, disregarding any meaning arising from the fact of the communication or the existence of the item of information or from any data relating to that fact.

(3) In subsection (2), "relevant system" means any system on or by means of which the data is held.

(4) For the meaning of "systems data" and "identifying data", see section 263.

[Investigatory Powers Act 2016, s 177.]

7.11231ZZ41 **178. Power to issue bulk equipment interference warrants** (1) The Secretary of State may, on an application made by or on behalf of the head of an intelligence service, issue a bulk equipment interference warrant if—

(a) the Secretary of State considers that the main purpose of the warrant is to obtain overseas-related communications, overseas-related information or overseas-related equipment data,

(b) the Secretary of State considers that the warrant is necessary—

(i) in the interests of national security, or

(ii) on that ground and on any other grounds falling within subsection (2),

(c) the Secretary of State considers that the conduct authorised by the warrant is proportionate to what is sought to be achieved by that conduct,

(d) the Secretary of State considers that—

(i) each of the specified operational purposes (see section 183) is a purpose for which the examination of material obtained under the warrant is or may be necessary, and

(ii) the examination of such material for each such purpose is necessary on any of the grounds on which the Secretary of State considers the warrant to be necessary,

(e) the Secretary of State considers that satisfactory arrangements made for the purposes of sections 191 and 192 (safeguards relating to disclosure etc) are in force in relation to the warrant, and

(f) except where the Secretary of State considers that there is an urgent need to issue the warrant, the decision to issue the warrant has been approved by a Judicial Commissioner.

For the meaning of "head of an intelligence service", see section 263.

(2) A warrant is necessary on grounds falling within this subsection if it is necessary—

(a) for the purpose of preventing or detecting serious crime, or

(b) in the interests of the economic well-being of the United Kingdom so far as those interests are also relevant to the interests of national security (but see subsection (3)).

(3) A warrant may be considered necessary on the ground falling within subsection (2)(b) only if the interference with equipment which would be authorised by the warrant is considered necessary for the purpose of obtaining information relating to the acts or intentions of persons outside the British Islands.

(4) An application for the issue of a bulk equipment interference warrant may only be made on behalf of the head of an intelligence service by a person holding office under the Crown.

[Investigatory Powers Act 2016, s 178.]

*Restrictions on use or disclosure of material obtained under warrants etc*

7.11231ZZ42 **191. Safeguards relating to retention and disclosure of material** (1) The Secretary of State must ensure, in relation to every bulk equipment interference warrant, that arrangements are in force for securing—

(a) that the requirements of subsections (2) and (5) are met in relation to the material obtained under the warrant, and

(b) that the requirements of section 193 are met in relation to that material.

This is subject to subsection (8).

(2) The requirements of this subsection are met in relation to the material obtained under the warrant if each of the following is limited to the minimum that is necessary for the authorised purposes (see subsection (3))—

(a) the number of persons to whom any of the material is disclosed or otherwise made available;

(b) the extent to which any of the material is disclosed or otherwise made available;

(c) the extent to which any of the material is copied;

(d) the number of copies that are made.

(3) For the purposes of subsection (2) something is necessary for the authorised purposes if, and only if—

(a) it is, or is likely to become, necessary in the interests of national security or on any other grounds falling within section 178(2),

(b) it is necessary for facilitating the carrying out of any functions under this Act of the Secretary of State, the Scottish Ministers or the head of the intelligence service to whom the warrant is or was addressed,

(c) it is necessary for facilitating the carrying out of any functions of the Judicial Commissioners or of the Investigatory Powers Tribunal under or in relation to this Act,

(d) it is necessary for the purpose of legal proceedings, or

(e) it is necessary for the performance of the functions of any person under any enactment.

(4) The arrangements for the time being in force under this section for securing that the requirements of subsection (2) are met in relation to the material obtained under the warrant must include arrangements for securing that every copy made of any of that material is stored, for so long as it is retained, in a secure manner.

(5) The requirements of this subsection are met in relation to the material obtained under the warrant if every copy made of any of that material (if not destroyed earlier) is destroyed as soon as there are no longer any relevant grounds for retaining it (see subsection (6)).

(6) For the purposes of subsection (5), there are no longer any relevant grounds for retaining a copy of any material if, and only if—

(a) its retention is not necessary, or not likely to become necessary, in the interests of national security or on any other grounds falling within section 178(2), and

(b) its retention is not necessary for any of the purposes mentioned in paragraphs (b) to (e) of subsection (3) above.

(7) Subsection (8) applies if—

(a) any material obtained under the warrant has been handed over to any overseas authorities, or

(b) a copy of any such material has been given to any overseas authorities.

(8) To the extent that the requirements of subsections (2) and (5) and section 193 relate to any of the material mentioned in subsection (7)(a), or to the copy mentioned in subsection (7)(b), the arrangements made for the purpose of this section are not required to secure that those requirements are met (see instead section 192).

(9) In this section—

"copy", in relation to any material obtained under a warrant, means any of the following (whether or not in documentary form)—

(a) any copy, extract or summary of the material which identifies the material as having been obtained under the warrant, and

(b) any record which is a record of the identities of persons who owned, used or were in possession of the equipment which was interfered with to obtain that material,

and "copied" is to be read accordingly;

"overseas authorities" means authorities of a country or territory outside the United Kingdom.

[Investigatory Powers Act 2016, s 191.]

**7.11231ZZ43 192. Safeguards relating to disclosure of material overseas** (1) The Secretary of State must ensure, in relation to every bulk equipment interference warrant, that arrangements are in force for securing that—

(a) any material obtained under the warrant is handed over to overseas authorities only if the requirements of subsection (2) are met, and

(b) copies of any such material are given to overseas authorities only if those requirements are met.

(2) The requirements of this subsection are met in the case of a warrant if it appears to the Secretary of State that requirements corresponding to the requirements of section 191(2) and (5) and section 193 will apply, to such extent (if any) as the Secretary of State considers appropriate, in relation to any of the material which is handed over, or any copy of which is given, to the authorities in question.

(3) In this section—

"copy" has the same meaning as in section 191;

"overseas authorities" means authorities of a country or territory outside the United Kingdom.

[Investigatory Powers Act 2016, s 192.]

**7.11231ZZ44 193. Safeguards relating to examination of material etc** (1) For the purposes of section 191, the requirements of this section are met in relation to the material obtained under a warrant if—

(a) the selection of any of the material obtained under the warrant for examination is carried out only for the specified purposes (see subsection (2)),

(b) the selection of any of the material for examination is necessary and proportionate in all the circumstances, and

(c) where any such material is protected material, the selection of the material for examination meets any of the selection conditions (see subsection (3)).

(2) The selection of material obtained under the warrant for examination is carried out only for the specified purposes if the material is selected for examination only so far as is necessary for the operational purposes specified in the warrant in accordance with section 183.

In this subsection "specified in the warrant" means specified in the warrant at the time of the selection of the material for examination.

(3) The selection conditions referred to in subsection (1)(c) are—

(a) that the selection of the protected material for examination does not breach the prohibition in subsection (4);

(b) that the person to whom the warrant is addressed reasonably considers that the selection of the protected material for examination would not breach that prohibition;

(c) that the selection of the protected material for examination in breach of that prohibition is authorised by subsection (5);

(d) that the selection of the protected material for examination in breach of that prohibition is authorised by a targeted examination warrant issued under Part 5.

(4) The prohibition referred to in subsection (3)(a) is that the protected material may not at any time be selected for examination if—

(a) any criteria used for the selection of the material for examination are referable to an individual known to be in the British Islands at that time, and

(b) the purpose of using those criteria is to identify protected material consisting of communications sent by, or intended for, that individual or private information relating to that individual.

It does not matter for the purposes of this subsection whether the identity of the individual is known.

(5) The selection of protected material ("the relevant material") for examination is authorised by this subsection if—

(a) criteria referable to an individual have been, or are being, used for the selection of material for examination in circumstances falling within subsection (3)(a) or (b),

(b) at any time it appears to the person to whom the warrant is addressed that there has been a relevant change of circumstances in relation to the individual (see subsection (6)) which would mean that the selection of the relevant material for examination would breach the prohibition in subsection (4),

(c) since that time, a written authorisation to examine the relevant material using those criteria has been given by a senior officer, and

(d) the selection of the relevant material for examination is made before the end of the permitted period (see subsection (7)).

(6) For the purposes of subsection (5)(b) there is a relevant change of circumstances in relation to an individual if—

(a) the individual has entered the British Islands, or

(b) a belief by the person to whom the warrant is addressed that the individual was outside the British Islands was in fact mistaken.

(7) In subsection (5)—

"senior officer", in relation to a warrant addressed to the head of an intelligence service, means a member of the intelligence service who—

(a) is a member of the Senior Civil Service or a member of the Senior Management Structure of Her Majesty's Diplomatic Service, or

(b) holds a position in the intelligence service of equivalent seniority to such a member;

"the permitted period" means the period ending with the fifth working day after the time mentioned in subsection (5)(b).

(8) In a case where the selection of protected material for examination is authorised by subsection (5), the person to whom the warrant is addressed must notify the Secretary of State that the selection is being carried out.

(9) In this Part, "protected material" means any material obtained under the warrant other than material which is—

(a) equipment data;

(b) information (other than a communication or equipment data) which is not private information.

[Investigatory Powers Act 2016, s 193.]

**7.11231ZZ45 194. Additional safeguards for items subject to legal privilege**

(1) Subsection (2) applies if, in a case where protected material obtained under a bulk equipment interference warrant is to be selected for examination—

(a) the selection of the material for examination meets any of the selection conditions in section 193(3)(a) to (c), and

(b) either—

(i) the purpose, or one of the purposes, of using the criteria to be used for the selection of the material for examination ("the relevant criteria") is to identify any items subject to legal privilege, or

(ii) the use of the relevant criteria is likely to identify such items.

(2) The material may be selected for examination using the relevant criteria only if a senior official acting on behalf of the Secretary of State has approved the use of those criteria.

(3) In deciding whether to give an approval under subsection (2) in a case where subsection (1)(b)(i) applies, a senior official must have regard to the public interest in the confidentiality of items subject to legal privilege.

(4) A senior official may give an approval under subsection (2) only if—

(a) the official considers that the arrangements made for the purposes of section 191 (safeguards relating to retention and disclosure of material) include specific arrangements for the handling, retention, use and destruction of items subject to legal privilege, and

(b) where subsection (1)(b)(i) applies, the official considers that there are exceptional and compelling circumstances that make it necessary to authorise the use of the relevant criteria.

(5) For the purposes of subsection (4)(b), there cannot be exceptional and compelling circumstances that make it necessary to authorise the use of the relevant criteria unless—

(a) the public interest in obtaining the information that would be obtained by the selection of the material for examination outweighs the public interest in the confidentiality of items subject to legal privilege,

(b) there are no other means by which the information may reasonably be obtained, and

(c) obtaining the information is necessary in the interests of national security or for the purpose of preventing death or significant injury.

(6) Subsection (7) applies if, in a case where protected material obtained under a bulk equipment interference warrant is to be selected for examination—

(a) the selection of the material for examination meets any of the selection conditions in section 193(3)(a) to (c),

(b) the purpose, or one of the purposes, of using the criteria to be used for the selection of the material for examination ("the relevant criteria") is to identify communications or other items of information that, if they were not communications made or (as the case may be) other items of information created or held with the intention of furthering a criminal purpose, would be items subject to legal privilege, and

(c) the person to whom the warrant is addressed considers that the communications or other items of information ("the targeted communications or other items of information") are likely to be communications made or (as the case may be) other items of information created or held with the intention of furthering a criminal purpose.

(7) The material may be selected for examination using the relevant criteria only if a senior official acting on behalf of the Secretary of State has approved the use of those criteria.

(8) A senior official may give an approval under subsection (7) only if the official considers that the targeted communications or other items of information are likely to be communications made or (as the case may be) other items of information created or held with the intention of furthering a criminal purpose.

(9) Where an item subject to legal privilege which has been obtained under a bulk equipment interference warrant is retained following its examination, for purposes other than the destruction of the item, the person to whom the warrant is addressed must inform the Investigatory Powers Commissioner as soon as is reasonably practicable.

(For provision about the grounds for retaining material obtained under a bulk equipment interference warrant, see section 191.)

(10) Unless the Investigatory Powers Commissioner considers that subsection (12) applies to the item, the Commissioner must—

(a) direct that the item is destroyed, or

(b) impose one or more conditions as to the use or retention of that item.

(11) If the Investigatory Powers Commissioner considers that subsection (12) applies to the item, the Commissioner may nevertheless impose such conditions under subsection (10)(b) as the Commissioner considers necessary for the purpose of protecting the public interest in the confidentiality of items subject to legal privilege.

(12) This subsection applies to an item subject to legal privilege if—

(a) the public interest in retaining the item outweighs the public interest in the confidentiality of items subject to legal privilege, and

(b) retaining the item is necessary in the interests of national security or for the purpose of preventing death or significant injury.

(13) The Investigatory Powers Commissioner—

(a) may require an affected party to make representations about how the Commissioner should exercise any function under subsection (10), and

(b) must have regard to any such representations made by an affected party (whether or not as a result of a requirement imposed under paragraph (a)).

(14) Each of the following is an "affected party" for the purposes of subsection (13)—

(a) the Secretary of State;

(b) the person to whom the warrant is or was addressed.

[Investigatory Powers Act 2016, s 194.]

7.11231ZZ46 **195. Additional safeguard for confidential journalistic material** Where—

(a) material obtained under a bulk equipment interference warrant is retained, following its examination, for purposes other than the destruction of the material, and

(b) it is material containing confidential journalistic material,

the person to whom the warrant is addressed must inform the Investigatory Powers Commissioner as soon as is reasonably practicable.

[Investigatory Powers Act 2016, s 195.]

7.11231ZZ47 **196. Offence of breaching safeguards relating to examination of material**

(1) A person commits an offence if—

(a) the person selects for examination any material obtained under a bulk equipment interference warrant,

(b) the person knows or believes that the selection of that material does not comply with a requirement imposed by section 193 or 194, and

(c) the person deliberately selects that material in breach of that requirement.

(2) A person guilty of an offence under this section is liable—

(a) on summary conviction in England and Wales—

(i) to imprisonment for a term not exceeding 12 months (or 6 months, if the offence was committed before the commencement of section 154(1) of the Criminal Justice Act 2003), or

(ii) to a fine,

or to both;

(b) on summary conviction in Scotland—

(i) to imprisonment for a term not exceeding 12 months, or

(ii) to a fine not exceeding the statutory maximum,

or to both;

(c) on summary conviction in Northern Ireland—
(i) to imprisonment for a term not exceeding 6 months, or
(ii) to a fine not exceeding the statutory maximum,
or to both;

(d) on conviction on indictment, to imprisonment for a term not exceeding 2 years or to a fine, or to both[1].

(3) No proceedings for any offence which is an offence by virtue of this section may be instituted—

(a) in England and Wales, except by or with the consent of the Director of Public Prosecutions;

(b) in Northern Ireland, except by or with the consent of the Director of Public Prosecutions for Northern Ireland.

[Investigatory Powers Act 2016, s 196.]

---

1 For procedure in respect of an offence triable either way, see the Magistrates' Courts Act 1980, ss 17A-21, In PART 1: MAGISTRATES' COURTS, PROCEDURE, ante

**7.11231ZZ48 197. Application of other restrictions in relation to warrants** Sections 132 to 134 (duty not to make unauthorised disclosures) apply in relation to bulk equipment interference warrants as they apply in relation to targeted equipment interference warrants, but as if the reference in section 133(2)(c) to a requirement for disclosure imposed by virtue of section 126(4) were a reference to such a requirement imposed by virtue of section 190(4).

[Investigatory Powers Act 2016, s 197.]

*Interpretation*

**7.11231ZZ49 198. Chapter 3: interpretation** (1) In this Chapter—

"communication" includes—

(a) anything comprising speech, music, sounds, visual images or data of any description, and

(b) signals serving either for the impartation of anything between persons, between a person and a thing or between things or for the actuation or control of any apparatus;

"equipment" means equipment producing electromagnetic, acoustic or other emissions or any device capable of being used in connection with such equipment;

"equipment data" has the meaning given by section 177;

"private information" includes information relating to a person's private or family life;

"protected material", in relation to a bulk equipment interference warrant, has the meaning given by section 193(9);

"senior official" means a member of the Senior Civil Service or a member of the Senior Management Structure of Her Majesty's Diplomatic Service;

"the specified operational purposes" has the meaning given by section 183(12).

(2) See also—

section 261 (telecommunications definitions);

section 263 (general definitions);

section 264 (general definitions: "journalistic material" etc);

section 265 (index of defined expressions).

[Investigatory Powers Act 2016, s 198.]

## PART 7[1]

## BULK PERSONAL DATASET WARRANTS

*Bulk personal datasets: interpretation*

**7.11231ZZ50 199. Bulk personal datasets: interpretation** (1) For the purposes of this Part, an intelligence service retains a bulk personal dataset if—

(a) the intelligence service obtains a set of information that includes personal data relating to a number of individuals,

(b) the nature of the set is such that the majority of the individuals are not, and are unlikely to become, of interest to the intelligence service in the exercise of its functions,

(c) after any initial examination of the contents, the intelligence service retains the set for the purpose of the exercise of its functions, and

(d) the set is held, or is to be held, electronically for analysis in the exercise of those functions.

(2) In this Part, "personal data" has the same meaning as in the Data Protection Act 1998 except that it also includes data relating to a deceased individual where the data would be personal data within the meaning of that Act if it related to a living individual.

[Investigatory Powers Act 2016, s 199.]

---

1 PART 7 contains ss 199–226. The omitted provisions concern: issue of warrants and their approval; requirements of warrants; duration, renewal, modification, cancellation of warrants.

*Requirement for warrant*

7.11231ZZ51 **200. Requirement for authorisation by warrant: general** (1) An intelligence service may not exercise a power to retain a bulk personal dataset unless the retention of the dataset is authorised by a warrant under this Part.

(2) An intelligence service may not exercise a power to examine a bulk personal dataset retained by it unless the examination is authorised by a warrant under this Part.

(3) For the purposes of this Part, there are two kinds of warrant—

(a) a warrant, referred to in this Part as "a class BPD warrant", authorising an intelligence service to retain, or to retain and examine, any bulk personal dataset of a class described in the warrant;

(b) a warrant, referred to in this Part as "a specific BPD warrant", authorising an intelligence service to retain, or to retain and examine, any bulk personal dataset described in the warrant.

(4) Section 201 sets out exceptions to the restrictions imposed by subsections (1) and (2) of this section.

[Investigatory Powers Act 2016, s 200.]

7.11231ZZ52 **201. Exceptions to section 200(1) and (2)** (1) Section 200(1) or (2) does not apply to the exercise of a power of an intelligence service to retain or (as the case may be) examine a bulk personal dataset if the intelligence service obtained the bulk personal dataset under a warrant or other authorisation issued or given under this Act.

(2) Section 200(1) or (2) does not apply at any time when a bulk personal dataset is being retained or (as the case may be) examined for the purpose of enabling any of the information contained in it to be destroyed.

(3) Sections 210(8), 219(8) and 220(5) provide for other exceptions to section 200(1) or (2) (in connection with cases where a Judicial Commissioner refuses to approve a specific BPD warrant, the non-renewal or cancellation of BPD warrants and initial examinations).

[Investigatory Powers Act 2016, s 201.]

7.11231ZZ53 **202. Restriction on use of class BPD warrants** (1) An intelligence service may not retain, or retain and examine, a bulk personal dataset in reliance on a class BPD warrant if the head of the intelligence service considers that the bulk personal dataset consists of, or includes, protected data.

For the meaning of "protected data", see section 203.

(2) An intelligence service may not retain, or retain and examine, a bulk personal dataset in reliance on a class BPD warrant if the head of the intelligence service considers—

(a) that the bulk personal dataset consists of, or includes, health records, or

(b) that a substantial proportion of the bulk personal dataset consists of sensitive personal data.

(3) An intelligence service may not retain, or retain and examine, a bulk personal dataset in reliance on a class BPD warrant if the head of the intelligence service considers that the nature of the bulk personal dataset, or the circumstances in which it was created, is or are such that its retention, or retention and examination, by the intelligence service raises novel or contentious issues which ought to be considered by the Secretary of State and a Judicial Commissioner on an application by the head of the intelligence service for a specific BPD warrant.

(4) In subsection (2)—

"health records" has the same meaning as in section 206;

"sensitive personal data" means personal data consisting of information about an individual (whether living or deceased) which is of a kind mentioned in section 2(a) to (f) of the Data Protection Act 1998.

[Investigatory Powers Act 2016, s 202.]

7.11231ZZ54 **203. Meaning of "protected data"** (1) In this Part, "protected data" means any data contained in a bulk personal dataset other than data which is one or more of the following—

(a) systems data;

(b) data which falls within subsection (2);

(c) data which is not private information.

(2) The data falling within this subsection is identifying data which—

(a) is contained in the bulk personal dataset,

(b) is capable of being logically separated from the bulk personal dataset, and

(c) if it were so separated, would not reveal anything of what might reasonably be considered to be the meaning (if any) of any of the data which would remain in the bulk personal dataset or of the bulk personal dataset itself, disregarding any meaning arising from the existence of that data or (as the case may be) the existence of the bulk personal dataset or from any data relating to that fact.

(3) For the meaning of "systems data" see section 263(4).

(4) In this section, "private information" includes information relating to a person's private or family life.

[Investigatory Powers Act 2016, s 203.]

*Further and supplementary provision*

7.11231ZZ55 **220. Initial examinations: time limits** (1) This section applies where—

(a) an intelligence service obtains a set of information otherwise than in the exercise of a power conferred by a warrant or other authorisation issued or given under this Act, and

(b) the head of the intelligence service believes that—

(i) the set includes, or may include, personal data relating to a number of individuals, and

(ii) the nature of the set is, or may be, such that the majority of the individuals are not, and are unlikely to become, of interest to the intelligence service in the exercise of its functions.

(2) The head of the intelligence service must take the following steps before the end of the permitted period.

*Step 1*

Carry out an initial examination of the set for the purpose of deciding whether, if the intelligence service were to retain it after that initial examination and hold it electronically for analysis for the purposes of the exercise of its functions, the intelligence service would be retaining a bulk personal dataset (see section 199).

*Step 2*

If the intelligence service would be retaining a bulk personal dataset as mentioned in step 1, decide whether to retain the set and hold it electronically for analysis for the purposes of the exercise of the functions of the intelligence service.

*Step 3*

If the head of the intelligence service decides to retain the set and hold it electronically for analysis as mentioned in step 2, apply for a specific BPD warrant as soon as reasonably practicable after making that decision (unless the retention of the dataset is authorised by a class BPD warrant).

(3) The permitted period begins when the head of the intelligence service first forms the beliefs mentioned in subsection (1)(b).

(4) The permitted period ends—

(a) where the set of information was created in the United Kingdom, 3 months after the day on which it begins;

(b) where the set of information was created outside the United Kingdom, 6 months after the day on which it begins.

(5) If the head of the intelligence service applies for a specific BPD warrant in accordance with step 3 (set out in subsection (2))—

(a) the intelligence service is not to be regarded as in breach of section 200(1) by virtue of retaining the bulk personal dataset during the period between the taking of the decision mentioned in step 2 and the determination of the application for the specific BPD warrant, and

(b) the intelligence service is not to be regarded as in breach of section 200(2) by virtue of examining the bulk personal dataset during that period if the examination is necessary for the purposes of the making of the application for the warrant.

[Investigatory Powers Act 2016, s 220.]

7.11231ZZ56 **221. Safeguards relating to examination of bulk personal datasets** (1) The Secretary of State must ensure, in relation to every class BPD warrant or specific BPD warrant which authorises examination of bulk personal datasets of a class described in the warrant or (as the case may be) of a bulk personal dataset described in the warrant, that arrangements are in force for securing that—

(a) any selection of data contained in the datasets (or dataset) for examination is carried out only for the specified purposes (see subsection (2)), and

(b) the selection of any such data for examination is necessary and proportionate in all the circumstances.

(2) The selection of data contained in bulk personal datasets for examination is carried out only for the specified purposes if the data is selected for examination only so far as is necessary for the operational purposes specified in the warrant in accordance with section 212.

(3) The Secretary of State must also ensure, in relation to every specific BPD warrant which specifies conditions imposed under section 207, that arrangements are in force for securing that any selection for examination of protected data on the basis of criteria which are referable to an individual known to be in the British Islands at the time of the selection is in accordance with the conditions specified in the warrant.

(4) In this section "specified in the warrant" means specified in the warrant at the time of the selection of the data for examination.

[Investigatory Powers Act 2016, s 221.]

7.11231ZZ57 **222. Additional safeguards for items subject to legal privilege: examination** (1) Subsections (2) and (3) apply if, in a case where protected data retained in reliance on a specific BPD warrant is to be selected for examination—

(a) the purpose, or one of the purposes, of using the criteria to be used for the selection of the data for examination ("the relevant criteria") is to identify any items subject to legal privilege, or

(b) the use of the relevant criteria is likely to identify such items.

(2) If the relevant criteria are referable to an individual known to be in the British Islands at the time of the selection, the data may be selected for examination using the relevant criteria only if the Secretary of State has approved the use of those criteria.

(3) In any other case, the data may be selected for examination using the relevant criteria only if a senior official acting on behalf of the Secretary of State has approved the use of those criteria.

(4) The Secretary of State may give approval for the purposes of subsection (2) only with the approval of a Judicial Commissioner.

(5) Approval may be given under subsection (2) or (3) only if—

(a) the Secretary of State or (as the case may be) the senior official considers that the arrangements mentioned in section 205(6)(d) include specific arrangements in respect of items subject to legal privilege, and

(b) where subsection (1)(a) applies, the Secretary of State or (as the case may be) the senior official considers that there are exceptional and compelling circumstances that make it necessary to authorise the use of the relevant criteria.

(6) In deciding whether to give an approval under subsection (2) or (3) in a case where subsection (1)(a) applies, the Secretary of State or (as the case may be) the senior official must have regard to the public interest in the confidentiality of items subject to legal privilege.

(7) For the purposes of subsection (5)(b), there cannot be exceptional and compelling circumstances that make it necessary to authorise the use of the relevant criteria unless—

(a) the public interest in obtaining the information that would be obtained by the selection of the data for examination outweighs the public interest in the confidentiality of items subject to legal privilege,

(b) there are no other means by which the information may reasonably be obtained, and

(c) obtaining the information is necessary in the interests of national security or for the purpose of preventing death or significant injury.

(8) In deciding whether to give approval for the purposes of subsection (4), the Judicial Commissioner must—

(a) apply the same principles as would be applied by a court on an application for judicial review, and

(b) consider the matter with a sufficient degree of care as to ensure that the Judicial Commissioner complies with the duties imposed by section 2 (general duties in relation to privacy).

(9) Subsections (10) and (11) apply if, in a case where protected data retained in reliance on a specific BPD warrant is to be selected for examination—

(a) the purpose, or one of the purposes, of using the criteria to be used for the selection of the data for examination ("the relevant criteria") is to identify data that, if the data or any underlying material were not created or held with the intention of furthering a criminal purpose, would be an item subject to legal privilege, and

(b) the person to whom the warrant is addressed considers that the data ("the targeted data") or any underlying material is likely to be data or underlying material created or held with the intention of furthering a criminal purpose.

(10) If the relevant criteria are referable to an individual known to be in the British Islands at the time of the selection, the data may be selected for examination using the relevant criteria only if the Secretary of State has approved the use of those criteria.

(11) In any other case, the data may be selected for examination using the relevant criteria only if a senior official acting on behalf of the Secretary of State has approved the use of those criteria.

(12) Approval may be given under subsection (10) or (11) only if the Secretary of State or (as the case may be) the senior official considers that the targeted data or the underlying material is likely to be data or underlying material created or held with the intention of furthering a criminal purpose.

(13) In this section, "underlying material", in relation to data retained in reliance on a specific BPD warrant, means any communications or other items of information from which the data was produced.

[Investigatory Powers Act 2016, s 222.]

7.11231ZZ58 223. **Additional safeguards for items subject to legal privilege: retention following examination** (1) Where an item subject to legal privilege is retained following its examination in reliance on a specific BPD warrant, for purposes other than the destruction of the item, the person to whom the warrant is addressed must inform the Investigatory Powers Commissioner as soon as is reasonably practicable.

(2) Unless the Investigatory Powers Commissioner considers that subsection (4) applies to the item, the Commissioner must—

(a) direct that the item is destroyed, or

(b) impose one or more conditions as to the use or retention of that item.

(3) If the Investigatory Powers Commissioner considers that subsection (4) applies to the item,

the Commissioner may nevertheless impose such conditions under subsection (2)(b) as the Commissioner considers necessary for the purpose of protecting the public interest in the confidentiality of items subject to legal privilege.

(4) This subsection applies to an item subject to legal privilege if—

(a) the public interest in retaining the item outweighs the public interest in the confidentiality of items subject to legal privilege, and

(b) retaining the item is necessary in the interests of national security or for the purpose of preventing death or significant injury.

(5) The Investigatory Powers Commissioner—

(a) may require an affected party to make representations about how the Commissioner should exercise any function under subsection (2), and

(b) must have regard to any such representations made by an affected party (whether or not as a result of a requirement imposed under paragraph (a)).

(6) Each of the following is an "affected party" for the purposes of subsection (5)—

(a) the Secretary of State;

(b) the person to whom the warrant is or was addressed.

[Investigatory Powers Act 2016, s 223.]

**7.11231ZZ59 224. Offence of breaching safeguards relating to examination of material**

(1) A person commits an offence if—

(a) the person selects for examination any data contained in a bulk personal dataset retained in reliance on a class BPD warrant or a specific BPD warrant,

(b) the person knows or believes that the selection of that data is in breach of a requirement specified in subsection (2), and

(c) the person deliberately selects that data in breach of that requirement.

(2) The requirements specified in this subsection are that any selection for examination of the data—

(a) is carried out only for the specified purposes (see subsection (3)),

(b) is necessary and proportionate, and

(c) if the data is protected data, satisfies any conditions imposed under section 207.

(3) The selection for examination of the data is carried out only for the specified purposes if the data is selected for examination only so far as is necessary for the operational purposes specified in the warrant in accordance with section 212.

In this subsection, "specified in the warrant" means specified in the warrant at the time of the selection of the data for examination.

(4) A person guilty of an offence under this section is liable—

(a) on summary conviction in England and Wales—

(i) to imprisonment for a term not exceeding 12 months (or 6 months, if the offence was committed before the commencement of section 154(1) of the Criminal Justice Act 2003), or

(ii) to a fine,

or to both;

(b) on summary conviction in Scotland—

(i) to imprisonment for a term not exceeding 12 months, or

(ii) to a fine not exceeding the statutory maximum,

or to both;

(c) on summary conviction in Northern Ireland—

(i) to imprisonment for a term not exceeding 6 months, or

(ii) to a fine not exceeding the statutory maximum,

or to both;

(d) on conviction on indictment, to imprisonment for a term not exceeding 2 years or to a fine, or to both[1].

(5) No proceedings for any offence which is an offence by virtue of this section may be instituted—

(a) in England and Wales, except by or with the consent of the Director of Public Prosecutions;

(b) in Northern Ireland, except by or with the consent of the Director of Public Prosecutions for Northern Ireland.

[Investigatory Powers Act 2016, s 224.]

---

[1] For procedure in respect of an offence triable either way, see the Magistrates' Courts Act 1980, s 17A-21, in PART 1: MAGISTRATES' COURTS, PROCEDURE, ante.

**7.11231ZZ60 225. Application of Part to bulk personal datasets obtained under this Act**

(1) Subject to subsection (2), this section applies where a bulk personal dataset has been obtained by an intelligence service under a warrant or other authorisation issued or given under this Act (and, accordingly, section 200(1) and (2) do not apply by virtue of section 201(1)).

(2) This section does not apply where the bulk personal dataset was obtained by the intelligence

service under a bulk acquisition warrant issued under Chapter 2 of Part 6.

(3) Where this section applies, the Secretary of State may, on the application of the head of the intelligence service, give a direction that—

(a) the intelligence service may retain, or retain and examine, the bulk personal dataset by virtue of the direction,

(b) any other power of the intelligence service to retain or examine the bulk personal dataset, and any associated regulatory provision, ceases to apply in relation to the bulk personal dataset (subject to subsection (5)), and

(c) section 201(1) also ceases to apply in relation to the bulk personal dataset.

(4) Accordingly, where a direction is given under subsection (3), the intelligence service may exercise its power by virtue of the direction to retain, or to retain and examine, the bulk personal dataset only if authorised to do so by a class BPD warrant or a specific BPD warrant under this Part.

(5) A direction under subsection (3) may provide for any associated regulatory provision specified in the direction to continue to apply in relation to the bulk personal dataset, with or without modifications specified in the direction.

(6) The power conferred by subsection (5) must be exercised to ensure that—

(a) where section 56 and Schedule 3 applied in relation to the bulk personal dataset immediately before the giving of the direction, they continue to apply in relation to it (without modification);

(b) where sections 57 to 59 applied in relation to the bulk personal dataset immediately before the giving of the direction, they continue to apply in relation to it with the modification that the reference in section 58(7)(a) to the provisions of Part 2 is to be read as including a reference to the provisions of this Part.

(7) The Secretary of State may only give a direction under subsection (3) with the approval of a Judicial Commissioner.

(8) In deciding whether to give approval for the purposes of subsection (7), the Judicial Commissioner must apply the same principles as would be applied by a court on an application for judicial review.

(9) Where a Judicial Commissioner refuses to approve a decision by the Secretary of State to give a direction under subsection (3), the Judicial Commissioner must give the Secretary of State written reasons for the decision.

(10) Where a Judicial Commissioner, other than the Investigatory Powers Commissioner, refuses to approve such a decision, the Secretary of State may ask the Investigatory Powers Commissioner to decide whether to approve the decision.

(11) A direction under subsection (3)—

(a) may not be revoked;

(b) may be varied but only for the purpose of altering or removing any provision included in the direction under subsection (5).

(12) Subsections (7) to (10) apply in relation to the variation of a direction under subsection (3) as they apply in relation to the giving of a direction under that subsection.

(13) The head of an intelligence service may, at the same time as applying for a direction under subsection (3), apply for a specific BPD warrant under section 205 (and the Secretary of State may issue such a warrant at the same time as giving the direction).

(14) In this section, "associated regulatory provision", in relation to a power of an intelligence service to retain or examine a bulk personal dataset, means any provision which—

(a) is made by or for the purposes of this Act (other than this Part), and

(b) applied in relation to the retention, examination, disclosure or other use of the bulk personal dataset immediately before the giving of a direction under subsection (3).

[Investigatory Powers Act 2016, s 225.]

**7.11231ZZ61 226. Part 7: interpretation** (1) In this Part—

"class BPD warrant" has the meaning given by section 200(3)(a);

"personal data" has the meaning given by section 199(2);

"senior official" means a member of the Senior Civil Service or a member of the Senior Management Structure of Her Majesty's Diplomatic Service;

"specific BPD warrant" has the meaning given by section 200(3)(b);

"the specified operational purposes" has the meaning given by section 212(12).

(2) See also—

section 263 (general definitions),

section 265 (index of defined expressions).

[Investigatory Powers Act 2016, s 226.]

## PART 8
## OVERSIGHT ARRANGEMENTS

*Part 8 (not reproduced) contains ss 227-247. It establishes the Investigatory Powers Commission and other Judicial Commissioners and defines their functions. Section 237 "Information gateway" allows people to provide information to a Judicial Commissioner, regardless of any other legal restrictions that might exist, except that the protections in the Data Protection Act 1998 still apply when information is provided to the Investigatory Powers Commissioner. Section 240 abolishes a number of existing bodies. Section 244 requires the Information Commission to audit compliance with requirements or restrictions imposed by virtue of Part 4 relating to the integrity, security or destruction of data retained by virtue of that Part.*

## PART 9[1]
## MISCELLANEOUS AND GENERAL PROVISIONS

### CHAPTER 1[2]
### MISCELLANEOUS

*Wireless telegraphy*

**7.11231ZZ62 259. Amendments of the Wireless Telegraphy Act 2006** (1) The Wireless Telegraphy Act 2006 is amended as follows.

(2) Section 48 (interception and disclosure of messages) is amended as follows.

(3) In subsection (1), for "otherwise than under the authority of a designated person" substitute "without lawful authority".

(4) After subsection (3) insert—

"(3A) A person does not commit an offence under this section consisting in any conduct if the conduct—

(a) constitutes an offence under section 3(1) of the Investigatory Powers Act 2016 (offence of unlawful interception), or

(b) would do so in the absence of any lawful authority (within the meaning of section 6 of that Act)."

(5) Omit subsection (5).

(6) Omit section 49 (interception authorities).

(7) In consequence of the repeal made by subsection (6)—

(a) in sections 50(5) and 119(2)(a), for "49" substitute "48";

(b) in section 121(2), omit paragraph (b).

[Investigatory Powers Act 2016, s 259.]

---

1 Part 9 contains ss 248–272.
2 Chapter 1 contains ss 248–259.

### CHAPTER 2[1]
### GENERAL

*Review of operation of Act*

**7.11231ZZ63 260. Review of operation of Act** (1) The Secretary of State must, within the period of 6 months beginning with the end of the initial period, prepare a report on the operation of this Act.

(2) In subsection (1) "the initial period" is the period of 5 years and 6 months beginning with the day on which this Act is passed.

(3) In preparing the report under subsection (1), the Secretary of State must, in particular, take account of any report on the operation of this Act made by a Select Committee of either House of Parliament (whether acting alone or jointly).

(4) The Secretary of State must—

(a) publish the report prepared under subsection (1), and

(b) lay a copy of it before Parliament.

[Investigatory Powers Act 2016, s 260.]

---

1 Chapter 2 contains ss 260–272.

*Interpretation*

**7.11231ZZ64 261. Telecommunications definitions** (1) The definitions in this section have effect for the purposes of this Act.

*Communication*

(2) "Communication", in relation to a telecommunications operator, telecommunications service or telecommunication system, includes—

(a) anything comprising speech, music, sounds, visual images or data of any description, and

(b) signals serving either for the impartation of anything between persons, between a person and a thing or between things or for the actuation or control of any apparatus.

*Entity data*

(3) "Entity data" means any data which—

(a) is about—

(i) an entity,

(ii) an association between a telecommunications service and an entity, or

(iii) an association between any part of a telecommunication system and an entity,

(b) consists of, or includes, data which identifies or describes the entity (whether or not by reference to the entity's location), and

(c) is not events data.

*Events data*

(4) "Events data" means any data which identifies or describes an event (whether or not by reference to its location) on, in or by means of a telecommunication system where the event consists of one or more entities engaging in a specific activity at a specific time.

*Communications data*

(5) "Communications data", in relation to a telecommunications operator, telecommunications service or telecommunication system, means entity data or events data—

(a) which is (or is to be or is capable of being) held or obtained by, or on behalf of, a telecommunications operator and—
  (i) is about an entity to which a telecommunications service is provided and relates to the provision of the service,
  (ii) is comprised in, included as part of, attached to or logically associated with a communication (whether by the sender or otherwise) for the purposes of a telecommunication system by means of which the communication is being or may be transmitted, or
  (iii) does not fall within sub-paragraph (i) or (ii) but does relate to the use of a telecommunications service or a telecommunication system,

(b) which is available directly from a telecommunication system and falls within sub-paragraph (ii) of paragraph (a), or

(c) which—
  (i) is (or is to be or is capable of being) held or obtained by, or on behalf of, a telecommunications operator,
  (ii) is about the architecture of a telecommunication system, and
  (iii) is not about a specific person,

but does not include any content of a communication or anything which, in the absence of subsection (6)(b), would be content of a communication.

*Content of a communication*

(6) "Content", in relation to a communication and a telecommunications operator, telecommunications service or telecommunication system, means any element of the communication, or any data attached to or logically associated with the communication, which reveals anything of what might reasonably be considered to be the meaning (if any) of the communication, but—

(a) any meaning arising from the fact of the communication or from any data relating to the transmission of the communication is to be disregarded, and

(b) anything which is systems data is not content.

*Other definitions*

(7) "Entity" means a person or thing.

(8) "Public telecommunications service" means any telecommunications service which is offered or provided to the public, or a substantial section of the public, in any one or more parts of the United Kingdom.

(9) "Public telecommunication system" means a telecommunication system located in the United Kingdom—

(a) by means of which any public telecommunications service is provided, or

(b) which consists of parts of any other telecommunication system by means of which any such service is provided.

(10) "Telecommunications operator" means a person who—

(a) offers or provides a telecommunications service to persons in the United Kingdom, or

(b) controls or provides a telecommunication system which is (wholly or partly)—
  (i) in the United Kingdom, or
  (ii) controlled from the United Kingdom.

(11) "Telecommunications service" means any service that consists in the provision of access to, and of facilities for making use of, any telecommunication system (whether or not one provided by the person providing the service).

(12) For the purposes of subsection (11), the cases in which a service is to be taken to consist in the provision of access to, and of facilities for making use of, a telecommunication system include any case where a service consists in or includes facilitating the creation, management or storage of communications transmitted, or that may be transmitted, by means of such a system.

(13) "Telecommunication system" means a system (including the apparatus comprised in it) that exists (whether wholly or partly in the United Kingdom or elsewhere) for the purpose of facilitating the transmission of communications by any means involving the use of electrical or electromagnetic energy.

(14) "Private telecommunication system" means any telecommunication system which—

(a) is not a public telecommunication system,

(b) is attached, directly or indirectly, to a public telecommunication system (whether or not for the purposes of the communication in question), and

(c) includes apparatus which is both located in the United Kingdom and used (with or without other apparatus) for making the attachment to that public telecommunication system.

[Investigatory Powers Act 2016, s 261.]

**7.11231ZZ65 262. Postal definitions** (1) The definitions in this section have effect for the purposes of this Act.

*Communication*

(2) "Communication", in relation to a postal operator or postal service (but not in the definition of "postal service" in this section), includes anything transmitted by a postal service.

*Communications data*

(3) "Communications data", in relation to a postal operator or postal service, means—

(a) postal data comprised in, included as part of, attached to or logically associated with a communication (whether by the sender or otherwise) for the purposes of a postal service by means of which it is being or may be transmitted,

(b) information about the use made by any person of a postal service (but excluding any content of a communication (apart from information within paragraph (a)), or

(c) information not within paragraph (a) or (b) that is (or is to be or is capable of being) held or obtained by or on behalf of a person providing a postal service, is about those to whom the service is provided by that person and relates to the service so provided.

*Postal data*

(4) "Postal data" means data which—

(a) identifies, or purports to identify, any person, apparatus or location to or from which a communication is or may be transmitted,

(b) identifies or selects, or purports to identify or select, apparatus through which, or by means of which, a communication is or may be transmitted,

(c) identifies, or purports to identify, the time at which an event relating to a communication occurs, or

(d) identifies the data or other data as data comprised in, included as part of, attached to or logically associated with a particular communication.

For the purposes of this definition "data", in relation to a postal item, includes anything written on the outside of the item.

*Other definitions*

(5) "Postal item" means—

(a) any letter, postcard or other such thing in writing as may be used by the sender for imparting information to the recipient, or

(b) any packet or parcel.

(6) "Postal operator" means a person providing a postal service to persons in the United Kingdom.

(7) "Postal service" means a service that—

(a) consists in the following, or in any one or more of them, namely, the collection, sorting, conveyance, distribution and delivery (whether in the United Kingdom or elsewhere) of postal items, and

(b) has as its main purpose, or one of its main purposes, to make available, or to facilitate, a means of transmission from place to place of postal items containing communications.

(8) "Public postal service" means a postal service that is offered or provided to the public, or a substantial section of the public, in any one or more parts of the United Kingdom.

[Investigatory Powers Act 2016, s 262.]

**7.11231ZZ66 263. General definitions** (1) In this Act—

"apparatus" includes any equipment, machinery or device (whether physical or logical) and any wire or cable,

"civil proceedings" means any proceedings in or before any court or tribunal that are not criminal proceedings,

"crime" means conduct which—

(a) constitutes one or more criminal offences, or

(b) is, or corresponds to, any conduct which, if it all took place in any one part of the United Kingdom, would constitute one or more criminal offences,

"criminal proceedings" includes proceedings before a court in respect of a service offence within the meaning of the Armed Forces Act 2006 (and references to criminal prosecutions are to be read accordingly),

"data" includes data which is not electronic data and any information (whether or not electronic),

"destroy", in relation to electronic data, means delete the data in such a way as to make access to the data impossible (and related expressions are to be read accordingly),

"enactment" means an enactment whenever passed or made; and includes—

(a) an enactment contained in subordinate legislation within the meaning of the Interpretation Act 1978,

(b) an enactment contained in, or in an instrument made under, an Act of the Scottish Parliament,

(c) an enactment contained in, or in an instrument made under, a Measure or Act of the National Assembly for Wales, and
(d) an enactment contained in, or in an instrument made under, Northern Ireland legislation,

"enhanced affirmative procedure" is to be read in accordance with section 268,
"functions" includes powers and duties,
"GCHQ" has the same meaning as in the Intelligence Services Act 1994,
"head", in relation to an intelligence service, means—
(a) in relation to the Security Service, the Director-General,
(b) in relation to the Secret Intelligence Service, the Chief, and
(c) in relation to GCHQ, the Director,

"Her Majesty's forces" has the same meaning as in the Armed Forces Act 2006,
"identifying data" has the meaning given by subsection (2),
"intelligence service" means the Security Service, the Secret Intelligence Service or GCHQ,
"the Investigatory Powers Commissioner" means the person appointed under section 227(1)(a) (and the expression is also to be read in accordance with section 227(13)(b)),
"the Investigatory Powers Tribunal" means the tribunal established under section 65 of the Regulation of Investigatory Powers Act 2000,
"items subject to legal privilege"—
(a) in relation to England and Wales, has the same meaning as in the Police and Criminal Evidence Act 1984 (see section 10 of that Act),
(b) in relation to Scotland, means—
(i) communications between a professional legal adviser and the adviser's client, or
(ii) communications made in connection with, or in contemplation of, legal proceedings and for the purposes of those proceedings,

which would, by virtue of any rule of law relating to the confidentiality of communications, be protected in legal proceedings from disclosure, and
(c) in relation to Northern Ireland, has the same meaning as in the Police and Criminal Evidence (Northern Ireland) Order 1989 (SI 1989/1341 (N.I. 12)) (see Article 12 of that Order),

"Judicial Commissioner" means a person appointed under section 227(1)(a) or (b) (and the expression is therefore to be read in accordance with section 227(13)(a)),
"legal proceedings" means—
(a) civil or criminal proceedings in or before a court or tribunal, or
(b) proceedings before an officer in respect of a service offence within the meaning of the Armed Forces Act 2006,

"modify" includes amend, repeal or revoke (and related expressions are to be read accordingly),
"person holding office under the Crown" includes any servant of the Crown and any member of Her Majesty's forces,
"premises" includes any land, movable structure, vehicle, vessel, aircraft or hovercraft (and "set of premises" is to be read accordingly),
"primary legislation" means—
(a) an Act of Parliament,
(b) an Act of the Scottish Parliament,
(c) a Measure or Act of the National Assembly for Wales, or
(d) Northern Ireland legislation,

"public authority" means a public authority within the meaning of section 6 of the Human Rights Act 1998, other than a court or tribunal,
"serious crime" means crime where—
(a) the offence, or one of the offences, which is or would be constituted by the conduct concerned is an offence for which a person who has reached the age of 18 (or, in relation to Scotland or Northern Ireland, 21) and has no previous convictions could reasonably be expected to be sentenced to imprisonment for a term of 3 years or more, or
(b) the conduct involves the use of violence, results in substantial financial gain or is conduct by a large number of persons in pursuit of a common purpose,

"source of journalistic information" means an individual who provides material intending the recipient to use it for the purposes of journalism or knowing that it is likely to be so used,
"specified", in relation to an authorisation, warrant, notice or regulations, means specified or described in the authorisation, warrant, notice or (as the case may be) regulations (and "specify" is to be read accordingly),
"statutory", in relation to any function, means conferred by virtue of this Act or any other enactment,
"subordinate legislation" means—
(a) subordinate legislation within the meaning of the Interpretation Act 1978, or

(b) an instrument made under an Act of the Scottish Parliament, Northern Ireland legislation or a Measure or Act of the National Assembly for Wales,

"systems data" has the meaning given by subsection (4),

"the Technical Advisory Board" means the Board provided for by section 245,

"the Technology Advisory Panel" means the panel established in accordance with section 246(1),

"working day" means a day other than a Saturday, a Sunday, Christmas Day, Good Friday or a bank holiday under the Banking and Financial Dealings Act 1971 in any part of the United Kingdom.

(2) In this Act "identifying data" means—

(a) data which may be used to identify, or assist in identifying, any person, apparatus, system or service,

(b) data which may be used to identify, or assist in identifying, any event, or

(c) data which may be used to identify, or assist in identifying, the location of any person, event or thing.

(3) For the purposes of subsection (2), the reference to data which may be used to identify, or assist in identifying, any event includes—

(a) data relating to the fact of the event;

(b) data relating to the type, method or pattern of event;

(c) data relating to the time or duration of the event.

(4) In this Act "systems data" means any data that enables or facilitates, or identifies or describes anything connected with enabling or facilitating, the functioning of any of the following—

(a) a postal service;

(b) a telecommunication system (including any apparatus forming part of the system);

(c) any telecommunications service provided by means of a telecommunication system;

(d) a relevant system (including any apparatus forming part of the system);

(e) any service provided by means of a relevant system.

(5) For the purposes of subsection (4), a system is a "relevant system" if any communications or other information are held on or by means of the system.

(6) For the purposes of this Act detecting crime or serious crime is to be taken to include—

(a) establishing by whom, for what purpose, by what means and generally in what circumstances any crime or (as the case may be) serious crime was committed, and

(b) the apprehension of the person by whom any crime or (as the case may be) serious crime was committed.

(7) References in this Act to the examination of material obtained under a warrant are references to the material being read, looked at or listened to by the persons to whom it becomes available as a result of the warrant.

[Investigatory Powers Act 2016, s 263.]

**7.11231ZZ67 264. General definitions: "journalistic material" etc** (1) The definitions in this section have effect for the purposes of this Act.

*Journalistic material*

(2) "Journalistic material" means material created or acquired for the purposes of journalism.

(3) For the purposes of this section, where—

(a) a person ("R") receives material from another person ("S"), and

(b) S intends R to use the material for the purposes of journalism,

R is to be taken to have acquired it for those purposes.

Accordingly, a communication sent by S to R containing such material is to be regarded as a communication containing journalistic material.

(4) For the purposes of determining whether a communication contains material acquired for the purposes of journalism, it does not matter whether the material has been acquired for those purposes by the sender or recipient of the communication or by some other person.

(5) For the purposes of this section—

(a) material is not to be regarded as created or acquired for the purposes of journalism if it is created or acquired with the intention of furthering a criminal purpose, and

(b) material which a person intends to be used to further such a purpose is not to be regarded as intended to be used for the purposes of journalism.

*Confidential journalistic material*

(6) "Confidential journalistic material" means—

(a) in the case of material contained in a communication, journalistic material which the sender of the communication—

(i) holds in confidence, or

(ii) intends the recipient, or intended recipient, of the communication to hold in confidence;

(b) in any other case, journalistic material which a person holds in confidence.

(7) A person holds material in confidence for the purposes of this section if—

(a) the person holds it subject to an express or implied undertaking to hold it in confidence, or

(b) the person holds it subject to a restriction on disclosure or an obligation of secrecy contained in an enactment.

[Investigatory Powers Act 2016, s 264.]

7.11231ZZ68 265. **Index of defined expressions** In this Act, the expressions listed in the left-hand column have the meaning given by, or are to be interpreted in accordance with, the provisions listed in the right-hand column.

| *Expression* | *Provision* |
|---|---|
| Apparatus | Section 263(1) |
| Bulk equipment interference warrant | Section 176(1) |
| Bulk interception warrant | Section 136(1) |
| Civil proceedings | Section 263(1) |
| Communication | Sections 261(2) and 262(2) |
| Communications data | Sections 261(5) and 262(3) |
| Confidential journalistic material | Section 264(6) and (7) |
| Content of a communication (in relation to a telecommunications operator, telecommunications service or telecommunication system) | Section 261(6) |
| Crime | Section 263(1) |
| Criminal proceedings | Section 263(1) |
| Criminal prosecution | Section 263(1) |
| Data | Section 263(1) |
| Destroy (in relation to electronic data) and related expressions | Section 263(1) |
| Detecting crime or serious crime | Section 263(6) |
| Enactment | Section 263(1) |
| Enhanced affirmative procedure | Section 263(1) |
| Entity | Section 261(7) |
| Entity data | Section 261(3) |
| Events data | Section 261(4) |
| Examination (in relation to material obtained under a warrant) | Section 263(7) |
| Functions | Section 263(1) |
| GCHQ | Section 263(1) |
| Head (in relation to an intelligence service) | Section 263(1) |
| Her Majesty's forces | Section 263(1) |
| Identifying data | Section 263(2) and (3) |
| Intelligence service | Section 263(1) |
| Interception of communication (postal service) | Sections 4(7) and 5 |
| Interception of communication (telecommunication system) | Sections 4(1) to (6) and 5(1) |
| Interception of communication in the United Kingdom | Section 4(8) |
| Internet connection record | Section 62(7) |
| Investigatory Powers Commissioner | Section 263(1) |
| Investigatory Powers Tribunal | Section 263(1) |
| Items subject to legal privilege | Section 263(1) |
| Journalistic material | Section 264(2) to (5) |
| Judicial Commissioner | Section 263(1) |
| Judicial Commissioners | Section 227(7) |
| Lawful authority (in relation to interception of communication) | Section 6 |
| Legal proceedings | Section 263(1) |
| Modify (and related expressions) | Section 263(1) |
| Person holding office under the Crown | Section 263(1) |
| Postal data | Section 262(4) |
| Postal item | Section 262(5) |
| Postal item in course of transmission by postal service | Section 4(7) |
| Postal operator | Section 262(6) |

| | |
|---|---|
| Postal service | Section 262(7) |
| Premises | Section 263(1) |
| Primary legislation | Section 263(1) |
| Private telecommunication system | Section 261(14) |
| Public authority | Section 263(1) |
| Public postal service | Section 262(8) |
| Public telecommunications service | Section 261(8) |
| Public telecommunication system | Section 261(9) |
| Serious crime | Section 263(1) (and paragraph 6 of Schedule 9) |
| Source of journalistic information | Section 263(1) |
| Specified and specify (in relation to an authorisation, warrant, notice or regulations) | Section 263(1) |
| Statutory (in relation to any function) | Section 263(1) |
| Subordinate legislation | Section 263(1) |
| Systems data | Section 263(4) and (5) |
| Technical Advisory Board | Section 263(1) |
| Technology Advisory Panel | Section 263(1) |
| Telecommunications operator | Section 261(10) |
| Telecommunications service | Section 261(11) and (12) |
| Telecommunication system | Section 261(13) |
| Working day | Section 263(1) |

[Investigatory Powers Act 2016, s 265.]

*Supplementary provision*

7.11231ZZ69 **266. Offences by bodies corporate etc** (1) This section applies if an offence under this Act is committed by a body corporate or a Scottish partnership.

(2) If the offence is proved to have been committed with the consent or connivance of, or to be attributable to any neglect on the part of—

(a) a senior officer of the body corporate or Scottish partnership, or

(b) a person purporting to act in such a capacity,

the senior officer or person (as well as the body corporate or partnership) is guilty of the offence and liable to be proceeded against and punished accordingly.

(3) In this section—

"director", in relation to a body corporate whose affairs are managed by its members, means a member of the body corporate,

"senior officer" means—

(a) in relation to a body corporate, a director, manager, secretary or other similar officer of the body corporate, and

(b) in relation to a Scottish partnership, a partner in the partnership.

[Investigatory Powers Act 2016, s 266.]

7.11231ZZ70 **267. Regulations** (1) Any power of the Secretary of State or the Treasury to make regulations under this Act—

(a) is exercisable by statutory instrument,

(b) may be exercised so as to make different provision for different purposes or different areas, and

(c) includes power to make supplementary, incidental, consequential, transitional, transitory or saving provision.

(2) See sections 72(3) and 73(6) for the procedure for a statutory instrument containing regulations under section 71 to which section 72 applies or (as the case may be) regulations under section 73(4) to which section 73(5) applies (enhanced affirmative procedure).

(3) A statutory instrument containing regulations under—

(a) section 12(4) or 271(2) which amend or repeal any provision of primary legislation,

(b) section 46(2),

(c) section 52(5),

(d) section 83,

(e) section 90(1),

(f) section 239,

(g) section 240(3),

(h) section 245,

(i) section 253,

(j) section 257(1), or

(k) paragraph 33 of Schedule 8,

may not be made unless a draft of the instrument has been laid before, and approved by a resolution of, each House of Parliament.

(4) A statutory instrument containing—

(a) regulations under section 12(4) or 271(2) to which subsection (3) does not apply,

(b) regulations under section 65(5), or

(c) regulations under paragraph 2(1)(b) of Schedule 5,

is (if a draft of the instrument has not been laid before, and approved by a resolution of, each House of Parliament) subject to annulment in pursuance of a resolution of either House of Parliament.

(5) A statutory instrument containing—

(a) regulations under section 10(3),

(b) regulations under section 52(3),

(c) regulations under section 58(8)(a),

(d) regulations under section 71 to which section 72 does not apply,

(e) regulations under section 73(4) to which section 73(5) does not apply,

(f) regulations under section 133(6)(a), or

(g) regulations under section 255(7),

is subject to annulment in pursuance of a resolution of either House of Parliament.

(6) A statutory instrument containing regulations under paragraph 4 of Schedule 5 is subject to annulment in pursuance of a resolution of the House of Commons.

(7) See paragraphs 4(4) and 5(5) of Schedule 7 for the procedure for a statutory instrument containing regulations about the coming into force of a code of practice under that Schedule or of any revisions to such a code of practice (affirmative procedure or, in the case of the coming into force of revisions, a choice between that procedure and laying before Parliament after being made).

(8) A statutory instrument containing regulations which are subject to a particular parliamentary procedure under this Act may also include regulations which are subject to a different or no parliamentary procedure under this Act (but this subsection does not apply to regulations mentioned in subsection (2), (4), (6) or (7)).

(9) A statutory instrument which, by virtue of subsection (8), contains regulations which are subject to different parliamentary procedures, or one or more parliamentary procedure and no parliamentary procedure, is subject to whichever procedure is the higher procedure; and the order is as follows (the highest first)—

(a) the procedure set out in subsection (3) (the affirmative procedure),

(b) the procedure set out in subsection (5) above (the negative procedure),

(c) no procedure.

(10) Provision is not prevented from being included in regulations made under this Act merely because the provision could have been included in other regulations made under this Act which would have been subject to a different or no parliamentary procedure.

[Investigatory Powers Act 2016, s 267.]

**7.11231ZZ71 268. Enhanced affirmative procedure** (1) For the purposes of regulations under section 71 to which section 72 applies and regulations under section 73(4) to which section 73(5) applies, the enhanced affirmative procedure is as follows.

(2) Subsection (3) applies if—

(a) the Secretary of State has consulted under section 72(2) or (as the case may be) 73(5) in relation to making such regulations,

(b) a period of at least 12 weeks, beginning with the day on which any such consultation first began, has elapsed, and

(c) the Secretary of State considers it appropriate to proceed with making such regulations.

(3) The Secretary of State must lay before Parliament—

(a) draft regulations, and

(b) a document which explains the regulations.

(4) The Secretary of State may make regulations in the terms of the draft regulations laid under subsection (3) if, after the end of the 40-day period, the draft regulations are approved by a resolution of each House of Parliament.

(5) But subsections (6) to (9) apply instead of subsection (4) if—

(a) either House of Parliament so resolves within the 30-day period, or

(b) a committee of either House charged with reporting on the draft regulations so recommends within the 30-day period and the House to which the recommendation is made does not by resolution reject the recommendation within that period.

(6) The Secretary of State must have regard to—

(a) any representations,

(b) any resolution of either House of Parliament, and

(c) any recommendations of a committee of either House of Parliament charged with reporting on the draft regulations,

made during the 60-day period with regard to the draft regulations.

(7) If after the end of the 60-day period the draft regulations are approved by a resolution of each House of Parliament, the Secretary of State may make regulations in the terms of the draft

regulations.

(8) If after the end of the 60-day period the Secretary of State wishes to proceed with the draft regulations but with material changes, the Secretary of State may lay before Parliament—

(a) revised draft regulations, and

(b) a statement giving a summary of the changes proposed.

(9) If the revised draft regulations are approved by a resolution of each House of Parliament, the Secretary of State may make regulations in the terms of the revised draft regulations.

(10) For the purposes of this section regulations are made in the terms of draft regulations or revised draft regulations if they contain no material changes to the provisions of the draft, or revised draft, regulations.

(11) References in this section to the "30-day", "40-day" and "60-day" periods in relation to any draft regulations are to the periods of 30, 40 and 60 days beginning with the day on which the draft regulations were laid before Parliament; and, for this purpose, no account is to be taken of any time during which Parliament is dissolved or prorogued or during which either House is adjourned for more than four days.

[Investigatory Powers Act 2016, s 268.]

**7.11231ZZ72 270. Transitional, transitory or saving provision** (1) Schedule 9 (which contains transitional, transitory and saving provision including a general saving for lawful conduct) has effect.

(2) The Secretary of State may by regulations make such transitional, transitory or saving provision as the Secretary of State considers appropriate in connection with the coming into force of any provision of this Act.

[Investigatory Powers Act 2016, s 270.]

**7.11231ZZ73 271. Minor and consequential provision** (1) Schedule 10 (which contains minor and consequential provision) has effect.

(2) The Secretary of State may by regulations make such provision as the Secretary of State considers appropriate in consequence of this Act.

(3) The power to make regulations under subsection (2) may, in particular, be exercised by modifying any provision made by or under an enactment.

(4) In subsection (3) "enactment" does not include any primary legislation passed or made after the end of the Session in which this Act is passed.

[Investigatory Powers Act 2016, s 271.]

*Final provision*

**7.11231ZZ74 272. Commencement, extent and short title** (1) Subject to subsections (2) and (3), this Act comes into force on such day as the Secretary of State may by regulations appoint;[1] and different days may be appointed for different purposes.

(2) Sections 260 to 269, 270(2), 271(2) to (4) and this section come into force on the day on which this Act is passed.

(3) Sections 227 and 228 come into force at the end of the period of two months beginning with the day on which this Act is passed.

(4) Subject to subsections (5) to (7), this Act extends to England and Wales, Scotland and Northern Ireland.

(5) An amendment, repeal or revocation made by this Act of an enactment has the same extent within the United Kingdom as the enactment amended, repealed or revoked.

(6) Her Majesty may by Order in Council provide for any of the provisions of this Act to extend, with or without modifications, to the Isle of Man or any of the British overseas territories.

(7) Any power under an Act to extend any provision of that Act by Order in Council to any of the Channel Islands may be exercised so as to extend there (with or without modifications) any amendment or repeal of that provision which is made by or under this Act.

(8) This Act may be cited as the Investigatory Powers Act 2016.

[Investigatory Powers Act 2016, s 272.]

[1] For details of commencement regulations made, see the Note to the title of the Act.

SCHEDULE 2

Abolition of Disclosure Powers

Section 12(1)

*Health and Safety at Work etc Act 1974*

7.11231ZZ75 1. In section 20 of the Health and Safety at Work etc Act 1974 (powers of inspectors), at end, insert—

"(9) Nothing in this section is to be read as enabling an inspector to secure the disclosure by a telecommunications operator or postal operator of communications data without the consent of the operator.

(10) In subsection (9) "communications data", "postal operator" and "telecommunications operator" have the same meanings as in the Investigatory Powers Act 2016 (see sections 261 and 262 of that Act)."

*Criminal Justice Act 1987*

2. In section 2 of the Criminal Justice Act 1987 (investigation powers of Director of Serious Fraud Office), after subsection (10), insert—

"(10A) Nothing in this section is to be read as enabling a person to secure the disclosure by a telecommunications operator or postal operator of communications data without the consent of the operator.

(10B) In subsection (10A) "communications data", "postal operator" and "telecommunications operator" have the same meanings as in the Investigatory Powers Act 2016 (see sections 261 and 262 of that Act)."

*Consumer Protection Act 1987*

**3.** In section 29 of the Consumer Protection Act 1987 (powers of search etc), at end, insert—

"(8) The officer may not exercise a power under this section to secure the disclosure by a telecommunications operator or postal operator of communications data without the consent of the operator.

(9) In subsection (8) "communications data", "postal operator" and "telecommunications operator" have the same meanings as in the Investigatory Powers Act 2016 (see sections 261 and 262 of that Act)."

*Environmental Protection Act 1990*

**4.** In section 71 of the Environmental Protection Act 1990 (obtaining of information from persons and authorities), at end, insert—

"(5) Nothing in this section is to be read as enabling a person to secure the disclosure by a telecommunications operator or postal operator of communications data without the consent of the operator.

(6) In subsection (5) "communications data", "postal operator" and "telecommunications operator" have the same meanings as in the Investigatory Powers Act 2016 (see sections 261 and 262 of that Act)."

*Social Security Administration Act 1992*

**5.** In section 109B of the Social Security Administration Act 1992 (power to require information)—

(a) in subsection (2A) omit paragraph (j),

(b) in subsection (2E) for the words from "for" to the end of the subsection substitute "so as to secure the disclosure by a telecommunications operator or postal operator of communications data without the consent of the operator.",

(c) omit subsection (2F), and

(d) in subsection (7)—

(i) after the definition of "bank" insert—

""communications data" has the same meaning as in the Investigatory Powers Act 2016 (see sections 261 and 262 of that Act);",

(ii) after the definition of "insurer" insert—

""postal operator" has the same meaning as in the Investigatory Powers Act 2016 (see section 262 of that Act);", and

(iii) for the definition of "telecommunications service" substitute—

""telecommunications operator" has the same meaning as in the Investigatory Powers Act 2016 (see section 261 of that Act)."

**6.** In section 109C of the Social Security Administration Act 1992 (powers of entry) for subsection (6) substitute—

"(6) Subsections (2E) and (5) of section 109B apply for the purposes of this section as they apply for the purposes of that section."

*Social Security Administration (Northern Ireland) Act 1992*

**7.** In section 103B of the Social Security Administration (Northern Ireland) Act 1992 (power to require information)—

(a) in subsection (2A) omit paragraph (i),

(b) in subsection (2E) for the words from "for" to the end of the subsection substitute "so as to secure the disclosure by a telecommunications operator or postal operator of communications data without the consent of the operator.",

(c) omit subsection (2F), and

(d) in subsection (7)—

(i) after the definition of "bank" insert—

""communications data" has the same meaning as in the Investigatory Powers Act 2016 (see sections 261 and 262 of that Act);",

(ii) after the definition of "insurer" insert—

""postal operator" has the same meaning as in the Investigatory Powers Act 2016 (see section 262 of that Act);", and

(iii) for the definition of "telecommunications service" substitute—

""telecommunications operator" has the same meaning as in the Investigatory Powers Act 2016 (see section 261 of that Act)."

**8.** In section 103C of the Social Security Administration (Northern Ireland) Act 1992 (powers of entry) for subsection (6) substitute—

"(6) Subsections (2E) and (5) of section 103B apply for the purposes of this section as they apply for the purposes of that section."

*Financial Services and Markets Act 2000*

**9.** In section 175 of the Financial Services and Markets Act 2000 (information gathering and investigations: supplemental provision), after subsection (5), insert—

"(5A) Nothing in this Part is to be read as enabling a person to secure the disclosure by a telecommunications operator or postal operator of communications data without the consent of the operator.

(5B) In subsection (5A) "communications data", "postal operator" and "telecommunications operator" have the same meanings as in the Investigatory Powers Act 2016 (see sections 261 and 262 of that Act)."

*Finance Act 2008*

**10.** In Schedule 36 to the Finance Act 2008 (information and inspection powers), in paragraph 19 (restrictions on powers: types of information), at end, insert—

"(4) An information notice does not require a telecommunications operator or postal operator to provide or produce communications data.

(5) In sub-paragraph (4) "communications data", "postal operator" and "telecommunications operator" have the same meanings as in the Investigatory Powers Act 2016 (see sections 261 and 262 of that Act)."

*Prevention of Social Housing Fraud (Power to Require Information) (England) Regulations 2014 (SI 2014/899)*

**11.** In regulation 4 of the Prevention of Social Housing Fraud (Power to Require Information) (England) Regulations 2014 (power to require information from persons who provide telecommunications services etc)—

(a) omit sub-paragraph (f) of paragraph (3),

(b) in sub-paragraph (g) of that paragraph for "(f)" substitute "(e)",

(c) omit paragraphs (6) and (7),

(d) after paragraph (10) insert—

"(10A) Nothing in this regulation is to be read as enabling a person to secure the disclosure by a telecommunications operator or postal operator of communications data without the consent of the operator.", and

(e) in paragraph (11)—

(i) after the definition of "bank" insert—

""communications data" has the same meaning as in the Investigatory Powers Act 2016 (see sections 261 and 262 of that Act);",

(ii) after the definition of "family" insert—

""postal operator" has the same meaning as in the Investigatory Powers Act 2016 (see section 262 of that Act);", and

(iii) for the definition of "telecommunications service" substitute—

""telecommunications operator" has the same meaning as in the Investigatory Powers Act 2016 (see section 261 of that Act)."

[Investigatory Powers Act 2016, Sch 2.]

## SCHEDULE 3

Exceptions to section 56

Section 56

*Introductory*

**7.11231ZZ76** **1.** This Schedule contains—

(a) exceptions to the exclusion by section 56(1) of certain matters from legal proceedings, and

(b) limitations on those exceptions where that exclusion will still apply.

*Disclosures of lawfully intercepted communications*

**2.** (1) Section 56(1)(a) does not prohibit the disclosure of any content of a communication, or any secondary data obtained from a communication, if the interception of that communication was lawful by virtue of any of the following provisions—

(a) sections 6(1)(c) and 44 to 52;

(b) sections 1(5)(c), 3 and 4 of the Regulation of Investigatory Powers Act 2000;

(c) section 1(2)(b) and (3) of the Interception of Communications Act 1985.

(2) Where any disclosure is proposed to be, or has been, made on the grounds that it is authorised by sub-paragraph (1), section 56(1) does not prohibit the doing of anything in, or for the purposes of, so much of any proceedings as relates to the question whether that disclosure is or was so authorised.

*Disclosures of convictions for certain offences*

**3.** Section 56(1)(b) does not prohibit the doing of anything that discloses any conduct of a person for which that person has been convicted of—

(a) an offence under section 3(1), 43(7), 59 or 155,

(b) an offence under section 1(1) or (2), 11(7) or 19 of the Regulation of Investigatory Powers Act 2000, or

(c) an offence under section 1 of the Interception of Communications Act 1985.

*Proceedings before the Investigatory Powers Tribunal etc*

**4.** Section 56(1) does not apply in relation to—

(a) any proceedings before the Investigatory Powers Tribunal,

(b) any proceedings on an appeal under section 67A of the Regulation of Investigatory Powers Act 2000 (appeal against decisions of the Tribunal etc), or

(c) any proceedings arising out of such an appeal.

*Proceedings before Special Immigration Appeals Commission*

**5.** (1) Section 56(1) does not apply in relation to—

(a) any proceedings before the Special Immigration Appeals Commission, or

(b) any proceedings arising out of proceedings before that Commission.

(2) But sub-paragraph (1) does not permit the disclosure of anything to—

(a) the appellant or (as the case may be) applicant to the Special Immigration Appeals Commission, or

(b) any person who—

(i) represents that appellant or applicant for the purposes of the proceedings, and

(ii) does so otherwise than by virtue of appointment under section 6 of the Special Immigration Appeals Commission Act 1997.

*Proceedings before Proscribed Organisations Appeal Commission*

**6.** (1) Section 56(1) does not apply in relation to—

(a) any proceedings before the Proscribed Organisations Appeal Commission, or

(b) any proceedings arising out of proceedings before that Commission.

(2) But sub-paragraph (1) does not permit the disclosure of anything to any of the following—

(a) the applicant to the Commission;

(b) the organisation concerned (if different);

(c) any person designated under paragraph 6 of Schedule 3 to the Terrorism Act 2000 to conduct the proceedings on behalf of that organisation;

(d) any person who—

(i) represents that appellant or that organisation for the purposes of the proceedings, and

(ii) does so otherwise than by virtue of an appointment under paragraph 7 of that Schedule.

*Closed material proceedings*

**7.** (1) Section 56(1) does not apply in relation to any section 6 proceedings within the meaning given by section 14(1) of the Justice and Security Act 2013 (certain civil proceedings in which closed material applications may be made).

(2) But sub-paragraph (1) does not permit a prohibited section 6 disclosure.

(3) In the case of section 6 proceedings where the only relevant person is the Secretary of State, a "prohibited section 6 disclosure" means a disclosure of anything to—

(a) any person, other than the Secretary of State, who is or was a party to the proceedings, or

(b) any person who—

(i) represents such a person for the purposes of the proceedings, and

(ii) does so otherwise than by virtue of appointment as a special advocate.

(4) In the case of section 6 proceedings where the Secretary of State is not the only relevant person, or is not a relevant person but is a party to the proceedings, a "prohibited section 6 disclosure" means a disclosure of anything to—

(a) any person, other than the relevant person concerned or the Secretary of State, who is or was a party to the proceedings, or

(b) any person who—

(i) represents a person within paragraph (a) for the purposes of the proceedings, and

(ii) does so otherwise than by virtue of appointment as a special advocate.

(5) In this paragraph "relevant person", in relation to section 6 proceedings, has the meaning given by section 14(1) of the Justice and Security Act 2013.

*TPIM proceedings*

**8.** (1) Section 56(1) does not apply in relation to—

(a) any TPIM proceedings, or

(b) any proceedings arising out of any TPIM proceedings.

(2) But sub-paragraph (1) does not permit the disclosure of anything to—

(a) any person, other than the Secretary of State, who is or was a party to the proceedings, or

(b) any person who—

(i) represents such a person for the purposes of the proceedings, and

(ii) does so otherwise than by virtue of appointment as a special advocate under Schedule 4 to the Terrorism Prevention and Investigation Measures Act 2011.

(3) In this paragraph "TPIM proceedings" has the same meaning as in the Terrorism Prevention and Investigation Measures Act 2011.

*TEO proceedings*

**9.** (1) Section 56(1) does not apply in relation to—

(a) any TEO proceedings, or

(b) any proceedings arising out of any TEO proceedings.

(2) But sub-paragraph (1) does not permit the disclosure of anything to—

(a) any person, other than the Secretary of State, who is or was a party to the proceedings, or

(b) any person who—

(i) represents such a person for the purposes of the proceedings, and

(ii) does so otherwise than by virtue of appointment as a special advocate under Schedule 3 to the Counter-Terrorism and Security Act 2015.

(3) In this paragraph "TEO proceedings" has the meaning given by paragraph 1 of Schedule 3 to the Counter-Terrorism and Security Act 2015 (temporary exclusion orders: proceedings).

*Proceedings relating to freezing of terrorist assets etc*

**10.** (1) Section 56(1) does not apply in relation to—

(a) any financial restrictions proceedings, or

(b) any proceedings arising out of such proceedings.

(2) In this paragraph "financial restrictions proceedings" has the meaning given by section 65 of the Counter-Terrorism Act 2008.

**11.** Section 56(1) does not apply in relation to any proceedings—

(a) on an appeal under section 26, or an application under section 27, of the Terrorist Asset-Freezing etc Act 2010 (appeals and reviews by the court), or

(b) on a claim arising from any matter to which such an appeal or application relates,

or any proceedings arising out of such proceedings.

**12.** But neither paragraph 10 nor paragraph 11 permits the disclosure of anything to—

(a) any person, other than the Treasury, who is or was a party to the proceedings, or

(b) any person who—

(i) represents such a person for the purposes of the proceedings, and

(ii) does so otherwise than by virtue of appointment as a special advocate.

*Proceedings relating to release of prisoners etc in Northern Ireland*

**13.** (1) Section 56(1) does not apply in relation to—

(a) any proceedings before—

(i) the Parole Commissioners for Northern Ireland, or

(ii) any Sentence Review Commissioners appointed under section 1 of the Northern Ireland (Sentences) Act 1998, or

(b) any proceedings arising out of such proceedings.

(2) But sub-paragraph (1) does not permit the disclosure of anything to—

(a) any person, other than the Secretary of State, who is or was a party to the proceedings, or

(b) any person who—

(i) represents such a person for the purposes of the proceedings, and

(ii) does so otherwise than by virtue of appointment as a special advocate.

*Employment or industrial tribunal proceedings*

**14.** (1) Section 56(1) does not apply in relation to any proceedings before an employment tribunal where the applicant, or the applicant's representatives, are excluded for all or part of the proceedings pursuant to—

(a) a direction to the tribunal by virtue of section 10(5)(b) or (c) of the Employment Tribunals Act 1996 (exclusion from Crown employment proceedings by direction of Minister in interests of national security), or

(b) a determination of the tribunal by virtue of section 10(6) of that Act (determination by tribunal in interests of national security).

(2) Section 56(1) does not apply in relation to any proceedings before an industrial tribunal in Northern Ireland where the applicant, or the applicant's representatives, are excluded for all or part of the proceedings pursuant to—

(a) a direction to the tribunal by virtue of Article 12(5)(b) or (c) of the Industrial Tribunals (Northern Ireland) Order 1996 (SI 1996/1921 (N.I. 18)) (exclusion from Crown employment proceedings by direction of Minister in interests of national security), or

(b) a determination of the tribunal by virtue of Article 12(6) of that Order (determination by tribunal in interests of national security).

(3) Section 56(1) does not apply in relation to any proceedings arising out of proceedings within sub-paragraph (1) or (2).

**15.** But paragraph 14 does not permit the disclosure of anything to—

(a) the person who is or was the applicant in the proceedings before the employment or industrial tribunal, or

(b) any person who—

(i) represents that person for the purposes of any proceedings within paragraph 14, and

(ii) does so otherwise than by virtue of appointment as a special advocate.

*Proceedings relating to dismissal for certain offences*

**16.** Section 56(1) does not prohibit anything done in, for the purposes of, or in connection with, so much of any legal proceedings as relates to the fairness or unfairness of a dismissal on the following grounds—

(a) any conduct constituting an offence under section 3(1), 43(7), 59 or 155;

(b) any conduct taking place before the coming into force of this paragraph and constituting—

(i) an offence under section 1(1) or (2), 11(7) or 19 of the Regulation of Investigatory Powers Act 2000, or

(ii) an offence under section 1 of the Interception of Communications Act 1985.

*Proceedings on appeals relating to claims of discrimination in Northern Ireland*

**17.** (1) Section 56(1) does not apply in relation to any proceedings on an appeal under Article 80(2) of the Fair Employment and Treatment (Northern Ireland) Order 1998 (SI 1998/3162 (N.I. 21)) where—

(a) the appeal relates to a claim of discrimination in contravention of Part 3 of that Order (employment cases) and to a certificate of the Secretary of State that the act concerned was justified for the purpose of safeguarding national security, and

(b) a party to the appeal, or the party's representatives, are excluded for all or part of the proceedings by virtue of section 91(4)(b) of the Northern Ireland Act 1998.

(2) Section 56(1) does not apply in relation to any proceedings arising out of proceedings within sub-paragraph (1).

**18.** But paragraph 17 does not permit the disclosure of anything to—

(a) any person who is or was excluded from all or part of the proceedings mentioned in paragraph 17(1), or

(b) any person who—

(i) represents such a person for the purposes of any proceedings within paragraph 17, and

(ii) does so otherwise than by virtue of appointment as a special advocate.

*Civil proceedings for enforcement of duty to assist with implementation of warrants*

**19.** Section 56(1) does not apply in relation to any civil proceedings under section 43(8) of this Act or section 11(8) of the Regulation of Investigatory Powers Act 2000 (enforcement of duty of operators to assist with implementation of warrants).

*Proceedings for certain offences*

**20.** (1) Section 56(1) does not apply in relation to any proceedings for a relevant offence.

(2) "Relevant offence" means—

(a) an offence under any provision of this Act;

(b) an offence under section 1 of the Interception of Communications Act 1985;

(c) an offence under any provision of the Regulation of Investigatory Powers Act 2000;

(d) an offence under section 47 or 48 of the Wireless Telegraphy Act 2006;

(e) an offence under section 83 or 84 of the Postal Services Act 2000;

(f) an offence under section 4 of the Official Secrets Act 1989 relating to any such information, document or article as is mentioned in subsection (3)(a) or (c) of that section;

(g) an offence under section 1 or 2 of the Official Secrets Act 1911 relating to any sketch, plan, model, article, note, document or information which—

(i) incorporates, or relates to, the content of any intercepted communication or any secondary data obtained from a communication, or

(ii) tends to suggest that any interception-related conduct has or may have occurred or may be going to occur;

(h) an offence of perjury committed in the course of any relevant proceedings;

(i) an offence of attempting or conspiring to commit an offence falling within any of paragraphs (a) to (h);

(j) an offence under Part 2 of the Serious Crime Act 2007 in relation to an offence falling within any of those paragraphs;

(k) an offence of aiding, abetting, counselling or procuring the commission of an offence falling within any of those paragraphs;

(l) contempt of court committed in the course of, or in relation to, any relevant proceedings.

(3) In this paragraph—

"intercepted communication" and "interception-related conduct" have the same meaning as in section 56;

"relevant proceedings" means any proceedings mentioned in paragraphs 4 to 19.

*Disclosures to prosecutors and judges*

**21.** (1) Nothing in section 56(1) prohibits—

(a) a disclosure to a person ("P") conducting a criminal prosecution that is made for the purpose only of enabling P to determine what is required of P by P's duty to secure the fairness of the prosecution, or

(b) a disclosure to a relevant judge in a case in which the judge has ordered the disclosure to be made to the judge alone.

(2) A relevant judge may order a disclosure under sub-paragraph (1)(b) only if the judge considers that the exceptional circumstances of the case make the disclosure essential in the interests of justice.

(3) Where in any criminal proceedings—

(a) a relevant judge orders a disclosure under sub-paragraph (1)(b), and

(b) in consequence of that disclosure, the judge considers that there are exceptional circumstances requiring the judge to make a direction under this sub-paragraph,

the judge may direct the person conducting the prosecution to make for the purposes of the proceedings any admission of fact which the judge considers essential in the interests of justice.

(4) But nothing in any direction under sub-paragraph (3) may authorise or require anything to be done in

contravention of section 56(1).

(5) In this paragraph "relevant judge" means—

(a) any judge of the High Court or of the Crown Court or any Circuit judge,

(b) any judge of the High Court of Justiciary or any sheriff,

(c) in relation to proceedings before the Court Martial, the judge advocate for those proceedings, or

(d) any person holding a judicial office that entitles the person to exercise the jurisdiction of a judge falling within paragraph (a) or (b).

*Disclosures to inquiries and inquests*

**22.** (1) Nothing in section 56(1) prohibits—

(a) a disclosure to the panel of an inquiry held under the Inquiries Act 2005, or

(b) a disclosure to a person appointed as legal adviser to such an inquiry,

where, in the course of the inquiry, the panel has ordered the disclosure to be made to the panel alone or (as the case may be) to the panel and any person appointed as legal adviser to the inquiry.

(2) The panel of an inquiry may order a disclosure under sub-paragraph (1) only if it considers that the exceptional circumstances of the case make the disclosure essential to enable the inquiry to fulfil its terms of reference.

(3) Any reference in this paragraph to a person appointed as legal adviser to an inquiry is a reference to a person appointed as solicitor or counsel to the inquiry.

**23.** (1) Section 56(1) does not apply in relation to any restricted proceedings of an inquiry held under the Inquiries Act 2005.

(2) Proceedings of an inquiry held under that Act are "restricted proceedings" for the purposes of this paragraph if restrictions imposed under section 19 of that Act are in force prohibiting attendance at the proceedings by any person who is not—

(a) a member of the panel of the inquiry,

(b) a person appointed as legal adviser to the inquiry,

(c) a person who is a relevant party to the proceedings,

(d) a person representing such a person for the purposes of the proceedings, or

(e) a person performing functions necessary for the proper functioning of the proceedings.

(3) But sub-paragraph (1) does not permit any disclosure which has not been made in accordance with paragraph 22(1).

(4) In this paragraph "relevant party", in relation to any proceedings of an inquiry, means—

(a) any person making a disclosure to the panel of the inquiry, or to a person appointed as legal adviser to the inquiry, in accordance with paragraph 22(1);

(b) any person giving evidence to the inquiry in circumstances where, in the absence of sub-paragraph (1), the prohibition imposed by section 56(1) would be breached;

(c) any person whose conduct is the interception-related conduct (within the meaning of section 56) to which the disclosure or evidence relates (whether or not that conduct has in fact occurred);

(d) any other person to whom the subject-matter of the disclosure or evidence has been lawfully disclosed in accordance with section 58.

(5) Any reference in this paragraph to a person appointed as legal adviser to an inquiry is to be read in accordance with paragraph 22(3).

**24.** (1) Nothing in section 56(1) prohibits—

(a) a disclosure to a person (the "nominated person") nominated under paragraph 3(1) of Schedule 10 to the Coroners and Justice Act 2009 (investigation by judge or former judge) to conduct an investigation into a person's death, or

(b) a disclosure to a person appointed as legal adviser to an inquest forming part of an investigation conducted by the nominated person,

where, in the course of the investigation, the nominated person has ordered the disclosure to be made to the nominated person alone or (as the case may be) to the nominated person and any person appointed as legal adviser to the inquest.

(2) The nominated person may order a disclosure under sub-paragraph (1) only if the person considers that the exceptional circumstances of the case make the disclosure essential in the interests of justice.

(3) In a case where a person who is not a nominated person is or has been conducting an investigation under Part 1 of the Coroners and Justice Act 2009 into a person's death, nothing in section 56(1) prohibits—

(a) a disclosure to the person that there is intercepted material in existence which is, or may be, relevant to the investigation;

(b) a disclosure to a person appointed as legal adviser to an inquest forming part of the investigation which is made for the purposes of determining—

(i) whether any intercepted material is, or may be, relevant to the investigation, and

(ii) if so, whether it is necessary for the material to be disclosed to the person conducting the investigation.

(4) In sub-paragraph (3) "intercepted material" means—

(a) any content of an intercepted communication (within the meaning of section 56), or

(b) any secondary data obtained from a communication.

(5) Any reference in this paragraph to a person appointed as legal adviser to an inquest is a reference to a person appointed as solicitor or counsel to the inquest.

[Investigatory Powers Act 2016, Sch 3.]

SCHEDULE 4
Relevant Public Authorities and Designated Senior Officers etc

Section 70(1)

## PART 1
## TABLE OF AUTHORITIES AND OFFICERS ETC

*Table*

**7.11231ZZ77**

| *(1)* *Relevant public authority* | *(2)* *DSO: minimum office, rank or position* | *(3)* *Type of communications data that may be obtained by DSO* | *(4)* *Paragraphs of section 61(7) specified for DSO* |
|---|---|---|---|
| Police force maintained under section 2 of the Police Act 1996 | Inspector | Entity data | (a), (b), (c), (d), (e), (g) and (i) |
| | Superintendent | All | (a), (b), (c), (d), (e), (g) and (i) |
| Metropolitan police force | Inspector | Entity data | (a), (b), (c), (d), (e), (g) and (i) |
| | Superintendent | All | (a), (b), (c), (d), (e), (g) and (i) |
| City of London police force | Inspector | Entity data | (a), (b), (c), (d), (e), (g) and (i) |
| | Superintendent | All | (a), (b), (c), (d), (e), (g) and (i) |
| Police Service of Scotland | Inspector | Entity data | (a), (b), (c), (d), (e), (g) and (i) |
| | Superintendent | All | (a), (b), (c), (d), (e), (g) and (i) |
| Police Service of Northern Ireland | Inspector | Entity data | (a), (b), (c), (d), (e), (g) and (i) |
| | Superintendent | All | (a), (b), (c), (d), (e), (g) and (i) |
| British Transport Police Force | Inspector | Entity data | (a), (b), (c), (d), (e), (g) and (i) |
| | Superintendent | All | (a), (b), (c), (d), (e), (g) and (i) |
| Ministry of Defence Police | Inspector | Entity data | (a), (b), (c) and (g) |
| | Superintendent | All | (a), (b), (c) and (g) |
| Royal Navy Police | Lieutenant Commander | Entity data | (a), (b), (c) and (g) |
| | Commander | All | (a), (b), (c) and (g) |
| Royal Military Police | Major | Entity data | (a), (b), (c) and (g) |
| | Lieutenant Colonel | All | (a), (b), (c) and (g) |
| Royal Air Force Police | Squadron Leader | Entity data | (a), (b), (c) and (g) |
| | Wing Commander | All | (a), (b), (c) and (g) |
| Security Service | General Duties 4 or any other level 4 officer | Entity data | (a), (b) and (c) |
| | General Duties 3 or any other level 3 officer | All | (a), (b) and (c) |
| Secret Intelligence Service | Grade 6 | All | (a), (b) and (c) |
| GCHQ | GC8 | All | (a), (b) and (c) |
| Ministry of Defence | Member of the Senior Civil Service or equivalent | All | (a) |
| | Grade 7 in the Fraud Defence Unit | All | (b) |
| Department of Health | Grade 7 in the Medicines and Healthcare Products Regulatory Agency | All | (b), (d) and (e) |
| | Grade 7 in the Anti-Fraud Unit | All | (b) |
| Home Office | Immigration inspector or equivalent with responsibility for investigations or other functions relating to immigration and border security | All | (b) |

| | | | |
|---|---|---|---|
| | Immigration inspector or equivalent with responsibility for anti-corruption in relation to investigations or other functions relating to immigration and border security | All | (b) |
| | Immigration inspector or equivalent with responsibility for asylum fraud investigations | All | (b) |
| | Immigration inspector or equivalent with responsibility for security and intelligence in the immigration detention estate | All | (b), (d) and (i) |
| Ministry of Justice | Manager in the security group of the National Offender Management Service responsible for intelligence | Entity data | (b) and (d) |
| | Senior manager in the security group of the National Offender Management Service responsible for intelligence | All | (b) and (d) |
| National Crime Agency | Grade 3 | Entity data | (b), (g) and (i) |
| | Grade 2 | All | (b), (g) and (i) |
| Her Majesty's Revenue and Customs | Higher officer | Entity data | (b) and (f) |
| | Senior officer | All | (b) and (f) |
| Department for Transport | Enforcement Officer in Maritime and Coastguard Agency | Entity data | (b) and (d) |
| | Head of Enforcement in Maritime and Coastguard Agency | All | (b) and (d) |
| | Maritime Operations Commander (grade 7) in the Maritime and Coastguard Agency | All | (g) |
| | Principal Inspector in the Air Accident Investigation Branch, the Marine Accident Investigation Branch or the Rail Accident Investigation Branch | All | (d) |
| Department for Work and Pensions | Senior Executive Officer in Fraud and Error Services | All | (b) |
| | Senior Executive Officer in the Child Maintenance Group Central Legal Services | All | (b) |
| An ambulance trust in England | Duty Manager of Ambulance Trust Control Rooms | All | (g) |
| Common Services Agency for the Scottish Health Service | Head of Counter Fraud Services | All | (b) |
| Competition and Markets Authority | Member of the Senior Civil Service with responsibility for cartels or criminal enforcement | All | (b) |
| Criminal Cases Review Commission | Investigations Adviser | All | (h) |
| Department for Communities in Northern Ireland | Deputy Principal | All | (b) |
| Department for the Economy in Northern Ireland | Deputy chief inspector in trading standards services | All | (b) |
| Department of Justice in Northern Ireland | Governor 4 in the Northern Ireland Prison Service | All | (b), (d) and (i) |
| Financial Conduct Authority | Head of department in the Enforcement and Market Oversight Division | All | (b) and (j) |

| | | | |
|---|---|---|---|
| A fire and rescue authority under the Fire and Rescue Services Act 2004 | Watch Manager (Control) | All | (g) |
| Food Standards Agency | Grade 6 | All | (b) |
| Food Standards Scotland | Head of the Scottish Food Crime and Incidents Unit | All | (b) |
| Gambling Commission | Senior manager | All | (b) |
| Gangmasters and Labour Abuse Authority | Head of operations | All | (b) |
| Health and Safety Executive | Band 1 inspector | All | (b), (d) and (e) |
| Independent Police Complaints Commission | Deputy Chair or Director | All | (b) and (i) |
| Information Commissioner | Group Manager | Entity data | (b) |
| | Head of enforcement or an equivalent grade | All | (b) |
| National Health Service Business Services Authority | Senior manager (of pay band 8b) in the Counter Fraud and Security Management Services Division | All | (b) |
| Northern Ireland Ambulance Service Health and Social Care Trust | Watch Manager (Control) | All | (g) |
| Northern Ireland Fire and Rescue Service Board | Watch Manager (Control) | All | (g) |
| Northern Ireland Health and Social Care Regional Business Services Organisation | Assistant Director Counter Fraud and Probity Services | All | (b) |
| Office of Communications | Senior associate | All | (b) |
| Office of the Police Ombudsman for Northern Ireland | Senior investigating officer | All | (b) |
| Police Investigations and Review Commissioner | Commissioner or Director of Operations | All | (b) and (i) |
| Scottish Ambulance Service Board | Watch Manager (Control) | All | (g) |
| Scottish Criminal Cases Review Commission | Investigations Adviser | All | (h) |
| Serious Fraud Office | Grade 6 | All | (b) |
| Welsh Ambulance Services National Health Service Trust | Watch Manager (Control) | All | (g) |

## PART 2
## INTERPRETATION OF TABLE

**1.** In the table in Part 1 of this Schedule—

"ambulance trust in England" means—

(a) an NHS trust all or most of whose hospitals, establishments and facilities are in England and which provides ambulance services, or

(b) an NHS foundation trust which provides such services,

"entity data" means any communications data which is entity data.

[Investigatory Powers Act 2016, Sch 4.]

## SCHEDULE 7
### Codes of Practice

Section 241

*Scope of codes*

7.11231ZZ78 **1.** (1) The Secretary of State must issue one or more codes of practice about the exercise of functions conferred by virtue of this Act.

(2) Sub-paragraph (1) does not apply in relation to—

(a) any functions conferred by virtue of this Act on—

(i) the Investigatory Powers Commissioner or any other Judicial Commissioner,

(ii) the Information Commissioner,

(iii) the Investigatory Powers Tribunal,

(iv) any other court or tribunal,

(v) the Technical Advisory Board, or

(vi) the Technology Advisory Panel,

(b) any function to make subordinate legislation which is conferred by virtue of this Act on the Secretary of State or the Treasury.

(3) A code may, in particular, contain provision about the training of people who may exercise functions in relation to which sub-paragraph (1) applies.

2. (1) Each code must include—

(a) provision designed to protect the public interest in the confidentiality of sources of journalistic information, and

(b) provision about particular considerations applicable to any data which relates to a member of a profession which routinely holds items subject to legal privilege or relevant confidential information.

(2) A code about the exercise of functions conferred by virtue of Part 2, Part 5 or Chapter 1 or 3 of Part 6 must also contain provision about when circumstances are to be regarded as "exceptional and compelling circumstances" for the purposes of any provision of that Part or Chapter that restricts the exercise of functions in relation to items subject to legal privilege by reference to the existence of such circumstances.

(3) The Investigatory Powers Commissioner must keep under review any provision included in a code by virtue of sub-paragraph (2).

(4) In this paragraph—

"relevant confidential information" means information which is held in confidence by a member of a profession and consists of—

(a) personal records or journalistic material which are (or would be if held in England and Wales) excluded material as defined by section 11 of the Police and Criminal Evidence Act 1984, or

(b) communications between Members of Parliament and their constituents,

and the references in this paragraph to a member of a profession include references to any person acting in the course of any trade, business, profession or other occupation or for the purposes of any paid or unpaid office.

3. (1) A code about the exercise of functions conferred by virtue of Part 3 must contain provision about communications data held by public authorities by virtue of that Part.

(2) Such provision must, in particular, include provision about—

(a) why, how and where the data is held,

(b) who may access the data on behalf of the authority,

(c) to whom, and under what conditions, the data may be disclosed,

(d) the processing of the data for purposes otherwise than in connection with the purposes for which it was obtained or retained,

(e) the processing of the data together with other data,

(f) the processes for determining how long the data should be held and for the destruction of the data.

*Procedural requirements*

4. (1) Before issuing a code the Secretary of State must—

(a) prepare and publish a draft of the code, and

(b) consider any representations made about it,

and may modify the draft.

(2) The Secretary of State must, in particular, consult the Investigatory Powers Commissioner and, in the case of a code relating to the exercise of functions conferred by virtue of Part 4, the Information Commissioner.

(3) A code comes into force in accordance with regulations made by the Secretary of State.

(4) A statutory instrument containing such regulations may not be made unless a draft of the instrument has been laid before, and approved by a resolution of, each House of Parliament.

(5) When a draft instrument is laid, the code to which it relates must also be laid.

(6) No draft instrument may be laid until the consultation required by sub-paragraphs (1) and (2) has taken place.

*Revision of codes*

5. (1) The Secretary of State may from time to time revise the whole or part of a code.

(2) Before issuing any revision of a code the Secretary of State must—

(a) prepare and publish a draft, and

(b) consider any representations made about it,

and may modify the draft.

(3) The Secretary of State must, in particular, consult the Investigatory Powers Commissioner and, in the case of a code relating to the exercise of functions conferred by virtue of Part 4, the Information Commissioner.

(4) A revision of a code comes into force in accordance with regulations made by the Secretary of State.

(5) A statutory instrument containing such regulations must be laid before Parliament if the regulations have been made without a draft having been laid before, and approved by a resolution of, each House of Parliament.

(6) When an instrument or draft instrument is laid, the revision of a code to which it relates must also be laid.

(7) No instrument or draft instrument may be laid until the consultation required by sub-paragraphs (2) and (3) has taken place.

*Effect of codes*

6. (1) A person must have regard to a code when exercising any functions to which the code relates.

(2) A failure on the part of a person to comply with any provision of a code does not of itself make that person liable to criminal or civil proceedings.

(3) A code is admissible in evidence in any such proceedings.

(4) A court or tribunal may, in particular, take into account a failure by a person to have regard to a code in determining a question in any such proceedings.

(5) A supervisory authority exercising functions by virtue of this Act may take into account a failure by a person to have regard to a code in determining a question which arises in connection with the exercise of those functions.

(6) In this paragraph "supervisory authority" means—

(a) the Investigatory Powers Commissioner or any other Judicial Commissioner,

(b) the Information Commissioner, or

(c) the Investigatory Powers Tribunal.

[Investigatory Powers Act 2016, Sch 7.]

## SCHEDULE 9

### Transitional, Transitory and Saving Provision

Section 270(1)

*Lawful interception of communications*

**7.11231ZZ79** **1.** Any agreement which, immediately before the day on which section 10 comes into force, is designated for the purposes of section 1(4) of the Regulation of Investigatory Powers Act 2000 is to be treated, on and after that day, as designated as an international mutual assistance agreement by regulations under section 10(3) of this Act.

*Authorisations for obtaining communications data*

**2.** The reference to the Gangmasters and Labour Abuse Authority in the table in Part 1 of Schedule 4 is to be read, in relation to any time before the day on which section 10(1) of the Immigration Act 2016 (renaming of Gangmasters Licensing Authority) comes into force, as a reference to the Gangmasters Licensing Authority.

*Retention of communications data*

**3.** (1) A retention notice under section 1 of the Data Retention and Investigatory Powers Act 2014 which is in force immediately before the commencement day is to be treated, on or after that day, as a retention notice under section 87 of this Act; and Part 4 of this Act is to be read accordingly but as if sections 87(1)(b), (4) and (8)(e), 89, 90(1) to (12), 91, 94(4)(b), (6), (10) and (12) and 96(2)(e) were omitted.

(2) In particular—

(a) anything which, immediately before the commencement day, is in the process of being done by virtue of, or in relation to, a retention notice under section 1 of the Act of 2014 may be continued as if being done by virtue of, or in relation to, a retention notice under section 87 of this Act, and

(b) anything done by virtue of, or in relation to, a retention notice under section 1 of the Act of 2014 is, if in force or effective immediately before the commencement day, to have effect as if done by virtue of, or in relation to, a retention notice under section 87 of this Act so far as that is required for continuing its effect on or after the commencement day.

(3) Sub-paragraphs (1) and (2) cease to apply, in relation to any retention notice under section 1 of the Act of 2014—

(a) at the end of the period of six months beginning with the commencement day, or

(b) if earlier, on the revocation in full of the notice;

but this is without prejudice to the continued operation of section 95(2) to (5) in relation to the notice.

(4) Section 249 applies in relation to costs incurred in complying with a retention notice under section 1 of the Act of 2014 which has continued in force on or after the commencement day as it applies in relation to costs incurred in complying with retention notices under section 87 of this Act but as if section 249(7) were omitted.

(5) The Secretary of State may revoke (whether wholly or in part) a retention notice under section 1 of the Act of 2014.

(6) The fact that a retention notice under section 1 of the Act of 2014 has, in relation to a particular description of data and a particular operator (or description of operators), ceased to have effect or been revoked does not prevent the giving of a retention notice under section 87 of this Act in relation to the same description of data and the same operator (or description of operators).

(7) In this paragraph "the commencement day" is the day on which section 1(1) of the Act of 2014 is repealed.

**4.** (1) Sub-paragraph (2) applies if any power to give, vary or confirm a retention notice under section 87 of this Act (excluding any power to vary a notice which has effect as such a notice by virtue of paragraph 3(1)) is brought into force without any requirement for approval by a Judicial Commissioner of the decision to give, vary or (as the case may be) confirm the notice.

(2) The notice as given, varied or confirmed ceases to have effect (so far as not previously revoked) at the end of the period of three months beginning with the day on which the requirement for approval comes into force.

**5.** (1) The repeal of section 1(7) of the Data Retention and Investigatory Powers Act 2014 does not affect the continued operation, during the transitional period mentioned in sub-paragraph (2), of regulations made under section 1(7) of that Act.

(2) The transitional period mentioned in this sub-paragraph is the period of six months beginning with the day on which section 1(7) of the Act of 2014 is repealed.

(3) In their continued operation by virtue of sub-paragraph (1), the regulations made under section 1(7) of the Act of 2014 have effect subject to such modifications (if any) as may be specified in regulations under section 270(2).

*Definitions of "other relevant crime" and "serious crime"*

**6.** (1) The definitions of—

(a) "other relevant crime" in section 62(6), and

(b) "serious crime" in section 263(1),

are to be read, until the appointed day, as if for the words "the age of 18 (or, in relation to Scotland or Northern Ireland, 21)" there were substituted "the age of 21".

(2) In sub-paragraph (1), "the appointed day" means the day on which the amendment made to section 81(3)(a) of the Regulation of Investigatory Powers Act 2000 by paragraph 211 of Schedule 7 to the Criminal Justice and Court Services Act 2000 comes into force.

*Savings for particular purposes*

**7.** Nothing in this Act affects any power conferred on a postal operator (within the meaning given by section 27(3) of the Postal Services Act 2011) by or under any enactment to open, detain or delay any postal packet (within the meaning given by section 125(1) of the Postal Services Act 2000) or to deliver any such packet to a person other than the person to whom it is addressed.

**8.** Nothing in Part 4 of this Act prevents the retention of data for the purposes of, or in connection with, legal proceedings (including proceedings which might arise in the future).

**9.** The amendments made to the Regulation of Investigatory Powers Act 2000 by sections 3 to 6 of the Data Retention and Investigatory Powers Act 2014 (and those sections) continue to have effect despite section 8(3) of the Act of 2014 (sunset provision for that Act) until the provisions they amend (and those sections) are repealed by this Act in connection with the coming into force of provisions of this Act.

*General saving for lawful conduct*

**10.** Nothing in any of the provisions of this Act by virtue of which conduct of any description is or may be authorised by any warrant, authorisation or notice, or by virtue of which information may be obtained in any manner, is to be read—

(a) as making it unlawful to engage in any conduct of that description which is not otherwise unlawful under this Act and would not be unlawful apart from this Act,

(b) as otherwise requiring—

(i) the issue, grant or giving of such a warrant, authorisation or notice, or

(ii) the taking of any step for or towards obtaining the authority of such a warrant, authorisation or notice,

before any such conduct of that description is engaged in, or

(c) as prejudicing any power to obtain information by any means not involving conduct that may be authorised under this Act.

[Investigatory Powers Act 2016, Sch 9.]

## SCHEDULE 10

Minor and Consequential Provision Section 271(1)

### Part 1
### General Amendments

7.11231ZZ80 **1.** *Police Act 1997*

In section 93(1A) of the Police Act 1997 (authorisations to interfere with property etc) after "this Part" insert "or the Investigatory Powers Act 2016".

*Northern Ireland Act 1998*

**2.** In paragraph 9(1) of Schedule 3 to the Northern Ireland Act 1998 (reserved matters) for paragraph (a) substitute—

"(a) the subject-matter of Parts 2 and 3 of the Regulation of Investigatory Powers Act 2000, so far as relating to the prevention or detection of crime (within the meaning of that Act) or the prevention of disorder;

(aa) the subject-matter of the following provisions of the Investigatory Powers Act 2016, so far as relating to the prevention or detection of serious crime (within the meaning of that Act)—

(i) sections 3 to 10 and Schedule 1,

(ii) Part 2, and

(iii) Chapter 1 of Part 6;

(ab) the subject-matter of section 11, Parts 3 and 4 and Chapter 2 of Part 6 of the Investigatory Powers Act 2016, so far as relating to the prevention or detection of crime (within the meaning of that Act) or the prevention of disorder;

(ac) the subject-matter of section 12 of, and Schedule 2 to, the Investigatory Powers Act 2016, so far as relating to the prevention or detection of crime (within the meaning of that Act);".

*Regulation of Investigatory Powers Act 2000*

**3.** The Regulation of Investigatory Powers Act 2000 is amended as follows.

**4.** In section 27(4)(a) (lawful surveillance etc: conduct to be dealt with under other enactments) after "Act" insert "or the Investigatory Powers Act 2016".

**5.** (1) Section 71 (issue and revision of codes of practice) is amended as follows.

(2) In subsection (2)(a), for "Parts I to III" substitute "Parts 2 and 3".

(3) Omit subsection (2A).

(4) In subsection (8) for "(2A)" substitute "(3)".

**6.** (1) Section 81(1) (general definitions) is amended as follows.

(2) For the definition of "apparatus" substitute—

""apparatus" has the same meaning as in the Investigatory Powers Act 2016 (see section 263(1) of that Act);".

(3) In paragraph (a) of the definition of "communication" omit "(except in the definition of "postal service" in section 2(1))".

(4) In the definition of "interception" and cognate expressions, for "section 2" substitute "sections 4 and 5 of the Investigatory Powers Act 2016".

(5) For the definitions of "postal service" and "public postal service" substitute—

""postal service" has the same meaning as in the Investigatory Powers Act 2016 (see section 262(7) of that Act);".

(6) Omit the definitions of "private telecommunication system", "public telecommunications service" and "public telecommunication system".

(7) In the definitions of "telecommunication system" and "telecommunications service", for "the meanings given by section 2(1)" substitute "the same meanings as in the Investigatory Powers Act 2016 (see section 261(11) to (13) of that Act)".

*Political Parties, Elections and Referendums Act 2000*

**7.** In paragraph 28(4) of Schedule 19C to the Political Parties, Elections and Referendums Act 2000 (civil sanctions: disclosure of information) for paragraph (b) substitute—

"(b) any of Parts 1 to 7 or Chapter 1 of Part 9 of the Investigatory Powers Act 2016."

**9.** *Social Security Fraud Act 2001*

In section 4(1)(b) of the Social Security Fraud Act 2001 (arrangements for payments in relation to persons providing a telecommunications service etc) for "the Regulation of Investigatory Powers Act 2000 (c 23)" substitute "the Investigatory Powers Act 2016".

**12.** *Proceeds of Crime Act 2002*

(1) The Proceeds of Crime Act 2002 is amended as follows.

(2) In section 436(3)(b) (disclosure of information to certain Directors) for "Part 1 of the Regulation of Investigatory Powers Act 2000 (c 23)" substitute "any of Parts 1 to 7 or Chapter 1 of Part 9 of the Investigatory Powers Act 2016".

(3) In section 438(8)(b) (disclosure of information by certain Directors) for "Part 1 of the Regulation of Investigatory Powers Act 2000 (c 23)" substitute "any of Parts 1 to 7 or Chapter 1 of Part 9 of the Investigatory Powers Act 2016".

(4) In section 439(3)(b) (disclosure of information to Lord Advocate and to Scottish Ministers) for "Part 1 of the Regulation of Investigatory Powers Act 2000" substitute "any of Parts 1 to 7 or Chapter 1 of Part 9 of the Investigatory Powers Act 2016".

(5) In section 441(7)(b) (disclosure of information by Lord Advocate and by Scottish Ministers) for "Part 1 of the Regulation of Investigatory Powers Act 2000 (c 23)" substitute "any of Parts 1 to 7 or Chapter 1 of Part 9 of the Investigatory Powers Act 2016".

*Police Reform Act 2002*

**13.** In paragraph 19ZA(2)(c) of Schedule 3 to the Police Reform Act 2002 (handling of complaints and conduct matters etc: power to serve information notice) for "Part 1 of the Regulation of Investigatory Powers Act 2000" substitute "any of Parts 1 to 7 or Chapter 1 of Part 9 of the Investigatory Powers Act 2016".

*Privacy and Electronic Communications (EC Directive) Regulations 2003 (SI 2003/2426)*

**14.** After regulation 5A(8) of the Privacy and Electronic Communications (EC Directive) Regulations 2003 (personal data breach) insert—

"(9) This regulation does not apply in relation to any personal data breach which is to be notified to the Investigatory Powers Commissioner in accordance with a code of practice made under the Investigatory Powers Act 2016."

*Audit and Accountability (Northern Ireland) Order 2003 (SI 2003/418 (N.I. 5))*

**15.** In Article 4C(3)(b) of the Audit and Accountability (Northern Ireland) Order 2003 (voluntary provision of data) for "Part 1 of the Regulation of Investigatory Powers Act 2000 (c 23)" substitute "any of Parts 1 to 7 or Chapter 1 of Part 9 of the Investigatory Powers Act 2016".

*Public Audit (Wales) Act 2004*

**16.** In section 64C(3)(b) of the Public Audit (Wales) Act 2004 (voluntary provision of data) for "Part 1 of the Regulation of Investigatory Powers Act 2000 (c 23)" substitute "any of Parts 1 to 7 or Chapter 1 of Part 9 of the Investigatory Powers Act 2016".

*Constitutional Reform Act 2005*

**17.** In section 107(3)(b) of the Constitutional Reform Act 2005 (disclosure of information to the Judicial Appointments Commission) for "Part 1 of the Regulation of Investigatory Powers Act 2000 (c 23)" substitute "any of Parts 1 to 7 or Chapter 1 of Part 9 of the Investigatory Powers Act 2016".

*Commissioners for Revenue and Customs Act 2005*

**18.** In section 22(b) of the Commissioners for Revenue and Customs Act 2005 (data protection, etc) for "Part 1 of the Regulation of Investigatory Powers Act 2000 (c 23)" substitute "any of Parts 1 to 7 or Chapter 1 of Part 9 of the Investigatory Powers Act 2016".

*Serious Crime Act 2007*

**19.** (1) The Serious Crime Act 2007 is amended as follows.

(2) In section 68(4)(b) (disclosure of information to prevent fraud) for "Part 1 of the Regulation of Investigatory Powers Act 2000 (c 23)" substitute "any of Parts 1 to 7 or Chapter 1 of Part 9 of the Investigatory Powers Act 2016".

(3) In section 85(8)(b) (disclosure of information by Revenue and Customs) for "Part 1 of the Regulation of Investigatory Powers Act 2000 (c 23)" substitute "any of Parts 1 to 7 or Chapter 1 of Part 9 of the Investigatory Powers Act 2016".

*Legal Services Act 2007*

**20.** In section 169(3)(b) of the Legal Services Act 2007 (disclosure of information to the Legal Services Board) for "Part 1 of the Regulation of Investigatory Powers Act 2000 (c 23)" substitute "any of Parts 1 to 7 or Chapter 1 of Part 9 of the Investigatory Powers Act 2016".

*Regulatory Enforcement and Sanctions Act 2008*

**21.** In section 70(4) of the Regulatory Enforcement and Sanctions Act 2008 (disclosure of information) for paragraph (b) substitute—

"(b) any of Parts 1 to 7 or Chapter 1 of Part 9 of the Investigatory Powers Act 2016."

*Counter-Terrorism Act 2008*

**22.** In section 20(2)(b) of the Counter-Terrorism Act 2008 (disclosure and the intelligence services: supplementary provisions) for "Part 1 of the Regulation of Investigatory Powers Act 2000 (c 23)" substitute "any of Parts 1 to 7 or Chapter 1 of Part 9 of the Investigatory Powers Act 2016".

*Borders, Citizenship and Immigration Act 2009*

**23.** In section 19(1)(b) of the Borders, Citizenship and Immigration Act 2009 (application of statutory provisions) for "Part 1 of the Regulation of Investigatory Powers Act 2000 (c 23)" substitute "any of Parts 1 to 7 or Chapter 1 of Part 9 of the Investigatory Powers Act 2016".

*Marine and Coastal Access Act 2009*

**24.** (1) The Marine and Coastal Access Act 2009 is amended as follows.

(2) In paragraph 13(5) of Schedule 7 (further provision about civil sanctions under Part 4: disclosure of information) for paragraph (b) substitute—

"(b) any of Parts 1 to 7 or Chapter 1 of Part 9 of the Investigatory Powers Act 2016."

(3) In paragraph 9(5) of Schedule 10 (further provision about fixed monetary penalties under section 142: disclosure of information) for paragraph (b) substitute—

"(b) any of Parts 1 to 7 or Chapter 1 of Part 9 of the Investigatory Powers Act 2016."

*Terrorist Asset-Freezing etc Act 2010*

**25.** In section 25(2)(b) of the Terrorist Asset-Freezing etc Act 2010 (application of provisions) for "Part 1 of the Regulation of Investigatory Powers Act 2000" substitute "any of Parts 1 to 7 or Chapter 1 of Part 9 of the Investigatory Powers Act 2016".

**27.** *Charities Act 2011*

In section 59(b) of the Charities Act 2011 (disclosure: supplementary) for "Part 1 of the Regulation of Investigatory Powers Act 2000" substitute "any of Parts 1 to 7 or Chapter 1 of Part 9 of the Investigatory Powers Act 2016".

*Prisons (Interference with Wireless Telegraphy) Act 2012*

**28.** In section 4(6) of the Prisons (Interference with Wireless Telegraphy) Act 2012 (meaning of "telecommunication system") for "Regulation of Investigatory Powers Act 2000" substitute "Investigatory Powers Act 2016 (see section 261(13) of that Act)".

*Crime and Courts Act 2013*

**29.** In paragraph 1(b) of Schedule 7 to the Crime and Courts Act 2013 (information: restrictions on disclosure) for "Part 1 of the Regulation of Investigatory Powers Act 2000" substitute "any of Parts 1 to 7 or Chapter 1 of Part 9 of the Investigatory Powers Act 2016".

*Marine Act (Northern Ireland) 2013 (c 10 (N.I.))*

**30.** In paragraph 8(5) of Schedule 2 to the Marine Act (Northern Ireland) 2013 (further provision about fixed monetary penalties under section 35: disclosure of information) for paragraph (b) substitute—

"(b) any of Parts 1 to 7 or Chapter 1 of Part 9 of the Investigatory Powers Act 2016."

*Local Audit and Accountability Act 2014*

**31.** In paragraph 3(3)(b) of Schedule 9 to the Local Audit and Accountability Act 2014 (data matching: voluntary provision of data) for "Part 1 of the Regulation of Investigatory Powers Act 2000" substitute "any of Parts 1 to 7 or Chapter 1 of Part 9 of the Investigatory Powers Act 2016".

*Anti-social Behaviour, Crime and Policing Act 2014*

**32.** In paragraph 7(4)(b) of Schedule 4 to the Anti-social Behaviour, Crime and Policing Act 2014 (ASB case reviews: information) for "Part 1 of the Regulation of Investigatory Powers Act 2000" substitute "any of Parts 1 to 7 or Chapter 1 of Part 9 of the Investigatory Powers Act 2016".

*Immigration Act 2014*

**33.** In paragraph 6(b) of Schedule 6 to the Immigration Act 2014 (information) for "Part 1 of the Regulation of Investigatory Powers Act 2000" substitute "any of Parts 1 to 7 or Chapter 1 of Part 9 of the Investigatory Powers Act 2016".

*Data Retention and Investigatory Powers Act 2014*

**34.** Omit sections 4(1), 7 and 8 of the Data Retention and Investigatory Powers Act 2014 (introductory, review and final provisions).

*Immigration Act 2016*

**35.** In section 7(2)(b) of the Immigration Act 2016 (information gateways: supplementary) for "Part 1 of the Regulation of Investigatory Powers Act 2000" substitute "any of Parts 1 to 7 or Chapter 1 of Part 9 of the Investigatory Powers Act 2016".

## PART 2
## LAWFUL INTERCEPTION OF COMMUNICATIONS

*Security Service Act 1989*

**36.** In section 1(5) of the Security Service Act 1989 (meaning of "prevention" and "detection") for the words from "the provisions" to the end substitute "that Act".

*Official Secrets Act 1989*

**37.** In section 4(3) of the Official Secrets Act 1989 (crime and special investigation powers) omit the "and" after paragraph (a) and after paragraph (b) insert "and

(c) any information obtained under a warrant under Chapter 1 of Part 2 or Chapter 1 of Part 6 of the Investigatory Powers Act 2016, any information relating to the obtaining of information under such a warrant and any document or other article which is or has been used or held for use in, or has been obtained by reason of, the obtaining of information under such a warrant."

*Intelligence Services Act 1994*

**38.** In section 11(1A) of the Intelligence Services Act 1994 (meaning of "prevention" and "detection") for the words from "apply" to the end substitute "apply for the purposes of this Act as it applies for the purposes of that Act, except that for the purposes of section 3 above it shall not include a reference to gathering evidence for use in any legal proceedings (within the meaning of that Act)."

*Criminal Procedure and Investigations Act 1996*

**39.** (1) The Criminal Procedure and Investigations Act 1996 is amended as follows.

(2) In section 3(7) (initial duty of prosecutor to disclose) for "section 17 of the Regulation of Investigatory Powers Act 2000" substitute "section 56 of the Investigatory Powers Act 2016".

(3) In section 7A(9) (continuing duty of prosecutor to disclose) for "section 17 of the Regulation of Investigatory Powers Act 2000 (c 23)" substitute "section 56 of the Investigatory Powers Act 2016".

(4) In section 8(6) (application by accused for disclosure) for "section 17 of the Regulation of Investigatory Powers Act 2000" substitute "section 56 of the Investigatory Powers Act 2016".

(5) In section 23 (code of practice) for subsection (6) substitute—

"(6) The code must be so framed that it does not apply to any of the following—

(a) material intercepted in obedience to a warrant issued under section 2 of the Interception of Communications Act 1985;

(b) material intercepted under the authority of an interception warrant under section 5 of the Regulation of Investigatory Powers Act 2000;

(c) material obtained under the authority of a warrant issued under Chapter 1 of Part 2 of the Investigatory Powers Act 2016;

(d) material obtained under the authority of a warrant issued under Chapter 1 of Part 6 of that Act."

*Police Act 1997*

**40.** In section 133A of the Police Act 1997 (meaning of "prevention" and "detection") for the words from "the provisions" to the end substitute "that Act".

**43.** *Financial Services and Markets Act 2000*

In section 394(7)(a) of the Financial Services and Markets Act 2000 (access to FCA or PRA material) for "section 17 of the Regulation of Investigatory Powers Act 2000" substitute "section 56 of the Investigatory Powers Act 2016".

*Regulation of Investigatory Powers Act 2000*

**44.** The Regulation of Investigatory Powers Act 2000 is amended as follows.

**45.** Omit Chapter 1 of Part 1 (interception of communications).

**46.** (1) Section 49 (investigation of electronic data protected by encryption etc: powers under which data obtained) is amended as follows.

(2) In subsection (1)(b) after "communications" insert "or obtain secondary data from communications".

(3) After subsection (9) insert—

"(9A) In subsection (1)(b) the reference to obtaining secondary data from communications is to be read in accordance with section 16 of the Investigatory Powers Act 2016."

**47.** In section 71 (issue and revision of codes of practice) omit subsection (10).

**48.** In section 78(3)(a) (affirmative orders) omit "12(10), 13(3),".

**49.** (1) Section 81 (general interpretation) is amended as follows.

(2) In subsection (1)—

(a) in the definition of "criminal", omit "or prosecution", and

(b) in the definition of "interception warrant", for "a warrant under section 5" substitute "—

(a) a targeted interception warrant or mutual assistance warrant under Chapter 1 of Part 2 of the Investigatory Powers Act 2016, or

(b) a bulk interception warrant under Chapter 1 of Part 6 of that Act".

(3) In subsection (4) omit the words from "; and references" to the end.
(4) In subsection (5) omit the words from ", except that" to the end.

**50.** In section 82 (amendments, repeals and savings etc) omit subsections (4) to (6).

## PART 3
## ACQUISITION OF COMMUNICATIONS DATA

*Regulation of Investigatory Powers Act 2000*

**53.** The Regulation of Investigatory Powers Act 2000 is amended as follows.

**54.** Omit Chapter 2 of Part 1 (acquisition and disclosure of communications data).

**55.** In section 49(1)(c) (investigation of electronic data protected by encryption etc: powers under which data obtained)—

(a) for the words from "section 22(3)" to "Part II" substitute "Part 3 of the Investigatory Powers Act 2016 or Part 2 of this Act", and

(b) for "under section 22(4)" substitute "in pursuance of an authorisation under Part 3 of the Act of 2016 or as the result of the issue of a warrant under Chapter 2 of Part 6 of the Act of 2016".

**56.** In section 71(2) (issue and revision of codes of practice) omit "23A or".

**57.** (1) Section 77A (procedure for order of sheriff under section 23A or 32A: Scotland) is amended as follows.

(2) In the heading and in subsection (1)—

(a) for "23A" substitute "75 of the Investigatory Powers Act 2016", and

(b) for "or 32A" substitute "or section 32A of this Act".

(3) In subsection (3) for "sections 23B and 32B and this section" substitute "this section, section 32B of this Act and section 75 of the Investigatory Powers Act 2016".

**58.** (1) Section 77B (procedure for order of district judge under section 23A or 32A: Northern Ireland) is amended as follows.

(2) In the heading and in subsections (1) and (4) for "section 23A or 32A" substitute "section 32A of this Act or section 75 of the Investigatory Powers Act 2016".

(3) In subsection (4) for "sections 23B and 32B" substitute "section 32B of this Act and section 75 of that Act".

**59.** In section 78(3)(a) (affirmative orders) omit "22(9), 23A(6), 25(5),".

**60.** In section 81(9) (general interpretation: certain references relating to Northern Ireland) omit "23A(7)(b),".

*Police Reform Act 2002*

**61.** (1) Paragraph 19ZA of Schedule 3 to the Police Reform Act 2002 (investigations by the IPCC: information notices) is amended as follows.

(2) In sub-paragraph (3) omit—

(a) the words from "(within the meaning of Chapter 2" to "2000)", and

(b) the words "(within the meaning of that Chapter)".

(3) After sub-paragraph (3) insert—

"(3A) In sub-paragraph (3) "communications data", "postal operator" and "telecommunications operator" have the same meanings as in the Investigatory Powers Act 2016 (see sections 261 and 262 of that Act)."

## PART 4
## RETENTION OF COMMUNICATIONS DATA

*Anti-terrorism, Crime and Security Act 2001*

**62.** Omit Part 11 of the Anti-terrorism, Crime and Security Act 2001 (retention of communications data).

*Data Retention and Investigatory Powers Act 2014*

**63.** Omit sections 1 and 2 of the Data Retention and Investigatory Powers Act 2014 (retention of relevant communications data).

## PART 5
## EQUIPMENT INTERFERENCE

*Regulation of Investigatory Powers Act 2000*

**64.** The Regulation of Investigatory Powers Act 2000 is amended as follows.

**65.** In section 48 (interpretation of Part 2), in subsection (3)(c)—

(a) omit the "or" at the end of sub-paragraph (i);

(b) after sub-paragraph (ii) insert "; or

(iii) Part 5, or Chapter 3 of Part 6, of the Investigatory Powers Act 2016 (equipment interference)."

**66.** (1) Paragraph 2 of Schedule 2 (persons having the appropriate permission where data obtained under warrant etc) is amended as follows.

(2) In sub-paragraph (1)—

(a) omit the "or" at the end of paragraph (a);

(b) after paragraph (b) insert "; or

(c) a targeted equipment interference warrant issued under section 106 of the Investigatory Powers Act 2016 (powers of law enforcement chiefs to issue warrants to law enforcement officers)."

(3) In sub-paragraph (5), at the end insert "or under a targeted equipment interference warrant issued under section 106 of the Investigatory Powers Act 2016."

(4) In sub-paragraph (6)—

(a) omit the "and" at the end of paragraph (b);

(b) after paragraph (c) insert "; and

(d) in relation to protected information obtained under a warrant issued under section 106 of the Investigatory Powers Act 2016, means the person who issued the warrant or, if that person was an appropriate delegate in relation to a law enforcement chief, either that person or the law enforcement chief."

(5) After sub-paragraph (6) insert—

"(6A) In sub-paragraph (6)(d), the references to a law enforcement chief and to an appropriate delegate in relation to a law enforcement chief are to be read in accordance with section 106(5) of the Investigatory Powers Act 2016."

**70.** *Crime and Courts Act 2013*

(1) In Schedule 1 to the Crime and Courts Act 2013 (the NCA and NCA officers), paragraph 6A

(investigatory activity in Northern Ireland) is amended as follows.

(2) In sub-paragraph (3)—

(a) in the opening words, omit "an authorisation granted under any of the following provisions";

(b) before paragraph (a) insert—

"(za) a targeted equipment interference warrant under Part 5 of the Investigatory Powers Act 2016;";

(c) in paragraph (a), for "in the" substitute "an authorisation granted under any of the following provisions of the";

(d) in paragraph (b), at the beginning insert "an authorisation granted under".

(3) After sub-paragraph (3) insert—

"(4) For the purpose of sub-paragraph (1), a relevant investigatory activity falling within sub-paragraph (3)(za) is to be regarded as carried out in Northern Ireland if (and to the extent that)—

(a) the equipment that is being interfered with under the warrant is in Northern Ireland, and

(b) at the time of the carrying out of the activity, the NCA officer knows that the equipment is in Northern Ireland.

(5) Sub-paragraph (6) applies where—

(a) in the carrying out by an NCA officer of a relevant investigatory activity falling within sub-paragraph (3)(za), equipment in Northern Ireland is interfered with under the warrant,

(b) at the time the interference begins, the NCA officer does not know that the equipment is in Northern Ireland, and

(c) at any time while the interference is continuing, the NCA officer becomes aware that the equipment is in Northern Ireland.

(6) The NCA officer is not to be regarded as in breach of sub-paragraph (1) if the interference continues after the NCA officer becomes aware that the equipment is in Northern Ireland, provided that the officer informs the Chief Constable of the Police Service of Northern Ireland about the interference as soon as reasonably practicable."

## PART 6
## JUDICIAL COMMISSIONERS

*Police Act 1997*

**71.** The Police Act 1997 is amended as follows.

**72.** In section 103(8) (appeals) for "the period" substitute "any period".

**73.** In section 105(1)(b)(iii) (reports of appeals dismissed) omit "under section 107(2),".

**74.** In section 108(1) (interpretation of Part 3) after the definition of "designated deputy" insert—

""the Investigatory Powers Commissioner" and "Judicial Commissioner" have the same meanings as in the Investigatory Powers Act 2016 (see section 263(1) of that Act);".

*Regulation of Investigatory Powers Act 2000*

**75.** The Regulation of Investigatory Powers Act 2000 is amended as follows.

**76.** In section 37(9)(a) (appeals against decisions of ordinary Surveillance Commissioners) for "the period" substitute "any period".

**77.** In section 39(3) (appeals: reports of Chief Surveillance Commissioner)—

(a) for "Subsections (3) and (4) of section 107 of the Police Act 1997" substitute "Subsections (6) to (8) of section 234 of the Investigatory Powers Act 2016", and

(b) for "subsection (2) of that section" substitute "subsection (1) of that section".

**78.** Omit section 40 (information to be provided to Surveillance Commissioners).

**79.** In section 51(7)(b) (notification to Intelligence Services Commissioner or Chief Surveillance Commissioner of certain directions relating to the disclosure of a key to protected information) for "the Commissioner in question" substitute "the Investigatory Powers Commissioner".

**80.** (1) Section 64 (delegation of Commissioners' functions) is amended as follows.

(2) In the heading for "Commissioners' functions" substitute "functions of the Investigatory Powers Commissioner for Northern Ireland".

(3) In subsection (1)—

(a) omit "or any provision of an Act of the Scottish Parliament", and

(b) for "a relevant Commissioner" substitute "the Investigatory Powers Commissioner for Northern Ireland".

(4) Omit subsection (2).

**81.** In section 71(2) (issue and revision of codes of practice) for "the Surveillance Commissioners" substitute "a Judicial Commissioner".

**82.** (1) Section 72 (effect of codes of practice) is amended as follows.

(2) In subsection (4) for paragraphs (c) to (e) (and the word "or" between paragraphs (d) and (e)) substitute—

"(ba) the Investigatory Powers Commissioner for Northern Ireland carrying out functions under this Act, or

(bb) the Investigatory Powers Commissioner or any other Judicial Commissioner carrying out functions under this Act, the Investigatory Powers Act 2016 or the Police Act 1997,".

(3) Omit subsection (5).

**83.** (1) Section 81(1) (general definitions) is amended as follows.

(2) Omit the definitions of "Assistant Surveillance Commissioner", "ordinary Surveillance Commissioner", "Surveillance Commissioner" and "Chief Surveillance Commissioner".

(3) After the definition of "interception warrant" insert—

""the Investigatory Powers Commissioner" and "Judicial Commissioner" have the same meanings as in the Investigatory Powers Act 2016 (see section 263(1) of that Act);".

**95.** *Terrorism Prevention and Investigation Measures Act 2011*

In section 21(3)(b) of the Terrorism Prevention and Investigation Measures Act 2011 (duty to consult certain persons before making an order for the continuation, repeal etc of TPIM powers) for "the Intelligence Services Commissioner" substitute "the Investigatory Powers Commissioner".

*Protection of Freedoms Act 2012*

**96.** The Protection of Freedoms Act 2012 is amended as follows.

**97.** (1) Section 29 (code of practice for surveillance camera systems) is amended as follows.

(2) In subsection (5)(d) (duty to consult certain persons in preparing code) for "the Chief

Surveillance Commissioner" substitute "the Investigatory Powers Commissioner".

(3) In subsection (7) omit the definition of "the Chief Surveillance Commissioner".

**98.** In section 33(8)(d) (duty to consult before making an order identifying who must have regard to the code) for "the Chief Surveillance Commissioner" substitute "the Investigatory Powers Commissioner".

## PART 7

## OTHER MINOR AND CONSEQUENTIAL PROVISION

*Telecommunications Act 1984*

**99.** Omit section 94 of the Telecommunications Act 1984 (directions in the interests of national security etc).

*Northern Ireland Act 1998*

**100.** In paragraph 17 of Schedule 2 to the Northern Ireland Act 1998 (excepted matters) after "subversion;" insert "the Technical Advisory Board provided for by section 245 of the Investigatory Powers Act 2016;".

*Communications Act 2003*

**101.** (1) The Communications Act 2003 is amended as follows.

(2) In section 401(5)(g), for "sections 47 to 49" substitute "section 47 or 48".

(3) In Schedule 18 (transitional provisions), omit paragraph 24 (which relates to section 94 of the Telecommunications Act 1984).

## PART 8

## REPEALS AND REVOCATIONS CONSEQUENTIAL ON OTHER REPEALS OR AMENDMENTS IN THIS ACT

*General amendments*

| *Title* | *Extent of repeal or revocation* |
|---|---|
| Serious Crime Act 2015 | Section 83. |
| | Section 86(12). |
| | In Schedule 4, paragraph 18. |


| *Title* | *Extent of repeal or revocation* |
|---|---|
| Serious Crime Act 2015 | Section 83. |
| | Section 86(12). |
| | In Schedule 4, paragraph 18. |


*Lawful interception of communications*

| *Title* | *Extent of repeal or revocation* |
|---|---|
| Regulation of Investigatory Powers Act 2000 | In Schedule 4, paragraphs 7(2) and 9. |
| Anti-terrorism, Crime and Security Act 2001 | Section 116(3). |
| Inquiries Act 2005 | In Schedule 2, paragraphs 20 and 21. |
| Terrorism Act 2006 | Section 32. |
| Wireless Telegraphy Act 2006 | In Schedule 7, paragraphs 22 and 23. |
| National Health Service (Consequential Provisions) Act 2006 | In Schedule 1, paragraph 208. |
| Armed Forces Act 2006 | In Schedule 16, paragraph 169. |
| Serious Crime Act 2007 | In Schedule 12, paragraph 6. |
| Counter-Terrorism Act 2008 | Sections 69 and 74. |
| Policing and Crime Act 2009 | Section 100. |
| Terrorist Asset-Freezing etc Act 2010 | Section 28(2) and (3). |
| Terrorism Prevention and Investigation Measures Act 2011 | In Schedule 7, paragraph 4. |
| Regulation of Investigatory Powers (Monetary Penalty Notices and Consents for Interceptions) Regulations 2011 (SI 2011/1340) | The whole Regulations. |
| Health and Social Care Act 2012 | In Schedule 5, paragraph 98. |
| Justice and Security Act 2013 | Section 16. |
| | In Schedule 2, paragraph 11. |
| Crime and Courts Act 2013 | In Schedule 8, paragraph 78. |
| | In Schedule 9, paragraph 125. |
| Data Retention and Investigatory Powers Act 2014 | Section 3(1) and (2). |
| | Section 4(2) to (7). |
| | Section 5. |
| Counter-Terrorism and Security Act 2015 | Section 15(3). |
| | In Schedule 8, paragraph 2. |

*Acquisition and retention of communications data*

| *Title* | *Extent of repeal or revocation* |
|---|---|
| Serious Organised Crime and Police Act 2005 | In Schedule 4, paragraph 135. |
| Serious Crime Act 2007 | In Schedule 12, paragraphs 7 and 8. |

| | |
|---|---|
| Police, Public Order and Criminal Justice (Scotland) Act 2006 (Consequential Provisions and Modifications) Order 2007 (SI 2007/1098) | In the Schedule, paragraph 4(5). |
| Policing and Crime Act 2009 | Section 7. |
| | In Schedule 7, paragraphs 13 and 14. |
| Protection of Freedoms Act 2012 | Section 37. |
| | In Schedule 9, paragraphs 7 and 8 and, in par sub-paragraph (i) (and the word "and" at the graph (i)). |
| Crime and Courts Act 2013 | In Schedule 8, paragraph 81. |
| Police and Fire Reform (Scotland) Act 2012 (Consequential Provisions and Modifications) Order 2013 (SI 2013/602) | In Schedule 2, paragraph 33(5) to (8) and (15 |
| Data Retention and Investigatory Powers Act 2014 | Section 3(3) and (4). |
| | Section 4(8) to (10). |
| Counter-Terrorism and Security Act 2015 | Section 21. |
| | Section 52(3)(a). |

*Judicial Commissioners*

| *Title* | *Extent of repeal or revocation* |
|---|---|
| Scotland Act 1998 (Cross-Border Public Authorities) (Adaptation of Functions etc) Order 1999 (SI 1999/1747) | In Schedule 6, paragraph 2(2) and (5). |
| Regulation of Investigatory Powers Act 2000 | In Schedule 4, paragraph 8(1), (10) and |
| Insolvency Act 2000 | In Schedule 4, paragraph 22(2). |
| Scotland Act 1998 (Transfer of Functions to the Scottish Ministers etc) (No 2) Order 2000 (SI 2000/3253) | In Schedule 3, paragraphs 9 to 12. |
| Insolvency Act 2000 (Company Directors Disqualification Undertakings) Order 2004 (SI 2004/1941) | In the Schedule, paragraph 10. |
| Constitutional Reform Act 2005 | In Schedule 17, paragraphs 27 and 30(2 |
| Tribunals, Courts and Enforcement Act 2007 | In Schedule 16, paragraph 11(2). |
| Serious Crime Act 2007 | In Schedule 12, paragraph 3. |
| Companies Act 2006 (Consequential Amendments, Transitional Provisions and Savings) Order 2009 (SI 2009/1941) | In Schedule 1, paragraph 169. |
| Police Reform and Social Responsibility Act 2011 | In Schedule 16, paragraph 222. |
| Protection of Freedoms Act 2012 | In Schedule 9, paragraphs 10 and 11. |
| Justice and Security Act 2013 | Section 5. |
| | In Schedule 2, paragraph 4. |
| Crime and Courts Act 2013 | In Schedule 8, paragraph 59. |
| | In Schedule 21, paragraph 4. |
| Police and Fire Reform (Scotland) Act 2012 (Consequential Provisions and Modifications) Order 2013 (SI 2013/602) | In Schedule 1, paragraph 6(6). |
| | In Schedule 2, paragraph 33(20) and (2 |
| Anti-social Behaviour, Crime and Policing Act 2014 | Section 150. |
| Data Retention and Investigatory Powers Act 2014 | Section 6. |

*Other minor and consequential provision*

| *Title* | *Extent of repeal or revocation* |
|---|---|
| Communications Act 2003 | In Schedule 17, paragraph 70. |

[Investigatory Powers Act 2016, Sch 10.]

## Telecommunications (Lawful Business Practice) (Interception of Communications) Regulations 2000[1]

(SI 2000/2699 amended by SI 2003/2426 and SI 2011/1208)

**7.11232** 1. *Citation and commencement* These Regulations may be cited as the Telecommunications (Lawful Business Practice) (Interception of Communications) Regulations 2000 and shall come into force on 24th October 2000.

[1] Made by the Secretary of State in exercise of the powers conferred by ss 4(2) and 78(5) of the Regulation of Investigatory Powers Act 2000.

**7.11233** 2. *Interpretation* In these Regulations—

(*a*) references to a business include references to activities of a government department, of any public authority or of any person or office holder on whom functions are conferred by or under any enactment;

(*b*) a reference to a communication as relevant to a business is a reference to—
(i) a communication—
(*aa*) by means of which a transaction is entered into in the course of that business, or
(*bb*) which otherwise relates to that business, or
(ii) a communication which otherwise takes place in the course of the carrying on of that business;
(*c*) "regulatory or self-regulatory practices or procedures" means practices or procedures—
(i) compliance with which is required or recommended by, under or by virtue of—
(*aa*) any provision of the law of a member state or other state within the European Economic Area, or
(*bb*) any standard or code of practice published by or on behalf of a body established in a member state or other state within the European Economic Area which includes amongst its objectives the publication of standards or codes of practice for the conduct of business, or
(ii) which are otherwise applied for the purpose of ensuring compliance with anything so required or recommended;
(*d*) "system controller" means, in relation to a particular telecommunication system, a person with a right to control its operation or use.

**7.11234** 3. *Lawful interception of a communication* (1) For the purpose of section 1(5)(*a*) of the Act, conduct is authorised, subject to paragraphs (2) and (3) below, if it consists of interception of a communication, in the course of its transmission by means of a telecommunication system, which is effected by or with the express consent of the system controller for the purpose of—
(*a*) monitoring or keeping a record of communications—
(i) in order to—
(*aa*) establish the existence of facts, or
(*bb*) ascertain compliance with regulatory or self-regulatory practices or procedures which are—
applicable to the system controller in the carrying on of his business or
applicable to another person in the carrying on of his business where that person is supervised by the system controller in respect of those practices or procedures, or
(*cc*) ascertain or demonstrate the standards which are achieved or ought to be achieved by persons using the system in the course of their duties, or
(ii) in the interests of national security, or
(iii) for the purpose of preventing or detecting crime, or
(iv) for the purpose of investigating or detecting the unauthorised use of that or any other telecommunication system, or
(v) where that is undertaken—
(*aa*) in order to secure, or
(*bb*) as an inherent part of,
the effective operation of the system (including any monitoring or keeping of a record which would be authorised by section 3(3) of the Act if the conditions in paragraphs (*a*) and (*b*) thereof were satisfied); or
(*b*) monitoring communications for the purpose of determining whether they are communications relevant to the system controller's business which fall within regulation 2(*b*)(i) above; or
(*c*) monitoring communications made to a confidential voice-telephony counselling or support service which is free of charge (other than the cost, if any, of making a telephone call) and operated in such a way that users may remain anonymous if they so choose.

(2) Conduct is authorised by paragraph (1) of this regulation only if—
(*a*) the interception in question is effected solely for the purpose of monitoring or (where appropriate) keeping a record of communications relevant to the system controller's business;
(*b*) the telecommunication system in question is provided for use wholly or partly in connection with that business;
(*c*) the system controller has made all reasonable efforts to inform every person who may use the telecommunication system in question that communications transmitted by means thereof may be intercepted; and
(*d*) in a case falling within—
(i) paragraph (1)(*a*)(ii) above, the person by or on whose behalf the interception is effected is a person specified in section 6(2)(*a*) to (*i*) of the Act;
(ii) paragraph (1)(*b*) above, the communication is one which is intended to be received (whether or not it has been actually received) by a person using the telecommunication system in question.

(3) Conduct falling within paragraph (1)(*a*)(i) above is authorised only to the extent that Article 5 of Directive 2002/58/EC of the European Parliament and of the Council of 12 July 2002 concerning the processing of personal data and the protection of privacy in the electronic communications sector so permits as amended by Directive 2009/136/EC of the European Parliament and of the Council of 25 November 2009 amending Directive 2002/22/EC on universal service and users' rights relating to electronic communications networks and services, Directive 2002/58/EC concerning the processing of personal data and the protection of privacy in the electronic communications sector and Regulation (EC) No 2006/2004 on cooperation between national

authorities responsible for the enforcement of consumer protection laws.

## Communications (Television Licensing) Regulations 2004[1]

(SI 2004/692 amended by SI 2005/606, SI 2006/619, SI 2007/718, SI 2008/643, SI 2009/505, SI 2010/640, SI 2011/2581, SI 2013/1854 and SI 2016/704[2])

### Part 1 General

7.11235 *1. Citation, commencement, extent and interpretation* (1) These Regulations may be cited as the Communications (Television Licensing) Regulations 2004 and shall come into force on 1st April 2004.

(2) These Regulations, except regulations 10 and 11, extend to the Channel Islands and the Isle of Man.

(3) In these Regulations "the Act" means the Communications Act 2003.

---

[1] Made by the Secretary of State, in exercise of the powers conferred by s 6(1) of the Wireless Telegraphy Act 1967 and ss 365(1) and (4), 368 and 402(3) of the Communications Act 2003, as extended by the Broadcasting and Communications (Jersey) Order 2004, the Communications (Bailiwick of Guernsey) Order 2004 and the Communications (Isle of Man) Order 2003, with the consent of the Treasury (to the extent that the Regulations are made in exercise of the powers conferred by s 365 of the Communications Act 2003).

[2] Reference is made only to those instruments which amend the provisions reproduced in this work.

### Part 2 TV Licence Fees

7.11236 *2. Interpretation of Part 2* (1) In this Part—

"caravan" means any structure designed or adapted for habitation which is capable of being moved from one place to another (whether by being towed, or by being transported on a motor vehicle or trailer) and any motor vehicle so designed or adapted;

"digital set top box" means a television receiver whose function is to receive television programmes in digital form, and which cannot itself display, or record or otherwise store such programmes;

"the due date" in relation to any TV licence means the date on which the licensee is required to obtain the licence in accordance with the Act whether in consequence of the expiry of a previous licence or otherwise; and

"touring caravan" means a caravan normally used for touring from place to place.

(2) Any reference to—

(*a*) the issue of a TV licence includes a reference to the renewal of such a licence;

(*b*) a person's residence includes any place provided for that person's private occupation.

7.11237 *3. TV licence fees* (1) Subject to regulations 5 and 6—

(*a*) on the issue of a TV licence of a type specified in an entry in column 1 of the table in Schedule 1, the fee payable shall be that specified in column 3 in relation to that type of licence;

(*b*) on the issue of a TV licence of a type specified in paragraph 1, 3 or 8 of Schedule 2, the person to whom the licence is issued shall be liable to make payments as provided by (as the case may be) Part 1, 2 or 3 of that Schedule;

(*c*) on the issue of a TV licence of a type specified in an entry in column 1 of the table in Part 1 of Schedule 3, the fee payable shall (subject to paragraph (2)) be determined in accordance with the entry in column 3 in relation to that type of licence;

(*d*) on the issue of a TV licence of the type specified in paragraph 1 of Schedule 4, the fee payable shall be determined in accordance with paragraph 2 of that Schedule;

(*e*) on the issue of a TV licence of the type specified in paragraph 2 of Schedule 5, the fee payable shall be determined in accordance with paragraph 3 of that Schedule.

(2) In relation to a TV licence of the type specified in the second entry in column 1 of the table in Part 1 of Schedule 3, the fee is to be payable in instalments in the circumstances specified in Part 2 of that Schedule; and the amount of each of the instalments, and the dates on which they are payable, are to be determined in accordance with that Part.

(3) Any sum payable by virtue of paragraph (1) or (2) shall be payable irrespective of the duration of the TV licence.

(4) In the first and third entries in column 2 of the table in Schedule 1, a reference to—

(*a*) installing a black and white television receiver includes a reference to installing a digital set top box in such a way that it can only be used to cause television programmes to be displayed on a television set or monitor that can display them in black and white only; and

(*b*) using a black and white television receiver includes a reference to using a digital set top box installed as described in this paragraph.

7.11238 *4. Duplicate licences* Where a TV licence has been lost or destroyed, the sum of £4.50 shall be paid on the issue of a duplicate of such a licence; but no such sum shall be payable on the issue of a duplicate of a TV licence that was issued free of charge.

7.11239 *5. Concessions for blind persons* (1) Where—

(*a*) a TV licence is issued to a blind person, authorising the installation or use of a television receiver at one or more places or in one or more vehicles, vessels or caravans specified in the licence; and

(*b*) each place, vehicle, vessel or caravan so specified is a residence of that person,

the fee payable (including the amount of any instalment payments) shall be 50 per cent of the amount which would otherwise be payable for the licence in accordance with regulation 3.

This reduction in the amount payable is referred to in this regulation as the "blind concession".

(2) In order to establish an entitlement to the blind concession a person must—

(*a*) show that he is registered as blind by means of a certificate or other document issued by or on behalf of—

(i) a local authority in Great Britain,

(ii) a Health and Social Services Trust in Northern Ireland, or

(iii) the Department of Health and Social Care for the Isle of Man; or

(*b*) provide evidence that he is blind by way of a certificate signed by an ophthalmologist.

(3) A person is not required to provide the evidence referred to in paragraph (2) to obtain the blind concession in respect of a TV licence where that person has previously established an entitlement to the concession by providing the evidence referred to in that paragraph and—

(*a*) the evidence was provided within the period of 5 years ending on the date on which the licence is issued, or

(*b*) the BBC are satisfied that the evidence previously provided is sufficient to establish the person's entitlement to the concession as at that date.

(4) This regulation does not apply where the TV licence is of a type and description specified in paragraph 1 of Schedule 4 or paragraph 2 of Schedule 5.

(5) In these Regulations—

"blind" means that the person concerned is so blind as to be unable to perform any work for which eyesight is essential;

"local authority" means—

(*a*) in England, a county council, a district council, a London borough council, the Common Council of the City of London, and the Council of the Isles of Scilly;

(*b*) in Wales, a county council or a county borough council;

(*c*) *Scotland*;

(*d*) *revoked*;

"ophthalmologist" means a doctor whose name is included in the register of specialists kept by the General Medical Council under article 8 of the European Specialist Medical Qualifications Order 1995 and in respect of whom that register indicates his speciality to be ophthalmology.

**7.11240** 6. *Concessions for persons aged 75 years or more* (1) No fee shall be payable for a TV licence of a type referred to in the first or second entry in column 1 of the table in Schedule 1 where—

(*a*) the licence is issued to a person aged 75 years or more or to a person who will attain that age in the calendar month in which the licence is issued; and

(*b*) the single place, vehicle, vessel or caravan specified in the licence is the sole or main residence of that person.

(2) Paragraph (1) only applies where the residence referred to in that paragraph is in the United Kingdom.

(2A) No fee shall be payable for a TV licence of a type referred to in the first or second entry in column 1 of the table in Schedule 1 where—

(*a*) a residence is in the Bailiwick of Guernsey (but excluding Sark);

(*b*) the licence is issued to a person who has attained the age of 75 before 1st September 2016; and

(*c*) the single place, vehicle, vessel or caravan specified in the licence is the sole or main residence of that person.

(3) Where a TV licence of the type referred to in paragraph 1 of Schedule 4 is issued in respect of accommodation for residential care, in calculating the fee payable no account shall be taken of any unit of accommodation or, as the case may be, residential care dwelling that is the sole or main residence of a resident who is aged 75 years or more on the date on which the licence is issued.

(4) In paragraph (3), the expressions "accommodation for residential care", "resident" and "residential care dwelling" shall have the meanings given to them by Part 2 of Schedule 4.

(5) Paragraph (3) only applies where the accommodation to which the licence relates is in the United Kingdom.

**7.11241** 7. *Revocation and savings*

## PART 3 DEFINITIONS FOR THE PURPOSES OF THE COMMUNICATIONS ACT 2003 AND THE WIRELESS TELEGRAPHY ACT 1967

**7.11242** 8. *Interpretation of Part 3* In this Part—

"digital set top box" has the same meaning as in Part 2;

"members of the public" means members of the public in the United Kingdom, the Channel Islands and the Isle of Man;

"on-demand programme service", and references to the provision of such a service by the BBC, have the same meanings as in the Communications Act 2003 (and, in the application of this Part to the Channel Islands and the Isle of Man, they are to have the meanings which they have in the United Kingdom). If an amendment of the Communications Act 2003 changes the meaning in the United Kingdom of "on-demand programme service" or the meaning of any reference to the provision of such a service by the BBC, the change to the meaning is also to have effect in the Channel Islands and the Isle of Man for the purposes of this Part;

"programme" has the same meaning as in the Act; and

"television programme service" has the same meaning as in Part 3 of the Act.

**7.11243** 9. *Meaning of "television receiver"* (1) Subject to paragraph (2), in Part 4 of the Act (licensing of TV reception), "television receiver" means any apparatus installed or used for the purpose of receiving (whether by means of wireless telegraphy or otherwise)—

(*a*) any television programme service, or

(*b*) an on-demand programme service which is provided by the BBC, whether or not the apparatus is installed or used for any other purpose.

(2) But a digital set top box is not a television receiver for the purposes of that Part if it is installed in such a way that it can be used only to cause the production of sound through a device whose functions are limited to the production, or the production and recording, of sound.

(3) In this regulation, any reference to receiving a television programme service includes a reference to receiving by any means any programme included in that service, where that programme is received at the same time (or virtually the same time) as it is received by members of the public by virtue of its being broadcast or distributed as part of that service.

SCHEDULE 1
Issue Fees for TV Licences

Regulation 3(1)()

**Table**

7.11244

| *Type of licence* | *Description of licence* | *Issue fee* |
|---|---|---|
| 1 TV licence (black and white only) General Form | A licence—<br>(*a*) to install and use black and white television receivers at the single place specified in the licence or, as the case may be, in the single vehicle, vessel or caravan so specified ("the specified location");<br>(*b*) to install and use black and white television receivers in any vehicle, vessel or caravan—<br>(i) being used or occupied by the licensee or by a person normally living with the licensee at the specified location, or<br>(ii) if the specified location is a business premises, being used or occupied for the purposes of the business by a person who normally works at that location,<br>being installation or use not covered by a licence described in Schedule 5, provided that, in a case falling within (i) above, a receiver may not be used in a caravan, other than a touring caravan, at the same time as a receiver is being used at the specified location; and<br>(*c*) for the use anywhere of any black and white television receiver powered solely by its own internal batteries by the licensee or by a person normally living with the licensee at the specified location. | £49.00 |
| 2 TV licence (including colour) General Form | A licence—<br>(*a*) to install and use television receivers at the single place specified in the licence or, as the case may be, in the single vehicle, vessel or caravan so specified ("the specified location");<br>(*b*) to install and use television receivers in any vehicle, vessel or caravan—<br>(i) being used or occupied by the licensee or by a person normally living with the licensee at the specified location, or<br>(ii) if the specified location is a business premises, being used or occupied for the purposes of the business by a person who normally works at that location,<br>being installation or use not covered by a licence described in Schedule 5, provided that, in a case falling within (i) above, a receiver may not be used in a caravan, other than a touring caravan, at the same time as a receiver is being used at the specified location; and<br>(*c*) for the use anywhere of any television receiver powered solely by its own internal batteries by the licensee or by a person normally living with the licensee at the specified location. | £145.50 |
| 3 TV licence (black and white only) Multiple Form | A licence—<br>(*a*) to install and use black and white television receivers at each of the places specified in the licence or, as the case may be, in each of the vehicles, vessels or caravans so specified ("the specified locations");<br>(*b*) to install and use black and white television receivers in any vehicle, vessel or caravan—<br>(i) being used or occupied by the licensee or by a person normally living at one of the specified locations, or<br>(ii) if a business is carried on from one or more of the specified locations, being used or occupied for the purposes of the business by a person who normally works at one of those locations, | £49.00 for each place, vehicle, vessel or caravan specified in the licence. |

| Type of licence | Description of licence | Issue fee |
|---|---|---|
| | being installation or use not covered by a licence described in Schedule 5, provided that, in a case falling within (i) above, a receiver may not be used in a caravan, other than a touring caravan, at the same time as a receiver is being used at the specified location at which the person using the receiver normally lives; and<br>(*c*) for the use anywhere of any black and white television receiver powered solely by its own internal batteries by the licensee or by a person normally living at one of the specified locations. | |
| 4TV licence (including colour) Multiple Form | A licence—<br>(*a*) to install and use television receivers at each of the places specified in the licence or, as the case may be, in each of the vehicles, vessels or caravans so specified ("the specified locations");<br>(*b*) to install and use television receivers in any vehicle, vessel or caravan—<br>(i) being used or occupied by the licensee or by a person normally living at one of the specified locations, or<br>(ii) if a business is carried on from one or more of the specified locations, being used or occupied for the purposes of the business by a person who normally works at one of those locations,<br>being installation or use not covered by a licence described in Schedule 5, provided that, in a case falling within (i) above, a receiver may not be used in a caravan, other than a touring caravan, at the same time as a receiver is being used at the specified location at which the person using the receiver normally lives; and<br>(*c*) for the use anywhere of any television receiver powered solely by its own internal batteries by the licensee or by a person normally living at one of the specified locations. | £145.50 for each place, vehicle, vessel or caravan specified in the licence. |

SCHEDULE 2
Fees for TV Licences Payable by Instalments — Regulation 3(1)(*b*)

SCHEDULE 3
Fees for Interim TV Licences — Regulation 3(1)(*c*)

SCHEDULE 4
Accommodation for Residential Care Licences — Regulation 3(1)(*d*)

SCHEDULE 5
TV Licence Fees for Hotels and Hospitality Areas and Mobile Units — Regulation 3(1)(*e*)

SCHEDULE 6
Revocations — Regulation 7(1)

# Regulation of Investigatory Powers (Extension of Authorisation Provisions: Legal Consultations) Order 2010[1]

(SI 2010/461)

**7.11245** 1. *Citation and commencement* This Order may be cited as the Regulation of Investigatory Powers (Extension of Authorisation Provisions: Legal Consultations) Order 2010 and shall come into force on the day after the day on which it is made.

[1] Made in exercise of the powers conferred on the Secretary of State by s 47(1)(*b*) of the Regulation of Investigatory Powers Act 2000.

**7.11246** 2. *Interpretation* In this Order—

(*a*) "legal consultation" means—

(i) a consultation between a professional legal adviser and his client or any person representing his client, or

(ii) a consultation between a professional legal adviser or his client or any such representative and a medical practitioner made in connection with or in contemplation of legal proceedings and for the purposes of such proceedings;

(*b*) "inquiry" means an inquiry under the Inquiries Act 2005;

(*c*) "medical practitioner" means a person registered under the Medical Act 1983; and

(*d*) "premises" has the meaning given in section 48(8) of the Regulation of Investigatory Powers Act 2000.

**7.11247** 3. *Extension of authorisation provisions: legal consultations* (1) Directed surveillance that is carried out in relation to anything taking place on so much of any premises specified in paragraph (2) as is, at any time during the surveillance, used for the purpose of legal consultations shall be treated for the purposes of Part II of the Regulation of Investigatory Powers Act 2000 as intrusive surveillance[1].

(2) The following premises are specified for the purposes of paragraph (1):

(*a*) any place in which persons who are serving sentences of imprisonment or detention, remanded in custody or committed in custody for trial or sentence may be detained;

(*b*) any place in which persons may be detained under paragraph 16(1), (1A) or (2) of Schedule 2 or paragraph 2(2) or (3) of Schedule 3 to the Immigration Act 1971 or section 36(1) of the UK Border Act 2007;

(*c*) any place in which persons may be detained under Part VI of the Criminal Procedure (Scotland) Act 1995, the Mental Health (Care and Treatment) (Scotland) Act 2003 or the Mental Health Act 2003;

(*d*) police stations;

(*e*) the place of business of any professional legal adviser; and

(*f*) any place used for the sittings and business of any court, tribunal, inquest or inquiry.

---

[1] For the application of this, see *R v Turner* [2013] EWCA Crim 642, [2013] Crim LR 993.

# THEATRE, CINEMATOGRAPH AND VIDEO

**Contents**



## LICENSING OF PLAYS, EXHIBITION OF FILMS, INDOOR SPORTING EVENTS, PERFORMANCE OF LIVE MUSIC, PLAYING OF RECORDED MUSIC ETC AND THE USE OF PREMISES FOR THE SUPPLY AND CONSUMPTION OF ALCOHOL

7.11248 Licensing by licensing authorities of "regulated entertainments" and premises for the supply and consumption of alcohol is now governed by the Licensing Act 2003 which is reproduced in this PART: title, LOCAL GOVERNMENT, ante.

## Cinematograph Films (Animals) Act 1937

(1 Edw 8 & 1 Geo 6 c 59)

7.11249 1. **Prohibition of films involving cruelty to animals** (1) No person shall exhibit to the public, or supply to any person for public exhibition (whether by him or by another person) any cinematograph film (whether produced in Great Britain or elsewhere) if in connection with the production of the film any scene represented in the film was organised or directed in such way as to involve the cruel infliction of pain or terror on any animal or the cruel goading of any animal[1] to fury.

(2) In any proceedings brought under this Act in respect of any film, the court may (without prejudice to any other mode of proof) infer from the film as exhibited to the public or supplied for public exhibition, as the case may be, that a scene represented in the film as so exhibited or supplied was organised or directed in such way as to involve the cruel infliction of pain or terror on an animal or the cruel goading of an animal to fury, but (whether the court draws such an inference or not) it shall be a defence for the defendant to prove that he believed, and had reasonable cause to believe, that no scene so represented was so organised or directed.

(3) Any person contravening the provisions of this section shall be liable on summary conviction to a fine not exceeding **level 3** on the standard scale, or to imprisonment for a term not exceeding **three months*** or to **both** such fine and imprisonment.

(4) For the purpose of this Act—

(*a*) a cinematograph film shall be deemed to be exhibited to the public when, and only when, it is exhibited in a place to which for the time being members of the general public as such have access, whether on payment of money or otherwise, and the expression "public exhibition" shall be construed accordingly; and

(*b*) in relation to England and Wales, the expression "animal" means a "protected animal" within the meaning of the Animal Welfare Act 2006; and

(*c*) *Scotland.*

[Cinematograph Films (Animals) Act 1937, s 1 as amended by the Criminal Law Act 1977, Sch 6, the Criminal Justice Act 1982, s 46 and the Animal Welfare Act 2006, Sch 3.]

* **Words substituted by the Criminal Justice Act 2003, Sch 26 from a date to be appointed.**

1 The expression "animal" means any domestic or captive animal (Protection of Animals Act 1911, s 15, in this PART: title ANIMALS, ante).

## Theatres Act 1968

(1968 c 54)

*Provisions with respect to performances of plays*

7.11250 2. **Prohibition of presentation of obscene performances of plays** (1) For the purposes of this section a performance of a play[1] shall be deemed to be obscene if, taken as a whole, its effect was such as to tend to deprave and corrupt persons who were likely, having regard to all relevant circumstances, to attend it[2].

(2) Subject to sections 3 and 7 of this Act, if an obscene performance of a play[1] is given, whether in public or private, any person who (whether for gain or not) presented[3] or directed[3] that performance shall be liable[4]—

(*a*) on summary conviction, to a fine not exceeding the prescribed sum or to imprisonment for a term not exceeding **six months**;

(*b*) on conviction on indictment, to a fine or to imprisonment for a term not exceeding **three years**, or **both**.

(3) A prosecution on indictment for an offence under this section shall not be commenced more than two years after the commission of the offence.

(4) No person shall be proceeded against in respect of a performance of a play[1] or any thing said or done in the course of such a performance—

(*a*) for an offence at common law where it is of the essence of the offence that the performance or, as the case may be, what was said or done was obscene, indecent, offensive, disgusting or injurious to morality; or

(*b*), (*c*) *repealed.*

and no person shall be proceeded against for an offence at common law of conspiring to corrupt public morals, or to do any act contrary to public morals or decency, in respect of an agreement to present or give a performance of a play, or to cause anything to be said or done in the course of such a performance.

[Theatres Act 1968, s 2 as amended by the Criminal Law Act 1977, s 28 and the Indecent Displays (Control) Act 1981, Sch.]

1 See s 18, post.
2 See note 2 to the Obscene Publications Act 1959, s 1, this PART: title OBSCENE PUBLICATIONS, ante.
3 See s 18, post.
4 For procedure in respect of an offence triable either way, see the Magistrates' Courts Act 1980, ss 17A–21, in PART I: MAGISTRATES' COURTS, PROCEDURE, ante. Proceedings may not be instituted except with the consent of the Attorney General (s 8, post).

7.11251 3. **Defence of public good** (1) A person shall not be convicted of an offence under section 2 of this Act if it is proved that the giving of the performance in question was justified as being for the public good on the ground that it was in the interest of drama, opera, ballet or any other art, or of literature or learning.

(2) It is hereby declared that the opinion of experts as to the artistic, literary or other merits of a performance of a play may be admitted in any proceedings for an offence under section 2 of this Act either to establish or negative the said ground[1].

[Theatres Act 1968, s 3.]

1 See note 4 to the Obscene Publications Act 1959, s 4, this PART: title OBSCENE PUBLICATIONS, ante.

7.11252 6. **Provocation of breach of peace by means of public performance of a play**
(1) Subject to section 7 of this Act, if there is given a public performance of a play[1] involving the use of threatening, abusive or insulting words or behaviour, any person who (whether for gain or not) presented[1] that performance shall be guilty of an offence under this section if—

(*a*) he did so with intent to provoke a breach of the peace; or

(*b*) the performance, taken as whole, was likely to occasion a breach of the peace.

(2) A person guilty of an offence under this section shall be liable on summary conviction to a fine not exceeding **level 5** on the standard scale or to imprisonment for a term not exceeding **six months** or to **both**.

[Theatres Act 1968, s 6 as amended by the Criminal Law Act 1977, Sch 1 and the Criminal Justice Act 1982, s 46.]

1 See s 18, post.

7.11253 7. **Exceptions for performances given in certain circumstances** (1) Nothing in sections 2 to 4 of this Act shall apply in relation to a performance of a play[1] given on a domestic occasion in a private dwelling.

(2) Nothing in sections 2 to 6 of this Act shall apply in relation to a performance of a play given solely or primarily for one or more of the following purposes, that is to say—

(*a*) rehearsal; or

(*b*) to enable—

(i) a record or cinematograph film to be made from or by means of the performance; or

(ii) the performance to be broadcast; or

(iii) the performance to be included in a programme service (within the meaning of the Wireless Telegraphy Act 2006) other than a sound or television broadcasting service;

but in any proceedings for an offence under section 2 or 6 of this Act alleged to have been committed in respect of a performance of a play if it is proved that the performance was attended by persons other than persons directly connected with the giving of the performance or the doing in relation thereto of any of the things mentioned in paragraph (*b*) above, the performance shall be taken not to have been given solely or primarily for one or more of the said purposes unless the contrary is shown.

(3) In this section—

"broadcast" means broadcast by wireless telegraphy (within the meaning of the Wireless Telegraphy Act 2006), whether by way of sound broadcasting or television;

"cinematograph film" means any print, negative, tape or other article on which a performance of a play or any part of such a performance is recorded for the purposes of visual reproduction;

"record" means any record or similar contrivance for reproducing sound, including the sound-track of a cinematograph film;

[Theatres Act 1968, s 7 as amended by the Cable and Broadcasting Act 1984, Schs 5 and 6, the Public Order Act 1986, Sch 3, the Broadcasting Act 1990, Sch 20, the Wireless Telegraphy Act 2006, Sch 7 and the Coroners and Justice Act 2009, Sch 23.]

1 See s 18, post.

7.11254 8. **Restriction on institution of proceedings** Proceedings for an offence under section 2 or 6 of this Act shall not be instituted in England and Wales except by or with the consent of the Attorney-General.

[Theatres Act 1968, s 8 as amended by the Public Order Act 1986, Sch 3 and the Coroners and Justice Act 2009, Sch 23.]

7.11255 9. **Script as evidence of what was performed** (1) Where a performance of a play[1] was based on a script, then, in any proceedings for an offence under section 2 or 6 of this Act alleged to have been committed in respect of that performance—

(*a*) an actual script on which that performance was based shall be admissible as evidence of what was performed and of the manner in which the performance or any part of it was given; and

(*b*) if such a script is given in evidence on behalf of any party to the proceedings then, except in so far as the contrary is shown, whether by evidence given on behalf of the same or any other party, the performance shall be taken to have been given in accordance with that script.

(2) In this Act "script", in relation to a performance of a play, means the text of the play (whether expressed in words or in musical or other notation) together with any stage or other directions for its performance, whether contained in a single document or not.

[Theatres Act 1968, s 9 as amended by the Public Order Act 1986, Sch 3.]

1 See s 18, post.

7.11256 10. **Power to make copies of scripts** (1) If a police officer of or above the rank of superintendent has reasonable grounds for suspecting—

(*a*) that an offence under section 2 or 6 of this Act has been committed by any person in respect of a performance of a play[1]; or

(*b*) that a performance of a play is to be given and that an offence under the said section 2 or 6 is likely to be committed by any person in respect of that performance,

he may make an order in writing under this section relating to that person and that performance.

(2) Every order made under this section shall be signed by the police officer by whom it is made, shall name the person to whom it relates, and shall describe the performance to which it relates in a manner sufficient to enable that performance to be identified.

(3) Where an order under this section has been made, any police officer, on production if so required of the order—

(*a*) may require the person named in the order to produce, if such a thing exists, an actual script[2] on which the performance was or, as the case may be, will be based; and

(*b*) if such a script is produced to him, may require the person so named to afford him an opportunity of causing a copy thereof to be made.

(4) Any person who without reasonable excuse fails to comply with a requirement under subsection (3) above shall be liable on summary conviction to a fine not exceeding **level 3** on the standard scale.

(5) Where, in the case of a performance of a play based on a script, a copy of an actual script on which that performance was based has been made by or on behalf of a police officer by virtue of an order under this section relating to that performance, section 9(1) of this Act shall apply in relation to that copy as it applies in relation to an actual script on which the performance was based.

[Theatres Act 1968, s 10 as amended by the Criminal Justice Act 1982, ss 38 and 46 and the Public Order Act 1986, Sch 3.]

1 See s 18, post.
2 See s 9(2), ante.

7.11257 11. **Delivery of scripts of new plays to British Museum** (1) Where after the coming into force of this section there is given in Great Britain a public performance of a new play[1], being a performance based on a script[2], a copy of the actual script on which that performance was based shall be delivered to the Trustees of the British Museum free of charge within the period of one month beginning with the date of the performance; and the Trustees shall give a written receipt for every script delivered to them pursuant to this section.

(2) If the requirements of subsection (1) above are not complied with in the case of any performance to which that subsection applies, any person who presented that performance shall be liable on summary conviction to a fine not exceeding **level 1** on the standard scale.

(3) In this section "public performance of a new play" means a public performance of a play of which no previous public performance has ever been given in Great Britain, but does not include a public performance of a play which—

(*a*) is based on a script substantially the same as that on which a previous public performance of a play given there was based; or (*b*) is based substantially on a text of the play which has been published in the United Kingdom.

(4) For the purposes of this section a performance of a play given solely or primarily for one or more of the purposes mentioned in section 7(2)(*a*) and (*b*) of this Act shall be disregarded.

[Theatres Act 1968, s 11 as amended by the Criminal Justice Act 1982, ss 38 and 46.]

---

1 See s 18, post.
2 See s 9(2), ante.

*Miscellaneous and general*

7.11258 **15. Powers of entry and inspection** (1) If a justice of the peace is satisfied by information on oath that there are reasonable grounds for suspecting, as regards any premises[1] specified in the information—

(*a*) that a performance of a play[1] is to be given at those premises, and that an offence under section 2 or 6 of this Act is likely to be committed in respect of that performance;

(*b*) *repealed*

the justice may issue a warrant under his hand empowering any police officer at any time within one month from the date of the warrant to enter the premises and—

(i) in a case falling within paragraph (*a*) above, to attend any performance of a play which may be given there;

(ii) in a case falling within paragraph (*b*) above, to inspect the premises.

(*Scotland*).

(2)–(7) *Repealed.*

[Theatres Act 1968, s 15 as amended by the Criminal Justice Act 1982, ss 38 and 46, the Police and Criminal Evidence Act 1984, Sch 6, the Public Order Act 1986, Sch 3, the Licensing Act 2003, Sch 6, SSI 2005/383 and SSI 2006/475.]

---

1 See s 18, post.

7.11259 **16. Offences by bodies corporate** Where any offence under this Act committed by a body corporate is proved to have been committed with the consent or connivance of, or to be attributable to any neglect on the part of, any director, manager, secretary or other similar officer of the body corporate, or any person purporting to act in any such capacity, he as well as the body corporate shall be guilty of that offence and shall be liable to be proceeded against and punished accordingly.

[Theatres Act 1968, s 16.]

7.11260 **18. Interpretation** (1) In this Act—

"licensing authority" means—

(*a*)–(*b*) *repealed*

(*c*) *Scotland*;

"play" means—

(*a*) any dramatic piece, whether involving improvisation or not, which is given wholly or in part by one or more persons actually present and performing and in which the whole or a major proportion of what is done by the person or persons performing, whether by way of speech, singing or action, involves the playing of a role; and

(*b*) any ballet given wholly or in part by one or more persons actually present and performing, whether or not it falls within paragraph (*a*) of this definition;

"police officer" means a member, or in Scotland a constable, of a police force;

"premises" includes any place;

"public performance" includes any performance in a public place within the meaning of the Public Order Act 1936, and any performance which the public or any section thereof are permitted to attend, whether on payment or otherwise;

"script" has the meaning assigned by section 9(2) of this Act.

(2) For the purposes of this Act—

(*a*) a person shall not be treated as presenting a performance of a play by reason only of his taking part therein as performer;

(*b*) a person taking part as a performer in a performance of a play directed by another person shall be treated as a person who directed the performance if without reasonable excuse he performs otherwise than in accordance with that person's direction; and

(*c*) a person shall be taken to have directed a performance of a play given under his direction notwithstanding that he was not present during the performance[1];

and a person shall not be treated as aiding or abetting the commission of an offence under section 2 or 6 of this Act in respect of a performance of a play by reason only of his taking part in that performance as a performer.

[Theatres Act 1968, s 18 as amended by the Local Government Act 1985, Sch 8, the Public Order Act 1986, Sch 3 and the Local Government (Wales) Act 1994, Sch 16 and the Licensing Act 2003, Sch 6.]

---

1 But under previous legislation a theatre licence did not "cause to be presented" an unauthorised interpolation for which a performer was solely responsible (*Lovelace v DPP* [1954] 3 All ER 481, 119 JP 21).

# Video Recordings Act 1984[1]

(1984 c 39)

*Preliminary*

7.11261 **1. Interpretation of terms** (1) The provisions of this section shall have effect for the interpretation of terms used in this Act.

(2) "Video work" means any series of visual images (with or without sound)—

(*a*) produced electronically by the use of information contained on any disc, magnetic tape or any other device capable of storing data electronically, and

(*b*) shown as a moving picture[2].

(3) "Video recording" means any disc, magnetic tape or any other device capable of storing data electronically containing information by the use of which the whole or a part of a video work may be produced.

(4) "Supply" means supply in any manner, whether or not for reward, and, therefore, includes supply by way of sale, letting on hire, exchange or loan; and references to a supply are to be interpreted accordingly.

[Video Recordings Act 1984, s 1 as amended by the Criminal Justice and Public Order Act 1994, Schs 9 and 11.]

---

[1] The provisions of this, the 1984 Act, apply only from the date of the coming into force of the Video Recordings Act 2010 which was on the date it received Royal Assent (21 January 2010).

The purpose of the 2010 Act was rectify an oversight whereby there was a failure to notify certain provisions of the 1984 Act in draft to the European Commission before that Act was passed in 1984 in accordance with Council Directive 83/189/EEC of 28 March 1983. Failure to notify provisions in accordance with the Technical Standards Directive had the effect that the provisions were not enforceable against individuals. Sections 1 to 17, 19, 21 and 22 of the 1984 Act were notified to the European Commission on 10 September 2009. The 2010 Act provided for those provisions to cease to be in force and then immediately to come into force again.

According to the Explanatory Notes issued with the 2010 Act transitional provisions are contained in the Schedule to the effect that the repeal and revival of the provisions does not change their effect or the effect of other enactments, instruments or documents that refer to them.

Convictions secured before the enactment of the 2010 Act remain, however, valid and the failure to comply with EU law does not justify setting them aside where no substantial injustice is caused by refusing such relief: *R v Budimir (Secretary of State for Culture, Media and Sport intervening); Interfact Ltd v Liverpool City Council* [2010] EWCA Crim 1486, [2010] EWHC 1604 (Admin), [2011] 3 All ER 206.

[2] It is inappropriate to take account of the brevity of the display. Provided the sequence is long enough to show continuing movement, it can properly be described as a moving picture (*Kent County Council v Multi Media Marketing (Canterbury) Ltd* (1995) Times, 9 May).

7.11262 **2. Exempted works** (1) Subject to subsection (1ZA) below, a video work other than a video game is for the purposes of this Act an exempted work if, taken as a whole—

(*a*) it is designed to inform, educate or instruct; or

(*b*) it is concerned with sport, religion or music.

(*c*) *repealed.*

(1ZA) A video work other than a video game is not an exempted work for those purposes if it does one or more of the following—

(*a*) it depicts or promotes violence or threats of violence;

(*b*) it depicts the immediate aftermath of violence on human or animal characters;

(*c*) it depicts an imitable dangerous activity without also depicting that the activity may endanger the welfare or health of a human or animal character;

(*d*) it promotes an imitable dangerous activity;

(*e*) it depicts or promotes activities involving illegal drugs or the misuse of drugs;

(*f*) it promotes the use of alcohol or tobacco;

(*g*) it depicts or promotes suicide or attempted suicide, or depicts the immediate aftermath of such an event;

(*h*) it depicts or promotes any act of scarification or mutilation of a person, or of self harm, or depicts the immediate aftermath of such an act;

(*i*) it depicts techniques likely to be useful in the commission of offences or, through its depiction of criminal activity, promotes the commission of offences;

(*j*) it includes words or images intended or likely to convey a sexual message (ignoring words or images depicting any mild sexual behaviour);

(*k*) it depicts human sexual activity (ignoring any depictions of mild sexual activity);

(*l*) it depicts or promotes acts of force or restraint associated with human sexual activity;

(*m*) it depicts human genital organs or human urinary or excretory functions (unless the depiction is for a medical, scientific or educational purpose);

(*n*) it includes swearing (ignoring any mild bad language); or

(*o*) it includes words or images that are intended or likely (to any extent) to cause offence, whether on the grounds of race, gender, disability, religion or belief or sexual orientation, or otherwise.

(1ZB) For the purposes of subsection (1ZA), a video work promotes something if the work is likely (to any extent) to stimulate or encourage that thing.

(1ZC) In subsection (1ZA)—

"human or animal character" means a character that is or whose appearance is similar to that of—

(*a*) a human being, or

(*b*) an animal that exists or has existed in real life,

but does not include a simple stick character or any equally basic representation of a human being or animal;

"imitable dangerous activity" means an activity which—

(*a*) if imitated by a person, may endanger the welfare or health of any person or animal, and

(*b*) may be easily imitated by a person; and

"violence" does not include any violence that is—

(*a*) mild, or

(*b*) not directed towards human or animal characters,

unless it is sexual violence.

(1A) Subject to subsection (2) or (3) below, a video game is for the purposes of this Act an exempted work if—

(*a*) it is, taken as a whole, designed to inform, educate or instruct;

(*b*) it is, taken as a whole, concerned with sport, religion or music; or

(*c*) it satisfies one or more of the conditions in section 2A.

(2) A video game is not an exempted work for those purposes if, to any significant extent, it depicts—

(*a*) human sexual activity[1] or acts of force or restraint associated with such activity;

(*b*) mutilation or torture of, or other acts of gross violence towards, humans or animals;

(*c*) human genital organs[1] or human urinary or excretory functions;

(*d*) techniques likely[1] to be useful in the commission of offences;

or is likely to any significant extent to stimulate or encourage anything falling within paragraph (*a*) or, in the case of anything falling within paragraph (*b*), is likely to any extent to do so.

(3) A video game is not an exempted work for those purposes if, to any significant extent, it depicts criminal activity which is likely to any significant extent to stimulate or encourage the commission of offences.

(4) The Secretary of State may by regulations amend this section—

(*a*) by adding or removing a case in which a video work is not an exempted work, or

(*b*) by amending a description of such a case.

[Video Recordings Act 1984, s 2 as amended by the Criminal Justice and Public Order Act 1994, s 89, the Digital Economy Act 2010, s 40 and Sch 2 and SI 2014/2097.]

---

1 Activity short of masturbation might amount to "human sexual activity". Female genitalia need not be confined to internal organs. In considering whether a work is designed to encourage human sexual activity it is unnecessary that any video clips be regarded as hard pornography or offensive (*Kent County Council v Multi Media Marketing (Canterbury) Ltd* (1995) Times, 9 May).

7.11263 **2A. Conditions relating to video games** (1) The conditions referred to in section 2(1A)(*c*) are as follows.

(2) The first condition is that the video game does not include any of the following—

(*a*) depictions of violence towards human or animal characters, whether or not the violence looks realistic and whether or not the violence results in obvious harm,

(*b*) depictions of violence towards other characters where the violence looks realistic,

(*c*) depictions of criminal activity that are likely, to any extent, to stimulate or encourage the commission of offences,

(*d*) depictions of activities involving illegal drugs or the misuse of drugs,

(*e*) words or images that are likely, to any extent, to stimulate or encourage the use of alcohol or tobacco,

(*f*) words or images that are intended to convey a sexual message,

(*g*) swearing, or

(*h*) words or images that are intended or likely, to any extent, to cause offence, whether on the grounds of race, gender, disability, religion or belief or sexual orientation or otherwise.

(3) In subsection (2) "human or animal character" means a character that is, or whose appearance is similar to that of—

(*a*) a human being, or

(*b*) an animal that exists or has existed in real life,

but does not include a simple stick character or any equally basic representation of a human being or animal.

(4) The second condition is that the designated authority, or a person nominated by the designated authority for the purposes of this section, has confirmed in writing that the video game is suitable for viewing by persons under the age of 12.

(5) The Secretary of State may by regulations amend this section—

(*a*) by amending the first condition, or

(*b*) by adding a further condition (or by amending or removing such a condition).

(6) Regulations under this section may make provision by reference to documents produced by the designated authority.

[Video Recordings Act 1984, s 2A as inserted by the Digital Economy Act 2010, s 40.]

7.11264 **3. Exempted supplies** (1) The provisions of this section apply to determine whether or not a supply of a video recording is an exempted supply for the purposes of this Act.

(2) The supply of a video recording by any person is an exempted supply if it is neither—

(*a*) a supply for reward, nor

(*b*) a supply in the course or furtherance of a business.

(3) Where on any premises facilities are provided in the course or furtherance of a business for supplying video recordings, the supply by any person of a video recording on those premises is to be treated for the purposes of subsection (2) above as a supply in the course or furtherance of a business.

(4) Where a person (in this subsection referred to as the "original supplier") supplies a video recording to a person who, in the course of a business, makes video works or supplies video recordings the supply is an exempted supply—

(*a*) if it is not made with a view to any further supply of that recording, or

(*b*) if it is so made, but is not made with a view to the eventual supply of that recording to the public or is made with a view to the eventual supply of that recording to the original supplier.

For the purposes of this subsection, any supply is a supply to the public unless it is—

(i) a supply to a person who, in the course of a business, makes video works or supplies video recordings,

(ii) an exempted supply by virtue of subsection (2) above or subsections (5) to (10) below, or

(iii) a supply outside the United Kingdom.

(5) Where a video work—

(*a*) is designed to provide a record of an event or occasion for those who took part in the event or occasion or are connected with those who did so,

(*b*) does not, to any significant extent, depict any of the following—

(i) human sexual activity or acts of force or restraint associated with such activity,

(ii) mutilation or torture of, or other acts of gross violence towards, humans or animals, or

(iii) human genital organs or human urinary or excretory functions, and

(*c*) is not designed—

(i) to any significant extent to stimulate or encourage anything falling within paragraph (*b*)(i), or

(ii) to any extent to stimulate or encourage anything falling within paragraph (*b*)(ii),

the supply of a video recording containing only that work to a person who took part in the event or occasion or is connected with someone who did so is an exempted supply.

(6) The supply of a video recording for the purpose only of the exhibition of any video work contained in the recording in premises other than a dwelling-house—

(*a*) being premises mentioned in subsection (7) below, or

(*b*) being an exhibition which in England and Wales or Scotland would be a film exhibition to which section 6 of the Cinemas Act 1985 applies (film exhibition to which public not admitted or are admitted without payment), or (*Northern Ireland*).

is an exempted supply.

(7) The premises referred to in subsection (6) above are—

(*za*) premises in England and Wales which, by virtue of an authorisation within the meaning of section 136 of the Licensing Act 2003, may be used for the exhibition of a film within the meaning of paragraph 15 of Schedule 1 to that Act,

(*a*)–(*c*) Scotland

(8) The supply of a video recording with a view only to its use for or in connection with a programme service (within the meaning of the Broadcasting Act 1990) is an exempted supply.

(8A) The supply of a video recording in the form of a machine of a type designed primarily for use in an amusement arcade is an exempted supply unless the video game (or, if more than one, any of the video games) that it contains—

(*a*) depicts, to any significant extent, anything falling within section 2(2)(*a*), (*b*), (*c*) or (*d*) or (3), or

(*b*) is likely to any significant extent to stimulate or encourage anything falling within section 2(2)(*a*) or, in the case of anything falling within section 2(2)(*b*), is likely to any extent to do so.

(8B) The supply of any other video recording is an exempted supply if the recording is supplied for the purpose only of its use in connection with a supply that is an exempted supply under subsection (8A).

(9) The supply of a video recording for the purpose only of submitting a video work contained in the recording for the issue of a classification certificate or otherwise only for purposes of

arrangements made by the designated authority is an exempted supply.

(10) The supply of a video recording with a view only to its use—

(*a*) in training for or carrying on any medical or related occupation,

(*b*) for the purpose of—

(i) services provided in pursuance of the National Health Service Act 2006, the National Health Service (Wales) Act 2006 or the National Health Service (Scotland) Act 1978, or

(ii) *Northern Ireland,*

(*c*) in training persons employed in the course of services falling within paragraph (*b*) above,

is an exempted supply.

(11) For the purposes of subsection (10) above, an occupation is a medical or related occupation if, to carry on the occupation, a person is required to be registered under the Health and Social Work Professions Order 2001, the Nursing and Midwifery Order 2001, the Medical Act 1983, the Osteopaths Act 1993 or the Chiropractors Act 1994.

(11A) But subsection (11) does not apply to a person in so far as the person is required to register under the Health and Social Work Professions Order 2001 as a member of the social work profession in England (within the meaning of section 60 of the Health Act 1999).

(12) The supply of a video recording otherwise than for reward, being a supply made for the purpose only of supplying it to a person who previously made an exempted supply of the recording, is also an exempted supply.

(13) The Secretary of State may by regulations amend this section and the regulations may, in particular—

(*a*) add a case in which the supply of a video recording is an exempted supply for the purposes of this Act, or

(*b*) repeal a provision of this section.

[Video Recordings Act 1984, s 3 as amended by the Cable and Broadcasting Act 1984, Sch 5, the Cinemas Act 1985, Sch 2, the Broadcasting Act 1990, Sch 20, the Chiropractors Act 1994, s 39, the Nurses, Midwives and Health Visitors Act 1997, Sch 4, SI 2002/254, the Licensing Act 2003, Sch 6, the National Health Service (Consequential Provisions) Act 2006, Sch 1, the Digital Economy Act 2010, ss 40, 41 and Sch 1, the Health and Social Care Act 2012, ss 213, 220 and SI 2014/2097.]

7.11265 4–7. *Classification and labelling of video works by authority designated by the Secretary of State.*

7.11266 8. **Requirements as to labelling etc** Secretary of State may make regulations[1] to labelling of video works.

[Video Recordings Act 1984, s 8—summarised.]

---

1 See the Video Recordings (Labelling) Regulations 2010, post.

*Offences and penalties*

7.11267 9. **Supplying video recording of unclassified work** (1) A person who supplies or offers to supply a video recording containing a video work in respect of which no classification certificate has been issued is guilty of an offence[1] unless—

(*a*) the supply is, or would if it took place be, an exempted supply, or

(*b*) the video work is an exempted work.

(2) It is a defence to a charge of committing an offence under this section to prove that the accused believed on reasonable grounds—

(*a*) that the video work concerned or, if the video recording contained more than one work to which the charge relates, each of those works was either an exempted work or a work in respect of which a classification certificate had been issued, or

(*b*) that the supply was, or would if it took place be, an exempted supply by virtue of section 3(4) or (5) of this Act.

(3) A person guilty of an offence under this section shall be liable[2]—

(*a*) on conviction on indictment, to imprisonment for a term not exceeding **two years** or a **fine or both,**

(*b*) on summary conviction, to imprisonment for a term not exceeding **six months** or a fine or **both**.

[Video Recordings Act 1984, s 9 as amended by the Criminal Justice and Public Order Act 1994, s 88 and SI 2015/664.]

---

1 The requirement for video works to be submitted for a classification certificate does not infringe art 34 of the Treaty on the Functioning of the European Union; its purpose is within the ambit of art 36 (prohibitions on grounds of public morality (etc), which qualifies art 34. The qualification of art 10(1) of the ECHR by art 10(2) raises the same issue as the qualification of art 34 by art 36. The provisions of VRA are lawful, necessary and justified for the protection of health and morals: *R v Dryzner and Play Media Distribution Ltd* [2014] EWCA Crim 2438, (2015) 179 JP 29.

2 For procedure in respect of this offence which is triable either way, see the Magistrates' Courts Act 1980, ss 17A–21, in PART I: MAGISTRATES' COURTS, PROCEDURE, ante.

7.11268 10. **Possession of video recording of unclassified work for the purposes of supply** (1) Where a video recording contains a video work in respect of which no classification certificate has been issued, a person who has the recording in his possession for the purposes of supplying it is guilty of an offence unless—

(*a*) he has it in his possession for the purpose only of a supply which, if it took place, would be an exempted supply, or

(*b*) the video work is an exempted work.

(2) It is a defence to a charge of committing an offence under this section to prove—

(*a*) that the accused believed on reasonable grounds that the video work concerned or, if the video recording contained more than one work to which the charge relates, each of those works was either an exempted work or a work in respect of which a classification certificate had been issued,

(*b*) that the accused had the video recording in his possession for the purposes only of a supply which he believed on reasonable grounds would, if it took place, be an exempted supply by virtue of section 3(4) or (5) of this Act, or

(*c*) that the accused did not intend to supply the video recording until a classification certificate had been issued in respect of the video work concerned.

(3) A person guilty of an offence under this section shall be liable[1]—

(*a*) on conviction on indictment, to imprisonment for a term not exceeding **two years** or a **fine** or **both**,

(*b*) on summary conviction, to imprisonment for a term not exceeding **six months** or a fine or **both**.

[Video Recordings Act 1984, s 10 as amended by the Criminal Justice and Public Order Act 1994, s 88 and SI 2015/664.]

---

1 For procedure in respect of this offence which is triable either way, see the Magistrates' Courts Act 1980, ss 17A–21, in PART I: MAGISTRATES' COURTS, PROCEDURE, ante.

**7.11269 11. Supplying video recording of classified work in breach of classification**

(1) Where a classification certificate issued in respect of a video work states that no video recording, or no video recording described in the certificate, that contains that work is to be supplied to any person who has not attained the age[1] specified in the certificate, a person who supplies or offers to supply such a video recording to a person who has not attained the age so specified is guilty of an offence unless—

(*a*) the video work is an exempted work, or

(*b*) the supply is, or would if it took place be, an exempted supply.

(2) It is a defence to a charge of committing an offence under this section to prove[2]—

(*a*) that the accused neither knew nor had reasonable grounds to believe that the classification certificate contained the statement concerned,

(*b*) that the accused neither knew nor had reasonable grounds to believe that the person concerned had not attained that age,

(*ba*) that the accused believed on reasonable grounds that the video work concerned or, if the video recording contained more than one work to which the charge relates, each of those works was an exempted work, or

(*c*) that the accused believed on reasonable grounds that the supply was, or would if it took place be, an exempted supply by virtue of section 3(4) or (5) of this Act.

(3) A person guilty of an offence under this section shall be liable, on summary conviction, to imprisonment for a term not exceeding **six months** or a fine not exceeding **level 5** on the standard scale or both.

[Video Recordings Act 1984, s 11 as amended by the Criminal Justice and Public Order Act 1994, s 88 and the Digital Economy Act 2010, Sch 1.]

---

1 Evidence of the 11-year-old son of a Trading Standards Officer acting under instructions to purchase an 18 category video was, in the absence of his acting as an agent provocateur, held to have been rightly admitted (*Ealing London Borough v Woolworths plc* [1995] Crim LR 58).

2 For this purpose, s 11(2) refers to the knowledge or reasonable grounds for belief of the employee through whom a company effects a supply (*Tesco Stores Ltd v Brent London Borough Council* [1993] 2 All ER 718, [1993] 1 WLR 1037, 158 JP 121).

**7.11270 12. Certain video recordings only to be supplied in licensed sex shops**

(1) Where a classification certificate issued in respect of a video work states that no video recording, or no video recording described in the certificate, that contains that work is to be supplied other than in a licensed sex shop, a person who at any place other than in a sex shop for which a licence is in force under the relevant enactment—

(*a*) supplies[1] such a video recording, or

(*b*) offers to do so[2],

is guilty of an offence unless the supply is, or would if it took place be, an exempted supply.

(2) It is a defence to a charge of committing an offence under subsection (1) above to prove—

(*a*) that the accused neither knew nor had reasonable grounds to believe that the classification certificate contained the statement concerned,

(*b*) that the accused believed on reasonable grounds that the place concerned was a sex shop for which a licence was in force under the relevant enactment, or (*c*) that the accused believed on reasonable grounds that the supply was, or would if it took place be, an exempted supply by virtue of section 3(4) of this Act or subsection (6) below.

(3) Where a classification certificate issued in respect of a video work states that no video recording, or no video recording described in the certificate, that contains that work is to be supplied other than in a licensed sex shop, a person who has such a video recording in his possession for the purpose of supplying it at any place other than in such a sex shop is guilty of an offence, unless he has it in his possession for the purpose only of a supply which, if it took place, would be an exempted supply.

(4) It is a defence to a charge of committing an offence under subsection (3) above to prove—

(*a*) that the accused neither knew nor had reasonable grounds to believe that the classification certificate contained the statement concerned,

(*b*) that the accused believed on reasonable grounds that the place concerned was a sex shop for which a licence was in force under the relevant enactment, or

(*c*) that the accused had the video recording in his possession for the purpose only of a supply which he believed on reasonable grounds would, if it took place, be an exempted supply by virtue of section 3(4) of this Act or subsection (6) below.

(4A) A person guilty of an offence under subsection (1) or (3) above shall be liable, on summary conviction, to imprisonment for a term not exceeding **six months** or a fine not exceeding **level 5** on the standard scale or both.

(5) In this section "relevant enactment" means Schedule 3 to the Local Government (Miscellaneous Provisions) Act 1982 or, in Scotland, Schedule 2 to the Civic Government (Scotland) Act 1982, and "sex shop" has the same meaning as in the relevant enactment.

(6) For the purposes of this section, where a classification certificate issued in respect of a video work states that no video recording, or no video recording described in the certificate, that contains that work is to be supplied other than in a licensed sex shop, the supply of such a video recording—

(*a*) to a person who, in the course of a business, makes video works or supplies video recordings, and

(*b*) with a view to its eventual supply in sex shops, being sex shops for which licences are in force under the relevant enactment,

is an exempted supply.

[Video Recordings Act 1984, s 12 as amended by the Criminal Justice and Public Order Act 1994, s 88 and the Digital Economy Act 2010, Sch 1.]

---

[1] The restriction is not directed simply to ensure a supply takes place "by" a licensed sex shop proprietor but to ensure that the "supply" of restricted material only takes place at licensed establishments. The customer must come face to face with the supplier. Accordingly, it is an offence to supply restricted videos by post in response to telephone, postal or internet orders (*Interfact Ltd v Liverpool City Council* [2005] EWHC 995 (Admin), [2005] 1 WLR 3118, 169 JP 353).

[2] The offence consists of the offer to make the supply, not to make the offer, other than in a licensed sex shop. As regards what amounts to an "offer", the issue is not whether a catalogue amounts to an offer to sell videos or an invitation to treat but whether it amounts to an offer to supply videos, namely to supply outside a licensed sex shop. An offer to supply under s 1(4) need not be underpinned by a contract of sale or contractually binding relationship. A gratuitous offer to supply without any consideration is equally an offer to supply a video recording (*Interfact Ltd v Liverpool City Council* [2005] EWHC 995 (Admin), [2005] 1 WLR 3118, 169 JP 353).

7.11271 **13. Supply of video recording not complying with requirements as to labels, etc**

(1) A person who supplies or offers to supply a video recording or any spool, case or other thing on or in which the recording is kept which does not satisfy any requirement imposed by regulations under section 8 of this Act is guilty of an offence unless —

(*a*) the video work is an exempted work, or

(*b*) the supply is, or would if it took place be, an exempted supply.

(2) It is a defence to a charge of committing an offence under this section to prove that the accused—

(*za*) believed on reasonable grounds that the video work concerned or, if the video recording contained more than one work to which the charge relates, each of those works was an exempted work,

(*a*) believed on reasonable grounds that the supply was, or would if it took place be, an exempted supply by virtue of section 3(4) or (5) of this Act, or

(*b*) neither knew nor had reasonable grounds to believe that the recording, spool, case or other thing (as the case may be) did not satisfy the requirement concerned.

(3) A person guilty of an offence under this section shall be liable, on summary conviction, to a fine not exceeding **level 5** on the standard scale.

[Video Recordings Act 1984, s 13 as amended by the Criminal Justice and Public Order Act 1994, Sch 10 and the Digital Economy Act 2010, Sch 1.]

7.11272 **14. Supply of video recording containing false indication as to classification**

(1) A person who supplies or offers to supply a video recording containing a video work in respect of which no classification certificate has been issued is guilty of an offence if the video recording or any spool, case or other thing on or in which the recording is kept contains any indication that a classification certificate has been issued in respect of that work unless—

(*a*) the video work is an exempted work, or

(*b*) the supply is, or would if it took place be, an exempted supply.

(2) It is a defence to a charge of committing an offence under subsection (1) above to prove—

(*a*) that the accused believed on reasonable grounds—

(i) that a classification certificate had been issued in respect of the video work concerned,

(ia) that the video work concerned or, if the video recording contained more than one work to which the charge relates, each of those works was an exempted work, or

(ii) that the supply was, or would if it took place be, an exempted supply by virtue of section 3(4) or (5) of this Act, or

(*b*) that the accused neither knew nor had reasonable grounds to believe that the recording, spool, case or other thing (as the case may be) contained the indication concerned.

(3) A person who supplies or offers to supply a video recording containing a video work in respect of which a classification certificate has been issued is guilty of an offence if the video recording or any spool, case or other thing on or in which the recording is kept contains any indication that is false in a material particular of any statement falling within section 7(2) of this Act[1] (including any advice falling within paragraph (*a*) of that subsection) contained in the certificate, unless—

(*a*) the video work is an exempted work, or

(*b*) the supply is, or would if it took place be, an exempted supply.

(4) It is a defence to a charge of committing an offence under subsection (3) above to prove—

(*a*) that the accused believed on reasonable grounds—

(i) that the supply was, or would if it took place be, an exempted supply by virtue of section 3(4) or (5) of this Act,

(ai) that the video work concerned or, if the video recording contained more than one work to which the charge relates, each of those works was an exempted work, or

(ii) that the certificate concerned contained the statement indicated, or

(*b*) that the accused neither knew nor had reasonable grounds to believe that the recording, spool, case or other thing (as the case may be) contained the indication concerned.

(5) A person guilty of an offence under subsection (1) or (3) above shall be liable, on summary conviction, to imprisonment for a term not exceeding **six months** or a fine not exceeding **level 5** on the standard scale.

[Video Recordings Act 1984, s 14 as amended by the Criminal Justice and Public Order Act 1994, s 88 and the Digital Economy Act 2010, Sch 1.]

1 Those requirements are that the certificate must contain:

(*a*) a statement that the video work concerned is suitable for general viewing and unrestricted supply (with or without any advice as to the desirability of parental guidance with regard to the viewing of the work by young children or as to the particular suitability of the work for viewing by children); or

(*b*) a statement that the video work concerned is suitable for viewing only by persons who have attained the age (not being more than eighteen years) specified in the certificate and that no video recording containing that work is to be supplied to any person who has not attained the age so specified; or

(*c*) the statement mentioned in paragraph (*b*) above together with a statement that no video recording containing that work is to be supplied other than in a licensed sex shop; (s 7(2), Video Recordings Act 1994).

7.11273 14A. **General defences to offences under this Act** Without prejudice to any defence specified in the preceding provisions of this Act in relation to a particular offence, it is a defence to a charge of committing any offence under this Act to prove—

(*a*) that the commission of the offence was due to the act or default of a person other than the accused, and

(*b*) that the accused took all reasonable precautions and exercised all due diligence[1] to avoid the commission of the offence by any person under his control.

[Video Recording Act 1984, s 14A as inserted by the Video Recording Act 1993, s 2.]

1 The "due diligence" defence was established where a company had been dealing with a reputable supplier for 20 years without problems which was clearly aware of its statutory obligations and it was not necessary for the company to make checks (*Bilon v WH Smith Trading Ltd* [2001] EWHC Admin 469, 165 JP 701, [2001] Crim LR 850).

7.11274 15. **Time limit for prosecutions** (1) No prosecution for an offence under this Act shall be brought after the expiry of the period of three years beginning with the date of the commission of the offence or one year beginning with the date of its discovery by the prosecutor, whichever is earlier.

(2)–(3) *Scotland.*

[Video Recordings Act 1984, s 15 as substituted by the Criminal Justice and Public Order Act 1994, Sch 10.]

*Miscellaneous and supplementary*

7.11275 16. **Offences by bodies corporate** (1) Where an offence under this Act committed by a body corporate is proved to have been committed with the consent or connivance of, or to be attributable to any neglect on the part of, any director, manager, secretary or other similar officer of the body corporate, or any person who was purporting to act in any such capacity, he as well as the body corporate shall be guilty of the offence and shall be liable to be proceeded against and punished accordingly.

(2) Where the affairs of a body corporate are managed by its members, subsection (1) above shall apply in relation to the acts and defaults of a member in connection with his functions of management as if he were a director of the body corporate.

[Video Recordings Act 1984, s 16.]

7.11276 **16A. Enforcement** (1) The functions of a local weights and measures authority include the enforcement in their area of this Act.

(1A) Subject to subsection (1B) below, the functions of a local weights and measures authority shall also include the investigation and prosecution outside their area of offences under this Act suspected to be linked to their area as well as the investigation outside their area of offences suspected to have been committed within it.

(1B) The functions available to an authority under subsection (1A) above shall not be exercisable in relation to any circumstances suspected to have arisen within the area of another local weights and measures authority without the consent of that authority.

(2) The following provisions of the Trade Descriptions Act 1968 apply in relation to the enforcement of this Act by such an authority as in relation to the enforcement of that Act—

section 27 (power to make test purchases),

section 28 (power to enter premises and inspect and seize goods and documents),

section 29 (obstruction of authorised officers), and

section 33 (compensation for loss, &c of goods seized under s 28).

(3) Nothing in this section shall be taken as authorising a local weights and measures authority in Scotland to initiate proceedings for an offence.

(4) *Northern Ireland.*

(4A) For the purposes of subsections (1A), (1B) and (2) above—

(*a*) offences in another area are "linked" to the area of a local weights and measures authority if—

(i) the supply or possession of video recordings in contravention of this Act within their area is likely to be or to have been the result of the supply or possession of those recordings in the other area; or

(ii) the supply or possession of video recordings in contravention of this Act in the other area is likely to be or to have been the result of the supply or possession of those recordings in their area; and

(*b*) "investigation" includes the exercise of the powers conferred by sections 27 and 28 of the Trade Descriptions Act 1968 as applied by subsection (2) above;

and sections 29 and 33 of that Act shall apply accordingly.

(5) Any enactment which authorises the disclosure of information for the purpose of facilitating the enforcement of the Trade Descriptions Act 1968 shall apply as if the provisions of this Act were contained in that Act and as if the functions of any person in relation to the enforcement of this Act were functions under that Act.

[Video Recordings Act 1984, s 16A as inserted by the Criminal Justice Act 1988, s 162 and amended by the Criminal Justice and Public Order Act 1994, s 91.]

7.11277 **16B. Extension of jurisdiction of magistrates' courts in linked cases** (1) A justice of the peace for an area to which section 1 of the Magistrates' Courts Act 1980 applies may issue a summons or warrant under and in accordance with that section as respects an offence under this Act committed or suspected of having been committed outside the area for which he acts if it appears to the justice that the offence is linked to the supply or possession of video recordings within the area for which he acts.

(2) Where a person charged with an offence under this Act appears or is brought before a magistrates' court in answer to a summons issued by virtue of subsection (1) above, or under a warrant issued under subsection (1) above, the court shall have jurisdiction to try the offence.

(3) For the purposes of this section an offence is "linked" to the supply or possession of video recordings within the area for which a justice acts if—

(*a*) the supply or possession of video recordings within his area is likely to be or to have been the result of the offence; or

(*b*) the offence is likely to be or to have been the result of the supply or possession of video recordings in his area.

[Video Recordings Act 1984, s 16B as inserted by the Criminal Justice and Public Order Act 1994, s 91.]

7.11278 **16C–16D.** *Scotland; Northern Ireland.*

7.11279 **17. Entry, search and seizure** (1) If a justice of the peace is satisfied by information on oath that there are reasonable grounds for suspecting—

(*a*) that an offence under this Act has been or is being committed on any premises, and

(*b*) that evidence that the offence has been or is being committed is on those premises,

he may issue a warrant under his hand authorising any constable to enter and search the premises.

(2) A constable entering or searching any premises in pursuance of a warrant under subsection (1) above may use reasonable force if necessary and may seize anything found there which he has reasonable grounds to believe may be required to be used in evidence in any proceedings for an

offence under this Act.

(3) Reference to Scotland and Northern Ireland.

[Video Recordings Act 1984, s 17 as amended by the Criminal Justice and Public Order Act 1994, Schs 9 and 11.]

**7.11280 19. Evidence by certificate** (1) In any proceedings in England and Wales or Northern Ireland for an offence under this Act, a certificate purporting to be signed by a person authorised in that behalf by the Secretary of State and stating—

(*a*) that he has examined—

(i) the record maintained in pursuance of arrangements made by the designated authority, and

(ii) a video work (or part of a video work) contained in a video recording identified by the certificate, and

(*b*) that the record shows that, on the date specified in the certificate, no classification certificate had been issued in respect of the video work concerned,

shall be admissible as evidence of the fact that, on that day, no classification certificate had been issued in respect of the video work concerned.

(2) A certificate under subsection (1) above may also state—

(*a*) that the video work concerned differs in such respects as may be specified from another video work examined by the person so authorised and identified by the certificate, and

(*b*) that the record shows that, on a date specified in the certificate under subsection (1) above, a classification certificate was issued in respect of that other video work;

and, if it does so, shall be admissible as evidence of the fact that the video work concerned differs in those respects from the other video work.

(3) In any proceedings in England and Wales or Northern Ireland for an offence under this Act, a certificate purporting to be signed by a person authorised in that behalf by the Secretary of State and stating—

(*a*) that he has examined—

(i) the record maintained in pursuance of arrangements made by the designated authority, and

(ii) a video work (or part of a video work) contained in a video recording identified by the certificate, and

(*b*) that the record shows that, on the date specified in the certificate under this subsection, a classification certificate was issued in respect of the video work concerned and that a document identified by the certificate under this subsection is a copy of the classification certificate so issued,

shall be admissible as evidence of the fact that, on that date, a classification certificate in terms of the document so identified was issued in respect of the video work concerned.

(3A) In any proceedings in England and Wales or Northern Ireland for an offence under this Act, a certificate purporting to be signed by a person authorised in that behalf by the Secretary of State and stating—

(*a*) that he has examined the record maintained in pursuance of arrangements made by the designated authority, and

(*b*) that the record shows that, on the date specified in the certificate, no classification certificate had been issued in respect of a video work having a particular title,

shall be admissible as evidence of the fact that, on that date, no classification certificate had been issued in respect of a work of that title.

(3B) In any proceedings in England and Wales or Northern Ireland for an offence under this Act, a certificate purporting to be signed by a person authorised in that behalf by the Secretary of State and stating—

(*a*) that he has examined the record maintained in pursuance of arrangements made by the designated authority, and

(*b*) that the record shows that, on the date specified in the certificate under this subsection, a classification certificate was issued in respect of a video work having a particular title and that a document identified by the certificate under this subsection is a copy of the classification certificate so issued,

shall be admissible as evidence of the fact that, on that date, a classification certificate in terms of the document so identified was issued in respect of a work of that title.

(4) Any document or video recording identified in a certificate tendered in evidence under this section shall be treated as if it had been produced as an exhibit and identified in court by the person signing the certificate.

(5) This section does not make a certificate admissible as evidence in proceedings for an offence unless a copy of the certificate has, not less than seven days before the hearing, been served on the person charged with the offence in one of the following ways—

(*a*) by delivering it to him or to his solicitor, or

(*b*) by addressing it to him and leaving it at his usual or last known place of abode or place of business or by addressing it to his solicitor and leaving it at his office, or

(*c*) by sending it in a registered letter or by the recorded delivery service addressed to him at his usual or last known place of abode or place of business or addressed to his solicitor at his office, or (*d*) in the case of a body corporate, by delivering it to the secretary or clerk of the body at its registered or principal office or sending it in a registered letter or by the recorded delivery service addressed to the secretary or clerk of that body at that office.

[Video Recordings Act 1984, s 19 as amended by the Video Recording Act 1993, s 4.]

7.11281 **21. Forfeiture** (1) Where a person is convicted of any offence under this Act, the court may order any video recording—

(*a*) produced to the court, and

(*b*) shown to the satisfaction of the court to relate to the offence,

to be forfeited.

(2) The court shall not order any video recording to be forfeited under subsection (1) above if a person claiming to be the owner of it or otherwise interested in it applies to be heard by the court, unless an opportunity has been given to him to show cause why the order should not be made.

(3) References in this section to a video recording include a reference to any spool, case or other thing on or in which the recording is kept.

(4) An order made under subsection (1) above in any proceedings in England and Wales or Northern Ireland shall not take effect until the expiration of the ordinary time within which an appeal may be instituted or, where such an appeal is duly instituted, until the appeal is finally decided or abandoned; and for this purpose—

(*a*) an application for a case to be stated or for leave to appeal shall be treated as the institution of an appeal; and

(*b*) where a decision on appeal is subject to a further appeal, the appeal is not finally decided until the expiration of the ordinary time within which a further appeal may be instituted or, where a further appeal is duly instituted, until the further appeal is finally decided or abandoned.

(5) *Scotland.*

[Video Recordings Act 1984, s 21.]

7.11282 **22. Other interpretation** (1) In this Act—

"business", except in section 3(4), includes any activity carried on by a club;

"premises" includes any vehicle, vessel or stall;

"video games authority" and "video works authority" have the meaning given in section 4ZA.

(2) For the purposes of this Act, and subject to regulations under subsection (2A)), a video recording contains a video work if it contains information by the use of which the whole or a part of the work may be produced; but where a video work includes any extract from another video work, that extract is not to be regarded for the purposes of this subsection as a part of that other work.

(2A) The Secretary of State may by regulations make provision about the circumstances in which, for the purposes of this Act, a video recording does or does not contain a video work.

(3) Where any alteration is made to a video work in respect of which a classification certificate has been issued, the classification certificate is not to be treated for the purposes of this Act as issued in respect of the altered work.

In this subsection, "alteration" includes addition.

[Video Recordings Act 1984, s 22 as amended by the Digital Economy Act 2010, Sch 1.]

7.11283 **22A. Regulations** (1) Regulations under this Act are to be made by statutory instrument.

(2) Every power of the Secretary of State to make regulations under this Act includes—

(*a*) power to make different provision for different purposes, and

(*b*) power to make transitional or saving provision.

(3) A statutory instrument containing regulations under section 2, 2A or 3 may not be made unless a draft of the instrument has been laid before, and approved by a resolution of, each House of Parliament.

(4) Any other statutory instrument containing regulations under this Act is subject to annulment in pursuance of a resolution of either House of Parliament.

[Video Recordings Act 1984, s 22A as inserted by the Digital Economy Act 2010, Sch 1.]

## Video Recordings (Labelling) Regulations 2012[1]

(SI 2012/1767)

7.11284 *1. Citation and Commencement* These Regulations may be cited as the Video Recordings (Labelling) Regulations 2012 and they come in to force on 30th July 2012.

[1] Made by the Secretary of State in exercise of the powers conferred by ss 8 and 22A of the Video Recordings Act 1984.

7.11285 *2. Interpretation* (1) In these Regulations—

(*a*) "the Act" means the Video Recordings Act 1984;

(*b*) "double-sided disc" means a disc containing on both faces the information by the use of which the whole or part of the video work may be produced;

(*c*) "unique title" means the title assigned to a video work under section 4(1)(*b*)(ia) of the Act;

(*d*) "case" means the case or cover in which a video recording is kept; and any reference to a case includes the case or cover in which a spool may be kept;

(*e*) "spool" means the device or article on which a magnetic tape is wound in order to be produced as a video recording but it does not mean the case or covering in which the spool may be kept;

(*f*) the "video works authority" and the "video games authority" are the persons designated by the Secretary of State under section 4 and 4ZA of the Act, as the authority responsible for making arrangements for the matters specified in that Act regarding video works and video games respectively;

(*g*) A "pre-commencement classification document" means a document issued by the video works authority or the video games authority prior to the coming into force date of these Regulations that contains the title of a video game and a statement that the video game concerned is only suitable for viewing by persons who have attained the age specified in the document (not being less than twelve years).

(2) A reference in these Regulations to a face of a case in which a video recording is kept is a reference to the outer face of such a case.

**7.11286** 3. *General labelling requirements* Where under these Regulations the classification symbol, the classification icon, the unique title or the explanatory statement, or any combination of them, is or are required to be shown, it or they shall be clearly legible and indelible and no part of it or them shall be hidden or obscured by any other written or pictorial matter or by any other sign or label.

**7.11287** 4. Where under these Regulations the classification symbol, the classification icon or the explanatory statement is or are required to be shown on a case in which a video recording is kept, it or they shall be shown in such manner as it remains, or they remain, clearly visible where that case is kept in a cover or covering.

**7.11288** 5. Where under these Regulations the classification symbol, the classification icon, the unique title or the explanatory statement, or any combination of them, is or are required to be shown it or they shall be shown by means of a label affixed to, or a marking on, the video recording which satisfies the requirements of these Regulations and any other requirements relating to the labelling of video recordings as may be determined by the authority, or authorities, responsible for making arrangements under section 4 of the Act.

**7.11289** 6. Where under these Regulations the explanatory statement and the classification symbol are required to be shown together on the same face of a case in which a video recording is kept, the symbol and the explanatory statement shall be shown within a single rectangular shaped frame.

**7.11290** 7. Where under these Regulations the classification symbol and classification icon are required to be shown together on the same face of a case in which a video game is kept, the symbol and the icon shall be shown within a single rectangular shaped frame.

**7.11291** 8. *Mixed content* For the purposes of these Regulations—

(*a*) where a video recording contains more than one video work and all or some of those works are works in respect of which classification certificates which are equally restrictive have been issued, those video works shall be taken to be one video work containing any one of them;

(*b*) Where a video recording contains more than one video work in respect of which classification certificates which are not equally restrictive have been issued, the video recording shall be taken to contain only the most restrictively classified video work of those works; and

(*c*) Where one or more video recordings are placed within a single case and those video recordings contain video works in respect of which classification certificates which are not equally restrictive have been issued, the indication required on the case is only that which applies by virtue of these Regulations to the most restrictively classified video work contained within that case.

**7.11292** 9. (1) For the purposes of paragraph (8) above—

(*a*) a classification certificate is equally restrictive as another such certificate if they both—

(i) contain an identical statement made within section 7(2)(*b*) of the Act;

(ii) contain an identical statement made within section 7(2)(*c*) of the Act;

(iii) contain a statement made within section 7(2)(*a*) of the Act with or without including advice as to the particular suitability of the work for viewing by children; or

(iv) contain a statement made within section 7(2)(*a*) of the Act with advice as to the desirability of parental guidance with regard to the viewing of the work by young children.

(*b*) "the most restrictively classified video work" means the work in respect of which the classification certificate issued in respect of it contains the most restrictive statement.

(2) For the purposes of these Regulations—

(*a*) The statements mentioned within sub-paragraphs (*a*), (*b*) and (*c*) of section 7(2) of the Act are to be regarded as progressively more restrictive so that a statement within sub-paragraph (*a*) is the least restrictive and the statement within sub-paragraph (*c*) is the most restrictive;

(*b*) A statement within sub-paragraph (*a*) of section 7(2) of the Act which includes advice as to the desirability of parental guidance with regard to the viewing of the video work by young children is to be regarded as more restrictive than a statement which includes advice as to the particular suitability of the video work for viewing by children or which includes no advice mentioned in sub-paragraph (*a*); and

(c) A statement within sub-paragraph (*b*) of section 7(2) of the Act is to be regarded, as more restrictive than another statement made within that sub-paragraph if the age included in the first statement is greater than the age included in the other statement.

7.11293 *10. Video works in respect of which classification certificates have been issued by the video works authority* Regulations 11 to 15 apply with respect to a video work for which a classification certificate is issued by the "video works authority".

7.11294 *11.* The "Explanatory Statement" is the following—

(*a*) With respect to a classification certificate containing a statement described in 7(2)(*a*) of the Act that the video work concerned is suitable for general viewing and unrestricted supply without any advice of a kind described in that section—

"UNIVERSAL. Suitable for all"

with the word "Universal" shown in capital letters.

(*b*) With respect to a classification certificate containing a statement described in section 7(2)(*a*) of the Act with advice as to the desirability of parental guidance with regard to the viewing of the work by young children—

"PARENTAL GUIDANCE. General viewing but some scenes may be unsuitable for young children"

with the words "parental guidance" shown in capital letters.

(*c*) With respect to a classification certificate containing a statement described in section 7(2)(*b*) of the Act without the other statement described in section 7(2)(*c*) of the Act—

"Suitable only for persons of . . . . . . . . . . .years and over. Not to be supplied to any person below that age"

with the age (in numbers) specified in the certificate in the explanatory statement before the word "years".

(*d*) With respect to a classification certificate containing the statements described in section 7(2)(*c*) of the Act—

"RESTRICTED. To be supplied only in licensed sex shops to persons of not less than . . . . . . . years"

with the age (in numbers) specified in the certificate in the explanatory statement before the word "years".

7.11295 *12.* (1) — Except in the case of a double-sided disc "the classification symbol" is the following—

(*a*) With respect to a classification certificate containing a statement described in section 7(2)(*a*) of the Act that the video work concerned is suitable for general viewing and unrestricted supply without any advice of a kind mentioned in that section, the capital letter "U".

(*b*) With respect to a classification certificate containing a statement described in section 7(2)(*a*) of the Act with advice as to the desirability of parental guidance with regard to the viewing of the work by young children, the capital letters "PG".

(*c*) With respect to a classification certificate containing a statement described in section 7(2)(*b*) of the Act without the other statement mentioned in section 7(2)(*c*) of the Act, the age (in numbers) specified in the certificate.

(*d*) With respect to a classification certificate containing the statements described in section 7(2)(*c*) of the Act, the word "restricted" in capital letters with the age (in numbers) specified in the certificate after a capital letter "R".

(2) In the case of a double-sided disc "the classification symbol" is the symbol specified within paragraphs (1)(*a*) to (*d*) above, with respect to the classification certificate referred to in those paragraphs, but with the letters "UK" in capitals inserted immediately before it.

7.11296 *13.* (1) Except in the case of a double-sided disc, "the classification symbol" must be of a minimum height of 5 millimetres and is required to be shown in the following manner—

(*a*) in the case of the symbol described in regulation 12(1)(*a*) it must be black or white, and set on a green coloured triangular shaped background;

(*b*) in the case of the symbol described in regulation 12(1)(*b*) it must be black or white, and set on a yellow coloured triangular shaped background;

(*c*) in the case of the symbol described in regulation 12(1)(*c*)—

(i) where the age specified in the classification certificate is 18 years, it must be black or white, and set on a red coloured circular shaped background;

(ii) where the age specified in the classification certificate is less than 18 years, it must be red and set on a white coloured circular shaped background;

(*d*) in the case of the symbol described in regulation 12(1)(*d*) it must be black or white, and set on a blue coloured rectangular shaped background.

(2) In the case of a double-sided disc where the classification symbol is required to be shown on one face of the disc it must be of a minimum height of 2 millimetres.

7.11297 *14.* (1) The classification symbol and the unique title must be clearly displayed on—

(*a*) one face of every video recording; and

(*b*) one face of every spool.

**7.11298** ***15.*** The classification symbol must be clearly displayed on one of the largest faces or the largest face of the case in which a video recording or spool is kept, and the explanatory statement and the classification symbol must be displayed together on another of the largest faces or another face of the case unless—

(*a*) The classification symbol is clearly visible through one of the largest faces or the largest face, as appropriate, of the case in which the video recording or spool is kept;

(*b*) The classification symbol and the explanatory statement are together clearly visible through another of the largest faces or another face of the case; and

(*c*) The classification symbol and the explanatory statement referred to in sub-paragraphs (*a*) and (*b*) are shown in the manner specified by these Regulations.

**7.11299** ***16.*** *Video works in respect of which classification certificates have been issued by the video games authority* Regulations 17 to 23 apply with respect to a video work for which a classification certificate is issued by the "video games authority" on or after the coming into force date of these Regulations.

**7.11300** ***17.*** The reference to a classification certificate in regulation 16 does not include a pre-commencement classification document.

**7.11301** ***18.*** "Classification icon" is the pictorial description of a kind of content (such as violence, sex or drugs) found within a video work, as may be determined by the video games authority to be suitable for pictorial description by virtue of the arrangements it makes under section 4 of the Act.

**7.11302** ***19.*** With respect to a classification certificate which contains a statement within section 7(2)(*b*) of the Act without the other statement within section 7(2)(*c*) of the Act, the "classification symbol" is the age in numbers specified in the certificate where the minimum age is 12 and the maximum age is 18.

**7.11303** ***20.*** Where under these Regulations the "classification symbol" is required to be shown on a video game it must be white, of a minimum height of 5 millimetres, and—

(*a*) where the age specified in the classification certificate is 18 years, the symbol must be set on a red background; or

(*b*) where the age specified in the classification certificate is less than 18 years, the symbol must be set on an orange background.

**7.11304** ***21.*** (1) The classification symbol referred to in regulation 19 may be required to be displayed together with one or more classification icons as may be specified by the video games authority by virtue of the arrangements that authority makes under section 4 of the Act.

(2) Where the classification icon is required to be displayed it may be white and set on a black rectangular background, or black and set on a white rectangular background.

**7.11305** ***22.*** The classification symbol and the unique title must be clearly displayed on one face of every video recording that contains information by the use of which the whole or part of a video game may be produced.

**7.11306** ***23.*** The classification symbol must be clearly displayed on one of the largest faces or the largest face of the case in which the video recording mentioned in regulation 22 is kept and the classification symbol together with its associated classification icon or icons must be displayed together on another of the largest faces or another face of the case unless—

(*a*) the classification symbol is clearly visible through one of the largest faces or the largest face, as appropriate, of the case in which the video game is kept;

(*b*) the classification symbol and the classification icon or icons are together clearly visible through another of the largest faces or another face of the case; and

(*c*) the classification symbol and the classification icon or icons referred to in sub-paragraphs (*a*) and (*b*) above are shown in the manner provided for by these Regulations.

**7.11307** ***24.*** *Revocation* The Video Recordings (Labelling) Regulations 2010 are revoked.

# THEFT AND FRAUD

**Contents**



## Introduction

**7.11308 Statutory definition of theft** A person is guilty of theft if he dishonestly appropriates property belonging to another with the intention of permanently depriving the other of it (Theft Act 1968, s 1).

The words "dishonestly", "appropriates" and "property" and the phrases "belonging to another" and "with the intention of permanently depriving the other of it" are amplified and partially defined in ss 2 to 6.

Much of the case law that built up over many years in respect of the offences under the Larceny Acts has no bearing on the offences against the Theft Act 1968 but those decisions which it is submitted remain appropriate have been annotated to the text of the Act.

**7.11309 The doctrine of recent possession is as applicable to offences of theft as it was to offences of larceny** Possession of stolen property recently after the date of the theft, if unexplained, is presumptive evidence that the possessor stole it or had received it well knowing that it had been previously stolen. Proof must be given that the property has actually been stolen. Where a person is found in possession of property recently stolen and there is no positive evidence of stealing, but the evidence is as consistent with theft as with receiving, he should be charged with both offences and the court will then determine whether he was the thief or the handler (*R v Seymour* [1954] 1 All ER 1006, 118 JP 311). For possession to be "recent", the time varies according to the nature of the article stolen. For articles that pass readily from hand to hand, the time must be short. Four months have been held to be recent for a debenture bond (*R v Livock* (1914) 10 Cr App Rep 264); but not six months for a horse (*R v Cooper* (1852) 3 Car & Kir 318), nor eight months for a bale of silk (*R v Marcus* (1923) 17 Cr App Rep 191). Any short time, ie twenty minutes after the theft will suffice (*R v Proctor* (1923) 17 Cr App Rep 124). Where the only evidence on a charge of handling stolen goods is that an accused person is in possession of property recently stolen, a court may infer guilty knowledge (*a*) if the accused offers no explanation to account for his possession, or (*b*) if the court is satisfied that the explanation he does offer is untrue. If, however, the explanation offered is one which leaves the court in doubt whether he believed the property was stolen the case has not been proved, and, therefore, the verdict should be not guilty (*R v Aves* [1950] 2 All ER 330, 114 JP 402; explaining *R v Schama, R v Abramovitch* (1914) 79 JP 184). See also *R v Garth* [1949] 1 All ER 773, 113 JP 222; *R v Norris* (1916) 86 LJKB 810; *R v Grinberg* (1917) 33 TLR 428; *R v Badash* (1917) 87 LJKB 732; *R v Sanders (No 2)* (1919) 14 Cr App Rep 11; *R v Currell* (1935) 25 Cr App Rep 116, CCA; *Mancini v DPP* [1942] AC 1, [1941] 3 All ER 272; *R v Smith* (1983) 148 JP 215. Therefore where the prisoner gives a reasonable explanation, it is incumbent on the prosecution to prove that such account is false unless there are other circumstances from which the jury may fairly infer the falsehood of the story (*R v Ritson* (1884) 48 JP 630; *R v Barnes* (1942) 86 Sol Jo 341), such as making different statements as to the manner in which he came by the property (*R v Harmer* (1848) 2 Cox CC 487). Although the alleged stolen property had not been seen by the owner for fifteen months before it was missed, where the prisoner admitted that it was in his possession immediately after the theft but alleged that he bought it some considerable time before at a sale, it was held that there was evidence of recent possession and the question was simply one of identity (*R v Evans* (1847) 2 Cox CC 270). On a charge of theft of Kruger gold sovereigns, evidence of similar sovereigns having been found in defendant's house is admissible (*R v Kurasch* [1937] 2 All ER 130).

**7.11310 Admissibility of documentary evidence** In any proceedings for an offence of theft of goods in the course of transmission (whether by post or otherwise) or of handling stolen goods from such a theft, a statutory declaration is admissible as proof of the fact that the goods were dispatched or received or not so received as the case may be, or that they were in a particular state or condition when dispatched or received.

(Theft Act 1968, s 27, post.)

**7.11311 Ownership** The word "owner" does not appear in the definition of theft but the decisions that have been made on the question of ownership can be regarded as appropriate in the consideration of the phrase "belonging to another". There can be no theft of things which have no owner at all, or perhaps more correctly where there is not such a possession as would support an action of trespass. Actual proof as to the ownership of goods may be dispensed with (*R v Fuschillo* [1940] 2 All ER 489). A prisoner may be indicted for stealing the property of some person unknown, if facts be proved from which the jury may fairly presume that the goods were stolen. Things of which the ownership has been abandoned are not capable of being stolen; where something is taken in the belief that it had been abandoned, the court must consider whether, according to the standards of reasonable and honest people, what was done was dishonest, and if it is so considered, whether the defendant himself must have realised that what he was doing was dishonest by those standards (*R v Small* [1988] RTR 32, 86 Cr App Rep 170, CA). Where the diseased carcases of pigs had been buried to prevent them being made use of, it was held that the ownership had not been abandoned (*R v Edwards and Stacey* (1877) 41 JP 212). If the evidence shows that the accused believed that they had been abandoned and belonged to nobody he is not guilty of theft (*R v White* (1912) 76 JP 384; *Ellerman's Wilson Line Ltd v Webster* [1952] 1 Lloyd's Rep 179). Running or standing water is not capable of being stolen, unlike water under control such as water in stand pipes (*Ferens v O'Brien* (1883) 11 QBD 21, 47 JP 472), as also gas (*R v Firth* (1869) LR 1 CCR 172, 33 JP 212; *R v White* (1853) Dears CC 203, 17 JP 391). At common law every co-owner is lawfully entitled to possession of the property and could not commit theft by taking it. Now he may be guilty of stealing from his co-owner (Theft Act 1968, s 5(1), post and see *R v Bonner* [1970] 2 All ER 97, 134 JP 429). A domestic servant left in charge of her master's property is included as she has the control of it (*R v Harding* (1929) 94 JP 55). Property stolen out of the possession of a bailee, pawnee, carrier or the like, may be described as the property of such bailee, etc, or of the actual owner. The property of a joint-stock company on winding up must not be described as belonging to the liquidator until he has taken actual possession of it (*R v Bell* (1877) 41 JP 455). A bailee has a special property in the article bailed even if the bailor had no intention of charging him with its loss; if the bailor fraudulently removes the goods from the possession of the bailee he may be charged with theft (*Rose v Matt* [1951] 1 KB 810, [1951] 1 All ER 361, 115 JP 122).

A person who obtains a mortgage advance by deception does not commit the offence of dishonestly obtaining property belonging to another contrary to s 15 of the Theft Act 1968. The original sum in the lender's bank account constitutes a chose in action enforceable by the lending institution against its own bank. Where the advance by way of mortgage is paid either by way of electronic transfer or by cheque to the borrower's or his solicitor's account, the lender's chose in action vis à vis its bank is extinguished pro tanto and a new chose in action is created owned by the borrower or his solicitor. Accordingly the defendant has not obtained the lender's chose in action, rather a new chose has been created which did not exist before. Similarly where a drawer writes a cheque in favour of the defendant a chose is thereby created in his favour. Prior to its drawing, the cheque did not constitute a chose in favour of the drawer and the defendant does not obtain a chose or property which belongs to another. Therefore whilst a third party might steal the chose belonging to the defendant, he did not obtain a chose belonging to the drawer (*R v Preddy* [1996] AC 815, [1996] 3 All ER 481, [1996] 2 Cr App Rep 524, HL)[1]. In such circumstances a dishonest defendant will commit an offence of obtaining a money transfer by deception contrary to s 15A of the Theft Act 1968 as inserted by the Theft (Amendment) Act 1996, s 1.

---

[1] In *R v Clark (Brian James Hemmings)* [2001] EWCA Crim 884, [2002] 1 Cr App Rep 14, the Court of Appeal, though sympathetic with the argument, held it was inappropriate to hold, in view of the observations of Lord Goff in *R v Preddy* (supra), that a cheque form was a tangible thing and was, therefore, property capable of being obtained.

## Theft Act 1968

(1968 c 60)

*Definition of "theft"*

7.11312 **1. Basic definition of theft** (1) A person is guilty of theft[1] if he[2] dishonestly[3] appropriates[4] property belonging to another[5] with the intention of permanently depriving the other of it[6]; and "thief" and "steal" shall be construed accordingly.

(2) It is immaterial whether the appropriation is made with a view to gain, or is made for the thief's own benefit.

(3) The five following sections of this Act shall have effect as regards the interpretation and operation of this section (and, except as otherwise provided by this Act, shall apply only for purposes of this section).

[Theft Act 1968, s 1.]

---

[1] This subsection and s 15(1) are not mutually exclusive (*Lawrence v Metropolitan Police Comr* [1972] AC 626, [1971] 2 All ER 1253).

[2] Appropriation can occur through the acts of innocent agents; see *R v Stringer and Banks* (1991) 94 Cr App Rep 13, [1991] Crim LR 639, CA.

[3] Defined in s 2. See note 5 to s 2(2), post. Where the accused gives evidence of his state of mind at the time of the alleged offence, the justices should give that evidence such weight as they think right in the circumstances and apply their own standards when deciding whether the appropriation was dishonest (*R v McIvor* [1982] 1 All ER 491, 146 JP 193).

[4] Defined in s 3. This subsection should not be read as if it contained the words "without the consent of the owner", and it is not necessary for the prosecution to prove that the taking was without the owner's consent; that is no longer an ingredient of the offence (*Lawrence v Metropolitan Police Comr*, supra). The issue of consent is dealt with in s 2(1) below.

[5] These words "belonging to another" signify no more than that at the time of appropriation the property belonged to another (*Lawrence v Metropolitan Police Comr*, supra). See further s 5, post. If a bookmaker pays out money in the mistaken belief that a horse has won it is unnecessary for the prosecution to rely on s 5(4), post, because the property in the money does not pass to the payee (*R v Gilks* [1972] 3 All ER 280, 136 JP 777). By virtue of s 18, r 5 of (what is now) the Sale of Goods Act 1979 the property in petrol passes from the garage to the customer when it is poured into the tank of his car, and the customer does not appropriate property belonging to another if he drives away without paying (*Edwards v Ddin* [1976] 3 All ER 705, 121 JP 27); but see now the Theft Act 1978, s 3, post (making off without payment). Where a purchaser returns an unsatisfactory video recorder to the seller for repair, and afterwards issues a summons claiming the return of money paid for defective goods, the court must have recourse to the civil law as to the passing of property,

rescission of contract etc in deciding ownership for the purpose of this section (*R v Walker* [1983] LS Gaz R 3238, [1984] Crim LR 112, CA).

In relation to goods in a supermarket, the general rule is that the property in them does not pass to a customer until he pays the price. This will normally be so even where goods have not only been bagged but also weighed according to the customer's requirements; see *Davies v Leighton* [1978] Crim LR 575, and commentary thereon; (1979) 68 Cr App Rep 4.

6 The essence of this offence is the dishonest appropriation of property. The "taking" required under previous law is not an element of the offence of theft. The words "dishonestly", "appropriates", "property" and the phrases "belonging to another" and "with the intention of permanently depriving the other of it" are amplified and partially defined in the following sections. See *R v Easom* [1971] 2 QB 315, [1971] 2 All ER 945; for a case in which a dishonest appropriation followed by replacement was held not to be theft but see also *R v Velumyl* [1989] Crim LR 299, CA, for an unauthorised temporary borrowing held to be dishonest.

The section does not distinguish between acts of essentially similar character which under previous law, would, according to circumstances, have been different offences. The offence of theft depends on the dishonest achievement of the accused and not on the means used to achieve it. If, when a person takes goods from a display stand in a supermarket, he intends to steal them, that is a dishonest appropriation; there can be a dishonest appropriation (and a theft) in a supermarket *before* the goods are taken past the point for payment; see *R v McPherson* [1973] Crim LR 191; distinguished in *Eddy v Niman* (1981) 73 Cr App Rep 237, where it was held that there had been no appropriation when goods were placed in a receptacle provided by the store. A cashier who received money from a customer without ringing it up on the till and intended to steal it was held guilty of a dishonest appropriation notwithstanding that she was arrested before the money could be removed from the till (*R v Monaghan* [1979] Crim LR 673).

7.11313 2. **"Dishonestly"** (1) A person's appropriation of property belonging to another is not to be regarded as dishonest—

(*a*) if he appropriates the property in the belief[1] that he has in law the right to deprive[2] the other of it, on behalf of himself or of a third person; or

(*b*) if he appropriates the property in the belief[3] that he would have the other's consent if the other knew of the appropriation and the circumstances of it; or

(*c*) (except where the property came to him as trustee or personal representative)[4] if he appropriates the property in the belief that the person to whom the property belongs cannot be discovered by taking reasonable steps.

(2) A person's appropriation of property belonging to another may be dishonest[5] notwithstanding that he is willing to pay for the property.

[Theft Act 1968, s 2.]

---

1 It is immaterial that there exists no basis in law for such belief; if the defendant believed he had a right, even if there were none, he would fall to be acquitted (*R v Turner (No 2)* [1971] 2 All ER 441, 135 JP 419).

2 Where such a defendant uses a knife in order to "recover" money owed to him, this will not be theft (nor robbery under s 9, post) even if he knew it was wrong to use the knife (*R v Robinson* [1977] Crim LR 173).

3 A defendant's "belief that he would have the other's consent . . . " must be an honest belief, and it must be an honest belief in a true consent, honestly obtained; see *A-G's Reference (No 2 of 1982)* [1984] QB 624, [1984] 2 All ER 216, 78 Cr App Rep 131).

4 This exception preserves the requirement that a trustee or personal representative is to obtain a direction of the court for the disposal of property coming to him in that capacity of which he believes that the owner cannot be traced.

5 See *R v Feely* [1973] QB 530, [1973] 1 All ER 341, 137 JP 157, and *Boggeln v Williams* [1978] 2 All ER 1061. "Dishonestly" in s 1 describes something in the mind of the accused and not his conduct; therefore, the test of dishonesty is subjective, but the standard of honesty to be applied is the standard of reasonable and honest people and not that of the accused (*R v Ghosh* [1982] QB 1053, [1982] 2 All ER 689, 75 Cr App Rep 154). The questions to be asked, based on *R v Feely* and *R v Ghosh* are (1) was what was done dishonest according to the ordinary standards of reasonable and honest people? And (2) must the defendant have realised that what he was doing was dishonest according to those standards? See however an article at [1985] Crim LR 341. An intention to repay or perform contractual obligations cannot of itself amount to a defence to deception, but may be some evidence of honesty (*R v O'Connell* (1991) 94 Cr App Rep 39, [1991] Crim LR 771).

7.11314 3. **"Appropriates"** (1) Any assumption by a person of the rights of an owner amounts to an appropriation[1], and this includes, where he has come by the property (innocently or not) without stealing it, any later assumption of a right to it by keeping or dealing with it as owner[2].

(2) Where property or a right or interest in property is or purports to be transferred for value[3] to a person acting in good faith, no later assumption by him of rights which he believed himself to be acquiring[4] shall, by reason of any defect in the transferor's title[5], amount to theft of the property.

[Theft Act 1968, s 3.]

---

1 The prosecution do not need to establish that the appropriation was without the owner's consent; even if consent is shown this will not mean that there was no dishonesty if consent was given without full knowledge of the circumstances; *Lawrence v Metropolitan Police Comr* [1972] AC 626, [1971] 2 All ER 1253, HL, taxi driver taking excessive fare out of foreigner's wallet. When theft is alleged and that which is alleged to be stolen passes to the defendant with the consent of the owner, but that consent has been obtained by a false representation, an appropriation within the meaning of s 1(1) of the Theft Act 1968 has taken place (*R v Gomez* [1993] 1 All ER 1 [1993] Crim LR 304, HL—owner of electrical goods induced by fraudulent misrepresentation, namely that cheques presented in payment were as good as cash, to consent to electrical goods being removed from his shop—cheques were in fact stolen and were dishonoured on presentation—held that there had been a dishonest appropriation of the goods). Appropriation is an objective description of the act done irrespective of the mental state either of the owner or the accused (*R v Gallasso* (1992) 98 Cr App Rep 284). For the relevance of a donor's mental capacity where the defendant maintains that the appropriation was the result of a gift *inter vivos*, see *R v Kendrick and Hopkins* [1997] 2 Cr App Rep 252, CA and *R v Hinks* [2001] 2 AC 241, [2000] 4 All ER 833, [2001] 1 Cr App Rep 1, HL; in the latter case, the House of Lords held that the acquisition of an indefeasible title to property from a person who no longer retained any proprietary interest or any right to resume or recover any proprietary interest in the property was capable of amounting to appropriation of that property.

A director can be guilty of theft from his own company where there is an appropriation within the meaning of s 3, provided the appropriation is dishonest ie directed at the company: *R (on the application of A) v Crown Court at Snaresbrook* (2001) 165 JPN 495, DC (director used resources of the company to bribe the managers of another company to secure an early renewal of a supply agreement; such conduct may be found not to be the conduct of the company, especially where the director does not own all the shares and the scheme involves concealment from the board of the company).

The use of a cheque card to guarantee payment of a cheque delivered to a payee and drawn on an account with inadequate funds was held not to be an assumption of the rights of the bank and thus not an appropriation within s 3(1), because the use of the cheque card and delivery of the cheque did no more than give the payee a contractual right, as against the bank, to be paid a specified sum from the banks' funds on presentation of the guaranteed cheque (*R v Navvabi* [1986] 3 All ER 102, [1986] 1 WLR 1311, 150 JP 474, CA).

"Appropriate" should be distinguished from obtains by deception. Where the defendant presented for payment cheques drawn by another person upon the credit balance of the drawer's account in respect of building work for which the defendant had dishonestly overbilled, the defendant had appropriated the chose in action by diminishing the relevant bank balance. (*R v Kohn* (1979) 69 Cr App Rep 395 *R v Williams* [2001] 1 Cr App Rep 23, [2001] Crim LR 253, CA). This should be contrasted with the situation in *R v Preddy* [1996] AC 815, where it had been difficult to discover the relevant obtaining of property belonging to another where on the facts a new chose in action had come into existence on the presentation of the relevant cheques (*R v Williams* [2001] 1 Cr App Rep 23, [2001] Crim LR 253, CA).

In a criminal enterprise involving theft there need not necessarily be only one "appropriation"; in the case of burglary in a dwelling house before any property is removed from the house there might be a number of appropriations by several persons at different times during the same incident, see *R v Gregory* (1982) 77 Cr App Rep 41, [1982] Crim LR 229, CA.

If goods have once been stolen, even if stolen abroad, they cannot be stolen again by the same thief exercising the same or other rights of ownership over the property. Accordingly, if a person steals property abroad and brings it into England for dishonest gain, the theft is nevertheless, committed abroad and cannot be charged with theft in England (*R v Atakpu* [1994] QB 69, [1993] 4 All ER 215, [1994] Crim LR 693). "Appropriate" connotes a physical act; thus, where a victim caused a payment to be made, in reliance on deceptive conduct by the defendant, there was no "appropriation" by the defendant; he had done no more than a remote act to trigger the payment: *R v Briggs* [2003] EWCA Crim 3662, [2004] Cr App R 34, [2004] Crim LR 495. Where money has been wrongly credited to the defendant's bank account in England and the defendant signs blank cheques and sends them to a person who lives in Scotland, appropriation takes place within the jurisdiction when the cheques are presented for payment in England (*R v Ngan* [1998] 1 Cr App Rep 331.).

[2] This subsection and s 5(4), post, together make it clear that a person coming into possession of property innocently can be guilty of theft if he later keeps it or otherwise deals with it as owner. But the position may be different if after discovering that the property was stolen, the defendant has not come to any decision as to what to do with it, and has not kept it for a long time or attempted to dispose of it; see *Broom v Crowther* (1984) 148 JP 592. The lacuna in the previous law which required the intention to deprive the owner to exist at the time of taking, is no longer present. An appropriation takes place where a bag is snatched and then immediately dropped, allowing the owner to recover it (*Corcoran v Anderton* (1980) 71 Cr App Rep 104, [1980] Crim LR 385). Where however there was no dishonesty at the time of acquisition and fitting of a gas cooker, there was a sale, and property passed; it was not possible to have a subsequent dishonest appropriation within s 3 (*R v Stuart* (1982) 147 JP 221). Drawing and issuing cheques on a company's account by a director who used the proceeds for his own purposes constitutes an appropriation; the fact that the cheques were honoured in contradiction of the terms of a mandate to the bank did not prevent the debt arising (*R v Wille* (1987) 86 Cr App Rep 296, CA). No offence was committed by a dealer who agreed to sell a medal and to keep it for the purchaser until later in the day and who then accepted the purchaser's cheque although meanwhile he has learnt that the medal was stolen (*R v Wheeler* (1990) 92 Cr App Rep 279).

[3] This subsection will not apply to property transferred as a gift.

[4] This refers to the moment when the person purchases for value (*R v Adams* [1993] Crim LR 72, CA).

[5] For example, because it was stolen.

7.11315 4. **"Property"** (1) "Property" includes money and all other property[1], real or personal, including things in action[2] and other intangible property[3].

(2) A person cannot steal land, or things forming part of land and severed from it by him or by his directions, except in the following cases, that is to say—

(*a*) when he is a trustee or personal representative, or is authorised by power of attorney, or as liquidator of a company, or otherwise, to sell or dispose of land belonging to another, and he appropriates the land or anything forming part of it by dealing with it in breach of the confidence reposed in him; or

(*b*) when he is not in possession of the land and appropriates anything forming part of the land by severing it or causing it to be severed, or after it has been severed; or

(*c*) when, being in possession of the land under a tenancy, he appropriates the whole or part of any fixture or structure let to be used with the land.

For purposes of this subsection "land" does not include incorporeal hereditaments; "tenancy" means a tenancy for years or any less period and includes an agreement for such a tenancy, but a person who after the end of a tenancy remains in possession as statutory tenant or otherwise is to be treated as having possession under the tenancy, and "let" shall be construed accordingly.

(3) A person who picks[4] mushrooms growing wild on any land, or who picks[4] flowers, fruit or foliage from a plant growing wild on any land, does not (although not in possession of the land) steal what he picks, unless he does it for reward or for sale or other commercial purpose.

For purposes of this subsection "mushroom" includes any fungus, and "plant" includes any shrub or tree.

(4) Wild creatures, tamed or untamed, shall be regarded as property; but a person cannot steal a wild creature not tamed nor ordinarily kept in captivity, or the carcase of any such creature, unless either it has been reduced into possession[5] by or on behalf of another person and possession of it has not since been lost or abandoned, or another person is in course of reducing it into possession.

[Theft Act 1968, s 4.]

---

[1] At common law a corpse and parts of a corpse are not property and therefore cannot be stolen. However they may become "property" within the meaning of s 4 if they have acquired different attributes by virtue of the application of skill, such as dissection and preservation techniques, for exhibition and teaching purposes: *R v Kelly* [1999] QB 621, [1998] 3 All ER 741, CA. In alcohol and driving cases there have been convictions for theft of urine and blood specimens: *R v Welsh* [1974] RTR 478; *R v Rothery* [1976] Crim LR 691. In *Oxford v Moss* (1978) 68 Cr App Rep 183, [1979] Crim LR 119; confidential information in an examination paper was held not to be intangible property for the purposes of this section.

What would otherwise constitute or be regarded as "property" for the purposes of the Theft Act 1968 does not cease to be so because its possession or control is, for whatever reason, unlawful or illegal or prohibited. The appropriation of drugs from a person who was in unlawful possession of prohibited Class A drugs by those who attacked him constituted theft: *R v Smith* [2011] EWCA Crim 66, [2011] 1 Cr App R 30, [2011] Crim LR 719.

[2] Where a cheque is made out in favour of the payee it constitutes a chose in action belonging to the payee which he can enforce against the payer and therefore constitutes "property" of the payee within s 4(1) (*R v Preddy* [1996] AC 815, [1996] 3 All ER 481, [1996] 2 Cr App Rep 524, HL). In *R v Clark (Brian James Hemmings)* [2001] EWCA Crim 884, [2002] 1 Cr App Rep 141, the Court of Appeal, though sympathetic with the argument, held it was inappropriate to hold, in view of the observations of Lord Goff in *R v Preddy* (supra), that a cheque form was a tangible thing and was, therefore, capable of being obtained. Theft of a bank debt may constitute theft of a chose in action (*R v Kohn* (1979) 69 Cr App R 395, [1979] Crim LR 675, CA, applied in *R v Graham* [1997] Crim LR 358). See also the *A-G's Reference (No 1 of 1983)* [1985] QB 182, [1984] 3 All ER 369, *Chan Man-sin v A-G of Hong Kong* [1988] 1 All ER 1, [1988] 1 WLR 196, 86 Cr App Rep 303, PC and *R v Stalham* [1993] Crim LR 310, CA.

[3] This subsection applies throughout this Act (s 34(1), post). However, electricity cannot be described as property; s 13, post, deals with the offence of dishonestly using electricity; see *Low v Blease* (1975) 119 Sol Jo 695. As to "intangible property" including patents, applications for patents, copyright, see commentary at [1983] Crim LR 332 on *R v Storrow and Poole*. Proof that only some of the property specified was stolen is enough for a conviction (*Machent v Quinn* [1970] 2 All ER 255, 134 JP 501); nor is it necessary to prove the precise sum of money involved (*Levene v Pearcey* [1976] Crim LR 63—taxi driver dishonestly taking longer route). It does not matter that theft of only part of the goods is charged and theft of the whole is proved (*Pilgram v Rice-Smith* [1977] 2 All ER 658, 141 JP 427).

[4] The expression "picks" would probably not include a complete uprooting of the plant.

[5] The ruling that there is no property in a swarm of bees until hived (*Kearry v Pattinson* [1939] 1 KB 471, [1939] 1 All ER 65) can be construed in the context of this section as meaning that until hived the swarm is not reduced into possession.

7.11316 **5. "Belonging to another[1]"** (1) Property[2] shall be regarded as belonging to any person having possession or control of it[3], or having in it any proprietary right or interest[4] (not being an equitable interest arising only from an agreement to transfer or grant an interest)[5].

(2) Where property is subject to a trust, the persons to whom it belongs shall be regarded as including any person having a right to enforce the trust, and an intention to defeat the trust shall be regarded accordingly as an intention to deprive of the property any person having that right.

(3) Where a person receives property[6] from or on account of another[7], and is under an obligation[8] to the other to retain and deal with that property or its proceeds in a particular way[9], the property or proceeds shall be regarded (as against him) as belonging to the other[10].

(4) Where a person gets property by another's mistake, and is under an obligation[11] to make restoration (in whole or in part) of the property or its proceeds or of the value thereof, then to the extent of that obligation the property or proceeds shall be regarded (as against him) as belonging to the person entitled to restoration, and an intention not to make restoration shall be regarded accordingly as an intention to deprive that person of the property or proceeds[12].

(5) Property of a corporation sole[13] shall be regarded as belonging to the corporation notwithstanding a vacancy in the corporation.

[Theft Act 1968, s 5.]

---

[1] See headnote to this title, ante, "Ownership".

[2] See s 4, ante.

[3] Such as a domestic servant left in charge of her master's property (*R v Harding* (1929) 94 JP 55). The words "possession or control" are not to be qualified in any way; it is sufficient if it is found that the person from whom the property was taken (or "appropriated") was at the time in fact in possession or control (*R v Turner (No 2)* [1971] 2 All ER 441, 135 JP 419). A person can be in possession or control of property without knowing of its existence (*R v Woodman* [1974] QB 754, [1974] 2 All ER 955, 138 JP 567). The lack of a coroner's inquisition determining the status and ownership of coins found does not prevent a conviction of theft of the coins as treasure trove if the jury determines that they were treasure trove (*R v Hancock* [1990] 2 QB 242, [1990] 3 All ER 183, 90 Cr App Rep 422, CA). Personal representatives appointed under a will do not have an interest in property under the will so as to enable a charge of theft of their property to be brought where it is said that the testator was induced to execute a new will by unlawful means (*R v Tillings and Tillings* [1985] Crim LR 393). It is possible in law for the directors and shareholders of a company to steal from their own company (*R v Philippou* (1989) 89 Cr App Rep 290, CA).

Where items were left by unknown donors outside a charity shop and were then dishonestly appropriated, while it could not be said that the charity had acquired possession or assumed control simply by reason of the items being left in close proximity, it was open to the court to infer that the items had not been abandoned; the donors had attempted to effect delivery but it would not be complete until the charity took up possession and, until then, the donors had not given up ownership; if, alternatively, the items had been placed in bins provided by the charity near their shop premises, the court could conclude that the bins were controlled by the charity with the result that anything put in them belonged to the charity in addition to the donors: *R (on the application of Ricketts) v Basildon Magistrates' Court* [2010] EWHC 2358, [2011] 1 Cr App Rep 202.

[4] The phrase "proprietory right or interest" was considered in *Re A-G's Reference (No 1 of 1985)* [1986] QB 491, [1986] 2 All ER 219. Where a bank mistakenly credits an account in another bank, and the defendant arranges for banker's drafts to be drawn in favour of himself, the bank retains rights by reason of the mistake, being an equitable proprietary interest, and on that basis the defendant is under a duty to make restoration of the instruments (*R v Shadrokh-Cigari* [1988] Crim LR 465).

[5] This subsection applies throughout this Act (s 34(1), post).

[6] Section 5(3) covers property received from another under an obligation short of actual trusteeship. Accordingly, provided that the obligation was one which clearly required the recipient to retain and deal with that property or its proceeds in a particular way, there is no good reason to introduce words of limitation in relation to the interest of the transferor, save that at the time of the handing over of the property he had lawful possession of it in circumstances which gave him a legal right vis-à-vis the recipient to require that it be retained or dealt with in a particular way for his benefit (*R v Arnold* [1997] 4 All ER 1, CA).

[7] Eg, a person acting as treasurer of a Christmas or holiday fund. An employee does not receive moneys *on account of* his employer when they are paid to him by customers for goods he has secretly obtained from someone other than his employer and sold to them, notwithstanding that the employee has contracted with the employer to sell only goods supplied by the employer (*Re A-G's Reference (No 1 of 1985)* [1986] QB 491, [1986] 2 All ER 219).

[8] Where money was collected for a charity, the defendant is under an obligation in the nature of a trust to the sponsors. Accordingly, he is under an obligation to retain, if not the actual notes and coins, at least their proceeds such as where he has credited the money to a bank account. Whether the defendant is a trustee is to be judged on an objective basis; it is not essential that he realised he was a trustee (*R v Wain* [1995] 2 Cr App Rep 660, CA). Where money is given by donors

to a charity collector, a trust is imposed and the money belongs to the beneficiaries of that trust (ie the charity) and property in the money passes from the donors to the charity when it is put into the tin; accordingly any subsequent misappropriation of the money by the collector is theft from the charity, not from the donors, and the charge should be so drafted (*R v Dyke and Munro* [2001] EWCA 2184, [2002] 1 Cr App Rep 404, [2002] Crim LR 153). The obligation is a legal, not a moral or social, obligation; see *DPP v Huskinson* (1988) 152 JP 582, [1988] Crim LR 620, and commentary thereto. Money received by a timeshare company from purchasers on implied terms that the money would be paid to a trust company which would act as a stakeholder to protect the purchasers, belonged to the purchasers when it was misapplied by the timeshare company. What was done was in breach of the obligation to deal with the money in a particular way so that s 5(3) applied. Although monies paid into the time share company's bank account might be replaced by a chose in action, s 5(3) deemed the money to belong to the purchasers. This situation is distinguishable from *R v Preddy* [1996] AC 815, HL where the money had been applied to the intended use, namely the purchase of property (*R v Klineberg* [1999] 1 Cr App Rep 427, CA).

[9] These words were considered in *R v Hall* [1973] 1 QB 126, [1972] 2 All ER 1009, 136 JP 593, *R v Hayes* (1976) 64 Cr App Rep 82 and *R v Wills* (1990) 92 Cr App Rep 297.

[10] And he will be guilty of theft if he misapplies it or the proceeds thereof. This will be so, even if the property had been acquired by the other (the bailor) illegally, if the defendant (as bailee) acts dishonestly (*R v Meech* [1974] QB 549, [1973] 3 All ER 939, 138 JP 6).

[11] The obligation must be a legal one; a social or moral obligation is not sufficient (*R v Gilks* [1972] 3 All ER 280 at 283).

[12] See note 2 to s 3, supra. This subsection was considered in detail in the *A-G's Reference (No 1 of 1983)* [1985] QB 182, [1984] 3 All ER 369, CA, where an opinion was expressed that a person who receives overpayment of a debt due to him by way of a credit to his bank account through the "direct debit" system and who knowing of that overpayment intentionally fails to repay the amount of the overpayment may be guilty of theft of the sum credited. When considering a financial consultant's treatment of money invested it has been said that the section applied if the defendant and the investor clearly understood that the investment or its proceeds was to be kept separate from the defendant's money or that of his business (*R v McHugh* (1993) 97 Cr App R 335).

[13] Eg, the Rector of a parish who holds parish property in that capacity.

7.11317 **6. "With the intention of permanently depriving the other of it"** (1) A person appropriating[1] property[2] belonging to another without meaning the other permanently to lose the thing itself is[3] nevertheless to be regarded as having the intention of permanently depriving the other of it if his intention is to treat the thing as his own to dispose of regardless of the other's rights[4]; and a borrowing[5] or lending of it may amount to so treating it if, but only if, the borrowing or lending is for a period and in circumstances making it equivalent to an outright taking or disposal.

(2) Without prejudice to the generality of subsection (1) above, where a person, having possession or control (lawfully or not) of property belonging to another, parts with the property under a condition as to its return which he may not be able to perform[6], this (if done for purposes of his own and without the other's authority) amounts to treating the property as his own to dispose of regardless of the other's rights.

[Theft Act 1968, s 6.]

[1] See s 3, ante.

[2] See s 4, ante.

[3] See s 5, ante.

[4] Thus a company director was properly convicted where he stole company cheques to pay his debts because even though they were company liabilities they had been incurred for his personal purposes and were unauthorised (*R v Sobel* [1986] Crim LR 261). A council tenant who removed doors which were the council's responsibility and substituted them for doors for which he was responsible had treated the doors as his own regardless of the council's rights (*DPP v Lavender* [1994] Crim LR 297). Section 6 may apply to a person in possession or control of another's property who, dishonestly and for his own purpose, deals with that property in such a manner that he knows he is risking its loss (*R v Fernandes* [1996] 1 Cr App Rep 175, CA (dishonest disposal of another's money on an obviously insecure investment)). A defendant who obtained used tickets for travel on London Underground whose usefulness had not been exhausted and sold them at a reduced price to persons intending to travel had an intention to treat the tickets as his own to dispose of regardless of the exclusive right of London Underground to sell tickets. The fact that the tickets might find their way back into the possession of London Underground Limited, albeit with their usefulness or "virtue" exhausted is not material (*R v Marshall* [1998] 2 Cr App Rep 282, 162 JP 488, [1999] Crim LR 317, CA).

The governing and general words of sub-s (1) are not limited to specific common law exceptions to the requirements of s 1. What s 6(1) requires is a state of mind in the defendant which Parliament regards as the equivalent of an intention permanently to deprive; it does not require the thing has been disposed of, nor does it require that the defendant intends to dispose of the thing in any particular way: *R v Vinall* [2011] EWCA Crim 6252, [2012] 1 Cr App Rep 400, 175 JP 517.

[5] Mere borrowing is insufficient to constitute the necessary guilty mind unless the intention is to return the thing in such a changed state that it has lost all its goodness or virtue; accordingly, feature films temporarily borrowed for copying in breach of copyright were held not to have been stolen since they had not diminished in value; see *R v Lloyd* [1985] QB 829, [1985] 2 All ER 661, CA.

[6] Eg, by pawning it.

*Theft, robbery, burglary, etc*

7.11318 **7. Theft** A person guilty of theft[1] shall on conviction on indictment be liable to imprisonment for a term not exceeding seven years[2].

[Theft Act 1968, s 7 as amended by the Criminal Justice Act 1991, s 26.]

[1] As defined in s 1, ante.

A person charged on indictment with theft of a conveyance (as defined in s 12(7)(*a*), post) may be convicted instead of an offence under s 12(1), post (s 12(4)).

[2] Triable either way; see the Magistrates' Courts Act 1980, s 17 and Sch 1, also ss 17A–21 (procedure) and s 32 (penalty) in PART I: MAGISTRATES' COURTS, PROCEDURE, ante. In respect of offences of stealing or attempting to steal a motor vehicle, see note to s 12(2) post, for the powers and duties of a Court as to endorsements and disqualifications.

A person who has in his possession any firearm or imitation firearm at the time of committing or at the time of his apprehension for this offence (or aiding and abetting or attempting to commit this offence) is subject to the provisions of the Firearms Act 1968, s 17(2), ante.

7.11319 **8. Robbery** (1) A person is guilty of robbery if he steals[1], and immediately before or at the time of doing so[2], and in order to do so, he uses force[3] on any person or puts or seeks to put any person[4] in fear of being then and there[5] subjected to force[6].

(2) A person guilty of robbery, or of an assault with intent to rob, shall on conviction on indictment be liable to imprisonment for life[7].

[Theft Act 1968, s 8.]

---

1 Where the "robbery" was an attempt to recover money owed, see *R v Robinson* [1977] Crim LR 173; an appropriate charge could be under s 21, blackmail, post.

2 It should be noted that force used after the theft is no longer within the offence of robbery. However, it should be noted that appropriation is a continuing act and accordingly a defendant who appropriated goods from the shelf of a shop and used violence on the shopkeeper when he approached, was guilty of robbery (*R v Hale* (1978) 68 Cr App Rep 415, CA, *R v Lockley* [1995] Crim LR 656). As to the stealing, the intent to permanently deprive must be at the time of the use of force. Subsequent 'disposal' of the property may be evidence either of an intention at the time of the taking or evidence of an intention at the time of the disposal. Although for an allegation of theft a later appropriation will suffice; when the allegation is robbery, it almost certainly will not: *R v Vinall* [2011] EWCA Crim 6252, [2012] 1 Cr App Rep 400, 175 JP 517.

3 It is not an acceptable proposition to seek to show that if one robber does violence, his confederates could not be held responsible for the consequences of that violence unless it was proved that they had agreed in advance to the use of that degree of violence to further their design (*R v Penfold* (1979) 71 Cr App Rep 4).

4 The person on whom the force is used or who is threatened need not be the person from whom the property is stolen. However, force on a person must be used or threatened. Where a cigarette was unexpectedly removed from between the fingers of the victim's hand this was not, on its own, the use of force on a person. The offence was similar to pick pocketing. It was simple theft: *P v DPP* (sub nom *DPP v RP*) [2012] EWHC 1657 (Admin), [2013] 1 WLR 2337, [2013] 1 Cr App Rep 109.

5 Ie immediately.

6 The assault is nothing more than an attempt to commit a robbery. It is not necessary to prove more than that the accused intended to rob the prosecutor and did some act in his presence with reference to him for that purpose.

7 A claim of right made in good faith was held to be defence to a charge of robbery under previous legislation (*R v Skivington* [1968] 1 QB 166, [1967] 1 All ER 483, 131 JP 265).

7.11320 **9. Burglary** (1) A person is guilty of burglary[1] if—

(*a*) he enters[2] any building[3] or part of a building[4] as a trespasser[5] and with intent[6] to commit any such offence as is mentioned in subsection (2) below; or

(*b*) having entered[2] any building[3] or part of a building[4] as a trespasser[5] he steals or attempts to steal anything in the building or that part of it or inflicts or attempts to inflict on any person therein any grievous bodily harm[7].

(2) The offences referred to in subsection (1)(*a*) above are offences of stealing anything in the building or part of a building in question, of inflicting on any person therein any grievous bodily harm therein, and of doing unlawful damage to the building or anything therein.

(3) A person guilty of burglary shall on conviction on indictment be liable to imprisonment for a term not exceeding—

(*a*) where the offence was committed in respect of a building or part of a building which is a dwelling, fourteen years[8];

(*b*) in any other case, ten years[8].

(4) References in subsections (1) and (2) above to a building, and the reference in subsection (3) above to a building which is a dwelling, shall apply also to an inhabited vehicle or vessel, and shall apply to any such vehicle or vessel at times when the person having a habitation in it is not there as well as at times when he is.

[Theft Act 1968, s 9 as amended by the Criminal Justice Act 1991, s 26 and the Sexual Offences Act 2003, Sch 6.]

---

1 The offence of burglary makes no distinction between offences committed during the night or in the daytime or between different types of buildings attacked. No element of breaking is required, instead it must be proved that entry was made as a trespasser.

2 The least degree of entry, with the hand or any part of the person is sufficient (*R v Davis* (1823) Russ & Ry 499) and does not require that the whole of the defendant's body be within the building (*R v Brown* [1985] Crim LR 212, CA). It would seem that the entry need not be effective (see *R v Brown* ante, and *R v Ryan* (1995) 160 JP 610, [1996] Crim LR 320, CA).

3 "Building" includes an inhabited vehicle or vessel (s 9(3), infra).

4 A person lawfully within one part of a building who enters another part as a trespasser is within the section; *R v Walkington* [1979] 2 All ER 716, 143 JP 542 (behind unattended counter in a shop).

5 In civil law an unauthorised, intentional, reckless or negligent entry into a building in another's possession is a trespass even though the entry is made, eg, in the mistaken impression that it is a different building. However, entry as a result of such a mistake will not amount to a trespass such as is contemplated by s 9 to form the basis of an offence of burglary. In criminal law "mens rea" is a necessary ingredient of trespass and therefore a knowledge of the fact of being a trespasser, or, at the very least, recklessness as to whether or not entering the premises of another is without that other's consent, is essential. The doctrine of "trespass ab initio" which in civil law renders an originally lawful entry into a trespass as a result of subsequent hostile action, has no place in consideration of the offence of burglary. The accused must be a trespasser at the actual time of entry. See *R v Collins* [1973] QB 100, [1972] 2 All ER 1105, 136 JP 605; and *R v John Jones* [1976] 3 All ER 54, 140 JP 515 (entry in excess of permission).

6 It is not necessary that the original intention should have been completed: it is enough that the intention existed at the time of entry. In *R v Walkington* [1979] 2 All ER 716, 143 JP 542, the fact that a till in a shop was empty did not destroy the defendant's intention to steal. In *Re A-G's Reference (Nos 1 and 2 of 1979)* [1980] QB 180, 143 JP 708, CA, it was held that the fact that the intention to steal was conditional on finding money in the house which had been unlawfully entered did not entitle a person to be acquitted of a charge under s 9(1)(*a*). Similar considerations apply where the charge relates to attempted burglary.

7 Under this paragraph the accused need not have had any specific intention at the time of entry if he commits such an offence having entered.

8 Triable either way unless burglary comprising the commission of, or an intention to commit, an offence which is

triable only on indictment, or burglary in a dwelling if any person in the dwelling was subjected to violence or the threat of violence; see the Magistrates' Courts Act 1980, s 17 and Sch 1; also ss 17A–21 (procedure) and s 32 (penalty) in PART I: MAGISTRATES' COURTS, PROCEDURE, ante. Burglary is also triable only on indictment where it is a "domestic" burglary and the accused has previously been convicted of on at least two occasions of relevant domestic burglaries see the Powers of Criminal Courts (Sentencing) Act 2000, s 111, in PART III: SENTENCING, ante. A person who has in his possession any firearm or imitation firearm at the time of committing or at the time of his apprehension for this offence (or aiding and abetting or attempting to commit this offence) is subject to the provisions of the Firearms Act 1968, s 17(2), ante.

7.11321 **10. Aggravated burglary** (1) A person is guilty of aggravated burglary if he commits any burglary[1] and at the time has with him[2] any firearm or imitation firearm, any weapon of offence[3], or any explosive; and for this purpose—

(*a*) "firearm" includes an airgun or air pistol, and "imitation firearm" means anything which has the appearance of being a firearm, whether capable of being discharged or not[4]; and

(*b*) "weapon of offence" means any article made or adapted for use for causing injury to or incapacitating a person, or intended by the person having it with him for such use[5]; and

(*c*) "explosive" means any article manufactured for the purpose of producing a practical effect by explosion, or intended by the person having it with him for that purpose.

(2) A person guilty of aggravated burglary shall on conviction on indictment be liable to imprisonment for life.

[Theft Act 1968, s 10.]

---

1 As defined in s 9, ante.

2 The gravamen of the offence is entry into a building with a weapon. Therefore where there is only one weapon and that weapon is with an accomplice who remains on the outside, although he may be guilty of aiding and abetting his co-accused who effects entry to the building, neither is guilty of the offence in its aggravated form (*R v Klass* [1998] 1 Cr App Rep 453, 162 JP 105, CA; followed in *R v Wiggins* [2012] EWCA Crim 885, 176 JP 305).

3 The time at which the defendant must be proved to have had with him a weapon of offence to make him guilty of aggravated burglary, is, in the case of a charge under s 9(1)(*a*) the time when he entered, and in the case of a charge under s 9(1)(*b*) the time at which he actually stole etc; see *R v O'Leary* (1986) 82 Cr App Rep 341. It is not necessary to prove intention to use the weapon during the course of the burglary (*R v Stones* [1989] 1 WLR 156, 89 Cr App Rep 26, CA).

4 Cf the definition in the Firearms Act 1968, s 57(4), ante.

5 Cf the definition of "offensive weapon" in the Prevention of Crimes Act 1953, s 1(4), ante.

7.11322 **11. Removal of articles from places open to the public** (1) Subject to subsections (2) and (3) below, where the public have access to a building[1] in order to view the building or part of it, or a collection or part of a collection housed in it, any person who without lawful authority removes[2] from the building or its grounds the whole or part of any article displayed or kept for display to the public in the building or that part of it or in its grounds shall be guilty of an offence. For this purpose "collection" includes a collection got together for a temporary purpose, but references in this section to a collection do not apply to a collection made or exhibited for the purpose of effecting sales or other commercial dealings.

(2) It is immaterial for purposes of subsection (1) above, that the public's access to a building is limited to a particular period or particular occasion; but where anything removed from a building or its grounds is there otherwise than as forming part of, or being on loan for exhibition with, a collection intended for permanent exhibition to the public[3] the person removing it does not thereby commit an offence under this section[4] unless he removes it on a day when the public have access to the building as mentioned in subsection (1) above.

(3) A person does not commit an offence under this section if he believes that he has lawful authority for the removal of the thing in question or that he would have it if the person entitled to give it knew of the removal and the circumstances of it.

(4) A person guilty of an offence under this section shall, on conviction on indictment, be liable to imprisonment for a term not exceeding five years[5].

[Theft Act 1968, s 11.]

---

1 Access to the grounds of a building is not thought to be sufficient: thus a person removing an article from a collection displayed in the grounds of a building to which the public have no access although there is access to the collection, is not liable to prosecution under this section, but might very well be liable under s 1, ante.

2 The offence under this section is "removes" and not "appropriates". It is not necessary that there is an intent to permanently deprive the owner of it. The building may either be open or closed to the public at the time of removal; see sub-s (2), post.

3 This means intended to be permanently *available* for exhibition to the public, and would therefore include pictures only intermittently on display in an art gallery (*R v Durkin* [1973] QB 786, [1973] 2 All ER 872).

4 But might very well be liable under s 1, ante.

5 Triable either way; see the Magistrates' Courts Act 1980, s 17 and Sch 1; also ss 17A–21 (procedure) and s 32 (penalty) in PART I: MAGISTRATES' COURTS, PROCEDURE, ante.

7.11323 **12. Taking motor vehicle or other conveyance without authority**[1] (1) Subject to subsections (5) and (6) below, a person shall be guilty of an offence[2] if, without having the consent[3] of the owner[4] or other lawful authority, he takes[5] any conveyance[5] for his own or another's use or, knowing that any conveyance[6] has been taken without such authority[7], drives[8] it or allows himself to be carried[9] in or on it.

(2) A person guilty of an offence under subsection (1) above shall be liable on summary conviction to a fine not exceeding **level 5** on the standard scale, to imprisonment for a term not exceeding **six months**, or to **both**[10].

(3) *Repealed.*

(4) If on the trial of an indictment[11] for theft the jury are not satisfied that the accused

committed theft, but it is proved that the accused committed an offence under subsection (1) above, the jury may find him guilty of the offence under subsection (1) and if he is found guilty of it, he shall be liable as he would have been liable under subsection (2) above on summary conviction.

(4A) Proceedings for an offence under subsection (1) above (but not proceedings of a kind falling within subsection (4) above) in relation to a mechanically propelled vehicle—

*(a)* shall not be commenced after the end of the period of three years beginning with the day on which the offence was committed; but

*(b)* subject to that, may be commenced at any time within the period of six months beginning with the relevant day.

(4B) In subsection (4A)*(b)* above "the relevant day" means—

*(a)* in the case of a prosecution for an offence under subsection (1) above by a public prosecutor, the day on which sufficient evidence to justify the proceedings came to the knowledge of any person responsible for deciding whether to commence any such prosecution;

*(b)* in the case of a prosecution for an offence under subsection (1) above which is commenced by a person other than a public prosecutor after the discontinuance of a prosecution falling within paragraph *(a)* above which relates to the same facts, the day on which sufficient evidence to justify the proceedings came to the knowledge of the person who has decided to commence the prosecution or (if later) the discontinuance of the other prosecution;

*(c)* in the case of any other prosecution for an offence under subsection (1) above, the day on which sufficient evidence to justify the proceedings came to the knowledge of the person who has decided to commence the prosecution.

(4C) For the purposes of subsection (4A)*(b)* above a certificate of a person responsible for deciding whether to commence a prosecution of a kind mentioned in subsection (4B)*(a)* above as to the date on which such evidence as is mentioned in the certificate came to the knowledge of any person responsible for deciding whether to commence any such prosecution shall be conclusive evidence of that fact.

(5) Subsection (1) above shall not apply in relation to pedal cycles; but, subject to subsection (6) below, a person who, without having the consent of the owner[12] or other lawful authority, takes a pedal cycle for his own or another's use, or rides a pedal cycle knowing it to have been taken without such authority, shall on summary conviction be liable to a fine not exceeding **level 3** on the standard scale.

(6) A person does not commit an offence under this section by anything done in the belief that he has lawful authority to do it or that he would have the owner's consent if the owner knew of his doing it and the circumstances of it.

(7) For purposes of this section—

*(a)* "conveyance" means any conveyance[13] constructed or adapted for the carriage of a person or persons whether by land, water or air, except that it does not include a conveyance constructed or adapted for use only under the control of a person not carried in or on it, and "drive" shall be construed accordingly; and

*(b)* "owner", in relation to a conveyance which is the subject of a hiring agreement or hire-purchase agreement, means the person in possession of the conveyance under that agreement.

[Theft Act 1968, s 12 as amended by the Criminal Justice Act 1982, ss 38 and 46, the Police and Criminal Evidence Act 1984, Sch 7, the Criminal Justice Act 1988, s 37 and the Vehicles (Crimes) Act 2001, s 37.]

---

1 For the offence of interference with a motor vehicle or trailer, see the Criminal Attempts Act 1981, s 9, in PART I: MAGISTRATES' COURTS, PROCEDURE, ante.

2 A person who has in his possession any firearm or imitation firearm at the time of committing or at the time of his apprehension for this offence (or aiding and abetting or attempting to commit this offence) is subject to the provisions of the Firearms Act 1968, s 17 (2), ante.

3 Consent is not vitiated by the fact that consent is obtained by a false pretence as to the destination and purpose of the journey (*R v Peart* [1970] 2 QB 672, [1970] 2 All ER 823, 134 JP 547). The consent of an owner to allow a vehicle to be hired was held not to have been vitiated where that consent was obtained by the fraudulent misrepresentations of the hirer as to his identity and the holding of a full driving licence (*Whittaker v Campbell* [1984] QB 318, [1983] 3 All ER 582, 77 Cr App Rep 267).

4 A person in possession of a conveyance under a hire purchase agreement is the owner for the purposes of this section. See also note 2 to s 5, ante.

5 Possession of a motor vehicle proved to have recently been "taken" would, no doubt, give rise to a rebuttable presumption (as in theft) of a "taking" for the purposes of this section. The evidence necessary to support a conviction where two or more persons are acting in concert was considered in *Ross v Rivenall* [1959] 2 All ER 376, 123 JP 352; and in *R v Stally* [1959] 3 All ER 814, 124 JP 65; in the latter case it was held that no offence was committed by a second defendant who was a passenger in a vehicle which had previously been taken by a first defendant, in his absence and without his knowledge; applied in *D (an infant) v Parsons* [1960] 2 All ER 493, 124 JP 375. However, the cases of a "second taking" need to be considered together with *DPP v Spriggs* [1993] Crim LR 622, [1994] RTR 1 when a defendant was convicted after taking a vehicle abandoned by an earlier taker. It should be noted that it is now not necessary that the conveyance taken should be "driven away". There still remains the need to show some movement, however small, of the conveyance, following the unauthorised taking of possession or control of it, before there can be a conviction of the completed offence rather than an attempt (*R v Bogacki* [1973] QB 832, [1973] 2 All ER 864, 137 JP 676). The offence does not require the propelling of the conveyance "in its own element"; thus a conviction was upheld where a defendant had loaded an inflatable rubber dinghy on a trailer which he then drove away (*R v Pearce* [1973] Crim LR 321). But in *R v Bow* [1977] RTR 6, [1977] Crim LR 176, where a vehicle which had caused an obstruction was moved 200 yards by allowing it to coast downhill, it was held that, as the vehicle was taken in a way which involved its use as a conveyance, the taker could not be heard to say that the taking was not for that use. An accidental movement of a vehicle is not a "taking",

see *Blayney v Knight* (1975) 60 Cr App Rep 269, [1975] Crim LR 237, nor did the moving of a motorcar round the corner as a practical joke where it was not established that anyone rode inside it (*R v Stokes* [1982] Crim LR 695).

An unauthorised deviation by an authorised driver was not an offence against previous corresponding legislation (*Mowe v Perraton* [1952] 1 All ER 423, 116 JP 739). A person having custody without authority to drive might have been guilty however (*R v Wibberley* [1966] 2 QB 214, [1965] 3 All ER 718, 130 JP 58). The circumstances of these two contrasting cases may be considered where a servant of the owner is charged. It will be no defence to prove that the conveyance was stolen rather than merely taken (*Tolley v Giddings* [1964] 2 QB 354, [1964] 1 All ER 201, 128 JP 182), nor is self-induced drunkenness a defence (*R v MacPherson* [1973] Crim LR 457).

6 Conveyance is defined at s 12(7)(*a*). See s 12(5) for the offence of taking pedal cycles without authority.

7 A memorandum of conviction by guilty plea of the driver to taking the vehicle without consent is sufficient prima facie evidence that the vehicle had been so taken: *R v Parker* (2006) Times, 7 June, DC.

8 The word "drive" is to be construed according to the nature of the conveyance taken, and would include for example rowing a boat or piloting an aircraft.

9 This involves some movement of the conveyance (*R v Miller* [1976] Crim LR 147).

10 Disqualification may be ordered (Road Traffic Offenders Act 1988, Sch 2, PART VI: TRANSPORT, ante). The defendant must deliver his driving licence to the clerk of the court prior to the hearing or have it with him at the hearing (Road Traffic Offenders Act 1988, ss 7 and 27, ante).

11 There is no power given to a magistrates' court to convict of an offence under this section in substitution of a conviction for theft. In such a court there may be no conviction under this section except where the accused has been charged with an offence thereunder.

12 Where there are admissions that a bicycle has been taken without the owner's consent and does not belong to the defendant, the court is entitled to find that the bicycle had not been abandoned and had an owner without the need of a formal statement from the owner (*Sturrock v DPP* (1995) Times, 9 February).

13 A horse to which a halter or bridle has been attached is not a conveyance for the purposes of this section (*Neal v Gribble* (1978) 68 Cr App Rep 9, [1978] Crim LR 500).

**7.11324 12A. Aggravated vehicle-taking**[1] (1) Subject to subsection (3) below a person is guilty of aggravated taking of a vehicle if—

(*a*) he commits an offence under section 12(1) above (in this section referred to as a "basic offence") in relation to a mechanically propelled vehicle; and

(*b*) it is proved that, at any time after the vehicle was unlawfully taken (whether by him or another) and before it was recovered, the vehicle was driven, or injury or damage was caused, in one or more of the circumstances set out in paragraphs (*a*) to (*d*) of subsection (2) below.

(2) The circumstances referred to in subsection (1)(*b*)[2] above are—

(*a*) that the vehicle was driven dangerously on a road or other public place;

(*b*) that, owing to the driving of the vehicle, an accident occurred by which injury was caused to any person[3];

(*c*) that, owing to the driving of the vehicle, an accident occurred by which damage was caused to any property, other than the vehicle;

(*d*) that damage[4] was caused to the vehicle.

(3) A person is not guilty of an offence under this section if he proves that, as regards any such proven driving, injury or damage as is referred to in subsection (1)(*b*) above, either—

(*a*) the driving, accident or damage referred to in subsection (2) above occurred before he committed the basic offence; or

(*b*) he was neither in nor on nor in the immediate vicinity of the vehicle when that driving, accident or damage occurred.

(4) A person guilty of an offence[5] under this section shall be liable on conviction on indictment to imprisonment for a term not exceeding **two years** or, if it is proved that, in circumstances falling within subsection (2)(*b*) above, the accident caused the death of the person concerned, **fourteen years**.

(5) If a person who is charged with an offence under this section is found not guilty of that offence but it is proved that he committed a basic[6] offence, he may be convicted of the basic offence.

(6) If by virtue of subsection (5) above a person is convicted of a basic offence before the Crown Court, that court shall have the same powers and duties as a magistrates' court would have had on convicting him of such an offence.

(7) For the purposes of this section a vehicle is driven dangerously[7] if—

(*a*) it is driven in a way which falls far below what would be expected of a competent and careful driver; and

(*b*) it would be obvious to a competent and careful driver that driving the vehicle in that way would be dangerous.

(8) For the purposes of this section a vehicle is recovered when it is restored to its owner or to other lawful possession or custody; and in this subsection "owner" has the same meaning as in section 12 above.

[Theft Act 1968, s 12A as inserted by the Aggravated Vehicle-Taking Act 1992, s 1 and amended by the Criminal Justice Act 2003, s 285.]

---

1 Nothing in s 12A applies to an offence under s 12(1) of the Theft Act 1968 which was committed before s 12A came into force on 1 April 1992, or to any driving, injury or damage which occurred before that date (Aggravated Vehicle-Taking Act 1992, s 1(3)).

2 Whilst of the four aggravating circumstances identified in subsection (2), (*a*) expressly imports a requirement of fault (the car must have been driven dangerously), (*b*), (*c*) and (*d*) do not operate independent of fault. In the case of (*b*) and (*c*), it is implicit in the requirement that the accident must have occurred "owing to the driving of the vehicle", that there will have been something wrong with the driving. The driving cannot be said to have caused the accident if it merely explained how the vehicle came to be in the place where the accident occurred. The essential point made in *R v Hughes* [2013] UKSC 56, [2013] 4 All ER 613, [2013] 1 WLR 2461 is common both to offences contrary to s 3ZB of the Road

Traffic Act 1988 and s 12A(2)(*b*) of the Theft Act 1968; both posit a direct causal connection between the driving and the injury. The one respect in which s 12A imposes strict liability is that the offence may be committed not only by the driver but by anyone else who was party to the basic offence under s 12(1) and is in or in the immediate vicinity of the vehicle at the time of the dangerous driving, injury or damage. The Act treats someone who has been party to the taking of a vehicle without authority as having control over it thereafter. He is in a position to take positive steps to ensure that it is driven safely and not in a manner which causes personal injury or damage to property. His responsibility continues to be engaged while he is present. However, while the legislation makes a person who has taken a car without authority responsible for the fault of another person who drives it in his presence; it does not make him responsible for personal injury or damage which could not have been prevented, because it occurred without fault or was entirely the fault of the victim. Accordingly, the test applicable in cases of aggravated vehicle taking is in the same terms as in *Hughes*. There must be at least some act or omission in the control of the car, which involves some element of fault, whether amounting to careless/inconsiderate driving or not, and which contributes in some more than minimal way to the injury or damage: *R v Taylor* [2016] UKSC 5, [2016] 4 All ER 617, [2016] 1 WLR 500, [2016] 1 Cr App R 27, [2016] RTR 28, (where the result was death of the other driver). See also, the Road Traffic Act 1988, s 3ZB in PART IV ROAD TRAFFIC, and notes thereto.

3 The term "accident" is concerned with the consequences of what occurred and not the way in which those consequences came about; thus, a deliberate result is included: *R v Branchflower* [2004] EWCA Crim 2042, [2005] RTR 165, [2005] 1 Cr App Rep 140.

4 Damage caused to a vehicle by a defendant in an attempt to escape from the vehicle is sufficient to establish the circumstances set out in paragraph (*d*) (*Dawes v DPP* [1994] RTR 209, [1995] 1 Cr App Rep 65).

5 This offence is triable either way (Magistrates' Courts Act 1980, s 17 and Sch 1, in PART I: MAGISTRATES' COURTS, PROCEDURE, ante. For procedure in relation to a triable either way offence, see the Magistrates' Courts Act 1980, ss 17A–21, ante, and for penalty, see the Magistrates' Courts Act 1980, s 32, ante. Nevertheless, if the only aggravating circumstances are damage, the total value of which is below the specified amount, ie £5,000, the offence is to be tried summarily (Magistrates' Courts Act 1980, s 22 and Sch 2, in PART I: MAGISTRATES' COURTS, PROCEDURE, ante.

When sentencing co-accused, differentiation should be made between a defendant who was the driver and a defendant passenger who had asked the driver to desist from the dangerous driving. (*R v Wiggins* (2000) 165 JP 210, [2001] RTR 37, CA). On conviction this offence carries obligatory disqualification; the court must order the offender to be disqualified for such period not less than 12 months as the court thinks fit, unless the court for special reasons thinks fit to order him to be disqualified for a shorter period. However, for the purposes of an offence of aggravated vehicle-taking the fact that the offender did not drive the vehicle in question at any particular time or at all shall not be regarded as a special reason; see the Road Traffic Offenders Act 1988, s 34(1)–(1A) and Sch 2, Pt II, in: title PART VI TRANSPORT, post. It is inappropriate to order the passenger convicted of an offence of aggravated vehicle taking to take an extended test (*R v Bradshaw* (1994) Times, 31 December).

6 This power is exercisable by the magistrates' court and for the court should generally indicate its intention as to the basic offence before dismissing the aggravated offence (*R on the application of H) v Liverpool City Youth Court* [2001] Crim LR 897, DC).

7 Subsection (7) reflects the meaning of "dangerous driving" provided by s 2A of the Road Traffic Act 1988 for the purposes of that Act; see PART VI: title TRANSPORT: ROAD TRAFFIC, post.

7.11325 **13. Abstracting of electricity** A person who dishonestly[1] uses without due authority, or dishonestly causes to be wasted or diverted, any electricity shall on conviction on indictment be liable to imprisonment for a term not exceeding **five years**[2].

[Theft Act 1968, s 13.]

1 See s 2, ante. It is sufficient for the prosecution to establish electricity was used without the authority of the Electricity Board and with no intention to pay (*R v McCreadie and Tume* (1992) 96 Cr App Rep 143, 157 JP 541, [1992] Crim LR 872 CA, where an officially disconnected meter was unlawfully reconnected by a third party and electricity used by squatters).

2 Triable either way; see the Magistrates' Courts Act 1980, s 17 and Sch 1; also ss 17A–21 (procedure) and s 32 (penalty) in PART I: MAGISTRATES' COURTS, PROCEDURE, ante.

7.11326 **14. Extension to thefts from mails outside England and Wales, and robbery, etc, on such a theft[1]** (1) Where a person—

(*a*) steals or attempts to steal any mail bag[2] or postal packet in the course of transmission as such between places in different jurisdictions in the British postal area, or any of the contents of such a mail bag or postal packet; or

(*b*) in stealing or with intent to steal any such mail bag or postal packet or any of its contents, commits any robbery, attempted robbery or assault with intent to rob;

then, notwithstanding that he does so outside England and Wales, he shall be guilty of committing or attempting to commit the offence against this Act as if he had done so in England or Wales, and he shall accordingly be liable to be prosecuted, tried and punished in England and Wales without proof that the offence was committed there.

(2) In subsection (1) above the reference to different jurisdictions in the British postal area is to be construed as referring to the several jurisdictions of England and Wales, of Scotland, of Northern Ireland, of the Isle of Man and of the Channel Islands.

(3) *Repealed.*

[Theft Act 1968, s 14 as amended by SI 2003/2908.]

1 Section 14 secures that theft from mail in transmission between different parts of the British postal areas and related offences against such mail will be criminal and so may be prosecuted even though the offence took place outside England and Wales.

2 See s 14(3), infra.

*Fraud and blackmail*

7.11327 **15. Obtaining property by deception[1]** (1) [2]A person who by any deception[3] dishonestly[4] obtains property[5] belonging to another[6], with the intention of permanently depriving the other of it[7], shall on conviction on indictment be liable to imprisonment for a term not exceeding **ten years**[8].

(2) For purposes of this section a person is to be treated as obtaining property if he obtains ownership, possession or control of it, and "obtain" includes obtaining for another[9] or enabling another to obtain or to retain.

(3) Section 6[10] above shall apply for purposes of this section, with the necessary adaptation of the reference to appropriating, as it applies for purposes of section 1[11].

(4) For purposes of this section "deception" means any deception (whether deliberate or reckless)[12] by words or conduct[13] as to fact or as to law, including a deception as to the present intentions of the person using the deception or any other person.

[Theft Act 1968, s 15.]

---

[1] **The repeal of this and other deception offences by the Fraud Act 2006 does not affect any liability, investigation, legal proceeding or penalty for or in respect of any offence partly committed before 15 January 2007: para 3 of Sch 2 to the Fraud Act 2006, in this PART, post, and the Fraud Act (Commencement) Order 2006, SI 2006/3200. As to the meaning of "partly committed", see sub-paras (2) and (3).**

[2] These sections replace previous law concerned with obtaining something by false pretences. Offences under s 15 are wider than in previous legislation applying to "property" generally including land. It is only necessary for the accused to obtain possession or control of property, not necessarily ownership as hitherto.

[3] See s 15(4), infra. The prosecution must prove that the deception acted on the mind of the person from whom the property was obtained (*R v Laverty* [1970] 3 All ER 432) unless there is a necessary inference that the deception was the cause of the obtaining (*Etim v Hatfield* [1975] Crim LR 234). A cheque is only dishonestly obtained from a company if a person whose state of mind stood for that of the company and who signed the cheque was actually deceived. It is not relevant that other employees who prepared the cheque were deceived (*R v Rozeik* [1996] 3 All ER 281, [1996] 1 WLR 159, [1996] Crim LR 271, CA). Defendants who sought by false representations to induce a person to have trees in her garden cut down, were held to have been properly convicted of attempting to obtain money by deception because the deception would have been an operative cause of obtaining the money, and not the work which they would have done if they had actually cut them down (*R v King* [1987] QB 547, [1987] 1 All ER 547). An excessively high quotation for work will not of itself amount to a false representation, but on the facts (where, for example there were circumstances of trust) it may be so (*R v Silverman* [1987] Crim LR 574). Where an exorbitant fare was paid by foreigners who had believed a defendant to be a taxi driver when entering his vehicle the offence was made out even though at the time money changed hands the victim knew the defendant to be lying (*R v Miller* [1993] RTR 6). A claim containing deliberate misrepresentations for housing benefit for which the claimant was qualified was a deception since the housing authority needed to know the truth before paying it (*R v Talbott* [1995] Crim LR 396, CA).

The basis of English courts' jurisdiction is that the physical acts of the accused, wherever they were done, had caused the intended consequence in England that property belonging to another had been obtained by deception, and *not* that the accused had done some physical act in England (*DPP v Stonehouse* [1977] 2 All ER 909); the *obtaining* must happen within the jurisdiction, thus where a computer in Kuwait had been programmed to debit a bank customers' accounts and credit accounts opened by the accused, the obtaining occurred when the bank transferred credit balance into English accounts by telex following the accused's letters requesting this (*R v Thompson* [1984] 3 All ER 565, [1984] 1 WLR 962, CA). The acquiring of ownership and control does not have to be tied to the physical location of the property in respect of a bank account. Therefore an English company obtained property at the place where it was registered where money was transferred into its account in a bank outside the jurisdiction (*R v Smith (Wallace Duncan)* [1996] 2 Cr App Rep 1, [1996] Crim LR 329, CA). See further the Criminal Justice Act 1993 ss 1–6 in PART I: MAGISTRATES' COURTS, PROCEDURE, ante.

[4] It should be noted that the partial definition of "dishonestly" in s 2 ante applies only for the purposes of s 1 (Theft Act 1968, s 1(3)). In general terms, however, the test to be applied in deciding whether someone had acted "dishonestly" is set out in *R v Ghosh* [1982] QB 1053, [1982] 2 All ER 689, 146 JP 376; the court must decide whether according to the ordinary standards of reasonable and honest people what was done was dishonest. If it was dishonest by those standards, the court must consider whether the defendant himself must have realised that what he was doing was by those standards dishonest. It is dishonest for a defendant to act in a way which he knows ordinary people consider to be dishonest, even if he asserts or genuinely believes that he is morally justified in acting as he did. This approach is likely to cover all occasions when a reference to s 2(1)(*a*) might otherwise (and but for s 1(3)) have been appropriate; see *R v Woolven*, [1983] Crim LR 623. The onus of proving that a false representation acted on the mind of the alleged victim falls on the prosecution and in the ordinary way should be proved by direct evidence (*R v Laverty* [1970] 3 All ER 432 but cf. *Etim v Hatfield* [1975] Crim LR 234).

[5] Section 4(1), ante (definition of "property") applies; see s 34(1), post. As to obtaining services, or evading liability by deception, or making off without payment, see the Theft Act 1978, post. Offences of fraud on the public purse were commented on in *R v Stewart* [1987] 2 All ER 383, [1987] 1 WLR 559, CA (noted in PART III: SENTENCING, para 3.136 ante).

[6] Section 5(1) ante defines "belonging to another"; see s 34(1), post.

[7] See s 6, ante.

[8] Even if the facts proved justify a conviction under this section, a conviction under s 1, ante, may still be sustained (*Lawrence v Metropolitan Police Comr* [1972] AC 626, [1971] 2 All ER 1253, HL; followed in *R v Hircock* (1978) 67 Cr App Rep 278, [1979] Crim LR 184). Triable either way; see Magistrates' Courts Act 1980, s 17 and Sch 1; also ss 17A–21 (procedure) and s 32 (penalty) in PART I: MAGISTRATES' COURTS, PROCEDURE, ante.

[9] It is irrelevant that there is no dishonesty or deception or knowledge thereof by the other person (*R v Duru* [1973] 3 All ER 715).

[10] Section 6 partially defines the expression "with the intention of permanently depriving the other of it".

[11] Section 1 is the general definition of the offence of theft.

[12] "Reckless" means more than being careless or negligent and involves an indifference to whether the statement is true or false (*R v Staines* (1974) 60 Cr App Rep 160).

[13] This can include "positive acquiescence" so that a defendant who had applied for and been granted a grant towards providing a downstairs bathroom at his house for his elderly and infirm mother, was guilty of deception in failing to notify the council of her death being aware that the council were still of the mind that the mother would occupy his premises, *R v Rai* [2000] 1 Cr App Rep 242, 164 JP 121, [2000] Crim LR 192, CA.

7.11328 **15A. Obtaining a money transfer by deception*** (1) A person is guilty of an offence if by any deception he dishonestly obtains a money transfer for himself or another.

(2) A money transfer occurs when—

(*a*) a debit[1] is made to one account,

(*b*) a credit[1] is made to another, and

(*c*) the credit results from the debit or the debit results from the credit[1].

(3) References to a credit and to a debit are to a credit of an amount of money and to a debit of an amount of money.

(4) It is immaterial (in particular)—

(*a*) whether the amount credited is the same as the amount debited;

(*b*) whether the money transfer is effected on presentment of a cheque or by another method;

(*c*) whether any delay occurs in the process by which the money transfer is effected;

(*d*) whether any intermediate credits or debits are made in the course of the money transfer;

(*e*) whether either of the accounts is overdrawn before or after the money transfer is effected.

(5) A person guilty of an offence under this section shall be liable on conviction on indictment to imprisonment for a term not exceeding **ten years**[2].

[Theft Act 1968, s 15A as inserted by the Theft (Amendment) Act 1996, s 1.]

---

*** The repeal of this and other deception offences by the Fraud Act 2006 does not affect any liability, investigation, legal proceeding or penalty for or in respect of any offence partly committed before 15 January 2007: para 3 of Sch 2 to the Fraud Act 2006, in this PART, post, and Fraud Act (Commencement) Order 2006, SI 2006/3200. As to the meaning of "partly committed", see sub-paras (2) and (3).**

1 "Credited" in that context of s 15A, means credited unconditionally and s 15A, furthermore, requires that, in addition to a credit to a bank account, there has to be a debit made to an account, and that the credit results from the debit or vice versa; however, the court is entitled to take judicial notice of invariable banking and accountancy practice that a money transfer cannot be made without an account being debited with the amount of the transfer and the debit and credit must be causally connected, and it is unnecessary to specify what account was debited as the concomitant to the credit or whether the former was overdrawn or in credit provided there was a debiting of an account and that debiting was causally connected with the credit: *Re Holmes* [2004] EWHC 2020 (Admin), [2005] 1 Cr App R 16, [2005] Crim LR 229.

2 Triable either way; see the Magistrates' Courts Act 1980, s 17 and Sch 1; also ss 17A–21 (procedure) and s 32 (penalty) in PART I: MAGISTRATES' COURTS, PROCEDURE, ante.

7.11329 **15B. Section 15A: supplementary** (1) The following provisions have effect for the interpretation of section 15A of this Act.

(2) "Deception" has the same meaning as in section 15 of this Act.

(3) "Account" means an account kept with—

(*a*) a bank; or

(*b*) a person carrying on a business which falls within subsection (4) below.

(4) A business falls within this subsection if—

(*a*) in the course of the business money received by way of deposit is lent to others; or

(*b*) any other activity of the business is financed, wholly or to any material extent, out of the capital of or the interest on money received by way of deposit;

and "deposit" here has the same meaning as in section 35 of the Banking Act 1987 (fraudulent inducement to make a deposit).

(5) For the purposes of subsection (4) above—

(*a*) all the activities which a person carries on by way of business shall be regarded as a single business carried on by him; and

(*b*) "money" includes money expressed in a currency other than sterling or in the European currency unit (as defined in Council Regulation No 3320/94/EC or any EU instrument replacing it).

[Theft Act 1968, s 15B as inserted by the Theft (Amendment) Act 1996, s 1 and amended by SI 2011/1043.]

---

*** The repeal of this and other deception offences by the Fraud Act 2006 does not affect any liability, investigation, legal proceeding or penalty for or in respect of any offence partly committed before 15 January 2007: para 3 of Sch 2 to the Fraud Act 2006, in this PART, post, and the Fraud Act (Commencement) Order 2006, SI 2006/3200. As to the meaning of "partly committed", see sub-paras (2) and (3).**

7.11330 **16. Obtaining pecuniary advantage by deception***[1] (1) A person who by any deception[2] dishonestly[3] obtains for himself or another any pecuniary advantage[4] shall on conviction on indictment be liable to imprisonment for a term not exceeding **five years**[5].

(2) The cases in which a pecuniary advantage within the meaning of this section is to be regarded as obtained for a person[6] are cases where—

(*a*) *Repealed*[7];

(*b*) he is allowed[8] to borrow by way of overdraft[9], or to take out any policy of insurance or annuity contract, or obtains an improvement of the terms on which he is allowed to do so; or

(*c*) he is given the opportunity to earn remuneration or greater remuneration in an office[10] or employment[11], or to win money by betting.

(3) For purposes of this section "deception" has the same meaning as in section 15 of this Act.

[Theft Act 1968, s 16 as amended by the Theft Act 1978, s 5.]

---

*** The repeal of this and other deception offences by the Fraud Act 2006 does not affect any liability, investigation, legal proceeding or penalty for or in respect of any offence partly committed before 15 January 2007: para 3 of Sch 2 to the Fraud Act 2006, in this PART, post, and the Fraud Act (Commencement) Order 2006, SI 2006/3200. As to the meaning of "partly committed", see sub-paras (2) and (3).**

1 See s 16(3), infra.

[2] Although there must be a causal connection between the deception used and the pecuniary advantage obtained, it is not necessary that the person deceived suffered any loss arising from the deception: see *R v Kovacs* [1974] 1 All ER 1236, 138 JP 425.

The drawer of a cheque represents to the payee (i) that he has an account with the bank, and (ii) that the cheque, as drawn, is a valid order for the payment of that amount (ie that it will be met on presentment). Where the drawer of a cheque uses a cheque card in compliance with the conditions endorsed on the card, he makes to the payee the representations mentioned above and further represents that he has the actual authority of the bank to create a contract with the payee on the bank's behalf that it will honour the cheque on presentment for payment (*Metropolitan Police Comr v Charles* [1977] AC 177, [1976] 3 All ER 112, 140 JP 531, HL). If the cheque given is post dated, the drawer impliedly represents that the state of facts existing at the date of delivery are such that in the ordinary course of events it will, on presentation for payment on or after the date specified in the cheque, be met (*R v Gilmartin* [1983] QB 953, [1983] 1 All ER 829, 147 JP 183, CA). The presentation of a credit card as a means of payment implies a representation on the part of the holder of the card that he has actual authority to make, on behalf of the bank or credit card company which issued the card, a contract with the payee to the effect that the bank or company will honour the voucher on presentation (*R v Lambie* [1982] AC 449, [1981] 2 All ER 776, 145 JP 364, HL).

Where no one can reasonably be expected to remember a particular transaction in detail, reliance on a dishonest representation may be established by proof of facts from which an irresistible inference of inducement can be drawn, see *R v Lambie*, supra.

[3] See s 2, ante, and *R v Royle* [1971] 3 All ER 1359; *R v Nordeng* [1975] Crim LR 194.

[4] Section 16(1) creates only one offence, which can be committed in the various ways specified in s 16(2): stating more than one such way (eg evasion *or* deferment) in the charge does not make it bad for duplicity (*Bale v Rosier* [1977] 2 All ER 160, 141 JP 292).

[5] Triable either way; see the Magistrates' Courts Act 1980, s 17 and Sch 1; also ss 17A–21 (procedure) and s 32 (penalty) in PART I: MAGISTRATES' COURTS, PROCEDURE, ante.

[6] This refers not only to the person using the deception but also to the other person mentioned in sub-s (1) for whom the pecuniary advantage is obtained (*Richardson v Skells* [1976] Crim LR 448).

[7] Section 16(2)(*a*) has been replaced by the Theft Act 1978, post, which makes separate provision for offences of obtaining services by deception, evasion of liability by deception, and making off without payment.

[8] A person may be so "allowed" even though a bank imposed limits on the use of a cheque book and cheque card which were breached by the person: the circumstances of s 12, ante are so different that the use of "allow" there does not help in defining its use in s 16(2)(*b*) (*R v Waites* [1982] Crim LR 369, [1982] LS Gaz R 535; such offence can be tried in England even when the use of the cheque card took place abroad (*R v Bevan* (1986) 84 Cr App Rep 143, [1987] Crim LR 129).

[9] A customer obtains the pecuniary advantage at the moment when the overdraft facility is granted to him, without need for proof that he drew on that facility (*R v Watkins* [1976] 1 All ER 578, 140 JP 197).

[10] A tenancy is not an "office" or "employment" within s 16(2)(*c*) (*R v McNiff* [1986] Crim LR 57).

[11] An independent contractor, who held himself out to be a self-employed accountant, and who was engaged to render services under a contract for services was held, for the purposes of s 16(2)(*c*), to have been "employed" by the person who engaged him (*R v Callender* [1992] 3 All ER 51, [1992] Crim LR 591).

7.11331 **17. False accounting** (1) Where a person dishonestly[1] with a view to gain[2] for himself or another or with intent to cause loss[2] to another—

(*a*) destroys, defaces, conceals or falsifies any account or any record[3] or document made or required[4] for any accounting purpose; or

(*b*) in furnishing information for any purpose produces or makes use of any account, or any such record or document as aforesaid, which to his knowledge is or may be misleading, false or deceptive in a material particular[5]

he shall, on conviction on indictment, be liable to imprisonment for a term not exceeding **seven years**[6].

(2) For purposes of this section a person who makes or concurs in making in an account or other document an entry which is or may be misleading, false or deceptive in a material particular, or who omits or concurs in omitting a material particular[7] from an account or other document, is to be treated as falsifying the account or document.

[Theft Act 1968, s 17.]

---

[1] "Dishonestly" is to be interpreted in the terms set out in *R v Ghosh* [1982] QB 1053, [1982] 2 All ER 689, 75 Cr App Rep 154 (*R v Wood* [1999] Crim LR 564, CA). See notes to s 2, ante.

[2] For definition of "gain" and "loss", see s 34(2)(*a*), post. The use of falsified bills of exchange with a view to securing a bank's forbearance from enforcing repayment of existing debts does not constitute falsification with a view to "gain" within the meaning of this section (*R v Golechha* [1989] 3 All ER 908, [1989] 1 WLR 1050, CA).

[3] A "record" may include a taximeter (*R v Solomons* [1909] 2 KB 980, 73 JP 467); a turnstile meter (*Edwards v Toombs* [1983] Crim LR 43).

[4] In *Re A-G's Reference (No 1 of 1980)* [1981] 1 All ER 366, [1981] 1 WLR 34; it was held, on the facts of that reference, that a personal loan proposal form was a document "required for any accounting purpose". See also *Osinuga v DPP* (1997) 162 JP 120, [1998] Crim LR 216. Failure to complete any documents when required can be an offence under this section (*R v Shama* [1990] 2 All ER 602, [1990] 1 WLR 661, CA). A claim form submitted in respect of a home insurance policy may be a document made or required for an accounting purpose in that the insurance company may use the form as a basis for keeping its accounting records but the court must receive some evidence that it is in fact used for this purpose and the court cannot draw its own conclusion from the nature and form of the claim form (*R v Sundhers* [1998] Crim LR 497, CA). A jury is entitled without any further direct evidence of the accounting practices of the lender, to conclude that an application for a mortgage or a loan made to a commercial institution is a document required for an accounting purpose (*R v O and B* [2010] EWCA Crim 2233, [2011] 2 All ER 656, [2011] 1 WLR 2936, [2011] 2 Cr App R 33, in this regard not following *Sundhers*). See also *R v Manning* [1999] QB 980, [1998] 4 All ER 876, [1998] 2 Cr App Rep 461, CA (court entitled to conclude that insurance cover note an accounting document as it set out on the document what was owed by the client), and *Re Baxter* [2002] All ER (D) 218 (Jan), (2002) JPN 99 (a certificate, included in an application pack for an investment scheme, by which an insurance company purportedly stood behind the investment programme concerned could be regarded as a document made or required for an accounting purpose, but another document that was a general solicitation, any response to which would have resulted in the issue of accounting documents, could not be so regarded).

[5] Where an accused has used a false instrument or furnished false information with a view to obtaining money or other property, the prosecution does not have to prove, either in relation to this offence or in relation to an offence under s 3 of the Forgery and Counterfeiting Act 1981, that the accused had no legal entitlement to the money or property in question (*A-G's Reference (No 1 of 2001)* [2002] EWCA Crim 1768, [2002] 3 All ER 840, [2002] Crim LR 844). Although the

document itself must be made or required for an accounting purpose, the material particular in question does not have to be one which is directly connected with the accounting purpose of the document (*R v Mallett* [1978] 3 All ER 10). This section applies generally to the falsification of accounting documents for the purpose of obtaining financial gain or causing financial loss. It does not require that such gain or loss should in fact result. It is to be contrasted to the statutory scheme under s 111A of the Social Security Administration Act 1992 where the mischief aimed at is not falsification of documents but dishonest failure by a recipient of public benefits to notify the relevant authority of a change of circumstances which would make a difference to the computation of his benefit (*R v Lancaster* [2010] EWCA Crim 370, [2010] 3 All ER 402, [2010] 2 Cr App R 7, [2010] Crim LR 776).

6 Triable either way; see the Magistrates' Courts Act 1980, s 17 and Sch 1; also ss 17A–21 (procedure) and s 32 (penalty) in PART I: MAGISTRATES' COURTS, PROCEDURE, ante.

7 As the subsection as a whole is concerned with documents which are or may be materially misleading either by reason of what they contain or by reason of what they should contain but fail to contain, in a non-disclosure case the omission will be material if it has the effect that the document is liable to mislead in a way which is significant (or to put it another way in a way which matters). It is a matter for the magistrates to judge for themselves, on the particular facts of the case, whether they regard the omission as significant (*R v Lancaster* [2010] EWCA Crim 370, [2010] 3 All ER 402, [2010] 2 Cr App R 7, [2010] Crim LR 776).

7.11332 **18. Liability of company officers for certain offences by company** (1) Where an offence committed by a body corporate under section 17 of this Act is proved to have been committed with the consent or connivance of any director, manager, secretary or other similar officer of the body corporate, or any person who was purporting to act in any such capacity, he as well as the body corporate shall be guilty of that offence, and shall be liable to be proceeded against and punished accordingly.

(2) Where the affairs of a body corporate are managed by its members, this section shall apply in relation to the acts and defaults of a member in connection with his functions of management as if he were a director of the body corporate.

[Theft Act 1968, s 18 as amended by the Fraud Act 2006, Schs 1 and 3.]

7.11333 **19. False statements by company directors, etc** (1) Where an officer of a body corporate or unincorporated association (or person purporting to act as such), with intent to deceive members or creditors of the body corporate or association about its affairs, publishes or concurs in publishing a written statement or account which to his knowledge is or may be misleading, false or deceptive in a material particular, he shall on conviction on indictment be liable to imprisonment for a term not exceeding **seven years**[1].

(2) For purposes of this section a person who has entered into a security for the benefit of a body corporate or association is to be treated as a creditor of it.

(3) Where the affairs of a body corporate or association are managed by its members, this section shall apply to any statement which a member publishes or concurs in publishing in connection with his functions of management as if he were an officer of the body corporate or association.

[Theft Act 1968, s 19.]

1 Triable either way; see the Magistrates' Courts Act 1980, s 17 and Sch 1; also ss 17A–21 (procedure) and s 32 (penalty) in PART I: MAGISTRATES' COURTS, PROCEDURE, ante.

7.11334 **20. Suppression, etc, of documents*** (1) A person who dishonestly[1], with a view to gain[2] for himself or another or with intent to cause loss[2] to another, destroys, defaces or conceals any valuable security[3], any will or other testamentary document or any original document of or belonging to, or filed or deposited in, any court of justice or any government department shall on conviction on indictment be liable to imprisonment for a term not exceeding **seven years**[4].

(2) A person who dishonestly[1], with a view to gain[2] for himself or another or with intent to cause loss[2] to another, by any deception[3] procures[5] the execution[6] of a valuable security shall on conviction on indictment be liable to imprisonment for a term not exceeding **seven years**[4], and this subsection shall apply in relation to the making, acceptance[7], indorsement, alteration, cancellation or destruction in whole or in part of a valuable security, and in relation to the signing or sealing of any paper or other material in order that it may be made or converted into, or used or dealt with as, a valuable security, as if that were the execution[8] of a valuable security.

(3) For purposes of this section "deception" has the same meaning as in section 15 of this Act, and* "valuable security"[9] means any document creating, transferring, surrendering or releasing any right to, in or over property, or authorising the payment of money or delivery of any property, or evidencing the creation, transfer, surrender or release of any such right, or the payment of money or delivery of any property, or the satisfaction of any obligation.

[Theft Act 1968, s 20.]

*** The repeal of the offence in sub-s (2) of procuring the execution of a valuable security (and words underlined in sub-s (3)) and other deception offences by the Fraud Act 2006 does not affect any liability, investigation, legal proceeding or penalty for or in respect of any offence partly committed before 15 January 2007: para 3 of Sch 2 to the Fraud Act 2006, in this PART, post, and the Fraud Act (Commencement) Order 2006, SI 2006/3200. As to the meaning of "partly committed", see sub-paras (2) and (3).**

1 "Dishonestly" is to be interpreted in the terms set out in *R v Ghosh* [1982] QB 1053, [1982] 2 All ER 689, 75 Cr App Rep 154 (*R v Wood* [1999] Crim LR 564, CA). See notes to s 2, ante.

2 The words "gain" and "loss" are defined in s 34(2)(*a*), post.

3 See s 20(3), infra.

4 Triable either way; see the Magistrates' Courts Act 1980, s 17 and Sch 1; also ss 17A–21 (procedure) and s 32 (penalty).

5 "Procure" for this purpose means to cause or bring about (*R v Beck* [1985] 1 All ER 571, [1985] 1 WLR 22, 149 JP 260, CA).

6 The execution of a valuable security contemplates acts done to or in connection with the document, and not the

giving effect to the document by carrying out the instructions which it might contain, such as the payment of money. Thus payment on a cheque or credit voucher is not such an execution (*R v Kassim* [1991] 3 All ER 713).

7 "Acceptance" is to be given its proper commercial meaning, derived from the Bills of Exchange Act 1882, s 17, of a written and signed signification by the drawee of his assent to the order of the drawer; accordingly, the mere handing over to and receipt of orders to a bank did not amount to an acceptance within s 20(2) (*R v Nanayakkara* [1987] 1 All ER 650, [1987] 1 WLR 265, 84 Cr App Rep 125, CA).

8 Where the final acceptance of a valuable security which was a traveller's cheque occurred in England, even though there had been an earlier acceptance abroad, that final acceptance constituted execution of the security within the jurisdiction (*R v Beck* [1985] 1 All ER 571, [1985] 1 WLR 22, 149 JP 260, CA). See also *R v Manning* [1999] QB 980, [1998] 4 All ER 876, [1998] 2 Cr App Rep 461 (actus reus of procuring of a valuable security by deception occurred in Greece where cheques were signed in Athens) not followed as to jurisdiction by *R v Smith (Wallace) (No 4)* [2004] EWCA Crim 631, [2004] Crim LR 951 and see the Criminal Justice Act 1993, Part I in PART I: MAGISTRATES' COURTS PROCEDURE, ante.

9 An irrevocable letter of credit is a valuable security within the meaning of this section (*R v Benstead and Taylor* [1982] Crim LR 456) as is a clearing house automated payment system ("CHAPS") order (*R v King* [1992] 1 QB 20, [1991] 3 All ER 705), but a telegraphic transfer of funds may be made without the execution of any document (*R v Manjdadria* [1993] Crim LR 73, CA).

7.11335 21. **Blackmail** (1) A person is guilty of blackmail[1] if, with a view to gain[2] for himself or another or with intent to cause loss[2] to another, he makes[3] any unwarranted demand with menaces[4]; and for this purpose a demand with menaces is unwarranted unless the person making it does so in the belief—

(*a*) that he has reasonable grounds for making the demand; and

(*b*) that the use of the menaces is a proper means of reinforcing the demand.

(2) The nature of the act or omission demanded is immaterial, and it is also immaterial whether the menaces relate to action to be taken by the person making the demand.

(3) A person guilty of blackmail shall on conviction on indictment be liable to imprisonment for a term not exceeding **fourteen years**.

[Theft Act 1968, s 21.]

1 This is a new offence replacing the offences of demanding property with menaces, the essence of this offence is that the accused knows either that he has no right to make the demand or that the use of menaces to reinforce it is improper.

2 The words "gain" and "loss" are defined in s 34(2)(*a*), post.

3 A person makes a demand when he utters threatening words, and when the demand is by letter it is made when the letter is posted. If posted in England to an intended victim abroad the offence is triable in England (*Treacy v DPP* [1971] AC 537, [1971] 1 All ER 110; distinguished by the Court of Appeal in *R v Baxter* [1972] 2 QB 1 [1971] 2 All ER 359; where the offence of attempting to obtain property by deception was held to be committed in England although the letters by which the attempt was made were posted abroad).

4 The word "menace" is not limited to threats of violence but includes threats of any action detrimental to or unpleasant to the person addressed, even if the accused is entitled to carry it out (*Thorne v Motor Trade Association* [1937] AC 797, [1937] 3 All ER 157; *R v Tomlinson* [1895] 1 QB 706 and *R v Boyle and Merchant* [1914] 3 KB 339, 78 JP 390, approved). The menaces may be not that the defendant would do something or allow others to do something but that the victim would suffer violence from others (*R v Lambert* [2009] EWCA Crim 2860, [2010] 1 Cr App R 21, [2010] Crim LR 576). It seems to be immaterial whether money was wholly or only in part obtained (*R v Robertson* (1864) 28 JP 821). A threat to injure a man's property may be a menace within the section (*R v Boyle and Merchant*, supra). The language used may be only a request; it need not necessarily be a specified demand. A request imposing conditions may be evidence of a demand (*R v Studer* (1915) 85 LJKB 1017). A threat to report a betting defaulter to Tattersalls was not a menace within corresponding legislation (*Burden v Harris* [1937] 4 All ER 559). It is submitted on the authority of *R v Moran* [1952] 1 All ER 803, 116 JP 216 that there can be no such offence as attempted blackmail.

Words or conduct are menaces if they are such as are likely to operate on the mind of a person of ordinary courage and firmness so as to make him accede unwillingly to the demand. It is not necessary that the intended victim is himself alarmed (*R v Clear* [1968] 1 QB 670, [1968] 1 All ER 75, 132 JP 103). See also *R v Garwood* [1987] 1 All ER 1032, [1987] 1 WLR 319.

### *Offences relating to goods stolen, etc*

7.11336 22. **Handling stolen goods** (1) [1]A person handles stolen[2] goods if (otherwise than in the course of the stealing[3]) knowing or believing[4] them to be stolen goods[5] he dishonestly receives[6] the goods, or dishonestly undertakes or assists[7] in their retention[8], removal, disposal or realisation[9] by or for the benefit of another person[10], or if he arranges to do so[11].

(2) A person guilty of handling stolen[2] goods shall on conviction on indictment be liable to imprisonment for a term not exceeding **fourteen years**[12].

[Theft Act 1968, s 22.]

1 This section replaces the previous offence of receiving stolen property. It creates only one offence, namely, handling stolen goods, and it is not necessary for the information to state whether the alleged handling was by receiving, undertaking retention or removal, etc but in the ordinary way these particulars should be given (*Griffiths v Freeman* [1970] 1 All ER 1117, 134 JP 394). See also *R v Willis* [1972] 3 All ER 797, [1972] 1 WLR 1605; *R v Deakin* [1972] 3 All ER 803, [1972] 1 WLR 1618; and *R v Pitchley* (1972) 57 Cr App Rep 30. But where the form of handling is particularised in the charge the defendant cannot be convicted of another form of handling with which he has not been charged (*R v Nicklin* [1977] 2 All ER 444, 141 JP 391). In the absence of evidence showing a preconcerted arrangement between husband and wife the receipt by the wife does not amount to a dishonest receiving by the husband of goods stolen (*R v Pritchard* (1913) 109 LT 911).

2 Goods obtained by deception or blackmail are within this offence (s 24(4), post). Goods are not to be regarded as stolen after they have been restored to the person from whom they were stolen: see s 24(3), post and note thereto.

3 If a person handles goods he has stolen subsequent to the theft he *may* be guilty of both theft and handling, though normally theft and handling will be alternative charges; see *R v Dolan* [1976] Crim LR 145 and *R v Sainthouse* [1980] Crim LR 506. See also *R v Pitham and Hehl* [1977] Crim LR 285, where the defendants were convicted of handling, having been taken to a house and sold furniture by the thief who thereby appropriated furniture left in his care: their buying was nevertheless not "in the course of the stealing". Where there are several charges of robbery and burglary, there are problems with one compendious charge of handling as an alternative: see *R v Smythe* (1980) 72 Cr App Rep 8.

In the ordinary case where there is no evidence that the defendant was the thief, the prosecution is not required to prove affirmatively that the defendant was not the thief, because handling the goods "otherwise than in the course of the stealing" is not an essential ingredient of the offence. However, where the defendant is in possession of stolen goods so recently after they are stolen that the inevitable inference is that he is the thief then, if he is charged only with handling, the words "otherwise than in the course of the stealing" are relevant since the prosecution can only prove the offence of handling if it proves affirmatively that the defendant was not the thief (*R v Cash* [1985] QB 801, [1985] 2 All ER 128, CA).

4 The question is a subjective one and it must be proved that the defendant was aware of the theft or that he believed the goods to be stolen. Suspicion that they were stolen, even coupled with the fact that he shut his eyes to the circumstances, is not enough, although those matters may be taken into account by a court when deciding whether or not the necessary knowledge or belief existed; see *R v Moys* (1984) 79 Cr App Rep 72. The prosecution need not go further and show that the defendant knew the identity of the goods (*R v McCullum* (1973) 117 Sol Jo 525).

The Court of Appeal has laid down guidelines to be followed on the approach to the phrase "knowing or believing" when directing juries. The guidelines, which will be equally relevant to justices, can be summarised as follows: A man may be said to know that goods are stolen when he is told by someone with first hand knowledge (ie such as the thief or burglar) that such is the case. Belief, which is something short of knowledge, may be said to be the state of mind of a person who says to himself, "I cannot say I know for certain that these goods are stolen, but there can be no other reasonable conclusion in the light of all the circumstances, in the light of all that I have heard and seen". Either of those two states of mind is enough to satisfy the words of the statute (*R v Hall* (1985) 81 Cr App Rep 260).

5 Section 27 post makes provision for evidence admissible for the purpose of proving that the accused knew or believed the goods to be stolen goods.

6 It has been stated that guilty knowledge must be proved at the moment of receipt and not at any time during the handling thereafter: see *Atwal v Massey* [1971] 3 All ER 881, *per* LORD WIDGERY, CJ at 882; and *R v Grainge* [1974] 1 All ER 928 at 932, *per* EVERLEIGH, J; but note s 3(1), ante, whereby a subsequent guilty knowledge might amount to a dishonest appropriation and, therefore, theft.

7 Assists means helping or encouraging amongst other things; there must be either affirmative or circumstantial evidence of help or encouragement (*R v Coleman* (1985) 150 JP 175, [1986] Crim LR 56. Something must be done by the defendant; a mere failure to act, where no duty to act existed in law, does not amount to an offence: *R v Burroughes* [2000] All ER (D) 2032, CA.

8 The words "by or for the benefit of another person", govern "retention", "removal", "disposal" and "realisation", and should be included in the charge where retention, removal, disposal or realisation is alleged (*R v Sloggett* [1972] 1 QB 430, [1971] 3 All ER 264, 135 JP 539). See *R v Deakin* [1972] 3 All ER 803, 137 JP 19. If the accused knows that the stolen goods are hidden on his property, mere failure to reveal their presence does not in itself amount to assisting in their retention but would afford strong evidence of providing accommodation for the goods which may amount to assisting in their retention (*R v Brown* [1970] 1 QB 105, [1969] 3 All ER 198, 133 JP 592). Merely using stolen goods in the possession of another does not constitute the offence of assisting in their retention, because something must be done by the offender, and done intentionally and dishonestly, for the purpose of enabling the goods to be retained (*R v Kanwar* [1982] 2 All ER 528, 146 JP 283; *R v Sanders* [1982] Crim LR 695).

9 "Realisation" merely involves the exchange of the goods for money; and he who pays is just as much involved in the realisation as he who receives the payment (*R v Deakin* [1972] 3 All ER 803, 137 JP 19).

10 A person who has *bona fide* acquired goods for value does not commit an offence of dishonestly undertaking the disposal or realisation of stolen property for the benefit of another if when he sells the goods he knows or believes them to be stolen, because it is the purchase, not the sale, which is for the purchaser's benefit (*R v Bloxham* [1983] 1 AC 109, [1982] 1 All ER 582, 146 JP 201). The word "another" in s 22(1) cannot be construed to embrace a co-accused on the same charge (*R v Gingell* (1999) 163 JP 648, [2000] 1 Cr App Rep 88, CA).

11 This does not cover the situation where the goods are not yet stolen (*R v Park* [1988] Crim LR 238).

12 Triable either way; see the Magistrates' Courts Act 1980, s 17 and Sch 1; also ss 17A–21 (procedure) and s 32 (penalty) in PART I: MAGISTRATES' COURTS, PROCEDURE, ante.

7.11337 **23. Advertising rewards for return of goods stolen or lost** Where any public advertisement of a reward for the return of any goods which have been stolen[1] or lost uses any words to the effect that no questions will be asked, or that the person producing the goods will be safe from apprehension or inquiry, or that any money paid for the purchase of the goods or advanced by way of loan on them will be repaid, the person advertising the reward and any person who prints or publishes the advertisement shall on summary conviction be liable[2] to a fine not exceeding **level 3** on the standard scale.

[Theft Act 1968, s 23 as amended by the Criminal Justice Act 1982, ss 35 and 46.]

---

1 See s 24(4), post.

2 This is an offence of strict liability requiring no *mens rea* (*Denham v Scott* [1983] Crim LR 558).

7.11338 **24. Scope of offences relating to stolen goods*** (1) The provisions of this Act relating to goods which have been stolen shall apply whether the stealing occurred in England or Wales or elsewhere, and whether it occurred before or after the commencement of this Act, provided that the stealing (if not an offence under this Act) amounted to an offence where and at the time when the goods were stolen; and references to stolen goods shall be construed accordingly.

(2) For purposes of those provisions references to stolen goods shall include, in addition to the goods originally stolen and parts of them (whether in their original state or not)—

(*a*) any other goods which directly or indirectly represent or have at any time represented the stolen goods in the hands of the thief[1] as being the proceeds of any disposal or realisation of the whole or part of the goods stolen[2] or of goods so representing the stolen goods; and

(*b*) any other goods which directly or indirectly represent or have at any time represented the stolen goods in the hands of a handler of the stolen goods or any part of them as being the proceeds of any disposal or realisation of the whole or part of the stolen goods handled by him or of goods so representing them.

(3) But no goods shall be regarded as having continued to be stolen goods after they have been restored[3] to the person from whom they were stolen or to other lawful possession or custody, or after that person and any other person claiming through him have otherwise ceased as regards those goods to have any right to restitution in respect of the theft.

(4) For purposes of the provisions of this Act relating to goods which have been stolen

(including subsections (1) to (3) above) goods obtained in England or Wales or elsewhere either by blackmail or, subject to subsection (5) below, by fraud (within the meaning of the Fraud Act 2006) in the circumstances described in section 15(1) of this Act shall be regarded as stolen; and "steal", "theft" and "thief" shall be construed accordingly.

(5) Subsection (1) above applies in relation to goods obtained by fraud as if—

(*a*) the reference to the commencement of this Act were a reference to the commencement of the Fraud Act 2006, and

(*b*) the reference to an offence under this Act were a reference to an offence under section 1 of that Act.*

[Theft Act 1968, s 24 as amended by the Fraud Act 2006, Sch 1.]

---

* **Subsection (5) was added by para 6(2) of Sch 1 to the Fraud Act 2006, but without affecting the operation of s 24 in relation to goods obtained in the circumstances described in s 15(1) where the obtaining was a result of a deception made before the commencement of para 6, namely 15 January 2007: para 4 of Sch 2 to the Fraud Act 2006, in this PART, post, and the Fraud Act (Commencement) Order 2006, SI 2006/3200.**

1 The words "in the hands of the thief" mean in the possession or under the control of the thief (*R v Forsyth* [1997] 2 Crim App Rep 299, CA).

2 Where a person is tried on a charge of handling stolen goods, the jury is not entitled to infer that a sum of money paid by cheque to the receiver by the thief represents stolen goods within s 24(2)(*a*), if the inference is to be drawn merely from the receiver's intention or belief that the money should or did represent stolen goods (*Re A-G's Reference (No 4 of 1979)* [1981] 1 All ER 1193, [1981] Crim LR 51).

3 This means taken into possession and not merely kept under observation: see *A-G's Reference (No 1 of 1974)* [1974] QB 744, [1974] 2 All ER 899, 138 JP 570. See also *Greater London Metropolitan Police Comr v Streeter* (1980) 71 Cr App Rep 113 (carton initialled by security officer and kept under observation).

7.11339 **24A. Dishonestly retaining a wrongful credit*** (1) A person is guilty of an offence[1] if—

(*a*) a wrongful credit has been made to an account kept by him or in respect of which he has any right or interest;

(*b*) he knows or believes that the credit is wrongful; and

(*c*) he dishonestly fails to take such steps as are reasonable in the circumstances to secure that the credit is cancelled.

(2) References to a credit are to a credit of an amount of money.

(2A) A credit to an account is wrongful to the extent that it derives from—

(*a*) theft;

(*b*) blackmail;

(*c*) fraud (contrary to section 1 of the Fraud Act 2006); or

(*d*) stolen goods.

(3) *Repealed.*

(4) *Repealed.*

(5) In determining whether a credit to an account is wrongful, it is immaterial (in particular) whether the account is overdrawn before or after the credit is made.

(6) A person guilty of an offence under this section shall be liable on conviction on indictment to imprisonment for a term not exceeding **ten years**[1].

(7) Subsection (8) below applies for purposes of provisions of this Act relating to stolen goods (including subsection (2A) above).

(8) References to stolen goods include money which is dishonestly withdrawn from an account to which a wrongful credit has been made, but only to the extent that the money derives from the credit.

(9) "Account" means an account kept with—

(*a*) a bank;

(*b*) a person carrying on a business which falls within subsection (10) below; or

(*c*) an issuer of electronic money (as defined for the purposes of Part 2 of the Financial Services and Markets Act 2000).

(10) A business falls within this subsection if—

(*a*) in the course of the business money received by way of deposit is lent to others; or

(*b*) any other activity of the business is financed, wholly or to any material extent, out of the capital of or the interest on money received by way of deposit.

(11) References in subsection (10) above to a deposit must be read with—

(*a*) section 22 of the Financial Services and Markets Act 2000;

(*b*) any relevant order under that section; and

(*c*) Schedule 2 to that Act;

but any restriction on the meaning of deposit which arises from the identity of the person making it is to be disregarded.

(12) For the purposes of subsection (10) above—

(*a*) all the activities which a person carries on by way of business shall be regarded as a single business carried on by him; and

(*b*) "money" includes money expressed in a currency other than sterling.

[Theft Act 1968, s 24A as inserted by the Theft (Amendment) Act 1996, s 2 and amended by the Fraud Act 2006, Sch 1.]

---

* **The omission of sub-s (3) and (4) and the insertion of sub-s (2A) made by para 7 of Sch 1 to the Fraud Act 2006 does not affect the operation of sub-s (7) and (8) in relation to credits falling within the now omitted provisions and made before the commencement of para 7, namely 15 January 2007: para 4 of Sch 2 to the Fraud Act 2006, in this PART, post, and the Fraud Act (Commencement) Order 2006, SI 2006/3200.**

1 Triable either way; see the Magistrates' Courts Act 1980, s 17 and Sch 1; also ss 17A–21 (procedure) and s 32 (penalty) in PART I: MAGISTRATES' COURTS, PROCEDURE, ante.

*Possession of housebreaking implements, etc*

7.11340 **25. Going equipped for stealing, etc**[1] (1) A person shall be guilty of an offence if, when not at his place of abode[2], he has with him[3] any article for use[4] in the course of or in connection with any burglary or theft.

(2) A person guilty of an offence under this section shall on conviction on indictment be liable to imprisonment for a term not exceeding **three years**.

(3) Where a person is charged with an offence under this section, proof that he had with him any article made or adapted for use in committing a burglary or theft shall be evidence that he had it with him for such use[5].

(4) *Repealed.*

(5) For purposes of this section an offence under section 12(1) of this Act of taking a conveyance shall be treated as theft.

[Theft Act 1968, s 25 as amended by the Serious Organised Crime and Police Act 2005, Sch 7.]

---

1 This offence can be committed at any time of the day or night.

2 The phrase "place of abode" means a site at which the occupier intends to abide. Therefore, a person who is living rough in a car is at his place of abode when on a site with the intention of abiding there, but not when the vehicle is in transit from one site to another (*R v Bundy* [1977] 2 All ER 382, 141 JP 345).

3 In a case under the equivalent provisions of previous legislation it was held that possession must be actual and not constructive and possession after arrest was not sufficient (*R v Harris* (1925) 89 JP 37); see also *R v Hatch* (1933) 24 Cr App Rep 100. A person in possession of counterfeit shirts at a bonded warehouse had them "with him" when in person he displayed them to undercover agents (*Re McAngus* [1994] Crim LR 602). The possession of housebreaking implements by one of two or more persons acting in concert was held to be possession by all (*R v Thompson* (1869) 33 JP 791).

4 The prosecution must prove that the defendant had the article for use in some *future* burglary, theft or cheat, though it is not necessary to prove that the defendant intended to use it himself (*R v Ellames* [1974] 3 All ER 130, 138 JP 682). There is no reason why a person should not be charged with an offence under this section as well as with attempted theft or theft where the circumstances in which he was in possession of the article were those of an attempt or of the completed crime; see *Minor v DPP* (1987) 152 JP 30, 86 Cr App Rep 378. A person who has not decided whether to use an article, which he has with him, should an opportunity present itself, does not have the necessary intention required for an offence under this section (*R v Hargreaves* [1985] Crim LR 243, CA).

5 Once possession of this sort of article has been proved the accused has an evidential burden to show that the article was in his possession for purposes other than burglary, theft or cheat.

*Enforcement and procedure*

7.11341 **26. Search for stolen goods** (1) If it is made to appear by information[1] on oath before a justice of the peace that there is reasonable cause to believe that any person has in his custody or possession or on his premises any stolen goods, the justice[2] may grant a warrant[2] to search for and seize the same[3]; but no warrant to search for stolen goods shall be addressed to a person other than a constable except under the authority of an enactment expressly so providing.

(2) *Repealed.*

(3) Where under this section a person is authorised to search premises for stolen goods, he may enter and search the premises accordingly, and may seize any goods[4], he believes to be stolen goods[5].

(4) *Repealed.*

(5) This section is to be construed in accordance with section 24 of this Act; and in subsection (2) above the references to handling stolen goods shall include any corresponding offence committed before the commencement of this Act[6].

[Theft Act 1968, s 26 as amended by the Criminal Justice Act 1972, Sch 6 and the Police and Criminal Evidence Act 1984, Sch 7.]

---

1 The information that a person has stolen goods in his possession may be sworn by any person. It is not necessary to state in the information that an offence has been actually committed (*Elsee v Smith* (1822) 1 Dow & Ry KB 97), or to specify the particular goods to be searched for (*Jones v German* [1897] 1 QB 374, 61 JP 180).

2 The issue and execution of this warrant must conform to the Police and Criminal Evidence Act 1984, ss 15 and 16 in PART I: MAGISTRATES' COURTS, PROCEDURE, ante.

3 See Precedent for search warrant in PART VIII: PRECEDENTS AND FORMS, post.

4 Even if they are not the suspected stolen goods. This provision preserves the law as laid down in *Chic Fashions (West Wales) Ltd v Jones* [1968] 2 QB 299, [1968] 1 All ER 229, 132 JP 175.

5 Section 26 is not limited solely to the purpose of enabling the police or other authorities to recover stolen property and the provisions are to be read as they are set out; the warrant is concerned primarily with search, seizure is permitted by subsection (3) and the fact that the warrant does not expressly state that property can be seized does not in any way invalidate it. The applicant is obliged to provide the material required by s 15 of PACE and it is that material which the justice has to consider in determining whether or not he is persuaded to grant the warrant: *R (on the application of R Cruickshank Ltd) v Chief Constable of Kent* [2001] EWHC Admin 123, [2001] Crim LR 990.

6 Ie, offences of receiving under the Larceny Act 1916.

7.11342 **27. Evidence and procedure on charge of theft or handling stolen goods** (1) Any number of persons may be charged in one indictment[1], with reference to the same theft, with having at different times or at the same time handled all or any of the stolen goods, and the persons so charged may be tried together.

(2) On the trial of two or more persons indicted[1] for jointly handling any stolen goods the jury may find any of the accused guilty if the jury are satisfied that he handled all or any of the stolen goods, whether or not he did so jointly with the other accused or any of them.

(3) Where a person is being proceeded against for handling stolen goods (but not for any offence other than handling stolen goods)[2], then at any stage of the proceedings, if evidence has been given of his having or arranging to have in his possession the goods the subject of the charge, or of his undertaking or assisting in, or arranging to undertake or assist in, their retention, removal, disposal or realisation, the following evidence shall be admissible for the purpose of proving that he knew or believed the goods to be stolen goods:

- (*a*) evidence that he has had in his possession[3], or has undertaken or assisted in the retention, removal, disposal or realisation of, stolen goods from any theft taking place not earlier than twelve months before the offence charged; and
- (*b*) (provided that seven days' notice in writing has been given to him of the intention to prove the conviction) evidence that he has within the five years preceding the date of the offence charged been convicted of theft or of handling stolen goods[4].

(4) In any proceedings for the theft of anything in the course of transmission (whether by post or otherwise), or for handling stolen goods from such a theft, a statutory declaration made by any person that he despatched or received or failed to receive any goods or postal packet, or that any goods or postal packet when despatched or received by him were in a particular state or condition, shall be admissible as evidence of the facts stated in the declaration, subject to the following conditions:

- (*a*) a statutory declaration shall only be admissible where and to the extent to which oral evidence to the like effect would have been admissible in the proceedings; and
- (*b*) a statutory declaration shall only be admissible if at least seven days before the hearing or trial a copy of it has been given to the person charged, and he has not, at least three days before the hearing or trial or within such further time as the court may in special circumstances allow, given the prosecutor written notice requiring the attendance at the hearing or trial of the person making the declaration.

(4A) Where the proceedings mentioned in subsection (4) above are proceedings before a magistrates' court inquiring into an offence as examining justices that subsection shall have effect with the omission of the words from "subject to the following conditions" to the end of the subsection.*

(5) This section is to be construed in accordance with section 24 of this Act; and in subsection (3)(*b*) above the reference to handling stolen goods shall include any corresponding offence committed before the commencement of this Act[5].

[Theft Act 1968, s 27 as amended by the Criminal Procedure and Investigations Act 1996, Sch 1.]

---

* **Subsection (4A) repealed by the Criminal Justice Act 2003, Schs 3 and 37 from a date to be appointed.**

1 These provisions do not apply to summary trial.

2 This exclusion preserves the principle laid down in *R v Davies* [1953] 1 QB 489, [1953] 1 All ER 341, 117 JP 121.

3 Proof may be by circumstantial evidence; see for example *R v Sbarra* (1919) 13 Cr App Rep 118 (goods delivered in the middle of the night to a side door); *R v Fuschillo* [1940] 2 All ER 489 ("This means going away"). A lie told by the accused as to where he acquired property is insufficient evidence that it was stolen (*Cohen v March* [1951] 2 TLR 402).

This section does not authorise the introduction of evidence as to the circumstances in which the stolen goods were found, nor explanations made by the defendant at that time (*R v Wood* [1987] 1 WLR 779). Such evidence ought not to be admitted if the real offence charged is theft and not handling, or if there is no evidence that the property found was stolen (*R v Girod and Girod* (1906) 70 JP 514; *R v Harding* (1909) 53 Sol Jo 762). Evidence of the thief that he has sold stolen property to the defendant at any previous time is admissible to prove guilty knowledge; it is not affected by the time limit in this subsection (*R v Powell* (1909) 3 Cr App Rep 1).

4 Admissibility under this subsection is directed to proof of guilty knowledge; if guilty knowledge is not a live issue in the trial the evidence may not be admitted (*R v Herron* [1967] 1 QB 107, [1966] 2 All ER 26, 130 JP 266); nor should it be admitted where it would be only of minimal assistance (*R v Perry* [1984] Crim LR 680 or where the only issue is one of dishonesty (*R v Duffus* (1993) 158 JP 224). Where the defence is based on a substantial additional point, eg, that the accused did not have possession of the property alleged to have been received or that property of which he had possession is not clearly identified as that which was stolen, evidence under this subsection may be excluded, at the court's discretion, on the ground that its prejudicial effect would outweigh its probative value (*R v Herron, supra*; *R v List* [1965] 3 All ER 710, 130 JP 30; *R v Wilkins* [1975] 2 All ER 734, 139 JP 543).

A certificate of a previous conviction adduced and admitted in evidence should, where the conviction was on indictment, state the substance and effect, omitting the formal parts, of the indictment and conviction, and where the previous indictment and conviction were for stealing or handling a car, the reference to the car is not a formal part but is of the substance of the indictment and the conviction. If a conviction on summary trial was for stealing or handling a car, the certificate should record that fact, and the whole of the certificate is admissible (*R v Hacker* [1995] 1 All ER 45, [1994] 1 WLR 1659, 159 JP 62, HL).

5 Ie offences of receiving under the Larceny Act 1916.

7.11343 **30. Spouses and civil partners** (1) This Act shall apply in relation to the parties to a marriage, and to property belonging to the wife or husband whether or not by reason of an interest derived from the marriage, as it would apply if they were not married and any such interest subsisted independently of the marriage[1].

(2) Subject to subsection (4) below, a person shall have the same right to bring proceedings against that person's wife or husband for any offence (whether under this Act or otherwise) as if they were not married[2], and a person bringing any such proceedings shall be competent to give evidence for the prosecution at every stage of the proceedings.*

(3) *Repealed.*

(4) Proceedings shall not be instituted against a person for any offence of stealing or doing unlawful damage to property[3] which at the time of the offence belongs to that person's wife or husband or civil partner, or for any attempt, incitement or conspiracy to commit such an offence, unless the proceedings are instituted by or with the consent[4] of the Director of Public Prosecutions. Provided that—

- (*a*) this subsection shall not apply to proceedings against a person for an offence—
  - (i) if that person is charged with committing the offence jointly with the wife or husband or civil partner;
  - (ii) if by virtue of any judicial decree or order (wherever made) that person and the wife or husband are at the time of the offence under no obligation to cohabit; or
  - (iii) an order (wherever made) is in force providing for the separation of that person and his or her civil partner.
- (*b*) *Repealed.*

(5) Notwithstanding section 6 of the Prosecution of Offences Act 1979[5] subsection (4) of this section shall apply—

- (*a*) to an arrest (if without warrant) made by the wife or husband or civil partner, and
- (*b*) to a warrant of arrest issued on an information laid by the wife or husband or civil partner.

[Theft Act 1968, s 30 as amended by the Criminal Jurisdiction Act 1975, Sch 5, the Prosecution of Offences Act 1979, Sch 1, the Police and Criminal Evidence Act 1984, Sch 7 and the Civil Partnership Act 2004, Sch 27.]

* **Words repealed by the Youth Justice and Criminal Evidence Act 1999, Sch 6, from a date to be appointed.**

1 The effect of this provision is to enable one spouse to prosecute the other for an offence under the Act even if they are living together.

2 The effect of this provision is to enable one spouse to prosecute the other for *any* offence (whether under the Theft Act or otherwise).

3 For example, under s 1(1) of the Criminal Damage Act 1971; see *R v Withers* [1975] Crim LR 647.

4 Consent is not required if the husband and wife are, by virtue of a judicial decree or order, no longer bound to cohabit (*Woodley v Woodley* [1978] Crim LR 629).

5 The effect of this would appear to be that the appropriate consent must be obtained before arrest, issue or execution of a warrant or remand. The 1979 Act has been repealed and replaced by the Prosecution of Offences Act 1985, s 25(2) in PART I: MAGISTRATES' COURTS, PROCEDURE, ante.

7.11344 **31. Effect on civil proceedings and rights** (1) A person shall not be excused, by reason that to do so may incriminate that person or the spouse or civil partner of that person of an offence under this Act—

- (*a*) from answering any question put to that person in proceedings for the recovery or administration of any property[1], for the execution of any trust or for an account of any property or dealings with property; or
- (*b*) from complying with any order made in any such proceedings;

but no statement or admission made by a person in answering a question put or complying with an order made as aforesaid shall, in proceedings for an offence under this Act, be admissible in evidence against that person or (unless they married or became civil partners after the making of the statement or admission) against thespouse or civil partner of that person.

(2) Notwithstanding any enactment to the contrary, where property has been stolen or obtained by fraud or other wrongful means, the title to that or any other property shall not be affected by reason only of the conviction of the offender[2].

[Theft Act 1968, s 31 as amended by the Civil Partnership Act 2004, Sch 27.]

1 Self-incriminating statements made by a bankrupt during his public examination can be used against him in criminal proceedings (*R v Kansal* [1993] QB 244, [1992] 3 All ER 844).

2 Under the provisions of this section, questions of title to property will be left to the Civil Law.

7.11345 **32. Effect on existing law and construction of references to offences** (1) The following offences are hereby abolished for all purposes not relating to offences committed before the commencement of this Act, that is to say—

- (*a*) any offence at common law of larceny, robbery, burglary, receiving stolen property, obtaining property by threats, extortion by colour of office or franchise, false accounting by public officers, concealment of treasure trove and, except as regards offences relating to the public revenue[1], cheating[2]; and
- (*b*) any offence under an enactment mentioned in Part I of Schedule 3 to this Act, to the extent to which the offence depends on any section or part of a section included in column 3 of that Schedule;

but so that the provisions in Schedule 1 to this Act (which preserve with modifications certain offences under the Larceny Act 1861 of taking or killing deer and taking or destroying fish) shall have effect as there set out.

(2) Except as regards offences committed before the commencement of this Act, and except in so far as the context otherwise requires—

- (*a*) references in any enactment passed before this Act to an offence abolished by this Act shall, subject to any express amendment or repeal made by this Act, have effect as references to the corresponding offence under this Act, and in any such enactment the expression "receive" (when it relates to an offence of receiving) shall mean handle, and "receiver" shall be construed accordingly; and

(*b*) without prejudice to paragraph (*a*) above, references in any enactment, whenever passed, to theft or stealing (including references to stolen goods), and references to robbery, blackmail, burglary, aggravated burglary or handling stolen goods, shall be construed in accordance with the provisions of this Act, including those of section 24.

[Theft Act 1968, s 32.]

1 The common law offence of cheating the revenue is still available even when the facts show that a statutory offence has ben committed; the common law offence may be satisfied by matters of omission, a positive act of deception directed against the revenue is not required (*R v Redford* (1988) 89 Cr App Rep 1, CA). See also *R v Mulligan* [1990] STC 220, [1990] Crim LR 427, CA.

2 This subsection is not to be construed as meaning that cheating at common law could not be charged where there was available a statutory offence; also, one can cheat by omission (*R v Redford* [1988] STC 845, 89 Cr App Rep 1, CA).

7.11346 **33. Miscellaneous and consequential amendments, and repeal** (1) *Repealed.*

(2) The enactments mentioned in Parts II and III of Schedule 2 to this Act shall have effect subject to the amendments there provided for, and (subject to subsection (4) below) the amendments made by Part II to enactments extending beyond England and Wales shall have the like extent as the enactment amended.

(3) The enactments mentioned in Schedule 3 to this Act (which include in Part II certain enactments related to the subject matter of this Act but already obsolete or redundant apart from this Act) are hereby repealed to the extent specified in column 3 of that Schedule; and, notwithstanding that the foregoing sections of this Act do not extend to Scotland, where any enactment expressed to be repealed by Schedule 3 does so extend, the Schedule shall have effect to repeal it in its application to Scotland except in so far as the repeal is expressed not to extend to Scotland.

(4) No amendment or repeal made by this Act in Schedule 1 to the Extradition Act 1870 or in the Schedule to the Extradition Act 1873 shall affect the operation of that Schedule by reference to the law of a British Possession; but the repeal made in Schedule 1 to the Extradition Act 1870 shall extend throughout the United Kingdom.

[Theft Act 1968, s 33 as amended by SI 2001/1149.]

*Supplementary*

7.11347 **34. Interpretation** (1) Sections 4(1) and 5(1) of this Act shall apply generally for purposes of this Act as they apply for purposes of section 1[1].

(2) For purposes of this Act—

(*a*) "gain" and "loss" are to be construed[2] as extending only to gain or loss in money or other property, but as extending to any such gain or loss whether temporary or permanent; and—

(i) "gain" includes a gain by keeping what one has, as well as a gain by getting what one has not; and

(ii) "loss" includes a loss by not getting what one might get, as well as a loss by parting with what one has;

(*b*) "goods", except in so far as the context otherwise requires, includes[3] money and every other description of property except land[4], and includes things severed from the land by stealing; and

(*c*) "mail bag" and "postal packet" have the meanings given by section 125(1) of the Postal Services Act 2000.

[Theft Act 1968, s 34 as amended by SI 2003/2908.]

1 Section 1 is the general definition of the offence of theft.

2 The definitions of "gain" and "loss" are material to the offences under ss 17(1) (destroying or defacing accounts or producing a false misleading or deceptive account), 20(1) and (2) (suppression, etc, of documents) and 21(1) (blackmail). A person who demands money that is undoubtedly owed to him does so with a view to gain by intending to obtain hard cash as opposed to a mere right of action in respect of the debt (*R v Parkes* [1973] Crim LR 358, followed in *A-G's Reference (No 1 of 2001)* [2002] EWCA Crim 1768, [2002] 3 All ER 840, [2002] Crim LR 844).

3 The definition of "goods" is material for the purposes of the offence of handling stolen goods under s 22 and the related ss 23, 24, 26 and 27. It also applies to the word "goods" in the provisions as to restitution orders in s 28.

4 Since land is excluded from the definition of goods, the offence of "handling" does not apply to land or the proceeds of stolen land.

## SCHEDULES

### SCHEDULE 1
OFFENCES OF TAKING, ETC DEER OR FISH — Section 32.

*(As amended by the Deer Act 1980, s 9, the Criminal Justice Act 1982, ss 35, 38 and 46 and the Marine and Coastal Access Act 2009, s 228, Sch 22.)*

*Taking or killing deer*

7.11348 **1.** *Repealed.*

*Taking or destroying fish*

**2.** (1) A person who unlawfully takes[1] or destroys, or attempts to take or destroy, any fish[2] in water which is private property[3] or in which there is any private[4] right of fishery shall on summary conviction be liable to a fine not exceeding level 5 on the standard scale.

(2) *Repealed.*

(3) The court by which a person is convicted of an offence under sub-paragraph (1) above may order the forfeiture of anything which, at the time of the offence, he had with him for use for taking or destroying fish.

(4) Any person may arrest without warrant anyone who is, or whom he, with reasonable cause, suspects to be, committing an offence under subparagraph (1) above, and may seize from any person who is, or whom he, with reasonable cause, suspects to be, committing any offence under this paragraph anything which on that person's conviction of the offence would be liable to be forfeited under subparagraph (3) above.*

* **Repealed by the Serious Organised Crime and Police Act 2005, Sch 7 in so far as it confers a power of arrest without warrant on a constable or persons in general.**

[1] There need be no "*mens rea*", no asportation: the taker may intend to keep the fish in a keep net and return them to the water at the end of his fishing (*Wells v Hardy* [1964] 2 QB 447, [1964] 1 All ER 953, 128 JP 238).

[2] Crayfish are included (*Caygill v Thwaite* (1885) 49 JP 614). So are winkles (*Leavett v Clark* [1915] 3 KB 9, 79 JP 396).

[3] The public cannot by prescription or otherwise obtain a legal right to fish in a non-tidal river even though it be navigable (*Smith v Andrews* [1891] 2 Ch 678). Proof of uninterrupted custom for sixty years and upwards to fish by angling from a public footpath running along the river bank of a non-navigable and non-tidal river did not support a claim on the part of the defendant, as one of the public, to fish in the river, as such a right could not possibly be acquired (*Hudson v MacRae* (1863) 4 B & S 585, 28 JP 436). But in *R v Stimpson* (1863) 4 B & S 301, where the defendant contended that he and the public had a right of fishing in a navigable *tidal* river, and proved by witnesses they had fished it for many years without interruption, it was held there was reasonable evidence to show that the question of title raised by the defendant was *bonâ fide*.

The public have no right to fish in a river made navigable by Act of Parliament but not tidal, although they have fished in it as of right for many years without interruption; the navigation is private property, subject to certain limited rights on the part of the public (*Hargreaves v Diddams* (1875) LR 10 QB 582, 40 JP 167). "That is called an arm of the sea where the sea flows and reflows and so far only as the sea flows and reflows;" "and only in such waters is there *prima facie* a right of fishing common to all" (HALE, *De jure Maris*, p 12). Upon exceptionally high tides the rising of the salt water in the lower part of the river Wye dammed back the fresh water and caused it to rise and fall with the flow and ebb of the tide, but the salt water did not reach the place where the public claimed a right to fish, and it was held that the place was not a tidal river within the meaning of the rule of law (*Reece v Miller* (1882) 8 QBD 626). KEKEWICH, J, held that a creek to be navigable in the legal sense of the term must be affected by the ebb and flow of ordinary or mean tides (*Earl of Ilchester v Raishleigh* (1890) 61 LT 477). Where there was some evidence to support the finding of the justices that the water of a Norfolk Broad (Wroxham) was not part of a tidal navigable river, the QB Division would not interfere with a conviction (*Blower v Ellis* (1886) 50 JP 326, Treat 338). A similar question was raised as to another Norfolk Broad (Hickling), when ROMER, J, held the public had a right of way over it, but no right to shoot or fish (*Mickelthwait v Vincent* (1892) 67 LT 225). It was expressly decided in the case of *Murphy v Ryan* (1868) IR 2 CL 143, that the public cannot acquire by immemorial usage any right to fish in a navigable river above the flow of the tide, and that the fishery belonged to the riparian owners, who could, if they pleased, prohibit the public any longer going there. But COCKBURN, CJ, in *R v Burrow* (1869) 34 JP 53, was not prepared to assent to that decision without further argument, and the conviction, which was for fishing in the Ullswater lake, was quashed. The QB Division has, however, since confirmed *Murphy v Ryan*, and held that *Hargreaves v Diddams, supra*, in which upon the argument reference was made to *Murphy v Ryan* and *R v Burrow*, put an end to any doubt thrown upon the Irish case (*Mussett v Burch* (1876) 41 JP 72). The last quoted case was for fishing from private land in the river Stour, a navigable river used by means of locks. The same rule of law was followed as to the Dee at Craigpool, Denbighshire, about 30 miles above the tidal flow, where the river is public and navigable for small craft; a *bonâ fide* claim of right was set up, and evidence was given that the public had not been interfered with for forty years and upwards when fishing in this part of the river, but the QB Division held justices were wrong in not convicting, for it was impossible that the public could acquire such a right (*Pearce v Scotcher* (1882) 9 QBD 162, 46 JP 248). The case of *R v Burrows, supra*, was again quoted and relied on, but was disregarded by the court: the *dictum* of COCKBURN, CJ, in that case may, therefore, be considered erroneous. The point has been, moreover, conclusively settled by *Reece v Miller, supra*, where the actual point argued was whether the river Wye was tidal at the spot in question, but the court being of opinion that the river was not tidal there, affirmed the conviction for unlawful fishing. An injunction was granted restraining a person from interfering with posts and chains which the owner of the bed of the river Mole, a non-tidal river running into the Thames, had placed in the river to stop the waterway. Evidence was given of the long use of the river for boating purposes, but the court held the use had been permissive (*Bourke v Davis* (1889) 44 Ch D 110).

The "dwellers" in a parish or manor cannot acquire a right of piscary, but the commoners of a manor, and probably the occupiers of their customary tenements may have such a right by custom of the manor (*Allgood v Gibson* (1876) 34 LT 883; see also *Lord Rivers v Adam* (1878) 3 Ex D 361); and it has been held by the House of Lords that the "uninterrupted enjoyment from time immemorial by the free inhabitants of ancient tenements", within a borough of dredging for oysters on certain days in a year, was sufficient to raise a presumption of the lawful origin of the usage (*Goodman v Saltash Corpn* (1882) 7 App Cas 633, 47 JP 276). As far back as living memory extended outfishing had been carried on in a tidal navigable river without interference from the plaintiff or his predecessors; but it was held this did not take away the right to a several fishery, which could only pass by deed (*Neill v Duke of Devonshire* (1882) 8 App Cas 135, HL).

The Crown has no *de jure* right to the soil or fisheries of an inland non-tidal lake (*Bristow v Cormican* (1878) 3 App Cas 641). The Court of Appeal has also held that the Crown never had anything to do with private fisheries; and as it could not exclude the owner of the soil from a private river, it certainly could not grant the fishery as a separate tenement to another. The presumption that half of the river fishery in a non-tidal river passes with the grant of the riparian lands may be rebutted (*Duke of Devonshire v Pattison* (1887) 20 QBD 263, 52 JP 276, Treat, 306). The executive right of fishing in tidal waters vested in the Crown is no more than an incidence of the soil over which the water flows (*Duke of Devonshire v Neill* (1876) 2 LR Ir 132). The grant of an exclusive right to fish in a river conveys the right irrespective of the ownership of the soil over which the water flows (*Foster v Wright* (1878) 4 CPD 438, 44 JP 7). The Crown or an individual can grant by deed a several fishery held by the Crown, or the individual before Magna Carta (*Neill v Duke of Devonshire, supra*). A several fishery in a navigable tidal river could only have been legally created by grant from the Crown before Magna Carta; the use of stop nets in such rivers was prohibited by 2 Hen 6, c 15, and such nets are illegal unless they were lawfully used before that statute. For an instance of such a grant, see *Stephens v Snell* [1939] 3 All ER 622. See *Holford v George* (1868) LR 3 QB 639, 32 JP 468; as to evidence of a several fishery in a public navigable river, see *Edgar v English Fisheries Special Comrs* (1870) 35 JP 822, and *Goodman v Saltash Corpn* (1882) 7 App Cas 633, 47 JP 276, HL; and as to evidence of a several fishery in the non-tidal part of a river, see *Powell v Heffernan* (1881) 8 LR Ir 130. The cases dealing with the right of owners of several fisheries were considered by the Court of Appeal in *Hindson v Ashby* [1896] 2 Ch 1, 60 JP 484, where a question was argued as to the ownership of the bed of a river upon recession of the water. See also *Hanbury v Jenkins* [1901] 2 Ch 401, 65 JP 631.

[4] A right of fishery can be conveyed only by deed; the ownership of the right must be proved (*Halse v Alder* (1874) 38 JP 407).

By a lease of land through which a river flows, the right of fishing, unless expressly reserved to the lessor, passes to the tenant, and the lessor cannot prosecute persons for unlawfully taking fish (*Jones v Davies* (1902) 66 JP 439).

# Theft Act 1978

(1978 c 31)

7.11349 1. **Obtaining services by deception*** (1) A person who by any deception dishonestly obtains services from another shall be guilty of an offence.

(2) It is an obtaining of services[1] where the other is induced to confer a benefit by doing some act, or causing or permitting some act to be done, on the understanding[2] that the benefit has been or will be paid for.

(3) Without prejudice to the generality of subsection (2) above, it is an obtaining of services where the other is induced to make a loan, or to cause or permit a loan to be made, on the understanding that any payment (whether by way of interest or otherwise) will be or has been made in respect of the loan.

[Theft Act 1978, s 1 as amended by the Theft (Amendment) Act 1996, s 4.]

---

* **The repeal of this and other deception offences by the Fraud Act 2006 does not affect any liability, investigation, legal proceeding or penalty for or in respect of any offence partly committed before 15 January 2007: para 3 of Sch 2 to the Fraud Act 2006, in this Part, post, and Fraud Act (Commencement) Order 2006, SI 2006/3200. As to the meaning of "partly committed", see sub-paras (2) and (3).**

[1] Obtaining a credit card or the opening of a bank account provides access to bank services which underlie the use of an account or a credit card. Therefore, the dishonest opening of a bank account or the obtaining of a credit card by deception can constitute obtaining services by deception as can the dishonest operation of a bank account over a period or the dishonest use of a credit card (*R v Sofroniou* [2003] EWCA Crim 3681, [2004] QB 1218, [2004] 1 Cr App R 35, [2004] Crim LR 381).

[2] This is intended to cover situations where nothing explicitly is said about payment, but where there is a common, objective, understanding that the service will not be provided gratuitously (even though the defendant might not have a subjective intention to make payment) (*R v Sofroniou* [2003] EWCA Crim 3681, [2004] QB 1218, [2004] 1 Cr App R 35, [2004] Crim LR 381).

7.11350 2. **Evasion of liability by deception*** (1) [1] Subject to subsection (2) below, where a person by any deception—

(*a*) dishonestly secures the remission of the whole or part of any existing liability to make a payment, whether his own liability or another's; or

(*b*) with intent to make permanent default in whole or in part on any existing liability[2] to make a payment, or with intent to let another do so, dishonestly induces the creditor or any person claiming payment on behalf of the creditor to wait for payment (whether or not the due date for payment is deferred) or to forgo payment; or

(*c*) dishonestly obtains any exemption from or abatement of liability to make a payment[3];

he shall be guilty of an offence.

(2) For purposes of this section "liability" means legally enforceable liability; and subsection (1) shall not apply in relation to a liability that has not been accepted or established to pay compensation for a wrongful act or omission.

(3) For purposes of subsection (1)(*b*) a person induced to take in payment a cheque or other security for money by way of conditional satisfaction of a pre-existing liability is to be treated not as being paid but as being induced to wait for payment.

(4) For purposes of subsection (1)(*c*) "obtains" includes obtaining for another or enabling another to obtain.

[Theft Act 1978, s 2.]

---

* **The repeal of this and other deception offences by the Fraud Act 2006 does not affect any liability, investigation, legal proceeding or penalty for or in respect of any offence partly committed before 15 January 2007: para 3 of Sch 2 to the Fraud Act 2006, in this Part, post, and the Fraud Act (Commencement) Order 2006, SI 2006/3200. As to the meaning of "partly committed", see sub-paras (2) and (3).**

[1] For consideration of the provisions of s 2(1), see *R v Holt* [1981] 2 All ER 854, [1981] 1 WLR 1000; considered in *R v Jackson* [1983] Crim LR 617.

[2] The fact that an agreement is not enforceable without a court order does not mean there is no existing liability (*R v Modupe* [1991] Crim LR 530—improperly executed consumer credit agreement). An offence may be committed by a defendant either intending to make permanent default in respect of a personal liability or by intending to enable another to make permanent default in respect of that other's liability (*R v Attewell-Hughes* [1991] 4 All ER 810, [1991] 1 WLR 955, 155 JP 828, CA).

[3] As to the relationship of paragraphs (*a*), (*b*) and (*c*), see *R v Sibartie* [1983] Crim LR 470. For the purpose of paragraph (*c*), the deception may take the form of an act of commission or omission; see *R v Firth* (1989) 154 JP 576, 91 Cr App Rep 217, CA.

7.11351 3. **Making off without payment** (1) Subject to subsection (3) below, a person who, knowing that payment on the spot for any goods supplied or service done is required or expected[1] from him, dishonestly makes off[2] without having paid as required or expected and with intent[3] to avoid payment of the amount due shall be guilty of an offence[3].

(2) For purposes of this section "payment on the spot" includes payment at the time of collecting goods on which work has been done or in respect of which service has been provided.

(3) Subsection (1) above shall not apply where the supply of the goods or the doing of the

service is contrary to law, or where the service done is such that payment is not legally enforceable[4].

(4) *Repealed.*

[Theft Act 1978, s 3 as amended by the Serious Organised Crime and Police Act 2005, Sch 7.]

---

[1] Where an agreement has been made to defer payment, that agreement will defeat the normal expectation of payment on the spot. As this subsection is intended to create a simple and straightforward offence, an analysis of whether the agreement was obtained by deception is neither required nor permitted. The fact that the agreement was obtained dishonestly does not reinstate the expectation (*R v Vincent* [2001] EWCA Crim 295, [2001] 1 WLR 1172, [2001] 2 Cr App Rep 150, CA).

[2] "Making off" involves a departure from the spot where payment is required (*R v Brooks* (1983) 76 Cr App Rep 66); a breach of contract by the party claiming payment may mean that the defendant may not have been in a situation in which he was bound to pay or even tender the money, thus cannot be charged with making off (*Troughton v Metropolitan Police* [1987] Crim LR 138). The words "dishonestly makes off without payment" are not qualified in any way; the words "makes off" involve a departure without paying from the place where payment would normally be made. In the case of a taxi, payment might be made while sitting in the taxi or standing by the window. Payment might be requested whilst the fares are still in the cab and at this stage the fares might be disputed. The fact that the taxi driver then drives off to a police station, or somewhere else, locking the door, does not mean that when the defendant runs off he could not be making off without having paid, dishonestly intending to avoid payment. It is the time at which he makes off which is critical at which he had to have formed the intention to avoid payment. But to apply the words too literally would be to misunderstand the legislation. Thus, if a passenger were to explain (honestly) to the taxi driver that he had to enter his house in order to obtain the fare, the moment for payment would be deferred for him to do so. A decision not to return to the taxi would mean that, from that moment, the passenger is making off without payment. See *R v Morris* [2013] EWCA Crim 436, [2014] 1 WLR 16, [2013] 2 Cr App R 89.

[3] There must be an intention permanently to avoid payment or to avoid payment altogether and not merely an intent to delay or defer payment (*R v Allen* [1985] AC 1029, [1985] 2 All ER 641, 149 JP 587, HL).

[4] For example, where the person providing a service is in breach of contract; see *Troughton v Metropolitan Police* [1987] Crim LR 138 (taxi driver not completing journey).

7.11352 4. **Punishments** (1) Offences under this Act shall be punishable either on conviction on indictment or on summary conviction.

(2) A person convicted on indictment shall be liable—

(*a*) for an offence under section 1 or section 2 of this Act, to imprisonment for a term not exceeding **five years**; and

(*b*) for an offence under section 3 of this Act, to imprisonment for a term not exceeding **two years**.

(3) A person convicted summarily of any offence under this Act shall be liable[1]—

(*a*) to imprisonment for a term not exceeding **six months**; or

(*b*) to a fine not exceeding **the prescribed sum** for the purposes of section 32 of the Magistrates' Courts Act 1980 (punishment on summary conviction of offences triable either way: £1,000[2] or other sum substituted by order under that Act), or to **both**.*

[Theft Act 1978, s 4 as amended by the Magistrates' Courts Act 1980, Sch 7.]

---

* **The repeal of subsection (2)(*a*) by the Fraud Act 2006 does not affect any penalty for or in respect of any offence partly committed before 15 January 2007: para 3 of Sch 2 to the Fraud Act 2006, in this Part, post, and the Fraud Act (Commencement) Order 2006, SI 2006/3200. As to the meaning of "partly committed", see sub-paras (2) and (3).**

[1] For procedure in respect of an offence triable either way, see the Magistrates' Courts Act 1980, ss 17A–21, in PART I: MAGISTRATES' COURTS, PROCEDURE, ante.

[2] For the current amount of "the prescribed sum", see the Magistrates' Courts Act 1980, s 32(9), in PART I: MAGISTRATES' COURTS, PROCEDURE, ante.

7.11353 5. **Supplementary** (1) For purposes of sections 1 and 2 above "deception" has the same meaning as in section 15 of the Theft Act 1968, that is to say, it means any deception (whether deliberate or reckless) by words or conduct as to fact or as to law, including a deception as to the present intentions of the person using the deception or any other person; and section 18 of that Act (liability of company officers for offences by the company) shall apply in relation to sections 1 and 2 above as it applies in relation to section 15 of that Act.*

(2) Sections 30(1) (husband and wife), 31(1) (effect on civil proceedings) and 34 (interpretation) of the Theft Act 1968, so far as they are applicable in relation to this Act, shall apply as they apply in relation to that Act.

(4)–(5) *Visiting Forces Act 1952; Repeal provisions.*

[Theft Act 1978, s 5 as amended by the Criminal Justice Act 1988, Sch 16 and the Extradition Act, Sch 2.]

---

* **Subsection (1) repealed by the Fraud Act 2006, Sch 3. See note to sections 1, 2 ante.**

# Fraud Act 2006[1]

(2006 c 35)

*Fraud*

7.11354 1. **Fraud** (1) A person is guilty of fraud if he is in breach of any of the sections listed in subsection (2) (which provide for different ways of committing the offence).

(2) The sections are—

(*a*) section 2 (fraud by false representation[2]),

(*b*) section 3 (fraud by failing to disclose information), and

(*c*) section 4 (fraud by abuse of position).

(3) A person who is guilty of fraud is liable—

(a) on summary conviction, to imprisonment for a term not exceeding 12 months or to a fine not exceeding the statutory maximum (or to both);

(b) on conviction on indictment, to imprisonment for a term not exceeding 10 years or to a fine (or to both)[3].

(4) Subsection (3)(a) applies in relation to Northern Ireland as if the reference to 12 months were a reference to 6 months.

[Fraud Act 2006, s 1.]

---

[1] This Act provides for a general offence of fraud, which may be committed by: (a) false representation; (b) failing to disclose information; and (c) abuse of position. It creates new offences of obtaining services dishonestly and of possessing, making and supplying articles for use in fraud. It also contains a new offence, which parallels the offence of fraudulent trading in s 458 of the Companies Act 1986 and extends it to non-corporate businesses.

The Act further repeals the deception offences contained in ss 15, 15A, 16 and 20(2) of the Theft Act 1968 (and the corresponding provisions in relation to Northern Ireland), and ss 1 and 2 of the Theft Act 1978 (and, again, the corresponding provisions in relation to Northern Ireland).

The Act was brought fully into force by the Fraud Act (Commencement) Order 2006, SI 2006/3200) with effect from 15 January 2007. As to transitional provisions and savings, see Sch 2 to the Act.

[2] In *Government of the United Arab Emirates v Allen* [2012] EWHC 1712 (Admin), [2012] 1 WLR 3419, The defendant, a British national, obtained a mortgage from a bank in the United Arab Emirates. The loan was for a period of 20 years, repayable by monthly instalments to be debited from the defendant's credit card account held with the bank. As security, the defendant provided the bank with an undated cheque in a sum approximately equal to the loan amount. Some 19 months later, the defendant defaulted on her loan payments and the bank presented the cheque for payment, but it "bounced". The defendant returned to the UK and thereafter was convicted in her absence in the UAE of an offence of issuing an uncovered cheque. The UAE sought her extradition, but this was refused on the basis that the "dual criminality" requirement was not satisfied since the default on a loan agreement supported by the security of an undated cheque could not of itself amount to an offence in the United Kingdom of fraud by false representation contrary to s 2 of the Fraud Act 2006 (the UK offence relied on by the UAE).

This decision was upheld on appeal. A "representation" for the purposes of s 2 had to be capable of being expressed as a statement of the past or present, and did not include a simple promise of future action. While the issue of a post-dated cheque can convey an implied representation of existing fact – see *R v Gilmartin* [1983] QB 953 – it was necessary to consider the commercial context and what a reasonable person would have understood from the defendant's conduct in so doing. The defendant's contractual promises to the bank were not representations for the purposes of s 2. By agreeing to provide an undated cheque as security against a default on her loan, the defendant had not thereby impliedly represented that her current financial circumstances were such as to be able to say with confidence that in the event of that contingency occurring, at any time during the term of the loan, the cheque would in the ordinary course be met. Furthermore, there was no basis for concluding that the defendant had made any implied representation as to her financial circumstances which continued at the time when the cheque was presented. The only representation which could be inferred from the defendant's conduct was that she intended, at the time the loan agreement had been entered into, to honour its terms, but it was not alleged that such representation had been false.

[3] As to procedure for offences triable either way, see the Magistrates' Courts Act 1980, s 17–21 in PART I: MAGISTRATES' COURTS, PROCEDURE, ante.

7.11355 2. **Fraud by false representation** (1) A person is in breach of this section if he—

(a) dishonestly[1] makes a false representation[2], and

(b) intends, by making the representation[3]—

(i) to make a gain for himself or another, or

(ii) to cause loss to another or to expose another to a risk of loss.

(2) A representation is false if—

(a) it is untrue or misleading, and

(b) the person[4] making it knows that it is, or might be, untrue or misleading.

(3) "Representation" means any representation as to fact or law, including a representation as to the state of mind of—

(a) the person making the representation, or

(b) any other person.

(4) A representation may be express or implied.

(5) For the purposes of this section a representation may be regarded as made if it (or anything implying it) is submitted in any form to any system or device designed to receive, convey or respond to communications (with or without human intervention).

[Fraud Act 2006, s 2.]

---

[1] As to the meaning of "dishonestly" see Note 3 to s 1 of the Theft Act 1968 in this PART, ante.

[2] It is a matter of fact in each case whether the required causative link between the intention and the false representation has been established: *R v Gilbert* [2012] EWCA Crim 2392, [2013] Lloyd's Rep FC, where G was party to providing false information to open a bank account, but it was not suggested that she was party to a subsequent scheme to obtain computer equipment by means of post-dated cheques drawn on that account which were subsequently stopped, causing a loss of £130,000 to the supplier. The need to be sure of the above causative link had not been properly addressed and the conviction was, therefore, quashed.

[3] See note 2, supra.

[4] The test is subjective, ie it is what the accused knows is or may be misleading and not what a reasonable person in his position would have known or suspected: ' . . . the safest course for a judge to adopt is to pose to the jury the question for them in words as close as possible to those of the statute. Elaboration will rarely assist. It may be that some direction as to the consequences of an accused wilfully shutting his eyes to the obvious may be required, but rarely will more be needed': (*R v Augunas* [2013] EWCA Crim 2046, [2014] 1 Cr App Rep 240(per McCombe LJ at para 19).

7.11356 3. **Fraud by failing to disclose information** A person is in breach of this section if he—

(a) dishonestly[1] fails to disclose to another person information which he is under a legal duty[2] to disclose, and

(*b*) intends, by failing to disclose the information—
(i) to make a gain for himself or another, or
(ii) to cause loss to another or to expose another to a risk of loss.

[Fraud Act 2006, s 3.]

[1] As to the meaning of "dishonestly" see Note 3 to s 1 of the Theft Act 1968 in this PART, ante.

[2] The Law Commission report on *Fraud* (Law Com No 276, Cm 5560, 2002) explained the concept of legal duty as "7.28 . . . Such a duty may derive from statute (such as the provisions governing company prospectuses), from the fact that the transaction in question is one of the utmost good faith (such as a contract of insurance), from the express or implied terms of a contract, from the custom of a particular trade or market, or from a fiduciary relationship between the parties (such as that of agent and principal). 7.29 For this purpose there is a legal duty to disclose information not only if the defendant's failure to disclose it gives the victim a cause of action for damages, but also if the law gives the victim a right to set aside any change in his or her legal position to which he or she may consent as a result of the non-disclosure. For example, a person in a fiduciary position has a duty to disclose material information when entering into a contract with his or her beneficiary, in the sense that a failure to make such disclosure will entitle the beneficiary to rescind the contract and to reclaim any property transferred under it."

7.11357 4. **Fraud by abuse of position**[1] (1) A person is in breach of this section if he—
(*a*) occupies a position in which he is expected[2] to safeguard, or not to act against, the financial interests of another person[3],
(*b*) dishonestly[4] abuses that position, and
(*c*) intends, by means of the abuse of that position—
(i) to make a gain for himself or another, or
(ii) to cause loss to another or to expose another to a risk of loss.

(2) A person may be regarded as having abused his position even though his conduct consisted of an omission rather than an act.

[Fraud Act 2006, s 4.]

[1] The Law Commission report on *Fraud* (Law Com No 276, Cm 5560, 2002) explained the meaning of "position" as:

"7.38 The necessary relationship will be present between trustee and beneficiary, director and company, professional person and client, agent and principal, employee and employer, or between partners. It may arise otherwise, for example within a family, or in the context of voluntary work, or in any context where the parties are not at arm's length. In nearly all cases where it arises, it will be recognised by the civil law as imposing fiduciary duties, and any relationship that is so recognised will suffice. We see no reason, however, why the existence of such duties should be essential. This does not of course mean that it would be entirely a matter for the fact-finders whether the necessary relationship exists. The question whether the particular facts alleged can properly be described as giving rise to that relationship will be an issue capable of being ruled upon by a judge and, if the case goes to the jury, of being the subject of directions."

[2] The meaning of 'expect' is objective. In situations where there was no formal legal duty of a fiduciary nature, it was for the courts to decide when s 4 of the 2006 Act applied. While s 4 did not apply in the general commercial area where individuals and businesses competed in markets of one kind or another, including labour markets and were entitled to and expected to look after their own interests, a gangmaster was subject to licensing standards not to withhold earnings, etc, and on that basis occupied a position in which he was expected to safeguard or not to act against the financial interests of another person, for the purposes of s 4: *R v Valujevs* [2014] EWCA Crim 2888, [2015] QB 745, [2015] 3 WLR 109.

[3] See for an example of the position in respect of joint bank accounts and equitable interests arising from the expenditure of monies from a joint account: *R v Pennock* [2014] EWCA Crim 598, [2014] 2 Cr App Rep 129.

[4] As to the meaning of "dishonestly" see note 3 to s 1 of the Theft Act 1968 in this PART, ante.

7.11358 5. **"Gain" and "loss"** (1) The references to gain and loss in sections 2 to 4 are to be read in accordance with this section.

(2) "Gain" and "loss"—
(*a*) extend only to gain or loss in money or other property;
(*b*) include any such gain or loss whether temporary or permanent;

and "property" means any property whether real or personal (including things in action and other intangible property).

(3) "Gain" includes a gain by keeping what one has, as well as a gain by getting what one does not have.

(4) "Loss" includes a loss by not getting what one might get, as well as a loss by parting with what one has.

[Fraud Act 2006, s 5.]

7.11359 6. **Possession etc of articles for use in frauds** (1) A person is guilty of an offence if he has in his possession[1] or under his control any article for use in the course of or in connection with any fraud[2].

(2) A person guilty of an offence under this section is liable—
(*a*) on summary conviction, to imprisonment for a term not exceeding 12 months or to a fine not exceeding the statutory maximum (or to both);
(*b*) on conviction on indictment, to imprisonment for a term not exceeding 5 years or to a fine (or to both)[3].

(3) *Northern Ireland.*

[Fraud Act 2006, s 6.]

[1] See *R v Montague* [2013] EWCA Crim 1781, [2014] Crim LR 615 and commentary thereto.

[2] When the words "or cheat" (repealed by this Act) appeared in the offence of going equipped for theft in s 25 of the Theft Act 1968, they were interpreted as follows. In *R v Rashid* [1977] 2 All ER 237, 141 JP 305, because of a misdirection to the jury, the defendant was held to have been wrongly convicted of possession of bread and tomatoes with which he intended to make sandwiches for sale to passengers on a train on which he was a steward. In that case the Court of Appeal,

in an obiter dicta, expressed the view that on the facts of the case there was probably no obtaining by deception and that it was not appropriate to exalt a breach of contractual duty owed to the defendant's employers into a criminal offence. But *R v Rashid* was distinguished in *R v Doukas* [1978] 1 All ER 1061, where a wine waiter in an hotel was held to have been properly convicted of having with him his own wine which he dishonestly intended to sell to customers as property of his employers. In the latter case it was held that it had to be assumed that the hypothetical customer against whom the intended deception was to be practised was reasonably honest and intelligent, and that it was unlikely that any customer to whom the true situation was made clear would willingly make himself a party to what was a fraud by the waiter on his employer. See also *R v Corboz* [1984] Crim LR 629 and *R v Whiteside; R v Antoniou* [1989] Crim LR 436, CA. It is submitted that such conduct clearly falls within "fraud by abuse of position" (s 4) and "fraud by false representation" (s 2) and, consequently, amounts to an offence under s 6. The article must be with the defendant for the purpose or intention that it will be used for fraud then or in the future; it is insufficient that the article may have been used for fraud in the past: *R v Sakalauskas* [2013] EWCA Crim 2278 [2014] 1 All ER 1231, [2014] 1 WLR 1204 (see also *R v Ellames* (1974) 60 Cr App R 7 noted to the Theft Act 1968, ante).

[3] As to procedure for offences triable either way, see Magistrates' Courts Act 1980, ss 17–21 in PART I: MAGISTRATES' COURTS, PROCEDURE, ante.

7.11360 7. **Making or supplying articles for use in frauds** (1) A person is guilty of an offence if he makes, adapts, supplies or offers to supply any article—

(*a*) knowing that it is designed or adapted for use in the course of or in connection with fraud, or

(*b*) intending it to be used to commit, or assist in the commission of, fraud.

(2) A person guilty of an offence under this section is liable—

(*a*) on summary conviction, to imprisonment for a term not exceeding 12 months or to a fine not exceeding the statutory maximum (or to both);

(*b*) on conviction on indictment, to imprisonment for a term not exceeding 10 years or to a fine (or to both)[1].

(3) *Northern Ireland.*

[Fraud Act 2006, s 7.]

[1] As to procedure for offences triable either way, see the Magistrates' Courts Act 1980, s 17–21 in PART I: MAGISTRATES' COURTS, PROCEDURE, ante.

7.11361 8. **"Article"** (1) For the purposes of—

(*a*) sections 6 and 7, and

(*b*) the provisions listed in subsection (2), so far as they relate to articles for use in the course of or in connection with fraud,

"article" includes any program or data held in electronic form.

(2) The provisions are—

(*a*) section 1(7)(*b*) of the Police and Criminal Evidence Act 1984 (c 60),

(*b*) section 2(8)(*b*) of the Armed Forces Act 2001 (c 19), and

(*c*) Article 3(7)(*b*) of the Police and Criminal Evidence (Northern Ireland) Order 1989 (SI 1989/1341 (NI 12));

(meaning of "prohibited articles" for the purposes of stop and search powers).

[Fraud Act 2006, s 8.]

7.11362 9. **Participating in fraudulent business carried on by sole trader etc** (1) A person is guilty of an offence if he is knowingly a party to the carrying on of a business to which this section applies.

(2) This section applies to a business which is carried on—

(*a*) by a person who is outside the reach of section 993 of the Companies Act 2006 (offence of fraudulent trading), and

(*b*) with intent to defraud creditors of any person or for any other fraudulent purpose.

(3) The following are within the reach of that section—

(*a*) a company (as defined in section 1(1) of the Companies Act 2006);

(*b*) a person to whom that section applies (with or without adaptations or modifications) as if the person were a company;

(*c*) a person exempted from the application of that section.

(4) *Repealed.*

(5) "Fraudulent purpose" has the same meaning as that section.

(6) A person guilty of an offence under this section is liable—

(*a*) on summary conviction, to imprisonment for a term not exceeding 12 months or to a fine not exceeding the statutory maximum (or to both);

(*b*) on conviction on indictment, to imprisonment for a term not exceeding 10 years or to a fine (or to both)[1].

(7) *Northern Ireland.*

[Fraud Act 2006, s 9 as amended by SI 2007/2194 and SI 2009/1941.]

[1] As to procedure for offences triable either way, see the Magistrates' Courts Act 1980, s 17–21 in PART I: MAGISTRATES' COURTS, PROCEDURE, ante.

*Obtaining services dishonestly*

7.11363 11. **Obtaining services dishonestly** (1) A person is guilty of an offence under this section if he obtains services for himself or another—

(*a*) by a dishonest[1] act, and
(*b*) in breach of subsection (2).

(2) A person obtains services in breach of this subsection if—
(*a*) they are made available on the basis that payment has been, is being or will be made for or in respect of them,
(*b*) he obtains them without any payment having been made for or in respect of them or without payment having been made in full, and
(*c*) when he obtains them, he knows—
(i) that they are being made available on the basis described in paragraph (*a*), or
(ii) that they might be,

but intends that payment will not be made, or will not be made in full.

(3) A person guilty of an offence under this section is liable—
(*a*) on summary conviction, to imprisonment for a term not exceeding 12 months or to a fine not exceeding the statutory maximum (or to both);
(*b*) on conviction on indictment, to imprisonment for a term not exceeding 5 years or to a fine (or to both)[2].

(4) Subsection (3)(*a*) applies in relation to Northern Ireland as if the reference to 12 months were a reference to 6 months.

[Fraud Act 2006, s 11.]

---

[1] As to the meaning of "dishonest" see Note 3 to s 1 of the Theft Act 1968 in this PART, ante.
[2] As to procedure for offences triable either way, see the Magistrates' Courts Act 1980, s 17–21 in PART I: Magistrates' COURTS, PROCEDURE, ante.

*Supplementary*

7.11364 **12. Liability of company officers for offences by company** (1) Subsection (2) applies if an offence under this Act is committed by a body corporate.

(2) If the offence is proved to have been committed with the consent or connivance of—
(*a*) a director, manager, secretary or other similar officer of the body corporate, or
(*b*) a person who was purporting to act in any such capacity,

he (as well as the body corporate) is guilty of the offence and liable to be proceeded against and punished accordingly.

(3) If the affairs of a body corporate are managed by its members, subsection (2) applies in relation to the acts and defaults of a member in connection with his functions of management as if he were a director of the body corporate.

[Fraud Act 2006, s 12.]

7.11365 **13. Evidence** (1) A person is not to be excused from—
(*a*) answering any question put to him in proceedings relating to property, or
(*b*) complying with any order made in proceedings relating to property,

on the ground that doing so may incriminate him or his spouse or civil partner of an offence under this Act or a related offence[1].

(2) But, in proceedings for an offence under this Act or a related offence, a statement or admission made by the person in—
(*a*) answering such a question, or
(*b*) complying with such an order,

is not admissible in evidence against him or (unless they married or became civil partners after the making of the statement or admission) his spouse or civil partner.

(3) "Proceedings relating to property" means any proceedings for—
(*a*) the recovery or administration of any property,
(*b*) the execution of a trust, or
(*c*) an account of any property or dealings with property,

and "property" means money or other property whether real or personal (including things in action and other intangible property).

(4) "Related offence" means—
(*a*) conspiracy to defraud;
(*b*) any other offence involving any form of fraudulent conduct or purpose.

[Fraud Act 2006, s 13.]

---

[1] This section is similar to s 31(1) of the Theft Act 1968, ante, but goes further by including "related" offences, which are defined in subs (4) infra.

7.11366 **14. Minor and consequential amendments etc** (1) Schedule 1 contains minor and consequential amendments.

(2) Schedule 2 contains transitional provisions and savings.

(3) Schedule 3 contains repeals and revocations.

[Fraud Act 2006, s 14.]

7.11367 **15. Commencement and extent** (1) This Act (except this section and section 16) comes into force on such day as the Secretary of State may appoint[1] by an order made by statutory instrument; and different days may be appointed for different purposes.

(2) Subject to subsection (3), sections 1 to 9 and 11 to 13 extend to England and Wales and Northern Ireland only.

(3) Section 8, so far as it relates to the Armed Forces Act 2001 (c 19), extends to any place to which that Act extends.

(4) Any amendment in section 10 or Schedule 1, and any related provision in section 14 or Schedule 2 or 3, extends to any place to which the provision which is the subject of the amendment extends.

[Fraud Act 2006, s 15.]

[1] The Act is fully in force, but with the transitional and savings provisions contained in Sch 2, infra.

7.11368 16. **Short title** This Act may be cited as the Fraud Act 2006.

[Fraud Act 2006, s 16.]

## SCHEDULE 1[1]

Minor and Consequential Amendments — Section 14(1)

[1] The following paragraphs containing repeals/amendments are reproduced here rather than shown in the Acts concerned because of the transitional provisions and savings contained in Sch 2.

*Abolition of various deception offences*

7.11369 1. Omit the following provisions—

(*a*) in the Theft Act 1968 (c 60)—
 (i) section 15 (obtaining property by deception);
 (ii) section 15A (obtaining a money transfer by deception);
 (iii) section 16 (obtaining pecuniary advantage by deception);
 (iv) section 20(2) (procuring the execution of a valuable security by deception);

(*b*) in the Theft Act 1978 (c 31)—
 (i) section 1 (obtaining services by deception);
 (ii) section 2 (evasion of liability by deception);

(*c*) in the Theft Act (Northern Ireland) 1969 (c 16 (NI))—
 (i) section 15 (obtaining property by deception);
 (ii) section 15A (obtaining a money transfer by deception);
 (iii) section 16 (obtaining pecuniary advantage by deception);
 (iv) section 19(2) (procuring the execution of a valuable security by deception);

(*d*) in the Theft (Northern Ireland) Order 1978 (SI 1978/1407 (NI 23))—
 (i) Article 3 (obtaining services by deception);
 (ii) Article 4 (evasion of liability by deception).

6. (1) In section 24(4) (meaning of "stolen goods") for "in the circumstances described in section 15(1) of this Act" substitute ", subject to subsection (5) below, by fraud (within the meaning of the Fraud Act 2006)".

(2) After section 24(4) insert—

"(5) Subsection (1) above applies in relation to goods obtained by fraud as if—

(*a*) the reference to the commencement of this Act were a reference to the commencement of the Fraud Act 2006, and

(*b*) the reference to an offence under this Act were a reference to an offence under section 1 of that Act."

7. (1) In section 24A (dishonestly retaining a wrongful credit), omit subsections (3) and (4) and after subsection (2) insert—

"(2A) A credit to an account is wrongful to the extent that it derives from—

(*a*) theft;

(*b*) blackmail;

(*c*) fraud (contrary to section 1 of the Fraud Act 2006); or

(*d*) stolen goods."

(2) In subsection (7), for "subsection (4)" substitute "subsection (2A)".

(3) For subsection (9) substitute—

"(9) "Account" means an account kept with—

(*a*) a bank;

(*b*) a person carrying on a business which falls within subsection (10) below; or

(*c*) an issuer of electronic money (as defined for the purposes of Part 2 of the Financial Services and Markets Act 2000).

(10) A business falls within this subsection if—

(*a*) in the course of the business money received by way of deposit is lent to others; or

(*b*) any other activity of the business is financed, wholly or to any material extent, out of the capital of or the interest on money received by way of deposit.

(11) References in subsection (10) above to a deposit must be read with—

(*a*) section 22 of the Financial Services and Markets Act 2000;

(*b*) any relevant order under that section; and

(*c*) Schedule 2 to that Act;

but any restriction on the meaning of deposit which arises from the identity of the person making it is to be disregarded.

(12) For the purposes of subsection (10) above—

(*a*) all the activities which a person carries on by way of business shall be regarded as a single business carried on by him; and

(*b*) "money" includes money expressed in a currency other than sterling."

SCHEDULE 2

Transitional Provisions and Savings

Section 14(2)

*Maximum term of imprisonment for offences under this Act*

**7.11370** **1.** In relation to an offence committed before the commencement of section 154(1) of the Criminal Justice Act 2003 (c 44), the references to 12 months in sections 1(3)(*a*), 6(2)(*a*), 7(2)(*a*), 9(6)(*a*) and 11(3)(*a*) are to be read as references to 6 months.

*Increase in penalty for fraudulent trading*

**2.** Section 10 does not affect the penalty for any offence committed before that section comes into force.

*Abolition of deception offences*

**3.** (1) Paragraph 1 of Schedule 1 does not affect any liability, investigation, legal proceeding or penalty for or in respect of any offence partly committed before the commencement of that paragraph.

(2) An offence is partly committed before the commencement of paragraph 1 of Schedule 1 if—

(*a*) a relevant event occurs before its commencement, and

(*b*) another relevant event occurs on or after its commencement.

(3) "Relevant event", in relation to an offence, means any act, omission or other event (including any result of one or more acts or omissions) proof of which is required for conviction of the offence.

*Scope of offences relating to stolen goods under the Theft Act 1968 (c 60)*

**4.** Nothing in paragraph 6 of Schedule 1 affects the operation of section 24 of the Theft Act 1968 in relation to goods obtained in the circumstances described in section 15(1) of that Act where the obtaining is the result of a deception made before the commencement of that paragraph.

*Dishonestly retaining a wrongful credit under the Theft Act 1968*

**5.** Nothing in paragraph 7 of Schedule 1 affects the operation of section 24A(7) and (8) of the Theft Act 1968 in relation to credits falling within section 24A(3) or (4) of that Act and made before the commencement of that paragraph.

*Powers of arrest under Asylum and Immigration (Treatment of Claimants, etc) Act 2004 (c 19)*

**11.** (1) Nothing in paragraph 35 of Schedule 1 affects the power of arrest conferred by section 14 of the Asylum and Immigration (Treatment of Claimants, etc) Act 2004 in relation to an offence partly committed before the commencement of that paragraph.

(2) An offence is partly committed before the commencement of paragraph 35 of Schedule 1 if—

(*a*) a relevant event occurs before its commencement, and

(*b*) another relevant event occurs on or after its commencement.

(3) "Relevant event", in relation to an offence, means any act, omission or other event (including any result of one or more acts or omissions) proof of which is required for conviction of the offence.

# Specialist Printing Equipment and Materials (Offences) Act 2015

(2015 c 16)

**7.113670A** **1. Offence of supplying specialist printing equipment knowing it will be used for criminal purposes** (1) A person commits an offence if—

(*a*) the person supplies any specialist printing equipment, and

(*b*) in making the supply, the person knows that the equipment will be or is intended to be used for the purposes of criminal conduct.

(2) "Criminal conduct" means conduct which constitutes—

(*a*) an offence under the law of England and Wales, or

(*b*) an offence under the law of a country outside England and Wales which, if it took place in England and Wales, would constitute an offence in England and Wales.

(3) An individual guilty of an offence under this section is liable on conviction on indictment to imprisonment for a term not exceeding 10 years, or to a fine, or to both.

(4) Any other person guilty of an offence under this section is liable on conviction on indictment to a fine.

(5) It is a defence for a person charged with an offence under this section to prove that the person's conduct was necessary for a purpose related to the prevention or detection of crime.

[Specialist Printing Equipment and Materials (Offences) Act 2015, s 1.]

**7.113670B** **2. Meaning of "specialist printing equipment"** (1) In this Act, "specialist printing equipment" means any equipment which is designed or adapted for, or is otherwise capable of being used for, the making of relevant documents (including any material or article that is used in the making of such documents).

(2) A "relevant document" is anything that is or purports to be—

(*a*) an identity document;

(*b*) a travel document;

(*c*) an entry document;

(*d*) a document used for verifying the holder's age or national insurance number;

(*e*) a currency note or protected coin, as defined by section 27(1) of the Forgery and Counterfeiting Act; 1981

(*f*) a debit or credit card;

(*g*) any other instrument to which section 5 of the Forgery and Counterfeiting Act 1981 applies (money orders, etc).

(3) In subsection (2)(*a*), "identity document" means—

(*a*) a document used for confirming the right of a person under the EU Treaties in respect of entry or residence in the United Kingdom;

(*b*) a document that is given in the exercise of immigration functions and records information about leave granted to a person to enter or remain in the United Kingdom;

(*c*) a registration card (within the meaning of section 26A of the Immigration Act 1971);

(*d*) a United Kingdom passport (within the meaning of the Immigration Act 1971);

(*e*) a passport, or other document used for the purposes of establishing identity, issued by or on behalf of the authorities of a country or territory outside the United Kingdom or by or on behalf of an international organisation;

(*f*) a document that can be used (in some or all circumstances) instead of a passport.

(4) In subsection (2)(*b*), "travel document" means—

(*a*) a licence to drive a motor vehicle granted under Part 3 of the Road Traffic Act 1988 or under Part 2 of the Road Traffic (Northern Ireland) Order 1981 (SI 1981/154 (NI 1));

(*b*) a driving licence issued by or on behalf of the authorities of a country or territory outside the United Kingdom or by or on behalf of an international organisation;

(*c*) a ticket or other document authorising travel on public passenger transport services;

(*d*) a permit authorising travel on public passenger transport services at a concession;

(*e*) a badge of a form prescribed under section 21 of the Chronically Sick and Disabled Persons Act 1970 (blue badge scheme) or a recognised badge for the purposes of section 21A of that Act.

(5) In subsection (2)(*c*), "entry document" means any document used for the purpose of authorising the holder to enter any premises (or part of premises), including—

(*a*) a security pass or other document used in that capacity, and

(*b*) a ticket, or other document used in that capacity, to a sporting or other event.

(6) In this section—

"equipment" includes any device, machinery or apparatus and any wire or cable, together with any software used with it;

"document" means information recorded in any form (including stamps or labels);

"immigration functions" means functions under the Immigration Acts (within the meaning of the Asylum and Immigration (Treatment of Claimants, etc) Act 2004);

"premises" includes any land;

"public passenger transport services" has the same meaning as in the Transport Act 1985 (see section 63(10) of that Act).

[Specialist Printing Equipment and Materials (Offences) Act 2015, s 2.]

**7.113670C 3. Offences by bodies corporate and partnerships etc** (1) For the purposes of section 1(1) a body (whether corporate or not) is to be treated as knowing a fact about a supply of equipment if a person who has responsibility within the body for the supply knows of the fact.

(2) Where an offence committed by a body corporate is proved—

(*a*) to have been committed with the consent or connivance of an officer of the body corporate, or

(*b*) to be attributable to neglect on the part of an officer of the body corporate,

that officer (as well as the body corporate) is guilty of the offence and is liable to be proceeded against and dealt with accordingly.

(3) "Officer", in relation to a body corporate, means—

(*a*) any director, manager, secretary or other similar officer of the body corporate, or

(*b*) any person purporting to act in any such capacity;

and for this purpose "director", in relation to a body corporate whose affairs are managed by its members, means a member of the body corporate.

(4) Proceedings for an offence alleged to have been committed by a partnership may be brought in the name of the partnership.

(5) Rules of court relating to the service of documents have effect in relation to such proceedings as if the partnership were a body corporate.

(6) For the purposes of such proceedings section 33 of the Criminal Justice Act 1925 and Schedule 3 to the Magistrates' Courts Act 1980 apply as they apply in relation to a body corporate.

(7) A fine imposed on a partnership on its conviction for an offence is to be paid out of the partnership assets.

(8) Where an offence committed by a partnership is proved—

(*a*) to have been committed with the consent or connivance of a partner, or

(*b*) to be attributable to neglect on the part of a partner,

the partner (as well as the partnership) is guilty of the offence and is liable to be proceeded against and dealt with accordingly.

(9) For the purposes of subsections (2)(*b*) and (8)(*b*), the commission of an offence is attributable to neglect on the part of an officer or partner only if that person ought reasonably to have known of the facts giving rise to the offence.

(10) In this section—

"offence" means an offence under section 1;

"partner" includes a person purporting to act as a partner.

[Specialist Printing Equipment and Materials (Offences) Act 2015, s 3.]

**7.113670D 4. Application to Crown** This Act applies to individuals in the public service of the Crown as it applies to other individuals.

[Specialist Printing Equipment and Materials (Offences) Act 2015, s 4.]

**7.113670E 5. Extent, commencement and short title** (1) This Act extends to England and Wales only.

(2) Her Majesty may by order in Council provide for this Act to extend with or without modifications to the Isle of Man.

(3) This Act comes into force two months after the day on which this Act is passed[1].

(4) Nothing in this Act applies in relation to supplies of specialist printing equipment before that day.

(5) This Act may be cited as the Specialist Printing Equipment and Materials (Offences) Act 2015.

[Specialist Printing Equipment and Materials (Offences) Act 2015, s 5.]

---

1 This Act was passed on 26 March 2015.

# TOWN AND COUNTRY PLANNING

**Contents**



## Caravan Sites and Control of Development Act 1960

(8 & 9 Eliz 2 c 62)

### Part I
### Caravan Sites

*Licensing of caravan sites*

7.11370A 1. **Prohibition of use of land as caravan site without site licence** (1) Subject to the provisions of this Part of this Act, no occupier[1] of land shall after the commencement of this Act[2] cause or permit any part of the land to be used as a caravan site[3] unless he is the holder of a site licence (that is to say, a licence under this Part of this Act authorising the use of land as a caravan site) for the time being in force as respects the land so used.

(1A) Subsection (1) does not apply in relation to a regulated site within the meaning of the Mobile Homes (Wales) Act 2013.

(2) If the occupier of any land contravenes subsection (1) of this section he shall be guilty of an offence and liable on summary conviction—

(*a*) where the land in question is in England, to a fine not exceeding **level 5** on the standard scale.

(*b*) where the land in question is in Wales, to a fine not exceeding **level 4** on the standard scale.

(3) In this Part of this Act the expression "occupier" means, in relation to any land, the person who, by virtue of an estate or interest therein held by him, is entitled to possession thereof or would be so entitled but for the rights of any other person under any licence granted in respect of the land: Provided that where land amounting to not more than four hundred square yards in area is let under a tenancy entered into with a view to the use of the land as a caravan site, the expression "occupier" means in relation to that land the person who would be entitled to possession of the land but for the rights of any person under that tenancy.

(4) In this Part of this Act the expression "caravan site" means land on which a caravan is stationed for the purposes of human habitation and land which is used in conjunction with land on which a caravan is so stationed.

[Caravan Sites and Control of Development Act 1960, s 1 as amended by the Criminal Justice Act 1982, ss 35, 38 and 46, the Mobile Homes (Wales) Act 2013, Sch 4 and the Mobile Homes Act 2013, s 13.]

---

1 "Occupier" is defined by s 1(3), *infra*.

2 This Act commenced on 29 August 1960.

3 "Caravan site" is defined by s 1(4), *infra*. "Caravan" means any structure designed or adapted for human habitation which is capable of being moved from one place to another whether by being towed, or by being transported on a motor vehicle or trailer, and any motor vehicle so designed or adapted, but does not include—(*a*) any railway rolling stock which is for the time being on rails forming part of a railway system, or, (*b*) any tent (s 29(1)). The definition of "caravan" contemplates that the structure has to be capable of being moved from one place to another as a single unit; accordingly, a prefabricated structure which was delivered to a site by lorry, had to be bolted together and which lacked wheels so that it had to be dismantled to be moved was held not to be a caravan; see *Carter v Secretary of State for the Environment* [1994] 1 WLR 1212.

7.11371 2. **Exemptions from licensing requirements** No site licence shall be required for the use of land as a caravan site in any of the circumstances specified in the First Schedule to this Act[1] and that Schedule shall have effect accordingly.

[Caravan Sites and Control of Development Act 1960, s 2.]

---

1 For the purposes of this work, the First Schedule may be summarised as follows: A licence is not required, in the circumstances set out in the Schedule, for: (1) use within curtilage of a dwelling-house, (2) use for not more than two nights, (3) use of holdings of five acres or more in certain circumstances, (4) sites occupied or approved by exempted organisations, (5) agricultural and forestry workers, (6), building and engineering sites, (7) travelling showmen, (8) sites occupied by local authority.

As to the exemption for travelling showmen, see *Holmes v Cooper* [1985] 3 All ER 114, [1985] 1 WLR 1060, CA.

7.11372 3, 4. Issue of site licences by local authorities.—The council of a borough or urban or rural district or the Common Council of the City of London may, and in prescribed circumstances shall[1] issue to applicants a site licence, the duration of which is unlimited except where permission to use the land as a caravan site has been granted under Part III of the Town and Country Planning

Act [1990], otherwise than by a development order. [Caravan Sites and Control of Development Act 1960, ss 3, 4, amended by the Local Government, Planning and Land Act 1980, Sch 3 *summarised*.] The application of the Act to Greater London is modified by the London Government Act 1963, 17th Sch, para 21.

[1] Where a local authority being required to issue a licence, fail to do so, no offence is committed under s 1 by a person by whom an application has been made (s 6).

7.11373 5. **Power of local authority to attach conditions to site licences** (1) A site licence issued by a local authority in respect of any land may be so issued subject to such conditions as the authority may think it necessary or desirable to impose on the occupier of the land in the interests of persons dwelling thereon in caravans, or of any other class of persons, or of the public at large; and in particular, but without prejudice to the generality of the foregoing, a site licence may be issued subject to conditions—

(*a*) for restricting the occasions on which caravans are stationed on the land for the purposes of human habitation, or the total number of caravans which are so stationed at any one time;

(*b*) for controlling (whether by reference to their size, the state of their repair or, subject to the provisions of subsection (2) of this section, any other feature) the type of caravan which are stationed on the land;

(*c*) for regulating the positions in which caravans are stationed on the land for the purposes of human habitation and for prohibiting, restricting, or otherwise regulating, the placing or erection on the land, at any time when caravans are so stationed, of structures and vehicles of any description whatsoever and of tents;

(*d*) for securing the taking of any steps for preserving or enhancing the amenity of the land, including the planting and replanting thereof with trees and bushes;

(*e*) for securing that, at all times when caravans are stationed on the land, proper measures are taken for preventing and detecting the outbreak of fire and adequate means of fighting fire are provided and maintained;

(*f*) for securing that adequate sanitary facilities, and such other facilities, services or equipment as may be specified, are provided for the use of persons dwelling on the land in caravans and that, at all times when caravans are stationed thereon for the purposes of human habitation, any facilities and equipment so provided are properly maintained.

(2) No condition shall be attached to a site licence controlling the types of caravans which are stationed on the land by reference to the materials used in their construction.

(2A) Where the Regulatory Reform (Fire Safety) Order 2005 applies to the land, no condition is to be attached to a site licence in so far as it relates to any matter in relation to which requirements or prohibitions are or could be imposed by or under that Order.[1]

(3) A site licence issued in respect of any land shall, unless it is issued subject to a condition restricting to three or less the total number of caravans which may be stationed on the land at any one time, contain an express condition that, at all times when caravans are stationed on the land for the purposes of human habitation, a copy of the licence as for the time being in force shall be displayed on the land in some conspicuous place.

(3A) The local authority shall consult the fire and rescue authority as to the extent to which any model standards relating to fire precautions which have been specified under subsection (6) of this section are appropriate to the land.

(3B) If—

(*a*) no such standards have been specified; or

(*b*) any standard that has been specified appears to the fire and rescue authority to be inappropriate to the land,

the local authority shall consult the fire and rescue authority as to what conditions relating to fire precautions ought to be attached to the site licence instead.

(3C) Subsections (3A) and (3B) of this section do not apply where the Regulatory Reform (Fire Safety) Order 2005 applies to the land.[1]

(4) A condition attached to a site licence may, if it requires the carrying out of any works on the land in respect of which the licence is issued, prohibit or restrict the bringing of caravans on to the land for the purposes of human habitation until such time as the local authority have certified in writing that the works have been completed to their satisfaction; and where the land to which the site licence relates is at the time in use as a caravan site, the condition may, whether or not it contains any such prohibition or restriction as aforesaid, require the works to be completed to the satisfaction of the authority within a stated period[2].

(5) For the avoidance of doubt, it is hereby declared that a condition attached to a site licence shall be valid notwithstanding that it can be complied with only by the carrying out of works which the holder of the site licence is not entitled to carry out as of right.

(6) The Minister[3] may from time to time specify for the purposes of this section model standards[4] with respect to the layout of, and the provision of facilities, services and equipment for, caravan sites or particular types of caravan site; and in deciding what (if any) conditions to attach to a site licence, a local authority shall have regard to any standards so specified.

(6A) No model standards may be specified under subsection (6) of this section in relation to land to which the Regulatory Reform (Fire Safety) Order 2005 applies in so far as the standards relate to any matter in relation to which requirements or prohibitions are or could be imposed by or under that Order.[1]

(7) The duty imposed on a local authority by subsection (6) of this section to have regard to standards specified under that subsection is to be construed, as regards standards relating to fire precautions which are so specified, as a duty to have regard to them subject to any advice given by the fire and rescue authority[2] under subsection (3A) or (3B) of this section.

(8) In this section "fire precautions" means precautions to be taken for any of the purposes specified in paragraph (*e*) of subsection (1) of this section for which conditions may be imposed by virtue of this section[1].

[Caravan Sites and Control of Development Act 1960, s 5 as amended by the Local Government (Miscellaneous Provisions) Act 1982, s 8, the Fire and Rescue Services Act 2004, Sch 1 and SI 2005/1541.]

---

1 Subsections (2A), (3C) and (6A) and words "this section" inserted in relation to England and Wales by SI 2005/1541.

2 Failure to complete the works after the end of the stated period is a continuing offence under s 9, post (*Penton Park Homes Ltd v Chertsey UDC* (1973) 72 LGR 115, 26 P & CR 531).

3 "The Minister" is the Secretary of State for the Environment (s 29(1)).

4 Model Standards were specified by the Minister of Housing and Local Government in 1960 and are obtainable from HM Stationery Office.

**7.11373A 5A. Relevant protected sites: annual fee**

**7.11374 7. Appeal against conditions attached to site licence** (1) Any person aggrieved by any condition (other than the condition referred to in s 5(3) of this Act) subject to which a site licence has been issued to him in respect of any land may, within twenty-eight days of the date on which the licence was so issued, appeal to a magistrates' court[1]; or, in a case relating to land in England, to a residential property tribunal; and the court or tribunal, if satisfied (having regard amongst other things[2] to any standards which may have been specified by the Minister under subsection (6) of the said section five[2]) that the condition is unduly burdensome[3], may vary or cancel the condition.

(1A) In a case where a residential property tribunal varies or cancels a condition under subsection (1), it may also attach a new condition to the licence in question.

(2) In so far as the effect of a condition (in whatever words expressed) subject to which a site licence is issued in respect of any land is to require the carrying out on the land of any works, the condition shall not have effect during the period within which the person to whom the site licence is issued is entitled by virtue of the foregoing subsection to appeal against the condition nor, thereafter, whilst an appeal against the condition is pending.

[Caravan Sites and Control of Development Act 1960, s 7 as amended by the Courts Act 2003, Sch 8 and the Mobile Homes Act 2013, s 3.]

---

1 Appeal is by way of complaint (Magistrates' Courts Rules 1981, r 34, in PART I: MAGISTRATES' COURTS, PROCEDURE, ante).

2 Visual amenity of an area is a matter to which magistrates can lawfully have regard (*Babbage v North Norfolk District Council* (1988) 153 JP 278).

3 The site licence must be confined within the limits of the planning permission: a magistrates' court has no jurisdiction to vary a condition of a site licence, beyond the scope of this permission (*R v Kent Justices, ex p Crittenden* [1964] 1 QB 144, [1963] 2 All ER 245, 127 JP 359). On the other hand, conditions which seek to impose a substantial limitation on the licensee, beyond the scope and object of the Act (ie control of the physical condition or use of the site) may be invalid and therefore unduly burdensome, see *Mixnam's Properties Ltd v Chertsey UDC* [1965] AC 735, [1964] 2 All ER 627, 128 JP 405, HL.

Section 17 of the Act contains provisions whereby planning permission is deemed to have been granted in respect of existing sites (defined in s 13, post). The licensing authority may not impose conditions derogating from existing user rights; *Minister of Housing and Local Government v Hartnell* [1965] AC 1134, [1965] 1 All ER 490, 129 JP 234, HL. Whether any such conditions are "unduly burdensome" is a question of fact for the magistrates (*Esdell Caravan Parks Ltd v Hemel Hempstead RDC* [1966] 1 QB 895, [1965] 3 All ER 737, 130 JP 66).

**7.11375 8. Power of local authority to alter conditions attached to site licences** (1) The conditions attached to a site licence may be altered at any time (whether by the variation or cancellation of existing conditions, or by the addition of new conditions, or by a combination of any such methods) by the local authority, but before exercising their powers under this subsection the local authority shall afford to the holder of the licence an opportunity of making representations.

(1A) Where the Regulatory Reform (Fire Safety) Order 2005 applies to the land to which the site licence relates, no condition may be attached to a site licence under subsection (1) of this section in so far as it relates to any matter in relation to which requirements or prohibitions are or could be imposed by or under that Order.[1]

(1B) A local authority in England may require an application by the holder of a site licence in respect of a relevant protected site in their area for the alteration of the conditions attached to the site licence to be accompanied by a fee fixed by the local authority.

(2) Where the holder of a site licence is aggrieved by any alteration of the conditions attached thereto or by the refusal of the local authority of an application by him for the alteration of those conditions[2], he may within twenty-eight days of the date on which written notification of the alteration or refusal is received by him, appeal to a magistrates' court[2]; or, in a case relating to land in England, to a residential property tribunal; and the court or tribunal may, if they allow the appeal,

give to the local authority such directions as may be necessary to give effect to their decision.

(3) The alteration by a local authority of the conditions attached to any site licence shall not have effect until written notification thereof has been received by the holder of the licence.

(5) The local authority shall consult the fire and rescue authority before exercising the powers conferred upon them by subsection (1) of this section in relation to a condition attached to a site licence for the purposes set out in section 5(1)(*e*) of this Act.

(5A) Subsection (5) of this section does not apply where the Regulatory Reform (Fire Safety) Order 2005 applies to the land.[1]

[Caravan Sites and Control of Development Act 1960, s 8 as amended by the Local Government (Miscellaneous Provisions) Act 1982, s 8, the Courts Act 2003, Sch 8, the Fire and Rescue Services Act 2004, Sch 1, SI 2005/1541 and the Mobile Homes Act 2013, ss 1, 3.]

---

1 Subsections (1A) and (5A) inserted in relation to England and Wales by SI 2005/1541.

2 The expression "those conditions" includes the conditions originally imposed on the grant of the licence and is not limited to the conditions that the local authority propose to alter (*Peters v Yiewsley and West Drayton UDC* [1963] 2 QB 133, [1963] 1 All ER 843, 127 JP 277).

7.11376 **9. Breach of condition: land other than relevant protected sites in England**

(1) If an occupier of land, other than land in England which is a relevant protected site, fails to comply with any condition for the time being attached to a site licence held by him in respect of the land, he shall be guilty of an offence and liable on summary conviction, to a fine not exceeding **level 4** on the standard scale.

(2) Where a person convicted under this section for failing to comply with a condition attached to a site licence has on two or more previous occasions been convicted thereunder for failing to comply with a condition attached to that licence, the court before whom he is convicted may, if an application in that behalf is made at the hearing by the local authority in whose area the land is situated, make an order for the revocation of the said site licence to come into force on such date as the court may specify in the order, being a date not earlier than the expiration of any period within which notice of appeal (whether by case stated or otherwise) may be given against the conviction[1] and if before the date so specified an appeal is so brought the order shall be of no effect pending the final determination or withdrawal of the appeal.

The person convicted or the local authority who issued the site licence may apply to the magistrates' court which has made such an order revoking a site licence for an order extending the period at the end of which the revocation is to come into force, and the magistrates' court may, if satisfied that adequate notice of the application has been given to the local authority or, as the case may be, the person convicted, make an order extending that period.

(3) Where an occupier of land, other than land in England which is a relevant protected site, fails within the time specified in a condition attached to a site licence held by him to complete to the satisfaction of the local authority in whose area the land is situated any works required by the condition to be so completed, the local authority may carry out those works, and may recover as a simple contract debt in any court of competent jurisdiction from that person any expenses reasonably incurred by them in that behalf.

[Caravan Sites and Control of Development Act 1960, s 9 as amended by the Courts Act 1971, Sch 8, the Criminal Justice Act 1982, ss 35, 38 and 46 and the Mobile Homes Act 2013, s 4.]

---

1 See the Magistrates' Court Act 1980, s 111(2), and the Crown Court Rules 1982 in PART I: MAGISTRATES' COURTS, PROCEDURE, ante.

7.11377 **9A. Breach of condition: relevant protected sites in England** (1) If it appears to a local authority in England who have issued a site licence in respect of a relevant protected site in their area that the occupier of the land concerned is failing or has failed to comply with a condition for the time being attached to the site licence, they may serve a compliance notice on the occupier.

(2) A compliance notice is a notice which—

(*a*) sets out the condition in question and details of the failure to comply with it,

(*b*) requires the occupier of the land to take such steps as the local authority consider appropriate and as are specified in the notice in order to ensure that the condition is complied with,

(*c*) specifies the period within which those steps must be taken, and

(*d*) explains the right of appeal conferred by subsection (3).

(3) An occupier of land who has been served with a compliance notice may appeal to a residential property tribunal against that notice (for further provision about appeals under this section, see section 9G).

(4) A local authority may—

(*a*) revoke a compliance notice;

(*b*) vary a compliance notice by extending the period specified in the notice under subsection (2)(*c*).

(5) The power to revoke or vary a compliance notice is exercisable by the local authority—

(*a*) on an application made by the occupier of land on whom the notice was served, or

(*b*) on the authority's own initiative.

(6) Where a local authority revoke or vary a compliance notice, they must notify the occupier of the land to which the notice relates of the decision as soon as is reasonably practicable.

(7) Where a compliance notice is revoked, the revocation comes into force at the time when it is made.

(8) Where a compliance notice is varied—

(*a*) if the notice has not become operative (see section 9H) when the variation is made, the variation comes into force at such time (if any) as the notice becomes operative in accordance with section 9H;

(*b*) if the notice has become operative when the variation is made, the variation comes into force at the time when it is made.

[Caravan Sites and Control of Development Act 1960, s 9A as inserted by the Mobile Homes Act 2013, s 4.]

**7.11378 9B. Compliance notice under section 9A: offence and multiple convictions**

(1) An occupier of land who has been served with a compliance notice which has become operative (see section 9H) commits an offence if the occupier fails to take the steps specified in the notice under section 9A(2)(*b*) within the period so specified under section 9A(2)(*c*).

(2) A person guilty of an offence under subsection (1) is liable on summary conviction to a fine not exceeding level 5 on the standard scale.

(3) In proceedings against an occupier of land for an offence under subsection (1), it is a defence that the occupier had a reasonable excuse for failing to take the steps referred to in subsection (1) within the period referred to in that subsection.

(4) Subsection (5) applies where—

(*a*) an occupier of land is convicted of an offence under subsection (1), and

(*b*) the occupier has been convicted on two or more previous occasions of an offence under subsection (1), or an offence under section 9 committed before the commencement of this section, in relation to the site licence to which the conviction mentioned in paragraph (*a*) relates.

(5) On an application by the local authority who served the compliance notice in question, the court before which the occupier of the land was convicted may make an order revoking the site licence in question on the date specified in the order.

(6) An order under subsection (5) must not specify a date which is before the end of the period within which notice of appeal (whether by case stated or otherwise) may be given against the conviction mentioned in subsection (4)(*a*).

(7) Where an appeal against the conviction mentioned in subsection (4)(*a*) is made by the occupier of the land before the date specified in an order under subsection (5), the order does not take effect until—

(*a*) the appeal is finally determined, or

(*b*) the appeal is withdrawn.

(8) On an application by the occupier of the land or by the local authority who issued the site licence, the court which made the order under subsection (5) may make an order specifying a date on which the revocation of the site licence takes effect which is later than the date specified in the order under subsection (5).

(9) But the court must not make an order under subsection (8) unless it is satisfied that adequate notice of the application has been given to the occupier of the land or to the local authority (as the case may be).

[Caravan Sites and Control of Development Act 1960, s 9B as inserted by the Mobile Homes Act 2013, s 4.]

**7.11379 9C. Compliance notice under section 9A: power to demand expenses**

(1) When serving a compliance notice on an occupier of land, a local authority may impose a charge on the occupier as a means of recovering expenses incurred by them—

(*a*) in deciding whether to serve the notice, and

(*b*) in preparing and serving the notice or a demand under subsection (3).

(2) The expenses referred to in subsection (1) include in particular the costs of obtaining expert advice (including legal advice).

(3) The power under subsection (1) is exercisable by serving the compliance notice together with a demand which sets out—

(*a*) the total expenses the local authority seek to recover under subsection (1) ("relevant expenses"),

(*b*) a detailed breakdown of the relevant expenses, and

(*c*) where the local authority propose to charge interest under section 9I, the rate at which the relevant expenses carry interest.

(4) Where a tribunal allows an appeal under section 9A against the compliance notice with which a demand was served, it may make such order as it considers appropriate—

(*a*) confirming, reducing or quashing any charge under this section made in respect of the notice, and

(*b*) varying the demand as appropriate in consequence.

[Caravan Sites and Control of Development Act 1960, s 9A as inserted by the Mobile Homes Act 2013, s 4.]

7.11380 **10. Transfer of site licences and transmission on death, etc** Provision is made for transfer of a site licence and for its devolution to a person becoming the occupier of the land.

[Caravan Sites and Control of Development Act 1960, s 10—summarised.]

7.11380A **10A. Powers to charge fees: supplementary**

7.11381 **11. Duty of licence holder to surrender licence for alteration** (1) A local authority who have issued a site licence may at any time require the holder to deliver it up so as to enable them to enter in it any alteration of the conditions or other terms of the licence made in pursuance of the provisions of this Part of this Act.

(2) If the holder of a site licence fails without reasonable excuse to comply with a requirement duly made under this section he shall be liable on summary conviction to a fine not exceeding **level 1** on the standard scale.

[Caravan Sites and Control of Development Act 1960, s 11 as amended by the Criminal Justice Act 1982, ss 38 and 46.]

*Caravans on commons*

7.11382 **23.** A district council may make an order with respect to prescribed commons in their area prohibiting the stationing of caravans on the land for the purposes of human habitation. Contravention of such an order is punishable on summary conviction by a fine not exceeding **level 1** on the standard scale.

[Caravan Sites and Control of Development Act 1960, s 23 as amended by the Local Government Act 1972, Sch 29, the Criminal Justice Act 1982, ss 38 and 46 and the Local Government (Wales) Act 1994, Sch 16—summarised.]

*Miscellaneous and supplemental*

7.11383 **26. Power of entry of officers of local authorities** (1) Subject to the provisions of this section, any authorised officer of a local authority shall, on producing, if so required, some duly authenticated document showing his authority, have a right at all reasonable hours to enter any land which is used as a caravan site or in respect of which an application for a site licence has been made—

(*a*) for the purpose of enabling the local authority to determine what conditions should be attached to a site licence or whether conditions attached to a site licence should be altered;

(*b*) for the purpose of ascertaining whether there is, or has been, on or in connection with the land any contravention of the provisions of this part of this Act;

(*c*) for the purpose of ascertaining whether or not circumstances exist which would authorise the local authority to take any action, or execute any work, under this Part of this Act;

(*d*) for the purpose of taking any action, or executing any work, authorised by this Part of this Act to be taken or executed by the local authority:

Provided that admission to any land shall not be demanded as of right unless twenty-four hours notice of the intended entry has been given to the occupier.

(2) If it is shown to the satisfaction of a justice of the peace—

(*a*) that admission to any land has been refused, or that refusal is apprehended, or that the occupier of the land is temporarily absent and the case is one of urgency, or that an application for admission would defeat the object of the entry; and

(*b*) that there is reasonable ground for entering on the land for any such purpose as is mentioned in subsection (1) of this section,

the justice may by warrant under his hand authorise the local authority by any authorised officer to enter the land, if need be by force:

Provided that such a warrant shall not be issued unless the justice is satisfied either that notice of the intention to apply for the warrant has been given to the occupier, or that the occupier is temporarily absent and the case is one of urgency, or that the giving of such notice would defeat the object of the entry.

(3) An authorised officer entering any land by virtue of this section, or of a warrant issued thereunder, may take with him such other persons as may be necessary.

(4) Every warrant granted under this section shall continue in force until the purpose for which the entry is necessary has been satisfied.

(5) A person who wilfully obstructs any person acting in the execution of this section, or of a warrant under this section, shall be liable on summary conviction—

(*a*) where the wilful obstruction occurs in relation to land in England, to a fine not exceeding level 4 on the standard scale;

(*b*) where the wilful obstruction occurs in relation to land in Wales, to a fine not exceeding level 1 on the standard scale.

[Caravan Sites and Control of Development Act 1960, s 26 as amended by the Criminal Justice Act 1982, ss 38 and 46 and the Mobile Homes Act 2013, s 13.]

7.11384 **26A. Liability of officers of bodies corporate** (1) This section applies to an offence under this Act committed in relation to land in England.

(2) Where a body corporate commits an offence to which this section applies and it is proved that—

(*a*) the offence was committed with the consent or connivance of an officer of the body corporate, or

(*b*) the offence was attributable to neglect on the part of an officer of the body corporate,

the officer, as well as the body corporate, is guilty of the offence and is liable to be proceeded against and punished accordingly.

(3) In subsection (2), "officer" means—

(*a*) a director, manager, secretary or similar officer of the body corporate,

(*b*) in the case of a body corporate whose affairs are managed by its members, a member of the body corporate, or

(*c*) a person purporting to act in a capacity mentioned in paragraph (*a*) or (*b*).

[Caravan Sites and Control of Development Act 1960, s 26A as inserted by the Mobile Homes Act 2013, s 14.]

# Caravan Sites Act 1968

(1968 c 52)

## Part I

## Provisions for Protection of Residential Occupiers

7.11385 **1. Application of Part I** (1) This Part of this Act applies in relation to any licence or contract (whether made before or after the passing of this Act) under which a person is entitled to station a caravan on a protected site (as defined by subsection (2) below) and occupy it at his residence, or to occupy as his residence a caravan stationed on any such site; and any such licence or contract is in this Part referred to as a residential contract, and the person so entitled as the occupier.

(2) For the purposes of this Part of this Act a protected site is any land in respect of which a site licence is required under Part I of the Caravan Sites and Control of Development Act 1960 or would be so required if paragraph 11 or 11A of Schedule 1 to that Act (exemption of gypsy and other local authority sites) were omitted, not being land in respect of which the relevant planning permission or site licence—

(*a*) is expressed to be granted for holiday use only; or

(*b*) is otherwise so expressed or subject to such conditions that there are times of the year when no caravan may be stationed on the land for human habitation.

(3) References in this Part of this Act to the owner of a protected site are references to the person who is or would apart from any residential contract be entitled to possession of the land.*

[Caravan Sites Act 1968, s 1 as amended by the Housing Act 2004, s 209.]

* **Reproduced as in force in England and Wales.**

7.11386 **3. Protection of occupiers against eviction and harassment** (1) Subject to the provisions of this section, a person shall be guilty of an offence under this section—

(*a*) if, during the subsistence of a residential contract, he unlawfully deprives the occupier of his occupation on the protected site of any caravan which the occupier is entitled by the contract to station and occupy, or to occupy, as his residence thereon;

(*b*) if, after the expiration or determination of a residential contract, he enforces, otherwise than by proceedings in the court, any right to exclude the occupier from the protected site or from any such caravan, or to remove or exclude any such caravan from the site;

(*c*) if, whether during the subsistence or after the expiration or determination of a residential contract, with intent to cause the occupier—

(i) to abandon the occupation of the caravan or remove it from the site, or

(ii) to refrain from exercising any right or pursuing any remedy in respect thereof,

he does acts likely to interfere with the peace or comfort of the occupier or persons residing with him, or withdraws or withholds or, if the site concerned is in Wales, persistently withdraws or withholds services or facilities reasonably required for the occupation of the caravan as a residence on the site.

(1A) Subject to the provisions of this section, the owner of a protected site or his agent shall be guilty of an offence under this section if, whether during the subsistence or after the expiration or determination of a residential contract—

(*a*) he does acts likely to interfere with the peace or comfort of the occupier or persons residing with him, or

(*b*) he withdraws or withholds or, if the site concerned is in Wales, persistently withdraws or withholds services or facilities reasonably required for the occupation of the caravan as a residence on the site,

and (in either case) he knows, or has reasonable cause to believe, that that conduct is likely to cause the occupier to do any of the things mentioned in subsection (1)(*c*)(i) or (ii) of this section.

(1AA) The owner of a protected site in England or the owner's agent is guilty of an offence under this section if, during the subsistence of a residential contract, the owner or (as the case may be) agent—

(*a*) knowingly or recklessly provides information or makes a representation which is false or misleading in a material respect to any person, and

(*b*) knows, or has reasonable cause to believe, that doing so is likely to cause—

(i) the occupier to do any of the things mentioned in subsection (1)(*c*)(i) or (ii), or
(ii) a person who is considering whether to purchase or occupy the caravan to which the residential contract relates to decide not to do so.

(1B) References in subsections (1A) and (1AA) of this section to the owner of a protected site include references to a person with an estate or interest in the site which is superior to that of the owner.

(2) References in this section to the occupier include references to the person who was the occupier under a residential contract which has expired or been determined and, in the case of the death of the occupier (whether during the subsistence or after the expiration or determination of the contract), to any person then residing with the occupier being—

(*a*) The widow, widower or surviving civil partner of the occupier; or
(*b*) in default of a widow, widower or surviving civil partner so residing, any member of the occupier's family.

(3) A person guilty of an offence under this section shall, without prejudice to any liability or remedy to which he may be subject in civil proceedings, be liable—

(*a*) on summary conviction, to a fine not exceeding the statutory maximum or to imprisonment for a term not exceeding 12 months, or to both;
(*b*) on conviction on indictment, to a fine or to imprisonment for a term not exceeding 2 years, or to both.

(4) In proceedings for an offence under paragraph (*a*) or (*b*) of subsection (1) of this section it shall be a defence to prove that the accused believed, and had reasonable cause to believe, that the occupier of the caravan had ceased to reside on the site.

(4A) In proceedings for an offence under subsection (1A) of this section it shall be a defence to prove that the accused had reasonable grounds for doing the acts or withdrawing or withholding the services or facilities in question.

(5) Nothing in this section applies to the exercise by any person of a right to take possession of a caravan of which he is the owner, other than a right conferred by or arising on the expiration or determination of a residential contract, or to anything done pursuant to the order of any court.*

[Caravan Sites Act 1968, s 3 as amended by the Criminal Justice Act 1982, ss 35, 38 and 46, the Housing Act 2004, s 210, the Civil Partnership Act 2004, Sch 27 and the Mobile Homes Act 2013, s 12.]

---

* **Reproduced as in force in England and Wales.**

## PART III

7.11387 **13. Twin-unit caravans** (1) A structure designed or adapted for human habitation which—

(*a*) is composed of not more than two sections separately constructed and designed to be assembled on a site by means of bolts, clamps or other devices; and
(*b*) is, when assembled, physically capable of being moved by road from one place to another (whether by being towed, or by being transported on a motor vehicle or trailer),

shall not be treated as not being (or as not having been) a caravan within the meaning of Part I of the Caravan Sites and Control of Development Act 1960 by reason only that it cannot lawfully be so moved on a highway when assembled.

(2) For the purposes of Part I of the Caravan Sites and Control of Development Act 1960, the expression "caravan" shall not include a structure designed or adapted for human habitation which falls within paragraphs (*a*) and (*b*) of the foregoing subsection if its dimensions when assembled exceed any of the following limits, namely—

(*a*) length (exclusive of any drawbar): 65.616 feet (20 metres);
(*b*) width: 22.309 feet (6.8 metres);
(*c*) overall height of living accommodation (measured internally from the floor at the lowest level to the ceiling at the highest level): 10.006 feet (3.05 metres).

(3) The Minister may by order made by statutory instrument after consultation with such persons or bodies as appear to him to be concerned substitute for any figure mentioned in subsection (2) of this section such other figure as may be specified in the order.

(4) Any statutory instrument made by virtue of subsection (3) of this section shall be subject to annulment in pursuance of a resolution of either House of Parliament.

[Caravan Sites Act 1968, s 13 as amended by SI 2006/2374 and SI 2007/3163.]

7.11388 **14. Offences** (1) Where an offence under this Act committed by a body corporate is proved to have been committed with the consent or connivance of or to be attributable to any neglect on the part of, any director, manager, secretary or other similar officer of the body corporate or any person who is purporting to act in any such capacity, he as well as the body corporate shall be guilty of that offence and shall be liable to be proceeded against and punished accordingly.

(2) Proceedings for an offence under this Act may be instituted by any local authority.

[Caravan Sites Act 1968, s 14.]

7.11389 **16. Interpretation** In this Act the following expressions have the following meanings that is to say—

"caravan" has the same meaning as in Part I of the Caravan Sites and Control of Development Act 1960, as amended by this Act;

"local authority" has the same meaning as in section 24 of the Caravan Sites and Control of Development Act 1960;

"the Minister" means, in England other than Monmouthshire, the Minister of Housing and Local Government, and in Wales and Monmouthshire the Secretary of State;

"planning permission" means permission under Part III of the Town and Country Planning Act 1990.

[Caravan Sites Act 1968, s 16 as amended by the Town and Country Planning Act 1971, Sch 23, the Planning (Consequential Provisions) Act 1990, Sch 2 and the Criminal Justice and Public Order Act 1994, Sch 11.]

# Town and Country Planning Act 1990

(1990 c 8)

## PART III

## CONTROL OVER DEVELOPMENT[1]

### *Meaning of development*

7.11390 55. **Meaning of "development" and "new development"** (1) Subject to the following provisions of this section, in this Act, except where the context otherwise requires, "development," means the carrying out of building, engineering, mining or other operations in, on, over or under land, or the making of any material change in the use of any buildings or other land.

(1A) For the purposes of this Act "building operations" includes—

(*a*) demolition of buildings;

(*b*) rebuilding;

(*c*) structural alterations of or additions to buildings; and

(*d*) other operations normally undertaken by a person carrying on business as a builder.

(2) The following operations or uses of land shall not be taken for the purposes of this Act to involve development of the land—

(*a*) the carrying out for the maintenance, improvement or other alteration of any building of works which—

(i) affect only the interior of the building, or

(ii) do not materially affect the external appearance of the building,

and are not works for making good war damage or works begun after 5th December 1968 for the alteration of a building by providing additional space in it underground;

(*b*) the carrying out on land within the boundaries of a road by a highway authority of any works required for the maintenance or improvement of the road but, in the case of any such works which are not exclusively for the maintenance of the road, not including any works which may have significant adverse effects on the environment;

(*c*) the carrying out by a local authority or statutory undertakers of any works for the purpose of inspecting, repairing or renewing any sewers, mains, pipes, cables or other apparatus, including the breaking open of any street or other land for that purpose;

(*d*) the use of any buildings or other land within the curtilage of a dwellinghouse for any purpose incidental to the enjoyment of the dwellinghouse as such;

(*e*) the use of any land for the purposes of agriculture or forestry (including afforestation) and the use for any of those purposes of any building occupied together with land so used;

(*f*) in the case of buildings or other land which are used for a purpose of any class specified in an order made by the Secretary of State under this section, the use of the buildings or other land or, subject to the provisions of the order, of any part of the buildings or the other land, for any other purpose of the same class;

(*g*) the demolition of any description of building specified in a direction given by the Secretary of State to local planning authorities generally or to a particular local planning authority.

(2A) The Secretary of State may in a development order specify any circumstances or description of circumstances in which subsection (2) does not apply to operations mentioned in paragraph (*a*) of that subsection which have the effect of increasing the gross floor space of the building by such amount or percentage amount as is so specified.

(2B) The development order may make different provision for different purposes.

(3) For the avoidance of doubt it is hereby declared that for the purposes of this section—

(*a*) the use as two or more separate dwellinghouses of any building previously used as a single dwellinghouse involves a material change in the use of the building and of each part of it which is so used;

(*b*) the deposit of refuse or waste materials on land involves a material change in its use, notwithstanding that the land is comprised in a site already used for that purpose, if—

(i) the superficial area of the deposit is extended, or

(ii) the height of the deposit is extended and exceeds the level of the land adjoining the site.

(4) For the purposes of this Act mining operations include—

(*a*) the removal of material of any description—

(i) from a mineral-working deposit;

(ii) from a deposit of pulverised fuel ash or other furnace ash or clinker; or

(iii) from a deposit of iron, steel or other metallic slags; and

(*b*) the extraction of minerals from a disused railway embankment.

(4A) Where the placing or assembly of any tank in any part of any inland waters for the purpose of fish farming there would not, apart from this subsection, involve development of the land below, this Act shall have effect as if the tank resulted from carrying out engineering operations over that land; and in this subsection—

"fish farming" means the breeding, rearing or keeping of fish or shellfish (which includes any kind of crustacean and mollusc);

"inland waters" means waters which do not form part of the sea or of any creek, bay or estuary or of any river as far as the tide flows; and

"tank" includes any cage and any other structure for use in fish farming.

(5) Without prejudice to any regulations made under the provisions of this Act relating to the control of advertisements, the use for the display of advertisements of any external part of a building which is not normally used for that purpose shall be treated for the purposes of this section as involving a material change in the use of that part of the building.

(6) *Repealed.*

[Town and Country Planning Act 1990, s 55 as amended by the Planning and Compensation Act 1991, ss 13, 14 and Sch 19, SI 1999/293 and the Planning and Compulsory Purchase Act 2004, s 49 and Sch 9.]

---

[1] Part III contains ss 55–106C.

7.11391 **65. Notice etc of applications for planning permission or permission in principle**

(1) A development order may make provision requiring—

(*a*) notice to be given of any application for planning permission or permission in principle, and

(*b*) any applicant for such permission to issue a certificate as to the interests in the land to which the application relates or the purpose for which it is used,

and provide for publicising such applications and for the form, content and service of such notices and certificates.

(2) Provision shall be made by a development order for the purpose of securing that, in the case of any application for planning permission, any person (other than the applicant) who on such date as may be prescribed by the order is an owner of the land to which the application relates, or an agricultural tenant of that land, is given notice of the application in such manner as may be required by the order.

(3) A development order may require an applicant for planning permission or permission in principle to certify, in such form as may be prescribed by the order, or to provide evidence, that any requirements of the order have been satisfied.

(3A) In subsections (1) and (3) references to any application for planning permission or any applicant for such permission include references to any application for approval under section 61L(2) or any applicant for such approval._

(a) any application for consent, agreement or approval as mentioned in section 61DB(2) or any applicant for such consent, agreement or approval, and

(b)

(4) A development order making any provision by virtue of this section may make different provision for different cases or different classes of development.

(5) A local planning authority shall not entertain an application for planning permission or permission in principle unless any requirements imposed by virtue of this section have been satisfied.

(6) If any person—

(*a*) issues a certificate which purports to comply with any requirement imposed by virtue of this section and contains a statement which he knows to be false or misleading in a material particular; or

(*b*) recklessly issues a certificate which purports to comply with any such requirement and contains a statement which is false or misleading in a material particular;

he shall be guilty of an offence.

(7) A person guilty of an offence under this section shall be liable on summary conviction to a fine not exceeding **level 5** on the standard scale.

(8) In this section—

"agricultural tenant", in relation to any land, means any person who—

(*a*) is the tenant, under a tenancy in relation to which the Agricultural Holdings Act 1986 applies, of an agricultural holding within the meaning of that Act any part of which is comprised in that land; or

(*b*) is the tenant, under a farm business tenancy (within the meaning of the Agricultural Tenancies Act 1995), of land any part of which is comprised in that land;

"owner" in relation to any land means any person who—

(*a*) is the estate owner in respect of the fee simple;

(*b*) is entitled to a tenancy granted or extended for a term of years certain of which not less than seven years remain unexpired; or (*c*) in the case of such applications as may be prescribed by a development order, is entitled to an interest in any mineral so prescribed,

and the reference to the interests in the land to which an application for planning permission or permission in principle relates includes any interest in any mineral in, on or under the land.

(9) Notwithstanding section 127 of the Magistrates' Courts Act 1980, a magistrates' court may try an information in respect of an offence under this section whenever laid.

[Town and Country Planning Act 1990, s 65 as substituted by the Planning and Compensation Act 1991, s 16 and amended by the Agricultural Tenancies Act 1995, Sch, the Localism Act 2011, Sch 12 and the Housing and Planning Act 2016, Sch 12.]

* **Words inserted by the Infrastructure Act 2015, Sch 4 from a date to be appointed.**

7.11392 **102. Orders requiring discontinuance of use or alteration or removal of buildings or works** [1] A local planning authority, if it appears expedient so to do in the interests of the proper planning, may by order require that any use of land should be discontinued, or that any conditions be imposed on the continuance thereof, or that any buildings or works should be altered or removed. Such an order requires to be confirmed by the Secretary of State after the owner and occupier and any other person affected has been given an opportunity of being heard. Where such an order involves the displacement of persons residing in any premises, provision is made for their being provided with alternative accommodation.

[Town and Country Planning Act 1990, s 102 as amended by the Planning and Compensation Act 1991, Schs 1, 7—summarised.]

1 Schedule 9 to this Act makes provision for the discontinuance of mineral working. For enforcement of orders under this section see s 172 et seq.

## PART VII
## ENFORCEMENT

### *Enforcement notices*[1]
### *Introductory*

7.11393 **171A. Expressions used in connection with enforcement**[2] (1) For the purposes of this Act—

(*a*) carrying out development without the required planning permission; or

(*b*) failing to comply with any condition or limitation subject to which planning permission has been granted,

constitutes a breach of planning control.

(2) For the purposes of this Act—

(*a*) the issue of an enforcement notice (defined in section 172); or

(*b*) the service of a breach of condition notice (defined in section 187A),

constitutes taking enforcement action.

(3) In this Part "planning permission" includes permission under Part III of the 1947 Act, of the 1962 Act or of the 1971 Act.

[Town and Country Planning Act 1990, s 171A as inserted by the Planning and Compensation Act 1991, s 4.]

1 Part VII contains ss 171A–196.

2 Control of development on Crown land is provided by s 294 of this Act.

7.11394 **171B. Time limits** (1) Where there has been a breach of planning control consisting in the carrying out without planning permission of building, engineering, mining or other operations in, on, over or under land, no enforcement action may be taken after the end of the period of four years beginning with the date on which the operations were substantially completed[1].

(2) Where there has been a breach of planning control consisting in the change of use of any building to use as a single dwellinghouse, no enforcement action may be taken after the end of the period of four years beginning with the date of the breach[2].

(3) In the case of any other breach of planning control, no enforcement action may be taken after the end of the period of ten years beginning with the date of the breach.

(4) The preceding subsections do not prevent—

(*a*) the service of a breach of condition notice in respect of any breach of planning control if an enforcement notice in respect of the breach is in effect; or

(*b*) taking further enforcement action in respect of any breach of planning control if, during the period of four years ending with that action being taken, the local planning authority have taken or purported to take enforcement action in respect of that breach[3].

[Town and Country Planning Act 1990, s 171B as inserted by the Planning and Compensation Act 1991, s 4.]

1 The purpose of this provision is to provide a single easily-applied limitation period for operations. In considering whether a building is "substantially completed" it is appropriate to adopt a holistic approach and the question is not confined to those aspects of the development which require planning consent and includes the remainder of the works, such as interior works, which fall outside the definition of development in s 55(2) of the Act (*Sage v Secretary of State for the Environment, Transport and the Regions* [2003] UKHL 22, [2003] 2 All ER 689).

2 If, in the case of any breach of planning control, the time for issuing an enforcement notice has expired, before the coming into force of this section, by virtue of section 172(4)(*b*) of the principal Act (as originally enacted), nothing in this section enables any enforcement action to be taken in respect of the breach; (Planning and Compensation Act 1991,

s 4(2)). There was no change of use where the defendant had deliberately concealed the construction of a dwelling house instead of the permitted barn: *Welwyn Hatfield Borough Council v Secretary of State for Communities and Local Government* [2011] UKSC 15, [2011] AC 304.

[3] The breach does not have to be identically described on both occasions. Accordingly where the first enforcement notice referred to a mobile home which the defendant subsequently transformed into a single storey dwelling, the second enforcement notice referring to it or such, was directed at the same development and was within the terms of the subsection (*Jarmain v Secretary of State for the Environment, Transport and the Regions* [1999] 15 LS Gaz R 30).

7.11395 **171BA. Time limits in cases involving concealment** (1) Where it appears to the local planning authority that there may have been a breach of planning control in respect of any land in England, the authority may apply to a magistrates' court for an order under this subsection (a "planning enforcement order") in relation to that apparent breach of planning control.

(2) If a magistrates' court makes a planning enforcement order in relation to an apparent breach of planning control, the local planning authority may take enforcement action in respect of—

(*a*) the apparent breach, or

(*b*) any of the matters constituting the apparent breach,

at any time in the enforcement year.

(3) "The enforcement year" for a planning enforcement order is the year that begins at the end of 22 days beginning with the day on which the court's decision to make the order is given, but this is subject to subsection (4).

(4) If an application under section 111(1) of the Magistrates' Courts Act 1980 (statement of case for opinion of High Court) is made in respect of a planning enforcement order, the enforcement year for the order is the year beginning with the day on which the proceedings arising from that application are finally determined or withdrawn.

(5) Subsection (2)—

(*a*) applies whether or not the time limits under section 171B have expired, and

(*b*) does not prevent the taking of enforcement action after the end of the enforcement year but within those time limits.

[Town and Country Planning Act 1990, s 171BA as inserted by the Localism Act 2011, s 124.]

7.11396 **171BB. Planning enforcement orders: procedure** (1) An application for a planning enforcement order in relation to an apparent breach of planning control may be made within the 6 months beginning with the date on which evidence of the apparent breach of planning control sufficient in the opinion of the local planning authority to justify the application came to the authority's knowledge.

(2) For the purposes of subsection (1), a certificate—

(*a*) signed on behalf of the local planning authority, and

(*b*) stating the date on which evidence sufficient in the authority's opinion to justify the application came to the authority's knowledge,

is conclusive evidence of that fact.

(3) A certificate stating that matter and purporting to be so signed is to be deemed to be so signed unless the contrary is proved.

(4) Where the local planning authority apply to a magistrates' court for a planning enforcement order in relation to an apparent breach of planning control in respect of any land, the authority must serve a copy of the application—

(*a*) on the owner and on the occupier of the land, and

(*b*) on any other person having an interest in the land that is an interest which, in the opinion of the authority, would be materially affected by the taking of enforcement action in respect of the apparent breach.

(5) The persons entitled to appear before, and be heard by, the court hearing an application for a planning enforcement order in relation to an apparent breach of planning control in respect of any land include—

(*a*) the applicant,

(*b*) any person on whom a copy of the application was served under subsection (4), and

(*c*) any other person having an interest in the land that is an interest which, in the opinion of the court, would be materially affected by the taking of enforcement action in respect of the apparent breach.

(6) In this section "planning enforcement order" means an order under section 171BA(1).

[Town and Country Planning Act 1990, s 171BB as inserted by the Localism Act 2011, s 124.]

7.11397 **171BC. Making a planning enforcement order** (1) A magistrates' court may make a planning enforcement order in relation to an apparent breach of planning control only if—

(*a*) the court is satisfied, on the balance of probabilities, that the apparent breach, or any of the matters constituting the apparent breach, has (to any extent) been deliberately concealed by any person or persons, and

(*b*) the court considers it just to make the order having regard to all the circumstances.

(2) A planning enforcement order must—

(*a*) identify the apparent breach of planning control to which it relates, and

(*b*) state the date on which the court's decision to make the order was given.

(3) In this section "planning enforcement order" means an order under section 171BA(1).

[Town and Country Planning Act 1990, s 171BC as inserted by the Localism Act 2011, s 124.]

*Planning contravention notices*

**7.11398 171C. Power to require information about activities on land** (1) Where it appears to the local planning authority that there may have been a breach of planning control in respect of any land, they may serve notice to that effect (referred to in this Act as a "planning contravention notice") on any person who—

(*a*) is the owner or occupier of the land or has any other interest in it; or

(*b*) is carrying out operations on the land or is using it for any purpose.

(2) A planning contravention notice may require the person on whom it is served to give such information as to—

(*a*) any operations being carried out on the land, any use of the land and any other activities being carried out on the land; and

(*b*) any matter relating to the conditions or limitations subject to which any planning permission in respect of the land has been granted,

as may be specified in the notice.

(3) Without prejudice to the generality of subsection (2), the notice may require the person on whom it is served, so far as he is able—

(*a*) to state whether or not the land is being used for any purpose specified in the notice or any operations or activities specified in the notice are being or have been carried out on the land;

(*b*) to state when any use, operations or activities began;

(*c*) to give the name and postal address of any person known to him to use or have used the land for any purpose or to be carrying out, or have carried out, any operations or activities on the land;

(*d*) to give any information he holds as to any planning permission for any use or operations or any reason for planning permission not being required for any use or operations;

(*e*) to state the nature of his interest (if any) in the land and the name and postal address of any other person known to him to have an interest in the land.

(4) A planning contravention notice may give notice of a time and place at which—

(*a*) any offer which the person on whom the notice is served may wish to make to apply for planning permission, to refrain from carrying out any operations or activities or to undertake remedial works; and

(*b*) any representations which he may wish to make about the notice,

will be considered by the authority, and the authority shall give him an opportunity to make in person any such offer or representations at that time and place.

(5) A planning contravention notice must inform the person on whom it is served—

(*a*) of the likely consequences of his failing to respond to the notice and, in particular, that enforcement action may be taken; and

(*b*) of the effect of section 186(5)(*b*).

(6) Any requirement of a planning contravention notice shall be complied with by giving information in writing to the local planning authority.

(7) The service of a planning contravention notice does not affect any other power exercisable in respect of any breach of planning control.

(8) In this section references to operations or activities on land include operations or activities in, under or over the land.

[Town and Country Planning Act 1990, s 171C as inserted by the Planning and Compensation Act 1991, s 1 and amended by SI 2003/956 and SI 2004/3156.]

**7.11399 171D. Penalties for non-compliance with planning contravention notice** (1) If, at any time after the end of the period of twenty-one days beginning with the day on which a planning contravention notice has been served on any person, he has not complied with any requirement of the notice, he shall be guilty of an offence.

(2) An offence under subsection (1) may be charged by reference to any day or longer period of time and a person may be convicted of a second or subsequent offence under that subsection by reference to any period of time following the preceding conviction for such an offence.

(3) It shall be a defence for a person charged with an offence under subsection (1) to prove that he had a reasonable excuse for failing to comply with the requirement.

(4) A person guilty of an offence under subsection (1) shall be liable on summary conviction to a fine not exceeding **level 3** on the standard scale.

(5) If any person—

(*a*) makes any statement purporting to comply with a requirement of a planning contravention notice which he knows to be false or misleading in a material particular; or

(*b*) recklessly makes such a statement which is false or misleading in a material particular,

he shall be guilty of an offence.

(6) A person guilty of an offence under subsection (5) shall be liable on summary conviction to a fine not exceeding **level 5** on the standard scale.

[Town and Country Planning Act 1990, s 171D as inserted by the Planning and Compensation Act 1991, s 1.]

**7.11400 171E. Temporary stop notice** (1) This section applies if the local planning authority think—

(*a*) that there has been a breach of planning control in relation to any land, and

(*b*) that it is expedient that the activity (or any part of the activity) which amounts to the breach is stopped immediately.

(2) The authority may issue a temporary stop notice.

(3) The notice must be in writing and must—

(*a*) specify the activity which the authority think amounts to the breach;

(*b*) prohibit the carrying on of the activity (or of so much of the activity as is specified in the notice);

(*c*) set out the authority's reasons for issuing the notice.

(4) A temporary stop notice may be served on any of the following—

(*a*) the person who the authority think is carrying on the activity;

(*b*) a person who the authority think is an occupier of the land;

(*c*) a person who the authority think has an interest in the land.

(5) The authority must display on the land—

(*a*) a copy of the notice;

(*b*) a statement of the effect of the notice and of section 171G.

(6) A temporary stop notice has effect from the time a copy of it is first displayed in pursuance of subsection (5).

(7) A temporary stop notice ceases to have effect—

(*a*) at the end of the period of 28 days starting on the day the copy notice is so displayed,

(*b*) at the end of such shorter period starting on that day as is specified in the notice, or

(*c*) if it is withdrawn by the local planning authority.

[Town and Country Planning Act 1990, s 171E as inserted by the Planning and Compulsory Purchase Act 2004, s 52.]

**7.11401 171F. Temporary stop notice: restrictions** (1) A temporary stop notice does not prohibit—

(*a*) the use of a building as a dwelling house;

(*b*) the carrying out of an activity of such description or in such circumstances as is prescribed.

(2) A temporary stop notice does not prohibit the carrying out of any activity which has been carried out (whether or not continuously) for a period of four years ending with the day on which the copy of the notice is first displayed as mentioned in section 171E(6).

(3) Subsection (2) does not prevent a temporary stop notice prohibiting—

(*a*) activity consisting of or incidental to building, engineering, mining or other operations, or

(*b*) the deposit of refuse or waste materials.

(4) For the purposes of subsection (2) any period during which the activity is authorised by planning permission must be ignored.

(5) A second or subsequent temporary stop notice must not be issued in respect of the same activity unless the local planning authority has first taken some other enforcement action in relation to the breach of planning control which is constituted by the activity.

(6) In subsection (5) enforcement action includes obtaining the grant of an injunction under section 187B.

[Town and Country Planning Act 1990, s 171F as inserted by the Planning and Compulsory Purchase Act 2004, s 52.]

**7.11402 171G. Temporary stop notice: offences** (1) A person commits an offence if he contravenes a temporary stop notice—

(*a*) which has been served on him, or

(*b*) a copy of which has been displayed in accordance with section 171E(5).

(2) Contravention of a temporary stop notice includes causing or permitting the contravention of the notice.

(3) An offence under this section may be charged by reference to a day or a longer period of time.

(4) A person may be convicted of more than one such offence in relation to the same temporary stop notice by reference to different days or periods of time.

(5) A person does not commit an offence under this section if he proves—

(*a*) that the temporary stop notice was not served on him, and

(*b*) that he did not know, and could not reasonably have been expected to know, of its existence.

(6) A person convicted of an offence under this section is liable on summary conviction, or on conviction on indictment, to a fine.

(7) In determining the amount of the fine the court must have regard in particular to any financial benefit which has accrued or has appeared to accrue to the person convicted in consequence of the offence.

[Town and Country Planning Act 1990, s 171G as inserted by the Planning and Compulsory Purchase Act 2004, s 52 and amended by SI 2015/664.]

7.11403 **171H. Temporary stop notice: compensation** (1) This section applies if and only if a temporary stop notice is issued and at least one of the following paragraphs applies—

(*a*) the activity which is specified in the notice is authorised by planning permission or by a development order, a local development order or a neighbourhood development order;

(*b*) a certificate in respect of the activity is issued under section 191 or granted under that section by virtue of section 195;

(*c*) the authority withdraws the notice.

(2) Subsection (1)(*a*) does not apply if the planning permission is granted on or after the date on which a copy of the notice is first displayed as mentioned in section 171E(6).

(3) Subsection (1)(*c*) does not apply if the notice is withdrawn following the grant of planning permission as mentioned in subsection (2).

(4) A person who at the time the notice is served has an interest in the land to which the notice relates is entitled to be compensated by the local planning authority in respect of any loss or damage directly attributable to the prohibition effected by the notice.

(5) Subsections (3) to (7) of section 186 apply to compensation payable under this section as they apply to compensation payable under that section; and for that purpose references in those subsections to a stop notice must be taken to be references to a temporary stop notice.*

[Town and Country Planning Act 1990, s 171H as inserted by the Planning and Compulsory Purchase Act 2004, s 52 and amended by the Localism Act 2011, Sch 12.]

* **Amended by the Infrastructure Act 2015, Sch 4 from a date to be appointed.**

7.11404 **172. Issue of enforcement notice** (1) The local planning authority may issue a notice (in this Act referred to as an "enforcement notice") where it appears to them—

(*a*) that there has been a breach of planning control[1], and

(*b*) that it is expedient to issue the notice, having regard to the provisions of the development plan and to any other material considerations.

(2) A copy of an enforcement notice shall be served[2]—

(*a*) on the owner[3] and on the occupier of the land[3] to which it relates; and

(*b*) on any other person having an interest in the land, being an interest which, in the opinion of the authority, is materially affected by the notice.

(3) The service[2] of the notice shall take place—

(*a*) not more than twenty-eight days after its date of issue; and

(*b*) not less than twenty-eight days before the date specified in it as the date on which it is to take effect.

[Town and Country Planning Act 1990, s 172 as substituted by the Planning and Compensation Act 1991, s 5.]

1 Control of development on Crown land is provided by s 294 of this Act. "Development" is defined by s 55 ante.

2 For mode of service see s 329 post, and *Moody v Godstone RDC* [1966] 2 All ER 696, 130 JP 332. The validity of an enforcement notice may generally be questioned only by way of an appeal; see s 285.

Notice must be served on all the occupiers (*Caravans and Automobiles Ltd v Southall Borough Council* [1963] 2 All ER 533, 127 JP 415), which may include squatters (*Scarborough Borough Council v Adams and Adams* (1983) 147 JP 449); this case also sanctioned the service of a notice on someone not categorised in sub-s (6)(*a*) or (*b*), although service on someone not within the definition of "owners" has been held to be invalid (*Courtney-Southan v Crawley UDC* [1967] 2 QB 930, [1967] 2 All ER 246, 131 JP 330. Failure to serve a notice in accordance with the Act's requirements may not render the notice a nullity (*R v Greenwich London Borough Council, ex p Patel* (1985) 84 LGR 241, 51 P & CR 232, CA).

3 "Owner" and "land" are defined in s 336, post. The phrase "multiple paying occupation" was considered in *Duffy v Pilling* (1976) 120 Sol Jo 504.

7.11405 **172A. Assurance as regards prosecution for person served with notice** (1) When, or at any time after, an enforcement notice is served on a person, the local planning authority may give the person a letter—

(*a*) explaining that, once the enforcement notice had been issued, the authority was required to serve the notice on the person,

(*b*) giving the person one of the following assurances—

(i) that, in the circumstances as they appear to the authority, the person is not at risk of being prosecuted under section 179 in connection with the enforcement notice, or

(ii) that, in the circumstances as they appear to the authority, the person is not at risk of being prosecuted under section 179 in connection with the matters relating to the enforcement notice that are specified in the letter,

(*c*) explaining, where the person is given the assurance under paragraph (*b*)(ii), the respects in which the person is at risk of being prosecuted under section 179 in connection with the enforcement notice, and

(*d*) stating that, if the authority subsequently wishes to withdraw the assurance in full or part, the authority will first give the person a letter specifying a future time for the withdrawal that will allow the person a reasonable opportunity to take any steps necessary to avoid any risk of prosecution that is to cease to be covered by the assurance.

(2) At any time after a person has under subsection (1) been given a letter containing an assurance, the local planning authority may give the person a letter withdrawing the assurance (so

far as not previously withdrawn) in full or part from a time specified in the letter.

(3) The time specified in a letter given under subsection (2) to a person must be such as will give the person a reasonable opportunity to take any steps necessary to avoid any risk of prosecution that is to cease to be covered by the assurance.

(4) Withdrawal under subsection (2) of an assurance given under subsection (1) does not withdraw the assurance so far as relating to prosecution on account of there being a time before the withdrawal when steps had not been taken or an activity had not ceased.

(5) An assurance given under subsection (1) (so far as not withdrawn under subsection (2)) is binding on any person with power to prosecute an offence under section 179.

[Town and Country Planning Act 1990, s 172 as inserted by the Localism Act 2011, s 125.]

7.11406 173. *Contents and effect of notice.*

7.11407 173A. *Variation and withdrawal of enforcement notices.*

7.11408 174–177. *Appeal against enforcement notice.*

7.11409 178. *Execution and costs of works required by enforcement notice.*

7.11410 179. **Offence where enforcement notice not complied with** (1) Where, at any time after the end of the period for compliance with an enforcement notice,[1] any step required by the notice to be taken has not been taken or any activity[2] required by the notice to cease is being carried on, the person who is then the owner of the land is in breach of the notice.

(2) Where the owner of the land is in breach of an enforcement notice he shall be guilty of an offence[3].

(3) In proceedings against any person for an offence under subsection (2), it shall be a defence for him to show that he did everything he could be expected to do to secure compliance with the notice[4].

(4) A person who has control of or an interest in the land to which an enforcement notice relates (other than the owner) must not carry on any activity which is required by the notice to cease or cause[5] or permit such an activity to be carried on.

(5) A person who, at any time after the end of the period for compliance with the notice, contravenes subsection (4) shall be guilty of an offence.

(6) An offence under subsection (2) or (5) may be charged by reference to any day or longer period of time and a person may be convicted of a second or subsequent offence under the subsection in question by reference to any period of time following the preceding conviction for such an offence.

(7) Where—

(*a*) a person charged with an offence under this section has not been served with a copy of the enforcement notice; and

(*b*) the notice is not contained in the appropriate register[6] kept under section 188,

it shall be a defence[7] for him to show that he was not aware of the existence of the notice.

(8) A person guilty of an offence under this section shall be liable[8] on summary conviction, or on conviction on indictment, to a fine.

(9) In determining the amount of any fine to be imposed on a person convicted of an offence under this section, the court shall in particular have regard to any financial benefit[9] which has accrued or appears likely to accrue to him in consequence of the offence.

[Town and Country Planning Act 1990, s 179 as substituted by the Planning and Compensation Act 1991, s 8 and amended by SI 2015/664.]

---

1 A defect in an enforcement notice does not render the notice invalid unless it amounts to a material error which causes an injustice: *Patel v Betts* (1977) 243 Estates Gazette 1003. An "enforcement notice" means a notice issued by a planning authority which on its face complies with the requirements of the Act and has not actually been quashed on appeal or by judicial review. Therefore a defendant in criminal proceedings is not entitled as a matter of right to put forward the defence that the decision to issue the enforcement notice was ultra vires such as where it is alleged the local authority's decision was influenced by bias or improper motives: *R v Wicks* [1997] 2 All ER 801, [1997] 2WLR 876, 161 JP 433, HL. (See also the decision of the Court of Appeal in the same case where it was held that so long as the enforcement notice is not a nullity, patently defective on its face, it will remain valid until quashed. The prosecutor is under no requirement to establish that the decision of the local planning authority to issue the notice was valid and within its powers. Only the High Court has power to quash the notice. In an exceptional case where proper ground to challenge the validity of the notice came to light as a prosecution was about to be pursued, the appropriate procedure would be for the defendant to apply for an adjournment of the trial on an undertaking to apply for judicial review to quash the notice. If there is a sound basis for such an adjournment the court in its discretion might grant it: *R v Wicks* (1995) 160 JP 46, CA). An information alleging an offence under sub-ss (1) and (6) must aver to the compliance period which is an essential element of the offence: *Maltedge Ltd v Wokingham District Council* [1993] Crim LR 400.

2 It is a matter of fact and not for expert evidence as to whether a particular site is being used in a particular way during the relevant period against a background of planning law, and in particular the law relating to use, change of use and the like. Where what is in issue is, for example, whether the use is as a 'builders' merchant with ancillary sales' the prosecution does not have to differentiate each time between trade sales and retail sales, it is the nature of the evidence overall: *Matsons Ltd v Leicester City Council* [2016] EWHC 642 (Admin), 180 JP 302.

3 The offence under s 179(2) is only complete and crystallises (subject to the various "knowledge defences") once the period for compliance has expired but thereafter the offence is a continuing one: *Sanger v Newham London Borough Council* [2014] EWHC 1922 (Admin), [2015] 1 WLR 332, [2014] 2 P &CR 263.

4 The court is permitted to take into account the defendant's personal and financial circumstances in determining whether he has done everything he could be expected to do to secure compliance with the notice: *Kent County Council v Brockman* [1994] Crim LR 296. The primary objective of the legislation is to ensure compliance with planning controls. The role played by the criminal law is a secondary one, in support of that primary objective. The threat or potential risk of criminal proceedings concentrates the mind of a person, who will then take steps to ensure that a breach of planning

control comes to an end. Accordingly, a defendant is able to rely on this defence if he did everything he could reasonably be expected to do but did so only after the date specified in the enforcement notice has expired: *Sanger v London Borough of Newham*, supra.

[5] To "cause" involves some express or positive mandate from the person causing: *McLeod (or Houston) v Buchanan* [1940] 2 All ER 179, approved in *Shave v Rosner* [1954] 2 QB 113, [1954] 2 All ER 280, 118 JP 364, but see *Sopp v Long* [1969] 1 All ER 855, 133 JP 261. To "permit" involves being in a position to forbid the user: *Goodbarne v Buck* [1940] 1 KB 771, [1940] 1 All ER 613. See introductory note to PART IV: ROAD TRAFFIC, ante on causing, permitting etc. A perpetual injunction was granted at the suit of the Attorney-General to restrain use of land in contravention of an enforcement notice after the defendant had been fined repeatedly by a magistrates' court: *A-G (on relation of Hornchurch UDC) v Bastow* [1957] 1 QB 514, [1957] 1 All ER 497, 121 JP 171; *A-G v Smith* [1958] 2 QB 173, [1958] 2 All ER 557, 122 JP 367. When deciding whether a failure to take legal action for eviction to prevent an unlawful use from continuing can be said to amount permitting that use, regard must be had to the reasonableness or otherwise of taking that action: *Ragsdale v Creswick* (1984) 148 JP 564. An offence under s 179(6) may be committed by anyone who contravenes the enforcement notice, whether they be occupiers, squatters or other trespassers: *Scarborough Borough Council v Adams and Adams* (1983) 147 JP 449.

[6] An entry which is incomplete because it does not set out all the particulars required by art 26 of the Town and Country Planning (General Development Procedure) Order 1995, SI 1995/419 may still be said to be contained in the register kept under s 188 if the crucial information which is needed to see that there was an enforcement notice in existence in respect of the relevant address was present: *Sanger v Newham London Borough Council*, supra.

[7] Parliament was prepared to provide a defence only if the lack of knowledge of the enforcement notice is accompanied by a failure to serve it and a failure to put it into the appropriate register. Lack of knowledge by itself under the Act is no defence to a prosecution. Where an enforcement notice had been served on a person who was out of the country until the notice had expired and a fresh notice was served but he again went abroad, subsequent criminal proceedings were not a breach of his art 6 rights to a fair trial as they are concerned with procedural fairness, not with the substance of the criminal law in a domestic jurisdiction. The issue was abuse of process to which the issue of whether the planning authority acted in good faith or not was relevant. Also, the defendant should reasonably have anticipated the service of a fresh enforcement notice on him: *Goodall v Peak District National Park Authority* [2008] EWHC 734 (Admin), [2008] 1 WLR 2705.

[8] For procedure in respect of an offence triable either way, see the Magistrates' Courts Act 1980, ss 17A–21 in PART I: MAGISTRATES' COURTS, Procedure, ante. As a general rule, the court should proceed to hear and determine an information alleging an offence under this section notwithstanding that a planning application has recently been submitted, unless there is a prospect that the planning application's fate will be known shortly; see *R v Beaconsfield Magistrates, ex p South Buckinghamshire District Council* (1993) 157 JP 1073.

Where a summons for failure to comply with an enforcement notice was marked withdrawn in contemplation of the imminent grant of a certificate of lawful development after a not guilty plea had been entered, but that certificate was later revoked due to non-disclosure and misrepresentation, the authority was entitled to bring identical, fresh proceedings and the principle of autrefois acquit did not arise: *Islington London Borough Council v Andreas Michaelides* [2001] EWHC 468, [2001] 26 LS Gaz R 46, [2001] Crim LR 84.

This subsection creates a continuing offence and hence a previous acquittal in respect of an earlier period will not bar proceedings in relation to a later period; see *Tandridge District Council v Powers* [1982] Crim LR 373. An information which alleges a failure to comply with an enforcement notice over a period of time is not bad for duplicity since subsection (5) creates a single offence; see *Hodgetts v Chiltern District Council* [1983] 2 AC 120, [1983] 1 All ER 1057, 147 JP 372, HL.

Section 175(4) provides that where an appeal is brought under that section, the enforcement notice shall be of no effect pending the final determination or the withdrawal of the appeal. Where however no such appeal has been brought, courts should beware of adjourning simply because planning permission is being sought. Section 180(3) of the Act makes it clear that even if planning permission is later granted, this is without prejudice to the liability of any person for an offence in respect of a failure to comply with an enforcement notice prior to that.

[9] Although failure to comply with an enforcement notice is a continuing offence, the prosecution of any one offence is limited to the period up to the date the information was laid. The requirement to have regard to financial benefit does not fetter the discretion of the court when sentencing and the court is not obliged to order the full amount or even part of it. Subsection (9) predates the Proceeds of Crime Act 2002 and it is common practice for the latter to be used to assess the benefit and make the appropriate confiscation order. Where such an order is made it is wrong in principle to impose a fine in respect of the financial benefit as this amounts to double-counting: *R v Kohali* [2015] EWCA Crim 1757, [2016] 1 Cr App R (S) 30.

7.11411 **180. Effect of planning permission, etc, on enforcement or breach of condition notice** (1) Where, after the service of—

(*a*) a copy of an enforcement notice; or

(*b*) a breach of condition notice,

planning permission is granted for any development carried out before the grant of that permission, the notice shall cease to have effect so far as inconsistent with that permission.

(2) Where after a breach of condition notice has been served any condition to which the notice relates is discharged, the notice shall cease to have effect so far as it requires any person to secure compliance with the condition in question.

(3) The fact that an enforcement notice or breach of condition notice has wholly or partly ceased to have effect by virtue of this section shall not affect the liability of any person for an offence in respect of a previous failure to comply, or secure compliance, with the notice.

[Town and Country Planning Act 1990, s 180 as substituted by the Planning and Compensation Act 1991, Sch 7.]

7.11412 **181. Enforcement notice to have effect against subsequent development** (1) Compliance with an enforcement notice, whether in respect of—

(*a*) the completion, removal or alteration of any buildings or works;

(*b*) the discontinuance of any use of land; or

(*c*) any other requirements contained in the notice,

shall not discharge the notice.

(2) Without prejudice to subsection (1), any provision of an enforcement notice requiring a use of land to be discontinued shall operate as a requirement that it shall be discontinued permanently, to the extent that it is in contravention of Part III; and accordingly the resumption of that use at any time after it has been discontinued in compliance with the enforcement notice shall to that extent be

in contravention of the enforcement notice.

(3) Without prejudice to subsection (1), if any development is carried out on land by way of reinstating or restoring buildings or works which have been removed or altered in compliance with an enforcement notice, the notice shall, notwithstanding that its terms are not apt for the purpose, be deemed to apply in relation to the buildings or works as reinstated or restored as it applied in relation to the buildings or works before they were removed or altered; and, subject to subsection (4), the provisions of section 178(1) and (2) shall apply accordingly.

(4) here, at any time after an enforcement notice takes effect—

(*a*) any development is carried out on land by way of reinstating or restoring buildings or works which have been removed or altered in compliance with the notice; and

(*b*) the local planning authority propose, under section 178(1), to take any steps required by the enforcement notice for the removal or alteration of the buildings or works in consequence of the reinstatement or restoration,

the local planning authority shall, not less than 28 days before taking any such steps, serve on the owner and occupier of the land a notice of their intention to do so.

(5) Where without planning permission a person carries out any development[1] on land by way of reinstating or restoring buildings or works which have been removed or altered in compliance with an enforcement notice—

(*a*) he shall be guilty of an offence and shall be liable on summary conviction to a fine not exceeding **level 5** on the standard scale, and

(*b*) no person shall be liable under section 179(2) for failure to take any steps required to be taken by an enforcement notice by way of removal or alteration of what has been so reinstated or restored.

[Town and Country Planning Act 1990, s 181 as amended by the Planning and Compensation Act 1991, Sch 7.]

[1] Purely internal works are not "development" by virtue of s 52(2)(*a*)(i), and positioning a new doorbell or a utility connection on the outside of a house are unlikely to materially affect the external appearance of the building; therefore, where a house was converted into flats without planning permission and an enforcement notice was issued to cease that use, remove one kitchen from each property and remove the duplicate utility connections and doorbells, and this was done but the property was then converted into flats again, the case was properly prosecuted under s 179 rather than s 181(5): *R v Ahmed* [2014] EWCA Crim 1270, [2015] 1 WLR 378.

7.11413 **182.** *Enforcement by the Secretary of State.*

*Stop notices*

7.11414 **183. Stop notices** (1) Where the local planning authority considers it expedient that any relevant activity should cease before the expiry of the period for compliance with an enforcement notice, they may, when they serve the copy of the enforcement notice or afterwards, serve a notice (in this Act referred to as a "stop notice") prohibiting the carrying out of that activity on the land to which the enforcement notice relates, or any part of that land specified in the stop notice.

(2) In this section and sections 184 and 186 "relevant activity" means any activity[1] specified in the enforcement notice as an activity which the local planning authority require to cease and any activity carried out as part of that activity or associated with that activity.

(3) A stop notice may not be served where the enforcement notice has taken effect.

(4) A stop notice shall not prohibit the use of any building as a dwellinghouse[2].

(5) A stop notice shall not prohibit the carrying out of any activity if the activity has been carried out (whether continuously or not) for a period of more than four years ending with the service of the notice; and for the purposes of this subsection no account is to be taken of any period during which the activity was authorised by planning permission.

(5A) Subsection (5) does not prevent a stop notice prohibiting any activity consisting of, or incidental to, building, engineering, mining or other operations or the deposit of refuse or waste materials.

(6) A stop notice may be served by the local planning authority on any person who appears to them to have an interest in the land or to be engaged in any activity prohibited by the notice.

(7) The local planning authority may at any time withdraw a stop notice (without prejudice to their power to serve another) by serving notice to that effect on persons served with the stop notice.

[Town and Country Planning Act 1990, s 183 as amended by the Planning and Compensation Act 1991, s 9.]

[1] "Activity" can be restricted in its meaning so as to comprehend merely a particular kind of advertisement; see *Arora v Hackney London Borough Council* (1990) 155 JP 808, DC.

[2] Although the exemption applies only to dwellinghouses and does not extend to caravans, whilst amounting indirectly to discrimination against gypsies and an infringement of their human rights, it is objectively justified and proportionate and thereby valid (*R (on the application of Wilson) v Wychavon District Council* [2007] EWCA Civ 52, [2007] QB 801, [2007] 2 WLR 798).

7.11415 **184. Stop notices: supplementary provisions** (1) A stop notice must refer to the enforcement notice to which it relates and have a copy of that notice annexed to it.

(2) A stop notice must specify the date on which it will take effect (and it cannot be contravened until that date).

(3) That date—

(*a*) must not be earlier than three days after the date when the notice is served, unless the local planning authority consider that there are special reasons for specifying an earlier date and a statement of those reasons is served with the stop notice; and

(*b*) must not be later than twenty-eight days from the date when the notice is first served on any person.

(4) A stop notice shall cease to have effect when—

(*a*) the enforcement notice to which it relates is withdrawn or quashed; or

(*b*) the period of compliance with the enforcement notice expires; or

(*c*) notice of the withdrawal of the stop notice is first served under section 183(7).

(5) A stop notice shall also cease to have effect if or to the extent that the activities prohibited by it cease, on a variation of the enforcement notice, to be relevant activities.

(6) Where a stop notice has been served in respect of any land, the local planning authority may display there a notice (in this section and section 187 referred to as a "site notice")—

(*a*) stating that a stop notice has been served and that any person contravening it may be prosecuted for an offence under section 187,

(*b*) giving the date when the stop notice takes effect, and

(*c*) indicating its requirements.

(7) If under section 183(7) the local planning authority withdraw a stop notice in respect of which a site notice was displayed they must display a notice of the withdrawal in place of the site notice.

(8) A stop notice shall not be invalid by reason that a copy of the enforcement notice to which it relates was not served as required by section 172 if it is shown that the local planning authority took all such steps as were reasonably practicable to effect proper service.

[Town and Country Planning Act 1990, s 184 as amended by the Planning and Compensation Act 1991, s 9 and Sch 7.]

**7.11416** **187. Penalties for contravention of stop notice** (1) If any person contravenes a stop notice after a site notice has been displayed or the stop notice has been served on him he shall be guilty of an offence.

(1A) An offence under this section may be charged by reference to any day or longer period of time and a person may be convicted of a second or subsequent offence under this section by reference to any period of time following the preceding conviction for such an offence.

(1B) References in this section to contravening a stop notice include causing or permitting its contravention.

(2) A person guilty of an offence under this section shall be liable[1] on summary conviction, or on conviction on indictment, to a fine.

(2A) In determining the amount of any fine to be imposed on a person convicted of an offence under this section, the court shall in particular have regard to any financial benefit which has accrued or appears likely to accrue to him in consequence of the offence.

(3) In proceedings for an offence under this section it shall be a defence for the accused to prove—

(*a*) that the stop notice was not served on him, and

(*b*) that he did not know, and could not reasonably have been expected to know, of its existence.

[Town and Country Planning Act 1990, s 187 as amended by the Planning and Compensation Act 1991, s 9 and SI 2015/664.]

---

1 For procedure in respect of an offence triable either way, see the Magistrates' Courts Act 1980, ss 17A–21 in PART I: MAGISTRATES' COURTS, PROCEDURE, ante. The defendant is entitled to attempt to establish that he is not in fact prohibited from carrying on his activities by the terms of the prohibition contained on the face of the stop order (*R v Jenner* [1983] 2 All ER 46, [1983] 1 WLR 873).

*Breach of condition*

**7.11417** **187A. Enforcement of conditions** (1) This section applies where planning permission for carrying out any development of land has been granted subject to conditions.

(2) The local planning authority may, if any of the conditions is not complied with, serve a notice (in this Act referred to as a "breach of condition notice") on—

(*a*) any person who is carrying out or has carried out the development; or

(*b*) any person having control of the land,

requiring him to secure compliance with such of the conditions as are specified in the notice.

(3) References in this section to the person responsible are to the person on whom the breach of condition notice has been served.

(4) The conditions which may be specified in a notice served by virtue of subsection (2)(*b*) are any of the conditions regulating the use of the land.

(5) A breach condition notice shall specify the steps which the authority consider ought to be taken, or the activities which the authority consider ought to cease, to secure compliance with the conditions specified in the notice.

(6) The authority may by notice served on the person responsible withdraw the breach of condition notice, but its withdrawal shall not affect the power to serve on him a further breach of condition notice in respect of the conditions specified in the earlier notice or any other conditions.

(7) The period allowed for compliance with the notice is—

(*a*) such period of not less than twenty-eight days beginning with the date of service of the notice as may be specified in the notice; or

(*b*) that period as extended by a further notice served by the local planning authority on the person responsible.

(8) If, at any time after the end of the period allowed for compliance with the notice—

(*a*) any of the conditions specified in the notice is not complied with; and

(*b*) the steps specified in the notice have not been taken or, as the case may be, the activities specified in the notice have not ceased,

the person responsible is in breach of the notice.

(9) If the person responsible is in breach of the notice he shall be guilty of an offence[1].

(10) An offence under subsection (9) may be charged by reference to any day or longer period of time and a person may be convicted of a second or subsequent offence under that subsection by reference to any period of time following the preceding conviction for such an offence.

(11) It shall be a defence for a person charged with an offence under subsection (9) to prove—

(*a*) that he took all reasonable measures to secure compliance with the conditions specified in the notice; or

(*b*) where the notice was served on him by virtue of subsection (2)(*b*), that he no longer had control of the land.

(12) A person who is guilty of an offence under subsection (9) shall be liable on summary conviction to a fine—

(*a*) not exceeding level 4 on the standard scale if the land is in England;

(*b*) not exceeding level 3 on the standard scale if the land is in Wales.

(13) In this section—

(*a*) "conditions" includes limitations; and

(*b*) references to carrying out any development include causing or permitting another to do so.

[Town and Country Planning Act 1990, s 187A as inserted by the Planning and Compensation Act 1991, s 2 and amended by the Localism Act 2011, s 126.]

1 A "breach of condition notice" means a breach of condition notice which has been served within the limits prescribed by s 171B, ante. Accordingly a defendant charged with failing to comply with such a notice is entitled by way of defence in criminal proceedings to challenge the validity of the notice on the ground that it was served out of time under s 171B(3), ante. Furthermore the defendant is also entitled by way of defence in such proceedings to challenge the lawfulness of the planning condition (*Dilieto v Ealing London Borough Council* [2000] QB 381, [1998] 2 All ER 885, [1998] 3 WLR 1403).

7.11418 **187B.** *Injunctions restraining breaches of planning control.*

*Enforcement of orders for discontinuance of use etc*

7.11419 **189. Penalties for contravention of orders under section 102 and Schedule 9**

(1) Any person who without planning permission—

(*a*) uses land, or causes or permits land to be used—

(i) for any purpose for which an order under section 102 or paragraph 1 of Schedule 9 has required that its use shall be discontinued; or

(ii) in contravention of any condition imposed by such an order by virtue of subsection (1) of that section or, as the case may be, sub-paragraph (1) of that paragraph; or

(*b*) resumes, or causes or permits to be resumed, development consisting of the winning and working of minerals or involving the depositing of mineral waste the resumption of which an order under paragraph 3 of that Schedule has prohibited; or

(*c*) contravenes, or causes or permits to be contravened, any such requirement as is specified in sub-paragraph (3) or (4) of that paragraph,

shall be guilty of an offence.

(2) Any person who contravenes any requirement of an order under paragraph 5 or 6 of that Schedule or who causes or permits any requirement of such an order to be contravened shall be guilty of an offence.

(3) Any person guilty of an offence under this section shall be liable[1]—

(*a*) on summary conviction to a fine not exceeding the **statutory maximum**; and

(*b*) on conviction on indictment, to a **fine**.

(4) It shall be a defence for a person charged with an offence under this section to prove that he took all reasonable measures and exercised all due diligence to avoid commission of the offence by himself or by any person under his control.

(5) If in any case the defence provided by subsection (4) involves an allegation that the commission of the offence was due to the act or default of another person or due to reliance on information supplied by another person, the person charged shall not, without the leave of the court, be entitled to rely on the defence unless, within a period ending seven clear days before the hearing, he has served on the prosecutor a notice in writing giving such information identifying or assisting in the identification of the other person as was then in his possession.

[Town and Country Planning Act 1990, s 189 as amended by the Planning and Compensation Act 1991, Sch 1.]

[1] For procedure in respect of an offence triable either way, see the Magistrates' Courts Act 1980, ss 17A–21, in PART I: MAGISTRATES' COURTS, PROCEDURE, ante.

*Certificate of lawful use or development*

7.11420 **191. Certificate of lawfulness of existing use or development** (1) If any person wishes to ascertain whether—

(*a*) any existing[1] use of buildings or other land is lawful;

(*b*) any operations which have been carried out in, on, over or under land are lawful; or

(*c*) any other matter constituting a failure to comply with any condition or limitation subject to which planning permission has been granted is lawful,

he may make an application for the purpose to the local planning authority specifying the land and describing the use, operations or other matter.

(2) For the purposes of this Act uses and operations are lawful at any time if—

(*a*) no enforcement action may then be taken in respect of them (whether because they did not involve development or require planning permission or because the time for enforcement action has expired or for any other reason); and

(*b*) they do not constitute a contravention of any of the requirements of any enforcement notice then in force.

(3) For the purposes of this Act any matter constituting a failure to comply with any condition or limitation subject to which planning permission has been granted is lawful at any time if—

(*a*) the time for taking enforcement action in respect of the failure has then expired; and

(*b*) it does not constitute a contravention of any of the requirements of any enforcement notice or breach of condition notice then in force.

(3A) In determining for the purposes of this section whether the time for taking enforcement action in respect of a matter has expired, that time is to be taken not to have expired if—

(*a*) the time for applying for an order under section 171BA(1) (a "planning enforcement order") in relation to the matter has not expired,

(*b*) an application has been made for a planning enforcement order in relation to the matter and the application has neither been decided nor been withdrawn, or

(*c*) a planning enforcement order has been made in relation to the matter, the order has not been rescinded and the enforcement year for the order (whether or not it has begun) has not expired.

(4) If, on an application under this section, the local planning authority are provided with information satisfying them of the lawfulness at the time of the application of the use, operations or other matter described in the application or that description as modified by the local planning authority or a description substituted by them, they shall issue a certificate to that effect; and in any other case they shall refuse the application.

(5) A certificate under this section shall—

(*a*) specify the land to which it relates;

(*b*) describe the use, operations or other matter in question (in the case of any use falling within one of the classes specified in an order under section 55(2)(*f*), identifying it by reference to that class);

(*c*) give the reasons for determining the use, operations or other matter to be lawful; and

(*d*) specify the date of the application for the certificate.

(6) The lawfulness of any use, operations or other matter for which a certificate is in force under this section shall be conclusively presumed.

(7) A certificate under this section in respect of any use shall also have effect, for the purposes of the following enactments, as if it were a grant of planning permission—

(*a*) section 3(3) of the Caravan Sites and Control of Development Act 1960;

(*b*) section 5(2) of the Control of Pollution Act 1974; and

(*c*) section 36(2)(*a*) of the Environmental Protection Act 1990.

[Town and Country Planning Act 1990, s 191 as substituted by the Planning and Compensation Act 1991, s 10 and amended by the Localism Act 2011, s 124.]

[1] The uses for which the certificate is requested may include uses which although not physically active at the time of the application, are dormant uses (*Panton and Farmer v Secretary of State for the Environment, Transport and the Regions* (1998) 78 P & CR 186).

7.11421 **192. Certificate of lawfulness of proposed use or development** (1) If any person wishes to ascertain whether—

(*a*) any proposed use of buildings or other land; or

(*b*) any operations proposed to be carried out in, on, over or under land,

would be lawful, he may make an application for the purpose to the local planning authority specifying the land and describing the use or operations in question.

(2) If, on an application under this section, the local planning authority are provided with information satisfying them that the use or operations described in the application would be lawful if instituted or begun at the time of the application, they shall issue a certificate to that effect; and in

any other case they shall refuse the application.

(3) A certificate under this section shall—

(*a*) specify the land to which it relates;

(*b*) describe the use or operations in question (in the case of any use falling within one of the classes specified in an order under section 55(2)(*f*), identifying it by reference to that class);

(*c*) give the reasons for determining the use or operations to be lawful; and

(*d*) specify the date of the application for the certificate.

(4) The lawfulness of any use or operations for which a certificate is in force under this section shall be conclusively presumed unless there is a material change, before the use is instituted or the operations are begun, in any of the matters relevant to determining such lawfulness.

[Town and Country Planning Act 1990, s 192 as substituted by the Planning and Compensation Act 1991, s 10.]

7.11422 **193.** *Certificates under sections 191 and 192: supplementary provisions.*

7.11423 **194. Offences** (1) If any person, for the purpose of procuring a particular decision on an application (whether by himself or another) for the issue of a certificate under section 191 or 192—

(*a*) knowingly or recklessly makes a statement which is false or misleading in a material particular;

(*b*) with intent to deceive, uses any document which is false or misleading in a material particular; or

(*c*) with intent to deceive, withholds any material information,

he shall be guilty of an offence.

(2) A person guilty of an offence under subsection (1) shall be liable[1]—

(*a*) on summary conviction, to a fine not exceeding the **statutory maximum**; or

(*b*) on conviction on indictment, to imprisonment for a term not exceeding **two years**, or a **fine**, or **both**

(3) Notwithstanding section 127 of the Magistrates' Courts Act 1980, a magistrates' court may try an information in respect of an offence under subsection (1) whenever laid.

[Town and Country Planning Act 1990, s 194 as substituted by the Planning and Compensation Act 1991, s 10.]

---

1 For procedure in respect of an offence triable either way, see the Magistrates' Courts Act 1980, ss 17A–21, in PART I: MAGISTRATES' COURTS, PROCEDURE, ante.

*Rights of entry for enforcement purposes*

7.11424 **196A. Rights to enter without warrant** (1) Any person duly authorised in writing by a local planning authority may at any reasonable hour enter any land—

(*a*) to ascertain whether there is or has been any breach of planning control on the land or any other land;

(*b*) to determine whether any of the powers conferred on a local planning authority by this Part should be exercised in relation to the land or any other land;

(*c*) to determine how any such power should be exercised in relation to the land or any other land;

(*d*) to ascertain whether there has been compliance with any requirement imposed as a result of any such power having been exercised in relation to the land or any other land,

if there are reasonable grounds for entering for the purpose in question.

(2) Any person duly authorised in writing by the Secretary of State may at any reasonable hour enter any land to determine whether an enforcement notice should be issued in relation to the land or any other land, if there are reasonable grounds for entering for that purpose.

(3) The Secretary of State shall not so authorise any person without consulting the local planning authority.

(4) Admission to any building used as a dwellinghouse shall not be demanded as of right by virtue of subsection (1) or (2) unless twenty-four hours' notice of the intended entry has been given to the occupier of the building.

[Town and Country Planning Act 1990, s 196A as inserted by the Planning and Compensation Act 1991, s 11.]

7.11425 **196B. Right to enter under warrant** (1) If it is shown to the satisfaction of a justice of the peace on sworn information in writing—

(*a*) that there are reasonable grounds for entering any land for any of the purposes mentioned in section 196A(1) or (2); and

(*b*) that—

(i) admission to the land has been refused, or a refusal is reasonably apprehended; or

(ii) the case is one of urgency,

the justice may issue a warrant authorising any person duly authorised in writing by a local planning authority or, as the case may be, the Secretary of State to enter the land.

(2) For the purposes of subsection (1)(*b*)(i) admission to land shall be regarded as having been refused if no reply is received to a request for admission within a reasonable period.

(3) A warrant authorises entry on one occasion only and that entry must be—

(*a*) within one month from the date of the issue of the warrant; and

(*b*) at a reasonable hour, unless the case is one of urgency.

[Town and Country Planning Act 1990, s 196B as inserted by the Planning and Compensation Act 1991, s 11.]

**7.11426 196C. Rights of entry: supplementary provisions** (1) A person authorised to enter any land in pursuance of a right of entry conferred under or by virtue of section 196A or 196B (referred to in this section as "a right of entry")—

(*a*) shall, if so required, produce evidence of his authority and state the purpose of his entry before so entering;

(*b*) may take with him such other persons as may be necessary; and

(*c*) on leaving the land shall, if the owner or occupier is not then present, leave it as effectively secured against trespassers as he found it.

(2) Any person who wilfully obstructs a person acting in the exercise of a right of entry shall be guilty of an offence and liable on summary conviction to a fine not exceeding **level 3** on the standard scale.

(3) If any damage is caused to land or chattels in the exercise of a right of entry, compensation may be recovered by any person suffering the damage from the authority who gave the written authority for the entry or, as the case may be, the Secretary of State.

(4) The provisions of section 118 shall apply in relation to compensation under subsection (3) as they apply in relation to compensation under Part IV.

(5) If any person who enters any land, in exercise of a right of entry, discloses to any person any information obtained by him while on the land as to any manufacturing process or trade secret, he shall be guilty of an offence.

(6) Subsection (5) does not apply if the disclosure is made by a person in the course of performing his duty in connection with the purpose for which he was authorised to enter the land.

(7) A person who is guilty of an offence under subsection (5) shall be liable[1] on summary conviction to a fine not exceeding the **statutory maximum** or on conviction on indictment to imprisonment for a term not exceeding **two years** or a **fine** or **both**.

(8) In sections 196A and 196B and this section references to a local planning authority include, in relation to a building situated in Greater London, a reference to the Historic Buildings and Monuments Commission for England.

[Town and Country Planning Act 1990, s 196C as inserted by the Planning and Compensation Act 1991, s 11.]

1 For procedure in respect of an offence triable either way, see the Magistrates' Courts Act 1980, ss 17A–21 in PART I: MAGISTRATES' COURTS, PROCEDURE, ante.

## PART VIII[1]
## SPECIAL CONTROLS

### CHAPTER I
### TREES

*Tree preservation orders*

**7.11427 198. Power to make tree preservation orders[2]** * (1) If it appears to a local planning authority that it is expedient in the interests of amenity to make provision for the preservation of trees or woodlands in their area, they may for that purpose make an order with respect to such trees, groups of trees or woodlands as may be specified in the order.

(2) An order under subsection (1) is in this Act referred to as a "tree preservation order"[3].

(3) A tree preservation order may, in particular, make provision—

(*a*) for prohibiting (subject to any exemptions for which provision may be made by the order) the cutting down, topping, lopping, uprooting, wilful damage or wilful destruction of trees except with the consent of the local planning authority, and for enabling that authority to give their consent subject to conditions;

(*b*) for securing the replanting, in such manner as may be prescribed by or under the order, of any part of a woodland area which is felled in the course of forestry operations permitted by or under the order;

(*c*) for applying, in relation to any consent under the order, and to applications for such consent, any of the provisions of this Act mentioned in subsection (4), subject to such adaptations and modifications as may be specified in the order.

(4) The provisions referred to in subsection (3)(*c*) are—

(*a*) the provisions of Part III relating to planning permission and to applications for planning permission, except sections 56, 62, 65, 69(3) and (4), 71, 91 to 96, 100 and 101 and Schedule 8; and

(*b*) sections 137 to 141, 143 and 144 (except so far as they relate to purchase notices served in consequence of such orders as are mentioned in section 137(1)(*b*) or (*c*));

(*c*) section 316.*

(5) A tree preservation order may be made so as to apply, in relation to trees to be planted pursuant to any such conditions as are mentioned in section 197(*a*), as from the time when those trees are planted.

(6) Without prejudice to any other exemptions for which provision may be made by a tree preservation order, no such order shall apply[4]—

(*a*) to the cutting down, uprooting, topping or lopping of trees which are dying or dead or have become dangerous[5], or

(*b*) to the cutting down, uprooting, topping or lopping of any trees in compliance with any obligations imposed by or under an Act of Parliament or so far as may be necessary for the prevention or abatement of a nuisance[6].*

(7) This section* shall have effect subject to—

(*a*) section 39(2) of the Housing and Planning Act 1986 (saving for effect of section 2(4) of the Opencast Coal Act 1958 on land affected by a tree preservation order despite its repeal); and

(*b*) section 15 of the Forestry Act 1967 (licences under that Act to fell trees comprised in a tree preservation order).

(8) In relation to an application for consent under a tree preservation order the appropriate authority may by regulations make provision as to—

(*a*) the form and manner in which the application must be made;

(*b*) particulars of such matters as are to be included in the application;

(*c*) the documents or other materials as are to accompany the application.

(9) The appropriate authority is—

(*a*) the Secretary of State in relation to England;

(*b*) the National Assembly for Wales in relation to Wales,

and in the case of regulations made by the National Assembly for Wales section 333(3) must be ignored.*

[Town and Country Planning Act 1990, s 198 as amended by the Planning and Compensation Act 1991, Sch 6.]

* **Subsections (3), (4), (6), (8), (9) are repealed and in sub-s (7) the words underlined are substituted by the words "Tree preservation regulations" by the Planning Act 2008, Schs 8 and 13 from 6 April 2012 (in relation to England and from a date to be appointed (in relation to Wales).**

1 Part VIII contains sections 197–225.

2 Additionally this section has effect subject to s 39(2) of the Housing and Planning Act 1986 (saving s 2(4) of the repealed Opencast Coal Act 1958) and s 15 of the Forestry Act 1967 (licence to fell) Town and Country Planning Act 1990, s 198(7).

3 For procedure in respect of the making of tree preservation orders see the Town and Country Planning (Trees) Regulations 1999, SI 1999/1892 amended by SI 2001/4050, SI 2008/2260 and 3202 and SI 2012/792 (W) (revoked in relation to England by SI 2012/605) and the Town and Country Planning (Tree Preservation) (England) Regulations 2012, SI 2012/605.

4 In proceedings alleging commission of an offence under s 210(1), post, it will be for the defendant to prove on the balance of probabilities that the conditions creating an exemption under this section existed at the time; see *R v Alath Construction Ltd* [1990] 1 WLR 1255, CA (decided under s 102(1) of the repealed 1971 Act).

5 The burden of proof on the issue of whether the tree was dying, or dead or had become dangerous, so as to justify its felling without the local authority's consent, falls on the defendant who asserts such exemption from the preservation order (*R v Alath Construction Ltd*, supra).

6 The intent of the section is that a protected tree should remain protected unless there was a real need to lift that protection. Effect is given to that intention by reading the expression "so far as may be necessary for the prevention or abatement of a nuisance" as "if and so far as may be necessary for the prevention or abatement of a nuisance" The first question is whether anything needs to be done to the tree or could, for example, alternative engineering solutions be considered. The test requires that whatever is done to the tree itself is *necessary*; it is not enough that whatever is done is *sufficient* (*Perrin v Northampton Borough Council* [2007] EWCA Civ 1353, [2008] 4 All ER 673, [2008] 1 WLR 1307).

**7.11428 202A. Tree preservation regulations: general** (1) The appropriate national authority may by regulations make provision in connection with tree preservation orders.

(2) Sections 202B to 202G make further provision about what may, in particular, be contained in regulations under subsection (1).

(3) In this section and those sections "tree preservation order" includes an order under section 202(1).

(4) In this Act "tree preservation regulations" means regulations under subsection (1).

(5) In subsection (1) "the appropriate national authority"—

(*a*) in relation to England means the Secretary of State, and

(*b*) in relation to Wales means the Welsh Ministers.

(6) Section 333(3) does not apply in relation to tree preservation regulations made by the Welsh Ministers.

(7) Tree preservation regulations made by the Welsh Ministers are subject to annulment in pursuance of a resolution of the National Assembly for Wales.

[Town and Country Planning Act 1990, s 202A as inserted by the Planning Act 2008, s 192.]

**7.11429 202B. Tree preservation regulations: making of tree preservation orders**

(1) Tree preservation regulations may make provision about—

(*a*) the form of tree preservation orders;

(*b*) the procedure to be followed in connection with the making of tree preservation orders;

(*c*) when a tree preservation order takes effect.

(2) If tree preservation regulations make provision for tree preservation orders not to take effect until confirmed, tree preservation regulations may—

(*a*) make provision for tree preservation orders to take effect provisionally until confirmed;

(*b*) make provision about who is to confirm a tree preservation order;

(*c*) make provision about the procedure to be followed in connection with confirmation of tree preservation orders.

[Town and Country Planning Act 1990, s 202B as inserted by the Planning Act 2008, s 192.]

**7.11430 202C. Tree preservation regulations: prohibited activities** (1) Tree preservation regulations may make provision for prohibiting all or any of the following—

(*a*) cutting down of trees;
(*b*) topping of trees;
(*c*) lopping of trees;
(*d*) uprooting of trees;
(*e*) wilful damage of trees;
(*f*) wilful destruction of trees.

(2) A prohibition imposed on a person may (in particular) relate to things whose doing the person causes or permits (as well as to things the person does).

(3) A prohibition may be imposed subject to exceptions.

(4) In particular, provision may be made for a prohibition not to apply to things done with consent.

(5) In this section "tree" means a tree in respect of which a tree preservation order is in force.

[Town and Country Planning Act 1990, s 202C as inserted by the Planning Act 2008, s 192.]

**7.11431 202D. Tree preservation regulations: consent for prohibited activities** (1) This section applies if tree preservation regulations make provision under section 202C(4).

(2) Tree preservation regulations may make provision—

(*a*) about who may give consent;
(*b*) for the giving of consent subject to conditions;
(*c*) about the procedure to be followed in connection with obtaining consent.

(3) The conditions for which provision may be made under subsection (2)(*b*) include—

(*a*) conditions as to planting of trees;
(*b*) conditions requiring approvals to be obtained from the person giving the consent;
(*c*) conditions limiting the duration of the consent.

(4) The conditions mentioned in subsection (3)(*a*) include—

(*a*) conditions requiring trees to be planted;
(*b*) conditions about the planting of any trees required to be planted by conditions within paragraph (*a*), including conditions about how, where or when planting is to be done;
(*c*) conditions requiring things to be done, or installed, for the protection of any trees planted in pursuance of conditions within paragraph (*a*).

(5) In relation to any tree planted in pursuance of a condition within subsection (4)(*a*), tree preservation regulations may make provision—

(*a*) for the tree preservation order concerned to apply to the tree;
(*b*) authorising the person imposing the condition to specify that the tree preservation order concerned is not to apply to the tree.

(6) "The tree preservation order concerned" is the order in force in relation to the tree in respect of which consent is given under tree preservation regulations.

(7) The provision that may be made under subsection (2)(*c*) includes provision about applications for consent, including provision as to—

(*a*) the form or manner in which an application is to be made;
(*b*) what is to be in, or is to accompany, an application.

(8) Tree preservation regulations may make provision for appeals—

(*a*) against refusal of consent;
(*b*) where there is a failure to decide an application for consent;
(*c*) against conditions subject to which consent is given;
(*d*) against refusal of an approval required by a condition;
(*e*) where there is a failure to decide an application for such an approval.

(9) Tree preservation regulations may make provision in connection with appeals under provision made under subsection (8), including—

(*a*) provision imposing time limits;
(*b*) provision for further appeals;
(*c*) provision in connection with the procedure to be followed on an appeal (or further appeal);
(*d*) provision about who is to decide an appeal (or further appeal);
(*e*) provision imposing duties, or conferring powers, on a person deciding an appeal (or further appeal).

[Town and Country Planning Act 1990, s 202D as inserted by the Planning Act 2008, s 192.]

**7.11432 202E. Tree preservation regulations: compensation** (1) Tree preservation regulations may make provision for the payment of compensation—

(*a*) where any consent required under tree preservation regulations is refused;
(*b*) where any such consent is given subject to conditions;
(*c*) where any approval required under such a condition is refused.

(2) Tree preservation regulations may provide for entitlement conferred under subsection (1) to

apply only in, or to apply except in, cases specified in tree preservation regulations.

(3) Tree preservation regulations may provide for entitlement conferred by provision under subsection (1) to be subject to conditions, including conditions as to time limits.

(4) Tree preservation regulations may, in relation to compensation under provision under subsection (1), make provision about—

(*a*) who is to pay the compensation;

(*b*) who is entitled to the compensation;

(*c*) what the compensation is to be paid in respect of;

(*d*) the amount, or calculation of, the compensation.

(5) Tree preservation regulations may make provision about the procedure to be followed in connection with claiming any entitlement conferred by provision under subsection (1).

(6) Tree preservation regulations may make provision for the determination of disputes about entitlement conferred by provision under subsection (1), including provision for and in connection with the referral of any such disputes to, and their determination by, the First-tier Tribunal or the Upper Tribunal.

[Town and Country Planning Act 1990, s 202E as inserted by the Planning Act 2008, s 192.]

**7.11433 202F. Tree preservation regulations: registers** Tree preservation regulations may make provision for the keeping of, and public access to, registers containing information related to tree preservation orders.

[Town and Country Planning Act 1990, s 202F as inserted by the Planning Act 2008, s 192.]

**7.11434 202G. Tree preservation regulations: supplementary** (1) Tree preservation regulations may provide for the application (with or without modifications) of, or make provision comparable to, any provision of this Act mentioned in subsection (2).

(2) The provisions are any provision of Part 3 relating to planning permission or applications for planning permission, except sections 56, 62, 65, 69(3) and (4), 71, 91 to 96, 100 and 101 and Schedule 8.

(3) Tree preservation regulations may make provision comparable to—

(*a*) any provision made by the Town and Country Planning (Tree Preservation Order) Regulations 1969 or the Town and Country Planning (Trees) Regulations 1999;

(*b*) any provision that could have been made under section 199(2) and (3).

(4) Tree preservation regulations may contain incidental, supplementary, consequential, transitional and transitory provision and savings.

[Town and Country Planning Act 1990, s 202G as inserted by the Planning Act 2008, s 192.]

**7.11435 207–209.** *Replacement of trees*[1].

[1] By s 209(6) any person wilfully obstructing the exercise of a power under s 209(1)(*a*) is punishable on summary conviction to a fine not exceeding **level 3** on the standard scale.

**7.11436 210. Penalties for non-compliance with tree preservation order** (1) If any person, in contravention of a tree preservation order—

(*a*) cuts down, uproots or wilfully destroys[1] a tree,

(*b*) wilfully damages, tops or lops a tree in such a manner as to be likely to destroy it, or

(*c*) causes or permits the carrying out of any of the activities in paragraph (*a*) or (*b*),

he shall be guilty of an offence.

(2) A person guilty of an offence under subsection (1) shall be liable[2] on summary conviction, or on conviction on indictment, to a fine.

(3) In determining the amount of any fine to be imposed on a person convicted of an offence under subsection (1), the court shall in particular have regard to any financial benefit[3] which has accrued or appears likely to accrue to him in consequence of the offence.

(4) If any person contravenes the provisions of a tree preservation order otherwise than as mentioned in subsection (1), he shall be guilty of an offence and liable on summary conviction to a fine not exceeding **level 4** on the standard scale.

(4A) Proceedings for an offence under subsection (4) may be brought within the period of 6 months beginning with the date on which evidence sufficient in the opinion of the prosecutor to justify the proceedings came to the prosecutor's knowledge.

(4B) Subsection (4A) does not authorise the commencement of proceedings for an offence more than 3 years after the date on which the offence was committed.

(4C) For the purposes of subsection (4A), a certificate—

(*a*) signed by or on behalf of the prosecutor, and

(*b*) stating the date on which evidence sufficient in the prosecutor's opinion to justify the proceedings came to the prosecutor's knowledge,

is conclusive evidence of that fact.

(4D) A certificate stating that matter and purporting to be so signed is to be deemed to be so signed unless the contrary is proved.

(4E) Subsection (4A) does not apply in relation to an offence in respect of a tree in Wales.

(5) *Repealed.**

[Town and Country Planning Act 1990, s 210 as amended by the Planning and Compensation Act 1991, s 23, the Localism Act 2011, s 126 and SI 2015/664.]

*** The following amendments are made by the Planning Act 2008, Sch 8 from 6 April 2012 (in relation to England) and from a date to be appointed (in relation to Wales): in the section heading the word underlined is substituted by the word "regulations", in sub-s (1) the words underlined are substituted by the words "tree preservation regulations", sub-s (1)(*c*) and the word preceding it is inserted and in sub-s (4) the words underlined are substituted by the words "tree preservation regulations".**

1 A tree is "destroyed" if it ceases to have any use as an amenity, or as something worth preserving, and if a competent forester, taking into account its situation, would decide it ought to be felled (*Barnet London Borough Council v Eastern Electricity Board* [1973] 2 All ER 319, 137 JP 486). It is not necessary for the prosecutor to prove that the accused knew of the existence of the preservation order (*Maidstone Borough Council v Mortimer* [1980] 3 All ER 552). The prosecutor must adduce evidence of the age of the tree to establish that it was subject to the tree preservation order and it is not permissible for the justices to act on personal knowledge of facts after looking at photographs tendered in evidence (*Carter v Eastbourne Borough Council* (2000) 164 JP 273).

2 For procedure in respect of an offence triable either way, see the Magistrates' Courts Act 1980, ss 17A–21, in PART I: MAGISTRATES' COURTS, PROCEDURE, ante.

3 See *R v Davey* [2013] EWCA Crim 1662, [2014] 1 Cr App R (S) 205. The appellant hired a tree surgeon to cut down a protected maritime pine tree on his neighbour's land because it obstructed his view of Poole harbour. The Crown Court made a confiscation order in the same of £50,000, representing the increase in value of the appellant's house in consequence of the tree's removal. The judge also imposed a fine of £75,000. It was argued on appeal that the confiscation order stripped the appellant of his benefit and that the fine was, consequently, too high. The Court of Appeal upheld the sentence. Although the confiscation order removed the financial benefit to the appellant, it did not remove the amenity benefit of the improved view that the appellant would enjoy while he remained in occupation of the property. It was a very serious aggravating feature that the tree was not owned by the appellant, but by his neighbour. Removal of the tree diminished the amenity value of other properties for which the tree would have been an attractive local feature and not an inconvenience. This was an offence that was one of the most serious of its type, and fines for this type of offence must include an element of deterrence.

*Trees in conservation areas*

7.11437 **211. Preservation of trees in conservation areas** (1) Subject to the provisions of this section and section 212[1], any person who, in relation to a tree to which this section applies, does any act which might by virtue of section 198(3)(*a*) be prohibited by a tree preservation order* shall be guilty of an offence.

(1A) Subsection (1) does not apply so far as the act in question is authorised by an order granting development consent.

(2) Subject to section 212, this section applies to any tree in a conservation area in respect of which no tree preservation order is for the time being in force.

(3) It shall be a defence for a person charged with an offence under subsection (1) to prove—

(*a*) that he served notice of his intention to do the act in question (with sufficient particulars to identify the tree) on the local planning authority in whose area the tree is or was situated; and

(*b*) that he did the act in question—

(i) with the consent of the local planning authority in whose area the tree is or was situated, or

(ii) after the expiry of the period of six weeks from the date of the notice but before the expiry of the period of two years from that date.

(4) Section 210 shall apply to an offence under this section as it applies to a contravention of a tree preservation order*.

(5) An emanation of the Crown must not, in relation to a tree to which this section applies, do an act mentioned in subsection (1) above unless—

(*a*) the first condition is satisfied, and

(*b*) either the second or third condition is satisfied.

(5A) Subsection (5) does not apply so far as the act in question is authorised by an order granting development consent.

(6) The first condition is that the emanation serves notice of an intention to do the act (with sufficient particulars to identify the tree) on the local planning authority in whose area the tree is situated.

(7) The second condition is that the act is done with the consent of the authority.

(8) The third condition is that the act is done—

(*a*) after the end of the period of six weeks starting with the date of the notice, and

(*b*) before the end of the period of two years starting with that date.

[Town and Country Planning Act 1990, s 211 as amended by the Planning and Compulsory Purchase Act 2004, s 86 and the Planning Act 2008, Sch 2.]

*** In sub-s (1) the words underlined are substituted by the words "which might by virtue of section 202C be prohibited by tree preservation regulations" and in sub-s (4) the words underlined are substituted by the words "tree preservation regulations", by the Planning Act 2008, Sch 8 from 6 April 2012 (in relation to England) and from a date to be appointed (in relation to Wales).**

1 Under s 212 the Secretary of State may disapply s 211 in specified cases. Exceptions are contained in the Town and Country Planning (Trees) Regulations 1999, SI 1999/1892 amended by SI 2001/4050, SI 2008/2260 and 3202 (revoked in relation to England by SI 2012/605)and SI 2012/792 (W) and the Town and Country Planning (Tree Preservation) (England) Regulations 2012, SI 2012/605.

7.11438 **214A.** *Injunctions.*

*Rights of entry*

7.11439 **214B. Rights to enter without warrant** (1) Any person duly authorised in writing by a local planning authority may enter any land for the purpose of—

(*a*) surveying it in connection with making or confirming a tree preservation order with respect to the land;

(*b*) ascertaining whether an offence under section 210 or 211 has been committed on the land; or

(*c*) determining whether a notice under section 207 should be served on the owner of the land,

if there are reasonable grounds for entering for the purpose in question.

(2) Any person duly authorised in writing by the Secretary of State may enter any land for the purpose of surveying it in connection with making, amending or revoking a tree preservation order with respect to the land, if there are reasonable grounds for entering for that purpose.

(3) Any person who is duly authorised in writing by a local planning authority may enter any land in connection with the exercise of any functions conferred on the authority by or under this Chapter.

(4) Any person who is an officer of the Valuation Office may enter any land for the purpose of surveying it, or estimating its value, in connection with a claim for compensation in respect of any land which is payable by the local planning authority under this Chapter (other than section 204).

(5) Any person who is duly authorised in writing by the Secretary of State may enter any land in connection with the exercise of any functions conferred on the Secretary of State by or under this Chapter.

(6) The Secretary of State shall not authorise any person as mentioned in subsection (2) without consulting the local planning authority.

(7) Admission shall not be demanded as of right—

(*a*) by virtue of subsection (1) or (2) to any building used as a dwellinghouse; or

(*b*) by virtue of subsection (3), (4) or (5) to any land which is occupied,

unless twenty-four hours' notice of the intended entry has been given to the occupier.

(8) Any right to enter by virtue of this section shall be exercised at a reasonable hour.

[Town and Country Planning Act 1990, s 214B as inserted by the Planning and Compensation Act 1991, s 23.]

7.11440 **214C. Right to enter under warrant** (1) If it is shown to the satisfaction of a justice of the peace on sworn information in writing—

(*a*) that there are reasonable grounds for entering any land for any of the purposes mentioned in section 214B(1) or (2); and

(*b*) that—

(i) admission to the land has been refused, or a refusal is reasonably apprehended; or

(ii) the case is one of urgency,

the justice may issue a warrant authorising any person duly authorised in writing by a local planning authority or, as the case may be, the Secretary of State to enter the land.

(2) For the purposes of subsection (1)(*b*)(i) admission to land shall be regarded as having been refused if no reply is received to a request for admission within a reasonable period.

(3) A warrant authorises entry on one occasion only and that entry must be—

(*a*) within one month from the date of the issue of the warrant; and

(*b*) at a reasonable hour, unless the case is one of urgency.

[Town and Country Planning Act 1990, s 214C as inserted by the Planning and Compensation Act 1991, s 23.]

7.11441 **214D. Rights of entry supplementary provisions** (1) Any power conferred under or by virtue of section 214B to 214C to enter land (referred to in this section as "a right of entry") shall be construed as including power to take samples from any tree and samples of the soil.

(2) A person authorised to enter land in the exercise of a right of entry—

(*a*) shall, if so required, produce evidence of his authority and state the purpose of his entry before so entering;

(*b*) may take with him such other persons as may be necessary; and

(*c*) on leaving the land shall, if the owner or occupier is not then present, leave it as effectively secured against trespassers as he found it.

(3) Any person who wilfully obstructs a person acting in the exercise of a right of entry shall be guilty of an offence and liable on summary conviction to a fine not exceeding **level 3** on the standard scale.

(4) If any damage is caused to land or chattels in the exercise of a right of entry, compensation may be recovered by any person suffering the damage from the authority who gave the written authority for the entry or, as the case may be, the Secretary of State.

(5) The provisions of section 118 shall apply in relation to compensation under subsection (4) as they apply in relation to compensation under Part IV.

[Town and Country Planning Act 1990, s 214D as inserted by the Planning and Compensation Act 1991, s 23.]

## Chapter II

## Land Adversely Affecting Amenity of Neighbourhood

7.11442 **215. Power to require proper maintenance of land** (1) If it appears to the local planning authority that the amenity of a part of their area, or of an adjoining area, is adversely affected by the condition of land in their area, they may serve on the owner and occupier of the land a notice under this section.

(2) The notice shall require such steps for remedying the condition of the land as may be specified in the notice to be taken within such period as may be so specified.

(3) Subject to the following provisions of this Chapter, the notice shall take effect at the end of such period as may be specified in the notice.

(4) That period shall not be less than 28 days after the service of the notice.

[Town and Country Planning Act 1990, s 215.]

7.11443 **216. Penalty for non-compliance with s 215 notice** (1) The provisions of this section shall have effect where a notice has been served under section 215.

(2) If any owner or occupier of the land on whom the notice was served fails to take steps required by the notice within the period specified in it for compliance with it, he shall be guilty of an offence and liable on summary conviction to a fine not exceeding **level 3** on the standard scale.

(3) Where proceedings have been brought under subsection (2) against a person as the owner of the land and he has, at some time before the end of the compliance period, ceased to be the owner of the land, if he—

(*a*) duly lays information to that effect, and

(*b*) gives the prosecution not less than three clear day's notice of his intention,

he shall be entitled to have the person who then became the owner of the land brought before the court in the proceedings.

(4) Where proceedings have been brought under subsection (2) against a person as the occupier of the land and he has, at some time before the end of the compliance period, ceased to be the occupier of the land, if he—

(*a*) duly lays information to that effect, and

(*b*) gives the prosecution not less than three clear days' notice of his intention,

he shall be entitled to have brought before the court in the proceedings the person who then became the occupier of the land or, if nobody then became the occupier, the person who is the owner at the date of the notice.

(5) Where in such proceedings—

(*a*) it has been proved that any steps required by the notice under section 215 have not been taken within the compliance period, and

(*b*) the original defendant proves that the failure to take those steps was attributable, in whole or in part, to the default of a person specified in a notice under subsection (3) or (4),

then—

(i) that person may be convicted of the offence; and

(ii) if the original defendant also proves that he took all reasonable steps to ensure compliance with the notice, he shall be acquitted of the offence.

(6) If, after a person has been convicted under the previous provisions of this section, he does not as soon as practicable do everything in his power to secure compliance with the notice, he shall be guilty of a further offence and liable on summary conviction to a fine not exceeding **one-tenth of level 3 on the standard scale for each day** following his first conviction on which any of the requirements of the notice remain unfulfilled.

(7) Any reference in this section to the compliance period, in relation to a notice, is a reference to the period specified in the notice for compliance with it or such extended period as the local planning authority who served the notice may allow for compliance.

[Town and Country Planning Act 1990, s 216 as amended by the Planning and Compensation Act 1991, Sch 7.]

7.11444 **217. Appeal to magistrates' court against s 215 notice** (1) A person on whom a notice under section 215 is served, or any other person having an interest in the land to which the notice relates, may, at any time within the period specified in the notice as the period at the end of which it is to take effect, appeal against the notice on any of the following grounds—

(*a*) that the condition of the land to which the notice relates does not adversely affect the amenity of any part of the area of the local planning authority who served the notice, or of any adjoining area;

(*b*) that the condition of the land to which the notice relates is attributable to, and such as results in the ordinary course of events from, the carrying on of operations or a use of land which is not in contravention of Part III;

(*c*) that the requirements of the notice exceed what is necessary for preventing the condition of the land from adversely affecting the amenity of any part of the area of the local planning authority who served the notice, or of any adjoining area;

(*d*) that the period specified in the notice as the period within which any steps required by the notice are to be taken falls short of what should reasonably be allowed.

(2) Any appeal under this section shall be made to a magistrates' court[1].

(3) Where such an appeal is brought, the notice to which it relates shall be of no effect pending

the final determination or withdrawal of the appeal.

(4) On such an appeal the magistrates' court may correct any informality, defect or error in the notice if satisfied that the informality, defect or error is not material.

(5) On the determination of such an appeal the magistrates' court shall give directions for giving effect to their determination, including, where appropriate, directions for quashing the notice or for varying the terms of the notice in favour of the appellant.

(6) Where any person has appealed to a magistrates' court under this section against a notice, neither that person nor any other shall be entitled, in any other proceedings instituted after the making of the appeal, to claim that the notice was not duly served on the person who appealed.

[Town and Country Planning Act 1990, s 217 as amended by the Courts Act 2003, Sch 8.]

---

[1] Appeal is by way of complaint (Magistrates' Courts Rules 1981, r 34 in PART I: MAGISTRATES' COURTS, PROCEDURE, ante. The appellant or the local planning authority who served the notice under s 215 may thereafter appeal to the Crown Court (s 218); the Magistrates' Courts Act 1980, ss 109 and 110 ante and the Crown Court Rules 1982 in PART I: MAGISTRATES' COURTS, PROCEDURE will apply.

As to the inference of receipt of the notice of appeal where it was sent by post, see *R (on the application of Latimer) v Chief Clerk to the Justices, Bury Magistrates' Court and Bury Metropolitan Council; R (on the application of Kotegaonkar) v Bury Magistrates' Court and Bury Metropolitan Borough Council* [2008] EWHC 2213 (Admin), 172 JP 555: " . . . in a case where it is common ground that (*a*) letter was sent, the appropriate inference is that it was received. This is not a presumption of law: it is a presumption based on the application of common sense. It is likely to be a particularly potent inference when the consequence of finding that a letter was not received is that the writer of the letter may be exposed to criminal prosecution and policy" (per Simon J at para 14).

## CHAPTER III
## ADVERTISEMENTS

**7.11445 220.** *Regulations controlling display of advertisements.*

**7.11446 221.** *Power to make different advertisement regulations for different areas.*

*Enforcement of control over advertisements*

**7.11447 224. Enforcement of control as to advertisements** (1) Regulations[1] under section 220 may make provision for enabling the local planning authority to require—

(*a*) the removal of any advertisement which is displayed in contravention of the regulations, or

(*b*) the discontinuance of the use for the display of advertisements of any site which is being so used in contravention of the regulations.

(2) For that purpose the regulations may apply any of the provisions of Part VII with respect to enforcement notices or the provisions of section 186, subject to such adaptations and modifications as may be specified in the regulations.

(3) Without prejudice to any provisions included in such regulations by virtue of subsection (1) or (2), if any person displays an advertisement in contravention of the regulations he shall be guilty of an offence[2] and liable on summary conviction to a fine of such amount as may be prescribed, not exceeding **level 4** on the standard scale and, in the case of a continuing offence, **one-tenth of level 4 on the standard scale for each day** during which the offence continues after conviction.

(4) Without prejudice to the generality of subsection (3), a person shall be deemed to display an advertisement for the purposes of that subsection if—

(*a*) he is the owner or occupier of the land on which the advertisement is displayed; or

(*b*) the advertisement gives publicity to his goods, trade, business or other concerns[3].

(5) A person shall not be guilty of an offence under subsection (3) by reason only—

(*a*) of his being the owner or occupier of the land on which an advertisement is displayed, or

(*b*) of his goods, trade, business or other concerns being given publicity by the advertisement,

if he proves either of the matters specified in subsection (6).

(6) The matters are that—

(*a*) the advertisement was displayed without his knowledge; or

(*b*) he took all reasonable steps to prevent the display or, after the advertisement had been displayed, to secure its removal.

(7) Proceedings for an offence under subsection (3) may be brought within the period of 6 months beginning with the date on which evidence sufficient in the opinion of the prosecutor to justify the proceedings came to the prosecutor's knowledge.

(8) Subsection (7) does not authorise the commencement of proceedings for an offence more than 3 years after the date on which the offence was committed.

(9) For the purposes of subsection (7), a certificate—

(*a*) signed by or on behalf of the prosecutor, and

(*b*) stating the date on which evidence sufficient in the prosecutor's opinion to justify the proceedings came to the prosecutor's knowledge,

is conclusive evidence of that fact.

(10) A certificate stating that matter and purporting to be so signed is to be deemed to be so

signed unless the contrary is proved.

(11) Subsection (7) does not apply in relation to an offence in respect of an advertisement in Wales.

[Town and Country Planning Act 1990, s 224 as amended by the Planning and Compensation Act 1991, Sch 7, the Anti-social Behaviour Act 2003, s 53, the Clean Neighbourhoods and Environment Act 2005, s 33 and the Localism Act 2011, s 126.]

---

1 See the Town and Country Planning (Control of Advertisements) Regulations 1992, post. For application of the predecessor regulations to advertisements on a petrol station forecourt, see *Heron Service Stations Ltd v Coupe* [1973] 2 All ER 110, 137 JP 415.

2 This is an absolute offence; see *Porter v Honey* [1988] 2 All ER 449. The display of different posters on a hoarding on different dates has been held to constitute separate offences for each display, contrary to reg 27 of the Town and Country Planning (Control of Advertisements) Regulations 1992, this PART, post (*Kingston-upon-Thames London Borough Council v National Solus Sites Ltd* (1993) 158 JP 70). The regulations under s 220 provide a code for control of advertisements which does not depend on the breach of planning and control and enforcement procedures under Pts III and VII of this Act. Accordingly, the defence in s 171B(3), ante, is not available in a prosecution under s 224(3) of the Act (*Torridge District Council v Jarrad* (1998) Times, 13 April.)

3 Whether an advertisement gives publicity to the "goods, trade, business or other concerns" of the defendant is a mixed question of fact and law (*Merton London Borough Council v Edmonds* (1993) 157 JP 1129).

7.11448 225. *Power to remove or obliterate placards and posters.*

7.11449 225A. **Power to remove structures used for unauthorised display** (1) Subject to subsections (2), (3) and (5) and the right of appeal under section 225B, the local planning authority for an area in England may remove, and then dispose of, any display structure—

(*a*) which is in their area; and

(*b*) which, in the local planning authority's opinion, is used for the display of advertisements in contravention of regulations under section 220.

(2) Subsection (1) does not authorise the removal of a display structure in a building to which there is no public right of access.

(3) The local planning authority may not under subsection (1) remove a display structure unless the local planning authority have first served a removal notice on a person who appears to the local planning authority to be responsible for the erection or maintenance of the display structure.

(4) Subsection (3) applies only if there is a person—

(*a*) who appears to the local planning authority to be responsible for the erection or maintenance of the display structure; and

(*b*) whose name and address are either known by the local planning authority or could be ascertained by the local planning authority after reasonable enquiry.

(5) If subsection (3) does not apply, the local planning authority may not under subsection (1) remove a display structure unless the local planning authority have first—

(*a*) fixed a removal notice to the display structure or exhibited a removal notice in the vicinity of the display structure; and

(*b*) served a copy of that notice on the occupier of the land on which the display structure is situated.

(6) Subsection (5)(*b*) applies only if the local planning authority know who the occupier is or could identify the occupier after reasonable enquiry.

(7) Where—

(*a*) the local planning authority has served a removal notice in accordance with subsection (3) or (5)(*b*), and

(*b*) the display structure is not removed by the time specified in the removal notice,

the local planning authority may recover, from any person on whom the removal notice has been served under subsection (3) or (5)(*b*), expenses reasonably incurred by the local planning authority in exercising the local planning authority's power under subsection (1).

(8) Expenses are not recoverable under subsection (7) from a person if the person satisfies the local planning authority that the person was not responsible for the erection of the display structure and is not responsible for its maintenance.

(9) Where in the exercise of power under subsection (1) any damage is caused to land or chattels, compensation may be recovered by any person suffering the damage from the local planning authority exercising the power, but compensation is not recoverable under this subsection or section 325(6)—

(*a*) for damage caused to the display structure; or

(*b*) for damage reasonably caused in removing the display structure.

(10) The provisions of section 118 apply in relation to compensation under subsection (9) as they apply in relation to compensation under Part 4.

(11) In this section "removal notice", in relation to a display structure, means notice—

(*a*) stating that in the local planning authority's opinion the display structure is used for the display of advertisements in contravention of regulations under section 220;

(*b*) stating that the local planning authority intend after a time specified in the notice to remove the display structure; and

(*c*) stating the effect of subsections (7) and (8).

(12) A time specified under subsection (11)(*b*) may not be earlier than the end of 22 days

beginning with the date of the notice.

(13) In this section "display structure" means (subject to subsection (14))—

(*a*) a hoarding or similar structure used, or designed or adapted for use, for the display of advertisements;

(*b*) anything (other than a hoarding or similar structure) principally used, or designed or adapted principally for use, for the display of advertisements;

(*c*) a structure that is itself an advertisement; or

(*d*) fitments used to support anything within any of paragraphs (*a*) to (*c*).

(14) Something is a "display structure" for the purpose of this section only if—

(*a*) its use for the display of advertisement requires consent under this Chapter, and

(*b*) that consent has not been granted and is not deemed to have been granted.

(15) In subsection (13) "structure" includes movable structure.

[Town and Country Planning Act 1990, s 225A as inserted by the Localism Act 2011, s 127.]

7.11450 **225B. Appeal against notice under section 225A** (1) A person on whom a removal notice has been served in accordance with section 225A(3) or (5)(*b*) may appeal to a magistrates' court on any of the following grounds—

(*a*) that the display structure concerned is not used for the display of advertisements in contravention of regulations under section 220;

(*b*) that there has been some informality, defect or error in, or in connection with, the notice;

(*c*) that the period between the date of the notice and the time specified in the notice is not reasonably sufficient for the removal of the display structure;

(*d*) that the notice should have been served on another person.

(2) For the purposes of subsection (3), a person is a "permitted appellant" in relation to a removal notice if—

(*a*) the removal notice has been fixed or exhibited in accordance with section 225A(5)(*a*);

(*b*) the person is an owner or occupier of the land on which the display structure concerned is situated; and

(*c*) no copy of the removal notice has been served on the person in accordance with section 225A(5)(*b*).

(3) A person who is a permitted appellant in relation to a removal notice may appeal to a magistrates' court on any of the following grounds—

(*a*) that the display structure concerned is not used for the display of advertisements in contravention of regulations under section 220;

(*b*) that there has been some informality, defect or error in, or in connection with, the notice;

(*c*) that the period between the date of the notice and the time specified in the notice is not reasonably sufficient for the removal of the display structure.

(4) So far as an appeal under this section is based on the ground mentioned in subsection (1)(*b*) or (3)(*b*), the court must dismiss the appeal if it is satisfied that the informality, defect or error was not a material one.

(5) If an appeal under subsection (1) is based on the ground mentioned in subsection (1)(*d*), the appellant must serve a copy of the notice of appeal on each person who the appellant considers is a person on whom the removal notice should have been served in accordance with section 225A(3) or (5)(*b*).

(6) If—

(*a*) a removal notice is served on a person in accordance with section 225A(3) or (5)(*b*), and

(*b*) the local planning authority bring proceedings against the person for the recovery under section 225A(7) of any expenses,

it is not open to the person to raise in the proceedings any question which the person could have raised in an appeal under subsection (1).

(7) In this section "removal notice" and "display structure" have the same meaning as in section 225A.

[Town and Country Planning Act 1990, s 225B as inserted by the Localism Act 2011, s 127.]

7.11451 **225C. Remedying persistent problems with unauthorised advertisements** (1) Subsections (2) and (3) apply if the local planning authority for an area in England have reason to believe that there is a persistent problem with the display of unauthorised advertisements on a surface of—

(*a*) any building, wall, fence or other structure or erection; or

(*b*) any apparatus or plant.

(2) The local planning authority may serve an action notice on the owner or occupier of the land in or on which the surface is situated.

(3) If after reasonable enquiry the local planning authority—

(*a*) are unable to ascertain the name and address of the owner, and

(*b*) are unable to ascertain the name and address of the occupier, the local planning authority may fix an action notice to the surface.

(4) For the purposes of this section "an action notice", in relation to a surface, is a notice requiring the owner or occupier of the land in or on which the surface is situated to carry out the measures specified in the notice by a time specified in the notice.

(5) A time may be specified in an action notice if it is a reasonable time not earlier than the end of 28 days beginning with the date of the notice.

(6) Measures may be specified in an action notice if they are reasonable measures to prevent or reduce the frequency of the display of unauthorised advertisements on the surface concerned.

(7) The time by which an owner or occupier must comply with an action notice may be postponed by the local planning authority.

(8) This section has effect subject to—

(*a*) the other provisions of the enactments relating to town and country planning;

(*b*) the provisions of the enactments relating to historic buildings and ancient monuments; and

(*c*) Part 2 of the Food and Environmental Protection Act 1985 (which relates to deposits in the sea).

(9) Subsection (10) applies if—

(*a*) an action notice is served under subsection (2) or fixed under subsection (3); and

(*b*) the measures specified in the notice are not carried out by the time specified in the notice.

(10) The local planning authority may—

(*a*) carry out the measures; and

(*b*) recover expenses reasonably incurred by the local planning authority in doing that from the person required by the action notice to do it.

(11) Power under subsection (10)(*a*) is subject to the right of appeal under section 225D.

(12) Where in the exercise of power under subsection (10)(*a*) any damage is caused to land or chattels, compensation may be recovered by any person suffering the damage from the local planning authority exercising the power, but compensation is not recoverable under this subsection for damage reasonably caused in carrying out the measures.

(13) The provisions of section 118 apply in relation to compensation under subsection (12) as they apply in relation to compensation under Part 4.

(14) The local planning authority may not recover expenses under subsection (10)(*b*) in respect of a surface that—

(*a*) forms part of a flat or a dwellinghouse;

(*b*) is within the curtilage of a dwellinghouse; or

(*c*) forms part of the boundary of the curtilage of a dwellinghouse.

(15) Each of sections 275 and 291 of the Public Health Act 1936 (provision for authority to agree to take the required measures at expense of owner or occupier, and provision for expenses to be recoverable also from owner's successor or from occupier and to be charged on premises concerned) applies as if the reference in that section to that Act included a reference to this section.

(16) In this section—

"dwellinghouse" does not include a building containing one or more flats, or a flat contained within such a building;

"flat" means a separate and self-contained set of premises constructed or adapted for use as a dwelling and forming part of a building from some other part of which it is divided horizontally;

"unauthorised advertisement" means an advertisement in respect of which an offence—

(*a*) under section 224(3), or

(*b*) under section 132 of the Highways Act 1980 (unauthorised marks on highway),

is committed after the coming into force of this section.

[Town and Country Planning Act 1990, s 225C as inserted by the Localism Act 2011, s 127.]

7.11452 **225D. Right to appeal against notice under section 225C** (1) A person on whom notice has been served under section 225C(2) may appeal to a magistrates' court on any of the following grounds—

(*a*) that there is no problem with the display of unauthorised advertisements on the surface concerned or any such problem is not a persistent one;

(*b*) that there has been some informality, defect or error in, or in connection with, the notice;

(*c*) that the time within which the measures specified in the notice are to be carried out is not reasonably sufficient for the purpose;

(*d*) that the notice should have been served on another person.

(2) The occupier or owner of premises which include a surface to which a notice has been fixed under section 225C(3) may appeal to a magistrates' court on any of the following grounds—

(*a*) that there is no problem with the display of unauthorised advertisements on the surface concerned or any such problem is not a persistent one;

(*b*) that there has been some informality, defect or error in, or in connection with, the notice;

(*c*) that the time within which the measures specified in the notice are to be carried out is not reasonably sufficient for the purpose.

(3) So far as an appeal under this section is based on the ground mentioned in subsection (1)(*b*) or (2)(*b*), the court must dismiss the appeal if it is satisfied that the informality, defect or error was not a material one.

(4) If an appeal under subsection (1) is based on the ground mentioned in subsection (1)(*d*), the appellant must serve a copy of the notice of appeal on each person who the appellant considers is a person on whom the notice under section 225C(2) should have been served.

(5) If—

(*a*) notice under section 225C(2) is served on a person, and

(*b*) the local planning authority bring proceedings against the person for the recovery under section 225C(10)(*b*) of any expenses,

it is not open to the person to raise in the proceedings any question which the person could have raised in an appeal under subsection (1).

[Town and Country Planning Act 1990, s 225D as inserted by the Localism Act 2011, s 127.]

7.11453 **225E. Applying section 225C to statutory undertakers' operational land**

(1) Subsection (2) and (3) apply where the local planning authority serves a notice under section 225C(2) requiring a statutory undertaker to carry out measures in respect of the display of unauthorised advertisements on a surface on its operational land.

(2) The statutory undertaker may, within 28 days beginning with the date of service of the notice, serve a counter-notice on the local planning authority specifying alternative measures which will in the statutory undertaker's reasonable opinion have the effect of preventing or reducing the frequency of the display of unauthorised advertisements on the surface to at least the same extent as the measures specified in the notice.

(3) Where a counter-notice is served under subsection (2), the notice under section 225C(2) is to be treated—

(*a*) as requiring the alternative measures specified in the counter-notice to be carried out (instead of the measures actually required by the notice under section 225C(2)); and

(*b*) as having been served on the date on which the counter-notice is served.

(4) The time by which a statutory undertaker must carry out the measures specified in a counter-notice served under subsection (2) may be postponed by the local planning authority."

[Town and Country Planning Act 1990, s 225E as inserted by the Localism Act 2011, s 127.]

## CHAPTER 4[1]

## REMEDYING DEFACEMENT OF PREMISES

7.11454 **225F. Power to remedy defacement of premises** (1) Subsections (2) and (3) apply if—

(*a*) premises in England include a surface that is readily visible from a place to which the public have access;

(*b*) either—

(i) the surface does not form part of the operational land of a statutory undertaker, or

(ii) the surface forms part of the operational land of a statutory undertaker and subsection (11) applies to the surface;

(*c*) there is a sign on the surface; and

(*d*) the local planning authority consider the sign to be detrimental to the amenity of the area or offensive.

(2) The local planning authority may serve on the occupier of the premises a notice requiring the occupier to remove or obliterate the sign by a time specified in the notice.

(3) If it appears to the local planning authority that there is no occupier of the premises, the local planning authority may fix to the surface a notice requiring the owner or occupier of the premises to remove or obliterate the sign by a time specified in the notice.

(4) A time specified under subsection (2) or (3) may not be earlier than the end of 15 days beginning the date of service or fixing of the notice.

(5) Subsection (6) applies if—

(*a*) a notice is served under subsection (2) or fixed under subsection (3); and

(*b*) the sign is neither removed nor obliterated by the time specified in the notice.

(6) The local planning authority may—

(*a*) remove or obliterate the sign; and

(*b*) recover expenses reasonably incurred by the local planning authority in doing that from the person required by the notice to do it.

(7) Power under subsection (6)(*a*) is subject to the right of appeal under section 225I.

(8) Expenses may not be recovered under subsection (6)(*b*) if the surface—

(*a*) forms part of a flat or a dwellinghouse;

(*b*) is within the curtilage of a dwellinghouse; or

(*c*) forms part of the boundary of the curtilage of a dwellinghouse.

(9) Section 291 of the Public Health Act 1936 (provision for expenses to be recoverable also from owner's successor or from occupier and to be charged on premises concerned) applies as if the

reference in that section to that Act included a reference to this section.

(10) For the purposes of this section, a universal postal service provider is treated as being the occupier of any plant or apparatus that consists of a universal postal service letter box or a universal postal service pouch-box belonging to it.

(11) This subsection applies to a surface if the surface abuts on, or is one to which access is given directly from, either—

(*a*) a street; or

(*b*) any place, other than a street, to which the public have access as of right.

(12) In this section—

"dwellinghouse" does not include a building containing one or more flats, or a flat contained within such a building;

"flat" means a separate and self-contained set of premises constructed or adapted for use as a dwelling and forming part of a building from some other part of which it is divided horizontally;

"premises" means building, wall, fence or other structure or erection, or apparatus or plant;

"sign"—

(*a*) includes any writing, letter, picture, device or representation, but

(*b*) does not include an advertisement;

"statutory undertaker" does not include a relevant airport operator (within the meaning of Part 5 of the Airports Act 1986);

"street" includes any highway, any bridge carrying a highway and any road, lane, mews, footway, square, court, alley or passage, whether a thoroughfare or not;

"universal postal service letter box" has the meaning given in section 86(4) of the Postal Services Act 2000;

"universal postal service pouch-box" has the meaning given in paragraph 1(10) of Schedule 6 to that Act.

[Town and Country Planning Act 1990, s 225F as inserted by the Localism Act 2011, s 127.]

[1] Chapter 4 comprises ss 225F–225J.

**7.11455 225G. Notices under section 225F in respect of post boxes** (1) The local planning authority may serve a notice under section 225F(2) on a universal postal service provider in respect of a universal postal service letter box, or universal postal service pouch-box, belonging to the provider only if—

(*a*) the authority has served on the provider written notice of the authority's intention to do so; and

(*b*) the period of 28 days beginning with the date of service of that notice has ended.

(2) In this section—

"universal postal service letter box" has the meaning given in section 86(4) of the Postal Services Act 2000;

"universal postal service pouch-box" has the meaning given in paragraph 1(10) of Schedule 6 to that Act.

[Town and Country Planning Act 1990, s 225G as inserted by the Localism Act 2011, s 127.]

**7.11456 225H. Section 225F powers as respects bus shelters and other street furniture** (1) The local planning authority may exercise the power conferred by section 225F(6)(*a*) to remove or obliterate a sign from any surface on a bus shelter, or other street furniture, of a statutory undertaker that is not situated on operational land of the statutory undertaker only if—

(*a*) the authority has served on the statutory undertaker notice of the authority's intention to do so;

(*b*) the notice specified the bus shelter, or other street furniture, concerned; and

(*c*) the period of 28 days beginning with the date of service of the notice has ended.

(2) In this section "statutory undertaker" does not include an airport operator (within the meaning of Part 5 of the Airports Act 1986).

[Town and Country Planning Act 1990, s 225H as inserted by the Localism Act 2011, s 127.]

**7.11457 225I. Right to appeal against notice under section 225F** (1) A person on whom notice has been served under section 225F(2) may appeal to a magistrates' court on any of the following grounds—

(*a*) that the sign concerned is neither detrimental to the amenity of the area nor offensive;

(*b*) that there has been some informality, defect or error in, or in connection with, the notice;

(*c*) that the time within which the sign concerned is to be removed or obliterated is not reasonably sufficient for the purpose;

(*d*) that the notice should have been served on another person.

(2) The occupier or owner of premises which include a surface to which a notice has been fixed under section 225F(3) may appeal to a magistrates' court on any of the following grounds—

(*a*) that the sign concerned is neither detrimental to the amenity of the area nor offensive;

(*b*) that there has been some informality, defect or error in, or in connection with, the notice;

(*c*) that the time within which the sign concerned is to be removed or obliterated is not reasonably sufficient for the purpose.

(3) So far as an appeal under this section is based on the ground mentioned in subsection (1)(*b*) or (2)(*b*), the court must dismiss the appeal if it is satisfied that the informality, defect or error was not a material one.

(4) If an appeal under subsection (1) is based on the ground mentioned in subsection (1)(*d*), the appellant must serve a copy of the notice of appeal on each person who the appellant considers is a person on whom the notice under section 225F(2) should have been served.

(5) If—

(*a*) notice under section 225F(2) is served on a person, and

(*b*) the local planning authority bring proceedings against the person for the recovery under section 225F(6)(*b*) of any expenses,

it is not open to the person to raise in the proceedings any question which the person could have raised in an appeal under subsection (1).

[Town and Country Planning Act 1990, s 225I as inserted by the Localism Act 2011, s 127.]

7.11458 **225J. Remedying defacement at owner or occupier's request** (1) Subsection (2) applies if—

(*a*) premises in England include a surface that is readily visible from a place to which the public have access;

(*b*) there is a sign on the surface; and

(*c*) the owner or occupier of the premises asks the local planning authority to remove or obliterate the sign.

(2) The local planning authority may—

(*a*) remove or obliterate the sign; and

(*b*) recover expenses reasonably incurred by the local planning authority in doing that from the person who asked the local planning authority to do it.

(3) In this section "premises" means building, wall, fence or other structure or erection, or apparatus or plant.

(4) In this section "sign"—

(*a*) includes—

(i) any writing, letter, picture, device or representation, and

(ii) any advertisement, but

(*b*) does not include an advertisement for the display of which deemed or express consent has been granted under Chapter 3.

[Town and Country Planning Act 1990, s 225J as inserted by the Localism Act 2011, s 127.]

## CHAPTER 5[1]

## APPLICATION OF PROVISIONS OF CHAPTERS 3 AND 4 TO STATUTORY UNDERTAKERS

7.11459 **225K. Action under sections 225A, 225C and 225F: operational land** (1) This section applies in relation to the exercise by the local planning authority of—

(*a*) power conferred by section 225A(1), or section 324(3) so far as applying for the purposes of section 225A(1), to—

(i) enter on any operational land of a statutory undertaker, or

(ii) remove a display structure situated on operational land of a statutory undertaker;

(*b*) power conferred by section 225C(10)(*a*), or section 324(3) so far as applying for the purposes of section 225C(10)(*a*), to—

(i) enter on any operational land of a statutory undertaker, or

(ii) carry out any measures to prevent or reduce the frequency of the display of unauthorised advertisements on a surface on operational land of a statutory undertaker; or

(*c*) power conferred by section 225F(6)(*a*), or section 324(3) so far as applying for the purposes of section 225F(6)(*a*), to—

(i) enter on any operational land of a statutory undertaker, or

(ii) remove or obliterate a sign on a surface of premises that are, or are on, operational land of a statutory undertaker.

(2) The authority may exercise the power only if—

(*a*) the authority has served on the statutory undertaker notice of the authority's intention to do so;

(*b*) the notice specified the display structure, surface or sign concerned and its location; and

(*c*) the period of 28 days beginning with the date of service of the notice has ended.

(3) If—

(*a*) a notice under subsection (2) is served on a statutory undertaker, and

(*b*) within 28 days beginning with the date the notice is served, the statutory undertaker serves a counter-notice on the local planning authority specifying conditions subject to which the power is to be exercised,

the power may only be exercised subject to, and in accordance with, the conditions specified in the counter-notice.

(4) The conditions which may be specified in a counter-notice under subsection (3) are conditions which are—

(*a*) necessary or expedient in the interests of safety or the efficient and economic operation of the undertaking concerned; or

(*b*) for the protection of any works, apparatus or other property not vested in the statutory undertaker which are lawfully present on, in, under or over the land upon which entry is proposed to be made.

(5) If—

(*a*) a notice under subsection (2) is served on a statutory undertaker, and

(*b*) within 28 days beginning with the date the notice is served, the statutory undertaker serves a counter-notice on the local planning authority requiring the local planning authority to refrain from exercising the power,

the power may not be exercised.

(6) A counter-notice under subsection (5) may be served only if the statutory undertaker has reasonable grounds to believe, for reasons connected with the operation of its undertaking, that the power cannot be exercised under the circumstances in question—

(*a*) without risk to the safety of any person; or

(*b*) without unreasonable risk to the efficient and economic operation of the statutory undertaker's undertaking.

(7) In this section "statutory undertaker" does not include an airport operator (within the meaning of Part 5 of the Airports Act 1986).

[Town and Country Planning Act 1990, s 225K as inserted by the Localism Act 2011, s 127.]

[1] Chapter 5 comprises s 225K.

## PART XII[1]

## VALIDITY

7.11460 **284. Validity of development plans and certain orders, decisions and directions** The validity of these is not to be questioned in any legal proceedings whatsoever; these matters include orders under ss 97, 102, 221(5), Sch 9, paras 1, 3, 5 and 6, a tree preservation order, a decision under ss 76A, 77,78, 95, 177(1)(*a*) or (*b*) or 195(1), and any decision relating—

(i) to an application for consent under a tree preservation order,

(ii) to an application for consent under any regulations made in accordance with sections 220, 221 or 293A, or

(iii) to any certificate or direction under any such order or regulations, whether it is a decision on appeal or a decision on an application referred to the Secretary of State for determination in the first instance.

[Town and Country Planning Act 1990, s 284 amended by the Planning and Compensation Act 1991, Schs 4, 7 and 19, the Planning and Compulsory Purchase Act 2004, s 82, the Planning Act 2008, s 191, Schs 8 and 13 and the Criminal Justice and Courts Act 2015, Sch 16—summarised.]

[1] Part XII contains ss 284–292.

7.11461 **285. Validity of enforcement notices and similar notices** (1) The validity of an enforcement notice shall not, except by way of an appeal under Part VII, be questioned in any proceedings whatsoever on any of the grounds on which such an appeal may be brought.

(2) Subsection (1) shall not apply to proceedings brought under section 179 against a person who—

(*a*) has held an interest in the land since before the enforcement notice was issued under that Part;

(*b*) did not have a copy of the enforcement notice served on him under that Part; and

(*c*) satisfies the court—

(i) that he did not know and could not reasonably have been expected to know that the enforcement notice had been issued; and

(ii) that his interests have been substantially prejudiced by the failure to serve him with a copy of it.

(3) Subject to subsection (4), the validity of a notice which has been served under section 215 on the owner and occupier of the land shall not, except by way of an appeal under Chapter II of Part VIII, be questioned in any proceedings whatsoever on either of the grounds specified in section 217(1)(*a*) or (*b*).

(4) Subsection (3) shall not prevent the validity of such a notice being questioned on either of those grounds in proceedings[1] brought under section 216 against a person on whom the notice was not served, but who has held an interest in the land since before the notice was served on the owner and occupier of the land, if he did not appeal against the notice under that Chapter.

(5)–(6) *Repealed.*

[Town and Country Planning Act 1990, s 285 as amended by the Planning and Compensation Act 1991, Sch 7.]

[1] "Proceedings" includes criminal proceedings (*R v Thomas George Smith* [1984] Crim LR 630). Section 285 of the 1990 Act does not, however, prevent the claimant from challenging via judicial review the validity of the notice on the ground that the notices was not been served within the time required by s 172(3): *R (on the application of Stern) v Horsham*

*District Council* [2013] EWHC 1460 (Admin), [2013] 3 All ER 798. A person who has no right of appeal to the Secretary of State against the enforcement notice may in subsequent criminal proceedings challenge the validity of the enforcement notice (*Scarborough Borough Council v Adams and Adams* (1983) 147 JP 449). In *R v Clayton* [2014] EWCA Crim 1030, [2014] 1 WLR 3994, [2014] 2 Cr App Rep 296 the defendants were prosecuted for allegedly breaching an enforcement notice by letting flats in a property owned by them as long-term residencies rather than holiday or short lettings. They received information from a former council employee that the enforcement notice was invalid because at the time it was issued the council had allegedly known that the property had been used as permanent residencies for more than four years. The informant alleged that there had been deliberate concealment of this information. At a hearing before the Crown Court the defendants submitted that the proceedings should be stayed as an abuse of processes. The judge ruled that the Crown Court lacked jurisdiction to hear the abuse argument because of s 285. The Court of Appeal upheld the conviction. The only challenge to the validity of the notice was by way of appeal, whether the basis was that it was invalid or that there had been deliberate concealment of information. See further, note 1 to s 179, ante.

7.11462 **286. Challenges to validity on ground of authority's powers** (1) The validity of any permission, determination or certificate granted, made or issued or purporting to have been granted, made or issued by a local planning authority in respect of—

(*a*) an application for planning permission or permission in principle;

(*aa*) an application for non-material changes to planning permission under section 96A;

(*b*) *repealed*;

(*c*) an application for a certificate under section 191 or 192;

(*d*) an application for consent to the display of advertisements under section 220; or

(*e*) a determination under section 302 or Schedule 15,

shall not be called in question in any legal proceedings, or in any proceedings under this Act which are not legal proceedings, on the ground that the permission, determination or certificate should have been granted, made or given by some other local planning authority.

(2) The validity of any order under section 97 revoking or modifying planning permission or permission in principle, any order under section 102 or paragraph 1 of Schedule 9 requiring discontinuance of use, or imposing conditions on continuance of use, or requiring the alteration or removal of buildings or works, or any enforcement notice under section 172 or stop notice under section 183 or a breach of condition notice under section 187A, being an order or notice purporting to have been made, issued or served by a local planning authority, shall not be called in question in any such proceedings on the ground—

(*a*) in the case of an order or notice purporting to have been made, issued or served by a district planning authority, that they failed to comply with paragraph 11(2) of Schedule 1;

(*b*) in the case of an order or notice purporting to have been made, issued or served by a county planning authority, that they had no power to make, issue or serve it because it did not relate to a county matter within the meaning of that Schedule.

[Town and Country Planning Act 1990, s 286 as amended by the Planning and Compensation Act 1991, Schs 7 and 19, the Planning Act 2008, s 190 and the Housing and Planning Act 2016, Sch 12.]

## PART XV[1]

## MISCELLANEOUS AND GENERAL PROVISIONS

### *Application of Act in special cases*

7.11463 **315. Power to modify Act in relation to minerals** Many provisions, including practically all those included in this work, may be subject to prescribed adaptations and modifications in relation to development consisting of the winning and working of minerals.

[Town and Country Planning Act 1990, s 315 amended by the Planning and Compensation Act 1991, Schs 1, 6 and 19 and the Coal Industry Act 1994, Schs 9 and 11—summarised.]

[1] Part XV comprises ss 315–337.

### *Rights of entry*

7.11464 **324.** *Rights of entry*[1].

[1] Section 324 enables the Secretary of State or a local planning authority to give written authority to enter land to survey it, or for the purposes of ss 207–209, or 225, or valuation purposes, or to ascertain compliance with an order or notice, or to ascertain the nature of the subsoil or the presence of minerals.

7.11465 **325. Supplementary provisions as to rights of entry**[1] (1) A person authorised under section 324 to enter any land—

(*a*) shall, if so required, produce evidence of his authority and state the purpose of his entry before so entering, and

(*b*) shall not demand admission as of right to any land which is occupied unless 24 hours notice of the intended entry has been given to the occupier.

(2) Any person who wilfully obstructs a person acting in the exercise of his powers under section 324 shall be guilty of an offence and liable on summary conviction to a fine not exceeding **level 3** on the standard scale.

(3) If any person who, in compliance with the provisions of section 324, is admitted into a factory, workshop or workplace discloses to any person any information obtained by him in it as to any manufacturing process or trade secret, he shall be guilty of an offence.

(4) Subsection (3) does not apply if the disclosure is made by a person in the course of

performing his duty in connection with the purpose for which he was authorised to enter the land.

(5) A person who is guilty of an offence under subsection (3) shall be liable[2] on summary conviction to a fine not exceeding the **statutory maximum** or on conviction on indictment to imprisonment for a term not exceeding **two years** or a **fine** or **both**.

(6)–(9) *Compensation for damage to land; notice required to search and bore; Minister's consent for land held by statutory undertakers.*

[Town and Country Planning Act 1990, s 325 as amended by the Planning and Compensation Act 1991, s 11 and Sch 7.]

---

[1] This section applies as well to s 88 of the Planning (Listed Buildings and Conservation Areas) Act 1990 (rights of entry under that Act), post.

[2] For procedure in respect of an offence triable either way, see the Magistrates' Courts Act, 1980, ss 17A–21, in PART I: MAGISTRATES' COURTS, PROCEDURE, ante.

**7.11465A 325A. Rights of entry: Crown land**

**7.11466 329. Service of notices** (1) Any notice or other document required or authorised to be served or given under this Act may be served or given either—

(*a*) by delivering it to the person on whom it is to be served or to whom it is to be given; or

(*b*) by leaving it at the usual or last known place of abode of that person or, in a case where an address for service has been given by that person, at that address; or

(*c*) by sending it in a prepaid registered letter, or by the recorded delivery service, addressed to that person at his usual or last known place of abode or, in a case where an address for service has been given by that person, at that address; or

(*cc*) in a case where an address for service using electronic communications has been given by that person, by sending it using electronic communications, in accordance with the condition set out in subsection (3A), to that person at that address (subject to subsection (3B)); or

(*d*) in the case of an incorporated company or body, by delivering it to the secretary or clerk of the company or body at their registered or principal office or sending it in a prepaid registered letter, or by the recorded delivery service, addressed to the secretary or clerk of the company or body at that office.

(2) Where the notice or document is required or authorised to be served on any person as having an interest in premises, and the name of that person cannot be ascertained after reasonable inquiry, or where the notice or document is required or authorised to be served on any person as an occupier of premises, the notice or document shall be taken to be duly served if—

(*a*) it is addressed to him either by name or by the description of "the owner" or, as the case may be, "the occupier" of the premises (describing them) and is delivered or sent in the manner specified in subsection (1)(*a*), (*b*) or (*c*); or

(*b*) it is so addressed and is marked in such a manner as may be prescribed for securing that it is plainly identifiable as a communication of importance and—

(i) it is sent to the premises in a prepaid registered letter or by the recorded delivery service and is not returned to the authority sending it, or

(ii) it is delivered to some person on those premises, or is affixed conspicuously to some object on those premises.

(3) Where—

(*a*) the notice or other document is required to be served on or given to all persons who have interests in or are occupiers of premises comprised in any land, and

(*b*) it appears to the authority required or authorised to serve or give the notice or other document that any part of that land is unoccupied,

the notice or document shall be taken to be duly served on all persons having interests in, and on any occupiers of, premises comprised in that part of the land (other than a person who has given to that authority an address for the service of the notice or document on him) if it is addressed to "the owners and any occupiers" of that part of the land (describing it) and is affixed conspicuously to some object on the land.

(3A) The condition mentioned in subsection (1)(*cc*) is that the notice or other document shall be—

(*a*) capable of being accessed by the person mentioned in that provision;

(*b*) legible in all material respects; and

(*c*) in a form sufficiently permanent to be used for subsequent reference;

and for this purpose "legible in all material respects" means that the information contained in the notice or document is available to that person to no lesser extent than it would be if served or given by means of a notice or document in printed form.

(3B) Subsection (1)(*cc*) shall not apply to—

(*a*) service of a planning contravention notice;

(*b*) service of a copy of an enforcement notice by a local planning authority;

(*c*) giving of notice under section 173A of the exercise of powers conferred by subsection (1) of that section;

(*d*) service under section 181(4) of notice of a local planning authority's intention to take steps required by an enforcement notice;

(*e*) service of an enforcement notice issued by the Secretary of State;
(*f*) service of a stop notice, or of notice of withdrawal of a stop notice, by a local planning authority;
(*g*) service of a stop notice by the Secretary of State;
(*h*) service of a breach of condition notice or of notice of withdrawal of a breach of condition notice;
(*i*) giving of notice of the making of a tree preservation order, or service of a copy of such an order, in accordance with regulations under section 199*;
(*j*) service of a notice under section 215 requiring steps to be taken to remedy the condition of any land;
(*k*) service of a notice under section 330 requiring information as to interests in land.

(4) This section is without prejudice to section 233 of the Local Government Act 1972 (general provisions as to services of notices by local authorities).

[Town and Country Planning Act 1990, s 329 as amended by the Planning and Compensation Act 1991, Sch 7, SI 2003/956 and SI 2004/3156.]

---

* **In sub-s (3B) the words underlined are substituted by the words "tree preservation regulations" by the Planning Act 2008, Sch 8 from 6 April 2012 (in relation to England) and from a date to be appointed (in relation to Wales).**

**7.11467 329A. Service of notices on the Crown** (1) Any notice or other document required under this Act to be served on the Crown must be served on the appropriate authority.

(2) Section 329 does not apply for the purposes of the service of such a notice or document.

(3) "Appropriate authority" must be construed in accordance with section 293(2).

[Town and Country Planning Act 1990, s 329A as inserted by the Planning and Compulsory Purchase Act 2004, Sch 3.]

**7.11468 330. Power to require information as to interests in land** (1) For the purpose of enabling the Secretary of State or a local authority to make an order or issue or serve any notice or other document which, by any of the provisions of this Act, he or they are authorised or required to make, issue or serve, the Secretary of State or the local authority may by notice in writing require the occupier of any premises and any person who, either directly or indirectly, receives rent in respect of any premises to give in writing such information as to the matters mentioned in subsection (2) as may be so specified.

(2) Those matters are—
(*a*) the nature of the interest in the premises of the person on whom the notice is served;
(*b*) the name and postal address of any other person known to him as having an interest in the premises;
(*c*) the purpose for which the premises are being used;
(*d*) the time when that use began;
(*e*) the name and postal address of any person known to the person on whom the notice is served as having used the premises for that purpose;
(*f*) the time when any activities being carried out on the premises began.

(3) A notice under subsection (1) may require information to be given within 21 days after the date on which it is served, or such longer time as may be specified in it, or as the Secretary of State or, as the case may be, the local authority may allow.

(4) Any person who, without reasonable excuse, fails to comply with a notice served on him under subsection (1) shall be guilty of an offence and liable on summary conviction to a fine not exceeding **level 3** on the standard scale.

(5) Any person who, having been required by a notice under subsection (1) to give any information, knowingly makes any misstatement in respect of it shall be guilty of an offence and liable[1] on summary conviction to a fine not exceeding the **statutory maximum** or on conviction on indictment to imprisonment for a term not exceeding **two years** or to a **fine**, or **both**.

(6) This section shall have effect as if the references to a local authority included references to a National Park authority.

[Town and Country Planning Act 1990, s 330 as amended by the Environment Act 1995, Sch 10, SI 2003/956 and SI 2004/3156.]

---

[1] For procedure in respect of an offence triable either way see the Magistrates' Courts Act 1980, ss 17A–21 in PART I: MAGISTRATES' COURTS, PROCEDURE, ante.

**7.11468A 330A. Information as to interests in Crown land**

**7.11469 331. Offences by corporations** (1) Where an offence under this Act[1] which has been committed by a body corporate is proved to have been committed with the consent or connivance of, or to be attributable to any neglect on the part of—
(*a*) a director, manager, secretary or other similar officer of the body corporate, or
(*b*) any person who was purporting to act in any such capacity,

he as well as the body corporate shall be guilty of that offence and be liable to be proceeded against accordingly.

(2) In subsection (1) "director", in relation to any body corporate—
(*a*) which was established by or under an enactment for the purpose of carrying on under national ownership an industry or part of an industry or undertaking, and

(*b*) whose affairs are managed by its members,

means a member of that body corporate.

[Town and Country Planning Act 1990, s 331.]

---

1 This section applies for the purposes of the Planning (Listed Buildings and Conservation Areas) Act 1990 post (with the exception of s 59 thereof) as well: Planning (Listed Buildings and Conservation Areas) Act 1990, s 89.

**7.11470 333.** *Regulations and orders.*

**7.11471 336. Interpretation**[1] (1) In this Act, except in so far as the context otherwise requires and subject to the following provisions of this section and to any transitional provision made by the Planning (Consequential Provisions) Act 1990—

"address", in relation to electronic communications, means any number or address used for the purposes of such communications;

"advertisement"[2] means any word, letter, model, sign, placard, board, notice, awning, blind, device or representation, whether illuminated or not, in the nature of, and employed wholly or partly for the purposes of, advertisement, announcement or direction, and (without prejudice to the previous provisions of this definition), includes any hoarding or similar structure used or designed, or adapted for use and anything else principally used, or designed or adapted principally for use, for the display of advertisements, and references to the display of advertisements shall be construed accordingly;

"agriculture" includes horticulture, fruit growing, seed growing, dairy farming, the breeding and keeping of livestock (including any creature kept for the production of food, wool, skins or fur, or for the purpose of its use in the farming of land), the use of land as grazing land, meadow land, osier land, market gardens and nursery grounds, and the use of land for woodlands where that use is ancillary to the farming of land for other agricultural purposes, and "agricultural" shall be construed accordingly;

"breach of condition notice" has the meaning given in section 187A;

"breach of planning control" has the meaning given in section 171A;

"building" includes any structure or erection, and any part of a building, as so defined, but does not include plant or machinery comprised in a building;

"buildings or works" includes waste materials, refuse and other matters deposited on land, and references to the erection or construction of buildings or works shall be construed accordingly and references to the removal of buildings or works include demolition of buildings and filling in of trenches;

"building operations" has the meaning given by section 55;

"depositing of mineral waste" means any process whereby a mineral-working deposit is created or enlarged and "depositing of refuse or waste materials" includes the depositing of mineral waste;

"development" has the meaning given in section 55, and "develop" shall be construed accordingly;

"development consent" means development consent under the Planning Act 2008;

"development plan" must be construed in accordance with section 38 of the Planning and Compulsory Purchase Act 2004;

"electronic communication" has the same meaning as in the Electronic Communications Act 2000;

"enforcement notice" means a notice under section 172;

"engineering operations" includes the formation or laying out of means of access to highways;

"land" means any corporeal hereditament, including a building, and, in relation to the acquisition of land under Part IX, includes any interest in or right over land;

"local authority" (except in section 252 and subject to subsection (10) below and section 71(7) of the Environment Act 1995) means—

(*a*) a billing authority or a precepting authority (except the Receiver for the Metropolitan Police District)**, as defined in section 69 of the Local Government Finance Act 1992 or the Mayor's Office for Policing and Crime;

(*aa*) a fire and rescue authority in Wales constituted by a scheme under section 2 of the Fire and Rescue Services Act 2004 or a scheme to which section 4 of that Act applies;

(*ab*) the London Fire and Emergency Planning Authority;

(*b*) a levying body within the meaning of section 74 of the Local Government Finance Act 1988; and

(*c*) a body as regards which section 75 of that Act applies;

and includes any joint board or joint committee if all the constituent authorities are local authorities within paragraph (*a*), (*b*) or (*c*);

"local highway authority" means a highway authority other than the Secretary of State or a strategic highways company;

"local planning authority" shall be construed in accordance with Part I;

"owner", in relation to any land, means a person, other than a mortgagee not in possession, who, whether in his own right or as trustee for any other person, is entitled to receive the rack rent of the land, or, where the land is not let at a rack rent, would be so entitled if it were so let;

"the planning Acts" means this Act, the Planning (Listed Buildings and Conservation Areas) Act 1990, the Planning (Hazardous Substances) Act 1990 and the Planning (Consequential Provisions) Act 1990;

"planning contravention notice" has the meaning given in section 171C;
"planning decision" means a decision made on an application under Part III or section 293A;
"planning permission" means permission under Part III;
"planning permission granted for a limited period" has the meaning given in section 72(2);
"restricted byway" has the same meaning as in Part 2 of the Countryside and Rights of Way Act 2000;
"spatial development strategy" shall be construed in accordance with Part VIII of the Greater London Authority Act 1999 (planning);
"stop notice" has the meaning given in section 183;
"strategic highways company" means a company for the time being appointed under Part 1 of the Infrastructure Act 2015;
"tree preservation order" has the meaning given in section 198;
"tree preservation regulations" means regulations under section 202A(1); *
"universal postal service provider" means a universal service provider within the meaning of Part 3 of the Postal Services Act 2011; and references to the provision of a universal postal service shall be construed in accordance with that Part;
"use", in relation to land, does not include the use of land for the carrying out of any building or other operations on it;
"waste" includes anything that—

(*a*) is waste within the meaning of Article 3(1) of Directive 2008/98/EC of the European Parliament and of the Council on waste, and
(*b*) is not excluded from the scope of that definition by Article 2(1), (2) or (3).

(1A) In this Act—

(*a*) any reference to a county (other than one to a county planning authority) shall be construed, in relation to Wales, as including a reference to a county borough;
(*b*) any reference to a county council shall be construed, in relation to Wales, as including a reference to a county borough council; and
(*c*) section 17(4) and (5) of the Local Government (Wales) Act 1994 (references to counties and districts to be construed generally in relation to Wales as references to counties and county boroughs) shall not apply.

(2)–(9) *Further references.*

(10) In section 90, Chapter I of Part VI, and sections 324(2) and 330 "local authority", in relation to land in the Broads, includes the Broads Authority.

[Town and Country Planning Act 1990, s 336, as amended by the Planning and Compensation Act 1991, s 24, Schs 1, 4, 7 and 19, the Local Government Finance Act 1992, Sch 13, the Police and Magistrates' Courts Act 1994, Sch 9, the Local Government (Wales) Act 1994, Sch 6, the Environment Act 1995, Sch 10, the Gas Act 1995, Sch 4, the Greater London Authority Act 1999, s 344 and Sch 27, SI 2001/1149, SI 2003/956, SI 2004/3156, the Planning and Compulsory Purchase Act 2004, Sch 6, the Fire and Rescue Services Act 2004, Sch 1, SI 2006/1177 and 1281, the Planning Act 2008, s 201 and Sch 2, SI 2011/988, the Postal Services Act 2011, Sch 12, the Police Reform and Social Responsibility Act 2011, Sch 16 and the Infrastructure Act 2015, Sch 1.]

---

* **Definition "tree preservation regulations" inserted by the Planning Act 2008, Sch 8 from 6 April 2012 (in relation to England) and from a date to be appointed (in relation to Wales).**

** **Words repealed by the Greater London Authority Act 1999, Sch 27 from a date to be appointed.**

[1] Only selected definitions are printed here, relevant to the parts of the Act appearing in this work.

[2] The very broad definition of "advertisement" facilitates control by guarding against the exploitation of loopholes. The local authority is enabled to control not just a sign etc but also the structure to which it is attached: *Butler v Derby City Council* [2006] 1 WLR 1346. That does not mean that a bare, unadorned structure remains an "advertisement" in circumstances where continual use is asserted, eg in Class 13 of Sch 3 to the 2007 Regulations. During the period of cessation, the unadorned structure is no longer 'in the nature of, and employed wholly or partly for the purposes of, advertisement' and it cannot feed the continuance required by class 13: *Winfield v Secretary of State for Communities and Local Government* [2012] EWCA Civ 1415, [2013] 1 WLR 948.

# Planning (Listed Buildings and Conservation Areas) Act 1990

(1990 c 9)

## Part I[1]

## Listed Buildings

### Chapter I

### Listing of special buildings

7.11472 **1. Listing of buildings of special architectural or historic interest**

(1)–(4) *Secretary of State to compile or approve lists*

(5) In this Act "listed building"[2] means a building which is for the time being included in a list compiled or approved by the Secretary of State under this section; and for the purposes of this Act—

(*a*) any object or structure fixed to the building;
(*b*) any object or structure within the curtilage of the building which, although not fixed to the building, forms part of the land and has done so since before 1st July 1948,

shall be treated as part of the building.

(6) *Former building preservation orders.*

[Planning (Listed Buildings and Conservation Areas) Act 1990, s 1.]

[1] Part I comprises ss 1–68.

[2] Notwithstanding the definition of "building" in s 336 of the Town and Country Planning Act 1990 which includes "any part of a building" unless the context otherwise requires, the term "listed building" in this Act is not required to include part of a building. Accordingly whether work amounts to alteration of a listed building has to be considered in the context of the whole, and not part only of the building. Since "demolition" means the complete destruction of a building, the pulling down of a part falls within the expression "alteration" for the purposes of the Act, *Shimizu (UK) Ltd v Westminster City Council* [1997] 1 All ER 481, [1997] 1 WLR 168, HL.

## CHAPTER II

### AUTHORISATION OF WORKS AFFECTING LISTED BUILDINGS

*Control of works in respect of listed buildings*

7.11473 7. **Restriction on works affecting listed buildings** (1) Subject to the following provisions of this Act, no person shall execute or cause to be executed any works for the demolition of a listed building or for its alteration or extension in any manner which would affect its character as a building of special architectural or historic interest, unless the works are authorised under section 8.

(2) Subsection (1) is subject to section 33(1) of the Planning Act 2008 (exclusion of requirement for other consents for development for which development consent required).

[Planning (Listed Buildings and Conservation Areas) Act 1990, s 7 as amended by the Planning Act 2008, Sch 2.]

7.11474 8. **Authorisation of works: listed building consent** (1) Works for the alteration or extension of a listed building are authorised if—

(*a*) written consent for their execution has been granted by the local planning authority or the Secretary of State; and

(*b*) they are executed in accordance with the terms of the consent and of any conditions attached to it.

(2) Works for the demolition of a listed building are authorised if—

(*a*) such consent has been granted for their execution;

(*b*) notice of the proposal to execute the works has been given to the Commission;*

(*c*) after such notice has been given either—

(i) for a period of at least one month following the grant of such consent, and before the commencement of the works, reasonable access to the building has been made available to members or officers of the Commission* for the purpose of recording it; or

(ii) the Secretary of the Commission*, or another officer of theirs with authority to act on their behalf for the purposes of this section, has stated in writing that they have completed their recording of the building or that they do not wish to record it; and

(*d*) the works are executed in accordance with the terms of the consent and of any conditions attached to it.

(3) Where—

(*a*) works for the demolition of a listed building or for its alteration or extension are executed without such consent; and

(*b*) written consent is granted by the local planning authority or the Secretary of State for the retention of the works,

the works are authorised from the grant of that consent.

(4) In this section "the Royal Commission" means—

(*a*) in relation to England, the Royal Commission on the Historical Monuments of England; and

(*b*) in relation to Wales, the Royal Commission on Ancient and Historical Monuments in Wales.

(5) The Secretary of State may by order provide that subsection (2) shall have effect with the substitution for the references to the Royal Commission of references to such other body as may be so specified.

(6) Such an order—

(*a*) shall apply in the case of works executed or to be executed on or after such date as may be specified in the order; and

(*b*) may apply in relation to either England or Wales, or both.

(7) Consent under subsection (1), (2) or (3) is referred to in this Act as "listed building consent".

[Planning (Listed Buildings and Conservation Areas) Act 1990, s 8.]

* **In relation to works for the demolition of a listed building executed or to be executed on or after 19 February 2001: see SI 2001/24, art 1(1).**

7.11475 9. **Offences** (1) If a person contravenes section 7 he shall be guilty of an offence[1].

(2) Without prejudice to subsection (1), if a person executing or causing to be executed any works in relation to a listed building under a listed building consent fails to comply with any

condition attached to the consent, he shall be guilty of an offence.

(3) In proceedings for an offence under this section it shall be a defence to prove the following matters—

(*a*) that works to the building were urgently necessary in the interests of safety or health or for the preservation of the building;

(*b*) that it was not practicable to secure safety or health or, as the case may be, the preservation of the building by works of repair or works for affording temporary support or shelter;

(*c*) that the works carried out were limited to the minimum measures immediately necessary; and

(*d*) that notice in writing justifying in detail the carrying out of the works was given to the local planning authority as soon as reasonably practicable.

(4) A person who is guilty of an offence under this section shall be liable[2]—

(*a*) on summary conviction, to imprisonment for a term not exceeding **six months** or a fine, or **both**; or

(*b*) on conviction on indictment, to imprisonment for a term not exceeding **two years** or a **fine**, or **both**.

(5) In determining the amount of any fine to be imposed on a person convicted of an offence under this section, the court shall in particular have regard to any financial benefit which has accrued or appears likely to accrue to him in consequence of the offence.[3]

[Planning (Listed Buildings and Conservation Areas) Act 1990, s 9 as amended by the Planning and Compensation Act 1991, Sch 3 and SI 2015/664.]

---

1 This is an offence of strict liability and does not require the prosecution to prove intent (*R v Wells Street Metropolitan Stipendiary Magistrate, ex p Westminster City Council* [1986] 3 All ER 4, [1986] 1 WLR 1046. Section 7 does not apply to the demolition of a redundant building in pursuance of a pastoral or redundancy scheme within the meaning of the Pastoral Measure 1968 (Redundant Churches and other Religious Buildings Act 1969, s 2).

2 For procedure in respect of an offence triable either way, see the Magistrates' Courts Act 1980, ss 17A–21 in PART I: MAGISTRATES' COURTS, PROCEDURE, ante.

3 The requirement is only to "have regard to"; the court is not obliged to impose a sum equal to the full amount of any financial benefit or even a large proportion of it: *R v Rance (Piers)* [2012] EWCA Crim 2023, [2013] 1 Cr App R (S) 123, [2013] Crim LR 74.

7.11476 **10.** *Making of applications for listed building consent[1].*

7.11477 **11. Certificates as to applicant's status etc** (1)–(5) *Applications may need to be accompanied by certificates as prescribed by regulations[1] as to ownership etc.*

(6) If any person—

(*a*) issues a certificate which purports to comply with the requirements of regulations made by virtue of this section and contains a statement which he knows to be false or misleading in a material particular; or

(*b*) recklessly issues a certificate which purports to comply with those requirements and contains a statement which is false or misleading in a material particular,

he shall be guilty of an offence and liable on summary conviction to a fine not exceeding **level 3** on the standard scale.

(7) Subject to subsection (5), in this section "owner" means a person who is for the time being the estate owner in respect of the fee simple or is entitled to a tenancy granted or extended for a term of years certain of which not less than seven years remain unexpired.

[Planning (Listed Buildings and Conservation Areas) Act 1990, s 11.]

---

1 The Planning (Listed Buildings and Conservation Areas) Act Regulations 1990, SI 1990/1519 amended by SI 2003/2048 (E), SI 2004/2210 (E) and 3341 (E), SI 2005/108 (E), SI 2006/1063 (E), 1388 (W) and 3316 (W), SI 2008/551 (E), SI 2009/1026 (W), 2262 (E) and 2711 (E), SI 2010/568 and 2185 (E), SI 2012/2275, SI 2013/1239, 2115 and 2146 (revoked in relation to Wales by SI 2012/793) and 2590 and SI 2015/807 (E) and the Planning (Listed Buildings and Conservation Areas) (Wales) Regulations 2012, SI 2012/793 amended by SI 2015/1332 and SI 2016/91 have been made. See also the Transport and Works Applications (Listed Buildings, Conservation Areas and Ancient Monuments Procedure) Regulations 1992, SI 1992/3138. See also the Transport and Works Applications (Listed Buildings, Conservation Areas and Ancient Monuments Procedure) Regulations 1992, SI 1992/3138.

## CHAPTER IV
## ENFORCEMENT

7.11478 **38. Power to issue listed building enforcement notice[1]** (1) Where it appears to the local planning authority—

(*a*) that any works have been or are being executed to a listed building in their area; and

(*b*) that the works are such as to involve a contravention of section 9(1) or (2),

they may, if they consider it expedient to do so having regard to the effect of the works on the character of the building as one of special architectural or historic interest, issue a notice under this section (in this Act referred to as a "listed building enforcement notice").

(2) A listed building enforcement notice shall specify the alleged contravention and require such steps as may be specified in the notice to be taken—

(*a*) for restoring the building to its former state; or

(*b*) if the authority consider that such restoration would not be reasonably practicable or would be undesirable, for executing such further works specified in the notice as they consider necessary to alleviate the effect of the works which were carried out without listed building consent; or

(*c*) for bringing the building to the state in which it would have been if the terms and conditions of any listed building consent which has been granted for the works had been complied with.

(3) A listed building enforcement notice—

(*a*) shall specify the date on which it is to take effect and, subject to sections 39(3) and 65(3A) shall take effect on that date, and

(*b*) shall specify the period within which any steps are required to be taken and may specify different periods for different steps,

and, where different periods apply to different steps, references in this Part to the period for compliance with a listed building enforcement notice, in relation to any step, are to the period within which the step is required to be taken.

(4) copy of a listed building enforcement notice shall be served, not later than 28 days after the date of its issue and not later than 28 days before the date specified in it as the date on which it is to take effect—

(*a*) on the owner and on the occupier of the building to which it relates; and

(*b*) on any other person having an interest in that building which in the opinion of the authority is materially affected by the notice.

(5), (6) *Withdrawal of notices.*

(7) Where a listed building enforcement notice imposes any such requirement as is mentioned in subsection (2)(*b*), listed building consent shall be deemed to be granted for any works of demolition, alteration or extension of the building executed as a result of compliance with the notice.

[Planning (Listed Buildings and Conservation Areas) Act 1990, s 38 as amended by the Planning and Compensation Act 1991, Sch 3.]

[1] There are similar provisions in s 172 of the Town and Country Planning Act 1990, ante.

7.11479 39–42. *Appeals, execution of works.*

7.11480 **43. Offence where listed building enforcement notice not complied with**

(1) Where, at any time after the end of the period for compliance with the notice, any step required by a listed building enforcement notice to be taken has not been taken, the person who is then owner of the land is in breach of the notice.

(2) If at any time the owner of the land is in breach of a listed building enforcement notice he shall be guilty of an offence.

(3) An offence under this section may be charged by reference to any day or longer period of time and a person may be convicted of a second or subsequent offence under this section by reference to any period of time following the preceding conviction for such an offence.

(4) In proceedings against any person for an offence under this section it shall be a defence for him to show—

(*a*) that he did everything he could be expected to do to secure that all the steps required by the notice were taken; or

(*b*) that he was not served with a copy of the listed building enforcement notice and was not aware of its existence.

(5) A person guilty of an offence under this section shall be liable[1] on summary conviction, or on conviction on indictment, to a fine.

(6) In determining the amount of any fine to be imposed on a person convicted of an offence under this section, the court shall in particular have regard to any financial benefit which has accrued or appears likely to accrue to him in consequence of the offence.

[Planning (Listed Buildings and Conservation Areas) Act 1990, s 43 as substituted by the Planning and Compensation Act 1991, Sch 3 and amended by SI 2015/664.]

[1] For procedure in respect of an offence triable either way, see the Magistrates' Courts Act 1980, ss 17A–21 in PART I: MAGISTRATES' COURTS, PROCEDURE, ante.

7.11481 **44. Effect of listed building consent on listed building enforcement notice**

(1) If, after the issue of a listed building enforcement notice, consent is granted under section 8(3)—

(*a*) for the retention of any work to which the notice relates; or

(*b*) permitting the retention of works without compliance with some condition subject to which a previous listed building consent was granted,

the notice shall cease to have effect in so far as it requires steps to be taken involving the works not being retained or, as the case may be, for complying with that condition.

(2) The fact that such a notice has wholly or partly ceased to have effect under subsection (1) shall not affect the liability of any person for an offence in respect of a previous failure to comply with that notice.

[Planning (Listed Buildings and Conservation Areas) Act 1990, s 44.]

## CHAPTER V

## PREVENTION OF DETERIORATION AND DAMAGE

*Compulsory acquisition of listed building in need of repair*

7.11482 **47–58.** *Compulsory acquisition of listed building in need of repair, compensation, acquisition of land by agreement, management of listed buildings, urgent works for unoccupied listed buildings, dangerous structures orders, etc.*

*Damage to listed buildings*

7.11483 **59. Acts causing or likely to result in damage to listed buildings** (1) If, with the intention of causing damage to a listed building, any relevant person does or permits the doing of any act which causes or is likely to result in damage to the building, he shall be guilty of an offence and liable on summary conviction to a fine not exceeding **level 3** on the standard scale.

(2) A person is a relevant person for the purpose of subsection (1) if apart from that subsection he would be entitled to do or permit the act in question.

(3) Subsection (1) does not apply to an act for the execution—

(*a*) of works authorised by planning permission granted or deemed to be granted in pursuance of an application under the principal Act; or

(*b*) of works for which listed building consent has been given under this Act; or

(*c*) of works for which development consent has been granted under the Planning Act 2008.

(4) If a person convicted of an offence under this section fails to take such reasonable steps as may be necessary to prevent any damage or further damage resulting from the offence, he shall be guilty of a further offence and liable on summary conviction to a fine not exceeding one-tenth of level 3 on the standard scale for each day on which the failure continues.

[Planning (Listed Buildings and Conservation Areas) Act 1990, s 59 as amended by the Planning and Compensation Act 1991, Sch 7 and the Planning Act 2008, Sch 2.]

## CHAPTER VI

## MISCELLANEOUS AND SUPPLEMENTAL

*Exceptions for church buildings and ancient monuments*

7.11484 **60. Exceptions for ecclesiastical buildings and redundant churches** (1) The provisions mentioned in subsection (2) shall not apply to any ecclesiastical building which is for the time being used for ecclesiastical purposes.

(2) Those provisions are sections 3, 4, 7 to 9, 47, 54 and 59.

(3) For the purposes of subsection (1), a building used or available for use by a minister of religion wholly or mainly as a residence from which to perform the duties of his office shall be treated as not being an ecclesiastical building.

(4) For the purposes of sections 7 to 9 a building shall be taken to be used for the time being for ecclesiastical purposes if it would be so used but for the works in question.

(5), (6) *Orders*[1] *of Secretary of State restricting or excluding sub-ss (1)–(3).*

(7) Sections 7 to 9 shall not apply to the execution of works for the demolition, in pursuance of a pastoral or redundancy scheme (within the meaning of the Pastoral Measure 1983), of a redundant building (within the meaning of that Measure) or a part of such a building.

[Planning (Listed Buildings and Conservation Areas) Act 1990, s 60.]

[1] The Ecclesiastical Exemption (Listed Buildings and Conservation Areas) Order 1994, SI 1994/1771 (revoked in relation to England by SI 2010/1806) and the Ecclesiastical Exemption (Listed Buildings and Conservation Areas) (England) Order 2010, SI 2010/1176 amended by SI 2010/1806 have been made.

7.11485 **61. Exceptions for ancient monuments etc** (1) The provisions mentioned in subsection (2) shall not apply to any building for the time being included in the schedule of monuments compiled and maintained under section 1 of the Ancient Monuments and Archaeological Areas Act 1979.

(2) Those provisions are sections 3, 4, 7 to 9, 47, 54 and 59.

[Planning (Listed Buildings and Conservation Areas) Act 1990, s 61.]

*Validity of instruments, decisions and proceedings*

7.11486 **62–65.** *Validity of certain orders, decisions, notices; appeals to High Court*[1].

[1] These provisions restricting challenges in legal proceedings to the validity of steps taken by various authorities are comparable with those contained in ss 284–290 of the Town and Country Planning Act 1990, ante.

7.11487 **88–88B.** *Rights of entry, warrants to enter land*[1].

[1] These provisions are similar to those in s 214C of the Town and Country Planning Act 1990, ante.

# Planning (Hazardous Substances) Act 1990

(1990 c 10)

7.11488 **4.** *Requirement of hazardous substances consent*[1].

[1] Sections 1–3 of the Act state who are the hazardous substances authorities for a variety of circumstances; in most instances the authority will be the council of the district or London Borough.

**7.11489 5.** *Power to prescribe hazardous substances*[1].

[1] The Planning (Hazardous Substances) Regulations 2015, SI 2015/627 amended by SI 2015/1359 and SI 2016/721 and the Planning (Hazardous Substances) (Wales) Regulations 2015, SI 2015/1597 amended by SI 2016/721 have been made.

**7.11490 8. Certificates as to applicant's status etc** (1)–(5) *Regulations may provide that applications for hazardous substances consent shall be accompanied by certificates in prescribed form.*

(6) If any person—

(*a*) issues a certificate which purports to comply with the requirements of regulations made by virtue of this section and contains a statement which he knows to be false or misleading in a material particular; or

(*b*) recklessly issues a certificate which purports to comply with those requirements and contains such a statement,

he shall be guilty of an offence and liable on summary conviction to a fine not exceeding **level 3** on the standard scale.

(7), (8) Regulations. Meaning of "owner".

[Planning (Hazardous Substances) Act 1990, s 8.]

*Contraventions of hazardous substances control*

**7.11491 23. Offences** (1) Subject to the following provisions of this section, if there is a contravention of hazardous substances control, the appropriate person shall be guilty of an offence.

(2) There is a contravention of hazardous substances control—

(*a*) if a quantity of a hazardous substance equal to or exceeding the controlled quantity is or has been present on, over or under land and either—

(i) there is no hazardous substances consent for the presence of the substance; or

(ii) there is hazardous substances consent for its presence but the quantity present exceeds the maximum quantity permitted by the consent;

(*b*) if there is or has been a failure to comply with a condition subject to which a hazardous substances consent was granted.

(3) In subsection (1) "the appropriate person" means—

(*a*) in relation to a contravention falling within paragraph (*a*) of subsection (2)—

(i) any person knowingly causing the substance to be present on, over or under the land;

(ii) any person allowing it to be so present; and

(*b*) in relation to a contravention falling within paragraph (*a*) or (*b*) of that subsection, the person in control of the land.

(4) A person guilty of an offence under this section shall be liable[1] on summary conviction, or on conviction on indictment, to a fine.

(4A) In determining the amount of any fine to be imposed on a person convicted of an offence under this section, the court shall in particular have regard to any financial benefit which has accrued or appears likely to accrue to him in consequence of the offence.

(5) In any proceedings for an offence under this section it shall be a defence for the accused to prove—

(*a*) that he took all reasonable precautions and exercised all due diligence to avoid commission of the offence, or

(*b*) that commission of the offence could be avoided only by the taking of action amounting to a breach of a statutory duty.

(6) In any proceedings for an offence consisting of a contravention falling within subsection (2)(*a*), it shall be a defence for the accused to prove that at the time of the alleged commission of the offence he did not know, and had no reason to believe—

(*a*) if the case falls within paragraph (*a*)(i)—

(i) that the substance was present; or

(ii) that it was present in a quantity equal to or exceeding the controlled quantity;

(*b*) if the case falls within paragraph (*a*)(ii), that the substance was present in a quantity exceeding the maximum quantity permitted by the consent.

(7) In any proceedings for an offence consisting of a contravention falling within subsection (2)(*b*), it shall be a defence for the accused to prove that he did not know, and had no reason to believe, that there was a failure to comply with a condition subject to which hazardous substances consent had been granted.

[Planning (Hazardous Substances) Act 1990, s 23 as amended by the Planning and Compensation Act 1991, Sch 3 and SI 2015/664.]

[1] For procedure in respect of an offence triable either way, see the Magistrates' Courts Act 1990, ss 17A–21 in PART I: MAGISTRATES' COURTS, ante.

7.11492 **24. Power to issue hazardous substances contravention notice**[1] (1) Where it appears to the hazardous substances authority that there is or has been a contravention of hazardous substances control, they may issue a notice—

(*a*) specifying an alleged contravention of hazardous substances control; and

(*b*) requiring such steps as may be specified in the notice to be taken to remedy wholly or partly the contravention,

if they consider it expedient to do so having regard to any material consideration.

(2) Such a notice is referred to in this Act as a "hazardous substances contravention notice".

(3) A hazardous substances authority shall not issue a hazardous substances contravention notice where it appears to them that a contravention of hazardous substances control can be avoided only by the taking of action amounting to a breach of statutory duty.

(4) A copy of a hazardous substances contravention notice shall be served—

(*a*) on the owner of the land to which it relates;

(*b*) on any person other than the owner who appears to the hazardous substances authority to be in control of the land; and

(*c*) on such other persons as may be prescribed.

(5) A hazardous substances contravention notice shall also specify—

(*a*) a date not less than 28 days from the date of service of copies of the notice as the date on which it is to take effect;

(*b*) in respect of each of the steps required to be taken to remedy the contravention of hazardous substances control, the period from the notice taking effect within which the step is to be taken.

(6) Where a hazardous substances authority issue a hazardous substances contravention notice the steps required by the notice may, without prejudice to the generality of subsection (1)(*b*), if the authority think it expedient, include a requirement that the hazardous substance be removed from the land.

(7) Where a notice includes such a requirement, it may also contain a direction that at the end of such period as may be specified in the notice any hazardous substances consent for the presence of the substance shall cease to have effect or, if it relates to more than one substance, shall cease to have effect so far as it relates to the substances which are required to be removed.

(8) The hazardous substances authority may withdraw a hazardous substances contravention notice (without prejudice to their power to issue another) at any time before or after it takes effect.

(9) If they do so, they shall immediately give notice of the withdrawal to every person who was served with a copy of the notice or would, if the notice were re-issued, be served with a copy of it.

[Planning (Hazardous Substances) Act 1990, s 24 as amended by the Planning and Compensation Act 1991, Sch 3.]

[1] Section 25 makes supplementary provision for hazardous substances contravention notices, in particular the making of regulations by the Secretary of State, which may direct that any of the provisions of ss 178(1) to (5) and (7), 179–181, 183, 184, 187 and 188 of the Town and Country Planning Act 1990 (ante) shall have effect, with appropriate modifications, to notices under this Act.

7.11493 **36–36B.** *Rights of entry, warrants to enter land*[1].

[1] These provisions are similar to those in s 214C of the Town and Country Planning Act 1990, ante.

## Planning Act 2008[1]

(2008 c 29)

7.11494 **53. Rights of entry** (1) Any person duly authorised in writing by the Secretary of State may at any reasonable time enter any land for the purpose of surveying and taking levels of it, or in order to facilitate compliance with the provisions mentioned in subsection (1A), in connection with—

(*a*) an application for an order granting development consent, whether in relation to that or any other land, that has been accepted by the Secretary of State,

(*b*) a proposed application for an order granting development consent, or

(*c*) an order granting development consent that includes provision authorising the compulsory acquisition of that land or of an interest in it or right over it.

(1A) Those provisions are any provision of or made under an Act for the purpose of implementing—

(*a*) Council Directive 85/337/EEC of 27 June 1985 on the assessment of the effects of certain public and private projects on the environment, as amended from time to time,

(*b*) Council Directive 92/43/EC of 21 May 1992 on the conservation of natural habitats and of wild fauna and flora, as amended from time to time, or

(*c*) any EU instrument from time to time replacing all or any part of either of those Directives.

(2) Authorisation may be given by the Secretary of State under subsection (1)(*b*) in relation to any land only if it appears to the Secretary of State that—

(*a*) the proposed applicant is considering a distinct project of real substance genuinely requiring entry onto the land,

(*b*) *repealed*

(*c*) *repealed.*

(3) Subject to subsections (9) and (10), power conferred by subsection (1) to survey land includes power to search and bore for the purpose of ascertaining the nature of the subsoil or the presence of minerals or other matter in it.

(3A) Power conferred by subsection (1) for the purpose of complying with the provisions mentioned in subsection (1A) includes power to take, and process, samples of or from any of the following found on, in or over the land—

(*a*) water,

(*b*) air,

(*c*) soil or rock,

(*d*) its flora,

(*e*) bodily excretions, or dead bodies, of non-human creatures, or

(*f*) any non-living thing present as a result of human action.

(4) A person authorised under subsection (1) to enter any land—

(*a*) must, if so required, produce evidence of the person's authority, and state the purpose of the person's entry, before so entering,

(*b*) may not demand admission as of right to any land which is occupied unless 14 days' notice of the intended entry has been given to the occupier, and

(*c*) must comply with any other conditions subject to which the Secretary of State's authorisation is given.

(5) A person commits an offence if the person wilfully obstructs a person acting in the exercise of power under subsection (1).

(6) A person guilty of an offence under subsection (5) is liable on summary conviction to a fine not exceeding level 3 on the standard scale.

(7) Where any damage is caused to land or chattels—

(*a*) in the exercise of a right of entry conferred under subsection (1), or

(*b*) in the making of any survey for the purpose of which any such right of entry has been conferred,

compensation may be recovered by any person suffering the damage from the person exercising the right of entry.

(8) Any question of disputed compensation under subsection (7) must be referred to and determined by the Upper Tribunal.

(9) No person may carry out under subsection (1) any works authorised by virtue of subsection (3) unless notice of the person's intention to do so was included in the notice required by subsection (4)(*b*).

(10) The authority of the appropriate Minister is required for the carrying out under subsection (1) of works authorised by virtue of subsection (3) if—

(*a*) the land in question is held by statutory undertakers, and

(*b*) they object to the proposed works on the ground that execution of the works would be seriously detrimental to the carrying-on of their undertaking.

(11) In subsection (10)—

"the appropriate Minister" means—

(*a*) in the case of land in Wales held by water or sewerage undertakers, the Welsh Ministers, and

(*b*) in any other case, the Secretary of State;

"statutory undertakers" means persons who are, or who are deemed to be, statutory undertakers for the purposes of any provision of Part 11 of TCPA 1990.

[Planning Act 2008, s 53 as amended by SI 2009/1307 and the Localism Act 2011, s 136 and Schs 13 and 25.]

---

[1] Provision is made for a new system of development consent for nationally significant infrastructure projects. The Infrastructure Planning Commission is given responsibility for examining such applications and for deciding any such application when there is in force a relevant national policy statement. Consent will be in the form of an order which may confer rights for the purpose of facilitating the project including compulsory purchase of land. There is a statutory timetable for examination of applications and decisions. In addition, Part 9 of the Act makes various alterations to the existing town and country planning regime (which continues to apply to other types of development).

The provisions of this Act referred to in this Manual come into force in accordance with orders made by the Secretary of State under s 241. At the date of going to press, the following orders had been made: (No 1 and Savings) SI 2009/400; (No 1) (England) SI 2010/1303; (No 2) SI 2009/2260; (No 3) SI 2009/3573; (No 4 and Saving) SI 2010/101; (No 5 and Saving) SI 2010/566; (No 6) SI 2011/705; (No 7) SI 2011/2054; (No 2) (England) SI 2012/601; (No 1) (Wales) SI 2012/802; (No 2) (Wales) SI 2014/1769; (No 3) (Wales) SI 2014/2780. Of the provisions reproduced here, ss 37–54 were fully in force by 1 October 2009; ss 161–170 fully in force by 1 March 2010.

**7.11495** **54. Rights of entry: Crown land** (1) Subsections (1) to (3A) of section 53 apply to Crown land subject to subsections (2) and (3) of this section.

(2) A person must not enter Crown land unless the person ("P") has the permission of—

(*a*) a person appearing to P to be entitled to give it, or

(*b*) the appropriate Crown authority.

(3) In section 53(3), the words "Subject to subsections (9) and (10)" must be ignored.

(4) Subsections (4) to (6) and (9) to (11) of section 53 do not apply to anything done by virtue of subsections (1) to (3) of this section.

[Planning Act 2008, s 54 as amended by the Localism Act 2011, s 136.]

7.11496 **161. Breach of terms of order granting development consent** (1) A person commits an offence if without reasonable excuse the person—

(*a*) carries out, or causes to be carried out, development in breach of the terms of an order granting development consent, or

(*b*) otherwise fails to comply with the terms of an order granting development consent.

(2) Subsection (1) is subject to section 149A(4).

(3) It is a defence for a person charged with an offence under this section to prove that—

(*a*) the breach or failure to comply occurred only because of an error or omission in the order, and

(*b*) a correction notice specifying the correction of the error or omission has been issued under paragraph 2 of Schedule 4.

(4) A person guilty of an offence under this section is liable on summary conviction, or on conviction on indictment, to a fine.

(5) *Repealed.*

[Planning Act 2008, s 161 as amended by the Marine and Coastal Access Act 2009, Sch 8 and SI 2015/664.]

7.11497 **162. Time limits** (1) A person may not be charged with an offence under section 160 or 161 after the end of—

(*a*) the relevant 4-year period, or

(*b*) if subsection (3) applies, the extended period.

(2) The "relevant 4-year period" means—

(*a*) in the case of an offence under section 160, the period of 4 years beginning with the date on which the development was substantially completed;

(*b*) in the case of an offence under section 161, the period of 4 years beginning with the later of—

(i) the date on which the development was substantially completed, and

(ii) the date on which the breach or failure to comply occurred.

(3) This subsection applies if during the relevant 4-year period—

(*a*) an information notice has been served under section 167, or

(*b*) an injunction has been applied for under section 171.

(4) The "extended period" means the period of 4 years beginning with—

(*a*) the date of service of the information notice, if subsection (3)(*a*) applies;

(*b*) the date of the application for the injunction, if subsection (3)(*b*) applies;

(*c*) the later (or latest) of those dates, if both paragraphs (*a*) and (*b*) of subsection (3) apply.

[Planning Act 2008, s 162.]

7.11498 **163. Right to enter without warrant** (1) This section applies in relation to any land if the relevant local planning authority has reasonable grounds for suspecting that an offence under section 160 or 161 is being, or has been, committed on or in respect of the land.

(2) A person authorised in writing by the relevant local planning authority may at any reasonable hour enter the land for the purpose of ascertaining whether an offence under section 160 or 161 is being, or has been, committed on the land.

(3) A person may enter a building used as a dwelling-house under subsection (2) only if 24 hours' notice of the intended entry has been given to the occupier of the building.

[Planning Act 2008, s 163.]

7.11499 **164. Right to enter under warrant** (1) This section applies if it is shown to the satisfaction of a justice of the peace on sworn information in writing—

(*a*) that there are reasonable grounds for suspecting that an offence under section 160 or 161 is being, or has been, committed on or in respect of any land, and

(*b*) that the condition in subsection (2) is met.

(2) The condition is that—

(*a*) admission to the land has been refused, or a refusal is reasonably apprehended, or

(*b*) the case is one of urgency.

(3) The justice of the peace may issue a warrant authorising any person who is authorised in writing for the purpose by the relevant local planning authority to enter the land.

(4) For the purposes of subsection (2)(*a*) admission to land is to be regarded as having been refused if no reply is received to a request for admission within a reasonable period.

(5) A warrant authorises entry on one occasion only and that entry must be—

(*a*) before the end of the period of one month beginning with the date of the issue of the warrant, and

(*b*) at a reasonable hour, unless the case is one of urgency.

[Planning Act 2008, s 164.]

7.11500 **165. Rights of entry: supplementary provisions** (1) A person authorised to enter land in pursuance of a right of entry conferred under or by virtue of section 163 or 164 ("a relevant right of entry")—

(*a*) must, if so required, produce evidence of the authority and state the purpose of entry before entering the land,

(*b*) may take on to the land such other persons as may be necessary, and

(*c*) must, if the person leaves the land at a time when the owner or occupier is not present, leave it as effectively secured against trespassers as it was found.

(2) A person commits an offence if the person wilfully obstructs a person acting in the exercise of a relevant right of entry.

(3) A person guilty of an offence under subsection (2) is liable on summary conviction to a fine not exceeding level 3 on the standard scale.

(4) If any damage is caused to land or chattels in the exercise of a relevant right of entry, compensation may be recovered by any person suffering the damage from the local planning authority that authorised the entry.

(5) Except so far as otherwise provided by regulations, any question of disputed compensation under subsection (4) is to be referred to and determined by the Upper Tribunal.

(6) In relation to the determination of any such question, the provisions of section 4 of the Land Compensation Act 1961 (c 33) apply subject to any necessary modifications and to any other prescribed modifications.

[Planning Act 2008, s 165 as amended by SI 2009/1307.]

7.11501 **166. Rights of entry: Crown land** Sections 163 and 164 do not apply to Crown land.

[Planning Act 2008, s 166.]

*Information notices*

7.11502 **167. Power to require information** (1) This section applies in relation to any land if it appears to the relevant local planning authority that an offence under section 160 or 161 may have been committed on or in respect of the land.

(2) The relevant local planning authority may serve an information notice.

(3) The information notice may be served on any person who—

(*a*) is the owner or occupier of the land or has any other interest in it, or

(*b*) is carrying out operations on the land or is using it for any purpose.

(4) The information notice may require the person on whom it is served to give such of the following information as may be specified in the notice—

(*a*) information about any operations being carried out in, on, over or under the land, any use of the land and any other activities being carried out in, on, over or under the land, and

(*b*) information about the provisions of any order granting development consent for development of the land.

(5) An information notice must inform the person on whom it is served of the likely consequences of a failure to respond to the notice.

(6) A requirement of an information notice is complied with by giving the required information to the relevant local planning authority in writing.

[Planning Act 2008, s 167.]

7.11503 **168. Offences relating to information notices** (1) A person commits an offence if without reasonable excuse the person fails to comply with any requirement of an information notice served under section 167 before the end of the period mentioned in subsection (2).

(2) The period referred to in subsection (1) is the period of 21 days beginning with the day on which the information notice is served.

(3) A person guilty of an offence under subsection (1) is liable on summary conviction to a fine not exceeding level 3 on the standard scale.

(4) A person commits an offence if the person—

(*a*) makes any statement purporting to comply with a requirement of an information notice which he knows to be false or misleading in a material respect, or

(*b*) recklessly makes such a statement which is false or misleading in a material respect.

(5) A person guilty of an offence under subsection (4) is liable on summary conviction to a fine not exceeding level 5 on the standard scale.

[Planning Act 2008, s 168.]

*Notices of unauthorised development*

7.11504 **169. Notice of unauthorised development** (1) Subsection (2) applies if a person is found guilty of an offence under section 160 committed on or in respect of any land.

(2) The relevant local planning authority may serve a notice of unauthorised development on the person requiring such steps as may be specified in the notice to be taken—

(*a*) to remove the development, and

(*b*) to restore the land on which the development has been carried out to its condition before the development was carried out.

(3) Subsection (4) applies if a person is found guilty of an offence under section 161 committed on or in respect of any land.

(4) The relevant local planning authority may serve a notice of unauthorised development on the person requiring the person to remedy the breach or failure to comply.

(5) A notice of unauthorised development—

(*a*) must specify the period within which any steps are required to be taken, and

(*b*) may specify different periods for different steps.

(6) Where different periods apply to different steps, references in this Part to the period for compliance with a notice of unauthorised development, in relation to any step, are to the period

within which the step is required to be taken.

(7) A notice of unauthorised development must specify such additional matters as may be prescribed.

[Planning Act 2008, s 169.]

7.11505 **170. Execution of works required by notice of unauthorised development**
(1) If any of the steps specified in a notice of unauthorised development have not been taken before the end of the period for compliance with the notice, the relevant local planning authority may—

(*a*) enter the land on which the development has been carried out and take those steps, and

(*b*) recover from the person who is then the owner of the land any expenses reasonably incurred by it in doing so.

(2) Where a notice of unauthorised development has been served in respect of development—

(*a*) any expenses incurred by the owner or occupier of the land for the purposes of complying with it, and

(*b*) any sums paid by the owner of the land under subsection (1) in respect of expenses incurred by the relevant local planning authority in taking steps required by it,

are to be deemed to be incurred or paid for the use and at the request of the person found guilty of the offence under section 160 or 161.

(3) Regulations[1] may provide that all or any of the following sections of the Public Health Act 1936 (c 49) are to apply, subject to such adaptations and modifications as may be specified in the regulations, in relation to any steps required to be taken by a notice of unauthorised development—

section 276 (power of local authorities to sell materials removed in executing works under that Act subject to accounting for the proceeds of sale);

section 289 (power to require the occupier of any premises to permit works to be executed by the owner of the premises);

section 294 (limit on liability of persons holding premises as agents or trustees in respect of the expenses recoverable under that Act).

(4) Regulations under subsection (3) applying all or any of section 289 of that Act may include adaptations and modifications for the purpose of giving the owner of land to which such a notice relates the right, as against all other persons interested in the land, to comply with the requirements of the notice.

(5) Regulations under subsection (3) may also provide for the charging on the land on which the development is carried out of any expenses recoverable by the relevant local planning authority under subsection (1).

(6) A person commits an offence if the person wilfully obstructs a person acting in the exercise of powers under subsection (1).

(7) A person guilty of an offence under subsection (6) is liable on summary conviction to a fine not exceeding level 3 on the standard scale.

[Planning Act 2008, s 170.]

[1] See the Infrastructure Planning (Compulsory Acquisition) Regulations 2010, SI 2010/104 amended by SI 2011/2055, SI 2012/2654 and 2732, SI 2013/522, SI 2014/469 and SI 2015/1682 and the Infrastructure Planning (Miscellaneous Prescribed Provisions) Regulations 2010, SI 2010/105 amended by SI 2012/630 and SI 2013/520.

# Town and Country Planning (Control of Advertisements) (England) Regulations 2007[1]

(SI 2007/783 amended by SI 2007/1739, SI 2011/2057 and 3058, SI 2012/2372 and SI 2013/2114)

## Part 1 General

7.11506 *1. Citation, commencement and application* (1) These Regulations may be cited as the Town and Country Planning (Control of Advertisements) (England) Regulations 2007 and shall come into force on 6th April 2007.

(2) These Regulations apply in relation to the display of advertisements on sites in England only.

(3) Parts 2 and 3 of these Regulations do not apply to the display of an advertisement of a description set out in column (1) of Schedule 1 to these Regulations so long as—

(*a*) the display complies with the conditions and limitations specified in column (2) of that Schedule as applicable to advertisements of that description; and

(*b*) except in the case of an advertisement within Class F, all the conditions specified in Schedule 2 are complied with;

(*c*) in the case of an advertisement within Class F, the requirements of paragraphs 1 to 3 and 5 of the standard conditions are complied with.

[1] Made by Secretary of State for Communities and Local Government, in exercise of the powers conferred by ss 220, 221, 223(1), 224(3) and 333(1) of the Town and Country Planning Act 1990. Equivalent provision is made for Wales by the Town and Country Planning (Control of Advertisements) Regulations 1992, SI 1992/666 amended by SI 1994/2351, SI 1996/252, SI 1996/525, SI 1999/1810, SI 2001/1149 and 4050, SI 2003/2155, SI 2005/3050 and SI 2012/791 (W).

7.11507 *2. Interpretation* (1) In these Regulations—

"the Act" means the Town and Country Planning Act 1990;

"advertisement" does not include—

(*a*) anything employed wholly as a memorial or as a railway signal; or (*b*) a placard or other object borne by an individual or an animal;

"advertiser", in relation to an advertisement, means—

(*a*) the owner of the site on which the advertisement is displayed;

(*b*) the occupier of the site, if different; and

(*c*) any other person who undertakes or maintains the display of the advertisement;

and any reference in these Regulations to the person displaying an advertisement shall be construed as a reference to the advertiser;

"amenity" includes aural and visual amenity;

"Area of Outstanding Natural Beauty" means an area designated as such by an order made under section 82 of the Countryside and Rights of Way Act 2000;

"area of special control" means an area designated by an order under regulation 20;

"balloon" means a tethered balloon or similar object;

"deemed consent" means consent granted by regulation 6;

"discontinuance notice" means a notice served under regulation 8;

"electronic communication" means an electronic communication within the meaning of the Electronic Communications Act 2000, the processing of which on receipt is intended to produce writing;

"electronic communications code operator" means—

(*a*) a provider of an electronic communications network in whose case the electronic communications code applies by virtue of a direction given by OFCOM under section 106 of the Communications Act 2003; and

(*b*) a person who, by virtue of paragraph 17(1) and (2) of Schedule 18 to that Act, is treated after the commencement of that section as a person in whose case that code applies by virtue of a direction given by OFCOM;

"electronically" means by electronic communication;

"express consent" has the meaning given by regulation 5;

"highway authority" has the meaning given by sections 1 to 3 of the Highways Act 1980;

"highway land" means any land within the boundaries of a highway;

"illuminated advertisement" means an advertisement which is designed or adapted to be illuminated by artificial lighting, directly or by reflection, and which is so illuminated (whether continuously or from time to time);

"local planning authority"—

(*a*) as regards land in a National Park, other than land within a metropolitan county, means the county planning authority for the area where the land is situated;

(*b*) as regards land in the area of an urban development corporation, means (except in regulation 20) that corporation where it is the local planning authority for the purposes of sections 220 and 224 of the Act; and

(*c*) as regards any other land, means the relevant district planning authority, metropolitan district or London borough council or urban development corporation;

"National Park" has the meaning given by section 5 of the National Parks and Access to the Countryside Act 1949;

"site" means any land or building, other than an advertisement, on which an advertisement is displayed;

"standard conditions" means the conditions specified in Schedule 2;

"statutory undertaker" includes, in addition to any person referred to in section 262(1) of the Act—

(*a*) any person deemed to be a statutory undertaker under subsection (3) or (6) of that section,

(*b*) the British Airports Authority,

(*c*) the Coal Authority or any licensed operator within the meaning of section 65(1) of the Coal Industry Act 1994,

(*d*) any electronic communications code operator, and

(*e*) any person who is a licence holder, or who has the benefit of a licence exemption, within the meaning of Part 1 of the Railways Act 1993,

and "statutory undertaking" shall be construed accordingly;

"traffic sign" has the meaning given by section 64(1) of the Road Traffic Regulation Act 1984;

"vehicle" includes a vessel on any inland waterway or in coastal waters; and

"working day" means a day which is not a Saturday or a Sunday, Christmas Day, Good Friday or a bank holiday in England and Wales under the Banking and Financial Dealings Act 1971.

(2) Except in Class 15 in Schedule 3, any reference in these Regulations to the building, the land, the premises or the site on which an advertisement is displayed includes, in the case of an advertisement which is displayed on, or which consists of, a balloon, a reference to the building, the land, the premises or the site to which the balloon is attached and to all buildings, land or premises normally occupied therewith.

**7.11508** 3. *Powers to be exercised in the interests of amenity and public safety* (1) A local planning authority shall exercise its powers under these Regulations in the interests of amenity and public safety, taking into account—

(*a*) the provisions of the development plan, so far as they are material; and

(*b*) any other relevant factors.

(2) Without prejudice to the generality of paragraph (1)(*b*)—

(*a*) factors relevant to amenity include the general characteristics of the locality, including the presence of any feature of historic, architectural, cultural or similar interest;

(*b*) factors relevant to public safety include—

(i) the safety of persons using any highway, railway, waterway, dock, harbour or aerodrome (civil or military);

(ii) whether the display of the advertisement in question is likely to obscure, or hinder the ready interpretation of, any traffic sign, railway signal or aid to navigation by water or air;

(iii) whether the display of the advertisement in question is likely to hinder the operation of any device used for the purpose of security or surveillance or for measuring the speed of any vehicle.

(3) In taking account of factors relevant to amenity, the local planning authority may, if it thinks fit, disregard any advertisement that is being displayed.

(4) Unless it appears to the local planning authority to be required in the interests of amenity or public safety, an express consent for the display of advertisements shall not contain any limitation or restriction relating to the subject matter, content or design of what is to be displayed.

**7.11509** 4. *Requirement for consent* (1) Subject to paragraph (2), no advertisement may be displayed unless consent for its display has been granted—

(*a*) by the local planning authority or the Secretary of State on an application in that behalf (referred to in these Regulations as "express consent"); or

(*b*) by regulation 6 (referred to in these Regulations as "deemed consent").

(2) An advertisement to which, by virtue of regulation 1(3), Parts 2 and 3 of these Regulations do not apply may be displayed without express consent or deemed consent.

(3) In determining an application for consent for the display of advertisements, the local planning authority may have regard to any material change in circumstances likely to occur within the period for which the consent is requested.

**7.11510** 5. *General effect of consent* A consent for the display of advertisements (whether deemed or express) shall have effect—

(*a*) as consent for the use of the site for the purposes of the display of advertisements, whether by the erection of structures or otherwise; and

(*b*) for the benefit of any person interested in the site.

## Part 2 Deemed Consent

**7.11511** 6. *Deemed consent for the display of advertisements* (1) Subject to regulations 7 and 8, and in the case of an area of special control also to regulation 21, consent is granted for the display of an advertisement of any class specified in Part 1 of Schedule 3, subject to—

(*a*) the standard conditions; and

(*b*) in the case of any class other than Class 12, the conditions and limitations specified in that Part in relation to that class.

(2) Part 2 of Schedule 3 applies for the interpretation of that Schedule.

**7.11512** 7. *Directions restricting deemed consent* (1) If the Secretary of State is satisfied, upon a proposal made to her by the local planning authority, that the display of advertisements of any class or description specified in Schedule 3, other than Class 12 or 13, should not be undertaken in any particular area or in any particular case without express consent, she may direct that the deemed consent for that class or description shall not apply in that area or in that case, for a specified period or indefinitely.

(2) Before making any such direction, the Secretary of State shall—

(*a*) where the proposal relates to a particular area, publish, or cause to be published, in at least one newspaper circulating in the locality, and on the same or a subsequent date in the London Gazette, a notice that such a proposal has been made, naming a place or places in the locality where a map or maps defining the area concerned may be inspected at all reasonable hours; and

(*b*) where the proposal relates to a particular case, serve, or cause to be served, on the owner and occupier of the land affected and on any other person who, to her knowledge, proposes to display on that land an advertisement of the class or description concerned, a notice that a proposal has been made, specifying the land and the class or description of advertisement concerned.

(3) A notice under paragraph (2) shall state that any representation about the making of a direction may be made to the Secretary of State in writing within such period, being not less than 21 days from the date when the notice was first published or served (as the case may be), as is specified in the notice.

(4) The Secretary of State shall not make a direction under this regulation until after the expiry of the specified period.

(5) In determining whether to make a direction, the Secretary of State—

(*a*) shall take into account any representation made in accordance with paragraph (3) (a "paragraph (3) representation");

(*b*) where any paragraph (3) representation consists of an objection, may give to the local planning authority and to any other person who has made a paragraph (3) representation, an opportunity of appearing before and being heard by a person appointed by her for the purpose; and

(*c*) may modify the proposal of the local planning authority if—

(i) she has given to that authority and every person who has made a paragraph (3) representation, notice in writing of her intention and the reasons for it and has given them a reasonable opportunity to respond; and

(ii) the intended modification does not extend the area of land specified in the proposal.

(6) Where the Secretary of State makes a direction, she shall send it to the local planning authority, with a statement of her reasons for making it, and shall send a copy of that statement to every person who has made a paragraph (3) representation.

(7) Notice of the making of any direction for a particular area shall be published by the local planning authority in at least one newspaper circulating in the locality and, unless the Secretary of State otherwise directs, on the same or a subsequent date in the London Gazette, and such notice shall—

(*a*) contain a full statement of the effect of the direction;

(*b*) name a place or places in the locality where a copy of the direction and of a map defining the area concerned may be seen at all reasonable hours; and

(*c*) specify a date when the direction shall come into force, being at least 14 and not more than 28 days after the first publication of the notice.

(8) Notice of the making of any direction for a particular case shall be served by the local planning authority on the owner and on any occupier of the land to which the direction relates, and on any other person who, to the knowledge of the authority, proposes to display on that land an advertisement of the class or description concerned.

(9) A direction for an area shall come into force on the date specified in the notice given under paragraph (7), and a direction for a particular case shall come into force on the date on which notice is served on the occupier or, if there is no occupier, on the owner of the land affected.

**7.11513** 8. *Discontinuance of deemed consent* (1) Subject to paragraph (2), the local planning authority may, if it is satisfied that it is necessary to do so to remedy a substantial injury to the amenity of the locality or a danger to members of the public, serve a notice requiring the discontinuance of—

(*a*) the display of a particular advertisement for which there is deemed consent; or

(*b*) the use of a particular site for the display of advertisements for which there is deemed consent.

(2) Paragraph (1) does not apply in relation to an advertisement that is within both Class 12 in Schedule 3 and Class E or Class F in Schedule 1.

(3) A discontinuance notice—

(*a*) shall be served on the advertiser;

(*b*) shall specify the advertisement or, as the case may be, the site to which the notice relates;

(*c*) shall specify a period within which the display or the use of the site, as the case may be, is to be discontinued;

(*d*) shall contain a statement of the reasons why the local planning authority—

(i) considers that a substantial injury to the amenity of the locality or a danger to members of the public, as the case may be, has been caused; and

(ii) considers it necessary to serve the notice; and

(*e*) shall include the names and addresses of all persons on whom the notice has been served.

(4) Subject to paragraphs (5) and (6), a discontinuance notice shall take effect at the end of the period (being at least 8 weeks after the date on which it is served) specified in the notice.

(5) If an appeal is made to the Secretary of State under section 78 of the Act (as applied by regulation 17(3)), the notice shall be of no effect until the appeal is finally determined or withdrawn.

(6) The local planning authority may, by notice served on every person on whom the discontinuance notice was served under paragraph (3)—

(*a*) withdraw the discontinuance notice at any time before it takes effect; or

(*b*) unless an appeal is made to the Secretary of State, from time to time vary the discontinuance notice by extending the period at the end of which the notice is to take effect.

(7) For the purposes of paragraph (5), an appeal is finally determined—

(*a*) if the period for bringing any further appeal has ended without an appeal having been made, or

(*b*) if it is withdrawn or otherwise ceases to have effect.

(8) In considering whether to serve a discontinuance notice, the local planning authority shall have regard to any material change in circumstances that has occurred.

## Part 3 Express Consent

**7.11514** 9. *Applications for express consent* (1) An application for express consent shall be made to the local planning authority.

(2) Subject to paragraphs (6) and (7), the application shall be made electronically or in hard copy on a form published by the Secretary of State or a form substantially to the same effect.

(3) The applicant shall—

(*a*) include the particulars specified in the form; and

(*b*) send with the application (whether electronically or otherwise) a plan which—

(i) is drawn to an identified scale,

(ii) shows the direction of North,

(iii) identifies the location of the site by reference to at least two named roads, and
(iv) identifies the proposed position of the advertisement.

(4) Unless an application is made electronically or the local planning authority indicates that a lesser number is required, three copies of the completed form and the plan shall accompany the application.

(5) Where the application is one to which directions given by the Secretary of State under regulation 11 apply, the applicant shall send with the application (whether electronically or otherwise) such particulars, plans or information specified or referred to in those directions as may have been notified to the applicant by the local planning authority.

(6) An application made on or after 6th April 2007 and before 1st October 2007, may be made in writing on a form devised by the local planning authority.

(7) An application made after 30th September 2007 and before 1st November 2007 otherwise than by a local planning authority or an interested planning authority, may be made in writing on a form devised by the local planning authority.

(8) Where an application is made electronically, the applicant shall be taken to have agreed—

(*a*) to the use by the authority of electronic communication for the purposes of his application;

(*b*) that his address for that purpose is the address incorporated into, or otherwise logically associated with, his application; and

(*c*) that his deemed agreement under this paragraph shall subsist until he gives notice in writing—

(i) withdrawing any address notified to the authority for that purpose, or
(ii) revoking that deemed agreement,

and such withdrawal or revocation shall be final and shall take effect on a date specified by the person in the notice but not less than seven days after the date on which the notice is given.

(9) An application made electronically shall, unless the contrary is proved, be treated as having been delivered at 9 a.m. on the next working day after the day on which it is transmitted.

(10) This regulation applies to applications for renewal of consent as it applies to applications for consent.

(11) An application for the renewal of an express consent may not be made more than 6 months before the date on which the consent is due to expire.

**7.11514A** *10. Application of section 77 of the Act to applications for express consent*

**7.11514B** *11. Secretary of State's directions*

**7.11514C** *12. Receipt of applications*

**7.11514D** *13. Duty to consult*

**7.11515** *14. Power to deal with applications* (1) Where an application for express consent is made to the local planning authority, the authority may—

(*a*) grant consent, in whole or in part, subject to the standard conditions and, subject to paragraphs (6) and (7), to such additional conditions as it thinks fit;

(*b*) refuse consent; or

(*c*) in a case to which paragraph (2) applies, decline to determine the application.

(2) This paragraph applies where the application relates to an advertisement to which section 70A of the Act, as modified as mentioned in paragraph (3), applies.

(3) For the purposes of this regulation, section 70A of the Act shall apply subject to the modifications specified in Part 1 of Schedule 4; and the provisions of that section as so modified are set out in Part 2 of that Schedule.

(4) Express consent may be granted—

(*a*) for the display of a particular advertisement or advertisements with or without illumination;

(*b*) for the use of a particular site for the display of advertisements in a specified manner, whether by reference to the number, siting, size or illumination of the advertisements, or the structures intended for such display, or the design or appearance of any such structure, or otherwise; or

(*c*) for the retention of any display of advertisements or the continuation of the use of a site begun before the date of the application.

(5) The conditions imposed under paragraph (1)(*a*) may, in particular, include conditions—

(*a*) regulating the display of advertisements to which the consent relates;

(*b*) regulating the use for the display of advertisements of the site to which the application relates or any adjacent land under the control of the applicant, or requiring the carrying out of works on any such land;

(*c*) requiring the removal of any advertisement or the discontinuance of any use of land authorised by the consent, at the end of a specified period, and the carrying out of any works required for the reinstatement of the land.

(6) In relation to the display of an advertisement within any class specified in Part 1 of Schedule 3, the local planning authority shall not impose any condition more restrictive than those imposed by regulation 6(1)(*b*) in relation to advertisements of that class.

(7) Subject to paragraph (6), an express consent shall be subject to the condition that it expires at the end of—

(*a*) such period as the local planning authority may specify in granting the consent; or (*b*) where no period is so specified, a period of 5 years.

(8) The local planning authority may specify, as the date on which the period under paragraph (7)(*a*) is to begin, whichever is the earlier of—

(*a*) the date of the commencement of the display; and

(*b*) a specified date not later than 6 months after the date on which the consent is granted.

**7.11515A** *15. Applications by interested planning authorities*

**7.11516** *16. Notification of decision* (1) The grant or refusal by a local planning authority of an application for express consent shall be notified in writing to the applicant within a period of 8 weeks from the date of the receipt of the application or such longer period as the applicant may, before the expiry of that period, agree in writing.

(2) The authority shall state in writing its reasons for—

(*a*) any refusal of consent in whole or in part;

(*b*) the imposition of any condition under regulation 14(1)(*a*), other than—

(i) a standard condition;

(ii) a condition specified in Part 1 of Schedule 3 in relation to a class within which the advertisement falls; and

(*c*) the imposition of a condition whereby the consent expires before the expiry of 5 years from the date on which it is granted, unless the period specified in the condition is a period proposed by the applicant.

*17. Appeals to the Secretary of State*

**7.11517** *18. Revocation or modification of express consent* (1) Subject to paragraphs (3) and (4), if a local planning authority is satisfied that it is expedient to do so, it may by order revoke or modify an express consent.

(2) Without prejudice to the generality of paragraph (1), a local planning authority may have regard to any material change in circumstances that has occurred since the consent was granted.

(3) An order under paragraph (1) shall not take effect without the approval of the Secretary of State.

(4) The power to make an order under this regulation may be exercised—

(*a*) in a case which involves the carrying out of building or other operations, at any time before those operations have been completed;

(*b*) in any other case, at any time before the display of advertisements is begun.

(5) When an authority submits an order under paragraph (1) to the Secretary of State for approval, it shall serve notice on the person who applied for the express consent, the owner and any occupier of the land affected and any other person who, in the authority's opinion, will be affected by the order, specifying a period of at least 28 days from the date of service of the notice within which objection may be made.

(6) If, within the period specified in the notice, an objection to the order is received by the Secretary of State from any person on whom notice was served, the Secretary of State shall, before considering whether to approve the order, give to that person and to the local planning authority an opportunity of appearing before and being heard by a person appointed by her.

(7) In considering whether to approve an order submitted to her under this regulation, the Secretary of State may have regard to any material change in circumstances that has occurred since the consent was granted.

(8) The Secretary of State may approve an order submitted to her under this regulation either without modification or subject to such modifications as she considers expedient.

(9) Where the Secretary of State approves an order submitted to her under this regulation, the local planning authority shall, within 14 days of the receipt of the Secretary of State's decision, send to every person notified under paragraph (5) notice of the Secretary of State's approval.

(10) An order which has been approved under this regulation shall take effect on the day after that on which the local planning authority complies with the requirements of paragraph (9).

(11) Where an order is made in a case to which paragraph (4)(*a*) applies, the revocation or modification of consent shall not affect such operations as have been carried out before the date on which, in accordance with paragraph (5), notice of the order is served.

**7.11517A** *19. Compensation for revocation or modification*

## PART 4 AREAS OF SPECIAL CONTROL

**7.11518** *20. Area of special control orders* (1) Every local planning authority shall from time to time consider whether any part or additional part of its area should be designated as an area of special control.

(2) An area of special control shall be designated by an area of special control order made by the local planning authority and approved by the Secretary of State, in accordance with the provisions of Schedule 5.

(3) An area of special control order may be revoked or modified by a subsequent order made by the authority and approved by the Secretary of State, in accordance with the provisions of Schedule 5.

(4) Where an area of special control order is in force the local planning authority shall consider at least once in every 5 years whether it should be revoked or modified.

(5) Before making an order under this regulation, a local planning authority shall consult—

(*a*) where it appears to the authority that the order will be likely to affect any part of the area of a neighbouring local planning authority, that authority;

(*b*) where the order will relate to any land in a National Park, other than land in a metropolitan county, any district planning authority within whose area any of that land is situated.

(6) A local planning authority shall not exercise its functions under this regulation in the interests of public safety and, in particular, shall disregard the factors mentioned in regulation 3(2)(*b*).

7.11519 *21. Control in areas of special control* (1) Subject to the provisions of this regulation, no advertisement may be displayed in an area of special control unless it falls within one or more of the following—

(*a*) any Class in Schedule 1;

(*b*) any of Classes 1 to 3, 5 to 7 and 9 to 14 in Schedule 3;

(*c*) paragraph (2).

(2) An advertisement falls within this paragraph if it is displayed with express consent and—

(*a*) it is a hoarding or similar structure to be used only for the display of notices relating to local events, activities or entertainments;

(*b*) it is—

(i) for the purpose of announcement or direction in relation to buildings or other land in the locality; and

(ii) reasonably required having regard to the nature and situation of such buildings or other land;

(*c*) it is required in the interests of public safety;

(*d*) it could be displayed by virtue of paragraph (1)(*b*) but for—

(i) a condition or limitation imposed by regulation 6(1)(*b*) as respects size, height from the ground, number or illumination; or

(ii) a direction under regulation 7; or

(*e*) it falls within Class 4A, 4B or 8 in Schedule 3.

(3) Express consent may not be granted for the display in an area of special control of an illuminated advertisement falling within paragraph (2)(*a*) or (*b*).

(4) Where an area is designated as an area of special control, advertisements of any description in column (1) of the Table below, which are being displayed in that area immediately before the area of special control order comes into force, may continue to be displayed, but only for the period specified in column (2) as applicable to advertisements of that description.

*Table*

| ***(1) Description*** | ***(2) Period*** |
|---|---|
| An advertisement within Class 4 in Schedule 3 (illuminated advertisements on business premises) for which express consent has not been granted. | 5 years from the date on which the area of special control order comes into force. |
| An advertisement within Class 8 in Schedule 3 (advertisements on hoardings) for which express consent has not been granted. | Whichever is the longer of—<br>(*a*) 1 year from the date on which the area of special control order comes into force; and<br>(*b*) 2 years from the date on which the advertisement was first displayed. |
| An advertisement for which express consent has been granted. | Whichever is the longer of—<br>(*a*) 6 months from the date on which the area of special control order comes into force; and<br>(*b*) the remainder of the period of the express consent. |

(5) Nothing in paragraphs (1) to (4) shall—

(*a*) affect a notice served at any time under regulation 8;

(*b*) override any condition, imposed on a consent, which requires the removal of an advertisement;

(*c*) restrict the powers of a local planning authority, or of the Secretary of State, in regard to any contravention of these Regulations;

(*d*) render unlawful the display, pursuant to—

(i) express consent; or

(ii) deemed consent by virtue of Class 14 in Schedule 3,

of an advertisement referred to in paragraph (2)(*d*) or (*e*).

## Part 5 Miscellaneous

**7.11520** *22. Documents in electronic form*

**7.11520A** *23. Repayment of expense of removing prohibited advertisements*

**7.11520B** *24. Register of applications*

**7.11520C** *25. Directions requiring information*

**7.11520D** *26. Exercise of powers by the Secretary of State*

**7.11521** *27. Discontinuance notice in respect of authority's advertisement* (1) If the Secretary of State is satisfied that it is necessary to remedy a substantial injury to the amenity of the locality or a danger to members of the public, she may serve a discontinuance notice under regulation 8 in relation to an advertisement displayed by an interested planning authority.

(2) Paragraphs (3) and (6) of regulation 8 shall apply in relation to a discontinuance notice served under paragraph (1) as they apply in relation to a discontinuance notice served by a local planning authority as if for references to the local planning authority there were substituted references to the Secretary of State.

(3) Paragraph (3) of regulation 17 shall apply in relation to a discontinuance notice served under paragraph (1) as it applies in relation to a discontinuance notice served by a local planning authority, with such modifications as may be necessary.

**7.11522** *28. Extension of time limits* The Secretary of State may, in any particular case, extend the time within which anything is required to be done under these Regulations or within which any objection, representation or claim for compensation may be made.

**7.11523** *29. Cancellation or variation of directions* Any power conferred by these Regulations to give a direction includes power to cancel or vary the direction by a subsequent direction.

**7.11524** *30. Contravention of Regulations* (1) Subject to paragraph (2), a person displaying an advertisement in contravention of these Regulations shall be liable, on summary conviction of an offence under section 224(3) of the Act, to a fine of an amount not exceeding level 4 on the standard scale and, in the case of a continuing offence, one tenth of level 4 on the standard scale for each day during which the offence continues after conviction.

(2) Paragraph (1) does not apply to the Crown.

*31. Transitional provisions*

*32. Principal Regulations ceasing to have effect in relation to England, with savings*

### SCHEDULE 1
### Classes of Advertisement to which Parts 2 and 3 Do Not Apply

Regulation 1(3)

**7.11525**

| *(1)* *Description of advertisement* | *(2)* *Conditions, limitations and interpretation* |
|---|---|
| CLASS A | |
| An advertisement displayed on enclosed land. | 1 The advertisement is not readily visible from outside the enclosed land or from any place to which the public have a right of access.<br>2 For the purposes of Class A, "enclosed land" includes—<br>(*a*) any railway station (and its yards) or bus station, together with its forecourt, whether enclosed or not; but does not include any public park, public garden or other land held for the use or enjoyment of the public, or (except as specified above) any enclosed railway land normally used for the carriage of passengers or goods by rail;<br>(*b*) any sports stadium; and<br>(*c*) any shopping mall or covered shopping arcade other than an historic shopping arcade.<br>3 In paragraph 2(*c*) "historic shopping arcade" means a group of buildings—<br>(*a*) of which more than 50%—<br>(i) are listed buildings within the meaning of the Planning (Listed Buildings and Conservation Areas) Act 1990 (whether listed individually or for their group value); or<br>(ii) are located within a conservation area within the meaning of that Act; and<br>(*b*) in more than 50% of which at least 75% of the ground floor is used for retail purposes. |
| CLASS B | |
| An advertisement displayed on or in a vehicle normally employed as a moving vehicle. | The vehicle is not used principally for the display of advertisements. |
| CLASS C | |
| An advertisement incorporated in the fabric of a building. | 1 The building or any external face of it is not used principally for the display of advertisements. |

| (1) *Description of advertisement* | (2) *Conditions, limitations and interpretation* |
|---|---|
| | 2 For the purposes of Class C— (*a*) an advertisement fixed to, or painted on, a building is not to be regarded as incorporated in its fabric; (*b*) a hoarding or similar structure is to be regarded as a building used principally for the display of advertisements. |
| CLASS D An advertisement displayed on an article for sale or on the container in, or from which, an article is sold. | 1 The advertisement refers only to the article for sale. 2 The advertisement may not be illuminated. 3 It may not exceed 0.1 square metre in area. 4 For the purpose of Class D, "article" includes a gas or liquid. |
| CLASS E An advertisement relating specifically to a pending Parliamentary, European Parliamentary or local government election or a referendum under the Political Parties, Elections and Referendums Act 2000. | The advertisement shall be removed within 14 days after the close of the poll in the election or referendum to which it relates. |
| CLASS F An advertisement required to be displayed by Standing Orders of either House of Parliament or by any enactment or any condition imposed by any enactment on the exercise of any function. | 1 If the advertisement would, if it were not within this Class, fall within any Class in Schedule 3, any conditions imposed on that Class as to size, height or number of advertisements displayed, shall apply to it. 2 In a case to which paragraph 1 does not apply, the size, height, and number of advertisements displayed shall not exceed what is necessary to achieve the purpose for which the advertisement is required. 3 The advertisement may not be displayed after— (*a*) the expiry of the period during which it is required or authorised to be displayed, or (*b*) if there is no such period, 14 days after its purpose has been satisfied. |
| CLASS G A traffic sign. | |
| CLASS H (*a*) Any country's national flag; | 1 Neither the flag nor the flagstaff may display any advertisement or subject matter additional to the design of the flag. |
| (*b*) The flag of the Commonwealth, the European Union or the United Nations; | 2 An advertisement within paragraph (*d*) of this Class may be displayed only in the county with which the saint is associated. |
| (*c*) The flag of any English county; | |
| (*d*) The flag of any saint. | |
| CLASS I An advertisement displayed inside a building. | 1 The advertisement may not be illuminated. 2 No part of the advertisement may be within 1 metre of any external door, window or other opening, through which it is visible from outside the building. |

## SCHEDULE 2

The Standard Conditions — Regulation 2(1)

7.11526 *1.* No advertisement is to be displayed without the permission of the owner of the site or any other person with an interest in the site entitled to grant permission.

*2.* No advertisement shall be sited or displayed so as to—

(*a*) endanger persons using any highway, railway, waterway, dock, harbour or aerodrome (civil or military);

(*b*) obscure, or hinder the ready interpretation of, any traffic sign, railway signal or aid to navigation by water or air; or

(*c*) hinder the operation of any device used for the purpose of security or surveillance or for measuring the speed of any vehicle.

*3.* Any advertisement displayed, and any site used for the display of advertisements, shall be maintained in a condition that does not impair the visual amenity of the site.

*4.* Any structure or hoarding erected or used principally for the purpose of displaying advertisements shall be maintained in a condition that does not endanger the public.

*5.* Where an advertisement is required under these Regulations to be removed, the site shall be left in a condition that does not endanger the public or impair visual amenity.

## SCHEDULE 3

Classes of Advertisement for which Deemed Consent is Granted — Regulation 6

Part 1 Specified Classes and Conditions

7.11527

| | |
|---|---|
| **Class 1** | **Functional advertisements of government departments and their agencies, local authorities, public transport undertakers, statutory undertakers and Transport for London** |
| Description | **1A** An advertisement displayed wholly for the purpose of announcement or direction in relation to any of the functions of a government department, an agency of a government department, a local authority or Transport for London, or to the operation of a statutory undertaking or a public transport undertaking, which—<br>(*a*) is reasonably required to be displayed for the safe or efficient performance of those functions, or operation of that undertaking, and<br>(*b*) cannot be displayed by virtue of any other specified class. |
| Conditions and Limitations | **1A**<br>(1) Illumination is not permitted unless reasonably required for the purpose of the advertisement.<br>(2) No advertisement may exceed 1.55 square metres in area. |
| Description | **1B** An advertisement displayed by a local planning authority on land in its area. |
| Conditions and Limitations | **1B** In an area of special control, the advertisement may be displayed only if the authority could have granted express consent for its display. |
| **Class 2** | **Miscellaneous advertisements relating to the premises on which they are displayed** |
| Description | **2A** An advertisement displayed for the purpose of identification, direction or warning, with respect to the land or building on which it is displayed. |
| Conditions and Limitations | **2A**<br>(1) No advertisement may exceed 0.3 square metre in area.<br>(2) Illumination is not permitted.<br>(3) No character or symbol on the advertisement may be more than 0.75 metre in height, or 0.3 metre in an area of special control.<br>(4) No part of the advertisement may be more than 4.6 metres above ground level, or 3.6 metres in an area of special control. |
| Description | **2B** An advertisement relating to any person, partnership or company separately carrying on a profession, business or trade at the premises where it is displayed. |
| Conditions and Limitations | **2B**<br>(1) No advertisement may exceed 0.3 square metre in area.<br>(2) No character or symbol on the advertisement may be more than 0.75 metre in height, or 0.3 metre in an area of special control.<br>(3) No part of the advertisement may be more than 4.6 metres above ground level, or 3.6 metres in an area of special control.<br>(4) Not more than one advertisement is permitted for each person, partnership or company or, in the case of premises with entrances on different road frontages, one advertisement at each of two such entrances.<br>(5) Illumination is not permitted unless—<br>(*a*) the advertisement states that the services of a practitioner in human health or a veterinary surgeon are available at the premises on which the advertisement is displayed, or that medical or veterinary supplies are available there;<br>(*b*) the illumination—<br>(i) is by static means,<br>(ii) includes no intermittent light source, flashing lights, moving parts or features, exposed cold cathode tubing, animation or retroflective material, and<br>(iii) is in a manner reasonably required to fulfil the purpose of the advertisement; and<br>(*c*) the levels of luminance do not exceed the levels set out in paragraph 2 of Part 2. |
| Description | **2C** An advertisement relating to any institution of a religious, educational, cultural, recreational or medical or similar character, or to any hotel, inn or public house, block of flats, club, boarding house, hostel or Bed and Breakfast establishment, at the premises where it is displayed. |
| Conditions and Limitations | **2C**<br>(1) Not more than one advertisement is permitted in respect of each premises or, in the case of premises with entrances on different road frontages, one advertisement at each of two such entrances.<br>(2) No advertisement may exceed 1.2 square metres in area.<br>(3) No character or symbol on the advertisement may be more than 0.75 metre in height, or 0.3 metre in an area of special control.<br>(4) No part of the advertisement may be more than 4.6 metres above ground level, or 3.6 metres in an area of special control.<br>(5) Illumination is not permitted unless—<br>(*a*) the advertisement states that the services of a practitioner in human health or a veterinary surgeon are available at the premises on which the advertisement is displayed, or that medical or veterinary supplies are available there;<br>(*b*) the illumination—<br>(i) is by static means,<br>(ii) includes no intermittent light source, flashing lights, moving parts or features, exposed cold cathode tubing, animation or retroflective material, and<br>(iii) is in a manner reasonably required to fulfil the purpose of the advertisement; and<br>(*c*) the levels of luminance do not exceed the levels set out in paragraph 2 of Part 2. |

**Class 3** **Miscellaneous temporary advertisements**

Description

**3A** An advertisement relating to the sale or letting, for residential, agricultural, industrial or commercial use or for development for such use, of the land or premises on which it is displayed.

Conditions and Limitations

**3A**

(1) Not more than one advertisement, consisting of a single board or two joined boards, is permitted; and where more than one advertisement is displayed, the first to be displayed shall be taken to be the one permitted.

(2) No advertisement may be displayed indicating that land or premises have been sold or let, other than by the addition to an existing advertisement of a statement that a sale or letting has been agreed, or that the land or premises have been sold or let, subject to contract.

(3) The advertisement shall be removed within 14 days after the completion of a sale or the grant of a tenancy.

(4) No advertisement may exceed in area—

(*a*) where the advertisement relates to residential use or development, 0.5 square metre or, in the case of two joined boards, 0.6 square metre in aggregate;

(*b*) where the advertisement relates to any other use or development, 2 square metres or, in the case of two joined boards, 2.3 square metres in aggregate.

(5) Where the advertisement is displayed on a building, the maximum projection permitted from the face of the building is 1 metre.

(6) Illumination is not permitted.

(7) No character or symbol on the advertisement may be more than 0.75 metre in height, or 0.3 metre in an area of special control.

(8) No part of the advertisement may be higher above ground level than 4.6 metres, or 3.6 metres in an area of special control or, in the case of a sale or letting of part only of a building, the lowest level of that part of the building on which display is reasonably practicable.

Description

**3B** An advertisement announcing the sale of goods or livestock, and displayed on the land where the goods or livestock are situated or where the sale is held, not being land which is normally used, whether at regular intervals or otherwise, for the purpose of holding such sales.

Conditions and Limitations

**3B**

(1) Not more than one advertisement may be displayed at any one time on the land concerned; and where more than one advertisement is displayed, the first to be displayed shall be taken to be the one permitted.

(2) No advertisement may be displayed earlier than 28 days before the day on which the sale is due to begin.

(3) The advertisement shall be removed within 14 days after the sale is completed or, if the sale is cancelled or postponed, within 14 days of the day on which it was due to begin.

(4) No advertisement may exceed 1.2 square metres in area.

(5) Illumination is not permitted.

(6) No character or symbol on the advertisement may be more than 0.75 metre in height, or 0.3 metre in an area of special control.

(7) No part of the advertisement may be more than 4.6 metres above ground level, or 3.6 metres in an area of special control.

Description

**3C** An advertisement relating to the carrying out of building or similar work on the land on which it is displayed, not being land which is normally used, whether at regular intervals or otherwise, for the purposes of carrying out such work.

Conditions and Limitations

**3C**

(1) Except in the case mentioned in paragraph (4), not more than one advertisement shall be displayed at any one time on each road frontage of the land, in respect of each separate development project; and where (otherwise than as authorised by paragraph (4)) more than one advertisement is displayed, the first to be displayed on any frontage shall be taken to be the one permitted.

(2) No advertisement may be displayed except while the relevant works are being carried out.

(3) No advertisement may exceed in aggregate—

(*a*) in the case of an advertisement referring to one person—

(i) if the display is more than 10 metres from a highway, 3 square metres in area; or

(ii) in any other case, 2 square metres;

(*b*) in the case of an advertisement referring to more than one person—

(i) if the display is more than 10 metres from a highway, 3 square metres plus 0.6 square metre for each person in excess of one; or

(ii) in any other case, 2 square metres plus 0.4 square metre for each person in excess of one, together with 0.2 of the area permitted under sub-paragraph (*a*) or (*b*) for the name, if any, of the development project.

(4) Where the advertisement does not refer to any person carrying out such work, that person may display a separate advertisement with a maximum area of 0.5 square metre, which does so refer, on each frontage of the land for a maximum period of 3 months.

(5) Illumination is not permitted.

(6) No character or symbol on the advertisement may be more than 0.75 metre in height, or 0.3 metre in an area of special control.

(7) No part of the advertisement may be more than 4.6 metres above ground level, or 3.6 metres in an area of special control.

Description

**3D**

An advertisement—

(*a*) announcing any local event of a religious, educational, cultural, political, social or recreational character, or

(*b*) relating to any temporary matter in connection with an event or local activity of such a character,

not being an event or activity promoted or carried on for commercial purposes.

Conditions and Limitations

**3D**

(1) No advertisement may exceed 0.6 square metre in area.

(2) No advertisement may be displayed earlier than 28 days before the first day on which the event or activity is due to take place.

(3) The advertisement shall be removed within 14 days after the end of the event or activity.

(4) Illumination is not permitted.

(5) No character or symbol on the advertisement may be more than 0.75 metre in height, or 0.3 metre in an area of special control.

(6) No part of the advertisement may be more than 4.6 metres above ground level, or 3.6 metres in an area of special control.

Description

**3E** An advertisement relating to any demonstration of agricultural methods or processes, on the land on which it is displayed.

Conditions and Limitations

**3E**

(1) Advertisements of this Class may not be displayed on any land for more than 6 months in any period of 12 months.

(2) The maximum area of display permitted in respect of each demonstration is 1.2 square metres.

(3) No single advertisement may exceed 0.4 square metre in area.

(4) No advertisement may be displayed earlier than 28 days before the day (or first day) on which the demonstration is due to take place and shall be removed within 14 days after the end of the demonstration.

(5) Illumination is not permitted.

(6) No character or symbol on the advertisement may be more than 0.75 metre in height, or 0.3 metre in an area of special control.

(7) No part of the advertisement may be more than 4.6 metres above ground level, or 3.6 metres in an area of special control.

Description

**3F** An advertisement relating to the visit of a travelling circus, fair or similar travelling entertainment to any specified place in the locality.

Conditions and Limitations

**3F**

(1) No advertisement may exceed 0.6 square metre in area.

(2) No advertisement may be displayed earlier than 14 days before the first performance or opening of the entertainment at the place specified.

(3) The advertisement shall be removed within 7 days after the last performance or closing of the specified entertainment.

(4) At least 14 days before the advertisement is first displayed, the local planning authority is to be notified in writing of the first date on which, and of the site at which, it is to be displayed.

(5) Illumination is not permitted.

(6) No part of the advertisement may be more than 4.6 metres above ground level, or 3.6 metres in an area of special control.

---

**Class 4** — **Illuminated advertisements on business premises**

Description

**4A** An illuminated advertisement displayed on the frontage of premises within a retail park, which overlook or face on to a communal car park wholly bounded by the retail park, where the advertisement refers wholly to any or all of the following: the business carried on, the goods sold or services provided, or the name or qualifications of the person carrying on the business, or supplying the goods or services, on those premises.

Conditions and Limitations

**4A**

(1) Subject to paragraph (2), no advertisement is permitted within a conservation area, an Area of Outstanding Natural Beauty, a National Park or the Broads.

(2) Paragraph (1) does not preclude the continued display of an advertisement that is displayed at the date of designation of the relevant area until the expiry of 5 years from that date.

(3) Not more than one advertisement of the prescribed description parallel to a wall and one projecting at right angles from a wall is permitted, and in the case of any projecting advertisement—

(*a*) no surface may be greater than 1 square metre in area;

(*b*) the advertisement may not project more than 1 metre from the wall; and

(*c*) the advertisement may not be more than 1.5 metres high.

(4) The lowest part of the advertisement must be at least 2.5 metres above ground level.

(5) No character or symbol on the advertisement may be more than 0.75 metre in height.

(6) No part of the advertisement may be higher above ground level than 4.6 metres or the bottom level of any first floor window in the wall on which the advertisement is displayed, whichever is the lower.

(7) Illumination is permitted only where—

(*a*) it is by static means,

(*b*) it includes no intermittent light source, flashing lights, moving parts or features, exposed cold cathode tubing, animation or retroflective material, and

(*c*) it is in a manner reasonably required to fulfil the purpose of the advertisement.

(8) may be—

(*a*) by halo illumination, or

(*b*) so long as no part of the background of the advertisement is illuminated, by illumination of each character or symbol of the advertisement from within.

(9) Where the method of illumination is that described in paragraph (8)(*b*), the luminance of the advertisement may not exceed the levels specified in paragraph 2 of Part 2.

(10) In the case of an advertisement consisting of a built-up box containing the light source, the distance between—

(*a*) the face of the advertisement and any wall parallel to which it is displayed, at the point where it is affixed, or

(*b*) the two faces of an advertisement projecting from a wall,

may not exceed 0.25 metre.

Description

**4B** An illuminated advertisement, other than one falling within Class 4A, displayed on business premises wholly with reference to any or all of the following: the business carried on, the goods sold or services provided, or the name or qualifications of the person carrying on the business, or supplying the goods or services, on those premises.

Conditions and Limitations

**4B**

(1) Subject to paragraph (2), no advertisement is permitted within a conservation area, an Area of Outstanding Natural Beauty, a National Park or the Broads.

(2) Paragraph (1) does not preclude the continued display of an advertisement that is displayed at the date of designation of the relevant area until the expiry of 5 years from that date.

(3) In the case of a shop, no advertisement may be displayed except on a wall containing a shop window.

(4) Not more than one advertisement parallel to a wall and one projecting at right angles from a wall is permitted, and in the case of any projecting advertisement—

(*a*) no surface may be greater than 0.75 square metre in area;

(*b*) the advertisement may not project more than 1 metre from the wall or two thirds of the width of any footway or pavement below, whichever is the less;

(*c*) the advertisement may not be more than 1 metre high; and

(*d*) it may not project over any carriageway.

(5) The lowest part of the advertisement shall be at least 2.5 metres above ground level.

(6) No surface of the advertisement may exceed one-sixth of the frontage on which it is displayed, measured up to a height of 4.6 metres from ground level or one-fifth of the frontage measured to the top of the advertisement, whichever is less.

(7) No character or symbol on the advertisement may be more than 0.75 metre in height.

(8) No part of the advertisement may be higher above ground level than 4.6 metres or the bottom level of any first floor window in the wall on which the advertisement is displayed, whichever is the lower.

(9) Illumination is permitted only where—

(*a*) it is by static means,

(*b*) it includes no intermittent light source, flashing lights, moving parts or features, exposed cold cathode tubing, animation or retroflective material, and

(*c*) it is in a manner reasonably required to fulfil the purpose of the advertisement.

(10) Illumination may be—

(*a*) by halo illumination, or

(*b*) so long as no part of the background of the advertisement is illuminated, by illumination of each character or symbol of the advertisement from within.

(11) Where the method of illumination is that described in paragraph (10)(*b*), the luminance of the advertisement may not exceed the levels specified in paragraph 2 of Part 2.

(12) In the case of an advertisement consisting of a built-up box containing the light source, the distance between—

(*a*) the face of the advertisement and any wall parallel to which it is displayed, at the point where it is affixed, or

(*b*) the two faces of an advertisement projecting from a wall,

may not exceed 0.25 metre.

**Class 5** — **Other advertisements on business premises**

Description

**5** Any advertisement which does not fall within Class 4A or 4B displayed on business premises wholly with reference to any or all of the following: the business carried on, the goods sold or services provided, or the name or qualifications of the person carrying on the business, or supplying the goods or services, on those premises.

Conditions and Limitations

**5**

(1) In the case of a shop, no advertisement may be displayed except on a wall containing a shop window.

(2) In an area of special control, the space occupied by the advertisement may not exceed one-tenth of the overall area of the face of the building on which it is displayed, up to a height of 3.6 metres from ground level; and the area occupied by the advertisement shall, notwithstanding that it is displayed in some other manner, be calculated as if the whole advertisement were displayed flat against the face of the building.

(3) Illumination is not permitted unless—

(*a*) the advertisement states that the services of a practitioner in human health or a veterinary surgeon are available at the premises on which the advertisement is displayed, or that medical or veterinary supplies are available there;

(*b*) the illumination—

(i) is by static means,

(ii) includes no intermittent light source, flashing lights, moving parts or features, exposed cold cathode tubing, animation or retroflective material, and

(iii) is in a manner reasonably required to fulfil the purpose of the advertisement; and

(*c*) the levels of luminance do not exceed the levels set out in paragraph 2 of Part 2.

(4) No character or symbol on the advertisement may be more than 0.75 metre in height, or 0.3 metre in an area of special control.

(5) No part of the advertisement may be higher above ground level than whichever is the lower of—

(*a*) 4.6 metres, or 3.6 metres in an area of special control; and

(*b*) the bottom level of any first floor window in the wall on which the advertisement is displayed.

(6) The area of an advertisement consisting of a single placard or poster shall not exceed 1.55 square metres.

---

**Class 6** — **An advertisement on a forecourt of business premises**

Description

**6** An advertisement displayed on any forecourt of business premises, wholly with reference to all or any of the matters specified in Class 5.

Conditions and Limitations

**6**

(1) Advertisements displayed on any forecourt or, in the case of a building with a forecourt on two or more frontages, on each of those frontages, shall not exceed in aggregate 4.6 square metres in area.

(2) Illumination is not permitted.

(3) No character or symbol on the advertisement may be more than 0.75 metre in height, or 0.3 metre in an area of special control.

(4) No part of the advertisement may be more than 4.6 metres above ground level, or 3.6 metres in an area of special control.

(5) No single advertisement may exceed 1.55 square metres in area.

---

**Class 7** — **Flag advertisements**

Description

**7A** An advertisement in the form of a flag attached to a single flagstaff projecting vertically from the roof of a building.

Conditions and Limitations

**7A**

(1) No advertisement is permitted other than one—

(*a*) bearing either the name or device, or both the name and device, of any person occupying the building; or

(*b*) referring to a specific event (other than the offering of named goods for sale) of limited duration, which is taking place in the building, for the duration of that event.

(2) No character or symbol on the flag may be more than 0.75 metre in height, or 0.3 metre in an area of special control.

Description

**7B** An advertisement in the form of a flag attached to a single vertical flagstaff erected on a site which forms part of an area of land in respect of which planning permission has been granted for development of which the only or principal component is residential development and on which—

(*a*) operations for the construction of houses are in progress pursuant to that permission, or

(*b*) such operations having been completed, at least one of the houses remains unsold.

Conditions and Limitations

**7B**

(1) No advertisement is permitted within a conservation area, an Area of Outstanding Natural Beauty, a National Park, the Broads or an area of special control.

(2) The number of advertisements on the land concerned shall not exceed—

(*a*) where the aggregate number of houses on that land does not exceed 10, one;

(*b*) where the aggregate number of houses on that land exceeds 10 but does not exceed 100, two;

(*c*) where the aggregate number of houses on that land exceeds 100, three.

(3) No part of the flagstaff may be more than 4.6 metres above ground level.

(4) No flag shall exceed 2 square metres in area.

(5) No advertisement shall be displayed after the expiration of the period of 1 year commencing on the day on which building operations on the land concerned have been substantially completed.

---

**Class 8** — **Advertisements on hoardings**

| | |
|---|---|
| Description | **8** An advertisement on a hoarding which encloses, either wholly or in part, land on which building operations are taking place or are about to take place, if those operations are in accordance with a grant of planning permission (other than outline permission) for development primarily for use for commercial, industrial or business purposes. |
| Conditions and Limitations | **8**<br>(1) Subject to paragraph (2), no advertisement shall be displayed in a conservation area, a National Park, an Area of Outstanding Natural Beauty or the Broads.<br>(2) Paragraph (1) does not preclude the continued display of an advertisement that is displayed at the date of designation of the relevant area until the expiry of 1 year from that date, or 2 years from the date of commencement of the display, whichever is the later.<br>(3) No advertisement may be displayed earlier than three months before the commencement of the building operations.<br>(4) No advertisement shall exceed 38 square metres in area.<br>(5) No part of the advertisement may be more than 4.6 metres above ground level.<br>(6) At least 14 days before the advertisement is first displayed, the person who proposes to display it shall notify the local planning authority in writing of the date on which it will first be displayed and shall send a copy of the relevant planning permission.<br>(7) No advertisement shall be displayed for more than 3 years.<br>(8) Illumination is not permitted unless it—<br>(*a*) is by static means,<br>(*b*) includes no intermittent light source, flashing lights, moving parts or features, exposed cold cathode tubing, animation or retroflective material, and<br>(*c*) is in a manner reasonably required to fulfil the purpose of the advertisement. |
| **Class 9** | **Advertisements on highway structures** |
| Description | **9** An advertisement displayed on a part of an object or structure designed to accommodate six-sheet panel displays, the use of which for the display of advertisements is authorised under section 115E(1)(*a*) of the Highways Act 1980. |
| Conditions and Limitations | **9**<br>(1) No advertisement may exceed 2.16 square metres in area.<br>(2) Illumination is not permitted.<br>(3) No character or symbol on the advertisement may be more than 0.75 metre in height or 0.3 metre in an area of special control.<br>(4) No part of the advertisement may be more than 4.6 metres above ground level, or 3.6 metres in an area of special control. |
| **Class 10** | **Advertisements for neighbourhood watch and similar schemes** |
| Description | **10** An advertisement displayed on or near highway land (but not in the window of a building), to give notice that a closed circuit television surveillance scheme, or a neighbourhood watch or similar scheme, established jointly by the local policing body and a local committee or other body of persons, is in operation in the area. |
| Conditions and Limitations | **10**<br>(1) No advertisement may exceed 0.2 square metre in area.<br>(2) No advertisement may be displayed on highway land without the consent of the highway authority.<br>(3) The local planning authority shall, at least 14 days before the advertisement is first displayed, be given particulars in writing of the place at which it is to be displayed and a certificate—<br>(*a*) that the scheme has been properly established;<br>(*b*) that the local policing body has agreed to the display of the advertisement; and<br>(*c*) where relevant, that the consent of the highway authority has been given.<br>(4) The advertisement shall be removed within 14 days after—<br>(*a*) the relevant scheme ceases to operate;<br>(*b*) the relevant scheme ceases to be approved by the local policing body; or<br>(*c*) the highway authority withdraws its consent to its display.<br>(5) Illumination is not permitted.<br>(6) No character or symbol on the advertisement may be more than 0.75 metre in height, or 0.3 metre in an area of special control.<br>(7) No part of the advertisement may be more than 3.6 metres above ground level. |
| **Class 11** | **Directional advertisement** |
| Description | **11** An advertisement on a single flat surface directing potential buyers and others to a site where residential development is taking place. |
| Conditions and Limitations | **11**<br>(1) No advertisement may exceed 0.15 square metre in area.<br>(2) No part of the advertisement may be of a retroflective material.<br>(3) The design of the advertisement may not be similar to that of a traffic sign.<br>(4) The advertisement is to be displayed on land adjacent to highway land, in a manner which makes it reasonably visible to an approaching driver, but not within 50 metres of a traffic sign intended to be observed by persons approaching from the same direction. |

(5) No advertisement may be more than two miles from the main entrance of the site.

(6) The person who proposes to display the advertisement shall notify the local planning authority, in writing, at least 14 days before the advertisement is first displayed, of the place at which, and the first date on which, it will be displayed.

(7) No advertisement may be displayed after the development of the site is completed or, in any event, for more than 2 years.

(8) Illumination is not permitted.

(9) No character or symbol on the advertisement shall be less than 0.04 metre high or more than 0.25 metre high.

(10) No part of the advertisement may be more than 4.6 metres above ground level, or 3.6 metres in an area of special control.

**Class 12** — **Advertisements inside buildings**

Description

12 An advertisement displayed inside a building, other than an advertisement—
(*a*) falling within Class I in Schedule 1; or
(*b*) displayed on the glazed surface of a telephone kiosk.

**Class 13** — **Advertisements on sites used for preceding ten years for display of advertisements without express consent**

Description

13 An advertisement displayed on a site that has been used continually for the preceding ten years for the display of advertisements without express consent.

Conditions and Limitations

13

(1) An advertisement does not fall within this description if, during the relevant 10-year period, there has been either a material increase in the extent to which the site has been used for the display of advertisements or a material alteration in the manner in which it has been so used.

(2) If any building or structure on which such an advertisement is displayed—

(*a*) is removed in compliance with a requirement of, or under, any enactment,

(*b*) is removed in any other circumstances, or

(*c*) is destroyed by any means,

the erection of any building or structure to continue the display is not permitted.

(3) Illumination is not permitted unless—

(*a*) the advertisement is displayed with illumination on 6th April 2007; or

(*b*) the advertisement is first displayed after that date, and the advertisement most recently displayed was illuminated.

(4) An advertisement that—

(*a*) comprises sequential displays; or

(*b*) otherwise includes moving parts or features; or

(*c*) features intermittent lighting in a manner designed to give the appearance of movement,

is not permitted unless—

(i) it is displayed on 6th April 2007 and falls within the description specified in any of sub-paragraphs (*a*) to (*c*); or

(ii) it is first displayed after that date, and the advertisement most recently displayed fell within any such description.

**Class 14** — **Advertisements displayed after expiry of express consent**

Description

14 An advertisement displayed after the expiry of express consent, unless—

(*a*) it would contravene a condition subject to which express consent was granted; or

(*b*) an application for renewal of consent has been refused.

Conditions and Limitations

14

(1) The terms of the express consent, including any conditions to which it was subject (to the extent that those terms and conditions are not incapable of performance by reason of the passage of time), shall be treated as applying to the continued display.

(2) No advertisement may be displayed under this class except on a site which has been continually used for the purpose since the expiry of the express consent.

(3) Unless authorised by the express consent, an advertisement that—

(*a*) comprises sequential displays; or

(*b*) otherwise includes moving parts or features; or

(*c*) features intermittent lighting in a manner designed to give the appearance of movement; or

(*d*) is illuminated,

is not permitted.

**Class 15** — **Advertisements on balloons**

Description

15 The display of an advertisement on, or consisting of, a balloon not more than 60 metres above ground level.

Conditions and Limitations

15

(1) The site of the advertisement is not in an Area of Outstanding Natural Beauty, a conservation area, a National Park, the Broads or an area of special control.

(2) Not more than one advertisement may be displayed on the site at any one time.

(3) The site may not be used for the display of advertisements on more than 10 days in total in any calendar year.

| | |
|---|---|
| **Class 16** | **Advertisements on telephone kiosks** |
| Description | **16** An advertisement displayed on the glazed surface of a telephone kiosk, other than a kiosk of type K2 (1927) or K6 (1935) designed by Giles Gilbert Scott. |
| Conditions and Limitations | **16**<br>(1) No advertisement may be displayed in an Area of Outstanding Natural Beauty, a conservation area, a National Park, the Broads or an area of special control.<br>(2) Illumination is not permitted.<br>(3) Subject to paragraph (4), with the exception of the name of the electronic communications code operator, its trading name or symbol, no advertisement may be displayed on more than one face of the kiosk.<br>(4) Where three or more kiosks are sited in a row or group, the display of an advertisement on any face of one kiosk shall preclude the display of an advertisement on the face of any adjacent kiosk. |
| **Class 17** | **Advertisements on a charging point for electric vehicles** |
| Description | **17** An advertisement displayed on a charging point for electric vehicles |
| Conditions and Limitations | (1) An advertisement may only be displayed by the person ("the relevant person") who—<br>(*a*) installed the charging point;<br>(*b*) supplies the electricity to the charging point; or<br>(*c*) does both of the above.<br>(2) Only one advertisement may be displayed on the charging point by the relevant person.<br>(3) The advertisement must only display—<br>(*a*) the name of the relevant person;<br>(*b*) the device of that person; or<br>(*c*) both of the above.<br>(4) No advertisement may exceed 70 square centimetres in area.<br>(5) Where the person who installed the charging point and the person who supplies the electricity to the charging point are different people, no more than two advertisements are permitted on the charging point.<br>(6) Where there are two advertisements on a charging point, those advertisements are to be placed, so far as is reasonably practicable, so as to face in opposite directions.<br>(7) Illumination is not permitted. |

## Part 2 Interpretation

*1.* (1) In this Schedule—

"business premises" means any building or part of a building normally used for the purpose of any professional, commercial, or industrial undertaking, or for providing services to members of the public or of any association, and includes a public restaurant, licensed premises and a place of public entertainment, but does not include—

(*a*) a building designed for use as one or more separate dwellings, unless—

(i) it has normally been used in each of the preceding ten years for the purpose of any professional, commercial, or industrial undertaking, or for providing services to members of the public or of any association; or

(ii) it has been adapted for use for any such purpose by the construction of a shop front or the making of a material alteration of a similar kind to its external appearance;

(*b*) a building used as an institution of a religious, educational, cultural, recreational, or medical or similar character;

(*c*) any forecourt or other land forming part of the curtilage of a building;

(*d*) any fence, wall or similar screen or structure, unless it forms part of the fabric of a building;

"electronic communications apparatus" means apparatus falling within the definition of that term in paragraph 1(1) of Schedule 2 to the Telecommunications Act 1984;

"electronic communications code operator" means—

(*a*) a provider of an electronic communications network in whose case the electronic communications code applies by virtue of a direction given by OFCOM under section 106 of the Communications Act 2003; and

(*b*) a person who is treated after the commencement of that section as a person in whose case that code applies by virtue of a direction given by OFCOM;

"electronic communications service" means a service falling within the definition of that term in section 32(2) of the Communications Act 2003;

"forecourt", in relation to any building or part of a building, means an area of land (whether or not enclosed) within the curtilage of the building or part, to which the public may have access only with the permission (express or implied) of the owner; and includes any fence, wall or similar screen or structure that defines the boundaries of that area;

"ground level", in relation to the display of advertisements on any building, means the ground-floor level of that building;

"highway land" means any land within the boundaries of a highway;

"joined boards" means boards joined at an angle, so that only one surface of each is usable for advertising;

"practitioner in human health" includes a chiropodist, chiropractor, dentist or doctor of medicine, an optician or osteopath, and a physiotherapist;

"public transport undertaking" means an undertaking engaged in the carriage of passengers in a manner similar to that of a statutory undertaking;

"retail park" means a group of 3 or more retail stores, at least one of which has a minimum internal floor area of 1,000 square metres and which—

(*a*) are set apart from existing shopping centres but within an existing or proposed urban area;

*(b) sell primarily goods other than food; and*

(*c*) share one or more communal car parks; and

"telephone kiosk" means any kiosk, booth, acoustic hood, shelter or similar structure which is erected or installed for the purpose of housing or supporting electronic communications apparatus and at which an electronic communications service is provided (or is to be provided) by an electronic communications code operator.

(2) Where a maximum area is specified, in relation to any class in this Schedule, in the case of a double-sided advertisement, the area of one side only shall be taken into account.

*2.* (1) The permitted levels of luminance for advertisements falling within Classes 2B, 2C, 4A, 4B or 5 are—

(*a*) where the illuminated area is not more than 10 square metres, 600 candela per square metre; and
(*b*) where the illuminated area is more than 10 square metres, 300 candela per square metre.
(2) In calculating an area for the purposes of paragraph (1)—
(*a*) each advertisement, or in the case of a double-sided projecting advertisement, each side of the advertisement, is to be taken separately; and
(*b*) no unilluminated part of the advertisement is to be taken into account.
*3.* In relation to advertisements within Class 4A or 4B, "halo illumination" means illumination of the background to the text of the advertisement, where the light source cannot be viewed directly from any angle.
*4.* (1) For the purposes of Class 7B—
"aggregate number" means the aggregate of the number of houses constructed, in the course of construction, or proposed to be constructed, on the land concerned;
"flat" means a separate and self-contained set of premises constructed for the purpose of a dwelling and forming part of a building from some other part of which it is divided horizontally;
"house" includes a flat;
"planning permission" does not include any outline planning permission in relation to which some or all of the matters reserved for subsequent approval remain to be approved; and
"the land concerned", in relation to any development, means—
(*a*) except in a case to which sub-paragraph (2) or (3) applies, the land to which the planning permission for the development relates;
(*b*) in a case to which sub-paragraph (2) applies, the land on which a particular phase of that development was or, as the case may be, is being or is about to be carried out;
(*c*) in a case to which sub-paragraph (3) applies, the part of the land to which the permission relates on which a person has carried out part of that development, or, as the case may be, is carrying it out or is about to carry it out.
(2) Subject to sub-paragraph (3), this sub-paragraph applies where the development is carried out in phases.
(3) This sub-paragraph applies where the development is carried out by two or more persons who each carry out part of it on a discrete part of the land to which the planning permission relates (whether the whole of the development or any part of it is carried out in phases or otherwise).
*5.* For the purposes of Class 15, "the site" means—
(*a*) in a case where the advertisement is being displayed by a person (other than the occupier of the land) who is using, or proposing to use, the land to which the balloon is attached for a particular activity (other than the display of advertisements) for a temporary period, the whole of the land used, or to be used, for that activity;
(*b*) in any other case, the land to which the balloon is attached and all land normally occupied with it.

## SCHEDULE 4
## Modifications of the Act

Regulations 14 and 17

### Part 1 Modifications of Section 70A of the Act

**7.11528** *1.* In section 70A of the Act—
(*a*) in subsection (1), for paragraph (*a*), substitute—
"(*a*) the condition in subsection (3) or (4) is satisfied, and";
(*b*) after subsection (1) insert the following subsection—
"(1A) A local planning authority may decline to determine a relevant application if, by virtue of regulation 21(1) of the Town and Country Planning (Control of Advertisements) (England) Regulations 2007, they have no power to grant the consent applied for.";
(*c*) omit subsection (2);
(*d*) in subsection (3), for "in that period", substitute "in the period of two years ending with the date on which the application mentioned in subsection (1) is received";
(*e*) for subsection (5) substitute—
"(5) A relevant application is an application under regulation 9 of the Town and Country Planning (Control of Advertisements) (England) Regulations 2007 for express consent to display an advertisement.";
(*f*) in subsection (6), at the end of paragraph (*b*), insert—
"including, in particular, the factors relevant to amenity and public safety that the local planning authority are required to take into account when exercising their powers under the Town and Country Planning (Control of Advertisements) (England) Regulations 2007";
(*g*) in subsection (7), in paragraph (*a*), for "subsections (2) and (4)", substitute "subsection (4)"; and
(*h*) in subsection (8)—
(i) for "planning permission", substitute "express consent"; and
(ii) for "the development", substitute "the subject matter of".

### Part 2 Section 70A of the Act as Modified

*1.* (1) A local planning authority may decline to determine a relevant application if—
(*a*) the condition in subsection (3) or (4) is satisfied, and
(*b*) the authority think there has been no significant change in the relevant considerations since the relevant event.
(1A) A local planning authority may decline to determine a relevant application if, by virtue of regulation 21(1) of the Town and Country Planning (Control of Advertisements) (England) Regulations 2007, they have no power to grant the consent applied for.
. . . . . . . . . . . . *subsection (2) omitted*
(3) The condition is that in the period of two years ending with the date on which the application mentioned in subsection (1) is received the Secretary of State has dismissed an appeal—
(*a*) against the refusal of a similar application, or
(*b*) under section 78(2) in respect of a similar application.
(4) The condition is that—
(*a*) in that period the local planning authority have refused more than one similar application, and
(*b*) there has been no appeal to the Secretary of State against any such refusal.
(5) A relevant application is an application under regulation 9 of the Town and Country Planning (Control of Advertisements) (England) Regulations 2007 for express consent to display an advertisement.
(6) The relevant considerations are—
(*a*) the development plan so far as material to the application; and
(*b*) any other material considerations including, in particular, the factors relevant to amenity and public safety that the local planning authority are required to take into account when exercising their powers under the Town and Country Planning (Control of Advertisements) (England) Regulations 2007.
(7) The relevant event is—
(*a*) for the purposes of subsection (4) the refusal of the similar application;

(*b*) for the purposes of subsection (3) the dismissal of the appeal.

(8) An application for express consent is similar to another application if (and only if) the local planning authority think that the subject matter of and the land to which the applications relate are the same or substantially the same.

PART 3 MODIFICATIONS OF SECTIONS 78 AND 79 OF THE ACT (APPLICATIONS FOR EXPRESS CONSENT)

*1.* In section 78 of the Act—

(*a*) in subsection (1), for paragraphs (*a*) to (*c*) substitute "refuse an application for express consent or grant it subject to conditions,";

(*b*) for subsection (2) substitute—

"(2) A person who has made an application for express consent may also appeal to the Secretary of State if within the period of 8 weeks from the date when the application was received by the local planning authority, that authority have neither given him notice of their decision on it nor given him notice that they have exercised their power under section 70A to decline to determine the application.";

(*c*) for subsection (3) substitute the following subsections—

"(3) An applicant who wishes to appeal under subsection (1) or (2) shall give notice of appeal to the Secretary of State by—

(*a*) serving on the Secretary of State within—

(i) 8 weeks from the date of receipt of the local planning authority's decision, or, as the case may be, within 8 weeks from the expiry of the period mentioned in subsection (2); or

(ii) such longer period as the Secretary of State may, at any time, allow, a completed appeal form, obtained from the Secretary of State; and

(*b*) serving on the local planning authority a copy of the completed appeal form mentioned in sub-paragraph (*a*) as soon as reasonably practicable.

(3A) The notice mentioned in subsection (3) shall be accompanied by a copy of each of the following documents—

(*a*) the application made to the local planning authority;

(*b*) all relevant plans and particulars submitted to them;

(*c*) the notice of the authority's decision (if any); and

(*d*) any other relevant correspondence with the authority.";

(*d*) omit subsection (4);

(*da*) omit subsections (4A) to (4D);

(*e*) in subsection (5), omit the references to sections 79(3), 253(2)(*c*) and 266(1)(*b*).

*2.* In section 79 of the Act—

(*a*) after subsection (1) insert—

"(1A) The Secretary of State may, in granting an express consent, specify that its term shall run for such longer or shorter period than 5 years as he considers expedient, having regard to the interests of amenity (including aural amenity) and public safety, and taking into account—

(*a*) relevant provisions of any applicable development plan;

(*b*) the factors referred to in regulation 3 of the Town and Country Planning (Control of Advertisements) (England) Regulations 2007; and

(*c*) any period specified in the application for consent.";

(*b*) omit subsection (4);

(*c*) in subsection (5), for "such an appeal shall be final", substitute "an appeal under section 78 shall be final, and shall otherwise have effect as if it were a decision of the local planning authority";

(*d*) in subsection (6)—

(i) omit "such"; and

(ii) for the words from "an application for planning permission" to "planning permission for that development", substitute "in respect of an application for express consent, the Secretary of State forms the opinion that, having regard to the Regulations mentioned in subsection (1A) and to any direction given under them, consent"; and

(*e*) in subsection (6A), after the word "appeal", the first time it appears, insert "as is mentioned in subsection (6)".

PART 4 SECTIONS 78 AND 79 OF THE ACT AS MODIFIED

*78.* (1) Where a local planning authority refuse an application for express consent or grant it subject to conditions, the applicant may by notice appeal to the Secretary of State.

(2) A person who has made an application for express consent may also appeal to the Secretary of State if within the period of 8 weeks from the date when the application was received by the local planning authority, that authority have neither given him notice of their decision on it nor given him notice that they have exercised their power under section 70A to decline to determine the application.

(3) An applicant who wishes to appeal under subsection (1) or (2) shall give notice of appeal to the Secretary of State by—

(*a*) serving on the Secretary of State within—

(i) 8 weeks from the date of receipt of the local planning authority's decision, or, as the case may be, within 8 weeks from the expiry of the period mentioned in subsection (2); or

(ii) such longer period as the Secretary of State may, at any time, allow, a completed appeal form, obtained from the Secretary of State; and

(*b*) serving on the local planning authority a copy of the completed appeal form mentioned in sub-paragraph (*a*) as soon as reasonably practicable.

(3A) The notice mentioned in subsection (3) shall be accompanied by a copy of each of the following documents—

(*a*) the application made to the local planning authority;

(*b*) all relevant plans and particulars submitted to them;

(*c*) the notice of the authority's decision (if any); and

(*d*) any other relevant correspondence with the authority.

(4) *Repealed.*

(5) For the purposes of the application of sections 79(1), 288(10)(*b*) and 319A(7)(*b*) in relation to an appeal under subsection (2), it shall be assumed that the authority decided to refuse the application in question.

*79.* (1) On appeal under section 78 the Secretary of State may—

(*a*) allow or dismiss the appeal, or

(*b*) reverse or vary any part of the decision of the local planning authority (whether the appeal relates to that part of it or not),

and may deal with the application as if it had been made to him in the first instance.

(1A) The Secretary of State may, in granting an express consent, specify that its term shall run for such longer or shorter period than 5 years as he considers expedient, having regard to the interests of amenity (including aural amenity) and public safety, and taking into account—

(*a*) relevant provisions of any applicable development plan;

(*b*) the factors referred to in regulation 3 of theTown and Country Planning (Control of Advertisements) (England) Regulations 2007; and
(*c*) any period specified in the application for consent.
(2) *Repealed.*
(3) *Repealed.*
(5) The decision of the Secretary of State on an appeal under section 78 shall be final, and shall otherwise have effect as if it were a decision of the local planning authority.
(6) If, before or during the determination of an appeal in respect of an application for express consent, the Secretary of State forms the opinion that, having regard to the Regulations mentioned in subsection (1A) and to any direction given under them, consent—
(*a*) could not have been granted by the local planning authority; or
(*b*) could not have been granted otherwise than subject to the conditions imposed,
he may decline to determine the appeal or to proceed with the determination.
(6A) If at any time before or during the determination of such an appeal as is mentioned in subsection (6) it appears to the Secretary of State that the appellant is responsible for undue delay in the progress of the appeal, he may—
(*a*) give the appellant notice that the appeal will be dismissed unless the appellant takes, within the period specified in the notice, such steps as are specified in the notice for the expedition of the appeal; and
(*b*) if the appellant fails to take those steps within that period, dismiss the appeal accordingly.
(7) Schedule 6 applies to appeals under section 78, including appeals under that section as applied by or under any other provision of this Act.

PART 5 MODIFICATIONS OF THE ACT (DISCONTINUANCE NOTICES)

*1.* In section 78, for subsections (1) to (5) substitute—
"(1) Where a discontinuance notice has been served on any person by a local planning authority under regulation 8 of theTown and Country Planning (Control of Advertisements) (England) Regulations 2007 that person may, if he is aggrieved by the notice, appeal by notice under this section to the Secretary of State.
(2) A person who wishes to appeal under subsection (1) shall give notice of appeal to the Secretary of State by—
(*a*) serving on the Secretary of State within—
(i) before the date on which the discontinuance notice is due to take effect under regulation 8(4), taking into account where appropriate of any extension of time under regulation 8(6), of those Regulations; or
(ii) such longer period as the Secretary of State may allow, a completed appeal form, obtained from the Secretary of State; and
(*b*) serving on the local planning authority a copy of the completed appeal form mentioned in sub-paragraph (*a*) as soon as reasonably practicable.
(3) A notice of appeal shall be accompanied by a copy of each of the following documents—
(*a*) the discontinuance notice;
(*b*) any notice of variation; and
(*c*) any relevant correspondence with the authority."
*2.* In section 79—
(*a*) for subsection (1) substitute—
"(1) Where an appeal is brought in respect of a discontinuance notice the Secretary of State may—
(*a*) allow or dismiss the appeal, or
(*aa*) omit subsections (2) and (3);
(*b*) subject to subsection (1A)—
(i) correct any defect, error or misdescription in the discontinuance notice; or
(ii) reverse or vary any part of the notice (whether the appeal relates to that part of it or not),
and deal with the matter as if an application for express consent had been made and refused for the reasons stated for the taking of discontinuance action.
(1A) The Secretary of State may take any action mentioned in subsection (1)(*b*) only if he is satisfied that the correction, reversal or variation will not cause injustice to the appellant or the local planning authority."
(*b*) for subsection (4) substitute—
"(4) On the determination of an appeal under section 78 the Secretary of State shall give such directions as may be necessary for giving effect to his determination including, where appropriate, directions for quashing the discontinuance notice or for varying its terms.";
(*c*) omit subsection (6); and
(*d*) in subsection (6A), after the word "appeal", the first time it appears, insert "in respect of a discontinuance notice".

SCHEDULE 5
Area of Special Control Orders

# TOWNS IMPROVEMENT; TOWN POLICE

**Contents**



## Towns Improvement Clauses Act 1847[1]

(10 & 11 Vict c 34)

OFFENCES

7.11529 **64. Defacing numbers etc** Every person who destroys, pulls down, or defaces any number of a house, or name of a street[2] put up by the local authority or puts up any number or name different from the number or name put up by the authority—*Penalty*, not exceeding **level 1** on the standard scale.

[Towns Improvement Clauses Act 1847, s 64 as amended by the Criminal Law Act 1977, s 31 as amended by the Criminal Justice Act 1982, s 46—summarised.]

---

[1] This Act was originally intended for incorporation in local Acts. The sections here contained were incorporated by the Public Health Act 1875, s 160, and are of general application except for Greater London. By virtue of the Highways Act 1959, Sch 25, s 160 of the Public Health Act 1875 now incorporates only the provisions of this Act relating to naming streets and numbering houses. Section 251 of the 1875 Act provides for summary procedure and remains in force for incorporated provisions although otherwise repealed by the Public Health Act 1936. S 253 of the 1875 Act, which required written consent of the Attorney General for proceedings to be taken by a person other than the party aggrieved or the local authority, was repealed by the Local Government (Miscellaneous Provisions) Act 1976, s 27. Where the Public Health Act 1875 is incorporated in a local Act, publication of bye-laws in conformity with that Act is sufficient (*Fielding v Rhyl Improvement Comrs* (1878) 3 CPD 272, 42 JP 311).

[2] Where Pt II of the Public Health Act 1925 is in force, see ss 17–19, thereof, ante. The local authority has a right to name a street, and if an owner or other person obliterates or removes the name affixed by the authority, he is liable to be convicted under this section. But the section does not give the local authority a right to alter the well-known name of an old street (*Collins v Hornsey UDC* [1901] 2 KB 180, 65 JP 600). For power to alter street name, and penalties for obliterating same, etc, see the Public Health Acts Amendment Act 1907, s 21 in this PART: title PUBLIC HEALTH, ante.

7.11530 **65. Renewing numbers** Every occupier who fails within one week after notice from the local authority to mark his house with a number approved by the authority, or to renew such number when obliterated—*Penalty*, not exceeding **level 1** on the standard scale, with power for the authority to do the work at the expense of the occupier.

[Towns Improvement Clauses Act 1847, s 65 as amended by the Criminal Justice Act 1967, Sch 3 as amended by the Criminal Justice Act 1982, ss 38 and 46—summarised.]

## Town Police Clauses Act 1847[1]

(10 & 11 Vict c 89)

7.11531 **1. Incorporation with special Act** This Act shall extend only to such towns or districts in England or Ireland as shall be comprised in any Act of Parliament hereafter to be passed which shall declare that this Act shall be incorporated therewith; and all the clauses of this Act, save so far as they shall be expressly varied or excepted by any such Act, shall apply to the town or district which shall be comprised in such Act, and to the commissioners appointed for improving and regulating the same, so far as such clauses shall be applicable thereto respectively, and shall, with the clauses of every other Act which shall be incorporated therewith, form part of such Act, and be construed therewith as forming one Act.

[Town Police Clauses Act 1847, s 1.]

---

[1] Although originally adoptive, this Act has had ss 21–36 applied throughout England and Wales by virtue of s 171 of the Public Health Act 1875, as amended by the Local Government Act 1972, s 179 and Sch 14, and by virtue of para 23 of the said Sch 14. Paragraph 24 of Sch 14 does, however, exclude s 171(4) of the 1875 Act (Hackney carriages) with the saving that those provisions will apply to those areas to which they applied immediately before 1 April 1974. Paragraph 25 takes this a stage further by enabling local authorities to apply or disapply provisions in para 24 to their area. Proceedings are those appropriate to summary jurisdiction; prosecutions must be taken before two or more justices (Public Health Act 1875, s 251). Since the nullifying of s 253 of the Public Health Act 1875 by s 27 of the Local Government (Miscellaneous Provisions) Act 1976, the power to prosecute is not limited to the local authority.

*Interpretation*

7.11532 **2. "The special Act"—"Prescribed"—"The commissioners"** And with respect to the construction of this Act, whether incorporated in whole or in part with any other Act, and of any Act incorporated therewith, be it enacted as follows:

The expression "the special Act" used in this Act shall be construed to mean any Act which shall be hereafter passed for the improvement or regulation of any town or district defined or comprised therein, and with which this Act shall be incorporated; and the word "prescribed" used in this Act in reference to any matter herein stated shall be construed to refer to such matter as the same shall be prescribed or provided for in the special Act, and the sentence in which such word shall occur shall be construed as if instead of the word "prescribed" the expression "prescribed for that purpose in the special Act" had been used; and the expression "the commissioners" shall mean the commissioners, trustees, or other persons or body corporate instrusted by the special Act with powers for executing the purposes thereof.

[Town Police Clauses Act 1847, s 2.]

7.11533 **3. Interpretations in this and the special Act** The following words and expressions in both this and the special Act, and any Act incorporated therewith, shall have the meanings hereby assigned to them, unless there be something in the subject or context repugnant to such construction; (that is to say,)

NUMBER: Words importing the singular number shall include the plural number, and words importing the plural number shall include the singular number:

GENDER: Words importing the masculine gender shall include females;

"PERSON": The word "person" shall include a corporation, whether aggregate or sole:

"LANDS": The words "lands" shall include messuages, lands, tenements, and hereditaments, of any tenure:

"STREET": The word "street" shall extend to and include any road, square, court, alley, and thoroughfare, or public passage, within the limits of the special Act:

"MONTH": The word "month" shall mean a calendar month:

"JUSTICE": The word "justice" shall mean justice of the peace acting for the place where the matter requiring the cognizance of any such justice arises; and where any matter shall be authorized or required to be done by two justices, the expression "two justices" shall be understood to mean two or more justices met and acting together:

"CATTLE": The word "cattle" shall include horses, asses, mules, sheep, goats, and swine.

[Town Police Clauses Act 1847, s 3 amended by the Courts Act 2003, Sch 8.]

*Obstructions and Nuisances in Streets*

7.11535 **21. Power to make orders for preventing obstructions in the streets during public processions, etc** The local authority may from time to time make orders[1] for the route to be observed by all carts, carriages, horses and persons, and for preventing obstruction of the streets in all times of public processions, rejoicings, or illuminations, and in any case when the streets are thronged or liable to be obstructed[2], and may also give directions to the constables for keeping order and preventing any obstruction of the streets in the neighbourhood of theatres and other places of public resort; and every wilful breach of any such order shall be deemed a separate offence against this Act, and every person committing any such offence shall be liable to a penalty not exceeding **level 3** on the standard scale.

[Town Police Clauses Act 1847, s 21 as amended by the Criminal Justice Act 1967, Sch 3 and the Criminal Justice Act 1982, ss 39 and 46 and Sch 3.]

---

[1] Where an order was made that constables stationed at certain crossings should give directions to drivers of vehicles, it was held that there was an implied obligation on the part of the drivers to obey such directions (*Dudderidge v Rawlings* (1912) 77 JP 167). For power to erect appropriate traffic signs, see the Road Traffic Regulation Act 1984, s 66, ante. See also the Road Traffic Regulation Act 1984, ss 1, 14 (orders restricting use of roads and for one way traffic), the Road Traffic Act 1988, ss 35, 36 (neglect of traffic directions by a police constable or traffic sign), ante, and the "Highway Code". Nothing contained in the Roman Catholic Relief Act 1926 shall affect any power conferred by any Act or byelaw upon any local authority to make byelaws or regulations relating to, or otherwise to control, any meeting or procession in streets or public places, or adjoining or abutting unfenced grounds (Roman Catholic Relief Act 1926, s 2). No local authority shall exercise these powers in relation to the Greater London area; see the Public Health Act 1875, s 171 and the Local Government Act 1972, Sch 14, para 26.

[2] This expression is limited to cases of the same class or *genus* as the three preceding instances; a more general order is invalid (*Brownsea Haven Properties Ltd v Poole Corpn* (supra), overruling *Teale v Williams* [1914] 3 KB 395, 78 JP 383; *Edwards v Wanstall* (1929) 94 JP 51; *Etherington v Carter* [1937] 2 All ER 528). A breach of an order must be alleged and proved to have been "wilful" (*Waring v Wheatley* (1951) 115 JP 630).

7.11536 **23. *Power to stage carriages to deviate from route under order of commissioners***

7.11537 **24. Power to impound stray cattle[1]** If any cattle be at any time found at large in any street within the limits of the special Act, without any person having the charge thereof, any constable or officer of police, or any person residing within the limits of the special Act, may seize and impound such cattle in any common pound within the said limits, or in such other place as the commissioners appoint for that purpose, and may detain the same therein until the owner thereof pay to the commissioners a penalty not exceeding level 1 on the standard scale, besides the reasonable expenses of impounding and keeping such cattle.

[Town Police Clauses Act 1847, s 24 as amended by the Criminal Law Act 1977, s 31 and the Criminal Justice Act 1982, s 46.]

---

[1] See the Protection of Animals Act 1911, s 7(1), title ANIMALS—*Protection*, ante (feeding impounded cattle); also this PART: title POUND BREACH, ante.

7.11538 **25. Power to sell cattle impounded for payment of penalty and expenses, after notice and advertisement** If the said penalty and expenses be not paid within three days after such impounding[1], the pound-keeper or other person appointed by the commissioners for that purpose may proceed to sell or cause to be sold any such cattle; but previous to such sale seven days notice thereof shall be given to or left at the dwelling house or place of abode of the owner of such cattle, if he be known, or if not, then notice of such intended sale shall be given by advertisement, to be inserted seven days before such sale in some newspaper published or circulated within the limits of the special Act; and the money arising from such sale, after deducting the said sums, and the expenses aforesaid, and all other expenses attending the impounding, advertising, keeping, and sale of any such cattle so impounded, shall be paid to the commissioners, and shall be by them paid, on demand, to the owner of the cattle so sold.

[Town Police Clauses Act 1847, s 25.]

[1] This time limit will not nowadays always fit the time-scale of the summary proceedings required by s 251 of the Public Health Act 1875.

7.11539 **26. Persons guilty of pound-breach to be committed for three months[1]** Every person who releases or attempts to release any cattle from any pound or place where the same are impounded under the authority of this or the special Act, or who pulls down, damages, or destroys the same pound or place, or any part thereof, with intent to procure the unlawful release of such cattle, shall, upon conviction of such offence before any two justices, be committed by them to some common gaol or house of correction for any time not exceeding three months.*

[Town Police Clauses Act 1847, s 26.]

* **Words substituted by the Criminal Justice Act 2003, Sch 32 from a date to be appointed.**

[1] By the provisions of the Magistrates' Courts Act 1980, s 34(3), may in the alternative impose a fine not exceeding **level 3** on the standard scale.

7.11540 **27.** ***Power to provide a pound***

7.11541 **28. Penalty on persons committing any of the offences herein named** Every person[1] who in any[2] street to the obstruction, annoyance[3] or danger[4], of the residents or[5] passengers[6], commits any of the following offences[7], shall be liable to a penalty not exceeding **level 3** on the standard scale for each offence, or, in the discretion of the justice[8] before whom he is convicted, may be committed to prison for a period not exceeding **fourteen days**; (that is to say,)*

Every person who suffers to be at large any unmuzzled ferocious[9] dog, or sets on or urges any dog or other animal to attack, worry, or put in fear any person or animal[10];

Every person who rides or drives furiously[10] any horse or carriage[13] or drives furiously any cattle[12];

Every person who causes any tree, or timber, or iron beam, to be drawn in or upon any carriage without having sufficient means of safely guiding the same;

Every person who wantonly discharges any firearm, or throws or discharges any stone, or other missile, or makes any bonfire, or throws or sets fire to any firework;

Provided always that it shall not be an offence to lay sand or other materials in any street in time of frost to prevent accidents, or litter or other suitable materials to prevent the freezing of water in pipes, or in case of sickness to prevent noise, if the party laying any such things causes them to be removed as soon as the occasion for them ceases;

[Town Police Clauses Act 1847, s 28 as amended by the Street Offences Act 1959, Sch, the Police Act 1964, Sch 9, the Criminal Justice Act 1967, Sch 3, the Rabies Act 1974, s 9, the Statute Law (Repeals) Act 1975, Sch, Part X, the Indecent Displays (Control) Act 1981, Sch, the Criminal Justice Act 1982, ss 39 and 46 and Sch 3, the Police and Criminal Evidence Act 1984, Sch 7, the Sexual Offences 2003, Schs 6 and 7 and the Deregulation Act 2015, Sch 23.]

* **Amended by the Criminal Justice Act 2003, Schs 32 and 37 from a date to be appointed.**

[1] "Person" includes a corporation, whether aggregate or sole (s 3).

[2] The word "street" includes any road, square, court, alley and thoroughfare, or public passage (s 3). The street includes the carriageway and the footways at the sides. The offence must be committed in the street, but the annoyance may be to "residents", meaning, it seems, the occupiers of houses in the street although they may not be in the street at the time. See *Mantle v Jordan* [1897] 1 QB 248, 61 JP 119. As to the definition of "street" for the purpose of certain offences within this section where the Public Health Acts Amendment Act 1907 is in force, see s 81 of that Act, ante.

[3] There is no offence merely for shouting in connection with selling newspapers without evidence that any person was annoyed (*Stanley v Farndale* (1892) 56 JP Jo 709). But see *Innes v Newman* [1894] 2 QB 292, 58 JP 543, where it was held that, as the act complained of was calculated to annoy the inhabitants generally, annoyance of one inhabitant by a similar outcry was sufficient to justify a conviction under a byelaw. See also *Brabham v Wookey* (1901) 18 TLR 99, where under a local Act the appellant was convicted for using indecent language "to the annoyance of the inhabitants or passengers", he at the time being inside his house, the door of which was open, and there being no evidence of annoyance save that of two constables.

[4] These words govern the whole of the section, and restrict the offences to cases where obstruction, annoyance, or danger can be proved (see *Stinson v Browning* (1866) LR 1 CP 321, 30 JP 312). But it will not be necessary to call any person who has been annoyed, etc, as a witness (*Woolley v Corbishley* (1860) 24 JP 773; *Read v Perrett* (1876) 1 Ex D 349, 41 JP 135) or to prove that any particular passenger was endangered (*West Riding Cleaning Co Ltd v Jowett* [1938] 4 All ER 21). Several of the offences mentioned in this section are punishable under the Highways, Vagrancy and other Acts.

[5] The conviction must specify against which class the offence has been committed (*Cotterill v Lamprière* (1890) 24 QBD 684, 54 JP 588).

[6] For the purposes of an information alleging that the defendant wilfully and indecently exposed his person, it was held that police officers who witnessed the defendant masturbating in a public lavatory were not "passengers" when they had been stationed in the lavatory following complaints (*Cheeseman v DPP* [1992] QB 83, 93 Cr App Rep 145, [1991] Crim LR 296).

[7] A failure on the part of any person to observe any provision of the "Highway Code", may in any proceedings be relied upon by any party to the proceedings as tending to establish or to negative any liability which is in question in those proceedings (Road Traffic Act 1988, s 38, ante).

[8] Where the provisions of this section are in force under the Public Health Act, the conviction must be by two justices (Public Health Act 1875, s 251). If the case is heard before one justice the sum adjudged to be paid must not exceed £1 (Magistrates' Courts Act 1980, s 121(5), ante).

[9] WILLS J, held in a civil action that it was not a necessary inference because a dog was accustomed to attack sheep that it was, *ipso facto*, liable to attack men (*Osborne v Chocqueel* [1896] 2 QB 109). It is not necessary to show that the dog has, to the knowledge of its owner, actually bitten or attempted to bite anybody. It is sufficient to prove that the dog is, to the knowledge of its master, ferocious, which may be of an intermittent character, as when a bitch has pups (*Barnes v*

*Lucille Ltd* (1907) 96 LT 680). Complaints to servants of owner at his house are some evidence of *scienter* (*Applebee v Percy* (1874) 38 JP 567). In the case of a corporation, knowledge of a servant is ineffectual, unless communicated to the directors or others in control. There is no absolute duty imposed on the occupier of premises because he allowed a dog to be kept there. It is the person who controls and harbours the dog who is liable (*Knott v LCC* [1934] 1 KB 126, 97 JP 335, CA). An opinion is given at 54 JP 639, that there must be evidence that the defendant suffered, ie knowingly permitted, the dog to be at large, but that it is not necessary to prove the defendant knew the dog to be ferocious. A dog on a lead is not "at large" (*Ross v Evans* [1959] 2 QB 79, [1959] 2 All ER 222, 123 JP 320). As to dangerous dogs, see the Dogs Act 1871, s 2, ante, under which proceedings may be taken in the proper case despite the dismissal of an information under this section. Cf *Keddle v Payn* [1964] 1 All ER 189, 128 JP 144.

[10] For extended meaning of "street" in relation to offences as to dogs, where the Public Health Acts Amendment Act 1907 is in force, see s 81 of that Act, ante.

[12] "Cattle" includes horses, asses, mules, sheep, goats and swine (s 3).

[13] A bicycle is a carriage (*Taylor v Goodwin* (1879) 4 QBD 228, 43 JP 653).

7.11542 **29. Penalty on persons guilty of riotous or indecent behaviour**[1] Every person guilty of any violent or indecent behaviour in any police office or any police station-house shall be liable to a penalty not exceeding **level 1** on the standard scale for every such offence, or, in the discretion of the justice before whom he is convicted to imprisonment for a period not exceeding **one month**.*

[Town Police Clauses Act 1847, s 29 as amended by the Penalties for Drunkenness Act 1962, s 1, the Criminal Justice Act 1967, Sch 7 and the Criminal Justice Act 1982, ss 38 and 46.]

* **Amended by the Criminal Justice Act 2003, Schs 32 and 37 from a date to be appointed.**

[1] The Criminal Justice Act 1967, s 91 in this PART: title PUBLIC MEETING AND PUBLIC ORDER, ante has effect in place of this section where a person is guilty whilst drunk of disorderly behaviour (Criminal Justice Act 1967, s 91(2)).

*Fires*

7.11543 **31. Penalty for accidentally allowing chimneys to catch fire** If any chimney accidentally catch or be on fire the persons occupying or using the premises in which such chimney is situated shall be liable to a penalty not exceeding **level 1** on the standard scale:
Provided always, that such forfeiture shall not be incurred if such person prove to the satisfaction of the justice before whom the case is heard that such fire was in no wise owing to omission, neglect, or carelessness of himself or servant.

[Town Police Clauses Act 1847, s 31 as amended by the Criminal Law Act 1977, s 31 and the Criminal Justice Act 1982, s 46.]

*Hackney Carriages*[1]

7.11544 **37. Local authority may licence hackney carriages** Local authority may from time to time license[2] to ply for hire within the prescribed distance[3] or if no distance is prescribed, within five miles from the General Post Office of the city, town, or place to which the special Act refers, (which in that case shall be deemed the prescribed distance,) hackney coaches or carriages of any kind or description adapted to the carriage of persons.

[Town Police Clauses Act 1847, s 37 as amended by the Transport Act 1985, s 16.]

[1] The 1847 Act is to be construed as one with the Town Police Clauses Act 1889; both Acts are incorporated with the Public Health Act 1875. The hackney carriage provisions were adoptive (Local Government Act 1972, Sch 14, para 25) and applied in conjunction with Part II of the Local Government (Miscellaneous Provisions) Act 1976, in this PART: title LOCAL GOVERNMENT, ante. The Transport Act 1985, s 15 has applied the hackney carriage provisions of the 1847 Act throughout England and Wales. The police are now, despite s 253 of the Public Health Act 1875, enabled to prosecute for hackney carriage offences under this Act. See the Public Health Act 1875, ss 171(4) and 253, the Local Government Act 1972, Sch 14, paras 23–25, and the Local Government (Miscellaneous Provisions) Act 1976, s 27. The 1847 Act provisions do not apply in London (see the Public Passenger Vehicles Act 1981, s 64, the Metropolitan Public Carriage Act 1869 and, as to the metropolitan traffic area the London Passenger Transport Act 1933, s 51(7)).

Sections 37–65 of the Act, to the extent to which they are part of the taxi code, shall apply, subject to modifications and exceptions, to a licensed taxi which is being used to provide a local service under a special licence under s 12 of the Transport Act 1985 (Local Services (Operation by Taxis) Regulations 1986, SI 1986/567).

Sections 52–59 of the Act are modified or disapplied in relation to the hiring of taxis at separate fares under ss 10 and 11 of the Transport Act 1985 (Licensed Taxis (Hiring at Separate Fares) Order 1986, SI 1986/1386).

[2] The Transport Act 1985, s 16 provides that where the hackney carriage provisions of the 1847 Act are incorporated in any enactment, the person considering licence applications may refuse only if satisfied that there is no significant unmet demand, as to which see *R v Reading Borough Council, ex p Egan and Sullman* [1990] RTR 399n (a note of 1987 cases); also *Stevenage Borough Council v Younas* [1990] RTR 405n (a note of a 1988 case) and *Ghafoor v Wakefield Metropolitan District Council* [1990] RTR 389. As to appeal, see the Public Health Acts Amendment Act 1890, s 7(1). A failure to determine an application for a hackney carriage licence amounts to "withholding" for the purpose of affording a right of appeal under s 107(1) of the 1890 Act, in this PART: title Public Health, ante. Where, on appeal, the crown court determines that there is a significant unmet demand, further inquiry must be made to determine its extent and how it is to be matched with all the current competing applications before granting the application before it. The crown court may do this itself or remit the matter to the local authority for reconsideration (*Kelly v Wirral Metropolitan Borough Council* (1996) Times, 13 May, CA). The policy of the legislation is that the authority licensing hackney carriage is the authority for the area in which those vehicles will generally be used; it is thus difficult for a local authority to justify the grant of a licence to an applicant whom the authority knows has no intention of using it to ply for hire within the authority's area: *R (on the application of Newcastle City Council) v Berwick-Upon-Tweed Borough Council* [2008] EWHC 2369 (Admin), [2009] LGR 195, [2009] RTR 413.

[3] The Public Health Act 1875, s 171, defines this as within any urban district.

7.11545 **38. What vehicles to be deemed hackney carriages** Every wheeled carriage[1], whatever may be its form or construction, used in standing or plying for hire[2] in any street[3] within the prescribed distance, and every carriage standing upon any street within the prescribed distance, having thereon any numbered plate required by this or the special Act to be fixed upon a hackney carriage, or having thereon any plate resembling or intended to resemble any such plate as aforesaid, shall be deemed to be a hackney carriage within the meaning of this Act; and in all proceedings at law or otherwise the term "hackney carriage" shall be sufficient to describe any such carriage: Provided always, that no stage coach[4] used for the purpose of standing or plying for passengers to be carried for hire at separate fares, and duly licensed for that purpose, and having thereon the proper numbered plates required by law to be placed on such stage coaches, shall be deemed to be a hackney carriage[4] within the meaning of this Act.

[Town Police Clauses Act 1847, s 38.]

---

[1] The Town Police Clauses Act 1889 provides:—The several terms "hackney carriages", "hackney coach", "carriages", and "carriage", whenever used in sections thirty-seven, forty to fifty-two (both inclusive), fifty-four, fifty-eight, and sixty to sixty-seven (both inclusive) of the principal Act shall, notwithstanding anything contained in section thirty-eight of that Act, be deemed to include every omnibus (s 4(1));

Notwithstanding the above provisions, it has been held that Parliament's intention must have been to attribute the same meaning to the term "hackney carriage" throughout the 1847 Act and this necessarily limited the meaning to that within s 38 of the 1847 Act without incorporation of the 1889 Act amendments. Accordingly, a trishaw was held to be a hackney carriage and not a stage coach for the purposes of the licensing provisions under s 37, ante and ss 47 and 59 of the Local Government (Miscellaneous Provisions) Act 1976 (*R v Cambridge City Council, ex p Lane* [1999] RTR 182).

The term "omnibus," where used in this Act, shall include—

Every omnibus, char-à-banc, wagonette, brake, stage coach, and other carriage plying or standing for hire by or used to carry passengers at separate fares, to, from, or in any part of the prescribed distance;

but shall not include—

Any tramcar or tram carriage duly licensed under the provisions of the Tramways Act 1870, or of any Provisional Order made thereunder and confirmed by Parliament, or under the provisions of any local Act of Parliament:

Any carriage starting from and previously hired for the particular passengers thereby carried at any livery stable yard (within the prescribed distance) whereat horses are stabled and carriages let for hire, the said carriage starting from the said stable yard and being bona fide the property of the occupier thereof, and not standing or plying for hire within the prescribed distance:

Any omnibus belonging to or hired or used by any railway company for conveying passengers and their luggage to or from any railway station of that company, and not standing or plying for hire within the prescribed distance:

Any omnibus starting from outside the prescribed distance, and bringing passengers within the prescribed distance, and not standing or plying for hire within the prescribed distance (s 3).

As to tramcars and trolley vehicles, see the Tramways Act 1870, s 48; and as to carriages as a light railway, see *Yorkshire (Woollen District) Electric Tramways Ltd v Ellis* [1905] 1 KB 396, 69 JP 67. The provisions of the 1847 Act do not apply to motor public service vehicles (Road Traffic Act 1930, ss 121(1), 122 and Sch 5), but do apply to a motor "contract carriage" (Road Traffic Act 1930). Note also the definition of "hackney carriage" for use purposes in the Vehicle Excise and Registration Act 1994, Sch 1, Part III.

[2] With regard to cases on the meaning of "plying for hire", see also footnote 3, post. "Plying for hire" involves being on view to the public and inviting the public to use it; it can be inferred from the appearance of the vehicle, the place where it was on view and its conduct; see *Rose v Welbeck Motors Ltd* [1962] 2 All ER 801, 126 JP 413, and cases quoted therein. See also *Cogley v Sherwood* [1959] 2 All ER 313, 123 JP 377; *Greyhound Motors Ltd v Lambert* [1928] 1 KB 322, 91 JP 198; *Sales v Lake* (1922) 1 KB 553, 86 JP 80; *Cocks v Mayner* (1894) 58 JP 104 ("voluntary contributions").

[3] The word "street" shall extend to and include any road, square, court, alley and thoroughfare, or public passage, within the limits of the special Act (Town Police Clauses Act 1847, s 3). A number of cases on the meaning of "plying for hire" were decided under London legislation; although the cases are relevant, the actual wording of the section differs from that in the 1847 Act and this should be duly noted; "any carriage for the conveyance of passengers which plies for hire within the limits of this Act, and is not a stage carriage" (Metropolitan Public Carriage Act 1869, s 4).

Special provision is made for railway premises by the Public Health Act 1925, s 76, as follows;

> "In any area within which the provisions of the Town Police Clauses Act 1847 with respect to hackney carriages are in force, those provisions and any byelaws of the local authority with respect to hackney carriages shall be as fully applicable in all respects to hackney carriages standing or plying for hire at any railway station or railway premises within such area, as if such railway station or railway premises were a stand for hackney carriages or a street:
>
> Provided that—
>
> (*a*) the provisions of this section shall not apply to any vehicle belonging to or used by any railway company for the purpose of carrying passengers and their luggage to or from any of their railway stations or railway premises, or to the driver or conductor of such vehicle;
>
> (*b*) nothing in this section shall empower the local authority to fix the site of the stand or starting place of any hackney carriage in any railway station or railway premises, or in any yard belonging to a railway company, except with the consent of that company."

The word "street" does not include an airport private road (*Young v Scampion* [1989] RTR 95, 87 LGR 240) but a vehicle positioned on private land in order to draw custom from the general public in an adjoining public street can be "plying for hire in any street" (*Eastbourne Borough Council v Stirling and Morley* [2001] RTR 65, [2001] Crim LR 42, DC).

[4] See note 1, ante.

7.11546 40. **Persons applying for licence to sign a requisition** Before any such licence is granted a requisition for the same, in such form as the commissioners from time to time provide for that purpose, shall be made and signed by the proprietor or one of the proprietors of the hackney carriage in respect of which such licence is applied for; and in every such requisition shall be truly stated the name and surname and place of abode of the person applying for such licence, and of every proprietor or part proprietor of such carriage, or person concerned, either solely or in partnership with any other person, in the keeping, employing, or letting to hire of such carriage; and any person who, on applying for such licence, states in such requisition the name of any person who is not a proprietor or part proprietor of such carriage, or who is not concerned as aforesaid in the keeping, employing, or letting to hire of such carriage, and also any person who wilfully omits to specify truly in such requisition as aforesaid the name of any person who is a proprietor or part proprietor of such carriage, or who is concerned as aforesaid in the keeping, employing, or letting to hire of such carriage, shall be liable to a penalty not exceeding **level 1** on the standard scale.

[Town Police Clauses Act 1847, s 40 as amended by the Criminal Justice Act 1967, Sch 3 and the Criminal Justice Act 1982, ss 38 and 46.]

7.11547 **41. What shall be specified in the licences** In every such licence shall be specified the name and surname and place of abode of every person who is a proprietor or part proprietor of the hackney carriage in respect of which such licence is granted, or who is concerned, either solely or in partnership with any other person, in the keeping, employing, or letting to hire of any such carriage, and also the number of such licence which shall correspond with the number to be painted or marked on the plates to be fixed on such carriage, together with such other particulars as the commissioners think fit.

[Town Police Clauses Act 1847, s 41.]

7.11548 **42. Licences to be registered** Every licence shall be made out by the clerk of the commissioners, and duly entered in a book to be provided by him for that purpose; and in such book shall be contained columns or places for entries to be made of every offence committed by any proprietor or driver or person attending such carriage; and any person may at any reasonable time inspect such book, without fee or reward.

[Town Police Clauses Act 1847, s 42.]

7.11549 **43. Licence to be in force for one year only** Every licence so to be granted shall be under the common seal of the commissioners, if incorporated, or, if not incorporated, shall be signed by two or more of the commissioners, and shall not include more than one carriage so licensed, and shall be in force for one year only from the day of the date of such licence or until the next general licensing meeting, in case any general licensing day be appointed by the commissioners.

[Town Police Clauses Act 1847, s 43.]

7.11550 **44. Notice to be given by proprietors of hackney carriage of any change of abode** So often as any person named in any such licence as the proprietor or one of the proprietors, or as being concerned, either solely or in partnership with any person, in the keeping, employing, or letting to hire of any such carriage, changes his place of abode, he shall, within seven days next after such change, give notice thereof in writing, signed by him, to the commissioners, specifying in such notice his new place of abode; and he shall at the same time produce such licence at the office of the commissioners, who shall by their clerk, or some other officer, endorse thereon and sign a memorandum specifying the particulars of such change; and any person named in any such licence as aforesaid as the proprietor, or one of the proprietors, of any hackney carriage, or as being concerned as aforesaid, who changes his place of abode and neglects or wilfully omits to give notice of such change, or to produce such licence in order that such memorandum as aforesaid may be endorsed thereon, within the time and in the manner limited and directed by this or the special Act, shall be liable to a penalty not exceeding **level 1** on the standard scale.

[Town Police Clauses Act 1847, s 44 as amended by the Criminal Law Act 1977, s 31 and the Criminal Justice Act 1982, s 46.]

7.11551 **45. Penalty for plying for hire without a licence**[1] If the proprietor or part proprietor of any carriage, or any person so concerned as aforesaid, permits the same to be used as a hackney carriage plying for hire within the prescribed distance without having obtained a licence as aforesaid for such carriage, or during the time that such licence is suspended as hereinafter provided, or if any person be found driving, standing, or plying for hire[2] with any carriage within the prescribed distance for which such licence as aforesaid has not been previously obtained, or without having the number of such carriage corresponding with the number of the licence openly displayed on such carriage, every such person so offending shall for every such offence be liable to a penalty not exceeding **level 4** on the standard scale.

[Town Police Clauses Act 1847, s 45 as amended by the Criminal Justice Act 1967, Sch 3 and the Criminal Justice Act 1982, ss 39 and 46 and Sch 3.]

---

1 In *Stockton-on-Tees Borough Council v Fidler* [2010] EWHC 2430 (Admin), 175 JP 49 it was held that, on a true construction of s 45 of the 1847 Act a person performing any of the acts prohibited by that section, namely, standing or plying for hire, was guilty of an offence unless licensed by the local authority for the area in which the acts took place. A hackney carriage licensed by authority B might not be used to stand or ply for hire outside the area of authority B. It was clearly an offence for a hackney carriage to stand or ply for hire outside the area for which it was licensed.

In *Dudley Metropolitan Borough Council v Arif* [2011] EWHC 3880 (Admin), [2012] RTR 261 the defendant private hire driver was outside a cinema when he was approached by two females. One of them asked him to take them to a particular destination. The defendant nodded, did not ask for her name or whether or not she had booked the taxi and took them to their specified destination and charged a £10 fare. During the journey he radioed his base to the effect that he had picked up a fare. The passengers were licensing investigators. When an enforcement officer visited the defendant's operator's office it was found that a booking had been made in the name of a female from the same cinema to the same destination at the same time, and this had been allocated to the defendant's vehicle. When he was interviewed under caution the defendant said the fare was pre-booked, but he conceded he had not asked for a name. The justices did not reject the booking evidence as "manufactured" and they were not persuaded that the defendant had been "plying for hire". In their view, given the way he had been approached it had been reasonable for him to assume that this was the fare that had been booked and it was unreasonable to expect him to have made any further inquiry.

It was held on appeal by way of case stated that the authorities showed that the question whether or not a particular vehicle is playing for hire is "largely one of degree and therefore fact". In *Nottingham City Council v Woodings* [1994] RTR 72, DC, the question posed was "Does the driver of a marked minicab . . . ply for hire . . . if he, without more, is approached by a member of the public and then enters into and/or concludes negotiation for the hire of the vehicle". The question was answered in the affirmative. There was this distinction, however, between the present case and *Woodings*. In the latter, the prospective passengers had asked the driver if he "was free to carry them" and he had answered affirmatively. Further, in *Woodings* there had been no question of a bona fide mistake. The court adopted the following formulation of the principles stated in *Woodings*:

(a) A carriage cannot accurately be said to ply for hire unless two conditions are satisfied.

(1) There must be a soliciting or waiting to secure passengers by the driver or other person in control without any previous contract with them, and
(2) The owner or person in control who is engaged or authorises the soliciting or waiting must be in possession of a carriage for which he is soliciting or waiting to obtain passengers: *Sales v Lake* [1922] 1 KB 553.
(b) A vehicle plies for hire if the person in control of the vehicle exhibits the vehicle and makes a present open offer to the public, an offer which can be accepted, for example, by a member of the public stepping into the vehicle: *Cogley v Sherwood* [1959] 2 QB 311 at 331.

The actus reus of the offence was "driving, standing or plying for hire with any carriage within the prescribed distance", and "what the driver thought he was doing relevant to whether he was 'plying for hire'". Otherwise, even if the driver, on being approached by the two females, had asked if they had pre-booked and they said that they had, and even if he had asked for their names, those questions and answers would have been relevant to sentence only if there had not, in fact, been a pre-booking.

2 The driver of a marked mini-cab, not licensed to ply for hire as a hackney carriage did ply for hire when telling a prospective passenger that he was free (*Nottingham City Council v Woodings* [1994] RTR 72).

7.11552 **46. Drivers not to act without first obtaining a licence** No person shall act as driver of any hackney carriage licensed in pursuance of this or the special Act to ply for hire within the prescribed distance without first obtaining a licence from the commissioners, which licence shall be registered by the clerk to the commissioners, and such fee as the commissioners may determine shall be paid for the same; and every such licence shall be in force until the same is revoked except during the time that the same may be suspended as after mentioned.

[Town Police Clauses Act 1847, s 46 as amended by the Local Government, Planning and Land Act 1980, s 1(6), Sch 6.]

7.11553 **47. Penalty on drivers[1] acting without licence, or proprietors employing unlicensed drivers** If any person acts as such driver as aforesaid without having obtained such licence, or during the time that his licence is suspended, or if he lend or part with his licence, except to the proprietor of the hackney carriage, or if the proprietor of any such hackney carriage employ any person as the driver thereof who has not obtained such licence, or during the time that his licence is suspended, as herein-after provided, every such driver and every such proprietor shall for every such offence respectively be liable to a penalty not exceeding **level 3** on the standard scale.

[Town Police Clauses Act 1847, s 47 as amended by the Criminal Justice Act 1967, Sch 3 and the Criminal Justice Act 1982, ss 35, 38 and 46.]

1 This offence is committed if the vehicle is licensed as a hackney carriage even if it is not, at the time, plying for hire (*Yates v Gates* [1970] 2 QB 27, [1970] 1 All ER 754, 134 JP 274). The Town Police Clauses Act 1889, s 4(2), provides that the word "driver" or "drivers", when used in ss 37, 40–52, 54, 58 and 60–67, shall be deemed to include every conductor of any omnibus.

7.11554 **48. Proprietor to retain licences of drivers,[1] and to produce the same before justices on complaint** In every case in which the proprietor of any such hackney carriage permits or employs any licensed person to act as the driver thereof, such proprietor shall cause to be delivered to him, and shall retain in his possession, the licence of such driver, while such driver remains in his employ; and in all cases of complaint, where the proprietor of a hackney carriage is summoned to attend before a justice, or to produce the driver, the proprietor so summoned shall also produce the licence of such driver, if he be then in his employ; and if any driver complained of be adjudged guilty of the offence alleged against him, such justice shall make an endorsement upon the licence of such driver, stating the nature of the offence and amount of the penalty inflicted; and if any such proprietor neglect to have delivered to him and to retain in his possession the licence of any driver while such driver remains in his employ, or if he refuse or neglect to produce such licence as aforesaid, such proprietor shall for every such offence be liable to a penalty not exceeding **level 1** on the standard scale.

[Town Police Clauses Act 1847, s 48 as amended by the Criminal Law Act 1977, s 31 and the Criminal Justice Act 1982, s 46.]

1 See definition of "driver" noted to s 47, ante.

7.11555 **49. Proprietor to return licence to drivers except in case of misconduct** When any driver leaves the service of the proprietor by whom he is employed without having been guilty of any misconduct, such proprietor shall forthwith return to such driver the licence belonging to him; but if such driver have been guilty of any misconduct, the proprietor shall not return his licence, but shall give him notice of the complaint which he intends to prefer against him, and shall forthwith summon such driver to appear before any justice to answer the said complaint; and such justice, having the necessary parties before him, shall inquire into and determine the matter of complaint, and if upon inquiry it appear that the licence of such driver has been improperly withheld, such justice shall direct the immediate re-delivery of such licence, and award such sum of money as he thinks proper to be paid by such proprietor to such driver by way of compensation.

[Town Police Clauses Act 1847, s 49.]

7.11556 **50. Revocation of licences of proprietors or drivers** The commissioners may, upon the conviction for the second time of the proprietor or driver of any such hackney carriage for any offence under the provisions of this or the special Act with respect to hackney carriages, or any byelaw made in pursuance thereof, suspend or revoke, as they deem right, the licence of any such proprietor or driver.

[Town Police Clauses Act 1847, s 50.]

7.11557 **51. Number of persons to be carried in a hackney carriage to be painted thereon[1]** No hackney carriage shall be used or employed or let to hire, or shall stand or ply for hire, within the prescribed distance, unless the number of persons to be carried by such hackney carriage, in words at length, and in form following, (that is to say,) "To carry . . . . . . . . . . . persons," be painted on a plate placed on some conspicuous place on the outside of such carriage, and in legible letters, so as to be clearly distinguishable from the colour of the ground whereon the same are painted, one inch in length, and of a proportionate breadth; and the driver of any such hackney carriage shall not be required to carry in or by such hackney carriage a greater number of persons than the number painted thereon.

[Town Police Clauses Act 1847, s 51.]

[1] The provisions in this section in relation to tramcars and trolley vehicles were repealed by the Transport Charges etc. (Miscellaneous Provisions) Act 1954, ss 14(1), 15(1) and Sch 2 Part IV (which provisions were in turn repealed by the Transport and Works Act 1992, s 68(1), Sch 4, Pt I as from 26 February 1998).

7.11558 **52. Penalty for neglect to exhibit the number, or for refusal to carry the prescribed number**[1] If the proprietor of any hackney carriage permit the same to be used, employed, or let to hire, or if any person stand or ply for hire with such carriage, without having the number of persons to be carried thereby painted and exhibited in manner aforesaid, or if the driver[2] of any such hackney carriage refuse, when required by the hirer thereof, to carry in or by such hackney carriage the number of persons painted thereon, or any less number, every proprietor or driver so offending shall be liable to a penalty not exceeding **level 1** on the standard scale.

[Town Police Clauses Act 1847, s 52 as amended by the Criminal Law Act 1977, s 31 and the Criminal Justice Act 1982, s 46.]

[1] The provisions in this section in relation to tramcars and trolley vehicles were repealed by the Transport Charges etc. (Miscellaneous Provisions) Act 1954, ss 14(1), 15(1) and Sch 2 Part IV (which provisions were in turn repealed by the Transport and Works Act 1992, s 68(1), Sch 4, Pt I as from 26 February 1998).

[2] See definition of "driver" noted to s 47 ante.

7.11559 **53. Penalty on driver for refusing to drive** A driver of a hackney carriage standing at any of the stands for hackney carriages appointed by the commissioners, or in any street, who refuses or neglects, without reasonable excuse, to drive such carriage to any place within the prescribed distance, or the distance to be appointed by any byelaw of the commissioners, not exceeding the prescribed distance, to which he is directed to drive by the person hiring or wishing to hire such carriage, shall for every such offence be liable to a penalty not exceeding **level 2** on the standard scale.

[Town Police Clauses Act 1847, s 53 as amended by the Criminal Justice Act 1967, Sch 3 and the Criminal Justice Act 1982, ss 39 and 46 and Sch 3.]

7.11560 **54. Penalty for demanding[1] more than the sum[2] agreed for** If the proprietor or driver of any such hackney carriage, or if any other person on his behalf, agree beforehand with any person hiring such hackney carriage to take for any job a sum less than the fare allowed by this or the special Act, or any byelaw made thereunder, such proprietor or driver shall be liable to a penalty not exceeding **level 1** on the standard scale if he exact or demand for such job more than the fare so agreed upon.

[Town Police Clauses Act 1847, s 54 as amended by the Criminal Law Act 1977, s 31 and the Criminal Justice Act 1982, s 46.]

[1] See definition of "driver" noted to s 47, ante.

[2] The Town Police Clauses Act 1889, s 4(3), provides that for the purposes of ss 54, 58 and 66, the fare is deemed to be that allowed by the 1847 Act or a byelaw thereunder.

7.11561 **55. Agreement to pay more than the legal fare** No agreement whatever made with the driver, or with any person having or pretending to have the care of any such hackney carriage, for the payment of more than the fare allowed by any byelaw made under this or the special Act, shall be binding on the person making the same; and any such person may, notwithstanding such agreement, refuse, on discharging such hackney carriage, to pay any sum beyond the fare allowed as aforesaid; and if any person actually pay to the driver of any such hackney carriage, whether in pursuance of any such agreement or otherwise, any sum exceeding the fare to which such driver was entitled, the person paying the same shall be entitled, on complaint made against such driver before any justice of the peace, to recover back the sum paid beyond the proper fare, and moreover such driver shall be liable to a penalty for such exaction not exceeding **level 3** on the standard scale[1]; and in default of the repayment by such driver of such excess of fare, or of payment of the said penalty, such justice shall forthwith commit such driver to prison, there to remain for any time not exceeding one month, unless the said excess of fare and the said penalty be sooner paid.

[Town Police Clauses Act 1847, s 55 as amended by the Criminal Law Act 1977, s 31 and the Criminal Justice Act 1982, ss 39 and 46 and Sch 3.]

[1] The excess fare is recoverable as a civil debt; provision in the section for imprisonment in default of paying the fine is now superseded by the provisions of the Magistrates' Courts Act 1980, Pt III. The power of fixing the fare is, by s 37 *and the Public Health Act 1875*, s 171, limited to the fare for drivers within the urban district. The offence of taking more than the proper fare is committed at the arrival point, which may be outside the jurisdiction of the justices (*Ely v Godfrey* (1922) 86 JP 82). As to public service vehicle fares, see the Public Passenger Vehicles Act 1981, s 33. In *House v Reynolds* [1977] 1 All ER 689, 141 JP 202, a defendant who required persons telephoning to hire a taxicab to pay a "booking fee" in addition to the fare was properly convicted under s 55, but his appeal allowed against a conviction under s 58.

7.11562 **56. Agreements to carry passengers a discretionary distance for a fixed sum** If the proprietor or driver of any such hackney carriage, or if any other person on his behalf, agree with any person to carry in or by such hackney carriage persons not exceeding in number the number so painted on such carriage as aforesaid, for a distance to be in the discretion of such proprietor or driver, and for a sum agreed upon, such proprietor or driver shall be liable to a penalty not exceeding **level 1** on the standard scale if the distance which he carries such persons be under that to which they were entitled to be carried for the sum so agreed upon, according to the fare allowed by this or the special Act, or any byelaw made in pursuance thereof.

[Town Police Clauses Act 1847, s 56 as amended by the Criminal Law Act 1977, s 31 and the Criminal Justice Act 1982, s 46.]

7.11563 **57. Deposit to be made for carriages required to wait** When any hackney carriage is hired and taken to any place, and the driver thereof is required by the hirer there to wait with such hackney carriage, such driver may demand and receive from such hirer his fare for driving to such place, and also a sum equal to the fare of such carriage for the period, as a deposit over and above such fare, during which he is required to wait as aforesaid, or if no fare for time be fixed by the byelaws, then the sum of 7p for every half hour during which he is so required to wait, which deposit shall be accounted for by such driver when such hackney carriage is finally discharged by such hirer; and if any such driver who has received any such deposit as aforesaid refuses to wait as aforesaid, or goes away or permits such hackney carriage to be driven or taken away without the consent of such hirer, before the expiration of the time for which such deposit was made, or if such driver on the final discharge of such hackney carriage refuse duly to account for such deposit, every such driver so offending shall be liable to a penalty not exceeding **level 1** on the standard scale.

[Town Police Clauses Act 1847, s 57 as amended by the Criminal Law Act 1977, s 31 and the Criminal Justice Act 1982, s 46.]

7.11564 **58. Penalty on proprietors etc convicted of overcharging** Every proprietor or driver[1] of any such hackney carriage who is convicted of taking as a fare a greater sum than is authorized[2] by any byelaw made under this or the special Act shall be liable to a penalty not exceeding **level 3** on the standard scale, and such penalty may be recovered before one justice; and in the conviction of such proprietor or driver an order may be included for payment of the sum so overcharged, over and above the penalty and costs; and such overcharge shall be returned to the party aggrieved.

[Town Police Clauses Act 1847, s 58 as amended by the Criminal Justice Act 1967, Sch 3 and the Criminal Justice Act 1982, ss 39 and 46 and Sch 3.]

1 See definition of "driver" noted to s 47, ante.

2 The excess fare is recoverable as a civil debt; provision in the section for imprisonment in default of paying the fine is now superseded by the provisions of the Magistrates' Courts Act 1980, Pt III. The power of fixing the fare is, by s 37 and the Public Health Act 1875, s 171, limited to the fare for drivers within the urban district. The offence of taking more than the proper fare is committed at the arrival point, which may be outside the jurisdiction of the justices (*Ely v Godfrey* (1922) 86 JP 82). As to public service vehicle fares, see the Public Passenger Vehicles Act 1981, s 33. In *House v Reynolds* [1977] 1 All ER 689, 141 JP 202, a defendant who required persons telephoning to hire a taxicab to pay a "booking fee" in addition to the fare was properly convicted under s 55, but his appeal allowed against a conviction under s 58.

7.11565 **59. Penalty for permitting persons to ride without consent[1] of hirer** Any proprietor or driver of any such hackney carriage which is hired who permits or suffers any person to be carried in or upon or about such hackney carriage during such hire, without the express consent of the person hiring the same, shall be liable to a penalty not exceeding **level 1** on the standard scale.

[Town Police Clauses Act 1847, s 59 as amended by the Criminal Law Act 1977, s 31 and the Criminal Justice Act 1982, s 46.]

1 This means positive consent not mere acquiescence (*Yates v Gates* [1970] 2 QB 27, [1970] 1 All ER 754, 134 JP 274).

7.11566 **60. No unauthorised person to act as driver** No person authorized by the proprietor of any hackney carriage to act as driver[1] of such carriage shall suffer any other person to act as driver of such carriage without the consent of the proprietor thereof; and no person, whether licensed or not, shall act as driver of any such carriage without the consent of the proprietor; and any person so suffering another person to act as driver, and any person so acting as driver without such consent as aforesaid, shall be liable to a penalty not exceeding **level 1** on the standard scale for every such offence.

[Town Police Clauses Act 1847, s 60 as amended by the Criminal Law Act 1977, s 31 and the Criminal Justice Act 1982, s 46.]

1 See definition of "driver" noted to s 47, ante.

7.11567 **61. Penalty on drivers for drunkenness, furious driving, etc** If the driver[1] or any other person having or pretending to have the care of any such hackney carriage be intoxicated while driving, or if any such driver or other person by wanton and furious driving, or by any other wilful misconduct, injure or endanger any person in his life, limbs, or property, he shall be liable to a penalty not exceeding **level 1** on the standard scale[2].

[Town Police Clauses Act 1847, s 61 as amended by the Criminal Law Act 1977, s 31, the Criminal Justice Act 1982, s 46 and the Statute Law (Repeals) Act 1989, Sch 1.]

1 See definition of "driver" noted to s 47, ante.

2 Provisions in the section, as originally enacted, for imprisonment in default of paying the fine, are now superseded by provisions in the Magistrates' Courts Act 1980, Pt III in PART I: MAGISTRATES' COURTS, PROCEDURE, ante.

7.11568 **62. Penalties in case of carriages being unattended at places of public resort** If the driver[1] of any such hackney carriage leave it in any street or at any place of public resort or entertainment, whether it be hired or not, without some one proper to take care of it, any constable may drive away such hackney carriage and deposit it, and the horse or horses harnessed thereto, at some neighbouring livery stable or other place of safe custody; and such driver shall be liable to a penalty not exceeding **level 1** on the standard scale for such offence; and in default of payment of the said penalty upon conviction, and of the expences of taking and keeping the said hackney carriage and horse or horses, the same, together with the harness belonging thereto, or any of them, shall be sold by order of the justice before whom such conviction is made, and after deducting from the produce of such sale the amount of the said penalty, and of all costs and expences, as well of the proceedings before such justice as of the taking, keeping, and sale of the said hackney carriage, and of the said horse or horses and harness, the surplus (if any) of the said produce shall be paid to the proprietor of such hackney carriage.

[Town Police Clauses Act 1847, s 62 as amended by the Criminal Law Act 1977, s 31 and the Criminal Justice Act 1982, s 46.]

1 See definition of "driver" noted to s 47, ante.

7.11569 **63. Compensation for damage done by driver** In every case in which any hurt or damage has been caused to any person or property as aforesaid by the driver[1] of any carriage let to hire, the justice before whom such driver has been convicted may direct that the proprietor of such carriage shall pay such a sum, not exceeding five pounds, as appears to the justice a reasonable compensation for such hurt or damage; and every proprietor who pays any such compensation as aforesaid may recover the same from the driver, and such compensation shall be recoverable from such proprietor, and by him from such driver, as damages.

[Town Police Clauses Act 1847, s 63 as amended by the Criminal Justice Act 1982, ss 38 and 46.]

1 See definition of "driver" noted to s 47, ante.

7.11570 **64.** Any driver of any hackney carriage who suffers the same to stand for hire across any street or alongside of any other hackney carriage, or who refuses to give way, if he conveniently can, to any other carriage, or who obstructs or hinders the driver of any other carriage in taking up or setting down any person into or from such other carriage, or who wrongfully in a forcible manner prevents or endeavours to prevent the driver[1] of any other hackney carriage from being hired, shall be liable to a penalty not exceeding level 1 on the standard scale.

[Town Police Clauses Act 1847, s 64 as amended by the Criminal Law Act 1977, s 31 and the Criminal Justice Act 1982, s 46.]

1 See definition of "driver" noted to s 47, ante.

7.11571 **65. Compensation to drivers attending to answer complaints not substantiated** If the driver of any such hackney carriage be summoned or brought before any justice to answer any complaint or information touching or concerning any offence alleged to have been committed by such driver against the provisions of this or the special Act, or any byelaw made thereunder, and such complaint or information be afterwards withdrawn or quashed or dismissed, or if such driver be acquitted of the offence charged against him, the said justice, if he think fit, may order the complainant or informant to pay to the said driver such compensation for his loss of time in attending the said justice touching or concerning such complaint or information as to the said justice seems reasonable;

[Town Police Clauses Act 1847, s 65 amended by the Statute Law (Repeals) Act 1989, Sch 1.]

7.11572 **66. Fare unpaid may be recovered as a penalty** If any person refuse to pay on demand to any proprietor or driver of any hackney carriage the fare allowed by this or the special Act, or any byelaw made thereunder, such fare may, together with costs, be recovered before one justice[1] as a penalty.

[Town Police Clauses Act 1847, s 66.]

1 The fare, though recoverable as a penalty, is really only a debt. The amount is recoverable as a civil debt under the Magistrates' Courts Act 1980, s 58, and not by conviction under s 76 (*R v Kerswill* [1895] 1 QB 1, 59 JP 342). See also *R v Master (or Martin)* (1869) LR 4 QB 285. The demand may be by the proprietor, driver or conductor to see note 1 to s 47, ante. The fare is deemed to be the fare allowed by the 1847 Act or byelaws thereunder (Town Police Clauses Act 1889, s 4(3)).

7.11573 **68. Byelaws for regulating hackney carriages[1]** The commissioners may from time to time (subject to the restrictions of this and the special Act) make byelaws[2] for all or any of the purposes following; (that is to say,)

For regulating the conduct of the proprietors and drivers of hackney carriages plying within the prescribed distance in their several employments, and determining whether such drivers shall wear any and what badges, and for regulating the hours within which they may exercise their calling:

For regulating the manner in which the number of each carriage, corresponding with the number of its licence, shall be displayed:

For regulating the number of persons to be carried by such hackney carriages, and in what manner such number is to be shown on such carriage, and what number of horses or other animals is to draw the same, and the placing of check strings to the carriages, and the holding of the same by the driver, and how such hackney carriages are to be furnished or provided:

For fixing the stands of such hackney carriages, and the distance to which they may be compelled to take passengers, not exceeding the prescribed distance:

For fixing the rates or fares, as well for time as distance, to be paid for such hackney carriages within the prescribed distance, and for securing the due publication of such fares:

For securing the safe custody and re-delivery of any property accidentally left in hackney carriages, and fixing the charges to be made in respect thereof.

---

[1] The provisions in this section in relation to tramcars and trolley vehicles were repealed by the Transport Charges etc. (Miscellaneous Provisions) Act 1954, ss 14(1), 15(1) and Sch 2 Part IV (which provisions were in turn repealed by the Transport and Works Act 1992, s 68(1), Sch 4, Pt I as from 26 February 1998).

[2] This section gives power to make byelaws, and it is supplemented by s 6 of the Town Police Clauses Act 1889. Maximum fine for a breach of the byelaws is **level 2** on the standard scale and in case of a continuing offence a further penalty not exceeding £2 for each day after written notice of the offence from the local authority (Public Health Act 1875, s 183, as amended by the Criminal Law Act 1977, s 31(2) and the Criminal Justice Act 1982, s 46. Some of these byelaws may relate to horse-drawn vehicles only and some to motor vehicles as well (*Neal v Guy* [1923] 2 KB 451, 92 JP 119). A committee of a town council have no power to cause summonses to be issued to cabdrivers to appear before them and answer complaints of offences against byelaws (*Wiseman v Manchester Corpn* (1886) 3 TLR 12). As to tramcars or trolley vehicles, see the Transport Charges, etc, (Miscellaneous Provisions) Act 1954, Sch 2, Pt IV. As to plying for hire while a vehicle is in a parking place, and byelaws as to persons waiting to enter public service vehicles, see the Road Traffic Regulation Act 1984, and the Public Health Act 1925, s 75.

# UNIFORMS

**Contents**



## Uniforms Act 1894

(57 & 58 Vict c 45)

7.11574 **2. Military uniforms not to be worn without authority** (1) It shall not be lawful for any person not serving in Her Majesty's military forces[1] to wear without Her Majesty's permission the uniform of any of those forces, or any dress having the appearance or bearing any of the regimental or other distinctive marks of any such uniform:

Provided that this enactment shall not prevent . . . any persons from wearing any uniform or dress in the course of a stage play performed in a place duly licensed or authorised for the public performance of stage plays, or in the course of a music hall or circus performance, or in the course of any *bona fide* military representation.

(2) If any person contravenes this section he shall be liable on summary conviction to a fine not exceeding **level 3** on the standard scale.

[Uniforms Act 1894, s 2 as amended by the Statute Law Revision Act 1908, Sch, the Criminal Justice Act 1967, Sch 3 and the Criminal Justice Act 1982, ss 38 and 46.]

---

1 Sections 2 and 3 apply also to the Air Force: Air Force (Application of Enactments) (No 2) Order 1918, SI 1918/548.

7.11575 **3. Penalty for bringing contempt on uniform** If any person not serving in Her Majesty's naval or military forces[1] wears without Her Majesty's permission the uniform of any of those forces, or any dress having the appearance or bearing any of the regimental or other distinctive marks of any such uniform, in such a manner and under such circumstances as to be likely to bring contempt upon that uniform, or employs any other person so to wear that uniform or dress, he shall be liable on summary conviction to a fine not exceeding **level 3** on the standard scale, or to imprisonment for a term not exceeding **one month**.

[Uniforms Act 1894, s 3 as amended by the Criminal Justice Act 1967, Sch 3 and the Criminal Justice Act 1982, ss 38 and 46.]

---

1 Sections 2 and 3 apply also to the Air Force: Air Force (Application of Enactments) (No 2) Order 1918, SI 1918/548.

7.11576 **4.** In this Act—

"Her Majesty's Military Forces" has the same meaning as in the Armed Forces Act 2006;

"Her Majesty's Naval Forces" does not include any Commonwealth force.

[Uniforms Act 1894, s 4 as substituted by the Armed Forces Act 1981, Sch 3 and amended by the Armed Forces Act 2006, Sch 16.]

## Other Uniforms

7.11577 **Official Secrets Act 1920** The unauthorised use of any official uniform used for gaining admission to a "prohibited place" is an offence under s 1 of this Act (this Part: title Official Secrets, ante).

7.11578 **Chartered Associations (Protection of Names and Uniforms) Act 1926** Unauthorised use of uniform, etc, of an association protected by Order in Council under this Act is prohibited (this Part: title Copyright, Designs and Patents, ante).

7.11579 **Ministry of Defence Police Act 1987** Impersonation of a member of the Ministry of Defence Police with intent to deceive etc is an offence against this Act (s 5).

7.11580 **Merchant Shipping Act 1995** Unauthorised wearing of merchant navy uniform is an offence under s 57 of this Act (see the Merchant Shipping Act 1995 in Part VI: Transport, title Merchant Shipping ante).

7.11581 **Police Act 1996, Railways and Transport Safety Act 2003** Impersonation of a member of a police force or the British Transport Police with intent to deceive etc is an offence against these Acts (ss 90 and 68 respectively, this Part: title Police, ante).

# VAGRANTS

## Vagrancy Act 1824

(5 Geo 4 c 83)

7.11582 **3. Persons committing certain offences, how to be punished** Every person wandering abroad, or placing himself or herself in any public[1] place, street, highway, court, or passage, to beg[2] or gather alms, or causing or procuring or encouraging any child or children[3] so to do; shall be deemed an idle and disorderly person within the true intent and meaning of this Act; and, subject to section 70 of the Criminal Justice Act 1982[4], it shall be lawful for any justice of the peace to commit such offender (being thereof convicted before him by his own view, or by the confession of such offender, or by the evidence on oath of one or more credible witness or witnesses) to imprisonment[5] for any time not exceeding **one calendar month**[4].*

[Vagrancy Act 1824, s 3 as amended by the Prison Act 1865, s 56, the Statute Law Revision (No 2) Act 1888, the National Assistance Act 1948, Sch 7, the Criminal Justice Act 1948, s 1, the Criminal Justice Act 1982, Sch 14 and the Statute Law (Repeals) Act 1989, Sch 1.]

* **Words substituted by the Criminal Justice Act 2003, Sch 32 from a date to be appointed.**

1 Any place of public resort or recreation ground belonging to, or under the control of, the local authority, and any unfenced ground adjoining or abutting upon any street in an urban district, shall be deemed to be an open and public space (Public Health Acts Amendment Act 1907, s 81).

2 Workmen on strike seeking assistance are not begging (*Pointon v Hill* (1884) 12 QBD 306, 48 JP 341; *Mathers v Penfold* [1915] 1 KB 514, 79 JP 225).

3 See also the Children and Young Persons Act 1933, s 4, ante. As to age and appearance of a child, see *R v Viasani* (1867) 31 JP 260.

4 For certain of the offences in this section the power to sentence a person to imprisonment has been abolished by the Criminal Justice Act 1982, s 70; see note 8 to s 4, post.

5 The Magistrates' Courts Act 1980, s 34(3), as amended, provides an alternative to imprisonment of a fine not exceeding **level 3** on the standard scale. If the conviction is before a single justice, s 121(5) of the 1980 Act limits imprisonment to fourteen days and a fine to £1. See also note 5 supra as to limitation of the power to imprison.

7.11583 **4. Persons committing certain offences to be deemed rogues and vagabonds** Every person committing any of the offences[1] herein-before mentioned, after having been convicted as an idle and disorderly person; every person wandering abroad and lodging[2] in any barn or outhouse, or in any deserted or unoccupied building, or in the open air, or under a tent, or in any cart or waggon[3] and not giving a good account of himself or herself; every person wilfully, openly, lewdly, and obscenely exposing his person, with intent to insult any female, every person wandering abroad, and endeavouring by the exposure of wounds or deformities to obtain or gather alms; every person going about as a gatherer or collector of alms, or endeavouring to procure charitable contributions of any nature or kind, under any false or fraudulent pretence; every person being found in or upon any dwelling house[4], warehouse, coach-house, stable, or outhouse, or in any enclosed[5] yard, garden, or area for any unlawful purpose[6] and every person apprehended as an idle and disorderly person, and violently resisting any constable, or other peace officer so apprehending him or her, and being subsequently convicted of the offence for which he or she shall have been so apprehended; shall be deemed a rogue and vagabond[7] within the true intent and meaning of this Act: and, subject to section 70 of the Criminal Justice Act 1982[8], it shall be lawful for any justice of the peace to commit such offender (being thereof convicted before him by the confession of such offender, or by the evidence on oath of one or more credible witness or witnesses) to imprisonment[9] for any time not exceeding **three calendar months**[9].* **

[Vagrancy Act 1824, s 4 as amended by the Prison Act 1865, s 56, the Prevention of Crimes Act 1871, s 15, the Statute Law Revision (No 2) Act 1888, the Criminal Justice Act 1925, Sch 3, the Vagrancy Act 1935, s 1(2), the National Assistance Act 1948, Sch 7, the Criminal Justice Act 1948, s 1(2), the Criminal Law Act 1967, Sch 2, the Theft Act 1968, Sch 3, the Indecent Displays (Control) Act 1981, Sch, the Criminal Attempts Act 1981, s 8 and Sch, the Criminal Justice Act 1982, Sch 14, the Public Order Act 1986 Sch 3 and the Statute Law (Repeals) Act 1989, Sch 1.]

* **Words substituted and sub-s (2) inserted by the Criminal Justice Act 2003, Sch 32 from a date to be appointed.**

** **Repealed in relation to Northern Ireland by the Sexual Offences Act 2003, Sch 6.**

1 This section can properly be applied to an occupier of premises in respect of an offence on those premises, if he falls within the language of the relevant charging provisions; see *Wood v Metropolitan Police Comr* [1986] 2 All ER 570, [1986] 1 WLR 796.

2 This section has been amended by the Vagrancy Act 1935 to have effect as follows; a person wandering abroad and lodging as aforesaid shall not be deemed by virtue of the said enactment a rogue and vagabond within the meaning of the said Act unless it is proved either:

(a) that, in relation to the occasion on which he lodged as aforesaid, he had been directed to a reasonably accessible place of shelter and failed to apply for, or refused, accommodation there;

(b) that he is a person who persistently wanders abroad and, notwithstanding that a place of shelter is reasonably accessible, lodges or attempts to lodge as aforesaid; or

(c) that by, or in the course of, lodging as aforesaid he caused damage to property, infection with vermin, or other offensive consequence, or that he lodged as aforesaid in such circumstances as to appear to be likely so to do.

In this subsection the expression "a place of shelter" means a place where provision is regularly made for giving (free of charge) accommodation for the night to such persons as apply therefor.

3 The Vagrancy Act 1935, s 1(4), provides that the reference to a person lodging under a tent or in a cart or waggon shall not be deemed to include a person lodging under a tent or in a cart or waggon with or in which he travels.

4 The occupier's name need not be given in the information but the address must be (*Hollyhomes v Hind* [1944] KB 571, [1944] 2 All ER 8, 108 JP 190). "Dwellinghouse" includes an entrance hall common to several dwellings (ibid).

5 A yard, garden or area may be enclosed although access can be gained through spaces left between buildings, an archway, an open gate, etc (*Goodhew v Morton* [1962] 2 All ER 771, 126 JP 369). Railway sidings or a railway yard a mile

long and a quarter mile wide are not within the section; the essential feature of a yard is that it should be a relatively small area ancillary to a building (*Knott v Blackburn* [1944] KB 77, [1944] 1 All ER 116, 108 JP 19; *Quatromini v Peck* [1972] 3 All ER 521, 136 JP 854). University grounds and buildings, the boundaries of which are punctuated by roads and paths, are much larger than that which was contemplated by the legislation and do not consist of an "enclosed" area within s 4; the word "area" must be read in the context of the preceding words "enclosed yard, garden or area" and not meaning any space, and the 1824 cannot be interpreted differently to take account of changes in the times: *Akhurst v Enfield Magistrates' Court* [2009] EWHC 806 (Admin), 173 JP 499.

The words "enclosed yard, garden or area" connote an area which is in the open air; accordingly, enclosed area does not include a room within a building (*Talbot v DPP* [2000] 1 WLR 1102, [2000] 2 Cr App Rep 60, 164 JP 169, DC).

6 The unlawful purpose must be the commission of some offence which would subject the party to criminal proceedings, and not an act of immorality (*Hayes v Stevenson* (1860) 25 JP 39). Hiding from the police to escape detection for a criminal offence which has already occurred cannot constitute an unlawful purpose; the defendant must, at the time he was seen, found or discovered, have had the necessary unlawful purpose (*L v Crown Prosecution Service* [2007] EWHC 1843 (Admin), [2008] Crim 216, 171 JP 635). The unlawful purpose need not be to commit a crime at the time or place where the defendant is found (*Re Joy* (1853) 22 LT Jo 80). The accused must be found on the premises but may be arrested elsewhere (*Moran v Jones* (1911) 75 JP 411; *R v Goodwin* [1944] KB 518, [1944] 1 All ER 506, 108 JP 159; *R v Lumsden* [1951] 2 KB 513, [1951] 1 All ER 1101, 115 JP 364). The actions of a man who at night looked through the windows of a ground floor bed sitting room with the intention of frightening a woman inside and causing her to fear some act of immediate violence were held to constitute an assault, and therefore amounted to an "unlawful purpose" (*Smith v Chief Superintendent, Woking Police Station* (1983) 76 Cr App Rep 234).

7 It is not necessary to constitute a man a rogue and vagabond that he should lead a wandering and vagabond life (*Monck v Hilton* (1877) 2 Ex D 268, 41 JP 214).

8 The Criminal Justice Act 1982, s 70 provides that where a person is convicted:

(a) under section 3 or 4 of this Act, of wandering abroad, or placing himself in any public place, street, highway, court, or passage, to beg or gather alms; or
(b) under section 4 of this Act—
 (i) of wandering abroad and lodging in any barn or outhouse, or in any deserted or unoccupied building, or in the open air, or under a tent, or in any cart or waggon, and not giving a good account of himself; or
 (ii) of wandering abroad, and endeavouring by the exposure of wounds and deformities to obtain or gather alms,

the court shall not have power to sentence him to imprisonment but shall have the power to fine him.

If a person deemed a rogue and vagabond by virtue of section 4 of the Act is thereafter guilty of an offence mentioned above, he shall be convicted of that offence under section 4 of the Act and accordingly—

(a) shall not be deemed an incorrigible rogue; and
(b) shall not be committed to the Crown Court,

by reason only of that conviction.

9 The Magistrates' Courts Act 1980, s 34(3), as amended, provided an alternative to imprisonment of a fine not exceeding **level 3** on the standard scale. If the conviction is before a single justice, s 121(5) of the 1980 Act limits imprisonment to fourteen days and a fine to £1. The Criminal Justice Act 1982, s 70, removes the power to imprison for certain offences under this section; see note 11 supra. The Criminal Justice Act 1991, s 26(5), limits the fine for sleeping rough (see s 70(*b*)(i) of the 1982 Act in note 11 supra) to **level 1** on the standard scale.

7.11584 **5. Who shall be deemed incorrigible rogues** Every person committing any offence against this Act which shall subject him or her to be dealt with as a rogue and vagabond, such person having been at some former time adjudged so to be, and duly convicted thereof[1]; shall, subject to section 70 of the Criminal Justice Act 1982[2], be deemed an incorrigible rogue within the true intent and meaning of this Act; and subject to section 70 of the Criminal Justice Act 1982[2], it shall be lawful for any justice of the peace to commit[3] such offender (being thereof convicted before him by the confession of such offender, or by the evidence on oath of one or more credible witness or witnesses,) to the Crown Court[4] either in custody or on bail.*

[Vagrancy Act 1824, s 5 as amended by the Criminal Justice Act 1948, Sch 10, the Criminal Justice Act 1967, s 20 and Sch 6, the Courts Act 1971, Sch 8, the Criminal Justice Act 1982, Sch 14 and the Statute Law (Repeals) Act 1989, Sch 1.]

---

* **Repealed by the Criminal Justice Act 2003, Sch 37 from a date to be appointed.**

1 Before a person can be dealt with as an incorrigible rogue, proof must be furnished of a previous conviction either for an offence for which he is deemed an idle and disorderly person, recording his previous conviction for a similar offence (*R v Johnson* [1909] 1 KB 439, 73 JP 135), or for an offence which brought him within the category of rogues and vagabonds (*R v Teesdale* (1927) 44 TLR 30, 91 JP 184). Two separate convictions as an idle and disorderly person without stating that the latter was for a second offence will not suffice (*R v Johnson* supra). Proof will usually be by an extract from the court register: Police and Criminal Evidence Act 1984, ss 73-75 (certificates of conviction etc.) and the Criminal Procedure Rules, Part 5; see also the Criminal Justice Act 1948, s 39, ante (fingerprints).

2 The Criminal Justice Act 1982, s 70 provides that where a person is convicted:

(a) under section 3 or 4 of this Act, of wandering abroad, or placing himself in any public place, street, highway, court, or passage, to beg or gather alms; or
(b) under section 4 of this Act—
 (i) of wandering abroad and lodging in any barn or outhouse, or in any deserted or unoccupied building, or in the open air, or under a tent, or in any cart or waggon, and not giving a good account of himself; or
 (ii) of wandering abroad, and endeavouring by the exposure of wounds and deformities to obtain or gather alms,

the court shall not have power to sentence him to imprisonment but shall have the power to fine him.

If a person deemed a rogue and vagabond by virtue of section 4 of the Act is thereafter guilty of an offence mentioned above, he shall be convicted of that offence under section 4 of the Act and accordingly—

(a) shall not be deemed an incorrigible rogue; and
(b) shall not be committed to the Crown Court,

*by reason only of that conviction.*

3 The Criminal Justice Act 1967, s 56, ante, applies; for documents see the Criminal Procedure Rules, r 28.10, in the *Key Materials*.

4 See s 10, post.

7.11585 **10. Power of Crown Court to punish rogues and vagabonds and incorrigible rogues** When any incorrigible rogues shall have been committed to the Crown Court, it shall be lawful for the Crown Court to examine into the circumstances of the case, and to order, if they think fit, that such offender be imprisoned[1] for any time not exceeding one year from the time of making such order.*

[Vagrancy Act 1824, s 10 as amended by the Criminal Justice Act 1948, Sch 10, the Criminal Justice Act 1967, Sch 7, the Courts Act 1971, Sch 8 and the Statute Law (Repeals) Act 1989, Sch 1.]

* **Repealed by the Criminal Justice Act 2003, Sch 37 from a date to be appointed.**

1 The Crown Court has no power to adjudge whether the accused is an incorrigible rogue; the magistrates will have decided that (*R v Evans* [1915] 2 KB 762, 79 JP 415). Nor will the Crown Court have power to sentence for the offences on which the defendant was deemed to be an incorrigible rogue (*R v Walters* [1969] 1 QB 255, [1968] 3 All ER 863, 133 JP 73). For observations as to limits of Crown Court powers see *R v Jackson* [1974] QB 517, [1974] 2 All ER 211, 138 JP 363. As to procedure in the Crown Court see *R v Cope* (1925) 89 JP 100; *R v Holding, R v Long* (1935) 98 JP 459; *R v Billington* (1942) 28 Cr App Rep 180. Although there is no appeal from the conviction by the magistrates under s 10 of the Criminal Appeal Act 1968; appeal will lie from the decision of the Crown Court; see *R v Brown* (1908) 72 JP 427; *R v Dean* (1924) 18 Cr App Rep 133; *R v Cadwell* (1927) 20 Cr App Rep 60. As to appeal to the Crown Court from the magistrates' court, see s 14, post.

7.11586 **14. Persons aggrieved may appeal to the Crown Court** Any person aggrieved by any act or determination of any justice or justices of the peace out of sessions[1], in or concerning the execution of this Act, may appeal[2] to the Crown Court.

[Vagrancy Act 1824, s 14 as amended by the Summary Jurisdiction Act 1884, Sch and the Courts Act 1971, Sch 8.]

1 That is, where the decision was of a single justice, or at an occasional court house, or in petty sessions.

2 See the Magistrates' Courts Act 1980, ss 108–110, ante; the Criminal Procedure Rules, Part 34, in the *Key Materials*.

# WAR CRIMES

## War Crimes Act 1991[1]

(1991 c 13)

7.11587 **1. Jurisdiction over certain war crimes** (1) Subject to the provisions of this section, proceedings for murder, manslaughter or culpable homicide may be brought against a person in the United Kingdom irrespective of his nationality at the time of the alleged offence if that offence—

(*a*) was committed during the period beginning with 1st September 1939 and ending with 5th June 1945 in a place which at the time was part of Germany or under German occupation; and

(*b*) constituted a violation of the laws and customs of war.

(2) No proceedings shall by virtue of this section be brought against any person unless he was on 8th March 1990, or has subsequently become, a British citizen or resident in the United Kingdom, the Isle of Man or any of the Channel Islands.

(3) No proceedings shall by virtue of this section be brought in England and Wales or in Northern Ireland except by or with the consent of the Attorney General or, as the case may be, the Attorney General for Northern Ireland.

(4) The Schedule[2] to this Act provides a procedure for use instead of committal proceedings where a person is charged in Northern Ireland with an offence to which this section applies.

[War Crimes Act 1991, s 1 as amended by the Criminal Procedure and Investigations Act 1996, s 46 and Sch 5.]

---

1 This Act is protected from challenge under art 7(1) of the European Convention on Human Rights (the prohibition on retrospective criminal penalties) by art 7(2) which provides for the trial and punishment of any person for any act or omission which, at the time when it was committed, was criminal according to the general principles of law recognised by civilised nations.

2 The Schedule has been repealed in so far as it applied to England and Wales by the Criminal Procedure and Investigations Act 1996, s 46.

# WATER

**Contents**



See also titles Fisheries ante, Public Health ante (cleansing and repairing etc of drains in Part II of the Public Health Act 1936, pollution in the Control of Pollution Act 1974 Part II).

The Water Act 1989 reorganised arrangements for water matters. Schedule 26 thereto made transitional provisions and savings with respect to water authorities, water and sewerage services, control of pollution, water resources, flood defence and fisheries as well as various miscellaneous matters.

## Reservoirs Act 1975

(1975 c 23)

**7.11588** The enforcement authority for the purposes of this Act is the local authority, with supervisory powers to the Secretary of State[1] [ss 2 and 3].

A qualified civil engineer must design and supervise the construction or enlargement of a reservoir, which can only then be filled in accordance with his certificate [s 6]. The undertakers are to carry into effect any safety recommendations of an engineer appointed in place of a construction engineer [s 8(3)]. Re-use of abandoned reservoirs is subject to inspection, supervision, certification and implementation of safety recommendations [s 9]. Undertakers must have any large raised reservoir inspected periodically by an independent qualified civil engineer, implement and have certified any safety recommendations in his report [s 10]. Water levels etc must be recorded [s 11]. A supervising engineer must be employed for any large raised reservoir to advise on safety and compliance with provisions [s 12(1)]. Discontinuance and abandonment of reservoirs must also be under qualified supervision and subject to a safety report [ss 13 and 14].

A person duly authorised in writing by an enforcement authority has power to enter on reservoir land at any reasonable time. A Justice may issue a warrant to enter in the event of refusal or apprehended refusal or in the occupier's absence, where there is reasonable ground for entry and where notice in writing of intention to apply has been given to the occupier. Warrant continues in force until purpose satisfied: penalty for wilful obstruction **level 3** on the standard scale [s 17 as amended by the Criminal Justice Act 1982, ss 38 and 46].

[1] An index of general definitions appears in Sch 1 to the Act. The Reservoirs Act 1975 (Registers, Reports and Records) Regulations 1985, SI 1985/177 amended by SI 1985/548 and SI 2016/80 have been made.

**7.11589 22. Criminal liability of undertakers and their employees** (1) If—

(*a*) by the wilful default of the undertakers any of the provisions of section 6, 8(3), 9(1), (2) or (3), 10(1) or (6), 11, 12(1), 13 or 14(1) or (2) above is not observed or complied with in relation to a large raised reservoir;

(*b*) the undertakers fail to comply with a notice from the enforcement authority under section 8, 9, 10, 12 or 14 above; or

(*c*) the undertakers fail to comply with a direction under section 12A above;

then unless there is reasonable excuse for the default or failure, the undertakers shall be guilty of an offence and liable on conviction[1] on indictment or on summary conviction to a **fine**, which on summary conviction shall not exceed the **prescribed sum**.

(1A) If the undertakers fail without reasonable excuse to comply with a notice under section 12B above, they shall be guilty of an offence and liable—

(*a*) on summary conviction, to a fine not exceeding the statutory maximum;

(*b*) on conviction on indictment, to imprisonment for a term not exceeding two years, or to a fine, or to both.

(2) If, in the case of any large raised reservoir, the undertakers fail without reasonable excuse to

give the enforcement authority in due time any notice required by this Act to be given by them to that authority, the undertakers shall be guilty of an offence and liable on summary conviction to a fine not exceeding **level 4** on the standard scale.

(3) If, in the case of any large raised reservoir, the undertakers or persons employed by them without reasonable excuse refuse or knowingly fail to afford to any person the facilities required by section 21(5) above or to furnish to any person the information and particulars so required, the undertakers shall be guilty of an offence and liable on summary conviction to a fine not exceeding **level 4** on the standard scale.

(4) If for the purposes of section 21(5) above a person makes use of any document or furnishes any information or particulars which he knows to be false in a material respect, or recklessly makes use of any document or furnishes any information or particulars which is or are false in a material respect, he shall be guilty of an offence and liable on summary conviction to a fine not exceeding **level 5** on the standard scale.

(5) Where an offence committed by a body corporate under this section is proved to have been committed with the consent or connivance of any director, manager, secretary or other similar officer of the body corporate, or any person who was purporting to act in any such capacity, he as well as the body corporate shall be guilty of that offence, and shall be liable to be proceeded against and punished accordingly.

Where the affairs of a body corporate are managed by its members, this section shall apply in relation to the acts and defaults of a member in connection with his functions of management as if he were a director of the body corporate.

(6) In England and Wales proceedings for an offence under this section may be instituted only by the Environment Agency or the Secretary of State or by or with the consent of the Director of Public Prosecutions.

[Reservoirs Act 1975, s 22 as amended by the Criminal Law Act 1977, s 28, the Magistrates' Courts Act 1980, s 32(2), the Criminal Justice Act 1982, ss 38 and 46 and the Water Act 2003, ss 74 and 79.]

---

1 For procedure in respect of an offence triable either way, see the Magistrates' Courts Act 1980, ss 17A–21 in PART I: MAGISTRATES' COURTS, PROCEDURE, ante.

7.11590 **22A. Service of notices by the Environment Agency** Section 123 of the Environment Act 1995 (service of documents) applies to any document authorised or required by virtue of any provision of this Act to be served or given by the Environment Agency as if it were authorised or required to be served or given by or under that Act.

[Reservoirs Act 1975, s 22A as inserted by the Water Act 2003, s 76.]

## Water Act 1989

(1989 c 15)

7.11591 This Act has been extensively repealed by the Water Consolidation (Consequential Provisions) Act 1991, Sch 3. Preserved sections include s 174 (General restrictions on disclosure of information), 175 (Making false statements etc), which have penal provisions providing for offences triable either way, 177 (Offences by bodies corporate), and 189 (General interpretation, of which definitions relevant to the above preserved sections are retained and listed in Sch 3 of the 1991 Act).

## Water Industry Act 1991

(1991 c 56)

### PART III [1]

### WATER SUPPLY

7.11592 **57. Duty to provide a supply of water etc for fire-fighting** Water undertaker to allow any person to take water for extinguishing fires from mains or pipes fitted with a fire-hydrant; duty to fix fire-hydrants at request of fire and rescue authority, to keep same in good working order and replace when necessary, to supply keys to fire and rescue authority; breach punishable on summary conviction with fine not exceeding **statutory maximum** or on conviction on indictment by **fine**[2]; defence of being unable to do something by reason of carrying out necessary works, also took all reasonable steps and exercised all due diligence.

[Water Industry Act 1991, s 57—summarised.]

---

1 Part III comprises ss 37–93.

2 For procedure in respect of an offence triable either way, see the Magistrates' Courts Act 1980, ss 17A–21 in PART I: MAGISTRATES' COURTS, PROCEDURE, ante.

*Disconnections*

7.11593 **60. Disconnections for the carrying out of necessary works** Water undertaker may disconnect or reduce supply if it is reasonable to do so for the carrying out of necessary works; it must serve reasonable notice on the consumer, carry out the works with reasonable dispatch, make available an emergency supply within a reasonable distance for domestic purposes.

[Water Industry Act 1991, s 60—summarised.]

7.11594 **61. Disconnections for non-payment of charges** Water undertaker may disconnect supply if occupier of premises liable to pay and has failed to do so within seven days beginning with the day he is served with a notice; provision is made for disputed liability and to preserve supply to other premises on same service pipe.

[Water Industry Act 1991, s 61—summarised.]

7.11595 **62.** *Disconnections at request of customer.*

7.11596 **63. General duties of undertakers with respect to disconnections** Where a water undertaker disconnects or cuts off supply of water to any inhabited house for longer than 24 hours, it must serve notice on the local authority within 48 hours; if it disconnects other than under powers in ss 60–62 above or s 75 or any other enactment or fails to comply with requirements under which it disconnects, it is liable of summary conviction to a fine not exceeding **level 3** on the standard scale.

[Water Industry Act 1991, s 63—summarised.]

*Use of limiting devices*

7.11597 **63A. Prohibition of use of limiting devices** (1) A water undertaker shall be guilty of an offence under this section if it uses a limiting device in relation to any premises specified in Schedule 4A to this Act, with the intention of enforcing payment of charges which are or may become due to the undertaker in respect of the supply of water to the premises.

(2) For the purposes of this section "a limiting device", in relation to any premises, means any device or apparatus which—

(*a*) is fitted to any pipe by which water is supplied to the premises or a part of the premises, whether that pipe belongs to the undertaker or to any other person, and

(*b*) is designed to restrict the use which may be made of water supplied to the premises by the undertaker.

(3) An undertaker does not commit an offence under this section by disconnecting a service pipe to any premises or otherwise cutting off a supply of water to the premises.

(4) An undertaker guilty of an offence under this section shall be liable on summary conviction to a fine not exceeding level 3 on the standard scale.

[Water Industry Act 1991, s 63A as inserted by the Water Industry Act 1999, s 2.]

*Means of supply*

7.11598 **65. Duties of undertakers as respects constancy and pressure** Duty of water undertaker to cause water in mains and pipes used for domestic purposes or fire-hydrants to be paid on constantly and at such pressure as will cause it to reach to top of every building except when necessary works being carried out; breach punishable on summary conviction by a fine not exceeding the **statutory maximum** or on conviction on indictment to a **fine**[1].

[Water Industry Act 1991, s 65 as amended by the Competition and Service (Utilities) Act 1992, Sch 1—summarised.]

---

1 For procedure in respect of an offence triable either way, see the Magistrates' Courts Act 1980, ss 17A–21 in PART I: MAGISTRATES' COURTS, PROCEDURE, ante.

*Standards of wholesomeness*

7.11598A **67. Standards of wholesomeness.** *Secretary of State may by regulations make provision that water that is supplied to any premises is or is not to be regarded as wholesome for the purposes of this Chapter if it satisfies or, as the case may be, fails to satisfy such requirements as may be prescribed*[1].

---

1 The Private Water Supplies (England) Regulations 2016, SI 2016/618 have been made.

*General obligations of undertakers and water supply licensees*

7.11599 **69.** *Regulations for preserving water quality*[1].

---

1 The Water Supply (Water Quality) Regulations 2016, SI 2016/614 have been made. (For Wales, see the Water Supply (Water Quality) Regulations 2010, SI 2010/994 amended by SI 2011/14, SI 2013/235 and 1387 and SI 2016/410). Consent of the Secretary of State (in Wales, the Welsh Ministers) or the DPP is required for prosecution of an offence contrary to reg 33(4) (but not reg 33(1) and 33(3)).

7.11600 **70. Offence of supplying water unfit for human consumption** (1) Subject to subsection (3) below, where a water undertaker's supply system is used for the purposes of supplying water to any premises and that water is unfit for human consumption, the relevant persons shall be guilty of an offence and liable[1] on summary conviction, or on conviction on indictment, to a fine.

(1A) For the purposes of subsection (1) above, the relevant persons are—

(*a*) the water undertaker whose supply system is used for the purposes of supplying the water (in this section referred to as the "primary water undertaker"); and

(*b*) any employer of persons, or any self-employed person, who is concerned in the supply of the water.

(2) For the purposes of section 210 below and any other enactment under which an individual is guilty of an offence by virtue of subsection (1) above the penalty on conviction on indictment of an offence under this section shall be deemed to include imprisonment (in addition to or instead of

a fine) for a term not exceeding two years.

(3) In any proceedings against any relevant person for an offence under this section it shall be a defence for that person to show that it—

(*a*) had no reasonable grounds for suspecting that the water would be used for human consumption; or

(*b*) took all reasonable steps and exercised all due diligence for securing that the water was fit for human consumption on leaving the primary water undertaker's pipes or was not used for human consumption.

(3A) For the purposes of paragraph (*b*) of subsection (3) above—

(*a*) in the case of proceedings against a primary water undertaker, showing that the undertaker took all reasonable steps and exercised all due diligence as mentioned in that paragraph includes (among other things) showing that the relevant arrangements were reasonable in all the circumstances; and

(*b*) in the case of proceedings against any other relevant person, showing that the person took all reasonable steps and exercised all due diligence as mentioned in that paragraph includes (among other things) showing that it took all reasonable steps and exercised all due diligence for securing that all aspects of the relevant arrangements for which it was responsible were properly carried out.

(3B) In subsection (3A) above, "relevant arrangements" means arrangements made by the primary water undertaker to ensure that all other relevant persons were required to take all reasonable steps and exercise all due diligence for securing that the water was fit for human consumption on leaving the undertaker's pipes or was not used for human consumption.

(4) Proceedings for an offence under this section shall not be instituted except by the Secretary of State or the Director of Public Prosecutions.

[Water Industry Act 1991, s 70 as amended by the Water Act 2003, s 60 and Sch 8 and SI 2015/664.]

---

[1] For procedure in respect of an offence triable either way, see the Magistrates' Courts Act 1980, ss 17A–21 in PART I: MAGISTRATES' COURTS, PROCEDURE, ante.

*Waste, contamination, misuse etc*

7.11601 71. **Waste from water sources** (1) Subject to subsections (2) and (3) below, a person shall be guilty of an offence under this section if—

(*a*) he causes or allows any underground water to run to waste from any well, borehole or other work; or

(*b*) he abstracts from any well, borehole or other work water in excess of his reasonable requirements.

(2) A person shall not be guilty of an offence by virtue of subsection (1)(*a*) above in respect of anything done for the purpose—

(*a*) of testing the extent or quality of the supply; or

(*b*) of cleaning, sterilising, examining or repairing the well, borehole or other work in question.

(3) Where underground water interferes or threatens to interfere with the carrying out or operation of any underground works (whether waterworks or not), it shall not be an offence under this section, if no other method of disposing of the water is reasonably practicable, to cause or allow the water to run to waste so far as may be necessary for enabling the works to be carried out or operated.

(4) A person who is guilty of an offence under this section shall be liable, on summary conviction, to a fine not exceeding **level 3** on the standard scale.

(5) On the conviction of a person under this section, the court may—

(*a*) order that the well, borehole or other work to which the offence relates shall be effectively sealed; or

(*b*) make such other order as appears to the court to be necessary to prevent waste of water.

(6) If any person fails to comply with an order under subsection (5) above, then, without prejudice to any penalty for contempt of court, the court may, on the application of the appropriate agency, authorise the appropriate agency to take such steps as may be necessary to execute the order; and any expenses incurred in taking any such steps shall be recoverable summarily as a civil debt from the person convicted.

(7) Any person designated for the purpose by the Environment Agency shall, on producing some duly authenticated document showing his authority, have a right at all reasonable times—

(*a*) to enter any premises for the purpose of ascertaining whether there is, or has been, any contravention of the provisions of this section on or in connection with the premises;

(*b*) to enter any premises for the purpose of executing any order of the court under this section which the Environment Agency has been authorised to execute in those premises.

(8) Part I of Schedule 6 to this Act shall apply to the rights of entry conferred by subsection (7) above.

[Water Industry Act 1991, s 71 as amended by the Environment Act 1995, Sch 22 and SI 2013/755.]

7.11602 72. **Contamination of water sources** (1) Subject to subsections (2) and (3) below, a person is guilty of an offence under this section if he is guilty of any act or neglect whereby the water in any waterworks which is used or likely to be used—

(*a*) for human consumption or domestic purposes; or

(*b*) for manufacturing food or drink for human consumption,

is polluted or likely to be polluted.

(2) Nothing in this section shall be construed as restricting or prohibiting any method of cultivation of land which is in accordance with the principles of good husbandry.

(3) Nothing in this section shall be construed as restricting or prohibiting the reasonable use of oil or tar on any highway maintainable at public expense so long as the highway authority take all reasonable steps for preventing—

(*a*) the oil or tar; and

(*b*) any liquid or matter resulting from the use of the oil or tar,

from polluting the water in any waterworks.

(4) A person who is guilty of an offence under this section shall be liable[1]—

(*a*) on summary conviction, to a fine not exceeding the **statutory maximum** and, in the case of a continuing offence, to a further fine not exceeding **£50 for every day during which the offence is continued** after conviction;

(*b*) on conviction on indictment, to imprisonment for a term not exceeding **two years** or to a **fine** or to **both**.

(5) In this section "waterworks" includes—

(*a*) any spring, well, adit, borehole, service reservoir or tank; and

(*b*) any main or other pipe or conduit of a water undertaker; and

(*c*) any pipe or conduit of a licensed water supplier.

[Water Industry Act 1991, s 72 as amended by the Water Act 2003, Sch 8.]

---

[1] For procedure in respect of an offence triable either way, see the Magistrates' Courts Act 1980, ss 17A–21 in PART I: MAGISTRATES' COURTS, PROCEDURE, ante.

7.11603 73. **Offences of contaminating, wasting and misusing water etc** (1) If any person who is the owner or occupier of any premises to which a supply of water is provided by a water undertaker or licensed water supplier intentionally or negligently causes or suffers any water fitting for which he is responsible to be or remain so out of order, so in need of repair or so constructed or adapted, or to be so used—

(*a*) that water in a water main or other pipe of a water undertaker, or in a pipe connected with such a water main or pipe, is or is likely to be contaminated by the return of any substance from those premises to that main or pipe;

(*b*) that water that has been supplied by the undertaker or supplier to those premises is or is likely to be contaminated before it is used; or

(*c*) that water so supplied is or is likely to be wasted or, having regard to the purposes for which it is supplied, misused or unduly consumed,

that person shall be guilty of an offence and liable, on summary conviction, to a fine not exceeding **level 3** on the standard scale.

(1A) In any proceedings under subsection (1) above it shall be a defence to prove—

(*a*) that the contamination or likely contamination, or the wastage, misuse or undue consumption, was caused (wholly or mainly) by the installation, alteration, repair or connection of the water fitting on or after 1st July 1999;

(*b*) that the works were carried out by or under the direction of an approved contractor within the meaning of the Water Supply (Water Fittings) Regulations 1999; and

(*c*) that the contractor certified to the person who commissioned those works that the water fitting complied with the requirements of those regulations.

(2) Any person who uses any water supplied to any premises by a water undertaker for a purpose other than one for which it is supplied to those premises shall, unless the other purpose is the extinguishment of a fire, be guilty of an offence and liable, on summary conviction, to a fine not exceeding **level 3** on the standard scale.

(3) Where a person has committed an offence under subsection (2) above, the water undertaker in question shall be entitled to recover from that person such amount as may be reasonable in respect of any water wasted, misused or improperly consumed in consequence of the commission of the offence.

(4) For the purposes of this section the owner or occupier of any premises shall be regarded as responsible for every water fitting on the premises which is not a water fitting which a person other than the owner or, as the case may be, occupier is liable to maintain.

[Water Industry Act 1991, s 73 as amended by SI 1999/1148 and the Water Act 2003, Sch 8.]

7.11604 74. *Regulations for preventing contamination, waste etc and with respect to water fittings.*

7.11605 75. **Power to prevent damage and to take steps to prevent contamination, waste etc** In specified circumstances the water undertaker may in an emergency cut off the supply, and serve notice on the customer as soon as reasonably practicable thereafter specifying steps to be taken before supply is restored; failure by undertaker to serve notice punishable summarily by a fine not exceeding **level 3** on the standard scale.

[Water Industry Act 1991, s 75—summarised.]

7.11606 **76. Temporary bans on use** (1) A water undertaker may prohibit one or more specified uses of water supplied by it if it thinks that it is experiencing, or may experience, a serious shortage of water for distribution.

(2) Only the following uses of water may be prohibited—

(*a*) watering a garden using a hosepipe;

(*b*) cleaning a private motor-vehicle using a hosepipe;

(*c*) watering plants on domestic or other non-commercial premises using a hosepipe;

(*d*) cleaning a private leisure boat using a hosepipe;

(*e*) filling or maintaining a domestic swimming or paddling pool;

(*f*) drawing water, using a hosepipe, for domestic recreational use;

(*g*) filling or maintaining a domestic pond using a hosepipe;

(*h*) filling or maintaining an ornamental fountain;

(*i*) cleaning walls, or windows, of domestic premises using a hosepipe;

(*j*) cleaning paths or patios using a hosepipe;

(*k*) cleaning other artificial outdoor surfaces using a hosepipe.

(3) The Minister may by order—

(*a*) add a non-domestic purpose to the list in subsection (2);

(*b*) remove a purpose from the list in subsection (2).

(4) A prohibition must specify—

(*a*) the date from which it applies, and

(*b*) the area to which it applies (which may be all or part of the undertaker's area).

(5) A person who contravenes a prohibition—

(*a*) is guilty of an offence, and

(*b*) is liable on summary conviction to a fine not exceeding level 3 on the standard scale.

(6) A water undertaker which issues a prohibition must make arrangements for a reasonable reduction of charges which are made in respect of prohibited uses (including arrangements for repayment or credit where charges are paid in advance).

(7) A water undertaker may vary or revoke a prohibition.

[Water Industry Act 1991, s 76 as substituted by the Flood and Water Management Act 2010, s 36.]

7.11607 **76A. Temporary bans: supplemental** (1) A prohibition may—

(*a*) apply to one or more specified uses of water generally or only in specified cases or circumstances (which may be specified by reference to classes of user, timing or in any other way);

(*b*) be subject to exceptions (which may be absolute or conditional, and may be specified by reference to classes of user, timing or in any other way).

(2) The Minister may by order[1]—

(*a*) provide for exceptions to a category of use in section 76(2) (whether or not added under section 76(3));

(*b*) provide that a specified activity, or an activity undertaken in specified circumstances, is to be or not to be treated as falling within a category of use in section 76(2) (whether or not added under section 76(3));

(*c*) define a word or phrase used in section 76(2) (whether or not added under section 76(3)).

(3) In particular, an order may—

(*a*) restrict a category of use by reference to how water is drawn;

(*b*) frame an exception by reference to ownership of land by a specified person or class of person;

(*c*) provide for a process that involves the use of a hosepipe at any point to be included in the meaning of "using a hosepipe";

(*d*) provide for a reference to a thing to include a reference to something that is or may be used in connection with it (such as, for example, for a reference to a vehicle to include a reference to a trailer).

(4) In this section and section 76 "the Minister" means—

(*a*) the Secretary of State in relation to prohibitions which may be issued by water undertakers whose areas are wholly or mainly in England, and

(*b*) the Welsh Ministers in relation to prohibitions which may be issued by water undertakers whose areas are wholly or mainly in Wales.

(5) Subject to provision under subsection (2), a reference to a hosepipe in section 76 includes a reference to anything designed, adapted or used to serve the same purpose as a hosepipe.

[Water Industry Act 1991, s 76A as substituted by the Flood and Water Management Act 2010, s 36.]

---

[1] The Water Use (Temporary Bans) Order 2010 has been made, in this title, post.

7.11608 **76B. Temporary bans: procedure** (1) A prohibition takes effect only if this section is complied with.

(2) Before the period for which a prohibition is to apply the water undertaker must give notice of the prohibition and its terms—

(*a*) in at least two newspapers circulating in the area to which it is to apply, and

(*b*) on the water undertaker's internet website.

(3) The notice must give details of how to make representations about the proposed prohibition.

(4) The variation of a prohibition is to be treated as a prohibition for the purposes of this section.

(5) A water undertaker must give notice of a revocation of a prohibition—

(*a*) in at least two newspapers circulating in the area to which it is to apply, and

(*b*) on the water undertaker's internet website.

(6) The revocation may not take effect until at least one notice under subsection (5) has been given.

[Water Industry Act 1991, s 76B as substituted by the Flood and Water Management Act 2010, s 36.]

**7.11609 76C. Orders under sections 76 and 76A** (1) Section 213 applies to orders under section 76(3) or 76A(2) as it applies to regulations.

(2) But—

(*a*) an order made by the Secretary of State under section 76(3) may not be made unless a draft has been laid before and approved by resolution of each House of Parliament,

(*b*) an order made by the Welsh Ministers under section 76(3) may not be made unless a draft has been laid before and approved by resolution of the National Assembly for Wales, and

(*c*) an order made by the Welsh Ministers under section 76A(2) shall be subject to annulment in pursuance of a resolution of the National Assembly for Wales.

[Water Industry Act 1991, s 76C as substituted by the Flood and Water Management Act 2010, s 36.]

*Local authority functions*

**7.11610 78–84.** *Local authorities are to keep themselves informed about the wholesomeness and sufficiency of water supplies and to give appropriate notice to water undertakers and exercise remedial powers. Similar duties and powers are given in relation to private supplies. Rights of entry are regulated by Sch 6.*

**7.11611 85. Local authority power to obtain information for the purposes of functions under Chapter III**[1] (1) Subject to subsection (2) below, a local authority may serve on any person a notice requiring him to furnish that authority, within a period or at times specified in the notice and in a form and manner so specified, with such information as is reasonably required by that authority for the purpose of exercising or performing any power or duty conferred or imposed on that authority by or under any of sections 77 to 82 above.

(2) The Secretary of State may by regulations make provision for restricting the information which may be required under subsection (1) above and for determining the form in which the information is to be so required.

(3) A person who fails without reasonable excuse to comply with the requirements of a notice served on him under subsection (1) above shall be guilty of an offence and liable, on summary conviction, to a fine not exceeding **level 5** on the standard scale.

[Water Industry Act 1991, s 85.]

1 Chapter III of Pt III of this Act comprises ss 67–86.

**7.11612 86. Assessors for the enforcement of water quality** (1) The Secretary of State may for the purposes of this section appoint persons to act on his behalf in relation to some or all of—

(*a*) the powers and duties conferred or imposed on him by or under sections 67 to 70 and 77 to 82 above; and

(*b*) such other powers and duties in relation to the quality and sufficiency of water supplied using a water undertaker's supply system as are conferred or imposed on him by or under any other enactments.

(1A) Subject to subsection (1B) below, the Secretary of State shall designate one such person as the Chief Inspector of Drinking Water.

(1B) If the function of the Secretary of State under subsection (1) above is transferred to any extent to the Assembly—

(*a*) subject to paragraph (*b*) below, the Assembly may designate one such person appointed by it as the Chief Inspector of Drinking Water for Wales; but

(*b*) if the person designated by the Assembly is the same as the person designated by the Secretary of State as the Chief Inspector of Drinking Water, he shall be known as such in both capacities.

(2) An inspector appointed under this section shall—

(*a*) carry out such investigations as the Secretary of State may require him to carry out for the purpose of—

(i) ascertaining whether any duty or other requirement imposed on that undertaker or a licensed water supplier by or under any of sections 68, 69 and 79 above or imposed on a relevant person (as defined in subsection (1A) of section 70 above) by or under that section is being, has been or is likely to be contravened; or

(ii) advising the Secretary of State as to whether, and if so in what manner, any of the powers of the Secretary of State in relation to such a contravention, or any of the powers (including the powers to make regulations) which are conferred on him by or under any of sections 67 to 70 and 77 to 82 above should be exercised;

and

(*b*) make such reports to the Secretary of state with respect to any such investigation as the Secretary of State may require.

(3) Without prejudice to the powers conferred by subsection (4) below, it shall be the duty of a water undertaker, licensed water supplier or other relevant person (as defined in section 70(1A) above)—

(*a*) to give an inspector appointed under this section all such assistance; and

(*b*) to provide an inspector so appointed with all such information,

as that person may reasonably require for the purpose of carrying out any such investigation as is mentioned in subsection (2) above.

(4) Any inspector appointed under this section who is designated in writing for the purpose by the Secretary of State may—

(*a*) enter any premises for the purpose of carrying out any such investigation as is mentioned in subsection (2) above;

(*b*) carry out such inspections, measurements and tests on premises entered by that inspector or of articles or records found on any such premises, and take away such samples of water or of any land or articles, as that inspector considers appropriate for the purpose of enabling him to carry out any such investigation; or

(*c*) at any reasonable time require—

(i) any water undertaker or licensed water supplier to supply him with copies of, or extracts from, the contents of any records kept for the purpose of complying with any duty or other requirement imposed on that undertaker or supplier by or under any of sections 68, 69 and 79 above; or

(ii) any relevant person (as defined in subsection (1A) of section 70 above) to supply him with copies of, or extracts from, the contents of any records kept for the purpose of complying with any duty or other requirement imposed on that person by or under that section.

(5) Part II of Schedule 6 to this Act shall apply to the rights and powers conferred by subsection (4) above.

(6) Any water undertaker, licensed water supplier or other relevant person which fails to comply with the duty imposed on it by virtue of subsection (3) above shall be guilty of an offence and liable[1] on summary conviction, or on conviction on indictment, to a fine.

(7) Proceedings by the Secretary of State for an offence under this section or in relation to the quality and sufficiency of water supplied using a water undertaker's supply system may be instituted and carried on in the name of the Chief Inspector of Drinking Water.

(8) Any such proceedings by the Assembly may be instituted and carried on in the name of the Chief Inspector of Drinking Water for Wales, if there is one (or, if subsection (1B)(*b*) above applies, in the name of the Chief Inspector of Drinking Water).

(9) In this section "inspector" means the Chief Inspector of Drinking Water or any other person appointed under subsection (1) above.

[Water Industry Act 1991, s 86 as amended by the Water Act 2003, s 57 and Sch 8 and SI 2015/664.]

---

[1] For procedure in respect of this offence which is triable either way, see the Magistrates' Courts Act 1980, ss 17A–21 in Part I: Magistrates' Courts, Procedure, ante

7.11613 **93. Interpretation of Part III** (1) In this Part—

"connection notice" shall be construed in accordance with section 45(8) above;

"consumer", in relation to a supply of water provided by a water undertaker to any premises, means (except in Chapter IV) a person who is for the time being the person on whom liability to pay charges to the undertaker in respect of that supply of water would fall;

"food production purposes" means the manufacturing, processing, preserving or marketing purposes with respect to food or drink for which water supplied to food production premises may be used, and for the purposes of this definition "food production premises" means premises used for the purposes of a business of preparing food or drink for consumption otherwise than on the premises;

"necessary works" includes works carried out, in exercise of any power conferred by or under any enactment, by a person other than a water undertaker;

"private supply" means, subject to subsection (2) below, a supply of water provided otherwise than by a water undertaker or by a licensed water supplier in accordance with Chapter 1A of Part 2 of this Act (including a supply provided for the purposes of the bottling of water), and cognate expressions shall be construed accordingly;

"private supply notice" shall be construed in accordance with section 80(7) above;

"water fittings" includes pipes (other than water mains), taps, cocks, valves, ferrules, meters, cisterns, baths, water closets, soil pans and other similar apparatus used in connection with the supply and use of water;

"wholesome" and cognate expressions shall be construed subject to the provisions of any regulations made under section 67 above.

(2) For the purposes of any reference in this Part to a private supply, or to supplying water by means of a private supply, water shall be treated as supplied to any premises not only where it is supplied from outside those premises, but also where it is abstracted, for the purpose of being used or consumed on those premises, from a source which is situated on the premises themselves; and for the purposes of this subsection water shall be treated as used on any premises where it is bottled on those premises for use or consumption elsewhere.

(3) For the purposes of this Part a service pipe shall be treated as connected with a water main other than a trunk main even if the connection is an indirect connection made by virtue of a connection with another service pipe.

(4) The rights conferred by virtue of this Part as against the owner or occupier of any premises shall be without prejudice to any rights and obligations, as between themselves, of the owner and occupier of the premises.

[Water Industry Act 1991, s 93 as amended by the Water Act 2003, Sch 8.]

## PART IV [1]

## SEWERAGE SERVICES

*Communication of drains and private sewers with public sewers*

7.11614 **106. Right to communicate with public sewers** (1) Subject to the provisions of this section—

(*a*) the owner or occupier of any premises, or

(*b*) the owner of any private sewer which drains premises,

shall be entitled to have his drains or sewer communicate with the public sewer of any sewerage undertaker and thereby to discharge foul water and surface water from those premises or that private sewer.

(1A) In this section, and in sections 107 to 109, 111, 113 to 116, 118, 119, 124, 127, 139 and 146 below—

(*a*) references (however expressed) to a public sewer include a public lateral drain which satisfies sewer standards; and

(*b*) for the purposes of paragraph (*a*) above—

(i) a "public lateral drain" is a lateral drain which either belongs to the sewerage undertaker or is vested in the sewerage undertaker by virtue of a declaration made under section 102 above or under an agreement made under section 104 above; and

(ii) "sewer standards" means such standards of construction and repair as the undertaker would require if the public lateral drain or part of it were to become a public sewer.

(2) Subject to the provisions of Chapter III of this Part[2], nothing in subsection (1) above shall entitle any person—

(*a*) to discharge directly or indirectly into any public sewer—

(i) any liquid from a factory, other than domestic sewage or surface or storm water, or any liquid from a manufacturing process; or

(ii) any liquid or other matter the discharge of which into public sewers is prohibited by or under any enactment; or

(*b*) where separate public sewers are provided for foul water and for surface water, to discharge directly or indirectly—

(i) foul water into a sewer provided for surface water; or

(ii) except with the approval of the undertaker, surface water into a sewer provided for foul water; or

(*c*) to have his drains or sewer made to communicate directly with a storm-water overflow sewer.

(3) A person desirous of availing himself of his entitlement under this section shall give notice of his proposals to the sewerage undertaker in question.

(4) At any time within twenty-one days after a sewerage undertaker receives a notice under subsection (3) above, the undertaker may by notice to the person who gave the notice refuse to permit the communication to be made, if it appears to the undertaker that the mode of construction or condition of the drain or sewer—

(*a*) does not satisfy the standards reasonably required by the undertaker; or

(*b*) is such that the making of the communication would be prejudicial to the undertaker's sewerage system.

(5) For the purpose of examining the mode of construction and condition of a drain or sewer to which a notice under subsection (3) above relates a sewerage undertaker may, if necessary, require it to be laid open for inspection.

(5A) Where the sewer or drain satisfies the standards reasonably required by it, a sewerage undertaker may, as a condition of permitting the communication to be made, require that the sewer or that part of the drain forming the lateral drain be vested in it by virtue of a declaration under section 102 above.

(6) Any question arising under subsections (3) to (5A) above between a sewerage undertaker and a person proposing to make a communication as to—

(*a*) the reasonableness of the undertaker's refusal to permit a communication to be made; or

(*b*) as to the reasonableness of any requirement under subsection (5) or (5A) above,

may, on the application of that person, be determined by the Authority under section 30A above (and, accordingly, section 105 above shall not apply to any requirement under subsection (5A) above).

(7) *Repealed.*

(8) Where a person proposes under this section to make a communication between a drain or sewer and such a public sewer in Greater London as is used for the general reception of sewage from other public sewers and is not substantially used for the reception of sewage from private sewers and drains—

(*a*) the grounds on which a sewerage undertaker may refuse to permit the communication shall be such grounds as the undertaker thinks fit; and

(*b*) no application to the Authority may be made under subsection (6) above in respect of any refusal under this subsection.

(9) In this section "factory" has the same meaning as in the Factories Act 1961.

[Water Industry Act 1991, s 106 as amended by the Competition and Service (Utilities) Act 1992, ss 35 and 43, and Sch 2 and the Water Act 2003, s 36 and 99.]

---

[1] Part IV comprises ss 94–141.

[2] Chapter II of Pt IV comprises ss 118–141.

7.11615 **107. Right of sewerage undertaker to undertake the making of communications with public sewers** (1) Where a person gives to a sewerage undertaker notice under section 106 above of his proposal to have his drains or sewer made to communicate with a public sewer of that undertaker, the undertaker may—

(*a*) within fourteen days after the receipt of the notice; or

(*b*) if any question arising under the notice requires to be determined by the Authority within fourteen days after the determination of that question,

give notice to that person that the undertaker intends itself to make the communication.

(2) If, after a notice has been given to any person under subsection (1) above, that person proceeds himself to make the communication, he shall be guilty of an offence and liable, on summary conviction, to a fine not exceeding **level 4** on the standard scale.

(3) Where a sewerage undertaker has given a notice under subsection (1) above—

(*a*) the undertaker shall have all such rights in respect of the making of the communication as the person desiring it to be made would have; but

(*b*) it shall not be obligatory on the undertaker to make the communication until either—

(i) there has been paid to the sewerage undertaker any such sum, not exceeding the undertaker's reasonable estimate of the cost of the work, as the undertaker may have required to be paid to it; or

(ii) there has been given to the undertaker such security for the payment of the cost of the work as it may reasonably have required.

(4) If any payment made to a sewerage undertaker under subsection (3) above exceeds the expenses reasonably incurred by it in the carrying out of the work in question, the excess shall be repaid by the undertaker; and, if and so far as those expenses are not covered by such a payment, the undertaker may recover the expenses, or the balance of them, from the person for whom the work was done.

(4A) *Referral of any dispute between a sewerage* undertaker and any other person to the Authority.

(5) Sections 291, 293 and 294 of the Public Health Act 1936 (which provide for the means of, and for limitations on, the recovery of expenses incurred by a local authority) shall apply in relation to the recovery by a sewerage undertaker of any sums under this section as they apply in relation to the recovery of expenses under that Act by a local authority.

(6) For the purposes of this section, the making of the communication between a drain or private sewer and a public sewer includes all such work as involves the breaking open of a street.

[Water Industry Act 1991, s 107 as amended by the Competition and Service (Utilities) Act 1992, s 35 and the Water Act 2003, s 36.]

7.11616 **108. Communication works by person entitled to communication** (1) Where a sewerage undertaker does not under section 107 above elect itself to make a communication to which a person is entitled under section 106 above, the person making it shall—

(*a*) before commencing the work, give reasonable notice to any person directed by the undertaker to superintend the carrying out of the work; and

(*b*) afford any such person all reasonable facilities for superintending the carrying out of the work.

(2) For the purpose—

(*a*) of exercising his rights under section 106 above; or

(*b*) of examining, repairing or renewing any drain or private sewer draining his premises into a public sewer, the owner or occupier of any premises shall be entitled to exercise the same powers as, for the purpose of carrying out its functions, are conferred on a sewerage undertaker by sections 158 and 161(1) below.

(3) The provisions of Part VI of this Act shall apply, with the necessary modifications, in relation to the power conferred by subsection (2) above as they apply in relation to the power conferred by sections 158 and 161(1) below.

[Water Industry Act 1991, s 108.]

**7.11617** **109. Unlawful communications** (1) Any person who causes a drain or sewer to communicate with a public sewer—

(*a*) in contravention of any of the provisions of section 106 or 108 above; or

(*b*) before the end of the period mentioned in subsection (4) of that section 106,

shall be guilty of an offence and liable, on summary conviction, to a fine not exceeding **level 4** on the standard scale.

(2) Whether proceedings have or have not been taken by a sewerage undertaker in respect of an offence under this section, such an undertaker may—

(*a*) close any communication made in contravention of any of the provisions of section 106 or 108 above; and

(*b*) recover from the offender any expenses reasonably incurred by the undertaker in so doing.

(3) Sections 291, 293 and 294 of the Public Health Act 1936 (which provide for the means of, and for limitations on, the recovery of expenses incurred by a local authority) shall apply in relation to the recovery by a sewerage undertaker of any sums under this section as they apply in relation to the recovery of expenses under that Act by a local authority.

[Water Industry Act 1991, s 109.]

*Provisions protecting sewerage system*

**7.11618** **111. Restrictions on use of public sewers** (1) Subject to the provisions of Chapter III of this Part, no person shall throw, empty or turn, or suffer or permit to be thrown or emptied or to pass, into any public sewer, or into any drain or sewer communicating with a public sewer—

(*a*) any matter likely to injure the sewer or drain, to interfere with the free flow of its contents or to affect prejudicially the treatment and disposal of its contents; or

(*b*) any such chemical refuse or waste steam, or any such liquid of a temperature higher than forty-three degrees Celsius, as by virtue of subsection (2) below is a prohibited substance; or

(*c*) any petroleum spirit or carbide of calcium.

(2) For the purposes of subsection (1) above, chemical refuse, waste steam or a liquid of a temperature higher than that mentioned in that subsection is a prohibited substance if (either alone or in combination with the contents of the sewer or drain in question) it is or, in the case of the liquid, is when so heated—

(*a*) dangerous;

(*b*) the cause of a nuisance; or

(*c*) injurious, or likely to cause injury, to health.

(3) A person who contravenes any of the provisions of this section shall be guilty of an offence and liable[1]—

(*a*) on summary conviction, to a fine not exceeding the **statutory maximum** and to a further fine not exceeding **£50 for each day on which the offence continues** after conviction;

(*b*) on conviction on indictment, to imprisonment for a term not exceeding **two years** or to a **fine** or to **both**.

(4) For the purposes of so much of subsection (3) above as makes provision for the imposition of a daily penalty—

(*a*) the court by which a person is convicted of the original offence may fix a reasonable date from the date of conviction for compliance by the defendant with any directions given by the court; and

(*b*) where a court has fixed such a period, the daily penalty shall not be imposed in respect of any day before the end of that period.

(5) In this section the expression "petroleum spirit" means any such—

(*a*) crude petroleum;

(*b*) oil made from petroleum or from coal, shale, peat or other bituminous substances; or

(*c*) product of petroleum or mixture containing petroleum,

as, when tested in the manner prescribed by or under the Petroleum (Consolidation) Act 1928, gives off an inflammable vapour at a temperature of less than twenty-three degrees Celsius.

[Water Industry Act 1991, s 111 as amended by the Water Act 2003, Sch 7.]

---

[1] For procedure in respect of an offence triable either way, see the Magistrates' Courts Act 1980, ss 17A–21 in PART I: MAGISTRATES' COURTS, PROCEDURE, ante.

*Interpretation of Chapter II[1]*

**7.11619 117. Interpretation of Chapter II** (1) In this Chapter[1], except in so far as the context otherwise requires—

"dock undertakers" means persons authorised by any enactment, or by any order, rule or regulation made under any enactment, to construct, work or carry on any dock, harbour, canal or inland navigation;

"domestic sewerage purposes", in relation to any premises, means any one or more of the following purposes, that is to say—

(*a*) the removal, from buildings on the premises and from land occupied with and appurtenant to the buildings, of the contents of lavatories;

(*b*) the removal, from such buildings and from such land, of water which has been used for cooking or washing; and

(*c*) the removal, from such buildings and such land, of surface water;

but does not, by virtue of paragraph (*b*) of this definition, include the removal of any water used for the business of a laundry or for a business of preparing food or drink for consumption otherwise than on the premises.

(2) References in this Chapter to the construction of a sewer or of any sewage disposal works include references to the extension of any existing sewer or works.

(3) In this Chapter "local authority", in relation to the Inner Temple and the Middle Temple, includes, respectively, the Sub-Treasurer of the Inner Temple and the Under-Treasurer of the Middle Temple.

(4) Every application made or consent given under this Chapter shall be made or given in writing.

(5) Nothing in sections 102 to 109 above or in sections 111 to 116 above shall be construed as authorising a sewerage undertaker to construct or use any public or other sewer, or any drain or outfall—

(*a*) in contravention of any applicable provision of the Water Resources Act 1991; or

(*b*) for the purpose of conveying foul water into any natural or artificial stream, watercourse, canal, pond or lake, without the water having been so treated as not to affect prejudicially the purity and quality of the water in the stream, watercourse, canal, pond or lake.

(6) A sewerage undertaker shall so carry out its functions under sections 102 to 105, 112, 115 and 116 above as not to create a nuisance.

[Water Industry Act 1991, s 117.]

[1] Chapter II comprises ss 98–117.

## Chapter 2A
## Duties Relating to Sewerage Services: Sewerage Licensees

*Offences*

**7.11619A 117P. Prohibition on unauthorised use of sewerage system** (1) No person may use the sewerage system of a sewerage undertaker whose area is wholly or mainly in England for the purpose of providing sewerage services to premises of—

(*a*) a customer,

(*b*) the person so using that system, or

(*c*) a person associated with that person.

(2) Subsection (1) is subject to subsections (3) and (4) and section 117R.

(3) Subsection (1) does not apply where that use of the system is made by—

(*a*) the sewerage undertaker, or

(*b*) a sewerage licensee in pursuance of its sewerage licence.

(4) The Secretary of State may by regulations specify further circumstances in which subsection (1) does not apply.

(5) A person who contravenes subsection (1) is guilty of an offence.

(6) An undertaking entered into which involves a contravention of subsection (1) is unenforceable.

(7) A person guilty of an offence under this section is liable—

(*a*) on summary conviction, to a fine not exceeding the statutory maximum;

(*b*) on conviction on indictment, to a fine.

(8) Proceedings for an offence under this section may not be instituted except by—

(*a*) the Secretary of State, or

(*b*) the Authority.

(9) For the purposes of this section, a person (A) is associated with another person (B) if they would be associated with each other for the purposes of Schedule 2B if A were a sewerage licensee.

(10) In this section and sections 117Q and 117R, references to the sewerage system of a sewerage undertaker are to be construed in accordance with section 17BA(7).

[Water Industry Act 1991, s 117P as inserted by the Water Act 2014, Sch 4 and amended by Sch 5 thereto, from a date to be appointed.]

**7.11619B 117Q. Prohibition on unauthorised removal of matter from sewerage system**

(1) No person other than the undertaker may remove matter from the sewerage system of a sewerage undertaker whose area is wholly or mainly in England.

(2) Subsection (1) is subject to subsections (3) and (4) and section 117R.

(3) Subsection (1) does not apply where—

(*a*) matter is removed by a sewerage licensee in pursuance of its sewerage licence, or

(*b*) matter is removed by another sewerage undertaker under a main connection agreement (within the meaning of section 110A).

(4) The Secretary of State may by regulations specify further circumstances in which subsection (1) does not apply.

(5) An undertaking entered into which involves a contravention of subsection (1) is unenforceable.

(6) A person who contravenes subsection (1) is guilty of an offence.

(7) A person guilty of an offence under this section is liable—

(*a*) on summary conviction, to a fine not exceeding £20,000;

(*b*) on conviction on indictment, to a fine.

(8) For the purposes of section 210, the penalty on conviction on indictment of an offence under this section is to be deemed to include imprisonment for a term not exceeding two years (in addition to or instead of a fine).

(9) Proceedings for an offence under this section may not be instituted except by—

(*a*) the Secretary of State, or

(*b*) the Authority.

[Water Industry Act 1991, s 117Q as inserted by the Water Act 2014, Sch 4 and amended by Sch 5 thereto, from a date to be appointed.]

**7.11619C 117R. Sections 117P and 117Q: exemptions** (1) The Secretary of State may by order made by statutory instrument grant exemption from section 117P(1) or 117Q(1) to—

(*a*) a person or persons of a class;

(*b*) generally or to such extent as may be specified in the order;

(*c*) unconditionally or subject to such conditions as may be specified in the order.

(2) Before making an order under subsection (1), the Secretary of State must give notice—

(*a*) stating that the Secretary of State proposes to make such an order and setting out the terms of the proposed order;

(*b*) stating the reasons why the Secretary of State proposes to make the order in the terms proposed; and

(*c*) specifying the time (not being less than 28 days from the date of publication of the notice) within which representations or objections with respect to the proposals may be made,

and must consider any representations or objections which are duly made and not withdrawn.

(3) The notice required by subsection (2) is to be given—

(*a*) by serving a copy of it on the Authority, and

(*b*) by publishing it in such manner as the Secretary of State considers appropriate for bringing it to the attention of those likely to be affected by the proposed order.

(4) Notice of an exemption granted to a particular person is to be given—

(*a*) by serving a copy of the exemption on the person, and

(*b*) by publishing the exemption in such manner as the Secretary of State considers appropriate for bringing it to the attention of other persons who may be affected by it.

(5) Notice of an exemption granted to persons of a particular class is to be given by publishing the exemption in such manner as the Secretary of State considers appropriate for bringing it to the attention of—

(*a*) persons of that class, and

(*b*) other persons who may be affected by it.

(6) An exemption may be granted—

(*a*) indefinitely, or

(*b*) for a period specified in, or determined by or under, the exemption.

(7) The conditions that may be specified may, in particular, require any person carrying on any activity allowed by the exemption—

(*a*) to comply with any direction given by the Secretary of State or the Authority as to such matters as are specified in the exemption or are of a description so specified;

(*b*) except in so far as the Secretary of State or the Authority consents to the person's doing or not doing them, not to do or to do such things as are specified in the exemption or are of a description so specified;

(*c*) to refer for determination by the Secretary of State or the Authority such questions arising under the exemption as are specified in the exemption or are of a description so specified.

[Water Industry Act 1991, s 117R as inserted by the Water Act 2014, Sch 4.]

**7.11619D 117S. Section 117R: supplementary** (1) The Secretary of State may by order made by statutory instrument revoke an order by which an exemption was granted to a particular person under section 117R(1) or vary an order by which more than one exemption was so granted so as to terminate any of the exemptions—

(*a*) at the person's request,

(*b*) in accordance with any provision of the order by which the exemption was granted, or

(*c*) if it appears to the Secretary of State inappropriate that the exemption should continue to have effect.

(2) The Secretary of State may by order made by statutory instrument revoke an order by which an exemption was granted to persons of a particular class under section 117R(1) or vary an order by which more than one exemption was so granted so as to terminate any of the exemptions—

(*a*) in accordance with any provision of the order by which the exemption was granted, or

(*b*) if it appears to the Secretary of State inappropriate that the exemption should continue to have effect.

(3) The Secretary of State may by direction withdraw an exemption granted to persons of a particular class under section 117R(1) from any person of that class—

(*a*) at the person's request,

(*b*) in accordance with any provision of the order by which the exemption was granted, or

(*c*) if it appears to the Secretary of State inappropriate that the exemption should continue to have effect in the case of the person.

(4) Before making an order under subsection (1)(*b*) or (*c*) or (2) or giving a direction under subsection (3)(*b*) or (*c*), the Secretary of State must—

(*a*) consult the Authority, and

(*b*) give notice—

(i) stating that the Secretary of State proposes to make such an order or give such a direction,

(ii) stating the reasons why the Secretary of State proposes to make such an order or give such a direction, and

(iii) specifying the time (not being less than 28 days from the date of publication of the notice) within which representations or objections with respect to the proposals may be made,

and must consider any representations or objections which are duly made and not withdrawn.

(5) The notice required by subsection (4)(*b*) is to be given—

(*a*) where the Secretary of State is proposing to make an order under subsection (1)(*b*) or (*c*), by serving a copy of it on the person to whom the exemption was granted;

(*b*) where the Secretary of State is proposing to make an order under subsection (2), by publishing it in such manner as the Secretary of State considers appropriate for bringing it to the attention of persons of the class of persons to whom the exemption was granted;

(*c*) where the Secretary of State is proposing to give a direction under subsection (3)(*b*) or (*c*), by serving a copy of it on the person from whom the Secretary of State proposes to withdraw the exemption.

(6) A statutory instrument containing—

(*a*) an order under subsection (1) or (2), or

(*b*) an order under section 117R(1),

is subject to annulment in pursuance of a resolution of either House of Parliament.

(7) The power to—

(*a*) make an order under subsection (1) or (2) or section 117R(1), or

(*b*) give a direction under subsection (3),

is exercisable by the Welsh Ministers (and not by the Secretary of State) in relation to any supply system of a sewerage undertaker whose area is wholly or mainly in Wales.

(8) Accordingly, subsections (1) to (5) and section 117R apply in relation to an order made or a direction given by the Welsh Ministers by virtue of subsection (7) as they apply in relation to an order made or direction given by the Secretary of State.

(9) A statutory instrument containing an order made by the Welsh Ministers by virtue of subsection (7) is subject to annulment in pursuance of a resolution of the Assembly.*

[Water Industry Act 1991, s 117S as inserted by the Water Act 2014, Sch 4.]

* **Amended by the Water Act 2014, Sch 5 from a date to be appointed**

## CHAPTER III[1]
## TRADE EFFLUENT

*Consent for discharge of trade effluent into public sewer*

**7.11620 118. Consent required for discharge of trade effluent into public sewer**

(1) Subject to the following provisions of this Chapter[1], the occupier of any trade premises in the area of a sewerage undertaker may discharge any trade effluent proceeding from those premises into the undertaker's public sewers if he does so with the undertaker's consent.

(2) Nothing in this Chapter shall authorise the discharge of any effluent into a public sewer

otherwise than by means of a drain or sewer.

(3) The following, that is to say—

(*a*) the restrictions imposed by paragraphs (*a*) and (*b*) of section 106(2) above; and

(*b*) section 111 above so far as it relates to anything falling within paragraph (*a*) or (*b*) of subsection (1) of that section,

shall not apply to any discharge of trade effluent which is lawfully made by virtue of this Chapter.

(4) Accordingly, subsections (3) to (8) of section 106 above and sections 108 and 109 above shall have effect in relation to communication with a sewer for the purpose of making any discharge which is lawfully made by virtue of this Chapter as they have effect in relation to communication with a sewer for the purpose of making discharges which are authorised by subsection (1) of section 106 above.

(5) If, in the case of any trade premises, any trade effluent is discharged without such consent or other authorisation as is necessary for the purposes of this Chapter, the occupier of the premises shall be guilty of an offence and liable[2]—

(*a*) on summary conviction, to a fine not exceeding the **statutory maximum**; and

(*b*) on conviction on indictment, to a **fine**.

[Water Industry Act 1991, s 118.]

[1] Chapter III of Pt IV comprises ss 118–141.

[2] For procedure in respect of an offence triable either way, see the Magistrates' Courts Act 1980, ss 17A–21 in PART I: MAGISTRATES' COURTS, ante.

**7.11621 119. Application for consent** (1) An application to a sewerage undertaker for a consent to discharge trade effluent from any trade premises into a public sewer of that undertaker shall be by notice served on the undertaker by the owner of occupier of the premises.

(2) An application under this section with respect to a proposed discharge of any such effluent shall state—

(*a*) the nature or composition of the trade effluent;*

(*b*) the maximum quantity of the trade effluent which it is proposed to discharge on any one day; and

(*c*) the highest rate at which it is proposed to discharge the trade effluent.*

[Water Industry Act 1991, s 119.]

* **Sub-ss (2)(ab), (3) inserted by the Water Act 2003, s 89 from a date to be appointed.**

**7.11622 120. Applications for the discharge of special category effluent** (1) Subject to subsection (3) below, where a notice containing an application under section 119 above is served on a sewerage undertaker with respect to discharges of any special category effluent, it shall be the duty of the undertaker to refer to the appropriate agency the questions—

(*a*) whether the discharges to which the notice relates should be prohibited; and

(*b*) whether, if they are not prohibited, any requirements should be imposed as to the conditions on which they are made.

(2) Subject to subsection (3) below, a reference which is required to be made by a sewerage undertaker by virtue of subsection (1) above shall be made before the end of the period of two months beginning with the day after the notice containing the application is served on the undertaker.

(3) There shall be no obligation on a sewerage undertaker to make a reference under this section in respect of any application if, before the end of the period mentioned in subsection (2) above, there is a refusal by the undertaker to give any consent on the application.

(4) It shall be the duty of a sewerage undertaker where it has made a reference under this section not to give any consent, or enter into any agreement, with respect to the discharges to which the reference relates at any time before the appropriate agency serves notice on the undertaker of his determination on the reference.

(5) Every reference under this section shall be made in writing and shall be accompanied by a copy of the notice containing the application in respect of which it is made.

(6) It shall be the duty of a sewerage undertaker, on making a reference under this section, to serve a copy of the reference on the owner or the occupier of the trade premises in question, according to whether the discharges to which the reference relates are to be by the owner or by the occupier.

(7)–(8) *Repealed.*

(9) If a sewerage undertaker fails, within the period provided by subsection (2) above, to refer to the appropriate agency any question which he is required by subsection (1) above to refer to the appropriate agency, the undertaker shall be guilty of an offence and liable[1]—

(*a*) on summary conviction, to a fine not exceeding the **statutory maximum;**

(*b*) on conviction on indictment, to a **fine**.

(10) If the appropriate agency becomes aware of any such failure as is mentioned in subsection (9) above, the appropriate agency may——

(*a*) if a consent under this Chapter to make discharges of any special category effluent has been granted on the application in question, exercise its powers to review under section 127 or 131 below, notwithstanding anything in subsection (2) of the section in question; or (*b*) in any other case, proceed as if the reference required by this section had been made.

[Water Industry Act 1991, s 120 as amended by the Environment Act 1995, Sch 22 and SI 2013/755.]

---

[1] For procedure in respect of this offence which is triable either way, see the Magistrates' Courts Act 1980, ss 17A–21, in PART I: MAGISTRATES' COURTS, PROCEDURE ante.

7.11623 **121. Conditions of consent** (1) The power of a sewerage undertaker, on an application under section 119 above, to give a consent with respect to the discharge of any trade effluent shall be a power to give a consent either unconditionally or subject to such conditions as the sewerage undertaker thinks fit to impose with respect to—

(*a*) the sewer or sewers into which the trade effluent may be discharged;

(*b*) the nature or composition of the trade effluent which may be discharged;*

(*c*) the maximum quantity of trade effluent which may be discharged on any one day, either generally or into a particular sewer; and

(*d*) the highest rate at which trade effluent may be discharged, either generally or into a particular sewer.

(2) Conditions with respect to all or any of the following matters may also be attached under this section to a consent to the discharge of trade effluent from any trade premises—

(*a*) the period or periods of the day during which the trade effluent may be discharged from the trade premises into the sewer;

(*b*) the exclusion from the trade effluent of all condensing water;

(*c*) the elimination or diminution, in cases falling within subsection (3) below, of any specified constituent of the trade effluent, before it enters the sewer;

(*d*) the temperature of the trade effluent at the time when it is discharged into the sewer, and its acidity or alkalinity at that time;

(*e*) the payment by the occupier of the trade premises to the undertaker of charges for the reception of the trade effluent into the sewer and for the disposal of the effluent;

(*f*) the provision and maintenance of such an inspection chamber or manhole as will enable a person readily to take samples, at any time, of what is passing into the sewer from the trade premises;

(*g*) the provision, testing and maintenance of such meters as may be required to measure the volume and rate of discharge of any trade effluent being discharged from the trade premises into the sewer;

(*h*) the provision, testing and maintenance of apparatus for determining the nature and composition of any trade effluent being discharged from the premises into the sewer;

(*i*) the keeping of records of the volume, rate of discharge, nature and composition of any trade effluent being discharged and, in particular, the keeping of records of readings of meters and other recording apparatus provided in compliance with any other condition attached to the consent; and

(*j*) the making of returns and giving of other information to the sewerage undertaker concerning the volume, rate of discharge, nature and composition of any trade effluent discharged from the trade premises into the sewer.

(3) A case falls within this subsection where the sewerage undertaker is satisfied that the constituent in question, either alone or in combination with any matter with which it is likely to come into contact while passing through any sewers—

(*a*) would injure or obstruct those sewers, or make the treatment or disposal of the sewage from those sewers specially difficult or expensive; or

(*b*) in the case of trade effluent which is to be or is discharged—

(i) into a sewer having an outfall in any harbour or tidal water; or

(ii) into a sewer which connects directly or indirectly with a sewer or sewage disposal works having such an outfall,

would cause or tend to cause injury or obstruction to the navigation on, or the use of, the harbour or tidal water.

(4) In the exercise of the power conferred by virtue of subsection (2)(*e*) above, regard shall be had—

(*a*) to the nature and composition and to the volume and rate of discharge of the trade effluent discharged;

(*b*) to any additional expense incurred or likely to be incurred by a sewerage undertaker in connection with the reception or disposal of the trade effluent; and

(*c*) to any revenue likely to be derived by the undertaker from the trade effluent.

(5) If, in the case of any trade premises, a condition imposed under this section is contravened, the occupier of the premises shall be guilty of an offence and liable[1]—

(*a*) on summary conviction, to a fine not exceeding the **statutory maximum**; and

(*b*) on conviction on indictment, to a **fine**.

(6) In this section "harbour" and "tidal water" have the same meanings as in the Merchant Shipping Act 1995.*

(7) This section has effect subject to the provisions of sections 133 and 135(3) below[2].

[Water Industry Act 1991, s 121 as amended by the Merchant Shipping Act 1995, Sch 13.]

* **Sub-s (1)(ba) and words inserted by the Water Act 2003, s 89 from a date to be appointed.**

1 For procedure in respect of an offence triable either way, see the Magistrates' Courts Act 1980, ss 17A–21 in PART I: MAGISTRATES' COURTS, PROCEDURE, ante.

2 Sections 133 and 135(3) deal respectively with the duty of an undertaker to secure compliance with conditions under this section or s 132, and to the fixing of charges only under a charges scheme.

7.11624 **132. Powers and procedure on references and reviews** (1) This section applies to—

(*a*) any reference to the appropriate agency under section 120, 123 or 130 above; and

(*b*) any review by [the appropriate agency under section 127 or 131 above.

(2) On a reference or review to which this section applies, it shall be the duty of the appropriate agency, before determining the questions which are the subject-matter of the reference or review—

(*a*) to give an opportunity of making representations or objections to the appropriate agency—

(ai) where the Environment Agency is the appropriate agency, to the NRBW if the discharge or proposed discharge of special category effluent is from trade premises in England;

(bi) where the NRBW is the appropriate agency, to the Environment Agency if the discharge or proposed discharge of special category effluent is from trade premises in Wales;

(i) to the sewerage undertaker in question; and

(ii) to the following person, that is to say, the owner or the occupier of the trade premises in question, according to whether it is the owner or the occupier of those premises who is proposing to be, or is, the person making the discharges or, as the case may be, a party to the agreement;

and

(*b*) to consider any representations or objections which are duly made to the appropriate agency with respect to those questions by a person to whom the appropriate agency is required to give such an opportunity and which are not withdrawn.

(3) On determining any question on a reference or review to which this section applies, the appropriate agency shall serve notice on [any person consulted under subsection (2)(*a*) above.

(4) A notice under this section shall state, according to what has been determined—

(*a*) that the discharges or operations to which, or to the proposals for which, the reference or review relates, or such of them as are specified in the notice, are to be prohibited; or

(*b*) that those discharges or operations, or such of them as are so specified, are to be prohibited except in so far as they are made or carried out in accordance with conditions which consist in or include conditions so specified; or

(*c*) that the appropriate agency has no objection to those discharges or operations and does not intend to impose any requirements as to the conditions on which they are made or carried out.

(5) Without prejudice to section 133 below, a notice under this section, in addition to containing such provision as is specified in sub-paragraph (4) above, may do one or both of the following, that is to say—

(*a*) vary or revoke the provisions of a previous notice with respect to the discharges or operations in question; and

(*b*) for the purpose of giving effect to any prohibition or other requirement contained in this notice, vary or revoke any consent under this Chapter or any agreement under section 129 above.

(6) Nothing in subsection (1) or (2) of section 121 above shall be construed as restricting the power of the appropriate agency, by virtue of subsection (4)(*b*) above, to specify such conditions as the appropriate agency considers appropriate in a notice under this section.

(7) *Repealed.*

(8) The appropriate agency shall send a copy of every notice served under this section to the Authority.

[Water Industry Act 1991, s 132 as amended by the Environment Act 1995, Schs 22 and 24 and the Water Act 2003, s 36 and SI 2013/755.]

7.11625 **133. Effect of determination on reference or review** (1) Where a notice under section 132 above has been served on a sewerage undertaker, it shall be the duty—

(*a*) of the undertaker; and

(*b*) in relation to that undertaker, of the Authority,

so to exercise the powers to which this section applies as to secure compliance with the provisions of the notice.

(2) This paragraph applies to the following powers, that is to say—

(*a*) in relation to a sewerage undertaker, its power to give a consent under this Chapter, any of its powers under section 121 or 124 above and any power to enter into or vary an agreement under section 129 above; and (*b*) in relation to the Authority, any of its powers under this Chapter.

(3) Nothing in subsection (1) or (2) of section 121 above shall be construed as restricting the power of a sewerage undertaker, for the purpose of complying with this section, to impose any condition specified in a notice under section 132 above.

(4) *Repealed.*

(5) A sewerage undertaker which fails to perform its duty under subsection (1) above shall be guilty of an offence and liable[1]—

(*a*) on summary conviction, to a fine not exceeding the **statutory maximum;**

(*b*) on conviction on indictment, to a **fine**.

(6) The appropriate agency may, for the purpose of securing compliance with the provisions of a notice under section 132 above, by serving notice on any person consulted under section 132(2)(*a*) above, vary or revoke—

(*a*) any consent given under this Chapter to make discharges of any special category effluent, or

(*b*) any agreement under section 129 above.

[Water Industry Act 1991, s 133 as amended by the Environment Act 1995, Sch 22 and the Water Act 2003, s 36 and SI 2013/755]

1 For procedure in respect of an offence which is triable either way, see the Magistrates' Courts Act 1980, ss 17A–21, in PART I: MAGISTRATES' COURTS, PROCEDURE, ante.

*Supplemental provisions of Chapter III*

7.11626 **135A. Power of the Environment Agency to acquire information for the purpose of its functions in relation to special category effluent** (1) For the purpose of the discharge of its functions under this Chapter, the Environment Agency may, by notice in writing served on any person, require that person to furnish such information specified in the notice as that Agency reasonably considers it needs, in such form and within such period following service of the notice, or at such time, as is so specified.

(2) A person who—

(*a*) fails, without reasonable excuse, to comply with a requirement imposed under subsection (1) above, or

(*b*) in furnishing any information in compliance with such a requirement, makes any statement which he knows to be false or misleading in a material particular, or recklessly makes a statement which is false or misleading in a material particular,

shall be guilty of an offence.

(3) A person guilty of an offence under subsection (2) above shall be liable[1]—

(*a*) on summary conviction, to a fine not exceeding the **statutory maximum;**

(*b*) on conviction on indictment, to a **fine** or to imprisonment for a term not exceeding **two years**, or to **both**.

[Water Industry Act 1991, s 135A as inserted by the Environment Act 1995, Sch 22.]

1 For procedure in respect of an offence which is triable either way, see the Magistrates' Courts Act 1980, ss 17A–21, in PART I: MAGISTRATES' COURTS, PROCEDURE, ante.

7.11627 **138. Meaning of "special category effluent"** (1) Subject to subsections (1A) and (2) below, trade effluent shall be special category effluent for the purposes of this Chapter if—

(*a*) such substances as may be prescribed[1] under this Act are present in the effluent or are present in the effluent in prescribed concentrations; or

(*b*) the effluent derives from any such process as may be so prescribed or from a process involving the use of prescribed substances or the use of such substances in quantities which exceed the prescribed amounts.

(1A) If trade effluent is produced, or to be produced, by operating any Part A installation or Part A mobile plant or otherwise carrying on any Part A activity, the operation or carrying on of which requires a permit, that effluent shall not be special category effluent for the purposes of this Chapter as from the determination date relating to the installation, plant or activity in question.

(1B) In subsection (1A)—

(*a*) "determination date", in relation to an installation, plant or activity, means—

(i) in the case of an installation, plant or activity in relation to which a permit is granted, the date on which it is granted, whether in pursuance of the application, or on an appeal, of a direction to grant it;

(ii) in the case of an installation, plant or activity in relation to which the grant of a permit is refused, the date of refusal or, on appeal, of the affirmation of the refusal,

and in this paragraph the references to an appeal are references to an appeal under the Environmental Permitting (England and Wales) Regulations 2007 ("the 2007 Regulations");

(aa) the expressions "Part A activity", "Part A installation" and "Part A mobile plant" have the same meaning as in the 2007 Regulations;

(*b*) "permit" means a permit granted under the 2007 Regulations.

(2) Trade effluent shall not be special category effluent for the purposes of this Chapter if it is produced, or to be produced, in any process which is a prescribed process designated for central

control as from the date which is the determination date for that process.

(3) In subsection (2) above "determination date", in relation to a prescribed process, means—

(*a*) in the case of a process for which authorisation is granted, the date on which the enforcing authority grants it, whether in pursuance of the application or, on an appeal, of a direction to grant it;

(*b*) in the case of a process for which authorisation is refused, the date of refusal or, on appeal, of the affirmation of the refusal.

(4) In subsection (2) and (3) above—

(*a*) "authorisation", "enforcing authority" and "prescribed process" have the meanings given by section 1 of the Environmental Protection Act 1990; and

(*b*) the references to designation for central control and to an appeal are references, respectively, to designation under section 4 of that Act and to an appeal under section 15 of that Act.*

(5) Without prejudice to the power in subsection (3) of section 139 below, nothing in this Chapter shall enable regulations under this section to prescribe as special category effluent any liquid or matter which is not trade effluent but falls to be treated as such for the purposes of this Chapter by virtue of an order under that section.**

[Water Industry Act 1991, s 138, as amended by SI 2000/1973 and SI 2007/3538.]

* **Sub-ss (2)–(4) repealed by the Pollution Prevention and Control Act 1999, Sch 3, from a date to be appointed.**

** **Sub-s (5) repealed by the Water Act 2003, Sch 9 from a date to be appointed.**

[1] See the Trade Effluent (Prescribed Processes and Substances) Regulations 1992, SI 1992/339.

**7.11628 139.** *Power to apply Chapter III to other effluents.*

*Interpretation of Chapter III*

**7.11629 141. Interpretation of Chapter III** (1) In this Chapter, except in so far as the context otherwise requires*—

"appropriate agency" means—

(a) in relation to the discharge or proposed discharge of special category effluent to a public sewer that directly or indirectly discharges or is to discharge (other than via a storm-water overflow sewer) that effluent to any controlled waters in England, the Environment Agency;

(b) in relation to the discharge or proposed discharge of special category effluent to a public sewer that directly or indirectly discharges or is to discharge (other than via a storm-water overflow sewer) that effluent to any controlled waters in Wales, the NRBW;

"special category effluent" has the meaning given by section 138 above;

"trade effluent"—

(*a*) means any liquid, either with or without particles of matter in suspension in the liquid, which is wholly or partly produced in the course of any trade or industry carried on at trade premises; and

(*b*) in relation to any trade premises, means any such liquid which is so produced in the course of any trade or industry carried on at those premises,

but does not include domestic sewage;

"trade premises" means, subject to subsection (2) below, any premises used or intended to be used for carrying on any trade or industry.

(2) For the purposes of this Chapter any land or premises used or intended for use (in whole or in part and whether or not for profit)—

(*a*) for agricultural or horticultural purposes or for the purposes of fish farming; or

(*b*) for scientific research or experiment,

shall be deemed to be premises used for carrying on a trade or industry; and the references to a trade or industry in the definition of "trade effluent" in subsection (1) above shall include references to agriculture, horticulture, fish farming and scientific research or experiment.

(3) Every application or consent made or given under this Chapter shall be made or given in writing.

(4) Nothing in this Chapter shall affect any right with respect to water in a river stream or watercourse, or authorise any infringement of such a right, except in so far as any such right would dispense with the requirements of this Chapter so far as they have effect by virtue of any regulations under section 138 above.

[Water Industry Act 1991, s 141 as amended by SI 2013/755.]

* **Words inserted by the Water Act 2003, s 88 from a date to be appointed.**

## PART V [1]

## FINANCIAL PROVISIONS

**7.11630** *The powers of undertakers include the power to fix charges for services including, in the case of a sewerage undertaker, charges for its trade effluent functions, and to demand and recover charges* (s 142). *Occupiers of premises are liable for charges for water supply and sewerage services; provision is made for notice on ceasing to occupy premises* (s 144). Charging by reference to volume (s 144A–144B).

*Provision is made for limiting connection charges* (s 146) *and emergency use of water* (s 147), *as well as restriction on charging for metering works* (s 148, amended by the Competition and Service (Utilities) Act 1992, s 53). *Regulations may be made relating to charging by volume* (s 149, amended by the Competition and Service (Utilities) Act 1992, s 53). *Billing disputes: Secretary of State may by regulations make provision for billing disputes to be referred to the Director for determination* (s 150A).

---

[1] Part V comprises ss 142–154. Water Industry (Charges) (Vulnerable Groups) (Consolidation) Regulations 2015, SI 2015/365 have been made which define vulnerable groups, ie persons who are in receipt of, or reside with a person in receipt of, certain benefits or tax credits, who are to be given assistance with water and sewerage charges by water and sewerage undertakers.

## Part VI[1]
## Undertakers' Powers and Works

**7.11631 157.** *Byelaws with respect of undertakers' waterways and land.*

---

[1] Part VI comprises ss 155–192.

*Powers to discharge water*

**7.11632 165. Discharges for works purposes** (1) Subject to the following provisions of this section and to section 166 below, where any water undertaker—

(*a*) is exercising or about to exercise any power conferred by section 158, 159, 161 or 163[1] above (other than the power conferred by section 161(3) above); or

(*b*) is carrying out, or is about to carry out, the construction, alteration, repair, cleaning, or examination of any reservoir, well, borehole, or other work belonging to or used by that undertaker for the purposes of, or in connection with, the carrying out of any of its functions,

the undertaker may cause the water in any relevant pipe or in any such reservoir, well, borehole or other work to be discharged into any available watercourse.

(2) Nothing in this section shall authorise any discharge which—

(*a*) damages or injuriously affects the works or property of any railway undertakers or navigation authority; or

(*b*) floods or damages any highway.

(3) If any water undertaker fails to take all necessary steps to secure that any water discharged by it under this section is as free as may be reasonably practicable from—

(*a*) mud and silt;

(*b*) solid, polluting, offensive or injurious substances; and

(*c*) any substances prejudicial to fish or spawn, or to spawning beds or food of fish,

the undertaker shall be guilty of an offence and liable, on summary conviction, to a fine not exceeding **level 3** on the standard scale.

(4) In this section "relevant pipe" means any water main (including a trunk main), resource main, discharge pipe or service pipe.

[Water Industry Act 1991, s 165.]

---

[1] Section 158 provides powers to lay pipes in streets, s 159 power to lay pipes in other land, s 161 power to deal with foul water and pollution (s 161(3) deals with the construction and maintenance of drains etc to deal with foul water or of otherwise preventing the pollution of waters, reservoir or underground strata from which the NRA or a water undertaker will take water) and s 163 is the power to fit stopcocks.

**7.11633 166. Consents for certain discharges under section 165** No discharge through any pipe exceeding 229 mm shall be made except with consent of the Environment Agency and any relevant navigation authority; water undertaker contravening is liable on summary conviction to fine not exceeding **level 3** on the standard scale.

[Water Industry Act 1991, s 166 amended by the Environment Act 1995, Sch 22—summarised.]

*Entry to land etc by water undertakers*

**7.11634 168–172.** *Entry to land etc*[1].

---

[1] Part II of Sch 6 applies for the purposes of ss 168, 169, 172 and Pt I thereof for ss 170 and 171.

**7.11635 173. Impersonation of persons entitled to entry** (1) A person who, without having been designated or authorised for the purpose by a relevant undertaker, purports to be entitled to enter any premises or vessel in exercise of a power exercisable in pursuance of any such designation or authorisation shall be guilty of an offence and liable, on summary conviction, to a fine not exceeding **level 4** on the standard scale.

(2) For the purposes of this section it shall be immaterial, where a person purports to be entitled to enter any premises or vessel, that the power which that person purports to be entitled to exercise does not exist or would not be exercisable even if that person had been designated or authorised by a relevant undertaker.

[Water Industry Act 1991, s 173.]

## Chapter II
## Protection of Undertakers' Works, Apparatus Etc
*Protection of apparatus in general*

**7.11636 174. Offences of interference with works etc** (1) Subject to subsection (2) below, if any person without the consent of the water undertaker—

(*a*) intentionally or recklessly interferes with any resource main, water main or other pipe vested in any water undertaker or with any structure, installation or apparatus belonging to any water undertaker; or

(*b*) by any act or omission negligently interferes with any such main or other pipe or with any such structure, installation or apparatus so as to damage it or so as to have an effect on its use or operation,

that person shall be guilty of an offence and liable, on summary conviction, to a fine not exceeding **level 3** on the standard scale.

(1A) Subject to subsection (2) below, if any person without the consent of the licensed water supplier—

(*a*) intentionally or recklessly interferes with any pipe or any structure, installation or apparatus which—

(i) is vested in any licensed water supplier (in the case of a pipe) or belongs to any such supplier (in any other case); and

(ii) is used in connection with the carrying on by the supplier of the activities authorised by its licence; or

(*b*) by any act or omission negligently interferes with any such pipe or with any such structure, installation or apparatus so as to damage it or so as to have an effect on its use or operation,

that person shall be guilty of an offence and liable, on summary conviction, to a fine not exceeding level 3 on the standard scale.

(2) A person shall not be guilty of an offence under subsection (1) or (1A) above—

(*a*) by reason of anything done in an emergency to prevent loss or damage to persons or property; or

(*b*) by reason of his opening or closing the stopcock fitted to a service pipe by means of which water is supplied to any premises by a water undertaker or licensed water supplier if—

(i) he has obtained the consent of every consumer whose supply is affected by the opening or closing of that stopcock or, as the case may be, of every other consumer whose supply is so affected; and

(ii) in the case of opening a stopcock, subsection (2A) below applies.

(2A) This subsection applies—

(*a*) in the case of a stopcock belonging to a water undertaker, if the stopcock was closed otherwise than by the undertaker;

(*b*) in the case of a stopcock belonging to a licensed water supplier—

(i) if the stopcock was closed otherwise than by the supplier; or

(ii) if the stopcock was closed by the supplier and the person in question for the purposes of subsection (2) above is the water undertaker whose supply system is used for the purpose of the supply made by the supplier,

and in this subsection the reference to the supply system of a water undertaker shall be construed in accordance with section 17B(5) above.

(3) Any person who, without the consent of the water undertaker—

(*a*) attaches any pipe or apparatus—

(i) to any resource main, water main or other pipe vested in a water undertaker; or

(ii) to any service pipe which does not belong to such an undertaker but which is a pipe by means of which water is supplied by such an undertaker to any premises;

(*b*) makes any alteration in a service pipe by means of which water is so supplied, or in any apparatus attached to any such pipe; or

(*c*) subject to subsection (4) below, uses *any pipe or apparatus* which has been attached or altered in contravention of this subsection,

shall be guilty of an offence and liable, on summary conviction, to a fine not exceeding **level 3** on the standard scale.

(3A) Any person who, without the consent of the licensed water supplier—

(*a*) attaches any pipe or apparatus to any pipe which is—

(i) vested in a licensed water supplier; and

(ii) used in connection with the carrying on by the supplier of the activities authorised by its licence;

(*b*) attaches any pipe or apparatus to any service pipe which does not belong to such a supplier or a water undertaker but which is a pipe by means of which water is supplied by such a supplier to any premises;

(*c*) makes any alteration in a service pipe by means of which water is so supplied, or in any apparatus attached to any such pipe; or

(*d*) subject to subsection (4) below, uses any pipe or apparatus which has been attached or altered in contravention of this subsection,

shall be guilty of an offence and liable, on summary conviction, to a fine not exceeding level 3 on the standard scale.

(4) In proceedings against any person for an offence by virtue of paragraph (*c*) of subsection (3) above or paragraph (*d*) of subsection (3A) above it shall be a defence for that person to show that he did not know, and had no grounds for suspecting, that the pipe or apparatus in question had been attached or altered as mentioned in subsection (3) or (3A) above (as the case may require).

(5) If any person wilfully or negligently injures or suffers to be injured any water fitting belonging to a water undertaker, he shall be guilty of an offence and liable, on summary conviction, to a fine not exceeding **level 1** on the standard scale.

(5A) If any person wilfully or negligently injures or suffers to be injured any water fitting which—

(*a*) belongs to a licensed water supplier; and

(*b*) is used in connection with the carrying on by the supplier of the activities authorised by its licence,

he shall be guilty of an offence and liable, on summary conviction, to a fine not exceeding level 1 on the standard scale.

(6) An offence under subsection (1) or (3) above shall constitute a breach of a duty owed to the water undertaker in question; and any such breach of duty which causes the undertaker to sustain loss or damage shall be actionable at the suit of the undertaker.

(7) The amount recoverable by virtue of subsection (6) above from a person who has committed an offence under subsection (3) above shall include such amount as may be reasonable in respect of any water wasted, misused or improperly consumed in consequence of the commission of the offence.

(8) A water undertaker may—

(*a*) do all such work as is necessary for repairing any injury done in contravention of subsection (5) above; and

(*b*) recover the expenses reasonably incurred by the undertaker in doing so from the offender summarily as a civil debt[1].

(8A) In this section "consumer"—

(*a*) in relation to a supply of water provided by a water undertaker to any premises, means a person who is for the time being the person on whom liability to pay charges to the undertaker in respect of that supply of water would fall;

(*b*) in relation to a supply of water provided by a licensed water supplier to any premises, means a person who is for the time being the person on whom liability to pay charges to the supplier in respect of that supply of water would fall.

(9) In this section "water fitting" has the same meaning as in Part III of this Act[2]; and in subsection (1) above the references to apparatus belonging to a water undertaker do not include references to any meter which belongs to such an undertaker and is used by it for the purpose of determining the amount of any charges which have been fixed by the undertaker by reference to volume.

[Water Industry Act 1991, s 174 as amended by the Water Act 2003, Sch 8.]

---

[1] For enforcement of a civil debt, see the Magistrates' Courts Act 1980, s 96, in PART I: MAGISTRATES' COURTS, PROCEDURE, ante.

[2] See s 93, ante.

*Protection of meters*

7.11637 **175. Offence of tampering with meter** (1) If any person—

(*a*) so interferes with a meter used by any relevant undertaker or licensed water supplier in determining the amount of any charges fixed in relation to any premises as intentionally or recklessly to prevent the meter from showing, or from accurately showing, the volume of water supplied to, or of effluent discharged from, those premises; or

(*b*) carries out any works which he knows are likely to affect the operation of such a meter or which require the disconnection of such a meter,

he shall be guilty of an offence and liable, on summary conviction, to a fine not exceeding **level 3** on the standard scale.

(2) A person shall not be guilty of an offence under this section in respect of anything done by him with the appropriate consent.

(3) *In subsection (2) above, the "appropriate consent" means*—

(*a*) if the meter is used by one relevant undertaker, the consent of that undertaker;

(*b*) if the meter is used by one licensed water supplier, the consent of that supplier;

(*c*) if the meter is used by two or more of the following persons—

(i) a relevant undertaker;

(ii) a licensed water supplier,

the consent of each of those persons.

(4) In subsection (3) above, references to the consent of a relevant undertaker are references to consent under section 176 below.

[Water Industry Act 1991, s 175 as amended by the Water Act 2003, Sch 8.]

7.11638 176. **Consent for the purposes of section 175** (1) Where an application is made to any relevant undertaker for a consent for the purposes of section 175 above, the undertaker—

(*a*) shall give notice of its decision with respect to the application as soon as reasonably practicable after receiving it; and

(*b*) subject to subsection (2) below, may make it a condition of giving any consent that the undertaker itself should carry out so much of any works to which the application relates as is specified in the notice of its decision.

(2) On such an application a relevant undertaker shall not refuse its consent, or impose any such condition as is mentioned in subsection (1)(*b*) above, unless it is reasonable to do so.

(3) Where any relevant undertaker has given a notice to any person imposing any such condition as is mentioned in subsection (1)(*b*) above, the undertaker—

(*a*) shall carry out those works as soon as reasonably practicable after giving the notice; and

(*b*) may recover from that person any expenses reasonably incurred by it in doing so.

(4) Any dispute between a relevant undertaker and any other person (including another such undertaker)—

(*a*) as to whether the undertaker or that other person should bear any expenses under subsection (3) above; or

(*b*) as to the amount of any expenses to be borne by any person under that subsection,

shall be referred to the arbitration of a single arbitrator appointed by agreement between the undertaker and that person or, in default of agreement, by the Authority.

(5) Subsection (3) above shall not apply where the person who was given the notice notifies the undertaker that the carrying out of the works to which the condition relates is no longer required.

[Water Industry Act 1991, s 176 as amended by the Water Act 2003, s 36.]

7.11639 177. **Financial obligations with respect to any interference with a meter** (1) A relevant undertaker which carries out any works made necessary by the commission of an offence under section 175 above shall be entitled to recover any expenses reasonably incurred in carrying out those works from the person who committed the offence.

(2) Any person who sustains any loss or damage in consequence of any failure by any relevant undertaker—

(*a*) to comply with any obligation imposed on it by section 176 above; or

(*b*) to exercise reasonable care in the performance of the duty imposed by subsection (3)(*a*) of that section,

shall be entitled to recover compensation from the undertaker.

(3) Any dispute between a relevant undertaker and any other person (including another such undertaker)—

(*a*) as to whether the undertaker or that other person should bear any expenses under this section;

(*b*) as to whether the undertaker should pay any compensation under this section; or

(*c*) as to the amount of any expenses to be borne by any person under this section or as to the amount of any such compensation,

shall be referred to the arbitration of a single arbitrator appointed by agreement between the undertaker and that person or, in default of agreement, by the Authority.

[Water Industry Act 1991, s 177 as amended by the Water Act 2003, s 36.]

*Obstruction of sewerage works etc*

7.11640 178. **Obstruction of sewerage works etc** (1) A person who wilfully obstructs any person acting in the execution of any of the relevant sewerage provisions shall be guilty of an offence and liable, on summary conviction, to a fine not exceeding **level 1** on the standard scale.

(2) If on a complaint made by the owner of any premises, it appears to a magistrates' court that the occupier of those premises is preventing the owner of those premises from carrying out any work which he is required to carry out by or under any of the relevant sewerage provisions, the court may order the occupier to permit the carrying out of the work.

(3) Sections 300 to 302 of the Public Health Act 1936 (which relate to the determination of questions by courts of summary jurisdiction and to appeals against such determinations) shall apply for the purposes of and in relation to the determination under subsection (2) above of any matter by a magistrates' court—

(*a*) as they apply for the purposes of or in relation to a determination by such a court under that Act; and

(*b*) in the case of section 302, as if the reference to a decision of a local authority included a reference to a decision of a sewerage undertaker.

[Water Industry Act 1991, s 178.]

## Chapter III
## Supplemental Provisions with respect to Undertakers' Powers

*Vesting of works in undertaker*

7.11641 **179. Vesting of works in undertaker** (1)-(3) ...

(4) If any water fittings let for hire by a water undertaker are suitably marked, they—

(*a*) shall continue to be the property of and removable by the undertaker, even if they are fixed to some part of the premises in which they are situated or are laid in the soil under any premises; and

(*b*) shall not be subject to distress or be liable to be taken control of under Schedule 12 to the Tribunals, Courts and Enforcement Act 2007, or to be taken in execution under any process of any court or in any proceedings in bankruptcy against a person in whose possession they are;

but nothing in this subsection shall affect the valuation for rating of any rateable hereditament.

(5) It is hereby declared that anything which, in pursuance of any arrangements under section 97 above, is done on behalf of a sewerage undertaker by a relevant authority within the meaning of that section is, subject to any provision to the contrary contained in any such arrangements, to be treated for the purposes of this section as done by the undertaker.

(6) he preceding provisions of this section are without prejudice, in relation to any company appointed to be a relevant undertaker, to the vesting of anything in that company by virtue of any scheme under Schedule 2 to this Act or of the exercise by any relevant undertaker of any power to acquire property by agreement or compulsorily.

(7) In this section—

"relevant pipe"—

(*a*) in relation to a water undertaker, means any water main (including a trunk main), resource main, discharge pipe or service pipe; and

(*b*) in relation to a sewerage undertaker, means any sewer, lateral drain or disposal main; and

"water fittings" has the same meaning as in Part III of this Act;

and water fittings let on hire by a water undertaker shall be treated as suitably marked for the purposes of this section if and only if they bear either such a distinguishing metal plate affixed to them or such a distinguishing brand or other mark conspicuously impressed or made on them as sufficiently indicates the undertaker as the actual owner of the fittings.

[Water Industry Act 1991, s 179 as amended by the Water Act 2003, Sch 8 and the Tribunals, Courts and Enforcement Act 2007, Sch 14.]

## Part VII
## Information Provisions

*Power to acquire and duties to provide information*

7.11642 **203. Power to acquire information for enforcement purposes** (1) Where it appears to the Secretary of State or the Authority—

(*a*) in the case of a company which holds an appointment as a relevant undertaker, that the company—

(i) may be contravening, or may have contravened, any condition of the appointment or any statutory or other requirement enforceable under section 18 above; or

(ii) may be causing or contributing to, or may have caused or contributed to, a contravention by a company holding a licence under Chapter 1A of Part 2 of this Act of any condition of the licence or any statutory or other requirement enforceable under section 18 above; or

(*b*) in the case of a company which holds a licence under that Chapter, that the company—

(i) may be contravening, or may have contravened, any condition of the licence or any statutory or other requirement enforceable under section 18 above; or

(ii) may be causing or contributing to, or may have caused or contributed to, a contravention by a company holding an appointment as a relevant undertaker of any condition of the appointment or any statutory or other requirement enforceable under section 18 above,

he may, for any purpose connected with such of his powers under Chapter II of Part II of this Act as are exercisable in relation to that matter, serve a notice under subsection (2) below on any person.

(2) A notice under this subsection is a notice signed by the Secretary of State or the Authority and—

(*a*) requiring the person on whom it is served to produce, at a time and place specified in the notice, to—

(i) the Secretary of State or the Authority; or

(ii) any person appointed by the Secretary of State or the Authority for the purpose,

any documents which are specified or described in the notice and are in that person's custody or under his control; or (*b*) requiring that person, if he is carrying on a business, to furnish, at the time and place and in the form and manner specified in the notice, the Secretary of State or the Authority with such information as may be specified or described in the notice.

(3) No person shall be required under this section to produce any documents which he could not be compelled to produce in civil proceedings in the High Court or, in complying with any requirement for the furnishing of information, to give any information which he could not be compelled to give in evidence in any such proceedings.

(4) A person who, without reasonable excuse, fails to do anything required of him by a notice under subsection (2) above shall be guilty of an offence and liable, on summary conviction, to a fine not exceeding **level 5** on the standard scale.

(5) A person who intentionally alters, suppresses or destroys any document which he has been required by any notice under subsection (2) above to produce shall be guilty of an offence and liable[1]—

(*a*) on summary conviction, to a fine not exceeding the **statutory maximum**;

(*b*) on conviction on indictment, to a **fine**.

(6) If a person makes default in complying with a notice under subsection (2) above, the High Court may, on the application of the Secretary of State or the Authority, make such order as the Court thinks fit for requiring the default to be made good; and any such order may provide that all the costs or expenses of and incidental to the application shall be borne by the person in default or by any officers of a company or other association who are responsible for its default.

(7) Nothing in this section shall be construed as restricting any power of the Secretary of State or the Authority under section 202 above or the conditions of an appointment under Chapter I of Part II of this Act or of a licence under Chapter 1A of that Part to require a company holding such an appointment or licence to produce any document to him or it or to furnish him or it with any information.

[Water Industry Act 1991, s 203 as amended by the Water Act 2003, s 36 and Sch 8.]

---

1 For procedure in respect of an offence triable either way, see the Magistrates' Courts Act 1980, ss 17A–21 in PART I: MAGISTRATES' COURTS, PROCEDURE, ante.

**7.11643 204. Provision of information to sewerage undertakers with respect to trade effluent discharges** (1) The owner or occupier of any land on or under which is situated any sewer, drain, pipe, channel or outlet used or intended to be used for discharging any trade effluent into a sewer of a sewerage undertaker shall, when requested to do so by the undertaker—

(*a*) produce to the undertaker all such plans of the sewer, drain, pipe, channel or outlet as the owner or, as the case may be, occupier possesses or is able without expense to obtain;

(*b*) allow copies of the plans so produced by him to be made by, or under the directions of, the undertaker; and

(*c*) furnish to the undertaker all such information as the owner or, as the case may be, occupier can reasonably be expected to supply with respect to the sewer, drain, pipe, channel or outlet.

(2) A request by a sewerage undertaker for the purposes of this section shall be made in writing.

(3) Every person who fails to comply with this section shall be guilty of an offence and liable, on summary conviction to a fine not exceeding **level 3** on the standard scale.

(4) Expressions used in this section and in Chapter III of Part IV of this Act have the same meanings in this section as in that Chapter; and, accordingly, section 139 above shall have effect for the purposes of this section as it has effect for the purposes of that Chapter.

[Water Industry Act 1991, s 204.]

*Restriction on disclosure of information*

**7.11644 206. Restriction on disclosure of information** (1) Subject to the following provisions of this section, no information with respect to any particular business which—

(*a*) has been obtained by virtue of any of the provisions of this Act; and

(*b*) relates to the affairs of any individual or to any particular business,

shall, during the lifetime of that individual or so long as that business continues to be carried on, be disclosed without the consent of that individual or the person for the time being carrying on that business.

(2) No person shall disclose any information furnished to him under section 204 above or under Chapter III of Part IV of this Act except—

(*a*) with the consent of the person by whom the information was furnished;

(*b*) in connection with the execution of that Chapter;

(*c*) for the purposes of any proceedings arising under that Chapter (including any appeal, application to the Secretary of State or the Authority or an arbitration);

(*d*) for the purposes of any criminal proceedings (whether or not so arising); or

(*e*) for the purposes of any report of any proceedings falling within paragraph (*c*) or (*d*) above.

(3) Subsection (1) above does not apply to any disclosure of information which is made—

(*a*) for the purpose of facilitating the carrying out by the Secretary of State, the Minister, the Environment Agency, the Scottish Environment Protection Agency, the Authority, the Council, the Competition Commission or a county council or local authority of any of his, its or, as the case may be, their functions by virtue of this Act, any of the other consolidation Acts, the Water Act 1989, Part I or* IIA of the Environmental Protection Act 1990, the Environment Act 1995, regulations under section 2 of the Pollution Prevention and Control Act 1999, or the Water Act 2003;

(*b*) for the purpose of facilitating the performance by a relevant undertaker of any of the duties imposed on it by or under this Act, any of the other consolidation Acts, the Water Act 1989 or the Water Act 2003 or by a licensed water supplier of any of the duties imposed on it by or under this Act;

(*c*) in pursuance of any duty imposed by section 27H above or section 197(1)(*a*) or (2) or 203(1), (1A), (2) or (2A) of the Water Resources Act 1991 (information about water flow and pollution);

(*d*) for the purpose of facilitating the carrying out by any person mentioned in Part I of Schedule 15 to this Act of any of his functions under any of the enactments or instruments specified in Part II of that Schedule;

(*e*) for the purpose of enabling or assisting the Secretary of State, the Treasury or the Financial Services Authority to exercise any powers conferred by or under the Financial Services and Markets Act 2000 or by the enactments relating to companies or insolvency;

(*ea*) for the purpose of enabling or assisting any inspector appointed under enactments relating to companies to carry out his functions;

(*f*) for the purpose of enabling an official receiver to carry out his functions under the enactments relating to insolvency or for the purpose of enabling or assisting a recognised professional body for the purposes of section 391 of the Insolvency Act 1986 to carry out its functions as such;

(*g*) for the purpose of facilitating the carrying out by the Health and Safety Executive of any of its functions under any enactment or of facilitating the carrying out by any enforcing authority, within the meaning of Part I of the Health and Safety at Work etc Act 1974, of any functions under a relevant statutory provision, within the meaning of that Act;

(*h*) for the purpose of facilitating the carrying out by the Comptroller and Auditor General of any of his functions under any enactment;

(*i*) in connection with the investigation of any criminal offence or for the purposes of any criminal proceedings;

(*j*) for the purposes of any civil proceedings brought under or by virtue of this Act, any of the other consolidation Acts, the Water Act 1989, the Water Act 2003 or any of the enactments or instruments specified in Part II of Schedule 15 to this Act, or of any arbitration under this Act, any of the other consolidation Acts, the Water Act 1989 or the Water Act 2003; or

(*k*) in pursuance of an EU obligation.

(4) Nothing in subsection (1) above shall be construed—

(*a*) as limiting the matters which may be published under section 38A, 95A or 201 above or may be included in, or made public as part of, a report of the Environment Agency, the Scottish Environment Protection Agency, the Authority, the Council (or any regional committee), or the Competition Commission under any provision of this Act, Part I or* IIA of the Environmental Protection Act 1990, the Water Resources Act 1991, the Environment Act 1995, regulations under section 2 of the Pollution Prevention and Control Act 1999, or the Water Act 2003; or

(*b*) as applying to any information which has been so published or has been made public as part of such a report or to any information exclusively of a statistical nature.

(5) Subject to subsection (6) below, nothing in subsection (1) above shall preclude the disclosure of information—

(*a*) if the disclosure is of information relating to a matter connected with the carrying out of the functions of a relevant undertaker, or with the carrying on by a licensed water supplier of activities under its licence, and is made by one Minister of the Crown or government department to another; or

(*b*) if the disclosure is for the purpose of enabling or assisting any public or other authority for the time being designated for the purposes of this section by an order made by the Secretary of State to discharge any functions which are specified in the order.

(6) The power to make an order under subsection (5) above shall be exercisable by statutory instrument subject to annulment in pursuance of a resolution of either House of Parliament; and where such an order designates an authority for the purposes of paragraph (*b*) of that subsection, the order may—

(*a*) impose conditions subject to which the disclosure of information is permitted by virtue of that paragraph; and

(*b*) otherwise restrict the circumstances in which disclosure is so permitted.

(7) Any person who discloses any information in contravention of the preceding provisions of

this section shall be guilty of an offence.

(8) A person who is guilty of an offence under this section by virtue of subsection (1) above shall be liable[1]—

(*a*) on summary conviction, to a fine not exceeding the **statutory maximum**;

(*b*) on conviction on indictment, to imprisonment for a term not exceeding **two years** or to a **fine** or to **both**.

(9) A person who is guilty of an offence under this section by virtue of subsection (2) above shall be liable, on summary conviction, to imprisonment for a term not exceeding **three months** or** to a fine not exceeding **level 3** on the standard scale or to both**.

(9A) Information obtained by the Authority in the exercise of functions which are exercisable concurrently with the OFT under Part I of the Competition Act 1998 is subject to Part 9 of the Enterprise Act 2002 (Information) and not to subsections (1) to (9) of this section.

(10) In this section "the other consolidation Acts" means the Water Resources Act 1991, the Land Drainage Act 1991 and the Water Consolidation (Consequential Provisions) Act 1991.

[Water Industry Act 1991, s 206 as amended by the Competition and Service (Utilities) Act 1992, Sch 1, the Environment Act 1995, Schs 22 and 24, the Competition Act 1998, Sch 10, SI 1999/506, the Pollution Prevention and Control Act 1999, Schs 2 and 3, SI 2001/3649, the Enterprise Act 2002, Sch 25, the Water Act 2003, s 36, SI 2008/960, SI 2011/1043 and the Deregulation Act 2015, Sch 23.]

* **Words repealed by the Pollution Prevention and Control Act 1999, Sch 3 from a date to be appointed.**

** **Words repealed by the Criminal Justice Act 2003, Sch 37 from a date to be appointed.**

1 For procedure in respect of an offence triable either way, see the Magistrates' Courts Act 1980, ss 17A–21 in PART I: MAGISTRATES' COURTS, PROCEDURE, ante.

*Provision of false information*

**7.11645 207. Provision of false information** (1) If any person, in furnishing any information or making any application under or for the purposes of any provision of this Act, makes any statement which he knows to be false in a material particular, or recklessly makes any statement which is false in a material particular, he shall be guilty of an offence and liable[1]—

(*a*) on summary conviction, to a fine not exceeding the **statutory maximum**;

(*b*) on conviction on indictment, to a **fine**.

(2) Proceedings for an offence under subsection (1) above shall not be instituted except by or with the consent of the Secretary of State or the Director of Public Prosecutions.

[Water Industry Act 1991, s 207 as amended by SI 2002/794.]

1 For procedure in respect of an offence triable either way, see the Magistrates' Courts Act 1980, ss 17A–21, in PART I: MAGISTRATES' COURTS, PROCEDURE, ante.

## PART VIII[1]

## MISCELLANEOUS AND SUPPLEMENTAL

*Miscellaneous*

**7.11646 208. Directions in the interests of national security** Person disclosing something when the Secretary of State has notified him that disclosure against the interests of national security: liable on conviction on indictment to two years imprisonment and/or a fine.

[Water Industry Act 1991, s 208(5), (6)—summarised.]

1 Part VIII comprises ss 208–223.

*Offences*

**7.11647 210. Offences by bodies corporate** (1) Where a body corporate is guilty of an offence under this Act and that offence is proved to have been committed with the consent or connivance of, or to be attributable to any neglect on the part of, any director, manager, secretary or other similar officer of the body corporate or any person who was purporting to act in any such capacity, then he, as well as the body corporate, shall be guilty of that offence and shall be liable to be proceeded against and punished accordingly.

(2) Where the affairs of a body corporate are managed by its members, subsection (1) above shall apply in relation to the acts and defaults of a member in connection with his functions of management as if he were a director of the body corporate.

[Water Industry Act 1991, s 210.]

**7.11648 211. Limitation on right to prosecute in respect of sewerage offences** Proceedings in respect of an offence created by or under any of the relevant sewerage provisions shall not, without the written consent of the Attorney-General, be taken by any person other than—

(*a*) a party aggrieved;

(*b*) a sewerage undertaker; or

(*c*) a body whose function it is to enforce the provisions in question.

[Water Industry Act 1991, s 211.]

*Judicial disqualification*

**7.11649 212. Judicial disqualification** No judge of any court or justice of the peace shall be disqualified from acting in relation to any proceedings to which a relevant undertaker is a party by reason only that he is or may become liable to pay a charge to that undertaker in respect of any service that is not the subject-matter of the proceedings.

[Water Industry Act 1991, s 212.]

**7.11650 216.** *Provisions relating to the service of documents.*

**7.11651 218. Meaning of "domestic purposes" in relation to water supply** (1) Subject to the following provisions of this section, in this Act references to domestic purposes, in relation to a supply of water to any premises or in relation to any cognate expression, are references to the drinking, washing, cooking, central heating and sanitary purposes for which water supplied to those premises may be used.

(2) Where the whole or any part of the premises are or are to be occupied as a house, those purposes shall be taken to include—

(*a*) the purposes of a profession carried on in that house or, where—

(i) that house and another part of the premises are occupied together; and

(ii) the house comprises the greater part of what is so occupied,

in that other part; and

(*b*) such purposes outside the house (including the washing of vehicles and the watering of gardens) as are connected with the occupation of the house and may be satisfied by a supply of water drawn from a tap inside the house and without the use of a hosepipe or similar apparatus.

(3) No such reference to domestic purposes shall be taken to include a reference—

(*a*) to the use of a bath having a capacity, measured to the centre line of overflow or in such other manner as may be prescribed, of more than two hundred and thirty litres;

(*b*) to the purposes of the business of a laundry; or

(*c*) to any purpose of a business of preparing food or drink for consumption otherwise than on the premises.

[Water Industry Act 1991, s 218.]

**7.11652 219. General interpretation** (1) In this Act, except in so far as the context otherwise requires—

"accessories", in relation to a water main, sewer or other pipe, includes any manholes, ventilating shafts, inspection chambers, settling tanks, wash-out pipes, pumps, ferrules or stopcocks for the main, sewer or other pipe, or any machinery or other apparatus which is designed or adapted for use in connection with the use or maintenance of the main, sewer or other pipe or of another accessory for it, but does not include any electronic communications apparatus unless it—

(*a*) is or is to be situated inside or in the close vicinity of the main, sewer or other pipe or inside or in the close vicinity of another accessory for it; and

(*b*) is intended to be used only in connection with the use or maintenance of the main, sewer or other pipe or of another accessory for it;

"the Assembly" means the National Assembly for Wales;

"the Authority" means the Water Services Regulation Authority;

"analyse", in relation to any sample of land, water or effluent, includes subjecting the sample to a test of any description, and cognate expressions shall be construed accordingly;

"conservancy authority" means any person who has a duty or power under any enactment to conserve, maintain or improve the navigation of a tidal water, and is not a harbour authority or navigation authority;

"contravention" includes a failure to comply, and cognate expressions shall be construed accordingly;

"the Council" means the Consumer Council for Water;

"damage", in relation to individuals, includes death and any personal injury, including any disease or impairment of physical or mental condition;

"disposal"—

(*a*) in relation to land or any interest or right in or over land, includes the creation of such an interest or right and a disposal effected by means of the surrender or other termination of any such interest or right; and

(*b*) in relation to sewage, includes treatment;

and cognate expressions shall be construed accordingly;

"disposal main" means (subject to subsection (2) below) any outfall pipe or other pipe which—

(*a*) is a pipe for the conveyance of effluent to or from any sewage disposal works, whether of a sewerage undertaker or of any other person; and

(*b*) is not a public sewer;

"domestic purposes", except in relation to sewers, shall be construed in accordance with section 218 above;

"drain" means (subject to subsection (2) below) a drain used for the drainage of one building or of any buildings or yards appurtenant to buildings within the same curtilage;

"effluent" means any liquid, including particles of matter and other substances in suspension in the liquid;

"enactment" includes an enactment contained in this Act or in any Act passed after this Act;

"engineering or building operations", without prejudice to the generality of that expression, includes—

(*a*) the construction, alteration, improvement, maintenance or demolition of any building or structure or of any reservoir, watercourse, dam, weir, well, borehole or other works; and

(*b*) the installation, modification or removal of any machinery or apparatus;

"harbour authority" means a person who is a harbour authority within the meaning of Chapter II of Part VI of the Merchant Shipping Act 1995 and is not a navigation authority;

"highway" and "highway authority" have the same meanings as in the Highways Act 1980;

"house" means any building or part of a building which is occupied as a dwelling-house, whether or not a private dwelling-house, or which, if unoccupied, is likely to be so occupied;

"information" includes anything contained in any records, accounts, estimates or returns;

"inland waters", has the same meaning as in the Water Resources Act 1991;

"lateral drain" means—

(*a*) that part of a drain which runs from the curtilage of a building (or buildings or yards within the same curtilage) to the sewer with which the drain communicates or is to communicate; or

(*b*) (if different and the context so requires) the part of a drain identified in a declaration of vesting made under section 102 above or in an agreement made under section 104 above;

"licensed water supplier" shall be construed in accordance with section 17B(9) above;

"limited company" means a company (as defined in section 1(1) of the Companies Act 2006) that—

(*a*) is registered in England and Wales or Scotland, and

(*b*) is limited by shares;

"local authority" means the council of a district or of a London borough or the Common Council of the City of London but, in relation to Wales, means the council of a county or county borough;

"local statutory provision" means—

(*a*) a provision of a local Act (including an Act confirming a provisional order);

(*b*) a provision of so much of any public general Act as has effect with respect to a particular area, with respect to particular persons or works or with respect to particular provisions falling within any paragraph of this definition;

(*c*) a provision of an instrument made under any provision falling within paragraph (*a*) or (*b*) above; or

(*d*) a provision of any other instrument which is in the nature of a local enactment;

"meter" means any apparatus for measuring or showing the volume of water supplied to, or of effluent discharged from, any premises;

"micro-organism" includes any microscopic biological entity which is capable of replication;

"modifications" includes additions, alterations and omissions, and cognate expressions shall be construed accordingly;

"navigation authority" means any person who has a duty or power under any enactment to work, maintain, conserve, improve or control any canal or other inland navigation, navigable river, estuary, harbour or dock;

"new towns residuary body" means—

(*a*) in relation to a new town in England, the Homes and Communities Agency so far as exercising functions in relation to anything transferred (or to be transferred) to it as mentioned in section 52(1)(*a*) or (*b*) of the Housing and Regeneration Act 2008 or the Greater London Authority so far as exercising its new towns and urban development functions (and references to the "English new towns residuary body" are to be read accordingly); and

(*b*) in relation to a new town in Wales, the Welsh Ministers so far as exercising functions in relation to anything transferred (or to be transferred) to them as mentioned in section 36(1)(*a*)(i) or (ii) of the New Towns Act 1981 (and references to the "Welsh new towns residuary body" are to be read accordingly);

"notice" means notice in writing;

"the OFT" means the Office of Fair Trading;

"owner", in relation to any premises, means the person who—

(*a*) is for the time being receiving the rack-rent of the premises, whether on his own account or as agent or trustee for another person; or

(*b*) would receive the rack-rent if the premises were let at a rack-rent,

and cognate expressions shall be construed accordingly;

"prescribed" means prescribed by regulations made by the Secretary of State;

"public authority" means any Minister of the Crown or government department, the Environment Agency, any local authority or county council or any person certified by the Secretary of State to be a public authority for the purposes of this Act;

"public sewer" means (subject to section 106 (1A) above) a sewer for the time being vested in a sewerage undertaker in its capacity as such, whether vested in that undertaker by virtue of a scheme under Schedule 2 to the Water Act 1989 or Schedule 2 to this Act or under section 179 above or otherwise, and "private sewer" shall be construed accordingly;

"railway undertakers" means the British Railways Board, Transport for London or any subsidiary (within the meaning of the Greater London Authority Act 1999) of Transport for London, or any other person authorised by any enactment, or by any order, rule or regulation made under any enactment, to construct, work or carry on any railway;

"records" includes computer records and any other records kept otherwise than in a document;

"regional committee" means a regional committee of the Council established under section 27A above;

"the relevant sewerage provisions" means the following provisions of this Act, that is to say—

(*a*) Chapters II and III of Part IV (except sections 98 to 101 and 110 and so much of Chapter III of that Part as provides for regulations under section 138 or has effect by virtue of any such regulations);

(*b*) sections 160, 171, 172(4), 178, 184, 189, 196 and 204 and paragraph 4 of Schedule 12; and

(*c*) the other provisions of this Act so far as they have effect for the purposes of any provision falling within paragraph (*a*) or (*b*) of this definition;

"relevant undertaker" means a water undertaker or sewerage undertaker;

"resource main" means (subject to subsection (2) below) any pipe, not being a trunk main, which is or is to be used for the purpose of—

(*a*) conveying water from one source of supply to another, from a source of supply to a regulating reservoir or from a regulating reservoir to a source of supply; or

(*b*) giving or taking a supply of water in bulk;

"service pipe" means (subject to subsection (2) below) so much of a pipe which is, or is to be, connected with a water main for supplying water from that main to any premises as—

(*a*) is or is to be subject to water pressure from that main; or

(*b*) would be so subject but for the closing of some valve,

and includes part of any service pipe;

"services" includes facilities;

"sewer" includes (without prejudice to subsection (2) below) all sewers and drains (not being drains within the meaning given by this subsection) which are used for the drainage of buildings and yards appurtenant to buildings;

"sewerage services" includes the disposal of sewage and any other services which are required to be provided by a sewerage undertaker for the purpose of carrying out its functions;

"special administration order" has the meaning given by section 23 above;

"statutory water company" means any company which was a statutory water company for the purposes of the Water Act 1973 immediately before 1st September 1989;

"stopcock" includes any box or pit in which a stopcock is enclosed and the cover to any such box or pit;

"street" has, subject to subsection (5) below, the same meaning as in Part III of the New Roads and Street Works Act 1991;

"subordinate legislation" has the same meaning as in the Interpretation Act 1978;

"substance" includes micro-organisms and any natural or artificial substance or other matter, whether it is in solid or liquid form or in the form of a gas or vapour;

"supply of water in bulk" means a supply of water for distribution by a water undertaker taking the supply;

"surface water" includes water from roofs;

"trunk main" means a water main which is or is to be used by a water undertaker for the purpose of—

(*a*) conveying water from a source of supply to a filter or reservoir or from one filter or reservoir to another filter or reservoir; or

(*b*) conveying water in bulk, whether in the course of taking a supply of water in bulk or otherwise, between different places outside the area of the undertaker, from such a place to any part of that area or from one part of that area to another part of that area;

"underground strata" means strata subjacent to the surface of any land;

"vessel" includes a hovercraft within the meaning of the Hovercraft Act 1968;

"water main" means (subject to subsection (2) below) any pipe, not being a pipe for the time being vested in a person other than the undertaker, which is used or to be used by a water undertaker or licensed water supplier for the purpose of making a general supply of water available to customers or potential customers of the undertaker or supplier, as distinct from for the purpose of providing a supply to particular customers;

"watercourse" includes all rivers, streams, ditches, drains, cuts, culverts, dykes, sluices, sewers and passages through which water flows except mains and other pipes which belong to the Environment Agency or a water undertaker or are used by a water undertaker or any other person for the purpose only of providing a supply of water to any premises.

(2) In this Act—

(*a*) references to a pipe, including references to a main, a drain or a sewer, shall include references to a tunnel or conduit which serves or is to serve as the pipe in question and to any accessories for the pipe; and

(*b*) references to any sewage disposal works shall include references to the machinery and equipment of those works and any necessary pumping stations and outfall pipes;

and, accordingly, references to the laying of a pipe shall include references to the construction of such a tunnel or conduit, to the construction or installation of any such accessories and to the making of a connection between one pipe and another.

(3) Nothing in Part III or IV of this Act by virtue of which a relevant undertaker owes a duty to any particular person to lay any water main, resource main or service pipe or any sewer, lateral drain, disposal main or discharge pipe shall be construed—

(*a*) as conferring any power in addition to the powers conferred apart from those Parts; or

(*b*) as requiring the undertaker to carry out any works which it has no power to carry out.

(4) References in this Act to the fixing of charges in relation to any premises by reference to volume are references to the fixing of those charges by reference to the volume of water supplied to those premises, to the volume of effluent discharged from those premises, to both of those factors or to one or both of those factors taken together with other factors.

(4A) In this Act, unless otherwise stated, references to the supply system of a water undertaker are to the water mains and other pipes which it is the undertaker's duty to develop and maintain by virtue of section 37 above.

(5) Until the coming into force of Part III of the New Roads and Street Works Act 1991, the definition of "street" in subsection (1) above shall have effect as if the reference to that Part were a reference to the Public Utilities Street Works Act 1950; but nothing in this section shall be taken—

(*a*) to prejudice the power of the Secretary of State under that Act of 1991 to make an order bringing Part III of that Act into force on different days for different purposes (including the purposes of this section); or

(*b*) in the period before the coming into force of that Part, to prevent references in this Act to a street, where the street is a highway which passes over a bridge or through a tunnel, from including that bridge or tunnel.

(6) For the purposes of any provision of this Act by or under which power is or may be conferred on any person to recover the expenses incurred by that person in doing anything, those expenses shall be assumed to include such sum as may be reasonable in respect of establishment charges or overheads.

(7) References in this Act to the later or latest of two or more different times or days are, in a case where those times or days coincide, references to the time at which or, as the case may be, the day on which they coincide.

(8) Where by virtue of any provision of this Act any function of a Minister of the Crown is exercisable concurrently by different Ministers, that function shall also be exercisable jointly by any two or more of those Ministers.

(9) Sub-paragraph (1) of paragraph 1 of Schedule 2 to the Water Consolidation (Consequential Provisions) Act 1991 has effect (by virtue of sub-paragraph (2)(*b*) of that paragraph) so that references in this Act to things done under or for the purposes of provisions of this Act or the Water Resources Act 1991 include references to things done, or treated as done, under or for the purposes of the corresponding provisions of the law in force before the commencement of this Act[1].

(10) If the Assembly designates a person as Chief Inspector of Drinking Water for Wales under section 86(1B) above, references in this Act to the Chief Inspector of Drinking Water, as respects anything to be done in relation to him, shall be taken as references to the person designated as the Chief Inspector of Drinking Water by the Secretary of State and also the person designated by the Assembly as the Chief Inspector of Drinking Water for Wales.

[Water Industry Act 1991, s 219 as amended by the Local Government (Wales) Act 1994, Sch 11, the Merchant Shipping Act 1995, Sch 13, the Environment Act 1995, Schs 22 and 24, SI 1999/506, the Enterprise Act 2002, Sch 25 SI 2003/1615, the Communications Act 2003, Sch 17 and the Water Act 2003, ss 57, 97, 99 and Sch 8, the Water Act 2003, Sch 7, the Housing and Regeneration Act 2008, Sch 8, SI 2009/1941 and the Localism Act 2011, Sch 19.]

[1] Definitions not relevant to the parts of this Act printed here have been omitted.

**7.11653 220.** *Effect of local Acts.*

**7.11654 221.** *Crown application.*

## SCHEDULE 4A

PREMISES THAT ARE NOT TO BE DISCONNECTED FOR NON-PAYMENT OF CHARGES — Section 63A

*(Inserted by the Water Industry Act 1999, Sch 1 and amended by the Care Standards Act 2000, s 116, the Health and Social Care (Community Health and Standards Act 2002, Sch 11, SI 2003/1016, the Fire and Rescue Services Act 2004, Sch 1, the Housing Act 2004, Sch 15, the National Health Service (Consequential Provisions) Act 2006, Sch 1 and the Childcare Act 2006, Sch 2, SI 2010/750 and 2224, the Criminal Justice and Courts Act 2015, Sch 9 and SI 2015/914.)*

**7.11655** 1. (1) Any dwelling which is occupied by a person as his only or principal home.

(2) In this paragraph "dwelling" means—

(*a*) a private dwelling-house (which may be a building or part of a building),

(*b*) a caravan within the meaning of Part I of the Caravan Sites and Control of Development Act 1960 (disregarding the amendment made by section 13(2) of the Caravan Sites Act 1968), or

(*c*) a boat or similar structure designed or adapted for use as a place of permanent habitation.

2. (1) Any house in multiple occupation which does not constitute a dwelling within the meaning of paragraph 1 above and in which any person has his only or principal home.

(2) In this paragraph "house in multiple occupation" means a house in multiple occupation as defined by sections 254 to 259 of the Housing Act 2004, as they have effect for the purposes of Part 1 of that Act (that is, without the exclusions contained in Schedule 14 to that Act).

**3.** (1) Accommodation for the elderly in which a person has his only or principal home.

(2) In this paragraph "accommodation for the elderly" means residential accommodation to which sub-paragraph (3) or (4) below applies, but which is not a dwelling within the meaning of paragraph 1 above or a house in multiple occupation within the meaning of paragraph 2 above.

(3) This sub-paragraph applies to residential accommodation—

(*a*) which is particularly suitable, having regard to its location, size, design, heating systems and other features, for occupation by elderly persons,

(*b*) which it is the practice of the landlord to let for occupation by persons aged 60 or more, and

(*c*) where the services of a warden are provided.

(4) This sub-paragraph applies to any building or part of a building designed or adapted for use as residential accommodation for elderly persons.

**4.** A hospital as defined by section 275 of the National Health Service Act 2006 in relation to England or section 206 of the National Health Service (Wales) Act 2006 in relation to Wales.

**5.** Premises used for the provision of medical services by a registered medical practitioner.

**6.** Premises used for the provision of dental services by a person who under the Dentists Act 1984 is permitted to practise dentistry.

**7.** Premises not falling within paragraph 5 or 6 above which are used for the provision of primary medical services or primary dental services under Part 1 of the National Health Service Act 2006 or the National Health Service (Wales) Act 2006.

**8.** (1) A care home or independent hospital.

(2) In this paragraph—

"care home" means—

(*a*) a care home within the meaning of the Care Standards Act 2000;

(*b*) a building or part of a building in which residential accommodation is provided under section 21 of the National Assistance Act 1948.

(*c*) a building or part of a building in which accommodation is provided under Part 1 of the Care Act 2014;

(3) In this paragraph "independent hospital", in relation to England, means—

(*a*) an establishment, not being a health service hospital as defined by section 275 of the National Health Service Act 2006,—

(i) the main purpose of which is to provide medical or psychiatric treatment for illness or mental disorder or palliative care; or

(ii) in which (whether or not other services are provided) any of the services listed in sub-paragraph (5) are provided; or

(*b*) any other establishment, not being a health service hospital as so defined, in which treatment or nursing (or both) are provided for persons liable to be detained under the Mental Health Act 1983.

(4) In this paragraph "independent hospital", in relation to Wales, means an independent hospital within the meaning of the Care Standards Act 2000.

(5) The services referred to in sub-paragraph (3)(*a*)(ii) are as follows—

(*a*) medical treatment under anaesthesia or intravenously administered sedation;

(*b*) dental treatment under general anaesthesia;

(*c*) obstetric services and, in connection with childbirth, medical services;

(*d*) termination of pregnancies;

(*e*) cosmetic surgery, other than—

(i) ear and body piercing,

(ii) tattooing,

(iii) the subcutaneous injection of a substance or substances into the skin for cosmetic purposes, or

(iv) the removal of hair roots or small blemishes on the skin by the application of heat using an electric current.

(6) In sub-paragraph (3)(*a*)(i)—

(*a*) "illness" includes any injury; and

(*b*) "mental disorder" has the same meaning as in the Mental Health Act 1983.

**9.** A children's home within the meaning of the Care Standards Act 2000.

**10.** A school within the meaning of the Education Act 1996.

**11.** (1) Premises used by an institution within the further education sector or an institution within the higher education sector for, or in connection with, the provision of education.

(2) In this paragraph the references to an institution within the further education sector or within the higher education sector are to be construed in accordance with section 91 of the Further and Higher Education Act 1992.

**12.** (1) Premises in England which are used for the provision of childcare by a person who is registered (otherwise than as a childminder) under Part 3 of the Childcare Act 2006 in respect of the premises.

(2) Premises in Wales which are used for the provision of day care for children by a person who is registered under Part 10A of the Children Act 1989 in respect of the premises.

**13.** (1) A prison or removal centre.

(2) In this paragraph "prison" means—

(*a*) any prison, young offender institution or remand centre* which is under the general superintendence of, or is provided by, the Secretary of State under the Prison Act 1952, including a contracted out prison within the meaning of Part IV of the Criminal Justice Act 1991,

(*b*) any secure training centre,

(*ba*) a secure college, or

(*c*) a naval, military or air force prison.

(3) In this paragraph "removal centre" means any premises which are used solely for detaining persons under the Immigration Act 1971 or the Nationality, Immigration and Asylum Act 2002, but which are not a part of a prison.

---

*** Words substituted by the Criminal Justice and Court Services Act 2000, Sch 7 from a date to be appointed.**

**14.** Premises occupied for the purposes of a police force.

**15.** Premises occupied for the purposes of a fire and rescue authority.

**16.** Premises occupied for the purposes of the provision of an ambulance service by a National Health Service trust established under Part I of the National Health Service Act 2006 or the National Health Service (Wales) Act 2006 or by an NHS foundation trust.

## SCHEDULE 6
### Supplemental Provisions Relating to Rights of Entry

*(As amended by SI 2009/1307)* Sections 71 to 84 and 162 to 172

### Part I
### Rights requiring Notice for Entry to Non-business Premises

*Notice of entry*

7.11656 **1.** (1) Where this Part of this Schedule applies to any right of entry conferred by a provision of this Act, admission to any premises which are not business premises shall not be demanded as of right by virtue of that provision, unless twenty-four hours notice of the intended entry has been given to the occupier of the premises.

(2) In this paragraph "business premises" means—

(*a*) any factory; or

(*b*) any place in which persons are employed otherwise than in domestic service;

and in this sub-paragraph "factory" has the same meaning as in the Factories Act 1961.

*Warrants to exercise right*

**2.** (1) Subject to sub-paragraph (3) below, if it is shown to the satisfaction of a justice of the peace, on sworn information in writing—

(*a*) that any one or more of the conditions specified in sub-paragraph (2) below is fulfilled in relation to any premises which a person is entitled to enter by virtue of a right of entry to which this Part of this Schedule applies; and

(*b*) that there is reasonable ground for entry to the premises for any purpose for which the right is exercisable,

the justice may by a warrant under his hand authorise that person to enter the premises, if need be by force.

(2) The conditions mentioned in sub-paragraph (1) above are—

(*a*) that admission to the premises has been refused to the person having the right to enter them;

(*b*) that such refusal is apprehended;

(*c*) that the premises are unoccupied or the occupier is temporarily absent;

(*d*) that the case is one of urgency;

(*e*) that an application for admission would defeat the object of the entry.

(3) A warrant under this Part of this Schedule shall not be issued by a justice of the peace in a case in which he is satisfied that the condition mentioned in paragraph (*a*) or (*b*) of sub-paragraph (2) above is fulfilled unless he is also satisfied—

(*a*) that notice of the intention to apply for a warrant has been given to the occupier;

(*b*) that a condition mentioned in either of paragraphs (*c*) and (*d*) of that sub-paragraph is also fulfilled in relation to the premises; or

(*c*) that the giving of such notice as is mentioned in paragraph (*a*) above would defeat the object of the entry.

(4) Every warrant under this Part of this Schedule shall continue in force until the purpose for which the entry is necessary has been fulfilled.

(5) A person leaving any unoccupied premises which he has entered by virtue of a warrant under this Part of this Schedule shall leave them as effectually secured against trespassers as he found them.

*Supplementary power of person making entry*

**3.** Any person entitled to enter any premises by virtue of a right to which this Part of this Schedule applies, or of a warrant under this Part of this Schedule, may take with him such other persons as may be necessary.

*Obstruction of person exercising right*

**4.** Any person who wilfully obstructs any person upon whom a right of entry has been conferred by virtue of—

(*a*) any provision of this Act relating to a right of entry to which this Part of this Schedule applies; or

(*b*) a warrant under this Part of this Schedule,

shall be guilty of an offence and liable, on summary conviction, to a fine not exceeding **level 1** on the standard scale.

*Duty of persons exercising rights to maintain confidentiality*

**5.** (1) Without prejudice to section 206 of this Act and subject to sub-paragraphs (2) and (3) below, any person who is admitted to any premises in compliance—

(*a*) with any provision of this Act relating to a right of entry to which this Part of this Schedule applies; or

(*b*) with a warrant under this Part of this Schedule,

shall be guilty of an offence under this paragraph if he discloses to any person any information obtained by him there with regard to any manufacturing process or trade secret.

(2) A person shall not be guilty of an offence under this paragraph in respect of any disclosure made in the performance of his duty.

(3) For the purposes of the application of this Part of this Schedule to the right conferred by section 171 of this Act, the reference to premises in subsection (1) above shall have effect as a reference only to business premises, within the meaning of paragraph 1 above.

(4) A person who is guilty of an offence under this paragraph, other than such a person as is mentioned in sub-paragraph (5) below, shall be liable[1]—

(*a*) on summary conviction, to imprisonment for a term not exceeding **three months** or to a fine not exceeding the **statutory maximum** or to **both**;

(*b*) on conviction on indictment, to imprisonment for a term not exceeding **three months** or to a **fine** or to **both**.*

(5) A person who is guilty of an offence under this paragraph by virtue of the application of this Part of this Schedule to the rights conferred by section 171 of this Act shall be liable, on summary conviction, to imprisonment for a term not exceeding **three months** or* to a fine not exceeding **level 3** on the standard scale or to **both***.

* **Words substituted and repealed by the Criminal Justice Act 2003, Schs 32 and 37 from a date to be appointed.**

[1] For procedure in respect of an offence triable either way, see the Magistrates' Courts Act 1980, ss 17A–21 in PART I: MAGISTRATES' COURTS, PROCEDURE, ante.

## PART II
## OTHER RIGHTS OF ENTRY AND RELATED POWERS

*Notice of entry*

**6.** (1) Without prejudice to any power exercisable by virtue of a warrant under this Part of this Schedule, no person shall make an entry into any premises by virtue of any right or power to which this Part of this Schedule applies except—

(*a*) in an emergency; or

(*b*) at a reasonable time and after the required notice of the intended entry has been given to the occupier of the premises.

(2) For the purposes of this paragraph the required notice is—

(*a*) in the case of the rights and powers conferred by virtue of any of sections 74(4), 84(2) and (3), 86(4) and 170(1)(*c*) and (3) of this Act, twenty-four hours' notice; and

(*b*) in any other case, seven days' notice.

(3) For the purposes of the application of this Part of this Schedule to any right or power conferred by section 168 of this Act the reference in sub-paragraph (1) above to an emergency—

(*a*) in relation to any entry to premises for the purposes of, or for purposes connected with, the exercise or proposed exercise of any power in relation to a street, includes a reference to any circumstances requiring the carrying out of emergency works within the meaning of Part III of the New Roads and Street Works Act 1991; and

(*b*) in relation to any other entry to premises, includes a reference to any danger to property and to any interruption of a supply of water provided to any premises by any person and to any interruption of the provision of sewerage services to any premises.

(4) Until the coming into force of section 52 of the New Roads and Street Works Act 1991, sub-paragraph (3)(*a*) above shall have effect as if the reference to Part III of that Act were a reference to the Public Utilities Street Works Act 1950; but nothing in this sub-paragraph shall be taken to prejudice the power of the Secretary of State under that Act of 1991 to make an order bringing that section 52 into force on different days for different purposes (including the purposes of this paragraph).

(5) For the purposes of the application of this Part of this Schedule to the rights and other powers conferred by section 172 of this Act sub-paragraph (1) above shall have effect as if the power in an emergency to make an entry to any premises otherwise than at a reasonable time and after the required notice were omitted.

*Warrant to exercise right or power*

**7.** (1) If it is shown to the satisfaction of a justice of the peace on sworn information in writing—

(*a*) that there are reasonable grounds for the exercise in relation to any premises of a right or power to which this Part of this Schedule applies; and

(*b*) that one or more of the conditions specified in sub-paragraph (2) below is fulfilled in relation to those premises,

the justice may by warrant authorise the relevant authority to designate a person who shall be authorised to exercise the right or power in relation to those premises in accordance with the warrant and, if need be, by force.

(2) The conditions mentioned in sub-paragraph (1)(*b*) above are—

(*a*) that the exercise of the right or power in relation to the premises has been refused;

(*b*) that such a refusal is reasonably apprehended;

(*c*) that the premises are unoccupied;

(*d*) that the occupier is temporarily absent from the premises;

(*e*) that the case is one of urgency; or

(*f*) that an application for admission to the premises would defeat the object of the proposed entry.

(3) A justice of the peace shall not issue a warrant under this Part of this Schedule by virtue only of being satisfied that the exercise of a right or power in relation to any premises has been refused, or that a refusal is reasonably apprehended, unless he is also satisfied—

(*a*) that notice of the intention to apply for the warrant has been given to the occupier of the premises; or

(*b*) that the giving of such a notice would defeat the object of the proposed entry.

(4) For the purposes of the application of this Part of this Schedule to the rights and powers conferred by section 169 of this Act in a case to which subsection (4) of that section applies, a justice of the peace shall not issue a warrant under this Part of this Schedule unless he is satisfied that the Secretary of State has given his authorisation for the purposes of that subsection in relation to that case.

(5) Every warrant under this Part of this Schedule shall continue in force until the purposes for which the warrant was issued have been fulfilled.

*Manner of exercise of right or power*

**8.** A person designated as the person who may exercise any right or power to which this Part of this Schedule applies shall produce evidence of his designation and other authority before he exercises the right or power.

*Supplementary powers of person making entry etc*

**9.** A person authorised to enter any premises by virtue of any right or power to which this Part of this Schedule applies shall be entitled, subject in the case of a right or power exercisable under a warrant to the terms of the warrant, to take with him on to the premises such other persons and such equipment as may be necessary.

*Duty to secure premises*

**10.** A person who enters any premises in the exercise of any right or power to which this Part of this Schedule applies shall leave the premises as effectually secured against trespassers as he found them.

*Compensation*

**11.** (1) Where any person exercises any right or power to which this Part of this Schedule applies, it shall be the duty of the relevant authority to make full compensation to any person who has sustained loss or damage by reason of—

(*a*) the exercise by the designated person of that right or power or of any power to take any person or equipment with him when entering the premises in relation to which the right or power is exercised; or

(*b*) the performance of, or failure of the designated person to perform, the duty imposed by paragraph 10 above.

(2) Compensation shall not be payable by virtue of sub-paragraph (1) above in respect of any loss or damage if the loss or damage—

(*a*) is attributable to the default of the person who sustained it; or

(*b*) is loss or damage in respect of which compensation is payable by virtue of any other provision of this Act.

(3) Any dispute as to a person's entitlement to compensation under this paragraph or as to the amount of any such compensation, shall be referred to the arbitration of a single arbitrator appointed by agreement between the relevant authority and the person who claims to have sustained the loss or damage or, in default of agreement—

(*a*) by the Upper Tribunal where the relevant authority is the Secretary of State; and

(*b*) by the Secretary of State, in any other case.

*Obstruction of person exercising right or power*

**12.** A person who intentionally obstructs another person acting in the exercise of any right or power to which this Part of this Schedule applies shall be guilty of an offence and liable, on summary conviction, to a fine not exceeding **level 3** on the standard scale.

*Interpretation of Part II*

**13.** (1) In this Part of this Schedule "relevant authority", in relation to a right or power to which this Part of this Schedule applies, means the person who, by virtue of—

(*a*) the provision by which the right or power is conferred; or

(*b*) (except in paragraph 7 above) the warrant,

is entitled to designate the person by whom the right or power may be exercised.

(2) References in this Part of this Schedule, except in paragraph 7 above, to a right or power to which this Part of this Schedule applies include references to a right or power exercisable by virtue of a warrant under this Part of this Schedule.

(3) For the purposes of paragraphs 10 and 11 above a person enters any premises by virtue of a right or power to which this Part of this Schedule applies notwithstanding that he has failed (whether by virtue of the waiver of the requirement by the occupier of the premises or otherwise) to comply with—

(*a*) any requirement to enter those premises at a reasonable time or after giving notice of his intended entry; or

(*b*) the requirement imposed by paragraph 8 above.

# Water Resources Act 1991

(1991 c 57)

## PART II[1]

## WATER RESOURCES MANAGEMENT

### CHAPTER II

### ABSTRACTION AND IMPOUNDING

*Restrictions on abstraction and impounding*

7.11657 **24. Restrictions on abstraction** No person shall, or cause or permit any other person, to abstract water or construct or extend any well, borehole or other work or install or modify machinery to abstract additional quantities of water, except with, and complying with conditions on, a licence; offence punishable on summary conviction, or on conviction on indictment, to a fine[2].

[Water Resources Act 1991, s 24 as amended by the Water Act 2003, s 60 and SI 2015/664—summarised.]

1 Part II comprises ss 19–81.

2 For procedure in respect of an offence triable either way, see the Magistrates' Courts Act 1980, ss 17A–21 in PART I: MAGISTRATES' COURTS, PROCEDURE, ante.

7.11658 **24A. Abstraction licences**

7.11659 **25. Restrictions on impounding** No person shall, or cause or permit any other person, to begin construct or alter impounding works at any point in any inland waters which are not discrete waters except with, and complying with requirements of, a licence; offence punishable on summary conviction, or on conviction on indictment, to a fine[1].

[Water Resources Act 1991, s 25 as amended by SI 2015/664—summarised.]

1 For procedure in respect of an offence triable either way, see the Magistrates' Courts Act 1980, ss 17A–21 in PART I: MAGISTRATES' COURTS, PROCEDURE, ante.

**7.11660 25A. Enforcement notices** (1) Subject to the following provisions of this section, where it appears to the appropriate agency that a person is—

(*a*) in breach of section 24(1) or (2) or section 25(1) above; or

(*b*) for the purposes of section 24 or 25 above a holder of a licence under this Chapter and has not complied with a condition or requirement imposed by the provisions, as for the time being in force, of that licence,

the appropriate agency shall be entitled to serve an enforcement notice on him if the condition in subsection (2) below is satisfied.

(2) The condition is that it appears to the appropriate agency that the breach or failure to comply is causing or is likely to cause significant damage to the environment.

(3) An enforcement notice is a notice requiring the person on whom it is served—

(*a*) to cease his breach of section 24(1) or (2) or section 25(1) above, or to comply with the condition or requirement in question; and

(*b*) to carry out any works or operations specified in the notice.

(4) The works or operations which may be specified are works or operations which it appears to the appropriate agency are appropriate for the purpose of remedying or mitigating the effects of the breach or failure to comply, and may include—

(*a*) works or operations for the purpose, so far as it is reasonably practicable to do so, of restoring any affected waters, including any flora and fauna dependent on them, to their state immediately before the breach or failure to comply; and

(*b*) in the case of a breach of section 25(1) above, the removal of any unauthorised impounding works or the reversal of any unauthorised alteration to impounding works.

(5) An enforcement notice must specify the periods within which the person on whom it is served must do each of the things specified in the notice.

(6) Before serving an enforcement notice on any person, the appropriate agency shall take reasonable steps to consult that person about the works or operations which are to be specified in the notice.

(7) The Secretary of State may by regulations make provision for or in connection with—

(*a*) the form or content of enforcement notices;

(*b*) requirements for consultation, before the service of an enforcement notice, with persons other than the person upon whom the notice is to be served;

(*c*) steps to be taken for the purposes of any consultation required under subsection (6) above or regulations made by virtue of paragraph (*b*) above;

(*d*) any other steps of a procedural nature which are to be taken in connection with, or in consequence of, the service of an enforcement notice.

(8) An enforcement notice is not invalid, or invalidly served, merely because of a failure to comply with subsection (6) above or with regulations made by virtue of subsection (7)(*b*) above.

(9) The Secretary of State may, if he thinks fit in relation to any person, give directions to the appropriate agency as to whether or how it should exercise its powers under this section.

(10) In proceedings for any offence under section 24 or 25 above against a person upon whom an enforcement notice has been served, the following are not to be taken as evidence that he has committed the offence—

(*a*) the fact that an enforcement notice has been served on him;

(*b*) the fact that he does not appeal against it;

(*c*) the fact that on an appeal against it the notice is confirmed (whether with or without modifications).

[Water Resources Act 1991, s 25A as inserted by the Water Act 2003, s 30 and amended by SI 2013/755.]

**7.11661 25B. Rights of entry and appeals** Sections 161B and 161C below (including any power to make regulations) shall apply in relation to enforcement notices as they apply in relation to works notices under section 161A below.

[Water Resources Act 1991, s 25B as inserted by the Water Act 2003, s 30.]

**7.11662 25C. Consequences of not complying with an enforcement notice** (1) If a person on whom the appropriate agency serves an enforcement notice fails to comply with any of its requirements, he shall be guilty of an offence.

(2) A person who commits an offence under subsection (1) above shall be liable on summary conviction, or on conviction on indictment, to a fine.

(3) If a person on whom an enforcement notice has been served fails to comply with any of its requirements, the appropriate agency may do what that person was required to do and may recover from him any costs or expenses reasonably incurred by appropriate agency in doing it.

(4) If the appropriate agency is of the opinion that proceedings for an offence under subsection (1) above would afford an ineffectual remedy against a person who has failed to comply with the requirements of an enforcement notice, the appropriate agency may take proceedings in the High Court for the purpose of securing compliance with the notice.

[Water Resources Act 1991, s 25C as inserted by the Water Act 2003, s 30 and amended by SI 2013/755 and SI 2015/664.]

*Rights to abstract or impound*

**7.11663 26.** *Rights of navigation, harbour and conservancy authorities.*

**7.11664 27. Rights to abstract small quantities** Exception for abstraction not exceeding 20 cubic metres if not part of a continuous operation or series of operations, or not exceeding 20 cubic metres in 24 hours.

[Water Resources Act 1991, s 27 as substituted by the Water Act 2003, s 6—summarised.]

**7.11665 29.** *Rights to abstract for drainage purposes etc.*

## CHAPTER III[1]
## DROUGHT

[1] Chapter III of Pt II comprises ss 73–81.

**7.11666 73–77.** *Power to make ordinary and emergency drought orders; provisions and duration of drought orders.*

**7.11667 78.** *Works under drought orders.*

**7.11668 79A.** *Drought permits.*

**7.11669 80. Offences against drought order** (1) If any person—

(*a*) takes or uses water in contravention of a prohibition or limitation imposed by or under any drought order or takes or uses water otherwise than in accordance with any condition or restriction imposed by or under any drought order or by any drought permit; or

(*b*) discharges water otherwise than in accordance with any condition or restriction imposed by or under such an order,

he shall be guilty of an offence under this section.

(2) If any person—

(*a*) fails to construct or maintain in good order a gauge, weir or other apparatus for measuring the flow of water which he was required to construct or maintain by any drought order or drought permit; or

(*b*) fails to allow some person authorised for the purpose by or under any such order or by virtue of any such permit to inspect and examine any such apparatus or any records made thereby or kept by that person in connection therewith or to take copies of any such records,

he shall be guilty of an offence under this section.

(3) In any proceedings against any person for an offence under this section it shall be a defence for that person to show that he took all reasonable precautions and exercised all due diligence to avoid the commission of the offence.

(4) A person who is guilty of an offence under this section shall be liable[1]—

(*a*) on summary conviction, to a fine not exceeding the **statutory maximum**;

(*b*) on conviction on indictment, to a **fine**.

[Water Resources Act 1991, s 80 as amended by the Environment Act 1995, Sch 22.]

[1] For procedure in respect of an offence triable either way, see the Magistrates' Courts Act 1980, ss 17A–21 in PART I: MAGISTRATES' COURTS, PROCEDURE, ante.

**7.11670 81. Interpretation of Chapter III** In this Chapter—

(*a*) references to the taking of water include references to the collection, impounding, diversion or appropriation of water; and

(*b*) references to an obligation or to a restriction include references to an obligation or, as the case may be, to a restriction which is imposed by or under any enactment or agreement.

[Water Resources Act 1991, s 81.]

## PART III[1]
## CONTROL OF POLLUTION OF WATER RESOURCES

*Consents for the purposes of sections 88 to 90*

**7.11679 91.** *Appeals in respect of consents under Chapter II.*

## CHAPTER IIA[1]
## ABANDONED MINES

**7.11680 91A. Introductory** (1) For the purposes of this Chapter, "abandonment", in relation to a mine,—

(*a*) subject to paragraph (*b*) below, includes—

(i) the discontinuance of any or all of the operations for the removal of water from the mine;

(ii) the cessation of working of any relevant seam, vein or vein-system;

(iii) the cessation of use of any shaft or outlet of the mine;

(iv) in the case of a mine in which activities other than mining activities are carried on (whether or not mining activities are also carried on in the mine)—

(A) the discontinuance of some or all of those other activities in the mine; and

(B) any substantial change in the operations for the removal of water from the mine; but

(b) does not include—

(i) any disclaimer under section 178 or 315 of the Insolvency Act 1986 (power of liquidator, or trustee of a bankrupt's estate, to disclaim onerous property) by the official receiver acting in a compulsory capacity; or

(ii) the abandonment of any rights, interests or liabilities by the Accountant in Bankruptcy acting as permanent or interim trustee in a sequestration (within the meaning of the Bankruptcy (Scotland) Act 1985);

and cognate expressions shall be construed accordingly.

(2) In this Chapter, except where the context otherwise requires—

"the 1954 Act" means the Mines and Quarries Act 1954;

"acting in a compulsory capacity", in the case of the official receiver, means acting as—

(a) liquidator of a company;

(b) receiver or manager of a bankrupt's estate, pursuant to section 287 of the Insolvency Act 1986;

(c) trustee of a bankrupt's estate;

(d) liquidator of an insolvent partnership;

(e) trustee of an insolvent partnership;

(f) trustee, or receiver or manager, of the insolvent estate of a deceased person;

"mine" has the same meaning as in the 1954 Act;

"the official receiver" has the same meaning as it has in the Insolvency Act 1986 by virtue of section 399(1) of that Act;

"prescribed" means prescribed in regulations;

"regulations" means regulations made by the Secretary of State;

"relevant seam, vein or vein-system", in the case of any mine, means any seam, vein or vein-system for the purpose of, or in connection with, whose working any excavation constituting or comprised in the mine was made.

[Water Resources Act 1991, s 91A as inserted by the Environment Act 1995, s 58.]

---

[1] Chapter IIA contains ss 91A and 91B.

7.11681 **91B. Mine operators to give the appropriate agency six months' notice of any proposed abandonment** (1) If, in the case of any mine, there is to be an abandonment at any time after the expiration of the initial period, it shall be the duty of the operator of the mine to give notice of the proposed abandonment to the appropriate agency at least six months before the abandonment takes effect.

(2) A notice under subsection (1) above shall contain such information (if any) as is prescribed[1] for the purpose, which may include information about the operator's opinion as to any consequences of the abandonment.

(3) A person who fails to give the notice required by subsection (1) above shall be guilty of an offence and liable[2]—

(a) on summary conviction, to a fine not exceeding the **statutory maximum;**

(b) on conviction on indictment, to a **fine**.

(4) A person shall not be guilty of an offence under subsection (3) above if—

(a) the abandonment happens in an emergency in order to avoid danger to life or health; and

(b) notice of the abandonment, containing such information as may be prescribed[1], is given as soon as reasonably practicable after the abandonment has happened.

(5) Where the operator of a mine is—

(a) the official receiver acting in a compulsory capacity, or

(b) the Accountant in Bankruptcy acting as permanent or interim trustee in a sequestration (within the meaning of the Bankruptcy (Scotland) Act 1985),

he shall not be guilty of an offence under subsection (3) above by reason of any failure to give the notice required by subsection (1) above if, as soon as reasonably practicable (whether before or after the abandonment), he gives to the appropriate agency notice of the abandonment or proposed abandonment, containing such information as may be prescribed[1].

(6) Where a person gives notice under subsection (1), 4(b) or (5) above, he shall publish prescribed[1] particulars of, or relating to, the notice in one or more local newspapers circulating in the locality where the mine is situated.

(7) Where the appropriate agency—

(a) receives notice under this section or otherwise learns of an abandonment or proposed abandonment in the case of any mine, and

(b) considers that, in consequence of the abandonment or proposed abandonment taking effect, any land has or is likely to become contaminated land, within the meaning of Part IIA of the Environmental Protection Act 1990,

it shall be the duty of the appropriate agency to inform the local authority in whose area that land is situated of the abandonment or proposed abandonment.

(8) In this section—

"the initial period" means the period of six months beginning with the day on which subsection (1) above comes into force;

"local authority" means—

(*a*) any unitary authority;

(*b*) any district council, so far as it is not a unitary authority;

(*c*) the Common Council of the City of London and, as respects the Temples, the Sub-Treasurer of the Inner Temple and the Under-Treasurer of the Middle Temple respectively;

"unitary authority" means—

(*a*) the council of a county, so far as it is the council of an area for which there are no district councils;

(*b*) the council of any district comprised in an area for which there is no county council;

(*c*) the council of a London borough;

(*d*) the council of a county borough in Wales.

[Water Resources Act 1991, s 91B as inserted by the Environment Act 1995, s 58 amended by SI 2013/755.]

---

1 See the Mines (Notice of Abandonment) Regulations 1998, SI 1998/892.

2 For procedure in respect of this offence which is triable either way, see the Magistrates' Courts Act 1980, ss 17A–21, in PART I: MAGISTRATES' COURTS, PROCEDURE, ante.

## CHAPTER IV

## SUPPLEMENTAL PROVISIONS WITH RESPECT TO WATER POLLUTION

7.11682 **101. Limitation for summary offences under Part III** Notwithstanding anything in section 127 of the Magistrates' Courts Act 1980 (time limit for summary proceedings), a magistrates' court may try any summary offence under this Part, or under any subordinate legislation made under this Part, if the information is laid not more than twelve months after the commission of the offence.

[Water Resources Act 1991, s 101.]

7.11683 **104. Meaning of "controlled waters" etc in Part III** (1) References in this Part to controlled waters are references to waters of any of the following classes—

(*a*) relevant territorial waters, that is to say, subject to subsection (4) below, the waters which extend seaward for three miles from the baselines from which the breadth of the territorial sea adjacent to England and Wales is measured;

(*b*) coastal waters, that is to say, any waters which are within the area which extends landward from those baselines as far as—

(*a*) the limit of the highest tide; or

(*b*) in the case of the waters of any relevant river or watercourse, the fresh-water limit of the river or watercourse,

together with the waters of any enclosed dock which adjoins waters within that area:

(*c*) inland freshwaters, that is to say, the waters of any relevant lake or pond or of so much of any relevant river or watercourse[1] as is above the fresh-water limit;

(*d*) ground waters, that is to say, any waters contained in underground strata;

and, accordingly, in this Part "coastal waters", "controlled waters", "ground waters", "inland freshwaters" and "relevant territorial waters" have the meanings given by this subsection.

(2) In this Part any reference to the waters of any lake or pond or of any river or watercourse includes a reference to the bottom, channel or bed of any lake, pond, river or, as the case may be, watercourse which is for the time being dry.

(3) In this section—

"fresh-water limit", in relation to any river or watercourse, means the place for the time being shown as the fresh-water limit of that river or watercourse in the latest map deposited for that river or watercourse under section 192 below;

"miles" means international nautical miles of 1,852 metres:

"lake or pond" includes a reservoir of any description:

"relevant lake or pond" means (subject to subsection (4) below) any lake or pond which (whether it is natural or artificial or above or below ground) discharges into a relevant river or watercourse or into another lake or pond which is itself a relevant lake or pond;

"relevant river or watercourse" means (subject to subsection (4) below) any river or watercourse (including an underground river or watercourse and an artificial river or watercourse) which is neither a public sewer nor a sewer or drain which drains into a public sewer.

(4)–(6) *Secretary of State's power to make orders.*

[Water Resources Act 1991, s 104.]

---

1 Waters which are within the definition of "controlled waters" for the purposes of this Act because they are "waters . . . of [a] . . . watercourse" do not cease to be controlled waters merely because they leave the watercourse as a result of diversion or flooding (*R v Dovermoss Ltd* (1995) 159 JP 448, CA).

# PART VII[1]
# LAND AND WORKS POWERS

## CHAPTER I
## POWERS OF THE AUTHORITY

*Restoration and improvement works for controlled waters*

7.11684 **161. Anti-pollution works and operations** (1) This section applies where it appears to the appropriate agency that any poisonous, noxious or polluting matter or any waste matter is or has been present in, or is likely to enter, any controlled waters.

(2) In a case where the matter appears to be or to have been present in the controlled waters, the appropriate agency shall be entitled to carry out works and operations for any of the following purposes—

(*a*) removing or disposing of the matter;

(*b*) remedying or mitigating any pollution caused by its presence in the waters; or

(*c*) restoring (so far as it is reasonably practicable to do so) the waters, including any flora and fauna dependent on the aquatic environment of the waters, to their state immediately before the matter became present in the waters.

(3) In a case where the matter appears to be likely to enter the controlled waters, the appropriate agency shall be entitled to carry out works and operations for the purpose of preventing it from doing so.

(4) The appropriate agency shall be entitled to carry out investigations for the purpose of establishing any of the following—

(*a*) the nature of the matter,

(*b*) the source of the matter;

(*c*) the nature and effects of any pollution caused or likely to be caused by the presence of the matter; and

(*d*) the identity of any responsible persons.

(5) Without prejudice to the power of the appropriate agency to carry out those investigations, the powers conferred by subsection (2) or (3) shall only be exercisable in a case where—

(*a*) the appropriate agency considers it necessary to carry out forthwith any works or operations falling within that subsection; or

(*b*) it appears to the appropriate agency, after reasonable enquiry, that no responsible person can be found on whom to serve a works notice.

(6) In this section "responsible person" means a person who has caused or knowingly permitted the matter—

(*a*) to be present in the controlled waters; or

(*b*) to be at a place from which it was likely, in the opinion of the appropriate agency, to enter the controlled waters.

[Water Resources Act 1991, s 161 as substituted by SI 2009/3104 and amended by SI 2013/755.]

---

[1] Part VII comprises ss 154–186.

7.11685 **161ZA. Other works and operations in respect of harm to controlled waters** (1) This section applies where it appears to the appropriate agency that any controlled waters are being or have been harmed, or are likely to be harmed, by any event, process or other source of potential harm (and it is immaterial whether the source of potential harm has been identified).

(2) In this section "harm" means any adverse impact on the condition of any hydromorphological quality element affecting the controlled waters that would be likely to prevent the achievement of the environmental objectives applicable to the controlled waters (whether by itself or in combination with other factors), other than an adverse impact caused by the entry into or presence in those waters of any poisonous, noxious or polluting matter or waste matter.

(3) In subsection (2) "environmental objectives" and "hydromorphological quality element" have the same meaning as in the Water Framework Directive.

(4) The appropriate agency shall be entitled to carry out works and operations for any of the following purposes (so far as it is reasonably practicable to achieve them)—

(*a*) removing the source of potential harm;

(*b*) preventing any harm or further harm being caused to the controlled waters;

(*c*) in a case where the controlled waters are being or have been harmed—

(i) remedying or mitigating the effects of the harm;

(ii) restoring the waters, including any flora and fauna dependent on the aquatic environment of the waters, to their state immediately before any harm was caused.

(5) The appropriate agency shall be entitled to carry out investigations for the purpose of establishing any of the following—

(*a*) the source of any harm or potential harm to the controlled waters;

(*b*) the nature and effects of any harm caused or likely to be caused to those waters; and (*c*) the identity of any responsible persons.

(6) Without prejudice to the power of the appropriate agency to carry out those investigations, the powers conferred by subsection (4) shall only be exercisable in a case where—

(*a*) the appropriate agency considers it necessary to carry out forthwith any works or operations falling within that subsection; or

(*b*) it appears to the appropriate agency, after reasonable enquiry, that no responsible person can be found on whom to serve a works notice.

(7) In this section "responsible person" means a person who has caused or knowingly permitted—

(*a*) any harm to be caused to the controlled waters; or

(*b*) a source of potential harm to exist that is likely, in the opinion of the appropriate agency, to cause harm to the controlled waters.

[Water Resources Act 1991, s 161ZA as substituted by SI 2009/3104 and amended by SI 2013/755.]

7.11686 **161ZB. Works and operations for improving controlled waters** (1) This section applies where it appears to the appropriate agency that—

(*a*) the condition of any hydromorphological quality element affecting any controlled waters is unsatisfactory; and

(*b*) it is possible to improve the hydromorphological quality element by carrying out works or operations.

(2) For the purposes of this section the condition of a hydromorphological quality element affecting the controlled waters is unsatisfactory if (whether by itself or in combination with other factors) if it is likely to prevent the waters from achieving the applicable environmental objectives.

(3) In this section "environmental objectives" and "hydromorphological quality element" have the same meaning as in the Water Framework Directive.

(4) The appropriate agency shall be entitled to carry out works and operations for the purpose of improving the condition of the hydromorphological quality element in question with a view to achieving (or contributing to the achievement of) the applicable environmental objectives.

(5) The appropriate agency shall be entitled to carry out investigations for the purpose of establishing why the condition of the hydromorphological quality element in question is unsatisfactory.

(6) Without prejudice to the power of the appropriate agency to carry out those investigations, the powers conferred by subsection (4) shall only be exercisable if it appears to the appropriate agency that it is unable to secure that the necessary works or operations are carried out by exercising its powers under section 161 or 161ZA or by serving a works notice on any responsible person.

[Water Resources Act 1991, s 161ZB as substituted by SI 2009/3104 and amended by SI 2013/755.]

7.11687 **161ZC. Sections 161 to 161ZB: supplementary** (1) Nothing in sections 161 to 161ZB shall entitle the appropriate agency to impede or prevent the making of any discharge in pursuance of an environmental permit.

(2) Where the appropriate agency carries out any works, operations or investigations under any of the powers conferred by section 161 or 161ZA it shall, subject to subsection (3), be entitled to recover the expenses reasonably incurred in doing so from any responsible person (within the meaning of the section conferring the powers in question).

(3) No expenses are recoverable from a person for any works, operations or investigations in respect of water from an abandoned mine or an abandoned part of a mine which that person permitted to enter any controlled waters or to reach a place from which it was likely, in the opinion of the appropriate agency, to enter any controlled waters.

(4) Subsection (3) does not apply to the owner or former operator of any mine or part of a mine if the mine or part in question became abandoned after 31st December 1999.

(5) *Repealed.*

(6) Nothing in sections 161, 161ZA and 161ZB—

(*a*) derogates from any right of action or other remedy (whether civil or criminal) in proceedings instituted otherwise than under any of those sections; or

(*b*) affects any restriction imposed by or under any other enactment, whether public local or private.

(7) In this section—

"expenses" includes costs;

"mine" has the same meaning as in the Mines and Quarries Act 1954;

"works notice" means a notice under section 161A.

(8) In sections 161, 161ZA and 161ZB and this section "controlled waters" has the same meaning as in Part 3 of this Act and in sections 161ZA and 161ZB, and "Water Framework Directive" has the same meaning as in section 93(7) of this Act.

[Water Resources Act 1991, s 161ZC as substituted by SI 2009/3104 and amended by SI 2010/675 and SI 2013/755.]

7.11688 **161A. Notices requiring persons to carry out works and operations** (1) Where it appears to the appropriate agency that—

(*a*) any poisonous, noxious or polluting matter or any waste matter is or has been present in, or is likely to enter, any controlled waters (so that section 161 applies), or

(*b*) any controlled waters are being or have been harmed, or are likely to be harmed, by any event, process or other source of potential harm (so that section 161ZA applies), the appropriate agency shall be entitled to serve a works notice on any responsible person.

(2) In this section "responsible person" has the same meaning as in section 161 or 161ZA) (as the case may be).

(3) For the purposes of this section a works notice is a notice requiring the person on whom it is served to carry out such works or operations as may be specified in the notice.

(4) The works or operations that may be so specified are works or operations which may be carried out under section 161(2) or (3) or section 161ZA(4) (as the case may be).

(5) Where the appropriate agency has carried out any such investigations as are mentioned in sections 161(4) or 161ZA(5) and serves a works notice on a responsible person in connection with the matters to which the investigations relate it shall (unless the notice is quashed or withdrawn) be entitled to recover from that person the costs or expenses reasonably incurred in carrying out those investigations.

(6) The appropriate national authority may, if it thinks fit in relation to any person, give directions to the appropriate agency as to whether or how it should exercise its powers under this section or section 161AA.

(7) In this section and sections 161AA and 161AB "controlled waters" has the same meaning as in Part 3 of this Act.

[Water Resources Act 1991, s 161A as substituted by SI 2009/3104 as amended by SI 2013/755.]

7.11689 **161AA. Works notices: form etc** (1) A works notice—

(*a*) must specify the periods within which the person on whom it is served is required to do each of the things specified in the notice; and

(*b*) is without prejudice to the powers of the appropriate agency to carry out any works or operations under section 161(5)(*a*) or 161ZA(6)(*a*).

(2) Before serving a works notice on any person, the appropriate agency shall reasonably endeavour to consult that person concerning the works or operations which are to be specified in the notice.

(3) The appropriate national authority may by regulations make provision for or in connection with—

(*a*) the form or content of works notices;

(*b*) requirements for consultation, before the service of a works notice, with persons other than the person on whom that notice is to be served;

(*c*) steps to be taken for the purposes of any consultation required under subsection (2) or regulations made by virtue of paragraph (*b*); or

(*d*) any other steps of a procedural nature which are to be taken in connection with or in consequence of the service of a works notice.

(4) A works notice shall not be regarded as invalid or as invalidly served by reason only of a failure to comply with the requirements of subsection (2) or of regulations made by virtue of paragraph (*b*) of subsection (3).

(5) In this section and section 161A, "appropriate national authority" means—

(*a*) in relation to England, the Secretary of State; and

(*b*) in relation to Wales, the Welsh Ministers.

(6) The power to make regulations under this section shall be exercisable by statutory instrument subject—

(*a*) in the case of regulations made by the Secretary of State, to annulment in pursuance of a resolution of either House of Parliament; and

(*b*) in the case of regulations made by the Welsh Ministers, to annulment in pursuance of a resolution of the National Assembly for Wales.

(7) In this section,—

(*a*) paragraph (1) of section 219 does not apply; and

(*b*) in paragraph (2) of that section, references to "the Ministers" or the "the Secretary of State" shall be taken to be references to the appropriate national authority.

[Water Resources Act 1991, s 161AA as substituted by SI 2009/3104 as amended by SI 2013/755.]

7.11690 **161AB. Works notices: exceptions etc** (1) Nothing in section 161A shall entitle the appropriate agency to require the carrying out of any works or operations which would impede or prevent the making of any discharge in pursuance of a consent given under Chapter 2 of Part 3 of this Act.

(2) No works notice shall be served on any person requiring him to carry out any works or operations in respect of water from an abandoned mine or an abandoned part of a mine which that person permitted to enter any controlled waters or to reach a place from which it was likely, in the opinion of the appropriate agency, to enter any controlled waters.

(3) Subsection (2) does not apply to the service of a notice on the owner or former operator of any mine or part of a mine if the mine or part in question became abandoned after 31st December 1999.

(4) Subsections (3B) and (3C) of section 89 apply in relation to subsections (2) and (3) as they apply in relation to subsections (3) and (4A) of that section.

(5) In this section "mine" has the same meaning as in the Mines and Quarries Act 1954.

[Water Resources Act 1991, s 161AB as substituted by SI 2009/3104 as amended by SI 2013/755.]

**7.11691 161B. Grant of, and compensation for, rights of entry etc** (1) A works notice may require a person to carry out works or operations in relation to any land or waters notwithstanding that he is not entitled to carry out those works or operations.

(2) Any person whose consent is required before any works or operations required by a works notice may be carried out shall grant, or join in granting, such rights in relation to any land or waters as will enable the person on whom the works notice is served to comply with any requirements imposed by the works notice.

(3) Before serving a works notice, the appropriate agency shall reasonably endeavour to consult every person who appears to it—

(*a*) to be the owner or occupier of any relevant land, and

(*b*) to be a person who might be required by subsection (2) above to grant, or join in granting, any rights,

concerning the rights which that person may be so required to grant.

(4) A works notice shall not be regarded as invalid, or as invalidly served, by reason only of any failure to comply with the requirements of subsection (3) above.

(5) A person who grants, or joins in granting, any rights pursuant to subsection (2) above shall be entitled, on making an application within such period as may be prescribed and in such manner as may be prescribed to such person as may be prescribed, to be paid by the person on whom the works notice in question is served compensation of such amount as may be determined in such manner as may be prescribed.

(6) Without prejudice to the generality of the regulations that may be made by virtue of subsection (5), regulations by virtue of that subsection may—

(*a*) provide for the basis on which any amount to be paid by way of compensation under this section is to be assessed;

(*b*) without prejudice to the generality of paragraph (*a*) above, provide for compensation under this section to be payable in respect of—

(i) any effect of any rights being granted, or

(ii) any consequence of the exercise of any rights which have been granted;

(*c*) provide for the times at which any entitlement to compensation under this section is to arise or at which any such compensation is to become payable;

(*d*) provide for the persons or bodies by whom, and the manner in which, any dispute—

(i) as to whether any, and (if so) how much and when, compensation under this section is payable, or

(ii) as to the person to or by whom it shall be paid,

is to be determined;

(*e*) provide for when or how applications may be made for compensation under this section;

(*f*) without prejudice to the generality of paragraph (*d*) above, provide for when or how applications may be made for the determination of any such disputes as are mentioned in that paragraph;

(*g*) without prejudice to the generality of paragraphs (*e*) and (*f*) above, prescribe the form in which any such applications as are mentioned in those paragraphs are to be made;

(*h*) make provision similar to any provision made by paragraph 8 of Schedule 19;

(*i*) make different provision for different cases, including different provision in relation to different persons or circumstances;

(*j*) include such incidental, supplemental, consequential or transitional provision as the Secretary of State considers appropriate.

(7) In this section—

"prescribed" means prescribed in regulations[1] made by the Secretary of State;

"relevant land" means—

(*a*) any land or waters in relation to which the works notice in question requires, or may require, works or operations to be carried out; or

(*b*) any land adjoining or adjacent to that land or those waters;

"works notice" means a works notice under section 161A above.

[Water Resources Act 1991, s 161B as inserted by the Environment Act 1995, Sch 22 and amended by SI 2007/3538 and SI 2013/755.]

[1] The Anti-Pollution Works Regulations 1999, SI 1999/1006 amended by SI 2009/1307 and 3104 and the Water Resources (Abstraction and Impounding) Regulations 2006, SI 2006/641 have been made.

**7.11692 161C. Appeals against works notices** (1) A person on whom a works notice is served may, within the period of twenty-one days beginning with the day on which the notice is served, appeal against the notice to the Secretary of State.

(2) On any appeal under this section the Secretary of State—

(*a*) shall quash the notice, if he is satisfied that there is a material defect in the notice; but

(*b*) subject to that, may confirm the notice, with or without modification, or quash it.

(3) The Secretary of State may by regulations[1] make provision with respect to—

(*a*) the grounds on which appeals under this section may be made; or (*b*) the procedure on any such appeal.

(4) Regulations[1] under subsection (3) above may (among other things)—

(*a*) include provisions comparable to those in section 290 of the Public Health Act 1936 (appeals against notices requiring the execution of works);

(*b*) prescribe the cases in which a works notice is, or is not, to be suspended until the appeal is decided, or until some other stage in the proceedings;

(*c*) prescribe the cases in which the decision on an appeal may in some respects be less favourable to the appellant than the works notice against which he is appealing;

(*d*) prescribe the cases in which the appellant may claim that a works notice should have been served on some other person and prescribe the procedure to be followed in those cases;

(*e*) make provision as respects—

(i) the particulars to be included in the notice of appeal;

(ii) the persons on whom notice of appeal is to be served and the particulars, if any, which are to accompany the notice; or

(iii) the abandonment of an appeal.

(5) In this section "works notice" means a works notice under section 161A above.

(6) This section is subject to section 114 of the 1995 Act (delegation or reference of appeals).

[Water Resources Act 1991, s 161C as inserted by the Environment Act 1995, Sch 22.]

[1] The Anti-Pollution Works Regulations 1999, SI 1999/1006 amended by SI 2009/1307 and 3104 and the Water Resources (Abstraction and Impounding) Regulations 2006, SI 2006/641 have been made.

7.11693 **161D. Consequences of not complying with a works notice** (1) If a person on whom the appropriate agency serves a works notice fails to comply with any of the requirements of the notice, he shall be guilty of an offence.

(2) A person who commits an offence under subsection (1) above shall be liable[1]—

(*a*) on summary conviction, to imprisonment for a term not exceeding **three months** or to a fine or to **both**;

(*b*) on conviction on indictment to imprisonment for a term not exceeding **two years** or to a **fine** or to **both**.

(3) If a person on whom a works notice has been served fails to comply with any of the requirements of the notice, the appropriate agency may do what that person was required to do and may recover from him any costs or expenses reasonably incurred by the appropriate agency in doing it.

(4) If the appropriate agency is of the opinion that proceedings for an offence under subsection (1) above would afford an ineffectual remedy against a person who has failed to comply with the requirements of a works notice, the appropriate agency may take proceedings in the High Court for the purpose of securing compliance with the notice.

(5) In this section "works notice" means a works notice under section 161A above.

[Water Resources Act 1991, s 161D as inserted by the Environment Act 1995, Sch 22 as amended by SI 2013/755 and SI 2015/664.]

[1] For procedure in respect of this offence which is triable either way, see the Magistrates' Courts Act 1980, ss 17A–21, in PART I: MAGISTRATES' COURTS, PROCEDURE, ante.

*Powers to discharge water*

7.11694 **163. Discharges for works purposes** The appropriate agency working on reservoir, well, borehole etc may discharge water into any available watercourse but must take steps to secure that the discharge is reasonably free from pollutants; failure punishable on summary conviction by fine not exceeding **level 3** on the standard scale[1].

[Water Resources Act 1991, s 163 as amended by the Environment Act 1995, Sch 22, SI 2003/1615 and SI 2013/755—summarised.]

[1] Section 163 is expressed in terms similar to s 165 of the Water Industry Act 1991, ante.

7.11695 **164.** *Consents for certain discharges under section 163.*

## CHAPTER II
## POWERS OF ENTRY

7.11696 **169. Powers of entry for enforcement purposes** (1) Any person designated in writing for the purpose by either of the Ministers, by the Agency, or by the NRBW, may—

(*a*) enter any premises or vessel for the purpose of ascertaining whether any provision of an enactment to which this section applies, of any subordinate legislation or other instrument made by virtue of any such enactment or of any byelaws made by the Agency or of any relevant byelaws made by the NRBW is being or has been contravened; and

(*b*) carry out such inspections, measurements and tests on any premises or vessel entered by that person or of any articles found on any such premises or vessel, and take away such samples of water or effluent or of any land or articles, as that Minister, the Agency, or the NRBW—

(i) considers appropriate for the purpose mentioned in paragraph (*a*) above; and

(ii) has authorised that person to carry out or take away.

(2) The powers conferred by subsection (1) above in relation to any premises shall include power, in order to obtain information for the purpose mentioned in subsection (1)(*a*) above—

(*a*) to carry out experimental borings or other works on those premises; and

(*b*) to install and keep monitoring and other apparatus there.

(3) Subject to subsection (4) below, this section applies to any enactment contained in this Act and to any other enactment under or for the purposes of which the Agency carries out functions or the NRBW carries out relevant transferred functions.

(4) The powers conferred by this section shall not have effect for the purposes of any of the Agency's pollution control functions, within the meaning of section 108 of the 1995 Act.

[Water Resources Act 1991, s 169 as amended by the Environment Act 1995, Sch 22, the Water Act 2003, s 71 and SI 2013/755.]

7.11697 **170. Power of entry for certain works purposes** (1) Any person designated in writing for the purpose by the Agency or by the NRBW may enter any premises for any of the purposes specified in subsection (2) below.

(2) The purposes mentioned in subsection (1) above are—

(*a*) the carrying out of any survey or tests for the purpose of determining—

(i) whether it is appropriate and practicable for the Agency or the NRBW to exercise any relevant works power; or

(ii) how any such power should be exercised;

(*b*) the exercise of any such power.

(3) The power by virtue of subsection (1) above of a person designated by the Agency or by the NRBW to enter any premises for the purposes of carrying out any survey or tests shall include power—

(*a*) to carry out experimental borings or other works for the purpose of ascertaining the nature of the sub-soil; and

(*b*) to take away and analyse such samples of water or effluent or of any land or articles as the Agency or the NRBW considers necessary for the purpose of determining either of the matters mentioned in subsection (2)(*a*) above and has authorised that person to take away and analyse.

(4) In this section "relevant works power" means any power conferred by any of the provisions of sections 159, 160, 162(2) and (3) and 163 above.

[Water Resources Act 1991, s 170 as amended by the Environment Act 1995, Sch 22 and SI 2013/755.]

7.11698 **171. Power to carry out surveys and to search for water** (1) Without prejudice to the rights and powers conferred by the other provisions of this Chapter, any person designated in writing under this section by the Agency or by the NRBW may enter any premises for any of the purposes specified in subsection (2) below.

(2) The purposes mentioned in subsection (1) above are the carrying out of any survey or tests for the purpose of determining—

(*a*) whether it would be appropriate for the Agency or the NRBW to acquire any land, or any interest or right in or over land, for purposes connected with the carrying out of its functions; or

(*b*) whether it would be appropriate for the Agency or the NRBW to apply for an order under section 168 above and what compulsory powers it would be appropriate to apply for under that section.

(3) The power by virtue of subsection (1) above of a person designated under this section to enter any premises for the purpose of carrying out any survey or tests shall include power—

(*a*) to carry out experimental borings or other works for the purpose of ascertaining the nature of the sub-soil, the presence of underground water in the sub-soil or the quantity or quality of any such water;

(*b*) to install and keep monitoring or other apparatus on the premises for the purpose of obtaining the information on which any such determination as is mentioned in subsection (2) above may be made; and

(*c*) to take away and analyse such samples of water or of any land or articles as the Agency or the NRBW considers necessary for any of the purposes so mentioned and has authorised that person to take away and analyse.

(4) The powers conferred by this section shall not be exercised in any case for purposes connected with the determination of—

(*a*) whether, where or how a reservoir should be constructed; or

(*b*) whether, where or how a borehole should be sunk for the purpose of abstracting water from or discharging water into any underground strata,

unless the Secretary of State has, in accordance with subsection (5) below, given his written authorisation in relation to that case for the exercise of those powers for those purposes.

(5) The Secretary of State shall not give his authorisation for the purposes of subsection (4) above unless—

(*a*) he is satisfied that notice of the proposal to apply for the authorisation has been given to the owner and to the occupier of the premises in question; and (*b*) he has considered any representation or objections with respect to the proposed exercise of the powers under this section which—

(i) have been duly made to him by the owner or occupier of those premises, within the period of fourteen days beginning with the day after the giving of the notice; and

(ii) have not been withdrawn.

(6) In relation to the NRBW, the reference to functions in subsection (2)(*a*) has effect as a reference to relevant transferred functions.

[Water Resources Act 1991, s 171 as amended by the Environment Act 1995, Sch 22 and SI 2013/755.]

7.11699 **172. Powers of entry for other purposes** (1) Any person designated in writing for the purpose by either of the Ministers, by the Agency, or by the NRBW may enter any premises or vessel for the purpose of—

(*a*) determining whether, and if so in what manner, any power or duty conferred or imposed on either of the Ministers, on the Agency, or on the NRBW, by virtue of any enactment to which this section applies (including a power of either or both of the Ministers to make subordinate legislation) should be exercised or, as the case may be, performed; or

(*b*) exercising or performing any power or duty which is so conferred or imposed.

(2) Any person designated in writing for the purpose by either of the Ministers, the Agency, or the NRBW, may—

(*a*) carry out such inspections, measurements and tests on any premises or vessel entered by that person under this section or of any articles found on any such premises or vessel; and

(*b*) take away such samples of water or effluent or of any land or articles,

as that Minister, the Agency, or the NRBW, considers appropriate for any purpose mentioned in subsection (1) above and has authorised that person to carry out or take away.

(3) Subject to subsection (3A) below, the powers which by virtue of subsections (1) and (2) above are conferred in relation to any premises for the purpose of enabling either of the Ministers, the Agency, or the NRBW, to determine whether or in what manner to exercise or perform any power or duty conferred or imposed on him or it by or under the water pollution provisions of this Act shall include power, in order to obtain the information on which that determination may be made—

(*a*) to carry out experimental borings or other works on those premises; and

(*b*) to install and keep monitoring and other apparatus there.

(3A) The powers conferred by this section shall not have effect for the purposes of any of the Agency's or the NRBW's pollution control functions, within the meaning of section 108 of the 1995 Act.

(4) This section applies to any enactment contained in this Act and to any other enactment under or for the purposes of which the Agency or the NRBW carries out functions.

(5) In relation to the NRBW, the reference to functions in subsection (4) has effect as a reference to relevant transferred functions.

[Water Resources Act 1991, s 172 as amended by the Environment Act 1995, Sch 22 and SI 2013/755.]

7.11700 **173. Powers of entry: supplemental provisions** Schedule 20[1] to this Act shall have effect with respect to the powers of entry and related powers which are conferred by the preceding provisions of this Chapter.

[Water Resources Act 1991, s 173.]

1 See Sch 20, post, for supplemental provisions including the issue of warrants.

7.11701 **174. Impersonation of persons exercising powers of entry** (1) A person who, without having been designated or authorised for the purpose by the Agency or by the NRBW, purports to be entitled to enter any premises or vessel in exercise of a power exercisable in pursuance of any such designation or authorisation shall be guilty of an offence and liable[1]—

(*a*) on summary conviction, to a fine not exceeding the **statutory maximum;**

(*b*) on conviction on indictment, to a **fine** or to imprisonment for a term not exceeding **two years**, or to **both**.

(2) For the purposes of this section it shall be immaterial, where a person purports to be entitled to enter any premises or vessel, that the power which that person purports to be entitled to exercise does not exist, or would not be exercisable, even if that person had been designated or authorised by the Agency or by the NRBW.

[Water Resources Act 1991, s 174 as amended by the Environment Act 1995, Sch 22 and SI 2013/755.]

1 For procedure in respect of an offence which is triable either way, see the Magistrates' Courts Act 1980, ss 17A–21, in PART I: MAGISTRATES' COURTS, PROCEDURE.

*Offence of interference with works etc*

7.11702 **176. Offence of interference with works etc** (1) Subject to subsection (2) below, if any person without the consent of the appropriate agency—

(*a*) intentionally or recklessly interferes with any resource main or other pipe vested in the appropriate agency or with any structure, installation or apparatus belonging to the appropriate agency; or

(*b*) by any act or omission negligently interferes with any such main or other pipe or with any such structure, installation or apparatus so as to damage it or so as to have an effect on its use or operation,

that person shall be guilty of an offence and liable, on summary conviction, to a fine not exceeding **level 3** on the standard scale.

(2) A person shall not be guilty of an offence under subsection (1) above—

(*a*) by reason of anything done in an emergency to prevent loss or damage to persons or property; or

(*b*) by reason of his opening or closing the stopcock fitted to a service pipe by means of which water is supplied to any premises by a water undertaker if—

(i) he has obtained the consent of every consumer whose supply is affected by the opening or closing of that stopcock or, as the case may be, of every other consumer whose supply is so affected; and

(ii) in the case of opening a stopcock, the stopcock was closed otherwise than by the undertaker.

(3) Any person who without the consent of the appropriate agency—

(*a*) attaches any pipe or apparatus to any resource main or other pipe vested in the appropriate agency; or

(*b*) subject to subsection (4) below, uses any pipe or apparatus which has been attached or altered in contravention of this section,

shall be guilty of an offence and liable, on summary conviction, to a fine not exceeding **level 3** on the standard scale.

(4) In proceedings against any person for an offence by virtue of paragraph (*b*) of subsection (3) above it shall be a defence for that person to show that he did not know, and had no grounds for suspecting, that the pipe or apparatus in question had been attached or altered as mentioned in that subsection.

(5), (6) *Action by appropriate agency for loss or damage.*

(7) In this section "service pipe" and "stopcock" have the same meanings as in the Water Industry Act 1991, and "consumer" has the same meaning as in Part III of that Act.

[Water Resources Act 1991, s 176 as amended by the Environment Act 1995, Sch 22 and SI 2013/755.]

*Interpretation of Part VII*

**7.11703** **186. Interpretation of Part VII** (1) In this Part—

"discharge pipe" means a pipe from which discharges are or are to be made under section 163 above;

"relevant transferred functions" means any functions which—

(*a*) were exercisable by the Agency before 1 April 2013, and

(*b*) are functions of the NRBW by virtue of the Natural Resources Body for Wales (Functions) Order 2013,

but this is subject to subsection (1A);

"resource main" means any pipe, not being a trunk main within the meaning of the Water Industry Act 1991, which is or is to be used for the purpose of—

(*a*) conveying water from one source of supply to another, from a source of supply to a regulating reservoir or from a regulating reservoir to a source of supply; or

(*b*) giving or taking a supply of water in bulk.

(1A) For the purposes of the definition of "relevant transferred functions"—

(*a*) a function of the Agency was exercisable before 1 April 2013 whether or not the enactment conferring it had come into force before that date, but

(*b*) a function is only a relevant transferred function when the enactment conferring the Agency function transferred to or conferred on the NRBW has come into force.

(2) In subsection (1) above—

"source of supply" shall be construed without reference to the definition of that expression in section 221 below; and

"supply of water in bulk" has the same meaning as in section 3 above[1].

(3) The powers conferred by Chapter I of this Part[2] shall be without prejudice to the powers conferred on the Agency or on the NRBW by any other enactment or by any agreement. shall be without prejudice to the powers conferred on the Agency by any other enactment or by any agreement.

[Water Resources Act 1991, s 186 as amended by the Environment Act 1995, Sch 22 and SI 2013/755.]

---

1 Section 3 defines "supply of water in bulk" as a supply of water for distribution by a water undertaker taking the supply.

2 Chapter I of Part VII comprises ss 154.

## PART VIII[1]
## INFORMATION PROVISIONS

*Provision and acquisition of information etc*

7.11704 198. **Information about underground water** Any person searching for or abstracting water by sinking a well or borehole deeper than 50 feet to notify, keep journal for, and supply particulars to the Natural Environment Research Council; he (and the occupier if different person) to allow access etc; failure is summary offence punishable by fine not exceeding **level 3** on the standard scale and a fine of £20 a day thereafter for continuing offence.

[Water Resources Act 1991, s 198—summarised.]

1 Part VII comprises ss 187–206.

7.11705 199. **Notice etc of mining operations which may affect water conservation** Failure to give notice or fail to comply with conservation notice is an offence punishable on summary conviction by a fine not exceeding the **statutory maximum** and on conviction on indictment by a **fine**[1].

[Water Resources Act 1991, s 199—summarised.]

1 For procedure in respect of an offence triable either way, see the Magistrates' Courts Act 1980, ss 17A–21 in PART I: MAGISTRATES' COURTS, PROCEDURE, ante.

7.11706 199A. **Appeals against conservation notices under section 199**

7.11707 200. **Gauges and records kept by other persons** Person proposing to install gauge on inland waters other than discrete waters to notify Agency, allow three months to elapse before installation, and state where records to be kept: contravention punishable on summary conviction by a fine not exceeding **level 1** on the standard scale.

[Water Resources Act 1991, s 200 as amended by the Environment Act, Sch 22—summarised.]

7.11708 201. **Power to require information with respect of water resouces functions** Person failing to comply with directions liable on summary conviction to fine not exceeding the statutory maximum and on conviction on indictment to a fine or imprisonment for a term not exceeding two years, or both.

[Water Resources Act 1991, s 201 as substituted by the Water Act 2003, s 70—summarised.]

7.11709 202. **Information and assistance required in connection with the control of pollution** (1) It shall be the duty of the Agency, if and so far as it is requested to do so by either of the Ministers, to give him all such advice and assistance as appears to it to be appropriate for facilitating the carrying out by him of his functions under the water pollution provisions of this Act.

(2) Subject to subsection (3) below, either of the Ministers of the Agency may serve on any person a notice requiring that person to furnish him or, as the case may be, it, within a period or at times specified in the notice and in a form and manner so specified, with such information as is reasonably required by the Minister in question or by the Agency for the purpose of carrying out any of his or, as the case may be, its functions under the water pollution provisions of this Act.

(3) Each of the Ministers shall have power by regulations to make provision for restricting the information which may be required under subsection (2) above and for determining the form in which the information is to be so required.

(4) A person who fails without reasonable excuse to comply with the requirements of a notice served on him under this section shall be guilty of an offence and liable[1]—

(*a*) on summary conviction, to a fine not exceeding the **statutory maximum;**

(*b*) on conviction on indictment, to a **fine** or to imprisonment for a term not exceeding **two years**, or to **both**.

(5) *Repealed.*

[Water Resources Act 1991, s 202 as amended by the Environment Act 1995, Schs 22 and 24.]

1 For procedure in respect of this offence which is triable either way, see the Magistrates' Courts Act 1980, ss 17A–21, in PART I: MAGISTRATES' COURTS, PROCEDURE, ante.

*Restriction on disclosure of information*

7.11710 204. **Restriction on disclosure of information** Subject to the following provisions of this section, no information with respect to any particular business which—

(*a*) has been obtained by virtue of any of the provisions of this Act; and

(*b*) relates to the affairs of any individual or to any particular business,

shall, during the lifetime of that individual or so long as that business continues to be carried on, be disclosed without the consent of that individual or the person for the time being carrying on that business.

(2) Subsection (1) above does not apply to any disclosure of information which is made—

(*a*) for the purpose of facilitating the carrying out by either of the Ministers, the Agency, the NRBW, the Scottish Environment Protection Agency, the Water Services Regulation Authority, the Consumer Council for Water, the Competition and Markets Authority or a local authority of any of his, its or, as the case may be, their functions by virtue of this Act, any of the other consolidation Acts, the Water Act 1989, Part I *or IIA* of the Environmental Protection Act 1990, the 1995 Act, regulations under section 2 of the Pollution Prevention and Control Act 1999, the Water Act 2003, or the Natural Resources Body for Wales (Establishment) Order 2012 (SI 2012/1903)*

(*b*) for the purpose of facilitating the performance by a water undertaker, sewerage undertaker or company holding a licence under Chapter 1A of Part 2 of the Water Industry Act 1991 of any of the duties imposed on it by or under this Act, any of the other consolidation Acts, the Water Act 1989 or the Water Act 2003;

(*c*) in pursuance of any duty imposed by section 197(1)(*a*) or (2) or 203(1), (1A), (2) or (2A) above or of any duty imposed by section 27H of the Water Industry Act 1991;

(*ca*) for the purpose of complying with a request under section 14 of the Flood and Water Management Act 2010;

(*d*) for the purpose of facilitating the carrying out by any person mentioned in Part I of Schedule 24 to this Act of any of his functions under any of the enactments or instruments specified in Part II of that Schedule;

(*e*) for the purpose of enabling or assisting the Secretary of State, the Treasury, the Financial Conduct Authority, the Prudential Regulation Authority or the Bank of England to exercise any powers conferred by or under the Financial Services and Markets Act 2000 or by the enactments relating to companies or insolvency;

(*ea*) for the purpose of enabling or assisting any inspector appointed under enactments relating to companies to carry out his functions;

(*f*) for the purpose of enabling an official receiver to carry out his functions under the enactments relating to insolvency or for the purpose of enabling or assisting a recognised professional body for the purposes of section 391 of the Insolvency Act 1986 to carry out its functions as such;

(*g*) for the purpose of facilitating the carrying out by the Health and Safety Executive of any of its functions under any enactment or of facilitating the carrying out by any enforcing authority, within the meaning of Part I of the Health and Safety at Work etc Act 1974, of any functions under a relevant statutory provision, within the meaning of that Act;

(*ga*) for the purpose of facilitating the carrying out by the Office for Nuclear Regulation of any of its functions under any enactment;

(*h*) for the purpose of facilitating the carrying out by the Comptroller and Auditor General of any of his functions under any enactment;

(*i*) in connection with the investigation of any criminal offence or for the purposes of any criminal proceedings;

(*j*) for the purposes of any civil proceedings brought under or by virtue of this Act, any of the other consolidation Acts, the Water Act 1989, the Water Act 2003 or any of the enactments or instruments specified in Part II of Schedule 24 to this Act, or of any arbitration under this Act, any of the other consolidation Acts, the Water Act 1989 or the Water Act 2003; or

(*k*) in pursuance of an EU obligation.

(3) Nothing in subsection (1) above shall be construed—

(*a*) as limiting the matters which may be included in, or made public as part of, a report of—

(i) the Agency;

(ia) the Scottish Environment Protection Agency;

(ib) the NRBW;

(ii) the Water Services Regulation Authority;

(iii) the Consumer Council for Water (or any regional committee of that Council established under section 27A of the Water Industry Act 1991); or

(iv) the Competition and Markets Authority,

under any provision of this Act, Part I or* IIA of the Environmental Protection Act 1990, that Act of 1991, the 1995 Act, regulations under section 2 of the Pollution Prevention and Control Act 1999, or the Water Act 2003;

(*b*) as limiting the matters which may be published under section 201 of that Act of 1991; or

(*c*) as applying to any information which has been made public as part of such a report or has been so published or to any information exclusively of a statistical nature.

(4) Subject to subsection (5) below, nothing in subsection (1) above shall preclude the disclosure of information—

(*a*) if the disclosure is of information relating to a matter connected with the carrying out of the functions of a water undertaker or sewerage undertaker, or with the carrying on by a company holding a licence under Chapter 1A of Part 2 of the Water Industry Act 1991 of activities under its licence, and is made by one Minister of the Crown or government department to another; or

(*b*) if the disclosure is for the purpose of enabling or assisting any public or other authority for the time being designated for the purposes of this section by an order made by the

Secretary of State to discharge any functions which are specified in the order.

(5) The power to make an order under subsection (4) above shall be exercisable by statutory instrument subject to annulment in pursuance of a resolution of either House of Parliament; and where such an order designates an authority for the purposes of paragraph (*b*) of that subsection, the order may—

(*a*) impose conditions subject to which the disclosure of information is permitted by virtue of that paragraph; and

(*b*) otherwise restrict the circumstances in which disclosure is so permitted.

(6) Any person who discloses any information in contravention of the preceding provisions of this section shall be guilty of an offence and liable[1]—

(*a*) on summary conviction, to a fine not exceeding the **statutory maximum**;

(*b*) on conviction on indictment, to imprisonment for a term not exceeding **two years** or to a **fine** or to **both**.

(7) In this section "the other consolidation Acts" means the Water Industry Act 1991, the Land Drainage Act 1991 and the Water Consolidation (Consequential Provisions) Act 1991.

[Water Resources Act 1991, s 204 as amended by the Environment Act 1995, Sch 22, SI 1999/506, the Pollution Prevention and Control Act 1999, Sch 2, SI 2001/3649, the Pollution Prevention and Control Act 1999, Sch 3, the Water Act 2003, Sch 7, SI 2008/960, the Flood and Water Management Act 2010, Sch 2, SI 2011/1043, SI 2013/755, SI 2014/892 and the Deregulation Act 2015, Sch 23.]

---

* **Words repealed by the Pollution Prevention and Control Act 1999, Sch 3, from a date to be appointed.**

1 For procedure in respect of an offence triable either way, see the Magistrates' Courts Act 1980, ss 17A–21 in PART I: MAGISTRATES' COURTS, PROCEDURE, ante.

7.11711 **205. Confidentiality of information relating to underground water etc** (1) The person sinking any such well or borehole as is mentioned in section 198 above or, if it is a different person, the owner or occupier of the land on which any such well or borehole is sunk may by notice to the Natural Environment Research Council require that Council to treat as confidential—

(*a*) any copy of or extract from the journal required to be kept under that section; or

(*b*) any specimen taken in exercise of the rights specified in subsection (5) of that section.

(2) Subject to subsections (3) and (4) below, the Natural Environment Research Council shall not, without the consent of the person giving the notice, allow any matter to which any notice under subsection (1) above relates to be published or shown to any person who is not an officer of that Council or of a department of the Secretary of State.

(3) Subsection (2) above shall not prohibit any matter from being published or shown to any person in so far as it contains or affords information as to water resources and supplies.

(4) If at any time the Natural Environment Research Council give notice to any person that in their opinion his consent for the purposes of subsection (2) above is being unreasonably withheld—

(*a*) that person may, within three months after the giving of the notice, appeal to the High Court for an order restraining that Council from acting as if consent had been given; and

(*b*) that Council may proceed as if consent had been given if either no such appeal is brought within that period or the High Court, after hearing the appeal, do not make such an order.

(5) Any person who fails to comply with any obligation imposed on him by the preceding provisions of this section shall be guilty of an offence and liable, on summary conviction—

(*a*) to a fine not exceeding **level 3** on the standard scale; and

(*b*) where the offence continues after conviction, to a further fine of £20 for every day during which it so continues.

(6) If any person who is admitted to any premises in compliance with section 198(2)(*c*) above discloses to any person any information obtained by him there with regard to any manufacturing process or trade secret, he shall, unless the disclosure is in performance of his duty, be guilty of an offence and liable[1]—

(*a*) on summary conviction, to imprisonment for a term not exceeding **three months** or to a fine not exceeding the **statutory maximum** or to **both**;*

(*b*) on conviction on indictment, to imprisonment for a term not exceeding **three months** or to a **fine** or to **both**.*

[Water Resources Act 1991, s 205.]

---

* **Words substituted by the Criminal Justice Act 2003, Sch 32, from a date to be appointed.**

1 For procedure in respect of an offence triable either way, see the Magistrates' Courts Act 1980, ss 17A–21 in PART I: MAGISTRATES' COURTS, PROCEDURE, ante.

*Making of false statements etc*

7.11712 **206. Making of false statements etc** (1) If, in furnishing any information or making any application under or for the purposes of any provision of this Act or of section 3, 4 or 10 of the Water Act 2003, any person makes a statement which he knows to be false or misleading in a material particular, or recklessly makes any statement which is false or misleading in a material particular, he shall be guilty of an offence under this section.

(2) *Repealed.*

(3) Where—

(*a*) the provisions contained in a licence under Chapter II of Part II of this Act in pursuance of paragraph (*b*) of subsection (2) of section 46 above, or of that paragraph as modified by subsection (6) of that section, require the use of a meter, gauge or other device; and

(*b*) such a device is used for the purposes of those provisions,

any person who wilfully alters or interferes with that device so as to prevent it from measuring correctly shall be guilty of an offence under this section.

(3A) If a person intentionally makes a false entry in any record required to be kept by virtue of a licence under Chapter II of Part II of this Act, or a consent under Chapter II of Part III of this Act, he shall be guilty of an offence under this section.

(4) If, in keeping any record or journal or in furnishing any information which he is required to keep or furnish under section 198 or 205 above, any person knowingly or recklessly makes any statement which is false in a material particular, he shall be guilty of an offence under this section.

(5) A person who is guilty of an offence under this section shall be liable[1]—

(*a*) on summary conviction, to a fine not exceeding the **statutory maximum;**

(*b*) on conviction on indictment, to a **fine** or to imprisonment for a term not exceeding **two years**, or to **both**.

[Water Resources Act 1991, s 206 as amended by the Environment Act 1995, Schs 19 and 24 and the Water Act 2003, Sch 7.]

---

[1] For procedure in respect of an offence triable either way, see the Magistrates' Courts Act 1980, ss 17A–21 in PART I: MAGISTRATES' COURTS, PROCEDURE, ante.

## PART IX[1]

## MISCELLANEOUS AND SUPPLEMENTAL

### *Miscellaneous*

7.11713 **209. Evidence of samples and abstractions** (1)–(2) *Repealed.*

(3) Where, in accordance with the provisions contained in a licence in pursuance of paragraph (*b*) of subsection (2) of section 46 above, or in pursuance of that paragraph as read with subsection (6) of that section, it has been determined what quantity of water is to be taken—

(*a*) to have been abstracted during any period from a source of supply by the holder of the licence; or

(*b*) to have been so abstracted at a particular point or by particular means, or for use for particular purposes,

that determination shall, for the purposes of any proceedings under Chapter II of Part II of this Act or any of the related water resources provisions, be conclusive evidence of the matters to which it relates.

(4) *Repealed.*

[Water Resources Act 1991, s 209 as amended by the Environment Act 1995, Sch 24.]

---

[1] Part IX comprises ss 207–225.

### *Byelaws*

7.11714 **210. Byelaw-making powers of the appropriate agency** (1) Schedule 25[1] to this Act shall have effect for conferring powers on the appropriate agency to make byelaws for purposes connected with the carrying out of its functions.

(2) Schedule 26[1] to this Act shall have effect in relation to byelaws made by the appropriate agency, whether by virtue of subsection (1) above or by virtue of any other enactment.

(3) Schedule 27 to this Act (emergency fisheries byelaws) shall have effect.

[Water Resources Act 1991, s 210 as amended by the Environment Act 1995, Sch 22, the Marine and Coastal Access Act 2009, s 225 and SI 2013/755]

---

[1] See, post.

7.11715 **211. Enforcement of byelaws** (1) If any person contravenes any byelaws made by virtue of paragraph 1 of Schedule 25[1] to this Act, he shall be guilty of an offence and liable, on summary conviction—

(*a*) to a fine not exceeding **level 1** on the standard scale; and

(*b*) if the contravention is continued after conviction, to a fine not exceeding **£5** for each day on which it is so continued.

(2) Byelaws made by virtue of paragraph 2 or 3 of that Schedule may contain provision providing for a contravention of the byelaws to constitute a summary offence punishable, on summary conviction, by a fine not exceeding **level 5** on the standard scale or such smaller sum as may be specified in the byelaws.

(3) A person who contravenes any byelaws made by virtue of paragraph 4 or 6 of that Schedule shall be guilty of an offence and liable, on summary conviction—

(*a*) in the case of byelaws made by virtue of paragraph 4, to a fine not exceeding level 4 on the standard scale or such smaller sum as may be specified in the byelaws;

(*b*) in the case of byelaws made by virtue of paragraph 6, to a fine.

(4) If any person acts in contravention of any byelaw made by virtue of paragraph 5 of that Schedule he shall be guilty of an offence and liable, on summary conviction—

(*a*) to a fine not exceeding **level 5** on the standard scale; and

(*b*) if the contravention is continued after conviction, to a further fine not exceeding **£40** for each day on which it is so continued.

(5) Without prejudice to any proceedings by virtue of subsection (1) or (4) above, the appropriate agency may—

(*a*) take such action as it considers necessary to remedy the effect of any contravention of byelaws made by virtue of paragraph 1 of Schedule 25 to this Act;

(*b*) take such action as may be necessary to remedy the effect of any person's contravention of byelaws made by virtue of paragraph 5 of that Schedule; and

(*c*) recover the expenses reasonably incurred by the appropriate agency in taking any action under paragraph (*a*) or (*b*) above from the person in default.

(6) So much of the Salmon and Freshwater Fisheries Act 1975[2] as makes provision with respect to or by reference to offences under that Act shall have effect as if an offence consisting in a contravention of byelaws made by virtue of paragraph 6 of Schedule 25 to this Act were an offence under that Act.

(7) Section 70 above shall apply in relation to any restrictions imposed by byelaws made by virtue of paragraph 1 of Schedule 25 to this Act as it applies in relation to restrictions imposed by the provisions of Chapter II of Part II of this Act which are mentioned in that section; and sections 100 and 101 above shall have effect in relation to contraventions of byelaws made by virtue of paragraph 4 of that Schedule as they have effect in relation to contraventions of provisions of Part III of this Act.

[Water Resources Act 1991, s 211 as amended by the Environment Act 1995, Sch 22, the Marine and Coastal Access Act 2009, s 226, SI 2013/755 and SI 2015/664.]

---

1 See, post.
2 See this Part: title, FISHERIES, ante.

*Offences etc*

7.11716 **216. Enforcement: powers and duties** (1) Without prejudice to its powers of enforcement in relation to the other provisions of this Act, it shall be the duty of the appropriate agency to enforce the provisions to which this section applies.

(2) No proceedings for any offence under any provision to which this section applies shall be instituted except—

(*a*) by the appropriate agency; or

(*b*) by, or with the consent of, the Director of Public Prosecutions.

(3) This section applies to Chapter II of Part II[1] of this Act and the related water resources provisions.

[Water Resources Act 1991, s 216 as amended by the Environment Act 1995, Sch 22 and SI 2013/755.]

---

1 Part II, Ch II comprises ss 24–72.

7.11717 **217. Criminal liabilities of directors and other third parties** (1) Where a body corporate is guilty of an offence under this Act or under section 4 of the Water Act 2003 and that offence is proved to have been committed with the consent or connivance of, or to be attributable to any neglect on the part of, any director, manager, secretary or other similar officer of the body corporate or any person who was purporting to act in any such capacity, then he, as well as the body corporate, shall be guilty of that offence and shall be liable to be proceeded against and punished accordingly.

(2) Where the affairs of a body corporate are managed by its members, subsection (1) above shall apply in relation to the acts and defaults of a member in connection with his functions of management as if he were a director of the body corporate.

(3) Without prejudice to subsections (1) and (2) above, where the commission by any person of an offence under the water pollution provisions of this Act is due to the act or default of some other person, that other person may be charged with and convicted of the offence whether or not proceedings for the offence are taken against the first-mentioned person.

[Water Resources Act 1991, s 217 as amended by the Water Act 2003, Sch 7.]

7.11718 **220.** *Provisions relating to service of documents.*

7.11719 **221. General interpretation[1]** (1) In this Act, except in so far as the context otherwise requires—

"the 1995 Act" means the Environment Act 1995;

"abstraction", in relation to water contained in any source of supply, means the doing of anything whereby any of that water is removed from that source of supply, whether temporarily or permanently, including anything whereby the water is so removed for the purpose of being transferred to another source of supply; and "abstract" shall be construed accordingly;

"accessories", in relation to a main, sewer or other pipe, includes any manholes, ventilating shafts, inspection chambers, settling tanks, wash-out pipes, pumps, ferrules or stopcocks for the main, sewer or other pipe, or any machinery or other apparatus which is designed or adapted for use in connection with the use or maintenance of the main, sewer or other pipe or of another accessory for it, but does not include any electronic communications apparatus unless it—

(*a*) is or is to be situated inside or in the close vicinity of the main, sewer or other pipe or inside or in the close vicinity of another accessory for it; and

(*b*) is intended to be used only in connection with the use or maintenance of the main, sewer or other pipe or of another accessory for it;

and in this definition "stopcock" has the same meaning as in the Water Industry Act 1991;

"the Agency" means the Environment Agency;

"agriculture" has the same meaning as in the Agriculture Act 1947 and "agricultural" shall be construed accordingly;

"analyse", in relation to any sample of land, water or effluent, includes subjecting the sample to a test of any description, and cognate expressions shall be construed accordingly;

"the appropriate agency" means—

(a) for the purposes of the flood risk management work provisions—

(i) in relation to flood risks (within the meaning of the Flood and Water Management Act 2010) in Wales, the NRBW;

(ii) in any other case, the Agency;

(b) for any other purpose—

(i) in relation to Wales, the NRBW;

(ii) in any other case, the Agency;

"conservancy authority" means any person who has a duty or power under any enactment to conserve, maintain or improve the navigation of a tidal water and is not a navigation authority or harbour authority;

"contravention" includes a failure to comply, and cognate expressions shall be construed accordingly;

"damage", in relation to individuals, includes death and any personal injury (including any disease or impairment of physical or mental condition);

"discrete waters" means inland waters so far as they comprise—

(*a*) a lake, pond or reservoir which does not discharge to any other inland waters; or

(*b*) one of a group of two or more lakes, ponds or reservoirs (whether near to or distant from each other) and of watercourses or mains connecting them, where none of the inland waters in the group discharges to any inland waters outside the group;

"disposal"—

(*a*) in relation to land or any interest or right in or over land, includes the creation of such an interest or right and a disposal effected by means of the surrender or other termination of any such interest or right; and

(*b*) in relation to sewage, includes treatment;

and cognate expressions shall be construed accordingly;

"drain" has, subject to subsection (2) below, the same meaning as in the Water Industry Act 1991;

"drainage" in the expression "drainage works" has the meaning given by section 113 above for the purposes of Part IV of this Act;

"drought order" means an ordinary drought order under subsection (1) of section 73 above or an emergency drought order under subsection (2) of that section;

"effluent" means any liquid, including particles of matter and other substances in suspension in the liquid;

"enactment" includes an enactment contained in this Act or in any Act passed after this Act;

"engineering or building operations", without prejudice to the generality of that expression, includes—

(*a*) the construction, alteration, improvement, maintenance or demolition of any building or structure or of any reservoir, watercourse, dam, weir, well, borehole or other works; and

(*b*) the installation, modification or removal of any machinery or apparatus;

"harbour authority" (except in the flood defence provisions of this Act, in which it has the same meaning as in section 313 of the Merchant Shipping Act 1995) means a person who is a harbour authority as defined in section 151 for the purposes of Chapter II of Part VI of that Act and is not a navigation authority;

"highway" has the same meaning as in the Highways Act 1980;

"information" includes anything contained in any records, accounts, estimates or returns;

"inland waters" means the whole or any part of—

(*a*) any river, stream or other watercourse (within the meaning of Chapter II of Part II of this Act), whether natural or artificial and whether tidal or not;

(*b*) any lake or pond, whether natural or artificial, or any reservoir or dock, in so far as the lake, pond, reservoir or dock does not fall within paragraph (*a*) of this definition; and

(*c*) so much of any channel, creek, bay, estuary or arm of the sea as does not fall within paragraph (*a*) or (*b*) of this definition;

"joint planning board" has the same meaning as in the Town and Country Planning Act 1990;

"local authority" means the council of any county, county borough, district or London borough or the Common Council of the City of London;

"local statutory provision" means—

(*a*) a provision of a local Act (including an Act confirming a provisional order);

(*b*) a provision of so much of any public general Act as has effect with respect to a particular area, with respect to particular persons or works or with respect to particular provisions falling within any paragraph of this definition;

(*c*) a provision of an instrument made under any provision falling within paragraph (*a*) or (*b*) above; or

(*d*) a provision of any other instrument which is in the nature of a local enactment;

"main river map" has, subject to section 194 above, the meaning given by section 193(2) above;

"micro-organism" includes any microscopic, biological entity which is capable of replication;

"the Minister" means the Minister of Agriculture, Fisheries and Food;

"the Ministers" means the Secretary of State and the Minister;

"modifications" includes additions, alterations and omissions, and cognate expressions shall be construed accordingly;

"navigation authority" means any person who has a duty or power under any enactment to work, maintain, conserve, improve or control any canal or other inland navigation, navigable river, estuary, harbour or dock;

"notice" means notice in writing;

"owner", in relation to any premises, means the person who—

(*a*) is for the time being receiving the rack-rent of the premises, whether on his own account or as agent or trustee for another person; or

(*b*) would receive the rack-rent if the premises were let at a rack-rent,

but for the purposes of Schedule 2 to this Act, Chapter II of Part II of this Act and the related water resources provisions does not include a mortgagee not in possession, and cognate expressions shall be construed accordingly;

"prescribed" means prescribed by regulations made by the Secretary of State or, in relation to regulations made by the Minister, by those regulations;

"public authority" means any Minister of the Crown or government department, the Authority, any local authority or any person certified by the Secretary of State to be a public authority for the purposes of this Act;

"public sewer" means a sewer for the time being vested in a sewerage undertaker in its capacity as such, whether vested in that undertaker by virtue of a scheme under Schedule 2 to the Water Act 1989, section 179 of or Schedule 2 to the Water Industry Act 1991 or otherwise;

"records" includes computer records and any other records kept otherwise than in a document;

"the related water resources provisions", in relation to Chapter II of Part II of this Act, means—

(*a*) the following provisions of this Act, that is to say, the provisions—

(i) of sections 21 to 23 (including Schedule 5);

(ii) of sections 120, 125 to 130, 158, 189, 199 to 201, 206(3), 209(3), 211(1) and 216; and

(iii) of paragraph 1 of Schedule 25; and

(*b*) the following provisions of the 1995 Act, that is to say, the provisions—

(i) of sections 41 and 42 (charging schemes) as they have effect by virtue of subsection (1)(*a*) of section 41 (licences under Chapter II of Part II of this Act); and

(ii) of subsections (1) and (2) of section 53 (inquiries and other hearings);

"sewage effluent" includes any effluent from the sewage disposal or sewerage works of a sewerage undertaker but does not include surface water;

"sewer" has, subject to subsection (2) below, the same meaning as in the Water Industry Act 1991;

"source of supply" means—

(*a*) any inland waters except, without prejudice to subsection (3) below in its application to paragraph (*b*) of this definition, any which are discrete waters; or

(*b*) any underground strata in which water is or at any time may be contained;

"street" has, subject to subsection (4) below, the same meaning as in Part III of the New Roads and Street Works 1991;

"subordinate legislation" has the same meaning as in the Interpretation Act 1978;

"substance" includes micro-organisms and any natural or artificial substance or other matter, whether it is in solid or liquid form or in the form of a gas or vapour;

"surface water" includes water from roofs;

"trade effluent" includes any effluent which is discharged from premises used for carrying on any trade or industry, other than surface water and domestic sewage, and for the purposes of this definition any premises wholly or mainly used (whether for profit or not) for agricultural purposes or for the purposes of fish farming or for scientific research or experiment shall be deemed to be premises used for carrying on a trade;

"underground strata" means strata subjacent to the surface of any land;

"vessel" includes a hovercraft within the meaning of the Hovercraft Act 1968;

"watercourse" includes (subject to sections 72(2) and 113(1) above) all rivers, streams, ditches, drains, cuts, culverts, dykes, sluices, sewers and passages through which water flows[2], except mains and other pipes which—

(*a*) belong to the Authority or a water undertaker; or

(*b*) are used by a water undertaker or any other person for the purpose only of providing a supply of water to any premises;

"water pollution provisions" in relation to this Act, means the following provisions of this Act—

(*a*) the provisions of Part III of this Act;

(*b*) sections 161 to 161D, 190, 202 and 203; and

(*c*) paragraph 4 of Schedule 25 to this Act and section 211 above so far as it relates to byelaws made under that paragraph.

and the following provisions of the 1995 Act, that is to say the provisions of subsections (1) and (2) of section 53.

(2) References in this Act to a pipe, including references to a main, a drain or a sewer, shall include references to a tunnel or conduit which serves or is to serve as the pipe in question and to any accessories for the pipe; and, accordingly, references to the laying of a pipe shall include references to the construction of such a tunnel or conduit, to the construction or installation of any such accessories and to the making of a connection between one pipe and another.

(3) Any reference in this Act to water contained in underground strata is a reference to water so contained otherwise than in a sewer, pipe, reservoir, tank or other underground works constructed in any such strata; but for the purposes of this Act water for the time being contained in—

(*a*) a well, borehole or similar work, including any adit or passage constructed in connection with the well, borehole or work for facilitating the collection of water in the well, borehole or work; or

(*b*) any excavation into underground strata, where the level of water in the excavation depends wholly or mainly on water entering it from those strata,

shall be treated as water contained in the underground strata into which the well, borehole or work was sunk or, as the case may be, the excavation was made.

(4) Until the coming into force of Part III of the New Roads and Street Works Act 1991, the definition of "street" in subsection (1) above shall have effect as if the reference to that Part were a reference to the Public Utilities Street Works Act 1950; but nothing in this section shall be taken—

(*a*) to prejudice the power of the Secretary of State under that Act of 1991 to make an order bringing Part III of that Act into force on different days for different purposes (including the purposes of this section); or

(*b*) in the period before the coming into force of that Part, to prevent references in this Act to a street, where the street is a highway which passes over a bridge or through a tunnel, from including that bridge or tunnel.

(5) For the purposes of any provision of this Act by or under which power is or may be conferred on any person to recover the expenses incurred by that person in doing anything, those expenses shall be assumed to include such sum as may be reasonable in respect of establishment charges or overheads.

(6) References in this Act to the later or latest of two or more different times or days are, in a case where those times or days coincide, references to the time at which or, as the case may be, the day on which they coincide.

(7) For the purposes of this Act—

(*a*) references in this Act to more than one Minister of the Crown, in relation to anything falling to be done by those Ministers, are references to those Ministers acting jointly; and

(*b*) any provision of this Act by virtue of which any function of a Minister of the Crown is exercisable concurrently by different Ministers, shall have effect as providing for that function also to be exercisable jointly by any two or more of those Ministers.

(8) Sub-paragraph (1) of paragraph 1 of Schedule 2 to the Water Consolidation (Consequential Provisions) Act 1991 has effect (by virtue of sub-paragraph (2)(*b*) of that paragraph) so that references in this Act to things done under or for the purposes of provisions of this Act, the Water Industry Act 1991 or the Land Drainage Act 1991 include references to things done, or treated as done, under or for the purposes of the corresponding provisions of the law in force before the commencement of this Act.

(9) Subject to any provision to the contrary which is contained in Schedule 26 to the Water Act 1989 or in the Water Consolidation (Consequential Provisions) Act 1991, nothing in any local statutory provision passed or made before 1st September 1989 shall be construed as relieving any water undertaker or sewerage undertaker from any liability arising by virtue of this Act in respect of any act or omission occurring on or after that date.

[Water Resources Act 1991, s 221 as amended by the Local Government (Wales) Act 1994, Sch 11, the Merchant Shipping Act 1995, Sch 13, the Environment Act 1995, Schs 22 and 24, the Communications Act 2003, Sch 17, SI 2010/675 and SI 2013/755.]

---

1 Section 221(1) is reproduced in an abridged form and contains only those definitions which are likely to be relevant to the provisions of the Act which are contained in this Manual.

2 The words "through which water flows" qualify only the words immediately preceding them ie "sewers and passages". Watercourses do not cease to be such because they are dry at the particular time (*R v Dovermoss Ltd* (1995) 159 JP 448, CA) and see s 104(2), this PART, ante.

*Other supplemental provisions*

7.11720 **222.** *Crown application.*

7.11721 **223.** *Exemption for visiting forces.*

SCHEDULE 20

SUPPLEMENTAL PROVISIONS WITH RESPECT TO POWERS OF ENTRY — Section 173

*(As amended by the Environment Act 1995, Sch 22, SI 2009/1307 and SI 2013/755.)*

*Notice of entry*

7.11723 **1.** (1) Without prejudice to any power exercisable by virtue of a warrant under this Schedule, no person shall make an entry into any premises or vessel by virtue of any power conferred by sections 169 to 172 of this Act except—

(*a*) in an emergency; or

(*b*) at a reasonable time and after the required notice of the intended entry has been given to the occupier of the premises or vessel.

(2) For the purposes of this paragraph the required notice is seven days' notice; but such notice shall not be required in the case of an exercise of a power conferred by section 169 or 172 above, except where the premises in question are residential premises, the vessel in question is used for residential purposes or the entry in question is to be with heavy equipment.

(3) For the purposes of the application of this paragraph to the power conferred by section 170 of this Act the reference in sub-paragraph (1) above to an emergency—

(*a*) in relation to any entry to premises for the purposes of, or for purposes connected with, the exercise or proposed exercise of any power in relation to a street, includes a reference to any circumstances requiring the carrying out of emergency works within the meaning of Part III of the New Roads and Street Works Act 1991; and

(*b*) in relation to any other entry to premises, includes a reference to any danger to property and to any interruption of a supply of water provided to any premises by any person and to any interruption of the provision of sewerage services to any premises.

(4) Until the coming into force of section 52 of the New Roads and Street Works Act 1991, sub-paragraph (3) above shall have effect as if the reference to Part III of that Act were a reference to the Public Utilities Street Works Act 1950; but nothing in this sub-paragraph shall be taken to prejudice the power of the Secretary of State under that Act of 1991 to make an order bringing that section 52 into force on different days for different purposes (including the purposes of this paragraph).

*Warrant to exercise power*

**2.** (1) If it is shown to the satisfaction of a justice of the peace on sworn information in writing—

(*a*) that there are reasonable grounds for the exercise in relation to any premises or vessel of a power conferred by sections 169 to 172 of this Act; and

(*b*) that one or more of the conditions specified in sub-paragraph (2) below is fulfilled in relation to those premises or that vessel,

the justice may by warrant authorise the relevant authority to designate a person who shall be authorised to exercise the power in relation to those premises, or that vessel, in accordance with the warrant and, if need be, by force.

(2) The conditions mentioned in sub-paragraph (1)(*b*) above are—

(*a*) that the exercise of the power in relation to the premises or vessel has been refused;

(*b*) that such a refusal is reasonably apprehended;

(*c*) that the premises are unoccupied or the vessel is unoccupied;

(*d*) that the occupier is temporarily absent from the premises or vessel;

(*e*) that the case is one of urgency; or

(*f*) that an application for admission to the premises or vessel would defeat the object of the proposed entry.

(3) A justice of the peace shall not issue a warrant under this Schedule by virtue only of being satisfied that the exercise of a power in relation to any premises or vessel has been refused, or that a refusal is reasonably apprehended, unless he is also satisfied—

(*a*) that notice of the intention to apply for the warrant has been given to the occupier of the premises or vessel; or

(*b*) that the giving of such a notice would defeat the object of the proposed entry.

(4) For the purposes of the application of this Schedule to the powers conferred by section 171 of this Act in a case to which subsection (4) of that section applies, a justice of the peace shall not issue a warrant under this Schedule unless he is satisfied that the Secretary of State has given his authorisation for the purposes of that subsection in relation to that case.

(5) Every warrant under this Schedule shall continue in force until the purposes for which the warrant was issued have been fulfilled.

*Manner of exercise of powers*

**3.** A person designated as the person who may exercise any power to which this Schedule applies shall produce evidence of his designation and other authority before he exercises the power.

*Supplementary powers of person making entry etc*

**4.** A person authorised to enter any premises or vessel by virtue of any power to which this Schedule applies shall be entitled, subject in the case of a power exercisable under a warrant to the terms of the warrant, to take with him on to the premises or vessel such other persons and such equipment as may be necessary.

*Duty to secure premises*

**5.** A person who enters any premises or vessel in the exercise of any power to which this Schedule applies shall leave the premises or vessel as effectually secured against trespassers as he found them.

*Compensation*

**6.** (1) Where any person exercises any power to which this Schedule applies, it shall be the duty of the relevant authority to make full compensation to any person who has sustained loss or damage by reason of—

(*a*) the exercise by the designated person of that power or of any power to take any person or equipment with him when entering the premises or vessel in relation to which the power is exercised; or

(*b*) the performance of, or failure of the designated person to perform, the duty imposed by paragraph 5 above.

(2) Compensation shall not be payable by virtue of sub-paragraph (1) above in respect of any loss or damage if the loss or damage—

(*a*) is attributable to the default of the person who sustained it; or

(*b*) is loss or damage in respect of which compensation is payable by virtue of any other provision of this Act.

(3) Any dispute as to a person's entitlement to compensation under this paragraph, or as to the amount of any such compensation, shall be referred to the arbitration of a single arbitrator appointed by agreement between the relevant authority and the person who claims to have sustained the loss or damage or, in default of agreement—

(*a*) by the Upper Tribunal where the relevant authority is one of the Ministers; and

(*b*) by one of the Ministers, where the Agency or the NRBW is the relevant authority.

*Obstruction of person exercising power*

**7.** A person who intentionally obstructs another person acting in the exercise of any power to which this Schedule applies shall be guilty of an offence and liable[1]—

(*a*) on summary conviction, to a **fine** not exceeding the **statutory maximum;**

(*b*) on conviction on indictment, to a **fine** or to imprisonment for a term not exceeding **two years**, or to **both**.

---

[1] For procedure in respect of this offence which is triable either way, see the Magistrates' Courts Act 1980, ss 17A–21, in PART I: MAGISTRATES' COURTS, PROCEDURE, ante.

*Interpretation*

**8.** (1) In this Schedule—

"relevant authority", in relation to a power to which this Schedule applies, means one of the Ministers, the Agency or the NRBW, according to who is entitled, by virtue of the provision by which the power is conferred or, as the case may be, the warrant, to designate the person by whom the power may be exercised; and

"sewerage services" has the same meaning as in the Water Industry Act 1991.

(2) References in this Schedule to a power to which this Schedule applies are references to any power conferred by Chapter II of Part VI of this Act, including a power exercisable by virtue of a warrant under this Schedule.

(3) For the purposes of paragraphs 5 and 6 above a person enters any premises or vessel by virtue of a power to which this Schedule applies notwithstanding that he has failed (whether by virtue of the waiver of the requirement by the occupier of the premises or otherwise) to comply with—

(*a*) any requirement to enter those premises at a reasonable time or after giving notice of his intended entry; or

(*b*) the requirement imposed by paragraph 3 above.

## SCHEDULE 25

### BYELAW-MAKING POWERS OF THE APPROPRIATE AGENCY

Section 210

*(As amended by the Environment Act 1995, s 103 and Schs 15 and 22, the Natural Environment And Rural Communities Act 2006, s 100, the Marine and Coastal Access Act 2009, s 224, Schs 11, 16 and 22, the Flood and Water Management Act 2010, Sch 2, SI 2013/755.)*

*Byelaws for regulating use of inland waters*

7.11724 **1.** (1) Subject to the following provisions of this paragraph but without prejudice to the powers conferred by the following provisions of this Schedule, where it appears to the appropriate agency to be necessary or expedient to do so for the purposes of any of the functions specified in sub-paragraphs (i), (iii) and (v) of section 2(1)(*a*) of the 1995 Act, the appropriate agency may make byelaws—

(*a*) prohibiting such inland waters as may be specified in the byelaws from being used for boating (whether with mechanically propelled boats or otherwise), swimming or other recreational purposes; or

(*b*) regulating the way in which any inland waters so specified may be used for any of those purposes.

(2) Byelaws made by the appropriate agency under this paragraph shall not apply to—

(*a*) any tidal waters or any discrete waters;

(*b*) any inland waters in relation to which functions are exercisable by a navigation authority, harbour authority or conservancy authority other than the appropriate agency; or

(*c*) any reservoir belonging to, and operated by, a water undertaker.

(3) Byelaws made in respect of any inland waters by virtue of this paragraph may—

(*a*) include provision prohibiting the use of the inland waters by boats which are not for the time being registered with the appropriate agency in such manner as the byelaws may provide; and

(*b*) authorise the appropriate agency to make reasonable charges in respect of the registration of boats in pursuance of the byelaws.

*Byelaws for regulating the use of navigable waters etc*

**2.** (1) The appropriate agency shall have power to make such byelaws as are mentioned in sub-paragraph (3) below with respect to any inland waters in relation to which—

(*a*) there is a public right of navigation; and

(*b*) the condition specified in sub-paragraph (2) below is satisfied, and with respect to any land associated with such waters.

(2) For the purposes of this paragraph the condition mentioned in sub-paragraph (1) above is satisfied in relation to any waters if navigation in those waters—

(*a*) is not for the time being subject to the control of any navigation authority, harbour authority or conservancy authority; or

(*b*) is subject to the control of such a navigation authority, harbour authority or conservancy authority as is prescribed for the purposes of this paragraph by reason of its appearing to the Secretary of State to be unable for the time being to carry out its functions.

(3) The byelaws referred to in sub-paragraph (1) above in relation to any inland waters or to any land associated with any such waters are byelaws for any of the following purposes, that is to say—

(*a*) the preservation of order in or on any such waters or land;

(*b*) the prevention of damage to anything in or on any such waters or land or to any such land:

(*c*) securing that persons resorting to any such waters or land so behave as to avoid undue interference with the enjoyment of the waters or land by others.

(4) Without prejudice to the generality of any of the paragraphs of sub-paragraph (3) above or to the power conferred on the appropriate agency by virtue of paragraph 4 below, the byelaws mentioned in that sub-paragraph include byelaws—

(*a*) regulating sailing, boating, bathing and fishing and other forms of recreation;

(*b*) prohibiting the use of the inland waters in question by boats which are not for the time being registered, in such manner as may be required by the byelaws, with the appropriate agency;

(*c*) requiring the provision of such sanitary appliances as may be necessary for the purpose of preventing pollution; and

(*d*) authorising the making of reasonable charges in respect of the registration of boats for the purposes of the byelaws.

(5) In this paragraph "boat" includes a vessel of any description, and "boating" shall be construed accordingly.

*Byelaws for regulating the use of the Authority's waterways etc*

**3.** (1) The appropriate agency shall have power to make such byelaws as are mentioned in sub-paragraph (2) below with respect to any waterway owned or managed by the appropriate agency and with respect to any land held or managed with the waterway.

(2) The byelaws referred to in sub-paragraph (1) above in relation to any waterway or to any land held or managed with any such waterway are byelaws for any of the following purposes, that is to say—

(*a*) the preservation of order on or in such waterway or land;

(*b*) the prevention of damage to anything on or in any such waterway or land or to any such land;

(*c*) securing that persons resorting to any such waterway or land so behave as to avoid undue interference with the enjoyment of the waterway or land by others.

(3) Without prejudice to the generality of any of the paragraphs of sub-paragraph (2) above or to the power conferred on the appropriate agency by virtue of paragraph 4 below, the byelaws mentioned in that sub-paragraph include byelaws—

(*a*) regulating sailing, boating, bathing and fishing and other forms of recreation;

(*b*) prohibiting the use of the waterway in question by boats which are not for the time being registered, in such manner as may be required by the byelaws, with the appropriate agency;

(*c*) requiring the provision of such sanitary appliances as may be necessary for the purpose of preventing pollution; and

(*d*) authorising the making of reasonable charges in respect of the registration of boats for the purposes of the byelaws.

(4) In this paragraph—

"boat" and "boating" have the same meanings as in paragraph 2 above; and

"waterway" has the same meaning as in the National Parks and Access to the Countryside Act 1949.

*Byelaws for controlling certain forms of pollution*

**4.** (1) The appropriate agency may by byelaws make such provision as the Authority considers appropriate—

(*a*) for prohibiting or regulating the washing or cleaning in any controlled waters of things of a description specified in the byelaws;

(*b*) for prohibiting or regulating the keeping or use on any controlled waters of vessels of a description specified in the byelaws which are provided with water closets or other sanitary appliances.

(2) In this paragraph—

"controlled waters" has the same meaning as in Part III of this Act; and

"sanitary appliance", in relation to a vessel, means any appliance which—

(*a*) not being a sink, bath or shower bath, is designed to permit polluting matter to pass into the water where the vessel is situated; and

(*b*) is prescribed for the purposes of this paragraph.

*Byelaws for flood defence and drainage purposes*

**5.** (1) The appropriate agencymay make such byelaws in relation to any particular locality or localities as it considers necessary for any of Purposes 1 to 4.

(1A) Purpose 1 is to secure the efficient working of a drainage system.

(1B) Purpose 2 is to regulate the effects on the environment of a drainage system.

(1C) Purpose 3 is to secure the effectiveness of flood risk management work within the meaning of section 165.

(1D) Purpose 4 is to secure the effectiveness of works done in reliance on section 38 or 39 of the Flood and Water Management Act 2010 (incidental flooding or coastal erosion).

(2) Without prejudice to the generality of sub-paragraph (1) above and subject to sub-paragraph (3) below, the appropriate agency may, in particular, make byelaws for any of the following purposes, that is to say—

(*a*) regulating the use and preventing the improper use of any watercourses, banks or works vested in the appropriate agency or under its control or for preserving any such watercourses, banks or works from damage or destruction;

(*b*) regulating the opening of sluices and flood gates in connection with any such works as are mentioned in paragraph (*a*) above;

(*c*) preventing the obstruction of any watercourse vested in the appropriate agency or under its control by the discharge into it of any liquid or solid matter or by reason of any such matter being allowed to flow or fall into it;

(*d*) compelling the persons having control of any watercourse vested in the appropriate agency or under its control, or of any watercourse flowing into any such watercourse, to cut the vegetable growths in or on the bank of the watercourse and, when cut, to remove them.

(3) No byelaw for any purpose specified in sub-paragraph (2)(*a*) above shall be valid if it would prevent reasonable facilities being afforded for enabling a watercourse to be used by stock for drinking purposes.

(3A) If, in any particular case,—

(*a*) a marine licence is needed for the carrying on of any activity,

(*b*) before that activity may be carried on, the consent of the appropriate agency would also be required (apart from this sub-paragraph) by virtue of any byelaw under this paragraph, and

(*c*) the appropriate agency considers that, in view of the terms and conditions that will be included in the marine licence, the requirement for the consent of the appropriate agency may be dispensed with, and issues a notice to that effect,

the requirement for the consent of the appropriate agency does not apply in relation to the carrying on of that activity.

(3B) In sub-paragraph (3A) "marine licence" has the same meaning as in Part 4 of the Marine and Coastal Access Act 2009.

(4) Notwithstanding anything in this Act, no byelaw made by the appropriate agency under this paragraph shall conflict with or interfere with the operation of any byelaw made by a navigation authority, harbour authority or conservancy authority.

(5) In this paragraph "banks", "drainage" and "watercourse" have the same meanings as in Part IV of this Act.

*Byelaws for purposes of fisheries functions*

**6.** (1) The appropriate agency shall have power, in relation to the whole or any part or parts of the area in relation to which it carries out its functions relating to fisheries under Part V of this Act, to make byelaws generally for the purposes of—

(*a*) the better execution of the Salmon and Freshwater Fisheries Act 1975; and

(*b*) the better protection, preservation and improvement of any fisheries of fish to which this paragraph applies.

(1A) This paragraph applies to—

(*a*) salmon, trout, eels, lampreys, smelt, shad and freshwater fish; and

(*b*) fish of such other description as may be specified for the purposes of this paragraph by order under section 40A of the Salmon and Freshwater Fisheries Act 1975.

(2) The appropriate agency shall have power, in relation to the whole or any part or parts of the area mentioned in sub-paragraph (1) above, to make byelaws for any of the following purposes, that is to say—

(*a*) prohibiting the taking or removal from any water without lawful authority, of any fish to which this paragraph applies, whether alive or dead;

(*aa*) specifying close seasons or times for the taking of any fish to which this paragraph applies by such means as may be prescribed by the byelaws;

(*b*) prohibiting or regulating—

(i) the taking of any fish to which this paragraph applies of a size greater or less than such as may be prescribed by the byelaw; or

(ii) the taking of fish to which this paragraph applies by any means within such distance as is specified in the byelaw above or below any dam or any other obstruction, whether artificial or natural;

(*c*) prohibiting the use for taking fish to which this paragraph applies of any instrument in such waters and at such times as may be prescribed by the byelaws;

(*d*) specifying the nets and other instruments which may be used for taking fish to which this paragraph applies, imposing requirements as to the use of such nets and other instruments and regulating the use, in connection with fishing with rod and line, of any lure or bait specified in the byelaw;

(*e*) authorising the placing and use of fixed engines at such places, at such times and in such manner as may be prescribed by the byelaws (including requiring fixed engines during close seasons or times to be removed or made incapable of taking or obstructing the passage of fish):

(*f*) imposing requirements as to the construction, design, material and dimensions of any such nets, instruments or engines as are mentioned in paragraphs (*d*) and (*e*) above, including in the case of nets the size of mesh:

(*g*) requiring and regulating the attachment to nets and instruments of marks, labels or numbers, or the painting of marks or numbers or the affixing of labels or numbers to boats, coracles or other vessels used in fishing;

(*h*) prohibiting the carrying in any boat or vessel whilst being used in fishing for fish to which this paragraph applies of any net which may not lawfully be used, or which is without the mark, label or number prescribed by the byelaws; and

(*i*) prohibiting or regulating the carrying in a boat or vessel during any close season or time for any description of fish to which this paragraph applies of a net capable of taking fish of that description, other than a net commonly used in the area to which the byelaw applies for sea fishing and carried in a boat or vessel commonly used for that purpose.

(3) *Repealed.*

(4) *Repealed.*

(5) The appropriate agency shall have power, in relation to the whole or any part of parts of the area mentioned in sub-paragraph (1) above, to make byelaws for the purpose of requiring persons to send to the appropriate agency returns, in such form, giving such particulars and at such times as may be specified in the byelaws—

(*a*) of the period or periods during which they have fished for fish to which this paragraph applies,

(*b*) of whether they have taken any; and

(c) if they have, of what they have taken.

(5A) A byelaw under this paragraph does not apply to a person (including an employee or agent of the appropriate agency) to the extent that he is acting—

(a) with the written authority of the appropriate agency; and

(b) in accordance with any conditions imposed by the appropriate agency in relation to that authority.

(5B) For the avoidance of doubt, a byelaw under this paragraph may apply to an historic installation as to any other fixed engine.

(6) Byelaws made under this paragraph may be made to apply to the whole or any part of parts of the year.

(7) Expressions used in this paragraph and in the Salmon and Freshwater Fisheries Act 1975 have the same meanings in this paragraph as in that Act.

*Fisheries byelaws for marine or aquatic environmental purposes*

**6A.** (1) Any power to make byelaws conferred by paragraph 6 above may be exercised for marine or aquatic environmental purposes.

(2) The power to make byelaws under paragraph 6 above by virtue of this paragraph is in addition to, and not in derogation from, the power to make byelaws under that paragraph otherwise than by virtue of this paragraph.

(3) In this paragraph "marine or aquatic environmental purposes" means—

(a) the conservation or enhancement of the natural beauty or amenity of marine or coastal, or aquatic or waterside, areas (including their geological or physiographical features) or of any features of archaeological or historic interest in such areas; or

(b) the conservation of flora or fauna which are dependent on, or associated with, a marine or coastal, or aquatic or waterside, environment.

**7.** *Repealed.*

## SCHEDULE 26

### PROCEDURE RELATING TO BYELAWS MADE BY THE APPROPRIATE AGENCY

*(As amended by the Environment Act 1995, Sch 22 and SI 2013/755.)* Section 210

*Confirmation of byelaws*

7.11725 **1.** (1) No byelaw made by the appropriate agency shall have effect until confirmed by the relevant Minister under this Schedule.

(2) At least one month before it applies for the confirmation of any byelaw, the appropriate agency shall—

(a) cause a notice of its intention to make the application to be published in the London Gazette and in such other manner as it considers appropriate for the purpose of bringing the proposed byelaw to the attention of persons likely to be affected by it; and

(b) cause copies of the notice to be served on any persons carrying out functions under any enactment who appear to it to be concerned.

(3) For at least one month before an application is made by the appropriate agency for the confirmation of any byelaw, a copy of it shall be deposited at one or more of the offices of the appropriate agency, including (if there is one) at an office in the area to which the byelaw would apply.

(4) The appropriate agency shall provide reasonable facilities for the inspection free of charge of a byelaw deposited under sub-paragraph (3) above.

(5) Every person shall be entitled, on application to the appropriate agency, to be furnished free of charge with a printed copy of a byelaw so deposited.

**2.** *Confirmation with or without modifications.*

*Commencement of byelaw*

**3.** (1) The relevant Minister may fix the date on which any byelaw confirmed under this Schedule is to come into force.

(2) If no date is so fixed in relation to a byelaw, it shall come into force at the end of the period of one month beginning with the date of confirmation.

*Availability of confirmed byelaws*

**4.** (1) Every byelaw made by the appropriate agency and confirmed under this Schedule shall be printed and deposited at one or more of the offices of the appropriate agency, including (if there is one) at an office in the area to which the byelaw applies; and copies of the byelaw shall be available at those offices, at all reasonable times, for inspection by the public free of charge.

(2) Every person shall be entitled, on application to the appropriate agency and on payment of such reasonable sum as the appropriate agency may determine, to be furnished with a copy of any byelaw so deposited by the appropriate agency.

**5.** *Revocation of byelaws by Minister.*

*Proof of byelaws*

**6.** The production of a printed copy of a byelaw purporting to be made by the appropriate agency upon which is endorsed a certificate, purporting to be signed on its behalf, stating—

(a) that the byelaw was made by the appropriate agency;

(b) that the copy is a true copy of the byelaw;

(c) that on a specified date the byelaw was confirmed under this Schedule; and

(d) the date, if any, fixed under paragraph 3 above for the coming into force of the byelaw,

shall be prima facie evidence of the facts stated in the certificate, and without proof of the handwriting or official position of any person purporting to sign the certificate.

**7.** *Meaning of "the relevant Minister".*

# Land Drainage Act 1991

(1991 c 59)

## PART II[1]

## PROVISIONS FOR FACILITATING OR SECURING THE DRAINAGE OF LAND

*Control of flow of watercourses etc*

7.11726 **23. Prohibition on obstructions etc in watercourses** Consent in writing of drainage board required before erection of mill dam, weir or other like obstruction or erection or alteration of culvert.

[Land Drainage Act 1991, s 23 amended by the Environment Act 1995, Sch 22—summarised.]

---

[1] Part II comprises ss 14–31.

7.11727 **24. Contraventions of prohibition on obstructions etc** (1) If any obstruction is erected or raised or otherwise altered, or any culvert is erected or altered, in contravention of section 23 above, it shall constitute a nuisance in respect of which the drainage board concerned may serve upon such person as is specified in subsection (2) below a notice requiring him to abate the nuisance within a period to be specified in the notice.

(2) The person upon whom a notice may be served under subsection (1) above is—

(*a*) in a case where the person by whom the obstruction has been erected or raised or otherwise altered has, at the time when the notice is served, power to remove the obstruction, that person; and

(*b*) in any other case, any person having power to remove the obstruction.

(3) If any person acts in contravention of, or fails to comply with, any notice served under subsection (1) above he shall be guilty of an offence and liable, on summary conviction—

(*a*) to a fine not exceeding **level 5** on the standard scale; and

(*b*) if the contravention or failure is continued after conviction, to a further fine not exceeding **£40 for every day on which the contravention or failure is so continued**.

(4) If any person acts in contravention of, or fails to comply with, any notice served under subsection (1) above, the drainage board concerned may, without prejudice to any proceedings under subsection (3) above—

(*a*) take such action as may be necessary to remedy the effect of the contravention or failure; and

(*b*) recover the expenses reasonably incurred by them in doing so from the person in default.

[Land Drainage Act 1991, s 24.]

7.11728 **25. Powers to require works for maintaining flow of watercourse** (1) Where any ordinary watercourse is in such a condition that the proper flow of water is impeded, then, unless the condition is attributable to subsidence due to mining operations (including brine pumping), the drainage board concerned may, by notice served on a person falling within subsection (3) below, require that person to remedy that condition.

(2) *Repealed.*

(*a*) the drainage board concerned is the drainage board for the internal drainage district in which the watercourse is situated; and

(*b*) the local authority concerned is the local authority for the area where the land as respects which the powers under this section are exercisable is situated;

but references in this section to the drainage board concerned shall, in relation to a watercourse which is not in an internal drainage district, be construed as references to the Agency.

(3) Subject to subsection (4) below, a notice under this section in relation to a watercourse may be served on—

(*a*) any person having control of the part of the watercourse where any impediment occurs; or

(*b*) any person owning or occupying land adjoining that part; or

(*c*) any person to whose act or default the condition of the watercourse mentioned in subsection (1) above is due.

(4) No notice under this section requiring any person to carry out any work on land not owned or occupied by him shall be served without the consent of the owner and the occupier of the land, except in a case where it is not practicable, after reasonable inquiry, to ascertain the name and address of the owner or occupier.

(5) A notice under this section shall indicate—

(*a*) the nature of the works to be carried out and the period within which they are to be carried out; and

(*b*) the right of appeal to a magistrates' court and the period within which such an appeal may be brought under section 27 below.

(6) Subject to the right of appeal provided by section 27 below, if the person upon whom a notice is served under this section fails to carry out the works indicated by the notice within the period so indicated—

(*a*) the drainage board concerned may themselves carry out the works and recover from that person the expenses reasonably incurred by them in doing so; and

(*b*) without prejudice to their right to exercise that power, that person shall be guilty of an offence and liable, on summary conviction, to a fine not exceeding **level 4** on the standard scale.

(7) In proceedings by the drainage board concerned for the recovery of any expenses under subsection (6) above it shall not be open to the defendant to raise any question which he could not have raised on an appeal under section 27 below.

(8) Nothing in this section shall affect the right of an owner or occupier to recover from the other, under the terms of any lease or other contract, the amount of any expenses incurred by him under this section or recovered from him by the drainage board concerned.

[Land Drainage Act 1991, s 25 as amended by the Environment Act 1995, Sch 22 and the Flood and Water Management Act 2010, Sch 2.]

7.11729 27. **Appeals against notices under section 25** (1) A person served with a notice under section 25 above may, within twenty-one days from the date on which the notice is served on him, appeal to a magistrates' court on any of the following grounds, that is to say—

(*a*) that the notice or requirement is not justified by that section;

(*b*) that there has been some informality, defect or error in, or in connection with, the notice;

(*c*) that the body which served the notice has refused unreasonably to approve the carrying out of alternative works, or that the works required by the notice to be carried out are otherwise unreasonable in character or extent, or are unnecessary;

(*d*) that the period within which the works are to be carried out is not reasonably sufficient for the purpose;

(*e*) that the notice might lawfully have been served on another person and that it would have been equitable for it to have been so served;

(*f*) that some other person ought to contribute towards the expenses of carrying out any works required by the notice.

(2) The procedure on an appeal under this section shall be by way of complaint for an order and in accordance with the Magistrates' Courts Act 1980.

(3) For the purposes of the time limit for bringing an appeal under this section the making of the complaint shall be treated as the bringing of the appeal.

(4) In so far as an appeal under this section is based on the ground of some informality, defect or error in, or in connection with, the notice, the court shall dismiss the appeal if it is satisfied that the informality, defect or error was not a material one.

(5) In the case of an appeal under this section, the appellant—

(*a*) may serve a copy of his notice of appeal on any person having an estate or interest in the part of the watercourse where the impediment occurs or land adjoining that part; and

(*b*) shall, where the grounds upon which the appeal under this section is brought include a ground specified in subsection (1)(*e*) or (*f*) above, serve a copy of his notice of appeal on each other person referred to.

(6) On the hearing of an appeal under this section the court may make such order as it thinks fit—

(*a*) with respect to the person by whom any work is to be carried out and the contribution to be made by any other person towards the cost of the work; or

(*b*) as to the proportions in which any expenses which may become recoverable by the body which served the notice are to be borne by the appellant and such other person.

(7) In exercising its powers under subsection (6) above the court shall have regard—

(*a*) as between an owner and an occupier, to the terms and conditions (whether contractual or statutory) of the tenancy and to the nature of the works required; and

(*b*) in any case, to the degree of benefit to be derived by the different persons concerned.

(8) A person aggrieved by an order, determination or other decision of a magistrates' court under this section may appeal to the Crown Court.

(9) Where upon an appeal under this section a court varies or reverses any decision of a body which has served a notice under section 25 above, it shall be the duty of that body to give effect to the order of the court.

[Land Drainage Act 1991, s 27.]

## PART IV[1]
## FINANCIAL PROVISIONS

7.11730 53. **Power to require information** (1) The drainage board for an internal drainage district may serve on the owner of any hereditament in the district in respect of which a drainage rate is levied a notice requiring him to state in writing the name and address of any person known to him as being an occupier of that hereditament.

(2) A person shall be guilty of an offence under this section if, where a notice is served on him under subsection (1) above, he—

(*a*) fails without reasonable excuse to comply with the notice; or

(*b*) in pursuance of the notice—

(i) makes any statement in respect of the information required which he knows to be false in a material particular; or
(ii) recklessly makes any statement in respect of that information which is false in a material particular.

(3) A person guilty of an offence under this section shall be liable, on summary conviction, to a fine not exceeding **level 4** on the standard scale.

(4) Where—
(*a*) a person is convicted of an offence under this section in respect of a failure to comply with a notice; and
(*b*) the failure continues after conviction,

then, unless he has a reasonable excuse for the continuance of the failure, he shall be guilty of a further offence under this section and shall be liable, on summary conviction, to be punished accordingly.

[Land Drainage Act 1991, s 53.]

1 Part IV contains ss 36–54.

7.11731 **54. Powers for enforcing payment** (1) Arrears of any drainage rates made under this Chapter may be recovered by the drainage board for an internal drainage district in the same manner in which arrears of a non-domestic rate may be recovered under the Local Government Finance Act 1988 by a charging authority.

(2) The drainage board for an internal drainage district may by resolution authorise any member or officer of the board, either generally or in respect of particular proceedings—
(*a*) to institute or defend on their behalf proceedings in relation to a drainage rate; or
(*b*) notwithstanding that he is not qualified to act as a solicitor, to appear on their behalf in any proceedings before a magistrates' court for the issue of a warrant of control for failure to pay a drainage rate.

(3) In proceedings for the recovery of arrears of a drainage rate the defendant shall not be entitled to raise by way of defence any matter which might have been raised on an appeal under section 45 or 51 above[1].

(4) The powers conferred by this section are in addition to, and not in substitution for, the powers conferred by any provision of any local Act on any drainage board in relation to arrears of drainage rates; and for the purposes of any such provisions a rate made under this Chapter shall be treated, subject to subsection (5) below, as a rate to which those provisions apply.

(5) Notwithstanding anything in any local Act—
(*a*) no distress for arrears of any rate made under this Chapter shall be levied on the goods or chattels of any person other than a person from whom the arrears may be recovered by virtue of subsection (1) above; and
(*b*) no proceedings shall be taken, whether by action or otherwise, for the enforcement of any charge on land created by a local Act for securing payment of arrears of any rate made under this Chapter.

(6) The drainage board for an internal drainage district shall not be required to enforce payment of any drainage rate in any case where the amount payable is, in their opinion, insufficient to justify the expense of collection.

[Land Drainage Act 1991, s 54 as amended by the Tribunals, Courts and Enforcement Act 2007, Sch 13.]

1 Sections 45 and 51 enable appeals against determinations of annual value by a valuation and community charge tribunal, and on any other ground to the Crown Court.

7.11732 **64. Powers of entry for internal drainage boards and local authorities** Authorised person may at all reasonable times enter etc after notice: penalty on summary conviction for person intentionally obstructing or impeding is fine not exceeding **level 4** on the standard scale.

[Land Drainage Act 1991, s 64—summarised.]

7.11733 **72. Interpretation[1]** (1) In this Act, unless the context otherwise requires—
"the Agency" means the Environment Agency;
"charging authority" has the same meaning as in the Local Government Finance Act 1988;
"drainage" includes—
(*a*) defence against water (including sea water);
(*b*) irrigation, other than spray irrigation;
(*c*) warping; and
(*d*) the carrying on, for any purpose, of any other practice which involves management of the level or water in a watercourse;

"drainage body" means the Agency, an internal drainage board or any other body having power to make or maintain works for the drainage of land;
"land" includes water and any interests in land or water and any easement or right in, to or over land or water;
"local authority" means the council of a county, county borough, district or London borough or the Common Council of the City of London;
"main river" has the same meaning as in the Water Resources Act 1991;
"the Minister" means the Minister of Agriculture, Fisheries and Food;

"the Ministers" means the Minister and the Secretary of State, and in relation to anything which falls to be done by the Ministers, means those Ministers acting jointly;

"ordinary watercourse" means a watercourse that does not form part of a main river;

"prescribed" means prescribed by regulations under section 65 above;

"qualified authority", in relation to an internal drainage district, means a charging authority for an area wholly or partly included in that district;

"qualified persons" shall be construed in accordance with subsection (2) below;

"the relevant Minister"—

(*a*) in relation to internal drainage districts which are neither wholly nor partly in Wales or to the boards for such districts, means the Minister;

(*b*) in relation to internal drainage districts which are partly in Wales or to the boards for such districts, means the Ministers; and

(*c*) in relation to internal drainage districts which are wholly in Wales or to the boards for such districts, means the Secretary of State;

"watercourse" includes all rivers and streams and all ditches, drains, cuts, culverts, dikes, sluices, sewers (other than public sewers within the meaning of the Water Industry Act 1991) and passages, through which water flows.

(2) Subject to the provisions of paragraph 19 of Schedule 2 to the Water Consolidation (Consequential Provisions) Act 1991 (which makes provision with respect to qualification under this subsection by reference to drainage rates levied on land in respect of years beginning before 1993), where any provision of this Act refers, in relation to an internal drainage district, to the making of any appeal or petition by a sufficient number of qualified persons—

(*a*) the persons who are qualified are the occupiers of any land in the district in respect of which a drainage rate is levied; and

(*b*) subject to subsection (3) below, their number shall be sufficient if (but only if)—

(i) they are not less than forty; or

(ii) they are not less than one-fifth of the number of persons who are qualified to make the petition or appeal; or

(iii) the assessable value for the purposes of the last drainage rate levied in the district of all the land in respect of which they are qualified persons is not less than one-fifth of the assessable value of all the land in respect of which that rate was levied.

(3) In relation to a district divided into sub-districts the persons qualified to make a petition under section 39 above as being the occupiers of land in one of the sub-districts shall also be sufficient in any case where the condition in subsection (2)(*b*)(ii) or (iii) above would be satisfied if the sub-district were an internal drainage district.

(4) The references to the assessable value of any land in paragraph (*b*) of subsection (2) above are references to the amount which for the purposes of the drainage rate mentioned in that paragraph would be the annual value of the land.

(5) References in this Act to the carrying out of drainage works include references to the improvement of drainage works.

(6) Nothing in this Act shall operate to release any person from an obligation to which section 21 above applies; and the functions of the Agency or any internal drainage board as respects the doing of any work under this Act are not to be treated as in any way limited by the fact that some other person is under an obligation, by reason of tenure, custom, prescription or otherwise, to do that work.

(7) Where by virtue of any provision of this Act any function of a Minister of the Crown is exercisable concurrently by different Ministers, that function shall also be exercisable jointly by any two or more of those Ministers.

(8) This Act so far as it confers any powers on the Agency shall have effect subject to the provisions of the Water Resources Act 1991.

(9) The powers conferred by this Act on the Common Council of the City of London shall be exercisable as respects that City.

(10) Sub-paragraph (1) of paragraph 1 of Schedule 2 to the Water Consolidation (Consequential Provisions) Act 1991 has effect (by virtue of sub-paragraph (2)(*b*) of that paragraph) so that references in this Act to things done under or for the purposes of provisions of this Act or the Water Resources Act 1991 include references to things done, or treated as done, under or for the purposes of the corresponding provisions of the law in force before the commencement of this Act.

[Land Drainage Act 1991, s 72, as amended by the Local Government (Wales) Act 1994, Sch 11, the Merchant Shipping Act 1995, Sch 13 and the Environment Act 1995, s 100 and Schs 22 and 24.]

---

[1] Only definitions relevant to the parts of this Act printed in this work are included here.

# Water Act 2003[1]

(2003 c 37)

## Part 1[2]

## Abstraction and Impounding

*Restrictions on abstraction and impounding*

7.11734 3. **Existing impounding works** (1) Except as provided in subsection (3), the restriction in section 25(1)(*b*) of the WRA (as substituted by section 2 of this Act) does not apply in respect of any existing unlicensed impounding works.

(2) With respect to any existing unlicensed impounding works to which, but for subsection (1), that restriction would apply, the Environment Agency may serve a notice on any relevant person requiring him to apply for a licence.

(3) If that person fails to apply for such a licence within—

(*a*) the period of 28 days beginning with—

(i) the date of service of the notice, or

(ii) if an appeal is brought under subsection (4) and the appeal is dismissed, the date when the decision of the appropriate authority is notified to that person, or

(*b*) such extended period as may be agreed in writing between the Agency and that person,

the restriction in section 25(1)(*b*) of the WRA applies in respect of the impounding works from the expiry of that period.

(4) If the relevant person on whom a notice is served under subsection (2) is aggrieved by the service of that notice, he may by notice appeal to the appropriate authority.

(5)–(13) *Appeals.*

[Water Act 2003, s 3.]

---

[1] This Act is to be brought into force in accordance with orders made under s 105. At the date of going to press the following commencement orders had been made: (No 1 and Transitional Provisions) 2004, SI 2004/641; (Wales) 2004, SI 2004/910; (No 2, Transitional Provisions and Savings) 2004, SI 2004/2528; (No 2) (Wales) SI 2004/2916; (No 3) (England) 2005, SI 2005/344; (No 4 Transitional Provisions and Savings) 2005, SI 2005/968; (No 5 Transitional Provisions and Savings) 2005, SI 2005/2714; (No 6, Transitional Provisions and Savings) 2006, SI 2006/984; (No 7 and Transitional Provisions) 2007, SI 2007/1021; (No 8) 2008, SI 2008/1922; (No 9 and Saving Provisions) (England) 2009, SI 2009/359; (No 10) SI 2010/975 (ss 58, 101(2) (part) and Sch 9 (part)); (No 11) (s 86); (No 3) (Wales) SI 2012/24 (s 86); (No 4) (Wales) SI 2017/88. Sections 3 and 4 were brought into force on 1 April 2006 by SI 2006/984.

[2] Part 1 comprises ss 1–33.

7.11735 4. **Existing impounding works: works notices** (1) Without prejudice to the Environment Agency's power under subsection (2) of section 3, where it appears to the Agency to be necessary for—

(*a*) the protection of the environment, or

(*b*) the performance of its functions in connection with the management of water resources,

the Agency may serve a works notice on any relevant person with respect to any existing unlicensed impounding works of the kind mentioned in subsection (2) of that section.

(2) For the purposes of subsection (1), a works notice is a notice requiring the person on whom it is served to carry out such works or operations in relation to the impounding works as—

(*a*) appear to the Environment Agency to be required for the purposes mentioned in subsection (1)(*a*) or (*b*), and

(*b*) are specified in the notice.

(3) The following provisions of the WRA apply in relation to works notices under this section as they apply in relation to notices referred to in those provisions—

(*a*) subsections (5) to (9) of section 25A (as inserted by section 30 of this Act), and

(*b*) sections 161B and 161C,

including any power to make regulations or give directions, but references in those provisions to the Secretary of State shall be treated as references to the appropriate authority.

(4) If a person on whom the Agency serves a notice under this section fails to comply with any of its requirements, he shall be guilty of an offence.

(5) A person who commits an offence under subsection (4) shall be liable on summary conviction, or on conviction on indictment, to a fine.

(6) If a person on whom a works notice has been served under this section fails to comply with any of its requirements, the Agency may do what that person was required to do and may recover from him any costs or expenses reasonably incurred by the Agency in doing it.

(7) If the Agency is of the opinion that proceedings for an offence under subsection (4) would afford an ineffectual remedy against a person who has failed to comply with the requirements of a works notice, the Agency may take proceedings in the High Court for the purpose of securing compliance with the notice.

(8) In this section, "the appropriate authority", "existing unlicensed impounding works" and "relevant person" have the meanings given in section 3.

[Water Act 2003, s 4 as amended by SI 2015/664.]

# Flood and Water Management Act 2010[1]

(2010 c 29)

PART 2[2]

MISCELLANEOUS

[1] This Act makes provision about water, including flood and coastal erosion risk management. Only the provisions reproduced below are relevant to magistrates' courts.

Section 36 of the Act came fully into force on 1 October 2010 (see the Flood and Water Management Act 2010 (Commencement No 1 and Transitional Provisions) Order 2010, SI 2010/2169).

[2] Part 2 contains ss 32–46.

SCHEDULE 1

Risk Management: Designation of Features Section 30

*Powers of entry*

7.11736 13. (1) A person authorised by the responsible authority may at any reasonable time enter land—

(*a*) to determine whether a person has contravened paragraph 5(1),

(*b*) to determine whether a person has complied with an enforcement notice,

(*c*) to take steps specified in accordance with paragraph 11(4), or

(*d*) to act in accordance with paragraph 12(2).

(2) A person authorised by a designating authority may at any reasonable time enter land for the purpose of determining whether a structure or feature may be designated by the authority under paragraph 4.

(3) A person may not demand entry to land which is occupied unless—

(*a*) at least 7 days' notice has been given to the occupier, specifying the purpose for which entry is required, or

(*b*) the entry is for the purpose mentioned in sub-paragraph (1)(*d*).

(4) A person seeking to enter land under this paragraph must on request produce evidence of authorisation.

(5) It is an offence to obstruct a person entitled to enter land under this paragraph.

(6) A person guilty of an offence under sub-paragraph (5) is liable—

(*a*) on conviction on indictment, to imprisonment for a term not exceeding 2 years, to a fine or to both, or

(*b*) on summary conviction, to a fine not exceeding the statutory maximum.[1]

[1] For procedure in respect of offences triable either way, see ss 17A–23 of the Magistrates' Courts Act 1980 in PART I: MAGISTRATES' COURTS, PROCEDURE, ante. At the date at which this work states the law, this para had not been brought into force.

# Water Act 2014[1]

(2014 c 21)

PART 3

ENVIRONMENTAL REGULATION

7.11736A 61. **Regulation of the water environment** (1) The Minister may by regulations make provision for any of the purposes listed in Part 1 of Schedule 8; and Part 2 of that Schedule has effect for supplementing Part 1.

(2) Except as provided in Schedule 8, any provision so made is to be provision for or in connection with—

(*a*) regulating the use of water resources,

(*b*) securing the drainage of land or the management of flood risk, or

(*c*) safeguarding the movement of fish through regulated waters.

(3) In making regulations under this section, the Minister is to have regard to the desirability of reducing burdens by ensuring that so far as is reasonably practicable any system established by regulations under this section is combined with, or is consistent with, systems for regulating activities or other matters that cause pollution.

(4) Regulations under this section may—

(*a*) contain such consequential, incidental, supplementary, transitional or saving provisions (including provisions amending, repealing or revoking enactments) as the Minister considers appropriate, and

(*b*) make different provision for different cases, including different provision in relation to different persons, circumstances, areas or localities.

(5) Before making any regulations under this section, the Minister is to consult—

(*a*) the Environment Agency;

(*b*) the Natural Resources Body for Wales;

(*c*) such bodies or persons appearing to the Minister to be representative of the interests of local government, industry, agriculture and small businesses respectively as the Minister may consider appropriate;

(*d*) such other bodies or persons as the Minister may consider appropriate.

(6) It is immaterial for the purposes of subsection (5) whether consultation is carried out before or after the coming into force of this section.

(7) The Secretary of State's power to make regulations under this section is subject to the consent of the Scottish Ministers so far as the regulations apply as mentioned in subsection (11)(*b*),

(8) In this section and Schedule 8 a reference to the use of water resources—

(*a*) includes a reference to taking, diverting or impounding water from any inland waters, or taking water contained in underground strata, and applying it to any purpose, and
(*b*) includes a reference to wasting water whether by action or omission, but
(*c*) does not include a reference to the use, by a person other than a water undertaker, of water drawn from a water mains or pipe forming part of a system used by a water undertaker in carrying out a duty under section 37 of the Water Industry Act 1991.

(9) In this section and Schedule 8—

"enactment" includes—
(*a*) an enactment contained in subordinate legislation within the meaning of the Interpretation Act 1978;
(*b*) an enactment contained in, or an instrument made under, an Act of the Scottish Parliament;
(*c*) an enactment contained in, or in an instrument made under, an Act or Measure of the National Assembly for Wales;

"fish" means freshwater fish and migratory fish;

"flood" has the meaning given in section 1 of the Flood and Water Management Act 2010;

"flood risk" has the meaning given in section 2 of that Act;

"freshwater fish" means any fish habitually living in fresh water;

"inland waters" has the meaning given by section 221(1) of the Water Resources Act 1991;

"migratory fish" means fish of a kind which migrates from fresh to salt water, or from salt to fresh water, in order to spawn;

"the Minister" means—
(*a*) the Secretary of State, in relation to England and in relation to so much of the River Esk and its banks and tributary streams as is mentioned in subsection (11)(*b*), and
(*b*) the Welsh Ministers, in relation to Wales;

"regulated waters" means—
(*a*) inland waters in England and Wales,
(*b*) the waters of so much of the River Esk and its tributary streams up to their source as is mentioned in subsection (11)(*b*), and
(*c*) waters adjoining the coast of England and Wales to a distance of six nautical miles measured from the baselines from which the breadth of the territorial sea is measured;

"Wales" has the meaning given in section 158(1) of the Government of Wales Act 2006.

(10) The reference in subsection (8)(*a*) to water contained in underground strata is to be read in accordance with section 221(3) of the Water Resources Act 1991, as if this section formed part of that Act.

(11) Regulations made in reliance on subsection (2)(*c*)—
(*a*) are not to apply in relation to the Tweed district (as defined in article 2(1) of the Scotland Act 1998 (River Tweed) Order 2006 (SI 2006/2913)), but
(*b*) may apply in relation to so much of the River Esk, with its banks and tributary streams up to their source, as is situated in Scotland.

(12) Regulations under this section may make provision applying in relation to (and to places above and below) the territorial waters adjacent to any part of England and Wales.

[1] The provisions reproduced here came into force on 14 July 2014 (s 94(2)).

**7.11736B 62. Environmental regulation: procedure** (1) The power to make regulations under section 61 is to be exercised by statutory instrument.

(2) A statutory instrument containing regulations made by the Secretary of State under section 61 is subject to annulment in pursuance of a resolution of either House of Parliament, subject as follows.

(3) A statutory instrument containing regulations made by the Welsh Ministers under section 61 is subject to annulment in pursuance of a resolution of the National Assembly for Wales, subject as follows.

(4) A statutory instrument containing any of the following regulations (whether alone or with other regulations) is subject to the affirmative resolution procedure—
(*a*) the first regulations to be made by the Secretary of State under section 61;
(*b*) the first regulations to be made by the Welsh Ministers under section 61;
(*c*) regulations under section 61 which create an offence or increase a penalty for an existing offence;
(*d*) regulations under section 61 which amend or repeal any provision of an Act, or an Act or Measure of the National Assembly for Wales.

(5) A statutory instrument containing regulations made by the Secretary of State under both section 61 above and section 2 of the Pollution Prevention and Control Act 1999 is subject to the affirmative resolution procedure if an instrument containing only—
(*a*) the regulations made by the Secretary of State under section 61 above, or

(b) the regulations made by the Secretary of State under section 2 of the Pollution Prevention and Control Act 1999,

would be subject to the affirmative resolution procedure.

(6) A statutory instrument containing regulations made by the Welsh Ministers under both section 61 above and section 2 of the Pollution Prevention and Control Act 1999 is subject to the affirmative resolution procedure if an instrument containing only—

(a) the regulations made by the Welsh Ministers under section 61 above, or

(b) the regulations made by the Welsh Ministers under section 2 of the Pollution Prevention and Control Act 1999,

would be subject to the affirmative resolution procedure.

(7) A statutory instrument containing regulations made by the Secretary of State that is subject to the affirmative resolution procedure may not be made unless a draft of the instrument has been laid before, and approved by a resolution of, each House of Parliament.

(8) A statutory instrument containing regulations made by the Welsh Ministers that is subject to the affirmative resolution procedure may not be made unless a draft of the instrument has been laid before, and approved by a resolution of, the National Assembly for Wales.

(9) Subsections (11) and (12) apply in relation to a statutory instrument containing both—

(a) regulations under section 61 made or to be made by the Secretary of State, and

(b) regulations under section 61 made or to be made by the Welsh Ministers.

(10) Subsections (11) and (12) also apply in relation to a statutory instrument containing—

(a) regulations under section 61 made or to be made by the Secretary of State,

(b) regulations under section 61 made or to be made by the Welsh Ministers, and

(c) regulations made under section 2 of the Pollution Prevention and Control Act 1999 (whether by the Secretary of State or the Welsh Ministers or both).

(11) If in accordance with subsection (2) or (3) (negative resolution procedure)—

(a) either House of Parliament resolves that an address be presented to Her Majesty praying that an instrument containing regulations made by the Secretary of State be annulled, or

(b) the National Assembly for Wales resolves that an instrument containing regulations made by the Welsh Ministers be annulled,

nothing further is to be done under the instrument after the date of the resolution and Her Majesty may by Order in Council revoke the instrument.

(12) If the statutory instrument contains any regulations which, on their own, would make the instrument subject to the affirmative resolution procedure, the instrument is subject to that procedure.

(13) In section 2 of the Pollution Prevention and Control Act 1999, after subsection (9) there is inserted—

"(10) See section 62 of the Water Act 2014 for further provision about the procedure applying to statutory instruments containing both regulations made under this section and regulations made under section 61 of that Act.".

7.11736C **63. Repeal of certain provisions about culverts** The following provisions of the Public Health Act 1936 are repealed—

(a) section 262 (power of local authority to require culverting of watercourses and ditches where building operations in prospect);

(b) section 263 (watercourses in urban districts not to be culverted except in accordance with approved plans).

## SCHEDULE 8
regulation of the Water Environment

Section 61

### Part 1
### Purposes for which Provision may be Made
*Interpretation*

7.11736D 1. In this Schedule—

"fish regulations" means regulations containing provision which—

(a) satisfies section 61(2)(c), or

(b) is for the purpose mentioned in paragraph 8(2) or 30(3);

"flood regulations" means regulations containing provision which—

(a) satisfies section 61(2)(b), or

(b) is for the purpose mentioned in paragraph 8(2) or 30(2);

"water regulations" means regulations containing provision which—

(a) satisfies section 61(2)(a), or

(b) is for the purpose mentioned in paragraph 8(2) or 30(1).

2. In this Schedule—

"functions" includes powers and duties;

"regulated activity" means—

(a) in relation to water regulations, the use of water resources;

(b) in relation to flood regulations, any activity that affects, or could affect, the drainage of land, flood risk or the management of flood risk;

(*c*) in relation to fish regulations, any activity that affects, or could affect, the movement of fish through regulated waters;

"regulated field" means—

(*a*) in relation to water regulations, regulating the use of water resources;

(*b*) in relation to flood regulations, securing the drainage of land or the management of flood risk;

(*c*) in relation to fish regulations, safeguarding the movement of fish through regulated waters;

"the regulations" means regulations under section 61;

"specified" means specified in the regulations.

**Preliminary**

**3.** (1) Establishing standards, objectives or requirements in relation to—

(*a*) regulated activities, and

(*b*) in the case of fish regulations, structures or obstructions that affect, or could affect, the movement of fish through regulated waters.

(2) In the case of water regulations, authorising the making of plans for—

(*a*) the setting of overall limits,

(*b*) the allocation of rights, or

(*c*) the progressive improvement of standards or objectives,

relating to the use of water resources.

(3) In the case of water regulations, authorising the making of schemes for the trading or other transfer of rights so allocated.

**4.** (1) Determining the authorities (whether public or local or the Minister) by whom functions conferred by the regulations—

(*a*) in relation to permits under the regulations, or

(*b*) otherwise for or in connection with the regulated field,

are to be exercisable (in this Schedule referred to as "regulators").

(2) Specifying any purposes for which any such functions are to be exercisable by regulators.

**5.** Enabling the Minister to give directions which regulators are to comply with, or guidance which regulators are to have regard to, in exercising functions under the regulations, including—

(*a*) directions providing for any functions exercisable by one regulator to be instead exercisable by another;

(*b*) directions given for the purpose of the implementation of any obligations of the United Kingdom under the EU treaties or under any international agreement to which the United Kingdom is a party;

(*c*) directions relating to the exercise of any function in a particular case or class of case (except functions in relation to the investigation or prosecution, in a particular case, of an offence under the regulations).

*Permits*

**6.** Prohibiting persons from carrying on any activities of any specified description, except—

(*a*) under a permit in force under the regulations, and

(*b*) in accordance with any conditions to which the permit is subject.

**7.** Specifying restrictions or other requirements in connection with the grant of permits (including provisions for restricting the grant of permits to those who are fit and proper persons within the meaning of the regulations); and otherwise regulating the procedure to be followed in connection with the grant of permits.

**8.** (1) Prescribing the contents of permits.

(2) Authorising permits to be granted subject to conditions imposed by regulators (the nature of any such condition not being restricted by section 61(2)).

(3) Securing that permits have effect subject to—

(*a*) conditions specified in the regulations; or

(*b*) rules of general application specified in or made under the regulations.

**9.** (1) Requiring permits or the conditions to which permits are subject to be reviewed by regulators (whether periodically or in any specified circumstances).

(2) Authorising or requiring the variation of permits or such conditions by regulators (whether on applications made by holders of permits or otherwise).

(3) Regulating the making of changes in the carrying on of the activities.

**10.** (1) Regulating the transfer or surrender of permits.

(2) Authorising the revocation of permits by regulators.

(3) Authorising the imposition by regulators of requirements with respect to the taking of preventive action (by holders of permits or other persons) in connection with the surrender or revocation of permits.

**11.** Authorising the Minister to make schemes for the charging by regulators of fees or other charges in respect of, or in respect of an application for—

(*a*) the grant of a permit,

(*b*) the variation of a permit or the conditions to which it is subject, or

(*c*) the transfer or surrender of a permit,

or in respect of the subsistence of a permit.

**12.** Authorising, or authorising the Minister to make schemes for, the charging by the Minister or public or local authorities of fees or other charges in respect of—

(*a*) any advice given, or

(*b*) any testing, assessment or investigation done or other action taken,

in cases where the advice or action is in any way in anticipation of, or otherwise in connection with, the making of applications for the grant of permits or is carried out in pursuance of conditions to which any permit is subject.

*Further regulation*

**13.** (1) Requiring persons who propose to carry out activities of a specified description to give notice of their proposals to regulators.

(2) Requiring owners or occupiers of land to give notice to regulators of any obstruction of a specified description occurring on the land.

**14.** Requiring persons to apply for a permit under the regulations in respect of activities of a specified description.

**15.** (1) Authorising a regulator, where a person is carrying on an activity of a specified description—

(a) to serve notice on the person requiring them to cease carrying on the activity or, at their own cost, to take such action in connection with the activity as may be specified in the notice, or
(b) to arrange itself for action to be taken in connection with the activity.
(2) Authorising a regulator to—
(a) to serve notice on persons of a specified description requiring them, at their own cost, to take such action as may be specified in the notice, or
(b) to arrange itself for action to be taken,
in respect of a structure or obstruction of a specified description.

**16.** Imposing requirements, or authorising regulators to impose requirements, on persons of a specified description in relation to the operation and maintenance of specified structures.

*Information, publicity and consultation*

**17.** Enabling persons of any specified description (whether or not they are holders of permits) to be required—
(a) to compile information about—
(i) regulated activities, and
(ii) in the case of fish regulations, structures or obstructions that affect, or could affect, the movement of fish through regulated waters;
(b) to provide such information in such manner as is specified in the regulations.

**18.** Securing—
(a) that publicity is given to specified matters;
(b) that regulators maintain registers of specified matters (but excepting information which under the regulations is, or is determined to be, commercially confidential and subject to any other exceptions specified in the regulations) which are open to public inspection;
(c) that copies of entries in such registers, or of specified documents, may be obtained by members of the public.

**19.** Requiring or authorising regulators to carry out consultation in connection with the exercise of any of their functions; and providing for them to take into account representations made to them on consultation.

*Enforcement and offences*

**20.** (1) Conferring on regulators functions with respect to the monitoring and inspection of—
(a) the carrying on of regulated activities, or
(b) regulated structures or obstructions.
(2) Authorising regulators to appoint suitable persons to exercise any such functions and conferring on persons so appointed powers such as those specified in—
(a) sections 169 to 174 of the Water Resources Act 1991;
(b) section 108(4) of the Environment Act 1995;
(c) regulation 26 of the Eels (England and Wales) Regulations 2009 (SI 2009/3344);
(d) sections 31 and 32 of the Salmon and Freshwater Fisheries Act 1975.
(3) Functions which may be conferred in reliance on sub-paragraph (1) include—
(a) power to take samples or to make copies of information;
(b) power to arrange for preventive or remedial action to be taken at the expense of holders of permits.
(4) In sub-paragraph (1) "regulated structures or obstructions" means structures or obstructions which—
(a) may be the subject of notices served by regulators under the regulations, or
(b) may be subject to requirements imposed under the regulations.

**21.** Authorising regulators to serve on holders of permits—
(a) notices requiring them to take remedial action in respect of contraventions, actual or potential, of conditions to which their permits are subject;
(b) notices requiring them to provide such financial security as the regulators serving the notices consider appropriate pending the taking of remedial action in respect of any such contraventions;
(c) notices requiring them to take steps to remove or reduce, or to mitigate the effect of the potential consequences of, the following imminent risks (whether or not arising from any such contraventions)—
(i) an imminent risk of a significant waste of water resources or of significant damage to the environment, in the case of water regulations;
(ii) an imminent risk of a significant impediment to drainage or of a flood, in the case of flood regulations;
(iii) an imminent risk of a significant impediment to the movement of fish through regulated waters, in the case of fish regulations.

**22.** Authorising regulators to suspend the operation of permits so far as having effect to authorise the carrying on of activities to which they relate.

**23.** Establishing a procedure for the resolution of disputes in relation to notices served by regulators under the regulations.

**24.** Providing for the enforcement of notices served by regulators under the regulations by proceedings in—
(a) the High Court, or
(b) in the case of fish regulations applying as mentioned in section 61(11)(b), the Sheriff Court.

**25.** Where action is required to be taken by a person under the regulations or pursuant to a notice served under the regulations, authorising regulators in specified circumstances to take action instead of that person; and making provision for the liability of that person in respect of reasonable costs incurred by the regulators in taking such action.

**26.** Creating offences and dealing with matters relating to such offences, including—
(a) the provision of defences, and
(b) evidentiary matters.

**27.** Enabling, where a person has been convicted of an offence under the regulations—
(a) a court dealing with that person for the offence to order the taking of remedial action (in addition to or instead of imposing any punishment), or
(b) a regulator to arrange for such action to be taken at that person's expense.

**28.** Where a person causes damage to any structure constructed, altered or maintained by a regulator under these regulations, authorising the regulator to require the person to pay the expenses of the regulator in repairing the damage and providing for the manner in which such expenses may be recovered.

*Appeals*

**29.** Conferring rights of appeal in respect of decisions made, notices served or other things done (or omitted to be done) under the regulations; and making provision for (or for the determination of) matters relating to the making, considering and determination of such appeals (including provision for or in connection with the holding of inquiries or hearings).

*Corresponding provision*

**30.** (1) Making provision which, subject to any modifications that the Minister considers appropriate, corresponds or is similar to any provision made by or under, or capable of being made under—

(*a*) section 71 of the Water Industry Act 1991 (waste from water sources);

(*b*) Chapter 2 of Part 2 of the Water Resources Act 1991 (abstraction and impounding);

(*c*) Part 1 of the Water Act 2003 (abstraction and impounding).

(2) Making provision which, subject to any modifications that the Minister considers appropriate, corresponds or is similar to—

(*a*) any provision made by section 339 of the Highways Act 1980 (saving for works etc of drainage authorities etc);

(*b*) any provision made by or under, or capable of being made under, sections 109 and 110 of the Water Resources Act 1991 (erecting structures over main rivers etc prohibited without consent);

(*c*) any provision made by any byelaw, or capable of being made by any byelaw, under paragraph 5 of Schedule 25 to that Act (byelaws for flood defence and drainage purposes).

(3) Making provision which, subject to any modifications that the Minister considers appropriate, corresponds or is similar to—

(*a*) sections 9 to 15 and 18 of the Salmon and Freshwater Fisheries Act 1975 (obstructions to passage of fish);

(*b*) Part 4 of the Eels (England and Wales) Regulations 2009 (SI 2009/3344) (passage of eels).

(4) Each reference to an enactment in sub-paragraph (1), (2) or (3) is a reference to that enactment as it has effect on the coming into force of that sub-paragraph.

(5) Provision made under this paragraph is not subject to the requirement in section 61(2).

*Crown application*

**31.** Making provision about the application of the regulations to the Crown.

## PART 2

## SUPPLEMENTARY PROVISION

*Water regulations trading schemes: penalties*

**32.** (1) The regulations may, if they are water regulations, authorise the inclusion in a trading scheme of—

(*a*) provision for penalties in respect of contraventions of provisions of the scheme;

(*b*) provision for the amount of any penalty under the scheme to be such as may be set out in, or calculated in accordance with—

(i) the scheme, or

(ii) the regulations (including regulations made after the scheme starts to operate).

(2) In this paragraph "trading scheme" means a scheme of the kind mentioned in paragraph 3(3).

**Determination of matters by regulators**

**33.** The regulations may make provision for anything which, by virtue of paragraphs 7 to 10, could be provided for by the regulations to be determined under the regulations by regulators.

*Delegation between regulators*

**34.** The regulations may make provision authorising regulators to arrange for specified functions to be exercised on their behalf by other regulators.

*Imposition of conditions*

**35.** In connection with the determination of conditions as mentioned in paragraph 8(3)(*a*) the regulations may in particular provide—

(*a*) for such conditions to be determined in the light of any specified general principles and any directions or guidance given under the regulations;

(*b*) for such guidance to include guidance sanctioning reliance by a regulator on any arrangements referred to in the guidance to operate to secure a particular result as an alternative to imposing a condition.

**Charging schemes**

**36.** The regulations may—

(*a*) require any such scheme as is mentioned in paragraph 11 or 12 to be so framed that the fees and charges payable under the scheme are sufficient, taking one year with another, to cover such expenditure (whether or not incurred by the regulator or other person to whom they are so payable) as is specified;

(*b*) authorise any such scheme to make different provision for different cases (and specify particular kinds of such cases).

*Offences*

**37.** (1) The regulations may provide for any such offence as is mentioned in paragraph 26 to be triable—

(*a*) only summarily, or

(*b*) either summarily or on indictment.

(2) The regulations may provide for any such offence to be punishable on summary conviction with—

(*a*) imprisonment for a term not exceeding such period as is specified in the regulations (which may not exceed the normal maximum term), or

(*b*) a fine not exceeding such amount as is so specified (which may not exceed £20,000),

or both.

(3) The "normal maximum term" means—

(*a*) in relation to England and Wales—

(i) in the case of an offence triable only summarily, 51 weeks, and
(ii) in the case of an offence triable either summarily or on indictment, twelve months;

(*b*) in relation to Scotland—
(i) in the case of an offence triable only summarily, 6 months, and
(ii) in the case of an offence triable either summarily or on indictment, twelve months.

(4) Regulations that—

(*a*) are made before the date on which section 281(5) of the Criminal Justice Act 2003 comes into force, and

(*b*) in relation to England and Wales, make provision for a summary offence to be punishable with a term of imprisonment exceeding six months,

must provide that, where the offence is committed before that date, it is punishable with imprisonment for a term not exceeding six months.

(5) Regulations that—

(*a*) are made before the date on which section 154(1) of the Criminal Justice Act 2003 comes into force, and

(*b*) in relation to England and Wales, make provision for an offence triable either summarily or on indictment to be punishable on summary conviction with a term of imprisonment exceeding six months,

must provide that, where the offence is committed before that date, it is punishable on summary conviction with imprisonment for a term not exceeding six months.

(6) The regulations may provide for such an offence to be punishable on indictment with—

(*a*) imprisonment for a term not exceeding such period as is specified (which may not exceed two years), or

(*b*) a fine,

or both.

*Restrictions on Crown application*

**38.** (1) To the extent that the regulations bind the Crown (by virtue of provision made under paragraph 31), they are subject to the following restrictions.

(2) No contravention of any provision of the regulations may make the Crown criminally liable; but the regulations may provide that the High Court may, on the application of a regulator, declare unlawful any act or omission of the Crown which constitutes such a contravention.

(3) Sub-paragraph (2) does not affect the criminal liability of persons in the service of the Crown.

(4) The regulations must provide that if the Secretary of State certifies that it appears to him, as respects any Crown premises and any relevant powers of entry, that it is requisite or expedient that, in the interests of national security, the powers should not be exercisable in relation to those premises, those powers shall not be exercisable in relation to those premises.

(5) Subject to sub-paragraph (6), where a power is conferred in relation to land by any provision of the regulations, the regulations must provide that—

(*a*) that power is to be exercisable in relation to any land in which there is a Crown or Duchy interest only with the consent of the appropriate authority, and

(*b*) that a consent for such purposes may be given on such financial and other conditions as the appropriate authority giving the consent may consider appropriate.

(6) But provision contained in the regulations in accordance with sub-paragraph (5) is not to require any consent to be given for the exercise of any power in relation to any land in which there is a Crown or Duchy interest to the extent that that power would be so exercisable apart from provision in the regulations made by virtue of paragraph 31.

(7) In this paragraph—

"the appropriate authority" has the same meaning as in section 293 of the Town and Country Planning Act 1990;

"Crown or Duchy interest" means an interest belonging to Her Majesty in right of the Crown or the Duchy of Lancaster, or to the Duchy of Cornwall, or belonging to a government department, or held in trust for Her Majesty for the purposes of a government department;

"Crown premises" means premises held by or on behalf of the Crown;

"relevant powers of entry" means powers of entry that are—

(*a*) contained in the regulations,
(*b*) exercisable in relation to the premises in question, and
(*c*) specified in the Secretary of State's certificate under sub-paragraph (4).

## Water Resources (Control of Pollution) (Silage, Slurry and Agricultural Fuel Oil) (England) Regulations 2010[1]

(SI 2010/639 amended by SI 2010/1091 and SI 2013/1001)

**7.11737** 1. *Citation, commencement and application* These Regulations—

(*a*) may be cited as the Water Resources (Control of Pollution) (Silage, Slurry and Agricultural Fuel Oil) (England) Regulations 2010;

(*b*) apply to England only; and

(*c*) come into force on 6th April 2010.

[1] Made by the Secretary of State in exercise of the powers conferred by ss 92 and 219(2)(*d*) to (*f*) of the Water Resources Act 1991. Similar provision is made in respect of Wales by the Water Resources (Control of Pollution) (Silage, Slurry and Agriculture Fuel Oil) (Wales) Regulations 2010, SI 2010/1493 amended by SI 2016/359.

**7.11738** 2. *Interpretation* (1) In these Regulations—

"construct" includes install;

"fuel oil" means oil intended for use as a fuel for the production of heat or power but does not include oil intended for use exclusively as a fuel for heating a farmhouse or other residential premises on a farm and stored separately from other oil;

"livestock" means—
(*a*) animals kept for the production of food or wool, or
(*b*) birds kept for the production of food;

"reception pit" means a pit used for the collection of slurry before it is transferred into a slurry storage tank or for the collection of slurry discharged from such a tank;

"silage" includes a crop being made into silage;

"silage effluent" means effluent from silage;

"silo" means a structure used for making or storing silage;

"slurry" means liquid or semi-liquid matter composed of—
(*a*) excreta produced by livestock while in a yard or building (including that held in wood chip corrals); or
(*b*) a mixture wholly or mainly consisting of livestock excreta, livestock bedding, rainwater and washings from a building or yard used by livestock,

of a consistency that allows it to be pumped or discharged by gravity at any stage in the handling process;

"slurry storage tank" includes a lagoon, a pit (other than a reception pit) or tower used for the storage of slurry.

(2) A reference in these Regulations to a slurry storage system includes a slurry storage tank and—
(*a*) any reception pit and any effluent tank used in connection with the tank; and
(*b*) any channels and pipes used in connection with the tank, any reception pit or any effluent tank.

(3) A requirement in these Regulations for a silo or slurry storage tank to conform to a British Standard (in whole or in part) is satisfied if the silo or tank conforms to a standard or specification that provides an equivalent level of protection and performance and is recognised for use in a member State, Iceland, Liechtenstein, Norway or Turkey.

**7.11739** 3. *Making or storage of silage* (1) Subject to paragraph (3), a person who has custody or control of silage that is being made or stored must ensure that—
(*a*) the silage is kept in a silo that satisfies the requirements of Schedule 1; or
(*b*) the silage is compressed into bales that—
(i) are wrapped and sealed into impermeable membranes, or enclosed in impermeable bags; and
(ii) are stored at least 10 metres from any inland freshwaters or coastal waters that effluent escaping from the bales could enter; or
(*c*) if the silage is a crop being made into field silage (that is, silage made on open land by a method different from the baling method referred to in paragraph (*b*)) or silage that is being stored on open land—
(i) the Agency is given notice of the place where the silage is to be made or stored at least 14 days before the place is first used for that purpose; and
(ii) the place is at least 10 metres from any inland freshwaters or coastal waters, and at least 50 metres from the nearest relevant abstraction point of any protected water supply source that silage effluent could enter if it escaped.

(2) For paragraph (1)(*c*)(ii), a water supply source is a protected water supply source if—
(*a*) any relevant water abstraction from the source is licensed under Part II of the Water Resources Act 1991; or
(*b*) the person making or storing the silage was aware of the source's location—
(i) before the making of the silage began; or
(ii) if the silage was made elsewhere, before it was stored on the land in question.

(3) Paragraph (1) does not apply to silage while it is stored temporarily in a container, trailer or vehicle in connection with its transport about the farm or elsewhere.

(4) A person who has custody or control of a silage bale must not open or remove the wrapping of the bale within 10 metres of any inland freshwaters or coastal waters which silage effluent could enter as a result.

(5) In this regulation—
(*a*) "relevant water abstraction" means the abstraction of water for use for—
(i) human consumption, or
(ii) domestic purposes (within the meaning given by section 218 of the Water Industry Act 1991) other than human consumption, or
(iii) manufacturing food or drink for human consumption; and
(*b*) "water supply source" means inland freshwaters or ground waters from which a relevant abstraction is made or licensed to be made.

**7.11740** 4. *Storage of slurry* (1) Subject to paragraph (2), a person having custody or control of slurry must store it only in a slurry storage system that satisfies the requirements of Schedule 2.

(2) Paragraph (1) does not apply to slurry while it is stored temporarily in a tanker that is used for transporting slurry on roads or about a farm.

**7.11741** 5. *Storage of fuel oil on farms* (1) Subject to paragraph (2), a person who has custody or control of fuel oil on a farm must ensure that it is stored—
(*a*) in a fuel storage tank within a storage area or facility that satisfies the requirements of Schedule 3;
(*b*) in drums within such a storage area; or

(*c*) in an underground fuel storage tank.

(2) Paragraph (1) does not apply—

(*a*) to the temporary storage of fuel oil in a tanker used for transporting fuel oil on roads or about a farm; or

(*b*) where the total quantity of fuel oil stored on the farm does not exceed 1,500 litres.

**7.11742** 6. *Exemptions* (1) Subject to paragraph (2), these Regulations do not apply to a silo, slurry storage system or fuel storage tank—

(*a*) which, before 1st March 1991, was being used for the purpose of making silage, storing slurry or, as the case may be, storing fuel oil;

(*b*) where it was not used before 1st March 1991 for that purpose, it was constructed before that date for such use; or

(*c*) in relation to which—

(i) a contract for its construction, substantial enlargement or substantial reconstruction was entered into before 1st March 1991, or

(ii) such work was commenced before that date, and

and in either case the work was completed before 1st September 1991.

(2) These Regulations apply to a silo, slurry storage system or fuel storage tank meeting the requirements of paragraph (1) if any requirement of a notice under regulation 7 is not complied with within the period stated in the notice.

(3) Any reference in paragraph (2) to the period stated in a notice is to that period as extended if it has been extended under regulation 7(5)(*b*) or by virtue of regulation 8(6) and any reference in those paragraphs to a requirement of a notice is to that requirement as modified if it has been modified under regulation 7(5).

**7.11743** 7. *Notice requiring works etc* (1) The Agency may serve, on a person who has custody or control of silage, slurry or fuel oil or is responsible for the silo, slurry storage system or fuel oil storage tank, in circumstances in which these Regulations apply, a notice ("regulation 7 notice") requiring the person to carry out works, or take precautions or other steps, specified in the notice.

(2) The works, precautions or other steps must be, in the opinion of the Agency, appropriate, having regard to the requirements of these Regulations, for reducing to a minimum any significant risk of pollution of controlled waters.

(3) The notice must—

(*a*) specify or describe the works, precautions or other steps that the person is required to carry out or take;

(*b*) state the period within which any such requirement is to be complied with; and

(*c*) inform the person of the effect of regulation 8.

(4) The period for compliance stated in the notice is—

(*a*) 28 days; or

(*b*) such longer period as is reasonable in the circumstances.

(4A) A person on whom a regulation 7 notice has been served must comply with the requirements of that notice.

(5) The Agency may at any time (including a time after the period for compliance has ended)—

(*a*) withdraw the notice;

(*b*) extend the period for compliance with any requirement of the notice; or

(*c*) with the consent of the person on whom the notice is served, modify the requirements of the notice.

(6) The Agency must withdraw the notice, extend the period for compliance, or modify the requirements of the notice if so directed by the Secretary of State under regulation 8(5).

**7.11744** 8. *Appeals against regulation 7 notices* (1) A person served with a regulation 7 notice may, within the period of 28 days beginning on the day after the date on which the notice is served (or such longer period as the Secretary of State allows), appeal to the Secretary of State against the notice.

(2) An appeal under this regulation must be made by the appellant serving notice on the Secretary of State.

(3) The notice must contain or be accompanied by a statement of the grounds of appeal.

(4) Before determining an appeal under this regulation, the Secretary of State must, if requested to do so by the appellant or the Agency, afford them an opportunity of appearing before and being heard by a person appointed by the Secretary of State for the purpose.

(5) On determining an appeal under this regulation, the Secretary of State may direct the Agency to—

(*a*) withdraw the regulation 7 notice;

(*b*) modify any of its requirements;

(*c*) extend the period for compliance with any requirement; or

(*d*) dismiss the appeal.

(6) The period for compliance with a regulation 7 notice against which an appeal has been made is, subject to any direction under paragraph (5), extended so that it expires on the date on which the Secretary of State finally determines the appeal or, if the appeal is withdrawn, the date on which it is withdrawn.

**7.11745** 9. *Notice of construction etc* (1) This regulation applies to any silo, slurry or fuel oil storage system whose construction is to be begun on or after 15th June 2013 ("a new or improved store").

(2) A person who proposes to have custody or control of silage, slurry or fuel oil that is to be kept

in a new or improved store must give the Agency notice specifying the type of silo or storage system and its location, at least 14 days before work constructing the new or improved store is to be begun.

(3) In this regulation, "construction" includes substantial enlargement and reconstruction.

7.11746 *10. Offences and penalties* (1) A person who contravenes regulation 3(1) or (4), 4(1), 5(1) or 7(4A) of these Regulations is guilty of an offence and liable—

(*a*) on summary conviction, to a fine not exceeding the statutory maximum;

(*b*) on conviction on indictment, to a fine.

(2) A person who contravenes regulation 9 is guilty of an offence and liable on summary conviction to a fine not exceeding level 2 on the standard scale.

*11. Revocations*

SCHEDULE 1

Requirements for Silos — Regulation 3(1)(**a**)

7.11747 *1.* The requirement to be satisfied in relation to a silo is that it complies with the following provisions of this Schedule.

*2.* The base of the silo must—

(*a*) extend beyond any walls of the silo;

(*b*) be provided at its perimeter with channels designed and constructed so as to collect any silage effluent that escapes from the silo; and

(*c*) have adequate provision for the drainage of that effluent from those channels to an effluent tank through a channel or pipe.

*3.* The capacity of the effluent tank must not be less than—

(*a*) in the case of a silo with a capacity of less than 1,500 cubic metres, 20 litres for each cubic metre of silo capacity; and

(*b*) in the case of a silo with a capacity of 1,500 cubic metres or more, 30 cubic metres plus 6.7 litres for each cubic metre of silo capacity in excess of 1,500 cubic metres.

*4.* (1) The base of the silo must be—

(*a*) designed in accordance with the code of practice for design of concrete structures for retaining aqueous liquids published by the British Standards Institution and numbered BS 8007: 1987; or

(*b*) constructed using appropriate hot-rolled asphalt in accordance with the code of practice for selection and use of construction materials published by the British Standards Institution and numbered BS 5502: Part 21: 1990.

(2) The base of the silo, the base and walls of its effluent tank and channels and walls of any pipes must be impermeable.

*5.* The base and walls of the silo, its effluent tank and channels and the walls of any pipes must, so far as reasonably practicable, be resistant to attack by silage effluent.

*6.* No part of the silo, its effluent tank or channels or any pipes may be situated within 10 metres of any inland freshwaters or coastal waters into which silage effluent could enter if it were to escape.

*7.* If the silo has retaining walls—

(*a*) the retaining walls must be capable of withstanding minimum wall loadings calculated on the assumptions and in the manner indicated by paragraphs 15.6 of the code of practice on buildings and structures for agriculture published by the British Standards Institution and numbered BS 5502: Part 22: 2003;

(*b*) the silo must at no time be loaded to a depth exceeding the maximum depth consistent with the design assumption made in respect of the loadings of the retaining walls; and

(*c*) notices must be displayed on the retaining walls in accordance with paragraph 18 of that code of practice.

*8.* Subject to paragraph 9, the silo, its effluent tank and channels and any pipes must be designed and constructed so that with proper maintenance they are likely to continue to satisfy the requirements of paragraphs 2 to 5 and, if applicable, paragraph 7(*a*) for at least 20 years.

*9.* If any part of an effluent tank is below ground level, the tank must be designed and constructed so that it is likely to continue to satisfy the requirements of paragraphs 4 and 5 for at least 20 years without maintenance.

SCHEDULE 2

Requirements for Slurry Storage Systems — Regulation 4

7.11748 *1.* The requirements to be satisfied in relation to a slurry storage system are as follows.

*2.* The base of the slurry storage tank, the base and walls of any effluent tank, channels and reception pit, and the walls of any pipes, must be impermeable.

*3.* The base and walls of the slurry storage tank, any effluent tank, channels and reception pit, and the walls of any pipes, must be protected against corrosion in accordance with paragraph 7 of the code of practice on buildings and structures for agriculture published by the British Standards Institution and numbered BS 5502: Part 50: 1993.

*4.* The base and walls of the slurry storage tank and of any reception pit must be capable of withstanding characteristic loads calculated on the assumptions and in the manner indicated by paragraph 5 of the code of practice on buildings and structures for agriculture published by the British Standards Institution and numbered BS 5502: Part 50: 1993.

*5.* (1) Any facilities used for the temporary storage of slurry before it is transferred to a slurry storage tank must have adequate capacity to store—

(*a*) the maximum quantity of slurry that (disregarding any slurry which will be transferred directly into a slurry storage tank) is likely to be produced on the premises in any two day period; or

(*b*) a lesser capacity that the Agency agrees in writing is adequate to avoid any significant risk of pollution of controlled waters.

(2) Where slurry flows into a channel before discharging into a reception pit and the flow of slurry out of the channel is controlled by means of a sluice, the capacity of the reception pit must be adequate to hold the maximum quantity of slurry that can be released by opening the sluice.

*6.* (1) Subject to sub-paragraph (2), the slurry storage tank must have adequate storage capacity for the likely quantities of slurry produced from time to time on the premises in question, taking into account—

(*a*) the proposed method of utilising the slurry, and the likely rates and times of utilisation; and

(*b*) the matters mentioned in sub-paragraph (3).

(2) If it is proposed to utilise the slurry on the premises by spreading it on the land, the tank need not have a greater storage capacity than is adequate, taking into account the matters mentioned in sub-paragraph (3), to hold the maximum quantity of slurry likely to be produced in any four month period.

(3) The matters to be taken into account for sub-paragraphs (1) and (2) are—

(*a*) the storage capacity of any other slurry storage tank on the premises;

(*b*) the likely quantities of rainfall (including snow, hail or sleet) that may fall or drain into the slurry storage tank during the likely maximum storage period; and (*c*) the need to provide at least 750 millimetres of freeboard in the case of a tank with walls made of earth and 300 millimetres of freeboard in all other cases.

*7.* No part of the slurry storage tank or any effluent tank, channels or reception pit may be situated within 10 metres of any inland freshwaters or coastal waters into which slurry could enter if it were to escape unless precautions are taken that the Agency agrees in writing are adequate to avoid any significant risk of pollution of controlled waters.

*8.* The slurry storage tank and any effluent tank, channels, pipes and reception pit must be designed and constructed so that with proper maintenance they are likely to continue to satisfy the requirements of paragraphs 2 to 4 for at least 20 years.

*9.* If the walls of the slurry storage tank are not impermeable, the base of the tank must—

(*a*) extend beyond the walls;

(*b*) be provided with channels designed and constructed so as to collect any slurry that escapes from the tank;

(*c*) have adequate provision for the drainage of the slurry from those channels to an effluent tank through a channel or pipe.

*10.* (1) Subject to sub-paragraph (3), if the slurry storage tank or any effluent tank or reception pit is fitted with a drainage pipe there must be two valves in series on the pipe with each valve separated from the other by a minimum distance of 1 metre.

(2) Each valve must be capable of shutting off the flow of slurry through the pipe and must be kept shut and locked in that position when not in use.

(3) Sub-paragraph (1) does not apply in relation to a slurry storage tank that drains through the pipe into another slurry storage tank if the other tank is of equal or greater capacity or if the tops of the tanks are at the same level.

*11.* In the case of a slurry storage tank with walls made of earth the tank must not be filled to a level that allows less than 750 millimetres of freeboard.

SCHEDULE 3

Requirements for Fuel Oil Storage Areas — Regulation 5(1)

**7.11749** *1.* The requirements to be satisfied in relation to a fuel oil storage area are as follows.

*2.* The storage area must be surrounded by a bund capable of retaining within the area—

(*a*) if there is only one fuel storage tank within the area and fuel oil is not otherwise stored there, a volume of fuel oil not less than 110 per cent of the capacity of the tank;

(*b*) if there is more than one fuel storage tank within the area and fuel oil is not otherwise stored there, a volume of fuel oil not less than the greater of—

(i) 110 per cent of the capacity of the largest tank within the area; or

(ii) 25 per cent of the total volume of such oil which could be stored in the tanks within the area;

(*c*) if there is no fuel storage tank within the area, a volume of fuel oil not less than 25 per cent of the total of such oil at any time stored within the area;

(*d*) in any other case, a volume of fuel oil not less than the greater of—

(i) 110 per cent of the capacity of the fuel storage tank or, as the case may be, of the largest tank within the area;

(ii) if there is more than one fuel storage tank within the area, 25 per cent of the total volume of such oil that could be stored in the tanks within the area; or

(iii) 25 per cent of the total volume of such oil at any time stored within the area.

*3.* The bund and the base of the area must be—

(*a*) impermeable to water and oil; and

(*b*) designed and constructed so that they are of sufficient strength and structural integrity so that with proper maintenance they are likely to remain so for at least 20 years.

*4.* Every part of any fuel storage tank must be within the bund.

*5.* Any tap or valve permanently fixed to the fuel storage tank through which fuel oil can be discharged to the open must—

(*a*) also be within the bund;

(*b*) be so arranged as to discharge vertically downwards; and

(*c*) be shut and locked in that position when not in use.

*6.* If fuel from the tank is delivered through a flexible pipe that is permanently attached to the tank, the pipe must be—

(*a*) fitted with a tap or valve at its end that closes automatically when not in use; and

(*b*) locked in a way that ensures that it is kept within the bund when not in use.

*7.* No part of the fuel storage area or the bund enclosing it may be situated within 10 metres of any inland freshwaters or coastal waters that fuel oil could enter if it were to escape.

# Water Use (Temporary Bans) Order 2010[1]

(SI 2010/2231)

## Part 1 Introduction

**7.11750** *1.* ***Citation and commencement*** This Order may be cited as the Water Use (Temporary Bans) Order 2010 and comes into force on 1st October 2010.

[1] Made by the Secretary of State and the Welsh Ministers in exercise of powers conferred by s 76A(2) of the Water Industry Act 1991.

**7.11751** *2.* ***Interpretation*** In this Order—

"the Act" means the Water Industry Act 1991;

"grow" includes cultivate or propagate;

"health or safety reasons" includes—

(*a*) removing or minimising any risk to human or animal health or safety; and

(*b*) preventing or controlling the spread of causative agents of disease;

"National Plant Collection" means a plant collection which is part of the National Council for the Conservation of Plants and Gardens' National Plant Collection scheme;

"outdoor pot" means a pot or other container that is outdoors or under cover;

"temporary garden or flower display" means a garden or flower display that is—

(*a*) at a show or exhibition; and

(*b*) on public display for a period not exceeding 7 days; and

"under cover" means in a greenhouse or outbuilding or under a permanent canopy.

## PART 2 CATEGORIES OF USE

**7.11752** 3. ***Definition of "using a hosepipe"*** (1) Using a hosepipe, in relation to a purpose in section 76(2) of the Act, includes the following—

(*a*) drawing relevant water through a hosepipe from a container and applying it for the purpose;

(*b*) filling or partly filling a container with relevant water by means of a hosepipe and applying it for the purpose.

(2) In paragraph (1), "relevant water" does not include water supplied by a water undertaker before the use of water to which the purpose relates was prohibited under section 76(1) of the Act.

**7.11753** 4. ***Watering a garden using a hosepipe*** (1) Using a hosepipe to water a garden for health or safety reasons is not to be treated as falling within the category of use in section 76(2)(*a*) of the Act.

(2) In that section, "a garden" includes any of the following—

(*a*) a park;

(*b*) gardens open to the public;

(*c*) a lawn;

(*d*) a grass verge;

(*e*) an area of grass used for sport or recreation;

(*f*) an allotment garden, as defined in section 22(1) of the Allotments Act 1922;

(*g*) any area of an allotment used for non-commercial purposes;

(*h*) any other green space.

(3) But "a garden" does not include—

(*a*) agricultural land, as defined in section 109(1) of the Agriculture Act 1947;

(*b*) other land used in the course of a business for the purposes of growing, for sale or commercial use, any crops, fruit, vegetables or other plants;

(*c*) land used for the purposes of a National Plant Collection;

(*d*) a temporary garden or flower display; or

(*e*) plants (including plant organs, seeds, crops and trees) which are in an outdoor pot or in the ground, under cover.

**7.11754** 5. ***Cleaning a private motor-vehicle using a hosepipe*** In section 76(2)(*b*) of the Act, "private motor-vehicle" means—

(*a*) a mechanically propelled vehicle designed, constructed or adapted for use on roads, except—

(i) a public service vehicle, as defined in section 1 of the Public Passenger Vehicles Act 1981, and

(ii) a goods vehicle, as defined in section 192 of the Road Traffic Act 1988; or

(*b*) a trailer designed, constructed or adapted for attachment to a vehicle falling within paragraph (*a*).

**7.11755** 6. ***Watering plants on domestic or other non-commercial premises using a hosepipe*** (1) The category of use in section 76(2)(*c*) of the Act—

(*a*) applies only to the watering of plants which are in an outdoor pot or in the ground, under cover; and

(*b*) does not include watering plants—

(i) grown or kept for sale or commercial use, or

(ii) that are part of a National Plant Collection or temporary garden or flower display.

(2) In that section—

"domestic or other non-commercial premises" means—

(*a*) any land, building or other structure used or enjoyed in connection with the use of any of the following which is used principally as a dwelling—

(i) a building or part of a building,

(ii) a caravan,

(iii) a boat; or

(*b*) any other land or premises which is not used principally for the purposes of a business; and

"plants" includes plant organs, seeds, crops and trees.

**7.11756** 7. ***Cleaning a private leisure boat using a hosepipe*** (1) The category of use in section 76(2)(*d*) of the Act does not include cleaning any area of a private leisure boat which, except for doors or windows, is enclosed by a roof and walls.

(2) Using a hosepipe to clean a private leisure boat for health or safety reasons is not to be treated as falling within the category of use in that section.

(3) In that section, "private leisure boat" means a vessel or other thing, other than a seaplane, which is designed, constructed or adapted to move through, in, on or over water and which is not—

(*a*) used in the course of a business; or

(*b*) made available or accessible to the public.

**7.11757** 8. ***Filling or maintaining a domestic swimming or paddling pool*** (1) The following are not to be treated as falling within the category of use in section 76(2)(*e*) of the Act—

(*a*) filling or maintaining a pool where necessary in the course of its construction;

(*b*) filling or maintaining a pool using a hand-held container which is filled with water drawn directly from a tap;
(*c*) filling or maintaining a pool that is designed, constructed or adapted for use in the course of a programme of medical treatment;
(*d*) filling or maintaining a pool that is used for the purpose of decontaminating animals from infections or disease;
(*e*) filling or maintaining a pool used in the course of a programme of veterinary treatment;
(*f*) filling or maintaining a pool in which fish or other aquatic animals are being reared or kept in captivity.

(2) In that section, "domestic swimming or paddling pool" means a swimming or paddling pool, other than a pool that is being used for the purposes of a business, which is—
(*a*) in a building, or part of a building, used principally as a dwelling; or
(*b*) on any land or in any building that is used or enjoyed in connection with a building, or part of a building, mentioned in sub-paragraph (*a*).

**7.11758** *9.* ***Drawing water, using a hosepipe, for domestic recreational use*** (1) Drawing water, using a hosepipe, to operate water slides or other recreational equipment is to be treated as falling within the category of use in section 76(2)(*f*) of the Act.

(2) In that section, "domestic recreational use" means—
(*a*) recreational use in connection with a domestic swimming or paddling pool within the meaning of section 76(2)(*e*) of the Act; or
(*b*) recreational use on land that is used or enjoyed in connection with a building, or part of a building, used principally as a dwelling, other than for the purposes of a business.

**7.11759** *10.* ***Filling or maintaining a domestic pond using a hosepipe*** (1) The category of use in section 76(2)(*g*) of the Act does not include filling or maintaining a domestic pond in which fish or other aquatic animals are being reared or kept in captivity.

(2) In that section, "domestic pond" means a pond, including a swimming pond, on land that—
(*a*) is used or enjoyed in connection with a building, or part of a building, used principally as a dwelling; and
(*b*) is not being used for the purposes of a business.

**7.11760** *11.* ***Filling or maintaining an ornamental fountain*** (1) The category of use in section 76(2)(*h*) of the Act does not include filling or maintaining an ornamental fountain which is in or near a fish-pond and whose purpose is to supply sufficient oxygen to the water in the pond in order to keep the fish healthy.

(2) In that section, "ornamental fountain" includes a cascade or any other display of moving water.

**7.11761** *12.* ***Cleaning walls, or windows, of domestic premises using a hosepipe*** (1) The category of use in section 76(2)(i) of the Act applies only to the cleaning of the external walls or windows of domestic premises.

(2) Using a hosepipe to clean the walls or windows of domestic premises for health or safety reasons is not to be treated as falling within the category of use in that section.

(3) In that section, "domestic premises" means—
(*a*) a building used principally as a dwelling or dwellings;
(*b*) a garage, shed, outbuilding or other building or structure used or enjoyed in connection with a building mentioned in sub-paragraph (*a*); or
(*c*) a wall or other means of enclosure within the curtilage of a building mentioned in sub-paragraph (*a*).

**7.11762** *13.* ***Cleaning paths or patios using a hosepipe*** Using a hosepipe to clean paths or patios for health or safety reasons is not to be treated as falling within the category of use in section 76(2)(*j*) of the Act.

**7.11763** *14.* ***Cleaning other artificial outdoor surfaces using a hosepipe*** (1) Using a hosepipe to clean an artificial outdoor surface for health or safety reasons is not to be treated as falling within the category of use in section 76(2)(*k*) of the Act.

(2) In that section, "artificial outdoor surface" means any of the following—
(*a*) any area outdoors which is paved or laid with hard or artificial material;
(*b*) timber decking;
(*c*) a quay;
(*d*) a trailer designed, constructed or adapted to launch boats or other vessels or craft into water, other than a private motor-vehicle within the meaning of section 76(2)(*b*) of the Act;
(*e*) the roof of any domestic premises within the meaning of section 76(2)(i) of the Act.

(3) In paragraph (2), "quay" includes jetty, pontoon, wharf and slipway.

# WEIGHTS AND MEASURES

**Contents**



## European Communities Act 1972: regulations

**7.11764** Within the scope of the title Weights and Measures would logically fall the subject matter of a number of regulations made under the very wide enabling powers provided in s 2(2) of the European Communities Act 1972. Regulations may validly be made under this provision for the purpose of implementing the "Metrication Directive" (Council Directive 80/181/EEC)[1]. Certain regulations are made under this provision and s 15 of the Weights and Measures Act 1985; these are noted to s 15, post.

The Units of Measurement Regulations 1995, are contained, post; other such regulations which create offences are noted below in chronological order:

- Measuring Container Bottles (EEC Requirements) Regulations 1977, SI 1977/932 amended by SI 1985/306;
- Taximeters (EEC Requirements) Regulations 1979, SI 1979/1379 amended by SI 1985/306 and SI 1988/1128;
- Units of Measurement Regulations 1986, SI 1986/1082 amended by SI 1994/2867, SI 1995/1804, SI 2001/55 and SI 2009/3046;
- Measuring Instruments (EC Requirements) (Electrical Energy Meters) Regulations 1995, SI 1995/2607 amended by SI 2002/3082;
- Weights and Measures (Revocations) Regulations 2015, SI 2015/356;
- Non-automatic Weighing Instruments Regulations 2016, SI 2016/1152;
- Measuring Instruments Regulations 2016, SI 2016/1153.

1 *Thoburn v Sunderland City Council* [2002] EWHC 195 (Admin), [2003] QB 151, [2002] 4 All ER 156, 166 JP 257.

## Weights and Measures Act 1985

(1985 c 72)

### Part I

### Units and Standards of Measurement

**7.11765** This Part prescribes units of measurement[1] and provides for the maintenance of United Kingdom, Board of Trade and Local standards, and the provision of working standards and texting and stamping equipment. It gives effect to Schedule 1.

1 Certain units of measurement are authorised by the Units of Measurement Regulations 1986, SI 1986/1082 amended by SI 1994/2867, SI 1995/1804 and SI 2001/55. See also the Units of Measurement Regulations 1995, this title, post.

### Part II[1]

### Weighing and Measuring for Trade

*General*

**7.11766 7. Meaning of "use for trade"** (1) In this Act "use for trade" means, subject to subsection (3) below, use in Great Britain in connection with, or with a view to, a transaction falling within subsection (2) below where—

(*a*) the transaction is by reference to quantity or is a transaction for the purposes of which there is made or implied a statement of the quantity of goods to which the transaction relates, and

(*b*) the use is for the purpose of the determination or statement of that quantity.

(2) A transaction falls within this subsection if it is a transaction for—

(*a*) the transferring or rendering of money or money's worth in consideration of money or money's worth, or

(*b*) the making of a payment in respect of any toll or duty.

(3) Use for trade does not include use in a case where—

(*a*) the determination or statement is a determination or statement of the quantity of goods required for despatch to a destination outside Great Britain and any designated country, and

(b) the transaction is not a sale by retail, and

(c) no transfer or rendering of money or money's worth is involved other than the passing of the title to the goods and the consideration for them.

(4) The following equipment, that is to say—

(a) any weighing or measuring equipment which is made available in Great Britain for use by the public, whether on payment or otherwise, and

(b) any equipment which is used in Great Britain for the grading by reference to their weight, for the purposes of trading transactions by reference to that grading, of hens' eggs in shell which are intended for human consumption,

shall be treated for the purposes of this Part of this Act as weighing or measuring equipment in use for trade, whether or not it would apart from this subsection be so treated.

(5) Where any weighing or measuring equipment is found in the possession of any person carrying on trade or on any premises which are used for trade, that person or, as the case may be, the occupier of those premises shall be deemed for the purposes of this Act, unless the contrary is proved, to have that equipment in his possession for use for trade.

[Weights and Measures Act 1985, s 7.]

---

[1] Part II comprises ss 8–17.

7.11767 **8. Units of measurement, weights and measures lawful for use for trade**

(1) No person shall—

(a) use for trade any unit of measurement which is not included in Parts I to V of Schedule 1 to this Act, or

(b) use for trade, or have in his possession for use for trade, any linear, square, cubic or capacity measure which is not included in Schedule 3 to this Act, or any weight which is not so included.

(2) No person shall use for trade—

(a) the ounce troy, except for the purposes of transactions in, or in articles made from, gold, silver or other precious metals, including transactions in gold or silver thread, lace or fringe, or

(b) the carat (metric), except for the purposes of transactions in precious stones or pearls, or

(c) a capacity measure of 35, 70, 125, 150 or 175 millilitres, except for the purposes of transactions in intoxicating liquor, or

(d) the pint except for—

(i) the purposes of the sale of draught beer or cider, or

(ii) the purposes of the sale of milk in returnable containers.

(e), (f) *repealed.*

(3) Subsection (1)(a) above shall not apply to the prescribing of, or the dispensing of a prescription for, drugs.

(4) A person who contravenes subsection (1) or (2) above shall be guilty of an offence[1], and any measure or weight used, or in any person's possession for use, in contravention of that subsection shall be liable to be forfeited.

(5) The preceding provisions have effect subject to—

(a) subsection (5A) below, and

(b) sections 9 and 89 below.

(5A) Nothing in this section precludes the use for trade up to and including 31 December 2009, of any supplementary indication; and for this purpose any indication of quantity ("the imperial indication") is a supplementary indication if—

(a) it is expressed in a unit of measurement other than a metric unit,

(b) it accompanies an indication of quantity expressed in a metric unit ("the metric indication") and is not itself authorised for use in the circumstances as a primary indication of quantity, and

(c) the metric indication is the more prominent, the imperial indication being, in particular, expressed in characters no larger than those of the metric indication.

(6) The Secretary of State may by order—

(a) amend Schedule 3 to this Act by adding to or removing from it any linear, square, cubic or capacity measure, or any weight;

(b) add to, vary or remove from subsection (2) above any restriction on the cases or circumstances in which, or the conditions subject to which, a unit of measurement, measure or weight may be used for trade or possessed for use for trade.

(7) An order under subsection (6) above may contain such transitional or other supplemental or incidental provisions as appear to the Secretary of State expedient.

(8) In this section "unit of measurement" means a unit of measurement of length, area, volume, capacity, mass or weight.

[Weights and Measures Act 1985, s 8 as amended by SI 1994/1883, 2866 and 2867, SI 2001/55 and 1322.]

---

[1] For penalty see s 84, post.

7.11768 **9. Dual marking and conversion charts** (1) The Secretary of State may make regulations—

(*a*) requiring or authorising a person who uses a metric unit for trade to afford, for explanatory purposes, information giving the equivalent in the imperial system of the relevant quantity in the metric system, and

(*b*) specifying the manner in which the information is to be given, and in particular specifying the cases in which any obligation to give information in metric units is to be extended to include the same information in imperial units.

(2) The Secretary of State may make regulations requiring or authorising the display on premises where metric units are used for trade of conversion tables or other material for converting metric units into imperial units.

(3) Regulations under this section—

(*a*) may prescribe the form and manner in which any information or other material is to be given or displayed,

(*b*) may prescribe appropriate conversion factors by reference to which, in prescribed cases or circumstances, an amount expressed in imperial units is to be treated as equivalent to a given amount expressed in metric units,

(*c*) may prescribe the persons to whom, and the cases and circumstances in which, the regulations apply and may make different provision for different persons, cases or circumstances,

(*d*) may contain such consequential, incidental or supplementary provisions as appear to the Secretary of State to be expedient.

(4) A person contravening regulations made under this section shall be guilty of an offence[1].

(5) In this section "unit" in the expressions "metric unit" and "imperial unit" means any unit of measurement of length, area, volume, capacity, mass or weight.

(6) Regulations under this section imposing obligations apply whether or not the relevant imperial unit may lawfully be used for trade, and regulations authorising, but not requiring, anything to be done authorise it to be done notwithstanding that the relevant imperial unit may not be lawfully used for trade, but do not in any other respect authorise what is unlawful.

[Weights and Measures Act 1985, s 9.]

---

1 For penalty see s 84, post.

7.11769 **10. Multiples and fractions of measures and units** (1) Except as may be prescribed[1], and subject to any regulations made under section 15 below—

(*a*) a linear measure specified in Part I of Schedule 3 to this Act may be marked in whole or in part with divisions and sub-divisions representing any shorter length or lengths; but

(*b*) no capacity measure specified in Part IV of that Schedule shall be used for trade by means of any division or sub-division marked on it as a capacity measure of any lesser quantity.

(2) Any person who contravenes paragraph (*b*) of subsection (1) above shall be guilty of an offence[2], and any measure used, or in any person's possession for use, in contravention of that paragraph, shall be liable to be forfeited.

(3) The Secretary of State may by regulations prescribe what may be treated for the purposes of use for trade as the equivalent of, or of any multiple or fraction of, any unit of measurement included in Schedule 1 to this Act in terms of any other such unit.

(4) Nothing in any regulations under subsection (3) above shall apply to any transaction in drugs.

(5) *Saving*[3] *for prescribing or dealing in drugs.*

[Weights and Measures Act 1985, s 10.]

---

1 See the Weights and Measures Regulations 1963 as amended (noted to s 15, post).

2 For penalty see s 84, post.

3 The Weights and Measures (Equivalents for Dealing with Drugs) Regulations 1970, SI 1970/1897 amended by SI 1976/1664 were made under s 10 of the 1963 Act which this replaces. See also exemptions in the Measuring Instruments (EEC Requirements) Regulations, post.

*Weighing or measuring equipment for use for trade*

7.11770 **11. Certain equipment to be passed and stamped by inspector** (1) The provisions of this section shall apply to the use for trade[1] of weighing or measuring equipment of such classes or descriptions as may be prescribed[2].

(2) No person shall use[3] any article for trade as equipment to which this section applies, or have any article in his possession for such use, unless that article, or equipment to which this section applies in which that article is incorporated or to the operation of which the use of that article is incidental—

(*a*) has been passed by an inspector or approved verifier as fit for such use, and

(*b*) except as otherwise expressly provided by or under this Act, bears a stamp indicating that it has been so passed which remains undefaced otherwise than by reason of fair wear and tear.

(3) If any person contravenes subsection (2) above, he shall be guilty of an offence[4] and any article in respect of which the offence was committed shall be liable to be forfeited.

(4)–(10) *Testing, stamping, marking (summarised).*

(11) Where a person submits equipment to an inspector under this section, the inspector may require the person to provide the inspector with such assistance in connection with the testing of the equipment as the inspector reasonably considers it necessary for the person to provide and shall not be obliged to proceed with the test until the person provides it; but a failure to provide the assistance shall not constitute an offence under section 81 below.

(12) If an inspector refuses to pass as fit for use for trade any equipment submitted to him under this section and is requested by the person by whom the equipment was submitted to give reasons for the refusal, the inspector shall give to that person a statement of those reasons in writing.

(13) In the case of any equipment which is required by regulations made under section 15 below to be passed and stamped under this section only after it has been installed at the place where it is to be used for trade, if after the equipment has been so passed and stamped it is dismantled and reinstalled, whether in the same or some other place, it shall not be used for trade after being so reinstalled until it has again been passed under this section.

(14) If any person—

(*a*) knowingly uses any equipment in contravention of subsection (13) above, or

(*b*) knowingly causes or permits any other person so to use it, or

(*c*) knowing that the equipment is required by virtue of subsection (13) above to be again passed under this section, disposes of it to some other person without informing him of that requirement,

he shall be guilty of an offence[4] and the equipment shall be liable to be forfeited[5].

(15), (16) *Validity of stamping (summarised).*

[Weights and Measures Act 1985, s 11 as amended by SI 1999/503.]

1 Defined by s 7, ante.

2 See the text of Regulations noted to s 15, post.

3 This included the use of a vehicle in *FE Charman Ltd v Clow* [1974] 3 All ER 371, [1974] 1 WLR 384, 138 JP 728. Use of unstamped equipment for the sale of intoxicating liquor by the licensee of a public house in the course of his employment was held *prima facie* to be use by the employers for the purposes of s 11(2) (*Evans v Clifton Inns Ltd* (1986) 150 JP 639, 85 LGR 119).

4 For penalty see s 84, post.

5 For disposal of forfeiture see the Magistrates' Courts Act 1980, s 140, ante.

**7.11771 11A. Approval of persons to verify equipment manufactured etc by them**

**7.11772 11B. Testing by official EEA testers**

**7.11773 12. Approved patterns of equipment** Secretary of State may examine any pattern of weighing or measuring equipment and issue a certificate of approval which may be revoked.

[Weights and Measures Act 1985, s 12—summarised.]

**7.11774 13. Offences in connection with approved patterns of equipment** (1) Where one or more conditions are imposed by the Secretary of State on the grant or renewal of a certificate of approval, then if any person—

(*a*) knowing that a condition, other than such a condition as is mentioned in section 12(6) above, has been imposed with respect to any equipment, uses, or causes or permits any other person to use, that equipment in contravention of that condition, or

(*b*) knowing that any condition has been imposed with respect to any equipment, disposes of that equipment to any other person in a state in which it could be used for trade without informing that other person of that condition,

he shall be guilty of an offence[1] and the equipment shall be liable to be forfeited[2].

(2) Where a certificate of approval in respect of any pattern of equipment—

(*a*) expires (whether at the end of a period or by virtue of a notice under section 12(9) above), or

(*b*) is revoked in a case falling within section 12(11)(*b*) above,

then if any person, knowing that the certificate has expired or has been so revoked, supplies to another person any equipment of the pattern in question which is marked with a stamp and which was not used for trade at a time when the certificate was in force otherwise than by virtue of section 12(11) above, he shall be guilty of an offence[1] and the equipment supplied shall be liable to be forfeited[2].

(3) Where a certificate of approval in respect of any pattern of equipment is revoked in a case not falling within section 12(11)(*b*) above, then if any person, knowing that the certificate has been so revoked (and except as may be permitted by any fresh certificate granted in respect of that pattern)—

(*a*) uses for trade, or has in his possession for such use, any equipment of that pattern,

(*b*) causes or permits any other person to use any such equipment for trade, or

(*c*) disposes of any such equipment to any such person in a state in which it could be used for trade without informing that other person of the revocation,

he shall be guilty of an offence[1] and the equipment shall be liable to be forfeited[2].

(4) In this section "certificate of approval" means a certificate of approval of a pattern of weighing or measuring equipment granted under section 12 above; and subsections (1) and (3) above have effect in relation to a certificate of approval remaining in force by virtue of subsection (9) or (11) of section 12 above as they have effect in relation to other certificates of approval.

[Weights and Measures Act 1985, s 13.]

1 For penalty see s 84, post.
2 For disposal of forfeiture see the Magistrates' Courts Act 1980, s 140, ante.

7.11775 14. **General specifications of equipment** (1) The Secretary of State may by regulations prescribe general specifications for the construction of equipment to which section 11 above applies and, subject to subsection (4) below, while any such specification is for the time being so prescribed no equipment which does not conform with it shall be passed or stamped by an inspector or approved verifier under that section unless it is of a pattern in respect of which a certificate of approval under section 12 above is in force.

(2) If the Secretary of State is satisfied that any pattern submitted to him under section 12(1) above conforms with any general specification for the time being prescribed under this section he may, instead of issuing a certificate of approval under that section, cause to be published a declaration to that effect together with particulars of that pattern.

(3) Where a specification prescribed by regulations under this section is varied or revoked by further regulations under this section, then if any person—

(*a*) uses for trade[1] any equipment which conformed with that specification but which to his knowledge no longer conforms with any specification prescribed by regulations under this section,

(*b*) has any such equipment in his possession for use for trade,

(*c*) causes or permits any other person to use any such equipment for trade, or

(*d*) disposes of any such equipment to any other person in a state in which it could be used for trade without informing that other person that it no longer conforms with any specification prescribed by regulations under this section,

he shall be guilty of an offence[2] and the equipment shall be liable to be forfeited[3].

(4) Where, in the case of any particular equipment, the Secretary of State is of opinion that there are special circumstances which make it impracticable or unnecessary for that equipment to comply with any particular requirement of any specification prescribed under this section, the Secretary of State may exempt that equipment from that requirement subject to compliance with such conditions, if any, as he thinks fit.

(5) If any person knowingly contravenes any condition imposed with respect to any equipment by virtue of subsection (4) above, he shall be guilty of an offence[2] and the equipment shall be liable to be forfeited[3].

(6) If any difference arises between an inspector and any other person as to the interpretation of any specification prescribed under this section, or as to whether or not any equipment conforms with such a specification, that difference may with the consent of that other person, and shall at the request of that other person, be referred to the Secretary of State, whose decision shall be final.

[Weights and Measures Act 1985, s 14 as amended by SI 1999/503.]

1 "Use for trade" is defined by s 7, ante.
2 For penalty see s 84, post.
3 For disposal of forfeiture see the Magistrates' Courts Act 1980, s 140, ante.

*Miscellaneous*

7.11776 15. **Regulations relating to weighing or measuring for trade** (1) The Secretary of State may make regulations[1] with respect to—

(*a*) the materials and principles of construction of weighing or measuring equipment for use for trade,

(*b*) the inspection, testing, passing as fit for use for trade and stamping of such equipment, including—

(i) the prohibition of the stamping of such equipment in such circumstances as may be specified in the regulations,

(ii) the circumstances in which an inspector may remove or detain any such equipment for inspection or testing,

(iii) the marking of any such equipment found unfit for use for trade,

(*c*) the circumstances in which, conditions under which and manner in which stamps may be destroyed, obliterated or defaced,

(*d*) where any stamp on weighing or measuring equipment is lawfully destroyed, obliterated or defaced, the circumstances in which, and conditions subject to which, the equipment may be used for trade without contravening section 11(2) above,

(*e*) the purposes for which particular types of weighing or measuring equipment may be used for trade,

(*f*) the manner of erection or use of weighing or measuring equipment used for trade,

(*g*) the abbreviations of or symbols for units of measurement which may be used for trade, and

(*h*) the manner in which the tare weight of road vehicles, or of road vehicles of any particular class or description, is to be determined.

(2) Regulations under subsection (1) above with respect to the testing of equipment may provide—

(*a*) that where a group of items of equipment of the same kind is submitted for testing and prescribed conditions are satisfied with respect to the group, the testing may be confined to a number of items determined by or under the regulations and selected in the prescribed manner, and

(*b*) that if items so selected satisfy the test other items in the group shall be treated as having satisfied it.

(3) Subject to subsection (5) below, if any person contravenes any regulation made by virtue of subsection 1(*e*), (*f*), (*g*) or (*h*) above, he shall be guilty of an offence[2], and any weighing or measuring equipment in respect of which the contravention was committed shall be liable to be forfeited[3].

(4) If any difference arises between an inspector and any other person as to the interpretation of any regulations made under this section or as to the method of testing any weighing or measuring equipment, that difference may with the consent or that other person, and shall at the request of that other person, be referred to the Secretary of State, whose decision shall be final.

(5) Where in the special circumstances of any particular case it appears to be impracticable or unnecessary that any requirement of any regulations made under this section should be complied with, the Secretary of State may if he thinks fit dispense with the observance of that requirement subject to compliance with such conditions, if any, as he thinks fit to impose; and if any person knowingly contravenes any condition imposed with respect to any equipment by virtue of this subsection he shall be guilty of an offence[2] and the equipment shall be liable to be forfeited[3].

[Weights and Measures Act 1985, s 15.]

---

[1] The Weights and Measures Regulations 1963, SI 1963/1710 amended by SI 1972/767, SI 1979/1612, SI 1983/914, SI 1986/1320 and 1682, SI 1988/876 and 120, SI 1994/1259, SI 1995/735, SI 2000/388, SI 2001/599 and 1208 and SI 2003/2454 and 2761 were made under s 14 of the Weights and Measures Act 1963 which this section replaces.

The following regulations were made under the Weights and Measures Act 1963 and now have effect under s 15:

Cubic Measures (Ballast and Agricultural Materials) Regulations 1978, SI 1978/1962 amended by SI 1988/765;

Measuring Equipment (Liquid Fuel Deliveries from Road Tankers) Regulations 1983, SI 1983/1390 amended by SI 1986/1210, SI 1994/1851, SI 1995/3117, SI 2001/85, SI 2003/214 and SI 2009/3045;

Measuring Equipment (Intoxicating Liquor) Regulations 1983, SI 1983/1656 amended by SI 1984/273, SI 1994/1851, SI 2001/85 and SI 2009/2463 and 3045;

The following regulations have been made under this section:

Weighing Equipment (Filling and Discontinuous Totalising Automatic Weighing Machines) Regulations 1986, SI 1986/1320 amended by SI 1994/1851, SI 1996/797, SI 2000/387, SI 2001/85, SI 2003/214 and SI 2009/3045;

Measuring Equipment (Measures of Length) Regulations 1986, SI 1986/1682 amended by SI 1986/2109, SI 1994/1851, SI 1996/2636 and 3020, SI 2001/85, SI 2003/214 and SI 2009/3045;

Weights Regulations 1986, SI 1986/1683 amended by SI 1994/1851;

Weights and Measures (Quantity Marking and Abbreviation of Units) Regulations 1987, SI 1987/1538 amended by SI 1988/627, SI 1994/1852, SI 2006/659 and SI 2014/2975;

Cold Water Meters Regulations 1988, SI 1988/997 amended by SI 2001/1229 and SI 2003/214;

Measuring Equipment (Capacity Measures and Testing Equipment) Regulations 1995, SI 1995/735 amended by SI 2001/599 amended by SI 2001/85, SI 2003/214, SI 2006/659, SI 2009/3045 and SI 2015/356;

Measuring Equipment (Liquid Fuel and Lubricants) Regulations 1995, SI 1995/1014 amended by SI 1998/2218, SI 2001/85, SI 2003/214 and 2110, SI 2006/2234, SI 2009/3045 and SI 2010/675;

Weighing Equipment (Automatic Gravimetric Filling Instruments) Regulations 2000, SI 2000/388 and SI 2001/85, SI 2003/214, SI 2006/659, SI 2009/3045, SI 2010/675 and SI 2016/1154;

Weighing Equipment (Non-automatic Weighing Machines) Regulations 2000, SI 2000/932 amended by SI 2000/3236, SI 2001/85, SI 2003/214 and 2761, SI 2006/659, SI 2009/3045 and SI 2015/356;

Weighing Equipment (Beltweighers) Regulations 2001, SI 2001/1208 amended by SI 2003/214 and SI 2009/3045;

Weighing Equipment (Automatic Rail-weighbridges) Regulations 2003, SI 2003/2454 amended by SI 2010/675;

Weighing Equipment (Automatic Catchweighing Instruments) Regulations 2003, SI 2003/2761 amended by SI 2009/3045 and SI 2010/675;

Weights and Measures (Packaged Goods) Regulations 2006, SI 2006/659 amended by SI 2013/1478, SI 2014/2975 and SI 2015/356;

Non-automatic Weighing Instruments Regulations 2016, SI 2016/1152;

Measuring Instruments Regulations 2016, SI 2016/1153.

[2] For penalty see s 84, post.

[3] For disposal of forfeiture, see the Magistrates' Courts Act 1980, s 140 ante.

7.11777 **15A. Pre-test stamping by certain manufacturers** (1) Subject to subsection (2) below, an approved verifier who is the manufacturer of any equipment to which section 11 above applies may apply the prescribed stamp to the equipment, notwithstanding that it has not been passed as fit for use for trade, if he is satisfied on reasonable grounds that it will not be used (whether for trade or otherwise) unless either—

(*a*) the equipment has been passed as fit for use for trade, or

(*b*) the stamp has been destroyed, obliterated or defaced.

(2) A prescribed stamp shall not be applied under subsection (1) above unless the stamp includes the approved verifier's number.

(3) If any person contravenes subsection (2) above, he shall be guilty of an offence and any equipment in respect of which the offence[1] was committed shall be liable to be forfeited.

(4) A prescribed stamp which has been duly applied to any equipment under subsection (1) above shall have effect as follows—

(*a*) at any time before the equipment is passed as fit for use for trade, as an indication that, at the time when the stamp was applied, the approved verifier was satisfied as mentioned in subsection (1) above, and

(*b*) at any time after the equipment is so passed, as evidence of the passing of the equipment as fit for such use.

(5) Where equipment to which a prescribed stamp has been duly applied under subsection (1) above is passed as fit for use for trade, nothing in section 11(4)(*c*) or (4A)(*c*) above shall require another such stamp to be applied to it.

(6) Where the approved verifier fails to pass as fit for use for trade equipment to which a prescribed stamp has been applied under subsection (1) above, he may destroy, obliterate or deface the stamp—

(*a*) in any case where there is a prescribed manner of doing so, in that manner, and

(*b*) in any other case, in such reasonable manner as will leave no doubt that the stamp has been intentionally destroyed, obliterated or defaced.

(7) References in subsections (4) to (6) above to prescribed stamps which have been applied do not include references to such stamps which have subsequently been destroyed, obliterated or defaced.

[Weights and Measures Act 1985, s 15A as inserted by SI 1999/503.]

---

1 For penalty see s 84, post.

7.11778 **16. Offences in connection with stamping of equipment** (1) Subject to subsection (2) below, any person who, in the case of any weighing or measuring equipment used or intended to be used for trade—

(*a*) not being an inspector or approved verifier or a person acting under the instructions of an inspector or approved verifier, marks in any manner any plug or seal used or designed for use for the reception of a stamp,

(*b*) forges, counterfeits or, except as permitted by or under this Act, in any way alters or defaces any stamp,

(*c*) removes any stamp and inserts it into any other such equipment,

(*d*) makes any alteration in the equipment after it has been stamped such as to make it false or unjust, or

(*e*) severs or otherwise tampers with any wire, cord or other thing by means of which a stamp is attached to the equipment,

shall be guilty of an offence[1].

(2) Paragraphs (*a*) and (*b*) of subsection (1) above shall not apply to the destruction or obliteration of any stamp, plug or seal, and paragraph (*e*) of that subsection shall not apply to anything done, in the course of the adjustment or repair of weighing or measuring equipment by, or by the duly authorised agent of, a person who is a manufacturer of, or regularly engaged in the business of repairing, such equipment.

(3) Any person who uses for trade, sells, or exposes or offers for sale any weighing or measuring equipment which to his knowledge—

(*a*) bears a stamp which is a forgery or counterfeit, or which has been transferred from other equipment, or which has been altered or defaced otherwise than as permitted by or under this Act, or

(*b*) is false or unjust as the result of an alteration made in the equipment after it has been stamped,

shall be guilty of an offence[1].

(4) Any weighing or measuring equipment in respect of which an offence under this section is committed, and any stamp or stamping implement used in the commission of the offence, shall be liable to be forfeited[2].

[Weights and Measures Act 1985, s 16 as amended by SI 1999/503.]

---

1 For penalty see s 84, post.
2 For disposal of a forfeiture, see the Magistrates' Courts Act 1980, s 140, ante.

7.11779 **17. Offences relating to false or unjust equipment or fraud** (1) If any person uses for trade, or has in his possession[1] for use for trade[2], any weighing or measuring equipment which is false or unjust, he shall be guilty of an offence[3] and the equipment shall be liable to be forfeited[4].

(2) Without prejudice to the liability of any equipment to be forfeited, it shall be a defence for any person charged with an offence under subsection (1) above in respect of the use for trade of any equipment to show—

(*a*) that he used the equipment only in the course of his employment by some other person, and

(*b*) that he neither knew, nor might reasonably have been expected to know, nor had any reason to suspect, the equipment to be false or unjust.

(3) If any fraud is committed in the using of any weighing or measuring equipment for trade, the person committing the fraud and any other person party to it shall be guilty of an offence[3] and the equipment shall be liable to be forfeited[4].

[Weights and Measures Act 1985, s 17.]

---

1 For a person to have weighing or measuring equipment "in his possession", he must have at least some degree of control over it; and the mere fact that, as licensee, he is the only person lawfully entitled by himself or his agents, to use the equipment in question for selling intoxicating liquor to customers does not necessarily, or of itself, create a situation in which he "has possession of" such equipment (*Bellerby v Carle* [1983] 2 AC 101, [1983] 1 All ER 1031).

[2] "Use for trade" is defined by s 7, ante.
[3] For penalty see s 84, post.
[4] For disposal of a forfeiture, see the Magistrates' Courts Act 1980, s 140.

## PART III[1]

## PUBLIC WEIGHING OR MEASURING EQUIPMENT

7.11780 **18. Keepers of public equipment to hold certificate** (1) No person shall attend to any weighing or measuring by means of weighing or measuring equipment available for use by the public, being a weighing or measuring demanded by a member of the public and for which a charge is made, other than a weighing or measuring of a person, unless he holds a certificate from a chief inspector that he has sufficient knowledge for the proper performance of his duties.

(2) Any person refused such a certificate by a chief inspector may appeal against the refusal to the Secretary of State, who may if he thinks fit direct the chief inspector to grant the certificate.

(3) Any person who contravenes, or who causes or permits any other person to contravene, subsection (1) above shall be guilty of an offence[2].

[Weights and Measures Act 1985, s 18.]

[1] Part III comprises ss 18–20.
[2] For penalty see s 84, post.

7.11781 **19. Provision of public equipment by local authorities** Local authority may provide and maintain weighing or measuring equipment.

[Weights and Measures Act 1985, s 19—summarised.]

7.11782 **20. Offences in connection with public equipment** (1) Subsection (2) below shall apply where any article, vehicle (whether loaded or unloaded) or animal has been brought for weighing or measuring by means of weighing or measuring equipment which is available for use by the public and is provided for the purpose of weighing or measuring articles, vehicles or animals of the description in question.

(2) If any person appointed to attend to weighing or measuring by means of the equipment in question—

(*a*) without reasonable cause fails to carry out the weighing or measuring on demand,

(*b*) carries out the weighing or measuring unfairly,

(*c*) fails to deliver to the person demanding the weighing or measuring or to his agent a statement in writing of the weight or other measurement found, or

(*d*) fails to make a record of the weighing or measuring, including the time and date of it and, in the case of the weighing of a vehicle, such particulars of the vehicle and of any load on the vehicle as will identify that vehicle and that load,

he shall be guilty of an offence[1].

(3) If in connection with any such equipment as is mentioned in subsection (1) above—

(*a*) any person appointed to attend to weighing or measuring by means of the equipment delivers a false statement of any weight or other measurement found or makes a false record of any weighing or measuring, or

(*b*) any person commits any fraud in connection with any, or any purported, weighing or measuring by means of that equipment,

he shall be guilty of an offence[1].

(4) If, in the case of a weighing or measuring of any article, vehicle or animal carried out by means of any such equipment as is mentioned in subsection (1) above, the person bringing the article, vehicle or animal for weighing or measuring, on being required by the person attending to the weighing or measuring to give his name and address, fails to do so or gives a name or address which is incorrect, he shall be guilty of an offence[1].

(5) The person making any weighing or measuring equipment available for use by the public (in this section referred to as "the responsible person") shall retain for a period of not less than two years any record of any weighing or measuring by means of that equipment made by any person appointed to attend to the weighing or measuring.

(6) An inspector, subject to the production of his credentials if so requested, may require the responsible person to produce any such record as is mentioned in subsection (5) above for inspection at any time while it is retained by him.

(7) If the responsible person fails to retain any such record as is mentioned in subsection (5) above in accordance with that subsection or fails to produce it in accordance with subsection (6) above, he shall be guilty of an offence[1].

(8) If any person wilfully destroys or defaces any such record as is mentioned in subsection (5) above before the expiration of two years from the date when it was made, he shall be guilty of an offence[1].

[Weights and Measures Act 1985, s 20.]

[1] For penalty see s 84, post.

## PART IV[1]

## REGULATION OF TRANSACTIONS IN GOODS

### *Transactions in particular goods*

**7.11783 21–24.** *Effect is given to Schedules 4–7 relating to transactions in goods. Secretary of State may make Orders[2] relating to transactions in particular goods and the information which is to be displayed: contravention is an offence[3]; provision is made for exemptions.*

[Weights and Measures Act 1985, ss 21–24—summarised.]

---

1 Part IV comprises ss 21–46.

2 The following regulations and orders have been made under s 21 of the Weights and Measures Act 1963 and now have effect under ss 21–24 of the 1985 Act: Weights and Measures (Solid Fuel) Regulations 1987, in this title, post; Weights and Measures (Milk and Solid Fuel Vending Machines) Regulations 1980, SI 1980/246; Weights and Measures Act 1963 (Cheese, Fish, Fresh Fruits and Vegetables, Meat and Poultry) Order 1984, in this title, post; Weights and Measures (Liquid Fuel Carried by Road Tanker) Order 1985, SI 1985/778; the following orders and regulations have been made under ss 21–24 of the following Act: Weights and Measures (Knitting Yarn) Order 1988, SI 1988/895 amended by SI 2009/663; Weights and Measures Act 1963 (Intoxicating Liquor) Order 1988, SI 1988/2039, in this title, post; Weights and Measures (Miscellaneous Foods) Order 1988, SI 1988/2040, in this title, post.

3 For penalty see s 84, post. The Weights and Measures (Intoxicating Liquor) Order 1988 and the Weights and Measures (Miscellaneous Foods) Order 1988 are also reproduced in this PART, post.

**7.11784 25. Offences relating to transactions in particular goods** (1) Subject to section 44 below, where any goods are required, when not pre-packed, to be sold only by quantity expressed in a particular manner[1] or only in a particular quantity, any person shall be guilty of an offence[2] who—

(*a*) whether on his own behalf or on behalf of another person, offers[3] or exposes for sale[4], sells or agrees to sell, or

(*b*) causes or suffers any other person to offer or expose for sale, sell or agree to sell on his behalf,

those goods otherwise than by quantity expressed in that manner or, as the case may be, otherwise than in that quantity.

(2) Any person shall be guilty of an offence[2] who—

(*a*) whether on his own behalf or on behalf of another person has in his possession for sale[5], sells or agrees to sell,

(*b*) except in the course of carriage of the goods for reward, has in his possession for delivery after sale, or

(*c*) causes or suffers any other person to have in his possession for sale or for delivery after sale, sell or agree to sell on behalf of the first-mentioned person,

any goods to which subsection (3) below applies, whether the sale is, or is to be, by retail or otherwise.

(3) This subsection applies to any goods—

(*a*) which are required to be pre-packed only in particular quantities but are not so pre-packed,

(*b*) which are required to be otherwise made up in or on a container for sale or for delivery after sale only in particular quantities but are not so made up,

(*c*) which are required to be made for sale only in particular quantities but are not so made,

(*d*) which are required to be pre-packed only if the container is marked with particular information but are pre-packed otherwise than in or on a container so marked,

(*e*) which are required to be otherwise made up in or on a container for sale or for delivery after sale only if the container is marked with particular information but are so made up otherwise than in or on a container so marked,

(*f*) which are required to be pre-packed only in or on a container of a particular description but are not pre-packed in or on a container of that description, or

(*g*) which are required to be otherwise made up in or on a container for sale or for delivery after sale only in or on a container of a particular description but are not so made up in or on a container of that description.

(4) In the case of any sale where the quantity of the goods sold expressed in a particular manner[1] is required to be made known to the buyer at or before a particular time and that quantity is not so made known, the person by whom, and any other person on whose behalf, the goods were sold shall be guilty of an offence[2].

(5) Where any goods required to be sold by means of, or to be offered or exposed for sale in, a vending machine only if certain requirements are complied with are so sold, offered or exposed without those requirements being complied with, the seller or person causing the goods to be offered or exposed shall be guilty of an offence[2].

(6) The preceding provisions of this section have effect subject to sections 33 to 37 below.

(7) For the purposes of this section the quantity of goods in a package, or of a loaf of bread, to which the packaged goods regulations apply shall be deemed to be the nominal quantity (within the meaning of those regulations) of the package or the loaf of bread.

(8) In this section "required" means required by or under this Part of this Act.

[Weights and Measures Act 1985, s 25 as amended by SI 2006/659.]

[1] For extended use of this expression, see s 44, post.
[2] For penalty see s 84, post.
[3] See *Fisher v Bell* [1961] 1 QB 394; [1960] 3 All ER 731; 125 JP 201.
[4] There is an exposure for sale when goods are sent to a purchaser who, by agreement, is entitled to accept or reject them, and he rejects them (*Ollett v Jordan* [1918] 2 KB 41, 82 JP 221).
[5] This means possession with a sale in contemplation (*Birkett v McGlassons Ltd* [1957] 1 All ER 369, 121 JP 126), not during an intermediate stage between the completion of manufacture and the time when, eg, in the case of loaves of bread, it has been decided after checking and sorting which particular goods are to be offered for sale (*Ben Worsley Ltd v Harvey* [1967] 2 All ER 507, 131 JP 376). Unascertained goods such as coal are in the possession for sale of the vendors or their agent until delivery of the goods is completed so as to perform the contract for sale (*Church v Lee and Co-operative Retail Services* (1985) 150 JP 300).

*Quantity to be stated in writing*

7.11785 **26. Quantity to be stated in writing in certain cases** (1) Subject to section 27 below, the provisions of this section shall have effect on any sale of goods—

(*a*) which is required by or under this Part of this Act to be a sale by quantity expressed in a particular manner[1],

(*b*) in the case of which the quantity of the goods sold expressed in a particular manner is so required to be made known to the buyer at or before a particular time, or

(*c*) which, being a sale by retail[2] not falling within paragraph (*a*) or (*b*) above, is, or purports to be, a sale by quantity expressed in a particular manner other than by number.

(2) Subject to subsections (4) to (6) below, unless the quantity of the goods sold expressed in the manner in question is made known to the buyer at the premises of the seller and the goods are delivered to the buyer at those premises on the same occasion as, and at or after the time when, that quantity is so made known to him, a statement in writing of that quantity shall be delivered to the consignee at or before delivery of the goods to him.

(3) If subsection (2) above is contravened then, subject to sections 33 to 37 below, the person by whom, and any other person on whose behalf, the goods were sold shall be guilty of an offence[3].

(4) If at the time when the goods are delivered the consignee is absent, it shall be sufficient compliance with subsection (2) above if the statement is left at some suitable place at the premises at which the goods are delivered.

(5) Subsection (2) above shall not apply to any sale otherwise than by retail where, by agreement with the buyer, the quantity of the goods sold is to be determined after their delivery to the consignee.

(6) Where any liquid goods are sold by capacity measurement and the quantity sold is measured at the time of delivery and elsewhere than at the premises of the seller, subsection (2) above shall not apply but, unless the quantity by capacity measurement of the goods sold is measured in the presence of the buyer, the person by whom the goods are delivered shall immediately after the delivery hand to the buyer, or if the buyer is not present leave at some suitable place at the premises at which the goods are delivered, a statement in writing of the quantity by capacity measurement delivered, and if without reasonable cause he fails so to do he shall be guilty of an offence[3].

[Weights and Measures Act 1985, s 26.]

[1] For extended use of this expression, see s 44, post.
[2] This means a sale to a consuming member of the public; contrasted with a sale wholesale to a purchaser who proposes himself to sell the goods by retail (*Chappell & Co Ltd v Nestlé Co Ltd* [1960] AC 87, [1959] 2 All ER 701, HL, *Treacher v Treacher* [1874] WN 4; *Phillips v Parnaby* [1934] 2 KB 299, 98 JP 388).
[3] For penalty see s 84, post.

7.11786 **27. Exemption from requirements of section 26** (1) The Secretary of State may by order grant, with respect to goods or sales of such descriptions as may be specified in the order, exemption, either generally or in such circumstances as may be so specified, from all or any of the requirements of section 26 above.

(2) Until otherwise provided by an order under subsection (1) above, nothing in section 26 above shall apply to —

(*a*) a sale by retail from a vehicle of—

(i) any of the following in a quantity not exceeding 110 kilograms, that is to say, any solid fuel within the meaning of Schedule 5 to this Act, and wood fuel, or

(ii) any of the following in a quantity not exceeding 25 litres, that is to say, liquid fuel, lubricating oil, and any mixture of such fuel and oil,

(*b*) a sale by retail of bread within the meaning of the Weights and Measures Act 1963 (Miscellaneous Foods) Order 1984,

(*c*) goods made up for sale (whether by way of pre-packing or otherwise) in or on a container marked with a statement in writing with respect to the quantity of the goods expressed in the manner in question, being a container which is delivered with the goods,

(*d*) a sale of goods in the case of which a document stating the quantity of the goods expressed in the manner in question is required to be delivered to the buyer or consignee of the goods by or under any other provision of this Part of this Act,

(*e*) any such goods or sales as are mentioned in section 24(2)(*a*) to (*d*) above, (*f*) a sale of intoxicating liquor for consumption at the premises of the seller,

(*g*) a sale by means of a vending machine, or

(*h*) goods delivered at premises of the buyer by means of an installation providing a connection of a permanent nature between those premises and premises of the seller.

(3) Nothing in section 26 above shall apply to goods that are subject to the FIC Regulation.

[Weights and Measures Act 1985, s 27 as amended by SI 1994/2867 and SI 2014/2975.]

*General offences*

**7.11787 28. Short weight, etc** (1) Subject to sections 33 to 37 below, any person who, in selling or purporting to sell any goods by weight or other measurement or by number, delivers or causes to be delivered[1] to the buyer—

(*a*) a lesser quantity than that purported to be sold, or

(*b*) a lesser quantity than corresponds with the price charged,

shall be guilty of an offence[2].

(2) For the purposes of this section—

(*a*) the quantity of goods in a package, or of a loaf of bread, to which the packaged goods regulations apply shall be deemed to be the nominal quantity (within the meaning of those regulations) of the package or the loaf of bread; and

(*b*) any statement, whether oral or in writing, as to the weight of any goods shall be taken, unless otherwise expressed, to be a statement as to the net weight of the goods.

(3) Nothing in this section shall apply in relation to any such goods or sales as are mentioned in section 24(2)(*a*) or (*b*) above.

[Weights and Measures Act 1985, s 28 as amended by SI 2006/659.]

---

1 The licensee is the only person who can sell intoxicating liquor and thus an absent licensee was rightly convicted of causing the delivery to a purchaser of a short measure of whisky which was supplied to a customer by his servant. Active causation or counselling the delivery of a short measure was not necessary for the offence to be complete (*Sopp v Long* [1970] 1 QB 518, [1969] 1 All ER 855, 133 JP 261). Where an order for 15 lbs of meat was made and joints were delivered with a delivery note stating the meat weight as 14.35 lbs whereas the lamb when delivered weighed just over 9.25 lbs, it was held that no offence had been committed because the defendants had, as was their normal practice, removed the bone and the customer was only entitled to expect what was delivered (*North Yorkshire County Council v Holmesterne Farm Co Ltd* (1985) 150 JP 124).

2 For penalty see s 84, post.

**7.11788 30. Quantity less than stated** (1) If, in the case of any goods that are pre-packed within the meaning of this Act or are prepacked food within the meaning of the FIC Regulation and (in either case) are in or on a container marked with a statement in writing with respect to the quantity of the goods, the quantity of the goods is at any time found to be less than that stated, then, subject to sections 33 to 37 below—

(*a*) any person who has those goods in his possession for sale shall be guilty of an offence[1], and

(*b*) if it is shown that the deficiency cannot be accounted for by anything occurring after the goods had been sold by retail and delivered to, or to a person nominated in that behalf by, the buyer, any person by whom or on whose behalf those goods have been sold or agreed to be sold at any time while they were pre-packed within the meaning of this Act or were prepacked food within the meaning of the FIC Regulation and (in either case) were in or on the container in question, shall be guilty of an offence[1].

(2) If—

(*a*) in the case of a sale of or agreement to sell any goods which, not being pre-packed within the meaning of this Act or prepacked food within the meaning of the FIC Regulation, are made up for sale or for delivery after sale in or on a container marked with a statement in writing with respect to the quantity of the goods, or

(*b*) in the case of any goods which, in connection with their sale or an agreement for their sale, have associated with them a document containing such a statement,

the quantity of the goods is at any time found to be less than that stated, then, if it is shown that the deficiency cannot be accounted for by anything occurring after the goods had been delivered to, or to a person nominated in that behalf by, the buyer, and subject to sections 33 to 37 below and paragraph 10 of Schedule 4 to this Act, the person by whom, and any other person on whose behalf, the goods were sold or agreed to be sold shall be guilty of an offence[1].

(3) Subsections (1) and (2) above shall have effect notwithstanding that the quantity stated is expressed to be the quantity of the goods at a specified time falling before the time in question, or is expressed with some other qualification of whatever description, except where—

(*a*) that quantity is so expressed in pursuance of an express requirement of this Part of this Act or any instrument made under this Part, or

(*b*) the goods, although falling within subsection (1) or subsection (2)(*a*) above—

(i) are not required by or under this Part of this Act to be pre-packed as mentioned in subsection (1) or required by the FIC Regulation to be prepacked food as mentioned in that subsection or, as the case may be, to be made up for sale or for delivery after sale in or on a container only if the container is marked as mentioned in subsection (2)(*a*), and

(ii) are not goods on a sale of which (whether any sale or a sale of any particular description) the quantity sold is required by or under any provision of this Part of this Act other than section 26 or required by the FIC Regulation, to be made known to the buyer at or before a particular time, or

(*c*) the goods, although falling within subsection (2)(*b*) above, are not required by or under this Part of this Act to have associated with them such a document as is mentioned in that provision.

(4) In any case to which, by virtue of paragraph (*a*), (*b*) or (*c*) of subsection (3) above, the provisions of subsection (1) or (2) above do not apply, if it is found at any time that the quantity of the goods in question is less than that stated and it is shown that the deficiency is greater than can be reasonably justified on the ground justifying the qualification in question, then, subject to sections 33 to 37 below—

(*a*) in the case of goods such as are mentioned in subsection (1) above, if it is further shown as mentioned in that subsection, then—

(i) where the container in question was marked in Great Britain, the person by whom, and any other person on whose behalf, the container was marked, or

(ii) where the container in question was marked outside Great Britain, the person by whom, and any other person on whose behalf, the goods were first sold in Great Britain,

shall be guilty of an offence[1];

(*b*) in the case of goods such as are mentioned in subsection (2) above, the person by whom, and any other person on whose behalf, the goods were sold or agreed to be sold shall be guilty of an offence if, but only if, he would, but for paragraph (*a*), (*b*) or (*c*) of subsection (3) above have been guilty of an offence under subsection (2).

(5) Subsection (2) of section 28 above shall have effect for the purposes of this section as it has effect for the purposes of that section.

(6) Nothing in this section shall apply in relation to any such goods or sales as are mentioned in section 24(2)(*a*) or (*b*) above.

[Weights and Measures Act 1985, s 30 as amended by SI 2014/2975.]

1 For penalty see s 84, post.

7.11789 **31. Incorrect statements** (1) Without prejudice to section 30(2) to (4) above, if in the case of any goods required by or under this Part of this Act to have associated with them a document containing particular statements, that document is found to contain any such statement which is materially incorrect, any person who, knowing or having reasonable cause to suspect that statement to be materially incorrect, inserted it or caused it to be inserted in the document, or used the document for the purposes of this Part of this Act while that statement was contained in the document, shall be guilty of an offence[1].

(2) Subsection (2) of section 28 above shall have effect for the purposes of this section as it has effect for the purposes of that section.

(3) Nothing in this section shall apply in relation to any such goods or sales as are mentioned in section 24(2)(*a*) or (*b*) above.

[Weights and Measures Act 1985, s 31.]

1 For penalty see s 84, post.

7.11789A **31A. Non-compliance with certain requirements of the FIC Regulation** (1) Subject to subsection (2) below, a food business operator to which Article 1(3) of the FIC Regulation applies is guilty of an offence if that food business operator fails to comply with—

(*a*) any of the provisions of Article 8 of the FIC Regulation (responsibilities of food business operators) applicable to the food business operator, to the extent that the provisions relate to net quantity;

(*b*) Article 9(1)(*e*) of the FIC Regulation (mandatory indication of net quantity of food), except to the extent that it relates to a failure to comply with Article 13(5) of the FIC Regulation; or

(*c*) Chapter V of the FIC Regulation (voluntary food information), to the extent that it imposes requirements in respect of net quantity.

(2) A food business operator is not guilty of an offence under subsection (1) if the food business operator acts in accordance with any of the following—

(*a*) an exception contained in Chapter IV of the FIC Regulation;

(*b*) national measures adopted under Article 40 of the FIC Regulation (milk and milk products);

(*c*) national measures maintained under Article 42 of the FIC Regulation (measures adopted before 12 December 2011);

(*d*) transitional measures under Article 54(1) of the FIC Regulation.

(3) In this section "food business operator" and "net quantity" have the same meanings as in the FIC Regulation.

[Weights and Measures Act 1985, s 31A as inserted by SI 2014/2975.]

7.11790 **32. Offences due to default of third person** Where the commission by any person of an offence under this Part of this Act (other than section 31A) or an instrument made under this Part is due to the act or default[1] of some other person, the other person shall be guilty of an offence and may be charged with and convicted[2] of the offence whether or not proceedings are taken against the first-mentioned person.

[Weights and Measures Act 1985, s 32 as amended by SI 2014/2975.]

1 The prosecution must identify the "act or default" of the third person to which the commission of the offence was said to be due. Where the third person was a company which owned a public house and an employee of the company caused a short measure of beer to be served to a purchaser, it was held that an assumption that the owner could not adequately have trained their staff was insufficient to establish the offence was due to the "act or default" of the company (*Allied Domecq Leisure Ltd v Cooper* (1998) 163 JP 1, [1999] Crim LR 230).

2 A person convicted, whether the original defendant or "third party" may appeal to the Crown Court; see *R v Epsom Justices, ex p Dawnier Motors Ltd* [1961] 1 QB 201, [1960] 3 All ER 635, 125 JP 40, in which previous decisions on the subject are reviewed. Where the "third party" appeals, he must serve notice on both the prosecutor and the defendant (*Oxo Ltd v Chappell and Turner* [1966] 2 QB 228, [1966] 3 All ER 1968, 130 JP 356).

*Defences*

7.11791 **33. Warranty** (1) Subject to the following provisions of this section, in any proceedings for an offence under this Part of this Act or any instrument made under this Part, being an offence relating to the quantity or pre-packing of any goods, it shall be a defence for the person charged to prove—

(*a*) that he bought the goods from some other person—

(i) as being of the quantity which the person charged purported to sell or represented, or which was marked on any container or stated in any document to which the proceedings relate, or

(ii) as conforming with the statement marked on any container to which the proceedings relate, or with the requirements with respect to the pre-packing of goods of this Part of this Act or any instrument made under this Part,

as the case may require, and

(*b*) that he so bought the goods with a written warranty from that other person that they were of that quantity or, as the case may be, did so conform, and

(*c*) that at the time of the commission of the offence he did in fact believe the statement contained in the warranty to be accurate and had no reason to believe it to be inaccurate, and

(*d*) if the warranty was given by a person who at the time he gave it was resident outside Great Britain and any designated country, that the person charged had taken reasonable steps to check the accuracy of the statement contained in the warranty, and

(*e*) in the case of proceedings relating to the quantity of any goods, that he took all reasonable steps to ensure that, while in his possession, the quantity of the goods remained unchanged and, in the case of such or any other proceedings, that apart from any change in their quantity the goods were at the time of the commission of the offence in the same state as when he bought them.

(2) A warranty shall not be a defence in any such proceedings as are mentioned in subsection (1) above unless, not later than three days before the date of the hearing, the person charged has sent to the prosecutor a copy of the warranty with a notice stating that he intends to rely on it and specifying the name and address of the person from whom the warranty was received, and has also sent a like notice to that person.

(3) Where the person charged is the employee of a person who, if he had been charged, would have been entitled to plead a warranty as a defence under this section, subsection (1) above shall have effect—

(*a*) with the substitution, for any reference (however expressed) in paragraphs (*a*), (*b*), (*d*) and (*e*) to the person charged, of a reference to his employer, and

(*b*) with the substitution for paragraph (*c*) of the following—

"(*c*) that at the time of the commission of the offence his employer did in fact believe the statement contained in the warranty to be accurate and the person charged had no reason to believe it to be inaccurate,".

(4) The person by whom the warranty is alleged to have been given shall be entitled to appear at the hearing and to give evidence.

(5) If the person charged in any such proceedings as are mentioned in subsection (1) above wilfully attributes to any goods a warranty given in relation to any other goods, he shall be guilty of an offence[1].

(6) A person who, in respect of any goods sold by him in respect of which a warranty might be pleaded under this section, gives to the buyer a false warranty in writing shall be guilty of an offence[1] unless he proves that when he gave the warranty he took all reasonable steps to ensure that the statements contained in it were, and would continue at all relevant times to be, accurate.

(7) Where in any such proceedings as are mentioned in subsection (1) above ("the original proceedings") the person charged relies successfully on a warranty given to him or to his employer, any proceedings under subsection (6) above in respect of the warranty may, at the option of the prosecutor, be taken either before a court having jurisdiction in the place where the original proceedings were taken or before a court having jurisdiction in the place where the warranty was

given.

(8) For the purposes of this section, any statement with respect to any goods which is contained in any document required by or under this Part of this Act to be associated with the goods or in any invoice, and, in the case of goods made up in or on a container for sale or for delivery after sale, any statement with respect to those goods with which that container is marked, shall be taken to be a written warranty of the accuracy of that statement.

[Weights and Measures Act 1985, s 33.]

1 For penalty see s 84, post.

7.11792 **34. Reasonable precautions and due diligence** (1) In any proceedings for an offence under this Part of this Act or any instrument made under this Part, it shall be a defence for the person charged to prove[1] that he took all reasonable precautions[2] and exercised all due diligence[3] to avoid the commission of the offence.

(2) If in any case the defence provided by subsection (1) above involves an allegation that the commission of the offence in question was due to the act or default of another person[4] or due to reliance on information supplied by another person, the person charged shall not, without the leave of the court, be entitled[5] to rely on the defence unless, before the beginning of the period of seven days ending with the date when the hearing of the charge began, he served on the prosecutor a notice giving such information identifying or assisting in the identification of the other person as was then in his possession.

[Weights and Measures Act 1985, s 34.]

1 The onus of proof is on the defendant; but is less than is required of the prosecution in proving case beyond reasonable doubt and may be discharged by evidence of probability (*R v Carr-Briant* [1943] 2 All ER 156, 107 JP 167). The somewhat narrow extent of this defence is illustrated by *Urwin v Toole* [1976] Crim LR 583.

2 The court must require proof of all the prescribed elements, not, eg, merely that the defendant in the court's opinion took all reasonable precautions; see *Marshall v Matthews* [1939] 1 All ER 156.

3 There is no legal standard of diligence; therefore the question of what is due diligence falls to be decided as a question of fact (*R C Hammett Ltd v Crabb, R C Hammett Ltd v Beldam* (1931) 95 JP 180). Due diligence of a limited company means that of those who represent the directing mind and will of the company and control what it does; it does not refer to that of a subordinate unless some part of the functions of management has been delegated to him, and it does not refer to shop managers who act under the control of directions from their superiors (*Tesco Supermarkets Ltd v Nattrass* [1972] AC 153, [1971] 2 All ER 127, 135 JP 289).

4 See *Melias Ltd v Preston* [1957] 2 QB 380, [1957] 2 All ER 449, 121 JP 444.

5 See *Thomas v Thomas Bolton & Sons Ltd* (1928) 92 JP 147; cf Factories Act 1961, s 162; *R v Derby Recorder, ex p Spalton* [1944] KB 611, [1944] 1 All ER 721, 108 JP 193; *R v Epsom Justices, ex p Dawnier Motors Ltd* [1951] 1 QB 201, [1960] 3 All ER 635, 125 JP 40; *Oxo Ltd v Chappell and Tunner* [1966] 2 QB 228, [1966] 3 All ER 168, 130 JP 356.

7.11793 **35. Subsequent deficiency** (1) This subsection applies to any proceedings for an offence under this Part of this Act, or any instrument made under this Part, by reason of the quantity—

(*a*) of any goods made up for sale or for delivery after sale (whether by way of pre-packing or otherwise) in or on a container marked with an indication of quantity,

(*b*) of any goods which, in connection with their sale or an agreement for their sale, have associated with them a document purporting to state the quantity of the goods, or

(*c*) of any goods required by or under this Part of this Act to be pre-packed, or to be otherwise made up in or on a container for sale or for delivery after sale, or to be made for sale, only in particular quantities,

being less than that marked on the container or stated in the document in question or than the relevant particular quantity, as the case may be.

(2) In any proceedings to which subsection (1) above applies, it shall be a defence for the person charged[1] to prove[2] that the deficiency arose—

(*a*) in a case falling within paragraph (*a*) of subsection (1) above, after the making up of the goods and the marking of the container,

(*b*) in a case falling within paragraph (*b*) of that subsection, after the preparation of the goods for delivery in pursuance of the sale or agreement and after the completion of the document,

(*c*) in a case falling within paragraph (*c*) of that subsection, after the making up or making, as the case may be, of the goods for sale,

and was attributable wholly to factors for which reasonable allowance was made in stating the quantity of the goods in the marking or document or in making up or making the goods for sale, as the case may be.

(3) In the case of a sale by retail of food, other than food pre-packed in a container which is, or is required by or under this Part of this Act or the FIC Regulation to be, marked with an indication of quantity, in any proceedings for an offence under this Part of this Act or any instrument made under this Part, by reason of the quantity delivered to the buyer being less than that purported to be sold, it shall be a defence for the person charged to prove[2] that the deficiency was due wholly to unavoidable evaporation or drainage since the sale and that due care and precaution were taken to minimise any such evaporation or drainage.

(4) If in any proceedings for an offence under this Part of this Act or any instrument made under this Part, being an offence in respect of any deficiency in the quantity of any goods sold, it is shown that between the sale and the discovery of the deficiency the goods were with the consent of the buyer subjected to treatment which could result in a reduction in the quantity of those goods for

delivery to, or to any person nominated in that behalf by, the buyer, the person charged shall not be found guilty of that offence unless it is shown that the deficiency cannot be accounted for by the subjecting of the goods to that treatment.

[Weights and Measures Act 1985, s 35 as amended by SI 2014/2975.]

---

1 The defence in this subsection is not restricted to the person who has packed and marked the goods but is also available to the retailer (*F W Woolworth & Co Ltd v Gray* [1970] 1 All ER 953, 134 P 324).

2 See note to "prove" in s 34 above.

**7.11794 36. Excess due to precautions** In any proceedings for an offence under this Part of this Act or any instrument made under this Part, being an offence in respect of any excess in the quantity of any goods, it shall be a defence for the person charged to prove[1] that the excess was attributable to the taking of measures reasonably necessary in order to avoid the commission of an offence in respect of a deficiency in those or other goods.

[Weights and Measures Act 1985, s 36.]

---

1 See note to "prove" in s 34 above.

**7.11795 37. Provisions as to testing** (1) If proceedings for an offence under this Part of this Act, or any instrument made under this Part, in respect of any deficiency or excess in the quantity—

(*a*) of any goods made up for sale (whether by way of pre-packing or otherwise) in or on a container marked with an indication of quantity, or

(*b*) of any goods which have been pre-packed or otherwise made up in or on a container for sale or for delivery after sale, or which have been made for sale, and which are required by or under this Part of this Act or the FIC Regulation to be prepacked, or to be otherwise so made up, or to be so made, as the case may be, only in particular quantities,

are brought with respect to any article, and it is proved that, at the time and place[1] at which that article was tested, other articles of the same kind, being articles which, or articles containing goods which, had been sold by the person charged or were in that person's possession for sale or for delivery after sale, were available for testing, the person charged shall not be convicted of such an offence with respect to that article unless a reasonable number[2] of those other articles was also tested.

(2) In any proceedings for such an offence as is mentioned in subsection (1) above, the court—

(*a*) if the proceedings are with respect to one or more of a number of articles tested on the same occasion, shall have regard to the average quantity in the articles tested,

(*b*) if the proceedings are with respect to a single article, shall disregard any inconsiderable[3] deficiency or excess, and

(*c*) shall have regard generally to all the circumstances of the case.

(3) Subsections (1) and (2) above shall apply with the necessary modifications to proceedings for an offence in respect of the size, capacity or contents of a container as they apply to proceedings for an offence in respect of the excess or deficiency in the quantity of certain goods.

(4) Where by virtue of section 32 above a person is charged with an offence with which some other person might have been charged, the reference in subsection (1) above to articles or goods sold by or in the possession of the person charged shall be construed as a reference to articles or goods sold by or in the possession of that other person.

[Weights and Measures Act 1985, s 37 as amended by SI 2014/2975.]

---

1 As to the time and place of the start of the test, see *Sears v Smith's Food Group Ltd* [1968] 2 QB 288, [1968] 2 All ER 721.

2 Where 56 loaves had been weighed, and evidence given of deficiency in weight of 37 of them but no evidence of the weight of the other 19, which were either of correct or excess weight, it was held that a reasonable number had been weighed (*Cave v Dudley Co-operative Society Ltd* (1934) 98 JP 265).

3 A deficiency of 2½ oz in a 2 lb loaf is not inconsiderable (*Cave v Dudley Co-operative Society Ltd* (1934) 98 JP 265).

*Miscellaneous and supplementary*

**7.11796 41. Check-weighing of certain road vehicles** Where any road vehicle is loaded with goods for sale by weight to a single buyer of the whole of the vehicle's load, or for delivery to the buyer after they have been so sold, the buyer or seller of the goods, or any inspector who shows that he is authorised so to do by the buyer or seller of the goods, may require the person in charge of the vehicle to have it check-weighed, and if that person fails without reasonable cause to comply with any such requirement he shall be guilty of an offence[1].

[Weights and Measures Act 1985, s 41.]

---

1 For penalty see s 84, post.

**7.11797 44. Selling by quantity** Where any goods are required by or under this Part of this Act to be sold only by quantity expressed in a particular manner—

(*a*) it shall be a sufficient compliance with that requirement in the case of any sale of, or agreement to sell, any such goods if the quantity of the goods expressed in the manner in question is made known to the buyer before the purchase price is agreed; and

(*b*) no person shall be guilty of an offence under section 25(1) above by reason of the exposing or offering for sale of such goods at any time if both the quantity of the goods expressed in the manner in question and the price at which they are exposed or offered for sale are made known at that time to any prospective buyer.

[Weights and Measures Act 1985, s 44.]

7.11798 **45. Making quantity known to a person** (1) For the purposes of this Part of this Act, without prejudice to any other method of making known to a person the quantity of any goods expressed in a particular manner, that quantity shall be taken to be made known to that person—

(*a*) if the goods are weighed or otherwise measured or counted, as the case may require, in the presence of that person,

(*b*) if the goods are made up in or on a container marked with a statement in writing of the quantity of the goods expressed in the manner in question and the container is readily available for inspection by that person, or

(*c*) upon such a statement in writing being delivered to that person.

(2) The Secretary of State may by order provide that subsection (3) below shall apply, in the case of such goods in such circumstances as are specified in the order, to any requirement so specified of, or of any instrument made under, this Part of this Act with respect to the making known to the buyer of the quantity by weight of such goods sold by retail.

(3) In any case to which this subsection applies, the requirement specified in the order shall be taken to be satisfied if the goods are bought at premises at which weighing equipment of such description as may be prescribed—

(*a*) is kept available by the occupier of those premises for use without charge by any prospective buyer of such goods for the purpose of weighing for himself any such goods offered or exposed for sale by retail on those premises, and

(*b*) is so kept available in a position on those premises which is suitable and convenient for such use of the equipment, and

(*c*) is reserved for use for that purpose at all times while those premises are open for retail transactions,

and a notice of the availability of the equipment for such use is displayed in a position on the premises where it may be readily seen by any such prospective buyer.

[Weights and Measures Act 1985, s 45.]

7.11799 **46. Weighing in presence of a person** For the purpose of this Part of this Act, a person shall not be taken to weigh or otherwise measure or count any goods in the presence of any other person unless he causes any equipment used for the purpose to be so placed, and so conducts the operation of weighing or otherwise measuring or counting the goods, as to permit that other person a clear and unobstructed view of the equipment, if any, and of the operation, and of any indication of quantity given by any such equipment as the result of that operation.

[Weights and Measures Act 1985, s 46.]

## PART VI
## ADMINISTRATION

7.11800 *This Part, comprising ss 69–78, is chiefly concerned with the functions of weights and measures authorities and the appointment of inspectors.*

7.11801 **75. Offences in connection with office of inspector** (1) Any inspector who—

(*a*) stamps any weighing or measuring equipment in contravention of any provision of this Act or the packaged goods regulations or of any instrument made under this Act or without duly testing it, or

(*b*) derives any profit from, or is employed in, the making, adjusting or selling of weighing or measuring equipment, or

(*c*) knowingly[1] commits any breach of any duty imposed on him by or under this Act or otherwise misconducts himself in the execution of his office,

shall be guilty of an offence[2].

(1A) Any approved verifier who—

(*a*) stamps any weighing or measuring equipment in contravention of any provision of this Act or of any instrument made under this Act or without duly testing it, or

(*b*) commits any breach of any duty imposed on him by or under this Act or the packaged goods regulations,

shall be guilty of an offence[2].

(2) If any person who is not an inspector, or is not an approved verifier, acts or purports to act as such, he shall be guilty of an offence.[1]

(3) Section 34 of this Act shall apply in relation to proceedings for an offence under subsection (1A)(*b*) above as it applies in relation to proceedings for an offence under Part IV of this Act.

[Weights and Measures Act 1985, s 75 as amended by SI 1999/503 and SI 2006/659.]

---

1 A person acts knowingly if, intending what is happening, he deliberately looks the other way (*Ross v Moss* [1965] 2 QB 396, [1965] 3 All ER 145, 129 JP 537.

2 For penalty see s 84, post.

## PART VII[1]
## GENERAL

*Enforcement and legal proceedings*

7.11802 **79. General powers of inspection and entry** (1) Subject to the production if so requested of his credentials, an inspector may, within the area for which he was appointed inspector, at all reasonable times—

(*a*) inspect and test any weighing or measuring equipment which is, or which he has reasonable cause to believe to be, used for trade or in the possession of any person or upon any premises for such use, or which has been, or which he has reasonable cause to believe to have been, passed by an approved verifier, or by a person purporting to act as such a verifier, as fit for such use,

(*b*) inspect any goods to which any of the provisions of Part IV of this Act or any instrument made under that Part for the time being applies or which he has reasonable cause to believe to be such goods, and

(*c*) enter any premises at which he has reasonable cause to believe there to be any such equipment or goods, not being premises used only as a private dwelling-house[2].

(2) Subject to the production if so requested of his credentials, an inspector may at any time within the area for which he was appointed inspector seize and detain—

(*a*) any article which he has reasonable cause to believe is liable to be forfeited under Parts II or IV of this Act, and

(*b*) any document or goods which the inspector has reason to believe may be required as evidence in proceedings for an offence under this Act.

(3) If a justice of the peace, on sworn information in writing—

(*a*) is satisfied that there is reasonable ground to believe that any such equipment, goods, articles or documents as are mentioned in subsection (1) or (2) above are on any premises, or that any offence under this Act or any instrument made under it has been, is being or is about to be committed on any premises, and

(*b*) is also satisfied either—

(i) that admission to the premises has been refused, or a refusal is apprehended, and that notice of the intention to apply for a warrant has been given to the occupier, or

(ii) that an application for admission, or the giving of such a notice, would defeat the object of the entry, or that the case is one of urgency, or that the premises are unoccupied or the occupier temporarily absent,

the justice may by warrant under his hand, which shall continue in force for a period of one month, authorise an inspector to enter the premises, if need be by force.

(4) *Scotland.*

(5) An inspector entering any premises by virtue of this section may take with him such other persons and such equipment as may appear to him necessary.

(6) An inspector who leaves premises which he has entered by virtue of a warrant under subsection (3) above and which are unoccupied or from which the occupier is temporarily absent shall leave the premises as effectively secured against trespassers as he found them.

(7) If any inspector or other person who enters any workplace by virtue of this section discloses to any person any information obtained by him in the work-place with regard to any secret manufacturing process or trade secret, he shall, unless the disclosure was made in the performance of his duty, be guilty of an offence[3].

(8) In exercising his functions under this Act at any mine of coal, stratified ironstone, shale or fire-clay, an inspector shall so exercise those functions as not to impede or obstruct the working of the mine.

(9) Nothing in this Act shall authorise any inspector to stop any vehicle on a highway.

[Weights and Measures Act 1985, s 79 as amended by SI 1999/503 and SI 2006/659.]

---

1 Part VII comprises ss 79–99.

2 He may not go on to private property to instruct a coal merchant not to tip a suspect sack he wants to weigh (*Brunner v Williams* [1975] Crim LR 250).

3 For penalty see s 84, post.

7.11803 **80. Obstruction of inspectors** Any person who wilfully obstructs[1] an inspector acting in pursuance of this Act or the packaged goods regulations shall be guilty of an offence[2].

[Weights and Measures Act 1985, s 80 as amended by SI 2006/659.]

---

1 Mere passive conduct is not obstruction unless there is a duty to act (*Swallow v LCC* [1916] 1 KB 224, 80 JP 164).

2 For penalty see s 84, post.

7.11804 **81. Failure to provide assistance or information** (1) Any person who—

(*a*) wilfully fails to comply with any requirement properly made of him by an inspector under section 38, 39 or 40 above, or

(*b*) without reasonable cause fails to give to any inspector acting in pursuance of this Act any other assistance or information which the inspector may reasonably require of him for the purposes of the performance by the inspector of his functions under Parts II, III, IV or VI of this Act or under this Part of this Act,

shall be guilty of an offence[1].

(2) If any person, in giving to an inspector any such information as is mentioned in subsection (1) above, gives any information which he knows to be false, he shall be guilty of an offence[1].

(3) Nothing in this section shall be construed as requiring a person to answer any question or give any information if to do so might incriminate him.

(4) Subsection (1) of section 14 of the Civil Evidence Act 1968 (which relates to the privilege against self-incrimination) shall apply to the right conferred by subsection (3) above as it applies to the right described in subsection (1) of that section; but this subsection does not extend to Scotland.

[Weights and Measures Act 1985, s 81.]

1 For penalty see s 84, post.

7.11805 **82. Offences by corporations** (1) Where an offence under, or under any instrument made under, this Act which has been committed by a body corporate is proved to have been committed with the consent or connivance of, or to be attributable to any neglect on the part of, any director, manager, secretary or other similar officer of the body corporate, or any person who was purporting to act in any such capacity, he as well as the body corporate shall be guilty of that offence and shall be liable to be proceeded against and punished accordingly.

(2) In subsection (1) above "director" in relation to any body corporate established by or under any enactment for the purpose of carrying on under national ownership any industry or part of an industry or undertaking, being a body corporate whose affairs are managed by its members, means a member of that body corporate.

[Weights and Measures Act 1985, s 82.]

7.11806 **83. Prosecution of offences** (1) In England and Wales, proceedings for any offence under this Act or any instrument made under this Act shall not be instituted except by or on behalf of a local weights and measures authority or the chief officer of police for a police area.

(2) *Repealed.*

(3) Proceedings for an offence under any provision contained in, or having effect by virtue of, Part IV or V of this Act, other than proceedings for an offence under section 33(6), 57(2) or 64 or proceedings by virtue of section 32, shall not be instituted—

(*a*) unless there has been served on the person charged a notice in writing of the date and nature[1] of the offence alleged where the proceedings are in respect of one or more of a number of articles of the same kind tested on the same occasion, of the results of the tests of all those articles; or

(*b*) except where the person charged is a street trader, unless the said notice was served before the expiration of the period of thirty days beginning with the date when evidence which the person proposing to institute the proceedings considers is sufficient to justify a prosecution for the offence came to his knowledge; or

(*c*) after the expiration of the period—

(i) of twelve months beginning with the date mentioned in paragraph (*a*) above, or

(ii) of three months beginning with the date mentioned in paragraph (*b*) above,

whichever first occurs.

(4) Such a notice as is mentioned in subsection (3)(*a*) above may be served on any person either by serving it on him personally or by sending it to him by post at his usual or last known residence or place of business in the United Kingdom or, in the case of a company, at the company's registered office.

(5) For the purposes of subsection (3) above—

(*a*) a certificate of a person who institutes proceedings for an offence mentioned in that subsection which states that evidence came to his knowledge on a particular date shall be conclusive evidence of that fact; and

(*b*) a document purporting to be a certificate of such a person and to be signed by him or on his behalf shall be presumed to be such a certificate unless the contrary is proved.

[Weights and Measures Act 1985, s 83 as amended by SI 2006/659.]

1 The section requires that "the nature", "not particulars", of the alleged offence shall be served on the defendant; see *Milner v Allen* [1933] 1 KB 698, [1933] All ER Rep 734, 97 JP 111.

7.11807 **84. Penalties** (1) A person guilty of an offence under any of the provisions of this Act specified in subsection (2) below shall be liable on summary conviction to a fine not exceeding **level 3** on the standard scale.

(2) The provisions of this Act to which subsection (1) above refers are—

section 8(4);
section 9(4);
section 10(2);
section 11(3);
section 11(14);
section 13(1);
section 13(2);
section 13(3);

section 14(3);
section 14(5);
section 15(3);
section 15(5);
section 15A(3);
section 18(3);
section 20(2);
section 20(4);
section 20(7);
section 20(8);
paragraphs 4 and 5 of Schedule 4;
paragraph 28(3) of Schedule 5.

(3) A person guilty of an offence under paragraph 24(4) of Schedule 5 to this Act shall be liable on summary conviction to a fine not exceeding **£2,000**.

(4) A person guilty of an offence—

(*a*) under section 17(3) or 20(3)(*b*) above, or

(*b*) under paragraph 10 of Schedule 5 to this Act,

shall be liable[1] on summary conviction to a fine not exceeding **level 5** on the standard scale or to imprisonment for a term not exceeding **six months** or to **both**.

(5) A person guilty of an offence under section 79(7) above shall be liable, on summary conviction, to a fine not exceeding the **statutory maximum** and, on conviction on indictment, to imprisonment for a term not exceeding **two years** or to a **fine** or to **both**.

(6) A person guilty of an offence under any provision of this Act other than those mentioned in subsections (1) to (5) above shall be liable on summary conviction to a fine not exceeding **level 5** on the standard scale.

(7) The Secretary of State may by order alter the penalty imposed by subsection (3) above but such an order shall not impose any penalty exceeding that provided by subsection (6) above.

[Weights and Measures Act 1985, s 84 as amended by SI 1999/503 and SI 2006/659.]

---

1 For procedure in respect of an offence triable either way see the Magistrates' Courts Act 1980, ss 17A–21 in PART I: MAGISTRATES' COURTS, PROCEDURE, ante.

**7.11808 85. Determination of certain questions by Secretary of State** (1) Where in any proceedings for an offence under this Act or any instrument made under it, any question arises as to the accuracy of any weighing or measuring equipment, the court shall at the request of any party to the proceedings, and may if it thinks fit without any such request, refer the question to the Secretary of State, whose decision shall be final.

(2) Except where in any particular proceedings the Secretary of State waives his rights under this subsection, any expenses incurred by the Secretary of State in making any test for the purpose of determining any question referred to him under subsection (1) above shall be paid by such of the parties to the proceedings as the court may by order direct.

[Weights and Measures Act 1985, s 85 as amended by SI 2006/659.]

*Miscellaneous and supplementary*

**7.11809 88. Application to Crown** (1) Her Majesty may by Order in Council provide for the application to the Crown of such of the provisions of this Act or of any instrument made under it as may be specified in the Order, with such exceptions, adaptations and modifications as may be so specified.

(2), (3) *Orders in Council.*

[Weights and Measures Act 1985, s 88.]

**7.11810 89. Saving for use of certain units in wholesale transactions** (1) Except as the Secretary of State may by order otherwise provide, and subject to subsection (2) below, nothing in this Act shall make unlawful the use in any transaction, by agreement between the parties to that transaction, of any unit of measurement which—

(*a*) was customarily used for trade in the like transactions immediately before 31st July 1963, and

(*b*) is not inconsistent with anything for the time being contained in Schedule 1 to this Act,

notwithstanding that the unit in question is not included in Parts I to V of that Schedule.

(2) Subsection (1) above shall not apply in relation to—

(*a*) any retail transaction, or

(*b*) any transaction with respect to which provision to the contrary effect is made by or under Part IV of this Act.

[Weights and Measures Act 1985, s 89.]

**7.11811 92. Spelling of "gram", etc** No provision contained in or made under this or any other Act prevents the use of "gram" or "gramme" as alternative ways of spelling that unit, and the same applies for other units in the metric system which are compounds of "gram".

[Weights and Measures Act 1985, s 92.]

**7.11812 94. General interpretation** (1) Except where the context otherwise requires, in this Act—

"approved verifier" has the meaning given by section 11(6A) above;
"capacity measurement" means measurement in terms of a unit of measurement included in Part IV of Schedule 1 to this Act;
"check-weighed", in relation to any vehicle, means weighed with its load by means of the nearest suitable and available weighing equipment, and weighed again after it has been unloaded by means of the same or other suitable weighing equipment;
"chief inspector" means a chief inspector of weights and measures appointed under section 72(1) above;
"container" includes any form of packaging of goods for sale as a single item, whether by way of wholly or partly enclosing the goods[1] or by way of attaching the goods to, or winding the goods round, some other article, and in particular includes a wrapper or confining band;
"contravention", in relation to any requirement, includes a failure to comply with that requirement, and cognate expressions shall be construed accordingly;
"credentials", in relation to an inspector, means authority in writing from the local weights and measures authority who appointed him for the exercise by that inspector of powers conferred on inspectors by this Act;
"Department for Business, Innovation and Skills standards" means the secondary, tertiary and coinage standards maintained by the Secretary of State under section 3 above;
"drugs" and "food" have the same meanings respectively as for the purposes of the Food Safety Act 1990;
"the FIC Regulation" means Regulation (EU) No 1169/2011 of the European Parliament and of the Council on the provision of food information to consumers;
"gross weight", in relation to any goods, means the aggregate weight of the goods and any container in or on which they are made up;
"indication of quantity", in relation to any container in or on which goods are made up, means a statement in writing to the effect that those goods are of, or of not less than, a specified quantity by net weight, gross weight or other measurement or by number, as the case may require;
"industrial use", in relation to any goods, means the use of those goods in the manufacture of, or for incorporation in, goods of a different description in the course of the carrying on of a business;
"inspector" means an inspector of weights and measures appointed under section 72(1) above;
"intoxicating liquor" means spirits, beer, wine, made-wine or cider as defined in section 1 of the Alcoholic Liquor Duties Act 1979;
"local standard" means a standard maintained under section 4 above;
"mark" includes label;
"occupier", in relation to any stall, vehicle, ship or aircraft or in relation to the use of any place for any purpose, means the person for the time being in charge of the stall, vehicle, ship or aircraft or, as the case may be, the person for the time being using that place for that purpose;
"packaged goods regulations" means the Weights and Measures (Packaged Goods) Regulations 2006;
"premises", except in section 45 above, includes any place and any stall, vehicle, ship or aircraft;
"pre-packed" means made up in advance ready for retail sale in or on a container;
"prescribed" means prescribed by the Secretary of State by regulations;
"secondary standard" means a standard maintained under section 3(2) above;
"ship" includes any boat and any other description of vessel used in navigation;
"stamp" means, subject to section 15A(4) above, a mark for use as evidence of the passing of weighing or measuring equipment as fit for use for trade, whether applied by impressing, casting, engraving, etching, branding, or otherwise, and cognate expressions shall be construed accordingly;
"tertiary standard" means a standard maintained under section 3(3) above;
"testing equipment" means testing equipment maintained under section 5 above;
"United Kingdom primary standard" means a standard maintained under section 2 above;
"use for trade" shall be construed in accordance with section 7 above;
"weighing or measuring equipment" means equipment for measuring in terms of length, area, volume, capacity, weight or number, whether or not the equipment is constructed to give an indication of the measurement made or other information determined by reference to that measurement;
"working standard" means a standard maintained under section 5 above.

(2) In any provision of this Act "designated country" means such, if any, of the following, that is to say, Northern Ireland, any of the Channel Islands and the Isle of Man, as the Secretary of State, having regard to the law for the time being in force there, thinks it proper to designate for the purposes of that provision by order.

(3) On any premises where articles of any description are—

(*a*) made up in advance ready for retail sale in or on a container, or

(*b*) kept or stored for sale after being so made up,

any article of that description found made up in or on a container shall be deemed to be pre-packed unless the contrary is proved; and it shall not be sufficient proof of the contrary to show that the container has not been marked in accordance with the requirements of this Act or any instrument made under it with respect to the pre-packing of such articles.

(4) Except where the context otherwise requires, any reference in this Act to any person, other than a reference to an inspector, shall be construed as a reference to that person or some other person acting on his behalf in the matter in question.

[Weights and Measures Act 1985, s 94 as amended by the Food Safety Act 1990, Sch 3, the Statute Law (Repeals) Act 1993, Sch 1, SI 1999/503, SI 2006/659, SI 2007/3224, SI 2009/2748 and SI 2014/2975.]

---

1 For a case in which a piece of greaseproof paper adhering to goods was held not to be "packaging", see *Lucas v Rushby* [1966] 2 All ER 302, 130 JP 279.

7.11813 **96. Transitional provisions and savings** (1) Schedule 11 to this Act (which contains transitional provisions and savings) shall have effect.

(2) The re-enactment—

(*a*) in section 84(3) of, and Part IV of Schedule 5 to, this Act, of provisions contained in the Weights and Measures (Solid Fuel) (Carriage by Rail) Order 1966, and

(*b*) in paragraphs 12 to 17, 22 and 25 of Schedule 11 to this Act, of provisions contained in the Units of Measurement Regulations 1978 and the Units of Measurement Regulations 1980,

shall be without prejudice to the validity of those provisions; and any question as to the validity of any of those provisions shall be determined as if the re-enacting provision of this Act were contained in a statutory instrument made under the powers under which the original provision was made.

(3) The provisions of Schedule 11 to this Act are without prejudice to the operation of sections 16 and 17 of the Interpretation Act 1978 (which relate to the effect of repeals).

[Weights and Measures Act 1985, s 96.]

# SCHEDULES

## SCHEDULE 1

## DEFINITIONS OF UNITS OF MEASUREMENT

Sections 1(2), 8(1)

7.11814

*(As amended by SI 1994/2867.)*

### PART I

### MEASUREMENT OF LENGTH

Metric units

Kilometre = 1000 metres.

METRE is the length of the path travelled by light in vacuum during a time interval of 1/299 792 458 of a second.

Decimetre = 1/10 metre.

Centimetre = 1/100 metre.

Millimetre = 1/1000 metre.

### PART II

### MEASUREMENT OF AREA

Metric units

Hectare = 100 ares.

Decare = 10 ares.

Are = 100 square metres.

SQUARE METRE = a superficial area equal to that of a square each side of which measures one metre.

Square decimetre = 1/100 square metre.

Square centimetre = 1/100 square decimetre.

Square millimetre = 1/100 square centimetre.

### PART III

### MEASUREMENT OF VOLUME

Metric units

Hectare = 100 ares.

Decare = 10 ares.

Are = 100 square metres.

SQUARE METRE = a superficial area equal to that of a square each side of which measures one metre.

Square decimetre = 1/100 square metre.

Square centimetre = 1/100 square decimetre.

Square millimetre = 1/100 square centimetre.

### PART IV

### MEASUREMENT OF CAPACITY

Imperial unit

PINT = 0.568 261 25 cubic decimetre.

Metric units

Hectolitre = 100 litres.

LITRE = a cubic decimetre.

Decilitre = 1/10 litre.

Centilitre = 1/100 litre.

Millilitre = 1/1000 litre.

## PART V
## MEASUREMENT OF MASS OR WEIGHT

Imperial unit

OUNCE TROY = 0.031 103 476 8 kilogram.

Metric units

Tonne, metric tonne = 1000 kilograms.
KILOGRAM is the unit of mass; it is equal to the mass of the international prototype of the kilogram.
Hectogram = 1/10 kilogram.
Gram = 1/1000 kilogram.
Carat (metric) = 1/5 gram.
Milligram = 1/1000 gram.

## PART VI
## DEFINITIONS OF CERTAIN UNITS WHICH MAY NOT BE USED FOR TRADE EXCEPT AS SUPPLEMENTARY INDICATIONS
### MEASUREMENT OF LENGTH

| | | |
|---|---|---|
| | Measurement of length | |
| Mile | = | 1760 yards. |
| Furlong | = | 220 yards. |
| Chain | = | 22 yards. |
| YARD | = | 0.9144 metre. |
| Foot | = | 1/3 yard. |
| Inch | = | 1/36 yard. |
| | Measurement of area | |
| Square mile | = | 640 acres. |
| Acre | = | 4840 square yards. |
| Rood | = | 1210 square yards. |
| Square yard | = | a superficial area equal to that of a square each side of which measures one yard. |
| Square foot | = | 1/9 square yard. |
| Square inch | = | 1/144 square foot. |
| | Measurement of volume | |
| Cubic yard | = | a volume equal to that of a cube each edge of which measures one yard. |
| Cubic foot | = | 1/27 cubic yard. |
| Cubic inch | = | 1/1728 cubic foot. |
| | Measurement of capacity | |
| Bushel | = | 8 gallons. |
| Peck | = | 2 gallons. |
| GALLON | = | 4.546 09 cubic decimetres. |
| Quart | = | 1/4 gallon. |
| Gill | = | 1/4 pint. |
| Fluid ounce | = | 1/20 pint. |
| Fluid drachm | = | 1/8 fluid ounce. |
| Minim | = | 1/60 fluid drachm. |
| | Measurement of mass or weight | |
| Ton | = | 2240 pounds. |
| Hundredweight | = | 112 pounds. |
| Cental | = | 100 pounds. |
| Quarter | = | 28 pounds. |
| Stone | = | 14 pounds. |
| POUND | = | 0.453 592 37 kilogram. |
| Ounce | = | 1/16 pound. |
| Dram | = | 1/16 ounce. |
| Grain | = | 1/7000 pound. |
| Pennyweight | = | 24 grains. |
| Ounce apothecaries | = | 480 grains. |
| Drachm | = | 1/8 ounce apothecaries. |
| Scruple | = | 1/3 drachm. |
| Metric ton | = | 1000 kilograms. |
| Quintal | = | 100 kilograms. |

## PART VII
## MEASUREMENT OF ELECTRICITY

1.

(*a*) AMPERE is that constant current which, if maintained in two straight parallel conductors of infinite length, of negligible circular cross-section and placed 1 metre apart in vacuum, would produce between these conductors a force equal to 2 x 10 (to the power of minus seven) newton per metre of length.

(*b*) OHM is the electric resistance between two points of a conductor when a constant potential difference of 1 volt, applied between the two points, produces in the conductor a current of 1 ampere, the conductor not being the seat of any electromotive force.

(*c*) VOLT is the difference of electric potential between two points of a conducting wire carrying a constant current of 1 ampere when the power dissipated between these points is equal to 1 watt.

(*d*) WATT is the power which in one second gives rise to energy of 1 joule.

2.

Kilowatt = 1000 watts.
Megawatt = one million watts.

## SCHEDULE 2
### EXISTING UNITED KINGDOM PRIMARY STANDARDS AND AUTHORISED COPIES

Section 2(3)

## SCHEDULE 3
### MEASURES AND WEIGHTS LAWFUL FOR USE FOR TRADE

Section 8(1)

**7.11815**

*(As amended by SI 1994/1883 and 2866 and SI 2001/1322.)*

## PART I
## LINEAR MEASURES

1. *Revoked*

*Metric system*

2. Measures of—

| | |
|---|---|
| 50 metres | 2 metres |
| 30 metres | 1.5 metres |
| 20 metres | 1 metre |
| 10 metres | 0.5 metre |
| 5 metres | 1 decimetre |
| 3 metres | 1 centimetre |

## PART II
## SQUARE MEASURES

1. *Revoked*

*Metric system*

2. Measures of, or of any multiple of, 1 square decimetre.

## PART III
## CUBIC MEASURES

*Metric system*

1. Measures of, or of any multiple of, 0.1 cubic metre.
2. Measures of—

| | |
|---|---|
| any multiple of 10 litres | |
| 10 litres | 100 millilitres |
| 5 litres | 50 millilitres |
| 2.5 litres | 25 millilitres |
| 2 litres | 20 millilitres |
| 1 litre | 10 millilitres |
| 500 millilitres | 5 millilitres |
| 250 millilitres | 2 millilitres |
| 200 millilitres | 1 millilitre |

## Part IV
## Capacity Measures
*Imperial system*

1. Measures of—

16 pints
8 pints
4 pints
2 pints
1 pint
1/2 pint
1/3 pint

*Metric system*

2. Measures of—

any multiple of 10 litres
10 litres
5 litres
2.5 litres
2 litres
1 litre
500 millilitres
250 millilitres
200 millilitres
175 millilitres
150 millilitres
125 millilitres
100 millilitres
70 millilitres
50 millilitres
35 millilitres
25 millilitres
20 millilitres
10 millilitres
5 millilitres
2 millilitres
1 millilitre

## Part V
## Weights
*Imperial system*

1. *Repealed.*
2. Weights of—

500 ounces troy
400 ounces troy
300 ounces troy
200 ounces troy
100 ounces troy
50 ounces troy
40 ounces troy
30 ounces troy
20 ounces troy
10 ounces troy
5 ounces troy
4 ounces troy
3 ounces troy
2 ounces troy
1 ounce troy
0.5 ounce troy
0.4 ounce troy
0.3 ounce troy
0.2 ounce troy
0.1 ounce troy
0.05 ounce troy
0.04 ounce troy
0.03 ounce troy
0.025 ounce troy
0.02 ounce troy
0.01 ounce troy
0.005 ounce troy
0.004 ounce troy
0.003 ounce troy
0.002 ounce troy
0.001 ounce troy

*Metric system*

3. Weights of—

25 kilograms
20 kilograms
10 kilograms
3 grams
2 grams
1 gram

| | |
|---|---|
| 5 kilograms | 500 milligrams |
| 2 kilograms | 400 milligrams |
| 1 kilogram | 300 milligrams |
| 500 grams | 200 milligrams |
| 200 grams | 150 milligrams |
| 100 grams | 100 milligrams |
| 50 grams | 50 milligrams |
| 20 grams | 20 milligrams |
| 15 grams | 10 milligrams |
| 10 grams | 5 milligrams |
| 5 grams | 2 milligrams |
| 4 grams | 1 milligram |

4. Weights of—

| | |
|---|---|
| 500 carats (metric) | 1 carat (metric) |
| 200 carats (metric) | 0.5 carat (metric) |
| 100 carats (metric) | 0.25 carat (metric) |
| 50 carats (metric) | 0.2 carat (metric) |
| 20 carats (metric) | 0.1 carat (metric) |
| 10 carats (metric) | 0.05 carat (metric) |
| 5 carats (metric) | 0.02 carat (metric) |
| 2 carats (metric) | 0.01 carat (metric) |

## SCHEDULE 3A
### Approvals under section 11A

Section 11A

7.11816

*(As inserted by SI 1999/503.)*

### PART I
### APPROVALS: GENERAL

## SCHEDULE 4
### SAND AND OTHER BALLAST

Section 21

7.11817

*(As amended by SI 1994/2866 and SI 2009/663.)*

### PART I
### GENERAL PROVISIONS

1. In this Schedule, "ballast" means any of the following materials, that is to say—
   (*a*) sand, gravel, shingle, ashes and clinker of any description,
   (*b*) broken slag, slag chippings, granite chippings, limestone chippings, slate chippings and other stone chippings (including such materials which have been coated with tar, bitumen or cement),
   (*c*) any other material commonly used in the building and civil engineering industries as a hardcore or an aggregate, and
   (*d*) any other material commonly known in those industries as ballast.

2. Subject to paragraphs 3 and 11 below, ballast—
   (*a*) if made up in advance ready for retail sale or wholesale in a securely closed container, shall be sold only by volume or by net weight, and
   (*b*) if not so made up, shall be sold only by volume in a multiple of 0.2 cubic metre or by net weight.

3. There shall be exempted from the requirements of paragraph 2 above—
   (*a*) ballast in a quantity both less than 1 tonne and less than one cubic metre.
   (*b*) any sale with a view to its industrial use of ballast of any description mentioned in paragraph 1(*b*), (*c*) or (*d*) above,
   (*c*) any sale in the case of which the buyer is to take delivery in or from a ship,
   (*d*) any sale as a whole of ballast produced in the demolition or partial demolition of a building where the buyer is responsible for the removal of the ballast from the site of the building, and
   (*e*) any sale in the state in which it was produced of clinker or ashes produced as a by-product, or of any other ballast produced as a casual product, of the carrying on of an industrial process on any premises or of the mining of coal where the buyer is responsible for the removal of the ballast from those premises or, as the case may be, from the colliery tip.

4. Without prejudice to section 15 of this Act, no article shall be used for trade as a cubic measure of ballast other than a receptacle (which may, if so desired, form part of a vehicle) which conforms with such requirements as to form, capacity, calibration and other matters as may be prescribed[1]; and any person who uses for trade, or has in his possession for use for trade, as a cubic measure of ballast any article other than such a receptacle shall be guilty of an offence[2].

5. In measuring any ballast against a calibration mark on such a receptacle as mentioned in paragraph 4 above, the ballast shall be filled into all parts of the receptacle as far as, and be levelled off against, that calibration mark as nearly as the nature of the ballast will permit; and where any ballast is measured for the purposes of trade in such a receptacle, any person who—

(*a*) being the person carrying out the measuring, fails so to level off the ballast when it is loaded into the receptacle, or

(*b*) causes or permits a heaped load to be sent out in the receptacle,

shall be guilty of an offence[2].

---

[1] See the Cubic Measures (Ballast and Agricultural Materials) 1978, SI 1978/1962 amended by SI 1988/765.

[2] For penalty see s 84, ante.

## PART II

## CARRIAGE OF BALLAST BY ROAD

**6.** This Part of this Schedule shall have effect with respect to the carriage of ballast by a road vehicle on a journey any part of which is along a highway.

**7.** (1) If any of the ballast is being carried for delivery to a buyer in pursuance of, or of an agreement for, its sale and paragraph 2 above applies to the sale, the following provisions of this paragraph shall have effect with respect to that ballast.

(2) There shall, before the journey begins, be delivered to the person in charge of the vehicle a document signed by or on behalf of the seller (in this paragraph referred to as "the delivery document") stating—

(*a*) the name and address of the seller,

(*b*) the name of the buyer, and the address of the premises to which the ballast is being delivered,

(*c*) the type of the ballast,

(*d*) subject to sub-paragraph (4) below, the quantity of the ballast either by net weight or by volume,

(*e*) sufficient particulars to identify the vehicle, and

(*f*) the place, date and time of the loading of the ballast in the vehicle.

(3) Where the quantity of the ballast is stated in the delivery document by volume, the ballast shall be carried on the vehicle only in such a receptacle as is mentioned in paragraph 4 above.

(4) The statement referred to in sub-paragraph (2)(*d*) above shall not be required at any time while the vehicle is travelling between the place where it was loaded and the nearest suitable and available weighing equipment if the whole of the vehicle's load is being delivered to the same person at the same premises and the delivery document states that the quantity of the ballast is to be expressed by net weight determined by means of that equipment and specifies the place at which the equipment is situated.

(5) In any case to which sub-paragraph (4) above applies, the person in charge of the vehicle at the time when the net weight of the ballast is determined shall forthwith add to the delivery document a statement of that net weight, and if he fails so to do he shall be guilty of an offence[1].

(6) If any of the provisions of sub-paragraph (2) or (3) above is contravened, the seller shall be guilty of an offence[1].

(7) If the vehicle is carrying ballast as mentioned in sub-paragraph (1) above for delivery to each of two or more persons, sub-paragraphs (1) to (3) above shall apply separately in relation to each of those persons; but this sub-paragraph shall not be construed as prohibiting the use of the same receptacle such as is mentioned in sub-paragraph (3) above for the carriage of ballast for delivery to two or more different persons.

**8.** (1) Subject to sub-paragraph (2) below, if all or any of the ballast on the vehicle is being carried in such circumstances that paragraph 7 above does not apply to it, there shall before the journey begins be delivered to the person in charge of the vehicle a document containing a statement to that effect signed by or on behalf of the person causing that ballast to be carried and giving the name and address of the last-mentioned person, and if this paragraph is contravened the last-mentioned person shall be guilty of an offence[1].

(2) Sub-paragraph (1) above shall not apply where all the ballast in the vehicle is being carried in such circumstances that paragraph 7 does not apply to it and is being so carried in a container which does not form part of the vehicle.

**9.** Any document required by paragraph 7 or 8 above shall at all times during the journey be carried by the person for the time being in charge of the vehicle and shall be handed over by him to any other person to whom he hands over the charge of the vehicle in the course of the journey; and in the case of any document such as is mentioned in paragraph 7 above, on the unloading of the ballast to which the document relates at the premises to which that ballast is to be delivered—

(*a*) before any of that ballast is so unloaded, the document shall be handed over to the buyer, or

(*b*) if the document cannot be so handed over by reason of the absence of the buyer, it shall be left at some suitable place at those premises;

and if at any time any of the provisions of this paragraph is contravened without reasonable cause, the person in charge of the vehicle at that time shall be guilty of an offence[1].

**10.** In the case of any document such as is mentioned in paragraph 7 above, if at any time during the journey or on unloading at the place of delivery the quantity of the ballast to which the document relates is found to be less than that stated in the document, the statement shall nevertheless be deemed for the purposes of this Act to be correct if, but only if, it is proved that the deficiency is solely attributable to the draining away of normal moisture from, or the consolidation of, the ballast during the journey.

## PART III

*Application to Scotland*

---

[1] For penalty see s 84, ante.

## SCHEDULE 5

Section 21

*(As amended by SI 1987/216, the Coal Industry Act 1987, Sch 1, the Coal Industry Act 1994, Schs 9 and 11, SI 1994/2866 and 2867 and SI 2009/663.)*

## SOLID FUEL

## PART I
## GENERAL

*Introductory*

**7.11818** **1.** This Schedule applies to goods of any of the following descriptions (in this Schedule referred to as "solid fuel"), that is to say—
(*a*) coal,
(*b*) coke, and
(*c*) any solid fuel derived from coal or of which coal or coke is a constituent.

*Sales by net weight*

**2.** (1) Subject to sub-paragraphs (2) and (3) below, solid fuel shall be sold only by net weight.
(2) There shall be exempted from the requirements of sub-paragraph (1) above—
(*a*) briquettes in a quantity not exceeding 7.5 kilograms, and
(*b*) any solid fuel pre-packed in a securely closed container marked with an indication of quantity by net weight.
(3) In the case of any area in Scotland which the Secretary of State may by order specify for the purposes of this sub-paragraph, solid fuel for delivery in that area may be sold by volume in a quantity of 0.2 cubic metre or a multiple of 0.2 cubic metre.

*Quantities in containers*

**3.** (1) Solid fuel—
(*a*) if made up in advance ready for retail sale or wholesale in a securely closed container, shall be sold only by net weight, and
(*b*) if not so made up, shall be sold only in one of the following quantities by net weight, namely—
(i) 25 kilograms;
(ii) 50 kilograms;
(iii) any multiple of 50 kilograms.
(2) *Repealed.*
(3) *Repealed.*
(4) This paragraph and paragraphs 4, 5 and 6 below have effect subject to the exemptions in paragraph 7.

*Indication of quantity*

**4.** (1) This paragraph applies to solid fuel made up in a container for sale, or for delivery after sale, except where it is made up in a container which is not securely closed.
(2) The solid fuel shall be made up in a container for sale, or for delivery after sale, only if the container is marked with an indication of quantity by net weight.
**5.** *Repealed.*

*Information about containers*

**6.** (1) This paragraph applies where solid fuel is carried on a road vehicle on a highway for sale, or for delivery after sale, and is made up in containers which are not securely closed or is delivered from the vehicle in such containers.
(2) There shall be displayed on the vehicle—
(*a*) an indication of the quantity, or quantities, by net weight of the fuel comprised in the containers (other than any securely closed containers) on, or delivered from, the vehicle, and
(*b*) a statement of the name and address of the seller.
(3) Regulations[1] under section 23 of this Act may prescribe the manner in which the information required by sub-paragraph (2) above is to be displayed, and a person who contravenes any such regulation shall be guilty of an offence[2].
(4) If this paragraph is contravened, the seller, and any other person who is in charge of the vehicle at the time of the contravention, shall each be guilty of an offence[2].

*Exemptions*

**7.** There shall be exempted from all the requirements of paragraphs 3, 4, 5 and 6 above—
(*a*) solid fuel supplied under arrangements made in the coal industry for the supply of solid fuel to persons who are or have been employed in that industry or to the dependants of such persons;
(*b*) solid fuel made up in a container only for ease of handling as part of the load of a vehicle or ship where the whole of that load so far as it consists of solid fuel is being delivered to a single buyer.

*Vending machines*

**8.** Solid fuel shall be sold by means of, or offered or exposed for sale in, a vending machine only if there is displayed on or in the machine—
(*a*) an indication of the quantity by net weight of the fuel comprised in each item for sale by means of that machine; and
(*b*) except where the machine is on premises at which the seller carries on business, a statement of the name and address of the seller.

*Byelaws*

**9.** A local weights and measures authority may make byelaws, subject to the confirmation of the Secretary of State—
(*a*) for securing that on any premises within their area on or from which solid fuel available for purchase in a quantity of 100 kilograms or less is sold or kept or exposed for sale there is displayed a notice specifying the price of the fuel;
(*b*) prohibiting the sale on or from any such premises of any such fuel at a higher price than that so displayed in relation to that fuel; and
(*c*) prescribing penalties not exceeding level 2[3] on the standard scale for any offence under such byelaws.

*Damping of fuel*

**10.** Any person who with intent to defraud or deceive[4] damps any solid fuel shall be guilty of an offence[2].

*Sale of fuel from vehicles*

**11.** (1) This paragraph applies to any vehicle which is used on highways for carrying solid fuel for sale, or for delivery after sale; and in this paragraph "container" means any container in which solid fuel is carried on such a vehicle, or is delivered from such a vehicle.

(2) The Secretary of State may by order make provision—

(*a*) for securing the display on any such vehicle of an indication of the quantities in which solid fuel is made up in containers;

(*b*) for requiring all containers carried on or delivered from any one vehicle to be made up in the same quantity, or for regulating in any other way the quantities in which they are made up;

(*c*) for imposing any requirement as to the loading of the vehicle, or the delivery of solid fuel from the vehicle, which appears to the Secretary of State appropriate for securing that purchasers are not misled as to the quantity of fuel they purchase.

(3) Any order under sub-paragraph (2) above may—

(*a*) make provision for any of the purposes mentioned in that sub-paragraph by means of amending, or of applying with or without modifications, or of excluding the application in whole or in part of, any of the preceding paragraphs of this Schedule;

(*b*) contain such consequential, incidental or supplementary provision, whether of such kinds as aforesaid or otherwise, as appear to the Secretary of State to be expedient;

(*c*) may in particular make provision, in respect of contraventions of the order for which no penalty is provided by this Act, for the imposition of penalties not exceeding those provided by section 84(6) of this Act for an offence under this Act.

**12.** An order under section 22 of this Act may amend or repeal any of the preceding paragraphs of this Schedule.

---

[1] The Weights and Measures (Solid Fuel) Regulations 1978, post, have been made.

[2] For penalty see s 84, ante.

[3] A byelaw in force at 17 July 1978 and then providing for a maximum fine of £20 now has a maximum of £50 (Criminal Law Act 1977, s 31(2) and (3). Where the maximum was an amount less than £20 it remains the same. This provision is continued in force by Sch 11, para 24 of this Act.

[4] To deceive is by falsehood to induce a state of mind; to defraud is by deceit to induce a course of action whether in doing something or refraining from something (*Re London and Globe Finance Corpn Ltd* [1903] 1 Ch 728, 82 JP Jo 447; *R v Wines* [1953] 2 All ER 1497, 118 JP 49). This statement of law was discussed at length in *Welham v DPP* [1961] AC 103, [1960] 1 All ER 805, 124 JP 280, HL; affg sub nom *R v Welham* [1960] 2 QB 445, [1960] 1 All ER 260, 124 JP 156, CCA, in which it was held that it was not an ingredient of an intent to defraud that there shall be economic loss; the intention may be by deceit to induce a person to act to his detriment in a manner contrary to his duty.

## Part II
## Weighing of Solid Fuel at Buyer's Request

**13.** If in the case of any solid fuel sold otherwise than by means of a vending machine the buyer so requests—

(*a*) with respect to any of that fuel the delivery of which has not at the time of the request been completed, or

(*b*) if the request is made before the departure from the premises at which the fuel is delivered of the person delivering it, with respect to any of that fuel the delivery of which has been completed but which is still capable of identification,

the seller shall cause the fuel to be weighed by means of suitable weighing equipment in the presence of the buyer and, in the case of any fuel such as is mentioned in sub-paragraph (*a*) of this paragraph, before the delivery of that fuel is completed; and if this paragraph is contravened, the seller shall be guilty of an offence.

**14.** Where a request under paragraph 13 above is made in respect of the whole load of a vehicle, the requirements of that paragraph shall be deemed to be satisfied, notwithstanding that the weighing is not done in the presence of the buyer, if the seller causes the vehicle to be check-weighed and the statements of the weights found by the person or persons attending to the check-weighing to be delivered to the buyer.

**15.** Where after any weighing in pursuance of a request under paragraph 13 above the weight of the solid fuel is found to be not less than that marked on any container in which the fuel was made up or than that stated by the seller in any document delivered to the buyer at or before the delivery of the fuel to him, the buyer shall be liable to repay to the seller all costs reasonably incurred by the seller in connection with the weighing.

## Part III
## Carriage of Solid Fuel by Road

**16.** This Part of this Schedule shall have effect with respect to the carriage by a road vehicle on a journey any part of which is along a highway of any solid fuel required by paragraph 2 above to be sold only by net weight (in this Part of this Schedule referred to as "relevant goods").

**17.** (1) If the vehicle is carrying any relevant goods for delivery to a buyer in pursuance of, or of an agreement for, a sale of a quantity exceeding 110 kilograms, then, subject to sub-paragraph (6) below, there shall before the journey begins be delivered to the person in charge of the vehicle a document signed by or on behalf of the seller (in this paragraph referred to as "the delivery document") stating—

(*a*) the name and address of the seller,

(*b*) the name of the buyer and the address of the premises to which the goods to which the document relates are being delivered,

(*c*) the type of those goods,

(*d*) subject to sub-paragraph (2) below, the aggregate net weight of those goods, and

(*e*) where any of those goods are made up in containers—

(i) the number of those containers, and

(ii) except where the whole of the relevant goods carried on the vehicle are for delivery to a single buyer, and except where the whole of the vehicle's load consists of such solid fuel as is mentioned in paragraph 7(*a*) above, the net weight of the goods in each of those containers;

and if this sub-paragraph is contravened the seller shall be guilty of an offence[1].

(2) Where the whole of the vehicle's load consists of relevant goods not made up in containers and is being delivered to the same person at the same premises, the statement referred to in sub-paragraph (1)(*d*) above shall not be required at any time while the vehicle is travelling between the place where it was loaded and the nearest suitable and available weighing equipment if the delivery document states that the quantity of the relevant goods is to be expressed by net weight determined by means of that equipment and specifies the place at which the equipment is situated.

(3) In any case to which sub-paragraph (2) above applies, the person in charge of the vehicle at the time when the net weight of the relevant goods is determined shall forthwith add to the delivery document a statement of that net weight, and if he fails so to do he shall be guilty of an offence[1].

(4) Subject to sub-paragraph (5) below, if the vehicle is carrying relevant goods to which sub-paragraph (1) above applies for delivery to each of two or more buyers—

(*a*) that sub-paragraph shall apply separately in relation to each of those buyers, and

(*b*) the relevant goods for delivery to each respectively of those buyers shall be carried on the vehicle made up separately in containers or in separate compartments;

and if paragraph (*b*) of this sub-paragraph is contravened the seller shall be guilty of an offence[1].

(5) Sub-paragraph (4)(*b*) above shall not apply where the vehicle is constructed or adapted for the mechanical making up in containers of the fuel carried thereon and incorporates weighing equipment approved by the Secretary of State for that purpose.

(6) Sub-paragraph (1) above shall not apply to any goods which to the knowledge of the seller are to be loaded into a ship before their delivery to the buyer.

**18.** (1) Subject to sub-paragraph (2) below, if all or any of the relevant goods on the vehicle are being carried in such circumstances that paragraph 17(1) above does not apply, there shall, before the journey begins, be delivered to the person in charge of the vehicle a document signed by or on behalf of the person causing the goods to be carried giving the name and address of the last-mentioned person and containing a statement to the effect that all or part of the relevant goods on the vehicle are goods to which paragraph 17(1) above does not apply, and if this paragraph is contravened the last-mentioned person shall be guilty of an offence[1].

(2) Sub-paragraph (1) above shall not apply where the total quantity of the relevant goods carried on the vehicle does not exceed 110 kilograms.

**19.** Any document required by paragraph 17 or 18 above shall at all times during the journey be carried by the person for the time being in charge of the vehicle and shall be handed over by him to any other person to whom he hands over the charge of the vehicle in the course of the journey; and in the case of any document such as is mentioned in paragraph 17 above, on the unloading of the goods to which the document relates at the premises to which those goods are to be delivered—

(*a*) before any of those goods are so unloaded, the document shall be handed over to the buyer, or

(*b*) if the document cannot be so handed over by reason of the absence of the buyer, it shall be left at some suitable place at those premises[2];

and if at any time any of the requirements of this paragraph is contravened without reasonable cause, the person in charge of the vehicle at that time shall be guilty of an offence[1].

---

[1] For penalty, see s 84, ante.

[2] In connection with this paragraph, reference may be made to the following cases decided under s 21 of the Weights and Measures Act 1889 (repealed and replaced by this Part of this Schedule); *Stangoe v Slatter* (1896) 60 JP 342; *Kyle v Dunsdon* [1908] 2 KB 293, 72 JP 293; *Lucas v Hodson* [1919] 1 KB 6, 83 JP 15.

## PART IV

## CARRIAGE OF SOLID FUEL BY RAIL

**20.** Where any seller of solid fuel causes that fuel to be loaded into a rail vehicle by way of, or for the purpose of, the delivery of that fuel to, or to a person nominated in that behalf by, the buyer, and the fuel is not carried on the vehicle made up in containers, then, except where at the time of loading it is known to the seller that before the fuel is delivered to the consignee it is to be loaded into a ship, paragraphs 21 to 25 below shall apply in relation to that vehicle.

**21.** Subject to paragraphs 22 and 28 below, the vehicle shall not be loaded until its tare weight has been determined or redetermined by means of suitable weighing equipment at the place of loading.

**22.** (1) Paragraph 21 above shall not apply to any rail vehicle which forms part of or is intended to form part of a train conveying only fuel destined for a particular generating station, gas works or other industrial undertaking if—

(*a*) the vehicle is loaded by equipment which weighs the fuel and discharges it directly into the vehicle, or

(*b*) the buyer has agreed with the seller that the weight of the load shall be ascertained at the vehicle's destination, or

(*c*) the buyer has agreed to accept as the tare weight of the vehicle a tare weight ascertained not more than three months before the time of loading and the vehicle has marked upon it in durable lettering a statement of the weight so ascertained and of the date and place at which it was ascertained, or

(*d*) all the vehicles comprised in the train are coupled together in such a manner that they may be weighed while in motion by equipment designed to determine the total weight of the train, and the buyer has agreed with the seller that the total net weight of fuel carried in the train shall be ascertained by deducting the total weight of the train so determined before loading from the total weight thereof so determined when loaded.

(2) Nothing in sub-paragraph (1)(*c*) above shall afford any exemption from the requirements of paragraph 21 above in the case of a vehicle which has undergone repairs or modification or has suffered substantial damage since its tare weight was last ascertained and marked as mentioned in that sub-paragraph.

**23.** (1) Subject to subparagraph (2) and paragraph 24 below, as soon as the loading has been completed and the seller has ascertained the weight of the vehicle with its load and the identity of the consignee, the seller shall cause to be attached to the vehicle a document stating—

(*a*) the name of the seller and the place and date of weighing,

(*b*) the name of the consignee and the destination of the vehicle,

(*c*) sufficient particulars to identify the vehicle,

(*d*) the tare weight of the vehicle as determined or redetermined in pursuance of paragraph 21 above or, if by virtue of paragraph 28 below paragraph 21 does not apply to the vehicle, the tare weight of the vehicle expressed to be as estimated by the seller,
(*e*) the weight attributed to the solid fuel in the vehicle by the seller for the purpose of calculating its purchase price, and
(*f*) the type of that fuel.

(2) Subparagraph (1) above shall not apply if, at the time of departure of the vehicle from the place of loading, the seller causes to be transmitted to the buyer, for receipt not later than the time of arrival of the vehicle at the buyer's premises, the information required by subparagraphs (*a*) to (*f*) of subparagraph (1) above: Provided that where such information is transmitted otherwise than in a legible form—
(*a*) the seller and the buyer have agreed in writing that the information may be so transmitted;
(*b*) the places of loading and destination of the vehicle are suitably equipped for the transmission and receipt of information in such form; and
(*c*) the information is capable of being reproduced in a permanent legible form by the system effecting the transmission, and is so reproduced if required by an inspector, subject to the production, if so requested, of his credentials.

**24.** (1) Paragraph 23 above shall not apply to any vehicle forming part or intended to form part of any such train as is mentioned in paragraph 22 above, but the seller shall either (*a*) before the departure of the train which includes that vehicle deliver to the authority responsible for railway traffic at the place of loading for carriage on that train a document (in this paragraph and paragraph 25 below referred to as "a train bill") giving the information specified in sub-paragraph (2) below or, in the case of any such train as is mentioned in paragraph 22(1)(*d*) above, sub-paragraph (3) below or (*b*) at the time of departure of the train which includes that vehicle transmit to the buyer, for receipt not later than the time of arrival of the train at the buyer's premises, the information required by subparagraph (2) or, as the case may be, subparagraph (3) below: Provided that where such information is transmitted otherwise than in a legible form—
(*a*) the seller and the buyer have agreed in writing that the information may be so transmitted;
(*b*) the places of loading and destination of the train are suitably equipped for the transmission and receipt of information in such form; and
(*c*) the information is capable of being reproduced in a permanent legible form by the system effecting the transmission, and is so reproduced if required by an inspector, subject to the production, if so requested, of his credentials.

(2) Except in a case to which sub-paragraph (3) below applies, the train bill shall contain the following information—
(*a*) the names of the seller and of the consignee and the destination of the train,
(*b*) sufficient particulars to identify each vehicle in the train,
(*c*) the date and place of loading of each vehicle,
(*d*) a statement of the type of fuel in each vehicle,
(*e*) except in the case of fuel which a buyer has agreed shall be weighed at the train's destination, the weight attributed by the seller to the fuel in each vehicle for the purpose of calculating its purchase price,
(*f*) where any vehicle is not exempted from paragraph 21 above, the tare weight of that vehicle,
(*g*) where any vehicle has been loaded by equipment which weighs fuel and discharges it directly into vehicles, a statement as to the vehicle which has been so loaded,
(*h*) where any vehicle is loaded with fuel the weight of which is to be ascertained at the train's destination, a statement as to the vehicle so loaded,
(*i*) where any vehicle is exempted from paragraph 21 above by reason of paragraph 22(1)(*c*) above, a statement of the tare weight and related particulars marked upon that vehicle, and
(*j*) where any vehicle is so exempt by reason of any certificate or direction under paragraph 28 below, a weight stated to be the seller's estimate of the tare weight of that vehicle.

(3) In the case of any such train as is mentioned in paragraph 22(1)(*d*) above, the train bill shall contain the following information—
(*a*) the names of the seller and the consignee and the destination of the train,
(*b*) the date and place of loading of the train,
(*c*) the number of vehicles in the train,
(*d*) the total net weight of fuel carried in the train,
(*e*) a statement of the type of fuel carried in the train, and
(*f*) a statement that the buyer has agreed that the total net weight of fuel carried in the train shall be ascertained in the manner mentioned in paragraph 22(1)(*d*) above.

(4) If the requirements of sub-paragraph (1) above are contravened, the seller shall be guilty of an offence[1].

**25.** (1) The following provisions of this paragraph apply—
(*a*) in a case where by virtue of paragraph 24 above a train bill is carried, when the train reaches its destination, and
(*b*) in any other case, when the vehicle in question reaches its destination.

(2) The authority responsible for railway traffic at the destination of the train or vehicle, as the case may be, shall—
(*a*) permit the consignee and, subject to the production if so requested of his credentials, any inspector to inspect the document required by paragraph 23 or, as the case may be, 24 above.
(*b*) permit the consignee either to take possession of that document after the train or vehicle is unloaded or to make a copy of the particulars stated therein, and
(*c*) if so requested by the consignee with respect to any such copy which the authority is satisfied is accurate, certify the accuracy thereof,

and if any of the provisions of this sub-paragraph is contravened the authority shall be guilty of an offence[1].

(3) Subject to sub-paragraphs (5) and (6) below, any of the following persons, that is to say—
(*a*) any inspector, subject to the production if so requested of his credentials, or
(*b*) the consignee, subject to his undertaking to pay any cost reasonably incurred,

may require the vehicle to be weighed either before or after or both before and after it is unloaded, and the vehicle shall be weighed accordingly unless it is certified by or on behalf of the authority mentioned in sub-paragraph (2) above that in the circumstances of the particular case the carrying out of the weighing would cause undue dislocation of railway traffic at the vehicle's destination; and any inspector who is present at any such weighing shall if so requested certify the weight found.

(4) If when the fuel is unloaded from the vehicle it is weighed accurately with accurate weighing equipment in the presence of an inspector, the inspector shall if so requested certify that it was so weighed and state in his certificate the weight found.

(5) Where by virtue of paragraph 24 above a train bill is carried and the buyer has agreed that the weight of the fuel in any vehicle is to be ascertained at the train's destination, sub-paragraph (3) above shall not apply in relation to that vehicle.

(6) In a case falling within paragraph 22(1)(*d*) above, sub-paragraph (3) above shall have effect—

(*a*) with the omission of paragraph (*b*), and

(*b*) as if any reference to a vehicle were a reference to a train.

**26.** Where, in the case of any rail vehicle used on a journey to carry solid fuel which is not made up in containers, paragraphs 21 to 25 above do not apply, the consignor shall cause to be attached to the vehicle before it starts on the journey a document stating the name of the consignor and the place of loading of the vehicle.

**27.** (1) If paragraph 21 or 23 above is contravened, the seller shall be guilty of an offence[1].

(2) If paragraph 26 above is contravened, the consignor shall be guilty of an offence[1].

(3) If, in the case of any rail vehicle used on a journey to carry solid fuel—

(*a*) the authority responsible for railway traffic at the place of loading or any person employed by that authority wilfully prevents or impedes the attachment to the vehicle of the document required by paragraph 23 or 26 above, or

(*b*) any person, being a person concerned in the sale, carriage or delivery of that fuel, wilfully removes, defaces or alters any such document attached to the vehicle,

that authority or person shall be guilty of an offence[1].

**28.** (1) *Repealed.*

(2) If any seller of solid fuel who uses any place, for causing solid fuel to be loaded as mentioned in paragraph 20 above makes representations to the Secretary of State that the provision at that place of weighing equipment suitable for determining the tare weight of rail vehicles is not reasonably practicable or would be unjustified on economic grounds and the Secretary of State is satisfied that there are grounds for those representations, the Secretary of State may direct, that subject to such conditions and for such period as may be specified in the direction, paragraph 21 above shall not apply to any vehicle loaded at that place.

(3) *Repealed.*

---

[1] For penalty, see s 84, ante.

## SCHEDULE 6

### Miscellaneous Goods other than Foods

Section 21

**7.11819**

*(As amended by SI 1994/1884 and 2866, SI 2009/663 and SI 2013/1478.)*

### Part I
### Liquid Fuel and Lubricants

**1.** This Part of this Schedule applies to—

(*a*) liquid fuel, lubricating oil and any mixture of such fuel and oil, and

(*b*) lubricating grease.

**2.** Subject to paragraph 3 below, goods to which this Part of this Schedule applies—

(*a*) unless pre-packed, shall be sold only by net weight or by capacity measurement,

(*b*) shall be pre-packed only if the container is marked with an indication of quantity either by net weight or by capacity measurement, and

(*c*) in the case of lubricating oil in a quantity of one litre or less, shall be made up in a container for sale otherwise than by way of pre-packing only if the container is marked with an indication of quantity by capacity measurement.

**3.** Notwithstanding anything in paragraph 2 above, liquid fuel—

(*a*) when not pre-packed may be sold by volume, and

(*b*) may be pre-packed in a container marked with an indication of quantity by volume,

being in either case the volume of the gas which would be produced from the fuel in question at such temperature and such atmospheric pressure as are specified in regulations made by the Secretary of State with respect to fuel of the type in question or, if no such regulations are in force, as may be made known by the seller to the buyer before he pays for or takes possession of the fuel; and there shall be exempted from all requirements of paragraph 2 above goods of any description in a quantity of less than 250 grams or of less than 250 millilitres.

### Part II
### Ready-Mixed Cement Mortar and Ready-Mixed Concrete

**4.** This Part of this Schedule applies to ready-mixed cement mortar and ready-mixed concrete.

**5.** (1) Subject to the following provisions of this Part of this Schedule, any goods to which this Part of this Schedule applies—

(*a*) if made up in advance ready for retail sale or wholesale in a securely closed container, shall be sold only by volume, and

(*b*) if not so made up, shall be sold only by volume in a multiple of 0.1 cubic metre.

(2) There shall be exempted from the requirements of this paragraph any goods in a quantity of less than one cubic metre.

**6.** Part II of Schedule 4 to this Act, except sub-paragraph (3) of paragraph 7, shall apply for the purposes of this Part of this Schedule as if—

(*a*) any reference in the said Part II to ballast included a reference to goods to which this Part of this Schedule applies; and

(*b*) the reference in sub-paragraph (1) of paragraph 7 to paragraph 2 of Schedule 4 were a reference to paragraph 5 of this Schedule.

**7.** Paragraphs 5 and 6 above shall not have effect in any area in Scotland specified by the Secretary of State by order.

## Part III

## Agricultural Liming Materials, Agricultural Salt and Inorganic Fertilisers

**8.** This Part of this Schedule applies—

(*a*) to agricultural liming materials, other than calcareous sand,

(*b*) to agricultural salt,

(*c*) to, and to any mixture consisting mainly of, inorganic fertilisers, other than such fertilisers or such a mixture made up into pellets or other articles for use as individual items, and

(*d*) to any mixture of any of the foregoing.

**9.** (1) Goods to which this Part of this Schedule applies which are not pre-packed, other than liquid fertilisers, shall be sold only by quantity, being—

(*a*) quantity by net weight; or

(*b*) if the goods are sold in a container which does not exceed the permitted weight and the gross weight of the goods is not less than 25 kilograms, quantity either by net weight or by gross weight; or

(*c*) quantity by volume.

(2) Goods to which this Part of this Schedule applies shall be pre-packed only if the container is marked with an indication of quantity, being—

(*a*) in the case of liquid fertilisers, quantity by capacity measurement;

(*b*) in any other case, quantity by net weight or, if the container does not exceed the permitted weight and the gross weight of the goods is not less than 25 kilograms, quantity either by net weight or by gross weight.

(3) In this paragraph, "the permitted weight" means a weight at the rate of 650 grams per 50 kilograms of the gross weight.

(4) There shall be exempted from all requirements of this paragraph any sale of goods with a view to their industrial use.

**10.** Paragraphs 4 and 5 of Schedule 4 to this Act shall have effect as if any reference in those paragraphs to ballast included a reference to any goods to which this Part of this Schedule applies.

## Part IV

## Wood Fuel

**11.** Subject to paragraphs 12 and 13 below—

(*a*) wood fuel which is not made up in a container for sale shall be sold by retail only by net weight;

(*b*) in the case of a sale by retail of wood fuel made up in a container for sale, the quantity by net weight of the fuel sold shall be made known to the buyer before he pays for or takes possession of it.

**12.** (1) Paragraph 11 above shall not have effect in any area unless the local weights and measures authority for that area so direct by byelaw.

(2) Not less than one month before making any byelaw by virtue of this paragraph, the local weights and measures authority shall give public notice of their intention to make it by advertisement in one or more newspapers circulating in the area to which the byelaw is to apply.

(3) The local weights and measures authority by whom any byelaw is made by virtue of this paragraph shall give notice of the making of the byelaw to the Secretary of State.

**13.** There shall be exempted from the requirements of paragraph 11 above any sale of wood fuel in a quantity which does not exceed 7.5 kilograms or which exceeds 500 kilograms.

**14.** Paragraphs 9 and 10 of Schedule 5 to this Act shall have effect as if any reference in those paragraphs to solid fuel included a reference to wood fuel.

## Part VI

## Soap

**16A.** (1) In this Part of this Schedule "soap" does not include any soap which is a cosmetic product.

(2) "Cosmetic product" has the same meaning as in Regulation (EC) 1223/2009 of the European Parliament and of the Council on cosmetic products (recast), as amended from time to time.

**17.** Subject to paragraph 18 below—

(*a*) soap in the form of a cake, tablet or bar shall be pre-packed only if the container is marked with an indication of quantity by net weight,

(*b*) liquid soap shall be pre-packed only if the container is marked with an indication of quantity by capacity measurement, and

(*c*) soap in any other form—

(i) unless pre-packed, shall be sold by retail only by net weight, and

(ii) shall be pre-packed only if the container is marked with an indication of quantity by net weight.

**18.** There shall be exempted from the requirements of this Part of this Schedule—

(*a*) liquid soap in a quantity of less than 125 millilitres, and

(*b*) soap in any other form in a quantity of less than 25 grams.

## Part VII

## Miscellaneous Goods to be Sold by or Marked with Length

**19.** This Part of this Schedule applies to goods of any of the following descriptions, that is to say, bias binding, elastic, ribbon, tape and sewing thread.

**20.** Subject to paragraph 21 below, goods to which this Part of this Schedule applies—

(*a*) unless pre-packed, shall be sold by retail only by length, and

(*b*) shall be pre-packed only if the container is marked with an indication of quantity by length.

**21.** There shall be exempted from all requirements of paragraph 20 above goods of any description in a quantity of less than one metre.

## Part VIII

## Miscellaneous Goods to be Sold by or Marked with Net Weight

**22.** This Part of this Schedule applies to—

(*a*) distemper,

(*b*) articles offered as feed for household pets, being manufactured feed or bird feed, other than animal feed in biscuit or cake form pre-packed in a quantity by number not exceeding sixteen,

(*c*) nails,

(*d*) paste paint,
(*e*) seeds, other than pea or bean seeds, and
(*f*) rolled oats.

**23.** Subject to paragraphs 24 and 25 below, goods to which this Part of this Schedule applies—
(*a*) unless pre-packed, shall be sold by retail only by net weight, and
(*b*) shall be pre-packed only if the container is marked with an indication of quantity by net weight.

**24.** The following shall be exempted from the requirements of this Part of this Schedule—
(*a*) distemper or paste paint in a quantity of less than 250 grams,
(*b*) bird seed in a quantity of less than 125 grams, and
(*c*) any other goods in a quantity of less than 25 grams.

**25.** Notwithstanding anything in paragraph 24 above, nails—
(*a*) when not pre-packed may be sold by retail by number, and
(*b*) may be pre-packed in or on a container marked with an indication of quantity by number.

## Part IX

## Miscellaneous Goods to be Marked when Pre-Packed with Net Weight

**26.** This Part of this Schedule applies to—
(*a*) Portland cement,
(*b*) cleansing powders and scouring powders,
(*c*) detergents, other than liquid detergents, and
(*d*) paint remover, other than liquid paint remover.

**27.** Subject to paragraph 28 below, goods to which this Part of this Schedule applies shall be pre-packed only if the container is marked with an indication of quantity by net weight.

**28.** There shall be exempted from the requirements of this Part of this Schedule goods of any description in a quantity of less than 25 grams.

## Part X

## Miscellaneous Goods to be Sold by or Marked with Capacity Measurement

**29.** This Part of this Schedule applies to antifreeze fluid for internal combustion engines, linseed oil, paint (other than paste paint), paint thinner, turpentine, turpentine substitute, varnish, and wood preservative fluid (including fungicides and insecticides).

**30.** Subject to paragraph 31 below, goods to which this Part of this Schedule applies—
(*a*) unless pre-packed, shall be sold by retail only by capacity measurement, and
(*b*) shall be pre-packed only if the container is marked with an indication of quantity by capacity measurement.

**31.** There shall be exempted from all requirements of this Part of this Schedule goods of any description in a quantity of less than 150 millilitres.

## Part XI

## Miscellaneous Goods to be Marked when Pre-Packed with Capacity Measurement

**32.** This Part of this Schedule applies to enamel, lacquer, liquid detergents, liquid paint remover, petrifying fluid and rust remover.

**33.** Subject to paragraph 34 below, goods to which this Part of this Schedule applies shall be pre-packed only if the container is marked with an indication of quantity by capacity measurement.

**34.** The following shall be exempted from the requirements of paragraph 33 above—
(*a*) liquid detergents in a quantity of less than 125 millilitres, and
(*b*) goods of any other description in a quantity of less than 150 millilitres.

## Part XII

## Miscellaneous Goods to be Sold by or Marked with Net Weight or Capacity Measurement

**35.** This Part of this Schedule applies to—
(*a*) polishes,
(*b*) dressings, analogous to polishes, and
(*c*) pea seeds and bean seeds.

**36.** Subject to paragraph 37 below, goods to which this Part of this Schedule applies—
(*a*) unless pre-packed, shall be sold by retail only by net weight or by capacity measurement, and
(*b*) shall be pre-packed only if the container is marked with an indication of quantity either by net weight or by capacity measurement.

**37.** The following shall be exempted from all the requirements of this Part of this Schedule, that is to say—
(*a*) pea or bean seeds in a quantity of less than 250 grams or of less than 250 millilitres, and
(*b*) any other goods in a quantity of less than 30 grams or of less than 30 millilitres.

## Part XIII

## Miscellaneous Goods to be Marked when Pre-Packed with Quantity by Number

**38.** This Part of this Schedule applies—
(*a*) to cheroots, cigarettes and cigars,
(*b*) to postal stationery, that is to say, paper or cards for use in correspondence, and envelopes,
(*c*) to, and to any mixture consisting mainly of, inorganic fertilisers, being such fertilisers or such a mixture made up into pellets or other articles for use as individual items, and
(*d*) to manufactured animal feed in biscuit or cake form pre-packed in a quantity by number of sixteen or less.

**39.** Subject to paragraphs 40 and 41 below, goods to which this Part of this Schedule applies shall be pre-packed only if the container is marked with an indication of quantity by number.

**40.** In relation to postal stationery, the reference to number in paragraph 39 above shall be construed as a reference to the number of sheets of paper, cards or envelopes, as the case may be, in the pad, confining band or other form of container; and postal stationery shall be exempted from the requirements of that paragraph if pre-packed as part of a collection of articles made up for sale together and including any article other than postal stationery and blotting or other paper.

41. There shall be exempted from the requirements of this Part of this Schedule any goods in a quantity by number of one.

SCHEDULE 7 Section 21

*(As amended by SI 1994/2866, SI 2009/663 and SI 2014/2975)*

COMPOSITE GOODS AND COLLECTIONS OF ARTICLES

7.11820 1. (1) This paragraph applies to any goods which, not being pre-packed, and not themselves being goods—

(*a*) required by or under Part IV of this Act, except this paragraph, to be sold (whether on any sale or on a sale of any particular description) only by quantity expressed in a particular manner, or

(*b*) on a sale of which (whether any sale or a sale of any particular description) the quantity of the goods sold expressed in a particular manner is required by or under Part IV of this Act, except this paragraph, to be made known to the buyer at or before a particular time, or

(*c*) expressly exempted by or under Part IV of this Act, except this paragraph, from all such requirements as mentioned in paragraph (*a*) or (*b*) above which would otherwise apply to them,

consist of a mixture constituted wholly or mainly of goods of one or more descriptions to which there applies any such requirement made by reference to any of the following (whether exclusively or otherwise), that is to say, weight, capacity measurement or volume.

(2) Subject to paragraph 5 below, goods to which this paragraph applies shall be sold only by net weight or by capacity measurement or by volume.

2. (1) This paragraph applies to any goods which, not being aerosol products and not themselves being goods—

(*a*) required by or under Part IV of this Act, except this paragraph, to be pre-packed only if the container is marked with an indication of quantity, or

(*aa*) that are subject to the FIC Regulation, or

(*b*) in the case of which when sold pre-packed (whether on any sale or on a sale of any particular description) the quantity of the goods sold expressed in a particular manner is required by or under Part IV of this Act, except this paragraph, to be made known to the buyer at or before a particular time, or

(*c*) expressly exempted by or under Part IV of this Act, except this paragraph, from all such requirements as mentioned in paragraph (*a*) or (*b*) above which would otherwise apply to them,

consist of a mixture constituted wholly or mainly of goods of one or more descriptions to which there applies any such requirement made by reference to any of the following (whether exclusively or otherwise), that is to say, weight, capacity measurement or volume.

(2) Subject to paragraph 5 below, goods to which this paragraph applies shall be pre-packed only if the container is marked with an indication of quantity either by net weight or by capacity measurement or by volume.

3. (1) This paragraph applies to aerosol products containing any goods required by or under Part IV of this Act, except this paragraph, to be pre-packed only if the container is marked with an indication of quantity expressed in a particular manner.

(1A) This paragraph does not apply to aerosol products containing goods that are subject to the FIC Regulation.

(2) Subject to paragraph 5 below, any aerosol product to which this paragraph applies shall be pre-packed only if the container is marked with

(*a*) an indication of the total capacity of the container (indicated in such a way as to avoid giving a false impression of the quantity of the goods in the container), and

(*b*) an indication of the quantity by net volume of the entire contents of the container.

4. (1) This paragraph applies to any collection of two or more items which, not itself being—

(*a*) required by or under Part IV of this Act, except this paragraph, to be pre-packed only if the container is marked with particular information, or

(*b*) expressly exempted by or under Part IV of this Act, except this paragraph, from any such requirement which would otherwise apply to it,

contains one or more articles to which any such requirement applies.

(1A) This paragraph does not apply to a collection containing any goods that are subject to the FIC Regulation.

(2) Any collection to which this paragraph applies shall be pre-packed only if—

(*a*) the container in which the collection is pre-packed is marked with an indication of the quantity of each of any such articles as mentioned in sub-paragraph (1) above contained in it, or

(*b*) each of any such articles contained in the container is made up in an individual container marked with an indication of quantity,

being in either case the like indication of the quantity of each respectively of those articles as would have been required if that article had itself been pre-packed.

5. There shall be exempted from any requirement of paragraph 1, 2 or 3(2)(*b*) above food of any description in a quantity of less than five grams or of less than five millilitres and goods of any other description in a quantity of less than 25 grams or of less than 25 millilitres.

## Weights and Measures (Solid Fuel) Regulations 1978[1]

(SI 1978/238)

**7.11821** *1, 2. Citation, operation, interpretation.*

[1] These Regulations are made under the Weights and Measures Act 1963, s 21(4) and Sch 6, para 3C (3), as amended. Reference should now be made to the 1985 Act.

**7.11822** *4.* (1) The information required by paragraph 3C (2) (*a*) shall be in the following terms—"All open sacks on this vehicle contain either 25kg or 50kg".

(2) The information—

(*a*) shall be marked on the vehicle or on a durable material securely affixed to the vehicle;

(*b*) shall be clearly and permanently inscribed in characters of a height of not less than 6 cm; and

(*c*) shall be easily read from either side of the vehicle.

**7.11823** 5. The statement required by paragraph 3C(2)(*b*) of the said Schedule 6, as so amended, to be displayed on a vehicle shall comply with the provisions of paragraph (2) of Regulation 4 above with the substitution in subparagraph (*b*) of that paragraph of 3 cm for 6 cm.

## Weights and Measures Act 1963 (Cheese, Fish, Fresh Fruits and Vegetables, Meat and Poultry) Order 1984[1]

(SI 1984/1315 amended by SI 1985/988 and 1980, the Weights and Measures Act 1985, Sch 13, the Criminal Justice Act 1988, s 52 and SI 2014/2975)

**7.11824** 1. *Citation, commencement, revocation.*

[1] Made under the Weights and Measures Act 1963, ss 21(2), (3) and (5) and 54(1) and (4). Reference should be made to the 1985 Act.

*Interpretation*

**7.11825** 2. (1) In this Order—

"cheese" means cheese, whether or not containing flavouring or colouring matter, and whether or not coated or mixed with other food for the purpose of giving the cheese a distinctive appearance or flavour, and includes processed cheese and cheese spread;

"countable produce" means fruit or vegetables specified in Part I of Schedule 1 to this Order;

"mass caterer" means any establishment (including a vehicle or a fixed or mobile stall), such as restaurants, canteens, schools, hospitals and catering enterprises in which, in the course of a business, food is prepared to be ready for consumption by the final consumer;

"meat" means any part of an animal of any of the following descriptions, that is to say, cattle, sheep and swine; and

"pre-packed", in relation to food to which this Order applies, means either or both of—

(*a*) made up for direct sale (within the meaning of Article 2(2)(e) of the FIC Regulation) by way of retail;

(*b*) made up in advance ready for retail sale in an open container;

"relevant wholesale", in relation to food to which this Order applies, means a sale by way of wholesale, but does not include any of the following:

(*a*) a sale to a mass caterer;

(*b*) a supply of food that is prepacked food within the meaning of the FIC Regulation intended for sale to the final consumer or to a mass caterer, or any other supply of food that is made up in advance ready for retail sale in an open container; or

(*c*) a supply to which Article 8(8) of the FIC Regulation applies;

"soft fruits" means fruits of the following descriptions, that is to say, bilberries, blackberries, blackcurrants, boysenberries, brambles, cherries, cranberries, gooseberries, loganberries, mulberries, raspberries, redcurrants, strawberries, tayberries and whitecurrants.

(2) References in this Order to items being "loose" include items packed at the request of the customer.

*Cheese, fish, meat and poultry*

**7.11826** 4. (1) This Article applies to food of any of the following descriptions that is to say—

(*a*) cheese;

(*b*) fish, meat or poultry of any description, whether fresh, chilled, frozen, salted, cooked or processed;

(*c*) sausage-meat in any form, whether cooked or uncooked; and

(*d*) any article which, though it also contains other food, consists substantially of cheese, fish, meat, poultry or sausage-meat,

other than dripping, lard, fish paste, meat paste, poultry paste and shredded suet, and any reference in this Article to poultry includes a reference to any part of any poultry.

(2) Subject to paragraphs (7) to (9) below, any food to which this Article applies which is sold loose must, if sold by retail, be sold only—

(*a*) by net weight; or

(*b*) if it is sold in a container which does not exceed the appropriate permitted weight specified in Table A of Schedule 2 to this Order, either by net weight or by gross weight.

(3) Subject to paragraphs (7) and (8), where food to which this article applies (other than cheese and fish) is sold in a relevant manner (as defined in paragraph (3A)), it must be sold only—

(*a*) by net weight; or

(*b*) if it is sold in a container which does not exceed the permitted weight specified in Table A of Schedule 2, either by net weight or gross weight.

(3A) For the purposes of paragraph (3), food is sold "in a relevant manner" if it is sold—

(*a*) pre-packed otherwise than by retail sale;

(*b*) loose to a mass caterer; or

(*c*) by relevant wholesale.

(4) Subject to paragraph (7) below, any food (other than cheese) to which this Article applies shall be pre-packed only if the container is marked with an indication of quantity by net weight:

Provided that there shall be exempted from the requirements of this paragraph any food in a quantity of less than 5 g.

(5) Subject to paragraph (9) below—

(*a*) processed cheese;

(*b*) cheese spread; and

(*c*) natural cheese of any of the following descriptions, that is to say, Caerphilly, Cheddar, Cheshire, Derby, Double Gloucester, Dunlop, Edam, Gouda, Lancashire, Leicestershire and Wensleydale,

shall be pre-packed only if the container is marked with an indication of quantity by net weight.

(6) On or after 1st January 1986, cheese of any description other than that specified in paragraph (5) above shall be pre-packed only if the container is marked with an indication of quantity by net weight:

Provided that there shall be exempted from the requirements of this paragraph—

(*a*) whole Stilton cheese;

(*b*) any cheese in a quantity of less than 25 g and more than 10 kg; and

(*c*) any cheese sold by gross weight in a container which does not exceed the appropriate permitted weight specified in Table A of Schedule 2 to this Order, if the quantity is made known to the buyer before he pays for or takes possession of the goods.

(7) There shall be exempted from the requirements of paragraphs (2) to (4) of this Article—

(*a*) bath chaps, cheese, fish, meat or poultry pies, puddings and flans and sausage rolls, provided that in the case of more than one item of food pre-packed in a container not marked with an indication of quantity by net weight the number of items in the container is marked on the container or is clearly visible and capable of being easily counted through the container;

(*b*) any other goods (other than cheese) in a quantity of less than 5 g.

(8) There shall be exempted from the requirements of paragraphs (2) and (3) of this Article—

(*a*) cooked poultry;

(*b*) shellfish in shell, jellied fish, pickled fish and fried fish;

(*c*) any sale of fish made otherwise than from a market, shop, stall or vehicle;

(*d*) single cooked sausages in natural casings less than 500 g in weight; and

(*e*) sausage-meat products other than in sausage form when offered or exposed for sale as a single item in a quantity of less than 500 g.

(9) There shall be exempted from the requirements of paragraphs (2) and (5) of this Article any cheese in a quantity of less than 25 g.

*Fresh fruits and vegetables other than potatoes*

**7.11827** *5.* (1) This Article applies to food consisting of fruits or vegetables of any description, other than potatoes—

(*a*) in the state in which they were harvested;

(*b*) in the said state apart from cleaning or trimming;

(*c*) in the case of beetroots, in the said state apart from having been cooked; or

(*d*) in the case of peas, in the said state apart from having been shelled.

(2) Where fruits or vegetables of any description to which this Article applies have been divided into pieces or have had part thereof removed or both, then, subject to paragraph 7 below, paragraph 6 shall apply to any food consisting of, or including any part of, any of those fruits or vegetables which have not been subjected to any further process.

(3) Subject to paragraphs (7) to (9) below, fruits and vegetables of any description, other than soft fruits and mushrooms, shall be pre-packed only if the container is marked with an indication of quantity by net weight or, in the case of countable produce, either by net weight or by number.

(4) Subject to paragraphs (7) and (9) below, fruits and vegetables of any description, other than soft fruits and mushrooms, which are sold loose must, if sold by retail, be sold only—

(*a*) by net weight;

(*b*) in the case of countable produce either by net weight or number; or

(*c*) if the food is sold in a container which does not exceed the appropriate permitted weight specified in Table A of Schedule 2 to this Order, either by net weight or by gross weight.

(5) Subject to paragraph (7) below, any fruits or vegetables consisting of soft fruits or mushrooms which are sold pre-packed or loose shall, if sold by retail, be sold only—

(*a*) by net weight; or

(*b*) if the food is sold in a container which does not exceed the appropriate permitted weight specified in Table B of Schedule 2 to this Order, either by net weight or by gross weight,

and the quantity shall be made known to the buyer before he pays for or takes possession of the food.

(6) Any food to which this paragraph applies by virtue of paragraph (2) above, shall—

(*a*) if sold loose and if sold by retail, be sold only by net weight or, in the case of countable produce, either by net weight or by number; or

(*b*) be pre-packed only if the container is marked with an indication of quantity by net weight or, in the case of countable produce, either by net weight or by number.

(7) The following shall be exempted from any requirement of paragraph (3), (4) or (5) above which would otherwise apply thereto, that is to say—

(*a*) food pre-packed in the same container with other goods (except potatoes) to which none of those requirements applies;

(*b*) food pre-packed in the same container with goods of two or more other descriptions to which some requirement of this Article would otherwise apply or which include potatoes;

(*c*) any food in a quantity of more than 5 kg;

and there shall be exempted from all requirements of this Article any goods in a quantity of less than 5 g.

(8) There shall be exempted from the requirements of paragraph (3) above a pre-packed collection of not more than eight articles of countable produce, if the container is such that all the articles can be clearly seen by a prospective buyer.

(9) There shall be exempted from the requirements of paragraphs (3) and (4) above any vegetables specified in Part II of Schedule 1 to this Order, if sold in a bunch.

(10) Where at any premises other than a vehicle or ship any food to which this Article applies has been sold by weight when made up in a container, and the sale is otherwise than by retail, the buyer may require all or any of the following weighings to be carried out at those premises, that is to say—

(*a*) a weighing of that container while the food is therein;

(*b*) a weighing of that container after the removal of the food therefrom;

(*c*) a weighing of a similar container which is empty,

and thereupon the seller shall either carry out or permit the buyer to carry out the weighing or weighings so required; and if the seller without reasonable cause contravenes this requirement he shall be guilty of an offence.

(11) The occupier of any premises at which any food to which this Article applies is made up in a container for sale by weight otherwise than by retail, or of any premises (other than a vehicle or ship) at which such food so made up is so sold, shall provide suitable weighing equipment and make that equipment available for any weighing or weighings required under the foregoing paragraph to be carried out at those premises; and if he without reasonable cause contravenes any of the requirements of this paragraph he shall be guilty of an offence.

(12) Except as provided in paragraph (13) below, any person guilty of an offence under paragraph (10) or (11) above shall be liable on summary conviction to a fine not exceeding **level 5** on the standard scale.

(13) Any person guilty of such an offence committed before 1st May 1984 shall be liable on summary conviction to a fine not exceeding **level 4** on the standard scale.

*Multipacks*

**7.11828** *6.* Nothing in the previous provisions of this Order shall require any container to be marked with any information if all the following provisions are satisfied—

(*a*) the contents of the container in which any foods to which this Order applies are pre-packed consist of two or more packs of goods;

(*b*) where any pack, if sold individually, would be required by the Order to be marked with an indication as to the quantity of the goods, the pack is so marked;

(*c*)

(i) the container is marked with a description of the goods in each pack, the total number of packs containing goods of each description and where paragraph (*b*) above applies with an indication as to the quantity of the goods in each such pack; or

(ii) where each pack to which paragraph (*b*) above applies contains the same quantity of identical goods, an indication as to the quantity of the goods in at least one such pack is clearly visible, and the total number of such packs is clearly visible and capable of being easily counted, through the container; or

(iii) where each pack does not contain goods of the same description or does contain such goods but does not contain them in the same quantity, an indication as to the quantity of any goods in each pack to which paragraph (*b*) above applies, or if there are two or more identical such packs an indication as to the quantity of the goods in at least one of them, is clearly visible, and the total number of such packs of each description is clearly visible and capable of being easily counted, through the container.

SCHEDULE 1 Articles 2 and 5(9)

PART I COUNTABLE PRODUCE

**7.11829**

| **COUNTABLE PRODUCE** | | |
|---|---|---|
| Apples | Garlic | Passion fruit |
| Apricots | Grapefruit | Pawpaw |
| Artichokes (globe) | Guavas | Peaches |
| Aubergines | | Pears |
| Avocados | Kiwi fruit | Pineapple |
| | Kohlrabi | Plums |
| Bananas | | Pomegranates |
| Beetroots (including cooked) | Lemons | Pomelo |
| | Lettuce | Pumpkins |
| Cabbage | Limes | |
| Cauliflower | | Radishes |

| COUNTABLE PRODUCE | | |
|---|---|---|
| Capsicum | Mangoes | |
| Celery | Marrows | Shaddock |
| Coconuts | Melons | Soft citrus fruits |
| Corn on the cob | | |
| Cucumber | Nectarines | Tomatoes |
| Fennel | Onions (other than spring) | Ugli |
| Figs (fresh) | Oranges | |

PART II VEGETABLES WHICH MAY BE SOLD BY THE BUNCH

| VEGETABLES WHICH MAY BE SOLD BY THE BUNCH | |
|---|---|
| Asparagus | Mustard and cress |
| Beetroots | Onions (including spring) |
| Carrots | Parsley |
| Chives | Radishes |
| Endives | Salad cress |
| Garlic | Turnips |
| Mint | Watercress |

SCHEDULE 2

TABLES OF PERMITTED WEIGHTS FOR CONTAINERS

Articles 4 and 5

7.11830

*TABLE A*

| Gross weight | Permitted weight of container |
|---|---|
| Not exceeding 500 g | 5 g |
| Exceeding 500 g | a weight at the rate of 10 g per kg of the gross weight. |

*TABLE B*

| Gross weight | Permitted weight of container |
|---|---|
| Not exceeding 250 g | a weight at the rate of 120 g per kg of the gross weight. |
| Exceeding 250 g but not exceeding 1 kg | a weight at the rate of 100 g per kg of the gross weight. |
| Exceeding 1 kg but not exceeding 3 kg | a weight at the rate of 90 g per kg of the gross weight. |
| Exceeding 3 kg | a weight at the rate of 60 g per kg of the gross weight. |

## Weights and Measures (Intoxicating Liquor) Order 1988[1]

(SI 1988/2039 amended by SI 1990/1550, SI 1994/1883 and 2868, SI 2009/663, SI 2011/2331, 2936, SI 2013/3235 and SI 2014/2975)

7.11831 *1.* (1) *Citation and commencement.*

(2) In this Order except where the context expressly otherwise requires—

"the 1979 Act" means the Alcoholic Liquor Duties Act 1979;

"beer" and "cider" have the same meanings respectively as in section 1 of the 1979 Act, but, in the case of "cider", as if the definition in section 1(6) did not include the words "(or perry)" in either place where they occur or "or pear";

"CN Code" means a code comprised in the Combined Nomenclature;

"the Combined Nomenclature" means the Combined Nomenclature of the European Community;

"made-wine" and "wine" have the same meanings respectively as in section 1 of the 1979 Act; and

references to a subheading are to a subheading of the Combined Nomenclature.

(3) *Revocations.*

[1] Made by the Secretary of State under ss 22(1) and (2), 24(1) and 86(1) of the Weights and Measures Act 1985.

**7.11832** *2.* (1) Unless pre-packed in a securely closed container and except when sold as a constituent of a mixture of two or more liquids, beer or cider shall be sold by retail—

(*a*) only in a quantity of 1/3 pint, 1/2 pint, 2/3 pint or a multiple of 1/2 pint; and

(*b*) subject to paragraph (2) below, where sold for consumption on the premises of the seller, only in a capacity measure of the quantity in question.

(2) Paragraph 1(*b*) above shall not apply where—

(*a*) the quantity of the intoxicating liquor the subject of the sale is ascertained by means of measuring equipment stamped in accordance with Regulation 16(2) of the Measuring Equipment (Intoxicating Liquor) Regulations 1983;

(*b*) the liquor in question is delivered directly from the measuring equipment into the container in which it is intended the buyer should receive it;

(*c*) the liquor in question is so delivered after the buyer has ordered it; and

(*d*) the measuring equipment (or that part of it from which the liquor is delivered) is installed in such a position that the delivery of the liquor into the container can readily be seen by customers in that part of the premises where the buyer ordered the liquor.

**7.11833** *3.* (1) Subject to paragraphs (2) and (3) below, unless pre-packed in a securely closed container intoxicating liquor of any of the following descriptions, that is to say, gin, rum, vodka and whisky, shall be sold by retail for consumption on the premises at which it is sold only—

(*a*) in, or in a multiple of, one of the following quantities, which shall be the same for those parts of any licensed premises or licensed canteen within the meaning of the Licensing Act 1964 or the Licensing (Scotland) Act 1976 of which any person is the licensee and for all those liquors, that is to say, 1/4 gill, 1/5 gill and 1/6 gill, 25 ml or 35 ml; and

(*b*) if there is displayed on those premises, in such a position and manner as to be readily available without special request for inspection by the buyer before the sale is made, a statement in writing showing in which of those quantities those liquors are offered for sale on those premises.

Provide that the quantities of 1/4 gill, 1/5 gill and 1/6 gill referred to in sub-paragraph (*a*) of this paragraph shall not be permitted after 31st December 1994.

(2) Any such liquor shall be exempted from the requirements of this Article when it forms a constituent of a mixture of three or more liquids.

(3) Nothing in this Article shall make unlawful the sale at the express request of the buyer of any mixture of liquids containing any of those liquors in a quantity not otherwise permitted by this Article.

**7.11834** *3A.* (1) Subject to paragraph (2), the intoxicating liquors specified in column 1 of Schedule A1 to this Order may be pre-packed only if they are made up in one of the quantities specified in column 3, subject to the exceptions specified in column 4.

(2) Paragraph (1) does not apply to the intoxicating liquors specified in column 1 of Schedule A1 to this Order when they are sold duty-free for consumption outside the European Union.

(3) Where two or more pre-packages make up a multi-pack, the quantities specified in column 3 of Schedule A1 to this Order apply to each pre-package.

(4) For the purposes of this article—

(*a*) "pre-package" means a combination of a product and the individual package in which it is pre-packed; and

(*b*) "pre-packed" means made up in advance ready for retail sale or wholesale in a securely closed container.

**7.11835** *4.* *Revoked.*

**7.11836** *5.* (1) Subject to paragraph (2) of this Article, wine and made-wine for consumption on the premises at which it is sold shall—

(*a*) be pre-packed only in one of the following quantities, that is to say, 25 cl, 50 cl, 75 cl, or 1 L;

(*b*) when not pre-packed, be sold only in those quantities; and

(*c*) whether pre-packed or not, be sold only if a statement in writing showing the quantities in which wine or made-wine is for sale is either displayed on those premises in such a position and manner as to be readily available without special request for inspection by the buyer before the sale is made, or is contained in every winelist and menu which is available to the buyer on those premises before the sale is made and which indicates that wine or made-wine is for sale for consumption on those premises.

(2) Paragraph (1) above shall not apply in the case of wine or made-wine which—

(*a*) is pre-packed in a securely closed container whether or not it is to be decanted at the request of the buyer before being served; or

(*b*) subject to article 5A below is sold in the glass or other vessel from which it is intended to be drunk.

**7.11837** *5A.* (1) For the purposes of this article—

(*a*) "wine" (except when used in the expression "wine fortified for distillation") means the intoxicating liquor and other liquids specified in column 1 of Part 1 of Schedule 1 to this Order, other than wine fortified for distillation; and

(*b*) "wine fortified for distillation" has the same meaning as in the additional notes to Chapter

22 of the Combined Nomenclature.

(2) Subject to paragraph (3), when sold in the glass or other vessel from which it is intended to be drunk, for consumption on the premises at which it is sold—

(*a*) wine shall be sold only in, or in a multiple of, the following quantities, that is to say, 125 ml and 175 ml; and

(*b*) wine fortified for distillation shall be sold only in, or in a multiple of, the following quantities, that is to say, 50 ml and 70 ml,

and, in either case, only if a statement in writing of the kind required by subparagraph (c) of article 5(1) is displayed or otherwise provided as required by that sub-paragraph.

(3) Nothing in this article shall make unlawful the sale—

(*a*) at the express request of the buyer, of any mixture of liquids containing, in a quantity not permitted by this article—

(i) wine; or

(ii) wine fortified for distillation; or

(*b*) of wine in a quantity of less than 75 ml, without the display or provision of a statement in writing of the kind referred to in paragraph (2).

**7.11838** *6.* (1) Where intoxicating liquor or other liquids specified in column 1 of Schedule 1—

(*a*) are pre-packed in a closed container for direct sale (within the meaning of Article 2(2)(e) of the FIC Regulation); or

(*b*) are, in the case of those specified in Part III of Schedule 1, made up in a closed container for relevant wholesale,

the container must, subject to the exemptions specified in column 4 of Schedule 1, be marked with an indication of quantity by volume.

(2) Intoxicating liquor of any other description shall be pre-packed for direct sale (within the meaning of Article 2(2)(e) of the FIC Regulation) in a closed container in a quantity of 5 ml or more but not exceeding 5 L only if the container is marked with an indication of quantity by volume.

(3) For the purposes of this article—

(*a*) "mass caterer" means any establishment (including a vehicle or a fixed or mobile stall), such as restaurants, canteens, schools, hospitals and catering enterprises in which, in the course of a business, food is prepared to be ready for consumption by the final consumer; and

(*b*) "relevant wholesale", in relation to food to which this article applies, means a sale by way of wholesale, but does not include any of the following:

(i) a sale to a mass caterer;

(ii) a supply of food that is prepacked food within the meaning of the FIC Regulation intended for sale to the final consumer or to a mass caterer, or any other supply of food that is made up in advance ready for retail sale in an open container; or

(iii) a supply to which Article 8(8) of the FIC Regulation applies.

**7.11839** *7.* (1) Without prejudice to the provisions of section 25 of the Weights and Measures Act 1985, if Article 2(1)(*b*), 3(1)(*b*), 5(1)(*c*) or 5A(2)(*b*) above is contravened, the occupier of the premises in question shall be guilty of an offence.

(2) Any person guilty of an offence under paragraph (1) above shall be liable on summary conviction to a **fine not exceeding £2,000**.

**7.11840** *8.* Nothing in this Order shall require any container to be marked with any information or to enclose intoxicating liquor or other liquids of a particular quantity if all the following provisions are satisfied—

(*a*) the contents of the container in which any intoxicating liquor or other liquids is pre-packed consist of two or more packs of goods;

(*b*) where the goods in any pack, if sold individually, would be required by the Order to be made up in a specified quantity, the goods in any such pack are so made up;

(*c*) where any pack, if sold individually, would be required by the Order to be marked with an indication as to the quantity of the goods, the pack is so marked;

(*d*)

(i) the container is marked with a description of the goods in each pack, the total number of packs containing goods of each description and, where paragraph (*c*) above applies with an indication as to the quantity of the goods in each such pack; or

(ii) where each pack to which paragraph (*c*) above applies contains the same quantity of identical goods, an indication as to the quantity of the goods in at least one such pack is clearly visible, and the total number of such packs is clearly visible and capable of being easily counted, through the container; or

(iii) where each pack does not contain goods of the same description or does contain such goods but does not contain them in the same quantity, an indication as to the quantity of any goods in each pack to which paragraph (*c*) above applies, or if there are two or more identical such packs an indication as to the quantity of the goods in at least one of them is clearly visible, and the total number of such packs of each description is clearly visible and capable of being easily counted, through the container.

SCHEDULE A1

**7.11841**

| *(1)* *Product* | *(2)* *Product Definition* | *(3)* *Specified Quantities* | *(4)* *Exceptions* |
|---|---|---|---|
| Still wine | wine as defined in point(1) of Part II of Annex VII to the Regulation of the European Parliament and of the Council adopted on 16 December 2013 establishing a common organisation of the markets in agricultural products and repealing Council Regulations (EEC) No 922/72, (EEC) No 234/79, (EC) No 1037/2001 and (EC) No 1234/2007, as amended from time to time | Only the following specified quantities: 100 ml 187 ml 250 ml 375 ml 500 ml 750 ml 1000 ml 1500 ml | Containers of a capacity of less than 100 ml or more than 1500 ml |
| Yellow wine | wine using the traditional term "vin jaune" listed and defined in the "E-Bacchus" database in accordance with Article 40(1) of Commission Regulation (EC) No 607/2009 laying down certain detailed rules for the implementation of Council Regulation (EC) No 479/2008 as regards protected designations of origin and geographical indications, traditional terms, labelling and presentation of certain wine sector products | Only the following specified quantity: 620 ml | Containers of a capacity of less than 100 ml or more than 1500 ml |
| sparkling wine, quality sparkling wine, quality aromatic sparkling wine, aerated sparkling wine, semi-sparkling wine and aerated semi-sparkling wine | as those wines are defined (respectively) in points (4) to (9) of Part II of Annex VII to the Regulation of the European Parliament and of the Council adopted on 16 December 2013 establishing a common organisation of the markets in agricultural products and repealing Council Regulations (EEC) No 922/72, (EEC) No 234/79, (EC) No 1037/2001 and (EC) No 1234/2007, as amended from time to time | Only the following specified quantities: 125 ml 200 ml 375 ml 750 ml 1500 ml | Containers of a capacity of less than 125 ml or more than 1500 ml |
| Liqueur wine | liqueur wine as defined in point (3) of Part II of Annex VII to the Regulation of the European Parliament and of the Council adopted on 16 December 2013 establishing a common organisation of the markets in agricultural products and repealing Council Regulations (EEC) No 922/72, (EEC) No 234/79, (EC) No 1037/2001 and (EC) No 1234/2007, as amended from time to time | Only the following specified quantities: 100 ml 200 ml 375 ml 500 ml 750 ml 1000 ml 1500 ml | Containers of a capacity of less than 100 ml or more than 1500 ml |
| Aromatised wine | Aromatised wine as defined in Article 2(1)(*a*) of Council Regulation (EEC) No 1601/91 of 10 June 1991 laying down general rules on the definition, description and presentation of aromatised wines, aromatised wine-based drinks and aromatised wine-product cocktails (OJ L 149, 14.6.1991, p 1) as last amended by the Treaty concerning the accession of the Republic of Bulgaria and Romania to the European Union (OJ L 157, 21.6.2005, p 1) (CN code 2205). | Only the following specified quantities: 100 ml 200 ml 375 ml 500 ml 750 ml 1000 ml 1500 ml | Containers of a capacity of less than 100 ml or more than 1500 ml |

| *(1)* **Product** | *(2)* **Product Definition** | *(3)* **Specified Quantities** | *(4)* **Exceptions** |
|---|---|---|---|
| Spirit drinks | Spirit drinks as defined in Article 1(2) of Council Regulation (EEC) No 1576/89 of 29 May 1989 laying down general rules on the definition, description and presentation of spirit drinks (OJ L 160, 12.6.1989, p 1) as last amended by the Treaty concerning the accession of the Republic of Bulgaria and Romania to the European Union (OJ L 157, 21.6.2005, p 1) (CN code 2208). | Only the following specified quantities: | Containers of a capacity of less than 100 ml or more than 2000 ml" |
| | | 100 ml | |
| | | 200 ml | |
| | | 350 ml | |
| | | 500 ml | |
| | | 700 ml | |
| | | 1000 ml | |
| | | 1500 ml | |
| | | 1750 ml | |
| | | 2000 ml | |

SCHEDULE

Articles 4 and 6

PART I

7.11843

| (1) Description and subheading | (4) Exemptions from quantity marking |
|---|---|
| Wine of fresh grapes; grape must with fermentation prevented or arrested by the addition of alcohol, including wine made of unfermented grape juice blended with alcohol, grape must in fermentation or with fermentation arrested otherwise than by the addition of alcohol, of subheadings 2204 21 21 to 2204 21 39 inclusive, 2204 29 21 to 2204 29 39 inclusive and 2204 30 10 | less than 5 ml, more than 10 L |
| "Yellow" wines entitled to use the following designations of origin: | |
| "Côtes du Jura", | |
| "Arbois", | |
| "L'Etoile" and | |
| "Château-Chalon" | |

PART II

| (1) Description and subheading | (4) Exemptions from quantity marking |
|---|---|
| Sparkling wine and wine in bottles with "mushroom" stoppers held in place by ties or fastenings, and wine otherwise made up with an excess pressure of not less than one bar but less than three bar, measured at a temperature of 20°C, of subheadings 2204 10 11, 2204 10 19, 2204 10 90, 2204 21 10 and 2204 29 10 | less than 5 ml, more than 10 L |

PART III

| (1) Description and subheading | (4) Exemptions from quantity marking |
|---|---|
| Spirits, liqueurs and other spirituous beverages and compound alcoholic preparations of a kind used for the manufacture of beverages, of subheadings 2208 1010 to 2208 90 79 inclusive | less than 5 ml, more than 10 L |

## Weights and Measures (Miscellaneous Foods) Order 1988[1]

(SI 1988/2040 amended by SI 1990/1550, SI 1994/2868, SI 2005/3057, SI 2006/659, SI 2009/663, SI 2011/2331 and SI 2014/2975)

7.11844 1. *Citation, commencement, revocation.*

[1] Made by the Secretary of State under ss 22(1) and (2), 24(1) and 86(1) of the Weights and Measures Act 1985.

*Interpretation*

7.11845 *2.* (1) In this Order, unless the context otherwise requires—

"the Act" means the Weights and Measures Act 1985;

"biscuits" includes wafers, rusks, crispbreads, extruded flatbread, oatcakes and matzos;

"bread" means bread in any form other than breadcrumbs and includes the following, and any part of the following, that is to say, fancy loaves and milk loaves and "loaf" in relation to bread includes a roll and a bap; and for the purposes of this Order any pre-packed sliced bread shall be deemed to be a whole loaf of bread and the pre-packing of sliced bread in any quantity by net weight shall be deemed to be the making for sale of a whole loaf of bread of that net weight;

"casein" and "caseinate" have the same meanings as they have in the Caseins and Caseinates Regulations 1985;

"chicory", "chicory extract paste", "coffee extract paste", "instant chicory", "instant coffee", "liquid chicory extract" and "liquid coffee extract", have the same meanings—

(*a*) in relation to the application of this Order to England, as in the Coffee Extracts and Chicory Extracts (England) Regulations 2000;

(*b*) in relation to the application of this Order to Scotland, as in the Coffee Extracts and Chicory Extracts (Scotland) Regulations 2001, and

(*c*) in relation to the application of this Order to Wales, as in the Coffee Extracts and Chicory Extracts (Wales) Regulations 2001;

"chocolate confectionery" means any food which is ready for consumption without further preparation, of which a characterising ingredient is chocolate, cocoa or non-fat cocoa solids, and includes food of which a characterising ingredient is carbohydrate sweetening matter and which has a chocolate or chocolate-flavoured coating, but does not include any biscuits, chocolate products, flour confectionery or edible ice;

"chocolate product" means—

(*a*) in relation to the application of this Order to England, any chocolate product to which the Cocoa and Chocolate Products (England) Regulations 2003 apply;

(*b*) in relation to the application of this Order to Scotland, any chocolate product to which the Cocoa and Chocolate Products (Scotland) Regulations 2003 apply; and

(*c*) in relation to the application of this Order to Wales, any chocolate product to which the Cocoa and Chocolate Products (Wales) Regulations 2003 apply;

"cocoa product" means—

(*a*) in relation to the application of this Order to England, any cocoa product to which the Cocoa and Chocolate Products (England) Regulations 2003 apply;

(*b*) in relation to the application of this Order to Scotland, any cocoa product to which the Cocoa and Chocolate Products (Scotland) Regulations 2003 apply; and

(*c*) in relation to the application of this Order to Wales, any cocoa product to which the Cocoa and Chocolate Products (Wales) Regulations 2003 apply;

"coffee" means the dried seed of the coffee plant whether such seed has been roasted or ground or both roasted and ground;

"coffee bag" means a permeable sealed bag, which is intended to be immersed in water or to have water percolated through it, containing coffee, or a coffee mixture, or a combination of either coffee or a coffee mixture (or both) with a lesser quantity of instant coffee;

"condensed milk" means milk, partly skimmed milk or skimmed milk or any combination thereof, whether with or without the addition of cream, dried milk or sucrose, which has been concentrated by the partial removal of water, but does not include dried milk;

"container", in relation to cocoa products, chocolate products and fancy chocolate products, includes any form of packaging of goods for sale as a single item, whether by way of wholly or partly enclosing the food or by way of attaching the food to some other article, and in particular includes a wrapper or confining band, but does not include any crimp case used to support the base or the base and sides of any chocolate product;

"dried milk" means milk, partly skimmed milk or skimmed milk or any combination thereof, whether with or without the addition of cream, which has been concentrated to the form of powder, granule or solid by the removal of water;

"fancy chocolate product" includes any chocolate product in the form of figurines, cigarettes or eggs or enclosed in a seasonal selection pack;

"flour confectionery" means any cooked food which is ready for consumption without further preparation (other than reheating), of which a characterising ingredient is ground cereal, including shortbread, sponges, crumpets, muffins, macaroons, ratafias, pastry and pastry cases, and also includes meringues, petits fours and uncooked pastry and pastry cases, but does not include bread, pizzas, biscuits, crispbread, extruded flat bread or any food containing a filling which has as an ingredient any cheese, meat, offal, fish or shellfish;

"liquid coffee and chicory products" means liquid coffee extract and liquid chicory extract, and blends thereof;

"mass caterer" means any establishment (including a vehicle or a fixed or mobile stall), such as restaurants, canteens, schools, hospitals and catering enterprises in which, in the course of a business, food is prepared to be ready for consumption by the final consumer;

"Member State" means a member State as defined in Part II of Schedule 1 to the European Communities Act 1972, Norway, Iceland or Liechtenstein;

"milk" means cows' milk in any liquid form other than that of condensed milk (including evaporated milk) or of cream;

"potatoes" means potatoes in the state in which they were harvested or in that state apart from cleaning;

"pre-packed", in relation to food to which this Order applies, means either or both of—

(*a*) made up for direct sale (within the meaning of Article 2(2)(*e*) of the FIC Regulation) by way of retail;
(*b*) made up in advance ready for retail sale in an open container;

"preserved milk" means condensed milk (including evaporated milk) or dried milk;

"relevant wholesale", in relation to food to which this Order applies, means a sale by way of wholesale, but does not include any of the following—
(*a*) a sale to a mass caterer;
(*b*) a supply of food that is prepacked food within the meaning of the FIC Regulation intended for sale to the final consumer or to a mass caterer, or any other supply of food that is made up in advance ready for retail sale in an open container; or
(*c*) a supply to which Article 8(8) of the FIC Regulation applies,

"solid and paste coffee and chicory products" means instant coffee, coffee extract paste, instant chicory, chicory extract paste, and blends thereof, and extracts of blends of roasted coffee and roasted chicory.

"sugar confectionery" means any food which is ready for consumption without further preparation, of which a characterising ingredient is carbohydrate sweetening matter, and includes sweetened liquorice and chewing gum, but does not include any chocolate confectionery, chocolate products, cocoa products, flour confectionery, edible ice, table jellies, slab marzipan or sugar.

(2) References in this Order to items being "loose" include items packed at the request of the customer.

*Scope of application*

**7.11846** *3.* (1) Subject to the following provisions of this Order, the following must be made up in a container marked with an indication of quantity by net weight—
(*a*) the foods specified in column 1 of Schedule 1, when pre-packed; and
(*b*) cocoa products and chocolate products, solid and paste coffee and chicory products and sugar, when made up in a container for relevant wholesale,

subject to the exemptions specified in column 2 of Schedule 1.

(2) Unless sold loose or packaged in a quantity of less than 5 g, honey must be made up in a container marked with an indication of quantity by net weight.

(3) Subject to the following provisions of this Order, the foods specified in column 1 of Schedule 1 must, when sold loose, if sold by retail be sold only by net weight.

(4) Paragraph (3) above shall not apply in relation to any of the following—
(*a*) biscuits (except to wafer biscuits which are not cream filled) when sold in a quantity of eight or less;
(*b*) bread;
(*c*) chunk honey; or
(*d*) comb honey.

*Provision for the containers of certain foods not sold by retail to be accompanied by a document indicating quantity*

**7.11847** *4.* (1) In the case of solid and paste coffee and chicory products, cocoa products and chocolate products, honey, caseins and caseinates or preserved milk for human consumption pre-packed or made up in a container for relevant wholesale, the information required by Article 3(2) above or, as the case may be 7, 9(2) or 12 below to be marked on the container may, if—
(*a*) the foods are not sold by retail; and
(*b*) the net weight of the foods is not less than the particular quantities specified in paragraph (2) below in relation to the foods,

be given at the time when they are sold in a document accompanying the container and containing an indication of quantity by net weight.

(2) The quantities referred to in paragraph (1) above are:

solid and paste coffee and chicory products 5 kg
cocoa products and chocolate products . . . . . . . . . . . . 10 kg
honey . . . . . . . . . . . . . 10 kg
caseins and caseinates . . . . . . . . . . . . 10 kg
preserved milk for human consumption . . . . . . . . . . . . 10 kg

*Special provisions in respect of particular foods*

*Biscuits and shortbread*

**7.11848** *5.* (1) Article 3(1) above shall not apply in relation to biscuits which have been pre-packed on the same premises as those on which they were produced, and either:—
(*a*) the biscuits are in the possession of the producer for sale by him by retail on those premises; or
(*b*) if the producer has agreed to sell or has sold the biscuits, he agreed to sell or sold them by retail on those premises.

(2) Biscuits to which paragraph (1) above applies (other than wafer biscuits which are not cream-filled) shall be pre-packed only if the container is marked with an indication of quantity by net weight:

Provided that there shall be exempted from the requirements of this paragraph biscuits pre-packed in a quantity not exceeding 100 g.

(3) Shortbread shall be pre-packed only if the container is marked with an indication of quantity by net weight:

Provided that there shall be exempted from the requirements of this paragraph shortbread—

(*a*) where made up in a quantity not exceeding 50 g; or

(*b*) consisting of a piece or pieces each weighing 200 g or more if the number of pieces in the container, if more than one, is marked on the container or is clearly visible and capable of being easily counted through the container.

(4) Wafer biscuits which are not cream-filled shall be pre-packed only if the container is marked with an indication of quantity by number.

(5) Wafer biscuits which are not cream-filled and which are sold loose must if sold by retail be sold only by number.

(6) Shortbread, when sold loose must, if sold by retail, be sold only by net weight, unless sold in a quantity of eight pieces or fewer.

*Bread*

**7.11849** *6.* (1) For the purposes of this article "unwrapped loaf of bread" means a loaf of bread which is not made up in advance ready for retail sale or wholesale in a securely closed container and includes bread offered for sale in a confining band.

(2) Subject to paragraph (3), an unwrapped loaf of bread may be made for sale only if—

(*a*) an indication of the quantity of the bread is given on a ticket displayed in immediate proximity to that loaf; or

(*b*) there is displayed, in such a position and manner as to be readily available without special request for inspection by a buyer before any sale is made, a notice—

(i) listing the forms in which unwrapped loaves of bread are made for sale; and

(ii) indicating the quantity or quantities in which each such form is made for sale.

(3) The following are exempt from the requirements of paragraph (2)—

(*a*) any unwrapped loaf of bread in a quantity of 400 g or a multiple of 400 g;

(*b*) any unwrapped loaf of bread weighing 300 g or less; and

(*c*) any sale under a contract for the supply of bread for consumption on the premises of the buyer if the contract provides for each delivery of bread to be of a specified aggregate quantity of not less than 25 kg and for the weighing of the bread on delivery.

*Caseins and Caseinates*

**7.11850** *7.* In the case of caseins and caseinates for human consumption, when pre-packed or made up in a container for relevant wholesale, the container must be marked with an indication of quantity by net weight.

*Cocoa and chocolate products*

**7.11851** *8.* (1) Subject to paragraph (2) below, in the case of cocoa products and chocolate products, when pre-packed or made up in a container for relevant wholesale, the container must be marked with an indication of quantity by net weight, unless sold in a quantity by net weight of less than 50g.

(2) Nothing in paragraph (1) above shall require a container to be marked with an indication of quantity by net weight if it is a container in which fancy chocolate products are pre-packed, except that when the products are on sale by retail the exemption provided by this paragraph shall apply only if an indication of quantity by net weight is given on a ticket or notice displayed on or in immediate proximity to the products.

(3) Except in the case of an article the net weight of which is less than 50 g cocoa products and chocolate products which are sold loose must, when sold by retail, be sold only by net weight.

*Coffee and chicory products*

**7.11852** *9.* (1) In the case of liquid coffee and chicory products, when pre-packed or made up in a container for relevant wholesale, the container must be marked with an indication of quantity by capacity measurement, unless sold in a quantity of less than 5 ml.

(2) Where the contents of a container in which solid and paste coffee and chicory products or liquid coffee and chicory products are pre-packed or made up for relevant wholesale consists of packs of such products not intended for individual sale, the container shall, in addition to any marking required by Article 3(2) and paragraph (1) above, be marked with the total number of such packs.

*Liquid edible oil*

**7.11853** *10.* Liquid edible oil shall be pre-packed only if the container is marked with an indication of quantity by volume:

Provided that there shall be exempted from the requirements of this Article liquid edible oil pre-packed in a quantity of less than 5 ml or more than 20 L.

*Milk*

**7.11854** *11.* (1) Milk which is sold loose or made up in a container for relevant wholesale shall be sold only by capacity measurement or by net weight.

(2) *Revoked.*

(3) Milk shall be sold by means of, or offered or exposed for sale in, a vending machine only if there is displayed on or in the machine—

(*a*) an indication of the quantity by capacity measurement of the milk comprised in each item for sale by means of that machine; and

(*b*) except where the machine is on premises at which the seller carries on business, a statement of the name and address of the seller.

*Preserved milk*

**7.11855** *12.* In the case of preserved milk for human consumption, when pre-packed or made up in a container for relevant wholesale, the container must be marked with an indication of quantity by net weight, unless sold in a quantity of less than 5g.

*Potatoes*

**7.11856** *13.* (1) Where at any premises other than a vehicle or ship any potatoes have been sold by weight when made up in a container, and the sale is otherwise than by retail, the buyer may require all or any of the following weighings to be carried out at those premises, that is to say—

(*a*) a weighing of that container while the potatoes are therein;

(*b*) a weighing of that container after the removal of the potatoes therefrom;

(*c*) a weighing of a similar container which is empty,

and thereupon the seller shall either carry out or permit the buyer to carry out the weighing or weighings so required; and if the seller without reasonable cause contravenes this requirement he shall be guilty of an offence.

(2) The occupier of any premises at which any potatoes are made up in a container for sale by weight otherwise than by retail, or of any premises (other than a vehicle or ship) at which such potatoes so made up are so sold, shall provide suitable weighing equipment and make that equipment available for any weighing or weighings required under the foregoing paragraph to be carried out at those premises; and if he without reasonable cause contravenes any of the requirements of this paragraph he shall be guilty of an offence.

(4) Any person guilty of an offence under this Article shall be liable on summary conviction to a fine not exceeding **£2,000**.

**7.11857** *14.* Potatoes, which are sold loose must, if sold by retail, be sold only—

(*a*) by net weight; or

(*b*) if the food is sold in a container which does not exceed the appropriate permitted weight specified in the Table in Schedule 2 to this Order, either by net weight or gross weight.

*Miscellaneous foods to be marked when pre-packed with quantity by number*

**7.11858** *15.* (1) Subject to paragraph (2) below, foods of any of the following descriptions, that is to say—

(*a*) cereal biscuit breakfast foods, other than foods in the case of which none of the biscuits weighs more than 10 g;

(*b*) flour confectionery, except when consisting of uncooked pastry or uncooked pastry cases, not containing any filling, or shortbread;

(*c*) fruit preservative tablets, rennet tablets, saccharin tablets, soft drink tablets and sweetening tablets;

(*d*) shell eggs;

(*e*) vanilla pods;

(*f*) capsule and tablet foods,

shall be pre-packed only if the container is marked with an indication of quantity by number.

(2) There shall be exempted from the requirements of this Article—

(*a*) flour confectionery, if the number of items in the container is clearly visible and capable of being easily counted through the container; and

(*b*) any foods in a quantity by number of one.

*Other pre-packed foods*

**7.11859** *16.* (1) This Article applies to foods of any description which are not goods—

(*a*) required by any other provision of this Order or under or by virtue of any other provision of the Act to be pre-packed only if the container is marked with an indication of quantity; or

(*b*) in the case of which when sold pre-packed (whether on any sale or on a sale of any particular description) the quantity of the goods sold expressed in a particular manner is required by or under any such provision to be made known to the buyer at or before a particular time; or

(*c*) expressly exempted by any such provision from all such requirements which would otherwise apply thereto.

(2) Subject to paragraph (3) below, foods to which this Article applies shall be pre-packed only if the container is marked with an indication of quantity either by net weight or by capacity measurement.

(3) The following shall be exempted from the requirements of this Article, that is to say—

(*a*) bread, including bun loaves, fruit loaves, malt loaves and fruited malt loaves;

(*b*) food to which Articles 4 and 5 of the Weights and Measures Act 1963 (Cheese, Fish, Fresh Fruits and Vegetables, Meat and Poultry) Order 1984 apply, other than dates;

(*c*) freeze drinks in a quantity of less than 50 ml;

(*d*) herbs, whole and sifted except saffron, in a quantity of less than 25 g;

(*e*) iced lollies and water ices;

(*f*) intoxicating liquor to which Article 6 of the Weights and Measures (Intoxicating Liquor) Order 1988 applies;

(*g*) milk;

(*h*) potato crisps and other similar products commonly known as snack foods in a quantity of less than 1 oz up to and including 30th June 1989 and thereafter in a quantity of less than 25 g;

(*i*) single portion vending machine beverage packs in a quantity of less than 25 g or of less than 25 ml whether or not they contain other foods to which this Article does not apply;

(*j*) single toffee apples;

(*k*) soft drinks of any description in a syphon;

(*l*) sugar confectionery consisting of rock or barley sugar in sticks or novelty shapes;

(*m*) sugar confectionery not included in paragraph (*l*) above, and chocolate confectionery, in a quantity of less than 50 g;

(*n*) goods of any other description, except saffron, in a quantity of less than 5 g or of less than 5 ml.

*Multipacks*

**7.11860** *17.* (1) Nothing in the previous provisions of this Order shall require any container to be marked with any information or to enclose foods of a particular quantity if all the following provisions are satisfied—

(*a*) the contents of the container in which any foods to which the Order applies are pre-packed or made up in the container for relevant wholesale consist of two or more packs of goods;

(*b*) where the goods in any pack, if sold individually, would be required by the Order to be made up in a specified quantity, the goods in any such pack are so made up;

(*c*) where any pack, if sold individually, would be required by the Order to be marked with an indication as to the quantity of the goods, the pack is so marked;

(*d*)

(i) the container is marked with a description of the goods in each pack, the total number of packs containing goods of each description and where paragraph (*c*) above applies with an indication as to the quantity of the goods in each such pack; or

(ii) where each pack to which paragraph (*c*) above applies contains the same quantity of identical goods, an indication as to the quantity of the goods in at least one such pack is clearly visible, and the total number of such packs is clearly visible and capable of being easily counted, through the container; or

(iii) where each pack does not contain goods of the same description or does contain such goods but does not contain them in the same quantity, an indication as to the quantity of any goods in each pack to which paragraph (*c*) above applies, or if there are two or more identical such packs an indication as to the quantity of the goods in at least one of them, is clearly visible, and the total number of such packs of each description is clearly visible and capable of being easily counted, through the container.

(2) Where the provisions of both Article 4 and paragraph (1) above apply in a particular case, the information permitted by paragraph (1)(*d*)(i) above to be marked on the container may be given in a document accompanying the container.

*Application of Section 25 of the Act as modified in relation to certain foods*

**7.11861** *18.* (1) Section 25(2) and (3) of the Act shall apply in the case of any solid and paste coffee and chicory products, cocoa products and chocolate products, honey, caseins and caseinates or preserved milk for human consumption pre-packed or made up in a container for relevant wholesale where the information required by Article 3(2), 7, 9(2) or 12, or permitted by Article 17(1)(*d*)(i), to be marked on the container is given in a document accompanying the container in accordance with Article 4 or 17(2) with the following modifications—

(*a*) in section 25(2) the words "whether the sale is, or is to be, by retail or otherwise" shall be omitted; and

(*b*) in paragraphs (*d*) and (*e*) of section 25(3)—

(i) after the word "information" there shall be inserted the words "or is accompanied by a document containing particular information"; and

(ii) after the words "so marked" there shall be inserted the words "or accompanied".

(2) Where subsections (2) and (3) of section 25 of the Act applies by virtue of paragraph (1) above, a person shall not be guilty of an offence under the said subsection (2) by reason only of—

(*a*) having in his possession for sale, or

(*b*) having in his possession for delivery after sale, or

(*c*) causing or suffering any other person to have in his possession for sale or for delivery after sale,

solid and paste coffee and chicory products, cocoa products and chocolate products, honey, caseins and caseinates or preserved milk for human consumption pre-packed or made up in a container for relevant wholesale otherwise than in a container so accompanied.

SCHEDULE 1
Foods

Article 3

7.11862

| (1) Foods | (2) Exemptions from quantity marking |
|---|---|
| Barley kernels, pearl barley, rice (including ground rice and rice flakes), sago, semolina and tapioca. | less than 5 g. |
| Biscuits, other than wafer biscuits which are not cream-filled. | 50 g or less |
| Bread in the form of a whole loaf. | where the net weight of each loaf is less than 300 g and the number of items (if more than one in the container) is marked on the container or is clearly visible and capable of being easily counted through the container. |
| Cereal breakfast foods in flake form, other than cereal biscuit breakfast foods. | less than 5 g. |
| Coffee, coffee mixtures and coffee bags. | less than 5 g. |
| Coffee extracts and chicory extracts consisting of solid and paste coffee and chicory products. | less than 5 g. |
| Dried fruits of any one or more of the following descriptions, that is to say, apples (including dried apple rings), apricots, currants, dates, figs, muscatels, nectarines, peaches, pears (including dried pear rings), prunes, raisins, sultanas and dried fruit salad. | less than 5 g. |
| Dried vegetables of any of the following descriptions, that is to say, beans, lentils and peas (including split peas). | less than 5 g. |
| Edible fats of any of the following descriptions— | less than 5 g. |
| (*a*) butter, margarine, any mixture of butter and margarine, and low fat spreads (butter or margarine substitutes); | |
| (*b*) dripping and shredded suet; | |
| (*c*) lard and compound cooking fat and substitutes therefor; | |
| (*d*) solidified edible oil (except in gel form). | |
| Flour, namely flour of bean, maize, pea, rice, rye, soya bean or wheat and flour products of any of the following descriptions, that is to say— | less than 5 g. |
| (*a*) cake flour, other than cake mixtures and sponge mixtures; | |

| (1) *Foods* | (2) *Exemptions from quantity marking* |
|---|---|
| (*b*) cornflour, other than blancmange powders and custard powders; | |
| (*c*) self-raising flour. | |
| Honey. | less than 5 g. |
| Jam and marmalade, other than diabetic jam or marmalade. Jelly preserves. | less than 5 g. |
| Molasses, syrup and treacle. | less than 5 g. |
| Oat products of any of the following descriptions: | less than 5 g. |
| (*a*) flour of oats; | |
| (*b*) oatflakes and oatmeal | |
| Pasta. | less than 5 g. |
| Potatoes. | (1) where the net weight of each potato is not less than 175 g and the container is marked with an indication of quantity by number and with a statement to the effect that each potato in the container is of a net weight not less than a weight specified in grams, whether the weight so specified is 175 g or a greater weight. |
| | (2) less than 5 g |
| Salt. | less than 5 g. |
| Sugar. | less than 5 g. |
| Tea in a tea bag, namely a permeable sealed bag, containing tea, which is intended to be immersed in water in the course of preparation to drink. | less than 5 g. |
| Tea, other than instant tea or tea in a tea bag. | less than 5 g. |

SCHEDULE 2

TABLE OF PERMITTED WEIGHTS FOR CONTAINERS

Article 14

7.11863

| Gross weight | Permitted weight of container |
|---|---|
| Not exceeding 500 g | 5 g |
| Exceeding 500 g | a weight at the rate of 10 g per kg of the gross weight |

# Units of Measurement Regulations 1995[1]

(SI 1995/1804)

**7.11864** *1. Citation and commencement* These Regulations may be cited as the Units of Measurement Regulations 1995 and shall come into force on 1st October 1995.

[1] Made by the Secretary of State, being a Minister designated for the purposes of s 2(2) of the European Communities Act 1972.

**7.11865** *2. Interpretation* In these Regulations—

"Act" includes a local and personal or private Act, an Act of the Parliament of Northern Ireland and a Measure of the Northern Ireland Assembly;

"the commencement date", subject to regulation 4 below, means 1st October 1995;

"corresponding metric unit", in relation to a relevant imperial unit, means the unit of measurement specified in relation to the relevant imperial unit in the second column of the Schedule to these Regulations;

"existing provision" means any of the following, namely—

(*a*) a provision of any Act passed, or of any subordinate legislation made, before the commencement date;

(*b*) a provision of any contract, agreement, licence, authority, undertaking or statement made or given before that date; and

(*c*) a provision of any deed, instrument or document made before that date;

"relevant imperial unit" means a unit of measurement specified in the first column of the Schedule to these Regulations;

"subordinate legislation" means Orders in Council, orders, rules, regulations, schemes, warrants, byelaws and other instruments made under any Act; and

"the Units of Measurement Directive" means the Directive of the Council of the European Communities dated 20th December 1979 (No 80/181/EEC) on the approximation of the laws of member States relating to units of measurement.

**7.11866** 3. *Conversion of imperial units of measurement* (1) Subject to the following provisions of these Regulations, where—

(*a*) an existing provision authorises or requires a measurement to be made, or an indication of quantity to be expressed, in a relevant imperial unit,

(*b*) the provision has effect for economic, public health, public safety or administrative purposes, and

(*c*) the provision has legal effect on or after the commencement date,

the provision shall, unless the context otherwise requires, be construed on or after that date as authorising or requiring the measurement to be made, or the indication of quantity to be expressed, in the corresponding metric unit.

(2) Subject to the following provisions of these Regulations, where—

(*a*) an existing provision contains a reference to an indication of quantity expressed in a relevant imperial unit,

(*b*) the provision has effect for economic, public health, public safety or administrative purposes, and

(*c*) the provision has legal effect on or after the commencement date,

the provision shall, unless the context otherwise requires, be construed on or after that date as if the indication of quantity concerned were expressed in the corresponding metric unit.

(3) Subject to paragraph (4) below, any conversion of an indication of quantity expressed in a relevant imperial unit which is required to be made by virtue of paragraph (2) above shall be made by using the metric equivalent specified in relation to the relevant imperial unit in the third column of the Schedule to these Regulations.

(4) Any conversion of an indication of quantity expressed in degrees Fahrenheit which is required to be made by virtue of paragraph (2) above shall be made by subtracting thirty-two and multiplying the result by five-ninths.

**7.11867** 4. *Later application of regulation 3 in relation to certain uses of imperial units* In relation to any of the following uses of relevant imperial units which are permitted by Article 1(*d*) of the Units of Measurement Directive, that is to say—

(*a*) the use of the fathom for marine navigation,

(*b*) the use of the pint or fluid ounce for beer, cider, water, lemonade and fruit juice in returnable containers,

(*c*) the use of the pound or ounce (avoirdupois) for goods sold loose from bulk, and

(*d*) the use of the therm for the supply of gas,

regulation 3 above shall be treated as coming into force on 1st January 2000 and that date shall be treated as the commencement date for the purposes of these Regulations.

**7.11868** 5. *Exceptions* (1) Nothing in these Regulations shall apply in relation to any supplementary indication; and in this paragraph "supplementary indication" has the same meaning as it has in section 8(5A) of the Weights and Measures Act 1985.

(2) Nothing in these Regulations shall apply in relation to any of the uses of relevant imperial units which are permitted by Article 1(*b*) of the Units of Measurement Directive, that is to say—

(*a*) the use of the mile, yard, foot or inch for road traffic signs, distance and speed measurement,

(*b*) the use of the pint for dispensing draught beer and cider;

(*c*) the use of the pint for milk in returnable containers;

(*d*) the use of the acre for land registration; and

(*e*) the use of the troy ounce for transactions in precious metals.

(3) Nothing in these Regulations shall apply in relation to any use of a relevant imperial unit which is permitted by Article 2(*b*) of the Units of Measurement Directive (use in the field of air and sea transport and rail traffic of units laid down in international conventions or agreements).

(4) Nothing in these Regulations shall apply in relation to any contract to which regulation 11(1) of the Units of Measurement Regulations 1986 applies.

**7.11869** *6. Revocation.*

SCHEDULE

RELEVANT IMPERIAL UNITS, CORRESPONDING METRIC UNITS AND METRIC EQUIVALENTS Regulations 2 and 3

**7.11870**

| Relevant imperial unit | Corresponding metric unit | Metric equivalent |
|---|---|---|
| **Length** | | |
| inch | centimetre | 2.54 centimetres |
| hand | metre | 0.1016 metre |
| foot | metre | 0.3048 metre |
| yard | metre | 0.9144 metre |
| fathom | metre | 1.8288 metres |
| chain | metre | 20.1168 metres |
| furlong | kilometre | 0.201168 kilometre |
| mile | kilometre | 1.609344 kilometres |
| nautical mile (UK) | metre | 1853 metres |
| **Area** | | |
| square inch | square centimetre | 6.4516 square centimetres |
| square foot | square metre | 0.09290304 square metre |
| square yard | square metre | 0.83612736 square metre |
| rood | square metre | 1011.7141056 square metres |
| acre | square metre | 4046.8564224 square metres |
| square mile | square kilometre | 2.589988110336 square kilometres |
| **Capacity** | | |
| fluid ounce | millilitre | 28.4130625 millilitres |
| gill | litre | 0.1420635125 litre |
| pint | litre | 0.56826125 litre |
| quart | litre | 1.1365225 litres |
| gallon | litre | 4.54609 litres |
| **Pressure** | | |
| inch of water | pascal | 249.08891 pascals |
| **Mass** | | |
| grain | gram | 0.06479891 gram |
| dram | gram | 1.7718451953125 grams |
| ounce (avoirdupois) | gram | 28.349523125 grams |
| troy ounce | gram | 31.1034768 grams |
| pound | kilogram | 0.45359237 kilogram |
| stone | kilogram | 6.35029318 kilograms |
| quarter | kilogram | 12.70058636 kilograms |
| cental | kilogram | 45.359237 kilograms |
| hundredweight | kilogram | 50.80234544 kilograms |
| ton | tonne | 1.0160469088 tonnes |
| **Force** | | |
| pound-force | newton | 4.4482216152605 newtons |
| ton-force | kilonewton | 9.96401641818352 kilonewtons |
| **Volume** | | |
| cubic inch | cubic centimetre | 16.387064 cubic centimetres |
| cran | cubic decimetre | 170.478375 cubic decimetres |
| cubic foot | cubic metre | 0.028316846592 cubic metre |
| bushel | cubic metre | 0.03636872 cubic metre |
| cubic yard | cubic metre | 0.764554857984 cubic metre |
| **Power** | | |
| horsepower | kilowatt | 0.74569987158227022 kilowatt |
| **Temperature** | | |
| degree Fahrenheit | degree Celsius | (See regulation 3(4)) |
| **Energy** | | |
| foot pound-force | joule | 1.3558179483314004 joules |
| British thermal unit | kilojoule | 1.05505585257348 kilojoules |
| therm | megajoule | 105.505585257348 megajoules |

| Relevant imperial unit | Corresponding metric unit | Metric equivalent |
|---|---|---|
| **Illuminance** | | |
| foot candle | lux | 10.763910416709 lux |
| **Speed** | | |
| knot (UK) | metres per second | 0.51477 metres per second |

# WITNESSES

**Contents**



## Witnesses (Public Inquiries)

7.11871 The **Witnesses (Public Inquiries) Protection Act 1892** (55 & 56 Vict c 64) protects witnesses who give evidence before any Royal Commission or any committee of either House of Parliament or other public inquiry. A person who threatens, or in any way punishes, damnifies or injures such a witness is liable to a penalty of **level 3** on the standard scale **or three months' imprisonment** (s 2). A prosecution for an offence under this Act may be heard and determined by a magistrates' court.

[Witnesses (Public Inquiries) Protection Act 1892, s 3, as amended by the Criminal Law Act 1977, Sch 13 and the Criminal Justice Act 1982, ss 38 and 46—summarised.]

## Inquiries Act 2005

(2005 c 12)

*Constitution of inquiry*

7.11872 **1. Power to establish inquiry** (1) A Minister may cause an inquiry to be held under this Act in relation to a case where it appears to him that—

(*a*) particular events have caused, or are capable of causing, public concern, or

(*b*) there is public concern that particular events may have occurred.

(2) In this Act "Minister" means—

(*a*) a United Kingdom Minister;

(*b*) the Scottish Ministers;

(*ba*) the Welsh Ministers;

(*c*) a Northern Ireland Minister.

(3) References in this Act to an inquiry, except where the context requires otherwise, are to an inquiry under this Act.

[Inquiries Act 2005, s 1 as amended by the Government of Wales Act 2006, Schs 10 and 12.]

*Inquiry proceedings*

7.11873 **17. Evidence and procedure** (1) Subject to any provision of this Act or of rules under section 41, the procedure and conduct of an inquiry are to be such as the chairman of the inquiry may direct.

(2) In particular, the chairman may take evidence on oath, and for that purpose may administer oaths.

(3) In making any decision as to the procedure or conduct of an inquiry, the chairman must act with fairness and with regard also to the need to avoid any unnecessary cost (whether to public funds or to witnesses or others).

[Inquiries Act 2005, s 17.]

7.11874 **18. Public access to inquiry proceedings and information** (1) Subject to any restrictions imposed by a notice or order under section 19, the chairman must take such steps as he considers reasonable to secure that members of the public (including reporters) are able—

(*a*) to attend the inquiry or to see and hear a simultaneous transmission of proceedings at the inquiry;

(*b*) to obtain or to view a record of evidence and documents given, produced or provided to the inquiry or inquiry panel.

(2) No recording or broadcast of proceedings at an inquiry may be made except—

(*a*) at the request of the chairman, or

(*b*) with the permission of the chairman and in accordance with any terms on which permission is given.

Any such request or permission must be framed so as not to enable a person to see or hear by means of a recording or broadcast anything that he is prohibited by a notice under section 19 from seeing or hearing.

(3) Section 32(2) of the Freedom of Information Act 2000 (c 36) (certain inquiry records etc exempt from obligations under that Act) does not apply in relation to information contained in documents that, in pursuance of rules under section 41(1)(*b*) below, have been passed to and are held by a public authority.

(4) Section 37(1)(*b*) of the Freedom of Information (Scotland) Act 2002 (asp 13) (certain inquiry records etc exempt from obligations under that Act) does not apply in relation to

information contained in documents that, in pursuance of rules under section 41(1)(*b*) below, have been passed to and are held by a Scottish public authority.

[Inquiries Act 2005, s 18.]

7.11875 **19. Restrictions on public access etc** (1) Restrictions may, in accordance with this section, be imposed on—

(*a*) attendance at an inquiry, or at any particular part of an inquiry;

(*b*) disclosure or publication of any evidence or documents given, produced or provided to an inquiry.

(2) Restrictions may be imposed in either or both of the following ways—

(*a*) by being specified in a notice (a "restriction notice") given by the Minister to the chairman at any time before the end of the inquiry;

(*b*) by being specified in an order (a "restriction order") made by the chairman during the course of the inquiry.

(3) A restriction notice or restriction order must specify only such restrictions—

(*a*) as are required by any statutory provision, enforceable Community obligation or rule of law, or

(*b*) as the Minister or chairman considers to be conducive to the inquiry fulfilling its terms of reference or to be necessary in the public interest, having regard in particular to the matters mentioned in subsection (4).

(4) Those matters are—

(*a*) the extent to which any restriction on attendance, disclosure or publication might inhibit the allaying of public concern;

(*b*) any risk of harm or damage that could be avoided or reduced by any such restriction;

(*c*) any conditions as to confidentiality subject to which a person acquired information that he is to give, or has given, to the inquiry;

(*d*) the extent to which not imposing any particular restriction would be likely—

(i) to cause delay or to impair the efficiency or effectiveness of the inquiry, or

(ii) otherwise to result in additional cost (whether to public funds or to witnesses or others).

(5) In subsection (4)(*b*) "harm or damage" includes in particular—

(*a*) death or injury;

(*b*) damage to national security or international relations;

(*c*) damage to the economic interests of the United Kingdom or of any part of the United Kingdom;

(*d*) damage caused by disclosure of commercially sensitive information.

[Inquiries Act 2005, s 18.]

7.11876 **20. Further provisions about restriction notices and orders** (1) Restrictions specified in a restriction notice have effect in addition to any already specified, whether in an earlier restriction notice or in a restriction order.

(2) Restrictions specified in a restriction order have effect in addition to any already specified, whether in an earlier restriction order or in a restriction notice.

(3) The Minister may vary or revoke a restriction notice by giving a further notice to the chairman at any time before the end of the inquiry.

(4) The chairman may vary or revoke a restriction order by making a further order during the course of the inquiry.

(5) Restrictions imposed under section 19 on disclosure or publication of evidence or documents ("disclosure restrictions") continue in force indefinitely, unless—

(*a*) under the terms of the relevant notice or order the restrictions expire at the end of the inquiry, or at some other time, or

(*b*) the relevant notice or order is varied or revoked under subsection (3), (4) or (7).

This is subject to subsection (6).

(6) After the end of the inquiry, disclosure restrictions do not apply to a public authority, or a Scottish public authority, in relation to information held by the authority otherwise than as a result of the breach of any such restrictions.

(7) After the end of an inquiry the Minister may, by a notice published in a way that he considers suitable—

(*a*) revoke a restriction order or restriction notice containing disclosure restrictions that are still in force, or

(*b*) vary it so as to remove or relax any of the restrictions.

(8) In this section "restriction notice" and "restriction order" have the meaning given by section 19(2).

[Inquiries Act 2005, s 20.]

7.11877 **21. Powers of chairman to require production of evidence etc** (1) The chairman of an inquiry may by notice require a person to attend at a time and place stated in the notice—

(*a*) to give evidence;

(*b*) to produce any documents in his custody or under his control that relate to a matter in question at the inquiry;

(*c*) to produce any other thing in his custody or under his control for inspection, examination or testing by or on behalf of the inquiry panel.

(2) The chairman may by notice require a person, within such period as appears to the inquiry panel to be reasonable—

(*a*) to provide evidence to the inquiry panel in the form of a written statement;

(*b*) to provide any documents in his custody or under his control that relate to a matter in question at the inquiry;

(c) to produce any other thing in his custody or under his control for inspection, examination or testing by or on behalf of the inquiry panel.

(3) A notice under subsection (1) or (2) must—

(*a*) explain the possible consequences of not complying with the notice;

(*b*) indicate what the recipient of the notice should do if he wishes to make a claim within subsection (4).

(4) A claim by a person that—

(*a*) he is unable to comply with a notice under this section, or

(*b*) it is not reasonable in all the circumstances to require him to comply with such a notice,

is to be determined by the chairman of the inquiry, who may revoke or vary the notice on that ground.

(5) In deciding whether to revoke or vary a notice on the ground mentioned in subsection (4)(*b*), the chairman must consider the public interest in the information in question being obtained by the inquiry, having regard to the likely importance of the information.

(6) For the purposes of this section a thing is under a person's control if it is in his possession or if he has a right to possession of it.

[Inquiries Act 2005, s 21.]

7.11878 22. **Privileged information etc** (1) A person may not under section 21 be required to give, produce or provide any evidence or document if—

(*a*) he could not be required to do so if the proceedings of the inquiry were civil proceedings in a court in the relevant part of the United Kingdom, or

(*b*) the requirement would be incompatible with an EU obligation.

(2) The rules of law under which evidence or documents are permitted or required to be withheld on grounds of public interest immunity apply in relation to an inquiry as they apply in relation to civil proceedings in a court in the relevant part of the United Kingdom.

[Inquiries Act 2005, s 22 as amended by SI 2011/1043.]

7.11879 23. **Risk of damage to the economy** (1) This section applies where it is submitted to an inquiry panel, on behalf of the Crown, the Financial Conduct Authority, the Prudential Regulation Authority or the Bank of England, that there is information held by any person which, in order to avoid a risk of damage to the economy, ought not to be revealed.

(2) The panel must not permit or require the information to be revealed, or cause it to be revealed, unless satisfied that the public interest in the information being revealed outweighs the public interest in avoiding a risk of damage to the economy.

(3) In making a decision under this section the panel must take account of any restriction notice given under section 19 or any restriction order that the chairman has made or proposes to make under that section.

(4) In this section—

"damage to the economy" means damage to the economic interests of the United Kingdom or of any part of the United Kingdom;

"revealed" means revealed to anyone who is not a member of the inquiry panel.

(5) This section does not prevent the inquiry panel from communicating any information in confidence to the Minister.

(6) This section does not affect the rules of law referred to in section 22(2).

[Inquiries Act 2005, s 23 as amended by the Financial Services Act 2012, Sch 18.]

*Supplementary*

7.11880 35. **Offences** (1) A person is guilty of an offence if he fails without reasonable excuse to do anything that he is required to do by a notice under section 21.

(2) A person is guilty of an offence if during the course of an inquiry he does anything that is intended to have the effect of—

(*a*) distorting or otherwise altering any evidence, document or other thing that is given, produced or provided to the inquiry panel, or

(*b*) preventing any evidence, document or other thing from being given, produced or provided to the inquiry panel,

or anything that he knows or believes is likely to have that effect.

(3) A person is guilty of an offence if during the course of an inquiry—

(*a*) he intentionally suppresses or conceals a document that is, and that he knows or believes to be, a relevant document, or (*b*) he intentionally alters or destroys any such document.

For the purposes of this subsection a document is a "relevant document" if it is likely that the inquiry panel would (if aware of its existence) wish to be provided with it.

(4) A person does not commit an offence under subsection (2) or (3) by doing anything that he is authorised or required to do—

(*a*) by the inquiry panel, or

(*b*) by virtue of section 22 or any privilege that applies.

(5) Proceedings in England and Wales or in Northern Ireland for an offence under subsection (1) may be instituted only by the chairman.

(6) Proceedings for an offence under subsection (2) or (3) may be instituted—

(*a*) in England and Wales, only by or with the consent of the Director of Public Prosecutions;

(*b*) in Northern Ireland, only by or with the consent of the Director of Public Prosecutions for Northern Ireland.

(7) A person who is guilty of an offence under this section is liable on summary conviction to a fine not exceeding level three on the standard scale or to imprisonment for a term not exceeding the relevant maximum, or to both.

(8) "The relevant maximum" is—

(*a*) in England and Wales, 51 weeks;

(*b*) in Scotland and Northern Ireland, six months.

[Inquiries Act 2005, s 35.]

7.11881 37. **Immunity from suit** (1) No action lies against—

(*a*) a member of an inquiry panel,

(*b*) an assessor, counsel or solicitor to an inquiry, or

(*c*) a person engaged to provide assistance to an inquiry,

in respect of any act done or omission made in the execution of his duty as such, or any act done or omission made in good faith in the purported execution of his duty as such.

(2) Subsection (1) applies only to acts done or omissions made during the course of the inquiry, otherwise than during any period of suspension (within the meaning of section 13).

(3) For the purposes of the law of defamation, the same privilege attaches to—

(*a*) any statement made in or for the purposes of proceedings before an inquiry (including the report and any interim report of the inquiry), and

(*b*) reports of proceedings before an inquiry,

as would be the case if those proceedings were proceedings before a court in the relevant part of the United Kingdom.

[Inquiries Act 2005, s 37.]

*General*

7.11882 43. **Interpretation** (1) In this Act—

"assessor" means an assessor appointed under section 11;

"chairman", in relation to an inquiry, means the chairman of the inquiry;

"the course of the inquiry" and similar expressions are to be read in accordance with subsection (2);

"date of conversion" has the meaning given by section 15(1);

"document" includes information recorded in any form (and see subsection (3));

"event", except in sections 13 and 46, includes any conduct or omission;

"inquiry", except where the context requires otherwise, means an inquiry under this Act;

"inquiry panel" is to be read in accordance with section 3(2);

"interested party", in relation to an inquiry, means a person with a particularly significant interest in the proceedings or outcome of the inquiry;

"interim report" means a report under section 24(3);

"joint inquiry" has the meaning given by section 32(2);

"member", in relation to an inquiry panel, includes the chairman;

"Minister" is to be read in accordance with section 1(2) (and see subsection (4) below);

"Northern Ireland Minister" includes the First Minister and the deputy First Minister acting jointly;

"public authority" has the same meaning as in the Freedom of Information Act 2000 (c 36);

"the relevant Parliament or Assembly" means whichever of the following is or are applicable—

(*a*) in the case of an inquiry for which the Treasury is responsible, the House of Commons;

(*b*) in the case of an inquiry for which any other United Kingdom Minister is responsible, or one for which the Secretary of State exercising functions by virtue of section 45(2) is responsible, the House of Parliament of which that minister is a member;

(*c*) in the case of an inquiry for which the Scottish Ministers are responsible, the Scottish Parliament;

(*d*) in the case of an inquiry for which the Welsh Ministers are responsible, the National Assembly for Wales;

(*e*) in the case of an inquiry for which a Northern Ireland Minister is responsible, the Northern Ireland Assembly;

"the relevant part of the United Kingdom", in relation to an inquiry, means the part specified under section 31(1);

"report" means a report under section 24(1);

"responsible", in relation to an inquiry, is to be read in accordance with subsection (5);

"Scottish public authority" has the same meaning as in the Freedom of Information (Scotland) Act 2002 (asp 13);

"setting-up date" means the date specified under section 5(1)(*a*);

"statutory provision" means a provision contained in, or having effect under, any enactment, Act of the Scottish Parliament or Northern Ireland legislation;

"terms of reference", in relation to an inquiry under this Act, has the meaning given by section 5(6);

"United Kingdom Minister"—

(*a*) means the holder of a Ministerial office specified in Part 1, 2 or 3 of Schedule 1 to the Ministerial and other Salaries Act 1975 (c 27) or a Parliamentary Secretary;

(*b*) also includes the Treasury.

But a reference to a United Kingdom Minister does not include a reference to the Secretary of State discharging functions by virtue of section 45(2).

(2) References in this Act to the course of an inquiry are to the period beginning with the setting-up date, or (in the case of an inquiry converted under section 15) the date of conversion, and ending with the date on which the inquiry comes to an end (which is given by section 14).

(3) References in this Act to producing or providing a document, in relation to information recorded otherwise than in legible form, are to be read as references to producing or providing a copy of the information in a legible form.

(4) References in this Act to "the Minister", in relation to an inquiry, are to the Minister or Ministers responsible for the inquiry.

(5) For the purposes of this Act a Minister is "responsible" for an inquiry if he is the Minister, or one of the Ministers, by whom it was caused to be held under section 1 or converted under section 15.

This is subject to section 34(2)(*a*).

[Inquiries Act 2005, s 43 as amended by the Government of Wales Act 2006, Sch 10.]

# PART VIII
# PRECEDENTS AND FORMS

## CONTENTS

**Precedents**



**Forms**



# PRECEDENTS

## MAGISTRATES' COURTS, PROCEDURE

### 8.1 1 Application to justices to state case[1]

Application to justices to state case

(Magistrates' Courts Act 1980, s 111(1); Magistrates' Courts Rules 1981, r 76). – TO [name and address of the Clerk to the Justices for the magistrates' court] Clerk of the [name] Magistrates' Court sitting at [place].

On the [*date*] an information (*or* complaint) wherein (I the undersigned) [*name and address*] was informant (*or* complainant) and (I the undersigned) [*name and address*] was defending was heard before and determined by the above magistrates' court as follows [*set out the information or complaint and the determination of the court*].

I am aggrieved by the conviction (*or* order *or* determination or [*specify other proceeding*] as being wrong in law (and/*or* in excess of jurisdiction) and I apply to the justices composing the said court to state a case for the opinion of the High Court. The question(s) of law (and/*or* jurisdiction) on which the opinion of the High Court is sought is/are [*specify*].

Dated the [*date*].

*Signed [signature of applicant]*.

[1] The form of a stated case is set out in the section of Forms as form 155. Procedural matters once the case has been stated are contained in Civil Procedure Rules 1998 Part 52, in PART I: MAGISTRATES' COURTS, PROCEDURE, ante.

### 8.2 2 Certificate of refusal to state case

(Magistrates' Courts Act 1980, s 111(5)). – [Name of county and of magistrates' court]. On the [date] an information (or complaint) was preferred by [name and address of informant or complainant] against [name and address of defendant] that [set out information or complaint] and was determined by us as follows [set out the determination of the court]

The said [name of informant or complainant or defendant] being aggrieved by the determination as being wrong in law (and/or in excess of jurisdiction) has applied to us to state a case for the opinion of the High Court.

We are of opinion that the application is frivolous and so refuse to state a case.

Dated the [*date*].

*[Signature of Justices of the Peace]*

*Justices of the Peace*

### 8.3 3 Endorsement for service

*(Summary Jurisdiction (Process) Act* 1881, *s* 4). – Proof on oath (*or* solemn declaration) having been produced before me that the name of [*name*] subscribed to the within summons (*or* warrant *or* order etc) is of the handwriting of the sheriff (*or* justice of the peace) within mentioned; I authorise this summons to be served (or warrant to be executed) within the County of [specify].

Dated the [*date*].

*[Signature of Justices of the Peace]*

*Justices of the Peace*

### 8.4 4 Affidavit[1]

Affidavit

– In the matter of ([*specify*] (and other matters)) (R *v [name of (first) defendant*] (and others)); I [*name*] of [*address, occupation or description*][2], make oath (*or* do solemnly and sincerely affirm) and say as follows [*state matter of affidavit in numbered paragraphs*][3].

Sworn (Affirmed) at *full address* this day of 19 .

*[signature of maker of affidavit]*

(I having first truly distinctly and audibly read over the contents of this affidavit to the deponent (he being blind) (and explained the nature and effect of the exhibits therein referred to) who appeared perfectly to understand the same and made his mark thereto in my presence).

Before me

*[Signature of Commissioner]*

*A Commissioner for Oaths*[4].

---

[1] This precedent may be used where for example the law envisages information being placed before the High Court by justices or by the justices' clerk by way of affidavit. Reference must be made to the detailed requirements of Civil Procedure Rules 1998 for example, the affidavit must be in book form, following continuously from page to page, both sides of the paper being used; dates, sums and other numbers must be expressed in figures and not words, alterations, interlineations, erasures etc must be initialled (and the alteration repeated in the margin and initialled). Any affidavit that does not comply with the Civil Procedure Rules 1998 and *Practice Note* [1983] 3 All ER 33, [1983] 1 W LR 922, amended by Practice Direction [1995] 2 All ER 511, may be rejected by the court or made the subject for an order for costs. The above Practice Direction makes provision in the following terms-

Affidavits

(a) *Marking* At the top right-hand corner or the first page of every affidavit, and also on the backsheet, there must be written in clear permanent dark blue or black marking (I) the party on whose behalf it is filed, (ii) the initials and surname of the deponent, (iii) the number of the affidavit in relation to the deponent, (iv) the identifying initials and number of each exhibit to the affidavit, and (v) the date when sworn. For example: "2nd Dft: EW Jones: 3rd: 24.7.82; EWJ 3, 4 and 5."

(b) *Binding* Affidavits must not be bound with thick plastic strips or anything else which would hamper filing.

[2] The description must be full; for example the following have been held to be insufficient; "gentleman", "esquire", "clerk", "articled clerk", "director of public company", "justice of the peace".

[3] Each paragraph should as far as possible be confined to a distinct portion of the subject. The jurat which follows the subject matter should follow immediately after the text and should never begin a fresh page.

[4] By the provisions of the Solicitors Act 1974, s 81(1); every solicitor who holds a current practising certificate has the powers of a Commissioner for Oaths under the Comrs for Oaths Act 1889 and 1891 and s 24 of the Stamp Duties Management Act 1891. He must not be a party to the proceedings.

### 8.5 5 Endorsement on exhibit[1]

Endorsement on exhibit

– In the matter of ([*specify*] (and other matters)) (R *v* [*name of (first) defendant*] (and others)); This is the [*name the exhibit*] marked [*specify distinguishing mark if any referred to in the affidavit*] which is referred to as being exhibited to the affidavit of [*name*] sworn (affirmed) on [*date*].

Certified by me

*[Signature of Commissioner]*

*A Commissioner for Oaths*[2].

---

[1] As to affidavits, exhibits and bundles of documents to be used in proceedings in the Court of Appeal or any division of the High Court, see *Practice Note* [1983] 3 All ER 33, [1983] 1 WLR 922. Failure to comply with this Practice Direction may result in the documents being rejected by the court or made the subject for an order for costs.

[2] By the provisions of the Solicitors Act 1974, s 81(1); every solicitor who holds a current practising certificate has the powers of a Commissioner for Oaths under the Comrs for Oaths Act 1889 and 1891 and s 24 of the Stamp Duties Management Act 1891. He must not be a party to the proceedings.

### 8.6 6 Statutory declaration[1]

Statutory declaration

(Statutory Declarations Act 1835[2]).

I [*name*] of [*address*] do solemnly and sincerely declare that:

[*specify matter to be declared*].

And I make this solemn declaration conscientiously believing the same to be true, and by virtue of the provisions of the Statutory Declarations Act 1835.

Dated the [*date*]

*[Signature of person making the declaration]*

Declared before me

[*Signature of Justice of the Peace*]

*Justice of the Peace*

[1] Any justice or other person administering an oath when not authorised by law so to do, contravenes the Statutory Declarations Act 1835, s 13, in PART II: EVIDENCE, ante. Justices are however empowered to take and receive the voluntary declaration of any person which may be necessary and proper for the confirmation or written instruments of allegations, or of the execution of deeds or other prescribed matters (ibid, s 18). For punishment for making a false declaration see Perjury Act 1911, s 5 in PART VII title PERJURY, ante.

[2] See STATUTES ON EVIDENCE AND INTERPRETATION IN PART II: EVIDENCE, ante.

## WARRANTS OF ENTRY, SEARCH WARRANTS AND OTHER WITHOUT NOTICE APPLICATIONS

### *MENTAL HEALTH*

**8.7 101 Search warrant (Mental Health Act 1983, s 135)[1]**

Search warrant

(*Mental Health Act 1983, s 135*). – TO [*name*] a constable of the [*name*] Police Force.

Information on oath (*or* affirmation) has this day been laid by [*name*] an approved social worker of [*name of local social services authority*], that there is reasonable cause to suspect that [*name if available*] a person believed to be suffering from mental disorder (has been or is being ill-treated, neglected or kept otherwise than under proper control) (being unable to care for himself/herself, is living alone at [*specify premises which must be within the justice's jurisdiction*]).

You are hereby authorised to enter, if need be by force, the premises specified herein, accompanied by an approved social worker and by a registered medical practitioner, and if it is thought fit, to remove the said person to a place of safety with a view to the making of an application in respect of him under Part II of the Mental Act 1983, or of other arrangements for his treatment or care.

Dated the [*date*].

[*Signature of Justice of the Peace*]

*Justice of the Peace*

[1] Note the power under s 135(5) of the Mental Health Act 1983, in PART VII, title MENTAL HEALTH, ante, to issue a warrant to take or retake a patient without naming him in the information or warrant: the warrant must be adapted to accord with that subsection if appropriate.

### *PUBLIC HEALTH*

**8.8 102 Warrant of removal of person in need of care and attention (National Assistance Act 1948, s 47)[1]**

Warrant of removal of person in need of care and attention

(National Assistance Act 1948, s 47; National Assistance (Amendment) Act 1951, s 1). – For the purposes of this Order,

the council is the [*name*] District Council,
the applicant is
the patient is
the registered medical practitioner is } [*name and addresses*]
the hospital is
the officer of the council is

The applicant, acting on behalf of (or being the proper officer[2] so authorised of) the council, has certified that in the opinion of the proper officer and of the registered medical practitioner it is in the interests of the patient to remove him without delay.

I am satisfied on the applicant's evidence that the patient is suffering from grave chronic disease (*or* being aged *or* infirm *or* physically incapacitated is living in insanitary conditions) and is unable to devote to himself and is not receiving from other people, proper care and attention; and that in the patient's interests (*or* to prevent injury to the health of *or* prevent serious nuisance to other persons) it is necessary and expedient to remove the patient from the premises in which he is residing; and that the manager of the hospital agrees to accommodate the patient.

I hereby order that the patient be removed to the hospital by the officer of the council, and that the patient be detained therein for the period of [*specify period not exceeding three weeks*] after his removal there.

Dated the [*date*]

[*Signature of Justice of the Peace*]

*Justice of the Peace*

[1] This form is for the emergency *ex parte* procedure provided for under the 1951 Act. It may be adapted for the court order made solely under the 1948 Act.

[2] The proper officer of a local authority replaces the Medical Officer of Health by reason of the Local Government Act 1972, Sch 29, para 4.

**8.9 103 Warrant of entry (Public Health Act 1936, s 287)**

(Public Health Act 1936, s 287). – TO any authorised officer of the [*name local authority*]:

Information on oath (or affirmation) and in writing has been laid this day by [*name and address of information*], an authorised officer of [*name of local authority*] that admission has been refused[1] (*or* it is apprehended that admission will be refused[1] *or* the premises are unoccupied *or* the occupier is temporarily absent *or* admission is a case of urgency *or* an application for admission would defeat the object of the entry) and that there is reasonable ground for entry, namely [*specify*].

You are hereby authorised to enter the premises named herein if need be by force.

Dated the [*date*].

*[Signature of Justice of the Peace]*

*Justice of the Peace*

[1] The justice should be satisfied that if admission has been refused or is apprehended, the occupier should have been given notice of the intention to apply for a warrant.

# FORMS

## MAGISTRATES' COURTS, CIVIL PROCEDURE

## CONTENTS

Civil Proceedings



Prescribed by the Magistrates' Courts (Forms) Rules 1981. Forms for use in proceedings are to be found in several sources. In relation to civil proceedings, forms relating to general procedure may be found in the Magistrates' Courts (Forms) Rules 1981, SI 1981/553 as amended. Forms in relation to particular proceedings may be found in rules made in respect of those proceedings (see the rules contained in PART I: STATUTORY INSTRUMENTS ON PRACTICE AND PROCEDURE, ante). Forms relating to criminal proceedings are to be found in Annex D to the *Practice Direction (criminal: consolidated)* [2002].

## MAGISTRATES' COURTS (FORMS) RULES 1981[1]

(SI 1981/553 amended by 1982/246, 1983/524, 1984/1542, 1985/1945, 1986/1333, SI 1990/336, SI 1992/729, SI 1994/1481, SI 1995/585 and 1909, SI 1997/707, SI 1997/2421, SI 2001/615, SI 2003/1236 and Courts Act 2003, Sch 8)

[1] Made by the Lord Chancellor in exercise of the power conferred on him by s 144 of the Magistrates' Courts Act 1980, as extended by s 145 of that Act. In Wales, bi-lingual forms may be used and in certain cases forms may be requested in Welsh; see Magistrates' Courts (Welsh Forms) Rules 1986, SI 1986/1079.

**8.10** *1.* (1) These Rules may be cited as the Magistrates' Courts (Forms) Rules 1981 and shall come into operation on 6th July 1981.

(2) The Rules mentioned in Schedule 1 to these Rules are hereby revoked, but where proceedings were commenced before 6th July 1981 and the old enactments within the meaning of paragraphs 1 and 2(2) of Schedule 8 to the Magistrates' Courts Act 1980 continue to apply by virtue of paragraph 2(1) of the said Schedule 8, the provisions of the Rules so mentioned continue to apply and nothing in these Rules affects those provisions.

**8.11** *2.* (1) The forms contained in Schedule 2 to these Rules or forms to the like effect may be used, with such variation as the circumstances may require, in connection with proceedings in magistrates' courts[1].

(2) Where a requirement is imposed by or under any Act for the use of a form prescribed by rules made under section 144 of the Magistrates' Courts Act 1980, and an appropriate form is contained in Schedule 2 to these Rules, that form or a form to the like effect shall be used.

[1] The forms in Sch 2 to the Magistrates' Courts (Children and Young Persons) Rules 1992, may be used in lieu of these forms in the youth court.

## Civil Procedure

**Schedule 2 Forms** Rule 2

### 8.12 Form 121[1] Recognizance to prosecute on appeal before the High Court on case stated and for bail pending appeal

***(MC Act 1980, s 114)***

***(The form of recognizance is the same as that for Form 118)***

The principal shall prosecute without delay the principal's appeal to the High Court from the following decision.
Magistrates' Court. . . . . . . . . . .
Offence/order and date . . . . . . . . . . .
Decision subject to appeal:
and shall submit to the judgment of the High Court and pay such costs as may be awarded by the High Court (and, unless the decision appealed against is reversed, appear before the above Magistrates' Court within ten days after the judgment is given*).This recognizance shall then be void but otherwise shall remain in force.
*Delete if the principal is not to be released on bail.

***GENERAL[2]***

[1] Form 118 was revoked by SI 2003/1236, rr 47 and 48.
[*] Revoked in relation to criminal proceedings, see now the Criminal Procedure Rules, in the *Key Materials. For forms in criminal proceedings, see the Practice Direction issued under the Courts Act 2003, s 74.*

### 8.13 Form 155 Case stated

***(MC Act 1980, s 111; MC Rules 1981, rr 78, 81)***

In the High Court of Justice
Queen's Bench Division
Between AB, . . . . . . . . . . . Appellant
. . . . . . . . . . . CD, and . . . . . . . . . . . Respondent.
Case stated by Justices for the (county of . . . . . . . . . . . , acting in and for the Petty Sessional Division of
. . . . . . . . . . . ), in respect of their adjudication as a Magistrates' Court sitting at . . . . . . . . . . .

***CASE***

1
On the . . . . . . day of . . . . . . . . . , 19. . . . . . . , an information (*or* complaint) was preferred by the appellant (or respondent) against the respondent (*or* appellant) that he/she (*state shortly particulars of information or complaint and refer to any relevant statutes*).
2
We heard the said information (*or* complaint) on the . . . . . . day of . . . . . . . . . , 19 . . . . . . , and found the following facts: — (*set out in separate lettered paragraphs*).
*(The following is a short statement of the evidence: — (set out so as to show relevant evidence given by each witness)). (*Insert only if the opinion of the High Court is sought whether there was evidence upon which the Magistrates' Court could come to its decision.)
**3
It was contended by the appellant that . . . . . . . . . . .
**4
It was contended by the respondent that . . . . . . . . . . .
(***Only a brief summary should be given.*)
5
We were referred to the following cases . . . . . . . . . . .
6
We were of opinion that (*state grounds of decision*) and accordingly (*state decision including any sentence or order*).
*Question*
7
The question for the opinion of the High Court is . . . . . . . . . . .
Dated the . . . . . . day of . . . . . . . . . , 19. . . . . . .

EF,. . . . . . . . . . .

GH,. . . . . . . . . . .

. . . . . . . . . . . Justices of the Peace for the (county) aforesaid (on behalf of all the Justices adjudicating).

# Magistrates' courts, criminal procedure

## CONTENTS



**8.14 Criminal Procedure Rules Forms**

### *(1) Introduction*

Criminal Practice Direction Part I General matters *5A Forms* provides that the forms at Annex D to the Consolidated Criminal Practice Direction [2002] (Annex D is preserved by CP 5A), or forms to that effect, are to be used in the criminal courts in accordance with CrimPRr 5.1. Similarly, forms at Annex E to the Consolidated Criminal Practice Direction [2002] (also preserved), the case management forms, must be used in the criminal courts, in accordance with the Criminal Procedure Rules r 5.1. The forms may be amended or withdrawn from time to time, or new forms added, under the authority of the Lord Chief Justice.

In this Manual we list the forms at Annexes D and E as preserved at the end of the Criminal Practice Directions in *Key Materials* but for convenience we reproduce an abbreviated list below of those forms made under the Criminal Procedure Rules. The forms are grouped and numbered to reflect the provisions of the Criminal Procedure Rules to which they relate. We do not reproduce the titles of forms in those Parts which have application only to the Court of Appeal. Other forms may be available, see Annexes D and E as reproduced in the *Key Materials*). These forms are available on the Ministry of Justice website: www.justice.gov.uk/courts/procedure-rules/criminal/formspage.

Some forms are available in the Welsh language.

### *General matters (including case management)*

#### Part 1 The overriding objective

*There are no forms for use with this Part.*

#### Part 2 Understanding and applying the Rules

*There are no forms for use with this Part.*

#### Part 3 Case Management

Preparation for Trial in a Magistrates' Court
Preparation for Trial in a Magistrates' Court: notes for guidance
Case sent to the Crown Court for trial – case management questionnaire
**Crown Court forms, for cases sent to the Crown Court before 5 January 2016**
(but cases sent to Better Case Management early adopter courts use PTPH forms)
Plea & Case Management Hearing (PCMH) form – single defendant
Plea & Case Management Hearing (PCMH) form – multiple defendants
**Crown Court forms, for cases sent to the Crown Court on or after 5 January 2016**
Plea & Trial Preparation Hearing (PTPH) introduction and guidance notes
Plea & Trial Preparation Hearing (PTPH) introduction to the online PTPH form
Plea & Trial Preparation Hearing (PTPH) form – 1 defendant plain version
Plea & Trial Preparation Hearing (PTPH) form – 2 to 5 defendants plain version

#### Part 4 Service of documents

*There are no forms for use with this Part.*

#### Part 5 Forms and court records

*There are no forms for use with this Part.*

#### Part 6 Reporting, etc. restrictions

*There are no forms for use with this Part.*

## *Preliminary proceedings*

### Part 7 Starting a prosecution in a magistrates' court

Information by a prosecutor

### Part 8 Initial details of the prosecution case

*There are no forms for use with this Part.*

### Part 9 Allocation and sending for trial

*There are no forms for use with this Part.*

### Part 10 The indictment

Form of indictment

Form of indictment (order for trial under section 17(2) of the Domestic Violence, Crime and Victims Act 2004)

### Part 11 Deferred prosecution agreements

*There are no forms for use with this Part.*

### Part 12 Discontinuing a prosecution

*There are no forms for use with this Part.*

## *Custody and bail*

### Part 13 Warrants for arrest, detention or imprisonment

*There are no forms for use with this Part.*

### Part 14 Bail and custody time limits

Application to magistrates' court to reconsider police bail, CrimPR 14.6

Notice of application for court to consider bail, CrimPR 14.7

Defendant's application or appeal to the Crown Court after magistrates' court bail decision, CrimPR 14.8

Draft order for conditional bail with residence in EU member State, CrimPR 14.16

Draft European supervision order certificate, CrimPR 14.16

Application for conditional bail with residence in EU member State – notes for use with the forms of draft order and draft certificate, CrimPR 14.7 & 14.16

Application for extension of pre-charge bail, CrimPR 14.21

Application for extension of pre-charge bail: confidential information supplement, CrimPR 14.21

Response to application for extension of pre-charge bail, CrimPR 14.21

## *Disclosure*

### Part 15 Disclosure

Defence statement, CrimPR 15.4

Defence witness notice, CrimPR 15.4

Defendant's application for prosecution disclosure, CrimPR 15.5

## *Evidence*

### Part 16 Written witness statements

Written witness statement, CrimPR 16.2

Prosecutor's notice to defendant of proof by written witness statement, CrimPR 16.4

### Part 17 Witness summonses, warrants and orders

Application for a witness summons, CrimPR 17.3, 17.4

Application for a witness summons: confidential information relating to another person, CrimPR 17.3, 17.4, 17.5

**Part 18 Measures to assist a witness or defendant to give evidence**

Application for a special measures direction, CrimPR 18.3, 18.10
Application for a witness to give evidence by live link, CrimPR 18.3, 18.24

**Part 19 Expert evidence**

*There are no forms for use with this Part.*

**Part 20 Hearsay evidence**

Notice to introduce hearsay evidence, CrimPR 20.2
Application to exclude hearsay evidence after notice, CrimPR 20.3
Application to exclude hearsay evidence where no notice required, CrimPR 20.3

**Part 21 Evidence of bad character**

Application to introduce evidence of a non-defendant's bad character, CrimPR 21.3(2)
Notice objecting to evidence of a non-defendant's bad character, CrimPR 21.3(4)
Notice to introduce evidence of a defendant's bad character, CrimPR 21.4(2)
Application to exclude evidence of a defendant's bad character, CrimPR 21.4(5)

**Part 22 Evidence of a complainant's previous sexual behaviour**

*There are no forms for use with this Part.*

**Part 23 Restriction on cross-examination by a defendant**

Prosecutor's notice of prohibition against cross-examination by defendant in person
Prosecutor's application for order prohibiting cross-examination by defendant in person
Court's notice of prohibition against cross-examination by defendant in person
Court's notice of appointment of advocate

***Trial***

**Part 24 Trial and sentence in a magistrates' court**

Statutory declaration of ignorance of proceedings, CrimPR 24.17

**Part 25 Trial and sentence in the Crown Court**

*There are no forms for use with this Part.*

**Part 26 Jurors**

Notice to jurors, CrimPR 26.3

**Part 27 Retrial after acquittal**

*There are no forms for use with this Part.*

***Sentencing***

**Part 28 Sentencing procedures in special cases**

*There are no forms for use with this Part.*

**Part 29 Road traffic penalties**

Statutory declaration under s. 72(2), Road Traffic Offenders Act 1988, CrimPR 29.4
Statutory declaration under s. 73(2), Road Traffic Offenders Act 1988, CrimPR 29.4
Notice of appeal against recognition of foreign driving disqualification, CrimPR 29.6

**Part 30 Enforcement of fines and other orders for payment**

*There are no forms for use with this Part.*

**Part 31 Behaviour orders**

Notice of intention to apply, and application, for a serious crime prevention order, CrimPR 31.3
Notice of intention to apply, and application, for a criminal behaviour order, CrimPR 31.3

Application to vary or revoke a behaviour order, CrimPR 31.5

## Part 32 Breach, revocation and amendment of community and other orders

*There are no forms for use with this Part.*

## *Confiscation and related proceedings*

## Part 33 Confiscation and related proceedings

*There are no forms for use with this Part.*

## *Appeal*

## Part 34 Appeal to the Crown Court

Appeal notice, CrimPR 34.3
Notice abandoning an appeal, CrimPR 34.9

## Part 35 Appeal to the High Court by case stated

Application to magistrates' court or Crown Court to state a case for an appeal to the High Court, CrimPR 35.2

## Part 36 Appeal to the High Court by case stated

[*Various forms*]

## Part 37 Appeal to the Court of Appeal against ruling at preparatory hearing

[*Various forms*]

## Part 38 Appeal to the Court of Appeal against ruling adverse to prosecution

[*Various forms*]

## Part 39 Appeal to the Court of Appeal about conviction or sentence

[*Various forms*]

## Part 40 Appeal to the Court of Appeal about reporting or public access restriction

[*Various forms*]

## Part 41 Reference to the Court of Appeal of point of law or unduly lenient sentencing

*There are no forms for use with this Part.*

## Part 42 Appeal to the Court of Appeal in confiscation and related proceedings

[*Various forms*]

## Part 43 Appeal or reference to the Supreme Court

[*Various forms*]

## Part 44 Request to the European Court for a preliminary ruling

*There are no forms for use with this Part.*

## *Appeal*

## Part 45 Costs

Application for a wasted, etc. costs order under CrimPR 45.8, 45.9 or 45.10
Appellant's notice on costs appeal to a Costs Judge, CrimPR 45.12

### *Other proceedings*

**Part 46 Representatives**

Application by person with legal aid to change solicitor

**Part 47 Investigation orders and warrants**

Application for a production order under PACE Schedule 1, paragraph 4, CrimPR 47.10
Notice of application for a PACE production order, CrimPR 47.10
Application for a production order and order to grant entry under TA Schedule 5, paragraph 5, CrimPR 47.12
Notice of application for a TA production order, CrimPR 47.12
Application for an explanation order under TA Schedule 5, paragraph 13, CrimPR 47.14
Notice of application for a TA explanation order, CrimPR 47.14
Application for a customer information order under TA Schedule 6, paragraph 1, CrimPR 47.15
Notice of application for a TA customer information order, CrimPR 47.15
Application for an account monitoring order under TA Schedule 6A, paragraph 2, CrimPR 47.16
Notice of application for a TA account monitoring order, CrimPR 47.16
Application for a production order and order to grant entry under POCA sections 345 and 347, CrimPR 47.18
Notice of application for a POCA production order, CrimPR 47.18
Application for a disclosure order under POCA section 357, CrimPR 47.20
Notice of application for a POCA disclosure order, CrimPR 47.20
Application for a customer information order under POCA section 363, CrimPR 47.21
Notice of application for a POCA customer information order, CrimPR 47.21
Application for an account monitoring order under POCA section 370, CrimPR 47.22
Notice of application for a POCA account monitoring order, CrimPR 47.22
Application for search warrant under s.8 Police and Criminal Evidence Act 1984, CrimPR 47.28
Application for search warrant under s.2 Criminal Justice Act 1987, CrimPR 47.29
Application for a search warrant under PACE Schedule 1, paragraph 12, CrimPR 47.30
Application for a search warrant under TA Schedule 5, paragraph 11, CrimPR 47.31
Application for a search warrant under POCA section 352, CrimPR 47.32
Application for search warrant under ss.15 & 16 Police and Criminal Evidence Act 1984, CrimPR 47.34

**Part 48 Contempt of court**

Application to punish for contempt of court by failure to comply with court order, etc., CrimPR 48.9

**Part 49 International co-operation**

*There are no forms for use with this Part.*

**Part 50 Extradition**

Appellant's notice, CrimPR 50.20
Appellant's notice guidance notes
Respondent's notice, CrimPR 50.21
Respondent's notice guidance notes
Application notice, CrimPR Part 50 Section 3 (Appeal to the High Court)

### *(2) Criminal procedure forms*

We reproduce below certain forms which might require immediate reference.

**Search warrants**

CrimPR Part 6 rule 6.30 (section 8, Police and Criminal Evidence Act 1984)

## APPLICATION FOR SEARCH WARRANT

*(Criminal Procedure Rules, rule 47.30; section 8, Police and Criminal Evidence Act 1984)*

Use this form ONLY for an application for a search warrant under section 8 of the Police and Criminal Evidence Act 1984 (PACE). There is a different form of application for the court to issue a search warrant under another power to which sections 15 & 16 of PACE apply. A magistrates' court cannot authorise a search for excluded or special procedure material. See also the notes for guidance at the end of this form.

**Application to** . . . . . . . . . . . **Magistrates' Court**

**This is an application by** . . . . . . . . . . . (name of applicant)

**of** . . . . . . . . . . . (name of police force or investigating agency)

Applicant's address:[1] . . . . . . . . . . .

Email address: . . . . . . . . . . .

Phone: Mobile:

**I am a constable** ☐ **or**

**another person authorised to apply for a search warrant**[2] ☐

**I estimate that the court should allow** . . . . . . . . . . . (time) **to read this application and** . . . . . . . . . . . (time) **for the hearing.**[3]

**I expect any warrant issued to be executed on** . . . . . . . . . . . (give the planned date).

**I wish to attend the hearing by live link** (if available) Yes ☐ No ☐

**1. Complete the box above and boxes 1 to 8 below**. If you use an electronic version of this form, the boxes will expand.[4] If you use a paper version and need more space, you may attach extra sheets.

**2. Complete the declaration in box 9 and the authorisation in box 10.**

**3. Attach the draft warrant(s) you are asking the court to issue.**

**4. Send or deliver a copy of the completed form and draft warrant(s) to the court**. You may send them by secure email. Make sure the court knows if the application is urgent. Your time estimates will help the court to allow enough time to prepare for the hearing.

**1) The offence(s) under investigation.**[5] Make sure the court has a copy of any legislation to which you want to refer, including any legislation which allows you to make this application if you are not a constable. If necessary, attach a copy of the legislation when you send or deliver this form to the court.

(a) What offence(s) are you investigating? Specify the legislation or other law which creates the offence.

(b) If you are not a constable, how does the legislation allow you to make this application?

**2) The investigation**. What you need to explain will depend on the offence(s) under investigation.

(a) What are you investigating? Explain briefly.

(b) Why do you believe that the offence(s) under investigation has/have been committed? Explain briefly.

**3) Material sought.**[6] Explain how what you are looking for meets the criteria set by section 8 of PACE.

(a) What are you looking for? Identify the material for which you want to search in as much detail as practicable.

(b) Why do you believe that the material for which you want to search is likely to be of substantial value to the investigation? Material may be of substantial value by itself or together with other material.

(c) Why do you believe that the material for which you want to search is likely to be relevant evidence? There may be nothing to add to the answer to (b) above.

(d) Is there any reason to think that the material for which you want to search consists of or includes items subject to legal privilege, excluded material or special procedure material?

**4) Premises to be searched which CAN be specified.** Use this box if you are applying for a search warrant in respect of one set of premises which you can specify. If you are applying for the issue of warrants in respect of more than one set of premises which you can specify, tick this box ☐ and complete the table at the end of this form instead. If you want to search premises that you CANNOT specify, see box 5 below.

(a) Address or other description of the premises:

(b) Why do you believe that the material you are looking for is on those premises? Explain briefly.

(c) At least one of the following four access conditions must apply. Tick to indicate which.

☐ (i) it is not practicable to communicate with any person entitled to grant entry to the premises.

☐ (ii) it is practicable to communicate with such a person but it is not practicable to communicate with any person entitled to grant access to the evidence sought.

☐ (iii) entry to the premises will not be granted unless a warrant is produced.

☐ (iv) the purpose of a search may be frustrated or seriously prejudiced unless a constable arriving at the premises can secure immediate entry to them.

Explain briefly why you believe that each condition you have ticked applies:

**5) Premises to be searched which CANNOT be specified.** Use this box only if you are applying for a search warrant in respect of premises that you cannot specify, which are occupied or controlled by a person you can identify (an 'all premises warrant'). If you want to search premises that you CAN specify, see box 4 above.

(a) Whose premises do you want to search? Name or describe the person in occupation or control of the premises.

(b) Why do you believe that the material you are looking for is on the premises? Explain briefly.

(c) Why do you believe that, because of the particulars of the offence under investigation, it is necessary to search more premises than you can specify?

(d) Why do you believe that it is not reasonably practicable to specify all the premises which might need to be searched?

**6) Search on more than one occasion.** Use this box only if you are applying for the court's authority to search premises on more than one occasion.

(a) Which premises do you want to search on more than one occasion? List them.

(b) Why is it necessary to search on more than one occasion in order to achieve the purpose for which the court issues the warrant?

(c) How many times do you want to be able to search those premises? Specify any maximum number of occasions, or state 'unlimited'.

**7) Search with additional persons.** Use this box only if you are applying for the court's authority to conduct the search with people who are not constables and who are not otherwise authorised by law to conduct or take part in the search.

(a) Which other persons do you want to take part in the search? Identify those people by function or description (e.g. scientists, IT experts, accountants).

(b) Why do you want those people to take part in the search?

**8) Duty of disclosure.**[7] See also the declaration in box 9.

| |
|---|
| Is there anything of which you are aware that might reasonably be considered capable of undermining any of the grounds of this application, or which for some other reason might affect the court's decision? Include anything that reasonably might call into question the credibility of information you have received, and explain why you have decided that that information still can be relied upon. |
| **9) Declaration**<br>To the best of my knowledge and belief:<br>(a) this application discloses all the information that is material to what the court must decide, including anything that might reasonably be considered capable of undermining any of the grounds of the application, and<br>(b) the content of this application is true.<br>Signed:[8] . . . . . . . . . . . [applicant]<br>Date: Time: . . . . . . . . . . . |
| **10) Authorisation**<br>I have reviewed this application and I authorise the applicant to make it.<br>Authorising officer's name: . . . . . . . . . . .<br>Rank or grade: . . . . . . . . . . .<br>Signed:[8] . . . . . . . . . . . [authorising officer]<br>Date: Time: . . . . . . . . . . . |
| **Decision**<br>I heard this application today.<br>The applicant satisfied me about his or her entitlement to make the application.<br>The applicant confirmed on oath or affirmation the declaration in box 9.<br>The applicant gave me additional information, the essence of which was:[9]<br><br>I [issued] [refused to issue] [a warrant] [warrants] because:[10]<br><br>Signed: . . . . . . . . . . .<br>Name: . . . . . . . . . . . [Justice of the Peace]<br>[District Judge (Magistrates' Court)]]<br>Date: Time: . . . . . . . . . . . |

1 See guidance note 2 at the end of this form.
2 E.g. an officer of HM Revenue and Customs or of the National Crime Agency. See guidance note 3 at the end of this form. In box 1, specify the legislation which allows you to apply.
3 See guidance note 4 at the end of this form.
4 Forms for use with the Rules are at: www.justice.gov.uk/courts/procedure-rules/criminal/formspage.
5 See guidance note 5 at the end of this form.
6 See guidance notes 6 to 10 at the end of this form.
7 See guidance note 11 at the end of this form.
8 If an electronic version of this form is used, instead of a signature it may be authenticated electronically (e.g. by sending it from an email address recognisable to the recipient). See Criminal Procedure Rules, rule 5.3.
9 Delete if not applicable.
10 Delete as applicable, and give brief reasons for your decision.

**List of specified premises to be searched**. See box 4. Use the table on this and the next page if you are applying for the issue of warrants in respect of more than one specified set of premises. **In column (a)**, give the address or other description of the premises. **In column (b)**, explain briefly why you believe the material you are looking for is on those premises.
The four access conditions are listed in box 4. **In column (c)**, indicate which applies. Explain briefly why you believe each condition you have indicated applies.

| (a) Address or description of premises | (b) Reasons for believing material is on those premises | (c) Reasons for believing access condition(s) met |
|---|---|---|
| | | |
| | | |
| | | |
| | | |

| (a) Address or description of premises | (b) Reasons for believing material is on those premises | (c) Reasons for believing access condition(s) met |
|---|---|---|
| | | |
| | | |
| | | |
| | | |

### *Notes for Guidance*

**1. Use of this form**

This form is for use in connection with an application for a search warrant under section 8 of the Police and Criminal Evidence Act 1984 (PACE). There is a different application form for a search warrant under other legislation to which sections 15 and 16 of PACE apply.

**2. Applicant's contact details**

The court may need to contact the applicant urgently. In choosing the address and telephone number(s) to give, applicants should be aware that details entered in this application form may be disclosed in subsequent legal proceedings, unless the court orders them to be withheld.

**3. Status of the applicant**

The applicant must satisfy the court about his or her entitlement to make the application. Officers of some other investigating authorities can apply for and execute warrants to enter, search and seize as if they were constables, under the legislation which applies to them. Examples include members of the National Crime Agency designated with the powers of a constable, and officers of HM Revenue and Customs.

**4. Making an application: time estimates and live links**

The court needs an estimate of how long to allow for reading and hearing the application. If in doubt, consult the justices' legal adviser.

To help assess the urgency of the application compared with others, the court also needs to know when it is expected that the warrant will be executed.

Where a live link is available, it can be used for the applicant to attend before the court, if the court so allows. The application must have been delivered to the court (delivery may be by email), and the applicant will be required to take an oath (or affirm) as required by the Criminal Procedure Rules.

**5. The offence(s) under investigation**

Section 8 of PACE applies where the investigation is into an indictable offence. An offence may be indictable under legislation or at common law. Section 8 of PACE also applies where the investigation is into a summary offence under the Immigration Act 1971 which is a 'relevant offence' as defined in section 28D(4) of that Act (e.g. illegal entry into the UK, contrary to section 24 of the 1971 Act).

**6. The material sought (see also notes 7, 8, 9 & 10)**

The applicant must explain what the search is for in as much detail as practicable. A corresponding description must be entered in the draft warrant for the court (and the applicant must take care that the words used in the warrant can be understood without reference to the rest of the application). The search may be unlawful if the warrant does not sufficiently identify the material for which it authorises search, or if it leaves the identification of that material to the discretion of those who conduct the search.

For the purposes of section 8 of PACE, 'relevant evidence', in relation to an offence, means anything that would be admissible in evidence at a trial for the offence.

Powers to seize additional material beyond the scope of the warrant are given by section 19 of PACE and section 50 of the Criminal Justice and Police Act 2001.

## APPLICATION FOR SEARCH WARRANT

*(Criminal Procedure Rules, rule 47.31; section 2, Criminal Justice Act 1987)*

Use this form ONLY for an application for a search warrant under section 2 of the Criminal Justice Act 1987. See the notes for guidance at the end of this form.

**Application to be heard at . . . . . . . . . . . [Magistrates'] [Crown] Court**[1]

**This is an application by** . . . . . . . . . . . (name of applicant),

**a member of the Serious Fraud Office.**

Applicant's address:[2] . . . . . . . . . . .

Email address: . . . . . . . . . . .

Phone: Mobile:

**I estimate that the court should allow** . . . . . . . . . . . (time) **to read this application and** . . . . . . . . . . . (time) **for the hearing.**[3]

**I expect any warrant issued to be executed on** . . . . . . . . . . . (give the planned date).

**I wish to attend the hearing by live link** (if available)[4] Yes ☐ No ☐

**1. Complete the box above and boxes 1 to 5 below.** If you use an electronic version of this form, the boxes will expand[5]. If you use a paper version and need more space, you may attach extra sheets.

**2. Complete the declaration in box 6 and the authorisation in box 7.**

**3. Attach the draft warrant(s) you are asking the court to issue.**

**4. Send or deliver a copy of the completed form and all supporting documents to the court.**

You may send them by secure email. Make sure the court knows if the application is urgent. Your time estimates will help the court to allow enough time to prepare for the hearing.

**1) The investigation**. Describe the investigation being conducted by the Director of the Serious Fraud Office (the Director). You must include an explanation of what is alleged and why, and a chronology of relevant events.

**2) Documents sought.**[6]

(a) What documents are you looking for?

(b) Why do you believe that those documents relate to a matter relevant to the investigation?

(c) Is there any reason to think that the person who has those documents would be entitled to refuse to disclose them on grounds of legal professional privilege?

(d) One of the following three conditions must apply. Tick to indicate which.

☐ (i) a person has failed to comply with a notice by the Director to produce the documents.

☐ (ii) it is not practicable to serve such a notice in relation to the documents.

☐ (iii) the service of such a notice in relation to the documents might seriously prejudice the investigation.

Explain briefly why you believe that the condition you have ticked applies:

**3) Premises to be searched**. Use this box only if you are applying for a search warrant in respect of one set of premises. If you are applying for the issue of warrants in respect of more than one set of premises, tick this box ☐ and complete the table at the end of this form instead.

(a) Address or other description of the premises:

(b) Why do you think the documents you are looking for are on those premises? Explain briefly.

**4) Preservation of documents**. Use this box only if you are applying for the court's authority to preserve documents without seizing them.

(a) What steps do you want the court's authority to take to preserve and prevent interference with any documents? Specify those steps.

(b) Why? Explain the reasons.

**5) Duty of disclosure.** See also the declaration in box 6.

Is there anything of which you are aware that might reasonably be considered capable of undermining any of the grounds of this application, or which for some other reason might affect the court's decision? Include anything that reasonably might call into question the credibility of information you have received, and explain why you have decided that that information still can be relied upon.

**6) Declaration**

To the best of my knowledge and belief:

(a) this application discloses all the information that is material to what the court must decide, including anything that might reasonably be considered capable of undermining any of the grounds of the application, and

(b) the content of this application is true.

Signed:[7] . . . . . . . . . . [applicant]

Date: Time: . . . . . . . . . . .

**7) Authorisation**

I have reviewed this application and I authorise the applicant to make it.

Authorising officer's name: . . . . . . . . . . .

Rank or grade: . . . . . . . . . . .

Signed:[7] . . . . . . . . . . . [authorising officer]

Date: Time: . . . . . . . . . . .

**Decision**

I heard this application today.

The applicant satisfied me about his or her entitlement to make the application.

The applicant confirmed on oath or affirmation the declaration in box 6.

The applicant gave me additional information, the essence of which was:[8]

I [issued] [refused to issue] [a warrant] [warrants] because:[9]

Name: . . . . . . . . . . . [Justice of the Peace]

[District Judge (Magistrates' Court)]

[Circuit judge]

Signed: . . . . . . . . . . .

Date: Time: . . . . . . . . . . .

1 See guidance note 2 at the end of this form.

2 See guidance note 3 at the end of this form.

3 See guidance note 4 at the end of this form.

4 See guidance note 4. Live link may not be appropriate to an application under CrimPR rule 6.31.

5 Forms for use with the Rules are at: www.justice.gov.uk/courts/procedure-rules/criminal/formspage.

6 See guidance notes 6, 7 & 8 at the end of this form.

7 If an electronic version of this form is used, instead of a signature it may be authenticated electronically (e.g. by sending it from an email address recognisable to the recipient). See Criminal Procedure Rules, rule 5.3.

8 Delete if not applicable.

9 Delete as applicable, and give reasons for your decision.

**List of premises to be searched.** See box 3. Use this table if you are applying for the issue of warrants in respect of more than one set of premises.

**In column (a)**, give the address or other description of the premises. **In column (b)**, explain briefly why you believe the documents you are looking for are on those premises.

| (a) Address or description of premises | (b) Reasons for believing documents are on those premises |
|---|---|
| | |
| | |
| | |
| | |

## *Notes for Guidance*

**1. Use of this form**

This form is for use in connection with an application by a member of the Serious Fraud Office for a search warrant under section 2 of the Criminal Justice Act 1987.

**2. The court**

The legislation allows an application to be made to a justice of the peace, a District Judge (Magistrates' Court), or a Circuit or other judge exercising the powers of a justice of the peace under section 66 of the Courts Act 2003.

**3. Applicant's contact details**

The court may need to contact the applicant urgently. In choosing the address and telephone number(s) to give, applicants should be aware that details entered in this application form may be disclosed in subsequent legal proceedings, unless the court orders them to be withheld.

**4. Making an application: time estimates and live links**

The court needs an estimate of how long to allow for reading and hearing the application. If in doubt, consult the court. To help assess the urgency of the application compared with others, the court also needs to know when it is expected that the warrant will be executed.

Where a live link is available, it can be used for the applicant to attend before the court, if the court so allows. The application must have been delivered to the court (delivery may be by email), and the applicant will be required to take an oath (or affirm) as required by the Criminal Procedure Rules. Applicants should be aware that the court may not consider live link a satisfactory method by which to receive explanations of material of great factual complexity, or by which to hear an application in which the court has to be referred to a substantial number of documents.

**5. Special features of applications by the Serious Fraud Office**

Investigations by the Director of the Serious Fraud Office are, by definition, of such complexity that it would be exceptional not to supplement this form with additional documents. In particular, rule 6.31 of the Criminal Procedure Rules requires that, if the court so directs, the applicant must make available to the court material on which is based the information given in this application. The nature of such investigations is likely to require the court to set aside a significant period for reading and hearing this application.

**6. The documents sought (see also notes 7 & 8)**

The applicant must explain what the search is for in as much detail as practicable. A corresponding description must be entered in the draft warrant for the court (and the applicant must take care that the words used in the warrant can be understood without reference to the rest of the application). The search may be unlawful if the warrant does not sufficiently identify the documents for which it authorises search, or if it leaves the identification of those documents to the discretion of those who conduct the search. Powers to seize additional material beyond the scope of the warrant are given by section 19 of the Police and Criminal Evidence Act 1984 and section 50 of the Criminal Justice and Police Act 2001.

**7. Legal privilege**

Under section 2(9) of the Criminal Justice Act 1967, neither the Director nor the court can require a person to produce any document which that person would be entitled to refuse to produce on grounds of legal professional privilege in proceedings in the High Court. However, a lawyer may be required to give the name and address of his or her client.

**APPLICATION FOR SEARCH WARRANT**

*(Criminal Procedure Rules, rule 47.32; sections 15 & 16, Police and Criminal Evidence Act 1984)*

Use this form ONLY for an application for a search warrant under a power to which sections 15 & 16 of the Police and Criminal Evidence Act 1984 (PACE) apply, other than section 8 of PACE. There is a different form of application for the court to issue a search warrant under section 8. A magistrates' court cannot authorise a search for excluded or special procedure material. See also the notes for guidance at the end of this form.

**Application to** . . . . . . . . . . . **Magistrates' Court**

**This is an application by** . . . . . . . . . . . (name of applicant)

**of** (name of police force or investigating agency)

. . . . . . . . . . .

Applicant's address:[1] . . . . . . . . . . .

Email address: . . . . . . . . . . .

Phone: Mobile:

**I am a constable** ☐ **or**

**another person authorised to apply for a search warrant**[2] ☐

**I estimate that the court should allow** . . . . . . . . . . . (time) **to read this application and** . . . . . . . . . . . (time) **for the hearing.**[3]

**I expect any warrant issued to be executed on** . . . . . . . . . . . (give the planned date).

**I wish to attend the hearing by live link** (if available) Yes ☐ No ☐

**1. Complete the box above and boxes 1 to 8 below**. If you use an electronic version of this form, the boxes will expand[4]. If you use a paper version and need more space, you may attach extra sheets.

**2. Complete the declaration in box 9 and the authorisation in box 10.**

**3. Attach the draft warrant(s) you are asking the court to issue.**

**4. Send or deliver a copy of the completed form and draft warrant(s) to the court**. You may send them by secure email. Make sure the court knows if the application is urgent. Your time estimates will help the court to allow enough time to prepare for the hearing.

**1) The main search power**. Make sure the court has a copy of the legislation which allows it to issue the warrant(s) for which you are applying (the main search power), and any legislation which allows you to make this application if you are not a constable. If necessary, attach a copy of the legislation when you send or deliver this form to the court.

(a) What legislation allows the court to issue the warrant(s) for which you are applying? This is the main search power.

(b) If you are not a constable, how does the legislation allow you to make this application?

**2) The investigation**. What you need to explain will depend on the terms of the main search power.

(a) What are you investigating? Explain briefly.

(b) Why do you think the offence or activity under investigation has taken place? Explain briefly. The main search power may require you to show that you 'suspect' or 'believe' it has taken place.

**3) Articles or person(s) sought.**[5] Identify what, or who, you are looking for in as much detail as practicable. Explain how those things, or people, meet the criteria for the issue of a search warrant prescribed by the main search power.

**4) Premises to be searched which CAN be specified**. Use this box if you are applying for a search warrant in respect of one set of premises which you can specify. If you are applying for the issue of warrants in respect of more than one set of premises which you can specify, tick this box ☐ and complete the table at the end of this form instead. If you want to search premises that you CANNOT specify, see box 5 below.

(a) Address or other description of the premises:

(b) Why do you think the articles or person(s) you are looking for is / are on those premises? Explain briefly. The main search power may require you to show that you 'suspect' or believe' they are there.

(c) How do the circumstances satisfy any access conditions prescribed by the main search power? What you need to explain depends on the terms of the main search power. For example, you may need to satisfy the court that entry will not be granted without a warrant, or that an attempt to search without a warrant would frustrate the investigation.

**5) Premises to be searched which CANNOT be specified**. Use this box only if you are applying for a search warrant in respect of premises that you cannot specify, which are occupied or controlled by a person you can identify (an 'all premises warrant'). Whether the court can issue an all premises warrant depends on the terms of the main search power. If you want to search premises that you CAN specify, see box 4 above.

(a) Whose premises do you want to search? Name or describe the person in occupation or control of the premises.

(b) If you have been able to specify some of that person's premises, why is it not reasonably practicable to specify all the premises which you want to search?

(c) Why is it necessary to search more premises than you can specify? There may be nothing to add to the answer to (b) above.

(d) Why do you think the articles or person(s) you are looking for are on those premises? Explain briefly. The main search power may require you to show that you 'suspect' or 'believe' they are there.

**6) Search on more than one occasion**. Use this box only if you are applying for the court's authority to search premises on more than one occasion. Whether the court can give that authority depends on the terms of the main search power.

(a) Which premises do you want to search on more than one occasion? List them.

(b) Why do you want to search on more than one occasion?

(c) How many times do you want to be able to search those premises? Specify any maximum number of occasions, or state 'unlimited'.

**7) Search with additional persons**. Use this box only if you are applying for the court's authority to conduct the search with people who are not constables and who are not otherwise authorised by law to conduct or take part in the search.

(a) Which other persons do you want to take part in the search? Identify those people by function or description (e.g. scientists, IT experts, accountants).

(b) Why do you want those people to take part in the search?

**8) Duty of disclosure.**[6] See also the declaration in box 9.

Is there anything of which you are aware that might reasonably be considered capable of undermining any of the grounds of this application, or which for some other reason might affect the court's decision? Include anything that reasonably might call into question the credibility of information you have received, and explain why you have decided that that information still can be relied upon.

**9) Declaration**

To the best of my knowledge and belief:

(a) this application discloses all the information that is material to what the court must decide, including anything that might reasonably be considered capable of undermining any of the grounds of the application, and

(b) the content of this application is true.

Signed:[7] . . . . . . . . . . . [applicant]

Date: Time: . . . . . . . . . . . .

**10) Authorisation**

I have reviewed this application and I authorise the applicant to make it.

Authorising officer's name: . . . . . . . . . . . .

Rank or grade: . . . . . . . . . . . .

| | |
|---|---|
| Signed:[7] . . . . . . . . . . . . [authorising officer] | |
| Date: Time: . . . . . . . . . . . | |
| **Decision**<br>I heard this application today.<br>The applicant satisfied me about his or her entitlement to make the application.<br>The applicant confirmed on oath or affirmation the declaration in box 9.<br>The applicant gave me additional information, the essence of which was:[8]<br><br>I [issued] [refused to issue] [a warrant] [warrants] because:[9]<br>Signed: . . . . . . . . . . .<br>Name: . . . . . . . . . . . [Justice of the Peace]<br>[District Judge (Magistrates' Court)]<br>Date: Time: . . . . . . . . . . . | |

[1] See guidance note 2 at the end of this form.

[2] E.g. an officer of HM Revenue and Customs or of the National Crime Agency. See guidance note 3 at the end of this form. In box 1, specify the legislation which allows you to apply.

[3] See guidance note 4 at the end of this form.

[4] Forms for use with the Rules are at: www.justice.gov.uk/courts/procedure-rules/criminal/formspage.

[5] See guidance notes 6 to 8 the end of this form.

[6] See guidance note 9 at the end of this form.

[7] If an electronic version of this form is used, instead of a signature it may be authenticated electronically (e.g. by sending it from an email address recognisable to the recipient). See Criminal Procedure Rules, rule 5.3.

[8] Delete if not applicable.

[9] Delete as applicable, and give brief reasons for your decision.

**List of specified premises to be searched**. See box 4. Use the table on this and the next page if you are applying for the issue of warrants in respect of more than one specified set of premises. **In column (a)**, give the address or other description of the premises. **In column (b)**, explain briefly why you think the articles or person(s) you are looking for is/are on those premises. (The main search power may require you to show that you 'suspect' or 'believe' they are there.) **In column (c)**, explain how the circumstances satisfy any conditions prescribed by the main search power. (What you need to explain depends on the terms of the main search power. For example, you may need to satisfy the court that entry will not be granted without a warrant, or that an attempt to search without a warrant would frustrate the investigation.)

| **(a) Address or description of premises** | **(b) Reasons for thinking articles / persons are on those premises** | **(c) Reasons why access conditions are met** |
|---|---|---|
| | | |
| | | |
| | | |
| | | |

| **(a) Address or description of premises** | **(b) Reasons for thinking articles / persons are on those premises** | **(c) Reasons why access conditions are met** |
|---|---|---|
| | | |
| | | |
| | | |
| | | |

## *Notes for Guidance*

**1. Use of this form**

This form is for use in connection with an application for a search warrant under legislation (the main search power) to which sections 15 and 16 of the Police and Criminal Evidence Act 1984 (PACE) apply, other than section 8 of PACE (for which there is a different application form).

By section 15(1), "This section and section 16 . . . have effect in relation to the issue to constables under any enactment, including an enactment contained in an Act passed after this Act, of warrants to enter and search premises; and an entry on or search of premises under a warrant is unlawful unless it complies with this section and section 16 . . . ."

Other search powers include section 26 of the Theft Act 1968, section 23 of the Misuse of Drugs Act 1971 and paragraph 1 of Schedule 5 to the Terrorism Act 2000.

**2. Applicant's contact details**

The court may need to contact the applicant urgently. In choosing the address and telephone number(s) to give, applicants should be aware that details entered in this application form may be disclosed in subsequent legal proceedings, unless the court orders them to be withheld.

**3. Status of the applicant**

The applicant must satisfy the court about his or her entitlement to make the application. Officers of some other investigating authorities can apply for and execute warrants to enter, search and seize as if they were constables, under the legislation which applies to them. Examples include members of the National Crime Agency designated with the powers of a constable; officers of HM Revenue and Customs; and, in the case of an application under section 26 of the Theft Act 1986, or under section 23 of the Misuse of Drugs Act 1971, a person designated as an investigating officer under section 38 of the Police Reform Act 2002, to whom relevant paragraphs of Part 2 of Schedule 4 to that Act apply.

**4. Making an application: time estimates and live links**

The court needs an estimate of how long to allow for reading and hearing the application. If in doubt, consult the justices' legal adviser.

To help assess the urgency of the application compared with others, the court also needs to know when it is expected that the warrant will be executed.

Where a live link is available, it can be used for the applicant to attend before the court, if the court so allows. The application must have been delivered to the court (delivery may be by email), and the applicant will be required to take an oath (or affirm) as required by the Criminal Procedure Rules.

**5. Special requirements of the main search power under which the warrant is issued**

The main search power may require the applicant to demonstrate either suspicion or belief as to the presence of the articles or persons sought on the premises to be searched, and either suspicion or belief as to other grounds or conditions about which the court must be satisfied. One of those other grounds is likely to be that nothing sought consists of or includes items subject to legal professional privilege. When completing box 3, applicants must take care to satisfy the court about these requirements, or it may not be possible for the court to issue the warrant.

The main search power may prescribe criteria that must be met in relation to the premises to be searched, for example that giving the occupant notice would frustrate the purpose of the search, or that access has been refused, or that a person who could and would allow access cannot be found. When completing box 4, or the table at pages 5 & 6, applicants must take care to satisfy the court about these requirements, or again it may not be possible for the court to issue the warrant.

**6. The articles or persons sought (see also notes 7 & 8)**

The applicant must explain what the search is for in as much detail as practicable. A corresponding description must be entered in the draft warrant for the court (and the applicant must take care that the words used in the warrant can be understood without reference to the rest of the application). The search may be unlawful if the warrant does not sufficiently identify the material for which it authorises search, or if it leaves the identification of that material to the discretion of those who conduct the search.

Powers to seize additional material beyond the scope of the warrant are given by section 19 of PACE and section 50 of the Criminal Justice and Police Act 2001.

**7. Legal privilege**

Unless, exceptionally, permitted by the main search power, the court cannot issue a warrant to search for items subject to legal privilege. Unless the items in question are held with the intention of furthering a criminal purpose, section 10 of PACE defines those items as:

- (a) communications between a professional legal adviser and his client or any person representing his client made in connection with the giving of legal advice to the client;
- (b) communications between a professional legal adviser and his client or any person representing his client or between such an adviser or his client or any such representative and any other person made in connection with or in contemplation of legal proceedings and for the purposes of such proceedings; and
- (c) items enclosed with or referred to in such communications and made—
  - (i) in connection with the giving of legal advice; or
  - (ii) in connection with or in contemplation of legal proceedings and for the purposes of such proceedings,

  when they are in the possession of a person who is entitled to possession of them.

**8. 'Seize and sift'**

Under section 50 of the Criminal Justice and Police Act 2001, if a person executing a search warrant (a) finds something which he or she has reasonable grounds to believe may be, or may contain, something for which that person has authority to search under the warrant, and (b) it is not reasonably practicable there and then to determine whether that is so; then that person can seize so much of what he or she has found as it is necessary to remove to enable that to be determined.

Under that same section, if such a person (a) finds something which he or she would be entitled to seize under the warrant but for its being comprised in something which he or she is not entitled to seize, and (b) it is not reasonably practicable there and then to separate the seizable property from the other property; then that person can seize both the seizable and the other property.

**9. Information that might undermine the grounds of the application**

Information that might undermine any of the grounds of the application must be included in the application, or the court's authority for the search may be ineffective. The court will not necessarily refuse to issue a warrant in every case in which there is information that undermines the grounds of the application.

The applicant must explain why information is thought to be credible where it comes from a source that cannot be tested (for example, a report from an anonymous informant).

The applicant must inform the court if there is anything else that might influence the court's decision to issue a warrant. This may include whether the premises have been searched before, and with what outcome, or whether there is any unusual feature of the investigation or of any potential prosecution.

**10. Other powers to issue search warrants**

This form can be adapted for use in connection with applications for search warrants under other legislation, but applicants must note that:

(a) they must give all the information required by that legislation to satisfy the court that the warrant sought should be issued; and

(b) the legislation under which the application is made will determine whether the court can authorise the search of more than one set of premises, the search of unspecified premises, or the search of premises on more than one occasion (and see sections 15 and 16 of PACE); and may determine the power to search persons found on the premises.

## APPEAL TO THE CROWN COURT FROM A MAGISTRATES' COURT

*(Criminal Procedure Rules, rule 34.3)*

**Case details**

Name of defendant:

Address If the defendant is in custody, give prison and prison number, if known.

Email address:

Phone: Mobile:

Appeal from Magistrates' Court

Magistrates' court case reference number:

Appeal to the Crown Court at

**This is an appeal to the Crown Court about:**

Give brief details of the magistrates' court decision about which you are appealing, including the date of that decision (e.g. 'my conviction for [offence] on [date]', or 'my sentence of [penalty] for [offence] on [date]').

**I have asked the magistrates' court to reconsider my case** ☐ Yes ☐ No

You may not need to appeal. Sometimes a magistrates' court can change a decision which it has made, under section 142 of the Magistrates' Courts Act 1980. Ask at the magistrates' court office.

**I need an extension of time for this appeal** ☐ Yes ☐ No

See the time limits listed below. If your appeal is late, you must answer question 1, on the other side of this form. Only the Crown Court can extend the 21 day time limit for appeal.

Use this form ONLY for an appeal to the Crown Court about conviction, sentence, etc. under Criminal Procedure Rules Part 63. There is a different form for applying or appealing to the Crown Court after a magistrates' court has made a decision about bail, under Criminal Procedure Rule 19.8.

**1. Complete the boxes above and give the details required in the boxes below**. If you use an electronic version of this form, the boxes will expand[1]. If you use a paper version and need more space, you may attach extra sheets.

**2. Sign and date the completed form.**

**3. Send a copy of the completed form to:**

**(a) the magistrates' court**, and

**(b) the other party to the case** (e.g. the prosecutor, if you are the defendant).

You must send this form so as to reach the recipients **not more than 21 days after:**

- the date you were sentenced or your sentence was deferred (whichever was earlier), if your appeal is against conviction or against a finding of guilt,
- the date you were sentenced, if your appeal is against sentence, or
- in any other case, the date of the order or failure to make an order about which you want to appeal.

**1) Extension of time** (if you need one: see the notes on the front page). **My appeal is late because:** Explain why your appeal is late. Attach copies of any letters or other documents you want the court to see.

**2) The issues in this case are:**

Summarise the matters of fact or law, or the reasons for sentence or other order, which are in dispute.

**3) Appeal against conviction: case management in the Crown Court.**

Only answer these questions if you are appealing against conviction or a finding of guilt.

How long did the trial last in the magistrates' court?

Which of the prosecution witnesses in the magistrates' court do you want to ask questions if they are witnesses again in the Crown Court? Name them:

How long do you expect the appeal to take in the Crown Court?

**4) Other applications. I am also applying for:**

☐ **pending my appeal, the suspension of my disqualification e.g. from driving**. You can ONLY apply for the suspension of a disqualification imposed in this case.

☐ **pending my appeal, bail**.

Give reasons for any application you are making:

**I want my application(s) considered by** ☐ the magistrates' court ☐ the Crown Court

Each court can consider these applications. You can apply to both.

Signed[2]: ______________

[defendant / defendant's solicitor]

Date

[1] Forms for use with the Rules are at: www.justice.gov.uk/courts/procedure-rules/criminal/formspage.

[2] If you use an electronic version of this form, you may instead authenticate it electronically (e.g. by sending it from an email address recognisable to the recipient). See Criminal Procedure Rules, rule 5.3.

**Notice of Abandonment of Appeal**

*(Criminal Procedure Rules, r 63.8)*

**Appellant**

Name:

Address:

**Details of appeal**

Appeal from Magistrates' Court

Case number:

Appeal to the Crown Court at:

Crown Court case number:

Crown Court hearing date:

**I abandon my appeal against:** *(specify the conviction or finding of guilt, the sentence or other order against which you are abandoning your appeal)*

HOW TO USE THIS FORM

You must:

**1. Fill in the box above.**

**2. Sign and date the completed form in the space below.**

**3. Send or give copies of the completed form to (a) the Crown Court office, (b) the magistrates' court office and (c) every other party to the case** (e.g. the prosecutor), **so they receive it before the hearing of the appeal begins.**

If you want to abandon your appeal after the hearing of the appeal begins, you need the permission of the Crown Court.

If you abandon your appeal, the court may make a costs order against you.

Signed: appellant / appellant's solicitor

Date:

# PART IX
# STOP PRESS: MISCELLANEOUS LEGISLATION

Material included in Part IX was received too late for inclusion under its correct part and title. The material is listed below in the order in which it would normally appear.



# STOP PRESS

## Criminal Justice (Electronic Monitoring) (Responsible Person) Order 2017

(2017 No 235)

9.2 *1.* ***Citation and commencement*** This Order may be cited as the Criminal Justice (Electronic Monitoring) (Responsible Person) Order 2017 and comes into force on 13th March 2017.

*2.* ***Person responsible for monitoring of persons on bail*** For the purposes of section 3AC(2) of the Bail Act 1976 (electronic monitoring: general provisions), a description of person who may be made responsible for the electronic monitoring of a person on bail is a person who is employed by Buddi Limited, Talbot House, 17 Church Street, Rickmansworth, Hertfordshire WD3 1DE (Company Number 05308826).

*3.* ***Person responsible for monitoring of persons subject to community orders and suspended sentence orders*** For the purposes of section 215(3) of the Criminal Justice Act 2003 (electronic monitoring requirement), a description of person who may be made responsible for the electronic monitoring of a person subject to a community order or suspended sentence order is a person who is employed by Buddi Limited, Talbot House, 17 Church Street, Rickmansworth, Hertfordshire WD3 1DE (Company Number 05308826).

## Policing and Crime Act 2017 (Possession of Pyrotechnic Articles at Musical Events) Regulations 2017[1]

(2017 No 306)

9.3 *1.* ***Citation, commencement and interpretation*** (1) These Regulations may be cited as the Policing and Crime Act 2017 (Possession of Pyrotechnic Articles at Musical Events) Regulations 2017 and come into force on 3rd April 2017.

(2) In these Regulations—

"premises licence" has the meaning given in section 11 of the Licensing Act 2003;

"the provision of regulated entertainment" has the meaning given in Schedule 1 to the Licensing Act 2003.

*2.* ***Specified description of event*** (1) For the purposes of section 134(5) of the Policing and Crime Act 2017, an event to which paragraph (2) applies is specified.

(2) This paragraph applies to an event that—

(a) is provided to any extent for members of the public or a section of the public; and

(b) takes place on premises in respect of which—

(i) a premises licence has been granted; and

(ii) the licence authorises the premises to be used for the provision of regulated entertainment in the form of a performance of live music.

[1] Made by the Secretary of State in exercise of the power conferred by s 134(5) of the Policing and Crime Act 2017.

## Specified Agreement on Driving Disqualifications Regulations 2017

(2017 No 628)

9.4 *1. **Citation and commencement*** These Regulations may be cited as the Specified Agreement on Driving Disqualifications Regulations 2017 and come into force on the 22nd day after the day on which they are made.

*2. **Specified agreement on driving disqualifications*** The Agreement on the Mutual Recognition of Driving Disqualifications between the United Kingdom of Great Britain and Northern Ireland and Ireland made on 30th October 2015 is specified for the purposes of Chapter 1 of Part 3 of the Crime (International Co-operation) Act 2003.

## Proscribed Organisations (Name Change) Order 2017[1]

(2017 No 615)

9.5 *1. **Citation and commencement*** This Order may be cited as the Proscribed Organisations (Name Change) Order 2017 and comes into force on the day after the day on which it is laid before Parliament.

*2. **Name change*** Hay'at Tahrir Al-Sham, being a name that is not specified in Schedule 2 to the Terrorism Act 2000 (proscribed organisations), is to be treated as another name for the organisation listed in that Schedule as Al-Qa'ida.

[1] Made by the Secretary of State in exercise of the powers conferred by s 3(6)(a) of the Terrorism Act 2000.

## Sexual Offences Act 2003 (Prescribed Police Stations) Regulations 2017[1]

(2017 No 573)

*1. **Citation, commencement and extent*** (1) These Regulations may be cited as the Sexual Offences Act 2003 (Prescribed Police Stations) Regulations 2017 and come into force on 12th May 2017.

(2) These Regulations extend to England and Wales only.

*2. **Prescribed police stations*** The police stations listed in the Schedule to these Regulations are prescribed for the purposes of section 87(1)(a) of the Sexual Offences Act 2003.

*3. **Revocation*** The Sexual Offences Act 2003 (Prescribed Police Stations) (No 2) Regulations 2015 are revoked.

[1] Made by the Secretary of State in exercise of the powers conferred by s 87(1)(a) of the Sexual Offences Act 2003.

SCHEDULE

Police Stations in England and Wales

Regulation 2

| Local Police Area | Police Station Name and Address | |
|---|---|---|
| Avon and Somerset | Broadbury Road Police Station<br>Broadbury Road<br>Knowle<br>West Bristol BS4 1JT | Yeovil Police Station<br>Horsey Lane<br>Yeovil<br>Somerset BA20 1SN |
| | Southmead Road Police Station<br>Southmead Road<br>Bristol BS10 5DW | Taunton Police Station<br>Shuttern<br>Taunton<br>Somerset TA1 3QA |
| | Chipping Sodbury<br>Police Station<br>High Street<br>Chipping Sodbury<br>Bristol BS37 6AH | Wellington Police Station<br>Victoria Street<br>Wellington<br>Somerset TA21 8HR |
| | Trinity Road Police Station<br>Trinity Road<br>Bristol BS2 0NW | Nailsea Police Station<br>Stockway South<br>Nailsea<br>Somerset BS48 2LE |
| | Minehead Police Station<br>32 Townsend Road<br>Minehead TA24 5RJ | Wells Police Station<br>18 Glastonbury Road<br>Wells |
| | Radstock Police Station | Somerset BA5 1TL |

| | | |
|---|---|---|
| | Wells Road<br>Radstock<br>Bath BA3 3SG<br><br>Bridgwater Police Centre<br>Express Park<br>Bristol Road<br>Bridgwater<br>Somerset TA6 4RR | The Bridewell Police Station<br>The Bridewell<br>1–2 Bridewell Street<br>Bristol BS1 2AA<br><br>Patchway Police Centre<br>Gloucester Road<br>Bristol BS34 6PY<br><br>Keynsham Police Centre<br>Ashmead Road<br>Keynsham<br>Bristol BS31 1SX |
| Bedfordshire | Force Headquarters<br>Woburn Road<br>Kempston<br>Bedfordshire MK43 9AX | Dunstable Police Station<br>West Street<br>Dunstable LU6 1SJ |
| | Luton Police Station<br>Buxton Road<br>Luton LU1 1SD | |
| Cambridgeshire | Thorpe Wood Police Station<br>Thorpe Wood<br>Longthorpe<br>Peterborough PE3 6SD<br><br>Parkside Police Station<br>Parkside<br>Cambridge CB1 1JG<br><br>March Police Station<br>Burrowmoor Road<br>March PE15 9RB<br><br>Huntingdon Police Station<br>Ferrars Road<br>Huntingdon PE29 3DQ | St Neots Police Station<br>Dovehouse Close<br>St Neots PE19 1DS<br><br>Wisbech Police Station<br>Nene Parade<br>Wisbech PE13 3BT<br><br>Ely Police Station<br>Nutholt Lane<br>Ely CB7 4PL |
| Cheshire | Ellesmere Port Police Station<br>4 Stannery Lane<br>Ellesmere Port CH65 9ER<br><br>Congleton Police Station<br>Market Square<br>Congleton CW12 1EU<br><br>Blacon Divisional HQ<br>Blacon Avenue<br>Blacon<br>Chester CH1 5BD<br><br>Runcorn Police Station<br>Halton Lea<br>Runcorn WA7 2HG<br><br>Northwich Police Station<br>Chester Way<br>Northwich CW9 5EP | Macclesfield DHQ<br>Brunswick Street<br>Macclesfield SK10 1HQ<br><br>Winsford Police Station<br>Collingham Way<br>Winsford CW7 2WA<br><br>Wilmslow Police Station<br>Hawthorn Street<br>Wilmslow SK9 5HQ<br><br>Crewe Police Station<br>Civic Centre<br>Crewe CW1 2DQ<br><br>Widnes Police Station<br>Jon Briggs House<br>Gerrard Street<br>Widnes WA8 6BE<br><br>Warrington Police Station |

| | | |
|---|---|---|
| | | Arpley Street<br>Warrington WA1 1LQ |
| Cleveland | Hartlepool Police Station<br>Avenue Road<br>Hartlepool TS24 8AB | Middlesbrough District HQ<br>Bridge Street West<br>Middlehaven<br>Middlesbrough TS2 1AB |
| Cumbria | Carlisle Division Headquarters<br>Brunel Way<br>Durranhill Industrial Estate<br>Carlisle CA1 3NQ<br><br>Penrith Police Station<br>Hunter Lane<br>Penrith CA11 7UT<br><br>Workington Police Station<br>Hall Brow<br>Workington CA14 4AP | Whitehaven Police Station<br>Scotch Street<br>Whitehaven CA28 7NN<br><br>Kendal Police Station<br>Busher Walk<br>Kendal LA9 4RJ<br><br>Barrow Police Station<br>Andrews Way<br>Barrow in Furness LA14 2UE |
| Derbyshire | Buxton Police Station<br>Silverlands<br>Buxton SK17 6QJ<br><br>Derby Police Station<br>St Mary's Wharf<br>Prime Parkway<br>Chester Green<br>Derby DE1 3AB | Chesterfield Police Station<br>Beetwell Street<br>Chesterfield S40 1QP |
| Devon & Cornwall | Camborne Police Station<br>South Terrace<br>Camborne<br>Cornwall TR14 8SY<br><br>Plymouth Police Station<br>Charles Cross<br>Plymouth<br>Devon PL4 8HG<br><br>Torquay Police Station<br>South Street<br>Torquay<br>Devon TQ2 5AH<br><br>Exeter Police Station<br>Heavitree Road<br>Exeter<br>Devon EX1 2LR | Barnstaple Police Station<br>North Walk<br>Barnstaple<br>Devon EX31 1DU<br><br>Crownhill Police Station,<br>Budshead Way,<br>Crownhill,<br>Plymouth,<br>Devon PL6 5HT (9–5 Mon–Fri)<br><br>Bodmin Police Station<br>Tollgate Road<br>Bodmin<br>North Cornwall<br>PL31 2FJ<br>(9–5 Mon–Fri) |
| | St Austell Police Station<br>1 Palace Road<br>St Austell<br>Restormel<br>Cornwall PL25 4AL | Truro Police Station, Courtleigh<br>House 74–75 Lemon Street<br>Truro<br>Cornwall TR1 2PN (9–5 Mon–Fri) |
| Dorset | Bournemouth Police Station | Bridport Police Station |

| | | |
|---|---|---|
| | Madeira Road<br>Bournemouth BH1 1QQ | Tannery Road<br>Bridport DT6 3TP |
| | Weymouth West<br>Police Station<br>Radipole Lane<br>Chickerell<br>Weymouth DT4 9WW | Sherborne Police Station<br>Digby Road<br>Sherborne DT9 3NL |
| | Poole Police Station<br>Wimborne Road<br>Poole BH15 2BP | Blandford Police Station<br>Salisbury Road<br>Blandford DT11 7HR |
| Durham | Darlington Police Station<br>St Cuthbert's Way<br>Darlington DL1 5LB | Durham City Police Station<br>New Elvet<br>Durham DH1 3AQ |
| | Bishop Auckland Police Station<br>Woodhouse Lane<br>Bishop Auckland DL14 6LB | Peterlee Police Station<br>St Aidan's Way<br>Peterlee SR8 1QR |
| | | Consett Police Station<br>Parliament Street<br>Consett DH8 5DL |
| Dyfed—Powys | Llanelli Police Station<br>Waunlanyrafon<br>Llanelli<br>Carmarthenshire SA15 3AD | Pembroke Dock Police Station<br>Water Street<br>Pembroke Dock<br>Pembrokeshire SA72 6DW |
| | Newtown Police Station<br>Park Lane<br>Newtown<br>Powys SY16 1EN | Carmarthen Police Station<br>Friars Park<br>Carmarthen<br>Carmarthenshire SA31 3AW |
| | Brecon Police Station<br>Plas-y-Ffynnon<br>Cambrian Way<br>Brecon<br>Powys LD3 7HP | Cardigan Police Station<br>Parc Teifi<br>Cardigan<br>Ceredigion SA43 1EW |
| | Llandrindod Wells Police Station<br>Noyadd Park<br>Llandrindod Wells<br>Powys LD1 5DF | Aberystwyth Police Station<br>Boulevard Saint Brieuc<br>Aberystwyth<br>Ceredigion SY23 1PH |
| | | Haverfordwest Police Station<br>Merlins Hill<br>Haverfordwest<br>Pembrokeshire SA61 1PF |
| Essex | Chelmsford Police Station<br>New Street<br>Chelmsford CM1 1NF | Colchester Police Station<br>10 Southway<br>Colchester CO3 3BU |
| | Clacton Police Station<br>8 Beatrix Road<br>Clacton CO15 1ET | Grays Police Station<br>Brooke Road<br>Grays RM17 5BX |
| | Braintree Police Station<br>Blyths Meadow<br>Braintree CM7 3DJ | Basildon Police Station<br>Great Oaks<br>Basildon SS14 1EJ |

| | | |
|---|---|---|
| | Harlow Police Station<br>The High<br>Harlow CM20 1HG | Southend Police Station<br>Victoria Avenue<br>Southend-on-Sea SS2 6ES |
| Gloucestershire | Gloucester Police Station<br>Bearland<br>Longsmith Street<br>Gloucester GL1 2JP<br><br>Hesters Way Police Station<br>Princess Elizabeth Way<br>Cheltenham GL51 7SG<br><br>Stroud Police Station<br>Parliament Street<br>Stroud GL5 1QQ | Coleford Police Station<br>Lords Hill<br>Coleford GL16 8BG<br><br>Cirencester Police Station<br>The Forum<br>Cirencester GL7 2QY<br><br>Stow Police Station<br>High Street<br>Stow on the Wold GL54 1AB |
| Greater Manchester | GMP Divisional Headquarters<br>Longsight Police Station<br>2 Grindlow Street<br>Manchester M13 0LL<br><br>GMP Divisional Headquarters<br>Ashton-under-Lyne Police Station<br>Manchester Road<br>Ashton-under-Lyne OL7 0BQ | GMP Divisional Headquarters<br>Oldham Police Station<br>Barn Street<br>Oldham OL1 1LR<br><br>GMP Divisional Headquarters<br>Swinton Police Station<br>208 Chorley Road<br>Swinton M27 6BA |
| | Bolton Divisional Headquarters<br>Bolton Police Station<br>Scholey Street<br>Bolton BL2 1HD<br><br>Cheadle Heath Police Station<br>Spectrum Way<br>Cheadle SK3 0SA<br><br>GMP Divisional Headquarters<br>Bury Police Station<br>Dunster Road<br>Bury BL9 0RD<br><br>Wythenshawe Police Station<br>Poundswick Lane<br>Manchester M22 9PQ<br><br>Leigh Police Station<br>Chapel Street<br>Leigh WN7 2PS<br><br>Bootle Street<br>City Centre<br>Manchester<br>M2 5GU | GMP Divisional Headquarters<br>Wigan Police Station<br>Robin Park Road<br>Wigan WN5 0UF<br><br>GMP Divisional Headquarters<br>Stretford Police Station<br>Talbot Road<br>Stretford M32 0XB<br><br>Rochdale Police Station<br>The Esplanade<br>Rochdale OL16 1AG<br><br>Chadderton Police Station<br>Broadgate<br>Chadderton<br>Oldham OL9 9XA<br><br>GMP Headquarters<br>Central Park<br>Northampton Road<br>Manchester M40 5BP<br><br>Pendleton Police Station<br>Broadwalk<br>Meyrick Road<br>Salford M6 5FX |
| Gwent | Newport Police Station<br>3 Cardiff Road<br>Newport NP20 2EH<br><br>Ebbw Vale Police Station<br>Bethcar Street<br>Ebbw Vale<br>Gwent NP23 6UY | Cwmbran Police Station<br>Tudor Road<br>Cwmbran NP44 3XH<br><br>Blackwood Police Station<br>Blackwood Road<br>Blackwood NP12 2XA |

| | | |
|---|---|---|
| Hampshire & Isle of Wight | Southampton Central Police Station<br>Southern Road<br>Southampton SO15 1AN<br><br>Aldershot Police Station<br>Wellington Avenue<br>Aldershot GU11 1NZ | Fareham Police Station<br>Quay Street<br>Fareham PO16 0NA<br><br>Andover Police Station<br>South Street<br>Andover SP10 2ED<br><br>Portsmouth Central Police Station<br>Winston Churchill Avenue<br>Portsmouth PO1 2DG |
| | Northern Police Investigation Centre<br>Jays Close<br>Viables Business Park<br>Basingstoke RG22 4BS<br><br>Winchester City Neighbourhood Police Office<br>Operational Headquarters<br>Tower Street<br>Winchester SO23 8ZD<br><br>Waterlooville Police Station<br>Swiss Road<br>Waterlooville<br>PO7 7FX | Newport Police Station<br>High Street<br>Newport<br>Isle of Wight PO30 1SZ<br><br>Havant Police Station<br>Civic Centre Road<br>Havant PO9 2AN<br><br>Lyndhurst Police Station<br>Pikes Hill<br>Lyndhurst SO43 7NR<br><br>Portswood Police Station<br>St Denys Road<br>Southampton<br>SO17 2GN |
| Hertfordshire | Stevenage Police Station<br>Lytton Way<br>Stevenage SG1 1HF | Hatfield Police Station<br>Comet Way<br>Hatfield AL10 9SJ |
| Humberside | Grimsby Police Station<br>Victoria Street<br>Grimsby DN31 1PE<br><br>Scunthorpe Police Station<br>Corporation Road<br>Scunthorpe DN15 6QB<br><br>Goole Police Station<br>Estcourt Terrace<br>Goole DN14 5AF<br><br>Beverley Police Station (HQ)<br>Sessions House<br>New Walk<br>Beverley HU17 7AF | Priory Road Police Station<br>Priory Road<br>Kingston upon Hull HU5 5SF<br><br>Bridlington Police Station<br>Ashville Street<br>Bridlington YO16 4EW<br><br>Clough Road Police Station<br>Clough Road<br>Kingston upon Hull HU5 1SW<br><br>Osborne Street Police Station<br>Osborne Street<br>Kingston Upon Hull HU1 2NW |
| Kent | Tunbridge Wells Police Station<br>Crescent Road<br>Tunbridge Wells TN1 2LU<br><br>Tonbridge Police Station<br>1 Pembury Road<br>Tonbridge TN9 2HS | Sittingbourne Police Station<br>Central Avenue<br>Sittingbourne ME10 4NR<br><br>Canterbury Police Station<br>Old Dover Road<br>Canterbury CR1 3JQ |
| | Maidstone Police Station | Margate Police Station |

| | | |
|---|---|---|
| | Palace Avenue<br>Maidstone ME15 6NF | Fort Hill<br>Margate CT9 1HL |
| | Ashford Police Station<br>Tufton Street<br>Ashford TN23 1BT | Folkestone Police Station<br>Bouverie House<br>Bouverie Road West<br>West Folkestone CT20 2SG |
| | Medway Police Station<br>Purser Way<br>Gillingham ME7 1NE | North Kent Police Station<br>Thames Way<br>Northfleet<br>Gravesend DA11 8BD |
| | Dover Police Station<br>Ladywell<br>Dover CT16 1DJ | Sheerness Police Station<br>Millennium Way<br>Sheerness ME12 1PA |
| | Swanley Police Station<br>London Road<br>Swanley BR8 7AJ | |
| Lancashire | Accrington Police Station<br>8/10 Broadway<br>Accrington BB5 1EY | Darwen Police Station<br>Union Street<br>Darwen BB3 0DA |
| | Blackpool Police Station<br>Bonny Street<br>Blackpool FY1 5RL | Clitheroe Police Station<br>King Street<br>Clitheroe BB7 2EU |
| | Lancaster Police Station<br>Thurnham Street<br>Lancaster LA1 1YB | Burnley Police Station<br>Parker Lane<br>Burnley BB11 2BT |
| | Morecambe Police Station<br>21 Poulton Street<br>Morecambe LA4 5PZ | Colne Police Station<br>Craddock Road<br>Colne BB 8 0JZ |
| | Fleetwood Police Station<br>North Church Street<br>Fleetwood FY7 6HJ | Leyland Police Station<br>Lancastergate<br>Leyland PR5 1EX |
| | Garstang Police Station<br>Garstang Road<br>Bowgreave<br>Garstang PR3 1YD | Blackburn Police Station<br>Greenbank Business Park<br>Whitebirk Drive<br>Blackburn BB1 3HT |
| | Skelmersdale Police Station<br>Southway<br>Skelmersdale WN8 6NH | Rossendale Police Station<br>Bacup Road<br>Waterfoot BB4 7JA |
| | Bispham Police Station<br>Red Bank Road<br>Bispham FY2 0HJ | St Anne's Police Station<br>St Andrew's Road North<br>St Anne's-on-Sea FY8 2JF |
| | Kirkham Police Station<br>Freckleton Street<br>Kirkham PR4 2SN | Blackburn Town Centre Police Station<br>The Boulevard<br>Railway Road<br>Blackburn BB1 1EX |
| | Preston Police Station<br>Lancaster Road North<br>Preston PR1 2SA | Ormskirk Police Station<br>1 Denby Street<br>Ormskirk<br>L39 2BJ |
| | Chorley Police Station<br>St Thomas's Road<br>Chorley PR7 1DR | |

| | | |
|---|---|---|
| | Nelson Police Station<br>Broadway<br>Nelson<br>BB9 9SJ | |
| Leicestershire | Keyham Lane Police Station<br>Colin Grundy Drive<br>Off Keyham Lane<br>Leicester LE5 1FY<br><br>Mansfield House Police Station<br>74 Belgrave Gate<br>Leicester LE1 3GG | Beaumont Leys Police Station<br>2 Beaumont Way<br>Leicester LE14 1DS |
| Lincolnshire | Lincoln Police Station<br>West Parade<br>Lincoln LN1 1YP<br><br>Grantham Police Station<br>Swingbridge Road<br>Grantham NG31 7XT<br><br>Spalding Police Station<br>Westlode Street<br>Spalding PE11 2AF<br><br>Skegness Police Station<br>Park Avenue<br>Skegness PE25 1BJ<br><br>Horncastle Police Station<br>The Wong<br>Horncastle LN9 6EB | Louth Police Station<br>Eastfield Road<br>Louth LN11 7AN<br><br>Sleaford Police Station<br>The Hoplands<br>Boston Road<br>Sleaford NG34 7LZ<br><br>Gainsborough Police Station<br>Morton Road<br>Gainsborough DN21 2SY<br><br>Boston Police Station<br>Lincoln Lane<br>Boston PE21 8QS<br><br>Stamford Police Station<br>North Street<br>Stamford PE9 2SF |
| City of London | Bishopsgate Police Station<br>182 Bishopsgate<br>London EC2M 4NP | |
| London Metropolitan | Barking and Dagenham<br>Dagenham Police Station<br>561 Rainham Road South<br>Dagenham<br>Essex RM10 7TU<br><br>Barnet (1)<br>Barnet Police Station<br>26–32 High Street<br>Barnet EN5 5RU<br><br>Barnet (2)<br>Colindale Police Station<br>Grahame Park Way<br>Colindale NW9 5TW<br><br>Bexley<br>Bexleyheath Police Station<br>2 Arnsberg Way<br>Bexleyheath DA7 4QS<br><br>Bromley<br>Bromley Police Station<br>High Street<br>Bromley BR1 1ER | Brent (1)<br>Kilburn Police Station<br>38 Salisbury Road<br>Kilburn NW6 6NN<br><br>Brent (2)<br>Wembley Police Station<br>603 Harrow Road<br>Wembley HA0 2HH<br><br>City of Westminster<br>Charing Cross Police Station<br>Agar Street<br>London WC2N 4JP<br><br>Croydon<br>Croydon Police Station<br>71 Park Lane<br>London CR9 1BP<br><br>Enfield<br>Edmonton Police Station<br>462 Fore Street<br>Edmonton<br>London N9 0PW |

| | | |
|---|---|---|
| | Camden (1)<br>Kentish Town Police Station<br>12a Holmes Road<br>London NW5 3AE | Greenwich<br>Plumstead Police Station<br>200 Plumstead High Street<br>London SE18 1JY |
| | Camden (2)<br>Holborn Police Station<br>10 Lambs Conduit Street<br>London WC1N 3NR | Hackney (1)<br>Stoke Newington Police Station<br>33 Stoke Newington High Street<br>London N16 8DS |
| | Ealing (1)<br>Southall Police Station<br>67 High Street<br>Southall<br>London UB1 3HG | Hackney (2)<br>Shoreditch Police Station<br>4–6 Shepherdess Walk<br>London N1 7LF |
| | Ealing (2)<br>Acton Police Station<br>250 High Street<br>London W3 9BH | Haringey (1)<br>Tottenham Police Station<br>398 High Road<br>Tottenham N17 0HQ |
| | Hammersmith and Fulham<br>Shepherds Bush Police Station<br>253 Uxbridge Road<br>London W12 7JA | Haringey (2)<br>Hornsey Police Station<br>98 Tottenham Lane<br>Hornsey<br>London N8 7EJ |
| | Hillingdon<br>Uxbridge Police Station<br>1 Warwick Place<br>Harefield Road<br>Uxbridge UB8 1PG | Islington<br>Islington Police Station<br>Tolpuddle Street<br>London N1 0YY |
| | Harrow<br>South Harrow Police Station<br>74 Northolt Road<br>London HA2 0DN | Lambeth<br>Brixton Police Station<br>367 Brixton Road<br>London SW9 7DD |
| | Havering<br>Romford Police Station<br>19 Main Road<br>Romford<br>Essex RM1 3BJ | Kensington & Chelsea<br>Notting Hill Police Station<br>101 Ladbroke Road<br>London W11 3PL |
| | Hounslow (1)<br>Hounslow Police Station<br>5 Montague Road<br>Hounslow<br>Middlesex TW3 1LB | Merton<br>Wimbledon Police Station<br>15 Queens Road<br>London SW19 8NN |
| | Hounslow (2)<br>Chiswick Police Station<br>209–211 High Rd<br>Chiswick W4 2DU | Newham (1)<br>Forest Gate Police Station<br>350–360 Romford Road<br>London E7 8BS |
| | Kingston upon Thames<br>Kingston Police Station<br>5–7 High Street<br>Kingston upon Thames<br>Surrey KT1 1LB | Newham (2)<br>Plaistow Police Station<br>444 Barking Station<br>London E13 8HJ |
| | Lewisham (1)<br>Lewisham Police Station<br>43 Lewisham High Street<br>London SE13 5JZ | Redbridge<br>Ilford Police Station<br>270–294 High Street<br>Essex IG1 1GT |
| | Lewisham (2)<br>Catford Police Station | Sutton<br>Sutton Police Station<br>6 Carshalton Road<br>Sutton<br>Surrey SM1 4RF |

| | | |
|---|---|---|
| | 333 Bromley Road<br>London SE6 2RJ<br><br>Richmond<br>Twickenham Police Station<br>41 London Road<br>Twickenham TW1 3SY | Waltham Forest<br>Chingford Police Station<br>1 King's Head Hill<br>London E4 7EA |
| | Southwark (1)<br>Southwark Police Station<br>323 Borough High Street<br>London SE1 1JL<br><br>Southwark (2)<br>Walworth Police Station<br>12–28 Manor Place<br>London SE17 3RL<br><br>Tower Hamlets (2)<br>Bethnal Green Police Station<br>12 Victoria Park Square<br>London E2 9NZ | Wandsworth<br>Lavender Hill Police Station,<br>176 Lavender Hill,<br>Battersea, SW11 1JX<br><br>Tower Hamlets (1)<br>Limehouse Police Station<br>29 West India Dock Road<br>London E14 8EZ |
| Merseyside | Huyton Police Station<br>Lathom Road<br>Huyton<br>Merseyside L36 9XU<br><br>Admiral Street Police Station<br>Admiral Street<br>Liverpool L8 8JN<br><br>Speke Police Station<br>Ganworth Road<br>Liverpool L24 2XQ<br><br>Marsh Lane Police Station<br>Marsh Lane<br>Bootle L20 5HJ<br><br>Wallasey Police Station<br>Manor Road<br>Wallasey<br>Wirral<br>CH44 1DA | St Helens Police Station<br>College Street<br>St Helens WA10 1TG<br><br>St Anne Street Police Station<br>St Anne Street<br>Liverpool L3 3HJ<br><br>Birkenhead Police Station<br>Mortimer Street<br>Birkenhead<br>Wirral CH41 5EU<br><br>Southport Police Station<br>Albert Road<br>Southport PR9 0LL<br><br>Kirkby Police Station<br>St Chads Drive<br>Kirkby<br>Merseyside<br>L32 8RF |
| Norfolk | Bethel Street Police Station<br>Bethel Street<br>Norwich NR2 1NN<br><br>Police Station<br>Howard Street North<br>Great Yarmouth NR30 1PH<br><br>Police Station<br>Yarmouth Road<br>North Walsham NR28 9AW | Police Station<br>Holt Road<br>Cromer NR27 9EB<br><br>Police Station<br>St James Road<br>King's Lynn PE30 5DE<br><br>Police Station<br>Norwich Road<br>Thetford IP24 2HU |
| | Police Station<br>30 Norwich Road<br>Fakenham NR21 8BB | Police Station<br>Commercial Road<br>East Dereham NR19 1AE<br><br>Police Station<br>63 London Road<br>Downham Market PE38 9BQ |

| | | |
|---|---|---|
| Northamptonshire | Daventry Police Station<br>New Street<br>Daventry NN11 4BS | Corby Police Station<br>Elizabeth Street<br>Corby NN17 1SH |
| | Weston Favell Police Station<br>Pyramid Close<br>Weston Favell<br>Northampton NN3 8NZ | Wellingborough Police Station<br>Midland Road<br>Wellingborough NN8 1HF |
| Northumbria | Alnwick Police Station<br>Prudhoe Street<br>Alnwick NE66 1UJ | North Shields Police Station<br>Upper Pearson Street<br>North Shields NE30 1AB |
| | Berwick Police Station<br>Church Street<br>Berwick TD15 1DZ | Wallsend Police Station<br>Middle Engine Lane<br>Wallsend<br>Tyne and Wear NE28 9NT |
| | Hexham Police Station<br>Shaftoe Leazes<br>Hexham NE46 3DG | Gateshead East Police Station<br>High West Street<br>Gateshead NE8 1BN |
| | Ashington Police Station<br>Lintonville Terrace<br>Ashington NE63 8HD | Whickham Police Station<br>Front Street<br>Whickham NE16 4HE |
| | Bedlington Police Station<br>Schalkesmuhle Road<br>Bedlington NE22 7LA | South Shields Police Station<br>Millbank Station Road<br>South Shields NE33 1RR |
| | Newcastle City Centre Police Station<br>Forth Banks<br>Newcastle upon Tyne NE31 3PH | Sunderland Police Station<br>Church Bank<br>Southwick<br>Sunderland<br>SR5 2DU |
| | Byker Police Station<br>Clifford Street<br>Newcastle upon Tyne NE6 1EA | Houghton-le-Spring Police Station<br>Dairy Lane<br>Houghton-le-Spring DH4 5BL |
| | Newcastle Area Command HQ<br>Etal Lane Police Station<br>Westerhope<br>Newcastle upon Tyne NE5 4AW | Washington Police Station<br>The Galleries<br>Washington NE38 7RY |
| North Wales | Holyhead Police Station<br>Stanley Street<br>Holyhead LL65 1HL | Mold Police Station<br>King Street<br>Mold<br>Flintshire CH7 1EF |
| | Caernarfon Police Station<br>Maesincla<br>Caernarfon<br>Gwynedd LL55 1BU | Divisional Police HQ<br>St Asaph Business Park<br>Ffordd William Morgan<br>St Asaph LL17 0HQ |
| | Dolgellau Police Station<br>Barmouth Road<br>Dolgellau<br>Gwynedd LL40 2YT | Wrexham Police Station<br>Bodhyfryd<br>Wrexham LL12 7BW |
| North Yorkshire | York Police Station<br>Fulford Road<br>York YO10 4BY | Northallerton Police Station<br>72 High Street<br>Northallerton DL7 8ES |
| | Harrogate Police Station<br>Beckwith Head Road<br>Harrogate | Skipton Police Station<br>Otley Road<br>Skipton BD23 1EZ |

| | | |
|---|---|---|
| | North Yorkshire HG3 1FR<br><br>Scarborough Police Station<br>Northway<br>Scarborough YO12 7AD | |
| Nottinghamshire | Bridewell Police Station<br>Magistrates Building<br>Carrington Street<br>Nottingham NG2 1EE<br><br>Mansfield Police Station<br>Great Central Road<br>Mansfield<br>Nottinghamshire NG18 2HQ<br><br>Carlton Police Station<br>Cavendish Road<br>Carlton<br>Nottingham NG4 3DZ<br><br>Central Police Station<br>Byron House<br>Maid Marion Way<br>Nottingham<br>NG1 6HS | Newark Police Station<br>Queen's Road<br>Newark<br>Nottinghamshire NG24 1LH<br><br>Worksop Police Station<br>Potter Street<br>Worksop<br>Nottinghamshire S80 2AL<br><br>Oxclose Lane Police Station<br>Oxclose Lane<br>Arnold<br>Nottinghamshire NG5 6FZ<br><br>Radford Road Police Station<br>Radford Road<br>Hyson Gree<br>Nottingham<br>NG7 5GX |
| South Wales | Merthyr Tydfil Police Station<br>Rhydycar Business Park<br>Merthyr Tydfil CF48 1DL<br><br>Pontypridd Police Station<br>Berw Road<br>Pontypridd CF37 2TR<br><br>Cardiff Central Police Station<br>King Edward VII Avenue<br>Cathays Park<br>Cardiff CF10 3NN<br><br>Barry Police Station<br>Gladstone Road<br>Barry CF63 1TD | Bridgend Police Station<br>Brackla Street<br>Bridgend CF31 1BZ<br><br>Neath Police Station<br>Gnoll Park Road<br>Neath SA11 3BW<br><br>Swansea Central Police Station<br>Grove Place<br>Swansea SA1 5EA<br><br>Cardiff Bay Police Station<br>James Street<br>Cardiff Bay<br>Cardiff CF10 5EW |
| South Yorkshire | Doncaster Police Station<br>College Road<br>Doncaster DN1 3HX<br><br>Rotherham Police Station<br>Main Street<br>Rotherham S60 1QY<br><br>Moss Way Police Station<br>Moss Way<br>Sheffield S20 7XX | Barnsley Police Station<br>Churchfields<br>Barnsley S70 2DL<br><br>Ecclesfield Police Station<br>321 The Common<br>Sheffield S35 9WL<br><br>South Yorkshire Police HQ<br>Snig Hill<br>Sheffield S3 8LY |
| Staffordshire | Burton Police Station<br>Horninglow Street<br>Burton-on-Trent DE14 1PA<br><br>Rugeley Police Station<br>Anson Street | Longton Police Station<br>Sutherland Road<br>Longton<br>Stoke-on-Trent ST3 1HH<br><br>Leek Police Station |

| | | |
|---|---|---|
| | Rugeley WS15 2BQ<br><br>Cannock Police Station<br>Wolverhampton Road<br>Cannock WS11 1AH<br><br>Burslem Police Station<br>Jackson Street<br>Burslem<br>ST6 1AF | Fountain Street<br>Leek ST13 6QT<br><br>Tamworth Police Station<br>Spinning School Lane<br>Tamworth B79 7BB<br><br>Wombourne Police Station<br>High Street<br>Wombourne WV5 9EE<br><br>Stafford Police Station<br>Eastgate Street<br>Stafford ST16 2DQ |
| Suffolk | Bury St Edmunds Police Station<br>Raingate Street<br>Bury St Edmunds IP33 2AP<br><br>Lowestoft Police Station<br>Old Nelson Street<br>Lowestoft NR32 1PE | Ipswich Police Station<br>10 Museum Street<br>Ipswich<br>Suffolk IP1 1HT |
| Surrey | Guildford Police Station<br>Margaret Road<br>Guildford<br>Surrey GU1 4QS<br><br>Staines Police Station<br>22 Kingston Road<br>Staines<br>Middlesex TW18 4LQ | Reigate Police Station<br>79 Reigate Road<br>Reigate<br>Surrey RH2 0RY<br><br>Woking Police Station<br>Station Approach<br>Woking<br>Surrey GU22 7SY |
| Sussex | Worthing Police Station<br>21 Chatsworth Road<br>Worthing<br>West Sussex BN11 1LY<br><br>Chichester Police Station<br>Kingsham Road<br>Chichester<br>West Sussex PO19 8AD<br><br>Littlehampton Police Station<br>County Buildings<br>East Street<br>Littlehampton<br>West Sussex BN17 6AR<br><br>Shoreham Police Station<br>Ham Road<br>Shoreham-by-Sea<br>West Sussex BN43 6PA<br><br>Bognor Police Station<br>London Road<br>Bognor<br>West Sussex PO21 1BA<br><br>Eastbourne Police Station<br>1 Grove Road<br>Eastbourne<br>East Sussex<br>BN21 4UF | Crawley Police Station<br>Northgate Avenue<br>Crawley<br>West Sussex RH10 8BF<br><br>Hastings Police Station<br>Bohemia Road<br>Hastings<br>East Sussex TN34 1JJ<br><br>Uckfield Police Station<br>New Town<br>Uckfield<br>East Sussex TN22 5DL<br><br>Police Patrol Centre<br>Hammonds Drive<br>Eastbourne<br>East Sussex BN23 6PW<br><br>Brighton Police Station<br>John Street<br>Brighton BN2 0LA<br><br>Haywards Heath Police Station<br>Bolnore Road<br>Haywards Heath<br>West Sussex RH16 4BA |

| | | |
|---|---|---|
| | Halisham Police Station<br>George Street<br>Halisham<br>East Sussex<br>BN27 1AB | Horsham Police Station<br>Hurst Road<br>Horsham<br>West Sussex<br>RH12 2DJ |
| | Seaford Police Station<br>Church Street<br>Seaford<br>East Sussex<br>BN25 1HG | Rye Police Station<br>Cinque Ports Street<br>Rye<br>East Sussex<br>TN13 7AN |
| | Lewes Police Station<br>6 North Street<br>Lewes<br>East Sussex<br>BN7 2PA | Battle Police Station<br>North Trade Road<br>Battle<br>East Sussex<br>TN33 0EX |
| | Crowborough Police Station<br>Crowborough Hill<br>Crowborough<br>East Sussex<br>TN6 2DA | Bexhill Police Station<br>Terminus Road<br>Bexhill-on-Sea<br>East Sussex<br>TN39 3NR |
| Thames Valley | Abingdon Police Station<br>Colwell Drive<br>Abingdon<br>Oxfordshire OX14 1AU | Maidenhead Police Station<br>Bridge Street<br>Maidenhead<br>Berks SL6 8LP |
| | Aylesbury Police Station<br>Wendover Road<br>Aylesbury<br>Bucks HP21 7LA | Milton Keynes Police Station<br>302 North Row<br>Witan Gate East<br>Milton Keynes<br>Bucks MK9 2DS |
| | Banbury Police Station<br>Warwick Road<br>Banbury<br>Oxon OX16 2AE | Newbury Police Station<br>Mill Lane<br>Newbury<br>Berks RG14 5QU |
| | Bicester Police Station<br>Queens Avenue<br>Bicester<br>Oxfordshire OX26 2NT | Oxford Police Station<br>St Aldates<br>Oxford OX1 1SZ |
| | Bracknell Police Station<br>The Broadway<br>Bracknell<br>Berks RG12 1AD | Reading Police Station<br>Castle Street<br>Reading<br>Berks RG1 7TH |
| | High Wycombe Police Station<br>Queen Victoria Road<br>High Wycombe<br>Bucks HP11 1BE | Slough Police Station<br>Windsor Road<br>Slough<br>Berks SL1 2HH |
| | Loddon Valley Police Station<br>Rushey Way<br>Lower Earley<br>Berks RG6 4PS | Witney Police Station<br>Welch Way<br>Witney<br>Oxfordshire OX28 6JN |
| | Amersham Police Station<br>Oxford Road<br>King George V Road<br>Amersham<br>Bucks HP6 5AL | Kidlington Police Station<br>Oxford Road<br>Kidlington<br>OX5 2NX |

| | | |
|---|---|---|
| Warwickshire | Rugby Police Station<br>Newbold Road<br>Rugby CV21 2DH | Stratford Police Station<br>Rother Street<br>Stratford upon Avon CV37 6RD |
| | Nuneaton Police Station<br>Warwickshire Justice Centre<br>Vicarage Street<br>Nuneaton CV11 4JU | Leamington Police Station<br>Warwickshire Justice Centre<br>Newbold Terrace<br>Leamington Spa CV32 4EL |
| West Mercia | Worcester Police Station<br>Castle Street<br>Worcester WR1 3QX | Kidderminster Police Station<br>Habberley Road<br>Kidderminster DY11 6AN |
| | Hereford Police Station<br>Bath Street<br>Hereford HR1 2HT | Redditch Police Station<br>Grove Street<br>Redditch<br>Worcestershire B98 8DD |
| | Shrewsbury Police Station<br>Clive Road<br>Monkmoor<br>Shrewsbury SY2 5RW | Malinsgate Police Station<br>Malinsgate<br>Telford TF3 4HW |
| West Midlands | Birmingham Central<br>Police Station<br>Steelhouse Lane<br>Birmingham B4 6NW | Stechford Police Station<br>338 Station Road<br>Stechford<br>Birmingham B33 8RR |
| | Sutton Coldfield Police Station<br>Lichfield Road<br>Sutton Coldfield B74 2NR | Solihull Police Station<br>Homer Road<br>Solihull<br>West Midlands B91 3QL |
| | Bournville Lane Police Station<br>341 Bournville Lane<br>Birmingham B30 1QX | Bloxwich Police Station<br>Station Street<br>Bloxwich WS3 2PD |
| | Coventry Central Police Station<br>Little Park Street<br>Coventry CV1 2JX | Brierley Hill Police Station<br>Bank Street<br>Brierley Hill DY5 3DH |
| | Wolverhampton Central<br>Police Station<br>Bilston Street<br>Wolverhampton WV1 3AA | West Bromwich Police Station<br>Moor Street<br>West Bromwich B70 8HS |
| West Yorkshire | Bradford South<br>Trafalgar House<br>Nelson Street<br>Bradford BD5 0EW | Dewsbury Police Station<br>Aldams Road<br>Dewsbury WF12 8AP |
| | Huddersfield Police Station<br>Castlegate<br>Huddersfield HD1 2NJ | Halifax Police Station<br>Richmond Close<br>Halifax HX1 5TW |
| | Leeds District Headquarters<br>Elland Road<br>Leeds LS11 8BU | Wakefield District Headquarters<br>Havertop Lane<br>Normanton WF6 1FD |
| Wiltshire | Marlborough Police Station<br>George Lane<br>Marlborough SN8 4DB | Trowbridge Police Station<br>Polebarn Road<br>Trowbridge BA14 7EP |
| | Gablecross Police Station<br>Shrivenham Road | Melksham Police Station<br>Divisional Police HQ |

| | | |
|---|---|---|
| | South Marston<br>Swindon SN3 4RB | Hampton Park<br>West Melksham SN12 6QQ<br><br>Warminster Police Station<br>Station Road<br>Warminster BA12 9BR |

# Table of Statutes, Conventions and Treaties

Paragraph references in this Table indicate where an Act is set out in part or in full.

**B**

## D

## E

**G**

## H

## I

## J

## K



## L

## P

## R

**W**

## Y



## Z

# Alphabetical Table of Statutory Instruments, Codes and EC Regulations

Paragraph references in this Table indicate where a Statutory Instrument, etc is set out in part or in full.

The Criminal Procedure Rules are in the *Key Materials*.

## B

## E



## F

## G

## H

## N

## S

## T

## Y

## Z

# Chronological List of Statutory Instruments

Paragraph references in this Table indicate where a Statutory Instrument is set out in part or in full.

The Criminal Procedure Rules are now in the *Key Materials*.

2010/675 Environmental Permitting (England and Wales) Regulations 2010 .... 7.10320

# Table of Cases

**Decisions of the European Court of Justice are listed below numerically. These decisions are also included in the preceding alphabetical Table.**

## C

## D

## E

## G

## H

Holden & Co (a firm) v Crown Prosecution Service (No 2) [1992] 2 All ER 642, sub nom Steele Ford & Newton v Crown Prosecution Service (No 2) [1992] 1 WLR 407, [1992] 1 LS Gaz R 32, 135 Sol Jo LB 196, CA; revsd [1994] 1 AC 22, [1993] 2 All ER 769, [1993] 2 WLR 934, [1993] 27 LS Gaz R 34, [1993] NLJR 847, 137 Sol Jo LB 152, HL .......... 1.338
Holden v Lancashire Justices (1998) 162 JP 789 .......... 7.1624
Holford v George (1868) LR 3 QB 639, 32 JP 468, 37 LJQB 185, 18 LT 817, 16 WR 1204 .. 7.11348
Holland v Phipp [1982] 1 WLR 1150, 126 Sol Jo 466, [1983] RTR 123 .......... 4.351
Hollington v Hewthorn & Co Ltd [1943] KB 587, [1943] 2 All ER 35, 112 LJKB 463, 169 LT 21, 59 TLR 321, 87 Sol Jo 247, CA .......... 2.5, 2.85, 2.322
Hollis v Marshall (1858) 2 H & N 755, 22 JP 210, 27 LJ Ex 235, 30 LTOS 334, 6 WR 365 ... 7.9756
Holloway v Cross [1981] 1 All ER 1012, 125 Sol Jo 46, [1981] RTR 146 .......... 7.1831
Holloway v DPP [2004] EWHC 2621 (Admin), (2004) 169 JP 14, [2004] All ER (D) 278 (Oct) .......... 7.10379
Hollyhomes v Hind [1944] KB 571, [1944] 2 All ER 8, 108 JP 190, 113 LJKB 285, 171 LT 175, 60 TLR 376, 42 LGR 238 .......... 1.167, 1.289, 7.11583
Holmes, Re [2004] EWHC 2020 (Admin), [2005] 1 All ER 490, [2005] 1 WLR 1857, [2005] 1 Cr App Rep 229, (2004) Times, 28 October, [2004] All ER (D) 111 (Aug) .......... 7.11328
Holmes v Campbell (1998) 162 JP 655 .......... 1.158, 1.164
Holmes v Chief Constable Merseyside Police [1976] Crim LR 125 .......... 7.8132
Holmes v Cooper [1985] 3 All ER 114, [1985] 1 WLR 1060, 129 Sol Jo 653, 84 LGR 225, 50 P & CR 437, CA .......... 7.11371, 7.11382
Holmes v DPP. See R v Holmes (1946)
Holmes v Pipers Ltd [1914] 1 KB 57, 78 JP 37, 83 LJKB 285, 109 LT 930, 30 TLR 28, 12 LGR 25, 23 Cox CC 689 .......... 7.1830
Holroyd v Berry [1973] RTR 145, [1975] Crim LR 118 .......... 4.466
Holt v DPP [1996] 2 Cr App Rep (S) 314, [1996] Crim LR 524 .......... 3.87
Home Office v Wainwright. See Wainwright v Home Office
Homolka v Osmond [1939] 1 All ER 154 .......... 1.537, 4.48, 4.130, 4.439
Hood v Lewis [1976] RTR 99, [1976] Crim LR 74 .......... 4.175
Hooper v Riddle & Co (1906) 70 JP 417, 95 LT 424, 21 Cox CC 277 .......... 7.1830
Hope v DPP [1992] RTR 305 .......... 4.246
Hopton v Thirlwall (1863) 27 JP 743, 9 LT 327, 12 WR 72 .......... 7.4617
Horn v Raine (1898) 62 JP 420, [1843.60] All ER Rep 481, 67 LJQB 533, 78 LT 654 .......... 7.5322
Horncastle v United Kingdom (App. No. 4184/10) (2015) Times, 21 January, [2014] ECHR 4184/10, [2014] All ER (D) 160 (Dec), ECtHR .......... 2.95
Hornchurch UDC v Webber [1938] 1 KB 698, [1938] 1 All ER 309, 102 JP 167, 107 LJKB 438, 158 LT 258, 54 TLR 358, 82 Sol Jo 157, 36 LGR 262 .......... 6.423
Horne v Gaygusuz [1979] Crim LR 594, [1979] LS Gaz R 705 .......... 7.6451
Horner v Cadman (1886) 50 JP 454, 55 LJMC 110, 54 LT 421, 34 WR 413, 16 Cox CC 51 ... 6.375
Horner v Sherwoods of Darlington Ltd (1989) 154 JP 299 .......... 7.1839
Horrix v Malam (1984) 148 JP 30, [1984] RTR 112 .......... 1.121
Horsfield v Brown [1932] 1 KB 355, 96 JP 123, 101 LJKB 177, 146 LT 280, 30 LGR 153, 29 Cox CC 422 .......... 1.622
Horton v Twells (1983) Times, 9 December .......... 4.239
Horwood v Goodall (1872) 36 JP 486 .......... 6.396
Horwood v Hill (1872) 36 JP 486 .......... 6.396
Hosier v Goodall [1962] 2 QB 401, [1962] 1 All ER 30, [1962] 2 WLR 157, 126 JP 52, 105 Sol Jo 1085, 60 LGR 500 .......... 2.201, 4.434
Hotchin v Hindmarsh [1891] 2 QB 18, 55 JP 775, 60 LJMC 146, 65 LT 149, 39 WR 607 .... 7.4739
Hough v Chief Constable of Staffordshire [2001] EWCA Civ 39, (2001) 165 JPN 54 .......... 1.738
Houghton v Mundy (1910) 74 JP 377, 103 LT 60, 48 LGR 838 .......... 7.4739
Houghton v Trafalgar Insurance Co Ltd [1954] 1 QB 247, [1953] 2 All ER 1409, [1953] 3 WLR 985, [1953] 2 Lloyd's Rep 503, 97 Sol Jo 831, CA .......... 4.384
Hounslow London Borough Council v Thames Water Utilities Ltd [2003] EWHC 1197 (Admin), [2004] QB 212, [2003] 3 WLR 1243, [2003] 27 LS Gaz R 37, [2003] 24 EG 162 (CS), [2003] All ER (D) 347 (May) .......... 7.10061
House v Reynolds [1977] 1 All ER 689, [1977] 1 WLR 88, 141 JP 202, 120 Sol Jo 820, 75 LGR 311, [1977] RTR 135 .......... 7.11561, 7.11564
Howard v Hallett [1984] RTR 353, [1984] Crim LR 565, [1984] LS Gaz R 2225 .......... 4.244, 4.447
Howes v Peake (1876) 33 LT 818, 24 WR 407, 3 Char Pr Cas 468; affd 35 LT 584, CA . 1.769, 1.326
Howey v Bradley (1969) 114 Sol Jo 37, [1970] Crim LR 223 .......... 2.13
Howker v Robinson [1973] QB 178, [1972] 2 All ER 786, [1972] 3 WLR 234, 136 JP 562, 116 Sol Jo 354 .......... 7.7341
Howlett v Holding [2006] EWHC 41 (QB) .......... 7.8697
Howley v Oxford (1985) 149 JP 363, 81 Cr App Rep 246, [1985] Crim LR 724 .......... 1.612, 3.353
Hoy v Smith [1964] 3 All ER 670, [1964] 1 WLR 1377, 129 JP 33, 108 Sol Jo 841, 62 LGR 661 .......... 4.162
Hoyle v Hitchman (1879) 4 QBD 233, 43 JP 430, 48 LJMC 97, 40 LT 252, 27 WR 487 .......... 7.4739
Huckerby v Elliott [1970] 1 All ER 189, 134 JP 175, 113 Sol Jo 1001 .......... 7.2682
Hudson v Bridge (1903) 67 JP 186, 88 LT 550, 20 Cox CC 425, 1 LGR 400 .......... 7.4739
Hudson v Bushrod [1982] RTR 87 .......... 4.283, 4.1508

## I

## J

Joy, Re (1853) 22 LT Jo 80 .......... 7.11583
Joy v Federation against Copyright Theft Ltd [1993] Crim LR 588 .......... 1.801
Joyce v Boots Cash Chemists (Southern) Ltd [1950] 2 All ER 719, 66 (pt 2) TLR 635, 94 Sol Jo 536, 43 R & IT 593; affd [1951] 1 All ER 682n, 115 JP 247n, 95 Sol Jo 172, CA .......... 7.5499
Joyce v DPP [1946] AC 347, [1946] 1 All ER 186, 115 LJKB 146, 174 LT 206, 62 TLR 208, 31 Cr App Rep 57, HL .......... 7.2584
Jubb v DPP [2002] EWHC 2317 (Admin), [2003] RTR 272, 167 JP 50 .......... 4.244, 4.448
Jukes v DPP [2013] EWHC 195 (Admin), 177 JP 212, [2013] Crim LR 773, [2013] All ER (D) 109 (Jan) .......... 7.10386
Julius v Lord Bishop of Oxford (1860) 5 App Cas 214, [1874.80] All ER Rep 43, 44 JP 600, 49 LJQB 577, 42 LT 546, 28 WR 726, HL .......... 2.136

## K

K (KJS) (an infant), Re [1966] 3 All ER 154, [1966] 1 WLR 1241, 110 Sol Jo 545 .......... 1.1983
K (minors), Re [1988] Fam 1, [1988] 1 All ER 214, [1987] 3 WLR 1233, 152 JP 185, [1988] 1 FLR 435, [1988] Fam Law 166, 131 Sol Jo 1697, [1987] LS Gaz R 3501 .......... 2.57
K (minors), Re [1994] 3 All ER 230, [1994] 2 FCR 805, [1994] 1 FLR 377, [1994] Fam Law 247, sub nom Kent County Council v K [1994] 1 WLR 912 .......... 7.4260
K (adoption) (permission to advertise), Re [2007] EWHC 544 (Fam), [2007] 1 WLR 2531, [2007] 2 FLR 326, [2007] Fam Law 681, (2007) Times, 20 April, [2007] All ER (D) 310 (Mar) .......... 7.4259
K (a child) (secure accommodation order: right to liberty), Re [2001] Fam 377, [2001] 2 All ER 719, [2001] 2 WLR 1141, [2001] 1 FCR 249, [2001] 1 FLR 526, [2001] Fam Law 99, [2000] 48 LS Gaz R 36, (2000) Times, 29 November, 144 Sol Jo LB 291, [2000] All ER (D) 1834, CA .......... 7.4237
K and H (Children), Re [2015] EWCA Civ 543, [2015] 1 WLR 3801, [2015] Fam Law 778, (2015) Times, 25 June, [2015] 5 Costs LO 607, [2015] All ER (D) 230 (May) .......... 1.1246, 1.1740,1 1761, 7.6401
K v K (1979). See Kokosinski v Kokosinski
K Ltd v National Westminster Bank plc (Revenue and Customs Prosecution Office and Serious Organised Crime Agency intervening) [2006] EWCA Civ 1039, [2006] 4 All ER 907, [2006] 2 All ER (Comm) 655, [2007] 1 WLR 311, [2006] 2 Lloyd's Rep 569, (2006) Times, 27 July, 150 Sol Jo LB 982, [2006] All ER (D) 269 (Jul) .......... 3.518
KK v DPP [2016] EWHC 1976 (Admin), [2016] 4 WLR 162, [2016] Crim LR 868 .......... 1.285, 2.48
KL and LK v DPP [2001] EWHC Admin 1112, (2001) 166 JP 369 .......... 1.44
Kajala v Noble (1982) 75 Cr App Rep 149, [1982] Crim LR 433 .......... 2.19, 2.27
Kakis v Government of the Republic of Cyprus [1978] 2 All ER 634, [1978] 1 WLR 779, 122 Sol Jo 400, HL .......... 7.3950, 7.3964
Kameswara Rao v Wyles [1949] 2 All ER 685, 113 JP 516, 65 TLR 659, 93 Sol Jo 679, 47 LGR 720 .......... 7.8114
Kanaris, Re [2003] UKHL 2, [2003] 1 All ER 593, [2003] 1 WLR 443, [2003] 2 Cr App Rep 1, 147 Sol Jo LB 146 .......... 1.936
Kandola v Generalstaatwaltschaft Frankfurt, Germany [2015] EWHC 619 (Admin), [2015] 1 WLR 5097 .......... 7.3948A
Kang v DPP [2016] EWHC 3014 (Admin), [2017] 4 WLR 3 .......... 1.324, 4.244, 4.447
Kapri v The Lord Advocate representing The Government of the Republic of Albania [2013] UKSC 48, [2013] 4 All ER 599, [2013] 1 WLR 2324, [2013] NLJR 14, (2013) Times, 21 August, 2013 SCCR 430, [2013] All ER (D) 123 (Jul) .......... 7.4029
Karamat v R [1956] AC 256, [1956] 1 All ER 415, [1956] 2 WLR 412, 100 Sol Jo 109, 40 Cr App Rep 13, sub nom Kamarat v R 120 JP 136, PC .......... 1.25
Karflex Ltd v Poole [1933] 2 KB 251, [1933] All ER Rep 46, 102 LJKB 475, 149 LT 140, 49 TLR 418 .......... 1.160
Karpinski v City of Westminster [1993] Crim LR 606 .......... 1.147
Karsten v Wood Green Crown Court [2014] EWHC 2900 (Admin), [2014] All ER (D) 286 (Oct) .......... 7.11121
Karuse AS v Politsei- ja Piirivalveamet: C-222/12 [2014] RTR 257, ECJ .......... 4.1198
Kashich v Kashich (1951) WN 557, 116 JP 6 .......... 1.295, 2.18
Kates v Jeffery [1914] 3 KB 160, 78 JP 310, 83 LJKB 1760, 111 LT 459, 24 Cox CC 324, 12 LGR 974 .......... 1.325
Katsonis v Crown Prosecution Service [2011] EWHC 1860 (Admin), 175 JP 396, [2011] All ER (D) 16 (Jul) .......... 7.8625
Kavanagh v Chief Constable of Devon and Cornwall [1974] QB 624, [1973] 3 All ER 657, [1973] 3 WLR 415, 137 JP 807, 117 Sol Jo 634; affd [1974] QB 624, [1974] 2 All ER 697, [1974] 2 WLR 762, 138 JP 618, 118 Sol Jo 347, CA .......... 7.7333
Kavanagh v Glorney (1876) IR 10 CL 210 .......... 1.325
Kay v Butterworth (1945) 110 JP 75, 173 LT 191, 61 TLR 452, 89 Sol Jo 381 .......... 4.9
Kay v Hibbert [1977] Crim LR 226, 141 JP Jo 157 .......... 7.9193

## L

## M

## N

## O

## P

## Q



## R

## S

## U

## V

## W

## X



## Y



## Z

**Decisions of the European Court of Justice are listed below numerically. These decisions are also included in the preceding alphabetical Table.**

# Index

## A

## C

## G

## H

**J**

K



L

## M

## P

## S

intention as to plea 1.521–1.523

## U

## X



## Y

## Z

# PENALTY POINTS

| | | | |
|---|---|---|---|
| RTRA 1984, | | | |
| ss: | 16(1) | Contravene temporary prohibition etc | 3–6 |
| | 17(4) | Contravene special road scheme or regulations | 3–6 |
| | 25(5) | Contravene pedestrian crossing regulations | 3 |
| | 28(3) | Not stopping at school crossing | 3 |
| | 29(3) | Contravene street playground order | 2 |
| | 89(1) | Exceeding speed limit | 3–6 |
| RTA 1988, | | | |
| ss: | 1 | Death by dangerous driving | 3–11* |
| | 1A | Causing serious injury by dangerous driving | 3–11* |
| | 2 | Dangerous driving | 3–11* |
| | 2B | Causing death by careless, or inconsiderate, driving | 3–11* |
| | 3 | Careless and inconsiderate driving | 3–9 |
| | 3ZB | Causing death by driving unlicensed or uninsured drivers | 3–11* |
| | 3ZC | Causing death by driving: disqualified drivers | 3–11* |
| | 3ZD | Causing serious injury by driving: disqualified drivers | 3–11* |
| | 3A | Causing death by careless driving when under influence of drink or drugs | 3–11* |
| | 4(1) | Driving/attempt when unfit through drink or drugs | 3–11* |
| | 4(2) | In charge when unfit through drink or drugs | 10 |
| | 5(1)(*a*) | Driving/attempt with excess alcohol | 3–11* |
| | 5(1)(*b*) | In charge with excess alcohol | 10 |
| | 5A(1)(*a*) | Driving/attempt with a concentration of a specified controlled drug in excess of the specified limit | 3–11* |
| | 5A(1)(*b*) | In charge with a concentration of a specified controlled drug in excess of the specified limit | 10 |
| | 6 | Fail co-operate with preliminary test | 4 |
| | 7 | Fail provide specimen for analysis | |
| | | (*a*) when driving or attempting to drive | 3–11* |
| | | (*b*) otherwise | 10 |
| | 7A | Failing to allow specimen to be subjected to laboratory test | |
| | | (*a*) when driving or attempting to drive | 3–11* |
| | | (*b*) otherwise | 10 |
| | 12 | Racing and speed trials on public highways | 3–11* |
| | 22 | Leave vehicle in dangerous position | 3 |
| | 23 | Carry passenger on motor cycle | 3 |
| | 35 | Fail comply with traffic directions | 3 |
| | 36 | Fail comply with traffic signs | 3 |
| | 40A | Using vehicle in dangerous condition | 3 |
| | 41A | Breach of requirement as to brakes, steering gear or tyres | 3 |
| | 41C | Breach of requirement as to speed assessment equipment detection device *(from date to be appointed)* | 3–6 |
| | 41D | Breach of requirement as to control of vehicle mobile phones, etc | 3 |
| | 87(1) | Drive otherwise than in accordance with licence (where offender's driving would not have been in accordance with any licence that could have been granted to him) | 3–6 |
| | 92(10) | Drive after making false declaration as to fitness | 3–6 |
| | 94(3A) | Drive after failure to notify disability | 3–6 |
| | 94A | Drive after licence refused | 3–6 |
| | 96 | Uncorrected defective eyesight, or refuse test | 3 |
| | 103(1)(*b*) | Driving while disqualified | 6 |
| | 143 | Using motor vehicle without insurance | 6–8 |
| | 170(4) | Fail stop, give particulars, report accident | 5–10 |
| | 172 | Fail give identity of driver | 6 |
| RTOA 1988, s 28(2) | | Aid, abet, counsel, procure, incite an offence involving obligatory disqualification | 10 |
| OAPA 1861, s 5 | | Manslaughter by driver of motor vehicle | 3–11* |
| OAPA 1861, s 35 | | Furious driving | 3–9 |
| Theft Act 1968, s 12A | | Aggravated vehicle-taking | 3–11* |

* These offences carry notional penalty points which will be ordered only if special reasons are found for not imposing the obligatory disqualification which the offences carry.

## ROAD TRAFFIC FIXED PENALTIES

| *Item Number* | *Offence* | *Fixed Penalty* |
|---|---|---|
| 1 | A fixed penalty offence under section 3 of the Road Traffic Act 1988 | £100 |
| 1A | A fixed penalty offence under s 41D(b) of the Road Traffic Act 1988 | £200 |
| 2 | A fixed penalty offence under section 143 of the Road Traffic Act 1988 | £300 |
| 3 | A fixed penalty offence under section 172 of the Road Traffic Act 1988 | £200 |
| 4 | Any other fixed penalty offence involving obligatory endorsement | £100 |
| 5 | A fixed penalty parking offence committed in Greater London on a red route | £60 |
| 6 | Any other fixed penalty parking offence committed in Greater London | £40 |
| 7 | fixed penalty offence under section 14 (seat belts: adults) of the Road Traffic Act 1988 | £100 |
| 8 | A fixed penalty offence under section 15(2) or 15(4) (restrictions on carrying children not wearing seat belts in motor vehicles) of the Road Traffic Act 1988 | £100 |
| 9 | A fixed penalty offence under section 47 of the Road Traffic Act 1988 | £100 |
| 10 | A fixed penalty offence under section 42(1) of the Vehicle Excise and Registration Act 1994 (driving or keeping a vehicle without required registration mark) | £100 |
| 11 | A fixed penalty offence under section 43(1) of the Vehicle Excise and Registration Act 1994 (driving or keeping a vehicle with registration mark obscured etc) | £100 |
| 12 | A fixed penalty offence under section 59 of the Vehicle Excise and Registration Act 1994 (failure to fix prescribed registration mark to a vehicle in accordance with regulations made under section 23(4)(a) of that Act) | £100 |
| 13 | A fixed penalty offence under section 98(4) of the Transport Act 1968 | £300 |
| 14 | A fixed penalty offence under section 99(4) of the Transport Act 1968 | £300 |
| 15 | A fixed penalty offence under section 99ZD(1) of the Transport Act 1968 | £300 |
| 16 | A fixed penalty offence under section 99C of the Transport Act 1968 | £300 |
| 17 | A fixed penalty offence under section 3(1) of the Road Traffic (Foreign Vehicles) Act 1972 | £300 |
| 18 | A fixed penalty offence under section 12(5) of the Public Passenger Vehicles Act 1981 | £300 |
| 19 | A fixed penalty offence under section 71(1) of the Road Traffic Act 1988 | £300 |
| 20 | A fixed penalty offence under section 90D(6) of the Road Traffic Offenders Act 1988 | £300 |
| 21 | A fixed penalty offence under section 2(5) of the Goods Vehicles (Licensing of Operators) Act 1995 | £300 |
| 22 | A fixed penalty offence under regulation 3 of the Goods Vehicles (Community Authorisations) Regulations 1992 | £100 |
| 23 | A fixed penalty offence under regulation 3 of the Public Service Vehicles (Community Licences) Regulations 1999 | £100 |
| 24 | A fixed penalty offence under regulation 3(1) of the Road Transport (Passenger Vehicles Cabotage) Regulations 1999 | £100 |
| 25 | A fixed penalty offence under regulation 4(1) of the Road Transport (Passenger Vehicles Cabotage) Regulations 1999 | £100 |
| 26 | A fixed penalty offence under section 11 of the HGV Road User Levy Act 2013 | £300 |
| 27 | Any other fixed penalty offence except for a fixed penalty parking offence | £50 |
| 28 | Any other fixed penalty parking offence | £30 |
| 29 | A fixed penalty offence under s 11 of the HGV Road User Levy Act 2015 | £300 |
| 30 | An offence of keeping a motor vehicle which does not meet insurance requirements, contrary to s 144A of the Road Traffic Act 1988 | £100, or £50 if the penalty is paid within 21 days |